Webster's New Biographical Dictionary

A Merriam-Webster®

MERRIAM-WEBSTER INC., Publishers

Springfield, Massachusetts

A GENUINE MERRIAM-WEBSTER

The name *Webster* alone is no guarantee of excellence. It is used by a number of publishers and may serve mainly to mislead an unwary buyer.

A Merriam-Webster® is the registered trademark you should look for when you consider the purchase of dictionaries or other fine reference books. It carries the reputation of a company that has been publishing since 1831 and is your assurance of quality and authority.

Library of Congress Cataloging in Publication Data
Main entry under title:

Webster's new biographical dictionary.

1. Biography—Dictionaries. I. Merriam-Webster, Inc. II. Title: New biographical dictionary.

CT103.W4 1988 920'.02 87-28302

ISBN 0-87779-543-6

Made in the United States of America

789RMcN91908988

Contents

Preface vii

Explanatory Notes ix

Guide to Pronunciation xii

Abbreviations in This Book xvi

Pronunciation Symbols xviii

Biographies 1

Pronouncing Lists of Name Elements, Titles, and Prenames 1091

Preface

It is forty years since Webster's Biographical Dictionary first appeared. It was the product of more than five years' work by a large staff of editors, and it quickly justified their efforts by becoming a standard reference. In those forty years the book has seen some 21 updated printings recording the accelerating changes of an increasingly complex and cosmopolitan world. The task of maintaining the book's currency, along with that of constantly improving its accuracy, has been made easier over the years by the thousands of readers and users who have written to offer criticisms, corrections, and suggestions and who are hereby publicly and sincerely thanked. But the task eventually demanded more than updating; hence, Webster's New Biographical Dictionary.

The present work, while based firmly on its predecessor, is wholly revised and reedited to meet new demands. A new typographic design has greatly simplified the appearance of the pages and will make the book easier to use. Numerous other changes in the arrangement and treatment of information are discussed in detail in the Explanatory Notes section. One major change in the coverage of the book should be noted here: Living persons, whose biographies are virtually impossible to keep up-to-date in a book of this nature, are not included. References such as Who's Who, Current Biography, encyclopedia yearbooks, and the like do an excellent job of reporting on current personalities. Webster's New Biographical Dictionary takes as its job to present in a single volume biographical information on important, celebrated, or notorious figures from the last five thousand years, beginning with Menes, king of Egypt c.3100 B.C., and continuing through some 30,000 more.

As befits a work aimed at today's and, we hope, tomorrow's readers, the coverage of the non-English-speaking part of the world, especially of Asia, Africa, and what are called variously the developing or Third World nations has been greatly increased. Yet as befits a work that will be used primarily by English-speaking consultants, the treatment afforded American, Canadian, and British subjects tends to be fuller and more detailed.

Webster's New Biographical Dictionary retains such useful features of its predecessor as the indication of end-of-line division and pronunciation of names (fully discussed in the Explanatory Notes) and the separate list of prenames appended to the main body of the book. To that list have been added lists of common titles and honorifics and of common connective name elements.

It cannot be pretended that this book is free of error or that the selection of names to be included is in any sense definitive. It is confidently expected that the correspondence of the last forty years with readers around the world will continue, with new grist for the mills of the sharp-eyed detectors of typographical errors and editorial infelicities. Nonetheless Webster's New Biographical Dictionary is offered as a worthy successor to its distinguished parent and an important addition to the line of Merriam-Webster reference books.

Webster's New Biographical Dictionary was planned and edited by Robert McHenry, assisted by Frank Calvillo, assistant editor. Valuable help was provided by Dr. Frederick C. Mish, Editorial Director of Merriam-Webster. Pronunciation was the work of Dr. John K. Bollard, associate editor, assisted by Susan M. McDonald, assistant editor, and Dru A. Whitten, editorial assistant. Proof was read and corrected by Eileen M. Haraty, editorial assistant, Peter D. Haraty, assistant editor, Daniel J. Hopkins, assistant editor, and Cynthia S. Ashby. The often demanding clerical work required by such a project was carried out under the direction of Gloria Afflitto. Acknowledgment is also due the staff of the first Webster's Biographical Dictionary, headed by William Allan Neilson, John P. Bethel, and Lucius H. Holt.

Explanatory Notes

In compiling and arranging this dictionary, the editors have striven to present information in as consistent a manner as was compatible with clarity and ease of use. The structure of individual entries and the significance of the various sorts of information included in them are in nearly every case self-evident, but the consultant will find useful a brief description and explanation of various devices and conventions adopted by the editors to achieve greater consistency, accuracy, or compression.

In general, entries in this book include the following elements: 1. Entry name, printed in bold type. 2. Pronunciation (unless carried over from a preceding entry). 3. Prenames. 4. Titles, epithets, pen names, nicknames, original names, etc. 5. Birth and death dates or other indication of historical period. 6. Nationality or, where more applicable, ethnic identification, followed by an occupational description and, for Americans, Canadians, and selected others, birthplace. 7. Pertinent details of the subject's career.

Variations of this basic arrangement occur in composite entries, for details of which see section 8 below.

1. Entry Names.

a. Boldface entry selection. The general practice in this book is to enter each subject under his or her family name, when there is one. Entries are not made at titles of nobility, at pseudonyms, nicknames, or other variants. Exceptions to the family-name rule are cases in which the subject adopted a living name (as opposed, for example, to a pen name) different from his family name. Thus, the writer George Orwell (a pseudonym) is entered at **Blair**, Eric Arthur, and a cross-reference at Orwell makes the entry readily accessible; on the other hand, John Wayne is entered at **Wayne**, John, as the name he lived under in spite of having been born Marion Michael Morrison. In cases of the common medieval and Renaissance practice of translating family names into Latin equivalents, the editors have preferred the original vernacular name unless it is clear that the Latin name was more than merely a pen name or unless the Latin name is firmly established in English usage. Thus, Georgius Agricola is entered at **Bauer**, Georg, while Michael Praetorius is entered at **Praetorius**; again cross-references assure that every entry is fully accessible.

Subjects lacking family names, including those whose surnames are not family names, are entered at their given names, as **Berengaria** or **George Pachymeres**. Rulers, even those with family names, are generally entered at the given names by which they are known in English, so that kings Friedrich and Wilhelm of Germany are entered at **Frederick** and **William**, King Istvan of Hungary is at **Stephen**, and so on. Where no English equivalent exists, the vernacular name is used, as **Władysław**. In the case of Chinese rulers, who have personal names, temple names, reign titles, and sometimes others, the use of personal names has placed most of them in composite dynastic entries (see 8 below).

Except for the case of rulers' names given in English, vernacular usage has governed spelling. For languages not written in the Roman alphabet, the following conventions have been adopted:

Chinese: Wade-Giles transliterations are used, with Pin-yin variants shown for some recent figures.

Russian and others using Cyrillic: the transcription system used in the Encyclopaedia Britannica has been adopted, making easier the use of this book in conjunction with a major English-language reference work.

Arabic: the transliteration system used in the Encyclopaedia Britannica has been adopted.

For simplicity, Chinese and Vietnamese names have been treated as units and printed entirely in boldface. In Japanese and Korean names, with few exceptions, the distinction between family and personal names is observed. (Note that in those languages normal name order places the family name first; hence, in this dictionary no comma appears between family and personal name as it would in, for example, an inverted English name. Hungarian names, which also use family–personal name order are, on the other hand, treated as English names and the comma is used.)

Major variant spellings or forms of names are given following the main entry name and printed in boldface to indicate their parallel status. Minor variants are usually given separately following the prenames (see 4 below).

In many languages, surnames are sometimes composed of two or more elements. The choice of element(s) for the boldface main entry has again been determined by vernacular usage. In the relatively simple cases of names containing such connective elements as *d'*, *de*, *de la*, *di*, *do*, *du*, *ten*, *van*, *van der*, *von*, *von der*, *zu*, etc., this means in general that in European names the element following the connective is chosen for entry, while in English names the connective itself is considered the first part of the surname. Individual usage, where it differs, is given precedence over these rules.

In French, Spanish, and Portuguese, compound surnames are common, as Alphonse-Marie-Louis de Prat de **Lamartine** or Lope Félix de **Vega Carpio**. Again vernacular usage has determined the selection of element for alphabetical entry, occasionally in contrast to English usage, as in Vasco **Núñez de Balboa**. In the case of French names the convention of hyphenating personal names has been adopted, but in all cases of compound surnames the surname status of any element is indicated by its being given a pronunciation in the entry.

b. Alphabetization. The order of entries is determined by ordinary rules of alphabetization applied to the boldface entry names and by the following additional rules:

i. Diacritical marks, marks of punctuation, and spaces within the boldface names are ignored, as are Roman numerals.

ii. Entries with the same boldface entry name are arranged alphabetically by prename; where prenames are the same or absent, they are ordered chronologically by birth date. In a few entries, chiefly of Scottish subjects, a qualifying phrase is a[illegible] tached to the surname, as "**Mackenzie** of Rosehaugh, George"; such phrases are ignored in alphabetizing.

iii. In series of entries in which the boldface entry name is [illegible] sonal name, as **Boniface** or **John**, the order is: (1) sa[illegible] popes; (3) rulers or members of ruling families, orde[illegible] betically by name of geographical entity; (4) others bearing only that name.

iv. Entries whose boldface entry name is followed by a period or by a pronunciation and a period precede those followed by a qualifying word or phrase, as "of Ceos" or "the Blind." The latter precede entries whose boldface entry name is the same but is a family name, followed by prenames.

v. Entries consisting of a personal name followed by a qualifying word or phrase not in English, as "de Lusignan" or "le Diable," are boldfaced throughout and follow entries in which only the first element is boldfaced.

vi. Names beginning with M', Mac, or Mc are alphabetized as though spelled Mac.

The following ordered list of fictitious names illustrates these rules:

Albert. Saint.
Albert. Pope.
Albert II. Duke of Austria.
Albert I. King of Lusatia.
Albert. Baron of Pomerania.
Albert. British chronicler.
Albert of Mainz.
Albert of Regensburg.
Albert the Lion-heart.
Albert, Franklin.
Albert, George. 1832–1863.
Albert of Edinburgh, George. 1833–1848.
Albert, George. 1835–1899.
Albert de Paris.
Alberti, Lorenzo.
Albert von Krankheit.

c. **End-of-line division**. The centered dots within boldface entry names indicate points at which a hyphen may be put at the end of a line of print or writing. The centered dots are not meant to separate the syllables of a name. (Syllables are indicated in the pronunciation transcriptions.) As far as possible, division of names has been shown according to principles consistent with those used in the language of origin. No division is shown after a single initial letter or before a single terminal letter because printers seldom isolate a single letter at the end or beginning of a line.

In cases where variation in pronunciation would call for variant end-of-line divisions on either side of a letter or digraph, the leftmost division is regularly shown, purely for the sake of consistency. There are acceptable alternative end-of-line divisions just as there are acceptable variant spellings and pronunciations; the divisions in this book are simply meant to provide printers, typists, and writers with a consistent set of divisions.

2. Pronunciation.

Pronunciation of names is shown immediately following boldface entries and between reversed virgules \ \ using the characters and conventions given in the list of Pronunciation Symbols and discussed in the Guide to Pronunciation. Boldface variants of main entry names are given pronunciations when they differ from that of the main entry; any main entry or boldface variant takes the first ronunciation appearing to its right, whether immediately following not.

hyphen is used in pronunciation transcriptions to show syllabic ion. The hyphens sometimes coincide with the centered dots name that indicate end-of-line division; sometimes they do

h-set mark /ˈ/ indicates primary (strongest) stress or ac- w-set mark /ˌ/ indicates secondary (medium) stress. The stands at the beginning of the syllable that receives he principle that before a syllable can be uttered the speaker must know whether to stress it or not. A third level of weak stress is left unmarked.

For some names variant pronunciations have been shown. A second place variant is not to be regarded as less acceptable than the pronunciation that is given first. All of the pronunciations shown in this book are considered to be in acceptable educated usage. When known, the pronunciation preferred by a person or family entered in this book has, of course, been given priority of place. Variant pronunciations are generally separated by commas. Semicolons are occasionally used to set off groups of variants. Where applicable in Spanish and Portuguese names, Latin American pronunciation variants are given following a semicolon.

Within the limits of an English-based pronunciation system, most foreign names have been given a pronunciation approximating that of the native language. Some foreign names frequently heard in English contexts are given a foreign pronunciation followed by an anglicized variant preceded by the abbreviation *Angl*\\. Other language labels may be used when variant pronunciations are common in two or more languages.

Symbols enclosed in parentheses represent elements that are present in the pronunciation of some speakers but are absent from the pronunciation of others, elements that are present in some but absent from other utterances by the same speaker, or elements whose presence or absence is uncertain. When a name has less than a full pronunciation shown, the missing part is to be supplied from a preceding variant within the same pair of reversed virgules or from a pronunciation at a preceding entry. Only the first in a sequence of identical boldface entries is given a pronunciation if their pronunciations are the same.

3. Prenames.

Prenames, also called given names, personal names, Christian names, etc., appear following the boldface entry name and its pronunciation, set off (except in Japanese and Korean names, as noted above) by a comma. Where a variant of or change in prename requires notice, it is generally signaled by an italicized word or phrase, as *or, known as, orig., called.* Pronunciations for prenames are given in a separate list at the end of the book, with end-of-line divisions and pronunciations appropriate for various languages clearly shown; where any ambiguity exists as to which language is the proper one for a particular entry, a superscript number following the prename indicates the correct numbered variant in the prenames list.

4. Titles and other Names.

Following the entry name, pronunciation, and prenames, and set off by periods, are indicated a subject's titles of dignity or rank, original name, nickname, pseudonym, or other identifications. The nature of these other names is clearly denoted by key phrases or in some cases lengthy explanations printed in italic type. Note that an entry reading "**Smith**, John, *orig.* George Jones." means that the subject's original name was George Jones Smith, while one reading "**Smith**, John. *Orig.* George Jones." means that his original name was George Jones. Pronunciations of principal elements are given in the entry; a list of common titles and their pronunciations appears in the back of the book. Titles of dignity in which the proper name element is the same as the subject's surname are frequently given in short form; thus, "**Lagrange**, Joseph-Louis. Comte." means that the subject's title is Comte Lagrange. A connective name element such as *de* or *von* is carried over into the title in such cases: "**Pocci**, Franz von. Graf." is the Graf von Pocci.

5. Dates.

Birth and death dates, if known, are given in full for each subject. Where information is uncertain or lacking, various devices are used to indicate that fact. A question mark immediately preceding or following a date indicates lack of certainty about the probable date cited; a lesser degree of certainty is indicated by the abbreviation c. (for *circa*) attached to a date. Entire uncertainty is indicated by use of the abbreviation fl. (Latin *floruit*, flourished) attached to a date or period associated with the subject's career or by the substitution of a century for specific dates. Where only a birth or death date is known, it is indicated by the abbreviation b. or d. Dates before the Common Era are always denoted B.C.; the term A.D. is used whenever needed for clarity.

6. Ascriptive identifier.

Most subjects are identified by a phrase combining a geographical or ethnic reference and a word or phrase suggesting a role, an occupation, or a field of endeavor. In some few cases where it is more to the point, the ascription may omit the geographical reference as implicit in the role description; *e.g.* "**Paul**. Saint. 1st century A.D. One of the twelve Christian apostles." In some other cases, no intelligible geographical or ethnic description is available; for those subjects what is known is made clear in the body of the entry. For Americans and Canadians, the subject's birthplace is appended to the ascription. For British subjects not born in England, for subjects who have both a native country and one of adoption, and for selected others of interest, country of origin is also given.

7. Career details.

Entries include, generally in the following order, such details of the subject's career as: major offices or positions, in chronological order; major actions or achievements; titles of works not previously mentioned in the entry. Entries may also contain indications of the subject's relation to other subjects entered in the book or suggestions to see (*q.v.*) or compare (*cf.*) other entries. Marital details are given when they contribute to an understanding of sequences of events, when marital partners are also subjects of entries in the dictionary or are otherwise prominent, or when for female subjects they explain and date changes of surname.

8. Composite entries.

Many entries treat more than one subject. Some treat members of a family linked by a common occupation; some treat major families or dynasties whose members are of individual importance but whose relationships are more easily comprehended in a single article. In both instances, each run-on, or additional, subject is marked for rapid location by the symbol ¶. A second form of composite entry typically lists popes or temporal rulers of a given country who share a common entry name regardless of familial relationships, as the kings Henry I through VIII of England. In these entries each new subject's name is given in boldface at the beginning of a new paragraph.

9. Cross-References.

Cross-references are used copiously throughout the book to direct the reader to entries placed at real names rather than at perhaps better known pseudonyms or titles and to refer the reader to related entries. In addition there are many fairly elaborate entries at dynastic names that are in essence extended cross-references to the various members of a dynasty entered at their personal names.

Guide to Pronunciation

A pronunciation transcription is given for each name in this book, with a few exceptions. All boldface entries are followed immediately by the pronunciation or else the pronunciation can be found at a preceding entry with the same spelling. Pronunciations for other names and name elements appear either after the first occurrence in the text of an entry or in one of the supplementary lists of particles, titles, and given names at the back of the book. The following are the main exceptions.

The full form of Arabic names is not usually given a pronunciation transcription since the full forms are rarely used in English speech and a transcription would take up an inordinate amount of space:

> **Ab·del·ka·der** \ˌäb-dəl-ˈkäd-ər\. *Arab. in full* ʻAbd al-Qādir ibn Muḥyī ad-Dīn ibn Muṣṭafā al-Ḥasanī al-Jazāʼirī.

American Indian names appearing in boldface are accompanied by a transcription but subsequent romanized forms of names in the native language are not:

> **Cra·zy Horse** \ˈkrā-zē-ˌhȯ(ə)rs\. *Indian name* Ta-sunko-witko *or* Tashunka-Uitco.

> **Ge·ron·i·mo** \jə-ˈrän-ə-ˌmō\. *Indian name* Goyathlay, *i.e.* One Who Yawns.

Variant forms of names in some archaic languages have not been given pronunciations since these are primarily written forms:

> **Pa·cor·us** \pə-ˈkōr-əs, -ˈkȯr-\. *Parthian* Pkwr.

The pronunciation transcriptions for non-English names in this book represent approximations of the pronunciation in the native language. The individual sounds of each language vary in some ways from the similar sounds of other languages. With the inclusion of a few symbols to represent some sounds not found in English, however, the Merriam-Webster pronunciation symbols allow us to represent the pronunciation of foreign names sufficiently accurately for English speakers in an English context. Classical names, such as in Greek and Latin, are given a pronunciation according to modern English usage. Modern Greek names, of course, are given a pronunciation approximating Modern Greek as closely as possible.

The following discussion sets out the signification and use of the …nunciation symbols in this book with special attention to varia… or departures from English in the transcriptions of non-En… names. The order of symbols explained below is the same as th…er in the list of Pronunciation Symbols, with the exception … symbols that are not letter characters are here listed first.

**\ ** All pronunciation information is printed between re…rsed virgules. Pronunciation symbols are printed in ro- man type… all other information, such as notes and language la- bels, is prin… in italics.

**\ ˈ ˌ ** A high set stress mark precedes a syllable with primary (strongest) stress; a low set mark precedes a syllable with secondary (medium) stress; a third level of weak stress requires no mark at all: *penmanship* \ˈpen-mən-ˌship\.

In some languages, such as French, Japanese, Korean, and Malay, all syllables receive equal stress or stress that varies somewhat according to sentence context. In accordance with the practice of most phoneticians, no stress is indicated in the pronunciation of names in such languages, except, of course, in the case of anglicized pronunciations. In some languages, such as Spanish, only primary stress is indicated; the stress of other syllables of names in these languages is relatively even. In some languages, such as Chinese, Norwegian, and Swedish, some words may be distinguished only by a difference in intonation rather than stress. Names, however, are not likely to be confused because of tone changes, especially in English contexts, and tone is not indicated in this book.

**\ - ** Hyphens are used in transcriptions to separate syllables. The placement of these hyphens is based on phonetic principles and may not match the end-of-line divisions indicated by centered dots in the entry itself.

**\ ( ) ** Parentheses are used in transcriptions to indicate that whatever is symbolized between them is present in some utterances but not in others; thus *factory* \ˈfak-t(ə-)rē\ is pronounced both \ˈfak-tə-rē\ and \ˈfak-trē\.

**\ , ; ** Variant pronunciations are separated by commas; groups of variants are separated by semicolons. In Spanish names, where applicable, Latin American pronunciation variants are given after a semicolon. Similarly, Brazilian Portugese variants follow a semicolon in Portugese names.

**\ ə ** in unstressed syllables as in banana, collide, abut. This neutral vowel may be represented orthographically by any of the letters *a, e, i, o, u, y* , and by many combinations of letters. The final vowel sound of Russian names ending in -y is a diphthong that varies somewhat in pronunciation and that is represented in this book as \əi\.

\ ˈə, ˌə ** in stressed syllables as in **humdrum, abut.

\ ᵊ ** immediately preceding \l\, \n\, \m\, \ŋ\, as in **battle, cotton, and one pronunciation of **open** \ˈōp-ᵊm\ and of **and** \ᵊŋ\, as in one pronunciation of the phrase *lock and key* \ˌläk-ᵊŋ-ˈkē\.

In the transcription of some French names \ᵊ\ is placed immediately after \l\, \m\, \r\, to indicate one nonsyllabic pronunciation of these consonants, as in the French words table "table," prisme "prism," and titre "title," each of which in isolation and in some contexts is a one syllable word.

\ər\ as in **further, urger, bird**.

\ˈər-, ˈə-r\ as in two different pronunciations of *hurry*. Most U.S. speakers pronounce \ˈhər-ē\ with the \ər\ representing the same sounds as in *bird* \ˈbərd\. Usually in metropolitan New York and southern England and frequently in New England and the southeastern U.S. the vowel of *hurry* is the same as the vowel of *hum* followed by a syllable-initial variety of \r\ as in *red* \ˈred\. This pronunciation of *hurry* is represented as \ˈhə-rē\. Both types of pronunciation are shown for English names where appropriate. The vowel represented as \œ\ in this book is often anglicized as \ə(r)\ with the vowel of *bird* with or without a following \r\ sound.

\a\ as in **mat, map, mad, gag, snap, patch**.

\ā\ as in **day, fade, date, aorta, drape, cape**. In most English speech this is actually a diphthong. In lowland South Carolina, Georgia, and Florida, in some British dialects, and occasionally elsewhere in English \ā\ is pronounced as a monophthong with the tongue more tense and somewhat higher in the mouth than for \e\. As a diphthong \ā\ has a first element \e\ or monophthongal \ā\ and a second element \i\.

In most other languages \ā\ is a monophthong. In some languages a diphthong \e\ + \i\ or \ā\ + \i\ occurs in some contexts, especially when spelled *ei* or *ej*. In this book \ā\ is used to represent all of these possibilities.

\ä\ as in **bother, cot**, and, with most American speakers, **father, cart**.

\ȧ\ as in **father** as pronounced by those who do not rhyme it with *bother*; also as in French *chat* "cat," *patte* "paw." In English the pronunciation of this vowel varies regionally. In eastern New England and southern England it is generally pronounced farther forward in the mouth than \ä\ but not as far forward as \a\. In New York City and the southeastern U.S. it may have much the same quality as \ä\ but somewhat greater duration. In areas in which \r\ is not pronounced before another consonant or a pause \ȧ\ occurs for the sequence transcribed in this book as \är\. In the transcription of foreign names \ȧ\ represents the vowel heard in French *patte* \pȧt\ and *chat* \shȧ, shȧt\. This vowel is intermediate between \a\ and \ä\ and is similar in quality to the \ȧ\ heard in eastern New England.

\au̇\ as in **now, loud, out**. The initial element of this diphthong may vary from \a\ to \ȧ\ or \ä\, the first being more common in Southern and south Midland speech in the U.S.

\b\ as in **baby, rib**.

\b̲\ as in Spanish **hablar** "to speak." Whereas for \b\ the lips are in contact and form a closure along their entire extent, for \b̲\ the lips are close together without complete closure. This voiced fricative sound can be approximated by pronouncing \v\ with both lips rather than with the upper teeth and the lower lip.

\ch\ as in **chin, nature** \ˈnā-chər\. Actually, this sound is \t\ + \sh\.

\d\ as in **did, adder**.

\e\ as in **bet, bed, peck**.

\ˈē, ˌē\ in stressed syllables as in **beat, nosebleed, evenly, easy**.

\ē\ in unstressed syllables as in **easy**. In some English dialects, such as in southern England and the southeastern U.S., \i\ is often, if not usually, pronounced instead of \ē\. In English names in this book only \ē\ is shown in final position, though for some foreign names a final \i\ is transcribed in order to represent the foreign pronunciation more accurately.

\f\ as in **fifty, cuff**.

\g\ as in **go, big, gift**.

\ḡ\ as in Spanish **leugo** "immediately." This is a voiced fricative sound pronounced with the tongue in approximately the position for \g\ but without complete closure at the roof of the mouth. \ḡ\ is the voiced equivalent of unvoiced \k̲\.

\h\ as in **hat, ahead**.

\hl\ as in Welsh **llan** "church," Icelandic **hlusta** "to listen." This sound is actually a voiceless \l\ which can be approximated by attempting to pronounce \h\ and \l\ simultaneously without vibration of the vocal cords.

\hw\ as in **whale** as pronounced by those who do not have the same pronunciation for both *whale* and *wail*. Most U.S. speakers distinguish these two words as \ˈhwā(ə)l\ and \ˈwā(ə)l\ respectively, though frequently in the U.S. and usually in southern England \ˈwā(ə)l\ is the pronunciation of both. Some linguists consider \hw\ to be a single sound, a voiceless \w\.

\i\ as in **tip, banish, active**.

\ī\ as in **site, side, buy, tripe**. Actually, this sound is a diphthong, usually composed of \ä\ + \i\ or \ȧ\ + \i\. In the southeastern U.S., especially before a pause or a voiced consonant, as in *shy* and *five*, the second element \i\ may not be pronounced.

\j\ as in **job, gem, edge, join, judge**. Actually, this sound is \d\ + \zh\.

\k\ as in **kin, cook, ache**.

\k̲\ as in German **ich** "I," **Buch** "book," and one pronunciation of English **loch**. Actually, there are two distinct sounds in German; the \k̲\ in *ich* is pronounced toward the front of the mouth and the \k̲\ in *Buch* is pronounced toward the back. In English, however, no two words otherwise identical are distinguished by these two varieties of \k̲\, and therefore only a single symbol is necessary. In English speech the front variety of \k̲\ is produced automatically to accompany a front vowel, such as \e\ or \i\, and the back variety of \k̲\ to accompany a back vowel, such as \ä\ or \ü\.

\l as in **lily**, **pool**. In some contexts, as in *battle* and *fiddle*, the \l\ is a syllabic consonant, transcribed as \ᵊl\ in this book. In Polish there are two distinct varieties of \l\ sounds. One is represented by the letter *l* and is pronounced toward the front of the mouth much as in the English word *lily*, and the other is represented by the letter ł and is pronounced toward the back of the mouth, much as in English *pool*. Both of these Polish sounds are transcribed as \l\ in this book.

\m as in **murmur**, **dim**, **nymph**. In some contexts \m\ may be pronounced as a syllabic consonant transcribed as \ᵊm\, as in one pronunciation of *open*\ˈōp-ᵊm\ and of *happen* \ˈhap-ᵊm\.

\n as in **no**, **own**. In some contexts, as in *cotton* and *sudden*, the \n\ is a syllabic consonant, transcribed as \ᵊn\ in this book.

\ⁿ indicates that a preceding vowel or diphthong is pronounced with the nasal passages open, as in French *un bon vin blanc* \œⁿ- bōⁿ-vaⁿ-bläⁿ\ "a good white wine."

\ŋ as in **sing**\ˈsiŋ\, **singer** \ˈsiŋ-ər\, **finger** \ˈfiŋ-gər\, **ink** \ˈiŋk\. In English \ŋ\ does not occur at the beginning of a word although it does in some other languages. In some contexts \ŋ\ may be a syllabic consonant, transcribed as \ᵊŋ\ in this book.

\ō as in **bone**, **know**, **beau**. Especially in positions of emphasis, as when it is word final, with primary stress, and before a pause, \ō\ tends to become diphthongal, moving from \ō\ toward a second element \u̇\. In southern England and in some U.S. speech the first element is often approximately \ə\. Thus many British phoneticians represent this sound as \əu̇\. In most other languages \ō\ is generally monophthongal. In this book \ō\ is used for all of the above variants.

\ȯ as in **saw**, **all**, **caught**.

\œ as in French **boeuf** "beef," German **Hölle** "hell." This non-English vowel can be approximated by attempting to pronounce the vowel \e\ with the lips moderately rounded as for the vowel \u̇\. This vowel is often anglicized as \ə(r)\ with the vowel of *bird* with or without an accompanying \r\ sound.

\œ̄ as in French **feu** "fire," German **Höhle** "hole." This non-English vowel can be approximated by attempting to pronounce a monophthongal \ā\ with the lips fully rounded as for the vowel \ü\.

\ȯi as in **coin**, **destroy**. In the southeastern U.S., especially before a consonant in the same word, the second element of this diphthong may disappear or be replaced by \ə\.

\p as in **pepper**, **lip**.

\r as in **red**, **rarity**, **car**, **beard**. In some dialects, especially in the southeastern U.S., eastern New England, New York City, and southern England, \r\ is not pronounced when another consonant or a pause follows immediately. In these dialects *r* is pronounced as a non-syllabic \ə\ when it occurs in these positions or there may be no sound corresponding to the *r*; thus *beard* may be pronounced as \ˈbiəd\ or, usually with some lengthening of the vowel sound, as \ˈbid\. In *car* and *card* those who do not pronounce \r\ generally have a vowel we would transcribe as \ȧ\, usually pronounced with some lengthening. Because it is determined by the phonetic context this "r-dropping" is not explicitly shown in this dictionary; speakers of these dialects will automatically substitute the sounds appropriate to their own speech.

In other languages \r\ is usually more vigorously articulated than in English. Two of the most common varieties of \r\ are the tongue-point trill and the uvular \r\. In the former the tip of the tongue is vibrated rapidly up and down against the back part of the teethridge by the outgoing breath; in the latter the voiced breath passes over the raised back of the tongue, either causing the uvula to vibrate (uvular trill) or producing a strong fricative sound (uvular scrape). Both the tongue-point trill and the uvular \r\ occur in French and German. Italian and Russian have only the tongue-point trill. Danish \r\ is usually uvular. In Spanish *rr* is a tongue-point trill, transcribed in this book as \r-r\ when it occurs between vowels. A single *r* in Spanish usually has only a single flip of the tongue against the teethridge, although *sr* and initial *r* are trilled. Portugese \r\ is much like Spanish except that the trill is frequently a uvular trill. Final *r* in Portugese may not be pronounced. In German *r* and *rr* before another consonant or a pause is pronounced as a non-syllabic \ə\ in much the same manner as by "r-dropping" speakers of English. In Czech and in Serbo-Croatian the tongue-point trill may serve as the vowel of an accented syllable, as in Czech *Brno* and Serbo-Croatian *Srbin*; in this book this is transcribed as \ər\. The Czech character ř represents a trilled fricative sound formed by the simultaneous production of a tongue-point trilled \r\ and \zh\; in this book this is transcribed as \r-zh\ between vowels as in *Dvorak*, and \rzh\ after consonants as in *Bedrich*.

\s as in **source**, **less**

\sh as in **shy**, **mission**, **machine**, **special**. Actually, this is a single sound, not two. When the two sounds \s\ and \h\ occur in sequence they are separated by a hyphen, as in *grasshopper* \ˈgras-ˌhäp-ər\.

\t as in **tie**, **attack**, **late**, **latter**. In some contexts, as when a stressed or unstressed vowel precedes and an unstressed vowel or \ᵊl\ follows, the sound represented by *t* or *tt* is pronounced in much American speech the same as the sound represented by *d* or *dd* in similar contexts. Thus, the pairs *ladder* and *latter*, *leader* and *liter*, *parody* and *parity* are often homophones. In such instances this dictionary shows \d\ at the end of a syllable spelled with *d* or *dd* and \t\ at the end of a syllable spelled with *t* or *tt*. In southern England, in some American speech, and in most other languages \t\ in these contexts is pronounced much like the syllable-initial \t\ of *attack*.

\th as in **thin**, **ether**. Actually, this is a single sound, not two. When the two sounds \t\ and \h\ occur in sequence they are separated by a hyphen, as in *knighthood* \ˈnīt-ˌhu̇d\.

\t̲h̲ as in **then**, **either**, **this**. Actually, this is a single sound, not two. The basic difference between \th\ and \t̲h̲\ is that the former is pronounced without and the latter with vibration of the vocal cords.

\ü in **rule**, **youth**, **union** \ˈyün-yən\, **few** \ˈfyü\.

\u̇ as in **pull**, **wood**, **book**, **curable** \ˈkyu̇r-ə-bəl\, **fury** \ˈfyu̇(ə)r-ē\.

\ue as in German **füllen** "to fill," **hübsch** "handsome." This vowel, which occurs only in foreign-derived terms and names, can be approximated by attempting to pronounce the vowel \i\ with the lips moderately rounded as for the vowel \u̇\.

\ue as in French rue "street," German fühlen "to feel." This vowel, which occurs only in foreign-derived terms and names, can be approximated by attempting to pronounce the vowel \ē\ with the lips fully rounded as for the vowel \ü\.

\v as in vivid, invite.

\w as in we, away, evaluate \i-ˈval-yə-ˌwāt\.

\y as in yard, young, cue \ˈkyü\, curable \ˈkyu̇r-ə-bəl\, few \ˈfyü\, fury\ˈfyu̇(ə)r-ē\, union \ˈyün-yən\. The sequences \lyü\, \syü\, and \zyü\ in the same syllable, as in *lewd, suit,* and *presume,* are common in southern British speech but are rare in American speech and, therefore, only \lü\, \sü\, and \zü\ are shown in this book.

In English \y\ does not occur at the end of a syllable after a vowel, though it does in some languages, such as French where it is often represented in the spelling *il* or *ille,* or Serbo-Croatian where it is represented by *j.* The sound \y\ transcribed afer a vowel, as in French *Corbeil* \kȯr-bey\, is much the same as the \y\ of English *yard.*

\ʸ indicates that during the articulation of the preceding consonant the tongue has substantially the position it has for the articulation of the \y\ of yard, as in French *digne* \dēnʸ\ "worthy." Thus \ʸ\ does not itself represent a sound but rather a modification of the preceding symbol. It is used only in the transcription of non-English names. The pronunciation of \tʸ\ and \dʸ\ may be approximated in English by the substitution of \ch\ and \j\, but since some languages maintain a significant distinction between \tʸ\ and \ch\ and between \dʸ\ and \j\ the transcriptions \tʸ\ and \dʸ\ are used in names from these languages.

\z as in zone, raise.

\zh as in vision, azure \ˈazh-ər\. Actually, this is a single sound, not two. When the two sounds \z\ and \h\ occur in sequence they are separated by a hyphen in this book, as in *hogshead* \ˈhȯgz-ˌhed, ˈhägz-ˌhed\.

Abbreviations in This Book

AAF	Army Air Forces
ABC	American Broadcasting Corporation
Acad.	Academy
A.D.	Anno Domini (in the year of our Lord)
ad int	ad interim
adj.	adjutant
adm.	Admitted
Adm.	Admiral
A.E.F.	American Expeditionary Force, or Forces
AFL-CIO	American Federation of Labor–Congress of Industrial Organizations
Afrik.	Afrikaans
Agric.	Agricultural; Agriculture
A.I.F.	Australian Imperial Forces
Ala.	Alabama
Alb.	Albanian
Alta.	Alberta
Am.	America(n)
A. & M.	Agricultural and Mechanical (College)
Amer.	America(n)
Angl.	Anglicized
anon.	anonymous, anonymously
ANZUS	Australia, New Zealand, United States Treaty Organization
Apr.	April
Arab.	Arabic
Ariz.	Arizona
Ark.	Arkansas
Arm.	Armenian
A.-S.	Anglo-Saxon
Assn.	Association
Aug.	August
A.V.	Authorized Version (of the Bible)
b.	born
Bab.	Babylonian
B.C.	before Christ; British Columbia
B.E.F.	British Expeditionary Force, or Forces
Belg.	Belgian
biog(s).	biography; biographies
Brig. Gen.	Brigadier General
Brit.	Britain; British
Bulg.	Bulgarian
B.W.I.	British West Indies
c.	circa (*Lat.*, about)
Cal. or Calif.	California
Calif. Inst. Tech.	California Institute of Technology
Can.	Canadian
Capt.	Captain
CBS	Columbia Broadcasting System
cc	cubic centimeter(s)
C.C.N.Y.	College of the City of New York
Celt.	Celtic
cf.	confer (*Lat.*, compare)
Chin.	Chinese
Cie	Compagnie (*French*, Company)
CIO	Congress of Industrial Organizations; before 1938, Committee for Industrial Organization
cm.	centimeter(s)
Co.	Company; County
Col.	Colonel
Coll.	College
Colo.	Colorado
Com.	Commander; Commodore
Comm.	Commission; Committee
Conn.	Connecticut
cont.	continued
Corp.	Corporation
cr.	created
Croat.	Croatian
cu.	cubic
d.	died
Dan.	Danish
D.A.R.	Daughters of the American Revolution
D.C.	District of Columbia
Dec.	December
Del.	Delaware
Den.	Denmark
dept(s).	department(s)
div.	divorced
Dr.	Doctor
D.-R.	Democratic-Republican
Du.	Dutch
E.	East
ed(s).	edition(s); editor, edited
educ.	educated
e.g.	exempli gratia (*Lat.*, for example)
Eng.	English
esp.	especially
Esq.	Esquire
est., estab.	established
Est.	Estonian
et al.	et alii *or* et aliae (*Lat.*, and others)
etc.	et cetera (*Lat.*, and others; and the rest; and so forth)
exc.	except; exception
f.	following
Feb.	February
ff.	following
Finn.	Finnish
fl.	floruit (*Lat.*, flourished)
Fla.	Florida
Flem.	Flemish
Fr.	French
freq.	frequently
ft.	foot; feet
Ft.	Fort
Ga.	Georgia
Gael.	Gaelic
gen.	generally
Gen.	General
Ger.	German
Gov.	Governor
Gr.	Greek
Gk.	Greek
Heb.	Hebrew
Hind.	Hindustani
H.M.S.	His (or Her) Majesty's Ship
Hon.	Honorable
hr(s).	hour(s)
Hung.	Hungarian; Hungary
I(s).	Island(s)
Ia.	Iowa
Icel.	Icelandic
i.e.	id est (*Lat.*; that is)
Ill.	Illinois
illust.	illustrated; illustration
in.	inch(es)
Inc.	Incorporated
Ind.	Indiana
Inst.	Institute; Institution
Ire.	Ireland
Ir. Gael.	Irish Gaelic
Ital.	Italian
I.W.W.	Industrial Workers of the World
Jan.	January
Jp.	Japanese
Jr., jr.	Junior
Kans.	Kansas
Kor.	Korean
Ky.	Kentucky
l.	line
La.	Louisiana
lat.	latitude
Lat.	Latin; Latinized
lb(s).	libra (*lat.*, pound)
Lieut.	Lieutenant
lit.	literature; literary; literal
Lith.	Lithuanian
ll.	lines
Lt.	Lieutenant
Ltd.	Limited
m.	married; mile(s)
M.	Monsieur
Maj.	Major
Man.	Manitoba
Mar.	March
Mass.	Massachusetts
MCC	Marylebone Cricket Club
Md.	Maryland
M.D.	Medicinae Doctor (Doctor of Medicine)
Me.	Maine
Med.	Medical
Messrs.	Messieurs
MGM	Metro-Goldwyn-Mayer Co.
Mich.	Michigan
Mil.	Military
min(s).	minute(s)
Minn.	Minnesota
Miss.	Mississippi
M.I.T.	Massachusetts Institute of Technology
Mlle	Mademoiselle
Mme	Madame
Mo.	Missouri
Mongol.	Mongolian
Mont.	Montana
M.P.	Member of Parliament
mph	miles per hour
Mr.	Mister
Mrs.	Mistress
MS., ms.	manuscript
MSS., mss	manuscripts
Mt(s).	Mount; Mountain(s)
N.	North
NATO	North Atlantic Treaty Organization
N.B.	New Brunswick
NBC	National Broadcasting Corporation
N.C.	North Carolina

N. Dak.	North Dakota
N.E.	Northeast
Neb., Nebr.	Nebraska
Neth.	Netherlands
Nev.	Nevada
Newf.	Newfoundland
Nfld.	Newfoundland
N.H.	New Hampshire
N.J.	New Jersey
N. Mex.	New Mexico
no(s).	numero (*Lat.*, number)
Norw.	Norwegian
Nov.	November
N.S.	Nova Scotia
N.S.W.	New South Wales
N.T.	New Testament
N.W.	Northwest
N.Y.	New York
N.Y.C.	New York City
N.Y.U.	New York University
N.Z.	New Zealand
O.	Ohio
Oct.	October
Okla.	Oklahoma
Ont.	Ontario
Ore.	Oregon
orig.	original; originally
O.T.	Old Testament
oz(s).	ounce(s)
p.	page
Pa.	Pennsylvania
pat.	patented
P.E.I.	Prince Edward Island
Penn. State	Pennsylvania State (College *or* University)
Pers.	Persian
P.I.	Philippine Islands
pl.	plural
P.O.	Post Office
Pol.	Polish
Poly.	Polytechnic (Institute *or* School)
Port.	Portuguese
pp.	pages
P.R.	Puerto Rico
Pres.	President
prob.	probably
Prof.	Professor
pron.	pronounced, pronunciation
pub.	published
qq.v.	quae vide (*Lat.*, which see)
Que.	Quebec
q.v.	quod vide (*Lat.*, which see)
R.A.F.	Royal Air Force
rev.	revised
Rev.	Reverend
R.I.	Rhode Island
Rom.	Romanian
R.R.	Railroad
Russ.	Russian
Ry.	Railway
S.	South; Saint (*Ital.*, Santo)
Sask.	Saskatchewan
S.C.	South Carolina
Sc. Gael.	Scottish Gaelic
Scot.	Scottish
S. Dak.	South Dakota
S.E.	Southeast
SEATO	South East Asia Treaty Organization
sec(s).	second(s)
Sem.	Seminary
sep.	separated
Sept.	September
Serb.	Serbian
Serb.-Cr.	Serbo-Croatian
Skt.	Sanskrit
Span.	Spanish
specif.	specific; specifically
sq.	square
Sr., sr.	Senior
SS	Saints (*Ital.*, Santi; *Lat.*, Sancti)
St.	Saint; Street
Ste.	Sainte (*French*, feminine of Saint)
Sts.	Saints
S.W.	Southwest
Swed.	Swedish
Tech.	Technical; (Institute *or* School of) Technology
Tenn.	Tennessee
Tex.	Texas
Theol.	Theological; Theology
Turk.	Turkish
U.	University
U.C.L.A.	University of California at Los Angeles
U.K.	United Kingdom
Ukrain.	Ukrainian
UN	United Nations (Organization)
UNESCO	United Nations Educational, Scientific, and Cultural Organization
Univ(s).	University; Universities
UNRRA	United Nations Relief and Rehabilitation Administration
U.S.	United States (of America)
U.S.A.	United States of America
U.S.S.	United States Ship
U.S.S.R.	Union of Soviet Socialist Republics
usu.	usual(ly)
v.	versus
Va.	Virginia
V.C.	Victoria Cross
V.I.	Virgin Islands
viz.	videlicet (*Lat.*, namely)
V.M.I.	Virginia Military Institute
vol(s).	volume(s)
V.P.I.	Virginia Polytechnic Institute
vs.	versus
Vt.	Vermont
W.	West
Wash.	Washington
W.I.	West Indies
Wis.	Wisconsin
W. Va.	West Virginia
Wyo.	Wyoming
Yid.	Yiddish
Y.M.C.A.	Young Men's Christian Association
Yugo.	Yugoslavian
Y.W.C.A.	Young Women's Christian Association

Pronunciation Symbols

For more information see Guide to Pronunciation

ə .... banana, collide, abut

ˈə, ˌə .... humdrum, abut

^{ə} .... immediately preceding \l\, \n\, \m\, \ŋ\, as in battle, mitten, eaten, and sometimes open \ˈōp-^{ə}m\, lock and key \-^{ə}ŋ-\; immediately following \l\, \m\, \r\, as often in French table, prisme, titre

ər .... further, urger, bird, opportunity

ˈər-, ˈə-r .... as in two different pronunciations of hurry \ˈhər-ē, ˈhə-rē\

a .... mat, map, mad, gag, snap, patch

ā .... day, fade, date, aorta, drape, cape

ä .... bother, cot, and, with most American speakers, father, cart

ȧ .... father as pronounced by speakers who do not rhyme it with *bother*; French patte

aů .... now, loud, out

b .... baby, rib

b̲ .... Spanish hablar

ch .... chin, nature \ˈnā-chər\ (actually, this sound is \t\ + \sh\)

d .... did, adder

e .... bet, bed, peck

ˈē, ˌē .... beat, nosebleed, evenly, easy

ē .... easy, mealy

f .... fifty, cuff

g .... go, big, gift

g̲ .... Spanish luego

h .... hat, ahead

hl .... Welsh llan, Icelandic hlusta

hw .... whale as pronounced by those who do not have the same pronunciation for both *whale* and *wail*

i .... tip, banish, active

ī .... site, side, buy, tripe (actually, this sound is \ä\ + \i\, or \ȧ\ + \i\)

j .... job, gem, edge, join, judge (actually, this sound is \d\ + \zh\)

k .... kin, cook, ache

k̲ .... German ich, Buch; one pronunciation of loch

l .... lily, pool

m .... murmur, dim, nymph

n .... no, own

^{n} .... indicates that a preceding vowel or diphthong is pronounced with the nasal passages open, as in French *un bon vin blanc* \œ^{n}-bō^{n}-va^{n}-blä^{n}\

ŋ .... sing \ˈsiŋ\, singer \ˈsiŋ-ər\, finger \ˈfiŋ-gər\, ink \ˈiŋk\

ō .... bone, know, beau

ȯ .... saw, all, gnaw, caught

œ .... French boeuf, German Hölle

œ̄ .... French feu, German Höhle

ȯi .... coin, destroy

p .... pepper, lip

r .... red, car, rarity

s .... source, less

sh .... as in shy, mission, machine, special (actually, this is a single sound, not two); with a hyphen between, two sounds as in *grasshopper* \ˈgras-ˌhäp-ər\

t .... tie, attack, late, latter

th .... as in thin, ether (actually, this is a single sound, not two); with a hyphen between, two sounds as in *knighthood* \ˈnīt-ˌhu̇d\

t̲h̲ .... then, either, this (actually, this is a single sound, not two)

ü .... rule, youth, union \ˈyün-yən\, few \ˈfyü\

u̇ .... pull, wood, book, curable \ˈkyu̇r-ə-bəl\

ue .... German füllen, hübsch

ue̅ .... French rue, German fühlen

v .... vivid, give

w .... we, away, evaluate \i-ˈval-yə-ˌwāt\

y .... yard, young, cue \ˈkyü\, union \ˈyün-yən\

^{y} .... indicates that during the articulation of the sound represented by the preceding character the front of the tongue has substantially the position it has for the articulation of the first sound of *yard*, as in French *digne* \dēn^{y}\

z .... zone, raise

zh .... with nothing between, as in vision, azure \ˈazh-ər\ (actually, this is a single sound, not two); with a hyphen between, two sounds as in *hogshead* \ˈhȯgz-ˌhed, ˈhägz-ˌhed\

\ .... slant line used in pairs to mark the beginning and end of a transcription: \ˈpen\

ˈ .... mark preceding a syllable with primary (strongest) stress: \ˈpen-mən-ˌship\

ˌ .... mark preceding a syllable with secondary (medium) stress: \ˈpen-mən-ˌship\

\- .... mark of syllable division

( ) .... indicate that what is symbolized between is present in some utterances but not in others: *factory* \ˈfak-t(ə-)rē\

A

Aa·ge·sen \'ō-gə-sən\, Svend. 12th century. Earliest Danish historian. Author of *Compendiosa historia regum daniae,* recording Danish history from 300 to 1185.

Aaḥmes. See AHMOSE.

Aak·jaer \'ōg-yer\, Jeppe. *Orig. surname* Jen·sen \'yen-sən\. 1866–1930. Danish poet and novelist. Verse published in *Fri felt* (1905), *Rugens sange* (1906); several of his poems have become popular folk songs, as "Jens Vejmand"; novels, including *Vredens børn* (1904) and *Gärende Kräfte* (1916), reflected social consciousness and regionalist movement.

Aal·to \'äl-tō\, Alvar, *in full* Hugo Alvar Henrik. 1898–1976. Finnish architect and designer. Major works included Sunila Pulp Mill at Kotka, hospitals, as sanatorium at Paimio, libraries, as library at Viipuri, town hall at Säynätsalo, theaters, stores, and private dwellings; noted for use of natural materials, esp. wood, irregular forms, light; designed laminated wood furniture. His wife ¶Aino (d. 1949) collaborated with him in architectural work and furniture designing.

Aan·rud \'ōn-rüd\, Hans. 1863–1953. Norwegian writer. Author of stories of peasant life and such comedies as *Storken* (1895), *Høit tilhest* (1901), *Hanen* (1906).

Aa·re·strup \'ō-rə-ˌstrüp\, Carl Ludvig Emil. 1800–1856. Danish lyric poet. Published *Digte* (1838).

Aar·on \'ar-ən, 'er-\. fl. c.14th century B.C. Traditional founder of Hebrew priesthood. Elder brother of Moses, with whom, according to biblical book of Exodus, he led the Israelites out of Egypt. Succeeded by his son Eleazar; another son, Ithamar, was ancestor of Eli.

Aaron ben Eli·jah \-ben-i-'lī-jə\. 1328 or 1330–1369. Jewish theologian. Lived in Constantinople; compiled three books of Karaite lore, *'Etz Ḥayyim* (1346), *Gan Eden* (1354), *Keter Torah* (1362), constituting main philosophical basis for Karaite movement.

Aaron ben Me·ir \-ˌben-mā-'ir\. 10th century. Palestinian Talmudist. Proposed (921) a radical calendar reform on which he was opposed by Sa'adia ben Joseph.

Aa·sen \'ō-sən\, Ivar Andreas. 1813–1896. Norwegian philologist. From Old Norwegian and various dialects constructed Landsmål (later called Nynorsk) language to replace official Dano-Norwegian; published *Det norske folkesprog grammatik* (1848), *Ordbog over det norske folkesprog* (1850).

Aba·hai \'ä-'bä-'hī\. *Reign titles* T'ien-ts'ung \tē-'ent-'sůŋ\ *and* Ch'ung-te \'chůŋ-'de\. 1592–1643. Manchu leader and emperor of China. Son of Nurhachi. After death of father (1626) eliminated brothers and other rivals and consolidated rule over Manchu tribes; conquered Inner Mongolia and Korea; perfected military organization called Eight Banners; in raids on northern China captured Chinese bureaucrats who reorganized Manchu government; established Ch'ing dynasty and began conquest of Ming dynasty completed in reign of his son Shun-chih.

Abailard, Pierre. See Peter ABELARD.

Aba·ka·no·wicz \ˌäb-ä-'kän-ō-ˌvits\, Bruno Abdank. 1852–1900. Lithuanian mathematician. Known for invention (c.1880) of integraph.

Abarbanel. See ABRABANEL.

Abar·ca de Bo·lea \ä-'b̲är-kä-t̲h̲ā-bō-'lā-ä\, Pedro Pablo. Conde de Aran·da \-t̲h̲ā-ä-'rän-t̲h̲ä\. 1718–1798. Spanish general and politician. Artillery officer; ambassador to Portugal (1755), Poland (1760); captain general of Valencia (1764); appointed president of Council of Castile by Charles III (1766–73); restored order and instilled public confidence in Charles's autocratic reforms; carried out expulsion of Jesuits (1767); ambassador to France (1773–87); prime interior minister to Charles IV (1792); dismissed from Council of State and banished (1794) for opposition to war with France.

Abas·cal y Sou·sa \äb̲-äs-'käl-ē-'sō-sä\, José Fernando. Marqués de la Con·cor·dia \-t̲h̲ā-läk-ōŋ-'kört̲h̲-yä\. 1743–1821. Spanish statesman and general. Governor of Cuba (1796); commander and intendant of Nueva Galicia (Mexico, 1799); viceroy of Peru (1804–16); successfully held Peru against revolutionaries (from 1810).

Aba·si·ya·nık \ˌäb-ä-si-'yän-ək\, Sait Faik. 1907–1954. Turkish writer. With short stories collected in *Semaver* (1936), *Lüzumsuz odam* (1948), *Kumpanya* (1951), *Alemdağda var bir yilan* (1953), etc., gained reputation as one of most important of modern Turkish writers; also wrote experimental novel *Bir takım insanlar* (1952).

Abate *or* **Abati,** Niccolò dell'. See ABBATE.

Abau·zit \å-bō-zēt\, Firmin. 1679–1767. French Protestant theologian and philosopher. Traveled widely; librarian of Geneva (from 1727); helped produce new French *New Testament,* contributed to *Encyclopédie.*

Ab·ba Ari·ka \'äb-bä-å-'rik̲-ä\. *Usually called* Rab *Heb* 'räv, *Angl* 'rab \. 2d–3d century A.D. Babylonian rabbi. Founded (c.220) Jewish Academy of Sura; a founder of systematic study of the Mishna.

'Ab·bād \ab-'bäd\. Name of several Muslim rulers in Andalusia: 'Abbād I, *orig.* Abū al-Qāsim Muḥammad ibn 'Abbād. d. 1042. Founder of 'Abbādid dynasty of Seville. As *qāḍī* of Seville, seized occasion of anarchy in Córdoba to secure control of Seville and establish new throne (1023). His son ¶'Abbād II, *orig.* al-Mu'taḍid (reigned 1042–69), poet and patron of letters; noted for cruelty; seized several Berber kingdoms; forced to pay tribute to Ferdinand I of Castile. His son ¶'Abbād III, *orig.* al-Mu'tamid (1040–1095), seized Córdoba (1071); held a gay court, giving rise to many legends; aroused enmity of Christians, esp. of Alfonso VI of Castile; called to his aid Ibn Tāshufīn of the Almoravid dynasty, who defeated Alfonso at Zallāqah (1086); later (1091) deposed by them and sent into exile.

'Ab·bād·ids \'ab-ə-didz\. Short-lived Muslim dynasty founded by 'Abbād I and ruling (1023–91) at Seville in southern Spain; overthrown by the Almoravids.

Ab·ba·die \å-bå-dē\, Antoine-Thomson d' (1810–1897) and his brother Arnaud-Michel d' (1815–1893). French explorers, b. Dublin. Conducted explorations in Ethiopia (1838–48); studied geology, geography, archaeology, natural history of country; Antoine published reports on topography (1860–73), geography (1890), and catalog of Ethiopian manuscripts (1859); Arnaud published *Douze ans de séjour dans la Haute Éthiopie* (1868).

Ab·ba Ma·ri ben Moses ben Joseph \'äb-bä-'mä-rē-\ of Lu·nel \lü-nel\. *Pseudonym* As·truc \ås-trœ̄k\. *Also called* ha-Ya·re·ḥa \hä-'yär-ä-k̲ä\. 1250?–after 1306. French Jewish theologian. Disturbed by spread of rationalist philosophy of Aristotelians, leading to heterodoxy and allegorical interpretation of scripture, wrote series of letters to Rabbi Solomon ben Abraham Adret that led to latter's public ban on study or teaching of science and philosophy by those under 25 (1305); settled in Perpignan after expulsion of Jews from France (1306); published correspondence with Adret as *Minḥat qenaot.*

'Ab·bās \ab-'bäs\. *In full* al-'Abbās ibn 'Abd al-Muṭṭalib. 566–c.653. Paternal uncle of Muḥammad. Rich merchant of Mecca; one of chief apostles of Islām; ancestor of dynasty of Abbasids.

'Ab·bās \ab-'bäs\. Name of two khedives (viceroys) of Egypt:

'Abbās I. 1813–1854. Khedive (1848–54). Grandson of Muḥammad 'Alī Pasha, whose reforms he opposed and in part reversed; blocked construction of Suez Canal; reduced army, but sent force to support Ottomans in Crimea (1853).

'Abbās II. *Called* 'Ab·bās Ḥil·mī Pa·sha \ab-'bäs-'hil-mi-'på-shä\. 1874–1944. Last khedive of Egypt (1892–1914). Son of Tawfiq Pasha. Attempted to rule independent of British influence; encouraged nationalist movement; allowed formation (1907) of National party under Muṣṭafā Kāmil; deposed when British protectorate over Egypt established (1914).

'Abbās. Name of three shāhs of Persia of the Ṣafavid dynasty:

'Abbās I. *Called* the Great. 1571–1629. Shāh (1588–1629). Son of Shāh Solṭān Moḥammad. Created Persia's first standing army; defeated the Uzbeks near Herat (1598) and drove them from Persia; transferred capital to Isfahan; fought long war (from 1603) with Ottoman Turks; defeated Turks at Basra

(1605) and at Sultanieh (1618) and regained lost Persian territory; besieged and took Baghdad (1623); made many reforms in the country, fostered trade with Europe, and patronized flowering of Persian arts.

'Abbās II. 1633–1666. Shāh (1642–66). Son of Safi I; regained Kandahar (1648).

'Abbās III. Shāh (1732–36). Son of Ṭahmāsp II; child ruler, last of the Ṣafavid dynasty; deposed by Nāder Shāh.

'Ab·bā·sids \'ab-bə-sidz\. Second great Muslim dynasty of the Caliphate, ruling 750–1258; founded by Abū al-'Abbās as-Saffāh, who overthrew Umayyad dynasty.

'Ab·bās Mīr·zā \ab-'bäs-'mēr-'zä\. 1789–1833. Persian prince. Son of Fatḥ 'Alī. Commanded Iranian army in war with Russia (1804–13); unsuccessful in preventing loss of Persian provinces in Caucasus; began reform of army on British model, sending students to England and translating European manuals; won against Turks at Erzurum (1821); after initial success, lost Armenia in second Russian war (1826–28).

Ab·ba·te \äb-'bä-tā\ *or* **Aba·te** \ä-'bä-\, Niccolò dell'. c.1512–1571. Italian painter. Painter, esp. of landscapes, of the Bolognese school; at court of Henry II and Charles IX of France (1552–71); helped introduce Mannerist painting to France.

Ab·be \'ab-ē\, Cleveland. 1838–1916. American meteorologist, b. New York City. Director, Cincinnati Observatory (1868); recruited corps of weather observers reporting by telegraph and began issuing weather reports (1869); influenced founding of U.S. Weather Service (1870) and served in it (1871–1916).

Ab·be \'äb-ə\, Ernst. 1840–1905. German physicist and industrialist. On faculty, U. of Jena (from 1863); directed research for optical firm of Carl Zeiss (from 1866); partner (1876); took over management of firm after death of Zeiss (1888) and reorganized it (1896) into a co-operative industry. Established (1891) with his own fortune the Carl-Zeiss-Stiftung for scientific research and social betterment. Noted for work in optics and improvements in optical glass and instruments, esp. the microscope; discovered Abbe sine condition, invented (1868) apochromatic lens.

Ab·bey \'ab-ē\, Edwin Austin. 1852–1911. American painter and illustrator, b. Philadelphia. *Harper's Weekly* staff illustrator (from 1871); to London (1878). Illustrated *Selections from the Poetry of Robert Herrick* (1882), *Old Songs* (1889), comedies of Shakespeare (from 1896). Executed panels, illustrating the *Quest of the Holy Grail,* for Boston Public Library (1890–1902). Painted coronation portrait for Edward VII (1902); executed group of murals at Pennsylvania State Capitol (1911).

Ab·bon \á-bōⁿ\ of Fleu·ry \flœ-rē\. Saint. *Lat.* Ab·bo Flo·ri·a·cen·sis \'ab-ō-,flō-rē-ə-'sen-səs\. c.945–1004. French religious and theologian. Established monastery school at Ramsey, England (985); elected abbot of Fleury (988); strong supporter of papal authority and monastic reform.

Abbot, Anthony. See Charles F. OURSLER.

Ab·bot \'ab-ət\, Charles Greeley. 1872–1973. American astrophysicist, b. Wilton, N.H. Assistant (1895), director (1907–44), Smithsonian Astrophysical Observatory; secretary, Smithsonian Institution (1928–44). Carried out research on solar radiation. Author of *The Sun* (1911), *The Earth and the Stars* (1925), *The Sun and the Welfare of Man* (1929).

Abbot, Ezra. 1819–1884. American biblical scholar, b. Jackson, Me. Professor, Harvard Divinity School (from 1872); member of New Testament Committee for Revision of English Bible (from 1871).

Abbot, Francis Ellingwood. 1836–1903. American clergyman and philosopher, b. Boston. Formed Free Religious Association (1869), National Liberal League (1876). Author of *Scientific Theism* (1881), *The Way Out of Agnosticism* (1890), *The Syllogistic Philosophy* (1906).

Abbot, George. 1562–1633. English prelate. Dean of Winchester (1600); bishop of Lichfield and Coventry (1609), of London (1610); recognized leader of English Calvinists; author of *A Brief Description of the Whole Worlde* (1599); archbishop of Canterbury (from 1611). One of translators of New Testament in King James Bible (1611).

Abbot, Henry Larcom. 1831–1927. American soldier and engineer, b. Beverly, Mass. Assisted Capt. Andrew A. Humphreys in investigating flood-protection questions of the lower Mississippi (1857–61); appointed to command Engineer Battalion at Willett's Point, N.Y. (1865); developed Engineer School of Application. Member (1904) of board of consulting engineers to determine plan of a Panama canal.

Ab·bott \'ab-ət\, Charles. 1st Baron Ten·ter·den \'ten-tər-dən\. 1762–1832. English jurist. Chief justice (from 1818).

Abbott, Grace. 1878–1939. American social worker, b. Grand Island, Nebr. Helped organize (1908) and head (1908–17) of Immigrants' Protective League, Chicago; chief of U.S. Children's Bureau, Washington, D.C. (1921–34). Author of *The Child and the State* (1938). Her sister ¶Edith (1876–1957), dean (1924–42) of School of Social Service Administration, U. of Chicago. Author of *Women in Industry* (1910), books on the immigration problem, *The Tenements of Chicago* (1936), *Public Assistance* (1939).

Abbott, Jacob. 1803–1879. American clergyman and author, b. Hallowell, Me. Father of Lyman Abbott. Founded in Boston (1829) Mount Vernon School for girls. Won success with *The Young Christian* (1832); became known as writer of juveniles, including the *Rollo* books (28 vols.: *Rollo at Play, Rollo's Travels,* etc., from 1834), *Franconia Stories* (10 vols.), etc.

Abbott, Sir John Joseph Caldwell. 1821–1893. Canadian politician. Dean of law faculty, McGill U. (1855–80); member of Legislative Assembly (1857–74, 1880–87); member of federal Senate (1887–92); minister without portfolio (1887–91); prime minister (1891–92). Mayor of Montreal (1887–89).

Abbott, Lyman. 1835–1922. American clergyman, author, and editor, b. Roxbury, Mass. Son of Jacob Abbott. Editor, *Illustrated Christian Weekly* (1870). Joined Henry Ward Beecher (1876) in editorship of *Christian Union,* succeeding him (1881) as editor in chief and continuing when paper changed to *The Outlook* (1893). Succeeded Beecher in pulpit of Plymouth Congregational Church in Brooklyn (1890–99). Author of *Christianity and Social Problems* (1897), *Henry Ward Beecher* (1903), *The Great Companion* (1904), *The Spirit of Democracy* (1910).

Abbott, Robert Sengstacke. 1868–1940. American publisher and editor, b. St. Simons Island, Ga. Founded (1905) and edited (1905–40) *Chicago Defender,* leading newspaper devoted to interests of Negro community; led in anti-lynching campaign.

Abbott, Samuel Warren. 1837–1904. American physician, b. Woburn, Mass. Secretary of Massachusetts Board of Health (1886–1904); leader in public health movement, esp. in establishing vital statistics as field of study and as government responsibility; wrote *Past and Present Condition of Public Hygiene and State Medicine in the United States* (1900).

'Abd al-. See also names beginning ABDUL.

'Abd al-'Azīz \əb-,dul-az-'ēz\. *In full* 'Abd al-'Azīz ibn Mūsa ibn Nuṣayr. d. 716. Son of Mūsa. First amir (713–716) of conquered region of southern Spain; made Seville his capital.

'Abd al-'Azīz *or* **'Abd al-'Azīz IV.** *In full* 'Abd al-'Azīz ibn al-Ḥasan ibn Muḥammad al-Ḥasanī al-'Alawī. 1878 or 1881–1943. Sultan of Morocco (1894–1908). His modern ideas, friendliness to foreigners, and attempts to introduce modern administrative methods led to unrest; last years of reign (1904–08) marked by exploits of bandit Raisuli; deposed by revolt led by his brother Moulay Abd al-Hafid, who succeeded him.

'Abd al-Azīz. See also IBN SA'ŪD.

'Abd al-Gha·nī ibn Is·mā·'īl an-Nā·bu·lu·sī \əb-dul-gän-ē-,ib-ən-,is-mä-'ēl-ə(n)-,nə-bul-u-'sē\. 1641–1731. Syrian mystic and poet. Author of accounts of his travels throughout Islāmic world, of works on Ṣūfī mysticism, etc.

'Abd al-Ilāh \əb-,dul-ē-'lä\. 1913–1958. Ruler of Iraq. Son of Hashemite king, 'Alī ibn Ḥusayn of the Hejaz; named regent for cousin Fayṣal II of Iraq (1939); fled pro-German revolt but restored with British help (1941); worked with Nuri as-Said to establish pro-Western policy; relinquished rule to King Fayṣal (1953); continued as crown prince and leading adviser to king.

Abd al-Karim Qasim. See Abdul KASSEM.

'Abd al-Karīm Quṭb ad-Dīn ibn Ibrāhīm al-Jīlī. See JĪLĪ.

'Abd Allāh. See also ABDULLAH.

'Abd Al·lāh \(,)əb-dul-'ä\. 9th–10th century. Umayyad ruler in Spain. Amir (888–912).

'Abd Allāh. *In full* 'Abd Allāh ibn Muḥammad at-Ta'ī'ishī. *Called* 'Ab·dul·la·hi \əb-,dul-ä-'hē\. 1846–1899. Sudanese Islāmic leader. Became (c.1880) a follower of Muḥammad Aḥmad, the Mahdī, who appointed him a caliph; succeeded (1885) to leadership of Mahdist movement; defeated in invasion of Egypt (1889); driven out of capital Omdurman by Anglo-Egyptian force (1896–98); killed in battle.

'Abd Allāh ibn al-'Ab·bās \-ib-ən-əl-əb-'bäs\. *Called* Ibn Ab·bās \,ib-ən-ab-'bäs\, al-Ḥibr \al-'hib(-ə)r\, *and* al-Baḥr \al-'bä-hər\. c.619–687 or 688. Islāmic scholar. Supported 'Alī in struggle for caliphate and was appointed governor of Baṣra; later fled to Mecca, thence to the Hejaz and aṭ-Ṭā'if. Known as first exegete of the Qur'ān.

'Abd Allāh ibn az-Zu·bayr \-ib-ən-ə(z)-zu-'bīr\. 624–692. Islāmic soldier and rebel. Took part in many military campaigns; appointed by caliph 'Uthmān to assist in compiling official recension of Qur'ān; opposed Umayyad rise to power and refused to pledge allegiance to caliph Yazīd (680); fled to Mecca and gathered army; withstood siege by Yazīd's army until latter's death (683); killed in new siege by caliph 'Abd al-Malik.

'Abd Allāh ibn Is·kan·dar \-is-kän-'där\. 1532 or 1533–1598. Shaybānid ruler. Conquered Bukhara (1557); placed father on throne of united Uzbek realm (1561) while retaining real power himself; campaigning almost continuously, captured Balkh (1573–74), Samarkand (1578), Tashkent (1582–83); succeeded father on throne; conducted raids against Shī'ite Iran (1593–94, 1595–96).

ʽAbd Allāh ibn Saʽd ibn Abī Sarḥ \-ˌib-ən-ˈsäd-ˌib-ən-äb-ˈē-ˈsärk̲\. d. c.656. Muslim ruler of Egypt. Under caliph ʽUthmān ruled as governor of Upper Egypt (644–656); with future caliph Muʽāwiyah I formed first Muslim navy, which seized Cyprus (647-649), Rhodes, and Cos and defeated Byzantine fleets off Alexandria (652) and Lycian coast (655); attacked Christian Nubian kingdom (651–652).

ʽAbd Al·lāh ibn Yā·sīn \əb-dů-ˈlä-ˌib-ən-yä-ˈsēn\. d. c.1060. Moroccan Islāmic scholar and reformer. Helped inspire and became leader of the Almoravids movement among Berber tribes in northwestern Africa.

ʽAbd al-Ma·lik ibn Mar·wān \əb-ˌdůl-mə-ˈlik-ˌib-ən-mär-ˈwän\. 646 or 647–705. Fifth Umayyad caliph (685–705). Son of Marwān I. Driven from Medina with father (683); spent first years of reign in putting down revolts of rival caliphs; with aid of his general al-Ḥajjaj, defeated Muṣʽab (691) and his brother, anticaliph Ibn az-Zubayr (692) and united Islām; at war with Byzantine emperors, esp. Justinian II, but results indecisive; captured North African territory, including (697) Carthage; first caliph to coin purely Arabic money; made improvements in administration and established Arabic as official language; built Dome of the Rock, Jerusalem.

ʽAbd al-Muʼ·min \-ˈmů-min\. *In full* ʽAbd al-Muʼmin ibn-ʽAlī ibn Makhlūf ibn Yuʽlā ibn Marwān. *Also called* Abū Muḥammad al-Kūmī. d. 1163. Berber leader and founder of Almohad dynasty. Became (c.1117) follower of Ibn Tūmart, founder of sect of Almohads; after Ibn Tūmart's death (1130) succeeded as leader of Almohads, assumed title of caliph, and began conquest of North Africa; with capture of Marrakesh put end to Almoravid dynasty (1147); conquered Tunis and Tripoli (1158–59); secured allegiance of most of Muslim Spain.

ʽAbd al-Muṭ·ṭa·lib \-ˈmůt-tə-lib\. d. 578. Grandfather of Muḥammad and his guardian for about two years.

ʽAbd al-Qā·dir al-Jī·lā·nī \-ˈkä-dir-əl-jē-ˈlän-ē\. d. 1166. Ṣūfī leader. Founder of Qādirīyah order of Ṣūfīs, a moderate order concerned with economic activity and humanitarian work; considered greatest of Ṣūfī saints.

ʽAbd al-Wah·hāb \-wa-ˈhäb\, Muḥammad ibn. 1703–1792. Islāmic reformer. While a teacher in Iran began (1736) enunciating doctrine of return to pure Islām; opposed all innovations in faith and practice; wrote *Kitāb at-tawḥīd,* principal text of what became Muwaḥḥidūn, or Wahhābī movement; teachings adopted by Ibn Saʽūd (1744), and spread by conquest to most of Arabia.

ʽAbd ar-Raḥ·mān \əb-ˌdůr-räk̲-ˈmän\. Name of several Umayyad rulers in Spain, including:

ʽAbd ar-Raḥmān I. *Called* Ad-Dākhil Raḥmān \əd-ˈdäk̲-ēl-\. 731–788. Grandson of Hishām. After overthrow of Umayyad caliphate by ʽAbbāsids (750), escaped massacre of members of family; made his way to Spain and exploited Arab rivalries to gain power; defeated rivals and established amirate in Córdoba (756); with other exiles of Umayyad caliphate established new administrative system; subdued Spanish Berbers, defeated armies of ʽAbbāsids and of Charlemagne (778).

ʽAbd ar-Raḥmān II. 788–852. Grandson of ʽAbd ar-Raḥmān I. Fourth amir (822–852). Patron of music and letters; built many fine structures in Córdoba.

ʽAbd ar-Raḥmān III an-Nā·ṣir \-ən-ˈnä-sir\. 891–961. Eighth amir (912–929); caliph (929–961). Succeeded grandfather ʽAbd Allāh as amir; revitalized strong central government; subdued rebels, capturing Seville (913), Bobastro (928), Toledo (933); seized part of Morocco in opposition to Fāṭimid caliphs; at war with kings of León and Navarre during much of his reign, defeating them esp. at Valdejunquera (920); assumed title of caliph (929); during his reign, Umayyad caliphate of Spain reached zenith of its power; made Córdoba most important center of learning in Europe.

ʽAbd ar-Raḥmān al-Ghā·fi·qī \-əl-ˈgäf-ik-ē\. Moorish soldier. d. 732. Led Saracen army through western Pyrenees into France (732); met Franks under Charles Martel at Tours, near Poitiers (732); defeated and killed in great battle.

ʽAbd ar-Raḥmān ibn Hi·shām \-ˌib-ən-hish-ˈäm\. 1789 or 1790–1859. Twenty-fourth ʽAlawid ruler of Morocco (1822–59). Involved in disputes with Austria, Spain, and England because of piracy practiced by his subjects; sided with Abdelkader (1844) in war against France; both badly defeated by Bugeaud in battle of Isly (1844); made peace with France.

Ab·del·ka·der \ˌäb-dəl-ˈkäd-ər\. *Arab. in full* ʽAbd al-Qādir ibn Muḥyī ad-Dīn ibn Muṣṭafā al-Ḥasanī al-Jazāʼirī. 1808–1883. Algerian leader. Elected (1832) to succeed father as head of Qādirīyah Muslim brotherhood; conducted war of harassment against French; won control of interior of Oran in Treaty of Desmichels (1834); expanded control in Treaty of Tafna (1837); organized modern Algerian state with capitals at Mascara and Tiaret (Tagdempt); conquered Saharan territory (1838–39); defeated by French in war of attrition conducted by Gen. Bugeaud (1840–47); surrendered himself from Moroccan exile and held prisoner in France (1847–52); later lived exemplary religious life in Bursa and Damascus.

Abd el-Krim \ˌab-dəl-ˈkrēm\. *Arab. in full* Muḥammad ibn ʽAbd al-Karīm al-Khaṭṭābī. 1882–1963. Berber leader. Abandoned career in Spanish colonial government in Morocco to begin organizing resistance (1919); defeated Spanish army at Annoual (1921); formed Republic of the Rif and served as its president (1921–26); organized modern state on traditional Berber tribal institutions; attacked French colonials and nearly captured Fez (1925); defeated by large Franco-Spanish force under Marshal Pétain (1926) and exiled to Réunion (1926–47); later lived in Egypt.

ʽAbd ol-Ba·hāʼ \ˌab-dəl-bä-ˈhä\. 1844–1921. Persian religious leader. Son of Bahāʼ Allāh. Succeeded father as leader of Bahāʼī sect (1892–1921); traveled extensively in Europe, Africa, America (1910–13).

ʽAb·dor·raḥ·mān Khān \ˌäb-dȯr-ˈäk̲-män-ˈk̲än\. c.1844–1901. Ruler of Afghanistan. Grandson of Dōst Moḥammad Khān. Driven into exile by Shīr ʽAlī (1869); returned (1880) and proclaimed amir; negotiated removal of British troops, while leaving Britain control of foreign affairs; consolidated rule by defeating Ayūb Khān, Isḥāq Khān, and rebel Ghilzai tribe; agreed on Durand Line as Afghanistan–Indian border (1893).

ʽAb·duh \ˈäb-(ˌ)dü, -(ˌ)dů\, Muḥammad. 1849–1905. Egyptian scholar and reformer. Follower (from 1872) of Jamāl ad-Dīn al-Afghānī's pan-Islāmic movement; exiled for participation in ʽUrābī Pasha's rebellion (1882); returned to Egypt (1888); appointed judge in National Courts of First Instance (1888), Court of Appeal (1891); named *muftī* of Egypt (1899); through decisions and other writings did much to reconcile modern civilization and liberal reform with Islāmic tradition and theology; fostered secular education.

Abdul. See also names beginning ABD AL-.

Ab·dül·a·ziz \ˌäb-dūel-ä-ˈzēz\. *In full* Abdülaziz Oglu Mahmud II. 1830–1876. Ottoman sultan (1861–76). Son of Mahmud II; brother and successor of Abdülmecid I. Continued brother's westernizing program; encouraged public education; promulgated first Ottoman civil code; first sultan to visit Western Europe (1867); after 1871 rule became more absolutist; turned to Russia; established Bulgarian exarchate (1870); revolt in Herzegovina and Bosnia (1875) spread to Turkey and he was deposed; committed suicide or murdered.

Ab·dül·hak Hâ·mid \ˌäb-dūel-ˈhäk-hä-ˈmēd\. 1852–1937. Turkish poet and playwright. Followed father in diplomatic service; member of Turkish senate (1908) and of Grand National Assembly (1928); wrote plays inspired by 19th century Tanzimat movement and by Western Romanticism, including *Tarik, Tezer, Eshber, Ibn-i Musa, Finten.*

Ab·dül·ha·mid \ˌäb-dūel-hä-ˈmēd\. Name of two Ottoman sultans:

Abdülhamid I. 1725–1789. Sultan (1774–89). Son of Ahmed III. Succeeded his brother Mustafa III. Forced to conclude war with Russia in Treaty of Küçük Kaynarca (1774), ceding territory and privileges; following Russian annexation of Crimea (1783), declared war again (1787).

Abdülhamid II. 1842–1918. Sultan (1876–1909). Son of Abdülmecid I; succeeded his brother Murad V. Promulgated first Ottoman constitution (1876) and appointed liberal Midhat Paşa as grand vizier; harsh suppression of insurrection in Balkans led to war with Russia (1877–78); lost most of his possessions in Europe by Treaty of San Stefano (1878); suspended constitution (1878) and ruled autocratically from seclusion; responsible for Armenian massacres (1895–96); driven to war with Greece by revolts in Crete (1896–97); maintained support largely through appeals to pan-Islāmism. His misgovernment led to prolonged period (1896–1908) of discontent and increasing strength of Young Turk movement; faced with their revolutionary activity, restored (1908) constitution of 1876; supported unsuccessful reactionary uprising (1909) and thereupon deposed.

Abdul Kasim. See ABŪ AL-QĀSIM.

Abdullah. See also ʽABD ALLĀH.

Ab·dul·lah \əb-dů-ˈlä\. *Arab. in full* ʽAbd Allāh ibn al-Ḥusayn. 1882–1951. King of Jordan (1946–51). Son of Ḥusayn ibn ʽAlī. Took lead in negotiations with British leading to Arab declaration of revolt against Ottomans (1916); declined throne of Iraq (1920); occupied (1920) and made amir of British mandate of TransJordan (1921); became king on independence of Jordan (1946); occupied (1948) and annexed (1950) West Bank of Jordan River; assassinated by Palestinian nationalist.

Ab·dul·lah bin Ab·dul Ka·dir \əb-dů-ˈlä-bin-əb-ˈdůl-kä-ˈdir\, Munshi. 1796–1854. Malay writer. Secretary and translator to Sir Thomas Raffles (1811); translated many Western works into Malay; in those and in his own travel writings, as *Kesah Pelayaran Abdullah* and autobiographical *Hikayat Abdullah,* transformed Malay literature by introduction of realism.

ʽAbdullahi. See ʽABD ALLĀH (1846–1899).

ʽAbdullahi ibn Muḥammad. See ʽABD ALLĀH.

Ab·dül·me·cid I \ˌäb-dūel-mej-ˈēd\. 1823–1861. Ottoman sultan (1839–61). Son of Mahmud II. Ascended throne following Ottoman defeat at Nizip by Egypt; his rights protected by powers in Treaty of London (1840). Began to carry out reforms of predecessors, aided by chief adviser, Reşid Paşa; issued decrees (1839, 1856) granting various rights to citizens, including Christians; reorganized army, courts; fostered education. Engaged in Crimean War (1853–56), securing alliance (1854) with England and France.

Abdülmecid II. 1868–1944. Last Ottoman caliph (1922–24). Son of Sultan Abdülaziz. Named crown prince (1918); proclaimed caliph in succession to his cousin Mehmed VI and after abolition of sultanate; to Switzerland on abolition (1924) of caliphate by Mustafa Kemal Atatürk.

Ab·dul Mu·is \əb-ˈdu̇l-mü-ˈēs\. 1890–1959. Indonesian nationalist. A leader of Sarekat Islām, religious-nationalist organization.

Ab·dul Rah·man \əb-ˌdu̇l-räk̲-ˈmän\. Tuanku (prince). 1895–1960. Malayan politician. Son of ruler of Negri Sembilan. Trained in law in England; succeeded father as ruler of Negri Sembilan (1933); chosen chief of state of newly independent Federation of Malaya (1957–60).

Ab·dul Ra·zak \-rä-ˈzäk\, Tun. 1922–1976. Malaysian politician. Deputy prime minister of Federation of Malaya (1957–63) and of Malaysia (1963–70); prime minister, minister of foreign affairs and of defense, Malaysia (1970–76); fostered economic development, nonaligned foreign policy.

ʽAbd-uṣ-Ṣa·mad \əb-du̇s-sa-ˈmad\, Khwāja. 16th century. Persian painter. To India (1549) at invitation of emperor Humāyūn; taught future emperor Akbar, also Dasvant; named master of the mint (1576), dewan of Multān (1584) by Akbar. A founder, with Mīr Sayyid ʽAlī, of Mughal school of miniature painting; helped supervise production of *Dāstān-e Amir Ḥamzeh* story series.

Abe \äb-e\ Isoo. 1865–1949. Japanese politician. Professor at Waseda U., Tokyo (1901–26); opposed Russo-Japanese War (1904–05) and published pacifist-Socialist magazine *Shinkigen;* formed Fabian Society of Japan (1921); secretary general of People's Socialist party (1926); member, House of Representatives (from 1928); chairman (1932–40) of reorganized opposition Social Mass party; remembered also for introducing baseball to Japan.

Abe Masahiro. 1819–1857. Japanese politician. Named head of *Rōjū,* i.e. Elders (1844); opposed Western contacts, but bowed to superior force of Commodore Matthew C. Perry and signed Treaty of Kanagawa (1854) establishing limited relations with U.S.; made similar treaties with Britain, Russia, Netherlands; subsequently forced to relinquish power.

Abe Nobuyuki. 1875–1953. Japanese soldier and politician. Commander in chief of Formosan army (1932); general (1933); supreme war councilor (1934–36); prime minister (1939–40); governor general of Korea (1944–45).

à Becket, Thomas. See BECKET.

à Beck·ett \ə-ˈbek-ət\, Gilbert Abbott. 1811–1856. English humorist and playwright. Member of original staff of *Punch* (from 1841); author of *Comic History of England* (1848), *Comic History of Rome* (1852), etc.

Abegg \ˈäb-eg\, Richard Wilhelm Heinrich. 1869–1910. German chemist. Taught at U. of Breslau (1897–99), Technische Hochschule, Breslau (from 1899); known for studies of valence and its relation to number of electrons in atom.

Abel \ˈá-bəl\. c.1218–1252. King of Denmark (1250–52). Son of Valdemar II. Made duke of South Jutland on accession of elder brother Erik (1232); deposed and killed Erik (1250); killed in attack on Frisians.

Abel \ˈā-bəl\, Sir Frederick Augustus. 1827–1902. English chemist. Chemist to War Department (1854–88); inventor (1889) of cordite (with Sir James Dewar), also of the Abel tester for determining flash point of petroleum; author of works on explosives.

Abel, John Jacob. 1857–1938. American pharmacologist and physiological chemist, b. Cleveland. Professor at U. of Michigan (1891–93), Johns Hopkins (1893–1932); known for research on endocrine glands; isolated adrenalin (1897); crystallized insulin (1926); developed artificial kidney (1914); did research on chemical composition of animal tissues and fluids; isolated compound known as epinephrine.

Abel \ˈäb-əl\, Karl von. 1788–1859. German politician. Of Ultramontane party; prime minister of Bavaria (1837–47); clerical policies damaged popularity of King Louis I.

Abel, Karl Friedrich. 1723–1787. German musician and composer. Virtuoso on viola da gamba; to London (1759); chamber musician to Queen Charlotte (1765); with Johann Christian Bach, conducted Bach-Abel Concerts in London (1765–82); wrote some 40 symphonies, one long attributed to Mozart (K. 18).

Abel, Niels Henrik. 1802–1829. Norwegian mathematician. Known for research in theory of elliptic functions, transcendental functions, theory of integrals; proved impossibility of general solution of quintic equation.

Abel, Rudolf Ivanovich. c.1902–1971. Soviet Russian spy. Entered U.S. illegally (1948), lived in New York City; arrested and convicted of espionage (1957); exchanged for U-2 pilot Francis Gary Powers (1962).

Ab·e·lard \ˈab-ə-ˌlärd\, Peter. *Fr.* Pierre Abé·lard *or* Abai·lard \á-bā-lár\. 1079–?1144. French philosopher and theologian. Student of logic under William of Champeaux in Paris and later of theology under Anselm of Laon (1113–17); much of early life passed as peripatetic teacher. Secretly married Héloïse, incurring anger of her uncle Fulbert, canon of Paris Cathedral, whose hirelings emasculated him. Withdrew to abbey of Saint-Denis; his nominalistic doctrines declared heretical by council of Soissons (1121). Elected abbot of Saint-Gildas-de-Rhuys (1125); soon returned to Paris; became abbot of the Paraclete, foundation of nuns headed by Héloïse; composed book of hymns and with Héloïse compiled collection of their correspondence; moved to Mont-Sainte-Geneviève (c.1135), where his teaching drew large numbers. Wrote *Sic et non,* compilation of biblical and patristic quotations with guide to resolving apparent contradictions, *Scito te ipsum, Theologia,* etc.; at urging of Bernard of Clairvaux, condemned by council at Sens (1140); retired to monastery of Cluny. Body given to Héloïse; she was buried beside him (1164); both entombed at Paris (1817).

Abell \ˈā-bəl\, Arunah Shepherdson. 1806–1888. American newspaper publisher and editor, b. East Providence, R.I. With two partners founded *Philadelphia Public Ledger* (1836), *Baltimore Sun* (1837); edited *Sun* (1837–88); sole owner (from 1868); established pioneering newsgathering system employing express riders, carrier pigeons, telegraph.

Abell \ˈá-bəl\, Kjeld. 1901–1961. Danish playwright and critic. Known esp. for plays *Melodien der blev vaek* (1935), *Anna Sophie Hedvig* (1939), *Silkeborg* (1946); made many innovations in scenic design and effects.

Abell \ˈā-bəl\, Sir Westcott Stile. 1877–1961. English naval architect. Professor at Liverpool (1910–14), Armstrong Coll. (1928–41); chief ship surveyor, Lloyd's Register (1914–28); designed Dover-Dunkirk ferries; author of *The Safe Sea* (1932), *The Shipwright's Trade* (1948).

Aben·cer·ra·jes \äb̲-än-ther-ˈrä-k̲ās\. A 15th-century family of Moors in Granada, famed in romance for their feud with the family of the Zegris; massacred at Alhambra Palace by Muḥammad XI (c.1485).

Abercorn, Earls, marquises, dukes of. See HAMILTON family.

Ab·er·crom·bie *or* **Ab·er·crom·by** \ˈab-ər-ˌkräm-bē, -ˌkrəm-\, James. 1706–1781. British general, b. Scotland. Commander of British forces in America early in French and Indian War; attacked French at Ticonderoga (1758); defeated; recalled to England (1758).

Abercrombie, Lascelles. 1881–1938. English poet and critic. Professor at Leeds (1922–29), U. of London (1929–35), reader at Oxford (1935–38). Author of *Interludes and Poems* (1908), *Mary and the Bramble* (1910), *Emblems of Love* (1912), *Deborah* (1912), *Speculative Dialogues* (prose, 1913), *The Sale of St. Thomas* (1931), and critical works *Essay Toward a Theory of Art* (1922), *Principles of English Prosody* (1924), *Romanticism* (1926), *Poetry, its Music and Meaning* (1932).

Abercrombie, Sir Patrick, *in full* Leslie Patrick. 1879–1957. English architect. Brother of Lascelles Abercrombie. Professor at Liverpool (1915–35), U. Coll., London (1935–46); pioneering specialist in town planning; prepared urban and regional plans for Dublin, Doncaster, Sheffield, Plymouth, Hull, Edinburgh, etc., and esp. known for *County of London Plan* (1943) and *Greater London Plan* (1944).

Ab·er·crom·by \ˈab-ər-ˌkräm-bē, -ˌkrəm-\, Sir Ralph. 1734–1801. British general, b. Scotland. Entered army (1756); M.P. (1774–80); major general (1787); served under Duke of York and commanded rear column in retreat from Netherlands (1793–95); commanded expeditionary force that conquered St. Lucia and Trinidad (1795–96); commander in Ireland (1797–98), Scotland (1798–1800); division commander in second Netherlands expedition (1799); commanded troops in Mediterranean (1800); defeated French under Menou at Alexandria (1801) and died of wounds received there. Credited with restoring discipline and efficiency to British army. His brother ¶Sir Robert (1740–1827), also a British general, served in America in French and Indian War and American Revolution; major general (1790); aided Cornwallis in conquering Tippu Sultan (1792); commanded in second Rohilla War. Sir Ralph's 3d son ¶James (1776–1858), 1st Baron Dun·ferm·line \dən-ˈfərm-lin, dəm-\, was called to bar at Lincoln's Inn (1801); M.P. (1807–30, 1832–39); judge advocate general (1827); chief baron of exchequer of Scotland (1830); master of the mint in Earl Grey's cabinet (1834); speaker of House of Commons (1835–39); created baron (1839).

Aberdare, Baron. See Henry Austin BRUCE.

Aberdeen, Earl of. See GORDON family.

Aberdeen and Temair, Marquis of. See GORDON family.

Ab·er·hart \ˈā-bər-ˌhärt\, William. 1878–1943. Canadian politician, b. near Kippen, Ont. Helped promote Social Credit theories and reforms of Clifford Douglas (from 1932); elected first Social Credit premier of Alberta (1935–43).

Ab·er·ne·thy \ˌab-ər-ˈnē-thē, -ˈneth-ē\, John. 1764–1831. English surgeon. Assistant surgeon (1787–1815), surgeon (1815–27) at St. Bartholomew's Hospital, London; lecturer at Coll. of Surgeons (1814–17); known esp. as an effective teacher; devised method for ligation of the external iliac artery (1797).

Abetz \ˈäb-ets\, Heinrich Otto. 1903–1958. German propagandist and diplomat. Worked for Franco-German rapprochement; propagandist for Nazis (from 1932); Ribbentrop's personal agent in Paris (1938); expelled (1939); ambassador in Paris (1940–45); imprisoned by French (1949–54).

Ab·gar \'ab-gär\. *Surnamed* Uk·ka·ma \ůk-'kä-mä\. 4 B.C.–50 A.D. King of Edessa. In popular legend dating from 4th century, reputed to have written a letter to Jesus asking to be cured of a serious infirmity.

Abh·di·sho bar Be·ri·kha \äb-'dē-shō-bär-bā-'rē-kä\. *Known also as* Eb·e·dje·sus \ˌeb-ej-'ā-sůs\ of Ni·si·bis \'nis-ə-bəs\. d. 1318. Syrian Christian theologian. Nestorian bishop of Shiggar and Beth-Arabaye (c.1285); metropolitan of Nisibis (Nusaybin; c.1291); author of *Margaritha vitae,* comprehensive summary of Nestorian thought on nature of Christ.

Abhi·na·va·gup·ta \ə-ˌbin-ə-və-'gůp-tə\. fl. 1014. Indian philosopher. Wrote on aesthetics and commentaries on Śaivite monist philosophy, including *Īśvara-pratyabhijñā-vimarśinī* and *Īśvara-pratyabhijñā-vivṛti-vimarśinī.*

Abi·jah \ə-'bī-jə\. *Hebrew* Abiyyah *and* Abiyyahu. 10th century B.C. Second king of Judah (c.915–913 B.C.). Son and successor of Rehoboam.

Abild·gaard \'ä-bil-ḡȯr\, Nikolai Abraham. 1743–1809. Danish painter. Director of Copenhagen Academy (from 1789); leading Danish painter of his day; known esp. for historical and literary works in Neoclassical style.

Ab·ing·ton \'ab-iŋ-tən\, Fanny, *nee* Frances Bar·ton \'bärt-ᵊn\. 1737–1815. English actress. m. (1759) her music master. Flower girl and street singer; stage debut at Haymarket (1755); great success in Dublin (1759–64); played at Drury Lane (1764–82) under Garrick until his death; at Covent Garden (1782–90); last appearances 1797–99. Created thirty characters, including Lady Teazle (1777); a leader of English fashion.

Ableiges \á-blezh\, Jacques d'. d. 1410 or 1411. French legal compiler. Compiled collection of old, chiefly customary, laws known as *Grand Coutumier de France* (c.1385).

Ab·ney \'ab-nē\, Sir William de Wiveleslie. 1843–1920. English chemist and educator. Inspector (1877), director (1893) of science schools for and assistant secretary (1899) of Board of Education. Specialist in photographic chemistry; developed photographic emulsion sensitive to infrared and used it to map solar spectrum; discovered (1880) developing properties of hydroquinone.

aboo- *or* **abou-**. See names beginning ABŪ.

Abool- *or* **Aboul-**. See names beginning ABŪ AL-, ABUL-.

About \á-bü\, Edmond-François-Valentin. 1828–1885. French journalist, novelist, and playwright. Author of polemical and satirical works, including *La Grèce contemporaine* (1854), *Tolla* (1855), *Le Roi des montagnes* (1856), *L'Homme à l'oreille cassée* (1862), *Le Nez d'un notaire* (1862), *Madelon* (1863), *L'Infâme* (1867), *Le Roman d'un brave homme* (1880).

Aboyné, Viscounts and 5th Earl of. See earls and marquises of Huntly under GORDON family.

Abra·ba·nel *Span* äb-rä-bä-'nel, *Port* əb-rə-bə-\ *or* **Abar·ba·nel** *Span* äb-är-bä-'nel, *Port* á-bər-bə-'nel\ *or* **Abra·va·nel** *Span* äb-rä-bä-'nel, *Port* á-brə-və-'nel\. Name of old Jewish family of southern Europe, esp. of Spain, Portugal, and Italy, distinguished as physicians, scholars, poets, and benefactors of Jewish people. Members included: Isaac ben Judah Abrabanel (1437–1508), theologian and statesman, b. Lisbon; treasurer of Afonso V of Portugal (to 1481); minister of state (1484–92) to Ferdinand and Isabella of Castile; unable to prevent expulsion of Jews from Spain (1492); and also to governments of Naples and Venice (1503–08); his commentaries on Bible exerted wide influence; wrote philosophical works and apologetics in defense of Jewish doctrine of the Messiah. His son ¶Judah León Abrabanel (c.1460–c.1521), physician and poet, known in Spanish literary history as Le·ón He·breo \lā-'ōn-ā-'brā-ō\ and in Italian as Le·o·ne Ebreo \lā-'ō-nā-ā-'brā-ō\, i.e. Leo the Hebrew; his *Dialoghi di amore* (in Italian) used in Castiglione's *Courtier.*

Ab·ra·ha \'äb-rä-ˌhä\ *or* **Ab·re·ha** \-re-ˌhä\. 6th century. Christian Ethiopian king of southern Arabia. Led expedition against Mecca in year of Muḥammad's birth (c.570); failure of expedition accounted a miracle by Muslims.

Abra·ham \'ā-brə-ˌham\ *or* **Abram** \'ā-bram\. Early 2d millennium B.C. Traditionally first Hebrew patriarch. Migrated from the Ur to Canaan; father of Isaac and Ishmael and grandfather of Jacob. Held as founder of faith by Jews, Christians, Muslims.

Abraham the Mighty. See Abraham KUYPER.

Ab·ra·ham \'äb-rä-ˌhäm\, Karl. 1877–1925. German psychoanalyst. Began practice in Berlin (1907); established there first branch of International Psychoanalytic Institute (1910); known esp. for studies of infant sexuality, treatment of manic-depressive psychoses; author of *Short Study of the Development of the Libido* (1924).

Abra·ham a Sanc·ta Cla·ra \'äb-rä-ˌhäm-ä-'zäŋk-tä-'klä-rä\. *Orig.* Johann Ulrich Me·ger·le \'mā-gər-lə\. 1644–1709. German friar and preacher. Augustinian friar (1662); court preacher at Vienna (1677); author of popular, often satiric, devotional works, including *Merk's Wien* (1680), *Auff, auff, ihr Christen* (1683), *Judas der Erzschelm* (1686–95).

Abra·ham bar Hiy·ya Sa·va·sor·da \'ā-brə-ˌham-bär-'hē-(y)ə-ˌsäv-ä-'sȯr-dä\. *Also known as* Abraham bar Hiyya Ha·na·si \-hän-'äs-ē\. c.1065–c.1136. Spanish Jewish philosopher and mathematician. Led revival of written Hebrew among western Jews; wrote geometry textbook, long used in Latin translation (1145), containing first European exposition of Arabic algebra.

Abraham ben Meir. See IBN EZRA.

Abraham ibn Daud. See IBN DAUD.

Abra·hams \'ā-brə-ˌhamz\, Israel. 1858–1925. English scholar. Reader at Cambridge (1902–25); author of *Jewish Life in the Middle Ages* (1896), *Chapters on Jewish Literature* (1899), *Book of Delight* (1913), *Studies in Pharisaism* (1917); coeditor of *Jewish Quarterly Review* (1888–1908).

Abra·mo·vich \(ˌ)ə-'brám(-əv)-ˌyich\ *or* **Broy·de** \'brȯid-ə\, Shalom Jacob. *Pseudonym* Men·de·le Mokh·er Sef·a·rim \'mȯk-ər-'men-də-ˌlā-ˌsef-ə-ˌrem\, i.e. Mendele the Itinerant Bookseller. 1835–1917. Russian Jewish writer. Author of humorous and satirical plays, stories, and novels in Yiddish and in Hebrew; responsible for developing modern written Hebrew; works included *Dos Vinschfingerl* (1865), *Ha-avot we-ha-vanim* (1868), *Fishke der Krumer* (1869).

Ab·ra·mo·witz \ə-'bräm-ə-vits\, Raphael. *Orig. surname* Rein \'rān\. 1880–1963. Russian revolutionary. Member of Jewish Bund and Menshevik faction; opposed Bolshevik revolution (1917); to U.S. (1920); worked as Socialist journalist; author of *The Soviet Revolution 1917–1939* (1962).

Abrams \'ā-brəmz\, Creighton Williams. 1914–1974. American army officer, b. Springfield, Mass. Rose to rank of major general (1965); commanded tank battalion during World War II, playing key role in relief of Bastogne; appointed vice-chief of U.S. army (1964–67); commanded U.S. troops in Vietnam (1968–72); implemented Vietnamization policy and oversaw U.S. withdrawal; served as army chief of staff (1972–74).

Abrantès, Duc d'. See Andoche JUNOT.

Abreha. See ABRAHA.

Abreu \ə-'breů\, António de. 16th century. Portuguese explorer. Discovered Banda Kepulavan islands, Indonesia (1512).

Abreu, João Ca·pis·tra·no de \kə-pē-'strá-nü-thē\. 1853–1927. Brazilian historian. Professor, Rio de Janeiro (1883–99); author of works dealing with early history of Brazil, including *Descobrimento do Brasil* (1883), *Capítulos da história colonial* (1907).

Abruzzi, Duke of the. See LUIGI AMEDEO.

Ab·sa·lom \'ab-sə-ləm\. fl. c.1020 B.C. Third and favorite son of King David of Israel. Stirred up rebellion against father, whom he temporarily drove from Jerusalem; killed by Joab in flight from battle.

Ab·sa·lon \'áp-sá-lȯn\. *Sometimes called* Ax·el \'ak-səl\. 1128–1201. Danish soldier, statesman, and prelate. Helped foster brother gain Danish throne as Valdemar I (1156–57); named bishop of Roskilde (1158); supported Valdemar's siding with Frederick I Barbarossa against Pope Alexander III; led campaign against Wends and captured Rügen (1169); founded fortress of Havn (Copenhagen; 1169); helped secure canonization of Canute Lavard and coronation of Canute VI (1170); elected archbishop of Lund (1177); led expedition that captured Pomerania and Mecklenburg (1184).

Abt \äpt\, Franz. 1819–1885. German composer. Kapellmeister in Brunswick (1852–82); composer of much vocal music, esp. choruses and part songs.

Abū 'Abd Allāh. See IBN AL-'ARABĪ.

Abū 'Abd Allāh al-Ḥarith ibn Asad al-'Anazī al-Muḥāsibī. See MUHASIBI.

Abū 'Abd Al·lāh al-Shī'ī \ə-ˌbü-əb-dů-'lä-al-'shē-ē\. d. 911. Muslim religious leader. As representative of Shī'ite sect, arranged overthrow of Aghlabid dynasty of North Africa (910) and establishment of Fāṭimids.

Abū 'Abd Allāh Mālik ibn Anas ibn al-Ḥārith al-Aṣbaḥī. See MĀLIK IBN ANAS.

Abū 'Abd Allāh Muḥammad XI. See MUḤAMMAD XI.

Abū 'Abd Allāh Muḥammad al-Quḍā'ī. See IBN AL-ABBĀR.

Abū 'Abd Allāh Muḥammad ibn 'Abd Allāh al-Lawātī aṭ-Ṭanjī ibn Baṭṭūṭah. See IBN BAṬṬŪṬAH.

Abū 'Abd Allāh Muḥammad ibn Idrīs ash-Shāfi'ī. See SHĀFI'Ī.

Abū 'Abd Allāh Muḥammad ibn Ismā'īl al-Bukhārī. See BUKHĀRĪ.

Abū 'Abd Allāh Muḥammad ibn Jābir ibn Sinān al-Battānī al-Ḥarrānī as-Ṣābi'. See BATTĀNĪ.

Abū 'Abd Allāh Muḥammad ibn 'Umar ibn al-Ḥusayn Fakhr ad-Dīn ar-Rāzī. See FAKHR AD-DĪN AR-RĀZĪ.

Abū 'Abdollāh Ja'far ebn Moḥammad. See RŪDAKĪ.

Abū al-. See also names beginning ABUL-.

Abū al-'Abbas al-Walīd ibn Yazīd ibn 'Abd al-Malik ibn Marwān. See WALĪD IBN YAZĪD.

Abū al-'Ab·bās as-Saf·fāḥ \ə-ˌbül-äb-'bas-ə-sáf-'fak\. 722–754. Muslim caliph. Descendant of 'Abbās, uncle of Muḥammad; led revolution against Umayyad dynasty (747–750); first caliph of 'Abbāsid dynasty (750–754); moved capital to Baghdad.

Abū al-'Abbās Muḥammad ibn Yazīd. See MUBARRAD.

\ə\ **abut** \ᵊ\ **kitten,** *Fr.* **table** \ər\ **further** \a\ **ash** \ā\ **ace** \ä\ **cot, cart** \aů\ **out** \ch\ **chin** \e\ **bet** \ē\ **easy** \g\ **go** \i\ **hit** \ī\ **ice** \j\ **job** \ŋ\ **sing** \ō\ **go** \ȯ\ **law** \ȯi\ **boy** \th\ **both** \th\ **the** \ü\ **loot** \ů\ **foot** \y\ **yet** \zh\ **vision** \á, b, ḡ, k, ⁿ, œ, œ̄, ue, ue̅, ʸ\ *see* **Guide to Pronunciation**

Abū al-ʽAlā'. See MA'ARRĪ.
Abū al-ʽAtā·hi·yah \ə-ˌbül-ä-ˈta-hi-yə\. *Orig.* Abū Isḥāq Ismāʽīl ibn al-Qāsim ibn Suwayd ibn Kaysān. 748–825 or 826. Arab poet. Lived in Baghdad in caliphate of Hārūn ar-Rashīd, whose favor he gained through his early love lyrics; later ascetic poems, collected (1071) in *Zuhdīyāt,* expressed social ideas and everyday observations in fresh language that helped free Arabic prosody.
Abū al-Fadl Aḥmad ibn al-Ḥusayn al-Hamadhānī. See HAMADHĀNĪ.
Abū al-Faraj. See BAR HEBRAEUS.
Abū al-Fa·raj al-Is·ba·hā·nī \ə-ˌbül-ˈfär-äj-əl-ˌis-bə-ˈha-nē\. *More completely* Abū al-Faraj ʽAlī ibn al-Ḥusayn al-Qurashī al-Iṣbahānī. 897–967. Arab scholar. Spent most of life in Baghdad; compiled *Kitāb al-aghānī,* collection of songs, information on Arab composers and poets, etc. from pre-Islāmic, Umayyad, and ʽAbbāsid periods.
Abū al-Fi·dā' \ə-ˌbül-fi-ˈda\. *More completely* Abū al-Fidā' Ismāʽīl ibn ʽAlī al-Mālik al-Mu'ayyad ʽImād ad-Dīn. *Also known as* Abul·fe·da \ə-ˌbu̇l-fi-ˈdä\. 1273–1331. Arab historian and geographer. Descendant of Ayyūb. Took part in campaigns against crusaders (1285–98); prince of Hamāh (1310–31); given rank of sultan (1320). Author of *Mukhtaṣar ta'rīkh al-bashar,* history of the world from Creation to 1329, and *Taqwīm al-buldān,* a geography; both works based on earlier writers.
Abū al-Ghā·zī Ba·hā·dur Khān \äb-ˈül-ˈgäz-ē-ˌbä-hä-ˈdur-ˈkän\. 1603–1663. Turkish historian and ruler of Khiva (Khwārezm). Son of Khan of Khiva; fled to Isfahan on outbreak of dynastic struggle following father's death (1629); succeeded to throne (1644 or 1645); carried on wars with Turkmen, Uzbeks, Kalmyks, Russia, Iran. Author of *Shajare-i Tarākime* or *Şecere-i Terakime,* a Turkish genealogy based on work of Rashīd ad-Dīn, and *Shajare-i Turk,* history of Shaybānid dynasty completed (1665) by his son.
Abū al-Ḥa·san \ə-ˌbu̇l-ha-ˈsan\. 17th century. Mughal painter. Served Emperor Jahāngīr, who gave him title Nādir-uz-Zamān, i.e. Wonder of the Age, and Emperor Shāh Jahān.
Abū al-Ḥasan al-Ashʽarī. See ASH'ARĪ.
Abū al-Ḥa·san ʽAlī \ə-ˌbül-ˈhä-sän-ä-ˈlē\. c.1297–1351. Sultan of Morocco (1331–51). Son and successor of Abū Saʽīd. Captured Algeciras and Gibraltar (1333); attacked Algerian territories, capturing Tlemcen (1337); won naval battle in Straits of Gibraltar (1340) but after defeat at Rio Salado (1340) gave up plan to conquer Spain; gained virtual sovereignty over Tunisia (1342) and captured Tunis (1347); defeated by Tunisian tribes (1348); short-lived North African empire ended in revolt of his son, in whose favor he abdicated (1351).
Abū al-Ḥasan ʽAlī al-Masʽūdī. See MAS'ŪDĪ.
Abū al-Ḥasan ʽAlī ibn Hilāl ibn al-Bawwāb. See IBN AL-BAWWĀB.
Abū al-Ḥasan ʽAlī ʽIzz ad-Dīn ibn al-Athīr. See IBN AL-ATHĪR.
Abū al-Ḥasan Yehuda ben Shemuel ha-Levi. See JUDAH HA-LEVI.
Abū al-Ḥusayn Muslim ibn al-Ḥajjāj al-Qushayrī. See MUSLIM IBN AL-ḤAJJĀJ.
Abū ʽAlī al-Ḥa·san ibn al-Hay·tham \ə-ˌbü-ä-ˈlē-əl-ˈhä-sän-ˌib-ən-əl-ˈhī-thəm\. *Known by Latinized name* Al·haz·en \al-ˈha-zən\. 965–1039. Arab mathematician and physicist. Spent much of life in Egypt, where apparently he failed in a plan presented to Caliph al-Hākim to control the flooding of the Nile; known for researches in optics, including work on refraction, reflection, lenses, parabolic and spherical mirrors, aberration, etc., related in *Kitāb fī al-Manāzir* (Lat. translation *Opticae Thesaurus Alhazeni libri vii,* 1270); first to explain vision as effect of light coming from object to eye; wrote also on astronomy, esp. critiques of Ptolemy. Work of great influence in Europe.
Abū ʽAlī Muḥammad ibn ʽAlī ibn Muqlah. See IBN MUQLAH.
Abū al-Khayr Khān \ə-ˌbu̇l-ˈkīr-ˈkän\. 1412–1468. Uzbek ruler. Descendant of Shaybān, youngest son of Jochi of the Golden Horde. As khān in Siberia, greatly expanded dominion; conquered Kipchak and (1430–31) Khwārezm; founder of Muslim Shaybānid dynasty.
Abū al-Majd Maj·dud ibn Adam \ə-ˌbu̇l-ˈmïd-ˈmī-du̇d-ˌib-ən-ä-ˈdäm\. *Pseudonym* Sanā'ī \sa-ˈnī\. 1050–1131. Persian poet. Court panegyrist at Ghaznavid court; later left in search of spiritual perfection. Author of *Ḥadīqeh ol-ḥaqīqat,* first great mystical poem in Persian; first to adopt traditional ode, lyric, and rhymed couplet forms to philosophical and ethical ideas of Ṣūfism.
Abū al-Mughīth al-Ḥusayn ibn Manṣūr al-Ḥallāj. See ḤALLĀJ.
Abū al-Mulūk. See ʽABD AL-MALIK IBN MARWĀN.
Abū al-Mundhir. See HISHĀM IBN AL-KALBĪ.
Abū al-Qā·sim \ə-ˌbül-ˈkäs-im\ *or* **Abul Kasim.** *In full* Abū al-Qāsim Khalaf ibn ʽAbbās az-Zahrāwī. *Lat.* Al·bu·ca·sis \ˌal-byü-ˈkä-səs\. c.936–c.1013. Spanish Arab physician. Court physician to ʽAbd ar-Raḥmān III; author of *at-Taṣrīf li-man ʽajaz ʽan at-Taʼālīf,* medical compendium partly based on earlier authors, esp. Paul of Aegina, but containing new material including remarkable illustrations of surgical instruments; work greatly influential on European surgery for 500 years.
Abū al-Wa·fā' al-Bū·za·jā·nī \ə-ˌbu̇l-wə-ˈfä-al-ˌbu̇-za-ˈjän-ē\ *or* **Abul We·fa** \ə-ˌbu̇l-wə-ˈfä\. *In full* Muḥammad ibn Muḥammad ibn Yaḥyā ibn Ismāʽīl ibn al-ʽAbbās Abū al-Wafā' al-Būzajānī. 940–998. Persian astronomer. Worked at observatory in Baghdad (from 959); constructed first wall quadrant there; calculated tangent and cotangent tables; devised new method for calculating sine tables; invented secant and cosecant functions; proved general sine theorem for spherical triangles; wrote widely used textbooks on arithmetic and geometry.
Abū al-Walīd Marwān ibn Janāh. See IBN JANĀH.
Abū aṭ-Ṭāhir Majd ad-Dīn al-Fīrūzābādī. See FĪRŪZĀBĀDĪ.
Abū aṭ-Ṭayyib Aḥmad ibn Ḥusayn al-Mutanabbī. See MUTANABBĪ.
Abū Ba·kar \ə-ˌbü-ˈbak-ər\. 1843?–1895. Sultan of Johore (1885–95). Became *temenggong* (ruler subject to sultan) of Johore (1862); assumed title of maharaja (1868) and of sultan (1885), displacing former dynasty; promoted trade and agricultural development, adopted Western administrative methods; successfully maintained limited independence of British colonial rule.
Abū Bakr \ə-ˌbü-ˈbak-ər\. *Called* aṣ-Ṣid·dīq \əs-sid-ˈdēk\, *i.e.* the Upright. c.573–634. First Muslim caliph. Reputedly Muḥammad's first male convert, became his closest companion and adviser; accompanied Muḥammad to Medina (622); conducted pilgrimage to Mecca (631) and led public prayers in Muḥammad's last illness (632); chosen *khalīfat rasūl Allāh,* i.e. deputy or successor to the Prophet of God (632); began expansion of Islām into central Arabia, Iraq, Syria.
Abū Bakr (1165–1240). See IBN AL-ʽARABĪ.
Abū Bakr ʽAbd al-Qāhir ibn ʽAbd ar-Raḥmān al-Jurjānī. See JURJĀNĪ.
Abū Bakr Muhammad ibn ʽAbd al-Malik ibn Muḥammad ibn Muḥammad ibn Ṭufayl al-Qaysī. See IBN ṬUFAYL.
Abū Bakr Mu·ḥam·mad ibn Yaḥ·yā ibn al-Sā·yigh al-Tu·jī·bī al-An·da·lu·sī al-Sa·ra·qus·ṭī \-mu̇-ˈham-məd-ˌib-ən-ya-ˈhyä-ˌib-ən-al-ˈsä-yiḡ-al-ˌtu̇j-ē-ˈbē-al-ˌan-da-lu̇-ˈsē-al-sä-rä-ˈkü-stē\. *Also known as* Ibn Bāj·jah \ˌib-ən-ˈba-jə\. *Lat.* Avem·pa·ce \ˌäv-əm-ˈpä-sä\. c.1095–1138 or 1139. Spanish Arab philosopher. First known Arabic philosopher of the Aristotelian-Neoplatonic school; forerunner of Ibn Ṭufayl and of Ibn Rushd (Averroës); author of *Tadbīr al-Mutawaḥḥid,* also songs, poems, etc.
Abū Bakr Muḥammad ibn Zakarīyā' ar-Rāzī. See RĀZĪ.
Abū Bishr ʽAmr ibn ʽUth·mān \ə-ˌbü-ˈbish-ər-ˈäm-ər-ˌib-ən-u̇th-ˈmän\. *Nicknamed* Sī·ba·wayh \ˈsē-bə-ˈwī\760?–?793. Grammarian of Baṣra, of Persian origin. Known for major work on Arabic grammar, *al-Kitāb fī an-naḥw* or simply *al-Kitāb.*
Abū Ḥāmid Muḥammad ibn Muḥammad aṭ-Ṭūsī al-Ghazālī. See GHAZĀLĪ.
Abū Ḥa·nī·fah \ə-ˌbü-han-ˈē-fä\. *In full* Abū Ḥanīfah an-Nuʽmān ibn Thābit. 699–767. Muslim jurist and theologian. Undertook a critical analysis of existing legal doctrine and practice and developed a rigorous and systematic body of doctrine, the first of the four orthodox Islāmic schools of law.
Abū Ḥudhayfah. See WĀṢIL IBN ʽAṬĀ'.
Abū ʽImram Mūsā ibn Maymūn ibn ʽUbayd Allāh. See Moses ben MAIMON.
Abū ʽĪsā Muḥammad ibn ʽĪsā ibn Sawrah ibn Shaddād at-Tirmidhī. See TIRMIDHĪ.
Abū Isḥāq Ibrāhīm ibn Sayyār ibn Hanī' an-Naẓẓām. See NAẒẒĀM.
Abū Isḥāq Ismāʽīl ibn al-Qāsim ibn Suwayd ibn Kaysān. See ABŪ AL-ʽATĀHIYAH.
Abū Kā·li·jār al-Mar·zu·bān ibn Sul·ṭān ad-Daw·lah \ə-ˌbü-ˈkä-lē-jär-al-ˈmär-zu̇-ˌbän-ˌib-ən-ˈsül-tän-ad-ˈdau̇-lä\. *Known also as* Mu·ḥyī' ad-Dīn \ˈmü-hyē-ad-ˈdēn\. 1009–1048. Būyid ruler of Iran and Iraq. Succeeded father on Būyid throne (1024); defeated his uncle, ruler of Kerman (1028); carried on civil war with Iraqi branch of dynasty (1027–37); succeeded uncle Jalāl ad-Dawlah as ruler of Būyid Iraq (1044); fortified capital Shīrāz against Seljuq Turks (1044); killed in battle with Seljuqs under Togrïl Beg.
Abu·la·fia \ə-ˌbu̇l-ə-ˈfē-ə\, Abraham ben Samuel. c.1240–after 1291. Jewish theologian. Founder of "prophetic Kabbala" school of Jewish mysticism.
Abulafia, Meir. c.1170–1244. Spanish Talmudist. His teachings contradicting certain tenets of Moses ben Maimon began prolonged controversy.
Abu-l-Fazl ʽAl·lā·mī \ə-ˌbu̇l-ˈfaz-əl-al-ˈlä-mē\. 1551–1602. Mughal historian, soldier, and theologian. Under patronage of Emperor Akbar (from 1574); helped develop new eclectic form of Islāmic worship; distinguished himself in military campaigns in the Deccan (1599); assassinated at instance of Akbar's rebellious son Salīm (later Emperor Jahāngīr). Author of *Akbar-nāmeh* and *Āīn-e Akbarī,* history of Akbar's family and description of his realm, government, and culture.
Abulfeda. See ABŪ AL-FIDĀ'.
Abul Wefa. See ABŪ AL-WAFĀ'.
Abu Ma·di \ə-ˌbu̇m-ä-ˈdē\, Iliya. c.1890–1957. Arab poet and journalist. Published first collection of poetry (1911) in Egypt; to U.S. (1912); worked as journalist in New York City (from 1916); founded (1929) *as-Samīr,* monthly magazine later (1936) expanded to daily newspaper; later collections of poetry included *al-Jadāwil* (1927), *al-Khamā'il* (1946), *Tibr wa-turāb* (1960).

Abū Manṣūr Muḥammad ibn Maḥmūd al-Ḥanafī al-Mutakallim al-Māturīdī as-Samargandī. See MĀTURĪDĪ.

Abū Manṣūr Sebüktigin. See SEBÜKTIGIN.

Abū Ma·'shar \ə-ˌbü-'mash-ar\. *Known as* Al·bu·ma·zar \ˌal-byü-'maz-ər\ *or* Al·bu·ma·sar \-'mas-\. 787–886. Muslim astrologer. The leading astrologer of his day; author of *Kitāb al-Madkhal al-Kabīr 'alā 'ilm aḥkām al-nujūm, Kitāb al-girānāt, Kitāb taḥāwīl sini al-ālam,* etc.; works widely circulated in Europe in Latin translation; inspired literary characters of astrologers in works of Giovanni della Porta, Thomas Tomkis, etc.

Abumeron. See IBN ZUHR.

Abū Muḥammad 'Abd Allāh ibn Muslim al-Dīnawarī ibn Qutaybah. See IBN QUTAYBAH.

Abū Muḥammad al-Ḥasan ibn Aḥmad al-Hamdānī. See HAMDĀNĪ.

Abū Muḥammad 'Alī ibn Aḥmad ibn Sa'īd ibn Ḥazm. See IBN ḤAZM.

Abū Muḥammad al-Kūmī. See 'ABD AL-MU'MIN.

Abū Muḥammad al-Qāsim ibn 'Alī al-Ḥarīrī. See ḤARĪRĪ.

Abū Mūsā Jabir ibn Ḥayyān. See JABIR IBN ḤAYYĀN.

Abū Naṣr. See AḤMAD SHĀH.

Abū Naṣr al-Fārābī. See FĀRĀBĪ.

Abū Nu·wās \ə-ˌbü-nü-'wäs\. *Also spelled* Abū Nu'ās. *In full* Abū Nuwās al-Ḥasan ibn Hānī' al-Ḥakamī. c.747 to 762–c.813 to 815. Arab poet. Known for poems marked by irony and cynicism and frequently on sensual topics; won favor of Hārūn ar-Rashīd and al-Amīn at Baghdad; considered one of the greatest poets of 'Abbāsid period.

Abū Sa'īd 'Abd al-Malik ibn Qurayb al-Aṣma'ī. See AṢMA'Ī.

Abu Sa'īd ibn Abī al-Ḥasan Yasār al-Baṣrī. See ḤASAN AL-BAṢRĪ.

Abū Tam·mām \ə-ˌbü-tam-'mäm\. *In full* Abū Tammām Ḥabīb ibn Aws. 804–c.845. Arab poet. A favorite at court of al-Mu'taṣim; known for panegyrics and decorative verse; most important work the compilation of the *Ḥamāsah,* anthology of early Arabic poetry.

Abū 'Ubādah al-Walīd ibn 'Ubayd Allāh al-Buḥturī. See BUḤTURĪ.

Abū ul-Fatḥ Jalāl-ud-Dīn Muḥammad Akbar. See AKBAR.

Abū 'Uthman 'Amr ibn Baḥr ibn Maḥbub al-Jāḥiẓ. See JĀḤIẒ.

Abū Ya'qūb al-Basir. See JOSEPH BEN ABRAHAM HA-COHEN.

Abū Yūsuf Ya'qūb al-Manṣūr. See Abū Yūsuf Ya'qūb al-MANṢŪR.

Abū Zayd 'Abd ar-Raḥmān ibn Khaldūn. See IBN KHALDŪN.

Aca·cius \ə-'kā-sh(ē-)əs\. 5th century. Patriarch of Constantinople (471–489). Appointed papal legate in the East (475) for his repudiation of Monophysitism; attempted to reconcile Christological dispute with *Henoticon* doctrine (482); deposed and excommunicated by Pope Felix III (484); removed references to Felix and to bishop of Rome from inscriptions and liturgy. Acacian Schism was formally healed (519) but left seed of ultimate breach between Eastern and Western churches (1054).

Ac·cia·iuo·li \ˌät-chī-'wò-lē\. Florentine family prominent in mercantile and political fields from 13th to 15th century, including: Niccolò (1310–1365), entered service of King Robert of Naples, who knighted him (1335) and gave him several fiefs in Apulia and Greece; conquered Achaea (1338–41); helped arrange marriage of Louis of Toranto and Queen Joan I of Naples (1347); named seneschal of Naples (1348); commanded defense of Louis and Joan against Louis I of Hungary and restored them to throne (1352); conquered most of Sicily (1356–1357); defended Achaea against Turks and Catalans (1358); named governor of Bologna and the Romagna (1360). His nephew and adopted son ¶Ranieri I, *called* Neri (d. 1394) acquired Corinth (1366) and conquered Catalans holding Athens (1388), becoming master of entire region; created duke of Athens (1394) by King Ladislas of Naples.

Ac·ci·us \'ak-shē-əs\ *or* **At·ti·us** \'at-ē-əs\, Lucius. 170–c.86 B.C. Roman tragic poet. Known esp. for his adaptations of Greek dramas; wrote *Decius* and *Brutus* on Roman historical materials; author also of *Didascalia* on Greek and Roman poetry.

Ac·col·ti \äk-'kòl-tē\, Benedetto. 1415–1466. Italian jurist and historian. Chancellor of Florentine Republic (1459); author (with his brother Leonardo) of a Latin history of the First Crusade, credited with being basis for Tasso's *Gerusalemme liberata.*

Ac·co·ram·bo·ni \ˌäk-kō-räm-'bò-nē\, Vittoria. 1557–1585. Italian woman whose first husband was murdered (1581) in order that she might marry the Duke of Bracciano. After the duke's death (1585), she was murdered at the instigation of a relative of his. Her story was used in John Webster's play *The White Divel* (1612) and in Ludwig Tieck's novel *Vittoria Accoramboni* (1840).

Ac·cur·sio \äk-'kür-syō\, Francesco. *Lat.* Franciscus Ac·cur·si·us \ə-'kər-sh(ē-)əs\. 1182–1260. Italian jurist. Professor at Bologna; compiled authoritative *Glossa ordinaria* or *Glossa magna* (1220–50) on Roman law.

Accursio *or* **Ac·cor·si** \äk-'kòr-sē\, Mariangelo. c.1480–1546. Italian poet and critic. Known for his satiric dialogues, including *Diatribae in Ausonium, Solinum, et Ovidium* (1524), and for *De anima* (1535), translation of letters of Cassiodorus.

Ace \'ās\, Goodman. 1899–1982. American humorist, b. Kansas City, Mo. Columnist for Kansas City *Journal Post;* began radio show "Easy Aces" (1928–45), conducted with his wife ¶Jane, *nee* Sherwood (1905–74), who became widely known for malapropisms; he wrote also for many television comedians (from 1952); later conducted a column in *Saturday Review.*

Acernus, Sebastian. See KLONOWIC.

Ace·ve·do Dí·az \äth-ā-'b̲ā-t̲h̲ō-'dē-äs\, Eduardo. 1851–1924. Uruguayan writer and politician. Considered Uruguay's first novelist; works included *Ismael* (1888), *Nativa* (1890), *Grito de gloria* (1894), *Soledad* (1894).

Acevedo y Zú·ñi·ga \-ē-'thün-yē-gä\, Gaspar de. Conde de Mon·ter·rey \-t̲h̲ā-mòn-ter-'rā\. c.1560–1606. Spanish colonialist. Viceroy of New Spain (1595–1603); dispatched explorers Juan da Oñate to New Mexico and Juan Vizcaíno to California; sent to Peru (1603–06). Monterey, Cal., named in his honor.

Achab. See AHAB.

Achad Haam. See Asher GINZBERG.

Achaem·e·nes \ə-'kem-in-ēz, -'kē-min-\. *Persian* Ha·kha·ma·nish \hä-'kä-mä-nish\. d. c.460 B.C. Persian governor of Egypt. Son of Darius I. Appointed satrap of Egypt (484 B.C.) by brother Xerxes I; commanded Egyptian contingent at battle of Salamis (480); killed in battle with Egyptian rebels.

Ach·ae·men·i·dae \ˌak-i-'men-ə-dē\ *or* **Ach·ae·men·ids** \ˌak-i-'men-idz\. *Persian* Ha·kha·ma·ni·shi·ya \hä-'kä-mä-ˌnish-i-yä\. Name of ruling house of ancient Persia, derived from its founder, Achaemenes, *Persian* Hakhamanish, of 7th century B.C. Early rulers were Teispes, Cyrus I, and Cambyses I, kings of Anshan (or Anzan); Cyrus II the Great, and Cambyses II; by a collateral line (according to Herodotus) from Teispes, Darius I and his successors down to Darius III, overthrown by Alexander the Great (330 B.C.). See individual biographies.

Achard \ä-shär\, Franz Karl, *orig.* François-Charles. 1753–1821. German chemist and physicist. Student and successor of A.S. Marggraf at Berlin Academy; developed (1799) method of crystallizing beet sugar; pioneer in beet-sugar industry.

Achen·bach \'äk̲-ən-ˌbäk̲\, Andreas. 1815–1910. German painter. Known for landscapes and seascapes; pioneer in German realist school. His brother and pupil ¶Oswald (1827–1905) was also a landscape painter.

Ach·e·son \'ach-ə-sən\, Archibald. 2d Earl of Gos·ford \'gäs-fərd\. 1776–1849. British politician. Member of Irish Parliament (1798–1800); M.P. (1800–07); representative peer for Ireland (1811–49); lord lieutenant of Armagh (1832); governor in chief of British North America (1835–37); alienated both English and French Canadians with policy of "conciliation without concession."

Acheson, Dean Gooderham. 1893–1971. American lawyer and statesman, b. Middletown, Conn. Entered U.S. Department of State (1941); undersecretary (1945–47), secretary of state (1949–53); formulated Truman Doctrine (1947); helped shape Marshall Plan (1947–48); promoted formation of NATO (1949). Author of *Power and Diplomacy* (1958), *Morning and Noon* (1965), *Present at the Creation* (1969; Pulitzer prize).

Acheson, Edward Goodrich. 1856–1931. American inventor, b. Washington, Pa. Assistant to Thomas Edison (1880–81); discovered silicon carbide, which he named carborundum (1891); devised new method for making graphite (1896).

Achil·les Paint·er \ə-'kil-ēz-'pānt-ər\. 5th century B.C. Name given to an Athenian vase painter known for red-figure work, as *Achilles and Briseis,* whence his name, and white-ground funerary vases.

Achilles Ta·ti·us \-'tā-sh(ē-)əs\. 2d century A.D. Greek rhetorician. Author of a romance, *Leucippe and Cleitophon.*

Achil·li·ni \ˌäk-ē-'lē-nē\, Alessandro. 1463–1512. Italian philosopher and physician. Professor at Bologna (1484–1512); follower of William of Ockham.

Achor·is \'ak-ə-rəs\. 4th century B.C. Egyptian king. Third ruler of 29th dynasty (reigned 393–380 B.C.).

Ack·er·mann \'äk-ər-ˌmän\, Konrad Ernst. 1710 or 1712–1771. German actor. Opened (1765) in Hamburg a theater, later regarded as setting standard for German acting.

Ack·er·mann \ä-ker-mån\, Louise-Victorine, *nee* Cho·quet \shò-ke\. 1813–1890. French poet. m. (1843) Paul Ackermann. Wrote *Contes en vers* (1855), *Contes et poésies* (1862), and deeply pessimistic *Poésies, premières poésies, poésies philosophiques* (1874).

Ack·er·mann \'ak-ər-mən\, Rudolph. 1764–1834. German inventor and art publisher. Established print shop, London (1795); patented (1801) method for waterproofing paper and cloth; credited with establishing art lithography in England.

Acon·cio \ä-'kòn-chō\ *or* **Acon·zio** \ä-'kònt-syō\, Giacomo. *Lat.* Jacobus Acon·tius \ə-'kän-shē-əs\. 1492–?1566. Italian engineer and religious writer.

Secretary to Cardinal Madruzzo; repudiated Roman Catholicism, made way to England (1559); wrote *Satanae stratagematum* (1565), notable attempt to find a basis of dogma common to all Christians.

Acos·ta \ä-'kō-stä\, Joaquín. 1800–1852. Colombian soldier and historian. Soldier in Bolívar's army (1819); wrote fully documented *Compendio histórico del descubrimiento y colonización de la Nueva Granada* (1848).

Acosta, José de. 1539–1600. Spanish missionary. Entered Jesuit order (1551); to Peru (1571); provincial (1576–81); theologian to council of Lima (1582); to Spain (1587); author of *Historia natural y moral de las Indias* (1590).

Acosta Gar·cía \-gär-'sē-ä\, Julio. 1872–1954. Costa Rican politician. President of Costa Rica (1920–24).

Acosta, Uriel. See Gabriel da COSTA.

Acquaviva, Claudio. See AQUAVIVA.

Acropolites, Georgius. See AKROPOLITES.

Ac·ton \'ak-tən\, John Emerich Edward Dal·berg \'dal-bərg\. 1st Baron Acton. 1834–1902. English historian. Grandson of Sir John F.E. Acton and of Emmerich Joseph, duc de Dalberg. Introduced to Whig circles by stepfather, Lord Granville; M.P. (1859–65); edited John Henry Newman's *Rambler* (1859–64); created baron (1869); professor of modern history, Cambridge (1895–1902). Leader of English liberal Roman Catholics hostile to dogma of papal infallibility. Planned, as editor, *Cambridge Modern History.*

Acton, Sir John Francis Edward. 1736–1811. English naval officer in service of Tuscany and Naples. Commanded Tuscan squadron against Algeria (1774); reorganized and made commander in chief of Neapolitan navy (1779); minister of navy, of war, of finance, and prime minister under Ferdinand IV of Naples; on entry of French into Naples fled to Sicily (1806).

Acu·ña \ä-'kün-yä\, Cristóbal de. 1597–?1676. Spanish missionary. To South America; accompanied Pedro Teixeira on trip down Amazon (1637–39); author of *Nuevo descubrimiento del gran río de las Amazonas* (1641).

Acuña, Hernando de. c.1520–1580. Spanish poet, soldier, and diplomat. Known esp. for translation of Olivier de La Marche's *Le Chevalier délibéré* into Spanish quintillas as *El caballero determinado* (1553).

Adad-ni·ra·ri \'ä-däd-nē-'rä-rē\. Name of several kings of Assyria: Adad-nirari I (reigned c.1307–c.1275 B.C.); defeated Kassites and the Mitanni; extended boundaries of empire; succeeded by his son Shalmaneser I. ¶Adad-nirari II (reigned 911–891 B.C.); resumed southeastern campaigns, annexing new regions along the Tigris; defeated Babylonian king (909); reconquered Aramaeans in northwest (907–903); made treaty with Babylonians; succeeded by his son Tukuliti-Ninurta II. ¶Adad-nirari III (reigned 810–783 B.C.), son of Shamshi-Adad V and of Sammu-ramat (Semiramis); extended conquests to west.

Adair \ə-'da(ə)r, -'de(ə)r\, John. c.1655–c.1772. Scottish surveyor and cartographer. Prepared (1680–86) maps of counties adjoining River Forth and charts of Forth, River Clyde, and the west country; published (1703) first part of *Description of the Sea-coast and Islands of Scotland, With Large and Exact Maps;* work established new standard of excellence in map-making.

Adal·be·ro \ä-däl-'ber-ō\. d. 989. Frankish prelate. Archbishop of Reims (from 969); intrigued against attempt of Lothair to recapture Lorraine; saved from trial by Hugh Capet (985); on death of Louis V (987), declared Frankish crown elective rather than hereditary, then supported and crowned Hugh Capet.

Adalbero. *Also called* As·ce·lin *or* As·se·lin \'äs-ə-(,)lin\. *Known as* the Old Traitor. d. 1030. Frankish prelate. Bishop of Laon (from 977); supported election of Hugh Capet to Frankish throne (987); plotted with Otto III of Germany against Hugh Capet (993); led unsuccessful revolt against Robert II (998). Author of several satirical poems.

Adal·bert \'äd-äl-,bert, *Angl* 'ad-ᵊl-(,)bərt\ *or* **Adel·bert** \'äd-əl-,bert, *Angl* 'ad-ᵊl-(,)bərt, ə-'del-\. Saint. *Orig.* Voj·těch \'vi-chek\. 956–997. Bohemian prince and prelate. Elected first native bishop of Prague (982); failing to convert his people, abandoned his diocese and retired (988) to monastery near Rome; sent back to Prague (992) by Pope John XV; again left (994) and preached gospel among Hungarians, Poles, and Prussians; murdered by a heathen priest. Known as "Apostle of the Prussians."

Adalbert. d. c.966. Lombard king of Italy (950–c.966). Great grandson of Berengar of Friuli and son of Berengar II of Ivrea. With father fought Hugh of Provence and his son Lothair (946–947); on Lothair's death crowned co-king of Italy with father (950); engaged in constant struggle with Emperor Otto I, who drove him from Italy (951, 962, 965).

Adalbert. c.1000–1072. German prelate. Archbishop of Hamburg-Bremen (1043); as papal legate (1053) under Pope Leo IX spread Christianity among the Wends; failed to form an independent northern patriarchate; guardian of and tutor to Henry IV and virtual ruler in Saxony (1064–66).

Adalbert. *In full* Heinrich Wilhelm Adalbert. 1811–1873. Prince of Prussia. Nephew of Frederick William III. Engaged in organizing first German fleet; chief of Prussian navy (1849); admiral (1854).

Ada·lo·ald \,äd-ä-'lō-äld\. 602–c.626. Lombard king of Italy (616–c.626). Son of King Agilulf. Undertook (c.624) campaign of murder against Lombard chiefs, on apparent pretext of combating Arianism; deposed and murdered.

Adam \'ad-əm\ of Bremen. *Ger.* Adam von Bre·men \'äd-äm-fōn-'brā-mən\. d. 1081–85. German ecclesiastical historian. Author of *Gesta Hammaburgensis ecclesiae pontificum* (c.1072–76), important for history, politics, geography, including earliest reference to Leif Ericsson's Vinland.

Adam \'äd-äm\. Family of Bavarian painters, including: Albrecht (1786–1862), painter of battle scenes and horses; and his sons ¶Benno (1812–1892), painter of the hunt and of animals, ¶Franz (1815–1886), painter of animals and battle scenes, ¶Eugen (1817–1880), genre painter and painter of battle scenes, and ¶Julius (1821–1874), lithographer and photographer.

Adam \á-däᵐ\. Family of French sculptors, including: Jacob Sigisbert (1670–1747) and his sons ¶Lambert Sigisbert, *called* Adam l'Aîné (1700–1759), who founded an influential atelier and executed pieces for Versailles, as *Neptune et Amphitrite,* for Choisy, and for Frederick II of Prussia; ¶Nicolas Sebastien, *called* Adam Cadet (1705–1778), best known for *Prométhée enchaîné* at the *Académie,* and ¶François Balthasar Gaspard (1710–1761), who executed many monuments in Potsdam and Sans Souci.

Adam, Adolphe-Charles. 1803–1856. French composer. Known for comic operas, esp. *Le Chalet* (1834) and *Le Postillion de Longjumeau* (1836), masses, vocal music and ballets, esp. *Giselle* (1841).

Adam, Juliette, *nee* Lam·ber \läⁿ-ber\. 1836–1936. French writer. Founded (1879) and edited *La Nouvelle Revue;* author of novels and miscellaneous works. Her second husband ¶Antoine-Edmond Adam (1816–1877), was prefect of police in Paris during Franco-Prussian War.

Adam, Paul. 1862–1920. French writer. Author of novels in naturalist manner, as *Chair molle* (1885), and in Symbolist manner, as *Le Thé chez Miranda* (1886); later known for historical novels, as *La Force* (1889), *La Ruse* (1903), *Au soleil de juillet* (1903), *Le Serpent noir* (1905); wrote *Vues d'Amérique* (1906), *Le Trust* (1910) on United States.

Ad·am \'ad-əm\, Robert. 1728–1792. Scottish architect. Studied under father and (1754–58) in Italy; established practice in London; executed Admiralty Screen (1760); appointed architect of the king's works (1761); with brother James (d. 1794) developed the light, airy Adam style that largely supplanted the Palladian version of Neoclassicism; other important works included Adelphi development, London (1768–72), Portland Place (1773), Derby House (1773–74), Register House, Edinburgh (1772–92), U. of Edinburgh (1789); also designed furniture in a style popularized by Hepplewhite.

Adam, Roi. See ADENET LE ROI.

Adam de la Halle \á-däⁿ-də-lá-ál\. *Called* Adam le Bos·su \lə-bò-sü̅\, *i.e.* Adam the Hunchback. c.1250–c.1306. French trouvère, musician, and playwright. Composed lyrics, love songs, motets, rondeaux, and dramatic pieces. Author of *Le Jeu de la feuillée,* known as the earliest French comedy, *Le Congé, Le Jeu de Robin et Marion,* earliest comic opera, *Jeu de pélérin.*

Ad·a·mic \'ad-ə-mik, ə-'dam-ik\, Louis. 1899–1951. American author, b. Blato, Carniola (now in Yugoslavia). To U.S. (1913); naturalized (1918). Author of *Dynamite* (1931), *The Native's Return* (1934), *Cradle of Life* (1936), *My America* (1938), *From Many Lands* (1940), *Two-Way Passage* (1942), etc.

Ad·am·nan \'ad-əm-,nan, ə-'dam-nən\ *or* **Ad·om·nan** \'ad-əm-,nan, ə-'däm-nən\ *or* **Eu·nan** \'ō-nən\. Saint. c.628–704. Irish ecclesiastic. Abbot of Iona (679–704); author of a biography *Vita S. Columba.*

Ada·mov \(,)ə-'dá-məv\, Arthur. 1908–1970. Armenian-Russian writer. To Germany (1912), Paris (1924); associated with Surrealists; wrote autobiographical *L'Aven* (1938–43); wrote plays that helped create Theatre of the Absurd, including *La Parodie* (1947), *L'Invasion* (1950), *La grande et la petite manoeuvre* (1950), *Le Professeur Taranne* (1953), *Le Ping-Pong* (1955), *Paolo Paoli* (1957), *Le Printemps 71* (1961), *La Politique des restes* (1963).

Ad·ams \'ad-əmz\, Abigail, *nee* Smith. 1744–1818. American writer, b. Weymouth, Mass. m. (1764) John Adams, second President of the United States. Her grandson Charles Francis Adams published her letters (1840).

Adams, Alvin. 1804–1877. American businessman, b. Andover, Vt. Formed (1840) Adams & Co., incorporated (1854) as Adams Express Co.

Adams, Andy. 1859–1935. American cowboy and writer, b. Whitley Co., Ind. Wrote stories and novels of cowboy life, including *The Log of a Cowboy* (1903), *Texas Matchmaker* (1904), *The Outlet* (1905), *Cattle Brands* (1906).

Adams, Ansel Easton. 1902–1984. American photographer, b. San Francisco. Known for his sharply focused photographs of the American landscape. Adopted Paul Strand's "straight photography" as medium of expression. Formed (1932) Group f/64 with Edward Weston and other exponents of straight photography, establishing photography as an art form; co-founded (1940) the collection of photographs at New York's Museum of Modern Art; established (1946) San Fransciso's California School of Fine Arts. An ardent conservationist, served as director of Sierra Club (1936–73). Published many portfolios of his work.

Adams, Brooks. 1848–1927. American historian, b. Quincy, Mass. Son of Charles Francis Adams (1807–86). Author of *Law of Civilization and Decay*

(1895), *America's Economic Supremacy* (1900), *The New Empire* (1902), *The Theory of Social Revolutions* (1913).

Adams, Charles Follen. 1842–1918. American poet, b. Dorchester, Mass. Author of German dialect poems, as in *Leedle Yawcob Strauss, and Other Poems* (1877) and *Dialect Ballads* (1888).

Adams, Charles Francis. 1807–1886. American diplomat and author, b. Boston. Son of John Quincy Adams. Member, U.S. House of Representatives (1858–61); minister to Great Britain (1861–68) through Civil War; one of U.S. arbitrators on commission to settle *Alabama* claims (1871–72). Edited letters of Abigail Adams (1840), *Works of John Adams* (1850–56), and *Memoirs of John Quincy Adams* (1874–77).

Adams, Charles Francis. 1835–1915. American railroad expert and historian, b. Boston. Son of Charles Francis Adams (1807–86). Member (1869–79) and chairman (1872–79), Massachusetts Board of Railroad Commissioners; chairman of government directors (1878) and president (1884–90), Union Pacific Railroad; forced out by Jay Gould. Author of *Chapters of Erie* (1871), *New Departure in the Common Schools* (1879), *Railroads: Their Origin and Problems* (1878), *Life of Charles Francis Adams* (1900). His nephew ¶ Charles Francis Adams (1866–1954), b. Quincy, Mass., was a noted yachtsman and U.S. secretary of the navy (1929–33).

Adams, Charles Kendall. 1835–1902. American educator, b. Derby, Vt. Professor of history, U. of Michigan (1867–85); president of Cornell (1885–92), of U. of Wisconsin (1892–1901).

Adams, Frank Dawson. 1859–1942. Canadian geologist, b. Montreal. Member of Geological Survey of Canada (1880–89); on faculty of McGill U. (1889–1931); known for studies of metamorphism and Precambrian crystalline rocks; author of *The Birth and Development of Geological Sciences* (1938).

Adams, Franklin Pierce. *Known as* F.P.A. 1881–1960. American journalist and humorist, b. Chicago. Conducted column "The Conning Tower," in New York *Tribune* (1914–22), *World* (1922–31), *Herald-Tribune* (1931–37), *Post* (1937–41). Author of *Tobogganing on Parnassus* (1911), *In Other Words* (1912), *By and Large* (1914), *So There!* (1922), *Christopher Columbus* (1931), *The Diary of Our Own Samuel Pepys* (1935), etc.; one of regular members of "Information Please" radio program (1938–48).

Adams, Hannah. 1755–1831. American author, b. Medfield, Mass. Compiler of *Alphabetical Compendium of the Various Sects* (1784); author of *Summary History of New-England* (1799).

Adams, Harriet Stratemeyer. See Edward STRATEMEYER.

Adams, Henry Brooks. 1838–1918. American historian, b. Boston. Son of Charles Francis Adams (1807–86). Secretary to his father in Washington (1860–61) and London (1861–68); teacher of history at Harvard, and editor of *North American Review* (1870–76). Author of *Essays in Anglo-Saxon Law* (1876), biographies of John Randolph and Albert Gallatin (1879, 1882), novels *Democracy* (1880) and *Esther* (1884), *History of the United States,* covering Jefferson and Madison administrations (1889–91), *Mont-Saint-Michel and Chartres* (1904), *The Education of Henry Adams* (1907; Pulitzer Prize 1919), *A Letter to American Teachers of History* (1910), *Degradation of Democratic Dogma* (1919).

Adams, Herbert Samuel. 1858–1945. American sculptor, b. West Concord, Vt. Executed busts of John Marshall, William Ellery Channing, William Cullen Bryant, Will Rogers, and Joseph Story; also the bronze doors of St. Bartholomew's Church, New York City, and those of the Library of Congress.

Adams, Herbert Baxter. 1850–1901. American historian, b. Shutesbury, Mass. Professor, Johns Hopkins (1876–1901); inaugurated *Johns Hopkins Studies in Historical and Political Science* series (1882). An organizer (1884) and first secretary (1884–1900), American Historical Association. Author of *Life and Writings of Jared Sparks* (1893), etc.

Adams, James Truslow. 1878–1949. American historian, b. Brooklyn, N.Y. New York stockbroker (1900–12); retired to study and write. Author of *Founding of New England* (1921; Pulitzer prize), *Revolutionary New England, 1691–1776* (1923), *The Epic of America* (1931), *The March of Democracy* (1932–33), *America's Tragedy* (1935), *Frontiers of American Culture* (1943), etc.; editor of *Dictionary of American History* (1940), *Atlas of American History* (1943), *Album of American History* (1944–48).

Adams, John. 1735–1826. Second president of the United States, b. Braintree (now Quincy), Mass. Defense counsel for British soldiers accused of Boston Massacre (1770); delegate to Continental Congress (1774–78); member of committee charged with drafting Declaration of Independence (1776); congressional commissioner to France (1778–79); minister to United Provinces (1780); negotiated a loan from Dutch bankers (1782). Joined Jay and Franklin in Paris (1782) to negotiate treaty of peace with Great Britain; minister to Great Britain (1785–88). Elected vice-president (1789, 1792) and president (1796) of United States; defeated by Jefferson for presidency (1800) and retired to private life. Author of *Dissertation on the Canon and Feudal Law* (1768), *Thoughts on Government* (1776), *A Defence of the Constitutions of Government of the United States of America* (1787–88).

Adams, John. *Alias* Alexander Smith. 1760?–1829. British seaman. Mutineer on H.M.S. *Bounty* (1789); founded colony on Pitcairn Island.

Adams, John Couch. 1819–1892. English astronomer. Deduced mathematically existence and location of the planet Neptune (1843–45). Professor at St. Andrews (1858), Cambridge (from 1859); director of Cambridge Observatory (from 1861); investigated lunar theory, Leonid meteors.

Adams, John Quincy. 1767–1848. Sixth president of the United States, b. Braintree (now Quincy), Mass. Son of John Adams (1735–1826). Minister to the Netherlands (1794–96), Germany (1796–1801); in U.S. Senate (1803–08); minister to St. Petersburg (1809–11). Appointed justice of Supreme Court (1811), but declined. One of negotiators (1814) of Treaty of Ghent ending War of 1812; minister to Great Britain (1815–17); secretary of state under Monroe (1817–25); negotiated northern U.S. boundary with Great Britain (1818); largely formulated Monroe Doctrine (1823). President of the United States (1825–29); defeated by Andrew Jackson for second term. Representative in Congress (1831–48); fought against congressional gag rule (1836–44).

Adams, Joseph Quincy. 1881–1946. American scholar, b. Greenville, S.C. Teacher at Cornell (1909–31); director, Folger Shakespeare Library, Washington, D.C. (1931–46). General editor, *The New Variorum Shakespeare.* Author of *Shakespearean Playhouses* (1917), *Life of William Shakespeare* (1923); editor of *Chief Pre-Shakespearean Dramas* (1924).

Adams, Maude Ewing. *Orig. surname* Kis·kad·den \kis-ˈkad-ən\. 1872–1953. American actress, b. Salt Lake City. Starred in *Little Minister* (1897–98), *L'Aiglon* (1900–01), *Quality Street* (1902), *Peter Pan* (1905–07), *What Every Woman Knows* (1908–09), *Chantecler* (1910–11), etc. Retired (1918); returned in *Merchant of Venice* (1931, with Otis Skinner), *Twelfth Night* (1934). Teacher of dramatics, Stephens Coll. (1937–43).

Adams, Robert. c.1791–1875. Irish physician. Known for studies of heart disease and gout; described (1827) Adams-Stokes disease or syndrome.

Adams, Roger. 1889–1971. American chemist, b. Boston. Taught at Illinois (1916–57); head of chemistry department (1926–54); conducted researches in organic chemistry; determined constitution of chaulmoogra oil, gossypol, marijuana, and many alkaloids; worked also in stereochemistry, synthesis of medical compounds, and platinum catalysis.

Adams, Samuel. 1722–1803. American revolutionary politician, b. Boston. Unsuccessful in business; tax collector of Boston (1756–64); member of Massachusetts legislature (1765–74). Organized opposition to Stamp Act (1765); organized Non-Importation Association (1768); helped found Boston Committee of Correspondence (1772) and instrumental in maintaining activities of similar committees among American colonies; leader in agitation that led up to Boston Tea Party (1773). Delegate (1774–75) to First and Second Continental Congresses; signed Declaration of Independence; member of Congress (to 1781); governor of Massachusetts (1794–97).

Adams, Samuel Hopkins. 1871–1958. American journalist, b. Dunkirk, N.Y. On staff New York *Sun* (1891–1900), *McClure's Magazine* (1900–05). Author of *The Great American Fraud* (1906), *Average Jones* (1911), *Success* (1921), *Revelry* (1926), *The Flagrant Years* (1929), *The Gorgeous Hussy* (1934), *The Harvey Girls* (1942), *The Pony Express* (1950), *The Erie Canal* (1953).

Adams, Sarah, *nee* Flow·er \ˈflau̇-(ə)r\. 1805–1848. English poet and hymn writer. m. W. B. Adams (1834). Author of *Vivia Perpetua* (dramatic poem; 1841), and the hymn "Nearer, My God, to Thee" (1840).

Adams, Sherman. 1899–1966. American government official, b. East Dover, Vt. Governor of New Hampshire (1949–53); White House chief of staff under Pres. Dwight Eisenhower (1953–58); directed day-to-day White House operations; established precedent for powerful presidential chiefs of staff; resigned (1958) under fire following disclosures that he had accepted expensive gifts from businessman seeking federal favors.

Adams, Walter Sydney. 1876–1956. American astronomer, b. Antioch, Syria. Astronomer (from 1904), director (1923–46), Mount Wilson Observatory, Calif.; studied stellar spectra; determined spectroscopically the differential rotation of the sun and presence of carbon dioxide in atmosphere of Venus; ascertained velocities and distances of thousands of stars; helped plan Mt. Palomar Observatory.

Adams, William. *Jp. title* An·jin Sa·ma \ˈän-jēn-sä-mä\, *i.e.* Mr. Pilot. 1564–1620. English navigator. Engaged (1598) as pilot major for Dutch fleet of five vessels bound for the Indies, one of which reached Kyushu (1600); as first Englishman to visit Japan, summoned to shogun at Ōsaka; because of his knowledge of ships, shipbuilding, navigation, etc., held by shogun as adviser (1600–20), rendering valuable services to the Japanese; helped establish English trading factory for East India Co. (c.1613).

Adams, William Taylor. *Pseudonym* Oliver Op·tic \ˈäp-tik\. 1822–1897. American author, b. Bellingham, Mass. Teacher in Boston public schools (1845–65); author of some 125 books, chiefly various series of books for boys.

Ad·am·son \ˈad-əm-sən\, Joy Friederike Victoria, *nee* Gess·ner \ˈges-nər\. 1910–1980. British naturalist and writer, b. Austria. m. (1943) George Adamson. Lived in Kenya (from 1937), studying and painting wildlife and tribesmen; author of *Born Free* (1960), *Elsa* (1961), *Forever Free* (1962), *Elsa and Her Cubs* (1965), etc.

Adamson, William Charles. 1854–1929. American politician, b. Bowdon, Ga. Member, U.S. House of Representatives (1897–1917); introduced Adamson Act (1916), making eight hours a normal day for railroad labor.

Adam von Ful·da \ˈäd-äm-fȯn-ˈfu̇l-dä\. c.1445–1505. German composer. Court music master and composer in Torgau; professor at Wittenberg (1502); author of *De musica* (1490).

Adan le Menestrel. See ADENET LE ROI.

Adan·son \a-dän-sōn\, Michel. 1727–1806. French naturalist. Author of *Les Familles naturelles des plantes* (1763) in which he proposed a system of classification and nomenclature later superseded by that of Linnaeus.

Ad·dams \ˈad-əmz\, Jane. 1860–1935. American social worker, b. Cedarville, Ill. With Ellen Gates Starr, opened social settlement of Hull-House, Chicago (1889); its resident head (1889–1935). Became acknowledged leader of social settlement work in U.S.; founder and first president (1911–35), National Federation of Settlements. President (1919–35), Woman's International League for Peace and Freedom; helped found (1920) American Civil Liberties Union. Shared Nobel peace prize with Nicholas Murray Butler (1931). Author of *Democracy and Social Ethics* (1902), *Twenty Years at Hull-House* (1910), *A New Conscience and an Ancient Evil* (1911), *Peace and Bread in Time of War* (1922), *The Second Twenty Years at Hull-House* (1930), etc.

Ad·dicks \ˈad-iks\, John Edward O'Sullivan. 1841–1919. American promoter and politician, b. Philadelphia. Pioneer in production of illuminating gas; president, Bay State Gas Co. (1884), Brooklyn Gas Co. (1892). Promoter, with Thomas W. Lawson, of Amalgamated Copper Co. Campaigned (1889–1906) to obtain U.S. senatorship from Delaware by bribery and corruption.

Ad·ding·ton \ˈad-iŋ-tən\, Henry. 1st Viscount Sid·mouth \ˈsid-məth\. 1757–1844. English politician. M.P. (1784–1805); speaker, House of Commons (1789–1801); prime minister, first lord of treasury, and chancellor of exchequer (1801–04); created viscount (1805); lord president of council (1805, 1806–07, 1812); lord privy seal (1806); as home secretary (1812–21) took strong measures against Luddite rioters, suspended habeas corpus (1817), introduced four of the Six Acts (1819), his repressive measures helping to provoke Peterloo Massacre (1819).

Ad·di·son \ˈad-ə-sən\, Christopher. 1st Viscount Addison. 1869–1951. English physician and politician. M.P. (1910–22, 1929–31, 1934–35); minister of munitions (1916–17); minister of reconstruction (1917); first minister of health (1919–21); minister without portfolio (1921); minister of agriculture and fisheries (1930–31); created baron (1937), viscount (1945); secretary of state for dominion affairs (1945–47); leader of House of Lords (1945–51); lord privy seal (1947–51).

Addison, Joseph. 1672–1719. English essayist, poet, and statesman. Early Latin verse commended by Dryden; attracted Whig patronage with "A Poem to His Majesty" (1695); traveled in Europe on pension in preparation for diplomatic service (1699–1704); succeeded John Locke in sinecure of commissioner of appeals in excise (1704). Wrote, at request of Lord Halifax, *The Campaign* (1704), celebrating Marlborough's victory at Blenheim. Undersecretary of state (1705–08); secretary to lord lieutenant of Ireland (1708–10); M.P. (from 1708). Started *Whig Examiner,* a periodical (1710). Contributed essays to Steele's *Tatler* (1709–11); with Steele produced the nonpolitical *Spectator,* writing half the 555 papers of social satire and literary criticism (1711–12). His tragedy *Cato,* produced at Drury Lane (1713), was successful, partly because of popular interpretation as a defense of the Whigs. Contributed a few papers to Steele's *Guardian* (1713) and to a revived *Spectator* (1714); issued the *Free-Holder* (1715–16); wrote comedy *The Drummer,* produced at Drury Lane (1716). Secretary for Ireland (1715). m. Charlotte, Countess Dowager of Warwick (1716). One of lords commissioners of trade (1716); secretary of state under Sunderland (1717–18). Considered one of the great masters of English prose, esp. of the periodical essay. See Sir Richard STEELE and Thomas TICKELL.

Addison, Thomas. 1793–1860. English physician. Physician to Guy's Hospital, London (from 1837); described (1849) Addison's disease and Addison's anemia.

Ade \ˈād\, George. 1866–1944. American humorist and playwright, b. Kentland, Ind. On staff of *Chicago Record* (1890–1900). Author of *Fables in Slang* (1899), *The Girl Proposition* (1902), *Breaking into Society* (1903), *Knocking the Neighbors* (1912), *Single Blessedness* (1922), *The Old-Time Saloon* (1931), and the plays *The Sultan of Sulu* (1902), *The County Chairman* (1903), *The College Widow* (1904), *Father and the Boys* (1907).

Ad·e·la \ˈad-ə-lə\. c.1062–1137. French noblewoman. Daughter of William the Conqueror; m. (1080) Stephen, Count of Blois and Chartres. Mother of Stephen, king of England, whose title to the throne derived through her.

Ade·laer *or* **Ade·ler** \ˈäd-ə-lər\, Cort Sivertsen. *Orig.* Cort Si·vert·sen \ˈsē-vərt-sən\. 1622–1675. Norwegian naval commander. In service of Dutch (1639–42), of Venice (1642–61); distinguished himself in battle at Dardanelles and forced Turkish surrender at Tenedos (1654); lieutenant admiral (1660); admiral of Danish fleet (1662).

Ad·e·laide \ˈad-ə-ˌlād\. Saint. *Ger.* Adel·heid \ˈäd-əl-ˌhīt\. 931–999. Holy Roman empress. Daughter of King Rudolf II of Burgundy; m. Lothair (947; d. 950), son of King Hugh of Italy. Imprisoned by Berengar II (951); appealed to Otto I, King of Germany, who came to her rescue and married her (951); crowned empress by Pope John XII (962). As queen mother during reign of Otto II (973–983), had much influence in administering state affairs. Joint regent with Empress Theophano for Otto III (983–991), sole regent (991–996).

Adelaide. *In full* Amelia Adelaide Louisa Theresa Caroline. 1792–1849. Queen of William IV of England. Daughter of George, Duke of Saxe-Coburg-Meiningen; m. (1818) William, Duke of Clarence, who became William IV of England (1830).

Adé·la·ïde \a-dā-la-ēd\. *In full* Adélaïde Eugénie Louise. Princess of Or·lé·ans \ȯr-lā-än\. 1777–1847. French noblewoman. Sister of Louis-Philippe; influential in persuading him to accept the crown (1830).

Ad·e·lard \ˈad-əl-ˌärd\ of Bath. 12th century. English traveler and philosopher. Author of Platonic *De eodem et diverso,* the *Quaestiones naturales* based on Arabic science, and Latin translation of Arabic version of Euclid's *Elements.*

Adelbert. See ADALBERT.

Adel·chis \ˈäd-əl-kis\. d. c.788. Lombard prince. Son of King Desiderius. Fled from Charlemagne's attacks on Pavia and Verona (773); with Byzantine and Greek support, attempted to regain control of Italy (788); either killed or captured in attempt, or retired to Constantinople.

Adeler. See ADELAER.

Ade·lung \ˈäd-ə-ˌlu̇ŋ\, Johann Christoph. 1732–1806. German philologist and grammarian. Court librarian at Dresden (1787–1806); author of highly influential *Versuch eines vollständigen grammatisch-kritischen Wörterbuches der hochdeutschen Mundart* (1774–86), *Über den deutschen Stil* (1785–86), *Mithridates, oder allgemeine Sprachenkunde* (1806–17); helped standardize German grammar, spelling, style.

Ade·nau·er \ˈäd-ə-ˌnau̇-ər; *Angl* ˈad-ən-ˌau̇(-ə)r, ˈäd-\, Konrad. 1876–1967. German politician. Lord mayor of Cologne (1917); member (1920–33) and speaker (1928–33) of Prussian Staatsrat; helped form Christian Democratic party (1945), chairman (1946–66); chairman of Parlamentarischer Rat (1946–49); member of Bundestag (1949–66) and first chancellor of postwar West Germany (1949–63).

Ade·net le Roi \äd-nel-ər-wä\. *Known also as* Roi Adam, Li Rois Adenes, Adan le Menestrel, Adam Rex Menestrallus. c.1240–c.1300. French trouvère. Chief minstrel to Guy of Dampierre (from c.1268); adapted chansons de geste to fashionable forms.

Ade·od·a·tus \ˌäd-ē-ˈäd-ət-əs\. Name of two popes:

Adeodatus I. See DEUSDEDIT.

Adeodatus II. *Sometimes known as* Deusdedit II. d. 676. Pope (672–676). First to date events in terms of his reign.

Ader \á-der\, Clément. 1841–1926. French engineer and inventor. Invented microphone, public-address device; built and flew for 50 meters the "Eole," bat-winged steam-powered airplane (1890).

Ad·hé·mar de Cha·bannes \á-dā-mär-də-shá-bán\. 988–1034. Frankish chronicler. Author of *Chronican Aquitanicum et Francicum,* history of Aquitania and the Franks from legendary times to 1028.

Adhémar de Mon·teil \-də-mōn-tāy\. *Called also* Ai·mar de Le Puy \em-ár-də-lə-pwyē\. d. 1098. French prelate. Bishop of Le Puy (1077); named papal legate (1095) by Pope Urban II to lead First Crusade; principal unifying force and military leader of Crusade; died of plague.

Ad·her·bal \ad-ˈhər-bəl\. d. 112 B.C. Numidian king. Son of King Micipsa. King of Numidia (118–112 B.C.) jointly with his brother Hiempsal (to c.117) and cousin Jugurtha; ousted and slain by Jugurtha.

Ad·ler \ˈäd-lər\, Alfred. 1870–1937. Austrian psychiatrist. Student and associate of Freud (1902–c.1911); advanced theory of the inferiority complex to explain psychopathic cases in *Studie über Minderwertigkeit von Organen* (1907); asserted primacy of aggressive instinct; developed school of individual psychology; wrote *Über den nervösen Charakter* (1912), *Menschenkenntnis* (1927); established first child-guidance clinic in Vienna (1921); taught in U.S. (1927–37).

Ad·ler \ˈad-lər\, Cyrus. 1863–1940. American scholar and educator, b. Van Buren, Ark. With Smithsonian Institution (1892–1908) and U.S. National Museum (1889–1908). President, Dropsie College, Philadelphia (1908–24); president, Jewish Theological Seminary of America, New York (1924–40).

Founded (1906) American Jewish Committee. Editor on *Jewish Encyclopedia;* editor of *American Jewish Year Book* (from 1899).

Adler, Dankmar. 1844–1900. American architect, b. Stadtlengsfeld, Germany. To U.S. (1854). Draftsman and architect in Detroit and Chicago (from 1857); in partnership with Louis Sullivan (1881–95). Built Auditorium, Gage Building, Chicago; Wainwright Building, St. Louis; Guaranty Building, Buffalo, N.Y.; in solo practice designed Chicago Stock Exchange.

Adler, Felix. 1851–1933. American educator, b. Alzey, Germany. To U.S. (1857). Founder (1876) and lecturer, N.Y. Society for Ethical Culture; founder (1880) of Workingmen's School, later called (from 1895) Ethical Culture School. Professor of political and social ethics, Columbia (from 1902). Author of *Creed and Deed* (1877), *Life and Destiny* (1905), *Religion of Duty* (1905), *An Ethical Philosophy of Life* (1918).

Adler, Nathan Marcus. 1803–1890. British rabbi, b. Hanover, Germany. Chief rabbi of Oldenburg (1829), of Hanover (1830); chief rabbi of London (1844); principal founder of Jews' Coll., London (1855); suggested United Synagogues Act (passed 1870). His son ¶Hermann (1839–1911) was also British chief rabbi (from 1891).

Ad·ler \ˈäd-lər\, Victor. 1852–1918. Austrian politician. Under influence of Engels and Bebel founded Socialist weekly *Gleichheit* (1886–89); led in founding Austrian Social Democratic party (1888); member of Lower Austrian diet (1905–18). His son ¶Friedrich (1879–1960), Socialist politician, assassinated (1916) Count Karl von Stürgkh; death sentence commuted.

Ad·ler·spar·re \ˈäd-lər-ˌspär-rə\, Georg. Count. 1760–1835. Swedish general, editor, and writer. Published (1797–1801) liberal journal *Läsningi blandade ämnen;* a leader of army faction in overthrow of Gustavus IX (1809); member of Council of State (1809–10); governor of Skaraborg (1810–24).

Ad·lum \ˈad-ləm\, John. 1759–1836. American viticulturist, b. York, Pa. Produced the Catawba grape; author of *Adlum on Making Wine* (1826).

Adolf. See also ADOLPHUS.

Adolf \ˈäd-ˌȯlf\ of Nas·sau \ˈnäs-ˌau̇\. *Lat.* Adol·phus \ə-ˈdäl-fəs, -ˈdȯl-\. c.1250–1298. King of Germany (1292–98). Son of Walram II, whom he succeeded as count of Nassau (1277). Elected to succeed Rudolf I of Habsburg; claimed title to Holy Roman Empire but never crowned; gained control of Meissen and Thuringia (1294–96); deposed (1298) in favor of Albert I and killed soon after in battle of Göllheim.

Adolf of Nassau. *Full name* Adolf (*or* Adolph) William Charles Frederick Augustus. 1817–1905. Duke of Nassau (1839–66). Forced to relinquish duchy as result of Prussian victory over Austria; renounced all claims to duchy (1867); grand duke and first ruler of autonomous Luxemburg (1890–1905).

Adolf Fred·er·ick \-ˈfred-(ə-)rik\. *Swed.* Adolf Fredrik. 1710–1771. King of Sweden (1751–71). Son of Christian Augustus, Duke of Schleswig-Holstein-Gottorp. Bishop of Lübeck (1727–50); favored by Empress Elizabeth of Russia; through her influence made heir to throne of Sweden (1743); m. (1744) Louisa Ulrica, sister of Frederick the Great. Deprived of power as ruler by council of state and by party factions.

Adol·phus Frederick \ə-ˈdäl-fəs-, -ˈdȯl-\. Duke of Cambridge. 1774–1850. Seventh son of George III of England. Served in Hanoverian and British armies (1793–1803); created duke (1801); privy councillor (1802); colonel of Coldstream guards (1805); field marshal (1813); viceroy of Hanover (1816–37).

Ador \á-dȯr\, Gustave. 1845–1928. Swiss politician. Member (1889–1917) and president (1902), National Council; president, Swiss Confederation (1919).

Ador·no \ä-ˈdȯr-nō\, Theodor. *Orig. surname* Weis·en·grund \ˈvēs-ən-ˌgru̇nt\. 1903–1969. German philosopher and music critic. Taught at Frankfurt (1931–33), Oxford (1934–37), Princeton (1938–50), Frankfurt (1950–69); under influence of Hegel and Marx, took sociological approach to philosophy and music; author of *Dialektik der Aufklärung* (1947, with M. Horkheimer), *Philosophie der neuen Musik* (1949), *Minima Moralia* (1951), *Versuch über Wagner* (1952), *Dissonanzen* (1956), *Mahler* (1960), *Drei Studien über Hegel* (1963), *Jargon der Eigentlichkeit* (1964).

Adret \ä-ˈdret\, Solomon ben Abraham. *Known in Hebrew as* Rabbi Shlomo ben Adret *or as* Rash·ba \räsh-ˈbä\. 1235–1310. Spanish rabbi. Widely influential as Talmudist; known esp. for decree (1305) threatening excommunication of all Jews under 30 who studied philosophy or science.

Adrets, Baron des. See François de BEAUMONT.

Adri·an \ˈā-drē-ən\. Name of six popes:

Adrian I. d. 795. Pope (772–795). Summoned Charlemagne to drive back Lombards under Desiderius, who were threatening Rome (773–774); secured temporal control of territories that remained the Papal States for 11 centuries; presided over Second Nicene Council (787) and won its condemnation of iconoclast heresy.

Adrian II. 792–872. Pope (867–872). Failed to maintain vigorous policies of St. Nicholas I; dominated by secretary, Anastasius the Librarian; readmitted Lothair II of Lorraine to communion and intervened ineffectually in his succession; rebuffed by Charles II the Bald and by Archbishop Hincmar of Reims; approved Slavic liturgy of Cyril and Methodius, but lost Bulgaria to Constantinople; dispatched legates to Council of Constantinople (869–870) and caused removal of Patriarch Photius.

Adrian III. Saint. d. 885. Pope (884–885). Died en route to Diet of Worms to aid Charles III the Fat in settling his succession.

Adrian IV. *Orig.* Nicholas Break·spear \ˈbrāk-ˌspi(ə)r\. 1100?–1159. Pope (1154–59), b. near St. Albans, England. Cardinal bishop of Albano (1149); legate to Scandinavia (1152); only English pope; crowned Frederick Barbarossa Holy Roman Emperor (1155); thereafter almost constantly in conflict with the emperor; excommunicated (1154), then accepted as liege (1156) William I the Bad of Sicily; supposed to have issued controversial bull giving Ireland to Henry II of England (1154).

Adrian V. *Orig.* Ottobono Fie·schi \ˈfyes-kē\. d. 1276. Pope (1276). Nephew of Pope Innocent IV, who created him cardinal deacon (1244); legate to England (1265–68); died five weeks after election as pope.

Adrian VI. *Orig.* Adrian Florensz Boey·ens \ˈbü-yəns\. 1459–1523. Pope (1522–23). Only Dutch pope. Chancellor of U. of Louvain; chosen tutor (1507) to Archduke Charles (later Charles V); bishop of Tortosa (1516); grand inquisitor of Aragon (1517) and Castile (1518); viceroy of Spain (1517); created cardinal (1517) by Leo X; as pope, failed in efforts to reform church and to oppose advances of Turks.

Adrian, Edgar Douglas. 1st Baron Adrian of Cambridge. 1889–1977. English physiologist. At Cambridge U. as professor (1937–51), master of Trinity Coll. (1951–65), chancellor (1968–75). Known for studies of electrical activity of nerves and brain; corecipient with Sir Charles Sherrington of the Nobel prize (1932) for medicine or physiology.

Adriano di Bologna. See Adriano BANCHIERI.

ʽAḍ·ud ad-Daw·lah \ə-ˌdu̇d-ad-dau̇-ˈlä\. 936–983. Ruler of Iran. Ruler of Fars province (from 944); succeeded to Būyid throne (949); extended rule to all southern Iran and most of Iraq; reign noted for public works, esp. dam near Shīrāz.

Ady \ˈä-dē\, Endre. 1877–1919. Hungarian poet. Worked as journalist in Hungary and Paris; with *Uj versek* (1906) emerged as leading poetic voice in Hungary; works rejuvenated Hungarian language and literature and were taken up by liberal and left-wing reformers; considered greatest Hungarian lyric poet of 20th century. Other volumes included *Vér és Arany* (1907), *Az Illés Szekerén* (1908), *Szeretném Ha Szeretnének* (1909), *Minden Titkok Versei* (1910), *A Magunk Szerelme* (1913).

AE *or* **A.E.** See George William RUSSELL.

Aedde. See EDDI.

Ae·de·sius \i-ˈdē-sē-əs\. d. 335 A.D. Greek philosopher. Founded school of Pergamum, emphasizing Neoplatonic theurgy and polytheism.

Aedilberct. See AETHELBERHT (d. 616).

Aegelbriht. See AETHELBERHT (d. 794).

Aegidius of Assisi. See GILES of Assisi.

Aegidius Romanus. See GILES of Rome.

Aeh·ren·thal \ˈe-rən-tal\, Alois Le·xa \ˈlek-sä\ von. Freiherr. 1854–1912. Austro-Hungarian statesman. Entered imperial foreign service (1877); ambassador to Bucharest (1895), to St. Petersburg (1899); foreign minister (1906–12). Instrumental in Austrian annexation of Bosnia and Herzegovina (1908); created count (1909).

Aeken, Jeroen van. See Hieronymus BOSCH.

Aelfgifu. See EMMA of Normandy.

Aelf·heah \ˈalf-ˌha-ək\. Saint. *Known also as* Al·phege \ˈal-ˌfej\, El·phege \ˈel-\, *or* Al·phage \ˈal-ˌfāj\. 954–1012. English prelate. Anchorite abbot at Bath; bishop of Winchester (984); archbishop of Canterbury (1005). Obtained from Olaf I Trygvasson promise not to invade England (994); captured (1011) and killed by Danes; early venerated as martyr.

Aelfled. See AETHELFLAED.

Aelfred. See ALFRED (849–901).

Ael·fric \ˈal-frik, *also* -frich\. *Called* Gram·mat·i·cus \grə-ˈmat-i-kəs\. c.955–c.1010. Anglo-Saxon abbot and writer. Abbot of Cernel (now Cerne Abbas), later of Eynsham. Author of a Latin and English grammar and glossary, two books of *Catholic Homilies* (990–992) and *Lives of the Saints;* considered greatest Anglo-Saxon prose writer of his time.

Ae·li·an·us \ˌē-lē-ˈā-nəs\ *or* **Ae·li·an** \ˈē-lē-ən\, Claudius. c.170–235 A.D. Roman rhetorician. Author, in Greek, of works commonly known by Latin titles, as *De natura animalium* and *Varia historia.*

Aelianus *or* **Aelian,** *known as* Tac·ti·cus \ˈtak-ti-kəs\. 2d century A.D. Greek writer in Rome. Author of *Taktikē theōria* (probably 106 A.D.), manual of tactics for armored infantry that was of great influence on Byzantine, Muslim, and post-15th century European military practice.

Aelius Donatus. See DONATUS.

\ə\ **abut** \ᵊ\ **kitten,** ***Fr.*** **table** \ər\ **further** \a\ **ash** \ā\ **ace** \ä\ **cot, cart** \au̇\ **out** \ch\ **chin** \e\ **bet** \ē\ **easy** \g\ **go** \i\ **hit** \ī\ **ice** \j\ **job** \ŋ\ **sing** \ō\ **go** \ȯ\ **law** \ȯi\ **boy** \th\ **both** \t͟h\ **the** \ü\ **loot** \u̇\ **foot** \y\ **yet** \zh\ **vision** \á, b̲, g̲, k̲, ⁿ, œ, œ̄, ue, ue̅, ʸ\ ***see*** **Guide to Pronunciation**

Aelius Herodianus. See Herodianus.

Aelius Stilo. See Stilo Praeconinus.

Ael•le \'al-ə\. 5th century A.D. Anglo-Saxon ruler. Supposed to have landed in West Sussex (477); defeated native Britons and founded kingdom of West Sussex; according to Bede, first king acknowledged by all English south of the Humber.

Aelred, Saint. See Aethelred.

Ae•mil•i•a•nus \i-,mil-ē-'ā-nəs\ *or* **Ae•mil•ian** \i-'mil-ē-ən\. *In full* Marcus Aemilius Aemilianus. d. 253 A.D. Roman emperor. Governor of Pannonia and Moesia in reign of Gallus; after successful campaign against barbarians on Danube, invaded Italy; on death of Gallus, recognized by Senate and imperial armies as emperor (253); assassinated three months later by own troops.

Aemilius Lepidus. See Lepidus.

Aemilius Papinianus. See Papinian.

Aemilius Paulus, Lucius. See Paulus.

Aeneas Silvius. See Pope Pius II.

Ae•nes•i•de•mus \i-,nes-ə-'dē-məs\. 1st century B.C. Greek Skeptic philosopher. Author of *Pyrrhonian Discourses.*

Aengus, Saint. See Oengus.

Ae•pi•nus \e-'pē-nus\, Franz Maria Ulrich Theodor Hoch. 1724–1802. German physicist. Professor at St. Petersburg (1757–98); conducted researches in electricity and magnetism; author of *Tentamen theoriae electricitatis et magnetismi* (1759), first attempt to apply mathematics systematically to those phenomena.

Aes•chi•nes \'es-ki-,nēz, 'ē-ski-\. 389–c.314 B.C. Athenian orator. Opponent of Demosthenes in Athenian assembly, advocating appeasement policy in dealing with Philip II of Macedon. Forced into exile (330).

Aes•chy•lus \'es-kə-ləs, 'ēs-, *also* -kyə-\. 525–456 B.C. Greek tragic dramatist. According to tradition, served in Athenian armies in Persian wars and was engaged at Marathon, Artemisium, Salamis, and Plataea. In annual competitions at Athens won first prize in tragedy thirteen times (between 484 and 468). Credited with creating the true drama of action; one of three great Greek tragic poets. Of his many plays (perhaps 90 in all) seven have survived: *Persai* (472 B.C.), *Hepta epi Thebas* (*Seven Against Thebes,* 467), *Hiketides* (*Suppliants,* 463), the *Oresteia* trilogy comprising *Agamemnon, Choephoroi,* and *Eumenides,* and *Prometheus desmotes* (*Prometheus Bound*).

Ae•sop \'ē-,säp, -səp, *sometimes* 'ā-\. Reputed Greek author of *Aesop's Fables.* Said variously to have been a slave and adviser to King Croesus of Lydia. Almost certainly a legendary figure.

Ae•so•pus \i-'sō-pəs\, Claudius *or* Clodius. 1st century B.C. Roman tragedian. Friend of Cicero; regarded by Horace the equal of Roscius.

Aethelbald. See also Eadbald.

Aeth•el•bald \'ath-əl-,bold, 'ath-\ *or* **Eth•el•bald** \'eth-, 'eth-\. d. 757. Anglo-Saxon ruler. King of Mercia (from 716); extended domain, taking in Kent (725) and Wessex (726); styled himself (from 736) "King of Britain"; liberal supporter of the church.

Aethelbald *or* **Ethelbald.** d. 860. Anglo-Saxon ruler. Son of Aethelwulf. Assumed throne of Wessex during father's pilgrimage to Rome (855) and refused to relinquish it on his return (856); m. (858) father's widow Judith, daughter of Charles the Bald.

Aeth•el•berht \'ath-əl-,berkt, 'ad-ᵊl-\. Saint. *Name also spelled* Eth•el•bert \'eth-əl-,bərt, 'eth-\, Aeg•el•briht \'a-(y)əl-'brikt\, Albert. d. 794. British king. King of East Angles; slain by Offa, King of Mercia; venerated as patron of Hereford cathedral.

Aethelberht *or* **Ethelbert** *or* **Aed•il•berct** \'ath-əl-,berkt, 'ad-ᵊl-\. d. 616. King of Kent (560–616). Received Augustine and other missionaries sent by Pope Gregory I (597); issued first surviving Anglo-Saxon code of laws (604); extended rule reputedly to all Britain south of the Humber.

Aethelberht *or* **Ethelbert.** d. 866. Anglo-Saxon ruler. Son of Aethelwulf. Became under-king of Kent (c.853); king (855–856); on death of older brother Aethelbald succeeded to throne of Wessex (860).

Aeth•el•flaed \'ath-əl-,flad, 'ath-\ *or* **Eth•el•fleda** \'eth-əl-,fled-ə, 'eth-\ *or* **Ael•fled** \'al-(,)fled\. d. 918. Anglo-Saxon ruler. Daughter of Alfred the Great; m. (c.880) Aethelred, ealdorman of the Mercians. Aided her brother, Edward the Elder, in repelling Danish invaders; led Mercian army against Danes (910–911); after death of Aethelred (911), ruled Mercia alone; fortified Mercia; subdued Welsh at Brecknock (916); in joint campaign with Edward against Danes, took Derby (917), Leicester (918). On her death Mercia passed to Edward.

Aeth•el•frith \'ath-əl-,frith, 'ath-\ *or* **Eth•el•frith** \'eth-, 'eth-\ *or* **Et•el•frid** \'eth-əl-,frid, 'eth-\ *or* **Aed•il•frid** \'ath-əl-,frid, 'ad-ᵊl-\. d. 616. Anglo-Saxon ruler. Succeeded to throne of Bernicia (593), then that of Deira, becoming King of all Northumbria; defeated Scottish King Aidan (603); killed in battle with King Raedwald of East Anglia.

Aeth•el•gar \'ath-əl-,gär, 'ath-\ *or* **Eth•el•gar** \'eth-, 'eth-\ *or* **Al•gar** \'al-,gär\. d. 990. Anglo-Saxon prelate. Named abbot of Newminster by Aethelwold (964); helped introduce Benedictine rule to England; bishop of Selsey (980); archbishop of Canterbury (988–990).

Aethehard. See Adelard.

Aeth•el•heard \'ath-əl-,ha(-ə)rd, 'ath-\ *or* **Eth•el•hard** \'eth-əl-,ha(ə)rd, 'eth-\ *or* **Ad•el•ard** \'ath-ə-,la(ə)rd, 'ad-ᵊl-,a(ə)rd\ *or* **Ed•el•red** \'eth-əl-,red, 'ed-ᵊl-\. d. 805. Mercian prelate. Elected archbishop of Canterbury (791); consecration delayed (to 793) by Kentish opposition to Mercian clergy; exiled to Mercia after death of his patron, King Offa (796); restored (798) and assured of primacy of Canterbury over other British sees by Pope Leo III (802).

Aeth•el•noth \'ath-əl-,noth, 'ath-, -,näth\ *or* **Eth•el•noth** \'eth-, 'eth-\. *Lat.* Egel•no•dus \,eg-əl-'nōd-əs\ *or* Ed•no•dus \ed-'nōd-əs\. d. 1038. Anglo-Saxon prelate. Grandson of Aethelweard. Monk at Glastonbury; archbishop of Canterbury (1020–38).

Aeth•el•red \'ath-əl-,red, 'ath-\ of Rie•vaulx \'rē-(,)vō, -(,)vōz, 'riv-əz\. Saint. *Name also spelled* Eth•el•red \'eth-, 'eth-\, Ael•red \'al-,red\, Ail•red \'al-, 'ā(ə)l-\. c.1110–1167. British historian and abbot. Entered Cistercian order (c. 1134); abbot of Revesby (1143–47), Rievaulx (1147–67); influential adviser to Henry II of England, Louis VII of France, David I of Scotland. Author of devotional works as *Speculum caritatis, De Jesu puero duodenui,* and *De spirituali amicitia,* and historical works as *Genealogia regum Anglorum* and *Vita S. Eduardi Confessoris.*

Aethelred I *or* **Ethelred.** d. 871. Anglo-Saxon ruler. Son of Aethelwulf. Originally intended to succeed brother Aethelbald as King of Wessex, but supplanted by Aethelberht (860); finally succeeded Aethelberht as king (866); drove Danes from Mercia (868–869); with brother Alfred defeated them soundly at Ashdown (871); died probably of wounds inflicted at Merton.

Aethelred II *or* **Ethelred.** *Called* the Unready. 968?–1016. King of England (978–1016). Son of King Edgar. Succeeded half-brother Edward the Martyr as king; suspected by many of complicity in Edward's murder; unable to defend country against Danish and Norse invaders, resorted to purchasing peace; attacked invaders' fleet (992); again bought off invasion army (994); made ineffectual resistance to new Danish invasion (999); ordered massacre of Danish settlers (1002); again forced to buy peace from consequent renewed invasions (1006, 1011); besieged in London as Danish King Sweyn I was acknowledged king in Britain (1013); fled to Normandy (1014); returned (1014); died in London as Canute was preparing new siege.

Aethelred *or* **Ethelred.** d. 889. Anglo-Saxon prelate. Archbishop of Canterbury (870–889).

Aeth•el•stan \'ath-əl-,stän, 'ath-, -,stan, -stən\ *or* **Athelstan.** d. 939. Anglo-Saxon ruler. Son of Edward the Elder, whom he succeeded as king of Mercia (924) and as king of Wessex (925); annexed Northumbria (926); firmly established rule over all England; defeated coalition of Scottish King Constantine, Owain of Strathclyde, and Olaf Guthfrithson at Brunanburh (937); issued several codes of laws, esp. dealing with theft and corruption.

Aeth•el•weard \'ath-əl-'wa(-ə)rd, 'ath-\ *or* **Eth•el•werd** \'eth-əl-,wa(ə)rd, 'eth-\. d. 998? Anglo-Saxon chronicler. Descendant of Aethelred I. Probably ealdorman of western provinces; wrote Latin history of the world down to 973.

Aeth•el•wold \'ath-əl-,wóld, 'ath-, -,wäld\. Saint. *Name also spelled* Eth•el•wold \'eth-, 'eth-\, Ad•el•wold \'ath-əl-, 'ad-ᵊl-\. c.908–984. Anglo-Saxon prelate. Monk at Glastonbury; reforming abbot of Abingdon (c.954); introduced Benedictine rule into England (c.960); bishop of Winchester (963); cooperated with his friend Bishop Dunstan in program of monastic reform; rebuilt many churches; built new cathedral at Winchester (dedicated by Dunstan, 980).

Aeth•el•wulf \'ath-əl-,wúlf, 'ath-\ *or* **Eth•el•wulf** \'eth-, 'eth-\ *or* **Ad•el•wulf** \'ath-əl-,wúlf, 'ad-ᵊl-\ *or* **Ath•ulf** \'ath-,úlf, 'ath-, -əlf\. d. 858. Anglo-Saxon ruler. Son of Egbert, whom he succeeded as King of West Saxons (839); won major victory over Danes at Ockley (851); formed alliance with Mercia by marrying his daughter to King Burgred (853); himself married daughter of Charles II the Bald of the West Franks (856); made pilgrimage to Rome (855–856), leaving Wessex to son Aethelbald; denied throne on return, but retained rule in Kent. Father also of Aethelberht and Alfred the Great.

Aë•tion \ā-'ē-sh(ē-)ən, -tē-ən\. 4th century B.C. Greek painter. Known esp. for painting of marriage of Alexander and Roxana.

Aë•ti•us \ā-'ē-sh(ē-)əs\. *Called* the Atheist *or* the Ungodly. d. c.366. Syrian prelate and heretic. Founder (c.350) of an extreme sect of Arians, known as Aetians, Anomoeans, or Eunomians (after Eunomius, his disciple); known as an extremely subtle logician; banished by Constantius II following Council of Seleucia (359) but brought back and made a bishop by Julian (361).

Aëtius, Flavius. d. 454. Roman general. Consul (432, 437, 446); in command of all Roman forces and dominating influence on Emperor Valentinian III (from 432); named patrician (433); defeated Armoricans (435–437), destroyed Burgundian kingdom at Worms (437); defeated Visigoths at Toulouse (437–439); won his most famous victory, over Attila and the Huns, at Châlons (451); put to death in Rome by Valentinian.

Afa·na·syev \ə-(ˌ)fə-ˈnás-yif\, Aleksandr Nikolayevich. 1826–1871. Russian scholar. Compiled *Narodnye russkie skazki* (1855–63), collection of Russian folk tales.

Afanasyev, Georgy Dmitriyevich. 1906–1975. Russian petrologist. Known esp. for studies of magnetic rocks of the Caucasus Mountains and of the origin of rocks.

Af·er \ˈaf-ər\, Domitius. d. c.59 A.D. Roman orator. Achieved renown with prosecution of Claudia Pulchra for Tiberius (26 A.D.); escaped prosecution himself by flattering Caligula (39); consul (39). Considered by Quintilian the greatest orator of his day.

Af·fleck \ˈaf-ˌlek\, Thomas. 1745–1795. American cabinetmaker, b. Aberdeen, Scotland. To U.S. (1763); settled in Philadelphia; one of the outstanding craftsmen in the Chippendale style.

Affonso. See AFONSO.

Af·fre \äfrᵊ\, Denis-Auguste. 1793–1848. French prelate. Vicar general of Luçon (1821), Amiens (1823), Paris (1834); archbishop of Paris (1840); during June Revolution of 1848 mortally wounded by stray bullet at barricades in Paris while attempting to persuade insurgents to submit to authority.

Afghānī, al-. See JAMĀL AD-DĪN AL-AFGHĀNĪ.

Afon·so \ə-ˈfōⁿ-sü\. Name of six kings of Portugal:

Afonso I. *Called also* Afonso Henriques. 1109?–1185. First king of Portugal (1143–85). Son of Henry of Burgundy, Count of Portugal (d. 1112) and grandson of Alfonso VI of León and Castile. Wrested control of Portugal from mother (1128); assumed title of king; by Treaty of Zamora (1143) recognized as autonomous ruler by cousin Alfonso VII; extended domain into Muslim territory, capturing Santarém and Lisbon (1147), Beja (1162), Évora (1165), Juromenha (1166).

Afonso II. *Called* Afonso o Gor·do \-ü-ˈgōr-dü\, *i.e.* the Fat. 1185?–1223. King (1211–23). Son of Sancho I. Defeated Muslims at Las Navas de Tolosa (1212) and Alcácer do Sol (1217); excommunicated along with entire court (1219).

Afonso III. 1210–1279. King (1248–79). Son of Afonso II. Named regent on deposing of brother Sancho II (1245); succeeded Sancho as king (1248); captured district of Faro from Muslims (1249); secured Algarve district (1250).

Afonso IV. *Called* Afonso o Bra·vo \-ü-ˈbrá-vü\, *i.e.* the Brave. 1291–1357. King (1325–57). Son of Dinis. Made war on son-in-law Alfonso XI of Castile (1336–40); joined Alfonso in war on Muslims, winning battle of Salado River (1340); provoked son Pedro into brief but devastating rebellion (1355).

Afonso V. *Called* Afonso o Afri·ca·no \-ˌü-ə-frē-ˈká-nü\. 1432–1481. King (1438–81). Son of Edward. Succeeded to throne under mother's regency; undertook campaigns in northern Africa, conquering Alcácer Ceguer (1458), Arzila and Tangier (1471); married cousin Joan, daughter of Henry IV of Castile, on whose death (1474) he claimed throne of León and Castile; defeated in Battle of Toro (1476) by Ferdinand and Isabella; surrendered claim to Castile in Treaty of Alcáçovas (1479).

Afonso VI. 1643–1683. King (1656–83). Son of John IV. Occupied throne under mother's regency (1656–62); reign marked by series of victories over Spain at Ameixal (1663), Castelo Rodrigo (1664), Montes Claros (1665), and by struggle with brother Pedro; forced to surrender power to regency of Pedro (1667); held prisoner until death.

Afonso I. *Called also* Nzin·ga Mbem·ba \en-ˈziŋ-əm-ˈbem-bə\. d. c.1550. Ruler of Kongo Kingdom. Became sixth manikongo, i.e. lord of the Kongo (1506 or 1507); adopted Christianity and encouraged Portuguese colonization; signed treaty (1512) with Manuel I of Portugal.

Afra·ni·us \ə-ˈfrā-nē-əs\, Lucius. d. 46 B.C. Roman general. Follower of Pompey, with whose aid he was elected consul (60 B.C.); defeated by Caesar in Spain (49); joined Pompey and was present at disastrous battles of Pharsalus (48) and Thapsus (46); captured and executed.

Africanus, Scipio. See SCIPIO AFRICANUS.

Af·ri·ca·nus \ˌaf-ri-ˈkā-nəs\, Sextus Julius. c.180–c.250. Christian traveler and historian. Author of *Chronographia,* a history of the world from creation, which he placed at 5499 B.C., to 221 A.D., in which he antedated Christ's birth by three years. His chronology (known as Alexandrian era) adopted by most Eastern churches.

Af·ze·li·us \áv-ˈsā-lē-əs\, Arvid August. 1785–1871. Swedish clergyman and folklorist. Collected Swedish folk songs in *Svenska folkvisor från forntiden* (with E.G. Geijer, 1814–16).

Aga·ja *or* **Aga·dja** \ä-ˈgäj-ə\. c.1673–1740. Ruler of Dahomey (1708–40). Expanded kingdom, conquering Allada (1724), Whydah (1727); forced to pay tribute to invading Oyos (1730); created centralized administration for kingdom.

Aga Khan \ˈäg-ə-ˈkän\. Title of heads of Ismāʻīlī sect of Shīʻite Muslims:

Aga Khan I. *Orig.* Hasan ʻAlī Shāh. 1800–1881. Traced descent from ʻAlī, son-in-law of Muḥammad; governor of Persian province of Kerman; first holder of title of *imām* of Ismāʻīlīs; granted title Aga Khan by Fatḥ ʻAlī; after quarrel with Moḥammed Shāh, emigrated to India (1838); greatly aided British in first Afghan War (1839–42), conquest of Sind (1842–43); granted style of "His Highness".

Aga Khan II. *Orig.* ʻAlī Shāh. d. 1885. Son of Aga Khan I, whom he succeeded as *imām* (1881).

Aga Khan III. *Orig.* Sultan Sir Mohammed Shah. 1877–1957. Son of Aga Khan II, whom he succeeded as *imām* (1885); headed Muslim deputation (1906) that led to Morley-Minto reforms (1909); took part in London Round Table conferences on Indian constitutional reform (1930–32); Indian representative at League of Nations (1932, 1934–37), president of Assembly (1937).

Āgā Moḥammad Khān. See ĀGHĀ MOḤAMMAD KHĀN.

Ag·a·pe·tus \ˌag-ə-ˈpēt-əs\. Name of two popes:

Agapetus I. Saint. d.536. Pope (535–536). Sent by Ostrogothic king Theodatus to dissuade Justinian I from invading Italy; while in Constantinople, deposed patriarch Anthimus for Monophysite beliefs and secured election of Mennas (536).

Agapetus II. d. 955. Pope (946–955).

Agar \ˈā-ˌgär\, Herbert Sebastian. 1897–1980. American journalist and writer, b. New Rochelle, N.Y. Correspondent (1929–35), columnist (1935–40), editor (1940–42), Louisville (Ky.) *Courier-Journal;* author of *Bread and Circuses* (1930), *The People's Choice* (1933; Pulitzer prize), *Land of the Free* (1935), *Pursuit of Happiness* (1938), *Price of Union* (1950), *The Saving Remnant* (1960), etc.

Aga·si·as \ə-ˈgā-shē-əs\. fl. 100 B. C. Either of two Greek sculptors of Ephesus. One is known for several portrait busts, the other for statue known as *Borghese Gladiator.*

Ag·as·siz \á-gá-sē, *Angl* ˈag-ə-(ˌ)sē\, Alexander Emmanuel Rodolphe. 1835–1910. American zoologist, b. Neuchâtel, Switzerland. Son of Jean Louis Agassiz. To U.S. (1849). Mine superintendent at Calumet, Mich. (1866–69); curator, Harvard Museum (1874–85). Made zoological exploration trips to west coast of S. America (1875), the Gulf Stream (1877), West Indies (1878), Hawaii (1885), S. America (1891), Bahamas (1892), Bermuda and Florida reefs (1894), Australian Great Barrier Reef (1896), etc. Author of *North American Acalephae* (1865), *Embryology of the Starfish* (1865), *Seaside Studies in Natural History* (with stepmother Elizabeth C. Agassiz, 1865), *North American Starfishes* (1877), etc.

Ag·as·siz \ˈag-ə-(ˌ)sē\, Elizabeth Cabot, *nee* Cary \ˈka(ə)r-ē, ˈke(ə)r-ē\. 1822–1907. American educator, b. Boston. m. (1850) Louis Agassiz. Conducted school for girls (1855–63); helped organize classes for women by Harvard teachers (1879); president of Society for Collegiate Instruction of Women (1882–94) and its successor, Radcliffe College (1894–99); honorary president (1899–1903). Author of *First Lesson in Natural History* (1859), *Seaside Studies in Natural History* (with A. Agassiz, 1865), *Journey in Brazil* (with L. Agassiz, 1867), *Louis Agassiz* (1885).

Ag·as·siz \á-gá-sē, *Angl* ˈag-ə-(ˌ)sē\, Louis, *in full* Jean Louis Rodolphe. 1807–1873. American naturalist, b. Môtier-en-Vully, Switzerland. To Paris (1832); associated with Cuvier and von Humboldt; published *Recherches sur les poissons fossiles* (1833–34); professor of natural history, Neuchâtel (1832–46). Published *Monographies d'échinodermes vivans et fossiles* (1838–42), *Études sur les glaciers* (1840), *Études critiques sur les mollusques fossiles* (1840–45). To U.S. (1846) for lectures at Cambridge; professor of natural history, Lawrence Scientific School, Harvard (1847–73); began collections now in Harvard Museum of Comparative Zoology (1859). Naturalized (1861). Undertook zoological expeditions to Brazil (1865), Cuban waters (1869), around Cape Horn to California (1871). Established (1873) Anderson School of Natural History, a summer school on Penikese Island. Published *Lake Superior* (1850), four of projected ten volumes of *Contributions to the Natural History of the United States* (1857–62), *Essay on Classification* (1859).

Agate \ˈā-gət, ˈag-ət\, James Evershed. 1877–1947. English dramatic critic. On staff of *Manchester Guardian* (1907–14); drama critic for *Saturday Review* (1921–23), *Sunday Times* (1923–47); reviews noted for wit, clarity, seriousness; published novels, including *Responsibility* (1919), *Blessed Are the Rich* (1924), many collections of reviews, and nine volumes of diary under title *Ego* (1935–49).

Ag·a·tha \ˈag-ə-thə\. Saint. 3d century A.D. Sicilian Christian martyr. According to legend, was tortured by Roman consul whose advances she had resisted.

Ag·a·thar·chi·des \ˌag-ə-ˈthär-kə-ˌdēz\. *Also* Ag·a·thar·chus \-ˈthär-kəs\. 2d century B.C. Greek historian and geographer. Wrote a history and geography of Europe and one of Asia and *On the Erythraean Sea.*

Agatharcus. fl. c.460–417 B.C. Athenian painter. Said to have originated scene painting with a scene for Aeschylus.

Aga·thi·as \ə-ˈgā-thē-əs, ə-ˈgath-ē-əs\. c.536–c.582. Byzantine writer. Author of love poems, epigrams, and a history of reign of Justinian I.

Ag·a·tho \'ag-ə-,thō\. Saint. c.577–681. Pope (678–681). Restored St. Wilfrid to see of York; regularized see of Ravenna; successfully opposed monothelitism at Council of Constantinople (680–681).

Agath·o·cles \ə-'gath-ə-,klēz\. 361–289 B.C. Tyrant of Syracuse (317–c.304 B.C.), king (304–289 B.C.). Served in army of Syracuse; with army aid became tyrant (317); subdued most of Sicily; broke through Carthaginian siege (310) and attacked Carthage, where he was finally repelled (307); consolidated rule and took title of king (c.304); invaded Italy and Corcyra (300–295).

Ag·a·thon \'ag-ə-,thän\. c.445–c.400 B.C. Athenian tragic poet. Friend of Euripides and Plato; scene of Plato's *Symposium* is his house on occasion of his victory in the Great Dionysia (416 B.C.).

Agaz·za·ri \,ä-gät-'tsär-ē\, Agostino. 1578–1640. Italian composer. Chapel master at Siena (1630–40); wrote madrigals, motets, etc., in both late Renaissance and early Baroque styles; known esp. for treatise *Del sonare sopra il basso* (1607).

Agee \'ā-(,)jē\, James. 1909–1955. American author, b. Knoxville, Tenn. Author of film criticism; film scripts, as for *African Queen* (1951), *Night of the Hunter* (1955); verse, as *Permit Me Voyage* (1934); nonfiction *Let Us Now Praise Famous Men* (with photographs by Walker Evans, 1941); novels *The Morning Watch* (1951), *A Death in the Family* (1957, Pulitzer prize).

Ag·e·la·das \,aj-ə-'lād-əs\ *or* **Hag·e·la·das** \,haj-\. 6th–5th century B.C. Greek sculptor. Reputed teacher of Myron, Phidias, and Polycletus.

Ager \'ā-jər\, Milton. 1893–1979. American songwriter, b. Chicago. Wrote "Ain't She Sweet," "Happy Days Are Here Again," etc.

Ag·e·san·der \,aj-ə-'san-dər\. 1st century B.C. Greek sculptor. According to Pliny, collaborated with Polydorus and Athenodorus in carving Laocoön group.

Ages·i·la·us II \ə-,jes-ə-'lā-əs\. c.444–360 B.C. King of Sparta (399–360 B.C.). Son of Archidamus II; succeeded Agis II; led Spartan forces against Phrygia (396–394), Lydia (395); recalled to fight Corinthian League (394–387); besieged Thebes (378, 377); provoked Theban war that ended in Spartan defeat at Leuctra (371); saved Sparta from Theban Sieges (370–369, 362); died in Egypt commanding Spartan mercenaries.

Aggeus. See HAGGAI.

Aghā Mo·ḥam·mad Khān \ä-'gä-mó-'ḳȧm-mȧd-'ḳän\. 1742–1797. Shah of Iran (1796–97); founder of the Qājār dynasty (1779–1925). Chief of Qavānlū clan (from 1758); political prisoner (1762–79); established rule in Astarābād (1779) and gradually gained control of northern Iran; conquered kingdom of Georgia (1796); crowned shāhanshāh (1796); conquered Khorāsān (1796).

Agh·lab·id \'ag-lə-bid, ag-'lab-id\. Muslim Arab dynasty, ruling (800–909) in eastern North Africa with capital at Kairouan. Founded by Ibrahim ibn al-Agh·lab \-al-ag-'lab\, sent out as governor by Hārūn ar-Rashīd; some of Aghlabid emirs harried coasts of Italy, France, Corsica, and Sardinia, conquered Sicily (827) and invaded southern Italy; dynasty destroyed by Fāṭimids.

Ag·ias \'ā-jē-əs\. 8th century B.C. Greek cyclic poet. Author of *Nostoi,* epic narrating story of homeward voyage of Achaean warriors from siege of Troy.

Agi·lulf \ä-'gē-,lu̇lf, -lə(l)f\. d. 616. King of the Lombards in Italy (590–616).

Agis \'ā-jəs\. Name of four kings of Sparta:

Agis I. 11th century B.C. Traditionally said to have been son of Eurysthenes, a founder of Sparta; progenitor of the Agiad royal line.

Agis II. d. 400 or 398 B.C. King (c.427–400 or 398). Son of Archidamus II. Commanded Spartan army in Peloponnesian War; defeated Athens and Argive alliance at Mantineia (418); occupied Deceleia (413); defeated Elis (400 or 398); succeeded by half-brother Agesilaus instead of son Leotychidas, reputedly really the son of Alcibiades.

Agis III. d. 331 B.C. King (338–331). Succeeded father Archidamus III; while Alexander was absent in Anatolia, raised revolt of Greek cities; revolt crushed by Antipater at Megalopolis (331), where Agis died.

Agis IV. c.263–241 B.C. King (244–241). Succeeded father Eudamidus II; proposed redistribution of land, cancellation of debts, and granting of citizenship to numbers of the Perioeci; reforms opposed by Leonidas II, who was deposed; tried and executed by ephors.

Agnel·li \än-'yel-lē\, Giovanni. 1866–1945. Italian manufacturer. Founded Fabbrica Italiana Automobili Torino, or Fiat (1899); president (1899–1920); senator (1923); chief mobilizer of Italian industry in World War II.

Ag·nes \'ag-nəs\. Saint. d. 304 A.D. Roman virgin martyr. According to legend, refused all suitors and at 12 or 13 was placed in brothel, where she remained unharmed; suffered martyrdom at Rome. Patron saint of young girls.

Agnes \ȧn-yes\ of Poi·tou \pwȧ-tü\. c.1024–1077. French noblewoman. Daughter of William V the Pious, duke of Aquitaine; m. (1043) Emperor Henry III; regent (1056–62) for son, Emperor Henry IV; politically ineffectual; lost control of government to Anno, archbishop of Cologne.

Agne·si \än-'yā-zē\, Maria Gaetana. 1718–1799. Italian mathematician. Professor, U. of Bologna (from 1750); author of *Propositiones philosophicae* (1738), *Instituzioni analitiche* (1748) on differential calculus; known esp. for discussion of cubic curve known through mistranslation as Witch of Agnesi.

Ag·new \'ag-,n(y)ü\, David Hayes. 1818–1892. American surgeon and educator, b. Lancaster Co., Pa. Professor, U. of Pennsylvania (1871–89); known as brilliant lecturer and demonstrator.

Ag·ni·hot·ri \,äg-nə-'hō-trē\, Shiv Narayan. 1850–1923. Indian reformer. Founder of Deva Samaj ethical society.

Agnolo, Baccio d'. See BACCIO D'AGNOLO.

Agno·lo \'än-yō-(,)lō\ *or* **An·gio·lo** \än-'zhō-lō\ **di Co·si·mo** \dē-'koz-ē-(,)mō\. *Called* Il Bron·zi·no \,ēl-brȯn-'zē-nō\. 1503–1572. Florentine painter. A chief exponent of Mannerist style, esp. in elegant and decorative portraits, as of Eleonor of Toledo, Maria de' Medici; also executed sacred and allegorical works.

Agnolo di Ventura. See under AGOSTINO DI GIOVANNI.

Ag·non \'äg-,nän\, Shmuel Yosef. *Orig.* Samuel Josef Czacz·kes \'chȧch-kās\. 1888–1970. Israeli author, b. Galicia. To Palestine (1907); author of stories and novels, including *Agunot* (1908), *Hakhnasat kala* (1919), *Ore'ah Nata Lalun* (1938), *'Tmol shilshom* (1945); often considered the greatest writer in modern Hebrew; shared Nobel prize for literature (1966) with Nelly Sachs.

Ago·bard \ȧ-gȯ-bȧr\. Saint. 769 or 779–840. Frankish prelate, b. Spain. Archbishop of Lyons (816–835, 838–840); removed from see on restoration of Louis the Pious (835), but reconciled and restored (838); wrote against Adoptionist heresy of Felix of Urgel.

Ag·o·rac·ri·tus \,ag-ə-'rak-rət-əs\. 5th century B.C. Greek sculptor. Studied under Phidias; sculptor of a statue of Nemesis (at Rhamonus).

Ago·sti·no di Duc·cio \,äg-ō-'stē-nō-dē-'düt-chō\. 1418–?1481. Italian sculptor and decorator. Best known for decorative sculpture in Tempio Malatestiano, Rimini, and for work on façade of Oratory of S. Bernardino in Perugia.

Agostino di Gio·van·ni \-dē-jō-'vän-nē\. 14th century. Italian sculptor. Best known for work, with Agnolo di Ventura, in Gothic style, on tomb of Guido Tarlati, Arezzo; on Porta Romana and church of S. Francesco, Siena; Agostino alone may have done monument of Cino dei Sigibuldi, Pistoia.

Agoult \ȧ-gü\, Marie-Catherine-Sophie d', *nee* de Fla·vi·gny \də-fla-vēn-yē\. Comtesse d'Agoult. *Pseudonym* Daniel Stern \'stern\. 1805–1876. French writer. m. (1927) Charles d'Agoult. Known first for liaison (c.1834–39) with Franz Liszt (of their three children, one became Cosima Wagner); became writer and held a salon in Paris; close friend of George Sand. Author of *Nélida* (1846), *Lettres républicaines* (1848), *Histoire de la révolution de 1848* (1850–53), *Jeanne d'Arc* (play, 1857), *Dante et Goethe* (1866), *Mes Souvenirs 1806–1833* (1877).

Agra·mon·te y Si·mo·ni \äg-rä-'mon-tā-ē-sē-'mō-nē\, Aristides. 1869–1931. American bacteriologist, b. Camagüey, Cuba. With Walter Reed, Jesse Lazear, and James Carroll, member U.S. army board that discovered transmission of yellow fever by mosquitoes (1900); professor, U. of Havana (1900–30), Louisiana (1931).

Agreda, María de. See María CORONEL.

Agri·co·la \ȧ-'grē-kō-,lȧ\, Alexander. 1446–1506. Dutch or Flemish composer. In service of Charles VII of France, Lorenzo de' Medici (1474), Philip the Fair of Burgundy (1500); wrote 9 masses, 25 motets, chansons, etc.

Agricola, Georgius. See Georg BAUER.

Agric·o·la \ə-'grik-ə-lə\, Gnaeus Julius. 40–93 A.D. Roman soldier. Father-in-law of Tacitus. With Suetonius Paulinus in Britain (59–61); quaestor in Asia (64); people's tribune (66); praetor (68); made patrician (73); governor of Aquitania (74–77); consul (77) and governor of Britain (77–84); conquered and pacified Britain to northern boundary of Perth and Argyll. Subject of Tacitus's *Agricola.*

Agricola, Johann. See Johann SCHNEIDER.

Agricola, Martin. See Martin SOHR.

Ag·ri·co·la \,äg-'rik-ȯ-lȧ\, Michael. 1509–1557. Finnish prelate and writer. Bishop of Åbo; one of first to write in Finnish vernacular; published version of New Testament in Finnish (1548) and helped thereby to establish Åbo dialect as basis of written Finnish.

Agricola, Rodolphus. See Roelof HUYSMAN.

Agrippa I and **II.** See HEROD AGRIPPA I and II.

Agrip·pa \ə-'grip-ə\. fl. c.200 A.D.? Greek Skeptic philosopher. Developed the "five tropes" (possibly derived from Aenesidemus) summarizing rigorous Skepticism.

Agrip·pa \ä-'grip-ä\, Heinrich Cornelius. *Called* Agrip·pa von Net·tes·heim \-fòn-'net-əs-,hīm\. 1486–1535. German physician, theologian, and philosopher. Served in army of Emperor Maximilian I (1501–07); lectured at Dôle (1509), Pavia (1515–18); public orator and advocate of Metz (1518–20); physician to Louise of Savoy (1524–27); historiographer to Emperor Charles V at Antwerp (1529–30). Author of *De occulta philosophia* (c.1510; pub. 1531), a cosmology based on cabalistic and Pythagorean analyses and magic that helped link his name to Faust legend; and of *De incertitudine et vanitate scientiarum et artium* (c.1526; pub. 1531), rejecting all scientific knowledge for simple biblical piety.

Agrip·pa \ə-'grip-ə\, Marcus Vipsanius. 63?–12 B.C. Roman general and statesman. Son-in-law and deputy of Emperor Augustus, whom he aided in gaining power; probably tribune of the plebs (43 B.C.); praetor urbanus (40); suppressed disorders in Gaul and Germany (38); consul (37). Appointed Augustus's naval commander; defeated Sextus Pompeius at Mylae and Naulochus (36); with Augustus in Dalmatian campaign (35–34); aedile (33); largely responsible for naval victory over Anthony at Actium (31); consul (28, 27). Succeeded Marcellus as chief minister (23); governor in the East (from 23); subdued Cantabrians in Spain (19–18); again imperial governor in the East (17–12).

Ag·rip·pi·na \ˌag-ri-ˈpī-nə\ the Elder. *Known also as* Vip·sa·nia Agrippina \vip-ˈsā-nē-ə-\. c.14 B.C.–33 A.D. Roman woman. Daughter of M. Vipsanius Agrippa and of Julia, daughter of Augustus; wife of Germanicus Caesar and mother of Caligula; regarded as one of noblest and most heroic women of antiquity; accompanied her husband on all his campaigns; on his death (19 A.D.) returned to Italy; incurred hatred of Tiberius and Sejanus; banished to Pandataria; died of starvation, perhaps voluntarily but under suspicious circumstances. Her daughter ¶Agrippina the Younger (15?–59 A.D.), b. at Oppidum Ubiorum, later named Colonia Agrippina after her (modern Cologne); m. 1st Domitius Ahenobarbus by whom she was mother of Nero, 2d Passienus Crispus, 3d (49 A.D.) her uncle Emperor Claudius, whom she may have poisoned (54) after persuading him to adopt Nero as his successor; sought to rule through her son Nero, but was put to death by him.

Agua·do \äg-ˈwäth-ō\, Alejandro María. Marqués de las Ma·ris·mas \thā-läs-mä-ˈrē-smäs\. 1784–1842. Spanish financier. Financial agent of Ferdinand VII; became naturalized French citizen (1828); amassed huge fortune; bequeathed valuable paintings to the Louvre.

Agues·seau \á-ges-ō\, Henri-François d'. 1668–1751. French jurist. Advocate general (1690–1700), attorney general (1700–17) to Parlement of Paris; resisted papal intervention in French religious affairs; under Louis XV chancellor of France (1717–18, 1720–22, 1727–50); continued codification of French law, improved court procedures; obtained from Louis XV ordinances on donations (1731), testaments (1735), successions (1747).

Agui·lar \äg-ē-ˈlär, *Angl* ə-ˈgwil-ər\, Grace. 1816–1847. English writer. Author of *The Spirit of Judaism* (1842), verse *The Magic Wreath* (1835), and the novels *Home Influence* (1847), *Vale of Cedars* (1850), *Days of Bruce* (1852), etc.

Agui·nal·do \äg-ē-ˈnäl-dō\, Emilio. 1869–1964. Filipino leader. Commander of Filipino forces in rebellion against Spain (1896–98); led insurrection against American authority (1899–1901); captured by Funston (1901); forced to take oath of allegiance to U.S.; retired from public life; named to Council of State (1950).

Aguir·re \ä-ˈgēr-rā\, Lope de. c.1518–1561. Spanish adventurer. To Peru (1544), where he took part in various conflicts among the conquistadors; joined Pedro de Ursúa's expedition in search of El Dorado (1560); gained control of expeditionary party through murder of Ursúa and of his successor, Guzmán (1561); led expedition down Amazon as pirate band; plundered Indian villages and island of Margarita.

Aguirre Cer·da \-ˈser-thä\, Pedro. 1879–1941. Chilean politician. Leader of Radical party; president of Chile (1938–41).

Agu·ja·ri \ˌäg-ü-ˈyä-rē\, Lucrezia. 1743–1783. Italian operatic soprano. Noted for the extreme range of her voice.

Ag·ung \ˈäg-ˌüŋ\. d. 1645. Sultan of Mataram. Extended and consolidated kingdom; failed to drive Dutch from Batavia (1629); conquered East Java, but failed to capture Bali. Under his rule Mataram reached its peak of power.

Agung, Abulfatah. d. 1692. Ruler of Bantam (1651–83). Resisted Dutch encroachment until his son, Sultan Haji, seized throne with Dutch aid (1683).

Agus·tín \äg-ü-ˈstēn\, Antonio. 1517–1586. Spanish jurist and prelate. Auditor of Roman Rota (1544); papal nuncio to Queen Mary Tudor (1545); bishop of Lérida (1561); archbishop of Tarragona (1576); author of *Emendationum et opinionum libri IV ad Modestinum* (1567), *Diálogos de las armas y linajes de la nobleza de España*.

Agus·ti·ni \äg-u-ˈstē-nē\, Delmira. 1886–1914. Uruguayan poet. One of chief Modernist poets of South America; author of *El libro blanco* (1907), *Cantos de la mañana* (1910), *Los calices vacios* (1913), *Los astros de abismo* (1924).

Aḥa \ˈäk-ä\ of Shab·ḥa \ˈshäb-ˌkä\. c.680–752. Rabbinical scholar. Author of *She'eltot,* first attempt to codify and explicate Babylonian Talmud.

Ahab \ˈā-ˌhab\ *or* **Achab** \ˈā-ˌkab\. c.874–c.853 B.C. 7th king of Israel (c.874–c.853 B.C.). Son and successor of Omri. Established friendly relations with foreign states, esp. by marriage with Jezebel, daughter of king of Sidon; their daughter Athaliah married Jehoram, King of Judah, thus strengthening alliance with southern kingdom; brought large force to join allies that withstood (853) Shalmaneser III of Assyria at Karkar; killed in battle against Ben-hadad of Demascus. Jezebel's worship of Baal aroused strong opposition in Israel, esp. from Elijah. Succeeded by sons Ahaziah and Jehoram.

Aḥad Ha'am. See Asher Ginzberg.

Ahaz \ˈā-ˌhaz\ *or* **Achaz** \ˈā-ˌkaz\. *Assyrian* Je·ho·a·haz \ji-ˈhō-ə-ˌhaz\. 8th century B.C. King of Judah. Threatened by siege of Jerusalem by kings of Syria and Israel; called upon Tiglath-pileser I of Assyria for aid, contrary to advice of prophet Isaiah; forced to pay tribute to Assyria.

Aha·zi·ah \ˌā-hə-ˈzī-ə\ *or* **Och·o·zi·as** \ˌäk-ə-ˈzī-əs\. Name of two kings in biblical history:

Ahaziah. d. 851? B.C. King of Israel (c.853–c.851 B.C.). Son of Ahab and Jezebel. Helpless before revolt of Moab; succeeded by brother Jehoram.

Ahaziah. d. 844? B.C. King of Judah (844? B.C.). Son of Jeham and Athaliah; slain by Jehu; succeeded by Athaliah.

Ahe·no·bar·bus \ə-ˌhē-nə-ˈbär-bas, ə-ˌhen-ə-\. Name of plebeian Roman family, including notably: Gnaeus Domitius Ahenobarbus, tribune (104 B.C.), pontifex maximus (103), consul (96), and censor (92). His son ¶Lucius Domitius (d. 48 B.C.) challenged unsuccessfully the triumvirate of Caesar, Pompey and Crassus; elected consul (54); successor to Caesar as governor of Gaul (49), an appointment that precipitated civil war; follower of Pompey in civil wars, slain in flight after battle of Pharsala (48). Lucius's son ¶Gnaeus Domitius (d. 31 B.C.) commanded fleet of Caesar's assassins against Mark Antony (44); became privateer after defeat at Philippi (42); reconciled with Antony (40); governor of Bithynia (40–35); consul (32); deserted from Antony to Octavius at Actium (31) and died shortly thereafter. His grandson ¶Gnaeus Domitius, m. Agrippina, daughter of Germanicus Caesar; father of Emperor Nero.

Ahith·o·phel \ə-ˈhith-ə-ˌfel\ *or* **Achit·o·phel** \ə-ˈkit-ə-ˌfel\. 11th century B.C. Hebrew courtier. Counselor of King David of Israel; played major role in revolt of Absalom; on failure of his advice to Absalom, killed himself.

Ahlgren, Ernst. See Victoria Benedictsson.

Ahl·mann \ˈäl-ˌmän\, Hans Jakob Konrad Wilhelmsson. 1889–1974. Swedish glaciologist. Professor at Uppsala (1921–29), Stockholm (from 1929); Swedish ambassador to Norway (1950); known for studies of glaciers and of climatic fluctuations.

Aḥmad. See also Ahmed or Ahmet.

Aḥmad, Abū ol-Qāsem. See Firdawsī.

Aḥmad, Mirza Ghulam. See Ghulam Ahmad.

Aḥ·mad al-Man·ṣūr \ˈäk-məd-ˌal-man-ˈsür\. *Known as* al-Dha·ha·bī \-dä-ˈhäb-ē\, *i.e.* the Golden. 1549–1603. Moroccan ruler. Sixth sultan (1578–1603) of Sa'dī dynasty; maintained independence by adroit diplomacy and largely mercenary and slave army; took Gao and Timbuktu from Sudanese (1591); built opulent palace in Mārrakush.

Aḥ·mad Bā·bā \ˈäk-məd-ˈbäb-ä\. *In full* Abū al-'Abbās Aḥmad ibn Aḥmad al-Takrūrī al-Massūfī. 1556–1627. Sudanese jurist and writer. Exiled from native Timbuktu and held in Mārrakush (1594–1603); noted for legal opinions and for biographical dictionary of jurists of the Mālikī school.

Aḥ·mad Bey \ˈam-ad-ˈbā\. *Known also as* Ahmad ibn Mus·ta·fa \-ˌib-ən-ˌmüs-tä-ˈfä\. 1806–1855. Tunisian ruler. Tenth ruler (1837–55) of Ḥusaynid dynasty; obtained European training for army, established modern navy; ended slavery (1846); instituted administrative reforms, established schools and hospitals; obtained Ottoman recognition of Tunisian independence (1845).

Aḥmad Ebn Buyeh. See Mu'izz ad-Dawlah.

Aḥ·mad Grāñ \ˈäk-məd-ˈgrän\. *Orig. name* Aḥmad ibn Ibrāhīm al-Ghāzī. c. 1506–1543. Muslim leader. Gained control of Somali state of Adal; organized army of Somali tribesmen reinforced by Turkish troops; launched holy war on Christian Ethiopia (1531); conquered southern and central Ethiopia; defeated Portuguese force sent to aid Ethiopia (1541); killed in later battle.

Aḥmad ibn Ḥan·bal \-ˌib-ən-ˈkän-bəl\. 780–855. Muslim theologian and jurist. Compiler of *Musnod,* the Traditions of the Prophet Muḥammad; heroically resisted inquisition (833–848) begun by caliph al-Ma'mūn to enforce Mu'tazilī doctrine of created Qur'ān; his huge popularity helped moderate and finally end inquisition; founder of the strictly traditionalist Ḥanbalī school of Islāmic law.

Aḥmad ibn Ṭū·lūn \-ˌib-ən-ˈtü-lün\. 835–884. Egyptian ruler. Rose from slavery to government service under 'Abbasīd caliph in Baghdad; assigned to service of governor of Egypt (868); gained control of finances and became vice governor, exercising full power (872); created large army personally loyal to him; annexed Syria (882); established virtual independence of Egypt from Baghdad, suspending tribute and putting own name on coinage. Ṭūlūnid dynasty lasted to 905.

Ah·mad Khan \ˈam-ad-ˈkän\, Sir Sayyid. 1817–1898. Indian educator, jurist, and author. Served in judicial department of East India Co. (1841–76); worked to revive Muslim society in India; founded several schools and the Scientific Society; founded reform journal *Tahdhīb al-Akhlāq* (1870); founded (1877) Muhammadan Anglo-Oriental College (later Alīgarh Muslim University); organized (1886) All-India Muhammadan Educational Conference; of great influence in rebirth of Urdu literature; knighted (1888).

Aḥmad Khān Abdālī. See AḤMAD SHĀH DURRĀNI.

Aḥ·mad Shāh \'äk-məd-'shä\. *In full* Aḥmad Shāh Bahādur Mujāhid-ud-Dīn Abū Naṣr. 1725–1775. Mughal emperor of India (1748–54). Son and successor of Muḥammad Shāh; ineffectual ruler; lost territory to Aḥmad Shāh Durrāni; deposed by own vizier in league with Marāthās.

Aḥmad Shāh. 1898–1930. Iranian ruler. Last shah of Iran (1909–25) of Qājār dynasty; son and successor of Moḥammad 'Alī; deposed by Constituent Assembly, which elected Reza Pahlavi to replace him.

Aḥmad Shāh Dur·rā·ni \-dür-'än-ē\. *Orig.* Aḥmad Khān Abdālī. 1722?–1773. Founder and first ruler of Afghanistan. Son of chief of Abdālī tribe and leader of Abdālī cavalry in army of Nāder Shāh of Persia; on Nāder Shāh's death elected shah by Afghan chiefs (1747); established capital at Qandahār, organized central government; invaded India 9 times, plundering Delhi, Āgra and other cities (1757) and conquering entire Punjab; made son Tīmūr viceroy of Punjab (1757); failed to conquer Sikhs.

Aḥmad Sir·hin·dī \-sir-'hin-dē\. *Also called* Shaykh Aḥmad Sirhindī, the Twelfth Renovator. 1593–1624. Indian Muslim theologian and educator. Opposed Ṣūfī mysticism and pantheistic influence of Hinduism; effective in reasserting Muslim orthodoxy in India.

Aḥmad 'Urābī Pasha al-Miṣrī. See 'URĀBĪ PASHA.

Aḥ·ma·du Se·ku \a-'mad-ü-'sä-kü\. d. 1898. West African ruler. Succeeded father al-Ḥājj 'Umar as ruler of Tukulor empire (1864); forced to accept French protectorate status in Treaty of Gouri (1887); left virtually powerless by further French advances (1891).

Ah·med \ä-'met\. Name of three Ottoman sultans:

Ahmed I. 1590–1617. Sultan (1603–17). Son and successor of Mehmed III. First part of reign humane and efficient; forced to sign peace treaty of Zsitvatörök with Austria (1606), which abolished annual tribute paid by her; concluded unsuccessful war with Persia (1602–12); forced to grant commercial privileges to European nations; built Blue Mosque, Istanbul.

Ahmed II. 1642–1695. Sultan (1691–95). Son of İbrahim and brother and successor of Süleyman II; his army defeated with great loss at Slankamen (1691) by Louis William I of Baden, resulting in loss of Hungary; further losses to Holy League were complicated by internal unrest.

Ahmed III. 1673–1736. Sultan (1703–30). Son of Mehmed IV and brother and successor of Mustafa II; afforded refuge to Charles XII of Sweden after his defeat at Poltava (1709); forced by this into war with Russia (1711–13); in Peace of the Pruth (1711) secured Azov and concessions. Took Morea and Ionian Islands from Venetians (1715); invaded Hungary, but army badly defeated (1716) at Peterwardein by Prince Eugene of Savoy; Belgrade occupied (1717); lost considerable territory by Treaty of Passarowitz (1718). In war with Persia (1730), defeated by Nāder Shāh. Deposed by revolt of Patrona Halil and died in prison.

Ahmed Bey Zogu. See ZOG I.

Ahmed Cevdet Paşa. See CEVDET PAŞA.

Ah·med Ha·şim \ä-'met-hä-'shēm\. 1884–1933. Turkish writer. Official in various Ottoman government departments; under influence of Baudelaire, Rimbaud, Mallarmé, etc., altered his orig. classical Ottoman poetic style to develop a Turkish Symbolist style; published *Göl saatleri* (1921), *Göl kuşlari,* etc.

Ah·me·di \,äm-e-'dē\, Taceddin *or* Taj al-Dīn. *In full* Taceddin İbrahim ibn Hizr Ahmedi. 1334?–1413. Turkish poet. Poet at courts of Bayezid I, Süleyman of Rumelia, Mehmed I; known esp. for *Iskendername,* containing valuable early Ottoman history, *Cemşid u Hürşid,* etc. Considered one of the greatest Anatolian poets of his time.

Ahmed Tevfik Paşa. See TEVFIK PAŞA.

Ah·med Ve·fik Pa·şa \ä-'met-vef-'ik-pä-'shä\. 1823–1891. Ottoman diplomat and scholar. Member of family of diplomats; imperial commissioner in Danubian principalities (1849); ambassador to Persia (1851), to France (1860–61); president of first Ottoman Parliament (1877); grand vizier (1878, 1882); governor to Bursa (1879–82). Editor of first *Salnâme* (Year Book) of Ottoman Empire (1847); founder at Bursa of first Ottoman theater, which produced his translations of Molière; compiled historical and geographical manuals and *Lehçe-i Osmanî* (1876), concise dictionary of Turkish. Under house arrest on orders of Sultan Abdülhamid II (1882–91).

Ahmed Ye·se·vi \-yes-e-'vē\ *or* **Ya·sa·vi** \-,yäs-ä-'vē\. *Arab.* Ah·mad Ya·sa·wī \'äk-məd-yə-'sä-wē\. d. 1166. Turkish poet and mystic. Studied with Ṣūfī masters and became widely popular as religious leader and as poet of the people; if the *Divan-i hikmet* is not his, as is generally thought, none of his poems is extant.

Ah·mes \'äm-,äs\. 18th century B.C. Egyptian scribe. Author of Rhind, or Anmes, papyri (c.1700 B.C.) containing earliest treatment of algebraic problems.

Ah·met Pa·şa Bur·sa·li \ä-'met-pä-'shä-,bür-sä-'lē\. d. 1496 or 1497. Turkish writer. Teacher in religious college in Bursa; qāḍī, or judge, of Edirna (1451); military judge and tutor to Sultan Mehmed II (from 1451); later served under Bayezid II; known esp. as author of odes, lyrics, and panegyrics; considered first master of classical Ottoman poetry; laid foundation of Turkish language and poetic style.

Ah·mose \'äm-,ōs\. *Gk.* Ama·sis \ə-'mā-səs\. Name of two kings of ancient Egypt:

Ahmose I. Brother and successor of Kamose; first king of 18th dynasty; reigned (c.1570–46 B.C.). Re-established government at Thebes; expelled the Hyksos from Egypt and Palestine; recovered Nubia. Father of Amenhotep I.

Ahmose II. Fifth king of the 26th dynasty; reigned (570–526 B.C.). General under Psamtik II and Apries; proclaimed king by army mutineers; reputedly conquered Cyprus; founded Naukratis as market city for the Greeks.

Aho, Juhani. See Johannes BROFELDT.

Aḥ·sā'ī, al- \,al-äk-'sä-ē, -'sī\. *More completely* Shaykh Aḥmad ibn Zayn ad-Dīn ibn Ibrāhīm al-Aḥsā'ī. 1741 or 1742 or 1753–1826. Muslim religious. Traveled widely before settling in Yazd, Persia; evolved heterodox view of the Mahdī, the Shī'ite messiah; founder of Shaykhī sect; formally denounced as infidel (1824).

Ahui·zotl \ä-'wē-sōt-əl\. d. 1503. Eighth king of the Aztecs (1486–1503). Completed great temple at Tenochtitlan; subdued neighboring tribes; built aqueduct from Chapultepec to Lake of Texcoco.

Ai·card \ā-kar\, Jean, *in full* François-Victor-Jean. 1848–1921. French poet, novelist, and playwright. Author of *Jeunes Croyances* (1867), *Les Rebellions et les apaisements* (1871), *Poèmes de Provence* (1874), *La Chanson de l'enfant* (1876), a play *Le Père Lebonnard* (1889), a novel *Maurin des maures* (1908), etc.

Aich·ing·er \'īk-iŋ-ər\, Gregor. 1564–1628. German composer. Wrote chiefly choral and ecclesiastical music for Latin texts; known esp. for motets; published *Cantiones ecclesiasticae* (1607).

Ai·dan \'ād-ᵊn\. Saint. d. 651. Irish monk. Monk of Iona; at request of King Oswald, set out to evangelize Northumbria (635); first bishop of Lindisfarne (635); founded churches, monasteries; later won favor of Oswin, last king of Deira.

Aiguillon, Duc d'. See VIGNEROT DU PLESSIS DE RICHELIEU.

Ai·ken \'ā-kən\, Conrad Potter. 1889–1973. American poet, critic, and writer, b. Savannah, Ga. Author of volumes of verse, as *The Jig of Forslin* (1916), *Charnel Rose* (1918), *House of Dust* (1920), *Priapus and the Pool* (1922), *Selected Poems* (1929, Pulitzer prize), *John Deth* (1930), *Landscape West of Eden* (1934), *Time in the Rock* (1936), *Brownstone Eclogues* (1942), *The Soldier* (1944), *The Kid* (1947), *Letter from Li-Po* (1955), *Morning Song of Lord Zero* (1963), *Collected Poems* (1953, 1970); novels, as *Blue Voyage* (1927), *Great Circle* (1933), *King Coffin* (1935), *Conversation* (1940); *Bring! Bring! and Other Stories* (1925), and *Collected Short Stories* (1950); *Ushant* (autobiography, 1952); *Scepticisms* (1919), *Reviewer's ABC* (1958), and *Collected Criticism* (1968).

Aiken, George L. 1830–1876. American actor and playwright, b. Boston. Dramatized *Uncle Tom's Cabin* (1852).

Aiken, Howard Hathaway. 1900–1973. American mathematician, b. Hoboken, N.J. At Harvard (1939–61); with C.D. Lake, B.M. Durfee, F.E. Hamilton, invented (1944) Harvard Mark I, pioneering electronic digital computer; built Mark II (1947).

Ail·ly \ā-yē\, Pierre d'. 1350–1420. French prelate and theologian. Master (1384) and later chancellor of College of Navarre; confessor and almoner to Charles VI (1389); named bishop of Le Puy (1395) and Cambrai (1397) by antipope Benedict XIII; broke with Benedict; prominent at Council of Pisa (1409), which adopted his view that councils could depose popes; appointed cardinal (1411) and legate (1413) by Pope John XXIII; prominent at Council of Custance (1414–18), which condemned Hussites and ended Great Schism in electing Pope Martin V; Martin's legate at Avignon.

Ailred, Saint. See AETHELRED.

Aimard, Gustave. See Olivier GLOUX.

Aimar de Le Puy. See ADHÉMAR DE MONTEIL.

Aime \em, *Angl* 'ām\, Valcour. 1798–1867. American planter, b. St. Charles Parish, La. Built first sugar refinery in U.S. on plantation; reputed the richest man in the South, his home called "Little Versailles."

Ai·moin \em-waⁿ\. 960–1010. French monk and chronicler. Monk at Fleury-sur-Loire; author of *Miracula Sancti Benedicti,* a life of abbot Abbon, and *Historia Francorum.*

Ain·mil·ler \'īn-,mil-ər\, Max Emanuel. 1807–1870. German artist. Known esp. for painting on glass and stained glass; executed works for cathedrals of Cologne, Regensburg, for St. Paul in London, etc.

Ains·lie \'ānz-lē\, Hew. 1792–1878. American poet, b. Ayrshire, Scotland. To U.S. (1822); author of *Pilgrimage to the Land of Burns* (1822), *Scottish Songs, Ballads, and Poems* (1855).

Ains·worth \'ānz-(,) wərth\, Henry. 1571–?1622. English Separatist clergyman and scholar. To Amsterdam (1593) where he was chosen teacher of a Separatist congregation; drew up confession of faith (1596); with Francis Johnson wrote

An Apology or Defence of Such True Christians as Are Commonly but Unjustly Called Brownists (1604); noted Hebrew scholar, author of *Annotations* on several Old Testament books.

Ainsworth, William Harrison. 1805–1882. English novelist. Editor of *Bentley's Miscellany* (1840–42); published *Ainsworth's Magazine* (1842–53), *New Monthly Magazine* (from 1853); author of popular historical romances, including *Rookwood* (1834), *Jack Sheppard* (1839), *Tower of London* (1840), *Old St. Paul's* (1841), *Guy Fawkes* (1841), *Windsor Castle* (1843), *St. James's* (1844), *Lancashire Witches* (1849), *The Flitch of Bacon* (1854), and *Boscobel* (1872), several illustrated by Cruikshank.

Aird \'a(ə)rd, 'e(ə)rd\, Sir John. 1833–1911. British contractor. Built reservoirs, canals, docks and other major works; with engineer Sir Benjamin Baker constructed Aswān and Asyūṭ dams (1898–1902); M.P. (1887–1905); created baronet (1901).

Aird, Thomas. 1802–1876. Scottish poet. Author of *Martzoufle* (1826), *Old Bachelor in the Scottish Village* (1845).

Air·lang·ga \ar-'läŋ-gə\. 991–?1049. Indonesian ruler. Son-in-law of Dharmavamsa; escaped destruction of Dharmavamsa's empire (1007); undertook to reunite empire; ruler of united eastern Javanese empire (1019–?49); subject of Javanese epic *Arjunavivāha.*

Airy \'a(ə)r-ē, 'e(ə)r-\, Sir George Biddell. 1801–1892. English astronomer. Astronomer royal (1835–81); equipped Royal Observatory at Greenwich with newly designed instruments; reduced all lunar and planetary observations made at Greenwich in 1750–1830 and otherwise organized work of observatory; invented cylindrical lens for correction of astigmatism (1827).

'Ā'i·shah \'ä-i-sha\. *In full* 'Ā'ishah bint Abī Bakr. 614–678. Third and favorite wife of Muḥammad. Daughter of Abū Bakr. Played little role in religious or political affairs during marriage or for a time after Muḥammad's death (632); helped foment opposition to caliph 'Uthmān; captured in Battle of the Camel against caliph 'Alī (656).

Aïs·sé \a-ē-sā\, Mlle. *Also called* Hai·dée \e-dā\. 1694?–1733. Circassian slave girl. Bought in infancy from Turks by French ambassador at Constantinople and educated at Paris; taken up by Regency society; her *Letters* (pub. 1787 with notes by Voltaire) depict social life in Paris at beginning of 18th century.

Ais·tulf \'ī-ˌstulf\ *or* **As·tolf** \'as-ˌtälf\. d. 756. King of the Lombards (749–756). Besieged and captured Ravenna from Byzantines (750–751); hostile to Rome and the pope, at whose urging he was besieged at Pavia by the Franks under Pepin (755); forced to promise return of Ravenna; besieged Rome (756) but defeated by Pepin.

Ait·ken \'āt-kən\, John. 1839–1919. Scottish physicist. Investigator of atmospheric dust, dew, cyclones, etc.; discovered role of microscopic particles (Aitken nuclei) in condensation of atmospheric water vapor.

Aitken, Robert. 1734–1802. American printer, b. Dalkeith, Scotland. Opened bookstore in Philadelphia (1769); published first complete English Bible printed in America (1781–82).

Aitken, Robert Grant. 1864–1951. American astronomer, b. Jackson, Calif. At U. of the Pacific (1891–95); on staff (1895–1935), director (1930–35), Lick Observatory; discovered over 3000 double stars.

Aitken, Robert Ingersoll. 1878–1949. American sculptor, b. San Francisco. Executed McKinley monuments in San Francisco and St. Helena, Calif., George Rogers Clark monument at U. of Virginia, busts of Thomas Jefferson, Daniel Webster, Benjamin Franklin, Henry Clay in Hall of Fame, equestrian statue of Gen. O. O. Howard in Gettysburg National Park, *The Four Elements, Fountain of the Earth,* west pediment of U.S. Supreme Court Building, etc.

Aitken, William Maxwell. 1st Baron Bea·ver·brook \'bē-vər-ˌbrůk\. 1879–1964. British politician and newspaper proprietor, b. Maple, Ont. Acquired fortune as Montreal stockbroker; to England (1910); M.P. (1911–16); created baron (1917); in Lloyd George cabinet as chancellor of duchy of Lancaster and minister of information (1918); in Churchill cabinet as minister for aircraft production (1940–41), of supply (1941–42), lord privy seal (1943–45). Bought control of *Daily Express* (1916); introduced *Sunday Express* (1918); acquired *Evening Standard* (1923) and later Glasgow *Evening Citizen.* Author of *Politicians and the Press* (1925), *Politicians and the War* (1928), *Don't Trust to Luck* (1954), *Men and Power* (1956), etc.

Ai·ton \'āt-ᵊn\, William. 1731–1793. Scottish botanist. Director of Kew Gardens (1759–93); published catalogue *Hortus Kewensis* (1789), an enlarged edition of which was brought out (1810–13) by his son and successor ¶William Townsend (1766–1849).

Ai·za·wa \ī-zä-wä\ Yasushi. *Also called* Aizawa Seishisai. 1782–1863. Japanese scholar. Author of strongly nationalist, pro-imperial works that helped spark imperial restoration (1868) and were later revived by ultranationalist militarists; works included *Shinron, Tekii-hen, Kagaku-Jigen.*

Ajal·bert \á-zhål-ber\, Jean. 1863–1947. French lawyer and writer. Author of volumes of impressionist verse, novels, and esp. books of travel, as *Notes sur Berlin* (1894), *Sao van Di* (1905), *Raffin Su-Su* (1911).

Ak·bar \'ak-bər, *Angl also* -ˌbär\. *In full* Abū-ul-Fatḥ Jalāl-ud-Dīn Muḥammad Akbar. 1542–1605. Mughal emperor of India (1556–1605). Son of Humāyūn, on whose regaining of throne (1555) Akbar became governor of Punjab; succeeded to father's reduced empire (1556); with chief minister Bayram Khān, won back empire from Hindus at Panipat (1556); ruled (1556–60) under regency of Bayram Khān; dismissed him (1560). Spent early years of reign in continual warfare; subjugated Rājput kingdoms (1561–69); conquered Gujarāt (1572–73) and later (1593) annexed it; conquered Bengal (1576) and Kashmir (1586); annexed Sind (1591), Qandahār (1595); conquered much of Deccan (1601); finally ruled empire comprising all of northern India. Excelled as organizer and administrator of conquered provinces; introduced many reforms, abolished extortion, developed trade, and was most tolerant toward the many religious faiths of India; conducted brilliant court; patron of arts. Built Fatehpur Sīkri as his capital (1570–86). Last years troubled by rebellious conduct of his son Prince Salīm (later Jahāngīr).

Ake·ley \'ā-klē\, Carl Ethan. 1864–1926. American taxidermist, sculptor, naturalist, and explorer, b. Clarendon, N.Y. On staff of Field Museum of Natural History, Chicago (1895–1909), American Museum of Natural History, New York (1909–26); made exploring and collecting trips to Africa (1896, 1905, 1909, 1921–22, 1926); developed method of applying skin over finely modelled mannequins to achieve unprecedented realism; inventor of the Akeley cement gun and of a naturalist's motion-picture camera; author of *In Brightest Africa* (1923).

Akeley, Mary L., *nee* Jobe \'jōb\. 1886–1966. American naturalist and author, b. Tappan, O. m. (1923) Carl Akeley; succeeded husband in charge of African expedition (1926) and as adviser to American Museum of Natural History in planning African (later Akeley) Hall; author of *Carl Akeley's Africa* (1929), *Lions, Gorillas and Their Neighbors* (1932), *Congo Eden* (1950).

à Kempis, Thomas. See THOMAS À KEMPIS.

Aken·side \'ā-kən-ˌsīd\, Mark. 1721–1770. English poet and physician. Practiced in London; physician to queen (1761). Author of *Pleasures of the Imagination,* philosophical poem patterned on Virgil and Horace (1744), *Odes on Several Subjects* (1745), *Hymn to the Naiads* (1746), and other verse.

Akhe·na·ton \ˌäk-(ə-) 'nät-ᵊn\. *Also written* Ikh·na·ton \ik-'nät-ᵊn\. *Called also* Amenhotep IV *or* Amenophis IV. 14th century B.C. King of Egypt (1379–1362 B.C.) of 18th dynasty. Son and successor of, possibly for a time coregent with, Amenhotep III; reigned for six years as Amenhotep IV; assumed name Akhenaton and built new capital of Akhetaton as part of new religion of Aton, the sun disk; reign noted for extraordinary vigor of art; preoccupation with Aton religion apparently permitted disintegration of empire and caused discontent among priestly and military classes. Sometimes considered the first monotheist. See also NEFERTITI, TUTANKHAMEN.

Akhmatova, Anna. See Anna GORENKO.

Akh·tal, al- \əl-'ak̲-tal\. *In full* Ghiyāth ibn Ghawth ibn aṣ-Ṣalt al-Akhṭal. c.640–710. Christian Arab poet. With Jarīr and al-Farazdaq, member of trio of great poets of Umayyad period; court poet to caliphs Yazīd I and 'Abd al-Malik.

Akh·toy \äk-'toi\. *Also written* Ach·thoes \äk-'tō-ˌēz\. 22nd century B.C. Egyptian king. Ruler of Heracleopolitan nome of Upper Egypt; proclaimed himself king (c.2160 B.C.), founding 9th dynasty.

Aki·ba ben Jo·seph \á-'kiv-ä-ben-'jō-zəf\. c.40–c.135 A.D. Jewish sage and martyr in Palestine. Founded great rabbinical school at Jaffa; developed exegetical method of Midrash; introduced new method of interpreting Jewish oral law (Halakha) which developed as foundation of the Mishna; as scholar and as jurist had very great impact on Judaism. May have supported Bar Kokhba in revolt against Hadrian (132); taken prisoner by Romans and suffered martyrdom by being flayed alive.

Akin·dy·nos \ˌä-kin-'dē-nōs\, Gregorios. c.1300–c.1349. Greek monk and theologian. Student of Gregory Palamas; sought to unite Hesychast monasticism with Neoplatonic thought; became critical of some Palamite doctrines, attracting support of Emperor John V Palaeologus; not supported by John VI; posthumously condemned by Byzantine church (1351).

Akins \'ā-kənz\, Zoë. 1886–1958. American poet and playwright, b. Humansville, Mo. Author of poetry, as *Interpretations* (1911), *The Hills Grow Smaller* (1937), and plays, as *Déclassée* (1919), *Daddy's Gone A-Hunting* (1921), *A Royal Fandango* (1923), *The Greeks Had a Word For It* (1930), *The Old Maid* (1935, Pulitzer prize), *The Little Miracle* (1936), and several film scripts.

Ak·ro·po·li·tes \ˌak-rə-pə-'līt-ēz\, Georgios. *Lat.* Georgius Ac·ro·po·li·ta \ˌak-rə-pə-'līt-ə\. 1217–1282. Byzantine historian and diplomat. In service of emperors John III Ducas, Theodore II Lascaris, Michael VII Palaeologus; grand logothete (1244); negotiated and at Second Council of Lyons (1274) signed pact reuniting Greek and Latin churches; author of *Chronikē syngraphē,* a history of Byzantine empire from 1204 to 1261.

Aksa·kov \(,)ək-'sä-kəf\, Sergey Timofeyevich. 1791–1859. Russian novelist. Author of realistic and humorous novels and valuable descriptions of contemporary life, including *Blizzard* (1834), *Semeynaya Khronika* (1856), *Vospominaniya* (1856), *Detskie gody bagrova-vnuka* (1858). His elder son ¶Konstantin Sergeyevich (1817–1860), poet and dramatist, was a principal theorist of the Slavophile movement. Another son ¶Ivan Sergeyevich (1823–1886), was a writer and leading Slavophile; founder and editor of Slavophile and Panslavist newspapers *Den* (1861–65), *Moskva* (1867–69), *Rus* (1880–86); author of *Brodyaga* (1852), first Russian narrative poem on peasant life; in Russo-Turkish War (1877–78), influential supporter of liberation of Balkan Slavs.

Ak·sel·rod \ək-syil-'rȯd\, Pavel Borisovich. *Known also as* Paul Axelrod. 1850–1928. Russian political leader. Founded Marxist Osvobozhdeniye Truda party (1883); became Menshevik (1903) and led "liquidationist" movement (from 1905); opposed Bolshevik Revolution (1917). Author of memoirs *Perezhitoye i Peredumanoye* (1923).

A·ku·ei \'äk-'ü-'ā\. 1717–1797. Chinese general. Led expeditions to put down rebellions in Szechwan and Kansu provinces; conquered Ili, Chinese Turkistan, Burma.

A·ku·ta \'äk-'ü-'tä\. *Posthumous title* T'ai Tsu \'tid-'zü\, *i.e.* Grand Progenitor. 1069–1123. Chinese ruler. Leader of nomadic Juchen tribes; repudiated allegiance to Mongol Liao dynasty (1112); declared himself emperor (1115); with Sung aid, conquered Liao and rest of northern China; founded Chin dynasty. Successor drove Sung court from its capital (1126).

Aku·ta·ga·wa \äk-ù-tä-gä-wä\ Ryūnosuke. *Pseudonyms* Cho·kō·do Shu·jin \chō-kō-dō-shùj-in\ *and* Ga·ki \gäk-ē\. 1892–1927. Japanese writer. Author of stylistically polished stories, often of old Japan; best known story "Rashomon" (1915).

'Alā' ad-Dīn Mu·ḥam·mad \ä-'lä-ed-'dēn-mù-'ḵam-məd\. d. 1220. Ruler of Khwārezm (1200–20). Under his rule as penultimate Khwārezm-Shāh, an empire reaching from India to Anatolia was created; after his death empire fell to Mongols.

Al·a·bas·ter \,al-ə-'bas-tər\ *or* **Ar·blas·tier** \är-'blas-tyər\, William. 1567–1640. English clergyman and poet. Converted to Catholicism (1597) but was condemned for mystical writings and returned to Anglican church; king's chaplain (1618). Author of Latin tragedy *Roxana* (1597), unfinished Latin epic on Elizabeth I *Elisaeis,* biblical commentaries, etc.

Ala·coque \á-lá-kȯk\, Saint Marguerite-Marie. 1647–1690. French religious. Entered Visitation order (1671); founder of devotion to Sacred Heart of Jesus. Canonized (1920) by Benedict XV.

Alain. See Émile-Auguste CHARTIER.

Alain de Lille \á-laⁿ-də-lēl\. *Lat.* Ala·nus ab In·su·lis \ə-'lä-nə-sab-'in-s(y)ù-ləs\ *or* de In·su·lis \dē-'in-\. *Called* the Universal Doctor. c.1128–1202. French philosopher, theologian, and poet. Author of *De planctu naturae,* verse satire on human vices, *Anticlaudianus,* verse treatise on morals and arts, *De arte seu de articulis catholicae fidei* on theology, *Contra haereticos,* etc.; forwarded a rationalist-mystical philosophy against scholasticism.

Alain-Fournier. See Henri-Alban FOURNIER.

'Alām, Shāh. See SHĀH 'ALĀM II.

Ala·mán \äl-ä-'män\, Lucas. 1792–1853. Mexican historian and politician. Represented Mexico in Spanish Cortes (1819–21); in independent Mexico, minister of interior and exterior relations (1823–25, 1830–32); promoted industrialization; recognized as leader of Mexican conservatives; engaged in frequent disputes with United States; founded Muséo Nacional and Archivo Général. Author of *Disertaciones sobre la historia de la republica mejicana* (1844–49), *Historia de México* (1848–52).

Ala·man·ni \,äl-ä-'män-nē\ *or* **Ale·man·ni** \,äl-ä-\, Luigi. 1495–1556. Italian poet. Conspired against Giulio de' Medici; fled to Venice, thence to France where he spent most of life, chiefly at court. His works included *Opere Toscane* (1532), *La Coltivazione* (1546), romance *Girone il Cortese* (1548), etc.

'Ālam·gīr \'äl-əm-,gēr\. Name of two Mughal emperors of India:

'Ālamgīr. *Given name* Muḥī-ud-Dīn Muhammad; *princely title* Aurangzeb. 1618–1707. Son of Shāh Jahān; commanded troops against Uzbeks and Persians (1646–47); viceroy of Deccan kingdoms (1636–44, 1654–58); engaged in struggle (1657–59) with elder brother Dārā Shukōh, the heir apparent; by military ability and ruthlessness won throne, deposing father (1658) and defeating Dārā (1659); began to impose Muslim orthodoxy on realm (from c. 1680), alienating Hindus and others; provoked rebellion by Sikhs, Satnamis, Jāṭs; engaged in long fruitless war against Marāthās; strained economy by difficult conquest of Deccan states (1686–87).

'Ālamgīr II. *In full* 'Azīz-ud-Dīn 'Ālamgīr. 1699–1759. Emperor (1754–59). Son of Jahāndār Shāh; succeeded Aḥmad Shāh at behest of vizier 'Imād ul-Mulk, who actually held power; became virtual puppet of Afghan ruler Aḥmad Shāh Durrāni, who invaded India (1756, 1759); during reign Marāthā power also reached zenith; murdered on order of vizier.

Ala·mi·nos \äl-ä-'mē-nōs\, Antonio. fl. 1493–1520. Spanish navigator. With Columbus (1493), Ponce de León (1512), Grijalva (1518), Cortés (1519) in voyages to New World; credited with discovery of Gulf Stream (1513).

Alan, William. See William ALLEN.

Alanbrooke, Viscount. See Sir Alan Francis BROOKE.

Alanus ab (*or* **de) Insulis.** See ALAIN DE LILLE.

Alar·cón \äl-är-'kȯn\, Hernando de. 16th century Spanish explorer. Commanded naval expedition in conjunction with Coronado's search for Cíbola (1540–41); explored Gulf of California, discovered mouth of Colorado River, established California not an island.

Alarcón, Pedro Antonio de. 1833–1891. Spanish writer. Edited liberal journal *El látigo;* participated as volunteer in Moroccan campaign (1859); member, council of state (1875–81); minister to Norway and Sweden. Known esp. for short stories and sketches of Spanish rustic life, as *El sombrero de tres picos* (1874) and *El niño de la bola* (1878). Other works included the chronicle *Diario de un testigo de la guerra de Africa* (1859); novels, as *El final de Norma* (1855), *El escándalo* (1875), *El capitán veneno* (1881), and *La pródiga* (1880); and *Historia de mis libros* (1889).

Alarcón y Mendoza, Juan Ruiz de. See Juan RUIZ DE ALARCÓN Y MENDOZA.

Al·a·ric \'al-ə-rik\. Name of two kings of the Visigoths:

Alaric. c.370–410. King (395–410). Under Emperor Theodosius, commanded Gothic auxiliaries (394); after Theodosius's death (395), left Roman service, was elected king of Visigoths; complaining promised subsidies had not been paid his people, marched toward Constantinople; turned aside, he invaded Greece (395–396), sacked Piraeus, attacked Corinth, Megara, Argos, Sparta; appointed governor in Illyricum by Emperor Arcadius as bribe. Invaded (401) and ravaged Italy until checked by Stilicho (402 and 403). Besieged Rome (408, 409), on latter occasion proclaiming Attalus emperor; appointed *magister utriusque militiae* by Attalus (409); deposed Attalus (410), besieged, occupied, and sacked Rome (410); died during Visigoth withdrawal northward.

Alaric II. d. 507 A.D. King (484–507). Son and successor of Euric. Issued (506) abstract of Roman laws and imperial decrees known as *Lex Romana Visigothorum* or *Breviarum Alaricianum.* Defeated and killed by Clovis and the Franks in Battle of Vouillé.

Alas \'äl-äs\, Leopoldo. *Pseudonym* Cla·rín \klä-'rēn\. 1852–1901. Spanish critic and novelist. Professor of law, U. of Oviedo (1883–1901); leading literary critic of the time in Spain, advocate of Naturalism; author of novels, including *La regenta* (1884–85), *Su único hijo* (1890), stories as in *Cuentos morales* (1896), *El gallo de Socrates* (1900).

à Lasco, Johannes. See Jan ŁASKI.

'Alā'-ud-Dīn \ə-'lä-ùd-'dēn\. Name of three sultans of India of the Bahmanī dynasty:

'Alā'-ud-Dīn Bah·man Shāh \-bä-'män-'shä\. *Orig. name* Ḥa·san Gan·gū \kä-'sän-gäŋ-'ü\. 14th century. Following revolt of Muslim nobles in the Deccan against Sultan Muḥammad ibn Tughlug of Delhi, founded (1347) Bahmanī dynasty; consolidated rule over Muslim western portion of the Deccan, attempted to subdue Hindu region; succeeded (1358) by son Muḥammad Shāh I.

'Alā'-ud-Dīn Mu·jā·hid \-,mü-jä-'hēd\. Sultan (1375–78). Son and successor of Muḥammad Shāh I; murdered by cousin Dā'ūd.

'Alā'-ud-Dīn Aḥ·mad II \-'äk-mäd\. Sultan (1436–58). Son of Shihāb-ud-Dīn Aḥmad I; reign marked by wars with Hindu powers.

Ala'ud'din \ə-'lä-ùd-'dēn\. d. c.1564. Sultan of Johore (1528–c.1564). Sometimes considered cofounder of kingdom of Johore with father Mahmud Shah, last sultan of Malacca; moved capital to Johore Lama; taken prisoner by Achinese (1564).

'Alā'-ud-Dīn Muḥammad Khal·jī \-käl-'jē\. d. 1316. Sultan of Delhi (1296–1316) of the Khaljī dynasty. Gained throne by assassinating uncle Jalāl-ud-Dīn; instituted central administration, reforms including heavy taxation; built standing army; conquered Gujarāt (1299), Ranthambhor (1301), Chitor (1303), Māndū (1305), Siwāna (1308), Jālor (1312); repelled numerous Mongol attacks from north; laid foundation for Muslim empire in Deccan and southern India.

Ala·ung·pa·ya \ä-,lä-ùŋ-'pī-ə\. *Known also as* Alompra *and* Aungzeya. 1714–1760. King of Burma (1752–60). Organized Burmese resistance following Mon capture of Ava and end of Toungoo dynasty (1752); proclaimed himself king (1752); recaptured Ava (1753); captured Mon capital at Pegu (1757); concluded treaty with British East India Co. (1757); led invasion of Siam (1760); died during retreat from siege of Ayutthaya.

Ála·va y Es·qui·vel \'äl-äv-ä-ē-es-kē-'bel\, Miguel Ricardo de. 1771–1843. Spanish soldier and statesman. Spanish commissary and aide-de-camp to Duke of Wellington in Peninsular War (1811 ff.); in service of Ferdinand VII as ambassador to Netherlands (1815–22); lost favor because of liberal ideas; president (1822) of the Cortes; aided in deposition of Ferdinand (1822); fled to England after restoration of Ferdinand by French (1823); in service of Maria Christina against Don Carlos; ambassador to London (1834), Paris (1835).

Alay·rac \á-le-räk\, Nicolas d'. 1753–1809. French composer. Wrote nearly 60 opéras-comiques, including *L'Eclipse totale* (1782), *Nina* (1786), *Camille* (1791), *Adolphe et Clara* (1799), *Maison à vendre* (1800), *Une heure de mariage* (1804), etc.

Alba, Duke of. See Fernando ÁLVAREZ DE TOLEDO.

Al·ba·leg \'äl-bäl-ˌeg\, Isaac. 13th century. Jewish philosopher of northern Spain or southern France. Made Hebrew translation, with commentary, of parts of al-Ghazālī's *Maqāṣid al-falāsifah.*

Al·ban \'ól-bən, 'al-\. Saint. 3d century A.D. First British martyr. According to Bede, served in Roman army; put to death (c.304) after changing clothes with Christian cleric who converted him.

Al·ba·ni \äl-'bän-ē\, Alessandro. 1692–1779. Italian prelate. Nephew of Pope Clement XI; cardinal (1721); built Villa Albani and formed famous art collection.

Al·ba·ni \äl-'bän-ē\, Dame Emma. *Orig.* Marie Louise Cécilie Emma La·jeu·nesse \lä-zhœ-nes\. 1847–1930. Canadian operatic singer, b. Chambly, Que. Made London debut in *La sonnambula* at Covent Garden (1872); toured Russia (1873, 1874), U.S. (1874, 1889), Canada (1883, 1889), etc.; greatly admired for warmth and beauty of voice; retired (1911).

Albani *or* **Al·ba·no** \äl-'bän-ō\, Francesco. 1578–1660. Italian painter. Known esp. for his representations of the Holy Family and for his frescoes on mythological subjects.

Albany, Duke of. English title held by members of Stewart family (*q.v.*), including royal Stuarts James I and Charles I and II of England. For Duke of York and Albany, see FREDERICK AUGUSTUS.

Albany, Countess of. See LOUISE MAXIMILIENNE CAROLINE.

Albategnius *or* **Albatenius.** See al-BATTĀNĪ.

Al·bee \'ól-(ˌ)bē, 'al-\, Edward Franklin. 1857–1930. American theater manager, b. Machias, Me. With B.F. Keith established Boston Bijou Theatre (1885); created Keith-Albee theater circuit, eventually controlling nearly 400 U.S. theaters; general manager (1885–1914), president (1914–28); president of United Booking Office (1900–28); circuit absorbed into RKO (Radio-Keith-Orpheum, 1928).

Albermarle, Duke of. See George MONCK.

Albemarle, Earls of. See Arnold Joost van KEPPEL.

Al·bé·niz \äl-'b̲ā-nēth\, Isaac Manuel Francisco. 1860–1909. Spanish pianist and composer. Virtuoso pianist; a leader of Spanish nationalist school; known for operas, zarzuelas, and piano pieces, including *Iberia* (1906–09), *Suite española, Cantos de España, Navarra, Tango in D.*

Al·ber·di \äl-'ber-t̲h̲ē\, Juan Bautista. 1810–1884. Argentine statesman, jurist, and philosopher. In exile in Uruguay and Chile (1838–52) until fall of Juan Manuel de Rosas; wrote *Bases y punto de partida para la organización política de la República Argentina* (1852), which strongly influenced Argentine constitution of 1853; minister to France, Spain, U.S., Great Britain; later again in exile in France. Author also of *Sistema económico y rentístico de la Confederación* (1854), *Ensayos sobre la sociedad* (1898).

Al·ber·dingk Thijm \'äl-bər-diŋk-'tīm\, Josephus Albertus. 1820–1889. Dutch author and art critic. Wrote fiction, poetry, drama and criticism from strongly Catholic viewpoint; works included *Karolingische verhalen* (1851), *Verspreide verhalen in proza* (1879–84). His son ¶Karel Joan Lodewijk (1864–1952), *pseudonym* Lodewijk van Deys·sel \-vän-'dā-səl\, was also a writer and critic; author of naturalistic and later impressionistic novels, including *Een liefde* (1887), and critical essays collected in *Verzamelde opstellen* (1894–1911).

Al·ber·ic I \'al-bər-ik\. d. 925? Lombard noble. Margrave of Camerino (from 891) and of Spoleto (from 897); with Theophylact restored Sergius III to papacy (904); played large part in Pope John X's victory over Saracens on Garigliano River (915). His son by Theophylact's daughter Marozia, ¶Alberic II (c.905–954), led uprising and imprisoned half-brother Pope John XI (932); ruled Rome under title of *princeps* (932–954); arranged election of illegitimate son Octavian as Pope John XII.

Al·be·ro·ni \ˌäl-bā-'rō-nē\, Giulio. 1664–1752. Italian prelate and politician in Spain. Canon at Parma (1698); in service of duc de Vendôme (1706); with Vendôme in Madrid (1711); representative of Parma in Madrid (1713); negotiated marriage of Philip V and Elizabeth Farnese; de facto prime minister of Spain (1716–19); introduced various reforms, reduced power of aristocracy; cardinal (1717); foreign policy led to war with Quadruple Alliance disastrous to Spain; banished from Spain (1719).

Al·bers \'äl-ˌbers, *Angl* 'al-bərz, 'äl-\, Josef. 1888–1976. American artist, b. Bottrop, Germany. Student and (from 1923) teacher at Bauhaus; to U.S. (1933), naturalized (1939); at Black Mountain Coll. (1934–49), Yale (1950–58); known esp. for carefully calculated experiments in color and geometry, as paintings in *Homage to the Square* series, drawings in *Structural Constellations* series; influenced Color Field and Op Art movements.

Albert, Saint. See AETHELBERHT.

Al·bert \'al-bərt\. *Ger.* Al·brecht \'äl-(ˌ)brek̲t\. Names of several dukes and archdukes of Austria, including:

Albert I. See ALBERT I, king of Germany.

Albert II. *Called* der Wei·se \der-'vī-zə\, *i.e.* the Wise, *or* der Lah·me \-'läm-ə\, *i.e.* the Lame. c.1298–1358. Son of King Albert I of Germany; succeeded brother Frederick I (III as king of Germany) as duke of Austria (1330); ruled jointly (1330–39) with younger brother Otto, later (1339–58) alone.

Albert III. c.1350–1395. Son of Albert II; with brother Leopold III succeeded elder brother Rudolf IV as joint ruler of Austrian lands (1365); quarrelled with Leopold and by Treaty of Neuberg (1379) divided Habsburg Austrian lands, himself taking Upper and Lower Austria; patron of arts; issued statute for U. of Vienna (1389).

Albert V. See ALBERT II, king of Germany.

Albert VII. *Known as* Albert the Pious. 1559–1621. Archduke of Austria. Son of Emperor Maximilian II; educated for church; archbishop of Toledo and cardinal (1577); viceroy of Portugal (1585–95); governor of Spanish Netherlands (1595); m. (1599) Isabella Clara Eugenia, daughter of Philip II of Spain, through whom he received nominal sovereignty over Netherlands; conducted inconclusive campaign against Dutch ending in 12-year truce (1609).

Albert. 1817–1895. Archduke of Austria and duke of Teschen. Son of Archduke Charles. Fought in Italian campaign (1848–49); governor of Hungary (1851–63); in war with Prussia commanded Italian front and won major victory at Custoza (1866); following Austrian defeat at Königgratz, named commander in chief of Austrian forces (1866); as inspector general (1869–95), worked to reform and modernize army.

Albert. *Ger.* Albrecht. Name of several dukes of Bavaria-Munich, including:

Albert III. *Called* der From·me \der-'fró-mə\, *i.e.* the Pious. 1401–1460. Duke (1438–60); promoted monastic reform.

Albert IV. *Called* der Wei·se \-'vī-zə\, *i.e.* the Wise. 1447–1508. Son and successor of Albert III; reunited long divided ducal territories; established primogeniture (1506); patron of artists and scholars.

Albert V. 1528–1579. Son and successor of William IV; duke (1550–79); founded state library, art museum, etc.

Albert I. 1875–1934. King of the Belgians (1909–34). Son of Philip, Count of Flanders; succeeded uncle Leopold II on throne; served in army (to 1909) and Senate (1893–98); reaffirmed Belgian neutrality and refused German demand for free passage of troops (1914); led Belgian army in retreat to Flanders (1914); led Belgian and French troops in final Allied offensive (Sept.–Nov. 1918); directed postwar reconstruction; introduced new monetary system (1926).

Albert. *Ger.* Albrecht. Name of several margraves and electors of Brandenburg, including:

Albert I. *Called* the Bear. c.1100–1170. Son of Otto the Rich, from whom he inherited (1123) Saxon estates; inherited (1142) Billung estates from mother. For services to Emperor Lothair II in Italy received North Mark (1134); campaigned against Wends; received Brandenburg on death of Pribislav, prince of Havelland, and took title of margrave (1150); revived bishoprics of Havelberg and Brandenburg (1151–52); carried on colonization and missionary work among Slavs; introduced Frisian and Saxon settlers in Brandenburg territories. Founder of Ascanian dynasty.

Albert III Achil·les \ä-'kil-es\. 1414–1486. Son of Frederick I, Elector of Brandenburg; succeeded (1440) to principality of Ansbach; inherited Bayreuth on death of brother John (1464); succeeded as elector of Brandenburg on abdication of brother Frederick II (1470); issued Disposito Achillea (1473), laying foundation for primogeniture in disposition of mark of Brandenburg; spent much of reign attempting to subdue rebellious cities, esp. Nürnberg.

Albert Al·ci·bi·a·des \-ˌält-sē-'bē-ä-ˌdes\. 1522–1557. Son of Margrave Casimir; became margrave of Kulmbach-Bayreuth (1541); supported cause of Emperor Charles V (to 1551); joined Maurice of Saxony and negotiated treaty of Chambord with Henry II of France, forming league against Charles V (1552); returned to Charles, who ratified Albert's seizure of large German territories; defeated by Maurice and Ferdinand at Sievershausen (1553); outlawed by Imperial Chamber at Speyer (1553); fled to France (1554).

Albert. *Ger.* Albrecht. Name of two kings of Germany:

Albert I. c.1255–1308. King (1298–1308). Son of King Rudolf I of Habsburg; created duke of Austria and of Styria (1282); made alliance with German electors to depose and succeed Adolf of Nassau (1298); formed alliance (1299) with Philip IV of France against Pope Boniface VIII; unsuccessful in claims of Holland, Zealand, and Frisia; suppressed rebellion of Rhineland electors (1300–02); finally obtained recognition of election from Boniface (1303); attempted to place son Rudolf on throne of Bohemia (1306); defeated in attempt to take Thuringia and Meissen (1307); assassinated by nephew John of Swabia, known as the Parricide.

Albert II. 1397–1439. King (1438–39). Son of Duke Albert IV of Austria, whom he succeeded as Albert V (1404); m. (1421) Elisabeth, daughter of Emperor Sigismund; on death of Sigismund crowned king of Hungary (1438) and of Bohemia (1438); elected king of Germany (1438); at diet at Nürnberg (1438) ended right of private warfare; instituted administrative reforms; died in campaign against Turks.

Albert. *Ger.* Albrecht. 1490–1545. Cardinal elector of Mainz. Son of Elector Johann Cicero of Brandenburg; archbishop of Magdeburg (1513); archbishop and elector of Mainz (1514); cardinal (1518); to gain Pope Leo X's consent to hold two dioceses, made large contribution to rebuilding of St. Peter's Basilica; repaid loan from banking house of Fugger by sale of indulgences, becoming object of Luther's condemnation in Ninety-Five Theses; patron of artists, notably Cranach, Dürer, Grünewald.

Albert. *Ger.* Albrecht. Name of several dukes of Mecklenburg, including:

Albert III. See ALBERT, king of Sweden.

Albert VII. 1486–1547. Duke (1503–47); opposed Reformation.

Albert I. *In full* Albert-Honoré-Charles Gri·mal·di \grē-mäl-dē\. 1848–1922. Prince of Monaco (1889–1922). Son of Prince Charles III; noted as sailor and amateur oceanographer; founded Oceanographic Museum of Monaco (1899), Oceanographic Institute of Paris (1906); introduced (1885) copper floats for tracking ocean currents.

Albert. *Ger.* Albrecht. *Called* der Ältere \der-'el-ter-ə\, *i.e.* the Elder. 1490–1568. First duke of Prussia (1525–68). Son of Frederick of Hohenzollern, Margrave of Ansbach-Bayreuth; named grand master of Teutonic Knights (1510); engaged in war with Poland (1519–21) over status of East Prussia; adopted suggestion of Martin Luther that Teutonic Knights' East Prussian holdings be transformed into hereditary dukedom (1525); reign marked by intrigues of political adventurers; established secular government and orthodox Lutheranism; fostered founding of U. of Königsberg (1544).

Albert. *Ger. in full* Friedrich Wilhelm Nikolaus Albrecht. 1837–1906. Prince of Prussia. General in Prussian campaigns (1866, 1870–71); general field marshal (1888); appointed by federal council regent of Duchy of Brunswick (1885–1906) to exclude claim of Ernest Augustus, Duke of Cumberland.

Albert. *Ger.* Albrecht. *Called* der Be·herz·te \der-bə-'hert-stə\, *i.e.* the Bold. 1443–1500. Duke of Saxony. Son of Frederick II the Gentle, Elector of Saxony; on death of father (1464) succeeded to rule jointly with elder brother Ernest; on division of duchy (1485) received eastern and western portions; governor of Netherlands for Holy Roman emperors (1488–93); governor of Friesland (1498–1500). Founder of Albertine, or Wittenberg, line of the Wettin family.

Albert. 1828–1902. King of Saxony (1873–1902). Son of King John; served in German campaign against Danes (1849); general of infantry (1857); member of upper house of Saxon parliament (1862); commanded Saxon army in Seven Weeks' War against Prussia (1866); commanded Saxon corps in Franco–Prussian War, distinguishing himself at Gravelotte and Sedan (1870); commanded German army of occupation in France (1871); field marshal and inspector general of imperial German army (1871).

Albert. *Ger.* Albrecht. 1340–1412. King of Sweden (1363–89). Duke of Mecklenburg as Albert III (1384–1412); nephew of Magnus Eriksson, whom he was elected to succeed (1363) as king of Sweden; power restricted by Council of Nobles (1371); defeated and captured by army of Margaret (1389); retired to Mecklenburg.

Albert. *Ger.* Albrecht. 1865–1939. Duke of Württemberg. Son of Philip, Duke of Württemberg; entered military service (1885); inspector general (1913); in World War I field marshal commanding German Fourth army (1917), army group in Alsace (1917–18).

Al·bert \àl-ber\ of Aix \eks\. fl. 1130. French chronicler. Canon of Aachen; compiled history of First Crusade and of Kingdom of Jerusalem to 1120.

Al·bert \'äl-,bert\ of Bux·hoev·den \'büks-,hœv-dən\. *Known also as* Albert of Ri·ga \'rē-(,)gä\. c.1165–1229. German prelate. Bishop of Livonia (1199); founded city of Riga (1201); founded Order of the Brothers of the Sword (1202).

Albert *or* **Al·er·ic** \'al-ə-rik\ of Sabina. 12th century. Antipope (1102). Bishop of Sabina; elected as successor to antipope Theodoric by Emperor Henry IV's faction opposing Pope Paschal II; imprisoned and later confined to monastery by Paschal.

Albert of Saxe-Coburg-Gotha. *In full* Franz Albrecht August Karl Emmanuel. 1819–1861. Prince consort of Queen Victoria of Great Britain. Son of Ernest, Duke of Saxe-Coburg-Gotha; m. (1840) Victoria, a first cousin. Diligent student of political affairs and tutor and adviser to Victoria; noted for high moral standards he set for household and for aristocracy; managed Great Exhibition at Crystal Palace (1851); with difficulty overcame early hostility of British public.

Albert of Saxony. *Known also as* Albert von Helm·stedt \-fòn-'helm-,shtet\. c. 1316–1390. German Scholastic philosopher. Rector of U. of Paris (1353–c. 1362), of U. of Vienna (1365–66); bishop of Halberstadt (1366); wrote on mathematics, physics, logic; helped spread nominalist logic of William of Ockham.

Albert the Great. See ALBERTUS MAGNUS.

Albert the Pious. See ALBERT VII of Austria.

Albert the Worker. See Albert-Alexandre MARTIN.

Al·bert \àl-ber\, Charles d'. Duc de Luynes \də-lwʸēn\. 1578–1621. French politician. Falconer to Louis XIII (1611); plotted murder of marquis d'Ancre (1617); chief minister to Louis XIII (from 1617); created duc de Luynes and named governor of Picardy (1619); constable of France (1621); worked to limit power of nobles and of queen mother Marie de Médicis; failed in attempt to conquer Huguenots of southern France (1621).

Albert, Eugen D'. See D'ALBERT.

Al·bert \'äl-,bert\, Heinrich. 1604–1651. German composer, poet, and organist. Cathedral organist at Königsberg (from 1631); composed operas, festival pieces, and esp. *Arien* (1638–50), vocal settings of sacred and secular texts, considered epitomes of German Baroque song.

Albert, Joseph. 1825–1886. German photographer. Discovered (1868) improved photogelatin engraving process (albertype) permitting more than a thousand copies to be made from one plate.

Al·ber·ti \äl-'ber-tē\, Domenico. c.1710–1740. Italian musician. Known esp. for harpsichord sonatas in which melody is supported by broken-chord bass accompaniment known as Alberti bass.

Alberti, Friedrich August von. 1795–1878. German geologist. Gave (1834) name of Trias or Triassic system to lowest major division of Mesozoic era.

Alberti, Leon Battista. 1404–1472. Italian mathematician, architect, painter, and writer. Secretary in papal chancery (1432–64). Author of dialogues on moral philosophy as *Della famiglia, Della pittura* (1436) in which laws of perspective were first set out scientifically, *De re aedificatoria* (1452), the fundamental work of Renaissance architecture, *De iciarchia* (1468), an epitome of Humanism; contributed to cartography, cryptography; wrote first Italian grammar; designed church of S. Andrea at Mantua, church of S. Francesco at Rimini, façade of Sta. Maria Novella and Palazzo Rucellai at Florence. Considered the type of the Renaissance man.

Alberti del Giu·di·ce \-del-jü-'dē-chā\, Niccolò di Jacopo. d. 1377. Florentine merchant and politician. At Avignon formed (1362) close banking ties with papacy; co-director (1369), director (1372) of family mercantile and banking activities; prior (1355) and gonfalonier of justice (1363) for Florence; captain of Guelph party; built Villa Paradiso. Family remained most powerful in Florence, noted for patronage of arts, until overcome by rival Albizzi family (1402).

Al·ber·tine line \'al-bər-tən, -,tēn\. *Also known as* Wit·ten·berg line \'vit-ən-,berk\. Younger line of Wettin family (*q.v.*), established (1485) by division of electoral duchy of Saxony between Ernest and Albert (*qq.v.;* see also ERNESTINE LINE), sons of Frederick the Gentle. At division received eastern and western portions; gained electoral dignity and much territory (1547) from Ernestine line when it was defeated in war of the League of Schmalkalden; acquired various lands and titles in Germany (1569–1815); retained Saxony, which later (1806) became a kingdom; electors of Saxony also kings of Poland (1697–1763). See especially electors of Saxony: MAURICE, AUGUSTUS, JOHN GEORGE I-IV, AUGUSTUS II and III of Poland, and kings of Saxony: FREDERICK AUGUSTUS I-III, JOHN, ALBERT.

Al·ber·ti·nel·li \,äl-ber-tē-'nel-lē\, Mariotto. 1474–1515. Florentine painter. Known esp. for *Visitation of the Virgin* and for many collaborations with Fra Bartolommeo.

Al·ber·ti·ni \,äl-ber-'tē-nē\, Luigi. 1871–1941. Italian journalist and politician. Joined staff of *Corriere della Sera* (1896), editor (1900–25); dismissed for opposition to Fascist government; senator (from 1914).

Albert l'Ouvrier. See Albert-Alexandre MARTIN.

Al·ber·tus Mag·nus \al-'bərt-ə-'smag-nəs\. Saint. *Real name* Albert, Graf von Boll·städt \-fòn-'bòl-,shtet\. *Called* Albert of Cologne, Albert the Great *and* Doc·tor Uni·ver·sa·lis \'däk-tər-,yü-nə-vər-'sā-ləs\. c.1200–1280. German scholastic philosopher, theologian, and scientist. Entered Dominican order (1223); taught in various German schools, at Paris (1245–48), and at Cologne (1248–54, 1257–59), where Thomas Aquinas was his pupil. Provincial of Dominicans in Germany (1254–57); with Thomas Aquinas and Bonaventure made notable defense of mendicant friars at Paris (1256); bishop of Regensburg (1260–62); papal legate for Urban IV (1263–64). Retired and spent rest of life (mostly at Cologne) in scholarly and scientific pursuits, notably in preparing commentaries on Aristotle and an attempt to unite theology and Aristotelianism; succeeded in establishing place for natural science in system of Christian studies; recognized in own lifetime as greatest scholar of the day. Author of *Summa theologiae* (incomplete), *De natura boni, Physica,* and many other writings. Beatified (1622); named doctor of the church, and canonized, by Pius XI (1931).

Al·bi·no·ni \ˌäl-bē-ˈnō-nē\, Tomaso Giovanni. 1671–1751. Italian composer. Chamber musician to duke of Mantua; wrote some 50 operas, *Sinfonie e Concerti a 5* (1707), concerti for violin, oboes, etc.

Al·bin·o·va·nus Pe·do \al-ˌbin-ə-ˈvā-nə-ˈspēd-ō\. 1st century A.D. Roman poet. Friend of Ovid; author of an epic on exploits of Germanicus Caesar in Germany, of which a fragment survives, and of the lost *Theseid* and epigrams.

Al·bi·nus \al-ˈbī-nəs\. 2d century A.D. Greek philospher. Author of *Epitome,* analysis of Plato's works through Stoic and Aristotelian methods that helped found Neoplatonic school.

Albinus. d. c.524. Roman politician. Senator, consul, and patrician under King Theodoric; accused of treasonable correspondence with Eastern Emperor Justin I; defended by philosopher Boethius; executed along with Boethius and Symmachus.

Al·bi·nus \äl-ˈbē-nəs\, Bernard Siegfried. 1697–1770. German anatomist. Professor at Leiden (1718–70); author of *Tabulaesceleti et musculorum corporus humani* (1747) noted for its excellent illustrations; first to demonstrate connection of vascular systems of mother and fetus.

Al·bi·nus \al-ˈbī-nəs\, Decimus Clodius Septimius. d. 197 A.D. Roman general. Became candidate for emperor on death of Pertinax (193); made peace with Lucius Septimius Severus but later broke it; proclaimed emperor by own army of Britain, set out for Rome; defeated by Severus near present Lyon (197).

Albinus, Spurius Postumius. 4th century B.C. Roman general. Consul (334, 321 B.C.); commander at defeat of Romans by Samnites in battle of Caudine Forks.

Al·biz·zi \äl-ˈbēt-tsē\, Rinaldo degli. 1370–1442. Florentine general. Succeeded father as head of oligarchy (1417); suffered defeats in wars with Milan (1423, 1434), Lucca (1430); exiled Cosimo de' Medici (1433); himself exiled on Cosimo's coming to power (1434).

Al·bo \ˈäl-ˌbō\, Joseph. c.1380–c.1444. Jewish philosopher in Spain. Author of *Ikkarim* (1485), classic work of Jewish dogmatics.

Al·boin \ˈal-ˌbȯin, -ˌbō-ən\. d. 572. King of the Lombards (c.565–572). Son and successor of King Audoin; in alliance with the Avars destroyed the Gepidae (c.566); killed Cunimund, king of the Gepidae, and married his daughter Rosamund. Led Lombards, Saxons, and others into northern Italy, establishing kingdom of Lombardy with capital at Pavia, captured after three-year siege (569–572). Aided Belisarius in his conquest of Italy. According to legend, murdered at behest of his wife.

Al·bor·noz \äl-bȯr-ˈnōth\, Gil Álvarez Carillo de. *Called* Egi·dio \ā-ˈk̲ē-t͟hēō\. c.1310–1367. Spanish soldier and prelate. Archbishop of Toledo (1338); participated in King Alfonso XI's campaigns against Moors; to court of Pope Clement VI at Avignon; created cardinal-priest (1350). Legate and vicar general to Rome in service of Innocent VI (1353); secured restoration of papal authority in Papal States (1353–62); codified laws of Papal States in *Liber constitutionum Sanctae Matris Ecclesiae* (1357); prepared way for papacy to return to Italy; legate to Bologna in service of Urban V (1367).

Albrecht. See ALBERT.

Al·brechts·ber·ger \ˈäl-brek̲ts-ˌber-gər\, Johann Georg. 1736–1809. Austrian composer and teacher. Deputy court organist in Vienna (1772–92); chapel master of St. Stephen's (1793–1809); famed as a teacher, his students including Beethoven; composed masses, string quartets, other religious and chamber music; noted esp. as a contrapuntist; author of *Gründliche Anweisung zur Komposition* (1790).

Al·bret \äl-bre\. Name of a Gascon family holding a lordship in the Landes from the 11th century, originating with Amanieu I d'Albret (fl. 1050) and including: Arnaud-Amanieu *or* Amanieu VIII (d. 1401), who fought in the Hundred Years' War and was rewarded by Charles V with lands and his sister-in-law Marguerite de Bourbon. His son ¶Charles, constable of France in command at Agincourt (1415); killed in the battle. Charles' grandson ¶Alain, *known as* Alain le Grand (1440–1522) ruled vast domain. His son ¶Jean (d. 1516), king of Navarre by his marriage (1484) with Catherine de Foix. Their son ¶Henri, king of Navarre (see HENRY II of Navarre); made a duke of France (1550); m. Margaret, sister of Francis I of France. ¶Charlotte, sister of Jean; m. (1499) Cesare Borgia. ¶Jeanne (1528–1572), queen of Navarre (1562–72), daughter of Henri, m. (1548) Antoine de Bourbon; son was Henry IV of France.

Al·bright \ˈȯl-ˌbrīt\, Ivan Le Lorraine. 1897–1983. American painter, b. North Harvey, Ill. Painted in the style of "magic realism" haunting, meticulously detailed pictures depicting obsession, corruption, and decay; worked for years on *The Door* and the disturbingly chaotic *The Window.* Other paintings included *Woman* (1928) and *Into the World Came a Soul Called Ida* (1930).

Albright, Jacob. 1759–1808. American preacher, b. near Pottstown, Pa. Converted to Methodism (1790). Organized classes (1800) among his converts. Annual conference (1807) adopted name "The Newly Formed Methodist Conference," and elected Albright a bishop. Methodists refused to recognize the movement, later known as the Evangelical Association, then as Evangelical Church, later merged into Evangelical United Brethren Church.

Albright, William Foxwell. 1891–1971. American archaeologist, b. Coquimbo, Chile, of American parents. Director (1921–29, 1933–36) American School of Oriental Research, Jerusalem; professor, Johns Hopkins U. (1929–58); noted for archaeological excavations of biblical sites. Author of *Archaeology of Palestine and the Bible* (1932), *From Stone Age to Christianity* (1940), *The Bible and the Ancient Near East* (1961), etc.

Albucasis. See ABŪ AL-QĀSIM.

Albumazar. See ABŪ MA'SHAR.

Al·bu·quer·que \ˌäl-bü-ˈker-kə\, Afonso de. *Called* Afonso o Gran·de \ü-ˈgraⁿ(n)-də\, *i.e.* the Great, *and* the Portuguese Mars. 1453–1515. Portuguese soldier. Spent youth at court of Afonso V; took part in expedition against Turks, in capture of Arzila and Tangier (1471), and in battle of Otranto (1481); master of horse to King John II (1481–95); served at Graciosa (1489). Made first journey to the East (1503–04) to establish trade in Cochin; built first Portuguese fortress in Asia; explored east coast of Africa (1506–07), built fort on Socotra, captured Hormuz; named governor to succeed Viceroy Dom Francisco de Almeida in India (1508); made prisoner at Cannanore by Almeida (1508–09) but released; captured Goa (1510) and made it chief Portuguese city in the East; gradually (1510–15) secured control of Malabar coast, Ceylon, Sunda Isles, Malacca; replaced and ordered home (1515). Died at sea near Goa.

Alburquerque, Duque de. See FERNÁNDEZ DE LA CUEVA.

Āl Bū Sa·ʽīd \ˈal-ˈbü-sa-ˈēd\. Muslim dynasty ruling Oman (c.1749 to present) and Zanzibar (c.1749–1964). Founded by Aḥmad ibn Saʽīd; he and successors ruled Oman and Zanzibar, Pemba and Kilwa in East Africa, and eventually Bahrain, Hormuz, and other possessions. ¶Sulṭān ibn Aḥmad (reigned 1792–1806) concluded treaty with British East India Co. ¶Saʽīd ibn Sulṭān (reigned 1806–56) established commercial relations with U.S. and France; on his death domain divided, Oman going to son ¶Thuwayn (reigned 1856–66), Zanzibar to son ¶Majīd (1856–70); Zanzibar line overthrown (1964) and island merged into United Republic of Tanzania.

Al·cae·us \al-ˈsē-əs\. c.620–c.580 B.C. Greek lyric poet. Wrote hymns, drinking and love songs, and political odes against tyrants; works known from fragments and quotation; reputedly invented the alcaic stanza.

Al·ca·lá Za·mo·ra \äl-kä-ˈlä-thä-ˈmō-rä\, Niceto. 1877–1949. Spanish politician. Member of Cortes (1905–31); minister of works (1917), of war (1922); joined republican movement (1930) and led revolutionary committee in calling for abdication of King Alfonso XIII (1931); prime minister of provisional government (April–Oct. 1931); president of Second Republic (1931–36); deposed after failure of attempt to steer middle course and end political violence; exiled to France and later Argentina.

Al·cam·e·nes \al-ˈkam-ə-ˌnēz\. 5th century B.C. Greek sculptor of Lemnos and Athens. Noted for delicacy and finish of such works as *Aphrodite of the Gardens, Hermes Propylaeus, Hephaestus.*

Alcester, Baron. See Frederick B. P. Seymour under marquises of Hertford in SEYMOUR family.

Al·cia·ti \äl-ˈchä-tē\ *or* **Al·cia·to** \-tō\, Andrea. 1492–1550. Italian jurist. Among first to make historical study of Roman law; author of legal works and *Emblemata,* a book of moral lessons in Latin verse (1522).

Al·ci·bi·a·des \ˌal-sə-ˈbī-ə-ˌdēz\. c.450–404 B.C. Athenian general and politician. In Peloponnesian War (431–404) persuaded Athenians to join alliance against Spartans; early served with Socrates at Potidaea (432), Delium (424); as general (420) a leader in unsuccessful expedition against Syracuse (415). Accused of mutilating statues of Hermes; escaped to Sparta and there induced revolt of Ionians (412) against Athens; lost confidence of Spartans and moved to Sardis; frustrated in plan to use Persian support to supplant Athenian oligarchs; offered command by Athenian fleet (411) and won victories over Sparta at Abydos (411) and Cyzicus (410); returned to Athens (407); appointed general but dismissed after defeat at Notium (407); murdered in Phrygia.

Al·cid·a·mas \al-ˈsid-ə-məs\. 4th century B.C. Greek rhetorician and sophist. Pupil of Gorgias; instructor at Athens and rival of Isocrates; author of *Peri sōphiston.*

Al·ci·phron \ˈal-sə-ˌfrän\. 2d or 3d century A.D. Greek rhetorician. Author of fictitious letters in imitation of pure Attic dialect of 4th century B.C., professedly written by common people in Athens, constituting character sketches and giving details of domestic life, manners, etc.

Alc·mae·on \alk-ˈmē-ən\. 6th century B.C. Greek physician and Pythagorean philosopher. First known to have made anatomical dissections of human bodies; perhaps first to attempt vivisection.

Alc·mae·on·i·dae \ˌalk-mē-ˈän-ə-ˌdē\. A powerful Athenian family, to which Cleisthenes, Alcibiades, and Pericles belonged, leaders in politics of 6th and 5th centuries B.C., opponents esp. of Peisistratus and Hippias.

Alc·man \'alk-mən\. 7th century B.C. Greek poet. Traditionally the founder of Doric lyric poetry; composed choral songs, hymns, paeans, etc.; work survives in fragments, esp. of a *parthenion* (choir song for girls).

Al·cock \'ȯl-ˌkäk\, John. c.1430–1500. English prelate. Bishop of Rochester (1472), Worcester (1476), and Ely (1486); twice lord chancellor (1475, 1486); first lord president of Wales (1476); founded Jesus College, Cambridge (1496).

Alcock, Sir John William. 1892–1919. English aviator. Served as captain in World War I; bombed Constantinople; captured by Turks (1917). Test pilot for Vickers Aircraft (1919); pilot of plane, with Arthur W. Brown as navigator, which made first nonstop transatlantic flight, Newfoundland to Ireland, in 16 hrs., 27 mins. (June 14, 1919).

Al·co·fo·ra·do \ˌäl-kü-fü-'rä-thü\, Mariana. 1640–1723. Portuguese nun. Long believed to be author of *Lettres portugaises,* five letters (pub. anonymously at Paris, 1669) to her deserting lover, identified as Comte de Chamilly; real author of widely popular letters shown (1926) to be Gabriel de Lavergne.

Al·cott \'ȯl-kət, 'al-, -ˌkät\, Amos Bronson. 1799–1888. American transcendentalist, teacher, and writer, b. Wolcott, Conn. Itinerant peddler in Virginia and Carolinas (1818–23); teacher in small towns of Connecticut (1823–27), Boston (1828–30), Germantown, Pa. (1831–33); operated unorthodox Temple School, Boston (1834–39). Established cooperative community, Fruitlands, near Harvard, Mass. (1844); abandoned (1845). Absorbed in transcendental philosophy, lectured at intervals (1853–59). Appointed superintendent of schools, Concord, Mass. (1859). Improvidence mitigated by support of friends, esp. Ralph Waldo Emerson; family poverty relieved by success of his daughter Louisa's *Little Women* (1868). Started Concord Summer School of Philosophy and Literature (1879) which continued until his death. Author of *Observations on the Principles and Methods of Infant Instruction* (1830), *The Doctrine and Discipline of Human Culture* (1836), *Ralph Waldo Emerson* (1865).

Alcott, Louisa May. 1832–1888. American author, b. Germantown, Pa. Daughter of A. Bronson Alcott. Nurse in Union hospital at Georgetown during Civil War. Her letters of this period, revised, were published as *Hospital Sketches* (1863); first novel *Moods* (1864) followed. Editor, *Merry's Museum,* a magazine for children (1867). Achieved great success with first volume of *Little Women* (1868), followed by second volume (1869). Other works included *An Old Fashioned Girl* (1870), *Little Men* (1871), *Aunt Jo's Scrap-Bag* (1872–82), *Jo's Boys* (1886).

Al·cuin \'al-(ˌ)kwin, -kwən\ *or* **Al·bi·nus** \al-'bī-nəs\. *Anglo-Saxon name* Ealh·wi·ne \'a-əlk-ˌwin-ə\. *Adopted surname* Flac·cus \'flak-əs\. c.732–804. Anglo-Saxon scholar. Headmaster of cathedral school of York (778); invited by Charlemagne to become head of Palatine school at Aachen (781); introduced Anglo-Saxon scholarship into Frankish schools, sparking Carolingian Renaissance. Revised Frankish liturgy; introduced sung creed; arranged votive masses for days of the week; edited Vulgate; upheld orthodoxy against adoptionist heresy at council held at Frankfort (794). Left court to become abbot of Tours (796); encouraged development of Carolingian minuscule script by monks of Tours. Author of manuals of instruction in grammar, rhetoric, and dialectics; theological, biblical, and hagiological works; metrical annals.

Al·da \'äl-dä\, Frances Jeanne. *Orig. surname* Davies. 1883–1952. New Zealand operatic soprano. Made debut at Opéra-Comique (1904); at Metropolitan Opera, New York (1908–29); m. (1910; div. 1928) Giulio Gatti-Casazza. Author of *Men, Women, and Tenors* (1937).

Aldanov, Mark Aleksandrovich. See Mark LANDAU.

Al·de·gre·ver \'äl-də-ˌgrā-vər\, Heinrich. 1502–after 1555. German painter, engraver, and goldsmith. Works included over 300 copper engravings showing influence of Dürer, two series of *The Wedding Dancers,* also historical, allegorical, and biblical subjects, ornaments, portraits, etc.

Al·den \'ȯl-dən\, John. 1599?–1687. American colonist, b. England. One of pilgrims on *Mayflower,* landing at Plymouth, Mass. (1620); a signer of Mayflower Compact; a founder of Duxbury. Governor's assistant (1633–41, 1650–86). Deputy governor (1664–65, 1677). Remembered for part in legend involving Priscilla Mullins and Myles Standish.

Al·der \'äl-dər\, Kurt. 1902–1958. German chemist. Professor at Kiel (1934–36), Cologne (1940–58); research director of I.G. Farbenindustrie (1936–40). For work in diene synthesis and discovery of Diels-Alder reaction shared Nobel prize for chemistry (1950) with Otto Diels.

Ald·frith \'ald-(ˌ)frith\ *or* **Eald·frith** \'a-əld-\ *or* **Eah·frith** \'a-ək-\. d. 704. King of Northumbria (685–704). Illegitimate son of King Oswin; succeeded brother Eagfrith; noted for piety and patronage of scholarship.

Ald·helm \'ald-ˌhelm\. c.639–709. Anglo-Saxon scholar. Abbot of Malmesbury (c.675); bishop of Sherborne (705); built churches and monasteries. Most learned teacher and most popular Latinist and poet of Wessex. Wrote Latin verse; a Latin treatise on celibate life later turned into hexameters; a treatise on Latin prosody, including his famous 100 riddles for King Aldfrith; as well as songs in English.

Al·ding·ton \'ȯl-diŋ-tən\, Richard, *orig.* Edward Godfree. 1892–1962. English poet and novelist. m. Hilda Doolittle (1913; div. 1937). Author of translations from Greek, French, and medieval Latin; poetry including *Images* (1915), *War and Love* (1918), *Images of Desire* (1919), *A Fool i' the Forest* (1925), *A Dream in the Luxembourg* (1930), *Life Quest* (1936); novels, as *Death of a Hero* (1929), *The Colonel's Daughter* (1931), *All Men Are Enemies* (1933), *Very Heaven* (1937), *Rejected Guest* (1939); biographies of Voltaire (1926), Wellington (1946), Lawrence of Arabia (1955); memoirs, etc.

Al·do·bran·di·ni \ˌäl-dō-brän-'dē-nē\. Noble family of Florence (from 12th century) including: Silvestro Aldobrandini (1499–1558); teacher of law at Pisa; led revolt against Medici; banished (1581) because of resistance of imperial army of Charles V; became advocate of Pope Paul III. His son Ippolito became Pope Clement VIII. Another son ¶Tommaso (c.1540–1572) was secretary of briefs to Pope Paul IV. Ippolito's nephews ¶Pietro (1571–1621) and ¶Cinzio (1551–1610) were together made cardinals (1593) and jointly papal secretary of state; Pietro became archbishop of Ravenna (1604).

Aldred. See EALDRED.

Al·drich \'ȯl-drich, *esp Brit* -drij\, Bess Genevra, *nee* Stree·ter \'strēt-ər\. 1881–1954. American writer, b. Cedar Falls, Iowa. m. (1907) Charles S. Aldrich (d. 1925). Author of short stories and novels, including *The Rim of the Prairie* (1925), *Lantern in Her Hand* (1928), *A White Bird Flying* (1931), *Miss Bishop* (1933), *Spring Came on Forever* (1935), *Song of Years* (1939), etc.

Aldrich, Henry. 1647–1710. English scholar. Dean, Christ Church, Oxford (1689–1710); designed Peckwater quadrangle of Christ Church; adapted anthems and church music; wrote humorous verse, notably the catch "Hark, the bonny Christ Church bells"; author of *Artis Logicae Compendium* (1691), long used as a textbook.

Aldrich, Nelson Wilmarth. 1841–1915. American politician, b. Foster, R.I. Member, U.S. House of Representatives (1879–81), Senate (1881–1911). Leading conservative and protectionist Republican; identified esp. with tariff and currency legislation; name attached to Aldrich-Vreeland Currency Act (1908) and Payne-Aldrich Tariff Act (1909); chairman of National Monetary Commission (1908–12).

Aldrich, Thomas Bailey. 1836–1907. American author and editor, b. Portsmouth, N.H. Editor, *Every Saturday,* Boston (1865–74), *Atlantic Monthly* (1881–90). Author of stories, as *The Story of a Bad Boy* (1870), *Marjorie Daw* (1873); novels including *Prudence Palfrey* (1874), *Queen of Sheba* (1877); and several volumes of poems.

Al·dridge \'ȯl-drij\, Ira Frederick. *Called* the African Ros·ci·us \'räsh-ē-əs\. 1805–1867. American actor, b. New York City or Belair, Md. Personal attendant to Edmund Kean and encouraged by him to study for stage; made debut in London as Othello (1826); successful in England and on Continent; probably never returned to U.S.

Al·dring·en \'äl-driŋ-ən\ *or* **Al·dring·er** \-ər\ *or* **Al·tring·er** \'äl-triŋ-ər\, Johann. Graf. 1588–1634. Austrian soldier. In Spanish service (1606–25); general in imperial German army during Thirty Years' War; succeeded Tilly as commander of Catholic League army (1632); as field marshal conducted successful campaign in Bavaria and Swabia against Swedes. Fell at Landshut.

Al·dro·van·di \ˌäl-drō-'vän-dē\, Ulisse. 1522–1605. Italian naturalist and physician. Taught at Bologna (1553–1605); director of botanical garden established (1568) at his instigation by senate of Bologna; introduced systematic study of natural history; author of beautifully illustrated volumes on ornithology, entomology, ichthyology, etc., and of *Antidotarii bononiensis epitome* (1574), official pharmacopoeia.

Ale·an·dro \ˌäl-ā-'än-drō\, Girolamo. *Lat.* Hieronymus Al·e·an·der \ˌal-ē-'an-dər\. 1480–1542. Italian scholar and cardinal. Rector of U. of Paris; papal representative on missions to Germany, Netherlands, and France; for Pope Leo X led opposition to Luther at Diet of Worms (1520); Clement VIII's nuncio at court of Francis I of France (1523); cardinal (1538). Compiler of Greek-Latin lexicon (1512); author of unfinished *De habendo Concilio* on Council of Trent, Latin verses.

Ale·ar·di \ˌäl-ā-'är-dē\, Aleardo, *orig.* Gaetano. Conte. 1812–1878. Italian poet and patriot. Took part in insurrection (1848) against Austria; imprisoned (1852, 1859). Veronese representative in Italian parliament (1866); later senator. Author of *Le lettere a Maria* (1846), *Le città italiane marinare e commercianti* (1856), *Itre fiumi* (1857), *I sette soldati* (1861), *Canti* (1864).

Alec·san·dri \ˌäl-ek-'sän-drē\, Vasile. c.1821–1890. Romanian lyric poet. Active in revolutionary movement (1848); fled to Paris. Romanian minister for foreign affairs (1859–60); minister to France (1885). Published first collection of Romanian folk songs (1844, 1852); author of lyrics in *Doine și lăcrimioare* (1853), *Pasteluri* (1868–75), *Cantul gintei latina* (1878) and poetic dramas *Despot Vodă, Ovidiu* (1885).

Ale·gria \ˌäl-ā-'grē-ä\, Ciro. 1909–1967. Peruvian novelist. Exiled for political activity on behalf of pro-Indian Aprista organization (1934–48). Author of novels reflecting lives of Peruvian Indians *La serpiente de oro* (1935), *Los perros hambrientos* (1938), *El mundo es ancho y ajeno* (1941).

Aleichem, Shalom *or* Sholem. See Sholem RABINOWITZ.

Aleijadinho. See Antônio LISBOA.

Aleix·an·dre \ˌäl-ek-ˈsän-dre\, Vicente. 1898–1984. Spanish poet. Remained in Spain during the Civil War and Franco's regime. Regarded as a Surrealist; wrote vivid and colorful poetry greatly influenced by Freud's works and expressing a pantheistic philosophy. Author of *Ámbito* (1928), *La destrucción o el amor* (1935), *En un vasto dominio* (1962). Awarded Nobel prize for literature (1977).

Aleksandr. See ALEXANDER.

Ale·khine *or* **Ale·khin** *or* **Alje·chin** \(ˌ)əl-ˈyo-k-yin\, Alexander. *Orig.* Aleksandr Aleksandrovich Alyokhin. 1892–1946. Russian chess master. Naturalized French citizen after Russian Revolution (1917); won world championship from Capablanca (1927); world champion (1927–35, 1937–46).

Alek·san·drov \a-ˈlek-sän-dröv\, Todor. 1881–1924. Macedonian separatist leader. Head of Internal Macedonian Revolutionary Organization (1920–24); directed terrorist campaigns against Yugoslavian and Bulgarian governments.

Alek·se·yev \(ˌ)əl-yik-ˈsyā-yif\, Mikhail Vasilyevich. 1857–1918. Russian general. Entered army (1876); took part in Russo–Japanese War (1904–05); general (1904); won victory in Galicia campaign early in Word War I (1914); commander on northwestern front (1915); chief of imperial general staff (1915–16); removed for political reasons; after abduction of Nicholas II, named commander in chief of Russian army (March–May 1917); organized anti-Bolshevik Volunteer army (1918) later commanded by Kornilov and Denikin.

Aleksey *or* **Alexei.** See ALEXIS.

Alem \ä-ˈlān\, Leandro. 1844–1896. Argentine politician. Organizer (1887) and leader of proletarian Unión Cívica party and of its radical successor Unión Cívica Radical (1892); banished (1893).

Ale·mán \ˌäl-ā-ˈmän\, Mateo. 1547–c.1614. Spanish novelist. Emigrated to Mexico (1608). His picaresque novel *Guzmán de Alfarache* (1599; part II, 1604) ran through about sixteen editions in five years and was translated into French (1600), English (1623), and Latin (1623).

Alemanni, Luigi. See ALAMANNI.

Alem·bert \á-lä^n-ber\, Jean Le Rond \lə-rō^n\ d'. 1717–1783. French mathematician, scientist, and philosopher. Son of Mme. de Tencin and of the chevalier Destouches; member of Academy of Sciences (1741); wrote *Traité de dynamique* (1743) containing "d'Alembert's principle," *Traité de l'équilibre et du mouvement des fluides* (1744), *Réflexions sur la cause générale des vents* (1747) containing his discovery of partial differential equations; explained precession of equinoxes, rotation of Earth's axis; associated with Diderot in editing the *Encyclopédie* (1746–54), writing *Discours préliminaire* for Vol. I (1751); member (1754) of French Academy; wrote six volumes of *Histoire des membres de l'Académie* (1785–87); author also of *Éléments de musique* (1752), *Mélanges de littérature, d'histoire et de philosophie* (1753); published collected *Opuscules mathématiques* (1761–80).

Alen·çon \á-lä^n-sō^n\. A French ducal title held originally by House of Bellême from the dukes of Normandy (10th century). Second House of Alençon descended from Mabile, dame d'Alençon (d. 1082) and Roger de Montgomery (d. 1094?) and held title until duchy was sold to Philip II Augustus (1219 or 1220). Third House began with Charles, Count of Valois (d. 1325); countship raised to dukedom (1414) for Jean I (d. 1415); Jean II (d. 1476) was companion of Joan of Arc; line ended with Jean II's grandson Charles IV (d. 1525) and title reverted to crown on death (1549) of his widow, Margaret of Angoulême. Title reestablished later for François, son of Henry II, who held the title (1566–74) until he became duc d'Anjou; for Gaston, duc d'Orléans (1608–60), brother of Louis XIII; for Charles, duc de Berry (d. 1714); for Louis XVIII before his accession; and for Ferdinard (1844–1910), grandson of Louis-Philippe.

Ale·ni \ä-ˈlā-nē\, Giulio. 1582–1649. Italian missionary. To Macao (1610), China (1613); first Christian missionary in Kiangsi and Fukien provinces; adopted Chinese manners, built many churches; wrote life of Christ (1635–37) and cosmography translated into Manchu as *Tchi fang wai ki* (1623).

Aler \ˈäl-ər\, Paul. 1656–1727. Belgian Jesuit and educator. Author of *Gradus ad Parnassum* (1702), dictionary of prosody once widely used in English schools as aid in Latin versification.

Ales·san·dri Pal·ma \ˌäl-ä-ˈsän-drē-ˈpäl-mä\, Arturo. 1868–1950. Chilean politician. Elected to chamber of deputies (1897); became a leader of the Liberal group; minister of industry and public works (1908), of finance (1913), and of the interior (1918); senator (1915); president of Chile (1920–25); attempted many social and political reforms, but forced out by the depression and an army revolt (1924); recalled from Europe (1925) but soon again expelled; again president (1932–38).

Ales·si \ä-ˈles-sē\, Galeazzo. 1512–1572. Italian architect. Friend and imitator of Michelangelo; built S. Maria di Carignano, and the Sauli, Lercari, and Cambiaso palaces, Genoa; San Paolo and Santa Vittoria, Milan, etc.

Al·ex·an·der \ˌal-ig-ˈzan-dər, ˌel-, *Brit also* -ˈzän-\. Saint. c.250–328. Patriarch of Alexandria (313–328). Supported for election to patriarchate by Arius, whom he named to an important parish; called local synod (c.318) which condemned and excommunicated Arius for heretical teachings; a leader of orthodox party at Council of Nicaea (325). Saint of the Coptic church.

Alexander. Name of seven popes:

Alexander I. Saint. d. c.115 or 119. Fifth pope in succession to Peter (reigned 105–115 or 109–119); said to have introduced holy water and custom of mixing sacramental wine with water; said to have been martyred.

Alexander II. *Known also as* Anselm of Lucca. d. 1075. Pope (1061–73). Bishop of Lucca (1057); known as a church reformer; election to papacy opposed by German court, which installed antipope Honorius II; recognized by German emperor (1064); carried on voluminous diplomatic correspondence; sanctioned military action against Muslims.

Alexander III. *Orig.* Rolando Ban·di·nel·li \ˌbän-dē-ˈnel-lē\. c.1105–1181. Pope (1159–81). Professor at Bologna (c.1140); cardinal deacon (1150), cardinal priest (1151), chancellor to Pope Eugene III (1153); helped negotiate Treaty of Constance (1153) and Concordat of Benevento (1156). As pope engaged in long struggle (1159–76) with Emperor Frederick I Barbarossa; excommunicated Frederick; opposed by three antipopes (elected 1159, 1164, 1168); forced to seek refuge in France (1162–65); organized Lombard League of supporters in northern Italy; victorious over Frederick at battle of Legnano (1176); also successful in contest with Henry II of England, finally winning recognition of papal supremacy and canonization of Thomas à Becket.

Alexander IV. *Orig.* Rinaldo *or* Rainaldo Con·ti \ˈkōn-tē\, Count of Se·gni \ˈsān-yē\. 1199–1261. Pope (1254–61). Nephew of Gregory IX; cardinal bishop of Ostia (1231); as pope almost continuously in conflict with Hohenstaufens, esp. with Manfred of Sicily, whom he excommunicated, giving Sicily to Edmund, son of Henry III of England; driven from Rome, spent last years at Viterbo; worked to reunite Eastern and Western churches; extended Inquisition in France.

Alexander V. See ALEXANDER V, antipope, below.

Alexander VI. *Orig.* Rodrigo de Bor·ja y Doms \-thä-ˈbór-kä-ē-ˈthōms\. *Ital.* Rodrigo Bor·gia \ˈbór-jä\. 1431–1503. Pope (1492–1503). Nephew of Pope Calixtus III. Made cardinal bishop (1476); amassed great wealth, had many mistresses, esp. Vannozza (Giovanna) dei Cattanei (1470–92), who bore him several children (see Cesare BORGIA and Lucrezia BORGIA), and Giulia Farnese; elected to papacy through simony; formed league against Naples (1493); issued bull (1493) dividing New World between Spain and Portugal; unsuccessfully opposed Charles VIII of France in his invasion of Naples (1494); joined (1495) Holy League with the emperor, Milan, Venice, and Spain to expel Charles; ordered execution of Savonarola (1498); aided in downfall of the Sforza (1500); destroyed power of houses of Orsini and Colonna; instituted censorship of books (1501). Directed all his efforts to increase temporal power of pope and to family aggrandizement; patron esp. of Bramante, Raphael, Michelangelo.

Alexander VII. *Orig.* Fabio Chi·gi \ˈkē-jē\. 1599–1667. Pope (1655–67). Papal nuncio at Cologne (1639–51); papal secretary of state (1651); created cardinal (1652); engaged in long conflict with Louis XIV; issued bull against Jansenists; a patron of literature and architecture; commissioned Bernini's colonnade in piazza of St. Peter's.

Alexander VIII. *Orig.* Pietro Vito Ot·to·bo·ni \ˌōt-tō-ˈbō-nē\. 1610–1691. Pope (1689–91). Cardinal (1652); bishop of Brescia (1654); as pope persuaded Louis XIV of France to restore Avignon; condemned Gallican Articles of French clergy (1690).

Alexander V. *Orig.* Petros Phi·lar·gos \fə-ˈlär-gəs\. *Ital.* Pietro di Can·dia \ˈkän-dē-(ˌ)ä\. c.1339–1410. Antipope (1409–10). Franciscan; archbishop of Milan (1402); cardinal (1405); papal legate to Lombardy under Innocent VII; elected pope by invalid Council of Pisa (1409) in hopes of ending Western Schism, but Gregory XII and antipope Benedict XIII refused to resign.

Alexander I. Prince. *In full* Alexander Joseph of Bat·tenberg \ˈbät-ən-ˌberk\. 1857–1893. First prince of autonomous Bulgaria (1879–86). Second son of Prince Alexander of Hesse and his morganatic wife, Countess von Haucke; nephew of Czar Alexander II of Russia. Served in Hessian army and (1877–78) in Russian army in Russo–Turkish War. Elected (1879) prince of new autonomous principality, Bulgaria; dissolved national assembly (1880) and suspended liberal constitution (1881), assuming plenary power; with deteriorating relations with Russia, restored (1883) constitution and encouraged development of political parties. Annexed Eastern Rumelia (1885) after revolution there; led army in war with Serbia (1885), winning several battles. Overthrown (1886) by conspiracy of army officers under Russian influence; formally abdicated; granted title of Count von Har·te·nau \ˈhär-tə-ˌnau̇\; retired to Austria.

Alexander. 870–913. Byzantine emperor (912–913). Son of Basil I; nominally, joint ruler of Eastern Roman Empire with his brother Leo VI (886–912), but took no part in affairs; coregent with heir and nephew, Constantine VII (912–913).

Alexander I and **II** of Egypt. See PTOLEMY X and XI.

Alexander. Name of two kings of Epirus:

Alexander I. d. c.330 B.C. Brother of Olympias, mother of Alexander the Great; made king of Epirus by Philip II of Macedon; during festivities at his marriage with Philip's daughter Cleopatra, Philip was slain by Pausanias (336); killed at battle of Pandosia against his former ally, Tarentum.

Alexander II. Succeeded his father Pyrrhus (272 B.C.); invaded Macedonia (264), but defeated by Demetrius II and later temporarily driven from Epirus.

Alexander. 1893–1920. King of Greece. Second son of King Constantine; succeeded to throne on father's deposition by Allies (1917); entrusted administration of government to Premier Venizélos; approved Greece's entry into World War I on side of Allies; in treaties of Neuilly (1919) and Sèvres (1920) gained territories of Thrace and Smyrna; died as result of bite from pet monkey.

Alexander. Name of five kings of Macedonia:

Alexander I. d. c.454 B.C. King (c.500–c.454 B.C.). Son and successor of Amyntas I; dependent of Persia; used by Mardonius of Persia as envoy to Athens (479).

Alexander II. d. 367 B.C. King (369–367 B.C.). Son and successor of Amyntas II and elder brother of Philip II.

Alexander III. *Known as* Alexander the Great. 356–323 B.C. King (336–323). Son and successor of Philip II. In youth tutored by Aristotle; commanded left wing in father's defeat of Greek alliance at Chaeronea (338); on accession conquered Thrace and Illyria, destroyed Thebes, and gained ascendancy over all Greece (335). Started expedition to East to attack Persia (334); won battle of Granicus (334) and after advancing through western Asia Minor defeated Darius III at Issus (333); conquered Tyre after long siege (332) and Gaza, occupied Egypt, and founded Alexandria (332); destroyed Persian power in battle of Gaugamela (331) and occupied Babylon; took Susa, Persepolis, where he burned palace of Xerxes, Ecbatana; invaded eastern Persia (330–327), defeating Bessus of Bactria, Spitamenes, and Oxyartes, whose daughter Roxana he married; established city of Alexandria Eschate at farthest boundary of empire; invaded northern India (326); defeated Porus on the Hydaspes (326); withdrew from India to Persia (325–324). Consolidated empire; executed many satraps and former companions; attempted to integrate subject peoples, esp. Persians, into government and army; died of fever in Babylon.

Alexander IV. 323–310 B.C. Posthumous son of Alexander the Great and Roxana; nominal ruler, jointly (323–317) with half-witted uncle Philip Arrhidaeus; put to death with his mother by order of Cassander.

Alexander V. d. 294 B.C. Third son of Cassander; shared throne (297–294 B.C.) with his brother Antipater; murdered by order of Demetrius.

Alexander I. *Orig.* Aleksander Ja·giel·loń·czyk \ˌyäg-ye-ˈlōnʸ-chik\. 1461–1506. King of Poland (1501–06). Son of Casimir IV; made grand prince of Lithuania (1492); succeeded elder brother John Albert as king (1501).

Alexander. Name of three emperors of Russia of Romanov dynasty:

Alexander I. *Russ.* Aleksandr Pavlovich. 1777–1825. Emperor (1801–25). Eldest son of Paul I; reared by grandmother Catherine the Great; m. (1793) Princess (Louise Marie) Elisabeth of Baden. Placed on throne by conspiracy against Paul; began reign with ideas for sweeping reforms; made senate the supreme high court (1801); established ministries (1802); encouraged education and science. Joined coalition against Napoléon (1805); present at Austerlitz (1805); joined with Prussia but, after defeats (1807) of Eylau and Friedland, signed Treaty of Tilsit with Napoléon. Briefly resumed interest in reform, sponsoring Speransky's legal work. Fought successful war against Turkey (1806–12); became rival of Napoléon, resulting in French invasion of Russia (1812); helped destroy Napoléon's army in retreat; present at battles of Dresden and Leipzig (1813); entered Paris with allies (1814); took part in Congress of Vienna (1815); obtained Poland and assumed its throne (1815); formed Holy Alliance (1815) and took part in conferences that followed it. Last years of reign (1820–25) marked by reactionary policies, embittered feelings, increasing popular discontent. Succeeded by his brother Nicholas I.

Alexander II. *Russ.* Aleksandr Nikolayevich. 1818–1881. Emperor (1855–81). Son of Nicholas I. Carefully educated, in part by Vasily Zhukovsky, and given military training; m. (1841) Marie, afterwards known as Maria Alexandrovna, daughter of Grand Duke Louis II of Hesse-Darmstadt. Signed Treaty of Paris (1856) terminating Crimean War. Had strong convictions for reforms; emancipated serfs (1861), his greatest achievement; reorganized army and government administration; established regular system of courts and local elective legislatures, reformed judicial system (1864), and founded schools; encouraged building of railroads throughout Russia. Put down Polish insurrection (1863–64); friendly to Germany in Franco-Prussian War (1870–71); waged war with Turkey (1877–78), winning the liberation of Bulgaria; extended boundaries of Russia in Caucasus and Central Asia (1868–81). Shortly after death of wife (1880), m. Yekaterina Dolgorukaya. In spite of good done by his reforms, many added burdens placed upon peasants; repressive measures following several assassination attempts increased unrest; repression reached height under authority of interior minister, Count Loris-Melikov; activity of Nihilists and terrorists increased (1879–81); killed by bomb in St. Petersburg.

Alexander III. *Russ.* Aleksandr Aleksandrovich. 1845–1894. Emperor (1881–94). Son and successor of Alexander II. Became heir apparent on death (1865) of his elder brother Nikolay; m. (1866) Dagmar, subsequently known as Maria Fyodorovna, daughter of Christian IX of Denmark. During years before accession (1865–81) showed open disapproval of some of father's policies; succeeded to throne on father's assassination; crowned (1883). Canceled liberal reforms of father's reign, instituting conservative regime based on Russian language and customs and Orthodox church; countenanced persecutions, esp. of Jews; continued Russian advance in Central Asia to frontier of Afghanistan (1884–85), bringing about crisis with England. Opposed any close union with Germany, but became virtual ally of France (1891–94); succeeded by his son Nicholas II.

Alexander. Name of three kings of Scotland:

Alexander I. c.1080?–1124. King (1107–24). Fourth son of Malcolm III Canmore. Succeeded his brother Edgar as king (1107), giving southern Scotland to younger brother and heir David; joined Henry I of England in Welsh campaigns; quelled insurrection of northern clans.

Alexander II. 1198–1249. King (1214–49). Succeeded his father, William I the Lion; entered into league with English barons to resist King John; invaded England (1215); m. (1221) Joan, eldest sister of Henry III; consolidated royal authority in Scotland; subdued Argyll (1222); by Peace of York (1237) abandoned claims to English territory; repelled Henry's demand for homage (1244); settled dispute at Newcastle (1244); died of fever on expedition to wrest Hebrides from Norway.

Alexander III. 1241–1286. King (1249–86). Son of Alexander II; m. (1251) Margaret, daughter of Henry III. Defeated Norwegian invasion by Haakon V (1263); united Hebrides and Isle of Man to kingdom (1266); assisted Henry III against barons (1264); induced recognition of granddaughter Margaret, daughter of Eric of Norway, called "Maid of Norway," as heir presumptive; subject of *Lament for Alisaundre,* one of earliest Scottish poems.

Alexander. Name of three rulers of the Serbs:

Alexander Kar·a·geor·ge·vić \ˌkar-ə-ˈjór-jə-vich\. *Serbian* Aleksandar Ka-ra·đor·đe·vić \ká-ˌrá-ˈdyór-dyev-ˌētʸ\. 1806–1885. Prince of Serbia (1842–58). Son of Karageorge. Officer in Russian army; chosen prince by Skupština (i.e. parliament) to succeed Michael Obrenović; weak and vacillating in his policy, at times pro-Russian and at others pro-Austrian; maintained neutrality of Serbia during Crimean War; deposed by Skupština (1858).

Alexander. *Serbian* Aleksandar Obre·no·vić \ó-ˌbren-ó-ˌvētʸ\. 1876–1903. King of Serbia (1889–1903). Son of Milan and Queen Natalie. On father's abdication proclaimed king under regency; assumed full authority (1893); abolished (1894) Constitution of 1889; curtailed freedoms of press and association in response to criticism of his authoritarianism; made unpopular marriage (1900) with Draga Mašín; after several arbitrary acts, murdered with Queen Draga by group of officers; last of Obrenović family. Succeeded by King Peter I.

Alexander I. 1888–1934. Son of Peter I and grandson of Alexander Karageorgević. Distinguished himself in Balkan War (1912–13); named by father prince regent of Serbia (1914–18); commander of Serbian forces in World War I; proclaimed Kingdom of Serbs, Croats, and Slovenes (1918); prince regent (1918–22), king (1922–29); m. (1922) Princess Marie of Rumania. Because of disturbed condition of kingdom, especially after assassination of Stjepan Radić (1928), abolished constitution of 1921 and dismissed parliament (1929); established royal dictatorship (1929) and adopted name Yugoslavia; king (1929–34). Worked to end ethnic, religious, regional prejudices, and to standardize national administration, holidays, schools; promulgated new constitution and restored Skupština (1931); entered Balkan Entente with Greece, Turkey, Rumania (1934); assassinated by Croatian separatists.

Alexander of **Aph·ro·dis·i·as** \ˌaf-rə-ˈdiz-ē-əs\. fl. c.200 A.D. Greek philosopher. Became (c.200) head of Lyceum in Athens; known for commentaries on Aristotle and for original works including *On Fate,* against Stoics, and *On the Soul.*

Alexander of **Hales** \ˈhā(ə)lz\. *Known as* Doctor Ir·re·fra·ga·bi·lis \-ir-ˌ(r)əf-rə-ˈgab-ə-ləs\. c.1170 or 1185–1245. English theologian and philosopher. Studied in Paris; archdeacon of Coventry (1235); entered Franciscan order (c.1236); founded in Paris Schola Fratrum Minorum; evolved a doctrine combining Augustinian thought with elements of Aristotelianism; influential teacher, an influence on St. Bonaventure and John of La Rochelle. Author of *Expositio regulae, Quaestiones disputatae antequam esset frater, Quodlibeta, Exoticon,* commentary on Peter Lombard's *Sententiae,* and parts of *Summa theologica* (largely the work of his followers).

Alexander of Phe·rae \'fi(ə)r-ē\. d. 358 B.C. Despot of Pherae, Thessaly (369–358 B.C.). Instituted tyrannical rule that prompted other Thessalian cities to appeal to Thebes; imprisoned a Theban emissary, Pelopidas, until compelled by large army to release him; defeated by Theban army (364) and compelled to acknowledge freedom of Thessalian cities.

Alexander of Tral·les \'tral-(,)ēz\. *Lat.* Alexander Tral·li·a·nus \,tral-ē-'ā-nəs\. c.525–c.605. Byzantine physician. Practiced in Rome; author of major work on pathology and therapy circulated in Greek, Arabic, and Latin (*Libri duodecim de re medica*) into the 16th century.

Alexander of Tunis, Earl. See Harold R.L.G. ALEXANDER.

Alexander the Paph·la·go·ni·an \,paf-lə-'gō-nē-ən\. 2d century A.D. Paphlagonian impostor. Established oracle of Asclepius in native town; instituted mystical rites; fame spread widely; amassed fortune through oracles and blackmail; exposed by satirist Lucian.

Alexander, Franz Gabriel. 1891–1964. American physician and psychoanalyst, b. Budapest. At Berlin Psychoanalytic Institute (1919–30); to U.S. (1930); professor at U. of Chicago (1930), U. of Illinois Medical School (1938–56); founded and directed (1932–56) Chicago Institute for Psychoanalysis; in research, Mt. Sinai Hospital, Los Angeles (1956–64). Author of *Psychoanalyse der Gesamtpersönlichkeit* (1927), *Fundamentals of Psychoanalysis* (1948), *Western Mind in Transition* (1960).

Alexander, Grover Cleveland. 1887–1950. American baseball player, b. Elba, Neb. Pitcher for Philadelphia (1911–17), Chicago (1918–26), St. Louis (1926–29) of National League; tied or broke Christy Mathewson's league record with 373 or 374 wins (lost 208); won 30 or more games (1915, 1916, 1917); record 16-shutout season (1916); 88 or 90 career shutouts; record career earned run average of 2.56; 440 complete games. Considered master of control, one of greatest right-handers. Elected to Baseball Hall of Fame (1938).

Alexander, Harold Rupert Leofric George. 1st Earl Alexander of Tu·nis \'t(y)ü-nəs\. 1891–1969. British general. Served in France (1914–18) and North-West frontier, India (1935); commander of 1st division (1938–40); in charge of evacuation of British army from Dunkirk (May–June 1940); lieutenant general (1940), general (1942); commander on Burma front (1942); commander in chief in Middle East (1942–43); deputy allied commander in chief in North Africa (Feb. 1943), then in Mediterranean theater, commanding invasions of Sicily (July 1943) and Italy (Sept. 1943); field marshal (1944) and allied commander in chief in Italy (1944–45); governor general of Canada (1946–52); minister of defense (1952–54); created viscount (1946), earl (1952).

Alexander, Jerome. 1876–1959. American chemist, b. New York City. Specialist in chemistry of colloids; pioneer in ultramicroscopy; author of *Colloid Chemistry* (1919), *Glue and Gelatin* (1923); edited *Colloid Chemistry, Theoretical and Applied* (1926–50).

Alexander, John White. 1856–1915. American painter, b. Allegheny, Pa. Illustrator on staff of *Harper's* (from 1874); kept studio at Paris (1890–1901), New York (1901–15). His works included portraits of Rodin, Grover Cleveland, Carnegie, Howells, Mark Twain, Alphonse Daudet, R.L. Stevenson, Hardy, Whitman, Joseph Jefferson, Maude Adams; six lunettes (*Evolution of the Book*) in Library of Congress; and paintings, as *The Pot of Basil, The Green Bow, Study in Black and Green, The Engagement Ring.*

Alexander, Samuel. 1859–1938. British philosopher, b. Australia. Professor of philosophy, Victoria U. of Manchester (1893–1924). Developed system of emergent evolution in major work *Space, Time, and Deity* (1920); author also of *Spinoza and Time* (1921), *Art and the Material* (1925), *Beauty and Other Forms of Value* (1933).

Alexander, William. 1st Earl of Stir·ling \'stər-liŋ\. 1567–1640. Scottish poet and courtier. Tutor to earl of Argyle, Prince Henry Frederick, and Prince Charles (later Charles I of England). Received grant of Nova Scotia and New Brunswick (1621); encouraged colonization, but with scant success; compelled to surrender territory by Treaty of Susa (1629) ending Anglo-French war; secretary of state for Scotland (1626 till death). Author of sonnet sequence *Aurora* (1604), *Monarchicke Tragedies* (1604), *Paraenesis to the Prince* (1604), *Doomesday* (1614).

Alexander, William. *Known as* Lord Stirling. 1726–1783. American Revolutionary officer, b. New York City. Unsuccessfully claimed earldom of Stirling (1756–62). Colonel, 1st New Jersey Regiment (1775); captured British transport at Sandy Hook (1776). Brigadier general in Continental army (1776); as commander in New York City, built Fort Lee and Fort Washington; captured in battle of Long Island (Aug. 1776); major general (1777); commanded left wing at Monmouth (1778); presided over court-martial of Gen. Charles Lee (1778); served on court of inquiry to decide fate of John André (1780).

Alexander, William. 1824–1911. Irish Anglican prelate. Bishop of Derry (1867–93); archbishop of Armagh and primate of all Ireland (1893–1911); author of *St. Augustine's Holiday* (poems, 1886) and theological works. His wife ¶Cecil Frances, *nee* Hum·phreys \'həm(p)-frēz\ (1818–1895; m. 1850), wrote tracts in connection with Oxford Movement and hymns, including "There Is a Green Hill Far Away," "All Things Bright and Beautiful," "Once in Royal David's City," and "Jesus Calls Us o'er the Tumult."

Alexander Ae·to·lus \i-'tō-ləs\. fl. c.280 B.C. Greek poet. Author of tragedies, all lost but for one title, *Astragalistae,* and of other works; arranged and catalogued tragedies in library of Alexandria for Ptolemy II Philadelphus.

Alexander Ba·las \'bā-ləs\. *Also called* Alexander Epiph·a·nes \-i-'pif-ə-,nēz\. d. 145 B.C. King of Syria and Pergamun (150–145). Of obscure origin; claimed to be son of Antiochus IV Epiphanes. Usurped Seleucid throne with help of Romans, killing Demetrius I Soter; m. Cleopatra Thea. Defeated and killed in battle near Antioch by Demetrius II Nicator and Ptolemy VI Philometor. Succeeded by his son Antiochus VI.

Alexander Jan·nae·us \-ya-'nī-əs\ *or* **Alexander Yan·nai** \-'yän-,ī\. d. 76 B.C. Hasmonean (Maccabean) King of Judea (103–76 B.C.). Succeeded brother Aristobulus I; extended rule to Palestinian coast and other areas; favored Sadducees over Pharisees.

Alexander Nev·sky \'nyäf-skəi\. *Russ.* Aleksandr. c.1220–1263. Russian hero. Son of Prince Yaroslav II Vsevolodovich of Vladimir; elected prince of Novgorod (1236); defeated Swedes (1240) in great battle near site of present Leningrad, on Neva river (whence his surname); defeated Teutonic knights (1242) on ice of Lake Peipus. On father's death (1246), became grand duke of Kiev and (1252) of Vladimir; vassal of Mongols throughout his rule, but on friendly terms with them; suppressed revolt in Novgorod against Mongol-imposed taxation census (1258). Canonized by Russian Orthodox Church (1547).

Alexander Poly·his·tor \-,päl-ē-'hist-ər\. *In full* Lucius Cornelius Alexander Polyhistor. d. c.35 B.C. Roman writer. Captured by Roman army in war with King Mithridates of Pontus; sold as slave in Rome; later freed; author of works, extant only in fragments, on history, geography, and esp. of paraphrases of many otherwise lost Hellenistic Jewish authors.

Alexander Severus. See SEVERUS ALEXANDER.

Al·ex·an·der·son \,äl-ək-'sän-dər-,sȯn, *Angl* ,al-ig-'zan-dər-sən, ,el-\, Ernst Frederik Werner. 1878–1975. American electrical engineer and inventor, b. Uppsala, Sweden. To U.S. (1901); associated with General Electric Co. (1902–48), RCA (from 1952). Inventions included a high-frequency alternator that greatly improved transoceanic radio, multiple-tuned antenna, vacuum-tube telephone transmitter, selective radio tuning circuit (1916), amplidyne automated control system, television (1927), color television (1955). Also a pioneer in electric ship propulsion and railroad electrification.

Al·ex·an·dra \,al-ig-'zan-drə, ,el-, *Brit also* -'zän-\. 1844–1925. Queen consort of Great Britain. Eldest daughter of Christian IX of Denmark and Louise, daughter of Landgrave William of Hesse. Queen consort of Edward VII of England whom she married (1863) when he was prince of Wales; founded (1902) Imperial Military Nursing Service; enjoyed great popularity.

Alexandra. *Russ.* Aleksandra Fyodorovna. *Orig.* Alix Victoria Helene Luise Beatrix. 1872–1918. Empress of Russia (1894–1917). Daughter of Grand Duke Louis IV of Hesse-Darmstadt; granddaughter of Queen Victoria; m. (1894) Nicholas II, Emperor of Russia. Superstitious and pious, caused scandals by her relations with the religious fanatic Rasputin; ruled arbitrarily during Nicholas's absence at the war front (1915); along with entire family, taken prisoner (1917) by Bolsheviks and killed.

Alexei *or* **Aleksey.** See ALEXIS.

Alexeyev. See ALEKSEYEV.

Alex·is \ə-'lek-səs\. *Russ.* Aleksey. Name of several members of Russian imperial family, including:

Alexis I Mikhaylovich. 1629–1676. Second czar of Romanovs (1645–76). Son of Czar Michael. First ten years of reign (1645–55) stormy period of internal troubles and insurrections. Gained control over eastern Ukraine (1654) by treaty with Chmielnicki; fought war against Poland in two campaigns (1654–56, 1660–67); secured Smolensk; waged unsuccessful war with Sweden (1656–61); suppressed with difficulty great peasant revolt (1667–71). Promulgated *Sobornoye Ulozheniye* (1649), code of laws legitimizing serfdom; approved church reforms of Nikon that precipitated schism (1666–67).

Alexis Petrovich. 1690–1718. Czarevitch. Eldest son of Peter the Great by Eudoxia (Lopukhina). Took part in Great Northern War; denied permission to renounce succession and enter monastery (1715); opposed father's reforms; fled to Vienna and Naples (1716); persuaded by father's agents to return; suspected of role in conspiracy to supplant Peter; seized, condemned to death, and tortured; died before execution.

Alexis Nikolayevich. 1904–1918. Czarevitch. Youngest child and only son of Emperor Nicholas II; his hemophilia was helped on several occasions by Rasputin, a circumstance that allowed Rasputin to gain great influence with

Czarina Alexandra. Seized with parents and sisters by Bolsheviks during revolution (1917); executed.

Alexis. 4th–3rd century B.C. Greek poet. Said to have been uncle of Menander; credited with writing 245 comedies in the Middle and New Comedy modes.

Alexis, Willibald. See Georg W. HÄRING.

Alex·i·us \ə-ˈlek-sē-əs\. Name of five rulers of Byzantine Empire:

Alexius I Com·ne·nus \käm-ˈnē-nəs\. 1048–1118. Emperor (1081–1118). Nephew of Emperor Isaac Comnenus; served ably against Turks; with aid of Ducas family seized throne (1081) from Nicephorus III; restored a measure of military and naval power and defended empire against Scythians, Turks, and Italian Normans; his domains invaded by First Crusade (1096–99). Founder of Comnenian dynasty; his life (*Alexiad*) written by his daughter Anna Comnena (*q.v.*).

Alexius II Comnenus. 1169–1183. Emperor (1180–83). Son and successor of Manuel I; ruled through regency of mother and uncle Alexis; deposed and murdered by his uncle Andronicus I.

Alexius III An·ge·lus \ˈan-jə-ləs\. d. 1211. Emperor (1195–1203). Son of Andronicus Angelus, grandson of Alexius I; proclaimed emperor by troops; deposed and imprisoned his brother, Emperor Isaac II; through military and diplomatic defeats lost Bulgaria; deposed by army of crusaders (1203) who besieged Constantinople and reinstated Isaac II and Alexius IV; died in exile.

Alexius IV Angelus. d. 1204. Emperor (1203–04). Son of Isaac II Angelus; imprisoned (1195) by Alexius III; escaped (1201) and enlisted aid of crusaders in restoring his father; overthrown and put to death by Alexius V.

Alexius V. *Known as* Alexius Du·cas Mur·tzu·phlus \ˈthü-käs-ˈmürt-sü-ˌflos\. d. 1204. Emperor (1204). Son-in-law of Alexius III Angelus; led revolt against Latin crusaders invited into Constantinople by Alexius IV; deposed and killed Alexius IV; fled crusader siege; captured and killed. Last Greek emperor of Byzantium.

Alexius I. *Called* Grand Comnenus. 1180?–1222. First emperor of Trebizond (1204–22). Grandson of Emperor Andronicus I; with his brother David Comnenus, seized Trebizond and coastland of northeastern Asia Minor when Constantinople was taken by crusaders (1204). Attacked Nicaean emperor, Theodore I Lascaris, in Bithynia, but defeated. Founded dynasty that lasted more than 250 years (1204–1461).

Al·fa·no \äl-ˈfän-ō\, Franco. 1875–1954. Italian composer. Wrote operas, including *Miranda* (1896), *Risurrezione* (1904), *Sakuntala* (1921); completed Puccini's unfinished *Turandot* (1925).

Alfarabius. See al-FĀRĀBĪ.

Al·fa·ro \äl-ˈfär-ō\, Eloy. 1864–1912. Ecuadorian general and politician. Led uprising against President Cordero (1893–95); declared himself anticlerical dictator (1895); constitutional president of Ecuador (1897–1901 and 1906–11). Led the revolt (1906) that deposed President Lisardo García. Reduced power of Roman Catholic church; completed railroad from Quito to Guayaquil (1908). Murdered in uprising of 1912.

Alfaro, Ricardo Joaquín. 1882–1971. Panamanian politician. Secretary of government and justice (1918–22); minister to U.S. (1922–30, 1933–36); member of the Hague Tribunal (1929–41); president of Panama (1931–32) following overthrow of President Arosemena; foreign minister (1945–47); member of International Court of Justice (1959–64).

Al·fa·si *or* **Al-Pha·si** \äl-ˈfäs-ē\, Isaac ben Jacob. *Called* RIF *from initials of* Rabbi Isaac Fasi. 1013–1103. Moroccan Talmudist. Author of *Sefer ha-Halakhot,* important codification of Talmudic law; fled to Spain (1088) and established Talmudic academy at Lucena.

Al·fie·ri \äl-ˈfyä-rē\, Vittorio. Conte. 1749–1803. Italian tragic poet. Traveled through England and Europe and became ardent liberal; settled (1772) in Turin; achieved great success with first tragedy, *Cleopatra* (produced 1775); moved to Florence (c.1776) to study Tuscan for his playwriting; there met Louise Maximilienne Caroline, Countess of Albany (*q.v.*), who became his mistress. Author of 19 tragedies, all classical in form, including *Filippo, Polinice, Agamemnone, Oreste, Mirra, Saul, Sofonisba, Antigone,* and *Maria Stuart;* an autobiography *Vita di Vittorio Alfieri scritta da eso;* sonnets; odes, esp. the five comprising *L'America libera;* a political treatise *Della tirannide* (1777); six comedies; and a satire against France, *Misogallo.* A precursor of the Risorgimento; his works served to revive the national spirit in Italy.

Alfonso. See also AFONSO.

Al·fon·so \äl-ˈfón-sō, *Angl* al-ˈfän(t)-(ˌ)sō, -ˈfän-(ˌ)zō\. Name of five kings of Aragon:

Alfonso I. *Called* el Ba·tal·la·dor \el-bä-täl-yä-ˈthȯr\, *i.e.* the Battler. c.1073–1134. King of Aragon and Navarre (1104–34). Son of Sancho V Ramírez; brother and successor of Peter I; m. (1109) Urraca, daughter of King Alfonso VI of León and Castile, and claimed that throne until her death (1126), when he abandoned it in favor of stepson Alfonso VII; continually at war with Castile and León; made count of Toulouse his vassal (1116); won Saragossa from Moors (1118); led spectacular raid into Andalusia (1125); killed in battle at Fraga.

Alfonso II. *Called* el Cas·to \-ˈkäs-tō\, *i.e.* the Chaste. 1152–1196. King (1164–96). Son of Queen Petronilla; succeeded father Ramón Berenguer IV as count of Barcelona (1162); undertook conquest of Valencia and made Cazorla Pact (1179) with Alfonso VIII of Castile, dividing regions of reconquest. A provision in his will alienated Provence from Aragonese crown.

Alfonso III. *Called* el Li·be·ral \-lē-bā-ˈräl\, *i.e.* the Generous. 1265–1291. King (1285–91). Son of Peter III; forced to grant wide powers to nobles (1287).

Alfonso IV. *Called* el Be·nig·no \-bā-ˈnēg-nō\, *i.e.* the Benign. 1299–1336. King (1327–36). Son of James II; reign marked by revolt in Sardinia, leading to war with Genoa.

Alfonso V. *Called* el Mag·ná·ni·mo \-mäg-ˈnän-ē-mō\, *i.e.* the Magnanimous. 1396–1458. King (1416–58). Son of Ferdinand I; as Alfonso I, king of Sicily (1416–58) and of Naples (1442–58). Made heir to throne of Naples by Joan II (1420); disinherited (1423). Captured Naples (1442) and transferred court there (1443); a restless military and diplomatic adventurer, left Iberian territories to regencies of wife and brother John (later John II).

Alfonso. Name of eleven kings of Asturias, León, and Castile:

Alfonso I. *Called* el Ca·tó·li·co \-kä-ˈtó-lē-kō\, *i.e.* the Catholic. c.693–757. King of Asturias (739–757). Probably son-in-law of Pelayo; drove Moors out of Galicia.

Alfonso II. *Called* el Cas·to \-käs-tō\, *i.e.* the Chaste. c.759–842. King of Asturias (791–842). Held court at Oviedo; restored Visigothic traditions; defended realm against Moors of Córdoba.

Alfonso III. *Called* el Mag·no \-ˈmäg-nō\, *i.e.* the Great. c.838–910. King of Asturias (866–910). Son of Ordoño I; extended realm to Duero River and Osma; founded Burgos.

Alfonso IV. *Called* el Mon·je \-ˈmón-kā\, *i.e.* the Monk. d. 933. King of León and Asturias (c.925–c.931). Son of Ordoño II; succeeded uncle Fruela II; reign marked by unrest; abdicated in favor of brother Ramiro II.

Alfonso V. 994–1028. King of León and Asturias (999–1028). Son of Bermudo II; in years following death of al-Manṣūr of Córdoba, was able to recapture lost Leónese territory.

Alfonso VI. *Called* el Bra·vo \-ˈbrä-bō\, *i.e.* the Valiant. 1040?–1109. King of León (1065–1109) and of Castile (1072–1109). Son of Ferdinand I; father of Teresa, wife of Henry of Burgundy; driven from León by elder brother Sancho II (1072), but on Sancho's death (1072) regained it and inherited Castile; occupied Galicia; recovered Toledo from Moors (1085); defeated by Almoravids (1086). Took title of "emperor of all Spain" (1077). Reign notable for exploits of Rodrigo Díaz de Vivar (el Cid).

Alfonso VII. c.1104–1157. King of León and Castile (1126–57). Acceded to throne on death of mother Urraca and abandonment of claim by stepfather, Alfonso I of Aragon; captured Almería (1147); defended against Almohad invasions (from 1146).

Alfonso VIII. c.1155–1214. King of Castile (1158–1214). Son of Sancho III; concluded Pact of Cazorla (1179) with Alfonso II of Aragon, agreeing on division of lands recaptured from Moors; defeated León and Navarre (1195); won great victory over Almohads at Navas de Tolosa (1212).

Alfonso IX. 1171–1230. King of León (1188–1230). Son of Ferdinand II of León; allied with Almohads to regain lands lost to cousin Alfonso VIII of Castile; as a result ordered by papal interdict to marry (1197) Berengaria of Castile; founded U. of Salamanca (1219); won victories against Almohads (1227–30).

Alfonso X. *Called* el Sa·bio \-ˈsäb-yō\, *i.e.* the Learned. 1221–1284. King of Castile and León (1252–84). Son of Ferdinand III; elected Holy Roman emperor (1257) but election not accepted by Pope Alexander IV; captured Cartagena and Cádiz from Moors; promulgated code of laws, *Las Siete Partidas,* basis of Spanish jurisprudence.

Alfonso XI. 1311–1350. King of Castile and León (1312–50). Son of Ferdinand IV; increased power of municipalities and the Cortes versus nobles; with Afonso IV of Portugal, defeated Marinid forces of Morocco at Río Salado (1340); recaptured Algeciras (1344); died while besieging Gibraltar.

Alfonso, dukes of Ferrara. See ESTE family.

Alfonso. Name of two kings of Naples:

Alfonso I. See ALFONSO V of Aragon.

Alfonso II. 1449–1496. King (1494–95). Son of Ferdinand I of Naples; unpopular ruler; resigned in favor of his son, Ferdinand II, on approach of French forces under Charles VIII.

Alfonso. Name of two Bourbon kings of Spain, numbered consecutively with those of Asturias, León, and Castile:

Alfonso XII. 1857–1885. King (1874–85). Son of Isabella II; proclaimed by army at end of civil war; suppressed Carlist opposition (1876); summoned Cortes which made new constitution (1876); enjoyed popular and largely peaceful reign under influence of prime minister, Cánovas del Castillo.

Alfonso XIII. 1886–1941. King (1886–1931). Posthumous son of Alfonso XII and María Cristina; under regency of his mother (1886–1902); reign marked by Alfonso's continued interference in parliamentary system and his increasing autocratic tendencies, Spanish neutrality in World War I, and defeat of Spanish in Morocco (1921) by Moors under Abd el-Krim. Associated himself with dictatorship of Primo de Rivera (1923–30); agreed to municipal elections (1931) which returned overwhelming Republican majority; lost support of army; refused to abdicate, but left Spain (1931); lived in exile.

Al·ford \'ȯl-fərd\, Henry. 1810–1871. English clergyman and scholar. Edited New Testament in Greek with collation of readings (1849–61); published sermons, hymns, and poems. Dean of Canterbury (1857–71). First editor of *Contemporary Review* (1866–70).

Al·fred *or* **Ael·fred** \'al-frəd, -fərd\. *Called* the Great. 849–899. King of Wessex (871–899). Fifth son of Aethelwulf. Assisted his elder brother Aethelred I against Danes in Mercia (868); succeeded Aethelred as king (871); fought Danes at Wilton (871). Met second invasion of Danes under Guthrum with victory at Edington in Wiltshire (878); repelled invasion of Danes of Kent (885) and captured London (886), received submission of Angles and Saxons, and recognized as sovereign of all England not under Danish rule. Repelled major invasion of Danes from Continent (892–896), using improved navy and aid from the Welsh. Compiled best laws of earlier kings; divided parts of Mercia according to shire system for first time; promoted learning, bringing to Wessex many famous scholars. Author of free translations from Latin of *Pastoral Care* by Pope St. Gregory I, St. Augustine's *Soliloquies,* and Boethius's *Consolation of Philosophy.*

Alfred. Prince. *In full* Alfred Ernest Albert. 1844–1900. Duke of Ed·in·burgh \'ed-ᵊn-ˌbər-ə, -ˌbə-rə, -b(ə-)rə\ (1866–93) and of Saxe-Coburg-Gotha (1893–1900). Second son and fourth child of Queen Victoria. Captain in British navy (1866); commander of Channel squadron (1883–84), in Mediterranean (1886–89); admiral (1887), admiral of the fleet (1893). Offered but refused crown of Greece (1863). Married (1874) Grand Duchess Marie Alexandrovna, daughter of Alexander II of Russia; had four daughters: (1) Marie, Queen of Romania, (2) Victoria Melita, who married Grand Duke Cyril of Russia, (3) Alexandra, Princess of Hohenlohe-Langenburg, and (4) Beatrice, who married Alfonso, infante of Spain.

Alf·vén \äl-'vän\, Hugo Emil. 1872–1960. Swedish composer. Musical director, U. of Uppsala (1910–39); composed 5 symphonies, choral music, songs, 3 orchestral rhapsodies, including *Midsommarvaka,* and ballet *Prodigal Son* (1957).

Al·gar·di \äl-'gär-dē\, Alessandro. 1595–1654. Italian sculptor. Studied with Lodovico Carracci; to Rome (1625); gained reputation for portraiture; succeeded Bernini as papal court sculptor under Pope Innocent X, whose statue he did (1645); executed *Meeting of Attila and Pope Leo,* one of largest alto-relievos in the world, and tomb of Pope Leo XI (both in St. Peter's); designed façade of Church of Sant'Ignazio at Rome, etc. Considered second only to Bernini among exponents of the Baroque style.

Al·ga·rot·ti \ˌäl-gä-'rȯt-tē\, Francesco. 1712–1764. Italian philosopher and critic. Popular in intellectual circles in Paris (from 1733); friend of Frederick the Great. Author of *Il Newtonianismo per le dame* (1737), essays on architecture, opera, etc.

Algazel. See al-GHAZĀLĪ.

Al·ger \äl-zhe\ of Liège \lyezh\. *Known also as* Alger of Clu·ny \klü̅-nē\ *and as* Al·ger·us Mag·is·ter \'al-jə-rə-'smaj-ə-stər\. c.1060–c.1131. French priest and writer. Author of *De misericordia et justitia, De Sacramentis corporis et sanguinis Dominici, Libellus de libero arbitrio, De sacrificio missae,* and a lost history of the church of Liège.

Al·ger \'al-jər\, Cyrus. 1781–1856. American industrialist and inventor, b. Bridgewater, Mass. Established foundry business, Boston (1809); formed (1827) South Boston Iron Co., which became largest foundry in U.S.; invented cylinder stove, improved foundry processes, rifled gun barrel.

Alger, Horatio, Jr. 1832–1899. American clergyman and author, b. Revere, Mass. Writer of more than 100 enormously popular books for boys, including the *Ragged Dick* (1867), *Luck and Pluck* (1869), and *Tattered Tom* (1871) series.

Alger, Russell Alexander. 1836–1907. American politician, b. Lafayette, Ohio. Served in Civil War; rose from ranks to colonelcy; national commander, Grand Army of the Republic (1889–90). Governor of Michigan (1885–86); U.S. secretary of war (1897–99); U.S. senator (1902–07).

Al·gir·das \'äl-gir-ˌdäs\ *or* **Ol·gierd** \'ȯl-ˌgyert\. d. 1377. Grand duke of Lithuania (1345–77) and Prince of Krevo and Vitebsk (1341–45). Son of Gediminas; made Lithuania one of largest European states of his day; defeated Teutonic Knights (1360); supported Michael of Tver in Russian civil conflicts; led his armies into southern Russia as far as Black Sea and defeated Tatars (1362–63), captured principality of Kiev; succeeded by his son Jagiełło.

Al·gren \'ȯl-grən\, Nelson. 1909–1981. American novelist, b. Detroit. Author of naturalistic novels of marked vitality including *Somebody in Boots* (1935), *Never Come Morning* (1942), *Man With the Golden Arm* (1949), *Walk on the Wild Side* (1956); also short stories in *Neon Wilderness* (1947), nonfiction *Chicago, City on the Make* (1951) and *Who Lost an American?* (1963).

Alhazen. See ABŪ ʿALĪ AL-ḤASAN IBN AL-HAYTHAM.

ʿAlī \a-'lē\. *In full* ʿAlī ibn Abī Ṭālib. c.600–661. Fourth caliph (656–661). Adopted son and, as husband of Fāṭima, son-in-law of Muḥammad and one of his first converts; followed him to Medina (622); disappointed at succession (632) of Abū Bakr as caliph; invited to become caliph after murder of ʿUthmān; his rule stormy and full of civil conflicts; put down rebellion headed by ʿĀʾishah, Muḥammad's widow, in "battle of the camel" at Basra (656); faced rebellion led by Muʿāwiyah, another by Khārijite sect; assassinated by one of latter. Revered by Shīʿite branch of Islām as true successor to Muḥammad.

Ali, Prophet Drew. See DREW ALI.

ʿAlī ar-Ri·ḍā \a-'lē-är-rē-'dä\. *In full* Abū al-Ḥasan ibn Mūsā ibn Jaʿfar ʿAlī ar-Riḍā. c.768–818. Eighth imām of the Twelver Shīʿah. Named successor to caliph al-Maʾmūn (817) in attempt to heal Sunnah-Shīʿah schism; died soon after.

ʿA·lī Bey \'äl-ē-'bā\. 1728–1773. Mamlūk governor and then ruler of Egypt (1750–72). In boyhood sold as slave into Egypt; became senior bey (1750); defied Ottoman sovereignty (1768) and assumed trappings of independence; conquered Syria and the Hejaz; forced by betrayals to flee (1772); killed attempting to regain power.

Al·ice Maud Mary \'al-ə-'smȯd-'me(ə)r-ē, -'ma(ə)r-ē, -'mā-rē\. 1843–1878. Princess of Great Britain and Ireland. Duchess of Saxony. Grand Duchess of Hesse-Darm·stadt \'hes-'därm-ˌstat, -ˌshtät\. Second daughter of Queen Victoria; m. (1862) Frederick William Louis of Hesse who became grand duke (as Louis IV) of Hesse-Darmstadt (1877–92). Their fourth daughter, Alix, married Czar Nicholas II of Russia. Founder of Women's Union for Nursing Sick and Wounded in War.

Alighieri, Dante. See DANTE.

ʿAlī ibn Muḥammad al-Jurjānī. See al-JURJĀNĪ.

ʿAlī Mo·ham·mad \a-'lē-mu̇-'kam-məd\, Mīrzā. *Called* the Bāb \'bab\ *and* ʿAlī Moḥammad of Shī·rāz \shi-'räz\. 1819 or 1820–1850. Iranian religious leader. Schooled in the Shaykhī school of Shīʿite Islām; declared himself the Bāb, i.e. Gateway, to the hidden 12th *imām* (1844); assembled 18 disciples; faced strong opposition from mullahs and other authorities; imprisoned (1847–50) and executed. Late in career abandoned title Bāb and declared himself the 12th *imām,* or *imām Mahdī.* The Bābī religion played a role in later Bahāʾī religion.

Alin·sky \ə-'lin(t)-skē\, Saul David. 1909–1972. American reformer, b. Chicago. Pioneer in field of community organization; formed Back of the Yards Council, Chicago (1938) to agitate for neighborhood improvement; founded Industrial Areas Foundation (1940) to further such work; organized in Detroit, Kansas City, Buffalo, Rochester, etc. Author of *Reveille for Radicals* (1947), *Rules for Radicals* (1971).

Ali Pa·şa \ä-'lē-pä-'shä\. *Called* the Lion of Ja·ni·na \'yän-ē-(ˌ)nä\. 1741–1822. Turkish brigand. By murder and intrigue became (1788) pasha of Janina (modern Ioànnina, Greece); held power over much of Albania, Macedonia, Thessaly, Epirus, and the Morea; intrigued as sovereign ruler with England and France; his barbarous though cultured court was described by Byron and others.

Âli Paşa \ä-'lē-\, Mehmed Emin. 1815–1871. Turkish diplomat and politician. Ambassador to Great Britain (1841–45); minister of foreign affairs (1846); delegate to Congress of Vienna (1855), of Paris (1856); grand vizier (1852, 1855–56, 1858–59, 1861, 1867–71); maintained peace in Serbia and Moldavia-Walachia; put down Cretan revolt (1868); maintained power of grand vizierate against Sultan Abdülaziz; a principal figure, with Reşid Paşa and Fuad Paşa, in the Tanzimat period of Turkish history.

Alī Shīr Navāʾī. See NAVĀʾĪ.

Al·i·son \'al-ə-sən\, Archibald. 1757–1839. Scottish clergyman. Author of *Essays on the Nature and Principles of Taste* (1790). His son ¶Sir Archibald (1792–1867) was a historian; called to Scottish bar (1814); as sheriff of Lanarkshire suppressed riots (1837); author of *History of Europe during the French Revolution* (1833–42, and in continuation 1852–59), biographies, and an autobiography.

Al·ka·betz \ˌal-kə-'bets\, Solomon ben Moses ha-Levi. c.1505–1574. Jewish Kabbalist poet. Author of *Lekha dodi,* recited to commence sabbath observances in synagogues.

Al·ka·lai \ˌal-kə-'lī\, Judah ben Solomon Hai. 1798–1878. Jewish rabbi in Croatia. Author of *Goral la-Adonai* (1857) and other works anticipating Zionist movement.

Al·kan \äl-kän\, Valentin. *Orig.* Charles-Valentin Mor·hange \mȯ-rä"zh\. 1813–1888. French pianist and composer. Virtuoso pianist in youth; friend of Chopin, George Sand; later appeared rarely in concert, becoming virtual recluse. Composed difficult, often brilliantly unorthodox piano works, including sets of preludes and études in all major and minor keys, étude *Chemin de fer* (1844), *Marche triomphale* (1846), sonata *Les Quatre Âges* (1848), *Les Mois* (c.1872).

Al·lan \'al-ən\, David. 1744–1796. Scottish painter. Director and master, Academy of Arts, Edinburgh (1780–96); illustrated Allan Ramsay's *Gentle Shepherd;* known as "Scottish Hogarth" for humorous descriptive paintings such as *Scotch Wedding, Highland Dance, Repentance Stool,* etc.

Allan, Sir Hugh. 1810–1882. Canadian financier and shipowner, b. Ayrshire, Scotland. To Canada (1826); founded Allan Line of steamships (1853); one of projectors of Canadian Pacific Railway, for which he was awarded a charter (1872); subsequent revelation of his huge financial contribution to Conservative party discredited his railway firm and brought down Sir John Macdonald's government (1873).

Allan, Sir William. 1782–1850. Scottish historical painter. Known esp. for scenes of Russian life, and scenes from Scottish history; president, Royal Scottish Academy (1838); painter to the Queen in Scotland (1841).

All·butt \'ȯl-bət, 'äl-\, Sir Thomas Clifford. 1836–1925. English physician. Regius professor, Cambridge (1892–1925). Invented short clinical thermometer (1866); described hyperpiesia (essential hypertension) apart from kidney disease (1895); demonstrated aortic origin of angina pectoris (1894). Author of *Systems of Medicine* (1896–99), *Diseases of the Arteries* (1915).

Al·lee \a(l)-'lē\, Warder Clyde. 1885–1955. American zoologist and ecologist, b. near Bloomington, Ind. On faculty of Lake Forest Coll. (1915–21), U. of Chicago (1921–50), U. of Florida (1950–55); known esp. for studies of animal social behavior, distribution, and aggregations. Author of *Animal Aggregations* (1931), *Social Life of Animals* (1938); co-author of *Principles of Animal Ecology* (1949).

Al·le·gri \äl-'lā-grē\, Antonio. *Known as* Cor·reg·gio \kōr-'rād-jō, *Angl* kə-'rej-(ē-,)ō\. 1494–1534. Italian painter, b. Correggio. Influenced by Andrea Mantegna and Leonardo da Vinci; studied under uncle Lorenzo Allegri and probably under Lorenzo Costa; employed at Correggio, Modena, and Parma. Works included *Holy Family, Madonna, Zingarella,* altarpiece *Madonna Blessing St. Francis,* frescoes in Convent of San Paolo at Parma, frescoes in cupola of San Giovanni at Parma, series of frescoes titled *Assumption of the Virgin* in Parma Cathedral, *Mystic Marriage of St. Catherine, Holy Night, Jupiter and Antiope, Danaë.* His sensuous use of color and space influenced later Baroque artists. His son ¶Pomponio Allegri (1521–c.1593) was a minor painter.

Allegri, Gregorio. 1582–1652. Italian composer. Member, Sistine choir (from 1629). His *Miserere* is sung annually in the Sistine Chapel on Good Friday.

Al·leine \'al-ən\, Joseph. 1634–1668. English Puritan clergyman. Ejected from Anglican living (1662) for nonconformity; frequently fined and imprisoned for evangelical preaching. Wrote *An Alarm to the Unconverted* (1672).

Al·len \'al-ən\, Edgar. 1892–1943. American anatomist, b. Canon City, Colo. Professor (1923–33) and dean of medical school (1929–33), U. of Missouri; professor, Yale (1933–43). Conducted research on reproduction and hormones with E. A. Doisy; discovered (1923) estrogen.

Allen, Elisha Hunt. 1804–1883. American politician, b. New Salem, Mass. Member, U.S. House of Representatives (1841–43). U.S. consul at Honolulu (1850–56); minister of finance under king of Hawaii (1856–57); chancellor and chief justice (1857–76); Hawaiian minister to U.S. (1876–83).

Allen, Elizabeth Anne, *nee* Chase. *Pseudonym* Florence Per·cy \'pər-sē\. 1832–1911. American poet, b. Strong, Me. m. B. P. Akers (1850; d. 1861), E. M. Allen (1865). Author of poem "Rock Me to Sleep" (1860).

Allen, Ethan. 1738–1789. American Revolutionary soldier, b. Litchfield, Conn. Served (1757) during French and Indian War. Associated with early Vermont (then known as New Hampshire grants) history (from 1769). Colonel commanding irregular Green Mountain Boys (1770–75). On orders from Connecticut, seized, with Benedict Arnold, Fort Ticonderoga (May 10, 1775); captured at Montreal and held prisoner (1775–78); exchanged; returned to Vermont; major general of militia. Presented to Congress Vermont's claims to independence and recognition (1778). Involved (1780–83) in negotiations with British, perhaps undertaken to force American Congress to recognize Vermont's claims. Author of *Narrative of Colonel Ethan Allen's Captivity* (1779), *Reason, the Only Oracle of Man* (1784).

Allen, Florence Ellinwood. 1884–1966. American judge, b. Salt Lake City. Judge, Ohio court of common pleas (1921–26), supreme court of Ohio (1922–34), U.S. circuit court of appeals (1934–59). First woman to sit on a court of last resort and first on a general federal bench.

Allen, Forrest Clare, *known as* Phog \'fȯg, 'fäg\. 1885–1974. American coach. Basketball coach, U. of Kansas (1919–56); career record 770 games won, 223 lost; Kansas team of 1951–52 won NCAA championship; secured addition of basketball to Olympic Games (1936); coached winning U.S. Olympic basketball team (1952).

Allen, Fred. *Orig.* John Florence Sullivan. 1894–1956. American humorist, b. Cambridge, Mass. In vaudeville, for a time as "Freddie James, World's Worst Juggler"; host of radio program "Allen's Alley" (1932–49); noted for sharply satirical humor. Author of autobiographical *Treadmill to Oblivion* (1954).

Allen, Frederick Lewis. 1890–1954. American editor and author, b. Boston. On staff (from 1923), editor (1941–53), *Harper's Magazine.* Author of *Only Yesterday* (1931), *The Lords of Creation* (1935), *Since Yesterday* (1940), *The Big Change* (1952).

Allen, Henry Watkins. 1820–1866. American soldier, b. Prince Edward Co., Va. Served in Sam Houston's Texas army (1842); enlisted in Louisiana regiment for Civil War service (1861); colonel of 4th Louisiana at Shiloh (1862); brigadier general (1863). Governor of Louisiana (1863–65); instituted fiscal and supply reforms, welfare system.

Allen, Hervey, *in full* William Hervey, Jr. 1889–1949. American author, b. Pittsburgh, Pa. Author of volumes of verse, a biography of E. A. Poe (1926), and the novels *Anthony Adverse* (1933), *Action at Aquila* (1938), *It Was Like This* (1940), etc.

Allen, Horatio. 1802–1890. American civil engineer, b. Schenectady, N.Y. Engineer with Delaware and Hudson Co. (1825–29); ran first locomotive on an American railroad at Honesdale, Pa. (Aug. 9, 1829). Designed *Best Friend of Charleston,* first American-built commercial locomotive (1830); devised pivoted trucks for running gear. President, Erie Railroad (1843–70); consulting engineer for Brooklyn Bridge, Panama Railroad.

Allen, Sir Hugh Percy. 1869–1946. English organist. Organist of New College, Oxford (1901–18); conductor, London Bach choir (1907–20); director, Royal College of Music (1918–37); professor of music, Oxford (1918–46); exerted great influence on music education.

Allen, Ira. 1751–1814. American Revolutionary politician, b. Cornwall, Conn. Brother of Ethan Allen. A leader in agitation to obtain statehood for Vermont; member of Green Mountain Boys; helped draw up constitution (1777); involved (1780–91) in negotiations with British. Assisted in founding U. of Vermont (1789).

Allen, Sir James. 1855–1942. New Zealand politician, b. Australia. M.P., New Zealand (1887–1920); leader of opposition (1892–1912); leader of Reform party (1912–20); minister of finance and education (1912–15), of defense (1912–20), of finance and external affairs (1919–20). High commissioner in London (1920–26); member, Legislative Council, N.Z. (1927–38).

Allen, James Lane. 1849–1925. American novelist, b. near Lexington, Ky. Engaged in school and college teaching (1872–85). Author of *Flute and Violin, and Other Kentucky Tales and Romances* (1891), *A Kentucky Cardinal* (1894), *Aftermath* (1895), *The Choir Invisible* (1897), *The Reign of Law* (1900), *The Mettle of the Pasture* (1903), etc.

Allen, John. 1810–1892. American dentist, b. Broome Co., N.Y. Devised modern denture, with porcelain teeth attached to platinum plate (patented 1851).

Al·len \'ál-ən\, Carl Ferdinand. 1811–1871. Danish historian. Author of unfinished but important *De tre nordiske Rigers Historie 1497–1536* (1864–72).

Al·len \'al-ən\, Ralph. *Called* the Man of Bath \'bȧth, *US* 'bath, 'bȧth\. 1694–1764. English philanthropist. Deputy postmaster, Bath. Amassed fortune by devising and forming new system of direct postal routes for England and Wales. Supposed original of Allworthy in Fielding's *Tom Jones.*

Allen, Richard. 1760–1831. American bishop, b. Philadelphia. Born a slave; purchased own freedom (1786); established (1787) in Philadelphia first church for Negroes in U.S.; first Negro ordained in Methodist church (1799); a founder of African Methodist Episcopal Church, and its bishop (1816–31).

Allen, Viola Emily. 1867–1948. American actress, b. Huntsville, Ala. Played in *Little Lord Fauntleroy* (1888), *Shenandoah* (1889), *The Christian* (1898), *In the Palace of the King* (1900), *Toast of the Town* (1906), *White Sister* (1909); toured with own Shakespearian company (1903–07).

Allen, William. 1532–1594. English cardinal. Refused to take oath of supremacy and fled England (1565); opened English Roman Catholic seminary at Douai (1568), later moved to Reims (1578); began work on Reims-Douai translation of the Bible; helped found English college in Rome (1576); organized first Jesuit mission to England (1580). Urged Philip II of Spain to conquer England, for which he was created cardinal (1587). At time of Armada urged Roman Catholics of England to rise against Elizabeth. Made librarian at Vatican; served on commission for revision of Vulgate.

Allen, Zachariah. 1795–1882. American inventor, b. Providence, R.I. Invented first hot-air house-heating system (1821) and an automatic steam-engine cutoff (1834).

Al·len·by \'al-ən-bē\, Edmund Henry Hynman. 1st Viscount Allenby. 1861–1936. English field marshal. Served in Bechuanaland (1884–85), Zululand (1888), and in cavalry operations in Boer War (1899–1902). Major general (1909). In World War I commanded cavalry (1914–15), Third army (1915–17) in France; commander in chief of Egyptian Expeditionary Force, took Beersheba and Gaza from Turks (1917), entered Jerusalem (1917), and won sweeping victory at Megiddo (1918) in last great mounted cavalry campaign. Raised to peerage as Viscount Allenby of Megiddo and Felixstowe and promoted field marshal (1919). High commissioner for Egypt (1919–25).

Al·len·de \ä(l)-ˈyān-dā; *Angl* ä(l)-ˈyen-dē, ə(l)-, -(ˌ)dā\, Salvador. *Full surname* Allende Gos·sens \ˈgō-sāns\. 1908–1973. Chilean politician. Trained as physician; a founder of Socialist party (1933); member of Chamber of Deputies (1937–45), Senate (1945–70; pres. 1965–69); several times candidate for president of Chile; elected president (1970). Believed to be first freely elected Marxist head of state. Overthrown in military coup (1973) during which he died.

Al·leyne \ˈal-ən; ˈal-ˌēn, -ˌān, al-ˈ\, Edward. 1566–1626. English actor. One of Earl of Worcester's players (1586), then with others; associated (from 1592) with Philip Henslowe; with Henslowe, built Fortune Theatre at Cripplegate (1600) and there directed Lord Admiral's company (1600–03). Rivalled only by Richard Burbage as leading actor of the day; made last appearances in *Tamburlaine, Jew of Malta,* and *Faustus* (1604). Founded and endowed Dulwich College (incorporated 1619). m. (1623) Constance, daughter of John Donne.

Al·li·bone \ˈal-ə-ˌbōn\, Samuel Austin. 1816–1889. American editor and librarian, b. Philadelphia. Compiler of *A Critical Dictionary of English Literature and British and American Authors* (1858–71).

Al·ling·ham \ˈal-iŋ-əm\, Margery Louise. 1904–1966. English writer. Creator of fictional detective Albert Campion; author of detective novels of great wit and ingenuity, including *Crime at Black Dudley* (1928), *Mystery Mile* (1929), *Police at the Funeral* (1931), *Sweet Danger* (1933), *Death of a Ghost* (1934), *Flowers for the Judge* (1936), *Traitor's Purse* (1941), *Coroner's Pidgin* (1945), *Tiger in the Smoke* (1952), *The China Governess* (1963), *The Mind Readers* (1965).

Allingham, William. 1824–1889. Irish poet. Author of *Day and Night Songs* (1854), *Laurence Bloomfield in Ireland* (1864), *Irish Songs and Poems* (1887), *Flower Pieces* (1888). Editor, *Fraser's Magazine* (1874–79).

Al·li·son \ˈal-ə-sən\, William Boyd. 1829–1908. American politician, b. near Ashland, O. Member from Iowa, U.S. House of Representatives (1862–70), U.S. Senate (1872–1908); coauthor of Bland-Allison Act of 1878. Chairman of committee on appropriations, U.S. Senate (1881–1908); with N.W. Aldrich, O.H. Platt, J.C. Spooner, one of "Big Four" Republican leaders.

Al·lon \ˈal-ən\, Henry. 1818–1892. English Congregational minister. Held London pastorate at Union Chapel (1844–92); published *Congregational Psalmist* (1858); edited *British Quarterly Review* (1877–86).

Al·lo·ri \äl-ˈlō-rē\, Alessandro. 1535–1607. Italian painter. Known for altarpieces, frescoes, paintings in mannerist style; frequently an imitator of Michelangelo. His son ¶Cristofano (1577–1621), also portrait painter of Florentine mannerist school, known esp. for *Judith and Holofernes, St. Julian,* and *Isabella of Aragon at the Feet of Charles VIII.*

Al·lott \ˈal-ət\, Robert. fl. 1600. English poet. Editor of miscellany of Elizabethan poetry entitled *England's Parnassus* (1600).

Al·lou·ez \äl-wā\, Claude-Jean. 1622–1689. French missionary in America. Entered Jesuit order (1639); to Quebec (1658); Jesuit vicar-general of the Northwest (1663–89); penetrated new regions about Lake Superior (1665–75) establishing missions; continued Marquette's work among the Illinois (1676–89).

All·port \ˈȯl-ˌpō(ə)rt, -ˌpȯ(ə)rt\, Gordon Willard. 1897–1967. American psychologist, b. Montezuma, Ind. Professor (1930–67), Harvard. Author of *Personality: A Psychological Interpretation* (1937), *Nature of Personality* (1950), *Nature of Prejudice* (1954), *Becoming* (1955), *Pattern and Growth in Personality* (1961), etc.

Al·lston \ˈȯl-stən\, Robert Francis Withers. 1801–1864. American planter and politician, b. All Saints' Parish, S.C. Developed great rice plantation; governor of South Carolina (1856–58); wrote valuable works on agriculture.

Allston, Washington. 1779–1843. American artist and author, b. Georgetown Co., S.C. Studied in Europe (1800–08); settled in Cambridgeport, Mass. (1830). Paintings included *Belshazzar's Feast, The Flood, Elijah in the Desert, Moonlit Landscape;* noted esp. for dramatic subject matter, use of light and atmospheric color; outstanding American Romantic. Author of *The Sylphs of the Seasons with other Poems* (1813), *Monaldi,* a Gothic novel (1841).

Al·mack \ˈȯl-ˌmak, ˈäl-\, William. d. 1781. Scottish clubman. Founder of famous Almack's Assembly Rooms, King St., St. James's, London (1765). His surname is said to be a syllabic transposition of an original patronymic McCaul or McCall.

Al·ma·gro \äl-ˈmäg̅-rō\, Diego de. 1475–1538. Spanish soldier. To Panama with Pedrarias Dávila (1514); took part in first voyage to south (1524–25). Took part in Pizarro's conquest of Peru, joining expedition at Cajamarca (1533); quarreled violently with Pizarro but soon reconciled; joined march on Cuzco; with Pizarro joint captain general of Nueva Castile. Led expedition of conquest to Chile (1535–36); returned (1537), claimed Cuzco, and captured it by surprise; imprisoned Pizarro's brothers; defeated (1538) in ensuing war with Alonso de Alvarado and Hernando Pizarro; captured and executed. His son ¶Diego (1518–1542), b. in Panama, of an Indian mother, accompanied him to Chile; made governor of Peru at Pizarro's death (1541); later defeated by royalists and executed.

Almansor *or* **Almanzor.** See al-MANṢŪR.

Al·ma-Tad·e·ma \ˈäl-mə-ˈtȧ-də-mȧ, *Angl* ˈal-mə-ˈtad-ə-mə\, Sir Lawrence. 1836–1912. British painter, b. Dronrijp, Netherlands. Studied at Academy of Antwerp and under Hendrik Leys. Settled in England (1870); naturalized (1873). Known for historic idylls and genre scenes that enjoyed great popularity; excelled at textures, architectural detail. Important works included *Tarquinius Superbus* (1867), *Danse pyrrhique* (1869), *Wine Shop* (1869), *Un Jongleur* (1870), *Roses of Heliogabalus* (1888), *Conversion of Paula* (1898).

Al·mei·da \äl-ˈmā-t̲h̲ə\, Antônio José de. 1866–1929. Portuguese physician and statesman. Deputy (from 1906); interior minister in provisional government (1910); prime minister (1916–17); president of Portugal (1919–23).

Almeida, Brites de. fl. 1385. Portuguese heroine. Led townspeople of Aljubarrota in resistance to Spanish invasion of Portugal and alone killed seven Spaniards with her baker's shovel.

Almeida, Francisco de. c.1450–1510. Portuguese soldier. First viceroy of Portuguese India (1505–09); established forts and trading posts in Cochin, Ceylon, and Sumatra; destroyed Arab-Egyptian fleet off Diu (1509); superseded by Afonso de Albuquerque (1509); killed in skirmish with Hottentots on voyage home. His son ¶Lourenço (d. 1508) served as his lieutenant; headed probably the first Portuguese expedition to Ceylon (1505) and founded settlement at Colombo; killed in engagement with Egyptian fleet.

Almeida, Guilherme de. 1890–1969. Brazilian poet. Author of *Danza de las horas* (1919), *Era uma vez* (1922), *Raza* (1925), *El ángel del sal* (1951), etc.

Almeida, Jose Valentim Fialho de. See FIALHO DE ALMEIDA.

Almeida, Manuel Antônio de. 1831–1861. Brazilian novelist. Author of *Memórias de um sargento de Milícias* (1854–55), a novel of advanced realism considered first great novel of Brazil.

Almeida Garrett, Visconde de. See João GARRETT.

Al·mo·hads \ˈal-mō-ˌhadz\. *Arab.* al-Mu·waḥḥi·dūn \ˌal-ˌmu̇-wa-hi-ˈdün\, *i.e.* Unitarians. Berber dynasty established in North Africa and Spain (1130–1269) by Islāmic sect of Almohads, founded by Ibn Tūmart (*q.v.*). His successor ʽAbd al-Mu'min (*q.v.*) conquered Morocco and southern Spain, overthrowing Almoravids (1147). Power of dynasty declined after disastrous defeat by Christians at Navas de Tolosa (1212); terminated in Spain (1232) and in Africa (1269).

Al·mon \ˈal-mən\, John. 1737–1805. English political writer. Achieved reputation with Whig pamphlets including *Conduct of a late Noble Commander Examined* (1759), *Review of Mr. Pitt's Administration* (1761), etc.; established bookseller's shop, London (1763); acquitted in prosecution for pamphlet *Juries and Libels* (1765); fined for selling *London Museum* issue containing Junius's "Letter to the King" (1770); championed right of printers to publish accounts of parliamentary debates; reported on Parliament for *London Evening Post* (1771); established *Parliamentary Register* (1774). Later imprisoned for libel and then forced to flee country. Published (1805) correspondence of his friend John Wilkes.

Al·mon·de \äl-ˈmȯn-də\, Phillips van. 1644–1711. Dutch admiral. Commanded fleet that bore William of Orange to England (1688); commander of Dutch fleet and second to English Adm. Edward Russell at victory at La Hogue (1692), and, with Sir George Rooke, of allied fleet that destroyed Spanish fleet in Bay of Vigo (1702).

Al·mon·te \äl-ˈmȯn-tā\, Juan Nepomuceno. 1804?–1869. Mexican general and politician. Minister to U.S. (1841–46, 1853), to France (1857, 1866); opposed liberal regime of Juárez; accompanied French expedition to Mexico (1862) and headed a regency government (1863–64) preparing way for Maximilian.

Al·mo·ra·vids \ˌal-mə-ˈräv-ədz\. *Arab.* al-Mu·rā·bi·tūn \ˌal-mu̇-ˌrä-bi-ˈtün\, *i.e.* the warrior hermits. A Berber dynasty established (c.1062) by Almoravid sect in North Africa; later ruled (1090–1147) in Spain. Its founder, YUSUF IBN TĀSHUFĪN, made Marrakech its African capital; in Spain its power centered in Seville; overcome by Almohads (1147).

Alm·qvist \ˈälm-ˌkvist\, Carl Jonas Love. 1793–1866. Swedish writer. Led unsettled life as exponent of Romanticism. Author of novels, stories, verse dramas, poems, much collected in two series of the *Törnrosens bok* (1832–51); individual volumes included *Jaktslottet* (1832), *Drottningens juvelsmycke* (1834), *Palatset* (1838), *Amorina* (1839), *Det går an* (1839).

A.L.O.E. See Charlotte Maria TUCKER.

Alompra. See ALAUNGPAYA.

Alon·so \ä-ˈlȯn-sō\, Amado. 1896–1952. Spanish linguist. Professor and director, language institute at U. of Buenos Aires (1927–46); professor at

Harvard (1946–52). Edited *Revista de filología hispánica* (1939–46); author of *El problema de la lengua en América* (1935), *Estudios linguisticos* (1951), etc.

Alon·so \ä-'lȯn-sō\, Mateo. 1878–1955. Argentine sculptor. His most notable work, *Christ of the Andes* (1902), monument molded in bronze from old Argentine cannon, at Uspallata Pass on Chile–Argentina border as symbol of perpetual peace between the two countries.

Aloysius Gonzaga, Saint. See GONZAGA.

Alp Ars·lan \'äl-pär-'slän\. c.1030–1072 or 1073. Second sultan of Seljuq Turks (1063–72). Great-grandson of Seljuq. Succeeded his father Chaghri Beg as ruler of Khorāsān (1061) and under Toghrïl Beg as leader of all Seljuqs (1063). Conquered Georgia and Armenia (1064); defeated Byzantine Emperor Romanus IV Diogenes at Manzikert (1071) and took him prisoner; released him for ransom; by this victory, established Seljuq sultanate of Rūm in Asia Minor. Administration of empire left to vizier, Niẓām al-Mulk. Succeeded by his son Malik-Shāh.

Alpharabius. See FĀRĀBĪ.

Alphege, Saint. See AELFHEAH.

Alphonsa, Mother. See Mary Alphonsa LATHROP.

Al·phonse I \al-fōⁿs\. *Surnamed* Jour·dain \zhür-dāⁿ\. 1103–1148. Count of Toulouse. Son of Count Raymond IV; succeeded brother Bertrand as count of Toulouse and marquis of Provence (1112); lost Toulouse to William IX, Duke of Aquitaine (1114) but recovered it (1123); accompanied King Louis VII on Second Crusade (1146); died at Caesarea.

Alphonse. *Called* Alphonse de France \-də-frāⁿs\. 1220–1271. Count of Poitiers and of Toulouse. Fifth son of Louis VIII of France, from whom he received (1241) Poitou and Auvergne; through marriage (1237) to Joan, daughter of Raymond VII, inherited (1249) countship of Toulouse; on Seventh Crusade stood hostage for brother Louis IX (1250); with Charles of Anjou regent of France in absence of Louis IX (1250–54); died on Eighth Crusade. Through him southern French kingdom reverted to the crown.

Al·pi·ni \äl'pē-nē\ *or* **Al·pi·no** \-nō\, Prospero. *Lat.* Prosper Al·pi·nus \al-'pī-nəs\. 1553–1616 or 1617. Italian botanist and physician. Professor at Padua (from 1593); author of *De medicina Aegyptorum* (1591), *De plantis Aegypti liber* (1593), *De praesagienda vita et morte aegrotontium* (1601); credited with introducing coffee and bananas to Europe.

Als·berg \'als-ˌbərg, 'alz-\, Carl Lucas. 1877–1940. American biochemist, b. New York City. On staff, U.S. Dept. of Agriculture (1908–21), Stanford U. Food Research Institute (1921–37); authority on food chemistry.

Al·sop \'ȯl-səp, 'al-ˌsäp, 'ȯl-\, Mary O'Hara. *Pseudonym* Mary O'Hara \ō-'har-ə\. 1885–1980. American novelist, b. Cape May Point, N.J. Author of *My Friend Flicka* (1941), *Thunderhead* (1943), *Green Grass of Wyoming* (1946), etc.

Alsop, Vincent. c.1630–1703. English Nonconformist clergyman. Lost living by Act of Uniformity (1662); gained reputation as effective pamphleteer with *Melius Inquirendum* (1679), *Mischief of Impositions* (1680), etc.

Al·ta·mi·ra y Cre·vea \äl-tä-'mē-rä-ē-krā-'vā-ä\, Rafael. 1866–1951. Spanish jurist and historian. Professor, Oviedo U. (1897–1910); professor, Madrid (1914–36), U. of Mexico (from 1944). Judge, Permanent Court of International Justice (1922–45). Author of *Historia de España y de la civilización española* (1900–11), *Historia del Derecho español* (1903), etc.

Altamsh. See ILTUTMISH.

Al·tan Khan \'äl-tän-k̲än\. *Known also as* An·da \'än-dä\. d. 1583. Mongol chief. Became chief of eastern Mongols (1543); led raid across Great Wall to outskirts of Peking (1550); established capital at Kuku-khoto; adopted Dge-lugs-pa (Yellow Hat) sect of Lamaism as official Mongol religion (1580); established title of Dalai Lama for head of sect and bestowed it on own grandson.

Alt·dor·fer \'ält-ˌdȯr-fər\, Albrecht. c.1480–1538. German painter. Citizen (1505) and public official in Regensburg; as artist a leader of the Danube school; pioneered in landscape painting and in depiction of scenes lighted by torches or twilight. Chief works included altar panels for St. Florian (1509–18), paintings *Alexanderschlacht, Geburt Mariä, Kreuzigung, Zwei Johannes,* wood carvings, drawings done with white and black lines on colored paper, copper engravings notable for sometimes fantastic imagination.

Al·ten \'äl-tən\, Karl August von. Graf. 1764–1840. Hanoverian general. In Hanoverian army (1776–1803), German Legion of British army (1803–15), serving under Wellington in Peninsular War and at Waterloo; Hanoverian minister of war (1832), foreign affairs (1833).

Al·ten·stein \'äl-tən-ˌshtīn\, Karl. Freiherr vom Stein \'shtīn\ zum Altenstein. 1770–1840. Prussian statesman. Minister of finance (1808–10), of public worship and education (1817–38); responsible for founding of U. of Bonn (1818) and for new building at U. of Halle, of Berlin, of Breslau; encouraged establishment of common schools, teacher training programs, etc.

Al·ter \'ȯl-tər\, David. 1807–1881. American physicist and physician, b. Westmoreland Co., Pa. Discovered, simultaneously with A.J. Angström, that elemental gases have characteristic spectra, thus making possible spectroscopic determination of chemical nature of gases.

Alt·geld \'ȯlt-'geld, 'ält-, 'alt-, -gelt\, John Peter. 1847–1902. American politician, b. Nassau, Germany. Governor of Illinois (1893–97), first Democratic governor of state since Civil War; aroused controversy by pardoning three convicted "conspirators" of 1886 Haymarket Riot, and by protesting use of federal troops to break Pullman strike (1894).

Alt·haus \'ält-ˌhaủs\, Johannes. *Lat.* Al·thu·sius \al-'thü-sē-əs, -sh(ē-)əs\. 1557–1638. Dutch jurist. Professor at Herborn (1586–1604); syndic of Emden (1604–38); evolved Calvinist idea of contract into complete theory of society and politics; considered father of theory of federalism. Author of *Jurisprudentiae Romanae libri duo* (1586), *Politica methodice digesta atque exemplis sacris et profanis illustrata* (1603).

Althrop, Viscounts. See Earls Spencer under SPENCER family.

Al·ti·chie·ro \ˌäl-tē-'kyā-rō\. c.1330–after 1390. Italian painter. Effective founder of Veronese school; known esp. for two fresco cycles in Padua.

Alt·man \'ȯlt-mən\, Benjamin. 1840–1913. American merchant and art collector, b. New York City. Opened (1865) drygoods store that developed into B. Altman & Co. department store (incorporated 1913); collection of Chinese and European art, valued at $20 million at death, left to Metropolitan Museum of Art.

Altringer, Count Johann. See ALDRINGEN.

Alva, Duke of. See ÁLVAREZ DE TOLEDO.

Al·va·ra·do \äl-b̲ä-'räth̲-ō\, Pedro de. c.1485–1541. Spanish soldier. Companion of Grijalva (1518) and of Cortés in conquest of Mexico (1519–21); in command of Mexico City (1520) when Cortés went against Narváez on coast; in "la Moche Triste," retreating from Aztec forces, said to have saved his own life by famous leap, "Salto de Alvarado." First *alcalde* of Mexico City (1522). Led expedition to Guatemala (1523–27) during which he conquered part of present El Salvador (1524). While in Spain (1527–29) named governor and captain general of Guatemala; led expedition (1534) against Quito, but persuaded by Pizarro to retire; later engaged in quest for Seven Cities of Cíbola.

Álvares Pereira, Nuno. See PEREIRA.

Ál·va·rez \'äl-b̲ä-rās\, Juan. 1790–1867. Mexican politician. Took part in revolutions for Mexican independence under Morelos (1811) and Iturbide (1821); joined Santa Anna to overthrow Iturbide (1823); fought in war with U.S. (1846–47); first governor of Guerrero (1849); leader in revolt against Santa Anna (1854); provisional president of Mexico (Oct.–Dec. 1855), resigning in favor of Comonfort; led reform movements; determined opponent of Maximilian and French invasion (1861–67).

Ál·va·rez de Cien·fue·gos \'äl-b̲ä-rāth-th̲ā-thyān-'fwā-gōs\, Nicasio. 1764–1809. Spanish poet. A founder and editor of journals *Gaceta de Madrid* and *Mercurio* (from 1798); author of *Poesías* (1798) and many plays, including *La Zorayda, La Condesa de Castilla, Idomeneo, Las hermanas generosas, Pítaco,* all published posthumously. Deported to France (1808) for liberal anti-French writings.

Álvarez de To·le·do \-th̲ā-tō-'lā-th̲ō\, Fernando. 3d Duque de Al·ba \'äl-b̲ä\ *or* Al·va. 1507–1582. Spanish soldier. Distinguished himself fighting French at Fuenterrabía and named its governor (1524); soon became outstanding military commander by mastery of discipline, tactics, logistics; commanded part of Charles V's Tunis campaign (1535); as commander of imperial armies defeated Schmalkaldic League at Mühlberg (1547); commander of imperial forces in Italy (1552–59) and viceroy of Naples (1556–59); a chief minister to Philip II. Sent by Philip to pacify Netherlands (1567); established Council of Troubles, later called Council of Blood, through which he exercised personal rule; executed Count Egmont and Count van Hoorne and supposedly 18,000 others; defeated William of Orange and other Protestant leaders; aroused further opposition with proposed sales tax; countenanced atrocities in campaign of 1572–73; recalled to Spain after failure of his fleet against Gueux. Later fell from Philip's favor and held in house arrest (1579–80). Released to command invasion of Portugal, which he completed brilliantly (1581).

Álvarez Ga·to \-'gä-tō\, Juan. between 1440 and 1450–1509. Spanish writer. Known esp. for religious, satirical, and love poems.

Álvarez Quin·te·ro \-kēn-'tā-rō\, Serafín (1871–1938) and his brother Joaquín (1873–1944). Spanish dramatists. Authors in collaboration of almost 200 comic plays dealing with Andalusian life, as *La reja* (1897), *El patio* (1900), *Los galeotos* (1900), *El amor que pasa* (1904), *El genio alegre* (1906), and *Malvaloca* (1912); their works extremely popular in Spain, and also in English-speaking world through translations published in 1928 by Helen and Harley Granville-Barker.

Al·ve·ar \äl-vā-'är\, Carlos Maria de. 1789–1852. Argentine revolutionary. A rival of San Martín; compelled surrender of Montevideo (1814); defeated by Artigas; succeeded Gervasio Posadas as dictator (1815). Governor of Buenos Aires; forced to flee to Brazil (1820); minister to U.S. (1824). Commanded Argentine army against Brazil in Uruguay (1826); won battle of Ituzaingó (1827). Banished by Rosas (after 1829); minister to U.S. (1838–52).

Alvear, Máximo Marcelo Torcuato de. 1868–1942. Argentine diplomat and politician. A cofounder of Unión Cívica Radical (1890); took part in revolutions (1890, 1893, 1905); minister of public works (1911); parliamentary deputy (1912–17); minister to France (1917–22); president of Argentina (1922–28); broke with UCR and Pres. Irigoyen (1928); exiled (1931–32).

Al·vens·le·ben-Erx·le·ben \'äl-vən-,slā-bən-'erk-,slā-bən\, Gustav von. Graf. 1803–1881. Prussian general. On Prussian general staff (1847–58); helped suppress revolts in Baden (1849), Rhineland (1854); adjutant general (1861); influential adviser to William I. Negotiated Alvensleben Convention (1863) with Russia on mutual suppression of Polish uprising; lieutenant general (1863), general of infantry (1868); commanded 4th Army Corps in Franco–Prussian War (1870). His brother ¶Konstantin von Alvensleben (1809–1892) commanded 3d Army Corps in Franco–Prussian War; retired as general of infantry (1873).

Alver, Amalie. See Bertha Amalie SKRAM.

Alves, Francisco de Paula Rodrigues. See RODRIGUES ALVES.

Al·ves de Li·ma y Sil·va \'äl-vis-thā-'lē-mȧ-ē-'sil-vȧ\, Luis. Duque de Ca·xi·as \kȧ-'shē-ȧs\. 1803–1880. Brazilian soldier and politician. Distinguished himself in war of independence in Bahia (1823); organized military police in Rio de Janeiro following abdication of Pedro I (1831); governor of Maranhão state (1837); elected deputy (1840). Pacified rebelling São Paulo, Minas Gerais, Rio Grande do Sul states (1841–45); commanded Brazilian troops helping to overthrow de Rosas in Argentina (1852); minister of war (from 1855); president of council of ministers (1866, 1875–78). Commanded Brazilian army (1867–70) in Paraguayan War; made duke for capture of Asunción (1869).

Al·y·at·tes \,al-ē-'at-ēz\. d. c.560 B.C. King of Lydia (c.619–c.560 B.C.). Carried on war against Miletus (c.619–614); fought war with Media (c.590–585); conquered Carians, drove off Cimmerians; captured and largely destroyed Smyrna; established Lydian empire, which he left to son Croesus.

Alyp·i·us \ə-'lip-ē-əs\. fl. c.360 A.D. Greek theorist and writer on music. Author of *Introduction to Music,* key to musical system of notation of ancient Greeks.

Al·zon \ȧl-zon\, Emmanuel-Marie-Joseph-Maurice Dau·dé \'dō-dā\ d'. 1810–1880. French ecclesiastic. Canon and vicar-general of Nîmes (1835–80); president of College of the Assumption in Nîmes (1844–80); founded (1845) order of Augustinians of the Assumption, called Assumptionists, to teach, publish, and work among Byzantine rite Catholics; cofounded (1865) Oblate Sisters of the Assumption.

Ama·deo \äm-ä-'thā-ō\. *Ital. in full* Amedeo Ferdinando Maria di Savoia \-dē-sä-'voi-(y)ə\. 1845–1890. King of Spain (1870–73). Son of King Victor Emmanuel II of Italy; duke of Aosta; elected by Spanish Cortes after unsuccessful attempt to persuade prince of Hohenzollern to accept crown; attempted to exercise authority but opposed by all factions and unable to form government; abdicated (1873) following outbreak of 2d Carlist civil war.

Ama·deo \äm-ä-'de-ō\ *or* **Omo·deo** \,ō-mō-'de-ō\, Giovanni Antonio. *Lat.* Am·a·de·us \,am-ə-'dē-əs, ,äm-, -'dā-\. 1447–1522. Italian sculptor and architect. Important figure in early Florentine Renaissance; works included sculptures in Colleoni Chapel at Bergamo, sarcophagus of St. Lanfrancus in church of St. Lanfrancus near Pavia. Aided in designing Milan cathedral.

Am·a·de·us \,am-ə-'dē-əs, ,äm-, -'dā-\. *Fr.* Amé·dée \ȧ-mā-dā\. Name of nine counts and dukes of Savoy including:

Amadeus III. 1095–1148. Count (1103–48). Brother-in-law of Louis VI; died on Second Crusade.

Amadeus V. d. 1323. Count (1285–1323). Expanded territory of Savoy, but granted the Piedmont to his nephew Philippe, prince of Achaea.

Amadeus VI. *Known as* the Green Count. 1334–1383. Count (1343–83). Early gained renown as knight and leader; expanded territory to nearly all of western Alps and regained some Piedmontese lands; mediated many disputes among Italian powers, esp. the Peace of Turin (1381); named imperial vicar by Emperor Charles IV (1365); at Pope Urban V's behest undertook crusade against Turks at Gallipoli (1366); fought Bulgarians and restored cousin John V Palaeologus to Greek throne (1366). Died during expedition to rescue Joan I of Naples.

Amadeus VII. *Known as* the Red Count. 1360–1391. Count (1383–91). Son of Amadeus VI; acquired Nice (1388) and other Provençal towns.

Amadeus VIII. *Called* the Peaceful. 1383–1451. Count (1391–1416) and first duke (1416–40). Son of Amadeus VII; m. (1393) Mary, daughter of Philip the Bold of Burgundy. Claimed Geneva (1401); acquired territory in Bresse (1402), Domo d'Ossola (1406), the Piedmont (1419). His holdings raised to duchy by Emperor Sigismund (1416); promulgated code of statutes for Savoy (1430). Retired to monastery (1434) but continued to exercise power through son Ludovico; finally abdicated (1440). Elected pope (1439) by rebellious Council of Basel; reigned as Felix V in opposition to Pope Eugenius IV; resigned (1449); cardinal (1449).

Amadeus IX. 1435–1472. Duke (1465–72). m. Yolande, sister of Louis XI; because of ill health, passed much authority to wife, through whom France gained influence over Savoy.

Ama·dor de los Rí·os \äm-ä-'thōr-thā-lōs-'rē-ōs\, José. 1818–1878. Spanish critic and historian. Known esp. for *História política, social y religiosa de los judíos de España y Portugal* (1875–76).

Amador Guer·re·ro \-ge-'re-rō\, Manuel. 1833–1909. Panamanian politician. Elected president of Colombia (1868) but prevented from taking power by Gen. Ponce; governor of Panama state (1886); a leader in Panama's struggle for independence; first president of republic (1904–08).

Amal·a·ric \ə-'mal-ə-rik\. 502–531 A.D. King of Visigoths (507–531). Son of Alaric II; held real power only from 526 in Spain and part of Languedoc.

Am·a·la·sun·tha \,am-ə-lə-'sən-thə\ *or* **Am·a·la·suen·tha** \-s(y)ü-'en-thə\ *or* **Am·a·la·swin·tha** \-'swin-thə\. 498–535 A.D. Queen of Ostrogoths (526–534). Daughter of Theodoric, King of Ostrogoths at whose death (526) she became regent for her son Athalaric; aroused opposition of nobles by pro-Byzantine policy; on death of son (534) shared throne with cousin Theodahad, who banished her.

Amalfi, Duke of. See Octavio in PICCOLOMINI family.

Ama·lia \ä-'mä-lē-ä, -'mäl-yə\. *In full* Anna Amalia. Duchess of Saxe-Wei·mar \'saks-'vī-,mär\. 1739–1807. Wife (m. 1756) of Ernest Augustus Constantine, Duke of Saxe-Weimar (d. 1758). Regent (1758–75) for son Duke Charles Augustus. Patroness of literature and art.

Ama·lie Frie·de·ri·ke Ma·rie Au·gu·ste \ä-'mäl-ē-ə-,frē-də-'rē-kə-mä-'rē-ə-aù-'güs-tə\. *Pseudonym* Amalie Hei·ter \'hīt-ər\. 1794–1870. Duchess of Saxony. Sister of King Frederick Augustus II and King John of Saxony. Author of plays including *Die Fürstenbraut, Der Majoratserbe,* and *Der Oheim.*

Amal·ric \ə-'mal-rik, 'am-əl-\ *or* **Amau·ry** \ə-'mȯr-ē, -'mōr-, *Fr* ȧ-mō-rē\. Name of two kings of Jerusalem:

Amalric I (1135–1174). King (1163–74). Count of Jaffa and Ascalon; succeeded brother Baldwin III as king; struggled (1163–74) with Nureddin for control of Egypt, three times invading it; attacked by Saladin (1170); formed alliance with Byzantine empire.

Amalric II (c.1155–1205). King of Cyprus (1194–1205) and of Jerusalem (1198–1205). Member of Lusignan family and brother of Guy de Lusignan (*qq.v.*); m. (1197) Isabella, daughter of Amalric I and half sister of Sibylla, Guy of Lusignan's wife; succeeded Guy as king of Cyprus; as king of Jerusalem secured truce with Muslims.

Amalric of Be·na \'bē-nə\. *Fr.* Amal·ric de Bène \ȧ-mȧl-rēk-də-ben\ *or* Amau·ri de Char·tres \ȧ-mō-rē-də-shȧrtrᵊ\. d. 1206 or 1207. French theologian and mystical philosopher, b. Bène, near Chartres. Pantheistic views, drawn in part from Aristotle, attracted followers known as Amalricians; doctrines condemned by Pope Innocent III (1204), by synod at Paris (1209), and by Lateran Council (1215).

Amān·ol·lāh Khān \'ə-mən-'ùl-lä-'kän\. 1892–1960. Ruler of Afghanistan (1919–29). Son of Ḥabībollāh Khān; assumed crown on murder of his father; declared Afghan independence from Great Britain (1919); introduced reforms which led to revolt (1928); forced to abdicate; lived in exile.

Ama·ra Sim·ha \'əm-ə-rə-'siⁿ-hə\. c. 4th–6th century A.D. Sanskrit grammarian and poet. Author of *Amara-kosa* (*Treasury of Amara*), collection of Sanskrit roots (in 3 books).

Amar Dās \'əm-är-'däs\. 1479–1574. Third Sikh Gurū. Appointed Gurū (1552) at advanced age; broadened Sikh doctrine, encouraged family life, sought to break down caste distinctions and eliminate Hindu practices from Sikhism; dispatched Sikh missionaries.

Amasias. See AMAZIAH.

Amasis. See AHMOSE.

Ama·sis Paint·er \ə-'mā-sə-'spān-tər\. fl. c.555–525 B.C. Greek vase painter. Real name unknown; with Exekias, one of leading black-figure painters in Archaic style.

Ama·ti \ä-'mä-tē\. Name of Italian family of violin-makers of Cremona in 16th and 17th centuries. Andrea Amati (c.1510–c.1578) founded Cremona school of violin making; set style for later works by family and, with modifications by Stradivari, for all modern violins. Andrea's sons ¶Antonio (c.1540–1638) and ¶Girolamo (1561–1630), *known as* the brothers Amati, made violins, violas, and violoncellos. Most famous member of family, Girolamo's son ¶Nicolò (1596–1684), teacher of Antonio Stradivari and of Andrea Guarneri, improved on violin and developed grand Amati. His son ¶Girolamo (1649–1740) was last of family to achieve distinction.

Amauri de Chartres. See AMALRIC of Bena.

Amaury. See AMALRIC.

Am·a·zi·ah \,am-ə-'zī-ə\ *or* **Am·a·si·as** \-sī-əs\. d. c.783 B.C. King of Judah (c.800–c.783 B.C.). Son of Joash. Conquered Edomites (798); extended rule over Philistia; challenged Joash, King of Israel; defeated and taken prisoner; assassinated.

Am•bed•kar \əm-ˈbād-kər\, Bhimrao Ramji. 1893–1956. Indian lawyer and social worker. Leader of Hindu untouchables; ardent worker for abolition of caste, finally forcing Gandhi to take up untouchables as political issue; law minister (1947–51); despairing of eliminating untouchability doctrine, led some 200,000 fellows in conversion to Buddhism (1956).

Am•bi•o•rix \am-ˈbī-ə-riks\. 1st century B.C. Chief of the Eburones of Belgian Gauls. Led campaigns against Romans (54–53 B.C.).

Am•boise \äⁿ-bwäz\, Georges d'. 1460–1510. French prelate. Bishop of Montauban (1474) and almoner to Louis XI; archbishop of Narbonne (1492), of Rouen (1493–98). On accession of Louis XII (1498) became cardinal and chief minister; introduced major tax and judicial reforms; active in French campaigns in northern Italy (1499–1503). Ambitious to become pope, but twice passed over; legate for life in France (1503); helped negotiate Treaty of Blois (1504).

Am•bro•gi•ni \ˌäm-brō-ˈjē-nē\, Angelo. *Known as* Po•li•tian \pə-ˈlish-ən\ *or* Angelo Po•li•zia•no \ˌpō-lēts-ˈyän-ō\. 1454–1494. Italian Humanist and poet. One of foremost classical scholars of the Renaissance. Protégé of Lorenzo de' Medici (1473 ff.); estranged from Medici household after quarrel with Lorenzo's wife (1479); in Mantua at court of Cardinal Gonzaga (1479–80); reconciled with Medicis and appointed canon of Florence cathedral (1480); lectured at Florentine university on Latin and Greek poetry (1282–86). Author of *Stanze per la giostra del Magnifico Giuliano de' Medici* (1475–78), *Detti piacevoli* (1477–79), *Favola d'Orfeo* (1480; first play in Italian), *Miscellanea* (1489; critical essays), Latin translations, as of the *Iliad* (books 2-5; 1470–75) and Epictetus' *Manual* (1479), and Latin elegies (as *In violas, In Lalagen*), odes (as *In puellam*), and epigrams.

Am•bros \ˈäm-ˌbrōs\, August Wihelm. 1816–1876. Bohemian musicologist and composer. Professor at Prague (1868), Vienna Conservatory (1871); composed Czech opera *Bretislaw a Jitka;* author of *Geschichte der Musik* (1862–78).

Am•brose \ˈam-ˌbrōs, -ˌbrōz\. *Lat.* Am•bro•si•us \am-ˈbrō-zhəs, -zē-əs\. Saint. 339–397. Roman prelate. Of noble family; governor of Aemilia-Liguria (c.370); proclaimed bishop of Milan (374). Powerful influence at imperial court; secured rejection of move for toleration of paganism (384); successfully opposed Empress Justina's attempts to set aside a church for Arians (385–386); successfully asserted authority over Emperor Theodosius in causing him to set aside punishment of a bishop (388) and to do public penance for ordering a massacre at Thessalonica (390); considered architect of medieval ideal of church-state relations. Greatly effective as preacher and author of classical Latin homilies, etc. Converted and baptized (386) Augustine, later bishop of Hippo. Works included exegesis, based on Philo, Origen, Plotinus, as *Hexaemeron, De Isaac at anima, De bono mortis;* moral works as *De officiis ministrorum, De virginitate;* orations as *De obitu Valentiniani, De obitu Theodosii, De excessu fratris;* hymns as "Deus Creator omnium," "Aeterne rerum conditor," "Iam surgit hora tertia." A Doctor of the Church.

Ambrose *or* **Am•broise d'Év•reux** \äⁿ-brwäz-dāv-rœ\. fl. c.1190. Norman poet and chronicler. Accompanied Richard I of England on Third Crusade; wrote account of crusade, now lost but the source of extant *Estoire de la guerre sainte* and of *Itinerarium Regis Ricardi* by Richard, canon of Holy Trinity, London.

Ambrose of Ca•mal•do•li \kä-mä-ˈdō-lē\. *Ital.* Am•bro•gio Tra•ver•sa•ri \äm-ˈbrō-jō-ˌträ-ver-ˈsä-rē\. 1386–1439. Italian Humanist and religious. Entered Camaldolese monastery (1400); prior general of Camaldolese order (1431). Expert translator of Latin and Greek, esp. of patristic works. Emissary of Pope Eugenius IV to Council of Basel (1435) and to Council of Ferrara-Florence (1438), where he received Byzantine Emperor John VIII and Patriarch Joseph; chief negotiator of decree of union of Latin and Greek churches (1439).

Am•da Tsey•on \ˈäm-dät-ˈsī-on\, *i.e.* Pillar of Zion. d. 1344? Ruler of Ethiopia (1314–1344?). Sometimes considered founder of Ethiopian state; successfully defended against Muslim kingdoms and enlarged own domain.

Amédée. See AMADEUS.

Ameer Ali. See AMIR ALI.

Ame•ghi•no \ä-mā-ˈgē-nō\, Florentino. 1854–1911. Argentine anthropologist and paleontologist. Professor at Córdoba (1884), La Plata National U. (1887–90, 1906–11); discovered over 6000 fossil species.

Amen, Jacob. See Jacob AMMANN.

Amen•do•la \ä-ˈmen-dō-(ˌ)lä\, Giovanni. 1882–1926. Italian politician. Professor of theoretical philosophy, Pisa; liberal journalist; elected to Parliament (1919); minister for colonies (1922); opposed Fascist policies; founded anti-Fascist newspaper *Il Mondo;* died as result of beatings inflicted by political opponents.

Amen•em•het \ˈäm-ən-em-ˈhet\ *or* **Amen•em•hat** \-ˈhät\. Name of four kings of Egypt of the 12th dynasty:

Amenemhet I. King (1991–62 B.C.). Vizier under Mentuhotep IV, whom he helped overthrow; founded new (12th) dynasty, moving capital from Thebes to al-Fayyūm; reunified Egypt, instituted strong administration, strengthened Amon worship; appointed son Sesostris I coregent (1971).

Amenemhet II. King (1929–1895 B.C.). Son of Sesostris I, who made him coregent (1929); sole ruler (from 1928); encouraged mining and trade with Nubia, Sinai, Syria, Punt, Crete, etc.

Amenemhet III. King (1842–1797 B.C.). Son of Sesostris III; built elaborate irrigation system around Lake Moeris at al-Fayyūm; increased mining, quarrying, and building; brought Middle Kingdom Egypt to peak of prosperity.

Amenemhet IV. King (1798–90 B.C.). Son of Amenemhet III.

Am•en•e•mo•pe \ˌäm-en-e-ˈmō-pā\. Egyptian writer. Fl. in late New Kingdom period (1567–1085 B.C.); author of "Instruction of Amenemope," believed to represent culmination of Egyptian tradition of wisdom literature.

Amen•ho•tep \ˌäm-ən-ˈhō-ˌtep\ *or* **Am•e•no•phis** \ˌam-ə-ˈnō-fis\. Name of four kings of Egypt of the 18th dynasty:

Amenhotep I. King (1546–26 B.C.). Son of Ahmose I; invaded Nubia and consolidated authority to Second Cataract; also fought war with Libyans.

Amenhotep II. King (1450–25 B.C.). Son of Thutmose III; coregent with his father for one year; put down revolt in Syria; settled relations with Mitanni, Babylon, Hittites; by firm rule kept Nubia under control.

Amenhotep III. King (1417–1379 B.C.). Son of Thutmose IV; m. Tiy; led successful expedition into Nubia above Second Cataract; held supremacy in Asia; contracted political marriages with Mitanni and Babylonian princesses. Reign an era of magnificence and prosperity; his capital, Thebes, developed into great monumental city; erected main part of Luxor temple, great pylon at Karnak, and mortuary temple including Colossi of Memnon.

Amenhotep IV. See AKHENATON.

Amenhotep. *Known as* Amenhotep, son of Hapu. c.1460–c.1380 B.C. Egyptian official. High official in service of Amenhotep III; in charge of regulating immigration in Nile Delta area; later in charge of all royal works; associated with Amon worship, leading to his deification by priests of 21st dynasty (1085–945 B.C.).

Amer•bach \ˈäm-ər-ˌbäk\, Johannes. c.1445–1513. German printer in Basel. Published (1480–1512) over 70 works including those of St. Augustine (1506) and St. Ambrose. His son ¶Bonifaz *or* Bonifatius (1495–1562), Swiss jurist and scholar, was professor and syndic in Basel; friend and heir of Erasmus. Bonifaz's son ¶Basilius (1533–1591) was a jurist and noted art collector.

Amerigo Vespucci. See VESPUCCI.

Amery \ˈā-mər-ē\, Leopold Charles Maurice Stennett. 1873–1955. British journalist and politician, b. India. On editorial staff, London *Times* (1899–1909); correspondent in Boer War (1899–1900); M.P. (1911–45); staunch conservative, advocating tariff reform, imperial preference. First lord of admiralty (1922–24); secretary of state for colonies (1924–29) and for dominion affairs (1925–29), for India (1940–45); remembered esp. for speech in Commons that helped bring down government of Neville Chamberlain (1940). Author of *The Empire in the New Era* (1928), *The Forward View* (1935), *My Political Life* (1953–55).

Ames \ˈāmz\, Fisher. 1758–1808. American politician, b. Dedham, Mass. Member, U.S. House of Representatives (1789–97). Supported Hamilton's Federalist policies; opposed commercial retaliation against Great Britain (1794); spoke in favor of Jay's Treaty (1796).

Ames, Joseph. 1689–1759. English bibliographer and antiquarian. Compiler of *Typographical Antiquities* (1749), regarded as foundation of English bibliography.

Ames, Joseph Sweetman. 1864–1943. American physicist, b. Manchester, Vt. Member (1915–39), chairman (1927–39), National Advisory Committee for Aeronautics. Professor (1898–1926), president (1929–35), Johns Hopkins U.

Ames, Oakes. 1804–1873. American financier and politician, b. Easton, Mass. Made fortune in Oliver Ames & Sons, shovel manufacturers. Member, U.S. House of Representatives (1863–73). Involved in affairs of Union Pacific Railroad construction and Crédit Mobilier; sold shares of Crédit Mobilier to members of Congress to forestall investigation (1868); exposed by investigating committee (1872–73) and censured by vote of House of Representatives (1873).

Ames, Oakes. 1874–1950. American botanist, b. North Easton, Mass. Grandson of Oakes Ames (1804–1873). On staff (1899–1922), director (1910–22), Harvard botanical garden; professor of botany, Harvard (1926–41); noted expert on and collector of orchids; pioneer in economic botany. Author of *Economic Annuals and Human Cultures* (1939).

Ames, William. *Lat.* Ame•si•us \ə-ˈmē-sē-əs\. 1576–1633. English Puritan theologian. Forced to move to Netherlands (1610); engaged in debates and pamphlet controversy with Arminians; observer at Synod of Dort (1618–19); professor at Franeker (1622–33). Author of *Medulla Theologiae* (1623), *De Conscientia et Ejus Jure vel Casibus* (1632).

Ames, Winthrop. 1871–1937. American theatrical producer, b. North Easton, Mass. Grandson of Oakes Ames (1804–1873). Managed theaters in Boston and New York (1904–32); manager of New Theater, New York (1909–11); built Little Theater (1912) and Booth Theater, New York (1913); wrote and produced *Snow White* (1913), first play in New York City especially for children; revived Gilbert and Sullivan operas (1926–29).

Am·frye \äⁿ-frü̅-ā\, Guillaume. Abbé de Chau·lieu \shō-lyœ̅\. 1639–1720. French cleric and poet. Known as the "Anacreon of the Temple"; poems included "Ode sur l'inconstance," "La Retraite," "La Goutte," "Solitude de Fontenay."

Am·herst \ˈam-(ˌ)ərst, -ˌhərst\, Jeffrey. Baron Amherst. 1717–1797. English soldier. Commander of expedition against French America; captured fortress of Louisbourg (1758); commander in chief in North America (1759); captured Ticonderoga and Crown Point (1759); captured Montreal (1760). Governor general of British North America (1760–63); commander in chief of British army (1772–95). Created baron (1776), field marshal (1796). Amherst Coll. and several U.S. towns were named after him.

Amherst, William Pitt. Earl Amherst of Ara·kan \ˌär-ä-ˈkän, ˌar-ə-ˈkan\. 1773–1857. English diplomat. Nephew of Jeffrey Amherst. Envoy to Naples (1809–11), Peking (1816–17); governor general of India (1823–28); conducted successful war on king of Burma (1824–26); created earl (1826).

Am·hurst \ˈam-(ˌ)ərst, -ˌhərst\, Nicholas. 1697–1742. English poet and publicist. Expelled from Oxford (1719) for Whig sympathies; published series of satirical papers *Terrae Filius* (1721); wrote numerous occasional poems; founded and edited journal *The Craftsman* (1726–37), which achieved great popularity; imprisoned for publishing letter purportedly by Colley Cibber, attacking censorship of plays (1737).

Ami·ci \ä-ˈmē-chē\, Giovanni Battista. 1786–1863. Italian astronomer and optician. Professor at Modena (1815–25); astronomer to grand duke of Tuscany and director of observatory of Royal Museum, Florence (1831–59); devised (1837) hemispherical frontal lens that greatly improved resolution of compound microscope; invented (1840) oil-immersion technique; improved reflecting telescopes; invented Amici roof prism and Amici compound prism.

Amicis, Edmondo De. See De Amicis.

Amiel \am-yel\, Henri Frédéric. 1821–1881. Swiss poet and philosopher. Professor of aesthetics (1849) and moral philosophy (1853) at Geneva; author of *Journal intime* (pub. in part, 1883–84), an introspective diary kept from 1847.

ʿĀm·i·lī, al- \ˌal-äm-i-ˈlē\, Muḥammad ibn Ḥusayn Bahāʾi ad-Dīn. *Known also as* Shaykh Bahāʾī \ˈshīk-bə-ˈhī\. c.1546–c.1622. Iranian theologian, astronomer, and writer. Appointed chief judge of Muslim court at Isfahan by Shāh ʿAbbās I; stimulated revival of mathematics in Iran with his *Khulāṣah fi al-ḥisāb,* a standard textbook for 3 centuries; author also of verse, as *Nān o-ḥalvā,* the *Jāmiʿe Abbāsī* on Shīʿite jurisprudence, and many other works; designed Shāh Mosque in Isfahan.

Amīn, al- \al-a-ˈmēn\. *In full* Muḥammad al-Amīn. 787–813. ʿAbbāsid caliph of Baghdad (809–813). Son and successor of Harūn ar-Rashīd; opposed by his brother al-Maʾmūn, whom he wished to bar from succession; declared al-Maʾmūn a rebel and sent army against him; besieged in Baghdad (812–813); surrendered and killed.

Amiot *or* **Amyot** \ȧm-yō\, Jean-Joseph-Marie. 1718–1793. French Jesuit. Missionary to China (from 1750); author of books on China, a Manchu grammar, and a Manchu-French dictionary.

Am·ir Ali \a-ˈmēr-a-ˈlē\, Sayyid. 1849–1928. Indian Muslim jurist and writer. Founder of National Mohammedan Association (1877); judge of High Court, Calcutta (1890–1904); resident of England (from 1904); member of judicial committee of Privy Council (1909). Favored continued British rule in India as alternative to Hindu dominance. Author of *Critical Examination of the Life and Teachings of Mohammed* (1873), *Spirit of Islam* (1891).

Am·īr Khos·row \a-ˈmēr-käs-ˈrau̇\. 1253–1325. Indian poet and historian. Son of Turkish officer; patronized by sultans of Delhi; works included historical poems *Nuh Sipihr* and *Tughluq-nāmah,* collection of five idylls called *Khamsah* in imitation of Neẓāmī, prose treatise *Khazāʾin al-futūh* or *Tārīkh-e ʿAlāʾī.* Considered one of greatest Persian-language poets of India.

Am·man \ˈäm-ˌän\, Jost. 1539–1591. Swiss painter and printmaker. Worked in Nürnberg; executed many woodcuts for editions of Bible (1564–71), 115 woodcuts for a book on arts and trades (1568, with poems by Hans Sachs), copperplate engravings of a series of kings of France, etc.

Am·man *or* **Am·mann** \ˈäm-ˌän\ *or* **Amen** \ˈäm-ən\, Jacob. c.1644–c.1730. Swiss Mennonite bishop. Led (1693–97) schism from Mennonite church in Switzerland and Alsace; followers known as Amish or Amish Mennonites.

Am·mann \ˈäm-ˌän\, Othmar Herman. 1879–1965. American engineer, b. Schaffhausen, Switzerland. To U.S. (1904); with Pennsylvania Steel Co. (1905–12); chief assistant to Gustav Lindenthal (1912–23); in private practice (1923–30). Helped Lindenthal design and build Hell Gate Bridge, New York City, and Ohio River Bridge, Sciotoville, O.; designed and built George Washington Bridge, New York (opened 1931). As chief engineer (1930–37) and director of engineering (1937–39) of Port of New York Authority, supervised building of Bayonne Bridge, Outerbridge Crossing, Goethals Bridge, Lincoln Tunnel, Bronx-Whitestone Bridge, Triborough Bridge; member of board of engineers in charge of construction of Golden Gate Bridge, San Francisco (opened 1937); in private practice (from 1939), designed with C.S. Whitney the Throgs Neck Bridge, Dulles International Airport, Washington, D.C., and Verrazano Narrows Bridge (opened 1965).

Am·man·na·ti \ˌäm-än-ˈnä-tē\, Bartolommeo. 1511–1592. Italian sculptor and architect. The leading exponent of Florentine Mannerism; principal works included the Ponta Sta. Trinità, Palazzo Giugni, Palazzo Griffoni, extension of Palazzo Pitti, and Fontana del Nettuno, all in Florence, and villa of Pope Julian and del Monte tomb in Rome.

Am·mers-Kül·ler \ˈäm-ər-ˈskᵫl-ər\, Johanna van. 1884–1966. Dutch writer. Author of plays, children's books, and novels including *De verzwegen strijd* (1916), *Maskerade* (1919), *De opstandigen* (1925), *Vrouwenkruistocht* (1930), *Heeren, knechten en vrouwen* (1934), *Elzelina* (1940), *Ma* (1942), *Het scharlaken wambuis* (1955).

Am·mi·a·nus Mar·cel·li·nus \ˌam-ē-ˈā-nəs-ˌmär-sə-ˈlī-nəs\. c.330–395. Roman soldier and historian. Of noble Greek family; served under Constantius II in Gaul and Persia. Author of *Rerum gestarum libri,* Latin history of Roman Empire from Nerva to death of Valens (96–378), constituting a continuation of Tacitus' history; of 31 original books, 18 are extant, covering period from 353 to 378.

Am·mo·ni·us Her·mi·ae \ə-ˈmō-nē-əs-ˈhər-mē-ˌī\. fl. c.550 A.D. Greek philosopher. Head of Alexandrian school; author of commentaries on Aristotle as *On the Categories,* on the *Organon,* on *Prior Analytics,* and on Porphyry's *Isagoge.*

Ammonius Sac·cas \-ˈsak-əs\. d. after 242 A.D.? Alexandrian philosopher. Founder of Neoplatonism; teacher of Longinus, Origen, and esp. of Plotinus; almost nothing is known of his doctrines.

Amon·tons \ȧ-mōⁿ-tōⁿ\, Guillaume. 1663–1705. French physicist. Studied friction, thermometry; invented a hygrometer (1687), a perfected barometer (1695), air-pressure thermometer (1702).

Amo·ry \ˈām-(ə-)rē\, Thomas. 1691?–1788. British author of Irish descent. Author of *Memoirs, Containing Lives of Several Ladies of Great Britain* (1755) and fictional autobiography *Life of John Buncle, Esq.* (1756–66).

Amos \ˈā-məs\. 8th century B.C. Hebrew prophet. Herdsman of Tekoa, near Bethlehem, whose reproofs, exhortations, and visions foretold destruction of kingdom of Israel; earliest prophet to have a book of the Bible named for him.

Am·père \äⁿ-per\, André-Marie. 1775–1836. French physicist. Professor at École Polytechnique, Paris (1805), U. of Paris (1820), Collège de France (1824); inspector general of French university system (1808–36). Following on Ørsted's discovery (1820), formulated mathematical basis of electrodynamics, including Ampère's law on force between two electric currents. Invented astatic needle, which made invention of astatic galvanometer possible. The ampere, unit of electric current, is named after him.

Ampère, Jean-Jacques-Antoine. 1800–1864. French historian and philologist. Son of André-Marie Ampère. Professor, U. of Paris (1830–33), Collège de France (1833–64); author of *De l'histoire de la poésie* (1830), *Histoire littéraire de la France avant le douzième siècle* (1839–40), *Histoire de la formation de la langue française* (1841), *Promenade en Amérique: États-Unis, Cuba et Mexique* (1855, on a journey with Prosper Mérimée), *L'Histoire romaine à Rome* (1861–64).

Am·ram bar Shesh·na \ˈam-rəm-ˈbär-ˈshēsh-nä\. d. 875? Jewish Talmudist. Head of Talmudic academy at Sura, Babylonia; composed *Siddur Rav Amram,* first complete domestic and synagogal liturgical cycle for the year.

Ampthill, Barons. See Russell family.

ʿAmri. See Omri.

ʿAmr ibn al-ʿAṣ \am-ˌrüb-nə-ˈläs\. d. 663 A.D. Arab general. Converted to Islām (629); sent by Muḥammad to convert Arabs of Oman; commanded one of caliph Abū Bakr's three military forces; conquered southwestern Palestine; undertook, perhaps on own initiative, conquest of Egypt (639); seized Pelusium and defeated Byzantines at Heliopolis (640); entered Alexandria (642); first Muslim governor of Egypt (642–644); founded city of al-Fusṭāt (now Cairo); sent to subdue Alexandria (645–646); later falsely accused of ordering destruction of Alexandrine Library; sided with Muʿāwiyah against ʿAlī in controversy over succession to caliphate; named governor of Egypt (661).

ʿAmr ibn Kul·thum \am-ˌrüb-nə-ku̇l-ˈthüm\. 6th century A.D. Pre-Islāmic Arab poet. Author of one of odes comprising the anthology *al-Muʿallaqāt.*

Ams·dorf \ˈäms-ˌdȯrf\, Nikolaus von. 1483–1565. German Protestant theologian. Professor at Wittenberg (1511); supported Luther; aided in translation of Bible; superintended Jena edition of Luther's works; opposed Melanchthon's later liberal views. Bishop of Naumburg (1541–47).

Amund·sen \ˈäm-u̇n-sən\, Roald. 1872–1928. Norwegian explorer. Navigated Northwest Passage and fixed position of North Magnetic Pole (1903–06); first to reach South Pole (Dec. 1911). Flew across North Pole with Lincoln

\ə\ **abut** \ᵊ\ **kitten,** *Fr.* **table** \ər\ **further** \a\ **ash** \ā\ **ace** \ä\ **cot, cart** \au̇\ **out** \ch\ **chin** \e\ **bet** \ē\ **easy** \g\ **go** \i\ **hit** \ī\ **ice** \j\ **job** \ŋ\ **sing** \ō\ **go** \ȯ\ **law** \ȯi\ **boy** \th\ **both** \t͟h\ **the** \ü\ **loot** \u̇\ **foot** \y\ **yet** \zh\ **vision** \ȧ, ḵ, ⁿ, œ, œ̅, ᵫ, ᵫ̅, ʸ\ *see* **Guide to Pronunciation**

Ellsworth and Umberto Nobile (1926); disappeared on flight to rescue Nobile who was lost returning from North Pole. Author of *North West Passage* (1908), *The South Pole* (1912), *The North East Passage* (1918–20), *Our Polar Flight* (with Lincoln Ellsworth; 1925), *First Crossing of the Polar Sea* (with Lincoln Ellsworth; 1927), *My Life as an Explorer* (1927).

Amyn·tas \ə-'min-təs\. Name of three kings of Macedonia:

Amyntas I. d. c.498 B.C. Fifth in descent from Perdiccas; acknowledged himself tributary vassal to Persian sovereign, Darius Hystaspis.

Amyntas II. d. 370 or 369 B.C. King (c.393–370 or 369). Laid foundation for emergence of Macedonia as Greek power, continued by son Philip II.

Amyntas III. d. 336 B.C. King (360–359). Grandson of Amyntas II; excluded from throne (359) by his uncle Philip II of Macedon; executed (336) by Alexander the Great for plotting against him.

Amyot \ám-yō\, Jacques. 1513–1593. French prelate and scholar. Professor at Bourges (1536–46); for his translation of *Aethiopica* of Heliodorus, given abbey of Bellozane by Francis I; named tutor to sons of Henry II (1557), grand almoner (1560), bishop of Auxerre (1570). Translated part of *Bibliotheca historica* of Diodorus Siculus (1554), *Daphnis et Chloé* of Longus (1559), *Bioi Paralleloi* of Plutarch (1559), *Opera Moralia* of Plutarch (1572). His French Plutarch, *Les Vies parallèles,* a great contribution to French Humanism and Renaissance idea of tragic hero; source of Sir Thomas North's English version (1579).

Amyot, Jean-Joseph-Marie. See AMIOT.

Amy·raut \á-mē-rō\, Moïse. 1596–1664. French Protestant theologian. Professor at Saumur (from 1633); propounded a liberal Calvinism; influential in public affairs.

Amyr·tae·us \ˌam-ēr-'tā-əs\ of Sa·is \'sā-əs\. d. 399 B.C. Egyptian king (404–399 B.C.). Led successful revolt (404) against Achaemenian rule in Delta; gained control of Upper Egypt (400); reign constituted whole of 28th dynasty.

An·a·char·sis \ˌan-ə-'kär-səs\. 6th? century B.C. Scythian prince and philosopher. Supposed to have visited Athens and become acquainted with Solon; reputed author of many epigrams and letters; remembered as type of primitive virtue; sometimes counted among Seven Wise Men.

Anacharsis Cloots. See VAL-DE-GRÂCE.

An·a·cle·tus \ˌan-ə-'klēt-əs\ *or* **Cle·tus** \'klēt-əs\ *or* **An·en·cletus** \ˌan-ən-\. Saint. d. 88 or 91. Second pope (76–88 or 79–91) following St. Peter.

Anacletus II. *Orig.* Pietro Pier·le·o·ni \ˌpyär-lā-'ō-nē\. d. 1138. Antipope (1130–38) in opposition to Innocent II. Cardinal (1116); elected pope by majority of cardinals and forced Innocent to flee to France; besieged in Rome by Lothair (1132); excommunicated (1134) by Council of Pisa convoked by Innocent.

Anac·re·on \ə-'nak-rē-ən\. c.582–c.485 B.C. Greek lyric poet. Said to have served in Greek forces resisting invasion of Cyrus the Great (545); reputed tutor and later courtier of Polycrates of Samos; after death of Polycrates, invited by Hipparchus to Athens. Famed for satires and esp. for lyrics celebrating love and wine. Only fragments of his verse are extant.

Anan ben Da·vid \á-'nän-ben-'dā-vəd\. 8th century A.D. Jewish religious leader in Persia. Unsuccessful candidate for exilarch (c.765); founded heretical antirabbinical sect Ananites, forerunner of Karaite sect; author of *Sefer ha-mitzwot,* code of Ananites, rejecting Talmud and rabbinate.

Ānan·da \'än-ən-də\. 6th century B.C. Favorite disciple of Buddha. Cousin and early convert of Buddha; later his personal attendant.

Ananda Mahidol. See RAMA VIII.

An·as·ta·sia \ˌan-ə-'stā-zh(ē-)ə, -sh(ē-)ə\. *Russ.* Anastasiya Nikolayevna. 1901–1918. Russian princess. Youngest daughter of Czar Nicholas II; imprisoned and assassinated with family. Various women later claimed to be she.

An·as·ta·si·us \ˌan-ə-'stā-zh(ē-)əs, -sh(ē-)əs\. Name of four popes:

Anastasius I. d. 401. Pope (399–401). Condemned writings of Origen.

Anastasius II. d. 498. Pope (496–498). Attempted to heal Acacian schism; received emissary from Byzantine supporter of Acacius, thus causing schism in Roman church; died before controversy was resolved.

Anastasius III. d. 913. Pope (911–913). Reigned during dominance of Theophylactus and thus wielded little authority.

Anastasius IV. *Orig.* Cor·ra·do di Su·bur·ra \kō-'rä-dō-dē-sü-'bür-rä\. 1073–1154. Pope (1153–54). Cardinal bishop of Sabina (from c.1126); as pope settled disputes with Frederick I Barbarossa over see of Magdeburg and with St. William of York.

Anastasius. Name of two rulers of Eastern Roman Empire:

Anastasius I. 430?–518. Emperor (491–518). Financial official and bodyguard under Emperor Zeno; chosen to succeed Zeno by latter's widow Ariadne, whom he shortly married; instituted tax reforms; resettled rebellious Isaurians in Thrace; put down revolt in Asia Minor (492–496); fought indecisive war with Persia (502–505); built Anastasian Wall (512) from Propontis (Sea of Marmara) to Euxine (Black Sea) to keep out Bulgarians and Slavs; forced to suppress riots and insurrections, esp. by his commander in Thrace, Vitalianus, caused by his Monophysite beliefs.

Anastasius II. *Orig.* Artemis. d. 721. Emperor (713–715). Chosen to succeed Philippicus; reversed Monothelite policies of Philippicus; organized strong army and navy; overthrown by mutiny led by Theodosius; retired to Thessalonica and became monk; slain by Leo III.

Anastasius. *Called* Anastasius Bib·li·o·the·car·i·us \ˌbib-lē-ō-thə-'kar-ē-əs\, *i.e.* the Librarian. c.810–c.878. Roman scholar. Cardinal priest of St. Marcellus, Rome (c.848); deposed (853); stood as antipope (855–858) to Benedict III; reconciled and made librarian of the Vatican (858–878); effectively disputed Photius of Constantinople and helped formulate anti-Byzantine doctrines; attended and translated *Acts* of Council of Constantinople (869–870).

Anastasius Si·nai·ta \-si-'nī-tä\. Saint. 7th century. Palestinian monk. Abbot of Monastery of St. Catherine on Mt. Sinai; author of works on dogma, on monastic life, on biblical exegesis, of a tract against the Jews, and works on heresy, esp. the *Ho dēgos* (c.685) against Monophysites.

An·a·to·li \á-ná-tó-lē\, Jacob. c.1194–1258. French Jewish philosopher. Practiced medicine; translated works of Averroës (Ibn Rushd); wrote *Malmad ha-Talmidim,* collection of philosophical homilies.

An·aw·rah·ta \ˌan-aù-'rät-ə\ *or* **An·i·rud·dha** \ˌan-i-'rüd-də\. d. 1077. First king of all Burma (1044–77). Originally king of Anya (Upper Burma); conquered Mon states of Lower Burma, extending Burmese dominion to Irawaddy delta, north to Bhamo, west to Arakan; converted to Theravāda Buddhism; built many pagodas and temples in capital Pagan.

An·ax·ag·o·ras \ˌan-ak-'sag-ə-rəs\. c.500–c.428 B.C. Greek philosopher. Taught in Athens for 30 years (c.480–450), his pupils including Pericles, Euripides, and possibly Socrates; charged with impiety (an indirect attack on Pericles) and banished from Athens for life. First to introduce dualistic explanation of universe: held that all natural objects are composed of infinitesimally small particles containing mixtures of all qualities, and that mind or intelligence (*nous*) acts upon masses of these particles to produce objects.

An·ax·an·dri·des \ˌan-ak-'san-drə-ˌdēz\. d. c.520 B.C. King of Sparta (c.560–c.520 B.C.). Co-king with Ariston; father of Cleomenes I.

Anax·i·man·der \ə-ˌnak-sə-'man-dər\. 610–c.547 B.C. Greek astronomer and philosopher. Thought to have been disciple of Thales. Credited with discovery of obliquity of the ecliptic, introduction of sundial, and invention of geographical maps. Taught that primary substance (*apeiron,* i.e. unlimited) is eternal and indestructible matter containing within itself all contraries, such as heat and cold, moist and dry, and that the phenomenal universe evolved through the separation and the creative reunion of these contraries.

An·ax·im·e·nes \ˌan-ak-'sim-ə-ˌnēz\ of Lamp·sa·cus \'lamp-sə-kəs\. c.380–c.320 B.C. Greek rhetorician and historian. Wrote histories of Philip of Macedon and of Greece, and an epic on Alexander; accompanied Alexander to Persia; probable author of *Rhetorica ad Alexandrum,* once attributed to Aristotle.

Anaximenes of Mi·le·tus \mī-'lēt-əs, mi-\. fl. c.545 B.C. Greek philosopher. Third of the three great thinkers of Miletus, following Thales and Anaximander; held that air is the primary substance and that all things are derived from it by varying degrees of compression or rarefaction.

An·chi·e·ta \ˌäⁿ-shē-'e-tə\, José de. 1534–1597. Portuguese missionary. Entered Society of Jesus (1551); to Brazil (1553); helped found São Paulo and Rio de Janeiro; helped found colleges at Rio, Bahia, Pernambuco; Jesuit provincial of Brazil (1577–87). Author of poetry, esp. mystical *De beata virgine dei matre Maria,* of religious plays, of a Tupí Indian grammar, and of works on Brazil. Called "Apostle of Brazil."

An Chung-shik \'än-'chüŋ-'shēk\. *Also known as* Shim·jon \'shēm-'jōn\, *i.e.* Spirit Field. 1861–1919. Korean painter. Trained in China; became master of popular Southern style; master calligrapher; adopted certain Western techniques, as perspective; helped found (1918) Korean Association of Painters and Calligraphers.

An·cil·lon \äⁿ-sē-yōⁿ\, Charles. 1659–1715. French jurist and writer. Argued unsuccessfully against revocation of Edict of Nantes and then moved to Brandenburg (1686); appointed judge of French Protestant exile community by Elector Frederick III (1686); director of Academy of Nobles (1687); historiographer to Elector Frederick (1699); helped Leibnitz found Academy of Berlin (1700). Author of *Réflexions politiques* (1686), *L'Irrévocabilité de l'édit de Nantes* (1688), *Histoire de l'établissement des Français réfugiés dans les états de S.A.E. Brandenbourg* (1690).

Ancillon, David. 1617–1692. French Protestant clergyman. Following revocation of Edict of Nantes (1685) became head of French Protestant exile communities in Frankfurt am Main and Berlin; author of *Traité de la tradition* (1657).

Ancillon, Johann Peter Friedrich, *called also* Jean-Pierre-Frédéric. 1767–1837. Prussian politician. Great-grandson of David Ancillon. Professor of history, Berlin Military Academy (from 1792); court historiographer (1803) and tutor to future Frederick William IV (1810); member (from 1814) and head (1832–37) of Prussian foreign ministry; worked to preserve Metternich's reactionary policies and to combat liberalism. Author of *Tableau des révolutions du système politique de l'Europe depuis le XVe siècle* (1803–05).

Anc·kar·ström \'äŋ-kär-ˌstrœm\, Jakob Johan. 1762–1792. Swedish army officer. Assassin of King Gustavus III of Sweden (1792).

Anc·kar·svärd \'äŋ-kärs-ˌverd\, Carl Henrik. Count. 1782–1865. Swedish politician. A leader of coup d'etat against King Gustav IV (1809); continued to champion liberal democratic principles in Riksdag.

Ancona, Allessandro d'. See D'ANCONA.

Ancre, Marquis d'. See CONCINI.

An·cus Mar·ci·us \'aŋ-kəs-'smär-sh(ē-)əs\. 7th century B.C. Fourth legendary king (642–617) of early Rome. A Latin, grandson of Numa Pompilius. Credited by Livy with settlement of Aventine Hill, founding of Ostia, etc.

Anda. See ALTAN KHAN.

An·ders \'än-ders\, Władysław. 1892–1970. Polish soldier. Served in Russian army in World War I; in Polish army in Russo–Polish War (1919–20); fought both Germany and Soviet Union at beginning of World War II (1939); captured by Soviet forces and imprisoned (1939–41); allowed to form Polish force, which he led into Iran and Iraq (1942); commanded Polish II Corps in Italy, capturing Monte Cassino (1944); to Great Britain (1945); a post-war leader of anti-Communist Polish exiles.

Andersen. See also ANDERSON, ANDERSSEN, and ANDERSSON.

An·der·sen \'än-ər-sən, *Angl* 'an-dər-sən\, Hans Christian. 1805–1875. Danish author. Born in poverty, educated by patrons; attracted attention with *Fodrejse fra Holmens Kanal til Østpynten af Amager* (1829), a tale in the style of E.T.A. Hoffmann; achieved success with novels *Improvisatoren* (1835), *O.T.* (1836), *Kun en spillemand* (1837) and play *Mulatten* (1840); best known for volumes of *Eventyr, fortalte for børn* ("Tales, Told for Children"; 1835, 1843, 1858, 1861) containing such tales as "Little Claus and Big Claus," "Princess and the Pea," "Tinderbox," "Ugly Duckling," "The Nightingale," "Snow Queen," "Emperor's New Clothes," "Steadfast Tin Soldier," "Little Fir Tree" written in homely vernacular; also wrote travel books and volumes of autobiography, esp. *Mit Lius Eventyr* (1855).

An·der·sen \'än-der-sən\, Tryggve. 1866–1920. Norwegian writer. A leader of Norwegian Neoromantic movement; known esp. for story cycle *I cancelliraadens dage* (1897) and novel *Mot kvaeld* (1900).

Andersen Nexø, Martin. See NEXØ.

Anderson. See also ANDERSEN and ANDERSSON.

An·der·son \'an-dər-sən\, Alexander. 1775–1870. American engraver, b. New York City. Made first wood engravings in America (1794), for *Looking Glass for the Mind.*

Anderson, Carl Thomas. 1865–1948. American cartoonist, b. Madison, Wis. Creator (1932) of comic strip "Henry."

Anderson, Sir Edmund. 1530–1605. English jurist. Lord chief justice of common pleas (1582); took part in trials of Mary, Queen of Scots (1586), and Sir Walter Raleigh (1603) among other notables; known for harshness toward Catholics.

Anderson, Elizabeth, *nee* Gar·rett \'gar-ət\. 1836–1917. English physician. m. (1871) J.G.S. Anderson. Studied medicine privately after being refused admission to medical schools; licensed (1865); general medical attendant to St. Mary's Dispensary, London (1866), later known as New Hospital, where she instituted medical courses for women. First English woman elected mayor (Aldeburgh, Suffolk, 1908). New Hospital renamed (1918) Elizabeth Garrett Anderson Hospital.

Anderson, Elizabeth, *nee* Mil·bank \'mil-ˌbaŋk\. 1850–1921. American philanthropist, b. New York City. m. (1887) Abram A. Anderson. Created Milbank Memorial Fund (1905) with eventual endowment of over $9 million, income to be used to "improve the physical, mental, and moral condition of humanity."

Anderson, James. 1739–1808. Scottish economist. Author of *An Inquiry into the Nature of the Corn Laws* (1777), anticipating Ricardo's theory of rent; edited *The Bee,* Edinburgh (1790–94); invented a two-horse plow without wheels, called Scotch plow.

Anderson, Sir John. Viscount Wa·ver·ley \'wā-vər-lē\. 1882–1958. British civil servant. Entered colonial office (1905); permanent undersecretary, Home Office (1922–32); governor of Bengal (1932–37); M.P. (1938–50); lord privy seal (1938–39); home secretary and minister of home security (1939–40) in charge of interning of enemy aliens, evacuations, and building of air-raid shelters (one type of shelter being named for him); lord president of the council (1940–43); chancellor of the exchequer (1943–45); created viscount (1952).

Anderson, John Henry. 1814–1874. Scottish magician. Began performing (1831) as "Professor Anderson, Wizard of the North"; to London (1840); toured U.S. (1851–53); devised "gun trick," appearing to catch bullet in teeth; first magician successfully to employ advertising.

Anderson, Joseph Reid. 1813–1892. American soldier and manufacturer, b. Botetourt Co., Va. Engineer, U.S. army (1836–37); agent (1841–48), owner (from 1848), Tredegar Iron Works, Richmond, Va.; brigadier general, Confederate army (1861–62); principal supplier of heavy ordnance to Confederacy (1861–65).

Anderson, Sir Kenneth Arthur Noel. 1891–1959. British general. Served in World War I, in India (1930–31), at Dunkirk (1940); commander, Allied 1st Army (1942–43); captured Tunis (1943); governor of Gibraltar (1947–52); general (1949).

Anderson, Margaret Caroline. 1893?–1973. American editor, b. Indianapolis. Founded (1914) *Little Review,* organ of "Chicago Renaissance," publishing works of Sandburg, Bodenheim, Hecht, Sherwood Anderson, W.C. Williams, Amy Lowell, Wallace Stevens, etc.; published *Little Review* in Paris (1924–29).

Anderson, Mary. 1859–1940. American actress, b. Sacramento, Calif. Made debut as Juliet (Louisville, Ky., 1875); New York debut in *Lady of Lyons* (1877); achieved great popular success in Shakespeare, *Guy Mannering, Ingomar* (London debut, 1883); retired in England (1890).

Anderson, Maxwell. 1888–1959. American playwright, b. Atlantic, Pa. Journalist until success of play *White Desert* (1923); author of *What Price Glory* (with Laurence Stallings, 1924), *First Flight* (1925), *The Buccaneer* (1925), *Elizabeth the Queen* (verse drama, 1930), *Mary of Scotland* (verse drama, 1933), *Both Your Houses* (1933, Pulitzer prize), *Valley Forge* (1934), *Winterset* (1935), *High Tor* (1936), *Knickerbocker Holiday* (musical with Kurt Weill, 1938), *Key Largo* (1939), *The Eve of St. Mark* (1942), *Anne of the Thousand Days* (1948), *Lost in the Stars* (1949), *The Bad Seed* (1954).

Anderson, Rasmus Björn. 1846–1936. American author, editor, and diplomat, b. Albion, Wis. Professor, U. of Wisconsin (1869–83); U.S. minister to Denmark (1885–89); president, Wisconsin Life Insurance Co. (1895–1922). Author of *The Scandinavian Languages* (1873), *America not Discovered by Columbus* (1874), *Norse Mythology* (1875), *Viking Tales of the North* (1877), etc.; translator of many Scandinavian works.

Anderson, Richard Heron. 1821–1879. American soldier, b. Statesburg, S.C. Confederate brigadier general (1861), major general (1862), lieutenant general, temporary (1864); saved Spotsylvania, Va. (1864).

Anderson, Robert. 1750–1830. Scottish editor. Edited *A Complete Edition of the Poets of Great Britain* (14 vols., 1792–1807).

Anderson, Robert. 1805–1871. American soldier, b. near Louisville, Ky. In command of Fort Sumter (Charleston, S.C.) at time of Confederate attack (April 1861).

Anderson, Sherwood. 1876–1941. American writer, b. Camden, O. Author of novels *Windy McPherson's Son* (1916), *Marching Men* (1917), *Poor White* (1920), *Many Marriages* (1922), *Dark Laughter* (1925), *Beyond Desire* (1932), *Kit Brandon* (1936); story collections *Winesburg, Ohio* (1919), *Triumph of the Egg* (1921), *Horses and Men* (1923), *Death in the Woods* (1933); autobiographical *Story Teller's Story* (1924), *Tar: A Midwest Childhood* (1926). A pioneer in psychological naturalism, use of vernacular prose.

An·ders·sen \'än-dər-sən\, Adolf. 1818–1879. German chess player. Considered world's strongest player from victory at first modern international tournament (London, 1851) to defeat by Paul Morphy (1858); again from 1861 to defeat by Steinitz (1866).

Andersson. See also ANDERSEN and ANDERSON.

An·ders·son \'än-dərs-ˌsȯn\, Dan, *in full* Daniel. 1888–1920. Swedish poet and writer. Author of *Kolarhistorier* (1914) and *Kolvaktarens visor* (1915), poems on charcoal burners that made them beloved folk figures; also of *Svarta ballader* (poems, 1917) and autobiographical novels *De tre hemlösa* (1918), *David Ramms arv* (1919).

Andersson, Karell Johan. 1827–1867. Swedish explorer. In southwestern Africa (1851–55), discovering Lake Ngami (1854); penetrated to Okavango River (1858–59).

Andersson, Johan Gunnar. 1874–1960. Swedish geologist and archaeologist. Discovered (1921) first evidence of Neolithic culture in Yellow River valley of China; predicted (1921) discovery (1927) of fossil hominid *Sinanthropus* (Peking man).

Andino, Tiburcio Carías. See CARÍAS ANDINO.

An·dō \än-dō\ Shōeki. fl. c.1700. Japanese philosopher. One of first Japanese to study European thought; criticized feudal society under shogunate; projected utopian peasant society that foreshadowed imperial restoration.

An·doc·i·des \an-'däs-ə-ˌdēz\. c.440–after 391 B.C. Athenian politician and orator. Exiled (415–403 B.C.) after informing on those responsible for mutilation of sacred herms; again exiled (392) on failure of peace mission to Sparta.

An·dra·da e Sil·va \aⁿ(n)-'drä-t͟hä-ē-'sil-vä\, José Bonifácio de. 1763?–1838. Brazilian statesman and geologist. Professor at Coimbra, secretary of Lisbon Academy (1812); returned to Brazil (1819); headed ministry of regent Dom

Pedro (1822); urged independence; prime minister under Emperor Pedro I (1822–23); exiled (1823–29) for opposition to emperor's Portuguese advisers; tutor to Pedro II.

An·drade \'an-ˌdrād\, Edward Neville da Costa. 1887–1971. English physicist. Professor, Artillery Coll., Woolwich (1920–28), U. of London (1928–50). Author of *The Structure of the Atom, The Mechanism of Nature,* etc.

An·dra·de \ȧ^{n}(n)-'drȧ-th̲ā\, Mario de. *In full* Mario Raul de Morais Andrade. 1893–1945. Brazilian poet, novelist, and critic. In volumes of poetry *Há uma gota de sangue en cada poema* (1917), *Paulicéia desvairada* (1922) introduced Brazilian vernacular and Modernism to Brazilian poetry; also wrote novels as *Macunaíma* (1928). As director of Department of Culture, São Paulo (1935–45), fostered research into Brazilian folklore and music.

Andrade, Oswald de. *In full* José Oswald de Sousa Andrade. 1890–1954. Brazilian poet and novelist. A leader of Modernist movement in Brazilian arts; issued Modernist-nationalist manifesto *Pau-Brasil* (1925); founded Antropofagia group; author of novels as *Memórias séntimentais de João Miramar* (1924), *Serafim Ponte Grande* (1934), *Marco Zero* (1943).

An·drag·o·ras \an-'drag-ə-rəs\. d. c.238 B.C. Seleucid satrap of Parthia. Assumed sovereign rule, issuing coinage bearing own image; overthrown by Parni tribesmen led by Arsaces.

An·drás·sy \'än-ˌdrȧ-shē\, Gyula. Count. 1823–1890. Hungarian politician. Follower of Kossuth; entered Diet (1847); exiled for participation in revolt of 1848; obtained amnesty (1857); again elected to diet (1861); vice-president of diet (1865); supported Deák's dual-realm compromise of 1867; first constitutional prime minister of Hungary (1867); foreign minister of Austria-Hungary (1871–79); maneuvered to check growth of Russian and Slavic power in Balkans; delegate to Congress of Berlin (1878), where he agreed to Austrian occupation of Bosnia and Hercegovina; signed Austro-German alliance (1879). His son ¶Count Gyula (1860–1929) entered Austrian Abgeordnetenhaus (1884); minister of interior (1906–09); foreign minister (1918); deputy in Hungarian National Assembly (1922); imprisoned (1921) for implication in attempt to restore Charles I to throne.

An·dré \'an-drē, 'än-(ˌ)drā\, John. 1750–1780. British soldier. To Canada (1774); aide-de-camp to General Grey and Gen. Sir Henry Clinton; made adjutant general by Clinton, with rank of major. Appointed to negotiate with Benedict Arnold for betrayal of West Point to British (1779–80); captured while returning toward New York in civilian clothes with incriminating papers in his boots; hanged as spy.

An·dreä \än-'drā-e\, Jakob. 1528–1590. German Lutheran theologian and writer. Active in organizing Lutheran Church throughout Germany and in producing *Formula of Concord,* second part of *Book of Concord,* published (1580) to end controversies among Lutheran groups.

An·drea da Bar·be·ri·no \än-'drā-ä-dä-ˌbär-bā-'rē-nō\. c.1370–c.1432. Italian writer and balladeer, b. Barberino. Author or compiler of epic tales, as *I reali di Francia* from Charlemagne legends and *Guerin meschino* or *Guerrino il meschino,* a picaresque narrative, and of romances as *Aspromonte, Le storie Narbonesi, La storia di Ugone, La discesa di Guerino all' inferno.*

Andrea da Fi·ren·ze \-fē-'ränt-sä\. *Known also as* Andrea di Bo·na·iu·ti \ˌbō-nä-'yü-tē\. fl. c.1337–77. Florentine painter. Follower of Giotto and of Andrea Orcagna; known chiefly for frescoes in Sta. Maria Novella, Florence (commissioned 1365); believed to have painted murals in Campo Santo cemetery, Pisa.

Andrea d'Agno·lo \-dän-'yō-lō\. *Known as* Andrea del Sar·to \-del-'sär-tō\. 1486–1530. Florentine artist. Associated esp. with church and convent of SS. Annunziata, for which he did frescoes (1509–14, 1525); received patronage of Francis I of France (1518–19) and Pope Leo X (1519–21) but little work resulted. Other works included series of frescoes on life of John the Baptist for Chiostro dello Scalzo, Florence (1511–26); *Noli Me Tangere* (1510); *Marriage of St. Catherine* (1512–13); *Madonna of the Harpies* (1517); *Pietà* (c.1520); many self-portraits and portraits of his wife. Concerned with atmosphere, color, expression of emotion; notable for increasing perfection of drawings. His work and workshop strongly influenced younger Florentine artists.

Andrea del Verrocchio. See VERROCCHIO.

Andrea di Bar·to·lo \-dē-'bär-tō-lō\. *In full* Andrea di Bartolo de Si·mo·ne \-dā-sē-'mō-nā\. *Known as* Andrea del Cas·ta·gno \del-käs-'tän-yō\. c.1421–1457. Florentine painter, b. near Castagno. Influenced by Masacchio; executed works in naturalistic manner with attention to modeling and light. Works included *Last Supper* and other frescoes in S. Apollonia, Florence; fresco portraits in Villa Pandolfini; portrait of Niccolò da Tolentino in Florence cathedral; *Trinity with St. Jerome, Assumption of the Virgin,* etc.

Andrea di Cione. See Andrea CIONE.

An·dre·a·ni \ˌän-drā-'än-ē\, Andrea. fl. c.1580–c.1625. Italian engraver on wood. Known esp. for his chiaroscuro printing; best known works included series of 12 prints on *Trionfo di Giulio Cesare,* and prints after Mantegna, Ligozzi, Beccafumi, etc.

Andreas Capellanus. See ANDRÉ LE CHAPELAIN.

An·dre·as-Sa·lo·mé \än-'drā-ä(s)-'zä-lō-ˌmā\, Lou, *nee* Salomé. 1861–1937. German writer. Daughter of German general in Russian service; m. (1887) F.C. Andreas; closely associated with Nietzsche, Rilke, Freud. Author of novels, stories, poems, nonfiction, including *Im Kampf um Gott* (1885), *Friedrich Nietzsche in seinen Werken* (1894), *Ruth* (1895), *Ma* (1901), *Die Erotik* (1910), *Das Haus* (1921), *Der Teufel und seine Grossmutter* (1922), *Rainer-Maria Rilke* (1928), *Mein Dank an Freud* (1931).

An·dree \'än-dre-ə\, Karl Theodor. 1808–1875. German geographer. Founded (1862) periodical *Globus;* author of *Nordamerika in geographischen und geschichtlichen Umrissen* (1854), *Geographische Wanderungen* (1859), *Geographie des Welthandels* (1862–77).

An·drée \ȧn-'drā\, Salomon August. 1854–1897. Swedish engineer and explorer. Lost while attempting flight in balloon to North Pole from Spitsbergen.

An·dre·i·ni \ˌän-drā-'ē-nē\, Francesco. 1548–1624. Italian actor. In company of Flaminio Scala, where he met his wife (m. 1578) ¶Isabella, *nee* Ca·na·li \kä-'nä-lē\ (1562–1604); together they formed Compagnia dei Gelosi, one of most famous commedia dell'arte troupes; toured Europe successfully. Their son ¶Giovambattista (c.1578–c.1654) was member of parents' company; formed (1601) Compagnia dei Fedeli and toured Italy (to 1613); wrote play *Adamo* (1613), from which Milton reputedly got idea for *Paradise Lost.*

An·dre·is \än-'drā-ēs\, Felix de, *in full* Andrew James Felix Bartholomew de. 1778–1820. Italian missionary in America. Entered Vincentian Order (1797); ordained (1802); to U.S. at head of group of missionaries (1816); to St. Louis as vicar general of Vincentians (1817); administered and taught in two colleges, established novitiate; gained reputation for sanctity.

An·dré le Chap·e·lain \ä^{n}-drā-lə-shȧp-la^{n}\. *Lat.* Andreas Ca·pel·la·nus \ˌkap-ə-'lā-nəs\. 12th century. French writer. Thought to have been chaplain at court of Marie, Countess of Champagne, at whose request he wrote *Liber de arte honeste amandi et reprobatione inhonesti amoris* (c.1185), codifying cult of courtly love.

An·drew \'an-ˌdrü\. Saint. d. 60 or 70 A.D. One of the twelve Christian apostles; brother of St. Peter; according to tradition, suffered martyrdom by crucifixion in Greece.

Andrew. *Hung.* En·dre \'en-dre\ *or* An·drás \'än-ˌdräsh\. Name of three kings of Hungary of Árpád dynasty:

Andrew I. d. 1060. King (1046–60). Banished by King Stephen, lived in Poland and Russia; overthrew King Peter (1046); engaged in three campaigns (1049–52) against Emperor Henry III; independence acknowledged (1052); dethroned by his brother Béla I.

Andrew II. 1175–1235. King (1205–35). Son of Béla III; succeeded László III. His extravagance and generosity brought financial troubles; forced to grant estates to nobles who reduced Hungary almost to anarchy. m. Gertrude of Meran, murdered (1213) by nobles. Set out with large army on crusade to Holy Land (1217); sailed to Acre, but expedition failed. On return nobles extorted from him (1222) the Golden Bull, which limited the monarchy, granted people annual assembly, and preserved rights of feudal nobles; during his reign Teutonic Knights expelled from Hungary (1225). Father of St. Elizabeth of Hungary.

Andrew III. *Called* Andrew the Venetian. d. 1301. Last king (1290–1301) of Árpád dynasty. Nephew of Andrew II. At beginning of reign forced to contest claims of Charles Martel, son of king of Naples, and of Albert of Habsburg, son of Emperor Rudolf; died without issue.

Andrew. *Russ. in full* Andrey Yuryevich Bo·gol·yub·sky \bəg-(ˌ)əl-'yüb-skəi\. c.1111–1174. Russian prince. Son of Yury Dolgoruky; succeeded as prince of Rostov-Suzdal (1157); extended domain; sacked Kiev (1169) and named grand prince of Vladimir (1169); placed subordinate princes in Kiev, Novgorod; increased power of grand prince; killed by nobles.

Andrew. *Russ. in full* Andrey Ya·ros·la·vo·vich \yə-(ˌ)rə-'slȧ-vəv-ˌyich\. 13th century. Russian prince. Younger brother of Alexander Nevsky; grand prince of Vladimir (1246–52); deposed by brother.

Andrew of Cae·sa·rea \ˌsē-zə-'rē-ə, ˌses-ə-, ˌsez-\. 6th–7th century. Greek prelate and theologian. Bishop of Caesarea; author of important commentary on biblical Book of Revelations, parts of which may have become incorporated into biblical text.

Andrew of Car·nio·la \ˌkär-nē-'ō-lə\. *Also called* Andrew of Krai·na \'krī-nä\. d. 1484. Slavic? prelate. Named bishop of Carniola (1476) with support of Emperor Frederick III; failed to win cardinalate (1478) and thereafter opposed Pope Sixtus IV; denounced Sixtus, convened council at Basel to consider formal indictment; failed to win support of other bishops; Basel placed under interdict (1482) for harboring him; imprisoned, reportedly took own life.

Andrew of Crete \'krēt\. Saint. c.660–740. Greek prelate. Archbishop of Gortyna; took part in Synod of Constantinople (712), subscribing to Monothelitism; recanted (713); credited with inventing canon form of hymnography (9 odes in stanzaic form, each sung to different melody) to replace Kontakion form; author of many hymns and canons.

Andrew of Lon·ju·mel \lō^n-zhü̅e-mel\ *or* Long·ju·meau *or* Lon·gu·meau \lō^n-zhü̅e-mō\. fl. 1238–1253. French religious and diplomat. Dominican friar; for King Louis IX undertook mission to Constantinople (1238) whence he returned with relic revered as Christ's crown of thorns; accompanied mission sent by Pope Innocent V to Mongol court at Kars, Armenia (1247); for Louis traveled to Mongol court of Güyük (1249–52); wrote account of journey.

Andrew of Wyntoun. See WYNTOUN.

Andrew, James Osgood. 1794–1871. American Methodist Episcopal bishop, b. in Wilkes County, Ga. Chosen bishop (1832). His holding of slaves was issue which, at general conference of the church (1844), resulted in division of Methodist Episcopal Church into northern and southern branches (1845); chosen one of first bishops of Methodist Episcopal Church, South (1846).

Andrew, John Albion. 1818–1867. American politician, b. Windham, Me. Helped organize Republican party in Massachusetts; governor (1860–66); Civil War leader, organized state troops before Lincoln's call for volunteers.

An·drewes \'an-ˌdrüz\, Lancelot. 1555–1626. English prelate and scholar. Bishop of Chichester (1605), Ely (1609), Winchester (1619); lord almoner (1605–19) and dean of chapels royal (1619–26); renowned as eloquent and vastly learned preacher. Effective defender of Anglican theology against Catholic and Calvinist doctrines. One of ten Westminster translators of Pentateuch and historical books for Authorized Version of Bible (1607).

Andrews, Charles McLean. 1863–1943. American historian, b. Wethersfield, Conn. Professor, Bryn Mawr (1889–1907), Johns Hopkins (1907–10), Yale (1910–31). Authority on colonial America. Author of *The Historical Development of Modern Europe* (1896–98), *Colonial Self-Government* (1904), *A Short History of England* (1912), *Fathers of New England* (1919), *The Colonial Background of the American Revolution* (1924), *Colonial Period of American History* (1934–38, of which vol. 1 won Pulitzer prize).

Andrews, Frank Maxwell. 1884–1943. American army officer, b. Nashville, Tenn. With aviation section of Signal Corps (1917–20), Air Service (1920–26), Army Air Corps (1926–43); organizer and first commander (temporary brigadier general) of G. H. Q. Air Force (1935–39); temporary lieutenant general, head of U.S. Caribbean defense command (1941–42); head of Middle East command (1942–43) and then of U.S. forces in Europe (1943).

Andrews, Roy Chapman. 1884–1960. American naturalist, explorer, and author, b. Beloit, Wis. Joined staff of American Museum of Natural History, New York City (1906); on expeditions to Alaska (1908), Borneo, etc. (1909–10), northern Korea (1911–12), Alaska (1913); headed expeditions (1916–30) to Tibet, China, Burma, Mongolia, and Central Asia, esp. the Gobi. Known esp. for discoveries of geological strata, dinosaur eggs, remains of Baluchitherium, largest known land mammals, and evidences of ancient human life. Director of American Museum (1935–42). Author of *Across Mongolian Plains* (1921), *On the Trail of Ancient Man* (1926), *The Ends of the Earth* (1929), *The New Conquest of Central Asia* (1932), *This Business of Exploring* (1935), *This Amazing Planet* (1940), *Under a Lucky Star* (1943), *An Explorer Comes Home* (1947), *Beyond Adventure* (1954).

Andrews, Stephen Pearl. 1812–1886. American philosopher and reformer, b. Templeton, Mass. Agitated for abolition of slavery in Texas and England; taught Pitman shorthand, urged spelling reform, edited magazines printed in phonetic alphabet; devised Alwato, international language; author of *Basic Outline of Universology* (1877), comprehensive philosophy.

Andrews, Thomas. 1813–1885. Irish physicist and chemist. Professor, Belfast (1849–79). By experiments in liquefaction of gases, established concepts of critical temperature and pressure; showed that ozone is form of oxygen.

An·dre·yev \(ˌ)ən-'dryā-yəf\, Leonid Nikolayevich. 1871–1919. Russian writer. Worked as lawyer and crime reporter; encouraged by Gorky. Published short stories notable for realism, pessimism, including "Zhili-blyi"; novels including *Gubernator* (1905), *Krasny smekh* (1905), *T'ma* (1907), *Rasskaz o semi poveshennykh* (1908); plays including *Zhizn cheloveka* (1907), *Tot kto poluchayet poshchyochiny* (He Who Gets Slapped, 1916).

An·drić \'än-drēt^y\, Ivo. 1892–1975. Serbo-Croatian writer. Member of Yugoslavian diplomatic corps; author of volume of lyrical meditations *Ex Ponto* (1918), novels *Travnička hronika* (1945), *Na Drini ćuprija* (Bridge on the Drina, 1945), *Gospođica* (1945), collections of stories *Put Alije Đerzeleza* (1920), *Pripovetka* (1924), *Nove Pripovetke* (1948), *Prokleta avlija* (1954). Awarded Nobel prize in literature (1961).

An·dri·eux \ä^n-drē-œ̅\, Francois-Guillaume-Jean-Stanislas. 1759–1833. French poet and playwright. Judge of revolutionary Cour de Cassation (1790–93); president of Tribunat (1800–02). Author of several comedies, as *Les Étourdis* (1787), *Helvétius* (1802), *Le Vieux fat* (1810), *La Comédienne* (1816), and of verse narratives, as *Le Meunier sans-souci* (1797).

An·dris·cus \an-'dris-kəs\. 2d century B.C. Greek adventurer. Passed himself off as son of Perseus, king of Macedon; seized throne (149 B.C.); conquered Thessaly; defeated by Metellus (148 B.C.); sent as captive to Rome and executed.

An·dro·clus \'an-drə-kləs\ *or* **An·dro·cles** \'an-drə-ˌklēz\. 1st century A.D. Roman slave. According to story of Apion and Aulus Gellius, spared in arena by lion from whose foot he had extracted a thorn years before in Africa.

An·dro·ni·cus \ˌan-drə-'nī-kəs, an-'drän-ə-kəs\. Name of four emperors of Eastern Roman Empire:

Andronicus I Com·ne·nus \käm-'nē-nəs\. 1118–1185. Emperor (1183–85); grandson of Alexius I Comnenus; raised army and entered Constantinople (1182), assuming role of regent for Emperor Alexius II; crowned co-emperor with Alexius, whom he killed (1183); instigated massacre of westerners in Constantinople and bitterly opposed western church; policies provoked invasion by Béla III of Hungary (1183) and Normans under William II of Sicily (1185); overthrown by Isaac II Angelus. Last of Comnenus dynasty.

Andronicus II Pa·lae·ol·o·gus \ˌpā-lē-'äl-ə-gəs, ˌpal-ē-\. 1260–1332. Emperor (1282–1328); son of Michael VIII Palaeologus. Disbanded navy, reduced army, allowing Ottoman Turks to take nearly all Anatolia; called Roger di Flor and his Catalan Grand Company to fight them; after defeating Turks, Roger's company pillaged Byzantine cities; deposed by grandson Andronicus III.

Andronicus III Palaeologus. 1296–1341. Emperor (1328–41); forced grandfather Andronicus II to recognize him as co-emperor (1325) and then to abdicate (1328); rebuilt navy; lost territory to Serbs and Ottomans, regained Greek islands, Epirus, Thessaly; influenced by John VI Cantacuzenus.

Andronicus IV. d. 1385. Emperor (1376–79); son of John V Palaeologus, whom he deposed and by whom he was in turn deposed.

Andronicus of Cyr·rhus \'sī-rəs\ *or* **Andronicus Cyr·rhes·tes** \-si-'res-tēz\. fl. c.100 B.C. Greek astronomer. Architect of Tower of the Winds, known in Middle Ages as Lantern of Demosthenes, a tower in Athens bearing a weather vane, eight sundials, and containing a water clock.

Andronicus of Rhodes \'rōdz\. 1st century B.C. Greek Peripatetic philosopher. Edited, arranged, catalogued, and published works of Aristotle.

Andronicus, Lucius Livius. See LIVIUS ANDRONICUS.

An·dro·pov \än-'drȯ-pəf\, Yuri Vladimirovich. 1914–1984. Soviet politician. Joined Communist party (1939); advanced to second secretary of the party Central Committee in Karelia (1947); to Moscow (1953); to Hungary (1954); instrumental in crushing Hungarian uprising (1956); recalled to Moscow (1957); appointed head of KGB (1967); nonvoting member of Politburo (1967), full member (1973); elected general secretary of Communist party (1982); member of Presidium (1982); as Soviet leader sought to improve domestic productivity and relations with China.

An·dros \'an-drəs\, Sir Edmund. 1637–1714. British colonial governor in America. Governor of province of New York and New Jersey (1674–81); appointed (1686) governor of "Dominion of New England," formed by uniting the several New England colonies and later New York and New Jersey; interfered with colonists' rights and customs; colonies revolted (1689), imprisoned him, and resumed separate existences. Sent to England for hearing, but charges not pressed. Governor of province of Virginia (1692–98), of Maryland (1693–94). Lieutenant governor of Guernsey (1704–06).

An·dro·ti·on \an-'drō-shē-ˌän\. 4th century B.C. Athenian orator. Pupil of Isocrates; attacked by Demosthenes.

Androuet. See DU CERCEAU.

Anei·rin \ə-'nī-rin, -'nā-\ *or* **Aneu·rin.** *Orig* Nei·rin \'nī-rin, 'nā-\. 6th century. Welsh bard. Author of core of epic *Y Gododdin* on defeat of Britons of northern kingdom of Manaw Gododdin by Saxons (c.600), one of earliest known poems in Welsh.

Ane·rio \ä-'ner-yō\, Felice. 1560?–1614. Italian composer of church music. Succeeded (1594) Palestrina as composer for the papal chapel; composed spiritual and secular madrigals, spiritual canzonettas, masses. His brother ¶Giovanni Francesco (1567?–1630) was also a composer, esp. of church music.

Ane·than \ȧn-tä^n\, Jules Joseph d'. Baron. 1803–1888. Belgian politician. Conservative Catholic leader; premier (1870–71); senate president (1884–86).

Ane·za·ki \än-ez-äk-ē\ Masaharu. *Also known as* Anezaki Chōfū. 1873–1949. Japanese scholar. Professor of science of religion, Tokyo Imperial U. (from 1903); a pioneer in critical historical study of Buddhism; author of *Nichiren the Buddhist Prophet* (1916), *History of Japanese Religion* (1930).

An·fos·si \än-'fȯs-sē\, Pasquale. 1727–1797. Italian composer. Maestro di capella, St. John Lateran (1792–97); composed 76 operas and 7 oratorios.

An·gad \äŋ-'gäd\. *Also called* Leh·na \'len-ä\ *or* La·hi·na \lə-'hē-nä\. 1504–1552. Second Sikh Gurū. Follower of Gurū Nānak, whom he succeeded (1539); established schools, promoted the *langur,* i.e. free kitchen; originated Gurmukhi, Punjabi script.

Angarita, Isaías Medina. See MEDINA ANGARITA.

An·gas \'aŋ-gəs\, George Fife. 1789–1879. English merchant and shipowner. Commissioner for formation of colony of South Australia (1834); emigrated to Adelaide (1851); regarded as a founder of South Australia.

Ang Chan \'äŋ-'chän\. Name of two kings of Cambodia:

Ang Chan. d. 1566. King (1516–66). Succeeded uncle Dharmarajadhiraja; ruled from Pursat and (from 1528) Lovek; secured kingdom against Thais.

Ang Chan II. 1791–1835. King (1802–35). Son of Ang Eng; recognized as king by dominant Thais; preserved peace by sending tribute to Siam and Vietnam; fled to Vietnam when briefly deposed by Thai-backed brother Ang Snguon (1811).

Ang Duong \'äŋ-də-wòŋ\. 1796–1860. King of Cambodia (1841–60). Brother of Ang Chan II; formally installed (1848) after truce between Siam and Vietnam recognizing dual hegemony; gradually rebuilt national unity and consciousness; last Cambodian king before imposition of French protectorate.

Angela Merici, Saint. See MERICI.

Angelico, Fra. See GUIDO DI PIETRO.

Angélique de Saint-Jean, Mère. See under ARNAULD family.

An·gell \'ān-jəl\, James Burrill. 1829–1916. American educator and diplomat, b. Scituate, R.I. Professor, Brown U. (1853–60); president, U. of Vermont (1866–71), Michigan (1871–1909). U.S. minister to China (1880–81), Turkey (1897–98).

Angell, James Rowland. 1869–1949. American educator and psychologist, b. Burlington, Vt. Son of James B. Angell. Professor (1894–1919), dean (1911–19), acting president (1918–19), U. of Chicago. President, Carnegie Corp. (1920–21). President, Yale U. (1921–37). Author of *Psychology* (1904), *American Education* (1937), etc.

Angell, Sir Norman. *Orig.* Ralph Norman Angell Lane \'lān\. 1872–1967. English author and lecturer. Editor, *Galignani's Messenger* (1899–1903), *Foreign Affairs* (1928–31); M.P. (1929–31). Invented The Money Game, series of card games designed to teach elements of economics. Author of *The Great Illusion* (1910), *The Great Illusion, 1933* (1933), *America's Dilemma* (1940), and other works on international affairs, finance, and peace. Awarded 1933 Nobel peace prize.

An·ge·lus \'an-jə-ləs\. Byzantine family that furnished rulers of Eastern Roman Empire: Isaac II Angelus, Alexius III Angelus, and Alexius IV Angelus. Family came to prominence when Constantine Angelus married Theodora, daughter of Alexius I Comnenus; took part in overthrow of Andronicus I Comnenus (1185). Michael VIII Palaeologus was direct descendant of family; another ruling house was established by Michael Angelus Comnenus as despots of Epirus and Thessaly (1204–1318).

Angelus Silesius. See Johannes SCHEFFLER.

An·gennes \äⁿ-zhen\, Catherine d', *nee* de Vi·vonne de Sa·vel·li \də-vē-vòn-də-sȧ-vā-yē\. Marquise de Ram·bouil·let \-də-räⁿ-bü-ye\. 1588–1665. French hostess. Established at her Paris townhouse, Hôtel de Rambouillet, salon devoted to literature and cultured conversation that exerted considerable influence on development of French literature.

Angers, David d'. See DAVID D'ANGERS.

An·ger·stein \'aŋ-gər-ˌstīn\, John Julius. 1735–1823. British merchant and philanthropist, b. Russia. Underwriter at Lloyd's (1756). Collected paintings, purchased at his death by British government as nucleus of National Gallery.

An·ghie·ra \äŋ-'gye-rä\, Pietro Martire d'. 1457–1526. Italian historian. To Spain (1487); chaplain, tutor to royal children, diplomatic representative of court of Ferdinand and Isabella of Spain; member of Charles V's Council of the Indies (1518); royal chronicler (1520). Author of *De Orbe Novo* (1530), giving first account of discovery of America, and of *Opus Epistolarum* (1530), 812 letters valuable as source material for the period.

An·gil·bert \'aŋ-gil-ˌbərt\. Saint. c.740–814. Frankish Latin poet and prelate. Privy councilor to Charlemagne; abbot of Centula, now Saint-Riquier, Picardy (794); friend of Alcuin; honored at court by name "Homer." Father, by Charlemagne's daughter Bertha, of the historian Nithard.

An·gio·lie·ri \ˌän-jōl-'ye-rē\, Cecco. c.1260–c.1312. Italian poet. Author chiefly of ribald, satirical, and autobiographical poems.

An·gio·li·ni \ˌän-jō-'lē-nē\, Gasparo. *Orig.* Domenico Maria Angiolo Gas·pa·ri·ni \ˌgäs-pä-'rē-nē\. 1731–1803. Italian choreographer and composer. Ballet master at court opera house, Vienna (1757–65), Imperial Theatre, St. Petersburg (1765–72); produced, with music by Gluck, ballets *Don Juan, ou le festin de pierre* (1761), *Orfeo ed Euridice* (1762), *Sémiramis* (1765), and to own music *L'Orfano della China* (1774), *Thésée et Ariane* (1776); with J.-G. Noverre, one of first to integrate dance, music, plot into balletic unity.

Anglesey, Marquis of. See Henry William PAGET.

An·glin \'aŋ-glən\, Margaret Mary. 1876–1958. American actress, b. Ottawa. New York debut in *Shenandoah* (1894); appeared in companies of Charles Frohman, Henry Miller, etc.; great success in W.V. Moody's *Great Divide* (1906); formed (1913) repertory company to present Shakespearean plays and Greek tragedies.

An·go *or* **An·got** \äⁿ-gō\, Jean. c.1480–1551. French shipowner. Built import-export business into 70-ship fleet; equipped explorers Verrazano, the Parmentiers, privateer Jean Fleury; loaned ships to Francis I for use against Spain and England; supported in privateering against Portugal by Francis I.

An·gou·lême \äⁿ-gü-lem\. French title of nobility derived from countship in southwest France dating from 9th century and held by several families, becoming crown appanage (1373) under Charles V and possession of House of Orléans. Among counts of Angoulême were John, a son of Louis I, Duc d'Orléans (see ORLÉANS), and John's son Charles. Countship was made a duchy (1515) by Charles's son Francis I, with whom Angoulême branch of House of Valois began to rule as kings of France (1515–89).

Angoulême, Duc d'. See (1) Louis-Antoine de BOURBON; (2) Charles de VALOIS.

Ång·ström \'òŋ-strœm\, Anders Jonas. 1814–1874. Swedish astronomer and physicist. Lecturer (1839), professor (1858), U. of Uppsala; known for studies in spectroscopy, of which he was a founder; angstrom unit of length named in his honor. Made spectral analyses, esp. of sun and aurora borealis; identified hydrogen in solar atmosphere (1862); published maps of solar spectrum (1868). His son ¶Knut Johan (1857–1910), also a physicist at Uppsala, investigated solar radiation and photographed infrared spectrum (1895).

An·guier \äⁿ-gyā\, François (c.1604–1669) and his brother Michel-André (c.1613–1686). French sculptors. Known for decorative work; François known esp. for funerary statue of Gasparde de la Châtre and, with brother, for tomb of Henri II, duc de Montmorency; Michel-André known for apartments of Anne of Austria in Louvre, chateau of Nicolas Fouquet, church of Val-de-Grâce in Paris, reliefs for Porte Saint-Denis, statue of Amphitrite.

An·gui·scio·la \äŋ-'gwē-shō-(ˌ)lä\ *or* **An·guis·so·la** \äŋ-'gwēs-sō-(ˌ)lä\, Sofonisba. 1527–1625. Italian portrait painter. Known esp. for her self-portraits and for portrait of Philip II.

Angus, Earls of. See (1) UMFRAVILLE; (2) DOUGLAS family.

An·halt \'än-ˌhält\. German duchy and its ruling house, which originated with Albert I the Bear (*q.v.*), Margrave of Brandenburg. On death (1252) of Albert's grandson Henry I, district (then a county) divided into three parts; succession of unions and redivisions (1570–1863); final unification effected (1863) under Leopold IV Frederick (1817–1871). Recent rulers: Leopold IV (1863–71), Frederick I (1871–1904), Frederick II (1904–abdicated 1918). Most important division (during 17th–19th centuries) was An·halt-Des·sau \-'des-ˌaù\ branch. Among princes of the line were Leopold I (1676–1747), Leopold II (1700–1751), and Moritz (1712–1760), all distinguished generals. See individual biographies.

An·i·ce·tus \ˌan-i-'sēt-əs\. Saint. 2nd century A.D. Pope (c.155–c.166). Combatted heresies, esp. those of Marcionites and Gnostics.

An·iel·lo \än-'yel-lō\, Tomasso *or* Tommaso. *Known as* Ma·san·iel·lo \ˌmäs-än-'yel-lō\. 1620–1647. Neapolitan insurrectionist. A fisherman, chosen to lead protest against fruit tax levied by nobles of Naples to pay tribute to Spain (1647); after success of protest lost control of himself, urging slaughter of nobles; assassinated.

Ani·muc·cia \ˌän-ē-'müt-chä\, Giovanni. c.1500–1571. Italian composer. Maestro di cappella at St. Peter's (1555–71). Instrumental in evolution of musical form of oratorio, developed from his *laudi spirituali,* religious part-songs performed in oratory of St. Philip Neri; also composed masses, madrigals, etc. His brother ¶Paolo (c.1500–c.1570), composer of motets and madrigals, was maestro di cappella at the Lateran (1550–52).

Aniruddha. See ANAWRAHTA.

An·jou \äⁿ-zhü, *Angl* 'an-ˌjü\. French noble family, established in 9th century and deriving name from county in western France. There have been several houses of Anjou:

FIRST HOUSE: Counts of Anjou from Fulk I to Geoffrey Plantagenet (*qq.v.*); Geoffrey's son Henry became king of England as Henry II.

SECOND HOUSE: Plantagenet kings of England, esp. first three: Henry II, Richard I, and John. Much English land in France lost by John to Philip II of France; English military campaign to retake land defeated (1214); countship of Anjou attached to France (1259). Other Plantagenets to Richard II also called Angevins, but none after John were counts of Anjou.

THIRD HOUSE: Kings of Naples and Sicily. Anjou given (1246) by King Louis IX as appanage to his brother Charles, Count of Provence, later (1266–85) king of Naples and Sicily; succeeded as king by his son Charles II (1285–1309). Charles II had five children, from whom descended five interrelated lines of European rulers: (1) HUNGARY—from oldest son, Charles Martel (1272?–1295), king in opposition (1290–95) to Andrew III. Other members of line included Charles Robert, founder of Anjou line of Hungary (1308–42); Louis the Great, King of Hungary (1342–82), Poland (1370–82); and Mary (ruled 1382–95), who married Sigismund, later Holy Roman Emperor. (2) NAPLES—from second son, Robert; succeeded his father, Charles II, as king of Naples (1309–43); succeeded in turn by granddaughter, Joanna I, Queen of Naples (1343–82), who adopted Louis of Anjou (see 4, below). (3) NAPLES—from third son, John, Duke of Du·raz·zo \dü-'rät-tsō\. His grandson was Charles III, King of Naples (1381–86), succeeded by his son Ladislas (1386–1414) and daughter Joanna II (1414–35), with whom direct line became extinct. (4) FRANCE, ANJOU, AND NAPLES—from fourth child, Margaret; m. Charles de Valois (see

VALOIS). Their son Philip chosen (1328), as Philip VI, first king of France of House of Valois; countship united to crown. Philip succeeded by son John II (1350–64); countship bestowed (1351) by John on his second son, Louis I, and raised to duchy (1360). Louis adopted by Joanna I as her successor to throne of Naples (1382–84); titular king only. Next two dukes also titular kings only: Louis II (reigned 1389–99) and Louis III (reigned 1417–34). Louis II's second son, René, last ruling duke of Anjou (1434–80); also king of Naples (1435–42) after death of Joanna II, but driven out by Alfonso I (see 5, below). René's daughter Margaret of Anjou married King Henry VI of England. (5) ARAGON AND NAPLES—from fifth child, Blanche; m. James II, King of Aragon. From them descended Alfonso V (1416–58), who as Alfonso I was king of Naples (1443–58). His natural son Ferdinand I succeeded as king of Naples (1458–94), followed by Alfonso II (ruled 1494–95) and Ferdinand II (ruled 1495–96), last of house of Anjou in Naples. Meanwhile, duchy of Anjou had reverted to French crown (1480); bestowed several times later, especially (1574–84) on François, son of Henry II, but on his death (1584) became definitively part of royal domain. Title duke of Anjou also borne by other French kings and members of royal family but without implying territorial sovereignty.

An·khe·se·na·men \äŋ-ˌkes-ə-ˈnäm-ən\. *Orig.* Ankhesenpaaten. 14th century B.C. Queen of Egypt (1362–c.1351 B.C.). Third daughter of Akhenaton and Nefertiti; m. her father and, on his accession, brother Tutankhamen; on husband's death offered throne to Hittite prince, who was murdered on way to Egypt; m. Ay, former vizier; removed as queen.

Anlaf Sihtricson. See OLAF SIHTRICSON.

An Lu-shan \ˈän-ˈlü-ˈshän\. *Orig. name* K'ang; *imperial name* Hsiung Wu; *canonized as* Yen La Wang. 703–757. Chinese general. Of Turkish-Iranian descent; rose rapidly in Chinese army; gained command of 3 frontier provinces; favorite at court of Hsüan Tsung; launched rebellion (755); proclaimed himself emperor of Great Yen dynasty (756); forces occupied Chinese capital Ch'ang-an (756); murdered by eunuch slave in conspiracy with son. Rebellion persisted to 763, seriously weakening T'ang dynasty.

Ann, Mother. See ANN LEE.

An·na Com·ne·na \ˈan-ə-käm-ˈnē-nə\. 1083–?1148. Byzantine author. Daughter of Emperor Alexius I Comnenus; m. (1097) Nicephorus Bryennius. Conspired (1118) against Emperor John II, her brother; retired with her mother, Irene, to convent, where she wrote *Alexiad,* a history of period 1069–1118, covering reigns from Isaac Comnenus to Alexius.

An·na Iva·nov·na \ˈán-nə-i-ˈvá-nəv-nə\. 1693–1740. Empress of Russia (1730–40). Younger daughter of Ivan V and niece of Peter the Great; m. (1710) Frederick William, Duke of Courland (d. 1711). Elected to throne by Supreme Privy Council under conditions practically vitiating her authority; foiled council by abolishing it; surrounded herself with German favorites, esp. Biron, Osterman, Münnich. Countenanced severely repressive regime; intervened successfully in War of Polish Succession (1733–35); in alliance with Austria, fought war against Turks (1736–39); secured Azov by treaty of Belgrade (1739); secured succession to her great-nephew Ivan VI.

Anna Le·o·pol·dov·na \-lyi-(ˌ)ə-ˈpól^{y}-dəv-nə\. *Orig.* Elisabeth Katharina Christine. 1718–1746. Regent of Russia (1740–41). Daughter of Charles Leopold, Duke of Mecklenburg-Schwerin; niece of Anna Ivanovna; m. (1739) Anthony Ulrich (1714–1776), Prince of Brunswick. Grand duchess; following arrest of Biron, named regent (1740–41) of Russia during reign of her infant son, Ivan VI; imprisoned (1741–46) with husband after Ivan's deposition by Elizabeth.

Anne \ˈan\. 1665–1714. Queen of Great Britain and Ireland (1702–14). Second daughter of James II and Anne Hyde; reared in Protestant faith; m. (1683) George, Prince of Denmark (d. 1708). Supported accession of William and Mary (1689) and placed in succession; signed Act of Settlement (1701), designating Hanoverian descendants of James I as her successors. After accession to throne suffered domination of Duke and Duchess of Marlborough (see Sarah Jennings Churchill under John CHURCHILL) till alienated from them because of their Whig sympathies; this estrangement (1710) followed by Tory ministry of Harley and St. John. Indulged in patronage of the church; granted crown revenues to form "Queen Anne's Bounty" (1704). Reign marked by bitter party disputes, War of Spanish Succession; most important public event of her reign was Act of Union with Scotland (1707).

Anne of Austria. *Fr.* Anne d'Au·triche \än-dō-trēsh, án-\. 1601–1666. Queen consort of France. Daughter of Philip III of Spain; m. (1615) Louis XIII of France; virtually separated (1620–43) through influence of Cardinal Richelieu; took some part in conspiracies against husband, esp. on behalf of her brother, Philip IV. Queen regent for her son Louis XIV (1643–51); chose Cardinal Mazarin as prime minister; successfully maintained autocratic power of throne against nobles; with Mazarin defeated Fronde rebellion.

Anne of Bohemia. 1366–1394. Queen consort of England. Daughter of Emperor Charles IV by Elizabeth of Pomerania; m. (1382) Richard II; interceded with Richard in behalf of City of London, which had been shorn of its privileges for refusing him a loan, and gained pardon (1392); died of pestilence.

Anne of Brittany. 1477–1514. Duchess of Brittany (1488–1514) and queen consort of France. Daughter of Duke Francis II of Brittany; sought to maintain autonomy of Brittany; sought alliance with Maximilian of Austria against Charles VIII of France (1490); forced to marry Charles (1491), thus laying foundation for union of crown and Brittany; m. (1499) Louis XII. Patron of artists and poets.

Anne of Cleves \ˈklēvz\. 1515–1557. Queen consort of England. Fourth wife of Henry VIII. Daughter of John, Duke of Cleves, leader of Protestants of western Germany; selected by Thomas Cromwell on death of Jane Seymour as wife for Henry, to ally him with German Protestants against emperor. m. Henry (1540); marriage annulled by Parliament at Henry's request a few months later.

Anne of Denmark. 1574–1619. Queen of James I of England. Daughter of Frederick II of Denmark and Norway; m. James (1589); patron of arts, appeared in masques by Jonson and Dekker; conducted extravagant court.

Anne of France. 1461–1522. French princess. Eldest daughter of Louis XI; m. (1474) Pierre de Bourbon, seigneur de Beaujeu (d. 1503); virtual regent for brother Charles VIII (1483–91); arranged his marriage to Anne of Brittany (1491) following successful conclusion of "Mad War" between crown and Francis II of Brittany with the duc d'Orléans.

An·ni·ce·ris \ˌan-ə-ˈser-əs\. 4th–3d century B.C. Greek philosopher. Dedicated to restoring Cyrenaic school of hedonism to original principles of Aristippus.

An·ning \ˈan-iŋ\, Mary. 1799–1847. English naturalist. Discovered skeleton of ichthyosaurus (1811), later first specimens of plesiosaurus and pterodactyl.

An·no \ˈan-(ˌ)ō\ *or* **Han·no** \ˈhan-(ˌ)ō\. Saint. c.1010–1075. German prelate. Confessor to Emperor Henry III, who named him archbishop of Cologne (1056); headed uprising of princes against regency of Agnes of Poitou (1062), kidnaped her son King Henry IV, taking him to Cologne, and usurped regency; shared regency with Archbishop Adalbert of Hamburg-Bremen; decisively influenced Council of Mantua (1064) in recognizing papacy of Alexander II against antipope Honorius II.

Annunzio, Gabriele D'. See D'ANNUNZIO.

An·que·til-Du·per·ron \ä^{n}k-tēl-dūē-pe-rō^{n}\, Abraham-Hyacinthe. 1731–1805. French scholar. Traveled to India (1755) to learn Avestan; acquired Zoroastrian manuscripts; made first translation of *Zend-Avesta* into modern European language (1771); author of works on India.

Anschar. Saint. See ANSCAR.

An·schütz-Kaemp·fe \ˈän-shuets-ˈkemp-fə\, Hermann. 1872–1931. German engineer. Inventor of gyrocompass (1908).

An·se·gis \ˈan-sə-jəs\ *or* **An·se·gi·sus** \ˌan-sə-ˈjī-səs\. Saint. c.770–833/34. Abbot of Fontanelle (from 823); collected laws and decrees of Charlemagne and Louis le Débonnaire in *Quatuor libri capitularium regum Francorum,* known commonly as *Capitularies* (completed 827).

An·selm \ˈan-ˌselm\ of Canterbury. Saint. 1033 or 1034–1109. Scholastic philosopher, b. Aosta, Italy. Entered Benedictine abbey of Bec (1060); elected abbot of Caen (1063), of Bec (1078). Wrote treatises *Monologion* on attributes of God and *Proslogion* on ontological argument for existence of God. Appointed archbishop of Canterbury by William II Rufus (1093); embroiled with William Rufus over his refusal to accept episcopal pall from king and with Henry I over his refusal to consecrate prelates invested by king; suffered exile by each in turn; reconciled with Henry through compromise (1107). During exile wrote treatise on the atonement, *Cur Deus Homo?* Canonized (1063?) and declared doctor of the church (1720).

Anselm of Laon. *Fr.* An·selme de Laon \ä^{n}-selm-də-lä^{n}\. d. 1117. French theologian. Studied at Bec; conducted famous school at Laon, students including Peter Abelard, William of Champeaux; author of *Glossa interlinearis,* interlinear gloss of Vulgate Bible, and of *Sententiae.*

Anselm II of Luc·ca \ˈlük-kä\. Saint. 1036–1086. Italian ecclesiastic. Nephew of Pope Alexander II; bishop of Lucca (from 1073); partisan of Gregory VII; known esp. for ecclesiastical reforms; author of *Liber contra Wibertum* and *Collectio canonum.*

An·selme \ä^{n}-selm\. *Known as* Father Anselme of the Virgin Mary. *Orig.* Pierre de Gui·bours \də-gē-bür\. 1625–1694. French friar and genealogist. Entered Discalced Hermits of St. Augustine (1644); author of *Le Palais de l'honneur* (1663–68), *Le Palais de la gloire* (1664), *La Science héraldique* (1675), and esp. *Histoire généalogique et chronologique de la maison royale de France, des pairs, des grands officiers de la couronne, et de la maison du roy et des anciens barons du royaume* (1674), later continued by Honoré Caille, seigneur du Fourny, and two other friars.

An·ser·met \äⁿ-ser-me\, Ernest. 1883–1969. Swiss orchestral conductor. Known for his interpretations of modern composers as Hindemith, Bartók, Prokofiev, and esp. Stravinsky; principal conductor of Diaghilev's Ballet Russe (1915 ff.); founder (1918) and conductor (1918–66), Orchestre de la Suisse Romande.

Ans·gar \'ans-ˌgär\ *or* **Ans·kar** *or* **Ans·char** \'ans-ˌkär\. Saint. *Fr.* Ans·chaire \äⁿs-ker\. *Lat.* Ans·gar·i·us \ans-'gar-ē-əs\. 801?–865. Frankish prelate and missionary. Entered Benedictine order (814?); at direction of Louis I the Pious, accompanied exiled King Harald back to Denmark to evangelize (826–829); preached in Sweden (829–831); named abbot of Corvey and first bishop of Hamburg (831); made archbishop and papal legate for all Scandinavian and Slavic missions (832); became known as "apostle of the North"; Scandinavian pagan revolt, with burning of Hamburg (845), ended work for a time; named bishop of Bremen (847) by Louis the German; converted King Haarik of Denmark (851), evangelized in Sweden (853–854). Canonized by Pope Nicholas I.

An·son \'an(t)-sən\, Adrian Constantine. *Known as* Cap *and later* Pop. 1851–1922. American baseball player, b. Marshalltown, Iowa. With National Association teams in Rockford, Ill. (1871), Philadelphia Athletics (1872–75); player (1876–97), manager (1879–97), National League team, Chicago; manager (1898), National League New York team; career batting average .329 or .339; believed to have hit over .400 in two years; led Chicago to 5 league championships. Elected to Baseball Hall of Fame (1939).

Anson, George. Baron Anson. 1697–1762. English admiral. Entered navy (1712); commanded squadron in Pacific, inflicted damage on Spanish commerce, circumnavigated world (1740–44); his *Centurion* first English warship in Chinese waters; rear admiral (1744); defeated French off Finisterre (1747); first lord of admiralty (1751–56, 1757–62); admiral of fleet (1761). Effected reforms in naval administration, raising navy to high efficiency.

Anson, Sir William Reynell. 3d Baronet Anson. 1843–1914. English jurist. Vinerian reader, Oxford (1874–81); warden, All Souls Coll. (1881–1914); M.P. (1899–1914). Author of standard texts, as *The Principles of the English Law of Contract* (1884), *The Law and Custom of the Constitution* (1886–92).

An·stey \'an-stē\, Christopher. 1724–1805. English poet. Fellow of King's Coll., Cambridge (1745–54). Published epistolary novel in verse, *New Bath Guide,* an immediate success, praised for original humor (1766).

Anstey, F. See Thomas Anstey GUTHRIE.

An·tal·ci·das \an-'tal-sə-dəs\. 4th century B.C. Spartan naval commander and diplomat. Negotiated successfully for Persian aid against Athens (388) and commanded Sparta's fleet in operations near the Hellespont; forced peace (Peace of Antalcidas, 386) on Athens by terms of which Asia Minor was acknowledged as subject to Persia, and other Greek cities (except islands of Lemnos, Imbros, and Skyros, which remained Athenian) were recognized as independent. Continued on friendly relations with Artaxerxes until Sparta's defeat at Leuctra (371).

'An·ta·rah ibn Shad·dād al-'Ab·si \ˌan-tä-'rä-ˌib-ən-shad-'däd-al-äb-'sē\. 6th century A.D. Arab warrior and poet. Took part in fierce war between two Arab tribes and became famous for his deeds of valor; wrote battle songs and love poems included in anthology *al-Mu'allaqāt;* hero of extremely popular Arabic romantic literature, esp. of a very large compilation, *Sirat 'Antar ibn Shaddād* or Romance of 'Antar.

An·te·la·mi \ˌän-tä-'lä-mē\, Benedetto. c.1150–1230. Italian sculptor and architect. Known for baptistery of Parma cathedral, decoration of S. Andrea at Vercelli.

An·te·nor \an-'tē-ˌnȯr, -nər\. fl. c.540–500 B.C. Athenian sculptor. Executed bronze group of tyrannicides Harmodius and Aristogiton placed by Athenians in the Akropolis, carried off by Xerxes to Susa, and said to have been returned to Athens by Alexander the Great.

An·ter·us \'an-tər-əs\ *or* **An·ter·os** \-ˌäs\ *or* **An·ther·us** \'an-thər-əs\. Saint. 3d century A.D. Pope (235–236); said to have been martyred.

An·theil \'an-ˌtīl\, George, *orig.* Georg Johann Carl. 1900–1959. American composer, b. Trenton, N.J. Known for ultramodern compositions as *Zingareska* (1921), *Ballet méchanique* scored for player pianos, automobile horns, airplane propeller, etc., which created sensation at Paris debut (1926), operas *Transatlantic* (1930), *Helen Retires* (1934), *Volpone* (1953), *The Wish* (1955), orchestral works, as *Archipelago* (1933), ballets *Dreams* (1935), *Capital of the World* (1953), chamber music, and motion picture scores.

An·the·mi·us \an-'thē-mē-əs\. d. 472. Roman emperor (467–472). Son-in-law of Marcian, Emperor of the East; appointed emperor by Emperor Leo I on advice of Ricimer; defeated Huns in Dacia (466, 468); his daughter married Ricimer (467); later, quarreled with Ricimer, who brought Olybrius and army and besieged Rome; killed in the assault.

Anthemius of Tral·les \'tral-ēz\. 6th century A.D. Lydian mathematician and architect. Planned (with Isidorus of Miletus) and built (532–537) church of Saint Sophia at Constantinople for Emperor Justinian.

An·thi·mus \'an(t)-thə-məs\. Name of several patriarchs of Constantinople, including:

Anthimus I. *Also called* Anthimus of Trebizond. 6th century. Patriarch (535–536). Bishop of Trebizond (533); raised to patriarchate at instance of Empress Theodora; although publicly pledged to orthodoxy, harbored Monophysite sympathies; deposed by council convened by Pope Agapetus I; event led to canonical condemnation of Monophysitism and its exponents by his successor, Mennas.

Anthimus VI. *Orig. surname* Jo·an·ni·des \yō-'än-i-thes\. c.1790–1878. Patriarch (1845–48, 1853–55, 1871–73). With patriarchs of Alexandria, Jerusalem, and Antioch composed *Encyclical of the Patriarchs* (1848) criticizing Roman church and Pope Pius IX's encyclical *In Suprema Petri Apostoli Sede*; convened synod (1872) which excommunicated Bulgarian national church.

Anthimus VII. *Orig. surname* Tsa·tsos \'tsät-sȯs\. c.1835–1913. Patriarch (1895–96). Author of encyclical (1894) rejecting encyclical *Praeclara Gratulationis* of Pope Leo XIII and its offer of ecumenism and criticizing many Roman Catholic doctrines.

Anthimus of Iberia. *Also called* Antim Ivi·re·a·nul \ē-ˌvē-rä-'än-ül\. d. 1716. Romanian prelate and writer. Bishop of Ramnic (1705); metropolitan of Walachia (1708); translated Gospels into Romanian (1697); wrote sermons, a collection of moral exhortations called *Didahii* in Romanian; compiled anthology *Margaritare.* Contributed greatly to development of Romanian language and literature by writings and by printing of books. Executed for anti-Turkish nationalist sympathies.

An·tho·ny \'an(t)-thə-nē, *chiefly Brit* 'an-tə-\. Name of several patriarchs of Constantinople, including:

Anthony III. *Surnamed* Stu·dite \'stü-ˌdīt\. d. 983. Patriarch (974–979). Monk; secretary to Patriarch Basil I; succeeded when Basil was deposed by Emperor John I Tzimisces; known as reformer and strong supporter of church authority; deposed for role in conspiracy of Bardas Sclerus. Author of *Monitum,* treatise on asceticism and monk's life.

Anthony IV. d. 1397. Patriarch (1389–90, 1391–97). Upheld unity of Orthodox churches and primacy of Constantinople; worked to resist Turkish power.

Anthony of Bour·bon \'bu̇(ə)r-bən, 'bō(ə)r-, 'bȯ(ə)r-\. *Fr.* An·toine de Bour·bon \äⁿ-twän-də-bür-bōⁿ\. 1518–1562. Duke of Vendôme and king consort of Navarre (1555–62). Son of Charles de Bourbon, duc de Vendôme; m. (1548) Jeanne d'Albret, heiress to throne of Navarre. Weak and irresolute on religious question; at first joined his brother Louis, prince de Condé; involved in conspiracy against Francis II (1560); after this joined Catholic forces; killed in assault on Rouen. Father of Henry IV of France.

Anthony *or* **An·to·ny** \'an-tə-nē\ of Egypt. Saint. c.250–355. First Christian monk. Ascetic from age of twenty; withdrew to solitude of a height near the Nile; emerged (c.305) to organize communities of hermits who had settled nearby; moved (c.313) to Eastern Desert; visited Alexandria (c.350) to preach against Arianism. Subject of legends recording temptations that beset him and his struggles against forces of evil. Regarded as founder of Christian monachism; rule and fame spread by *Vita Antonii* of St. Athanasius.

Anthony of Ki·ev \'kē-yif\. *Also called* Anthony of Pe·cher·sky \pyi-'cher-skəi\. d. 1073. Russian religious. Entered Greek monastery on Mt. Athos (c.1028); returned to Kiev and settled on Mt. Berestov; organized followers into community, built monastery of Pechersky Lavra, instituted modified Athonite rule; considered founder of Russian monasticism.

Anthony of Nov·go·rod \'nȯv-gə-rəd\. *Orig.* Dobrynia Jad·rej·ko·vič \(ˌ)yə-'drä-kə-ˌvyich\. 13th century. Russian prelate. Archbishop of Novgorod (1211); established diplomatic and commercial ties with West. Author of *Pilgrim's Book,* account of visit to Constantinople and of mystical wonders of the city, esp. Hagia Sophia and its liturgy.

Anthony *or* **An·to·ny** \'an-tə-nē\ of Pad·ua \'paj-ə-wə\. Saint. 1195–1231. Portuguese religious. Joined Augustinian canons (1210), Franciscans (1220); to Italy (1221) where he taught theology and preached to heretics, esp. the Albigenses; named first Franciscan professor of theology by St. Francis (1223). Canonized (1232) by Pope Gregory IX; named doctor evangelicus (1946) by Pope Pius XII.

Anthony of Tag·rit \'täg-ˌrēt\. 9th century. Syrian theologian. Member of Jacobite sect of Eastern Syriac church; author of *Misron,* theological work, and of earliest known Syriac treatise on rhetoric; first to use rhyme in Syriac verse.

Anthony, Mark. See Marcus ANTONIUS.

Anthony, Susan Brownell. 1820–1906. American reformer, b. Adams, Mass. Active in temperance, abolitionist, and woman suffrage movements (from c.1850); with Elizabeth Cady Stanton organized National Woman Suffrage Association (1869); traveled, campaigned, wrote tirelessly on behalf of suffrage; president, National American Woman Suffrage Association (1892–1900). Author, with Stanton and M.J. Gage, of *History of Woman Suffrage* (1881–1902).

Anthony Mel·is·sa \-ˈmel-ə-sə\. 11th century. Byzantine monk and writer. Author of *Melissa* (whence surname), compilation of teachings and maxims on contemplative spirituality drawn from scripture and early Christian and secular authors.

An·tig·o·nus \an-ˈtig-ə-nəs\. Name of two kings of Judea:

Antigonus I. 135?–104 B.C. Coregent (105–104) with his brother Aristobulus. Killed as result of court intrigue.

Antigonus II. *Called* Mat·ta·thi·as \ˌmat-ə-ˈthī-əs\. 80?–37 B.C. King (40–37), last of the Hasmonaean dynasty. Son of Aristobulus II. Taken by Pompey as prisoner to Rome (63); escaped, but again prisoner (56); failed to secure Caesar's aid to throne of Judea; defeated by Herod (42); with help of Parthians, became king (40); drove Herod from Jerusalem; overcome by Romans (37) and put to death at Antioch.

Antigonus. Name of three kings of Macedonia:

Antigonus I. *Called* Antigonus Cy·clops \-ˈsī-ˌkläps\ *or* Mon·oph·thal·mus \ˌmän-əf-ˈthal-məs\, *i.e.* the One-Eyed. 382–301 B.C. King (306–301). One of generals of Alexander the Great, who made him satrap of Phrygia (333); after death of Alexander (323), received provinces of Lycia and Pamphylia; with others of *diadochoi* made war against Perdiccas (322); commander in chief of Antipater's army (321), which he led against Eumenes; gained control of Asia Minor; fought wars (315–311, 310–301) against coalition of other *diadochoi* Ptolemy, Lysimachus, Cassander, Seleucus; gained Aegean, eastern Mediterranean, Near East; proclaimed king by army (306); invaded Egypt (305); revived pan-Hellenic league (302); with his son Demetrius Poliorcetes, overwhelmed at Ipsus (301) by Lysimachus and Seleucus; killed in the battle.

Antigonus II Gon·a·tas \ˈgän-ət-əs\. c.319–239 B.C. King (276–239). Assumed title on death of his father, Demetrius I Poliorcetes (283) but counted reign from 276, following his defeat of the Celts in Macedonia; lost much of kingdom to Pyrrhus of Epirus (274), but regained it on his death (272); defeated Sparta and Athens in Chremonidean War (267–261); with Antiochus II fought Ptolemy II (261–255); maintained control over Aegean despite Greek revolts and Egyptian opposition.

Antigonus III Do·son \ˈdō-ˌsän\. c.263–221 B.C. King (227–221). Nephew of Antigonus Gonatas and cousin of Demetrius II, whom he succeeded, marrying his widow; created Hellenic League (224); supported Achaean League of Aratus, in alliance with whom he defeated Spartans under Cleomenes III at Sellasia (222).

Antigonus of Ca·rys·tus \kə-ˈris-təs\. 3d century B.C. Greek sculptor and author. Wrote *Lives of Philosophers, Collection of Wonderful Tales.*

An·tim·a·chus \an-ˈtim-ə-kəs\ of Col·o·phon \ˈkäl-ə-ˌfän\ *or* of Clar·os \ˈklar-ˌäs\. fl. c.400 B.C. Greek poet. Author of epic *Thebais* and elegy *Lydē,* both praised by Plato.

An·tin \ˈan-tən\, Mary. 1881–1949. American writer, b. Polotsk, Russia. To U.S. (1894); m. (1901) A. W. Grabau. Author of *From Plotzk to Boston* (1899), *The Promised Land* (1912), and *They Who Knock at Our Gates* (1914).

An·tin·o·üs \an-ˈtin-ə-wəs\. c.110–130 A.D. Roman courtier. Page and favorite of Emperor Hadrian; noted for his beauty; drowned in Nile; subject of many works of art.

An·ti·o·chus \an-ˈtī-ə-kəs\. Name of four kings of Commagene, reigning during period 62 B.C.–72 A.D.; at war with or under control of Rome; Commagene finally made part of Roman province of Syria by Vespasian.

Antiochus. Name of thirteen kings of the Seleucid kingdom of Syria, forming dynasty reigning 280–64 B.C.:

Antiochus I. *Called* Antiochus So·ter \-ˈsōt-ər\, *i.e.* Savior. 324–261 B.C. King (280–261 B.C.). Son of Seleucus I Nicator. Fought at Ipsus (301); associated with father as ruler (292); m. his stepmother, Stratonice (*q.v.*); put down Syrian revolts; won great victory over Gauls in Asia Minor (275); waged indecisive war (276–273) against Ptolemy II of Egypt; made alliance with Antigonus II Gonatas of Macedonia; had difficulty in keeping great Seleucid empire intact; waged war against Eumenes I of Pergamum (263–261).

Antiochus II. *Called* Antiochus The·os \-ˈthē-ˌäs\, *i.e.* the God. c.287–246 B.C. King (261–246 B.C.). Son of Antiochus I. Waged long war with Ptolemy II (259–255), regaining much of Anatolia and Phoenician coast; allied with Antigonus II of Macedonia; expelled tyrant Timarchus from Miletus (258) and was given surname Theos for this deliverance; lost (c.250) Bactria (Balkh) to Diodotus and Parthia to the Arsacids (*q.v.*); m. 1st Laodice, by whom he was father of Seleucus II (who succeeded him) and Antiochus Hierax, 2d (c.253) Berenice, daughter of Ptolemy II, as token of peace with Egypt.

Antiochus III. *Called* Antiochus the Great. 242–187 B.C. King (223–187 B.C.). Younger son of Seleucus II; succeeded brother Seleucus III. Suppressed revolts in Media and Persia (220); at war with Ptolemy IV Philopator (219–217), who defeated him at Raphia (217); faced with attempt to make Asia Minor independent, finally overcame usurper Achaeus after two-year siege of Sardis (215–213); recovered Armenia (212); made successful invasion of Parthia, Media, and Bactria and reached Hindu Kush (210–205); formed coalition (202) with Philip V of Macedon against Egypt; reduced all of southern Syria (202), defeated Egyptians at Paneas (198); took most Egyptian holdings in Asia Minor and by marriage of his daughter Cleopatra to Ptolemy V established influence over Egypt; invaded Thrace (196–194). Warned by Rome to stay out of Europe; aggravated situation by giving refuge to Hannibal (195); invited to invade Greece by anti-Roman Achaean League (192); defeated by Romans at Thermopylae (191) and his fleets beaten twice (191, 190) off western and southern coasts of Asia Minor; completely defeated (190) by Romans under P. Scipio Africanus at Magnesia (Manisa), near Ephesus; made peace in Treaty of Apamea (188), giving up all Asia Minor; killed while plundering temple in Elymaïs. Succeeded by his sons Seleucus IV and Antiochus IV.

Antiochus IV. *Called* Antiochus Epiph·a·nes \-i-ˈpif-ə-ˌnēz\, *i.e.* God Manifest. c.215–164 B.C. King (175–164). Son of Antiochus III; sent as hostage to Rome (189); educated there; seized throne when his brother Seleucus IV was murdered; waged war with Egypt (171–168); captured Pelusium (169); defeated both Ptolemy VI and VII; declared Judaism illegal (168); took Cyprus (168); undertook second campaign against Egypt (168) but forced by Rome to give it up. Fostered Hellenic culture throughout realm; his intolerance and stringent methods against Jewish religion, esp. his placing altar to Zeus Olympios in Temple of Jerusalem, brought on Wars of the Maccabees (166–160); lost Jerusalem, but made successful expedition to Armenia and Persia.

Antiochus V. *Called* Antiochus Eu·pa·tor \-ˈyü-pə-ˌtȯr\, *i.e.* of a good father. 173–162 B.C. Son of Antiochus IV. King (163–162) under regency of Lysias; made peace with Jews; overthrown and killed by his cousin Demetrius I Soter.

Antiochus VI. *Called* Antiochus Theos *and* Antiochus Epiphanes Di·o·ny·sus \-ˌdī-ə-ˈnī-səs\. d. 142 B.C. Boy king (145–142), under regent at Antioch, in opposition to Demetrius II Nicator. Son of Alexander Balas and Cleopatra Thea.

Antiochus VII. *Called* Antiochus Si·de·tes \-sī-ˈdēt-ēz\. c.159–129 B.C. King (139/138–129). Son of Demetrius I and brother of Demetrius II; after capture of Demetrius II he married his queen Cleopatra Thea (her 3d husband), and drove out usurper Tryphon (139); at war with Jews (138–134); destroyed Jerusalem (133); killed in Parthian War.

Antiochus VIII. *Called* Antiochus Gry·pus \-ˈgrī-pəs\, *i.e.* the Hook-Nosed. d. 96 B.C. King (125–96 B.C.). Son of Demetrius II Nicator and Cleopatra Thea. Joint ruler with his mother (125–121); sole king (121–115); forced to divide realm with Antiochus IX (115–96).

Antiochus IX. *Called* Antiochus Cyz·i·ce·nus \-ˌsiz-i-ˈsē-nəs\. d. 95 B.C. King (115–95). Seleucid pretender; son of Antiochus VII. As rival ruler, at war with Antiochus VIII; drove him from Antioch, but lost it (112).

Antiochus X. *Called* Antiochus Eu·se·bes \-ˈyü-si-ˌbēz\, *i.e.* the Pious. d. 92 B.C. Son of Antiochus IX. King (95–93) in opposition to his cousin Demetrius III.

Antiochus XI. *Called* Antiochus Epiphanes Phil·a·del·phus \-ˌfil-ə-ˈdel-fəs\. d. 92 B.C. Son of Antiochus VIII. King (92). Defeated by Antiochus X.

Antiochus XII. *Called* Antiochus Dionysus. d. 85 B.C. King (88–85). Son of Antiochus VIII; succeeded Demetrius III.

Antiochus XIII. *Called* Antiochus Asi·at·i·cus \-ˌā-zhē-ˈat-ə-kəs, -ˌā-shē-\. King (69–64 B.C.). Son of Antiochus X. Received large part of Syria from Lucullus after the defeat of Tigranes (69), losing it when it was made a Roman province (64) by Pompey. Last of Seleucids.

Antiochus of As·ca·lon \ˈas-kə-ˌlän\. 1st century B.C. Greek philosopher. Succeeded Philo as head of Academy; strongly influenced by Stoics; works no longer extant.

Antiochus of Syracuse. 5th century B.C. Greek historian. His writings on history of Syracuse and colonizing of Italy used as source material by later historians, esp. by Thucydides.

Antiochus Hi·er·ax \-ˈhī-ər-ˌaks\. fl. c.263–226 B.C. Seleucid prince. Son of Antiochus II and Laodice. Sent to rule Asia Minor while elder brother Seleucus II fought Third Syrian War (246–241) with Egypt; attempted to take throne (241); fought War of the Brothers (239–236) with Seleucus; in alliance with Celts, defeated Seleucus at Ancyra (236); expelled from Asia Minor in war with Attalus I of Pergamum (236–228); exiled to Thrace (227).

An·tip·a·ter \an-ˈtip-ət-ər\. c.397–c.319 B.C. Macedonian general. Ambassador of Philip II of Macedon to Athens (346); negotiated peace after battle of Chaeronea (338); regent of Macedonia during Alexander's expedition in East (334–323); suppressed Spartan revolt under Agis III by victory at Megalopolis (331); at division of empire after Alexander's death, left in command in Macedonia and Greece; associated with his son-in-law Craterus (323–321) in rule; on death of Perdiccas, regent of empire (321–319) for Philip III and Alexander IV.

Antipater. *Called* Antipater the Id·u·mae·an \ˌij-ə-ˈmē-ən\. d. 43 B.C. Procurator of Judea (47–43). Supported Hyrcanus II against Aristobulus II; gained influence in Judea after Pompey seized Jerusalem (63); later, on decline of Pompey's power, made friends with Caesar; aided him at Alexandria (47); rewarded with Roman citizenship and appointment as procurator; assassinated. Founder of Herodian dynasty through son, Herod the Great.

Antipater. d. 4 B.C. Judaean prince. Son of Herod the Great; conspired to win throne, arranged execution of half-brothers Aristobulus and Alexander (6 or 7 B.C.); tried and executed for plotting against father.

An·tiph·a·nes \an-ˈtif-ə-ˌnēz\. c.388–c.311 B.C. Greek playwright. With Alexis, principal representative of Middle Comedy; of 134 titles known, fragments extant.

An·ti·phon \ˈan-tə-ˌfän\. c.480–411 B.C. Athenian orator. Writer of speeches for litigants, especially in murder cases; condemned to death (411) for his part in conspiracy of the Four Hundred (wealthy citizens) to maintain control of Athens.

An·tis·the·nes \an-ˈtis-thə-ˌnēz\. c.445–c.365 B.C. Athenian philosopher. Studied under Socrates; founder of the Cynic school, teaching that happiness depends on moral virtue.

An·toine \äⁿ-twän\, André. 1858–1943. French actor and theater manager. Founded (1887) Théâtre-Libre, where new methods of dramatic presentation were tried; opened (1897) Théâtre-Antoine where he produced many contemporary plays; managed the Odéon (1906–13).

Antoine, Jacques-Denis. 1733–1801. French architect. Designer of the mint in Paris (1771–77).

Antoine de Bourbon. See ANTHONY of Bourbon.

An·to·kol·ski \ən-(ˌ)tə-ˈkōlʸ-skəi\, Mark Matveyevich. 1843–1902. Russian sculptor. Specialized in portrait statues, as of Ivan the Terrible, Peter the Great, Turgenev.

An·to·ku \än-to-kü\. 1178–1185. 81st emperor of Japan (1180–85). Placed on throne by Taira clan; driven from Kyōto by Minamoto forces (1181); died in naval battle of Dannoura, in which great sword, one of Three Imperial Regalia, was lost.

An·tom·mar·chi \ˌän-tōm-ˈmär-kē\, Francesco. 1780–1838. Corsican physician. Physician to Napoléon at St. Helena (from 1819); exhibited (1822) alleged Napoleonic death mask; wrote *Les derniers moments de Napoléon* (1823).

An·to·nel·li \ˌän-tō-ˈnel-lē\, Giacomo. 1806–1876. Italian prelate. Minister of finance, Papal States (1845); created cardinal (1847); prime minister (1848); accompanied Pius IX to Gaeta (1848) and, on return to Rome (1850), reestablished absolute power of papal administration; secretary of foreign affairs (from 1850); opponent to Italian unification.

An·to·nel·lo da Mes·si·na \ˌän-tō-ˈnel-lō-däm-äs-ˈsē-nä\. c.1430–1479. Sicilian painter. Reputed to have introduced oil painting into Italy; studied Flemish techniques; worked in Venice, where he profoundly influenced other artists; work noted for luminous color, meticulous realism, psychological insight; among his works were *St. Jerome, Salvator Mundi, Madonna del Rosario, Crucifixion, St. Sebastian, Portrait of a Condottiere, Virgin Annunciate.*

An·to·ne·scu \ˌän-tō-ˈnes-kü\, Ion. 1882–1946. Romanian general. Served in Romanian army in World War I; military attaché in Paris and London; general; chief of staff (1934); minister of defense (1937–38); suspended from army (1938) and imprisoned for Fascist sympathies; appointed prime minister (1940); on abdication of King Carol II, established Fascist dictatorship; entered war against Russia as German ally (1941); removed from office in coup d'état of King Michael (1944); executed as war criminal.

An·to·nia \an-ˈtō-nē-ə, -ˈtōn-yə\. *Called* Antonia Ma·jor \-ˈmā-jər\. 1st century A.D. Roman noblewoman. Daughter of Marcus Antonius and Octavia; m. L. Domitius Ahenobarbus; grandmother of Nero. Her younger sister ¶Antonia, *called* Antonia Minor (36 B.C.–37 A.D.), m. Nero Claudius Drusus; mother of Emperor Claudius, Germanicus Caesar, and Livilla; grandmother of Caligula.

An·to·ni·nus \ˌan-tə-ˈnī-nəs\. Saint. *Orig. given name* Antonio *or* Antonino; *surname* Pie·roz·zi \pyā-ˈrōt-tsē\ *or* De' For·ci·glio·ni \dā-ˌfōr-chēl-ˈyō-nē\. 1389–1459. Italian prelate and theologian. Entered Dominican order (1405); vicar general of Observants (1432–45); founded convent of San Marco, Florence (1436); prior of San Marco (1439–44); theologian at Council of Florence (1439); archbishop of Florence (1446). Known esp. for preaching, compassion, moral leadership. Among his works were *Summa Confessionum* (1472) and *Summa Theologica* or *Summa Moralis* (1477). Canonized by Pope Adrian VI (1523).

Antoninus, Marcus Aurelius. See also MARCUS AURELIUS.

Antoninus, Marcus Aurelius. *Called* Ca·ra·cal·la \kə-ˈrak-ə-lə\. *Orig.* Bas·si·a·nus \ˌbas-ē-ˈā-nəs\. 188–217 A.D. Roman emperor (211–217). Son of Lucius Septimius Severus; named caesar (196), assuming then the family name Antoninus; augustus (198); on death of father (211) murdered brother Geta to gain sole possession of throne. Conducted expeditions against German tribes (212–213), Parthians (216–217), marked by cruel excess and treachery; identified himself closely with Alexander the Great and had himself represented on coins and in statues as a god or pharaoh. Issued Constitutio Antoniniana de Civitate (212), granting Roman citizenship to all free inhabitants of the empire; ordered construction of the Thermae Antoninianae or Baths of Caracalla in Rome. Nicknamed Caracalla for Gallic cloak he allegedly designed and introduced.

Antoninus Pi·us \-ˈpī-əs\. *Full name* Ti·tus Au·re·li·us Ful·vus Boi·o·ni·us Ar·ri·us Antoninus \ˈtīt-əs-ȯ-ˈrē-lē-əs-ˈfəl-vəs-bȯi-ˈō-nē-əs-ˈar-ē-əs-\. 86–161 A.D. Roman emperor (138–161). Consul (120); proconsul in Asia (133–136); adopted (138) by Emperor Hadrian and succeeded him (138); m. (138) Annia Galeria Faustina, in whose memory he founded (141) charitable institution Puellae Faustinianae. Enjoyed remarkably peaceful and prosperous reign; principal disturbance of peace occurred in Britain, where earthen Wall of Antonine built by Roman governor from Forth to Clyde to keep out Pict and Scot invasions. Reformed harsh laws, observed sound fiscal policy. His daughter Faustina married his nephew Marcus Aurelius, whom he adopted as successor; also adopted Lucius Verus.

An·to·nio \əⁿ(n)-ˈtȯn-yü\. *Called* Dom Antonio. *Known as* the Prior of Crato. 1531–1595. Portuguese pretender. Natural son of Luís, Duke of Beja, second son of King Emanuel; became head of Order of St. John in Portugal and (1555) prior of Crato; accompanied King Sebastian to North Africa and on his death there (1578) claimed throne; claim rejected by Henry and then by ruling council (1580); acclaimed king by supporters, but defeated (1580) by Duke of Alba; with French aid mounted naval expeditions to Azores (1582, 1583); English fleet under Drake and Norris supported him but was defeated (1589).

An·to·nio \än-ˈtōn-yō\, Nicolás. 1617–1684. Spanish bibliographer. Author of *Bibliotheca Hispana* (1672–96), index of Spanish authors from reign of Augustus to 1670.

An·to·ni·us \an-ˈtō-nē-əs, -ˈtōn-yəs\, Marcus. 143–87 B.C. Roman orator. Consul (99); censor (97); as follower of Sulla, executed by order of Marius and Cinna (87). Praised by Cicero, who portrayed him in *De Oratore.*

Antonius, Marcus. *Known in English as* Mark, *or* Marc, An·to·ny \ˈan-tə-nē\ *or* An·tho·ny \ˈan(t)-thə-nē, ˈan-tə-nē\. 82 or 81–30 B.C. Roman orator, triumvir, and soldier. Grandson of Marcus Antonius (143–87); member of old patrician family related through his mother to Julius Caesar. To Greece (58); took part in campaigns (58–54) against Aristobulus II and in Palestine and Egypt; aided Caesar in Gaul (54–50); through Caesar's influence became successively quaestor, augur, and tribune of the plebs; master of horse in charge of Italy (49, 48–47); commanded left wing of Caesar's army at Pharsalus (48); consul with Caesar (44). After Caesar's death (44), influenced Romans by his oratory to drive out the assassins; governor of Transalpine and Cisalpine Gaul (44–39); found Octavian a rival; defeated by forces of senate (43); with Octavian and Lepidus formed (43) second triumvirate to rule Rome, Antonius receiving Asia as his command; with Octavian defeated republican forces at Philippi (42). Visited Asia to punish Cleopatra; succumbed to her charms and followed her to Egypt (41); in division of Roman world by triumvirate, took East (40–36); m. (40) Octavia as second wife, but returned to Cleopatra; suffered serious defeat by Parthians (36); settled in Alexandria, alienating his Roman support (34); bestowed extravagant titles on Cleopatra and her children (34). Rivalry with Octavian increased; deprived of his power (32) by senate; with Cleopatra, completely defeated by Octavian in naval battle at Actium (31); fled to Egypt; deserted by army, committed suicide.

Antony, Mark *or* Marc. See Marcus ANTONIUS.

An·to·ny Khra·po·vit·shy \(ˌ)ən-ˈtȯn-yəi-krə-(ˌ)pə-ˈvit-shəi\. *Orig.* Aleksey Pavlovich Krha·po·vit·sky \-ˈvit-skəi\. 1863–1936. Russian prelate. Rector of Orthodox academies in St. Petersburg, Moscow, Kazan (1890–97); bishop of Vohynia (1902); suppressed Ukrainian Catholic and nationalist Orthodox tendencies; elected to Holy Synod (1912); archbishop of Kharkov (1914); metropolitan of Kiev (1918). Fled Bolshevik revolution to Yugoslavia; leader of Russian Orthodox church in exile (from 1920). Noted polemicist, disputed papal authority and Western theology; promulgated ethical allegorical interpretation of Christian doctrine.

Antrim, Marquess of. See Randal MACDONNELL.

Ant·schel \ˈänt-shəl\, Paul. *Pseudonym* Paul Ce·lan \ˈtsel-än\. 1920–1970. German poet, b. Romania. In labor camp during World War II; lived in Bucharest, Vienna, and (from 1948) Paris. Author of verse influenced by Symbolists and expressing profound uncertainty of modern age, including *Der Sand aus den Urnen* (1848), *Mohn und Gedächtnis* (1952), *Von Schwelle zu Schwelle* (1955), *Sprachgitter* (1959), *Niemandrose* (1963), *Atemwende* (1967), *Lichtzwang* (1970).

Anūshīrvan. See KHOSROW I.

Anvarī. See AWHAD.

An·ville \äⁿ-vēl\, Jean-Baptiste Bour·gui·gnon \bür-gēn-yōⁿ\ d'. 1697–1782. French geographer and cartographer. Royal geographer (1719); produced 211 maps considered finest of their day, including important ones of China (1735), Italy (1743), Africa (1749), Asia (1751), India (1752); published historical atlases and wrote on ancient geography and meteorology.

Any·te \än-'ē-tā\. 3d century B.C. Greek poet. Wrote lyrics, epitaphs, epigrams, some extant; highly esteemed, esp. by Meleager, who honored her in his "Garland," and by Antipater of Thessalonica, who called her "a woman Homer."

Any·tus \än-'ēt-əs\. 5th–4th century B.C. Athenian politician. Chiefly responsible for conviction and condemnation (399 B.C.) of Socrates for "corruption of the young."

An·za \'än-sä\, Juan Bautista de. 1735–after 1788. Spanish explorer, b. Fronteras, Mexico. Established land route from Arizona to Monterey (1774); founded San Francisco (1776); governor of New Mexico (1778–88).

An·zen·gru·ber \'änt-sən-ˌgrü-bər\, Ludwig. 1839–1889. Viennese playwright and novelist. Wrote realistic plays of peasant life, including *Der Pfarrer von Kirchfeld* (1870), *Der Meineidbauer* (1871), *Die Kreuzelschreiber* (1872), *Der G'wissenswurm* (1874), *Das vierte Gebot* (1877); novels included *Der Schandfleck* (1876), *Dorfgänge* (1879), *Der Sternsteinhof* (1884).

An·zi·lot·ti \ˌänt-sē-'lȯt-tē\, Dionisio. 1869–1950. Italian jurist. Professor at Palermo, Bologna, and (1911–37) Rome; judge (1921–30) and president (1928–30), Permanent Court of International Justice.

Apa·fi *or* **Apaf·fy** \'äp-äf-ē\, Michael. 1632–1690. Prince of Transylvania (1661–90). Ruled as vassal of the Porte (1661–86); recognized suzerainty of Emperor Leopold I. His son ¶Michael II Apafi (1677–1713) succeeded him as prince (1690–97); acknowledged vassalage to Habsburgs, Transylvania becoming part of Hungary; abdicated (1697).

A-pao-chi \'ä-'paů-'jē\. d. 926. Mongol leader. Elected leader of Khitan tribes, declared himself king; on fall of T'ang dynasty (907) took title of emperor; aided Chin in conquest of North China and was given a region encompassing site of present Peking (926).

Ape. See Carlo PELLEGRINI.

Apel·les \ə-'pel-ēz\. 4th century B.C. Greek painter. Worked under Pamphilus at Dorian school of Sicyon; court painter of Philip II of Macedon and Alexander the Great. His paintings (no copies of which are extant) included one of Alexander grasping a thunderbolt, Artemis with a chorus of maidens, Aphrodite rising from the sea, and portraits of Clitus, Archelaus, and Antigonus. His reputation as greatest painter of antiquity has endured.

Apel·li·con \ə-'pel-i-ˌkän\ of Te·os \'tē-ˌäs\. d. c.84 B.C. Athenian bibliophile. Acquired libraries of Aristotle and Theophrastus; said to have published with corrections works of Aristotle; collection later carried to Rome after Sulla's capture of Athens and formed basis for edition of Andronicus of Rhodes.

Ap·gar \'ap-ˌgär\, Virginia. 1909–1974. American physician, b. Westfield, New Jersey. Professor, Columbia U. (1938–59); with National Foundation–March of Dimes (1960–74). Devised (1952) Apgar Score system for medical evaluation of newborn infants.

Aphra·a·tes \a-'frā-ə-ˌtēz\. *Syriac* Afra·hat \ä-'frä-ät\. 4th century A.D. Syrian Christian ascetic and writer. Monk and possibly bishop; author of many biblical commentaries, earliest known in Syriac church, expressing primitive Christian theology.

Apianus, Petrus. See Peter BENNEWITZ.

Api·ci·us \ə-'pish-ē-əs\, Marcus Gavius. 1st century A.D. Roman epicure. Said to have spent vast fortune in satisfying desire for rare foods.

Api·on \'ā-pē-ˌän, 'ap-ē-\, 1st century A.D. Greek grammarian. Head of school at Alexandria; led deputation sent by citizens of Alexandria to Emperor Caligula to complain against Jews (38); his strictures against the Jews were refuted by Josephus in *Contra Apionem.* Settled in Rome and taught rhetoric. Tale of Androcles and the lion is from his *Aiguptiaka.*

Apol·li·naire \á-pȯl-ē-ner\, Guillaume. *Orig.* Wilhelm Apollinaris de Kos·tro·wit·zki \kò-strò-'vēt-skē\. 1880–1918. French poet of Polish-Italian parentage, b. Rome? To Paris (1900); associated with advanced literary and artistic groups; wrote variously in fantastic, symbolic, whimsical manners, often with bizarre typography. Verse included *L'Enchanteur pourrissant* (1909), *Le Bestiaire* (1911), *Alcools* (1913), *Calligrammes* (1918); also wrote stories in *L'Hérésiarque et Cie* (1910) and *Le Poète assassiné* (1916), *Peintures cubistes* (1913, with aid of Picasso), and play *Les Mamelles de Tirèsias* (1917) for which he coined term surrealism.

Apol·li·nar·is \ə-ˌpäl-ə-'nar-əs\ *or* **Apol·li·nar·i·us** \-'nar-ē-əs\ of La·od·i·cea \lā-ˌäd-ə-'sē-ə\. *Also called* Apollinaris the Younger. c.310–c.390. Syrian prelate and theologian. Bishop of Laodicea, Syria (from c.361). When Emperor Julian prohibited Christians from teaching the classics, collaborated with his father Apollinaris the Elder in converting Old Testament into Homeric and Pindaric poems and New Testament into dialogues in imitation of Plato; opposed Arianism; set forth his own beliefs (Apollinarianism) that Christ had no rational soul; resulting sect condemned as heretical by several church councils; author of poems and religious works, most of which have been lost.

Apollinaris the Apologist. Saint. 2d century A.D. Phrygian prelate. Bishop of Hierapolis; championed orthodoxy, esp. against the Montanists.

Apollinaris Si·do·ni·us \-sī-'dō-nē-əs, -sə-\, Gaius Sollius. c.430–487 or 488. Roman prelate and writer in Gaul, b. Lyon. As a favorite of Emperor Anthemius, appointed governor of Rome (467); bishop of Averna (Clermont; 472). Author of *Panegyrics* on several emperors, nine books of letters and poems valued as source material for 5th-century political and literary history.

Apol·lo·do·rus \ə-ˌpäl-ə-'dȯr-əs, -'dōr-\. *Known as* Sci·ag·ra·phos \skī-'ag-rə-ˌfäs\, *i.e.* Shadow Painter. 5th century B.C. Athenian painter. Said to have introduced technique of shading by gradations of color.

Apollodorus. fl.140 B.C. Athenian grammarian. Author of verse *Chronicle* covering Greek history from fall of Troy to 119 B.C., of treatise *On the Gods,* and works on grammar, etc.

Apollodorus of Ca·rys·tus \kə-'ris-təs\. 3d century B.C. Greek playwright. Author of 47 comedies in New Comedy manner, and five times winner of prize for comedy.

Apollodorus of Damascus. 2d century A.D. Greek architect. A favorite of Emperor Trajan; designed Forum Trajanum and its Trajan's Column at Rome and triumphal arches at Benevento and Ancona; banished and put to death by Emperor Hadrian.

Ap·ol·lo·ni·us \ˌap-ə-'lō-nē-əs\. *Known as* Apollonius Mo·lon \-'mō-ˌlän\. 1st century B.C. Greek rhetorician. Teacher at Rhodes, particularly of Cicero and Caesar.

Apollonius. *Surnamed* Dys·co·lus \'dis-kə-ləs\, *i.e.* the Crabbed. 2d century A.D. Alexandrian scholar. One of greatest of Greek grammarians; made first critical study of Greek syntax; only four of his many works extant.

Apollonius of Per·ga \'pər-gə\. c.262–c.190 B.C. Greek mathematician. Called "the great geometer" for brillance and originality; principal work *Conics* in 8 books fully developed field of conic sections and introduced terms ellipse, parabola, hyperbola; also wrote treatises, most lost, on tangency, spherical and parabolic mirrors, proportion, irrational numbers, value of pi, etc.; introduced systems of eccentric and epicyclic motions later used by Ptolemy.

Apollonius of Rhodes \'rōdz\ *or* **Apollonius Rho·di·us** \'rō-dē-əs\. 3d century B.C. Greek epic poet. Author of an epic, *Argonautica,* based on legend of the Argonauts; librarian at Alexandria (perhaps c.260–c.247).

Apollonius of Tral·les \'tral-ēz\. 2d century B.C. Greek sculptor. Collaborated with his brother Tauriscus in executing marble group known as *Farnese Bull.*

Apollonius of Ty·a·na \'tī-ə-nə\. 1st century A.D. Greek Neo-Pythagorean philosopher. Traveled in India, visiting Babylon and Nineveh en route; regarded by many contemporaries as magician; biography of him by Philostratus, commissioned by Empress Julia Domna, attributed miracles and other Christ-like attributes to him.

Apollonius the Athenian. 1st century B.C. Greek sculptor. Known only from signatures on Belvedere torso and bronze *Boxer,* both apparently copied from lost 2d century B.C. originals.

Apo·pi \ä-'pō-pē\ *or* **Ap·o·phis** \'ap-ə-(ˌ)fis\. Name of several Hyksos kings in Egypt, esp. AUSERRE APOPI I (*q.v.*).

Ap·pert \a-per\, Nicolas-François. c.1750–1841. French chef and inventor. Invented process for preserving food in hermetically sealed containers, winning thereby (1810) award from interior ministry; published *L'Art de conserver, pendant plusieurs années, touts les substances animales et végétales* (1810); established (1812) House of Appert, first commercial cannery; also invented bouillon tablet, an autoclave, etc.

Ap·pia \'äp-pyä\, Adolphe. 1862–1928. Swiss stage designer. Pioneer in developing modern realistic stage lighting and setting; designed sets and lighting for La Scala, Basel, and other opera houses. Author of *La Mise en scène du drame Wagnérien* (1895), *Die Musik und die Inszenierung* (1899), *L'Oeuvre d'art vivant* (1921).

Ap·pia·ni \äp-'pyä-nē\, Andrea. 1754–1817. Italian painter. Known esp. for his frescoes at Monza and in Church of Santa Maria, Milan; called "Painter of the Graces"; first court painter to Napoléon.

Ap·pi·a·nos \ˌap-ē-'ā-nəs\ *or* **Ap·pi·an** \'ap-ē-ən\. 2d century A.D. Greek historian. Official in Alexandria; later moved to Rome, becoming citizen. Author in Greek of *Romaica,* history of Rome and its conquests; of the original 24 books, 11 complete books and fragments of others are extant.

Appius Claudius. See CLAUDIUS.

Ap·ple·by \'ap-əl-bē\, John Francis. 1840–1917. American inventor, b. Westmoreland, N.Y. Invented a cartridge magazine and automatic feed device for rifles (pat. 1864) and a grain binder and knotter (pat. 1878, 1879).

Ap·ple·gate \'ap-əl-ˌgāt\, Jesse. 1811–1888. American pioneer, b. Kentucky. Surveyor; to Oregon in wagon train (1843); led exploring party that opened southern route to Oregon (1845); influential in Oregon politics. Author of Western classic "A Day with the Cow-Column" (1876).

Appleseed, Johnny. See John CHAPMAN.

Ap·ple·ton \ˈap-əl-tən, -əlt^{ə}n\, Daniel. 1785–1849. American publisher, b. Haverhill, Mass. With his son William Henry (1814–1899) founded D. Appleton & Co., book publishers (1838).

Appleton, Sir Edward Victor. 1892–1965. English physicist. Professor, King's Coll., London (1924–36), Cambridge (1936–39); secretary, Dept. of Scientific and Industrial Research (1939–49); principal, vice chancellor, U. of Edinburgh (1949–65). Known for research in propagation of electromagnetic waves; awarded Nobel prize for physics (1947) for discovery of an electrically charged layer in the ionosphere (Appleton layer or F region) that reflects radio waves.

Appleton, Victor. See Edward STRATEMEYER.

Ap·po·nyi \ˈäp-pȯn-yē\. Name of Hungarian noble family including: Count György (1808–1899), chancellor (1846–48), Conservative party leader (to 1848) and, later, Nationalist party leader supporting Deák in efforts to negotiate Austro-Hungarian Ausgleich. His son ¶Count Albert György (1846–1933), member of Parliament (1872–1918), becoming leader of Hungarian nationalists; minister of education (1906–10, 1917–18), latterly in Esterházy and Wekerle cabinets; head of Hungarian peace delegation in Paris (1919–20); several times Hungarian delegate to League of Nations.

Apra·ksin *or* **Aprax·in** \(ˌ)ə-ˈpräk-syin\, Fyodor Matveyevich. Count. 1661–1728. Russian admiral. Entered service of Peter the Great (1682); became favorite of Peter; governor of Archangel (1692), of Azov (1700); one of most influential members of imperial court; admiral (1707); built ships, wharves, fortresses; defeated Swedes (1708), saving St. Petersburg from destruction. Created count (1709). Captured Viborg (1710), Åbo (1713), Helsinki (1714); defeated Swedish fleet (1713), with result that Baltic provinces by Treaty of Nystad (1721) became Russian; won several other naval victories in Turkey and Persia. His nephew ¶Count Stepan Fyodorovich Apraksin (1702–1760), general, served in war against Turks (1737); made general in chief (1746) and marshal (1756); strongly opposed to German influence; in Seven Years' War, defeated Prussians at Gross-Jägersdorf (1757); died in prison.

Ap·ri·es \ˈap-rē-ēz\. *Also written* Ouaphris. *Egyptian* Haaibra Wahibra; *Hebrew* Hophra. d. 567 B.C. King of Egypt (589–570 B.C.) of 26th dynasty. Son of Psamtik II. Failed to aid ally King Zedekiah of Judah against Nebuchadrezzar; later took Sidon; defeated in expedition against Cyrene, whereupon he was deposed by army in favor of Ahmose II.

Ap·u·le·ius \ˌap-yə-ˈlē-(y)əs\, Lucius. *Known sometimes as* Apuleius of Madaura. c.124–after 170? A.D. North African philosopher and rhetorician. Traveled widely; taught rhetoric in Rome; author of commentaries on Plato, of *Apologia,* and of literary works, esp. *Metamorphoses,* or *The Golden Ass,* Latin novel of many adventurous, bizarre, dignified, or ludicrous episodes that provided material for such later authors as Boccaccio, Cervantes, Robert Bridges.

Āqā Mī·rak \ä-ˈkä-ˈmē-räk\. *Also known as* Āghā Mī·rak \ä-ˈgä-\. 16th century. Persian painter. Pupil of Behzād; patronized by Shāh Ṭahmāsp I.

Āqā Re·zā \ä-kä-rä-ˈzä\. 16th–17th century. Persian painter. Court painter and calligrapher to Shāh ʿAbbās I; noted for mannered figure studies, miniatures.

ʿAq·qād \ä-ˈkäd\, ʿAbbās Maḥmud al-. 1889–1964. Egyptian journalist, poet, and critic. Author of verse, a novel *Sarāh* (1938), works on political philosophy, religion, and literature, biographies, and essays; influential innovator of modern Arabic poetic and critical styles.

Aqua·vi·va \ˌäk-wä-ˈvē-vä\ *or* **Ac·qua·vi·va** \ˌäk-kwä-\, Claudio. 1543–1615. Italian ecclesiastic. Entered Jesuit order (1567); fifth general of Society of Jesus (1581–1615); fostered Jesuit scholarship; drew up *Ratio atque institutio studiorum* (1586), unified code for Jesuit schools.

Aq·ui·la \ˈak-wə-lə\. *Called* Aquila of Pon·tus \ˈpän-təs\ *or* Aquila Pon·ti·cus \ˈpän-ti-kəs\. 2d century A.D. Jewish translator of Old Testament. According to some, related to Emperor Hadrian; became Christian; later, returned to Judaism and reputedly disciple of Rabbi Akiba ben Joseph. Translated Old Testament from Hebrew into Greek (c.140 A.D.), extant only in fragments.

Aquin, Louis Claude d'. See DAQUIN.

Aquinas, Saint Thomas. See THOMAS AQUINAS.

ʿArabī, Ibn al-. See IBN AL-ʿARABĪ.

Arabi Pasha. See ʿURĀBĪ PASHA.

Ara·go \á-rá-gō, *Angl* ˈar-ə-ˌgō\, François, *in full* Dominique-François-Jean. 1786–1853. French physicist. Professor, École Polytechnique, Paris (1809–30); director of Paris observatory (from 1830). Minister of war and marine in provisional government (1848); responsible for abolition of slavery in French colonies; opposed election of Louis-Napoléon as president of France; refused to take oath of allegiance after coup d'état of 1851. Known for demonstrations of production of magnetism by rotation, contributions to discovery of laws of light polarization; devised experiment by which wave nature of light was demonstrated through its reduced speed through dense media; encouraged Le Verrier to investigate anomalous motion of Uranus. His son ¶Emmanuel (1812–1896), vigorous opponent of Louis-Napoléon, was minister of justice (1870), later of the interior; member, National Assembly (1871–76); senator (1876–80); ambassador to Switzerland (1880–94).

Ara·gon \á-rá-gō^{n}\, Louis. 1897-1982. French writer and political activist. Attracted to Communism (1927); visited Soviet Union (1930); joined underground resistance after fall of France; became French national hero for his resistance poems; member of French Communist party (1950–60). Leader of Surrealist movement; co-founder of Surrealist review *Littérature* (1919); editor of *Les Lettres Françaises* (1953–72). Author of such books of poetry as *Feu de joie* (1920), *Le Mouvement perpétuel* (1925), *La Grande Gaite* (1929), *Le Front Rouge* (1931), *Le Crève-Coeur* (1941). Published *Le Monde réel,* a series of novels about the class struggle, starting with *Les Cloches de Bale* (1934).

Arai \ä-rī\ Hakuseki. 1657–1725. Japanese politician, historian, and philosopher. Chief adviser to Tokugawa shoguns Ienobu and Ietsugu (1709–16); devised stringent fiscal and trade policies, attempted to halt corruption in government. Author of important historical studies *Dokushi yoron* and *Koshi tsū.*

Arak·che·yev \ə-(ˌ)rək-ˈchā-yif\, Aleksey Andreyevich. Count. 1769–1834. Russian soldier and statesman. Favorite of Czar Paul and commander of his bodyguard; made count (1799); political adviser to Alexander I (1801–25); as inspector general, reorganized artillery branch of army (1803); minister of war (1808–10); led attack on Åland Islands (1809) in Russo-Swedish War; Alexander's chief military adviser in Napoleonic War (1812); his dominance of domestic affairs (1815–25) gave decade the name Arakcheyevshchina.

Ara·ki \ä-rä-kē\ Sadao. 1877–1966. Japanese general. Member of ultranationalist army faction; minister of war (1932–34); minister of education (1938–40); sentenced as war criminal to life imprisonment in 1948; released in 1955.

Ar·am \ˈar-əm, ˈer-\, Eugene. 1704–1759. English schoolmaster and murderer. Self-taught philologist; recognized in advance of scholars the Indo-European affinities of Celtic, and disputed the derivation of Latin from Greek. Convicted of murder on evidence by an accomplice; executed. Subject of a romance by Bulwer-Lytton and a ballad by Thomas Hood.

Aram·bu·ru \är-äm-ˈbü-rü\, Pedro Eugenio. 1903–1970. Argentine soldier and politician. Member of military junta that overthrew Pres. Juan Perón (1955); acting president (1955–58).

Aranda, Conde de. See ABARCA DE BOLEA.

Aranha, José Pereira da Graça. See GRAÇA ARANHA.

Ara·nha \á-ˈrán-yá\, Oswaldo. 1894–1960. Brazilian lawyer and diplomat. A leader in Vargas coup d'état (1930); minister of justice (1930–31) and finance (1931–34); ambassador to U.S. (1934–38); minister of foreign affairs (1938–44); delegate to United Nations (1947–48); president, UN General Assembly (1947); again finance minister (1953–54); agriculture minister (1954).

Arany \ˈär-än^{y}\, János. 1817–1882. Hungarian poet. Professor at Nagykörös Gymnasium (1851–60); member (from 1858), secretary (1865–79), Hungarian Acad.; close friend of Sándor Petőfi. Achieved fame with epic trilogy *Toldi* (1847), *Toldi szerelme* (1848–79), *Toldi estéje* (1854); also wrote incomplete epics *Bolond Istók* (1850), *Buda halála* (1864), and many ballads and lyrics.

Ará·nyi \ä-ˈrán-yē\, Jelly Eva d'. 1895–1966. Hungarian violinist. Debut, Vienna (1909); to London (1913); known esp. for playing of contemporary works; dedicatee of Bartok's sonatas for violin and piano, Ravel's *Tzigane for Violin and Orchestra,* Vaughan Williams' *Violin Concerto.*

Ara·son \ˈär-ä-ˌsȯn\, Jón. c.1484–1550. Icelandic prelate and poet. Roman Catholic bishop of Hólar (1522); resisted imposition of Lutheranism; seized Lutheran see of Bishop Marteinn (1549–50); arrested and beheaded; last Catholic bishop in Iceland. Author of religious and satirical verse.

Ara·tor \ə-ˈrāt-ər, -ˈrā-ˌtȯr\. 6th century A.D. Ligurian Christian poet. Author of *De Actibus Apostolorum* (544 A.D.), an apostolic history in verse.

Ara·tus \ə-ˈrāt-əs\ of Sic·y·on \ˈsis(h)-ē-ˌän\. 271–213 B.C. Greek general and statesman. Liberated and established democracy in Sicyon (251); strategos of Achaean League (alternate years from 245); captured Acrocorinth (243); defeated Aetolians at Pellene (241); helped liberate Athens from Macedonia (229); fought Spartans under Cleomenes, finally, with aid from Antigonus Doson of Macedonia, defeating Cleomenes at Sellasia (222). Waged defensive war with Aetolians (221–217).

Aratus of So·li \ˈsō-lē\. c.315–c.245 B.C. Greek physician and poet. Author of didactic poems *Phaenomena* and *Diosēmeia* on astronomy and meteorology, later popular in Rome; quoted by St. Paul in speech on Mars' Hill, Athens.

Arbeau, Thoinot. See Jehan TABOUROT.

Ar·benz Guz·mán \ˈär-bāns-güs-ˈmän\, Jacobo. 1913–1971. Guatemalan politician. Took part in overthrow of dictator Jorge Ubico (1944); minister of war (1949–50); president of Guatemala (1950–54); policies of land redistribution, labor organization, expropriation of foreign holdings led to overthrow by Col. C. Castillo Armas (1954); in exile in Mexico, Uruguay, Cuba.

Ar·ber \ˈär-bər\, Agnes, *nee* Rob·ert·son \ˈräb-ərt-sən\. 1879–1960. English botanist. m. (1909) E.A.N. Arber (son of Edward Arber). Author of *Herbals, Their Origin and Evolution* (1912), *Water Plants* (1920), *Monocotyledons* (1925), *The Gramineae* (1934), *The Natural Philosophy of Plant Form* (1950).

Arber, Edward. 1836–1912. English scholar. Professor, Birmingham (1881–94); editor of *English Reprints* (1868–71), a series of accurate texts of works previously accessible only in rare editions, of *An English Garner* of old tracts and poems (1877–96), *English Scholar's Library of Old and Modern Works* (1878–84), etc.

Arblastier, William. See William ALABASTER.

Arblay, Madame d'. See Fanny BURNEY.

Ar·bo·gast \ˈär-bō-ˌgast\. d. 394 A.D. Frankish general in Roman army. Rose to master of cavalry in western Roman army; sent by Gratian (380) to aid Theodosius against Goths; sent by Theodosius against usurper Maximus (388 A.D.); defeated Maximus' son Flavius Victor; pacified Rhenish frontier (389); count and regent in Gaul (391); resisted dismissal by Valentinian; probably killed Valentinian (392), proclaimed his own candidate, Eugenius, emperor, and began campaign to restore paganism; defeated by Theodosius (394); committed suicide.

Ar·bois de Ju·bain·ville \år-bwå-də-zhüe-baⁿ-vēl\, Marie-Henri d'. 1827–1910. French historian. Professor, Collège de France (from 1882); author of *Les Premiers habitants de l'Europe* (1889–94), *Les Celtes* (1903).

Ar·buth·not \är-ˈbəth-nət, ˈär-bəth-ˌnät\, John. 1667–1735. Scottish physician and writer. Physician in ordinary to Queen Anne (1705–14). Close friend of Swift, Pope, Gay, and a founder with them of Scriblerus Club. Author of witty political pamphlets, including one (*The History of John Bull,* 1727, a satire against the duke of Marlborough) which popularized and fixed modern conception of John Bull as the typical Englishman; chief contributor to *Memoirs of Martinus Scriblerus* (1713–14; pub. 1741); also author of medical and scientific papers.

Arc, Joan of. See JOAN of Arc.

Ar·ca·delt \ˈär-kå-ˌdelt\, Jacques. *Name also given as* Jacob *or* Jakob, Arcadel, Archadelt, Archadente, Archadet, *or* Harchadelt. c.1505–1568. Dutch or Flemish composer. Choirmaster of papal chapel, Rome (1539–49); member of French royal chapel (1557). Composed more than 200 madrigals in Italian mode, which strongly influenced evolution of the form; some 120 chansons; motets; masses.

Ar·ca·di·us \är-ˈkād-ē-əs\. c.377–408. Emperor of Eastern Roman Empire (383–408). Son of Emperor Theodosius I; named augustus, or co-ruler, in East (383); succeeded to sole rule on death of father (395); lived in luxury and indifference to affairs of empire, while government administered by ministers Rufinus (praetorian prefect, murdered 395) and Eutropius (eunuch, deposed and beheaded, 399); associated his son Theodosius II with throne (402). Reign marked by rise of Gothic power; persecution of St. John Chrysostom by consort Eudoxia.

Arce, Gaspar Núñez de. See NUÑEZ DE ARCE.

Ar·ce \ˈär-sā\, Manuel José. d. 1847. Salvadorean soldier and politician. First president of United Provinces of Central America (1825–29); forced to resign and exiled in liberal revolt.

Ar·ces·i·la·us \är-ˌses-ə-ˈlā-əs\ *or* **Ar·ces·i·las** \är-ˈses-ə-ləs\. 316 or 315–c.241 B.C. Athenian philosopher. Succeeded Crates as head of Academy; in his teachings reacted against Stoic dogmatism and taught a skeptical "suspension of judgment."

Arch \ˈärch\, Joseph. 1826–1919. English reformer and politician. Agricultural laborer; founded National Agricultural Laborers' Union (1872); M.P. (1885–86, 1892–1902).

Archadelt, Archadente, *or* Archadet, Jakob. See ARCADELT.

Arch·bold \ˈärch-ˌbōld\, John Dustin. 1848–1916. American businessman, b. Leesburg, Ohio. Identified with Standard Oil Co. (1882–1911), a dominant figure in its organization; after dissolution forced by U.S. Supreme Court decision (1911), became president of Standard Oil Co. of New Jersey (1911–16).

Ar·che·la·us \ˌär-kə-ˈlā-əs\. d. 399 B.C. King of Macedonia (413–399 B.C.). Natural son of Perdiccas II; seized throne on murder of half-brother and other legitimate claimants; strengthened Macedonian economy and defense; patron of Greek art and literature.

Archelaus. 5th century B.C. Greek philosopher. Pupil of Anaxagoras; reputedly a teacher of Socrates.

Archelaus. Name of three Cappadocians:

Archelaus. 1st century B.C. A general of Mithridates VI Eupator. Sent by Mithridates (88–87 B.C.) with large fleet and army to hold Greece against Romans; won Athens and other Greek peoples to his aid; occupied Piraeus; defeated by Sulla at Chaeronea (86) and Orchomenus (85); discredited by Mithradates, became friend and ally of Rome.

Archelaus. d. 55 B.C. Son of the preceding. High priest at Comana (63); m. Berenice, daughter of Ptolemy Auletes of Egypt; king of Egypt for a few months (56); killed in battle against Aulus Gabinius, proconsul of Syria.

Archelaus. *Called* Archelaus Si·si·nes \-sə-ˈsī-nēz\. d. 17 A.D. Grandson of Archelaus of Comana. King of Cappadocia (40 B.C.–c.14 A.D.); made king by Mark Antony, whom he deserted after Actium (31 B.C.); his kingdom extended by Octavian (20 B.C.); deposed by Tiberius and died in prison in Rome, Cappadocia being made Roman province.

Archelaus. See HEROD ARCHELAUS.

Ar·chen·holz \ˈär-kən-ˌhōlts\, Johann Wilhelm von. 1743–1812. German historian and editor. Author of *England und Italien* (1785), *Annalen der britischen Geschichte* (1789–1800), *Geschichte des Siebenjährigen Krieges* (1793); edited political-literary journal *Minerva* (1792–1809).

Ar·cher \ˈär-chər\, Frederick. 1857–1886. English jockey. Foremost jockey of his day; rode 2,748 winners in career (1870–86).

Archer, Frederick Scott. 1813–1857. English photographer and sculptor. Invented wet collodion process in photography (1850), first by which multiple prints could be made; invented ambrotype portrait process.

Archer, Thomas. c.1668–1743. English architect. Leading English exponent of Baroque manner; designed Chatsworth House, Derbyshire (1705), Heythorpe Hall, Oxfordshire (c.1705), Roehampton House, Surrey (1712), St. Paul's Church, Deptford (1712), St. John's, Westminster (1714).

Archer, William. 1856–1924. Scottish dramatic critic and playwright. Dramatic critic on London *Figaro* (1879–81), later for *World, Nation, Manchester Guardian,* etc.; many reviews collected in *The Theatrical World* (1893–97). Introduced Ibsen to English stage by translation of *The Pillars of Society* (produced 1880) and other Ibsen plays. Author of *Masks or Faces?* (1888) and *Play-making* (1912); wrote *The Green Goddess* (1923), a successful melodrama.

Ar·cher·mus \är-ˈkər-məs\. 6th century B.C. Greek sculptor of Chios. Known esp. for treatment of draped female figures; said to have been first to depict Love and Victory as winged.

Ar·chi·as \ˈär-kē-əs\. 8th century B.C. Greek colonizer, from Corinth. By tradition, on command of Delphic oracle founded (734) Syracuse, Sicily.

Archias. *In full* Aulus Licinius Archias. c.120–after 61 B.C. Greek poet. To Rome (102 B.C.); defended by Cicero (*Pro Archia,* 61) against charge that he had obtained citizenship illegally.

Ar·chi·da·mus \ˌär-kə-ˈdā-məs\. Name of five kings of Sparta of Eurypontid house, including:

Archidamus II. d. 427 B.C. King (c.469–427 B.C.). Succeeded grandfather Leotychides; attempted to prevent war with Athens; commanded Spartan forces at beginning of Peloponnesian War (431–427).

Archidamus III. d. 338 B.C. King (360–338 B.C.). Son of Agesilaus II; commanded forces in Peloponnesian War; defeated Arcadians (367), defeated by them (364); defended Sparta against Epaminondas (363); supported Phocians in Sacred War (355–346), and commanded mercenary army in Italy protecting the Tarentines (338).

Ar·chil·o·chus \är-ˈkil-ə-kəs\. 7th century B.C. Greek lyric poet. Among works were hymns, elegies, and verses of bitter invective; used trochaic and iambic measure, credited with introducing epode form.

Ar·chi·me·des \ˌär-kə-ˈmēd-ēz\. c.287–212 B.C. Greek mathematician and inventor. Known especially for work in mechanics and hydrostatics; credited with devising Archimedian screw for raising water. Discovered principle of buoyancy, that a body immersed in fluid loses weight equal to the weight of the fluid displaced; according to legend, he was seeking method for determining purity of gold in King Hieron's crown, and shouted "*Eureka*" (I have found it) on discovering method determined by above principle. Wrote treatises on volumes of spheres and cylinders, on value of pi, on spirals, on center of gravity, etc.

Ar·chi·pen·ko *Ukrain* ər-k̲-yip-ˈyän-kō, *Russ* (ˌ)ər-k̲-ˈyēp-yən-kə, *Angl* ˌär-ki-ˈp(y)eŋ-(ˌ)kō\, Aleksandr Porfiryevich. 1887–1964. American sculptor, b. Kiev, Russia. Resident of Paris (1908–21), Berlin (1921–23), and U.S. (from 1923); U.S. citizen (1928). Worked in Cubist, later purely abstract manner; revolutionized sculpture through use of nonrepresentational forms in voids and solids.

Ar·chy·tas \är-ˈkīt-əs\ of Ta·ren·tum \tə-ˈren-təm\. fl. 400–350 B.C. Greek Pythagorean philosopher, scientist, and mathematician. Friend of Plato; solved problem of doubling the cube; advanced the study of acoustics and music by his investigations; first to distinguish harmonic progression from arithmetical and geometric progression; credited with inventing pulley.

Ar·cim·bol·do \ˌär-chēm-ˈbōl-dō\ *or* **Ar·cim·bol·di** \-dē\, Giuseppe. c.1530–1593. Milanese painter. Court painter to Maximilian II, Rudolph II in Prague; painted theatrical settings; known esp. for grotesque compositions of fruits, vegetables, and other objects, often representing allegorical figures.

Ar·çon \år-sōⁿ\, Jean-Claude-Éléonore Le Mi·chaud \mē-shō\ d'. 1733–1800. French military engineer. Inventor of unsinkable floating batteries used at siege of Gibraltar (1782); technical adviser to Committee of Public Safety and to Directory.

\ə\ **abut** \ᵊ\ **kitten,** *Fr.* **table** \ər\ **further** \a\ **ash** \ā\ **ace** \ä\ **cot, cart** \aů\ **out** \ch\ **chin** \e\ **bet** \ē\ **easy** \g\ **go** \i\ **hit** \ī\ **ice** \j\ **job** \ŋ\ **sing** \ō\ **go** \ȯ\ **law** \ȯi\ **boy** \th\ **both** \t̲h̲\ **the** \ü\ **loot** \ů\ **foot** \y\ **yet** \zh\ **vision** \å, b̲, g̲, k̲, ⁿ, œ, œ̄, ue, ue̅, ʸ\ *see* **Guide to Pronunciation**

Arc·ti·nus \ärk-'tī-nəs\ of Mi·le·tus \mī-'lēt-əs\. 8th century B.C. Greek cyclic poet. Author of *Aethiopis,* continuing story of Trojan War from *Iliad,* of *Iliu Persis* on sack of Troy, and perhaps of *Titanomachia.*

Ar·culf \'är-(,)kəlf\. 7th century A.D. Frankish prelate and traveler. Bishop perhaps of Périgueux; made pilgrimage to Holy Land (c.680) in which he became first major Western Christian observer of rise of Islām; first to relate story of St. George.

Ar·da·shīr \'är-də-shər\. *Later Persian form of* Artakhshathra. Name of three kings of Persia of Sāsānian dynasty:

Ardashīr I. 3d century A.D. King (224–241). Descendant of Sāsān; succeeded father Papak as king of Persis (208); began war against Persis and Carmania; defeated and killed Artabanus V, the Parthian king, at Hormizdagān (224); founded Sāsānian empire with Ctesiphon as its capital; established orthodox Zoroastrianism as official religion; extended kingdom but not successful against Armenia; at war with Rome (231–233); defeated by Alexander Severus (233); associated his son Shāpūr I on throne with him (241).

Ardashīr II. 4th century. King (379–383). Son of Hormizd II; succeeded brother Shāpūr II, during whose reign he was governor (or king) of Adiabene; quarreled with court nobles; deposed.

Ardashīr III. 621–630. King (628–630). Son of Kavadh II; raised to throne at age of seven during period of chaos following murder of Khosow II; murdered.

Ar·den \'är-dᵊn\, Elizabeth. *Orig.* Florence Nightingale Gra·ham \'grā-əm, 'gra(-ə)m\. 1884–1966. American businesswoman, b. Woodbridge, Ont. To New York City (c.1908); opened beauty salon (1910); adopted personal and corporate name Elizabeth Arden; opened luxury salons in cities in U.S., Europe, South America; developed line of cosmetics.

Ar·di·gò \,är-dē-'gō\, Roberto. 1828–1920. Italian positivist philosopher. Professor, Padua (1881–1909); author of *Psicologia come scienza positiva* (1870), *La morale dei positivisti* (1878), *Il vero* (1891), etc.

Ardilaun, Baron. See under GUINNESS family.

Ar·drey \'är-drē\, Robert. 1908–1980. American writer, b. Chicago. Author of plays as *Star-Spangled* (1936), *Thunder Rock* (1939); screenplays as *They Knew What They Wanted* (1940), *Three Musketeers* (1947), *Madame Bovary* (1948); novels as *Brotherhood of Fear* (1952); popular scientific works as *African Genesis* (1961), *Territorial Imperative* (1966), *Social Contract* (1970).

Ar·du·in \'är-də-,wēn\ *or* **Har·du·in** \'här-\. Marquis of Ivrea \ēv-'re-ä\. d. 1015. Lombard prince and king (1002–14). Raised revolt in northern Italy against Otto III (997–1000); on Otto's death, proclaimed by nobles king of the Lombards (1002); waged wars against Emperor Henry II (1004, 1013–14); deposed (1014).

Ar·du·i·no \,är-dü-'ē-nō\, Giovanni. 1714–1795. Italian geologist. Mining expert; consultant on agriculture and industry for Republic of Venice; laid foundation of stratigraphic chronology by identifying and naming Primary, Secondary, Tertiary, and Quaternary layers of earth's crust.

Arendt \ə-'rent\, Hannah. 1906–1975. American political scientist, b. Hanover, Germany. To U.S. (1940); research director, Conference on Jewish Relations (1944–46); chief editor, Schocken Books (1946–48); executive secretary, Jewish Cultural Reconstruction (1949–52); visiting professor, Princeton (1959), Columbia (1960); professor, U. of Chicago (1963–67), New School for Social Research (1967–75). Author of *Origins of Totalitarianism* (1951), *The Human Condition* (1958), *On Revolution* (1963), *Eichmann in Jerusalem* (1963), *On Violence* (1970), etc.

Arène \á-ren\, Paul-Auguste. 1843–1896. French writer and Provençal poet. Works included tales of Provence as *La Gueuse parfumée* (1876), *Contes de Paris et de Provence* (1887), novels as *La Chèvre d'or* (1889), *Domnine* (1894); plays, verse, etc.

Aren·sky \(,)ər-'yän-skəi, *Angl* ə-'ren-skē\, Anton Stepanovich. 1861–1906. Russian composer. Taught at Moscow Conservatory (1882–95); director, Imperial Chapel (1895–1901). Composer of operas *A Dream on the Volga* (1892), *Raphael* (1894), and *Nal and Damayanti* (1899), two symphonies, and songs, choruses, and piano pieces.

Ar·e·tae·us \,ar-ə-'tē-əs\ of Cap·pa·do·cia \,kap-ə-'dō-sh(ē-)ə\. 2d century A.D. Greek physician and writer. Practised in Rome and Alexandria; described many diseases and conditions; named diabetes; considered second only to Hippocrates among ancient physicians.

Aretino, Guido. See GUIDO of Arezzo.

Aretino, Leonardo. See Leonardo BRUNI.

Are·ti·no \,ä-rā-'tē-nō\, Pietro. *Real surname unknown.* 1492–1556. Italian satirist, b. Arezzo. Studied literature and painting, Perugia; to Rome (1517); protégé of Leo X, Clement VII; left Rome, in part because of his *Sonetti lussuriosi* ("Lewd Sonnets," 1524); settled in Venice (1527), where he became great friend of Titian. Known esp. for satirical attacks on powerful contemporaries, winning his nickname of Scourge of Princes. Among his works were *Ragionamenti* (1534–36), *Orazia* (tragedy in verse, 1546), the comedies *La cortigiana* (1534) and *La talanta* (1550), and six volumes of letters (1537–57).

Arezzo, d'. See (1) GUIDO of Arezzo; (2) GUITTONE D'AREZZO.

Ar·fe \'är-fā\. Name of family of Spanish silversmiths and goldsmiths of German origin, including Enrique de Arfe (fl. 1500–1543), known esp. for silver altarpieces in Gothic style for Córdoba and Toledo cathedrals; his son ¶Antonio de Arfe (fl. 1566), also known for altarpieces; and Antonio's son ¶Juan de Arfe y Vil·la·fa·ñe \-ē-bēl-yä-'fän-yā\ (1535–1603), known as "the Spanish Cellini"; worked in gold and bronze in classical style; made altarpieces for cathedrals of Avila, Seville, Burgos.

Ar·gall \'är-,gȯl, -gəl\, Sir Samuel. c.1572–c.1626. English mariner and adventurer. First to sail northern route direct to Virginia (1609); admiral of Virginia (1610); captured Pocahontas (1613), took her to Jamestown. Broke up French settlements on Maine and Nova Scotia coast, capturing Port Royal (Annapolis Royal, 1614); deputy governor, Virginia (1616–19); member of Council of New England (1622). Admiral, British naval force sent unsuccessfully against Cádiz (1625).

Ar·gand \ár-gäⁿ, *Angl* 'är-,gand\, Aimé. 1755–1803. Swiss physicist. Inventor (1784) of a lamp (Argand lamp), widely used in lighthouses, with a smokeless burner that produced brighter illumination by means of current of air introduced through a circular wick.

Argand, Émile. 1879–1940. Swiss geologist. Professor, Neuchâtel (1911–40); known for extensive studies of tectonics and evolution of Alps; author of *La Tectonique de l'Asie* (1922).

Argand, Jean Robert. 1768–1822. Swiss mathematician. Devised (1806) Argand diagram, a method of graphic portrayal of complex numbers.

Ar·ge·ad \är-'gē-əd\. Name of ruling house of Macedonia founded (c.700 B.C.) by Perdiccas I and remaining in power until dissolution of empire of Alexander the Great under his successors Philip III and Alexander IV (c.311 B.C.).

Ar·ge·lan·der \,är-gə-'län-dər\, Friedrich Wilhelm August. 1799–1875. Prussian astronomer. Astronomer, Åbo Observatory (1823), Helsinki Observatory (1832); professor, Bonn (1837). Introduced study of variable stars as independent branch of astronomy; studied progressive motion of solar system in space; published celestial atlas *Bonner Durchmusterung* (1859–62), cataloguing 324,188 stars.

Argens, Marquis d'. See Jean-Baptiste de BOYER.

Ar·gen·so·la \är-kän-'sō-lä\, Lupercio Leonardo de (1559–1613) and his brother Bartolomé Leonardo de (1562–1631). *Sometimes called* the Spanish Horaces. Spanish poets. Protégés of Maria of Austria; historiographers of Aragon (Lupercio, 1599–1613; Bartolomé, 1613 ff.); in retinue of count of Lemos, viceroy of Naples (1610); wrote in imitation of the classics; among Bartolomé's works was *Conquista de las Islas Molucas* (1609); Lupercio's works included dramas, as *Isabela* and *Alejandra,* and a continuation of Zurita y Castro's *Anales de la Corona de Aragón* (completed in part by Bartolomé).

Argenson, Comtes and marquises d'. See VOYER family.

Argenteau. See MERCY D'ARGENTEAU.

Argentina, La. See Antonia MERCÉ.

Ar·ghūn \är-'gün\. 13th century. Persian ruler (1284–91) of Il-Khan dynasty. Succeeded uncle Aḥmad; reversed Aḥmad's pro-Islāmic policies.

Ar·gue·das \är-'gwā-thäs\, Alcides. 1879–1946. Bolivian writer, sociologist, and diplomat. Held diplomatic posts in Paris, London, Colombia, Venezuela (from 1910); elected deputy (1916); minister of agriculture (1940); a leader of liberal party. Author of novels concerned esp. with plight of Bolivian Indians, including *Pisagua* (1903), *Wata-Wara* (1904), *Vida criolla* (1912), *Raza de bronce* (1919), histories, including *Historia general de Bolivia* (1922); sociological studies, as *Pueblo enfermo* (1909).

Ar·güel·lo \är-'gā(l)-yō\, Luis Antonio. 1784–1830. Californian politician, b. San Francisco. Governor of California under Mexican rule (1822–25), first native-born Californian to hold this post.

Argyll, Earls, marquises, and dukes of. See CAMPBELL family.

Ar·gy·ro·pou·los \,är-ji-rō-'pü-ləs, *mod Gk* ,är-yē-'rȯ-pü-lȯs\, Johannes *or* John. 1415–1487. Byzantine Humanist scholar. Taught in Florence, Padua, Constantinople, and (from 1471) Rome, his students including Lorenzo de' Medici, Angelus Politian, Johann Reuchlin, Constantine Lascaris. Translated parts of Aristotle's works into Latin.

Ar·i·a·ram·nes \,är-ē-är-'äm-,nēz\. *Also spelled* Ar·i·ya·ram·na \-'äm-nə\. 7th century B.C. King of Persia (c.640–c.615) of Achaemenian dynasty. Son of Teispes, whose kingdom he apparently divided with brother Cyrus I; defeated and made vassal by Medes.

Ar·i·a·ra·thes \,ar-ē-ə-'rā-thēz\. Name of nine Persian rulers of northern Cappadocia, the last seven forming an independent dynasty ruling from c.255 to 36 B.C.

Arias \'är-yäs\, Harmodio. *Full surname* Arias Mad·rid \mäth-'rēth\. 1886–1962. Panamanian politician. Held various ministerial posts; provisional president of Panama (1931) after revolution that deposed President Arosemena; elected president (1932–36).

Arias Dá·vi·la \-'thä-bē-lä\, Pedro. *Often contracted to* Pe·dra·ri·as \pā-'thrär-yäs\ *or* Pedrarias Dávila. 1440?–1531. Spanish soldier and administrator. As captain general of Spanish lands in the New World (from 1513), established colonies in Panama (1514) and Nicaragua (1522); founded Panama City (1519); governor of Panama (1514–26) and Nicaragua (1514–26); quarreled with Nuñez de Balboa and had him tried and executed (1519); sent out expeditions of conquest, esp. Pizarro and Almagro to conquer Incan Empire in Peru (1524).

Arias de Sa·a·ve·dra \-thā-sä-ä-'bā-thrä\, Hernando. *Called* Her·nan·da·rias \er-nän-'där-yäs\. c.1561–c.1634. Spanish colonist, b. present Paraguay. Governor of Río de la Plata district (1597–99, 1602–09, 1615–18); encouraged Jesuit missions; helped develop Buenos Aires, Santa Fe, and other cities.

Arias Mon·ta·no \-mōn-'tän-ō\, Benito. *Lat.* Benedictus Ar·i·as Mon·ta·nus \'ar-ē-əs-män-'tā-nəs\. 1527–1598. Spanish theologian and linguist. Theologian to Council of Trent (1562); chaplain to Philip II (1566); known esp. as editor of Antwerp Polyglot Bible (1569–73).

Ari·bau \ä-'rē-baù\, Buenaventura Carles. 1798–1862. Spanish economist and writer. Banker in Madrid (1830–41); director of the treasury (1847). Edited Romantic periodicals *El europeo, El vapor;* edited, with Rivadeneyra, first 4 volumes of *Biblioteca de autores españoles;* known esp. for poem "Oda a la patria" (1832), which sparked renaissance in Catalan literature.

Ari·ber·to da An·ti·mia·no \,är-ē-'ber-tō-dä-,än-tēm-'yän-ō\. *Also called* Heribert of Antimiano. d. 1045. Italian prelate. Archbishop of Milan (1018); led Milanese armies in service of Holy Roman emperors (1027, 1034); put down rebellion of Lombard nobles (1035); arrested and tried by Emperor Conrad II (1037); escaped to Milan, which under his leadership defied Conrad's military and diplomatic tactics (1037–39); driven from Milan by revolt of commoners (1040), in exile (1040–44).

Ari·chis \ä-'rē-kēs\. Name of two Lombard dukes of Benevento:

Arichis. d. c.641. Duke (c.591–c.641). Named by King Agilulf to succeed Duke Zotto; launched war on Greeks on Italian coast; besieged Naples; war ended by intervention of Pope Gregory I (598); resumed war in Campania (599–603); seized Spoleto (616).

Arichis II. 735?–788. Last duke of Benevento (758–788). Given duchy by King Desiderius to succeed deposed Liutprand; by astute diplomacy maintained independence of Benevento from papacy and Franks; adopted title prince (775); divised various schemes to unite Lombard duchies in alliance with Byzantines against Franks; defeated by Charlemagne (786), whose vassal he became, retaining title of prince; died during attempt to reassert independence.

Ar·ig·bö·ge \,ar-əg-'bō-gə\. *Also spelled* Ar·ik·bö·ge \,ar-ək-\ *or* Ar·i·böx \,ar-ə-'bōk\. d. 1266. Mongol leader. Brother of Kublai Khan; on death of Khan Mangu (1259) in Kublai's absence, declared himself chief Mongol leader; defeated in series of battles with Kublai (1260–64).

Ar·i·o·bar·za·nes \,ar-e-,ō-bär-'zā-nēz\. Name of three kings of Cappadocia:

Ariobarzanes I Philoromaios. 1st century B.C. King (c.95–63). Driven out (c.90, c.85) by King Tigranes of Armenia and restored by Romans; abdicated in favor of son.

Ariobarzanes II Philopator. d. 51 B.C. King (63–51). Son of Ariobarzanes I.

Ariobarzanes III Eusebes Philoromaios. d. 42 B.C. King (51–42). Deeply in debt to several leading Romans; friend of Caesar, Pompey, Cicero; sided with Pompey against Caesar (49–46); killed by Gaius Cassius Longinus for refusing to aid struggle against Caesar's supporters.

Ariobarzanes. d. c.360 B.C. Persian satrap of Phrygia (c.387–c.360). Led unsuccessful revolt of satraps of western Anatolia against Artaxerxes II of Persia.

Ariobarzanes. Name of three rulers of Pontus:

Ariobarzanes I. 5th century B.C. Persian satrap of Pontus; father of Mithradates I.

Ariobarzanes II. 4th century B.C. King of Pontus (363–337). Son of Mithradates I; revolted (362) against Artaxerxes II of Persia and established independence of Pontus.

Ariobarzanes III. 3d century B.C. King (266–c.240). Son of Mithradates III.

Ari·on \ə-'rī-ən\. 7th century B.C. Semilegendary Greek poet and musician of Lesbos. Resident at court of Periander, Tyrant of Corinth; reputedly first poet to use dithyramb.

Ari·o·sto \,är-ē-'ò-stō\, Ludovico. 1474–1533. Italian poet. Entered diplomatic and military service of Cardinal Ippolito d'Este (1503); to glorify house of Este, began (1506) best known work, a sequel to Boiardo's *Orlando innamorato,* the chivalric epic poem *Orlando Furioso* (pub. in 40 cantos, 1516; in 46 cantos, 1532), generally considered the most perfect poetic expression of Italian Renaissance. Broke with Cardinal d'Este (1517) and entered service of cardinal's brother Alfonso, Duke of Ferrara; appointed governor of Garfagnana (1522–25); retired to Ferrara (1525–33). Author also of comedies, as *La Cassaria* (1508), *I suppositi* (1509), *Il negromante* (1520), and *La lena* (1529), series of *Satire* (1517–25) modelled on Horace, sonnets, odes, Latin poems, etc.

Ar·i·o·vis·tus \,ar-ē-ō-'vis-təs\. fl. 71–58 B.C. Germanic tribal chief. Leader of the Suebi; crossed Rhine into Gaul (c.61); aided Sequani against Aedui; defeated (58) by Caesar at Vesontio (Besançon).

Ari·shi·ma \ä-rē-shē-mä\ Takeo. 1878–1923. Japanese novelist. Expressed deep concern for underprivileged in journal *Shirakaba,* edited with brother and others, in novels *Kain no matsuei* (1917), *Meiro* (1918), *Aru onna* (1919), and manifesto *Sengen hitotsu* (1922).

Aris·ta \ä-'rē-stä\, Mariano. 1802–1855. Mexican general and politician. Took part in Mexican attempt to overcome Texan Revolution (1836); commander of Mexican army; defeated by Zachary Taylor at Palo Alto and Resaca de la Palma (1846); minister of war and marine under Herrera (1848–51); president of Mexico (1851–53).

Ar·is·tag·o·ras \,ar-ə-'stag-ə-rəs\. d. 497 B.C. Tyrant of Miletus. Regent while his father-in-law Histiaeus was at court of Darius; unsuccessfully attacked Naxos (499 B.C.); incited Ionian cities to revolt against Persia; secured Athenian aid and burned Sardis (499); driven out by Persians and fled to Thrace.

Ar·is·tar·chus \,ar-ə-'stär-kəs\ of Samos. fl. c.270 B.C. Greek astronomer. First to maintain that earth rotates on its own axis and revolves about sun; showed method of estimating relative distances of sun and moon from earth from observations.

Aristarchus of Samothrace. c.217–145 B.C. Greek grammarian and critic. Chief librarian (from c.153 B.C.) in Alexandria; edited Homer, Hesiod, Pindar, Archilochus, Alcaeus, Anacreon; wrote commentaries on Herodotus, Aristophanes, Aeschylus, Sophocles, and other Greek authors; first to arrange *Iliad* and *Odyssey* in 24 books. Known as the Coryphaeus of Grammarians; his school of followers known as Aristarcheans.

Ar·is·ti·des *or* **Ar·is·tei·des** \,ar-ə-'stīd-ēz\. *Called* the Just. c.530–c.468 B.C. Athenian statesman. Commanded contingent at Marathon (490 B.C.); elected chief archon (489–488). Urged maintenance of Athens as military instead of naval power, opposing Themistocles; ostracized (482). Returned to Athenian service (480); as strategos (480–479), loyally supported Themistocles in Salamis campaign; commanded Athenian contingent at Plataea (479). Commanded Athenian squadron off Byzantium (478); entrusted by members of Delian League with fixing assessments of states in confederacy; arranged alliance of League with Athens. Remained influential in Athenian policy until his death.

Aristides *or* **Aristeides.** 2d century A.D. Greek Christian apologist. Author of *Apology for the Christian Faith,* earliest extant.

Aristides *or* **Aristeides** of Miletus. c.150–100 B.C. Greek writer. Author of *Milesiaca,* collection of often erotic tales very popular in Latin translation.

Aristides *or* **Aristeides,** Publius Aelius. *Surnamed* The·o·do·rus \thē-ə-'dōr-əs\. c.120–c.180 A.D. Greek rhetorician. Resident in Smyrna; after destruction of Smyrna by earthquake (178), wrote to Emperor Marcus Aurelius Antoninus and persuaded him to rebuild city.

Aristides *or* **Aristeides,** Quintilianus. 2d or 3d century A.D. Greek writer. Author of *Perì musikês,* treatise on music regarded as most important ancient book on this subject.

Ar·is·tip·pus \,ar-ə-'stip-əs\. c.435–366 B.C. Greek philosopher. Studied under Socrates; founded Cyrenaic school of hedonism, teaching that pleasure is chief end of life and that prudence should regulate its pursuit.

Aristo. See ARISTON.

Aris·to·bu·lus \ə-,ris-tə-'byü-ləs, ,ar-ə-stə-\. Name of two kings of Judaea of the Hasmonean family:

Aristobulus I. *Also called* Judas Aristobulus. d. 103 B.C. King (104–103). Seized throne from mother soon after death of Hyrcanus I; supposed to have conquered and converted Ituraeans of Lebanon; first Hasmonean ruler to adopt title *basileus* (king).

Aristobulus II. d. 49 B.C. King (67–63). Succeeded mother Salome Alexandra, widow of Alexander Jannaeus; fought with brother and rival Hyrcanus II; dispute ended by intervention of Romans under Pompey (63), who took control of Judaea; attempted unsuccessfully to regain power (56); imprisoned in Rome. Last Hasmonean king.

Aristobulus. 4th century B.C. Greek historian. Accompanied Alexander the Great and wrote account of his campaigns.

Aristobulus of Paneas. 2d century B.C. Jewish Hellenistic philosopher. Used Stoic allegorizing technique in interpreting Old Testament; also attempted to prove Greek indebtedness to Jewish religious ideology.

Aristogiton. See HARMODIUS.

Ar·is·tom·e·nes \,ar-ə-'stäm-ə-,nēz\. 7th century B.C. Semilegendary national hero of Messenia. Leader of revolt (c.650 B.C.) of enslaved Messenians against Sparta; credited with marvelous deeds of valor in the war.

Ar·is·ton \'ar-ə-,stän\ *or* **Ar·is·to** \'ar-ə-,stō\ of Chios. 3d century B.C. Greek philosopher. Studied under Zeno; combined Stoic and Cynic thought.

Ar·is·toph·a·nes \,ar-ə-'stäf-ə-,nēz\. c.450–c.388 B.C. Athenian playwright. Regarded as one of greatest writers of comedies of all time; only extant representative of Athenian Old Comedy. Of his more than 40 comedies, which gave satiric expression to his strong, conservative prejudices against certain trends and personalities in the Athens of his day, 11 are extant: *Acharneis* (425 B.C.; attack on war), *Hippeis* (424; attack on demagoguery), *Nephelai* ("The Clouds," 423; satire on Sophists, including Socrates), *Sphekes* ("The Wasps," 422; satire on courts of law), *Eirene* ("The Peace," 421), *Ornithes* ("The Birds," 414), *Lysistrate* (411; antiwar comedy), *Thesmophoriazousai* (411; satire on Euripides), *Batrachoi* ("The Frogs," 405; comedy involving Euripides and Aeschylus), *Ekklesiazousai* ("Parliament of Women," 391; parody of Plato), *Ploutos* (388).

Aristophanes of Byzantium c.257–180 B.C. Greek scholar. Chief librarian in Alexandria (c.195); edited works of Hesiod, Homer, Anacreon, Pindar, Aristophanes, Euripides, Alcaeus; revised and continued *Pinakes* of Callimachus; introduced innovations in criticism; believed to have organized Alexandrian Canon of literary genres; compiled lists of foreign and rare words.

Ar·is·tot·le \'ar-ə-,stät-ᵊl, *also* ,ar-ə-'\. 384–322 B.C. Greek philosopher. Son of court physician of Amyntas III of Macedonia; studied (367–347) under Plato at Academy in Athens; taught in Mytilene (c.344–342); tutored Alexander the Great (c.342–c.339); taught in Athens as head of Lyceum, also known as the Peripatetic school (335–323); withdrew (323) to Chalcis during anti-Macedonian reaction following Alexander's death. Works published by Aristotle now lost but for fragments included *Eudemus, De philosophia,* etc. Extant works are largely edited compilations of notes for and of lectures delivered to his disciples in Athens. Wrote on logic, metaphysics, natural science, ethics and politics, rhetoric and poetics. Among his writings on logic (called later the *Organon*) were *Categories, Prior Analytics, Posterior Analytics* and *Sophistical Refutations.* His great philosophical work was *Metaphysics.* In field of natural science were *Physics, On the Heavens, Parts of Animals, Generation of Animals, History of Animals, On the Soul (De Anima),* and *On Plants.* In field of ethics and politics were *Nicomachean Ethics* and *Politics.* Also wrote *Rhetoric* and *Poetics.* One of greatest thinkers of history, and a principal shaper of Western rationalism and scientific spirit.

Ar·is·tox·e·nus \,ar-ə-'stäk-sə-nəs\. 4th century B.C. Greek Peripatetic philosopher. Disciple of Aristotle; author of *Elements of Harmony, Elements of Rhythm,* extant in part, earliest authorities on classical musical theory.

Ari Thor·gils·son \'är-i-'thȯr-gyils-sȯn\. *Called* the Learned. c.1067–1148. Icelandic priest and historian. Author of *Íslendingabók,* first vernacular history of Iceland, from settlement to 1120; believed to have written much of *Landnámabók,* source of many family sagas.

Ari·ulf \'är-ē-,ülf\. d. 601. Second duke of Spoleto (c.591–601). Made duke apparently by Lombard king Agilulf; in alliance with Arichis I of Benevento, attacked Rome (592); made peace with Pope Gregory I.

Ari·us \ə-'rī-əs; 'ar-ē-əs, 'er-\. c.250–336 A.D. Greek ecclesiastic at Alexandria. Taught Neoplatonic doctrine that God is alone, unknowable, and separate from every created being, that Christ is a created being and not God in the fullest sense but a secondary deity, and that in the incarnation the Logos assumed a body but not a human soul. Principal written work *Thalia* (c.323). Growing dispute over his teaching led Emperor Constantine I to call Council of Nicaea (325), where Arianism was declared heresy.

Ari·yo·shi \,är-i-'yō-shē\, Sawako. 1931–1984. Japanese writer. Noted for works exploring the culture, traditions, social structure, and domestic problems of the Japanese people. Author of *Jiuta* (*Ballads,* 1956), *Kinokawa* (*The River Ki,* 1959), *Hanoaka Seishu No Tsuma* (*The Doctor's Wife,* 1961), *Kokotsu No Hito* (*The Twilight Years,* 1972), etc.

Ar·jun \'är-jən\ *or* **Arjun Mal** \-'mäl\. 1563–1606. Indian religious. Fifth Gurū of Sikh religion (1581–1606); succeeded father Rām Dās; compiled *Ādi Granth* or *Granth Sahib* (1604), Sikh sacred scripture; persecuted by Emperor Jahāngīr; first Sikh martyr.

Ar·kell \'är-,kel, -kəl\, William Joscelyn. 1904–1958. English paleontologist. Research fellow at New College (1933–40), Trinity College (1947–58), Cambridge; authority on rocks and fossils of Jurassic system. Author of *Jurassic System in Great Britain* (1933), *Geology of Oxford* (1947), *Jurassic Geology of the World* (1956), and monographs esp. on classification of ammonites.

Ark·wright \'ärk-,rīt\, Sir Richard. 1732–1792. English inventor and manufacturer. Inventor of water-powered spinning frame (pat. 1769), first machine capable of producing cotton thread of the firmness and hardness required in the warp; opened cloth factories; introduced all-cotton calico (1773).

Ar·landes \är-'läⁿd\, François d'. Marquis. 1742–1809. French soldier and aeronaut. With Pilâtre de Rozier, made first free balloon ascension (Nov. 21, 1783), over Paris.

Ar·len \'är-lən\, Harold. 1905–1986. American composer, b. Buffalo, N.Y. Created some of America's most enduring popular music; arranged and composed for Broadway shows and, later, musical films; collaborated with E.Y. Harburg, Johnny Mercer, et al. on over 500 songs, including "Get Happy," "Stormy Weather," "Over the Rainbow," "That Old Black Magic," etc.

Arlen, Michael. *Orig.* Dikran Kou·youm·djian \kü-'yüm-,j(ē-)än\. 1895–1956. British novelist and playwright, b. Bulgaria of Armenian parents. Naturalized British subject (1922). Author of *The London Venture* (1920), *These Charming People* (1923), *The Green Hat* (1924), *Men Dislike Women* (1931), *Man's Mortality* (1933), *Hell! Said the Duchess* (1934), *The Crooked Coronet* (1937), *The Flying Dutchman* (1939), etc.

Arlington, Earl of. See Henry BENNET.

Ar·liss \'är-ləs\, George. *Orig.* Augustus George An·drews \'an-,drüz\. 1868–1946. English actor. Made debut at London (1886); appeared on N.Y. stage (1901) with Mrs. Patrick Campbell; enjoyed great success in *The Second Mrs. Tanqueray* (1902), *Disraeli* (1911). Began career in motion pictures in U.S. (1920); played leading roles in *Green Goddess* (1930), *Old English* (1930), *Disraeli* (1930, Academy Award), *Alexander Hamilton* (1931), *House of Rothschild* (1934), *Cardinal Richelieu* (1935), etc. Author of autobiographies *Up the Years from Bloomsbury* (1927), *My Ten Years in the Studios* (1940).

Ar·ma·gnac \är-män-yäk\. Noble French house (from 10th century) which included powerful dukes of Armagnac. See BERNARD VII.

Ar·mans·perg \'är-mäns-,perk\, Joseph Ludwig von. Graf. 1787–1853. German politician. Bavarian minister of interior, foreign affairs, finance (1826–31); accompanied King Otto to Greece; served as member of regency (1832–35) and chancellor of state (1835–37), in Greece.

Ar·men·dá·riz \är-män-'där-ēth\, José de. Marqués de Cas·tel·fuer·te \käs-tel-'fwer-tā\. d. 1736. Spanish soldier. Commander in War of Spanish Succession (1701–14); viceroy of Peru (1724–36).

Arm·felt \'ärm-felt\, Gustaf Mauritz. Count. 1757–1814. Swedish statesman and general. Engaged by King Gustavus III in negotiations with Russia (1783), Denmark (1787); distinguished himself in war against Russia (1788–90); member of regency council after death of Gustavus III (1792); sent by duke-regent Charles to Naples; secretly asked Catherine II of Russia to support Gustavian faction; charged with treason; fled to Russia; later restored by Gustavus IV; ambassador to Vienna (1802–04); commander of Swedish forces in Pomerania (1805–07); expelled from Sweden for supporting crown prince Gustavus (1811); to Russia, where he gained influence over Czar Alexander I.

Ar·min \är-'mēn\ *or* **Her·mann** \'her-,män\. *Lat.* Ar·min·ius \är-'min-ē-əs\. 18 B.C.?–19 A.D. German tribal leader and national hero. Chief of the Cherusci; served in Roman armies (1–6 A.D.) and became Roman citizen; returned home and organized rebellion of Cherusci against Roman governor Varus; annihilated three Roman legions in attack in Teutoburger Wald (9 A.D.), forcing back Roman frontier from Elbe to Rhine; fended off attack by Germanicus Caesar (16 A.D.). Fought against Maroboduus, king of the Marcomanni.

Arminius, Jacobus. See Jacob HARMENSEN.

Ar·mi·stead \'är-mə-,sted, -stəd\, George. 1780–1818. American army officer, b. New Market, Va. Defended Fort McHenry against British (1814), and saved Baltimore.

Armistead, Lewis Addison. 1817–1863. American army officer, b. New Bern, N.C. In U.S. army (1839–61), Confederate army (1861–63); brigadier general (1862). Killed in Pickett's charge at Gettysburg.

Ar·mi·tage \'är-mət-ij\, Edward. 1817–1896. English painter. Known for biblical and historical paintings; executed frescoes in House of Lords.

Ar·mour \'är-mər\, John Douglas. 1830–1903. Canadian judge, b. near Peterborough, Ont. Chief justice of court of Queen's Bench (1887); chief justice, Ontario (1900); judge of supreme court of Canada (1902).

Armour, Philip Danforth. 1832–1901. American industrialist, b. Stockbridge, N.Y. Made fortune in pork futures at end of Civil War; joined (1865) Milwaukee grain commission house established by his brother Herman Ossian (1837–1901); added pork-packing plant (1868); business reorganized as Armour & Co. (1870); Philip became head of Armour & Co. with headquarters in Chicago (1875); responsible for improved meat-packing methods; founded Armour Institute of Technology (1892; later Illinois Institute of Technology).

Arm·stead \'ärm-,sted, -stəd\, Henry Hugh. 1828–1905. English sculptor. Works included reliefs and bronze statues for Albert Memorial, fountain at King's College, Cambridge, reredos in Westminster Abbey.

Arm·strong \'ärm-'strȯŋ\, Archibald, *called* Archie. d. 1672. Scottish court jester to James I and Charles I of England. Enjoyed royal favor and political influence; dismissed for insult to Archbishop Laud (1637).

Armstrong, Edward. 1846–1928. English historian. Lecturer (from 1869), bursar (1878–1911), pro-provost (1911–22), Queen's Coll., Oxford; expert on Dante and Italian Renaissance. Author of *French Wars of Religion* (1892), *Lorenzo de' Medici* (1896), *Emperor Charles V* (1902).

Armstrong, Edwin Howard. 1890–1954. American electrical engineer, b. New York City. Instructor, assistant to M.I. Pupin (1913–17, 1919–35), professor (1935–54), Columbia U.; served in Signal Corps, U.S. army (1917–19). His inventions in field of radio included regenerative circuit (1912), superheterodyne circuit (1918), superregenerative circuit (1920); developed frequency-modulation system of radio (1933).

Armstrong, Hamilton Fish. 1893–1973. American journalist, b. New York City. Founder (1922), managing editor (1922–28), editor (1928–72), *Foreign Affairs.* Author of *The New Balkans* (1926), *We or They* (1937), *Calculated Risk* (1947), etc., and a memoir, *Those Days* (1963).

Armstrong, Henry Edward. 1848–1937. English chemist. Taught at St. Bartholomew's Hospital (1870–82), London Institution (1871–84), Central Institution (later Central Technical Coll., 1884–1913). Known for research on substitution reactions of naphthalene, composition of camphor and other terpenes, water purification, organic crystallography.

Armstrong, Henry Worthington, *called* Harry. 1879–1951. American composer, b. Somerville, Mass. Wrote music for "Sweet Adeline" (1903, words by Richard G. Husch), "Nellie Dean," "I Love My Wife, But Oh You Kid!," "Frisco Rag," etc.

Armstrong, John *or* Johnnie. d. 1528. Scottish freebooter. Leader of gang of highwaymen along Scottish border; appeared before James V (of Scotland) and offered to aid in suppressing border marauders; seized and hanged; became subject of a number of ballads.

Armstrong, John. 1709–1779. Scottish physician and poet. Author of largely indecent *Oeconomy of Love* (1736) and blank-verse *Art of Preserving Health* (1744).

Armstrong, John. 1755–1816. American army officer and explorer, b. New Jersey. Served in Revolution; commander of Fort Pitt (1785–86); undertook largely secret explorations of Old Northwest and trans-Mississippi region (1790–91); took part in Harmar's and St. Clair's expeditions (1790, 1791); treasurer of Northwest Territory (1796).

Armstrong, John. 1758–1842. American army officer and politician, b. Carlisle, Pa. Served through American Revolution; wrote a series of anonymous letters, known as Newburgh letters (1783), in effort to force Congress to pay arrears to army officers. Member of Congress (1787–89); U.S. senator (1800–02, 1803–04); U.S. minister to France (1804–10); as secretary of war (1813–14), held in large part responsible for military failures in War of 1812.

Armstrong, Louis Daniel. *Called* Satch•mo \ˈsach-(ˌ)mō\. 1900–1971. American jazz musician, b. New Orleans. Second trumpet with Joe "King" Oliver's Creole Jazz Band (1922–25); led own Hot Five and Seven groups (1925–28); later solo performer, band leader, film performer, international celebrity. First great jazz virtuoso; invented scat singing style; composed "Dipper Mouth Blues," "Sister Kate," "Gut Bucket Blues," etc.

Armstrong, Paul. 1869–1915. American playwright, b. Kidder, Mo. Wrote popular melodramas, including *Heir to the Hoorah* (1905), *Salomy Jane* (1907), *Going Some* (1908, with Rex Beach), *Via Wireless* (1908, with Winchell Smith), *Alias Jimmy Valentine* (1909), *The Greyhound* (1912, with Wilson Mizner), etc.

Armstrong, Samuel Chapman. 1839–1893. American educator, b. Hawaii. Founded (1868) and headed (1868–93) Hampton Normal and Industrial Institute.

Armstrong, William George. Baron Armstrong. 1810–1900. English inventor and industrialist. Invented hydroelectric machine which produced frictional electricity (1843), a hydraulic crane (1846), hydraulic accumulator to power machinery (1850), the Armstrong breech-loading gun made of successive rings of metal shrunk upon an inner steel barrel with rifle bore (1855), prototype of all modern artillery, a breech-loading gun with wire-wound cylinder (1880). Created baron (1887). Founder (1847) of Elswick Engineering Works; merged (1927) its armament and shipbuilding with Vickers' Sons and Co. to form Vickers Armstrong, Ltd.

Arnaldo da Brescia. See ARNOLD of Brescia.

Ar•nau de Vil•la•no•va \ˈär-naù-t͟hā-b͟ē(l)-yä-ˈnȯb͟-ä\. *Fr.* Ar•naud de Vil•le•neuve \är-nō-də-vēl-nœv\. *Lat.* Ar•nal•dus Vil•la•no•va•nus \är-ˈnal-dəs-ˌvil-ə-nō-ˈvā-nəs\. c.1235–1312. Catalan physician, astrologer, alchemist. Taught at Barcelona, Montpellier, Paris; councillor to Pope Clement V; discovered poisonous property of carbon monoxide and of decayed meat.

Ar•naud \är-nō\, Henri. 1641–1721. French Waldensian pastor and soldier. Led group of Waldenses against allied French and Savoyard armies to regain native Vaudois valleys (1689–90); secured repatriation of Waldenses (1690–98); lived in Württemberg (1698–1721); wrote *Histoire de la glorieuse rentrée des Vaudois dans leurs vallées* (1710).

Ar•nauld \är-nō\. *Also spelled* Arnault *or* Arnaut. French family, orig. from Auvergne, closely associated with history of Jansenism and of Port-Royal; members included: Antoine (1560–1619), lawyer famous for his speech (1594) against Jesuits and in favor of U. of Paris. His 20 children included: ¶Robert Arnauld d'An•dil•ly \dä^n-dē-yē\(1588–1674), lawyer, theological writer; retired from affairs to Port-Royal on the rise of Cardinal Richelieu (1643); published collection of poems as *Oeuvres chrétiennes* (1642). ¶Jacqueline-Marie-Angélique Arnauld (1591–1661), *known as* Mère An•gé•lique \mer-ä^n-zhā-lēk\, abbess of Port-Royal, Paris (1602–30); instituted harsh reforms (from 1608); influenced by St. Francis de Sales, Saint-Cyran. ¶Jeanne-Catherine-Agnès Arnauld (1593–1672), *known as* Mère Agnès, Jansenist nun, abbess of Saint-Cyr (1600–08), of Port-Royal (1636–42, 1658–61); author of *Le Chaplet secret du Saint Sacrement* (1627). ¶Henri Arnauld (1597–1692), lawyer; in Rome (1621–25); lived in retirement during Richelieu's era; employed as diplomat by Mazarin (1645); bishop of Angers (1649); one of four bishops refusing to sign acceptance of pope's bull condemning Jansen's *Augustinus.* ¶Antoine Arnauld (1612–1694), *known as* the Great Arnauld, lawyer, philosopher, and Jansenist theologian; famed for his controversial writings, notably *De la fréquente communion* (1643); succeeded Saint-Cyran (1643) as head of Jansenist sect in France; expelled from faculty of Sorbonne (1656), reinstated (1669); retired to Brussels (1682). Author of *La Perpétuité de la Foi* (with Nicole, 1669–79), etc. A daughter of Robert Arnauld d'Andilly, ¶Angélique Arnauld d'Andilly, *called* Mère Angélique de Saint-Jean \sa^n-zhä^n\(1624–1684), abbess of Port-Royal (1678–84); author of *Mémoires pour servir à l'histoire de Port-Royal.* A son of Robert ¶Simon Arnauld, marquis de Pom•ponne \pō^n-pȯn\ (1618–1699), was secretary of state for foreign affairs (1671–79, 1696–99) and minister of state (1672–79) under Louis XIV; negotiated treaty that ended war (1672–78) with Dutch.

Ar•naut Da•niel \är-nō-dän-yel\. fl. 1180–1200. Provençal poet. Known esp. for mastery of difficult verse forms; credited with inventing sestina.

Arnd *or* **Arndt** \ˈärnt\, Johann. 1555–1621. German Lutheran theologian. Major figure in Eucharist controversy; author of *Vier Bücher vom wahren Christentum* (1606–10).

Arndt \ˈärnt\, Ernst Moritz. 1769–1860. German patriot and author. His *Versuch einer Geschichte der Leibeigenschaft in Pommern und Rügen* (1803) led to abolition of serfdom by Swedish king. Professor of history, Greifswald (1806; 1810–12); attacked Napoléon in *Geist der Zeit* (1806 ff.); fled Napoleonic army to Stockholm (1806–09); associated in Russia with Baron vom Stein against Napoléon (1812). Returned to Germany and fired German spirit against oppressors with songs, including "Der Gott, der Eisen wachsen liess" and "Was ist des Deutschen Vaterland," pamphlets, and patriotic poems. Professor, Bonn (1818, 1840–48); deputy to national assembly (1848). Author also of *Erinnerungen aus dem äusseren Leben* (1840).

Arne \ˈärn\, Thomas Augustine. 1710–1778. English composer. Wrote music for Joseph Addison's *Rosamund,* containing air "Rise, Glory, Rise" (1733), Fielding's *Tom Thumb* (1733), Milton's *Comus* (1738), Thomson and Mallet's *Masque of Alfred,* including song "Rule Britannia" (1740). Composer to Drury Lane Theatre and Vauxhall Gardens (from c.1744); composed settings for many songs of Shakespeare including "Under the Greenwood Tree," "Blow, Blow, thou Winter Wind"; wrote oratorio *Judith* (1761), opera *Artaxerxes* (1762), stage music for *Fairy Prince* (1771), *Elfrida* (1772), *Caractacus* (1776). His sister ¶Susannah Maria (1714–1766), m. (1734) Theophilus Cibber and known thereafter as Mrs. Cibber; appeared in her brother's *Rosamund* (1733); became noted oratorio singer, for whom Handel wrote contralto parts in *Messiah* and *Samson;* later turned to drama, won reputation as great emotional actress; associated with Garrick at Drury Lane (1753–66).

Ar•neth \ˈär-(ˌ)net\, Alfred von. Ritter. 1819–1897. Austrian historian. Keeper of state archives (from 1868); president, Imperial Academy of Sciences (1879). Author of *Prinz Eugen von Savoyen* (1858), *Geschichte Maria Theresias* (1863–79), *Aus meinem Leben* (1891–92), etc.

Arngrímur the Learned. See Arngrímur JÓNSSON.

Ar•ni•ches \är-ˈnē-kās\, Carlos. *Full surname* Arniches y Bar•re•ra \-ē-bär-ˈrā-rä\. 1866–1943. Spanish dramatist. Known esp. for comedies and comic sketches, including *Sandías y melones* (1900), *Gazpacho andaluz* (1902), *La pena negra* (1906), *La señorita de Trévelez* (1910), *La sobrina del cura* (1914), *Es mi hombre* (1921), *La risa de Juana* (1925), *Las doce en punto* (1933); published collection of sketches (sainetes) as *Del Madrid castizo* (1917).

Ar•nim \ˈär-nim\, Achim von, *orig.* Karl Joachim Friedrich Ludwig von. 1781–1831. German poet, dramatist, folklorist. With Clemens Brentano published *Des Knaben Wunderhorn* (1806–08), collection of folk poetry; own writings marked by Romantic and fantastic imagination. Published verse, *Trösteinsamkeit* (1808); novels and tales *Gräfin Dolores* (1810), *Isabella von Ägypten* (1812), *Die Kronenwächter* (1817–54), *Die Majorats-Herren* (1819); dramas *Halle und Jerusalem* (1811), *Schaubühne* (1813), *Die Gleichen* (1819). m. (1811) Brentano's sister Elisabeth.

Arnim, Bettina von. *Orig.* Elisabeth Katharina Ludovica Magdalena Brentano. 1785–1859. German writer. Sister of Clemens Brentano; m. (1811) Achim von Arnim. Representative woman of German Romantic movement; published records of correspondence in *Goethes Briefwechsel mit einem Kinde* (1835), *Die Günderode* (1840), *Clemens Brentanos Frühlingskranz* (1844), displaying vivid, unconventional style and imagination; expressed social-political views in *Dies Buch gehört dem König* (1843), *Gespräche mit Dämonen* (1852), both addressed to King Frederick William IV of Prussia.

Arnim *or* **Arn·heim** \'ärn-ˌhīm\, Hans Georg von. 1581–1641. German diplomat and general. Successively in the service of Sweden (1613), Poland (1621), the emperor (1626), and Saxony (1631).

Arnim, Harry Karl Kurt Eduard von. Graf. 1824–1881. German diplomat. Ambassador in Lisbon (1862), Rome (1864–70); supported German bishops opposing dogma of papal infallibility. Participated (1871) in peace negotiations between Germany and France. Ambassador at Paris (1872–74); arrested for allowing publication of confidential documents (1874); published defense in *Pro Nihilo* (1875) critical of Bismarck; sentenced to five years' imprisonment. Case led to addition of *Arnim Paragraphs* to German criminal code.

Arniston, Lord. See DUNDAS of Arniston.

Arno, Peter. See Curtis Arnoux PETERS.

Ar·no·bi·us \är-'nō-bē-əs\. *Called* the Elder. 4th century A.D. Christian apologist in northern Africa. Converted from paganism; wrote *Adversus nationes,* attacking various forms of paganism in often brilliant invective.

Arnobius. *Called* the Younger. 5th century A.D. Christian writer in Gaul. Author of *Commentarii in Psalmos,* mystical-allegorical commentary on the Psalms first published (1522) by Erasmus; author also of criticisms of St. Augustine of Hippo, tract against Monophysites.

Ar·nold \'ärn-əld\ of Brescia. *Ital.* Ar·nal·do da Bre·scia \är-'näl-dō-dä-'brā-shä\. c.1100–1155. Italian religious reformer. Student of Abelard; prior of monastery of Augustinian canons in Brescia; combated corruption of clergy; led popular revolt against bishop of Brescia; silenced by 2d Lateran Council (1139); condemned (with Abelard) by council of Sens (1141); defiantly continued to teach at Paris until exiled by King Louis VII; fled to Switzerland and then Germany; briefly reconciled with Pope Eugenius III (1145), who sent him to Rome; joined republican party that forced Eugenius into exile; patterned reformed government after Roman republic; excommunicated (1148); forced to flee by Adrian IV (1155); betrayed by Frederick I; executed at Rome.

Arnold of Villanova. See ARNAU DE VILLANOVA.

Arnold, Benedict. 1741–1801. American army officer, traitor, b. Norwich, Conn. With Ethan Allen, captured Fort Ticonderoga (1775); leader, with Richard Montgomery, of unsuccessful campaign to capture Quebec (1775); brigadier general in Continental army (1776); stopped British thrust from Canada down Lake Champlain (1776); major general (1777); repulsed British force in Mohawk Valley (1777); aided in forcing Burgoyne's surrender at Saratoga (1778). In command at Philadelphia (1778–79); court-martialed for financial irregularities and reprimanded; m. (1779) Margaret Shippen (*q.v.*) of Loyalist family. Began treasonable correspondence with British (1779); in command at West Point (1780); arranged to surrender West Point to British; plot discovered (1780). Fled to British; as brigadier general of provincial troops, led raids in Virginia (1780) and Connecticut (1781). To England (1781), where he died in disgrace and poverty.

Arnold, Sir Edwin. 1832–1904. English poet and journalist. Principal, Deccan Coll., Bombay, India (1856–61). Editor of *Daily Telegraph* (1873–1901). Author of epic poem *The Light of Asia* on life and teachings of Buddha (1879), a sequel *Light of the World* on Christian theme (1901), and other poems and translations on life and thought of the East.

Arnold, Henry Harley, *called* Hap. 1886–1950. American airman, b. Gladwyne, Pa. Received pilot's license (1911); won Mackay Trophy for 30-mile flight (1912) and as commander of U.S. army Alaskan flight (1934); major general, chief of U.S. Army Air Corps (1938); chief of Army Air Forces (1941); lieutenant general (1941); commander of AAF (1942–46); general (1943), general of the army (1944); general of the air force (1949). Author of *This Flying Game* (with Ira Eaker, 1936), *Winged Warfare* (with Eaker, 1941), *Army Flyer* (with Eaker, 1942), *Global Mission* (1949).

Arnold, Matthew. 1822–1888. English poet and critic. Son of Thomas Arnold; uncle of Mary Augusta Ward (*q.v.*). Inspector of schools (1851–86). Professor of poetry, Oxford (1857–67). His poetical works included *The Strayed Reveller* (1849), *Empedocles on Etna* (1852), *Poems* (containing "Sohrab and Rustum," "Scholar-Gipsy," and "Requiescat," 1853), *New Poems* (containing "Thyrsis" and "Dover Beach," 1867). Essays included *On Translating Homer* (1861–62), *On the Study of Celtic Literature* (1867), *Essays in Criticism* (1865, 1888), *Culture and Anarchy* (1869), *Literature and Dogma* (1873).

Arnold, Samuel. 1740–1802. English organist and composer. Composer to Covent Garden Theatre (c.1763–69); lessee of Marylebone Gardens (1769–72); organist and composer to Chapel Royal (from 1783); organist at Westminster Abbey (1793). Compositions included opera *Maid of the Mill* (1765), afterpieces, pantomimes, and oratorios. Published 36-volume edition of Handel's works (1786–97), first complete edition of a composer's works.

Arnold, Thomas. 1795–1842. English educator. Father of Matthew Arnold. Headmaster of Rugby (1828–42); introduced mathematics, modern history, and modern languages to curriculum; introduced prefect system; strongly influenced development of modern public schools in England. Regius professor of history at Oxford (1841). Author of five volumes of sermons, edition of Thucydides, and three-volume history of Rome.

Arnold, Thurman Wesley. 1891–1969. American lawyer, b. Laramie, Wyo. Professor, Yale (1930–37). Asst. attorney general of U.S. (1938–43); notable esp. as prosecutor of some 230 antitrust cases; judge, U.S. court of appeals for D.C. (1943–45). Author of *The Folklore of Capitalism* (1937), *Democracy and Free Enterprise* (1942), etc.

Ar·nold·son \'ar-nu̇ld-so̊n\, Klas Pontus. 1844–1916. Swedish writer, politician, and pacifist. Member of Riksdag (1881–87); advocated permanent neutrality; helped found (1883) Swedish Association for Peace and Conciliation; played large role in preserving peace between Sweden and Norway (1890–1905). Co-winner (with Fredrik Bajer) of 1908 Nobel peace prize.

Ar·nol·fo di Cam·bio \är-'nȯl-fō-dē-'käm-byō\. c.1245–1302. Florentine sculptor and architect. Pupil of Nicola Pisano; assisted in work on pulpit for Siena cathedral; to Rome (1277); produced tomb of Pope Adrian V at Viterbo, monument to Cardinal de Braye at Orvieto (1282), altar canopies for S. Paolo Fuori le Mura (1285) and Sta. Cecilia, Trastavere (1293) both in Rome; undertook rebuilding of Duomo, Florence (1296); credited also with design of Palazzo Vecchio and church of Sta. Croce.

Arn·stein \'ärn-ˌstīn, -ˌshtīn\, Karl. 1887–1974. American airship designer and builder, b. Prague, Bohemia. With Zeppelin Co., Germany (1919–24). To U.S. (1924); naturalized (1930). Technical director of aircraft construction, Goodyear Tire and Rubber Co., Akron, Ohio (1924); vice president and chief engineer, Goodyear-Zeppelin Corp. (1925–39); vice president, Goodyear Aircraft Corp. (1940–57). Designer of numerous commercial and military airships, including the U.S.S. *Akron* and *Macon*.

Ar·nulf \'är-ˌnu̇lf\. c.850–899. King of Germany (887–899) and crowned Holy Roman emperor (896). Son of Carloman of Bavaria and nephew of Charles the Fat; deposed Charles and elected king of Germany (887); acquired as vassals Odo of Paris, Berengar of Italy, Rudolph of Burgundy; won great victory over Vikings at Louvain (891); led successful expedition against Moravians (892); invaded Italy (893, 895) and stormed Rome (896); crowned emperor by Pope Formosus in opposition to Lambert; failed to defeat Lambert at Spoleto.

Arnulf. d. 937. Duke of Bavaria (907–937). Succeeded father Luitpold; refused to acknowledge supremacy of King Conrad I or of Henry I until 921.

Arnulf. c.580–641. Frankish prelate. Bishop of Metz (611 or 612–641); ruled Austrasia with Pepin I of Landen for King Dagobert I (622–c.627); retired to eremitic life. Considered a founder of Carolingian dynasty; his son married Pepin's daughter, from which union sprang Pepin II of Herstal.

Arnulf of Rohea. *Sometimes called* Arnulf Male·corne \-'mal-(ə-)ˌkȯrn\. d. 1118. Latin patriarch of Jerusalem (1099, 1112–18). Chaplain to Robert I, Duke of Normandy, in First Crusade; forced Latin rite on Christians of Jerusalem (1099); celebrated bigamous marriage of King Baldwin I (1113).

Aron \á-rōⁿ\, Raymond-Claude-Ferdinand. 1905–1983. French philosopher. Taught at Le Havre and Toulouse. With de Gaulle during World War II; edited resistance paper *La France Libre* (1940–44); professor of sociology at the Sorbonne (1955–68); professor at Collège de France (from 1970). A contributor to *Le Figaro* and *L'Express.* Author of *L'Opium des Intellectuels* (1955), *La Tragédie algérienne* (1957), *La République impériale* (1973), *Mémoires* (1983). A leader of France's center-right.

Aron·hold \'är-ōn-ˌhōlt\, Siegfried Heinrich. 1819–1884. German mathematician. Professor at Berlin (1863–83); a founder of mathematical theory of invariants and investigator of plane curves of third and fourth orders.

Aro·se·me·na \är-ō-sā-'mā-nä\, Florencio Harmodio. 1872–1945. Panamanian politician. President of Panama (1928–31). His brother ¶Juan Demóstenes (1879–1939) was also president of Panama (1936–39).

Arouet, François-Marie. See VOLTAIRE.

Arp, Bill. See Charles Henry SMITH.

Arp \ärpt\, Jean *or* Hans. 1887–1966. French artist and poet. Associated with Kandinsky and Der Blaue Reiter group, Munich (1912); a founder of Dada, Zürich (1916); member of surrealist group of painters, Paris (from 1925), later member of Cerole et Carré group. Experimented with "torn paper" and "crumpled paper" constructions. Author of verse *Der vogel selbdritt* (1920), *Des taches dans le vide* (1937), *Wortträume und schwarze Sterne* (1953), etc.

Ár·pád \'är-ˌpäd\. d. 907. National hero of Hungary. Magyar chief (from c.890); founder of first Magyar dynasty of Hungary; led Magyars into Hungary from Black Sea region (c.896); conquered much territory from Bulgars, Khazars, Vlachs, Moravians; founder of dynasty of Árpád, whose first crowned king was St. Stephen (997–1038) and last, Andrew III (d. 1301).

Arpino, Cavaliere d'. See Giuseppe CESARI.

Arran, Earls of. See HAMILTON family.

Ar·rest \ä-'re\, Heinrich Louis d'. 1822–1875. German astronomer. Professor, Leipzig (1852) and Copenhagen (1858); known for his discoveries of comets and asteroids and for his studies of nebulae.

Ar·rhe·ni·us \är-ˈrā-nē-əs\, Svante August. 1859–1927. Swedish physicist and chemist. Professor, Royal Institute of Technology, Stockholm (1895); director, Nobel Institute for Physical Chemistry (from 1905). Established electrolytic dissociation theory, for which he received 1903 Nobel prize for chemistry; a pioneer in field of physical chemistry. Author of works on biological chemistry, electrochemistry, physical chemistry, and astronomy.

Arrhidaeus. See PHILIP III of Macedonia.

Ar·ria·ga \är-ˈryäg-ä\, Juan Crisóstomo Jacobo Antonio. *Full surname* Arriaga y Bal·zo·la \-ē-bäl-ˈthō-lä\. 1806–1826. Spanish composer. After production of opera *Los esclavos felices* (1820) studied in Paris; assistant professor, Paris Conservatory (1824). Other works included octet *Nada y mucho* (1817), 3 string quartets, a symphony, cantatas, etc.

Ar·ria·ga \ər-ˈryá-gə\, Manuel José de. 1842–1917. Portuguese politician. Member of Liberal party and deputy during reign of Luís I; actively engaged in revolutionary movement (1910) that overthrew King Manuel and established republic; first elected president of Republic of Portugal (1911–15).

Ar·ri·an \ˈar-rē-ən\. *Lat.* Flavius Ar·ri·a·nus \ˌar-ē-ˈā-nəs\. 2d century A.D. Greek historian. Governor of Cappadocia (131–137); archon of Athens (147–148, 171). Author of *Anabasis of Alexander* (life of Alexander the Great), *Indica* (description of India), *Periplus of the Euxine,* and *Encheiridion* and *Diatribai* on teachings of Epictetus.

Ar·ria·za y Su·per·vie·la \är-ˈryä-thä-ē-sü-per-ˈbyā-lä\, Juan Bautista de. 1770–1837. Spanish poet. Author of *Las primicias* (1797), *Ensayos poéticos* (1799), didactic poem *Emilia* (1803), *Poesías patrióticas* (1810).

Ar·ri·ghi \är-ˈrē-gē\, Ludovico degli. *Also known as* Ludovico il Vi·cen·ti·no \ēl-ˌvē-chān-ˈtī-nō\. fl. 1522. Italian calligrapher and printer. Author of *La operina da imparare di scrivere littera cancellarescha* (1522), first writing manual for popular use; designed italic typefaces.

Ar·rol \ˈar-əl\, Sir William. 1839–1913. Scottish bridge builder. Constructed new Tay bridge (1882–87), Forth bridge (1883–90), Tower bridge, London (1886–94), Nile bridge at Cairo; M.P. (1892–1906).

Ar·row·smith \ˈar-ō-ˌsmith, ˈar-ə-\, Aaron. 1750–1823. English geographer and cartographer. Published major world maps (1790, 1794); maps of North America (1796), Pacific Ocean (1798); published *Atlas of South India* (1822). His nephew ¶John Arrowsmith (1790–1873) became head of the business (1839); published outstanding *London Atlas* (1834).

Ar·royo del Río \ä-ˈrȯi-ō-thäl-ˈrē-ō\, Carlos Alberto. 1893–1969. Ecuadorian politician. Lawyer and Liberal party leader; president of Ecuador (1940–44); overthrown as result of Peruvian invasion (1941).

Arruza, Carlos. See Carlos RUIZ CAMINO.

Ars, Curé of. See Jean-Baptiste-Marie VIANNEY.

Ar·sa·ces \ˈär-sə-ˌsēz\. 3d century B.C. Founder of Parthian state. Chief of Parni tribe; led confederation of tribes in struggle against Seleucids (from c.247); established kingdom of Parthia with capital at Hecatompylos; founded cities Asaak, Dara, Nisa. Founder of Arsacid dynasty, sometimes called Arshakuni, which ruled Parthian Empire (247 B.C.–224 A.D.) Name Arsaces with numerals sometimes attached to subsequent ruler: see ARTABANUS, MITHRADATES, ORODES, PHRAATES.

Ar·se·ni·us \är-ˈsē-nē-əs\. *Called* the Great. *Also known as* Arsenius of Rome. c.354–c.455. Roman religious. On recommendation of Pope Damasus, became tutor to sons of Emperor Theodosius I (c.383–394); retired to Mount Scete in Libyan Desert, later to Troe, Egypt; renowned as ascetic monk, coming to be numbered among the Desert Fathers as influence on development of contemplative monasticism.

Arsenius Au·to·ri·a·nus \-ə-ˌtȯr-ā-ˈā-nəs\ *Orig. name* George; *later monk as* Gen·na·dius \gə-ˈnād-ē-əs\. c.1200–1273. Patriarch of Constantinople. Adopted name Arsenius on becoming patriarch of Nicaea (1255); patriarch of Constantinople (1255–59), retiring after crowning Michael VIII Palaeologus; again patriarch (1261–65) until banished by Michael, whom he had excommunicated. Deposition caused schism in Eastern Church, as Arsenite faction opposed Michael's pro-Latin policy.

Ar·ses \ˈär-(ˌ)sēz\. *In some sources called* Xerxes III. d. 336 B.C. King of Persia (338–336 B.C.). Son of Artaxerxes III; placed on throne and later murdered by eunuch Bagoas.

Arshakan. See SANATRUCES.

Ar·sin·oë \är-ˈsin-ō-ˌē\. Name of several women prominent in Egyptian history:

Arsinoë. 4th century B.C. Concubine of Philip of Macedon; m. Lagus, founder of dynasty of Ptolemies; mother of Ptolemy I of Egypt.

Arsinoë I. 3d century B.C. Daughter of Lysimachus of Thrace; m. (c.282) as 1st wife, Ptolemy II Philadelphus, by whom she was mother of Ptolemy III, Lysimachus, and Berenice; accused of conspiring against Ptolemy (c.278) and banished to Coptos.

Arsinoë II. c.316–270 B.C. Daughter of Ptolemy I and Berenice; m. 1st (300) Lysimachus, King of Thrace; attempted to disgrace heir apparent Agathocles in favor of own son, precipitating war between Thrace and Seleucid King Seleucus I Nicator; on death of Lysimachus (281) fled Thrace; m. 2d Ptolemy Ceraunus, but immediately exiled by him and her children slain; fled to Egypt and m. 3d (c.277) her brother Ptolemy II Philadelphus as second wife; a nome of Egypt and several cities named after her.

Arsinoë III. c.235–c.204 B.C. Daughter of Ptolemy III Euergetes and Berenice II; m. (217) her brother Ptolemy IV Philopator; mother of Ptolemy V Epiphanes, murdered by courtiers soon after husband's death.

Arsinoë IV. c.63–41 B.C. Daughter of Ptolemy XII Auletes and sister of Cleopatra VII and Ptolemy XIII and XIV; with Ganymedes led Egyptian forces against Julius Caesar (48); captured by Romans and led in triumph through Rome; killed by order of Cleopatra and Mark Antony.

Ar·son·val \är-sōⁿ-väl\, Arsène d', *in full* Jacques-Arsène d'. 1851–1940. French biophysicist. Director, laboratory of biological physics, Collège de France (1882–1910). Devised first reflecting galvanometer containing a moving coil (d'Arsonval galvanometer); invented highly accurate calorimeter; investigated electrical character of muscle action; laid foundation for physical therapy and invented diathermy apparatus.

Ar·ta·ba·nus \ˌär-tə-ˈbā-nəs\. Name of five kings of Parthia of Arsacid dynasty:

Artabanus I. *Known also as* Arsaces II. 3d–2d century B.C. King (c.211–191). Son and successor of Arsaces; lost territory to Antiochus III of Syria but secured recognition of Parthian kingdom.

Artabanus II. 2d century B.C. King (c.128–124 or 123). Succeeded nephew Phraates II.

Artabanus III. 1st century A.D. King (c.12– c.38 A.D.). Originally king of Media Atropatene; chosen by nobles to succeed deposed Vonones I; restored central authority, reduced power of nobles; attempted to place son on throne of Armenia (c.34), angering Rome, which sent pretender Tiridates III to depose him (35); regained throne (37).

Artabanus IV. 1st century A.D. King (79–80 or 81). Ruled briefly in opposition to Pacorus II.

Artabanus V. 3d century A.D. King (c.213–224). Son of Vologases IV; ruled Median provinces (207–213); rebelled against brother Vologases V and established rival throne; attacked by Caracalla (216); counterattacked and forced Rome to sue for peace; extracted indemnity from Emperor Macrinus; killed in battle with Ardashīr, ending Arsacid line and Parthian Empire.

Artabanus, *i.e.* Protector of Right. *Later called* Ar·da·ban \ˈär-də-ˌbän\. d. 465 or 464 B.C. Persian minister. Minister to Xerxes I, whom he murdered (465 B.C.); either killed Darius earlier or induced Artaxerxes I to do so later; in confusion, effective ruler of Achaemenian state; killed by Artaxerxes.

Ar·ta·ba·zus \är-tə-ˈbā-zəs\. 5th century B.C. Persian general. Under Xerxes, commanded Parthians and Chorasmians in expedition against Greece (480 B.C.); warned Mardonius not to fight at Plataea (479); after Persian defeat, led his part of army (40,000 men) in retreat to Byzantium.

Artabazus. 4th century B.C. Persian general. Satrap of Phrygia; rebelled (c.356 B.C.) against Artaxerxes III; pardoned (c.349); fought under Darius at Gaugamela (331); made satrap of Bactria by Alexander the Great.

Ar·ta·pher·nes \ˌärt-ə-ˈfər-nēz\. *Also* Ar·taph·re·nes \är-ˈtaf-rə-ˌnēz\. 6th–5th century B.C. Persian general. Brother of Darius I the Great; satrap of Sardis; took active part in suppressing Ionian revolt (499–498). His son ¶Artaphernes (5th century B.C.) was a Persian general; with Datis, commanded Persian army that invaded Greece and was defeated at Marathon (490); led Lydians in expedition of Xerxes I against Greece (481).

Artashēs. See ARTAXIAS.

Ar·taud \är-tō\, Antonin. 1896–1948. French dramatist, actor, poet. Involved in Surrealist movement; wrote Surrealist verse in *L'Ombilic des limbes* (1925), *Le Pèse-nerfs* (1927); actor in Dada-Surrealist Théâtre de l'Oeuvre; helped found (1926) Théâtre Alfred Jarry; published theoretical works *Manifeste du théâtre de la cruauté* (1932), *Le Théâtre et son double* (1938); chief experimental play *Les Cenci* (1935) was a failure; other works included *Heliogabale, ou l'anarchiste couronné* (1934), *Mexico* (1936), *Van Gogh, le suicidé de la societé* (1947).

Ar·ta·vas·des III \ärt-ə-ˈvas-dēz\. 1st century B.C. King of Armenia (c.55–34 B.C.). Son and successor of Tigranes I the Great; abandoned Roman allegiance in favor of Parthia, giving sister to Pacorus in marriage; forced to submit to Rome by Mark Antony (36); captured in Antony's second invasion (34), taken to Alexandria, killed by Cleopatra.

Ar·ta·xer·xes \ˌärt-ə(g)-ˈzərk-sēz, -ə(k)-ˈsərk-\. *Greek form of Pers.* Ar·takh·shath·ra \ˈär-täk-ˌshät-ˈrä\, *later* Ardashir (see ARDASHIR). Name of three Persian kings of Achaemenid dynasty:

Artaxerxes I. *Called in Greek* Ma·cro·cheir \ˈmak-rō-ˌkī(ə)r, ˈmā-krō-\, *Lat.* Lon·gim·a·nus \län-ˈjim-ə-nəs\, *i.e.* Long-hand. d. 425 B.C. King (465–425). Son of Xerxes I; father of Xerxes II, Sogdianus, and Darius II. Killed his father's murderer, the vizier Artabanus (464). Enjoyed peaceful reign; put down

\ə\ abut \ᵊ\ kitten, *Fr.* table \ər\ further \a\ ash \ā\ ace \ä\ cot, cart \aù\ out \ch\ chin \e\ bet \ē\ easy \g\ go \i\ hit \ī\ ice \j\ job \ŋ\ sing \ō\ go \ȯ\ law \ȯi\ boy \th\ both \th\ the \ü\ loot \ù\ foot \y\ yet \zh\ vision \á, b, g, k, ⁿ, œ, œ̄, ue, ue̅, ʸ\ *see* Guide to Pronunciation

rebellion in Bactria and more serious one in Egypt (460–454); kept Persia neutral during Samian and Peloponnesian wars; sanctioned practice of Jewish religion in Jerusalem (458); appointed Nehemiah governor of Judea (445).

Artaxerxes II. *Called* Mne·mon \'nē-män\, *i.e* the Mindful. d. 359 or 358 B.C. King (404–359/358). Son of Darius II. Near beginning of his reign lost Egypt to revolt and then faced by revolt of his brother Cyrus the Younger, whom he defeated and killed at Cunaxa (401). Reign marked by many rebellions; concluded with Sparta peace of Antalcidas (386); his expeditions against Egypt (385–383, 374–372) failed completely; succeeded in subduing revolt of Anatolian satraps (c.366). Rebuilt royal palace at Susa; effected changes in Persian religion, restoring worship of early gods.

Artaxerxes III. *Orig.* Ochus \'ō-kəs\. d. 338 B.C. King (359 or 358–338). Son of Artaxerxes II. At accession, murdered most of his relatives; attempted to subjugate Egypt; failed at first; defeated by princes of Sidon, Cyprus, etc., and (346) by Greek generals in Egypt; later, with great cruelty and aided by Mentor of Rhodes, succeeded in subduing Nectanebo of Egypt (343); slain by eunuch Bagoas, an Egyptian who had been put in authority; succeeded by his son Arses.

Artaxerxes IV. See BESSUS.

Ar·tax·ias \är-'tak-shəs\ *or* **Ar·tash·es** \är-'tash-əs\. 2d century B.C. Armenian ruler. Satrap of Armenia for Antiochus III; on defeat of Antiochus by Romans (190), joined fellow satrap Zariadres in establishing Kingdom of Greater Armenia; considered founder of historical Armenia; established capital at Artaxata.

Ar·te·di \år-'te-dē\, Peter. 1705–1735. Swedish naturalist. Left materials for scientific study of fishes, edited by his friend Linnaeus (1738).

Ar·te·mi·do·rus \,ärt-ə-mə-'dōr-əs, -'dȯr-\ of Ephesus. fl. 100 B.C. Greek geographer. Author of a systematic geography (11 books), extant only in fragments, much relied on by Strabo and others.

Artemidorus Dal·di·a·nus \-,dal-dē-'ā-nəs\. 2d century A.D. Greek soothsayer. Author of *Oneirocritica* ("The Interpretation of Dreams"), which throws light on religious rites, myths, and opinions of the ancients.

Ar·te·mis·ia \,ärt-ə-'miz-ē-ə, -'mish-(ē-)ə\. 5th century B.C. Queen of Halicarnassus and Cos. Subject to Persian king Xerxes; joined fleet of Xerxes in expedition against Greece (480 B.C.); showed much bravery and skill in battle of Salamis.

Artemisia. d. c.350 B.C. Queen of Caria. m. her brother Mausolus; succeeded as ruler (352–350) at his death; in his memory, erected Mausoleum at Halicarnassus (completed c.350), one of the Seven Wonders of the (ancient) World.

Ar·te·vel·de \'är-tə-,vel-də\, Jacob van. c.1295–1345. Flemish statesman. Leader in declaring neutrality of Ghent in Anglo-French disputes (1338); chosen chief of five captains governing Ghent; sided with England (1340) and probably encouraged Edward III to declare himself king of France in Ghent; aided in siege of Tournai; murdered during riot. His son ¶ Philip (1340–1382) headed revolt of Ghent against count of Flanders (1382); defeated and killed at Roosebeke (1382).

Artha, Ritter von. See Leopold HASNER.

Ar·thur \'är-thər\. 6th century. Traditionally, King of the Britons. Legendary figure possibly based on 6th century military leader of Britons, believed by some to have defeated invading Saxons at Mons Badonicus (516?); said to have died at battle of Camlan (537). As central figure of great cycle of romance, said to have held court, with his wife Guinevere, at Caerleon on the Usk, and to have instituted order of Knights of the Round Table.

Arthur. Duke *or* Count of Brit·ta·ny \'brit-ᵊn-ē\. 1187–1203. Posthumous son of Geoffrey, 4th son of Henry II, by Constance of Brittany. Claimant to throne of England on death of King Richard (1199); captured by his uncle King John (1202); murdered at Rouen, probably by John's order.

Arthur. 1486–1502. Prince of Wales. Eldest son of Henry VII of England; m. (1501) Catherine of Aragon. His death led to accession of younger brother as Henry VIII, who married his widow.

Ar·thur \är-tœr\. Comte de Riche·mont \də-rēsh-mōⁿ\. 1393–1458. Breton soldier. Son of John IV the Valiant, duke of Brittany. Captured at Agincourt and imprisoned in England (1415–20); appointed constable of France and took control of French army (1425); banished from French court (1427–32); fought under Joan of Arc (1429); allied Burgundy with France (1435); reformed French army and led it to final expulsion (1449–53) of English from France at end of Hundred Years' War. Became (1457) Duc de Bretagne.

Ar·thur \'är-thər\. *In full* Arthur William Patrick Albert. Prince. Duke of Connaught. 1850–1942. British prince and soldier. Third son of Queen Victoria; created duke of Connaught and Strathearn (1874); served in India (1866–90); general (1893); commander in chief in Ireland (1900–04); inspector general (1904–07); commander in chief in Mediterranean (1907–09); governor general of Canada (1911–16). His son ¶Prince Arthur Frederick Patrick Albert (1883–1938) served in army (1901–20); governor general of Union of South Africa (1920–23).

Arthur, Chester Alan. 1829–1886. Twenty-first president of the United States, b. Fairfield, Vt. Collector of port of New York (1871–79). Vice-president, United States (Mar.–Sept. 1881); president (1881–85) on death of Garfield.

Arthur, Sir George. 1784–1854. English colonialist. In army in Napoleonic Wars in Europe and Egypt (1804–14); lieutenant governor of British Honduras (1814–22); governor of Van Diemen's Land (Tasmania, 1825–36); attempted unsuccessfully to save Tasmanian aborigines from extinction, fought bushrangers; lieutenant governor of Upper Canada (Ontario, 1837–41); governor of Bombay (1842–46).

Arthur, Joseph Charles. 1850–1942. American botanist, b. Lowville, N.Y. Professor, Purdue U. (1887–1915); an editor of *Botanical Gazette* (1882–1900). Known for discoveries in life history of rust fungi; author of *Manual of the Rusts in the United States and Canada* (1934).

Arthur, Julia. *Orig.* Ida Lewis. 1869–1950. American actress, b. Hamilton, Ont. On stage (from 1880); played in A. M. Palmer's company in New York (1891–92) and in Henry Irving's company in London (1895–97).

Arthur, Timothy Shay. 1809–1885. American writer, b. near Newburgh, N.Y. Advocate of temperance; achieved immense popularity with *Ten Nights in a Barroom and What I Saw There* (1854).

Ar·ti·gas \är-'tē-gäs\, José Gervasio. 1764–1850. Uruguayan general. Captain in Spanish army in Uruguay; joined Buenos Aires junta in revolt for independence (1810); defeated Spanish at Las Piedras and besieged Montevideo; led retreat into Banda Oriental; turned against central power of Buenos Aires; defended Uruguayan independence against Argentines and Brazilians; captured Montevideo from Argentines (1815) and lost it to Portuguese (1817); defeated by Portuguese at Tacuarembó (1820); fled to Paraguay (1820 ff.). Considered father of Uruguayan independence.

Ar·tin \'är-tən, 'ärt-ᵊn\, Emil. 1898–1962. Austrian mathematician. Taught at U. of Hamburg (1923–37), Notre Dame (1937–38), Indiana U. (1938–46), Princeton (1946–58), Hamburg (1958–62); known for contributions to class field theory, theory of braids (1925), discovery (1944) of Artin rings, etc.

Artois, Comte d'. Title granted (1757) by Louis XV of France to his grandson Charles-Philippe (later Charles X).

Ar·tôt \år-tō\. Professional name of Belgian musical family, originally surnamed Mon·ta·gney \mōⁿ-tån-yā\, including: Maurice Montagney Artôt (1772–1829), horn player and conductor; his sons ¶Jean-Désiré (1803–1887), horn player, and ¶Alexandre Joseph (1815–1845), violinist and composer; Jean-Désiré's daughter ¶Marguerite-Joséphine-Désirée (1835–1907), operatic singer; enjoyed great success at Paris Opéra (1858), London (1859), etc.; briefly engaged to Tchaikovsky (1868). Her daughter ¶Lola Artôt de Padilla (1876–1933), also a singer; with Berlin Royal Opera (1909–27).

Ar·tsy·ba·shev *or* **Ar·tzy·ba·sheff** \ər-tsi-'bå-shif\, Mikhail Petrovich. 1878–1927. Russian novelist. Author of grimly pessimistic and immoral novels *Sanin* (1907) and *The Breaking Point* (1915) and plays *The Law of the Savage, Jealousy, Enemies,* and *War* (Russian *Voina,* 1918).

Ar·tu·si \är-'tü-sē\, Giovanni Maria. c.1545–1613. Italian composer and musical theorist. Combated innovations in music; composed *Canzonette* (for 4 voices, 1598) and *Cantate Domino;* wrote *L'arte del contrappunto ridotta in travole* (1586), *Delle imperfezioni della musica moderna* (1600), *Considerazioni musicali* (1607), etc.

Ar·tzy·ba·sheff \ər-tsi-'bå-shif\, Boris. 1899–1965. American illustrator and writer, b. Kharkov, Russia. Son of Mikhail Artsybashev (*q.v.*); to U.S. (1919); naturalized (1926). Illustrator of books by Edmund Wilson, Padraic Colum, Tagore, Balzac, and Nansen; did cover illustrations for *Time, Life, Fortune,* etc. Author of *Poor Shaydullah* (1931), *Seven Simeons* (1937), *As I See* (1954).

Arundel, Earls of. See FITZALAN family; HOWARD family.

Ar·un·del \'ar-ən-dəl\, Thomas. 1353–1414. English prelate. Son of Richard Fitzalan, 3d Earl of Arundel. Bishop of Ely (1374); chancellor of England (1386–89, 1391–96); archbishop of York (1388); archbishop of Canterbury (1396). Banished (1397) for assisting in movement for regency in derogation of Richard II's authority; returned with Henry IV, whom he crowned (1399); resumed see; again chancellor (1399, 1407, 1412); bitter opponent of Lollards.

Ar·un·dell \'ar-ən-,del\, Lady Blanche. 1583–1649. English noblewoman. Daughter of Earl of Worcester; m. Thomas Arundell of Wardour in Wiltshire; defended Wardour Castle for nine days against Parliamentary army attacks (1643). Her son ¶Henry Arundell (1606?–1694), 3d Baron Arundell of War·dour \'wȯr-dər\, fought for Charles I, dislodged Parliamentary forces from Wardour Castle (1644); privy councilor (1686); lord privy seal (1687).

Arung Sing·kang \'är-u̇ŋ-'siŋ-,käŋ\. *Orig.* La Ma·'du·kel·leng \lə-,mä-dü-'kel-əŋ\. c.1700–1765. Buginese leader. Gained control of native state of Wadjo, Celebes (1737); created federation of Buginese states; forced from power (1754) but left strong federation that resisted Dutch for over a century.

Aruq·tai \ə-'rük-,tī\. 15th century. Mongol leader. Chief of As, or Alan, Mongols; proclaimed himself grand Khan of all Mongols (1423); directed devastating raids into North China; deposed by rebellion (c.1425).

Ār·ya·bha·ṭa I \'är-yə-'bət-ə\. 476–c.550. Indian mathematician and astronomer. Maintained theory of rotation of earth round its axis and explained cause of eclipses of sun and moon; his only work, *Āryabhaṭiya,* written in versed couplets, treated of astronomy and mathematics (quadratic equations, table of sines, and other rules of algebra and plane and spherical trigonometry).

Ar·ya·de·va \'är-yə-'dā-və\. 170–270 A.D. Indian Buddhist philosopher. Disciple of Nāgārjuna and with him a founder of Mādhyamika school of Buddhism.

Arz von Straus·sen·burg \ärts-fȯn-'shtrau̇-sən-ˌbu̇rk\, Arthur. Baron. 1857–1935. Austro-Hungarian general. Distinguished himself in World War I as commander of 6th army corps on Russian front; chief of general staff (1917–18).

Asa \'ā-sə\. 10th–9th century B.C. 3d king of Judah (c.913–c.873). Successor and son of Abijah. Purged Judah of Canaanite and other cults.

Asa·chi \ä-'säsh-ē\, Gheorghe. 1788?–?1869. Romanian writer. Author of verse and stories in Romanian; creator of the historical short story; founded (1829) periodical *Albina Românească.*

Asam \'äz-äm\. Family of Bavarian artists, including: Hans Georg (1649–1711), known for frescoes and stucco work; his sons ¶Cosmas Damian (1686–1739) and ¶Egid Quirin (1692–1750), known for their frescoes in Bavarian churches; designed late Baroque rooms and churches, esp. Johann-Nepomuk-Kirche, Munich (1743–46).

Asanga \ə-'säŋ-gə\. 4th–5th century. Indian Buddhist philosopher. Established Yogācāra school of Buddhist idealism; author of *Mahāyāna–samgraha* and other works.

Asa·no \ä-sä-nō\ Sōichirō. 1848–1930. Japanese businessman. In cement business; acquired (1883) Asano Cement Co., on which he built the Asano *zaibatsu,* or industrial combine, one of largest in Japan.

Asbaje, Juana Inés de. See Juana Inés de la CRUZ.

As·bjørn·sen \'äs-bycern-sən\, Peter Christen. 1812–1885. Norwegian writer, naturalist, and folklorist. Tutor and later forester in eastern Norway; with lifelong friend Jørgen Moe (*q.v.*) collected Norwegian folktales and published them in *Nor* (1837), *Norske folkeventyr* (1841); alone published collection of folktales *Norske huldreeventyr og folkesagn* (1845–48) and translated Darwin's *Origin of Species* (1860).

As·bury \'az-ˌber-ē, -b(ə-)rē\, Francis. 1745–1816. American prelate, b. Handsworth, England. Missionary of Methodism to U.S. (1771); recalled (1775) but refused to return; became citizen of Delaware (1778). Prominent in formation of Methodist Episcopal church in U.S. (1770–84); repudiated John Wesley's authority over American churches; consecrated as superintendent at conference in Baltimore (1784); assumed title of bishop (1785); ruled new church in U.S. until his death.

Asbury, Herbert. 1891–1963. American journalist and author, b. Farmington, Mo. On staff of New York *Sun* (1916–20), *Herald* (1920–24), *Herald Tribune* (1924–28), *Collier's Weekly* (1942–48). Author of *A Methodist Saint* (a life of Bishop Francis Asbury, 1927), *The Gangs of New York* (1928), *Life of Carry Nation* (1929), *The Barbary Coast* (1933), *The French Quarter* (1936), *Sucker's Progress* (1938), *Gem of the Prairie* (1940), *The Great Illusion* (1950), etc.

Ascanian dynasty. Line of German princes descended from Albert I the Bear; principal line were margraves of Brandenburg (*q.v.*).

As·ca·ri \äs-'kä-rē\, Alberto. 1918–1955. Italian racing driver. Raced for teams Maserati (1946–48), Ferrari (1949–54), Lancia (1955); world champion driver (1952, 1953); won Mille Miglia (1954); killed at Monza.

As·cá·su·bi \äs-'käs-ü-b̲ē\, Hilario. 1807–1875. Argentine poet, b. Spain. To Argentina (1821); took part in civil war against Rosas regime; under Pres. Urquiza served as minister to France (1864). Author of *Santos Vega, Paulino Lucero,* poems depicting gaucho life.

Asch \'äsh, *Angl* 'ash\, Sholem *or* Shalom. 1880–1957. Polish novelist and playwright, b. Kutno, Poland. Began writing in Hebrew, turned to Yiddish with *Dos Shtetl* (1904); to U.S. (1914), naturalized (1920); later lived in Paris, Russia, London. Author of plays including *The God of Vengeance* (1910), and fiction including *Kiddush Hashem* (1920), *The Mother* (1930), *The Three Cities* (1933), *Mottke the Thief* (1935), *The War Goes On* (1936), *The Nazarene* (1939), *Children of Abraham* (1942), *The Apostle* (1943), *East River* (1946), *Mary* (1949), *Moses* (1951), *The Prophet* (1955). His son ¶Nathan (1902–1964), b. Warsaw; to U.S. (1915); author of *The Office* (1925), *Love in Chartres* (1927), *Pay Day* (1930), *The Valley* (1935), *The Road* (1937), and many motion-picture scripts.

As·cham \'as-kəm\, Roger. 1515–1568. English writer and Humanist scholar. Reader in Greek, St. John's, Cambridge (c.1538); tutor to Princess Elizabeth (1548–50); secretary to Sir Richard Moryson, ambassador to Emperor Charles V (1550–53). Latin secretary to Queen Mary; tutor, and later secretary, to Queen Elizabeth. Prebendary of York (1559). Author of *Toxophilus,* first English treatise on archery (1545), and esp. of *The Scholemaster,* treatise on practical education (pub. 1570).

Asch·off \'äsh-ˌȯf\, Karl Albert Ludwig. 1866–1942. German pathologist. Professor, Marburg (1903–05), Freiburg (1906–35); described inflammatory nodules (Aschoff's bodies) in rheumatic heart muscle (1904), and system of phagocytic cells in various tissues which he named reticuloendothelial system (1924).

As·cle·pi·a·des \ˌas-klə-'pī-ə-ˌdēz\ of Bi·thyn·ia \bə-'thin-ē-ə\. 2d–1st century B.C. Greek physician. Opposed Hippocrates's theory of disease; taught that disease results from unharmonious motion of corpuscles of which body is composed; recommended simple treatments, as diet, bathing, and exercise; credited with being first to distinguish between acute and chronic diseases; pioneered humane treatment of mental disorders.

Asclepiades of Sa·mos \'sā-mäs\. 3d century B.C. Greek poet and epigrammatist. Reputedly friend of Theocritus; author of graceful love poems. A variety of logaoedic verse is called Asclepiadean after him.

Ascoli, Cecco d'. See Francesco STABILI.

Asco·li \'äs-kō-lē\, Graziadio Isaia. 1829–1907. Italian philologist. Professor, Milan (from 1860); founder and editor of *Archivio glottologico italiano* (1873–1912); pioneer in study of dialects.

As·co·ni·us Pe·di·a·nus \ə-'skō-nē-əs-pē-dē-'ā-nəs, -ped-ē-\, Quintus. 9 B.C.–76 A.D. Roman scholar. Prepared commentaries on Cicero's speeches.

Asel·li \ä-'sel-lē\ *or* **Asel·lio** \ä-'sel-lyō\, Gasparo. *Lat.* Gaspar Asel·li·us \ə-'sel-ē-əs\. 1581–1625. Italian physician and anatomist. Discovered the lacteal vessels of the intestine while dissecting a dog (1622).

Asen *or* **As·sen** \á-'sän\. Medieval Bulgarian dynasty (1186–1257), probably of Kuman-Bulgar origin:

Ivan Asen I. d. 1196. With his brother Peter Asen (d. 1197), boyars in control of fortresses near Tŭrnovo; revolted against Byzantine rule and established Bulgarian independence (1186); founded second Bulgarian empire; ruled jointly, though with Ivan taking precedence as czar; defeated Byzantine Emperor Isaac Angelus near Stara Zagora (1190). Rule taken over (1197) by younger brother, Kaloyan (*q.v.*).

Ivan Asen II. d. 1241. King (1218–41). Son of Ivan Asen I; gained throne by deposing Boril; greatest of family; soldier and able monarch; added Epirus, Macedonia, and part of Albania to his realm; conquered Serbia, and assumed title of czar of the Greeks and Bulgars. Succeeding rulers of dynasty were Kaliman I, Michael I, and Kaliman II (*qq.v.*).

Ás·gríms·son \'au̇s-grēm-sȯn\, Eysteinn. c.1310–1361. Icelandic monk and poet. Author of vivid religious poem *Lilja,* recounting Christian history from Creation to Last Judgment.

A'shā, al- \ˌal-ash-'ä\. *In full* Maymūn ibn Qays al-A'shā. before 570–c.625. Arab poet. Traveled widely; known as author of panegyrics and of an ode included in pre-Islāmic anthology *Mu'allaqāt.*

Ash·'a·rī, al- \ˌal-ash-a-'rē\. *In full* Abū al-Ḥasan al-Ash'arī. 873 or 874–935 or 936. Muslim Arab theologian. Joined school of Mu'tazilites in native Basra; became noted controversialist; began composition of major work, *Maqālāt;* at 40 abandoned Mu'tazilites; completed *Maqālāt,* wrote *Kitāb al-Luma';* moved (915) to Baghdad; associated with disciples of Ibn Ḥanbal, whom he praised in parts of his *Ibānah 'an uṣūl ad-diyānah;* attracted disciples and gradually evolved own school of theology.

Ash·bee \'ash-bē\, Charles Robert. 1863–1942. English architect and designer. A leading figure of Arts and Crafts Movement; founder and director, Guild of Handicraft (1888); noted as a silverworker. Author of *Book of Cottages and Little Houses* (1906), *Craftsmanship in Competitive Industry* (1908), *Should We Stop Teaching Art?* (1911), *Caricature* (1928).

Ashbourne, 1st Baron. See Edward GIBSON.

Ash·bur·ner \'ash-bər-nər\, Charles Edward. 1870–1932. American engineer and administrator, b. Bombay, India. Civil engineer; named city manager of Staunton, Va. (1908–11), first such post in U.S.; later city manager of Springfield, Ohio (1914–18), Norfolk, Va. (1918–23), Stockton, Cal. (1923–29).

Ashburton, 1st Baron. See John DUNNING.

Ashburton, 1st Baron of 2d creation. See BARING family.

Ashe \'ash\, John. 1720?–1781. American revolutionary commander, b. Grovely, N.C. His defeat at Briar Creek, Ga. (Mar. 4, 1778) enabled British to gain Georgia and access to the Carolinas.

Ash·er ben Je·hiel \'ash-ər-ben-jə-'hē-əl\. *Known also as* Rosh \'rȯsh\. c.1250–1327. German Talmudist. Fled persecution to Spain; aided by Rabbi Solomon ben Adret, became rabbi of Toledo; succeeded ben Adret as leader of European Jewry. Compiled (1307–14) *Piske Halachot,* principal compendium of law and commentary based on Palestinian Talmud.

Ash·ford \'ash-fərd\, Bailey Kelly. 1873–1934. American surgeon, b. Washington, D.C. Army surgeon in Puerto Rico in Spanish–American War. Known for his discovery of the hookworm and subsequent campaign against hookworm disease in Puerto Rico.

Ashford, Margaret Mary, *known as* Daisy. 1881–1972. English author. Known particularly for *The Young Visiters; or Mr. Salteena's Plan* (written at age of 9; pub. 1919).

Ashi \á-'shē\. c.352–c.427 A.D. Hebrew scholar of Babylon. At early age head of rabbinical school at Sura, Babylonia; one of two chief editors who fixed canon of Babylonian Talmud; considered preeminent Babylonian interpreter of the Mishna; may have redacted Babylonian Gemara.

Ashi·ka·ga \ä-shē-kä-gä\. Japanese noble family, holders of the office of shogun (1338–1573) in what is known as the Muromachi Period. Prominent members included:

¶Ashikaga Takauji (1305–1358), warrior, was sent (1333) by the Hōjō regency government to reinforce Kyōto against attack by Emperor Daigo II; switched allegiance to emperor and helped Daigo reestablish imperial rule; defeated Hōjō uprising (1335); turned against emperor, defeating imperial army and capturing Kyōto; driven out of Kyōto but raised new army and recaptured capital, driving Daigo to southern mountains (1338); installed puppet emperor and took title shogun. His brother ¶Tadayoshi (1306–1352) was a leading commander of imperial forces under Takauji; switched allegiance with brother (1333); led in revolt against Daigo II (1335); assumed many administrative tasks of shogun; following a quarrel, joined Daigo's supporters in south; captured and imprisoned by Takauji.

¶Ashikaga Yoshimitsu (1358–1408), grandson of Takauji, became shogun (1368); became inner minister (1381), minister of state (1394); effective administrator, reorganized civil service. Concluded treaty (1392) with rival southern court of Yoshino; suppressed feudal pirate lords of southwest; fostered cultural renaissance. Retired as shogun (1394) in favor of son.

¶Ashikaga Yoshimasa (1435–1490), shogun (1449–73); came to power in period of hardship and weak government control; disagreement over succession, to his younger brother or infant son, touched off Ōnin War (1467–77), which devastated region around Kyōto; abdicated in favor of son (1473); on son's death (1489) named brother's son to succeed. Famed as patron of arts, the cultural renaissance of his reign known as Higashiyama period; sponsored pottery, Nō drama, and himself developed tea ceremony into fine art; built Silver Pavilion near Kyōto.

¶Ashikaga Yoshiaki (1537–1597), shogun (1568–73); last of his line; installed and later deposed and banished by Oda Nobunaga.

Ashkenazi, Elijah. See Elijah LEVITA.

Ash·ley \'ash-lē\, William Henry. c.1778–1838. American fur trader and explorer, b. Powhatan Co., Va. To Missouri (1802); lieutenant governor (1820). Organized Rocky Mountain Fur Co. (1822) with Andrew Henry; led expeditions to upper Missouri River region (1822–23), Green River, Wyoming (1824–25), and westward nearly to Great Salt Lake (1826); developed annual rendezvous of trappers (from 1825). In U.S. House of Representatives (1831–37).

Ashley, Sir William James. 1860–1927. English economist. Professor, U. of Toronto (1888–92), Harvard (1892–1901), U. of Birmingham (1901–25). Author of *Introduction to English Economic History and Theory* (1888–93), *Tariff Problem* (1903), *Gold and Prices* (1912).

Ashley Cooper. See Anthony Ashley COOPER.

Ash·mead \'ash-,mēd\, Isaac. 1790–1870. American printer, b. Germantown, Pa. Founded (1819) Sunday and Adult School Union, which became (1824) American Sunday School Union.

Ash·mun \'ash-mən\, Jehudi. 1794–1828. American colonial agent, b. Champlain, N.Y. Episcopal clergyman; accompanied party of freed slaves to Liberia (1822); official agent in Liberia of American Colonization Society (1824–28).

Ash·mole \'ash-,mōl\, Elias. 1617–1692. English antiquarian. Royalist in Civil War. Published (1672) exhaustive history of Order of the Garter. Presented collection of rarities to Oxford (1677), nucleus of Ashmolean Museum.

Ash·ton \'ash-tən\, Winifred. *Pseudonym* Clemence Dane \'dān\. 1888–1965. English novelist and playwright. Author of novels including *Regiment of Women* (1917), *Legend* (1919), *Wandering Stars* (1924), *Broome Stages* (1931), *He Brings Great News* (1944), *The Flower Girls* (1954); plays including *Bill of Divorcement* (1921), *Will Shakespeare* (1921), *The Way Things Happen* (1925), *Granite* (1926), *Adam's Opera* (1928), *Come of Age* (1934), *Cousin Muriel* (1940), *Call Home the Heart* (1947), *Eighty in the Shade* (1958); volumes of essays *The Women's Side* (1927), *Tradition and Hugh Walpole* (1930).

Ashur·ba·ni·pal \,äsh-ůr-'bän-ē-,päl\. *Also spelled* As·sur·bani·pal *and* Asur·ba·ni·pal \,äs-\. *Assyrian* Assur-bani-apli. 7th century B.C. King of Assyria (668–627 B.C.). Son of Esarhaddon. Seized control of delta region and Memphis in Egypt (667) defeating rebel king Taharqa; recognized Necho I as chief of lords of delta region in Egypt (664) and Necho's son Psamtik as regent (663); lost Egypt to Psamtik (c.660–654); defeated (c.652) Cimmerians, who had overrun Asia Minor; overcame revolt of his older half-brother, Shamash-shum-ukin, ruler over Babylon (648); subdued Elam (642–639). Records of his reign remain very full for 30 years (669–639), but none exist for latter part. Last years marked by attacks of Scythians on north and northeast and by rapid rise of Media and Chaldea. Able administrator; devoted to art and literature; raised Assyria to height of power; collected great library of tablets. Remains of his palace at Nineveh, inner walls of which were lined with remarkable sculptures in relief, were unearthed at Kuyunjik, near Mosul.

Ashur·na·sir·pal \,äsh-ůr-'näz-ir-päl\. *Also spelled* As·sur·na·sir·pal *or* Asur·na·zir·pal \,äs-ůr-\. *Assyrian* Assur-na-sir-apli. Name of two kings of Assyria:

Ashurnasirpal I. 11th century B.C. King (1050–32 B.C.). Son of Shamshi-Adad IV. Reign marked a low ebb of Assyrian power and prosperity; at war constantly with nomads of western desert.

Ashurnasirpal II. 9th century B.C. King (883–859 B.C.). Son of Tukulti-Ninurta II. Extended and consolidated conquests of his father; ruthless in putting down rebellions; created new Assyrian Empire; rebuilt Calah (now Nimrūd) and made it capital.

Ash·ur·ubal·lit \'äsh-ůr-(y)ü-'bäl-ət\. Name of two kings of Assyria:

Ashur-uballit I. 14th century B.C. King (c.1365–30 B.C.). Created first Assyrian Empire and initiated Middle Assyrian period; with Hittite help destroyed Mitanni power; drove out Hittites and Hurrians; gained influence over Kassite dynasty of Babylon.

Ashur-uballit II. 7th century B.C. King (611–609 B.C.). Army commander; assumed title of king on death of Sin-shar-ishkun; harried by Medes, Scythians, Babylonians; defeat of his army (609) marked end of historical Assyria.

Ash·well \'ash-,wel, -wəl\, Lena. *Orig.* Lena Margaret Po·cock \'pō-,käk\. 1872–1957. English actress and theatrical manager. Achieved success in *Mrs. Dane's Defence* (1900), *Resurrection* (1903), *Darling of the Gods* (1903), *Leah Kleschna* (1905); managed Kingsway Theatre (1907–15); organized concerts and dramatic entertainments for troops in World War I; organized Once-a-Week Players, later Lena Ashwell Players (1919–29).

As·ık Pa·şa \'äs-ək-pä-'shä\. *More fully* Alâeddin Ali Asık Paşa. c.1272–1333. Turkish poet. Author of mystical-religious verse expressing orthodox Islāmic theology, among earliest literary works in Ottoman Turkish, including *Gharībnāmeh* and *Faqrnāmeh*.

As·ık·pa·şa·zâ·de \'äsh-ək-pä-'shäz-ä-'dä\. *Also called* Aş·ı·ki \äsh-ə-'kē\. *In full* Dervis Ahmet ibn Şeyh Yahya ibn Şeyh Salman ibn Aşık Paşa. 1400–after 1484. Turkish historian. Great grandson of Aşık Paşa. Author of *Tevarih-i Al-i Osman,* drawn partly from personal observation, an invaluable chronicle of early Ottoman history.

Asinius Pollio, Gaius. See POLLIO.

As·kew \'as-,kyü\, Anne. 1521–1546. English Protestant martyr. Burned at stake at Smithfield for refusing to recant her opinions on transubstantiation.

Aṣ·maʽī, al- \al-'as-ma-ē\. *In full* Abū Saʽīd ʽAbd al-Malik ibn Qurayb al-Aṣmaʽī. c.740–828. Iraqi scholar. A leader of Basra school of philology; tutor to son of Hārūn ar-Rashīd; compiled numerous anthologies of pre-Islāmic Arab poetry with learned commentaries.

Asmus. See Matthias CLAUDIUS.

As·nyk \'äs-nik\, Adam. *Pseudonym* Ely \'el-ē\. 1838–1897. Polish poet and dramatist. Active in Polish revolutionary government (1863). Author of philosophical verse published as *Poezje* (1869), frequently republished.

Aśo·ka \ə-'sō-kə\. *Skt.* Açо·ka \ə-'shō-kə\. d. 238 or 232 B.C. King of India (c.265–238 or c.273–232 B.C.) of Maurya dynasty. Son of Bindusara and grandson of Chandragupta. Brought kingdoms of Bengal and Orissa into his domain, which encompassed nearly all of modern India, Afghanistan, and Baluchistan; brought Kalinga war to successful close (261); converted to Buddhism (about 261); became zealous supporter of Buddhism, making it the state religion; endeavored to rule according to *dharma;* left edicts on Buddhism engraved on rocks and pillars in various parts of India that are today records of great value.

As·par \'as-pər\, Flavius Ardaburius. d. 471 A.D. Roman general. Led fleet of Eastern empire against Vandals in Africa but was defeated (434); consul (434); defeated Persians (441); defeated by Attila outside Constantinople (443); made patrician by Emperor Marcian (450); on Marcian's death arranged accession of own protégé as Leo I (457); as Leo attempted to assert independence, enlisted support of Isaurians against Aspar's Goths; killed in conspiracy of Leo and Isaurians.

As·pa·sia \as-'pā-sh(ē-)ə, -zh(ē-)ə\. 470?–410 B.C. Greek adventuress and consort of Pericles, b. probably at Miletus. Noted for her beauty, wit, and learning; at Athens won affection and esteem of Pericles, with whom she lived (c.445–429); attacked for supposed great influence over him in many of his public acts; bore one son named Pericles.

Aspasia. *Called* the Younger. *Real name, according to Plutarch,* Mil·to \'mil-(,)tō\. 5th–4th century B.C. Greek beauty. Presented to Cyrus the Younger, who placed her in his harem and named her Aspasia after the wife of Pericles; on death of Cyrus, became property of Artaxerxes; later claimed by Darius when he was named heir to Persian throne; created priestess by Artaxerxes to prevent her transfer to Darius.

Asp·din \'asp-dən\, Joseph. 1799–1855. English bricklayer and stonemason. Credited with invention (1824) of portland cement.

As·pin·wall \'as-pən-ˌwȯl\, William Henry. 1807–1875. American merchant, b. New York City. Promoter of Pacific Mail Steamship Co. (1848) and Panama Railroad (1850–55).

Asp·lund \'äsp-lənd\, Erik Gunnar. 1885–1940. Swedish architect. A leading exponent of modern design; major works included Woodland Chapel (1912–20), Skandia Cinema (1922–23), City Library (1924–27), Bredenberg store (1933–35), State Bacteriological Laboratory (1933–35), Woodland Crematorium (1935–40), all in Stockholm; Law Courts (1934–37), Göteborg; planned Stockholm Exposition (1930).

As·quith \'as-ˌkwith, -kwəth\, Herbert Henry. 1st Earl of Ox·ford \'äks-fərd\ and Asquith. 1852–1928. English politician. Liberal M.P. (1886–1918, 1920–24); home secretary (1892–95); chancellor of the exchequer (1905–08); prime minister (1908–16). Obtained passage of Parliament Act (1911), abolishing veto power of House of Lords, Home Rule Bill for Ireland, and Welsh Disestablishment Act. Formed (1915) coalition cabinet with Unionists; forced out by Lloyd George (1916). Created earl (1925). Author of *Genesis of the War* (1923), *Fifty Years of Parliament* (1926), *Memories and Reflections* (1928). His second wife ¶Margot, *orig.* Emma Alice Margaret, *nee* Tennant (1864–1945; m. 1894), wrote *Autobiography* (1920–22), *Lay Sermons* (1927), a novel *Octavia* (1928), *More Memories* (1933), and *Off the Record* (1943).

As·se·ma·ni \ˌäs-sä-'män-ē\, Joseph Simonius. 1687–1768. Syrian Maronite Orientalist. Custodian in Vatican Library; made two extensive journeys (1715, 1735) in East collecting Oriental manuscripts for Vatican; created titular archbishop of Tyre and librarian of Vatican Library; author of several works on Oriental manuscripts, esp. *Bibliotheca Orientalis Clementino-Vaticana* (1719–28). His nephew ¶Stephen Evodius (1707–1782), Orientalist and author, was custodian in Vatican Library; titular archbishop of Apamea; assisted uncle in compiling *Bibliothecae Apostolicae Vaticanae Codicum Manuscriptorum Catalogus* (1756–59). Another nephew ¶Joseph Aloysius (1710–1782) was professor of Oriental languages at Rome. A grandnephew ¶Simon (1752–1821), missionary in Syria, was appointed (1785) professor of Oriental languages at Padua; wrote valuable treatise on numismatics (1787) and a work (1787) on pre-Islāmic Arabic culture.

Assen. See ASEN.

As·ser \'as-ər\. d. c.909. Welsh monk. Called to household of Alfred the Great (886) as Alfred's Latin tutor for half of each year; wrote life of Alfred. Bishop of Devon and Cornwall, later of Sherborne.

As·ser \'äs-ər\, Tobias Michael Carel. 1838–1913. Dutch jurist. Professor of law, Amsterdam (1862–93); a founder of *Revue de droit international et de législation comparée* (1869) and of Institut de Droit International (1873); member, Dutch council of state (1893). Promoter of Hague Conference (1893); delegate to Hague Peace Conferences (1899, 1907), at first of which he promoted establishment of Permanent Court of Arbitration. Corecipient, with A. H. Fried, of 1911 Nobel peace prize.

Assisi, Saint Francis of. See FRANCIS of Assisi.

As·sol·lant \ȧ-sȯ-läⁿ\, Jean-Baptiste-Alfred. 1827–1886. French writer. Spent some years in U.S. and wrote *Scènes de la vie aux États-Unis* (1858); author also of popular juveniles, as *La Mort de Roland* (1860), *Marcomin* (1861), *Aventures merveilleuses du capitaine Corcoran* (1867), etc.

Assurbanipal. See ASHURBANIPAL.

Assurnasirpal. See ASHURNASIRPAL.

Ast·bury \'as(t)-ˌber-ē, -b(ə-)rē\, John. *Called* Astbury of Shelton. 1688–1743. English potter. Established pottery at Shelton (1725); became renowned for quality of wares; produced utilitarian wares and decorative pieces; developed sprigging method of decoration; first to use flint in clay for greater whiteness; also produced marble and agate wares. Considered first of great Staffordshire potters.

As·tell \'as-tᵊl\, Mary. 1668–1731. English author. Wrote (1694) *A Serious Proposal to Ladies,* proposing establishment of Anglican sisterhood; attacked in *Tatler* under name of Mad·o·nel·la \ˌmad-ᵊn-'el-ə\.

As·tle \'as-əl\, Thomas. 1735–1803. English antiquary and paleographer. Keeper of records, Tower of London (1783); author of *The Origin and Progress of Writing* (1784).

Ast·ley \'ast-lē\, Sir Jacob. Baron Astley. 1579–1652. English Royalist general. Served in Thirty Years' War; in Civil War commanded infantry at Edge Hill, Gloucester, Naseby; taken prisoner at Stow (1646), and paroled; author of battle prayer "O Lord, Thou knowest how busy I must be this day. If I forget Thee, do not Thou forget me."

Astley, Philip. 1742–1814. English equestrian. Joined British regiment of light horse (1759); proprietor of circus and hippodrome (known simply as "Astley's"), London (1770); opened Astley's Royal Amphitheatre, London (1798); established Astley Amphitheatre, Paris (1782) and 18 other circuses in Europe.

Astolf. See AISTULF.

As·ton \'as-tən\, Francis William. 1877–1945. English physicist. Assistant to J.J. Thomson (1910–19); fellow of Trinity College, Cambridge (from 1919). Discovered number of isotopes in several nonradioactive elements by means of mass spectrograph of his own devising (1919); in all discovered 212 of the 287 natural isotopes; awarded 1922 Nobel prize for chemistry. Author of *Isotopes* (1922), *Mass Spectra and Isotopes* (1933), and papers on electric discharge in gases.

As·tor \'as-tər\, John Jacob. 1763–1848. American fur trader and financier, b. Walldorf, Duchy of Baden, Germany. To U.S. (1784); entered fur trade (c.1786); by 1800 the dominant figure in American fur trade; incorporated American Fur Co. (1808), Pacific Fur Co. (1810). Founded (1811) Astoria, at mouth of Columbia River, as trading post, but lost it to British (1813). Made large and profitable loans to U.S. government (1814); invested heavily in New York real estate; monopolized Mississippi Valley (by 1817) and upper Missouri (1822–34) fur trade. Sold fur interests (1834); devoted himself to administering his fortune. His son ¶William Backhouse (1792–1875) administered Astor estate (1848–75); his grandson ¶John Jacob (1822–1890) served on McClellan's staff in Civil War, and administered Astor estate (1875–90); his great-grandson ¶John Jacob (1864–1912) managed Astor estate (from 1890); built Astoria section of later Waldorf-Astoria Hotel, New York City; served in Spanish–American War; lost his life in *Titanic* disaster.

Astor, William Waldorf. 1st Viscount Astor of He·ver \'hē-vər\ Castle. 1848–1919. British financier and journalist, b. New York City. Great-grandson of John Jacob Astor. Defeated in campaign (1881) for governor of New York State; U.S. minister at Rome (1882–85); published novels *Valentino* (1886) and *Sforza* (1889). To England (1890); naturalized (1899); proprietor, *Pall Mall Gazette* and *Pall Mall Magazine, Observer* (1911); created baron (1916), viscount (1917). His eldest son ¶Waldorf (1879–1952), 2d viscount, M.P. (1910–19); parliamentary secretary to Prime Minister Lloyd George (1917), to ministry of food (1918), and to ministry of health (1919–21); owner of *Observer* (1919–45). His wife ¶Nancy Witcher, *nee* Lang·horne \'laŋ-ərn\ (1879–1964), b. Danville, Va., m. 1st (1897; divorced 1903) Robert Gould Shaw, 2d (1906) Waldorf Astor; M.P. (1919–45), succeeding her husband in House of Commons when he entered House of Lords as 2d Viscount Astor, thus first woman to sit in British Parliament; noted hostess at country seat Cliveden, where the "Cliveden set" in 1930s included Neville Chamberlain, Sir Samuel Hoare, etc. Their son ¶William Waldorf (1907–1966), 3d viscount, was M.P. (1935–45, 1951–52); parliamentary private secretary to Sir Samuel Hoare (1936–39). The 2d viscount's brother ¶John Jacob (1886–1971), 1st Baron Astor of Hever (created 1956), army officer, aide-de-camp to viceroy of India (1911–14); M.P. (1922–45); proprietor of *Times* of London (1922–66).

Astorga, Baron d'. See Emanuele RINCÓN.

Astrea. See Aphra BEHN.

As·trid \'as-trəd, *Swed* 'äs-\. *In full* Astrid So·fia Lo·vi·sa Thy·ra \-sü-'fē-ȧ-'lü-vis-ˌȧ-'tu̅e-rȧ\. 1905–1935. Queen of the Belgians. Daughter of Prince Charles, brother of king of Sweden; m. (1926) Prince Leopold (later Leopold III) of Belgium.

Astruc. See ABBA MARI.

As·truc \as-tru̅ek\, Jean. 1684–1766. French physician. Physician to king of Poland, consultant to Louis XV. Besides medical works, wrote *Conjectures sur les mémoires originaux dont il paraît que Moïse s'est servi pour composer le livre de la Genèse* (1753), beginning of modern scholarly textual investigation of sources of Pentateuch.

As·tu·rias \äs-'tür-yäs\, Miguel Angel. 1899–1974. Guatemalan writer. Author of *Leyendas de Guatemala* (1930), verse *Sonetos* (1936), *El señor presidente* (1946), *Hombres de maíz* (1949), and epic trilogy comprising *Viento fuerte* (1950), *El papa verde* (1954), *Los ojos de los enterrados* (1960). In Guatemalan diplomatic service (from 1946); ambassador to France (1966–70). Awarded Lenin Peace prize (1966), Nobel prize for literature (1967).

As·ty·a·ges \as-'tī-ə-ˌjēz\. *Babylonian* Ishtumegu. 6th century B.C. Last king of Media (reigned c.584–550 B.C.). Son of Cyaxares. According to Herodotus, Astyages's daughter Mandane married Cambyses and was mother of Cyrus the Great. Attacked Cyrus; seized by his own troops in mutiny; held captive by Cyrus, who seized kingdom. See HARPAGUS.

Asurbanipal. See ASHURBANIPAL.

Aś·vag·ho·sa \'äsh-vəg-hō-sə\. 80?–?150 A.D. Indian philosopher and poet. Convert from Brahminism to Buddhism; great explicator of Mahāyāna Buddhism, as at fourth Buddhist council. Author of works on Mahāyāna, a verse life of Buddha *Buddhacarita,* the *Mahālankara,* etc.; considered father of Sanskrit drama; popularized Sanskrit *kāvya* verse form.

Aś·va·lā·ya·na \ˌäsh-və-ˈlä-yə-nə\. fl. 400 B.C.? Indian theologian. Author of Vedic manuals and texts including *Āśvalāyana-srauta-sūtra,* the *Grhya-sūtra,* and the four *Āraṇyaka* texts.

ʻAtāhiyah. See ABU AL-ʻATĀHIYAH.

Ata·hual·lpa *or* **Ata·hual·pa** \ä-tä-ˈwäl-pä, *Angl* ˌat-ə-ˈwäl-pə\ *or* **Ata·ba·li·pa** \ä-tä-ˈbä-lē-pä\. c.1502–1533. Last Inca king of Peru. On death (1525) of his father, Huayna Capac, disputed kingdom with his half-brother Huascar, whom he deposed (1530); arrested (1532) by Pizarro on his refusal to become a Christian; executed on charge of complicity in death of Huascar.

ʻAtā·sī \a-ˈtä-sē\, Hāshim al-. 1875–1960. Syrian politician. Served in Ottoman government of Syria and in Syrian Congress (1919); opposed French occupation; helped negotiate Franco-Syrian treaty of independence (1936); president of Syrian republic (1936–39, 1950–51, 1954–55).

Ata·türk \ä-tä-ˈtuerk, *Angl* ˈat-ə-ˌtərk\, Kemal. *Orig.* Mustafa; *in school adopted surname* Ke·mal \kä-ˈmäl\, *i.e.* maturity and perfection. 1881–1938. Turkish soldier and statesman. Distinguished himself in Turkish–Italian war in Tripoli (1911), defense of Gallipoli against British (1915), repulse of Russians in the east (1916); brigadier general (1916); commanded Ottoman 7th army in Palestine (1918). Disillusioned by terms of armistice, which dissolved Ottoman army; resolved on goal of Turkish state; in defiance of occupying forces and sultan, called National Congress of Turkish provinces at Erzurum (1919); resigned from army, elected president by Congress (1919); established headquarters of nationalist movement at Ankara; called and elected president of Grand National Assembly of Turkey at Ankara after British occupation of Istanbul (1920); proclaimed state of Turkey with himself as president and prime minister; directed campaigns against Armenians, Georgians, French to regain lost territories; as commander in chief decisively defeated Greeks (1922); secured British withdrawal; secured recognition of Turkish independence and national borders in Treaty of Lausanne (1923). Formed ruling People's Republican party (1923); proclaimed republic and elected president (1923). Abolished caliphate (1924); closed Islāmic monasteries and other institutions; instituted civil and cultural reforms; fostered secular education, western dress; adopted Roman alphabet for Arabic (1928); abolished polygamy; promulgated law requiring use of family names (1933), under which he was given name Atatürk, i.e. Father of Turks. Continued as president (1923–38).

At·a·ul·phus \ˌat-ä-ˈəl-fəs\. *Also written* At·a·wulf \ˈat-ə-ˌwu̇lf\ *or* At·a·ulf \ˈat-ä-ˌu̇lf\. d. 415 A.D. King of the Visigoths. Brother-in-law and successor (410) of Alaric. Withdrew Goths from Italy into Gaul (412); made alliance with Emperor Honorius, whose half-sister Galla Placidia he married (414); led army across Pyrenees into Spain; assassinated at Barcelona.

Atch·i·son \ˈach-ə-sən\, David Rice. 1807–1886. American politician, b. Frogtown, Ky. In Missouri legislature (1834–38); federal judge (1841–43); U.S. senator from Missouri (1843–56) and during that time president pro tem on 16 occasions. Held by some to have been president of the U.S. for one day (March 4, 1849), when Zachary Taylor declined to be inauguarated on the Sabbath.

At·get \át-zhe\, Eugène, *in full* Jean-Eugène-Auguste. 1856–1927. French photographer. An actor in provincial touring company; took up photography (c.1898); devoted rest of life to photographing Paris, esp. historic buildings, architectural decoration, shopfronts, tradespeople, etc., often achieving remarkable feats of composition and mood.

Athal·a·ric \ə-ˈthal-ə-rik\. 516–534. King of Ostrogoths in Italy (526–34). Grandson and successor (526) of Theodoric, under regency of mother Amalasuntha.

Athan·a·gild \ə-ˈthan-ə-ˌgild\. d. 567. King of Visigoths in Spain (554–567). Father of Brunhilde (*q.v.*).

Athan·a·ric \ə-ˈthan-ə-rik\. d. 381. Chief of Visigoths in Dacia (c.364–376). Defeated (369) by Roman Emperor Valens, and (376) by Iluns; carried on fierce persecutions of Christians (369–372); died in Byzantium while seeking aid from Emperor Theodosius.

Ath·a·na·si·us \ˌath-ə-ˈnā-zh(ē-)əs, -ˈnā-sh(ē-)əs\. Saint. *Called* Athanasius the Great. c.293–373. Greek theologian and prelate in Egypt. Lifelong opponent of Arianism; controversialist, for many years referred to as "Athanasius contra mundum"; also known as "Father of Orthodoxy." Early a student of theology; attended Council of Nicaea (325) as deacon. Bishop of Alexandria (328–373). Refused to obey command of emperor to reinstate Arius; tried by partisan Council of Tyre (335) and exiled by Emperor Constantine to Trier, Germany; advocated Homoousian doctrine; allowed to return to Alexandria (337) by Constantius; again exiled (338) by powerful Arians; found asylum with Pope Julius I; vindicated (343) by Western Council at Sardica; allowed to return to his see (346); wrote *Apology against the Arians;* exiled third time (356–362); lived mostly with Egyptian hermits; during this exile wrote, among other books, his greatest doctrinal work, *Four Orations against the Arians;* in Alexandria (362) but soon exiled for fourth time (362) by Julian; brought back (363) by Jovian and driven out a fifth time (365) by Valens; soon restored and during last years (366–373) continued his labors at Alexandria. Author of *History of the Arians, On the Decrees of the Nicene Synod,* and a series of festal epistles. Not author of Athanasian Creed, which originated later (5th or 6th century).

Athanasius I. 1230–1310. Byzantine prelate. Monk and later priest; founded monastery on Mt. Athos; led opposition to union of Latin and Greek churches decreed by Second Council of Lyons (1274); in exile in Palestine (1275–82); named patriarch of Constantinople (1289) by anti-unionist emperor Andronicus II; instituted sweeping disciplinary reforms, provoking enmity of clergy; expelled Franciscans from Constantinople (1307); forced to retire (1310).

Athanasius the Athonite. Saint. *Also called* Athanasius of Trebizond. *Orig. name* Abraham. c.920–c.1000. Byzantine monk. Retired to Mt. Athos and, with support of his spiritual protege, Emperor Nicephorus II Phocas, organized scattered monks there into Great Laura community and introduced rule for cenobitic life (963).

Athelstan. See AETHELSTAN.

Ath·e·nae·us \ˌath-ə-ˈnē-əs\. fl. c.200 A.D. Greek grammarian of Naucratis, Egypt. His only extant work, *Deipnosophistai* (15 books), contains much miscellaneous information about foods, music, dances, games, and other social diversions and quotes from some 800 ancient authors.

Ath·e·nag·o·ras \ˌath-ə-ˈnag-ə-rəs\. 2d century A.D. Greek Christian apologist. Possibly a convert from Platonism; established Christian school in Alexandria; wrote *Presbeia peri Christianōn* (c.177), first known work to adapt Neoplatonic concepts to Christianity; addressed to Emperor Marcus Aurelius Antoninus, it defended Christians against charges of atheism, incest, and cannibalism.

Athenagoras I. 1886–1972. Byzantine prelate. Metropolitan of Corfu (1923–30); archbishop of North and South America (1930–48); ecumenical patriarch of Constantinople (1948–72). Joined Pope Paul VI (1965) in nullifying anathemas pronounced in 1054 at outset of East–West church schism.

Athe·nas \á-tā-nás\, Georges. 1877–1955. French writer. With ¶Aimé Mer·lo \mer-lō\(1880–1958) published under pseudonyms Marius and Ary Le·blond \lə-blōⁿ\ novels including *Vies parallèles* (1902), *Les Sortilèges* (1905) *L'Oued* (1907), *En France* (1909, Goncourt prize), *Ulysse Cafre* (1926), *Histoire d'Afrique* (1937), *Le Paradis perdu* (1939).

Athe·no·dor·us \ə-ˈthē-nə-ˈdōr-əs, -ˈdȯr-\ of Cleitor. fl. c.405 B.C. Greek sculptor. Executed statues of Apollo and Zeus dedicated at Delphi after Spartan victory at Aegospotami (405 B.C.).

Athenodorus of Rhodes. 2d? century B.C. Greek sculptor. Collaborated with Agesander and Polydorus on *Laocoön* group.

Athenodorus Ca·na·ni·tes \-ˌkā-nə-ˈnīt-ēz\. c.74 B.C.–c.7 A.D. Greek Stoic philosopher. Tutor of Octavian; established government of property-holders favorable to Rome in native Tarsus.

Athenodorus Cor·dyl·io \-kȯr-ˈdil-ē-ˌō\. 1st century B.C. Greek Stoic philosopher. Keeper of library at Pergamum.

Ath·er·ton \ˈath-ər-tən, ˈath-ərt-ᵊn\, Gertrude Franklin, *nee* Horn \ˈhȯ(ə)rn\. 1857–1948 . American novelist, b. San Francisco. m. (1876) George H. B. Atherton (d.1887). Author of *The Californians* (1898), *The Conqueror* (1902), *Tower of Ivory* (1910), *Mrs. Balfame* (1916), *Black Oxen* (1923), *The Sophisticates* (1931), *Golden Peacock* (1936), *The House of Lee* (1940), *The Horn of Life* (1942), etc.

Athlone, 1st Earl of. See Godart van GINKEL; Alexander CAMBRIDGE.

Atholl, Earls, marquises, and dukes of. See under STEWART family; MURRAY family.

Atholstan, Baron. See Hugh GRAHAM.

Atī·śa \ə-ˈtē-shə\. *Known also as* Dī·pan·ka·ra \ˈdē-pəŋ-kər-ə\. 982–1054. Indian religious. Traveled to Tibet (1038 or 1042) and established monasteries; wrote treatises on Theravāda, Mahāyāna, and Vajrayāna Buddhism; his teachings formed basis of Tibetan Bka'-gdams-pa sect of Buddhism.

At·kin·son \ˈat-kən-sən\, Eleanor, *nee* Stack·house \ˈstak-ˌhau̇s\. 1863–1942. American writer, b. Rensselaer, Ind. m. (1891) Francis B. Atkinson. Author of *Mamzelle Fifine* (1903), *Greyfriars Bobby* (1912), *Johnny Appleseed* (1915), *Poilu, a Dog of Roubaix* (1918), etc.

Atkinson, Sir Harry Albert. 1831–1892. New Zealand politician, b. England. To N.Z. (1853); distinguished himself in Maori wars (1860, 1863); minister of defense (1864–65); colonial treasurer (1879–82, 1882–83). Prime minister (1876–77, 1883–84, 1887–91); successful in abolition of provinces and in introduction of economies in public expenditure.

Atkinson, Henry. 1782–1842. American soldier, b. North Carolina. Commanded exploring expeditions and frontier posts in West (1819–26); established Jefferson Barracks, St. Louis (1826); army commander in Black Hawk War (1832), defeating Black Hawk at Bad Axe (Aug. 2, 1832).

At·las \ˈat-ləs\, Charles. *Orig.* Angelo Si·cil·ia·no \ˌsē-chēl-ˈyän-ō\. 1894–1972. American physical culturist, b. Acri, Italy. To U.S. (1904); developed "dynamic tension" method of muscle-building; sculptor's model; declared "World's Most

Perfectly Developed Man" by *Physical Culture* magazine (1922); founded mail-order physical culture business.

Atli. See ATTILA.

Atos·sa \ə-'täs-ə\. 6th century B.C. Persian queen. Daughter of Cyrus the Great; wife of (1) her brother Cambyses, (2) of the Magian Smerdis, and (3) of Darius I Hystaspis; mother of Xerxes I. Exerted great influence over Darius.

At·tai·gnant *or* **At·tain·gnant** \à-ten-yä^{n}\, Pierre. c.1480–1552. French printer and publisher. Established printing business, Paris (1514); experimented with movable music type and used it to print *Chansons nouvelles* (1528), one of earliest examples of single-impression music printing; music printer and bookseller to the king (1538).

At·ta·lus \'at-ə-ləs\. Name of three kings of Pergamum, the Attalids:

Attalus I. *Surnamed* So·ter \'sōt-ər\. 269–197 B.C. Ruled (241–197). Succeeded uncle Eumenes I; refused tribute to Gauls of Galatia; defeated them decisively (before 230); took title of king; became master of all Asia Minor west of Mt. Taurus, defeating Antiochus Hierax in three battles (229–228); ally of Rome against Philip V of Macedon in First Macedonian War (214–205) and of Rhodes and Rome in Second (200–196); patron of arts.

Attalus II. *Surnamed* Phil·a·del·phus \,fil-ə-'del-fəs\. 220–138 B.C. King (159–138). Son of Attalus I; succeeded older brother Eumenes II. Before accession an able soldier; frequently sent as ambassador to Rome. Ally of Rome, which aided him in war against Prusias II of Bithynia (156–154); helped Alexander Balas overthrow Demetrius I (150). As patron of arts, kept Pergamum a center of Hellenistic culture.

Attalus III. *Surnamed* Phil·o·me·tor Eu·er·ge·tes \,fil-ə-'mēt-ər-yü-'er-jət-,ēz\. c.170–133 B.C. King (138–133). Son of Eumenes II; nephew and successor of Attalus II. Eccentric sovereign, represented as dilletante in literature and art; bequeathed his kingdom to Rome.

Attalus, Flavius Priscus. d. after 416. Emperor of Rome (409–410, 414). Prefect of Rome when it was besieged by Alaric (409); proclaimed emperor by Alaric in place of Honorius; deposed by Alaric (410); again named emperor by Ataulphus (414); banished by Honorius (416).

ʿAṭ·ṭār \ät-'tär\, Farīd od-Dīn Moḥammad ebn Ebrāhīm. *Also called* Farīd od-Dīn Abū Ḥamīd Moḥammad. c.1142–c.1220. Persian mystical poet. Traveled widely in early years; studied Ṣūfism; author of *Manṭeq oṭ-ṭeyr* (Conference of the Birds), a Ṣūfī allegory, *Elāhī-nāmeh, Moṣībat-nāmeh,* and prose work on early Ṣūfism *Tazkerat ol-owlīyā.*

At·ter·bom \'ät-ter-,büm\, Per Daniel Amadeus. 1790–1855. Swedish poet, philosopher, and literary historian. A leader of Swedish Romantic movement; professor at Uppsala (from 1828); a founder of society Musis Amici (1807), later called Auroraförbundet, and of its periodical *Phosphorus* (1810–13). Author of verse *Blommarna* (1812–37), fairy tale play *Lycksalighetens ö* (1824–27), and six-volume *Svenska siare och skalder* (1841–55).

At·ter·bury \'at-ər-,ber-ē, -b(ə-)rē\, Francis. 1663–1732. English ecclesiastic and controversialist. Dean of Carlisle (1704); bishop of Rochester and dean of Westminster (1713); a leader of Tory High Church party; helped defend Henry Sacheverell (1710); deprived and banished for complicity in Jacobite plots (1723).

At·ter·idge \'at-ər-əj\, Harold Richard. 1886–1938. American playwright and librettist, b. Lake Forest, Ill. Wrote esp. for Broadway revues, including the series *The Passing Show* (10 annual editions, 1912 ff.) and *Artists and Models.*

Atticus, Herodes. See HERODES ATTICUS.

At·ti·cus \'at-ə-kəs\, Titus Pomponius. 109–32 B.C. Roman man of letters. Original name Titus Pomponius; surname Atticus added because of his long residence in Athens (88–65 B.C.) to escape Roman civil war; amassed large library; wrote histories of Greece and Rome; intimate friend and correspondent of Cicero; edited Cicero's letters written to him.

At·ti·la \'at-^{ə}l-ə, ə-'til-ə\. 406?–453. King of the Huns (434–453). At first (434–441) occupied with wars with other barbarian tribes; extended his power over central Europe; exacted large tribute from Eastern Roman empire; on failure of tribute, drove Eastern Roman armies into Constantinople and occupied all Gallipoli (443); murdered co-ruling older brother Bleda (c.445); overran Balkan countries and northern Greece (447–450), causing great destruction. Claimed Honoria, sister of Emperor Valentinian III, for wife and half of Western empire as dowry (450); planned conquest of Visigoths and invaded Gaul (451) but forced to give up siege of Orléans; retired to Catalaunian Plains; defeated there (June 451), one of decisive battles of history, by combined armies of Romans under Aetius and Visigoths under Theodoric and Thorismond; pursued across Rhine. Invaded northern Italy (452), devastating region and destroying Aquileia; yielded to intercession of Pope Leo I and recrossed Alps; died suddenly on eve of new invasion of Italy. Appears under name Et·zel \'et-səl\ as legendary king in *Nibelungenlied* and as At·li \'ät-lē\ in *Völsunga Saga.*

Attius, Lucius. See ACCIUS.

Att·lee \'at-lē\, Clement Richard. 1st Earl Attlee and Viscount Prest·wood \'pres-,twu̇d\. 1883–1967. English politician. Settlement house worker (1907–22); lecturer (1913–22), London School of Economics; M.P. (1922–55); undersecretary for war (1924); postmaster general (1931); leader of Labour opposition in Commons (1935–40); member of war cabinet, as lord privy seal (1940–42), secretary of state for dominion affairs (1942–43), deputy prime minister (1942–45), lord president of the council (1943–45); prime minister (1945–51). Directed nationalization of industry, formation of welfare state, transformation of British Empire into Commonwealth. Again leader of Labour opposition (1951–55). Created earl and viscount (1955).

At·to Ad·al·bert \'at-(')ō-'ad-^{ə}l-,bərt\. *Ital.* Az·zo Adal·ber·to \'ät-tsō-,äd-äl-'ber-tō\. d. 988. Count of Canossa. Son of Siegfried, Baron of Lucca; given Canossa by bishop of Reggio for military services; rescued Adelaide, widow of Lothair II, from prison (951), provoking attack by Berengar II, whom he repulsed; made count of Canossa and marquis of Canossiana by Emperor Otto I (962); ruled Modena, Reggio, Ferrara. Founder of house of Canossa.

At·tucks \'at-əks\, Crispus. 1723?–1770. American patriot. Probably mulatto, possibly a runaway slave; member of mob in "Boston Massacre" (March 5, 1770) and one of three men killed by fire of British troops.

Att·wood \'at-,wu̇d\, Thomas. 1765–1838. English musician and composer. Pupil under Mozart (1785); organist (1796–1838), St. Paul's Cathedral; founding member of Philharmonic Society (1813); professor, Royal Academy of Music (1823–38); musician in ordinary to king (1825); organist to Chapel Royal (1836). Composed many theatrical works including *The Prisoner* (1792), *The Smugglers* (1796), *True Friends* (1800); liturgical music; songs; chamber music; coronation anthems for George IV and William IV.

Attwood, Thomas. 1783–1856. English economist and reformer. Organized Birmingham Political Union (1830) for reform of franchise; M.P. (1832–39); supported Chartists.

At·wa·ter \'at-,wȯt-ər\, Wilbur Olin. 1844–1907. American agricultural chemist, b. Johnsburg, N.Y. Professor, Wesleyan U. (1873–1907); director (1875–77), first state agricultural station in U.S., Middletown, Conn. Founder and chief, Office of Experiment Stations, U.S. Dept. of Agriculture (1888–1907). Discovered nitrogen-fixing ability of legumes (1881); conducted experiments in calorimetry.

At·wood \'at-,wu̇d\, George. 1746–1807. English mathematician. Author of mathematical works and inventor of Atwood's machine for verifying laws of acceleration of motion.

Atwood, Wallace Walter. 1872–1949. American geologist and geographer, b. Chicago. Professor, Harvard (1913–20); president of Clark U. (1920–46). Founder and editor of *Economic Geography* (1925). Author of *The World At Work* (1931), *The Growth of Nations* (1936), *The Rocky Mountains* (1945), etc.

Au·ba·nel \ō-bà-nel\, Théodore. 1829–1886. French poet. A leader of group (Félibrige) of Provençal writers striving to preserve Provençal as a literary language. Author of verse *La Miougrano entreduberto* (1860), *Li Fiho d'Avignoun* (1885), and plays including *Lou Pan dou pecat* (1878).

Au·ber \ō-ber\, Esprit, *in full* Daniel-François-Esprit. 1782–1871. French composer. Pupil of Cherubini. Influenced development of opéra comique with *La Bergère châtelaine* (1820) and, in collaboration with Eugène Scribe, *Leicester* (1823), *Le Maçon* (1825), *Fra Diavolo* (1830), *Les Diamants de la couronne* (1841), *Manon Lescaut* (1856); considered creator of French grand opera with *Muette de Portici* (1828; also called *Masaniello);* other grand operas included *Le Philtre* (1831), *Gustave III* (1833).

Au·bert \ō-ber\, Jacques. 1689–1753. French violinist and composer. Author of opera *La Reine des Péris* (1725) and violin sonatas, ballets, etc.

Aubignac, Abbé d'. See François HÉDELIN.

Au·bi·gné \ō-bēn-yā\, Françoise d'. Madame de Main·te·non \ma^{n}t-nō^{n}\. 1635–1719. Wife of Louis XIV of France. Granddaughter of Theodore-Agrippa d'Aubigné. After impoverished childhood m. (1652) Paul Scarron, over whose literary salon she presided; on his death (1660) left penniless; entered convent; governess of children of her friend the marquise de Montespan by Louis XIV (1669–79); with king's help bought Château de Maintenon (1674); granted title to lands (1675); secretly married Louis (1683 or 1697); accused by enemies of wielding great influence over Louis; founded (1686) Maison Royale de Saint-Louis, known as Saint-Cyr, school for impoverished noblewomen.

Aubigné, Jean-Henri Merle d'. See MERLE D'AUBIGNÉ.

Aubigné, Théodore-Agrippa d'. 1552–1630. French Huguenot commander and author. Served under Condé and Henry of Navarre; in exile at Geneva (from 1620). Wrote poetical works, esp. *Tragiques* (1616), satirical *Aventures du baron de Faeneste* (1617), and *Confession catholique du sieur de sancy* (pub. 1660), and a *Histoire universelle* (1616–20).

Aubigny, Seigneurs of. See earls and dukes of Lennox, under STEWART family.

Au·brey \ˈō-brē\, John. 1626–1697. English antiquary. Author of *Miscellanies* (1696), consisting of ghost stories and folklore, and of *Lives of Eminent Men* (1813) based on notes he made for Anthony à Wood's *Athenae Oxonienses* and including vivid portrayals of Bacon, Milton, Raleigh, Hobbes, and others.

Au·bus·son \ō-bü̅e-sō^{n}\, Pierre d'. 1423–1503. French soldier. Grand master of Knights of St. John of Jerusalem (from 1476); defended Rhodes against Turks (1480); created cardinal (1489) for turning over to Pope Innocent VIII his prisoner Jem, brother of Sultan Bayezid II; expelled Jews from Rhodes.

Au·chin·leck \ˌȯk-ən-ˈlek, ˌȯk-\, Sir Claude John Eyre. 1884–1981. English soldier. Entered army (1903); served in India, Egypt, Mesopotamia, etc.; commanded unsuccessful raid on Narvik, Norway (1940); commander in chief in India (1941), Middle East (1941–42); revived 8th army offensive in North Africa, capturing Cyrenaica (1941) and halting German drive on Egypt (1942); removed by Churchill for opposing early counteroffensive; commander-in-chief in India (1943–46); field marshal (1946); supreme commander in India and Pakistan (1947).

Auch·mu·ty \ȯk-ˈmyüt-ē\, Sir Samuel. 1756–1822. British general, b. New York. Served in British army during American Revolution, in India (1783–97), at Cape, in Egypt, in campaign against Buenos Aires (1806–08), and in Java; major general (1808), lieutenant general (1815); commander in chief in Ireland (1821).

Auckland, Baron, and Earl of. See William and George EDEN.

Au·den \ˈȯd-ən\, Wystan Hugh. 1907–1973. American poet, b. York, England. To U.S. (1939); naturalized (1946); returned to England (1972). Author of *Poems* (1930), *The Orators* (1932). *The Dance of Death* (1933), *Look, Stranger!* (1936), *Spain* (1937), *Another Time* (1940), *The Double Man* (1941), *For the Time Being* (1944), *Collected Poetry* (1945), *Age of Anxiety* (1947), *Nones* (1951), *Shield of Achilles* (1955), *Homage to Clio* (1960), *About the House* (1965), *Collected Shorter Poems* (1966), *Collected Longer Poems* (1968), *City Without Walls* (1969). Criticism and other prose included *Journey to a War* (1939, with Christopher Isherwood), *The Enchafèd Flood* (1950), *The Dyer's Hand* (1962), *Secondary Worlds* (1968), *A Certain World* (1970). Editor of *Oxford Book of Light Verse* (1938). Collaborated with Isherwood in plays *The Dog Beneath the Skin* (1935), *The Ascent of F6* (1936), *On the Frontier* (1938); collaborated with Louis MacNeice in *Letters from Iceland* (1937); with Chester Kallman, wrote opera librettos, as for Stravinsky's *Rake's Progress* (1951).

Au·di·ber·ti \ō-dē-ber-tē\, Jacques. 1899–1965. French poet, playwright, novelist. Verse, showing influence of Mallarmé, included *Race des hommes* (1937), *Des tonnes de semence* (1941), *La Nouvelle origin* (1942), *Toujours* (1944), *Rempart* (1953); novels included *Abraxas* (1938), *Carnage* (1942), *Le Maître de Milan* (1950); plays, influenced by opera, included *Quoat-Quoat* (1946), *Le Mal court* (1947), *Pucelle* (1950), *Les Naturels du Bordelais* (1953), *La Hobereaute* (1957).

Au·dif·fret-Pas·quier \ō-dē-fre-pä-kyā\, Edme-Armand-Gaston d'. Duc. 1823–1905. French politician. Elected to National Assembly (1871); president of National Assembly (1875); appointed senator for life (1875); president of senate (1876–79).

Aud·ley *or* **Aude·ley** \ˈȯd-lē\, Sir James. 1316?–1386. English knight. One of original knights companions of Order of the Garter, instituted (c.1344) by Edward III. Fought under Black Prince in France, distinguishing himself esp. at Poitiers (1356); governor of Aquitaine (1367); grand seneschal of Poitou (1369).

Audley, Thomas. Baron Audley of Wal·den \ˈwȯl-dən\. 1488–1544. English lord chancellor. Presided as speaker of "black parliament" (1529); lord chancellor (1533–44) after supporting Henry VIII in divorcing Catherine of Aragon; presided at trial of Sir Thomas More (1535); tried Anne Boleyn (1536); carried through Parliament attainders of Thomas Cromwell (1540) and of Catherine Howard (1542) and dissolution of Henry's marriage with Anne of Cleves (1540). Created baron (1538); founded Magdalene College, Cambridge (1542).

Au·dran \ō-drä^{n}\. Family of French artists and engravers including the brothers Charles (1594–1674) and Claude I (1597–1677), engravers. Their nephew ¶Claude II (1639–1684), painter, decorated Salon de Diane and Salon de Mars, Versailles. His brother ¶Gérard II (1640–1703), engraver and best known of the family; engraver to the king (1670); notable works included *Les Batailles d'Alexandre, La Coupole du Val-de-Grâce*. A nephew ¶Claude III (1658–1734) was a painter, tapestry designer, and curator of the Luxembourg palace. His brother ¶Benoît I (1661–1721), engraver, noted esp. for his *Daphnis et Chloé* (1718). Benoît's son ¶Benoît II (1698–1772) achieved fame as engraver of Watteau.

Audran, Edmond. 1842–1901. French composer. Known esp. for operettas and vaudeville pieces including *Le Grand Mogol* (1877), *Les Noces d'Olivette* (1879), *La Mascotte* (1880), *La Cigale* (1886), *Miss Hélyett* (1890), *La Poupée* (1896).

Au·du·bon \ˈȯd-ə-bən, -ˌbän\, John James. 1785–1851. American ornithologist and artist, b. Haiti. Natural son of Jean Audubon, a French mercantile agent, and a Creole woman. To America (1803); settled near Philadelphia. To Kentucky (1808); opened general store in Louisville, transferring later to various other cities; began painting birds from life; bankrupt in business (1819); voyaged down Mississippi observing and painting birds; took his work to England, seeking a publisher (1826). *Birds of America* (1827–38), *Ornithological Biography* (1831–39), and (with MacGillivray) *Synopsis of the Birds of North America* (1839) established his reputation. Settled (1841–51) on his estate, now Audubon Park, New York City, working at but not completing *The Viviparous Quadrupeds of North America* (with Bachman, 1845–53).

Aue, Hartmann von. See HARTMANN VON AUE.

Au·en·brug·ger von Au·en·brugg \ˈau̇-ən-ˌbru̇g-ər-fȯn-ˈau̇-ən-ˌbru̇k\, Leopold. 1722–1809. Austrian physician. Discoverer of percussion method of detecting diseases of thorax and lungs, published in *Inventum novum* (1761).

Au·er \ˈau̇-ər\, Carl. Freiherr von Wels·bach \-fȯn-ˈvels-ˌbäk\. 1858–1929. Austrian chemist. Discovered (1885) elements neodymium and praseodymium; invented (1885) Welsbach gas mantle, greatly improving gas illumination; invented (1898) first metallic filament for incandescent lamps; also invented (1904) misch metal and Auer's metal.

Auer, Leopold. 1845–1930. Hungarian violinist and teacher. Professor (1868–1917), Conservatory of Music, St. Petersburg; director (1887–92), Russian Imperial Music Society symphony concerts. To N.Y. (1918); became famed as teacher; among pupils were Heifetz, Milstein, Mischa Elman, and Zimbalist.

Au·er·bach \ˈau̇-ər-ˌbäk\, Berthold. *Orig.* Moses Baruch Auer·bach·er \-ər\. *Pseudonym* Theobald Chau·ber \ˈshau̇-bər\. 1812–1882. German novelist and story writer. Known esp. for his pictures of life in Black Forest. His fiction included *Spinoza* (1837), *Schwarzwälder Dorfgeschichten* (1843–54), *Barfüssele* (1856), *Edelweiss* (1861), *Auf der Höhe* (1865).

Auerbach, Erich. 1892–1957. German scholar. Librarian of Prussian State Library (1923–29); professor at Marburg (1929–36), Istanbul (1936–47), Pennsylvania State U. (1948–49), Institute for Advanced Study, Princeton (1949–50), Yale (1950–57). Author of *Dante als Dichter der irdischen Welt* (1929), *Mimesis* (1946), etc.

Au·ers·perg \ˈau̇-ər-sperk\, Anton Alexander von. Graf. *Pseudonym* Anastasius Grün \ˈgrü̅en\. 1806–1876. Austrian poet and politician. Represented Carniola at Diet in Laibach (from 1831); member of German National Assembly (1848); outspoken leader of liberal sentiment; named life member of Austrian Herrenhaus (1861). Verse included *Blätter der Liebe* (1830), *Der letzte Ritter* (1830), *Spaziergänge eines Wiener Poeten* (1831), *Schutt* (1836), and ironic epics *Die Nibelungen im Frack* (1843) and *Der Pfaff vom Kahlenberg* (1850); also published translations of popular Slovene songs of Carniola in *Volkslieder aus Krain* (1850).

Auersperg, Carlos. Fürst. 1814–1890. Austrian statesman. Member, Bohemian diet; president, Austrian upper chamber (Herrenhaus, 1861); defended constitutional system against clerical and feudal reaction, and championed unity of the empire; president, Austrian ministry (1867–68). His brother ¶Prince Adolf Karl Daniel (1821–1885), Herzog von Gottschee; cavalry officer; elected to Bohemian Landtag (1860); supreme provincial marshal of Bohemia (1867); provincial president of Salzburg (1870); prime minister of western half of empire (1871–79); promoted reforms and anticlerical legislation; last major liberal leader in empire.

Auersperg, Johann Weikhart. Fürst. 1615–1677. Austrian diplomat and politician. Helped negotiate Peace of Westphalia (1648); adviser to Emperor Leopold I; chief privy councillor (1665–69); concluded (1668) secret treaty with France for partition of Spanish territories. Banished by Leopold to Carniola (1669).

Auerstädt, Duc d'. See Louis-Nicolas DAVOUT.

Auer von Welsbach, Carl. See AUER.

Auf·fen·berg \ˈau̇f-ən-ˌberk\, Joseph von. Freiherr. 1798–1857. German dramatist. Author of *Die Flibustier* (1819), *Pizarro* (1823), *Die Löwe von Kurdistan* (1827), trilogy *Alhambra* (1829–30), and novel *Die Furie von Toledo* (1832).

Auf·fen·berg von Ko·ma·rów \ˈau̇f-ən-ˌberk-fȯn-kō-ˈmär-üf\, Moritz. Freiherr. 1852–1928. Austro-Hungarian general. Commanding general, Sarajevo (1909); minister of war (1911–12); commanded 4th Austrian army at beginning of World War I; victorious at Komarów (1914); imprisoned (1915) on charges of irregularities as war minister; acquitted.

Au·ge·reau \ōzh-rō\, Pierre-François-Charles. Duc de Ca·sti·glio·ne \ˌkäs-tēl-ˈyō-nā\. 1757–1816. French soldier. Distinguished himself at Lodi and Castiglione (1796); carried through coup d'état of 18 Fructidor (Sept. 4, 1797); made commander of VII Corps by Directory; secretary of assembly (1798); at first opposed Napoléon's coup (1799); commander of French and Dutch armies (1800–01); suffered defeats in Austria, Germany, Spain; named duke, marshal of France (1808); after defeat at Lyons (1814) declared for monarchy; retired on Restoration.

Au·gier \ōzh-yā\, Émile, *in full* Guillaume-Victor-Émile. 1820–1889. French poet and dramatist. Grandson of C. A. G. Pigault-Lebrun. His plays, chiefly comedies of manners and social satires, included *Gabrielle* (1849), *Le Gendre de Monsieur Poirier* (with Jules Sandeau, 1854), *Le Mariage d'Olympe* (1855), *Les Lionnes pauvres* (1858), *Les Effrontés* (1861), *Maître Guérin* (1864), *Lions et Renards* (1869), *Madame Caverlet* (1876), *Les Fourchambault* (1878).

Au·gu·sta \aù-'gùs-tä\. *In full* Maria Luise Katharina Augusta. 1811–1890. Queen consort of Prussia (1861–88). Daughter of Grand Duke Charles Frederick of Saxe-Weimar-Eisenach; m. (1829) Crown Prince William. Influence in favor of liberalism, Catholicism, friendship with England.

Au·gus·ta Vic·to·ria \ò-'gəs-tə-vik-'tōr-ē-ə, ə-'gəs-, -vik-'tòr-\. *Ger.* Au·gu·ste Vik·to·ria \au-'gus-tə-vik-'tō-rē-,ä\. 1858–1921. Queen consort of Germany (1888–1918). Daughter of Duke Frederick VIII of Schleswig-Holstein; m. (1881) Crown Prince William, later William II.

Augustenberg, Prince of. See FREDERICK CHRISTIAN AUGUSTUS.

Au·gus·tine \'ò-gəs-,tēn; ò-'gəs-tən, ə-\. Saint. *Known as* Saint Augustine of Hippo. *Lat.* Aurelius Au·gus·ti·nus \ò-gə-'stī-nəs\. 354–430. Early Christian church father and philosopher, b. Tagaste (Souk-Ahras) in eastern Numidia. Originally a Manichaean; to Rome as teacher of rhetoric (c.383); professor at Milan; came under influence of Bishop Ambrose of Milan; after passing through spiritual crisis, converted to Christianity and baptized (Easter 387). Returned to Tagaste and ordained priest (391); bishop of Hippo (396–430). By sermons, pastoral letters, and books, came to exercise enormous influence throughout Christian world; stood forth esp. as champion of orthodoxy against Manichaeans, Donatists, and Pelagians. Works included *De vera religione* (c.390), *De doctrina Christiana* (397–428), *De Trinitate* (400–416), *Confessiones* (c.400), *De civitate Dei* (413–426), many scriptural commentaries, esp. on Psalms, etc.

Augustine. Saint. *Also* Aus·tin \' òs-tən\. d. 604. First archbishop of Canterbury. Benedictine prior in Rome; sent (596), with forty monks, as missionary to the English by Pope Gregory I; baptized Aethelberht I, King of Kent (597); consecrated bishop of the English (597) at Arles; archbishop (601); founded Christ Church and monastery of SS. Peter and Paul, Canterbury; established sees of London and Rochester (604).

Augustinus, Antonius. See Antonio AGUSTÍN.

Augustulus, Romulus. See ROMULUS AUGUSTULUS.

Au·gus·tus \ò-'gəs-təs, ə-\. *Original name* Gaius Oc·ta·vi·us \äk-'tā-vē-əs\. *After his adoption* Gaius Julius Caesar. *Sometimes known in early life as* Oc·ta·vi·a·nus \äk-,tā-vē-'ā-nəs\, *Eng.* Oc·ta·vi·an \äk-'tā-vē-ən\. 63 B.C.–14 A.D. First Roman emperor (27 B.C.–14 A.D.). Son of Octavius and Atia (daughter of Julia, youngest sister of Julius Caesar). Talents brought him into favor of his great-uncle Julius Caesar, who adopted him as son and heir (45 B.C.). After death of Caesar (44), gained control in Italy, aided by Cicero; joined Mark Antony and Lepidus in establishing Second Triumvirate (43 B.C.); with Antony, defeated Brutus and Cassius at Philippi (42); after Philippi, received Italy as his portion. His sister Octavia married Antony (40). Fought Sicilian War against Sextus Pompeius (38–36) and won decisively with aid of admiral Marcus Agrippa; disarmed and deposed Lepidus (36); fought successful wars in Illyricum and Dalmatia (35–33). Rivalry with Antony finally settled by defeat of Antony and Cleopatra at battle of Actium (31). Became sole ruler of Roman world, cloaking autocracy in trappings of ancient republic; received title of "Augustus" (exalted, sacred), conferred by senate (27 B.C.), and, later, other titles; retained consular office, but sometimes granted it to others for certain periods; also granted power of tribune; inaugurated reforms and beneficial laws. Created imperial system of administration, established new coinages, encouraged trade. Became pontifex maximus on death of Lepidus (12 B.C.). Made his stepson Tiberius his heir and successor (4 A.D.); added to empire by victories in Spain, Pannonia, Dalmatia, and Gaul, but his legions suffered terrible defeat (9 A.D.; see ARMINIUS) when army of Publius Quintilius Varus (*q.v.*) was totally destroyed by Germans; died on journey to Campania. A ruler of great administrative ability and initiative; promoted agriculture and the arts, his reign (Augustan age) marking golden age of Latin literature. Married (1) Claudia, who had no children; (2) Scribonia, whose daughter Julia married three times and had five children by her second husband (see AGRIPPINA); (3) Livia Drusilla (divorced wife of Tiberius Claudius Nero), who had two sons (stepsons of Augustus), Tiberius, later emperor, and Drusus (d. 9 B.C. at age of 30). Met with domestic sorrows throughout his life, esp. because of conduct of his daughter Julia, who was banished for her excesses, and because he had no son, and his nephew, grandsons, and favorite stepson, Drusus, all died young.

Augustus. *Ger.* Au·gust \'aù-gùst\. 1526–1586. Elector of Saxony (1553–86). Son of Henry the Pious; brother of Maurice, whom he succeeded. Embraced Lutheranism (1574) through influence of his wife (m. 1584) Anna, daughter of Christian III of Denmark; instrumental in securing adoption (1580) of *Formula concordiae,* a creed of Lutheran orthodoxy; as ruler, introduced many reforms and improvements.

Augustus. Name of three kings of Poland:

Augustus I. See SIGISMUND II AUGUSTUS.

Augustus II. *Called* the Strong. 1670–1733. King (1697–1704, 1709–33). Son of Elector John George III of Saxony; succeeded brother John George IV as elector of Saxony (1694–1733) under name of Frederick Augustus I. As king, concluded Turkish War by Treaty of Carlowitz (1699), gaining Podolia and western Ukraine; attempted to wrest Livonia from Sweden, precipitating Great Northern War (1700–21); defeated by Charles XII of Sweden at Kliszów (1702) and at Charles' behest deposed by Polish Diet (1704); forced to recognize Stanisław Leszczyński (1706); with support of Peter I of Russia, restored to throne after Russian defeat of Sweden at Poltava (1709). Subsequently saw Poland decline to Russian protectorate.

Augustus III. 1696–1763. King (1734–63). Son of Augustus II; elector of Saxony (1733–63) under name of Frederick Augustus II. Elected king by small minority (1733); crowned (1734); established rule in War of Polish Succession (1733–35) against Stanisław Leszczyński. Supported Prussia in first Silesian War (1740–42) but sided with Austria in War of Austrian Succession (1742); defeated and forced to pay indemnity; electorate occupied by Prussians during Seven Years' War (1756–63).

Augustus William. *Ger.* August Wilhelm. 1722–1758. Prince of Prussia, of Hohenzollern line. Brother of Frederick the Great. Not successful as military leader; deprived of command (1757) by Frederick. Father of Frederick William II, who succeeded Frederick the Great as king of Prussia.

Auk·rust \'aùk-rüst\, Olav. 1883–1929. Norwegian poet. Wrote verses as *Himmelvarden* (1916), *Hamar i Hellom* (1926) in dialect of Gudbrandsdalen; contributed to development of Nynorsk as literary language.

Au·lard \ō-lår\, Francois-Alphonse. 1849–1928. French historian. Professor, Sorbonne (1887–1922). Known esp. as historian of the French Revolution. Author of *Histoire politique de la Révolution française* (1910) and editor of *Receuil des actes du comité de salut public* (1889–1904), *La Societé des Jacobins* (1889–97), *Paris pendant la réaction thermidorienne et sous le directoire* (1898–1902); founded journal *La Révolution française.*

Auletes. See PTOLEMY XII.

Aulis Caecina Alienus. See CAECINA.

Aulnoy, Comtesse d'. See LE JUMEL DE BARNEVILLE.

Au·male \ō-mål\. Name of French family of nobility derived from a town in Normandy near Dieppe, which became a county (11th century), later a duchy (1547). Dukedom of Aumale was first granted by King Henry II to Claude I and François de Lorraine, ducs de Guise (see LORRAINE). Duchy passed (1618) to ducal house of Nemours (Savoy), thence to Louis XIV by purchase (1675), and finally to House of Orléans. See also Henri-Eugene under LOUIS-PHILIPPE.

Aun·ger·ville *or* **Aun·ger·vyle** \'aùn-jər-,vil, -vəl\, Richard. *Known as* Richard de Bury \'ber-ē\. 1281–1345. English bibliophile. Benedictine monk; tutor to Edward of Windsor (later Edward III); dean of Wells and bishop of Durham (1333); high chancellor of England (1334–35), treasurer (1336); ambassador at Paris, Hainaut, Germany; commissioner to negotiate truce with Scotland (1342). A passionate collector of books and manuscripts; author of *Philobyblon* (pub. 1473), handbook on care of books and a valuable historical resource.

Aung San \aùŋ-sän\. 1914?–1947. Burmese nationalist hero. Student nationalist leader with U Nu; secretary general of revolutionary Dobama Asi-ayone group (1939); fled to Japan; returned with Japanese invasion (1941); led "Burma Independence Army" against British; minister of defense in Japanese puppet regime (1943–45); threw support to Allies (1945); as leader of Anti-Fascist People's Freedom League became de facto prime minister (1946–47); negotiated agreement for Burmese independence with Clement Atlee (1947); assassinated on order of rival U Saw.

Aungzeya. See ALAUNGPAYA.

Aunoy. See AULNOY.

Aurangzeb. See 'ĀLAMGĪR.

Au·re·lian \ò-'rēl-yən\. *Full Latin name* Lucius Domitius Au·re·li·a·nus \ò-,rē-lē-'ā-nəs\. *Called* Res·ti·tu·tor Or·bis \,res-tə-'t(y)üt-ər-'ór-bəs\, *i.e.* Restorer of the World. c.215–275. Roman emperor (270–275). From common soldier rose to high military positions under emperors Valerian, Gallienus, and Claudius; helped overthrow Gallienus and establish Claudius; elected emperor by army on death of Quintillus (270). Drove back Vandals, Sarmatians, Juthungi in north; drove Goths across Danube, but gave up Dacia; in war with Palmyra (271–273), defeated its queen, Zenobia, destroyed city, and carried Zenobia as prisoner to Rome; reconquered Egypt (273); recovered Gaul and Britain from Tetricus (274); began fortification walls of Rome. Killed by conspirators among his officers.

Aurelianus, Caelius. See CAELIUS AURELIANUS.

Aurelius. See (1) Commodus; (2) Constantine I (Roman emperor); (3) Numerian; (4) Probus.

Aurelius, Marcus. *In full* Marcus Aurelius Antoninus. See (1) Marcus Aurelius; (2) Marcus Aurelius Antoninus.

Aurevilly, Jules Barbey d'. See Barbey d'Aurevilly.

Aurifaber. See Goldschmied.

Au·riol \ȯr-yȯl\, Vincent. 1884–1966. French politician. Elected to Chamber of Deputies (1914); Socialist leader; minister of finance (1936–37), of justice (1937–38). Interned (1940–43). Member, Constituent Assembly (1945); minister of state; first president of Fourth Republic (1947–54).

Au·ri·spa \aù-'rē-spä\, Giovanni. 1369?–1459. Sicilian scholar and Humanist. Traveled in Near East (1414 ff.); returned with 238 manuscripts of classical Greek authors, as Homer, Aristophanes, Arrian, Pindar, Xenophon, Plato, Sophocles, Strabo, Aeschylus; published many translations.

Au·ro·bin·do \'ȯr-ō-'bin-(,)dō\, Sri. *Orig.* Sri Aurobindo Gho·se \'gō-sə\. 1872–1950. Indian poet and philosopher. In youth imprisoned for nationalist agitation; fled to French Pondicherry, founded ashram to promote spiritual development in his scheme of cosmic salvation. Author of *The Life Divine* (1940), *Synthesis of Yoga* (1948), *The Human Cycle* (1949), *Savitri* (1950), *On the Veda* (1956), etc.

Au·ser·re Ap·o·pi I \ō-'ser-ə-'äp-ə-,pē\. 17th–16th century B.C. Hyksos king of Egypt (c.1607–c.1566 B.C.). Quarreled with his vassal Seqenenre, the Theban king, whose successor Kamose declared open war on Hyksos kingdom; plan to have Nubian allies attack Theban rear foiled; domain reduced to region of capital Avaris in Delta; died before final expulsion of Hyksos by Ahmose I.

Aus·lan·der \'ō-,slan-dər\, Joseph. 1897–1965. American poet, b. Philadelphia. Instructor, Harvard (1919–23); lecturer in poetry, Columbia U. (from 1929). Author of *Sunrise Trumpets* (1924), *Cyclops' Eye* (1926), *Hell in Harness* (1930), *No Traveler Returns* (1933), *More Than Bread* (1936), *The Unconquerables* (1943); coeditor, *The Winged Horse* (poetry anthology, 1927).

Au·so·ni·us \ȯ-'sō-nē-əs\, Decimus Maximus. c.310–c.395 A.D. Latin poet and rhetorician of Gaul. Teacher in Bordeaux; tutor to Gratian, who named him prefect of Africa, Italy, and Gaul and (379) consul. Author of verse works such as *Technopaegnion, Praefatiunculae, Eclogae, Ordo nobilium urbium, Ludus septem sapientum, Parentalia, Professores Burdigalenses.*

Austen. See Godwin-Austen; Roberts-Austen.

Aus·ten \'ȯs-tən, 'äs-\, Jane. 1775–1817. English novelist. Considered the creator of English novel of manners and one of greatest novelists in English; works notable for psychological insight. During the period 1795 to 1798 wrote *Pride and Prejudice* (pub. 1813), *Sense and Sensibility* (1811), and *Northanger Abbey* (posthumously, 1817); desisted from writing because of discouragement over inability to find a publisher; during period 1811 to 1816 wrote *Mansfield Park* (1814), *Emma* (1815), and *Persuasion* (posthumously, 1817).

Austin, Saint. See Augustine (d. 604).

Aus·tin \'ȯs-tən, 'äs-\, Alfred. 1835–1913. English poet laureate. Joint editor (with W. J. Courthope), later editor, of *National Review* (1883–95); poet laureate (1896). Author of 20 volumes of verse including *The Season* (1861), *The Human Tragedy* (1862), *Savonarola* (1881), *Conversion of Winckelmann* (1897), *Sacred and Profane Love* (1908).

Austin, Frederic. 1872–1952. English singer and composer. Principal baritone, Beecham Opera Co.; artistic director of National Opera Co. (from 1924). Arranged music for first modern productions of *Beggar's Opera* (1920) and *Polly* (1922); composed choral and orchestral works, chamber music, etc.

Austin, Herbert. 1st Baron Austin. 1866–1941. English motorcar manufacturer. In engineering work in Australia (1884–93); with Wolseley Sheep Shearing Machine Co. (1890 ff.), chairman (1911); built Wolseley three-wheel car (1895); started manufacture of Austin motorcars (1905); introduced popular Austin Seven (1922). M.P. (1918–24); created baron (1936).

Austin, John. 1790–1859. English jurist. Professor of jurisprudence, University College, London (1828–32); author of *Province of Jurisprudence Determined* (1832), *Lectures on Jurisprudence* (1861–63). m. (1820) ¶Sarah, *nee* Taylor (1793–1867), who translated and edited German and French historical texts, including Ranke's *History of the Popes* (1840) and *History of the Reformation in Germany* (1845), and Guizot's *English Revolution* (1850). See also Lucie Duff-Gordon.

Austin, Mary, *nee* Hunter. 1868–1934. American writer, b. Carlinville, Ill. m. Stafford W. Austin (1891). Author of novels and story collections *The Land of Little Rain* (1903), *The Basket Woman* (1904), *Isidro* (1905), *The Flock* (1906), *A Woman of Genius* (1912), *The Ford* (1917), *The Land of Journeys' Ending* (1924), *Starry Adventure* (1931), the plays *The Arrow Maker* (1911), *The Man Who Didn't Believe in Christmas* (1916), an autobiography, *Earth Horizon* (1932), etc.

Austin, Stephen Fuller. 1793–1836. American colonizer in Texas, b. Austinville, Va. Carried out (1822) colonization plans of his father, Moses (1761–1821); directed (1822–32) government in the colony, encouraging immigration from U.S., maintaining peace and order. Imprisoned in Mexico City (1833–34) for urging Texas statehood and separation from Coahuila. Secretary of state, Republic of Texas (1836).

Aut·char·i·us \ōt-'kar-ē-əs\. 8th century A.D. Frankish noble. An envoy from Pepin III the Short to escort Pope Stephen II to France (753–754); supporter of Carloman after Pepin's death; escorted Pepin's widow Gerberga to refuge with Lombard court; reconciled with Charlemagne (773). Supposed prototype of legendary Ogier the Dane.

Au·tol·y·cus \ȯ-'täl-ə-kəs\. fl. c.310 B.C. Greek astronomer and mathematician. Author of earliest entirely preserved Greek mathematical work on motion of points on a revolving sphere; also wrote treatise on apparent rising and setting of fixed stars.

Au·tran \ō-trä^{n}\, Joseph. 1813–1877. French poet and dramatist. Author of *La Fille d'Eschyle* (1848), *Le Cyclope* (1863), etc.

Auvergne. See La Tour d'Auvergne.

Au·wers \'aù-vərs\, Arthur Julius Georg Friedrich von. 1838–1915. German astronomer. Astronomer, Imperial Academy of Sciences, Berlin (from 1866); made observations on transits of Venus (1874, 1882), proper motion of fixed stars, positions of stars, etc.

Aux·en·ti·us \ȯk-'sen-shē-əs\. d. 374? Cappadocian prelate. Leading Arian theologian; installed by Constantine as bishop of Milan (c.370); prominent in opposing Nicene Creed.

Ava·ku·mo·vić \ä-vä-'kü-mȯ-,vēt^{y}\, Jovan. 1841–1928. Serbian statesman. Minister of justice (1887); premier (1892–93). President of provisional government (1903).

Ávа·los \'äb-äl-ōs\, Fernando Francesco de. Marqués de Pe·sca·ra \pā-'skä-rä\. 1490–1525. Spanish soldier. m. (1509) Vittoria Colonna; commander (1512–25) of Spanish forces in Italy in service of Charles V; engaged at Ravenna (1512), Padua (1514), Milan (1521), Genoa and La Biocca (1522), Pavia (1525); approached by Girolamo Morone, chancellor of Duke Francesco Sforza of Milan, in conspiracy against Charles V; joined conspirators and, later, disclosed plans to Charles.

Avebury, Baron. See Sir John Lubbock.

Avel·lan·e·da \äb-ā(l)-yä-'nā-thä\, Alonso Fernández de. 17th century. Spanish writer. Pseudonymous and unknown author of spurious second part of *Don Quixote* (1614). Cervantes' genuine second part was published in 1615.

Avel·la·ne·da \äb-ā-zhä-'nā-thä\, Nicolás. 1836–1885. Argentine politician. In government of Sarmiento; president of Argentina (1874–80).

Avellaneda, Gertrudis Gómez de. See Gómez de Avellaneda.

Avempace. See Abū Bakr Muḥammad ibn Yaḥyā.

Ave·na·ri·us \,äv-ä-'när-ē-ùs\, Richard Heinrich Ludwig. 1843–1896. German philosopher. Professor, Zürich (1877–96); set forth principle of empiriocriticism, a doctrine of undivided pure experience in relation to environment and knowledge. Author of *Kritik der reinen Erfahrung* (1888–90), *Der menschliche Weltbegriff* (1891), etc. His brother ¶Ferdinand (1856–1923), poet and writer on art, founded art journal *Kunstwarts* (1887); wrote *Wandern und Werden* (1881), *Lebe!* (1883), *Stimmen und Bilder* (1897), etc.; compiled anthologies of poems.

Ave·nel \äv-nel\, Georges d'. Vicomte. 1855–1939. French economist and historian. Works included *Richelieu et la monarchie absolue* (1884–90), *Histoire économique de la propriété, 1200–1800* (1894–1909), *L'Évolution des moyens de transport* (1920), etc.

Avennasar. See Fārābī.

Ave·nol \äv-nȯl\, Joseph Louis Anne. 1879–1952. French diplomat. Financial delegate of France in London (1916–23); deputy secretary-general (1923–32) and secretary-general (1933–40), League of Nations.

Aventinus. See Johannes Turmair.

Avenzoar. See Ibn Zuhr.

Ave·re·scu \,äv-e-'res-kü\, Alexandru. 1859–1938. Romanian general and politician. Served in war for Romanian independence (1877–78); as minister of war (1907) responsible for harsh suppression of peasant revolt; undertook reorganization of Romanian army. Chief of general staff (1912); commanded attack on Bulgaria (1913); in World War I repelled Germans at Mărăşeşti (1917). As prime minister (1918), conducted peace negotiations with Central Powers; again prime minister of Romania (1920–21, 1926–27).

Aver·li·no \,äv-er-'lē-nō\ *or* **Ave·ru·li·no** \,äv-ā-rü-'lē-nō\, Antonio di Pietro. *Known as* Fi·la·re·te \,fē-lä-'re-tā\. c.1400–c.1469. Florentine architect and sculptor. Important esp. as disseminator of Renaissance style. Executed bronze doors (1433–45) of St. Peter's, Rome, for Pope Eugenius IV; in service of duke of Milan (from 1451); designed Ospedale Maggiore (1457–65). Author of influential *Trattato d'architettura* (1460–64), containing plans for model city Sforzinda.

Averroës. See Ibn Rushd.

Avery \'āv-(ə-)rē\, Milton. 1885–1965. American painter, b. Sand Bank, N.Y. Known esp. for landscapes and figure studies featuring flat color masses reminiscent of Matisse. Works included *Mother and Child* (1944), *Sea and*

Sand Dunes (1955), *Moon Path* (1958), *White Gull* (1958), *Sailfish in Fog* (1959), *Beach Blankets* (1960), *Bathers by the Sea* (1960).

Avery, Oswald Theodore. 1877–1955. American bacteriologist, b. Halifax, N.S. On staff of Rockefeller Institute Hospital (1913–48); known esp. for studies in immunology; laid foundation for immunochemistry by showing relation of immunological specificity to chemical products of bacteria; discovered role of DNA in transfer of heritable characteristics in bacteria (1944).

Avery, Samuel Putnam. 1822–1904. American artist and patron, b. New York City. Copper and wood engraver; established gallery (1865); U.S. commissioner at Paris International Exposition (1867); established Avery architectural library and Teachers' College library, Columbia U.; a founder of Metropolitan Museum of Art; gave collection of prints to N.Y. Public Library.

Avi·a·nus \ˌā-vē-ˈā-nəs\ *or* **Avi·a·nius** \-ˈā-nē-əs, -ˌān-yəs\, Flavius. fl. 4th century A.D. (or later). Latin writer. Author of fables, many similar to those of Babrius, much read in Middle Ages.

Avicebron. See IBN GABIROL.

Avicenna. See IBN SĪNĀ.

Avid·i·us Cas·sius \ə-ˈvid-ē-ə-ˈskash-əs\, Gaius. d. 175 A.D. Roman soldier. Commanded Roman forces against Parthia (161–165), sacking Ctesiphon and Seleucia (164–165); made commander of all Roman forces in East; suppressed revolt in Egypt (172); proclaimed himself emperor (175), apparently on basis of false rumor of death of Marcus Aurelius; assassinated by one of own soldiers.

Avi·e·nus \ˌā-vē-ˈē-nəs\, Rufus Festus. 4th century A.D. Roman poet. Translated Aratus's *Phainomena* and paraphrased Dionysius's *Periegesis* under title *Descriptio Orbis Terrae;* wrote also descriptions of coasts of Mediterranean, Black, and Caspian seas.

Ávila, John of. See JOHN of Avila.

Ávila, Pedro Arias de *or* Pedrarius de. See ARIAS DÁVILA.

Ávi·la Ca·ma·cho \ˈäb̲-ē-lä-kä-ˈmäch-ō\, Manuel. 1897–1955. Mexican soldier and politician. Entered army of Carranza (1914); minister of war and navy (1932–34), of national defense (1937–39); president of Mexico (1940–46). His term a period of stability and moderately progressive legislation.

Ávila y Zú·ñi·ga \-ē-ˈthün-yē-gä\, Luis de. 1500–1573. Spanish historian. Author of *Comentario de la guerra de Alemania hecha por Carlos V en 1546 y 1547* (1548).

Avilés, Pedro Menendez de. See MENENDEZ DE AVILÉS.

Avi·son \ˈā-və-sən\, Charles. 1709–1770. English organist and composer. Author of *Essay on Musical Expression* (1752); composed sonatas, string quartets, etc., in late Baroque style.

Avi·tus \ə-ˈvīt-əs\. *In full* Marcus Maecilius Avitus. *Also called* Eparchius Avitus. d. 456 A.D. Roman emperor of the West (455–456). Persuaded Theodoric I of Visigoths to join Aetius in repelling Attila (451); appointed master of armies of Gaul by Emperor Petronius Maximus (455); chosen emperor with help of Visigoths; deposed by Ricimer; became bishop of Placentia.

Aviz *or* **Avis** \ˈá-vēsh\. Name of Portuguese dynasty (1385–1580) derived from order of knighthood founded by King Afonso I and named from town in eastern Portugal. House founded by John the Great (John I), Grand Master of Order of Aviz, natural son of Peter I of house of Burgundy; succeeding rulers were: Edward, Afonso V, John II, Emanuel, John III, Sebastian, and Henry (d. 1580).

Avo·ga·dro \ˌäv-ō-ˈgä-drō\, Amedeo. Conte di Qua·re·gna e Ce·ret·to \-dē-kwä-ˈrān-yä-ā-chā-ˈret-tō\. 1776–1856. Italian chemist and physicist. Professor, Coll. of Vercelli (1809–20), Turin (1820–22, 1834–50); author of Avogadro's hypothesis (1811) that equal volumes of all gases at same temperature and pressure contain equal numbers of molecules; deduced molecular nature of oxygen, hydrogen, nitrogen, etc.

Avon, Earl of. See Anthony EDEN.

Av·va·kum Pe·tro·vich \(ˌ)əv-ˈvá-kim-pyi-ˈtrȯv-ˌyich\. 1620 or 1621–1682. Russian clergyman. A leader of resistance to Patriarch Nikon's reforms of Russian Orthodox liturgy (1652–53); leader of Old Believer sect; exiled to East (1653–63); again exiled and, after Synod of Moscow (1666–67) imprisoned; burned at stake. Author of several works, esp. *Zhitie,* first Russian autobiography and one of major works of early Russian literature.

Awde·lay *or* **Awde·ley** \ˈȯd-(ˌ)lā\, John. fl. 1559–1577. English printer. Reputed author of *Fraternitye of Vacabondes* (1565).

Aw·ḥad ad-Dīn ʻAli \au̇-ˈhäd-ad-ˈdēn-a-ˈlē\ ibn Vāḥid ad-Dīn Muḥammad Khāvarānī. *Also known as* Awḥad ad-Dīn Muḥammad ibn Muḥammad *or* Awḥad ad-Dīn ʻAlī ibn Maḥmūd. *Pseudonym* An·va·rī \ən-və-ˈrē\. c.1126–c.1189. Persian poet. Court poet to Sultan Sanjar; excelled in composition of odes and lyrics; considered one of greatest Persian panegyrists.

Aw·il-Mar·duk \ˈäv-ēl-ˈmär-ˌdük\. *Known in Bible as* Evil-Mer·o·dach \ˈē-vəl-ˈmer-ə-ˌdak, -mə-ˈrō-dak\. d. 560 B.C. King of Babylonia (561–560 B.C.). Son and successor of Nebuchadrezzar.

à Wood, Anthony. See Anthony WOOD.

Axa·ya·catl \ˌäsh-ä-ˈyäk-ät-ᵊl\ *or* **Axa·ya·ca·tzin** \ˌäsh-ä-yäˈkät-sin\. 15th century. Aztec emperor (1469–81). Nephew of Montezuma I and father of Montezuma II.

Axel. See ABSALON.

Ay \ˈī\. 14th century B.C. King of Egypt (c.1352–48 B.C.) of the 18th dynasty. Courtier and military leader under Akhenaton; principal adviser to Tutankhamen; made chancellor and vizier; succeeded Tutankhamen, marrying his widow; chose Horemheb as his successor.

Aya·la \ä-ˈyä-lä\, Eusebio. 1875–1942. Paraguayan politician. Held various official positions (1910–21); provisional president of Paraguay (1921–23); forced to resign; minister to U.S. (1925); again president (1932–36); deposed by Col. Rafael Franco.

Ayala, Juan Manuel de. 18th century. Spanish explorer. Commander of ship that made first exploration of Bay of San Francisco (1775).

Ayala, López de. See LÓPEZ DE AYALA.

Ayala, Ramón Pérez de. See PÉREZ DE AYALA.

Ay·bak \ˈī-ˌbäk\, ʻIzz ad-Dīn Abū al-Manṣūr. d. 1257. Sultan of Egypt (1250–57). Mamlūk military commander in Egypt; became regent on assassination of Sultan Tūrān-Shāh; shared reign with Musa, but retained power; first Mamlūk sultan in Egypt.

Ay·de·lotte \ˈā-də-ˌlät\, Frank. 1880–1956. American educator, b. Sullivan, Ind. Professor of English, M.I.T. (1915–21). President, Swarthmore Coll. (1921–40); president, Institute of Advanced Study, Princeton (1939–47). American secretary, Rhodes trustees (1917–53). Author of *Elizabethan Rogues and Vagabonds* (1913), *The Oxford Stamp* (1917), etc.

Ayer \ˈa(ə)r, ˈe(ə)r\, Francis Wayland. 1848–1923. American advertiser, b. Lee, Mass. Established (1869) N.W. Ayer & Son, Philadelphia; built it into first modern advertising agency.

Aylesford, Earl of. See FINCH family.

Ayl·lón \īl-ˈyȯn\, Lucas Váz·quez \ˈväth-kāth\ (*or* Vás·quez \ˈväs-kāth\) de. c.1475–1526. Spanish explorer. In Santo Domingo (1502–20); attempted settlement on American mainland, probably at Winyah Bay on South Carolina coast (1526); died there.

Ayl·mer \ˈāl-mər\, John. 1521–1594. English prelate. Tutor to Lady Jane Grey; archdeacon of Stow (1553); because of opposition to doctrine of transubstantiation had to flee to Continent until accession of Elizabeth (1558); bishop of London (1577); notorious for rigorous and harsh enforcement of Act of Uniformity against Puritans and Roman Catholics; assailed in Martin Marprelate tracts. Author of *An Harborowe for Faithfull and Trewe Subjectes* (1559) in reply to John Knox.

Ay·mé \em-ā\, Marcel. 1902–1967. French writer. Author of novels as *Brûlebois* (1926), *La Table-aux-crevés* (1929), *La Jument verte* (1933), *La Vouivre* (1943), *Le Chemin des écoliers* (1946); short stories notable for light irony and fantasy and including three series of *Contes du chat perché* (1939, 1950, 1958); plays including *Lucienne et le boucher* (1947), *Clérambard* (1950), *La Tête des autres* (1952).

Aymer de Valence. See VALENCE.

Ay·rer \ˈī-rər\, Jakob. 1543–1605. German dramatist. Author of over 100 pieces, including comedies, tragedies, *Fastnachtsspiele, Singspiele,* etc.

Ayres \ˈa(ə)rz, ˈe(ə)rz\, Anne. 1816–1896. American religious, b. London, England. To U.S. (1836); consecrated (1845) Sister Anne; followers organized (1852) as Sisterhood of the Holy Communion; first woman in America to become a Protestant sister.

Ayr·ton \ˈa(ə)rt-ᵊn, ˈe(ə)rt-\, William Edward. 1847–1908. English electrical engineer and inventor. In Indian telegraph service (1868); taught physics in Tokyo and London; professor of electrical engineering, South Kensington (1884–1908); invented numerous electrical measuring instruments and other devices. His second wife ¶Hertha, *nee* Marks \ˈmärks\ (1854–1923; m. 1885), awarded medal for researches on electric arc and on sand ripples (1906); collaborated with husband on admiralty reports on electric searchlights; invented an antigas fan (1915).

Ays·cue \ˈas-ˌkyü, ˈā-ˌskyü\, Sir George. d. 1671. British admiral. Sent by Parliament to reduce Barbados and visit Virginia (1651–52); lost his command after indecisive battle with Dutch off Plymouth (1652); naval adviser to Sweden till Restoration; served in second Dutch war (1664–66), becoming admiral of the white; prisoner in Holland (1666–67).

Ay·ton *or* **Ay·toun** \ˈāt-ᵊn\, Sir Robert. 1570–1638. Scottish poet. Author of lyrics and many Latin and English panegyrics; one of first Scottish poets to write in standard English.

Ay·toun \ˈāt-ᵊn\, William Edmondstoune. 1813–1865. Scottish poet and parodist. On staff of *Blackwood's* (1844); professor of rhetoric and belles lettres, U. of Edinburgh (1845). Author of *Poland, Homer, and Other Poems* (1832),

Lays of the Scottish Cavaliers (1848), *Firmilian, a Spasmodic Tragedy* (1854); collaborated with Sir Theodore Martin in *The Bon Gaultier Ballads* (1845) and *Poems and Ballads of Goethe* (1858); annotated collection of *Ballads of Scotland* (1858).

Ayūb Khān \ä-'üb-'kän, ī-\. 1855–1914. Amīr of Afghanistan (1880–81). Youngest son of Shīr 'Alī. After father's death, took possession of Herat (1879); after preliminary victory over the British, was defeated at Qandahār (1880); defeated by 'Abdorraḥmān (1881) and driven from Herat; lived in exile in Persia and (1887–1914) as state prisoner at Rawalpindi.

Ayub Khan, Mohammad. 1907–1974. Pakistani politician. Served in British Indian army (1928–47), in army of Pakistan (1947–58); commander in chief (1951–58), minister of defense (1954). Named martial law administrator by Pres. Iskander Mirza (1958); seized presidency (1958); instituted agrarian, economic, political reforms; resigned (1969).

Ay·yūb·id \ī-'yüb-id\. Muslim dynasty (1169–1250) established in Egypt (1173) by Ṣalāḥ ad-Dīn and named from his father, Ayyūb (d. 1173), a Kurd who served as a general in Syria and Mesopotamia; extended its power over Nubia, Hejaz, and Yemen; fought Europeans in Third, Fourth, and Fifth crusades; overthrown by Mamlūks.

Aza·ïs \á-zá-ēs\, Pierre-Hyacinthe. 1766–1845. French philosopher. Author of *Des compensations dans les destinées humaines* (1809), *Système universel* (1809–12).

Aza·ña y Dí·az \ä-'thän-yä-ē-'dē-äth\, Manuel. 1880–1940. Spanish politician. Editor and author; wrote biography of Juan Valera (1926). Active in republican opposition to Primo de Rivera; member of revolutionary committee (1930); active in overthrow of Alfonso XIII (1931); minister of war in first republican ministry; premier (1931–33); attempted many reforms; arrested and imprisoned (1934); again premier (1936); elected president (1936); continued in office, with declining power, until victory of Gen. Franco in civil war drove him into exile in France (1939).

Azariah. See UZZIAH.

Az·a·ri·ah \,az-ə-'rī-ə\, Vedanayakam Samuel. 1874–1945. Indian prelate. First Indian bishop of Anglican church as bishop of Dornakal (1912); directed missionary work in Madras; chairman of National Christian Council of India, Burma, and Ceylon (1929–45).

Azeglio, Marchese d'. See Massimo TAPARELLI.

Aze·ve·do \ə-zə-'vā-thü\, Aluízio. 1857–1913. Brazilian writer. Author of Naturalistic novels *O Mulato* (1881), *Casa de Pensão* (1884), *O Cortiço* (1890), etc.; later in diplomatic service.

Azh·a·rī \äzh-ä-'rē\, Ismā'īl al-. 1900–1969. Sudanese politician. President of Graduates' General Congress (1940); organized Ashiqqā' party (1943); president of National Union party (1952); prime minister (1954–56); turned against union with Egypt in favor of Sudanese independence; lost power after independence (1956); again head of National Union party (1964); president of Supreme Council of The Sudan (1965–69); overthrown by military coup.

'Azīz, al- \ə-lä-'zēz\. *Also called* al-'Azīz Bi'l·lāh \-bil-'lä\. *In full* al-'Azīz Bi'llāh Nizār Abū Manṣūr. 955–996. Caliph (975–990) of Fāṭimid dynasty. Son and successor of al-Mu'izz; for most of reign campaigned against Byzantines and rival 'Abbāsid caliphs.

Azorín. See José MARTÍNEZ RUIZ.

Az·ue·la \äs-'wā-lä\, Mariano. 1873–1952. Mexican writer. Army doctor with Pancho Villa (1915); wrote novels chronicling revolution and criticizing subsequent regime, including *Los de abajo* (1916), *Los caciques* (1917), *Las moscas* (1918), *Las tribulaciones de una familia decente* (1918), *La malhora* (1923), *La luciérnaga* (1932), *Avanzada* (1940), *La mujer donada* (1946).

Azzo. See ATTO.

Azzo d'Este. See ESTE family.

Az·zo·ne \ät-'tsō-nā\. *Also called* Azo \'ät-sō\, Az·zo \'at-tsō\, *or* Azzo dei Por·ci \-'pōr-chē\. *Lat.* Az·o·li·nus Por·cius \,az-ə-'lī-nəs-'pòr-shəs\ *or* Azo Sol·dan·us \'az-ō-sōl-'dän-əs\. c.1150–1230. Italian jurist. Professor at Bologna (from 1190); author of systematic summaries of Roman law; a leader of Bolognese school of jurists.

B

Baa·de \ˈbä-də\, Walter. 1893–1960. German astronomer. Member of staff, Hamburg observatory (1919–31); astronomer at Mount Wilson observatory, Pasadena, Cal. (1931–1958) and Mt. Palomar (1948–58); revised luminosity scale of Cepheid variable stars (1952), doubling estimated cosmic distances; professor, Göttingen (1959–60).

Baa·der \ˈbä-dər\, Franz Xaver von. 1765–1841. German Roman Catholic philosopher and writer. Professor, Munich (1826–41); lay theologian and proponent of ecumenism; contributed to creation of Holy Alliance (1815).

Ba'al Shem Tov. See ISRAEL BEN ELIEZER.

Ba·a·sha \ˈbā-ə-shə\ *or* **Ba·a·sa** \-sə\. 9th century B.C. King of Israel (c.900–877 B.C.). Succeeded, perhaps having killed, Nadab, son of Jeroboam I; waged war with Asa of Judah.

Bāb, the. See 'ALĪ MOHAMMAD.

Baba, Meher. See MEHER BABA.

Bā·bā Ṭā·her \bä-ˈbä-ˈtä-her\. *Called* 'Or·yān \òr-ˈyän\. c.1000–after 1055. Persian poet. Possibly a wandering dervish; by tradition an illiterate woodcutter to whom truths were revealed in a vision; author of highly regarded double distich verses on spiritual and philosophical themes.

Bab·bage \ˈbab-ij\, Charles. 1792–1871. English mathematician and inventor. Professor, Cambridge (1828–39). Devoted large part of fortune and government grants to perfecting a calculating machine; conceived analytical engine (1834), forerunner of computer, employing punched cards, memory elements, etc.; work suspended on withdrawal of government support (1842). Invented an ophthalmoscope, speedometer, locomotive cowcatcher. Instrumental in founding the Astronomical and Statistical societies. Author of *On Economy of Machines and Manufactures* (1832) and *Ninth Bridgewater Treatise* (1837).

Bab·bitt \ˈbab-ət\, Irving. 1865–1933. American scholar and educator, b. Dayton, Ohio. On staff (1894–1933), professor of French literature (from 1912), Harvard. Founder (with Paul Elmer More) of Neohumanistic movement. Author of *Literature and the American College* (1908), *The New Laokoön* (1910), *The Masters of Modern French Criticism* (1912), *Rousseau and Romanticism* (1919), *Democracy and Leadership* (1924), *On Being Creative* (1932).

Babbitt, Isaac. 1799–1862. American inventor, b. Taunton, Mass. Made first britannia-metal ware in U.S. (1824); invented a journal box (pat. 1839); suggested that it be lined with an alloy now known as Babbitt metal.

Bab·cock \ˈbab-ˌkäk\, Harold Delos. 1882–1968. American astronomer, b. Edgerton, Wis. Member of staff, Mount Wilson observatory, Pasadena, Cal. (from 1909); specialist in spectroscopy; invented (1951) solar magnetograph.

Babcock, Orville E. 1835–1884. American army officer, b. Franklin, Vt. Served through Civil War; aide-de-camp (1864–65) to General Grant. Private secretary (1869–77) to President Grant. Accused of involvement in Whisky Ring; acquitted (1876) as result of Grant's deposition regarding his excellent character.

Babcock, Stephen Moulton. 1843–1931. American agricultural chemist, b. Bridgewater, N.Y. Professor, U. of Wisconsin (1887–1913). Specialist in chemistry of milk; deviser of Babcock test (1890) for determining amount of fat in milk.

Ba·bel \ˈbá-byilʸ\, Isaac Emmanuilovich. 1894–1941. Russian writer. Gained reputation with morbid *Odessa Tales* (1916), published by Maksim Gorky; also wrote stories of war in *Konarmiya* (1926), plays *Zakat* (1928) and *Mariya* (1935). Exiled to Siberia (c.1937).

Ba·bell \ˈbā-bəl\, William. c.1690–1723. English organist and composer. Reputation as performer surpassed contemporaries, including Handel; remembered for harpsichord transcriptions from Handel's *Rinaldo* and other operas; also wrote sonatas for violin, oboe, flute.

Babenberg. Name of Franconian family that held margraviate (976–1156) and duchy (1156–1246) of Austria. See LEOPOLD; FREDERICK.

Ba·beş \ˈbäb-ēsh\, Victor. 1854–1926. Romanian physician and bacteriologist. Professor, Bucharest (1887–1926); discovered genus (*Babesia*) of protozoans in blood of animals, one species of which causes Texas or tick fever in cattle.

Ba·beuf \bá-bœf\, François-Noël. *Pseudonym* Gracchus Babeuf. 1760–1797. French agitator. Journalist during French Revolution; founded (1789) *Le Correspondent Picard* and (1794) *Le Tribun de Peuple;* arrested for attack on Thermidorian reaction (1795); evolved egalitarian doctrine (Babouvism) and formed secret Committee of Six to plan insurrection; joined Jacobins and others in conspiracy (1796) to overthrow Directory and reestablish constitution of 1793; guillotined.

Ba·bić \ˈbá-bēch\, Ljubomir. *Pen name* Ksa·ver Šan·dor Djal·ski \ˈksá-ver-ˈshán-dòr-ˈdyál-skē\. 1854–1935. Croatian poet. Advocate of Yugoslav unity; author of *Pod starim krovovima* (1886).

Ba·bi·net \bá-bē-ne\, Jacques. 1794–1872. French physicist. Known for researches in optics, meteorology; invented instruments as a goniometer, polariscope, hygrometer.

Bab·ing·ton \ˈbab-iŋ-tən\, Anthony. 1561–1586. English conspirator. Served as page to Mary, Queen of Scots; member (from (1580) of secret London society supporting Jesuit missionaries; induced (1586) by John Ballard, a priest, to organize a conspiracy to murder Elizabeth, lead a general Catholic uprising, and release Mary; detected by Walsingham's spies; executed with Ballard and a dozen others. His letters to Mary were ground of her trial and execution.

Ba·bin·ski \bá-baⁿ-skē, *Angl* bə-ˈbin-skē\, Joseph-François-Felix. 1857–1932. French neurologist. Discovered diagnostic value of Babinski reflex of big toe; with Alfred Fröhlich investigated adiposogenital dystrophy, called Babinski-Fröhlich syndrome.

Ba·bits \ˈbäb-its\, Mihály. 1883–1941. Hungarian writer. Major contributor to periodical *Nyugat* and editor (from 1929); author of intellectual verse, novels, essays, volumes including *A Gólyakalifa* (1916), *Mythológia* (1918), *Karácsonyi madonna* (1920), *Timár Virgil fia* (1922), *Halálfiai* (1927); translated Sophocles, Dante, Shakespeare, Goethe.

Ba·bo \ˈbäb-ˌō\, Joseph Marius von. 1756–1822. German dramatist. Author of *Otto von Wittelsbach* (1782).

Ba·bri·us \ˈbā-brē-əs\. 2d? century A.D. Writer of Greek fables. Probably an Italian living in Eastern empire; wrote fables after Aesop in scazon meter.

Bab·son \ˈbab-sən\, Roger Ward. 1875–1967. American financial statistician, b. Gloucester, Mass. Founder of Babson Business Statistical Organization (1904) and also of Babson Institute (1919); lecturer and columnist on statistics and economics.

Bābur. See ẒAHĪR-UD-DĪN MUḤAMMAD.

Ba·bu·ren \bä-ˈbü̅e-rən\, Dirck van. c.1590–1624. Dutch painter. While studying in Rome (1612–20) decorated chapel of S. Pietro, Montorio; returned home to become leading member of Utrecht school, influenced by Caravaggio; painted religious works as *Christ Crowned with Thorns,* genre pieces.

Bac·cel·li \bät-ˈchel-ē\, Guido. 1832–1916. Italian physician and politician. Taught medicine, U. of Rome; researches on malaria helped prompt reclamation of Roman marshes. Member, chamber of deputies (from 1874); minister of public instruction (1880–84, 1893–96, 1898–1900), of agriculture, industry, commerce (1901–03).

Bacchus, Saint. See SERGIUS.

Bac·chyl·i·des \bə-ˈkil-ə-ˌdēz\. 5th century B.C. Greek lyric poet. Nephew of Simonides and rival of Pindar. Only fragments of works are extant, containing dithyrambs and epinician odes.

Baccio. See Baccio BANDINELLI.

Bac·cio d'Agnolo \ˈbät-chō-ˈdän-yō-(ˌ)lō\. *More fully* Bartolomeo d'Agnolo Ba·glio·ni \bäl-ˈyō-nē\. 1462–1543. Florentine wood-carver. Executed much decorative work for church of Sta. Maria Novella, Palazzo Vecchio (1491–1502); planned Villa Borghese, Bartolini palace; designed campanile of Sta. Spirito.

Baccio della Porta. See BARTOLOMMEO.

Bach \'bäk\. Family of German musicians and composers, including: Johann(es), *known as* Hans (c.1550–1626), a professional musician; and his sons ¶Johann(es), *also called* Hans (1604–1673), organist and town musician at Erfurt; ¶Christoph (1613–1661), organist and town musician at Weimar, Erfurt, and Arnstadt; ¶Heinrich (1615–1692), organist and town musician at Arnstadt. Christoph's son ¶Johann Ambrosius (1645–1695), director of town music at Eisenach; and his sons ¶Johann Christoph (1671–1721), organist at Ohrdruf; and Johann Sebastian (for J. S. Bach and his sons and grandson see entry Johann Sebastian BACH). Another ¶Johann Christoph (1642–1703), son of Heinrich, organist at Eisenach (from 1665) and composer, esp. of vocal music; his work included motets, 44 chorales with preludes, a saraband with 12 variations for clavier, the vocal concerto *Es erhub sich ein Streit,* etc. His son ¶Johann Nicolaus (1669–1753), organist and director of university music at Jena; composer of a mass, sacred concerto, organ music, student music. ¶Johann Michael (1648–1694), another son of Heinrich, organist at Gehren (from 1673); composer of vocal and instrumental music; father-in-law of Johann Sebastian Bach.

Bach, Alexander von. Freiherr. 1813–1893. Austrian politician. Minister of justice (1848); of interior (1849–59); succeeded Schwarzenberg (1852) as leader of Austrian ministry. Established centralized administrative authority for Austrian empire; negotiated concordat with pope (1855); ambassador to Holy See (1859–67).

Bach, Johann Sebastian. 1685–1750. German organist and composer. Son of Ambrosius Bach and brother of Johann Christoph Bach (1671–1721), his first music teachers. Student and chorister, Michaelisschule, Lüneburg (1700–03); organist, Arnstadt (1703–07); studied organ under Buxtehude, Lübeck (1705); organist of Blasiuskirche, Mühlhausen (1707–08); court organist, Weimar (1708–17); court concertmeister, Weimar (1714–17); court Kapellmeister, Köthen (1717–23); cantor, Thomasschule, and director of university music, Leipzig (from 1723); honorary court composer, Dresden (1736). Visited Frederick the Great at Potsdam (1747); improvised there on the various newly invented pianos and tried the chief church organs; died totally blind (1750). Composed very large library of church, vocal, and instrumental music, including: *Vocal:* about 200 church cantatas and 24 secular cantatas; a Mass in B minor; Christmas, Easter, and Ascension oratorios; Passions according to St. Matthew and St. John; a Magnificat, motets, hymns, etc. *Organ music:* 140 choral preludes including *Orgelbüchlein,* 18 preludes and fugues including "St. Anne," various toccatas, fantasies, sonatas, etc. *Harpsichord: Clavierübung, Goldberg Variations, Well-Tempered Clavier* containing 48 preludes and fugues, two- and three-part inventions, etc. *Orchestral:* six *Brandenburg Concertos,* a *Sinfonia,* etc. Also wrote chamber music and unfinished *Art of the Fugue.* The premier composer of late German Baroque and one of greatest in history. Four of his sons and a grandson were musicians of importance. ¶Wilhelm Friedmann (1710–1784), called "the Halle Bach"; organist at Dresden (1733–46), at Halle (1747–64); composer of concertos, sonatas, fantasias for organ and clavier, an opera, symphonies, etc. ¶Carl Philipp Emanuel (1714–1788); composer and pioneer in establishing the sonata form; chamber musician to Frederick the Great, Berlin (1740–67); director of church music, Hamburg (from 1767); works included numerous concertos and sonatas for the clavier and piano, songs, church and chamber music, and a treatise called *The True Art of Clavier Playing* (1753–62), long influential. Most important composer of pre-Classical period, strong influence on Haydn, Mozart, Beethoven. ¶Johann Christoph Friedrich (1732–1795); chamber musician (1750) and Kapellmeister (c.1758) at Bückeburg; composer of motets, church and secular cantatas, 3 oratorios, 6 quartets for flute and stringed instruments, clavier sonatas, and symphonies. ¶Johann Christian (1735–1782); called "the English Bach"; cathedral organist, Milan (1760); composer to King's Theatre and then music master to Queen Charlotte Sophia, London (1762); cofounder of Bach-Abel concerts (1765); composer of operas, oratorios, many arias and cantatas, clavier concertos, chamber music, symphonies, overtures, etc. A leading exponent of Italianate Rococo style; influenced Mozart. ¶Wilhelm Friedrich Ernst (1759–1845); son of J. C. F. Bach; organist, pianist, and composer; Kapellmeister at Berlin (1789), and later music teacher of royal family; works included cantatas, songs, and piano pieces.

Bach, Julius Carl von. 1847–1931. German engineer. Known for studies of strength of materials, stress, machine design.

Ba·chau·mont \bá-shō-mōⁿ\, François Le Coi·gneux de \lə-kwán-yœ̄-də-\. 1624–1702. French politician and wit. As member of Paris Parlement, gave name Fronde (sling) to series of uprisings against Cardinal Mazarin. Author with Chapelle of *Voyage de Chapelle et Bachaumont* (1663).

Bachaumont, Louis Pe·tit de \pə-tē-də-\. 1690–1771. French publicist. From conversations in salon of Mme Doublet, recorded secret journal later published as part of chronicle *Mémoires secrets pour servir à l'histoire de la république des lettres* (1777–87).

Bache \'bāch\, Alexander Dallas. 1806–1867. American physicist, b. Philadelphia. Nephew of B.F. Bache. Professor, Pennsylvania (1828–36, 1842–43). President, Girard College (1836–42). Superintendent, U.S. Coast Survey (1843–67). First president, National Academy of Sciences (1863); one of incorporators of Smithsonian Institution (1846).

Bache, Benjamin Franklin. 1769–1798. American journalist, b. Philadelphia. Grandson of Benjamin Franklin. Founded the Philadelphia *General Advertiser* (1790; later known as the *Aurora*), Jeffersonian organ; attacked Washington and Adams; his anti-Federalist tirades a principal target of Sedition Act (1798); arrested (1798) for libeling president; released on parole.

Bachelin, Olivier. See Olivier BASSELIN.

Bach·el·ler \'bach-(ə-)lər\, Irving Addison. 1859–1950. American novelist, b. Pierpont, N.Y. Journalist in New York (1882–1900); editor of *New York World* (1898–1900). Author of *The Master of Silence* (1892), *Eben Holden* (1900), *D'ri and I* (1901), *Keeping Up With Lizzie* (1911), *The Light in the Clearing* (1917), *A Man for the Ages* (1919), *The Oxen of the Sun* (1935), *A Boy for the Ages* (1937), etc., and autobiographical *Coming Up the Road* (1928).

Bach·man \'bak-mən\, John. 1790–1874. American clergyman and naturalist, b. Rhinebeck, N.Y. Lutheran pastor in Charleston, S.C. (from 1815); associated with J.J. Audubon (from 1831); collaborator in *The Viviparous Quadrupeds of North America* (1845–49); author of *Unity of the Human Race* (1850).

Bacho, John. See BACONTHORPE.

Bach·o·fen \'bäk-,ō-fən\, Johann Jakob. 1815–1887. Swiss jurist and anthropologist. Professor, Basel (1841–45); judge, Basel criminal court (1842–66). Author of *Das Mutterrecht* (1861), *Die Sage von Tanaquil* (1870), works on Greek and Roman thought and customs.

Baciccia. See Giovanni GAULLI.

Back \'bak\, Sir George. 1796–1878. English explorer. Sailed with Franklin on arctic expeditions of discovery (1819–22, 1825–27); led two expeditions to explore remaining North American coastline (1833, 1836). Admiral (1857). Wrote *Narrative of the Arctic Land Expedition to the Mouth of the Great Fish River* (1836), *Narrative of Expedition in H.M.S. Terror* (1838).

Back·haus \'bäk-,haůs\, Wilhelm. 1884–1969. German pianist. Concert debut at 8 (1892); taught in England, Germany, U.S.; known esp. as interpreter of Beethoven.

Back·huy·sen *or* **Bak·huy·sen** *or* **Backhuizen** \'bäk-,hȯi-sən\, Ludolf. 1631–1708. Dutch painter and etcher. Known esp. for seascapes of intense realism.

Back·us \'bak-əs\, Isaac. 1724–1806. American clergyman, b. Norwich, Conn. Separatist from Congregational church (1746); New Light minister (1748–56). Organizer (1756) and pastor (1756–1806), Baptist church, Middleborough, Mass. Champion of religious liberty. Author of *A History of New England, with Particular Reference to the Denomination of Christians Called Baptists* (1777–96).

Back·well \'bak-wəl, -,wel\, Edward. d. 1683. English goldsmith and banker. Principal originator of bank-note system; intermediary in financial transactions between Charles II and Louis XIV.

Ba·con \'bā-kən\, Delia Salter. 1811–1859. American writer, b. Tallmadge, Ohio. Sister of Leonard Bacon. Worked in England (1853–57) to prove theory that Shakespearean plays were written by group headed by Francis Bacon. Author of *Philosophy of the Plays of Shakspere Unfolded* (1857), origin of so-called Baconian theory.

Bacon, Francis. 1st Baron Ver·u·lam \'ver-(y)ə-ləm\ *and* Viscount St. Al·bans \sənt-'ȯl-bənz, (,)sānt-\. 1561–1626. English philosopher and author. Son of Nicholas Bacon. Trained in law; M.P. (1584 ff.). Attached himself to Earl of Essex, Elizabeth's favorite (1591); despite Essex's recommendations, failed to win preferment from Elizabeth; instrumental in conviction of Essex on charge of treason (1601). Paid court to James I; commissioner for arranging union with Scotland (1604); solicitor general (1607); attorney general (1613); lord keeper (1617); lord chancellor and raised to peerage (1618); promoted increase of monopoly patents which enabled Buckingham's brothers to acquire wealth; confessed himself guilty of bribery and corrupt dealing in chancery suits (1621); fined £40,000 (later remitted by king), banished from Parliament and court (1621). Chief literary works included *Essayes* (1597 ff.; complete collection of 58 pub. 1625), concise expressions of practical wisdom and full of shrewd observations; *De Sapientia Veterum* (1609); *Apophthagmes new and old* (1624), a collection of anecdotes and witticisms. Chief philosophical and scientific works included *Advancement of Learning* (1605), a survey in English of state of knowledge, as an introduction to a projected (but never completed) *Instauratio Magna,* or encyclopedia of all knowledge; *Novum Organum* (1620), in Latin, key to his system for the new systematic analysis of knowledge, intended to replace the deductive logic of Aristotle with inductive method in interpreting nature; *Historia Ventorum* (1622), *Historia Vitae et Mortis* (1623), *De Augmentis Scientiarum* (1623), a completion in Latin of the *Advancement.* Other writings included *Sylva Sylvarum* and *New Atlantis* (1627), *Maxims of the Law* (1630), *Reading on the Statute of Uses* (1642).

Bacon, Henry. 1866–1924. American architect, b. Watseka, Ill. Designed (1911) Lincoln Memorial, Washington, D.C.; Public Library, Paterson, N.J.; Court of the Four Seasons, Panama-Pacific Exposition, San Francisco. Collaborated with Daniel Chester French in various memorials to famous Americans.

Bacon, John. See BACONTHORPE.

Bacon, John. 1738–1820. American clergyman and politician, b. Canterbury, Conn. Minister, Old South Church, Boston (1771–75); assoc. judge (1779–1807), presiding judge (1807–11), Berkshire Co. court of common pleas; U.S. representative in Congress (1801–03). Early advocate of civil and religious liberty; effective in opposing provision in new state constitution (1778) denying suffrage to Negroes, Indians, and mulattoes.

Bacon, John. 1740–1799. English sculptor. Perfected method of working in artificial stone; invented improved device for transferring design from model to marble; won first gold medal awarded for sculpture by Royal Academy (1769); A.R.A. (1770). Works included monuments to Pitt in Westminster Abbey and to Dr. Johnson in St. Paul's Cathedral.

Bacon, Leonard. 1802–1881. American clergyman, b. Detroit, Mich. Brother of Delia Bacon. Pastor, First Church, New Haven, Conn. (from 1825). One of founders and editor of *The Independent* (1848 ff.). Advocate of liberal orthodoxy and a leader in antislavery movement. Author of *Slavery Discussed in Occasional Essays* (1846), *The Genesis of the New England Churches* (1874).

Bacon, Leonard. 1887–1954. American poet, b. Solvay, N.Y. Author of *Ulug Beg* (1923), *Animula Vagula* (1926), *Guinea Fowl and Other Poultry* (1927), *Lost Buffalo* (1930), *The Furioso* (1932), *Sunderland Capture and Other Poems* (1940, Pulitzer prize).

Bacon, Nathaniel. 1647–1676. American colonial leader, b. England. Emigrated to America (1673); settled in Virginia; led expedition against Indians in defiance of Governor Berkeley; declared by Berkeley to be a rebel. At head of colonial force, captured Jamestown (1676), burned it; as leader of Bacon's Rebellion, controlled nearly all Virginia; died at height of power.

Bacon, Sir Nicholas. 1509–1579. English lawyer. Father of Francis Bacon. Lord keeper of great seal (1558–79) under Queen Elizabeth; received full jurisdiction of lord chancellor (1559); managed church matters with Cecil; advocated strict measures against Mary, Queen of Scots.

Bacon, Roger. c.1220–1292. English philosopher and scientist. Studied at Oxford and Paris; settled at Oxford as Franciscan monk (1247). Known esp. for his advocacy of experimentalism in search for truth. Experimented in alchemy and optics; knew how to make gunpowder; described spectacles and made a camera obscura for observing solar eclipses; accused of dealing in black magic. Prepared on request of Pope Clement IV encyclopedic *Opus majus* (1268), embracing treatises on grammar, logic, mathematics, physics, philology, and philosophy. Confined by Franciscans on suspicion of heresy (c.1278–?). Other works included *Communia naturalium* and *Communia mathematica* (c.1268), *Compendium philosophiae* (1272). Known to posterity as Doctor Mirabilis, i.e. wonderful teacher.

Ba·con·thorpe \'bā-kən-ˌthȯrp\ *or* **Bacon** *or* **Ba·cho** \'bā-(ˌ)kō\, John. *Known also as* Johannes de An·gli·cus \'an-gli-kəs\ *and as* Doc·tor Res·o·lu·tus \'däk-tə(r)-ˌrez-ə-'l(y)üt-əs\. c.1290–1346. English scholar. Grandnephew of Roger Bacon. Reared in Carmelite monastery; provincial of English Carmelites (1329–33); taught at Cambridge. Author of commentaries on Aristotle and Averroës that earned him title of Princeps Averroistarum, i.e. prince of Averroists; also wrote commentaries on Peter Lombard, St. Augustine of Hippo, St. Anselm, Pauline epistles, etc.

Ba·dā'ū·nī \bə-ˌdä-ü-'nē\, 'Abd al-Qādir. 1540–c.1615. Indo-Persian historian. Under patronage of Emperor Akbar (from 1574). Author of *Muntakhab at-tawārīkh* or *Tārīkh-e Badā'ūnī*, a history of Muslim India; contributed to *Tārīkh-e alfī*, millenial history of Islām; translated Sanskrit and Hindu works.

Bad·de·ley \'bad-lē,'bad-^{ə}l-ē\, Robert. c.1732–1794. English actor. Identified with Drury Lane and Haymarket theatres; in will bequeathed property to found home for aged and impoverished actors and also to provide wine and cake in green room of Drury Lane on Twelfth Night, a ceremony still observed.

Bade \bȧd\, Josse. *Lat.* Jod·o·cus Ba·di·us Ascen·sius \'jäd-i-kəs-'bād-ē-əs-ə-'sen-shəs\. 1462–1537. Flemish printer. Professor of Greek and Latin, Lyon; established printshop, Paris (c.1500); published Greek and Latin classics, Erasmus, etc.; editions noted for textual accuracy, typographic excellence.

Ba·den \'bäd-ən\. German dynasty of 800 years' duration, originating with Hermann, Duke of Carinthia, who assumed title of margrave of Baden (1112); lands of family, frequently divided and reunited, became electorate (1803) and grand duchy (1806). Recent rulers (with dates of reigns): Charles Frederick (1738–1811), Charles (1811–18), Louis (1818–30), Leopold (1830–52), Frederick I (1852–1907), Frederick II (1907–1918).

Ba·de·ni \bä-'dä-nē\, Kasimir Felix. Graf. *Pol.* Kazimierz Feliks Badeni. 1846–1909. Austrian statesman, b. Galicia. Governor of Galicia (1888); prime minister of Austrian half of dual monarchy of Austria-Hungary (1895–97); attempted by ordinance to place Czech language on par with German in Bohemia and Moravia; violently opposed by German-speaking deputies and forced to resign (1897).

Ba·den-Pow·ell \'bād-^{ə}n-'pō-əl\, Robert Stephenson Smyth. 1st Baron Baden-Powell of Gil·well \'gil-ˌwel\. 1857–1941. English soldier. Entered army (1876); served in India, Bechuanaland, Ashanti; became expert scout; chief staff officer, Matabele campaign (1896–97); held Mafeking through 217-day siege by Boers until relieved (1900); made major general; inspector general of cavalry (1903); lieutenant general (1908); retired (1910). Inaugurated Boy Scouts (1908) and, with his sister Agnes (1858–1945), the Girl Guides (1910). Published *Scouting for Boys* (1908) based on his army manual *Aids to Scouting* (1899); initiated Wolf Cubs (1916). Acclaimed Chief Scout of the World at first Boy Scout jamboree (1920). Created baron (1929).

Badī 'az-Zamān. See HAMADHĀNĪ.

Ba·din \bȧ-da^{n}, *Angl* 'bad-^{ə}n\, Stephen Theodore. 1768–1853. American clergyman, b. Orléans, France. Fled revolutionary France to U.S. (1792); first Roman Catholic priest ordained in U.S., by Bishop John Carroll at Baltimore (1793); itinerant priest in Kentucky (1793–1819); in France (1819–22); missionary to French Canadians and Potawatomi Indians and itinerant in Midwest (1822–53).

Badius, Jodocus. See Josse BADE.

Ba·do·glio \bä-'dȯl-yō\, Pietro. 1871–1956. Italian soldier. Officer in World War I; directed capture of Monte Sabotino (1916); defeated at Caporetto (1917); headed Italian armistice delegation (1918–19); promoted general and named chief of staff (1919–21). Ambassador to Brazil (1924). Chief of general staff (1925–28, 1933–40); field marshal (1926); governor general of Libya (1928–33); commanded Italian forces in Ethiopian campaign (1935–36); viceroy of Ethiopia (1936); commanded army early in World War II (1939–40); resigned in disagreement with Mussolini. Succeeded Mussolini as premier (1943–44); arranged armistice with Allies (1944).

Badr al-Ja·mā·lī \'bädr^{ə}-äl-jə-'mäl-ē\. d. 1094. Fāṭimid ruler of Egypt. Orig. an Armenian slave; rose to command in army; sent by caliph (1073) to take control of Egypt; temporarily reversed decline of Fāṭimid dynasty.

Badr Khā·nī Jā·la·dat \'bädr^{ə}-k̲ä-'nē-'jä-lə-dät\. 1893–1951. Kurdish leader. Active in Kurdish nationalist agitation (from c.1912); president, Kurdish National League (1927); editor (from 1932) of Kurdish review *Ḥawār*.

Baduila. See TOTILA.

Baeck \'bek\, Leo. 1873–1956. German rabbi and theologian. Rabbi in Berlin (1912–42); leader of National Agency of Jews in Germany (1933–42), arranging for emigration, charity, education, etc.; in concentration camp (1942–45). Author of *Das Wesen des Judentums* (1905), *Dieses Volk; Jüdische Existenz* (1955), etc.

Baeda. See BEDE.

Bae·de·ker \'bed-ə-kər, *Angl* 'bād-i-\, Karl. 1801–1859. German publisher. Established in Coblenz (1827); issued (1829) a guidebook to Coblenz, followed by a series of travel handbooks in German, later also in French and English, for most European countries, parts of North America and the Orient, etc.

Baeke·land \'bā-kə-ˌlänt, *Angl* 'bāk-(ə-)lənd\, Leo Hendrik. 1863–1944. American chemist and inventor, b. Ghent, Belgium. To U.S. (1889); manufacturer of photographic papers of his own invention; known esp. for discovery of the synthetic resin Bakelite (1907).

Baer \'ba(ə)r, 'be(ə)r\, Arthur, *nicknamed* Bugs. 1886–1969. American journalist, b. Philadelphia. Sports columnist, *Washington* (D.C.) *Times;* columnist, *New York World* (1914–19), *New York American* and Hearst King Features Syndicate (1919–69).

Baer, George Frederick. 1842–1914. American lawyer and industrialist, b. near Lavansville, Pa. President (1901 ff.), Reading Company; headed resistance to United Mine Workers of America in great strike (1902).

Baer \'ber\, Karl Ernst von. 1792–1876. German embryologist, b. Estonia. Professor, Königsberg (1817–34); with Academy of Sciences, St. Petersburg (from 1834). Pioneer of descriptive and comparative embryology; showed that the various organs of vertebrates are derived from germ layers by differentiation; discovered mammalian ovum (1827), notochord, etc.; elucidated principle of epigenesis. In Russia a naturalist, geologist, ethnologist, esp. in far North. Author of *Über Entwicklungsgeschichte der Thiere* (1828–37), *Untersuchungen über die Entwicklung der Fische* (1835), etc.

Baer \'ba(ə)r, 'be(ə)r\, Max, *in full* Maximilian Adelbert. 1909–1959. American boxer, b. Omaha, Neb. Won 65 of 79 fights in career (1929–41); world heavyweight champion (1934–35).

Baer, William Jacob. 1860–1941. American painter, b. Cincinnati, Ohio. Known for portraits, genre pictures, and esp. miniatures.

\ə\ abut \\$^{ə}$\ kitten, *Fr.* **table \ər\ further \a\ ash \ā\ ace \ä\ cot, cart \au̇\ out \ch\ chin \e\ bet \ē\ easy \g\ go \i\ hit \ī\ ice \j\ job \ŋ\ sing \ō\ go \ȯ\ law \ȯi\ boy \th\ both \t̲h̲\ the \ü\ loot \u̇\ foot \y\ yet \zh\ vision \ȧ, b̲, g̲, k̲, ^{n}, œ, œ̄, ue, ue̅, ^{y}\ *see* Guide to Pronunciation**

Baert·son \'bärt-son\, Albert. 1866–1922. Belgian painter. Known for landscapes and village scenes in Flanders.

Bae·yer \'be-yər\, Adolf von, *in full* Johann Friedrich Wilhelm Adolf von. 1835–1917. German organic chemist. Professor at Munich (1875–1915). Known esp. for synthesis of indigo (1880) and formulation of its structure (1883), synthesis of phthalein dyes, discovery of uric acid derivatives, investigation of polyacetylenes, etc. Awarded 1905 Nobel prize for chemistry.

Bá·ez \'bä-äs\, Buenaventura. 1810–1884. Dominican politician. Led revolt against Haiti (1843); president of Dominican Republic (1849–53, 1856–58, 1865–66, 1868–74, 1876–78); attempted to secure U.S. annexation (1850, 1869), invited Spanish intervention (1861); frequently exiled.

Baf·fin \'baf-ən\, William. c.1584–1622. English navigator. Pilot on several expeditions in search of Northwest Passage (1612–16); discovered Baffin Bay (1616); sailed to latitude 77° 45′, a record not surpassed for 236 years. First on record to determine longitude at sea by lunar observation.

Bage·hot \'baj-ət\, Walter. 1826–1877. English economist and journalist. Entered father's shipowning and banking business (1852); editor of *Economist* (1860–77). Author of *The English Constitution* (1867), *Lombard Street* (1873), *Physics and Politics* (1872); a pioneer in applying sociology and evolutionary thought to business and economic topics; known also for perspicuous and still valuable literary essays.

Bag·ge·sen \'bäg-ə-sən, *Ger* 'bäg-ə-zən\, Jens Immanuel. 1764–1826. Danish poet. Traveled in Germany, Switzerland, and France; adopted German as second language. Argued against romanticism, esp. against Oehlenschläger. Author of *Comiske fortaellinger* (1785), *Labyrinthen* (1792–93), *Parthenais* (in German, 1802), *Rimbreve* (1807), *Gengangeren* (1807), etc.

Bag·ley \'bag-lē\, William Chandler. 1874–1946. American educator, b. Detroit. Professor of education, U. of Illinois (1908–17), Teachers Coll., Columbia (1917–40); president, National Council of Education (1931–37). Author of *The Educative Process* (1905), *Craftsmanship in Teaching* (1911), *School Discipline* (1915), *Determinism in Education* (1925), *Education and Emergent Man* (1934), etc.; critic of progressive education.

Ba·glio·ni \bäl-'yō-nē\. Name of family of Umbrian nobles and soldiers of fortune who dominated Perugia (1488–1534), including: Malatesta (1389–1437), with tyrant of Perugia opposed Pope Martin V; later supported Martin and became virtual ruler of Perugia. ¶Giampaolo *or* Giovan Paolo (c.1470–1520) escaped attempt by Carlo and Grifonetto Baglioni to assassinate rest of family (1500) and emerged ruler of Perugia; preferred life of condottiere, left administration to Morgante Baglioni; driven from power (1502) but recaptured city (1503); acknowledged Pope Julius II as overlord (1506); killed by order of Pope Leo X. ¶Malatesta (1491–1531) commanded forces of both Venice and Florence; defended Florence against Pope Clement VII (1529) but betrayed city to him (1530). ¶Rodolfo (1518–54) ruled Perugia (1531–34) until defeated and banished by Pope Paul III.

Baglioni, Bartolomeo d'Agnolo. See BACCIO D'AGNOLO.

Bagnacavallo, Il. See Bartolommeo RAMENCHI.

Bag·nold \'bag-nəld\, Enid. 1889–1981. English writer. Author of novels including *Happy Foreigner* (1920), *Serena Blandish* (1924), *National Velvet* (1935), *The Squire* (1938), *The Girl's Journey* (1956), and plays including *National Velvet* (1945), *Poor Judas* (1951), *The Chalk Garden* (1956), *The Last Joke* (1960), *Call Me Jacky* (1967), *A Matter of Gravity* (1975).

Ba·go·as \bə-'gō-əs\. 4th century B.C. Persian courtier and soldier. A eunuch; commanded Achaemenid forces in conquest of Egypt (343 B.C.); chief adviser to Artaxerxes III, whom he came to dominate; murdered Artaxerxes (338) and placed Arses on throne; murdered Arses (336) and placed Darius III on throne; murdered by Darius on failure of attempt to murder him.

Bag·ot \'bag-ət\, Sir Charles. 1781–1843. English diplomat. M.P. (1807); minister to France (1814), U.S. (1815–1820); ambassador to St. Petersburg (1820), The Hague (1824). Governor general of British North America (1841–43).

Ba·gram·yan \,bä-,gräm-'yän\, Ivan Kristoforovich. 1897–1982. Soviet army commander. Commanded the Soviets' 11th Guard Army, which decisively figured in Battle of Kursk (July 1943), last German offensive on Russian front; commanded 1st Baltic Front which defeated Germans in Latvia and Lithuania (1944); served as Soviet deputy minister of defense (1958–68).

Ba·gra·ti·on \bə-grə-tyi-'yȯn\, Pyotr Ivanovich. Prince. 1765–1812. Russian general, of noble Georgian family. Entered Russian army (1782); at siege of Ochakov (1788) and in Polish campaign (1792, 1794); in campaigns in Italy and Switzerland (1799), distinguishing himself with capture of Brescia, and in Austro–Russian War (1805) against French; noted for resistance to greatly superior force at Hollabrunn near Vienna (1805); fought at Austerlitz (1805), Eylau and Friedland (1807); captured Åland Islands from Sweden (1808); in campaign against Turks (1809–10); in war with French (1812), defeated at Mogilyov and, while commanding left wing, mortally wounded at Borodino.

Bagritsky, Edward. See Edward DZYUBIN.

Bag·yi·daw \'bäg-yi-'dau̇\. 19th century. King of Burma (1819–37). Grandson and successor of Bodawpaya; with general, Maha Bandula, conquered Assam, Manipur, provoking First Anglo–Burmese War (1824–26); lost Assam, Manipur, Arakan, Tenasserim to British; abdicated in favor of brother, Tharrawaddy Min.

Bahā' ad-Dīn. See IBN SHADDĀD.

Bahā' ad-Dīn Zu·hayr \bə-'hä-u̇-'dēn-zu̇-'hir\. *More completely* Abū al-Faḍl Zuhayr ibn Muḥammad al-Muhallaī. 1186–1258. Arab poet. Secretary in Egyptian government and court poet of the Ayyūbids; vizier (1240); noted for polished and delicate verses, including panegyric odes, poems on love.

Ba·hā' Al·lāh \bə-'hä-al-'lä\ *or* **Ba·ha·ul·lah** \-u̇l-'lä\, *i.e.* Glory of God. *Orig.* Mīrzā Ḥoseyn Alī Nūrī. 1817–1892. Persian religious leader. Became follower of Mīrzā 'Alī Moḥammad, known as the Bāb (1844); persecuted and imprisoned (1852); exiled to Baghdad; preached Bābī religion in Baghdad; exiled to Constantinople and finally to Acre; claimed (1863) to be leader promised by the Bāb; took title Bahā' Allāh as head of new Bahā'ī faith.

Ba·hā·dur Shāh \bə-'hä-du̇r-'shä\. Name of two emperors of India of Mughal dynasty:

Bahādur Shāh I. *Orig.* Prince Mu'azzam. 1643–1712. Emperor (1707–12). Son and successor of Aurangzeb; led father's army against Marāthās in Goa and was defeated (1683–84); governor of Kābul (1699–1707); gained throne by killing brothers. Drove Sikhs into Punjab hills (1710–12).

Bahādur Shāh II. 1775–1862. Last Mughal emperor of India (1837–58). Son and successor of Akbar Shāh II; ineffectual ruler, largely a client of British; forced by rebel troops who seized Delhi to assume nominal leadership of Sepoy Mutiny (1857); exiled by British to Burma (1858).

Ba·hār \bə-'här\, Moḥammad Taqī. 1885–1951. Iranian poet. Followed father as poet and miniature painter to Qajar court; supported revolution (1907); edited liberal democratic newspaper *Now bahār;* member of Iranian parliament (1916–21); minister of national education (1946). Author of verse in classical Persian style, essays, a novel, etc.

Bah·ma·nī \bam-a-'nē\. Muslim dynasty of the Deccan, founded by 'Alā'-ud-Dīn Bahman Shāh (*q.v.*). Its fourteen sultans ruled (1347–1518) all provinces south of the Vindhya Hills.

Bahr \'bär\, Hermann. 1863–1934. Austrian journalist, playwright, and theater manager. Champion successively of Naturalism, Romanticism, and Symbolism; manager of Deutsches Theater, Berlin (1903), Burgtheater, Vienna (1918). Author of essays *Zur Kritik der Moderne* (1890); plays *Wienerinnen* (1900), *Der Krampus* (1901), *Das Konzert* (1909); novels *Die Rahl* (1908), *Drut* (1909), *Oh Mensch!* (1910), *Der inwendige Garten* (1927), etc.

Bah·rām \bä-'räm\. *Also* Va·rah·ran \,vär-ä-'rän\ *from older* Verethragna. Name of six Sāsānian kings of Persia:

Bahrām I. 3d century A.D. King (273–276). Son of Shāpūr I, who made him governor of Gilan province; succeeded brother Hormizd I; fostered Zoroastrianism and persecuted Manichaeans, Christians, Buddhists.

Bahrām II. 3d century. King (276–293). Son and successor of Bahrām I; survived Roman invasion and seizing of capital Ctesiphon (283).

Bahrām III. 3d century. King (293). Son and successor of Bahrām II; lost crown to Narses.

Bahrām IV. 4th century. King (388–399). Son of Shāpūr II; succeeded brother Shāpūr III.

Bahrām V. *Called* Gor \'gȯr\, *i.e.* wild ass. 5th century. King (420–438). Son of Yazdegerd I and father of Yazdegerd II. Began persecution of Christians, which led to war with Rome; defeated (422). Great hunter; a favorite in Persian tradition.

Bahrām VI. *Called* Bahrām Chū·bīn \-chü-'bēn\. 6th century. King (590–591). Master of household to Hormizd IV; as commander in Khorāsān, repelled Turkish invasion; defeated by Romans (589); rebelled against Hormizd; with aid of mutinous royal troops defeated Khosrow II and proclaimed himself king; deposed by Khosrow (591), fled to Turkistan.

Bahrdt \'bärt\, Carl Friedrich. 1741–1792. German theologian. Dismissed from professorship (1766–75) at Leipzig and Erfurt because of profligacy and at Giessen because of his *Neueste Offenbarungen Gottes in Briefen and Erzählungen,* heretical translation of New Testament (1773–75); imprisoned (1789) because of his satire *Das Religionsedikt;* spent last ten years of life as innkeeper. Other works included *Briefe über die Bibel im Volkston* (1782).

Bahur, Elija. See Elijah LEVITA.

Ba·hū·tī, al- \äl-bä-'hü-tē\. *More completely* Shaykh Manṣūr ibn Yūnus al-Bahūtī. *Known also as* al-Bahūtī al-Miṣrī. d. 1641. Egyptian jurist. Last major exponent in Egypt of Ḥanbalī school of Islāmic law.

Bah·ya ben Jo·seph ibn Pa·ku·da \'bä-yä-ben-'jō-zəf-,ib-ən-pä-'kü-dä\. 11th century. Spanish Jewish jurist and writer. Judge of rabbinical court in Muslim Spain. Influenced by Sūfīs and Neoplatonists, wrote in Arabic *al-Hidāyah ilā farā' id al-gulūb* ("Duties of the Heart," c.1080), which in Ibn Tibbon's Hebrew translation *Ḥovot ha-levavot* became classic of Jewish devotional literature.

Bai *or* **Baj** \'bä-ē\, Tommaso. c.1650–1714. Italian tenor and composer. Maestro di cappella, Vatican (1713–14); wrote a celebrated *Miserere.*

Baibars. See BAYBARS.

Ba·ïf \bȧ-ēf\, Jean-Antoine de. 1532–1589. French poet. One of La Pléiade; author of sonnets and epicurean lyrics in *Les Amours de Méline* (1552) and *L'Amour de Francine* (1555), drama *Le Brave, ou Taillebras* adapted from Plautus (1567), *Euvres en rime* (1573), *Etrénes de poezie fransoèze en vers mezurés* on his theory of "quantitative verse" (1574), *Mimes, enseignemens et proverbes* (1576), etc.

Bai·kie \'bā-kē\, William Balfour. 1825–1864. Scottish naturalist and philologist. Naval surgeon (1848); on Niger expedition (1854), taking command on death of captain; wrecked on second expedition (1857); settled at Lokoja; opened navigation of Niger, built roads. Compiled vocabularies of 50 native dialects; translated portions of Bible into Hausa.

Bailén, Duque de. See Francisco de CASTAÑOS.

Bai·ley \'bā-lē\, Florence Augusta, *nee* Mer·ri·am \'mer-ē-əm\. 1863–1948. American ornithologist, b. Locust Grove, N.Y. Sister of Clinton Hart Merriam; m. (1899) Vernon Bailey. Author of *Birds Through an Opera Glass* (1889), *Handbook of Birds of the Western United States* (1902), etc.

Bailey, Gamaliel. 1807–1859. American reformer, b. Mount Holly, N.J. Edited (1836–43) Cincinnati *Philanthropist,* first antislavery paper in West, and (1847–59) *National Era,* a Washington (D.C.) weekly journal under auspices of American and Foreign Anti-Slavery Society; serialized *Uncle Tom's Cabin* (1851–52).

Bailey, Henry Christopher. 1878–1961. English writer. Creator of fictional amateur detective Reggie Fortune, as in *Mr. Fortune Speaking, Clue for Mr. Fortune, The Bishop's Crime,* and of the criminal lawyer Joshua Clunk, as in *Orphan Ann.*

Bailey, James Anthony. *Orig.* James Mc·Gin·niss \mə-'gin-əs\. 1847–1906. American circus owner, b. Detroit. With circuses from boyhood; partner (1872) in Cooper & Bailey Circus; combined (1881) his circus with that of P. T. Barnum. See also RINGLING.

Bailey, James Montgomery. 1841–1894. American journalist, b. Albany, N.Y. Bought (1865) *Danbury Times,* Danbury, Conn., and merged it (1870) with the *Jeffersonian* to form the *Danbury News,* a weekly paper that became famous for humor with which real and fictitious news items were presented.

Bailey, Liberty Hyde. 1858–1954. American horticulturist and botanist, b. South Haven, Mich. Professor of horticulture, Michigan State (1884–88), Cornell (1888–1903); dean, N.Y. State College of Agriculture and director of agricultural experiment station (1903–13), Cornell; founder (1920) and director (1935–51), Bailey Hortorium. Known for research on North American sedges, blackberries, raspberries, and New World palms, as well as work on rural problems and education. Editor of *Cyclopedia of American Horticulture* (1900–02), *Cyclopedia of American Agriculture* (1907–09), *Standard Cyclopedia of Horticulture* (1914), *Manual of Cultivated Plants* (1923).

Bailey, Nathan *or* Nathaniel. d. 1742. English lexicographer. Author of *An Universal Etymological English Dictionary* (1721), an interleaved copy of which formed basis of Dr. Johnson's dictionary.

Bailey, Philip James. 1816–1902. English poet. Associated with the "spasmodic school." Author of *Festus* (1839), based on story of Faust, greatly altered in later editions; also *The Angel World* (1850), *The Mystic* (1855), *The Universal Hymn* (1867).

Bailey, Samuel. 1791–1870. English economist and philosopher. Founded Sheffield Banking Co. (1831); unsuccessfully sought Parliamentary seat as "Utilitarian radical." Author of *Essays on the Formation and Publication of Opinions* (1821), *Critical Dissertation on the Nature, Measures, and Causes of Value* in which he criticized Ricardian economics (1825), and *Essay on the Pursuit of Truth* (1829).

Bailey, Solon Irving. 1854–1931. American astronomer, b. Lisbon, N.H. Professor of astronomy (1893–1925), Harvard. Selected site (1888) and supervised work of Harvard observatory station at Arequipa, Peru (1893–1931).

Bail·lie \'bā-lē\, Lady Grizel. 1665–1746. Scottish poet. As a child, carried food to her father, Sir Patrick Hume, who had been forced into hiding, and messages to the imprisoned patriot Robert Baillie of Jerviswood (whose son George she married, 1692); shared parents' exile in Utrecht (1684–88). Wrote several songs and ballads, of which two are extant.

Baillie, Joanna. 1762–1851. Scottish dramatist and poet. From youth, lived in London. Author of *Fugitive Verses* (1790), a series of *Plays on the Passions* (1798, 1802, 1812), three volumes of dramas (1836). Her play *De Montfort* was produced (1800) by Kemble and Mrs. Siddons; *The Family Legend* (1810) was most successful. Her brother ¶Matthew (1761–1823) was a physician; author of *Morbid Anatomy of Some of the Most Important Parts of the Human Body* (1793), first systematic treatise on pathology.

Baillie, Robert. 1599–1662. Scottish clergyman. Member of Glasgow Assembly (1638); chaplain of Covenanting army (1639); professor of divinity, Glasgow U. (1642); sent to Westminster Assembly (1643); principal, Glasgow U. (1661).

Baillie, Robert. *Known as* Baillie of Jerviswood. c.1634–1684. Scottish nationalist leader. Active in struggle to free Scottish Presbyterian church from Anglican domination; in London (1683) met with duke of Monmouth and Lord William Russell, who subsequently implicated him in Rye House plot against Charles II; hanged, drawn, and quartered in Edinburgh.

Bail·lot \bȧ-yō\, Pierre-Marie-François de Sales \sȧl\. 1771–1842. French violinist. Toured Europe and Russia; led orchestra of Paris Opéra (1821–31); composed orchestral and chamber works for violin. Author of *Méthode de violon* (with Rode and Kreutzer, 1803), *L'Art du violon* (1834).

Bail·lou \bȧ-yü\ *or* **Bail·lon** \bȧ-yō^{n}\, Guillaume de. *Lat.* Bal·lo·ni·us \bə-'lō-nē-əs\. 1538–1616. French physician. Dean of medical faculty, U. of Paris (from 1580); physician to dauphin; revived Hippocratic medical practice in France. Described whooping cough (1578), gave modern definition of rheumatism; pioneer in epidemiology in *Epidemiorum* (1640), survey of epidemics 1570–79.

Bail·ly \bȧ-yē\, Jean-Sylvain. 1736–1793. French astronomer and politician. Computed orbit for Halley's Comet, studied Jupiter's major satellites; author of histories of ancient, modern, and East Indian astronomy. President of Third Estate in Estates-General (1789); president of National Assembly (1789); led proceedings in Tennis Court (June 20, 1789); first mayor of Paris (1789); imposed martial law and called out National Guard to keep order, leading to massacre of Champ de Mars; retired (1791); guillotined.

Bai·ly \bā-lē\, Edward Hodges. 1788–1867. English sculptor. Established reputation with *Eve at the Fountain* (1818); executed figures on Marble Arch, and statue of Nelson in Trafalgar Square, London.

Baily, Francis. 1774–1844. English astronomer. Made fortune on stock exchange and retired from business (1825). A founder of Royal Astronomical Society (1820); revised several star catalogues and improved *Nautical Almanac;* first to describe fully (1836) the phenomenon called Baily's beads observed during total eclipse of sun. Author of *Account of the Rev. John Flamsteed* (1835) and works on life annuities.

Bain, Alexander. 1818–1903. Scottish philosopher and psychologist. Secretary, London board of health (1848–50); examiner in logic and moral philosophy, U. of London (1857–62); member of the circle including Grote and J. S. Mill; professor, U. of Aberdeen (1860–80). Known for his application to psychology of the findings of physiology and for elevating standard of education in Scotland. Author of *The Senses and the Intellect* (1855), *Emotions and the Will* (1859), *Mental and Moral Science* (1868), *Logic* (1870), *Mind and Body* (1872), *Education as a Science* (1879), biographies of James and J. S. Mill (1882), and works on grammar and rhetoric; edited Grote's minor works (1873); founded the periodical *Mind* (1876).

Bain·bridge \'bān-brij\, John. 1582–1643. English astronomer. Professor, Oxford (1619–43); known esp. for studies of comets. Author of *Astronomical Description of the Comet of 1618* (1619) and *Antiprognosticon* (1642), in which he denounced superstitious view of comets as omens of disaster.

Bainbridge, William. 1774–1833. American naval officer, b. Princeton, N.J. Captain (1800); imprisoned after loss of *Philadelphia* in Tripoli harbor (1803); commanded *Constitution* in victory over *Java* (1812).

Baines \'bānz\, Thomas. 1822–1875. English artist, naturalist, explorer. To Cape Colony (1842); official artist in Eighth Frontier War (1850–53); took part in expeditions to northern Australia (1855), up the Zambezi with Livingstone (1858), to Victoria Falls (1861); explored goldfields in Matabeleland (1868). Author and illustrator of *Explorations in South-West Africa* (1864).

Ba·i·ni \bä-'ē-nē\, Giuseppe Giacobbe Baldassarre. 1775–1844. Italian clergyman and composer. Musical director of Sistine Chapel, Vatican (1819 ff.); composed a *Miserere* (1821) still used in Sistine Chapel; wrote *Memorie storico-critiche della vita e delle opere di Giovanni Pierluigi da Palestrina* (1828).

Bain·ville \ba^{n}-vēl\, Jacques. 1879–1936. French publicist and historian. Joined royalist movement; associated with royalist journals *Gazette de France* and *L'Action Française.* Author of *La République de Bismarck* (1905), *Histoire de deux peuples* (1915), *Les Consequences politiques de la paix* (1920), *Histoire de France* (1920), *Napoléon* (1931), *Les Dictateurs* (1935), *La Troisième République 1870–1935* (1935).

Baird \'ba(ə)rd, 'be(ə)rd\, Cora, *nee* Ei·sen·berg \'īz-ᵊn-,bərg\. 1912–1967. American puppeteer, b. New York City. m. (1937) William B. Baird. With husband led revival of puppet theater in U.S.; appeared in films, on television in such programs as "Life with Snarky Parker" (1950), "Bil Baird Show" (1953),

"Art Carney Meets Peter and the Wolf" (1958, lyrics by Ogden Nash); toured successfully; opened Bil Baird Theatre, N.Y.C. (1967).

Baird, Sir David. 1757–1829. Scottish soldier. Served as captain in India; prisoner there (1780–84); returned to last war against Tippu (1791–99); served in campaigns in Egypt (1801–02), Cape of Good Hope (1805–06), Copenhagen (1807); second in command in Spain (1808); baronet (1810); general (1814). Commander in chief in Ireland (1820–22).

Baird, John Logie. 1888–1946. Scottish inventor. Produced first televised picture of moving objects (1926); developed color television (1928); helped BBC begin experimental television service (1929); his system later replaced (1937) by a rival. Experimented with stereoscopic television.

Baird, John Lawrence. 1st Baron Stone·ha·ven \'stōn-,hā-vən\. 1874–1941. British diplomat and politician. In diplomatic service (from 1896); M.P. (1910–25); minister of transport (1922–24); governor general of Australia (1925–30).

Baird, Spencer Fullerton. 1823–1887. American zoologist, b. Reading, Pa. Asst. secretary (1850–78), secretary (1878 ff.), Smithsonian Institution, Washington, D.C. First U.S. commissioner of fish and fisheries (1871 ff.). Works included *Catalogue of North American Mammals* (1857), *Catalogue of North American Birds* (1858), *A History of North American Birds* (with T.M. Brewer and R. Ridgway, 1874).

Bairns·fa·ther \'ba(ə)rnz-,fäth-ər, 'be(ə)rnz-\, Bruce, *in full* Charles Bruce. 1888–1959. English soldier and cartoonist, b. India. Served in France (from 1914); captain (1915); transferred to war office (1916) for work abroad. Creator of famous "Old Bill" cartoons, orig. for *Bystander* (from 1915). Published several collections of cartoons; wrote play *The Better 'Ole* (1917).

Baius, Michael. See Michel de BAY.

Baj, Tommaso. See BAI.

Bajazet. See BAYEZID.

Baj·er \'bī-ər\, Fredrik. 1837–1922. Danish politician and writer. Member of Folketing (1872–95); worked for women's emancipation, Scandinavian cooperation, peace; founder of Danish Peace Society (1882); a founder (1891) and president (1891–1907), International Peace Bureau, Bern. Author of *The Scandinavian Neutrality System* (1906) and other works on neutrality. Co-winner (with Klas Arnoldson) of 1908 Nobel peace prize.

Bā·jī Rāo \'bä-jē-'rä-u\. Name of two Marāthā peshwas:

Bājī Rāo I. d. 1740. Second peshwa (1720–40). Son of Bālājī Vishvanāth. Organized his nation against Muslim powers in north; came to terms with his southern rival, the Nizām of Hyderābād (1731); conquered Gujarāt, Mālwa, and Bundelkhand, and (1737) threatened Delhi; made league with Rājputs against Mughals (1739).

Bājī Rāo II. d. 1852. Seventh and last peshwa (1796–1818). Son of Raghunath Rāo. Opposed by Holkar dynasty; forced to seek aid from British, signed Treaty of Bassein (1802); after Second Marāthā War (1802–04) in which other Marāthā houses were defeated, retained rule at Poona as British subsidiary; later, in Third Marāthā War (1817–18), defeated by British; retired as pensioner at Bithur.

Bajus, Michael. See Michel de BAY.

Baj·za \'bī-zä\, József. 1804–1858. Hungarian journalist and poet. Contributed to and succeeded Kisfaludy as editor (1830–37) of literary journal *Aurora;* director of National Theater at Pest (1837).

Ba·ker \'bā-kər\, Augustine, *orig.* David. 1575–1641. Welsh religious. Entered Benedictine order (1605); spiritual director of English Benedictine nuns at Cambrai (1624–33). Author of numerous treatises on asceticism, mystic theology, etc., many collected as *Sancta Sophia* (1657); also wrote *Holy Practices* (1657).

Baker, Sir Benjamin. 1840–1907. English civil engineer. In association with Sir John Fowler (from 1862; partner from 1875) planned underground railways of London (1869 ff.), designed bridge over Firth of Forth (1882–90); consulting engineer (1898–1902) on construction of Aswan and Asyut dams, Egypt; Hudson River tunnel, New York (1888–91), etc. Designed vessel that transported Cleopatra's Needle from Egypt to England (1877).

Baker, George. *Known as* Father Divine. 1877–1965. American religious leader, b. near Savannah, Ga. Began preaching (c.1900); to New York City (c.1915); founded Peace Mission movement (1919), communal religious society with branches in other cities.

Baker, George. 1915–1975. American cartoonist, b. Lowell, Mass. In U.S. army in World War II, attached to *Yank* magazine (1942–45); created "Sad Sack" character, representing the beleaguered enlisted man; continued "Sad Sack" cartoons in civilian life.

Baker, George Fisher. 1840–1931. American financier, b. Troy, N.Y. A founder (1863), president (from 1877), board chairman (from 1909), First National Bank, New York City. Endowed Harvard's Graduate School of Business Administration.

Baker, George Pierce. 1866–1935. American educator, b. Providence, R.I. Taught English at Harvard (1888–1924; professor from 1905); made reputation as teacher of dramatic composition in his course in play writing (English 47) and its associated 47 Workshop; students included O'Neill, Sidney Howard, George Abbott, Thomas Wolfe, Philip Barry, S.N. Behrman. Professor and director of the university theater, Yale (1925–35). Author of *The Development of Shakespeare as a Dramatist* (1907), *Dramatic Technique* (1919).

Baker, Henry. 1698–1774. English naturalist. Invented a system of instruction for deaf-mutes. Conducted, with his father-in-law, Daniel Defoe, *Universal Spectator and Weekly Journal* (1728–31). Received Copley gold medal (1744) for microscopical experiments on saline particles.

Baker, Sir Herbert. 1862–1946. English architect. Designed Groote Schuur for Cecil Rhodes, Government House and Union buildings for South African government at Pretoria, cathedrals at Capetown, Pretoria, and Salisbury in Rhodesia. With Sir E.L. Lutyens designed New Delhi, India (1912 ff.). Designed Rhodes House at Oxford, Bank of England buildings, India House at Aldwych, and Winchester College war memorial.

Baker, Josephine. *Orig.* Freda Josephine Mc·Don·ald \mək-'dän-ᵊld\. 1906–1975. American entertainer, b. St. Louis. Starred in *Shuffle Along* (1923), *Chocolate Dandies* (1924) on Broadway; sensation in Paris in *La Revue Nègre* (1925) and at Théâtre des Champs-Élysées; renowned for jazz singing and dancing, exotic costumes, and extravagant gestures; naturalized French citizen (1937); worked with Resistance in World War II.

Baker, Newton Diehl. 1871–1937. American lawyer and politician, b. Martinsburg, W. Va. City solicitor (1902–12) and mayor (1912–16), Cleveland. U.S. secretary of war (1916–21). Member, Permanent Court of Arbitration at The Hague (1928).

Baker, Ray Stannard. *Pseudonym* David Gray·son \'grā-sən\. 1870–1946. American journalist and author, b. Lansing, Mich. On staff of Chicago *Record* (1892–97), *McClure's Magazine* (1897–1905); with Lincoln Steffens, Ida M. Tarbell, W.A. White, etc. founded and co-edited (1906–15) *American Magazine;* director of press bureau for American Commission to Negotiate Peace, Paris (1919). Authorized biographer of Woodrow Wilson. Author of *Seen in Germany* (1901), *Following the Color Line* (1908), *The Spiritual Unrest* (1910), *Woodrow Wilson—Life and Letters* (1927–39, Pulitzer prize), the autobiographical *Native American* (1941), and, under pseudonym, *Adventures in Contentment* (1907), *Adventures in Friendship* (1910), *Adventures in Understanding* (1925), *Adventures in Solitude* (1931).

Baker, Sir Richard. c.1568–1645. English writer. M.P. (1593, 1597); imprisoned for debt (c.1635–45). Author of a widely used *Chronicle of the Kings of England* from Roman period to 1625 (1643).

Baker, Sir Samuel White. 1821–1893. English explorer. Founded agricultural colony in Ceylon (1848); supervised construction of railway from Danube to Black Sea (1859–60); explored Nile tributaries in Abyssinia (1861–62); discovered Lake Albert (1864); as governor general of equatorial regions of Nile on appointment by Ismā'īl Pasha, viceroy of Egypt, took steps to suppress slave trade and establish administration (1869–73). Author of *The Rifle and the Hound in Ceylon* (1854), *Nile Tributaries of Abyssinia* (1867), *Ismailia* (1874), *Wild Beasts and Their Ways* (1890), etc. His younger brother ¶Valentine (1827–1887), *known as* Baker Pa·sha \pä-'shä\, served in Kaffir War (1852–53) and Crimean War (1854–56); in sultan's service in Russo-Turkish War (1877–78); in Egyptian service and commander of police (1882–87); defeated (1884) by Osman Digna near Suakin; author of *Clouds in the East* (1876), *War in Bulgaria* (1879).

Baker, Sara Josephine. 1873–1945. American pediatrician, b. Poughkeepsie, N.Y. Director, Division of Child Hygiene, New York City (1908–23); organized first bureau of child hygiene under government control and thus aided in establishing in New York City lowest infant mortality rate of any large city. Author of *Healthy Mothers* (1920), *Healthy Babies* (1920), *Child Hygiene* (1925), *Fighting for Life* (1939), etc.

Baker, Valentine. See under Sir Samuel White BAKER.

Bake·well \'bāk-,wel, -wəl\, Robert. 1725–1795. English agriculturist. A pioneer in practice of systematic inbreeding; produced Leicestershire breed of sheep and Dishley, or New Leicestershire Longhorn, breed of cattle; first to establish on a large scale the letting of rams for breeding.

Bakht Khan \'bäkt-'kän\. c.1797–1859. Indian soldier and rebel. Served in army of British East India Co.; joined Indian or Sepoy Mutiny (1857), occupied Delhi, emerging as dominant figure in rebel government; driven from Delhi (1857); killed in battle.

Bak·hui·zen van den Brink \'bäk-,hœi-zən-vän-dən-'briŋk\, Reinier Cornelis. 1810–1865. Dutch historian and writer. Coeditor of *De Gids* (1837–43); government archivist (from 1854). Author of *Studien en schetsen over vaderlandsche geschiedenis en letteren* (1860 ff.).

Bakhuysen, Ludolf. See BACKHUYSEN.

Bâ·kî \'bäk-ē\. *Arab.* Bā·qī \'bäk-ē\. *More completely* Mahmud Abdülbâkî. 1526–1600. Turkish poet. Gained favor of Sultan Süleyman I with panegyric ode (1555); known esp. for lyrics, whose fresh vitality rejuvenated Turkish lyric poetry and won him title of "king of poets."

Bakin. See TAKIZAWA.

Bakst \'bäkst\, Léon. *Orig.* Lev Samoylovich Ro•sen•berg \'rō-zən-,berk\. 1866–1924. Russian artist. Painted religious, genre, portrait works, in St. Petersburg and Moscow; tutor to children of Grand Duke Vladimir; took up stage design (1900) at Hermitage court theater; in Paris (1908 ff.) achieved fame as scenic designer for Diaghilev's ballet productions; later designed sets for works of D'Annunzio, for Pavlova, for Paris Opéra, etc.

Ba•ku•nin \(,)bə-'kün-yin\, Mikhail Aleksandrovich. 1814–1876. Russian anarchist and writer. Served in Russian army (to 1835); traveled in Germany, France, and Switzerland (1841–47). Refused to return to Russia at government's demand and lost his property and passport (1842); in Paris associated with Proudhon, Marx, Herzen, etc.; active in European revolutionary movements (1848–49); arrested for participation in Dresden insurrection (1849); held in Austria but handed over (1851) to Czarist government; sent to eastern Siberia (1857); escaped, returning to Europe via Japan and U.S. (1861). Leading anarchist in Europe (1861–76); expelled (1872) by Marx from First International for his militant views; organized many secret revolutionary societies, esp. among Slavic groups. Author of *Appeal to the Slavs* (1848), *The Knouto-Germanic Empire* (1871), *State and Anarchy* (1873), etc.

Ba•lā•dhu•rī, al- \al-bä-'la-thü-'rē\. *In full* Aḥmad ibn Yaḥyā al-Balādhurī. d. c.892. Arab historian. Author of *Futūḥ al-buldān,* history of formation of the Arab Muslim empire, and *Ansāb al-ashrāf,* on Arab aristocracy.

Ba•la•guer \bäl-ä-'ger\, Victor. 1824–1901. Spanish poet and politician. A leader in developing Catalan nationalism; wrote poetic works in Catalan, esp. *Lo trobador de Montserrat* (1850), *Oda á la Verge de Montserrat* (1857); restored Juegos Florales festival (1859). Author of *Historia de Cataluña* (1860). Member of revolutionary council of Barcelona (1868); elected to national cortes (1869); minister of colonies (1871), of finance (1872).

Bā•lā•jī \'bäl-äj-ē\. Name of two Marāthā peshwas:

Bālājī Vis•va•nāth \-'vis-və-,nät\. d. 1720. Peshwa (1714–20). Became actual head of Marāthā confederacy, as nominal ruler Shāhū lost power; first ruling peshwa; marched to Delhi to support usurpers (1718); secured imperial grant of revenues of the Deccan (1720); succeeded by his son Bājī Rāo I.

Bālājī Rāo \-'raü\. c.1721–1761. Third peshwa (1740–61). Son of Bājī Rāo I; strengthened the confederacy, making Poona the capital (1750); ruled during zenith of Marāthā power; renewed invasion of upper India (1758–59); crushed in great battle at Pānīpat (1761) by Afghans under Aḥmad Shāh Abdālī.

Ba•la•ki•rev \(,)bə-'läk-yir-yif\, Mily Alekseyevich. 1837–1910. Russian composer. After early career as concert pianist turned to composition; with disciples Cui, Mussorgsky, Rimsky-Korsakov, Borodin formed "The Five"; cofounder (1862) of the Free School of Music at St. Petersburg; director (1883–94) of Imperial Capella. Composer of symphonic poems *Rus'* (1887), *Tamara* (1867–82), symphonies, music for *King Lear* (1856–61), piano fantasy *Islamey* (1869) and much other piano music; published Russian folk songs.

Ba•lard \bä-lär\, Antoine-Jérôme. 1802–1876. French chemist. Professor, Sorbonne (1842–51), Collège de France (1851 ff.); discoverer of bromine (1826); devised process for extracting sodium sulphate from sea water.

Bal•an•chine \,bal-ən-'shēn, 'bal-ən-,\, George. *Orig.* Georgy Melitonovich Bal•lan•chi•vadze \bä-,län-chi-'vädzə\. 1904–1983. American choreographer, b. St. Petersburg, Russia. Studied at the Imperial School of Ballet (later the Soviet State School of Ballet); joined Sergey Diaghilev's Ballets Russes in Paris as ballet master (1924); to U.S. (1933); co-founded School of American Ballet (1934) and American Ballet Company (1935); choreographed four movies and 19 Broadway musicals, including *On Your Toes* (1936); co-founded New York City Ballet (1948), serving as artistic director. Created over 200 ballets, including *Apollo* (1928), *The Prodigal Son* (1929), *Serenade* (1935), *The Four Temperaments* (1946), *The Nutcracker* (1954), *Agon* (1957), *Square Dance* (1957), *Don Quixote* (1965). Hailed as the century's greatest choreographer, whose plotless, streamlined, neoclassical ballets revolutionized dance in U.S.

Ba•lāsh \bə-'läsh\ *or* **Va•lākhsh** \və-'läksh\. 5th century A.D. King of Iran (484–488) of Sāsānian dynasty. Succeeded brother Fīrūz I; reign troubled by rebellions and invading nomads; deposed and succeeded by Kavadh I.

Ba•las•si \'bäl-äsh-ē\ *or* **Ba•las•sa** \-ä\, Bálint. Baron. 1554–1594. Hungarian lyric poet. A soldier and adventurer; author of patriotic and martial poems, love lyrics, religious hymns, and adaptations from Latin and German literature.

Bal•ban \'bəl-bən\. *In full* Ghiyās-ud-Dīn Balban. d. 1287. Next-to-last sultan of Slave Dynasty of Delhi (1266–87). Able general and minister (1246–66) of sultan Naṣīr-ud-Dīn Maḥmūd; campaigned against Rājputs. Warred with Mongols, wild tribes of India, and Rājputs; crushed revolt in Bengal.

Bal•bi \'bäl-bē\, Adriano. 1782–1848. Italian geographer. Author of *Atlas ethnographique du globe* (1826), *Abrégé de géographie* (1832).

Bal•bi•nus \bal-'bī-nəs\, Decimus Caelius Calvinus. d. 238 A.D. Roman emperor (238). Salian priest under Commodus; consul and proconsul of Asia under Septimius Serverus; again consul (213). Chosen co-emperor with Pupienus Maximus (238) in Senate's revolt against Maximinus; quarrelled with Maximus; murdered with him by praetorian guard.

Bal•bo \'bäl-bō\, Cesare. Conte di Vi•na•dio \dē-vē-'näd-yō\. 1789–1853. Italian politician and writer. In Piedmontese army (until 1821); accused of complicity in revolution of 1821; fled to France (to 1826). Associated with Cavour in founding of Risorgimento. Appointed first premier of Piedmont-Sardinia (1848). His works included *Storia d'Italia sotto ai Barbari* (1830), *Vita di Dante* (1839), *Meditazioni storiche* (1842), *Delle speranze d'Italia* (1844), *Lettere di politica e letteratura edite ed inedite* (1847).

Balbo, Italo. 1896–1940. Italian aviator and politician. Led Fascist Blackshirt militia in march on Rome (1922); general of national militia (1923); first minister of aviation (1929–33). Commanded mass transatlantic flights to Brazil (1929) and U.S. (1933). Promoted air marshal (1933); governor of Libya (1933). Shot down, apparently by mistake, by Italian guns in Tobruk harbor.

Balboa, Vasco Núñez de. See NÚÑEZ DE BALBOA.

Bal•bue•na \bäl-'bwā-nä\, Bernardo de. c.1562–1627. Spanish poet and prelate. Lived in Mexico, Spain, and West Indies; bishop of Puerto Rico (1620–27). Author of epic on national hero Bernardo del Carpio, *El Bernardo o la victoria de Roncesvalles* (1624); also of epic *La grandeza mejicana* (1604).

Bal•bus \'bal-bəs\, Lucius Cornelius. *Called* Major. 1st century B.C. Roman politician, b. Gades (Cádiz). Admitted to Roman citizenship by Pompey for services in Spain against rebel Quintus Sertorius; aided in forming 1st triumvirate (60 B.C.); accompanied Caesar to Spain (61) and Gaul (58). Acquitted (56) of charge of illegally exercising citizenship rights. Secretary to Caesar (46–44); praetor (43 or 42); first provincial to serve as consul (40).

Balcarres, Earls of. See LINDSAY family.

Balch \'bölch\, Emily Greene. 1867–1961. American economist and sociologist, b. Jamaica Plain, Mass. Taught (1896–1918), professor (1913), Wellesley Coll.; a founder and international secretary (1919–22, 1934–35), Women's International League for Peace and Freedom. Shared with John R. Mott 1946 Nobel prize for peace. Author of *Outline of Economics* (1899), *Our Slavic Fellow-Citizens* (1910), *Approaches to the Great Settlement* (1918), *Refugees as Assets* (1939), *Toward Human Unity* (1952).

Bal•chin \'bol-chin\, Nigel Martin. 1908–1970. English writer. Author of novels notable for psychological insight as *The Small Back Room* (1943), *Mine Own Executioner* (1945), *A Sort of Traitors* (1949), *The Fall of a Sparrow* (1955).

Bal•con \'bol-kən\, Sir Michael. 1896–1977. English film producer. Founded (1928) Gainsborough Pictures; director (1931) of Gaumont-British Picture Corp.; producer with MGM (1936–38); executive producer (1938–59) of Ealing Films, Ltd.; produced *Passport to Pimlico* (1949), *Kind Hearts and Coronets* (1949), *Whisky Galore* (1949), *Lavender Hill Mob* (1951).

Bal•der•ston \'bol-dər-stən\, John Lloyd. 1889–1954. American playwright, b. Philadelphia. Collaborator in writing *Dracula* (1927), *Frankenstein* (1931), etc., and scenarios for motion pictures *Lives of a Bengal Lancer, Berkeley Square, Prisoner of Zenda, Gone With the Wind, Gaslight,* etc.

Bal•di•nuc•ci \,bäl-dē-'nüt-chē\, Filippo. c.1624–1696. Florentine art historian. Author of first history of copper engraving, first lexicon of technical terms, and (pub. 1681–1728) *Notizie dei professor del disegno da Cimabue in qua.*

Bal•do•mir \bäl-dō-'mēr\, Alfredo. 1884–1948. Uruguayan soldier and politician. Minister of national defense, with rank of general (1935); president of Uruguay (1938–43); instituted new constitution (1942).

Bal•do•vi•net•ti \,bäl-dō-vē-'nāt-tē\, Alesso *or* Alessio. 1425?–1499. Florentine painter. Known esp. for his frescoes in Santa Trinità, Florence, Pisa Cathedral, SS. Annunziata, Florence, etc.; canvases included *Marriage at Cana, Madonna and Child, Nativity;* contributed to development of landscape depiction.

Bal•dung \'bäl-düŋ\, Hans. *Called* Hans Grien \'grēn\ *or* Grün \'grue̅n\. c.1484–1545. German painter, engraver, and designer. Assistant to Dürer (1503–06). Works included an altarpiece and stained glass windows for Freiburg Cathedral (1512–16); paintings as *Tod und die Frau* (1517), *Geburt Christi* (1520); woodcuts, tapestry designs, portraits.

Bald•win \'bol-dwən\. *Fr.* Bau•douin \bō-dwaⁿ\. Name of two emperors of Constantinople:

Baldwin I. 1172-1205. Emperor (1204–05). Son of Baldwin V, Count of Hainaut; count of Flanders as Baldwin IX and of Hainaut as Baldwin VI (1195–1205). A leader of the Fourth Crusade (1200–04); took part in capture of Constantinople by crusaders (1203) and in installation of Emperor Alexius IV Angelus; on fall of Alexius (1204) elected first Latin emperor. Beaten by Greeks and Bulgarians under Kaloyan at Adrianople (1205); captured and slain.

Baldwin II. 1217–1273. Emperor (1228–61). Nephew of Baldwin I and son of Peter of Courtenay; succeeded brother Robert (1228); reigned under regency of John of Brienne during minority (1228–37). Kingdom greatly reduced by incursions of Greeks and Bulgars; to finance defense of

Constantinople sold holy relics of Byzantium to Louis IX of France; driven out of Constantinople by Michael VIII Palaeologus (1261).

Baldwin. *Fr.* Baudouin. Name of nine counts of Flanders and six of Hainaut, including:

Baldwin I. *Called* Bras de Fer \brà-də-fer\, *i.e.* Iron Arm. d. 879. m. Judith, sister of Charles the Bald, who created him first count of Flanders (862).

Baldwin II. d. 918. Count of Flanders (879–918).

Baldwin V. *Called* le Pieux \le-pyœ̄\, *i.e.* the Pious. d. 1067. Count of Flanders (1030–67). m. Adélaïde, daughter of Robert II of France; regent (1060–66) for Philip I; married his daughter Mahaut or Mathilde to William of Normandy, whom he accompanied to England (1066).

Baldwin VI. d. 1070. Count of Flanders (1067–70). m. (1055) Richilde, countess of Hainaut. His son ¶Baldwin II (d. 1098), count of Hainaut (1070–98), was deprived of countship of Flanders by Robert le Frison; died on First Crusade.

Baldwin IV. 1099–1171. Count of Hainaut (1120–71). Attempted to regain Flanders after death (1127) of Count Charles the Good.

Baldwin V. 1150-1195. Count of Hainaut (1171– 95). m. Marguerite, sister of Count Philip of Flanders; on death of Philip (1191) became count of Flanders as Baldwin VIII. For their son Baldwin VI of Hainaut, IX of Flanders, see BALDWIN I of Constantinople.

Baldwin. *Fr.* Baudouin. Name of five kings of Jerusalem, belonging to family of counts of Flanders:

Baldwin I. *Known also as* Baldwin of Boulogne. 1058?–1118. King (1100–18). Son of Eustace II, count of Boulogne, and brother of Godfrey of Bouillon; accompanied Godfrey on First Crusade (1096–99); took Edessa (1098); elected by nobles to succeed Godfrey (1100); increased Latin kingdom by taking Acre (1104), and other coastal cities; built Krak de Montréal (1115).

Baldwin II. *Known as* Baldwin du Bourg \dūē-bür(k)\. d. 1131. King (1118–31). Cousin of Baldwin I; took part in First Crusade (1096–99); named by Baldwin I count of Edessa (1100–18); captured by Turks on way to aid Edessa (1123); released (1124); left his kingdom greatly enlarged to his son-in-law Fulk V of Anjou (see ANJOU).

Baldwin III. 1131–1162. King (1143-62). Grandson of Baldwin II and son of Fulk V of Anjou; Second Crusade in his reign (1147–49); captured Ascalon (1153), lost Damascus (1154).

Baldwin IV. 1161–1185. King (1174–85). Called the "Leper king." Son of Amalric I; reigned (1174–77) under regency of Raymond III, Count of Tripoli; reign marked by encirclement of Jerusalem by Saladin; crowned nephew Baldwin V (1183) in order to fix succession.

Baldwin V. 1177–1186. King (1185–86). Associated on throne with uncle Baldwin IV (1183); ruled under regency of Raymond III of Tripoli.

Baldwin. *Fr.* Baudouin. Count of Luxembourg. d. 1354. French prelate and politician. Bishop of Trier (1307); largely responsible for election of brother Henry as Holy Roman emperor (1308).

Baldwin, Abraham. 1754–1807. American politician, b. North Guilford, Conn. To Georgia (1783); a founder of U. of Georgia, orig. Franklin Coll. Member, Congress of the Confederation (1785), U.S. House of Representatives (1790–99), U.S. Senate (1799–1807).

Baldwin, Frank Stephen. 1838–1925. American inventor, b. New Hartford, Conn. Invented calculator called arithmometer (1875); developed Baldwin computing engine (1890), Baldwin calculator (1902); in association with J.R. Monroe perfected Monroe calculator (1912).

Baldwin, Henry. 1780–1844. American jurist, b. New Haven, Conn. Member (from Pennsylvania), U.S. House of Representatives (1817–22). Associate justice, U.S. Supreme Court (1830–44).

Baldwin, James Mark. 1861–1934. American psychologist, b. Columbia, S.C. Professor, U. of Toronto (1889–93), Princeton (1893–1903), Johns Hopkins (1903–09), National U. of Mexico (1909–13), École des Hautes Études, Paris (1918–19). Specialist in child psychology and social psychology. Founder with J. M. Cattell and editor (1894–1909), *Psychological Review.* Author of *Handbook of Psychology* (1889–91), *Mental Development in the Child and the Race* (1895), *Genetic Logic* (1906–11); editor of *Dictionary of Philosophy and Psychology* (1901–06).

Baldwin, Loammi. 1745–1807. American engineer, b. North Woburn, Mass. Built Middlesex Canal (1794–1804); first grower of Baldwin apples. His son ¶Loammi (1780–1838) was also a civil engineer; constructor of dry docks at the Charlestown (Mass.) and Norfolk (Va.) navy yards; built Union Canal, Pa.; designed Bunker Hill Monument, Boston.

Baldwin, Matthias William. 1795–1866. American industrialist, b. Elizabethtown, N.J. Manufactured stationary steam engines (from 1827) and locomotives (from 1831). Formed M.W. Baldwin Co., now the Baldwin Locomotive Works.

Baldwin, Robert. 1804–1858. Canadian politician, b. York (Toronto). Member of legislature of Upper Canada (1829–30); executive council (1836, 1840); solicitor general (1840). With L.H. Lafontaine formed first Liberal ministry (1842–43); with Lafontaine formed second Liberal government (1848–51).

Baldwin, Roger Nash. 1884–1981. American reformer, b. Wellesley, Mass. Secretary, Civic League of St. Louis (1910–17); founder (1920), director (1920–50), American Civil Liberties Union.

Baldwin, Stanley. 1st Earl Baldwin of Bewd·ley \'byüd-lē\. 1867–1947. English politician. Headed family heavy industries; M.P. (1908–37); financial secretary to treasury (1917–21); president, Board of Trade (1921–22); as chancellor of exchequer (1922–23), arranged with aid of Montagu Norman funding of British debt to U.S. (1922). Conservative prime minister and first lord of the treasury (1923–24, 1924–29, 1935–37); proclaimed state of emergency during general strike (1926); secured passage of Trade Disputes Act (1927); secured peaceful abdication of Edward VIII (1936); lord president of the council (1931–35). Created earl (1937). Author of *Classics and the Plain Man* (1926), *This Torch of Freedom* (1935), *Service of Our Lives* (1937).

Bale \'bā(ə)l\, John. 1495–1563. English prelate and author. Carmelite until becoming Protestant (c.1533); in exile (1540–48); bishop of Ossory (1548); prebendary of Canterbury Cathedral (1560). Author of controversial works in Protestant cause, of a Latin history of English literature, and of *Kynge Johan,* considered the first English historical play.

Ba·len \'bä-lən\, Hendrick van. 1575–1632. Flemish painter. First master of van Dyck. His works included altarpieces, historical scenes.

Ba·len·cia·ga \bäl-en-'thyäg-ä\, Cristóbal. 1895–1972. Spanish couturier. Successful in Spain (1915–37), Paris (1937–68); known esp. for elegant ball gowns.

Bales \'bā(ə)lz\, Peter. *Lat.* Ba·le·si·us \bə-'lē-sē-əs\. 1547–c.1610. English calligrapher. Famed for microscopic writing; employed by Sir Francis Walsingham for skill in imitating handwriting; opened school of penmanship (1590). Author of *Writing Schoolmaster* (1590), *Arte of Brachygraphie* which introduced one of earliest forms of shorthand (1590).

Ba·le·wa \bä-'lā-wä\, Sir Abubakar Tafawa. 1912–1966. Nigerian politician. Member of Northern House of Assembly (1946), federal Assembly (1951–66); minister of works (1952–54), transport (1954–57); first prime minister of Nigeria (1957–66); guided Nigeria to independence (1961); killed in military coup.

Balfe \'balf\, Michael William. 1808–1870. Irish composer and singer. Appeared as Figaro in Rossini's *Barbiere di Siviglia* in Paris (1827); produced his first opera, *I rivali di se stessi,* at Palermo (1829), his first in England being *Siege of Rochelle* (1835). Sang Papageno in first English production of *Magic Flute* (1838). Other operas included *Maid of Artois* (1836); *Falstaff* (1838); *The Bohemian Girl,* including the well known song "I dreamt I dwelt in marble halls" (1843); *The Sicilian Bride* (1852); and *Rose of Castille* (1857).

Bal·four \'bal-fər, -ˌfōr, -ˌfȯr\, Arthur James. 1st Earl of Balfour. 1848–1930. British politician. Conservative M.P. (1874–1911); one of so-called "Fourth party" (1880). To Berlin Congress (1878) as secretary to uncle Lord Salisbury; president, Local Government Board (1885–86); secretary for Scotland (1886–87); chief secretary for Ireland (1887–91); first lord of the treasury (1891, 1895, 1900) and government leader in Commons (1891, 1895). Prime minister (1902–05); concluded Anglo–French entente (1904). Leader of opposition (1906–11). First lord of admiralty, succeeding Winston Churchill (1915–16), foreign secretary (1916–19); made Balfour Declaration (Nov. 1917) that British government favored establishment in Palestine of national home for Jewish people, without prejudice to civil and religious rights of existing non-Jewish communities; attended Paris Peace Conference as foreign secretary; leading British delegate to Washington Disarmament Conference (1921–22); lord president of the council (1919–22, 1925–29). Created earl (1922). Author of *A Defence of Philosophic Doubt* (1879), *Theism and Humanism* (1915), *Theism and Thought* (1923).

Balfour, Francis Maitland. 1851–1882. British zoologist. Brother of A. J. Balfour. At Naples zoological station (1873–76); lecturer (1876–82), first professor of animal morphology (1882), Cambridge. Author of *Treatise on Comparative Embryology* (1880–81), first comprehensive text in field.

Balfour of Pit·ten·dreich \'pit-ᵊn-ˌdrīk\, Sir James. c.1525–1583. Scottish jurist. A follower of John Knox; implicated in assassination of Cardinal David Beaton (1546); taken prisoner with Knox by French at St. Andrews Castle (1547); freed on renouncing Protestantism (1549); shifted allegiance several more times, serving Mary of Lorraine, Mary Stuart in turn; probably helped arrange murder of Darnley (1567); deserted Mary and Bothwell; lord president of Court of Session (1567); testified against James Douglas, Earl of Morton (1581).

Balfour, Robert. 1550–after 1625. Scottish philosopher. Driven from Scotland by Reformation; taught Latin and Greek at U. of Paris, Collège de Guyenne. Author of a volume of commentaries on Aristotle (1618–20), a translation of Gelasius, etc.

Bal·iol *or* **Bal·liol** \'bāl-yəl\. Anglo-Norman family founded by Guido *or* Guy, holder of Ballieul and other fiefs in Normandy, and including: ¶John de Baliol

(d. 1269); great-great-grandson of Guido; regent for minor Alexander III (1251–55); founder of Balliol College, Oxford, by gift of lands (c.1263) and by gifts in his will and from his widow Devorguila. His son ¶John de Baliol (1249–1315) claimed Scottish throne on death (1290) of Margaret, Maid of Norway, by right of his maternal grandmother, daughter of David, Earl of Huntington, grandson of David I; claim allowed over rivals Robert Bruce and John Hastings by Edward I of England, whose overlordship was acknowledged; crowned at Scone (1292); rebelled against English overlordship; made alliance with Philip IV of France; brought to submission and forced to resign crown by Edward (1296); died in exile in Normandy. His son ¶Edward de Baliol (d. 1364) invaded Scotland (1332) with aid of Edward III of England and barons disinherited by Robert Bruce; defeated Earl of Mar, regent for David II, at Dupplin Moor; crowned king (1332); defeated by Sir Archibald Douglas at Annan, but returned (1333) and defeated Douglas and supporters of David II at Halidon Hill; unseated by Scottish patriots (1334); restored to throne by Edward III, but his hold on power continued precarious; surrendered kingdom to Edward III (1356).

Ball \ˈbȯl\, Albert. 1896–1917. English airman. Ace pilot in Royal Flying Corps; destroyed 43 enemy planes during World War I.

Ball, Sir Alexander John. 1757–1809. British naval officer. Took part in Sir George Rodney's victory in West Indies (1782); captain (1783); served in Mediterranean under Nelson; saved Nelson's flagship *Vanguard* (1798); engaged at Abukir Bay (1798) and in reduction of Malta (1798–1800); governor of Malta (1802–09); rear admiral (1805).

Ball, Frances. *Known as* Mother Frances Mary Theresa. 1794–1861. English religious. Entered (1814) Institute of Blessed Virgin Mary; established (1822) as Irish branch of Institute the Loretto, or Loreto, nuns, also called Ladies of Loretto; order spread to England, India, Canada, and the United States.

Ball \ˈbäl\, Hugo. 1886–1927. German writer. An actor, later one of founders of Dadaism. Author of *Kritik der deutschen Intelligenz* (1919), *Byzantinisches Christentum* (1923), *Die Folgen der Reformation* (1924), biography *Hermann Hesse* (1927), *Die Flucht aus der Zeit* (1927).

Ball \ˈbȯl\, John. d. 1381. English rebel. A priest, excommunicated (c.1366) for inflammatory sermons; a leader of Peasant Revolt (or Wat Tyler's Rebellion); hanged.

Ball, John. 1818–1889. Irish alpinist and politician. First president, Alpine Club (founded 1857); author of *Alpine Guide* (1863–68). Undersecretary for colonies (1855–57).

Ball, John. 1861–1940. British golfer. Amateur champion a record eight times between 1888 and 1912; first amateur to win open championship (1890) and to win both amateur and open championships in one year (1890).

Ball, Thomas. 1819–1911. American sculptor, b. Charlestown, Mass. Chief works included a life-size bust of Daniel Webster, busts of Rufus Choate, William H. Prescott, and Henry Ward Beecher; equestrian statue of George Washington (Public Garden, Boston); statue of St. John the Evangelist (1875); *Emancipation,* a group with Lincoln and a kneeling slave (1875); and statues of Daniel Webster (1876, Central Park, New York), Sumner (1878, Public Garden, Boston), Josiah Quincy (1879, Boston).

Bal·la \ˈbäl-lä\, Giacomo. 1871–1958. Italian artist. Early a Pointillist; under influence of Marinetti evolved Futurist doctrine of painting; an author of "Technical Manifesto of Futurist Painting" (1910). Works included *Street Light, Dynamism of a Dog on a Leash, Swifts.*

Bal·lance \ˈbal-ən(t)s\, John. 1839–1893. New Zealand politician, b. Ireland. To New Zealand (1865); served in Maori war (1867); M.P. (1875–93); colonial treasurer (1878–79); minister of lands and native affairs (1884–87); leader of Liberal opposition (1889–91); as prime minister (1891–93) imposed progressive land tax and progressive income tax and carried out other reform measures.

Bal·lanche \bá-läⁿsh\, Pierre-Simon. 1776–1847. French philosopher. Member of salon of Mme. Récamier; influenced Romantics with views on religion, sentiment. Author of *Du sentiment considéré dans ses rapports avec la littérature et les arts* (1801), *Essai sur les institutions sociales* (1814), *L'Homme sans nom* (1820), etc.

Bal·lan·tine \ˈbal-ən-ˌtīn\, William. 1812–1887. English lawyer. Prosecuted murderer Franz Müller (1864); led case for Tichborne Claimant (1871); defended gaekwar of Baroda (1875).

Bal·lan·tyne \ˈbal-ən-ˌtīn\, James. 1772–1833. Scottish printer. Proprietor and editor of *Kelso Mail* (1796–1802); moved to Edinburgh and published Walter Scott's works (1802 ff.); with brother John (1774–1821), associated with Walter Scott in printing and publishing (from 1808) until ruined by bankruptcy of Constable and Co. (1826); thereafter editor of *Weekly Journal.*

Ballantyne, John. See John BELLENDEN.

Ballantyne, Robert Michael. 1825–1894. Scottish writer. Nephew of James Ballantyne. Author of books for young people, beginning with *Hudson's Bay* (1848), based upon his service with Hudson's Bay Co. (1841–48) and including *Snowflakes and Sunbeams, or, The Young Fur Traders* (1855), *Ungava* (1857), *The Coral Island* (1858), *The Gorilla Hunters* (1862), *The Life Boat* (1864), *Deep Down* (1868), *Black Ivory* (1873), etc.

Bal·lard \bá-lár\. Family of French music printers who virtually monopolized the business (1560–1750), including: Robert (d. 1588), cousin of Adrian Le Roy; received patent from Henry II (1553); printed from movable type cut by Guillaume Le Bé. Robert's son ¶Pierre (d. 1639) continued business, receiving new patent from Louis XIII (1633); published Mersenne's *Harmonie universelle.* Pierre's son ¶Robert II (d. 1673) was succeeded at head of firm by Robert II's son ¶Christophe (1641–1715), under whom operas of Lully, Destouches, Desmarets, etc. were published. His son ¶Jean-Baptiste-Christophe (1663–1750) published Couperin, Charpentier, Delalande, Philidor, Rameau. After his death firm no longer had monopoly but continued under Jean's son ¶Christophe-Jean-François (d. 1765) and his son ¶Pierre-Robert-Christophe (d. 1812) to 1788.

Ballenden, John. See BELLENDEN.

Bal·lin \ˈbäl-ēn\, Albert. 1857–1918. German shipowner. Associated with Hamburg-American Steamship Line as director of passenger traffic (1886) and director general (from 1899); close adviser of William II; sought to rationalize North Atlantic shipping; worked for Anglo-German cooperation.

Bal·lin·ger \ˈbal-in-jər\, Richard Achilles. 1858–1922. American lawyer, b. Boonesboro, Iowa. U.S. secretary of interior under Taft (1909–11). Became center of attack by conservation group headed by Gifford Pinchot; accused by a subordinate of impeding investigation of certain coal land claims in Alaska; controversy investigated by Congress; cleared by investigating committee; resigned.

Balliol. See BALIOL.

Bal·li·vián \bä-yēb̠-ˈyän\, José. 1805–1852. Bolivian general and politician. Took part in campaign for independence from Spain and in war with Peru (1835–36); defeated new Peruvian invasion at Ingaví (1841). President of Bolivia (1841–47). His son ¶Adolfo (1831–1874) was a soldier, statesman, and diplomat; president of Bolivia (1873–74).

Ballon, Jean. See BALON.

Ballot, C. H. D. Buys. See BUYS BALLOT.

Bal·lou \bə-ˈlü\, Adin. 1803–1890. American clergyman, b. Cumberland, R.I. Founder (1841) and president (1841–52) of a Utopian community, Hopedale Community, Milford, Mass.; after its dissolution (1856), remained (to 1880) as pastor of Hopedale (Unitarian) Parish. Author of *Practical Christian Socialism* (1854), *Primitive Christianity and Its Corruptions* (1870).

Ballou, Hosea. 1771–1852. American clergyman, b. Richmond, N.H. One of early leaders of Universalism in U.S. Editor of *Universalist Magazine* (1819–28), *Universalist Expositor* (1830–40). Author of *Treatise on Atonement* (1805).

Bal·lu·et d'·Es·tour·nelles \bá-lu̅e-e-dā-tu̇r-nel\, Paul-Henri-Benjamin. *Full surname* Balluet d'Estournelles de Constant de Rebecque. *Known as* Paul d'Estournelles de Constant. 1852–1924. French politician and diplomat. Member of Chamber of Deputies (1895–1904), of Senate (from 1904); French delegate to The Hague conferences (1899, 1907); worked ceaselessly for international cooperation and peace, esp. through Hague Court of Arbitration; awarded, with A. Beernaert, Nobel prize for peace (1909). Author of *La Conciliation internationale* (1906), *Le Rapprochement franco-allemand* (1909), *Pour la Société des Nations* (1921).

Bal·ma·ce·da \bäl-mä-ˈsā-t̠h̠ä\, José Manuel. 1840–1891. Chilean politician. Deputy in congress (from 1870); minister to Argentina (1878–81); minister of foreign affairs (1881–86). President of Chile (1886–91); conflict with congress led to civil war (1891) in which he was defeated; committed suicide.

Bal·mer \ˈbäl-mər\, Johann Jakob. 1825–1898. Swiss mathematician and physicist. Discoverer of Balmer's formula (1885) which yielded wavelengths of main spectral lines of hydrogen (Balmer series).

Balmerino, Barons. See ELPHINSTONE family.

Bal·mes \ˈbäl-mās\, Jaime Luciano. 1810–1848. Spanish philosopher. Ordained priest (1834); professor of mathematics at Vich (1836–40); edited various periodicals, including *La sociedad;* founded (1844) *El pensamiento de la nación.* Author of *El protestantismo comparado con el catolicismo en sus relaciones con la civilización Europea* (1842–44), *El criterio* (1845), *Filosofía fundamental* (1846), *Curso de filosofía elemental* (1847), etc.

Bal·mont \ˈbálʸ-mənt\, Konstantin Dmitriyevich. 1867–1943. Russian Symbolist poet. Traveled widely; resident in Paris (after 1918). Translator of many English and other writers into Russian, esp. Shelley. Verse included *Pod severnym nebom* (1894), *V bezbrezhnosti* (1895), *Tishina* (1898), *Goryashchie zdanya* (1900), *Budem, kak solntse* (1903).

Bal·nav·es \bal-ˈnav-əs\, Henry. c.1512–1579. Scottish politician. Lord of session under James V (1538); secretary of state under Arran regency (1543);

imprisoned on account of his Protestantism (1543–44); captured with John Knox at St. Andrews (1547); in prison in Rouen wrote *Confession of Faith* (1548). Returned to Scotland (1557); lord of session (1564).

Ba·lo·dis \'bäl-ō-dis\, Janis. 1881–1965. Latvian soldier and politician. Served in Russian army (1902–18); commander in chief of Latvian army (1919–25); directed war of liberation against Germany and Russia. Member of Latvian parliament (1925–40); minister of war (1931); deputy prime minister (1934–36); vice president of Latvia under Ulmanis (1936–40). Deported by occupying Soviet force (1940).

Ba·lon *or* **Bal·lon** \bá-lōⁿ\, Jean. 1676–1739. French ballet dancer. Member of Paris Académie, forerunner of Paris Opéra (from 1691); noted for extraordinary leaps, hence term "ballon."

Bal·sa·mon \'bȯl-sə-,mȯn\, Theodore. c.1105–c.1195. Byzantine legal scholar and prelate. While law chancellor to patriarch of Constantinople wrote commentary (c.1170) on nomocanon which helped preserve early Byzantine records; patriarch of Antioch (c.1185–95).

Bal·ta \'bäl-tä\, José. 1814–1872. Peruvian soldier and politician. One of leaders in revolution that deposed Prado (1868); president of Peru (1868–72); murdered in army mutiny following his attempt to annul results of new election.

Bal·tard \bál-tár\, Victor. 1805–1874. French architect. Best known as architect of Halles Centrales, huge iron and glass structure housing general market of Paris; also built church of Saint-Augustin; appointed architect (1853) of Hôtel de Ville.

Baltimore, Baron. See George CALVERT.

Ba·lue \bá-lü̅\, Jean. c.1421–1491. French prelate and politician. Patronized by Louis XI, who appointed him almoner; bishop of Evreux (1464); cardinal (1467); intrigued with Charles the Bold and imprisoned (1469–80).

Ba·luze \bá-lü̅z\, Étienne. 1630–1718. French historian. Secretary to archbishop of Toulouse (1654–62), to bishop of Auch (1662–67); librarian to Jean-Baptiste Colbert (1667–1700); professor (1670–1708), director (1707–08), Collège Royal. Author of *Concilia Galliae Narbonensis* (1668), *Capitularia regum Francorum* (1677), *Vitae Paparum Avenionensium* (1693); exiled (1708) for making use of forgeries in a genealogy of Cardinal de Bouillon.

Bal·zac \bál-zák, *Angl* 'bȯl-,zak, 'bal-,\, Honoré de. *Orig. family name* Bal·sa \bál-sá\. 1799–1850. French novelist. To Paris (1818); studied law for three years; worked as editor, printer, typefounder, etc., while writing under various pseudonyms and in collaboration with others; achieved first success (1829) with *Le Dernier chouan,* a tale of Brittany in 1799 and anonymous *La Physiologie du mariage.* Associate of Hugo, Vigny, Lamartine, and George Sand; m. (1850) Madame Eveline Hanska, Polish lady and owner of estates in Russia. Considered greatest novelist of France and founder of the realistic novel; through his novels (with their more than 2000 characters from all phases of contemporary life) sought to demonstrate molding effect of social environment on raw material of human personality; conceived plan of presenting comprehensive picture of contemporary French society under general title *La Comédie humaine* (first series pub. 1842; pub. posthumously in 47 vols.), comprising *Études philosophiques, Études analytiques,* and *Études de moeurs,* last including such subdivisions as "Scènes de la vie privée," "Scènes de la vie de province," "Scènes de la vie parisienne," "Scènes de la vie militaire." Among individual works were *La Maison du chat-qui-pelote* (1830), *La Vendetta* (1830), *Gobseck* (1830), *Un Épisode sous la Terreur* (1830), *La Peau de chagrin* (1831), *Le Colonel Chabert* (1832), *Louis Lambert* (1832), *Eugénie Grandet* (1833), *La Recherche de l'absolu* (1834), *Le Père Goriot* (1834), *La Fille aux yeux d'or* (1835), *Le Lis dans la vallée* (1835), *L'Enfant maudit* (1836), *Illusions perdues* (trilogy, 1837–43), *Le Curé de village* (1839), *Une ténébreuse affaire* (1841), *Un Début dans la vie* (1842), *La fausse maîtresse* (1842), *Splendeurs et misères des courtisanes* (1839–47), *Modeste Mignon* (1844), *Les Paysans* (1845), *L'Envers de l'histoire contemporaine* (1842–48), *La Cousine Bette* (1846), *Le Cousin Pons* (1847), plays, as *Mercadet* (1838) and *Vautrin* (1840), and *Contes drolatiques* (1832–37).

Balzac, Jean-Louis Guez de \gez-də\. 1597–1654. French writer. Regarded as a master of classic French prose style; original member of Académie Française (1634). Author of *Lettres* (1624), *Le Prince* (1631), *Discours* (1644), *Le Barbon* (1648), *Le Socrate chrétien* (1652), *L'Aristippe* (1658).

Ba Maw \'bäm-'aü\. 1893–1977. Burmese politician. Lawyer; opposed, then (from 1934) supported separation of Burma from India; Burmese minister of education (1934). Formed Sinyetha Wunthann (Proletarian) party (1936); first prime minister of separate Burma (1937–39). Imprisoned (1940–42); head of state under Japanese occupation (1942–44). Later headed Mahabamma (Great Burma) party.

Bam·ber·ger \'bäm-,ber-gər\, Ludwig. 1823–1899. German politician and economist. Implicated in Revolution of 1848 as editor of radical *Mainzer Zeitung;* participated in republican uprising in Palatinate; forced to live in exile; banker, Paris (1853–66). Returned to Germany after amnesty (1866); member of Reichstag (1871–93); helped found Reichsbank; defended gold standard; opposed doctrinaire socialism and Bismarck's protectionist policy. Leader of secessionists from National Liberal party (1880); cofounder of German Liberal party (1884). Author of *Erlebnisse aus der Pfälzischen Erhebung* (1849), *Monsieur de Bismarck* (1868), *Die Fünf Milliarden* (1873), *Erinnerungen* (1899), etc.

Bamboccio, Il. See Pieter van LAER.

Bam·ford \'bam-fərd\, Samuel. 1788–1872. English reformer and poet. Author of verses in support of working class as *The Weaver Boy* (1819), *Homely Rhymes* (1843); also wrote *Passages in the Life of a Radical* (1840–44), *Early Days* (1849), etc.

Bamp·ton \'bam(p)-tən\, John. 1690?–1751. English clergyman. Endowed Bampton lectures, 8 divinity sermons delivered annually (from 1779; since 1895 every other year) at Oxford.

Bā·ṇa \'bän-ə\ *or* **Bā·na·bhaṭ·ṭa** \'bän-əb-hət-tə\. 7th century A.D. Sanskrit author. Resident at court of Emperor Harṣa. Wrote lyric poems, dramas, and romances, esp. *Kādambarī,* relating the fortunes of a princess of that name, and *Harṣacarita* (i.e. Deeds of Harṣa), an account of Harṣa's reign.

Ba·nach \'bá-näk\, Stefan. 1892–1945. Polish mathematician. Lecturer at Institute of Technology, Lvov (1919–22), U. of Lvov (1922–27); professor (1927–45). Developed modern functional analysis and theory of topological vector spaces; wrote *Théorie des opérations linéaires* (1932), etc.

Banbury, Earl of. See William KNOLLYS.

Ban·ces y Lo·pez-Can·da·mo \'bän-thā-sē-'lō-pāth-kän-'däm-ō\, Francisco Antonio de. 1662–1704. Spanish dramatic poet. Successor to Calderón de la Barca as official poet. Works included *El esclavo en grillos de oro, El duelo contra su dama, Por su rey y por su dama.*

Ban·chie·ri \bäy-'kye-rē\, Adriano, *orig.* Tomaso. 1568–1634. Italian composer. Monk and abbot (from 1620), San Michele, Bosco. Composer of church music, symphonies, and esp. dramatic pieces in madrigal style, forerunners of opera; author of works on organ playing and on counterpoint; founded Accademia de' Floridi, Bologna.

Banco, Nanni di. See NANNI DI BANCO.

Ban·croft \'baŋ-,krȯft, 'ban-\, Edward. 1744–1821. American scientist and secret agent, b. Westfield, Mass. Settled in Dutch Guiana; author of *Natural History of Guiana* (1769). Settled in England; discovered important dyes for use in textile manufacture. During American Revolution, served as secret agent for American commissioners in Paris; alleged also to have sold information on American affairs to British government.

Bancroft, George. 1800–1891. American historian, b. Worcester, Mass. Teacher (1822–31); publication of first three volumes (1834–40) of his *History of the United States* brought public recognition; appointed (1837) collector of the port, Boston; U.S. secretary of the navy (1845–46); established United States Naval Academy, Annapolis. U.S. minister to Great Britain (1846–49). Supported Lincoln through Civil War; wrote Andrew Johnson's first annual message as president (1865). U.S. minister to Germany (1867–74). Published seven more volumes of *History* (1852–74); also *Literary and Historical Miscellanies* (1855), *History of the Formation of the Constitution of the United States* (1882).

Bancroft, Hubert Howe. 1832–1918. American historian, b. Granville, Ohio. To California (1852); began (1859) collecting historical materials; assembled library and staff and edited and published 39-volume *History of the Pacific States of North America* (1875–90).

Bancroft, Richard. 1544–1610. English prelate. Leader of Anglicans; sponsored canons against Puritanism among clergy. Bishop of London (1597); archbishop of Canterbury (1604).

Bancroft, Sir Squire. *Orig. surname* Butterfield. 1841–1926. English actor and theatrical manager. London debut (1865); m. (1867) Marie Effie Wilton; managed jointly with wife Prince of Wales's Theatre, London (1867–79), producing and acting in plays of T. W. Robertson as a specialty; also produced Bulwer-Lytton's *Money,* Boucicault's *London Assurance,* etc.; rebuilt and managed Haymarket Theatre (1880–85). Credited with greatly raising production standards.

Bancroft, Wilder Dwight. 1867–1953. American chemist, b. Middletown, R.I. Taught physical chemistry at Cornell (1895–1937). Founder and editor (1896–1932), *Journal of Physical Chemistry.* Author of *The Phase Rule* (1897), *Applied Colloid Chemistry* (1932), etc.

Ban·da·ra·nai·ke \,bən-də-rə-'nī-kə\, Solomon West Ridgeway Dias. 1899–1959. Ceylonese politician. Member of State Council (1931–47), House of Representatives (1947–59); minister of health and local government (1947–51); left ruling United National party (1951), formed nationalist Sri Lanka Freedom party (1952); formed nationalist-socialist coalition Mahajana Eksath Peramuna (1956); prime minister (1956–59); established Sinhalese as official language; maintained neutralist foreign policy; assassinated.

Ban·dā Singh Ba·hā·dur \bən-'dä-siŋ-bə-'hä-dür\. *Also known as* Lachman Dās \'läk-mən-'däs\, Lachman Dev \-'dev\, *or* Madho Dās \'mäd-hō-'däs\. 1670–1716. Sikh military leader. Led (1709) first Sikh offensive campaign against Mughal empire; pillaged the Deccan; captured in fall of Gurdas Nangol (1715); tortured to death.

Bandeira, Bernardo de Sá da. See SÁ DA BANDEIRA.

Ban·dei·ra \bäⁿ(n)-'dā-rä\, Manuel. *In full* Manuel Carneiro de Sousa Bandeira Fi·lho \-'fēl-yü\. 1886–1968. Brazilian poet, translator, educator. With verse in *A Cinza das horas* (1917), *Carnaval* (1919), emerged as leader of Modernist movement in South America; subsequent volumes included *Oritmo dissoluto* (1924), *Libertinagem* (1930), *Estrêla da manhã* (1936), *Lira dos cincuent'anos* (1940), *Flauta de papel* (1956).

Ban·del \'bän-dəl\, Ernst von. 1800–1876. German sculptor. Known esp. for colossal statue (unveiled 1875) of the national hero Arminius (near Detmold).

Ban·de·lier \,ban-də-'li(ə)r\, Adolph Francis Alphonse. 1840–1914. American explorer and archeologist, b. Bern, Switzerland. To U.S. (1848); published (1877–79) studies of Aztecs; undertook field research in New Mexico and Arizona (1880–89) and in Peru and Bolivia (1892–1903). On staff of Museum of Natural History, N.Y. (1904–11). Author of monographs on Pueblo and South American Indians, esp. *Islands of Titicaca and Koati* (1910).

Ban·del·lo \bän-'del-lō\, Matteo. 1485–1561. Italian monk, soldier, and writer. Tutor of Lucrezia Gonzaga (Mantua, 1515–21). Lived at Milan (1521–25) until its fall to Spanish forced him to flee to France; bishop of Agen (1550). Author of *Rime* (1537) and *Lodi* (1545), both in honor of Lucrezia; known esp. for his *Novelle,* 214 stories in 4 volumes (1554–73). The novelle were translated into French and English; they provided source material for several Shakespearean and other Elizabethan plays and for Lope de Vega, Byron, and others.

Ban·die·ra \bän-'dyer-ä\, Attilio (1810–1844) and his brother Emilio (1819–1844). Italian patriots. Sons of Italian admiral in Austrian navy; served also in navy; attempted to spark revolt against Austrian rule in Kingdom of Naples (1844); betrayed, captured, executed.

Ban·di·nel·li \,bän-dē-'nel-lē\, Baccio *or* Bartolommeo. *Orig. surname* de' Bran·di·ni \,dā-brän-'dē-nē\. 1493?–1560. Florentine sculptor. Patronized by Cosimo I de' Medici; exponent of Mannerist style; works included *Hercules and Cacus, Adam and Eve* and bas-reliefs in choir of cathedral of Florence.

Ban·do \bän-dō\ Mitsugoro VIII. *Orig.* Mo·ri·ta \mō-rē-tä\ Toshirō. 1906–1975. Japanese actor. Son of Mitsugoro VII; debut on Kabuki stage under name Yasosuke (1912); succeeded to professional name Bando Minosuke VI (1928) at Meijiza Theater; gained fame in Osanai Kaoru Troupe, Toho Company, Kansai Shochiku Company; headmaster of Bando School of Dance; succeeded to father's professional name; designated National Living Treasure (1973).

Ban·du·la \bən-'dü-lə\, Maha. d. 1825. Burmese general. Under King Bagyidaw, commanded conquest of Assam (1821); made governor of Assam; led invasion of Arakan (1824); invaded Bengal, but forced to withdraw by British landing at Rangoon; attempted to encircle British; killed in British capture of Danubyu.

Ba·nér \bá-'nār\, Johan. 1596–1641. Swedish general. In Thirty Years' War served under Gustavus Adolphus against Russia and Poland; commander of right wing, Breitenfeld (1631); commander, Swedish forces in south Germany (1632); field marshal (1634); gained victories at Wittstock (1636) and Chemnitz (1639).

Ba·ner·jea \'bá-nȯr-jē\, Sir Surendranath. 1848–1925. Indian politician. Founded (1876) Indian Association in Bengal; editor, *The Bengalee* (1879–1919); twice president, Indian National Congress. Founded Ripon College, Calcutta (1882). Member of Bengali and imperial legislative councils (1913–24); minister of local self-government (1921–24). A founder of Indian nationalism.

Bang \'báŋ\, Bernhard Lauritz Frederik. 1848–1932. Danish veterinarian. Originated (1892) method of eradicating tuberculosis from dairy herds; discovered bacterium of infectious abortion, or Bang's disease (1897).

Bang, Hermann Joachim. 1857–1912. Danish writer. Author of Impressionist novels dealing esp. with lonely and unsuccessful people: *Håbløse slaegter* (1880), *Stuk* (1887), *Tine* (1889), *Ludvigsbakke* (1896), *Det grå hus* (1901), *Mikael* (1904), *De uden faedreland* (1906), etc.

Bang Klang Thao \'bäŋ-'kläŋ-'taü\. *Also spelled* Bang Klang T'ao. *Known as* Srī In·dra·dit·ya \,in-drə-'dēt-yə\ *or* In·dra·pa·tin·dra·dit·ya \,in-drə-,pät-,in-drə-'dēt-yə\. fl. 1220–1250. Thai chieftain. With Pha Muong, expelled Khmers from Sukhothai (c.1238) and established first independent Thai kingdom.

Bangs \'baŋz\, John Kendrick. 1862–1922. American humorist, b. Yonkers, N.Y. Humor editor, *Harper's Magazine* (1888–99); editor, *Harper's Weekly* (1899–1907). Author of *Tiddledywink Tales* (1891), *Coffee and Repartee* (1893), *The Idiot* (1895), *A House-boat on the Styx* (1896), and lectures, as *The Evolution of a Humorist, From Adam to Ade, Salubrities I Have Met.*

Ba·nim \'bā-nəm\, John. 1798–1842. Irish poet, playwright, and novelist. His blank verse tragedy *Damon and Pythias* produced (1821) at Covent Garden. Author, in conjunction with his brother ¶Michael (1796–1874), of series of *Tales of the O'Hara Family* (1825–26), depicting somber side of Irish peasant life. John also wrote *The Boyne Water* (1826), *The Denounced* (1830), and *The Smuggler* (1831). Michael also wrote *The Croppy* (1828), *Father Connell* (1842), *Clough Fion* (1852), *Town of the Cascades* (1864).

Ban·is·ter \'ban-ə-stər\, John. c.1625–1679. English musician and composer. Violinist in King's band (1660); leader of court violinists; gave public concerts, first in England (1672 ff.). Composed songs for plays of Dryden, Wycherley, Shadwell, etc.

Bankes \'baŋ(k)s\, Sir John. 1589–1644. English jurist. Attorney general (1634–40); chief justice of common pleas (1640–44). His wife ¶Lady Mary Bankes, *nee* Haw·trey \'hȯ-trē\ (d. 1661), won renown for heroic defense of Corfe Castle, Dorset, against Parliamentary forces (1643, 1645).

Bank·head \'baŋk-,hed\, Tallulah Brockman. 1903–1968. American actress. b. Huntsville, Ala. Daughter of W.B. Bankhead. Broadway debut in *Squab Farm* (1918); appeared in *The Green Hat* (London, 1925), *They Knew What They Wanted* (London, 1926), *Rain* (1935), *Little Foxes* (1939), *The Skin of Our Teeth* (1942), *Foolish Notions* (1945), *Private Lives* (1948), etc., and films *Lifeboat* (1944), *A Royal Scandal* (1945), etc.

Bankhead, William Brockman. 1874–1940. American politician, b. Moscow, Ala. Member U.S. House of Representatives (1917–40; speaker 1936–40).

Banks \'baŋks\, Isabella, *nee* Var·ley \'vär-lē\. *Known as* Mrs. Linnaeus Banks. 1821–1897. English novelist. m. (1846) George Linnaeus Banks, whom she assisted in editing various journals. Author of *God's Providence House* (1865), *The Manchester Man* (1873), *Caleb Booth's Clerk* (1878), *Forbidden to Marry* (1883), etc.

Banks, Sir Joseph. 1743–1820. English naturalist. Accompanied Cook's expedition round the world in the *Endeavour,* equipped by himself (1768–71); visited Hebrides and Iceland (1772). President of Royal Society (1778–1820). Aided settlement in New South Wales. His library and collections now in British Museum.

Banks, Nathaniel Prentiss. 1816–1894. American politician and army officer, b. Waltham, Mass. Member of Congress (1853–57), speaker (1854–57); governor of Massachusetts (1858–61). Served through Civil War as major general; commander of Department of the Gulf (1862–65); captured Port Hudson (1863). Again in Congress (1865–73, 1875–79, 1889–91).

Banks, Thomas. 1735–1805. English sculptor. Exponent of Neoclassicism; executed *Armed Neutrality* for Empress Catherine of Russia (1781) and sold to her *Cupid Catching a Butterfly;* other works included *Falling Titan, Rape of Proserpine, Thetis Comforting Achilles,* and *Shakespeare Attended by Painting and Poetry* in Stratford on Avon.

Ban·na·tyne \'ban-ə-,tīn\, George. 1545–?1608. Scottish anthologist. Compiled (1568) *Bannatyne Manuscript,* containing Scottish poetry of 15th and 16th centuries.

Bannatyne, John. See John BELLENDEN.

Ban·ne·ker \'ban-i-kər\, Benjamin. 1731–1806. American mathematician and astronomer, b. Ellicott, Md. Helped survey site of District of Columbia (1790); published almanac (1791–1802); defended intellectual equality of Negro in correspondence with Thomas Jefferson.

Bannerman, Sir Henry Campbell-. See CAMPBELL-BANNERMAN.

Ban·ting \'ban-tiŋ\, Sir Frederick Grant. 1891–1941. Canadian physician, b. Alliston, Ont. Working at U. of Toronto, under J.R.R. Macleod, on pancreatic secretions, discovered (with Charles H. Best) the hormone insulin (1921), specific remedy for diabetes. Awarded jointly with Macleod the 1923 Nobel prize for physiology or medicine, which was shared with Best and J.B. Collip for their part in discovery. Professor, U. of Toronto (1923–41).

Ban·tock \'ban-tək\, Sir Granville. 1868–1946. English composer. Operatic conductor (1896); director, School of Music, Birmingham and Midland Institute (1900); professor, Birmingham U. (1908–34); founder and editor (1893–96) *New Quarterly Music Review.* Prolific composer of operas as *The Pearl of Iran* (1894), symphonic poems, overtures, as well as a drama *Rameses II* (1891), choral works including *Omar Khayyam* (1906) and *Atalanta in Calydon* (1911).

Ban·vard \'ban-,värd\, John. 1815–1891. American painter and writer, b. New York City. Drifted down Mississippi in a flatboat (1840) painting scenes along the way for his *Panorama,* reputedly three miles long, exhibited throughout U.S. and in England. Painted *The Orison* (1861), from which first American chromolithograph was made.

Ban·ville \bäⁿ-vēl\, Théodore de, *in full* Étienne-Claude-Jean-Baptiste-Théodore-Faullain de. 1823–1891. French writer. Author of pieces for the theater, including *Les Fourberies de Nérine* (1864), *Diane au Bois* (1863), *Gringoire* (1866), *Riquet à la houppe* (1884). His volumes of verse included *Les Cariatides* (1842), *Les Stalactites* (1846), *Odes funambulesques* (1857),

Trente-six ballades joyeuses (1873), *Occidentales, Rimes dorées, Rondels* (1875), etc. In verse a leader of Parnassians, influenced Symbolists; revived old forms as ballade, rondeau. Also author of *Petit traité de poésie française* (1872), and tales, as *Contes héroiques* (1884) and *Contes bourgeois* (1885).

Ba·our Lor·mian \bá-ür-lór-myäⁿ\, Pierre-Marie-François-Louis. 1770–1854. French poet and playwright. Translated Tasso's *Gerusalemme Liberata* (1795), poems of Ossian (1801); wrote tragedies *Omasis* (1806) and *Mahomet II* (1810) and anti-Romantic essays *Le Classique et le Romantique* (1825), *Encore un mot* (1826).

Bap·tie \'bap-tē\, Norval. c.1879–1966. American athlete, b. Bathgate, N.D. World champion speed skater (1905–07); later starred in ice revues.

Bap·tiste \bá-tēst\. *Known as* Baptiste the Elder. *Orig.* Nicolas An·selme \äⁿ-selm\. 1761–1835. French actor. At Comédie-Française (1799–1828); a leading actor in sentimental comedy; associated esp. with Destouche's *Le Glorieux.*

Ba·que·ri·zo Mo·re·no \bä-kā-'rē-sō-mō-'rā-nō\, Alfredo. 1859–1951. Ecuadorian politician. President of Ecuador (1916–20); provisional president (1931–32).

Bar \bár\, François de. 1538–1606. French historiographer. Prior of Benedictine abbey of Anchin (from 1576); compiled historical documents and papers on ecclesiastical law from abbey library.

Bara \'bar-ə\, Theda. *Orig.* Theodosia Good·man \'gu̇d-mən\. 1885–1955. American actress, b. Cincinnati, Ohio. Aided by massive publicity, became sensation in silent films *A Fool There Was* (1915), *Cleopatra* (1917), *DuBarry* (1917), *Salome* (1918), etc.; created image of "vamp."

Baradai, Jacob. *Lat.* Jacobus Baradaeus. See Jacob BURD'ĀNĀ.

Ba·ra·guay d'Hil·liers \bá-rá-gā-dēl-yā\, Louis. 1764–1813. French general. Under Napoléon distinguished himself in Italy, Egypt, Spain and at Austerlitz. His son ¶Achille (1795–1878) fought in Spain, Algeria; lieutenant general (1843); commander of army of Paris under Louis Napoléon; senator and marshal of France (1854).

Ba·ra·ho·na de So·to \bär-ä-'kō-nä-thā-'sō-tō\, Luis. 1548?–1595. Spanish poet. Author of *Primera parte de la Angélica,* also called *Las lágrimas de Angélica* (1586), continuation of Ariosto's *Orlando furioso.*

Ba·rak·zāi \bə-rək-'zä-ē\. Ruling dynasty in Afghanistan (1826–1973), founded by Dōst Moḥammad Khān and including Shīr 'Alī Khān, Ya'qūb Khān, 'Abdor Raḥmān Khān, Ḥabībollāh Khān, 'Amānollāh Khān, Nāder Khān.

Ba·ra·naus·kas \,bä-rä-'nau̇s-käs\, Antanas. 1835–1902. Lithuanian prelate and writer. Professor, St. Petersburg (1865–67), Kaunas (1867–84); bishop of Seinai (1897). Author of poem *Anykščiu šilelis* (1858–59), considered one of greatest works in Lithuanian literature.

Ba·ra·nī \bə-rə-'nē\ *or* **Bar·ni** \'bär-nē\, Ẕiyā'-ud-Dīn. 1285–after 1357. Indian Muslim historian. Resident at court of Sultan Muḥammad ibn Tughlug; wrote *Tārīkh-e Fīrūz Shāhī* and *Fatawā-ye jahāndāri,* earliest known works of Muslim history of India.

Ba·ra·nov \(,)bə-'rá-nəf\, Aleksandr Andreyevich. 1746–1819. Russian fur trader. In Alaska 28 years (1790–1818); first governor of Russian America.

Barante, Baron de. See BRUGIÈRE.

Bá·rány \'bär-änʸ\, Robert. 1876–1936. Austrian physician. Taught at U. of Uppsala (1917–36). Investigated physiology and pathology of balancing apparatus in inner ear. Awarded 1914 Nobel prize for physiology or medicine.

Ba·rat \bá-rá\, Madeleine-Sophie. Saint. 1779–1865. French religious. Founded (1800) Society of the Sacred Heart of Jesus; superior of first house at Amiens (1802); superior general for life (1806). Canonized by Pope Pius XI (1925).

Ba·ra·tie·ri \,bär-ä-'tyer-ē\, Oreste. 1841–1901. Italian general. Served under Garibaldi in Sicily (1860); commander of Italian troops in Eritrea (1891); governor of Eritrea (1893); undertook campaign of conquest against Ethiopians; defeated decisively at battle of Adowa (1896); retired from army (1896); author of *Memorie d'Africa* (1897).

Ba·ra·tyn·sky *or* **Bo·ra·tyn·sky** \bə-(,)rə-'tin-skəi\, Yevgeny Abramovich. 1800–1844. Russian poet. In early life a soldier; author of elegant, melancholy philosophic verse including *Eda* (1826), *Bal* (1828), *Nalozhnitsa* (1831).

Bar·ba·ra \'bär-b(ə-)rə\. Saint. d. c.200 A.D. Christian virgin martyr. According to doubtful tradition, killed by her own pagan father for professing Christianity; one of 14 Holy Helpers; patron saint of artillerymen.

Bar·ba·ri \'bär-bär-ē\, Jacopo de'. *Known in Germany as* Jakob Walch \'välk\. 1440–1516. Venetian painter and engraver. Painter to Elector Frederick the Wise (1503–05); court painter at Brussels (from 1510) to Archduchess Margaret. Credited with first signed, dated (1504) pure still life; consulted by Dürer on copper engraving techniques.

Barbarossa. See FREDERICK I, Holy Roman Emperor.

Barbarossa. See KHAYR AD-DĪN.

Bar·bauld \'bär-,bō(ld)\, Anna Letitia, *nee* Ai·kin \'ā-kən\. 1743–1825. English author. m. Rev. Rochemont Barbauld (1774); with him conducted boys' boarding school in Suffolk (1774–85). Author of volumes of verse, anthologies, etc., and of *Hymns in Prose for Children.*

Barbellion, W. N. P. See Bruce Frederick CUMMINGS.

Bar·bé-Mar·bois \bár-bā-márb-wä\, François de. Marquis. 1745–1837. French politician. Intendant of Santo Domingo (1785–89); member of Council of Ancients (1795–97); exiled as monarchist (1797–99); as minister of finance under Napoléon (1801–06) negotiated sale of Louisiana to U.S. (1803). Created peer of France by Louis XVIII (1814), marquis (1817); became minister of justice (1815–16).

Bar·ber \'bär-bər\, Donn. 1871–1925. American architect, b. Washington, D.C. Works included National Park Bank, New York; Travelers Insurance Building, Aetna Life Insurance Building, and Supreme Court Building, Hartford, Conn.; Department of Justice Building, Washington, D.C.

Barber, Samuel. 1910–1981. American composer, b. West Chester, Pa. Works included setting of *Dover Beach* (1931), overture for *School for Scandal* (1933), *Music for a Scene from Shelley* (1935), *String Quartet* (1936, including the very popular "Adagio for Strings"), two *Essays for Orchestra* (1938, 1942), *First Symphony* (1936), *Second Symphony* (1942, commissioned by U.S. Army Air Forces), ballet *Medea* (1947), *Piano Sonata* (1949), opera *Vanessa* (1958, Pulitzer prize), *Andromache's Farewell* (1962), *Piano Concerto* (1962, Pulitzer prize), opera *Antony and Cleopatra* (1966).

Bar·be·ri \bär-'bā-rē\, Domenico. *Called* Dominic of the Mother of God. 1792–1849. Italian religious. Entered Passionist order (1814); ordained (1818); lecturer at Passionist college (1821–31); superior at Lucca (1831–33); provincial for southern Italy (1833); established first Passionist houses in Belgium (1840), in England (1841); received John Henry Newman into Catholic church (1845).

Bar·be·ri·ni \,bär-bā-'rē-nē\. Powerful Tuscan family, prominent in history of papacy in 17th century; rose to power in 16th century through commerce; excited jealousy of other noble families, esp. the Farnese; forced to flee to France after defeat by duke of Parma (1641–44); reestablished in Rome (1652). Prominent members included Maffeo (1568–1644), who became Pope Urban VIII (*q.v.*), and his nephews the three brothers ¶Francesco (1597–1679), cardinal (1623), papal secretary of state (1628), founder of Barberini Library, ¶Taddeo (1603–1647), commander of papal forces, prefect of Rome, prince of Palestrina (from 1631), and ¶Antonio (1607–1671), cardinal (1628), archbishop of Reims; high chamberlain to Urban VIII; patron of Bernini.

Barberino, Francesco da. See FRANCESCO DA BARBERINO.

Bar·bey d'Au·re·vil·ly \bár-bā-dór-vē-yē\, Jules-Amédée. 1808–1889. French writer. Literary critic succeeding Sainte-Beuve on *Le Constitutionnel* (1869–89); author of *Du dandyisme et de Georges Brummell* (1844), novels *Une vieille maîtresse* (1851), *L'Ensorcelée* (1854), *Le Chevalier des touches* (1864), *Un Prêtre marié* (1865), *Une Histoire sans nom* (1884), tales *Les Diaboliques* (1874), etc.

Bar·bier \bár-byā\, Antoine-Alexandre. 1765–1825. French bibliographer. Librarian to Directoire, to Conseil d'État, and (1807) to Napoléon; compiler of *Dictionnaire des ouvrages anonymes et pseudonymes* (1806–09); author of *Nouvelle bibliothèque d'un homme de goût* (1808–10).

Bar·bie·ri \bär-'byā-rē\, Giovanni Francesco. *Called* Il Guer·ci·no \,ēl-gwär-'chē-nō\, *i.e.* Squinting One. 1591–1666. Italian painter. Known for frescoes, esp. illusionistic ceiling *Aurora* in Casino Ludovisi, Rome (1621); other works included *Sta. Petronilla, Death of Dido,* fresco *Hercules and Antaeus* in Palazzo Sampieri, Bologna.

Bar·bi·rol·li \,bär-bə-'räl-ē, -'rō-lē\, Sir John, *orig.* Giovanni Battista. 1899–1970. British conductor. Violoncellist with International String Quartet (1924); guest conductor, Covent Garden (1929–33); conductor, Scottish Orchestra (1931–34); succeeded Toscanini as conductor of New York Philharmonic Orchestra (1936–42); conductor, Hallé Orchestra (1943–70), Houston Symphony (1961–67).

Bar·bon \'ba(ə)r-,bōn, 'be(ə)r-\, Nicholas. c.1640–1698. English economist. Probably son of Praise-God Barbon. First to institute fire insurance in England (c.1680); author of treatises on money.

Barbon, Praise-God. *Nicknamed* Bare·bone \'ba(ə)r-,bōn, 'be(ə)r-\ *or* Barebones \-,bōnz\. c.1596–?1680. English clergyman. Prosperous leather seller; preached to Independent congregation; summoned by Cromwell to sit for London in "Nominated Parliament" (1653), also called "Barebones Parliament"; opposed restoration of Charles II (1660); imprisoned in Tower (1661–62). It has been said, but without proof, that he had two brothers named (1) Christ-came-into-the-world-to-save Barebone and (2) If-Christ-had-not-died-thou-hadst-been-damned Barebone, the latter shortened to Damned Barebone.

Barbosa du Bocage, Manuel Maria. See BOCAGE.

Bar·bou \bár-bü\. Name of family of French printers, including: Jean (1490–1543), of Lyon, who printed (1539) a fine edition of works of Clément Marco. His son ¶Hugues (1538–1603), of Limoges, who printed (1580) an edition of Cicero's *Letters to Atticus.* ¶Jean-Joseph (1683–1752) established the firm in Paris. His nephew ¶Joseph-Gérard (1715–1813) printed (about 1750) a series of Latin classics.

Bar·bour \'bär-bər\, James. 1775–1842. American politician, b. Barboursville, Va. Governor of Virginia (1812–15); U.S. senator (1815–25); U.S. secretary of war (1825–28); U.S. minister to Great Britain (1828–29). His brother ¶Philip Pendleton (1783–1841), American jurist, b. Barboursville, Va., was member of Congress (1814–25, 1827–29); speaker (1821–23); president of Va. constitutional convention (1829–30); federal district judge (1830–36); associate justice of U.S. Supreme Court (1836–41).

Barbour *or* **Bar·bere** \'bär-bər\ *or* **Bar·bier** \'bärb-yər\, John. 1325?–1395. Scottish poet. Archdeacon of Aberdeen (by 1357). Author of the *Brus* (1376), titled more fully *The Actes and Life of the most Victorious Conqueror, Robert Bruce King of Scotland,* a national epic about Robert Bruce, the war of independence, and the battle of Bannockburn. *Legends of the Saints* and a translation *The Buik of Alexander* have been attributed to him.

Bar·busse \bar-bües\, Henri. 1873–1935. French editor and author. Served in World War I, from which he drew novel of trenches *Le Feu* (1916, Goncourt prize); among his other works were *Pleureuses* (poetry, 1895), the novels *Les Suppliants* (1903), *L'Enfer* (1908), *Clarté* (1919), and *Les Enchaînements* (1925), and political works *Lénine* (1934), *Staline* (1935).

Barca *or* **Barcas.** See HAMILCAR BARCA.

Bar·clay \'bär-klē, -(,)klā\, Alexander. c.1476–1552. British priest and poet, possibly of Scottish birth. Benedictine, later Franciscan, at Ely and Canterbury; rector of All Hallows, London (1552). Author of *The Ship of Fools* (*The Shyp of Folys,* 1509), part translation, part imitation, of Sebastian Brant's *Narrenschiff* (1494); also wrote *The Castell of Laboure, Egloges* (the first eclogues in English).

Barclay, Florence Louisa, *nee* Charles·worth \'chärlz-(,)wərth\. 1862–1921. English novelist. m. (1881) Rev. C. W. Barclay. Author of sentimental romances, including *The Rosary* (1909), *Mistress of Shenstone* (1910), *The Broken Halo* (1913), *White Ladies of Worcester* (1917).

Barclay, Sir George. fl. 1696. British conspirator. Instigator of assassination plot against King William III (1696).

Barclay, John. 1582–1621. Scottish satirical poet. Author of *Euphormionis Lusinini Satyricon* (1603–07), politico-satirical romance directed against Jesuits, medical profession, etc.; a supplement *Icon Animorum* (1614); *Argenis,* a Latin poem of adventure with allegory alluding to political faction and conspiracy (1621).

Barclay, John. 1734–1798. Scottish clergyman. Author of *Without Faith, Without God* (1769). Founded (1773) a sect called Church of the Berean Assembly, or Barclayites.

Barclay, Robert. 1648–1690. Scottish Quaker. Joined Society of Friends (1666); imprisoned several times; received, with William Penn and other Quakers, patent of East Jersey, and made nominal governor (1682–88). Author of *Theses Theologicae* (1675) and *Apology* (1678), standard exposition of Quaker tenets.

Barc·lay de Tol·ly \(,)bər-'klī-də-'tòl-yi\, Mikhail Bogdanovich. Prince. 1761–1818. Russian field marshal, of Scottish descent. Entered army (1786), serving in Turkish War (1788–89), against Sweden (1790), and Poland (1792, 1794); major general under Bennigsen at Pułtusk (1806); lieutenant general after Eylau (1807); commander in campaign against Swedes in Finland (1808–09); minister of war (1810–12); commander in chief of Army of the West (1812); his defeat at Smolensk forced him to yield command to Kutuzov, but his Fabian tactics, unpopular with Russians, finally brought about defeat of Napoléon; commanded right wing at Borodino (1812); after brilliant service at Bautzen (1813) again made commander in chief; took part in capture of Paris (1814) and promoted field marshal; commanded second invasion of France (1815); created prince (1815).

Bard \'bärd\, John. 1716–1799. American physician, b. Burlington, N.J. Introduced (1750, with Peter Middleton) systematic dissection of corpses for purposes of instruction. First to report a case of extrauterine fetus (1759). His son ¶Samuel (1742–1821), b. Philadelphia, was a physician to George Washington in New York after American Revolution and was instrumental in establishing first New York medical school and the New York hospital (1791). Samuel's son ¶William (1778–1853), b. Philadelphia, organized and headed New York Life Insurance and Trust Co. (1830–47).

Bar·de·sa·nes \,bärd-i-'sā-,nēz\ *or* **Bar·dai·san** \,bär-dī-'sän\. 154–c.222. Syrian Christian poet and theologian. Active in introducing Christianity into Edessa (from 179); blended Christian and Gnostic ideas; author of *Dialogue of Destiny, or Book of the Laws of the Countries,* oldest known composition in Syriac; wrote many hymns long used in Christian churches.

Bar·di \'bär-dē\, Giovanni. Conte del Ver·nio \dāl-'vern-yō\. 1534–1612. Italian scholar and music patron. Founded (c.1580) Florentine Camerata, group including Giulio Caccini, Jacopo Peri, Emilio del Cavaliere, Vincenzo Galilei, Ottavio Rinuccini, which played major role in evolution of opera; author of theoretical work on musical drama *Discorso mandato a Caccini sopra la Musica Antica* (1580). Chamberlain to Pope Clement VIII (1592).

Bar·di·ya \'bär-dē-(y)ə\. *Known by Greek name used by Herodotus* Smer·dis \'smərd-əs\. 6th century B.C. Persian noble. Son of Cyrus the Great; according to Darius, murdered by brother Cambyses and later successfully impersonated by Gaumata, a Magian, who seized throne (522 B.C.) and was killed by Darius; believed by many scholars, following Aeschylus, to have lived to seize throne from absent Cambyses (522) and be killed by Darius.

Bard·sley \'bärdz-lē\, Warren. 1884–1954. Australian cricketer. Member of Australian test match team (1909, 1912, 1921, 1926); first man to score century (100 runs) in each of two innings of test match (1909).

Barebone *or* **Barebones,** Praise-God. See BARBON.

Ba·rents \'bär-ənts\, Willem. c.1550–1597. Dutch navigator. Commanded expeditions (1594, 1595) that reached Novaya Zemlya in searching for a northeast passage to Asia; discovered Spitsbergen (1596). Barents Island and Barents Sea named in his honor.

Ba·rère de Vieu·zac \bá-rer-də-vyœ-zák\, Bertrand. 1755–1841. French revolutionist. Member of Estates-General (1789); conducted liberal journal *Le Point du jour;* jointed Jacobin Club (1789); member of National Convention (1792); helped form first Committee of Public Safety (1793); formulated much propaganda of and defended the Terror, becoming known, because of his eloquence, as "The Anacreon of the Guillotine." Lost power after fall of Robespierre (1794); escaped to Bordeaux (1795); served Napoléon; proscribed at Restoration as regicide; in exile until amnesty of 1830.

Ba·ret·ti \bä-'rät-tē\, Giuseppe Marc'Antonio. 1719–1789. Italian critic. Lived in England (1751–60, 1766 ff.); friend of Johnson, Burke, Garrick, Reynolds. Published journal *Frusta letteraria* (1763–65) in which, under pseudonym Aristarco Scannabue, he criticized contemporary writers. Author of *Dissertation upon the Italian Poetry* (1753), *Dictionary and Grammar of the Italian Language* (1760), *Lettere Familiari* (1762–63; published in English as *A Journey from London to Genoa,* 1770), *Discours sur Shakespeare et sur M. de Voltaire* (1777).

Bar·ghash \'bär-gāsh\. *In full* Barghash ibn Sa'īd. c.1834–1888. Sultan of Zanzibar (1870–88). Son of Sa'īd ibn Sultān; succeeded brother Mājid; forced by British consul to sign antislavery treaty (1873); relied on British protection and support; unable to prevent Anglo–German partition (1886).

Bar·gonne \bár-gòn\ *or* **Bar·gone** \-gòn\, Frédéric-Charles. *Pseudonym* Claude Far·rère \fá-rer\. 1876–1957. French novelist. In naval service (1899–1919). Author of exotic novels as *Fumée d'opium* (1904), *Les Civilisés* (1906), *L'Homme qui assassina* (1907), *La Bataille* (1909), *La Maison des morts vivants* (1911), *Thomas l'Agnelet* (1913), *La Dernière Déesse* (1920), *Cent Millions d'or* (1927), *Le Chef* (1930), *L'Homme seul* (1942).

Bar·ham \'bar-əm\, Richard Harris. *Pseudonym* Thomas In·golds·by \'iŋ-gəl(d)z-bē\. 1788–1845. English humorous writer. Priest in ordinary of Chapel Royal (1824). Author of *The Ingoldsby Legends,* drolly ironic metrical tales first published in *Bentley's Miscellany* and later collected (1840, 1842, 1847).

Bar He·brae·us \,bär-hē-'brē-əs\. *Arabic* ibn al-'Ibrī *or* Abū al-Faraj. 1226–1286. Syrian scholar. Son of Jewish convert to Christianity; became hermit at 17, bishop at 20, archbishop at 26; assistant patriarch of Eastern Jacobite (Monophysite) church (1264); compiled collections of texts in philosophy, theology, science etc.; wrote *Hē'wath ḥekkmthā,* encyclopedia of philosophy showing influence of Avicenna; greatly broadened scope of Syriac literature by own writings and translations from Arabic. Worked for mutual Muslim–Christian toleration.

Bar·ing \'ba(ə)r-iŋ, 'be(ə)r-\. Name of English family and financial and commercial house. Sir Francis (1740–1810), grandson of German Lutheran immigrant and cloth manufacturer, established (1763) with his brother John, banking house of John & Francis Baring & Co., London; director of East India Company (1779 ff.). His son ¶Alexander (1774–1848), 1st Baron Ash·bur·ton \'ash-(,)bərt-ᵊn\, extended firm's banking operations in U.S.; succeeded father as head of firm (1810); M.P. (1806–35); opposed Reform Bill (1832); president, Board of Trade (1834–35). Created baron (1835). Negotiated settlement of boundary between Maine and Canada (in Webster-Ashburton Treaty, 1842). One grandson of Sir Francis, ¶Charles Thomas (1807–1879) was bishop of Durham (1861–79); another, ¶Sir Francis Thornhill (1796–1866), Baron North·brook \'nò(ə)rth-,brùk\, was M.P. (1826–65); chancellor of the exchequer (1839–41); first lord of the admiralty (1849–52); created baron (1866). ¶Thomas George (1826–1904), 1st Earl of Northbrook, son of the preceding, was a statesman; M.P. (1857–66); undersecretary of state for war (1861, 1868–72); governor general of India (1872–76). Created earl (1876). First lord of admiralty (1880–85). ¶Edward Charles (1828–1897), 1st Baron Rev·el·stoke \'rev-əl-,stōk\, a third grandson of Sir Francis, followed Thomas as head of firm; weathered threat of bankruptcy following Argentina's default on bonds (1890). His 5th son ¶Maurice (1874–1945), journalist and author; in Foreign Office (1898–1904); foreign correspondent for *Morning Post, Times* (1904–14); in Royal Flying Corps (1914–18). Author of *Puppet*

Show of Memory (1922), verse, novels including *C* (1924), *Cat's Cradle* (1925), *Daphne Adeane* (1926). Another grandson of Sir Francis, ¶Evelyn (1841–1917), 1st Earl Cro·mer \'krō-mər\, in army (1858–72); secretary to cousin Lord Northbrook in India (1872–76); British agent and consul general with plenipotentiary diplomatic rank in Egypt (1883–1907); created "Veiled Protectorate" in dominating khedive; reformed public administration and finances; obtained loan to spend on irrigation (1885), which increased revenue and forestalled bankruptcy. Created earl (1901).

Bar·ing-Gould \-'güld\, Sabine. 1834–1924. English author. Rector of Lew Trenchard, North Devon (from 1881). Author of *Lives of the Saints* (15 vols., 1872–77), theological works, and hymns, including "Onward Christian Soldiers"; *Book of Were-Wolves* (1865) and other studies in legend and folklore; travel books as *In Troubador Land* (1891); one opera, *The Red Spider* (1898); and numerous novels including *Mehalah* (1880), *John Herring* (1883), *Cheap Jack Zita* (1893), *The Broom Squire* (1896).

Bar·ker \'bär-kər\, Sir Ernest. 1874–1960. English historian. Fellow and lecturer, Oxford (1898–1920); principal, King's College, London (1920–27); professor of political science, Cambridge (1928–39). Author of *Political Thought of Plato and Aristotle* (1906); *Political Thought in England from Herbert Spencer to To-day* (1915), *Greek Political Theory* (1918), *National Character* (1927), *Church, State, and Study* (1930), *Oliver Cromwell and the English People* (1937), *Traditions of Civility* (1948), etc.

Barker, Harley Granville-. See GRANVILLE-BARKER.

Barker, Robert. 1739–1806. Irish painter. Reputed inventor of panoramas.

Barker, Thomas. 1769–1847. English painter. Known for landscapes and rustic scenes, including *The Woodman* and *Old Tom.* His son ¶Thomas Jones (1815–1882) was a painter of portraits and military subjects; known for scenes of Franco-Prussian and Crimean wars.

Bark·hau·sen \'bärk-hau̇-zən\, Heinrich. 1881–1956. German physicist and electrical engineer. Discovered (1919) Barkhausen effect, discontinuities in magnetization of ferrous materials.

Bark·la \'bärk-lə\, Charles Glover. 1877–1944. English physicist. Professor, U. of Liverpool (1902–09), U. of London (1909–13), Edinburgh (1913–44). Investigated X-rays; developed X-ray scattering analysis of materials; used it to determine number of electrons in carbon atom (1906). Awarded Nobel prize for physics (1917).

Bar·kley \'bär-klē\, Alben William. 1877–1956. American politician, b. Graves Co., Ky. Member, U.S. House of Representatives (1913–27); U.S. Senate (1927–49, 1955–56), majority leader (1937–47); U.S. vice-president (1949–53).

Bar·kly \'bär-klē\, Sir Henry. 1815–1898. English colonial governor. M.P. (1845–48); governor of British Guiana (1848–53), Jamaica (1853–56), Victoria (1856–63), Mauritius (1863–70), Cape of Good Hope (1870–77).

Bar Kokhba. See KOKHBA.

Bar·laam \'bär-ˌläm\ the Ca·la·bri·an \kə-'lā-brē-ən\. c.1290–c.1350. Italo-Greek prelate, theologian, Humanist. Noted teacher; opponent of Hesychasm; disputed with Gregory Palamas and with Hesychast monks of Mt. Athos (1334–37); envoy of Byzantine court to Pope Benedict XII at Avignon (1339); taught Greek to Petrarch, who aided his conversion to Roman church; bishop of Gerace (1342); influenced Renaissance study of Greek culture.

Bar·lach \'bär-ˌläk\, Ernst. 1870–1938. German sculptor, playwright, and poet. Noted sculptor in Expressionist manner and modern Gothic style; wrote symbolist-realist plays *Der tote Tag* (1912), *Der arme Vetter* (1918), *Der Findling* (1922), *Die Sündflut* (1924), *Der blaue Boll* (1926).

Bar·low \'bär-(ˌ)lō\, Joel. 1754–1812. American poet and diplomat, b. Redding, Conn. Served as chaplain in American Revolution; U.S. consul to Algiers (1795–97); arranged treaties with Tunis, Algiers, and Tripoli; U.S. minister to France (1811). Works included epic poem, *The Vision of Columbus* (1787) revised as *The Columbiad* (1807), essay *Advice to the Privileged Orders* (1792), mock epic *The Hasty Pudding* (1796).

Barlow, Peter. 1776–1862. English mathematician and optician. Taught at Royal Military Academy, Woolwich (1801–47). Devised means of rectifying errors in ships' compasses (1819); invented (1833) Barlow achromatic lens. Published long-used *New Mathematical Tables* (1814).

Bar·ma·kids \'bär-mə-ˌkidz\ *or* **Bar·me·cides** \-mə-ˌsīdz\. Priestly family of Iranian origin that achieved great influence in 8th-9th centuries under 'Abbāsid caliphs. Members included: Khālid ibn Barmak \'kä-lēd-ib-ən-'bär-mäk\ (d. 781 or 782); converted to Islām after Arab conquest of native Balkh; became supporter of 'Abbāsid revolt; minister to caliph; governor of Fars and of Ṭabaristān (767–775) under caliph al-Manṣūr. His son ¶Yaḥ·yā \'yäk-yä\ (d. 805) was appointed secretary and tutor to Hārūn, son of caliph (778); intrigued to secure succession to Hārūn after death of Mūsā al-Hādī (786); named vizier by Hārūn; controlled government and treasury (786–797). His son ¶al-Faḍl \al-'fäd-əl\ (d. 808) was also named vizier (786); quelled revolt in Daylam (792); governor of Khorāsān (793); succeeded father in control of government (797); tutor to caliph's son al-Amīn. A second son of Yaḥya ¶Ja'far \'jä-fär\ (d. 803) was also named vizier (786); quelled revolt in Syria (796); director of bureaus of post, textiles, and mint (796). Family's great power and wealth evidently caused sudden downfall: Ja'far was executed (803), Yaḥyā and al-Faḍl died in prison (805, 808).

Bar·na·bas \'bär-nə-bəs\. Saint. *Orig.* Joseph the Levite *or* Jo·ses \'jō-(ˌ)sēz, -zəz\ the Levite. 1st century A.D. Apostolic Father of church. Cyprian Levite early converted to Christianity; assisted in work of church at Antioch; accompanied Paul on his first missionary journey, but later, after a disagreement, separated from him and went to Cyprus.

Bar·nack \'bär-ˌnäk\, Oskar. 1879–1936. German engineer. Employed by Ernst Leitz optical firm; designed (1913; introduced 1924) Leica I, first commercial miniature camera; determined standard 35-mm film picture size.

Bar·nard \'bär-nərd\, Lady Anne, *nee* Lindsay. 1750–1825. Scottish author. m. (1793) Sir Andrew Barnard, colonial secretary at Cape of Good Hope (1797–1802); author of ballad "Auld Robin Gray," published anonymously (1771).

Barnard, Chester Irving. 1886–1961. American businessman and sociologist, b. Malden, Mass. With American Telephone and Telegraph Co. (1909–48); president New Jersey Bell Telephone Co. (1927–48). Directed New Jersey state relief in Great Depression; president, United Services Organization (1942–45); president, Rockefeller Foundation (1948–52); chairman, National Science Foundation (1952–54). Pioneering student of business organization as sociological entity; author of *Functions of the Executive* (1938), *Organization and Management* (1948).

Barnard, Edward Emerson. 1857–1923. American astronomer, b. Nashville, Tenn. Astronomer, Lick Observatory (1887–95), Yerkes Observatory (1895–1923); professor, U. of Chicago (1895–1923). Discovered 5th satellite of Jupiter (1892), Barnard's star (1916); pioneer in celestial photography.

Barnard, Frederick Augustus Porter. 1809–1889. American educator, b. Sheffield, Mass. Professor of mathematics and natural history, U. of Alabama (1838–54), U. of Mississippi (1854–56); president, U. of Mississippi (1856–58); chancellor (1858–61). President, Columbia U. (1864–89); favored opening of Columbia's educational opportunities to women; Barnard College, Columbia, named in his honor.

Barnard, George Grey. 1863–1938. American sculptor, b. Bellefonte, Pa. Chief works included *Struggle of Two Natures in Man* (1894), two groups containing 31 statues commissioned for Pennsylvania Capitol (1910), *God Pan, Rising Woman, Adam and Eve,* controversial statue of Abraham Lincoln for Cincinnati (1917), *Mother Earth and Her Child, Refugee, Prodigal Son* (a group), and *Builder.*

Barnard, Henry. 1811–1900. American educator, b. Hartford, Conn. Active in improving public-school system, esp. in Connecticut and Rhode Island (1837–55). Chancellor, U. of Wisconsin (1858–60); president, St. John's College, Annapolis, Md. (1866–67). First U.S. commissioner of education (1867–70). Editor, *American Journal of Education* (1855–82).

Bar·nar·do \bär-'när-(ˌ)dō, (ˌ)bər-\, Thomas John. 1845–1905. British physician and philanthropist, b. Ireland. Known for his establishment (from 1870) in England and British possessions of over 90 Dr. Barnardo's Homes for orphaned and destitute children.

Bar·nato \bär-'nät-(ˌ)ō\, Barney. *Orig.* Barnett Isaacs \'ī-ziks, -zəks\. 1852–1897. English speculator. With brother formed diamond brokerage, Cape of Good Hope (1874); formed Barnato Diamond Mining Co. (1880); at first rival of, then joined interests with Cecil Rhodes (1888) as De Beers Consolidated Mines; later became interested in Witwatersrand goldfields; engineered Kaffir boom in mining stocks (1895); suicide at sea.

Bar·nave \bȧr-nȧv\, Antoine-Pierre-Joseph-Marie. 1761–1793. French politician. Elected to Estates-General (1789); member of National Assembly (1789); opposed Mirabeau frequently in debate; president of Assembly (1790); helped reorganize Jacobin club; lost favor by support of colonial interests and of constitutional monarchy; impeached for treasonable correspondence with king (1792); guillotined.

Barnes \'bärnz\, Barnabe. 1569?–1609. English lyric poet. Author of *Parthenophil and Parthenophe* (1593), *A Divine Centurie of Spirituall Sonnets* (1595), a tragedy *The Divil's Charter* (1607).

Barnes, Djuna. 1892–1982. American writer and painter, b. Cornwall-on-the-Hudson, N.Y. Her one-act plays *Three From the Earth, An Irish Triangle,* and *Kurzy of the Sea* produced by Provincetown players (1919–20); best known for avant-garde, psychological novel *Nightwood* (1936); also wrote *Ryder* (novel, 1928), *A Night Among the Horses* (stories and poems, 1929), *The Antiphon* (verse play, 1958), and *Creatures in an Alphabet* (poems, 1982).

Barnes, Ernest William. 1874–1953. English clergyman and mathematician. Taught mathematics at Cambridge (1902–15); ordained (1903); bishop of Birmingham (1924). Controversial proponent of theological modernism and of pacifism. Author of *Scientific Theory and Religion* (1933), *Rise of Christianity* (1947).

Barnes, George Nicoll. 1859–1940. British labor leader, b. Scotland. General secretary, Amalgamated Society of Engineers (1896–1908); led national engineers' strike (1897–98); a founder (1900), chairman (1910), Labour party; M.P. (1906–22); minister of pensions (1916–17), without portfolio (1917–20); member of war cabinet (1917–19); British delegate to Paris peace conference (1919) and first assembly of League of Nations (1921); principal founder, International Labor Organization (1919). Author of *From Workshop to War Cabinet* (1923), *Industrial Conflict: The Way Out* (1924), *The History of the International Labour Organization* (1926).

Barnes *or* **Bernes** \'bərnz, 'be(ə)rnz\ *or* **Ber·ners** \'bər-nərz\, Juliana. 15th century. English religious and author. Prioress in St. Albans; author of treatise on hunting, a verse adaptation of Anglo-Norman *Art de Venerie,* which forms part of *Boke of St. Albans* (pub. 1486).

Barnes, Robert. 1495–1540. English martyr. Prior, Austin friars, Cambridge; examined by Wolsey for Puritanical preaching (1526); abjured under pressure; fled to Wittenberg (1528) and met Luther; under safe conduct from Thomas Cromwell returned to England (1531); conducted diplomatic negotiations for Henry VIII; on fall of Cromwell, burnt for heresy under the Six Articles.

Barnes, Thomas. 1785–1841. English journalist. Contributed to Leigh Hunt's *Reflector* and *Examiner* and other journals; editor of *The Times* (1817–41), building it into foremost British journal; earned for himself and paper nickname "The Thunderer."

Barnes, William. 1801–1886. English poet, philologist, and clergyman. Master of a Dorchester boys' school; ordained (1847) and held various livings. Author of *Poems of Rural Life* (1844) and *Hwomely Rhymes* (1859), both in Dorset dialect; *Philological Grammar* (1854); *Outline of English Speechcraft* (1878).

Bar·nett \'bär-nit, -net\, John. 1802–1890. English singer and composer. Son of a Prussian immigrant (named Beer). Composed operas *Mountain Sylph* (Lyceum Theatre, 1834), *Fair Rosamond* (Drury Lane, 1837), *Farinelli* (Drury Lane, 1839); much incidental music, religious cantatas and masses, etc. His nephew ¶John Francis Barnett (1837–1916) was a pianist, professor of music, and composer; known for cantatas *The Ancient Mariner* (1867), *Eve of St. Agnes* (1913), oratorio *The Raising of Lazarus* (1873).

Barnett, Samuel Augustus. 1844–1913. English clergyman. Aided in founding (1884) Toynbee Hall, a university settlement in Whitechapel district, London, the first social settlement house; its first warden (1884–96); instrumental in educational and housing reform; canon of Bristol (1894–1906), Westminster (1906–13).

Barnevelt, Jan van Olden. See OLDENBARNEVELT.

Bar·ney \'bär-nē\, Joshua. 1759–1818. American naval officer, b. Baltimore. Served through American Revolution; captured three times by British; captured British frigate *General Monk* (1782). In French service (1796–1802). Privateer during War of 1812. Joined force at Bladensburg defending Washington; defeated after heroic resistance, wounded, and captured (1814).

Barn·field \'bärn-ˌfē(ə)ld\, Richard. 1574–1627. English poet. Author of *The Affectionate Shepherd* (1594), and of sonnets in the style of Shakespeare.

Bar·num \'bär-nəm\, Phineas Taylor. 1810–1891. American showman, b. Bethel, Conn. Opened Barnum's American Museum of curios, New York City (1841); exhibited the dwarf Tom Thumb (see Charles S. STRATTON) with great success in U.S. and England. Brought Jenny Lind to U.S. for concert tour (1850). Opened "The Greatest Show on Earth" in Brooklyn (1871); combined with James A. Bailey (1881) to form Barnum and Bailey Circus; imported Jumbo, a huge African elephant bought from Royal Zoological Society.

Ba·roc·ci \bä-'rot-chē\ *or* **Ba·roc·cio** \bä-'rot-chō\, Federico. *Sometimes called* Fi·ori da Ur·bi·no \fē-'ȯr-ē-dä-u̇r-'bē-nō\. c.1526–1612. Italian painter. Influenced by Raphael and esp. by Correggio; a leading exponent of central Italian Mannerist style; among his works were *Madonna del Popolo, Christ Crucified, Burning of Troy, Nativity.*

Ba·ro·ja \bä-'rō-kä\, Pío. *Full surname* Baroja y Nes·si \-ē-'näs-ē\. 1872–1956. Spanish author. Physician in Basque country; baker and journalist. Member of "Generation of '98"; wrote nearly 100 novels, beginning with *La casa de Aizgorri* (1900) and including trilogy *La lucha por la vida* (1904–05), *El árbol de la ciencia* (1911), *César o nada* (1911), *El mundo es ansi* (1912), and *Memorias de un hombre de acción,* cycle of 22 novels on 19th-century revolutionary Spain (1913–35).

Ba·ron \bá-rōⁿ\, Michel. *Orig.* Michel Boy·ron \bwá-rōⁿ\. 1653–1729. French actor. Member of Molière's company (1670–73), company of Hôtel de Bourgogne and of Comédie-Française; created many roles in works of Racine; master of French stage. Author of *L'Homme à bonnes fortunes* (1686).

Ba·ro·nio \bä-'rȯn-yō\, Cesare. *Lat.* Caesar Ba·ro·ni·us \bə-'rō-nē-əs\. 1538–1607. Italian ecclesiastical historian. Joined Oratory of St. Philip Neri (1557); superior (1593); confessor to Clement VIII; apostolic prothonotary (1595); cardinal (1596); Vatican librarian (1597). Commissioned by St. Philip Neri to write Roman Catholic reply to Protestant *Magdeburg Centuries,* the *Annales Ecclesiastici* (1588–1607).

Ba·roz·zi \bä-'rȯt-tsē\ *or* **Ba·ro·zio** \bä-'rōz-yō\, Giacomo. *Known as* Giacomo da Vi·gno·la \vēn-'yō-lä\. 1507–1573. Italian architect. At court of Francis I at Fontainebleau (1541–43); built Palazzo Bocchi, Bologna; architect to Pope Julius III (1551–55); with Giorgio Vasari and Bartolommeo Ammannati built papal Villa Giulia (1551–55); built church of S. Andrea, Rome, first with oval dome (1554); built Sta. Anna dei Palafrenieri (c.1572), the Gesú (begun 1568); for Farnese family completed Villa Farnese, Caprarola (1559–72). With Palladio and Giulio Romano, leader of Mannerist architecture in Italy. Author of *Regola delli cinque ordini d'architettura* (1562), long a standard text.

Barr \'bär\, Amelia Edith, *nee* Hud·dle·ston \'həd-ᵊl-stən\. 1831–1919. American novelist, b. Ulverston, Lancashire, England. m. Robert Barr (1850); to U.S. (1853). Popular novels included *Cluny McPherson* (1883), *Jan Vedder's Wife* (1885), *The Bow of Orange Ribbon* (1886), *Remember the Alamo* (1888), *Lion's Whelp* (1901), *The House on Cherry Street* (1909).

Barr, Archibald. 1855–1931. Scottish engineer and inventor. Professor, Glasgow U. (1889–1913); with William Stroud invented naval and military range finders, height finders, naval gunfire-control instruments, pressure pumps, etc.; chairman of company formed for manufacturing these instruments.

Barr, Stringfellow. 1897–1982. American educator, b. Suffolk, Va. President of St. John's College, Annapolis, Md. (1937–46); president of Foundation for World Government (1948–58). Known for academic reforms; instituted curriculum requiring study of some 100 classics, including works by Plato, Copernicus, Darwin, and Marx.

Bar·ra \'bär-ä\, Francisco León de la. 1863–1939. Mexican diplomat and politician. Ambassador to U.S. (1908–11); minister of foreign affairs (1911); ex officio provisional president from resignation of Gen. Porfirio Díaz to inauguration of Francisco Madero (May–Nov. 1911); in Huerta cabinet (1913); in Europe (from 1914), taught at Sorbonne.

Bar·rande \bá-räⁿd\, Joachim. 1799–1883. French geologist and paleontologist. Authority on Silurian formation of Bohemia; author of *Système silurien du centre de la Bohême* (1852–94), in which he identified over 4000 new fossil species.

Bar·ras \bá-rás\, Paul-François-Jean-Nicolas de. Vicomte. 1755–1829. French revolutionist. In army (1771–83); joined Jacobin Club; member of National Convention (1792); commissar in French army in Italy; organized Alpes-Maritimes department for captured territory of Var and Nice; voted for execution of Louis XVI; defeated anti-Jacobin forces in Toulon. Took prominent part in overthrow of Robespierre (1794). As commander in chief of Army of Interior and of police, appointed by Convention, called Napoléon Bonaparte to keep order in Paris. With Napoléon accomplished coup d'état establishing Directory (1795); a member (1795–99); chief power in state (1797–99); overthrown in Napoléon's coup (1799); thereafter suspected by Napoléon of plotting to restore monarchy; exiled from Paris (1799–1815).

Bar·rell \'bar-əl\, Joseph. 1869–1919. American geologist, b. New Providence, N.J. Professor of geology (from 1908), Yale. Known for work relating to igneous intrusions, non-marine origins of sedimentary rocks, isostasy, and origin of the earth.

Bar·rère \bá-rer\, Camille-Eugène-Pierre. 1851–1940. French diplomat. Ambassador to Italy (1897–1924); influenced Italy to join Allies in World War I.

Bar·rès \bá-res\, Maurice, *in full* Auguste-Maurice. 1862–1923. French writer and politician. Boulangist member, Chamber of Deputies (1889–93). Author of trilogy on his own self-analysis *Le Culte du moi,* comprising *Sous l'oeil des Barbares* (1888), *Un Homme libre* (1889), *Le Jardin de Bérénice* (1891); of nationalist trilogy *Le Roman de l'énergie nationale,* comprising *Les Déracinés* (1897), *L'Appel du soldat* (1900), *Leurs figures* (1902); of *Du Sang, de la volupté et de la mort* (1894); of an intensely nationalistic series "Les Bastions de l'Est" including *Au service de l'Allemagne* (1905), *Colette Baudoche* (1909); and of *La Colline inspirée* (1913), *La Grande Pitié des églises de France* (1914), *Un Jardin sur l'Oronte* (1922), etc.

Bar·rett \'bar-it, -ət\, Charles Simon. 1866–1935. American organizer of farmers, b. Pike County, Georgia. Leading organizer and president, National Farmers' Union (1906–28).

Barrett, Elizabeth. See BROWNING.

Barrett, John. 1866–1938. American journalist and diplomat, b. Grafton, Vt. U.S. minister to Siam (1894–98), Argentina (1903–04), Panama (1904–05), Colombia (1905–06). Director-general, Pan American Union (1907–20).

Barrett, Lawrence. 1838–1891. American actor, b. Paterson, N.J. New York debut in *The French Spy* (1857); played Boston, Philadelphia, San Francisco, London, and toured; noted for roles in Shakespeare, *Francesca da Rimini, Man o' Airlie,* etc.; by dint of technique one of leading American actors of the day.

Barrett, Wilson. 1846–1904. English actor, playwright, and theater manager. Manager in London of Court Theatre (1879–81), Princess Theatre (1881–86), Olympic Theatre (1890–96), Lyric Theatre (1896–99), Lyceum Theatre (1899). Author of *Nowadays* (1889), *The Sign of the Cross* (1895), etc.

Barri, Gerald *or* Giraldus de. See GERALD DE BARRI.

Bar·rie \'bar-ē\, Sir James Matthew. 1860–1937. Scottish novelist and dramatist. Editorial writer, *Nottingham Journal* (1883–85), began career as man of letters with *Auld Licht Idylls* (1888), *A Window in Thrums* (1889), *Little Minister* (1891), *Sentimental Tommy* (1896). Turned to theater; first play *Walker, London* (1893) a success, followed by *Professor's Love Story* (1894), *Quality Street* (1901), *The Admirable Crichton* (1902), *Peter Pan* (1904), *Alice-Sit-by-the-Fire* (1905), *What Every Woman Knows* (1908), *The Twelve Pound Look* (1910), *The Will* (1913), *A Kiss for Cinderella* (1916), *Dear Brutus* (1917), *Mary Rose* (1920), and *Shall We Join the Ladies?* (1921). Noted esp. for bringing supernatural and sentimental ideas to stage successfully in an era of social criticism; novels gave impetus to "kailyard" school of Scottish fiction.

Bar·ring·ton \'bar-iŋ-tən\, George. *Orig.* George Wal·dron \'wȯl-drən\. 1755–1804. Irish adventurer and writer. Joined actors' troupe under name Barrington (1771); transported to New South Wales as an incorrigible pickpocket (1790); pardoned (1796), made superintendent of convicts of Parramatta, N.S.W. (1796–1800). Reputed author of *Voyage to New South Wales* (1803), *History of New South Wales* (1802).

Barrington, John Shute. *Orig.* John Shute \'shüt\. 1st Viscount Barrington. 1678–1734. English lawyer and politician. Emissary to Scotland (1705) to win Presbyterian support for union with England; M.P. (1715–23). Author of pamphlets *Rights of Protestant Dissenters* (1704), *Dissuasive from Jacobitism* (1713). Created viscount in Irish peerage (1720). His son ¶William Wildman (1717–1793), 2d Viscount Barrington, was M.P. (1740 ff.); secretary at war (1755–61, 1765–78); chancellor of exchequer (1761–65); joint postmaster general (1782). Another son ¶Daines (1727–1800) was a lawyer and naturalist. Another son ¶Samuel (1729–1800) was a naval officer; rear admiral (1778); commander in chief in West Indies (1778–82); admiral (1787). Another son ¶Shute (1734–1826) was bishop of Llandaff (1769–82), Salisbury (1782–91), Durham (1791–26).

Bar·rios \'bär-yōs\, Justo Rufino. 1835–1885. Guatemalan general and politician. Commander in chief of army (1871–73); president of Guatemala (1873–85); instituted liberal reforms, expelled Jesuits, built highways, railroads, etc.; promulgated new constitution (1876); advocated use of force to create Central American union; killed in action in war with El Salvador.

Bar·ron \'bar-ən\, Clarence Walker. 1855–1928. American editor and publisher, b. Boston. On staff of Boston *Transcript* (1875–87). Founder (1887) and president, Boston News Bureau; founder, Philadelphia News Bureau (1897). Acquired Dow, Jones & Co., New York, publishers of *Wall Street Journal* (1901); founded (1921) *Barron's Business and Financial Weekly.* Author of *The Federal Reserve Act* (1914), *War Finance* (1919), *A World Remaking* (1920).

Barron, James. 1768–1851. American naval officer, b. Norfolk, Va.? Captain of *Chesapeake* when she was taken by British *Leopard* (1807); killed Stephen Decatur in duel (1820).

Bar·ros \'bȧr-rüsh\, João de. c.1496–1570. Portuguese historian. Governor of Portuguese Guinea (1522–25); royal treasurer (1525–28); crown agent in Portuguese India (1533–67). Author of grammatical and pedagogical works; known esp. for *Décadas da Ásia* (1552–1615), monumental history of Portuguese exploration and colonization.

Bar·ros Ara·na \'bär-rō-sä-'rä-nä\, Diego. 1830–1907. Chilean historian. Professor, dean of humanities, U. of Santiago (1863 ff.); ambassador to Argentina and Uruguay (1876), Brazil (1876); known esp. as authority on history of Chile. Author of *Historia de la Guerra del Pacífico* (1880–81), *Historia General de Chile* (1884–1902), etc.

Barros Lu·co \-'lü-kō\, Ramón. 1835–1919. Chilean politician. President of Chile (1910–15).

Bar·rot \bȧ-rō\, Odilon, *in full* Camille-Hyacinthe-Odilon. 1791–1873. French politician. Leader of "dynastic opposition" in Chamber of Deputies (1830–48); one of leaders of reform movement of 1847; appointed president of Council of State (1848) by Thiers. Chief minister and minister of justice (1848–49) during presidency of Louis Napoléon. Councilor of state (1870).

Bar·row *or* **Bar·rowe** \'bar-(,)ō\, Henry. c.1550–1593. English church reformer and martyr. Influenced by Brownists; imprisoned (1586) with John Greenwood for denying authority of ecclesiastical dignitaries; hanged at Tyburn for seditious writings, as *True Description out of the Word of God, of the Visible Church* (1589) and *Brief Discovery of the False Church* (1590).

Barrow \'bar-(,)ō\, Isaac. 1614–1680. English prelate. Bishop of Sodor and Man (1663–70), St. Asaph (1670–80); as only celibate bishop of the day, suspected by some of popery.

Barrow, Isaac. 1630–1677. English mathematician and theologian. Professor of Greek, Cambridge (1660–63); first Lucasian professor of mathematics at Cambridge (1663), resigned (1669) in favor of his pupil Isaac Newton. Chaplain to Charles II (1670); master of Trinity Coll , Cambridge (1673). Translated Euclid (1660). Author of *Lectiones Geometricae* (1670) in which he approached the calculus, controversial pieces including *Pope's Supremacy* (1680), and *Sermons.*

Barrow, Sir John. 1764–1848. English traveler. Secretary to ambassador to China (1792), and to governor of Cape of Good Hope (1797). Secretary of the admiralty (1804–06, 1807–45). Founder of Royal Geographical Society (1830). Promoted Arctic exploration; Cape Barrow, Point Barrow, Barrow Strait named for him.

Barry, Ann Street. See under Spranger BARRY.

Bar·ry \'bar-ē\, Sir Charles. 1795–1860. English architect. Built St. Peter's, Brighton (c.1826), Travellers' Club (1831), Reform Club (1837), and Bridgewater House (1847), London; won competition for best designs for Houses of Parliament (1836); occupied, with A. W. Pugin, in building them (1840–60). His son ¶Edward Middleton (1830–1880), also an architect, built new Covent Garden Theatre (1857), completed father's design for Parliament (1860 ff.), Charing Cross Hotel (1863–65), extensions to National Gallery (1871–75). Another son ¶Sir John Wolfe Wolfe-Barry \(')wu̇lf-'bar-ē\ (1836–1918), was a civil engineer; planned and directed extensions of London's electric railway systems; built Barry docks at Barry, near Cardiff, the Tower bridge and new Kew bridge over the Thames; British representative on International Suez Commission (1892–1906).

Barry, Elizabeth. 1658–1713. English actress. Coached by her lover the earl of Rochester, appeared successfully as Queen Isabella in *Mustapha* (1673); created over one hundred different roles in comedy, including Lady Brute in *Provoked Wife* and Belvidera in *Venice Preserved.*

Barry, James. 1741–1806. Irish historical painter. Brought to London by Edmund Burke (1764); executed six pictures on "Progress of Human Knowledge" on walls of Society of Arts (1777–83); professor of painting at Royal Academy (1782–99). Known for *Adam and Eve, Venus Rising from the Sea, Death of General Wolfe.*

Bar·ry \bȧ-rē, *Angl* 'bar-ē\, Jeanne du, *nee* Bé·cu \bā-kü̅\. Comtesse du Barry. 1743–1793. French courtier. Shopgirl in Paris until introduced by Jean du Barry to aristocratic society; became mistress of Louis XV (1768); m. (1768) Guillaume du Barry, brother of Jean, in order to qualify as official royal mistress; presented at court (1769); joined faction that brought about fall of the duc de Choiseul (1770); otherwise exercised little political influence, but her unpopularity contributed to decline of prestige of crown and court; banished to nunnery (1774–76) on accession of Louis XVI; lived at her estate, Louveciennes, with duc de Brissac; made several trips to London to aid French emigrés (1792); arrested and guillotined by Revolutionary Tribunal.

Bar·ry \'bar-ē\, John. 1745–1803. American naval officer, b. County Wexford, Ireland. Settled in Philadelphia (1760); entered naval service in American Revolution; performed brilliant exploits; recalled to service as senior captain (1794).

Barry, Leonora Marie, *nee* Kear·ney \'kər-nē, 'kär-\. *Known also as* Mother Lake \'lāk\. 1849–1930. American labor leader, b. County Cork, Ireland. To U.S. (1852); m. W. E. Barry (1871; d. 1881); joined Knights of Labor (1884); in charge of Knights' department of women's work (1886–90); organized women workers and fought for labor legislation. m. O. R. Lake (1890); later a Chautauqua lecturer on labor and temperance.

Barry, Martin. 1802–1855. English physician and embryologist. Demonstrated penetration of ova by spermatozoa (1842).

Barry, Philip James Quinn. 1896–1949. American playwright, b. Rochester, N.Y. Author of *You and I* (1922), *In a Garden* (1925), *White Wings* (1926), *Paris Bound* (1927), *Holiday* (1928), *Hotel Universe* (1930), *Tomorrow and Tomorrow* (1931), *The Animal Kingdom* (1932), *The Joyous Season* (1933), *Bright Star* (1935), *Here Come the Clowns* (1938), *The Philadelphia Story* (1939), *Without Love* (1942), etc.

Barry, Sir Redmond. 1813–1880. Irish colonial judge. To Australia (1839); first solicitor general of Victoria (1851); justice of Victoria supreme court (1852–80); founder and first chancellor of U. of Melbourne (1853–80).

Barry, Spranger. 1719–1777. Irish actor. Made London debut (1746) at Drury Lane as Othello; alternated with Garrick as Hamlet and Macbeth; with Mrs. Cibber as Juliet, rivaled Garrick's Romeo; built theaters in Dublin (1758) and Cork (1761); returned to Drury Lane under Garrick (1767); to Covent Garden (1774) with wife. His wife (m. 1768) ¶Ann, *nee* Street (1734–1801), Mrs. Dancer by an early marriage, played Cordelia to Barry's Lear in Dublin (1758); made last appearance in most successful part, as Lady Randolph in *Douglas* (1798).

Bar·ry·more \'bar-i-,mō(ə)r, -,mȯ(ə)r\. Name of a family of American actors founded by Maurice, *orig.* Herbert Blythe \'blīth\ (1847–1905), b. Fort Agra, India, son of British army officer; made London debut (1872); to U.S. (1875); with Augustin Daly's company (1875–78); toured with own company (1878–79); subsequently appeared with companies of A. M. Palmer, Lester Wallack. His wife (m. 1876) ¶Georgiana Emma, *nee* Drew \'drü\ (1854–1893), b. Philadelphia, daughter of John and Louisa Lane Drew (*qq.v.*); joined Daly company, New York City (1875); appeared opposite husband, Lawrence

Barrett, Edwin Booth, John McCullough, etc.; with husband played *Romeo and Juliet* in last production at New York Booth Theatre (1883). Their three children continued on stage: ¶Lionel (1878–1954), b. Philadelphia; appeared on stage in *Peter Ibbetson* (1917), *The Copperhead* (1918), *The Jest* (1919), etc., and in films *Mysterious Island* (1929), *Free Soul* (1931, Academy Award), *Grand Hotel* (1932), *Rasputin and the Empress* (with John and Ethel Barrymore, 1932), *Captains Courageous* (1937), *Duel in the Sun* (1947), the "Dr. Kildare" series, etc. ¶Ethel (1879–1959), b. Philadelphia, made debut with grandmother Louisa Lane Drew in *The Rivals* (1894); in London in *The Bells* and *Peter the Great* (1897–98); appeared in *Captain Jinks of the Horse Marines* (1901), *Alice-Sit-by-the-Fire* (1905), *Mid-Channel* (1910), *Trelawney of the Wells* (1911), *Déclassée* (1919), *The Second Mrs. Tanqueray* (1924), *Kingdom of God* (1928, opening Ethel Barrymore Theatre, N.Y.), *Scarlet Sister Mary* (1931), *Whiteoaks* (1938), *The Corn is Green* (1942); in films *The Nightingale* (1914), *Rasputin and the Empress* (1933, with brothers), *None but the Lonely Heart* (1944, Academy Award), *Spiral Staircase* (1946). ¶John (1882–1942), b. Philadelphia, known as "the Great Profile"; notable stage appearances in *Justice* (1910), *Peter Ibbetson* (1917), *The Jest* (1919) and esp. *Richard III* (1920), *Hamlet* (1922); in films *Dr. Jekyll and Mr. Hyde* (1920), *Beloved Rogue* (1927), *Moby Dick* (1930), *Grand Hotel* (1932), *Rasputin and the Empress* (1933), *Dinner at Eight* (1933), *The Great Profile* (1940).

Bar-Sa·li·bi \ˈbär-sä-ˈlē-bē\, Jacob. d. 1171. Syrian prelate and theologian. Bishop of Marash (1154–66) and of Mabbog (1155–66) under name Dionysius; metropolitan of Amid (1166–71); leading spokesman of Syrian Jacobite (Monophysite) church; author of numerous biblical commentaries, homilies, liturgies, prayers, etc. in Syriac.

Bar Sa·u·ma \ˈbär-sä-ü-ˈmä\, Rabban. c.1220–1294. Turkish Nestorian Christian prelate and traveler, b. China. Became monk (c.1243); gained fame as ascetic; traveled to Baghdad; Nestorian emissary to Mongol ruler of Persia; sent by Mongol ruler Arghun to western Europe (1287) to gain support for crusade against Muslims in Holy Land; met kings of Constantinople, France, England, Pope Nicholas IV.

Bar·sot·ti \bär-ˈsȯt-tē, *Angl* -ˈsät-ē\, Charles. 1850–1927. American newspaper editor, b. near Pisa, Italy. To New York City (1872); established *Il Progresso* (1880), first Italian daily newspaper in U.S.

Bart \bår\ *or* **Barth** \bårt\, Jean. 1650–1702. French privateer and naval officer. Commanded fleet of coastal privateers in war against Dutch (1672–78), capturing 81 prizes; commissioned lieutenant by King Louis XIV; as captain engaged against English at Beachy Head (1690); defended Dunkerque (1694–95); captured 96-ship wheat convoy (1696) to relieve French famine; ennobled; conducted Prince de Conti safely to Danzig (1697).

Bartas, Seigneur du. See Guillaume de SALLUSTE.

Bar·ten·stein \ˈbär-tən-ˌshtīn\, Johann Christoph von. Freiherr. 1689–1767. Austrian statesman. Secretary of state and advisor of Charles VI and Maria Theresa (1733–53); conducted Austrian foreign affairs during struggle for recognition of Pragmatic Sanction; vice-chancellor, political and financial affairs (1753).

Barth \ˈbärt\, Heinrich. 1821–1865. German explorer. Traveled through North Africa and Nile Valley, Palestine, Syria, Asia Minor, and Greece (1845–47), through the Sahara and Sudan (1850–55), and again in Greece, Asia Minor, and Turkey. Published comprehensively detailed *Reisen und Entdeckungen in Nord- und Zentralafrika* (1855–58). Professor, Berlin (1863–65).

Barth, Jean. See Jean BART.

Barth \ˈbärt\, Karl. 1886–1968. Swiss theologian. Reformed pastor, Safenwil (1911–21); professor, Göttingen (1921), Münster (1925), Bonn (1930), Basel (1935–62); with Martin Niemöller organized anti-Nazi Synod of Barmen (1934). Champion of dialectic theology and opponent of liberal rationalism. Author of *Der Römerbrief* (1919), *Das Wort Gottes und die Theologie* (1924), *Die Theologie und die Kirche* (1928), *Kirchliche Dogmatik* (1932), *Credo* (1935), *Gotteserkenntnis und Gottesdienst* (1938), etc.

Barth, Paul. 1858–1922. German philosopher and sociologist. Professor, Leipzig (1897–1922); edited *Quarterly of Scientific Philosophy* (1899–1916). Author of *Die Geschichtsphilosophie Hegels* (1890), *Philosophie der Geschichte als Soziologie* (1897), *Die Stoa* (1903), *Die Elemente der Erziehungs- und Unterrichtslehre* (1906), *Geschichte der Erziehung* (1911), etc.

Barth \ˈbärt\, Thomas Fredrik Weiby. 1899–1971. Norwegian petrologist and geochemist. At Geophysical Laboratory, Carnegie Institution, Washington, D.C. (1929–36); director of mineralogy, Geological Museum, and professor, U. of Oslo (1936–71). Known for studies of hot springs and geysers; author of *Theoretical Petrology* (1952).

Bar·thé·le·my \bår-tā-lə-mē, -tel-mē, -tāl-mē\, Auguste Mar·seille \mår-seʸ\. 1796–1867. French poet and satirist. Collaborated (1824–34) with Joseph Méry in political satires, including *La Villéliade* (against the minister Villèle, 1827), *La Peyronnéide* (against the minister Peyronet), *Napoléon en Égypte* (1828), *Waterloo* (1829); also collaborated in founding and editing weekly journal, *Némésis,* attacking (1831–32) government of Louis-Philippe.

Barthélemy, François de. Marquis. 1747–1830. French politician. Negotiated treaties of Basel (1795); member of Directory (1797); transported to Guiana for royalist sympathies (1797–99). Created senator by Napoléon; deserted Napoléon and favored (1814) Louis XVIII; created peer of France by Louis XVIII.

Barthélemy, Jean-Jacques. 1716–1795. French abbé and scholar. Author of *Voyage du Jeune Anacharsis en Grèce* (1788), an account of the government, customs, and buildings of ancient Greece as they might have appeared to a traveler in ancient times.

Barthélemy-Saint-Hi·laire \-saⁿ-tē-ler\, Jules. 1805–1895. French journalist, philosopher, and politician. Helped found (1830) journal *Le Bons Sens;* professor, Collège de France (1838); member of Chamber of Deputies (1848–51); secretary of Suez Canal construction company (1855–58); again deputy (1869–75); senator (1875); minister of foreign affairs (1880–81). Known esp. for 35-volume translation of Aristotle (1833–95).

Barthema, Lodovico de. See Lodovico de VARTHEMA.

Barthes \bårt\, Roland. 1915–1980. French critic. Author of *S/Z* (1970), *L'Empire des signes* (1970), *Sade, Fourier, Loyola* (1971), *Le Plaisir du texte* (1973).

Bar·thez \bår-tes, -tez\, Paul-Joseph. 1734–1806. French physician and philosopher. Collaborator with Diderot and d'Alembert on the *Encyclopédie;* a founder of vitalism; author of *Nouveaux éléments de la science de l'homme* (1778).

Barthold, Wilhelm. See Vasily BARTOLD.

Bar·thol·di \bår-tȯl-dē, *Angl* bär-ˈt(h)ȯl-dē, -t(h)äl-\, Frédéric-Auguste. 1834–1904. French sculptor. Known esp. for his colossal figures, as the Statue of Liberty (*Liberté éclairant le monde* or *Liberty Enlightening the World),* presented (1885, unveiled 1886) by the French people to the U.S. and located in New York harbor, and *Le Lion de Belfort* (1880), commemorating defense of Belfort in Franco–Prussian War.

Bar·tho·lin \bär-ˈtu̇l-in\, Caspar Berthelsen. *Lat.* Bar·tho·li·nus \ˌbärt-ᵊl-ˈī-nəs\. 1585–1629. Danish physician. Professor of medicine (1613), then of divinity (1624), U. of Copenhagen. First to describe olfactory nerve as first cranial nerve. Author of *Anatomicae Institutiones Corporis Humani* (1611), widely used manual of anatomy. His son ¶Thomas (1616–1680), known for his observations of the lymphatics, was professor of mathematics (1646–48), of anatomy (1648–61), at Copenhagen; physician to King Christian V (1670–80); enlarged his father's *Institutiones Anatomicae,* and defended Harvey's doctrine of the circulation of the blood. Another son ¶Erasmus (1625–1698), physician, mathematician, and physicist, was professor of medicine, Copenhagen (1657–98); discovered in Icelandic feldspar the phenomenon of double refraction of light.

Bar·thol·o·mae·us An·gli·cus \(ˌ)bär-ˌthȯl-ə-ˈmē-ə-ˈsaŋ-gli-kəs, -ˌtäl-, -ˈmā-\ *or* **Bar·thol·o·mew** \bär-ˈthäl-ə-ˌmyü\ the Englishman. fl. c.1220–1240. English Franciscan friar. Professor of theology, Paris; author of *De proprietatibus rerum* (first printed c.1495; Eng. transl. by Trevisa, 1398), a widely used encyclopedia of the Middle Ages.

Bar·tho·lo·mé \bår-tȯ-lȯ-mā\, Albert, *in full* Paul-Albert. 1848–1928. French sculptor. Known esp. for funerary pieces as *Jeune fille pleurant, Jeune fille priant, Monument aux morts* in Pére-Lachaise cemetery, and *La Victoire* in the Place du Carrousel.

Bar·thol·o·mew \bär-ˈthäl-ə-ˌmyü\. Saint. 1st century A.D. One of 12 Christian apostles, identified sometimes with Nathanael. Traditionally, missionary to India, Armenia, Mesopotamia, Ethiopia, Parthia.

Bartholomew, John George. 1860–1920. Scottish cartographer. Produced atlases of Scotland (1895), England and Wales (1903), *Atlas of Meteorology* (1899), *Atlas of Zoogeography* (1911); introduced layer system of contour coloring in topographic maps; his best known work, the [London] *Times Survey Atlas of the World,* completed (1921) after his death.

Bar·thou \bår-tü\, Jean-Louis. 1862–1934. French politician. Deputy (from 1889); held appointments in various cabinets, as minister of public works (1895, 1906, 1909–10), interior (1896–98), justice (1913). As premier of France (Mar.–Dec. 1913), secured passage of act to extend term of compulsory army service from two years to three. Minister of war under Briand (1920–22), of justice (1922) under Poincaré; headed French delegation to Genoa conference; elected senator (1922); appointed president of reparation commission. Again minister of justice under Poincaré (1926) and Briand (1929). As minister of foreign affairs (1934), directed efforts to secure French security by means of accords with Little Entente, Soviet Russia, Great Britain. Killed in assassination of King Alexander of Yugoslavia.

Bart·lett \ˈbärt-lət\, Sir Frederic Charles. 1886–1969. English psychologist. Professor, Cambridge (1931–52); director, Cambridge Psychological Laboratory (1922–52); editor, *British Journal of Psychology* (1924–48). Author of *Psychology and Primitive Culture* (1923), *The Problem of Noise* (1934), *Political Propaganda* (1941), *Thinking* (1958), etc.

Bartlett, John. 1820–1905. American publisher, b. Plymouth, Mass. Proprietor, Harvard U. Book Store (1849–63); with Little, Brown & Co. (from 1863); compiled *Familiar Quotations* (1855), *Complete Concordance to Shakespeare's Dramatic Works and Poems* (1894).

Bartlett, John Russell. 1805–1886. American bibliographer and librarian, b. Providence, R.I. Bookdealer, New York (1836–50); U.S. commissioner of Mexican boundary survey (1850–53); secretary of state, Rhode Island (1855–72). Aided in collection and care of library of John Carter Brown, Providence. Works included *Dictionary of Americanisms* (1848), *Records of the Colony of Rhode Island, 1636–1792, John Carter Brown Catalogue* (1865–82).

Bartlett, Josiah. 1729–1795. American physician and Revolutionary leader, b. Amesbury, Mass. Delegate to Continental Congress (1775–76, 1778–79); signer of Declaration of Independence. Associate justice (1782–88), chief justice (1788–90), superior court of New Hampshire. "President" of New Hampshire (1790, 1791, 1792) and its first governor (1793–94).

Bartlett, Paul Wayland. 1865–1925. American sculptor, b. New Haven, Conn. Among his notable works were *Bear Tamer, Columbus* and *Michelangelo* (Library of Congress, Washington), allegorical figures for New York Public Library, pediment of House wing of U.S. Capitol (1916), *Lafayette* (Louvre, Paris, 1908), *Puritans* (Connecticut Capitol).

Bartlett, Robert Abram. *Known as* Captain Bob Bartlett. 1875–1946. American explorer, b. Brigus, Nfld. On Peary expedition to Kane Basin (1898–99); commanded the *Roosevelt* on Peary's Arctic voyages (1905–09). On Canadian Arctic expedition under Stefansson (1913–14) commanded the *Karluk,* which was crushed by ice near Wrangel Island; crossed ice to Siberia, with one Eskimo, and returned with rescuers. Commanded third Croker Land Relief expedition to north Greenland (1917); in U.S. navy, World War I; on expeditions to N.W. Alaska and Arctic Ocean (1925), north Greenland and Ellesmere Land (1926), Siberia (1928), Labrador (1929), Greenland (1930 ff.); on own vessel *Morrissey* sought sites for U.S. military and naval bases in Arctic (1942–45). Author of *Last Voyage of the Karluk* (1916), *Log of Bob Bartlett* (1928), *Sails over Ice* (1934), etc.

Bar·tók \'bär-tōk\, Béla. 1881–1945. Hungarian composer. Professor, Academy of Music, Budapest (1907–34); to U.S. (1940). Noted as pianist and teacher. Published collections of over 6,000 Hungarian, Romanian, and Arabian folk tunes. Compositions included symphonic poem *Kossuth* (1903), orchestral suites, piano concertos (1926, 1930–31, 1945), violin concertos (1907–08, 1937–38), six string quartets (1908–09, 1915–17, 1927, 1928, 1934, 1939), *Piano Quintet* (1904), sonatas for violin and piano (1921, 1922), *Rhapsodies for Violin and Piano* (1928), piano pieces including *Mikrokosmos* (1926–39), opera *Duke Bluebeard's Castle* (1918), pantomime *Miraculous Mandarin* (1926), *Cantata Profana* (1930), *Music for Strings, Percussion and Celesta* (1936), *Sonata for Two Pianos and Percussion* (1937), *Concerto for Orchestra* (1943), *Sonata for Solo Violin* (1944).

Bar·told \'bȧr-təld\, Vasily Vladimirovich. *Also known as* Wilhelm Bar·thold \'bȧr-təld\. 1869–1930. Russian anthropologist. Professor, U. of St. Petersburg (later Leningrad, 1901–30); known for studies of Turkic peoples, Tadzhik Iranians, history and culture of Islām.

Bar·to·li \'bär-tō-lē\, Adolfo. 1833–1894. Italian literary scholar. Author of *I primi secoli della letteratura Italiana* (1870–79), *Storia della letteratura Italiana* (1878–89), etc.

Bartoli, Daniello. 1608–1685. Italian religious and historian. Entered Jesuit order (1623); wrote religious novel *L'uomo di lettere* (1645), *Dell'istoria della compagnia di Gesù* (1653–73).

Bartoli, Matteo Giulio. 1873–1946. Italian linguist. Professor, Turin (1908–46); developed theory of neolinguistics or areal linguistics. Author of *Das Dalmatische* (1906), *Introduzione alla neolinguistica* (1925), *Saggi di linguistica spaziale* (1945).

Bar·to·li·ni \ˌbär-tō-'lē-nē, *Angl* ˌbärt-ᵊl-'ē-(ˌ)nē\, Lorenzo. 1777–1850. Italian sculptor. Sent by Napoléon to found school of sculpture at Carrara (1808). Works included bas-reliefs on Column of Vendôme, the group *Charity* (Florence) and portrait busts, as of Napoléon, Mme. de Staël, Lord Byron, Liszt.

Bar·to·lo \bär-tō-lō\. *Lat.* Bar·to·lus \bär-'tō-ləs\. *Known also as* Bartolo of Saxoferrato. 1314–1357. Italian jurist. Professor at Perugia (1343–57); chief of post-glossators. Author of commentary on Justinian's Corpus Juris Civilis.

Bar·to·lom·meo \ˌbär-tō-lōm-'mā-ō\, Fra. *Orig.* Bartolommeo di Pa·go·lo del Fat·to·ri·no \dē-'päg-ō-lō-dāl-ˌfät-tō-'rē-nō\. *Also called* Bac·cio del·la Por·ta \'bät-chō-ˌdā-lä-'pȯr-tä\. 1472–1517. Florentine painter. Follower of Savonarola; retired to Dominican convent of San Marco (1500–04); visited Venice (1508); influenced by Leonardo, Bellini, Giorgione. Works included *Annunciation* (Volterra cathedral), *Vision of St. Bernard, God the Father with SS. Catherine of Siena and Mary Magdalene, Mystic Marriage of St. Catherine,* colossal *Jonah, Isaiah,* and *St. Mark,* and *Pietà.* Leading Florentine exponent of High Renaissance classicism in his day.

Bar·to·loz·zi \ˌbär-tō-'lōt-tsē\, Francesco. 1727–1815. Italian engraver. Engraved after works of Guercino, Annibale Carracci, Giordano, Reynolds, Gainsborough, Cosway, Angelica Kauffmann. To England (1764); engraver to king; one of original members of British Royal Academy (1769). Head of Royal Academy at Lisbon (1802–15).

Bar·ton \'bärt-ᵊn\, Andrew. d. 1511. Scottish naval officer. Cleared Scottish coast of Flemish pirates (1506), signalizing his success by sending James IV three barrels filled with pirates' heads. Accused of piracy.

Barton, Bernard. 1784–1849. English poet. Bank clerk, Woodbridge (1809–49); friend of Southey and Lamb; author of *Metrical Effusions* (1812), *Poems* (1820), etc.

Barton, Bruce. 1886–1967. American businessman, author, and politician, b. Robbins, Tenn. In magazine editorial work (1907–18); a founder and head of Batton, Barton, Durstine and Osborn advertising agency, New York City (1918–67); member, U.S. House of Representatives (1937–41). Author of *More Power to You* (1917), *Better Days* (1924), *The Man Nobody Knows* (1925), *The Book Nobody Knows* (1926), *What Can a Man Believe?* (1927), *On the Up and Up* (1929).

Barton, Clara, *in full* Clarissa Harlowe. 1821–1912. Founder of American Red Cross, b. Oxford, Mass. Schoolteacher (1836–54); clerk in patent office, Washington, D.C. (1854–57). During Civil War, solicited and distributed supplies for the wounded. In Europe (1869–73), gave aid during Franco–Prussian War, in association with International Red Cross. Campaigned (1877–82) to have U.S. sign Geneva agreement; became first president (1882–1904) of American Red Cross.

Barton, Sir Edmund. 1849–1920. Australian politician. Member of legislative assembly, New South Wales (1879–87, 1891–94, 1898–1900); speaker (1883–87); attorney general (1889, 1891–93); led delegation presenting Australian Commonwealth Constitution bill to British Parliament (1900); first prime minister of Australian Commonwealth (1901–03); judge of Australian high court (1903–1920).

Barton, Elizabeth. *Called* the Maid of Kent *or* Nun of Kent. c.1506–1534. English prophet. Tavern servant at Aldington; after nervous illness (1525) uttered prophecies and rebukes of those in power, which were believed by many to be divinely inspired; examined by ecclesiastical commission which pronounced her professions sincere. Inveighed against Henry VIII's divorce from Catherine of Aragon; her denunciations adjudged treasonable; condemned, executed at Tyburn.

Barton, Frances *or* Fanny. See Frances ABINGTON.

Bar·tram \'bär-trəm\, John. 1699–1777. American botanist, b. near Darby, Pa. Self-taught botanist; started garden (1728) near Philadelphia; made experiments in hybridizing. Corresponded and exchanged plants with English horticulturist Peter Collinson (from 1733) and with Linnaeus; botanist in colonies to George III (1765); traveled widely to collect plants. His son ¶William (1739–1823) was also a naturalist; continued father's horticultural work; published *Travels* (1791), an account of his travels through southeastern U.S. in search of plant and animal specimens; book influenced Romantic writers.

Bartsch \'bärch\, Karl. 1832–1888. German philologist and critic. Professor, Rostock (1858–71), Heidelberg (1871–88). Editor, *Germania* (1866–77); compiler of selections of Old French and Provençal literature; translator and editor of the *Nibelungenlied;* editor of *Parzival* (1870–71) and other medieval works.

Bartsch, Rudolf Hans. 1873–1952. Austrian novelist. Author of *Zwölf aus der Steiermark* (1906), *Schwammerl* (1912), etc.

Ba·ruch \bə-'rük\, Bernard Mannes. 1870–1965. American businessman and statesman, b. Camden, S.C. In brokerage business, New York City. Appointed by President Wilson member of Advisory Commission of Council for National Defense (1916); chairman of War Industries Board (1918–19). Member of Supreme Economic Council with American Commission to Negotiate Peace in Paris (1919). Adviser to President Roosevelt on economic mobilization in World War II. U.S. representative on United Nations Atomic Energy Commission (1946). Known as adviser to presidents and popular sage.

Bar·wick \'bar-ik, -ək\, John. 1612–1664. English clergyman. Royalist in sympathy; settled in London (1642) and with brothers supplied Charles I and Charles II with news of rebel plans. Imprisoned in Tower of London (1650–52). Royal chaplain (1660); dean of Durham (1660), St. Paul's (1661).

Bary, Heinrich Anton de. See DE BARY.

Ba·rya·tin·ski \(ˌ)bər-'yät-yin-skəi\, Aleksandr Ivanovich. Prince. 1814–1879. Russian field marshal. Entered army (1833); served in Caucasus, Poland, Turkey; general, chief of staff (1853); given command of army in Caucasus (1856) and made viceroy (1856) by Emperor Alexander II, conducting three successful campaigns against Caucasian tribes (1856–59); appointed field marshal.

Ba·rye \bä-rē\, Antoine-Louis. 1795–1875. French sculptor. Known for animal figures as *Centaure et le Lapithe, Jaguar dévorant un lièvre, Eléphant d'Afrique.*

Ba·ry·lo·vicz \ˌbär-ə-'lò-vits\, Dimitry. *Known as* Do·sof·tei \dò-'sȯf-ˌtā\. 1624–1693 or 1705. Moldavian prelate. Named metropolitan of Moldavia (1671); refugee in Poland (1673–76); author of verse psalter in Romanian, first verse in that language (1673), *Vieața și petreccere sfinților* ("Lives of the Saints," 1682–86).

Ba·sa·na·vi·čius \ˌbä-sä-'näv-i-chùs\, Jonas. 1851–1927. Lithuanian scholar and politician. Physician in Bulgaria (1879–1904); published (from 1875) works on Lithuanian mythology and folklore. Founded and edited (1883) first number of Lithuanian magazine *Aušra.* At time of Russian troubles (1905) settled at Vilna; chairman of national assembly (1905); member, Lithuanian national council (1917–18).

Ba·sa·rab \bä-sä-'räb\. Romanian princely dynasty ruling Walachia (1330–1658), including: Basarab I (d. 1352), defeated Hungarians at Posada (1330) and won independence of Walachia. ¶Mircea \'mērch-yä\, *called* cel Băt·rîn \chel-'bœ-trin\, *i.e.* the Old (ruled 1386–1418) was forced to recognize Ottoman suzerainty. ¶Vlad Dracul \'vläd-drä-'kül\, *i.e.* Vlad the Devil (ruled 1436–47), and ¶Vlad Țepeș \'vläd-'tsep-esh\, *i.e.* Vlad the Impaler (ruled 1456–62, 1476–77), were both notorious for cruel depravities; often cited as historical basis for legendary Dracula. ¶Michael the Brave, *Rom.* Mi·hai Vi·tea·zul \mē-'hī-vēt-yä-'zül\ (ruled 1593–1601) conquered Transylvania and Moldavia and for a time united all Romanian lands. ¶Ma·tei \mä-'tā\ (d. 1654) ruled (1632–54); defeated invasions by rival prince Vasile Lupu of Moldavia (1637, 1639); introduced many reforms, including first code of laws (1652); patron of arts and learning, introduced first printing press (1634). His successor ¶Constantin Șerban \ˌkȯn-stän-'tēn-'sher-bän\ (d. 1658) was last of line.

Ba·sā·sī·rī, al- \al-ˌbas-äs-'ē-rē\. *In full* Abū al-Ḥarith Arslān al-Muẓaffar al-Basāsīrī. d. 1060. Būyid military commander. With Arab help, attempted (1058–59) to seize power from 'Abbāsid caliph al-Qā'im in Baghdad; killed by Seljuq Turks under Toghril Beg.

Ba·sa·va \'bä-sä-vä\. 12th century. Indian religious reformer. Royal treasurer to Cālukya king Bijjala I; revived Lingāyat sect; subject of Lingāyat sacred text *Basava-Purāṇa.*

Ba·sā·van \bä-'säv-än\. 16th century. Mughal painter. Renowned for skill in characterization and as colorist.

Basch·et \bò-she\, Marcel. 1862–1941. French painter. Known esp. as portraitist, as of Ambroise Thomas, Claude Debussy, Francisque Sarcey.

Bascio, Matteo da. See MATTEO DA BASCIO.

Ba·se·dow \'bäz-ə-(ˌ)dō\, Johann Bernhard. 1724–1790. German educational reformer. Established the Philanthropinum, a model school for children, at Dessau (1774); advocated nature study, physical education, manual training. Author of *Methodenbuch* (1770), *Elementarwerk* (1774), etc.

Ba·shīr Shi·hāb II \ba-'shir-shē-'häb\. 1767–1850. Lebanese ruler. Chosen amir of Lebanon (1788); while remaining under Ottoman suzerainty, ruthlessly consolidated power in Lebanon, killing rivals and destroying Druze princely houses; ally of Muḥammad 'Alī; pitted Druzes and Christians against each other; driven out by Druze–Christian coalition supported by British (1840).

Bash·kir·tseff \(ˌ)bəsh-'kyirt-səf\, Marie. *Russ.* Marya Konstantinovna Bash·kir·tse·va \-sə-və\. 1860–1884. Russian painter and diarist. Acquainted with best society in European cities; studied painting at Paris; exhibited in the Salon (1880). Author of candid, sensitive *Journal,* covering most of her life.

Ba·sie \'bā-sē\, William. *Known as* Count Basie. 1904–1984. American bandleader and composer, b. Red Bank, N.J. Formed his own band (1935); became one of the most influential big band leaders of 1930s and 1940s; created hits including "One O'Clock Jump," "Swingin' the Blues," "Jumpin' at the Woodside," "Taxi War Dance," etc.; a swing style that emphasized a light, driving rhythm and ensemble playing.

Basho. See MATSUO Munefusa.

Basil. See also VASILY.

Bas·il \'baz-əl, 'bās-, 'bas-, 'bāz-\. *Lat.* Ba·sil·i·us \bə-'sil-ē-əs, -'zil-\. Saint. *Known as* Basil the Great. c.329–379 A.D. Early church father, b. Caesarea, Cappadocia. Brother of Gregory of Nyssa (*q.v.*). Studied at Byzantium and Athens; visited Syria and Egypt to learn from hermits there and led monastic life for a time (c.357); ordained (c.365); bishop of Caesarea (370). Devoted himself to stamping out heresies, esp. Arianism; improved liturgy and organized monastic institutions on basis of hard work, charitable services, and communal life to replace asceticism of hermits. Works included *De Spiritu Sancto, Moralia, Hexaëmeron,* and *Regulae.*

Basil. Name of two rulers of Eastern Roman Empire:

Basil I. *Called* the Macedonian. 812?–886. Emperor (867–886). Official and companion of Michael III; joint ruler with him (866–867); caused Michael's death. Founder of Macedonian dynasty (867–1056). Reformed finances; began recodification of laws with handbooks *Procheiron* and *Epanagoge;* generally successful with armies and fleets against Muslims in Asia Minor and Mediterranean; strengthened Byzantine hold on southern Italy and in Bulgaria.

Basil II. *Called* Bul·ga·roc·to·nus \ˌbùl-gə-'räk-tə-nəs\, *i.e.* Slayer of the Bulgars. c.958–1025. Emperor (976–1025). Son of Romanus II; crowned co-emperor with brother Constantine at age of two (960); empire ruled in fact by his mother, Theophano (963), by Nicephorus Phocas (963–969), and by John I Tzimisces (969–976) as guardians. Nominally joint emperor (976–1025) with his brother Constantine VIII, but latter took no part in government. Waged incessant warfare for 50 years; expanded empire into Georgia, Armenia, Mesopotamia; fought long, successful war (986–1014) against Bulgarians.

Basil of Ancyra. d. c.364 A.D. Greek prelate and theologian. Semi-Arian bishop of Ancyra (336); leader of Semi-Arian party; deposed by Arian Bishop Acacius of Caesarea (360); banished to Illyria. Author of *Synodal Letter,* clearest exposition of Semi-Arian position, and *On Virginity.*

Basil the Chamberlain. d. 985. Byzantine courtier. Eunuch and minister of Byzantine court; on death of Emperor John I Tzimisces (976) controlled throne occupied by great-nephews Basil II and Constantine; after lengthy struggle, overthrown by Basil.

Basil the Wolf. See VASILE.

Ba·si·le \bä-'sē-lā\, Giambattista. c.1575–1632. Neapolitan soldier and writer. Soldier, later official of Gonzaga court in Mantua; governor of succession of small states; collected Neapolitan folktales and fairy tales in *Lo cunto de li cunti* (1634), which influenced Grimms, Perrault, etc.

Bas·i·li·des \ˌbas-ə-'lī-ˌdēz, ˌbaz-\. 2d century A.D. Syrian mystic. Founded Gnostic sect in Alexandria called Basilidians.

Bas·i·lis·cus \ˌbas-ə-'lis-kəs, ˌbaz-\. d. 477. Eastern Roman emperor (475–476). Brother-in-law of Emperor Leo I. Sent by Leo (468) in command of expedition to Carthage against Vandals under Gaiseric; defeated and banished; deposed Zeno (475); after 20 disastrous months deposed by Zeno (476).

Ba·sin \ba-za^{n}\, Thomas. 1412–1491. French prelate and historian. Professor at Caen; bishop of Lisieux (1447); counsellor to Charles VII; opposed revolt of Louis the dauphin and later the policies of Louis XI; renounced see and went into exile (1470); named titular archbishop of Caesarea by Pope Sixtus IV (1474). Author of Latin history of reigns of Charles and Louis signed by pseudonym Amel·gard \á-mel-gár\.

Basir, Abū Ya'qub al-. See JOSEPH BEN ABRAHAM HA-COHEN.

Ba·sire \bə-'zi(ə)r, ba-\, James. 1730–1802. English engraver. Member of family of celebrated engravers; engraver to Society of Antiquaries (c.1763); teacher of William Blake; works included *Pylades and Orestes* (1771), *South View of Christ Church* (1799).

Bas·ker·ville \'bas-kər-ˌvil, -vəl\, John. 1706–1775. English printer and typographer. Worked as stone carver, writing master, and manufacturer of japanned goods; began to study typefounding (1750); pioneer manufacturer of fine printing paper and inks; produced quarto of Virgil (1757) and editions of Milton (1758), the Bible (1763), and Latin authors (1772–73); printer to Cambridge U. (1758–68). Designed Baskerville type.

Bas·nage \bä-názh\, Jacques. 1653–1725. French Protestant theologian and historian. Pastor in Rouen; exiled in Holland after revocation of Edict of Nantes (1685); aided diplomatically in arranging Triple Alliance at The Hague (1717); author of *Histoire de l'Eglise* (1699).

Bass \'bas\, George. 1771–1803. English explorer. Explored coast of New South Wales and discovered Bass Strait (1798).

Bass, Michael Thomas. 1799–1884. English brewer. Took control of firm founded (1777) by grandfather William Bass for brewing Burton beer; Liberal M.P. (1848–83).

Bass, Sam. 1851–1878. American outlaw, b. near Mitchell, Ind. Enjoyed brief but spectacular career as stagecoach and train robber (1877–78) in South Dakota, Nebraska, Kansas, Texas; killed by Texas Rangers during robbery.

Bas·sa·ni \bäs-'sä-nē\, Giovanni Battista. c.1657–1716. Italian composer. Composed operas, masses, sacred and secular cantatas, trio sonatas, etc.

Bassano, Duc de. See Hughes MARET.

Bas·sa·no \bäs-'sä-nō\, Jacopo *or* Giacomo da. *Also known as* Jacopo *or* Giacomo da Pon·te \-'pōn-tā\. c.1517–1592. Venetian painter. Known esp. as one of earliest Italian genre painters; works included genre paintings, lush landscapes, portraits, and biblical scenes. His sons ¶Francesco Bassano (1549–1592) and ¶Leandro Bassano (1557–1622) were also painters.

Basse \'bas\, William. d. 1653? English poet. Author of *Sword and Buckler* (1602); best known for *Epitaph on Shakespeare* and *Angler's Song.*

Bas·se·lin \bäs-la^{n}\ *or* **Ba·che·lin** \bäsh-la^{n}\, Olivier. c.1400–1450. French poet. Author esp. of drinking songs called *vaux-de-vire.*

Bas·ser·mann \'bäs-ər-,män\, Albert. 1867–1952. German actor. Member of Meiningen court theater (1890–95), Otto Brahm's company, Berlin (1899–1909), Max Reinhardt's (1909–15); toured successfully; in U.S. (1938–46). Noted esp. for interpretations of Ibsen roles.

Bassermann, Ernst. 1854–1917. German politician. Member of Reichstag (1893–1903, 1903–17); parliamentary leader of National Liberal party (1898–1917), president of party executive council (1905–17).

Bas·set \bȧ-se\, René. 1855–1924. French orientalist. Director, École Supérieure des Lettres in Algiers (from 1894). Author of *Études sur les dialectes berbères* (1894), *Nouveaux contes berbères* (1897), etc.

Bas·sett \'bas-ət, -it\, John Spencer. 1867–1928. American historian, b. Tarboro, N.C. Professor, Trinity Coll. (now Duke U., 1893–1906), Smith Coll. (1906–28). Founded *South Atlantic Quarterly* (1902), *Smith College Studies in History* (1906). Author of *Life of Andrew Jackson* (1911), *Short History of the United States* (1913), *Expansion and Reform* (1926).

Bas·si \'bäs-sē\, Agostino Maria. 1773–1856. Italian bacteriologist. Investigated (1807–35) muscardine disease of silkworms; announced in *Del mal del segno, calcinaccio o moscardino* (1835) that disease is caused by parasitic fungus; theorized that many diseases are caused by parasites, anticipating Pasteur and Koch in formulating germ theory.

Bassi, Matteo di. See MATTEO DA BASCIO.

Bas·si \'bäs-sē\, Ugo. 1801–1849. Italian priest and patriot. Entered Barnabite order (1819); ordained (1833); known as stirring preacher; joined Garibaldi at Rieti as chaplain (c.1848); captured by Austrians near Comacchio; tortured and executed.

Bassianus. See (1) Marcus Aurelius ANTONINUS; (2) ELAGABALUS.

Bas·so \'bas-(,)ō\, Hamilton, *in full* Joseph Hamilton. 1904–1964. American novelist, b. New Orleans. Author of *Cinnamon Seed* (1934), *Courthouse Square* (1936), *Days Before Lent* (1939), *The View from Pompey's Head* (1954), etc.

Bas·som·pierre \bȧ-sōⁿ-pyer\, François de. 1579–1646. French soldier and statesman. Favorite of Henry IV; member of party adhering to cause of Marie de Médicis (from 1610); created marshal of France (1622). Ambassador to Spain and to Switzerland; on diplomatic mission in England (1626). Known for amours. Confined by Richelieu in Bastille (1631–43); wrote there influential *Journal de ma vie* (1665).

Bass·ville \bȧs-vēl\, Nicolas-Jean Hu·gou de \ᵫē-gü-də-\. 1753–1793. French diplomat. Editor, *Mercure national* (1789–91); secretary to ambassador to Naples (1792–93); assassinated in Rome during anti-French demonstration. His death occasioned French demand for reparations secured from papacy in Peace of Tolentino (1797).

Bas·ta \'bäs-tä\, Giörgio. 1550–1607. Transylvanian soldier. Supported rebellion against Prince Michael the Brave of Wallachia (1601) and had him killed; commanded imperial Habsburg troops occupying Transylvania; persecuted Protestants, provoking rebellion (1604–06) of István Bocskay.

Bas·ta·ble \'bast-ə-bəl\, Charles Francis. 1855–1945. Irish economist. Professor, Dublin U. (1882–1932). Author of books on international commerce and public finance.

Ba·sti·an \'bäs-tē-,än\, Adolf. 1826–1905. German ethnologist. Traveled in every continent (1851–66). Professor, Berlin (after 1866) and director of its ethnological museum (1886). Developed theory of underlying psychic unity of mankind. Author of *Der Mensch in der Geschichte* (1860), *Die Völker des östlichen Asien* (1866–71), etc.

Bas·ti·at \bȧs-tyȧ\, Claude-Frédéric. 1801–1850. French economist. Advocate of free trade and opponent of Socialism; author of *Sophismes économiques* (1845), and of pamphlets including *Propriété et loi, Protectionnisme et Communisme, Capital et rente,* and *Gratuité du crédit* (all 1849–50). Member of Constituent Assembly and National Assembly (1848).

Bas·ti·das \bäs-'tē-t͟häs\, Rodrigo de. 1460–1526. Spanish explorer. Companion of Balboa; explored northern coast of South America (1500–02); discovered mouths of Magdalena River; founded Santa Marta, Colombia (1525).

Bas·ti·en-Le·page \bȧs-tyaⁿ-lə-pȧzh\, Jules. 1848–1884. French painter. Known for sentimental rustic and genre scenes.

Bast·wick \'bast-(,)wik\, John. 1593–1654. English physician. Author of polemics in Latin, Greek, and English against Catholic church and in favor of Presbyterianism; convicted and fined for seditious libel (1634); fined, sentenced to lose ears and to life imprisonment (1636); released by Long Parliament (1640).

Ba·t'a \'bȧt-yȧ\, Tomáš. 1876–1932. Czech industrialist. Founder of large shoe manufactory, Zlín.

Ba·taille \bȧ-täy\, Henry, *in full* Félix-Henry. 1872–1922. French playwright. His plays included *La Lépreuse* (1896), *L'Enchantement* (1900), *Maman Colibri* (1904), *La Marche nupitiale* (1905), *Poliche* (1905), *La Femme nue* (1908), *La Vierge folle* (1910), *Les Flambeaux* (1913), *Les Soeurs d'amour* (1919), etc.

Bate·man \'bāt-man\, Alan Mara. 1889–1971. Canadian geologist, b. Kingston, Ont. Member of Geological Survey of Canada (1905–12); professor, Yale (1915–59); known for work in economic geology and formation of ore deposits. Author of *Economic Mineral Deposits* (1942), *Formation of Mineral Deposits* (1951).

Bateman, Henry Mayo. 1887–1970. Australian cartoonist. Contributor of humorous drawings to *Punch* and other publications; known esp. for depiction of embarrassing situations, as "The Guardsman Who Dropped his Rifle."

Bateman, Hester, *nee* Need·ham \'nēd-am\. 1709–1794. English silversmith. m. John Bateman (d. 1760), and continued his smithing business with sons; produced domestic silverware of great elegance and grace.

Bateman, Hezekiah Linthicum. 1812–1875. American actor and manager, b. Baltimore. m. (1839) Sidney Frances Cowell (1823–1881); gave up acting to manage daughters ¶Ellen (1844–1936) and ¶Kate Josephine (1842–1917), who toured as the Bateman Children; they toured Great Britain under P.T. Barnum's management (1851); with father in New York, San Francisco, St. Louis; Ellen retiring, Kate starred on New York stage, esp. in Augustin Daly's production *Leah the Forsaken* (1863); played opposite Henry Irving at Lyceum Theatre, London, leased (1871–75) by her father, who earlier (1867–69) introduced *opéra bouffe* to New York.

Bates \'bāts\, Blanche. 1873–1941. American actress, b. Portland, Ore. In David Belasco's company starred in *Madame Butterfly* (1900), *Under Two Flags* (1901), *Darling of the Gods* (1902), *The Girl of the Golden West* (1903), etc.; appeared in *Witness for the Defense* (1913), *Molière* (1919), etc.; retired (1926). m. (1912) George Creel.

Bates, Henry Walter. 1825–1892. English naturalist. Journeyed to upper Amazon with Alfred Wallace (1848); returned to England (1859) with 8000 species of insects new to science; published important paper on mimicry (1861). Author of *The Naturalist on the Amazons* (1863).

Bates, Herbert Ernest. 1905–1974. English novelist and short-story writer. Author of *The Two Sisters* (1926), *The Poacher* (1935), *A House of Women* (1936), *My Uncle Silas* (1940); wrote war tales *The Greatest People in the World* (1942) and *How Sleep the Brave* (1943) as "Flying Officer X"; wrote novels and stories *Fair Stood the Wind for France* (1944), *The Purple Plain* (1946), *The Jacaranda Tree* (1948), *Love for Lydia* (1952), *Nature of Love* (1954), *Darling Buds of May* (1958), *A Moment in Time* (1964), *Triple Echo* (1970), etc.

Bates, Katharine Lee. 1859–1929. American educator and author, b. Falmouth, Mass. Professor of English at Wellesley (1891–1925). Author of *College Beautiful and Other Poems* (1887), *Rose and Thorn* (1888), *Sunshine and Other Verses for Children* (1890), *Hermit Island* (1891), *Fairy Gold* (1916), etc. Best known for poem "America the Beautiful" (1893; revised 1904, 1911).

Bates, Marston. 1906–1974. American zoologist, b. Grand Rapids, Mich. With International Division, Rockefeller Foundation (1937–52); professor, U. of Michigan (1952–71). Author of *Butterflies of Cuba* (1934), *Natural History of Mosquitos* (1949), *The Nature of Natural History* (1950), *Where Winter Never Comes* (1952), *Prevalence of People* (1955), *Coral Island* (1958), *The Forest and the Sea* (1960), *Gluttons and Libertines* (1968), *Jungle in the House* (1970).

Bates, Sir Percy Elly. 4th Baronet Bates. 1879–1946. English shipowner. Entered family shipping firm (1900); joined Cunard Line (1910), chairman (1930); negotiated acquisition of White Star Line (1934); instituted plan for two large passenger liners on North Atlantic run; launched *Queen Mary* (1934), *Queen Elizabeth* (1938).

Bate·son \'bāt-sən\, William. 1861–1926. English biologist. Champion of Darwinian evolution; proposed (1885) evolution of chordates from primitive echinoderms. At Cambridge conducted experiments in hybridization and morphology (c.1887–c.1900); published (1900) first English translation of Gregor Mendel's reports and experimentally confirmed them; coined term genetics for new field; demonstrated genetic linkage (1905–08); opposed chromosome theory of T.H. Morgan. First professor of genetics, Cambridge (1908–10); director of John Innes Horticultural Institution (1910–26). Author of *Material for the Study of Variation* (1894), *Mendel's Principles of Heredity. A Defence* (1902), *Problems of Genetics* (1913).

Bath, Earl of. See William PULTENEY.

Bath, 1st Marquis of. See Thomas THYNNE.

Bá·tho·ry *or* **Bá·tho·ri** \'ba-tōr-ē\. Noble family of Hungary originating in 13th century, including: Stephen (see STEPHEN BÁTHORY), king of Poland; succeeded as prince of Transylvania (1575–81) by his brother ¶Christoph, who invited Jesuits into his lands. Christoph's son ¶Sigismund², *Hung.* Zsigmond (1572–1613), Prince of Transylvania (1581–99); joined princes of Moldavia and Walachia against Turks (1594); defeated Ottoman army at Giurgiu (1595); under influence of Jesuits, abdicated in favor of Emperor Rudolf (1599) in order to enter priesthood; unsuccessfully sought to regain lands from Michael the Brave of Walachia (1600, 1601); forced to flee to Bohemia (1602).

Bath·urst \'bath-(,)ərst\, Allen. 1st Earl Bathurst. 1684–1775. English politician. Tory M.P. (1705–12); created baron (1712); in House of Lords opposed Sir Robert Walpole; defended Bishop Atterbury; privy councillor (1742); created earl (1772). Friend of Pope, Swift, Congreve, Sterne. His uncle ¶Ralph Bathurst (1620–1704) was a clergyman and physician; ordained (1644); compelled to abandon active public ministry by Civil War; practiced medicine during Commonwealth; for some time physician to navy; one of originators of Royal Society; chaplain to Charles II (1663); as president (from 1664) rebuilt Trinity College; vice-chancellor of Oxford (1673–76). ¶Henry, 2d earl (1714–1794), son of the 1st earl; M.P. (1735–54); judge of common pleas (1754–71); lord chancellor (1771–78) as Baron Aps·ley \'ap-slē\; lord president of the council (1779–82). His son ¶Henry, 3d earl (1762–1834), M.P. (1783–94); lord of Admiralty (1783–89), of the Treasury (1789–91); on Board of Control for India (1793–1802); president of Board of Trade and master of mint (1807–12); foreign secretary (1809); secretary for war and colonies (1812–27); lord president of the council (1828–30).

Bathurst, Charles. 1st Viscount Bled·is·loe \'bled-ə-,slō\. 1867–1958. English agriculturist and administrator. A founder of Central Land Association (1907); M.P. (1910–18); parliamentary secretary to Ministry of Food (1916–17); created baron (1918); parliamentary secretary to Ministry of Agriculture (1924–26). Governor general of New Zealand (1930–35). Created viscount (1935).

Bath·y·cles \'bath-i-,klēz\. 6th century B.C. Greek sculptor. Commissioned by Spartans to carve marble throne for statue of Apollo at Amyclae.

Ba·tis·ta y Zal·dí·var \bä-'tē-stä-ē-säl-'dē-vär\, Fulgencio. 1901–1973. Cuban soldier and dictator. Soldier in national army (1921–33); led coup that deposed Céspedes (1933); made colonel and commander of Cuban constitutional army (1933). As dictator, controlled provisional and de facto governments (1933–40); held title of president (1940–44); retired; returned to power by army coup (1952); regime marked by brutal repression and his personal embezzlement of huge sums; regime overthrown by Fidel Castro (1959).

Bat·lle \'bät-yā\, Lorenzo. 1810–1887. Uruguayan general and politician. President of Uruguay (1868–72). His son ¶José Batlle y Or·dó·ñez \ē-ȯr-'thōn-yās\ (1856–1929), journalist and politician; founded newspaper *El Día* (1886); became leader of Liberals (Colorados); president of Uruguay (1903–07, 1911–15); instituted liberal democratic reforms; president of national executive council (1920–26).

Batlle Ber·res \-'ber-rās\, Luis. 1897–1964. Uruguayan journalist and politician. Nephew of Batlle y Ordóñez; editor of *El Día;* in exile (1930–36); president of chamber of deputies (1942–46); vice president (1946–47); president of Uruguay (1947–51, 1955–56).

Bat·man \'bat-mən\, John. 1801–1839. Australian colonizer. Principal founder of Melbourne (1835).

Ba·to·ni \bä-'tō-nē\ *or* **Bat·to·ni** \bät-'tō-nē\, Pompeo Girolamo. 1708–1787. Italian painter. Known esp. for his portraits, as of Emperor Joseph II, Leopold II, Clement XII; invented the "grand tourist" portrait popular with English travelers.

Bat·sán·yi \'bät-sän-yē\, János. 1763–1845. Hungarian poet. Edited *Magyar Museum* (1787–96), becoming leader of Hungarian literary nationalist movement; wrote political verse as *A franciaországi változásokra* (1789), *Látó* (1793).

Bat·tā·nī, al- \al-ba-'ta-nē\. *In full* Abū 'Abd Allāh Muḥammad ibn Jābir ibn Sinān al-Battānī al-Ḥarrānī aṣ-Ṣabt. *Lat.* Al·ba·te·gni \,al-bə-'tän-yē\ *or* Al·ba·te·mi·us \,al-bə-'tē-mē-əs\. c.858–929. Arab astronomer and mathematician. Using trigonometric methods calculated improved values for length of year, precession of equinoxes, inclination of ecliptic; showed possibility of annular solar eclipses; best known of Arab astronomers among Europeans in Middle Ages.

Bat·ten·berg \'bät-ən-,berk, *Angl* 'bat-ən-,bərg\. Title of family of German counts; title died out (c.1314) and was revived (1851) for issue of morganatic marriage of Countess Julia Theresa von Haucke to Prince Alexander (1823–1888, younger son of Louis II, Grand Duke of Hesse-Darmstadt); title raised to prince (1858). Title renounced (1917) by members living in England in favor of the surname Mountbatten (*q.v.*). Second son Alexander became Alexander I of Bulgaria (*q.v.*).

Bat·ter·son \'bat-ər-sən\, James Goodwin. 1823–1901. American businessman, b. Wintonbury (now Bloomfield), Conn. In stonecutting business (to 1863). Founder (1863) and president (1863–1901) of Travelers Insurance Co., Hartford, the first accident-insurance company in America.

Bat·thyány \'bät-tyänʸ\. An old noble family of Hungary, including: Károly József (1698–1772), Prince of Batthyány; field marshal in Austrian service; distinguished himself in War of Austrian Succession, esp. at Pfaffenhofen (1745); ban of Croatia and prince of empire (1764). ¶Lajos (1806–1849), Count of Batthyány; member of upper house of Hungarian assembly (1830); leader of independence movement (1845); premier of first Hungarian ministry (1848); sought vainly to avoid breach with Austria; arrested and executed by Austrians. ¶Kázmér (1807–1854), Count of Batthyány; minister of foreign affairs (1849); fled with Kossuth to Turkey after insurrection; in France (1851–54).

Bat·ti·shill \'bat-ə-,shil, -shəl\, Jonathan. 1738–1801. English composer. Wrote popular songs, theatrical music as for opera *Almena* (1764), psalms, hymns, madrigals, etc.

Bat·ti·sti \bät-'tēs-tē\, Cesare. 1875–1916. Italian journalist and patriot. Founded (1900) journal *Il Popolo* in Trentino, attacking Austrian dictatorship; member of Austrian assembly (1911); to Italy on outbreak of World War I (1914); joined Alpine chasseurs; captured, condemned as a traitor, and hanged by the Austrians.

Battoni, Pompeo Girolamo. See BATONI.

Ba·tu Khan \'bä-tü-'kän\. d. 1255. Mongol ruler. Grandson of Genghis Khan and son of Jochi; under Ögödei led army that conquered Russia, Poland, and Hungary (1237–41); sacked Kiev (1240); aided by the great general Subotai; defeated Henry, Duke of Silesia, near Liegnitz (1241) and captured Pest; recalled to Karakorum by death of Ögödei; established khanate of the Golden Horde, or Western Kipchaks (1241), his realm extending from Lake Balkhash to Hungary. Succeeded by his brother Berke.

Ba·ty \bȧ-tē\, Gaston, *in full* Jean-Baptiste-Marie-Gaston. 1885–1952. French playwright and producer. Producer at Théâtre Montparnasse (1930), Comédie-Française (1936); productions noted for beautiful settings and groupings. His plays included *Dulcinée* (1938).

Ba·tyush·kov \'bȧt-yəsh-,kȯf\, Konstantin Nikolayevich. 1787–1855. Russian poet and essayist. Author of elegies and lyrics of notable sweetness and musicality, said to have influenced Pushkin.

Batz \bȧts\, Jean de. Baron. 1760–1822. French royalist. Attempted to rescue Louis XVI and royal family (1793).

Bau·de·laire \bōd(-ə)-ler\, Charles-Pierre. 1821–1867. French poet. Successful as art critic and as translator of tales of Edgar Allen Poe; author of a novel *La Fanfarlo* (1847), essays in *Les Paradis artificiels* (1860), *Curiosités esthétiques* (1868), and *Petits poèmes en prose* (1869), and esp. of a single celebrated and influential volume of verse, *Les Fleurs du mal* (1857, expanded 1861; definitive edition 1868), which led to his prosecution for obscenity and blasphemy. Life dogged by debt, drug addiction, venereal disease. Regarded as the earliest and finest poet of modernism in French, harbinger of later Symbolists.

Bau·dis·sin \'baů-dis-ən\, Wolf Heinrich von. Graf. 1789–1878. German literary critic and translator. In Danish diplomatic service (1810–14); with Dorothea Tieck translated 13 plays of Shakespeare; also translated Jonson, Molière, Gozzi, Goldoni.

Bau·dot \bō-dō\, Jean-Maurice-Émile. 1845–1903. French engineer. Devised telegraph code (pat. 1874) that largely supplanted Morse code in 20th century; invented a multiplex system (1894).

Baudouin. See BALDWIN.

Bau·douin de Cour·te·nay \bōd-wan-də-kůr-tə-ne\, Jan Niecisław. 1845–1929. Polish linguist. Professor at Kazan, Dorpat, Kraków (1893–1900), St. Petersburg (1901–14), Warsaw (1915–29); pioneer in structural analysis of speech; introduced term "phoneme". Author of *Versuch einer Theorie phonetischer Alternationen* (1895).

Bau·dry \bōd-rē\, Paul-Jacques-Aimé. 1828–1886. French painter and muralist. Known esp. for frescoes in Château de Chantilly, the Palais de Justice, and in foyer of Paris Opéra.

Bau·er \'baů-ər\, Andreas Friedrich. 1783–1860. German engineer. Cofounder with Friedrich Koenig of Koenig & Bauer, manufacturers of steam printing presses.

Bauer, Bruno. 1809–1882. German theologian and historical writer. Lecturer on theology (1834–42); deprived of license (1842) for radical literary criticism of Bible; later an avowed atheist and socialist. Author of *Kritik der evangelischen Geschichte des Johannes* (1840), *Kritik der evangelischen Geschichte der Synoptiker* (1840), *Christus und die Cäsaren* (1877), etc.

Bauer, Georg. *Lat.* Georgius Ag·ric·o·la \ə-'grik-ə-lə\. 1494–1555. German mineralogist and scholar. Friend of Erasmus. Physician in Joachimsthal (1527–33), Chemnitz (1533–55); bürgermeister of Chemnitz (1546–55). Studied mining methods, laws, customs, etc., in Saxony; wrote *Bermannus* (1530), *De natura fossilium* on classification of minerals (1546), *De natura eorum quae effluunt ex terra* (1546), *De orta et causis subterraneorum* (1546), and *De re metallica,* his major work, treating entire science and practice of mining and metallurgy (1556). Considered one of first to base writings on observation and inquiry rather than received opinion; considered also father of mineralogy.

Bauer, Gustav Adolf. 1870–1944. German politician. Labor organizer (1895 ff.); national chairman of Generalkommission der Gewerkschaften (1908–18);

member of Reichstag (1912–33); labor minister (1919); chancellor (1919–20) charged with securing ratification of Versailles treaty; vice chancellor and minister of treasury (1921–22).

Bauer, Harold. 1873–1951. American pianist, b. London, England. Made debut as pianist in Paris (1893); first appeared in U.S. with Boston Symphony Orchestra (1900); naturalized (1921). Helped introduce music of Debussy, Ravel, Franck to U.S.

Bauer, Otto. 1881–1938. Austrian politician. Leader of left wing of Social Democratic party; editor of *Arbeiter Zeitung* (from 1907); as foreign minister (1918–19) signed secret *Anschluss* treaty with Germany (1919); member of National Front (1929–34); in exile following abortive Socialist revolt in Vienna (1934).

Bauer, Sebastian Wilhelm Valentin. 1822–1875. German inventor. Pioneer in submarine development; built *Le Plongeur-Marin* (1850), from which he made first underwater escape (1851); from treadmill-driven *Le Diable-Marin* took what was probably the first underwater photographs (1855).

Bau·ern·feld \'bau̇-ərn-ˌfelt\, Eduard von. 1802–1890. Viennese playwright. Author of *Das Liebes-Protokoll* (1834), *Die Bekenntnisse* (1834), *Bürgerlich und romantisch* (1835), *Grossjährig* (1846), *Krisen* (1852), *Aus der Gesellschaft* (1867), and many other comedies, drawing-room pieces, etc.

Bau·hin \bō-a^{n}\, Gaspard *or* Caspar[3]. 1560–1624. Swiss botanist and anatomist. Professor, Basel (from 1582); one of first to describe ileocecal (Bauhin's) valve (1588); compiled *Theatrum Anatomicum* (1605), finest anatomical textbook of the day; introduced a binomial system of nomenclature for botany in *Pinax theatri botanica* (1623). His brother ¶Jean (1541–1613), physician and botanist at Basel; physician to duke of Württemberg (from 1571); compiled *Historia plantarum universalis* (1650–51).

Baum \'bäm, 'bȯm\, Lyman Frank. 1856–1919. American writer, b. Chittenango, N.Y. On editorial staff of newspapers in South Dakota and Chicago (1880–1902). Author of highly successful children's books *Father Goose* (1899), *Wonderful Wizard of Oz* (1900; produced as musical comedy 1901), 13 more "Oz" books, *Life and Adventures of Santa Claus* (1902), *Magical Monarch of Mo* (1903), etc.

Baum \'bau̇m\, Vicki, *orig.* Hedvig. 1888–1960. American novelist, b. Vienna, Austria. Contributed stories to magazines and engaged in editorial work (1906–31); wrote novels *Frühe Schatten* (1919), *Der Eingang zur Bühne* (1920), *Der Weg* (1925), *Studi chem. Helene Willfür* (1928), *Menschen im Hotel* (1929); last, as *Grand Hotel,* a best seller in English and basis of play and motion picture. To U.S. (1931); naturalized (1938). Later novels included *Falling Star* (1934), *Men Never Know* (1935), *Shanghai '37* (1939), *Weeping Wood* (1943), *Headless Angel* (1948), *The Mustard Seed* (1953).

Bau·mann \'bau̇-ˌmän\, Oskar. 1864–1899. Austrian explorer. Geographer, Congo expedition (1885); explored Fernando Po (1886), Usambara (1888), German East Africa, etc. (1890–95); ascertained source of Kagera river.

Baum·bach \'bau̇m-ˌbäk\, Rudolf. 1840–1905. German poet. Author of narrative verse of the vagabond school, as *Frau Holde* (1881), *Spielmannslieder* (1882), *Von der Landstrasse* (1882); known also for student drinking songs, esp. "Die Lindenwirtin."

Bau·mé \bō-mā\, Antoine. 1728–1804. French chemist. Discovered improvements in processes for purifying saltpeter, bleaching, making sal ammoniac, etc. Invented an improved hydrometer (1768).

Bäu·mer \'bȯi-mər\, Gertrud. 1873–1954. German writer and reformer. A leader of feminist movement in Germany; with Helene Lange published newspaper *Die Frau* (1893–1944); author of *Handbuch der Frauenbewegung* (1901 ff.), etc.

Bau·mes \'bȯm-əs\, Caleb Howard. 1863–1937. American politician, b. Bethlehem, N.Y. Member, New York State assembly (1909–13) and New York State senate (1919–37). Chairman of N.Y. State joint legislative committee (1926) to draft changes in code of criminal procedure and penal law; his name is associated with the several statutes passed (1926) esp. that mandating life imprisonment for fourth conviction for a felony.

Baum·gar·ten \'bau̇m-ˌgär-tən\, Alexander Gottlieb. 1714–1762. German philosopher. Professor, Frankfurt an der Oder (from 1740); considered founder of aesthetics as distinct field and coiner of term. Author of *Metaphysica* (1739), *Aesthetica Acroamatica* (1750–58, unfinished), *Philosophia generalis* (1770), etc.

Baumgarten, Michael. 1812–1889. German theologian. Professor, Rostock (1850). Opposed Lutheran hierarchy; removed from professorship for liberal views (1858).

Baumgarten, Siegmund Jakob. 1706–1757. German theologian. Professor, Halle (from 1734); moderated influence of Pietism on evangelical theology. Author of *Evangelische Glaubenslehre* (1759–60).

Baur \'bau̇r\, Ferdinand Christian. 1792–1860. German theologian and scholar. Professor, Tübingen (1826–60); founder of Tübingen school of biblical criticism, inspired by Hegel's metaphysics of history. Author of *Die christliche Gnosis* (1835), *Paulus, der Apostel Jesu Christi* (1845), *Lehrbuch der christlichen Dogmengeschichte* (1847), *Geschichte der christliche Kirche* (1863–77), etc.

Bausch \'bau̇sh\, John Jacob. 1830–1926. American businessman, b. Süssen, Germany. To U.S. (1849); founder (1853, with Henry Lomb) and president, Bausch & Lomb Optical Co., Rochester, N.Y.

Baux, Princes of. See ORANGE.

Bavaria, House of. See WITTELSBACH.

Ba·vi·us \'bā-vē-əs\. d. 35 B.C. Roman poet. Of inferior talent and malicious nature; enemy of Virgil and Horace.

Bavli, David ha-. See David al-MUKAMMAS.

Bax \'baks\, Sir Arnold Edward Trevor. 1883–1953. English composer. Compositions included symphonic poems, as *In the Faëry Hills* (1909), *The Garden of Fand* (1916), *Tintagel* (1917), and *November Woods* (1917), 7 symphonies, ballet *The Truth About the Russian Dancers* (scenario by J.M. Barrie; produced 1920 by Diaghilev), piano and chamber works. Master of the king's music (1941).

Bax, Ernest Belfort. 1854–1926. English writer. Helped William Morris to found Socialist League (1885) and edited with Morris its organ, *The Commonweal;* with Morris, wrote *Socialism, its Growth and Outcome* (1894); author of *Religion of Socialism* (1886), *The Problem of Reality* (1893), *The Real, the Rational and the Alogical* (1920).

Bax·ter \'bak-stər\, Andrew. 1686 or 1687–1750. Scottish philosopher. Metaphysical rationalist; author of *Enquiry Into the Nature of the Human Soul* (1733), *Matho, sive cosmotheoria puerilis* (1738), and papers published posthumously as *Evidence of Reason in Proof of the Immortality of the Soul* (1779).

Baxter, James. 1926–1972. New Zealand poet. Author of *Beyond the Palisade* (1944), *Blow, Wind of Fruitfulness* (1948), *The Fallen House* (1953), *Iron Breadboard* (1957), and critical study *Recent Trends in New Zealand Poetry* (1951).

Baxter, John. 1781–1858. English bookseller and printer. First to use ink roller; publisher of the illustrated "Baxter's Bible." His son ¶ George (1804–1867) invented oil-color printing process capable of high quality reproduction (pat. 1835).

Baxter, Richard. 1615–1691. English Puritan clergyman and writer. Ordained (1638); became moderate nonconformist; minister at Kidderminster (1641–60); chaplain in Cromwell's army (1645–47); forced out of Church of England by Act of Uniformity (1662). Suffered persecution climaxed by imprisonment by chief justice Jeffreys (1685) on charge of libeling the church in his *Paraphrase on the New Testament;* released after 18 months. Author of *Aphorismes of Justification* (1649), *Saints' Everlasting Rest* (1650), *Call to the Unconverted* (1657), a number of theological works, and the autobiographical *Reliquiae Baxterianae* (1696).

Bay \'bī\, Michel de. *Lat.* Michael Bai·us *or* Baj·us \'bī-əs\. 1513–1589. Belgian theologian. Taught at Louvain; wrote numerous treatises broaching new doctrines of original sin and grace that anticipated Jansenism; ideas condemned by Pope Pius V (1567) and Pope Gregory XIII (1580).

Ba·yan \'bī-'yän\. 14th century. Mongol official. Assumed virtual control of government under Emperor Togon-temür; instituted anti-Chinese policies; proposed virtual extermination of Chinese; provoked rebellions among Chinese; deposed (1339).

Ba·yard \bȧ-yȧr, *Angl* 'bā-ərd\, Pierre Ter·rail \te-ray\. Seigneur de Bayard. c.1473–1524. French hero. Renowned for knightly character; known as "Chevalier sans peur et sans reproche." Distinguished himself in Italian campaigns of Charles VIII, Louis XII, and Francis I, esp. in victory of Marignano (1515) and in defense of Mézières (1521); lieutenant general of Dauphiné (1515); killed in battle at Sesia River in Italy.

Bay·ard \'bī-ˌärd, -ərd\, James Asheton. 1767–1815. American politician, b. Philadelphia. Member, U.S. House of Representatives (1797–1803); in Jefferson–Burr disputed election (1800), intermediary who secured understanding with Jefferson resulting in Jefferson's election. U.S. senator from Delaware (1805–13). One of three Americans chosen by President Madison to negotiate terms of treaty of peace with Great Britain (1813–14), resulting in Treaty of Ghent (1814). His grandson ¶Thomas Francis (1828–1898) was U.S. senator from Delaware (1869–85), U.S. secretary of state (1885–89), and first U.S. ambassador to Great Britain (1893–97).

Bay·bars \'bī-bars\. Name of two Mamlūk sultans of Egypt and Syria:

Baybars I. *In full* al-Malik aẓ-Ẓāhir Rukn ad-Dīn Baybars. 1223–1277. Sultan (1260–77). Turkish slave, sold into Damascus; made commander in bodyguard by Ayyūbid sultan aṣ-Ṣāliḥ; defeated Crusaders under Louis IX at al-Manṣūrah (1250); led Mamlūk officers in revolt against Sultan Tūrān Shāh, murdering him (1250); led Mamlūk troops in defeat of Mongols at Nābulus (1260); assassinated Sultan Quṭuz and assumed throne (1260); founder of Mamlūk power; made Egypt center of Islāmic world; broke strength of Crusaders in Syria, capturing Arsūf (1265), Safed (1266), Jaffa (1268), Antioch (1268) and other points; successful in wars against Armenians and Seljuqs, capturing

Caesarea (1276); destroyed Syrian branch of order of Assassins (1272).

Baybars II. d. 1310. Sultan (1309–10). Circassian slave of Sultan Qalawun; seized throne, interrupting long rule of an-Nāṣir.

Bay·er \'bī-ər, *Angl* 'bā-ər, 'be(-ə)r\, Friedrich. 1825–1880. German industrialist. Founded (1863) Friedrich Bayer & Co., later Farbenfabriken Bayer AG.

Bay·er \'bī-ər\, Johann. 1572–1625. German astronomer. Published *Uranometria* (1603), 51 astronomical maps based on observations of his predecessors; introduced use of Greek and Latin characters to distinguish stars of a constellation in the order of their brightness.

Bayes \'bāz\, Nora. *Orig.* Dora Gold·berg \'gōl(d)-ˌbərg\. 1880–1928. American actress and singer. Starred in vaudeville and musical comedy; identified with songs "Down Where the Wurzburger Flows" and "Shine On, Harvest Moon" (which she wrote with husband Jack Norwood, 1908).

Bayes, Thomas. 1702–1761. English mathematician. Published tracts defending Newtonian calculus; first to establish method of probability inference.

Ba·yeu \'bä-yeü\, Francisco. *Full surname* Bayeu y Su·bí·as \-ē-sü-'bē-äs\. 1734–1795. Spanish painter. Brother-in-law of Goya. Court painter to Charles III; contributed to decoration of royal palace, Madrid (1763 ff.); executed frescoes in El Pilar cathedral, Saragossa, Toledo cathedral, palaces at El Pardo, La Granja, Aranjuez.

Bayeux, Thomas of. See THOMAS of Bayeux.

Ba·ye·zid \bī-(y)ə-'zēd\. *Also spelled* Baj·a·zet \ˌbaj-ə-'zet\. Name of two sultans of Ottoman Empire:

Bayezid I. *Called* Yil·di·rim \yil-di-'rim\, *i.e.* Thunderbolt. c.1360–1403. Sultan (1389–1402). Son and successor of Murad I; followed father's conquests in Balkans with defeat of Turkmen principalities (1390–91); put down Balkan revolt (1390–93) and besieged Constantinople; defeated Hungarian-Venetian crusade at Nicopolis (1396); first Ottoman ruler to be given title sultan. Organized centralized state based on Turkish and Muslim traditions. Annexed Karaman (1397), provoking Turkmen nobles to seek aid of Timur; defeated and captured by Timur at Ankara (1402).

Bayezid II. *Called* Ad·lî \äd-'lē\, *i.e.* the Just. c.1447–1512. Sultan (1481–1512). Son and successor of Mehmed II; restored Islāmic religious properties seized by father and reversed Mehmed's Europeanizing bias; consolidated Ottoman power in Balkans; defeated Venice, taking possession of Morea and other strongholds (1499–1503); carried on inconclusive war with Mamlūks of Egypt; last years marked by growing conflict with Ṣafavīds of Persia and struggle over succession between sons; abdicated in favor of son Selim.

Bay·in·naung \'bī-(y)in-'naùⁿ, -'naùŋ\. d. 1581. King of Burma (1551–81) of Toungoo dynasty. On death of brother-in-law Tabinshwehti, proclaimed himself king; suppressed Mon rebellion (1551); campaigned against Shans, recapturing Ava (1555); invaded Siam (1563), capturing capital Ayutthaya and royal family (1564); again invaded Siam (1568–69) and installed puppet king.

Bayle \bel\, Pierre. 1647–1706. French philosopher and critic. Born in Protestant faith; converted to Roman Catholicism; returned (1670) to Protestantism. Professor, Rotterdam (1681); defender of liberty of thought and religious toleration; removed because of skeptical beliefs (1693). Compiled (1697) *Dictionnaire historique et critique,* in which he analyzed and criticized accepted historical and philosophical tenets. Regarded as founder of 18th-century rationalism.

Baylebridge, William. See Charles BLOCKSIDGE.

Bay·ley \'bā-lē\, Richard. 1745–1801. American physician, b. Fairfield, Conn. Made valuable observations on diphtheria and yellow fever during New York City epidemics (1774, 1795); reduced mortality rates; secured passage of quarantine laws.

Bay·lis \'bā-ləs, -lis\, Lillian Mary. 1874–1937. English theater manager. Lessee of Old Vic Theatre, London (from 1898), where she created world famous Shakespearian repertory, and Sadler's Wells Theatre, London (from 1931), which she made a center for opera and ballet.

Bay·liss \'bā-ləs, -lis\, Sir William Maddock. 1860–1924. English physiologist. Taught physiology, University Coll., London (1888–1924); in collaboration with Ernest H. Starling conducted research on venous and capillary pressures (1894), innervation of the intestine (1898–99); discovered the hormone secretin manufactured by glands of the small intestine (1902) and coined term "hormone". His use of saline injections for amelioration of surgical shock was widely adopted among troops in 1918. Author of *Nature of Enzyme Action* (1908), *Principles of General Physiology* (1915), *The Vaso-motor System* (1923).

Bay·lor \'bā-lər\, Robert Emmet Bledsoe. 1793?–1873. American jurist and clergyman, b. Kentucky. Member of Congress from Alabama (1829–31); in Texas (from 1839). Associate justice, Texas supreme court (1841–45); district judge (1845–61). Instrumental in obtaining charter (1845) for first Baptist college in Texas, named Baylor University in his honor.

Bay·ly \'bā-lē\, Ada Ellen. *Pseudonym* Edna Ly·all \'lī(-ə)l\. 1857–1903. English novelist. Author of *Won by Waiting* (1879), *Donovan* (1882), *We Two* (1884), *In the Golden Days* (1885), *Doreen* (1894), *The Hinderers* (1902).

Bayly, Thomas Haynes. 1797–1839. English author and song writer. Author of songs and ballads, as "I'd Be a Butterfly," "She Wore a Wreath of Roses," "Welcome Me Home," "Oh, Pilot! 'tis a Fearful Night," "Oh, No, We Never Mention Her," etc.; dramatic pieces including the farce *Perfection,* and five novels including *The Aylmers.*

Baynes \'bānz\, Thomas Spencer. 1823–1887. English philosopher. Taught at U. of London (1856–64); professor, St. Andrews (1864–87). Editor of ninth edition of *Encyclopaedia Britannica* (1873–87). See William Robertson SMITH.

Bay·rak·dar Mus·ta·fa Pa·ṣa \bī-räk-'där-mùs-tä-'fä-pä-'shä\. 1775–1808. Ottoman politician, of Bulgarian origin. Led army on Constantinople to restore Sultan Selim III (1807); deposed usurper Mustafa IV and, Selim having been killed, placed Mahmud II on throne; grand vizier (1807–08); began reforms; killed by rebellious janissaries.

Ba·zaine \bä-zen, bȧ-\, Achille-François. 1811–1888. Marshal of France. Served in Crimean War (1854–56); in war with Austria captured Solferino, Italy (1859); head of French army in Mexico (1863). Appointed marshal (1864). Commander in chief in Franco–Prussian War; defeated at Vionville, Mars-la-Tour, and Gravelotte; besieged in Metz; surrendered to Bismarck (Oct. 27, 1870). Court-martialed (1873); sentence of death commuted to twenty years' imprisonment. Escaped from prison (1874); fled to Spain and lived there in exile.

Baz·al·gette \'baz-əl-ˌjet, -jit\, Sir Joseph William. 1819–1891. English civil engineer. Carried out construction of London's main drainage system (1858–75) and Thames embankment (1860–74).

Ba·zán \bä-'thän\, Álvaro de. Marqués de San·ta Cruz \sän-tä-'krüth\. 1526–1588. Spanish admiral. Foremost Spanish naval commander of his day. Distinguished himself in victory over Turks at Lepanto (1571); aided Duke of Alba's conquest of Portugal (1580); defeated French naval squadron at 2d Battle of Terceira (1583); made captain-general of the ocean (1583); proponent and planner of the Spanish Armada.

Bazán, Emilia Pardo. See PARDO BAZÁN.

Ba·zard \bȧ-zär\, Amand. 1791–1832. French Socialist. Organizer of French Carbonari; condemned for part in Belfort conspiracy (1822); leader of Saint-Simonians (1825–31).

Ba·zille \bä-zēy, bȧ-\, Jean-Frédéric. 1841–1870. French painter. Associate of Impressionists; works noted esp. for coloring. Paintings included *Réunion de famille, La Robe rose, Forêt de Fontainebleau.*

Ba·zin \bä-zaⁿ, bȧ-\, Henri-Émile. 1829–1917. French engineer. Member of Corps des Ponts et Chaussées; continued Darcy's studies of water flow in channels; studied wave propagation, fluid flow through orifices; suggested construction of suction dredgers. Chief engineer of Corps (1875–86), inspector general (1886–1900).

Bazin, René-François-Nicolas-Marie. 1853–1932. French novelist. His novels included *Stéphanette* (1884), *Une Tache d'encre* (1888), *La Terre qui meurt* (1899), *Les Oberlé* (1901), *Donatienne* (1903), *L'Isolée* (1905), *Le Blé qui lève* (1907); also wrote short stories, travel books, etc.

Baz·i·o·tes \'baz-ē-ˌōt-əs\, William. 1912–1963. American painter, b. Pittsburgh. A leading Abstract-Expressionist; works noted for formal structure, subtle coloration.

Baz·na \'bäz-nä\, Elyesa. *Pseudonym* Cic·e·ro \'sis-ə-ˌrō\. 1904–1970. Albanian spy. While employed (1943–44) as valet to Sir H.M. Knatchbull-Hugessen, British ambassador to Turkey, photographed secret Allied documents for Nazi Germany; paid in counterfeit British money. Author of *Ich war Cicero* (with Hans Nogly, 1962).

Baz·zi \'bät-sē\, Giovanni Antonio. *Known as* Il So·do·ma \ˌēl-sō-'dō-mä\. 1477–1549. Italian painter. Influenced by Leonardo da Vinci and esp. by Raphael; worked mainly in Siena (from 1501); works, reflecting transition from High Renaissance to Mannerist style, included decoration of Stanza della Segnatura, Vatican, for Pope Julius II (1508–09), fresco *Marriage of Alexander and Roxane* (c.1511–12) in Villa Farnesina, Rome.

Beach \'bēch\, Amy Marcy, *nee* Che·ney \'chē-nē\. 1867–1944. American pianist and composer, b. Henniker, N.H. m. (1885) Henry H. A. Beach (d. 1910). Appeared with Boston Symphony Orchestra and other orchestras. Among her compositions were *Mass in E-flat major* (1892), aria "Eilende Wolken" (1892), *Festival Jubilate* (1893), *Gaelic Symphony* (1896), *Panama Hymn* (1915), chamber works, songs, cantatas including *Rose of Avontown, Chambered Nautilus, Sylvania.*

Beach, Moses Yale. 1800–1868. American journalist and inventor, b. Wallingford, Conn. Bought New York *Sun* (1838) from brother-in-law Benjamin Day; its editor (1838–48); noted for efforts to speed collection of news; originated syndication of news stories; retired (1848). His son ¶Moses Sperry (1822–1892), b. Springfield, Mass., joined brother Alfred in taking over *Sun* (1848); remained in control until selling paper to Charles A. Dana (1868); invented a web press and cutter. Another son ¶Alfred Ely (1826–1896), b. Springfield, was associated with Moses S. in management of *Sun* (1848–52); publisher of *Scientific American* (1846–96), building it into a major magazine; invented a typewriter, cable railway, pneumatic passenger subway system. Alfred's son ¶Frederick Converse (1848–1918), b. Brooklyn, N.Y., was a director of *Scientific American* (from 1896); founded (1889) and edited *American Amateur Photographer*; editor (1902–18) *Encyclopedia Americana*.

Beach, Rex Ellingwood. 1877–1949. American writer, b. Atwood, Mich. Author of stories and novels of adventure, including *Pardners* (1905), *The Spoilers* (1906), *The Barrier* (1907), *Going Some* (1910), *The Ne'er-do-Well* (1911), *The Net* (1912), *The Auction Block* (1914), *Oh, Shoot* (1921), *The Goose Woman* (1925), *Don Careless* (1928), *Son of the Gods* (1929), *Alaskan Adventures* (1933), *Jungle Gold* (1935), etc.

Beach, Sylvia Woodbridge. 1887–1962. American bookseller and publisher, b. Baltimore. Opened bookshop Shakespeare and Co., Paris (1919); published James Joyce's *Ulysses* (1922), *Pomes Penyeach* (1927); shop closed by German occupation (1941). Wrote memoir *Shakespeare and Company* (1959).

Bea·dle \'bēd-^{ə}l\, Erastus Flavel. 1821–1894. American publisher, b. near Cooperstown, N.Y. Formed printing business (1852); with Robert Adams formed Beadle & Adams (1856); introduced Dime Novel series beginning with *Malaeska* (1860) by Anne S. Stephens; published 631 Dime Novels, 1103 Dime Library titles, 1168 Half Dime Library titles, including "Nick Carter," "Deadwood Dick," "Buffalo Bill," and other hero series.

Beaconsfield, Earl of. See DISRAELI.

Beal \'bē(ə)l\, Gifford Reynolds. 1879–1956. American painter, b. New York City. Known esp. for landscapes and coastal scenes, as *Across the Valley, Freight Yards, Hudson River, The Puff of Smoke.*

Beale \'bē(ə)l\, Dorothea. 1831–1906. English educator. Head teacher (1857) of Clergy Daughters' School, Casterton, Westmorland (the "Lowood" of *Jane Eyre*); principal of Cheltenham Ladies' College (1858–1906); helped found St. Hilda's College at Cheltenham (1885) for women secondary-school teachers, and St. Hilda's Hall at Oxford (1893) for women teachers.

Bean \'bēn\, Roy. 1825?–1903. American frontiersman, b. Mason Co., Ky. To Texas (c.1875); settled at Vinegaroon on lower Pecos River (1882); as unofficial justice of the peace, assumed role of "law west of the Pecos"; noted for devotion to Lillie Langtry, for whom his settlement was renamed.

Beard \'bi(ə)rd\, Charles Austin. 1874–1948. American historian, b. Knightstown, Ind. Professor of politics, Columbia (1907–17). Director of Training School for Public Service, New York City (1917–22); helped found New School for Social Research (1919). Leading Progressive historian and a founder of economic determinist method. Author of *Development of Modern Europe* (with J. H. Robinson, 1907), *American Government and Politics* (1910), *Supreme Court and the Constitution* (1912), *Economic Interpretation of the Constitution* (1913), *Economic Origins of Jeffersonian Democracy* (1915), *Economic Basis of Politics* (1922), *American Party Battle* (1928), *The Open Door at Home* (1934), *The Devil Theory of War* (1936), *American Foreign Policy in the Making 1932–1940* (1946), *President Roosevelt and the Coming of War 1941* (1948), etc. m. (1900) ¶Mary Rit·ter \'rit-ər\(1876–1958), b. Indianapolis; active in woman suffrage campaign; author of *Woman's Work in Municipalities* (1915), *Short History of the American Labor Movement* (1920), *On Understanding Women* (1931), *Woman as Force in History* (1946), etc.; collaborated with husband on *American Citizenship* (1913), *History of the United States* (1921), *The Rise of American Civilization* (1927), *America in Mid-Passage* (1939), etc.

Beard, Daniel Carter, *known as* Dan. 1850–1941. American illustrator, author, and outdoorsman, b. Cincinnati. Teacher of animal drawing, Woman's School of Applied Design (1893–1900); founded (1905) Sons of Daniel Boone, boys' club merged (1910) into Boy Scouts of America, of which he was an organizer and (1910–41) a national commissioner. Mt. Beard, a peak adjoining Mt. McKinley, was named in his honor. Author of *American Boys' Handy Book* (1882), *Outdoor Handy Book* (1900), *Boy Pioneers and Sons of Daniel Boone* (1909), *Shelters, Shacks, and Shanties* (1914), *Signs, Signals, and Symbols* (1918), *American Boys' Book of Camplore and Woodcraft* (1920), *Wisdom of the Woods* (1927), etc.

Beards·ley \'bi(ə)rdz-lē\, Aubrey Vincent. 1872–1898. English illustrator. A leader of the Aesthetic movement and a principal artist in the Art Nouveau manner. Art editor and illustrator for *The Yellow Book* quarterly (1894–96), illustrator for *The Savoy* magazine (1896–98); illustrated books *Morte D'Arthur* (1893), Oscar Wilde's *Salomé* (1894), *Lysistrata* (1896), *Rape of the Lock* (1896). Drawings noted for tendency to the grotesque and morbidly erotic.

Bearsted, Viscount. See Marcus SAMUEL.

Bea·ton \'bēt-^{ə}n\, Sir Cecil Walter Hardy. 1904–1980. British photographer and designer. Outstanding photographer of fashion and celebrities for *Vanity Fair, Vogue,* and other magazines; stage and costume designer for theatrical productions as *Lady Windermere's Fan, My Fair Lady, Grass Harp.* Published many books of photographs including *Book of Beauty* (1930), *Time Exposure* (with Peter Quennell, 1941), *Winged Squadrons* (1942), *Near East* (1943), *Far East* (1945), *Portrait of New York* (1949), *Persona Grata* (with Kenneth Tynan, 1953), *It Gives Me Great Pleasure* (1955), *Quail in Aspic* (1962), etc.

Beaton *or* **Be·thune** \'bēt-^{ə}n\, David. c.1494–1546. Scottish prelate and statesman. Sent by James V on missions to France; keeper of privy seal (1528); bishop of Mirepoix (1537); appointed cardinal under the title of St. Stephen in the Coelian Hill (1538); succeeded his uncle as archbishop of St. Andrews (1539); led party committed to French alliance and opposed to English alliance; upon failure in attempt to assume regency, put in custody by regent Arran (1543); chancellor and virtual ruler of Scotland (1543); undertook rigorous persecutions of Protestants; appointed papal legate (1544); had George Wishart, preacher of Reformation, arrested, tried for heresy, and burned at stake (1546); murdered in revenge by John and Norman Leslie and William Kirkcaldy. His uncle ¶James Beaton (1470?–1539) was lord treasurer (1505–09), chancellor (1513–26); archbishop of Glasgow (1509); archbishop of St. Andrews and primate of Scotland (1522); influenced James V to ally himself with France rather than England; initiated persecution of Scottish Protestants with burning of Patrick Hamilton (1528). David's nephew ¶James Beaton (1517–1603) was a trusted adviser of the queen regent, widow of James V; last Roman Catholic archbishop of Glasgow of the old hierarchy (1552); lived in Paris as Scottish ambassador (1560–1603).

Beatrice Portinari. See PORTINARI.

Bé·at·rix \bā-ȧ-trēks\. d. 1184. French noblewoman. Daughter of Renaud III, count of Burgundy; m. (1146) Emperor Frederick I Barbarossa, bringing as dowry Provençe and part of Burgundy.

Beat·tie \'bēt-ē\, James. 1735–1803. Scottish poet. Professor of moral philosophy, Marischal Coll., Aberdeen (1760–97). Author of *Original Poems and Translations* (1760), *Essay on the Nature and Immutability of Truth* against Hume (1770), and *The Minstrel* (1771–74), highly popular descriptive poem on progress of genius, in Spenserian stanzas, which inspired many early Romantics.

Beat·ty \'bēt-ē\, Clyde. 1903–1965. American animal trainer, b. Bainbridge, Ohio. Joined circus (1918); developed animal act that featured dangerous mixes of lions, tigers, pumas, bears, hyenas, etc.; with Ringling Bros. until taking partnership in Cole Brothers-Clyde Beatty Circus (1935); bought own circus (1945), later merged (1958) with Cole Brothers to form largest tent show on the road in the U.S.

Beatty, David. 1st Earl Beatty of the North Sea and of Brooks·by \'brůks-bē\. 1871–1936. British admiral. Entered navy (1884); distinguished himself in Egypt (1896), China (1899); captain (1900); rear admiral (1910); in command of battle cruiser squadron at Heligoland Bight (1914) and Dogger Bank (1915), where *Blücher* was sunk; vice admiral (1915); led squadron against German fleet in battle of Jutland (1916); succeeded Jellicoe as commander of Grand Fleet (1916); admiral of the fleet (1919); 1st sea lord of admiralty (1919–27); created earl (1919).

Beatus Rhenanus. See BILD AUS RHEINAU.

Beauchamp, Barons. See Edward Seymour (1539?–1621, 1561–1612), under SEYMOUR family.

Beau·champ \bō-shä^{n}\, Alphonse de. 1767–1832. French historian. Official in Revolutionary government (1793–1806); used official documents to compile popular *Histoire de la Vendée et des Chouans* (1806).

Beauchamp, Pierre. c.1636–c.1719. French ballet dancer. Director of Académie Royale de Danse (1661–87); considered first choreographer of Paris Opéra. Appeared as female lead opposite Louis XIV in Lully's *Le Triomphe de l'amour* (1681). Developed form of dance notation and defined basic five positions of feet.

Beau·champ \'bē-chəm\, Richard de. Earl of War·wick \'wär-ik, *US also* 'wȯr-ik, 'wȯr-(,)wik\. 1382–1439. English soldier. Son of Thomas de Beauchamp. Defeated Owen Glendower (1403); fought Percys for Henry IV at Shrewsbury (1403); visited Holy Land (1408); named captain of Calais (1414); suppressed Lollard uprising (1414); represented Henry V at Council of Constance (1414); took part in Henry V's French campaigns (1417–22), for which he was awarded Aumale (1419); had charge of education of Henry VI (1428–36). Defeated French at Beauvais (1431); lieutenant of France and Normandy (1437).

Beauchamp, Thomas de. Earl of Warwick. 1345?–1401. English nobleman. Named by Parliament governor of the king (1379); joined Gloucester and Arundel in overthrowing Richard II (1387); convicted of treason and imprisoned in Tower (1397–99); released by Henry IV.

Beau·che·min \bōsh(-e)-maⁿ\, Nérée. 1850–1931. French-Canadian poet, b. Yamachiche, Que. Leader of Le Terroir school of regionalists; published collections *Les Floraisons matutinales* (1897), *Patrie intime* (1928).

Beau·clerk \'bō-ˌkle(ə)r\, Topham. 1739–1780. English dandy. Descendant of Charles II and Nell Gwyn; intimate friend (after 1757) of Dr. Johnson. m. (1768) ¶Lady Diana Spen·cer \'spen (t)-sər\ (1734–1808), an amateur painter and illustrator of Dryden's *Fables,* immediately after her divorce from Lord Bolingbroke.

Beau de Ro·chas \bōd-ə-rō-shä\, Alphonse-Eugène. 1815–1893. French engineer. Patented (1862) plan for four-cycle internal combustion engine, but never built one.

Beau·fort \'bō-fərt, *also* -ˌfȯ(ə)rt\. Name of an English noble family which sprang from liaison of John of Gaunt and Catherine, the widow of Sir Hugh Swynford; their 4 children were legitimized by Parliament (1397), but excluded from royal succession. See Henry BEAUFORT; Thomas BEAUFORT. Other members included: ¶John Beaufort (1373?–1410), Earl of Som·er·set \'səm-ər-ˌset, -sət\; eldest of 3 sons of John of Gaunt and Catherine; assisted Richard II against the lords appellants (1397); made marquis of Dor·set \'dȯr-sət\ by Richard II; became admiral of the fleet. His daughter ¶Jane *or* Joan (d. 1445) married (1424) James I of Scotland, whose murderers she punished fiercely. His older son ¶John (1403–1444), 1st Duke of Somerset, commanded Henry V's forces in France (1439 ff.); with his younger brother ¶Edmund (cr. earl of Dorset, 1442; killed at St. Albans, 1455), recaptured Harfleur (1440). For Margaret, daughter of the 1st Duke, see Margaret BEAUFORT. ¶Henry (1436–1464), 3d Duke of Somerset, son of Edmund, shared in the struggle against Richard, Duke of York; defeated by Yorkists at Newnham Bridge (1460) but successful at Wakefield (1460); shared attainder of Henry VI (1461); captured and beheaded (1464).

Beaufort, Dukes of. See SOMERSET family.

Beaufort, Duc de. See François de Vendôme de BOURBON.

Beau·fort \'bō-fərt, *also* -ˌfȯ(ə)rt\, Sir Francis. 1774–1857. English naval officer. Entered navy (1787); saw much active service and survey duty; hydrographer to the navy (1829–55); rear admiral (1846). Devised "Beaufort's scale" (1805) for indicating wind velocities.

Beaufort, Henry. c.1374–1447. English cardinal and statesman. Second son of John of Gaunt by Catherine Swynford and half-brother of Henry IV. Bishop of Lincoln (1398), Winchester (1404). Chancellor (1403–04); leader of opposition in council to Thomas Arundel. Again chancellor under Henry V (1413–17); cardinal and papal legate (1417) but forced by Henry to resign offices; chancellor again (1424–26); cardinal and papal legate (1426); repelled attempt of Gloucester to deprive him of his see (1432). In virtual control of government of Henry VI (c.1435–43). Failed in missions of peace to France (1435, 1439, 1440).

Beaufort, Margaret. Countess of Rich·mond and Der·by \'rich-mən-dən-'där-bē, *chiefly US* -'dər-\. 1443–1509. English noblewoman. Daughter of John Beaufort, 1st Duke of Somerset; m. (1455) Edmund Tudor, Earl of Richmond, by whom she became mother of Henry VII. After triumph of Yorkists (1461), confined at Pembroke; m. (c.1464) Henry Stafford, son of Duke of Buckingham; m. (c.1473) Thomas Stanley, 1st Earl of Derby. Remembered as "Lady Margaret," generous patron of education; endowed divinity professorships at Oxford and Cambridge; enriched foundation that opened as Christ's Coll., Cambridge (1505), and corporation that refounded monastic house as St. John's Coll., Cambridge (1508); early patron of Caxton and Wynkyn de Worde.

Beaufort, Sir Thomas. Duke of Ex·e·ter \'ek-sət-ər\. d. 1427. English soldier. 3d son of John of Gaunt by Catherine Swynford. Admiral of fleet in the north (1403); commanded royal forces in Scrope's rebellion (1405); captain of Calais (1407); chancellor (1410–12); engaged in wars with French (1412–27); created earl of Dorset (1412), duke (1416); lieutenant of Aquitaine (1413), of Normandy (1416); member of council under Gloucester's protectorate (1422 ff.).

Beau·fre \bō-frā\, André. 1902–1975. French soldier. Served in Morocco, in Free French army (1942–45), and Indochina; commanded French forces in Suez campaign (1956); chief of general staff, Allied forces in Europe (1958); French NATO representative (1960); general of the army (1960). Proponent of French independent nuclear force. Author of *Introduction à la strategie* (1963), *L'O.T.A.N. et l'Europe* (1966), *La Nature de l'histoire* (1974).

Beau·har·nais \bō-är-ne\. Name of a noble French family of Orléanais. Prominent members include: Alexandre, vicomte de Beauharnais (1760–1794), army officer, fought under Rochambeau in American Revolution; deputy of nobility to Estates-General (1789); general in chief, army of the Rhine (1793); charged with responsibility for surrender of Mainz; guillotined. His wife ¶Joséphine de Beauharnais, *nee* Marie-Josèphe-Rose Ta·scher de la Pa·ge·rie \tä-sher-də-lä-päzh(-ə)-rē\ (1763–1814); b. in Martinique; m. 1st Alexandre de Beauharnais (1779), 2d Napoléon Bonaparte (1796); imprisoned briefly after Alexandre's fall from favor, but soon became leader of Paris society; worked to advance Napoléon's career; crowned empress of the French at Napoléon's coronation (1804); marriage annulled at instance of Napoléon (1810). A son of Alexandre and Joséphine, ¶Eugène de Beauharnais (1781–1824), served with Napoléon in Egypt (1798–99); created prince (1804); made by Napoléon viceroy of Italy (1805); m. Princess Amalie Auguste of Bavaria (1806); formally adopted by Napoléon and made heir apparent to crown of Italy (1806); distinguished himself in Austrian campaign (1809) and commanded army corps in Russian campaign (1812); retired to Bavaria (after 1814) and became (1817) duke of Leuch·ten·berg \'lȯik-tən-ˌberk\ and prince of Eich·stätt \'īk-shtet\. Eugène's children formed connections with several royal families: ¶Auguste, *Ger.* August (1810–1835), Duke of Leuchtenberg (1824–35); m. (1835) Queen Maria of Portugal. ¶Maximilien, *Ger.* Maximilian (1817–1852), duke (1835–52); m. (1839) Marya Nikolayevna, daughter of Czar Nicholas I of Russia; their descendants held title Prince Romanovski. ¶Joséphine (1807–1876), m. (1823) Oscar I, king of Sweden. ¶Eugénie-Hortense (1808–1847) m. Frederick William, prince of Hohenzollern-Hechingen. ¶Amélie (1812–1873) m. (1829) Dom Pedro I, emperor of Brazil. ¶Théodelinde (1814–1857) m. William, Count of Württemberg. Eugène's sister ¶Hortense de Beauharnais, *in full* Eugénie-Hortense (1783–1837), m. (1802) Louis Bonaparte, who became (1806) king of Holland; mother of Charles-Louis (later Napoléon III); center of Bonapartist intrigue (from 1814); banished from France (1815).

Beau·joy·eulx *or* **Beau·joy·eux** \bōzh-wä-yœ̄\, Balthasar de. *Ital.* Baldassare di Bel·gio·io·so \ˌbel-jō-'yō-sō\. d. 1587. Italian composer and choreographer. Violinist at French court (from 1555); created spectacle *Ballet comique de la reine* (1581), involving patterned group dance, poetry, dialogue, recitative, music; a forerunner of both opera and dramatic ballet.

Beau·ma·noir \bō-män-wär\, Jean de. Sire de Beaumanoir. d. 1366 or 1367. On behalf of Charles of Blois commanded 30 Breton knights in Battle of the Thirty (1351) against 30 knights under John Bramborough.

Beaumanoir, Philippe de Ré·mi \də-rā-mē\ de. Sire de Beaumanoir. c.1246–1296. French jurist. Author of *Coutumes de Beauvaisis* (c.1280–83), an early codification of French law.

Beau·mar·chais \bō-mär-she, *Angl* ˌbō-mär-'shā\, Pierre-Augustin Ca·ron \kä-rōⁿ\ de. 1732–1799. French playwright. At first, a clockmaker; invented an escapement mechanism; later engaged in commerce; attracted public attention when, in connection with litigation, he published in his own vindication four *Mémoires,* wittily attacking judicial injustice. Financed purchase of supplies for American colonies during American Revolution. Chiefly known as author of *Le Barbier de Séville* (first performed 1775) and *Le Mariage de Figaro* (first performed 1784), comedies which later inspired operas by Rossini and Mozart.

Beaumont, Charles. Chevalier d'Éon. See ÉON DE BEAUMONT.

Beau·mont \bō-mōⁿ\, Élie de, *in full* Jean-Baptiste-Armand-Louis-Léonce-Élie de. 1798–1874. French geologist. Professor, Collège de France (1832); published with O. P. Dufrénoy *Carte géologique de France* (1841), *Notice sur les systèmes de montagnes* (1852), etc.

Beaumont, Éon de. See ÉON DE BEAUMONT.

Beau·mont \'bō-mənt, -ˌmänt\, Francis. 1584–1616. English dramatist. Wrote commendatory verses for plays of Ben Jonson (1607–11); began (c.1606) intimate collaboration with fellow bachelor John Fletcher (*q.v.*) in composition of comedies and tragedies; probably sole author of *The Knight of the Burning Pestle* (c.1607); collaborations with Fletcher included *The Woman Hater* (1606), *Phylaster* (1608–10), *The Coxcombe* (1608–10), *The Maides Tragedy* (1608–11), *The Captaine* (1609–12), *A King and No King* (1611), *Cupids Revenge* (1611), *The Scornful Ladie* (1613–17), *Loves Pilgrimage* (1616?), *The Noble Gentleman* (c.1625). With Fletcher and Philip Massinger wrote *Thierry and Theodoret* (?), *The Beggars Bush* (1622?), *Loves Cure* (?).

Beau·mont \bō-mōⁿ\, François de. Baron des Adrets \-dā-zä-dre\. 1513–1587. French soldier. Served under Condé in Huguenot army (1562); assumed title of lieutenant general of the Dauphiné; became legendary for cruelty; abandoned Protestantism and fought his former coreligionists (1567).

Beau·mont \'bō-mənt, -ˌmänt\, Sir John. 1583–1627. English poet. Elder brother of Francis, the dramatist. Known chiefly for *Metamorphosis of Tobacco* (1602), *Bosworth Field* (1629) in which he introduced heroic couplet into English, and unpublished *Crown of Thorns.*

Beaumont, Robert de. Earl of Leices·ter \'les-tər\. 1104–1168. Chief justiciar of England. With his twin brother, Waleran (1104–1166), Count of Meu·lan \mœ̄-läⁿ\, aided and advised Stephen (1137). Made his peace with Henry II (1154); chief justiciar (from 1154) and viceroy of kingdom in king's absences in France.

Beau·mont \'bō-ˌmänt\, William 1785–1853. American surgeon, b. Lebanon, Conn. Army surgeon (1812–15, 1820–39); studied process of digestion by experiments with patient Alexis St. Martin, whose stomach was exposed by gunshot wound (1822). Published pioneering *Experiments and Observations on the Gastric Juice and the Physiology of Digestion* (1833).

Beau·mont de la Bon·ni·nière \bō-mōⁿ-də-lá-bò-nēn-yer\, Gustave-Auguste de. 1802–1866. French publicist. Author, with Tocqueville, of *Du système pénitentiaire aux États-Unis* (1833) and alone of *Marie, ou l'esclavage aux États-Unis* (1835), etc.

Beau·ne·veu \bōn(-ə)-vœ̄\, André. c.1330–c.1410. French sculptor and miniaturist. Sculptor of the tombs of Philip VI and Charles V of France; in service of duc de Berry.

Beau·re·gard \'bō-rə-ˌgärd, *Fr* bōr(-ə)-gár\, Pierre Gustave Toutant. 1818–1893. American army officer, b. near New Orleans. Served in Mexican War. Superintendent, U.S.M.A., West Point, on eve of Civil War (1861); resigned to enter Confederate army as brigadier general. In command at bombardment of Fort Sumter (April 12, 1861); commanded at Bull Run; general (1861); commander, Army of Mississippi; in command at Shiloh (1862); engaged in coastal defense (1862–64), defense of Richmond, Va. (1864–65).

Beauvais, Vincent of. See VINCENT of Beauvais.

Beauvoir, Roger de. See Edouard ROGER DE BULLY.

Beau·voir \bōv-wär\, Simone Bertrand de. 1908–1986. French writer and political activist. Known for polemical works including *The Second Sex* (1949), angry attack on oppressed state of women in Western society; also wrote novel *The Mandarins* (1954) and memoirs; shared existentialist philosophy and leftist politics of Jean-Paul Sartre.

Beaux \'bō\, Cecilia, *in full* Eliza Cecilia. 1863–1942. American painter, b. Philadelphia. Excelled in portraiture, especially in painting women and children; works included portraits of Mrs. Theodore Roosevelt, Mrs. Andrew Carnegie, Adm. David Beatty, Clemenceau, and *Last Days of Infancy, Mother and Daughter, The Dreamer, A New England Woman.*

Beaverbrook, 1st Baron. See William M. AITKEN.

Be·bel \'bā-bəl\, August. 1840–1913. German Social Democratic leader and writer. Joined German labor movement (1861); converted to socialism by Liebknecht; chairman, committee of German workingmen's unions (1867); cofounder of Social Democratic Labor party (1869). Entered North German Reichstag (1867); member of Imperial Reichstag (1871–81, 1883–1913). Sentenced with Liebknecht to imprisonment (1872–74) for high treason and lese majesty against German emperor, and later (1886) on further charges. Leader of Social Democratic party and (1912–13) of parliamentary opposition; editor of party organ *Vorwärts.* Author of *Unsere Ziele* (1870), *Der deutsche Bauernkrieg* (1876), *Die Frau und der Sozialismus* (1883), *Christentum und Sozialismus* (1892), *Aus meinem Leben* (1910–14), etc.

Bec·ca·fu·mi \ˌbāk-kä-'fü-mē\, Domenico. *Orig.* Domenico di Pa·ce \dē-'pä-chā\. *Called* Il Mec·che·ri·no \ēl-ˌmāk-kä-'rē-nō\. c.1486–1551. Italian painter and sculptor. Known esp. for his designs of scenes from the Old Testament for pavement in cathedral of Siena (1517–46); with Sodoma decorated Palazzo Borghese, Siena (1512); also decorated Palazzo Bindi Sergardi and Pinacoteca, Siena, executed frescoes in Siena city hall, and sculpture as bronze angels and marble figures of the apostles for cathedral of Siena.

Bec·ca·ria \ˌbāk-kä-'rē-ä\, Cesare Bo·ne·sa·na \ˌbō-nā-'sän-ä\. Marchese di Beccaria. 1738–1794. Italian economist and jurist. Professor of law and economy, Milan (1768–70); anticipated in his lectures economic theories of Adam Smith, and theories of Malthus on population and subsistence. Member of Supreme Economic Council of Milan (1771–94). Author of *Dei deletti e delle pene* (1764), first systematic treatment of rational criminal punishment; work was widely translated and influential. Economic lectures published as *Elementi di economia pubblica* (1804).

Beccaria, Giambatista, *orig.* Francesco. 1716–1781. Italian physicist. Professor, Turin (1748–69); experimented with atmospheric electricity and spread knowledge of Franklin's electrical researches; wrote *Dell' elettricismo artificiale et naturale* (1753), *Lettere al Beccari* (1758).

Beche, Sir Henry Thomas de la. See DE LA BECHE.

Bech·er \'bek-ər\, Johannes Robert. 1891–1958. German poet and critic. Active in Expressionist literary movement and Communist politics; elected to Reichstag (1933); in Moscow edited German-language newspaper (1935–45); to East Germany (1945); minister of culture (1954–58). Verse included *Der Ringende* (1911), *An Europa* (1916), *Verbrüderung* (1916), *An Alle!* (1919), *Am Grabe Lenins* (1924), *Heimkehr* (1946), *Sonett-Werk* (1956), etc.

Becher, Johann Joachim. 1635–1682. German chemist and physician. Physician to elector of Mainz (1663), elector of Bavaria (1664); commercial counsellor to Emperor Leopold I (1666); suggested establishment of German colonies in South America and building of Rhine–Danube canal. Carried on experiments for transmuting the Danube sand into gold. Advanced a theory of combustible earth that influenced Stahl's phlogiston theory of combustion. Author of *Physica subterranea* (1669), on the nature of minerals and other substances.

Be·chet \bə-'shā\, Sidney. 1897–1959. American musician, b. New Orleans. Clarinettist with Clarence Williams, Joe "King" Oliver, and other jazz bands; turned to soprano saxophone, becoming its only great jazz exponent; played with Duke Ellington, Noble Sissle; lived in Paris (from late 1940s).

Bech·stein \'bek-ˌshtīn\, Ludwig. 1801–1860. German poet, novelist, and folklorist. Author of poems *Die Haimonskinder* (1830) and *Faustus* (1833), the novel *Das tolle Jahr* (1833), the tale *Fahrten eines Musikanten* (1836–37), and collections of folk tales and fairy stories.

Bech·tel \'bek-təl\, Friedrich. 1855–1924. German scholar. Professor, Halle (1895–1924). Known for work on Greek dialectology and Homeric criticism; author of *Die griechischen Personennamen* (with August Fick, 1894), *Die griechischen Dialekte* (1921–24); edited *Sammlung der griechischen Dialektinschriften* (with Hermann Collitz, 1884–1915).

Bechterev. See BEKHTEREV.

Beck \'bek\, Józef. 1894–1944. Polish soldier and politician. Served in Piłsudski's Polish legion in World War I; military attaché at Paris (1922–23); Piłsudski's chief of cabinet (1926–30); as minister of foreign affairs (1932–39) signed alliance with Great Britain that brought her into World War II (1939).

Beck, Ludwig. 1880–1944. German general. Chief of general staff (1935–38); opposed Hitler's occupation of Rhineland and Sudetenland; central figure in generals' plot against Hitler (1944).

Beck, Martin. 1868?–1940. American theater manager and impresario, b. Liptószentmiklós, Hungary. Stranded by vaudeville troupe in Chicago (c.1890); manager, Orpheum Concert Saloon, San Francisco (from 1895), from which developed (1903) Orpheum Vaudeville Circuit of some 60 theaters in Midwest and West; managed circuit (1903–23), president (1920–23). Built Palace Theatre, chief U.S. vaudeville house, New York City (1913); built legitimate Martin Beck Theatre (1924).

Beck, Max Wladimir von. Freiherr. 1854–1943. Austrian politician. Entered ministry of agriculture (1880), chief of department (1900); premier of Austria (1906–08); secured enactment of universal male suffrage in Austria (1907); dismissed for opposition to annexation of Bosnia.

Becke \'bek-ə\, Friedrich Johann Karl. 1855–1931. Austrian mineralogist and geologist. Professor, Vienna (1898–1927); known esp. for investigations of schists and metamorphic rocks; inventor of a method for determining minerals by means of their light-refractive properties.

Beck·er \'bek-ər\, Carl Heinrich. 1876–1933. German scholar and politician. Professor, Hamburg (1908) and Bonn (1913). Prussian minister of culture (1921, 1925–30). Author of *Islamstudien* (1924–32), *Vom Wesen der Universität* (1925), etc.

Becker, Carl Lotus. 1873–1945. American historian, b. near Waterloo, Iowa. Professor, U. of Kansas (1902–16), Cornell (1917–41). Author of *Beginnings of the American People* (1915), *The Eve of Revolution* (1918), *The Declaration of Independence* (1922), *Our Great Experiment in Democracy* (1924), *Modern History* (1931), *The Heavenly City of the Eighteenth-Century Philosophers* (1932), *Progress and Power* (1936).

Becker, George Ferdinand. 1847–1919. American geologist, b. New York City. On staff of U.S. Geological Survey (1879–1919); studied western mining districts, South African goldfields (1896), mineral resources of the Philippines (1898). Also contributed to theoretical geophysics. Author of *Geology of the Comstock Lode and Washoe District* (1882), etc.

Becker, Nikolaus. 1809–1845. German poet. Known for his song of the Rhine (1840) beginning "Sie sollen ihn nicht haben, den freien deutschen Rhein," which inspired notably Alfred de Musset's answer "Nous l'avons eu, votre Rhin allemand" (1841).

Becker, Wilhelm Adolf. 1796–1846. German classical archaeologist. Professor, Leipzig (from 1842). Author of *Gallus* (1838) and *Charikles* (1840), romances of ancient everyday Greek and Roman life, *Handbuch der kömischen Altertümer* (begun 1843; revised later by Marquardt and Mommsen).

Becker-Modersohn, Paula. See MODERSOHN-BECKER.

Beck·et \'bek-ət\, Frederick Mark. 1875–1942. American metallurgist, b. Montreal. To U.S. (1895); joined (1906) Electro Metallurgical Co., predecessor of Union Carbide Corp., of which he became chief metallurgist (1906) and later vice-president. Developed (c.1904) silicon reduction process for mass production of low-carbon ferroalloys and stainless steels.

Becket, Thomas. *Called also* Thomas à Becket, Thomas of London, *and* Saint Thomas Becket. c.1118–1170. English prelate. Sent by Theobald, archbishop of Canterbury, to study canon law at Bologna and Auxerre; archdeacon of Canterbury (1154–62). Vigorous chancellor under Henry II (1155–62); organized campaign and fought in war with Toulouse (1159). Made archbishop of Canterbury (1162) by Henry and became uncompromising defender of rights of Church against lay power; refused to seal Constitutions of Clarendon, and fled to France (1164); persuaded Pope Alexander III to suspend bishops who crowned Prince Henry in his absence, and forced king to reconciliation (1170); refused absolution of bishops; murdered by four overzealous knights of

Henry's court. Canonized (1173). Shrine plundered by Henry VIII (1538) and name of saint expunged from English church calendar.

Beck·ett \ˈbek-ət\, Sir Edmund. *Orig. surname* Beckett Den·i·son \-ˈden-ə-sən\. 1st Baron Grim·thorpe \ˈgrim-ˌthȯ(ə)rp\. 1816–1905. English lawyer, architect, and horologist. After accumulating fortune at the bar, interested himself in church architecture, clockmaking, and religious controversies. Designed new escapement for Big Ben clock, Parliament (1859). Created baron (1886). Author of *A Rudimentary Treatise on Clock and Watch Making* (1850), *A Book on Building, Civil and Ecclesiastical* (1876), etc.

Beckett, Gilbert Abbott à. See À BECKETT.

Beck·ford \ˈbek-fərd\, William. 1760–1844. English writer, dilettante, and art collector. Wrote classic Gothic novel *Vathek,* written in French (1782), best known in the anonymous and unauthorized English translation which was published (1786) the year before the French original. Secluded himself in magnificent residence, "Fonthill," a Gothic "abbey" with a 260-foot tower. Author of travel sketches including *Dreams, Waking Thoughts and Incidents* (1783) and satires on the minor novel.

Beck·mann \ˈbek-ˌmän\, Max. 1884–1950. German painter. Associated with Sezession, later Neue Sachlichkeit groups; influenced by Edvard Munch. Works noted for grotesque, often violent depiction of scenes of horror, social commentary; a leader of Expressionist school. To U.S. (1947).

Beck·nell \ˈbek-nᵊl\, William. 1796?–1865. American pioneer, b. Amherst Co., Va. Traced Santa Fe trail (1822), which became main commercial route to Southwest.

Beck·with \ˈbek-(ˌ)with\, Sir George. 1753–1823. English army officer and colonial governor. Lieutenant general (1805); governor of Bermuda (1797), St. Vincent (1804), Barbados (1808); conquered Martinique (1809) and Guadaloupe (1810); general (1814); commanded English troops in Ireland (1816–20). His brother ¶Sir Thomas Sydney (1772–1831) served in Denmark (1807) and Peninsular campaign (1808–11); commander in chief at Bombay, India (1829); lieutenant general (1830); remembered as outstanding commander of light infantry. Their nephew ¶John Charles Beckwith (1789–1862), an army officer; served in Peninsular campaign in uncle's light division and at Waterloo (1815); settled in Piedmont among Waldenses, established some 120 schools, and endeavored to reawaken evangelical faith.

Beckx \ˈbeks\, Pierre-Jean. 1795–1887. Belgian ecclesiast. Entered Society of Jesus (1819); confessor to Duke Ferdinand of Anhalt-Köthen; Jesuit procurator in Austria (1847). General of Society of Jesus (1853–84). Author of *Der Monat Maria.*

Becque \bek\, Henry-François. 1837–1899. French dramatist. Author of *Les Corbeaux* (1882) and *La Parisienne* (1885) which marked rise of Naturalistic school in the French drama.

Béc·quer \ˈbek-ər\, Gustavo Adolfo. 1836–1870. Spanish poet. Author of the prose tales *Leyendas españolas,* essays *Cartas literarias a una mujer* (1864), and verse, including *Rimas* (1860–61).

Bec·que·rel \bek-rel\. Family of French physicists, including: Antoine-César (1788–1878); professor, Musée d'Histoire Naturelle (1837–78); one of creators of science of electrochemistry; invented thermoelectric needle for determining internal bodily temperatures; investigated atmospheric electricity, galvanometers, and electric conductivity of metals. His son ¶Alexandre-Edmond (1820–1891) succeeded to his professorship (1878–91); investigated light, phosphorescence, photochemistry, spectroscopy, magnetism. Alexandre-Edmond's son ¶Antoine-Henri (1852–1908) was professor at the Musée d'Histoire Naturelle (1892), École Polytechnique (1895); investigated magnetic rotation of plane of polarization of light; discovered (1896) natural radioactivity; awarded (together with Pierre Curie and Madame Curie) the Nobel prize for physics (1903).

Be·daux \bə-ˈdō\, Charles Eugène. 1886–1944. American efficiency engineer, b. Charenton-le-Pont, France. To U.S. (1906); originator of the Bedaux, or point, system of productivity measurement and wage payment.

Bed·does \ˈbed-(ˌ)ōz\, Thomas. 1760–1808. English physician and scientific writer. Established at Clifton a "pneumatic institution" for treatment of diseases by inhalation of gases (1798), with Humphry Davy as superintendent.

Beddoes, Thomas Lovell. 1803–1849. English poet. Son of Thomas Beddoes. Author of *The Bride's Tragedy* (1822) and of *Death's Jest-Book; or, The Fool's Tragedy,* which he worked at revising until his death; the Gothic-Romantic work, in part brilliant, appeared posthumously (1850).

Bede \ˈbēd\ *or* **Bae·da** \ˈbed-ə\ *or* **Be·da** \ˈbēd-ə\. Saint. *Known as* The Venerable. 672 or 673–735. Anglo-Saxon scholar, historian, and theologian. Ordained (703); associated with monastery of St. Paul at Jarrow throughout life; taught Greek, Latin, Hebrew, and theology. Concluded (731 or 732) his ecclesiastical history of England, *Historia ecclesiastica gentis Anglorum.* Author also of scriptural commentaries, of *De Temporum ratione* (725) on reckoning Easter, of grammatical works, of *Historia abbatum* (c.725), a history of the abbots of Wearmouth and Jarrow, and of *De natura rerum,* on physical science. Introduced custom of dating events from birth of Christ. Canonized (1899).

Be·del \bə-del\, Maurice. 1883–1954. French novelist. Author of *Jérôme 60° latitude Nord* (1927, Goncourt prize), *Molinoff, Indre-et-Loire* (1928), *Philippine* (1930), *Zulfu* (1933), *Le Laurier d'Apollon* (1937), *Le Mariage des couleurs* (1951), *Voyage de Jérôme aux Etats-Unis* (1953).

Bedford, Earls and dukes of. See JOHN of Lancaster; Jasper TUDOR; and RUSSELL family.

Bé·dier \bād-yā\, Joseph, *in full* Charles-Marie-Joseph. 1864–1938. French author and scholar. Professor, Collège de France (1903–38); published prose adaptation of *Roman de Tristan et Iseult* (1900), critical editions of *Roman de Tristan* (1902–05) and of *Chanson de Roland* (1921), and a study *Les Légendes épiques* (1908–13), advancing the theory that the medieval epic cycles developed along the routes followed by pilgrims.

Bē·dil \ˈbād-il\, Mīrzā. *In full* Mīrzā ʿAbd-ul-Qadir ibn ʿAbd-ul-Khāliq Arlās Bēdil. 1644–1721. Indian Muslim poet. Author of some 90,000 mystic verses; popular in Afghanistan, Chinese Turkistan.

Bedmar, Marqués de. See Alfonso de la CUEVA.

Bedny, Demyan. See Yefim PRIDVOROV.

Bed·ra·ja \bed-ˈrī-ä\. *Also known as* P'ra P'et·ra·ja \ˈprä-pe-ˈtrī-ä\ *and* Phra Pet·ra·cha \ˈprä-pe-träk-ä\. d. 1703. King of Siam (1688–1703). Reputedly foster brother of King Narai, whom he succeeded; began persecution of Christians and French; executed Constantine Phaulkon; closed Siam to European influence; reorganized civil and military administration; reign marked by harsh rule, military ventures, frequent revolts.

Bed·red·din \ˌbed-red-ˈdēn\. *Also known as* Badr ad-Dīn ibn Qāḍī Samāwnā. 1358 –1416 or 1420. Ottoman theologian and jurist. Convert to Ṣūfism (1381); tutor to Mamlūk crown prince of Egypt (1383); later Ṣūfī missionary in Asia Minor and Rumelia; evolved communalistic social doctrine that inspired popular revolt in İznik (1416).

Bed·well \ˈbed-wəl, -ˌwel\, William. 1561?–1632. English scholar. Considered father of Arabic studies in England; translator of mathematical works; compiler of an Arabic lexicon; one of translators of King James Bible (1604–11).

Bee \ˈbē\, Barnard Elliott. 1824–1861. American soldier, b. Charleston, S.C. Commissioned in U.S. army (1845); entered Confederate army (1861); brigadier general (1861); at Bull Run, gave nickname "Stonewall" to Gen. Thomas J. Jackson.

Bee·be \ˈbē-(ˌ)bē\, Charles William. 1877–1962. American naturalist and explorer, b. Brooklyn, N.Y. Curator of ornithology (from 1899) and director of department of tropical research (1919), N.Y. Zoological Society. Headed scientific expeditions to Nova Scotia, Mexico, S. America, the Himalayas, Borneo, etc.; with Otis Barton made bathysphere descent to record depth of 3028 feet off Bermuda (1934). Author of *Two Bird Lovers in Mexico* (1905), *Jungle Peace* (1918), *Galápagos, World's End* (1923), *Jungle Days* (1925), *The Arcturus Adventure* (1925), *Pheasants—Their Lives and Homes* (1926), *Beneath Tropic Seas* (1928), *Nonesuch: Land of Water* (1932), *Half Mile Down* (1934), *Book of Naturalists* (1944), *High Jungle* (1949), *Edge of the Jungle* (1950), *Unseen Life of New York* (1953).

Beebe, Lucius Morris. 1902–1966. American journalist, b. Wakefield, Mass. On staff of New York *Herald-Tribune* (1929–50), wrote column "This New York" (1933–44); published Virginia City, Nev., *Territorial Enterprise* (1950–60); wrote column "This Wild West" for *San Francisco Chronicle* (1960–66). Author of *Fallen Stars* (1921), *Boston and the Boston Legend* (1935), *High Iron* (1938), *Highliners* (1940), *Highball* (1945), *Saga of Wells Fargo* (1949), *The American West* (1955), etc.

Bee·cham \ˈbē-chəm\, Sir Thomas. 2d Baronet. 1879–1961. English conductor and impresario. Initiated (1906) and conducted (1907–09) New Symphony and Beecham Symphony concert orchestras in London, introducing works of Frederick Delius; produced and conducted operas, many for the first time in London, as Strauss's *Salome;* associated with first appearance of Diaghilev's Ballets Russes (1911–12); produced Russian operas (1913), in which Chaliapin made his first English appearances; founded British National Opera Co. (1919), London Symphony Orchestra (1932), Royal Philharmonic Orchestra (1947); toured frequently in U.S. A leading interpreter of Mozart, Haydn, Sibelius.

Bee·cher \ˈbē-chər\, Henry Ward. 1813–1887. American clergyman, b. Litchfield, Conn. Son of Lyman Beecher. Pastor, Plymouth Congregational Church, Brooklyn, N.Y. (1847–87); powerful and convincing speaker of wide influence throughout country. Against slavery; favored moderate Reconstruction, woman suffrage, etc. Edited Congregational *Independent,* founded (1870) *Christian Union* (later *Outlook*). Author of *Seven Lectures to Young*

\ə\ abut \ᵊ\ kitten, *Fr.* **table \ər\ further \a\ ash \ā\ ace \ä\ cot, cart \au̇\ out \ch\ chin \e\ bet \ē\ easy \g\ go \i\ hit \ī\ ice \j\ job \ŋ\ sing \ō\ go \ȯ\ law \ȯi\ boy \th\ both \t͟h\ the \ü\ loot \u̇\ foot \y\ yet \zh\ vision \à, k̲, g̃, k̲, ⁿ, œ, œ̄, ue, ue̅, ʸ** *see* **Guide to Pronunciation**

Men (1844), *Evolution and Religion* (1885). Acquitted (1875) by civil jury and ecclesiastical tribunals of charges of adultery that created national sensation.

Beecher, Lyman. 1775–1863. American clergyman, b. New Haven, Conn. Held Presbyterian pastorates in East Hampton, N.Y. (1799–1810), Litchfield, Conn. (1810–26), Boston (1826–32), and Cincinnati (1832–42). President, Lane Theological Seminary, Cincinnati (1832–50). Among his thirteen children were: ¶Catharine Esther (1800–1878), b. East Hampton, N.Y.; conducted girls' schools in Hartford, Conn. (1824–32) and Cincinnati (1832–37); propagandist for female higher education and antisuffragist. ¶Edward (1803–1895), b. East Hampton, N.Y.; Congregational clergyman and educator; president, Illinois College (1830–44); founded *The Congregationalist* (1849). ¶Thomas Kinnicut (1824–1900); Congregational clergyman at Elmira, N.Y. (1854–1900); pioneer in "institutional church" movement. Also Harriet Beecher STOWE, Henry Ward BEECHER.

Bee·chey \'bē-chē\, Sir William. 1753–1839. English painter. Made portrait painter to Queen Charlotte (1793); works included *Brother and Sister* and *Cavalry Review in Hyde Park.* His son ¶ Frederick William (1796–1856), naval officer and geographer, accompanied Franklin's scientific polar expedition (1818) and Parry's (1819); surveyed coasts of North Africa (1821–23), South America (1835), and Ireland (1837); author of geographical works.

Bee·croft \'bē-ˌkrȯft\, John. 1790–1854. English adventurer. To British base on Fernando Po (1829); unofficial ruler of population of liberated slaves (1834–43); named governor by Spain (1843), acted also as unofficial British consul; British consul for Bight of Benin (1849–54); laid groundwork for policy of active intervention in native affairs.

Beer \'bi(ə)r\, George Louis. 1872–1920. American historian, b. Staten Island, N.Y. Successful tobacco merchant (1893–1903); retired to devote himself to historical study. Author of *British Colonial Policy, 1754–1765* (1907), *Origins of the British Colonial System, 1578–1600* (1908), *The Old Colonial System* (1912), *The English-Speaking Peoples* (1917), etc.

Beer, Jakob Liebmann. See Giacomo MEYERBEER.

Beer \'bār\, Michael. 1800–1833. German playwright. Brother of Giacomo Meyerbeer. His most successful play was the tragedy *Struensee* (1829), for which Meyerbeer wrote an overture and incidental music.

Beer \'bi(ə)r\, Thomas. 1889–1940. American author, b. Council Bluffs, Iowa. Author of *Fair Rewards* (1922), *Stephen Crane* (1923), *Sandoval* (1924), *The Mauve Decade* (1926), *The Road to Heaven* (1928), *Hanna* (1929), *Mrs. Egg and Other Barbarians* (1933).

Beer \'bār\, Wilhelm. 1797–1850. German banker and astronomer. Brother of Giacomo Meyerbeer. Established an observatory in the Tiergarten of Berlin, and (with J.H. von Mädler) made studies of Mars and the moon (1828–40); their *Mappa selenographica* (1836) remained best map of moon for over 50 years.

Beer·bohm \'bi(ə)r-ˌbōm, -bəm\, Sir Max, *in full* Henry Maximilian. 1872–1956. English critic and caricaturist. Half-brother of Sir Herbert Beerbohm Tree. Succeeded G. B. Shaw as dramatic critic of *Saturday Review* (1898); resident in Rapallo, Italy (from 1910). Author of essays *The Works of Max Beerbohm* (1896), *The Happy Hypocrite* (1897), *More* (1899), *And Even Now* (1920), *Variety of Things* (1928); satirical novel *Zuleika Dobson* (1911); *A Christmas Garland,* a collection of parodies of contemporary authors (1912); and among the volumes of pictorial caricatures, *Twenty-five Gentlemen* (1896), *The Poet's Corner* (1904), *Rossetti and His Circle* (1922), *Observations* (1925).

Beerbohm Tree, Sir Herbert. See TREE.

Beer-Hof·mann \'bār-'hōf-ˌmän\, Richard. 1866–1945. Austrian poet, playwright, and novelist. Author of *Der Tod Georgs* (1900), *Der Graf von Charolais* (1904), and a trilogy comprising *Jaákobs Traum* (1918), *Der junge David* (1933), *Vorspiel auf dem Theater zu König David* (1936), etc.

Beer·naert \'bār-ˌnärt\, Auguste Marie François. 1829–1912. Belgian politician. Elected deputy (1873); minister of public works (1873–78), agriculture and industry (1884); prime minister and minister of finance (1884–94); president of Chamber of Deputies (1895–1900). Member of International Peace Conference, The Hague (1899, 1907). Recipient, with Baron d'Estournelles de Constant, of Nobel peace prize (1909).

Beers \'bi(ə)rz\, Clifford Whittingham. 1876–1943. American reformer, b. New Haven, Conn. In business, New York City (1898–1900, 1904–06). Suffered mental breakdown; entered sanitarium; made careful study of his own case and of his mental recovery; published famous book, *A Mind That Found Itself* (1908). Devoted himself thereafter to mental hygiene movement; founded (1908) Connecticut Society for Mental Hygiene, first society of its kind; founded National Commission for Mental Hygiene (1909), American Foundation for Mental Hygiene (1928), International Commission for Mental Hygiene (1930), and International Foundation for Mental Hygiene (1931).

Beers, Ethel Lynn. *Nee* Ethelinda Eliot. 1827–1879. American poet, b. Goshen, N.Y. m. (1846) William H. Beers. Author of poem "All Quiet Along the Potomac" (1861) and volume of verse under that title (1879).

Beery \'bi(ə)r-ē\, Wallace. 1886–1949. American actor, b. Kansas City, Mo. In youth an elephant trainer with Ringling Bros. circus; went on stage with brother Noah; joined Mack Sennett's Keystone film company (1917); later played at MGM. Films included *The Champ* (1931, Academy Award), *Min and Bill* (1931), *Tugboat Annie* (1933), *Dinner at Eight* (1934), *Viva Villa* (1934), *Ah! Wilderness* (1935).

Bees·ly \'bēz-lē\, Edward Spencer. 1831–1915. English historian. Professor of history, U. Coll., London (1860–93), Bedford Coll. (1860–89); editor, *Positivist Review* (1893). Author of translations and biography of Comte.

Bee·ston \'bē-stən\, Christopher. 1570?–1638. English actor and manager. Appeared with Shakespeare, Burbage, Augustine Phillips in *Every Man In his Humour* (1598); joined Worcester's Men (1602), remained as company became Queen Anne's Men (1603), becoming manager (1612); established company (1616) at his theater the Cockpit (later Phoenix); established company known as Beeston's Boys (1637); produced many of Thomas Heywood's plays.

Bee·tho·ven \'bāt-ˌhō-vən; *Angl* 'bā-ˌtō-vən, 'bāt-ˌō-\, Ludwig van. 1770–1827. German composer, of Flemish descent. Received early musical education from his father and from Neefe. Held various positions in Bonn (1783–92) as second court organist, opera band conductor, etc.; formed friendships in exclusive circles of Bonn, notably with Count Ferdinand von Waldstein and von Breuning family. In Vienna briefly (1787) to study with Mozart; again to Vienna (1792); studied with Haydn, Albrechtsberger, and Salieri. Resident in Vienna (from 1792) as pianist and composer; made public debut as pianist in his Concerto in C major (1795) and published three trios for piano, violin, and violoncello (opus 1); appeared for first time in his own concert (1800). Suffered from defective hearing (from c.1798); became totally deaf (c.1819); last years clouded by illness and worry. Often considered the greatest of composers; developed forms as symphony, quartet, sonata, to virtual perfection; raised instrumental music to unprecedented power of expression; principal inspiration of musical Romantics though himself strongly a classicist. Works included: 9 symphonies (1, 1800; 2, 1802; 3 or *Eroica,* 1804; 4, 1806; 5, 1808; 6 or *Pastoral,* 1808; 7, 1812; 8, 1812; 9 or *Choral,* 1824); 5 piano concertos including No. 3 (1800) and No. 5 or *Emperor* (1809); 32 piano sonatas, esp. *Moonlight* and *Appassionata* (1801, 1804); 20 sets of piano variations, as *Diabelli Variations* (1823); 17 string quartets along with trios, quintets, etc.; 10 sonatas for piano and violin as the *Kreutzer* (1803); music for theater including opera *Fidelio* (1805, revised 1806, 1814), and music for *Egmont* (1810); vocal music including oratorio *Christus am Ölberg* (1803), *Mass in C Major* (1807), *Missa Solemnis* (1823).

Beets \'bāts\, Nicolaas. 1814–1903. Dutch clergyman and writer. Professor of theology, Utrecht (1874–84). Author of Romantic verse *José* (1834), *Kuser* (1835), *Guy de Vlaming* (1837), of Dutch classic *Camera Obscura* (1839), a collection of tales and sketches of life and manners in Holland written under pseudonym Hil·de·brand \'hil-də-ˌbränt\, of literary criticism and works on theology, etc.

Bef·froy de Rei·gny \bāf-rwȧ-də-rān-yē\, Louis-Abel. *Pseudonym* Cou·sin Jacques \kü-zaⁿ-zhäk\. 1757–1811. French dramatist. Author of farces, as *Nicodème dans la lune* (1790), *La Petite Nanette* (1796), *Turlututu* (1797).

Be·gas \'bā-ˌgäs\, Karl. 1794–1854. German painter. Adherent successively of Nazarene (German Pre-Raphaelite), romanticist, and realist schools; court painter to king of Prussia; professor, Royal Academy, Berlin (from 1824). Works included frescoes in various Berlin churches; religious and historical paintings; portraits of Jacob Grimm, Meyerbeer, von Humboldt, and other contemporaries. His son ¶Oskar (1828–1883) was a portrait, genre, and historical painter; painted *Descent from the Cross* for Michaeliskirche, Berlin; later works included landscapes, portraits of Peter von Cornelius, Crown Prince Frederick, General von Moltke, and William I, and mural decorations in Berlin Rathaus. Another son ¶Reinhold (1831–1911) was a sculptor; works included *Pan Consoling a Deserted Nymph,* colossal group *Borussia* surmounting Berlin Bourse, Schiller monument in Berlin, *Mercury and Psyche,* monument of Alexander von Humboldt, portrait busts of William I, Frederick III, William II, Bismarck, and Moltke, marble sarcophagi of Frederick III and his empress (in Potsdam), and a bronze group *Germania* surmounting Reichstag building.

Bé·gin \bā-zhaⁿ\, Louis Nazaire. 1840–1925. Canadian prelate, b. La Pointe-Lévis, Que. Ordained (1865); professor of theology, Laval U. (1868–84); bishop of Chicoutimi (1888); coadjutor to Cardinal Taschereau (1891); archbishop of Quebec (1898); led a campaign of social action (1907 ff.); cardinal (1914).

Be·ha·ghel \bā-'häg-əl\, Otto. 1854–1936. German philologist. Professor at Heidelberg, Basel, and Giessen (from 1888); editor in chief (1888–92) of *Germania;* author of books on German language, including *Die deutsche Sprache* (1886), *Geschichte der deutschen Sprache* (1901), *Deutsche Syntax* (1923–32).

Be·haim \'bā-ˌhīm\ *or* **Be·hem** \-ˌhem\, Martin. c.1436–1507. German navigator and geographer. Traveled through Europe as merchant (1476–84); to Portugal (1484), said to have introduced various improvements in nautical instruments there; constructed (1492) a terrestrial globe, still preserved at Nürnberg, showing erroneous geographical conceptions previous to the discovery of America.

Be·haim \'bā-,hīm\ *or* **Be·ham** \-,häm\ *or* **Be·heim** \-,hīm\, Michel. 1416–c.1472. German Meistersinger. Soldier and court singer in Hungary, Norway, the Palatinate, and elsewhere. Author of *Buch von den Wienern* dealing with siege (1462) of imperial palace at Vienna.

Béhaine, Pierre Pigneau de. See PIGNEAU DE BÉHAINE.

Bé·haine \bā-en\, René. 1880–1966. French novelist. Author of *Histoire d'une société* (1904–59), cycle of 16 novels including *La Conquête de la vie, Les Survivants, Si jeunesse savait, L'Enchantement du feu, Avec les yeux de l'esprit.*

Be·ham \'bā-,häm\, Hans Sebald. 1500–1550. German painter and engraver. One of "Little Masters"; settled in Frankfurt (1531); works included miniatures for two prayer books of Cardinal Albert of Mainz, hundreds of woodcuts designed esp. as illustrations for history books and Bibles, 252 copper engravings, and 18 etchings. His brother and pupil ¶Barthel (1502–1540), likewise a painter and engraver and one of the "Little Masters," was court painter to Duke William IV of Bavaria in Munich; works included 17 portraits of Bavarian dukes and 92 engravings.

Be·han \'bē-ən\, Brendan Francis. 1923–1964. Irish author and playwright. Author of plays *The Quare Fellow* (1954), *An Giall* (Eng. *The Hostage,* 1958); novel *The Scarperer* (1964); memoirs *Borstal Boy* (1958), *Confessions of an Irish Rebel* (1965).

Behm \'bām\, Ernst. 1830–1884. German geographer and statistician. Founder (1866) and editor (1866–78) of *Geographische Jahrbuch;* editor in chief (from 1878) of *Petermanns Mitteilungen;* statistician (from 1876) of *Der Gothaische Hofkalender,* the Almanach de Gotha.

Behmen, Jakob. See Jakob BÖHME.

Behn \'bān, 'ben\, Aphra *or* Ayfara. *Orig. surname unknown. Called* the Incomparable Astrea. 1640–1689. English dramatist and novelist. Lived from childhood (to 1658) in Surinam, West Indies; m. merchant named Behn (d. 1666); served as spy in Antwerp; unrewarded; imprisoned for debt. First English woman professional writer; author of vivacious, rather coarse comedies including *Forc'd Marriage* (1671), *The Rover* (1677), *False Count* (1682), *The Roundheads* (1682), of poems and translations, of novels and tales, esp. *Oroonoko* (1688), drawn from her Surinam experiences.

Behn, Sosthenes. 1882–1957. American businessman, b. St. Thomas, V.I. To U.S. (1898); established sugar brokerage, Puerto Rico (1904); acquired Puerto Rican Telephone Co. (1914), Cuban Telephone Co. (1916); incorporated International Telephone and Telegraph Corp. (1920); built or acquired telephone systems in Spain, France, England, Italy, Rumania, Norway, South America; directed I.T.T. as president (1920–48), chairman (1948–56).

Beh·rens \'bā-rəns\, Peter. 1868–1940. German architect. Director of Düsseldorf art and craft school (1903–07); professor, Düsseldorf Academy (1921–22), Vienna Academy (1922–27). Artistic adviser to AEG manufacturing firm (1907 ff.); designed turbine assembly works, Berlin (1909), Mannesmann-Werke, Düsseldorf (1911–12), Farbwerke at Höchst (1920–24), German embassy, St. Petersburg (1911–12), state tobacco factory, Linz (1930), etc. A pioneer in modern architecture and industrial design.

Beh·ring \'bā-riŋ\, Emil Adolf von. 1854–1917. German bacteriologist. At Koch Institute of Hygiene, Berlin (1889–94); professor at Halle (1894–95), Marburg (from 1895); pioneer in immunology. With Shibasaburo Kitasato discovered principle of antitoxic immunity in work on tetanus (1890); developed diphtheria antitoxin (1892). Awarded 1901 Nobel prize for physiology or medicine.

Behr·man \'ber-mən\, Samuel Nathaniel. 1893–1973. American playwright, b. Worcester, Mass. Author of plays including *The Second Man* (1927), *Serena Blandish* (1928), *Brief Moment* (1932), *Biography* (1933), *Love Story* (1934), *End of Summer* (1936), *Wine of Choice* (1938), *No Time for Comedy* (1939), *The Talley Method* (1940), *Jacobowsky and the Colonel* (with Franz Werfel, 1944), *Fanny* (1954); screenplays; *Portrait of Max* (1960), *The Burning Glass* (1968).

Beh·zād \bez-'äd\. *In full* Ostād Kamāl od-Dīn Behzād. c.1455–c.1536. Persian painter. Head of academy at Herāt (1486–1506); court painter to Shāh Esmā'īl I (1506–22); director of royal library (1522–c.1536). Considered greatest of Persian painters and a teacher of lasting influence; noted esp. as miniaturist; master of color and composition; works included illustrations for works of poet Sa'dī.

Bei·der·becke \'bīd-ər-,bek\, Bix, *orig.* Leon Bismarck. 1903–1931. American musician, b. Davenport, Iowa. Self-taught cornettist and pianist; in brief career (1923–31) became first white musician to contribute significantly to techniques and style of jazz; best known recordings included "I'm Coming, Virginia," "Singin' the Blues," "In a Mist."

Beil·by \'bēl-bē\, Sir George Thomas. 1850–1924. Scottish industrial chemist. Improved process of distillation of shale oil and invented a synthetic process of manufacturing alkaline cyanides. Advanced original hypothesis on crystalline and vitreous states of solids, in *Aggregation and Flow of Solids* (1921).

Beil·stein \'bīl-,shtīn\, Friedrich Konrad. 1838–1906. German chemist. Professor, Institute of Technology, St. Petersburg (from 1866). Author of *Handbuch der organischen Chemie* (1880–83), a standard and indispensable reference work.

Beis·sel \'bī-səl\, Johann Conrad. 1690–1768. American clergyman, b. Eberbach, Germany. To Pennsylvania (1720); founded (c.1730) at Ephrata, Pa., "Economy," a community of Solitary Brethren of the Community of Seventh-Day Baptists (known as Dunkards). His hymns and melodies, as in *Göttliche Liebes und Lobes Gethöne* (1730), influenced American hymnology.

Beit \'bīt\, Alfred. 1853–1906. British financier and philanthropist, b. Hamburg. To South Africa (1875); entered diamond business; associated (from 1880) with Cecil Rhodes in South African diamond fields, amassed enormous fortune; developed Witwatersrand goldfields; trustee under Rhodes's will to carry out South African projects, including a university. His brother ¶Sir Otto (1865–1930) moved to England (1888); succeeded Alfred in administration of South African holdings and philanthropies; created baronet (1924).

Beith \'bēth\, John Hay. *Pseudonym* Ian Hay \'hā\. 1876–1952. British novelist and playwright. School teacher (1901–12). Novels included *Pip* (1907), *The Right Stuff* (1908), *A Man's Man* (1909), *The First Hundred Thousand* (1915), *Carrying On* (1917), *The Last Million* (1918), *Paid, With Thanks* (1925); plays included *Tilly of Bloomsbury* (1919), *A Safety Match* (1921), *Damsel in Distress* (with P.G. Wodehouse, 1928), *Leave it to Psmith* (with Wodehouse, 1930), *Housemaster* (1936).

Bé·jart \bā-zhȧr\. Family of French actors in comedy, including: Madeleine (1618–1672), ¶Joseph (c.1617–1659), ¶Louis (c.1630–1678), and ¶Geneviève (c.1624–1675); strolling players and members of family company; joined Molière in forming Illustre Théâtre company (1643); associated with his plays thereafter. Madeleine's other sister or perhaps daughter ¶Armande-Grésinde-Claire-Élisabeth (1642–1700), wife of Molière (1662 until his death) and of the actor Guérin d'Estriché (1677); kept company together after Molière's death (1673) under name *troupe du roi;* with additions, became company of Comédie Française.

Bek \'bek\, Anthony. 1240–1311. English prelate. Bishop of Durham (1285); trusted adviser of Edward I; held virtual royal authority in the north of England; renowned for wealth and liberality.

Beke \'bēk\, Charles Tilstone. 1800–1874. English geographer. Explored Abyssinia (1840–43), becoming first to determine course of Blue Nile; traveled in Syria, Palestine, Egypt (1861–62); explored alleged position of Mt. Sinai (1873). Wrote *Origines Biblicae* (1834), *Nile and its Tributaries* (1847), *Sources of the Nile* (1860), *Discoveries of Sinai in Arabia and of Midian* (1878).

Bé·ké·sy \'bā-,kā-shē, *Angl also* -kə-\, Georg von. 1899–1972. American physiologist, b. Budapest. On staff of Hungarian Telephone System Research laboratory (1923–46), U. of Budapest (1932–46); to U.S. (1947); on faculty, Harvard U. (1947–66), U. of Hawaii (1966–72). Studied detection and analysis of sound by human ear; demonstrated mechanics of frequency discrimination in basilar membrane; helped distinguish and find treatments for various forms of deafness. Awarded 1961 Nobel prize for physiology or medicine.

Bekh·te·rev \'byāk-tyir-yif\, Vladimir Mikhaylovich. 1857–1927. Russian neuropathologist. Professor, Kazan, then at Military Medical Academy, St. Petersburg (1893); director (1905–06); founded there psychoneurological institute (1907). Contributed to study of conditioned reflex. Author of *The Nerve Currents in Brain and Spinal Cord* (1882), *The Functions of the Nervous Centers* (1909), *Nervous System Diseases* (1911), etc.

Bek·ker \'bek-ər\, August Immanuel. 1785–1871. German classical scholar. Professor, Berlin (from 1810); prepared critical editions of Plato, Aristotle, Aristophanes, Photius, Livy, Tacitus; edited Byzantine, Provençal, and Old French authors; wrote *Anecdota Graeca* (1814–21), *Corpus Scriptorum Historiae Byzantinae* in 25 volumes (1850), etc.

Bekker, Balthasar. 1634–1698. Dutch theologian. Pastor, Amsterdam (1679–92); suspected of Cartesianism and deposed (1692) following publication of his *De Betoverde Wereld* (1691–93) condemning belief in witchcraft, the devil, and magical powers.

Bekker, Elisabeth. See Elisabeth WOLFF-BEKKER.

Bél \'bāl\, Mátyás. *Lat.* Matthias Be·li·us \'bē-lē-əs\. 1684–1749. Hungarian scholar. Historiographer to Emperor Charles VI; author of *Notitia Hungariae novae historico-geographica* (1735–42); founded (1721) *Nova Posoniensia,* first regular Hungarian journal.

Bé·la \'bā-lä\. Name of four kings of Hungary of the Árpád dynasty:

Béla I. d. 1063. King (1060–63). Deposed brother Andrew I (1060) to gain throne; killed in battle with supporters of Andrew's son Salomon.

Béla II. *Called* the Blind. d. 1141. King (1131–41). Nephew of Kálmán, by whom he was blinded in infancy; succeeded Kálmán's son Stephen II.

Béla III. d. 1196. King (1173–96). Gained throne with aid of Byzantine emperor Manuel I Comnenus; favored and introduced Byzantine customs and culture; m., as 2d wife, Margaret, sister of Philip Augustus of France; fought two wars (1181–88, 1190–91), only partly successful, against Venice to recover Dalmatia; aided Isaac II Angelus against Bulgarians.

Béla IV. 1206–1270. King (1235–70). Son of Andrew II; inherited much-disturbed kingdom from his father; spent most of reign in attempt to restore peace and order; m. Maria, daughter of Nicaean emperor, Theodore Lascaris. Major event of reign was his overwhelming defeat by Mongol invaders under Batu Khan (1241), all Hungary being overrun and devastated; forced to flee to Adriatic; after Mongol withdrawal, defeated (1246) Frederick of Austria, who had seized western provinces of Hungary; fought off other foreign enemies (Serbs, Tatars); engaged in war (1265–70) with Otakar II of Bohemia over possession of Styria.

Bé·lain d'·Es·nam·buc \bə-la^{n}-də-nä^{n}-büek\, Pierre. 1585–1637. French trader. Founded first French colonies in West Indies on St. Kitts (1625 or 1627); claimed Martinique for France (1635).

Béla Kun. See Béla KUN.

Be·lal·cá·zar \bā-läl-ˈkäth-är, -ˈkäs-\ *or* **Be·nal·cá·zar** \bā-näl-\, Sebastián de. *Orig.* Sebastián Mo·ya·no \mō-ˈyän-ō\. c.1495–1551. Spanish conquistador. To America (1519); conquered Nicaragua (1524); participated in Pizarro's conquest of Peru (1532); defeated Inca chief Rumiñahui at Quito (1533); established cities of Quito and Guayaquil; invaded Popayán (now southwestern Colombia) in search for El Dorado; founder (1537) and governor of Popayán.

Be·las·co \bə-ˈlas-(ˌ)kō\, David. 1853–1931. American playwright and producer, b. San Francisco. Child actor; manager of various theaters; wrote *Hearts of Oak* (1879) and toured in it with James A. Herne; stage manager, Madison Square Theater, New York City (1880–87) and later of the Lyceum; owner and manager of Belasco Theater, New York City (from 1906). Widely known for his success in developing talents of actors and for his methods of stage setting and lighting. Author of or collaborator in: *May Blossom* (1884), *Lord Chumley* (1887), *The Heart of Maryland* (1895), *Madame Butterfly* (1900; source of Puccini's opera), *Du Barry* (1901), *Music Master* (1905), *The Girl of the Golden West* (1905), *The Return of Peter Grimm* (1911), *Laugh, Clown, Laugh* (1923), *Lulu Belle* (1926), etc.

Be·la·ún·de \bā-lä-ˈün-dā\, Víctor Andrés. 1883–1966. Peruvian diplomat. Professor, U. of San Marcos (1915 ff.); member of constitutional assembly (1930–33); ambassador to Colombia and Switzerland; delegate to United Nations (1949–66), president of General Assembly (1959).

Bel·cher \ˈbel-chər\, Sir Edward. 1799–1877. English naval officer. Employed on coastal surveys of Africa, western America, East Indies (1830–47); commanded Arctic expedition in search of Sir John Franklin (1852–55); admiral (1872). Author of narratives of voyages.

Belcher, Jonathan. 1682–1757. American colonial governor, b. Cambridge, Mass. Governor of Massachusetts and New Hampshire (1730–41); governor of New Jersey (1746–57).

Bel·cre·di \bel-ˈkrā-dē\, Richard. Graf. 1823–1902. Austrian statesman. Governor of Silesia (1860); imperial representative at Prague (1864); succeeded Schmerling as minister of state and prime minister (1865–67); instituted conciliatory policy toward Slavs; forced to resign in aftermath of defeat in Seven Weeks' War with Prussia and Italy (1866); president of administrative court (1881–95).

Belesme *or* **Bellême,** Robert of. See ROBERT of Belesme.

Belgioioso, Baltazarini di. See Balthazar de BEAUJOYEULX.

Bel·gio·io·so \ˌbāl-jō-ˈyō-sō\, Cristina, *nee* Tri·vul·zio \trē-ˈvülts-yō\. Princess. 1808–1871. Italian patriot and author. m. (1824) Prince Emilio de Belgioioso. Lived in Paris (1830–48); founded (1843) and edited *La Gazzetta Italiana* in behalf of Italian nationalism. Raised at own expense volunteer corps for Charles Albert (c.1848); exiled (1849–61). Among her works were *Souvenirs d'exil* (1850), *Histoire de la Maison de Savoie* (1860), *Réflexions sur l'etat actuel de l'Italie et sur son avenir* (1869).

Bel·grand \bel-grä^{n}\, Marie-François-Eugène. 1810–1878. French hydrographic engineer. Installed sewerage system in Paris and built reservoirs of Montsouris.

Bel·gra·no \bel-ˈgrän-ō\, Manuel. 1770–1820. Argentine general and patriot. Member of ruling junta of Rio de la Plata (1810); in command of northern forces, defeated royalists in battles of Tucumán (1812) and Salta (1813); was defeated (1813) in campaigns in north and replaced (1814) by San Martín.

Belhaven, Barons. See under HAMILTON family.

Be·li·dor \bā-lē-dȯr\, Bernard Fo·rest de \fó-re-də\. 1698–1761. French engineer. Professor, École de Artillerie; inspector of artillery. Author of classic *Architecture hydraulique* (1737–53).

Be·lin \bə-la^{n}\, Edouard. 1876–1963. French engineer. Invented apparatus and made first telephoto transmission (Paris–Lyon–Bordeaux–Paris, 1907) and first transatlantic telephoto transmission (Annapolis, Md.–Malmaison, France, 1921).

Be·lin·sky \byəl-ˈyēn-skəi\, Vissarion Grigoryevich. 1811–1848. Russian literary critic. Turned to journalism after expulsion (1832) from Moscow U.; in critical articles expounded nationalist doctrine of Schelling; later became Hegelian; literary critic for *Otechestvennye zapiski* (1839–46), *Sovremennik* (1846–48); despite shifting viewpoint, staunch champion of Russian culture and character; author of famous letter critical of Gogol (1847).

Bel·i·sar·i·us \ˌbel-i-ˈsar-ē-əs, -ˈser-\. c.505–565. Byzantine general. Served in bodyguard of Emperor Justinian I; appointed (c.525) to command in eastern armies; hero of victory at Dara (530); m. (531) Antonina, favorite of Empress Theodora. Saved Justinian by suppressing Nika riot (532). Led expedition that overthrew Vandal kingdom in North Africa (533–534). Sent by emperor to subdue Ostrogoths in Italy; conquered Sicily (535) and southern Italy (536–537); occupied Rome (536) and defended it for a year (537–538). Lost Justinian's trust by entertaining offer of kingship by Goths; saved by favor of Theodora. Led forces against Persians (541–542). Sent again to Italy (544–548) but with inadequate forces and without Justinian's full support; replaced by Narses (548). In Constantinople in retirement (548–559). Recalled to service to repel Hun invaders (559). In later years in disfavor.

Belisha, Leslie Hore-. See HORE-BELISHA.

Bel·knap \ˈbel-ˌnap\, William Worth. 1829–1890. American army officer and politician, b. Newburgh, N.Y. Served through Civil War; brigadier general (1864). Secretary of war in Grant's cabinet (1869); impeached for malfeasance in office (1876); resigned.

Bell, Adam Schall von. See SCHALL VON BELL.

Bell \ˈbel\, Alexander Graham. 1847–1922. American inventor and educator, b. Edinburgh, Scotland. Son of Alexander M. Bell; assistant to father at U. Coll., London (1868–70); to Canada (1870) and U.S. (1871) as teacher of father's visible speech system; opened school for training teachers of the deaf, Boston (1872). Experimented with electrical and acoustical devices; invented telegraph multiplexing system (pat. 1875); produced first intelligible telephonic transmission of voice (June 3, 1875) to assistant Thomas A. Watson; patented telephone (1876); successfully defended patent against Elisha Gray's claims and others. With Gardiner G. Hubbard and others formed (1877) Bell Telephone Co. Moved to Washington, D.C. (1879); naturalized (1882). Established (1880) Volta Laboratory, where experiments led to photophone, audiometer, improvements in phonograph, induction balance for locating metallic objects in body, etc. Founded journal *Science* (1883), American Association to Promote Teaching of Speech to the Deaf (1890), Aerial Experiment Association (1907). President, National Geographic Society (1896–1904).

Bell, Alexander Melville. 1819–1905. American educator, b. Edinburgh, Scotland. A teacher of elocution, U. of Edinburgh (1843–65), U. Coll., London (1865–70), Queens Coll., Ontario (1870–81). Developed idea of a physiological alphabet which would present visually the articulating position of the vocal organs for each sound. Moved to Washington, D.C. (1881); naturalized (1897). Author of *Visible Speech: The Science of Universal Alphabetics* (1867).

Bell, Andrew. 1726–1809. Scottish engraver and publisher. With Colin Macfarquhar projected and published the *Encyclopaedia Britannica* (1st ed., 1768–71); furnished engraved plates for first three editions.

Bell, Andrew. 1753–1832. Scottish clergyman and educator. While superintendent of an orphanage in Madras, India (1789–96), originated monitorial system (Bell, or Madras, system) of school education, in which older pupils instruct the younger.

Bell, Sir Charles. 1774–1842. Scottish anatomist. Surgeon to Middlesex hospital (1812–36); professor of surgery, Edinburgh (1836). Discovered distinct functions of sensory and motor nerves and dual nature of spinal nerves. Author of *New Idea of Anatomy of the Brain* (1811), expanded into *Nervous System of the Human Body* (1830).

Bell, Charles Frederic Moberly. 1847–1911. English journalist. Founded *Egyptian Gazette* (1880); correspondent of London *Times* on Egyptian questions (1875); manager, London *Times* (1890–1911); published *Encyclopaedia Britannica,* 9th ed. (1898); started literary organ (1897–1901), later *The Times Literary Supplement;* established The Times Book Club (1905).

Bell, Clive, *in full* Arthur Clive Howard. 1881–1964. English critic. Author of *Art* (1914), *Peace at Once* (1915), *Since Cézanne* (1922), *Civilization* (1928), *Proust* (1929), *Account of French Painting* (1931). m. (1907) ¶Vanessa (1879–1961), daughter of Sir Leslie Stephen and fellow member of Bloomsbury group. Their son ¶Julian (1908–1937), poet, author of *We did not Fight* (1935), *Work for the Winter* (1936), was fatally wounded while driving ambulance for loyalists in Spanish civil war.

Bell, George Kennedy Allen. 1883–1958. English prelate. Ordained (1907); dean of Canterbury cathedral (1924); bishop of Chichester (1929). Organized acceptance of refugees from Nazi Germany; supported German Confessing church. A leader of Life and Work movement, and a leading ecumenist. Author of *Documents on Christian Unity* (1924–58), *Christianity and World Order* (1940), *Kingship of Christ* (1953).

Bell, Gertrude Margaret Lowthian. 1868–1926. English traveler, archaeologist, and government official. Traveled to Iran (1892–93), Palestine (1899), Syria and Cilicia (1905), Asia Minor (1907), Arabia (1913); engaged in military intelligence and political information work (1915–26); secretary to Sir Percy Cox; helped mold postwar administration of Mesopotamia, siding with forces bringing Faisal to throne of Iraq (1921). Author of *The Desert and the Sown* (1907), *Amurath to Amurath* (1911), and the archaeological work *The Palace and Mosque of Ukhaidir* (1914).

Bell, Henry. 1767–1830. Scottish engineer. Designed, and ran successfully on the Clyde (1812–20), the three-horsepower steamboat *Comet,* first commercially successful steamboat in Europe.

Bell, Henry Glassford. 1803–1874. Scottish lawyer and man of letters. Founded *Edinburgh Literary Journal* (1828). Author of a vindication of Mary, Queen of Scots (1830), *Summer and Winter Hours* (1831), *My Old Portfolio* (1832).

Bell, Sir Isaac Lowthian. 1816–1904. Scottish metallurgical chemist and industrialist. Founded, with his brothers, the Clarence iron-smelting works on the Tees (1854); M.P. (1875–80); created baronet (1885). Author of *Chemical Phenomena of Iron Smelting* (1872), etc.

Bell, John. 1691–1780. Scottish traveler. To St. Petersburg (1714); accompanied Russian embassies to Persia, China, and Constantinople; author of *Travels* (1763).

Bell, John. 1745–1831. British publisher. One of first to organize book-publishing firm on joint-stock basis; issued 109-volume *Poets of Great Britain complete from Chaucer to Churchill* (1777 ff.); introduced use of commissioned illustrations.

Bell, John. 1797–1869. American politician, b. near Nashville, Tenn. Member, U.S. House of Representatives (1827–41); speaker (1834–35); U.S. secretary of war (1841). Member, U.S. Senate (1847–59). Nominee (1860) of the Constitutional Union party for president of the United States; gained electoral votes of Tennessee, Kentucky, and Virginia.

Bell, John. 1811–1895. English sculptor. Chief works, all in London, included Wellington Monument at the Guildhall (1855–56), Guards' Memorial in Waterloo Place (1858–60), and American group in Albert Memorial (1873).

Bell, John Joy. 1871–1934. Scottish journalist and author. Established reputation as humorist with his *Wee MacGreegor* (1902; dramatized 1912). Other works included *Mistress M'Leerie* (1903), *Courtin' Christina* (1913), *Mr. Craw* (1924).

Bell, Julian. See under Clive BELL.

Bell, Lawrence Dale. 1894–1956. American aircraft designer, b. Mentone, Ind. Joined Glenn L. Martin (1913), rising to vice president of his firm; vice president of Consolidated Aircraft Co. (1929–35); president of Bell Aircraft Co. (1935–56). Produced P-39 Airacobra, P-63 Kingcobra fighters for World War II; built P-59 Airacomet, first U.S. jet aircraft (flown 1942); built Bell X-1, first aircraft to break sound barrier (1947).

Bell, Thomas. 1792–1880. English dental surgeon and naturalist. Lectured on dental surgery and comparative anatomy at Guy's Hospital, London (1817–61). Professor of zoology, King's College, London (1836). Author of books on British animals, esp. *History of British Stalk-eyed Crustacea* (1853); edited Gilbert White's *Natural History of Selborne* (1877).

Bell, Vanessa. See Clive BELL.

Bel·la \'bel-lä\, Giano della. d. c.1305. Florentine political leader. Wealthy aristocrat; became leader of democratic faction during Secondo Popolo (1292–93); instigated and promulgated Ordinamenti di Giustizia (1293), basis of Florentine constitution; attacked by magnate class, forced into exile (1295).

Bella, Stefano della. *Known in France as* Étienne de la Belle \də-lȧ-bel\. 1610–1664. Italian designer and engraver. Known esp. for his engravings of military episodes, executed for Richelieu, as *Siege of Arras, Siege of Saint-Omer,* etc.

Bellamont *or* **Bellomont,** Earl of. See Richard COOTE.

Bel·la·my \'bel-ə-mē\, Edward. 1850–1898. American author, b. Chicopee Falls, Mass. His Utopian romance *Looking Backward* (1888) presented a method of economic organization, socialistic in nature, guaranteeing material equality. Its enormous success inspired Nationalist clubs dedicated to realization of the scheme; also wrote an unsuccessful sequel, *Equality* (1897).

Bel·la·my \'bel-ȧ-mē\, Jacobus. 1757–1786. Dutch poet. Author of sentimental, patriotic, and Anacreontic poems, in *Gezangen mijner jeugd* (1782), *Roosje* (1784), *Vaderlandsche Gezangen* (1785).

Bel·lar·mine \'bel-,är-mən, -,mēn\, Robert. Saint. *Ital.* Roberto Francesco Romolo Bel·lar·mi·no \,bāl-lär-'mē-nō\. 1542–1621. Italian prelate and controversialist. Entered Society of Jesus (1560); professor of theology, Louvain (1569–76), Roman Coll. (1576–88); aided in revision of Vulgate (1591); rector, Roman Coll. (1592); theologian to Pope Clement VIII (1597); cardinal (1599); archbishop of Capua (1602–05). Champion of Catholic orthodoxy against Reformation; led in condemning work of Galileo. Author of *Disputationes de controversiis Christianae fidei huius temporis haereticos* (1586–93), *Dottrina cristiana breve* (1597), and *De potestate Summi Pontificis in rebus temporalibus* (1610) against William Barclay of Aberdeen, who had denied temporal power of pope.

Bel·lay \bā-le, be-\, Guillaume du. Seigneur de Lan·gey \də-lä^{n}-zhā\. 1491–1543. French general and diplomat. Fought in Flanders, Italy; captured with Francis I at Pavia (1525); employed by Francis I on missions to England (1529–30 and later), in negotiations for purpose of uniting German princes against Charles V (1532–36); governor of Turin (1537–39), of Piedmont (1539–43). His work on contemporary history, *Ogdoades,* largely lost; fragment inserted in *Mémoires* (1569) of his brother Martin.

Bellay, Jean du. c.1492–1560. French prelate and diplomat. Brother of Guillaume du Bellay; bishop of Bayonne (1526), of Paris (1532); undertook several missions to England for Francis I (1527–34) and to Rome (1534) to attempt to win papal acquiescence in divorce of Henry VIII; cardinal (1535); named by Francis lieutenant general (1536–37), archbishop of Bordeaux (1544), bishop of Mans (1546). After death of Francis (1547) retired to Rome; bishop of Ostia and dean of Sacred College of Cardinals (1553).

Bellay, Joachim du. c.1522–1560. French poet. Nephew of Guillaume and Jean du Bellay. Became friend of Ronsard and leader of the group of poets known as The Pléiade, whose ideas he embodied in his *Défense et illustration de la langue française* (1549). His volumes of sonnets included *Olive* (1550) and especially *Les Antiquités de Rome* and *Les Regrets* (both 1558). Other works included *Vers lyriques, Divers poèmes* (1552), *Les Jeux rustiques.*

Bel·leau \bā-lō, be-\, Rémy *or* Remi. 1528–1577. French poet and scholar. Member of The Pléiade. Author of descriptive and pastoral poetry, including *Petites inventions* (1556), *Bergerie* (1565, 1572), didactic *Les Amours et nouveaux échanges des pierres précieuses* (1576), comedy *La Reconnue* (1577); translated Anacreon's *Odes* (1556).

Bellecour. See Jean-Claude-Gilles COLSON.

Belle·garde \bel-'gärd\, Heinrich Joseph Johannes von. Graf. 1756–1845. Austrian general and statesman. General chief of staff of Austrian army in Italy (1800); president of war council (1805); field marshal (1806); governor general of Galicia (1809–13). Commander in chief of Austrian forces in Italy (1813–15); governor general of Lombardy and Venetia (1814). President of war council and minister of state (1820–25).

Belle-Isle \bel-ēl\, Charles-Louis-Auguste Fou·quet \fü-ke\ de. Duc de Gi·sors \-də-zhē-zȯr\. 1684–1761. Marshal of France. Grandson of Nicolas Fouquet. Served in War of the Spanish Succession (1701–14), Spanish War (1718), War of the Polish Succession (1733); marshal (1741). Made fortune in speculation in John Law's Mississippi Scheme. Led anti-Austrian faction at court, forcing France into War of the Austrian Succession; French delegate at Frankfurt, influential in election of Emperor Charles VII (1742), for which he was created duke. Commanded withdrawal of French troops from Prague (1742), defended Provence against Austrians and Sardinians (1746–47). As minister of war (1758–60) introduced useful reforms in army administration during Seven Years' War.

Bellême, Robert of. See ROBERT of Belesme.

Bel·len·den \'bel-ən-dən\ *or* **Bal·len·den** \'bal-\ *or* **Bal·len·tyne** *or* **Bal·lan·tyne** \'bal-ən-,tīn\ *or* **Ban·na·tyne** \'ban-ə-,tīn\, John. fl. 1533–1587. Scottish ecclesiastic and poet. Translator of Livy and of Boece's *Scotorum Historiae* into Scottish vernacular (1536).

Bellenden, William. c.1555–1633. Scottish classical scholar. Diplomatic agent in France of James VI and Mary, Queen of Scots; author of treatises illustrating Roman history by extracts from Latin authors, esp. *De tribus luminibus romanorum* (1634).

Bel·li \'bel-lē\, Giuseppe Gioacchino. 1791–1863. Italian poet. Wrote over 2000 satirical sonnets on Roman life, as *I sonetti romaneschi* (pub. 1886–96).

Belli, Pierino. 1505–1575. Italian soldier and jurist. Commander of army of Holy Roman Empire in Piedmont; councilor of state under duke of Savoy (1560). Author of *De re militari et de bello* (1563), pioneering treatise on military law and rules of war.

Bel·lings·hau·sen \'bel-iŋs-,hau̇-zən\, Fabian Gottlieb von. *Russ.* Faddey Faddeyevich Bel·lins·gau·zen \bəl-yiŋs-'gau̇z-yin\. 1778–1852. Russian admiral and explorer. Joined Russian navy (1788); officer on first Russian circumnavigation of globe (1803); given command by Emperor Alexander I of expedition of exploration to Antarctic which circumnavigated continent and discovered and named Peter I Island and Alexander I Island (1819–21).

Bel·li·ni \bāl-'lē-nē\. Venetian family of painters including:

Jacopo. c.1400–c.1470. Pupil of Gentile da Fabriano; to Venice (1429), initiator of Venetian school of painting. Works included *Annunciation,*

Crucifixion, Adoration of the Kings, and two sketchbooks including drawings as *Nativity, Crucifixion, Flagellation,* showing experiments in linear perspective.

¶Gentile. c.1429–1507. Son of Jacopo; influenced also by brother-in-law Andrea Mantegna; official painter to the Venetian state (1474); to Constantinople (1479–80) to paint for sultan; introduced oil painting in Venetian mural decoration. His works included decoration of organ of Scuola di San Marco; *Portrait of Mohammad II;* huge detailed Venetian scenes for Scuola di San Giovanni Evangelista, as *Procession in St. Mark's Square, Recovery of the Holy Cross;* and *St. Mark Preaching in Alexandria,* completed by his brother.

¶Giovanni. c.1430–1516. Son of Jacopo; leading painter of Venetian school; master of Giorgione, Titian, Palma Vecchio, etc.; known esp. for his altarpieces as *St. Vincent Ferrer* at SS. Giovanni e Paolo, *Coronation of the Virgin, St. Jerome at Meditation* at Sta. Maria dei Miracoli; executed other devotional works, including *Agony in the Garden, Blood of the Redeemer, Sacred Allegory, St. Francis in Ecstasy,* many madonnas. Master of light; in later years developed landscape element in pictures, becoming one of greatest of landscape artists.

Bellini, Lorenzo. 1643–1704. Italian physician and anatomist. Professor, Pisa (1663–93); physician to Duke Cosimo III and Pope Clement XI (1693 ff.). Discovered complex of tubules comprising kidney (subsequently Bellini's tubules) and described mechanical theory of excretion in *Exercitatio anatomica de usu renum* (1662); investigated sense of taste; published comprehensive mechanical-hydraulic theory in *De urinis et pulsibus et missione sanguinis* (1683) and *Opuscula aliquot* (1695).

Bellini, Vincenzo. 1801–1835. Italian composer. Composed melodic operas including *Adelson e Salvina* (1825), *Bianca e Fernando* (1826), *Il pirata* (1827), *I Capuleti e i Montecchi* (1830), *La sonnambula* (1831), *Norma* (1831), and *I puritani* (1835), also sacred music, various instrumental and choral works, etc.; one of the great composers of bel canto music.

Bell·mann \'bel-màn\, Carl Michael. 1740–1795. Swedish poet. Author of parodic song cycles *Fredmans Epistlar* (1790), *Fredmans Sånger* (1791), and other religious poems, improvisations, satires, parodies, and esp. drinking and love songs.

Bel·lo \'bā-yō\, Andrés. 1781–1865. Venezuelan scholar and author. London agent of Venezuelan revolutionary government (1810–29); while in London established reputation with two Virgilian poems on South America published as *Silvas americanas* (1826–27); joined Chilean ministry of foreign affairs (1829); founded (1843) U. of Chile, of which he was thereafter rector; principal author of Chilean Civil Code (1855), subsequently adopted also by Colombia and Ecuador. Author of *Gramática de la lengua castellana* (1847), and works on philosophy, law, literature, etc.

Bel·loc \'bel-ˌäk, -ək\, Hilaire, *in full* Joseph Hilaire Pierre René. *Called* Hilary Belloc. 1870–1953. English author. Son of French barrister and English mother; naturalized British subject (1902). Newspaper and magazine writer; M.P. (1906–10). Author of essays, verse, novels, history, biography, criticism, including *Verses and Sonnets* (1895), *Bad Child's Book of Beasts* (1896; nonsense verse), *The Modern Traveller* (1898, verse), *Danton* (1899), *Lambkin's Remains* (1900, novel), *Robespierre* (1901), *The Path to Rome* (1902, travel memoir), *Emmanuel Burden* (1904, novel), *Cautionary Tales* (1907, children's verse); further novels *Mr. Clutterbuck's Election* (1908), *The Girondin* (1911), *The Green Overcoat* (1912), and *The Man Who Made Gold* (1930); *Europe and the Faith* (1920) and *History of England* (1925–31); *Marie Antoinette* (1910), *James II* (1928), *Richelieu* (1929), *Wolsey* (1930), *Cranmer* (1931), *Cromwell* (1934), *Characters of the Reformation* (1936); essays and other nonfiction as *Historic Thames* (1907), *The Four Men* (1912), *The Contrast* (1923), *Cruise of the "Nona"* (1925), *The Crisis of Our Civilization* (1937), *The Great Heresies* (1938). Considered a master of English prose style.

Belloc, Marie Adelaide. *Pen name* Mrs. Belloc Lowndes \'laùn(d)z\. 1868–1947. English novelist. Sister of Hilary Belloc; m. Frederic S. Lowndes. Author of historical works, novels as *The Philosophy of a Marquise* (1899), and esp. murder and mystery stories, as *The Chink in the Armour* (1912), *The Lodger* (1913), *Who Rides on a Tiger* (1936), and the autobiographical *I, too, have lived in Arcadia* (1941).

Bel·lo·ri \bäl-'lò-rē\, Giovanni Pietro. c.1615–1696. Italian art historian. Author of *Le vite de'pittori, scultori ed architetti moderni* (1672).

Bel·lot·to \bel-'lòt-tō\, Bernardo. *Also called* Canaletto Be·lot·to \bā-'lòt-tō\. 1720–1780. Italian painter. Nephew and student of Antonio Canaletto; painted in Venice (to 1742); court painter to Frederick Augustus II in Dresden (1747–54), Empress Maria Theresa (1758–60); to St. Petersburg (1767); court painter to Stanisław II in Warsaw (1767–80). Known esp. for precisely drawn (often by means of a camera obscura) topographic views of European cities.

Bel·lows \'bel-(ˌ)ōz, -əz\, George Wesley. 1882–1925. American artist and lithographer, b. Columbus, Ohio. Associated with realist group The Eight, esp. with Robert Henri; known for paintings of sporting scenes and landscapes. Works included *42 Kids, Stag at Sharkey's, Both Members of this Club, Polo Game, Up the Hudson.*

Belloy, Dormont de. See Pierre-Laurent BUYRETTE.

Bellune, Duc de. See Claude PERRIN.

Bel·mont \'bel-ˌmänt, -mənt\, Alva Ertskin, *nee* Smith. 1853–1933. American socialite and reformer, b. Mobile, Ala. m. William K. Vanderbilt (1875; div. 1895), 2d O.H.P. Belmont (1896; d. 1908). Leader of New York and Newport society; arranged marriage of daughter Consuelo to Duke of Marlborough (1895). Became suffragist; sponsored U.S. tour of Christabel Pankhurst (1914); president, National Woman's party (1921–33).

Belmont, August.[1] 1816–1890. American banker, b. Alzey, Rhenish Palatinate (now Germany). To U.S. (1837); established banking house, August Belmont & Co. (1837). Consul general for Austria in U.S. (1844–50); U.S. minister to the Netherlands (1853–57); chairman, Democratic National Committee (1860–72). Noted art connoisseur and sportsman. He was succeeded as head of house of Belmont by his son ¶August (1853–1924).

Belmont, Eleanor Elise, *nee* Rob·son \'räb-sən\. 1879–1979. American actress and philanthropist, b. Wigan, England. To U.S. (1887); successful actress as Eleanor Robson in New York and London; captivated G.B. Shaw, who wrote *Major Barbara* for her; m. (1910) August Belmont and retired from stage. Devoted herself to worthy causes, esp. the Red Cross (from 1917) and N.Y. Metropolitan Opera.

Bel·mon·te y Gar·cía \bel-'mōn-tā-ē-gär-'sē-ä\, Juan. 1892–1962. Spanish bullfighter. Introduced (c.1914) technique of standing erect through bull's pass, diverting bull by dexterous capework; appeared in record 109 corridas (1919); retired (1935).

Bel·mon·tet \bel-mōⁿ-te\, Louis. 1799–1879. French poet. Wrote poems celebrating Napoléon, as *Les Funérailles de Napoléon* (1821), *Les Napoléoniennes* (1859), tragedy *Une fête sous Néron* (with A. Soumet, 1829).

Be·loch \'bā-lōk\, Karl Julius. 1854–1929. German historian. Professor, U. of Rome (1879–1912, 1913–18, 1924–29), Leipzig (1912–13). Author of *Griechische Geschichte* (1893–1904), *Römische Geschichte bis zum Beginn der punischen Kriege* (1926), etc.

Be·lon \bə-lōⁿ\, Pierre. 1517–1564. French naturalist. Author of *Histoire naturelle des éstranges poissons marins* (1551), containing pioneering work in comparative anatomy and embryology, *Les Observations de plusieurs singularitez et choses mémorables* (1553) on his tour of eastern Mediterranean, and *Histoire de la nature des Oyseaux* (1955).

Belotto, Bernardo. See BELLOTTO.

Be·low \'bā-(ˌ)lō\, Fritz von. 1853–1918. Prussian general. In World War I, commanded 2d army at St. Quentin (1915–16), 1st army at Cambrai and Rethel (1916–18), and 9th army on the Somme (1918). His brother ¶Otto (1857–1944) commanded 8th army at Tannenberg and Masurian Lakes (1915–16), 6th, and later the 14th, army, against Italy (1917), and the 17th army and new 1st army in France (1918).

Bel·shaz·zar \bel-'shaz-ər\. *Gk.* Bal·ta·sar \bäl-'täs-är\ *or* Bal·tha·sar \bäl-'thäs-är\. *Akkadian* Bel-shar-usur. d. c.539 B.C. Crown prince of Babylonia. Son of Nabonidus; occupied throne and commanded army during father's exile (550–c.540); died after fall of Babylon to Persian general Gobryas (539).

Bel·ter \'bel-tər\, John Henry, *orig.* Johann Heinrich. 1804–1863. American furniture maker, b. Germany. To New York City (1844); created a Rococo revival furniture style featuring rich carving, molding, bold asymmetry, heavy brocades; enjoyed fashionable patronage and inspired imitators.

Bel·tra·mi \bäl-'träm-ē\, Eugenio. 1835–1899. Italian mathematician. Professor at Bologna (1862–64, 1866–73), Pisa (1864–66), Rome (1873–76, 1891–99), Pavia (1876–91); known esp. for research in non-Euclidean geometry.

Bely, Andrey. See Boris BUGAEV.

Bel·ya·yev \byil-'yá-yif\, Pavel Ivanovich. 1925–1970. Russian cosmonaut. Pilot of Voskhod 2 spacecraft, from which first walk in space was made by copilot Aleksey Leonov (1965).

Bel·zo·ni \bält-'sō-nē\, Giovanni Battista. 1778–1823. Italian explorer and archaeologist. Explored Egyptian antiquities (1815–19); opened temple of Abu-Simbel (1817); discovered tomb of Seti I, Thebes (1817); opened pyramid of Khafra at Giza; brought colossal head of Ramses II and other items to England.

Bem \'bem\, Józef. 1794–1850. Polish general. Took part in Napoléon's Russian campaign (1812) and defense of Danzig (1813); distinguished himself in Polish revolution (1830–31); fled to Paris. Took part in insurrection in Vienna (1848), joining Hungarian army; commanded army of Transylvania (1848); made brilliant campaign with small force, defeating Austrians at Piski (1849); drove Austrians and Russians into Walachia but was badly defeated (1849) by superior forces at Schässburg (Sighişoara); escaped to Turkey; embraced Islām and as Murad Pasha became governor of Aleppo.

Bem·bo \ˈbem-bō\, Pietro. 1470–1547. Italian prelate and scholar. Secretary to Leo X (1513–21); historiographer of Venetian republic (1529); created cardinal (1539). Restored classic tradition in Italian language and literature. Author of Latin and vernacular verses, of *Gli Asolani* (1505), and of *Prose della volgar lingua* (1525), in which he codified Italian orthography and grammar.

Be·mel·mans \ˈbē-məl-mənz\, Ludwig. 1898–1962. American painter, illustrator, and writer, b. Meran, Austria (now Merano, Italy). To U.S. (1914); naturalized (1918). Author and illustrator of *Hansi* (1934), *My War with the U.S.* (1937), *Life Class* (1938), *Madeline* (1939), *Small Beer* (1939), *Hotel Splendide* (1939), *I Love You, I Love You, I Love You* (1942), *Now I Lay Me Down to Sleep* (novel, 1943), *Dirty Eddie* (novel, 1947), *How to Travel Incognito* (1952), *On Board Noah's Ark* (1962), etc.

Be·mis \ˈbē-məs\, Samuel Flagg. 1891–1973. American historian, b. Worcester, Mass. Professor, George Washington U. (1924–34), Yale (1935–1960). Author of *Jay's Treaty* (1923), *Pinckney's Treaty* (1926, Pulitzer prize), *A Diplomatic History of the United States* (1936), *John Quincy Adams and the Foundation of American Foreign Policy* (1949, Pulitzer prize), etc.

Bé·mont \bā-mōⁿ\, Charles. 1848–1939. French historian. Author of works on English and European history as *Simon de Montfort* (1884), *Chartes des libertés anglaises* (1892).

Benadad. See BENHADAD.

Benalcázar, Sebastián de. See BELALCÁZAR.

Bé·nard \bā-nȧr\, Abraham-Joseph. *Known as* Fleu·ry \flœ̄-rē, flœ-rē\. 1750–1822. French actor. Joined Comédie-Française (1778); doyen of company there to retirement (1818); accounted greatest comic actor of the day, noted esp. for role of Alceste in Molière's *Misanthrope.*

ben Ash·er \ben-ˈash-ər, -ˈäsh-\, Aaron ben Moses. *Arabic* Abū Saʿīd \ä-ˈbü-sä-ˈēd\. 10th century. Hebrew grammarian and scholar. Produced (c.930) corrected and annotated edition of Aleppo Codex of Old Testament.

Be·na·ven·te y Mar·tí·nez \bā-nä-ˈvān-tā-ē-mär-ˈtē-nāth\, Jacinto. 1866–1954. Spanish dramatist. Wrote plays notable for realism, social criticism, reliance on ideas and dialogue rather than action; works included *Gente conocida* (1896), *La comida des las fieras* (1898), *Lo cursi* (1901), *La noche del sábado* (1903), *Los intereses creados* (1907), *Señora Ama* (1908), *La malquerida* (1913), *Para el cielo y los altares* (1928), *La infanzona* (1948), *El lebrel del cielo* (1952). Awarded Nobel prize for literature (1922).

Be·na·vi·des \bā-nä-ˈvē-t͟hās\, Alonzo de. 1580?–? Spanish missionary. To Mexico (1603); entered Franciscan order (1603); as Father Custodian of Provinces and Conversions of New Mexico (1621–29) worked to convert Hopi and Apache Indians, founding 10 missions and convents; wrote *Memorial* presented to King Philip IV (1630); later archbishop of Goa.

Benavides, Oscar Raimundo. 1876–1945. Peruvian soldier and politician. Entered army (1894); chief of general staff, Peru (1913); chief of governing junta during revolution (1914); provisional president of Peru (1915). Minister to Italy (1917–20); Spain (1931), England (1932–33). Chief of national defense (1933); president of Peru (1933–39); ambassador to Spain (1940) and to Argentina (1941).

Ben·bow \ˈben-(ˌ)bō\, John. 1653–1702. English naval officer. Captain (1689); master of fleet under Adm. Edward Russell at La Hougue (1692); bombarded Saint-Malo (1693); commander of squadron in blockade of Dunkirk (1696) and in West Indies (1698–1700); vice admiral (1701); failed in pursuit of French naval commander Ducasse (1702) because of mutiny of officers; died of wounds.

Bench·ley \ˈbench-lē\, Robert Charles. 1889–1945. American humorist, b. Worcester, Mass. Drama critic for *Life* (1920–29), *New Yorker* (1929–40); appeared in motion pictures and short features, including *How to Sleep* (1935, Academy Award). Author of *Of All Things* (1921), *Love Conquers All* (1922), *The Early Worm* (1927), *The Treasurer's Report* (1930), *No Poems* (1932), *From Bed to Worse* (1934), *My Ten Years in a Quandary* (1936), *After 1903, What?* (1938), etc.

Ben·ci·vie·ni di Pe·po \ˌbān-chē-ˈvyā-nē-dē-ˈpā-pō\. *Known as* Ci·ma·bue \chē-ˈmäb-wā\. c.1240–c.1302. Italian painter. Known to have worked in Rome, Pisa, Assisi; considered greatest and culminating artist of medieval Byzantine style in Italy and first of modern artists; noted esp. for concern with rendering space, as in figure modeling or architectural portrayal. May have been teacher of Giotto, his later rival. Works included *Crucifix* in S. Domenico, Arezzo; *Four Evangelists, Great Crucifixion, St. Peter Healing the Lame, St. Peter Healing the Sick,* scenes from life of the Virgin, scenes of Apocalypse, all frescoes in Upper Church of S. Francesco, Assisi; *Madonna Enthroned with St. Francis* in Lower Church; *Sta. Trinita Madonna; St. John the Evangelist,* mosaic in Pisa cathedral.

Benck·en·dorff \ˈbeŋ-kən-ˌdȯrf\ *or* **Ben·ken·dorf** \ˈbyāŋk-yin-ˌdȯrf\. Russian family of German origin, settled in Livonia in 16th century, including: Aleksandr Khristoforovich (1783–1844); general and politican; took part in assassination of Czar Paul I (1801); engaged in campaigns against Napoléon (1813–15); aide-de-camp to Alexander I (1819–21); suppressed Dekabrist uprising (1825); head of police and member of chancellery (1826–44). ¶Aleksandr Konstantinovich (1849–1917) entered diplomatic service (1868); at Rome (1869–77); in retirement (1877–86); first secretary at Vienna (1886–97); minister at Copenhagen (1897–1903); ambassador in London (1903–16); influential in furthering Anglo–Russian friendship and forming Triple Entente (1907).

Ben·da \ˈben-dä\. Family of Bohemian musicians in Germany, whose chief members include: Franz *or* František (1709–1786), violinist and composer for violin; member of orchestra (from 1733), concertmaster (1771) of Frederick II the Great; composed symphonies, violin solos, concerti, and sonatas, etc. His brother ¶Georg Anton *or* Jiří Antonín (1722–1795), clavierist, violinist, and oboist; introduced music drama with spoken text; member of Frederick II's orchestra (1742–49); Kapellmeister to duke of Gotha (1750–78); composed operettas, cantatas, masses, etc., melodramas including *Ariadne auf Naxos* (1775), *Medea* (1775), *Pygmalion* (1779), and Singspiele including *Der Dorfjahrmarkt* (1775). Two sons of Franz, ¶Friedrich Wilhelm Heinrich (1745–1814), violinist and clavierist, royal chamber musician (1765–1810), composer of 3 operas, 2 oratorios, cantatas, and instrumental music; and ¶Karl Hermann Heinrich (1748–1836), violinist and composer of chamber music, concertmaster of royal opera (from 1802). Georg's son ¶Friedrich Ludwig (1752–1792), director of concerts at Königsberg (1789) and composer of comic operas, violin concertos, an oratorio, etc.

Ben·da \baⁿ-dȧ\, Julien. 1867–1956. French philosopher and writer. Leader of anti-Romantic movement in French criticism. Works included several attacks on philosophy of Bergson, as *Le Bergsonisme* (1912), *Sur le succès du bergsonisme* (1914); novel *L'Ordination* (1913); essays and philosophical tracts *Belphégor* (1919), *La Trahison des clercs* (1927), *La Fin de l'Éternel* (1929), *La France byzantine* (1945), *Du style d'idées* (1948); memoirs *La Jeunesse d'un clerc* (1937), *Mémoires d'infra-tombe* (1952).

Bendigo. See William THOMPSON.

Ben·dix \ˈben-diks\, Vincent. 1882–1945. American inventor and industrialist, b. Moline, Ill. Formed Bendix Co. in Chicago (1907) to manufacture automobiles; firm failed (1909); developed Bendix electric self-starter (1912); formed (1912) Bendix Brake Co., manufacturers of self-starters, brakes, carburetors, etc., for automobiles, and Bendix Aviation Corp. (1929). Established Bendix Transcontinental Air Race (1931).

Bendl \ˈben-dᵊl\, Karel. 1838–1897. Czech composer. Composed numerous operas on national or Hussite themes, as *Lejla* (1868), *Břetislav* (1869), *Černohorci* (1881), *Dítě Tábora* (1886–88); choral works as *Umírající husita* (1869); masses, cantatas, orchestral works, and many Czech songs.

Be·ne·dek \ˈbā-nā-ˌdek\, Ludwig August von. Ritter. 1804–1881. Austrian general. Served with distinction in Galician, Italian, and Hungarian campaigns (1846–49) and as a commander, 8th army corps, at Solferino (1859); chief of general staff and military governor of Hungary (1860); commander of Austrian army in Venetia and Alpine provinces (1861–66); commander, army of the north (1866); disastrously defeated by Prussians at Königgrätz (Sadowa) (July 3, 1866); suspended from command.

Be·ne·den \bə-ˈnā-dən\, Pierre-Joseph van. 1809–1894. Belgian zoologist. Professor at Catholic U. of Louvain (from 1835); discovered life cycle of tapeworm; studied fossil history of whales. Author of *Les Commensaux et les parasites dans la règne animal* (1875), *Ostéographie des cétacés, vivants et fossiles* (with Paul Gervais, 1868–80).

Benédette, Le. See Giovanni Benedetto CASTIGLIONI.

Be·ne·det·ti \bā-nā-de-tē, bā-nā-ˈdāt-tē\, Vincente. Comte. 1817–1900. French diplomat. Ambassador at Berlin (1864–70); in famous interview with Emperor William I at Ems (July 1870) attempted to secure renunciation of candidacy of Prince Leopold of Hohenzollern-Sigmaringen to throne of Spain; his failure, artfully misrepresented, gave Bismarck the casus belli necessary to precipitate Franco–Prussian War.

Be·ne·det·to da Ma·ia·no \bā-nā-ˈdāt-tō-dä-mä-ˈyä-nō\ *or* **Ma·ja·no.** 1442–1497. Italian sculptor. Executed works in early Renaissance manner marked esp. by elegance, realistic detail, and technical virtuosity. Works included shrine of S. Savino in Faenza cathedral; altar of Sta. Fina in S. Gimignano; pulpit of Sta. Croce, Florence; tomb of Filippo Strozzi, Florence; altar of S. Bartolo in S. Agostino at S. Gimignano.

Be·ne·dict \ˈben-ə-ˌdikt\. Name of fourteen or fifteen popes, two or three antipopes, and two counter-antipopes:

Benedict I. d. 579. Pope (575–579). Reign troubled by siege of Rome by Lombards.

Benedict II. Saint. d. 685. Pope (684–685). Secured from Emperor Constantine IV Pogonatus remission of requirement for imperial confirmation of papal elections; ordered restoration of Bishop Wilfrid of York.

Benedict III. d. 858. Pope (855–858). Imprisoned briefly after election, on order of Emperor Louis II the Bavarian, who established Athanasius the Librarian as antipope; supported hierarchy of church against civil powers; condemned clerical abuses, esp. in Frankish church. Restored many Roman churches damaged by Saracens.

Benedict IV. d. 903. Pope (900–903). Excommunicated Baldwin II, Count of Flanders, for murder of Fulk, archbishop of Reims; crowned Louis III the Blind as Holy Roman emperor (901).

Benedict V. d. 966. Pope or antipope (964). Elected on death of John XII, who, however, had been declared deposed by Emperor Otto I and replaced by Leo VIII; deposed and degraded after one month by synod convened by Otto after his forced entry into Rome.

Benedict VI. d. 974. Pope (973–974). Lacking a protector after death of Emperor Otto I (973), imprisoned by Roman nobility led by Crescentius I and replaced by antipope Boniface VII, who ordered him strangled.

Benedict VII. d. 983. Pope (974–983). Bishop of Sutri; elected to succeed Benedict VI at behest of Emperor Otto II, whose delegate, Count Sicco, drove out antipope Boniface VII; fostered monasticism; issued encyclical against simony (981).

Benedict VIII. *Orig.* The·o·phy·lac·tus \ˌthē-ō-fə-ˈlak-təs\. d. 1024. Pope (1012–24). First pope from the Tusculani family; ousted candidate of the declining Crescenti, antipope Gregory VI; crowned Emperor Henry II (1014); defeated Saracens in northern Italy (1016–17); encouraged clerical and monastic reform; convened synod of Pavia (1020), which degraded uncelibate higher clergy. Succeeded by his brother Romanus as John XIX.

Benedict IX. *Orig.* Theophylactus. d. 1055 or 1056. Pope (1032–45, 1047–48). Last of the Tusculani popes, succeeding his uncle John XIX; led violent and licentious personal life, excommunicated ecclesiastical leaders hostile to him; provoked Roman insurrection that elected John, bishop of Sabina, as Sylvester III (1045); after his brothers drove Sylvester from Rome (1045), sold papacy to godfather, Giovanni Graziano, who became Gregory VI (1045); attempted to reclaim papacy (1046) but formally deposed by Council of Sutri; on death of Clement II (1047) reclaimed papacy in Rome; driven from Rome on order of Emperor Henry III by Boniface of Tuscany and replaced by Damasus II.

Benedict X. *Orig.* John Min·cius \ˈmin-sh(ē-)əs, -sē-əs\. d. c.1080. Antipope (1058–59). Bishop of Velletri; on death of Stephen IX (X) placed on throne by Tusculani family; expelled by efforts of Hildebrand (later St. Gregory VII); expulsion followed by reform in papal elections through establishment (1059) of body that became Sacred College of Cardinals.

Benedict XI. *Orig.* Niccolò Boc·ca·si·ni \bȯk-kä-ˈsē-nē\. 1240–1304. Pope (1303–04). Entered Dominican order (1254); provincial of Lombardy (1282–96); general of order (1296); cardinal (1298); one of two cardinals who stood with Pope Boniface VIII when he was seized at Anagni (1303); in brief reign resolved conflict of papacy with Philip IV of France.

Benedict XII. *Orig.* Jacques Four·nier \fu̇rn-yā\. d. 1342. Pope (1334–42). Member of Cistercian order; abbot of Fontfroide (1311); bishop of Pamiers (1317), Mirepoix (1326); cardinal (1327); zealous opponent of heretics; elected third of the Avignon popes; settled theological controversy of the Beatific Vision (1336); imposed stringent new constitutions on religious orders.

Benedict XIII. *Orig.* Pierfrancesco Or·si·ni \ȯr-ˈsē-nē\. 1649–1730. Pope (1724–30). Entered Dominican order (1667); cardinal (1672); archbishop of Manfredonia (1675), Cesena (1680), Benevento (1686); principally a scholar, unsuited to administration; reign marred by abuses of Cardinal Niccolò Coscia.

Benedict XIII. *Orig.* Pedro de Lu·na \ˈlü-nä\. c.1328–1423. Antipope (1394–1423). Professor of canon law, Montpellier; cardinal (1375); at Great Western Schism (1378) followed antipope Clement VII to Avignon; succeeded Clement; refused to attempt seriously to end schism; lost support of Charles VI of France and other princes (1398) and deserted by most of his cardinals; prisoner in besieged papal palace at Avignon (1398–1403); escaped to Provence (1403) and regained support of cardinals and of France; refused to acknowledge acts deposing him by Council of Pisa (1409), Council of Constance (1417).

Benedict XIV. *Orig.* Prospero Lam·ber·ti·ni \ˌläm-ber-ˈtē-nē\. 1675–1758. Pope (1740–58). Promoter of the Faith under Clement XI and Innocent XIII (1708–27); archbishop of Ancona (1727); cardinal (1728); archbishop of Bologna (1731); enlightened ruler of Papal States; enlarged Vatican Library and U. of Rome; by concessions settled concordats with Savoy and Naples (1741), Spain (1753); condemned retention of native rites by Indian and Chinese converts (1742, 1744).

Benedict XIV. Name of two successive counter-antipopes: (1) Bernard Gar·nier \gȧrn-yā\ (d. 1433?), sacristan of Rodez, France; chosen pope (1425) by Jean Carrier, a fanatical follower of antipope Benedict XIII, in opposition to Benedict's successor, Clement VIII; in hiding throughout reign; abdicated (1430), naming one cardinal. (2) Jean Car·rier \kȧr-yā\ (?–?), antipope Benedict XIII's faithful cardinal, refused to recognize Pope Martin V or the Avignon antipope Clement VIII; under protection of the count of Armagnac, elected and kept hidden his chosen counter-antipope, Benedict XIV; captured and imprisoned at Foix (1433); elected by Benedict XIV's single cardinal to succeed, also as Benedict XIV.

Benedict XV. *Orig.* Giacomo del·la Chie·sa \ˌdāl-lä-ˈkyez-ä\. 1854–1922. Pope (1914–22). Ordained (1878); in papal diplomatic service (from 1880); undersecretary of state (1901–07); archbishop of Bologna (1907); cardinal (1914); during World War I maintained neutrality, organized relief work; unsuccessfully attempted to mediate a peace settlement (1917).

Benedict of Nur·sia \ˈnər-sh(ē-)ə\. Saint. c.480–547. Italian religious. Gained fame for sanctity as hermit near Subiaco; founded 12 monasteries in the region; founded monastery at Monte Cassino that became fountain of European monasticism; author of Benedictine Rule governing monastic life and discipline. Considered father of Western monasticism; declared patron saint of all Europe by Pope Paul VI (1964).

Ben·e·dict \ˈben-ə-ˌdikt\, Ruth, *nee* Fulton. 1887–1948. American anthropologist, b. New York City. m. (1914) Stanley R. Benedict. On faculty, Columbia U. (from 1924), professor (1948); under influence of Franz Boas, studied Pueblo, Apache, Blackfeet, Serrano, Zuñi, and other Indian groups. Author of *Tales of the Cochiti Indians* (1931), *Patterns of Culture* (1934), *Zuñi Mythology* (1935), *Race: Science and Politics* (1940), *The Chrysanthemum and the Sword* (1946).

Benedict Bi·scop \-ˈbish-ˌäp\. Saint. *Also called* Ben·et \ˈben-et\ Biscop. *Orig.* Biscop Ba·du·cing \-ˈbäd-u̇-ˌchiŋ(g)\. c.628–690. Anglo-Saxon ecclesiastic. Orig. a thane of King Oswin of Northumbria; undertook monastic life (653); on third journey to Rome, conducted Theodore of Tarsus from Rome to Canterbury (669); built monasteries of St. Peter at Wearmouth (674), and St. Paul at Jarrow (682). Father of Benedictine monasticism in Britain; patron of learning; teacher of Bede; said to have introduced stone-built church and art of glassmaking into England.

Ben·e·dicts·son \ˌben-e-ˈdik(t)(s)-sȯn\, Victoria Maria, *nee* Bru·ze·li·us \brü-ˈzā-lē-əs\. *Pseudonym* Ernst Ahl·gren \ˈäl-ˌgrān\. 1850–1888. Swedish writer. Author of stories of Swedish folk life, collected in *Från Skåne* (1884), and novels dealing esp. with women's role, as *Pengar* (1885), *Fru Marianne* (1887).

Ben·e·dikts·son \ˌben-e-ˈdik(t)(s)-sȯn\, Einar. 1864–1940. Icelandic poet. Devoted to Icelandic development and independence; author of Symbolist verse *Sögur og kvaedi* (1897), *Hafblik* (1906), *Hrannir* (1913), *Vogar* (1921), *Hvammar* (1930).

Be·ne·dix \ˈbā-nā-ˌdiks\, Roderich Julius. 1811–1873. German writer. Author of comedies *Das bemooste Haupt* (1841), *Doktor Wespe* (1843), etc.; novel *Bilder aus dem Schauspielerleben* (1847); volumes of *Deutsche Volkssagen* (1839 ff.).

Be·nel·li \bā-ˈnel-lē\, Sem. 1877–1949. Italian dramatist. Known esp. for *La Cena delle Beffe* (1909) and *L'Amore dei Tre Re* (1909), which was source of Montemezzi's opera.

Be·neš \ˈben-esh\, Edvard. 1884–1948. Czechoslovak statesman. Professor in Prague (1909–15); disciple of Masaryk; worked in Switzerland, Paris (1915–19) with Masaryk in Czech nationalist movement; member of provisional government (1918); Czech delegate at Versailles peace conference (1919–20). Foreign minister of new state of Czechoslovakia (1918–35); prime minister (1921–22); member of Council of League of Nations (1923–27); a cofounder of Little Entente with Romania and Yugoslavia (1921). President of Czechoslovakia (1935–38); resigned on German occupation of Sudetenland. In exile (1938–45); president of the Czechoslovak government in England (1940–45); resumed government in Prague (1945); resigned (1948) rather than sign new Communist constitution.

Be·nét \bə-ˈnā, ben-ˈā\, Stephen Vincent. 1898–1943. American writer, b. Bethlehem, Pa. Author of verse *Five Men and Pompey* (1915), *Ballad of William Sycamore, 1790–1880* (1923), *Tiger Joy* (1925), *John Brown's Body* (1928, Pulitzer prize), *A Book of Americans* (1933), *Western Star* (Book I of planned 5; 1943, Pulitzer prize), etc.; novels and tales including *Jean Huguenot* (1923), *Thirteen O'Clock,* including "The Devil and Daniel Webster" (1937), *Tales Before Midnight* (1939), *Nightmare at Noon* (1940).

Benét, William Rose. 1886–1950. American poet, novelist, and editor, b. Fort Hamilton, N.Y. Brother of Stephen V. Benet. On staff of *Century Magazine* (1911–18), New York *Evening Post Literary Review* (1920–24), *Saturday Review of Literature* (1924–50). Verse included *Merchants from Cathay* (1913), *The Falconer of God* (1914), *Perpetual Light* (1919), *Starry Harness* (1933), *Golden Fleece* (1935), *The Dust Which Is God* (1941, Pulitzer prize). Novels included *The First Person Singular* (1922). m. as 2d wife Elinor Wylie (1923).

Bé·né·zet \bā-nā-ze\. Saint. *Lat.* Benedictus. c.1165–?1184. French religious. A shepherd, claimed to be divinely commanded to build bridge over Rhône at Avignon, an engineering task that had discouraged Romans; convinced bishop of Avignon, who ordered work begun (1177); reputedly performed miracles in overcoming engineering difficulties. Pont d'Avignon opened (1188).

Bé·né·zit \bā-nā-zē\, Emmanuel. 1854–1920. French writer on art. Author of standard *Dictionnaire des peintres, dessinateurs, sculpteurs et graveurs de tous les temps et de tous les pays* (1911–21).

Ben·fey \'ben-ˌfī\, Theodor. 1809–1881. German Sanskrit scholar and philologist. Professor, Göttingen (1848–81). Author of translations of the *Sāmaveda* (1844), *Pañca-tantra* (1859); Sanskrit grammars and dictionary.

Beng·el \'beŋ-əl\, Johann Albrecht. 1687–1752. German theologian and scholar. Master of theological seminary, Denkendorf (1713–41). Author of a critical study of New Testament (1734), *Ordo Temporum* (1741), and *Gnomon Novi Testamenti* (1742), an exegetical commentary; founder of Swabian pietism.

Bengts·son \'bāŋ(k)t(s)-sȯn\, Frans Gunnar. 1894–1954. Swedish writer. Author of verse *Tärningskast* (1923), *Legenden om Babel* (1925); novel *Röde Orm* (1941–45); biographies; and informal essays, a genre he largely introduced into Swedish literature.

Ben-Gu·rion \ˌben-gu̇r-'yȯn; *Angl* -'yän, -'yōn, -'gu̇r-ˌ, -'gu̇r-ē-ən\, David. *Orig.* David Gruen. 1886–1973. Israeli politician, b. Poland. To Palestine (1906); expelled by Turkish authorities for Zionist activity (1914); returned with British Jewish Legion (1918); founded Histadrut labor organization (1920); head of Mapai labor party (1930–65); chairman of Zionist Executive (1935); proclaimed independence of Israel (1948); head of provisional government (1948–49); member of Knesset (1948–70); prime minister (1949–53; 1955–63).

Ben-ha·dad I \ben-'hā-ˌdad\ *or* **Ben·a·dad** \-'ā-\. *Also called* Adad-Id·ri \ā-'dad-id-'rē\. d. c.841 B.C. King of Damascus. Led coalition against Assyrian invasion under Shalmaneser III, defeating him at Karkar (853); battled King Ahab of Israel (853).

Be·nin·ca·sa \bā-nēŋ-'käs-ä\, Ursula. 1547–1618. Italian religious. Founded (1583) Oblate Sisters of the Immaculate Conception, known also as Theatine Sisters; founded (1617) Contemplative Hermit Sisters.

Ben·i·off \'ben-ē-ˌȯf\, Hugo, *in full* Victor Hugo. 1899–1968. American geophysicist, b. Los Angeles. With Carnegie Institution (1924–37); professor, California Inst. of Technology (1937–60). Known for studies of earthquakes, seismograph design, mountain formation, terrestrial magnetism.

Be·ni·vie·ni \bā-nēv-'yā-nē\, Girolamo. 1453–1542. Italian poet. Member of Medici circle of Florence; influential in spreading doctrine of Platonism through his versification of Ficino's translation of and commentary on Plato; later a follower of Savonarola, under whose influence he wrote religious verse.

Ben·ja·min \'ben-jə-mən\ of Tudela. 12th century. Spanish rabbi and traveler. Journeyed through Italy, Greece, Palestine, Persia to western border of China, returning through Egypt, Sicily (1159–73); wrote historically valuable record of travels, *Massa'ot.*

Benjamin, Arthur. 1893–1960. British pianist and composer, b. Australia. Professor, Royal College of Music, London (from 1926). Composed operas as *The Devil Take Her* (1931), *Tale of Two Cities* (1949–50), *Mañana* (1956); orchestral and piano works; songs reflecting South American and Caribbean influence, as popular "Jamaican Rumba" (1938).

Benjamin, Asher. 1773–1845. American architect, b. Greenfield, Mass. Author of *American Builder's Companion* (1806), *Practical House Carpenter* (1830), etc., which spread late colonial designs throughout New England.

Benjamin, Judah Philip. 1811–1884. American lawyer, b. St. Thomas, V.I. To Charleston, S.C., while a child; U.S. senator from Louisiana (1853–61); attorney general in Jefferson Davis's cabinet (1861); Confederate secretary of war (1861–62), of state (1862–65); extremely unpopular because of plan to arm slaves for Confederate service. Escaped to England (1865); built up large legal practice; queen's counsel (1872–83).

Ben·ja·min \baⁿ-zhä-maⁿ\, René. 1885–1948. French writer. Author of novel *Gaspard* (1915, Goncourt prize).

Ben·kei \ben-kā\. d. 1189. Japanese warrior-monk. In service of warrior Minamoto Yoshitsune; subject of numerous legends involving superhuman feats; popular figure in literature.

Benkendorf. See BENCKENDORFF.

Ben·lowes \'ben-(ˌ)lōz\, Edward. 1602–1676. English poet. Author of metaphysical poem *Theophila or Loves Sacrifice* (1652).

Benn \'ben\, Sir Ernest John Pickstone. 2d baronet. 1875–1954. English publisher. Joined father's publishing firm (1891); published several trade papers and journals; formed book publishing firm of Ernest Benn, Ltd. (1923); published paperback series of Augustan Poets, Sixpenny Poets, Sixpenny Library, etc. Author of *Confessions of a Capitalist* (1925), *The State the Enemy* (1953), etc.

Benn, Gottfried. 1886–1956. German poet and essayist. Physician in army in World Wars I and II. Author of Expressionist verse *Morgue* (1912), *Fleisch* (1917), *Schutt* (1924), *Statische Gedichte* (1948), *Fragmente* (1951), *Destillationen* (1953); essays *Nach dem Nihilismus* (1931), *Kunst und Macht* (1934), *Ausdruckswelt* (1949), etc.

Benn, William Wedgwood. Viscount Stans·gate \'stanz-ˌgāt\. 1877–1960. English politician. Brother of Sir Ernest J.P. Benn. Liberal M.P. (1906–27), Labour M.P. (1928–31, 1937–42); secretary of state for India (1929–31); created viscount (1942); secretary of state for air (1945–46). President of Inter-Parliamentary Union (1947–57).

Ben·net \'ben-ət\, Henry. 1st Earl of Ar·ling·ton \'är-liŋ-tən\. 1618–1685. English politician. Fought with Royalists in Civil War; in service of exiled royal family (from 1654); secretary of state under Charles II (1662–74); effectively chief minister after fall of Clarendon (1667); member of Cabal (1667–74); created "court party" (later the Tories) in House of Commons; created baron (1665); with Sir William Temple negotiated Triple Alliance with United Provinces and Sweden (1668); helped arrange secret Anglo-French treaties of Dover (1670); created earl (1672); denounced by Buckingham and impeached by Commons (1674); resigned as secretary of state; lord chamberlain, without further influence (1674–85).

Ben·nett \'ben-ət\, Arnold, *in full* Enoch Arnold. 1867–1931. English novelist, dramatist, and critic. Author of novels in Realistic manner depicting provincial or lower class life, including *A Man from the North* (1898), *Grand Babylon Hotel* (1902), *Buried Alive* (1908); known esp. for novels set in the "Five Towns," centers of the pottery industry, including *Anna of the Five Towns* (1902), *Old Wives' Tale* (1908), and trilogy *Clayhanger* (1910), *Hilda Lessways* (1911), *These Twain* (1916). Dramatized *Buried Alive* as *Great Adventure* (1913) and wrote, with Edward Knoblock, the play *Milestones* (1912). Other works included *Riceyman Steps* (1923), *Lord Raingo* (1926), *Accident* (1929), and *The Journals of Arnold Bennett, 1896–1928* (1932–33).

Bennett, Charles Edwin. 1858–1921. American Latin scholar, b. Providence, R.I. Professor, Cornell (1892–1921); author of *A Latin Grammar* (1895, with many later editions), *Appendix to Bennett's Latin Grammar* (1895), numerous other textbooks, and translations.

Bennett, Edward Herbert. 1874–1954. American architect, b. Cheltenham, England. To U.S. (1890); with Chicago firm of Daniel H. Burnham (1904–19), collaborating on Chicago Plan (1909); created city plans for Minneapolis, Detroit, Brooklyn, Portland, Ore., etc.; helped design U.S. Capitol grounds, Washington, D.C.; designed several buildings for Century of Progress Exposition, Chicago (1933).

Bennett, Floyd. 1890–1928. American aviator, b. near Warrensburg, N.Y. With Byrd in MacMillan expedition to northwestern Greenland (1925); pilot with Byrd in flight over North Pole (May 9, 1926).

Bennett, James Gordon. 1795–1872. American editor, b. Newmill, Banffshire, Scotland. To Nova Scotia (1819); on staff of *New York Enquirer* (1826–28), and its successor, *Morning Courier and New York Enquirer* (1829–32). Started New York *Herald* (1835), one-cent daily newspaper; remained its editor until his retirement (1867); pioneered in publishing Wall Street financial news, society news, etc., and in using telegraph, European correspondents. His son ¶James Gordon (1841–1918), b. New York City, succeeded him; established *New York Evening Telegram* (1867); sent Stanley to Africa to find Livingstone (1869–71); financed expedition (1875) to search for a northwest passage and expedition (1879–81) of George W. DeLong to the Arctic; established (1887) Paris edition of New York *Herald;* joined John W. Mackay in Commercial Cable Co. which laid transatlantic cables and broke Gould monopoly. Resident in Paris (from 1877); noted sportsman and eccentric. Established Gordon Bennett international trophies in yachting and automobile and aeronautical racing.

Bennett, John Hughes. 1812–1875. English physician. Introduced systematic lectures on histology, Edinburgh (1841); professor of institutes of medicine, Edinburgh (1843–74). Pioneer in use of microscope in clinical pathology.

Bennett, Richard. 1872–1944. American actor and producer, b. Deacons Mills, Ind. Appeared in many Charles Frohman productions (from 1897); also in *What Every Woman Knows* (1908), *Damaged Goods* (1913), *Beyond the Horizon* (1920), *The Hero* (1921), *He Who Gets Slapped* (1922), *They Knew What They Wanted* (1924), *Winterset* (1935). Father of actresses Constance and Joan Bennett.

Bennett, Richard Bedford. Viscount Bennett. 1870–1947. Canadian politician, b. Hopewell, N. B. Entered House of Commons (1911); minister of justice and attorney general (1921); leader of Conservative party (1927–38); prime minister (1930–35); organized Imperial Economic Conference, Ottawa (1932). Created viscount (1941).

Bennett, Robert Russell. 1894–1981. American musician, b. Kansas City, Mo. Composer and conductor, but known esp. as orchestrator of some 300 Broadway musicals including *Wildflower* (1923), *Rose Marie* (1924), *Show*

Boat (1927), *Of Thee I Sing* (1931), *Anything Goes* (1934), *Oklahoma!* (1943), *Carmen Jones* (1943), *Annie Get Your Gun* (1946), *Kiss Me Kate* (1948), *South Pacific* (1949), *The King and I* (1951), *My Fair Lady* (1956), *Flower Drum Song* (1958), *Sound of Music* (1959), *Camelot* (1960).

Bennett, Sir William Sterndale. 1816–1875. English pianist and composer. Intimate friend (from 1832) of Mendelssohn; professor of music at Cambridge (1856); principal, Royal Academy of Music (1866). Founded (1849) London Bach Society and conducted (1854) English premiere of *St. Matthew Passion.* Composed *Naiads* (overture, 1837), *The May Queen* (cantata, 1858), *Paradise and Peri* (overture, 1862), *Symphony in G Minor* (1864), *Woman of Samaria* (oratorio, 1867), *Ajax* (1872).

Ben·ne·witz \'ben-ə-ˌvits\ *or* **Bie·ne·witz** \'bē-nə-ˌvits\, Peter. *Lat.* Petrus Api·a·nus \ˌäp-ē-'än-us, *Angl* ˌap-ē-'ā-nəs, ˌā-pe-\. 1501–1552. German astronomer and geographer. Professor at Ingolstadt (from 1527); author of *Cosmographia* (1524), *Astronomicum Caesareum* (1540).

Ben·nig·sen \'ben-ik-sən\, Leonty Leontyevich, *orig.* Levin August Theophil. Count. 1745–1826. Russian general, b. Brunswick. Served in Hanoverian army (to 1764); entered Russian service (1773); fought against Turks (1774, 1778), in Poland (1793–94), and at Derbent in Persian War (1796); active in conspiracy that led to assassination of Emperor Paul (1801); governor general of Lithuania (1801); general of cavalry (1802); in Napoleonic Wars, fought at Pułtusk (1806), commanded at Eylau (1807), defeated at Friedland (1807); retired (1807). Returned to service (1812), commanded center at Borodin, defeated Murat at Tarutino (1812), but retired because of difference with Kutuzov; later, commanded Russian army on right wing at Leipzig (1813); made count by the emperor.

Bennigsen, Rudolf von, *in full* Karl Wilhelm Rudolf. 1824–1902. German politician. Leader of liberal opposition in lower chamber of Hanoverian assembly (1856–67); cofounder and leader of German National Verein (1859–67), which joined National Liberal party. Member (1867–83) and president (1873–79), Prussian Assembly; member (1871–83, 1887–97) of German Reichstag and leader of National Liberal party; warmly supported Bismarck; later (1878 ff.) opposed Bismarck's economic policy and laws against Socialists; president, Province of Hanover (1888–97).

Ben·no \'ben-(ˌ)ō\. Saint. c.1010–1106. German prelate. Bishop of Meissen (1066); deposed (1085) by Synod of Mainz for supporting Pope Gregory VII against Emperor Henry IV; restored by antipope Clement III (1085). His canonization (1523) by Pope Adrian VI violently attacked by Luther in *Wider den neun Abgott und alten Teufel.* Patron saint of Bavaria and of Munich.

Ben·ny \'ben-ē\, Jack. *Orig.* Benjamin Ku·bel·sky \kə-'bel-skē\. 1894–1974. American comedian, b. Chicago. Entered vaudeville (1911); star of Earl Carroll's *Vanities* (1931); conducted regular show on radio (1932–55), on television (1950–65); appeared in many movies from *Hollywood Revue of 1929.* Known for air of bemused annoyance, legendary miserliness, permanent age of 39, seriocomic violin playing.

Be·nois \byi-nȯi\, Aleksandr Nikolayevich, *Fr.* Alexandre. 1870–1960. Russian painter. With Diaghilev and Bakst founded (1899) magazine *Mir iskusstva;* scenic designer at Maryinsky Theatre, St. Petersburg (c.1901), later in Paris; known esp. for scenery and costumes for Stravinsky's ballet *Petruchka* and for ballets of Diaghilev.

Be·noît \bən-wä\, Pierre. 1886–1962. French novelist. Author of *Koenigsmark* (1918), *L'Atlantide* (1919), *Le Lac salé* (1921), *La Châtelaine du Liban* (1924), *Le Soleil de minuit* (1930), *Lunegarde* (1942), *Aïno* (1948), *Les Plaisirs du Voyage* (1950), *Ville perdue* (1954), *Fabrice* (1956), etc.

Benoît, Pierre Léonard Léopold, *also known as* Peter. 1834–1901. Belgian composer. Founder (1867) and director, Flemish School of Music (later Royal Flemish Conservatory); leader of Flemish nationalist movement in music. Works included operas, as *Het dorp in't gebergte* (1857), *Pompeja* (1895); oratorios as *Lucifer* (1866), *De waereld* (1878); *Rubens-cantata* (1877); religious compositions as *Quadrilogie religieuse* (1864), masses, motets.

Benoît de Sainte-Maure *or* **Sainte-More** \-də-saⁿ-mȯr\. 12th century. French trouvère. Author of a verse *Chronique des ducs de Normandie* for his patron, Henry II of England, and esp. of *Roman de Troie,* founded on works of Dares Phrygius and Dictys Cretensis.

Ben·se·rade \baⁿs-räd\, Isaac de. 1612 or 1613–1691. French poet and dramatist. Author of minor dramas, romantic verses, libretti for ballets at courts of Louis XIII and Louis XIV. Best known for a sonnet, *Job,* taken as rivaling a sonnet by Voiture entitled *Uranie* and initiating a court literary debate between adherents (Jobelins and Uranins) of the two poets.

Ben·so \'ben-sō\, Camillo. Conte di Ca·vour \käv-'ůr\. 1810–1861. Italian statesman. Served in army engineers (1826–31); in youth openly espoused republican ideals, compromising his career and future as member of leading nobility; retired to native Piedmont and devoted himself to agricultural projects and travel (1831–47); founded newspaper *Il Risorgimento* (1847) in which he urged King Charles Albert to grant liberal constitution and to undertake war with Austria. Elected to Piedmont parliament (1848); minister of agriculture (1850–52), finance (1850–52); established trade treaties with France, Belgium, England, aimed at anti-Austrian alliance; prime minister (1852–59); forced to accept alliance with France and England against Russia in Crimean War (1854); succeeded in raising Italian question at Congress of Paris (1856); made secret alliance with Napoléon III for war against Austria (1858); resigned after Napoléon's armistice with Austria and failure of war to produce Italian liberation (1859); resumed prime ministry (1860–61); ceded Savoy and Nice to France to placate Napoléon III, annexed several Italian duchies to Piedmont; sent army south, ostensibly to defend Rome against Garibaldi but in fact to effect unification of northern, central, and southern Italy; began negotiations with Pope Pius IX for end of temporal power of papacy and establishment of Rome as Italian capital.

Ben·son \'ben(t)-sən\, Edward Frederic. 1867–1940. English writer. Son of Edward W. Benson. Author of satirical novels of society, including *Dodo* (1893), *The Luck of the Vails* (1901), *Scarlet and Hyssop* (1902), *Mrs. Ames* (1912), *Dodo the Second* (1914), *Queen Lucia* (1920), *Dodo Wonders* (1921), *Miss Mapp* (1922), *Colin II* (1927), *Lucia in London* (1927); also wrote tales of the macabre, biographies, and volumes of reminiscence as *Account Rendered* (1911), *As We Were* (1930), *As We Are* (1932), *Final Edition* (1940).

Benson, Edward White. 1829–1896. English prelate. First head master of Wellington College (1859–72); bishop of Truro (1877); archbishop of Canterbury (1882); sponsored legislation reforming church patronage and discipline; opposed Welsh disestablishment (1893); delivered historically important Lincoln Judgment at trial of Dr. Edward King, Bishop of Lincoln, charged with ritual offenses (1889–90). Author of *Cyprian* (1897) and *The Apocalypse* (1900). His eldest son ¶Arthur Christopher (1862–1925), master at Eton (1885–1903), master of Magdalene College, Cambridge (1915–25); editor with Viscount Esher of *Correspondence of Queen Victoria* (1907); author of a biography of his father, monographs (in *English Men of Letters Series,* 1904–06) on Rossetti, FitzGerald, and Pater, and *From a College Window* (1906), *Beside Still Waters* (1907), *Memories and Friends* (1924). His third son was Edward F. Benson (*q.v.*). His fourth son ¶Robert Hugh (1871–1914), clergyman; took Anglican orders (1894); received into Roman Catholic Church (1903), ordained (1904); private chamberlain to Pope Pius X (1911). Author of semimystical fiction, as *The Light Invisible* (1903), historical fiction, as *By What Authority* (1904), and modern novels.

Benson, Sir Frank Robert. 1858–1939. English actor-manager. As student at Oxford produced *Agamemnon* in original Greek; made professional debut under Sir Henry Irving in *Romeo and Juliet* (1882); founded touring repertory company and school of acting; produced many of Shakespeare's plays; organized 26 of annual Stratford-on-Avon Shakespeare festivals. His brother ¶Godfrey Rathbone Benson (1864–1945), 1st Baron Charn·wood \'chärn-ˌwůd\, was M.P. (1892–95); created baron (1911). Author of biographies of Abraham Lincoln (1916), Theodore Roosevelt (1923); religious reflections *According to St. John* (1926), *A Personal Conviction* (1928).

Benson, Frank Weston. 1862–1951. American painter, b. Salem, Mass. Teacher at Museum of Fine Arts in Boston (1889–1912). Known esp. for paintings of women and children, often in outdoor scenes of brilliant light and color. Among well known paintings were *My Little Girl, In the Spruce Woods, Pomona, Moonlight at Sea, Eleanor.* Painted the murals *The Seasons* and *The Three Graces* (in Congressional Library at Washington, D.C.).

Benson, Richard Meux. 1824–1915. English ecclesiastic. Founded at Oxford (1866) an Anglican Society of Mission Priests of St. John the Evangelist, often called "Cowley Fathers"; superior (1866–90); established branch in Boston, Mass. (1870–71).

Benson, William Shepherd. 1855–1932. American naval officer, b. Bibb Co., Ga. Promoted through the grades to captain (1909), rear admiral (1915), admiral (1916); first chief of naval operations (1915–19); served on special commissions abroad during World War I and as naval adviser to American Commission to Negotiate Peace; retired (1919). Chairman, U.S. Shipping Board (1920–28).

Bent \'bent\, Charles. 1799–1847. American pioneer, b. Charleston, Va. (now W.Va.). Fur trader in Colorado and New Mexico (1823–47). With his brother ¶William (1809–1869), built trading post, Bent's Fort, near present La Junta (1833–49); civil governor of New Mexico (1846–47). William became first permanent white settler in Colorado and that state's most prominent citizen.

Bent, James Theodore. 1852–1897. English explorer and archaeologist. Made archaeological journeys to Greece, Asia Minor, Abyssinia, Arabia, the Bahrein Islands, South Africa. Made excavations of ruins of the Great Zimbabwe burial houses; wrote *Ruined Cities of Mashonaland* (1892).

Ben·tham \'ben(t)-thəm, -təm\, George. 1800–1884. English botanist. Nephew and secretary (1826–32) of Jeremy Bentham; donated large collection of plants to Kew Gardens (1854); compiled *Handbook of British Flora* (1858), *Flora Hongkongensis* (1861), *Flora Australiensis* (1863–78). Exhaustively studied, catalogued, and described over 92,000 species of seed-bearing plants for *Genera Plantarum* (with Sir Joseph Hooker, 1862–83).

Bentham, Jeremy. 1748–1832. English jurist and philosopher. Called to bar (1772); wrote *Fragment on Government,* criticism of Blackstone's *Commentaries* as showing antipathy to reform (1776). Made recommendations in *View of the Hard Labour Bill* (1778) for improvement in mode of criminal punishment, published later in *Rationale of Reward* (1825) and *Rationale of Punishment* (1830; the two orig. published as one in French, 1811). Made trip to Russia (1785–88) to visit his brother Samuel, there wrote *Defence of Usury* (printed 1787), following the principles of Adam Smith. Published *Introduction to the Principles of Morals and Legislation* (1789), expounding doctrine that morality of actions is determined by utility, that is, the capacity for rendering pleasure or preventing pain, and that the object of all conduct and legislation is "the greatest happiness of the greatest number." In "Panopticon" scheme pioneered in penal reform; promoted Parliamentary reforms. Wrote several treatises developed in *Rationale of Judicial Evidence* (edited by J. S. Mill, 1825). Aided in establishing *Westminster Review* (1823) to spread philosophical radicalism; working on codification of laws and *Constitutional Code* (1st vol., 1830) at his death.

Bentham, Sir Samuel. 1757–1831. English naval engineer and architect. Brother of Jeremy Bentham; in Russian service (1783–91); fitted out fleet of barges and boats and defeated larger Turkish force (1788); introduced shell guns to naval warfare; made brigadier general. Returned to England (1791); consultant to admiralty (from 1795); invented steam dredge, developed Arrow class sloop; commissioner of the navy (1807–12).

Ben·tinck \'ben-(,)tiŋk\, William. 1st Earl of Port·land \'pōrt-land, 'pȯrt-\ (2d creation). 1649–1709. English soldier and diplomat, b. in Holland. Trusted soldier and agent of William III; made privy councilor (1689); commanded troops in Ireland (1689); helped arrange treaty of Ryjswijk (1697); negotiated and signed treaties of partition (1698, 1700). His eldest son ¶Henry (1680–1724) was created 1st duke of Portland (1716). His great grandson ¶William Henry Cavendish Bentinck (1738–1809), 3d Duke of Portland; assumed by license additional name Cavendish. M.P. (1761–62); lord chamberlain under Rockingham (1765–66) and lord lieutenant of Ireland (1782); prime minister (1783); home secretary (1794–1801) and lord president of the council (1801–05) under Pitt; again prime minister (1807–09), when, owing to age, he was dominated by Castlereagh and Canning. His 2d son ¶Lord William Cavendish Bentinck (1774–1839), a lieutenant colonel at Marengo, was M.P. (1796–1803); governor of Madras (1803); recalled (1807) on account of a Sepoy mutiny at Vellore (1806); served in Peninsular campaign (1808–11); commander and virtual governor of Sicily (1811–14); again M.P. (1812–14, 1816–26). Governor general of Bengal (1828–33), effecting financial and judicial reform, supression of Thugs, and abolition (1829) of satī (suttee); first governor general of India (1833–35). ¶Lord William George Frederic Cavendish Bentinck, known as Lord George (1802–1848), son of 4th duke, was a devotee of horse racing; M.P. (1828–48); leader of anti-Peel protectionists (1846–47).

Ben·ti·vo·glio \ben-tē-'vōl-yō\. Prominent Bolognese family that largely controlled the city in latter 15th century; members included Giovanni I (?–?), signore of Bologna (1401–02) until defeated by the Visconti of Milan. His son ¶Anton Galeazzo (d. 1435) seized power briefly (1420) but was forced to yield to Pope Martin V. Anton's son ¶Annibale (d. 1445) was signore (1443–45); assassinated. A cousin ¶Sante (1424–1463) succeeded as signore (1445–63); secured recognition of Bologna's independence of papal rule (1447); established alliance with Sforza family of Milan. He was succeeded by a son of Annibale ¶Giovanni II (1443–1508), signore (1463–1506); built or improved public works; resisted papal authority but grew tyrannical; Bentivoglio family driven from Bologna (1506) by Pope Julius II.

Bentivoglio, Guido. 1579–1644. Italian prelate, diplomat, and historian. Papal nuncio to Flanders (1607–15), France (1616–21); cardinal (1621). Author of important historical records *Relazioni in tempo delle sue nunziature* (1629), *Della guerra di Fiandra* (1632–39).

Bent·ley \'bent-lē\, Arthur Fisher. 1870–1957. American political scientist and philosopher, b. Freeport, Ill. Teacher and journalist until retiring to orchardry and writing (1910). Author of *The Process of Government* (1908), seminal work in a behavioral approach to politics; also *Relativity in Man and Society* (1926), *Linguistic Analysis of Mathematics* (1932), *Behavior, Knowledge, Fact* (1935), *Knowing and the Known* (with John Dewey, 1949), *Inquiry into Inquiries* (1954).

Bentley, Edmund Clerihew. 1875–1956. English writer. Contributor to *Punch;* on staff of *Daily News* (1901–12), *Daily Telegraph* (1912–34). Known as author of detective stories esp. *Trent's Last Case* (1912), *Trent Intervenes* (1938) and as originator of a type of humorous pseudo-biographical verse known as clerihews, published in *Biography for Beginners* (1905), *More Biography* (1929), *Baseless Biography* (1939).

Bentley, John Francis. 1839–1902. English architect. Developed an English form of Gothic in building and decorating churches and convents; designed and built in Byzantine style the Roman Catholic cathedral in Westminster (1894 ff.).

Bentley, Phyllis Eleanor. 1894–1977. English writer. Author esp. of novels and stories of Yorkshire, as *Spinner of Years* (1928), *The Partnership* (1928), *Carr* (1929), *Trio* (1930), *Inheritance* (1932), *The Whole of the Story* (1935), *Freedom, Farewell!* (1936), *Take Courage* (1940), *Rise of Henry Morcar* (1946), *Quorum* (1950), *Love and Money* (1957); also wrote works on Brontë sisters and critical works as *The English Regional Novel* (1941), *Art of Narrative* (1946).

Bentley, Richard. 1662–1742. English clergyman, scholar, and critic. Won reputation as classical scholar by *Epistola ad Joannem Millium* (1691), treatise addressed to John Mill. Delivered first Boyle lectures, *A Confutation of Atheism* (1692). Proved in controversy (1697–99) with Charles Boyle spuriousness of *Epistles of Phalaris,* evoking Jonathan Swift's *Battle of the Books.* Master of Trinity College, Cambridge (1700–42); tried and nearly ejected for despotic rule; regius professor of divinity (1717–42). Known for critical texts of classical authors.

Bentley, Richard. 1794–1871. English publisher. Founder of *Bentley's Miscellany* (1837–68), of which Dickens was first editor, succeeded by Ainsworth.

Ben·ton \'bent-ᵊn\, Thomas Hart. 1782–1858. American politician, b. Hillsborough, N.C. To St. Louis, Mo. (1815); editor, *St. Louis Enquirer* (1818–20); member, U.S. Senate (1821–51); defender of sound money and of distribution of public lands to encourage western settlement; Democratic leader in Senate; supported Jackson in his campaign against the national bank; often called "Old Bullion." Opposed extension of slavery to territories; defeated (1850) for reelection because of stand on slavery issue. Member, U.S. House of Representatives (1853–55). Author of *Thirty Years' View* (1854–56), his political autobiography. Father of Jessie Benton Frémont.

Benton, Thomas Hart. 1889–1975. American painter, b. Neosho, Mo. Grandnephew of Sen. Thomas Hart Benton. A leader of American Regionalist school; known for vigorous and realistic portraiture of people representing ordinary life and occupations of American Middle West; among well known paintings were *Cotton Pickers, Lonesome Road, Meal, Homestead,* and *Susanna and the Elders;* his murals included *The Arts of Life in America* (Whitney Museum of American Art, New York City), *Arts of the West* (New Britain, Conn., Museum), *History of Indiana* for Indiana Building at Century of Progress Exhibition, Chicago (1933), and *History of Missouri* for State House at Jefferson City, Mo.

Benton, William. 1900–1973. American businessman, politician, and publisher, b. Minneapolis. Founded (1929) with Chester Bowles advertising firm of Benton and Bowles; vice president, U. of Chicago (1937–45); U.S. assistant secretary of state (1945–47); U.S. senator from Conn. (1949–52); U.S. representative to UNESCO (1963–69). Owner and publisher, *Encyclopaedia Britannica* (1942–73). Author of *This Is the Challenge* (1958), *Voice of Latin America* (1961).

Benz \'ben(t)s\, Carl Friedrich. 1844–1929. German engineer. Pioneer in construction of motor-driven vehicles; built three-wheeler driven through streets of Munich (1885). Founded (1883) firm of Benz & Co., Mannheim, to manufacture stationary engines; began manufacture of motor cars (1893); left firm (1906), which later (1926) merged with Daimler Co.

Ben-Zvi \bents-'vē\, Itzhak. *Orig.* Isaac Shim·shel·e·vich \shim-'shel-ev-,yich\. 1884–1963. Israeli politician, b. Ukraine. A founder (1905) of Poale Zion group in Russia and of Poale Zion World Federation (1907); to Palestine (1907); an organizer (1908) and director (1908–20) of Hashomer self-defense organization; founded (1909) first Hebrew high school in Palestine. Exiled (1915); with Ben-Gurion organized Jewish Legion and returned to Palestine (1918). Helped form Histadrut labor group (1920); with Ben-Gurion formed Mapai party (1929); a founder, chairman (1931–44), president (1944–49) of Vaad Leumi national council. Member of Knesset (1949–63); second president of Israel (1952–63).

Be·ol·co \bā-'ōl-kō\, Angelo. *Called* Il Ruz·zan·te \ēl-rüt-'sän-tā\. 1502–1542. Italian actor and playwright. Organized one of earliest acting troupes in Italy; author of Plautine comedies, as *La Vaccaria* and *La Piovana,* and esp. comedies in Paduan dialect depicting rural life, as *La Fiorina;* some of his character types are forerunners of commedia dell'arte characters.

Be·rain \bā-raⁿ\, Jean. *Known as* The Elder. 1637–1711. French artist and engraver. Royal designer to Louis XIV (from 1674); designed interiors, furniture, tapestries, faience, wall panels, etc. in florid, often grotesquely fanciful style; with patronage of French court, influenced craftsmen and artists throughout Europe and the later Rococo school. His son ¶Jean, *called* the

Younger (1678–1726), succeeded as royal designer but was best known as an engraver.

Ber·an \'ber-än\, Josef. 1888–1969. Czechoslovak prelate. Archbishop of Prague (1946); interned by Communist regime (1949–65); cardinal (1963).

Bé·ran·ger \bā-rä^{n}-zhā\, Pierre-Jean de. 1780–1857. French poet. Clerk at U. of Paris (1809–21); did literary hackwork. Author of highly popular chansons expressing liberal and humanitarian sympathies and satirizing Bourbon restoration; songs included "Le Roi d'Yvetot," "Le Dieu des pauvres gens," "La Grand-Mére," "Le Vieux Sergent."

Bé·raud \bā-rō\, Henri. 1885–1958. French novelist. Author of *Le Vitriol de la lune* (1921, Goncourt prize), *Le Martyre de l'obèse* (1922), *Les Lurons de sabolas* (1932), *Ciel de suie* (1934); author also of political pamphlets; imprisoned for collaboration in World War II (1944–50).

Berceo, Gonzalo de. See GONZALO DE BERCEO.

Ber·chem *or* **Ber·ghem** \'ber-kəm\, Claes *or* Nicolaes Pietersz. 1620–1683. Dutch painter and etcher. Known esp. for landscapes of Italy.

Ber·chet \bār-'shā\, Giovanni. 1783–1851. Italian poet. Political exile in England, France, Germany (1821–47); his works included *Lettera semiseria di Crisostomo* (manifesto of the Romantic movement in Italy, 1816), political and patriotic poems, and a collection of ballads.

Berch·told \'berk-,tōlt\, Leopold Anton Johann Sigismund Joseph Korsinus Ferdinand. Graf. 1863–1942. Austro-Hungarian politician. Ambassador at St. Petersburg (1907–11); foreign minister (1912–15); signed Austrian ultimatum to Serbia (1914) preceding World War I.

Berck·hey·de \berk-'hīd-ə\, Gerrit (1638–1698) and his brother Job (1630–1693). Dutch painters. Gerrit's paintings included chiefly street scenes and views of public places; Job's paintings, chiefly landscapes and architectural and genre subjects.

Ber·co·vici \'ber-kō-,vēch, *Angl* ,bər-kə-'vē-sē\, Konrad. 1882–1961. American writer, b. Braila, Rumania. To U.S. (1916); author of *Ghitza* (1919), *The Story of the Gypsies* (1928), *That Royal Lover* (1931), *The Incredible Balkans* (1933), *Exodus* (1947), *The Savage Prodigal* (1948), etc., and many articles and tales about gypsies.

Ber·di·chev·sky \'ber-di-'chev-skē\, Micah Joseph. *Pseudonym* Micah Joseph bin Go·rion \bin-gȯr-'yōn\. 1865–1921. German-Jewish writer, b. Podolia. Author of novels, stories, essays critical of dead tradition or expressing dilemma of tradition versus assimilation; many stories collected in *me-ḥutz le-taḥum* (1922–23), *Ben ha-ḥomot;* published retelling of tales from Aggada in *me-otzar ha-Aggada* (1913–14).

Ber·dya·yev \byird-'yä-yif\, Nikolay Aleksandrovich. 1874–1948. Russian philosopher. A Marxist and Russian Orthodox layman critical of both systems; professor, Moscow (1920–22); expelled for criticism of state (1922); a founder of Academy of Philosophy and Religion, Berlin (1922); moved academy to Paris (1924); founded journal *Put'* (1925–40); under influence of Kant and Böhme developed Christian Existentialism. Author of *Dukh i realnost* (1927, *Freedom and the Spirit*), *O naznachemi cheloveka* (1931, *Destiny of Man*), *Istoki i smysl russkogo kommunizma* (1937), *Essai de métaphysique eschatologique* (1946).

Be·ren·gar \'ber-ən-,gär\. Name of two kings of Italy:

Berengar of Friuli. d. 924. King (888–924) and Holy Roman emperor (915–924). Grandson of Louis I the Pious; elected king at Pavia under overlordship of East Frankish king Arnulf; confined to northeastern Italy until deaths of Guy of Spoleto (894) and his son Lambert (898) enabled him to extend rule to rest of Italy. Defeated at Brenta River by Magyars (899); expelled Louis III the Blind from Italy (902); captured him upon his return and blinded him (905); crowned emperor by Pope John X; defeated by Rudolf II of Burgundy (923); murdered by own men.

Berengar II. Marchese d' Ivrea. c.900–966. King (950–952). Grandson of Berengar of Friuli; seized throne on death of Lothair, and held his widow Adelaide captive (951); deposed by future Emperor Otto I; attacked Pope John XII (960), provoking Otto's reoccupation of Rome and coronation as emperor (962); imprisoned in Germany (963–966).

Ber·en·gar \'ber-ən-,gär\ *or* **Ber·en·ger** \-gər\ of Tours. *Lat.* Ber·en·gar·ius \,ber-ən-'gar-ē-əs\. c.999–1088. French theologian. Canon of Tours and head of School of Saint-Martin (1029); archdeacon of Angers (c.1040). Excommunicated (c.1050) by Pope Leo II for supporting doctrine of transsignification against transsubstantiation; imprisoned by Henry I at Paris (1050); condemned by synod at Paris (1051); forced to sign orthodox statement (1054) but later recanted; examined by councils at Rome (1059), Poitiers (1076), synods of Rome (1078, 1079); tried at Bordeaux (1080); silent thereafter.

Ber·en·gar·ia \,ber-ən-'gar-ē-ə\. *Span.* Be·ren·gue·la \bā-reŋ-'gā-lä\. 1108–1149. Queen of León and Castile (1128–49). Daughter of Ramón Berenguer IV, Conde de Barcelona; m. (1128), as 2d husband, Alfonso VII of León and Castile; defended Toledo against Moors (1139); famous for her beauty.

Berengaria. *Span.* Berenguela. 1165–1230. Queen of Richard I of England. Daughter of Sancho VI of Navarre; joined Richard at Reggio, Italy (1191), when on Crusade to Holy Land; m. Richard (1191) at Limassol, Cyprus; accompanied him to Acre; resided there (1191–92) during campaign against Saracens; lived at Poitou during Richard's imprisonment (1192–94) in Germany; possibly estranged after his release; after Richard's death (1199) lived mostly at Le Mans in Maine.

Berengaria. *Span.* Berenguela. c.1180–1246. Queen of Léon and Castile (1197–1246). Daughter of Alfonso VIII of Castile and Eleanor, daughter of Henry II of England; 2d wife of Alfonso IX of León; marriage (1197) stopped wars, but annulled (1214) by Pope Innocent III on ground of kinship; after death of her father Alfonso (1214) and her brother Henry I (1217), queen for a few months (1217); proclaimed her son Ferdinand III king (1217).

Be·ren·gar·io da Car·pi \ba-rān-'gär-ē-ō-dä-'kär-pē\, Giacomo *or* Jacopo. *Surname orig.* Ba·ri·gaz·zi \bar-ē-'gät-tsē\. c.1460–1530. Italian physician and anatomist. Professor, Bologna (1502–27); physician to Medici family. Author of important treatise *Commentaria* (1521) and its condensed version *Isagogae breves* (1522), containing original anatomical descriptions.

Bé·ren·ger \bā-rä^{n}-zhā\, Alphonse-Marie-Marcellin-Thomas. 1785–1866. French magistrate and politician. Deputy (1815, 1828–39); member of chamber of peers; active in promoting humanitarian reforms in law. Author of *De la justice criminelle en France* (1818), *De la répression pénale* (1853).

Bérenger, René. 1830–1915. French jurist and politician. Deputy (1871–75); elected senator for life (1875). Author of "Bérenger laws" favoring or granting immunity to first offenders; prominent in move to suppress exhibition of indecent pictures and inscriptions (hence his nickname "Père la Pudeur").

Berenguela. See BERENGARIA.

Be·ren·guer \bā-reŋ-'ger\, Dámaso. 1873–1953. Spanish soldier and politician, b. Cuba. Entered army (1889); served in Cuba, North Africa; general (1909); minister of war (1918); high commissioner of Morocco (1918–24); premier of Spain (1930–31) after fall of Primo de Rivera; failed to stabilize country for return of constitutional rule; minister of war (1931); imprisoned during second Republic (1931–34).

Berenguer, Ramón. See RAMÓN BERENGUER.

Ber·e·ni·ce \,ber-ə-'nī-sē\. Name of five Egyptian princesses:

Berenice I. fl. c.317–c.275 B.C. A Macedonian, member of retinue of Eurydice, second queen of Ptolemy I Soter; m. Ptolemy (c.317); mother by him of Ptolemy II Philadelphus and Arsinoë II; named queen by Ptolemy I (290).

Berenice. d. c.246 B.C. Daughter of Ptolemy II Philadelphus and his sister Arsinoë II; m. (c.252) Antiochus II Theos and persuaded him to renounce former wife Laodice and her children; after death of Antiochus, killed by supporters of Laodice, thus provoking her brother Ptolemy III Euergetes into Third Syrian War against Laodice and Seleucus II.

Berenice II. c.269–221 B.C. Daughter of Magas, king of Cyrene; despite mother's machinations, m. (c.245) Ptolemy III Euergetes of Egypt; dedicated lock of her hair to Aphrodite for safe return of husband from Third Syrian War, leading court astronomer to proclaim new constellation Coma Berenices; poisoned by son Ptolemy IV Philopator.

Berenice III. d. 80 B.C. Daughter of Ptolemy IX; m. (before 101) uncle Ptolemy X; became queen on death of dowager Cleopatra III (101); m. 2d Ptolemy XI, on whose death (80) she became sole ruler of Egypt. Murdered by Ptolemy Alexander when she refused to marry him and surrender authority.

Berenice IV. d. 55 B.C. Daughter of Ptolemy XII Auletes and elder sister of famous Cleopatra; ruled Egypt in father's absence (58–55); executed by him upon his restoration.

Berenice. Name of two princesses of the Jewish Idumean dynasty:

Berenice. 1st century B.C. Daughter of Salome and niece of Herod I; m. (c.17 B.C.) cousin Aristobulus; mother of Herod of Chalcis, Herod Agrippa I, Aristobulus, Herodias, Mariamne.

Berenice. c.28–after 79 A.D. Daughter of Herod Agrippa I; m. 2d her uncle Herod of Chalcis; lived later at court of brother Herod Agrippa II; sat on tribunal at Caesarea Palestinae before which St. Paul appeared (c.60); remained loyal to Rome during Jewish rebellion (66 ff.); became mistress of Titus, son of Emperor Vespasian.

Ber·en·son \'ber-ən-sən\, Bernard. 1865–1959. American art critic, b. Vilnius, Lithuania. To U.S. (1875); later settled in villa I Tatti near Florence; became foremost authority on art of Italian Renaissance. Author of *Venetian Painters of the Renaissance* (1894), *Drawings of the Florentine Painters* (1903), *Italian Painters of the Renaissance* (1906), etc.

Be·rent \'ber-ent\, Wacław. 1873–1940. Polish novelist. Member of Young Poland movement. Author of modernist novels *Fachowiec* (1895), *Próchno* (1903), *Ozimina* (1911), *Żywe kamienie* (1918), *Nurt* (1934).

Ber·es·ford \'ber-əz-fərd, -əs-\, Charles William de la Poer. 1st Baron Beresford. *Nicknamed* Lord Charles. 1846–1919. British naval officer, b. Ireland. Entered navy (1859); took part in bombardment of Alexandria (1882) and Nile expedition (1884–85); captain (1882). M.P. (1874–80, 1885–89, 1897–1900, 1902–03, 1910–16); advocate of big navy program in Parliament. Rear admiral (1897), vice admiral (1902), admiral (1906); commanded

Channel squadron (1903–05), Mediterranean fleet (1905–07), Channel fleet (1907–09). Author of *The Betrayal,* a protest against Lord Fisher's shipbuilding policy (1912).

Beresford, John. 1738–1805. Irish politician. Member of Irish parliament (1760–1805); Irish privy councillor (from 1768); subordinate commissioner (1770–80) and first commissioner (1780–1802) of Irish revenue; member of British privy council (from 1786). Opposed Pitt and later supported Earl Camden in maintaining repressive measures against Irish Catholic peasantry and retaining power of Protestant landowners.

Beresford, John Davys. 1873–1947. English novelist. Author of trilogy *Jacob Stahl* (1911), *A Candidate for Truth* (1912), *The Invisible Event* (1915). Other works included *God's Counterpoint* (1918), *The Monkey Puzzle* (1925), *Love's Illusion* (1930), *Cleo* (1937), *Snell's Folly* (1939), *Strange Rival* (1940).

Beresford, William Carr. Viscount Beresford. 1768–1854. British general. Natural son of 1st marquis of Waterford; entered army (1785); served in Nova Scotia (1786) and in Europe; made reputation as brigade commander in Egypt (1801–03) and at taking of Cape of Good Hope (1805); captured Buenos Aires (1806). Served through Peninsular War; distinguished himself at Corunna (1809); reorganized Portuguese army, of which he was made marshal (1809); lieutenant general in British army (1812); won victory of La Albuera (1811); commanded center of army in battles of Nivelle, the Nive, and Orthez (1814). Created duque de Elvas in Spanish peerage and viscount in English (1823); general (1825); made master general of ordnance by Wellington (1828–30).

Berg \ˈberk\, Alban Maria Johannes. 1885–1935. Austrian composer. Pupil of Arnold Schoenberg (1904–10); under his influence and that of Wagner and Mahler developed into master of atonal style, successfully marrying it to classical forms. Works included *Piano Sonata* (1908), *String Quartet* (1910), *Five Orchestral Songs* (1912), *Four Pieces for Clarinet and Piano* (1913), *Three Pieces for Orchestra* (1914), *Chamber Concerto* (1924), opera *Wozzeck* (1925), *Lyric Suite* (1925–26), concert aria *Der Wien* (1929), *Violin Concerto* (1935), incomplete opera *Lulu* (1937; first full performance 1979).

Berg, Max. 1870–1947. German architect. Exponent of German Expressionist school; known esp. for huge reinforced concrete dome of Jahrhunderthalle, Breslau (now Wrocław, Poland; 1912–13), Messehof exhibition hall (1925) and hydroelectric station, both also in Breslau.

Bergamasco, Il. See Giovanni Battista CASTELLO.

Berg·bom \ˈberg-bȯm\, Kaarlo. 1843–1906. Finnish author and theatrical producer. Founded (1872) Finnish National Theater; produced premiere of Ibsen's *John Gabriel Borkman* (1897).

Ber·gen \ˈbər-gən\, Edgar John. 1903–1978. American ventriloquist, b. Chicago. Achieved success on radio (from 1936) and in motion pictures with famous dummy Charlie McCarthy and later also with Mortimer Snerd; films included *Goldwyn Follies* (1938), *Letter of Introduction* (1938, special Academy Award), *You Can't Cheat an Honest Man* (1939), etc. McCarthy long noted for feud with W.C. Fields.

Ber·ger \ˈbər-gər\, Victor Louis. 1860–1929. American Socialist editor and politician, b. Nieder-Rehbach, Transylvania (now Rumania). To U.S. (1878); editor, Milwaukee *Wisconsin Vorwaerts* (1892–98), *Social Democratic Herald* (1901–11), Milwaukee *Leader* (1911–29). Member, U.S. House of Representatives (1911–13), first Socialist elected to Congress; elected again (1918 and 1919) but excluded by Congress on ground of disloyalty; finally elected and seated (1923–29). Sentenced to prison for 20 years on charge of giving aid and comfort to the enemy in time of war (1918); sentence reversed by U.S. Supreme Court (1921).

Bergerac, Cyrano de. See CYRANO DE BERGERAC.

Ber·gey \ˈbər-gē\, David Hendricks. 1860–1937. American bacteriologist, b. Skippack, Pa. On faculty (1895–1932), professor (1926–32), director of laboratory of hygiene (1929–31), U. of Pennsylvania. Authority on classification of bacteria. Author of *The Principles of Hygiene* (1901), etc.; principal author, *Bergey's Manual of Determinative Bacteriology.*

Bergh \ˈbərg\, Henry. 1811–1888. American reformer, b. New York City. Founded (1866) American Society for the Prevention of Cruelty to Animals; president (1866–88); helped found (1875) Society for Prevention of Cruelty to Children.

Berg·haus \ˈberk-ˌhau̇s\, Heinrich. 1797–1884. German geographer and cartographer. Produced widely used *Physikalischer Atlas* (1838–48). His nephew ¶Hermann (1828–1890) was also a cartographer; prepared new edition of *Physikalischer Atlas* (1886–92).

Berghem. See BERCHEM.

Ber·gi·us \ˈber-gē-u̇s\, Friedrich. 1884–1949. German chemist. Investigated effect of high pressure on chemical actions; developed processes for production of motor fuels by hydrogenation of coal under pressure and for production of sugar from wood. Awarded (with Carl Bosch) 1931 Nobel prize for chemistry.

Berg·man \ˈberʸ-mȧn\, Bo Hjalmar. 1869–1967. Swedish poet. Author of lyric verse expressing first pessimism and later a militant humanism; works included *Marionetterna* (1903), *Trots allt* (1931), *Gamla gudar* (1939), *Riket* (1944).

Bergman, Hjalmar Fredrik Elgérus. 1883–1931. Swedish writer. Author of plays as *Maria, Jesu moder* (1905), *Hans Nåds testamente* (1910), *Swedenhielms* (1925); short stories as in *Amourer* (1910); novels as *Vi Bookar, Krokar och Rothar* (1912), *En döds memoarer* (1918), *Markurells i Wad köping* (1919), *Farmor och vår Herre* (1921), *Chefen Fru Ingeborg* (1924).

Berg·man \ˈberʸ-mȧn, *Angl* ˈbərg-mən\, Ingrid. 1915–1982. Swedish actress. Known for performances in films as *Intermezzo* (1938), *Casablanca* (1942), *Gaslight* (1944, Academy Award), *Spellbound* (1945), *Bells of St. Mary's* (1945), *Notorious* (1946), *Stromboli* (1950), *Anastasia* (1956, Academy Award), *Indiscreet* (1958), *Inn of the Sixth Happiness* (1958), *Murder on the Orient Express* (1974, Academy Award), *Autumn Sonata* (1978); also appeared on stage.

Berg·man \ˈberʸ-mȧn\, Torbern Olof. 1735–1784. Swedish chemist and physicist. Professor, U. of Uppsala (1761–84); made many contributions to development of qualitative and quantitative analysis; a pioneer investigator of crystal structure. Another of *Disquisitio de attractionibus electivis* (1775), *De analysi aquarum* (1778), *De minerarum docimasia humida* (1780), *De praecipitatis metallicis* (1780), etc.

Berg·mann \ˈberk-ˌmän\, Ernst Gustav Benjamin von. 1836–1907. German surgeon. Professor, Dorpat, Würzburg, and (from 1882) Berlin; specialist in brain surgery; pioneered in aseptic methods. Author of classic *Die chirurgische Behandlung der Hirnkrankheiten* (1888).

Berg·son \berg-sōⁿ, *Angl* ˈbərg-sən\, Henri-Louis. 1859–1941. French philosopher. Professor, École Normale Supérieure (1897–1900), Collège de France (1900–21). Developed a humanistic philosophy of process to counter positivism; writing notable for grace and lucidity. Works included *Essai sur les données immédiates de la conscience* (1889), *Matière et mémoire* (1896), *Le Rire* (1900), *Introduction à la metaphysique* (1903), *L'Évolution créatrice* (1907), *Les Deux Sources de la morale et de la religion* (1932). Awarded Nobel prize for literature (1928).

Be·ria *or* **Be·ri·ya** \ˈbyār-yä\, Lavrenty Pavlovich. 1899–1953. Russian politician. Head of security police in Georgia (1921–31); political head of Transcaucasian republics (1931–38); head of Commissariat for Internal Affairs or NKVD (from 1938); deputy prime minister (1941–53); marshal (1945); member of Politburo (from 1946). Controlled vast security network, oversaw purges of political enemies; apparently attempted to succeed Stalin (1953); tried and executed.

Be·ring \ˈbā-rēŋ; *Angl* ˈbi(ə)r-iŋ, ˈbe(ə)r-\, Vitus Jonassen. 1681–1741. Danish navigator. Employed by Czar Peter the Great on expeditions (from 1724) to discover whether Asia and North America were connected; sailed through Bering Strait (1728); on second voyage (1741) explored Alaskan coast, discovered Aleutian Islands. Bering Sea and Bering Strait named in his honor.

Ber·ke \ˈber-kə\ *or* **Ba·ra·kah** \ˈbär-ə-ˌkä\. d. 1267. Mongol ruler. Grandson of Genghis Khan; first Mongol leader to adopt Islām; succeeded brother Batu as ruler of Golden Horde (1257–67).

Berke·ley \ˈbər-klē\, Busby. *Orig.* William Berkeley Enos \ˈē-nəs\. 1895–1976. American film director and choreographer, b. Los Angeles. Known for lavish production numbers involving large ensembles, costumes, inventive camera techniques, etc., in films as *Whoopee* (1930), *Forty-second Street* (1933), the *Gold Diggers* series (1933–37), *Babes in Arms* (1939).

Berke·ley \ˈbär-klē, ˈbər-\, George. 1685–1753. Irish philosopher. Fellow (1707–24), librarian (1709), lecturer in divinity, Greek, and Hebrew (1721–24), Dublin U.; ordained (1710); presented by Swift at English court (1713); dean of Derry (1724); obtained (1725) charter for college in Bermudas, but government grant never paid; lived in America (1728–31); made bishop of Cloyne (1734); retired to Oxford (1752). Developed philosophy of immaterialism and subjective idealism epitomized in motto "to be is to be perceived"; also evolved theory of sense perception. Works included *Essay towards a New Theory of Vision* (1709), *A Treatise concerning the Principles of Human Knowledge* (1710), *Three Dialogues between Hylas and Philonous* (1713), *De Motu* against Newtonian physics (1721), *Alciphron; or, the Minute Philosopher,* defense of Christianity and theism (1732), *The Analyst* (1734).

Berkeley, Sir William. 1606–1677. English colonial governor. Governor of Virginia (1641–77) except for Commonwealth period (1649–60); his policies led to Bacon's Rebellion (1676).

Ber·ken \ˈber-kən\, Ludwig van. *Also* Louis de Ber·quen \də-ber-ken\. 15th century. Flemish lapidary. Credited with establishing (c.1470) guild of lapidaries and with discovering (c.1476) the method of cutting diamond with diamond and use of diamond-powder rouge for polishing.

Berk·ley \ˈbär-klē, ˈbər-\, James John. 1819–1862. English engineer. Constructed first railway line in India, from Bombay to Thana, 20 miles (1853); completed Bombay–Calcutta–Madras–Nagpur line (1856).

Berk·man \'berk-män, *Angl* 'bərk-mən\, Alexander. 1870–1936. American anarchist, b. Vilna, Russia. To U.S. (1887); associated with Emma Goldman (from 1889); during Homestead (Pa.) strike disorders, stabbed Henry Clay Frick; confined in penitentiary (1892–1906); convicted with Emma Goldman of obstructing conscription (1917), imprisoned (1917–19) and deported to Russia (1919). Later resided in France; suicide. Author of *Prison Memoirs of an Anarchist* (1912).

Berk·ner \'bərk-nər\, Lloyd Viel. 1905–1967. American physicist and engineer, b. Milwaukee, Wis. Naval officer; served in Bureau of Lighthouses (1927–28), on Byrd Antarctic expedition (1928–30); with U.S. Bureau of Standards (1930–33), Carnegie Institution (1933–51). Known for study of atmosphere, esp. ionosphere, and of radio propagation; helped develop radar systems, esp. the Distant Early Warning system; proposed (1950) International Geophysical Year (1957–58).

Berkshire, Earls of. See under HOWARD family.

Ber·la·ge \'ber-läk-ə\, Hendrik Petrus. 1856–1934. Dutch architect. Designed Diamond Workers' Union hall (1900), Amsterdam Bourse (1903), Holland House, London (1914), Gemeentemuseum, The Hague (1934); introduced modern functional style to Holland; also involved in city planning.

Ber·lan·ga \ber-'läŋ-gä\, Tomás de. d. 1551. Spanish prelate. Entered Dominican order (1508); to New World; bishop of Panama (1530); en route by sea to Peru, discovered (1535) Galápagos Islands.

Ber·le \'bər-lē\, Adolf Augustus. 1895–1971. American lawyer and diplomat, b. Boston. Professor, Columbia U. (1927–63); member of Pres. Franklin D. Roosevelt's "Brains Trust"; assistant secretary of state (1938–44); ambassador to Brazil (1945–46); chairman, Twentieth Century Fund (1951–71). Author of *The Modern Corporation and Private Property* (with Gardiner C. Means, 1932), *New Directions in the New World* (1940), *Latin America* (1962), *American Economic Republic* (1963), *Power* (1969).

Ber·lich·ing·en \'ber-lik-iŋ-ən\, Götz *or* Gottfried von. 1480–1562. German knight. Fought in service of various princes (from 1497); at siege of Landshut (1504), lost his right hand, for which an iron one was substituted—hence the nickname "Götz of the Iron Hand"; led numerous feuds, notably against Nürnberg and Electorate of Mainz; twice (1512, 1518) put under ban for private warfare and robbery. Served Duke Ulrich of Württemberg against Swabian League and in defense of Möckmühl (1519); imprisoned at Heilbronn (1519–22). Forced by rebels to lead them in Peasants' Revolt (1525); imprisoned at Augsburg by Swabian League (1528–30). Fought under Charles V against Turks (1542) and France (1544). His autobiography (pub. 1731) used by Goethe as a source for the drama *Götz von Berlichingen* (1773).

Ber·lier \berl-yā\, Jean-Baptiste. 1843–1911. French engineer. Known esp. for his proposed underground railway system in Paris (realized in the Metro) including passage under Seine, and for installation of city-wide pneumatic system for delivery of telegrams and letters.

Ber·lin \byerl-'yēn\, Naphtali Zevi Judah. *Known by acronym* ha-Neziv. 1817–1893. Russian Jewish scholar. Developed yeshiva at Volozhin into spiritual center of Russian Jewry; one of first rabbis to join Zionist movement.

Ber·li·ner \'bər-lə-nər\, Emile. 1851–1929. American inventor, b. Hanover, Germany. To U.S. (1870); invented the Berliner loose-contact telephone transmitter or microphone (1877); perfected various features of telephone; introduced (pat. 1878) use of induction coil in transmitter. Invented gramophone talking machine (1887) and a method of duplicating disk records; invented and first used (1908) lightweight internal-combustion motor later used for airplanes; invented (1925) acoustic tile and acoustic cells for insuring good acoustics in halls, etc.

Ber·lin·ghie·ri \ber-liŋ-'gyā-rē\, Bonaventura. fl. 1235–1244. Italian painter. Known esp. for scenes depicting life of St. Francis of Assisi in S. Francesco, Pescia.

Ber·lin Paint·er \(,)bər-'lin-'pānt-ər\. Name given Greek vase painter (fl. 500–460 B.C.) who, with Kleophrades, was outstanding exponent of Late Archaic style; best known for amphora (now in Berlin) depicting satyrs; over 200 other unsigned works attributed to him.

Ber·lioz \ber-lyōz; *Angl* 'ber-lē-,ōz, *also* -,ōs *or* -,ō\, Hector, *in full* Louis-Hector. 1803–1869. French composer. Dedicated to creation and dissemination of new style of music, inspired by Beethoven, Gluck, and Weber, notable for dramatic expressiveness; considered first among French Romantic composers. Also a conductor of note, instilling new standards of precision and flexibility. Works included *Symphonie fantastique* (1830–31); overtures to *Waverly* (1823), *Les Francs-Juges* (1827), *Le Roi Lear* (1831), *Le Corsair* (1831), *Le Carnaval romain* (1844); choral works *Huit Scènes de Faust* (1829), *Lélio ou Le Retour à la vie* (1831), *Requiem* (1837), *Roméo et Juliette* (1839), *Symphonie funèbre et triomphale* (1840), *La Damnation de Faust* (1846), *L'Enfance du Christ* (1854), *Te Deum* (1855); operas *Benvenuto Cellini* (1838), *Les Troyens* in two parts (1855–58), *Béatrice et Bénédict* (1862); also *La Mort de Cléopâtre* (1829), *La Captive* (1834), *Les Nuits d'été* (1834–41), *La Mort d'Ophélie* (1850). m. (1833; d. 1854) actress Harriet Smithson.

Ber·me·jo \ber-'mā-kō\, Bartolomé. *Also called* Bartolomé de Cárdenas \-thā-'kär-thā-näs\. fl. 1474–95. Spanish painter. Considered finest Spanish painter before El Greco; introduced Flemish manner into Spain; best known work *La Piedad,* Barcelona cathedral.

Ber·mu·do \ber-'mü-thō\. *Span.* Ver·mu·do \ber-\. Name of three kings of Asturias, Galicia, or León:

Bermudo I. *Called* el Diá·co·no \el-dē-'ä-kō-nō\, *i.e.* the Deacon. d. 797? King of Asturias (788 or 789–791). Nephew of Alfonso I; abdicated in favor of Alfonso II following defeat by Moors.

Bermudo II. *Called* el Go·to·so \el-gō-'tō-sō\, *i.e.* the gouty one. 956–999. King of Galicia (982–999) and of León (985–999). Illegitimate son of Ordoño III; with aid of Abū ʿĀmir al-Manṣūr quelled civil war in León (984); later (989) broke with and fought against al-Manṣūr; reign marked by constant conflicts with Muslim forces.

Bermudo III. 1016–1037. King of León (1027–37). Son of Alfonso V; under regency of stepmother Urraca (1027–32); at war with Sancho III of Navarre until Sancho's death (1035); died at battle of Tamarón while attempting to recover territories from his brother-in-law Ferdinand I of Castile.

Bern, Dietrich von. See THEODORIC the Great.

Ber·na·dette \ber-nà-det, *Angl* ,bər-nə-'det\ of Lourdes. Saint. *Orig.* Marie-Bernarde Sou·bi·rous \sü-bē-rü\. 1844–1879. French religious. Experienced series of visions of Immaculate Conception (1858); joined Sisters of Charity at Nevers (1866). Her visions of Our Lady at Lourdes, instructing her to make known miraculous healing powers, led to establishment of Lourdes as a shrine. Canonized (1933).

Ber·na·dotte \ber-nà-dȯt, *Angl* 'bər-nə-,dät\. Name of family of old lineage of Béarn, France, whose earliest known member (17th century) owned estate in Pau known as "Bernadotte." Most prominent member Jean-Baptiste-Jules, who became King Charles XIV John (*q.v.*) of Sweden.

Ber·na·dot·te af Wis·borg \ber-nä-'dȯt-ə-äv-'vēs-bor^y\, Folke. Count. 1895–1948. Swedish soldier. Nephew of King Gustav V; vice president (1943–46), president (1946–48), Swedish Red Cross; saved thousands from Nazi concentration camps. United Nations mediator in Palestine (1948); secured ceasefire agreement between Israel and Arab states; murdered by Israeli extremists.

Ber·nal \(,)bər-'nal, 'be(ə)r-nᵊl\, John Desmond. 1901–1971. British physicist, b. Ireland. Professor, London U. (1938–63); known for work in X-ray crystallography.

Ber·na·nos \ber-nà-nōs, -nȯs\, Georges. 1888–1948. French novelist. Author of novels informed by deeply felt morality and Catholicism, including *Sous le soleil de Satan* (1926), *La Joie* (1929), *Journal d'un curé de campagne* (1936), *Nouvelle histoire de Mouchette* (1937), *Monsieur Ouine* (1943); known also for vehement polemics as *La grande peur des bien-pensants* (1931), *Les grands cimetières sous la lune* (1938), *Lettre aux Anglais* (1942).

Bernard. See also BERNHARD.

Ber·nard \'ber-närd; *Angl* (,)bər-'närd, 'bər-,närd, 'bər-nərd\. c.797–818. King of Italy (813–817). Illegitimate son of Pepin, son of Charlemagne; deposed after rebellion against uncle Louis I the Pious.

Bernard VII. Comte d'Ar·ma·gnac \-dàr-màn-yàk\. d. 1418. French noble. Constable of France; led Armagnac forces in civil war with Burgundians; in virtual control of government (c.1413–1418) under Charles VI; murdered.

Bernard *or* **Bern·hard** \'bern-,härt\ of An·halt \'än-,hält\. 1140–1212. Son of Albert I the Bear; inherited Ascanian lands in Saxony (1170), becoming count of Aschersleben, or Anhalt; duke of Saxony following overthrow of Henry the Lion (1180). Founder of the line of princes of Anhalt.

Bernard of Aosta. See BERNARD of Montjoux.

Ber·nard \ber-nàr, *Angl* (,)bər-'närd, 'bər-,närd, 'bər-nərd\ of Chartres \shärtrᵊ, *Angl* 'shärt(rᵊ)\. d. c.1130. French Humanist and philosopher. Brother of Thierry de Chartres. Teacher in cathedral school of Chartres (from 1114), chancellor of school (from 1119); also taught in Paris. Evolved Platonic philosophy from Pseudo-Dionysius, attempted to reconcile it with Aristotelianism; author of *De expositione Porphyrii* and a comparative study of Plato and Aristotle; works extant only in fragments but known through *Metalogicon* of his pupil John of Salisbury.

Bernard of Clair·vaux \kler-vō\. Saint. 1090–1153. French religious. Entered Cistercian abbey of Cîteaux (1112); established monastery at Clairvaux (1115); renowned for piety, charity, mystical faith. Vigorous opponent of Scholasticism and esp. Abelard; member of numerous civil and ecclesiastical councils and confidant of bishops and popes; one of the most influential churchmen of the day; instrumental in condemnations of Abelard and Gilbert de La Porrée. At urging of Pope Eugenius III and King Louis VII, vigorously promoted Second Crusade (1147–49). Author of epistles, sermons, treatises on Mariology, asceticism, polemics, etc.; character of his writings won him title of *doctor mellifluus* from Pope Pius XII (1953). Canonized (1174), declared doctor of the church (1830).

Bernard of Clu·ny \klüe̅nē\. *Also called* Bernard of Mor·laix \mȯr-le\. 12th century. French monk and poet. Perhaps orig. a monk of Saint-Sauveur d'Aniane; monk at Cluny (from c.1125). Author of *De contemptu mundi* (c.1140), a verse treatise on Neoplatonism and a criticism of moral decay in the church; also compiled *Consuetudines Cluniacenses,* compendium of monastic rules, customs, and practices at Cluny.

Bernard of Mont·joux \mōⁿt-zhü\. Saint. *Also called* Bernard of Men·thon \mäⁿ-tōⁿ\ *or* of Ao·sta \ȯ-stȧ, ȧ-ȯ-stȧ\. d. 1081? Italian religious. Vicar general of Aosta diocese; reestablished hospices of summits of Great and Little St. Bernard passes, giving them into care of clerics and laymen who later became Canons Regular of St. Augustine; canonized (c.1115–21); named patron saint of alpinists by Pope Pius XI (1923). St. Bernard dog named for him.

Bernard of Pisa. See EUGENIUS III.

Ber·nard \ber-nȧr\, Claude. 1813–1878. French physiologist. Professor, Sorbonne (1854), Collège de France (1855–68), Musée d'Histoire Naturelle (1868–78); named senator (1869). Investigated chemical phenomena of digestion, discovering role of pancreas in digestion of fat and the glycogenic function of the liver; discovered regulation of blood supply by vasomotor nerves. Author of *Introduction à la médecine expérimentale* (1865). Awarded grand prize in physiology three times by Académie des Sciences.

Bernard, Émile. 1868–1941. French painter. A leader of school of Pont-Aven, sometimes credited with founding Cloisonist style; known for friendships and correspondence with van Gogh, Cézanne, Gauguin, Redon.

Bernard, Jean-Jacques. 1888–1972. French playwright and novelist. Son of Tristan Bernard. Chief representative of "school of silence" in which nonverbal expression is paramount; plays included *Le Feu qui reprend mal* (1921), *Martine* (1922), *Le Printemps des autres* (1924), *L'Âme en peine* (1926), *À la recherche des coeurs* (1931), *Jeanne de Pantin* (1933). Also wrote novels *Le Roman de Martine* (1929), *Madeleine Landier* (1933), memoirs *Le Camp de la morte lente* (1944), *Mon ami le théâtre* (1958).

Bernard, Simon. 1779–1839. French military engineer. In French army (1797–1814); aide-de-camp to Napoléon (1813–14); with Napoléon at Waterloo (1815). To U.S. (1815); brevet brigadier general of engineers (1816); planned coast defenses (1815–30). Returned to France (1830); French minister of war (1834, 1836–39).

Bernard, Tristan, *orig.* Paul. 1866–1947. French playwright and novelist. Author of popular boulevard comedies including *L'Anglais tel qu'on le parle* (1899), *Triplepatte* (1905), *Monsieur Codomat* (1907), and the novels *Mémoires d'un jeune homme rangé* (1899), *La Féerie bourgeoise* (1924).

Bernard de Ven·ta·dour \də-väⁿ-tȧ-dür\. *Also spelled* Ber·nart de Ven·ta·dorn \ber-nȧrt-də-väⁿ-tȧ-dȯrn\. d.1195? Provençal troubadour. At various times at courts of Eleanor of Aquitaine, Toulouse; author of love lyrics, considered finest in Provençal, and melodies.

Ber·nar·des \bər-'nȧr-dēs(h), -des(h)\, Artur da Sil·va \də-'sēl-və\. 1875–1955. Brazilian politician. Deputy (1909), later senator; president of Brazil (1922–26); suppressed revolution in São Paulo; political exile (1932–34); professor, U. of Lisbon (1934).

Ber·nar·des \bər-'nȧr-dēsh\, Diogo. c.1530–1605. Portuguese poet. Known esp. for pastoral lyrics, elegies, and idyls; author of *Varias Rimas ao Bom Jesús* (1594), *O Lima* (1596), and *Flores do Lima* (1596).

Ber·nar·din de Saint-Pierre \ber-nȧr-daⁿ-də-saⁿ-pyer\, Jacques-Henri. 1737–1814. French writer. Precursor of French romantic movement; wrote *Voyage à l'Île de France* (1773), *Études de la nature* (1784–88) to which he appended his widely read pastoral romance *Paul et Virginie* (1788), and *La Chaumière indienne* (1790).

Ber·nar·di·no \,bär-när-'dē-nō\ of Siena. Saint. 1380–1444. Italian religious and theologian. Entered Observant Franciscans (1402); ordained (1404); became known esp. as a preacher and evangelizer in Lombardy; influenced devotion to Holy Name; vicar-general of Observants in Italy (1438–42); canonized (1450).

Ber·nau·er \'ber-,nau-ər\, Agnes. d.1435. German victim. Daughter of an Augsburg baker; m. (1432) Albert, son of Ernest, Duke of Bavaria-Munich; when Albert acknowledged the marriage, Ernest had her seized, convicted of witchcraft, and drowned in Danube. The tale is material for several German dramas.

Berners, 2d Baron. See John BOURCHIER.

Berners, 14th Baron. See TYRWHITT-WILSON.

Berners *or* **Bernes,** Juliana. See BARNES.

Bern·hard \'bern-,härt\. Duke of Saxe-Wei·mar \'saks-'vī-,mär\. 1604–1639. German general. Son of John, Duke of Weimar; brother of Ernest I the Pious. Served in Protestant cause in Thirty Years' War, in armies of Rhenish Palatinate, Baden, Denmark, and (from 1631) Gustavus II Adolphus of Sweden; commanded at Lützen (1632) after death of Gustavus Adolphus; with Gustav Horn, defeated at Nördlingen (1634); abandoned by Sweden, made alliance with Richelieu; won victory at Rheinfelden (1638) and captured Breisach (1638).

Bernhard. 1649–1706. German noble. Third son of Ernest I the Pious; founder (1680) of Saxe-Meiningen branch of Ernestine line of Saxony.

Bern·hardt \ber-nȧr, *Angl* 'bərn-,härt\, Sarah. *Orig.* Henriette-Rosine Ber·nard \ber-nȧr\. 1844–1923. French actress. With Odéon theater (1866–72), Comédie Française (1872–80); played successful roles in *Kean, Le Passant, Zaïre, Le Sphinx, Phèdre, Hernani, Ruy Blas.* Formed own company (1880); on tour in England, U.S., and European countries, acting chiefly in *Adrienne Lecouvreur, Froufrou,* and *La Dame aux camélias* (1880–82). Starred in a series of Sardou's plays, including *Fédora, Théodora, La Tosca, Cléopâtre* (1883–93). Became proprietress of Théâtre de la Renaissance (1893); leased (1899) Théâtre des Nations (renamed Théâtre Sarah-Bernhardt); acted in Rostand's *L'Aiglon* and a French rendition of *Hamlet.* Leg amputated (1915), but continued her career. Noted for remarkable voice, emotional acting, unconventional personal life. Author of memoirs *Ma double vie* (1907).

Ber·ni \'ber-nē\, Francesco. 1497 or 1498–1535. Italian satirist and poet. Translated Boiardo's *Orlando innamorato* into Tuscan dialect; author of farce *La Caterina;* known esp. for burlesques, in a style called *bernesco* after him.

Bernice. See BERENICE.

Ber·ni·ni \bār-'nē-nē\, Gian *or* Giovanni Lorenzo. 1598–1680. Italian sculptor, architect, and painter. Son of Pietro Bernini. Highly precocious sculptor; attracted patronage of Cardinal Borghese and esp. of Urban VIII and succeeding popes. Dominant influence on European sculpture for more than century; creator of Baroque style in sculpture. Succeeded Maderna as architect of St. Peter's (1629). Sculptures, notable esp. for capturing subtle emotional states, included *Aeneas, Anchises and Ascanius, Neptune and Triton, Pluto and Proserpina, Apollo and Daphne, David, St. Longinus, Cardinal Borghese, Ecstasy of St. Teresa, Constantine, Louis XIV, Gabriele Fonseca;* sculptural works included tombs of Urban VIII and Alexander VII, fountains of Triton, Four Rivers, Barcaccia. Architectural works, often combining architecture, sculpture, painting into dramatic settings, included the baldachin (1624–33), piazza and colonnade (1656–57), Cathedra Petri (1657–66), all in St. Peter's; Cornaro Chapel, Sta. Maria della Vittoria (1645–52); churches of S. Tomaso da Villanova (1658–61) and S. Andrea al Quirinale (1658–70); Altieri Chapel, S. Francesco a Ripa (c.1674).

Bernini, Pietro. 1562–1629. Italian sculptor. Worked in Naples (1584–c.1605), Rome (from c.1605), to which he was called by Pope Paul V; works, in late Mannerist style, included *Coronation of Clement VIII* and *Assumption* for Sta. Maria Maggiore, *St. John* for Barberini Chapel, S. Andrea della Valle.

Ber·nis \ber-nēs\, François-Joachim de Pierre de \pyer-də-\. 1715–1794. French cardinal and statesman. Member of Mme. de Pompadour's retinue; ambassador to Venice (1752–55); councilor of state (1755); represented France in diplomatic negotiations with Austria before Seven Years' War. Created cardinal (1758), archbishop of Albi (1764). Ambassador to Rome (1769–94); obtained (1773) from Pope Clement XIV suppression of Jesuits; opposed ecclesiastical reforms of French Revolution. Called, from his little poems and "bouquets poetiques," Ba·bet la Bou·que·tière \bȧ-bel-ȧ-bük-tyer\.

Ber·noul·li *Ger* ber-'nül-ē, *Fr* ber-nü-yē\. Name of a family of mathematicians and scientists of Basel, Switzerland, including: Jakob I (1654–1705); professor of mathematics at U. of Basel (from 1687); pioneer in application of Leibnizian calculus to variety of problems; introduced term "integral"; studied catenary and applied calculus to bridge design. Author of *Conamen novi systematis cometarum* (1682), *Dissertatio de gravitate aetheris* (1683), *Ars conjectandi* (pub. posthumously), etc. His brother ¶Johann I (1667–1748); professor of mathematics at U. of Basel (from 1705); pioneer in exponential calculus; in competition with brother developed calculus of variation. Teacher of Euler, and collaborator of L'Hospital. Their nephew ¶Nikolaus (1687–1759); professor of mathematics at Padua (1716–22), then of law and logic at U. of Basel; contributed to probability theory and infinite series. Johann's sons: ¶Daniel (1700–1782), professor of mathematics at St. Petersburg (1724–32), of anatomy, botany, and physics, and then of philosophy, at U. of Basel; discovered Bernoulli's principle relating fluid velocity and pressure; contributed to probability, kinetic theory of gases, celestial mechanics; author of *Hydrodynamica* (1738) and works on acoustics, astronomy, etc.; and ¶Johann II (1710–1790), professor of eloquence and of mathematics, known for his contribution to theories of heat and light. Two sons of the last named: ¶Johann III (1744–1807), astronomer to the Academy of Berlin, author of *Recueil pour les astronomes* (1772–76); and ¶Jakob II (1759–1789), professor of mathematics at St. Petersburg. ¶Christoph (1782–1863), grandson of Johann II and nephew of Johann III and Jakob II, was naturalist and professor at U. of Basel (from 1818); author of *Vademecum des Mechanikers* (1829), etc.

Bern·stein \'bern-ˌshtīn\, Aaron. 1812–1884. German writer. Author of classic Jewish tales *Vögele der Maggid* and *Mendel Gibbor;* also of political works. Founded (1853) and edited *Berliner Volks-Zeitung.*

Bernstein, Eduard. 1850–1932. German writer and politican. Nephew of Aaron Bernstein. Joined Social Democrats (1872); coeditor of *Sozialdemokrat* (1879–90), in Zurich (until 1888) then as exile in London; associate of Engels; proponent of revisionism (1889) which aimed at a modified Marxian socialism, evolutionary rather than revolutionary. Returned to Germany (1901); member of Reichstag (1902–06, 1912–18, 1920–28); joined Independents following split in Social Democratic party (1916); rejoined Majority Socialists (1919). Author of *Die Voraussetzungen des Sozialismus und die Aufgaben der Sozialdemokratie* (1899), etc.

Bern·stein \bern-sten\, Henry-Léon-Gustave-Charles. 1876–1953. French dramatist. Author of popular melodramas and later serious works, including *Le Marché* (1900), *Le Bercail* (1904), *Frère Jacques* (with Pierre Véber, 1904), *La Rafale* (1905), *La Griffe* (1906), *Le Voleur* (1906), *Samson* (1907), *Israël* (1908), *Après Moi* (1911), *Le Secret* (1913), *Judith* (1922), *Galerie des glaces* (1924), *Félix* (1926), *Mélo* (1929), *Le Jour* (1931), *Espoir* (1934), *Le Voyage* (1937), *Elvire* (1940), *La Soif* (1949), etc.

Bern·stein \'bərn-ˌstīn\, Herman. 1876–1935. American journalist and writer, b. Russia. To U.S. (1893); European correspondent, New York *Times* (1908–12); founder (1914) and editor (1914–16) of Yiddish daily *The Day;* editor, *American Hebrew* (1916–19). Published (1917) "Willy-Nicky" telegrams (messages between German kaiser and Russian emperor in 1904–07). Editor of weekly *Jewish Tribune* (1925–29). U.S. minister to Albania (1930–33). Author of *The Flight of Time* (poems, 1899), *In the Gates of Israel* (1902), *History of a Lie* (1921), *Celebrities of Our Time* (interviews, 1924).

Bern·storff \'bern-ˌshtȯrf\, Graf von. Title of several members of a German family of statesmen and diplomats in Danish, Prussian, and German service, including: Johann Hartwig Ernst (1712–1772); entered Danish service (1733); ambassador at Paris (1744–50); foreign minister (1751–70); preserved neutrality of Denmark in Seven Years' War; advocated friendly alliance with Sweden; concluded treaties with France (1758) and Russia (1767); furthered trade and commerce, a public health program, emancipation of peasants, and other reforms; dismissed (1770) as a result of Struensee's intrigues. His nephew ¶Andreas Peter (1735–1797) entered Danish service (1758); dismissed (1770) and recalled (1772); foreign minister (1773–80); concluded defensive anti-Swedish alliance with Russia (1773); joined unwillingly armed neutrality compact (1780) with Russia, Prussia, and Sweden and a separate agreement with Great Britain; dismissed (1780); again foreign minister (1784–97); took part in reform movements, including emancipation of Danish peasants (1788). Andreas's son ¶Christian Günther (1769–1835); in Danish service (1787–1818); ambassador at Berlin (1789–94) and Stockholm (1794–97); secretary of state (1797–1800), foreign minister (1800–10); Danish ambassador at Vienna (1811) and Berlin (1816). Entered Prussian diplomatic service as foreign minister (1818–32); frequently followed policies of Metternich, but helped found *Zollverein* and supported Russia's war against Turkey (1828). Christian's nephew ¶Albrecht (1809–1873); Prussian ambassador successively at Munich, Vienna, and Naples (1845–54); at London (1854–61, 1862–73); foreign minister (1861–62). Albrecht's son ¶Johann Heinrich (1862–1939) entered German diplomatic service (1889); consul general, Cairo (1906); ambassador at Washington (1908–17); endeavored, without support from his government, to further President Wilson's attempts at mediation preceding America's entry into World War I; ambassador at Constantinople (1917–18); member, Democratic party in Reichstag (1920–28); German delegate to disarmament conferences (1929–31).

Be·ros·sus \bə-'räs-əs\ *or* **Be·ro·sus** \-'rō-səs\ *or* **Be·ros·sos** \-'räs-əs, -(ˌ)ōs\ *or* **Be·ro·sos** \-'rō-səs, -(ˌ)sōs\. fl. c.290 B.C. Babylonian priest. Author of a history of Babylonia (in Greek), parts of which have been preserved as extracts in works of Josephus and Eusebius.

Berr \ber\, Henri. 1863–1954. French historian and philosopher. Professor, Lycée Henri IV, Paris (1896–1925); founded (1900) *Revue de synthèse historique;* founded journal *Science* (1936); edited 65 volumes of *L'Évolution de l'humanité* (1920–54). Author of numerous historical and political works and a novel, *L'Hymne à la vie* (1942).

Berrettini, Pietro. See PIETRO DA CORTONA.

Ber·ru·gue·te \ber-rü-'gā-tā\, Alonso. c.1488–1561. Spanish sculptor and painter. Son of Pedro Berruguete; studied in Italy; named court painter to Charles V (1518). Known mainly as sculptor in Mannerist style, noted for capturing anguish and ecstasy. Major works included tomb of Juan Selvagio, Zaragossa; *Resurrection* in cathedral of Valencia (c.1517); several altarpieces for monasteries; *Transfiguration* and choir stalls in Toledo cathedral (1539–48).

Berruguete, Pedro. *Also known as* Pedro Es·pa·ñol \es-pän-'yōl\. *Ital.* Pietro Spa·gnuo·lo \ˌspän-yə-'wō-lō\. d. 1504. Spanish painter. Considered first great Renaissance painter in Spain; produced works for cathedrals of Toledo (1483–99) and Avila (1499–1504) and altarpiece of convent of San Tomás, Avila.

Ber·ry \be-rē\. Duchy of central France which became (1360) an appanage of French reigning house; reabsorbed (1601) into royal domain. See JEAN DE FRANCE; Charles-Ferdinand de BOURBON.

Ber·ry \'ber-ē\, Edward Wilber. 1875–1945. American paleobotanist, b. Newark, N.J. On faculty, Johns Hopkins U. (1907–42), dean ot college of arts and sciences (1929–42), provost (1935–42); with U.S. Geological Survey (1910–42), senior geologist (1917–42). Authority on classification of ancient plants, esp. of southeastern North America, equatorial America, and South America. Author of *Tree Ancestors* (1923), *Paleontology* (1929).

Berry, Martha McChesney. 1866–1942. American educator, b. near Rome, Ga. Founder (from 1902) of Berry schools for underprivileged children of rural districts in Georgia and vicinity.

Ber·ryer \ber-yā\, Pierre-Antoine. 1790–1868. French lawyer and politician. Aided father in defense of Marshal Ney (1815); won acquittal of Lamennais (1826); defender of monarchy and papal power. Deputy (1830–48); mainstay of Catholic legitimists; defended Louis-Napoléon (1840) but opposed his coup d'etat (1851); briefly imprisoned. Opponent of empire in Legislative Assembly (1863–68).

Ber·ry·man \'ber-i-mən\, John. 1914–1972. American poet, b. McAlester, Okla. Taught at Wayne State U., Harvard, Princeton (1943–49), U. of Minnesota (1955–72). Author of *Poems* (1942), *The Dispossessed* (1948), *Homage to Mistress Bradstreet* (1956), *77 Dream Songs* (1964, Pulitzer prize), *Berryman's Sonnets* (1967), *His Toy, His Dream, His Rest* (1968), *Love & Fame* (1970).

Bert \ber\, Paul. 1833–1886. French physiologist and politician. Professor, Sorbonne (1869–86); studied effects of air pressure on physiology; discovered mechanism of caisson disease, explicated it in classic *La Pression barométrique* (1878). Deputy (1872–86), minister of education (1881–82). Governor general of Annam and Tonkin (1886).

Ber·ta·ni \ber-'tän-ē\, Agostino. 1812–1886. Italian physician and revolutionary. Took part in Milan insurrection (1848); organized republicans' ambulance system in Rome (1849); surgeon with Garibaldi in Austro-Sardinian War (1859); helped plan March of the Thousand on Sicily and Naples (1860); Garibaldi's secretary general in Naples (1860); directed Garibaldi's medical service in Austrian war (1866). In parliament (1861–86); leader of extreme left; founded journal *La Riforma* (1866).

Ber·taut \ber-tō\, Jean de Caen. 1552–1611. French prelate and poet. Bishop of Séez (1606); held various posts at court. Author of polished verses in *Recueil des oeuvres poétiques* (1601), *Recueil des quelques vers amoureux* (1602).

Ber·tha \'ber-tə, *Angl* 'bər-thə\. *Also spelled* Berta, Berte, Berthe, *or* Ber·tra·da \ber-'träd-ə\. d. 783. Carolingian queen. Daughter of Caribert, count of Laon; m. Pepin III the Short; mother of Charlemagne and Carloman.

Ber·the·lier \ber-təl-yā\, Philibert. c.1465–1519. Swiss patriot. Leader of Eidguenots, faction struggling to maintain independence of Geneva from domination by Charles III, Duke of Savoy; formed (1515) Enfants de Genève to resist temporal powers of Savoyard puppet John, bishop of Geneva; summarily executed.

Ber·the·lot \ber-tə-lō\, Philippe-Joseph-Louis. 1866–1934. French diplomat. Son of Marcelin Berthelot. Entered diplomatic service (1889); adviser to Briand and active in Allied liaison during World War I; secretary general of ministry of foreign affairs (1920–21, 1925–32).

Berthelot, Marcelin, *in full* Pierre-Eugène-Marcelin. 1827–1907. French chemist. Professor, Collège de France (1865); inspector of higher education (1876); elected senator for life (1881); minister of public instruction (1886–87); minister of foreign affairs (1895–96). Best known for his researches in explosives, dyestuffs, the synthesis of organic compounds, and esp. thermochemistry. Author of *Chimie organique fondée sur la synthèse* (1860), *Mécanique chimique* (1878), *Thermochimie* (1897), works on history of chemistry and alchemy, translations, etc.

Ber·thier \ber-tyā\, Louis-Alexandre. Prince de Neu·châ·tel \nœ-shä-tel\. Prince de Wa·gram \vá-grám, *Ger* 'vä-ˌgräm\. 1753–1815. Marshal of France. Served under Lafayette in American Revolution; chief of staff under Luckner (1792) and with Napoléon in Italy and Egypt; minister of war (1800–07); created marshal (1804); sovereign prince of Neuchâtel (1806); chief of staff, major general, in Grand Armée (1805–14). Created prince de Wagram (1809). Submitted to Louis XVIII (1814).

Bert·hold I \'ber-tōlt\ *or* **Berch·told I** \'berk-tōlt\. d. 1078. German noble. Held several Swabian countships; styled (from 1061) duke of Carinthia; helped Henry IV suppress rebellion in Saxony (1073–75); supported Pope Gregory VII against Henry (1075–77), and joined in deposing Henry (1077) in favor of Rudolf of Rheinfelden.

Berthold of Hen·ne·berg \'hen-ə-ˌberk\. *Also called* Berthold of Mainz \'mīn(t)s\. 1442–1504. German noble and prelate. Archbishop of Mainz (1484); active in election of Maximilian I as king of the Romans (1486);

imperial chancellor under Emperor Maximilian (1493); responsible for reform program presented at Diet of Worms (1495), including creation of high court (1495), council of regency (1500).

Berthold von Re·gens·burg \'rā-gəns-,bu̇rk\. c.1220–1272. German preacher. Franciscan; famed for preaching religion of the heart; his sermons chief exemplars of Middle High German prose style.

Ber·tho·let \ber-tȯ-le\, Alfred. 1868–1951. Swiss cleric and scholar. Professor, Basel (1899–1912), Tübingen (1913), Göttingen (1914–27), Berlin (1929–43), Basel (1945–51). Author of *Apokryphen und Pseudepigraphen* (1906), *Biblische Theologie* (1911), *Kulturgeschichte Israels* (1920), *Dynamismus und Personalismus in der Seelenauffassung* (1930), *Götterspaltung und Göttervereinigung* (1933), *Das Geschlecht der Gottheit* (1934), etc.

Ber·thol·let \ber-tȯ-le\, Claude-Louis. Comte. 1748–1822. French chemist. Superintendent of dyeing processes in France (1784); discovered composition of ammonia (1785); devised method of bleaching with chlorine (1789). One of founders of l'École Polytechnique; professor of chemistry there. One of savants with Napoléon in Italy and Egypt; named senator by Napoléon (1804); created count. Debated Lavoisier on phlogiston theory; showed that acids do not necessarily contain oxygen; investigated and systematized chemical affinity, anticipating law of mass action; with Lavoisier and others, devised system of chemical nomenclature that serves as basis of system still in use. His works included *Éléments de l'art de la teinture* (1791) and *Essai de statique chimique* (1803).

Ber·til·lon \ber-tē-yō^n, *Angl* (,)bər-'til-ən\, Alphonse. 1853–1914. French criminologist. As chief of department of identification in prefecture of police, Paris, devised system (Bertillonage) of identifying criminals by anthropometric measurements. His brother ¶Jacques (1851–1922), statistician, head of Paris bureau of vital statistics (1883–1913); introduced "Bertillon classification" of causes of death, adopted by many nations. Author of *La Statistique humaine en France* (1880), *L'Alcoolisme* (1904), *La Dépopulation de la France* (1911).

Ber·tin \ber-ta^n\. Family of French journalists, including: Louis-François Bertin (1766–1841) and his brother ¶Louis-François Bertin de Vaux \vō\ (1771–1842), purchased and revived (1800) the *Journal des débats* (changed by Napoléon I to *Journal de l'empire,* 1805–14); the younger Louis was minister of police (1815–18), deputy (1820), councillor of state (1827). Two sons of the older Louis-François ¶François-Édouard (1797–1871) and ¶Louis-Marie-Armand (1801–1854), continued editorship of *Journal des débats* (Armand, 1841–54; Édouard, 1854–71).

Ber·ton \ber-tō^n\, Pierre-Montan. 1727–1780. French musician. Orchestra leader (from 1755), co-manager (1767), director general (1775–78) of the Opéra, Paris. His son ¶Henri-Montan Berton (1767–1844), was a composer of light operas including *Ponce de León* (1797), *Montano et Stéphanie* (1799), *Le Délire* (1799), *Aline* (1803), *Françoise de Foix* (1809). Henri's natural son ¶Henri, *known as* François Berton (1784–1832), composed several operas presented at the Opéra-Comique, as *Monsieur Desbosquets* (1810), *Ninette à la cour* (1811), *Les Casquets* (1821).

Ber·to·ni \bār-'tō-nē\, Ferdinando Gasparo. 1725–1813. Italian organist and composer. Organist (1752–85), maestro di cappella (1785–1808), St. Mark's, Venice. Composed 50 operas as *La vedova accorta* (1745), *La pescatrici* (1751), *Orfeo ed Euridice* (1776), *Quinto Fabio* (1778); over 50 oratorios, and much church music.

Ber·trand \ber-trä^n\, Gabriel-Émile. 1867–1962. French biochemist. At Pasteur Institute (from 1900), professor (1908–37); coined term "oxidase" in studies of enzymes; discovered biological requirement for trace elements.

Bertrand, Henri-Gratien. Comte. 1773–1844. French engineer and general. With Napoléon in all campaigns of the empire; brigadier general (1800); built bridges for crossing of Danube at Wagram (1809); grand marshal of the palace (1813); accompanied Napoléon into exile on Elba (1814–15), St. Helena (1815–21).

Bertrand, Louis-Jacques-Napoléon. *Called* Aloysius Bertrand. 1807–1841. French writer. Liberal journalist in Dijon and Paris; author of *Gaspard de la nuit* (pub. 1842), which introduced prose poem into French literature and influenced later Symbolists.

Bertrand, Louis-Marie-Émile. 1866–1941. French writer. Author of novels and other works on North Africa, including *Le Sang des races (1899), Pépète le Bien-Aimé* (1904), *L'Invasion* (1907), *Saint Augustin* (1913), *Jean Perbal* (1926), *La Méditerranée* (1929), *Les Martyrs africains* (1930), etc.

Bertrand, Marcel-Alexandre. 1847–1907. French geologist. Taught at École des Mines (from 1886), Académie des Sciences (1896); developed theory of orogeny based on massive folding of the Earth's crust; developed orogenic wave theory whereby successive Caledonian, Hercynian, Alpine periods of orogeny built up European mountain system north to south.

Bertrand de Bar-sur-Aube \-də-bär-sūēr-ōb\. 13th century. French poet. Author of chansons de geste, esp. *Girart de Vienne* and *Aymeri de Narbonne.*

Ber·tran de Born \ber-trä^n-də-bȯrn\. Vicomte de Haute·fort \dōt(-ə)-fȯr\. d. c.1202–15. French soldier and troubador. Encouraged sons of Henry II of England to rebel. Wrote satires, lyrics of war and love.

Ber·tuch \'ber-,tu̲k\, Friedrich Justin. 1747–1822. German writer and publisher. Translator of *Don Quixote* (1775–76); with Wieland edited *Teutschem Merkur* (1782–86); with Wieland and Schütz founded (1785) *Allgemeine Literaturzeitung.*

Bé·rulle \bā-rūēl\, Pierre de. 1575–1629. French prelate. Founder (1611) of Congregation of the Oratory, in France; founded numerous colleges; cardinal (1627); principal adviser to Marie de Médicis; vigorously anti-Protestant, broke with Richelieu over proposed alliance against Spain.

Ber·wald \'ber-,vält\, Franz Adolf. 1796–1868. Swedish composer. Professor, Stockholm Academy (1864–67), Stockholm Conservatory (1867–68). Considered founder of Romanticism in Swedish music and first major symphonist; wrote 6 symphonies, 5 cantatas, concerti, operas as *Estrella di Soria* (1841), choral and chamber works.

Berwick, Duke of. See James FITZJAMES.

Berwick, Mary. See Adelaide Procter under Bryan Waller PROCTER.

Ber·wiń·ski \ber-'vēn^y-skē\, Ryszard Wincenty. 1819–1879. Polish poet. Achieved early fame with *Poezje* (1844); examined universality of folk traditions in *Studia o literaturze* (1854). Lifelong revolutionary, twice imprisoned, spent last years in exile in Constantinople.

Ber·ze·li·us \ber-'sā-lē-əs, *Angl* (,)bər-'zē-lē-əs\, Jöns Jakob. 1779–1848. Swedish chemist. Taught medicine and pharmacy at Stockholm (from 1807) and chemistry (1815–32). Created baron (1835). Determined atomic and molecular weights of thousands of substances, using oxygen as a standard; experimented in electrolysis and developed the dualistic theory originated by Lavoisier; discovered the elements cerium (1803), selenium (1817), and thorium (1828), and first isolated silicon (1823), zirconium (1824), titanium (1825); introduced present system of writing chemical symbols and formulas; improved analytical methods, esp. the blowpipe method; studied and named phenomena of isomerism and catalysis.

Ber·zsen·yi \'ber-zhen-yē\, Dániel. 1776–1836. Hungarian poet. Introduced classical meters and themes to Hungarian poetry; wrote esp. odes and elegies on Hungarian subjects, as "A magyacrokhoz" and "Fohász."

Bes·ant \'bez-ənt\, Annie, *nee* Wood. 1847–1933. English theosophist and Indian political leader. m. Rev. Frank Besant (1867). Associated, under pseudonym Ajax \'ā-,jaks\, with Charles Bradlaugh in propaganda for free thought and limitation of population; later associated with Fabian Socialists; joined Theosophical Society (1889); devoted pupil of Madame Blavatsky; president of society (1907–33). Founded Central Hindu College at Benares (1898); organized India Home Rule League (1916); president, Indian National Congress (1917). Author of *Reincarnation* (1892), *Karma* (1895), *Theosophy and the New Psychology* (1904), etc.

Be·sant \bi-'zant, 'bez-ənt\, Sir Walter. 1836–1901. English novelist. Coauthor, with James Rice, of a series of novels, including *Ready-Money Mortiboy* (1872), *Golden Butterfly* (1876), and *The Seamy Side* (1881). Sole author of novels upon social conditions, including *All Sorts and Conditions of Men* (1882) and *Children of Gibeon* (1886), and of critical and biographical works.

Be·se·ler \'bā-zə-lər\, Wilhelm Hartwig. 1806–1884. Prussian politician. President, provisional government of Schleswig-Holstein (1848); defended independence of the duchies; governor, with Count Friedrich von Reventlow, of the duchies (1849–51). His nephew ¶Hans Hartwig von Beseler (1850–1921), general; in World War I led siege of Antwerp (1914) and Novogeorgievsk (1915); as governor general of Poland (1915–18) and colonel general, attempted to organize a Polish government and army under German control.

Besht. See ISRAEL BEN ELIEZER.

Bes·nard \bā-när\, Albert, *in full* Paul-Albert. 1849–1934. French painter and etcher. Known for portraits, Impressionist landscapes, and for architectural decoration as in Hôtel de Ville de Paris, Sorbonne, Peace Palace at The Hague, Théâtre-Français; director of École Nationale Supérieur des Beaux-Arts (1922); first painter admitted to the Académie Française (1925).

Bess of Hardwick. See Elizabeth TALBOT.

Bessaraba. See BASARAB.

Bes·sar·i·on \bes-'er-ē-ən\. *Orig.* Basil. 1403–1472. Byzantine theologian and Humanist. Took name Bessarion on entering monastery (1423); archbishop of Nicaea (1437). Exerted himself to effect union of Greek and Latin churches; supported Roman Church in councils of Ferrara and Florence. Named cardinal by Pope Eugenius IV (1439); invested with title of Latin patriarch of Constantinople (1463). With Gemistus Plethon founded Accademia Platonica, Florence (1442). Papal governor of Bologna (1450–55). Translated Aristotle's *Metaphysics* and Xenophon's *Memorabilia;* collected library of

Greek manuscripts that became nucleus of library of St. Mark.

Bessborough, Earl of. See John William PONSONBY.

Bes·sel \'bes-əl\, Friedrich Wilhelm. 1784–1846. German astronomer. Professor, Königsberg (from 1810); supervised construction and director (1813–46) of observatory at Königsberg. Calculated orbit of Halley's comet (1804); made (1838) first authenticated determination of distance of a star (61 Cygni) from the earth; introduced consideration of the personal equation of observers and worked out theory of instrumental errors; invented Bessel functions (1817) used in physics and astronomy; calculated ellipticity of earth (1841).

Bes·se·mer \'bes-ə-mər\, Sir Henry. 1813–1898. English engineer and inventor. Obtained patents (1855 ff.) for manufacture of steel by decarbonization of melted pig iron by means of a blast of air (Bessemer process); established steel works at Sheffield (1859) making a specialty of gunmaking and, later, steel rails. Cf. William KELLY.

Bes·se·nyei \'besh-en-yā\, György. 1747–1811. Hungarian playwright and poet. Translated Pope's *Essay on Man* into Hungarian (1772); author of *Tragedy of Agis* (1772), first true comedy in Hungarian, and *Tarimenes' Journey* (1802–04), considered first Hungarian novel. Influential in introducing Enlightenment thought into Hungarian literature.

Bes·sey \'bes-ē\, Charles Edwin. 1845–1915. American botanist, b. near Milton, Ohio. Professor, Iowa State (1870–84), U. of Nebraska (1884–1915); introduced classification of angiosperms according to evolutionary divergences; pioneered in laboratory teaching methods and wrote numerous textbooks.

Bes·sières \bes-yer\, Jean-Baptiste. Duc d'Is·trie \dē-strē\. 1768–1813. Marshal of France. Entered army (1792); captain of Napoléon's escort in Italy (1796); distinguished himself at Aboukir (1798), Marengo (1800), Austerlitz (1805); marshal and commander of imperial guard (1804); won victory of Medina de Ríoseco, Spain (1808); commanded cavalry in Austria (1809); made duke (1809); again in Spain (1811), in Russia (1812).

Bes·son \bes-ōⁿ\, Jacques. 1540–1576. French engineer. Invented improvements to lathe, as cams and templates, described in his *Theatrum instrumentorum* (1569); also invented improved waterwheel.

Bes·sus \'bes-əs\. d. c.329 B.C. Ruler of Bactria and Sogdiana. Satrap under Darius III; murdered Darius (330) and assumed throne as Artaxerxes IV; attempted to oppose Alexander the Great; captured and killed for regicide.

Best \'best\, Charles Herbert. 1899–1978. Canadian physiologist, b. West Pembroke, Me. Head of department of physiology (1929–65), director of medical research (1941–67), U. of Toronto. Associated with F. G. Banting and others in discovery of insulin (1921); discovered choline, histaminase; introduced use of anticoagulant heparin. Author of *Internal Secretions of the Pancreas* (with Banting, 1922).

Bes·tia \'bes(h)-ch(ē-)ə, 'bes-tē-ə\, Lucius Calpurnius. 2d century B.C. Roman politician. Leading opponent of Gaius Sempronius Gracchus; tribune (120 B.C.); consul (111); led army against Jugurtha, but accepted unfavorable peace terms for a bribe and fled into exile (109).

Bes·tu·zhev-Ryu·min \byis-'tü-zhif-'ryüm-yin\, Aleksey Petrovich. Count. 1693–1766. Russian diplomat and politician. In service of Elector George of Hanover (1712–14); Russian minister in Copenhagen (1721–40); influential during reign of Elizabeth (1741–62); vice chancellor (1741–44), chancellor (1744–58); favored alliance of Russia, Austria, England, and Saxony to offset that of France and Prussia; achieved Austrian treaty (1746), British treaty (1755); his influence reduced by Anglo–Prussian alliance (1756); dismissed (1758); recalled on Catherine II's accession (1762) and created field marshal. His brother ¶Mikhail Petrovich (1688–1760) was a diplomat; represented Russia at several European capitals, esp. Copenhagen (1708), London (1720–21), Stockholm (1721–26, 1732–39), Warsaw (1726–30), and Berlin (1730–32); instrumental in bringing about Swedish–RussianWar (1741–43); successful in mission to Versailles (1757–60).

Be·tan·court \bā-'tän-kürt\, Rómulo. 1908–1981. Venezuelan politican. Active in liberal agitation (from 1928); several times imprisoned or exiled; organized Acción Democrática party (1941); took part in army coup that overthrew Gen. Angarita (1945); head of ruling junta (1945–48) with title of president; again exiled (1948–58); elected president (1959–64).

Beth·ell \'beth-əl\, Richard. 1st Baron West·bury \'wes(t)-b(ə-)rē\.1800–1873. English judge. M.P. (1852–61); attorney general (1856–58, 1859–61); lord chancellor (1861–65); advocate of law reform and codification.

Bé·then·court \bā-täⁿ-kür\, Jean de. c.1360–c.1422. French navigator. Conqueror of Canary Islands (1402–06).

Beth·len \'bet-lēn\, Gábor *or* Gabriel. *Full surname* Bethlen von Ik·tár \-fōn-'ik-tär\. 1580–1629. Prince of Transylvania (1613–29) and king of Hungary (1620–21). Member of prominent Protestant family; with Ottoman backing, overthrew Gábor Báthory (1613) and was chosen his successor; at beginning of Thirty Years' War (1618), took up arms against Austrian Emperor Ferdinand II; captured much of northern Hungary and threatened Vienna; elected king of Hungary by Diet (1620) but declined to be crowned; after defeat of Bohemians at White Mountain (1620), made peace (1621) with Ferdinand; named prince of the Holy Roman Empire. Renewed war (1623) but ended it with no gain (1624); again occupied Hungary (1626), withdrew.

Bethlen, István. Count. 1874–?1947. Hungarian politician. Elected to parliament as Liberal (1901); active in counterrevolutionary movement against Béla Kun (1918–19); his estates confiscated by Rumania (1920). Prime minister (1921–31) by appointment of Regent Horthy; sought to restore conservative government; settled dispute with Austria over Burgenland (1921); secured aid of League of Nations in financial reconstruction (1923); made treaty of friendship with Italy (1927); reportedly died in captivity in Russia.

Beth·mann Holl·weg \'bāt-,män-'hōl-,vāk\, Theobald Theodor Friedrich Alfred von. 1856–1921. German politician. Prussian minister of interior (1905), state secretary in Imperial Office of Interior (1907); succeeded von Bülow as chancellor (1909–17). Dominated in foreign affairs by military and expansionist factions; during World War I failed to restrict submarine warfare. Forced to resign over question of Prussian electoral reforms.

Bethune, David and James. See BEATON.

Be·thune \bə-'th(y)ün\, Mary, *nee* Mc·Leod \mə-'klaud\. 1875–1955. American educator, b. Mayesville, S.C. Taught in various mission schools in Georgia and Florida (1895–1904); opened (1904) at Daytona Beach, Fla., the Daytona Normal and Industrial Institute for girls, which merged (1923) with Cookman Institute into coeducational Bethune-Cookman College; president of college (1923–42, 1946–47); director of Division of Negro Affairs of the National Youth Administration (1936–44); founder and 1st president (1935–49), National Council of Negro Women.

Bé·thune \bā-tüen\, Maximilien de. Duc de Sully \süel-lē\. 1560–1641. French statesman. Reared a Huguenot; member of court of Henry of Navarre; barely escaped St. Bartholomew's Day massacre (1572); soldier and agent of Henry during Civil Wars of Religion; helped arrange Henry's marriage (1600) to Marie de Médicis; helped negotiate Peace of Savoy (1601); ambassador to James I of England (1603). Superintendent of royal finances (from c.1598); instituted reforms in administration, taxation, etc. Held numerous royal preferments; captain general of queen's men of arms; governor of Poitou (1603); created duke and peer of France (1606). Promoted system of national improvements, agriculture, frontier defense. Resigned offices (1611).

Bet·je·man \'bech-ə-mən\, Sir John. 1906–1984. British author. Known for humorous verse, written in traditional meters and rhyme schemes, that celebrated and satirized the English; demonstrated extensive knowledge of Victorian architecture. Author of *Vintage London* (1942), *A Few Late Chrysanthemums* (1954), *Collected Poems* (1958), *Summoned by Bells* (1960), etc. Poet laureate (from 1972).

Bet·ter·ton \'bet-ər-tən, -ərt-ᵊn\, Thomas. c.1635–1710. English actor. Joined Sir William Davenant's company (1661); managed Dorset Garden Theatre (1671); at Drury Lane (1682–95); later played Lincoln's Inn Fields and Haymarket. Remarkably versatile, created some 130 new roles and played many established ones as Sir Toby Belch, Hamlet, Lear, Macbeth, Mercutio, Othello.

Bet·ti \'bāt-tē\, Enrico. 1823–1892. Italian mathematician. Professor, Pisa (1857–92); known for rigorous development of theory of equations of Galois, and for pioneering work in topology.

Betti, Ugo. 1892–1953. Italian playwright. Magistrate (1920–30), judge (1930–44) in Rome; librarian of Ministry of Justice (1944–53). Author of poems *Il re pensieroso* (1922), plays *La padrona* (1927), *Frana allo scalo Nord* (1933), *Corruzione al palazzo di giustizia* (1949), *Delitto all' Isola delle Capre* (1950), *La regina e gli insorte* (1951), *La fuggitiva* (1953), etc.

Bet·ti·nel·li \,bāt-tē-'nel-lē\, Saverio. 1718–1808. Italian writer and critic. Entered Society of Jesus (1736); attacked Dante's literary reputation in *Lettere Dieci di Virgilio agli Arcadi* (1756); also wrote *Il risorgimento d'Italia dopo il mille* (1773), volumes of verse, etc.

Bet·to di Bia·go \'bāt-tō-dē-'byäj-ō\, Bernadino di. *Known as* Pin·tu·ric·chio \,pēn-tü-'rēk-kyō\. c.1454–1513. Italian painter. Leading historical painter of Umbrian school. Collaborated with Perugino in painting frescoes in Sistine Chapel (1481); other frescoes included decorations for Appartamento Borgia in Vatican (1492–94) and scenes in Siena cathedral (1503–08).

Bet·ty \'bet-ē\, William Henry West. 1791–1874. English actor. Debut at 11 in Voltaire's *Zaïre;* London debut (1804) caused sensation; star at Covent Garden and Drury Lane; attempt to perform as adult (1812) a failure.

Beuck·el·son \'bœ-kəl-,sȯn\ *or* **Bock·el·son** \'bȯk-əl-,sȯn\ *or* **Bock·old** \'bȯk-ōlt\, Jan. *Known as* John of Leiden. c.1509–1536. Dutch religious leader. An Anabaptist, led Protestant rebellion in Münster (1534) and proclaimed himself king; brief theocratic rule marked by lawlessness, pomp; deposed by prince-bishop of Münster (1535); executed.

Beust \'bȯist\, Friedrich Ferdinand von. Graf. 1809–1886. German politician. In Saxon diplomatic service (1830–49); minister of foreign affairs (1849–53), of interior (1853–66) of Saxony; frequently opposed Bismarck. Forced to resign by Bismarck (1866); appointed Austrian foreign minister (1866); imperial chancellor and minister president (1867); negotiated compromise that reorganized empire as a dualistic Austro-Hungarian union (1867); failed to prevent emergence of Prussia as dominant German state; dismissed (1871); ambassador to London (1871–78) and Paris (1878–82).

Beuys \'bòis\, Joseph. 1921–1986. West German sculptor, performance artist, and political activist. Created stationary sculptures and enigmatic performances known as "actions." Radical ideologue, crusader for "direct democracy," and founder of several political groups, including the Green Party.

Bev·an \'bev-ən\, Aneurin. 1897–1960. British politician, b. Wales. M.P. (1929–39, 1939–60); as Labour minister of health (1945–51) introduced National Health Service (1948); minister of labor (1951); leader of radical wing of Labour party. Noted as orator.

Bev·er·idge \'bev-(ə-)rij\, Albert Jeremiah. 1862–1927. American politician and historian, b. Highland Co., Ohio. Member, U.S. Senate (1899–1911); a leader of Progressive Republicans. Author of *The Life of John Marshall* (1916–19, Pulitzer prize).

Beveridge, William Henry. 1st Baron Beveridge of Tug·gal \'təg-əl\. 1879–1963. English economist. Director of labor exchanges (1909–16); 2d secretary (1916–18), permanent secretary (1919), ministry of food; director, London School of Economics (1919–37); master, U. Coll., Oxford (1937–45). M.P. (1944–45). As chairman of Inter-Departmental Committee on Social Insurance and Allied Services (1941–42) brought out (1942) comprehensive report embodying proposals for postwar social security in Great Britain. Created baron (1946). Author of *Unemployment: A Problem of Industry* (1909), *Insurance for All* (1924), *Planning Under Socialism* (1936), *Full Employment in a Free Society* (1944), *Pillars of Security (1948), etc.*

Bev·in \'bev-ən\, Ernest. 1881–1951. British labor leader. Active in labor union organization (from 1908); rose in hierarchy of Dockers' Union; gained prominence by speech before Transport Workers Court of Inquiry (1920); negotiated merger of 14 unions into national Transport and General Workers' Union (1922), and became general secretary (1922–40); member (from 1925), chairman (1936–37), general council of Trades Union Congress. Minister of labor and national service (1940–45); secretary of state for foreign affairs (1945–51); negotiated Brussels Alliance treaty (1948), largely responsible for NATO treaty (1949); initiated Colombo Plan for South Asia (1951). Lord privy seal (1951).

Bew·ick \'byü-ik\, Thomas. 1753–1828. English illustrator and wood engraver. Rediscovered and made improvements in techniques of wood engraving; illustrated Gay's *Fables* (1779), *General History of Quadrupeds* (1790), *History of British Birds* (1797–1804), *The Chillingham Bull* (1789).

Bey·er \'bī-(y)ər\, Absalon Pederssøn. 1528–1575. Norwegian Humanist. Lecturer at Cathedral School, Bergen; chief work *Om Norgis rige* (1567), seminal work on Norwegian history and national consciousness.

Bey·ers \'bī-ərs\, Christiaan Frederik. 1869–1914. South African soldier and politician. Lawyer in Transvaal; joined Boer forces (1899); general in command of northern Transvaal. In Transvaal Parliament as speaker (1907). Commandant general of Union Defence Force (1912–14).

Beyle \bel\, Marie-Henri. *Pseudonym* Sten·dhal \staⁿ-dȧl, *Angl* sten-'dȧl, stan-\. 1783–1842. French novelist. Served in Napoléon's army in Italy, Germany, Russia (1800–12); French consul at Trieste (1830), Civitavecchia (1831–42). Early enchanted by Italy and wrote his first books there. Works included biographies and travel books as *Vies de Haydn, de Mozart et de Métastase* (1814), *Rome, Naples et Florence* (1817), *De l'amour* (1822), *Vie de Rossini* (1823), *Promenades dans Rome* (1829); chiefly known for Romantic novels, among most important in French, as *Armance* (1827), *Le Rouge et le noir* (1830), *La Chartreuse de Parme* (1839). Also wrote autobiography *Vie de Henri Brulard* (1890), *Souvenirs d'égotisme* (1892).

Bezanson, Hugues. See Bezanson HUGUES.

Bez·bo·rod·ko \byiz-(,)bə-'ród-kə\, Aleksandr Andreyevich. Prince. 1747–1799. Russian politician. Appointed secretary of petitions to Catherine the Great (1775), later postmaster general and plenipotentiary in Foreign Office; named to Senate (1786); negotiated Treaty of Jassy (1792) with Turks; advised on partitions of Poland (1793, 1795); made prince and imperial chancellor (1796) by Czar Paul I.

Bèze \bez\, Théodore de. *Lat.* Theodorus Be·za \'bē-zə\. 1519–1605. French theologian. Paris lawyer; earned reputation as leading Latin poet with *Juvenilia* (1548); converted to Protestantism and joined Calvin in Geneva (1548); professor at Lausanne (1549); with Calvin founded Geneva academy (1559); succeeded Calvin (1564) as leader of Geneva church and Protestant movement. Author of *De jure magistratum* (1574), *Histoire ecclésiastique des Églises réformées au royaume de France* (1580); his Greek editions and Latin translations formed basis of Geneva Bible and King James Bible.

Bezrůc, Petr. See Vladimir VASEK.

Bha·dra·bā·hu I \,bə-drə-'bä-hü\. d. 298 B.C. Indian religious leader. Spiritual head of Jainas; after 12-year famine led community from northeast India to Mysore in the southwest (310 B.C.); believed to be author of 3 of the 12 Jaina sacred books and of commentaries on others.

Bhai Jetha. See RĀM DĀS.

Bha·ra·ta \'bä-rə-tə\ *or* **Bharata Mu·ni** \-'mü-nē\. 2d century A.D. Indian sage. Author of *Nāṭya-śāstra,* basic work on Indian dance and acting.

Bharatendu. See HARISHCHANDRA.

Bhā·ra·vi \'bä-rə-vē\. 7th century. Indian poet. Author of epic *Kiratarjuniya.*

Bhar·trha·ri \'bär-trə-rē\. 570?–?651. Indian philosopher and poet. Author of *Vākyapadīya,* classic work in Hindu philosophy of language, of Sanskrit verse *Śṛngāra-śataka,* and perhaps of *Nīti-śataka* and *Vairāgya-śataka.*

Bhā·sa \'bäs-ə\. 2d or 3d century A.D. Indian dramatist. Earliest known dramatist in Sanskrit; chief work *Svapnavāsavadattā.*

Bhās·ka·ra II \'bäs-kə-rə\. *Also known as* Bhās·ka·rā·cār·ya \,bäs-kə-rä-'kär-yə\ *or* Bhāskara the Learned. 1114–c.1185. Indian mathematician. Head of astronomical observatory at Ujjain; in such works as *Līlāvatī, Bījaganita,* and *Siddhāntaśiromani,* systematically developed decimal number system, anticipated modern sign conventions, solved quadratic equations, obtained good value of pi, made astronomical calculations.

Bhaṭṭa. See KUMĀRILA.

Bha·va·bhū·ti \,bə-və-'bü-tē\. fl. 700 A.D. Indian dramatist and poet. Plays in Sanskrit included *Mahāvīracarita, Mālatī Mādhava,* and *Uttararāmacarita.*

Bhu·min·da·ra·ja \,bům-in-də-'rä-jə\. *Also known as* Phra Chao Thai Sa \'prä-'jaů-'tī-'sä\ *or* Thai Sra \'tīs-'rä\. d. 1733. King of Siam (1709–33). Son and successor of Phra Chao Sua; failed in several attempts to capture Cambodian territory contested by Vietnamese.

Bhut·to \'bü-tō\, Zulfikar Ali. 1928–1979. Pakistani politician. Headed various ministries (1958–65), minister of foreign affairs (1963–66); founded People's party (1967); led movement against Pres. Ayub Khan (1968); deputy prime minister and minister of foreign affairs (1971); president (1971–77) and prime minister (1973–77); ousted by coup (1977); executed.

Biago, Bernadino di Betto di. See BETTO DI BIAGO.

Bia·lik *or* **Bya·lik** \'byä-lik\, Hayyim Nahman. 1873–1934. Jewish poet, b. Ukraine. Considered leading poet in Hebrew of modern times; poems included "ha-Matmid," "Mete midbar," "ha-Berekha," and "be-'Ir he-harega" ("City of Slaughter") on 1903 pogrom at Kishinyov. Also translated *Don Quixote, William Tell, Der Dybbuk,* etc. into Hebrew.

Bian·chi·ni \byäŋ-'kē-nē\, Francesco. 1662–1729. Italian astronomer. Observed spots on planet Venus; asserted that it rotates in 24 1/3 days; also observed lunar surface, discovered 3 comets; named by Clement XI to commission to reform calendar, for which he wrote *De Kalendario et Cyclo Caesaris* (1703); also wrote *Hesperi et Phosphori Nova Phaenomena* (1728).

Bian·co \'byäŋ-kō\, Margery, *nee* Williams. 1881–1944. English writer. m. (1904) Francesco Bianco; author of fiction, esp. for children, as *The Velveteen Rabbit* (1922).

Bian·dra·ta \byän-'drä-tä\, Giorgio. *Lat.* Georgius Blan·drata \blan-'drät-ə\. c.1515–1588. Italian physician and theologian. Physician to queen of Poland (1540–52); fled Italian Inquisition to Geneva (1556); joined, then left Calvinist church; joined Minor church in Poland (1558); called to Transylvania as physician to John Sigismund I (1563); with Ferenc Dávid proselytized for Unitarian church; later broke with Dávid and took more moderate position.

Bi·as of Pri·e·ne \'bī-ə-səv-prī-'ē-nē\. 6th century B.C. Greek sage. One of so-called Seven Wise Men of Greece, or Seven Sages; known esp. for maxims.

Bi·baud \bē-bō\, Michel. 1782–1857. French Canadian historian and poet, b. Côte des Neiges, Que. Schoolteacher and journalist; wrote *Histoire du Canada, sous la domination française* (1837–44), first major history of French Canada, and *Epîtres, satires, chansons, épigrammes, et autre pièces de vers* (1830), first volume of verse in French Canada.

Bi·ber \'bē-bər\, Heinrich Ignaz Franz von. 1644–1704. German violinist and composer. Virtuoso at court of archbishop of Salzburg, musical director (1676). Composed sonatas including 15 *Mystery Sonatas,* concerti, *Passacaglia in G Minor,* opera *Chi la dura, la vince* (1687), etc.

Bi·bes·cu \bē-'bes-kü\, Gheorghe Dimitrie. 1804–1873. Romanian politician. Led opposition to government of Alexandru II Ghica in Walachia; elected to succeed as hospodar, or prince (1842–48); fled nationalist-liberal uprising (1848). His brother ¶Barbu Dimitrie (1801–1869) took surname of an uncle, Ştir·bei \'shtir-bā\; took part in uprising under Ypsilanti (1821); minister of justice (1831–37) under Ghica; minister of interior (1844) under brother; hospodar of Walachia (1849–56) after Russo-Turkish suppression of uprising of 1848.

Bi·bie·na \bēb-'yen-ä\ *or* **Bib·bie·na** \bēb-'byen-ä\, Gal·li \'gäl-lē\ da. Italian family of architects and artists: Giovanni Maria Galli (1625–1665), b. Bibiena, studied under Albani; established family tradition of theatrical decoration. His son ¶Ferdinando Galli da Bibiena (1657–1743) built villa and garden of Colorno for duke of Parma; in charge of decoration for wedding of future emperor Charles VI in Barcelona (1708); in charge of scenery and decoration at court and opera, Vienna (1711–17); built royal theater, Mantua (1731). Author of *L'Architettura civile* (1711), *Varie opere di prospettiva* (1703–08). A second son ¶Francesco Galli (1659–1739) built theaters in Vienna, Nancy, the Teatro Filarmonico in Verona, Teatro Alibert in Rome. Ferdinando's three sons: ¶Alessandro Galli (1687–1769), architect and painter at court of elector of the Palatinate (from 1719); built opera house, part of royal castle. ¶Antonio Galli (1700–1774), architect of Academia Virgiliana in Mantua and of Teatro Communale in Bologna. ¶Giuseppe Galli (1696–1757), most distinguished of family; designed court festivities in Vienna; worked also in Munich, Prague; designed interior of theater at Bayreuth (1748); renovated Dresden Opera (1750); published engravings of stage settings in *Alcina* (1716), *Costanza e Fortezza* (1723), *Architetture e prospettive* (1740–44). Guiseppe's son ¶Carlo Galli (1728–1787), in opera set design in Germany, France, Netherlands, London, Naples, Stockholm, St. Petersburg; last of line.

Bib·u·lus \'bib-yə-ləs\, Marcus Calpurnius. d. 48 B.C. Roman politician. Opponent of Julius Caesar; consul with Caesar (59 B.C.); endeavored to block all measures sponsored by Caesar; in civil war, commanded Pompey's fleet in Ionian Sea; failed to prevent Caesar's crossing to Epirus (49).

Bi·chat \bē-shä\, Marie-François-Xavier. 1771–1802. French anatomist and physiologist. Pioneered in histological study of human tissues; completed 4th volume of *Journal de chirurgie* of his teacher, Pierre-Joseph Desault; author of *Traité des membranes* (1800), *Récherches physiologiques sur la vie et la mort* (1800), *Anatomie générale* (1801), *Anatomie descriptive* (1801–03).

Bick·er·dyke \'bik-ər-ˌdīk\, Mary Ann, *nee* Ball. 1817–1901. American relief worker, b. Knox Co., Ohio. m. Robert Bickerdyke (1847; d. 1859); volunteer nurse and collector of medical supplies early in Civil War; organized army hospital at Cairo, Ill. (1861); secured support of Gen. U.S. Grant; established hospitals and field services for Grant's army and later for Gen. W.T. Sherman's army.

Bick·er·staff \'bik-ər-ˌstaf\, Isaac. A pseudonym adopted by (1) Jonathan SWIFT in pamphlet (1708) chronicling death of John Patridge; (2) Richard STEELE in the *Tatler* (1709–11); (3) Benjamin WEST, American mathematician, in almanacs pub. (from 1768) in Boston.

Bick·er·staffe \'bik-ər-ˌstaf\, Isaac. c.1735–c.1812. Irish playwright. Author esp. of comedies and comic operas, as *Love in a Village* (1762), *Maid of the Mill* (1765), *The Padlock, The Hypocrite;* fled charges of capital offense (1772).

Bick·er·steth \'bik-ər-ˌsteth, -stəth\, Edward. 1786–1850. English evangelical clergyman. Collector of over 700 hymns in *Christian Psalmody* (1833). His son ¶Edward Henry (1825–1906), bishop of Exeter (1885–1900), wrote *Yesterday, To-day, and For Ever* (1866) and many hymns.

Bid·dle \'bid-ᵊl\, Francis. 1886–1968. American lawyer, b. Paris, France. Special assistant U.S. attorney (1922–26); judge, U.S. Circuit Court of Appeals (1939–40); solicitor general of U.S. (1940); attorney general of U.S. (1941–45); judge on International Military Tribunal, Nürnberg (1945–46). Author of *Mr. Justice Holmes* (1942), *Fear of Freedom* (1951), *In Brief Authority* (1962).

Biddle, James. 1783–1848. American naval officer, b. Philadelphia. First lieutenant of *Wasp* (1812), which captured *Frolic;* given command of *Hornet* (1813–15); commanded *Ontario,* entered Columbia River and claimed Oregon country for U.S. (1817); negotiated (1845) first treaty between U.S. and China.

Biddle, John. 1615–1662. English theologian. Schoolmaster, Gloucester; several times imprisoned for publishing *Twelve Arguments Against the Deity of the Holy Ghost* (c.1644); released by decree of oblivion (1652); imprisoned for *A Twofold Catechism* (1654); banished by Cromwell to Scilly Isles (1655), to save his life; returned (1658); again arrested (1662); died in prison. Known as father of English Unitarianism.

Biddle, Nicholas. 1786–1844. American financier, b. Philadelphia. Editor of *Port Folio* (1812–14); appointed by President Monroe a director of Bank of the United States (1819); elected its president (1822); followed policy of stable money supply, restricted credit. Center of attack by Jackson against bank; new charter refused (1836); secured state charter for Bank of the United States of Pennsylvania; resigned (1839) and retired. Author of *History of the Expedition of Captains Lewis and Clark* (1814).

Bid·lack \'bid-ˌlak\, Benjamin Alden. 1804–1849. American diplomat, b. Paris, N.Y. Member, U.S. House of Representatives from Pennsylvania (1841–45); U.S. chargé d'affaires in New Granada (1845–49); negotiated (1846) with New Granada a treaty including right of way across Isthmus of Panama.

Bidyasagar, Isvarcandra. See VIDYASAGAR.

Bid·well \'bid-ˌwel, -wəl\, John. 1819–1900. American pioneer, b. Chautauqua Co., N.Y. To Missouri (1839); joined first wagon train from Independence, Mo., to California (1841); took part in Bear Flag revolt (1846); served under Frémont and Stockton in conquest of California (1846–47); first to find gold on Feather River (1848); member of U.S. House of Representatives (1865–67); Prohibition candidate for U.S. president (1892).

Biel \'bēl\, Gabriel. c.1420–1495. German scholastic philosopher. Preacher at Mainz (c.1460); entered Brothers of Common Life (1468); prior at Butzbach (1470), Urach (1479); professor, Tübingen (1484); prior, Schönbuch (1492). Author of *Collectorium circa IV libros Sententiarum,* commentary on Peter Lombard and exposition of method of William of Ockham; also wrote *De potestate et utilitate monetarum.*

Bie·la \'bē-lä\, Wilhelm von. 1782–1856. German astronomer. Observed (1826) periodic comet (Biela's comet) which separated (1846) into two comets.

Biel·ski \'byel-skē\, Marcin. 1495–1575. Polish historian and poet. Wrote first history in Polish language (1551); his history of Poland (*Polnische Chronik,* 1597) completed by his son ¶Joachim (1540–1599).

Bien·court \byeⁿ-kür\, Charles de. Baron de Saint-Just \saⁿ-zhüest\. 1591 or 1592–1623 or 1624. French colonizer. To New France (1606); made commander of Port Royal (1611) by father, vice admiral of the seas of New France; suffered destruction of settlement by Sir Samuel Argall (1613–14); rebuilt but failed to prosper.

Bie·nerth \'bē-nərt\, Richard von. Frieherr. Graf von Bie·nerth-Schmer·ling \'bē-nərt-'shmer-liŋ\. 1863–1918. Austrian politician. In ministry of education (1886–1906), director (1905–06); minister of interior for Austria (1906–08); prime minister (1908–11); failed to achieve Czech–German reconciliation; governor of lower Austria (1911–15); made count (1915).

Bienewitz, Peter. See BENNEWITZ.

Bienville, Sieur de. See Jean-Baptiste under Charles LE MOYNE.

Bierce \'bi(ə)rs\, Ambrose Gwinnett. 1842–?1914. American journalist and writer, b. Meigs Co., Ohio. Served through Civil War. Journalist in San Francisco and (1872–75) London; reputation as witty and caustic writer established by *The Fiend's Delight* (1872), *Nuggets and Dust Panned Out in California* (1872), *Cobwebs from an Empty Skull* (1874). Contributed column of "Prattle" in San Francisco *Examiner* (1887–96). Later work became cynical, often bitter and gruesome. Disappeared into Mexico (1913) and fate unknown. Other works included *Tales of Soldiers and Civilians* (1891), *Can Such Things Be?* (1893), *Devil's Dictionary* (1906).

Bier·stadt \'bēr-ˌshtät, *Angl* 'bi(ə)r-ˌstat\, Albert. 1830–1902. American painter, b. Solingen, Germany. To U.S. (1831); one of last generation of Hudson River school of landscape painters; traveled through West painting such pictures as *Rocky Mountains, Mount Corcoran, Estes Park, Laramie Peak;* painted *Discovery of the Hudson River* and *Settlement of California* for U.S. Capitol.

Bie·rut \'byā-rüt\, Bolesław. 1892–1956. Polish politician. Communist organizer and propagandist (from 1918); frequently imprisoned; in Russia (1938–43); president of Poland (1945–52); secretary of Polish Workers' party, reorganized as Polish United Workers' party (1948); premier of Poland (1952–54). Imposed Soviet organization and policies on Poland.

Big·e·low \'big-ə-ˌlō\, Erastus Brigham. 1814–1879. American inventor, b. West Boylston, Mass. Invented power looms for use in manufacturing gingham, silk brocatel, and pile fabrics; established gingham mill (1843); invented power loom for weaving Brussels and Wilton carpets (1845–51); a founder of Massachusetts Inst. of Technology (1861).

Bigelow, Jacob. 1786–1879. American physician and botanist, b. Sudbury, Mass. Author of *Florula Bostoniensis* (1814), long the standard manual of New England botany, *American Medical Botany* (1817–20), etc.

Bigelow, John. 1817–1911. American writer and diplomat, b. Bristol (now Malden), N.Y. Coeditor and co-owner, with William Cullen Bryant, of New York *Evening Post* (1848–61). U.S. consul general at Paris (1861–65); U.S. minister to France (1865–66). Discovered and edited (1868) Benjamin Franklin's *Autobiography;* author of *France and the Confederate Navy, 1862–68* (1888), *Life of Benjamin Franklin* (1874), etc.

Bigelow, Poultney. 1855–1954. American traveler, journalist, and author, b. New York City. Son of John Bigelow; founded *Outing* (1885), first American magazine devoted esp. to amateur sport. Correspondent for London *Times* in Spanish–American War (1898). Author of *History of the German Struggle for Liberty, 1806–1848* (1896–1905), *Children of Nations* (1901), *Prussianism and Pacifism* (1919), *Japan and Her Colonies* (1923), etc.

Big·gers \'big-ərz\, Earl Derr. 1884–1933. American writer, b. Warren, Ohio. Creator of "Charlie Chan," a Chinese detective in several novels including *House without a Key* (1925), *Chinese Parrot* (1926), *Behind that Curtain* (1928), *Black Camel* (1929) and later used in stage and motion-picture versions. Author also of popular *Seven Keys to Baldpate* (1913, later dramatized and filmed), *The Agony Column* (1916), etc.

Biglow, Hosea. See James Russell LOWELL.

Bi·god \'bī-ˌgäd\ *or* **Bi·got** \'bī-ˌgät\. English noble family, prominent in 12th and 13th centuries and including: Hugh (d. 1177), created by King Stephen 1st Earl of Norfolk (1135); active in rebellions against Stephen and Henry II. His son ¶Roger (d. 1221), 2d earl; royal steward to Richard I; joined barons against John (1215) and had part in securing Magna Charta. His grandson ¶Roger (d. 1270), 4th earl, at first supported Henry III against Simon de Montfort but later joined de Montfort's party in Barons' War (1264–67). His nephew ¶Roger (1245–1306), 5th and last earl, took arms in protest against taxation without national consent and, with Humphrey Bohun, earl of Hereford, forced Edward I to confirm charter of liberties (1297).

Bi·gor·di \bē-'gōr-dē\, Domenico di Tom·ma·so \dē-tōm-'mäz-ō\. *Known as* Domenico Ghir·lan·da·jo *or* Ghir·lan·da·io \ˌgir-län-'dī-ō\. 1449–1494. Florentine artist. Known esp. for frescoes, often containing portraits of contemporaries, including series on *Life of Sta. Fina* in church of San Gimignano (1475), *St. Jerome* in Church of Ognissanti, Florence (1480), fresco on calling of Apostles in Sistine Chapel, Vatican (1481–82), series on life of St. Francis of Assisi in Sassetti Chapel, Sta. Trinità, Florence (1482–85), series on Virgin Mary and John the Baptist in Sta. Maria Novella, Florence (1485–94).

Bi·got \bē-gō\, François. 1703–c.1777. French administrator. Commissary at Louisbourg, N.S., Canada (1739–44), partly responsible for its loss; led unsuccessful expedition against Nova Scotia (1746); intendant of New France (1748–60); perpetrated numerous commercial frauds, seriously weakening colony; after fall of New France to British, returned to France; tried, imprisoned, banished.

Bigs·by \'bigz-bē\, John Jeremiah. 1792–1881. English physician and geologist. To Canada (1818); with Canadian International Boundary Commission (1822–27); returned to England (1827). Known for stratigraphic and paleontological discoveries in Canada. Author of *Thesaurus Siluricus* (1868), *Thesaurus Devonico-Carboniferus* (1878).

Bil·bo \'bil-(ˌ)bō\, Theodore Gilmore. 1877–1947. American politician, b. near Poplarville, Miss. Governor of Mississippi (1916–20, 1928–32), administrations marked by fiscal irresponsibility; U.S. senator (1935–47), noted as filibuster, demagogue, racist.

Bild aus Rhei·nau \'bil-taùs-'rī-ˌnaù\. *Known as* Be·at·us Rhe·na·nus \bē-'at-əs-rē-'nan-əs\. 1485–1547. Alsatian Humanist. Settled in Basel as editor for printer Johann Froben (1511–27); published editions of many classical writers, as Tacitus (1519–33), Pliny the Younger (1526), and the editio princeps of Velleius Paterculus, whose manuscript he discovered (1520); wrote first history of Germanic peoples, *Rerum Germanicarum libri tres* (1531). Became intimate with Erasmus and superintended printing of his works.

Bil·der·dijk \'bil-dər-ˌdīk\, Willem. 1756–1831. Dutch poet, scholar, and critic. As poet, a forerunner of Romanticism in Netherlands; works included religious verse *Gebed* (1796), translation of Ossian ballads (1803), *De kunst der poëzij* (1809), *De ondergang der eerste wareld* (1810), *De geestenwareld* (1811).

Bil·fing·er \'bil-ˌfiŋ-ər\, Georg Bernhard. 1693–1750. German philosopher and mathematician. Professor at Tübingen (1721–25, 1731–50), St. Petersburg (1725–31); developed philosophical position he called Leibniz-Wolffian. Author of *Dilucidationes Philosophicae* (1725), an exposition of Wolffian metaphysics, and *De causa gravitatis physica general* (1728).

Bil·ge \'bil-gə\ *or* **Bilge Ka·gan** \-'käg-än\. *Chin.* Mo-ki-lien \'mō-'kē-'lē-en\. d. 734. Mongolian ruler. Leader of Turk tribe T'u-chüeh; ruler of Mongolia (716–734); defeated Chinese forces of Emperor Hsüan Tsung (721).

Bil·laud-Va·renne \bē-yō-vȧ-ren\, Jean-Nicolas. 1756–1819. French revolutionary politician. Joined Jacobin club (1789); member of Commune and influential in instigating September Massacres (1792); elected to National Convention (1792); moved declaration of Republic (Sept. 1792); with Collot d'Herbois promoted harsh measures against counter-revolutionaries; appointed to Committee of Public Safety (1793); supported Robespierre against Hébert and Danton but later aided in his overthrow (1794). Prosecuted as Terrorist; transported to Guiana (1795); refused pardon offered by Napoléon; released (1816); to Haiti, where he died.

Bil·ling·hurst \bē-lēŋ-'gürst, *Angl* 'bil-iŋ-ˌhərst\, Guillermo Enrique. 1851–1915. Peruvian politician. Leader of radical democratic movement; president of Peru (1912–14); ousted by military coup d'état; exiled.

Bil·lings \'bil-iŋz\, Frederick. 1823–1890. American businessman, b. Royalton, Vt. Lawyer and politician in California (1849–64); associated with Northern Pacific Railway (from 1866), president (1879–81); largely responsible for reorganization and growth of the line. Billings, Mont., named for him.

Billings, John Shaw. 1838–1913. American physician and librarian, b. Switzerland Co., Ind. In medical service, U.S. army (1861–95); fostered growth of surgeon general's library in Washington; with Dr. Robert Fletcher, prepared *Index-Catalogue* (16 vols., 1880–95) and published *Index Medicus* (1879–95), a monthly guide to current medical literature. First director, New York Public Library (1896–1913).

Billings, Josh. See Henry Wheeler SHAW.

Billings, Warren K. See under T. J. MOONEY.

Billings, William. 1746–1800. American composer, b. Boston. Foremost composer of early American period; wrote hymns, psalms, anthems, fuguing tunes, etc., including "The Lord is Risen Indeed," "David's Lamentation," "Rose of Sharon," "When Jesus Wept," and "Chester," considered hymn of the Revolution; works collected in *New-England Psalm Singer* (1770), *Singing Master's Assistant* (1778), *Continental Harmony* (1794), etc.

Bil·lings·ley \'bil-iŋz-lē\, William. 1758–1828. British artist. Known esp. for flower paintings on porcelain vases.

Bil·ling·ton \'bil-iŋ-tən\, Elizabeth, *nee* Weich·sell \'vīk-səl\. 1768–1818. English opera singer. m. (1783) James Billington; sensation at Covent Garden (1786); toured Italy (1794 ff.); appeared at Covent Garden and Drury Lane on alternate nights (1801), and at King's Theatre in Italian opera (1802–11).

Bill·roth \'bil-(ˌ)rōt\, Theodor, *in full* Christian Albert Theodor. 1829–1894. German surgeon. Professor at Zürich (1860–67), Vienna (from 1867); made important contributions to histology and pathology; through use of antisepsis greatly advanced abdominal surgery. Author of *Allgemeine chirurgische Pathologie und Therapie* (1863).

Billy the Kid. See William BONNEY.

Bil·ney *or* **Byl·ney** \'bil-nē\, Thomas. c.1495–1531. English clergyman and martyr. Denounced prayers to saints as image worship; burned as heretic.

Bim·bi·sā·ra \ˌbim-bi-'sär-ə\. c.543–491 B.C. Indian ruler. An early king of Magadha; regarded as founder of the greatness of the kingdom; friend and protector of Gautama Buddha.

Bin·chois \baⁿ-shwȧ\ *or* **De Binche** \də-baⁿsh\, Gilles, *Lat.* Egidius. c.1400–1460. Flemish composer. Member of chapel of Philip the Good (1430–60); composed church music and secular chansons embodying both English and French styles.

Bin·du·sā·ra \ˌbin-dù-'sär-ə\. *Also known as* Amit·ro·cha·tes \ə-ˌmi-trō-'kāt-(ˌ)ēz\. d. 272 B.C. Second king of Magadha (c.297–272) of Maurya dynasty. Son of Candragupta and father of Aśoka.

Bi·net \bē-ne, *Angl* bə-'nā\, Alfred. 1857–1911. French psychologist. Director (1897–1911), laboratory of physiological psychology, Sorbonne; pioneered in experimental psychology, esp. in projective testing and intelligence testing; collaborated with Théodore Simon in establishing standardized Binet, or Binet-Simon, tests for measuring intelligence. Author of *La Psychologie du raisonnement* (1886), *Introduction à la psychologie expérimentale* (1894), *L'Étude expérimentale de l'intelligence* (1903), *Les Idées modernes sur les enfants* (1910), etc.

Bin·ger \baⁿ-zhā\, Louis-Gustave. 1856–1936. French explorer and administrator. Explored (1887–89) West African region north of Ivory Coast and established French protectorate; governor of Ivory Coast (1893).

Bing·ham \'biŋ-əm\, Eugene Cook. 1878–1945. American chemist, b. Cornwall, Vt. Professor, Richmond (Va.) Coll. (1906–15), Lafayette Coll. (1916–45). Considered founder of science of rheology. Author of *Fluidity and Plasticity* (1921), etc.

Bingham, George Caleb. 1811–1879. American painter, b. Augusta Co., Va. Known for portrait and genre paintings of frontier as *County Election, Verdict of the People, Jolly Flatboatmen, Fur Traders Descending the Missouri.*

Bingham, George Charles. 3d Earl of Lu·can \'lü-kən\. 1800–1888. English soldier. Commanded division in Crimea; given ambiguous orders by Lord Raglan, ordered charge of light brigade, followed by heavy brigade of cavalry at Balaklava (1854); covered with two regiments retirement of light brigade; censured by Lord Raglan (1855); general (1865); field marshal (1887).

Bingham, Hiram. 1789–1869. American missionary, b. Bennington, Vt. Missionary at Honolulu (1820–40). Reduced Hawaiian language to writing; with associates, translated Bible into Hawaiian. His son ¶Hiram (1831–1908) was missionary to Gilbert Islands (1857–64, 1873–75) and did for Gilbert language what his father had done for Hawaiian. The latter's son ¶Hiram (1875–1956) explored Bolívar's route across Venezuela and Colombia (1906–07), Spanish trade route from Buenos Aires to Lima (1908–09), Inca ruins in Peru (1911–15); discovered Inca capital Vilcabamba (1911) at Machu Picchu. Governor of Connecticut (1924), resigned to become U.S. senator from Conn. (1924–33). Author of *Inca Land* (1922), *Machu Picchu* (1930), *Lost City of the Incas* (1948).

Bingham, William. 1752–1804. American banker and politician, b. Philadelphia. Founder and director, Bank of North America (1781), first bank in the country. Served in Continental Congress (1786–89), Pennsylvania Assembly (1790–95), U.S. Senate (1795–1801). Founder of Binghamton, N.Y.

Bin·kis \'biŋ-kis\, Kazys. 1893–1942. Lithuanian poet. Leader of "Four Winds" movement introducing Futurism into Lithuanian verse. Author of verse *Eilėraščiai* (1920) and *Šimtas pavasari* (1926), plays *Atžalynas* (1938) and *Generalinė repeticija* (1948), children's stories, etc.

Bin·ney \'bin-ē\, Horace. 1780–1875. American lawyer, b. Philadelphia. Leader of Pennsylvania bar; member, U.S. House of Representatives (1833–35); edited *Reports of Cases Adjudged in the Supreme Court of Pennsylvania* (1809–15).

Binney, Thomas. 1798–1874. English clergyman. Noted pulpit orator; sought reunion of Congregational church with Church of England.

Bin·nya Da·la \ˈbin-nyä-ˈdäl-ä\. d. 1774. Ruler of Mon kingdom of Lower Burma (1747–57). Chief minister and successor of Smim Htaw Buddhaketi; led large Mon army into Upper Burma (1751), captured capital Ava (1752), executed last Toungoo king of Burma (1754). Deposed on capture of Mon capital Pegu (1757) by Alaungpaya; held captive until execution. Last Mon king.

Bin·swang·er \ˈbins-ˌväŋ-ər\, Ludwig. 1881–1966. Swiss psychiatrist. Applied Heidegger's existential phenomenology to psychotherapy. Author of *Grundformen und Erkenntnis menschlichen Daseins* (1942), *Erinnerungen an Sigmund Freud* (1956), *Der Mensch in der Psychiatrie* (1957), *Melancholie und Manie* (1960).

Bin·yon \ˈbin-yən\, Laurence, *in full* Robert Laurence. 1869–1943. English poet and art historian. On staff of British Museum (1893–1933), in charge of Oriental prints and drawings (1913–33). Author of works on Chinese, Japanese, and Indian art, including *Painting in the Far East* (1908), *Flight of the Dragon* (1911), of verse *The Sirens* (1924), *The Idols* (1928), *Collected Poems* (1931), *The North Star* (1941), of blank verse dramas including *Attila* (1907), *Arthur* (1923), *The Young King* (1934), and a verse translation of Dante's *Divina commedia.*

Bi·on \ˈbī-ən\. *Also called* Bion of Borysthenes. 325?–?255 B.C. Greek philosopher. Author of *Diatribae,* popular satires directed against gods, scientists, and men of wealth.

Bion. fl. 100 B.C. Greek bucolic poet. Author of *Bucolica,* extant in fragments, and of *Epitaphios Adonidos* (*Lament for Adonis*).

Bion·do \ˈbyōn-dō\, Flavio. *Lat.* Flavius Blon·dus \ˈblän-dəs\. 1392–1463. Italian Humanist and historian. In service of papacy (from 1433). Author of careful and critical histories of Rome and of European Christendom, including *De Roma instaurata* (1444–46), *De Roma triumphante* (1459), *Italia illustrata* (pub. 1474), *Historiarum ab inclinatione Romanorum imperii decades* (pub. 1483); linked papacy to ancient empire; first suggested notion of 1000-year Middle Ages.

Biot \byō\, Jean-Baptiste. 1774–1862. French mathematician, physicist, and astronomer. Professor, Beauvais (1797–1800), Collège de France (1800 ff.). With Gay-Lussac made balloon ascension (1804) to study upper atmosphere, terrestrial magnetism; with Arago studied optical properties of gases; with Félix Savart discovered (1820) Biot-Savart law describing strength of magnetic fields; investigated polarized light and became (1835) founder of saccharimetry by use of polariscope.

Bi·ran \bē-räⁿ\, Marie-François-Pierre Gon·thier de \gōⁿ-tyā-də-\. *Known as* Maine de Biran \men-də-\. 1766–1824. French politician, philosopher, and writer. As member of king's lifeguard, defended Louis XVI at Versailles (1789); retired to study; administrator in Dordogne district (1794); member of Five Hundred (1797); member and treasurer, Chamber of Deputies (1814); councillor of state (1816). From criticism of philosophy of sensation of the Idéologues, developed philosophy centered on consideration of will as source of human freedom. Author of *L'Influence de l'habitude* (1802), *La Décomposition de la pensée* (1805), *Essai sur les fondements de la psychologie* (1812), *Nouveaux essais d'anthropologie* (1823–24), etc.

Birch \ˈbərch\, Thomas. 1705–1766. English historian. Author of biographies of Boyle, Tillotson, John Ward, etc.; edited volumes of correspondence, state papers, etc., esp. *Papers of John Thurloe* (1742).

Bird *or* **Birde.** See also BYRD.

Bird, Isabella Lucy. See BISHOP.

Bird \ˈbərd\, Kenneth, *in full* Cyril Kenneth. *Pseudonym* Fou·gasse \fü-ˈgäs\. 1887–1965. British cartoonist. Contributor to *Punch* (from 1916), art editor (1937–49), editor (1949–53); known for cartoons on comic social situations, also for posters during World War II.

Bird, Robert Montgomery. 1806–1854. American writer, b. New Castle, Del. Author of plays as *The Gladiator* (1831), *Oralloosa* (1832), *The Broker of Bogota* (1834), all produced by Edwin Forrest, and novels as *Calavar* (1834), *The Infidel* (1835), *Nick of the Woods* (1837).

Birds·eye \ˈbərdz-ˌī\, Clarence. 1886–1956. American businessman and inventor, b. Brooklyn, N.Y. Developed (1916–28) methods of quick-freezing foods to preserve freshness; formed (1924) General Foods Co., sold (1929) to Postum Co. and becoming General Foods Corp., using "Birdseye" trademark for frozen foods; held some 300 patents for items as recoilless harpoon gun, infrared heat lamp, etc.

Birdseye, Claude Hale. 1878–1941. American topographic engineer, b. Syracuse, N.Y. With U.S. Geological Survey (1901–07, 1909–29, 1932–41), chief topographical engineer (1919–29); noted for work in mapping Kilauea volcano, Hawaii (1912), Mt. Ranier, Washington (1912), Marble and Grand canyons (1923), etc.

Bird·wood \ˈbər-ˌdwu̇d\, William Riddell. 1st Baron Birdwood. 1865–1951. British soldier, b. India. Entered army (1883); served in India, Boer War; military secretary to Lord Kitchener (1905–09); major general (1911). Commander of Australian and New Zealand Army Corps (ANZAC, 1914–18), taking part in Gallipoli campaign (1915); general (1917); commanded Fifth Army, France (1918). Commander in chief in India (1925–30); field marshal (1925); created baron (1938).

Bir·ger Jarl \ˈbir-yər-ˈyärl\. d. 1266. Swedish noble. Member of noble Folkung family; m. Ingeborg, sister of King Erik Eriksson; named jarl (1248); on death of Erik (1250) obtained election of own minor son Valdemar as king and retained real power as regent (1250–66). Defeated rebellious nobles, issued new laws, esp. those concerning the king's peace, strengthened ties with other Scandinavian countries, encouraged trade. Credited by many with founding Stockholm.

Birger Mag·nus·son \-ˈmäŋ-nu̇s-sȯn\. 1280–1321. King of Sweden (1290–1318). Son of Magnus I; nominal king under regency (1290–1302); engaged in civil war with brothers (1306–10); had brothers imprisoned and killed (1317); driven into exile in Denmark by revolt of nobles (1318).

Birgit *or* **Birgitta.** Saint. See BRIDGET.

Bi·rin·guc·cio \bē-rēŋ-ˈgüt-chō\, Vannoccio. 1480–c.1539. Italian metallurgist. Metallurgist and armorer in Siena, Parma, Ferrara, Venice; director of papal arsenal (from 1438). Author of *De la pirotechnia* (1540), first clear, comprehensive treatise on metallurgy.

Birk·beck \ˈbər(k)-ˌbek\, George. 1776–1841. English physician and educator. Professor in Glasgow (1799–1804); founder and first president (1823–41) of London Mechanics' Institute (later Birkbeck Coll.).

Birkenhead, 1st Earl of. See Frederick Edwin SMITH.

Birk·hoff \ˈbər-ˌkȯf, -ˌkäf\, George David. 1884–1944. American mathematician, b. Overisel, Mich. Professor of mathematics, U. of Wisconsin (1907–09), Princeton (1909–12), Harvard (1912–44). Known for researches in dynamics and on systems of differential equations; formulated ergodic theorem. Author of *Relativity and Modern Physics* (1923), *The Origin, Nature, and Influence of Relativity* (1925), *Dynamical Systems* (1928), *Aesthetic Measure* (1933), *Basic Geometry* (coauthor, 1941).

Birmingham, George A. See James Owen HANNAY.

Bir·ney \ˈbər-nē\, James Gillespie. 1792–1857. American antislavery leader, b. Danville, Ky. Founded Kentucky Anti-Slavery Society (1835); published antislavery paper *Philanthropist* (1836–37); executive secretary, American Anti-Slavery Society (1837 ff.). Liberty party candidate for president (1840, 1844). Policy was to accomplish abolition of slavery by political means and moral suasion.

Biron, Baron de. See Armand de GONTAUT.

Bi·ron \ˈbyē-rən, byi-ˈrȯn\, Ernst Johann. *Orig. surname* Büh·ren \ˈbu̅e-rən\. Duke of Kur·land \ˈku̇r-lənd\. 1690–1772. German politician. Entered service of Anna Ivanovna in Kurland and became (c.1727) her lover; accompanied her to Russia; chamberlain and virtual ruler of Russia during her reign (1730–40); head of coterie of German courtiers who excluded Russian nobles from government; period of his influence known as *Bironovshchina.* Elected duke of Kurland (1737). On death of Empress Anna, assumed regency for infant Ivan VI (1740); as result of palace revolution, was imprisoned (1740) and banished to Siberia (1741–42); restored to ducal throne of Kurland (1762) by Catherine the Great; abdicated in favor of son Peter (1769).

Bir·rell \ˈbir-əl\, Augustine. 1850–1933. English politician and writer. Liberal M.P. (1889–99, 1907–18); president, national board of education (1905–07); chief secretary for Ireland (1907–16); responsible for creation of National U. of Ireland (1908); resigned following Easter uprising (1916) for which he was totally unprepared. Author of volumes of essays *Obiter Dicta* (1884, 1887) and *More Obiter Dicta* (1924), and of biographies of Charlotte Brontë (1885), William Hazlitt (1902), and Frederick Locker-Lampson (1920).

Bī·rū·nī, al- \ˌal-bē-ˈrü-nē\. *More completely* Abū ar-Rayḥān Muḥammad ibn Aḥmad al-Bīrūnī. 973–1048. Arab scholar. Conversant in several languages; corresponded with Avicenna; studied culture of India. Author of historical chronicle *Āthār al-bāqīyah,* astrological treatise *at-Tafhīm,* astronomical work *al-Qanūn al-Mas'ūdī,* history of India *Tā'rīkh al-Hind,* medical treatise *Kitāb as-Saydalah,* etc.

Bi·schof \ˈbish-(ˌ)ȯf\, Werner. 1916–1954. Swiss photographer. Photojournalist for Zürich magazine *Du* (1942–54); traveled widely and became noted for photography displaying keen understanding and artistic sensibility.

Bis·cop \ˈbis-kōp\ *or* **Bis·chop** *or* **Biss·chop** \-kōp\, Simon. *Known as* Simon Ep·is·co·pi·us \ˌep-i-ˈskō-pē-əs\. 1583–1643. Dutch theologian. Professor, Leiden (1612–18); student of Arminius; represented Remonstrants at synods at The Hague (1611), Delft (1613), Dort (1618); expelled from church and banished (1618); head of Remonstrant Seminary, Amsterdam (from 1634); leader of Remonstrants after death of Arminius and systematizer of Arminian theology; author of *Confessio* (c.1622), *Apologia* (1629), *Institutiones Theologiae* (pub. 1650), etc.

Biscop Baducing. See BENEDICT BISCOP.

Bi·shan·dās \ˌbish-ən-ˈdäs\. 17th century. Indian painter. Leading portraitist of the Jahāngīr school of Mughal art; sent by Jahāngīr to Persia to paint shāh and nobles.

Bish·op \'bish-əp\, Elizabeth. 1911–1979. American poet, b. Worcester, Mass. Traveled widely; lived in Brazil (1951–67). Author of *North & South: A Cold Spring* (1955, Pulitzer prize), *Questions of Travel* (1965), *Complete Poems* (1969), *Geography III* (1976).

Bishop, Sir Henry Rowley. 1786–1855. English conductor and composer. Conducted at Covent Garden (1810), King's Theatre, Haymarket (1816–17), Drury Lane (from 1825), etc.; professor, Edinburgh (1841), Oxford (1848). Composer of operas, burlettas, and incidental music to Shakespeare's plays; remembered esp. for his glees and songs; introduced air of "Home, Sweet Home" into *Clari* (1823); first musician to be knighted (1842).

Bishop, Isabella Lucy, *nee* Bird. 1832–1904. English traveler, lecturer, and writer. m. (1881) Dr. John Bishop. Author of *Englishwoman in America* (1856), *The Hawaiian Archipelago* (1875), *Unbeaten Tracks in Japan* (1880), *The Yangtse Valley and Beyond* (1899), etc. First woman fellow of Royal Geographical Society (1892).

Bishop, John Peale. 1892–1944. American writer, b. Charles Town, W.Va. Resided in France (1922–33), Cape Cod, Mass. (from 1938); became chief poetry reviewer for *The Nation* (1940). Author of books of verse *Green Fruit* (1917), *Now with His Love* (1933), *Minute Particulars* (1935), novel *Act of Darkness* (1935), short-story collection *Many Thousands Gone* (1931), and essays.

Bishop, William Avery. 1894–1956. Canadian aviator, b. Owen Sound, Ont. Member of Canadian Expeditionary Force in France (1914); transferred to Royal Flying Corps (1915); awarded Victoria Cross (1917); officially credited with bringing down 72 enemy aircraft. Air vice marshal (1936); air marshal (1938); director, Royal Canadian Air Force (1939–45).

Bis·marck \'biz-,märk, *Angl* 'biz-\, *in full* Bis·marck-Schön·hau·sen \-shœn-'haù-zən\, Otto Eduard Leopold von. Fürst. *Called* the Iron Chancellor. 1815–1898. Prussian statesman and first chancellor of German Empire. Studied law at Göttingen and Berlin (1832–35). In Prussian civil (1836–39) and military service. Member, United Diet of Prussia (1847), second chamber of Prussian Diet (1849), and Erfurt Parliament (1850). Prussian ambassador to Germanic Diet at Frankfurt (1851–58); strongly opposed Austrian predominance and advocated consolidation of German people under conservative Prussian leadership. Ambassador to Russia (1859–62) and France (1862). Minister-president (prime minister) of Prussian cabinet, and foreign minister (1862–71); engaged in struggle with diet over army reorganization, the budget, and prerogatives of the crown; declared (1862) that German problems must be solved by "blood and iron." Worked for alliance with France and Russia. Defeated Denmark (with cooperation of Austria) in Schleswig-Holstein war (1864); created count (1865); broke again with Austria over Schleswig-Holstein question in Seven Weeks' War, and with Italy's help gained decisive victory (1866) at Königgrätz (Sadowa). Reorganized German Bund, excluding Austria, as North German Confederation under leadership of Prussia (1866). Gained triumphs in Franco-Prussian War (1870–71); succeeded in winning over south German states to join confederation, and gained prestige among German people. Became first chancellor (1871–90) of new German Empire and created prince (1871). Engaged in unsuccessful struggle (*Kulturkampf,* 1872 ff.) with Roman Catholics; put through many economic and social reforms, including workmen's compulsory insurance and government ownership of industrial enterprises; advocated strong colonial and international policy, and protective tariff. Presided over international Congress of Berlin (1878); concluded alliance with Austria-Hungary (1879), and the Triple Alliance (Dreibund) of Germany, Italy, and Austria-Hungary (1882) to make Germany secure against France and Russia. Disagreed with William II on several issues, esp. anti-Socialist laws, and resigned (1890). Author of brilliantly self-serving *Gedanken und Erinnerungen* (1898). His son ¶Prince Herbert Nikolaus von Bismarck-Schönhausen (1849–1904) served in Franco-Prussian War (1870); entered diplomatic service (1874); private secretary to his father (1877–81); counselor of German legation, London (1882) and St. Petersburg (1884); secretary of state (1886); Prussian minister of state (1888); presided at Samoan conference, Berlin, between Germany, England, and U.S. (1889); retired from diplomatic service after resignation of his father (1890). Member of Reichstag (1881–89, 1893, 1898).

Bis·sell \'bis-əl\, George Henry. 1821–1884. American petroleum pioneer, b. Hanover, N.H. Organized (1854) first oil company in U.S., to develop oil lands in Pennsylvania; firm reorganized (1855) as Pennsylvania Rock Oil Co. with Benjamin Silliman, Jr., as president; engaged Edwin L. Drake to drill experimental oil well (1859).

Bissell, Melville Reuben. 1843–1889. American inventor, b. Hartwick, N.Y. Invented (1876) carpet sweeper that became great commercial success.

Bissell, Richard Pike. 1913–1977. American writer, b. Dubuque, Iowa. Author of novels *A Stretch on the River* (1950), *The Monongahela* (1952), *7½ Cents* (1953), which he adapted for musical stage as *The Pajama Game* (1954), *Say, Darling* (1957), which he adapted for musical stage (1958, with wife Marian Bissell and Abe Burrows), *Good Bye, Ava* (1960), *Still Circling Moose Jaw* (1965).

Bis·so·la·ti-Ber·ga·ma·schi \,bēs-sō-'lä-tē-,bär-gä-'mäs-kē\, Leonida. 1857–1920. Italian politician. Editor of Socialist organ *Avanti* (1896); leader of revisionist group of Social Democratic party; seceded and founded Reformist Socialist party (1912); favored freedom of Libya and Italy's participation in World War I on side of entente; minister without portfolio (1916–17), minister of war (1917).

Bit·ter \'bit-ər\, Karl Theodore Francis. 1867–1915. American sculptor, b. Vienna. To U.S. (1889). His four figures *Architecture, Sculpture, Painting, Music,* adorn front of Metropolitan Museum, N.Y.C.; other works included decoration for World's Columbian Exposition, Chicago, Pennsylvania Station in Philadelphia, "Biltmore" estate at Ashville, N.C.; bronze gate for Trinity Church, N.Y.C.

Bit·zer \'bit-sər\, George William, *called* G. W. *or* Billy. 1874–1944. American motion-picture cameraman, b. Boston. Cameraman for D.W. Griffith on *Birth of a Nation* (1914), *Intolerance* (1916), *Broken Blossoms* (1919), *Way Down East* (1920), etc.; developed new techniques in composition, lighting, as soft-focus, fade-out, iris shot.

Bit·zi·us \'bit-sē-ùs\, Albert. *Pseudonym* Jeremias Gott·helf \'gòt-,helf\. 1797–1854. Swiss writer. Author esp. of novels and stories depicting village life in Switzerland, as *Der Bauernspiegel* (1837), *Leiden und Freuden eines Schulmeisters* (1838), *Die Armennot* (1840), *Uli der Knecht* (1841).

Bix·by \'biks-bē\, Horace Ezra. 1826–1912. Mississippi River pilot, b. Geneseo, N.Y. Friend, and for a time partner, of Samuel Clemens (Mark Twain).

Bix·io \'bēks-yō\, Nino, *in full* Girolamo Nino. 1821–1873. Italian soldier. Commanded Roman troops against French (1849); commanded vessel in Sicilian campaign (1860); captured Reggio (1860); promoted lieutenant general; forced surrender of Civitavecchia (1870). Elected to chamber of deputies (1861); senator (1870).

Bi·zet \bē-ze; *Angl* biz-'ā, bē-'zā\, Alexandre-César-Léopold, *called* Georges. 1838–1875. French composer. Studied under Gounod and Halévy; composed operas *Les Pêcheurs de perles* (1863), *La Jolie fille de Perth* (1867), and *Carmen* (1875), music for *Djamileh* (1872) and Daudet's *L'Arlésienne* (1872), *Symphony in C major* (1855), *Petite suite* (1871), piano duet *Jeux d'enfants* (1871).

Biz·zo·ze·ro \bēt-tsōt-'sā-rō\, Giulio Cesare. 1846–1901. Italian pathologist. Professor at Pavia (1867–72), Turin (1872–1901); appointed senator (1890). Pioneer in microscopic histology; made Turin a center of medical research.

Bjerk·nes \'byerk-nās\, Jacob Aall Bonnevie. 1897–1975. American meteorologist, b. Stockholm. Son of Vilhelm Bjerknes; assisted father in studies leading to theory of polar fronts; discovered origin of cyclones; to U.S. (1939); professor, UCLA (1940–75).

Bjerknes, Vilhelm Friman Koren. 1862–1951. Norwegian physicist. Professor, Stockholm (1895–1907), Kristiania (1907–12), Leipzig (1912–17), Bergen (1917–26), Oslo (1926–51). Known esp. for study of large-scale thermodynamics of oceanic and atmospheric masses; proposed theory of air masses fundamental to modern weather forecasting.

Bjørn·son \'byœrn-sòn\, Bjørnstjerne Martinius. 1832–1910. Norwegian poet, dramatist, novelist, and political and social leader. Theater manager, Bergen (1857–59); editor of *Bergenposten* (1858–59), *Aftenbladet,* Christiania (1859); director, Christiania theater (1865–67); editor of *Norsk Folkeblad* (1866–71). Author of verse *Digte og sange* (1870), including the national anthem "Ja, vi elsker dette landet"; an epic cycle, *Arnljot Gelline* (1870); the novels and tales *Synnøve Solbakken* (1857), *Arne* (1858), *En glad gut* (1860), *Fiskerjenten* (1868), *Det flager i byen og på havnen* (1884), *På Guds veje* (1889), *Mary* (1906); plays *Mellen Slagene* (1857), *Halte-Hulda* (1858), *Kong Sverre* (1861), *Sigurd Slembe* (1862), *Maria Stuart i Skotland* (1864), *De nygifte* (1865), *En fallit* (1874), *Redaktøren* (1874), *Kongen* (1877), *Det ny system* (1879), *En handske* (1883), *Over Aevne I og II* (1883, 1895), etc. In literature and politics, worked to link Norwegian history and legend to modern ideals. Awarded 1903 Nobel prize for literature.

Björns·son \'byœd-ᵊns-sòn\, Sveinn. 1881–1952. Icelandic politician and diplomat. Member of Althing (1914–16, 1920); special envoy to U.S. (1914), Great Britain (1915); minister to Denmark (1920–24, 1926–41). Three times regent of Iceland (1941–43) during occupation of Denmark; first president of Republic of Iceland (1944–52).

Black \'blak\, Adam. 1784–1874. Scottish publisher. Acquired copyrights of *Encyclopaedia Britannica* (1827), Scott's Waverley novels (1851), and De Quincey's works (1861). M.P. (1856–65).

Black, Davidson. 1884–1934. Canadian physician and anthropologist, b. Toronto. Professor, Peking Union Medical Coll. (1920–35); discovered (1927) hominid molar from which he inferred existence of *Sinanthropus pekinensis,* or Peking man.

Black, George. 1890–1945. English theatrical manager. Acquired circuit of theaters and music halls; took over Moss Empires Theaters (1933); inaugurated annual "Crazy Gang" shows at London Palladium (1935).

Black, Greene Vardiman. 1836–1915. American dentist, b. near Winchester, Ill. Professor, Missouri Dental Coll. (1870–80), Chicago Coll. of Dental Surgery (1883–89), U. of Iowa (1890–91), Northwestern U. (1891–1915; dean of dental school from 1897). Contributed much to dental technique and equipment, wrote *Dental Anatomy* (1891), *Operative Dentistry* (1908), etc.

Black, Hugo LaFayette. 1886–1971. American politician and jurist, b. Harlan, Ala. U.S. senator from Alabama (1927–37). Associate justice, U.S. Supreme Court (1937–71); known as a champion of Bill of Rights and strong constitutionalist.

Black, Jeremiah Sullivan. 1810–1883. American lawyer, b. near Stony Creek, Pa. U.S. attorney general in Buchanan's cabinet (1857–60); exposed California land title frauds; secretary of state (1860–61) during difficult months just preceding Civil War.

Black, Joseph. 1728–1799. Scottish chemist. Wrote doctoral thesis on causticization, by which process he rediscovered carbon dioxide; taught at Glasgow (1756–66), Edinburgh (from 1766); evolved theory of latent heat; measured latent heat of steam; founded doctrine of specific heats (1760).

Black, William. 1841–1898. Scottish journalist and novelist. War correspondent during Seven Weeks' War (1866). Author of *A Daughter of Heth* (1871), *A Princess of Thule* (1874), *Madcap Violet* (1876), *White Heather* (1885), etc.

Blackbeard. See Edward TEACH.

Black•burn \'blak-(,)bərn\, Gideon. 1772–1838. American clergyman, b. Augusta Co., Va. Ordained in Presbyterian ministry (c.1794); missionary to Cherokee Indians (1804–11); president, Centre Coll. (1827–33); founded (1836) Blackburn Theological Seminary, later Coll., Carlinville, Ill.

Blackburn, Helen. 1842–1903. British reformer, b. Ireland. Secretary, National Society for Women's Suffrage (from 1874); edited *Englishwoman's Review* (1881–90). Author of *Condition of Working Women and the Factory* (1896), *Women's Suffrage: A Record of the Movement in the British Isles* (1902), *Women under the Factory Acts* (1903).

Blackburn, Joseph. c.1730–after 1774? English painter. Worked in Bermuda (c.1752–53), New England (c.1753–64); introduced decorative Rococo manner of portraiture to colonies.

Blackburn, Thomas. 1916–1977. English poet and critic. Author of verse *The Holy Stone* (1954), *A Smell of Burning* (1961), *A Breathing Space* (1964), *Selected Poems* (1976); criticism *The Price of an Eye* (1961); *Robert Browning* (1967); musical drama *Judas Tree* (1967); autobiographical novel *A Clip of Steel* (1969).

Black•burne \,blak-(,)bərn\, Francis. 1782–1867. Irish lawyer. Attorney general for Ireland (1830–34, 1841); lord chancellor of Ireland (1852, 1866); prosecuted O'Connell and presided at trial of Smith O'Brien.

Black•ett \'blak-ət\, Patrick Maynard Stuart. 1897–1974. Baron Blackett. British physicist. Professor, U. of London (1933–37), Manchester U. (1937–53), and Imperial College of Science and Technology, London (1953–67); created life peer (1969). Known for work on cosmic rays, and esp. on the meson; helped develop the cloud chamber; a discoverer of the positron (1933). Awarded Nobel prize for physics (1948).

Black Hawk \'blak-,hȯk\. *Indian name* Ma-ka-ta-i-me-she-kia-kiak. 1767–1838. American Indian leader, b. near present Rockford, Ill. A leader of Sauk and Fox tribe; ally of British in War of 1812; rival of pro-U.S. Keokuk; returned from Iowa to original Illinois lands with 1,000 followers (1832); failed to gain assistance of other tribes; defeated by Illinois militia and U.S. army troops at Bad Axe River, Wis. (Aug. 2, 1832). Ward of Keokuk (1833–38).

Black•ie \'blak-ē\, John Stuart. 1809–1895. Scottish scholar and man of letters. Made translations in verse of *Faust* (1834), Aeschylus (1850), and the *Iliad* (1886); professor of Greek, Edinburgh (1852–82); founded and endowed Celtic chair, Edinburgh (1882).

Black•more \'blak-,mō(ə)r, -,mȯ(ə)r\, Sir Richard. 1654–1729. English physician and writer. Physician in ordinary to William III and Anne; author of epics *Prince Arthur* (1695), *King Arthur* (1697), *Eliza* (1705), *Alfred* (1723), also verse *Satyr Against Wit* (1700) and *Creation* (1712).

Blackmore, Richard Doddridge. 1825–1900. English novelist. Author of *Lorna Doone* (1869), *Springhaven* (1887), etc.

Black Prince, the. See EDWARD, Prince of Wales (1330–1376).

Black•stone \'blak-stən, *US usu* -,stōn\, Sir William. 1723–1780. English jurist. Fellow of All Souls Coll., Oxford (1744); gave first university lectures on English law (1753); first Vinerian professor of common law (1758–66); his lectures formed basis for famed *Commentaries on the Laws of England* (1765–69). M.P. (1761–70); solicitor general to queen (1763); judge of Common Pleas (1770–80).

Black•ton \'blak-tən\, James Stuart. 1875–1941. American film director, b. Sheffield, England. In New York formed (1896, with Albert E. Smith) Vitagraph film studio; produced *Burglar on the Roof* (1897), followed by films based on Shakespeare, the Bible, Dickens, etc.; introduced animation; sold Vitagraph to Warner Bros. (1925).

Black•wel•der \'blak-,wel-dər\, Eliot. 1880–1969. American geologist, b. Chicago. With U.S. Geological Survey (1906–18); head of geology dept., U. of Illinois (1916–19); chief geologist, Argus Oil Co. (1919–22); professor, Stanford (1922–45). Known for studies of desert geomorphology, structure and history of Rocky Mountains.

Black•well \'blak-,wel, -wəl\, Antoinette Louisa, *nee* Brown. 1825–1921. American reformer, b. Henrietta, N.Y. Congregational pastor in South Butler, N.Y. (1852–54), first U.S. woman formally engaged as pastor; m. (1856) Samuel C. Blackwell, a brother of Elizabeth Blackwell.

Blackwell, Elizabeth. 1821–1910. American physician, b. Counterslip, Bristol, England. To. U.S. (1832). M.D., Geneva Medical School of Western N.Y. (1849). First woman doctor of medicine in modern times. Opened private dispensary in New York (1853), which became incorporated (1857) into New York Infirmary for Women and Children; Woman's Medical Coll. established there (1868). Settled in England (1869); professor of gynecology in London School of Medicine for Women (1875–1907). Her sister ¶Emily (1826–1910) took an M.D. from Western Reserve U. (1854); joined sister's dispensary in New York City (1856); director of dispensary (1869–1910) and dean of Women's Medical Coll. (1869–1899).

Blackwell, Henry Brown. 1825–1909. American editor, b. Bristol, England. Brother of Elizabeth Blackwell. Pioneer woman suffrage advocate; m. (1855) Lucy Stone (*q.v.*); coeditor of *Woman's Journal* (1872–1909). His daughter ¶Alice Stone Blackwell (1857–1950), b. East Orange, N.J.; also an advocate of woman's suffrage; assisted in editing *Woman's Journal* (from 1881), chief editor (1893–1917); author of *Armenian Poems* (1896), *Songs of Russia* (1906), etc.

Blackwell, John. *Pseudonym* Alun \'äl-in\. 1797–1840. Welsh poet. Considered father of modern Welsh secular lyric; editor of magazine *Y Cylchgrawn* (1834–35). Collected works published as *Ceinion Alun* (1851).

Blackwell, Lucy Stone. See Lucy STONE.

Black•wood \'blak-,wu̇d\, Algernon Henry. 1869–1951. English novelist and traveler. Farmed in Canada; ran hotel in Toronto; journalist in New York. Author of novels and tales of occult and supernatural, as *The Empty House* (1906), *John Silence* (1908), *The Human Chord* (1910), *The Wave* (1916), *Tales of the Uncanny and Supernatural* (1949).

Blackwood, Frederick Temple Hamilton-Temple-. 1st Marquis of Duf•fer•in and Ava \'dəf(-ə)-rən-ən-'(d)äv-ə\. 1826–1902. British diplomat and administrator. Entered House of Lords (1850) as Baron Clan•de•boye \'klan-də-,bȯi\; lord in waiting to Queen Victoria (1849–52, 1854–58); undersecretary for India (1864–66), for war (1866–68); created earl of Dufferin (1871). As governor general of Canada (1872–78), quieted agitators and strengthened imperial connection; ambassador at St. Petersburg (1879–81), Constantinople (1881–82); commissioner in Egypt (1882–83) to establish reorganization after Pasha's defeat at at-Tall al-Kabīr; as governor general of India (1884–88), settled land question tactfully, settled crisis with Russia by delimiting northwest frontier, and annexed Upper Burma (1886); created marquis (1888); ambassador at Rome (1889–91), Paris (1891–96).

Blackwood, William. 1776–1834. Scottish publisher. Founder of *Edinburgh Encyclopaedia* (1810); founder and editor of *Edinburgh Monthly Magazine* (1817), which soon became *Blackwood's Magazine.* Founded publishing house of William Blackwood & Sons (c.1816). His son ¶John (1818–1879) succeeded an elder brother as editor (1845) of *Blackwood's* and as head of publishing business (1852); published George Eliot's *Scenes of Clerical Life* in *Blackwood's,* and most of her novels in book form.

Blaeu \'blau̇\, Willem Janszoon. 1571–1638. Dutch mathematician, geographer, and astronomer. Founder of a publishing firm at Amsterdam, known esp. for its terrestrial and celestial globes and maps; author of *Novus Atlas* (1634–62). His sons ¶Cornelius (d. 1650) and ¶Jan (d. 1673) continued the firm; Jan published *Atlas Magnus* (11 vols., 1650–62).

Bla•ga \'blä-gä\, Lucian. 1895–1961. Romanian poet and playwright. Known esp. for his dramatization of Romanian folk myths, as in *Meşterul Manole* (1927); verse included *Peomele luminii* (1919), *În marea trecere* (1924), *Laudă somnului* (1929).

Bla•ho•slav \'blä-hȯ-,släv\, Jan. 1523–1571. Czech prelate and writer. Bishop of Bohemian church; wrote *Muzica* on musical theory (1558), collection of hymns *Kancional v. Šamotuly* (1561), a pioneering *Gramatika českâ* (1571); translated New Testament into Czech (1564).

Blaich \'blīḵ\, Hans Erich. *Pseudonyms* Dr. Owl•glass \'au̇l-,glas\ *and* Ra•ta•tös•kr \'rä-tä-,tœs-kər\. 1873–1945. German writer and translator. Author of folk tales, often humorous; editor of *Simplicissimus* (1912–24, 1933–35); translator of Rabelais, Aristophanes, Montaigne, Cervantes, etc. Author of verse *Der saure Apfel* (1904), *Der Tintenkuli* (1924), *Stunde um Stunde* (1933), *Seitensprünge* (1942), etc.

Blaine \ˈblān\, James Gillespie. *Called* the Plumed Knight. 1830–1893. American politician, b. West Brownsville, Pa. Newspaper editor, Augusta, Me. (1854–60). Member, U.S. House of Representatives (1863–76); speaker (1869–75). U.S. senator (1876–81). Unsuccessful candidate for Republican presidential nomination (1876, 1880). U.S. secretary of state (1881). Republican nominee for president (1884); in campaign, Rev. S. D. Burchard called Democratic party "the party whose antecedents are rum, Romanism, and rebellion," losing many votes for Blaine; lost election to Grover Cleveland. U.S. secretary of state (1889–92).

Blain·ville \bla^{n}-vēl\, Henri-Marie Du·cro·tay de \dü̅e-krō-tā-də\. 1777–1850. French zoologist and physician. Succeeded Cuvier (1832) as professor in Muséum d'Histoire Naturelle, Paris; did valuable paleontological work by way of gathering evidence for his theory of a chain of creation.

Blair \ˈbla(ə)r, ˈble(ə)r\, Eric Arthur. *Pseudonym* George Or·well \ˈȯr-ˌwel, -wəl\. 1903–1950. English writer, b. India. Experiences as asst. district superintendent, Indian Imperial Police, in Burma (1922–27) recounted in *Burmese Days* (1935); became Socialist; lived in self-imposed poverty in Paris and London, described in *Down and Out in Paris and London* (1933) and *The Road to Wigan Pier* (1937); fought (1936–37) and wounded in Spanish Civil War on Republican side, basis for *Homage to Catalonia* (1938); wrote essays, reviews, and articles; gained fame with novels *Animal Farm* (1944) and *1984* (1949). Other works included *Coming Up for Air* (1939), *Inside the Whale* (1940), *The Lion and the Unicorn* (1941), *Shooting an Elephant and Other Essays* (1950), and *Such, Such Were the Joys* (1953).

Blair, Francis Preston. 1791–1876. American journalist and politician, b. Abingdon, Va. Established (1830) Jacksonian paper *Globe* in Washington, D.C.; member of Jackson's "kitchen cabinet"; published *Congressional Globe.* Helped organize Republican party (1856); valuable supporter of Lincoln's candidacy (1860); arranged unsuccessful peace conference at Hampton Roads, Va. (Feb. 1875). His son ¶Francis Preston, Jr. (1821–1875), b. Lexington, Ky.; helped organize Free-Soil party (1848) in Missouri; member of U.S. House of Representatives (1857–59); led formation of Missouri Republican party (1858); again in Congress (1860, 1861–62, 1863–64). Brigadier and major general of volunteers on staff of Gen. William T. Sherman (1862–63). Unsuccessful Democratic candidate for vice president (1868). Appointed to complete term in U.S. Senate (1871–73). His brother ¶Montgomery (1813–1883), b. Franklin Co., Ky., was U.S. district attorney for Missouri (1839–41), mayor of St. Louis (1842–43), judge of court of common pleas (1845–49). Attorney for Dred Scott before Supreme Court (1857). Postmaster general in Lincoln's cabinet (1861–64). Counsel of Samuel J. Tilden before Electoral Commission (1876).

Blair, Hugh. 1718–1800. Scottish Presbyterian clergyman. Professor of rhetoric, Edinburgh U. (1762–83); defended authenticity of Macpherson's Ossianic poems; author of *Lectures on Rhetoric* (1783).

Blair, James. 1656–1743. American educator, b. Edinburgh? To America (1685); rector of Varina Parish, Va. (1685); founder and first president of College of William and Mary (1693–1743).

Blair, John. 1732–1800. American jurist, b. Williamsburg, Va. Member of Constitutional Convention (1787); associate justice, U.S. Supreme Court (1789–96).

Blair, Robert. 1699–1746. Scottish clergyman and poet. Author of *The Grave* (1743), a poem in blank verse, later illustrated by William Blake.

Blaise *or* **Blaize** \ˈblāz\, *or* **Bla·sius** \ˈblā-zē-əs, -zhəs\. Saint. *Known also as* Blaise of Sebastia. d. c.316 A.D. Armenian prelate and martyr. Bishop of Sebastia; imprisoned, tortured, beheaded during persecutions of Emperor Licinius. Subject of many legends and of cult (from c. 6th century); one of Fourteen Holy Helpers in Germany; patron of throat sufferers.

Blake \ˈblāk\, Edward. 1833–1912. Canadian politician, b. Adelaide, Ont. Member of Ontario Legislative Assembly (1867–72), prime minister of Ontario (1871–72); member of federal House of Commons (1867–90); minister of justice (1875–77); leader of opposition Liberal party (1880–87). To Ireland (1890); M.P. (1892–1907); helped draft Home Rule bill (1893).

Blake, George. 1893–1961. Scottish journalist and novelist. Author of *Vagabond Papers* (1922), *The Shipbuilders* (1935), *David and Joanna* (1936), *Down to the Sea* (1937), *Late Harvest* (1938), etc.

Blake, James Hubert, *known as* Eubie. 1883–1983. American pianist and composer, b. Baltimore. One of the first blacks to perform without minstrel makeup; with lyricist Noble Sissle created *Shuffle Along* (1921, "I'm Just Wild About Harry"), one of the first musicals to be written, produced, and directed by blacks; also wrote score for innovative *Chocolate Dandies* (1929); had long career as recording and concert artist; was subject of Broadway musical *Eubie* (1978).

Blake, Nicholas. See Cecil DAY-LEWIS.

Blake, Robert. 1599–1657. English admiral. As Parliamentarian in Civil War, took part in defense of Bristol (1643), Lyme (1643–44), Taunton (1644–45). As admiral and general of the sea, pursued Prince Rupert's fleet to the Mediterranean and destroyed bulk of it (1650); captured Scilly Isles (1651); member of Council of State (1651–57). Fought engagements, breaking naval supremacy of Holland (1652–53). Destroyed Barbary pirate fleet (1655); destroyed Spanish West Indian fleet at Santa Cruz (1657). Introduced Articles of War, basis of naval discipline, and "Fighting Instructions," on tactics.

Blake, William. 1757–1827. English artist, poet, and mystic. Apprenticed to an engraver (1772–79); employed new process of printing from etched copper plates in series of his own lyrical poems, hand-illustrated and colored, beginning with *Songs of Innocence* (1789) and *Songs of Experience* (1794). Illustrated Mary Wollstonecraft's works (1791) and Young's *Night Thoughts* (1797). Executed and engraved many religious designs, his best *Inventions to the Book of Job* (1820–26); occupied at time of death in engraving designs for Dante's *Divina Commedia.* Author of mystical and metaphysical works including *Marriage of Heaven and Hell* (1793), *America: A Prophecy* (1793), *Europe: A Prophecy* (1794), *Book of Urizen* (1794), *Book of Ahania* (1795), *Book of Los* (1795), and of symbolic poems terminating with *Milton* (1808) and *Jerusalem* (1820); made illustrations for Bible, *Paradise Lost,* Blair's *The Grave, Pastorals of Virgil,* etc.

Blake·lock \ˈblā-ˌkläk\, Ralph Albert. 1847–1919. American painter, b. New York City. Among his works, mainly landscapes, were *Pipe Dance, From St. Ives to Lelant, Colorado Plains, October Sunshine, Indian Encampment.*

Bla·lock \ˈblā-ˌläk\, Alfred. 1899–1964. American surgeon, b. Culloden, Ga. Taught at Vanderbilt U. Hospital (1925–41), Johns Hopkins Medical School (1941–63). Specialized in vascular surgery; with Dr. Helen Taussig developed pulmonary artery bypass operation (1944) that saved many "blue babies."

Bla·mey \ˈblā-mē\, Sir Thomas Albert. 1884–1951. Australian soldier. Served in World War I (1914–18), on Turkish front. Lieutenant general, commanding Australian Army Corps in Middle East (1940); engaged in Greece (1941); deputy commander in chief of British forces in Middle East (1941); commander in chief, Australian Army (1941–45); field marshal (1950).

Blanc \blä^{n}\, Louis, *in full* Jean-Joseph-Charles-Louis. 1811–1882. French Socialist. Journalist; founded (1839) *Revue du Progrès,* organ for his Socialist doctrines. Gained prominence through his *Organisation du travail* (1840) and *Histoire de dix ans, 1830–1840* (1841–44), the latter an attack upon policies and methods of Louis-Philippe's government. Member of provisional government in revolution of 1848; forced government to adopt principle of guarantee of employment to workingmen; discredited by failure of policies as put into effect by politicians unfriendly to him; took refuge in England (1848–70). Returned to France; elected to Chamber of Deputies (1871). Author of *Histoire de la Révolution française* (1847–62) and many political pamphlets.

Blan·chard \blä^{n}-shȧr\, Jean-Pierre-François. 1753–1809. French aeronaut. Began making balloon ascents (1784); made first balloon ascent in England (1784); with John Jeffries (*q.v.*) made first aerial crossing of English Channel (Jan. 7, 1785); invented and used a parachute (1785); made first ascent over North America (Philadelphia, 1793).

Blan·chard \ˈblan-chərd, -shərd\, Thomas. 1788–1864. American inventor, b. Sutton, Mass. Invented automatic tack-manufacturing machine, a lathe for turning gun barrels, a method of turning irregular forms from a pattern, etc.

Blanche \blä^{n}sh, *Angl* ˈblanch\ of Castile. 1188–1252. Queen of France. Daughter of Alfonso VIII of Castile and granddaughter of Henry II of England; m. (1200) Louis, son of Philip II Augustus, King of France. With husband's help attempted unsuccessfully to seize English throne on death of King John (1216). Queen of France during Louis VIII's reign (1223–26); queen regent during minority (1226–36) of her son Louis IX and again (1248–52) during his absence on a crusade.

Blanche \blä^{n}sh\, Jacques-Émile. 1861–1942. French painter. Known esp. as portraitist; subjects included Loüys, Beardsley, Yvette Guilbert, Hardy, Proust.

Blan·chet \blä^{n}-she\. Name of a family of French harpsichord makers including: Nicolas (c.1660–1731), founded business in Paris (before 1685); took into partnership (1722) his son ¶François-Étienne, *called* the Elder (c.1695–1761), who became one of finest makers of Baroque harpsichords. Firm joined by ¶Pascal Tas·kin \tȧs-ka^{n}\ (1723–1793), his brother-in-law.

Blanco, Antonio Guzmán. See GUZMÁN BLANCO.

Blan·co Fom·bo·na \ˈbläŋ-kō-fōm-ˈbō-nä\, Rufino. 1874–1944. Venezuelan writer and publisher. Exiled from Venezuela (1910–35) for opposition to Pres. Gómez; resident in Madrid (1914). Author of *Cuentos de poeta* (1900), *Cuentos americanos* (1904), *El hombre de hierro* (1907), *El hombre de oro* (1915), *Tragedias grotescas* (1928), critical work *El modernismo y los poetas modernistas* (1929), and *Camino de imperfeccion* (1929).

Blanco White, Joseph. See WHITE.

Blan·co y Ere·nas \ˈbläŋ-kō-ē-ā-ˈrā-näs\, Ramón. Marqués de Pe·ña Pla·ta \t͟hā-ˈpān-yä-ˈplä-tä\. 1831–1906. Spanish soldier. Participated in Spanish annexation of Santo Domingo; governor of Mindanao; colonel general in

Spanish civil war (1871). Governor general of Cuba (1879–81, 1897–98); resisted invasion of U.S. troops.

Bland \ˈbland\, James A. 1854–1911. American songwriter, b. Flushing, N.Y. Member of Original Georgia Minstrels troupe; wrote "Carry Me Back to Old Virginny," "Oh, Dem Golden Slippers," "In the Evening by the Moonlight" (1878–79).

Bland, Richard Parks. 1835–1899. American politician, b. near Hartford, Ky. Member, U.S. House of Representatives from Missouri (1873–95, 1897–99). Leader of congressional free silver bloc of Democratic party; coauthor of Bland-Allison Act (1878) remonetizing silver. Defeated by W. J. Bryan (1896) for presidential nomination.

Blandrata, Georgius. See Giorgio BIANDRATA.

Blane \ˈblān\, Sir Gilbert. 1749–1834. Scottish physician. Accompanied Admiral Rodney to West Indies (1779, 1782); introduced use of lime juice in navy as a scurvy preventive, subsequently (1795) made obligatory; improved sanitary conditions in navy; instrumental in framing rules (1799), that became basis of modern quarantine regulations.

Blan·qui \blän-kē\, Adolphe, *in full* Jérôme-Adolphe. 1798–1854. French economist. Author of pioneering *Histoire de l'économie politique en Europe* (1837–38).

Blanqui, Auguste, *in full* Louis-Auguste. 1805–1881. French Socialist and revolutionary. Brother of Adolphe Blanqui. Theoretician of insurrection by trained guerilla groups and establishment of state socialism under temporary revolutionary dictatorship. Founded numerous secret societies and became inspiration of others, generally known as Blanquists. Took part in revolutions of 1830, 1848, 1871 and led unsuccessful insurrections (1839, 1870, 1871). Spent more than 33 years in prison (esp. 1831, 1836, 1839–48, 1849–59, 1861–65, 1871–79); elected president of Paris Commune (1871) and deputy for Bordeaux (1879) while in prison.

Blasch·ka \ˈbläsh-kä, *Angl* ˈblash-kə\, Leopold (d. 1895) and his son Rudolph (1857–1939). Bohemian artists in glass. Worked in Dresden; created (from 1887) thousands of glass models of flora, marine life, etc.

Blasch·ke \ˈbläsh-kə\, Wilhelm Johann Eugen. 1885–1962. German mathematician. Professor at Prague (1913–15), Leipzig (1915–17), Königsberg (1917–19), Hamburg (1919 ff.); known for contributions to differential and integral geometry and to kinematics, esp. discovery of kinematic mapping. Author of *Kreis und Kugel* (1916), *Differentialgeometrie* (1921–29), *Integralgeometrie* (1935–37), etc.

Blas·co Ibá·ñez \ˈbläs-kō-ē-ˈbän-yāth, -yās\, Vicente. 1867–1928. Spanish novelist. As ardent republican, forced to flee to Paris (1889) and Italy (1895); founded republican journal *El Pueblo* (1891); several times imprisoned; member of Cortes (1901–07); voluntary exile (1923 ff.). Works included *Arroz y tartana* (1894), *Flor de mayo* (1895), *La barraca* (1898), *Entre naranjos* (1900), *Cañas y Barro* (1902), *La catedral* (1903), *El intruso* (1904), *La bodega* (1906), *La maja desnuda* (1906), *Sangre y arena* (1908), *Los argonautas* (1915), *Los cuatro jinetes del Apocalipsis* (1916), *Mare nostrum* (1917), *Los enemigos de la mujer* (1919), *El Papa del Mar* (1925), and *A los pies de Venus* (1926).

Blash·field \ˈblash-ˌfēld\, Edwin Howland. 1848–1936. American painter, b. New York City. Known esp. for genre pictures, portraits, and murals. Decorated interiors for World's Columbian Exposition, Chicago (1893), central dome of Library of Congress (1896), and parts of the capitol buildings in Minnesota, Iowa, South Dakota, and Wisconsin.

Bla·sis \ˈblä-sēs\, Carlo. 1803–1878. Italian ballet teacher. Dancer and choreographer, King's Theatre, London (1826–30); ballet director, La Scala (1837 ff.). Taught many leading dancers; credited with creating *attitude* position. First codified ballet technique in *Traité élémentaire, théoretique et pratique de l'art de la danse* (1820); also wrote *Code of Terpsichore* (1830).

Blasius. See BLAISE.

Blas·ko·witz \ˈbläs-kō-ˌvits\, Johannes. 1883–1948. German general. Commanded Eighth Army in Poland (1939–40); protested to Hitler atrocities committed by Nazi police; commanded army groups in France (1940–44), Netherlands (1945); tried as war criminal, committed suicide.

Blas·ta·res \blas-ˈtär-(ˌ)ēz, -ˈtar-\, Matthew. 14th century. Byzantine monk and jurist. Priest-monk of Esaias monastery, Thessalonica; compiled (1335) *Syntagma kata stoicheion,* systematic history and compendium of civil and ecclesiastical laws, esp. influential in Slavic nations.

Blatch \ˈblach\, Harriot Eaton, *nee* Stan·ton \ˈstant-ᵊn\. 1856–1940. American woman suffrage leader, b. Seneca Falls, N.Y. Daughter of Elizabeth Cady Stanton; m. (1882) William H. Blatch. Founded (1907) Equality League of Self-Supporting Women. Author of *Mobilizing Woman Power* (1918), *A Woman's Point of View* (1920), *Elizabeth Cady Stanton* (1922).

Blatch·ford \ˈblach-fərd\, Samuel. 1820–1893. American jurist, b. New York City. Associate justice, U.S. Supreme Court (1882–93).

Bla·vat·sky \blə-ˈvat-skē\, Helena Petrovna, *nee* Hahn \ˈhän\. 1831–1891. American theosophist, b. Ekaterinoslav (Dnepropetrovsk), Russia. m. (1848) Gen. Nikifor V. Blavatsky; soon left him; visited Egypt and Europe; became interested in spiritism and occult sciences; to U.S. (1873); with Henry Steel Olcott, organized (1875) Theosophical Society; organized branch in India (1879); established official journal, *The Theosophist* (1879); won many distinguished converts, notably Annie Besant (*q.v.*); some of the psychic phenomena attributed to her were allegedly disproven (1885) in a report presented to the Society for Psychical Research. Author of *Isis Unveiled* (1877), *The Secret Doctrine* (1888), *The Key to Theosophy* (1889), and *The Voice of Silence* (1889).

Blaz·na·vac \bläz-ˈnä-väts\, Milivoje Petrović. 1824–1873. Serbian soldier and politician. Probably natural son of Miloš Obrenović; fought against Hungary (1849); minister of war (1865–72); on death of Prince Michael (1868), refused to recognize regency council appointed by the Skupština and proclaimed Milan Obrenović prince; one of three regents for Milan (1868–72); prime minister (1872–73).

Blease \ˈblēz\, Coleman Livingston. 1868–1942. American politician, b. near Newberry Courthouse, S.C. Governor of South Carolina (1911–15); U.S. senator (1925–31); notable as demagogic representative of agrarian revolt.

Ble·chen \ˈblek-ən\, Karl. 1798–1840. German painter. Professor at Berlin Academy (from 1831); known for theatrical decoration and esp. for Romantic landscapes.

Bledisloe, 1st Viscount. See Sir Charles BATHURST.

Bleek \ˈblāk\, Wilhelm Heinrich Immanuel. 1827–1875. German philologist. Pioneer in study of South African languages. Author of *The Language Mosambique* (1856), *Comparative Grammar of South African Languages* (1862–69), etc.

Ble·gen \ˈblā-gən\, Carl William. 1887–1971. American archaeologist, b. Minneapolis. On staff of American School of Classical Studies, Athens (1913–27); professor, U. of Cincinnati (1927–57). By excavations at site of Troy (1932–38) found evidence confirming Homeric account of sack of Troy and dating it to c.1250 B.C.; discovered earliest known examples of written Greek at site he identified (1939) as King Nestor's Pylos. Author of *Troy and the Trojans* (1963), *The Palace of Nestor at Pylos* (1966).

Blen·kin·sop \ˈbleŋ-kən-ˌsäp\, John. 1783–1831. English inventor. Patented (1811) a double-cylinder locomotive working by means of a racked rail and a toothed wheel, successfully tested (1812) and used thereafter. Cf. Richard TREVITHICK.

Blé·riot \blā-ryō, *Angl* ˈbler-ē-ˌō\, Louis. 1872–1936. French aviator. Manufactured a monoplane and in it was first to fly the English Channel in a heavier-than-air machine, taking off from Calais and landing near Dover (July 25, 1909).

Blessington, Countess of. See Marguerite GARDINER.

Blest Ga·na \ˈbläst-ˈgän-ä\, Alberto. 1830–1920. Chilean novelist. Held various political and diplomatic posts. Author of realistic social novels including *Una escena social* (1853), *El primer amor* (1858), *La aritmética en el amor* (1860), *Un drama en el campo* (1861), *Martín Rivas* (1862), *El ideal de una calavera* (1863), *Durante la Reconquista* (1897), *Los transplantados* (1905), *El loco Estero* (1910).

Bleu·ler \ˈblȯi-lər\, Eugen. 1857–1939. Swiss psychiatrist. Professor and director of Burghölzli Asylum, Zürich (1898–1927); introduced (1908) term schizophrenia and described several types; contended that some were treatable. Author of *Der geborene Verbrecher* (1896), *Dementia praecox oder Gruppe der Schizophrenien* (1911), *Lehrbuch der Psychiatrie* (1916), *Autistisch-undisziplinierte Denken in der Medizin und seine Überwindung* (1919).

Bli·cher \ˈblē-kər\, Steen Steensen. 1782–1848. Danish poet and writer. Author of novels and tales of Jutland, including *Jyllandsrejse; 6 Døgn* (1817), *En Landsbydegns Dagbog* (1824), *E Bindstouw* (1842), verse as *Traekfuglene* (1838), etc.

Bligh \ˈblī\, William. 1754–1817. English naval officer. Accompanied Captain Cook as sailing master on third voyage (1776–80); commanded *Bounty* on voyage to Tahiti (1787) to obtain breadfruit plants for introduction in West Indies; cast adrift in open boat with 18 men by mutinous crew led by Fletcher Christian (1789); reached Timor, in East Indies, after voyage of 4000 miles. Sailed again (1791) for breadfruit and succeeded in establishing the plant in the West Indies. Governor, New South Wales (1805–08); imprisoned by mutinous soldiers (1808–10). Vice admiral (1814).

Blind Harry. See HARRY the Minstrel.

Bliss \ˈblis\, Sir Arthur Edward Drummond. 1891–1975. English composer. Master of the Queen's Musick (1953–75). Composer esp. of choral and theatrical works, including: operas *The Olympians* (with J.B. Priestly, 1949), *Tobias and the Angel* (for television, 1960); ballets *Checkmate* (1937), *Miracle in the Gorbals* (1944), *Adam Zero* (1946), *Lady of Shallott* (1958); music for plays and for films *Things to Come* (1935), *Men of Two Worlds* (1945); vocal or choral works *Rhapsody* (1919), *Pastoral: Lie Strewn with White Flocks* (1928), *Morning Heroes* (1930), *Shield of Faith* (1975); orchestral *Colour Symphony* (1922), etc.

Bliss, Nathaniel. 1700–1764. English astronomer. Savilian professor of mathematics, Oxford (1742–64); astronomer royal (1762–64).

Bliss, Tasker Howard. 1853–1930. American army officer, b. Lewisburg, Pa. Engaged in Cuba and Puerto Rico in Spanish–American War (1898); first commandant, Army War Coll. (1903–05); chief of staff with rank of general (1917–18). Member of supreme war council in France (1917–18) and of American Commission to Negotiate Peace (1918–19).

Blitz·stein \ˈblit-ˌstīn\, Marc. 1905–1964. American composer, b. Philadelphia. Composed ballet *Jig Saw* (1927); operas *Triple Sec* (1928), *Parabola and Circula* (1929), *Regina* (1949), *Reuben, Reuben* (1951), *Juno* (1959); translated and adapted Brecht and Weill's *Threepenny Opera* (on Broadway 1954–60); other works included musical play *The Cradle Will Rock* (1937), choral *Freedom Morning* (1943), *Airborne Symphony* (1946).

Blixen, Baroness. See Karen C. DINESEN.

Bloch \blȯk, *Angl* ˈbläk\, Ernest. 1880–1959. American composer, b. Geneva, Switzerland. Taught at Geneva Conservatory (1911–15); to U.S. (1916); naturalized (1924). Founder and director (1920–25), Cleveland Inst. of Music; director (1925–30), San Francisco Cons. of Music. Compositions included works on Jewish themes, as *Trois poèmes juifs* (1913), *Israel* symphony (1916), tone poem *Schelomo* (1916), suite *Baal Shem* (1923), liturgy *Avodath Hakodesh* (1933); other works included symphonic works *Hiver-printemps* (1905), *America* (1926), *Suite symphonique* (1944), *Scherzo fantasque* (1948); opera *Macbeth* (1910); chamber works *Quintet for Piano and Strings* (1923), *Suite for Viola and Piano* (1919), string quartets, violin suites, etc.

Bloch \ˈblȯk\, Ernst. 1885–1977. German philosopher. Professor, Leipzig (1918–33, 1948–57), Tübingen (from 1961); in exile in Switzerland and U.S. (1933–48). From Marxism developed a "philosophy of hope"; broke with orthodox Marxist line, forbidden to publish (1953); fled East Germany to West Germany (1961). Works included *Geist der Utopie* (1918), *Erbschaft dieser Zeit* (1935), *Das Prinzip Hoffnung* (1954–59), etc.

Bloch \ˈbläk\, Felix. 1905–1983. American physicist, b. Zurich, Switzerland. To U.S. (1933); professor of physics, Stanford U. (1934–71); made contributions to solid-state physics; devised method for polarizing neutrons, separating them according to the direction of their intrinsic spins. Awarded 1952 Nobel prize for physics with Edward Mills Purcell for discovery of nuclear magnetic resonance (NMR) and its development as a means of studying solids and liquids by measuring the magnetic behavior of their atomic nuclei.

Bloch \blȯk\, Jean-Richard. 1884–1947. French novelist and playwright. Author of novels *Lévy* (1912), *Et Cie* (1918), *La Nuit kurde* (1925), etc.; plays *Le Dernier Empereur* (1926), *Toulon* (1945), etc.; known esp. for Communist polemics, as essay "Naissance d'une culture" (1936).

Bloch \ˈblȯk\, Joseph Samuel. 1850–1923. Austrian rabbi and politician. Achieved prominence disputing public charges that blood of Christians was used in Passover rituals (1882); member of Austrian parliament (1883–85, 1891–95); published (1884–1921) *Österreichische Wochenschrift.*

Block·sidge \ˈbläk-sij\, Charles William. *Pseudonym* William Bayle·bridge \ˈbā(ə)l-ˌbrij\. 1883–1942. Australian poet and story writer. Author of collections of verse and tales, mostly privately printed, including *Songs o' the South* (1908), *The New Life* (1910), *Selected Poems* (1919), *An Anzac Muster* (1921), *Love Redeemed* (sonnet cycle, 1934), *This Vital Flesh* (1939).

Blod·gett \ˈbläj-ət\, Katherine Burr. 1898–1979. American physicist and chemist, b. Schenectady, N.Y. Received first Ph.D. in physics awarded a woman by Cambridge U. (1926); invented (1938) nonreflecting glass used in windshields, telescopes, periscopes, cameras, etc.; invented color gauge to measure thickness of film and a smokescreen widely used in World War II.

Bloe·maert \ˈblü-ˌmärt\, Abraham. 1564–1651. Dutch painter and engraver. Known esp. for landscapes and religious and mythological pieces.

Bloe·men \ˈblü-mən\, Pieter van. *Called* Stan·daert \ˈstän-ˌdärt\. 1657–1719. Flemish battle and animal painter. His brother ¶Jan Frans van Bloemen (1662–?1748), landscape painter, was called in Italian O·riz·zon·te \ō-rēd-ˈdzōn-tā\, from the beautiful horizons in his landscapes.

Blois. See HENRY of Blois; PETER of Blois.

Blois \blwä\. A countship of north central France, originating c. 9th century; countships of Tou·raine \tü-ren\ and Char·tres \shärtrᵊ\ added (11th to 13th century). First count, as vassal of dukes of France, Thibaut I, *called* the Old *or* the Cheat (d. c.977); his successors vassals and rivals of Capetian kings of France. Countship gained with acquisition of Champagne (c.1023) by Eudes II. ¶Thibaut IV (d. 1152), brother of King Stephen of England and Bishop Henry of Winchester, brought countship to zenith of power. Countship sold (1397) to Louis I, Duc d'Orléans; united (1498) with crown.

Blois, François-Louis de. *Lat.* Franciscus Ludovicus Blo·si·us \ˈblō-zh(ē-)əs, -zē-əs\. 1506–1566. Flemish religious and mystical writer. Became a Benedictine (1520) and abbot of Liessies monastery in Hainaut (1530). Wrote in Latin; works translated into nearly all European languages. Among his best known works were *Institutio Spiritualis, Consolatio Pusillanimium, Sacellum Animae Fidelis,* and *Speculum Monachorum.*

Blok \ˈblȯk\, Aleksandr Aleksandrovich. 1880–1921. Russian poet. Much influenced by Vladimir Solovyov and Pushkin and by Bolshevik Revolution (1917). Verse characterized by violent Romanticism; chief Russian exponent of Symbolism. Works included *Vozmezdiye* (1908–13, unfinished), *Rodina* (1907–16), *Skify* (1918), *Dvenadtsat* (1918).

Blom \ˈblōm\, Frans Ferdinand. 1893–1963. Danish archaeologist. Known for explorations and discovery of several lost Mayan cities.

Blom·berg \ˈblȯm-ˌberk\, Werner Eduard Fritz von. 1878–1946. German army officer. In Hitler's cabinet, minister of defense (1933–35), minister of war and commander in chief of Wehrmacht (1935–38); field marshal (1936).

Blom·field \ˈblüm-ˌfēld\, Charles James. 1786–1857. English prelate. Bishop of London (1828–56); mediator in Tractarian movement. Edited plays of Aeschylus and Greek lyric poets. His son ¶Sir Arthur William (1829–1899) was architect to Bank of England (1883); associated with Arthur Edmund Street in erection of Law Courts in London (1881); known as a restorer of churches and for his revived Gothic. Sir Arthur William's nephew ¶Sir Reginald Theodore (1856–1942), architect and author, worked chiefly in domestic and civil architecture and garden designs; designed Menin Gate and Lambeth Bridge; author of *The Formal Garden in England* (1892), *A History of Renaissance Architecture in England* (1897).

Blon·del \blōⁿ-del\. *Also* Blondel de Nesle \-də-nel\. 12th century. French trouvère. According to unfounded legend, located imprisoned Richard, Cœur de Lion, in a castle by means of a song they had jointly composed.

Blondel, François. Sieur des Croi·settes \dāk-rwä-zet\. 1618–1686. French architect. Builder of Porte St. Denis, Paris (1672); author of *Cours d'architecture* (1675–83).

Blondel, Georges. 1856–1948. French scholar. Professor at Lyon, Lille, Collège de France. Specialist in German and Austrian studies; author of *L'Essor industriel et commercial du peuple allemand* (1898), *L'Ouvrier allemand* (1899), *L'Education économique du peuple allemand* (1908), *Le triomphe du germanisme* (1934), etc.

Blondel, Jacques-François. 1705–1774. French architect. Designed city reconstruction in Metz and Strasbourg. Author of treatises on architecture, esp. historically valuable *L'Architecture française* (1752–56).

Blondel, Maurice-Édouard. 1861–1949. French philosopher. Formulated dialectical "philosophy of action" from elements of neo-Platonism, Pragmatism, and Christianity. Author of *L'Action* (1893), *L'Illusion idéaliste* (1898), *La Pensée* (1934), *Exigences philosophiques du Christianisme* (1950).

Blon·din \blōⁿ-daⁿ, *Angl* ˈblän-dēn\, Charles. *Orig.* Jean-François Gra·ve·let \gräv(-ə)-le\. 1824–1897. French tightrope walker. Achieved fame with tightrope crossings of Niagara Falls (1859 ff.).

Blondus, Flavius. See Flavio BIONDO.

Blood \ˈbləd\, Thomas. c.1618–1680. Irish adventurer. Attempted to assassinate Duke of Ormonde (1670). Arrested for stealing English crown (1671); pardoned by Charles II.

Bloom·er \ˈblü-mər\, Amelia, *nee* Jenks \ˈjeŋks\. 1818–1894. American reformer, b. Homer, N.Y. m. (1840) Dexter C. Bloomer. Wrote articles on education, unjust marriage laws, woman's suffrage. Founded and edited (1849–55) feminist paper *Lily.* Notorious as advocate of dress reform; wore the full trousers for women now known as "bloomers."

Bloom·field \ˈblüm-ˌfēld\, Leonard. 1887–1949. American linguist, b. Chicago. Nephew of Maurice Bloomfield. Professor, U. of Illinois (1914–21), Ohio State U. (1921–27), U. of Chicago (1927–40), Yale (from 1940). Studied esp. American Indian and Polynesian languages; developed behavioristic approach to language. Author of *Introduction to the Study of Language* (1914), *Menomini Texts* (1928), *Language* (1933), etc.

Bloomfield, Maurice. *Orig. surname* Blu·men·feld \ˈblü-mən-ˌfelt\. 1855–1928. American philologist, b. Bielitz, Austria. To U.S. (1859). Professor of Sanskrit and comparative philology, Johns Hopkins (1881–1926). Author of *Vedic Concordance* (1907), etc.

Bloomfield, Robert. 1766–1823. English shoemaker and poet. Author of *The Farmer's Boy* (1800), and of *Rural Tales* (1802), *Wild Flowers* (1806), *The Banks of the Wye* (1811).

Bloor \ˈblu̇(ə)r\, Ella, *nee* Reeve \ˈrēv\. *Called* Mother Bloor. 1862–1951. American Communist leader and writer, b. near Mariners Harbor, N.Y. Took name Mrs. Richard Bloor (c.1905). Joined Social Democratic party (1897); active in labor organizing; helped Upton Sinclair gather information for *The Jungle* (1906); helped organize Communist Labor party (1919); member of central committee, U.S. Communist party (1932–48). Author of *We Are Many* (1940).

Blosius, Franciscus Ludovicus. See François-Louis de BLOIS.

Blou·et \blü-e\, Paul. *Pseudonym* Max O'Rell \ó-rel\. 1848–1903. French writer. In England (from 1872). Author of *John Bull et son Île* (1883), *Les Chers Voisins* (1885), *Jonathan et son Continent* (1889), *Un Français en Amérique* (1891), etc.

Blount \'blənt\, Charles. Earl of Dev·on·shire \'dev-ən-ˌshi(ə)r, -shər\. 8th Baron Mount·joy \ˌmau̇nt-'jói\. c.1562–1606. English soldier. Fought in Netherlands; accompanied Essex and Raleigh on Azores expedition (1597); lord deputy of Ireland (1600); put down earl of Tyrone's rebellion with victory at Kinsale (1601) and subdued most of Ireland (1603). Created earl (1603).

Blount, Charles. 1654–1693. English deist and writer. Author of *Anima Mundi* (1679), *The Two First Books of Apollonius Tyaneus* (1680), etc.

Blount *or* **Blunt** \'blənt\, Edward. c.1565–after 1632. English printer. Publisher of Florio's *Italian and English Dictionary* (1596), Florio's translation of Montaigne's *Essays* (1603), first English version of *Don Quixote* (1607), and, with Isaac Jaggard, of First Folio edition of Shakespeare's works (1623).

Blount, Thomas. 1618–1679. English antiquarian and lexicographer. Author of *Glossographia* (1656), a dictionary of difficult words; *Boscobel* (1660); *Nomolexicon* (1670), a dictionary of obscure legal terms; *Ancient Tenures of Land and Jocular Customs of some manors* (1679), etc.

Blount, Sir Walter. d. 1403. English soldier. Accompanied Black Prince to Spain (1367) and, probably, John of Gaunt to Castile (1386); killed at battle of Shrewsbury when mistaken for Henry IV. Character (called "Blunt") in Shakespeare's *Henry IV.*

Blount, William. 1749–1800. American politician, b. Bertie Co., N.C. Member, Continental Congress (1782, 1783, 1786, 1787); delegate to Constitutional Convention (1787). Governor of trans-Allegheny Southwest Territory (1790–96); leader in organizing state of Tennessee; first U.S. senator from Tennessee (1796–97); expelled from Senate on charge of plotting to aid British to get control of Spanish Florida and Louisiana.

Blow \'blō\, John. 1649?–1708. English composer. Organist in Westminster Abbey (1668–79, 1695–1708); first composer to Chapel Royal (1699). Composed liturgical services, anthems, etc., including: *Ode for St. Cecilia's Day* (1684); *Ode on the Death of Mr. Henry Purcell* (1696); *Lift up your heads, O ye gates; My days are gone like a shadow; Be merciful unto me, O Lord; I was glad when they said unto me;* motet *Salvator mundi.* Also composed *Venus and Adonis* (1685), considered first true English opera.

Blow, Susan Elizabeth. 1843–1916. American educator, b. St. Louis, Mo. Opened in St. Louis first public kindergarten in U.S. (1873); translated Froebel's *Mother Play* (1895).

Bloy \blwȧ\, Léon. 1846–1917. French novelist and critic. Convert to and proselytizer for Roman Catholic church; sharp critic of modern society and a noted polemicist; friend and adviser of Huysmans, Maritain, Rouault. Works included novels *Le Désespéré* (1886), *La Femme pauvre* (1897), *Belluaires et porchers* (1905), *Le Sang du pauvre* (1909); volumes of his *Journal.*

Blü·cher \'blu̅e̅k-ər; *Angl* 'blü-kər, -chər\, Gebhard Leberecht von. Prince of Wahl·statt \'väl-ˌshtät\. *Nicknamed* Mar·schall Vor·wärts \'mär-shäl-'fōr-ˌverts, -'fòr-\, *i.e.* Marshal Forward. 1742–1819. Prussian field marshal. Entered Swedish service (1756), Prussian service (1760); discharged from army by Frederick the Great (1770); engaged in farming in Pomerania. Rejoined army as major (1787); took part in Dutch campaign; distinguished himself in campaigns against France (1793–94); lieutenant general (1801); governor of Münster (1803). Served in campaign of 1805–06, notably at Auerstedt; surrendered to French (1806) at Ratkow, near Lübeck; general and commander in Pomerania (1809–11). After outbreak of War of Liberation, led Prussian troops under Russian command at Lützen, Bautzen, Haynau, etc. (1813); commander in chief of Silesian army (Prussians and Russians). Served (1813) in war against Napoléon; defeated Macdonald at Katzbach and Marmont at Möckern; crossed the Elbe at Wartenburg; first to enter Leipzig; field marshal general. Crossed Rhine (1814) and besieged Napoléon at La Rothière; suffered defeats and forced to retreat (1814); defeated Napoléon at Laon and entered Paris (1814); created Prince of Wahlstatt. Commander of Prussian forces in Belgium (1815); defeated at Ligny; aided Wellington in victory at Waterloo.

Blü·cher \'blyük-yər\, Vasily Konstantinovich. *Orig. surname* Gu·rov \'gü-rəv\. *Pseudonym* Ga·len \'gäl-yin\. 1889–1938. Russian general. Took part in Russian Revolution (1917) and fought against Kolchak and Wrangel (1919–20); commander of forces in Russian Far East (1921–22); drove Japanese out of Vladivostok (1922); military adviser to Kuomintang, Canton (1924–27); aided Chiang Kai-shek in northern campaign (1926–28) but left him when Chiang repudiated Communists; given command in eastern Siberia (1929); developed Khabarovsk; dismissed (1938) and disappeared.

Bluh·me \'blü-mə\, Christian Albrecht. 1794–1866. Danish politician. Prime minister (1852–53, 1864–65); leader of Conservative party; signed Treaty of Vienna (1864), ceding Schleswig and Holstein to Prussia and Austria.

Blum \blüm\, Léon. 1872–1950. French politician. Joined Socialist party under Jaurès (1904); contributed political articles, drama criticism to periodicals; deputy (1919–28, 1929–40); refused association with Third International; developed program of pacifism, economic development; joined Radical-Socialists and Communists in Popular Front (1936); premier (1936–37, 1938). Arrested (1940) and imprisoned (1940–45) by Vichy government; special ambassador to U.S. (1946); head of provisional government (1946–47).

Blum \'blüm\, Robert. 1807–1848. German political agitator, writer, and orator. Liberal leader in Leipzig; organized Liberal party of Saxony; vice president, Frankfurt National Assembly (1848) and leader of leftists; addressed democrat insurgents, Vienna (1848); sentenced to death (1848).

Blu·men·bach \'blü-mən-ˌbäk\, Johann Friedrich. 1752–1840. German zoologist and anthropologist. Professor of medicine, Göttingen (1778–1835). As pioneer in study of man as species, called founder of modern anthropology; pioneer in craniology; first to classify human species as Caucasian, Mongolian, Ethiopian, American and Malayan. Author of *De generis humani varietate nativa liber* (1776), *Handbuch der Naturgeschichte* (1779), etc.

Blu·men·thal \'blü-mən-ˌtäl\, Leonhard von. Graf. 1810–1900. Prussian general. Chief of staff, Austro-Prussian forces against Denmark (1849–50, 1864), army of Crown Prince Frederick against Austria (1866), and in Franco-Prussian war (1870–71).

Blumenthal, Oskar. 1852–1917. German playwright and critic. Drama critic and editor, *Berliner Tageblatt* (1875–87); founder and director (1888–97), Lessing Theater, Berlin.

Blun·den \'blən-dən\, Edmund Charles. 1896–1974. English poet. Fellow and tutor in English literature, Merton Coll., Oxford (1931–43); professor, Tokyo U. (1924–27), Hong Kong U. (1953–64), Oxford (1966–68). Author of verse collected in *Poems, 1914–30* (1930), *Poems, 1930–40* (1940), *After the Bombing* (1948), *Poems of Many Years* (1957), *A Hong Kong House* (1962), etc., and of prose works *Undertones of War* (1928), *Life of Leigh Hunt* (1930), *The Face of England* (1932), *Charles Lamb and His Contemporaries* (1934), *English Villages* (1941), *Thomas Hardy* (1942), *Cricket Country* (1944), etc.

Blundeville, Ranulf de. See Ranulf.

Blunt. See also Blount.

Blunt \'blənt\, Anthony Frederick. 1907–1983. British art historian and spy. Surveyor of Queen's pictures (1945–72); director of Courtauld Institute (1947–74); authority on Renaissance art, Baroque architecture, and Nicolas Poussin. Spied for U.S.S.R. while with British military intelligence in World War II; exposed (1979) and stripped of knighthood.

Blunt \'blənt\, Wilfrid Scawen. 1840–1922. English poet and traveler. After travels in Near East and India, became ardent anti-imperialist and active supporter of Muslim aspirations and of nationalism in Egypt, Ireland, and India. Author of the poems *Love Sonnets of Proteus* (1880) and *Esther* (1892); a novel in verse, *Griselda* (1893); *The Future of Islam* (1882) and *Ideas About India* (1885); and *My Diaries* (1919, 1920). m. (1858) ¶Lady Anne Isabella, *nee* No·el \'nō-əl, -(ˌ)el\ (1837–1917), who traveled through North Africa, Arabia, Asia Minor with him in search of horses for their stud farm; author of *Bedouin Tribes of the Euphrates* (1879), *A Pilgrimage to Nejd* (1881).

Bluntsch·li \'blu̇nch-lē\, Johann Kaspar. 1808–1881. Swiss legal scholar. Professor, Zürich (1833–48), Munich (1848–61), Heidelberg (from 1861). One of founders (1873) of Inst. of International Law, Ghent. Chief works, *Allgemeines Staatsrecht* (1852), *Das moderne Kriegsrecht* (1866), and *Das moderne Völkerrecht* (1868), etc.

Bly, Nellie. See Elizabeth Seaman.

Blyth \'blī, 'blīth, 'blīth\, Edward. 1810–1873. English naturalist. Curator of natural history museum, Calcutta (1841–62); author of numerous papers on Indian and Burmese fauna; in articles (1833–37) for *Magazine of Natural History* anticipated Darwin by suggesting possibility of organic evolution.

Blythe, Herbert. See Maurice Barrymore.

Boabdil. See Muḥammad XI of Granada.

Boadicea. See Boudicca.

Bo·as \'bō-(ˌ)as\, Franz. 1858–1942. American anthropologist, b. Minden, Westphalia, Germany. To America (1886); carried on investigations in North America, Mexico, and Puerto Rico (1886–1931); taught at Columbia U. (from 1896; professor from 1899); curator of anthropology, American Museum of Natural History (1896–1905). Pioneer in general anthropology of 20th century; established cultural relativism as dominant viewpoint. Author of *The Mind of Primitive Man* (1911), *Kultur und Rasse* (1913), *Anthropology and Modern Life* (1928), *Race, Language and Culture* (1940), etc.

Bo·ba·di·lla \bō-bä-'thē(l)-yä\, Francisco de. d. 1502. Spanish officer. Succeeded Columbus as viceroy of Indies (1499); imprisoned Columbus (1500), sending him back to Spain in chains; recalled, under arrest, to Spain (1502).

Bob·ri·kov \'bob-ryi-kəf\, Nikolay Ivanovich. 1839–1904. Russian general. As governor general (1898–1904), ruthless in Russification of Finland.

Bo·brzyń·ski \bòb-'zhinʸ-skē\, Michał. 1849–1935. Polish historian and politician. Professor, Cracow (1877–1908); leader of pessimistic or "Cracow" school of Polish historiography. Member of diet of Galicia and of Vienna

Reichsrat; viceroy of Galicia (1908–13); Galician minister in Vienna (1916–17). Author of *Dzieje Polski* (1879), etc.

Bo·ca·ge \bü-ˈkä-zhə\, Manuel Maria Bar·bo·sa du \bär-ˈbó-zə-t͟hü-\. *Academic name* Elmano Sa·di·no \sä-ˈt͟hē-nü\. 1765–1805. Portuguese poet. Served in navy in India; joined (c.1790) Nova Arcádia group of poets; works included revolutionary and antireligious poems for which he was imprisoned (1797); published *Rimas* (1791–1804).

Boc·cac·cio \bōk-ˈkät-chō, *Angl* bō-ˈkäch-(ē-ˌ)ō\, Giovanni. 1313–1375. Italian writer, b. Paris. To Naples (by 1328) to study accounting; frequented court of Robert d'Anjou. To Florence (c.1340); lived subsequently at Ravenna (1346), Forlì (1347); formed close friendship with Petrarch, at Florence (1350); engaged in diplomatic missions for Florence (1351, 1354, 1365, 1367); appointed lecturer on Dante, in Florence (1373). Known as father of classic Italian prose, because of his celebrated collection of 100 novelle, the *Decameron* (first pub. 1353). Other works included the romance *Il filocolo* (c.1336), the verse narratives *Il filostrato* (c.1338), *Teseida* (c.1341), and *Il ninfale fiesolano* (c.1345), the pastoral romances *Il ninfale d'Ameto* (1342), *L'amorosa visione* (1342–43), and *Fiammetta amorosa* (1343–44), the prose romance *Il corbaccio* (c.1354), sonnets, a *Life of Dante* with commentary (1354–55). Helped lay foundation of Humanist scholarship with the Latin prose works *De genealogia deorum gentilium* (1351–60), *De casibus virorum illustrium* (1355–74), *De claris mulieribus* (c.1360–74), *De montibus, sylvis,* etc., and a volume of Latin eclogues. His writings have been used as source books by many subsequent writers, as Chaucer, Shakespeare, D'Annunzio.

Boc·ca·li·ni \bōk-kä-ˈlē-nē\, Traiano. 1556–1613. Italian satirist. In papal service (1584–1612). Author of satiric *ragguagli* (reports) on contemporary men and events as *Ragguagli di Parnasso* (1612–13), *Pietra del paragone* (1614); also wrote Macchiavellian work *Commentarii sopra Cornelio Tacito.*

Boc·ca·ne·gra \ˌbōk-kä-ˈnā-grä\. Wealthy and influential family of Genoa, including: Guglielmo (13th century), elected captain of the people (1257) after popular insurrection against aristocracy; concluded Treaty of Nymphaeum (1261) with Byzantine emperor Michael VIII Palaeologus; sent fleet under his brother Marino to help Byzantines recover Constantinople from Venice (1261); overthrown by Genoese nobles (1262) and exiled. A descendant of his brother Lanfranco, ¶Simon (d. 1363?), was elected first doge of Genoa (1339) following another popular insurrection; deposed (1344), regained office (1356) with aid of Visconti of Milan; according to tradition, poisoned at a banquet. His brother ¶Egidio (d. 1372) was grand admiral of Castile under Alfonso XI; defeated Moroccan fleet off Algeciras (1344). Succeeded by his son ¶Ambrogio (?–?), who defeated Portuguese at mouth of Tagus (1371) and English under earl of Pembroke at La Rochelle (1371).

Boc·che·ri·ni \bōk-kā-ˈrē-nē\, Luigi, *in full* Ridolfo Luigi. 1743–1805. Italian composer and violoncellist. Enjoyed success in Vienna (1760), Paris (1767); invited to Spanish court by Infante Don Luis (1768). Known esp. as a composer of chamber works; helped develop form of string quartet, of which he wrote 102; created string quintet, of which he wrote 125, and string and piano quintet, of which he wrote 12; also wrote 60 string trios, 27 violin sonatas, 6 cello sonatas, 18 quintets for wind and strings, 4 cello concerti, 20 symphonies, opera *La Clementina* (1786), *Stabat Mater* (1781, 1800), etc.

Boc·chus \ˈbäk-əs\. Name of two Mauretanian kings:

Bocchus. 2d–1st century B.C. King (c.118–91 B.C.). At first supported, then betrayed son-in-law Jugurtha of Numidia in war with Rome; helped Lucius Cornelius Sulla capture Jugurtha (105).

Bocchus. d. c.33 B.C. Son of Bocchus; ruled eastern Mauretania (49–c.38); supported Caesar against Pompey and rewarded (46) with control of much of Numidia; supported Mark Antony against Octavian (from 44); seized western Mauretania from brother Bogud (c.38), ruling all of country thereafter.

Boc·cio·ni \bōt-ˈchō-nē\, Umberto. 1882–1916. Italian painter and sculptor. Associated (from 1907) with Marinetti; became leading theoretician of Futurism in visual arts. Notable paintings included *Riot in the Gallery, The City Rises, States of Mind;* sculptures included *Development of a Bottle in Space, Unique Forms of Continuity in Space.*

Bo·chart \bó-shár\, Samuel. 1599–1667. French theologian and philologist. Pastor of Reformed church; author of *Geographia Sacra seu Phaleg et Chanaan* (1646), *Hierozoicon sive Bipertitum de animalibus opus Sacrae Scripturae* (1663).

Bock \ˈbók\, Fedor von. 1880–1945. German general. Commanded army groups in Poland (1939), Belgium and Netherlands (1940), Russia (1941–42); relieved by Hitler on failure to capture Moscow; again relieved after failure at Stalingrad.

Bock, Hieronymus. *Lat.* Tra·gus \ˈtrā-gəs, *Ger* ˈträ-gùs\. 1498–1554. German botanist and physician. Regarded as one of founders of science of botany. Author of *Neu Kreütterbuch* (1539), pioneering classic in descriptive botany.

Bockelson *or* **Bockold,** Jan. See BEUCKELSON.

Böckh \ˈbœ̄k\, August. 1785–1867. German classical philologist. Professor, Berlin (from 1811). Author of *Pindar* (1811–21), *Corpus Inscriptionum Graecarum* (1825–43), by which he established science of Greek epigraphy, *Zur Geschichte der Mondzyklen bei den Hellenen,* on ancient chronology (1855), etc.

Böck·lin \ˈbœk-lēn\, Arnold. 1827–1901. Swiss painter. Known for paintings of moody landscapes, sinister allegories, morbid works presaging Symbolist and Surrealist art.

Bocs·kay \ˈbōch-kói\, István. 1557–1606. Hungarian national leader and prince of Transylvania (1605–06). Led Hungarian revolutionists against Emperor Rudolf (1604–05); secured Treaty of Vienna (1606) with religious freedom to Protestants of Hungary; said to have been poisoned.

Bo·daw·pa·ya \ˌbō-dó-ˈpī-ə\. *Also known as* Min·ta·yag·yi Pa·ya \ˌmin-tä-ˈyäg-yē-ˈpī-ə\. d. 1819. King of Burma (1782–1819). Son of Alaungpaya; deposed and executed grandnephew Maung Maung; invaded Arakan (1784) and made it a province of Burma; unsuccessfully attacked Siam (1785); crushed revolt in Arakan (1794); exacerbated tension with British India by campaign in Assam. Fervent Buddhist; persecuted heterodox sects, built many pagodas.

Bo·de \ˈbōd-ə\, Johann Elert. 1747–1826. German astronomer. Director of Berlin observatory (1786–1825); author of *Uranographia* (1801), a collection of star maps and a catalogue of 17,240 stars and nebulae. Bode's law, which expresses the relative distances of the planets from the sun, though named after him, had been previously discovered by J. D. Tietz (*q.v.*).

Bode, Wilhelm von. 1845–1929. German art critic and museum director. General director of all royal museums in Prussia (1905–20). Published historical studies, notably of Dutch and Flemish paintings, Italian and German sculpture, and crafts.

Bo·del \bó-del\, Jehan. c.1167–1210. French trouvère. Author of a chanson de geste, *Chanson des Saisnes,* on the conquest of Saxony by Charlemagne; *Jeu de Saint Nicholas,* first French miracle play; pastourelles and fabliaux; and the poem *Les Congés,* a farewell to his friends and patrons as he was about to be confined in a lepers' colony.

Bo·den·heim \ˈbōd-^{ə}n-ˌhīm\, Maxwell. 1893–1954. American writer, b. Hermanville, Miss. Author of poetry, as *Minna and Myself* (1918), *Against This Age* (1925), *Bringing Jazz* (1930); fiction, as *Blackguard* (1923), *Crazy Man* (1924), *Replenishing Jessica* (1925), *Georgie May* (1927), *Naked on Roller Skates* (1931), and volumes of essays. Known esp. as literary bohemian.

Bo·den·stedt \ˈbōd-ən-ˌshtet\, Friedrich Martin von. 1819–1892. German poet and writer. Professor, Munich (from 1854); director of court theater, Meiningen (1867–73). Author of *Tausend und ein Tag im Orient* (1850), *Lieder des Mirza Schaffy* (1851), translations from Russian (Lermontov, Pushkin, Turgenev), Persian (Hafiz, Omar Khayyám) and English (Shakespeare), etc.

Bo·den·stein \ˈbōd-ən-ˌshtīn\, Andreas Rudolf. *Known as* Bodenstein von Karl·stadt \-fón-ˈkärl-ˌshtät\. c.1480–1541. German theologian. Professor, Wittenberg (1505–21); early associate and supporter of Luther; disputed Johann Eck in Leipzig (1519); mentioned in papal bull excommunicating Luther (1520); invited to Denmark by Christian II (1521). Began advocating more radical reforms; issued tract *Von Abtuhung der Bylder* (1522); as "Brother Andreas" became for a time a mystic; engaged in controversy with Luther over Eucharist, laying foundation for later Anabaptists; nonetheless harbored by Luther at Wittenberg (1525–29); professor at Basel (from 1534).

Bo·dhi·dhar·ma \ˌbōd-i-ˈdər-mə\. *Known in Chinese as* Ta-Mo \ˈtä-ˈmō\, *Japanese* Da·ru·ma \dä-rùm-ä\. 6th century. Indian Buddhist monk. To China (520) as Buddhist missionary; known as founder and first patriarch of Ch'an (Zen) sect of Buddhism.

Bo·di·chon \bó-dē-shō^{n}\, Barbara Leigh, *nee* Smith. 1827–1891. English reformer. m. (1857) Dr. Eugène Bodichon. Advocate of women's rights; a founder of Girton College, Cambridge.

Bo·din \bó-da^{n}\, Jean. 1530–1596. French political philosopher. Author of *Methodus ad facilem historiarum cognitionem* (1566) and *Six livres de la République* (1576), outlining ideal state.

Bod·ley \ˈbäd-lē\, Sir Thomas. 1545–1613. English diplomat and bibliophile. Founder of Bodleian library at Oxford (opened 1602).

Bod·mer \ˈbōd-mər\, Johann Georg. 1786–1864. Swiss mechanic and inventor. Established firearms factory (1803) using interchangeable parts; in England established factory to manufacture textile machinery (1824), machine shop (1833); patented over 40 types of machine tools including gear-cutter, steam-engine devices; credited with inventing cylinder with opposed pistons.

Bodmer, Johann Jakob. 1698–1783. Swiss scholar and critic. Professor, Zürich (1725–75); member of canton legislature (1737–83). Edited, with Breitinger, *Die Diskurse der Mahlern* (1721–23), a weekly critical journal modeled after Addison's *Spectator.* Awakened interest in Germany in Middle High German and English literature, notably by his editions of *Paradise Lost* (1732) and part of *Nibelungenlied* (1757) and his studies on the Minnesingers (1758–59). Author of *Von dem Einfluss und Gebrauche der Einbildungskraft* (1727), *Von dem Wunderbaren in der Poesie* (1740), etc.

Bo·do·ni \bō-'dō-nē\, Giambattista. 1740–1813. Italian printer and type designer. Directed Stamperia Reale, press of Duke of Parma (from 1768). Among first to design modern typefaces; designed type known as Bodoni (1790); published editions of Homer's *Iliad,* Virgil, Horace, and multilingual edition of Lord's Prayer.

Boë, Franz de le. See DELEBOE.

Boé \bō-ā\, Jacques. *Pseudonym* Jacques Jas·min \zhä-smaⁿ\. 1798–1864. French poet. Barber and wigmaker by trade; attracted wide attention with touching verses in his native langue d'oc dialect on homely subjects, esp. "L'Abuglo de Castel-Culié" contained in first volume of his *Papillotos* (1835, 1842, 1851, 1863); other collections were *Lou Chilibari* (1825), *Mous soubenis* (1830); popular as public reader of his verse.

Boece. See also BOETHIUS.

Bo·ece \bō-'ēs\ *or* **Bo·e·thi·us** \bō-'ē-thē-əs\, Hector. *Also sometimes* Boyce \'bȯis\. *Family name* Boyis \'bȯis\. c.1465–c.1536. Scottish historian. Friend of Erasmus; first principal, U. of Aberdeen (1505). Known for his fabulous and legendary *Scotorum historiae a prima gentis origine* (1527).

Boehm. See also BÖHM.

Boehm \'bām, 'bœm\, Sir Joseph Edgar. 1834–1890. British sculptor, b. Vienna. Removed to London (1862) as portrait sculptor; produced busts, figures, and equestrian statues, including sarcophagus of Dean Stanley in Westminster Abbey and Wellington statue at Hyde Park Corner; designed queen's likeness on coinage (1887).

Boehme *or* **Boehm,** Jakob. See Jakob BÖHME.

Boe·ing \'bō-iŋ, 'bȯ(-)iŋ\, William Edward. 1881–1956. American industrialist, b. Detroit. Founded (1916) Pacific Aero Products Co., renamed (1917) Boeing Airplane Co.; firm grew into a major manufacturer of military and commercial aircraft, including Clipper flying boat (1938), B-17 Flying Fortress (1935), B-29 Superfortress (1942), B-52 Stratofortress (1952), Boeing 707 commercial jetliner (1957), etc.

Boer·haa·ve \'bür-,hä-və\, Hermann. 1668–1738. Dutch physician. Professor, Leiden (from 1708); renowned as a teacher, credited with founding modern system of clinical instruction. Author of *Institutiones medicae in usus annuae exercitationis domesticos digestae* (1708) and *Aphorismi de cognoscendis et curandis morbis* (1709), encyclopedic medical books widely translated; *Elementa chemiae* (1724); etc.

Bo·e·thi·us \bō-'ē-thē-əs\, Anicius Manlius Severinus. c.480–524. Roman philosopher. Friend of Theodoric, Ostrogoth ruler of Rome, who made him consul (510); head of government and court services (c.520); later, accused of conspiring against Theodoric, arrested, imprisoned at Pavia, and finally executed without trial. His greatest work, *De consolatione philosophiae* (*The Consolation of Philosophy*), written in prison at Pavia. Translated and wrote commentaries on several of Aristotle's works and wrote independent treatises on logic, arithmetic, music, and theology.

Boethius, Hector. See BOECE.

Bo·ë·thus \bō-'ē-thəs\. 2d century B.C. Greek sculptor. Known for his genre pieces, esp. for a group representing a boy struggling with a goose.

Boétie, Étienne de la. See Étienne de LA BOÉTIE.

Bof·frand \bȯ-fräⁿ\, Germain, *in full* Gabriel-Germain. 1667–1754. French architect. Architect to the king (1690); inspector general of roads and bridges in France (1732). Decorated Hôtel de Soubise, enlarged Palais Bourbon, restored Hôtel des Premiers Presidents; for duke of Lorraine restored ancient palace of Nantes and planned new one; directed construction of Paris Arsenal (1718–28), restored chamber of Palais de Justice; built episcopal palace of Würzburg (1724), Hospice des Enfants for Paris Hospital (1727); restored rose window in transept of Notre-Dame de Paris (1725–27); directed construction of bridges at Sens and Montereau; built many chateaux and houses.

Bo·gan \'bō-,gan\, Louise. 1897–1970. American poet, b. Livermore Falls, Me. Author of *Body of This Death* (1923), *Dark Summer* (1929), *The Sleeping Fury* (1937), *Collected Poems* (1954), *Blue Estuaries* (1968), *A Poet's Alphabet* (1970); also criticism *Achievement in American Poetry* (1951), *Selected Criticism* (1955).

Bo·gan·da \bō-'gän-də, -'gan-\, Barthélémy. 1910–1959. African politician. Nationalist leader in Oubangi-Chari; member of French National Assembly (from 1946); president of grand council, French Equatorial Africa (1957); laid groundwork for creation of Central African Republic (1958).

Bo·gar·dus \bō-'gärd-əs\, James. 1800–1874. American inventor, b. Catskill, N.Y. Inventor of a dry gas meter, engraving machines, and esp. a system of building construction based on cast-iron load-bearing columns; built first such building (1848) and manufactured prefabricated cast-iron frames for others.

Bo·gart \'bō-,gärt, -gərt\, Humphrey De Forest. 1899–1957. American actor, b. New York City. Starred on Broadway in *Petrified Forest* (1934); in films *Petrified Forest* (1936), *San Quentin* (1937), *High Sierra* (1941), *Maltese Falcon* (1942), *Casablanca* (1942), *To Have and Have Not* (1944), *The Big Sleep* (1946), *Key Largo* (1948), *Treasure of the Sierra Madre* (1948), *The African Queen* (1951, Academy Award), *The Caine Mutiny* (1954), *The Harder They Fall* (1956).

Bog·da·no·vich \bəg-(,)də-'nȯv-,yich\, Ippolit Fyodorovich. 1744–1803. Russian poet. Known esp. for sentimental poem *Duschenka* (1778–83).

Bo·go·raz \bə-(,)gə-'räz\, Vladimir Germanovich. *Pseudonyms* N. A. Tan \'tän\ *and* V.G. Tan. 1865–1936. Russian ethnographer. Exiled to Siberia for political activity (1886); began study of Siberian peoples and languages; contributed studies to Russian Geographical Society (1895–97), U.S. Jessup North Pacific Expedition (1900–01); to U.S. as a curator, American Museum of Natural History (1901–04); on return to Russia helped organize first peasant congress and Duma; professor and curator, Petrograd (from 1918). Author of *The Chukchee* (1904–09), *Chukchee Mythology* (1910), grammars, dictionary, textbooks, etc. of and for Chukchi.

Bo·gu·sław·ski \bȯ-gü-'släf-skē\, Wojciech. 1757–1829. Polish actor and playwright. Regarded as creator of the Polish theater; director of Polish National Theater, Warsaw (1783–1814); wrote some 80 plays, esp. comedies as *Cud czyli, Krakowiacy i górale* (1794).

Bo·he·mond \bȯ-ā-mōⁿ, *Angl* 'bō-ə-mənd\. Name of seven princes of Antioch:

Bohemond I. *Orig. name* Marc. c.1050 or 1058–1111. Son of Robert Guiscard; fought in father's wars; captured Avlona (1081); engaged (from 1081) in struggle with Byzantines under Alexius I Comnenus; joined First Crusade (1096); distinguished himself in capture of Antioch (1098) and became de facto ruler; remained after departure of other Crusaders; captured in unsuccessful attack on emir of Sebastea (1099); released (1103); journeyed to Rome, France (1105–06) enlisting support for struggle against Greeks; m. (1106) Constance, daughter of Philip I of France; commenced war on Greeks at Avlona, Durazzo, etc. (1107); offered peace by Alexius, becoming recognized prince of Antioch in return for vassalage (1107).

Bohemond II. 1109–1130. Prince (1126–30). Son of Bohemond I; succeeded to principality after regency of Baldwin II of Jerusalem. Died in battle with Turks.

Bohemond III. *Called* le Bègue \lə-beg\, *i.e.* the Stammerer. 1145–1201. Prince (1163–1201). Son of Raymond I of Poitiers and grandson of Bohemond II.

Bohemond IV. *Called* le Borgne \lə-bȯrnʸ\, *i.e.* the One-Eyed. d.1233. Prince (1201–33). Son of Bohemond III; adopted by Raymond III of Tripoli, whom he succeeded as count of Tripoli (1187); forcefully succeeded to Antioch, excluding his nephew Raymond Rhupen, grandson of Leo II of Armenia.

Bohemond V. c.1198–1252. Prince (1233–51) and count of Tripoli (1233–51). Son of Bohemond IV.

Bohemond VI. *Called* le Beau \lə-bō\, *i.e.* the Fair. c.1235–1275. Prince (1251–68) and count of Tripoli (1255–75). Son of Bohemond V; weak ruler; lived in Tripoli; lost Antioch to Turks (1268).

Bohemond VII. c.1255–1287. Count of Tripoli (1275–87) and titular prince of Antioch. Son of Bohemond VI; died shortly before Mamlūk conquest of Tripoli.

Böh·lau \'bœ-,lau̇\, Helene. 1859–1940. German novelist. Works included *Ratsmädelgeschichten* (1888), *Im frischen Wasser* (1891), *Der Rangierbahnhof* (1895), *Das Recht der Mutter* (1897), *Halbtier* (1899).

Boh·len \'bō-lən\, Charles Eustis. 1904–1974. American diplomat, b. Clayton, N.Y. Entered U.S. foreign service (1929); expert on Russian affairs; ambassador to U.S.S.R. (1953–57), to the Philippines (1957–59), and to France (1962–68). Author of memoir, *Witness to History 1929–1969* (1973).

Böhl de Fa·ber \'bœl-t͟hā-'fä-b͟er\, Cecilia. *Pseudonym* Fernán Ca·ba·lle·ro \kä-b͟äl-'yā-rō\. 1796–1877. Spanish novelist. Daughter of Johann Böhl von Faber. Lived in Spain (from 1813); helped found literary realism in Spanish. Works included *La gaviota* (1849), *La familia de Alvareda* (1856), *Relaciones* (1857), and volume of sketches *Cuadros de costumbres populares andaluzas* (1852).

Böhl von Faber \'bœl-fȯn-'fäb-ər\, Johann Nikolaus. 1770–1836. German merchant and critic. Published collection of Spanish verse *Floresta de rimas antiguas castellanas* (1821–25) and *Teatro español anterior a Lope de Vega* (1832).

Böhm \'bœm\, Georg. 1661–1733. German organist and composer. Church organist at Lüneburg (from 1698); composed works for harpsichord and organ; strongly influenced Bach.

Böhm, Karl. 1894–1981. Austrian conductor. Conductor at Munich Staatsoper (1921–27); musical director, Darmstadt (1927–31), Hamburg (1931–34), Dresden (1934–43), Vienna Staatsoper (1943–45, 1954–56); won international reputation esp. as interpreter of Mozart, Wagner, Strauss; conducted premieres of Strauss's *Die schweigsame Frau* (1935), *Daphne* (1938).

Böhm, Theobald. 1794–1881. German flutist and composer. Court musician, Munich (1818); began manufacturing woodwind instruments (1828); developed Böhm flute (1832) featuring key and ring mechanisms that made possible acoustically superior flutes; also introduced fingering system later improved by Auguste Buffet; introduced new cylindrical flute design (1847) that became standard.

Böhm-Ba·werk \'bœm-'bä-,verk\ *or* **Böhm von Bawerk,** Eugen. 1851–1914. Austrian economist and politician. Minister of finance (1895, 1897–98, 1900–04). Cofounder of so-called Austrian school, which advanced theory of a system of value based upon the final utility; introduced theory of interest. Author of *Kapital und Kapitalzins* (1884–89), etc.

Böh·me \'bœ-mə\, Jakob. 1575–1624. German mystic. Settled in Görlitz as shoemaker (c.1594). Underwent mystical experience (1600); read works of alchemists, Paracelsus, etc. Author of *Aurora, oder die Morgenröte im Aufgang* (1612; pub. 1634), manuscript of which condemned as heretical by ecclesiastical authorities, and of *Die drei Prinzipien des göttlichen Wesens* (1619), *Mysterium Magnum* (1623), *Von der Gnadenwahl* (1623), *Der Weg zu Christo* (1624), etc. His philosophy, concerned especially with problem of evil, rested on thesis of dualism of God. His writings translated into other languages, notably English; strongly influential on development of idealism, Romanticism, theology esp. of Quakers and Pietists.

Böh·mer \'bœ-mər\, Johann Friedrich. 1795–1863. German historian. Archivist (1825), head librarian (1830) of Frankfurt. Compiled 6-volume *Regesta imperii* (1831 ff.), annotated collection of documents of imperial Germany from 911 A.D.; also *Fontes rerum germanicarum* (1843–68).

Böhm-Er·mol·li \'bœm-'er-mō-lē\, Eduard von. Freiherr. 1856–1941. Austrian general. Led army in Serbia and Galicia during World War I; distinguished himself at Lemberg (1915); led summer offensive against Russians (1917); field marshal general (1918); commanded forces in Ukraine and later France (1918).

Bohn \'bōn\, Henry George. 1796–1884. English publisher. Issued "guinea catalog" of old books (1841); republished at cheap rate "libraries" of standard works and translations in history, science, philosophy, theology, etc. (1846 ff.); revised Lowndes's *Bibliographer's Manual of English Literature* (1864).

Bo·ho·mo·lec \bō-kō-'mō-lets\, Franciszek. 1720–1784. Polish writer and scholar. Jesuit priest; professor at Jesuit college, Warsaw (from 1752); wrote several student plays and (from 1766) comedies for Warsaw Theater, as *Małżeństwo 2 kalendarza, Czary,* and *Pan dobry.* Edited literary magazine *Monitor* (1764–84).

Bohr \'bōr, *Angl* 'bō(ə)r, 'bȯ(ə)r\, Harald August. 1887–1951. Danish mathematician. Brother of Niels Bohr. Professor, Polytechnic Inst., Copenhagen (1915–30), U. of Copenhagen (1930 ff.); formulated Bohr-Landau theorem (1914, with E. Landau) on Riemann zeta functions; formulated theory of almost periodic functions.

Bohr, Niels Henrik David. 1885–1962. Danish physicist. Professor, Copenhagen (1916); head of Institute of Theoretical Physics (1920–62). Proposed a theory of atomic structure utilizing Planck's quantum theory; explained spectral lines of hydrogen by proposing nuclear atom whose electrons could exist only in discrete energy states, the transitions from state to state yielding emissions of specific wavelength. Awarded 1922 Nobel prize for physics. Renowned as a teacher.

Böht·lingk \'bœt-,liŋk\, Otto von. 1815–1904. German scholar. Member of Russian Imperial Academy of Sciences (from 1842); published edition of Sanskrit grammar of Pāṇini (1839–42); author of *Über die Sprache der Jakuten* (1851); with Rudolf von Roth, Albrecht Weber, et al., compiled 7-volume *Sanskrit-Wörterbuch* (1853–73).

Bohun, de \də-'bün\. Name of an Anglo-Norman family, long resident on the Welsh Marches, including Humphrey de Bohun (d. 1187), supporter of Henry II in the rebellion of Prince Henry, "the Young King" (1173). His grandson ¶Henry (1176–1220), made (1199) 1st earl of Her·e·ford \'her-ə-fərd\; one of barons who obtained Magna Carta from King John (1215); died on pilgrimage to Holy Land (1220). His successors fluctuated between loyalty to the king and defiance of the king in baronial cause. The 2d earl, ¶Humphrey V (d. 1274), created earl of Es·sex \'es-iks\, joining federation of barons (1258) and joining king against de Montfort (1263). His grandson the 3d earl, ¶Humphrey VII (d. 1298), joined earl of Norfolk in refusing to serve in Gascony (1297). The 4th earl, ¶Humphrey VIII (1276–1322), also 3d earl of Essex, was taken prisoner as a follower of king at Bannockburn (1314) and slain as a baronial supporter at Boroughbridge. The male line was extinguished on death of ¶Humphrey X (d. 1373), who had inherited earldom of Northampton from his father.

Bo·iar·do \bō-'yär-dō\, Matteo Maria. Conte di Scan·dia·no \skän-'dyä-nō\. 1441?–1494. Italian poet. Known esp. for his uncompleted historical epic *Orlando Innamorato* (1487) in which he treated Carolingian epic material in the style of the Arthurian cycle of romances and which served as point of departure for Ariosto's *Orlando Furioso;* wrote other works in Latin and Italian, as *Amorum libri tres* (1499).

Boie \'bȯi-ə\, Heinrich Christian. 1744–1806. German writer. Member of Göttinger Dichter-Bundes group of poets; founded (1776) *Deutsche Museum* (from 1789 *Neue Deutsche Museum*) literary journal.

Bo·iel·dieu \bȯ-yel-dyœ\, François-Adrien. 1775–1834. French composer. Professor, Paris Conservatory (1798–1804, 1820–34); director of opera, St. Petersburg (1804–10); director of music to Louis XVIII (1816 ff.). Composer of piano music and esp. of musical scores of comic operas, as *Les Deux Lettres* (1796), *La Famille suisse* (1797), *Le Calife de Bagdad* (1800), *Ma Tante Aurore* (1803), *Jean de Paris* (1812), *Le Petit Chaperon rouge* (1818), *La Dame blanche* (1825), etc. Frequent collaborator with Cherubini, Isouard, Kreutzer, and others.

Boi·leau \bwȧ-lō\, Nicolas. *Called* Boileau-Des·pré·aux \-dā-prā-ō\. 1636–1711. French critic and poet. Author of *Satires* (1666), several volumes of *Épîtres* (beginning 1669), and *L'Art poétique* (1674), considered definitive statement of principles of classic French verse.

Boil·ly \bwȧ-yē\, Louis-Léopold. 1761–1845. French painter and lithographer. Known for genre scenes, satirical depictions of Parisian manners, portraits, as *Triomphe de Marat, Jardin des Tuileries, Le Sculpteur Houdon dans son atelier.*

Boisbaudran, Lecoq de. See LECOQ DE BOISBAUDRAN.

Bois·guil·le·bert \bwȧ-gē(-yə)-ber\, Pierre Le Pe·sant de \lə-pə-zäⁿ-də-\. Sieur de Boisguillebert. 1646–1714. French economist. Anticipated principal teachings of 18th-century Physiocrats; opposed Colbert.

Bois-Reymond, Du. See DU BOIS-REYMOND.

Bois·ro·bert \bwȧ-rō-ber\, François Le Mé·tel de \lə-mā-tel-də-\. Seigneur de Boisrobert. 1589–1662. French poet. Friend of Richelieu; assisted in establishment of French Academy (1634). Author of paraphrase of Psalms (1627), novel *Histoire indienne d'Anaxandre et d'Orazie* (1627), tragicomedy *Pyrandre et Zysimène* (1633), panegyric verse, etc.

Bois·sy d'An·glas \bwȧ-sē-däⁿ-gläs\, François-Antoine de. Comte. 1756–1826. French politician. Member of Estates-General (1789); member of Convention (1792), voted against death of king and aided in overthrow of Robespierre; member of Committee of Public Safety (1795); president of Council of Five Hundred; senator (1805) under Napoléon and peer of France (1814) under Louis XVIII.

Bo·i·to \'bō-ē-tō\, Arrigo, *orig.* Enrico Giuseppe Giovanni. 1842–1918. Italian composer and librettist. Known chiefly for his opera *Mefistofele* (1868; rev. 1875); wrote texts for Verdi's *Hymn of the Nations* (1862), *Otello* (1887), *Falstaff* (1893), for Ponchielli's *La gioconda* (1876), etc. Author also of several novels under the anagram To·bio Gor·ria \tō-'bē-ō-'gȯr-ryä\.

Bojangles. See Bill ROBINSON.

Bojardo. See BOIARDO.

Boj·er \'bȯi-ər\, Johan. 1872–1959. Norwegian novelist. Novels included *Et folketog* (1896), *Troens magt* (1903), *Den store hunger* (1916), *Den siste viking* (1921), *Vor egen stamme* (1924), *Folk ved sjøen* (1929).

Bo·jo Guk·sa \'bōz-'yō-'gu̇k-'sä\. *Secular name* Chi-nui \'shē-'nü-ē\. 1158–1210. Korean Buddhist leader. Founded (1200) Chogye-jong sect, strongly influenced by Zen Buddhism.

Bok \'bäk\, Edward William. 1863–1930. American editor, b. Den Helder, Netherlands. To U.S. (1870); organized (1886) Bok Syndicate to handle publication of Henry W. Beecher's sermons; developed "Bok page" of syndicated women's features; editor in chief, *The Ladies' Home Journal* (1889–1919). Led campaigns against patent medicines, for public beautification, pure food and drug regulation, public health, etc. Established (1923) Bok peace prize. Author of autobiography *The Americanization of Edward Bok* (1920, Pulitzer prize).

Bokelson, Jan. See BEUCKELSON.

Bok·e·nam *or* **Bok·en·ham** \'bək-ə-nəm\, Osbern. 1392?–?1447. English poet. Author of verse *Legends of Holy Women,* based on Latin originals.

Bol·den \'bōl-dən\, Charles Joseph, *called* Buddy. 1877–1931. American musician, b. New Orleans. Cornettist and leader of several New Orleans bands in 1890s; sometimes regarded as father of jazz.

Bol·di·ni \bōl-'dē-nē\, Giovanni. 1845–1931. Italian painter. In France (from c.1867) a fashionable portraitist.

Boldrewood, Rolf. See Thomas Alexander BROWNE.

Bo·le·slav \'bō-lə-,släf\. Name of three princes of Bohemia:

Boleslav I. *Sometimes called* the Cruel. d. 967. Prince (929–967). Arranged murder of elder brother Vaclav (St. Wenceslas) to gain throne; promoted Christianity; gained control of Moravia, Slovakia, Silesia; forced to acknowledge suzerainty of Emperor Otto I (950); aided Otto against Magyars, esp. at Lechfeld (955).

Boleslav II. d. 999. Prince (967–999). Son of Boleslav I; engaged in rebellion against Otto II (975–978).

Boleslav III. d. 1037. Prince (999–1003).

Bo·le·slav·sky \ˌbō-lə-ˈsläv-skē, -ˈsläf-\, Richard. *Orig.* Bo·le·sław·ski \bó-le-ˈsláf-skē\. 1889–1937. American film and stage director, b. Warsaw, Poland. To U.S. (1920); staged *Vagabond King* (1925), *White Eagle* (1927), *Ballyhoo* (1927), *Mr. Moneypenny* (1928); directed films including *Rasputin and the Empress* (1932), *Les Misérables* (1935).

Bo·le·sław \bó-ˈle-sláf\. Name of four rulers of Piast dynasty of Poland:

Bolesław I. *Called* Chro·bry \ˈk̲rô-bri\, *i.e.* the Brave. 966 or 967–1025. Succeeded father Mieszko as prince of Great Poland (992); conquered Pomerania and Kraków (996); crowned first king of Poland by Emperor Otto III (1000); obtained independent archdiocese for Polish church; after Otto's death (1002) seized Lusatia, Meissen, Bohemia; after lengthy war against Emperor Henry II, made peace of Bautzen (1018), much to Poland's advantage; placed son-in-law Svyatopolk on throne of Kiev (1018).

Bolesław II. *Called* the Bold *and* the Generous. 1039–1081. King (1058–81). Son of Casimir I; ally of Béla I of Hungary and Pope Gregory VII against Emperor Henry IV; placed relative Izyaslav on throne of Kiev (1069); following second intervention in Kiev (1077) faced revolt of nobles; executed St. Stanisław, bishop of Cracow (1079); forced into exile.

Bolesław III. *Called* Krzy·wo·us·ty \kshi-vó-ˈü-sti\, *i.e.* the Wry-mouthed. 1085–1138. Prince of Poland (1102–38). Son of Władysław I Herman; fought long war with brother Zbigniew for control of Poland; attempted to conquer Pomerania (1113–35), gaining control only on swearing fealty to Emperor Lothair II (1135). Devised seniority system for dividing realm among sons.

Bolesław IV. *Called* Ked·zie·rza·wy \kädz-yā-ˈzhá-vi\, *i.e.* the Curly. d. 1173. Duke or king of Mazovia. Son of Bolesław III; assumed seniority among Polish princes on exile of elder brother Władysław II (1146); lost Silesia to Frederick I Barbarossa; succeeded as senior by another brother (1073).

Bol·eyn \bu̇-ˈlin, ˈbu̇l-ən\ *or* **Bul·len** \ˈbu̇l-ən\, Anne. 1507?–1536. Second queen of Henry VIII. Attached to service of Queen Claude of France (c.1519–22); became mistress of Henry (1527); secretly married to him (1533), whereupon Henry's marriage to Catherine of Aragon declared null by Archbishop Cranmer; gave birth to future Queen Elizabeth I (Sept. 1533). Charged with adultery, convicted, and beheaded.

Bolingbroke, 1st Viscount. See Henry St. John.

Bo·lí·var \bō-ˈlē-b̲är; *Angl* bə-ˈlē-ˌvär, ˈbäl-ə-vər\, Simon. *Known as* El Li·ber·ta·dor \el-lē-b̲er-tä-ˈt͟hȯr\, *i.e.* the Liberator. 1783–1830. South American soldier, statesman, and revolutionary leader, b. Caracas, Venezuela. Fought under Miranda in revolt against Spanish in Venezuela (1811–12); compelled to flee to New Granada; raised army, planned and led expedition, and seized Caracas (1813); finally defeated in Venezuela and left for Cartagena (1814); captured Bogotá (1814) but defeated and went into exile in Jamaica. Fled to Haiti and planned another revolution; raised small army, including many English and Irish soldiers, and won allegiance of other rebel groups, notably those led by José Antonio Páez and Francisco de Paula Santander; entered New Granada and defeated Spanish at Boyacá (Aug. 1819); made president and military dictator of new republic of Colombia and given almost supreme power (1819); won battle of Carabobo (June 1821), final victory for independence of Venezuela, which became a province of Gran Colombia. Marched south to Quito (1821) and Peru; arrived in Callao (Sept. 1823) after Gen. San Martín had resigned and left the country; defeated Spanish in battle of Junín (Aug. 1824), which victory, with that of Sucre at Ayacucho (Dec. 1824), freed Peru from Spain. President (actually dictator) of Peru (1824–27); visited Upper Peru (1825), organizing new republic (named Bolivia after him); organized general congress of American states at Panama (1826). On outbreak of New Granada–Venezuela civil war (1827) returned to Bogotá; resumed presidency of Colombia (1828) and called constitutional convention; assumed dictatorial powers; escaped assassination (1828); faced revolts, Peruvian invasion, Venezuelan secession; resigned as supreme chief of Colombia (1830).

Böll \ˈbœl\, Heinrich Theodor. 1917–1985. West German author. Leading literary figure in postwar West Germany; joined (1950) Gruppe 47 writers, who strove to restore German literature to its pre-Nazi traditions. Author of novels *Der Zug war pünktlich* (1949), *Billard um halb zehn* (1959), *Ansichten eines Clowns* (1963), *Ende einer Dienstfahrt* (1966), *Gruppenbild mit Dame* (1971), *Die verlorene Ehre der Katherina Blum* (1975); also wrote short stories, radio plays, essays, translations. Critical of postwar materialism and consumerism and collective amnesia about Nazism. Awarded Nobel prize for literature (1972).

Bol·land \ˈbäl-änt, *Fr* bȯ-läⁿ, *Angl* ˈbäl-ənd\, Jean de. *Lat.* Bollandus. 1596–1665. Flemish Jesuit hagiologist. Editor (from 1629) of *Acta Sanctorum,* or *Lives of the Saints;* issued parts for *January* (1643), *February* (1658); work continued by his collaborators and successors, known as Bollandists.

Bologna, Giovanni da. See Giambologna.

Bolton, Dukes and Duchess of. See Paulet; Lavinia Fenton.

Bol·ton *or* **Boul·ton** \ˈbōlt-ᵊn\, Edmund. 1575?–?1633. English poet and antiquarian. Author of history *Nero Caesar* (1624), historiographic treatise *Hypercritica,* and verses included in miscellany *Englands Helicon* (1600).

Bolton, Guy Reginald. 1884–1979. English playwright. Author of plays and musical comedies, often in collaboration with P. G. Wodehouse, including *Sally, Dark Angel, Lady Be Good, Polly Preferred, Anything Goes, Seeing Stars, Swing Along, Magyar Melody, Hold Onto Your Hats, Follow the Girls, Music at Midnight, Girl Crazy, Anastasia, Simple Simon,* etc.; also wrote film scripts as *'Till the Clouds Roll By, Words and Music, Jennie Kissed Me.*

Bolton, Herbert Eugene. 1870–1953. American historian, b. Wilton Township, Wis. Professor at U. of Texas (1901–09), Stanford (1909–11), U. of Calif., Berkeley (1911–53); director, Bancroft Library (1916–40). Works included *Colonization of North America 1492–1783* (1920, with T. M. Marshall), *Spanish Borderlands* (1921), *Outpost of Empire* (1931), *Rim of Christendom* (1936), *Coronado on the Turquoise Trail* (1949).

Bolt·wood \ˈbōlt-ˌwu̇d\, Bertram Borden. 1870–1927. American scientist, b. Amherst, Mass. Professor, Yale (1897–1900, 1910–27). Specialist in field of radioactivity; discoverer of ionium, isotope of thorium; developed radiometric dating method for uranium-bearing rocks (1907).

Boltz·mann \ˈbōlt-ˌsmän\, Ludwig Eduard. 1844–1906. Austrian physicist. Won recognition in Germany of Maxwell's electromagnetic theory of light; deduced (1884) Stefan's, or Stefan-Boltzmann, law relating to radiation from a black body; known esp. for development of statistical mechanics relating thermodynamic laws to probability analyses of atomic or molecular motion; derived (1871) Maxwell-Boltzmann law of equipartition of energy.

Bo·lyai \ˈbȯl-yȯi\, Farkas. 1775–1856. Hungarian mathematician. Professor, Evangelical-Reformed College of Marosvásárhely (1804–53); spent entire life attempting to prove Euclid's parallel-line postulate; wrote *Tentamen Juventutem Studiosam in Elementa Matheseos Purae Introducendi* (1832–33) in which fundamentals of geometry treated in new way. His son ¶ János (1802–1860) concluded (1820) the parallel-line postulate could not be proved and then developed consistent non-Euclidean geometry outlined in *Appendix Scientiam Spatii Absolute Veram Exhibens* (1823).

Bol·za·no \bȯlt-ˈsä-nō\, Bernhard, *in full* Bernardus Placidus Johann Nepomuk. 1781–1848. Austrian theologian, philosopher, and mathematician. Professor, Prague (1805–19); known esp. for contributions to theory of mathematical proofs and fundamental theorems of geometry, arithmetic, analysis.

Bom·bast von Ho·hen·heim \ˈbȯm-ˌbäst-fȯn-ˈhō-ən-ˌhīm\, Philippus Aureolus Theophrastus. *Known as* Par·a·cel·sus \ˌpar-ə-ˈsel-səs\. 1493–1541. German alchemist and physician, b. Einsiedeln, Switzerland. Investigated mechanics of mining, minerals, and diseases of miners, in mines of Tirol; wandered (c.1510–24) throughout Europe, Russia, and Middle East; forced to leave U. of Basel because of his defiance of tradition, as lecturing in German and criticizing classical writers (1527–28); practiced at various places in Germany and Switzerland, finally settling in Salzburg; opposed humoral theory of disease, believing that diseases are specific entities and can be cured by specific remedies; emphasized value of observation and experience; first to connect goiter with minerals in drinking water; first to describe silicosis and the congenital form of syphilis; introduced use of therapeutic mineral baths and of opium, mercury, lead, sulphur, iron, arsenic, and copper sulphate as medicinal substances, thus establishing the role of chemistry in medicine. Author of medical and occult works, esp. *Die grosse Wundartzney* (1536).

Bom·berg \ˈbȯm-berk̲\, Daniel. 1470 or 1480–?1550. Dutch printer. Established printing business in Venice (1515); issued great *Biblia rabbinica* (1516–17) and first full text of Babylonian Talmud.

Bo·nac·cor·si \bō-näk-ˈkȯr-sē\, Pietro. *Known as* Pe·ri·no del Va·ga \pe-ˈrē-nō-del-ˈvä-gä\. 1501–1547. Italian painter. Associated with Raphael in Rome; instrumental in transmitting Roman style to Genoa.

Bo·nald \bȯ-náld\, Louis-Gabriel-Ambroise de. Vicomte. 1754–1840. French publicist and philosopher. An émigré during French Revolution; returned to France; member of council of public instruction (1814), viscount (1821), peer (1823); a leader of Legitimists. Author of *Théorie du pouvoir politique et religieux* (1796), *Essai analytique sur les lois naturelles de l'ordre social* (1800), *Réflexions sur l'intérêt général de l'Europe* (1815), etc.

Bo·na·parte \bȯ-ná-párt, *Angl* ˈbō-nə-ˌpärt\. *It.* Buo·na·par·te \ˌbwȯn-ä-ˈpär-tā\. A Corsican family of Italian origin to which belonged Napoléon I, Emperor of the French. Napoléon's parents were ¶Carlo Buonaparte (1746–1785), a Corsican lawyer, and Maria Letizia Ra·mo·li·no \rä-mō-ˈlē-nō\ (1750–1836). Their children (in chronological order) were:

(1) ¶Joseph (1768–1844); took part in Italian campaign (1796), French recovery of Corsica (1796); minister to court of Parma (1797); member of Council of Five Hundred (1798); councilor of state (1799); presided over diplomatic negotiations with U.S. (1800), Austria (1801), Britain (1802). Wished to be named Napoléon's heir. Head of French government in Napoléon's absence (1805–06); made by Napoléon king of Naples (1806–08), king of Spain (1808–14); resident in U.S. (1815–32) under name of Comte de Sur·vil·liers \sür-vēl-yā\.

(2) ¶Napoléon (1769–1821); see NAPOLÉON I.
(3) ¶Maria-Anna, *called* Élisa (1777–1820); made by Napoléon princess of Luc·ca \'lük-kä\ and Piom·bi·no \pyōm-'bē-nō\ (1805), grand duchess of Tus·ca·ny \'təs-kə-nē\ (1809).
(4) ¶Lucien (1775–1840); active in Jacobin cause on Corsica (from 1789); as president of Council of Five Hundred (1799) ensured Napoléon's election as consul of France; ambassador to Madrid (1800); negotiated peace treaty between Spain and Portugal (1801); exiled for opposing Napoléon's policies and for marrying against Napoléon's wish; on way to U.S., captured by English (1810); held as prisoner of state in England; created prince of Ca·ni·no \kä-'nē-nō\ (1814). Among his eleven children were:
(a) ¶Charles-Lucien-Jules-Laurent (1803–1857), Prince of Canino and of Mu·si·gna·no \mü-zēn-'yä-nō\; naturalist; resident of Philadelphia (1822–28); took part in Roman uprising against Austria (1848). Author of *American Ornithology* (1825–33), *Conspectus systematis* (1850), *Tableau des oiseaux-mouches* (1854), *Ornithologie fossile* (1858).
(b) ¶Louis-Lucien (1813–1891); phonetician and philologist; investigator of English and Basque languages; created prince (1863) by Napoléon III.
(c) ¶Pierre-Napoléon (1815–1881); declared himself a republican; leftist member of Chamber of Deputies (1848); nonetheless accepted coup d'état of cousin Napoléon III (1851); created prince (1852) by Napoléon III; shot journalist Victor Noir (1870) but acquitted of murder. Pierre's son ¶Prince Roland (1858–1924) was a geographer.
(5) ¶Louis (1778–1846); took part in Italian (1796–97) and Egyptian (1798–99) campaigns; m. (1802) Hortense de Beauharnais, daughter of Joséphine; general (1804); governor of Paris (1805); made by Napoléon king of Holland (1806); failed to enforce Continental System in Holland; abdicated (1810) and assumed title of comte de St.-Leu \də-sa^{n}-lœ\. His third son, Charles-Louis-Napoléon, was Emperor Napoléon III (*q.v.*).
(6) ¶Maria-Paulette, *called* Pauline, *orig.* Carlotta (1780–1825); m. 1st (1797) Charles V. E. Leclerc; 2d (1803) Prince Camillo Borghese (*q.v.*) and became duchess of Gua·stal·la \gwäs-'täl-lä\.
(7) ¶Marie-Annonciade, *later called* Caroline (1782–1839); m. (1800) Marshal Joachim Murat; exercised considerable ambition and skill at intrigue in favor of husband; reigned as queen of Naples (1808–15); lived (from 1815) in Trieste as Comtesse Li·po·na \lē-'pō-nä\.
(8) ¶Jérôme (1784–1860); lieutenant on expedition to Haiti (1803); took refuge from British in U.S.; m. (1803) Elizabeth Patterson (1785–1879) of Baltimore; marriage annulled (1805) by French council of state; m. (1807) Princess Catherine of Württemberg; made by Napoléon king of Westphalia (1807–13); distinguished himself at Waterloo (1815); after Napoléon's abdication, settled in Florence; returned to France (1848); created marshal of France (1850); president of the Senate (1852). His daughter ¶Mathilde-Letizia-Wilhelmine (1820–1904), m. Prince Anatole Demidov (1841).
¶Napoléon-Joseph-Charles-Paul (1822–1891); called Prince Napoléon; also known as Plon-Plon \plō^{n}-plō^{n}\; son of Jérôme and Princess Catherine; named successor to Napoléon III (1851); representative of liberal democratic opinion at court; general in Crimean war; minister for colonies and Algeria (1858); m. (1859) Princess Clotilde, daughter of Victor Emmanuel II of Sardinia; corps commander in war of 1859; occupied Tuscany; his liberal political views caused conflict with Napoléon III; death of prince imperial made him head of family (1879); as pretender to throne, exiled from France (1886) with his son ¶Prince Napoléon-Victor (1862–1926).

Bo·na·parte \'bō-nə-,pärt\, Charles Joseph. 1851–1921. American lawyer, b. Baltimore, Md. Son of Jérôme Bonaparte; grandson of Jérôme, King of Westphalia and Elizabeth Bonaparte. U.S. secretary of navy (1905–06); U.S. attorney general (1906–09).

Bonaparte, Elizabeth, *nee* Patterson. 1785–1879. American socialite, b. Baltimore. m. (1803) Jérôme Bonaparte, youngest brother of Napoléon I; marriage not recognized by Napoléon and annulled by French council of state (1805); lived most of the time in Europe (1815–40).

Bon·ar \'bän-ər\, Horatius. 1808–1889. Scottish clergyman. Author of three series of *Hymns of Faith and Hope* (1857–66), including "I heard the voice of Jesus say."

Bo·nard \bò-nár\, Louis-Adolphe. 1805–1867. French admiral. In command of French territory in Oceania (1849); governor of Guiana (1853); commander of French forces in Cochin China (Vietnam, 1861); first military governor of French possessions in Cochin China (1861–63); secured additional territory.

Bonar Law, Andrew. See Bonar LAW.

Bon·a·ven·tu·ra \,bō-nä-vān-'tü-rä, *Angl* ,bän-ə-,ven-'t(y)ùr-ə\ *or* **Bon·a·ven·ture** \,bän-ə-'ven-chər, 'bän-ə-,\. Saint. *Orig. name* Giovanni. c.1217–1274. Italian scholastic philosopher. Called "the Seraphic Doctor." Entered Franciscan order (1243); professor of theology, Paris (1253–57); minister general of Franciscans (1257–74); named cardinal bishop of Albano by Gregory X (1273). Renowned for piety, wisdom; effectively revitalized Franciscan order. Canonized by Sixtus IV (1482); declared doctor of the church by Sixtus V (1587). His works included *Itinerarium mentis in Deum* (1259), *De reductione artium in theologiam, Biblia pauperum* (1270), *Speculum Mariae Virginis, Breviloquium.*

Bon·com·pa·gni di Mom·bel·lo \,bōŋ-kōm-'pän-yē-dē-mōm-'bel-lō\, Carlo. Conte di Lam·po·ro \dē-läm-'pò-rō\. 1804–1880. Italian jurist and politician. Minister of justice (1848–53); president of chamber (1853–56); active in cause of Italian unification. Author of *Introduzione alla scienza del diritto* (1848).

Bon·com·pa·gno da Si·gna \,bōŋ-kōm-'pän-yō-dä-'sēn-yä\. c.1165–c.1240. Italian rhetorician. Noted as a teacher of rhetoric and letter writing; author of treatises *Rhetorica antiqua* (or *Boncompagnus*) and *Rhetorica novissima.*

Boncour, Joseph Paul-. See PAUL-BONCOUR.

Boncourt, Chamisso de. See CHAMISSO.

Bond \'bänd\, Carrie, *nee* Jacobs. 1862–1946. American song writer, b. Janesville, Wis. m. (1887) Dr. Frank L. Bond (d. 1895). Among her widely successful songs were "The End of a Perfect Day," "Just A-wearyin' for You," "I Love You Truly," "God Remembers When the World Forgets," "Do You Remember?"

Bond, Sir Robert. 1857–1927. Canadian politician, b. St. John's, Nfld. Member of Newfoundland Assembly (1882–1914), speaker (1884–89); colonial secretary (1889–94, 1895–97); negotiated fishing-rights and reciprocal trade agreement with U.S.; prime minister and colonial secretary (1900–09).

Bond, Thomas. 1712–1784. American physician, b. Calvert Co., Md. Practiced in Philadelphia (from 1734); planned and established (1752) Pennsylvania Hospital, first in America; helped found (1765) medical school of College of Philadelphia (now U. of Pennsylvania).

Bond, William Bennett. 1815–1906. Canadian prelate, b. England. To Canada (c.1835); curate of St. George's, Montreal (1848–78); bishop of Montreal (1878); archbishop and metropolitan (1901); primate of all Canada (1904).

Bond, William Cranch. 1789–1859. American astronomer, b. Falmouth (now Portland), Me. Took charge of construction of Harvard Observatory (1839); first director (1847–59). His son ¶George Phillips (1825–1865), b. Dorchester, Mass., was assistant director (1845–59) and then director of Harvard Observatory (1859–65). Together they pioneered in use of photography in mapping the sky, measuring brightness of stars and double stars; discovered (1848) Hyperion, satellite of Saturn, and the crepe ring.

Bon·de \'bòn-də\, Gustaf. Count. 1620–1667. Swedish politician. Governor of Södermanland (1648); privy councillor (1653); lord treasurer and member of regency council (1660); proposed conservative budget aimed at eliminating need for foreign subsidies, but overruled by supporters of Magnus De La Gardie; withdrew from service (1665).

Bond·field \'bän(d)-,fēld\, Margaret Grace. 1873–1953. English trade unionist and politician. First woman chairman of Trades Union Congress (1923); M.P. (1923–31); parliamentary secretary to ministry of labor (1924); minister of labor (1929–31); first woman minister in British government.

Bone \'bōn\, Henry. 1755–1834. English artist. Enamel painter to George III, George IV, and William IV; one of outstanding miniaturists of his day. His son ¶Henry Pierce (1779–1855) was also an enamel painter.

Bone, Sir Muirhead. 1876–1953. Scottish etcher and painter. Official artist in both World Wars; known esp. for drypoint architectural views, as series *Glasgow Fifty Drawings* (1911); published *Old Spain* (1936), containing drawings and watercolors.

Bonehill, Captain Ralph. See Edward STRATEMEYER.

Boner, Edmund. See BONNER.

Bo·ner \'bō-nər\, Ulrich. *Lat.* Bo·ne·ri·us \bō-'nir-ē-əs\. fl. 1324–49. Swiss writer. Dominican monk; collected verse fables under title *Der Edelstein* (c.1350; printed 1461), one of first German books to be printed.

Bon·fils \'bän-(,)filz\, Frederick Gilmer. 1860–1933. American newspaper publisher, b. Troy, Mo. To Denver (1895); with ¶Harry Heye Tam·men \'tam-ən\ (1856–1924) bought *Evening Post,* renaming it *Denver Post;* built it into sensational crusading journal of national influence.

Bong \'bäŋ, 'bòŋ\, Richard Ira. 1920–1945. American army officer and aviator, b. Superior, Wis. Leading American ace of World War II; in 3 tours of duty in Pacific shot down 40 enemy aircraft; awarded Medal of Honor (1944); died in test flight of P-80 jet fighter.

Bon·gars \bō^{n}-gár\, Jacques. Seigneur de Baul·dry et de la Ches·naye \də-bō-drē-ā-də-lə-shā-ne, -she-ne\. 1554–1612. French diplomat and scholar. In service of Henry of Navarre, later Henry IV (from 1586); minister in Germany (1593–1610). Published annotated edition of works of Justin (1581), collection of historical works on Hungary (1600), and *Gesta Dei per Francos* (1611), collection of contemporary accounts of Crusades.

Bon·ghi \'bòŋ-gē\, Ruggiero *or* Ruggero. 1826–1895. Italian scholar, writer, and politican. Member, chamber of deputies (1860 ff.); minister of education (1874–76). Founded newspaper *La Stampa,* Turin (1863).

Bon·heur \bò-nœr\, Rosa, *in full* Marie-Rosalie. 1822–1899. French painter. Known esp. for her paintings of animals, including *Tillage in Nivernais, Studies of Animals,* and *Horse Fair;* first woman awarded Grand Cross of Légion d'Honneur (1865).

Bon·hoef·fer \'bòn-,hœf-ər\, Dietrich. 1906–1945. German theologian. Lecturer at U. of Berlin (1931–33); active in anti-Nazi work (from 1933); organized and directed (1935–37) seminary for German Confessing church; leader of ecumenical movement. Arrested (1943); executed for involvement in plot to assassinate Hitler. Propounded a theology based on ethics, ascetic acceptance of burdens, active witness to secular world. Author of *Sanctorum Communio* (1930), *Akt und Sein* (1931), *Gemeinsames Leben* (1939), and posthumous *Ethik* (incomplete, 1949), *Widerstand und Ergebung* (1951).

Bo·ni \'bō-,nī\, Albert. 1892–1981. American publisher, b. New York City. Opened bookshop (1912); with Lawrence Langner founded (1915) Washington Square Players, later the Theatre Guild; with Horace Liveright formed publishing firm Boni & Liveright (1917); introduced "Modern Library" series of reprints; published works of Dreiser, Thornton Wilder, Ford Madox Ford, Trotsky; sold out to Liveright (1919); later pioneered in publishing paperback books; founded (1950) Readex Microprint Corp., president (1950–74).

Bon·i·face \'bän-ə-fəs, -,fās\. Saint. *Orig. name* Wyn·frid \'win-frəd\ *or* Wyn·frith \'win-()frith\. *Called* Apostle of Germany. c.675–754. English Benedictine missionary. Authorized by Pope Gregory II, preached and organized church in Frisia, Hesse, Bavaria, Thuringia (719 ff.); bishop (722); archbishop (732); entrusted with reformation of Frankish church (740); archbishop of Mainz (751); set upon, with his followers, by a mob and killed while evangelizing in Frisia.

Boniface. Name of eight popes and an antipope:

Boniface I. Saint. d. 422. Pope (418–422). Recognized by Emperor Honorius after schism caused by election of antipope Eulalius; supported St. Augustine, esp. against Pelagians.

Boniface II. d. 532. Pope (530–532). Designated successor by Pope Felix IV. Roman clergy opposed to him because of his Ostrogothic descent elected antipope Dioscorus, who died shortly thereafter; received submission of former opponents. At Roman synod (531) secured right to appoint successor, but renounced it at following synod; condemned Semi-Pelagianism.

Boniface III. d. 607. Pope (607). Legate to Constantinople (603); obtained from Emperor Phocas edict recognizing pope as head of all churches.

Boniface IV. Saint. d. 615. Pope (608–615). Converted Pantheon of Rome into church of Sancta Maria ad Martyres (609); held Council of Rome (610) for restoration of monastic discipline; faced uprising of Monophysites led by Heraclius, exarch of Africa.

Boniface V. d. 625. Pope (619–625). Attempted to conform canon and civil law; established right of asylum; encouraged evangelization of Britain, sending pallium to Justus, archbishop of Canterbury.

Boniface VI. d. 896. Pope (896). Died 15 days after election, either by gout or perhaps murdered by party of Spoleto.

Boniface VIII. *Orig.* Benedetto Ca·e·ta·ni \,kä-ä-'tä-nē\. c.1235 or 1240–1303. Pope (1294–1303). Cardinal priest (1291); as pope, endeavored to end wars, esp. those between England and France and between Aragon and Naples. Issued (1296) the bull *Clericis laicos* directed against Philip IV of France, forbidding collection of taxes on church property without consent of Holy See; issued (1301) the bull *Ausculta Fili,* reproach against Philip, and (1302) *Unam Sanctam* asserting temporal as well as spiritual supremacy of pope; as a result of quarrel with Philip, made prisoner at Anagni (1303) by Guillaume de Nogaret and members of Colonna family; died within a month.

Boniface IX. *Orig.* Pietro To·ma·cel·li \,tō-mä-'chel-lē\. c.1355–1404. Pope (1389–1404). Elected to succeed Urban VI during Great Western Schism; excommunicated antipope Clement VII; used every means to raise great sums necessary to win and hold allies against Avignon antipopes.

Boniface VII. d. 985. Antipope (974, 984–985). Murdered Pope Benedict VI and installed in papacy by Crescentius I; expelled at behest of Emperor Otto II; exiled in Constantinople; recalled (984) by Crescentii; imprisoned and probably murdered John XIV (984); murdered by Roman mob.

Boniface. Margrave of Ca·nos·sa \kä-'nòs-sä\. d. 1052. Italian ruler. Grandson of Atto Adalbert; ruled Canossa jointly with father Tedaldo, then with brother, and (from 1030) alone; for support of Emperor Conrad II, esp. at battle of Coviolo (1030), given marches of Attonia and Tuscia; led Italian forces in Conrad's occupation of Burgundy (1033).

Boniface. d. 1207. Margrave of Montferrat. Joined Fourth Crusade (1202) and succeeded Theobald of Champagne as its leader; led conquest of Constantinople (1204); king of Thessalonica (1204–07).

Boniface of Querfurt, Saint. See Saint BRUNO of Querfurt.

Boniface of Sa·voy \sə-'vòi\. d. 1270. Archbishop of Canterbury. Son of count of Savoy; although not ordained, elected archbishop (1241) through influence of his niece Eleanor, queen of Henry III of England; consecrated (1245). Initiated visitation of Canterbury (1250); supported bishops against exactions by king and pope (1256), but shifted to side of king and (1263) confirmed papal excommunication of rebel barons.

Bo·ni·fa·cio \bō-ni-'fāth-yō, -'fās-\, Andres. 1863–1897. Philippine insurrectionist. Founded (1892) nationalist Katipunan society; began insurrection against Spanish on Luzon (1896); suffered several defeats; replaced as leader by Emilio Aguinaldo (1897); attempted to establish rival leadership; arrested, tried, executed on orders of Aguinaldo.

Bon·i·fa·cius \,bän-ə-'fā-sh(ē-)əs\. d. 432 A.D. Roman general. Governor of Africa (425–431); reputed to have invited Vandals into that province (c.429); later, warred upon Vandals and defended city of Hippo from them. Died from wounds received in duel with Aëtius.

Bo·nin \bō-'nēn\, Eduard von. 1793–1865. Prussian general. Commanded Prussian troops against Denmark in Schleswig-Holstein (1848); commanding general of troops of the duchy (1848); war minister (1852–54, 1858–59).

Bon·ing·ton \'bän-iŋ-tən\, Richard Parkes. 1801–1828. English painter. Influenced by Constable and Turner; with Delacroix helped introduce English fashion for historical paintings to France; known esp. for brightly colored Romantic landscapes; made many innovations in oil and watercolor technique.

Bo·ni·vard \bò-nē-vår\, François. 1494?–1570. Swiss religious and patriot. Head of Cluniac priory of St. Victor; opposed attempts of Duke Charles III of Savoy and bishop of Geneva to curtail liberties of the city; imprisoned at Gex (1519–21); led Genevese revolt (1528); imprisoned at castle of Chillon (1530–36), held in underground dungeon (1532–36). (Episode formed basis of Lord Byron's poem "Prisoner of Chillon".) Later became Protestant; compiled *Chroniques de Genève* (pub. 1831).

Bon·nard \bò-når\, Abel. 1883–1968. French writer. Established reputation with books of travel, as *En Chine* (1923), essays as *L'Enfance* (1927), *L'Amitié* (1929), *Pensées dans l'action* (1941); minister of education in Vichy government (1942–44); fled to Spain (1944); sentenced to death in absentia (1945) and expelled from French Academy; returned to France (1958); sentenced to 10 years' banishment (1960).

Bonnard, Pierre. 1867–1947. French painter. A leading member of Nabis group of artists (1890s) and later an Intimiste; contributed illustrations to *Petites scènes familières* (1893) and *Petit sol fège illustré* (1893) of his brother-in-law Claude Terasse, to Verlaine's *Parallèlement* (1900), and to *La Revue blanche;* later turned to landscapes inspired by Mediterranean region; also painted still lifes, nude studies, self portraits, etc. Known as brilliant, subtle colorist, master of light; experimented with emotive effects of abstract color forms.

Bon·nas·sieux \bò-nås-yœ̄\, Jean-Marie. 1810–1892. French sculptor. Carved colossal statute *Notre-Dame de France* at Le Puy (1857).

Bon·nat \bò-nå\, Léon-Joseph-Florentin. 1833–1922. French painter. Attained great success with religious paintings; later a noted portraitist of Victor Hugo, Puvis de Chavannes, Pasteur, Dumas fils, Grévy, Renan, Thiers, Taine, etc.

Bonne \bòn\, François de. Duc de Les·di·guières \les-dig-yer, lā-, le-\. 1543–1626. French soldier. Joined Huguenot troops in Dauphiné, becoming leader (by 1575); gave allegiance to Henry of Navarre (1585) and secured submission of Dauphiné; continued defensive war against Spain and Savoy. Governor of Dauphiné (1591), marshal of France (1609), duke (1611). Abjured Protestantism (1622); constable of France (1622).

Bon·ner *or* **Bon·er** \'bän-ər\, Edmund. c.1500–1569. English prelate. Sent to Rome (1533) to appeal in behalf of Henry VIII, who had been excommunicated after marriage with Anne Boleyn (1533). Bishop of London (1540); deprived and imprisoned (1549–53) for insistence that royal supremacy was in abeyance during Edward VI's minority. Restored at accession of Mary (1553) and became agent in Marian persecution of Reformers; refused oath of supremacy at accession of Elizabeth and was deposed (1559); died in prison.

Bonner, Robert. 1824–1899. American newspaper publisher, b. near Londonderry, Ireland. To U.S. (1839); bought *New York Ledger* (1851) and built it into highly successful family and story newspaper; noted for ingenious promotions; owned a famous racing stable.

Bon·net \bò-ne\, Charles. 1720–1793. Swiss naturalist and philosopher. Discovered (1746) parthenogenesis while studying aphids; studied regeneration, photosynthesis. Author of *Essai de psychologie* (1754), *Considérations sur les corps organisés* (1761) in which he argued for preformation, *Contemplation de la nature* (1764), and *Palingénésie philosophique* (1769) in which he argued for catastrophic theory of evolution.

Bonnet, Georges-Étienne. 1889–1973. French politician and diplomat. Member of Chamber of Deputies (1924–40); held various cabinet posts (1926 ff.); ambassador to U.S. (1936); finance minister (1937–38); minister of foreign affairs (1938–39) at time of Munich conference; minister of justice (1939–40); member of National Council (1941–42). Again deputy (1956–68).

Bonne·val \bȯn(-ə)-väl\, Claude-Alexandre de. Comte. 1675–1747. French soldier. In French army (1691–1704), colonel (1701); court martialled (1704); entered Austrian service, serving in Netherlands as lieutenant field marshal and chief of artillery; left in disgrace (1724); entered Turkish service (1729) as Ah·med Pa·şa \ä-'med-pə-'shä\; served against Russia and Persia; reorganized Turkish artillery.

Bon·ne·ville \'bän-ə-,vil\, Benjamin Louis Eulalie de. 1796–1878. American army officer, b. Paris, France. To U.S. (1803); on duty on frontier (from 1821); on leave, explored northwestern country (1832–35); served in Mexican War and Civil War. Subject of Washington Irving's *Adventures of Captain Bonneville* (1837).

Bonne·ville \bȯn(-ə)-vēl\, Nicolas de. 1760–1828. French writer. Appointed president of one of Paris districts at outbreak of French Revolution (1789); reputed to be first to suggest formation of Garde Nationale; imprisoned during Terror and persecuted under Empire. Among his books were *Histoire de l'Europe moderne* (1789–92), *De l'esprit des religions* (1791).

Bon·ney \'bän-ē\, William. *Orig.* Henry Bonney *or perhaps* Mc·Car·ty \mə-'kärt-ē\. *Known as* Billy the Kid. 1859?–1881. American outlaw, b. New York City? Lived in New Mexico (from 1868); reputedly a killer by age 12; gunman in "Lincoln County War" between cattle barons (1878); refused to honor truce arranged by Gov. Lew Wallace; shot by Sheriff Pat Garrett after career of 21 murders.

Bon·nier \bȯn-yā\, Gaston. 1853–1922. French botanist. Professor, Sorbonne (from 1887); investigated photosynthesis and respiration; demonstrated symbiote nature of lichens. Author of *Flore complète ... de France, Suisse et Belgique* (1912–34).

Bono, Michele di Taddeo. See GIAMBONO.

Bo·no·mi \bō-'nȯ-mē\, Ivanoe. 1873–1951. Italian politician. Member of Parliament (1909 ff.); leader of moderate Reformist Socialists; minister of public works (1916–17), of war (1920), of treasury (1920–21); prime minister (1921–22); leader of anti-Fascist movement (from 1942); prime minister (1944–45) on fall of Mussolini; president of Senate (1948–51).

Bo·non·ci·ni \,bō-nōn-'chē-nē\ *or* **Buo·non·ci·ni** \,bwȯ-\. Italian family of musicians, including: Giovanni Maria (1642–1678), musical theorist and composer; author of *Musico prattico* (1673). His son ¶Giovanni (1670–1747) was operatic composer; known for his rivalry with Handel (1720–32); composer of some 300 cantatas, operas including *Il trionfo di Camilla* (1696), *Mutio Scevola* (1710), *Astarto* (1715), *Crispo* (1721), *Griselda* (1722), *Amore per amor* (1732), and much chamber music. Another son ¶Antonio Maria (1677–1726), composer of operas, cantatas, and oratorios.

Bon·pland \bōⁿ-pläⁿ\, Aimé-Jacques-Alexandre. *Orig. surname* Gou·jaud \gü-zhō\. 1773–1858. French naturalist. Traveled with von Humboldt (1799–1804) in Mexico, the Andes, etc., and collected many new species of plants; professor of natural sciences in Buenos Aires (1818–21). Author of *Plantes équinoxiales* (1805), etc.

Bon·por·ti \bōn-'pȯr-tē\, Francesco Antonio. 1672–1749. Italian composer. Composed many trio sonatas, violin sonatas and concertos; known esp. for 10 instrumental *Invenzioni* (1712) featuring rich harmonies and unconventional rhythms and recitative style; title borrowed by J.S. Bach, to whom 4 of the *Invenzioni* were mistakenly attributed.

Bon·stet·ten *Fr* bȯn-stā-ten, -ste-; *Ger* 'bōn-,shtet-ən\, Charles Victor de *or* Karl Viktor von. 1745–1832. Swiss writer. Among his works were *Über Nationalbildung* (1802), *Études de l'homme* (1821), *L'Homme du midi et l'homme du nord* (1824), *Souvenirs* (1832).

Bon·tem·pel·li \,bōn-tem-'pel-lē\, Massimo. 1878–1960. Italian writer. Author of traditional and Futurist verse; of novels including *La vita intensa* (1920), *La vita operosa* (1921), *Il figlio di due madri* (1929), *Gente nel tempo* (1937), *Giro del sole* (1941), *L'amante fedele* (1953); plays including *La guardia alla luna* (1916), *Siepe a nordovest* (1919), *Nostra dea* (1925); critical works *L'avventura novecentista* (1939), *Introduzioni e discorsi* (1945). Founded review *900* (1926); founder of *novecentismo* school of criticism.

Bon·temps \bän-'täm\, Arna Wendell. 1902–1973. American writer, b. Alexandria, La. Author of verse, esp. "Southern Mansion" and "A Black Man Talks of Reaping"; novels including *God Sends Sunday* (1931), *Black Thunder* (1935), *Drums at Dusk* (1939); nonfiction including *Story of the Negro* (1948), *Chariot in the Sky* (1951), *Frederick Douglass* (1959); edited anthologies of Negro verse, folklore, etc.

Bon·ve·sin da la Ri·va \bōn-'vā-sēn-dä-lä-'rē-vä\. c.1240–c.1315. Italian poet. Member of Humiliati order of Milan. Author of *De quinquaginta curialitatibus ad mensam* on contemporary social usages and mores, *De magnalibus urbis Mediolani* on city of Milan, and *Libro delle tre scritture* (1274) on hell, heaven, and the Passion, sometimes compared to Dante's *Divina commedia*.

Bon·vi·ci·no \,bōn-vē-'chē-nō\ *or* **Buon·vi·ci·no** \,bwȯn-\, Alessandro. *Known as* Mo·ret·to \mȯ-'ret-tō\ *or* Moretto da Bres·cia \-dä-'bresh-ä\. c.1498–1554. Italian painter. Leading painter of Brescian school; works noted for cool and harmonious coloring.

Boole \'bül\, George. 1815–1864. English mathematician and logician. Self-taught; professor, Queen's College, Cork (from 1849). Author of *Treatise on Differential Equations* (1859), *Treatise on the Calculus of Finite Differences* (1860), other mathematical works, and esp. *An Investigation of the Laws of Thought* (1854), in which he elaborated his method of applying algebraic operations to logic, yielding Boolean algebra, pioneer form of symbolic logic.

Boone \'bün\, Daniel. c.1734–1820. American pioneer, b. Berks Co., Pa. Moved to North Carolina (1750); made trips through Cumberland Gap to Kentucky region (1767, 1769–71). Guided settlers into Kentucky (1775); erected fort (1775) on site of what is now Boonesboro; his land titles there invalidated (after 1780). After some years in western Virginia (1788–99), moved into what is now Missouri.

Boorde *or* **Borde** \bō(ə)rd, bȯ(ə)rd\, Andrew. c.1490–1549. English physician and writer. Traveled widely in Europe (1529–34, c.1534, c.1538–42); author of *Fyrst Boke of the Introduction of Knowledge* (1548), earliest English guidebook to the Continent.

Boos \'bōs\, Martin. 1762–1825. German clergyman. During pastorate of Catholic church at Gallneukirchen, Austria (1806–12) began evangelical movement akin to Lutheran Pietism; opposed by church hierarchy.

Booth \'büth, *chiefly Brit* 'büṯẖ\. Family of actors on American stage, including: Junius Brutus (1796–1852), b. London; acted at Covent Garden (1817–20), and, in support of Edmund Kean, at Drury Lane (1820); on U.S. stage (from 1821) with occasional tours to England; chief roles, Othello, Iago, Richard III, Shylock; in later years a noted eccentric. His son ¶Junius Brutus (1821–1883), actor and manager. Another son ¶Edwin Thomas (1833–1893), b. near Belair, Md.; debut, Boston (1849); toured California (1852–54), Australia and Hawaii (1854–55); on New York stage (from 1857); toured England and Continent (1880–82), appearing with Henry Irving in *Othello* (1880); formed partnership with Lawrence Barrett (1886). Founded Players Club, New York (1888). Renowned as greatest Hamlet of the day. Another son ¶John Wilkes (1838–1865), b. near Belair, Md., achieved success in Shakespearean roles (1860–63); intrigued to kidnap Lincoln (1864) and then to assassinate him; shot and killed Lincoln at Ford's Theater, Washington (Apr. 14, 1865); escaped, but was shot, or killed himself.

Booth, Agnes. *Nee* Marian Agnes Land Rookes \'rüks\. 1846–1910. American actress, b. Sydney, Australia. To U.S. in childhood; m. 2d (1867) Junius Brutus Booth (d. 1883); appeared in support of Edwin Forrest, Edwin Booth, E. A. Sothern, Lawrence Barrett; leading woman in Palmer's company, at Madison Square Theater, New York (1885–97).

Booth, Ballington. See under William BOOTH.

Booth, Barton. 1681–1733. English tragic actor. Engaged by Betterton (1700); his best roles included Ghost to Wilks's Hamlet, Cato in Addison's tragedy, Brutus, Lear, Othello, Henry VIII, Hotspur.

Booth, Charles. 1840–1916. English shipowner and sociological writer. Began shipping service to Brazil (1866) reorganized as Booth Steamship Co. (1901); chairman (1901–12). Author of *Life and Labour of the People in London* (1891–1903); instrumental in obtaining passage of Old Age Pensions Act (1908).

Booth, Evangeline Cory. See under William BOOTH.

Booth, Sir Felix. 1775–1850. English distiller. Chief contributor to Capt. James Clark Ross's Arctic expedition of discovery (1829–33); after him Boothia Felix peninsula is named.

Booth, George. 1st Baron Del·a·mere \'del-ə-,mi(ə)r\ *or* de la Mer \'del-ə-,mär\. 1622–1684. English political and military leader. Member of Long Parliament (1645) and parliaments of 1654 and 1656; treasurer at war (1655); leader of New or Presbyterian Royalists, who joined with Cavaliers in attempt to effect the Restoration (1659); seized Cheshire but captured and imprisoned in Tower; released (1660); one of twelve members of Parliament sent to The Hague to summon Charles II. Created baron (1661). His second son ¶Henry (1652–1694), 2d Baron Delamere and 1st Earl of War·ring·ton \'wȯr-iŋ-tən, 'wär-\, was imprisoned for implication in Rye House Plot (1683); acquitted of charge of complicity in Monmouth's rebellion (1685); took up arms for William of Orange (1688); chancellor of exchequer (1689–90); created earl (1690).

Booth, William. *Known as* General Booth. 1829–1912. English religious leader and founder of Salvation Army. Preacher of Methodist New Connexion (1852–61); became independent itinerant revivalist; m. (1855) Catherine Mum·ford \'məm(p)-fərd\ (1829–1890), a preacher in public (1860) and later known as "Mother of the Salvation Army"; founded mission in Whitechapel, London (1865), which became (1878) the Salvation Army, with a program of social reforms and charities in city slums and among paupers and criminals;

introduced the army in America, Australia, Europe, Asia. General of the army (to 1912). Author of *In Darkest England and the Way Out* (1890).

His eldest son ¶Bramwell, *in full* William Bramwell (1856–1929), chief organizer and chief of staff of Salvation Army (1880–1912) and on father's death general of the army (1912–29); with W. T. Stead exposed white-slave traffic in England (1885); author of *Echoes and Memories* (1925). m. (1882) ¶Florence Eleanor So·per \'sō-pər\ (1861–1957), a worker in the army (from 1880), and organizer of Women's Social Work (1883) and of rescue work among women (1912).

¶Ballington (1857–1940), second son of William, was co-commander of Salvation Army in Australia (1883–85); commander of army in U.S. (1887–1896); withdrew from army after disagreement with father on method of operation in America; organized similar body, the Volunteers of America (1896); general (1896–1940). m. (1886) ¶Maud Elizabeth Charles·worth \'chä(ə)rlz-ˌwərth\ (1865–1948), who had worked with army in France and Switzerland and who on marriage adopted both husband's names, becoming known as Maud Ballington Booth; with him naturalized in U.S. (1895); aided her husband in founding of the Volunteers and directed its auxiliary Volunteer Prison League devoted to prison work; general of Volunteers of America (1940–48); one of founders of Parent-Teachers Association; author of *Branded* (1897) and *After Prison, What?* (1903).

¶Emma Moss Booth-Tuck·er \-'tək-ər\ (1860–1903), another daughter of William Booth; in charge of training homes of the army (1880–88); m. (1888) ¶Frederick St. George de Lautour Booth-Tucker (1853–1929; assumed name Booth in 1888), who resigned from Indian civil service to inaugurate Indian branch of Salvation Army (1882); secretary of international work in London (1891–96) and commander in U.S. (1896–1904); author of *Life of General William Booth* (1898) and *Farm Colonies of the Salvation Army* (1903).

¶Evangeline, *orig.* Eva, Cory Booth (1865–1950), seventh child of William Booth, was commander of the army in London (1889–96); took charge of army in U.S. on resignation of Ballington Booth (1896); commander of army in Canada (1896–1904), in U.S. (1904–34); established servicemen's canteens in World War I, "Evangeline Homes" for working mothers; elected general of international organization (1934). Author of *Love is All* (1908), *Songs of the Evangel* (1927), *Towards a Better World* (1928), *Woman* (1930).

Bopp \'bōp\, Franz. 1791–1867. German philologist. Carried on researches, esp. in Sanskrit mss., at Paris and London (1812 ff.); professor, Berlin (1821–64). Author of a Sanskrit grammar (1827) and glossary (1830); *Vergleichende Grammatik,* a comparative grammar of Indo-European languages (1833–52); established importance of Sanskrit for studies of Indo-European languages.

Bo·ra \'bō-ˌrä\, Katharina von. 1499–1552. German religious. Cistercian nun in Nimbschen, Saxony (1515–23); adopted Lutheran doctrines and fled to Wittenberg (1523); married Martin Luther (1525).

Bo·rah \'bōr-ə, 'bȯr-\, William Edgar. 1865–1940. American politician, b. near Fairfield, Ill. U.S. senator from Idaho (1907–40); chairman, Senate foreign relations committee (1924–33). A maverick Republican and isolationist; strongly opposed World Court and entrance of United States into League of Nations; advocated disarmament conference (1920–21); supported most of New Deal program; supported Neutrality Act (1935).

Boratynsky. See BARATYNSKY.

Borbón. Spanish form of BOURBON.

Bor·chard \'bȯr-chərd\, Edwin. 1884–1951. American lawyer, b. New York City. Law librarian of Congress (1911–13, 1914–16); professor of law, Yale (1917–50). Chief counsel to Peru in Tacna-Arica dispute (1923–25); U.S. technical adviser at Conference on Codification of International Law (1930).

Bor·chardt \'bȯr-ˌkärt\, Ludwig. 1863–1938. German Egyptologist. First director, German Archaeological Institute, Egypt (from 1907); during excavation at Amarna (1911–14) discovered bust of Nefertiti.

Borch·gre·vink \'bȯrk-grā-viŋk\, Carsten Egeberg. 1864–1934. Norwegian naturalist and explorer. Member of first party to land on Antarctic Continent (1894); in command of Sir George Newnes's *Southern Cross* expedition (1898–1900), first to winter on the Antarctic Continent.

Bor·da \bȯr-dȧ\, Jean-Charles de. 1733–1799. French mathematician and nautical astronomer. Studied fluid mechanics, geodesy; developed instruments for navigation; designed standard platinum meter bar, second pendulum.

Borde, Andrew. See BOORDE.

Bordeaux, Duc de. See DIEUDONNÉ D'ARTOIS.

Bor·deaux \bȯr-dō\, Henry. 1870–1963. French novelist. Known esp. for cycle of novels, including *Le Pays natal* (1900), *La Peur de vivre* (1902), *Les Yeux qui s'ouvrent* (1908), *La Niege sur les pas* (1911), *La Chartreuse du Reposoir* (1924), *La Fille du prisonnier* (1954), *Le Flambeau renversé* (1961).

Bor·den \'bȯrd-ᵊn\, Sir Frederick William. 1847–1917. Canadian politician, b. Cornwallis, N.S. Member of House of Commons (1874–82, 1887–1911); minister of militia and defense (1896–1911); played major role in creation and development of Canadian navy.

Borden, Gail. 1801–1874. American inventor, b. Norwich, N.Y. To Texas (1829); made first topographical map of Texas; surveyed site of Galveston (1838). Invented a meat biscuit (1851); condensed milk (1853; patented 1856); founded (1857) New York Condensed Milk Co. (later Borden Co.).

Borden, Lizzie Andrew. 1860–1927. American accused murderess, b. Fall River, Mass. Accused of murdering her wealthy father and stepmother (1892); acquitted in sensational trial.

Borden, Sir Robert Laird. 1854–1937. Canadian politician, b. Grand Pré, N.S. M.P. (from 1896); leader of Conservative opposition (1901–11); prime minister (1911–20); member of Imperial War Cabinet (1917–18); delegate of Canada at Paris Peace Conference (1919); representative of Canada on Council of League of Nations.

Bor·det \bȯr-de\, Jules-Jean-Baptiste-Vincent. 1870–1961. Belgian bacteriologist. Director, Pasteur Institute, Brabant (1901–40); professor, U. of Brussels (1907–35). Known for work in immunology and serology; discovered (1895) antibody and complement in blood serum; discovered (1898) process of hemolysis; with Octave Gengou discovered (1906) agent of whooping cough and laid basis for serological tests for various diseases; received 1919 Nobel prize for physiology or medicine.

Bor·do·ne \bōr-'dō-nā\, Paris. 1500–1571. Venetian painter. Worked in Venice, Augsburg, France, etc.; known for religious, mythological, historical works, as *Fisherman and Doge, Daphnis and Chloe, Chess Players, Christ Among the Doctors,* and esp. as portraitist.

Bo·ré \bōr-'ā, bȯr-\, Jean Étienne. 1741–1820. American planter, b. Louisiana. On failure of indigo crop, pioneered in planting sugar cane; invented granulating process (1794–95); mayor of New Orleans (1803–04).

Bo·rel \bȯ-rel\, Émile, *in full* Félix-Édouard-Justin-Émile. 1871–1956. French mathematician. Professor, École Normale Superieure (1896–1909), Sorbonne (1909 ff.); member of Chamber of Deputies (1924–36); minister of navy (1925–40); active in Resistance in World War II. Known for theory of measure of sets of points, pioneering work in theory of functions of real variable, theory of divergent series, pioneering work in game theory, etc.

Borel, Joseph-Pierre. *Known as* Petrus Borel *and later* Borel d'Haute·rive \-dō-trēv\. *Pseudonym* Ly·can·thrope \lē-käⁿ-trȯp\, *i.e.* Wolf-Man. 1809–1859. French writer. Extreme Romantic, a leader of group Les Bousingos. Author of verse *Rhapsodies* (1832), tales of horror *Champavert, contes immoraux* (1833), *Madame Putiphar* (1839).

Bo·rel·li \bō-'rel-lē\, Giovanni Alfonso, *orig.* Giovanni Francesco Antonio Alonso. 1608–1679. Italian physicist and physiologist. Professor, Messina (1649–56, 1667–74), Pisa (1656–67). In *Del movimento della cometa* (1665), published under pseudonym Pier Maria Mutoli, first suggested parabolic path for celestial object; postulated attractive force in *Theorica mediceorum planetarum* (1666) on motion of Jupiter's satellites; founded iatrophysical school with attempt to explain movements of animal bodies on mechanical principles in *De mota animalium* (1680–81).

Bo·re·ni·us \bȯ-'rē-nē-əs, bə-\, Tancred. 1885–1948. Finnish art historian, b. Vyborg, Russia. Taught at U. Coll., London (1914–48). Author of *Painters of Vicenza* (1909), *English Primitives* (1924), *Florentine Frescoes* (1930), *English Painting in the XVIIIth Century* (1938).

Bor·ges \'bȯr-ˌhās\, Jorge Luis. 1899–1986. Argentine author. One of Latin America's foremost men of letters. Wrote poetry, essays, and esp. short stories rich in fantasy and metaphysical allegory. Author of *Fervor de Buenos Aires* (1923), *Evaristo Carriego* (1930), *Ficciones, 1935–1944* (1944), *El Aleph* (1949), *Otras inquisiciones, 1937–1952* (1952), *El libro de arena* (1955), *El hacedor* (1960), *El libro de los seres imaginarios* (1967), *El informe de Brodie* (1970), etc. Credited with establishing the modernist Ultraist movement in South America.

Bor·ghe·se \bōr-'gā-sā\. Family of Italian noblemen, orig. from Siena, including: Camillo (1552–1621); elected to papacy as Paul V (*q.v.*). His nephew ¶Scipione Caf·fa·rel·li \ˌkäf-fä-'rel-lē\ (1576–1633) took name Borghese on being adopted by Camillo; named cardinal (1606) and given numerous other honors; amassed fortune, built Villa Borghese, and founded its celebrated art collection; patron of Bernini. Another nephew ¶Marcantonio II (1601–1658) was created prince of Sulmona (1610) and later of Vivaro; general of the church (1620). A descendant ¶Prince Camillo Filippo Lodovico Borghese (1775–1832) m. (1803) Maria-Paulette, sister of Napoléon; aided French in invasion of Italy and governed Piedmont (1807–14) under French rule; sold to Napoléon Borghese art collection (returned in part, 1815).

Bor·gia \'bȯr-jə, -zhə\. *Orig. Span. form* Bor·ja \'bȯr-ḵä\. Italian family of Spanish origin, influential in the papacy and in Italy in 15th and 16th centuries, from time of election (1455) of Alfonso as Pope Calixtus III (*q.v.*). His nephew Rodrigo, who became (1492) Pope Alexander VI (*q.v.*), was, before election as pope, father by Roman woman, Vannozza Cattanei, of four children:

¶Juan *or* Joan (1476–1497), duke of Gandía (1488); murdered, possibly at instigation of brother Cesare. ¶Jofré (1481–1517), prince of Squillace (1502).

¶Cesare. 1475 or 1476–1507. Created bishop of Pamplona (1491), archbishop of Valencia (1492), and cardinal (1493); sent as papal legate (1497) to Naples to crown Frederick of Aragon; relinquished cardinal's office (1498); to France as legate (1498) to carry to Louis XII pope's bull annulling Louis's marriage; granted duchy of Valentinois; m. (1499) Charlotte d'Albret, sister of king of Navarre. Captain general of papal army (1499); with French aid, began conquest of Romagna and Marches; captured Imola, Forlì, Rimini, Pesaro, Faenza (1499–1501); made duke (1501) by his father; seized Urbino, acting with extreme cruelty and treachery, spreading terror in all Italy; opposed by enemies, esp. Pope Julius II (elected 1503); forced to surrender castles to pope; arrested in Naples by Gonsalvo di Córdoba and sent to Spain (1504); imprisoned (1504–06); escaped, fled to Navarre, and killed in siege of castle at Viana. His character favorably portrayed by Machiavelli in his *Principe*. ¶Lucrezia. 1480–1519. Duchess of Fer·ra·ra \fār-'rä-rä\. Married three times for political reasons: (1) to Giovanni Sforza (1493), lord of Pesaro; marriage annulled (1497) when pope's friendliness to Naples made alliance with Sforzas undesirable; (2) to Alfonso of Aragon (1498), Duke of Bisceglie and illegitimate son of late Alfonso II of Naples; murdered (1500) by order of her brother Cesare; (3) with great splendor in Rome to Alfonso d'Este, son and heir to Ercole I, duke of Ferrara (1501), who became duke (1505). Set up at Ferrara brilliant court where gathered learned men, poets, and artists, among them Ariosto, Cardinal Bembo, Titian, Dosso Dossi, and Aldus Manutius; devoted rest of her life to education and charity.

Borgia, Francis. Saint. *Orig.* Francisco de Bor·ja y Ara·gón \dā-'bōr-kä-ē-är-ä-'gōn\. 1510–1572. Spanish noble and prelate. Son of 3d duke of Gandía and Joanna of Aragon; held various offices at court of Charles V of Spain; viceroy of Catalonia (1539–43); succeeded to duchy of Gandía (1543); on death of wife (1546) entered Society of Jesus; commissary general of Spanish provinces (1554). Third general of Jesuits (1565–72); expanded order, sent missions to Americas. Canonized (1671).

Bor·glum \'bór-gləm\, Gutzon, *in full* John Gutzon de la Mothe. 1867–1941. American sculptor, b. Bear Lake, Idaho. Among works were equestrian statue of Sheridan, large head of Lincoln (Capitol, Washington, D.C.), bronze group *Mares of Diomedes,* and statues of Beecher, Altgeld, Huntington, William Jennings Bryan, and figures of apostles for Cathedral of St. John the Divine, New York City. Designed and began carving Confederate memorial on face of Stone Mountain, Ga.; resigned (1925; work later resumed by others). Under commission of state of South Dakota (1927) designed and carved figures of Presidents Washington, Jefferson, Lincoln, and T. Roosevelt, on Mt. Rushmore in the Black Hills (completed 1939).

Borgo, Luca di. See Luca PACIOLI.

Borgognone, Il. See Jacques COURTOIS.

Bor·gon·gi·ni-Du·ca \,bór-gón-'jē-nē-'dü-kä\, Francesco. 1884–1954. Italian prelate. Professor, Urban Coll. of Propaganda, Rome (1907–21); negotiated and wrote Lateran Treaty (1929), establishing independence and sovereignty of Vatican City; named titular archbishop of Heraclea (1929), cardinal (1952), cardinal protector of Ursuline Nuns (1953).

Bo·ril \'bōr-əl, 'bór-\. 13th century. Czar of Bulgarian Empire (1207–18) of Asen dynasty. Nephew and successor of Kaloyan; incompetent ruler; deposed by Ivan Asen II.

Bo·ring \'bōr-iŋ, 'bór-\, Edwin Garrigues. 1886–1968. American psychologist, b. Philadelphia. Professor, Clark U. (1919–22), Harvard (1922–57); known for work on theoretical psychology, psychophysics, and sensation. Author of *History of Experimental Psychology* (1929), *Physical Dimensions of Consciousness* (1933), *History, Science and Psychology* (1966).

Bo·ris \'bōr-əs, 'bór-\. Name of three rulers of Bulgaria:

Boris I. d. 907. Czar (852–889). Son and successor of Pressian; converted to Christianity (865) after persuasion by Michael III, Byzantine emperor; accepted (866–870) primacy of Rome; succeeded in establishing national church under independent archbishop (870); promoted spread of faith, scholarship, Slavic language; abdicated (889) and retired to monastery; returned briefly (893) to depose his son Vladimir and place third son Symeon on throne.

Boris II. Czar (969–972). Forced to abdicate by Byzantine emperor John I Tzimisces, who conquered eastern Bulgaria.

Boris III. 1894–1943. King (czar) of Bulgaria (1918–43). Eldest son of Ferdinand I; succeeded on his father's abdication; m. (1930) Princess Giovanna, daughter of Victor Emmanuel III of Italy. Sought ties with Germany, Yugoslavia; survived assassination attempts and establishment (1934) of military dictatorship; himself ruled as virtual dictator (1938–43).

Boris Godunov. See GODUNOV.

Borja, Saint Francisco de. See Francis BORGIA.

Bor·ja y Ara·gón \'bōr-kä-ē-är-ä-'gōn\, Francisco de. c.1577–1658. Spanish colonial and poet. Took title of prince of Esquilache on marriage (1602) to Ana, Princess of Esquilache; viceroy of Peru (1614–21). Author of *La Pasión de N.S. Jesucristo en tercetos* (1638), *Obras en verso* (1648), *Nápoles recuperada por el rey don Alonso* (1651).

Bor·mann \'bór-(,)män\, Martin Ludwig. 1900–?1945. German Nazi leader. Joined Nazi party (1925); member of governing body of the Nazi party (from 1933); Rudolf Hess's chief of staff (1933–41) and successor as Hitler's 3d deputy; secretary to Hitler with great influence on domestic policy. Declared to have died in Hitler's bunker (1945) but without evidence; frequently reported alive in South America, also without evidence.

Born, Bertran de. See BERTRAN DE BORN.

Born \'bórn\, Ignaz von. 1742–1791. Austrian mineralogist and metallurgist. Introduced process of extracting gold and silver from ores by amalgamation.

Born, Max. 1882–1970. German physicist. Professor at Berlin (1915–19), Frankfurt (1919–21), Göttingen (1921–33), Cambridge (1933–36), Edinburgh (1936–53); known for work on the theory of relativity, the quantum theory, the space-lattice theory of crystals, and atomic structure. For statistical description of Schrödinger's wave functions (1926) awarded Nobel prize in physics (1954) with W. Bothe.

Bör·ne \'bœr-nə\, Ludwig. *Orig.* Löb Ba·ruch \'bär-ük\. 1786–1837. German political writer and satirist, of Jewish descent. Embraced Christianity and changed name (1818); to Paris to support July Revolution (1830). Published journals in which he criticized German stage and politics; became a leader of literary party "Young Germany"; engaged in bitter controversy with Heine. Author of *Briefen aus Paris* (1832–34), *Menzel, der Franzosenfresser* (1837), etc.

Borneil, Guiraut de. See GUIRAUT.

Bor·no \bór-nō\, Louis-Eustache-Antoine-François-Joseph. 1865–1942. Haitian lawyer and politician. Member of Permanent Court of International Justice at The Hague (1919–22); president of Haiti (1922–30).

Bo·ro·din \bə-(,)rəd-'yēn, *Angl* ,bór-ə-'dēn, 'bór-ə-,\, Aleksandr Porfiryevich. 1833–1887. Russian composer and chemist. Professor of chemistry, Medico-Surgical Academy (1862 ff.); noted for research on aldehydes and amarine. Devoted much leisure time to study of music and was stimulated by friendship with Balakirev and Liszt; member of The Five; composer of opera *Prince Igor* (begun 1869; completed by Rimsky-Korsakov and Glazunov, 1889), containing the popular "Polovtsian dances"; three symphonies (1867, 1869, 1887); much chamber and vocal music; and symphonic poem *In the Steppes of Central Asia* (1880).

Borodin, Mikhail Markovich. *Orig. surname* Gru·zen·berg \grüz-yin-'byerk\. 1884–1951. Russian diplomat. Joined Bolshevik party (1903); in exile in U.S. (1906–17); after Russian Revolution (1917), became active Communist worker; called to Canton (1923) by Sun Yat-sen as political adviser to Kuomintang; head of Communist government (1924–27) established at Hankow; broke with Chiang Kai-shek (1927) and forced to return to Russia; edited *Moscow Daily News* (1932–49); purged and sent to Siberia (1949).

Bo·ro·e·vić von Boj·na \'bōr-ō-yev-ēch-fón-'bói-nä\, Svetozar. Baron. 1856–1920. Austrian general of Croatian descent. Commanding general of army (1912); in World War I, commander of 3d army at Przemyśl (1914), commander of 5th army in 11 battles on Isonzo front culminating in Caporetto (Dec. 1917); field marshal general and commander in chief on the Italian front (1918).

Boron, Robert de. See BORRON.

Bor·ough *or* **Bur·rough** *or* **Bur·rowe** \'bər-(,)ō, 'bə-(,)rō\ *or* **Bor·rows** \'bər-(,)ōz, 'bə-(,)rōz; 'bär-(,)ōz, 'bór-\, Stephen. 1525–1584. English navigator. Master of *Searchthrift,* first English ship to sail around North Cape (named by him) to Russia (1553); discovered entrance to Kara Sea (1557); in charge of three ships sent to open trade relations with Muscovy (1560). His brother ¶William (1536–1599), comptroller of queen's navy; vice admiral under Drake in Cádiz expedition (1587); in command of ship against Armada (1588). ¶Christopher (fl. 1579–1587), son of Stephen, was interpreter of Russian for the Muscovy Company's expedition to Media and Persia (1579).

Borovský, Havel. See Karel HAVLÍČEK.

Bor·ro·meo \,bōr-rō-'mā-ō\, Carlo. Saint. 1538–1584. Italian prelate. Created cardinal and archbishop of Milan by uncle, Pope Pius IV (1560); helped plan Council of Trent (1562–63) and responsible for executing its decrees; brought out Roman catechism (1566); fostered clerical education in see of Milan; known esp. for his ecclesiastical reforms. Founded order of Oblates of St. Ambrose (1578). His cousin ¶Federigo (1564–1631), also a cardinal (1587) and archbishop of Milan, founded Ambrosian Library at Milan (1609).

Bor·ro·mi·ni \,bōr-rō-'mē-nē\, Francesco. *Orig. surname* Cas·tel·li \käs-'tel-lē\. 1599–1667. Italian architect and sculptor. Associated with Maderno and Bernini, esp. in building of Palazzo Barberini (1620–31), and designing Baldacchino in St. Peter's (1631–33); alone built S. Carlo alle Quattro Fontane (1638–41), S. Ivo della Sapienza (1642–60), Collegio di Propaganda Fide and its Re Magi chapel (1662–64), S. Agnese in Agone (1652 ff.), S. Andrea delle

Fratte (1653–65). Noted for novel and brillant use of space and geometric forms.

Bor·ron *or* **Bo·ron** \bò-rō^{n}\, Robert de. 12th–13th century. French poet. Known for Holy Grail trilogy comprising *Joseph d'Arimathie, Merlin,* and *Perceval.*

Bor·row \'bär-(,)ō, 'bòr-\, George Henry. 1803–1881. English author and linguist. Early acquired several languages; during law apprenticeship produced *Celebrated Trials* (1825). Tramped through England, met gypsies; as agent of Bible Society, toured Russia, Spain, Portugal, Morocco (1833–40); published *Romantic Ballads* translated from Danish (1826) and *Targum,* translations from thirty languages and dialects (1835); compiled lexicon of Romany (1874). Author of *The Zincali, or the Gypsies in Spain* (1841), *The Bible in Spain,* which made him famous (1843), *Lavengro* (1851) and its sequel *Romany Rye* (1857), both dealing with gypsy life, and *Wild Wales* (1862).

Borsa, Roger. See Roger, Duke of Apulia.

Bort, Léon Philippe Teisserenc de. See Teisserenc de Bort.

Bort·nyan·sky \bərt-'nyän-skəi\, Dmitry Stepanovich. 1751–1825. Russian composer. Kapellmeister (1779–1825), director (from 1796), Imperial Chapel Choir; composed church music, operas, chamber music.

Boru, Brian. See Brian.

Bo·san·quet \'bō-zən-,ket, -kət\, Bernard. 1848–1923. English philosopher. Fellow and tutor, Oxford (1870–81); professor, St. Andrew's (1903–08). Author of works on logic inspired by Lotze, as *Knowledge and Reality* (1885), *Essentials of Logic* (1895), *Implication and Linear Inference* (1920); on ethics and aesthetics influenced by Hegel, as *History of Aesthetic* (1892), *Philosophical Theory of the State* (1899), *Some Suggestions in Ethics* (1918).

Bos·boom-Tous·saint \,bòz-bōm-tü-'sa^{n}\, Anna Louisa Geertruida, *nee* Toussaint. 1812–1886. Dutch novelist. Author of historical romances as *Het Huis Lauernesse* (1840), *Majoor Frans* (1874). m. (1851) ¶Johannes Bos·boom \'bòz-bōm\ (1817–1891), Dutch church and architectural painter.

Bos·cán Al·mo·ga·ver \bòs-'kän-äl-mō-gä-'ver\, Juan. c.1490–1542. Spanish poet. At court of Charles V, Granada (1519 ff.); adapted Italian meters and verse forms to Spanish poetry; credited with founding Italian school of poetry in Spain.

Bos·caw·en \bäs-'kō-ən, -'kò-(w)ən\, Edward. *Known as* Old Dreadnought. 1711–1761. English naval officer. Won distinction at taking of Porto Bello (1739) and siege of Cartagena (1741); won victory of Finisterre (1747); intercepted French squadron off Newfoundland, capturing 2 ships and 1500 men (1755); admiral (1758); assisted at taking of Louisburg and island of Cape Breton (1758); defeated French Toulon fleet in Lagos Bay (1759).

Bosch \'bòsh\, Carl. 1874–1940. German chemist. Joined Badische Anilin- und Sodafabrik firm (1899); president of successor I.G. Farbenindustrie (1925). Developed Haber-Bosch process for commercial production of ammonia (1909 ff.); awarded with F. Bergius Nobel prize for chemistry (1931).

Bosch \'bòs, *Angl* 'bäsh, 'bòsh\, Hieronymus. *Also known as* Jeroen van Ae·ken \'ä-kən\ *or* van Aken. 1450–1516. Dutch painter. Painter of religious pictures marked by use of symbols and allegory and often employing fantastic representations of devils, monstrosities, and the like; works included *Ecce Homo, Seven Deadly Sins, Garden of Earthly Delights, Temptation of St. Anthony, Hay Wain, The Crowning with Thorns, Carrying of the Cross.*

Bosch, Johannes van den. Count. 1780–1844. Dutch colonialist. In army in Batavia (1798–1810); rejoined army, becoming chief of general staff; as commissary general of Antilles and Surinam (1827–28) introduced Dutch East Indies Culture System of enforced agricultural production and labor, greatly increasing output and exports; governor general of Dutch East Indies (1830–33); minister for colonies (1835–39).

Bosch, Robert August. 1861–1942. German engineer and industrialist. Founder (1886) of Robert Bosch Co., Stuttgart, manufacturers of magnetos, igniters, automatic lubricators, and other equipment for power-driven engines and vehicles; produced Bosch spark plug invented (1902) by colleague G. Honold.

Bo·sco \'bòs-kō, *Angl* 'bäs-(,)kō, 'bòs-\, Giovanni Melchior. Saint. 1815–1888. Italian priest. Began working with boys in Turin; founded (1859) Society of St. Francis de Sales, or Salesian Fathers; with St. Maria Mazzarello founded (1872) Salesian Sisters. Canonized (1934).

Bos·co·vich \'bòs-kō-vēch\, Ruggiero Giuseppe. *Orig.* Rudjer Josip Boš·ko·vić \'bòsh-kō-vēch\. 1711–1787. Croatian mathematician, astronomer, and physicist. Joined Jesuits (1725); taught in Rome (1740), Pavia (1764), Milan (1770); director of optics for French navy (1773–83). First in Italy to write in advocacy of Newton's theories; developed methods for calculating orbits, rotation of celestial objects; improved geodetic surveys, led international project to measure meridian arcs.

Bose \'bōs, 'bòs, 'bòsh\, Sir Jagadis Chandra. 1858-1937. Indian physicist and plant physiologist. Professor, Presidency College, Calcutta (1885–1915); founder and director (1917–37) of Bose Research Institute, Calcutta. Invented improved form of wireless coherer, an instrument for indicating the refraction of electric waves, and an instrument (the crescograph) sensitive to extremely slight movements in plants; used last to study plant responses to mechanical stimuli. Author of *Response in the Living and Non-Living* (1902), *The Nervous Mechanism of Plants* (1926), etc.

Bose, Satyendra Nath. 1894–1974. Indian mathematician and physicist. Professor, Dacca (1921–45), Calcutta (1945–56); known for work in quantum mechanics, esp. development (1924–45) of Bose-Einstein statistics.

Bose, Subhas Chandra. 1897–1945. Indian politician. Supported Gandhi and joined Swaraj party (1923); chief executive officer of Calcutta (1924); president of Bengal Congress (1927); led Bengal delegation to National Congress (1928); advocated complete independence for India; many times imprisoned; wrote *The Indian Struggle* (1935); president of the Indian National Congress (1938).

Bo·sel·li \bō-'sel-lē\, Paolo. 1838–1932. Italian politician. Professor of economic science, Rome; deputy (1870–1921); senator (1921–32); held various ministerial posts including education (1888), treasury (1899); premier (1916–17); declared war on Germany (1916).

Bö·sen·dor·fer \'bœ-zən-,dòr-fər\, Ignaz. 1796–1859. Austrian piano maker. Founded (1828) Viennese piano firm that produced variety of prized pianos, including 8-octave imperial grand.

Bo·sio \bōz-yō, bòz-\, François-Joseph. 1768–1845. French sculptor. Carved bas-reliefs of Column Vendôme in Paris, statue of Louis XIV in Paris, and portrait busts of Napoléon, Joséphine, Louis XVIII, etc.

Bos·quet \bòs-ke\, Pierre-Jean-François. 1810–1861. French army officer. Division commander in French army in Crimea; won victory at Alma; saved British army at Inkerman; wounded in assault on the Malakoff (1855); created senator and marshal of France (1856).

Boss \'bäs, 'bòs\, Lewis. 1846–1912. American astronomer, b. Providence, R.I. Director, Dudley Observatory, Albany, N.Y. (from 1876). Compiler of two catalogues of stars (1910, 1937).

Bosse \bòs\, Abraham. 1602–1676. French painter, engraver, and architect. Professor of perspective, Academy of Painting (1648–61); known esp. for satirical prints lampooning various trades and public personages, which contributed to development of art of caricature; works included *The Ages of Man* (1631), *Marriage of Ladislas IV* (1645).

Bos·sert \'bòs-ərt\, Helmuth Theodor. 1889–1961. German philologist and archaeologist. Professor, Berlin (1934–61), Istanbul (1934–61); excavated Hittite site at Karatepe, Turkey (1946 ff.) and discovered bilingual inscriptions permitting translation of Hittite. Author of *Geschichte des Kunstgewerbes aller Völker und Zeiten* (1928–35), *Die Ausgrabungen auf dem Karatepe* (1950), *Altsyrien* (1951).

Bossu, Adam le. See Adam de la Halle.

Bos·suet \bò-sw̅e-e\, Jacques-Bénigne. 1627–1704. French prelate. Achieved fame as sermonist and controversialist; bishop of Condom (1669–70); tutor to the dauphin (1670–81); bishop of Meaux (1681). Took lead in settling Gallican controversy (1681–82); attacked Quietism, obtained condemnation of Fénelon (1699). Known for funerary orations, classics of French Baroque prose, and for tracts supporting absolutism, as *Politique tirée des propres paroles de l'Ecriture sainte* (pub. 1709).

Bos·ton \'bò-stən\, John. *Known as* John Boston of Bury \'ber-ē\; *also called* Boston Bur·i·en·sis \-,ber-ē-'en-səs, -,bùr-\. 15th century. English bibliographer. Benedictine monk; compiled catalog of Latin writers, *Catologus Scriptorum Ecclesiae.*

Boston, Thomas. 1676–1732. Scottish clergyman. Promoted publication (1718) in Scotland of Calvinist work *The Marrow of Modern Divinity* by "E.F." Author of *The Fourfold State* (1720), and *Crook in the Lot,* once a favorite in rural Scotland.

Bos·well \'bäz-,wel, -wəl\, James. 1740–1795. Scottish lawyer and biographer of Samuel Johnson. Son of Alexander Boswell, laird of Au·chin·leck \'af-(,)lek; ,òk-ən-'lek, ,òk-\, lord justiciary. Acquainted with Voltaire, Rousseau, Wilkes, General Paoli. Met Dr. Johnson in London (1763), visited him frequently (1772–84), toured Hebrides with him (1773), was elected member of Literary Club (1773); took notes unceasingly of Dr. Johnson's conversations. Succeeded to father's estate (1782); called to English bar (1786). Author of *Account of Corsica* (1768), *Journal of Tour to Hebrides* (1785), *Life of Samuel Johnson,* masterpiece of biography (1791); his journal published as *Private Papers of James Boswell from Malahide Castle* (1928–34). His eldest son ¶Sir Alexander (1775–1822), antiquary and poet, issued reprints of old poems from his private press; author of songs as "Good night, and joy be wi' ye a'," "Jenny's Bawbee," "Jenny dang the Weaver"; Conservative M.P. (1818–21). A younger son ¶James (1778–1822), lawyer, assisted E. Malone with second edition of Shakespeare, and edited third variorum Shakespeare (1821).

Bos·worth \'bäz-(,)wərth\, Joseph. 1789–1876. English clergyman and philologist. Professor, Oxford (1858–76). Author of *An Anglo-Saxon Dictionary* (1838).

Bo·tev \'bò-tef\, Khristo. 1848–1876. Bulgarian poet and patriot. Active in Bulgarian literary nationalist movement (from 1867); in exile in Rumania (1867–76); returned leading group of rebels to join anti-Turkish uprising

(1876), killed by Turkish troops. Author of patriotic verses *Pesni u stihove* (1875).

Boteville, Francis and William. See William THYNNE.

Both \'bōt\, Jan. c.1618–1652. Dutch painter. Introduced Italianate trend into Dutch landscape painting; known also for genre works.

Both, Pieter. c.1550–1615. Dutch colonialist. First governor general of Dutch East India Co. (1609–14); established (1610) trading posts at Bantam and Jacatra (later Batavia and later still Djakarta).

Bo·tha \'bō-tä\, Louis. 1862–1919. South African soldier and politician. Helped form New Republic (1884) in present Natal; elected to Volksraad of South African Republic (1897). Commanded Boer army before Ladysmith (1899); defeated British at Colenso, Spioenkop, Vaalkrams; succeeded Joubert as commander in chief (1900). Carried on peace negotiations; became first prime minister of Transvaal (1907); headed Transvaal delegation at union convention (1908–09); first prime minister of Union of South Africa (1910–19); established South African party (1911). Put down Afrikaner revolt against intervention in World War I, and won surrender of German forces in South West Africa (1915); with Jan Smuts attended Paris peace conference as representative of South Africa (1919).

Bo·the \'bō-tə\, Walther Wilhelm Georg Franz. 1891–1957. German physicist. Professor, Berlin (1920–31), Giessen (1931–34); director of Max Planck Institute, Heidelberg (1934–57). With H. Geiger demonstrated (1925) particle nature of photons; devised new particle detection method, by which he showed (1929) that cosmic rays are particles; detected (1930) new radiation later shown to be neutron. Awarded Nobel prize in physics (1954) with Max Born.

Bothwell, 4th Earl of. See James HEPBURN.

Bot·sa·ris \bōt-'sär-ēs\, Markos. *Ital.* Marco Boz·za·ri \bōt-tsär-ē\. c.1788–1823. Greek patriot. Active in struggle of Souliots against brigand Ali Pasha (to 1803); fled to Corfu, where he served (1803–19) in Albanian regiment under French command; joined patriotic society Philikì Etaireía (1814); with Souliots joined Ali Pasha against Turkish government (1820); with Souliots joined Greek independence struggle (1821); led Souliots in defense of Missolonghi (1822–23) and in attack on Albanians at Karpenisíon (Aug. 21, 1823), where he was killed. Command of Souliot guerillas passed to Lord Byron.

Bot·ta \'bōt-tä, *Fr* bō-tà\, Carlo Giuseppe Guglielmo. 1766–1837. Italian physician and historian. Exiled to France (1795); served as surgeon in French army; member of Corps Législatif. Author of *Storia della guerra dell'indipendenza degli Stati Uniti d'America* (1809), *Storia d'Italia* (1832). His son ¶Paul-Émile (1802–1870), French archaeologist; appointed consul at Mosul (1842); discovered (1843) at Khorsabad palace of Sargon II. Author of *Monuments de Ninève* (1849–50).

Bot·te·si·ni \bōt-tā-'zē-nē\, Giovanni. 1821–1889. Italian musician and composer. Virtuoso double-bassist. Composed works for double bass; operas including *Cristoforo Colombo* (1847), *Marion Delorme* (1862), *Vinciguerra il bandito* (1870), *Ali Babà* (1871); oratorio *Garden of Olivet* (1887); symphonies, a quartet, and overtures.

Bött·ger \'bœt-gər\ *or* **Böt·ti·ger** \'bœt-i-gər\, Johann Friedrich. 1682–1719. German ceramist. With E. von Tschirnhaus, produced white china and a reddish-brown stoneware called Böttger and later Meissen ware; established factory at Dresden, later (1710) removed to Meissen.

Botticelli, Sandro. See Alessandro FILIPEPI.

Bot·tome \bə-'tōm\, Phyllis. 1884–1963. English writer. Works included novels *Raw Material* (1905), *Wind in His Fists* (1931), *Private Worlds* (1934), *Level Crossing* (1936), *Mortal Storm* (1937), *London Pride* (1941), *Within the Cup* (1943), *Under the Skin* (1950), *Not in Our Stars* (1955); short stories; *Alfred Adler: Apostle of Freedom* (1939); memoirs, etc.

Bot·tom·ley \'bät-əm-lē\, Gordon. 1874–1948. English poet and dramatist. Author of verse dramas including *A Vision of Giorgione* (1910), *King Lear's Wife* (1915), *Gruach* (1921), *The White Widow* (1936). Author also of lyric verse, as *Chambers of Imagery* (1907, 1912), *Poems of Thirty Years* (1925).

Bottomley, Horatio William. 1860–1933. English journalist and financier. Made fortune floating speculative stocks; established weekly *John Bull* (1906), vehicle of rabid patriotism during World War I; M.P. (1906–12, 1918–22). Bankrupt (1911); regained fortune in lotteries, etc.; finally convicted of misappropriation of funds held in trust (1922), and imprisoned for 5 years.

Botyov, Khristo. See BOTEV.

Botzaris, Markos. See BOTSARIS.

Bou·char·don \bü-shär-dōⁿ\, Edme. 1698–1762. French sculptor. Transitional figure from Rococo to Neoclassicism. Works included 8 figures of Apostles for Saint-Sulpice, Paris; *Christ à la colonne, Mère des douleurs, L'Amour taillant son arc;* equestrian statue of Louis XV; decoration for Neptune fountain, Versailles, etc.

Bou·cher \bü-shā\, Auguste-Gaspard-Louis. Baron Des·noy·ers \dān-wà-yā\. *Called* Boucher-Desnoyers. 1779–1857. French engraver. Engraver to the king (1825); best known for engravings after Raphael.

Boucher, François. 1703–1770. French painter. Director of Royal Academy and chief court painter (1765); favorite of Mme. de Pompadour; paintings in soft colors on generally frivolous subjects considered zenith of French Rococo art; also designed tapestries for Beauvais factory and porcelains for Gobelins.

Bou·cher \'baù-chər\, Jonathan. 1738–1804. English clergyman. In Virginia and Maryland (1759–75); forced to return to England for royalist views. Author of *A View of the Causes and Consequences of the American Revolution* (1797). His glossary of obsolete and provincial words was published (1807) as *A Supplement to Dr. Johnson's Dictionary of the English Language.*

Bou·cher de Crève·coeur de Perthes \bü-shā-də-krev-kœr-də-pert\, Jacques. 1788–1868. French archaeologist and writer. While director of customhouse of Abbeville (1825 ff.) excavated gravel deposits of Somme Valley, discovering Stone Age tools, etc.; first to bring scientific attention to such evidence of man's antiquity; attracted notice of Charles Lyell. Author of *Antiquités celtiques et antédiluviennes* (1847–64).

Boucher-Desnoyers. See Auguste BOUCHER.

Bou·chor \bü-shòr\, Maurice. 1855–1929. French poet and playwright. Author of *Chansons joyeuses* (1875), *Le Faust moderne* (1878), *Les Symboles* (1888–95), *Trois mystères* (1892), *Chants populaires* (1895–1909), *Saynètes et farces* (1913), etc.

Bou·ci·cault \'bü-si-,kō\ *or* **Bour·ci·cault** \'bùr-si-,kō\, Dion. *Orig.* Dionysius Lardner Bour·si·quot \'bùr-si-,kō\. 1820 or 1822–1890. American actor and playwright, b. Dublin, Ireland. On stage (1837); to New York (1853), with reputation already established. A leading figure on N.Y. stage (1853–62; again 1872–90). Among his plays were *London Assurance* (with John Brougham, 1841), *Old Heads and Young Hearts* (1844), *The Corsican Brothers* (1852), *The Poor of New York* (1857), *The Octoroon* (1859), *The Colleen Bawn* (1860), *Arrah-na-Pogue* (1864), an adaptation of *Rip Van Winkle* (1865) for Joseph Jefferson, *The O'Dowd* (1873), *The Shaughraun* (1874); last appearance (1886) in his play *The Jilt.*

Boucicaut. See Jean le MEINGRE.

Bou·dic·ca \bü-'dik-ə\. *Also called* Bo·a·di·cea \,bō-əd-ə-'sē-ə\. d. 60 A.D. British queen. Wife of Prasutagus, king of Iceni, who left fortune to daughters and to Emperor Nero; humiliated by Romans, who annexed kingdom on husband's death (60). Raised rebellion; burned towns, including mart of London, and army camps, massacred 70,000 (according to Tacitus), destroyed 9th Legion in battle; defeated by provincial governor Suetonius Paulinus; died of shock or perhaps took poison.

Bou·din \bü-daⁿ\, Eugène-Louis. 1824–1898. French painter. Known esp. for sea and beach scenes in manner prefiguring Impressionists; master of light; one of first painters to work in open air directly from nature.

Bou·di·not \'büd-ᵊn-,ō\, Elias. 1740–1821. American Revolutionary politician, b. Philadelphia. Member from N.J., Continental Congress (1777, 1778, 1781–84), president (1782, 1783); U.S. House of Representatives (1789–95). Director, U.S. mint (1795–1805).

Boué \bwā\, Ami, *in full* Amédée. 1794–1881. Austrian geologist. Began study of geology while a medical student in Edinburgh; helped found (1830) Société Géologique de France. Author of *Essai géologique sur l'Écosse* (1820), *Mémoires géologiques et paléontologiques* (1832), *La Turquie d'Europe* (1840), *Essai de carte géologique du globe terrestre* (1845).

Bouf·flers \bü-fler\, Louis-François de. Duc. 1644–1711. French soldier. Distinguished himself as commander of dragoons in Dutch War (1672–78); marshal of France (1693); created duke (1694); commanded defense of Namur against William III of Orange (1695). Commanded French forces in Spanish Netherlands in War of Spanish Succession (1701–11); defeated Dutch at Nijmegen (1702) before being driven back by duke of Marlborough; commander of royal bodyguard (1704); defended Lille against Prince Eugene (1708); on death of Marshal Villars executed masterly retreat from Malplaquet (1709).

Boufflers, Stanislas-Jean de. Chevalier. 1738–1815. French soldier, poet, and courtier. Refusing church career, joined Knights of Malta; brigadier of infantry (1780) and field marshal (1784). Governor of Senegal (1785–88); deputy to Estates-General (1789); émigré in Prussia (1791–1800); lived in retirement on his estates (from 1800). Author of romance *Aline, reine de Golconde* (1761), *Poésies et pièces fugitives* (1782), *Le Derviche* (1810).

Bou·gain·ville \bü-gaⁿ-vēl\, Louis-Antoine de. 1729–1811. French navigator. Aide-de-camp to Montcalm in Canada (1756); served in Germany in Seven Years' War (1761–63); entered navy (1763); made unsuccessful attempt to colonize Falkland Islands; commanded first French expedition around the world (1766–69) and visited Tuamotu, Tahiti, Samoa, New Hebrides, the Louisiade and New Britain archipelagoes. Secretary to Louis XV (1772); commodore in French fleet aiding in American Revolution; made a senator and count by Napoléon I. An island of Solomon group, two straits in Solomon and New Hebrides groups, and tropical vine bougainvillaea bear his name.

Bough·ton \ˈbau̇t-ᵊn\, George Henry. 1833–1905. English painter. Brought up at Albany, N.Y.; resided (after 1861) in London. Known for landscapes and genre scenes drawn from Dutch life and early American colonial life; illustrator of *Rip Van Winkle* (1893) and *Knickerbocker History* (1886).

Boughton, Rutland. 1878–1960. English composer. Known esp. for romantic operas including *The Immortal Hour* (1913), *Queen of Cornwall* (1924), *The Lily Maid* (1934), *Galahad* (1944); also wrote 3 symphonies, chamber music, choral works, etc.

Bou·guer \bü-ger\, Pierre. 1698–1758. French hydrographer and mathematician. Professor of hydrography, Havre (1713); measured intensity of light of sun as compared with that of moon and thus helped found photometry; studied variations in gravity at elevations; sent to Peru (with Godin, La Condamine, and Jussieu, 1735) to measure a degree of the meridian near the equator.

Bou·gue·reau \bü-g(ə-)rō\, Adolphe-William. 1825–1905. French painter. Known for academic works on religious and allegorical themes as *La Vierge consolatrice, Triomphe du martyr, La Naissance de Vénus.*

Bou·il·het \bü-ye\, Louis-Hyacinthe. 1822–1869. French poet and playwright. Close friend of Flaubert. Author of Parnassian verse in *Melaenis* (1851), *Fossiles* (1854), and plays *Madame de Montarcy* (1856), *L'Oncle million* (1860), *Faustine* (1864), *La Conjuration d'Amboise* (1866).

Bouil·lé \bü-yā\, François-Claude-Amour de. Marquis. 1739–1800. French general. Governor of Gaudeloupe (1768); served in American Revolution; brutally suppressed mutinies at Metz and Nancy (1789–90); plotted with Louis XVI to get him out of France (1791), but failed and fled to England.

Bouil·lon \bü-yōⁿ\. French family of nobility, deriving its name from medieval duchy and town of Bouillon, now part of Luxembourg province, Belgium. The duchy once belonged to the crusader Godefroy (see GODFREY of Bouillion); later it came under the houses of La Marck and La Tour d'Auvergne (*qq.v.*).

Bou·lain·vil·liers \bü-laⁿ-vēl-yā\, Henri de. Comte de Saint-Saire \saⁿ-ser\. 1658–1722. French historian. Developed view of history based on broad analysis of cultural and institutional change. Author of *État de la France* (1727–28), *Essai sur la noblesse de France* (1732), etc.

Bou·lan·ger \bü-läⁿ-zhā\, Georges-Ernest-Jean-Marie. 1837–1891. French general and politician. Served at seige of Metz (1870); helped suppress Paris Commune (1871); brigadier general (1880); director of infantry (1882); commanded army of occupation in Tunis (1884–85). Minister of war (1886–87); became figurehead for revanchists including Bonapartists, royalists, and leftists; dismissed from army (1888); elected deputy (1888); resigned on refusal of chamber to pass his program of constitutional reforms, but reelected (1889); aroused popular enthusiasm among elements antagonistic to government; called "Man on Horseback" because he often appeared mounted before Paris crowds. Boulangist movement aroused fears of a coup d'etat; accused of conspiracy by Tirard ministry; fled abroad (1889); committed suicide.

Boulanger, Gustave-Rodolphe-Clarence. 1824–1888. French painter. Best known for his Greek, Roman, and Oriental scenes.

Boulanger, Louis. 1806–1867. French painter. Painted portraits of Hugo, Balzac, Dumas père, and other notables; religious pictures *Saint Marc, Mater Dolorosa,* etc.; historical subjects as *L'Assassinat de Louis d'Orléans.*

Boulanger, Nadia-Juliette. 1887–1979. French music teacher. Associated (from 1921) with Conservatoire Américaine (director from 1950); taught also at Conservatoire de Paris (1945–57) and privately. Pupils included Aaron Copland, Roy Harris, Darius Milhaud, Walter Piston, Roger Sessions, Virgil Thomson, Leonard Bernstein. Noted also as a conductor.

Boule, André-Charles. See BOULLE.

Boule \bül\, Marcellin, *in full* Pierre-Marcellin. 1861–1942. French paleontologist. Professor, Musée National d'Histoire Naturelle (1902–36); known for work on geology of mountains of central France and on human and other mammalian fossils; reconstructed (1908) first complete Neanderthal skeleton. A founder of journal *L'Anthropologie* (1890; editor 1893–1940); author of *Les Hommes fossiles* (1921).

Boulle *or* **Boule** \bül\, André-Charles. *Surname also appears in English as* Buhl. 1642–1732. French cabinetmaker. Succeeded Macé as cabinetmaker to king (from 1672); created much of the furnishing for Versailles; also supplied pieces to Philip V of Spain and other royalty. Introduced furniture decorated by inlaying brass and tortoise shell on ebony or ebonized wood, a style called boulle or buhl work that was widely imitated.

Boul·lée \bü-lā\, Étienne-Louis. 1728–1799. French architect. Designed mansions, esp. Hôtel de Brunoy (1772); best known for unexecuted designs for often colossal buildings and monuments in severely geometric Neoclassical style, as designs for "Chapel of the Dead" (1775–90) and for cenotaph of Sir Isaac Newton (1784).

Boul·longne *or* **Bou·logne** \bü-lōnʸ\. Family of French artists including: Louis, *called* le Père *or* le Vieux (1609–1674); an original member of Academy of Painting and Sculpture (1648); works included *Les Enfants de Sciva, Le Martyre de saint Simon, La Décollation de saint Paul.* His son ¶Bon, *called* l'Aîné (1649–1717), was known for decoration in Grand Trianon, Versailles, and chapels of Saint-Jérôme and Saint-Ambroise in the Invalides. Another son ¶Louis, *called* le Jeune (1654–1733), professor (1693) and director (1722) of the Academy; first painter to Louis XV (1724). Sisters of Bon and the younger Louis, ¶Geneviève (1645–1710) and ¶Madeleine (1646–1709), were also painters, known for still lifes esp. of trophies of war or the hunt.

Boulogne, Jean. See GIAMBOLOGNA.

Boul·so·ver \ˈbōl-ˌzō-vər\, Thomas. 1706–1788. English cutler. Discovered (1743) fusibility of copper and silver and that thus fused they could be worked as one; began manufacturing various items from this "old Sheffield plate."

Boult \ˈbōlt\, Sir Adrian Cedric. 1899–1983. English conductor. Launched conducting career with Royal Philharmonic Society (1918); appointed conductor of Birmingham Orchestra (1924); assumed conductorship of London Bach Choir (1927); founded and served (1930–50) as director of music for British Broadcasting Corporation Symphony Orchestra; championed works of Elgar, Holst, Vaughan Williams, and other English composers; conducted at coronations of King George VI and Queen Elizabeth II; knighted (1937).

Boul·ter \ˈbōl-tər\, Hugh. 1672–1742. English prelate. Chaplain to George I (1719); archbishop of Armagh (1724); lord justice in Ireland (1724–42); virtual ruler of Ireland in period of Protestant Ascendancy; increased stringency of anti-Catholic laws.

Boul·ton \ˈbōlt-ᵊn\, Matthew. 1728–1809. English manufacturer and engineer. Invented process of steel inlay; began financing (1769) and became partner of James Watt (1775) and with him established plant for manufacturing steam engines; patented steam-powered coin press (1790); established new copper coinage for Great Britain (1797).

Bou·mé·dienne \bü-mād-yen\, Houari. *Orig.* Mohammed ben Bra·him Bou·khar·rou·ba \ben-ˈbrä-hēm-bük-ä-ˈrü-bä\. 1927–1978. Algerian soldier and politician. Joined guerilla war for Algerian independence from France (1955); chief of staff of National Liberation Army (1960); led successful invasion from Tunisia (1962). Minister of defense and vice president (1962–65); deposed Pres. Ben Bella (1965); president of Algeria (1965–78).

Bou·quet \bü-ˈkā\, Henry. 1719–1765. British officer in America, b. Switzerland. Served in Dutch army; to America (1756); served (1758) in expedition against Fort Duquesne and built Forbes's Road; naturalized by Maryland and Pennsylvania. Instrumental in crushing the Indian rebellion under Pontiac (1763); brigadier general (1765).

Bou·quet \bü-ke\, Martin, *called* Dom Martin. 1685–1754. French religious. Benedictine monk; began editing of *Rerum gallicarum et francicarum scriptores* (1738–1904), a collection of historical documents.

Bou·ras·sa \bü-rȧ-sȧ\, Henri, *in full* Joseph-Napoléon-Henri. 1868–1952. French-Canadian journalist and politician, b. Montreal. Contributor to *Le Nationaliste* in Montreal (from 1897); founder and editor of independent newspaper *Le Devoir* (from 1910). Member of Dominion House of Commons (1896–99, 1900–07, 1925–35); Nationalist party leader (from 1900). Opposed Canadian participation in World War I.

Bour·ba·ki \bür-bȧ-kē\, Charles-Denis-Sauter. 1816–1897. French general. Served in Algeria (1840–42), Crimean War (1854–55), and Italian campaign; aide-de-camp to Napoléon III (1869); commanded Imperial Guard at Metz (1870); failed to raise seige of Belfort (1871), replaced; retired (1881).

Bour·bon \bür-bōⁿ, *Angl* ˈbu̇(ə)r-bən\. *Span.* Bor·bón \bȯr-ˈbȯn\. French royal family, named from a castle and seigniory in central France, whose descendants formed ruling dynasties in France, Spain, and Naples. Its remote ancestor (9th century) was Baron Ai·mar \ˈī-ˌmär, e-mȧr\, one of whose descendants, Béatrix de Bourbon, m. (1272) ¶Robert de France (1256–1318), comte de Cler·mont \kler-mōⁿ\, 6th son of Louis IX.

DUCS DE BOURBON: Robert was succeeded by his son ¶Louis I (1279–1342), for whom the lordship was raised to a duchy (1327); Louis also acquired La Marche (1322) in exchange for Clermont. Duchy of Bourbon descended directly through ¶Pierre I (1311–1356), whose daughters Blanche and Jeanne married respectively Pedro of Castile and Charles V of France; ¶Louis II (1337–1410); ¶Jean I (c.1381–1434), who married Marie de Berry, comtesse de Montpensier, and thus added that title to family; ¶Charles I (1401–1456), whose daughter Isabella married Charles the Bold; ¶Jean II (1427–1488), from whom title passed to his brother ¶Pierre II (1439–1503) and thence to ¶Charles de Bourbon-Mont·pen·sier \-mōⁿ-päⁿ-syā\ (1490–1527), great-grandson of Jean I; comte de Montpensier (from 1501); m. Suzanne, daughter of Pierre II; became duc de Bourbon (1503); named constable of France by Francis I (1515); lost favor of king, who moved to confiscate his lands; initiated treasonable negotiations with Henry VIII of England and Emperor Charles V; escaped France and entered service of Charles V (1523); unsuccessfully invaded France (1524); killed at head of German-Spanish assault on Rome. His lands confiscated in France (1527). Headship of House of Bourbon passed to line of La Marche-Vendôme.

La Marche-Vendôme: Jacques I (c.1315–1361), 4th son of Louis I, duc de Bourbon, became (1327) comte de La Marche \lə-märsh\; he was succeeded by sons ¶Pierre (d. 1362) and ¶Jean (1337–1393), latter of whom m. Catherine de Vendôme; their children included ¶Charlotte (d. 1434), who married John II of Cyprus, ¶Jacques II (1367–1438), comte de La Marche, who m. 2d Joan II of Naples, and ¶Louis (c.1376–1446), comte de Ven•dôme \vä^{n}-dōm\. Louis was succeeded by his son ¶Jean (1429–1478), after whom the line divided.
Junior line ran from Jean's second son ¶Louis (d. c.1520), prince de La Roche-sur-Yon \lá-rȯsh-sᵫr-yō^{n}\, who married Louise, sister of Constable Charles, last direct duc de Bourbon; through her, their descendants gained the Montpensier title: ¶Louis (1513–1582), duc de Montpensier, whose daughter Charlotte m. William the Silent, prince of Orange, and whose son ¶François (1543–1592) succeeded as duc de Montpensier; thence to ¶Henri (1573–1608) and ¶Marie (1605–1627), duchesse de Montpensier, who m. Gaston, duc d'Orléans.
Senior line ran from Jean's elder son ¶François (1470–1495), comte de Vendôme, through ¶Charles (1489–1537), for whom Vendôme was raised to a duchy (1515), ¶Antoine (1518–1562), who m. (1548) Jeanne d'Albret, titular queen of Navarre, and ¶Henry (1553–1610), who became titular king of Navarre (1572) and king of France as Henry IV (1589). From Henry descended all Bourbon kings of France. Another son of Charles, ¶Louis (1530–1509), founded House of Condé (*q.v.*).

Bourbon Kings of France: On the extinction of the male line of Valois (1589), the throne passed to the senior Bourbon, Henry of Navarre, who became Henry IV (*q.v.*); in direct descent from him were all kings of France to 1792 and 1814–48: Louis XIII, Louis XIV, Louis XV, Louis XVI, Louis XVII, Louis XVIII, Charles X, Louis-Philippe (*qq.v.*).
For Henry's brother Gaston, duc d'Orléans, see Orléans III; Philippe I, son of Louis XIII, founded last House of Orléans (see Orléans IV).
Other notable members of royal Bourbon line included: ¶César de Bourbon (1594–1665), illegitimate son of Henry IV; legitimized (1595), created duc de Vendôme (1598); m. (1609) daughter of Philippe de Lorraine, duc de Mer•coeur \mer-kœr\; took part in aristocratic revolts (1614, 1616, 1620), incurring enmity of half-brother Louis XIII and of Cardinal Richelieu; distinguished himself in war against Huguenots (1621); implicated in Chalais conspiracy against Richelieu and imprisoned (1626–30); exile in England (1640–43) following accusation of second plot against Richelieu; supported Mazarin against Fronde and commanded troops against rebels in Burgundy (1650–53); later served against Spain. His son ¶Louis (1612–1669), duc de Mercoeur and (1665) duc de Vendôme, m. niece of Mazarin; helped pacify Toulon and Aix as governor of Provence (1652); took orders (1657); cardinal (1667). A second son ¶François (1616–1669), duc de Beau•fort \bō-fȯr\, was a distinguished soldier; fled France to escape questioning about conspiracy of Cinq-Mars (1642); returned after death of Richelieu (1642); imprisoned for conspiracy by Mazarin (1643–48); general of the Fronde (1648–49). Named admiral; allied with Cardinal de Retz; involved in second Fronde (1650–52); banished after defeat of Condé (1652); restored to favor (1658); led French naval forces in Algeria (1664); sent to aid Venetians against Turks in Crete, where he died in battle. Louis's son ¶Louis-Joseph (1654–1712), duc de Pen•thièvre \pa^{n}-tyevr^{ə}\ and (1669) duc de Vendôme, entered army (1672); lieutenant general (1688); in War of Grand Alliance distinguished himself at Steenkirke (1692) and in capturing Barcelona (1697); in War of Spanish Succession commanded in northern Italy (1702); fought Eugene of Savoy at Luzzara (1702), captured Vercelli (1704), defeated Eugene at Cassano (1705); in Flanders defeated by Eugene and Marlborough at Oudenaarde (1708); failed to relieve besieged Lille (1708); named commander of army of Philip V of Spain (1710); recaptured Madrid and forced surrender of Stanhope (1710); defeated Austrians at Villaviciosa (1710). His brother ¶Philippe (1655–1727), *called* le Prieur de Ven•dôme \lə-prē-œr-də-va^{n}-dōm\, joined Knights of Malta (1666); grand prior of France (1678); field marshal (1691), lieutenant general (1693); disgraced for inaction at Cassano (1705).
An illegitimate son of Louis XIV ¶Louis-Auguste de Bourbon (1670–1736), son of Marquise de Montespan; legitimized and created duc du Maine \men\ (1673); distinguished himself in War of Grand Alliance (1689–97); named prince of the blood with right of succession (1714); despite provisions in will of Louis XIV, deprived of place on council of regency and of command of royal guards by Philippe II, duc d'Orléans (1715); deprived of princely status (1717); embroiled by his wife, Louise-Bénédicte de Bourbon-Condé, in plot to kidnap Orléans and install Philip V of Spain as regent for Louis XV (1718); arrested and imprisoned (1718–20); retired from public life.
Two sons of Charles X: ¶Louis-Antoine (1775–1844), duc d'An•gou•lême \ä^{n}-gü-lem\, fled Revolution (1789); returned with Royalist forces (1814); commanded Royalist army in southern Rhône valley (1815); commanded expedition against anti-Bourbon uprising in Spain (1823). Last dauphin of France; on abdication of father (1830) renounced throne. His brother ¶Charles-Ferdinand (1778–1820), duc de Ber•ry \be-rē\; in exile during Revolution and Empire (1789–1815), serving in army of Prince de Condé and then Russian army and living in England (1801–14); returned to France (1814), retiring to Ghent during Hundred Days; assassinated by Bonapartist fanatic. His wife (m. 1816) ¶Marie-Caroline-Ferdinande-Louise (1798–1870), daughter of Francis I of the Two Sicilies; mother of Louise (m. Charles III of Parma) and ¶Henri (1820–1883), duc de Bor•deaux \bȯr-dō\ and later comte de Cham•bord \shä^{n}-bȯr\; attempted to secure succession for Henri on overthrow of Charles X (1830) and exiled; secretly returned to France (1832), instigated insurrection in favor of Henri at Vendée; imprisoned (1832–33).

Bourbons of Spain: The childless Charles II named as his successor the second grandson of Louis XIV of France and his consort, the infanta Marie-Thérèse, Philippe, duc d'Anjou, who reigned as Philip V (*q.v.*); the House of Borbón ruled Spain 1700–1808, 1814–68, 1874–1931, and from 1975; rulers were Louis, Ferdinand VI, Charles III, Charles IV, Ferdinand VII, Isabella II, Alfonso XII, and Alfonso XIII (*qq.v.*).

Bourbons of Naples: The infante Don Carlos, future Charles III of Spain, succeeded by right of his mother to duchy of Parma (1731) and conquered kingdom of Naples-Sicily (1734); on becoming king of Spain (1759) he resigned Naples-Sicily to his third son Ferdinand I (*q.v.*), whence throne descended to Francis I, Ferdinand II, and Francis II (*qq.v.*).

Bourbons of Parma: The infante Don Carlos of Spain was obliged to renounce Parma (1735), which passed to his brother Philip (*q.v.*), duke (1748–65), and thence to Ferdinand (*q.v.*), at whose death it was annexed to France (1802); Ferdinand's son Louis (*q.v.*) and grandson Charles (*q.v.*) ruled short-lived kingdom of Etruria; Charles subsequently ruled as duke of Lucca (1824–47) and was restored to Parma (1847–49), where he was succeeded by Charles III (*q.v.*) and Robert (1848–1907), last duke (1854–59).

Bourbon-Orléans. See Orléans IV.

Bour•cet \bür-se\, Pierre-Joseph de. 1700–1780. French general. Served in Italy, Germany, Corsica; lieutenant general (1766). Author of *Reconnaissances ... et les plans de campagne* and *Principes de la guerre de montagne;* devised strategy later adopted by Napoléon.

Bour•chier \ˈbau̇-chər\, John. 2d Baron Ber•ners \ˈbər-nərz\. c.1469–1533. English writer and soldier. Served Henry VII and Henry VIII; helped suppress Perkin Warbeck's partisans in Cornwall (1497); chancellor of the exchequer (1516); helped negotiate alliance with Charles I of Spain (1518); present at Field of Cloth of Gold (1520); deputy of Calais (1520–26, 1531–33). Known esp. for translation of Froissart's *Chroniques* (1523–25), *Boke Huon de Bordeuxe* which introduced figure of Oberon into English literature, *Golden boke of Marcus Aurelius* of Antonio de Guevara, etc.

Bourchier, Thomas. c.1412–1486. English prelate. Descendant of King Edward III. Bishop of Worcester (1435–43), of Ely (1443–54); archbishop of Canterbury (1454–86); lord chancellor (1455–56). Maintained stability of church during Wars of the Roses. Crowned Edward IV (1461) and his queen, Elizabeth Woodville (1465). Installed as cardinal (1467). Crowned Richard III (1483), and Henry VII (1485), and married Henry VII to Elizabeth of York (1486).

Bourcicault. See Boucicault.

Bour•da•loue \bür-dá-lü\, Louis. 1632–1704. French cleric. Entered Jesuit order (1648); gained renown as preacher; called to preach at Saint-Louis, Paris (1669); court preacher (from 1670), known for saintly character and fervid eloquence.

Bour•deille \bür-dey\, Pierre de. Abbé and seigneur de Bran•tôme \brä^{n}-tōm\. c.1540–1614. French soldier and chronicler. Author of chronicles of his times, comprising *Les Vies des dames illustres, Les Vies des dames galantes, Les Vies des hommes illustres et grands capitaines français,* and *Les Vies des hommes illustres et des grands capitaines étrangers,* published posthumously as *Mémoires de Messire Pierre de Bourdeilles* (1665–66).

Bour•delle \bür-del\, Antoine, *in full* Émile-Antoine. 1861–1929. French sculptor. Studied under Rodin; noted for works combining classic Greek manner with style of exaggeration conveying heroic energies. Works included a head of Apollo (1900), *Héraklès archer* (1910), *Rodin at Work* (1910), *Dying Centaur* (1914); executed sculptural decorations on "Apollo and His Thought" for Théâtre des Champs-Élysées (1912); later noted as a teacher.

Bour•det \bür-de\, Édouard. 1887–1945. French dramatist. Author of satirical and psychological studies of contemporary society, including *La Prisonnière* (1926), *Vient de paraître* (1928), *Le Sexe faible* (1929), *La Fleur des pois* (1932), *Les Temps difficiles* (1934), *Fric-frac* (1936), *Hyménée* (1941), *Père* (1943). Director of Comédie-Française (1936–40).

Bourdin, Maurice. See Antipope Gregory VIII.

Bour·don \bür-dō^{n}\, Eugène. 1808–1884. French inventor and industrialist. Founded machine shop, Paris (1835) for manufacture of steam engines; invented (1849) Bourdon tube pressure gauge.

Bourdon, Sébastien. 1616–1671. French painter. A founder of Academy of Painting and Sculpture (1648) and subsequently professor there; painter to Queen Christina of Sweden (1652). Known for landscapes, historical and religious scenes, including *Martyrdom of St. Andrew,* decoration for Notre-Dame, Hôtel de Grammont, and Hôtel de Bretonvilliers, *Dead Christ* for Saint-Benoît, *Fall of Simon Magus* for cathedral of Montpellier.

Bour·gault-Du·cou·dray \bür-gō-dü̅-kü-drā\, Louis-Albert. 1840–1910. French composer and musicologist. Composed operas and choral works; compiled collections of folk tunes that had large influence on Debussy and others.

Bour·ge·lat \bür-zhə-lȧ\, Claude. 1712–1779. French veterinarian. Founded and directed at Lyon (1761) first veterinary school in Europe.

Bour·geois \bür-zhwȧ\, Léon-Victor-Auguste. 1851–1925. French politician. Deputy (from 1888); held various ministerial posts; premier of France (1895–96); senator (1905–23; president 1920–23). Headed French delegation to Hague Peace Conferences (1899, 1907); member (from 1903), Permanent Court of Arbitration at The Hague. One of drafters of the Covenant of the League of Nations (1919); chairman of first meeting of League. Awarded Nobel peace prize (1920).

Bourgeois, Louis *or* Loys. c.1510–after 1561. French composer. Lived in Geneva (1541–57); close friend of Calvin; composed 4- and 6-part settings for Psalms; contributed about 85 melodies to *Genevan Psalter* (1562), including "Old Hundredth"; one of first to promote singing instruction by solfeggio.

Bour·get \bür-zhe\, Paul-Charles-Joseph. 1852–1935. French critic, poet, and novelist. Author of verse, as *La Vie inquiète* (1874), *Les Aveux* (1882), several poems set to music by Debussy. Wrote on causes of French pessimism. Novels included *L'Irréparable* (1884), *Cruelle énigme* (1885), *Un Crime d'amour* (1886), *André Cornélis* (1887), *Le Disciple* (1889), *Un Cœur de femme* (1890), *Cosmopolis* (1893), *L'Étape* (1902), *Un Divorce* (1904), *Le Sens de la mort* (1915), *Le Danseur mondain* (1926), *Nos actes nous suivent* (1927).

Bourgogne. See BURGUNDY.

Bourguignon, Le. See Jacques COURTOIS.

Bour·gui·gnon \bür-gēn-yō^{n}\, Louis-Dominique. *Known as* Car·touche \kȧr-tüsh\. 1693–1721. French criminal. Chief of band of Parisian thieves and robbers (c.1717–21); arrested and broken on the wheel; his exploits became legendary and he a figure of romance in popular literature.

Bou·ri·gnon \bü-rēn-yō^{n}\, Antoinette. 1616–1680. Flemish religious. Believed herself in direct communion with God and divinely appointed to criticize religious organizations and restore the spirit of the gospel. Bourignianism spread through Holland and esp. into Scotland.

Bourke, de. See BURGH.

Bourke \'bərk\, Sir Richard. 1777–1855. British soldier and colonialist, b. Ireland. Served in Netherlands and Peninsular campaigns (1798–1814); major general (1821). Governor of New South Wales (1831–37); freed press, sponsored education and church acts, fostered emigration and by impartiality united parties of free convicts and emigrants.

Bourke, Richard Southwell. 6th Earl of Mayo \'mā-(,)ō\. 1822–1872. British politician and colonialist, b. Ireland. M.P. (1847–67); chief secretary for Ireland (1852–67). Viceroy of India (1869–72); secured closer ties with Afghanistan; promoted public works; reformed public finance; founded Mayo Coll., Ajmer.

Bourke-White \'bərk-,(h)wīt\, Margaret. *Orig. surname* White. 1906–1971. American photographer, b. New York City. Associate editor, *Fortune* magazine (1929–33); on staff of *Life* (1936–69). Known for photographs of industrial and monumental sites, displayed often in photomural form; created photo essays on Russia, World War II (as first official woman photojournalist), India, South Africa, etc. Books included *Eyes on Russia* (1931), *U.S.S.R.* (1934), *They Called It Purple Heart Valley* (1944), *Halfway to Freedom* (1946), and with Erskine Caldwell (her husband 1939–42) *You Have Seen Their Faces* (1937), *North of the Danube* (1939), *Say! Is This the U.S.A.?* (1941).

Bour·mont \bür-mō^{n}\, Louis-Auguste-Victor de Ghaisnes de \də-gen-də-\. Comte. 1773–1846. French soldier and politician. An émigré (1789), but returned to France with the Royalist forces (1795); later served under Napoléon; wounded at Lützen (1813); commissioned general of division (1814); went over to Louis XVIII's side four days before Waterloo (1815). Minister of war (1829); commander in chief of Algerian expedition (1830); created marshal of France. Refused to support Louis-Philippe; supported plot of Duchesse de Berry (1832); exiled in Portugal and Rome (1832–40).

Bourne \'bō(ə)rn, 'bȯ(ə)rn, 'bu̇(ə)rn, 'bərn\, Francis Alphonsus. 1861–1935. English prelate. Archbishop of Westminster (1903); cardinal (1911).

Bourne, Hugh. 1772–1852. English preacher. Enthusiastic lay preacher; cut off from Wesleyan connection (1808); founder of the first society of Primitive Methodists (1810).

Bourne, Randolph Silliman. 1886–1918. American essayist and critic, b. Bloomfield, N.J. Contributor to liberal and radical journals; remembered esp. for opposition to American entry into World War I. Author of *Youth and Life* (1913), *Education and Living* (1917), *Untimely Papers* (1919), *History of a Literary Radical* (1920).

Bour·non·ville \'bōr-nōn-,vē-lə\, Auguste. 1805–1879. Danish dancer and choreographer. Director of Royal Danish Ballet and choreographer to Royal Theatre, Copenhagen (1830–77); also directed Swedish Royal Opera (1861–64). Created new and influential style based on bravura dancing and mime. Choregraphed works included *La Sylphide* (1836), *Napoli* (1842), *Konservatoriet* (1849), *La Ventana* (1854).

Bour·rienne \bür-yen\, Louis-Antoine Fau·ve·let de \fōv-le-də-\. 1769–1834. French diplomat. Private secretary of Napoléon (1797); helped draft Treaty of Campo Formio (1797); diplomat in Germany (1804–13). Offered services to Louis XVIII; minister of state and later deputy. Author of *Mémoires sur Napoléon* (1829).

Bour·sault \bür-sō\, Edme. 1638–1701. French playwright. Author of verse *Délices de la poésie galante* (1663); plays *Le Portrait du peintre* (1663) attacking Moliére, *Le Mercure galant* (1683), *Esope à la cour* (1701), etc.; romance *Le Prince de Condé* (1675).

Bous·set \bü-'se\, Wilhelm. 1865–1920. German scholar and theologian. Professor, Göttingen (1896–1916), Giessen (1916–20); a founder of Religionsgeschichtliche school of biblical scholarship. Author of *Die Religion des Judentums im neutestamentlichen (späthellenistischen) Zeitalter* (1903), etc.

Bous·sin·gault \bü-sa^{n}-gō\, Jean-Baptiste-Joseph-Dieudonné. 1802–1887. French agricultural chemist. Professor, Conservatory of Arts and Crafts, Paris (1839–87); conducted pioneering experiments in nitrogen fixation by legumes (1834–54). Author of *Economie rurale* (1843–44), *Agronomie, chimie agricole, et physiologie* (1860–74).

Bou·tens \'bü-tənz\, Pieter Cornelis. 1870–1943. Dutch poet and mystic. Author of verse *Verzen* (1898), *Stemmen* (1907), *Beatrijs* (1908), *Lentemaan* (1916), and of translations from Homer, Sophocles, Goethe, etc.

Bou·ter·wek \'büt-ər-,vek\, Friedrich. 1766–1828. German philosopher and critic. Professor, Göttingen (1797–1828); revised Kantian formalism under influence of Idealists. Author of *Apodiktik* (1799), *Ästhetik* (1806), *Geschichte der Poesie und Beredsamkeit* (1801–19), *Religion und Vernunft* (1824), etc.

Bou·ton \bü-tō^{n}\, Noël. Comte de Cha·mil·ly \shȧ-mē-yē\. 1636–1715. French soldier. Rose to marshal of France (1703); long believed to be the one addressed in the famed but spurious *Lettres portugaises,* attributed to the Portuguese nun Mariana Alcoforado.

Bou·troux \bü-trü\, Étienne-Émile-Marie. 1845–1921. French philosopher. Professor, École Normale Superieure (1878), Sorbonne (1885). Author of *De la contingence des lois de la nature* (1874), *De Pidée de loi naturelle* (1895), etc.

Bouts \'bau̇ts\, Dirck *or* Dierick *or* Dieric *or* Dirk *or* Thierry. c.1400–1475. Dutch painter. Known for landscapes, portraits, and religious scenes, as *Lamentation over Christ, The Entombment,* triptych for Cathedral of Granada, triptych on Last Supper for St. Peter, Louvain, etc.

Bout·well \'bau̇t-wəl, -,wel\, George Sewall. 1818–1905. American politician, b. Brookline, Mass. Governor of Massachusetts (1851, 1852). Member of Congress (1863–69); a leader in impeachment of Andrew Johnson. U.S. secretary of the treasury (1869–73). U.S. senator (1873–77).

Bou·vard *or* **Bou·vart** \bü-vȧr\, Alexis. 1767–1843. French astronomer. Discovered eight comets; may have been first to observe irregularities in motion of planet Uranus (1821) that led to discovery of Neptune.

Bou·vi·er \'bü-vē-,ā; bü-'vyā, -'vi(ə)r\, John. 1787–1851. American lawyer, b. Codogno, Italy, of French parentage. To U.S. (1802). Best known for his *Law Dictionary* (1839) and *The Institutes of American Law* (1851).

Bo·ve·ri \bō-'vā-rē\, Theodor Heinrich. 1862–1915. German zoologist. Professor, Würzburg (1893 ff.); known for researches in cytology, esp. on fertilization in ascarids and sea-urchin eggs; demonstrated separate and continuous existence of chromosomes; discovered centrosome.

Bow \'bō\, Clara. 1905–1965. American actress, b. Brooklyn, N.Y. Famous for portrayal of flappers in such films as *Down to the Sea in Ships* (1925), *The Plastic Age* (1925), *Mantrap* (1926), *Kid Boots* (1926), *Dancing Mothers* (1927); dubbed the "It girl" for role in film version of Elinor Glynn's *It* (1927); also appeared in *Wings* (1927), *The Fleet's In* (1928), *Dangerous Curves* (1928), *Saturday Night Kid* (1929), etc.

Bow·dich \'bau̇d-ich\, Thomas Edward. 1791–1824. English traveler. For African Company of Merchants negotiated (1817) treaty with kingdom of Ashanti; wrote *Mission from Cape Coast Castle to Ashantee* (1819), which influenced British government to take over direct control of Gold Coast.

Bow·ditch \'bau̇d-ich\, Henry Pickering. 1840–1911. American physiologist, b. Boston. Grandson of Nathaniel Bowditch. Taught at Harvard (1871–1906); dean of medical faculty (1883–93). Established first teaching laboratory of physiology in U.S. (1871). Known esp. for discovery of "all-or-none" law of muscle contraction (1871), indefatigability of nerves (1890).

Bowditch, Nathaniel. 1773–1838. American mathematician and astronomer, b. Salem, Mass. Self-educated mathematical prodigy. Prepared (1799) 1st American edition of J. H. Moore's standard work, *The Practical Navigator,* which he expanded and published as *The New American Practical Navigator* (1802). Translated, with commentaries, first four volumes of Laplace's *Celestial Mechanics* (1829–39).

Bowd·ler \'bau̇d-lər, 'bōd-\, Thomas. 1754–1825. English physician and editor. Published *Family Shakespeare* (10 vols., 1818), an expurgated version omitting or modifying parts "which cannot with propriety be read aloud in a family"—which gave rise to the opprobrious word *bowdlerize.*

Bow·doin \'bōd-ᵊn\, James. 1726–1790. American politician, b. Boston. Governor of Mass. (1785–87). A founder (1780) and first president, American Academy of Arts and Sciences. Bowdoin College (chartered 1794) is named in his honor.

Bow·ell \'bō(-ə)l\, Sir Mackenzie. 1823–1917. Canadian politician, b. England. To Canada (1833). Editor, Belleville (Ont.) *Intelligencer.* Member of Canadian Parliament (1867–92); prime minister (1894–96). Member of Senate, and leader of Conservative opposition (1896–1906).

Bow·en \'bō-ən\, Charles Synge Christopher. Baron Bowen. 1835–1894. English jurist. Junior counsel against claimant in famous Tichborne Case; judge of queen's bench and knighted (1879); lord of appeal in ordinary (1893).

Bowen, Elizabeth Dorothea Cole. 1899–1973. Irish novelist and short-story writer. Author of novels *The Hotel* (1927), *The Last September* (1929), *To the North* (1932), *The House in Paris* (1935), *The Death of the Heart* (1938), *The Heat of the Day* (1949), *A World of Love* (1955), *A Time in Rome* (1960), *The Little Girls* (1964), *Eva Traut* (1969); story collections *Encounters* (1923), *The Cat Jumps* (1934), *The Demon Lover* (1945); also *Bowen's Court* (1942), *The Shelbourne* (1951), *Pictures and Conversations* (1975).

Bowen, Sir George Ferguson. 1821–1899. English colonialist. First governor of Queensland (1859–67); conciliated Maoris and settlers as governor of New Zealand (1868–72); governor of Victoria, Australia (1872–79), Mauritius (1879–82), Hong Kong (1882–85); privy councilor (1886).

Bowen, Ira Sprague. 1898–1973. American astronomer, b. Seneca Falls, N.Y. Professor, Cal. Inst. Tech. (1926 ff.); director, Mt. Wilson Observatory (1946–48), combined Mt. Wilson–Mt. Palomar observatories (1948–64). Known for work on atomic structure, cosmic rays, and nebular spectra; explained "forbidden lines" in nebular spectra.

Bowen, Marjorie. See Gabrielle Margaret LONG.

Bowen, Norman Levi. 1887–1956. American petrologist and chemist, b. Kingston, Ont. Professor, Queens U., Kingston (1919–21), U. of Chicago (1937–47); with Geophysical Laboratory, Carnegie Inst., Washington, D.C. (1912–19, 1921–37, 1947–56). Pioneer in experimental petrology, known esp. for studies of silicate systems. Author of *Evolution of the Igneous Rocks* (1928).

Bow·er \'bau̇(-ə)r\, Frederick Orpen. 1855–1948. English botanist. Associated with T. Huxley at U. of London (1880–85); professor, Glasgow (1885–1925). Known for studies of ferns, mosses, etc. Author of *Origin of a Land Flora* (1908), *Ferns* (1923–28), *Primitive Land Plants* (1935).

Bow·er \'bō(-ə)r\ *or* **Bow·ma·ker** \'bō-ˌmā-kər\, Walter. 1385–1449. Scottish chronicler. Author of *Scotichronicon,* completed 1447, first connected history of Scotland (pub. 1722).

Bow·er·bank \'bau̇(-ə)r-ˌbaŋk\, James Scott. 1797–1877. English naturalist and paleontologist. One of founders of London Clay Club (1836), an organization for study of fossils of Tertiary period; founded Paleontographical Society (1847). Author of *History of Fossil Fruits and Seeds of London Clay* (1840), *Monograph of British Spongiadae* (1864–82).

Bow·ie \'bü-ē, 'bō-ē\, James. 1796–1836. American soldier, b. Logan Co., Ky. Settled in Texas (1828); naturalized Mexican citizen (1830). Leader in opposition to central Mexican government (1832). Colonel in Texas army (1835–36). Killed at the Alamo (Mar. 6, 1836). Credited with invention of bowie knife.

Bowie, William. 1872–1940. American geologist, b. Annapolis Junction, Md. With U.S. Coast and Geodetic Survey (1895–1937), chief of division of geodesy (1909–37); known for theoretical studies of isostasy and for construction of formulae and tables relating topography and isostatic compensation to intensity of gravity.

Bow·ker \'bau̇-kər\, Richard Rogers. 1848–1933. American editor and author, b. Salem, Mass. A founder (with F. Leypoldt and Melvil Dewey) and editor of *The Library Journal* (from 1876); publisher (from 1879), editor (from 1884) of *Publishers' Weekly;* a founder of American Library Association (1876). Author of *Work and Wealth* (1883), *Electoral Reform* (1889), *Of Business* (1901), *Of Politics* (1901), *Of Religion* (1903), *Economic Peace* (1923), etc.

Bowles \'bōlz\, Chester Bliss. 1901–1986. American government official, b. Springfield, Mass. Founded and directed own advertising agency (1925–40); director U.S. office of price administration and member of war production board (1943–46); director office of economic stabilization (1946); Democratic governor of Conn. (1949–51); U.S. ambassador to India and Nepal (1951–53, 1961–69); U.S. representative from Conn. (1959–61); U.S. undersecretary of state (1961). A leading liberal statesman of his time.

Bowles, Samuel. 1797–1851. American newspaper editor, b. Hartford, Conn. Published Hartford *Times* (1819–22); founded Springfield *Republican,* Springfield, Mass. (weekly, 1824–44; daily from 1844). His son ¶Samuel (1826–1878), b. Springfield, succeeded to control of paper at father's death; by vigor and independence of his policies and excellence of news reports made the *Republican* eminent among newspapers of the time. His son ¶Samuel (1851–1915) took over control of paper (1878).

Bowles, William Lisle. 1762–1850. English clergyman and poet. Broke away from commonplaces of 18th-century poetry in *Fourteen Sonnets* (1789), hailed as revival of natural poetry by Wordsworth, Coleridge, Southey. Aroused controversy with Campbell and Byron over Pope's poetical merits.

Bow·ley \'bō-lē\, Sir Arthur Lyon. 1869–1957. English statistician. Taught at London School of Economics and U. Coll., Reading (1895–1919), U. of London (1919–36); director of Oxford U. Inst. of Statistics (1940–44). Noted for development of social sampling techniques. Co-author of *Livelihood and Poverty* (1915), *Has Poverty Diminished?* (1925).

Bowmaker, Walter. See BOWER.

Bow·man \'bō-mən\, Isaiah. 1878–1950. American geographer and educator, b. Waterloo, Ont. Taught at Yale (1905–15); director, American Geographical Society, N.Y. (1915–35); president, Johns Hopkins (1935–48). Advisor to Pres. Wilson at Paris Peace Conference (1919). Author of *Forest Physiography* (1911), *South America* (1915), *Desert Trails of Atacama* (1923), *Geography in Relation to the Social Sciences* (1934).

Bowman, Sir William. 1816–1892. English histologist and surgeon. Made pioneering histological studies of various tissues; discovered Bowman's capsules in kidney and determined mechanism of urine production by filtration; with Richard B. Todd published *Physiological Anatomy and Physiology of Man* (1843–56). Also studied striated muscle, liver. Turned to ophthalmic surgery; devised new instruments and techniques, among first to adopt ophthalmoscope; described Bowman's membrane of cornea.

Bow·ring \'bau̇-riŋ\, Sir John. 1792–1872. English diplomat, writer, and linguist. Literary executor of Jeremy Bentham, edited works (1838–43); edited *Westminster Review* (from 1825). M. P. (1835–37, 1841–49). Superintendent of trade in China (1849); governor of Hong Kong (1854); negotiated treaty of commerce with Siam (1855). Translator and compiler of anthologies of eastern European poetry; author of poems and hymns.

Bow·yer \'bō-yər, 'bȯi-ər\, William, *called* the Younger. 1699–1777. English printer. Called "the learned printer." Printer to Society of Antiquaries (1736), to Royal Society (1761), to House of Commons and House of Lords (1767); published Greek Testament, translated Caesar's *Commentaries* (1750), Rousseau's *Discourse* (1751), etc.

Boy. Pseudonym of Tadeusz ŻELEŃSKI.

Boyce, Hector. See Hector BOECE.

Boyce \'bȯis\, William. 1711–1779. English composer. Composer (1736) and organist (1758) to Chapel Royal; master of King's Band of Music (1755). Composed numerous symphonies, concerti, overtures; theatrical music for plays and masques by Shakespeare and others; settings for many odes; church services and anthems. Published collection of *Cathedral Music* (1760–73).

Boy·cott \'bȯi-ˌkät, -kət\, Charles Cunningham. 1832–1897. English estate manager. Retired army captain, agent for estates in County Mayo (1873); conspicuous victim (1880) of the economic and social ostracizing practice of Irish Land League agitators which came to be called a "boycott."

Boyd \'bȯid\, James. 1888–1944. American novelist, b. Harrisburg, Pa. Author of *Drums* (1925), *Marching On* (1927), *Long Hunt* (1930), etc.

Boyd, Linn. 1800–1859. American politician, b. Nashville, Tenn. Member from Kentucky of U.S. House of Representatives (1835–37, 1839–55), speaker (1851–55).

Boyd, William. 1898–1972. American actor, b. Hendrysburg, Ohio. Best known for role as cowboy Hopalong Cassidy in series of films (from 1935) and on television (1948–53).

Boyd, Zachary. 1585?–1653. Scottish minister. Author of *The Last Battle of the Soul in Death* (1629); *Zion's Flowers,* quaint scriptural poems.

Boy·den \'bȯid-ᵊn\, Seth. 1788–1870. American inventor, b. Foxboro, Mass. Invented process for making patent leather (1819); malleable cast iron (1826, patent 1831); sheet iron; a hat-shaping machine. Developed Hilton strawberry.

Manufactured locomotives, stationary steam engines. His brother ¶Uriah Atherton (1801–1879) devised an improved turbine water wheel (1844).

Boyd Orr \'bòid-'ō(ə)r\, John. Baron Boyd-Orr of Brechin Mearns. 1880–1971. Scottish nutritionist. Director, Inst. of Animal Nutrition, Aberdeen (1914 ff.); founder, Imperial Bureau of Animal Nutrition (1929); professor, U. of Aberdeen (1942–45). M.P. (1945–46). First director of UN Food and Agriculture Organization (1945–48); awarded Nobel peace prize (1949). Created baron (1949). Author of *Food, Health, and Income* (1936), *Food—Foundation of World Unity* (1948), etc.

Bo·ye \'bò-yə\, Karin Maria. 1900–1941. Swedish poet. A leader of Clarté Socialist movement and of modernism in Swedish poetry. Author of verse collections *Moln* (1922), *För trädets skull* (1935), *De sju dödssynderna* (1941), etc., and novels including *Kris* (1934), *Kallocain* (1940).

Boy·en \'bòi-ən \, Hermann von. 1771–1848. Prussian general. Director of War Department (1810–12); general chief of staff in War of Liberation. Minister of war (1814–19); instituted numerous reforms in army organization. Recalled as war minister (1841–47); general field marshal (1847).

Boy·er \bwá-yā\, Alexis. 1757–1833. French surgeon. Imperial family surgeon to Napoléon (1804); consulting surgeon to Louis XVIII, Charles X, and Louis Philippe. Author of *Traité complet d'anatomie* (1797–99), etc.

Boyer, Jean-Baptiste de. Marquis d'Ar·gens \dár-zhäⁿs\. 1703–1771. French writer. Chamberlain in service of Frederick the Great (from 1744); author of polemical writings influential in disseminating Enlightenment thought. Works included *Mémoires secrètes de la république des lettres* (1737–39), *Lettres juives* (1738), *Lettres chinoises* (1739–40), *Lettres cabalistiques* (1741).

Boyer, Jean-Pierre. 1776–1850. Haitian politician. A free mulatto; joined Pétion and Christophe in move to establish republic; succeeded Pétion (1818) as president of southern portion; after death of Christophe (1820), brought whole island under his control; driven out by revolution (1843).

Boyle \'bòi(ə)l\. Family name of earls of Cork \'kòrk\ and of Or·rery \'ór-ər-ē, 'är-\, including: Richard (1566–1643), 1st Earl of Cork, founder of house of Cork and Orrery. Called the "Great Earl of Cork". Tried his fortunes in Ireland (1588); purchased Sir Walter Raleigh's Irish possessions (1602); introduced manufactures, built bridges and harbors; amassed fortune; created earl (1620); a lord justice (1629) and lord high treasurer (1631) of Ireland; helped to bring about impeachment of Strafford, his rival in Ireland; suppressed Irish rebellion of 1641. His 7th son was the famous physicist and chemist (see Robert BOYLE). His 3d son ¶Roger (1621–1679), Baron Brog·hill \'bräg-,hil, 'bròg-\ and 1st Earl of Orrery, soldier and dramatist, held general's command in Ireland under Cromwell (1650) and membership in Cromwell's privy council; became convinced of hopelessness of Richard Cromwell's cause and secured Ireland for Charles II; created earl (1660). Author of *Parthenissa,* a romance (1665–67), *A Treatise on the Art of War* (1677), and rhymed tragedies. ¶Charles (1676–1731), 4th Earl of Orrery, after whom as patron George Graham named his astronomical invention the orrery; grandson of Roger Boyle, 1st Earl of Orrery, edited *Epistles of Phalaris,* which were shown spurious by Richard Bentley, satirized by Swift in his *Battle of the Books* (1704); fought at Malplaquet; a negotiator of Treaty of Utrecht; imprisoned in Tower of London as a Jacobite (1721). ¶Richard (1695–1753), 3d Earl of Bur·ling·ton \'bər-liŋ-tən\ and 4th Earl of Cork; great grandson of 1st Earl of Cork; privy councilor (1714); lord high treasurer of Ireland (1715); patron of literature and art. ¶John (1707–1762), 5th Earl of Cork and 5th Earl of Orrery, son of 4th Earl of Orrery, was a friend of Swift, Pope, and Dr. Johnson; known chiefly for his rancorous and grudgingly commendatory *Remarks on the Life and Writings of Jonathan Swift* (1751) and a translation of the letters of Pliny the Younger (1751).

Boyle, Robert. 1627–1691. British physicist and chemist, b. Ireland. See BOYLE family. Settled at Oxford (1656) and devoted himself to chemistry and natural philosophy; one of first members of group that became the Royal Society. With Robert Hooke improved air pump and invented a compressed-air pump; experimented in pneumatics; investigated specific gravities, refractive powers, crystals, electricity, etc.; discovered importance of air in propagation of sound; held that atoms of one kind of matter constitute all substances, the atoms having different arrangements and movements in different substances. Author of *New Experiments Physico-Mechanical touching the Spring of the Air and its Effects* (1660); answered criticism of this work with his *Defense Against Linus* (1662), in which he enunciated Boyle's law that the volume of a gas varies inversely as the pressure; author also of *The Sceptical Chymist* (1661), *Origin of Forms and Qualities According to the Corpuscular Philosophy* (1666), *Memoirs for the Natural History of the Human Blood* (1684), and of moral and religious essays. By his will founded Boyle Lectures, for defense of Christianity against unbelievers.

Boylesve, René. See René TARDIVAUX.

Boyl·ston \'bòil-stən\, Zabdiel. 1679–1766. American physician, b. Brookline, Mass. Influenced by Cotton Mather, inoculated patients against smallpox (1721), first such practice in America.

Boyron, Michel. See Michel BARON.

Boys \'bòiz\, Sir Charles Vernon. 1855–1944. English physicist and inventor. Known for work with quartz fibers; invented quartz-torsion radio micrometer (1888), automatic recording calorimeter (1905), high speed cameras.

Boz. See Charles DICKENS.

Boze·man \'bōz-mən\, John M. 1835–1867. American pioneer, b. Georgia. Opened (1862) Rocky Mountain trail now known as Bozeman Trail (or Powder River road).

Bozzari, Marco. See Markos BOTSARIS.

Braak \'bräk\, Menno ter. 1902–1940. Dutch critic. Known for incisive criticism of cult of aestheticism; with Edgar du Perron founded magazine *Forum* (1931). Author of *Het carnaval der burgers* (1930), *Politicus zonder partij* (1934), *Van oude en nieuwe Christenen* (1937), etc.

Braa·ten \'bròt-ᵊn\, Oskar. 1881–1939. Norwegian novelist and dramatist. Author of works on working-class life, including novels *Kring fabrikken* (1910), *Ulvenhiet* (1919), *Matilde* (1920), *Masken* (1933), plays *Urgen* (1911), *Borgen* (1915), *Den store barnedåpen* (1925).

Brab·a·zon \'brəb-ə-zən\, John Theodore Cuthbert Moore- \'mō(ə)r-, 'mò(ə)r-, 'mu̇(ə)r-\. 1st Baron Brabazon of Tara \'tar-ə\. 1884–1964. British aviator. First British aviator to fly over own country (1909); first licensed by Royal Aero Club; helped develop aerial photography in Royal Flying Corps, World War I. M.P. (1918–29, 1931–42); minister of transport (1940–41), of aircraft production (1941–42). Created baron (1942).

Brabazon, Reginald. 12th Earl of Meath \'mēth, 'mēth\. 1841–1929. British philanthropist. Initiated recognition of Empire Day (May 24).

Brac·cio da Mon·to·ne \'brät-chō-dä-mōn-'tō-nā\. 1368–1424. Italian condottiere. Secured sovereignty of Perugia (1416); captured Rome (1417); created count of Foggia (1421); crowned prince of Aquila and Capua (1423); commanded Aragonese forces against forces of Naples under his lifelong rival Sforza (1424).

Brac·cio·li·ni \,brät-chō-'lē-nē\, Francesco. 1566–1645. Italian ecclesiastic and poet. Known esp. for his satire *Lo scherno degli Dei* (1618–26) and for *La croce riconquistata* (1605–11), an imitation of Tasso's *Gerusalemme liberata.*

Bracciolini, Poggio. See POGGIO BRACCIOLINI.

Brac·co \'bräk-kō\, Roberto. 1862–1943. Italian playwright. Author of *Maschere* (1893), *L'infedele* (1894), *Il frutto acerbo* (1904), *I fantasmi* (1906), *Il piccolo santo* (1911).

Brace \'brās\, Charles Loring. 1826–1890. American social-service worker, b. Litchfield, Conn. Instrumental in establishing Children's Aid Society (1853).

Brace·gir·dle \'brās-,gərd-ᵊl\, Anne. c.1663 or c.1673–1748. English actress. Appeared at Drury Lane (1688) as Lucia in Shadwell's *Squire of Alsatia;* closely associated with plays of Congreve; created Almeria in *Mourning Bride* (1697), and Belinda in Vanbrugh's *Provoked Wife;* played tragic roles in Shakespearean adaptations; retired (1707).

Brack·en·ridge \'brak-ən-,rij\, Hugh Henry. 1748–1816. American writer, b. Kintyre, Argyll, Scotland. To U.S. (1753); served in Revolution; founded *Pittsburgh Gazette* (1781), first newspaper in Old West; helped found U. of Pittsburgh. Author of poem "Rising Glory of America" (with Philip Freneau, 1771), verse dramas *Battle of Bunkers-Hill* (1776) and *Death of General Montgomery* (1777); known esp. for *Modern Chivalry* (1792–1815), picaresque novel of frontier.

Brackley, Viscounts of. See EGERTON family.

Brac·que·mond \bràk-mōⁿ\, Félix-Joseph-Auguste. 1833–1914. French painter and etcher. Credited with reviving art of etching in France (from c.1848); known also as decorator of porcelains for Sevres, Haviland, Limoges.

Brac·ton \'brak-tən\ *or* **Brat·ton** \'brat-ᵊn\ *or* **Bret·ton** \'bret-ᵊn\, Henry de. d. 1268. English ecclesiastic and judge. Author of *De legibus et consuetudinibus Angliae,* first systematic treatise on laws of England in Middle Ages.

Brad·bury \'brad-b(ə-)rē, *US usu* -,ber-ē\, John Swanwick. 1st Baron Bradbury. 1872–1950. English treasury official. Joint permanent secretary to the treasury (1913–19); principal British representative on reparations commission, Paris (1919–25). Created baron (1925). Treasury notes issued during World War I bearing his signature sometimes called "Bradburies."

Brad·dock \'brad-ək\, Edward. 1695–1755. British soldier. Major general and commander in chief of British forces in America (1754); led expedition against Fort Duquesne (1755); surprised by attack of force of French and Indians (July 9, 1755) and defeated with loss of over half his force; died of wounds.

Braddock, James Joseph. 1905–1974. American boxer, b. New York City. Defeated Max Baer to become world heavyweight champion (1935–37); lost crown to Joe Louis.

Brad·don \'brad-ᵊn\, Mary Elizabeth. 1837–1915. English novelist. Won success as novelist with *Lady Audley's Secret* (1862); author of over 70 other novels and many plays.

Brad·ford \'brad-fərd\, Gamaliel. 1863–1932. American biographer, b. Boston. Author of *Lee the American* (1912), *Confederate Portraits* (1914), *Union*

Portraits (1916), *Portraits of Women* (1916), *Damaged Souls* (1923), *Darwin* (1926), *D.L. Moody—A Worker in Souls* (1927), *Daughters of Eve* (1930), *The Quick and the Dead* (1931), etc.

Bradford, John. 1510?–1555. English Protestant martyr. Chaplain to Bishop Ridley (1550) and to Edward VI (1553). Accused of sedition on accession of Queen Mary; condemned as heretic and burned at Smithfield.

Bradford, Roark Whitney Wickliffe. 1896–1948. American writer, b. Lauderdale Co., Tenn. Among his books were *Ol' Man Adam an' His Chillun* (1928; successfully dramatized as *Green Pastures,* 1930, by Marc Connelly), *This Side of Jordan* (1929), *John Henry* (1931), *Let the Band Play Dixie* (1934), *The Three-Headed Angel* (1937).

Bradford, William. 1590–1657. American religious and colonial leader, b. Austerfield, Yorkshire, England. Joined a separatist group, the Brownists (1606); went with this group to Amsterdam (1609), seeking freedom of worship; moved to Leiden (1609), and became citizen of that city. Sailed with Pilgrims for New World (1620); a signer of the Mayflower Compact (1620). Governor of Plymouth Colony (1621–32, 1635, 1637, 1639–43, 1645–56). Author of *History of Plimoth Plantation* (pub. in full, 1856).

Bradford, William. 1663–1752. American printer, b. Barnwell, Leicestershire, England. To Pennsylvania (1685); associated in founding of first paper mill in America (1690); established printing press in Philadelphia; moved to New York (1693); crown printer (1693–1742); official printer to New Jersey (almost continuously 1703–33). His press turned out first legislative proceedings published in America, first New York paper money (1709), first American Book of Common Prayer (1710), first drama written in American colonies (1714), first history of New York (1727), first newspaper to appear in New York, *New York Gazette* (1725). His son ¶Andrew (1686–1742), appointed (about 1715) official printer to the province, founded and published *American Weekly Mercury,* first newspaper in Philadelphia (1719). Andrew's nephew ¶William (1722–1719), known as "patriot printer of 1776," founded and edited *Weekly Advertiser, or Pennsylvania Journal* (1742); printer to Continental Congress (1775); served in Revolution. His son ¶Thomas (1745–1838) founded *Merchants' Daily Advertiser,* Philadelphia (1797).

Brad·laugh \ˈbrad-ˌlȯ\, Charles. 1833–1891. English freethinker and reformer. Free-thought lecturer under name of "Iconoclast." Editor of *National Reformer* (1860); prosecuted (1877) with Mrs. Annie Besant for republishing birth-control pamphlet *Fruits of Philosophy.* Associated with Mrs. Besant's work (1874–85). M. P. (1880), asserted his right to affirm instead of swearing on Bible; reelected, but excluded by the house, each year until 1886; championed bill permitting members to affirm, which became law (1888).

Brad·ley \ˈbrad-lē\, Andrew Cecil. 1851–1935. English literary critic. Professor, Liverpool (1882–90), Glasgow (1890–1900), Oxford (1901–06). Author of *Shakespearean Tragedy* (1904), classic studies in dramatic construction and character interpretation, *Oxford Lectures on Poetry* (1909). His brother ¶Francis Herbert (1846–1924), philosopher, fellow, Merton Coll., Oxford (from 1870); attacked utilitarianism in *Ethical Studies* (1876); pointed out limitations in J. S. Mill's system in *Principles of Logic* (1883); expounded in *Appearance and Reality* (1893) and *Essays on Truth and Reality* (1914) metaphysical basis of his absolute idealism. A half-brother ¶George Granville Bradley (1821–1903), clergyman and scholar; headmaster of Marlborough (1858–70); master of U. Coll., Oxford (1870–81); succeeded Stanley as dean of Westminster (1881); biographer of Dean Stanley (1892).

Bradley, Edward. *Pseudonym* Cuthbert Bede \ˈbēd\. 1827–1889. English clergyman and writer. Author and illustrator of *Adventures of Mr. Verdant Green, an Oxford Freshman* (1853–56); illustrated his own verse and prose.

Bradley, Henry. 1845–1923. English philologist and lexicographer. Joint editor (1889), senior editor (1915–23), on death of Sir James Murray, of *Oxford English Dictionary.* Cofounder of Society for Pure English (1913). Author of "The Goths" (1888) for the *Story of the Nations* series, *Making of English* (1904), *English Place-names* (1910).

Bradley, James. 1693–1762. English astronomer. Professor, Oxford (1721); succeeded Halley as astronomer royal (1742). Discovered aberration of light (announced 1728) and nutation of earth's axis (announced 1748).

Bradley, Joseph P. 1813–1892. American jurist, b. near Albany, N.Y. Associate justice, U.S. Supreme Court (1870–92).

Bradley, Milton. 1836–1911. American publisher and manufacturer, b. Vienna, Me. Devised board game "Checkered Game of Life" (1860); founded Milton Bradley Co. (1864) to publish kindergarten materials and manufacture games and toys; helped popularize croquet.

Bradley, Omar Nelson. 1893–1981. American general, b. Clark, Mo. Brigadier general (1941); commanded II Corps, Tunisia (1943), Sicily (1943); commander First Army (Jan. 1944), 12th Army Group (Aug. 1944), largest force ever commanded by field commander. General (1945). Head of Veterans' Administration (1945–47); chief of staff, U.S. Army (1948–49); chairman, U.S. joint chiefs of staff (1949–53). General of the army (1950).

Brad·shaw \ˈbrad-ˌshȯ\, George. 1801–1853. English printer. Originator of railway timetables (1839), developed into well known series of Bradshaw's railway guides.

Bradshaw, John. 1602–1659. English judge. Presided at trial of Charles I and pronounced sentence (1649); president of Council of State (1649–53).

Brad·street \ˈbrad-ˌstrēt\, Anne, *nee* Dudley. c.1612–1672. American poet, b. Northampton, England. Daughter of Thomas Dudley, steward to earl of Lincoln; m. (1628) Simon Bradstreet; to America (1630). Author of poems published without her knowledge as *The Tenth Muse Lately Sprung Up in America* (London, 1650) and including "To My Dear and Loving Husband," "The Flesh and the Spirit," etc. Considered earliest English poet of merit in America. Her husband ¶Simon (1603–1697) served as commissioner of New England Confederation (1646–79); governor (1679–86, 1689–92).

Brad·war·dine \ˈbrad-wər-ˌdēn\, Thomas. *Called* the Profound Doctor. c.1290–1349. English prelate and mathematician. Chaplain and confessor to Edward III (1338); archbishop of Canterbury (1349); died of plague. Author of *De Causa Dei,* directed against Pelagianism, and of treatises on geometrical problems.

Brady, Alice. See under William A. BRADY.

Bra·dy \ˈbrād-ē\, James Buchanan, *called* Diamond Jim. 1856–1917. American financier, b. New York City. Bellboy; employee of New York Central R.R.; salesman for railroad supply house (1879); successful as financier; best known as Broadway bon vivant, celebrated for collections of diamonds and other jewels; endowed James Buchanan Brady Urological Institute, Johns Hopkins (1912).

Brady, Mathew B. 1823?–1896. American photographer, b. Warren Co., N.Y. Learned daguerreotypy from Samuel F.B. Morse; established studio, New York City (1844). Accompanied Union armies, taking photographs (1861–65) which became basis for *Brady's National Photographic Collection* (1870), pictorial history of Civil War.

Brady, Nicholas. 1659–1726. Irish Anglican clergyman. Collaborator with Nahum Tate in metrical version of Psalms (licensed 1696).

Brady, William Aloysius. 1863–1950. American theatrical producer and manager, b. San Francisco. Toured with repertory companies; managed boxer James J. Corbett (1890–92); leased Manhattan Theater, New York (1896); proprietor of the Playhouse, New York (1910); president, National Assembly of the Motion Picture Industry (1915–20); m. (1899, as 2d wife) ¶Grace George (1879–1961), actress, b. New York City, who made her New York debut in *The New Boy* (1894), subsequently starring in *The Turtle* (1898), *Sauce for the Goose* (1911), *Major Barbara* (1915), *Captain Brassbound's Conversion* (1916), *The First Mrs. Fraser* (1929), *Kind Lady* (1935), *Velvet Glove* (1949). His daughter ¶Alice Brady (1892–1939), also an actress, appeared successfully in Gilbert and Sullivan opera; starred on the stage in *Little Women* (1912), *Forever After* (1918), *Zander the Great* (1923), *Mourning Becomes Electra* (1931), and in motion pictures as *Gay Divorcee* (1934), *My Man Godfrey* (1936), *In Old Chicago* (1937, Academy Award).

Bra·ga \ˈbrä-gə\, Teófilo, *in full* Joaquim Teófilo Fernandes. 1843–1924. Portuguese scholar and writer. Professor, Lisbon (1872 ff.); wrote prolifically on literature, history, politics, etc.; noted controversialist, and anticlericalist republican. Head of provisional government (1910–11) after dethronement of King Manuel; interim president of Portugal (1915). Author of *Visão dos Tempos* (1864), *História da Poesia Popular Portuguesa* (1867), comprehensive *História da Romantismo en Portugal* (1880), *A Arcádia Lusitana* (1899), etc.

Bra·gan·ça \brə-ˈgäⁿ-sə\. *Also spelled* Bra·gan·za \brə-ˈgan-zə\. Name of a dynasty of Portugal (1640–1910) and of the collateral house of Brazil (1822–1889), derived from name of district in northern Portugal.

The Portuguese dynasty derived from ducal house founded by Afonso (d.1461), illegitimate son of John I; Duke João II ascended throne (1640) as John IV, who was followed by Afonso VI, Peter II (whose sister Catherine married Charles II of England), John V, Joseph, Maria I and Peter III, Maria I (alone), John VI (regent 1792–1816; king 1816–26), Peter IV, Maria II, Peter V, Louis I, Carlos I, and Manuel (*qq.v*).

The Brazilian house (1822–1889) was established (1815) when John VI (then regent) of Portugal declared the colony of Brazil a kingdom under the Portuguese monarchy. John's son Dom Pedro I (*q.v.*) was chosen (1822) "Constitutional Emperor and Perpetual Defender" of the new independent state in South America; abdicated (1831) and was succeeded by his son Pedro II (1831–89; *q.v.*).

Bragg \ˈbrag\, Braxton. 1817–1876. American army officer, b. Warrenton, N.C. Distinguished himself at Buena Vista (1847); retired (1856). Entered Confederate army (1861); general (1862). Won battle of Chickamauga over

Rosecrans (1863); unsuccessfully besieged Chattanooga; relieved of field command (Dec. 1863); military adviser to President Davis (1864–65).

Bragg, Sir William Henry. 1862–1942. English physicist. Professor, Adelaide U., South Australia (1886–1908), Leeds U. (1909–15), U. of London (1915–23); professor at Royal Institution and director of Davy-Faraday research laboratory (from 1923); president, Royal Society (1935–40). Pioneered, with his son William as associate, in the study of crystalline structure by means of X-rays; co-winner, with son William, of 1915 Nobel prize in physics. Author of *Studies in Radioactivity* (1912), *X-rays and Crystal Structure* (with his son, 1915), *The World of Sound* (1920), *Concerning the Nature of Things* (1925), *The Universe of Light* (1933). His son ¶Sir William Lawrence (1890–1971), b. South Australia; professor of physics, Victoria U., Manchester (1919–37); Cavendish professor of experimental physics, Cambridge (1938–54); director of Royal Institution (1954–65); discovered Bragg's law describing reflection of electromagnetic waves by atomic planes. Author of *The Crystalline State* (1934), *Atomic Structure of Minerals* (1937).

Bra·he \\'brä(-ə), 'brä-hə\\, Per, *called* the Younger. Count. 1602–1680. Swedish soldier and statesman. Served under Gustavus II Adolphus in Prussia (1626–28); marshal of nobility (1629); privy councillor (1630); a regent (1632–44, 1660–72); directed peace negotiations with Poland (1635). Governor general of Finland (1637–40, 1648–54). Founder (1640) and chancellor (1646–80) of U. of Åbo. Lord high chancellor (1641–80).

Bra·he \\'brä-hə, *Angl* 'brä(-hē)\\, Tycho. 1546–1601. Danish astronomer. Established with royal aid Uraniborg observatory on island of Hven (now Ven) in The Sound (1576); in Bohemia under patronage of Rudolph II (1599), where he had Kepler as assistant (1600). Amassed records of most accurate astronomical observations made to date in Europe. Proved nova (1572) was a star. Rejected Copernican system and held that the five planets revolved about the sun, which in turn revolved about the earth. His observations published by Kepler in the *Rudolphine Tables.* Author of *De nova stella* (1573), *Astronomiae instauratae mechanica* (1598) describing his life, discoveries, etc., and *Astronomiae instauratae progymnasmata* (1602–03, edited by Kepler).

Brahm \\'bräm\\, Otto. 1856–1912. German critic and theatrical director. Established (1889) and directed Freie Bühne company; established (1890) periodical *Freie Bühne* (later *Neue deutsche Rundschau*); director of Deutsche-theater, Berlin (1894–1904), Lessingtheater (1904–12); principal founder of German realist school.

Brah·ma·gup·ta \\,brə-mə-'gu̇p-tə\\. 598–c.665. Indian astronomer. Wrote (628) *Brahma-sphuṭa-siddhānta,* in verse, chief work of Hindu astronomy, containing important chapters on mathematics.

Brahms \\'bräms, *Angl* 'brämz\\, Johannes. 1833–1897. German composer and pianist. Early encouraged by Robert and Clara Schumann; director of court concerts and of a choral society in Detmold (1857–60); lived in Vienna (from 1862); conductor of the Singakademie (1863–64) and concerts of the Gesellschaft der Musikfreunde (1872–75). His compositions included orchestral works: 4 symphonies (1876, 1877, 1883, 1885), *Variations on a Theme by Haydn* (1873), the *Academic Festival* and *Tragic* overtures (1880), two piano concertos (1854–58, 1881), a violin concerto (1878), and a double concerto for violin and cello (1887); chamber music: 7 sonatas for piano and violin, cello, or clarinet; 5 trios, 3 quartets, and a quintet, for piano and other instruments; 3 string quartets; 2 string quintets; 2 string sextets; a quintet for clarinet and other instruments; piano works: 3 sonatas (1852–53), a scherzo, numerous variations, two rhapsodies, 4 sets of *Hungarian dances,* waltzes, and smaller pieces; organ works: preludes for chorales, a fugue in A-flat minor; vocal works: *German Requiem* (1868), *Rinaldo,* a cantata (1869), *Rhapsody* (1870), *Schicksalslied* (1871), *Triumphlied* (1872), *Nänie* (1881), *Gesang der Parzen* (1883), choruses, and songs.

Braid \\'brād\\, James. 1795–1860. British surgeon, b. Scotland. Practiced in Manchester; investigated mesmerism, proving its subjective nature and demonstrating that no magnetic influence passed from operator into subject; originated term *neurohypnotism,* later shortened to *hypnotism.*

Braid, James. 1870–1950. British golfer, b. Scotland. Winner of 5 British Opens (1901, 1905–06, 1908, 1910), 4 *News of the World* tournaments (1903, 1905, 1907, 1911), French championship (1910).

Braid·wood \\'brā-,dwu̇d\\, Thomas. 1715–1806. Scottish teacher. Opened in Edinburgh first school for deaf mutes in the British Empire (1760).

Braille \\bräy, bråy, *Angl* 'brā(ə)l, 'brī\\, Louis. 1809–1852. French teacher. Blind from age of three; devoted himself to study of music; organist in Paris. Teacher of the blind (from 1826); devised (1829) system of raised-point writing for literature and music (known as *Braille*), which has been widely adopted for instruction of the blind throughout the world.

Brai·nerd \\'brā-nərd\\, David. 1718–1747. American missionary, b. Haddam, Conn. Associated with Scottish Society for Propagation of Christian Knowledge (1742–47); missionary among Seneca and Delaware Indians (1744–47); gained fame through publication of his diary (1749) by Jonathan Edwards.

Brai·thwaite \\'brāth-,wāt\\, John. 1797–1870. English engineer. Built first practical steam fire engine (c.1829).

Brakelond. See JOCELIN DE BRAKELOND.

Bramah, Ernest. See Ernest B. SMITH.

Bra·mah \\'bram-ə, 'bräm-ə\\, Joseph. 1748–1814. English engineer. Inventor of a pick-proof lock (1784) and a hydraulic press (1795), both named for him; best known as designer, with Henry Maudslay, of precision machine tools.

Bra·man·te \\brä-'män-tā\\, Donato *or* Donino *or* Donnino. *Orig.* Donato d'A·gno·lo \\'dän-yō-lō\\ *or* d'An·ge·lo \\'dän-jā-lō\\. 1444–1514. Italian architect. Worked chiefly in Milan (1477–99) and in Rome (1499–1514); patronized by Sforza family; in Milan executed Sta. Maria presso S. Satiro (c.1481), helped plan Pavia cathedral, worked with Leonardo da Vinci on problems of Milan cathedral; began rectory of S. Ambrogio (1492); worked on Castel Sforzesco. In Rome employed by Popes Alexander VI and Julius II; designed new Basilica of St. Peter (begun 1506); also designed Belvedere courtyard; strongly influenced Julius's city plan for Rome (from c.1508); designed Palazzo dei Tribunali (1508), Palazzo Caprini (c.1510), also tempietto of S. Pietro in Montorio (1502), choir of Sta. Maria del Popolo (1505–09). Evolved style known as High Renaissance; influence felt for centuries.

Bram·hall \\'bram-,hȯl\\, John. 1594–1663. English prelate. Anglican bishop of Derry (1634); archbishop of Armagh (1661); speaker, Irish House of Lords (1661). Argued against Hobbes on freedom of the will.

Bram·lette \\'bram-lət\\, Milton Nunn. 1896–1977. American geologist, b. Bonham, Tex. With U.S. Geological Survey (1921–24, 1931–41); professor, U.C.L.A. (1941–51), Scripps Inst. of Oceanography (1951–62). Known for work in sedimentary petrology, submarine geology, micropaleontology, etc.

Brampton, Baron. See Sir Henry HAWKINS.

Branco, Castelo. See CASTELO BRANCO.

Brancovan, Princesse. See Anna-Elisabeth de NOAILLES.

Brân·co·vea·nu \\,brin-kōv-'yän-ü\\ *or* **Brîn·co·vea·nu** \\,brin-\\, Constantin. 1654–1714. Walachian ruler. Hospodar of Walachia (1688–1714), a vassal of Turks; defeated Austrians at Zărneşti (1690); executed by Turks for secretly negotiating with Czar Peter I of Russia. Built many churches and palaces.

Bran·cuşi \\'brän-küsh, *Angl* bran-'kü-sē\\, Constantin. 1876–1957. Romanian sculptor. Trained as woodworker and carver; to Paris (1904); first exhibited at Salon (1906). Evolved sculptural style emphasizing geometrical aspects of forms and progressively approaching pure abstraction; worked and reworked certain themes, as *Sleeping Muse* (1910–12), egg form as in *The New-Born* (1915) and *Beginning of the World* (1924), bird in *Maiastra* (1912) and *Bird in Space* (1919–40), *Endless Column* (1918 ff.), *Fish* (1922); other works included *The Kiss, Mademoiselle Pogany, Table of Silence, Gate of the Kiss, Flying Turtle.* Considered a principal figure in modern sculpture.

Brand \\'bränt\\, Hennig. *Also* Brandt. d. c.1692. German alchemist. Discovered the element phosphorus (1669).

Brand \\'bränt\\, Sir Johannes Henricus *or* Jan Hendrik. 1823–1888. South African politician. President, Orange Free State (1864–88); defeated Basutos (1865–68); declined to desert policy of friendship towards British to become president of Transvaal (1871).

Brand \\'brand\\, John. 1744–1806. English clergyman and antiquary. Author of *Observations on Popular Antiquities* (1777), etc.

Brand, Sir Quintin, *in full* Christopher Joseph Quintin. 1893–1968. British aviator, b. South Africa. Served in Royal Flying Corps, World War I; with Sir Pierre van Ryneveld made first London–Cape Town flight (1920); director general of aviation in Egypt (1932–36); served in World War II (1939–43) commanding fighter group; air vice-marshal.

Brandan, Saint. See BRENDAN.

Brande \\'brand\\, William Thomas. 1788–1866. English chemist. Successor of Sir Humphry Davy at Royal Institution (1813–52); author of *Manual of Chemistry* (1819) and *Dictionary of Pharmacy and Materia Medica* (1839).

Bran·deis \\'bran-,dīs\\, Louis Dembitz. 1856–1941. American jurist, b. Louisville, Ky. Appeared (1907–14) as special counsel in legal proceedings involving constitutionality of several state hours-and-wages laws, antimonopoly cases, etc.; developed "Brandeis brief" marshalling sociological statistics, expert opinion, etc.; devised savings bank insurance plans (1907); became known as the "people's attorney"; influenced Clayton Anti-Trust Act (1914), Federal Trade Commission. Associate justice, U.S. Supreme Court (1916–39); noted for devotion to free speech. Author of *Other People's Money* (1914).

Bran·den·burg \\'brän-dən-,bu̇rk, *Angl* 'bran-dən-,bərg\\, House of. German royal family (Ascanian dynasty) founded (1150) by Margrave Albert I the Bear (*q.v.*), whose descendants added territory (12th–13th centuries); especially prosperous during joint reign (1220–67) of John I and Otto III and reign of Waldemar (1303–19); became extinct (1320). Possession of the mark disputed by several claimants; acquired (1323) by Louis of Bavaria, only to be lost by his successors; declined greatly in influence; by treaty, all rights transferred (1373) to Emperor Charles IV; reverted (1411) to Emperor Sigismund, by whom it was conferred (1415) on Burgrave Frederick of Hohenzollern.

Bran·des \'brän-dəs\, Edvard, *in full* Carl Edvard. *Orig. surname* Co·hen \'kō-ən\. 1847–1931. Danish writer and politician. Brother of Georg Brandes. Member of Folketing (1880–1894), Landesting (1906–27) houses of parliament; minister of finance (1913–20); leader of Left Reform and (from 1905) of Radical party. Author of dramas, esp. *Une visite* (1882), criticism.

Brandes, Georg Morris. *Orig. surname* Cohen. 1842–1927. Danish literary critic and historian. Disciple of Comte, Taine, Renan, Mill, and Spencer; champion of materialism, esp. in literature. Taught at U. of Copenhagen (1872–77); accused of radicalism; journalist, writer, and lecturer, Berlin (1877–83); public lecturer, Copenhagen (from 1883); professor of aesthetics, U. of Copenhagen (from 1902). Author of *Hovedstrømninger i det 19de aarhundredes litteratur* (1871–87, Main Currents in 19th Century Literature), *Danske Digtere* (1877), *Det moderne gjennembruds maend* (1883), *Indtryk fra Polen* (1888), *Indtryk fra Russland* (1888), *Sagnet om Jesus* (1925), works on Lassalle (1877), Lord Beaconsfield (1879), Shakespeare (1895–96), Goethe (1915), Voltaire (1916–17), Julius Caesar (1918), Michelangelo (1921).

Brandon, Dukes of. Title of dukes of Hamilton, first bestowed on 4th duke. See MARQUISES AND DUKES OF HAMILTON under DOUGLAS family.

Brandon, Viscount. See Charles GERARD.

Bran·don \'bran-dən\, Charles. 1st Duke of Suf·folk \'səf-ək\. c.1484–1545. English soldier. Served Henry VIII as squire and on various diplomatic missions; created duke (1514); commanded unsuccessful invasion of France (1523) and at capture of Boulogne (1544).

Brandon, Richard. d. 1649. English executioner. Executioner of Charles I, Sir Thomas Wentworth, Bishop Laud, etc.

Brandt. See also BRAND and BRANT.

Brandt \'bränt\, Alfred. 1846–1899. German engineer. Designed hydraulic drill used to drive Arlberg tunnel; devised double-gallery system successfully employed in driving Simplon tunnel (1898–1905).

Brandt \'brant\, Bill. 1904?–1983. British photographer. Worked for British, French, and American publications; famous for candid photos of British social life, also for British landscapes, artists, and esp. female nudes; accorded retrospectives at New York's Museum of Modern Art (1961) and Britain's National Centre of Photography (1981). Works included *The English at Home* (1936), *The Land* (1975), *Shadow of Light* (1977), and *Nudes 1945–1980* (1980).

Brandt \'brånt\, Georg. 1694–1768. Swedish chemist. Director of chemistry for Swedish Council of Mines (1727); discovered and named cobalt (1730).

Brang·wyn \'braŋ-(g)wən\, Sir Frank. 1867–1956. British painter and decorator. Known for richness of color and bravura technique in his decorative panels, typically very large; executed designs for stained glass, tapestry, book decoration, pottery, and metalwork.

Bra·nic·ki \brȧ-'nēt-skyē\ *or* **Bra·nec·ki** \-'net-\, Ksawery Franciszek. c.1730–1819. Polish soldier. Hetman (commander) of forces of Stanisław II Poniatowski; led troops against Confederation of Bar (1768); established Confederation of Targowica (1792) to overthrow liberal constitution of 1791.

Bran·ly \brän-lē\, Édouard-Eugéne. 1844–1940. French physicist. Inventor (1890) of coherer, primitive form of radio detector that made wireless telegraphy possible.

Bran·nan \'bran-ən\, Samuel. 1819–1889. American pioneer, b. Saco, Me. Adopted Mormon faith (1842); led colony of Mormons to California (1846). Published *California Star* (1847), first newspaper in San Francisco; a founder (1851) and first president of Committee of Vigilance.

Bran·ner \'brän-ər\, Hans Christian. 1903–1966. Danish writer. Author of novels *Legetöj* (1936), *Drömmen om en kvinde* (1941), *Historien om Börge* (1942), *Ingen kender natten* (1955); story collections *Om lidt er vi borte* (1939), *To minutters stilhed* (1944), *Angst* (1947), *Bjergene* (1953); plays *Rytteren* (1949), *Söskende* (1952), *Thermopylae* (1958).

Brans·field \'bran(t)s-,fēld, 'branz-\, Edward. c.1795–1852. English naval officer. Sent (1820) to chart South Shetland Islands; southward, sighted mountains, possibly Mts. Bransfield and Jacquinot; believed thereby to have been first to sight Antarctica.

Brant \'brant\, Joseph. *Indian name* Thayendanegea. 1742–1807. Mohawk Indian chief. Associate of Sir William Johnson; served British in French and Indian War, Pontiac's War; in American Revolution given captain's commission by British, honored on trip to England; commanded Indian forces cooperating with St. Leger's expedition, fought fiercely at battle of Oriskany (Aug. 6, 1777); responsible for the Cherry Valley massacre (1778); with Tories ravaged Mohawk Valley. Assigned land in Canada after Revolution; persuaded British (1785) to indemnify Iroquois for their losses in the war; established first Episcopal church in upper Canada (1786).

Brant *or* **Brandt** \'bränt\, Sebastian. 1458?–1521. German Humanist and poet. Professor of law, Basel (to 1499); syndic (1500), city clerk (1503) of Strassburg. Author of satirical didactic poem *Das Narrenschiff* (1494; The Ship of Fools).

Bran·ting \'brån-tiŋ\, Karl Hjalmar. 1860–1925. Swedish Socialist leader and statesman. Editor of journals *Tiden* (1883–86), *Socialdemokraten*, Stockholm (1886–1917). Co-founder (1889), Social Democratic party; member, lower chamber of the Riksdag (from 1897); leader of Social Democrats (from 1907); minister of finance, Liberal Socialist cabinet (1917–18); advocated neutrality for Sweden but sympathized with Allies in World War I; delegate to Paris peace conference (1919); first Swedish delegate to League of Nations (1922–25). Prime minister (1920, 1921–23, 1924–25).

Brantôme, Seigneur de. See Pierre de BOURDEILLE.

Braque \bråk\, Georges. 1882–1963. French painter. Follower of Fauves (1905–07); with Picasso developed Cubism (c.1908); credited with first *papier collé* picture (1912); later developed various personal styles, as white-line drawings incised into blackened plaster plaques, series of paintings of mantelpieces, pedestal tables, billiard tables, birds.

Bras de Fer. See François de LA NOUE.

Bras·i·das \'bras-ə-dəs\. d. 422 B.C. Spartan general. Distinguished himself in Archidamian War (431–422); relieved Methone (431 B.C.), repulsed Athenian attack on Megara (424) and captured Athenian colony of Amphipolis (424); defeated Cleon before Amphipolis (422).

Bras·saï \brȧ-sī\. *Orig.* Gyula Ha·lász \'hä-,läs\. 1899–1984. French photographer, b. Brasso, Hung. Paris correspondent (1924) for Hungarian newspapers; entered photography (1930); photographer for *Harper's Bazaar* (1946–65). Recorded nightlife of Paris streets, theaters, bars, prostitutes, etc. Books included *Paris de nuit* (1933), *Séville en fête* (1954), *Graffiti de Brassaï* (1961).

Bras·sey \'bras-ē\, Thomas. 1805–1870. English railway contractor. Built sections of Grand Junction and London–Southampton lines; with W. Mackenzie built Paris–Rouen line (1841–43) and lines in Netherlands, Italy, Prussia, Spain; with Sir S.M. Peto and E.L. Betts built Grand Trunk railway, Canada (1853–59), Crimean railway (1854); also built in India, Australia, South America. His eldest son ¶Thomas (1836–1918), Earl Brassey, became civil lord (1880–83) and secretary (1884–85) of the admiralty; governor of Victoria, Australia (1895–1900); author of an encyclopedic work, *The British Navy* (1882–83); founder of the *Naval Annual* (1886); created earl (1911).

Brath·waite *or* **Brath·wait** *or* **Brath·wayte** \'brath-,wāt\, Richard. 1588–1673. English poet. Author of *The Golden Fleece* (1611), *A Strappado for the Devil* (1615), a collection of satires, and, under pseudonym Corymbaeus, *Barnabae Itinerarium* or *Barnabees Journal,* doggerel verse in English and Latin (1638).

Bră·tia·nu \brə-'tyän-ü\. Name of politically prominent Romanian family, including: Ion Constantin (1821–1891), active in Romanian rebellion against Russia and Turkey (1848); forced to take refuge in France; returned to Romania (1856) and founded and led Liberal party; aided in fall of Cuza and election of Prince Charles of Hohenzollern as king; held various ministerial posts (1866–70); prime minister (1876–88); credited, with King Carol, with creation of modern Romania. His son ¶Ionel, *known as* Ion I.C. (1864–1927), was minister of interior (1907–09); prime minister (1909–11, 1913–18, 1918–1919, 1922–26, 1927) and virtual dictator of country (from 1922); devoted to notion of Greater Romania through territorial acquisition; promoted agrarian reform. He was succeeded by his brother ¶Vintilă (1867–1930), who had been his minister of finance (1922–27); prime minister (1927–28). Another brother ¶Constantin, *also called* Dinu (1866–?1952), deputy in parliament (from 1895); succeeded to leadership of Liberal party (1933); minister of finance (1933–34); opposed dictatorial policies of Carol II; helped plan coup against Fascist government of Antonescu (1944); minister without portfolio (1944–45); arrested by Communist powers, died in prison.

Brat·tle \'brat-ᵊl\, Thomas. 1658–1713. American merchant, b. Boston. Treasurer, Harvard (1693–1713); chief organizer (1698) of Brattle Street Church, Cambridge, Mass.; condemned Salem witchcraft proceedings (1692).

Bratton, Henry de. See BRACTON.

Brau·chitsch \'braů-ḵich\, Walther von, *in full* Heinrich Alfred Hermann Walther von. 1881–1948. German army officer. Major general (1931); commander of East Prussian military area (1933); colonel general and commander in chief of German army (1938). Planned and carried out German occupation of Austria and Czechoslovakia, conquest of Poland, and campaigns against Netherlands, Belgium, and France (1940), Balkans (1941), France and Russia (1941); relieved of command (1941); interned by British (1945).

Braun \'braůn\, Alexander Carl Heinrich. 1805–1877. German botanist. Professor, Freiburg (1846–50), Berlin (1851–77); director of botanical gardens, U. of Berlin (1851–77); contributed to development of plant morphology; leading representative of *Naturphilosophie* school of teleological and vitalistic interpretation. Author of *Betrachtungen über die Erscheinung der Verjüngung in der Natur* (1849–50).

Braun, Eva. 1912–1945. German woman. Mistress of Adolf Hitler (from 1930s); married him and died with him in Berlin bunker.

Braun, Karl Ferdinand. 1850–1918. German physicist. Professor, Tübingen (1885–95), professor and director of Physical Institute at Strassburg (from 1895). Discovered method in wireless telegraphy of increasing energy of sending station; discovered crystal rectifier (1874); invented a cathode-ray tube oscilloscope (1897). Awarded (jointly with Marconi) the 1909 Nobel prize for physics.

Braun, Lily, *nee* von Kretsch·man \fön-'krech-,män\. 1865–1916. German reformer and writer. m. 2d (1896) Heinrich Braun, Social Democratic journalist and politician; helped publish *Die neue Gesellschaft;* with Minna Caver founded feminist newspaper *Die Frauenbewegung.* Author of *Aus Goethes Freundeskreisen* (1892), *Die Frauenfrage* (1901), *Im Schatten der Titanen* (1908), *Memoiren einer Sozialistin* (1909–11), etc.

Braun, Otto. 1872–1955. German politician. Social Democratic member of Prussian Chamber of Deputies (1913), of National Assembly, Weimar (1919–20), and of Reichstag (1920 ff.); minister of agriculture (1918–21); prime minister of Prussia (1920–21, 1921–25, 1925–32); in Switzerland (from 1933).

Braun, Wernher von. 1912–1977. American engineer, b. Wirsitz, Germany (now in Poland). Pioneer experimenter with rockets; associated with army rocket research (from 1932); technical director, Peenemünde test facility (1936–45); developed V-2 ballistic missile. To U.S. (1945, naturalized 1955); developed rockets for army, including Redstone, Jupiter-C, Juno, Pershing; led group that orbited Explorer I (1958); director, Marshal Space Flight Center (1960–70); deputy administrator, National Aeronautics and Space Administration (1970–72); developed Saturn V rocket used in Apollo flights. Author of *Conquest of the Moon* (1953, with Fred Whipple, Willy Ley), *Exploration of Mars* (1956), *First Men to the Moon* (1960), *Space Frontier* (1967).

Braunschweig. See BRUNSWICK.

Bra·vais \brá-ve\, Auguste. 1811–1863. French physicist. Served in navy (1831–57); professor, École Polytechnique (1845–56); known for work in lattice theory of crystals; demonstrated (1850) the 14 possible lattice configurations, known as Bravais lattices.

Bravo, Luis González. See GONZÁLES BRAVO.

Bra·vo \'brä-bō\, Nicolás. c.1786–1854. Mexican general and politician. Joined rebel Morelos (1811); commanded Mexican independence forces (1811–21); in government of Itúrbide (1821–23) and then one of leaders who overthrew him (1823); a founder of Republic of United Mexican States (1823); vice president of Mexico (1824–27); led rebellion against President Guadalupe Victoria (1827); defeated and banished (1828). Acting president (1839, 1842–43), also president for a few days (1846).

Bravo Mu·ril·lo \-mü-'rē(l)-yō\, Juan González. 1803–1873. Spanish politician. Member of Cortes (1837, 1839); proscribed as enemy of Espartero and fled to France (1840–43). Minister of justice (1847), public instruction and finance (1849); prime minister (1851–52); exiled (1854–56); engaged in diplomatic missions (1856–68).

Brax·ton \'brak-stən\, Carter. 1736–1797. American Revolutionary leader, b. Newington, Va. Member, Continental Congress (1775–76, 1777–83, 1785); signer of the Declaration of Independence.

Bray \'brā\, Thomas. 1656–1730. English clergyman. Sent by bishop of London to organize Anglican church in Maryland (1699); founder of Society for the Propagation of the Gospel in Foreign Parts (1701).

Bray·ley \'brā-lē\, Edward Wedlake. 1773–1854. English topographer and archaeologist. Collaborator with John Britton in beginning series *Beauties of England and Wales* (25 vol.; 1801–16).

Bray-Stein·burg \'bri-'shtīn-,bùrk\, Otto Camillus Hugo von. Graf. 1807–1899. German politician. Bavarian foreign minister (1846–47, 1848–49); minister to St. Petersburg and Vienna; as prime minister (1870) signed treaty of North German Federation incorporating Bavaria into German empire; ambassador in Vienna (1871–96).

Braz Pe·rei·ra Go·mes \'brás-pə-'rā-rá-'gō-mēs\, Wenceslau. 1868–1966. Brazilian politician. Vice president of Brazil (1910–14), president (1914–18).

Braz·za \brá(d)-zá\, Pierre-Paul-François-Camille Sa·vor·gnan de \sá-vórn-yäⁿ-də\. *Orig. surname* Braz·za Sa·vor·gna·ni \'brät-sä-sä-vórn-'yä-nē\. 1852–1905. French explorer. Born an Italian count; became French citizen (1874). Explored region of Ogowe River (1875–78); later, traversed Gabon, reached Stanley Pool; established French protectorate for region (1880); founded Brazzaville (1883); established colony (from 1891 French Equatorial Africa) and served as commissioner-general (1886–97).

Breakspear, Nicholas. See Pope ADRIAN IV.

Breas·ted \'bres-təd\, James Henry. 1865–1935. American Orientalist, archaeologist, and historian, b. Rockford, Ill. On staff of U. of Chicago (1894–1935), professor (1905–33); organized Oriental Inst. (1919). Director of various archaeological expeditions to Egypt and Mesopotamia. Author of *A History of Egypt* (1905), *Development of Religion and Thought in Ancient Egypt* (1912), *Ancient Times* (1916), *The Dawn of Conscience* (1933).

Bré·au·té \brā-ō-tā\, Falkes de. d. 1226. Norman soldier. In service of King John of England; seneschal of household (1215); a chief commander in John's war with barons (1215–16); forced to surrender castles and holdings to Henry III (1223–24); exiled (1224).

Bré·beuf \brā-bœf\, Jean de. Saint. 1593–1649. French missionary. Entered Jesuit order (1617); to New France (1625) as missionary to Huron Indians; forced to return to France by English (1629), returned to Huronia (1634); put to death by Iroquois; canonized (1930).

Brecht \'brekt\, Arnold. 1884–1977. German civil servant and political scientist. Served in ministry of justice (1910–18), ministry of economics (1918), chancellery (1918–21), ministry of interior (1921–27); Prussian delegate to Reichsrat (1927–32); fled to U.S. (1933); professor, New School for Social Research (1933–54). Author of *Prelude to Silence* (1944), *Political Philosophy of Arnold Brecht* (1954), *Political Theory* (1959), etc.

Brecht, Bertolt, *orig.* Eugen Berthold Friedrich. 1898–1956. German playwright and poet. Influenced by Symbolists and Expressionists, evolved theater of political and social criticism often involving cynicism and irony for antibourgeois and anarchist effect; later adopted Marxism; fled Nazi regime to Denmark (1933), Sweden (1939), Finland (1940), U.S. (1941); settled in East Germany (1949). Works included *Baal* (1922), *Trommeln in der Nacht* (1923), *Im Dickicht der Städte* (1923), *Mann ist Mann* (1926), *Die Dreigroschenoper* (music by Kurt Weill, 1928), *Aufstieg und Fall Der Stadt Mahagonny* (with Weill, 1930), *Die heilige Johanna der Schlachthöfe* (1932), *Die sieben Todsünden der Kleinbürger* (with Weill, choreographed by George Balanchine, 1933), *Die Gewehre der Frau Carrar* (1937), *Leben des Galilei* (music by Hanns Eisler, 1943), *Mutter Courage und ihre Kinder* (music by Paul Dessau, 1941), *Der gute Mensch von Sezuan* (with Dessau, 1943), *Der kaukasische Kreidekreis* (with Dessau, 1948), *Der aufhaltsame Aufstieg der Arturo Ui* (1958).

Breck·in·ridge \'brek-ən-(,)rij\, John. 1760–1806. American politician, b. near Staunton, Va. Elected to U.S. House of Representatives (1792) but resigned to move to Kentucky; state attorney general (1795–97), state legislator (1798–1800); sponsored Kentucky Resolutions (1798–99) on nullification; U.S. senator (1801–05); U.S. attorney general (1805–06).

Breckinridge, John Cabell. 1821–1875. American politican, b. near Lexington, Ky. Grandson of John Breckinridge. Member, U.S. House of Representatives (1851–55); vice president of U.S. (1857–61); presidential candidate, southern faction Democratic party (1860); U.S. senator (1861). Joined Confederate army (1861); major general (1862); secretary of war, Confederate States of America (1865).

Brecknock, Earl of. See John J. PRATT.

Bre·de·ro \'brā-də-,rō\, Gerbrand Adriaenszoon. 1585–1618. Dutch playwright and poet. Author of humorous lyrics of street life *Groot Liedt-Boeck* (1622); farces *Klucht van de Koe* (1612), *Klucht van den Molenaar* (1613), *Klucht van Symen sonder Soetigheyd* (1612 or 1613); comedies *Het Moortje* (1615), *De Spaanschen Brabander* (1617).

Bre·de·ro·de \'brā-də-,rō-də\, Hendrick van. Count. 1531–1568. Dutch nobleman. Leader (1565) of lesser nobles ("les Gueux," or "The Beggars") in struggle against Spanish rule in the Netherlands; took part (1566) in drawing up the "Compromise" of nobles, at Breda, and the petition of grievances presented to Margaret of Parma; made unsuccessful attempt to raise army at Antwerp; fled to Germany (1567).

Bre·feld \'brā-,felt\, Oscar, *in full* Julius Oscar. 1839–1925. German botanist. Professor, Forest Academy of Eberswalde (1878–84), Royal Botanical Inst., Münster (1884–98), Breslau (1898–1907); known for studies in mycology and development of pure culture techniques. Author of *Botanische Untersuchungen über Schimmelpilze* (1872–1912).

Bre·gen·dahl \'brig-ən-dál \, Marie. 1867–1940. Danish writer. m. (1893, div. 1900) Jeppe Aakjaer. Author of novel *En dødsnat* (1912), tales *Billeder of Sødalsfolkenes liv* (1914–23).

Bre·guet \brā-ge\, Abraham-Louis. 1747–1823. French mechanician and watchmaker. Established Paris shop (1775); built instruments of great accuracy, including astronomical clocks and marine chronometers; made improvements in watches, as the use of the ruby as a bearing. His grandson ¶Louis-François-Clément (1804–1883), physicist and watchmaker, was in charge of building first electric telegraph line along Rouen railway; invented an electric clock (1839), electric thermometer (1840), induction coil (1842), revolving mirror apparatus for Fizeau's speed-of-light experiments (1843), and system of electric clocks for transmitting time to a distance (1856). His son ¶Antoine (1851–1882) was an electrical engineer and industrialist; inventor of an electrical recording anemometer. A descendant ¶Louis-Charles (1880–1955), manufacturer of airplanes; built his first plane (1909); built hydroplane (1912) and a "gyroplane," forerunner of helicopter (1917); founded (1919) Compagnie des Messageries Aériennes, later Air France.

Brehm \'brām\, Alfred Edmund. 1829–1884. German zoologist. Founder (1867) and director (1867–75), Berlin Aquarium. Author of *Tierleben* (1864–69).

Brei·ting·er \'brī-tiŋ-ər\, Johann Jakob. 1701–1776. Swiss scholar. Professor, Collegium Carolinum, Zürich; founded weekly *Discoursen der Mahlern* (1721–23) under influence of *Spectator,* conducting it in collaboration with Bodmer and opposing in it literary influence of Gottsched and the rationalists; in *Critische Dichtkunst* (1740) influenced literary ideals of Klopstock, Goethe, and Schiller through championship of non-rational elements of poetry, esp. English. His *Fabeln aus den Zeiten der Minnesinger* (1757) helped pave way for later interest of romanticists in literature of Middle Ages.

Breit·kopf \'brīt-,köpf\. Family of German printers and publishers, including: Bernhard Christoph (1695–1777), founder of Leipzig printing (1719) and publishing (from 1725) firm, known (from 1795) as Breitkopf and Härtel. His son and successor (from 1745) ¶Johann Gottlob Immanuel (1719–1794), developed (1754–55) movable music type; improved musical notation and German characters; devised method of printing maps and Chinese characters from movable pieces; wrote several treatises on printing. Johann's son ¶Christoph Gottlob (1750–1800) gave up the business (1796) to G. C. Härtel.

Bre·mer \'brā-mər\, Fredrika. 1801–1865. Swedish novelist, b. Finland. To Sweden (1804). Introduced domestic novel into Swedish. Author of *Familjen H.* (1831), *Grannarna* (1837), *Hemmet* (1839); *Hertha* (1856), *Fader och dotter* (1858); also wrote *Hemmen i den nya verlden* (1853–54) on her impressions of America.

Bre·mond \brā-mōⁿ\, Henri. 1855–1933. French literary critic and historian. Entered Jesuit order (1882); left it (1904). Author of *L'Inquiétude religieuse* (1901–09), *Newman* (1906–32), *Apologie pour Fénelon* (1910), *Pour le romantisme* (1923), *La Poésie pure* (1926), *Prière et poésie* (1927), and esp. uncompleted *Histoire littéraire du sentiment religieux en France* (1916–33).

Bren·dan \'bren-dən\ *or* **Bren·ainn** \'bren-in\ *or* **Bran·dan** *or* **Bran·don** \'bran-dən\. Saint. *Ir. Gael.* Brén·aind \'bren-in\. *Also called* Brendan of Clon·fert \'klän-fərt\ *or* Brendan the Voyager. c.484 or 486–578. Irish religious and traveler. Abbot of Ardfert, Co. Kerry; established monasteries throughout Ireland and Scotland, esp. that at Clonfert (561). Hero of a legendary voyage (565–573) to the promised land of saints on western islands, basis of popular medieval legend *Navigatio Brendani.*

Bren·nan \'bren-ən\, Christopher John. 1870–1932. Australian poet. Professor of German and comparative literature, U. of Sydney (1920–32). Author of *XVIII Poems* (1897), *XXI Poems: Towards the Source* (1897), *Poems* (1914), *A Chant of Doom* (1915).

Bren·ner \'bren-ər\, Victor David. 1871–1924. American sculptor, b. Shavli, Russia. To U.S. (about 1890); designed Lincoln cent (issued 1909).

Brennglas, Adolf. See Adolf GLASSBRENNER.

Bren·nus \'bren-əs\. 4th century B.C. Gallic chieftain. According to legend, generally accepted, led an invasion of Italy, defeated Roman army, and plundered and burned city of Rome (c.390 B.C.); besieged capitol until bought off by offer of 1000 pounds of gold. According to legend, during weighing of gold, a Roman tribune protested against use of false weights by the Gauls, whereupon Brennus cast his sword on the scale with the exclamation, "Vae Victis!" *i.e.* "Woe to the vanquished!"

Brennus. d. 279 B.C. Gallic chieftain. Leader in invasion of Greece (279 B.C.); passed around Thermopylae; defeated before Delphi; said to have killed himself.

Brent \'brent\, Margaret. 1600?–?1671. American colonial, b. Gloucester, England. To America (1638); took up first grant of land made to a woman in Maryland; became a principal landowner in colony; raised troop of soldiers for defense (1644–46); executor of estate of Gov. Leonard Calvert (1647); requested but denied votes in colonial assembly (1648); moved to Virginia (1650).

Bren·ta·no \bren-'tä-nō\, Clemens. 1778–1842. German dramatist, novelist, and poet. Brother of Bettina von Arnim. Became fervid Roman Catholic (1818) and withdrew to monastery of Dülmen, near Münster (1818–24) to be near the nun Anna Katharina Emmerich (*q.v.*), whose revelations he recorded. Compiled (1805–08), with his brother-in-law Ludwig von Arnim, *Des Knaben Wunderhorn,* a collection of German folk songs. Author of tales, as *Gockel, Hinkel und Gackeleia* (1838); plays as *Ponce de Leon* (1801), *Die Gründung Prags* (1815); novel *Godwi* (1801); patriotic and spiritual verse. A central figure of "Heidelberg school" of German Romanticism.

Brentano, Franz. 1838–1917. German philosopher. Nephew of Clemens Brentano. Roman Catholic priest (1864–73); professor, Würzburg (1872), Vienna (1874–80); resident largely in Florence (from 1895). Author of *Psychologie von empirischen Standpunkte* (1874), *Untersuchungen zur Sinnespsychologie* (1907), *Von der Klassifikation der psychische Phänomene* (1911), and other works in which he set forth doctrines of act psychology or intentionalism; also wrote on Aristotle, logic, ethics.

Brentano, Heinrich von. 1904–1964. German politician. A founder of Christian Democratic Union party in Hesse (1946); member of federal Bundestag (1949–64); parliamentary leader of party (1949–55, 1961–64); foreign minister (1955–61) in Adenauer government. President (1952–53) of Schuman Plan committee to draft European constitution.

Brentano, Lujo. 1844–1931. German economist. Brother of Franz Brentano. Professor, Berlin, Breslau, Strassburg, Vienna, Leipzig, Munich. Author of *Die Arbeitergilden der Gegenwart* (1871–72), *Der wirtschaftende Mensch in der Geschichte* (1923), etc. A leading pacifist and opponent of German militarism; awarded Nobel prize for peace (1927).

Brentford, Earl of. See Patrick RUTHVEN.

Brenz \'brents\, Johannes. 1499–1570. German reformer. Stout supporter of Luther. Author of *Syngramma Suevicum* (1525), upholding Luther's view of Eucharist; coauthor of Württemberg Confession (1551).

Bre·qui·gny \brā-kēn-yē\, Louis-Georges-Oudart Feud·rix de \fœ-drēks-də-\. 1714–1794. French scholar. Sent to England (1764), copied 700,000 documents from English archives bearing on history of western France in Middle Ages; collection published in 109 volumes.

Brere·ton \'bre(ə)rt-ᵊn\, Lewis Hyde. 1890–1967. American army officer, b. Pittsburgh. In military aviation (from 1912); served in World War I; head of air force in Philippines (1941) and Middle East (1942) and of all U.S. forces in Middle East (1943); lieutenant general (1944); commander of First Allied Airborne Army, Europe (1944–45).

Brescia, Arnold of. See ARNOLD of Brescia.

Brescia, Moretto da. See BONVICINO.

Bres·din \brez-daⁿ\, Rodolphe. 1825–1885. French etcher and lithographer. Known for complex, detailed prints often touched with the bizarre or fantastic.

Bress·lau \'bres-,laù\, Harry. 1848–1926. German historian and paleographer. Professor, Berlin and Strassburg; edited *Monumenta Germaniae historica* (1890–1913).

Bře·ti·slav I \'brzhä-tē-släv\. 1005?–1055. Prince of Bohemia (1034–55). Grandson of Boleslav II; led permanent reconquest of Moravia; invaded Poland unsuccessfully (1039); forced to swear fealty to King Henry III of Germany (1041).

Bre·ton \brə-tōⁿ\, André. 1896–1966. French poet, essayist, and critic. Member of the Dadaists (c.1916) and cofounder of Dada magazine *Littérature* (1919); became leader of Surrealists (1922); in exile in U.S. (1941–46). Author of *Manifeste du surréalisme* (1924) and *Second manifeste* (1930); and of *Mort de piété* (1919), *Nadja* (1928), *L'Amour fou* (1937), *Anthologie de l'humour noir* (1940), *Fata Morgana* (1942), *Poèmes* (1948), *L'Art magique* (1957).

Bret·on \'bret-ᵊn\ *or* **Brit·ton** *or* **Brit·taine** \'brit-ᵊn\, Nicholas. 1553?–?1625. English poet. Author of satirical, religious, romantic, and pastoral works in prose and verse, including the pastoral *Passionate Shepheard* (1604), character books *Fantasticks* (1604?) and *The Good and the Badde,* and an idyll in prose, *Wits Trenchmour* (1597).

Bre·ton de los Her·re·ros \brā-'tōn-dā-lō-ser-'re-rōs\, Manuel. 1796–1873. Spanish dramatist. Director, Biblioteca Nacional (1847–73). Author of some 180 plays, including *A la vejez viruelas* (1824), *Me voy de Madrid* (1828), *Marcela* (1831), *A Madrid me vuelvo* (1836), *Muérete y verás* (1837), *Escuela del matrimonio* (1852), and lyric and satiric poems.

Bre·ton·neau \brə-tò-nō\, Pierre-Fidèle. 1778–1862. French physician. Known for descriptions of typhoid fever and diphtheria; credited with performing first successful tracheotomy (1825); first used the term *diphthérie* (1826); enunciated a theory of specific causes of infectious diseases.

Bret·schnei·der \'bret-,shnīd-ər\, Carl Gottlieb. 1776–1848. German Protestant theologian. Edited Melanchthon's works (1834–48) in *Corpus Reformatorum;* author of *Handbuch der Dogmatik* (1814), *Probabilia* (1820).

Brett \'bret\, John Watkins. 1805–1863. English pioneer in submarine telegraphy. Established submarine telegraphic communication between England and France (1850); associated in syndicate with Cyrus Field in laying first transatlantic cable (1858).

Brett, Reginald Baliol. 2d Viscount Esh·er \'esh-ər\. 1852–1930. English military reformer. M.P. (1880–85); secretary of Office of Works (1895–1902). Superintended Queen Victoria's diamond jubilee (1897) and funeral (1901). Member of Earl of Elgin's committee on military preparedness (1902); chairman of War Office Reconstruction Committee (1903–04) that created army general staff; member of Committee of Imperial Defence (1905–30). An editor of *Correspondence of Queen Victoria* (1907); wrote *Girlhood of Queen Victoria* (1912), *Tragedy of Lord Kitchener* (1921).

Bretton, Henry de. See BRACTON.

Breu·er \'brȯi-ər\, Josef. 1842–1925. Austrian physician. Successfully treated neurotic patient "Anna O." by hypnotic recall of early trauma (1880);

collaborated with Freud on *Studien über Hysterie* (1895). Also known for discovery (1873) of positional sensory function of semicircular canals of ear.

Breuer, Marcel Lajos. 1902–1981. American architect, b. Pécs, Hungary. Student and instructor, Bauhaus School in Germany (1920–28); in private practice (from 1928), with Walter Gropius (1938–41); to England (1936), U.S. (1937); taught at Harvard (1937–46). Leading and influential exponent of International Style; works included Dolderthal Apartments, Zürich (1934–36), Sarah Lawrence Coll. Theater, Bronxville, N.Y. (1952), UNESCO headquarters, Paris (1953–58), St. John's Abbey, Collegeville, Minn. (1953–61), IBM Research Center, La Gaude, France (1960–61), Whitney Museum of American Art, N.Y.C. (1963–66), U.S. Dept. of Housing and Urban Development headquarters, Washington, D.C. (1963–68). Known also for chair designs as Wassily chair (1925), Cesca chair (1929), utilizing tubular steel frames.

Breughel. See BRUEGHEL.

Breuil \brœy\, Henri-Édouard-Prosper. 1877–1961. French archaeologist. Ordained abbé (1897); professor, Inst. de Paléontologie Humaine (1910 ff.), Collége de France (1929–47). Author of works on paleolithic art including *La Caverne de Altamira* (1906), *La Caverne de Font-de-Gaume* (1910), *Four Hundred Centuries of Cave Art* (1952, with Capitan and Peyrony).

Brew·er \'brü-ər, 'brů(-ə)r\, David Josiah. 1837–1910. American jurist, b. Smyrna, Asia Minor. Associate justice, U.S. Supreme Court (1889–1910); member Venezuela boundary and arbitration commissions (1895–98).

Brewer, Ebenezer Cobham. 1810–1897. English clergyman and schoolmaster. Compiler of *Dictionary of Phrase and Fable* (1870).

Brew·ster \'brü-stər\, Sir David. 1781–1868. Scottish physicist. Principal, St. Salvator and St. Leonard's Coll., St. Andrew's U. (1838–59); principal, U. of Edinburgh (1859–68); known for studies of optics and polarized light; discovered Brewster's law of polarization (1811); invented kaleidoscope (1816).

Brewster, William. 1567–1644. American colonial, b. Nottinghamshire, England. Bailiff and postmaster, Scrooby, Eng. (1590–1608); joined Separatist church; led Separatist emigration to Holland (1608), settled at Leiden (1609); in printing business (1609–19). Sailed to America on the *Mayflower* (1620). Leader of church and influential in affairs of Plymouth Colony.

Brezh·nev \'brezh-ˌnef\, Leonid Ilyich. 1906–1982. Soviet leader. Full member of Communist party of Soviet Union (1931); served in tank regiment of Red Army; during World War II served in military as political commissar; attained rank of major gen. (1943). To Moldavia (1950) to sovietize Romanians; elected to Central Committee of Communist party (1952), but later lost seats on Politburo and Secretariat; reelected full Politburo member (1957); chairman of Presidium of the Supreme Soviet (1960–64); engineered ouster of Khrushchev (1964); first secretary of Communist party (1964–66); general secretary (1966–82); regained post of chairman of Presidium (1977). Established (1968) Brezhnev Doctrine entitling Soviet Union to interfere in affairs of Warsaw Pact countries. Sought to normalize relations with West and promote détente; later presided over Soviet invasion of Afghanistan (1979).

Březina, Otakar. See Václav JEBAVÝ.

Bri·al·mont \brē-äl-mō^n\, Henri-Alexis. 1821–1903. Belgian military engineer. Rose to major general, inspector general of fortifications; devised system of detached perimeter forts, disappearing guns, and steel turrets to defend against modern rifled artillery; undertook fortification of Bucharest (1877–85); inspector general of Belgian general staff corps (1885).

Brian \'brēn, *Angl* 'brī-ən\. *Known also as* Brian Bo·ru \-bə-'rü\. 941–1014. High king of Ireland (1002–14). King of Dál Cais and of Munster (976); invaded Ossory (983); displaced Maelsechlainn II as high king (1002); slain while defeating forces of Leinster and Norse Dublin at battle of Clontarf.

Bri·an \'brī-ən\, Havergal, *in full* William Havergal. 1876–1972. English composer. Worked in isolation and often neglect; composed 33 symphonies, including *Gothic* (1919–27); 5 operas including partly lost *The Tigers* (begun 1916); lyric drama *Prometheus Unbound;* cantatas, concerti, over 100 songs.

Bri·an·chon \brē-ä^n-shō^n\, Charles-Julien. 1783–1864. French mathematician. Professor, École d'Artillerie de la Garde Royal (from 1818); discovered theorem named for him, concerning a hexagon circumscribed to a conic, set forth in his *Sur les surfaces courbes du second degré* (1808).

Bri·and \brē-ä^n\, Aristide. 1862–1932. French statesman. Contributor to Radical and Socialist journals; deputy (1902–32); founded *L'Humanité* (1904) with Jean Jaurès; chiefly responsible for draft of law separating church and state (1905–06); held numerous ministerial posts. Prime minister (1909–10); lost left wing support by breaking railroad strike (1910); formed new government (1910–11); again prime minister (1913); minister of justice in Viviani's cabinet (1914–15); head of coalition government (1915–17). Again prime minister (1921–22); French representative at Washington Arms Limitation Conference (1921–22); delegate to League of Nations (1924); minister of foreign affairs (1925–32); prime minister (1925–26, 1929); influential as foreign minister in policy of rapprochement with Germany as marked by Locarno treaties (1925) and in entry of Germany into the League of Nations; with Secretary Kellogg of U.S. developed Kellogg-Briand Pact for renunciation of war (1927–28); issued memorandum for plan for "United States of Europe" (1930). With Gustav Stresemann awarded Nobel prize for peace (1926).

Brice \'brīs\, Fanny. *Orig.* Fannie Bo·rach \'bōr-ək, 'bȯr-\. 1891–1951. American singer and comedienne, b. New York City. Star of *Ziegfeld Follies* (1910 ff.); also appeared in *Honeymoon Express* (1913), *Music Box Revue* (1924), *Sweet and Low* (1930), *Crazy Quilt* (1931) and films including *The Great Ziegfeld* (1936). Known for "Baby Snooks" on radio (1936–51).

Bri·çon·net \brē-sȯ-ne\, Guillaume. c.1472–1534. French prelate. Son of counselor to Charles VIII; bishop of Lodève (1489), abbot of Saint-Germain-des-Prés (1507), bishop of Meux (1516); encouraged religious revival and reform in Meux, becoming leader of notable group of evangelicals.

Bride of Kildare, Saint. See BRIGIT.

Bri·del \brē-del\, Philippe-Sirice. 1757–1845. Swiss clergyman and man of letters. Encouraged unity of French- and German-speaking Swiss in developing indigenous literature. Author of *Étrennes helvétiennes* (1783–87), *Conservateur suisse* (1813–31), *Glossaire du patois de la Suisse romande* (1866).

Bridge \'brij\, Frank. 1879–1941. English composer and conductor. Virtuoso violist with Joachim and English String quartets; composed chamber music.

Bridg·er \'brij-ər\, James, *called* Jim. 1804–1881. American pioneer and scout, b. Richmond, Va. Fur trapper and mountain man (from 1822); first white man known to have visited Great Salt Lake (1824); established Ft. Bridger (1843).

Bridg·es \'brij-əz\, Calvin Blackman. 1889–1938. American geneticist, b. Schuyler Falls, N.Y. Student and assistant of T.H. Morgan at Columbia U. (1910–28), California Inst. of Tech. (1928–38); helped prove chromosome theory of heredity and began work of mapping chromosomes.

Bridges, Robert Seymour. 1844–1930. English poet. Abandoned medicine for poetry. Author of verse dramas *Nero* (1885), *Achilles in Scyros* (1890); narrative poems *Eros and Psyche* (1885), *Demeter* (1905); lyrics in *Shorter Poems* (1890–94); *Collected Poems* (1898–1905); wartime anthology *Spirit of Man* (1916); *New Verse* (1925); *Testament of Beauty* (1929). Edited verse of Gerard Manley Hopkins (1918). Poet laureate (1913–30).

Bridges, Styles, *in full* Henry Styles. 1898–1961. American politician, b. West Pembroke, Me. U.S. senator from New Hampshire (1937–61); a leader of and spokesman for conservative wing of Republican party.

Bridg·et \'brij-ət\ *or* **Brig·id** \'brig-əd\ *or* **Bir·git** \'bir-gət\ *or* **Bir·git·ta** \bir-'git-tȧ\. Saint. c.1303–1373. Swedish religious and mystic. Daughter of governor of Uppland; subject from early age to mystical visions; m. (1316) Ulf Gudmarsson; mother of St. Catherine of Sweden. After husband's death (1344) devoted herself to religion and asceticism; founded (1344; estab. 1370) the Bridgettine order, or Order of the Most Holy Saviour, for men and women, on basis of Augustinian rule; lived mainly in Rome (from 1350); visited Holy Land (1372). Author of *Revelationes,* accounts of visions she had had from early childhood. Canonized by Boniface IX (1391); patron saint of Sweden.

Bridget of Kildare, Saint. See BRIGIT.

Bridgewater, Earls and dukes of. See EGERTON family.

Bridg·man \'brij-mən\, Laura Dewey. 1829–1889. American blind deaf-mute, b. Hanover, N.H. Educated by use of a raised alphabet devised by Samuel G. Howe (*q.v.*); first blind deaf-mute educated by systematic means.

Bridgman, Percy Williams. 1882–1961. American physicist, b. Cambridge, Mass. Taught physics, Harvard (1910–54); professor (1919); known for studies of materials at extremely high pressures. Author of *The Nature of Physical Theory* (1936), *Logic of Modern Physics* (1946), *Reflections of a Physicist* (1950). Awarded 1946 Nobel prize for physics.

Bridie, James. See Osborne MAVOR.

Bridport, Viscount. See HOOD family.

Brienne, John of. See JOHN of Brienne.

Brienne, Loménie de. See LOMÉNIE DE BRIENNE.

Bri·eux \brē-œ\, Eugène. 1858–1932. French dramatist. Leading exponent of Realist drama of social criticism. Plays included *Blanchette* (1892), *Les Bienfaiteurs* (1896), *L'Évasion* (1896), *Les Trois filles de M. Dupont* (1897), *La Robe rouge* (1900), *Les Avariés* (1901), *Maternité* (1903), *Les Hannetons* (1906), *La Femme seule* (1912), *L'Avocat* (1922), *La Famille Lavolette* (1926).

Briggs \'brigz\, Charles Augustus. 1841–1913. American clergyman and biblical scholar, b. New York City. Professor, Union Theological Seminary (1874–1913). Vigorous proponent of higher criticism, for which he was tried for heresy by Presbytery of N.Y. (1892); suspended from Presbyterian ministry; became Episcopal clergyman (1900). His suspension caused Union Theological Seminary to become independent and undenominational.

Briggs, Clare A. 1875–1930. American cartoonist, b. Reedsburg, Wis. Staff member, *Chicago Tribune* (1907–14), New York *Tribune* (from 1914); created *The Days of Real Sport, When a Feller Needs a Friend, Mr. and Mrs,* etc.

Briggs, Henry. 1561–1630. English mathematician. Professor of geometry, Gresham College, London (1596–1620), Oxford U. (1619–31). Proposed decimal system of common (or Briggsian) logarithms now universally used;

calculated and published logarithmic tables. His works included *Arithmetica Logarithmica* (1624) and *Trigonometria Britannica* (1633, completed by Henry Gellibrand).

Brig·house \'brig-ˌhau̇s\, Harold. 1882–1958. English dramatist. Author of *Hobson's Choice* (1916), *The Game* (1920), and other plays, and of several novels, including *Fossie For Short* (1917).

Bright \'brīt\, Sir Charles Tilston. 1832–1888. English telegraph engineer. With Cyrus Field and J.W. Brett formed Atlantic Telegraph Company (1856); engineer in charge of laying first transatlantic cable, between Ireland and Newfoundland (1858); consulting engineer in laying of Atlantic cables of 1865 and 1866; with Josiah Latimer Clark, improved method of applying asphalt covering to submarine cables. M.P. (1865–68).

Bright, John. 1811–1889. English politician and orator. Took part in opposition to principle of church rates (1834–41); a founder of Anti-Corn Law League (1839); M.P. (almost continuously, 1843–89); with Richard Cobden contributed to defeat of corn laws (1846), and engaged in free-trade agitation and in movements for financial reform, electoral reform, and religious freedom. Denounced Crimean War (1854); advocated Irish disestablishment (1868). President of Board of Trade under Gladstone (1868–70); chancellor of duchy of Lancaster (1873–74, 1880–82), resigned (1882) on British intervention in Egyptian affairs. Last spoke in House of Commons (1887) in opposition to Gladstone's Irish home-rule policy.

Bright, Richard. 1789–1858. English physician. At Guy's Hospital, London (1820–43); published *Reports of Medical Cases* (vol. 1, 1827), containing first description and diagnosis of Bright's disease.

Bright, Timothy. 1551?–1615. English clergyman and inventor. Abandoned medical profession to take holy orders; invented system of English shorthand called "Characterie"; granted by Queen Elizabeth (1588) exclusive privilege for fifteen years of teaching and of printing shorthand according to his system.

Bright Eyes. See Susette LA FLESCHE.

Bright·man \'brīt-mən\, Edgar Sheffield. 1884–1953. American philosopher, b. Holbrook, Mass. Professor at Nebraska Wesleyan (1912–15), Wesleyan U. (1915–19), Boston U. (1919–53); exponent of personalist psychology and a theism based on idealism and consciousness. Author of *Religious Values* (1925), *Philosophy of Ideals* (1928), *Problem of God* (1930), *Personality and Religion* (1934), *Philosophy of Religion* (1940), *Nature and Values* (1945).

Brigid of Sweden, Saint. See BRIDGET.

Brig·it \'brij-ət, 'brē-ət\ of Kil·dare \kil-'da(ə)r, -'de(ə)r\ *or* of Ireland. Saint. *Also* Bridg·et, Brig·id \brij-əd, 'brē-əd\, Brighid \'brēd\, Bride \'brīd\ *or* Ffraid \'frȯid\. d. c.524–528. Irish religious. Daughter of a prince of Ulster; freed from parental control by King of Ulster because of extraordinary piety; founded four monasteries, the chief of these at Kildare, the first in Ireland.

Bril *or* **Brill** \'bril\, Paul *or* Paulus. 1554–1626. Flemish painter. Worked in Rome (from c.1575); known for popular landscapes in Mannerist and later in classical style and for fresco cycles as in S. Maria Maggiore, Clementina Gallery of the Vatican, etc. His brother ¶Matthäus (1550–1583) painted frescoes in the Vatican (1575 ff.).

Bril·lat-Sa·va·rin \brē-yá-sá-vá-ra^{n}\, Anthelme. 1755–1826. French politician and writer. Member of the National Assembly; fled to Switzerland during the Terror (1792); returned to Paris (1796); judge of the Court of Cassation during the Consulate. Best known for his *Physiologie du goût* on gastronomy (1825).

Bril·louin \brē-y-wa^{n}\, Marcel-Louis. 1854–1948. French physicist. Professor, Collège de France (1900–31); known for work on structure of crystals, kinetic theory, viscosity of liquids and gases. His son ¶Léon-Nicolas (1889–1969), also a physicist; professor, Paris (1928–32), Collège de France (1932–39); to U.S. (1941); professor, Brown U. (1942–43), Harvard (1946–49); director of research, International Business Machines, Inc. (1949–54). Known for work in quantum theory, electromagnetic waves; discovered Brillouin scattering of light.

Brind·ley \'brin-(d)lē\, James. 1716–1772. English canal engineer. For Duke of Bridgewater constructed (1759) 10-mile canal from Manchester to coal mines of Worsley; subsequently built some 360 miles of canals, including Grand Trunk, Coventry, Oxford, Chesterfield, etc.

Bri·nell \bri-'nel\, Johan August. 1849–1925. Swedish metallurgist. Introduced at Paris International Exposition (1900) the Brinell apparatus for measuring the hardness of metals and alloys.

Brink \'briŋk\, Bernhard ten. 1841–1892. Dutch philologist. Professor, Marburg (1870–73), Strassburg (from 1873). Author of *Chaucer: Studien* (1870), *Geschichte der englischen Literatur* (1877–93), *Chaucers Sprache und Verskunst* (1884), *Beowulf-Untersuchungen* (1888).

Brink·man \'briŋk-män\, Johannes Andreas. 1902–1949. Dutch architect. With Cornelis van der Vlugt designed van Nelle tobacco factory, Rotterdam (1928–30), and with van der Vlugt and W. van Tijen the Bergpolder apartment building, Rotterdam (1933–34), both outstanding examples of modern design.

Bri·non \brē-nō^{n}\, Fernand de. 1885–1947. French journalist and politician. Editor, *Journal des Débats* (1920–32); political editor, *L'Information* (1939); leading advocate of Franco-German reconciliation. Vichy representative to German-occupied French territories (1940); secretary of state (1942); headed collaborationist "government commission" at Belfort after fall of Pétain-Laval government (1944); fled to Germany; executed as collaborator.

Brin·ton \'brint-^{ə}n\, Daniel Garrison. 1837–1899. American anthropologist, b. Thornbury, Pa. Professor, Academy of Natural Sciences, Philadelphia (1884–86), U. of Pennsylvania (1886–99); pioneer in American anthropology. Author of *Myths of the New World* (1868), *Aboriginal American Authors* (1882–90), *The American Race* (1891).

Brin·vil·liers \bra^{n}-vēl-yā\, Marie-Madeleine-Marguérite de. Marquise. *Nee* d'Au·bray \dō-brā\. c.1630–1676. French poisoner. m. (1651) Antoine Gobelin de Brinvillers; with paramour, poisoned father and two brothers; failed in attempt to poison husband; discovered and beheaded (1676).

Bri·ón \brē-'ón\, Luis. 1782–1821. Colombian naval commander, b. Curaçao, of Dutch parentage. Joined Bolívar (1812 ff.), commanding rebel fleet in Venezuelan and Colombian revolutions; supplied, outfitted, and commanded fleet for Bolívar's later campaigns (1815, 1816); defeated Spaniards on Margarita Island.

Bri·o·schi \brē-'ós-kē\, Francesco. 1824–1897. Italian mathematician. Professor, Pavia (1852–61); founder, director, and professor, Istituto Tecnico Superiore, Milan (1863–97); senator (1865). Known esp. for work on theory of invariants, fifth-degree and sixth-degree equations, and elliptic functions.

Briosco. See Andrea RICCIO.

Bri·ot \brē-ō\, Nicolas. 1579 or 1580–1646. French engraver and medallist. Chief engraver of French mint (1609–25); in service of Charles I of England (1625–46); introduced machinery into coin- and medal-making.

Bris·bane \'briz-bən, -ˌbān\, Albert. 1809–1890. American reformer, b. Batavia, N.Y. Became (from 1834) chief American advocate of Fourierism, or Associationism; founded Fourierist phalanx at Red Bank, N.J. (1843). Author of *Social Destiny of Man* (1840), *Association* (1843). His son ¶Arthur (1864–1936), b. Buffalo, N.Y., was a journalist; began on staff of New York *Sun* (1884); editor of New York *Evening Journal* (1897–1921) and Chicago *Herald and Examiner* (from 1918); influential as an editorial writer and columnist in these and other Hearst journals.

Brisbane, Sir Thomas Makdougall. 1773–1860. Scottish soldier and astronomer. Major general (1813); commanded at Plattsburg in War of 1812; governor of New South Wales (1821–25). Established observatory at Paramatta, near Sydney (1822), and a magnetic observatory at Makerstoun, Scotland (1841); general (1841). Brisbane, Australia, is named after him.

Brissac, Comte de. See Charles de COSSÉ.

Bris·son \brē-sō^{n}\, Henri, *in full* Eugène-Henri. 1835–1912. French politician. Republican journalist; member of Chamber of Deputies (1871–1912), president (1900–12); premier of France (1885, 1898). Strongly anticlerical.

Bris·sot de War·ville \brē-sōd-ə-vár-vēl\, Jacques-Pierre. 1754–1793. French journalist and Revolutionary leader. Author of two works on philosophy of law (1781, 1782); imprisoned in Bastille; founded antislavery society (1788); one of the mob that stormed the Bastille (July 14, 1789); elected to first municipality of Paris (1789); obtained equality of rights for Negroes; elected to Legislative Assembly (1791); member of diplomatic committee of the Assembly and influential in decision for war (1792); a moderate in the Convention; leader of the Girondins, or Brissotins; guillotined in Paris.

Bristol, Earls of. See John DIGBY.

Bris·tol \'bris-t^{ə}l\, Mark Lambert. 1868–1939. American naval officer, b. Glassboro, N.J. Rear admiral (1918); U.S. high commissioner to Turkey (1919–27); commander of Asiatic fleet with rank of admiral (1927–29); chairman of navy general board (1930–32).

Bris·tow \'bris-(ˌ)tō\, Benjamin Helm. 1832–1896. American lawyer, b. Elkton, Ky. U.S. solicitor general (1870–72); secretary of treasury (1874–76); obtained evidence and convictions against the Whisky Ring.

Bri·tan·ni·cus \bri-'tan-i-kəs\. *Orig.* Claudius Tiberius Ger·man·i·cus \(ˌ)jər-'man-i-kəs\. 41–55 A.D. Roman noble. Son of Emperor Claudius and Messalina; surnamed Britannicus in honor of his father's triumph in Britain (43 A.D.). Considered heir to throne until execution of his mother (48); through influence of Agrippina, set aside in succession in favor of her son Nero; poisoned by Nero.

Brit·tain \'brit-^{ə}n\, Vera Mary. 1896?–1970. English writer. Author of feminist and pacifist works as *Testament of Youth* (1933), *Testament of Friendship* (1940), *Lady into Woman* (1953), *Testament of Experience* (1957).

Brit·ta·ny \'brit-^{ə}n-ē\, Duke or count of. English title held by Geoffrey (1158–1186), son of Henry II, by Geoffrey's son Arthur (1187–1203), and by Geoffrey's widow's second husband, Ranulf de Blundevill, earl of Chester; by

Charles de Blois (1319–1364), who married the daughter of, and succeeded, Guy of Brittany (d. 1331); lastly by Francis II of Brittany (1459–1488).

Brit·ten \ˈbrit-ᵊn\, Benjamin, *in full* Edward Benjamin. Baron Britten of Alde·burgh \ˈȯl(d)-ˌbər-ə, -ˌbə-rə, -b(ə-)rə\. 1913–1976. English composer. Known esp. as outstanding composer of English opera since Purcell. Operas included *Paul Bunyan* (1941, libretto by W. H. Auden), *Peter Grimes* (1945), *Rape of Lucretia* (1946), *Albert Herring* (1947), *Little Sweep or Let's Make an Opera* (1949), *Billy Budd* (1951), *Gloriana* (1953), *Turn of the Screw* (1954), *Midsummer Night's Dream* (1960), *Golden Vanity* (1967), *Death in Venice* (1973); composed church pageants and parables *Noye's Fludde* (1958), *Curlew River* (1964), *Burning Fiery Furnace* (1966), *Prodigal Son* (1968); choral works *A Boy Was Born* (1933), *Hymn to St. Cecilia* (1942, text by Auden), *Rejoice in the Lamb* (1943), *St. Nicolas* (1948), *Spring Symphony* (1949), *War Requiem* (1962); song cycles *Our Hunting Fathers* (1936), *Seven Sonnets of Michelangelo* (1940), *Serenade* (1943), *Holy Sonnets of John Donne* (1945), *Winter Words* (1953), *Hölderlin Fragment* (1958), *Poet's Echo* (1965); instrumental works *Simple Symphony* (1925), *Variations on a Theme of Frank Bridge* (1937), *Young Person's Guide to the Orchestra* (1945), piano and violin concertos, etc. Created life peer (1976).

Brit·ton \ˈbrit-ᵊn\, John. 1771–1857. English antiquary. Created popular taste for books on topography. Author, with F.W. Brayley, of first nine volumes of *The Beauties of England and Wales* (1801–16); author of *Cathedral Antiquities of England* (14 vols., 1814–35), etc.

Britton, Nathaniel Lord. 1859–1934. American botanist, b. Staten Island, N.Y. Professor, Columbia U. (1890 ff.); a founder and first director (1896–1929), New York Botanical Garden. Author of *Illustrated Flora of the Northern United States, Canada, and the British Possessions* (1896–98, with Addison Brown), *Flora of Bermuda* (1918).

Britton, Thomas. 1644–1714. English coal dealer. Known as the "musical small-coal man"; had a famous musical club over his shop, where Handel and other performers took part in concerts (1678).

Bri·zeux \brē-zœ̄\, Auguste, *in full* Julien-Auguste-Pélage. 1803–1858. French poet. Known esp. for his Breton verse, as *Primel et Nola* (1842), *Bretons* (1845); translated Dante's *Divina commedia.*

Broad \ˈbrȯd\, Charlie Dunbar. 1887–1971. English philosopher. Professor, Cambridge (1933–53); president, Society for Psychical Research (1935, 1959). Author of *Perception, Physics, and Reality* (1914), *Scientific Thought* (1923), *Five Types of Ethical Theory* (1930), *Religion, Philosophy and Psychical Research* (1953), etc.

Broad·wood \ˈbrȯd-ˌwu̇d\, John. 1732–1812. British piano manufacturer, b. Scotland. m. (1769) daughter of Burkat Shudi; partner (1770) with Shudi, and (1773) with Shudi's son; sole proprietor (1782–95); admitted to partnership (1795, 1807) his sons ¶James (1772–1851) and Thomas, the firm becoming John Broadwood & Sons. Manufactured (1781) first grand piano in England; introduced improvements in piano mechanism, as did his grandson ¶Henry Fowler Broadwood (1811–1893).

Bro·ca \brō-kä\, Paul, *in full* Pierre-Paul. 1824–1880. French surgeon and anthropologist. Founder of Société d'Anthropologie (1859), *Revue d'anthropologie* (1872), École d'Anthropologie, Paris (1876). Discovered seat of motor control of speech in the brain (1861); authority on aphasia.

Bro·card \brō-kär\, Henri, *in full* Pierre-René-Jean-Baptiste-Henri. 1845–1922. French mathematician. Army officer (1867–1910); known for work on geometry of triangle and discovery of Brocard's circle.

Broch \ˈbrōk\, Hermann. 1886–1951. Austrian novelist. Author of complex experimental novels including trilogy *Die Schlafwandler* (1931–32), *Die unbekannte Grösse* (1933), *Der Tod des Vergil* (1945), *Die Schuldlosen* (1950), *Der Versucher* (1953); also wrote critical essays. Lived in the U.S. (1940–51).

Brock \ˈbräk\, Sir Isaac. 1769–1812. British soldier. Commanded garrison at Quebec (1806–10), all troops in Upper Canada (1810–12); major general (1811); forced surrender of General William Hull at Detroit (1812); killed at battle of Queenston Heights.

Brock, Sir Thomas. 1847–1922. English sculptor. Executed statues of Queen Victoria before Buckingham Palace (1911), Captain Cook in the Mall (1914), busts of Longfellow (1884) and Gladstone (1902) in Westminster Abbey, etc.; portrait of Victoria on 1897 coinage.

Brock·dorff-Rant·zau \ˈbrȯk-ˌdȯr-ˈfränt-ˌsau̇\, Ulrich von. Graf. 1869–1928. German politician and diplomat. Minister in Copenhagen (1912–18); foreign minister (1919) and leader of German peace delegation at Versailles; resigned (1919) because of his opposition to Germany's signing of Treaty of Versailles. Ambassador to Moscow (1922–28); consolidated German–Soviet understanding in Treaty of Berlin (1926); opposed membership in League of Nations and the Locarno Pact.

Brock·es \ˈbrȯk-əs\, Barthold Heinrich. 1680–1747. German poet. Author of *Irdisches Vergnügen in Gott* (1721–48), influential collection of religious and nature poems, and of translations of Pope's *Essay on Man* (1740) and Thomson's *Seasons* (1745).

Brock·haus \ˈbrȯk-ˌhau̇s\, Friedrich Arnold. 1772–1823. German publisher. Founded (1805) book business in Amsterdam, organized as firm of F. A. Brockhaus, printers and publishers; transferred to Leipzig (1817). Publications of firm included encyclopedia *Brockhaus' Konversations-Lexikon* (begun 1796 by R. G. Löbel, from whom copyright bought 1808); second edition, titled *Der grosse Brockhaus,* begun (1812); later (1966–74) became *Brockhaus Enzyklopädie;* firm also published Ersch and Gruber's *Allgemeine Enzyklopädie der Wissenschaften und Kunste* (from 1831), as well as yearbooks, pocket editions, and books on popular science and travel. Friedrich Arnold's sons ¶Friedrich (1800–1865) and ¶Heinrich (1804–1874) and later Heinrich's sons and grandsons carried on the business. Another son of Friedrich Arnold ¶Hermann (1806–1877), was an Orientalist; professor, Leipzig (from 1841); edited various Sanskrit and Persian works; also edited journal of German Oriental Society (1852–65) and Ersch and Gruber's *Allgemeine Enzyklopädie* (from 1856, vols. 62–99).

Brock·way \ˈbräk-ˌwā\, Howard. 1870–1951. American composer, b. Brooklyn, N.Y. Works included *Sylvan Suite* (1900), chamber works for piano, violin; composer also of choral music, songs, and piano pieces.

Brod \ˈbrōt\, Max. 1884–1968. Austrian writer, b. Prague. Author of novels as *Tycho Brahes Weg zu Gott* (1916), *Die Frau* (1927), *Zauberreich* (1928); also wrote biographies of Janáček (1925), Heine (1934), poems, a play, and works on pacifism and Zionism; best known as friend and editor of works of Franz Kafka.

Bro·die \ˈbrōd-ē\, Sir Benjamin Collins. 1st Baronet Brodie. 1783–1862. English surgeon. Promoted conservative treatment of diseases of the joints, which effected reduction in number of amputations. Author of *Pathological and Surgical Observations on Diseases of the Joints* (1818).

Brodribb, John Henry and Sydney. See Sir Henry IRVING.

Bro·dziń·ski \brō-ˈjēnʸ-skē\, Kazimierz. 1791–1835. Polish poet and scholar. Professor of Polish literature, Warsaw (from 1822); best known poetical work, *Wieslaw* (1820); introduced Romanticism in *O klasyczności i romantyczności* (1818).

Bro·feldt \ˈbrü-ˌfelt\, Johannes. *Pseudonym* Juhani Aho \ˈä-kō\. 1861–1921. Finnish writer. Author of realistic stories and novels and, later, works of romantic nationalism; helped introduce modernism into Finnish literature. Books included *Rautatie* (1884), *Papin tytär* (1885), *Papin rouva* (1893), *Panu* (1897), *Kevät ja takatalvi* (1906), *Juha* (1911), and stories collected in 8 series of *Lastuja* (1891–1921).

Bro·gan \ˈbrō-gən\, Sir Denis William. 1900–1974. British political scientist. Professor, Cambridge (1939–68). Author of *The American Political System* (1933), *Development of Modern France* (1940), *American Problem* (1944), *Introduction to American Politics* (1954), etc.

Brøg·ger \ˈbrœg-gər\, Waldemar Christofer. 1851–1940. Norwegian geologist and mineralogist. Professor, Stockholm (1881–90), Oslo (1890–1917); known for studies of Permian igneous rocks and tectonics of Norway.

Broghill, Baron. See BOYLE family.

Bro·glie \brō-glē, *Ital* ˈbrȯl-yä\, de. Name of a noble French family of Piedmontese origin, including comtes, ducs, and princes de Broglie: Victor-Maurice (1646–1727), comte, army commander under Louis XIV; suppressed Protestant activities in the Cévennes; marshal of France (1724). His son ¶François-Marie (1671–1745), comte, and (1742) duc, also a soldier; led campaigns in Flanders, Germany, and Italy, under Louis XIV; marshal of France (1734); commanded army of Bohemia (1741). His son ¶Victor-François (1718–1804), 2d duc, also a soldier, in Seven Years' War in command at battle of Bergen (1759), won battle of Corbach (1760); prince of the Holy Roman Empire (1759) and marshal (1762); commanded troops assembled near Versailles at outbreak of French Revolution (1789); withdrew to Germany (1790); commanded force of émigrés operating in Champagne (1792); in British service (1794) and Russian service (1797). His son ¶Charles-Louis-Victor (1756–1794), prince, also a soldier; favored Revolutionary cause (1789) and was president of Constituent Assembly (1791); adjutant general, army of the Rhine (1792); guillotined, Paris (1794). His son ¶Achille-Charles-Léonce-Victor (1785–1870), 3d duc, statesman; member of Chamber of Peers (1814); defended Marshal Ney; minister of the interior and of public worship and instruction (1830), of foreign affairs (1832–34); president of the council (1835–36); deputy (1849–51); retired from political life (after 1851); author of four volumes of *Souvenirs.* His son ¶Jacques-Victor-Albert (1821–1901), prince, then 4th duc, statesman and historian; member of National Assembly (1871); ambassador to Great Britain (1871); premier and minister of foreign affairs (1873–74); lost support by extreme conservatism and by attempt to strike compromise between Legitimists and Bonapartists; again premier and minister of justice (1877); retired (1885). Author of *L'Église et l'empire romain au IVe siècle* (1856–66), *Frédéric II et Marie Thérèse* (1883), *Frédéric II et Louis XV* (1885), *Marie Thérèse Impératrice* (1888).

A grandson of the 4th duc ¶Maurice, *in full* Louis-César-Victor-Maurice (1875–1960), 6th duc, physicist; served in navy (1895–1908); established private laboratory; conducted pioneering research into X-ray diffraction and absorption spectra. His brother ¶Louis-Victor-Pierre-Raymond (1892–1987), 7th duc, physicist; showed mathematically (1923) that particles should exhibit wavelike properties; his prediction was confirmed experimentally (1927) by others and led to development of field of wave mechanics; awarded 1929 Nobel prize for physics.

Broke *or* **Brooke** \ˈbru̇k\, Arthur. d. 1563. English poet and translator. Author of *Tragicall Historye of Romeus and Juliet* (1562), first English version of story and Shakespeare's main source.

Broke \ˈbru̇k\, Sir Philip Bowes Vere. 1776–1841. English naval officer. Commander of the *Shannon* (1806–13), in which he captured American frigate *Chesapeake* off Boston (June 1, 1813), receiving severe wound in the action; rear admiral (1830).

Brome \ˈbrüm, ˈbrōm\, Alexander. 1620–1666. English poet. Known esp. for Royalist drinking songs and satires against Rump Parliament; published *Songs and Other Poems* (1661).

Brome, Richard. d. c.1652. English dramatist. Servant, later friend, of Ben Jonson; collaborator with Ben Jonson's son and with Thomas Heywood. Made reputation with *The Northern Lass* (1632); considered best of minor Jacobean dramatists. His *Jovial Crew* (1641) last play to be acted before closing of theaters by Cromwell (1642).

Brom•field \ˈbräm-ˌfēld\, Louis. 1896–1956. American writer, b. Mansfield, O. Author of *The Green Bay Tree* (1924), *Early Autumn* (1926, Pulitzer prize), *The Strange Case of Miss Annie Spragg* (1928), *The Farm* (1933), *The Rains Came* (1937), *Night in Bombay* (1939), *Wild is the River* (1941), *Mrs. Parkington* (1943), *Pleasant Valley* (1945), *Malabar Farm* (1948), etc.

Brom•ley \ˈbrəm-lē, ˈbräm-\, Sir Thomas. 1530–1587. English judge. M.P. (1558–62); solicitor general (1569–79); as lord chancellor (1579–87) presided over trial of Mary, Queen of Scots (1586).

'Brom-ston \ˈbrȯm-ˈstȯn\. 1008–1064. Tibetan Buddhist leader. Translated much Buddhist sacred literature into classic Tibetan; possibly made definitive arrangement of collections *Kanjur* and *Tanjur* (c.1060).

Bronck \ˈbräŋk, ˈbrȯŋk\, Jonas[1]. *Also* Bronk \ˈbräŋk, ˈbrȯŋk\ *or* Brunk \ˈbrəŋk\. d. 1643? Danish pioneer in America. First settler in upper New York City (1639), in district now the borough of Bronx, named after him.

Bron•gniart \brōⁿ-yär\, Alexandre. 1770–1847. French mineralogist and geologist. Professor, École Central des Quatre-Nations (1797), Sorbonne (1808), Museum of Natural History (1822); director of Sèvres porcelain factory (from 1800), where he revived art of painting on glass and developed ceramic chemistry. Author of *Classification naturelle des reptiles,* making the division into saurians, batrachians, chelonians, ophidians (1800), *Essai sur la géographie minéralogique des environs de Paris* introducing method of geologic dating by fossils (with Cuvier, 1811), *Traité des arts céramiques* (1844). Also determined and described chronological order of formations of the Tertiary Period; studied trilobites. His son ¶Adolphe-Théodore (1801–1876), botanist, was professor at the Museum of Natural History (1833–76); authority on pollen and on classification and distribution of fossil plants and seeds; pioneer in plant physiology; author of a catalogue of plants in the museum, the basis for the system of classification used in Germany.

Bronk \ˈbräŋk, ˈbrȯŋk\, Detlev Wulf. 1897–1975. American physiologist and educator, b. New York City. Professor, Swarthmore (1926–29), U. of Pennsylvania (1929–49), head of Inst. of Neurology there (1936–40, 1942–49); president of Johns Hopkins U. (1949–53), Rockefeller Inst. for Medical Research, now Rockefeller U. (1953–68). Chairman, National Research Council (1946–50); president, National Academy of Sciences (1950–62).

Bronn \ˈbrȯn\, Heinrich Georg. 1800–1862. German zoologist and paleontologist. Author of long-standard *Letheae geognostica* (1835–38), *Handbuch einer Geschichte der Natur* (1841–43), and translator of Darwin's *Origin of Species.*

Bron•sart von Schel•len•dorf \ˈbrȯn-ˌzärt-fȯn-ˈshel-ən-ˌdȯrf\, Paul. 1832–1891. German soldier and politician. Entered Prussian army (1849); chief of division in Franco-Prussian War (1870–71); made preliminary negotiations with Napoléon III for French surrender at Sedan; Prussian minister of war (1883–89); increased and modernized standing army and introduced magazine rifle; general, 1st army corps, Königsberg (1889). His brother ¶Walter (1833–1914) served in Prussian army in campaigns of 1864 and 1866, and as chief of general staff, 9th army corps, in war of 1870–71; commanding general of 3d (1888) and 10th (1890) army corps; war minister (1893–96).

Brøn•sted \ˈbrœ̄n-steth\, Johannes Nicolaus. 1879–1947. Danish chemist. Professor, Copenhagen (1908–47); known for studies of electrolyte solutions, catalysis, chemical affinities, thermodynamics; published simultaneously with T.M. Lowry a theory of acids and bases (1923). Author of *Blandingsaffiniteten* (1908), *Laerebog i fysisk kemi* (1936).

Bronstein, Lev. See Leon TROTSKY.

Bron•të \ˈbränt-ē, ˈbrän-(ˌ)tā\. Name of a family of English novelists, daughters of Patrick (1777–1861), Irish Anglican clergyman; named, before coming to England, Brunty or Prunty; perpetual curate of Haworth, Yorkshire (from 1820); eccentric in habits; m. (1812) Maria Branwell of Penzance, Cornwall. Their three daughters ¶Charlotte (1816–1855), ¶Emily Jane (1818–1848), and ¶Anne (1820–1849), after attending an oppressive boarding school for clergymen's daughters and teaching for a time, took to literature, publishing a volume of poems (1846) under the respective pseudonyms of Currer, Ellis, and Acton Bell \ˈbel\; produced novels reflecting the domestic unhappiness and the penury of their lives. Charlotte returned to Roehead as teacher (1835–38), governess (1839, 1841); studied languages, with Emily, in Brussels (1842); taught in Brussels (1843); had her first novel *The Professor* rejected (published posthumously, 1857); achieved success with *Jane Eyre* (1847); produced *Shirley* (1849) and *Villette* (1853). Emily produced only one novel, *Wuthering Heights* (1847). Anne produced *Agnes Grey* (1847), and *The Tenant of Wildfell Hall* (1848). The only son ¶Patrick Branwell (1817–1848) showed early promise as a painter but died a drunkard and opium addict.

Bronzino, Il. See AGNOLD DI COSIMO.

Brooke, Baron. See Sir Fulke GREVILLE.

Brooke \ˈbru̇k\, Sir Alan Francis. 1st Viscount Al•an•brooke \ˈal-ən-ˌbru̇k\. 1883–1963. British soldier. Entered army (1902); served in World War I; expert in gunnery and anti-aircraft warfare; major general (1935), lieutenant general (1938); director of military training (1936–37); in command of Mobile Division (1937–38), Anti-Aircraft Corps (1938–39), Anti-Aircraft Command (1939), 2d Army Corps, British Expeditionary Force (1939–40); covered evacuation of Dunkirk; commander in chief of home forces (1940–41); chief of Imperial General Staff (1941–46); field marshal (1944); created viscount (1946).

Brooke, Arthur. See BROKE.

Brooke, Basil Stanlake. 1st Viscount Brooke•bor•ough \ˈbru̇k-ˌbər-ə, -ˌbə-rə, -b(ə-)rə\. 1888–1973. Irish politician. Senator in Northern Ireland parliament (1921–22), M.P. (1929–68); minister of agriculture (1933–41), of commerce (1941–45); prime minister of Northern Ireland (1943–63).

Brooke, Henry. c.1703–1783. Irish poet and novelist. Author of philosophical poem *Universal Beauty* (1728), said to have suggested Darwin's *Botanic Garden;* tragedy *Gustavus Vasa* (1739); and two novels, *Juliet Grenville* (1774) and *The Fool of Quality* (1765–70).

Brooke, Sir James. 1803–1868. English soldier, raja of Sarawak, b. India. Set out (1838) in private schooner to bring civilization to Malay Archipelago; aided Raja Muda Hassim in suppressing rebellion of Dayak tribes; made governor of Sarawak with title of raja (1841); reformed government, suppressed headhunting; governor of British colony Labuan; left Sarawak (1863). His nephew ¶Sir Charles Anthony Johnson Brooke (1829–1917), name orig. Johnson, joined him (1852), assumed name Brooke, and succeeded him as second raja (1868); largely kept out Western investment and influence; succeeded in turn by his son ¶Sir Charles Vyner (1874–1963), third raja (1917–46), who continued the program of benevolent government; proclaimed constitution (1941); ceded Sarawak to Great Britain (1946).

Brooke, John Rutter. 1838–1926. American army officer, b. Montgomery Co., Pa. Served through Civil War; major general in command of 1st Corps at Chickamauga Park, Ga. (1897); led troops in skirmishes in Puerto Rico; military governor of Puerto Rico, and of Cuba (Jan. to Dec., 1899).

Brooke, Rupert. 1887–1915. English poet. Traveled in America and New Zealand (1913–14); commissioned in Royal Navy (1914); died on hospital ship; long considered type of gifted youth lost in World War I. Author of *Poems* (1911), *1914 and other Poems* (1915), *Letters from America* (1916).

Brookes \ˈbru̇ks\, Sir Norman Everard. 1877–1968. Australian tennis champion and businessman. Member of Australasian Davis Cup tennis team (1905–20); Wimbledon singles and doubles champion (1907, 1914).

Brook•ings \ˈbru̇k-iŋz\, Robert Somers. 1850–1932. American merchant and philanthropist, b. Cecil Co., Md. Successful in woodenware business, St. Louis (1867–96); president of corporation, Washington U. (1897–1928). A founder of Institute for Government Research (1916), Institute of Economics (1922), and Robert Brookings Graduate School of Economics and Government (1924), all of which were merged (1927) into the Brookings Institution, Washington, D.C., devoted to public service through the social sciences.

Brooks \ˈbru̇ks\, Alfred Hulse. 1871–1924. American geologist, b. Ann Arbor, Mich. With U.S. Geological Survey (1894–1918, 1919–24); head of Alaska Branch (1903–18, 1919–24); engaged in exploration and field work in Alaska (1898–1916); discovered Rainy Pass. Author of *Geography and Geology of Alaska* (1906). The Brooks Range, Brooks River, Mt. Brooks named for him.

Brooks, Charles William Shirley. 1816–1874. English journalist and novelist. Joined staff of *Punch* (1851), editor (1870–74). Author of several novels including *Aspen Court* (1855) and *Sooner or Later* (1868).

Brooks, Maria. *Nee* Abigail Gow·en \ˈgau̇-ən\. *Pen name* Maria del Oc·ci·den·te \-ˌdel-ˌäk-sə-ˈden-(ˌ)tā\. 1794?–1845. American poet, b. Medford, Mass. m. John Brooks (1810). Author of *Judith, Esther, and Other Poems* (1820), *Zóphiël* (1833), *Idomen* (1843).

Brooks, Phillips. 1835–1893. American clergyman, b. Boston. Served Episcopal pastorates at Philadelphia (1859–69); Trinity Church, Boston (1869–91). Bishop of Massachusetts (1891). Author of the hymn "O Little Town of Bethlehem" (1868); renowned for sermons.

Brooks, Van Wyck. 1886–1963. American critic and writer, b. Plainfield, N.J. Author of *The Wine of the Puritans* (1909), *America's Coming-of-Age* (1915), *The Ordeal of Mark Twain* (1920), *The Pilgrimage of Henry James* (1925), *The Life of Emerson* (1932), *The Flowering of New England* (1936, Pulitzer prize), *New England: Indian Summer* (1940), *On Literature Today* (1941), *World of Washington Irving* (1944), *Times of Melville and Whitman* (1947), *The Confident Years* (1952), *The Writer in America* (1953).

Brooks, William Keith. 1848–1908. American zoologist, b. Cleveland, O. Professor, Johns Hopkins (1876–1908); founded Chesapeake Zoological Laboratory (1878); known for studies of marine animals. Author of *The Oyster* (1891).

Broom \ˈbrüm\, Robert. 1866–1951. South African paleontologist, b. Scotland. To South Africa as physician (1897); professor of zoology and geology, Victoria College, South Africa (1903–10); known for studies of mammalian and hominid evolution. Author of *The Coming of Man* (1933), *Finding the Missing Link* (1950).

Broome \ˈbrüm\, William. 1689–1745. English scholar and poet. Translated about a third of text and provided most of the notes for Pope's *Odyssey* (1722–26). Wrote *Poems on Several Occasions* (1727).

Broon·zy \ˈbrün-zē\, William Lee Conley, *called* Big Bill. 1893–1958. American singer, b. Scott, Miss. Guitarist and blues singer in Chicago (from 1920); appeared at Carnegie Hall (1938); later toured U.S. and Europe; considered outstanding exponent of folk blues.

Bro·que·ville \brȯk-vēl\, Charles de. Comte. 1860–1940. Belgian politician. Deputy (1892–1919); prime minister (1911, 1912–17), minister of war (1912–17); senator (1919–40); again prime minister (1932–34).

Bror·son \ˈbrȯr-sȯn\, Hans Adolf. 1694–1764. Danish clergyman and hymnist. Pietist pastor in Jutland; bishop of Ribe (1741). Published *Troens rare klenodie* (1739), containing translations of German hymns and 82 original ones, and similar *Svanesang* (1765).

Broschi, Carlo. See FARINELLI.

Bro·sio \ˈbrȯz-yō\, Manlio. 1897–1980. Italian diplomat. Member, anti-Fascist Committee of National Liberation (1943–44); ambassador to U.S.S.R. (1946–52), Great Britain (1952–54), U.S. (1955–61), France (1961–64); secretary general, NATO (1964–71); senator (1972–80).

Brosse \brȯs\, Salomon de. 1571–1624 or 1626. French architect. Architect of Marie de Médicis (1614); designed Luxembourg Palace (1615–20), portal of Church of Saint Gervais (1616), the main hall of the Palais de Justice (1618), Château Blérancourt (1619), Protestant temple at Charenton-le-Pont (1623).

Brosses \brȯs\, Charles de. 1709–1777. French scholar. Established geographical divisions Australasia and Polynesia in *Histoire des navigations aux terres australes* (1756); also wrote *Lettres sur Herculaneum* (1750), *Formation mécanique des langues* (1765).

Bros·so·lette \brȯ-sȯ-let\, Pierre. 1902–?1944. French journalist. As radio commentator and later contributor to *Le Populaire,* opposed appeasement policy; joined army (1940); entered Resistance (1942), becoming a chief organizer and adviser to de Gaulle; captured by Gestapo and died in prison.

Bros·trom \ˈbrȯ-strȯm\, Axel Ludvig. 1838–1905. Swedish shipowner. Converted sailing ship to steamship (1870) and subsequently founded Ferm steamship company, which became largest shipping firm in Scandinavia; pioneered in construction of ore boats.

Broth·ers \ˈbrəth-ərz\, Richard. 1757–1824. British religious leader, b. Newfoundland. Naval officer; discharged on half pay (1783). Self-announced apostle of new religion, claiming crown of England as descendant of David and "nephew of the Almighty" (1793); developed theory of British Israel; committed to Newgate (1795), later to a lunatic asylum (till 1806).

Brougham \ˈbrüm, ˈbrü(-ə)m, ˈbrō(-ə)m\, Henry Peter. 1st Baron Brougham and Vaux \ˌbrüm-ən-ˈvȯks\. 1778–1868. British jurist and politican, b. Scotland. Founder, with Sydney Smith and Jeffrey, of *Edinburgh Review* (1802); admitted to English bar (1808); M.P. (1810–12, 1816–30); carried measure making slave trade felony (1810); proposed measure for freedom of press (1816); defended Queen Caroline as her attorney general in trial (1820); sponsored Public Education Bill (1820); a founder of London University (1828). Created baron (1830) and persuaded by Whigs to accept chancellorship under Grey (1830–34); by famous speech (1831) helped pass Reform Bill; remodeled judicial committee of privy council (1833), a lasting reform; estranged from Whigs. Continued for 30 years to hear appeals before privy council and House of Lords. Designed (c.1838) the one-horse brougham carriage.

Brougham, John. 1814–1880. American playwright, b. Dublin, Ireland. Made debut as actor, London (1830); manager of Lyceum Theatre (1840–42); to U.S. (1842); continued to act, manage, and write. Author of over 75 popular plays including *London Assurance* (with Dion Boucicault, 1841), *Life in the Clouds, Love's Livery, Enthusiasm, Tom Thumb the Second, Columbus,* etc.

Brough·ton \ˈbrȯt-ᵊn\, John, *called* Jack. c.1704–1789. English boxer. Third heavyweight champion of England (?–1750); operated boxing school and arena, London (1742–89); prepared first set of boxing rules (1743; in effect to 1838); invented "mufflers," precursor of boxing gloves.

Broughton, Rhoda. 1840–1920. English novelist. Made reputation for audacity with *Cometh Up as a Flower* (1867) and *Not Wisely but Too Well* (1867).

Broughton de Gyfford, Baron. See John Cam HOBHOUSE.

Broun \ˈbrün\, Heywood, *in full* Matthew Heywood Campbell. 1888–1939. American journalist, b. Brooklyn, N.Y. On staff, New York *Morning Telegraph* (1908–09, 1910–12), *Tribune* (1912–21), *World* (1921–28), *World-Telegram* (1929–39), *Post* (1939); writer of column "It Seems to Me" (1921–39). Among his books were *Pieces of Hate* (1922), *Gandle Follows His Nose* (1926).

Brounck·er \ˈbrəŋ-kər\, William. 2d Viscount Brouncker of Cas·tle Ly·ons \ˌkas-əl-ˈlī-ənz\. 1620–1684. Irish mathematician. M.P. (1660); a founder and first president of Royal Society (1662–77); known for studies of continued fractions and infinite series.

Brous·sais \brü-se\, François-Joseph-Victor. 1772–1838. French physician. Professor, U. of Paris (1831–38). Author of *Examen des doctrines médicale* (1816), which set forth theory that disease is result of spread of irritation in gastrointestinal tract by physiological sympathy to other parts; advocate of bleeding and fasting.

Brou·wer *or* **Brau·wer** \brau̇-(w)ər\, Adriaen. 1605 or 1606–1638. Flemish painter. Known for genre and landscape works, including *Peasants Brawling, Peasants Feasting, The Smoker, The Drinker, Tavern Interior.*

Brouwer, Dirk. 1902–1966. American astronomer, b. Rotterdam, Netherlands. To U.S. (1927); taught at Yale (1928–66); known for work in celestial mechanics, pioneered in application of computers to orbital problems.

Brouwer, Luitzen Egbertus Jan. 1881–1966. Dutch mathematician. Professor, Amsterdam (1912–51); known for fundamental work in topology, of which he is sometimes considered the founder, and logical structure of mathematics, to which he contributed doctrine of mathematical Intuitionism. Author of *Over de Grondslagen der Wiskunde* (1907), *Over de Onbetrouwbaarheid der logische Principes* (1908), etc.

Brow·der \ˈbrau̇d-ər\, Earl Russell. 1891–1973. American Communist politician, b. Wichita, Kans. Joined Communist party (1921); its general secretary (1930–45); its nominee for president of the United States (1936, 1940); expelled from party (1946) for advocacy of peaceful coexistence.

Brown. See also BROUN and BROWNE.

Brown \ˈbrau̇n\, Alice. 1856–1948. American writer, b. Hampton Falls, N.H. Author of *Fools of Nature* (1887), *Tiverton Tales* (1899), *The Mannerings* (1903), *Children of Earth* (play, 1914), *The Black Drop* (1919), *The Willoughbys* (1935), etc.

Brown, Sir Arthur Whitten. 1886–1948. British aviator, b. Scotland. Served in World War I; navigator of airplane piloted by John W. Alcock (*q.v.*) on first nonstop airplane flight across Atlantic Ocean (June 14, 1919).

Brown, Benjamin Gratz. 1826–1885. American lawyer, b. Lexington, Ky. Edited *Missouri Democrat* (1854–59); identified with Free-Soil movement in Missouri, and later in formation of Republican party. U.S. senator (1863–67); governor of Missouri (1871–73); Horace Greeley's Liberal Republican vice-presidential nominee (1872).

Brown, Capability. See Lancelot BROWN.

Brown, Charles Brockden. 1771–1810. American novelist, b. Philadelphia. Author of Gothic romances *Wieland* (1798), *Ormond* (1799), *Edgar Huntly* (1799), *Arthur Mervyn* (1799–1800). First American novelist to gain international reputation.

Brown, Crum, *in full* Alexander Crum. 1838–1922. Scottish chemist. Professor, Edinburgh (1869–1908); developed modern system of graphical chemical notation; discovered (1892) substitution rule for benzene; studied equilibrium sensing of inner ear.

Brown, Ernest William. 1866–1938. American mathematician, b. Hull, England. To U.S. (1891); professor, Haverford (1891–1907), Yale (1907–32); completed G.W. Hill's work on theory of lunar motion, published (1919) highly accurate lunar tables.

Brown, Ford Madox. 1821–1893. English painter. Grandson of John Brown (1735–1788). Accepted Dante Gabriel Rossetti as pupil (1848) and thereafter allied with Pre-Raphaelite group; known for subtly colored, highly finished historical and literary paintings and for works as *Work, The Infant's Repast, Last of England;* executed twelve wall paintings for Manchester town hall, illustrating town's history (1878).

Brown, George. 1818–1880. Canadian journalist and politician, b. Edinburgh. To U.S. (1837), Toronto (1843); founder of Toronto *Globe* (1844). Member of Canadian Parliament (1857–65); prime minister (1858); senator (1873–80); advocated secularization of Ontario schools, representation by population, federation of British colonies in North America, and purchase of northwest territories.

Brown, George Douglas. *Pen name* George Douglas. 1869–1902. Scottish novelist. Author of *The House with the Green Shutters* (1901), depicting harsher aspects of Scottish life in dissent from sentimentality of kailyard school.

Brown, Henry Billings. 1836–1913. American jurist, b. South Lee, Mass. U.S. district judge, eastern Michigan (1875–90); associate justice, U.S. Supreme Court (1890–1906).

Brown, Henry Kirke. 1814–1886. American sculptor, b. Leyden, Mass. Works included *Indian and Panther,* Washington (equestrian) and Lincoln (both Union Square, New York), Gen. Winfield Scott and Gen. Nathanael Greene (both Washington, D.C.), *Angel of the Resurrection.*

Brown, Jacob Jennings. 1775–1828. American army officer, b. Bucks County, Pa. Brigadier general of N.Y. militia (1810); in War of 1812, defended American base at Sacket's Harbor, on Lake Ontario (May 1813); commissioned brigadier general, U.S. army (1813); major general (1814); commanded invasion of Canada (1814), battles of Chippewa and Lundy's Lane (July 5, 25); commanding general of army (1821–28).

Brown, James. 1800–1855. American publisher, b. Acton, Mass. Organized partnership with Charles C. Little (1837) which developed (1847) into Little, Brown & Co., of Boston.

Brown, John. 1715–1766. English clergyman. Author of an *Essay on the Characteristics of Lord Shaftesbury,* defending utilitarian philosophy (1751), *An Estimate of the Manners and Principles of the Times,* a bitter satire (1757–58), as well as tragedies, odes, and writings on music.

Brown, John. 1735?–1788. Scottish physician. Founder of the Brunonian system of medicine, based on the doctrine that disease consists in excess or deficiency of excitation of the body by external agents; declared practice of bloodletting erroneous. Author of *Elementa Medicinae* (1780).

Brown, John. *Called* Old Brown of Osa·wat·o·mie \ˌō-sə-ˈwät-ə-mē\. 1800–1859. American abolitionist, b. Torrington, Conn. Obsessed with idea of abolishing slavery by force (from c.1849); joined antislavery forces in Kansas (1855); in revenge for a proslavery massacre at Lawrence, Kans., massacred five slavery adherents at Pottawatomie (May 24, 1856); made stand at Osawatomie (August 1856) against raid by proslavery adherents from Missouri. Conceived plan of establishing new state as refuge for Negroes and base of operations for freeing slaves; received financial aid from Massachusetts abolitionists; with 21 followers seized Harpers Ferry, Va., and government arsenal there (Oct. 16–17, 1859), intending action as signal for general insurrection of slaves. Overpowered, convicted of treason, hanged. Regarded by northern sympathizers as a martyr, and commemorated in marching song "John Brown's Body."

Brown, John. 1810-1882. Scottish physician and essayist. Author of *Horae subsecivae* (1858–61), *Rab and His Friends* (1859), *John Leech and other Papers* (1882).

Brown, Sir John. 1816–1896. English steel manufacturer. Established Atlas works at Sheffield (1856); originated use of rolled-steel armor plating for war vessels (1860).

Brown, John Carter. See Nicholas BROWN.

Brown, John Mason. 1900–1969. American critic, b. Louisville, Ky. Drama critic, New York *Evening Post* (1929–41), *World-Telegram* (1941–42); associate editor, drama critic, *Saturday Review* (1944 ff.). Author of *Modern Theatre in Revolt* (1929), *Art of Playgoing* (1936), *Two on the Aisle* (1938), *Seeing Things* (1946), etc.

Brown, Lancelot. *Nicknamed* Capability Brown. 1715–1783. English landscape gardener. Laid out gardens at Kew and Blenheim; noted for use of few and simple elements to achieve naturally harmonious effects.

Brown, Martha, *nee* Mc·Clel·lan \mə-ˈklel-ən\. 1838–1916. American temperance organizer, b. Baltimore. m. (1858) W. Kennedy Brown. An organizer of the Prohibition party (1869), and a founder of National Woman's Christian Temperance Union (1874).

Brown, Nicholas. 1729–1791. American businessman, b. Providence, R.I. With his brothers in foreign trading and domestic manufacture, as Nicholas Brown & Co. (from 1762). Revolutionary cannon made from iron ore taken from their deposits of bog ore at Scituate and cast in their furnace. Supplied clothing and munitions to American army. Instrumental in locating, in Providence, Rhode Island College, later (1804) named Brown University. His grandson ¶John Carter Brown (1797–1874) assembled library of Americana, now at Brown University.

Brown, Olympia. 1835–1926. American minister and suffragist, b. Prairie Ronde, Mich. Ordained (1863) minister of Universalist Church, first woman in America in ministry of a regular denomination. President, Wisconsin Woman Suffrage Assn. (1884–1912); founder (1892), president (1903–20), Federal Suffrage Assn.

Brown, Robert. 1773–1858. Scottish botanist. Naturalist on Flinders's expedition to Australia (1801–05); collected some 1700 new plant species; curator of botanical dept. in British Museum (1827). His adoption of Jusiaean system of classification furthered its general adoption in place of Linnaean; distinguished (1827) angiosperms and gymnosperms; noted streaming of protoplasm and recognized (1831) nucleus as constituent of plant cells. Noted (1827) continuous random movement of particles suspended in fluid (Brownian movement).

Brown, Thomas, the younger. See Thomas MOORE.

Brown, Thomas. 1663–1704. English writer. Author of satires, lampoons; translated works from Latin and French. Best known for reputedly extemporaneous translation of Martial's 33d epigram on demand of Dr. John Fell, dean of Christ Church, Oxford: "I do not love thee, Dr. Fell, ..."

Brown, Thomas. 1778–1820. Scottish metaphysician. Coadjutor (from 1810) of Dugald Stewart as professor of moral philosophy, Edinburgh; developed form of common-sense philosophy based in sense perception; defended Hume's doctrine of causality as not inconsonant with religion; made advances toward associational psychology. Author of *Observations on the Zoonomia of Erasmus Darwin* (1798), *Observations on the Nature and Tendency of the Doctrine of Mr. Hume* (1804).

Brown, Thomas Edward. 1830–1897. English poet, b. Isle of Man. Author of *Fo'c'sle Yarns* (1881), including "Betsey Lee," and other volumes of verse, much in Anglo-Manx dialect.

Brown, William Hill. 1765–1793. American writer, b. Boston. Author of *The Power of Sympathy* (1789), considered first American novel; the book was long attributed falsely to Mrs. Sarah W. Morton.

Browne. See also BROUN and BROWN.

Browne \ˈbrau̇n\, Charles Farrar. *Orig.* Brown. *Pseudonym* Artemus Ward. 1834–1867. American humorist, b. near Waterford, Me. Learned printer's trade. First of his humorous articles in Cleveland (Ohio) *Plain Dealer* (1858). On staff of *Vanity Fair,* New York (1859); lectured through country (1861–66); on English tour (1866–67). Author of *Artemus Ward, His Book* (1862), *Artemus Ward, His Travels* (1865).

Browne, Edward Granville. 1862–1926. English philologist. Professor, Cambridge (1902–26). Author of *Literary History of Persia* (1902–24).

Browne, Edward Harold. 1811–1891. English theologian and prelate. Professor of divinity, Cambridge (from 1854); bishop of Ely (1864), of Winchester (1873). Author of standard *Exposition of the Thirty-nine Articles* (1850–53).

Browne, Hablot Knight. *Pseudonym* Phiz \ˈfiz\. 1815–1882. English illustrator. Abandoned line engraving for etching and water-color painting; preferred to his rival applicant, W. M. Thackeray, as illustrator, in succession to Robert Seymour (d. 1836), of *Pickwick Papers;* illustrated other Dickens novels and those of Lever and Ainsworth.

Browne, Isaac Hawkins. 1705–1760. English poet. Author of parodies on contemporary poets, as *A Pipe of Tobacco,* and of Latin poem *De Animi Immortalitate* (1754). Called by Dr. Johnson one of first wits of the country.

Browne, Maximillian Ulysses von. Graf. Baron Ca·mus und Moun·ta·ny \ˈkäm-ü-u̇nt-mōn-tän-ē\. 1705–1757. Austrian field marshal, b. Switzerland. Son of Irish Jacobite exile in service of Emperor Charles VI; commanded and skillfully withdrew Maria Theresa's army in Silesia during War of Austrian Succession; commander in Bohemia (1751); field marshal (1753); defeated by Frederick the Great at Lobositz (1756) and Prague (1757).

Browne, Robert. c.1550–1633. English clergyman. Founder of a separatist congregation in Norwich (1580); founder of sect called Brownists, predecessors of the Independents, or Congregationalists. Emigrated with followers to Middelburg, Zeeland (1581); issued books enunciating Independency, circulation of which was punishable in England by death. Returned to England (1584); after qualified submission to bishop, appointed master of Stamford grammar school (1586); accepted episcopal ordination (1591); rector of Achurch, Northamptonshire (1591–1631).

Browne, Sir Samuel James. 1824–1901. British army officer, b. India. Served in Sepoy Mutiny, Afghan wars; general (1888); inventor of the sword belt called the "Sam Browne belt."

Browne, Sir Thomas. 1605–1682. English physician and author. Practiced medicine, Norwich (from 1637). Author of *Religio Medici,* confessions of a skeptic (1643, following surreptitious edition published without his knowledge in 1642), which was widely translated; *Pseudodoxia Epidemica,* storehouse of out-of-the-way learning (1646); *Hydriotaphia: Urne-Buriall* (1658); and a mystical treatise, *The Garden of Cyrus* (1658), showing how the quincunx pervades the universe.

Browne, Thomas Alexander. *Pseudonym* Rolf Bol•dre•wood \'bōl-dər-,wu̇d\. 1826–1915. Australian novelist, b. London. Son of one of founders of Melbourne. Author of *Robbery under Arms* (1888), *The Squatter's Dream* (1890), *Old Melbourne Memories* (1895), *The Babes in the Bush* (1900), *In Bad Company* (1901), and other novels of Australian life.

Browne, William. 1591?–?1645. English poet. Author of *Britannia's Pastorals* (1613–16) and *The Shepheards Pipe,* including eclogues by other poets (1614); also wrote *Inner Temple Masque* (published 1772).

Browne, William George. 1768–1813. English traveler. Traveled through Central Africa and Middle East; captive in Dāfūr, Sudan (1793–96); murdered en route to Samarkand. Author of *Travels in Africa, Egypt and Syria* (1799).

Brow•nell \brau̇-'nel, 'brau̇-,nel\, William Crary. 1851–1928. American journalist and literary critic, b. New York City. On staff New York *World* (1871–79), *The Nation* (1879–81); editor and literary adviser, Charles Scribner's Sons (1888–1928). Author of *French Traits* (1889), *French Art* (1892), *Victorian Prose Masters* (1901), *American Prose Masters* (1909), *Criticism* (1914), *Standards* (1917), *The Genius of Style* (1924), *Democratic Distinction in America* (1927).

Brow•ning \'brau̇-niŋ\, Elizabeth Barrett. *Nee* Elizabeth Moul•ton \'mōlt-ᵊn\. *Name Barrett assumed by father, Edward Moulton, on succeeding to estate in Jamaica.* 1806–1861. English poet. As result of injury to spine at fifteen, semi-invalid for years. Published *The Seraphim and Other Poems* (1838), *Poems, by E. Barrett Barrett* (1844), which attracted attention of Robert Browning; married him (1846). Produced her best work, *Sonnets from the Portuguese* (1850). Sympathized with struggle of Florentines for freedom in *Casa Guidi Windows* (1851). Completed *Aurora Leigh* (1857), expressing her "highest convictions in work and art"; last work *Poems before Congress* (1860).

Browning, John Moses. 1855–1926. American inventor, b. Ogden, Utah. Patented (1879) breech-loading single-shot rifle; designed sporting firearms manufactured by Winchester, Remington, Stevens, and Colt companies; organized with brother a gunmaking firm. Inventor of Browning automatic pistol (1911), Browning machine gun (1917), Browning automatic rifle (1918) which remained standard army shoulder weapon for 40 years.

Browning, Robert. 1812–1889. English poet. Showed Shelleyan influence in first published work, *Pauline* (anon., 1833); published long dramatic narrative poems *Paracelsus* (1835) and *Sordello* (1840). Urged by Macready, wrote tragedy *Strafford,* produced at Covent Garden (1837), followed by other plays, including *Pippa Passes* (1841), *Return of the Druses* (1843), *Blot in the 'Scutcheon* (1843), *Colombe's Birthday* (1844); published these plays along with *Dramatic Romances and Lyrics* under the title *Bells and Pomegranates* (1841–46), which included poems "My Last Duchess," "Pied Piper of Hamelin," "Home Thoughts from Abroad"; contributed to *Hood's Magazine* (1844–45) six poems including "The Bishop Orders his Tomb at Saint Praxed's" and "The Flight of the Duchess." m. (1846) Elizabeth Barrett (see Elizabeth Barrett BROWNING) and lived for next fifteen years more or less in seclusion, mainly in Italy; published only *Christmas-Eve and Easter Day* (1859) and *Men and Women* (1855, including "Fra Lippo Lippi," "Love Among the Ruins," "Bishop Blougram's Apology"). Returned to London upon wife's death (1861), and in psychological monologues of *Dramatis Personae* (1864; including "Prospice," "Rabbi Ben Ezra," "A Death in the Desert," "Caliban upon Setebos") found his best form; wrote *The Ring and the Book* (1868–69), story of a Roman murder case in 12 books, often regarded as his masterpiece. Turned increasingly to speculation and analytical disquisition in later writings on variety of subjects, including *Balaustion's Adventure* (1871), *Fifine at the Fair* (1872), *Red Cotton Nightcap Country* (1873), *The Inn Album* (1875); returned to direct narrative in *Dramatic Idylls* (1879, 1880). Showed failing powers of objectivity in last works; for example, *Jocoseria* (1883), *Ferishtah's Fancies* (1884), *Asolando* (1889, appearing the day of his death).

Brown•lee \'braün-lē\, John Edward. 1884–1961. Canadian politician, b. Port Ryerse, Ont. Attorney general of Alberta (1921–24); member of Alberta legislature (1921–34); prime minister (1924–34); secured provincial control of natural resources.

Brown•low \'braün-(,)lō\, William Gannaway. *Called* the Fighting Parson. 1805–1877. American political leader, b. Wythe Co., Va. Methodist itinerant preacher (1826–36); editor, Jonesboro (Tenn.) *Whig and Independent* (1839–49), Knoxville (Tenn.) *Whig* (1849–61), when it was suppressed because of Union sympathies. Governor of Tennessee (1865–69); U.S. senator (1869–75).

Brown•rigg \'braün-(,)rig\, Sir Robert. 1759–1833. British soldier. Served in Netherlands, Germany, and in Walcheren expedition (1809); governor of Ceylon (1811–20); conquered Kandyan kingdom (1814–15); general (1819).

Brown-Sé•quard \braün-sā-k(w)är\, Charles-Édouard. 1817–1894. French physiologist, b. Mauritius, of American and French parentage. Professor, Harvard (1864–68), Collège de France (1878–94); known esp. for investigations of physiology and pathology of spinal cord and discovery of essentiality of adrenal glands; late in life advocated injection of a fluid prepared from testicles of sheep as means of rejuvenation.

Brown•son \'braün-sən\, Orestes Augustus. 1803–1876. American clergyman and writer, b. Stockbridge, Vt. Universalist minister (1826–31); Unitarian minister (1832–44); converted to Roman Catholicism (1844); published *Brownson's Quarterly Review* (1844–65, 1872–75). Author of *The Spirit-Rapper* (1854), *The Convert* (1857), *The American Republic* (1865), etc.

Broz, Josip. See TITO.

Bruce \'brüs\ *or in early use* **de Bruce.** Surname of old Scottish family of Norman descent founded by Robert de Bruce I, *also* Braose *or* Breaux *or* Brus (d. 1094?), from Bruis, a castle near Cherbourg, follower of William the Conqueror. It included:

¶Robert II (d. 1141), son of Robert I; companion of King David I, from whom he received (c.1124) grant of Annandale.

¶Robert VI (1210–1295), son of Robert V (d. 1245) and Isabel, niece of the Scottish king William the Lion; recognized as heir presumptive (1238–41); one of fifteen regents during minority of Alexander III; fought on side of Henry III against barons; at arbitration of Edward I lost his claim to crown to Baliol (1292).

For Robert VIII (1274–1329) see ROBERT I of Scotland; for David (1324–1371) see DAVID II of Scotland.

Bruce. Name of English family holding earldom of El•gin \'el-gən\. Prominent members of family included Robert (d. 1685), 2d earl; created also earl of Ailesbury (1664); lord chamberlain of England (1685). His son ¶Thomas (1655?–1741), 3d earl; imprisoned as Jacobite (1696); resided in Brussels (1696–1741). ¶Thomas (1766–1841), 7th earl of Elgin and 11th earl of Kin•car•dine \kin-'kärd-ᵊn, kiŋ-\; British diplomat; envoy to Brussels (1790), Berlin (1792); arranged while envoy to the Ottoman Sultan (1799–1803) for conveyance of collection called the "Elgin marbles," including the Parthenon frieze, from the Acropolis of Athens to British Museum (1803–12). His son ¶James (1811–1863), 8th earl of Elgin and 12th earl of Kincardine; diplomat; governor of Jamaica (1842–46); governor general of Canada (1847–54); worked to develop responsible government; incurred Tory opposition with support of Rebellion Losses Act (1849); negotiated reciprocity treaty with U.S. (1854). Special envoy to China and Japan to negotiate treaties (1857–59, 1860–61); postmaster general (1859–60); first viceroy of India directly appointed by the crown (1862). His son ¶Victor Alexander (1849–1917), 9th earl of Elgin and 13th earl of Kincardine; b. Canada; viceroy of India during period of frontier uprisings (1894–99); chairman of royal commission to examine conduct of Boer War; colonial secretary in Campbell-Bannerman's ministry (1905–08).

Bruce, Blanche Kelso. 1841–1898. American politician, b. Farmville, Va. Originally a slave; studied at Oberlin Coll. (1866–68); became planter and politician in Mississippi; U.S. senator (1875–81), first Negro to serve full term; U.S. register of treasury (1881–89, 1895–98); recorder of deeds for District of Columbia (1889–95).

Bruce, Sir David. 1855–1931. British physician and bacteriologist, b. Australia. Entered Royal Army Medical Corps (1883); first described (1887) the bacterium that causes undulant fever (brucellosis), later placed in genus Brucella named for him. Served in South Africa (1894–1901); discovered trypanosome organism that causes nagana and that tsetse fly is its vector (1895); medical officer at siege of Ladysmith (1899–1900). To Uganda to investigate sleeping sickness (1903, with Nabarro and Castellani; again 1908–10); demonstrated agency of trypanosome and tsetse fly; to Nyasaland to investigate connection between human and animal diseases (1911–14); commandant, Royal Army Medical Coll. (1914–19). Major general (1912).

Bruce, Everend Lester. 1884–1949. Canadian geologist, b. Toledo, Ont. Member of Geological Survey of Canada (1913–19); professor, Queen's U., Kingston, Ont. (1919–49). Known for studies of Canadian regional geology; author of *Mineral Deposits of the Canadian Shield* (1933).

Bruce, Henry Austin. 1st Baron Ab•er•dare \,ab-ər-'da(ə)r, -'de(ə)r\. 1815–1895. English politician. M.P. (1852–73). Home secretary (1869–73); lord president of council (1873–74); responsible for Liquor Licensing Act (1872) which cost support for Liberal party and led to fall of Gladstone's ministry. Created baron (1873). First chancellor, U. of Wales (1894).

Bruce, James. 1730–1794. Scottish explorer. British consul, Algiers (1763–65); rediscovered source of Blue Nile (1770). Author of *Travels to Discover the Source of the Nile* (1790).

Bruce, Michael. 1746–1767. Scottish poet and schoolmaster. His poems published by Rev. John Logan as *Poems on Several Occasions* (1770), but several apparently withheld and published as Logan's own in *Poems* (1781), including "Ode to the Cuckoo."

Bruce, Stanley Melbourne. Viscount Bruce of Melbourne. 1883–1967. Australian politician. M.P. (1918–29, 1931–33); prime minister of Australia (1923–29). Representative on council of League of Nations (1933–36), and president of council (1936). High commissioner for Australia in London (1933–45); Australian representative in British war cabinet (1942–45); minister to Netherlands (1942–45). Chairman, World Food Council (1947). Created viscount (1947), first Australian in House of Lords.

Bruce, William Speirs. 1867–1921. Scottish explorer and naturalist. On polar expeditions (1892–99); leader of Scottish national Antarctic expedition to explore Weddell Sea (1902–04); visited Spitsbergen seven times (1906–20).

Bruch \'brük\, Max Karl August. 1838–1920. German composer. Known esp. for violin concertos; also composed operas *Scherz, List und Rache* (1858), *Die Loreley* (1863), *Hermione* (1872); sacred and secular choral works as *Odysseus* (1872), *Das Lied von der Glocke* (1879), *Das Feuerkreuz* (1889); songs, symphonies, chamber works, etc.

Bru·cio·li \brü-'chō-lē\, Antonio. d. 1566. Italian Humanist. Made Italian translation of Bible (1532); accused of Lutheranism, tried by Inquisition (1548, 1555, 1558–59), finally imprisoned for refusal to retract. His translation (printed in Geneva, 1562) became Bible of Italian Protestants.

Bruck \'brük\, Karl Ludwig von. 1798–1860. Austrian politician. Delegate to National Assembly, Frankfurt (1848); minister of commerce (1848–51); helped carry out many commercial and customs reforms; minister of finance (1855–60); failed in contemplated reforms and in meeting obligations resulting from Italian war of 1859; committed suicide.

Brücke \'brœk-ə\, Ernst Wilhelm von. 1819–1892. German physician and physiologist. Professor, Vienna (1849–91); established influential school of physiology dedicated to physicochemical explanations of phenomena; known for researches in histology and the physiology of the circulation of the blood, studies of digestion, nervous system, sense organs, and speech.

Bruck·er \'brük-ər\, Johann Jakob. 1696–1770. German philosopher. Author of *Historia Critica Philosophiae* (1742–44), first German history of philosophy.

Bruck·ner \'brük-nər\, Anton, *in full* Josef Anton. 1824–1896. Austrian composer. Organist, Sankt Florian Abbey (1848–56), Linz Cathedral (1856–68), Imperial chapel (1878–96); professor, Vienna Conservatory (1871), U. of Vienna (1875). Works included 10 symphonies, the last unfinished; a string quintet (1878–79); cantatas *Preiset den Herrn* (1862), *Germanenzug* (1863), *Das deutsche Lied* (1892), *Helgoland* (1893); and much sacred music, including *Requiem* (1848–49), *Te Deum* (1881), *Psalm CL* (1892).

Brück·ner \'brœk-nər\, Eduard. 1862–1927. German geographer and meteorologist. Professor, Bern (1888–1904), Halle (1904–06), Vienna (1906–27); specialist in climatology and glaciology; discovered (1887) 35-year Brückner climatic cycle.

Bru·de·nell \'bräd-ᵊn-əl, 'brüd-nəl\, James Thomas. 7th Earl of Car·di·gan \'kärd-ə-gən\. 1797–1868. English general. M.P. (1819–37); entered army (1824) and purchased colonelcy (1832) of 15th Hussars; succeeded to earldom (1837); lavished money on 11th Hussars (1836–54); major general (1854); in Crimean War commanded light brigade that, through his error, was decimated in charge at Balaclava. Received at home as hero; inspector general of cavalry (1855); lieutenant general (1861).

Brue·ghel *or* **Brue·gel** *or* **Breu·ghel** \'brœ̄-gəl, *Angl* 'brȯi-gəl\. Family of Flemish painters, including: Pieter the Elder (c.1525 or 1530–1569), called "Peasant Brueghel" and "the Droll"; known for drawings and engravings, often landscapes and mountain scenes, and paintings of peasant scenes, biblical episodes, and fantastic compositions similar to those of Bosch; for range of subject, wit and skill of treatment, considered greatest Flemish painter of 16th century. His sons ¶Pieter the Younger (1564–1638), called "Hell Brueghel," painter of rural and genre subjects in his father's style and esp. of paintings of rustic grotesques, infernal regions, devils, and flames; and ¶Jan the Elder (1568–1625), called "Velvet Brueghel" and "Flower Brueghel," painter esp. of flowers and of landscapes with biblical and mythological figures and animals, and of landscapes and background for many figure painters, notably Rubens. Jan's sons ¶Jan the Younger (1601–1678), pupil of his father and painter of landscapes and flowers, and ¶Ambrose (1617–1675), painter of flowers and fruits. ¶Abraham (1631–?1690), son of Jan the Younger, painter of still lifes in the Italian-Flemish style. ¶Jan Baptist (1670–1719), great-grandson of Jan the Elder, painter of flowers and fruits.

Bru·eys \brue̅-es\, David-Augustin de. 1640–1723. French writer. Collaborator with Palaprat on comedies, as *Le Concert ridicule* (1689), *Le Grondeur* (1691), *Le Muet* (1693), *L'Avocat Patelin* (1706).

Brug·gen \'brüg-ən\, Jochem van. 1881–1957. South African novelist. Author in Afrikaans of *Ampie* (trilogy, 1924–32), *Booia* (1931), *Die noodlot* (1939), *Kranskop* (1943).

Bru·gière \brue̅zh-yer\, Amable-Guillaume-Prosper. Baron de Ba·rante \bä-räⁿt\. 1782–1866. French politician and historian. Auditor to Council of State (1806); prefect of Vendée (1809), of Loire-Inférieure (1815); councillor of state and secretary general of interior (1815); peer (1819); ambassador to Turin (1830), St. Petersburg (1835). Author of *Histoire des ducs de Bourgogne* (1824–28), *Histoire de la Convention Nationale* (1851–53), *Histoire du Directoire de la République française* (1855).

Brug·mann \'brüg-,män\, Karl, *in full* Friedrich Karl. 1849–1919. German philologist. Professor of Sanskrit and comparative philology, Freiburg (1884) and Leipzig (1887); a leading exponent of *Junggrammatiker* (Neogrammarian) school. Author of *Nasalis Sonans in der indogermanischen Grundsprache* (1876), *Morphologische Untersuchungen* (with Osthoff, 1878–90, 1910), *Grundriss der vergleichenden Grammatik der indogermanischen Sprachen* (1886–93).

Bru·gnon \brue̅n-yōⁿ\, Jacques. *Called* To·to \tō-tō\. 1895–1978. French tennis player. One of "four musketeers" (Borotra, Cochet, Lacoste) who won Davis Cup for France 6 times (1927–32); French doubles champion (1922, 1928, 1930, 1932, 1934); Wimbledon doubles champion (1926, 1932, 1933); with Suzanne Lenglen won French mixed doubles 5 times (1921–26).

Brugsch \'brüksh\, Heinrich Karl. 1827–1894. German Egyptologist. Prussian consul in Egypt (1864); professor, Göttingen (1868); director of school of Egyptology, Cairo (1870–79). Pioneer in deciphering of demotic script. Author of hieroglyphic-demotic dictionary (1867–82), Egyptian grammar, and writings on geography, history, religion, etc., of ancient Egypt.

Brühl \'brue̅l\, Heinrich von. Graf. 1700–1763. Saxon politician. Won favor of Augustus III; prime minister in virtual control of Saxony and Poland (1746–63); failed in attempt to have Polish crown of Augustus made hereditary; as means of obtaining Silesia, induced Augustus to side against Prussia in Seven Years War, and fled with him to Warsaw after loss of Saxon army (1756); returned to Dresden (1763).

Bruhn \'brün\, Erik Belton Evers. 1928–1986. Danish ballet dancer and director. Debuted with Royal Danish Ballet (1946); danced with major international companies, including American Ballet Theatre, Royal Ballet, and Bolshoi Ballet; artistic director Royal Swedish Ballet (1967–72), National Ballet of Canada (1983–86). Regarded as premier danseur noble of his generation.

Bru·lé \brue̅-lā\, Étienne. 1592?–1633. French adventurer in America. To Quebec (1608) with Champlain; went into western wilderness (1610), becoming first European to see Great Lakes; lived with Huron Indians, assembling furs for the French (1618–29).

Brum \'brüm\, Baltasar. 1883–1933. Uruguayan jurist and politician. Minister of public education (1913–15), foreign affairs (1914–15); president of Uruguay (1919–23); director of newspaper *El Día* (1923–29); president, Council of National Administration (1929–31).

Bru·mel \brue̅-mel\, Antoine. *Surname also spelled* Brum·mel, Brom·mel \brō-\, Bru·nel \brue̅-nel\, Bru·nel·lo \brü-'nel-lō\. c.1460–c.1515. French composer. Attached to St. Peter's, Geneva (1486–92), Notre Dame, Paris (1498–1500); maestro di cappella to Duke Alfonso I d'Este of Ferrara (1506–10). Composed several masses and other sacred music, and some vocal and instrumental secular music.

Bru·mi·di \'brü-mēd-ē\, Constantino. 1805–1880. American painter, b. Rome, Italy. To U.S. (1852); chief work, frescoes in Capitol, Washington, D.C. (1855–80).

Brum·mell \'brəm-əl\, George Bryan. *Called* Beau Brummell \'bō-\. 1778–1840. English dandy. Friend of Prince of Wales, afterward George IV; leader of fashion in London; a gambler, fled from creditors to Calais (1816); British consul at Caen (1830–32); died in French asylum for insane.

Brun, Saint. See BRUNO.

Brun, Charles Le. See Charles LE BRUN.

Brun \'brün\, Johan Nordahl. 1745–1816. Norwegian prelate and writer. Bishop of Bergen (1804). Author of verse, including "For Norge, kjaempers fødeland," Norway's first national anthem (1771), dramas including *Zarine* (1772) and *Einer Tambeskielver* (1772), and many hymns.

Brun \'brün\, Rudolf. c.1300–1360. Swiss politician. Helped overthrow oligarchic rule in Zürich (1336); drafted new constitution and created office of mayor; chosen mayor for life (1336); forced to fight former ruling nobles of house of Rapperswil (1337, 1350), leading to war with Austria (1350); war forced Zürich into Swiss Confederation (1351).

Brun·dage \'brən-dij\, Avery. 1887–1975. American businessman and sports leader, b. Detroit. Member of U.S. Olympic team (1912); amateur all-round champion of America (1914, 1916, 1918). In construction business (from 1915). President, U.S. Olympic Association and Committee (1929–53); vice president (1945–52), president (1952–72), International Olympic Committee.

Brune \brue̅n\, Guillaume-Marie-Anne. 1763–1815. French army officer. Associated with Danton (1792); in Revolutionary army; general of division (1797); defeated Anglo-Russian army at Bergen and Castricum (1799); marshal of France (1804); drove Swedes from Stralsund (1807); during Hundred Days sent to hold Provence; murdered by royalist mob at Avignon.

Bru·neau \brue̅-nō\, Alfred, *in full* Louis-Charles-Bonaventure-Alfred. 1857–1934. French composer and music critic. Critic on staff of *Revue Indépen-*

dante, Gil Blas, Figaro, Le Matin; composer of operas notable for realism, many after works of Zola, including *Kérim* (1887), *Le Rêve* (1891), *L'Attaque du moulin* (1893), *Messidor* (1897), *L'Ouragan* (1901), *L'Enfant-roi* (1905), *Naïs Micoulin* (1907), *Angelo* (1928), *Virginie* (1931); also composed ballets *Les Bacchantes* (1912), *L'Amoureuse leçon* (1913), choral symphonies, a *Requiem* (1896), songs, etc.

Brunechildis *or* **Brunehilde** *or* **Brunehaut.** See BRUNHILDE.

Bru·nel \brü̅-nel, *Angl* brü-'nel\, Sir Marc Isambard. 1769–1849. British inventor and engineer, b. France. To New York (1793) as refugee of French Revolution; practiced as architect and engineer; to England (1799); invented method of making ships' blocks and installed machinery at Portsmouth dockyard (1803–06); erected many sawmills; experimented with steam navigation; invented knitting machine, timber-bending machine, etc.; invented tunnelling shield (1818) and with it constructed Thames Tunnel (1825–43). His son ¶Isambard Kingdom (1806–1859) was a designer and builder of railroads, bridges, tunnels, steamships, docks, etc.; as chief engineer, build most of Great Western Railway (from 1833) and introduced broad gauge; built the *Great Western,* first steamship for regular transatlantic trips (1838), *Great Britain,* first ocean screw steamship (1845), and *Great Eastern,* largest steamship of its time (1858).

Brunel, Oliver. c.1540–1585. Flemish merchant and explorer. Established trading post at site of Archangel, Russia (1565); as agent of Stroganovs established regular trade between Russia and Netherlands (1570); made several unsuccessful attempts to sail northeast to China and Indies.

Bru·nel·le·schi \,brü-näl-'läs-kē\ *or* **Bru·nel·le·sco** \-kō\, Filippo. 1377–1446. Florentine architect. First to establish soundly scientific theory of perspective (codified by Alberti in *Della pittura,* 1435). Designed and constructed dome of Santa Maria del Fiore cathedral in Florence, which in some measurements exceeds St. Peter's, Rome (1420 ff.). Among his other works were the church of San Lorenzo, church of S. Spirito, Capella dei Pazzi, and Ospedale degli Innocenti (all in Florence). Considered greatest architect and engineer of his day, a precursor of Renaissance.

Bru·net \brü̅-ne\, Jean. 1823–1894. French poet. One of the seven poets who founded Félibrige (1854).

Brunet, Jacques-Charles. 1781–1867. French bibliographer. Published standard *Manuel du libraire et de l'amateur de livres* (1810).

Bru·ne·tière \brü̅n-(ə-)tyer\, Ferdinand, *in full* Vincent de Paul-Marie-Ferdinand. 1849–1906. French critic. Professor of literature, École Normale, Paris (1886); lecturer at the Sorbonne (1893); editor, *Revue des Deux Mondes* (1893). Author of *Études critiques* (1880–1907), *Le Roman naturaliste* (1883), *L'Évolution de la poésie lyrique* (1894), etc.

Brunetto Latini. See Brunetto LATINI.

Brun·fels \brůn-,fels\, Otto. c.1488–1534. German physician and botanist. Carthusian monk (1514–21). Author of *Herbarum vivae eicones* (1530–36) and *Contrafayt Kreüterbuch* (1532–37), first of 16th-century herbals featuring illustrations of great accuracy.

Brun·hil·de \brün-'hil-də\ *or* **Bru·ne·hil·de** \,brü-nə-'hil-də\ *or* **Bru·ne·chil·dis** \,brü-nə-'kil-dəs\ *or* **Bru·ne·haut** \brü̅-nə-ō\. d. 613. Frankish queen. Daughter of Athanagild, king of Visigoths; queen of Austrasia by virtue of marriage (567) to Sigebert, king of Austrasia. Induced Sigebert to war against Chilperic, king of Neustria, who had murdered his wife Galswintha (Brunhilde's sister) in order to marry his mistress Fredegund, who later (575) murdered Sigebert. Sought to rule Austrasia as regent for her son Childebert II; opposed by nobles and forced to flee to Burgundy; continued to be troublemaker until, at age of 80, she was captured by Chlotar II and executed by being dragged to death by a wild horse.

Brun·hoff \brü̅-nôf\, Jean de. 1899–1937. French children's writer. Author and illustrator of children's stories, notably a series on Babar, the little elephant.

Bru·ni \brü-nē\, Antoine-Raymond-Joseph de. Chevalier d'En·tre·cas·teaux \äⁿ-trə-kȧs-tō\. 1737–1793. French navigator. Commander of French fleet in East Indies (1785); governor of Mauritius and Mascarenes (1787–89); rear admiral (1789); commanded expedition sent to find La Pérouse (1791–93); explored coasts of New Caledonia, Tasmania, New Holland; surveyed D'Entrecasteaux Channel, discovered d'Entrecasteaux Island, Bruny (Bruni) Island.

Bru·ni \'brü-nē\ *or* **Bru·no** \'brü-nō\, Leonardo. *Sometimes called* Leonardo Are·ti·no \,ä-rā-'tē-nō\. c.1370–1444. Italian Humanist, b. Arezzo. Apostolic secretary; chancellor of Florentine Republic (1427–44). Known esp. as promoter of Greek learning by literal translations into Latin of Plutarch, Demosthenes, Aristotle, and Plato. Author, in Italian, of biographies of Dante and Petrarch and of *Historiarum Florentini populi libri XII* (1610), first critical history of Florence.

Brü·ning \'brü̅-niŋ\, Heinrich. 1885–1970. German politician. Member (1924–33) and leader (1929), Catholic Center party in Reichstag; proponent of the "Lex Brüning," dealing with tax reforms (1925). Chancellor (1930–32) and foreign minister (1931–32); governed by emergency decree; forced to resign over failure to deal with economic distress. To U.S. (1934); taught at Harvard.

Brunne, Robert de. See Robert MANNYNG.

Brun·ner \'brůn-ər\, Emil, *in full* Heinrich Emil. 1889–1966. Swiss theologian. Professor, Zürich (1924–53); a leading exponent of Neo-orthodoxy and Protestant ecumenism. Author of *Erlebnis, Erkenntnis und Glaube* (1921), *Der Mittler* (1928), *Das Gebot und die Ordnungen* (1932), *Natur und Gnade* (1934), *Das Wort Gottes und der moderne Mensch* (1937), *Der Mensch in Widerspruch* (1938), *Wahrheit als Begegnung* (1941), *Dogmatik* (1946–60), *Missverständnis der Kirche* (1951), *Gott und sein Rebell* (1958).

Brunner, Heinrich. 1840–1915. German jurist and historian. Professor (1866–72) successively at Lemberg, Prague, and Strassburg, and (from 1873) at Berlin. Author of *Deutsche Rechtsgeschichte* (1887–92), etc.

Brunner, Johann Conrad. 1653–1727. Swiss anatomist. Professor, Heidelberg (from 1687); discovered Brunner's glands in the duodenum.

Brün·now \'brœn-ō\, Franz Friedrich Ernst. 1821–1891. German astronomer. Author of *Lehrbuch der sphärischen Astronomie* (1851).

Bru·no I \'brü-(,)nō\ *or* **Brun** \'brün\. Saint. *Also called* Bruno the Great. 925–965. German prelate. Son of Henry I the Fowler, and brother of Otto I the Great. Imperial chancellor (940); distinguished himself in victory (953) over Conrad of Lorraine in the latter's rebellion against Otto; named archbishop of Cologne and duke of Lorraine (953).

Bruno of Co·logne \kə-'lōn\. Saint. c.1030–1101. German religious. Head of cathedral school, Reims (1057); chancellor at Reims (1075); influential in obtaining removal of Archbishop Manasses de Gournai for misdeeds (1080), refused offer of see of Reims; resolved to withdraw from world and, aided by St. Hugh of Châteauneuf, established monastery at Chartreuse (1084), founding Carthusian order under modified Benedictine rule; refused see of Reggio, Italy (1090); founded hermitage at La Torre, Calabria. Canonized viva voce by Pope Leo X (1514).

Bruno *or* **Brun** \'brün\ of Quer·furt \'kvär-,fůrt\. Saint. *Also known as* Boniface. c.974–1009. German prelate and missionary. Attached to household of Otto III and accompanied him to Rome (997); entered monastery (997); given own monastery at Ravenna by Otto (1001); undertook missionary work to Poland; archbishop of missions (1004); evangelized in Hungary, Ukraine; massacred with 18 companions by Prussians.

Bru·no \'brü-nō\, Giordano, *orig.* Filippo. *Early called* Il No·la·no \ēl-nō-'lä-nō\. 1548–1600. Italian philosopher, b. Nola. Entered (1565) but forced to leave Dominican order because of unorthodoxy (c.1576); traveled widely, lecturing, teaching, and writing; settled in Paris (1581); to England (1583), where he lectured at Oxford and attended court of Elizabeth I. Again itinerant in France, Germany, Italy (1585–92). Arrested by Inquisition (1592) and burned at stake. A critic of Aristotelian logic and champion of Copernican cosmology, which he extended with notion of infinite universe. Author of philosophical dialogues *Cena de la Ceneri, De la causa, principio e uno, De l'infinito universo e mondi, Spaccio de la bestia trionfante, Cabala del cavallo Pegaseo, Degli eroici furori* (1584–85); *Centum et viginti articuli* against Aristotelianism (1586); comedy *Il Candelaio* (1582); works on mathematics, physics, etc.

Bruno, Leonardo. See BRUNI.

Brun·schvicg \brœⁿsh-vik\, Léon. 1869–1944. French philosopher. Professor, Sorbonne (1909–40); cofounder of *Revue de Métaphysique et de Morale* (1893) and of Société Française de Philosophie (1901). Idealist philosopher who regarded mathematical judgment as highest form of thought. Author of *La Modalité du jugement* (1897), *L'Idéalisme contemporain* (1905), *Les Étapes de la philosophie mathématique* (1912), etc.

Bruns·wick \'brənz-(,)wik\. *Ger.* Braun·schweig \'braůn-,shvīk\. A princely German house, descended from the Welf family (see WELF). The German duchy of Brunswick, with Lüneburg, which was created (1235) in the Welf family, was divided at the death of Duke Ernst (1546) into: (1) elder branch, Brunswick-Wol·fen·büt·tel \-'vòl-fən-,bœt-əl\, later Brunswick; and (2) younger branch, Brunswick-Lü·ne·burg \-'lœ-nə-,bůrk\, or Hanover (*q.v.*). Seat of duchy transferred from Wolfenbüttel to Brunswick (1754). A branch line, Brunswick-Be·vern \-'bā-vərn\, founded (1666) by Ferdinand Albert I, succeeded the direct line (1735). Rulers thenceforward were Karl I (1713–1780), Karl Wihelm Friedrich (*q.v.*), Friedrich Wilhelm (1771–1815), Karl II (1804–1873), and Wilhelm (1806–1884), at whose death duchy passed to junior line represented by Ernest Augustus (1845–1923), Duke of Cumberland (*q.v.*). See also HENRY JULIUS.

Brun·ton \'brənt-ᵊn\, Sir Thomas Lauder. 1st baronet. 1844–1916. Scottish physician. Did research on circulation, physiological action of drugs, etc.; discovered value of amyl nitrate in treatment of angina pectoris (1867).

Brusasorci, Il. See Domenico RICCIO.

Bru·se·witz \'brü-zə-vits\, Axel Karl Adolf. 1881–1950. Swedish political scientist and historian. Professor, Uppsala (1923–47); authority on Swedish constitutional history and Swiss democracy. Author of *Representationsfragan* *vid 1809–10 ars Riksdag* (1913), *Studier ofver 1809 ars forfattinngkris* (1917), *Folkomrostningsinstitutet i den schweiziska demokratien* (1923).

Brush \'brəsh\, Charles Francis. 1849–1929. American inventor, b. Euclid, Ohio. Pioneer investigator of methods of electric lighting; inventor of Brush electric arc light system (installed Wanamaker's store, Philadelphia, 1879; streets of Cleveland, 1879; New York City, 1880), a storage battery, etc.

Brush, George de Forest. 1855–1941. American painter, b. Shelbyville, Tenn. Known esp. for portraits of Indians and of family groups.

Bru·si·lov \brü-'syē-ləf\, Aleksey Alekseyevich. 1853–1926. Russian soldier. In World War I, led army invading Galicia (1914) and counterattacking in Volhynia (1915); succeeded (1916) Gen. Ivanov in command of all Russian armies south of Pripet marshes; made successful offensive (June–Aug. 1916) against Austrians; appointed to supreme command by coalition cabinet (1917); under Bolshevik regime directed war against Poland (1920).

Brusius. See PETER of Bruys.

Brus·to·lon \brü-'stō-lōn\, Andrea. 1662–1732. Italian woodcarver. Worked in Venice (1680–85) and native Belluno (from 1685); noted esp. for lavishly ornamented carved furniture for churches and residences.

Bru·tus \'brüt-əs\, Decimus Junius. *Surnamed* Al·bi·nus \al-'bī-nəs\. d. 43 B.C. Roman general. Served under Caesar in Gaul; defeated Veneti in naval battle (56); commanded fleet in siege of Massilia in Civil War (49); governor of Transalpine Gaul (48). Joined conspiracy against Caesar and one of his assassins (not to be confused with Marcus Junius BRUTUS); pursued Antony into Gallia Narbonensis (43); deserted by soldiers and captured; executed.

Brutus, Lucius Junius. 6th century B.C. Roman consul (509 B.C.), one of first two in Roman history. According to legend, took leading part in expulsion of Tarquins, sentenced own two sons to death when they conspired to restore Tarquins; killed in single combat with Aruns, a son of Tarquinius Superbus.

Brutus, Marcus Junius. *Known also as* Quintus Caepio Brutus. 85–42 B.C. Roman politician and conspirator. Sided with Pompey against Caesar, but pardoned by Caesar after Pompey's defeat at Pharsala (48 B.C.); governor of Cisalpine Gaul (46); praetor in Rome (44). Headed conspiracy against Caesar and was one of his assassins. After Caesar's death (44), raised army in Macedonia with Cassius; defeated at Philippi (42) by combined forces of Antony and Octavian. Committed suicide.

Bruyère, Jean de La. See Jean de LA BRUYÈRE.

Bruys, Pierre de. See PETER of Bruys.

Bry·an \'brī-ən\, Kirk. 1888–1950. American geologist, b. Albuquerque, N.M. With U.S. Geological Survey (1912–26); professor, Harvard (from 1926). Known for studies in evolution of landforms, effects of cold climate on soil, etc.

Bryan, William Jennings. *Known as* the Commoner. 1860–1925. American lawyer and politician, b. Salem, Ill. Member from Nebraska, U.S. House of Representatives (1891–95); allied himself with free-silver advocates (1894–96); editor of *Omaha World-Herald* (1894–96). Famous "Cross of Gold" speech in Democratic convention, Chicago, won him nomination for presidency (1896); defeated by McKinley. Nominated again (1900); campaigned as antiexpansionist and anti-imperialist; defeated by McKinley-Roosevelt ticket. Edited (from 1901) the *Commoner,* weekly paper. Nominated third time for the presidency (1908); defeated by Taft. In Democratic convention of 1912, instrumental in swinging nomination to Woodrow Wilson. U.S. secretary of state (1913–15); resigned because, as a pacifist, he opposed Wilson's policy after sinking of *Lusitania.* Lecturer on Chautauqua circuit and at religious assemblies; one of prosecuting attorneys in case against schoolteacher John T. Scopes (*q.v.*) and engaged in notable courtroom debate with Clarence Darrow (1925). His brother ¶Charles Wayland (1867–1945) was governor of Nebraska (1923–25, 1931–35) and Democratic candidate for vice president of the United States. (1924). See also Ruth Bryan ROHDE.

Bry·ant \'brī-ənt\, Paul William. *Known as* Bear Bryant. 1913–1983. American football coach, b. Kingsland, Ark. Coached football at U. of Alabama (1936–40), Vanderbilt U. (1940–41), U. of Maryland (1945–46), U. of Kentucky (1946–53), Texas A. & M. (1954–58), U. of Alabama (1958–1983). Coached Alabama to 25 winning seasons, 24 bowl games, and six national championships; at his death had won more games (323) than any other collegiate football coach.

Bry·ant \'brī-ənt\, William Cullen. 1794–1878. American poet and editor, b. Cummington, Mass. Practiced law, Great Barrington, Mass. (1816–25); retired to devote himself to writing. Early works, "Thanatopsis" and "To a Waterfowl," published in *North American Review* (1817); published volume *Poems* (1821). Co-owner and editor, New York *Evening Post* (1829–78), which he made a Democratic and later Free-Soil and then Republican organ. Published *The Fountain, and Other Poems* (1842), *The White-Footed Doe, and Other Poems* (1844).

Bry·ax·is \bri-'ak-səs\. 4th century B.C. Greek sculptor. Collaborated in executing mausoleum at Halicarnassus.

Bryce \'brīs\, James. 1st Viscount Bryce. 1838–1922. British jurist, historian, and diplomat, b. Ireland of a Scottish family. Regius professor of civil law, Oxford (1870–93); M.P. (1880–1907); undersecretary for foreign affairs under Gladstone (1886), president of Board of Trade (1894–95), and chief secretary for Ireland in Campbell-Bannerman cabinet (1905–06). Ambassador to the U.S. (1907–13); signer of Anglo-American arbitration treaty (1911). Created viscount (1914); named to International Court of Justice (1914). Author of *Holy Roman Empire* (1864), *The American Commonwealth* (1888), *Modern Democracies* (1922), and of studies of South Africa and South America.

Brydg·es \'brij-əz\. Name of an English family holding the titles of barons and dukes of Chan·dos \'shan-,däs, *also* 'chan-\ and including: John Brydges (c.1490–1557), served under Henry VIII in France; knighted (1513); helped suppress Wyat's rebellion (1554); as lieutenant of Tower of London (1553–54) had custody of such prisoners as princess Elizabeth. Created baron (1554). ¶James (1673–1744), son of 8th baron, amassed a large fortune and was given numerous titles; raised to duke of Chandos (1719); built Canons, great house in Middlesex. Known for patronage of Handel.

Brydges, Sir Samuel Egerton. Baronet. 1762–1837. English writer and genealogist. Known for editions of Elizabethan and 17th-century texts, esp. Edward Phillips' *Theatrum Poetarum* (1800) and Robert Greene's *Greenes groatsworth of witte* (1813).

Bry·en·ni·os \brē-'en-ē-ȯs\, Philotheos. 1833–1914. Greek prelate. Professor (1861), director (1863) of school at Khálki; head of Great School of the Nation, Istanbul (1867–75); metropolitan of Sérrai (1875), of Nicomedia (1877). Discovered (1873) *Didachè* manuscript, epistles of St. Clement, etc.

Bry·en·ni·us \brī-'en-ē-əs\, Nicephorus. 1062–1137. Byzantine soldier and historian. Defended Constantinople against Godfrey of Bouillon (1097); aided in defeat of Malik Shah, Seljuq sultan of Iconium (1116); m. Anna Comnena, daughter of Alexius I Comnenus; wrote history of period 1057–1079, completed by his wife.

Brygg·man \'brig-màn\, Erik. 1891–1955. Finnish architect. Known for work in introducing Functionalist architecture to Finland; works included library of Turku Academy (1935), chapel of Turku cemetery (1938–41), Water Tower at Riihimäki (1951–52).

Bry·gos \'brī-,gäs\. 6th–5th century B.C. Name appearing on several pieces of Greek red-figure pottery and applied to both the potter and the painter. Work of Brygos Painter esp. notable, as in kylix depicting *Sack of Troy.*

Bryu·sov \'briü-səf\, Valery Yakovlevich. 1873–1924. Russian poet, playwright, and novelist. Translated Verlaine, Rimbaud, Mallarmé, Maeterlinck, D'Annunzio, etc. into Russian, helping introduce modernism; edited Symbolist journal *Vesy* (1904–09). Author of verse *Russkie simvolisty* (1894), *Tertia vigilia* (1900), *Urbi et orbi* (1903), *Stephanos* (1906); novels *Ognenny angel* (1908), *Altar pobedy* (1911–12); stories *Nochi i dni* (1913); plays, etc.

Brzo·zow·ski \bzhȯ-'zȯv-skē\, Tadeusz. 1749–1820. Polish religious. Entered Society of Jesus (1765); superior (1805); first general of Jesuits after their restoration by Pope Pius VII (1814).

Bu·ache \bue̅-àsh\, Philippe. 1700–1773. French geographer and cartographer. Royal geographer (1729). Introduced 4-basin theory of physiography; pioneered in use of contour lines.

Bu·ade \bue̅-àd\, Louis de. Comte de Fron·te·nac et Pal·luau \frōⁿt-nàk-ā-pà-lwʸō\. 1622–1698. French soldier and colonialist. Colonel of Régiment de Normandie (1643); marechal de camp (1646); governor general of New France (1672–82); encouraged exploration and fur trade in west, but failed to deal with hostile Iroquois and was recalled. Reappointed governor and given command of expedition against New York (1689); defended Quebec against English under Sir William Phips (1690); subdued Iroquois (1696).

Bubb Dod·ing·ton \'bəb-'däd-iŋ-tən\, George. Baron Mel·combe \'mel-kəm\. *Orig. surname* Bubb. 1691–1762. English politician. Adopted name Dodington on inheriting uncle's estate (1720). M.P. (1715–61); envoy to Spain (1715–17); a lord of the treasury (1724–40); treasurer of the navy (1744, 1755); noted for assiduous cultivation of various patrons and bartering his parliamentary votes. Bravely spoke against execution of Adm. Byng (1757). One of "Mad Monks of Medmenham" (see Francis DASHWOOD). Raised to peerage (1761).

Bu·ben·berg \'bü-bən-,berk\, Adrian von. 1431?–1479. Swiss soldier. Magistrate of Bern (1468–69, 1473–74, 1477–79); opposed war with Burgundy (1474) but led Bernese forces in heroic defense of Morat (June 22, 1476).

Bu·ber \'bü-bər\, Martin. 1878–1965. German Jewish scholar, philosopher, and writer. Editor of Zionist weekly *Die Welt* (1901); founded and edited monthly *Der Jude* (1916–24); head of Freies Jüdisches Lehrhaus, Frankfurt (1933) and director of Jewish teacher retraining program in Germany (1934); emigrated to Palestine (1938); professor, Hebrew U., Jerusalem (1938–51). Evolved philosophy inspired by study of Hasidism, based on encounter of man with nature, man, and God. Author of *Daniel* (1913), *Ich und Du* (1923), *Die chassidischen Bücher* (1927), *Moshe* (1945), *Netivot be-uṭopya* (1947), *Bilder* *von Gut und Böse* (1952), *Elijah* (1963), etc.; made German translation of Hebrew Bible (1926?–37).

Bub·na von Lit·titz \'bůb-nä-fón-'lit-its\, Ferdinand von. *Czech.* Bub·na z Li·tic \'bůb-náz-'lit-yits\. Graf. 1768–1825. Austrian soldier. Served in Turkish War (1787–92), against France (1792–1814); distinguished himself at Austerlitz (1805), Wagram (1809); field marshal (1809); minister to Paris (1812–13); fought in battle of Leipzig (1813); governor general of Lombardy (1818).

Bu·ca·re·li y Ur·súa \bü-kä-'rā-lē-ē-ür-'sü-ä\, Antonio María. 1717–1779. Spanish general and administrator. Viceroy of Cuba (1760–71); viceroy of New Spain (1771–79); noted for fiscally prudent and humane administration; pacified Indians, promoted settlement of California, fostered arts and sciences.

Buccleuch, Duke of. See James SCOTT.

Bu·cer \'büt-sər\ *or* **But·zer** \'bůt-sər\, Martin. *Orig. surname* Kuh·horn \'kü-,hórn\. 1491–1551. German Protestant reformer. In Dominican order (1506–21); influenced by Erasmus and Luther (from 1518); engaged in spreading doctrines of Reformation in Strasbourg (1523), Ulm, and Cologne; mediated in differences between Luther and Zwinglians; helped draw up Tetrapolitan Confession for Diet of Augsburg (1530); with Melanchthon brought about Wittenberg Concordat between Luther and south Germans (1536); one of theologians called by Emperor Charles V to discuss Protestant–Catholic unity at Colloquy of Regensburg (1541); refused to sign Augsburg Interim (1548). Professor of theology, Cambridge U. (1549–51), at Cranmer's invitation; worked for Reformation in England.

Buch, Captal de. See Jean III de GRAILLY.

Buch \'bük\, Leopold von, *in full* Christian Leopold von. Freiherr. 1774–1853. German geologist and paleontologist. Traveled in Alps, Italy, Scandinavia, Canary Islands, Scotland, etc.; disproved neptunist theory, proving basalt of volcanic origin; contended Alps originated in upthrust of crust.

Buch·an \'bək-ən, 'bək-\. One of the seven original Scottish earldoms, held first by the Comyn family (*q.v.*); for a century and a half by the Stewart family; and after 1617 by the Erskine family (see David Steuart ERSKINE, 11th earl).

Buchan, Alexander. 1829–1907. Scottish meteorologist. Secretary (1860) of Scottish Meteorological Society, which inaugurated observatory on summit of Ben Nevis (1883); observed (1857–66) "Buchan spells" of abnormal temperatures. Author of *The Handy Book of Meteorology* (1867), *Report on Atmospheric Circulation* (1889), etc.

Buchan, Elspeth, *nee* Simpson. 1738–1791. Scottish religious. m. Robert Buchan. Founder (1783) of a fanatical sect, the Buchanites; persuaded followers that she was the woman of Revelation xii.

Buchan, Sir John. 1st Baron Tweeds·muir \'twēdz-,myů(ə)r\. 1875–1940. Scottish author and administrator. Director of information under Lloyd George (1917–18); M. P. (1927–35); created baron (1935); governor general of Canada (1935–40). Author of many novels of adventure, including *John Burnet of Barns* (1898), *Prester John* (1910), *Thirty-Nine Steps* (1915), *Greenmantle* (1916), *Mr. Standfast* (1919), *Huntingtower* (1922), *Three Hostages* (1924), *John Macnab* (1925), *Courts of the Morning* (1929), *Island of Sheep* (1936), *Sick Heart River* (1941), historical and biographical studies, as of Montrose (1928), Sir Walter Scott (1932), Cromwell (1934), Augustus (1937), and autobiography, *Memory Hold-The-Door* (1940).

Buchan, William. 1729–1805. Scottish physician. Author of *Domestic Medicine; or The Family Physician* (1769), a popular work on medicine.

Bu·chan·an \byü-'kan-ən, bə-\, Franklin. 1800–1874. American naval officer, b. Baltimore. Submitted plan for naval school at Annapolis; became first superintendent, U.S. Naval Academy (1845–47); served in Mexican War (1847–48); in command of Perry's flagship (1853) on expedition to Japan. Joined navy of the Confederacy (1861); admiral (1862); in command, captured by Farragut at battle of Mobile Bay (Aug. 5, 1864).

Buchanan, George. 1506–1582. Scottish Humanist and author. Satirized Franciscan friars in *Somnium* (1535) and *Franciscanus et fratres* (1537); imprisoned by Cardinal Beaton; fled to Bordeaux, where he taught in different colleges; had Montaigne as student; taught at Coimbra, Portugal; imprisoned by Portuguese Inquisition (1547–52); openly took side of Calvinists on return to Scotland (1561); moderator of General Assembly (1567). Vouched that Casket Letters were in handwriting of Mary, Queen of Scots; charged Mary, in *Detectio Mariae Reginae,* with murder of Darnley; tutor to James VI (1570–78); occupied last years with *De juri regni apud Scotos* (1579), confuting absolutism with doctrine that kings exist by will of people, and *Rerum Scoticarum historia* (1582). Author of tragedies as *Baptistes* (1534) and *Jepthes* (1578) and much Latin verse, including *De sphaera* (1555), *Epithalamium* (1558), and a paraphrase of the Psalms.

Buchanan, James. 1791–1868. Fifteenth president of the United States, b. near Mercersburg, Pa. Member, U.S. House of Representatives (1821–31); U.S. minister to Russia (1832–34); U.S. senator (1834–45); secretary of state (1845–49); minister to Great Britain (1853–56); helped draft Ostend Manifesto (1854). President (1857–61); failed to stem abolitionism, to settle Kansas question, or to meet challenge of South Carolina's secession (Dec. 20, 1860), and endeavored to avoid the issue of civil conflict.

Buchanan, Robert Williams. 1841–1901. British poet and novelist. Attacked Swinburne in "Session of the Poets" (in *Spectator,* 1866) and Pre-Raphaelites in "The Fleshly School of Poetry" (in *Contemporary Review,* 1871). Author of *London Poems* (1866), *Ballads of Life, Love, and Humour* (1882), and a series of novels and plays including *Shadow of the Sword* (1876), *Alone in London* (1884).

Bu·cher \'bük-ər\, Lothar, *in full* Adolf Lothar. 1817–1892. German publicist and diplomat. Member of Prussian national assembly (1848); fled prosecution to London (1850); there edited *National Zeitung* (1850–61); member of Bismarck's foreign ministry (1864–86); drew up constitution of North German Confederation (1867), helped negotiate Treaty of Frankfurt (1871); secretary-archivist at Congress of Berlin (1878). Collaborated on Bismarck's *Gedanken und Erinnerungen* (1898).

Bu·cher \'byü-kər\, Walter Herman. 1888–1965. American geologist, b. Akron, Ohio. Professor, U. of Cincinnati (1913–40), Columbia U. (1940–56); known for studies of orogeny, megatectonics, etc. Author of *Deformation of the Earth's Crust* (1933).

Buch·man \'bůk-mən, 'bək-\, Frank Nathan Daniel. 1878–1961. American evangelist, b. Pennsburg, Pa. As director of Christian work, Penn. State College (1909–15), evolved art of "changing" lives of students; missionary under Y.M.C.A. auspices in Japan, Korea, India; extension lecturer, Hartford Theological Foundation (1916–21). At Oxford U. organized Oxford Group, later called Buchmanism and Moral Re-Armament; organized similar groups in South Africa, South America, Canada, U.S., Scandinavian countries.

Buch·ner \'bük-nər\, Eduard. 1860–1917. German chemist. Assistant to Adolf von Baeyer (1890–93); at U. of Kiel (1893–96), Tübingen (1896–98), Berlin (1898–1917). Demonstrated that alcoholic fermentation of sugars is due to action of enzymes contained in yeast and not to physiological processes in yeast cells; awarded 1907 Nobel prize for chemistry. His brother ¶Hans (1850–1902), bacteriologist; professor, Munich (1880–1902); director, Hygienisches Institut (from 1894); pioneer investigator of gamma globulins; discovered bactericidal alexins in the blood.

Büch·ner \'bœk-nər\, Georg. 1813–1837. German dramatist. Influenced by Naturalism and Sturm und Drang school; forerunner of Expressionism. Author of dramatic *Dantons Tod* (1835), satire *Leonce und Lena* (1836), tragedy *Woyzeck* (1836).

Büchner, Ludwig, *in full* Friedrich Karl Christian Ludwig. 1824–1899. German physician and philosopher. Brother of Georg Büchner. Lecturer at Tübingen (1854–55); founded Deutschen Freidenkerbund (1881). Evolved philosophy of consistent, determinist materialism; roused controversy with view of mind and consciousness as epiphenomena of physical brain. Author of *Kraft und Stoff* (1855), *Natur und Geist* (1857), *Aus Natur und Wissenschaft* (1862), etc.

Buck \'bək\, Frank. 1884–1950. American hunter, b. Gainesville, Tex. Captured wild animals in South America, Africa, Asia, Australia, etc. (from 1911) to supply zoos, circuses, etc.; associated with Ringling Brothers and Barnum & Bailey circus (1937–38); popular lecturer. Author of *Bring 'Em Back Alive* (with E. Anthony, 1930), *Wild Cargo* (with Anthony, 1931), *Fang and Claw* (with F.L. Fraser, 1935), *On Jungle Trails* (with Fraser, 1937), *Animals Are Like That!* (with C. Weld, 1939).

Buck, Pearl Comfort, *nee* Sy·den·strick·er \'sīd-ᵊn-,strik-ər\. 1892–1973. American novelist, b. Hillsboro, W.Va. m. John L. Buck (1917; div. 1934). Author of *The Good Earth* (1931; Pulitzer prize), *Sons* (1932), *A House Divided* (1935), the three forming triology called *The House of Earth;* also *The Exile* (1936), *Fighting Angel* (1936), *The Patriot* (1939), *Other Gods* (1940), *Dragon Seed* (1942), *Dragon Fish* (1944), *Peony* (1948), *Imperial Woman* (1956), *Living Reed* (1963), etc.; also wrote *The Townsman* (1945) under pseudonym John Sedges, stories, memoirs, etc. Awarded Nobel prize for literature (1938).

Buck, Sir Peter Henry. *Orig.* Te Ran·gi Hi·roa \'tā-'räŋ-(g)ē-hē-'rō-ə\. 1880–1951. New Zealand anthropologist and politician. Son of English father, Maori mother; medical officer to Maoris for New Zealand health dept. (1905–08); with Sir Maui Pomare led campaign for improved medical care for Maoris (1905–14); member of parliament (1909–14), minister of Maori race (1912–14). Researcher in Polynesian ethnology at Bishop Museum, Honolulu (1927–51). Author of *Vikings of the Sunrise* (1938), *Coming of the Maori* (1947).

Buckhurst, Baron. See Thomas SACKVILLE.

Buck·ing·ham \'bək-iŋ-əm, *US also* -iŋ-,ham\, Earls, marquises, and dukes of. Title of earl in English peerage first conferred upon Walter Giffard of Normandy by William the Conqueror (or perhaps by William Rufus), held subsequently by Giffard's son Walter and then by Richard de Clare, earl of Pembroke, and returned to crown (1176); conferred (1377) on Thomas of Woodstock, son of Edward III, borne by his son Humphrey; at Humphrey's death it passed, through his sister Anne, to her son Humphrey Stafford, who was created duke of Buckingham (1444); remained in Stafford family until attainder and execution of Edward, 3d duke (1521). (See THOMAS of Woodstock; Humphrey, Henry, and Edward STAFFORD.) Title of earl (second creation) conferred (1617) by James I on George Villiers, followed by titles of marquis (1618) and duke (1623), latter two titles becoming extinct with death of 2d duke, that of earl claimed by line of doubtful legitimacy (till 1774). (See George VILLIERS, 1st and 2d dukes.) Title of duke of Buckingham and Normandy conferred (1703) on John Sheffield and became extinct on death of his son in 1735. (See John SHEFFIELD.)

Buckingham, Marquis of. See George Nugent-Temple-Grenville under Richard T. GRENVILLE.

Buck·land \'bək-lənd\, William. 1784–1856. English clergyman and geologist. Professor of mineralogy, Oxford (from 1813); dean of Westminster (from (1845); attempted to reconcile geologic evidence with Bible; denied evolution. Author of *Reliquiae Diluvianae* (1823) and the Bridgewater Treatise *Geology and Mineralogy considered with Reference to Natural Theology* (1836).

Buck·le \'bək-əl\, George Earle. 1854–1935. English journalist. Editor, *The Times,* London (1884–1912). Author of vols. 3-6 (1914–20) of *Life of Disraeli* begun by W.F. Monypenny; editor of letters of Queen Victoria.

Buckle, Henry Thomas. 1821–1862. English historian. Author of incomplete *History of Civilization in England* (1857–61), marked by scientific bent and vast erudition.

Buck·ner \'bək-nər\, Simon Bolivar. 1823–1914. American army officer, b. near Munfordville, Ky. Served through Mexican War; joined Confederate army as brigadier general (1861); surrendered to Grant at Fort Donelson (1862); major general (1862) with Bragg; lieutenant general (1864). Editor, Louisville *Courier* (1868); governor of Kentucky (1887–91). His son ¶Simon Bolivar, Jr. (1886–1945), army officer, b. Munfordville, Ky.; commandant of cadets, West Point (1933–36); commander of Alaska Defense Force (later Command; 1940–44); repelled Japanese landing at Unalaska, Attu, Kiska (1942–43); lieutenant general (1943); commanded Tenth Army (1944–45); killed in capture of Okinawa.

Buck·stone \'bək-ˌstōn, -stən\, John Baldwin. 1802–1879. English comedian and playwright. Author of some 150 plays and farces, including *Uncle Tom, Our Mary Anne, Luke the Labourer,* and *Ellen Wareham.* First London appearance in 1823; lessee and actor-manager, Haymarket Theatre (1853–78).

Budaeus. See Guillaume BUDÉ.

Budd \'bəd\, William. 1811–1880. English physician. Advocated disinfection to prevent spread of contagious diseases; recommended measures that stamped out Asiatic cholera in Bristol (1866); argued contagious nature of cholera in *Malignant Cholera* (1849) and of typhoid fever in *Typhoid Fever* (1873).

Buddha. See SIDDHĀRTHA GAUTAMA.

Bud·dha·gho·sa \'bu̇d-də-'gō-s(h)ə\. 5th century A.D. Indian Buddhist scholar. Went to Ceylon to study Buddhist texts; translated many Sinhalese commentaries into Pāli. Author of many works, esp. *Visuddhimagga* ("The Path of Purity"), a long summary of Buddhist doctrine.

Bud·dha·pā·li·ta \'bu̇d-də-'pä-lē-tä\. 5th century A.D. Indian Buddhist. Founder of Prāsangika school of Buddhism.

Bu·dé \bᵫē-dā\, Guillaume. *Lat.* Guglielmus Bu·dae·us \byu̇-'dē-əs\. 1467–1540. French scholar. Appointed royal librarian by Francis I (1515); responsible for Francis's foundation of library at Fontainebleau, later moved to Paris as Bibliothèque National; responsible also for Francis's foundation of Collège de France (1530). By his writings, as *Commentarii linguae Graecae* (1529), influenced revival of interest in Greek language and literature.

Bu·den·ny \büd-'yón-ē\, Semyon Mikhaylovich. 1883–1973. Russian soldier. Entered Russian army (1903); active in Revolution of 1917; joined Red army (1918); cavalry leader; active in campaign against Denikin and Wrangel (1919–20) and in Polish War (1920); inspector of cavalry (1924–37); marshal of Soviet Union (1935); commander of Moscow Military District (1937–40); member of Central Committee of Communist party (1939–61); first deputy commissar of defense (1940); in command of southern front (July–Nov. 1941) in war with Germany.

Bu·des \bᵫē-dā\, Jean-Baptiste. Comte de Gué·bri·ant \gā-brē-äⁿ\. 1602–1643. French soldier. Commanded (1635–39) French contingent in army of Bernhard of Saxe-Weimar; on Bernhard's death succeeded to command; made bold attack on Regensburg (1640); defeated imperial armies at Wolfenbüttel (1641), Kempen (1642); marshal of France (1642); mortally wounded at Rottweil.

Budge \'bəj\, Sir Wallis, *in full* Ernest Alfred Thompson Wallis. 1857–1934. English archaeologist. With British Museum (from 1883); keeper of Egyptian and Assyrian antiquities (1894–1924); conducted excavations in Egypt, the Sudan, and Mesopotamia and collected vast number of tablets, papyri, manuscripts.

Budg·ell \'bəj-əl\, Eustace. 1686–1737. English writer. Cousin of Joseph Addison; after Addison and Steele, principal contributor to *The Spectator;* edited own weekly *Bee* (1733–35); lost fortune in South Sea Bubble; drowned himself in Thames.

Bueil \bwʸey\, Honorat du. Seigneur de Ra·can \rá-käⁿ\. 1589–1670. French poet. Page at court of Henry IV; served in army; disciple of François de Malherbe; one of earliest members of Académie Française (1635); retired to his estate in Touraine (1639). Author of bucolic and religious poems; known esp. for *Stances sur la retraite* (c.1618) and pastoral drama *Les Bergeries* (performed 1620; published 1625).

Bu·ell \'byü(-ə)l\, Abel. 1742–1822. American metalworker and inventor, b. Killingworth, Conn. Silversmith, engraver; produced (1769) first American-designed font of type; engraved and printed (1784) first map of U.S. showing Treaty of Paris boundaries.

Buell, Don Carlos. 1818–1898. American army officer, b. near Marietta, Ohio. Served in Mexican War; brigadier general of volunteers at outbreak of Civil War; major general (1862); joined Grant at Shiloh (1862); defended Kentucky against Gen. Braxton Bragg but relieved of command after battle of Perryville (October 8, 1862), for failure to pursue Confederate force; resigned (1864).

Buff \'bu̇f\, Charlotte. 1753–1828. German woman. Friend and companion of Goethe in Wetzlar (1772); the original of Lotte in *Die Leiden des jungen Werthers.* Subject of Thomas Mann's novel *Lotte in Weimar.*

Buffalo Bill. See William F. CODY.

Buf·fier \bᵫēf-yā\, Claude. 1661–1737. French philosopher. Entered Jesuit order (1679); taught at Rouen and Paris; exiled (1696–1701) for opposition to his Jansenist archbishop; adapted Cartesian method in philosophy, influenced later common-sense school. Author of *Traité des vérités premières* (1724), *Éléments de métaphysique* (1725), *Cours de sciences* (1732), etc.

Buf·fon \bᵫē-fōⁿ\, Georges-Louis Le·clerc de \lə-kler-də-\. Comte. *Orig. surname* Leclerc; *adopted* Buffon (c.1732). 1707–1788. French naturalist. Director of Jardin du Roi (now Jardin des Plantes) and of royal museum (1739). Admitted to French Academy (1753), his inaugural address being the celebrated *Discours sur le style.* Author (with others) of *Histoire naturelle* (44 vols., 1749–1804), completed by B. G. E. de Lacépède.

Bū·ga \'bü-gä\, Kazimieras. 1879–1924. Lithuanian linguist. Professor, Perm (1917–22), Kaunas (1922–24); known for studies of Slavic and Baltic etymology, personal names, place names. Began comprehensive Lithuanian dictionary *Lietuviu Kalbos Žodynas.*

Bu·ga·ev *or* **Bu·ga·yev** \bü-'gá-yəf\, Boris Nikolayevich. *Pseudonym* Andrey Be·ly \'byā-lē\. 1880–1934. Russian poet and novelist. Leading theorist and exponent of Russian Symbolism; influenced by Solovyov. Author of several prose poems called by him "symphonies" and of verse *Zoloto v lazuri* (1904), *Pepel* (1908), *Urna* (1908), *Petersburg* (1912); novel *Serebryany golub* (1908); autobiographical *Kotik Letayev* (1917); etc.

Bu·gat·ti \bü-'gät-tē\, Ettore Arco Isidoro. 1881–1947. Italian automobile builder. Established factory (1909) in Alsace; known for racers and for luxury cars, esp. Type 41 "Golden Bugatti" or "La Royale."

Bu·geaud de la Pi·con·ne·rie \bᵫē-zhō-də-lá-pē-kón-rē\, Thomas-Robert. Duc d'Is·ly \dēs-lē\. 1784–1849. French soldier. Served in Napoleonic army; supported Restoration; served in Africa (1836–47); developed effective tactics against Arabs; governor of Algeria (1841–47); marshal of France (1843); won battle of Isly, in Morocco (1844); created duke (1844). Commanded Louis-Philippe's troops in Paris (1848).

Bu·gen·ha·gen \'bü-gən-ˌhäg-ən\, Johannes. *Called* Pom·er·a·nus \ˌpäm-ə-'rā-nəs\ *or* Dr. Pom·mer \'pόm-ər\. 1485–1558. German Protestant reformer, b. Pomerania. Won over to Luther (1520); professor (1535), Wittenberg; organized Protestant church in Brunswick (1528), Hamburg (1529), Lübeck (1531), Pomerania (1534), Denmark (1537), and Schleswig-Holstein (1542); general superintendent, electorate of Saxony (1539). Assisted Luther in translating Bible; translated Bible into Low German (1533); drew up Leipzig Interim with Melanchthon (1548).

Bug·ge \'büg-gə\, Sophus, *in full* Elseus Sophus. 1833–1907. Norwegian philologist. Professor, Christiania (from 1866). Author of critical works on the Edda songs and the northern, Celtic, Romance, and Etruscan languages; published *Norraen fornkvaedi,* edition of the *Edda* (1867).

Buhl, André-Charles. See André-Charles BOULLE.

Buhl \'bül\, Vilhelm. 1881–1954. Danish politician. Member of parliament (from 1937); finance minister (1937–42); prime minister (1942) until forced to resign by German occupation forces; again prime minister (1945); minister of economic coordination (1947–50), of justice (1950).

Buḥ·tu·rī, al- \al-'bu̇k-tu̇r-ē\. *In full* Abū 'Ubādah al-Walīd ibn 'Ubayd Allāh al-Buḥturī. 821–897. Muslim poet. Introduced to court at Baghdad by Abū Tammām; patronized by several caliphs; known for finely detailed, highly lyrical panegyrics.

Bu·ick \ˈbyü-ik\, David Dunbar. 1854–1929. American automobile manufacturer, b. Arbroth, Scotland. To U.S. (1856); sold plumbing supply business (1899) and formed (1902) Buick Manufacturing Co. to build engines; built first car (1903); with Buick Motor Co. (1903–06).

Bu·il \bü-ˈēl\, Bernardo. c.1450–1520. Spanish Benedictine monk. Accompanied Columbus on 2d trip to America as apostolic vicar of New World (1493); joined opponents of Columbus, returning to Spain (1494) to prefer charges against him; abbot of Cuxa Convent (c.1495–1520).

Bu·is·son \bu̅e̅-ē-sōⁿ\, Ferdinand-Édouard. 1841–1932. French educator. Successively inspector, inspector general, and director (1879–96) of elementary teaching; helped secure establishment of free, compulsory, secular primary schools (1881–86); professor, Sorbonne (1896–1902); deputy (1902–14, 1919–23). A founder (1898) and president (1913–26), Ligue des Droits de l'Homme; awarded (with Ludwig Quidde) Nobel peace prize (1927).

Bu·khā·rī, al- \al-bu̇-ˈk̲är-ē\. *In full* Abū ʿAbd Allāh Muḥammad ibn Ismāʿīl al-Bukhārī. 810–870. Muslim scholar. Traveled widely to collect, sift, and verify accounts of words and deeds of prophet Muḥammad; compiled *al-Jāmiʿ aṣ-ṣaḥīh,* esteemed by Sunnī Muslims second only to Qur'ān in authority; also wrote *at-Tārīkh al-kabīr,* biographical history of Ḥadīth traditions.

Bu·kha·rin \bü-ˈk̲är-yēn\, Nikolay Ivanovich. 1888–1938. Russian Communist leader and editor. Joined Social Democratic party (1906); his activities brought many arrests, imprisonments, and banishments (1906–17); with Lenin, published *Pravda* in Austria; edited (1916) *Novy Mir* (*New World*) in New York City; after Russian Revolution (1917), member of Central Committee of Communist party in Russia; editor of *Pravda* (1917–29); member of Politburo (1924–29); head of Third International (1926–29); expelled by Stalin from Comintern and Politburo posts (1929); editor of *Izvestia* (1934); again expelled (1937), arrested, and tried; executed with other Bolshevik leaders.

Buk·ka I \ˈbək-kə\. d. 1377. Hindu king. With brother Harihara I founded (1336) Vijayanagar Kingdom in India; sole ruler (1355–77); made war on Muslim Bahmanī sultanate.

Bul·finch \ˈbu̇l-ˌfinch\, Charles. 1763–1844. American architect, b. Boston. Considered first professional architect in U.S.; introduced Adam style. Works included Massachusetts State House (built 1795–98), Connecticut State House (1792–96), Maine State Capitol (1828–31); also built India Wharf and New South Church, Boston, and directed improvements on Boston Common and city streets. Succeeded Latrobe as architect of National Capitol (1817–30). His son ¶Thomas (1796–1867), b. Newton, Mass., was author of *The Age of Fable* (1855), usually known as *Bulfinch's Mythology.*

Bul·ga·kov \bül-ˈgä-kəf\, Macarius, *orig.* Mikhail Petrovich. 1816–1882. Russian prelate and scholar. Professor (1842), rector (1850), Academy of St. Petersburg; bishop (1851); bishop of Tambov (1857), Kharkov (1859), Vilna (1868); metropolitan of Moscow (1879). Author of *Orthodox Dogmatic Theology* (1847–53), *History of the Russian Church* (1857–82), etc.

Bulgakov, Mikhail Afanasyevich. 1891–1940. Russian novelist and playwright. Author of works of penetrating humor and satire; prohibited from publishing (1930); works revived and final novel *Master i Margerita* published (1966–67).

Bulgakov, Sergey Nikolayevich. 1871–1944. Russian economist and theologian. Professor, Kiev (1901–06), Moscow (1906–18); abandoned Marxism for Orthodox church; ordained (1918); expelled from Soviet Union (1923); professor and dean, Russian Orthodox Theological Institute, Paris (1925–44). Developed mystical theology of sophiology. Author of *The Unburning Bush* (1927), *Ladder of Jacob* (1929), *Lamb of God* (1933), *The Comforter* (1936).

Bul·ga·nin \bül-ˈgän-yin\, Nikolay Aleksandrovich. 1895–1975. Russian politician. Joined Communist party (1917); administrator in various state departments; premier of Russian republic (1937–38); chairman of Soviet state bank (1938–41); deputy premier of Soviet Union (1938–41); member of Central Committee (1939–61); minister of armed forces (1947); member of Politburo (1948); deputy premier and minister of defense (1953–55); premier (1955–58); demoted for opposition to Khrushchev (1958).

Bul·ga·ris \ˈvül-gär-ēs\, Eugenius. 1716–1806. Greek theologian. Entered monastery on Mt. Athos (1749); librarian and scholar to Catherine II, St. Petersburg; bishop of Kherson (1776); retired to monastery, Novgorod (1779). Contributed to development of Modern Greek with translations of classics; helped introduce Western thought to Orthodox world; author of *Orthodox Confession* (1767), *Treatise on Tolerance* (1768), *Dogmatic Theology* (c.1800), *History of the Christian Church in the First Century* (1805), etc.

Bul·ga·rus \ˈbəl-gə-rəs\. d. 1166 or 1167. Italian jurist. First among the so-called Four Doctors of Bologna, renowned for knowlege of Roman law, the other three being Martinus Gosia, Hugo da Porta Ravennate, Jacobus de Voragine. Adviser of Emperor Frederick I Barbarossa; author of *De regulis iuris.*

Bulgya, Aleksandr A. See Aleksandr FADEYEV.

Bulke·ley *or* **Bulk·ley** \ˈbəlk-lē\, Peter. 1583–1659. American clergyman, b. Odell, England. To Massachusetts (1635); founder and first minister of Concord, Mass. (1635).

Bulkeley, Richard. 1717–1800. Canadian soldier and politician, b. Dublin, Ireland. Entered British army (1727); to Nova Scotia (1749); provincial secretary (1757–92); editor of *Royal Gazette* (1758); member of Executive Council (1759) and its secretary (1763); judge of court of admiralty (1775–1800); acting governor (1791–92).

Bull \ˈbu̇l\, Ephraim Wales. 1806–1895. American horticulturist, b. Boston. Developed the Concord grape, first exhibited in 1853.

Bull, John. c.1562–1628. English organist and composer. Organist of Hereford cathedral (1582–85), Chapel Royal (1591–1613); professor, Gresham Coll. (1596–1607). Fled England (1613); organist of Antwerp cathedral (1617–28). Composed large number of keyboard works. Credited with composition of an early form (1619) of the air of *God Save the King.*

Bull \ˈbül\, Olaf Jacob Martin Luther. 1883–1933. Norwegian poet. Author of *Digte* (1909), *Digte og noveller* (1916), *Stjernerne* (1924), *Metope* (1927), *De hundrede år* (1928), *Oinos og Eros* (1930), *Ignis ardens* (1932).

Bull, Ole Bornemann. 1810–1880. Norwegian violinist. Toured as virtuoso throughout Europe and five times (1843–79) through North America; founded a national theater, Bergen (1849); lost fortune in attempt to found Norwegian colony in Pennsylvania (1852). His violin compositions included solos, concertos, and esp. fantasias on national themes as *Et saeterbesøg* (1848).

Bul·lant \bu̅e̅-läⁿ\, Jean. 1520?–1578. French architect. Architect for Catherine de Médicis (1570), for whom he enlarged châteaux at Saint-Maur and Chenonceau; also added wing to Tuileries, built Château d'Écouen, Petit-Château at Chantilly.

Bul·lard \ˈbu̇l-ərd, -ˌärd\, Sir Edward Crisp. 1907–1980. English geophysicist. Professor, Toronto (1946–49), Cambridge (1964–74); director of National Physical Laboratory (1950–55). Noted for studies of marine geophysics, seismic measurement, geomagnetism, dating of rocks; helped develop theory of continental drift.

Bul·ler \ˈbu̇l-ər\, Sir Redvers Henry. 1839–1908. British general. Entered army (1858); lieutenant general (1894); commander in chief in Boer War until coming of Roberts; relieved Ladysmith (1900); retired (1901).

Bul·lett \ˈbu̇l-ət\, Gerald William. 1893–1958. English novelist. Author of *History of Egg Pandervil* (1928), *Nicky, Son of Egg* (1929), *The Jury* (1935), *Cricket in Heaven* (1949), *Daughters of Mrs. Peacock* (1957).

Bul·ling·er \ˈbu̇l-iŋ-ər\, Heinrich. 1504–1575. Swiss reformer. Disciple of Zwingli; at Zwingli's death (1531) succeeded as pastor at Zürich and as head of Reformation in German Switzerland; shared in drawing up first Helvetic Confession (1536); concluded (1549) with Calvin the Consensus Tigurinus, on the Lord's Supper; prepared second Helvetic Confession (1566).

Bul·litt \ˈbu̇l-ət\, William Christian. 1891–1967. American diplomat, b. Philadelphia. Assistant in U.S. Department of State (1917–18); U.S. ambassador to Russia (1933–36), to France (1936–41), at large (1941–42); special assistant to secretary of the navy (1942).

Bul·lo·kar \ˈbu̇l-ə-ˌkär\, John. 1580?–?1641. English lexicographer. Published *An English Expositor* (1616), one of the earliest English dictionaries, long a rival of Cockeram's *Dictionarie.*

Bully, Édouard Roger de. See Édouard ROGER DE BULLY.

Bul·nes \ˈbül-nās\, Manuel. 1799–1866. Chilean soldier and politician. In command of Chilean army at Yungay (1839) and at capture of Lima; president of Chile for two terms (1841–51); encouraged development and cultural activities; suppressed revolt to establish his picked successor, Manuel Montt.

Bü·low \ˈbu̅e̅-lō\, Adam Heinrich Dietrich von. Freiherr. 1757–1808. Prussian soldier. Brother of Friedrich Wilhelm von Bülow. Served in army (1773–90); proposed adoption of French infantry tactics and his own strategic system based on mathematics in *Geist des neueren Kriegssystems* (1799), etc.

Bülow, Bernhard Heinrich Martin Karl von. Fürst. 1849–1929. Prussian politician. Son of Bernhard Ernst von Bülow (1815–1879), Bismarck's imperial secretary of state for foreign affairs. Served in war of 1870–71; served (1876–88) with embassies at Rome, Vienna, Athens, Paris, and St. Petersburg; secretary of Berlin Congress (1878); minister at Bucharest (1888–93) and ambassador at Rome (1893–97); through Holstein's influence became secretary of state for foreign affairs, Berlin (1897–1900); negotiated purchase of Caroline Islands and Samoa (1897–1900); promoted Baghdad Railway; created count (1899). Succeeded Hohenlohe as imperial chancellor (1900–09) and Prussian minister president (from 1900); effected fall of French foreign minister Delcassé (1905) and brought about the Algeciras conference (1906) following the Moroccan crisis; created prince (1905); forced European acceptance of Austria-Hungary's annexation of Bosnia-Hercegovina (1908); failed to prevent Anglo–French–Russian alliance against Germany; lost confidence of Emperor William II and resigned as chancellor (1909) following split on budget question; ambassador extraordinary to Rome (1914).

Bülow, Friedrich Wilhelm von. Count Bülow von Den·ne·witz \ˈden-ə-ˌvits\. 1755–1816. Prussian general. Brother of Adam von Bülow. Entered army (1768); served in Rhine campaigns (1792–95), Napoleonic campaign (1806–07); governor general of East and West Prussia (1812); lieutenant general

(1813); defeated Oudinot at Luckau and Grossbeeren, Ney at Dennewitz (1813); distinguished himself at Leipzig (1813); commanded campaign in Netherlands and Belgium; joined Blücher and took part at Laon (1814); general and count (1814); Prussian commander in chief (1814–15); at Waterloo.

Bülow, Hans Guido von. Freiherr. 1830–1894. German pianist and conductor. Studied under Hauptmann, Richard Wagner, and Liszt; made first concert tour (1853); teacher, Stern Conservatory, Berlin (1855–64); m. (1857) Liszt's daughter Cosima, who later married Wagner. As conductor of royal opera, Munich (1864), directed first performances of *Tristan* (1865) and *Die Meistersinger* (1868); director of Royal Conservatory, Munich (1867); conducted in Hanover (1877–80), Meiningen (1880–85). Edited works of Beethoven, Cramer, Chopin.

Bülow, Karl Wilhelm Paul von. 1846–1921. German general. Brother of Bernhard von Bülow. Entered army (1864); commanding general (1903–12); in command of 2d Army at outbreak of World War I, directed campaign in Belgium and invasion of France (1914); relieved after failure at the Marne but promoted field marshal (1915).

Bu·loz \bu̅e̅-lō\, François. 1804–1877. French journalist. Editor of *Revue des Deux Mondes* (1831–77). His son ¶Charles (1843–1905) succeeded him as editor of *Revue des Deux Mondes* (1877–93).

Bult·mann \'bu̇lt-ˌmän\, Rudolf Karl. 1884–1976. German theologian. Professor, Breslau (1916–20), Giessen (1920), Marburg (1921–51); evolved controversial theology, utilizing Existentialist philosophy, aimed at "demythologizing" New Testament and recasting its message in modern terms. Author of *Geschichte der synoptischen Tradition* (1921), *Jesus* (1926), *Glaube und Verstehen* (1933), *Geschichte und Eschatologie* (1964), etc.

Bul·wer \'bu̇l-wər\, William Henry Lytton Earle. Baron Dal·ling and Bulwer \'dal-iŋ-\. *Known as* Sir Henry Bulwer. 1801–1872. English diplomat. Brother of Edward Bulwer-LYTTON. Entered foreign service (1829); served in Vienna, Brussels, etc.; M. P. (1830–37); as secretary of legation, concluded Ponsonby commercial treaty at Constantinople (1837); ambassador at Madrid (1843–48); in U.S. (1849–52); concluded Clayton–Bulwer Treaty (1850) between U.S. and Britain guaranteeing mutual control and protection of Isthmian canal; ambassador at Constantinople (1858–65); created baron (1871).

Bulwer-Lytton. See LYTTON.

Bu·nau-Va·ril·la \bu̅e̅-nō-vȧ-rē-yȧ\, Philippe-Jean. 1859–1940. French engineer. Engaged in early French endeavors to construct a Panama canal (1884–89, 1894); minister from new republic of Panama to U.S. (1903); negotiated treaty by which U.S. acquired control of Panama Canal Zone (Hay–Bunau-Varilla Treaty, 1903).

Bunche \'bənch\, Ralph Johnson. 1904–1971. American diplomat, b. Detroit, Mich. Professor, Howard U. (1928–50); collaborated with Gunnar Myrdal on *American Dilemma* (1944); with Office of Strategic Services (1941–44), State Dept. (1944–47). Director of Trusteeship Department, United Nations, (1947–57); undersecretary (1955), secretary (1957) for special political affairs. Succeeded Count Folke Bernadotte as chief UN mediator in Palestine (1948); awarded Nobel prize for peace (1950). Helped mediate disputes in Suez Canal region (1956), Congo (1960), Yemen (1963), Cyprus (1964).

Bu·nin \'bün-yin\, Ivan Alekseyevich. 1870–1953. Russian poet and novelist. Lived in Paris (from 1919). Author of verse; short stories collected in *Gospodin iz San-Frantsisko* (1916), *Tyomnye alley* (1949), etc.; novels including *Derevnya* (1910), *Mitina lyubov* (1925), *Zhizn Arsenyeva* (1930), *Lika* (1939); memoirs *Okayannye dni* (1926), *Vospominaniya* (1950); works on Tolstoy, Chekhov; translated Longfellow's *Hiawatha,* Byron's *Manfred* and *Cain,* and Tennyson's *Lady Godiva.* Awarded Nobel prize for literature (1933).

Bun·ker \'bəŋ-kər\, Ellsworth. 1894–1984. American diplomat, b. Yonkers, N.Y. Executive with sugar company (1927–66); ambassador to Argentina (1951), Italy (1952–53), India (1956–61), Nepal (1956–59), South Vietnam (1967–73). Negotiated disputes between Netherlands and Indonesia (1962), Egypt and Saudi Arabia (1963), and Panama Canal treaties (1973–78).

Bun·nag \'bu̇n-'näg\, Chuang. *Known as* Chao Phra·ya Si Su·ri·ya·wong·se \'jau̇-'prī-ä-'sē-'sü-'rē-ä-'wȯŋ-'sā\. 1809–1883. Siamese politician. Succeeded his father as prime minister (1852); largely responsible for Treaty of Friendship and Commerce with Great Britain (1855); regent for King Chulalongkorn (1855–60); promoted modernizing reforms and education; lost power after Chulalongkorn reached majority (1873) and thereafter engaged in palace intrigues in attempt to undermine his power.

Bun·ner \'bən-ər\, Henry Cuyler. 1855–1896. American writer, b. Oswego, N.Y. On staff and later editor of humorous weekly *Puck* (1877–96); contributor of light familiar verse and short stories to magazines. Author of collections of tales and sketches *Short Sixes* (1890), *Zadoc Pine* (1891), *"Made in France"* (1893), *Love in Old Cloathes* (1896), *Jersey Street and Jersey Lane* (1896); novels *The Midge* (1886), *Story of a New York House* (1887).

Bunny. See Carl Emil SCHULTZE.

Bun·sei \bu̇n-sā\. 15th century. Japanese artist. Possibly a priest of Daitoku-ji, Tokyo; known for portraits of monks, of Yuima Koji, and a landscape.

Bun·sen \'bu̇n-zən, *Angl* 'bən(t)-sən\, Christian Karl Josias von. Freiherr. 1791–1860. Prussian diplomat, theologian, and scholar. Through Niebuhr's influence became (1818–38) successively Prussian secretary of embassy, chargé d'affaires, and resident minister at Rome; obtained (1830) from Pope Pius VIII brief making concessions on mixed marriages in Prussian dominions; recalled from Rome (1838). Minister to Switzerland (1838–41), to England (1842–54); defended German rights in Schleswig-Holstein against Denmark, reluctantly signed London protocol (1852). Created baron (1857).

Bunsen, Robert Wilhelm. 1811–1899. German chemist. Professor, Heidelberg (1852–89). Invented carbon-zinc electric Bunsen cell (1841), grease-spot photometer (1844), filter pump (1868), the ice calorimeter (1870); introduced Bunsen burner (1855). Formulated (with Roscoe) photochemical reciprocity law; with Kirchhoff pioneered in spectrum analysis (from 1859) and discovered the elements cesium and rubidium (1860).

Buntline, Ned. See Edward Z. C. JUDSON.

Bu·ñu·el \ˌbün-yü-'wel\, Luis. 1900–1983. Spanish film director. Came under influence of surrealists in Paris in 1920s; with Salvador Dali made *Un Chien andalou* (1928), surrealist film with shocking images drawn from the subconscious; second film, *L'Age d'or* (1930), an assault on conventional morality that caused a riot in Paris. Created films noted for bold surrealism and scathing attacks on the Establishment, middle class, and church. Films included *Los Olvidados* (1950), *Nazarin* (1958), *Viridiana* (1961), *El Angel Exterminador* (1962), *Belle de Jour* (1967), *Tristana* (1970), *Le Charme Discret de la Bourgeoisie* (1973), *Cet Obscur Objet du Désir* (1977).

Bun·yan \'bən-yən\, John. 1628–1688. English preacher and writer. Enlisted in Parliamentary army (1644–47); moved by two devotional books of his wife's, gave up amusements and swearing and joined nonconformist church in Bedford (c.1655); began to preach and published first writings against Quakers (1656, 1657); imprisoned for preaching without license (1660–72) until released by Charles II's Declaration of Indulgence; in prison, preached to prisoners, wrote nine of his books, including *Grace Abounding to the Chief of Sinners* (1666), *The Holy City* (1666); licensed and chosen pastor of Bedford Separatist congregation (1672); imprisoned again for short time (1677) during which his *Pilgrim's Progress* (pub. 1678) is supposed to have been written; continued to preach and write. Later works: *The Life and Death of Mr. Badman* (1680), *The Holy War* (1682), *Pilgrim's Progress, Second Part* (1684).

Buol-Schau·en·stein \'bül-'shau̇-ən-ˌshtīn\, Karl Ferdinand von. Graf. 1797–1865. Austrian politician. Ambassador to Baden (1828), Württemburg (1838), Piedmont (1844), Russia (1848), Great Britain (1851); minister of foreign affairs (1852–59); weakened Holy Alliance but failed to achieve ties with France and England.

Buonaccorsi, Pietro. See BONACCORSI.

Buonaparte. See BONAPARTE.

Buonarroti, Michelangelo. See MICHELANGELO.

Buo·na·rot·ti \ˌbwȯ-nä-'rȯt-tē, *Fr* bwȯ-nȧ-rȯ-tē\, Philippe, *orig.* Filippo Michele. 1761–1837. French revolutionary, b. Italy. Associate of Babeuf. Author of *Histoire de la Conspiration pour l'égalité, dite de Babeuf* (1828).

Buoninsegna, Duccio di. See DUCCIO DI BUONINSEGNA.

Buononcini. See BONONCINI.

Buon·ta·len·ti \ˌbwȯn-tä-'len-tē\, Bernardo. 1536?–1608. Florentine theatrical architect and designer. Patronized by Medici; built court stage for Uffizi Palace and directed court fêtes; invented elaborate stage machinery and effects. Also built numerous palaces, fortresses, villas.

Buonvicino. See BONVICINO.

Bur·bage \'bər-bij\, James. 1531–1597. English actor. One of earl of Leicester's players (1574); erected first English playhouse, The Theatre, in Shoreditch (1576); converted a house into Blackfriars Theatre (1596). His son ¶Richard (c.1567–1619), member of earl of Leicester's company and (from 1603) its successor the King's Men; played chief parts in plays of Shakespeare, Ben Jonson, Thomas Kyd, and Beaumont and Fletcher (1595–1618), excelling in tragedy; with his brother, removed fabric of The Theatre from Shoreditch to the Bankside (1598) and, taking Shakespeare, Heming, and Condell as partners, established Globe Theatre as a summer playhouse.

Bur·bank \'bər-ˌbaŋk\, Luther. 1849–1926. American horticulturist, b. Lancaster, Mass. Took up market gardening (1870); developed the Burbank potato, first practical result of his experiments with plants. Moved to Santa Rosa, California (1875); began experiments to develop more and better varieties of cultivated plants; developed new and improved varieties of plums, berries, lilies, roses, tomatoes, corn, squash, the Shasta daisy and Fire poppy. Author of *Luther Burbank, His Methods and Discoveries* (1914–15), *How Plants Are Trained to Work for Man* (1921).

Bur·chard \'bər-chərd\, Samuel Dickinson. 1812–1891. American clergyman, b. Steuben, N.Y. Presbyterian pastor, New York City (1839–85). In speech in support of Blaine (1884) he used the words: "We are Republicans and don't propose to leave our party and identify ourselves with the party whose antecedents are rum, Romanism, and rebellion." These words probably responsible for Blaine's loss of New York State's vote and the election.

Burch·field \'bərch-,fēld\, Charles Ephraim. 1893–1967. American painter, b. Ashtabula Harbor, Ohio. Known for imaginative landscapes, for town- and city-scapes imbued with dreary loneliness, and later for highly personal depictions of nature as *The Sphinx and the Milky Way, Three Trees, April Mood.*

Burchiello. See DOMENICO DI GIOVANNI.

Burck·hardt \'bu̇rk-,härt\, Georg. *Known as* Georg Spa·la·tin \'späl-ə-tən\. 1484–1584. German Humanist, b. Spalt. Joined circle of Humanists led by Mutianus Rufus (1505); ordained priest and made tutor to heir of Frederick III, elector of Saxony (1508); met Luther at Wittenberg (1511) and thereafter associated with him in advancing the Protestant Reformation; persuaded Frederick to protect Luther during controversy over indulgences (1518). Helped establish the Reformation in Saxony; aided Melanchthon in preparing Augsburg Confession (1530) and in establishing Schmalkaldic League (1531). Author of historical works (esp. *Annales Reformationis*) and translations of Luther and Melanchthon.

Burckhardt, Jakob Christopher. 1818–1897. Swiss historian of art and culture. Edited *Basler Zeitung* (1843–45) and lectured in Basel; professor, Zürich (1855–58), Basel (1858–93). Known as a profound scholar, a pioneer in history of culture; studied esp. the Renaissance. Author of *Die Zeit Konstantins des Grossen* (1853), *Der Cicerone* (1855), *Die Kultur der Renaissance in Italien* (1860), *Die Geschichte der Renaissance in Italien* (1867), etc.

Burckhardt, Johann Ludwig. *Known also as* Ib·rā·hīm ibn 'Abd Al·lāh \ē-'brä-hē-,mib-ən-ab-'dəl-ə\. 1784–1817. Swiss traveler. To Syria (1809); en route to Cairo discovered (1812) archaeological site of Petra; discovered Abu Simbel (1812); visited Mecca (1815). Author of *Travels in Nubia* (1819), *Travels in Syria and the Holy Land* (1822), *Travels in Arabia* (1829).

Bur·dach \'bu̇r-,däk\, Karl Friedrich. 1776–1847. German physiologist. Professor, Dorpat (1811–14), Königsberg (1814–47); founder and head of Royal Anatomical Institute (1817–47). Known esp. for work on anatomy of brain and nervous system. Author of *Vom Baue und Leben des Gehirn* (1819–26), *Die Physiologie als Erfahrungswissenschaft* (1826–40), *Blicke ins Leben* (1844).

Būrd·'ā·nā \bu̇r-'dän-ə\, Jacob. *Also called* Jacob Ba·ra·dai \,bär-ə-'dī\. *Lat.* Jacobus Bar·a·dae·us \,bar-ə-'dē-əs, -'dā-\. d. 578. Syrian prelate. A Monophysite; named titular bishop of Edessa (542 or 543); consecrated many Syrian Monophysites, creating new hierarchy that evolved into Syrian Jacobite church, so named for him.

Bur·dett \(,)bər-'det\, Sir Francis. 5th baronet. 1770–1844. English politician. M.P. (1796–1806, 1807–47); opposed war with France, urged parliamentary reform, prison reform, removal of Catholic disabilities, abolition of flogging in the army; championed free speech; imprisoned (1810, 1820) for parliamentary criticisms; later a Conservative.

Burdett-Coutts \-'küts\, Angela Georgina. Baroness Burdett-Coutts. 1814–1906. English philanthropist. Daughter of Sir Francis Burdett (*q.v.*) and granddaughter of Thomas Coutts (*q.v.*). Inherited grandfather's fortune (1837) and assumed surname Coutts. Built and endowed churches and schools; endowed three colonial bishoprics; established industries to relieve distress; established shelter for fallen women; presented market to London for supplying fish in poor district; built model dwellings; aided emigration schemes; raised Turkish relief fund (1877–78). Created peeress (1871); first woman presented with freedom of city of London (1872).

Bur·e·bis·tas \,bu̇r-ə-'bis-təs\ *or* **Bur·e·bis·ta** \-tə\. d. c.44 B.C. King of Dacia (c.60–c.44 B.C.). Established unified kingdom; defeated Boii and Tauri and threatened Roman possessions in Balkans. After his assassination kingdom disintegrated into at least 4 parts.

Bür·ger \'bu̇er-gər\, Gottfried August. 1747–1794. German poet. Associated at Göttingen with literary circle Göttinger Hainbund, including Voss and two Stolbergs, and became leading contributor and editor (from 1778) of their publication *Musenalmanach;* extraordinary professor, Göttingen (1789–94). Influential in revival of interest in folksong and a founder of German Romantic ballad literature. Translated Thomas Percy's *Reliques of Ancient English Poetry.* Author of ballads *Lenore* (1773), *Die Kuh* (1784), *Der wilde Jäger* (1785), *Der Kaiser und der Abt* (1785), and *Lenardo und Blandine.* Editor of first German version of *Baron Munchausen* (see R. E. RASPE).

Bur·gers \'bu̇r-gərs\, Thomas François. 1834–1881. South African theologian and politician. Aroused controversy by unorthodox theological views as clergyman in Cape Colony; president of Transvaal (1872–77); promoted railroad to Delagoa Bay, resulting in financial distress and disastrous war with Pedi tribe; acquiesced in British annexation of Transvaal (1877).

Bur·ges \'bər-jəz\, William. 1827–1881. English architect. A leader of Gothic Revival. Works included cathedrals of Lille, France, of Brisbane, Australia, of St. Finbar in Cork, Ireland; restoration of Cardiff Castle, Castle Coch.

Burgess \'bər-jəs\, Edward. 1848–1891. American yacht designer, b. West Sandwich, Mass. Designed the America's Cup yacht race winners *Puritan* (1885), *Mayflower* (1886), *Volunteer* (1887).

Burgess, Gelett, *in full* Frank Gelett. 1866–1951. American humorist and illustrator, b. Boston. Editor, *Lark,* San Francisco (1895–97), where first appeared his well known "Purple Cow" jingle. Author and illustrator of *Goops and How to Be Them* (1900), *Are You a Bromide?* (1907), *Why Men Hate Women* (1927), *Look Eleven Years Younger* (1937).

Burgess, Hugh. c.1825–1892. American inventor, b. Reading, England. With his partner Charles Watt invented soda process for wood pulp for paper (1851–54); to U.S. (1854) and built plant at Royersford, Pa., for making paper pulp from wood by this process; with Morris L. Keen founded (1863) American Wood Paper Co.

Burgess, Thornton Waldo. 1874–1965. American writer, b. Sandwich, Mass. Successful in writing nature stories and animal tales for children, including *Burgess Bedtime Stories* in daily press. Author of *Old Mother West Wind* series (1910–18), *Old Briar-Patch* (1947), *Nature Almanac* (1949), *Aunt Sally's Friends in Fur* (1955), and hundreds of "Peter Rabbit" stories.

Burgh \'bərg, 'bər-ə, 'bə-rə\, de. *Also spelled* Bourke \'bərk\, Burke \'bərk\, Bur·go \'bər-(,)gō\. Anglo-Irish family of Connaught, founded by William de Burgh (d. 1206), who was granted (1199) large holdings in Ireland by King John. His grandson ¶Walter (d. 1271) obtained (c.1255) a grant of Ulster, later styling himself earl of Ul·ster \'əl-stər\. He and his son ¶Richard (1259?–1326), 2d earl of Ulster, carried on continuous warfare with one or another branch of the native ruling O'Connor family. Richard served Edward I and Edward II of England in campaigns in France and Scotland; married (1304) his daughter Elizabeth to Robert Bruce (later Robert I of Scotland). He was succeeded by his grandson ¶William (1312–1333), who inherited the de Burgh lands and, through his mother, the Clare lands; died without male heir, but his daughter m. Lionel, son of Edward III; title earl of Ulster reverted to crown with ascension of their descendant Edward IV (1461).

Male de Burghs managed to hold much of their territory and became virtually native chieftains. Among them were ¶Ulick (d. 1544) who was created (1543) 1st earl of Clan·ric·arde \klan-'rik-ərd\. ¶Richard (1568?–1635), 4th earl, supported Queen Elizabeth against O'Neill rebellion and was made (1628) earl of St. Al·bans \sənt-'ȯl-bənz, sānt-\; m. Frances Walsingham, widow of Sir Philip Sidney. His son ¶Ulick (1604–1657) was supporter of Charles I; commanded English army in Connaught (1644); created marquis (1645); subdued Galway (1648); forced to capitulate to Parliamentary forces (1652). A second branch of the de Burgh family acquired title of viscounts of Mayo.

Burgh, Hubert de. d. 1243. English politician. Brother of William de Burgh (d. 1206). Chamberlain to King John (1197); jailer, according to the chronicler Ralph of Coggeshall, of Arthur, Duke of Brittany; made justiciar (1215); aided John against barons; a leader in expulsion of French from England (1216–17); regent and chief minister of Henry III; created earl of Kent (1227) and justiciar for life (1228); called to render account of administration by Henry III, charged with treason (1232) and outlawed; pardoned and restored to his estates and title (1234).

Burghley, Barons. See CECIL family.

Bür·gi \'bu̇er-gē\, Joost *or* Jobst. *Lat.* Justus Byr·gius \'bir-gē-əs\. 1552–1632. Swiss mathematician. Court watchmaker to Duke Wilhelm IV of Hesse (1579–92); made instruments for Kassel observatory; imperial clockmaker to Rudolf II at Prague (from c.1603); assisted Kepler. Helped develop decimal and exponential notation; invented logarithms, compiled tables (before 1603) but did not publish until after John Napier (1614).

Burgk·mair \'bu̇rk-,mīr\, Hans. 1473–c.1531. German painter and wood engraver. Friend of Dürer; helped introduce Italian Renaissance style into Germany, esp. with frescoes on facade of Jacob Fugger's house, Augsburg; executed some 700 woodcuts, including series of 135 on Maximilian I. Assisted by his son ¶Hans the Younger (c.1500–1559), produced *Turnierbuch.*

Burgmein. See RICORDI family.

Bur·gos \'bür-gōs\, José. 1837–1872. Philippine clergyman and patriot. Catholic priest, chaplain to U. of Manila; advocated reform of Spanish rule; executed in retaliation for mutiny of Filipino soldiers at Cavite; became martyr of nationalist movement.

Bur·goyne \'bər-,gȯin, (,)bər-'\, John. 1722–1792. British army officer. Served in Seven Years' War; M.P. (1761, 1768); as major general commanded expedition from Canada against American colonies (1776); captured Ticonderoga but forced to surrender to Gen. Horatio Gates at Saratoga (1777); commander in chief in Ireland (1782–83). Author of plays including *The Maid of the Oaks,* brought out by Garrick (1775), and *The Heiress* (1786). His natural son ¶Sir John Fox Burgoyne (1782–1871), military engineer; inspector general of fortifications (1845–68); general (1855); field marshal (1868).

Bur·gun·dy \'bər-gən-dē\. *Fr.* Bour·gogne \bür-gôn^{y}\. Name of two ruling houses:

I. Ducal house of Burgundy, a region in western central Europe which from 5th century to 15th had varying boundaries, was at different times a county, duchy, kingdom, etc., and was often divided, most of it becoming finally (end of 15th century) a part of France. Two lines of ducal house: (1) Capetian line (1032–1361), from Robert I (d. 1075), Duke of Burgundy, son of King Robert II of France, through eleven rulers to Duke Philip de Rouvres with whose death the line became extinct. See EUDES, HUGH, PHILIP, ROBERT. (2) Cadet or Valois line (1363–1477) reestablished by King John II of France, whose mother Jeanne de Bourgogne was a daughter of Robert II of Burgundy (Capetian line). This second line comprised dukes of Burgundy at height of their power; Philip the Bold, John the Fearless, Philip the Good, and Charles the Bold (see individual biographies; see also MARY of Burgundy). On the death of Charles (1477), the duchy proper passed to France. Dukedom revived for Louis (1682–1712), dauphin of France, grandson of Louis XIV.

II. A dynasty of Portugal originating with Henry of Burgundy (1057–?1112), grandson of Robert I, 1st Duke of Burgundy. See also AFONSO, DINIS, FERDINAND, PETER, SANCHO. Line became extinct with Ferdinand I (d. 1383) and was succeeded by the House of Aviz.

Bu·ri·án von Ra·jecz \'bùr-i-än-fôn-'rä-yets\, Stephan von. Count. 1851–1922. Austro-Hungarian politician. Succeeded von Berchtold as foreign minister (1915–16); again foreign minister (Apr.–Oct. 1918).

Bu·ri·dan \bu̅e-rē-dän^{n}, *Angl* 'byùr-əd-^{ə}n\, Jean. *Lat.* Joannes Bu·ri·da·nus \ˌbyùr-ə-'dā-nəs\. 1300–1358. French scholastic philosopher. Student, under William of Ockham, and then professor, U. of Paris; condemned Ockham's nominalist views (1340); posed famous problem that has become known as "Buridan's ass," used to prove the inability of the will to act except randomly between two equally powerful motives; also did work in mechanics, optics.

Burk *or* **Burke** \'bərk\, Martha Jane, *nee* Can·nary \'kan-ə-rē\. *Known as* Calamity Jane. 1852?–1903. American frontierswoman, b. Princeton, Mo. Grew up in Montana and acquired skills at riding, shooting, cussing; reputedly scouted for Col. George A. Custer; settled in Deadwood, S.D. (1876), becoming companion of Wild Bill Hickok; m. (1885) Clinton Burk or Burke; fancifully depicted in many Dime Novels.

Burke \'bərk\, Billie. 1886–1970. American actress. m. (1914) Florenz Ziegfeld. Leading woman in John Drew's company presenting *My Wife* (1907); also starred in several editions of *Ziegfeld Follies,* and in *Love Watches* (1908), *Suzanne* (1911), *Caesar's Wife* (1919), *Happy Husbands* (1929), *Vinegar Tree* (1931), and in motion pictures as *Wizard of Oz* (1939).

Burke, Edmund. 1729–1797. British statesman and orator, b. Dublin. Entered Middle Temple (1750) but abandoned legal studies for literary work; published *Vindication of Natural Society,* satire upon Bolingbroke (1756), and *On the Sublime and Beautiful* (1757); began *Annual Register* (1758) and edited it for some 30 years. Became secretary to Marquis of Rockingham and entered Parliament (1765); gained high position among Whigs through eloquence on American question and vigorous opposition to George III's policy of court domination and arbitrary rule; issued political pamphlets *On the Present State of the Nation* replying to Grenville on commerce and finance (1769), and *Thoughts on the Cause of the Present Discontents,* accusing Tory government of suppressing public opinion, as in Wilkes case (1770); advocated liberal treatment of colonies in speeches *American Taxation* (1774) and *Conciliation with the Colonies* (1775); championed free trade with Ireland and Catholic emancipation. Paymaster of the forces under Rockingham (1782) and in succeeding coalition government; took active part in investigation of East India Company and urged impeachment of Warren Hastings, opening the case (1788), and delivering nine-day speech in reply to defense (1794); supported Wilberforce in advocating abolition of slave trade (1788–89); appeared as champion of tradition and constitutionalism in conservative English mold in opposition to speculative innovation and mere democracy in *Reflections on the French Revolution* (1790) and a series of writings mounting in passionate denunciation and reaching climax in *Letters on a Regicide Peace* (1795–97); quarreled with Fox and Whigs (1791); retired from Parliament on pension (1794), defending its acceptance in the *Letter to a Noble Lord* (1796).

Burke, John. 1787–1848. Irish genealogist. Compiler (1826) of the first dictionary of baronets and peers in alphabetical order, known as *Burke's Peerage,* and of a dictionary of commoners, later known as *Burke's Landed Gentry* (1833–38). His son ¶Sir John Bernard (1814–1892), genealogist and expert in heraldry; Ulster king-of-arms (1853); keeper of state papers in Ireland (1855); re-edited his father's *Peerage* annually (1847–92), also his *Landed Gentry;* published *Vicissitudes of Families* (1859–63).

Burke, Robert O'Hara. 1820–1861. Irish explorer. To Australia (1853); led exploratory expedition for Royal Society of Victoria (1860); with companion, W.J. Wills (*q.v.*), made first crossing of Australian continent from south to north; died of exhaustion on return trip.

Burke, Thomas. 1886–1945. English writer. First popular success *Limehouse Nights* (1916); wrote further Limehouse stories, autobiographical novel *The Wind and the Rain* (1924), *Flower of Life* (1929), *Night Pieces* (1935), *Murder at Elstree* (1936), *The Real East End* (1932), *Living in Bloomsbury* (1939), *Streets of London* (1940), *English Inns* (1944).

Burke, William. 1792–1829. Irish criminal. To Scotland (c.1818); with accomplice William Hare began robbing graves to supply cadavers to medical schools; turned to murder, suffocated some 15 travelers; hanged after Hare turned king's evidence. (Hence the verb *burke,* meaning to murder by suffocation).

Burleigh, Barons. See CECIL family.

Bur·leigh \'bər-lē\, Harry Thacker. 1866–1949. American singer and composer, b. Erie, Pa. While a student at National Conservatory of Music (1892–94) introduced Dvořák to Negro spirituals. Soloist, St. George's Episcopal choir, New York City (1894–1946), Temple Emanu-El (1900–25). Composed over 200 songs; arranged over 100 spirituals, including "Deep River," "Go Down, Moses," "Oh, Didn't it Rain," "Steal Away," "Swing Low, Sweet Chariot," "Go Tell it On the Mountain."

Bur·lin·game \'bər-lən-ˌgām\, Anson. 1820–1870. American diplomat, b. New Berlin, N.Y. Member, U.S. House of Representatives (1855–61). U.S. minister to China (1861–67); appointed (1868) by Chinese government head of delegation to visit U.S. and Europe, and make treaties; concluded Burlingame Treaty (1868), establishing reciprocal rights of citizens of U.S. and China.

Burlington, Earl of. See BOYLE family.

Bur·na·by \'bər-nə-bē\, Frederick Gustavus. 1842–1885. English soldier and traveler. As correspondent for *The Times* of London, traveled with Gordon in the Sudan (1875); made journey on horseback across Russian steppes in midwinter (1875), and across Armenia and Asia Minor (1876), described in *Ride to Khiva* (1876), and *On Horseback through Asia Minor* (1876).

Bur·nand \(ˌ)bər-'nand\, Sir Francis Cowley. 1836–1917. English playwright. Editor of *Punch* (1880–1906). Author of many burlesques, including *Black-eyed Susan* (1866), *Cox and Box* (with music by Sir Arthur Sullivan, produced 1867), *The Colonel* (1881), and *Happy Thoughts* (1866).

Burne-Jones \'bərn-'jōnz\, Sir Edward Coley. Baronet. *Orig. surname* Jones. 1833–1898. English painter and designer. While at Oxford met William Morris and D.G. Rossetti; began executing large pseudo-medieval paintings in late Pre-Raphaelite manner; little known until he exhibited large oil paintings (1877–78), *Le Chant d'Amour, Days of Creation, The Beguiling of Merlin, The Mirror of Venus;* other works included *Merlin and Nimue* (1858–59), *The Golden Stairs* (1880), *King Cophetua and the Beggar Maid* (1884), *The Depths of the Sea* (1886); as pioneer with Morris in Arts and Crafts movement, designed decoration for furniture, tapestries, books; furnished many stained-glass designs, as for Christ Church cathedral, Oxford (1859).

Bur·nell \(ˌ)bər-'nel\, Robert. d. 1292. English bishop. Trusted agent of Henry III; a regent on death of Henry (1272) until return of Edward I (1274); lord chancellor and chief adviser of Edward I (1274–92); bishop of Bath and Wells (1275).

Burnes \'bərnz\, Sir Alexander. 1805–1841. British traveler and diplomat, b. Scotland. Entered Indian army (1821); explored up Indus River (1831); traveled through Afghanistan, Hindu Kush, Turkestan Balkh, Meshed, and Teheran (1832–33); political resident at Kabul (1839–41). Author of *Travels into Bokhara* (1834).

Bur·net \(ˌ)bər-'net, 'bər-nət\, Gilbert. 1643–1715. British prelate and historian, b. Edinburgh. Professor of divinity, Glasgow (1669–74); strongly anti-Catholic; reproved Charles II for his dissolute living; fled to Holland on accession of James II; outlawed (1687). Counseled William and Mary, accompanied them to England (1688), and preached their coronation sermon. Bishop of Salisbury (1689), influential at court during life of Queen Mary; his pamphlet defending Broad Church position, the *Exposition of the Thirty-nine Articles* (1699), condemned as heterodox; as member of an ecclesiastical commission appointed, after Mary's death, to distribute vacant church livings, devised the scheme known (after 1704) as Queen Anne's Bounty. Author of *History of the Reformation* (1679–1714), *History of His Own Time* (1724–34).

Burnet, Sir Macfarlane, *in full* Frank Macfarlane. 1899–1985. Australian virologist. Assistant director (from 1928), director (from 1944) of institute of medical research, Melbourne; professor of experimental medicine at U. of Melbourne (1946–65). Contributor to knowledge about viruses. Awarded (with Peter Medawar) Nobel prize for physiology or medicine (1960) for discovery of acquired immunological tolerance to tissue transplants. Author of *Biological Aspects of Infectious Disease* (1940), *Viruses and Man* (1953).

Burnet, Thomas. c.1635–1715. English clergyman. Master of Charterhouse (1685–1715). Author of *Telluris Theoria Sacra* (1681–89), a fanciful cosmogony praised by Addison; his *Archaeologiae Philosophicae* (1692), treating

Mosaic account of fall of man as allegory, gave great offense and precluded his clerical advancement.

Bur·nett \(,)bər-ˈnet, ˈbər-nət\, Frances Eliza, *nee* Hodg·son \ˈhäj-sən\. 1849–1924. American writer, b. Manchester, England. To U.S. (1865); settled near Knoxville, Tenn.; m. (1873; div. 1898) Dr. Swan Moses Burnett. Chief works, *That Lass o' Lowrie's* (1877), *Through One Administration* (1883), *Little Lord Fauntleroy* (1886), *Sara Crewe* (1888), *The Pretty Sister of José* (1889), *Little Saint Elizabeth* (1890), *A Lady of Quality* (1896), *Secret Garden* (1910), *T. Tembarom* (1913); plays *Esmeralda* (with William Gillette, 1881), *A Lady of Quality* (1896), *The First Gentleman of Europe* (1897), *Little Princess* (1905).

Burnett, James. Lord Mon·bod·do \män-ˈbäd-(,)ō\. 1714–1799. Scottish jurist and anthropologist. Admitted to Faculty of Advocates, Edinburgh (1737); made ordinary lord of session (1767). An acknowledged wit and eccentric. Pioneer student of origins of language and society. Author of *Of the Origin and Progress of Language* (1773–92) which in some respects anticipated Darwin.

Burnett, Whit. 1899–1973. American editor, b. Salt Lake City. Journalist and foreign correspondent in Europe (1927–31); founder and editor (1931–71), *Story* magazine; edited numerous anthologies of stories, essays, humor, etc.

Burnett, Sir William. 1779–1861. Scottish physician. Physician general of British navy; physician in ordinary to king (1835); patentee of disinfecting Burnett's fluid, a strong solution of zinc chloride with which wood, fabrics, etc., were impregnated (or burnettized) to prevent decay.

Bur·ney \ˈbər-nē\, Charles. 1726–1814. English organist, composer, and musical historian. Composed *Alfred, Robin Hood,* and *Queen Mab* for Drury Lane Theatre (1745–50); organist at King's Lynn (1751–60), Chelsea Hospital (1783–1814). Author of *Present State of Music in France and Italy* (1771), *Present State of Music in Germany, the Netherlands and the United Provinces* (1773), and esp. his *General History of Music* (1776–89). His eldest son ¶James (1750–1821), naval officer, twice sailed with Captain Cook; wrote histories of discoveries in the Pacific and *History of the Buccaneers of America* (1816). Charles' second son ¶Charles (1757–1817), classical scholar, collected rare books and manuscripts ultimately bought for British Museum.

Burney, Fanny, *orig.* Frances. *Known also as* Madame d'·Ar·blay \dȧr-blā, ˈdär-,blā\. 1752–1840. English novelist. Daughter of Charles Burney. Author of *Evelina* (anonymously, 1778), which won her European fame when her authorship was revealed, *Cecilia* (1782), *Camilla* (1796), *The Wanderer* (1814); appointed to royal household (1786–91); m. (1793) General Alexandre d'Arblay, a French refugee; with husband in Paris (1802–12); after Waterloo, passed rest of life in England. Edited her father's *Memoirs* (1832).

Burnham, Baron and Viscount. See Edward LEVY-LAWSON.

Burn·ham \ˈbər-nəm\, Daniel Hudson. 1846–1912. American architect, b. Henderson, N.Y. With John W. Root, organized Burnham & Root, architects (1873); after death of Root (1891), formed firm of D. H. Burnham & Co. Chief of construction for Chicago World's Fair (1893); chairman, commission of experts appointed for planning development of Washington, D.C. (1901); consultant on city planning for Cleveland, San Francisco, Manila. Submitted (1909) a plan of Chicago, later largely carried out. Among his buildings: Montauk Building, Chicago (first building called a skyscraper); Rookery (1886), Reliance (1890), Monadnock (1891) buildings, all Chicago; Flatiron Building, New York (1901); Union Railroad Station, Washington, D.C. (1909); Filene's Store, Boston (1912).

Burnham, Frederick Russell. 1861–1947. American explorer, b. near Mankato, Minn. Scout in South Africa (from 1893); discovered buried treasure in ruins of ancient civilization in Rhodesia; chief of scouts of British army in Boer War (1900–01); on surveys on Volta River, West Africa (1902); explored Congo basin region (1903–04). Discovered remains of Maya civilization, Mexico (1908). Author of *Scouting on Two Continents* (1926), *Taking Chances* (1944).

Burnham, Sherburne Wesley. 1838–1921. American astronomer, b. Thetford, Vt. On staff of Lick Observatory (1888–92); senior astronomer at Yerkes Observatory (1897–1914). Known for catalogues of 1290 new double stars that he discovered and of all known double stars (13,665) visible in Northern Hemisphere.

Bur·nouf \bu̇ēr-nüf\, Jean-Louis. 1775–1844. French philologist. Author of *Méthode pour étudier la langue grecque* (1814), *Méthode pour étudier la langue latine* (1840). His son ¶Eugène (1801–1852) was an Orientalist; professor, Collège de France (1832–52); noted for studies of Old Iranian and Zoroastrianism; author of *Essai sur le Pali* (with C. Lassen, 1826), *Commentaire sur le Yaçna* (1833–45), *Le Bhâgavata Purâṇa* (1840), etc. Eugène's cousin ¶Émile-Louis Burnouf (1821–1907) was also an Orientalist; author of *Méthode pour étudier la langue sanskrite* (1859), *Essai sur le véda* (1863), a collaborator on *Dictionnaire classique sanskrit-français* (1863–64).

Burns \ˈbərnz\, Anthony. 1834–1862. American slave, b. Stafford Co., Va. Arrested in Boston (May 1854) on charge of theft; recognized as fugitive slave. Protests against his return to Virginia culminated in riots and calling out of armed troops. Returned to Virginia; bought out of slavery; studied at Oberlin College (1857–62); pastor of a Negro Baptist church, St. Catherine's, Canada.

Burns, Sir George. Baronet. 1795–1890. Scottish shipowner. With Hugh Matthie began (1824) Glasgow–Liverpool–Belfast line of sailing ships; with Samuel Cunard, Robert Napier, David MacIver and others founded (1839) British and North American Royal Mail Steam Packet Co., later known as Cunard Line; retired (1858); created baronet (1889). Succeeded in management of firm by his son ¶Sir John (1829–1901); chairman of Cunard Line (1880–1901); created baron In·ver·clyde \,in-vər-ˈklīd\ (1897).

Burns, John Elliot. 1858–1943. English labor leader. At work from age ten; became with Tom Mann a leader of "New Unionism" of unskilled labor; joined Social Democratic Federation (1883); acquitted of sedition (1886); a leader of London dock strike (1889); elected to London County Council (1889); Socialist M. P. (1892–1918); as president of local government board (1905–14) and president of Board of Trade (1914), first British Cabinet member from working class; resigned on declaration of war.

Burns, Robert. 1759–1796. Scottish national poet. Son of tenant farmer and himself one (1784–89); began writing poems (1783) under influence of Scottish traditional verse, folksongs, genteel English verse, and own often satirical view of life; published in Kilmarnock *Poems, Chiefly in the Scottish Dialect* (1786) including "Cotter's Saturday Night," "To a Mountain Daisy," "To a Louse," "The Twa Dogs, " "Scotch Drink," "To a Mouse," "Address to the Devil," etc. On proceeds of second edition (1787) traveled through border towns; took farm at Ellisland (1788–91); became exciseman at Dumfries. Contributed 200 songs to James Johnson's *Scots Musical Museum* (1787–1803); supplied about 70 songs to George Thomson's *Select Collection of Original Scotish Airs for the Voice* (1793–1818); his songs, both wholly original or restorations of ancient songs, included "Green Grow the Rashes, O," "John Anderson, My Jo," "I'm O'er Young to Marry Yet," "Auld Lang Syne," "Comin' thro' the Rye," "Red, Red Rose."

Burns, Tommy. *Orig.* Noah Brus·so \ˈbrəs-(,)ō\. 1881–1955. Canadian boxer, b. Hanover, Ont. World heavyweight champion (1906–08), losing to Jack Johnson after 11 successful defenses of title.

Burns, William John. 1861–1932. American detective, b. Baltimore. With U.S. Secret Service (1889–1909), solving many major counterfeit and corruption cases; founder and president (1909–21), William J. Burns International Detective Agency; chief of Federal Bureau of Investigation (1921–24).

Burn·side \ˈbərn-,sīd\, Ambrose Everett. 1824–1881. American army officer, b. Liberty, Ind. Brigadier general (1861); captured Roanoke Island (Feb. 1862); major general (1862); in command of Army of Potomac (1862); unsuccessful in Fredericksburg campaign (Dec. 1862) and relieved of command (1863); assigned to Department of the Ohio. With Army of the Potomac, under Grant, before Petersburg (1864), failed to follow up advantage after explosion of a mine; blamed by court of inquiry; resigned (1865). Governor of Rhode Island (1866–69); U.S. senator (1875–81). Lent his name to type of side whiskers such as he wore —"burnsides."

Bur·pee \ˈbər-(,)pē\, Washington Atlee. 1858–1915. American seedsman, b. Sheffield, N.B. To U.S. as a child; started in seed business (1876) and developed W. Atlee Burpee & Co., which became world's largest mail-order seed house.

Burr \ˈbər\, Aaron. 1756–1836. American politicial leader, b. Newark, N.J. Grandson of Jonathan Edwards. Served in army from outbreak of Revolution (until 1779); practiced law, New York City (from 1782). U.S. senator (1791–97). In election of 1800, tied with Jefferson for the presidency; through opposition of Alexander Hamilton, defeated in Congress on 36th ballot; vice president of the United States (1801–05). Mortally wounded Alexander Hamilton in duel (July 11, 1804), at Weehawken, N.J. Conspired with Gen. James Wilkinson and others to seize territory from Spanish America and created a new republic in Southwest; arrested (1807); tried for treason; acquitted (1807). Went abroad (1808), and failed to interest authorities in France and England in his schemes; returned to U.S. (1812); resumed practice of law in New York.

Bur·ritt \ˈbər-ət, ˈbə-rət, ˈbu̇r-ət\, Elihu. *Called* the Learned Blacksmith. 1810–1879. American pacifist, b. New Britain, Conn. Blacksmith by trade and an autodidact; became public lecturer; founded *Christian Citizen* (1844), advocating international peace; edited it (1844–51). Founded (1846) League of Universal Brotherhood; organized (1848) "Friends of Peace" Congress, Brussels; U.S. consul, Birmingham, England (1863–70).

Burrough. See BOROUGH.

Bur·roughs \ˈbər-(,)ōz, ˈbə-(,)rōz\, Edgar Rice. 1875–1950. American writer, b. Chicago. Creator of Tarzan in *Tarzan of the Apes* (1914) and some 30 sequels; wrote series of adventure tales of Mars beginning with *Princess of Mars* (1917), other series on Venus, land at the Earth's core, etc.

Burroughs, John. 1837–1921. American naturalist, b. near Roxbury, N.Y. Teacher (1854–63); clerk in Treasury Dept., Washington, D.C. (1863–73); lived (from 1873) on a farm near Esopus, N.Y.; built a secluded cabin, called

"Slabsides" (1895), and spent much time there. Friend (from 1863) of Walt Whitman, whom he honored in *Notes on Walt Whitman as Poet and Person* (1867). His nature essays appeared in the *Atlantic Monthly* (from 1865). Author of *Wake-Robin* (1871), *Winter Sunshine* (1875), *Birds and Poets* (1877), *Locusts and Wild Honey* (1879), *Pepacton* (1881), *Fresh Fields* (1884), *Signs and Seasons* (1886), *Indoor Studies* (1889), *Literary Values* (1902), *Ways of Nature* (1905), *Bird and Bough* (1906), *Camping and Tramping with Roosevelt* (1907), *The Summit of the Years* (1913), *The Breath of Life* (1915), *Under the Apple Trees* (1916), *Field and Study* (1919).

Burroughs, William Seward. 1855–1898. American inventor, b. Auburn, N.Y. Developed mechanical calculating machine (1885); organized (1886) American Arithmometer Co.; patented practical recording adding machine (1892). American Arithmometer became (1905) Burroughs Adding Machine Corp.

Bur·rows \ˈbər-(ˌ)ōz, ˈbə-(ˌ)rōz\, Ronald Montagu. 1867–1920. English archaeologist. Professor, U. Coll., Cardiff (1898–1908), U. of Manchester (1908–13); principal, King's Coll., London (1913–20); conducted archaeological excavations at Pylos and Sphacteria (1895–96) and in Boeotia (1905, 1907).

Bur·rus \ˈbər-əs, ˈbə-rəs\, Sextus Afranius. d. 62 A.D. Roman general. Prefect of Praetorian Guard (51 A.D.), associated with Seneca in education of Nero and, after death of Claudius (54), used influence with Praetorian Guard to assure Nero's undisputed succession to throne.

Burt \ˈbərt\, Sir Cyril Lodowic. 1883–1971. English psychologist. Professor, U. of London (1924–31), U. Coll., London (1931–50); known for work on mental testing, standardization of tests, factor analysis; later shown to have falsified some of his statistical materials. Author of *Handbook of Tests* (1923), *The Young Delinquent* (1925), *Measurement of Mental Capacities* (1927), *Subnormal Mind* (1935), *Factors of the Mind* (1940), etc.

Burt, Struthers, *in full* Maxwell Struthers. 1882–1954. American writer, b. Baltimore. Cattle rancher in Wyoming (from 1908). Author of *In the High Hills* (1914), *Chance Encounters* (1921), *Interpreter's House* (1924), *Diary of a Dude Wrangler* (1924), *Delectable Mountains* (1926), *Festival* (1931), *Powder River* (1938), *Along These Streets* (1942), *Philadelphia* (1945).

Burt, William Austin. 1792–1858. American surveyor and inventor, b. Petersham, Mass. Patented (1829) "Typographer," forerunner of typewriter; solar compass (1836); equatorial sextant (1856). Discovered iron ore deposits in Upper Peninsula of Michigan (1844); promoter of Sault Sainte Marie Canal.

Bur·ton \ˈbərt-ᵊn\, Harold Hitz. 1888–1964. American jurist, b. Jamaica Plain, Mass. Practiced law in Cleveland (from 1919); mayor of Cleveland (1935–40); U.S. senator (1941–45); associate justice, U.S. Supreme Court (1945–58).

Burton, John Hill. 1809–1881. Scottish historian. Achieved reputation with *Life of David Hume* (1846); editor, with Sir John Bowring, of Bentham's works. Author also of *History of Scotland* (1853–70); edited *Registers of the Privy Council of Scotland* (1877–78).

Burton, Richard. *Orig.* Richard Jenkins. 1925–1984. British actor. Son of Welsh miner. Made London stage debut in *Druid's Rest* (1944), New York debut in *The Lady's Not for Burning* (1950). Other stage plays included *Othello* (1956), *Camelot* (1960, 1980–81), *Hamlet* (1964), *Equus* (1976). His films included *My Cousin Rachel* (1952), *The Robe* (1953), *The Desert Rats* (1953), *Alexander the Great* (1956), *Bitter Victory* (1958), *Cleopatra* (1963), *Becket* (1964), *The Spy Who Came in From the Cold* (1965), *Who's Afraid of Virginia Woolf?* (1966), *The Taming of the Shrew* (1967), *1984* (1984).

Burton, Sir Richard Francis. 1821–1890. British explorer and Orientalist. Mastered some 40 languages and dialects; joined Indian army (1842); recorded experiences in *Sind, and the Races That Inhabit the Valley of the Indus* (1851) and *Sind, or the Unhappy Valley* (1851); made pilgrimage to Mecca (1853) disguised as Pathan, which he described in *Pilgrimage to El-Medinah and Mecca* (1855–56); entered forbidden city of Harer, Somaliland (1854); with Speke, explored Somaliland (1854), Lake Tanganyika region (1858), described in *First Footsteps in East Africa* (1856); visited Salt Lake City (1860) and described Brigham Young and Mormons in *City of the Saints* (1861); British consul at Fernando Po (1861–65), Santos, Brazil (1865–69), Damascus (1869–71), Trieste (1872). Published translations of Camões (1880) and of *Arabian Nights* (1885–88); also wrote *Book of the Sword* (1884).

Burton, Robert. *Pseudonym* De·moc·ri·tus Junior \di-ˈmäk-rət-əs-\. 1577–1640. English clergyman and author. Vicar, St. Thomas's, Oxford (1616–40). Author of Latin comedy *Philosophaster* (1606; acted 1618) and of *The Anatomy of Melancholy* (1621), a treatise upon the causes, symptoms, and cure of melancholy, including a storehouse of miscellaneous learning, a picture of contemporary life and thought, and a sketch of a Utopia.

Burton, William Meriam. 1865–1954. American chemist, b. Cleveland. With Standard Oil Co. (from 1890); president (1918–27). Developed thermal process of cracking petroleum (1912).

Bury \ˈber-ē, ˈbyu̇r-ē\, John Bagnell. 1861–1927. British historian, b. Ireland. Professor (1893–1902), Regius professor (1902–27), Cambridge. Edited *Byzantine Texts* (1898–1904), Gibbon's *Rise and Fall of the Roman Empire* (1896–1900), *Cambridge Ancient History*. Author of *History of the Later Roman Empire* (1889), *History of the Roman Empire from its Foundation* (1893), *Ancient Greek Historians* (1909), *History of the Eastern Roman Empire* (1912), *History of Freedom of Thought* (1914), *Idea of Progress* (1920).

Bury, Richard de. See Richard AUNGERVILLE.

Bus·becq *or* **Bus·beck** \bǖz-bek\ *or* **Bous·becq** \büz-bek\ *or* **Bou·se·becque,** Ghislain de. 1522–1592. Flemish diplomat. Ambassador of Emperor Ferdinand I to sultan at Constantinople (1555–62); ambassador of Emperor Rudolph II at Paris. Collected Greek inscriptions and manuscripts; introduced many Middle Eastern plants to western Europe.

Bus·by \ˈbəz-bē\, Richard. 1606–1695. English clergyman and schoolmaster. Headmaster of Westminster (1638–95), numbering among his pupils South, Dryden, Locke, Prior, Atterbury; traditionally a severe disciplinarian.

Busch \ˈbu̇sh\, Adolphus. 1839–1913. American businessman and philanthropist, b. Mainz, Germany. To U.S. (1857); joined St. Louis brewery of Eberhard Anheuser (1861); president of Anheuser-Busch Brewing Association (1879–1913); introduced Budweiser brand; pioneered in pasteurization of beer.

Busch, Wilhelm. 1832–1908. German illustrator and poet. Illustrator for *Fliegende Blätter* (1859–71); author of humorous and satirical illustrated verse, including *Max und Moritz* (1865), *Der heilige Antonius von Padua* (1870), *Die fromme Helene* (1872), *Dideldum* (1874), *Herr und Frau Knopp* (1876), *Fipps der Affe* (1879), *Plisch und Plum* (1882).

Bu·sche \ˈbu̇sh-ə\, Hermann von dem. *Called* Pa·si·phi·lus \pä-ˈzē-fē-lu̇s, *Angl* pə-ˈsif-ə-ləs\. 1468–1534. German scholar and Humanist. Professor, Heidelberg (1523), Marburg (1527). Author of *Vallum Humanitatis,* 3 books of epigrams in defense of Humanism (1518); *Hypanticon* (1520).

Bü·sching \ˈbǖ-shiŋ\, Anton Friedrich. 1724–1793. German geographer. Author of the unfinished *Neue Erdbeschreibung* (1754–92) that laid foundation of modern statistical geography.

Busch·mann \ˈbu̇sh-ˌmän\, Johann Karl Eduard. 1805–1880. German philologist. Collaborated with the brothers von Humboldt and helped edit Alexander von Humboldt's *Kosmos*. Author of comparative grammar of dialects of Malaysia and Polynesia (1840).

Bu·sen·baum \ˈbü-zən-ˌbau̇m\ *or* **Bu·sem·baum** \-zəm-\, Hermann. 1600–1668. German Jesuit theologian. Entered Jesuit order (1619). Author of widely popular *Medulla theologiae moralis* (1650), which was later condemned for its sections on regicide and publicly burned (1757) by the Parliament of Toulouse.

Bush \ˈbu̇sh\, Vannevar. 1890–1974. American electrical engineer, b. Everett, Mass. Professor (1919–38), dean of engineering and vice president (1932–38), M.I.T.; president, Carnegie Institution of Washington (1939–55); director, Office of Scientific Research and Development (1941–46). Built differential analyzer, pioneering analog computer (1928).

Bush-Brown \ˈbu̇sh-ˈbrau̇n\, Henry Kirke. *Orig. surname* Bush. 1857–1935. American sculptor, b. Ogdensburg, N.Y. Works included *Buffalo Hunt* (1893), equestrian statues of Generals Meade, Reynolds, and Sedgwick at Gettysburg, Anthony Wayne at Valley Forge.

Bush·man \ˈbu̇sh-mən\, Francis Xavier. 1883–1966. American actor, b. Baltimore. Broadway debut in *Queen of the Moulin Rouge* (1907); starred in films including *Magic Wand* (1912), *Graustark* (1915), *Under Royal Patronage* (1916), *Red, White and Blue Blood* (1917), *Ben Hur* (1926), etc.

Bush·mil·ler \ˈbu̇sh-ˌmil-ər\, Ernest, *known as* Ernie. 1905–1982. American cartoonist, b. New York City. Took over from Larry Whittington comic strip "Fritzi Ritz" (1925), which he developed into "Nancy" (1940).

Bush·nell \ˈbu̇sh-nəl\, David. 1742?–1824. American inventor, b. Saybrook, Conn. Invented submarine boat "Bushnell's Turtle" (1775), first to be used in warfare and predecessor of modern submarine.

Bushnell, Horace. 1802–1876. American clergyman, b. Bantam, Conn. Congregational pastor, Hartford, Conn. (1833–59); considered father of American religious liberalism. Author of *Christian Nurture* (1847), *God in Christ* (1849); *Christ in Theology* (1851), *Nature and the Supernatural* (1858), *Vicarious Sacrifice* (1866), etc.

Bū·ṣī·rī, al- \al-bü-sē-ˈrē\. *More completely* Sharaf ad-Dīn Muḥammad ibn Sa'īd al-Būṣīrī aṣ-Ṣanhājī. c.1212–c.1295. Arab poet, of Berber descent. Author of *al-Burdah* ("Poem of the Mantle") in praise of Muḥammad, a poem much venerated and often used as lamentation for dead and in amulets by Muslims.

Bus·ken Hu·et \ˈbœs-kən-ˈhǖ-wet\, Conrad. 1826–1886. Dutch literary critic and writer. Editor of literary magazine *De gids* (1862–65). Author of *Littararische fantasiën en kritieken* (1868–88), *Het land van Rembrandt* (1882–84).

Bu·son \bůs-ōn\. *Orig. surname* Ta·ni·guchi \tän-ē-gůch-ē\; *later surname* Yo·sa \yō-sä\. 1716–1783. Japanese painter and poet. Master of haiku.

Bu·so·ni \bü-'zō-nē\, Ferruccio Benvenuto. 1866–1924. Italian pianist and composer. Taught at Helsinki (1889–90), Moscow (1890–91), Boston (1891–93), Berlin (1894 ff.). Considered greatest piano technician after Liszt and Rubinstein. Among his works were operas *Turandot* (1917), *Arlecchino* (1917), *Doktor Faust* (unfinished); *Konzertstück* (1890), *Indianische Fantasie* (1913) for piano and orchestra; six sonatinas (1910–20), *Fantasia contrappuntistica* (1910) for piano.

Bus·se \'bůs-ə\, Hermann Eris. 1891–1947. German novelist. Author of *Das schlafende Feuer* (1929), *Markus und Sixta* (1929), *Der letzte Bauer* (1930), *Der Trauträger* (1938), *Girlegig* (1941), etc.

Bus·so·ne \büs-'sō-nā\, Francesco. *Known as* Car·ma·gno·la \ˌkär-män-'yō-lə\ *or* Il Carmagnola \ēl-\ *or* Conte di Carmagnola. c.1385–1432. Italian condottiere. In service of Filippo Maria Visconti, whose army he rose to command and whom he helped regain duchy of Milan; defected to Venice; commanded combined Venetian-Florentine forces against Milan; heavily defeated; suspected by Venetians of duplicity, arrested, tortured, beheaded.

Bussy, Comte de. See Roger de RABUTIN.

Bus·sy \bue-sē\, Antoine-Alexandre-Brutus. 1794–1882. French chemist. Director, School of Pharmacy, Paris (1844–73); first prepared elements magnesium and beryllium (1828).

Bussy-d'Am·boise \-dän-bwäz\, Louis de Cler·mont de \də-kler-mōn-də-\. c.1549–1579. French nobleman. Took advantage of St. Bartholomew's Massacre (1572) to murder one of his relatives; pillaged Anjou, of which he was governor (1576); assassinated by jealous husband.

Bussy-Castelnau, Marquis de. See Charles-Joseph PATISSIER.

Bussy-Rabutin. See Roger de RABUTIN.

Bus·ta·man·te \büs-tä-'män-tā\, Anastasio. 1780–1853. Mexican general and politician. Fought in Spanish army against revolutionists (as early as 1808), but (1821) supported Iturbide and Plan of Iguala; vice president of the republic under Guerrero (1829) but, with Santa Anna, led revolt against him. President of Mexico (1830–32); driven out by Santa Anna but, after latter's downfall (1836), again president (1837–39; nominally until 1841).

Bustamante y Sir·vén \-ē-sēr-'bān\, Antonio Sánchez de. 1865–1951. Cuban jurist. Professor of international law, Havana (1884 ff.); senator (1902–18); delegate to 2d Hague International Conference (1907) and to World War I Peace Conference at Paris (1919); member of Permanent Court of Arbitration, The Hague (1908 ff.); judge of Permanent Court of International Justice (1921–39); drew up Bustamante Code of international private law (adopted 1928). Author of *Tratado de derecho internacional privado* (1896), *Derecho internacional público* (1933–38), etc.

Bus·tā·nī \bůs-'tän-ē\, Buṭrus al-. 1819–1883. Arabic scholar. Founded political-literary review *al-Jinan* (1870); worked for revitalization of Arabic culture. Compiled Arabic dictionary, 6 volumes of an Arabic encyclopaedia.

Bus·tel·li \bůs-'tel-ē\, Franz Anton. 1723–1763. Swiss sculptor. Known for porcelain sculptures and figurines in light, decorative Rococo style, modeled for Nymphenberg porcelain works, Germany (1754–63).

Bu·ta·des \byů-'tād-(ˌ)ēz\ of Sicyon. *Called also, incorrectly,* Di·bu·ta·des \ˌdī-byů-'tād-(ˌ)ēz\. fl. 600 B.C. ? Greek sculptor. Reputedly first Greek modeler in clay.

Butch·er \'bůch-ər\, Samuel Henry. 1850–1910. British scholar. Fellow, U. Coll., Oxford (1875–82); professor, Edinburgh (1882–1903); M.P. (1906–10). Collaborated with Andrew Lang in prose translation of *Odyssey* (1879), one of the best translations extant. Author of *Aristotle's Theory of Poetry and Fine Art* (1895) and other works on Greek subjects.

Bute, Earls of. See under STEWART family.

But·ler \'bət-lər\. Name of an Irish family holding the earldom (from 1328), the dukedom (1682–1758), and marquisate (extinct in 1758, revived 1825) of Or·monde \'ȯ(ə)r-mənd\. The name derived from the hereditary office of chief butler of Ireland given to Theobald Walter (d. c.1206). From late Middle Ages to 1688 Ireland was controlled by the Butlers or their rivals, the Fitzgeralds (*q.v.*). Members included: James Butler (c.1305–1338), created earl of Ormonde chiefly because his wife, Eleanor de Bohun, was granddaughter of Edward I. His son ¶James (1331–1382), 2d earl, several times viceroy of Ireland, as was his great-grandson ¶James (c.1392–1452), 4th earl, soldier and scholar. ¶James (1420–1461), 5th Earl of Ormonde and Earl of Wilt·shire \'wilt-ˌshi(ə)r, 'wil-chər, 'wilt-shər\ (English peerage), eldest son of 4th earl; lord high treasurer of England (1455, 1458); captured by Yorkists after battle of Towton (1461) and beheaded; and his brothers John and Thomas, 6th and 7th earls, English ambassadors to Continental courts. ¶Sir Piers *or* Pierce (1467?–1539), 8th earl (cousin of 7th earl) and 1st earl of Os·sory \'äs-ə-rē\; lord treasurer of Ireland, as was his son ¶James (1490?–1546), 9th earl, and his grandson ¶Thomas (1531–1614), 10th earl, a Protestant, who took side of Queen Elizabeth against Irish rebels; vice admiral of Ireland (1612). ¶James (1610–1688), 12th earl and 1st duke, created marquis (1642) and duke in Irish peerage (1661) and in English peerage (1682); m. cousin Elizabeth Preston, ending feud with Fitzgerald family, to which she belonged; supported Thomas Wentworth against Irish rebels (from 1640); as lord lieutenant of Ireland (1644) concluded peace with Catholic Confederacy (1649); fled to Paris (1650–60) with Charles II after Cromwell's conquest of Ireland; commissioner for treasury and navy (1660); as lord lieutenant of Ireland (1662) encouraged Irish commerce and industry; dismissed (1669) but reappointed (1677) lord lieutenant of Ireland. His son ¶Thomas (1634–1680) became lord deputy of Ireland (1664–65, 1668–9); distinguished himself in Dutch war; general of forces in Holland (1678). Thomas's son ¶James (1665–1745), 2d duke, fought in wars of William III; lord lieutenant of Ireland (1703–07, 1710–13); succeeded John Churchill as commander of British forces (1711–14); impeached (1715) by Whigs for Jacobite ties and complicity in secret Tory negotiations with France in War of Spanish Succession; settled in Spain.

Butler, Alban. 1710–1773. English hagiographer. Taught at English Coll., Douai, France (1734–49). Author of *Lives of the Saints* (1756–59).

Butler, Benjamin Franklin. 1818–1893. American army officer and politician, b. Deerfield, N.H. Entered Union service at outbreak of Civil War; occupied Baltimore (1861); major general; defined freed slaves as "contraband of war"; commanded land forces in capture of New Orleans (May 1, 1862); military governor, New Orleans (May–Dec. 1862); by his arbitrary government, caused protest and charges of corruption. In command, districts of eastern Virginia and North Carolina (1863); commanded Army of the James (1864). Member, U.S. House of Representatives (1867–75, 1877–79). Governor of Massachusetts (1882–84). Candidate of Anti-Monopoly and National (Greenback) parties for president (1884).

Butler, Ellis Parker. 1869–1937. American humorist, b. Muscatine, Iowa. Made first great success with *Pigs is Pigs* (1906). Among other books were *Great American Pie Co.* (1907), *Confessions of a Daddy* (1907), *That Pup* (1908), *Jibby Jones* (1923), *Pigs, Pets, and Pies* (1927), and *Hunting the Wow* (1934).

Butler, George. 1774–1853. English clergyman and educator. Headmaster of Harrow (1805–29); chancellor of Peterborough (1836), dean (1842). His son ¶Arthur Gray (1831–1909), was master at Rugby (1858–62), first headmaster of reconstituted Haileybury College (1862–67), and dean and tutor at Oriel College, Oxford (1875–97). Another son ¶Henry Montague (1833–1918) was headmaster of Harrow (1859–85), where he reformed and modernized curriculum; dean of Gloucester (1885–86), and master of Trinity College, Cambridge (1886–1918).

Butler, John. 1728–1796. American Loyalist, b. New London, Conn. At outbreak of American Revolution, recruited (1777–78) force of Indians and rangers, "Butler's Rangers," who invaded Wyoming Valley, Pa. (1778); defeated Continentals there, with atrocities committed by the Indians (Wyoming Massacre, July 3, 1778). Defeated (1779) by Gen. John Sullivan near Elmira, N.Y. British commissioner of Indian affairs at Niagara, Canada, following Revolutionary War. His son ¶Walter N. (d. 1781) commanded Butler's Rangers in attack, with Joseph Brant's Indians, on Cherry Valley, N.Y. (Cherry Valley Massacre, Nov. 11, 1778).

Butler, Joseph. 1692–1752. English theologian. Joined Church of England as a youth; rector of Stanhope (1725–40); clerk of the closet to queen (1736); to king (1746); bishop of Bristol (1738); dean of St. Paul's (1740); bishop of Durham (1750). Author of *Fifteen Sermons* (1726) and of *The Analogy of Religion* (1736).

Butler, Josephine Elizabeth, *nee* Gray. 1828–1906. English reformer. m. (1852) George Butler. Supported higher education for women; campaigned for repeal of Contagious Diseases Act (1869–86) and against licensed brothels and white-slave trade.

Butler, Nicholas Murray. 1862–1947. American educator, b. Elizabeth, N.J. Professor of philosophy and education, Columbia (1890–1901); president of Columbia (1901–45), Barnard (1904–45), Bard (1928–45), New York Post-Graduate Med. School (1931–45). An organizer and first president (1886–91) of New York Coll. for the Training of Teachers, now Teachers Coll., Columbia. President, Carnegie Endowment for International Peace (1925–45). Awarded, with Jane Addams, Nobel peace prize (1931).

Butler, Pierce. 1866–1939. American jurist, b. near Northfield, Minn. Practiced law in St. Paul (from 1897); associate justice, U.S. Supreme Court (1922–39).

Butler, Richard Austen. *Called* Rab \'rab\. Baron Butler of Saf·fron Wal·den \ˌsaf-rən-'wȯl-dən\. 1902–1982. British politician. Member of parliament (1929–65); first minister of education (1944–45), achieving a major reform of British educational system; chancellor of the exchequer (1951–55); secretary of state for foreign affairs (1963–64). Revitalized Conservative party after World War II and later served as its chairman (1959–61).

Butler, Samuel. 1612–1680. English poet. Page to countess of Kent (c.1628); clerk to puritan justices of the peace; secretary (1661) to 2d earl of Carbery, who appointed him steward of Ludlow Castle. Author of *Hudibras* (1663–78), mock heroic poem satirizing the Presbyterians and Independents.

Butler, Samuel. 1835–1902. English writer. Sheep rancher in New Zealand (1859–64); wrote *A First Year in Canterbury Settlement* (1863); dabbled in musical composition and painting and exhibited at Royal Academy regularly (1868–76). First important literary work anonymous *Erewhon* (1872), a utopian novel of a land divested of machinery; wrote *The Fair Haven* (1873), ironical defense of Christianity; *Life and Habit* (1878); *Evolution, Old and New* (1879), *Unconscious Memory* (1880), *Luck or Cunning* (1886), all attacking Darwinism; topographical works *Alps and Sanctuaries of Piedmont and the Canton Ticino* (1882) and *Ex Voto* (1888); *The Way of All Flesh* (1903), an iconoclastic philosophical novel largely autobiographical, satirizing family life in mid-Victorian England.

Butler, Smedley Darlington. 1881–1940. American marine officer, b. West Chester, Pa. Entered Marine Corps (1898); served in Philippines, China, Nicaragua; engaged at capture of Veracruz (1914) and awarded Medal of Honor; engaged at capture of Ft. Rivière, Haiti (1915) and awarded 2d Medal of Honor; organized and commanded (1916–19) Haitian constabulary; brigadier general (1921); commanded expeditionary force in Nanking, China (1927–29); major general (1929).

Butler, Walter N. See John BUTLER.

Butler, Sir William Francis. 1838–1910. British army officer, b. Ireland. Served in India (1860), Canada (1867–73), Ashanti War (1873–74), Zulu War (1879), the Sudan (1884–85). Commanded British troops at Alexandria (1890–93); ordered home from command in Boer War because of expression of views not approved by government (1899); lieutenant general (1900). His wife (m. 1877) ¶Elizabeth Southerden, *nee* Thompson (1850–1933) was a Swiss-born English painter of military and battle scenes.

But·le·rov \'büt-lyi-rəf\, Aleksandr Mikhaylovich. 1828–1886. Russian chemist. Professor, Kazan U. (1852–68), St. Petersburg (1868–85); known esp. for theory of chemical structure (1860); predicted and demonstrated isomerism; synthesized isobutane (1866).

Bütsch·li \'bu̇ech-lē\, Otto. 1848–1920. German zoologist. Professor, Heidelberg (1878–1918); investigated developmental history of invertebrates, anatomical structure of nematodes, and constitution of protoplasm; pioneered in study of nuclear and cell division.

Butt \'bət\, Dame Clara Ellen. 1872–1936. English contralto. Known esp. for performances of ballads and oratorios; cycle *Sea Pictures* composed specially for her by Sir Edward Elgar (1899).

Butt, Isaac. 1813–1879. Irish lawyer and nationalist leader. Professor, Dublin (1836–41); defended Young Ireland leaders (1848), Fenians (1865–69); M.P. (1852–65, 1871–79). Formed Home Government Association (1870); president, Home Rule Confederation (1873–77); generally credited with coining term Home Rule.

But·ter·field \'bət-ər-ˌfēld\, John. 1801–1869. American businessman, b. Berne, N.Y. Formed express company (1849); merged it (1850) with Wells & Co. and Livingston, Fargo & Co. to form American Express Co.; organized Overland Mail Co. (1857); mayor of Utica, N.Y. (1865).

Butterfield, William. 1814–1900. English architect. A leading exponent of Gothic revival, associated with Oxford Movement. Works, notable for contrasts of mass and texture, included All Saints', Margaret St., and St. Alban's, Holborn, both London; St. Augustine's, Bournemouth; Keble Coll., Oxford.

But·ter·ick \'bət-ə-(ˌ)rik\, Ebenezer. 1826–1903. American inventor, b. Sterling, Mass. Tailor and shirtmaker by trade; invented (1859) standardized paper patterns for shirts, suits, dresses, etc.

But·ton \'bət-ᵊn\, Stephen Decatur. 1803–1897. American architect, b. Preston, Conn. Pioneer in metal-frame construction with 241 Chestnut St. and Leland buildings, Philadelphia (1852, 1855).

Button, Sir Thomas. d. 1634. English navigator. Sent on expedition to search for Northwest Passage; first European to enter present Manitoba, first to reach west coast of Hudson Bay (1612–13).

Butzer, Martin. See BUCER.

Bux·te·hu·de \ˌbu̇k-stə-'hüd-ə, *Angl also* 'bu̇k-stə-ˌ\, Dietrich. 1637–1707. Danish organist and composer. Organist in Lübeck (1668–1707), renowned throughout Germany as virtuoso. Composed church music, including over 100 cantatas and much keyboard music esp. for organ, as preludes, fugues, toccatas, chaconnes.

Bux·ton \'bək-stən\, Sir Thomas Fowell. 1st Baronet. 1786–1845. English philanthropist. Accumulated fortune in brewing business. M.P. (1818–37); advocated amelioration of criminal law and prison discipline; advocated abolition of slavery in British dominions; helped form British and Foreign Anti-Slavery Society (1823) and succeeded Wilberforce as leader of campaign in Parliament (1822–37). Author of *Inquiry into Prison Discipline* (1818), *African Slave Trade and its Remedy* (1839). His son and biographer ¶Charles (1823–1871) was M.P. (1857–71); advocate of church reform, disestablishment, and security of tenure in Ireland; urged clemency for mutineers after Sepoy mutiny, and opposed retributive measures against Governor Eyre of Jamaica for his conduct in the uprising of 1865. Charles's son ¶Sydney Charles (1853–1934), 1st Earl Buxton, was M.P (1883–85, 1886–1914); undersecretary for colonies (1892–95); postmaster general (1905–10); president of Board of Trade (1910–14); largely responsible for writing and enactment of acts on copyright, unemployment insurance, pilotage, bankruptcy; governor general of South Africa (1914–20); created earl in 1920.

Bux·torf \'bu̇k-stȯrf\, Johann. *Called* the Elder. 1564–1629. German Hebraist. Professor, Basel (1590–1629). Author of *Lexicon hebraicum et chaldaicum* (1615), *Biblia hebraica rabbinica* (1618–19). His son ¶Johann, *called* the Younger (1599–1664), also a Hebraist, completed and published his *Concordantiae bibliorum hebraicorum* (1639) and *Lexicon chaldaicum, talmudicum, et rabbinicum* (1639).

Bu·yan·tu \bü-'yän-tü\. *Chin.* Chi Yen-tsung \'jē-'yen-'dzu̇ŋ\. 14th century. Mongol emperor (1311–20) of Yüan dynasty. Known for fostering commerce with Europe and patronizing literature.

Bū·yids \'bü-yidz\ *or* **Bu·way·hids** \bü-'wī-hidz\. A Persian Shī'ite dynasty (945–1055) founded by the Daylamites. It seized Baghdad and controlled caliphs until overthrown by Seljuqs. Chief representative 'ADUD AD-DAWLAH.

Buy·rette \bœy-ret, bwʸē-ret\, Pierre-Laurent. *Pseudonym* Dormont de Bel·loy \də-bā-lwȧ, -be-\. 1727–1775. French dramatist. Among first to create tragedies based on national history rather than on classics. Works included *Le Siège de Calais* (1765), *Gaston et Bayard* (1771), *Pierre le Cruel* (1772), *Gabrielle de Vergy* (1777).

Buys \'bœis\, Paulus. 1531–1594. Dutch politician. Pensionary of Leiden (1561); helped plan revolt of northern provinces against rule of Duke of Alba; elected advocate of Holland (1572); adviser to William I the Silent; resigned as advocate (1585); helped negotiate Treaty of Westminster with England (1585); opposed Earl of Leicester's plan for Calvinist government.

Buys Bal·lot \'bœis-bä-'lȯt\, Christoph Hendrik Diederik. 1817–1890. Dutch meteorologist. Director, Royal Dutch Meteorological Institute, Utrecht (from 1854); professor, Utrecht (from 1847); formulated (1857) Buys Ballot's law for determining from the direction of the wind the location of the area of lower barometric pressure.

Buys·se \'bœis-ə\, Cyriel. 1859–1932. Flemish novelist and playwright. Founded literary journal *Van nu en straks* (1893) to foster Flemish literature; a leading exponent of Naturalism in Flemish. Author of novels *Het recht van den sterkste* (1893), *Sursum Corda* (1894), *'n Leeuw van Vlaandern* (1901), *Het leven van Rozeke van Dalen* (1905), *De nachtelijke aanranding* (1912), *Kerels* (1927); plays *Het gezin van Paemel* (1893), *De plaatsvervangende vrederechter* (1895).

Buz·za·ti \büd-'dzä-tē\, Dino. 1906–1972. Italian journalist and writer. Known for works combining elements of surrealism, symbolism, absurdity, including novels *Barnabò delle montagne* (1933), *Il secreto del bosco vecchio* (1935), *Il deserto dei tartari* (1940), *Il grande retrato* (1960), *Un amore* (1963); novellas *I sette messaggeri* (1942), *Paura alla scala* (1949); stories *Sessanta racconti* (1958).

By \'bī\, John. 1781–1836. English engineer. Entered Royal Engineers (1799); in Canada designed and built (1826–32) Rideau Canal from Ottawa River to Kingston on Lake Ontario; settlement at Ottawa and Rideau rivers, originally Bytown, later became Ottawa.

Byalik, Chaim Nachman. See BIALIK.

Bylney, Thomas. See BILNEY.

Byng \'biŋ\, George. 1st Viscount Tor·ring·ton \'tȯr-iŋ-tən\. 1663–1733. British admiral. Captain (1688), rear admiral (1703); commanded taking of Gibraltar (1704); captured French fleet of Pretender (1708); repelled Pretender's second attempt (1715) and created baronet; admiral of the fleet (1718); destroyed Spanish fleet off Cape Passero (1718); viscount (1721); first lord of admiralty (1727–33). His fourth son ¶John (1704–1757) was in navy (from 1718); rear admiral (1745); his squadron was defeated in defending Minorca by French fleet (1756); sentenced by court martial for neglect of duty (1757) and shot.

Byng, Julian Hedworth George. 1st Viscount Byng. 1862–1935. British field marshal. Entered army (1883); served in Boer War; made skillful withdrawal from Dardanelles (1915); commanded Canadian Corps at capture of Vimy Ridge (Apr. 1917); commanding Third Army, executed on Cambrai front first large-scale tank attack (Nov. 1917); later broke Hindenburg line (Sept. 1918); governor general of Canada (1921–26); created viscount (1926); commissioner of London Metropolitan Police (1928–31); field marshal (1932).

Byn·kers·hoek \'biŋ-kərs-ˌhük\, Cornelis van. 1673–1743. Dutch jurist. Member (from 1703) and president (from 1724), Supreme Court of Holland, Zeeland, and West Friesland. Author of works on international and Roman and Dutch civil law, including *De dominio maris* (1703), *De foro legatorum* (1721), *Quaestiones juris publici* (1737).

Byrd \'bərd\, Richard Evelyn. 1888–1957. American naval officer and explorer, b. Winchester, Va. In charge of aviation unit, Navy-MacMillan Polar Expedition (1924–25); with Floyd Bennett flew by airplane over North Pole and back to Kings Bay, Spitzbergen (1926), for which both were awarded Medal of Honor; with three companions, made 42-hour transatlantic flight from New York to France (1927); established Antarctic base "Little America" and flew over South Pole (1929); rear admiral (1930); on second Antarctic expedition (1933–35) discovered Marie Byrd Land, Edsel Ford Mountains; third expedition (1939–40); commanded Operation High Jump (1946–47) and Operation Deep Freeze (1955–56) expeditions. Author of *Skyward* (1928), *Little America* (1930), *Discovery* (1935), *Alone* (1938). His brother ¶Harry Flood (1887–1966) was governor of Virginia (1926–30); U.S. senator (1933–65).

Byrd, William. 1543–1623. English organist and composer. Pupil and protégé of Thomas Tallis; organist at Lincoln cathedral (1563), with Tallis of Chapel Royal (1572–77); granted, with Tallis, 21-year monopoly of issuing printed music and music paper (1575). Composed 3 masses, much original keyboard music, motets, madrigals, songs, etc. published in *Cantiones sacrae* (1575), *Psalms, Sonets, & songs of sadnes & pietie* (1588), *Songs of sundrie natures* (1589), more *Cantiones sacrae* (1589, 1591), *Gradualia* (1605, 1607), *Psalms, Songs and Sonnets* (1611).

Byrd, William. *Known as* William Byrd of Westover. 1674–1744. American planter, b. Virginia. Managed large estate in Virginia (from 1705); king's councilor (1709); a commissioner to survey Virginia–North Carolina border (1728); laid out city of Richmond (1737); built mansion Westover and assembled largest library in colonial America; kept diary of great value for social and political history.

Byrgius, Justus. See Joost BÜRGI.

Byrne \'bərn\, Barry, *in full* Francis Barry. 1883–1967. American architect, b. Chicago. Trained in office of Frank Lloyd Wright; developed individual style esp. in school and church designs. Works included Immaculata High School, Chicago (1921–22), St. Patrick's, Racine, Wis. (1923), Church of Christ the King, Tulsa (1926), Church of Christ the King, Cork, Ireland (1928), Church of St. Francis Xavier, Kansas City (1948), St. Benedict's Abbey, Atchison, Kans. (1955).

Byrne, Donn. See Brian Oswald DONN-BYRNE.

Byrnes \'bərnz\, James Francis. 1879–1972. American politician, b. Charleston, S.C. Member, U.S. House of Representatives (1911–25); U.S. senator from S.C. (1931–41); associate justice, U.S. Supreme Court (1941–42); director, Office of Economic Stabilization (1942–43), of War Mobilization (1943–45); secretary of state (1945–47). Governor of S.C. (1951–55). Author of *Speaking Frankly* (1947).

Byrns \'bərnz\, Joseph Wellington. 1869–1936. American politician, b. Cedar Hill, Tenn. Member, U.S. House of Representatives (1909–36), majority leader (1932–35), speaker (1935–36).

By·rom \'bī-rəm\, John. 1692–1763. English poet. Contributed to development of shorthand in *Universal English Shorthand* (1767); his verse collected as *Miscellaneous Poems* (1773); author of hymns including "Christians, Awake! Salute the Happy Morn."

By·ron \'bī-rən\, George Gordon. 6th Baron Byron. *Known as* Lord Byron. 1788–1824. English poet. Grandson of John Byron. Lived with mother at Aberdeen until on the death of his great uncle (1798) he succeeded to barony; while at Cambridge published (1807) volume of poems, *Hours of Idleness,* which was fiercely assailed by *Edinburgh Review;* replied in witty satirical poem *English Bards and Scotch Reviewers* (1809). Traveled in Portugal, Spain, Greece, Turkey, swimming the Hellespont (1810); sprang into fame with publication of first two cantos of *Childe Harold's Pilgrimage,* a narrative poem of travels through southern Europe by an imaginary pilgrim (1812); published (1813–14) Turkish tales in verse *The Giaour, The Bride of Abydos, The Corsair, Lara,* which were as popular as *Childe Harold;* m. (1815) Anne Isabella Mil·banke \'mil-ˌbaŋk\ (1792–1860), a mathematician and heiress who gave birth (1815) to Augusta Ada, returned to her father's protection (1816), and became Baroness Wentworth (1856). Signed deed of separation from wife and left England (1816), never to return; traveled in Switzerland with Shelley; wrote *Childe Harold,* canto iii (1816) and "The Prisoner of Chillon" (1816); lived at or near Venice (1816–19); published brooding poetic drama *Manfred* (1817); finished canto iv of *Childe Harold* and began *Don Juan* (1819–24), a satirical epic poem narrating adventures of a handsome libertine; published satire *Beppo* (1818). Took Teresa, Countess Guiccioli, from her husband (1819); composed historical dramas *Marino Faliero, Sardanapalus, The Two Foscari,* and *Cain, a Mystery* (1821); satirized Southey with *The Vision of Judgment;* present at the cremation of Shelley (1822). Joined Carbonari (1820) and in the *Prophecy of Dante* (1821) denounced tyranny and spoke out as champion of liberty for oppressed in Italy; accepted invitation of Prince Mavrokordátos to join Greek insurgents in struggle for independence, enlisted a regiment, advanced large sums; died at Missolonghi of a fever. Other works included *Siege of Corinth* (1816), *Lament of Tasso* (1817), *Mazeppa* (1819).

Byron, John. *Called* Foul-weather Jack. 1723–1786. English navigator. Grandfather of the poet Byron. As midshipman with Anson, shipwrecked on Chile coast (1741); his account of this shipwreck used by Lord Byron in *Don Juan;* commanded exploratory voyage round the world (1764–66); governor of Newfoundland (1769–72); rear admiral (1775); worsted off Grenada (1779).

C

Ca·ma·ño \kä-äm-ˈän-yō\, José María Plácido. 1838–1901. Ecuadorian politician. Banished (1882) for conspiring against dictator Veintemilla; led expedition against Guayaquil (1883) and drove out Veintemilla. Provisional president of Ecuador (1883–84), president (1884–88); minister to Washington (1889–90); lived in Spain (1895–1901).

Caballero, Fernán. See Cecilia BÖHL DE FABER.

Caballero, Francisco Largo. See LARGO CABALLERO.

Ca·ba·nel \ká-bá-nel\, Alexandre. 1823–1889. French painter. Professor, École des Beaux-Arts (from 1863); known as historical, genre, and portrait painter. His works included *La Naissance de Vénus, Le Repos de Ruth, Françoise de Rimini, Christ au Jardin des Oliviers.*

Ca·ba·ni·lles \kä-b̲ä-ˈnē(l)-yās\, Juan Bautista José. 1644–1712. Spanish organist and composer. Organist, Valencia cathedral (from 1665); composed much keyboard music including tientos, toccatas, gallardas, pasacalles.

Ca·ba·nis \ká-bá-nēs\, Pierre-Jean-Georges. 1757–1808. French physician and philosopher. Professor of hygiene (1794), of legal medicine and history of medicine (1799), Medical School of Paris; sympathizer with Revolutionists; physician to Mirabeau; member of Council of Five Hundred (1797); senator (1799). Evolved radically mechanistic and materialistic theory of life processes, including thought. Author of *Rapports du physique et du moral de l'homme* (1802).

Ca·bar·rus \kä-b̲ä-ˈrüs\, Francisco de. Conde. *Fr.* François Ca·bar·rus \ká-bá-rue̅\. 1752–1810. Spanish financier, b. France. Settled in Madrid (c.1772); naturalized (1781); became adviser to Charles III; promoted currency and tax reforms; created count (1789); imprisoned by Charles IV (1790–92); represented Spain at Congress of Rastatt (1797); developed trade with Philippines; served as minister of finance under Ferdinand VII and Joseph Bonaparte (1808–10).

Cab·a·si·las \ˌkab-ə-ˈsī-ləs\, Nilus. c.1298–c.1363. Greek prelate and theologian. To Constantinople (c.1345), where he became court official; authority on writings of Church Fathers; encouraged Demetrios Cydones in translation of Aquinas; undertook to refute Latin church on points of doctrine, his *De processione Spiritus Sancti* becoming definitive statement of Orthodox position; supported Hesychast mysticism of Gregory Palamas in *Tomos hagioreitikos,* adopted (1351) by synod; criticized Nicephorus Gregoras in *Antigramma;* named metropolitan of Thessaloníki (1361). His nephew ¶Nicolas Cabasilas (c.1320–c.1390) was a lay theologian; wrote much in support of Gregory Palamas and Hesychasm; also wrote *Commentary on the Divine Liturgy* and *Life in Christ.*

Cab·ell \ˈkab-əl\, James Branch. 1879–1958. American novelist and essayist, b. Richmond, Va. First came to notice with the novel *Jurgen* (1919), attacked for immorality and temporarily suppressed; other volumes in his 18-volume *Biography of Manuel,* set in imaginary medieval province of Poictesme, included *Cream of the Jest* (1917), *Beyond Life* (1919), *Figures of Earth* (1921), *The High Place* (1923), *Way of Ecben* (1929). Other works included *The Eagle's Shadow* (1904), *Gallantry* (1907), *Chivalry* (1909), *The Cords of Vanity* (1909), *The Rivet in Grandfather's Neck* (1915), autobiographical *These Restless Heads* (1932), a trilogy *Smirt* (1934), *Smith* (1935), and *Smire* (1937), criticism *Preface to the Past* (1936).

Ca·bet \ká-be\, Étienne. 1788–1856. French Socialist. Involved in revolution of 1830; elected deputy (1831); exiled for radical articles (1834–39); published utopian novel *Voyage en Icarie* (1840). Influenced by Robert Owen, led a group to Nauvoo, Ill. (1849), to found a utopian community, called Icaria; withdrew from community after dissension (1856).

Ca·be·za de Va·ca \kä-ˈb̲ā-thä-t̲h̲ä-ˈb̲ä-kä\, Álvar Núñez. c.1490–c.1560. Spanish explorer. Treasurer of expedition to Florida of Narváez (1527–28); wrecked on island on Texas coast and imprisoned by Indians (1528); escaped and finally reached Mexico City via northern Mexico (1530–36); returned to Spain (1537). Led expedition to Río de la Plata region, across southern Brazil 1000 miles to Asunción (1541–42); colonial governor in Paraguay (1542–44); deposed and sent to Spain (1544–45); banished to service in Africa. Recounted adventures and tales of El Dorado in *Naufragios* (1542), *La Relación y Comentarios* (1555). His reports of Narváez expedition led directly to expeditions of Niza (1539) and Coronado (1540–42).

Ca·be·zón \kä-b̲ā-ˈt̲h̲ōn\, Antonio de. 1510–1566. Spanish composer. Blind from infancy; organist to Empress Isabel (1526); in service of Philip II (from 1548). Earliest major Spanish keyboard composer; works included tientos, psalm settings, variations on popular songs and on motets and chansons, dance pieces.

Ca·ble \ˈkā-bəl\, George Washington. 1844–1925. American author, b. New Orleans. After success of first book, *Old Creole Days* (1879), made writing his profession; other works in realistic local-color vein included *The Grandissimes* (1880), *The Creoles of Louisiana* (1884), *Dr. Sevier* (1885), *Bonaventure* (1888), *Strange True Stories of Louisiana* (1889), *The Cavalier* (1901), *Posson Jone and Père Raphael* (1909), *The Flower of the Chapdelaines* (1918).

Ca·boche \ká-bōsh\, Simon. *Also called* Simon le Cous·tel·lier \lə-kü-təl-yā\. 15th century. French merchant. Leader of merchant guilds protesting official corruption and taxation (from 1407); gained support of U. of Paris and of Duke John the Fearless of Burgundy; led riotous mob that seized Bastille (1413); won from King Charles VI *Ordonance Cabochienne* (1413), providing elections for Council, Parlement, and Chambre des Comptes; continued rioting suppressed by Charles, duc d'Orléans, rival of Burgundy, and *Ordonance* was withdrawn.

Cab·ot \ˈkab-ət\, George. 1752–1823. American businessman and politician, b. Salem, Mass. In shipping business (1768–94); U.S. senator (1791–96); leading member of Federalist group called the Essex Junto and president of secret Hartford Convention (Dec. 1814).

Cabot, John. *Ital.* Giovanni Ca·bo·to \kä-ˈbō-tō\. c.1450–c.1499. Italian navigator and explorer. Naturalized citizen of Venice (1476); visited Mecca; moved to England (c.1484); sailed from Bristol (1497) in the *Mathew,* under patent from Henry VII, in search of route to Asia; landed after 52 days at spot variously identified as Labrador, Newfoundland, or Cape Breton Island; made second voyage (1498); may have been lost at sea. His son ¶Sebastian (1476?–1557), b. Bristol, made map of Gascony and Guienne for Henry VIII of England (1512); map maker to Ferdinand II of Aragon (1512–16); prepared to sail on voyage of discovery, which was canceled (1516); pilot major to Emperor Charles V (1518–28, 1533–48); commanded Spanish expedition to La Plata region of South America (1525–28); published engraved map of world (1544); granted pension by Edward VI (1549); founded, and made governor of, company of Merchant Adventurers of London (1551), which sent expeditions (1553, 1555–56) to search for northeast passage to the east, effecting trade with Russia as result.

Cabot, Richard Clarke. 1868–1939. American physician, b. Brookline, Mass. With Mass. General Hospital (from 1898), chief of medical staff (1912–21); teacher (from 1899), professor of clinical medicine (1919–33), Harvard Medical School; professor of social ethics, Harvard (1920–34). Pioneer in field of medical social service. Author of *Clinical Examination of the Blood* (1897), *Social Service and the Art of Healing* (1909), *Differential Diagnosis* (1911–14), *What Men Live By* (1914), *Social Work* (1919), *The Meaning of Right and Wrong* (1933), etc.

Ca·bral \kə-ˈbräl\, Amílcar. 1921–1973. Guinean politician. Founded (1956) Partido Africano da Independência da Guiné e Cabo Verde; initiated open rebellion for independence of Guinea from Portugal (1962); de facto ruler of unoccupied portions of Guinea; assassinated.

Cabral, Pedro Álvars. 1467 or 1468–1520. Portuguese navigator. After da Gama's return, sent by King Manuel I of Portugal in command of fleet of 13 vessels to establish trade with India (1500–01). Took westward course; carried by wind and current to coast of Brazil (Apr. 22, 1500) and took possession of it in name of Portugal. Continued voyage to East; lost four ships in storm off

Cape of Good Hope; reached Calicut, India; established trading post there and at Cochin; returned to Portugal with 4 ships.

Cabrera, Manuel Estrada. See ESTRADA CABRERA.

Cab·re·ra \kä-'brā-rä\, Ramón. Conde de Mo·rel·la \mō-'rā(l)-yä\. *Full surname* Cabrera y Gri·ñó \-ē-grēn-'yō\. 1806–1877. Spanish insurgent. Joined Carlist revolt (1833) and became leader of Carlist bands; noted for cruelty; created count after victory at Morella (1838); driven into France (1840); again commander of Carlists in Catalonia (1846–49); lived in England (from 1860).

Ca·bril·ho \kȧ-'brēl-yü\, João Ro·dri·gues \rü-'thrē-gēs\. *Sp.* Juan Ro·drí·guez Ca·bril·lo \rȯth-'rē-gath-kȧ-'bre(l)-yō\. d. 1543. Portuguese explorer in service of Spain. To Mexico with Narváez (1520); with Cortés at capture of Mexico City (1521); founded Oaxaca. Discovered (1542) California, exploring much of its coast and entering San Diego and Monterey bays.

Ca·bri·ni \kə-'brē-nē\, Frances Xavier, *orig.* Maria Francesca. Saint. *Known as* Mother Cabrini. 1850–1917. American religious, b. Sant'Angelo, Lodigiano, Italy. Founded Missionary Sisters of the Sacred Heart (1880); superior general for life (1910). To U.S. (1889); naturalized (1909); founded schools, orphanages, hospitals throughout U.S., South America. Canonized (1946), becoming first American saint.

Ca·brol \kȧ-brȯl\, Fernand. 1855–1937. French religious. Entered Benedictine order (1877); abbot of monastery at Farnborough, England (1903–37). Author of *Livre de la prière antique* (1900); completed (1907) first volume of *Dictionnaire d'archéologie chrétienne et de liturgie.*

Cac·ci·ni \kät-'chē-nē\, Giulio. *Called also* Giulio Ro·ma·no \rō-'män-ō\. c.1545–1618. Italian singer and composer. Pioneer in monody, dramatic recitative, and operatic style. In Florence in service of Cosimo I de' Medici (before 1574); member of Giovanni Bardi's Camerata. His works included operas *Il rapimento di Cefalo* (1600) and *Euridice* (1602), and esp. the collection of canzonets and madrigals *Nuove Musiche* (1602).

Cá·ce·res \'käs-ā-rās\, Andrés Avelino. 1833–1923. Peruvian general and politician. Fought in War of the Pacific (1879–83); after capture of Lima by Chileans, head of provisional government (1883); led Peruvians who refused to accept Treaty of Ancón (1884) and overcame President Iglesias; president of Peru (1886–90); minister to France and Great Britain (1890–94); again president (1894–95) but defeated by party of Piérola; minister to Austria, Germany, and Italy (1905–11).

Ca·dal·so y Váz·quez \käth-'äl-sō-ē-'bäth-käth\, José de. 1741–1782. Spanish writer. Author of neoclassical drama *Sancho García, Conde de Castilla* (1771), *Eruditos a la violeta* (satire, 1772), and verse, including anacreontic *Ocios de mi juventud* (1773), *Noches lúgubres* (1798) and esp. *Cartas marruecas* (1793).

Ca'da Mo·sto *or* **Ca·da·mo·sto** \ˌkäd-äm-'ō-stō\, Alvise. 1432–1488. Venetian navigator and explorer. Explored west coast of Africa under commission from Prince Henry of Portugal (1455–56); discovered Cape Verde Islands (1456). Author of *Il Libro della prima navigazione per oceano alle terre de'negri della bassa etiopia* (1507).

Cad·bury \'kad-ˌber-ē, -ˌb(ə-)rē\, George. 1839–1922. English industrialist and reformer. Joined (1856) father's firm of Cadbury Brothers, cocoa and chocolate manufacturers; with brother ¶Richard (1836?–1899) took over management (1861); chairman (1899–1922); promoted welfare, educational work, and improved housing for employees, esp. with building of workers' town at Bournville (1894 ff.), deeded (1900) to Bournville Village Trust.

Cade \'kād\, John, *known as* Jack. d.1450. British rebel, b. Ireland. Fled Sussex to France (1449) to escape murder prosecution; returned under name John Aylmer. Led revolt of Kentish smallholders (1450) against high taxation, claiming name of Mortimer, that of Henry VI's rival Richard, duke of York; defeated Henry VI's forces at Sevenoaks; entered London; forced lord mayor and judges to condemn to death James Fiennes, the lord treasurer, and William Crowmer, sheriff of Kent; refused readmission to city on exaction of forced contributions; repulsed at London Bridge; hunted down after dispersion of army under amnesty and killed at Heathfield.

Cad·ell \'kad-ᵊl\, Francis. 1822–1879. Scottish explorer. Served East India Company and in Opium War (1840–41); explored Murray River and tributaries in Australia (1848–59); opened Murray to steam navigation (1853).

Cadillac, Sieur de. See Antoine de LA MOTHE.

Cad·man \'kad-mən\, Charles Wakefield. 1881–1946. American composer, b. Johnstown, Pa. Music critic, Pittsburgh *Dispatch* (1908–10); organist in Pittsburgh churches, and for Pittsburgh Male Chorus. Made special study of North American Indian songs. Composed operas on Indian themes, including *Land of the Misty Water* (1909–12), *Shanewis* (1918), *Sunset Trail* (1922); other operas as *Witch of Salem* (1926), *Willow Tree* (for radio, 1933); orchestral works *Thunderbird Suite* (1914), *Oriental Rhapsody* (1929), *Hollywood Suite* (1932), *Aurora Borealis* (1944); choral works as *Vision of Sir Launfal* (1909), *Father of Waters* (1928), hundreds of songs including "At Dawning" (1906), "From the Land of Sky-Blue Water" (1908).

Ca·dog·an \kə-'dəg-ən\, William. 1st Earl Cadogan. 1672–1726. British soldier, b. Ireland. Entered army (1690); quartermaster general to Marlborough (1702–11); distinguished himself at Blenheim (1704) and in crossing at Oudenarde and at Ramillies (1706); lieutenant general (1709). Under Jacobite party, resigned rank and emoluments (1712); restored to lieutenant generalship under George I (1714); lieutenant of ordnance (1714–18); waged last campaign against Jacobite insurrection (1715–16); general (1717), earl (1718); commander in chief (1722).

Cadore, Duc de. See Jean-Baptiste Nompère de CHAMPAGNY.

Ca·dor·na \kä-'dȯr-nä\, Raffaele. 1815–1897. Italian general. Took part in national movements (1848, 1859, 1866) and in Crimean War (1854–56); deputy in Sardinian parliament (1848 ff.); minister of war, Tuscany (1859); crushed insurrection in Sicily as military commandant (1866); captured and occupied Rome (Sept. 20, 1870); senator (1871 ff.); commanding general in Turin (1873–77). Author of *La liberazione di Roma nel 1870* (1889). His son ¶Luigi (1850–1928), soldier; on general staff (1896); chief of general staff (1914–17); commander in chief of Italian armies (1915–17); conducted operations on the Isonzo; captured Gorizia (1916); removed from command after defeat at Caporetto (Oct. 1917); field marshal (1924).

Ca·dou·dal \kȧ-dü-dȧl\, Georges. 1771–1804. French conspirator. A leader of Breton royalists and peasants in Chouan uprising (1799); implicated in plot formed by Pichegru and Moreau (1803); guillotined.

Cad·wal·adr \kad-'wäl-əd-ər\. d. 1172. Welsh prince. Son of Gruffudd, king of Gwynedd (North Wales). With older brother Owain Gwynedd conquered Aberystwyth, Ceredigion, Carmarthen (1136–38); expelled by Owain (1143); fled to Ireland; returned with army of Irish Danes but was reconciled to Owain without fighting; after further strife, fled to England; restored to his lands (1157) by Henry II.

Cad·wal·lon \kȧd-'wȧ-(h)lȯn, *Angl* kad-'wäl-ən\. d. 633. Welsh king of Gwynedd (c.625–633). Son of Cadfan; with Penda, king of Mercia, invaded Northumbria (632) and killed king Edwin in battle at Heathfield; ravaged the land; at Hexham slain by Edwin's nephew Oswald of Bernicia (633).

Cae·cil·ius \sə-'sil-ē-əs, -'sil-yəs\. 1st century A.D. Greek rhetorician. Only fragments of his works are extant, including *On the Style of the Ten Orators, History of the Servile Wars, On Rhetoric, On the Sublime, Against the Phrygians.*

Caecilius Sta·tius \-'stā-sh(ē-)əs\ *or* **Statius Caecilius.** c.219–166 B.C. Roman comic poet. Perhaps a slave by birth. His plays, extant only in fragments, were apparently mainly adapted from Menander; highly regarded by contemporaries.

Cae·ci·na \si-'sī-nə\. *In full* Aulus Caecina A·li·e·nus \ˌā-lē-'ē-nəs, ˌal-ē-\. d. 79 A.D. Roman general. After death of Nero (68 A.D.), supported Galba, and later Vitellius; commanded part of army of Vitellius in campaign in Italy and defeated Marcus Salvius Otho (69); consul (69); when confronted with Vespasian's army, turned traitor and attempted unsuccessfully to induce his contingents to desert to Vespasian. Involved in plot against Vespasian (79 A.D.); executed by Titus.

Caecus, Appius Claudius. See CLAUDIUS gens.

Caed·mon \'kad-mən\. fl. 658–680. English poet. A herdsman who, according to Bede, received divine call in a dream to sing of "the beginning of things"; put into verse Scriptural passages translated for him; accepted by Abbess Hilda as inmate of monastery at Whitby, where he continued to write poetry on sacred themes; earliest known English Christian poet, credited with paving way for English vernacular poetry. Original 9-line poem on Creation extant in several versions; other works doubtfully attributed to him, as *Genesis, Exodus, Daniel, Christ and Satan.*

Cae·li·us \'sē-lē-əs\. *In full* Marcus Caelius Ru·fus \'rü-fəs\. 82–48 B.C. Roman politician. Tribune (52 B.C.); aedile (50); friend and correspondent of Cicero, a number of his letters being preserved. Supported Caesar against Pompey; made praetor (48); deprived of office by Senate for unwise actions; joined Milo in insurrection against Caesar, in which he was killed. Best known from Cicero's defense of him in oration *Pro Caelio* against charge of attempted poisoning brought by Catullus's mistress.

Caelius Au·re·li·a·nus \ȯ-ˌrē-lē-'ā-nəs\. 5th century A.D. Roman physician of North Africa. Probably practiced in Rome. Author of *De morbis acutis et chronicis,* thorough exposition of classical medicine adapted in large part from Soranus of Ephesus; considered second only to Galen in line of Greco-Roman physicians and second only to Celsus as Latin medical writer.

Caesalpinus, Andreas. See Andrea CESALPINO.

Caesar, Crispus. See CRISPUS.

Caesar, Drusus. See DRUSUS gens.

Cae·sar \'sē-zər\, Gaius. 20 B.C.–4 A.D. Roman noble. Grandson of Emperor Augustus and son of M. Vipsanius Agrippa; adopted by Augustus (17 B.C.), making him probable successor to throne; proconsul on mission to Armenia (1 B.C.); mortally wounded while suppressing uprising there.

Caesar, Gallus. See GALLUS CAESAR.

Caesar, Germanicus. See GERMANICUS CAESAR.

Caesar, Julius, *in full* Gaius Julius. 100 B.C.–44 B.C. Roman general and statesman. Patrician by birth; m. (84 B.C.) Cornelia (d. 68?), daughter of Lucius Cinna, head of popular party in Rome; identified himself with popular party and became chief rival of Sulla, head of oligarchic party. Quaestor (68 B.C.); curule aedile (65); pontifex maximus (63); praetor (62); propraetor in Spain (61); m. Pompeia, a relative of Pompey. Succeeded in reconciling the two influential statesmen in Rome, Pompey and Crassus, and with them formed an alliance (First Triumvirate, 60); elected consul (59) and proconsul in Gaul and Illyricum (58); m. (59) Calpurnia. Made military reputation in Gaul (58–50), defeating the Helvetii and Ariovistus (58) and the Belgi (57), invading Britain (55, 54), crossing Rhine (55, 53), and subduing revolt under Vercingetorix (52). When senate, induced by Pompey, voted that he should disband his army by a given date or be regarded as an enemy to the state, led army across the Rubicon (49), small river that separated his province from Italy, and moved against Pompey in Rome, beginning actual fighting of civil war; quickly mastered all Italy; pursued Pompey to Thessaly and decisively defeated him at Pharsalus (48). Roman dictator (from 49); aided Cleopatra (49) and brought her to Rome; defeated Pharnaces at Zela (47) and remnants of Pompey's forces at Thapsus (46) and Munda (45). Offered the crown (Feb. 15, 44), but refused it. Murdered by group of nobles, including Brutus and Cassius, in senate building on ides of March (Mar. 15, 44). Renowned also as orator and writer; his works on the Gallic wars, *Commentarii de bello Gallico,* and civil war, *Commentarii de bello civili,* regarded as models of clear, concise, and vigorous historical composition. While head of Roman state, effected many reforms, including reform of the calendar (Julian calendar, introduced 46 B.C.); prevented by death from completing other reforms he planned, including codifying the law, draining Pontine marshes, enlarging harbor at Ostia, building canal through Isthmus of Corinth.

Caesar, Lucius Julius. d. 87 B.C. Roman politician. Consul (90 B.C.); secured passage of Julian Law, granting Roman citizenship to Italian allies. Distant cousin of Julius Caesar and grandfather of Mark Antony.

Cae·sar·i·us \sē-ˈzar-ē-əs\ of Arles \ˈär(-ə)l\. Saint. c.470–542. Gallic prelate. Took habit at Lérins (489); named bishop of Arles (502) by Pope Symmachus and thereby apostolic vicar of Gaul and Spain; presided over councils of Agde (506), Arles (524), Carpentras (527), Vaison and Orange (529), the last of which defended Augustinian doctrines and condemned Semi-Pelagianism; introduced many ecclesiastical reforms and founded several monasteries.

Caesarius of **Hei·ster·bach** \ˈhī-stər-ˌbäk\. c.1170–c.1240. German religious. Cistercian monk of Cologne; author of works on history of Cologne, as *Catalogus archiepiscoporum Coloniensium,* biographies of St. Elizabeth of Hungary and Archbishop Engelbert of Cologne, collections of miscellaneous stories, as *Dialogus Miraculorum* and *VIII Libri Miraculorum.*

Ca·e·ta·ni \ˌkä-ā-ˈtän-ē\ *or* **Ga·e·ta·ni** \ˌgä-\. Italian noble family, prominent since election (1294) of Benedetto Caetani to papacy (see BONIFACE VIII). The Anagni branch of family gained titles as dukes of Anagni, Sermoneta, Fondi, and Piedmont. Prominent members included: ¶Onorato I (1337–1408), count of Fon·di \ˈfōn-dē\; host to conclave of dissident French cardinals who elected antipope Clement VII (1378); held virtually absolute power until defeated by Pope Boniface IX and King Ladislas of Naples (1400). ¶Michelangelo (1804–1852), duke of Ser·mo·ne·ta \ˌsār-mō-ˈnā-tä\; minister of police in papal government (1848); noted Dante scholar, author of *La materia della Divina Commedia* (1865). His grandson ¶Leone (1869–1935), duke of Sermoneta and prince of Te·ano \tā-ˈän-ō\; noted scholar of Islām, author of *Annali del'Islam* (1904–26); deputy in parliament (1909–13).

Caf·fa·ro di Cas·chi·fel·lone \kä-ˈfär-ō-dē-ˌkäs-kē-fāl-ˈlō-nā\. c.1080–1166. Genoese soldier and chronicler. In First Crusade took part in siege of Caesarea (1101); later served in wars with Pisa, Saracens; 5 times consul of Genoese commune; ambassador to pope, Barcelona, Castile, Frederick I Barbarossa. Author of chronicle of Genoese affairs (1101–63) and of histories of Genoese campaigns in First Crusade and in Spain.

Caf·fié·ri \käf-yā-rē\. Family of French sculptors of Italian origin, including: Filippo *or* Philippe (1634–1716); in service of Pope Alexander VII and (from 1660) Cardinal Mazarin and then Louis XIV. His son ¶Jacques (1678–1755) executed vigorous Rococo decorations for Versailles and other royal residences (from 1736). Succeeded as royal sculptor by his son ¶Philippe (1714–1774); executed new altar furniture for Notre Dame de Paris (1759). Philippe's younger brother ¶Jean-Jacques (1725–1792) was sculptor to Louis XV; executed ornamental metalwork for staircase of Palais Royale, busts of Molière, Corneille, etc.; rival of Houdon in popularity.

Ca·glio·stro \käl-ˈyȯs-trō\, Alessandro di Conte. *Orig.* Giuseppe Bal·sa·mo \ˈbäl-sä-(ˌ)mō\. 1743–1795. Italian adventurer. Traveled throughout Europe selling an "elixir of long life"; practiced various forms of soothsaying and charlatanry; assumed title of count; in Italy, married Lorenza Feliciani, who accompanied and assisted him. In London, posed as founder of a kind of freemasonry; in Paris, involved, with Cardinal de Rohan (*q.v.*) and others, in affair of the diamond necklace and confined in Bastille; imprisoned in Rome.

Cag·ney \ˈcag-nē\, James. 1904–1986. American actor, b. New York City. Known esp. for playing gangsters and cocky tough guys. Among his films were *Public Enemy* (1931), *The Crowd Roars* (1932), *Angels with Dirty Faces* (1938), *The Fighting 69th* (1940), *Strawberry Blonde* (1940), *Yankee Doodle Dandy* (1942), *Mister Roberts* (1955), *One, Two, Three* (1961), *Ragtime* (1981).

Ca·gniard de la Tour \kån-yår-də-lå-tür\, Charles. 1777–1859. French engineer and physicist. Inventor of the *cagniardelle,* a forced-draft blowing machine, and of a siren used for determining number of vibrations corresponding to sounds of various pitches.

Ca·gno·la \kän-ˈyō-lä\, Luigi. 1762–1833. Italian architect. Known esp. for his two triumphal arches in Milan, Porta Di Marengo and Arco della Pace, the latter surpassed in size only by Arc de Triomphe, Paris; other works included the campanile at Urgnano and chapel of Santa Marcellina in Milan.

Ca·han \ˈkä-hån, *Angl* ˈkä-ˌhan\, Abraham. 1860–1951. American journalist and author, b. Vilna, Lithuania. To U.S. (1882); with Morris Hillquit founded New York Yiddish weekly *Arbeiter Zeitung* (1886), editor (1890–97); helped found (1897), editor (1897, 1902, 1903–51), *Jewish Daily Forward.* Author of novels *Yekl: A Tale of the New York Ghetto* (1896), *The Imported Bridegroom* (1898), *The White Terror and the Red* (1905), *Rise of David Levinsky* (1917); autobiography *Bleter fun mayn lebn* (1926–31).

Ca·hill \ˈkā-ˌhil\, Thaddeus. 1867–1934. American inventor, b. Mt. Zion, Iowa. Invented electric typewriter and the telharmonium (built 1895–1906), pioneer attempt to produce music electronically.

Cail·laux \kå-yō\, Joseph-Marie-Auguste. 1863–1944. French politician. Joined finance ministry (1886); member of chamber of deputies (1898–1917); minister of finance (1899–1902, 1906–09, 1911); premier of France (1911–12); negotiated for French protectorate over Morocco in exchange for concessions to Germany in Central Africa; again minister of finance (1913–14); accused of financial irregularities in office by editor of *Le Figaro,* Gaston Calmette, who was afterwards shot and killed in his office by Caillaux's wife (1914); opposed war preparations and advocated policy of making peace with Germany during World War I; arrested (Dec. 1917) and convicted (1920) of having had correspondence with the enemy; in prison (1920–23); granted amnesty (1924); again finance minister (1925); senator (1927–40), head of Commission of Finance (1927–40). Author of *Les Responsables* (1915), *Devant l'histoire, ma procès* (1921), *Où va la France, où va l'Europe?* (1922).

Cail·la·vet \kå-yå-ve\, Gaston Ar·man de \år-mäⁿ-də-\. 1869–1915. French journalist and playwright. Collaborator with R. de Flers in a number of comic operas and comedies, including *Les Travaux d'Hercule* (1901), *Paris ou le Bon Juge* (1906), *Le Roi* (also with E. Arène, 1908), *Le Bois sacré* (1910), *L'Habit vert* (1912), *La Belle aventure* (1913).

Cail·le·tet \kåy-te\, Louis-Paul. 1832–1913. French physicist. Made notable studies in metallurgy, esp. of gases produced in blast furnaces; first succeeded (1877–78) in liquefying oxygen, nitrogen, hydrogen, etc.

Cail·lié *or* **Cail·lé** \kå-yā\, René-Auguste. 1799–1838. French explorer. In order to reach Timbuktu from Senegal, learned Arabic, studied as convert to Islām, posed as Arab from Egypt, and joined caravan going inland; reached Timbuktu a year later (1827–28); first European to return from Timbuktu.

Cain \ˈkān\, James Mallahan. 1892–1977. American journalist and novelist, b. Annapolis, Md. Author of violent melodramas in "hard-boiled" manner, including *The Postman Always Rings Twice* (1934; dramatized 1936, filmed 1946), *Double Indemnity* (1936, film 1944), *Serenade* (1937), *Mildred Pierce* (1941, film 1945), *The Butterfly* (1947), *The Moth* (1948), *Root of His Evil* (1954), *Magician's Wife* (1965), *Rainbow's End* (1975).

Cain, Richard Harvey. 1825–1887. American clergyman and politician, b. Greenbrier Co., Va. Joined African Methodist Episcopal Church (about 1844); ordained (1862). Member, U.S. House of Representatives (1873–75, 1877–79). Bishop (1880) of Louisiana and Texas diocese.

Caine \ˈkān\, Sir Hall, *in full* Thomas Henry Hall. 1853–1931. English novelist. Secretary to Dante G. Rossetti (1881–82). Author of *Shadow of a Crime* (1885), *Son of Hagar* (1886), *The Deemster* (1887), *The Bondman* (1890), *The Manxman* (1894), *The Christian* (1897), *Eternal City* (1901), *Prodigal Son* (1904), *The Woman Thou Gavest Me* (1913), *The Master of Man* (1921), and *Life of Christ* (1938).

Caird \ˈka(ə)rd, ˈke(ə)rd\, Edward. 1835–1908. Scottish philosopher and theologian. Professor of moral philosophy, Glasgow (1866–93); succeeded Jowett as master of Balliol Coll., Oxford (1893–1907); with T. H. Green, founded English neo-Hegelian school of philosophy; advocate of higher education for women. Author of *Philosophy of Kant* (1877), *Hegel* (1883), *Social Philosophy and Religion of Comte* (1885), *Evolution of Religion* (1893), *Evolution of Theology in the Greek Philosophers* (1904). His brother ¶John

(1820–1898), clergyman and philosopher; professor of theology, Glasgow (1862); principal (1873); author of *An Introduction to the Philosophy of Religion* (1880) and *Fundamental Ideas of Christianity* (1899), expounding Hegel, and *Spinoza* (1888).

Cairnes \'ka(ə)rnz, 'ke(ə)rnz\, John Elliott. 1823–1875. Irish economist. Professor of political economy at Dublin (1856–61), Galway (1861–66), U. Coll., London (1866–72); sometimes regarded as last of classical economists. Author of *Character and Logical Method of Political Economy* (1857), *The Slave Power* (1862), *Essays in Political Economy* (1873).

Cairns \'ka(ə)rnz, 'ke(ə)rnz\, Hugh McCalmont. 1st Earl Cairns. 1819–1885. British politician, b. Ireland. M.P. (1852–67); solicitor general (1858); in Parliament won reputation by brilliant speeches (1858); attorney general and lord justice of appeal (1866); created baron (1867); lord chancellor (1868–69), leader of Conservative party in House of Lords (1869–74); opposed disestablishment of Irish church and Irish land bill (1870); again lord chancellor (1874–80); raised to earl (1878).

Cai·ro·li \kī-'rȯ-lē\, Benedetto. 1825–1889. Italian politician. Served with Garibaldi; deputy (1860–69, 1867–70); prime minister of Italy (1878, 1879, 1880–81); a leader of, but unable to control, extreme left; forced to resign following loss of Tunisia to France in Treaty of Bardo (1881).

Cai·tan·ya \kī-'tän-yə\. *Also known as* Gau·ran·ga \gau̇-'rəŋ-gə\. *Orig.* Viś-vam·bha·ra Miś·ra \vish-'vəm-bə-rə-'mish-rə\. 1485–1533. Indian Hindu mystic. A Brahmin; underwent mystic experience (1507); formally initiated as ascetic and took name Śrī Kṛṣṇa Caitanya (1510); settled at Puri, attracted many disciples to his emotionally intense form of worship of Lord Kṛṣṇa; movement continued to flourish.

Caithness, Earls of. See SINCLAIR family.

Caius. See GAIUS.

Caius \'kēz, 'kāz\, John. *Surname also spelled* Kees \'kāz\, Keys \'kāz\, Kay \'kā\, *or* Kaye \'kā\. 1510–1573. English physician and Humanist. Educ. Gonville Hall, Cambridge. Studied medicine under Vesalius at Padua; lecturer on anatomy, London (1544–64); one of physicians to Edward VI, Mary Tudor, Elizabeth. Enlarged and refounded his old college as Gonville and Caius College (1557); master (1559–73). Author of critical, antiquarian, and scientific works, esp. classic *Boke or Counseill against the Disease commonly called the Sweate, or Sweatyng Sicknesse* (1552).

Cajetan. See Tommaso de VIO.

Caj·e·tan \'kaj-ə-,tan\ of Thie·ne \'tyen-(,)ā\. Saint. *Ital.* Ga·e·ta·no da Thie·ne \,gä-ā-'tän-ō-dä-'tyen-ā\. 1480–1547. Italian religious. Prothonotary in Roman Curia (1506); ordained (1516); member of Oratory of Divine Love; with Gian Pietro Carafa (later Pope Paul IV) and others founded (1524) Congregation of Clerics Regular, later known as Theatines; superior of Theatines in Naples (from 1533). Canonized (1671).

Ca·ji·gal de la Ve·ga \kä-ke-'gäl-dā-lä-'bā-gä\, Francisco Antonio. 1695–1777. Spanish colonial governor. Governor of Santiago, Cuba (1738–47); repelled attack of English fleet under Admiral Vernon (1741); governor general of Cuba (1747–60); viceroy pro tem of Mexico (1760–61).

Ca·jo·ri \kī-'ōr-ē\, Florian. 1859–1930. American mathematician, b. St. Aignan, Switzerland. To U.S. (1875); professor, Tulane (1885–88); professor of physics (1889–98), mathematics (1898–1918), dean of engineering (1903–18), Colorado Coll.; professor of history of mathematics, U. of California (from 1918). Author of *History of Mathematics* (1919), *History of Mathematical Notations* (1928–29), etc.

Çak·mak \chäk-'mäk\, Fevzi. 1876–1950. Turkish soldier and politician. Entered army (1895); commander of Ottoman troops in Dardanelles, Caucasus, Syria in World War I; general (1914); minister of war (1920); resigned to join nationalist movement of Kemal Attatürk; prime minister and minister of defense of Grand National Assembly government (1920–22); marshal (1921); chief of staff of army (1922–44); member of assembly (1946–48).

Čak·ste \'chäk-ste\, Janis. 1859–1927. Latvian politician. Chairman of people's council (1918) after proclamation of Latvian republic; president, Latvian constituent assembly (1920). Unanimously elected first president of Latvia (1922); reelected (1925).

Calabrese, Il (Cavaliere). See Mattia PRETI.

Cal·a·mis \'kal-ə-məs\. 5th century B.C. Greek sculptor. Carved statues of various deities, as Apollo, Aphrodite, Hermes; noted for equestrian statues.

Calamity Jane. See Martha Jane BURK.

Cal·a·my \'kal-ə-mē\, Edmund. 1600–1666. English clergyman. Attached himself to Calvinist party; resigned church office on enforcement of ceremonial observances (1636); active defender of Presbyterian cause; one of principal authors of *Smectymnuus* (1641), assailing Bishop Joseph Hall's claim of divine right of episcopacy; opposed execution of Charles I; declined bishopric at Restoration; expelled from ministry under Act of Uniformity (1662). His grandson ¶ Edmund (1671–1732), also a Nonconformist minister, wrote *Account of the Ejected Ministers* (1702).

Ca·las \kȧ-läs\, Jean. 1698–1762. French merchant. A Huguenot; on basis of much hearsay evidence, judicially convicted on a charge of murdering his son Marc-Antoine (a suicide) to prevent the son from becoming a Roman Catholic; executed by being broken on the wheel. Through efforts of Voltaire, case became a cause célèbre.

Cal·a·sanz \'kal-ə-,sänz\ *or* **Ca·la·san·za** \kä-lä-'sän-thä\, José. Saint. *Lat.* Joseph Cal·a·sanc·tius \,kal-ə-'saŋ(k)-sh(ē-)əs\. 1556–1648. Spanish cleric and educator. Ordained (1583); to Rome (1592); opened (1597) first free school for poor children in Europe; gathered community of teaching religious and formed (1617) Order of Poor Clerks Regular of the Mother of God of the Pious Schools, known as Piarists; superior of order (1621–43). Canonized (1767) by Clement XIII; patron saint of all Roman Catholic schools.

Cal·car *or* **Kal·kar** \'käl-kär\, Jan Stephan van. c.1499–after 1545. Flemish painter and woodcut artist. His works included illustrations for anatomical work of Vesalius *De humani corporis fabrica* (1543), and imitations of works of Titian and Raphael.

Cal·da·ra \käl-'dä-rä\, Antonio. 1670–1736. Italian composer. Assistant Kapellmeister, under Fux, to Emperor Charles VI in Vienna (from 1716); composed over 70 operas, much other theatrical music, 43 oratorios, chamber and church music, etc.

Caldara, Polidoro. *Known as* Polidoro da Ca·ra·vag·gio \dä-,kä-rä-'väd-jō\. c.1500–1543. Italian painter, b. Caravaggio. Known esp. as painter of frescoes and other decorations; with Maturino da Firenze decorated S. Silvestro al Quirinale, Rome; considered an authority on idealized landscape.

Caldecote, Viscount. See Thomas INSKIP.

Cal·de·cott \'kȯl-də-kət\, Randolph. 1846–1886. English artist and illustrator. Did illustrations for Washington Irving's *Old Christmas* (1876) and *Bracebridge Hall* (1877), *The House That Jack Built* (1878), *Aesop's Fables* (1883) and other children's books; contributed to *Punch* and *Graphic*. Caldecott Medal named for him (1938).

Cal·der \'kȯl-dər\, Alexander Milne. 1846–1923. American sculptor, b. Aberdeen, Scotland. Orig. a stonecutter; worked on Albert Memorial, London; to U.S. (1868); works included colossal statue of William Penn for Philadelphia City Hall (1894), equestrian statue of Gen. Meade, etc. His son ¶Alexander Stirling (1870–1945), b. Philadelphia, also a sculptor; known esp. for portrait studies and memorial statues, as of Marcus Whitman, George Washington for Washington Square Arch, New York City, *St. George of Princeton,* Leif Ericsson in Reykjavik, Iceland, Walt Whitman. His son ¶Alexander (1898–1976), b. Philadelphia, also a sculptor; developed wire sculpture, esp. in a collection of circus animals and performers; developed motor-driven (c.1931) and then (1932) freely moving constructions of sculptured elements termed (by Marcel Duchamp) mobiles; made non-moving similar works termed (by Jean Arp) stabiles; created mobiles and stabiles in monumental size for numerous public commissions.

Calderón, Francisco García. See GARCÍA CALDERÓN.

Cal·de·rón \käl-dā-'rōn\, Rodrigo. Conde de Oli·va \ō-'lē-bä\, Marqués de Sie·te Igle·si·as \sē-'ā-tā-ē-'glā-zē-əs\. 1576?–1621. Spanish courtier. Follower of the duque de Lerma, royal favorite of Philip III; became object of enemies of Lerma; on Lerma's death (1618) imprisoned and tortured; after Philip's death (1621), hanged. His haughty behavior on scaffold became proverbial.

Calderón, Serafín Estébanez. See ESTÉBANEZ CALDERÓN.

Calderón de la Bar·ca \-dā-lä-'bär-kä\, Pedro. 1600–1681. Spanish dramatist and poet. Began writing plays for royal court (1623); created knight, Order of Santiago (1636), by Philip IV; served in campaign against Catalan rebels (1640–42); in service of Duke of Alba (1645–50). Entered Order of St. Francis (1650), priest (1651); honorary chaplain to Philip IV (1663). Successor to Lope de Vega as chief Spanish dramatist of the day. Works included over 100 *comedias,* including several *zarzuelas* and operas, as: *La cisma de Ingalaterra* (c.1627), *El principe constante* (1629), *La dama duende* (1629), *Casa con dos puertas, mala es de guardar* (1629), *La banda y la flor* (1632), *Amar después de la muerte* (1633), *La vida es sueño* (1635), *Las tres justicias en una* (c.1637), *El mágico prodigioso* (1637), *No hay cosa como callar* (1639), *No siempre lo peor es cierto* (c.1640), *El pintor de su deshonra* (c.1645), *El jardín de Falerina* (1648), *La hija del aire* (1653), *La púrpura de la rosa* (1660), *Celos, aun del aire matan* (1660); also wrote 76 known autos sacramentales, allegorical religious plays for Madrid's feast of Corpus Christi.

Cal·der·wood \'kȯl-dər-,wu̇d\, David. 1575–1650. Scottish clergyman. Banished to Holland (1619–24) for refusing to surrender roll of signatures to a remonstrance; defended Presbyterianism in *The Altar of Damascus* (1621); author of a *History of the Kirk of Scotland* (abridged edition pub. 1678).

Ca·le·nus \kə-'lē-nəs\, Quintus Fufius. d. 41 B.C. Roman general. Tribune of people (61 B.C.); praetor (59); served under Julius Caesar in Gaul (51) and Spain (49); consul (47). Joined Mark Antony after Caesar's death and commanded Antony's forces in north Italy; died while preparing to attack Octavian.

Ca·le·pi·no \,kä-lā-'pē-nō\, Ambrogio. c.1440–1510. Italian lexicographer. Augustinian monk; his Latin–Italian dictionary (1502) developed in successive editions and enlargements into a polyglot of eleven languages including Polish and Hungarian (1590), re-edited by Facciolati (*q.v.*) as a seven-language polyglot (1718) and by Egidio Forcellini as *Totius Latinitatis Lexicon* (1771). Hence the term *calepin* for a dictionary.

Calgacus. See Galgacus.

Cal·houn \\(ˈ)kal-ˈhün\\, John Caldwell. 1782–1850. American politician, b. Abbeville district, S.C. Member, U.S. House of Representatives (1811–17); associate of Clay and a leader of "War Hawks"; U.S. secretary of war (1817–25). Vice president of U.S. (1825–32). Champion of states' rights; instrumental in guiding South Carolina policy during nullification crisis (1832–33); resigned vice presidency to enter Senate (1832–43). U.S. secretary of state (1844–45). U.S. senator (1845–50). Champion of slavery and southern cause in Senate debates. Author of "South Carolina Exposition and Protest" (1828), *Disquisition on Government* (1851), *Discourse on the Constitution and Government of the United States* (1851).

Ca·lia·ri \\käl-ˈyä-rē\\, Paolo. *Known as* Paolo Ve·ro·ne·se \\ˌvā-rō-ˈnā-zā\\. 1528–1588. Italian painter, b. Verona. To Venice (1553); engaged in decoration of Palazzo Ducale, priory of S. Sebastiano; collaborated with Palladio on Villa Barbaro at Maser (1561). A chief painter of Venetian school; works notable for large scale, large number of figures, rich color, illusionist composition, frequently for architectural frames. Paintings included *Marriage at Cana, Anointment of David, Pilgrims of Emmaus, Feast in the House of Levi, Adoration of the Magi, Choice of Hercules, Mars and Venus.*

Ca·lig·u·la \\kə-ˈlig-yə-lə\\. *Orig.* Gaius Caesar. 12 A.D.–41 A.D. Roman emperor (37–41). Youngest son of Germanicus Caesar (nephew of Tiberius) and Agrippina; brought up in camps among soldiers; nicknamed Caligula, i.e. Little Boots, in youth. Declared heir to throne by Tiberius; for a short time ruled with moderation; restored treason trials (38), executed Naevius Sertorius Macro, prefect of Praetorian Guard; exhibited erratic and cruel behavior, later exaggerated by historians; murdered by members of praetorian cohorts led by Chaerea.

Că·li·ne·scu \\kə-lē-ˈnes-kü\\, Armand. 1893–1939. Romanian politician. Leader in National Peasant party; minister of interior (1937–39); under orders from King Carol, endeavored to suppress fascist Iron Guards; premier of Romania (March 1939); slain by Iron Guardists.

Calippus. See Callippus.

Ca·lix·tus \\kə-ˈlik-stəs\\ *or* **Cal·lis·tus** \\kə-ˈlis-təs\\. Name of three popes and an antipope:

Calixtus I. Saint. d. 222. Pope (217/218–222). Orig. a slave in Sardinian mines; ordained by Pope St. Zephyrinus, whom he succeeded; election opposed by Hippolytus, who became first antipope; condemned and excommunicated Sabellius; established Catholic Cemetery of Calixtus; martyred.

Calixtus II. *Orig.* Guido di Bor·gogne \\bȯr-gōnʸ, bu̇r-\\. d. 1124. Pope (1119–24). Son of William, Count of Burgundy; archbishop of Vienne (1088); opposed policies of Emperor Henry V; presided over synod at Vienne that excommunicated Henry; elected at Cluny, France, to succeed Pope Gelasius II (1119); at synod in Reims again excommunicated Henry and Henry's antipope Gregory VIII (1119); made Concordat of Worms (1122) with Henry; convoked first Lateran Council (1123).

Calixtus III. *Orig.* Alfonso de Bor·gia *or* Bor·ja \\ˈbȯr-jə\\. 1378–1458. Pope (1455–58). Bishop of Valencia (1429); made cardinal (1444) by Pope Martin V for having reconciled pope and King Alfonso V of Aragon; elected pope as compromise between Orsini and Colonna families; strove to raise crusade to capture Constantinople from Turks; instituted (1457) feast of the Transfiguration; lavished preferments on nephew Rodrigo Borgia (later Pope Alexander VI).

Calixtus III. *Orig.* Giovanni di Stru·mi \\ˈstrü-mē\\. 12th century. Antipope (1168–78). Successor to antipope Paschal III in opposition to Pope Alexander III; refused to abdicate following Treaty of Anagni (1176) between his patron Frederick I Barbarossa and Alexander; finally submitted to Alexander.

Ca·lix·tus \\kä-ˈlik-stu̇s\\ *or* **Ca·lixt** \\kä-ˈlikst\\, Georg. *Orig. surname* Cal·li·sen \\ˈkäl-ē-zən\\. 1586–1656. German Lutheran theologian. Traveled extensively in Europe and England and became acquainted with leading reformers; professor of theology, Helmstedt (after 1614). Upheld reunion of Lutheran and Reformed Protestant sects with each other and with Roman Catholic Church, and became a central figure in syncretistic controversy with orthodox opponents.

Cal·kins \\ˈkȯ-kənz\\, Mary Whiton. 1863–1930. American philosopher and psychologist, b. Hartford, Conn. Taught at Wellesley (1891–1930); her works included *Der doppelte Standpunkt in der Psychologie* (1905), *The Persistent Problems of Philosophy* (1907), *The Good Man and the Good* (1918).

Cal·las \\ˈkal-əs, ˈkäl-\\, Maria. *Orig.* Maria Anna Sofia Cecilia Ka·lo·ge·ro·pou·los \\ˌkä-lò-yer-ˈò-pü-lòs\\. 1923–1977. American singer, b. New York City. Debuts in Athens (1947), La Scala (1950), Chicago (1954), New York (1956); noted esp. for dramatic force; revived art of coloratura soprano and helped restore bel canto repertoire.

Call·cott \\ˈkȯl-kət\\, Sir Augustus Wall. 1779–1844. English painter. Surveyor of royal pictures (1834). Exhibited landscapes, as *The Mouth of the Tyne* (1818), and figure paintings as *Milton Dictating to his Daughter* (1840). His brother ¶John Wall (1766–1821), musician and composer; author of *Musical Grammar* (1806); known for his glees and catches, as *O beauteous fair* and *Dull repining sons of care.*

Cal·le·ja del Rey \\kä(l)-ˈyek-ä-t͟hel-ˈre-ē\\, Félix María. Conde de Cal·de·rón \\käl-dā-ˈrȯn\\. 1755?–1828. Spanish general. To Mexico (1789); defeated Hidalgo at Puente de Calderón, near Guadalajara (1811), and Hidalgo's successor Morelos; known for his cruel treatment of prisoners; viceroy of Mexico (1813–16).

Cal·len·dar \\ˈkal-ən-dər\\, Hugh Longbourne. 1863–1930. English physicist. Professor, McGill U., Montreal (1893–98), University Coll., London (1898–1902), Imperial Coll. of Science, London (1902–30). Known for investigations relating to steam and to thermometry; invented platinum resistance thermometer (1886), compensated air thermometer (1891), and a radio balance (1910). Author of *Callendar Steam Tables* (1915) and *Properties of Steam and Thermodynamic Theory of Turbines* (1920).

Cal·les \\ˈkä-yās\\, Plutarco Elías. 1877–1945. Mexican soldier and politician. Schoolteacher, farmer, and tradesman in Sonora; soldier under Obregón and Carranza (1913–15); effective in reorganization and modernization of army; governor of Sonora (1917–19); held cabinet positions under Carranza (1919–20) and Obregón (1920–24). President of Mexico (1924–28); carried out agrarian reforms; administration marked by struggle between church and state; founded (1929) Partido Nacional Revolucionario and through it controlled succeeding presidents; broke with Pres. Cárdenas; in exile in U.S., (1936–41).

Cal·li·as \\ˈkal-ē-əs\\. 5th century B.C. Athenian soldier and diplomat. Fought at Marathon (490 B.C.); credited with negotiating Peace of Callias with Persia (449/448); perhaps also helped negotiate Thirty Years' Treaty (445) between Athens and Sparta. His grandson ¶Callias commanded Athenian infantry in victory at Corinth (390 B.C.); headed mission to Sparta which negotiated peace (371); ridiculed in youth by Aristophanes for his extravagance.

Cal·lic·ra·tes *or* **Kal·lik·ra·tes** \\kə-ˈlik-rə-ˌtēz\\. 5th century B.C. Greek architect. Collaborated with Ictinus in designing the Parthenon (completed 438 B.C.); designed temple of Athena Nike on Acropolis (completed 424).

Cal·li·crat·i·das \\ˌkal-ə-ˈkrat-əd-əs\\. d. 406 B.C. Spartan admiral. Succeeded Lysander (406 B.C.); killed at battle of Arginusae.

Cal·lières \\kȧl-yer\\, François de. 1645–1717. French diplomat. Undertook numerous diplomatic missions for Louis XIV; made cabinet secretary (1698). Author of classic treatise on diplomacy, *De la manière de négocier avec les souverains* (1716). His brother ¶Louis-Hector (1648–1703), soldier, was governor of Montreal (1684–99), governor of New France (1699–1703).

Cal·lim·a·chus \\kə-ˈlim-ə-kəs\\. 5th century B.C. Greek sculptor. Reputed inventor of the Corinthian column; also reputedly first to use the running drill in carving folds in drapery, etc.

Callimachus. c.305–c.240 B.C. Greek scholar and poet. Cataloguer of royal library of Alexandria. Author of *Hymns,* some 60 extant *Epigrams,* small-scale epic *Hecale,* polemical *Ibis,* elegies, narrative *Aetia* later the model for Ovid's *Metamorphoses;* also influenced Catullus.

Callinicus. See Seleucus II.

Cal·li·ni·cus \\ˌkal-ə-ˈnī-kəs\\. *Also known as* Callinicus of Heliopolis. 7th century A.D. Syrian Jewish architect. Credited with invention of Greek fire, used in burning Saracen fleet in battle of Cyzicus, off Constantinople (c.673).

Cal·li·nus \\kə-ˈlī-nəs\\. 7th century B.C. Greek poet. Author of political and martial elegies. Only a few fragments extant.

Cal·lip·pus *or* **Ca·lip·pus** \\kə-ˈlip-əs\\. 4th century B.C. Greek astronomer. Improved on Eudoxus's studies of planetary motion; instituted Callippic cycle, a period of 76 years, equal to 4 Metonic cycles minus a day, harmonizing solar and lunar cycles.

Callisen, Georg. See Georg Calixtus.

Cal·lis·the·nes \\kə-ˈlis-thə-ˌnēz\\. *Also called* Callisthenes of Olynthus. c.360–328 B.C. Greek philosopher and historian. Nephew and disciple of Aristotle; accompanied Alexander the Great on eastern expedition; criticized Alexander for adopting Oriental ways; imprisoned; died in prison. Author of a history of Greece from 386 to 355, and other historical works, none extant.

Cal·lis·tra·tus \\kə-ˈlis-trət-əs\\. d. 355 B.C. Athenian orator and general. His brilliant defense of his policy in allowing the Thebans to occupy Oropus on their promise (later violated) to surrender it on demand influenced Demosthenes to study oratory; executed.

Callistus. See also Calixtus.

Cal·lis·tus I \kə-ˈlis-təs\. d. 1363. Greek prelate. Monk of Mt. Athos; adherent of Hesychasm; patriarch of Constantinople (1350–53); convened synod (1351) that approved Hesychasm; forced to resign on refusal to crown Matthew Cantacuzenus; resumed patriarchate (1354–63); excommunicated Stefan Dušan and reasserted authority over churches of Serbia, Bulgaria, Hungary.

Cal·lot \ka-lō\, Jacques. 1592 or 1593–1635. French painter and engraver. Portrayed pageants of Medici court of Florence; employed by Duke of Lorraine (from c.1612); etched genre sketches; first artist to raise etching to an independent art; noted also for landscape drawings. His famous etchings included *Pont-Neuf, Madonna of the Impruneta,* the series *Capricci* and *Le Gueux,* and two series of *Misères de guerre* (1632, 1633).

Cal·mette \kàl-met\, Albert-Léon-Charles. 1863–1933. French bacteriologist. Founder (1891) and director (1891–93) of Pasteur bacteriological institute at Saigon; founder (1896) and director (1896–1919) of Pasteur Institute at Lille; with Camille Guérin developed (c.1921) Bacillus Calmette-Guérin (BCG) vaccine for vaccination of children against tuberculosis. His brother ¶Gaston (1858–1914) was editor of *Figaro* (1903–14); launched editorial campaign against Joseph Caillaux (1914) and threatened to publish letters of Mme. Caillaux, formerly his mistress; shot by Mme. Caillaux.

Ca·lo·mar·de \kä-lō-ˈmär-thā\, Francisco Tadeo. 1773–1842. Spanish politician. Staunch supporter of Ferdinand VII; occupied posts in council for Indies and in ministry of justice (1814–15); minister of justice (1823–32); fled to France (1833) after unsuccessful attempt to insure succession of Don Carlos to Spanish throne.

Ca·lonne \kà-lȯn\, Charles-Alexandre de. 1734–1802. French politician. Intendant of Metz (1768) and Lille (1774); controller general of finance (1783); found state treasury in hopeless disorder; began policy of display and new loans which after three years (1784–86) reached absolute limits; opened Assembly of Notables (1787) to consider his proposed taxation of nobles and clergy; opposed, removed from office. Lived in England (1787–1802); chief adviser to émigrés (1790–92); allowed by Napoléon to return to France (1802).

Ca·lov \ˈkäl-ˌȯf\, Abraham. *Orig. surname* Ka·lau \ˈkäl-ˌau̇\. *Lat.* Ca·lo·vi·us \kə-ˈlō-vē-əs\. 1612–1686. German theologian. Professor, Wittenberg (from 1650); championed Lutheran orthodoxy; attacked esp. the syncretism of Calixtus; opposed Calvinists, Arminians, Socinians, and Pietists. Author of *Systema locorum theologicorum* (12 vols., 1655–77).

Calprenède. See La Calprenède.

Cal·pur·nia \kal-ˈpər-nē-ə\. 1st century B.C. Roman noblewoman. Daughter of L. Calpurnius Piso; m. (59 B.C.) Julius Caesar; endeavored to dissuade him from going to senate on day of his assassination.

Calpurnius Bestia. See Bestia.

Calpurnius Piso. See Piso.

Cal·pur·ni·us Sic·u·lus \kal-ˈpər-nē-ə-ˌsik-yə-ləs\, Titus. 1st century A.D. Roman poet. Of his works, 7 pastoral eclogues, a panegyric on Gaius Calpurnius Piso (perhaps his father), and a few fragments are extant.

Cā·luk·ya \ˈkä-(ˌ)lək-yə\. Name of two dynasties of ancient India. Western Cālukyas reigned as emperors in the Deccan (543–757 and c.975–c.1189); see Pulakeśin. Eastern Cālukyas reigned in Vengi (c.624–c.1070).

Cal·vaert *or* **Cal·vart** \ˈkäl-värt\, Denis *or* Denys. *Called in Fr.* De·nis le Fla·mand \də-nē-lə-flä-mäⁿ\; *Ital.* Dionisio Fi·am·min·go \ˌfē-ä-ˈmiŋ-gō\. 1540–1619. Flemish painter. Worked in Bologna and Rome; influential as a teacher.

Cal·vé \kàl-vā\, Emma. *Orig.* Rosa-Noémie-Emma Cal·vet de Ro·quer \kàl-ved-ə-rȯ-kā\. 1858–1942. French singer. Made debut at Brussels (1881) as Marguerite in *Faust;* sang thereafter in Paris, Italy, England, Spain, Russia, and U.S.; especially successful in roles in *Cavalleria rusticana, Sapho, Carmen.*

Cal·ver·ley \ˈkal-vər-lē\, Charles Stuart. 1831–1884. English poet and parodist. Best known for his humorous verse, as in *Verses and Translations* (1862) and *Fly Leaves* (1872); rendered Theocritus into scholarly English verse (1869).

Cal·vert \ˈkal-vərt\, George. 1st Baron Bal·ti·more \ˈbȯl-tə-ˌmō(ə)r, -ˌmȯ(ə)r, -mər\. 1580?–1632. English politician and colonialist. M.P. (1609–25); secretary of state and member of Privy Council (1619); announced conversion to Roman Catholic faith (1625); resigned secretaryship of state; created baron (1625). Founded colony in Ferryland in Newfoundland (1621); obtained charter for renamed Avalon (1623) and bought family there (1628); objected to it because of climate; granted territory comprising what is now Maryland (1632), but died before charter was issued. Charter issued (1632) to his son ¶Cecilius (1605–1675), 2d baron, who established Maryland colony. George's second son ¶Leonard (1606–1647) brought out two shiploads of colonists (1634); governor of Maryland province (1634–47). Cecilius's son ¶Charles (1637–1715), 3rd baron, was governor of Maryland (1661–75) and proprietor (1675–89); deprived on accession of William and Mary.

Cal·vin \ˈkal-vən\, John. *Orig.* Jean Cau·vin \kō-vaⁿ\. 1509–1564. French theologian and reformer. Published (1532) edition of Seneca's *De clementia* with commentary; adopted Protestantism and left Paris (1534); settled in Basel, Switzerland, where he published his famous *Christianae religionis Institutio* (1536; translated as *Institutes of the Christian Religion*). To Geneva (1536); joined Farel in trying to establish theocratic government over city; driven out by popular revolt (1538); retired to Strassburg as professor and pastor of its French church. Recalled to Geneva (1541), succeeded in establishing organized Reformed church and a theocratic government; held no civil office but as head of Company of Pastors and of Consistory held effective power. Had controversies with various heretics, one of whom, Servetus, was burned at the stake (1553). Founded at Geneva (1559) theological academy that became U. of Geneva. With Consensus Tigurinus (1549) formed alliance with Zwinglian Protestantism of Zürich. His Genevan government served as focal point for defense of Protestantism throughout Europe, and his zeal and his writings brought into one body of doctrine the scattered and unsystematic reformed opinions of the period; encouraged Protestant churches elsewhere and supplied pastors and organizational support, esp. to France.

Calvisius, Sethus. See Seth Kalwitz.

Cal·vo \ˈkäl-bō\, Carlos. 1824–1906. Argentine diplomat and jurist. In consular service (1852–58); deputy (1859); minister plenipotentiary to Berlin (1883), Russia (1889), Austria (1890), Paris (1899). Formulated Calvo doctrine on jurisdiction of governments over aliens and use of force to collect indemnities (cf. Luis María Drago). Author of *Derecho internacional teórico y práctico de Europa y América* (1863), *Annales historiques de la révolution de l'Amérique latine* (1864–75).

Cal·vus \ˈkal-vəs\, Gaius Licinius Macer. 82–c.47 B.C. Roman orator and poet. Leader of Attic school of oratory in opposition to florid Asiatic school. Little of his work has survived.

Cal·za·bi·gi \ˌkält-sä-ˈbē-jē\, Raniero Simone Francesco Maria de. 1714–1795. Italian poet. Collaborator with Gluck in reform of opera; contributed libretti to Gluck's *Orfeo ed Euridice* (1762), *Alceste* (1767), *Paride ed Elena* (1770); collaborated with Boccherini on comic operas *Le donne letterate* (1770), *L'amor innocente* (1770).

Cam, Diogo. See Cão.

Camacho, Manuel Ávila. See Ávila Camacho.

Ca·mar·go \kà-màr-gō\, Marie-Anne de Cu·pis de \də-kü̅e̅-pēd-ə-\. 1710–1770. Belgian ballerina. Danced with Paris Opéra (1726–35, 1741–51); noted for speed and agility and command of jumping steps as entrechat and cabriole; introduced shortened skirt, heelless slippers and set fashions in coiffure, etc.; reputedly established basic turned-out leg position.

Cam·ba·cé·rès \käⁿ-bà-sā-res\, Jean-Jacques-Régis de. Duc de Parme \pàrm\. 1753–1824. French jurist and statesman. Member of the Convention (1792); member of Committee of Public Safety (1794) and Committee of Five Hundred (1796); minister of justice (1799); second consul (1799). Friend and chief counselor of Napoléon; archchancellor of the Empire (1804); instrumental in formulation of Code Napoléon (1804); created duke (1808); recalled by Napoléon to direct ministry of justice and preside over Chamber of Peers during Hundred Days (1814); exiled to Belgium (1815–18).

Cam·bert \käⁿ-ber\, Robert. c.1627–1677. French composer. Musical superintendent to Anne of Austria (1662); composed *La Pastorale* (1659; text by Pierre Perrin), regarded as first French comedy in music; associated with Perrin as director of Académie Royale de Musique of the Paris opera house (patent obtained by Perrin, 1669); with him produced *Pomone* (1671), regarded as first real French opera; took refuge in London (1672) following dispossession of Perrin's right by Lully.

Cam·bia·so \käm-ˈbyä-zō\ *or* **Cam·bia·si** \-zē\, Luca. *Sometimes called* Il Lu·chet·to \ēl-lü-ˈchāt-tō\. 1527–1585. Genoese painter. Achieved reputation for frescoes in Genoese churches; called to Spain by Philip II to assist in frescoing the Escorial (1583).

Cam·bi·ni \käm-ˈbē-nē\, Giuseppe Maria Gioacchino. 1746–1825. Italian violinist and composer. Settled in Paris (c.1770); composed over 60 symphonies, 144 string quartets, duos and sonatas, theatrical works including operas, ballets, etc., concertos, and vocal music.

Cambio, Arnolfo di. See Arnolfo di Cambio.

Cam·bon \käⁿ-bōⁿ\, Joseph, *in full* Pierre-Joseph. 1756–1820. French financier and politician. Member of the Legislative Assembly (1791–92) and the Convention (1792); voted for execution of Louis XVI; secured passage of decree expropriating property of church and nobility in conquered territories (1792). Member of Committee of Public Safety (1793); worked to stabilize public finance; head of committee on finance (1793–95); exiled after Restoration (1815).

Cambon, Paul, *in full* Pierre-Paul. 1843–1924. French diplomat. In home government service (1870–82) and diplomatic service (1882–1920); ambassador at Madrid (1886), Constantinople (1891), London (1898–1920); instrumental in negotiating Entente Cordiale (1904). His brother ¶Jules-Martin (1845–1935), diplomat; governor general of Algeria (1891–97); ambassador at Washington (1897–1902), Madrid (1902–07), Berlin (1907–14); secretary general of foreign ministry (1915); chairman of Council of Ambassadors (1919–31).

Cambrensis, Giraldus. See GERALD DE BARRI.

Cam·bridge \'kām-brij\, Duke of. A title of English nobility held by: (1) Three infant sons of James II (title cr. 1661), none of whom lived to maturity. (2) George II, prior to accession as king (title held 1706–27). (3) Adolphus Frederick (1774–1850), and his son George William Frederick Charles (*qq.v.*).

Cambridge, Earl of. A title of English nobility, originally united with earldom of Huntingdon and held by Plantagenet kings, which was bestowed: (1) on other Plantagenets, including Edmund of Langley and several dukes of York; (2) in 1619 on James Hamilton, 2d Marquis of Hamilton, and held by his sons James and William, 1st and 2d dukes of Hamilton (see HAMILTON family); (3) in 1659 on Henry, Duke of Gloucester, brother of Charles II.

Cambridge, Alexander Augustus Frederick William Alfred George. 1st Earl of Ath·lone \ath-'lōn\ (2d creation). 1874–1957. British soldier. Brother of Queen Mary; m. (1904) Princess Alice, granddaughter of Queen Victoria. Served in Matabele War (1896–97), Boer War (1899–1900), World War I; brigadier general (1915). Took title of earl (1917). Governor general of and high commissioner to Union of South Africa (1923–31); governor general of Canada (1940–45).

Cambridge, Richard Owen. 1717–1802. English poet. Author of mock epic poem, the *Scribleriad* (1751), with Martinus Scriblerus hero.

Cam·bronne \kän-brōn\, Pierre-Jacques-Étienne. Vicomte. 1770–1842. French general. Served with distinction in campaigns of 1812, 1813, 1814; accompanied Napoléon to Elba; commanded division of Imperial Guard at Waterloo (1815).

Cam·by·ses I \kam-'bī-ˌsēz\. *Old Persian* Kam·bu·jia \käm-'bü-j(ē-)ə\. 6th century B.C. King of Anshan (c.600–559 B.C.). Son of Cyrus I; according to Herodotus, m. daughter of King Astyages of Media; father of Cyrus II the Great.

Cambyses II. d. 522 B.C. King of Persia (529–522 B.C.). Son of Cyrus the Great; secretly murdered younger brother Smerdis before setting out to conquer Egypt; defeated Psamtik III at Pelusium (525); added Nile Valley as far as Nubia to Persian Empire; failed in expeditions against Amon and Ethiopia; died while returning to Persia (522) after learning of usurpation of his throne by "false Smerdis."

Camden, Earls and marquis of. See Sir Charles PRATT.

Cam·den \'kam-dən\, William. 1551–1623. English antiquary and historian. Traveled in various parts of England collecting archaeological material; second master of Westminster School (1575); headmaster (1593–97). Compiled *Britannia,* topographical account in Latin of British Isles from earliest times (first pub. 1586); printed list of epitaphs found in Westminster Abbey (1600); wrote a history of reign of Queen Elizabeth (1615, 1625).

Ca·me·rar·i·us \ˌkä-mā-'rä-rē-ùs, *Angl* ˌkam-ə-'rar-ē-əs\, Joachim. *Orig. surname* Kam·mer·mei·ster \'käm-ər-ˌmī-stər\. 1500–1574. German classical scholar. Embraced Reformation and became friend of Melanchthon at Wittenberg (1521); attended Diet of Augsburg and helped formulate Augsburg Confession (1530); helped develop Latin and Greek studies as professor at Tübingen (1535) and Leipzig (from 1541). Author of handbooks of grammar, translations and editions of Plautus, Sophocles, Herodotus, Homer, Xenophon, an edition of Melanchthon's letters (1569), biographies of Eobanus Hessus (1553) and of Melanchthon (1566), *Epistolae Familiares,* a contribution to the history of his time, etc.

Camerarius, Rudolf Jakob. 1665–1721. German physician and botanist. Professor, Tübingen (from 1688); demonstrated sexuality in plants (reported 1694).

Cameron, Donald. See CAMERON of Lochiel.

Cam·er·on \'kam-(ə-)rən\, Duncan. 1764–1848. Canadian fur trader, b. Glenmoriston, Inverness-shire, Scotland. To U.S. as child; joined North West Co. as trapper (1784), becoming partner (c.1800); in charge of firm's Red River depot (1814–16); clashed with colonists of Earl of Selkirk's Hudson Bay Co., attacked Ft. Gibraltar (1816); captured, sent to England for trial; acquitted; member of Legislative Assembly of Upper Canada (1824 ff.).

Cameron, Sir Ewen *or* Evan. See CAMERON of Lochiel.

Cameron, John. c.1579–1625. Scottish theologian. Protestant minister, Bordeaux (1608–17); professor of divinity, Saumur (1618–20, 1623–24), Montaubon (1624); principal, Glasgow U. (1620–21); disliked in Scotland and France for his doctrine of passive obedience; stabbed in street in Montaubon. Called founder of moderate Calvinistic school of Saumur, often called Cameronites.

Cameron, Julia Margaret. 1815–1879. British photographer, b. India. Known esp. for portraits, as of Tennyson, Longfellow, Carlyle, Darwin, Ellen Terry, Sir John Herschel; also made allegorical, genre, and illustrative photographs, as for Tennyson's *Idylls of the King.*

Cameron, Richard. 1648–1680. Scottish Covenanter. Schoolmaster; on return from Holland (1680) resisted reinstatement of Episcopal church in Scotland; preached in fields; founded sect of Reformed Presbyterians called Cameronians; in Sanquhar Declaration (1680) renounced allegiance to Charles II; killed in skirmish in hills of Ayrshire, the survivors of which were amnestied and formed nucleus of the famous Cameronian regiment of British army.

Cameron, Simon. 1799–1889. American financier and politician, b. Lancaster Co., Pa. U.S. senator (1845–49, 1857–61, 1867–77); controlled Republican political machine in Pennsylvania (1857–77). U.S. secretary of war (1861–62); criticized for manner of awarding army contracts. U.S. minister to Russia (1862). His son ¶James Donald (1833–1918) succeeded him in control of Republican machine in Pennsylvania; U.S. secretary of war (1876–77); senator (1877–97).

Cameron, Verney Lovett. 1844–1894. English explorer. Served in British navy (1857–83); in Abyssinian campaign (1868); leader of Royal Geographic Society's expedition to aid Livingstone (1873); sent Livingstone's papers to England; explored southern half of Lake Tanganyika; first European to cross equatorial Africa sea to sea (1875). Author of *Across Africa* (1877) and, with Sir R. F. Burton, *To the Gold Coast for Gold* (1883).

Cameron of Loch·iel \lä-'kē(ə)l, -'k̲ē(ə)l\, Sir Ewen. 1629–1719. Scottish highland chieftain. Chief of clan Cameron (from c.1647); renowned for feats of strength; led clan against forces of Commonwealth (1652); submitted to Monck and was received at Charles II's court (1660); raised his clan to join John Graham of Claverhouse in battle of Killiecrankie (1689); sent clan to join in Earl of Mar's uprising (1715); said to have killed last wolf in Scotland. His grandson ¶Donald Cameron (1695?–1748), called "the Gentle Lochiel," chieftain of clan Cameron; reluctantly supported Prince Charles Edward (1745); took Edinburgh (1745); fought at Prestonpans; captured Falkirk; wounded at Culloden (1746); escaped with Prince Charles Edward to France (1746).

Ca·mil·lo de Lel·lis \kä-'mēl-lō-dā-'lel-lēs\. Saint. 1550–1614. Italian religious. Soldier of fortune; converted (1575) and became servant at St. James's Hospital, Rome; ordained (1584); founded (1586) congregation of priests that gained papal approval (1591) as order of Ministers of the Sick; general of order (1591–1607). Canonized (1746); with St. John of God, patron saint of the sick.

Ca·mil·lus \kə-'mil-əs\, Marcus Furius. d. 365 B.C. Roman soldier and statesman. Captured Veii (396 B.C.) after ten-year siege; saved Rome from complete destruction in Gallic invasion under Brennus; five times elected dictator; aided in securing passage of Licinian laws (367 B.C.).

Cam·maerts \'käm-ärts\, Émile. 1878–1953. Belgian poet and writer. Settled in England (1908) but remained Belgian subject; professor, London U. (1931–47). Translator of Ruskin and Chesterton into French. Author of *Chants patriotiques* (1915), verse written during World War I, translated into English as *Belgian Poems* (1915), *New Belgian Poems* (1916), *Messines and Other Poems* (1918), *Poèmes intimes* (1922), and of *Discoveries in England* (1930), *The Laughing Prophet* (1937), *The Child of Divorce* (1938), *Flemish Painting* (1945), *The Cloud and the Silver Lining* (1952), etc.

Cam·ma·ra·no \ˌkäm-mä-'rä-nō\, Salvatore. 1801–1852. Italian librettist. Wrote libretti of Donizetti's *Lucia di Lammermoor, Roberto Devereux, Belisario,* etc., Verdi's *Alzira, Luisa Miller,* most of *Il trovatore,* etc.

Ca·mões \kə-'mōĩⁿsh\, Luíz Vaz de \'vȧzh-t̲h̲ə\. *Also spelled* Camoëns. 1524 or 1525–1580. Portuguese poet. Member of impoverished noble family; early life undocumented and subject of much legend; supposed to have been in Morocco (c.1550); in military service in Far East (c.1555–72); gained patronage of King Sebastian; reinstated at court. Author of *Os Lusíadas* (1572), his masterpiece, an epic treating in ottava rima the chief episodes in Portuguese history; wrote also sonnets, odes, elegies, satires, epigrams, and comedies, including *Amphitriões* and *Filodemo;* many pieces included in posthumous editions of his *Rimas* (1595 ff.) doubtless incorrectly attributed. Notable for his development of Portuguese lyric to its highest point and for his influence on national drama.

Camp \'kamp\, Walter Chauncey. 1859–1925. American football coach, b. New Britain, Conn. In employ of New Haven Clock Co. (from 1883). Football coach, Yale (1888–92); influential in shaping American football rules; invented set scrimmage, 11-man team, gridiron field, quarterback position, signal calling, 4th-down rule; with Casper Whitney originated annual All-American football team (from 1889). Deviser of the "Daily Dozen," a series of simple calisthenic exercises.

Cam·pa·gna \käm-'pän-yä\, Gerolamo. 1552?–1623. Venetian sculptor. Works included statue of Doge Leonardo Loredano, statue of St. Justina over portal of Arsenal, altar of San Giorgio Maggiore, statue of St. Anthony in church of San Giacomo di Rialto (all in Venice), statue of Duke Federico Montefeltro (at Urbino), and bronze statues on façade of Palazzo del Consiglio (at Verona).

Cam·pa·gno·la \ˌkäm-pän-'yō-lä\, Domenico. c.1484–c.1563. Italian painter and printmaker. Worked chiefly in Padua; assisted Titian in decoration of

Scuola del Santo, Padua. His paintings included frescoes in Scuola del Santo and Scuola del Carmine (Padua), engravings, woodcuts, and many pen-and-ink drawings.

Campagnola, Giulio. c.1482–after 1514. Italian engraver and painter. Engraved chiefly after Giorgione, as *The Astrologer, The Samaritan, Two Nude Women;* his technique of engraving anticipated stippling.

Cam·pan \kä^n-pä^n\, Jeanne-Louise-Henriette, *nee* Ge·net \zhə-ne\. 1752–1822. French educator. First lady of the bedchamber to Marie Antoinette (c.1769–89). Opened girls' boarding school at Saint-Germain (1794); appointed by Napoléon (1806) head of a school for daughters, sisters, and nieces of officers of the Legion of Honor. Author of *Mémoires sur la vie privée de Marie Antoinette* (1823).

Cam·pa·na \käm-ˈpän-ä\, Giampietro. Marchese di Ca·vel·li \kä-ˈvel-lē\. 1808–1880. Italian antiquarian. Director of state pawnshop Monte di Pietà, Rome (1833–58); assembled large collection of antiquities, esp. Etruscan; discovered Grotta Campana, Veii (1842), Grotta dei Rilievi, Cerveteri (1850); exiled for peculation, collection seized and sold to foreign governments.

Campaña, Pedro. See Pieter de KEMPENEER.

Cam·pa·nel·la \ˌkäm-pä-ˈnel-lä\, Tommaso, *orig.* Giovanni Domenico. 1568–1639. Italian philosopher. Dominican monk (from 1583); taught at Rome and Naples; evolved anti-Scholastic philosophy; imprisoned for heresy on publication of *Philosophia sensibus demonstrata* (1591); developed idea of religious reformation and social regeneration in *De monarcha Christianorum* (1593) and *Dialogo politico contra Luterani, Calvinisti ed altri eretici* (1595); again imprisoned (1599–1626) on charges of heresy and conspiracy against Spanish rule; forced to flee to France (1634); protégé of Louis XIII and Richelieu. Known especially for his *La Città del Sole* (1602), written during imprisonment, a description of a utopian state similar to that of Plato's *Republic.* Other works included *Apologia pro Galilaeo* (1616), lyric verse in *Scelta* (1622), *Metafisica* (1638).

Cam·pa·ni \käm-ˈpän-ē\, Giuseppe. 1635–1715. Italian optician. Invented (1664) lens-grinding lathe to grind and polish spherical lenses; built numerous telescopes; made observations of Jupiter's moons and Saturn's rings; invented screw-barrel microscope.

Cam·pa·ni·us \kam-ˈpā-nē-əs\, John. 1601–1683. Swedish clergyman. Ordained in Lutheran ministry (1633); to Swedish settlement at Fort Christina (now Wilmington), Delaware (1643); preached among Delaware Indians; devised phonetic alphabet for Delaware language and translated Luther's *Shorter Catechism;* returned to Sweden (1648).

Cam·pa·nus \käm-ˈpän-əs\ of No·va·ra \nō-ˈvär-ä\. *Lat.* Cam·pa·nus No·va·ri·en·sis \kam-ˈpā-nəs-ˌnō-ˌvar-ē-ˈen-səs\. *Also called* Johannes Campanus. d.1296. Italian mathematician. Chaplain to popes Urban IV, Nicholas IV, Boniface VIII. Author of edition of Euclid used as standard textbook for 3 centuries, of astronomical works based on Ptolemy as *Theorica planetarum* and *Tractatus de spera,* and of *Computus major* on time and calendrical computation.

Camp·bell \ˈkam-bəl, *US also* ˈkam-əl\. Ancient Scottish family holding (from 1457) titles of earl and duke of Ar·gyll \är-ˈgī(ə)l\. Prominent members included: Colin Campbell (d. 1493), succeeded his grandfather as Lord Campbell (1453); created earl of Argyll (1457) by James II; lord justiciary of Scotland (1465); lord high chancellor (1483). His son ¶Archibald (d. 1513), 2d earl, was lord high chancellor (1494); killed at Flodden. His son ¶Colin (d. 1530), 3d earl, was appointed (1528) justiciar of Scotland, office becoming hereditary. His son ¶Archibald (d. 1558), 4th earl, was first among Scottish nobles to embrace the Reformation. His son ¶Archibald (1530–1573), 5th earl, deserted party of John Knox to espouse cause of Mary, Queen of Scots; co-conspirator in murder of Darnley (1567); commanded Mary's forces at Langside (1568); submitted to James VI's party (1571); lord high chancellor (1572). At his death title passed to his younger half-brother ¶Colin (d. 1584), 6th earl, who was lord high chancellor (1579). His son ¶Archibald (1576?–1638), 7th earl, as king's lieutenant was defeated by earls of Huntly and Erroll at Glenlivet (1594); largely responsible for virtual extermination of Macgregors (1608) and Macdonalds (1615); converted to Catholicism and served king of Spain (1618). His son ¶Archibald (1607–1661), 8th earl, joined Covenanters (1638); ravaged lands of Royalist earls of Atholl and Mar and of Ogilvies (1640); negotiated compromise with Charles I and created marquis of Argyll (1641); struck alliance with English Parliament; defeated by Royalists under Earl of Montrose at Inverlochy and Kilsyth (1645), took part in defeat of Royalists at Philiphaugh (1645); after final defeat of Scottish Royalists, formed new government in Edinburgh (1648); formed alliance with Cromwell; forced by execution of Charles I to repudiate Cromwell and accept proclamation in Scotland of Charles II (1649); crowned Charles at Scone (1651); after defeat of Charles's army at Worcester (1651), submitted to Cromwell; arrested at Restoration (1660) and beheaded. His son ¶Archibald (1629–1685), 9th earl, fought at Dunbar as Highland Royalist; submitted, at Charles's direction, to Cromwell (1655); imprisoned for suspected Royalist plot (1657–60); restored to father's forfeited title and holdings (1663); commissioned to disarm Highlands (1667); opposed persecutions of Covenanters; commissioned to disarm Highlanders suspected of Catholic sympathies (1679); opposed Scottish test act (1681); incurred enmity of James, Duke of York; imprisoned on charge of treason and sentenced to death (1681); escaped to Holland; planned invasion of Scotland with Rye House conspirators (1683); led unsuccessful invasion of western Highlands (1685); captured and beheaded. His son ¶Archibald (d. 1703) joined William of Orange at The Hague and accompanied him to England (1688); restored to father's estate and the earldom (1689); together with John Campbell, Earl of Breadalbane, and Sir John Dalrymple, responsible for massacre of Macdonalds of Glencoe for nonsubmission (1692); created duke of Argyll (1701). His son ¶John (1678–1743), 2d Duke of Argyll, was lord high commissioner to Scottish parliament (1705); strongly promoted Act of Union; served as brigadier general under Marlborough at Oudenarde (1708); major general commanding siege of Ghent (1708–09); lieutenant general (1709); captured Tournay (1709); distinguished himself at Malplaquet (1709); ambassador to and commander of British troops in Spain (1711–12); governor of Minorca (1712–16); put down Jacobite uprising in Scotland (1715–16); created duke of Green·wich \ˈgrin-ij, ˈgren-, -ich\ in English peerage (1719); field marshal (1736). On his death without male heir his English titles became extinct; Scottish titles passed to his brother ¶Archibald (1682–1761), 3d Duke of Argyll; lord high treasurer of Scotland (1705); commissioner of union (1706); created earl of Is·lay \ˈī-(ˌ)lā, ī-lə\ (1706); representative peer of Scotland (1706–61); justice-general of Scotland (1710) and lord register (1714); Walpole's chief adviser in Scotland; keeper of great seal (1733–61). On his death without issue, title passed to his cousin John, a grandson of the ninth earl, of the Campbells of Mamore. A descendant ¶George John Douglas (1823–1900), 8th duke, entered House of Lords as a follower of Peel (1847); lord privy seal (1853–55, 1859–66); postmaster general (1855–58); secretary of state for India (1868–74); staunchly opposed Tory foreign policy on "Eastern question" (1877–80); lord privy seal under Gladstone (1880–81); broke with Gladstone in opposing Irish home rule (1886); author of *The Eastern Question* (1879), *Scotland As It Was and As It Is* (1887), *Unseen Foundations of Society* (1893), etc. His son ¶John Douglas Sutherland (1845–1914), 9th duke, m. (1871) Princess Louise, 4th daughter of Queen Victoria; M.P. (1868–71); governor general of Canada (1878–83); M.P. (1895–1900).

Campbell, Alexander. See under Thomas CAMPBELL (1763–1854).

Campbell, Sir Archibald. 1739–1791. British soldier, b. Scotland. Entered army (1757); served under Simon Fraser in French and Indian War in America (1757–63), in India (1764–73); M.P. (1774); to America (1775); captured and exchanged for Ethan Allen (1776); brigadier general (1776); captured Savannah, Ga., and held it (1778–82); major general (1782); governor of Jamaica (1782–85), of Madras, India (1785–89); M.P. (1789–91).

Campbell, Sir Archibald. 1769–1843. British army officer, b. Scotland. Served in India (1788–99), in Portugal (1808–20); Portuguese commander at Lisbon (1816–20); conducted Burmese War (1824–26); major general (1825); governor of British Burma (1826–29); lieutenant governor of New Brunswick, Canada (1831–37); lieutenant general (1838).

Campbell, Sir Colin. Baron Clyde \ˈklīd\. 1792–1863. British army officer, b. Glasgow. Original surname Mac·li·ver \mə-ˈklē-vər\ changed through error of Duke of York (1807). Served in Peninsular War (1810–13), in American War of 1812 (1813–14), in West Indies (1819–26), in China (1842–46), in India (1846–53); commanded first division in Crimean War (1854–55); lieutenant general (1856). Commander in chief in India (1857–60); relieved Lucknow (1857); suppressed Sepoy Mutiny (1857–58); created baron and promoted general (1858); field marshal (1862).

Campbell, Donald Malcolm. See under Sir Malcolm CAMPBELL.

Campbell, Douglas Houghton. 1859–1953. American botanist, b. Detroit. Professor, Stanford (1891–1925). Author of *Elements of Structural and Systematic Botany* (1890), *Structure and Development of Mosses and Ferns* (1895), *Plant Life and Evolution* (1911), *Outline of Plant Geography* (1926), *Evolution of the Land Plants* (1940), etc.

Campbell, George. 1719–1796. Scottish theologian. Principal of Marischal Coll., Aberdeen (1759–92) and professor of divinity (1771–92). Author of *Dissertation on Miracles* (1762) and of *Philosophy of Rhetoric* (1776).

Campbell, John. 1653–1728. American colonial journalist, b. Scotland. Emigrated to Massachusetts (c.1695); postmaster at Boston (1702–18). Publisher of Boston *News-Letter* (1704–22), first regular newspaper in America.

Campbell, John. 1st Baron Campbell. 1779–1861. British jurist, b. Scotland. Called to bar in England (1806); M.P. (1830–49); took active part in law reform, largely by abolition of obstructive technicalities; solicitor general (1832); attorney general (1834–41); chief justice of queen's bench (1850); lord chancellor (1859). Author of *Lives of the Lord Chancellors* (1845–47), *Lives of the Chief Justices* (1849, 1857).

Campbell, John Archibald. 1811–1889. American jurist, b. Washington, Ga. Associate justice, U.S. Supreme Court (1853–61); assistant secretary of war in Confederate cabinet (1862–65).

Campbell, John Francis. *Known as* John Campbell of Islay. 1822–1885. Scottish folklorist and government official. Gaelic scholar. Author of *Popular Tales of the West Highlands* (1860–62).

Campbell, Lewis. 1830–1908. Scottish scholar. Professor of Greek and Gifford lecturer, St. Andrews (1863–94). Edited Sophocles, translated Sophocles and Aeschylus into English verse, completed Jowett's translation of Plato's *Republic* (1894).

Campbell, Sir Malcolm. 1885–1948. English racer. Set first land speed record of 146.16 mph (1924); raised record 8 times, culminating in 301.13 mph (1935); set water speed records of 129.5 mph (1931), 130.93 (1938), 141.74 (1939); all set in autos and hydroplanes named "Bluebird." Author of *Speed* (1931), *Romance of Motor-Racing* (1936), etc. His son ¶Donald Malcolm (1921–1967), also a racer; set water speed records of 202.32 mph (1955), 276.33 (1964); in jet-powered automobile set record of 403.1 mph (1964).

Campbell, Mrs. Patrick. *Nee* Beatrice Stella Tan·ner \'tan-ər\. 1865–1940. English actress. m. 1st, Patrick Campbell (1884; d. 1900), 2d, George Cornwallis-West (1914). On professional stage (from 1888); appeared in *The Second Mrs. Tanqueray, The Masqueraders, The Notorious Mrs. Ebbsmith, Little Eyolf, Magda, Hedda Gabler, Pygmalion;* well known in roles of Ophelia, Lady Teazle, Lady Macbeth, and Juliet.

Campbell, Reginald John. 1867–1956. English clergyman. Ordained in Congregational ministry (1895); minister of City Temple, London (1903–15), where his sermons were credited with teaching a new theology; ordained in Church of England (1916). Author of *New Theology* (1907), *Christianity and the Social Order* (1908), *The War and the Soul* (1916), *Problems of Life* (1919), *The Call of Christ* (1933), *The Peace of God* (1936).

Campbell, Robert. See Robert MACGREGOR.

Campbell, Robert. 1808–1894. Canadian trader and explorer, b. Glenlyon, Perthshire, Scotland. To Canada with Hudson's Bay Co. (1830); established first post in Yukon (1842); explored Yukon and Pelly rivers; discovered Upper Yukon River (1848); retired (1871).

Campbell, Roy, *in full* Ignatius Roy Dunnachie. 1901–1957. British poet, b. South Africa. War correspondent of the *Tablet;* served in Spanish Civil War. Author of vigorous, often satirical verse including *The Flaming Terrapin* (1924), *The Wayzgoose* (1928), *Adamastor* (1930), *Georgiad* (1931), *Flowering Reeds* (1933), *Talking Bronco* (1946); autobiographical *Broken Record* (1934), *Light on a Dark Horse* (1951).

Campbell, Thomas. 1763–1854. American religious leader, b. Ireland. Ordained in Scottish church (1798), becoming a "seceder," or independent congregationalist; to U.S. (1807) and settled at Washington, Pa.; assisted son in establishing Disciples; preached in Ohio, Pennsylvania, Vermont. His son ¶Alexander (1788–1866), b. Ballymena, Ireland; to U.S. (1809); pastor at Brush Run, Pa. (1812); followed father into Thomas Corey's Christian Association, took it into alliance with Baptists; followers became known as Disciples; published newspaper *Christian Baptist* (1823–30), changed to *Millennial Harbinger* (1830 ff.) on expulsion of Disciples by Baptists; Disciples, known also as Campbellites, merged with Barton Stone's followers to form (1832) Disciples of Christ. Alexander and father traveled and preached widely; Alexander founded (1840) Bethany Coll., Bethany, W.Va.; president (1840–66).

Campbell, Thomas. 1777–1844. British poet, b. Glasgow. Studied law in Edinburgh (1797) and worked as tutor; published didactic poem *The Pleasures of Hope* (1799), treating of contemporary subjects, including French Revolution, partition of Poland, Negro slavery, which scored a success; published *Specimens of the British Poets* (1819), selections with short lives; edited *New Monthly Magazine* (1820–30); lord rector of Glasgow (1826–29). Remembered chiefly for his stirring patriotic and war lyrics, including "Hohenlinden," "Ye Mariners of England," "Soldier's Dream," "Battle of the Baltic" (mostly written 1800–01).

Campbell, William Edward March. *Pseudonym* William March \'märch\. 1893–1954. American writer, b. Mobile, Ala. Served in World War I; pursued successful business career. Critical and popular success with short stories collected in *Little Wife* (1935), *Some Like Them Short* (1939), *Trial Balance* (1945), novels *Company K* (1933), *Come In at the Door* (1934), *The Tallons* (1936), *Looking-Glass* (1943), *The Bad Seed* (1954; dramatized by Maxwell Anderson, 1954).

Campbell, William Ellsworth. *Stage name* Chung Ling Soo \'jəŋ-'liŋ-'sü\. 1861–1918. American conjurer, b. New York City. Successful stage performer in U.S. and England; adopted (1900) Chinese guise modeled on Chinese conjurer Ching Ling Foo; admitted masquerade (1904) but continued a popular performer; killed while performing bullet-catching trick.

Campbell, William Wallace. 1862–1938. American astronomer, b. Hancock Co., Ohio. Astronomer (1891–1930), director (1901–30), Lick Observatory, Calif.; president, U. of Calif. (1923–30). In charge of 7 eclipse expeditions (1898–1922); made spectrographic studies of stellar radial velocities; established Sun's motion in galaxy. Author of *Elements of Practical Astronomy* (1899), *Stellar Motions* (1913).

Campbell, William Wilfred. 1861–1918. Canadian poet, b. Berlin (now Kitchener), Ont. Anglican clergyman (1885–91); entered Canadian civil service (1891). Author of *Lake Lyrics* (1889), *Dread Voyage* (1893), *Beyond the Hills of Dream* (1899), *Collected Poems* (1905), *Poetic Tragedies* (1908), *Sagas of Vaster Britain* (1914); also wrote plays, novels, etc.; editor, *Oxford Book of Canadian Verse* (1906).

Campbell-Ban·ner·man \-'ban-ər-mən\, Sir Henry. *Orig. surname* Campbell. 1836–1908. British politican, b. Glasgow. Assumed name Bannerman under maternal uncle's will (1872). Liberal M.P. (1868–1908); financial secretary to war office (1871–74, 1880–82); chief secretary for Ireland (1884–85); secretary for war (1886, 1892–95); supported Gladstone's home-rule policy for Ireland; leader of Liberals in House of Commons (1899); advocated conciliatory measures toward conquered Boers, and denounced British "methods of barbarism" in South Africa (1901). Prime minister (1905–08), on Balfour's resignation; ended importation of indentured Chinese labor into South Africa; granted responsible government to Transvaal (1906), Orange River Colony (1907).

Cam·pe \'käm-pə\, Joachim Heinrich. 1746–1818. German educator. Helped reorganize school system as educational adviser in Brunswick (1786–1805); took over Brunswick educational book house (1787–1808), which he developed largely through publication of his own works. Author of juveniles, including *Robinson der Jüngere* (1779–80, based on Defoe), works on education, and works on German language, including *Wörterbuch der deutschen Sprache* (1807–11).

Cam·peg·gio \käm-'päd-jō\, Lorenzo. 1474–1539. Italian prelate. Bishop of Feltri (1512); cardinal (1517); papal nuncio in Germany (1511, 1513); sent to England (1518) to urge crusade against Turks; made bishop of Salisbury by Henry VIII (1524–34); archbishop of Bologna (1524); as colegate with Wolsey to hear Henry VIII's suit to divorce Catherine of Aragon (1528–29), was under papal instructions not to offend Catherine's nephew Charles V; legate at diets of Regensburg (1524), Augsburg (1530); assisted at coronation of Charles V (1530).

Cam·pen \'käm-pən\, Jacob van. 1595–1657. Dutch architect. Leader of Palladian classical revival in Netherlands. Works included Mauritshuis (1633–44) and royal palace Huis ten Bosch (1645, with Pieter Post), both The Hague; Town Hall (1648–55; now Royal Museum), Amsterdam; Nieuwe Kerk (1645–49), Haarlem.

Cam·pen·hout \'käm-pən-ˌhau̇t\, François van. 1779–1848. Belgian violinist and composer. His works included several operas, cantatas, choruses, religious music, and songs, notably the music of the Belgian national air, *La brabançonne* (written during revolution of 1830).

Cam·per \'käm-pər\, Pieter. 1722–1789. Dutch anatomist. Professor at Franeker (1750), Amsterdam (1755), Groningen (1763–73). Known for work in human and comparative anatomy, also in surgery and obstetrics; attempted to determine the degree of human intelligence by measuring the facial angle; discovered the large air content of the bones of birds.

Camperdown, Earl of. See Adam DUNCAN.

Cam·pe·ro \käm-'pā-rō\, Narciso. 1813–1896. Bolivian soldier and politician. Minister of war (1872); president of Bolivia (1880–84); in War of the Pacific with Chile, commanded Peruvian and Bolivian armies at Tacna; defeated (1880).

Camp·huy·sen \'kämp-ˌhȯi-s^{ə}n\, Dirk Rafaelszoon. 1586–1627. Dutch painter, poet, and theologian. Preacher in Vleuten, near Utrecht (1616); deprived of post because of Arminian views (1619); lived subsequently in poverty, and resided in Dokkum as dealer in flax; author of a translation of the Psalms, the volume of devotional verse *Stichtelijke rijmen* (1624), etc.

Cam·pi \'käm-pē\. 16th-century Italian family of painters in Cremona, including: Galeazzo (1477–1536), pupil and imitator of Boccaccino, painter chiefly of religious pictures. His son ¶Giulio (1502–1572), pupil of Giulio Romano in Mantua; chief works included high altar in San Abbondio at Cremona (1527) and frescoes in Santa Margherita at Cremona (1547). Another son ¶Antonio (1536–c.1591), known also as an architect and writer; imitator of Correggio; employed in several Italian cities and by Phillip II in Madrid; works included the painting *Birth of Christ* in church of San Paolo in Milan and a chronicle of Cremona decorated with original engravings. A third son ¶Vincenzo (1536–1591), pupil of his brother Giulio, painter chiefly of portraits and of still life and genre scenes. Their cousin ¶Bernardino Campi (1522–c.1591), pupil of Giulio Campi, influenced chiefly by Giulio Romano

\ə\ **abut** \$^{ə}$\ **kitten,** *Fr.* **table** \ər\ **further** \a\ **ash** \ā\ **ace** \ä\ **cot, cart** \au̇\ **out** \ch\ **chin** \e\ **bet** \ē\ **easy** \g\ **go** \i\ **hit** \ī\ **ice** \j\ **job** \ŋ\ **sing** \ō\ **go** \ȯ\ **law** \ȯi\ **boy** \th\ **both** \t̲h̲\ **the** \ü\ **loot** \u̇\ **foot** \y\ **yet** \zh\ **vision** \á, b̲, g̲, k̲, ^{n}, œ, œ̄, ue, ue̅, ^{y}\ *see* **Guide to Pronunciation** and Correggio; chief work frescoes in cupola of San Sigismondo at Cremona; author of *Parere sopra la Pittura* (1584).

Cam·pin \'käm-pin\, Robert. c.1378–1444. Flemish painter. One of earliest and greatest of Flemish masters; principal works included altarpieces as the *Mérode Altarpiece* (c.1428). Identified by most scholars as creator of works attributed to the "Master of Flémalle," although by some the works are attributed to Campin's pupil Rogier van der Weyden (*q.v.*).

Cam·pi·on \'kam-pē-ən, -pyən\, Edmund. 1540–1581. English Jesuit martyr. Anglican deacon (1568); suspected of papist leanings, escaped to Douai; joined Jesuits (1573); professor of rhetoric, Prague. Sent to England (1580) with Robert Parsons (*q.v.*) on mission to suppressed Catholics; distributed at Oxford service his "Decem rationes" (1581), attack on Anglican church; indicted for conspiracy to dethrone queen; racked three times; executed as traitor. Beatified (1886).

Campion, Thomas. 1567–1620. English poet and composer. Practiced medicine in London (from 1606). Wrote masques and composed music for them, for court occasions (1607–13); wrote *Poemata,* a collection of epigrams, elegies, etc., in Latin (1595), *Observations on the Arte of English Poesie* advocating rhymeless verse on model of classical quantitative verse (1602), and a textbook on counterpoint (1613). Remembered chiefly for graceful and musical lyrics published in 4 *Bookes of Ayres* (1601–17).

Cam·pis·tron \kän-pē-strōn\, Jean Galbert de. 1656–1723. French playwright. Author of tragedies *Virginie* (1683), *Andronic* (1685), *Alcibiade* (1686), *Tiridate* (1691); also comedies and lyric works.

Cam·po·a·mor y Cam·po·o·so·rio \käm-pō-ä-'mòr-ē-käm-pō-ō-'sōr-yō\, Ramón de. 1817–1901. Spanish poet. Deputy to Cortes; governor of Alicante (1847) and Valencia (1851); councilor of state (after 1874); senator. Author of political tracts, as *Polémicas con la democracia* (1862); philosophical treatises, as *La filosofía de las leyes* (1846) and *La metafísica y la poética* (1891); poems, as *Ternezas y flores* (1840), *Ayes del alma* (1842), *Fábulas* (1842), *Doloras* (1846), *Colón* (16 cantos, 1853, 1857), *El drama universal* (1869), *Pequeños poemas* (1872–74), *Humoradas* (1886–88).

Campomanes, Conde de. See Pedro RODRÍGUEZ CAMPOMANES Y PÉREZ.

Campos, Arsenio Martínez de. See MARTÍNEZ DE CAMPOS.

Cam·pos Sal·les \'känm-püs-'säl-ēs\, Manuel Fer·raz de \fər-'ráz-thə-\. 1841–1913. Brazilian politician. Deputy (1884–89); minister of justice (1889 ff.); governor of São Paulo (1896–1898). President of Brazil (1898–1902).

Cam·pra \kän-prá\, André. 1660–1744. French composer. Master of music, Toulon cathedral (1679), Arles (1681), Toulouse (1683–94), Notre-Dame, Paris (1694–1700); one of four masters of royal chapel (from 1723). Known esp. for his creation of the *opéra-ballet,* as in *L'Europe galante* (1697) and *Les fêtes vénitiennes* (1710). Also composed lyric tragedies as *Hésione* (1700), *Tancrède* (1702), *Indomenée* (1712), five books of motets (1695–1720), three books of cantatas (1708–28), a mass (1700), psalms, etc.

Ca·mus \ká-mǖ\, Albert. 1913–1960. French novelist, essayist, and playwright, b. Algeria. Journalist in Algiers; active in Resistance during World War II; editor of daily *Combat* in Paris (1945–47). Became leading exponent of postwar disillusionment and analyst of nihilism and morality. Author of novels *L'Étranger* (1942, *The Stranger*), *La Peste* (1947, *The Plague*), *La Chute* (1956, *The Fall*); stories collected as *L'Exil et le royaume* (1957); philosophical, political, personal essays including *Le Mythe de Sisyphe* (1942), *L'Homme révolté* (1951, *The Rebel*), and collections *L'Envers et l'endroit* (1937), *Actuelles* (1950–58); plays including *Le Malentendu* (1944), *Caligula* (1945), *L'État de siège* (1948). Awarded Nobel prize for literature (1957).

Ca·nal \kä-'näl\, Giovanni Antonio. *Called* Ca·na·let·to \,kä-nä-'lāt-tō\. 1697–1768. Venetian painter. Chief among Venetian school of topographical painters, painted innumerable views of Venice with great skill in depicting light, shadow, etc.; works popular throughout Europe; worked in England (1746–55); in later years also painted idealized and imaginary landscapes and architectural scenes.

Ca·na·le·jas y Mén·dez \kä-nä-'le-käs-ē-'mān-dāth\, José. 1854–1912. Spanish politician. Member of Cortes (from 1881); minister of public works and of justice (1888), of finance (1894–95), of agriculture, industry, commerce (1902); president of Cortes (1906); premier (1910–11); accomplished separation of church and state, securing passage of anticlerical measures; consolidated Spanish position in Morocco.

Canaletto. See Giovanni CANAL.

Canaletto Belotto. See Bernardo BELLOTTO.

Ca·na·li·zo \kä-nä-'lē-sō\, Valentín. 1794–1850. Mexican general. Acting president of Mexico during Santa Anna's absences (1843, 1844); served in war against U.S. (1847); in command of Mexican retreat after Cerro Gordo.

Ca·na·ris \kä-'när-əs\, Wilhelm Franz. 1887–1945. German naval officer. Head of *Abwehr* (military intelligence, 1935–44); admiral (1940); engaged in anti-Hitler conspiracies; following assassination attempt (1944), arrested and executed.

Can·by \'kan-bē\, Henry Seidel. 1878–1961. American author and editor, b. Wilmington, Del. Teacher of English, Yale (from 1900, professor from 1922); editor, "Literary Review" of New York *Evening Post* (1920–24); editor, *Saturday Review of Literature* (1924–36). Author of *The Short Story in English* (1909), *Everyday Americans* (1920), *American Estimates* (1929), *Classic Americans* (1931), *The Age of Confidence* (1934), *Alma Mater* (1936), *Thoreau* (1939), *Walt Whitman* (1943), *Family History* (1945), *Turn West, Turn East* (1951), etc.

Cancrin, Georg von. See Yegor KANKRIN.

Candamo, Francisco de Bances. See BANCES Y LOPEZ-CANDAMO.

Can·da·mo \kän-'dä-mō\, Manuel. 1842–1904. Peruvian journalist and politician. Provisional president (1895), president (1903–04; died in office).

Can·did \'kän-dēd\, Pieter. *Ital.* Pietro Can·di·do \kän-'dē-dō\. *Orig. surname* de Wit \də-'vit\ *or* de Wit·te \də-'vit-ə\. c.1548–1628. Flemish painter. Studied under Vasari in Italy; court painter at Munich (from 1568). Best known for his murals (as in the Residenz, Munich) and altarpieces.

Can·dī·dās \(,)kən-'dē-däs\. 14th–15th century. Indian poet. According to own poems, a Brahmin who broke caste rules by falling in love with a washerwoman, Rāmī, to whom his love poems were addressed; his story and verse influenced Bengali art, literature, and theology, esp. the Vaiṣṇava and Sahajiyā movements.

Candish, Thomas. See CAVENDISH.

Can·dler \'kan-dlər\, Asa Griggs. 1851–1929. American manufacturer, b. near Villa Rica, Ga. Bought formula for Coca-Cola (1887); built Coca-Cola Co. into major business, retiring as president (1916); mayor of Atlanta (1917–18); benefactor of Atlanta and Emory U. His brother ¶Warren Akin (1857–1941), Methodist Episcopal clergyman; president, Emory Coll. (1888–98); bishop, Methodist Episcopal Church, South (from 1898).

Can·dlish \'kan-dlish\, Robert Smith. 1806–1873. Scottish clergyman. Minister of St. George's, Edinburgh (1834–73); took a leading part (from 1843) in formation of independent Free Church, and succeeded Thomas Chalmers as its leader (1847); principal of New College, Edinburgh (1862).

Can·dolle \kän-dòl\, Augustin-Pyrame de. 1778–1841. Swiss botanist. To Paris (1796); professor, Montpellier (1808–17), Geneva (1817–41). His *Plantarum historia succulentarum* (1799–1803) and *Astragalogia* (1802) attracted notice of Cuvier and J. B. Lamarck, who entrusted him with publication of third edition of *Flore française* (1805–15), the introduction to which contained first exposition of his natural system of plant classification; made botanical and agricultural survey of France in six summers for French government (1806–12). Introduced new scientific method of classifying plants by structure in *Théorie élémentaire de la botanique* (1813); developed and applied method in *Regni vegetabilis systema naturale* (1818–21) and *Prodromus systematis naturalis regni vegetabilis* (1824–39); coined term "taxonomy" for such classification. His son ¶Alphonse-Louis-Pierre-Pyrame de Candolle (1806–1893) succeeded him as professor at Geneva (1842–93); continued *Prodromus systematis* to 17 volumes (to 1873); author of *Géographie botanique raisonnée* (1855), *Origine des plantes cultivées* (1883).

Can·dra·gup·ta \,kən-drə-'gùp-tə\ *or* **Chan·dra·gup·ta** \,chən-\. *Also known as* Candragupta Maur·ya \-'maùr-yə\. d. c.297 B.C. Indian emperor (c.321–c.297 B.C.). Son of impoverished Maurya family; sold as slave; trained by a Brahmin politician, learned military arts; raised mercenary army, overthrew Nanda dynasty, and assumed throne of Magadha (c.325); after withdrawal of agents of Alexander the Great took over Punjab (c.322) and founded Maurya dynasty of unified kingdom (c.321); extended realm to Persian border, defeating Seleucus (c.305), and to rest of India to the south; established efficient administration; converted to Jainism; fasted to death in sorrow for famine.

Can·dra Gup·ta \'kən-drə-'gùp-tə\. *Also spelled* Chan·dra Gup·ta \'chən-\. Name of two Indian rulers of the Gupta dynasty:

Candra Gupta I. 4th century A.D. King (320–c.330). Grandson of Sri Gupta, founder of line; succeeded to throne of Magadha; married princess of ruling house of Licchavi tribe, increasing power and realm; imperial rule (from 320 A.D.) began traditional Gupta chronology; apparently abdicated in favor of son Samudra Gupta (*q.v.*).

Candra Gupta II. 4th–5th century. Emperor (c.380–c.415). Son of Samudra Gupta; reputedly achieved throne by assassinating elder brother; extended Gupta influence by matrimonial alliances and conquest, esp. of Gujarāt, Saurāṣṭra, Mālawa; fostered prosperity, learning.

Cand·ra·kīr·ti \,kən-drə-'kir-tē\. fl. 600–650 A.D. Indian Buddhist philosopher. Author of authoritative Sanskrit commentary on Nāgārjuna's *Prasannapadā;* representative of Prāsangika school of logic.

Cañete, Marqués de. See Andres HURTADO DE MENDOZA.

Canfield, Dorothy. See Dorothy Canfield FISHER.

Can·ga Ar·güel·les \'käŋ-gä-är-gwā(l)-yās\, José. 1770–1843. Spanish politician. Deputy to constituent Cortes (1812); exiled by Ferdinand VII (1814);

minister of finance (1820–21); exile in England (1823–29). Author of *Elementos de la ciencia de hacienda* (1825), *Diccionario de hacienda* (1827).

Cange, du. See DU CANGE.

Cangrande. See under SCALA.

Canice, Saint. See Saint KENNETH.

Canino, Prince of. See under BONAPARTE.

Ca·ni·sius \kə-'nish(-ē)-əs\, Peter, *Lat.* Petrus. Saint. *Orig.* Pieter Ka·ni·us \'kän-ē-œs\ *or* Ka·nijs \'kän-əs\. 1521–1597. Dutch religious and theologian. Entered Jesuit order (1543), and founded at Cologne first house of that order in Germany; influential in reestablishing Roman Catholicism in parts of Germany and in Poland and called therefore "second apostle of Germany" by Pope Leo XIII; first provincial of Jesuit order in Germany (1556–69); established numerous colleges as at Munich (1559), Würzburg (1567), Fribourg (1580); adviser to Emperor Ferdinand I. Prepared a catechism in Latin, *Summa doctrinae christianae* (1555). Canonized and declared doctor of the church (1925).

Ca·nitz \'kän-its\, Friedrich Rudolf Ludwig von. Freiherr. 1654–1699. Prussian diplomat and poet. Minister plenipotentiary in peace negotiations at Rijswijk. Author of odes, satires, and elegies, chiefly imitations of Latin and French models, as in *Nebenstunden unterschiedener Gedichte* (1700).

Can·kar \'tsän-kär\, Ivan. 1876–1918. Slovene writer and patriot. Helped develop modern Slovenian prose. Author of social criticism, psychological novels, satires, stories, verse, etc.; volumes included *Hiša Marije Pomočnice* (1904), *Hlapec Jernej in njegova pravica* (1907), *Martin Kačur* (1907).

Canmore. See MALCOLM III (of Scotland).

Can·ning \'kan-iŋ\, George. 1770–1827. British politician. Reared and educated by wealthy uncle; entered politics under sponsorship of William Pitt; M.P. (1793–1827); brilliant orator; undersecretary for foreign affairs in Pitt's administration (1796–99); supported ministry by his periodical the *Anti-Jacobin* (1797–98); barred from advancement because of poverty and direction of merciless wit against Whigs, yet influential as chief confidant of Pitt; left office of treasurer of navy (from 1804) on Pitt's death (1806). Foreign secretary (1807–09); planned seizure of Danish fleet; fought duel with Castlereagh (1809), occasioned by latter's failure to cooperate in vigorous war policy. President, Board of Control (1817–20); succeeded Castlereagh as foreign secretary and leader of House of Commons (1822); promoted policy of nonintervention and fostered liberal and nationalist movements in Europe; acknowledged independence of Spanish colonies in America (1823); shielded Greece against Turkish aggression (1825–27); established British independence of Holy Alliance; contended for Catholic emancipation and laid groundwork for repeal of corn laws. Prime minister (1827).

His third son ¶Charles John (1812–1862), Earl Canning; M.P. (1836–56); undersecretary of state for foreign affairs (1841); postmaster general (1853–55); governor general of India (1856–58); brought war with Persia to successful conclusion (1857); on own responsibility, intercepted troops en route to China for service against Taiping rebels, and diverted them to India to help quell Sepoy Mutiny (1857); nicknamed "Clemency Canning" because of refusal to make reprisals; oversaw transfer of India to crown (1858) and reorganized government; first viceroy of India (1858–62); created earl (1859).

Canning, Sir Samuel. 1823–1908. English engineer. Engineer in chief of Atlantic cable-laying expeditions (1865–66, 1869) in steamship *Great Eastern;* laid cables from England to Malta and Alexandria.

Canning, Sir Stratford. 1st Viscount Strat·ford de Red·cliffe \'strat-fərd-də-'red-klif\. 1786–1880. British diplomat. Cousin of George Canning. Minister plenipotentiary at Constantinople (1810–12); negotiated treaty of Bucharest between Russia and Turkey (1812). As minister to Switzerland (1814–18), aided in establishing federal government there. Minister to U.S. (1820–23). Ambassador to Constantinople (1825–28, 1831); attempted to obtain general recognition of Greek independence from Turkey (1825), to negotiate settlement of Greek affairs with French and Russian envoys (1828). M.P. (1828–41). Again ambassador at Constantinople (1842–58); viscount (1852).

Can·niz·za·ro \,kän-nēd-'dzä-rō\, Stanislao. 1826–1910. Italian chemist. Assistant in chemistry at Pisa, later at Turin; took part in Sicilian Revolution (1848); fled to Paris (1849); professor, Alexandria (1851), Genoa, (1855), Palermo (1861), Rome (1871); senator (1871). Discovered Cannizzaro reaction; clearly defined distinction between molecular and atomic weights; amplified Avogadro's hypothesis and applied it to the atomic theory; showed method of deducing atomic weights of elements in volatile compounds from molecular weights of the compounds.

Can·non \'kan-ən\, Annie Jump. 1863–1941. American astronomer, b. Dover, Del. Assistant (1896–1911), curator of astronomical photographs (1911–40), professor (1938–40), Harvard Observatory. Observed visually many variable stars of long period; in photographic work, discovered 300 variable stars, 5 novae; catalogued over 225,000 stellar spectra for *Henry Draper Catalogue* (1918–24) and more for *Henry Draper Extension* (1924, 1949).

Cannon, Harriet Starr. 1823–1896. American religious, b. Charleston, S.C. Founder and mother superior, Episcopal Sisterhood of St. Mary (1865); founded many hospitals, schools.

Cannon, James. 1864–1944. American clergyman, b. Salisbury, Md. Admitted to Virginia Conference of the Methodist Episcopal Church, South (1888); president, Blackstone Coll. for Girls (1894–1918); bishop (1918–38). Member of executive committee, Anti-Saloon League of America (from 1902), and of its administrative committee (from 1927), chairman of its national legislative committee (from 1914); leader of Southern Democrats opposed to Alfred E. Smith in presidential campaign of 1928.

Cannon, Joseph Gurney. *Called* Uncle Joe. 1836–1926. American politician, b. Guilford Co., N.C. Member from Illinois, U.S. House of Representatives (1873–91, 1893–1913, 1915–23); speaker (1903–11). Leader of the reactionary Republicans. As speaker, accused of autocratic methods in controlling House procedure; power of speaker overthrown (1910) by combination of Democrats and insurgent Republicans.

Cannon, Walter Bradford. 1871–1945. American physiologist, b. Prairie du Chien, Wis. Teacher (from 1899), professor (1906–42), Harvard Medical School. Known for work on movements of stomach and intestines, including pioneer X-ray studies, and on effects of emotions on bodily processes, the autonomic nervous system, etc.; discovered (1931) sympathin, produced by stimulation of sympathetic nerves, which causes stimulation of certain organs. Author of *Mechanical Factors in Digestion* (1911), *Traumatic Shock* (1923), *Bodily Changes in Pain, Hunger, Fear, and Rage* (1929), *The Wisdom of the Body* (1932), *Autonomic Neuro-effector Systems* (with A. Rosenblueth, 1937), autobiography *Way of an Investigator* (1945), etc.

Ca·no \'kä-nō\, Alonso. *Sometimes called* El Gra·na·di·no \el-grä-nä-'thē-nō\. 1601–1667. Spanish painter, sculptor, and architect, b. Granada. Court painter, Madrid (1638–44); canon of Granada (1652 ff.); chief architect, Granada cathedral (1667 ff.). Works included design for Granada cathedral façade, polychromed wood statues of the Virgin, San Diego, etc., busts of Adam and Eve, and a cycle of paintings, *Seven Joys of the Virgin.*

Cano, Juan Sebastián del. See Juan de ELCANO.

Cano, Melchor *or* Melchior. c.1509–1560. Spanish theologian. Entered Dominican order (1523); professor, Valladolid (1533–42), Alcalá (1542–46), Salamanca (1546–52); theologian to Council of Trent (1551); bishop of Canary Islands (1552–54); adviser to Philip II and bitter opponent of Jesuits; rival of Bartolomé de Carranza; elected Dominican provincial of Castile (1557, 1559, but not confirmed until 1560). Author of *De locis theologicis,* inquiry into sources of theological knowledge.

Ca·non·i·cus \kə-'nän-i-kəs\. 1565?–1647. American Indian leader. Sachem of Narragansett Indians; friendly with English; ceded land comprising present state of Rhode Island to Roger Williams.

Ca·no·va \kä-'nō-vä\, Antonio. 1757–1822. Italian sculptor. Established studio, Venice (1775); to Rome (1779) on pension from Venetian government; called to Paris to execute commissions for Napoléon (1802, 1805, 1810); sent to Paris (1815) by Pius VII to recover art treasures taken from Rome; created marquis of Ischia; perpetual president, Academy of St. Luke (from 1810). Outstanding figure in development of Neoclassical sculpture; works included *Orpheus, Eurydice, Daedalus and Icarus, Theseus Vanquishing the Minotaur, Cupid and Psyche,* monuments to Clement XIV and Clement XIII in Rome, *Venus and Adonis, Hebe Pouring Nectar, Pauline Borghese as Venus Victrix, Napoléon as First Consul, Three Graces, Venus Borghese, Theseus and the Centaur, Mars and Venus.*

Cá·no·vas del Cas·til·lo \'kä-nō-bäs-thel-käs-'tē(l)-yō\, Antonio. 1828–1897. Spanish politician and writer. Deputy to Cortes (1854); chargé d'affaires, Rome (1855–57); minister of interior (1864), of colonies (1865); banished (1868–69). A leader in securing restoration of Bourbons (Alfonso XII, 1874); premier (1875–79, 1879–81, 1884–85, 1890–92, 1895–97); wrote new constitution (1876); resisted reforms in Cuban administration; assassinated by anarchist. Author of verse, several volumes of literary studies, a life of Estébanez Calderón (1883), and of *Problemas contemporáneos* (1884–90), *Estudios del reinado de Felipe IV* (1888–90), etc.

Can·ro·bert \kän-rō-ber\, Certain, *in full* François-Certain. 1809–1895. French army officer. Distinguished himself in Algeria (1835–51), esp. at Zaatcha (1847); general and aide-de-camp to Louis-Napoléon (1851); active in coup d'état (Dec. 2, 1851). French commander in Crimean War (1854–55); marshal of France (1856). Commanded Army of Rhine (1870); taken prisoner at Metz (1870). Elected senator (1876).

Can·ta·cu·zi·no \,kän-tä-kü-'zē-nō\. Name of a Byzantine family, including Emperor John VI Cantacuzenus (*q.v.*), later prominent in Romania; members included: Serban Cantacuzino (c.1640–1688), hospodar of Walachia (1679–

88); compelled to serve under Turks at siege of Vienna (1683); national benefactor; introduced Indian corn; influential in substituting Romanian for Slavonic language in liturgy. His cousin ¶Dumitrașcu (1648–1685) was prince of Moldavia (1673–75, 1684–85); unpopular ruler. Another cousin ¶Ștefan (d. 1716) succeeded Constantin Brîncoveanu as prince of Walachia (1714–16); deposed and executed for intrigues with Habsburgs; fall marked end of indigenous rule in Walachia. A descendant ¶Constantin Cantacuzino (1793–1877) was secretary of state (1842–48) to Prince Alexandru II Ghica of Walachia; governor of Walachia (1848–49) following nationalist uprising; head of council of administration (1854). Another member ¶Gheorghe Grigore (1837–1913), Romanian public official; head of Conservative party (1899–1905); premier of Romania (1905–07).

Can·te·lupe or **Can·ti·lupe** \ˈkant-ə-ˌlüp\, Walter de. d. 1266. English prelate. Justice itinerant (1231); bishop of Worcester (1236–66); defended pluralities against papal legate Otho (1237); opposed archbishop Boniface's claim of right of visitation (1251) and papal demands for money (1252, 1255); took part in excommunicating infringers of Magna Carta (1253); one of 24 representatives who set up Provisions of Oxford (1258); supported Simon de Montfort's cause and won over Oxford University to popular side. His nephew ¶Thomas de Cantelupe (c.1218–1282), prelate and saint; taught canon law at Oxford; favored Montfort party in dispute with Henry III over Provisions of Oxford; chancellor of England (Feb.–Aug. 1265); bishop of Hereford (1275–82); chief adviser of Edward I; led opposition to Archbishop Peckham (1279); appealed against Peckham to Rome in dispute over jurisdiction; excommunicated by Peckham (1282); went to Rome; died at Orvieto. Canonized by Pope John XXII (1320).

Cantemir. See KANTEMIR.

Canterbury, Viscounts. See MANNERS-SUTTON.

Canth \ˈkänt\, Ulrika Vilhelmina, *called* Minna. *Nee* Johns·son \ˈyȯns-sȯn\. 1844–1897. Finnish writer and feminist. m. J.F. Canth (1865; d. 1879). Author of plays *Työmiehen vaimo* (1885), *Kovan onnen lapsia* (1888), *Papin perhe* (1891), *Anna Liisa* (1895); stories *Novelleja ja Kertomuksia* (1878), *Kauppa-Lopo* (1889); also novels.

Cantilupe. See CANTELUPE.

Can·ton \ˈkant-ᵊn\, John. 1718–1772. English physicist. Schoolmaster, London (1745–72); elected to Royal Society for paper on making artificial magnets (1749); first in England to verify Franklin's hypothesis of identity of lightning and electricity; invented an electroscope and an electrometer; demonstrated compressibility of water (1762); discovered phosphorescent substance known as Canton's phosphorus (1768).

Can·tor \ˈkant-ər\, Eddie. *Orig.* Edward Israel Is·ko·witz \ˈis-kə-ˌvits\. 1892–1964. American comedian, b. New York City. In vaudeville and burlesque, including *Ziegfeld Follies* (1917–19); musical comedy as *Kid Boots* (1923), *Whoopee* (1928); films as *Kid Boots* (1926), *Roman Scandals* (1933), *Strike Me Pink* (1936); on radio (1931–39) and television (1950–53); active in many charitable drives, as the March of Dimes.

Can·tor \ˈkän-ˌtȯr\, Georg Ferdinand Ludwig Philipp. 1845–1918. German mathematician. Professor, Halle (from 1872); pioneer in set theory; developed a theory of irrational numbers, an arithmetic of the infinite; introduced transfinite numbers.

Cantor, Moritz Benedikt. 1829–1920. German mathematician. Professor at Heidelberg (1863–1913); author of *Vorlesungen über Geschichte der Mathematik* (1880–1908), a history of mathematics to 1799.

Can·tù \kän-ˈtü\, Cesare. 1804?–1895. Italian historian. Known especially for his historical works, as *La Lombardia nel secolo XVII* (1832), *Storia universale* (35 vols., 1838–47), *Storia degli Italiani* (1854); author also of the historical romance *Margherita Pusterla,* describing prison life (1838), and a volume of poems (1870).

Ca·nute or **Cnut** \kə-ˈn(y)üt\ or **Knud** \ˈknüth\ or **Knut** \kə-ˈn(y)üt\. Name of six kings of Denmark, two of whom were also kings of England, including:

Canute of Denmark. *Known as* the Great. d. 1035. King of England (1016–35) and of Denmark (1018–35). Son of Sweyn I Forkbeard; fled to Denmark (1014); returned and waged war with Edmund II Ironside (1015–16); defeated Edmund at Assandun in Essex but allowed him to rule in the south (1016); thoroughly conquered all England after Edmund's death (1016–18); chosen by witan as king of all England (1017); m. (1017) Emma of Normandy, widow of King Aethelred; in Denmark for a few months (1019) to strengthen his hold there; at first cruel, but during most of reign (1020–35) an able, just, and popular ruler; strongly supported the church; defeated attempt (1026) of kings of Norway and Sweden to conquer Denmark; overcame Swedish fleet and damaged their combined fleet; made pilgrimage to Rome (1026–27); drove out Olaf II Haraldsson and became king of Norway (1028–35); subject of many legends. Father of Harold and Hardecanute (*qq.v.*).

Canute III. See HARDECANUTE.

Canute IV. Saint. c.1043–1086. King (1080–86). Son of Sweyn II Estrithson; succeeded brother Harold Hen; strong supporter of the church; tried to invade England (1085); murdered by rebels. Canonized (1101); patron saint of Denmark.

Canute V. d. 1157. King (1147–57). Son of Magnus the Strong; ruled in Jutland; waged civil war with Sweyn III; assassinated.

Canute VI. 1163–1202. King (1182–1202). Son of Valdemar I the Great; crowned as coregent (1170); extended Danish dominion over Pomerania, Mecklenburg, and Holstein; under influence of Archbishop Absalon, came into conflict with Emperor Frederick I Barbarossa.

Ca·nute La·vard \kən-ˈyüt-ˈlä-vär\. 1094?–1131. Prince of Denmark. Son of Eric I; became duke of Sles·vig \ˈslis-vē\ (1115); brought German culture to Denmark; conquered Wendish tribes on frontier; killed by Magnus the Strong.

Cão \ˈkaùⁿ\, Diogo. *Name also spelled* Cam \ˈkaùⁿ\. fl. 1480–86. Portuguese navigator. Discovered mouth of Congo River (1482); granted honors by King John II (1484); on second voyage (1485–86) followed coast of Africa south to Cape Cross.

Capa \ˈkap-ə\, Robert. *Orig.* Andrei Fried·mann \ˈfrēd-ˌmän\. 1913–1954. American photographer, b. Budapest, Hungary. Established reputation in Paris; later to U.S.; known esp. as photographer of war; covered Spanish Civil War, World War II, Palestine, French Indochina (where he was killed); helped found (1947) Magnum Photos agency.

Ca·pa·blan·ca \kä-pä-ˈbläŋ-kä\, José Raúl. 1888–1942. Cuban chess master. Official in Cuban foreign office (from 1913). Defeated Lasker in match for world's championship at Havana (1921); defeated by Alekhine (1927); author of books on chess.

Capac, Manco. See MANCO CAPAC.

Cape \ˈkāp\, Jonathan, *in full* Herbert Jonathan. 1879–1960. English publisher. Bookseller; with G.W. Howard founded (1921) Jonathan Cape publishing firm; succeeded with lines of general and quality literary works, children's books, Travellers' Library of reprints, etc.

Ča·pek \ˈchä-ˌpek\, Karel. 1890–1938. Czech journalist and writer. On staff of *Národní Listy,* Prague (1919–23) and *Lidové Noviny* (from 1923). Author of plays, including *R.U.R.* (1920), *Ze života hmyzu* (with his brother Josef, 1921), *Bílá nemoc* (1937), *Matka* (1938), satirizing modern science, industrialism, militarism, totalitarianism; stories collected as *Zářivé hlubiny* (with Josef, 1916), *Krakonošova zahrada* (with Josef, 1918), *Trapné povídky* (1921), *Povídky z jedné kapsy* and *Povídky z druhé kapsy* (both 1929); novels *Továrna na absolutno* (1922), *Krakatit* (1924), trilogy comprising *Hordubal* (1933), *Provětroň* (1934), and *Obyčejný život* (1934), *Válka s mloky* (1936), *Prvni parta* (1937).

Ca·pel \ˈkā-pəl\, Arthur. Lord Capel of Had·ham \ˈhad-əm\. 1610?–1649. English Royalist leader. Member of Short and Long Parliaments (1640); created baron (1641); lieutenant general of Shropshire, Cheshire, and North Wales (1643); escorted queen to Paris (1646); aided Charles I's escape to Isle of Wight (1647); one of leaders of Second Civil War (1648); captured in siege of Colchester (1648) and beheaded. His son ¶Arthur (1631–1683), Earl of Essex (from 1661); lord lieutenant of Hertfordshire (1660), of Wiltshire (1668), of Ireland (1672–77); opposed grants to Charles II's favorites and opposed his Catholic leanings; first lord of treasury (1679); joined Shaftesbury in support of exclusion of James II (1680); on discovery of Rye House Plot (1683) sent to Tower; found with throat cut, possibly a suicide.

Ca·pell \ˈkā-pəl\, Edward. 1713–1781. English scholar. Deputy inspector of plays (1737); published edition of Shakespeare's plays based on collation of Folio and Quarto texts (10 vols., 1768) and a complete commentary, *Notes and Various Readings to Shakespeare* (1779–83).

Ca·pel·la \kə-ˈpel-ə\, Martianus Minneus Felix. 4th–5th century A.D. North African writer. Lawyer in Carthage; author of a prose and verse introduction to the liberal arts that was influential into the Middle Ages, but whose overall title is lost.

Capellanus, Andreas. See ANDRÉ LE CHAPELAIN.

Ca·pel·le \kä-ˈpel-ə\, Eduard von. 1855–1931. German naval officer. Admiral (1913); succeeded von Tirpitz as secretary of the navy (1916–18); put in effect (1917) unrestricted submarine warfare against Allies, esp. Great Britain.

Ca·pel·len \kä-ˈpel-ən\, Godert Alexander Gerard Philip van der. Baron. 1778–1848. Dutch colonialist. Minister of interior (1809–10); helped draft new colonial policy (1814); governor general of Dutch East Indies (1816–26); attempted to implement liberal policies, but disruption and inequities led to economic stagnation, Java War (1825–30); dismissed after mortgaging Indies to Britain.

Ca·pel·lo \kä-ˈpel-ō, -ˈpäl-\ or **Cap·pel·lo** \käp-\, Bianca. 1542?–1587. Italian noblewoman and adventuress. Mistress of Francesco de' Medici, Duke of Tuscany; simulated pregnancy and palmed off on him as his own son a child of a commoner; m. Francesco (1578) and was proclaimed grand duchess of Tuscany four months later; died within a day of Francesco, possibly poisoned at instance of his brother Cardinal Ferdinando I de' Medici.

Capet, Hugh. See HUGH CAPET.

Ca·pe·tian \kə-ˈpē-shən\ dynasty. *Fr.* Ca·pé·tien \kä-pās-yaⁿ\. The third dynasty of French kings, derived from its first ruler, Hugh Capet; ruled (987–1328) through 14 kings in the direct line: Robert II, Henry I, Louis VI through X, Philip I through V, John I, Charles IV; followed by Valois dynasty (1328). For collateral branches see BURGUNDY, ANJOU, VALOIS, ORLÉANS, BOURBON. Members of family earlier than Hugh Capet included Robert the Strong, the counts of Paris Eudes and Robert I, and Hugh the Great (*qq.v.*).

Cap·grave \ˈkap-ˌgrāv\, John. 1393–1464. English chronicler and hagiographer. Joined order of Augustinian hermits and resided most of life in friary at King's Lynn, Norfolk; provincial of order in England. Author of *The Chronicle of England* (from Creation to 1417) in English, *Liber de illustribus Henricis, Solace of Pilgrims, Life of St. Katherine;* formerly believed to have written *Nova Legenda Angliae* on English saints.

Ca·pi·to \ˈkä-pē-ˌtō, *Lat* ˈkap-ə-ˌtō\, Wolfgang Fabricius. *Orig. surname* Köp·fel \ˈkœp-fəl\. 1478–1541. German clergyman and reformer. Roman Catholic priest at Basel (1515) and in service of Archbishop Albert at Mainz (1519); conferred with Erasmus, Zwingli, Luther; adopted Reformation. To Strasbourg (1523); became leader, with Martin Bucer, of Reformation movement in that vicinity; endeavored to reconcile Lutherans and Swiss reformers. With Bucer wrote (1530) Tetrapolitan Confession submitted to Diet of Augsburg; also wrote *Berner Synodus* (1532).

Cap·ma·ny Su·rís y de Mon·pa·lau \käp-ˈmänʸ-sü-ˈrē-sē-t͟hā-mōm-pä-ˈlä-ü\, Antonio. 1742–1813. Spanish philologist and politician. Officer in Spanish army; member of Cortes at Cádiz (1812–13); fought against Napoleonic domination. Author esp. of works on Castilian philology and on history of Barcelona; compiled literary anthology *Teatro histórico-crítico de la elocuencia española* (1786–94) and a French-Spanish dictionary (1805).

Capnio. See Johann REUCHLIN.

Capo d'Istrias. See KAPODÍSTRIAS.

Ca·pone \kə-ˈpōn\, Alphonse. *Nicknamed* Scarface. 1899–1947. American gangster, b. Naples, Italy. To U.S. as a child; to Chicago (1920) as lieutenant to bootlegger Johnny Torrio; fought with rival O'Banion gang (1924–26), winning control of bootlegging and vice in Chicago; controlled political campaigns, police, etc.; ordered St. Valentine's Day Massacre of Bugs Moran gang (1929); convicted of income-tax evasion (1931); imprisoned (1931–39).

Ca·pote \kə-ˈpō-tē\, Truman. 1924–1984. American writer, b. New Orleans. A leading American man of letters of post-World War II period. Pioneered genre of "nonfiction novel" with *In Cold Blood* (1966), an exhaustively researched account of a Kansas mass murder. Author of novels *Other Voices, Other Rooms* (1948), *The Grass Harp* (1951), stories *Breakfast at Tiffany's* (1958), *A Christmas Memory* (1966), play *House of Flowers* (1954), screenplay *Beat the Devil* (1954), etc. Noted as an enfant terrible and tireless socialite.

Capp \ˈkap\, Al. *Orig.* Alfred Gerald Cap·lin \ˈkap-lən\. 1909–1979. American cartoonist, b. New Haven, Conn. Assistant to Ham Fisher in drawing comic strip "Joe Palooka" (1932–34); introduced own strip "L'il Abner" (1934–77), concerning hillbilly characters in Dogpatch; strip noted for satirical commentary on current events and public figures.

Cap·pel \kä-pel\, Louis. *Lat.* Ludovicus Cap·pel·lus *or* Ca·pel·lus \kə-ˈpel-əs\. 1585–1658. French Protestant clergyman. Professor of Hebrew (1613–33) and of theology (from 1633) at theological seminary at Saumur; known for his critical studies of Old Testament texts, especially their orthography and pointing. Author of *Critica Sacra* (1634).

Cappello, Bianca. See CAPELLO.

Cap·po·ni \käp-ˈpō-nē\, Gino Marchese. 1792–1876. Florentine statesman and scholar. Prime minister of Tuscany (1848); instrumental in securing liberal constitution from Leopold III; senator in Tuscan assembly (1859); head of council of state (1859) which prepared union of Tuscany and Piedmont; created senator by King Victor Emmanuel of Italy (1860). Author of *Storia della repubblica di Firenze* (1875).

Capps \ˈkaps\, Edward. 1866–1950. American classicist, b. Jacksonville, Ill. Professor of Greek, U. of Chicago (1892–1907), of classics, Princeton (1907–36); American editor of Loeb Classical Library; managing editor of *Classical Philology* (1906–07); chairman of managing committee, American School of Classical Studies, Athens (1919–39). Author of *From Homer to Theocritus* (1901), *Introduction of Comedy into the City Dionysia* (1903), *Four Plays of Menander* (1910), etc.

Ca·pra·ra \kä-ˈprä-rä\, Giovanni Battista. 1733–1810. Italian ecclesiastical diplomat. Nuncio to Cologne, Lucerne, Vienna (1767–92); cardinal (1792); bishop of Jesi (1793); legate to France to implement terms of Concordat of 1801; an ineffectual representative of church's position; archbishop of Milan (1802); officiated at coronation of Napoléon as king of Italy (1805).

Ca·pré·o·lus \kä-prā-ō-lüᵊ\, Jean. c.1380–1444. French religious and scholar. Dominican; lectured at U. of Paris. Author of *Libri defensionum theologiae divi Thomae de Aquino* (1408–33; pub. 1483–1589), commonly called the *Defensiones,* which revived interest in Thomistic philosophy and earned him title of "Prince of Thomists."

Ca·pri·vi \kä-ˈprē-vē\, Leo von, *in full* Georg Leo von. Graf. 1831–1899. German soldier and politician. Entered Prussian army (1849); chief of staff of 10th army corps in Franco-Prussian War (1870–71). Appointed chief of the admiralty (1883–88); reorganized German navy. Commanding general, 10th army corps, in Hanover (1888). Succeeded Bismarck as imperial chancellor (1890–94) and president of ministry (1890–92); renewed Triple Alliance but vacillated between European allies and Russia; strengthened army.

Ca·pro·li \kä-ˈprō-lē\ *or* **Ca·pri·o·li** \ˌkä-prē-ˈō-lē\, Carlo. *Also called* Carlo del Vi·o·li·no \ˌvē-ō-ˈlē-nō\. c.1615/20–c.1692/95. Italian composer. Composed large number of cantatas and canzoni, of which some 70 are extant; for Jules Mazarin composed *Le nozze di Peleo e di Theti* (1654, libretto by Francesco Buti), one of first Italian operas performed in France.

Ca·pro·ni \kä-ˈprō-nē\, Giovanni Battista. Conte di Ta·lie·do \täl-ˈyād-ō\. 1886–1957. Italian airplane builder. Established (from 1908) and acquired several aircraft firms; noted for Caproni bomber of World War I.

Ca·pua·na \kä-ˈpwä-nä\, Luigi. 1839–1915. Italian writer and critic. Leader with Verga of Realist movement in Italy. Author of novels and short stories including *Profili di donne* (1877), *Giacinta* (1879), *C'era una volta* (1882), *Il Profumo* (1890), *Le appassionate* (1893), *Le paesane* (1894), *Fausto Bragia* (1897), *Il marchese di Roccaverdina* (1901); of plays, as *Malia* (1895), *Lu cavalieri Pidagno* (1903), *Lu paraninfa* (1914); and of critical works, as *Teatro Italiano contemporaneo* (1865), *Studi sulla letteratura contemporanea* (1879–82), *Cronache letterarie* (1899).

Ca·pus \kä-püᵊ\, Alfred. 1858–1922. French journalist and playwright. Political editor of *Figaro* (1914–22). His plays included *La Veine* (1901), *La Châtelaine* (1902), *Notre jeunesse* (1904), *Monsieur Piégeois* (1905), *Les deux hommes* (1908), *L'Aventurier* (1910), *Hélène Ardouin* (1913).

Caracalla. See Marcus Aurelius ANTONINUS.

Caracci. See CARRACCI.

Ca·rac·cio·la \kä-rät-ˈchō-lə\, Rudolf. 1901–1959. German race driver. In racing career (1922–52) won over 100 races including 20 Grand Prix.

Ca·rac·cio·li \kä-ˈrät-chō-lē\ *or* **Ca·rac·cio·lo** \-(ˌ)lō\. Neapolitan noble family, including: Marino Caraccioli (1468–1538), diplomat; bishop of Catania (1524); cardinal (1535); imperial governor of Milan. ¶Giovanni (1487–1550), prince of Melfi, marshal of France, governor of Piedmont (1545 ff.). ¶Saint Francesco, *orig.* Ascanio (1563–1608), founder of Clerici Regulares Minores (1588); rector general (1591–98). ¶Domenico, Marchese di Caraccioli (1715–1789), Neapolitan ambassador to Turin (1754–64), London (1764–71), Paris (1771–81); viceroy of Sicily (1781–86). ¶Francesco (1752–1799), admiral; served with British in American Revolution, under Nelson at Toulon (1793); in service of Ferdinand IV of Naples (to 1798); in service of Parthenopean Republic (1799); successfully prevented landing of British and Sicilian fleet; arrested at capture of Naples and hanged by Nelson.

Caractacus. See CARATACUS.

Ca·ra·fa \kä-ˈrä-fä\, Michele Enrico Francesco Vincenzo Aloisio Paolo. 1787–1872. Italian composer. Cavalry officer under Murat, King of Naples; took part in Russian campaign (1812); lived in Naples (1814–27), Paris (1827–72); professor of composition, Paris Conservatory (1840). His operas included *Gabriella di Vergy* (1816), *Jeanne d'Arc à Orléans* (1821), *Le Solitaire* (1822), *Le Valet de chambre* (1823), *Masaniello* (1827), *Le Nozze di Lammermoor* (1829), *La Prison d'Edimbourg* (1833), *Thérèse* (1838).

Ca·ra·gia·le \ˌkä-rä-ˈjä-le\, Ion Luca. 1852–1912. Romanian writer. Author of comedies as *Conul Leonida* (1879), *O noaple furtunoasă* (1880), *O scrisoare pierdută* (1884); created peasant drama with *Năpasta* (1890); wrote short stories including *O făclie de Paşte* (1889), *Kir Ianulea* (1909).

Caran d'Ache. See Emmanual POIRÉ.

Ca·rat·a·cus \kə-ˈrat-ə-kəs\. *Also called* Ca·rac·ta·cus \-ˈrak-tə-\. *Welsh* Ca·ra·doc *or* Ca·ra·dog \kə-ˈrád-ōg\. 1st century A.D. British chieftain. Son of Cunobelinus; joint chieftain with brother Togodumnus (from c.42); resisted Roman invasion of Emperor Claudius; defeated by Aulus Plautius at Medway River (43); rallied Silures and Ordovices of Wales; defeated by Ostorius Scapula (50); captured, exhibited in Rome, pardoned.

Ca·ra·thé·o·do·ry \ˈkä-rä-t͟he-ō-t͟hō-ˈrē\, Constantin. 1873–1950. Greek mathematician. Professor, Hannover (1909), Breslau (1910–13), Göttingen (1913–18), Berlin (1918–20), Smyrna (1920–22), Athens (1922–24), Munich (1924–50); known for work on calculus of variations, on theory of real functions, and theory of point-set measure. Author of *Vorlesungen über reelle Funktionen* (1918), *Geometrische Optik* (1937), *Funktionen theorie* 1950).

Ca·rau·si·us \kə-ˈró-zhē-əs\, Marcus Aurelius. d.293. Roman general. Originally a Menapian pilot on Scheldt; served Roman Emperor Maximian against rebelling Gauls (286); put in command of Roman fleet at Boulogne to ward off Frankish and Saxon pirates, enriched himself by plunder; set himself up as emperor in Britain (286); defeated Maximian's fleet (289); murdered by Allectus, one of his ministers.

Caravaggio. See Michelangelo MERISI.

Caravaggio, Polidoro da. See Polidoro CALDARA.

Car•a•way \'kar-ə-ˌwā, 'ker-\, Hattie Ophelia, *nee* Wy•att \'wī-ət\. 1878–1950. American politician, b. Bakersville, Tenn. m. Thaddeus H. Caraway (1902; d. 1931). Appointed to complete husband's term in Senate (1931–32); first woman to be elected to the U.S. Senate (1932); served as senator from Arkansas (1931–45).

Car•bo \'kär-(ˌ)bō\, Gaius Papirius. d. 119 B.C. Roman politician. Tribune (131 B.C.); member of land commission of Gracchus (130–122); deserted Gracchus for party of Optimates (122); consul (120); defended Lucius Optimius for murder of Lucius Gracchus; impeached, committed suicide.

Carbo, Gnaeus Papirius. c.130–82 B.C. Roman general. Leader of forces of Gaius Marius against those of Sulla; blockaded and forced capitulation of Rome (87); consul with Cinna (85); illegally usurped consulship (84, 83); defeated by Sulla's general Metellus Pius (82); executed.

Carco, Francis. See CARCOPINO-TUSOLI.

Car•co•pi•no-Tu•so•li \kȧr-kȯ-pē-nō-tü̅e̅-sō-lē\, François. *Pseudonym* Francis Car•co \kȧr-kō\. 1886–1958. French poet and novelist. Author of verse *La Bohème et mon coeur* (1912), *Poésies complètes* (1955); novels *Jésus la Caille* (1914), *Les Innocents* (1917), *L'Equipe* (1919), *L'Homme traqué* (1922), *Perversité* (1925), *La Rue* (1930), *Les Hommes en cage* (1936), *Les belles manières* (1945), *Campagnons de la mauvaise chance* (1954); books on Parisian life.

Car•da•no \kär-'dä-nō\, Geronimo *or* Gerolamo *or* Girolamo. *Eng.* Jerome Car•dan \'kär-ˌdan, 'kärd-ᵊn\. *Lat.* Hieronymus Car•da•nus \kär-'dā-nəs\. 1501–1576. Italian mathematician, physician, and astrologer. Public lecturer in geometry at Milan (1534); rector of college of physicians, Milan; professor of medicine, Pavia (1543–60), Bologna (1562); arrested for heresy or debt or both (1570); on release, moved to Rome (1571); pensioned by Pope Pius V. Successful as a physician, being summoned to Scotland, where he cured the archbishop (1552). In *Ars Magna* (1545), gave as his own the cubic solution which he had obtained from Tartaglia, its discoverer, thus giving rise to a controversy; published *De subtilitate rerum* (1550) and *De rerum varietate* (1557) containing scientific speculation and information on contemporary physical knowledge; also wrote *Liber de ludo alaea* (pub. 1663), first systematic work on probability, and works on astronomy, astrology, rhetoric, medicine, etc., and an autobiography, *De propria vita* (1576).

Cárdenas, Bartolemé de. See Bartolomé de BERMEJO.

Cárdenas, García López de. See LÓPEZ DE CÁRDENAS.

Cár•de•nas \'kär-t͟hā-näs\, Lázaro. 1895–1970. Mexican soldier and politician. Joined revolutionary forces of Carranza (1913); general (1923); governor of Michoacán (1928–32); national chairman, Partido Nacional Revolucionario (1930); minister of interior (1931); minister of war and marine (1933). President of Mexico (1934–40); launched Six-Year Plan involving massive redistribution of land, industrial and transportation development, renewal of struggle with Roman Catholic Church, and expropriation (1938) of foreign-owned oil properties; reorganized and enlarged ruling party as Partido de la Revolución Mexicana (1938). Commander, forces on Pacific coast (1941), Mexican army (1945); minister of defense (1943–45).

Cardi de Cigoli, Ludovico. See CIGOLI.

Cardigan, Earl of. See James Thomas BRUDENELL.

Car•do•zo \kär-'dō-zō\, Benjamin Nathan. 1870–1938. American jurist, b. New York City. Practiced law, New York City (from 1891); judge of New York Court of Appeals (1914–32), chief judge (1926–32); associate justice, U.S. Supreme Court (1932–38). Author of *Nature of the Judicial Process* (1921), *Growth of the Law* (1924), *Paradoxes of Legal Science* (1928), etc.

Car•duc•ci \kär-'düt-chē\, Bartolommeo. *Span.* Bartolomé Car•du•cho \kär-t͟hü-chō\. 1560–c.1610. Italian painter, sculptor, and architect. Accompanied his master Federigo Zuccaro to Spanish court (1585); protégé of Philip II and III; painted frescoes in Escorial library and several altarpieces in church of San Felipe el Real. His works included *Holy Eucharist, Descent from the Cross, St. Francis Receiving the Stigmata, Adoration of the Kings.* His brother ¶Vincenzo, *Span.* Vicente (1576–1638), accompanied him to Spain (1585); painter to Spanish court (1609 ff.); protégé of Philip III and IV; leading artist of Madrid until Velázquez. His works included *Martyrdom of St. Andrew* (in cathedral at Toledo), and 54 paintings for the El Paular monastery (now in the Prado). Author of *Diálogos de la Pintura* (1633).

Carducci, Giosuè. *Early pseudonym* E•no•tri•o Ro•ma•no \ā-'nō-trē-ō-rō-'mä-nō\. 1835–1907. Italian poet. Professor of literary history, Bologna (1861–1904). Awarded Nobel prize for literature (1906). Staunch classicist; attempted to introduce classical metrical schemes into Italian poetry; considered national poet of modern Italy. Author of many volumes of verse, including *Rime* (1857), *Giambi ed epodi* (1867–69), *Levia gravia* (1868), *Satana e polemiche sataniche* (1879), *Odi barbare* (1887–89), *Rime e ritme* (1899); also of critical and historical works.

Card•well \'kärd-wəl, -ˌwel\, Edward. Viscount Cardwell. 1813–1885. English politician. M.P. (1842–74); supported Peel and free-trade policy; president of Board of Trade in Aberdeen's coalition ministry (1852–55); carried Merchant Shipping Act (1854); secretary for Ireland (1859–61); secretary for colonies (1864–66); refused to keep British troops in colonies during peacetime unless colonies paid for them; abolished penal transportation (1868); laid foundations for federation in Canada; secretary for war under Gladstone (1868–74); abolished flogging as peacetime punishment and commissions by purchase, and instituted short-service system and the reserve in army; created viscount (1874).

Careless, William. See William CARLOS.

Ca•rew \kə-'rü\, George. Baron Carew of Clop•ton \'kläp-tən\ *and* Earl of Tot•nes \'tät-nəs\. 1555–1629. English soldier. Served in Irish wars against Earl of Desmond (1574–83); master of ordnance in Ireland (1588–92); lieutenant general of ordnance in England (1592); on Essex's expeditions to Cádiz (1596) and Azores (1597); ambassador to France (1598). President of Munster, Ireland (1600–03); after failure of Essex, repressed rebellion of Earl of Tyrone with ruthlessness. Created baron (1605); master general of ordnance (1608–17); governor of Guernsey (1610–21); earl (1626).

Carew, Richard. 1555–1620. English poet and antiquary. M.P. (1584); high sheriff of Cornwall (1586). Translator of five cantos of Tasso's *Gerusalemme liberato* (1594); published *Survey of Cornwall* (1602).

Carew, Thomas. 1595?–?1640. English poet. Secretary to Lord Herbert of Cherbury (1619); served in court of Charles I (from 1630); friend of Sir John Suckling, Ben Jonson, Davenant; admirer of Donne. Author chiefly of short brilliant amatory or occasional lyrics; considered first of Cavalier poets; also wrote masque *Coelum Britannicum* for court (1634).

Car•ey \'ka(ə)r-ē, 'ke(ə)r-ē\, Henry. 1st Baron Huns•don \'hənz-dən\. 1524?–1596. English soldier and diplomat. Son of Anne Boleyn's sister; M.P. (1547, 1554, 1555); created baron (1559); envoy to France (1564, 1591), to Scotland (1587); governor of Berwick (1568–87); commissioner on treason trials (1585–95) and to try Mary, Queen of Scots (1586). His youngest son ¶Robert (1560?–1639), 1st Earl of Mon•mouth \'män-moth, 'mən-\, soldier; M.P. (1586, 1588, 1593); fought in Netherlands (1587), against Armada (1588), in Normandy (1591); warden of Scottish border (1593–1603); by sixty hours of riding carried news of Queen Elizabeth's death to James VI of Scotland (1603); followed Charles, Prince of Wales, to Spain (1623); created earl (1626).

Carey, Henry. c.1687–1743. English poet and composer. Reputed illegitimate son of George Savile, Marquis of Halifax. Published first poems (1713); wrote farces, burlesques, and songs, and often the accompanying music, for London stage (1715–39), including *Chrononhotonthologos,* a burlesque of contemporary theatrical bombast (1734), and *A Wonder; or the Honest Yorkshireman,* a ballad opera (1735). Author and composer of "Sally in our Alley" (pub. in *The Musical Century,* 1737); without basis often reputed to be author of words and music of *God Save the King.*

Carey, James. 1845–1883. Irish nationalist. Dublin builder and town councilor, originally a bricklayer; a founder of the Invincibles (1881); directed assassination (1882) of Lord Frederick Cavendish and T.H. Burke in Phoenix Park, Dublin; betrayed Fenians and by his evidence caused execution of five associates; shot at sea on way to Natal by assassin sent by the Invincibles to avenge the deaths.

Carey, Mathew. 1760–1839. American publisher, b. Dublin, Ireland. Edited anti-British *Freeman's Journal* (1780–83), *Volunteer's Journal* (1783–84). Fled to America (1784) to escape prosecution; founded *Pennsylvania Herald* (1785), *Columbian Magazine* (1786), *American Museum* (1787); publisher and bookseller in Philadelphia (from 1790). His son ¶Henry Charles (1793–1879), b. Philadelphia, became partner in publishing house (1817); gave up business (1835) to study and write on economics. Author of *Essay on the Rate of Wages* (1835), *Principles of Political Economy* (1837–40), *The Past, the Present, and the Future* (1848), *Harmony of Interests* (1851), *Principles of Social Science* (1858–60), *Unity of Law* (1872).

Carey, William. 1761–1834. English Orientalist and missionary. Helped found Baptist Missionary Society (1792); one of the first missionaries to go to India (1793); established church, school, and printing press at Serampore (1799–1801); professor of Sanskrit in college at Fort William near Calcutta (1801–30); issued translations (known as *Serampore versions)* of the Scriptures in some 35 languages and dialects; compiled grammars and dictionaries of Marathi, Sanskrit, Punjabi, and other native languages; helped translate an edition of the *Rāmāyaṇa* (1806–10).

Car•gill \'kär-(ˌ)gil\, Donald. 1619?–1681. Scottish Covenanter. Ejected from his parish for rebuking Charles II (1662); wounded at Bothwell Bridge (1679) during insurrection by Scottish Covenanters; with Richard Cameron (*q.v.*) declared Charles II deposed and excommunicated (1680); beheaded for treason.

Cargill, Oscar. 1898–1972. American critic, b. Livermore Falls, Me. Professor, New York U. (1930–66); consulting editor, Macmillan Co. (1935–63). Author and editor of numerous textbooks and editions; wrote *Intellectual America* (1941), *Toward a Pluralistic Criticism* (1965).

Ca·rí·as An·di·no \kä-'rē-ä-sän-'dē-nō\, Tiburcio. 1876–1969. Honduran general and politician. President of Honduras (1933–49); promulgated new constitution (1937) in order to remain in office; ruled dictatorially, suppressed several rebellions.

Carignano. The cadet, or Savoy-Carignan, branch of house of Savoy (*q.v.*).

Ca·ri·nus \kə-'rī-nəs\, Marcus Aurelius. d. 285. Roman emperor (283–285). Elder son of emperor Carus; appointed (282) caesar and governor of western provinces; on death of Carus (283) left joint emperor with brother Numerianus; indulged in violent excesses, but displayed some bravery and military skill against barbarians; defeated Aurelius Julianus (285); fought with Diocletian; won battle near Margus in Moesia; killed by one of his officers.

Ca·ris·si·mi \kä-'rēs-sē-mē\, Giacomo. 1605–1674. Italian composer. Maestro di cappella, Collegio Germanico of S. Apollinare, Rome (1629–74). Composed masses and motets, but best known for oratorios and secular cantatas; an originator of oratorio form, his including *Jephte, Judicium extremum, Baltazar, Judicium Salomonis, Jonah.* Through music and students exerted long-lived influence.

Ca·ri·tat \kȧ-rē-tȧ\, Marie-Jean-Antoine-Nicolas de. Marquis de Con·dor·cet \kōⁿ-dȯr-se\. 1743–1794. French mathematician, philosopher, and revolutionary. Protégé of d'Alembert; assisted on *Encyclopédie;* welcomed Revolution; member and secretary of Legislative Assembly (1791–92); drew up call for and member of National Convention (1792); fled persecution of moderate Girondins; in hiding (1792–94); arrested, died in prison. Author of *Essai sur l'application de l'analyse à la probabilité des décisions rendues à la pluralité des voix* on probability (1785), biographies of Turgot (1786) and Voltaire (1789), and *Esquisse d'un tableau historique des progrès de l'esprit humain* (1795).

Carl. See Charles.

Carle·ton \'kär(-ə)l-tən, 'kär(-ə)lt-ᵊn\, Sir Guy. 1st Baron Dor·ches·ter \'dȯr-,ches-tər, -chəs-\. 1724–1808. British soldier and administrator, b. Ireland. Served in America (from 1758); lieutenant governor (1766–70), acting governor (1767–70) of Quebec; major general (1773); governor of Quebec and commander of British forces in Canada (1775–77); repelled attack of Montgomery and Benedict Arnold on Quebec (1775–76); defeated Arnold on Lake Champlain and took Crown Point (1776); superseded as commander by Burgoyne (1777); lieutenant general (1777); succeeded Sir Henry Clinton as commander in chief in America (1782–83); governor of Quebec (1786–91), Lower Canada (1791–96); general (1793).

Carleton, Will, *in full* William McKendree. 1845–1912. American poet, b. near Hudson, Mich. Author of *Farm Ballads* (1873), *City Ballads* (1885); best known poem, "Over the Hill to the Poor House."

Carleton, William. 1794–1869. Irish novelist. Tutor in Dublin. Author of stories delineating Irish peasant life, including two series of *Traits and Stories of the Irish Peasantry* (1830, 1833) and a long powerful novel *Fardorougha the Miser* (1839); alienated many Irishmen by unsparing criticism in later stories, including *The Tithe Proctor* (1849), *The Squanders of Castle Squander* (1852).

Car·li \'kär-lē\, Gian Rinaldo. 1720–1795. Italian economist and antiquary. Professor of astronomy and navigation, Padua (1744); president, council of commerce, Milan (1753); president, school of finance, Milan (1771). Author of *Della moneta e dell'istituzione delle zecche d'Italia* (1754–60), *Antichità italiche* (1788–90), etc.

Car·lile \kär-'lī(ə)l, 'kär-,\, Richard. 1790–1843. English freethinker and reformer. Journeyman tinsmith in London; disciple of Thomas Paine; vendor of *Black Dwarf,* a prohibited radical weekly (1817); printed Southey's *Wat Tyler* and other free-thought papers; imprisoned for publishing his *Political Litany* and again (1819–25) for publishing Paine's works; published journal *The Republican* (1819–26), despite imprisonment of his wife, sister, and shopmen as his accomplices; edited weeklies *The Lion* and *The Gorgon;* imprisoned for refusing to pay church rates (1830–33, 1834–35).

Carlile, Wilson. 1847–1942. English clergyman. Founded (1882) Church Army, organization of Anglican lay evangelists.

Carlingford, Baron. See Chichester Samuel FORTESCUE.

Carlisle, Countess of. See Lucy HAY.

Carlisle, Earls of. See HOWARD family.

Car·lisle \kär-'lī(ə)l, 'kär-,\, John Griffin. 1835–1910. American politician, b. Campbell (now Kenton) Co., Ky. Member, U.S. House of Representatives (1877–90); speaker (1883–89); identified with movement for tariff reform; U.S. senator (1890–93); U.S. secretary of the treasury (1893–97); noted for sound-money policy.

Carlo. See CHARLES.

Car·lo·man \'kär-lō-,man, *Fr* kȧr-lȯ-mäⁿ\. *Ger.* Karl·mann \'kärl-,män\. c.715–754. Frankish prince. Son of Charles Martel; mayor of the palace (741–745) jointly with his brother Pepin the Short; administered eastern Frankish kingdom; fought wars with Germans and strengthened power of church; retired to a monastery (745) and later to Monte Cassino (750).

Carloman. *Ger.* Karlmann. 751–771. Frankish prince. Son of Pepin the Short; co-king of Franks with elder brother Charlemagne (754); king of Eastern Franks (768–771).

Carloman. *Ger.* Karlmann. 828–880. Carolingian prince. Son of Louis the German and father of the Emperor Arnulf; duke of Bavaria (865–876); king of Bavaria and Carinthia (876–880); proclaimed but not crowned king of the Lombards (877); relinquished rule to brother Louis the Younger (879).

Carloman. *Ger.* Karlmann. d. 884. King of the West Franks. Son of Louis II; joint ruler with his brother Louis III (879–882); sole ruler (882–884); reigned in south (Aquitaine and Burgundy).

Carlos. See also CHARLES.

Car·los \'kär-lōs, *Angl* -ləs\, Don. Name of several princes of Spain:

Don Carlos de Aus·tria \-thā-'au̇s-trē-ä\. 1545–1568. Eldest son of Philip II and Maria of Portugal; prince of Asturias and heir to Spanish throne; showed signs of instability; barred from succession by father; attempted to flee to Flanders (1567); imprisoned (1568) for plotting with Dutch leaders against father; died in prison. Subject of Schiller's tragedy *Don Carlos* (1801) and of dramas by Alfieri, Chénier, Otway, Núñez de Arce, etc.

Don Carlos de Borbón. See CHARLES III of Spain.

Don Carlos. *Full name* Carlos María Isidro de Bor·bón \bōr-'bōn\. Conde de Mo·li·na \mō-'lē-nä\. 1788–1855. Second son of Charles IV and brother of Ferdinand VII; became pretender to Spanish throne when Ferdinand, persuaded by his wife Maria Christina, abrogated (1830) Salic Law of Succession in favor of male heirs and secured throne to his daughter Isabella II; proclaimed king by supporters as Charles V; revolted, but in Carlist wars (1833–39) overcome by government forces; fled to France (1839); resigned pretensions (1845) to his son Don Carlos 2d.

Don Carlos. *Full name* Carlos Luis Fernando de Borbón. Conde de Mon·te·mo·lín \mōn-tā-mō-'lēn\. 1818–1861. Recognized by Carlists as Charles VI (1845); fought hopeless war in Catalonia (1846–48); made prisoner during insurrection (1860); released on signing renunciation of claims; died without issue, claims passing to youngest brother, Don Juan.

Don Carlos. *Full name* Carlos María de los Dolores de Borbón. 1848–1909. Son of pretender Don Juan; succeeded as pretender (1868); published proclamation claiming Spanish throne as Charles VII (1872); waged Second Carlist civil war (1872–76); fled to France; gave up struggle, but did not relinquish claims; expelled from France (1881) for Orléanist sympathies; abdicated (1909) in favor of his son Don Jaime of Madrid.

Car·los *or* **Car·les** *or* **Care·less** \'ke(ə)r-ləs, 'ka(ə)r-\, William. d. 1689. English Royalist officer. After battle of Worcester, shared with Prince Charles (later Charles II) his hiding place in a hollow oak (the "Royal Oak") at Boscobel, Shropshire (Sept. 6–7, 1651); escaped to France; later in service of Charles II.

Car·lo·ta \kär-'lō-tä\. *Full name* Marie-Charlotte-Amélie-Augustine-Victoire-Clémentine-Léopoldine. 1840–1927. Empress of Mexico (1864–67). Only daughter of Leopold I of Belgium; m. (1857) Maximilian, Archduke of Austria; accompanied him to Mexico (1864) when he was given imperial crown; sent by Maximilian (1866) to Europe to secure aid from Napoléon III and the pope against Mexican republicans; realizing failure of her husband's cause became hopelessly insane; confined in château near Brussels.

Carl·son \'kär(-ə)l-sən\, Anton Julius. 1875–1956. American physiologist, b. Bohuslan, Sweden. To U.S. (1891); taught at U. of Chicago (1904–40); did research on nervous excitation of the heart, the thyroid and parathyroids, the pancreas, immune bodies, also on metabolism, gastric secretion, and hunger.

Carlson, Chester Floyd. 1906–1968. American inventor, b. Seattle, Wash. Worked for Bell Telephone Co. and P. R. Mallory Co.; on his own worked on problem of making copies of documents; developed electrostatic "xerography" process (1938; pat. 1940 ff.); licensed development to Battelle Memorial Inst., Columbus, Ohio (1944) and commercial rights to Haloid Co. (1947, later the Xerox Corp.)

Carlson, Evans Fordyce. 1896–1947. American soldier, b. Sidney, N.Y. Served in China (1927–29), Nicaragua (1930–33), in China and Japan (1933–36); as observer traveled with Chinese 8th Route Army (1937–39); recorded experiences and observations in *Twin Stars of China* and *The Chinese Army* (1940). As lieutenant colonel trained and led (1942–43) 2d Marine Raider Battalion, known as "Carlson's Raiders"; took part in operations on Makin Island and Guadalcanal; retired as brigadier general (1946).

Carlstadt, Bodenstein von. See BODENSTEIN.

Carl·ton \'kär(-ə)l-tən, 'kärlt-ᵊn \, Effie, *nee* Crock·ett \'kräk-ət\. 1857–1940. American actress. Author, under pen name Effie Can·ning \'kan-iŋ\, of the lullaby "Rock-a-Bye Baby" (orig. copyright, 1887).

Car·lyle \kär-'lī(ə)l, 'kär-,\, Thomas. 1795–1881. Scottish essayist and historian. Taught mathematics, Annan (1814); schoolmaster at Kirkcaldy (1816). Wrote articles for Brewster's *Edinburgh Encyclopaedia;* translated Legendre's *Geometry* and Goethe's *Wilhelm Meister;* wrote *Life of Schiller* (1825). Met Coleridge, Hazlitt, and other literary men in London (1824); m. (1826) Jane Baillie Welsh; settled in Edinburgh; wrote essays for *Edinburgh Review;* formed friendship with Jeffrey. Moved to Craigenputtock (1828); wrote the autobiographical *Sartor Resartus* (pub. in *Fraser's Magazine,* 1833–34), a speculative discussion of creeds and systems of philosophy under guise of a philosophy of clothes; settled in London (1834). His *French Revolution* (1837), published despite burning of manuscript for most of first volume by John Stuart Mill's servant, established his reputation as one of foremost men of letters; published *Chartism* (1840), *On Heroes, Hero-Worship, and the Heroic in History* (1841), *Past and Present* (1843), *Latter-Day Pamphlets* (1850); in *Oliver Cromwell* (1845) revolutionized contemporary estimate of Cromwell; biographized his friend John Sterling (1851); devoted himself (1851–65) to his *History of Frederick the Great;* installed as rector of Edinburgh U. (1866), publishing address as *On the Choice of Books* (1866). Self-styled prophet, one of great sages of era.

Carmagnola. See Francesco BUSSONE.

Car·man \'kär-mən\, Bliss, *in full* William Bliss. 1861–1929. Canadian poet, b. Fredericton, N.B. On staff successively of New York *Independent, Current Literature, Atlantic Monthly.* His many volumes of verse included *Low Tide on Grand Pré* (1893), *A Seamark* (1895), *Ballads of Lost Haven* (1897), *By the Aurelian Wall* (1898), *Sappho* (1902), *Pipes of Pan* (1903–05); collaborated with Richard Hovey in *Songs from Vagabondia* (1894), *More Songs from Vagabondia* (1896), and *Last Songs from Vagabondia* (1900). Prose essays collected in *Kinship of Nature* (1904), *The Poetry of Life* (1905), etc.

Carmarthen, Marquis of. See Thomas OSBORNE.

Carmen Sylva. See ELIZABETH, Queen of Romania.

Carmichael \'kär-,mī-kəl, kär-'\, Hoagland Howard, *called* Hoagy. 1899–1981. American songwriter, b. Bloomington, Ind. Pianist and arranger with various bands, including his own; appeared in films. Songs included "Riverboat Shuffle," "Washboard Blues," "Stardust," "Rockin' Chair," "Georgia on My Mind," "The Nearness of You," "I Get Along Without You Very Well," "Two Sleepy People," "Lazy River," "In the Cool, Cool, Cool of the Evening" (Academy Award, 1951), "Lazy Bones" (with Johnny Mercer).

Carmichael, Leonard. 1898–1973. American psychologist, b. Philadelphia. Professor, Brown U. (1924–36), U. of Rochester (1936–38); president, Tufts U. (1938–52); secretary of Smithsonian Inst. (1953–64); vice president for research and exploration, National Geographic Society (1964–73), sponsoring work of L.S.B. Leakey, J.-Y. Cousteau, etc.

Car·mo·na \kər-'mō-nə\, António Óscar de Fra·go·so \də-frə-'gō-zü\. 1869–1951. Portuguese general and politician. Entered army (1888); general (1922); took part in military coup (1926); made prime minister and minister of war by military decree (1926); virtually dictator; put down revolts in Oporto and Lisbon (1927); elected president by plebiscite (1928); remained president (1928–51); named António Salazar premier (1932).

Carmontelle, Louis. See Louis CARROGIS.

Car·nap \'kär-,näp, *Angl* -,nap\, Rudolf. 1891–1970. American philosopher, b. Ronsdorf, Germany. Professor, Vienna U. (1926–31), German U. of Prague (1931–35), U. of Chicago (1936–52), Inst. for Advanced Study (1952–54), UCLA (1954–70); a member of Vienna Circle of logical positivists (1926ff.). One of leading logicians of the time. Author of *Der logische Aufbau der Welt* (1928), *Abriss der Logistik* (1929), *Logische Syntax der Sprache* (1934), *Meaning and Necessity* (1947), *Logical Foundations of Probability* (1950).

Carnarvon, Earls of. See HERBERT family.

Car·ne·a·des \kär-'nē-ə-,dēz\. 214?–?129 B.C. Greek skeptic philosopher. Founder in Athens of the New, or Third, Academy. Cf. CLEITOMACHUS.

Car·ne·gie \'kär-nə-gē, kär-'neg-ē\, Andrew. 1835–1919. American industrialist and humanitarian, b. Dunfermline, Scotland. To U.S. (1848); settled in Allegheny, Pa. Held minor positions in cotton textile factory and telegraph company; secretary to superintendent, Pittsburgh division, Pennsylvania Railroad. Entered iron and steel business (1865); concentrated on steel industry (from 1873); chief owner, Homestead Steel Works, by 1888; controlled seven other manufactories; consolidated his interests into Carnegie Steel Co. (1899); merged this company with United States Steel Corp. (1901), and retired. Devoted rest of life to distribution of huge fortune for benefit of society, in accordance with views expressed in his article "Wealth" in *North American Review* (1889). Benefactions included large contributions for public libraries, public education, and international peace; founded Carnegie Institute of Technology, Pittsburgh (1900), Carnegie Institution of Washington, D.C. (1902), Carnegie Foundation for the Advancement of Teaching (1905), Hero Funds in U.S. (1904), Great Britain (1908); built Temple of Peace, The Hague (1903); endowed Carnegie Corporation of New York (1911) with $125,000,000 to support his benefactions after his death.

Carnegie, Dale. *Surname orig.* Car·na·gey \'kär-nə-gē, kär-'nā-ge\. 1888–1955. American writer and speaker, b. Maryville, Mo. Worked as traveling salesman (1908–12); began teaching public speaking at YMCA, New York City (1912); organized public and private courses and chain of schools. Author of *Art of Public Speaking* (1915), *Lincoln, the Unknown* (1932), best-selling *How to Win Friends and Influence People* (1936), etc.

Car·ne·ra \kär-'ner-ə, -'ni(ə)r-ə\, Primo. 1906–1967. American boxer, b. Sequals, Italy. To U.S. (1930); compiled 87–13 record in boxing career (1928–37); won heavyweight championship of world from Jack Sharkey (1933), lost it to Max Baer (1934); noted for great size and strength; became professional wrestler (1946); naturalized U.S. citizen (1953).

Car·ne·sec·chi \,kär-nā-'sek-kē\, Pietro. 1508–1567. Italian Humanist. Secretary to Pope Clement VII; became follower of Juan de Valdés (1540) and later adopted some Lutheran tenets; fled to Paris (1546) and protection of Catherine de Médicis; condemned (1558) for failing to answer summons of Pope Paul IV; absolved (1559); returned to Rome; investigated by Inquisition under Pius V (1566), burned and beheaded.

Car·ni·cer y Bat·lle \kär-nē-'sā-rē-'b̲ät-(l)yā\, Ramón. 1789–1855. Spanish composer. Professor of composition, Madrid conservatory (1831–55). Contributed to formation of national opera in Spain. Composer of operas including *Adele di Lusignano* (1819), *Elena e Constantino* (1821), *Elena e Malvina* (1829), *Cristoforo Columbo* (1831), *Ismalia* (1838); also of symphonies, religious works, and songs including Chilean national anthem "Dulce patria" (1828).

Car·not \kȧr-nō\, Lazare-Nicolas-Marguerite. *Called* le Grand Carnot *and* l'Organisateur de la Victoire. 1753–1823. French soldier and administrator. Entered army as engineer (1773); deputy to Legislative Assembly (1791) and National Convention (1792); member, Committee of Public Safety (1793); in charge of organization and direction of the armies (1793–95); president of the Convention (1795); member of the Directory (1795–97), and twice its president; fled to Switzerland and Germany at coup d'état of Fructidor (1797) to escape proscription on account of supposed Royalist sympathies; minister of war (1800–01); member of Tribunat (1802–07), opposed making Napoléon consul for life and opposed establishment of empire; governor of Antwerp (1814); Napoléon's minister of interior during Hundred Days (1815); exiled by Louis XVIII (1815).

Carnot, Sadi, *in full* Nicolas-Léonard-Sadi. 1796–1832. French physicist and engineer. Son of Lazare Carnot; served in engineer corps (1814–28); engaged in research; published (1824) his famous essay on heat, *Réflexions sur la puissance motrice du feu;* his theory, later developed by other scientists, notably Lord Kelvin, was in substance the second law of thermodynamics; devised a reversible engine to investigate theories on energy produced and heat applied under ideal conditions; elucidated the Carnot, or heat cycle of idealized heat engine.

Carnot, Sadi, *in full* Marie-François-Sadi. 1837–1894. French politician. Grandson of Lazare Carnot; entered engineering profession; made prefect of Department of Seine-Inférieure (1871); elected to Chamber of Deputies (1876); minister of public works (1880–81), of finance (1885–87); elected fourth president of the republic to succeed Grévy (1887–94); administration marked by his tact and ability, especially in meeting crises of Boulangist agitation (1889) and Panama scandals (1892); assassinated by an Italian anarchist.

Ca·ro \'kä-rō\, Annibale. 1507–1566. Italian poet and translator. Author of sonnets, lyrics, satires published as *Rime* (1569), of comedy *Straccioni* (1544), etc.; best known for translation of Virgil's *Aeneid* (1581) in which he perfected the 11-syllable line, free verse form called *endecasillabi sciolti.*

Caro, Heinrich. 1834–1910. German industrial chemist. Worked in England (1859–66); with Badische Anilin und Sodafabrik (1868–1910); one of the founders of the coal-tar dye industry.

Caro, Joseph ben Ephraim. See KARO.

Caro, Miguel Antonio. 1843–1909. Colombian politician and author. Editor of conservative journal and partly responsible for 1886 constitution. Vice president of Colombia (1892–94), and president (1894–98) at death of Núñez. Writer on philosophy, politics, and history; known esp. for poetry, as in collection *Horas de amor.*

Carobert. See CHARLES I of Hungary.

Ca·rol \'kä-rȯl, *Angl* 'kar-əl\. Name of two kings of Romania;

Carol I. *Orig.* Karl Eitel Friedrich. 1839–1914. Prince of Romania (1866–81); first king of Romania (1881–1914). Second son of Prince Charles Anthony of Hohenzollern-Sigmaringen and brother of Leopold; entered military service; m. (1869) Elizabeth (*q.v.*), Princess of Wied; elected prince (1866) after deposition of Alexandru Cuza; aided Russia in war against Turkey (1877), independence of Romania being recognized by Treaty of Berlin (1878);

proclaimed king (1881); made secret alliance with Austria (1883); promoted economic development of country but failed to act on rural problems, leading to peasant rebellion (1907); declared war on Bulgaria (1913) in Second Balkan War; proclaimed neutrality at beginning of World War I (1914), though sympathizing with Germany. Succeeded by his nephew Ferdinand I.

Carol II. 1893–1953. King (1930–40). Eldest son of Ferdinand I; contracted morganatic marriage (1917) with Zizi Lambrino; divorced her to marry (1921) Princess Helen of Greece, by whom he was father of King Michael. Renounced (1925) right of succession to throne, deserted wife, and went to Paris to live in exile with Magda Lupescu; formally divorced Princess Helen (1928). Returned to Romania (1930); supplanted his son Michael as king; reign marked by continued attempts to please both Russia and Germany; abolished political parties, established corporatist dictatorship, created Front of National Rebirth (1938); driven from throne (1940) by German influence; fled to Spain.

Carolan, Turlough. See O'Carolan.

Car·o·line of Ans·bach \ˈkar-ō-līn-əv-ˈanz-pak\. *In full* Wilhelmina Carolina. 1683–1737. Queen of Great Britain and Ireland, wife of George II. Daughter of John Frederick, Margrave of Brandenburg-Ansbach; m. (1705) George Augustus, Electoral Prince of Hanover; went to England on accession of George I (1714); gathered distinguished circle including Pope, Gay, Chesterfield, and Lord Hervey; connived at husband's amour with Henrietta Howard; crowned queen (1727); kept Sir Robert Walpole in power; regent during absence of king on four occasions.

Caroline of Bruns·wick \ˈbrənz-(ˌ)wik\. *In full* Karoline Amalie Elisabeth. 1768–1821. Queen of Great Britain and Ireland, wife of George IV. Daughter of Charles William Ferdinand, Duke of Brunswick-Wolfenbüttel. Forced as bride (1795) upon prince of Wales by George III; deserted by profligate husband after birth of Princess Charlotte Augusta (1796); censured for improprieties and unguarded speech (1806); traveled on Continent; on death of George III (1820) refused offer of settlement on condition of renouncing title of queen; held popular support and secured abandonment of bill in House of Lords divorcing her on ground of adultery (1820); forcibly excluded from Westminster on coronation day (1821).

Caroline Ma·til·da \-mə-ˈtil-də\. 1751–1775. Queen of Denmark. Daughter of Frederick Louis and sister of George III of England; m. (1766) Christian VII of Denmark; driven by his neglect into affair with court physician Count Johann Streuensee; divorced by Christian after Streuensee's execution (1772).

Car·o·lin·gi·an \ˌkar-ə-ˈlin-j(ē-)ən\ *or* **Car·lo·vin·gi·an** \ˌkär-lə-ˈvin-j(ē-)ən\ dynasty. Second Frankish dynasty of kings and emperors, succeeding Merovingian dynasty; ruled in France from Pepin the Short (751) to death of Louis V (987) and in Germany to death of Louis III the Child (911).

Carolsfeld. See Schnorr von Carolsfeld.

Carolus Magnus. See Charlemagne.

Ca·ron \kä-rō^{n}, kȧ-\, Antoine. c.1515–1593. French painter. A Mannerist, leading French painter of the day; helped decorate Château Fontainebleau; associated with Valois court (from 1561), patronized esp. by Catherine de Médicis; painted allegorical symbolic, festive scenes, as *Triumph of the Seasons, Massacre Under the Triumvirate, Augustus and the Tiburtine Sibyl;* his series for Catherine on history of Artemis made into tapestries.

Caron, Pierre-Augustin. See Beaumarchais.

Ca·ron·de·let \kä-rȯn-dā-ˈlet, *Angl* kə-ˌrän-də-ˈlet\, Francisco Luis Hector de. Baron. c.1748–1807. Spanish administrator in America. Governor of Louisiana and West Florida (1791–95); fortified Yazoo strip, intrigued with Indians, with Gen. James Wilkinson and others, against U.S.; after sale of West Florida to France, continued as governor of Louisiana (1795–97); governor general of Quito, Ecuador (1799–1807).

Ca·ros·sa \kä-ˈrȯ-sä\, Hans. 1878–1956. German poet and novelist. Physician in Bavaria. Verse included *Stella Mystica* (1902), *Gedichte* (1910), *Stern über der Lichtung* (1946); novels *Doktor Bürgers Ende* (1913), *Eine Kindheit* (1922), *Verwandlungen einer Jugend* (1928), *Der Arzt Gion* (1931), *Geheimnisse des reifen Lebens* (1936), *Das Jahr der schönen Täuschungen* (1941), *Ungleiche Welten* (1951), many of them autobiographical as were *Rumanisches Tagebuch* (1924), a war diary, and *Der Tag des jungen Arztes* (1955).

Ca·roth·ers \kə-ˈrəth-ərz\, Wallace Hume. 1896–1937. American chemist, b. Burlington, Iowa. Teacher (1921–28); director of organic chemical research, E. I. Du Pont de Nemours and Co., Wilmington, Del. (from 1928); conducted research on polymerization; patented (1937) synthetic material nylon, patent being issued posthumously and assigned to du Pont company.

Ca·ro·to \kä-ˈrȯ-tō\, Gian Francesco. c.1480–1555. Veronese painter. Pupil of Liberale and Mantegna. His works included frescoes in church of Sant'Eufemia, *Annunication* in San Girolamo, *St. Ursula* in San Giorgio, altar of San Fermo Maggiore.

Car·pac·cio \kär-ˈpät-chō\, Vittore. c.1460–1525/26. Venetian painter. Noted esp. for compositional and narrative power. Works included series on St. Ursula for Sculoa di Sta. Orsola, on St. Jerome for Scuola di S. Giorgio degli Schiavoni, on the Virgin for Scuola degli Albanese; altarpiece *Presentation in the Temple* for S. Giobbe.

Car·peaux \kȧr-pō\, Jean-Baptiste. *Also called* Jules Carpeaux. 1827–1875. French sculptor. Leading French sculptor of his time. Notable works included *Ugolin et ses enfants* (1861) for the Tuilleries, *La Danse* (1865–69) for façade of Opéra, Paris, *Les Quatre Parties du monde* (1872) in gardens of Luxembourg, and portrait busts of Napoléon III, Alexandre Dumas fils, Princess Mathilde, the painter Gérome, Gounod, Jules Grévy, etc.

Car·pen·ter \ˈkär-pən-tər, ˈkärp-^{ə}m-tər\, Edward. 1844–1929. English writer. In Anglican ministry (1869–74); visited U.S. (1877) and met Emerson, Holmes, Lowell, Bryant, and Whitman; settled in Derbyshire (1883); became interested in Socialist and crafts movements inspired by Hyndman and William Morris; lectured on Socialism. Author of *Towards Democracy* (poem, 1883), *England's Ideal* (1887), *Chants of Labour* (1888), *Civilization, its Cause and Cure* (1889), *Love's Coming of Age* (1896), *Angels' Wings* (1898), *Iolaus* (1902), *The Art of Creation* (1904), *My Days and Dreams* (1916).

Carpenter, John Alden. 1876–1951. American composer, b. Park Ridge, Ill. Vice president of family industrial firm (1909–36). Works included *Adventures in a Perambulator* (suite, 1914), *Piano Concerto* (1915), *Birthday of the Infanta* (ballet, 1917–18), *Krazy Kat* (jazz pantomime, 1921), *Skyscrapers* (ballet, 1923–24), *Jazz Orchestra Pieces* (1925–26), *Sea Drift* (tone poem after Whitman, 1933), *Danza* (1937), symphonies (1940, 1942), *Song of Freedom* (chorus and orchestra, 1941), *The Seven Ages* (suite, 1945).

Carpenter, Mary. 1807–1877. English educator and reformer. Opened girls' school at Bristol (1829); organized a "working and visiting society" (1835); founded a ragged school, Bristol (1846), reformatories, an industrial school (1859); visited India in interests of female education and prison management (1866, 1868, 1869, 1875); author of treatises on reformatories, juvenile delinquents, young convicts.

Carpenter, William Benjamin. 1813–1885. English physiologist. Brother of Mary Carpenter. Professor of physiology at Royal Institution, London (1844); professor of forensic medicine, University Coll., London (1844); took part in expedition for deep-sea exploration (1868–71). Author of *Principles of General and Comparative Physiology* (1839), *The Microscope and Its Revelations* (1856), *Zoology* (1857), *Principles of Mental Physiology* (1874).

Car·pen·tier \kȧr-pä^{n}-tyā; *Angl* ˌkär-pən-ˈti(ə)r\, Georges. 1894–1975. French pugilist. Won light-heavyweight championship of the world by knocking out Battling Levinsky in four rounds (1920); defeated by Dempsey in fourth round of fight for heavyweight championship (1921); lost light-heavyweight crown to Battling Siki (1922).

Carpi, Jacopo Berengario da. See Berengario da Carpi.

Car·pi \ˈkär-pē\, Ugo da. c.1480–between 1520 and 1532. Italian wood engraver. Claimed to be inventor of wood-block printing in chiaroscuro (c.1516); actually, improved original German technique and originated the term *chiaroscuro.* His prints, chiefly after Raphael and Parmigianino, included *Sybil, Descent from the Cross, Massacre of the Innocents, Diogenes.*

Car·pi·ni \kär-ˈpē-nē\, Giovanni da Pian del. c.1180–1252. Italian religious and traveler. Companion and disciple of St. Francis of Assisi; head of Catholic mission sent by Pope Innocent IV to the khan to protest against Mongols' invasion of Christian lands and to gain information about them; met Batu at camp on Volga (April 1246); proceeded to Sira Ordu near Karakorum, arriving after election of Güyük as supreme khan of Mongols (July 1246); dismissed by khan with letter to pope bearing information of no significance; returned to Kiev (June 1247) and finally to pope at Lyon. First notable European to travel in Mongol lands; his *Liber Tartarorum,* containing information concerning the regions and peoples visited, was not published in its entirety until 1839.

Car·poc·ra·tes \kär-ˈpäk-ra-ˌtēz\. 2d century A.D. Greek religious. Founded Gnostic sect of Carpocratians; taught doctrine that men can attain to a state of illumination; revered Plato, Pythagoras, Aristotle, Jesus.

Carp·zov \ˈkärpt-sȯf\, Benedikt. 1595–1666. Saxon jurist. Professor at Leipzig (1645); author of *Practica nova Imperialis Saxonica rerum criminalium* (1638), *Jurisprudentia forensis Romano-Saxonica* (1638), and *Jurisprudentia ecclesiastica seu consistorialis* (1649).

Carr \ˈkär\, Emily. 1871–1945. Canadian painter and writer, b. Victoria, B.C. Known esp. for paintings of western Indians and landscapes. Author of autobiographical volumes including *Klee Wyck* (1941), *House of All Sorts* (1944), *Growing Pains* (1946), *Pause* (1953).

Carr, Robert. Viscount Roch·es·ter \ˈräch-ə-stər, -ˌes-tər\. Earl of Som·er·set \ˈsəm-ər-ˌset, -sət\. c.1590–1645. Scottish courtier. Commended to James I by good looks and high spirits; substituted by James for his constitutional adviser; given Sir Walter Raleigh's manor of Sherborne (1609); created viscount Rochester (1611), earl of Somerset and treasurer of Scotland (1613). Enamored of Lady Frances Howard, wife of Earl of Essex; opposed in his marriage to Countess of Essex upon her obtaining of a decree of nullity, by his confidant in the intrigue, Sir Thomas Overbury, who was found poisoned in the Tower (1613); married Countess of Essex (1613); lord chamberlain (1614); dislodged as favorite by George Villiers (1614). With his wife (who pleaded guilty and was pardoned, 1616) accused of murdering Overbury (1615); prosecuted by Francis Bacon; imprisoned in Tower (until 1621); later pardoned.

Car·rà \kä(r)-'rä\, Carlo. 1881–1966. Italian painter. Associated with Futurists (1909–14), with De Chirico in Metaphysical School (1917–18); later known for figurative paintings of monumental, simplified realism, usually imbued with mood of melancholy.

Car·rac·ci *or* **Car·rac·ci** \kä(r)-'rät-chē\. Bolognese family of painters; founders of the Accademia degli Incamminati; pupils included Guido Reni, Francesco Albani, Domenichino, Alessandro Algardi; influenced Rubens. Their joint works included frescoes, esp. series from Ovid in Palazzo Farnese at Rome, story of Jason in Palazzo Fava, story of Romulus in Palazzo Magnani, and at Palazzo Sampieri at Bologna.

¶Lodovico Carracci (1555–1619), pupil of Prospero Fontana at Bologna; studied works of Italian masters at Parma, Mantua, and Venice; worked chiefly at Bologna; noted teacher. Works included *Mystical Marriage of a Saint, Vision of St. Anthony of Padua, Madonna and Child with St. Francis, St. Joseph and Donors,* frescoes in life of St. Benedict at S. Michele in Bosco, Bologna.

¶Annibale (1560–1609), Lodovico's cousin; began work at Palazzo Farnese (1595); works included lunettes *Flight into Egypt* and *Entombment* for Palazzo Aldobrandini, *St. Roch Giving Alms, Dead Christ Mourned;* also worked in copper engraving.

¶Agostino (1557–1602), Annibale's brother; known also as an engraver; popular court painter, esp. to Duke Ranuccio Farnese of Parma; works included *Bacchus and Ariadne, Communion of St. Jerome, Pluto, Christ and the Adulteress.*

Car·ran·za \kär-'rän-thä\, Bartolomé de. *Also known as* Bartolomé de Mi·ran·da \mē-'rän-dä\. 1503–1576. Spanish theologian. Entered Dominican order (c.1520); professor of theology at Valladolid (1530–39), Rome (1539 ff.); confidant of Charles V and Phillip II; confessor to Mary Tudor; theologian at Council of Trent; archbishop of Toledo (1557); imprisoned (1559–67) by Inquisition on charges of heresy evinced in his *Comentarios sobre el catechismo cristiano;* reimprisoned at Rome (1567–76).

Car·ran·za \kär-'rän-sä\, Venustiano. 1859–1920. Mexican revolutionist and politician. Took part in local revolt in Coahuila (1893); held various state offices; governor of Coahuila at time of Madero revolution (1911), in which he supported Madero; after Madero's assassination (1913), became leader of Constitutionalists; successful in opposition to Victoriano Huerta; proclaimed "First Chief" by coalition of revolutionary bands including those of Villa, Zapata (1914); adopted program of social and economic reform; unfriendly to U.S.; attacked by forces of Villa and Emiliano Zapata; provisional president (1915–17); accepted Constitution of 1917; elected president (1917–20); kept Mexico neutral in World War I; forced to leave capital by Obregón; defeated in battle and murdered.

Car·ra·ra \kär-'rä-rä\. Italian family that ruled Padua in 14th century; members included: Marsiglio (d. 1338), established power of family; leader of Guelfs, fought Ghibelline leader Cangrande della Scala of Verona; defeated (1329); after della Scala's death gained throne (1337) with Venetian aid. ¶Francesco (d. 1393), known as Il Vec·chio \ēl-'vek-kyō\; succeeded uncle Giacomino as ruler of Padua (1355–88); sided with Visconti family of Milan against traditional ally Venice; betrayed, forced to abdicate in favor of son Francesco II; prisoner until death.

Car·ras·quil·la \kär-räs-'kē-yä\, Tomás. 1858–1941. Colombian novelist. Author of novels of remote Antioquia, including *Frutos de mi tierra* (1896), *Salve Regina* (1903), *Grandeza* (1910), *El Padre Casafús* (1914), *Ligia Cruz* (1926), *La Marquesa de Yolombó* (1928), *Hace tiempo* (1935–36).

Car·rel \kȧ-rel; *Angl* kə-'rel, 'kar-əl\, Alexis. 1873–1944. French surgeon and biologist. Prosector, U. of Lyon (1900–02); to U.S. (1904); on staff of Rockefeller Institute for Medical Research (1906–38). Developed methods for suturing blood vessels and transplantation of organs; awarded 1912 Nobel prize for physiology or medicine; successful in cultivating chicken heart tissue outside of the body for period of many years; developed the Carrel-Dakin treatment of wounds by regular intermittent irrigation with Dakin's solution (see H. D. DAKIN); assisted by Charles A. Lindbergh on construction of the perfusion pump, used in keeping organs alive outside of the body. Author of *Man, the Unknown* (1935), *The Culture of Organs* (with Lindbergh, 1938).

Car·re·ño de Mi·ran·da \kär-'ren-yō-thā-mē-'rän-dä\, Juan. 1614–1685. Spanish painter. Assisted Velázquez in decoration of Alcázar; court painter and portraitist (1671). Works included portraits, as of Charles II, and religious paintings, as *Founding of Trinitarian Order* (1666).

Car·re·ra \kär-'rer-ä\, José Miguel. 1785–1821. Chilean revolutionist. Served in Europe in Spanish army; joined revolutionary movement in Chile (1810) with his brothers Juan José and Luis (both shot as rebels at Mendoza, 1818); overthrew conservative junta (1811); dissolved congress and established new government, ruling as military dictator (1811–13); replaced by Bernardo O'Higgins (1813); made pretense of aiding O'Higgins at Rancagua (1814); fled to Buenos Aires and U.S.; after return to Buenos Aires (1816), attempted to stir up rebellion against Chile; captured and executed at Mendoza.

Carrera, Rafael. 1814–1865. Guatemalan revolutionist and politician. Active against anticlerical Liberal revolt (1837); led Guatemalan insurgents and finally destroyed Central American Federation (1839); proclaimed Guatemala independent (1839); dominated Guatemala as dictator (1840–65) and, for much of the time, Central American states also; established conservative ascendancy, restored Catholic church; president of Guatemala (1844–48, 1854–65); made president for life (1854).

Car·rère \kə-'re(ə)r\, John Merven. 1858–1911. American architect, b. Rio de Janeiro, Brazil. In office of McKim, Mead and White, New York (1883–84). With Thomas Hastings, formed firm of Carrère and Hastings, New York (1886). Examples of their work: hotels Ponce de Leon (1887) and Alcazar (1888), St. Augustine, Fla.; Royal Bank of Canada, Montreal (1906); Carnegie Institution, Washington, D.C. (1906); Memorial Hall, Yale Univ. (1906); U.S. Senate and U.S. House of Representatives office buildings, Washington, D.C.; New York Public Library (completed 1911).

Car·rier \kȧr-yā\, Jean-Baptiste. 1756–1794. French revolutionist. Helped establish Tribunal (1793); member of the Convention; sent on mission to Normandy and Brittany; notorious for his cruelty in executing sentences of revolutionary tribunal in Nantes (1793–94); helped bring about fall of Robespierre (1794); guillotined in Paris.

Car·ri·er \'kar-ē-ər\, Willis Haviland. 1876–1950. American engineer and inventor, b. Angola, N.Y. Designed temperature-humidity control systems (from 1902); developed basic engineering standards for air conditioning (1911); formed Carrier Engineering Corp. (1915), president (1915–30), chairman (1930–48); invented air conditioning system for high-rise buildings (1939).

Car·ri·e·ra \ˌkär-rē-'ā-rä\, Rosalba. 1675–1757. Italian painter. Worked chiefly in Venice; lionized during visit to Paris (1720–21); known chiefly for flattering portraits and miniatures in Rococo style; first to paint miniatures on ivory.

Car·rier-Bel·leuse \kȧr-yā-bel-ūez\, Albert-Ernest. *Surname orig.* Carrier de Belleuse. 1824–1887. French sculptor. Studied under David d'Angers; among his works were *L'Amour et l'Amitié, Jupiter et Hébé, Bacchante;* teacher of Rodin (1864–70).

Car·rière \kȧr-yer\, Eugène. 1849–1906. French painter and lithographer. Known for domestic scenes and groups and for portraits as of Daudet, Anatole France, Verlaine, Goncourt; late works notable for soft gray tonalities.

Car·ri·llo \kär-'rē-yō\, Braulio. 1800–1845. Costa Rican politician. Chief justice of supreme court; president of Costa Rica (1834–37, 1838–41); declared Costa Rica's independence of United Provinces of Central America (1838); assumed dictatorial power; deposed (1841). To Salvador and practiced law; assassinated (1845).

Carrillo, Julián Antonio. 1875–1965. Mexican violinist and composer. Director, National Conservatory of Music, Mexico City (1913–14, 1920–24); director, American Symphony Orchestra, New York (1915–18), and National Orchestra of Mexico, Mexico City (1919). Introduced theory of microtonal music which he called *Sonido 13* (1925 ff.); author of many musical treatises. Compositions included 3 symphonies, 2 masses, vocal and chamber music in microtones; 3 symphonies, 3 masses, operas *Ossian* (1902), *Xulitl* (1920), orchestral, vocal, and chamber music in non-microtonal mode.

Car·ri·llo y So·to·ma·yor \kär-'ē(l)-yō-ē-sō-tō-mä-'yōr\, Luis. 1583?–1610. Spanish poet. Known as exponent of cultism, deliberate rhetorical obscurity based on work of Luis de Góngora. Author of *Fábula de Acis y Galatea* and other verse and treatise *Libro de la erudición poética.*

Carrington, Lord. See Sir Archibald Primrose (1616–1679), under PRIMROSE family.

Car·ring·ton \'kar-iŋ-tən\, Henry Beebee. 1824–1912. American soldier, b. Wallingford, Conn. Served through Civil War; established posts on Bozeman Trail (1866); fought Sioux under Red Cloud, losing many men at Fetterman Massacre (1866).

Carrington, Richard Christopher. 1826–1875. English astronomer. Observer to Durham U. (1849–52); built private observatory near Reigate, Surrey (1853); published (1857) catalogue of circumpolar stars; first to make systematic observations of sunspots; discovered sun's differential rotation; first to observe solar flare (1859).

Car·ro·gis \kȧ-rō-zhē\, Louis. *Pseudonym* Louis Car·mon·telle \kȧr-mōⁿ-tel\. 1717–1806. French writer and painter. In service of Philippe d'Orléans, duc de Chartres. Author of *Proverbes dramatiques* (1768–81), *Théâtre de campagne* (1775); executed portraits of Philidor, Boufflers, Grimm, etc.

Car·roll \ˈkar-əl\, Anna Ella. 1815–1893. American political writer, b. near Pocomoke City, Md. Wrote *Great American Battle* (1856), *Star of the West* (1857) and campaigned for Know-Nothing party; in support of Union cause wrote *War Powers of the General Government* (1861), *Relation of the National Government to the Revolted Citizens Defined* (1862), outlining what became President Lincoln's constitutional theory; later claimed to be author of Gen. Grant's Tennessee River strategy.

Carroll, Charles. *Known as* Charles Carroll of Carrollton. 1737–1832. American Revolutionary leader, b. Annapolis, Md. Member, committee of correspondence and committee of safety (1775), Maryland convention (1776), Continental Congress (1776–78); signer of Declaration of Independence. U.S. senator (1789–92).

Carroll, Earl. 1893–1948. American theatrical producer, b. Pittsburgh. Wrote lyrics and music for some 400 songs, including "Dreams of Long Ago," "So Long, Letty," "Canary Cottage"; wrote and produced Broadway shows as *The Love Mill, The Land of the Lamp,* etc. Producer of lavish, gaudy revues, the Earl Carroll *Vanities* (1923–35); built own theaters (1923, 1931); later produced revues and movies in Hollywood.

Carroll, James. 1854–1907. American physician, b. Woolwich, England. To Canada (1869) and shortly afterwards to U.S.; in U.S. army (1883–1907); took medical degree (1891). Assisted Walter Reed in Cuba in investigations of yellow fever; for scientific purposes, allowed himself to be bitten by mosquito and thus contracted first experimental case of yellow fever (1900). Professor of bacteriology and pathology, Columbian (now George Washington) U. and Army Medical School (1902–07).

Carroll, John. 1735–1815. American prelate, b. Upper Marlboro, Md. Entered Jesuit order (1753); after suppression of Jesuit order (1773), returned to America (1774); bishop of Baltimore (1789), first Roman Catholic bishop in U.S.; founded forerunner of Georgetown U. (1789); his see being created an archdiocese (1811), became first archbishop of Baltimore.

Carroll, Lewis. See Charles Lutwidge DODGSON.

Carroll, Paul Vincent. 1900–1968. Irish playwright. Author of *The Watched Pot* (1931), *Things That Are Caesar's* (1932), *Shadow and Substance* (1937), *White Steed* (1939), *The Strings, My Lord, Are False* (1942), *The Old Foolishness* (1945), *The Devil Came From Dublin* (1952), *The Wayward Saint* (1955).

Carr-Saun·ders \ˈkär-ˈsȯn-dərz, -ˈsän-\, Sir Alexander Morris. 1886–1966. British sociologist and educator. Social worker in London; professor, U. of Liverpool (1923–37); director, London School of Economics (1937–56); instrumental in establishing colonial university colleges that became universities of Khartoum, Malaya, Ibadan, West Indies, East Africa. Author of *The Population Problem* (1922), *Survey of Social Structure of England and Wales* (with D.C. Jones, 1927), *The Professions* (with P.A. Wilson, 1933), *New Universities Overseas* (1961).

Carrucci, Jacopo. See Jacopo da PONTORMO.

Car·son \ˈkärs-ᵊn\, Christopher, *known as* Kit. 1809–1868. American trapper, scout, and Indian agent, b. Madison Co., Ky. Ran away to join Santa Fe expedition (1826); joined expedition to California (1829–31); trapper (1831–42); guide, Frémont's expeditions (1842, 1843, 1845); after battle of San Pascual (Dec. 6, 1846), when Kearny's force was surrounded, crawled at night through investing troops and summoned aid from San Diego. Appointed Indian agent to Utes (1853–61); raised and commanded 1st New Mexico Volunteers in southwest against Indians during Civil War.

Carson, Edward Henry. Baron Carson of Dun·cairn \(ˌ)dən-ˈka(ə)rn, -ˈke(ə)rn\. 1854–1935. British jurist and politician, b. Dublin. Queen's counsel at Irish bar (1889) and English bar (1894); defended Marquis of Queensberry against Oscar Wilde's libel charge (1895). M.P. (1892–1921); solicitor general for Ireland (1892); solicitor general (1900–05); leader of Irish Unionists (1910–21); opposed Irish home rule, encouraged Ulster separatism; attorney general (1915–16); first lord of admiralty (1917); member of war cabinet, without portfolio (1917–18); created baron (1921); lord of appeal in ordinary (1921–29).

Carson, Rachel Louise. 1907–1964. American biologist and author, b. Springdale, Pa. Taught at U. of Maryland (1931–36); with U.S. Bureau of Fisheries (1936–52). Author of *Under the Sea Wind* (1941), *The Sea Around Us* (1951), *Edge of the Sea* (1955), *Silent Spring* (1962).

Car·stares *or* **Car·stairs** \ˈkär-ˌsta(ə)rz, -ˌste(ə)rz\, William. 1649–1715. Scottish clergyman. To Utrecht (1669–72) on father's outlawry as Covenanter; arrested as agent of William of Orange (1675) and again after Rye House Plot (1683); put to torture of boot and thumbscrew; on release (1685) became chaplain to William of Orange, whom he accompanied to England (1688); king's chief adviser in Scottish affairs (1693–1702). Principal of Edinburgh U. (1703–15).

Car·stens \ˈkär-stəns\, Asmus Jakob. 1754–1798. German painter and designer. Professor, Academy of Art, Berlin (1790); lived in Rome (from 1792). Among his works were scenes from Greek mythology, Dante's *Divina commedia,* Ossian's poems, and Shakespeare's plays; influential in infusing classical spirit into German art of the day.

Car·tan \kȧr-täⁿ\, Elie-Joseph. 1869–1951. French mathematician. Professor, Montpelier (1894–96), Lyons (1896–1903), Nancy (1903–12), Sorbonne (from 1912); known for work on theory of Lie groups, subalgebras, etc.; discovered spinors (1913). Author of *La Géométrie des espaces de Riemann* (1925), *La Théorie des groupes continus et des espaces généralisées* (1935).

Carte \ˈkärt\, Richard D'·Oy·ly \ˈdȯi-lē\. 1844–1901. English impresario. Joined his father, a flutist, in musical instrument business (1861); composed operettas. Became successful concert and lecture agent; produced Gilbert and Sullivan's *Trial by Jury* (1875), *Sorcerer* (1877), *H.M.S. Pinafore* (1878); formed partnership with Gilbert and Sullivan; often had five companies performing Gilbert and Sullivan operas in U.S.; built Savoy Theatre, first public building in England lighted by electricity (1881), where rest of Gilbert and Sullivan operas and other operas were performed; organized touring companies that continued to operate after his death; built an unsuccessful Royal English Opera House (1891).

Carte, Thomas. 1686–1754. English historian. Strong Jacobite; resigned as reader at Bath Abbey rather than take oaths to George I (1715); secretary to Bishop Atterbury, fled to France (1722–28); published his *Life of Ormonde* (1736) and *General History of England* (1747–55).

Car·ter \ˈkärt-ər\, Alvin Pleasant, *known as* A.P. 1891–1960. American musician, b. Maces Spring, Va. Formed Carter Family singers, who in recording career (1927–43) and on radio were instrumental in popularizing and preserving much Appalachian folk music. Group also featured his sister-in-law ¶Maybelle Carter, *nee* Ad·ding·ton \ˈad-iŋ-tən\ (1909–1978).

Carter, Caroline Louise, *nee* Dud·ley \ˈdəd-lē\. *Known as* Mrs. Leslie Carter. 1862–1937. American actress, b. Lexington, Ky. m. Leslie Carter (1880; div.); made New York debut (1890); starred in series of David Belasco productions including *Heart of Maryland* (1895), *Zaza* (1899), *Madame Du Barry* (1901), *Adrea* (1905); retired (1916).

Carter, Elizabeth. 1717–1806. English poet and translator. Contributed verse to *Gentleman's Magazine;* published *Poems upon Particular Occasions* (1738), *Poems on Several Occasions* (1762); expert linguist; translator from French and Italian; translator of Epictetus (1758); friend of Dr. Johnson, who praised her Greek scholarship.

Carter, Henry. See Frank LESLIE.

Carter, Hodding. 1907–1972. American journalist and author, b. Hammond, La. Editor and publisher, *Delta Democrat-Times,* Greenville, Miss. (1939–72); spokesman for progressive "New South"; Pulitzer prize (1946). Author of *Lower Mississippi* (1942), *Winds of Fear* (1945), *Flood Crest* (1947), *Southern Legacy* (1950), *Angry Scar* (1959), *First Person Rural* (1963), etc.

Carter, Howard. 1873–1939. English archaeologist. On archaeological survey work in Egypt (from 1890); assisted Flinders Petrie at Tell el-Amarna (1892); served Egyptian government as inspector-general of antiquities department; discovered tombs of Hatshepsut and Thutmose IV (1902). Associated with Earl of Carnarvon in Egyptian excavations (1907–12, 1919–23) culminating (1922) in discovery of tomb of Tutankhamen. Author of *Thoutmôsis IV* (with P.E. Newberry, 1904), *Tomb of Tut-ankh-Amen* (with A.C. Mace, 1923–33).

Carter, Mrs. Leslie. See Caroline CARTER.

Carter, Samuel Powhatan. 1819–1891. American army and naval officer, b. Elizabethton, Tenn. In navy (1840–62); assigned to recruit and train militia in Tennessee (1861); brigadier general of volunteers (1862); successful cavalry commander (1862–65); returned to naval service (1866–81); commandant of midshipmen, U.S. Naval Academy (1870–73); made rear admiral, retired (1882); only person to hold flag or general rank in both army and navy.

Car·ter·et \ˈkärt-ə-ˌret\, Sir George. c.1610–1680. British naval officer and colonial proprietor. Second in command against Sallee pirates (1637); comptroller of English navy (1639); succeeded his uncle as bailiff of his native island of Jersey (1643); lieutenant governor (1643); subdued Parliamentary party on island and sent out privateers in Royalist cause; surrendered Jersey to Parliamentary force (1651); vice admiral in French navy. At Restoration, M.P. (1661–69) and privy councilor; treasurer of navy (1661–67); censured by House of Commons for mismanagement of navy funds (1669); one of eight to receive grant of Carolina (1663); proprietor (from 1664), with Lord John Berkeley, of territory between Hudson and Delaware rivers, named New Jersey for his birthplace; deputy treasurer of Ireland (1667–73).

Carteret, John. Earl Gran·ville \ˈgran-(ˌ)vil\. 1690–1763. English diplomat and politician. Grandson of Sir George Carteret; succeeded father as 2d Baron Carteret (1695). Entered House of Lords (1711); bailiff of Jersey (1715); lord lieutenant of Devonshire (1716–21). Envoy to Sweden (1719); gained access to Baltic for British commerce, arranged peace treaties among Baltic powers

\ə\ abut \ᵊ\ kitten, *Fr.* **table \ər\ further \a\ ash \ā\ ace \ä\ cot, cart \au̇\ out \ch\ chin \e\ bet \ē\ easy \g\ go \i\ hit \ī\ ice \j\ job \ŋ\ sing \ō\ go \ȯ\ law \ȯi\ boy \th\ both \th\ the \ü\ loot \u̇\ foot \y\ yet \zh\ vision \ȧ, ḵ, g̅, k̲, ⁿ, œ, œ̄, ue, ue̅, ʸ** *see* **Guide to Pronunciation**

(1719–20). Secretary of state under Walpole (1721–24). As lord lieutenant of Ireland (1724–30), ordered prosecution of publisher of *Drapier's Letters;* despite this became friend of Jonathan Swift. Opposed Walpole (1730–42); real head of administration (1742–44), though only secretary of state, with policy of supporting Maria Theresa against France; hated for his partiality to house of Hanover; inherited Granville title from mother (1744); advised George II to exclude William Pitt from office (1746); failed to form ministry (1746); lord president of council (1751–63).

Carteret, Philip. 1639–1682. English colonialist. Distant cousin of Sir George Carteret. Governor of New Jersey (1665–76), and, after division of province, of East New Jersey (1676–82); had early difficulties collecting rents for the proprietors; in conflict with Andros, governor of New York, over collections of customs duties (1680–81).

Carteret, Philip. d. 1796. English navigator. Commanded *Swallow* in Wallis's expedition for exploration of Southern Hemisphere (1766); separated from first vessel in Straits of Magellan; discovered Pitcairn Island and Queen Charlotte Islands, explored St. George's Channel (1767); retired as admiral (1794).

Carteromaco. See Niccolò FORTEGUERRI.

Cartesius, Renatus. See René DESCARTES.

Car·tier \kȧr-tyā\, Sir George Étienne. Baronet. 1814–1873. Canadian politician, b. St. Antoine, Que. Practiced law (from 1835); took part in Papineau's rebellion (1837); Conservative member of legislature (1848–72); attorney general (1856). Joint prime minister with Sir John Macdonald (1858–62); supported building of Grand Trunk Railway and Canadian Pacific; carried his native province into federation (1867). Minister of militia and defense under Sir John Macdonald (1867–73); defeated by Roman Catholic clerical influence (1872).

Cartier, Jacques. 1491–1557. French sailor and explorer. Made three voyages to Canada for Francis I, exploring (1534) Gulf of St. Lawrence, sailing (1535) up St. Lawrence River to site of Montreal, and with Jean-François de Roberval attempting to colonize (1541–42) in Canada. Known as the discoverer of the St. Lawrence River.

Cartier, Raymond-Marcel-Ernest. 1904–1975. French journalist. On staff of conservative *Echo de Paris* (1929–37); editor in chief of daily *L'Époque* (1937–40); served with Free French army in World War II; founder and editor (1949–75) of weekly *Paris-Match.*

Car·ti·man·dua \ˌkärt-ə-ˈman-jə-wə\. 1st century A.D. British tribal ruler. Queen of the Brigantes; made alliance with Roman forces (43 A.D.), with whose help she retained power; arrested Caratacus and turned him over to Romans (51); with Roman aid suppressed rebellions of husband Venutius (57, 69).

Car·ton de Wiart \kȧr-tō^{n}-dəv-yȧr\, Henri Victor. Comte. 1869–1951. Belgian politician. Member of Chamber of Representatives (from 1896); instrumental in securing passage of law providing for proportional representation (1899); minister of justice (1911–18); prime minister (1920–21); minister of social welfare (1932–34), without portfolio (1949–50), of justice (1950). Belgian delegate to League of Nations (1928–35); organized Social Christian party (1950). Founded literary journal *Durendal* (1894); author of novels including *La Cité ardente* (1905), *Les Vertus bourgeoises* (1910).

Cartouche. See Louis BOURGUIGNON.

Cart·wright \ˈkärt-ˌrīt\, Alexander Joy. 1820–1892. American sportsman, b. New York City. A founder of Knickerbocker Baseball Club, New York City; chairman of committee that drew up code of rules (1845) for baseball, including provision for tagging runner out instead of hitting him with thrown ball; credited with fixing base paths at 90 feet. Elected to Baseball Hall of Fame (1938).

Cartwright, Edmund. 1743–1823. English inventor. Country clergyman; after visit to cotton-spinning mill (1784), conceived idea of applying machinery to weaving; patented a power loom (1785–87), which was improved and developed into the modern power loom; built a weaving mill (1787); patented a wool-combing machine (1789); bankrupt (1793); patented an alcohol engine (1797); rewarded with £10,000 by Parliament (1809).

Cartwright, John. *Called* Major Cartwright. 1740–1824. English politician and reformer. Brother of Edmund Cartwright. Served in navy (1758?–70); chief magistrate in Newfoundland (1765–70); warm supporter of American colonists in resistance to taxation (1774–75); major of militia (1775–90); devoted himself to writing in favor of strengthening the navy, manhood suffrage, annual parliaments, abolition of slavery, emancipation of Greece; indicted for sedition and fined (1820).

Cartwright, Peter. 1785–1872. American clergyman, b. Amherst Co., Va. Itinerant Methodist preacher (from 1803) in Kentucky and (1824) Illinois; noted for fiery revivalist sermons. Author of *Autobiography* (1856), *Fifty Years as a Presiding Elder* (1871).

Cartwright, Sir Richard John. 1835–1912. Canadian politician, b. Kingston, Ont. M.P. (1863–1904); minister of finance (1873–78), of trade and commerce (1896); chief financial spokesman of Liberal opposition (1878–96); Canada's representative on Anglo-American joint high commission at Quebec (1898–99); senator (1904–12); acting prime minister in absence of Laurier at imperial conference in London (1907).

Cartwright, Thomas. 1535–1603. English Puritan clergyman. Left Cambridge on Queen Mary's accession (1553); attacked use of surplice (1565); professor of divinity, Cambridge (1569–70); deprived of post by John Whitgift, vice chancellor; lectured against constitution of Church of England; imprisoned for nonconformity; clergyman to English residents at Antwerp and Middelburg; author of exegetical treatises.

Cartwright, William. 1611–1643. English dramatist. A florid preacher in university; junior proctor at Oxford (1643). Author of *The Ordinary* (1635?), a play ridiculing Puritans, and of fantastic plays, including *The Royal Slave* (1636).

Car·ty \ˈkärt-ē\, John Joseph. 1861–1932. American electrical engineer, b. Cambridge, Mass. Chief engineer, New York Telephone Co. (1889–1907); chief engineer (1907–19), vice president (1919–30), American Telephone and Telegraph Co. Pioneer in switchboard construction and the development of the telephone, for which he made many inventions.

Ca·rus \ˈkär-u̇s\, Carl Gustav. 1789–1869. German physician and philosopher. Professor, Dresden (from 1814); royal physician (1827). Adherent of Schelling in philosophy; sought to explain consciousness and the development of the soul. Noted also as a painter. Author of *Vorlesungen über Psychologie* (1831), *Goethe* (1843), *Psyche* (1846), *Symbolik des menschlichen Gestalt* (1853), etc.

Car·us \ˈkar-əs\, Marcus Aurelius. 223?–283. Roman emperor (282–283). Either a Gaul or an Illyrian; prefect of Praetorian Guard; chosen emperor by soldiers (282) on murder of Probus; successful in campaign against Sarmatians in Illyricum; proceeded against Persians; killed on the Tigris. Succeeded by his two sons, Carinus and Numerian (*qq.v.*).

Ca·rus \ˈkär-u̇s\, Paul. 1852–1919. American editor and philosopher, b. Ilsenburg, Germany. To U.S. (c.1884); settled in Chicago. Editor (from 1887) of philosophical journal *Open Court,* also (from 1888) the *Monist;* established Open Court Publishing Co. to publish philosophical and scientific treatises. Author of *Monism and Meliorism* (1885), *Soul of Man* (1891), *Religion and Science* (1893), *The Surd of Metaphysics* (1903), *God* (1908), *The Principle of Relativity* (1913), etc.

Ca·ru·so \kä-ˈrü-zō, *Angl* kə-ˈrü-(ˌ)sō, -(ˌ)zō\, Enrico, *orig.* Errico. 1873–1921. Italian singer. Appeared on Italian stage (1894–98); at St. Petersburg and Buenos Aires (1898–99); at La Scala, Milan (1900–01); debut at Covent Garden (1902). First appeared at Metropolitan Opera House, New York (Nov. 1903) in *Rigoletto,* with great success; established as leading tenor of Metropolitan company. Had large repertoire, comprising more than forty operas, esp. *Rigoletto, I Pagliacci, La Bohème;* noted for warm, appealing lyric tenor voice of great emotive power.

Car·va·jal \kär-b̠ä-ˈk̠äl\, Francisco de. 1464–1548. Spanish soldier. Possibly a son of César Borgia; fought under Gonzalo de Córdoba and was at Ravenna and Pavia (1525) and sack of Rome (1527); to Mexico (1536); sent by Hernando Cortes to Peru (1536) to aid Francisco Pizarro; as field marshal under Vaca de Castro, overcame Diego de Almagro at Chupas (1542); joined Gonzalo Pizarro against Pedro de la Gasca; taken prisoner and executed.

Carvajal y Men·do·za \-ē-mān-ˈdō-thä\, Luisa de. 1568–1614. Spanish missionary. Following execution of Henry Walpole (1595) founded college for English Jesuits at Louvain; college moved to Watten, near St. Omer (1612). To England (1605); under protection of Spanish ambassador carried on missions to English Catholics; ministered to Gunpowder Plot prisoners; arrested (1608) but released because of king's desire not to offend Spain.

Car·va·lho e Mel·lo \kər-ˈväl-yü-ä-ˈmel-ü\, Sebastião José de. Marquês de Pom·bal \pəm-ˈbäl\. 1699–1782. Portuguese politician. Envoy extraordinary to London (1738–45), to Vienna (1745–49). On accession of Joseph Emanuel, appointed minister for foreign affairs (1750–56); gained complete ascendancy over Joseph that lasted till end of reign (1777); active in aid of sufferers from great earthquake at Lisbon (1755). Prime minister (1756–77); instituted administrative reforms; encouraged development of industry and commerce; under him colonies developed, native slaves in Brazil liberated (1755); reduced power of Inquisition; engaged in long controversy with Jesuits (1754–59), who were finally expelled from all Portuguese dominions; reorganized finances and defenses. Dismissed on death of Joseph (1777).

Car·ver \ˈkär-vər\, George Washington. c.1864–1943. American botanist, b. near Diamond Grove, Mo. Son of slave parents; led wandering early life, obtaining education by own efforts; B.S. (1894), M.S. Agr. (1896), Iowa State. Director of agriculture department and of agricultural research, Tuskegee Institute (from 1896); promoted crop diversification among Southern farmers, esp. adoption of peanuts, soybeans, and other soil-enriching crops; developed over 300 derivative products from peanuts, 118 from sweet potatoes. Spingarn Medal (1923).

Carver, John. 1576–1621. English colonist. Emigrated to Holland (1609); joined Pilgrims at Leiden; contributed liberally to finance the group. Agent of

Pilgrims (1617–20) in getting charter and financial aid in England for expedition to New World. Chartered the *Mayflower,* gathered the London Pilgrims together, and sailed from London (July 1620). Elected first governor of Plymouth colony under Mayflower Compact (Nov. 21, 1620).

Carver, Jonathan. 1710–1780. American explorer, b. Weymouth, Mass. Began his travels (1766) at suggestion of Major Robert Rogers; traveled from Mackinac to Green Bay; explored Fox and Wisconsin rivers; ascended Mississippi to Falls of St. Anthony; on second trip (1767–68) explored Lake Superior to Grand Portage; went to England (1769) and published his *Travels Through the Interior Parts of North America* (1778) and a treatise on tobacco (1779).

Carver, Robert. c.1490–after 1546. Scottish composer. Composer of remarkable body of polyphonic vocal music including two motets and five masses as *Missa "Dum sacrum mysterium"* (1513), *Missa "L'Homme armé"* (c.1520), *Missa "Pater creator omnium"* (1546).

Cary \ˈka(ə)r-ē, ˈke(ə)r-ē\, Alice (1820–1871) and her sister Phoebe (1824–1871). American poets, b. near Cincinnati. Authors of *Poems of Alice and Phoebe Cary* (1849); settled in New York City (1850); contributed to magazines. Alice published *Clovernook Papers* (1852, 1853), *Hagar* (1852), *Lyra and Other Poems* (1852), *Pictures of Country Life* (1859), *Ballads, Lyrics, and Hymns* (1866), etc. Phoebe published *Poems and Parodies* (1854), *Poems of Faith, Hope, and Love* (1868); best known for her hymn "Nearer Home."

Cary, Edward. 1840–1917. American journalist, b. Albany, N.Y. Editor, *New York Times* (1871–1917).

Cary, Henry Francis. 1772–1844. English clergyman and translator, b. Gibraltar. Published translation in blank verse of Dante's *Inferno* (1805) and of *Purgatorio* and *Paradiso* (1812); translated Aristophanes' *Birds* (1824), and Pindar (1832).

Cary, Joyce, *in full* Arthur Joyce Lunel. 1888–1957. British novelist, b. N. Ireland. With Red Cross in Montenegro (1912–13), colonial service in Nigeria (1914–20). Author of *Aissa Saved* (1932), *American Visitor* (1933), *African Witch* (1936), *Mister Johnson* (1939), *Charley Is My Darling* (1940), *House of Children* (1941), *Moonlight* (1946), *Fearful Joy* (1949), *Captive and the Free* (1959); trilogies *Herself Surprised* (1941), *To Be a Pilgrim* (1942), *Horse's Mouth* (1944), and *Prisoner of Grace* (1952), *Except the Lord* (1953), *Not Honour More* (1955).

Cary, Lucius. 2d Viscount Falk·land \ˈfȯ(l)-klənd\. c.1610–1643. English Royalist. Son of Sir Henry Cary, lord deputy of Ireland (1622–29); succeeded to viscountcy and fortune (1633); member of Long Parliament (1640); opposed policies and ministers of Charles I but sought compromise between factions in Parliament; broke with Parliament over Puritan control; secretary of state (1642); killed at Newbury. Best known from *History of the Rebellion* by his friend Edward Hyde.

Cary, Phoebe. See Alice CARY.

Ca·sa \ˈkä-sä\, Giovanni della. 1503–1556. Italian prelate and writer. Protégé of Alessandro Farnese (Paul III); archbishop of Benevento (1544); papal nuncio to Venice (1544–49); papal secretary of state under Paul IV (1555–56). Author of manual of polite conduct *Il Galateo ovvero De' Costumi,* his best known work (1558), translations of Thucydides, and many poems notable for their style.

Ca·sal \kä-ˈsäl\, Julián del. *Full surname* Casal y de la Las·tra \-ē-t͟hā-lä-ˈlä-strä\. 1863–1893. Cuban poet. Influenced by Parnassians, esp. Baudelaire; forerunner of Modernists in Latin America. Author of verse *Hojas al viento* (1890), *Nieve* (1892), *Bustos y rimas* (1893).

Ca·sals \kä-ˈsäls, *Angl* kə-ˈsälz, -ˈzälz\, Pablo, *Catalan* Pau. 1876–1973. Spanish violoncellist, conductor, and composer. Professor, conservatory of music, Barcelona (1897); debut as soloist (1898); achieved worldwide renown as virtuoso, toured frequently (from 1901); founded (1919) Orquesta Pau Casals to play for Catalan working people; noted esp. as interpreter of Bach. After Spanish Civil War settled in Prades, France (1936); to Puerto Rico (1956); in both places established annual music festivals. Composer of works for violoncello and piano, violin and piano, and orchestral and choral works.

Ca·sa·no·va \ˌkä-sä-ˈnȯ-vä, *Angl* ˌkas-ə-ˈnō-və, ˌkaz-\, Francesco. 1727–1802. Italian painter and etcher. Brother of Giovanni Giacomo Casanova. Painter to the king at Paris and member of the Academy (1763); known for his battle paintings, including *Hannibal Crossing the Alps* and series painted for Catherine of Russia. Another brother ¶Giovanni Battista (1730–1795), also a painter, was director of the Dresden Academy (from 1764).

Casanova, Giovanni Giacomo. Chevalier de Sein·galt \sa^{n}-gȧl\. 1725–1798. Italian adventurer. Expelled for scandalous conduct from Seminary of St. Cyprian (1741); secretary in household of Cardinal Aquaviva; entered Venetian army at Corfu; by turns preacher, abbé, alchemist, cabalist, gambler, violin player, for nearly 20 years visiting capitals of Europe, as far as Constantinople, alternately in fortune and in distress; skeptic and sensualist; involved in one intrigue after another. Imprisoned as magician on return to Venice (1755) but made a marvelous escape (1756); director of state lotteries in Paris, accumulated fortune; acquired title of chevalier in Netherlands (1759); agent of Louis XV; declined post offered by Frederick II in Berlin (1764); made acquaintance of the great, including the Pope, Empress Catherine, Voltaire, von Haller, Mme. de Pompadour, Cagliostro. Traveled to Russia, whence forced to flee because of a scandal and a duel; police spy for Venetian inquisitors (from 1774); exiled for satirical libel upon one of patrons (1782); librarian for Count von Waldstein at Dux Castle in Bohemia (from 1785). Translated *Iliad;* author of adventure tale *Icosameron* (1788) and esp. of witty, cynical autobiography *Histoire de ma vie* (full publication 1960–62).

Casas, Bartolomé de las. See LAS CASAS.

Ca·sau·bon \kȧ-zō-bō^{n}, *Angl* kə-ˈsȯ-bən\, Isaac. 1559–1614. French theologian and scholar, b. Geneva. Son of refugee Huguenot parents; professor of Greek at Geneva (1581–96), Montpellier (1596–99); corresponded with Joseph Scaliger; summoned to Paris by Henry IV but prevented from receiving professorship by Catholic opposition; sublibrarian in royal library (1604–10). Feeling insecure after murder of king, crossed to England (1610); favorably received by James I and made prebendary of Canterbury and Westminster; welcomed by Anglican bishops as having reached theological position midway between Puritanism and Romanism; forced to share increasing unpopularity of James and bishops; spent last years on assignment by king and bishops to refute the *Annales* of Baronius. With Scaliger and Lipsius, member of famous triumvirate of 16th-century classical scholars. Author of commentaries on Theophrastus (1592), Suetonius (1595), Persius (1605), Polybius (1609, unfinished till 1617), of a revision, with commentary, of Athenaeus (his most ambitious work, 1600), of a diary *Ephemerides* (pub. 1850).

Cas·ca \ˈkas-kə\, Publius Servilius. d. after 42 B.C. Roman politician. First among the assassins of Julius Caesar to strike him (44 B.C.).

Cas·ca·ri·o·lo \ˌkäs-kä-rē-ˈō-lō\, Vincenzo. 1571–1624. Italian alchemist. Cobbler by trade; while searching for philosopher's stone, discovered luminescing property of mineral barite, naming it *lapis solaris.*

Case \ˈkās\, Leonard. 1820–1880. American lawyer and philanthropist, b. Cleveland. Founder (1880) and benefactor of Case School of Applied Science (later Case Inst. of Technology; now Case Western Reserve U.).

Case, Shirley Jackson. 1872–1947. American theologian and scholar, b. Hatfield Point, N.B. Professor, Bates Coll. (1906–08), U. of Chicago (1908–38); dean of U. of Chicago School of Divinity (1933–38). Author of *Evolution of Early Christianity* (1914), *Jesus: A New Biography* (1927), *Social Triumph of the Ancient Church* (1933), *Christian Philosophy of History* (1943), *Origins of Christian Supernaturalism* (1946), etc.

Ca·sel·la \kä-ˈsel-lä\, Alfredo. 1883–1947. Italian pianist and composer. Professor of piano, Liceo di Santa Cecilia, Rome (1915–22); founded Società Italiana di Musica Moderna (1917); leader of Italian Modernist movement in music. Composer of ballets as *Le Couvent sur l'eau* (1912–13), *La giara* (1924), *La camera dei disegni* (1940); operas as *La donna serpente* (1928–31); orchestral works including 2 symphonies, rhapsody *Italia* (1909), *Elegia eroica* (1916), *Pagine di guerra* (1918), *Concerto romano* (1926), *Scarlattiana* (1926), *Paganiniana* (1942); a *Missa solemnis* (1944); chamber and vocal music. Author of *L'evoluzione della musica* (1924), *Igor Stravinski* (1926), a collection of essays *21 + 26* (1931), *Il Pianoforte* (1937).

Caselli, Jean. See Henry CAZALIS.

Case·ment \ˈkas-mənt\, Sir Roger David. 1864–1916. British consular agent and Irish rebel. Distinguished himself in investigation for British government of conduct of rubber trade of Upper Congo (1903) and in investigation of atrocities by Anglo-Peruvian Amazon Company (1910); knighted. Joined Irish Nationalists and helped organize National Volunteers (1913); to Berlin (1914) to seek assistance in gaining Irish independence; landed from German submarine near Tralee (1916); hanged as traitor.

Cases, Las. See LAS CASES.

Ca·sey \ˈkā-sē\, Richard Gardiner. Baron Casey. 1890–1976. Australian politician. In Australian foreign service (1927–31); M.P. (1931–40, 1949–60); federal treasurer (1935–39); minister for supply and development (1939–40). Australian minister to United States (1940–42); British minister of state in the Middle East (1942–43); governor of Bengal (1944–46). Minister of works (1949–51), of development (1950–51), for external affairs (1951–60). Created baron (1960). Governor general of Australia (1965–69).

Cash·in \ˈkash-ən\, Sir Michael Patrick. 1864–1926. Canadian politician, b. Cape Broyle, Nlfd. Member of Newfoundland assembly (1893–1919); helped found People's party (1908); minister of finance and customs (1909–19); managed Victory Loan for World War I (1917); prime minister of Newfoundland (1919).

Cas·i·mir \'kaz-ə-,mi(ə)r\. *Pol.* Ka·zi·mierz \kä-'zēm-yesh\. Name of four rulers of Poland:

Casimir I. *Called* Od·no·wi·ciel \òd-nò-'vē-chel\, *i.e.* the Restorer. 1016–1058. King (1034–37, 1040–58). Son of Mieszko II; took monastic orders but with papal dispensation succeeded father on throne (1034); deposed by revolt of nobles (1037); with aid of Conrad II and Henry III of Germany regained throne (1040); supported by brother-in-law Yaroslav the Great of Kiev, reclaimed Mazovia and Pomerania (1047); took Silesia from Bohemia (1050); restored central government and church.

Casimir II. *Called* Spra·wied·li·wy \spräv-yed-'lē-vi\, *i.e.* the Just. 1138–1194. Grand prince (1177–94). Son of Bolesław III; prince of Sandomierz (1166); succeeded brother Mieszko III as senior prince of Piast family, ruling from Cracow (1177); acquired Mazovia (1186).

Casimir III. *Called* Wiel·ky \'vyel-kyi\, *i.e.* the Great. 1310–1370. King (1333–70). Son of Władysław I; by dynastic marriages and firm diplomacy greatly increased Poland's territory and prestige; settled disputes with Bohemia and Teutonic Knights; occupied Red Russia (1340, 1349); issued Magdeburg Law for town governments; codified laws of Great Poland and Little Poland in *Liber juris Teutonici;* founded U. of Cracow (1364). Last of Piast dynasty.

Casimir IV. *Also called* Casimir Ja·giel·loń·czyk \yäg-yel-'lòn^y-chik\. 1427–1492. King (1447–92). Son of Władysław II Jagiełło; named to succeed Sigismund as grand duke of Lithuania (1440); proclaimed successor to brother Władysław III (1444), finally crowned king of Poland (1447); m. (1454) Elizabeth of Habsburg and successfully placed several sons and daughters on thrones or in advantageous dynastic marriages throughout Europe; defeated Teutonic Knights in Thirteen Years' War (1454–66) and by Treaty of Toruń (Thorn, 1466) secured East Pomerania.

Casimir, John. See JOHN II of Poland.

Ca·si·mir-Pé·rier \kä-zē-mēr-pär-yā\, Jean-Paul-Pierre. 1847–1907. French politician. Son of Auguste-Casimir Périer (see PÉRIER). Decorated for conduct in Franco–Prussian War (1870–71); elected to Chamber of Deputies (1876); vice president (1890–93), president (1893), Chamber of Deputies; prime minister (1893–94); again president of Chamber (1894). Elected president of Third Republic after assassination of Carnot (1894–95); unexpectedly resigned under pressure from leftists and of Dreyfus affair and retired to private business.

Caskoden, Sir Edwin. See Charles MAJOR.

Cas·lon \'kaz-lən\, William. 1692–1766. English typefounder. Opened engraving shop, London (1716); designed "English Arabic" typeface (1720); cut typefaces for printer William Bowyer; designed (1720–26) Caslon typeface, used in England and America and on Continent till about 1800, revived about 1845 by Chiswick Press. His son ¶William (1720–1778) became partner (1742) and carried on his father's business.

Cass \'kas \, Lewis. 1782–1866. American politician, b. Exeter, N.H. Served through War of 1812 to brigadier general; governor of Michigan Territory (1813–31); responsible for constructive administration in opening up territory. U.S. secretary of war (1831–36); directed conduct of Black Hawk and Seminole wars; U.S. minister to France (1836–42); U.S. senator (1845–48). Democratic candidate for president (1848); defeated by Taylor. U.S. senator (1849–57); U.S. secretary of state (1857–60).

Cas·sag·nac \kä-sän-yäk\, Paul Gra·nier de \grän-yā-də-\. 1843–1904. French journalist and politican. Contributor to various journals; director of *Le Pays;* ardent Bonapartist; elected deputy (1871–93, 1896–1904); founded journal *L'Autorité* (1886), in which he supported Boulangist movement; a noted duellist.

Cas·san·der \kə-'san-dər\. c.358–297 B.C. King of Macedonia (305–297 B.C.). Son of Antipater; failed to be named successor on Antipater's death (319); supported by many Greek states, waged successful war (319–317) against Macedonian regent Polyperchon; seized Olympias, mother of Alexander, and put her to death (316); m. (316) Alexander's half-sister Thessalonica, for whom he built and named a city in Macedonia. Engaged in war with Antigonus (315–311); caused murder of Roxana and her son (310); joined forces with Lysimachus, Ptolemy, and Seleucus against Antigonus, who was defeated and slain at Ipsus (301); lost Athens (307), other Greek possessions (303–302); took title king of Macedonia (305).

Cassandre. See Adolphe MOURON.

Cas·satt \kə-'sat\, Mary Stevenson. 1844–1926. American painter, b. Allegheny City, Pa. To Paris (1866); first exhibited at Salon (1872); associated with Impressionists, esp. Degas and Courbet; exhibited with Impressionists (1879, 1880, 1881, 1886); first solo exhibit (1891); produced oils, pastels, prints, etchings; known esp. for figure studies and portrayals of mothers and children.

Casse·grain \käs-gra^n\, N. 17th century. French inventor. Possibly a physician and professor, Collège de Chartres; inventor of the Cassegrainian form of reflecting telescope (1672); author of a treatise on the megaphone.

Cas·sel \'kas-əl\, Sir Ernest Joseph. 1852–1921. British financier and philanthropist, b. Cologne, Germany. Member (1870–84) of house of Bischoffscheim and Goldschmidt in London; naturalized (1878). Set up own business (1884); reorganized finances of Uruguay and of railroads in Sweden, Mexico, and U.S.; issued Mexican and Chinese government loans; financed Nile dams and irrigation work and founded National Bank of Egypt; created State Bank of Morocco and National Bank of Turkey; privy councilor (1902). In life a philanthropist to extent of £2,000,000.

Cas·sel \'käs-səl\, Gustav, *in full* Karl Gustav. 1866–1945. Swedish economist. Professor, Stockholm (1904–33); financial expert with Swedish delegation at Genoa conference (1922); Swedish delegate at international economic conference, Geneva (1927); called in by League of Nations (1920–21) for opinion on currency problems; delegate, World Economic Conference, London (1933). Author of *Das Recht auf den vollen Arbeitsertrag* (1900), *Nature and Necessity of Interest* (1903), *Theoretische Sozialökonomie* (1918), *Das Stabilisierungsproblem* (1926), *Der Zusammenbruch der Goldwährung* (1937), *Världsekonomien efter kriget* (1941), etc.

Cas·sell \'kas-əl\, John. 1817–1865. English publisher. Apprenticed to carpenter; to London (1836) as temperance advocate; started publishing business to supply reading for instruction of working classes (1850), issued educational magazines and *Cassell's Magazine* (from 1852); formed partnership (1859) with T.D. Galpin and G.W. Petter.

Cas·se·rio \,käs-'sā-rē-ō\, Giulio. *Lat.* Julius Cas·se·ri·us \kə-'sir-ē-əs\. 1552?–1616. Italian anatomist. Servant and student of Fabrici; substitute teacher of anatomy for Fabrici (from 1604) at Padua; appointed lecturer in surgery, Padua (1609). First to give detailed and comparative descriptions of human organs of voice and hearing in *De vocis auditusque organis historia anatomica* (1600–01); described organs of five senses in *Pentaestheseion* (1609); compiled complete atlas of human anatomy as *Tabulae anatomicae* (1627).

Cas·si·an \'kas(h)-ē-ən\, John. Saint. *Lat.* Johannes Cas·si·a·nus \,kas(h)-ē-'ā-nəs\. *Also known as* Johannes Mas·sil·i·en·sis \mə-,sil-ē-'en-səs\ *and* Johannes Er·e·mi·ta \,er-i-'mīt-ə\. 360–435. Monk and theologian, b. Scythia Minor. Entered monastery in Bethlehem as youth; lived in Egypt as anchorite (385–399); disciple of St. John Chrysostom in Constantinople (399–404); founded Monastery of St. Victor and convent at Marseilles (415); abbot (415–35); a leading exponent of Semi-Pelagianism and of eastern monasticism in West. Author of *De Institutis coenobiorum* on monasticism, *Collationes,* dialogues of Desert Fathers.

Cas·sin \kä-sa^n\, René-Samuel. 1887–1976. French jurist and statesman. Professor at Aix, Lille, Paris; on staff of League of Nations (1924–38); member of De Gaulle's government in exile (1940–44); president of supreme court of arbitrage (1950), of provisional constitutional committee (1958). Delegate to United Nations (1945); a founder of UNESCO (1945); principal author of UN Universal Declaration of Human Rights (1948); president, UN Human Rights Commission (1955–57) and of European Court of Human Rights (1965–68). Awarded Nobel prize for peace (1968).

Cas·si·ni \kä-sē-nē\. Family of French astronomers including: Gian Domenico, *later* Jean-Dominique (1625–1712), b. Italy; professor at Bologna (1650–68); invited to join French Royal Academy of Sciences (1668); naturalized French citizen (1673); first director of the Paris observatory. Observed comets, planetary surfaces; constructed tables of Jovian satellites; discovered four of Saturn's satellites (1671–84); observed a dark division in Saturn's ring; made earliest systematic observation of zodiacal light; determined parallax of sun, obliquity of ecliptic, and eccentricity of earth's orbit; in mathematics, discovered Cassinian oval. His son ¶Jacques (1677–1756) succeeded him as director of Paris observatory (1712); known for work to determine figure of the earth; measured meridian of Paris (1718); published *De la grandeur et de la figure de la terre* (1722), celestial tables, etc. His son ¶César-François Cassini de Thu·ry \tuē-rē\ (1714–1784), his successor as director of the Paris observatory (1756); began topographical map of France (1744); specialized in geodesy. ¶Jacques-Dominique de Cassini (1748–1845), son of César and his successor as director of Paris observatory (1784–93); completed César's map of France (pub. 1793); created count by Napoléon.

Cas·si·o·do·rus \,kas(h)-ē-ə-'dōr-əs\, Flavius Magnus Aurelius. c.490–c.585. Roman statesman and writer. Government official under Theodoric and Athalaric; quaestor (507–511), consul (514), praetorian prefect (533); retired (c.540) to devote himself to study and writing. Founded monasteries, in which he required the monks to copy and translate Greek, Christian, pagan, and other works to preserve culture of Rome. Among his works were panegyrics on the Gothic kings and queens; a philosophical treatise *De Anima; Variae,* a collection of the decrees of Theodoric and his successors; *Chronicon,* a universal history to 519; *Institutiones divinarum et saecularium litterarum,* on learning and the liberal arts; etc. His *Historia Gothica* is lost.

Cas·si·rer \kä-'sēr-ər, *Angl* -'si(ə)r-\, Ernst. 1874–1945. German philosopher. Taught at Berlin U. (1905–19), Hamburg U. (1919–33), Oxford (1933–35), Göteborg (1936–41), Yale (1941–44), Columbia (1944–45). His works chiefly neo-Kantian examinations of foundations of scientific and cultural values, including *Das Erkenntnisproblem* (1906–20); *Substanzbegriff und Funktions-*

begriff (1910), *Freiheit und Form* (1916), *Philosophie der symbolischen Formen* (1923–29), *Sprache und Mythos* (1925), *Die Philosophie der Aufklärung* (1932), *Essay on Man* (1944), *Myth of the State* (1946).

Cassius, Avidius. See AVIDIUS CASSIUS.

Cassius Dio. See DIO CASSIUS.

Cas·sius Di·o·ny·sius \'kash-(ē-)əs-dī-ə-'nish-(ē-)əs, 'kas-ē-, -'nis-ē-, -'nī-sē-\. 1st century A.D. North African writer. Translated Columella's treatise on agriculture from Punic (c.88 A.D.); fragments of this translation are only remains of Columella's work.

Cassius Lon·gi·nus \-län-'jī-nəs, -lȯn-\, Gaius. d. 42 B.C. Roman general and conspirator. Distinguished himself in Parthian War (53 B.C.); tribune (49); sided with Pompey against Caesar and fought at Pharsalus (48); pardoned by Caesar; praetor (44). Headed conspiracy against Caesar (44) and was one of the actual assassins. Raised army in Syria and defeated Dolabella (43); defeated at Philippi, he ordered his freedman to kill him.

Cassius Longinus, Gaius. 1st century A.D. Roman jurist. Consul (30 A.D.); governor of Syria (45–49); banished by Nero (65), recalled by Vespasian. Author of *Libri juris civilis.*

Cassius Longinus, Quintus. d. 47 B.C. A relative of Cassius Longinus the conspirator; quaestor (54 B.C.), tribune and governor (49) of Further Spain, notorious for severity of his administration.

Cassius Par·men·sis \-pär-'men-səs\, Gaius. d. after 31 B.C. Roman politician. One of the assassins of Julius Caesar (44 B.C.). After battle of Philippi (42), joined Sextus Pompeius in Sicily; after Pompeius's defeat at Naulochus, joined Antony and fought at Actium (31); fled to Athens; captured and executed by Octavian. Author of satires, epigrams, elegies, and plays.

Cassius Vec·el·li·nus \-ˌves-ə-'lī-nəs\ *or* **Vic·el·li·nus** \ˌvis-\, Spurius. 6th–5th century B.C. Roman political and military leader. As consul (502 B.C.) defeated Sabines; again consul (493, 486); supposedly executed by patricians for supporting agrarian law favorable to plebeians.

Cas·si·ve·lau·nus *or* **Cas·si·vel·lau·nus** \ˌkas-ə-və-'lȯ-nəs, -(ˌ)vel-'ȯ-\. *Also known as* Cas·wal·lawn \kȧs-'wȧ-ˌ(h)lau̇n\ *or* Cas·wal·lon \-(h)ȯn\. fl. 54 B.C. British prince. Chief of Catuvellauni (in Hertfordshire, Buckinghamshire, Berkshire); opposed Julius Caesar's second expedition into Britain (54 B.C.); made effective use of guerilla and chariot warfare, but ultimately defeated.

Castagno, Andrea del. See ANDREA DI BARTOLO.

Ca·stal·di \käs-'täl-dē\, Pamfilo. 1398–?1490. Italian physician and printer. Thought by some to have invented printing from movable types, the invention later supposedly revealed to Gutenberg by Castaldi's pupil Johann Fust.

Castalion. See CHATEILLON.

Castañeda, Jorge Ubico. See UBICO CASTAÑEDA.

Cas·ta·ños \käs-'tän-yōs\, Francisco Javier de. Duque de Bai·lén \bī-'lān\. 1756–1852. Spanish soldier. Defeated by Godoy at Badajoz (1799); lieutenant general (1802); defeated French under General Dupont de l'Étang at Bailén (1808); commanded Spanish army, under Wellington, at Vitoria (1813); president, council of Castile (1833); opponent of Carlists; became the guardian of Queen Isabella (1843).

Cas·tel \kȧs-tel\, Charles-Irénée. *Known as* Abbé de Saint-Pierre \saⁿ-pyer\. 1658–1743. French reformer. Abbot of Tiron (from 1795); secretary to Cardinal de Polignac (1712–14). Proposed reforms in law, politics, and social institutions, esp. the creation of a "European Republic" and a peace-keeping international organization outlined in *Le Projet de paix perpétuelle* (1713).

Cas·te·lar y Ri·poll \käs-tä-'lär-ē-rē-'pȯlʸ\, Emilio. 1832–1899. Spanish politician and writer. Professor of history, Madrid (1856–65, 1868–75); exiled to France (1866–68); deputy to the Cortes (1869); advocate of republic and separation of church and state; minister of foreign affairs after proclamation of republic (1873); president (1873–74); strengthened army, suppressed revolts, conciliated church; ousted by Republican opposition; in exile following military coup; deputy (1876–93). Author of *La civilización en los cinco primeros siglos del cristianismo* (1859), *Historia del movimiento republicano en europa* (1873–74), biographies of Byron and Fra Filippo Lippi.

Cas·te·leyn \ˌkäs-tə-'līn\, Matthijs de. c.1488–1550. Flemish poet and critic. Member of the Rederijkerskammers, or Chambers of Rhetoric. Author of many plays and of *Const van rhetoriken* (1555), first treatise on Flemish versification, containing also ballads, songs, etc.

Castelfranco, Giorgione da. See GIORGIONE.

Ca·stel·li \käs-'tel-ē\, Ignaz Franz. 1781–1862. Austrian journalist, poet, and dramatist. Wrote, translated, or adapted, chiefly from French originals, over 200 plays chiefly satirizing Viennese fables; also wrote "Kriegslied für die österreichische Armee" (1809), banned by Napoléon.

Castellion. See CHATEILLON.

Ca·stel·lo \käs-'tel-lō\, Giovanni Battista. *Called* Il Ber·ga·ma·sco \ēl-ˌbär-gä-'mäs-kō\. 1509?–1569. Italian painter and architect, b. at or near Bergamo. Associated with Genoese school; called to Madrid by Phillip II (1567); aided in restoration of the Alcázar (Madrid) and in construction of Escorial.

Cas·tel·nau \kȧs-tel-nō\, Michel de. Sieur de la Mau·vis·sière \də-lȧ-mō-vēs-yer\. 1520?–1592. French soldier and diplomat. Served in Piedmont and Picardy; in service of king (from 1559); ambassador to England (1575–85); attempted to negotiate marriage between Queen Elizabeth and duc d'Alençon. Author of historically valuable *Mémoires.*

Castelnau, Noël-Marie-Joseph-Édouard de Cu·rières de \də-kūēr-yer-də-\. 1851–1944. French general. Commanded 3d army in Lorraine (1914) and group of armies constituting French center (1915); chief of staff to General Joffre (Dec. 1915); had share in early defense of Verdun (1916); commanded group of armies in eastern France at time of armistice. Member, Chamber of Deputies (1919–24).

Castelnuovo, Conte di. See Francesco BUSSONE.

Cas·tel·nuo·vo-Te·des·co \ˌkäs-tāl-nə-'wȯ-vō-tā-'dās-kō\, Mario. 1895–1968. American composer, b. Florence, Italy. Early achieved recognition; to U.S. (1939), naturalized (1946). Composed works in neo-Romantic manner including operas as *La mandragola* (1920–23), *Merchant of Venice* (1956), *All's Well that Ends Well* (1955–58); ballets as *Bacco in Toscana* (1925–26), *Octoroon Ball* (1947); orchestral works as overtures to 12 Shakespearian plays, concertos for violin, for cello, for guitar; choral, vocal, and chamber music; much music for piano; film scores, etc.

Cas·te·lo Bran·co \kȧs-'tā-lü-'brȧŋ-kü\, Camilo. Visconde de Cor·reia Bo·te·lho \thā-kȯr-'rā-ə-bȯ-'tel-yü\ (cr.1885). 1825–1890. Portuguese writer. Led passionate life mirrored in his novels, which ranged in style from romantic melodrama to realism; best known included *Anathema* (1851), *Onde está la felicidade?* (1856), *Vingança* (1858), *O Romance d'un homem rico* (1861), *Amor de perdição* (1862), *Amor de salvação* (1864), *O Retrato de Richardina* (1868), *Eusébio Macário* (1879), *A Corja* (1880); also wrote stories and tales as *Novellas de Minho* (1875–77), verse, polemics, plays.

Castelo Branco, Humberto de Alen·car \ä-'lāⁿ(n)-kȧr\. 1900–1967. Brazilian soldier and politician. Served in Brazilian expeditionary force in Italy (1943–45); major general (1958), lieutenant general (1962); chief of army staff. Led military coup that overthrew Pres. João Goulart (1964); president of Brazil (1964–67); acquired dictatorial powers.

Castelo Melhor, Conde de. See VASCONCELOS E SOUSA.

Ca·stel·ve·tro \ˌkäs-tāl-'vā-trō\, Lodovico. c.1505–1571. Italian critic and philologist. Forced to flee Italy on charges of heresy (1561), stemming from a literary quarrel with poet Annibale Caro. His works included *La Poetica di Aristotele vulgarizzata* (1570), influential translation and exposition of Aristotle's *Poetics;* commentaries on Cicero's *Rhetorica* (1553), Dante, and Petrarch.

Ca·sti \'käs-tē\, Giovanni Battista. 1724–1803. Italian poet and adventurer. Abandoned holy orders to frequent court of Joseph II; visited Russian court (1778); imperial court poet under Francis I (Vienna); settled at Paris (1798). His works included *Poema tartaro* (1787), satire on court of Catherine II, *Novelle galanti* in ottave rime (1793), the political satire *Gli animali parlanti* (1802), and librettos for operas of Paisiello, as *Il re Teodora* (1784).

Castiglione, Duc de. See Pierre-François-Charles AUGEREAU.

Ca·sti·glio·ne \ˌkäs-tēl-'yō-nā\, Baldassare. 1478–1529. Italian diplomat and writer. Attached to courts of Milan (1496–99), Mantua (1499–1507), and Urbino (1507–13); ambassador of duke of Urbino at papal court (1513–24); apostolic prothonotary (1524); commander of papal troops; sent by Clement VII on diplomatic mission to Spain (1525); after sack of Rome by Bourbons (1527), accused of treachery; settled in Spain. Known particularly for his celebrated dialogue on ideal courtly life *Il cortegiano.*

Castiglione, Giovanni Benedetto. *Called* Il Gre·chet·to \ēl-grā-'kāt-tō\ *and* Le Be·né·det·te \lā-ˌbā-nā-'dāt-tā\. c.1616–1670. Italian painter and etcher. Court painter to duke of Mantua (1664 ff); known especially for his paintings of rural and market scenes, biblical scenes, animals; technical innovator in printmaking, one of first to make chiaroscuro woodcuts; first known practitioner of monotype printing.

Ca·sti·glio·ni \ˌkäs-tēl-'yō-nē\, Virginia Ve·ra·sis di \vā-'rä-sēs-dē-\. Contessa. *Nee* Ol·do·ini \ˌōl-dō-'ē-nē\. 1835–1899. Italian courtier. m. (1854) Conte Francesco Verasis di Castiglioni; noted for wit and charm; sent (1856) by Cavour to Paris; captivated court of Napoléon III; reputed to have influenced Franco–Sardinian alliance.

Cas·ti·lho \kəsh-'tēl-yü\, Antônio Feliciano de. 1800–1875. Portuguese poet. Early became a leader of Portuguese Romantic movement. Gained recognition with verse *Cartas de Eco e Narciso* (1821), *Primavera* (1822), *Amor e melancolia* (1828), *A Noite do Castelo* (1836), *Ciúmes de Bardo* (1838); editor of journals *O Panorama* (1837), *Revista Universal Lisbonense* (1842). In later years his position as literary arbiter and his increasing traditionalism gave rise to revolt of younger poets and celebrated polemic exchange. Translated Greek and Latin writers including Ovid, Virgil; also translated Shakespeare, Molière, Goethe.

Cas·ti·lla \käs-'tē-yä\, Ramón. *Full surname* Castilla Mar·que·sa·do \-mär-kä-'sä-thō\. 1797–1867. Peruvian general and politician, b. Chile. Joined San Martín's expedition to Peru (1820); rose to chief of staff under Gamarra and Orbegozo; minister of war (1837); in anarchy and civil war following Gamarra's death, seized power (1845); president of Peru (1845–51); led revolution which overthrew President José Echenique, becoming president for second term (1855–62); abolished slavery and Indian head tax (1856); promoted economic stability, church; proclaimed new constitution (1860).

Cas·ti·lle·jo \käs-tē(l)-'ye-kō\, Cristóbal de. 1490?–?1550. Spanish poet. Entered Cistercian monastery; left to become secretary to Ferdinand I at Vienna (1525–?50). His works (collected edition, expurgated by Inquisition, 1573) included ballads, *Diálogo entre el autor y su pluma,* erotic verse *Sermón de amores* (1542), and satirical poems, as *Contra los que dejan los metros castellanos y siguen los italianos* championing traditional Spanish verse forms against Italianate innovations (c.1540), *Diálogo de mujeres* (1544).

Castillejos, Marqués de los. See Juan PRIM Y PRATS.

Castillo, Bernal Díaz del. See DÍAZ DEL CASTILLO.

Cas·ti·llo \käs-'tē-zhō\, Ramón S. 1873–1944. Argentine politician. Senator (1932–35); minister of public instruction and interior (1936); vice president (1938–40); acting president in illness of Pres. Ortiz (1940–42); proclaimed Argentine neutrality in World War II (1941); president (1942–43); overthrown by military coup.

Cas·ti·llo Ar·mas \käs-'tē(l)-yō-'är-mäs\, Carlos. 1914–1957. Guatemalan soldier and politician. Took part in overthrow of Ubico (1944); led unsuccessful coup attempt (1950) and fled; with covert U.S. aid invaded Guatemala and overthrew leftist government of Pres. Arbenz (1954); president (1954–57); promulgated new constitution, banned left wing parties, unions; assassinated.

Castillo So·lór·za·no \-sō-'lōr-thä-nō\, Alonso de. 1584–?1648. Spanish writer. Author of humorous poems, plays, and esp. short stories in *Tardes entretenidas* (1625), *Jornadas alegres* (1626), *Huerta de Valencia* (1629), *Noches de placer* (1631), *Sala de recreación* (1649), etc., and picaresque novels, as *La niña de los embustes* (1632) and *La garduña de Sevilla* (1642).

Cas·tle \'kas-əl\, Vernon Blythe. *Orig.* Vernon Blythe \'blīth\. 1887–1918. British dancer and aviator. To U.S. (1906); on stage (from 1907); assumed name Castle. His dancing popular in Paris (1912), and later in New York; originated the one-step, turkey trot, Castle walk. Aviator in Royal Flying Corps (1916–18). His wife (m. 1911) ¶Irene, *nee* Foote \'fu̇t\ (1893–1969), dancer; sometimes credited with starting fad for bobbed hair; founded Orphans of the Storm animal shelter (1928); author of *Modern Dancing* (with Vernon Castle, 1914), *My Memories of Vernon Castle* (1918).

Castle, William Ernest. 1867–1962. American zoologist, b. Alexandria, Ohio. Teacher at Harvard (from 1897; professor 1908–36); known for experimental studies of heredity. Author of *Heredity in Relation to Evolution and Animal Breeding* (1911), *Genetics and Eugenics* (1916), etc.

Castlemaine. (1) Earl of. See Roger PALMER. (2) Countess of. See Barbara VILLIERS.

Castlemon, Harry. See Charles Austin FOSDICK.

Castlereagh, Viscount. See Robert STEWART.

Cas·trén \'käs-,trān\, Matthias Alexander. 1813–1852. Finnish ethnologist and philologist. Professor of Finnish language and literature (1851), chancellor (1852), Helsinki; determined relation of Finnish to other language groups; ardent nationalist and proponent of Pan-Turanism. Regarded as founder of Ural-Altaic philology.

Castriota, George. See KASTRIOTI.

Cas·tro \'käs-trō\, Cipriano. 1858–1924. Venezuelan general and dictator. From exile in Colombia led insurrection against President Ignacio Andrade (1899); became "supreme military leader" (1899–1901); provisional president (1901–02); elected president (1902–08); his administration marked by many revolts and by despotic acts; involved Venezuela in serious difficulties with foreign powers, notably with Germany, England, Italy, and Belgium as creditor nations (1902–07; their blockade of Venezuelan ports bringing about U.S. intervention, 1902), with U.S. (1904–08) because of confiscation of American properties in Venezuela, and with Colombia and France (1905); known also for dissolute life. During absence in Paris, deposed by vice president Gómez (1908); in exile thereafter.

Cas·tro \'kash-trü\, Eugénio de. 1869–1944. Portuguese poet. Professor, Coimbra (1914–39). Author of *Oaristos* (1890), *Horas* (1891), *Sagramor* (1895), *Salomé* (1896), *El rey Galaor* (1897), *Constança* (1900); chief Portuguese exponent of Symbolism.

Cas·tro \'käs-trō\, Inés de. 1320?–1355. Spanish noblewoman. Descendant of royal family of Castile; became mistress of Dom Pedro (future Peter I); murdered at Coimbra by order of Dom Pedro's father Afonso IV. Episode was celebrated by novelists and poets.

Cas·tro \'kash-trü\, João de. 1500–1548. Portuguese naval commander. Sailed to India, helped break siege of Diu (1538); in command of fleet to rid European seas of pirates (1543); to Portuguese India (1545) as viceroy ad interim; again relieved city of Diu; subdued Malacca; appointed viceroy (1547) by John III. First noted deflection of compass by nearby iron; wrote three valuable pilot books.

Cas·tro \'käs-trō\, José María. 1818–1893. Costa Rican politician. President of Costa Rica (1847–49) at time of declaration of independence (1848) and therefore called "Founder of the Republic"; again president (1866–68).

Castro, Rosalía de. 1837–1885. Spanish writer. Champion of Galician language. Author of verse *Cantares gallegos* (1863), *Follas novas* (1880), *En las orillas del Sar* (1884); novels *La hija del mar* (1859), *Ruinas* (1866), *El primer loco* (1881), etc.

Cas·tro Al·ves \'kash-trü-'äl-vās\, Antônio de. 1847–1871. Brazilian poet. A Romantic, leader of the Condoreira group; noted esp. for verse directed against slavery. Author of *Espumas flutuantes* (1870), *Os escravos* (1876), *Vozes d'Africa* (1880).

Cas·tro y Bell·vís \'käs-trō-ē-belʸ-'vēs\, Guillén de. 1569–1631. Spanish dramatist. Best known for *Las mocedades del Cid* (1599?), source for Corneille's *Le Cid.*

Castro y Velasco, Antonio Acisclo Palomino de. See PALOMINO.

Ca·struc·cio Ca·stra·ca·ni \käs-'trüt-chō-,käs-trä-'kä-nē\, *surnamed* de·gli An·tel·mi·nel·li \,dāl-yē-,än-tāl-mē-'nel-lē\. 1281–1328. Italian soldier and Ghibelline leader. Condottiere in service of English, Lombards, Emperor Henry VII; with Uguccione della Faggiuola, conquered Lucca (1314); vicar of Sargana (1314); overthrew Uguccione, becoming lord of Lucca (1316); carried on war with Florentine Guelphs; imperial vicar (1320), duke of Lucca (1324).

Caswallawn *or* **Caswallon.** See CASSIVELAUNUS.

Cas·well \'kaz-,wel, -wəl\, Richard. 1729–1789. American Revolutionary officer, b. Cecil Co., Md. Delegate to Continental Congress (1774–76); colonel in Revolutionary army; won battle of Moore's Creek (Feb. 27, 1776); governor of North Carolina (1776–80, 1785–87).

Cat \'kat\, Christopher. fl. 1703–1733. English tavern keeper. Proprietor of The Cat and Fiddle in London, meeting place of the Kit-cat Club, a social club for Whigs.

Ca·ta·la·ni \,kä-tä-'lä-nē\, Alfredo. 1854–1893. Italian composer. Professor, Milan Conservatory (1886–93). Composed operas *La falce* (1875), *Elda* (1880; revised as *Loreley,* 1890), *Dejanice* (1883), *Edmea* (1886), *La Wally* (1892); also wrote piano and orchestral works, songs.

Ca·tar·giu \,kä-tär-'jü\, Lazăr. 1823–1899. Romanian politician. Helped plan creation of united Romania (1858); helped overthrow Prince Alexandru Cuza (1866); member of regency (1866); prime minister of Romania (1866, 1871–76, 1889, 1891–95); leader in Senate of Conservative opposition to Brătianu (1876–88).

Ca·te·na \kä-'tā-nä\, Vincenzo di Bia·gio \dē-'byä-jō\. c.1470–1531. Venetian painter. His works included *Holy Trinity* (San Simeone Grande, Venice), *Judith, Knight Adoring the Christ Child, Christ Giving the Keys to St. Peter.*

Caterina. See CATHERINE.

Cates·by \'kāts-bē\, Mark. 1679?–1749. English naturalist and traveler. In America (1712–19, 1722–25), studying flora and fauna. Author of *The Natural History of Carolina, Florida, and the Bahama Islands* (1731–48).

Catesby, Robert. 1573–1605. English conspirator. Took part in rebellion of Earl of Essex (1601); named accomplice in Rye Plot (1603) to seize James I and force concessions of religious tolerance; chief instigator of Gunpowder Plot (1604–05); betrayed by Francis Tresham; killed resisting arrest.

Catharine. See CATHERINE.

Cath·cart \'kath-kərt, -,kärt\, Sir William Schaw. 10th Baron and 1st Earl Cathcart. 1755–1843. English soldier and diplomat. Commanded an irregular corps, the "British legion," in America (1777–80); served in Low Countries (1793–95); commander in chief in Ireland (1803–05); bombarded Copenhagen (1807); general (1812); ambassador at St. Petersburg (1814–20); created earl (1814).

His son ¶Charles Murray (1783–1859), 2d earl, styled Lord Green·ock \'grin-ək\; soldier; served in Italy and Sicily (1805–06), at Walcheren (1809), in Iberian Peninsula (1810–12), as quartermaster general (1814–23), at Waterloo; commander in chief in Canada (1846–49); general (1854); discovered new mineral, greenockite (1841). Charles's brother ¶George (1794–1854) was aide-de-camp to Wellington at Waterloo and in France (1815–18); governor and commander in chief in South Africa (1852–54); conquered Kaffirs and Basutos; killed at battle of Inkerman.

Ca·the·li·neau \kät-lē-nō\, Jacques. 1759–1793. French Royalist. Leader of Vendeans in uprising of 1793; died of wounds received leading assault on Nantes.

Cath·er \'kath-ər\, Willa Sibert. 1873–1947. American novelist, b. Winchester, Va. On staff of Pittsburgh *Daily Leader* (1898–1901); associate editor of *McClure's Magazine* (1906–12). Author of *April Twilights* (verse, 1903); the novels *Alexander's Bridge* (1912), *O Pioneers!* (1913), *Song of the Lark* (1915), *My Ántonia* (1918), *Youth and the Bright Medusa* (1920), *One of Ours* (1922, Pulitzer prize), *A Lost Lady* (1923), *The Professor's House* (1925), *My Mortal Enemy* (1926), *Death Comes for the Archbishop* (1927), *Shadows on the Rock* (1931), *Lucy Gayheart* (1935), *Sapphira and the Slave Girl* (1940); stories *Obscure Destinies* (1932); essays *Not Under Forty* (1936).

Cath·er·ine \'kath-(ə-)rən\. Saint. *Orig.* Caterina del Ric·ci \'rēt-chē\, *earlier* Alessandra dei Ricci. 1522–1590. Italian religious. Entered Dominican convent at Prato (1535); prioress (1560–90); widely known for her visions of the Passion and for her stigmata. Canonized (1746).

Catherine. Name of three wives of king Henry VIII of England. See (1) CATHERINE of Aragon; (2) Catherine HOWARD; (3) Catherine PARR.

Catherine. *Russ.* Ye·ka·te·ri·na \yik-ət-yir-'yē-nə\. Name of two empresses of Russia:

Catherine I. *Russ.* Yekaterina Alekseyevna. *Orig.* Marta Skow·ron·ska \(,)skəv-'rón-skə\. 1684–1727. Empress (1725–27). Of Livonian peasant origin; m. a Swedish dragoon; taken prisoner at Marienburg (1702); became serf of Prince Menshikov. Attracted attention of Peter I the Great and became his mistress (1702); received into Orthodox church and rechristened (1703); exerted influence over Peter and became his adviser; saved his life in campaign against Turks on the Prut (1711); m. Peter as his second wife (1712); crowned empress consort (1724). Succeeded Peter as Catherine I (1725); during short peaceful reign, relied upon Prince Menshikov; established Supreme Privy Council (1726), thus undercutting authority of Senate and Holy Synod; founded Russian Academy of Sciences (1725). Succeeded by grandson Peter II.

Catherine II. *Called* Catherine the Great. *Russ.* Yekaterina Alekseyevna. *Orig.* Sophie Friederike Auguste von An·halt-Zerbst \'än-,hält-'(t)serpst\. 1729–1796. Empress (1762–96). Married (1745) Grand Duke Peter (later Peter III), nephew of Empress Elizabeth; soon became estranged from Peter, both being subjects of much court scandal; soon after Peter's accession (1762), deposed him with help of her paramour Grigory Orlov and others; had herself proclaimed empress (1762). During her reign, serfdom and misery among peasants increased but frontiers of empire extended by large conquests; secularized property of clergy (1762); established a paramour, Stanisław Poniatowski, as king of Poland (1764); participated in partitions of Poland (1772, 1793, 1795); won victories over Turks in war (1768–74); put down rebellion of Yemelyan Pugachov and Cossacks (1774); reduced much of free peasantry to serfdom. Aided in policies by Grigory Potemkin (from 1774). Annexed Crimea (1783); engaged in second war with Turks (1787–92), concluding favorable Treaty of Jassy (1792); although German, identified herself completely with Russian people.

Catherine of Alexandria. Saint. d. early 4th century. Egyptian religious. Of questionable historicity; by legend, a learned girl; disputed with philosophers; converted wife of Emperor Maxentius; beheaded after failure of attempt to torture her on a spiked wheel.

Catherine of Ar·a·gon \'ar-ə-,gän\. 1485–1536. 1st Queen of Henry VIII of England. Daughter of Ferdinand and Isabella of Spain; m. Arthur, Prince of Wales (1501; d. 1502); betrothed (1503) to Prince Henry, with papal dispensation, but unmarried while Henry VII extorted new demands from her father. Married Henry VIII (1509); mother of Mary (later Mary I); regent during Henry's invasion of France (1513). Informed by Henry (1527) that cohabitation must cease pending decision of validity of marriage with brother's widow; appeared before legatine court of Cardinals Campeggio and Wolsey (1529), after which case was revoked to Rome; abandoned by Henry (1531) and separated from her daughter Princess Mary. Refused to yield title of queen for princess-dowager after Archbishop Cranmer's declaration of nullity of her marriage (1533); passed rest of life in religious devotion, a prisoner.

Catherine of Bo·lo·gna \bə-'lōn-yə\. Saint. *Orig.* Caterina Vi·gri \'vē-grē\. 1413–1463. Italian religious. Entered order of Poor Clares (1432); founded (1456) convent in Bologna; abbess (1456–63); subject throughout life to visions and revelations.

Catherine of Bra·gan·za \brə-'gan-zə\. 1638–1705. Queen of Charles II of England. Daughter of John IV, Duke of Braganza and (after 1640) King of Portugal; m. (1662) to Charles II; forced by Charles to receive his mistress Lady Castlemaine and to live in retirement; subjected to schemes for dissolution of marriage because of childlessness (1667–70); accused by Titus Oates of design to poison king and by Whigs of complicity in Popish Plot (1678–80); shielded from these attacks by king; abandoned for duchess of Portsmouth; reconciled Charles on his deathbed with Catholic church (1685). Retired to Lisbon (1692); regent of Portugal for her brother Peter II (1704–05), gaining successes over Spain.

Catherine of Gen·oa \'jen-ə-wə\. Saint. *Orig.* Caterina Fie·schi \'fyās-kē\. 1447–1510. Italian mystic. Converted by mystical experience (1473); undertook service to sick, joined by husband whom she converted. Author of *Trattato del Purgatorio* and *Dialogo* (both printed 1551), records of mystical life.

Catherine of Sie·na \'syen-ä, *Angl* sē-'en-ə\. Saint. *Orig.* Caterina Be·nin·ca·sa \,bā-nēn-'kä-sä\. 1347–1380. Italian religious. Became Dominican tertiary (1363); gained reputation for holiness, asceticism, visions and revelations; urged a crusade; visited Pope Gregory XI at Avignon in interest of peace with Florence; influenced his return to Rome (1376); in Rome assisted Pope Urban VI in reorganization of church (1378–80). Author of devotional letters published (c.1475) as *Dialogo.* Canonized (1461); declared patron saint of Italy (1939).

Catherine of Sweden. Saint. *Orig.* Katarina Ulfs·dot·ter \'ülfs-,dót-tər\. 1331/32–1381. Swedish religious. Daughter of Saint Bridget, whom she succeeded as abbess of the convent of the Brigittines at Vadstena.

Catherine of Va·lois \vál-wá\. 1401–1437. Queen of Henry V of England. Daughter of Charles VI of France; m. Henry (1420); crowned in Westminster Abbey (1421); mother of Henry VI. After Henry's death in France (1422) was secretly married (c.1429) to Owen Tudor (*q.v.*) by whom she was mother of three sons and a daughter, the eldest son (Edmund, cr. earl of Richmond 1453) being father of Henry VII; retired to nunnery (1436).

Catherine de Foix. See FOIX.

Ca·the·rine de Mé·di·cis \ká-trēn-də-mā-dē-sēs\. *Ital.* Ca·te·ri·na de' Me·di·ci \,kä-tā-'rē-nä-dā-'med-ē-(,)chē, *Angl* -'med-ə-(,)chē\. 1519–1589. Queen of Henry II of France. Daughter of Lorenzo de' Medici; m. (1533) Henry, son of Francis I of France; became queen of France (1547). Had four sons, three of whom became kings of France; began to assert herself when eldest, Francis II, became king (1559); regent during minority of Charles IX (1560–63) and had practically complete control during his entire reign (1560–74); exerted some influence over Henry III (1574–89). Struggled with Guise faction for control of government; attempted to mediate Catholic–Protestant conflict and worked to establish legal toleration for Protestants; by edicts ended civil wars of religion (1562–63, 1567–68). Traditionally implicated in St. Bartholomew's Day Massacre (Aug. 23–24, 1572) but on unclear evidence.

Catherine Howard. See Catherine HOWARD.

Cat·i·line \kat-ᵊl-,īn\. *Full Lat. name* Lucius Sergius Cat·i·li·na \'kat-ᵊl-'ī-nə\. c.108–62 B.C. Roman politician. Quaestor (77 B.C.); praetor (68); governor of Africa (67–66); defeated in election for consul (64, 63). Entered into conspiracy to assassinate the consuls and plunder Rome (63); foiled by Cicero, then a consul. Attacked by Cicero in speeches in senate and forum; fled to army of Manlius, his ally in Etruria; defeated (62) and slain.

Ca·ti·nat \ká-tē-ná\, Nicolas. 1637–1712. French soldier. Field marshal (1680), lieutenant general (1688); commanded Italian army (1690–96) and forced duke of Savoy to sue for peace; created marshal of France (1693).

Cat·lin \'kat-lən\, George. 1796–1872. American artist and author, b. Wilkes-Barre, Pa. Gave up law for painting (1823); devoted himself (from 1829) to study of American Indians; executed series of Indian portraits (painted 1829–38) now in National Museum, Washington, D.C., and of Indian sketches, in American Museum of Natural History, New York. Author of *Letters and Notes on the Manners, Customs and Condition of the North American Indians* (1841), *Life Amongst the Indians* (1867), etc.

Ca·to \'kāt-(,)ō, 'kā-,tō\, Dionysius. 3d–4th century A.D. Roman writer. Supposed author of *Dionysii Catonis disticha de moribus ad filium,* collection of moral apothegms much admired in Middle Ages.

Cato, Marcus Porcius. *Known as* Cato the Censor *and* Cato the Elder. 234–149 B.C. Roman politician. Quaestor (204 B.C.); aedile (199); praetor (198); consul (195); censor (184). Endeavored to restore by legislation what he believed to be the high morals and simplicity of life characteristic of early days of the republic; fought Hellenist influence; champion of anti-Carthaginian policy and chiefly responsible for bringing on Third Punic War. Noted orator; writer of great influence on development of Latin literature; author of *Origines,* a history of Rome, of *Praecepta,* book of maxims; only extant work is *De agri cultura,* or *De re rustica.*

His great-grandson ¶Marcus Porcius Cato, *surnamed* Uti·cen·sis \,ət-ə-'sen(t)-səs\ *from Utica, city of his death. Known as* Cato the Younger. 95–46 B.C. Roman politician. Reared in house of M. Livius Drusus; served against Spartacus (72 B.C.); military tribune in Macedonia (67); quaestor (65 or 64); tribune of the people (62); praetor (54). A leader of conservative, aristocratic Optimate faction; supported Cicero against Catiline, and Pompey against Caesar; failed to hold Sicily for Pompey; committed suicide on learning of Caesar's decisive victory at Thapsus (46).

Cato, Publius Valerius. 1st century B.C. Roman scholar and poet. Leader of "new" school of poetry; author of mythological epics, lyrics, elegies.

Ca·tron \'kā-trən\, John. 1786?–1865. American jurist, b. probably in Wythe Co., Va. To Tennessee (1812); first chief justice of Tennessee (1831–34); associate justice, U.S. Supreme Court (1837–65).

Ca·troux \kȧ-trü\, Georges. 1877–1969. French general. Served in World War I, Morocco, Algeria; governor general of Indochina (1939–40); Free French high commissioner and General de Gaulle's representative in Near East (1940); commander in chief in Levant (1941–43); proclaimed independence of Syria and Lebanon (1941); governor general of Algeria (1943–44); ambassador to Russia (1945–48).

Cats \ˈkäts\, Jakob. 1577–1660. Dutch poet and official. Grand pensionary of Holland (1636–51) and keeper of the great seal (1648–51). Author of Calvinist didactic verse published in popular emblem-books as *Sinn'-en minne-beelden* (1618), *Spieghel van den ouden ande nieuwen Tijdt* (1632); verse on love and marriage as *Houwelyck* (1625), *Trou-Ringh* (1637).

Catt \ˈkat\, Carrie Clinton Chapman, *nee* Lane \ˈlān\. 1859–1947. American reformer, b. Ripon, Wis. High school principal, and superintendent of schools, Mason City, Iowa; m. Leo Chapman (1885; d. 1886), 2d George W. Catt (1890; d. 1905). State lecturer and organizer, Iowa Woman Suffrage Association (1890–92); on staff of National American Woman Suffrage Association (from 1892), president (1900–04, 1915–47); also, president International Woman Suffrage Alliance (1904–23). A leader in campaign resulting in adoption of 19th Amendment to U.S. Constitution (1920).

Cat·ta·neo \ˌkät-tä-ˈnā-ō\, Carlo. 1801–1869. Italian writer. A leader of Risorgimento; wrote on arts, sciences, language, reform, politics; edited journal *Il Politecnico* in Milan; chosen to revolutionary council after Milanese revolt (1848); forced to flee to Switzerland by Austrian reoccupation. Works included *Notizie naturali e civili su la Lombardia* (1844), *L'insurrection de Milan* (1848), *Dell'Insurrezione di Milano* (1849).

Cat·tell \kə-ˈtel\, James McKeen. 1860–1944. American psychologist, b. Easton, Pa. Professor and head of department of psychology, U. of Penn. (1888–91), Columbia (1891–1917); founded Psychological Corp. (1921); known for studies of reaction time, mental testing, individual differences; noted esp. for development of experimental methods in psychology. Editor of *Psychological Review* (1894–1904), *Science* (from 1894), *Scientific Monthly* (from 1900), *American Naturalist* (from 1907), *School and Society* (1915–39), also of *American Men of Science* (from 1906), *Leaders in Education* (from 1932).

Cat·ton \ˈkat-ᵊn\, Bruce, *in full* Charles Bruce. 1899–1978. American writer and editor, b. Petoskey, Mich. Journalist, Washington, D.C. (1926–41); information officer, various government departments (1942–52); editor, *American Heritage* magazine (1954–59). Author of *War Lords of Washington* (1948); trilogy *Mr. Lincoln's Army* (1951), *Glory Road* (1952), *A Stillness at Appomattox* (1953, Pulitzer prize); *This Hallowed Ground* (1956), *America Goes to War* (1958), *Grant Moves South* (1960); Centennial History of Civil War, comprising *The Coming Fury* (1961), *Terrible Swift Sword* (1963), *Never Call Retreat* (1965).

Ca·tul·lus \kə-ˈtəl-əs\, Gaius Valerius. c.84–c.54 B.C. Roman poet. Author of 113 to 116 extant poems, comprising elegies, miniature epics, epithalamia, lyrics, epigrams; several love poems are addressed to "Lesbia," tentatively identified as Clodia, notorious sister of Clodius, and wife (63–59 B.C.) of Quintus Metellus Celer. Regarded as one of the greatest lyric poets in Rome's literary history.

Cat·u·lus \ˈkach-ə-ləs\. Name of a family of ancient Rome, including notably: Gaius Lutatius (3d century B.C.); consul (242 B.C.), commander of fleet (241 B.C.) that defeated Carthaginian fleet of the Aegates (Aegadian Isles). ¶Quintus Lutatius (d. 87? B.C.), consul with Marius (102 B.C.), and his colleague in defeating (101) the Cimbri at Vercellae (Vercelli); committed suicide. His son ¶Quintus Lutatius (c.120–61/60 B.C.); follower of Sulla, and a leader of ultraconservative Optimates; consul (78); joined Pompey in defeating Lepidus (77); censor (65); defeated by Caesar in election for pontifex maximus (63); supporter of Cicero in his attack against Catiline (63).

Cau·chon \kō-shōⁿ\, Pierre. 1371–1442. French prelate. Bishop of Beauvais (1420–32), of Lisieux (from 1432); judge at trial of Joan of Arc (1431).

Cau·chy \kō-shē\, Augustin-Louis. Baron. 1789–1857. French mathematician. Held professorships at Faculté des Sciences, Collège de France, and École Polytechnique (1816–30); refused to take oath required by Louis-Philippe and went into exile (1830); taught at Turin; returned to Paris (1838); professor again at École (1838) and at Sorbonne (1848). Established modern mathematical rigor; founded theory of elasticity, theory of functions of complex variables, theory of substitution groups; reorganized calculus on concepts of limit and continuity; contributed to theory of wave propagation, optics, error theory, etc. Author of *Cours d'analyse de l'École Royale Polytechnique* (1821), *Résumé des leçons sur le calcul infinitésimal* (1823), *Leçons sur les applications du calcul infinitésimal à la géométrie* (1826–28).

Cauchy, Eugène-François. 1802–1877. French jurist. Brother of Augustin Cauchy. Authority on maritime law and author of *Le Droit maritime international* (1863).

Cau·lain·court \kō-laⁿ-kür\, Armand-Augustin-Louis de. Marquis. 1773–1827. French soldier and diplomat. Colonel of cavalry (1799); distinguished himself at Hohenlinden (1800); general and aide-de-camp to Napoléon (1802); master of horse (from 1804); ambassador to Russia (1807–11). Created duc de Vicence (1808) and a senator (1813); minister of foreign affairs (1813–14, and during the Hundred Days). His brother ¶Auguste-Jean-Gabriel (1777–1812), general; aide-de-camp to Berthier (1804); general of brigade (1806); served in Spain, Portugal, and Russia; killed in battle of Moscow.

Cauliaco, Guido de. See GUY DE CHAULIAC.

Caul·le·ry \kōl-(ə-)rē\, Maurice-Jules-Gaston-Corneille. 1868–1958. French biologist. Professor, Marseilles (1900–03); lecturer, Paris (1903–09); professor, Faculté des Sciences (1909–39). Known for research on embryology, evolution, ecology of tunicates and annelids; discovered marine worm *Siboglinum Weberi,* representing a new phylum of invertebrates. Author of *La Parasitisme et la symbiose* (1922), *Le Problème de l'évolution* (1931), *Organisme et sexualité* (1942).

Cau·mont La Force \kō-mōⁿ-lȧ-fôrs\, Antonin-Nompar de. Duc de Lau·zun \lō-zœⁿ\. 1633–1723. French soldier. Colonel of foreign dragoons (1658); imprisoned by Louis XIV (1665) in quarrel over mistress; colonel general of dragoons (1668); again briefly imprisoned for criticizing king's mistress (1669); imprisoned by Louis (1671–81) to prevent his marriage to the Duchesse de Montpensier, richest heiress in Europe; released on renouncing her gifts to him; possibly secretly married her (1682); separated (1684). Commanded French troops in Ireland (1690); created duc (1692).

Caunt \ˈkȯnt\, Benjamin. 1815–1861. British pugilist. Defeated Bendigo (William Thompson, 1838) and claimed English championship; sought opponents in U.S. so as to claim world title (1841); managed Charles Freeman of U.S. in English tour; lost title to Bendigo (1845).

Cau·po·li·cán \ˌkau̇-pō-li-ˈkän\. *Also spelled* Que·po·li·cán \ˌkā-\. d. 1558. Indian leader. Chief of Araucanian people; leader of resistance to Spanish occupation of present-day Chile; with Lautaro, defeated Pedro de Valdivia (1553); defeated Spanish at Villagrán (1557); heavily defeated by Don García Hurtado de Mendoza in 3 battles; retreated to mountains; captured and murdered.

Caus *or* **Cauls** *or* **Caulx** *or* **Caux** \kō\, Salomon de. 1576–1626. French engineer. Exiled as Protestant; active in England and Germany. Author of *Les Raisons des forces mouvantes* (1615), in which he anticipated steam engine.

Cavafy, Constantine. See KAVÁFIS.

Ca·vai·gnac \kȧ-ven-yȧk\, Jean-Baptiste. 1762–1829. French lawyer and revolutionist. As member of National Convention (1792), voted for death of Louis XVI; agent for dechristianization campaign; member of Council of Five Hundred; exiled as regicide after Restoration. His son ¶Godefroy, *in full* Éléonore-Louis-Godefroy (1801–1845), journalist and politician, active in revolutionary events and intrigues (1830–34); imprisoned, escaped to England; returned to France (1841); president, Society of the Rights of Man (1843). Another son ¶Louis-Eugène (1802–1857), army commander; dismissed from army (1831) for republicanism but restored and served in Algeria (1832–48); as minister of war (1848), suppressed uprising in Paris; chief of the executive body (June–Dec. 1848); unsuccessful candidate for president of France (Dec. 1848); leader of opposition to Louis-Napoléon.

Ca·vail·lé-Coll \kə-vȧ-yā-kȯl\, Aristide. 1811–1899. French organ builder. Built organ at Saint-Denis, Paris (completed 1841); given several rebuilding commissions by Napoléon III; built or rebuilt some 600 organs in France and England; made improvements in mechanism and pipework, developed distinctive voicing for which Franck, Saint-Saëns, Widor, etc. composed.

Ca·val·can·ti \ˌkä-väl-ˈkän-tē\, Guido. c.1255–1300. Florentine poet. Leading Florentine poet before Dante, who called him his "first friend"; wrote in *dolce stil nuovo;* author of some 50 poems including deeply moving love lyrics, sonnets, ballads, canzoni.

Ca·val·ca·sel·le \ˌkä-väl-kä-ˈsel-lā\, Giovanni Battista. 1820–1897. Italian art historian and critic. Took part in revolution (1848) in Venice; with Garibaldi; captured (1849), taken to Paris; later to London; inspector of Museo Nazionale, Florence (1867), and general director of fine arts in Rome. His works, written in collaboration with Joseph Archer Crowe (*q.v.*), included *Early Flemish Painters* (1857), *New History of Italian Painting* (1864), *Titian* (1877), and *Raphael* (1882–85).

Ca·va·lier \kȧ-vȧl-yā\, Jean. 1681–1740. French insurgent. Son of a peasant; baker at Geneva; led Huguenot insurgents (Camisards) in the Cévennes and Languedoc (1702); defeated superior forces but made submission (1704), failing to obtain liberty of conscience; served under duke of Savoy and with English in Spain (1706).

Ca·va·lie·ri \ˌkä-väl-ˈyer-ē\, Emilio de'. *Also* Emilio del Ca·va·lie·re \-ˈyer-ā\. c.1550–1602. Italian composer. Inspector general of arts at Medici court (1587 ff.); member of Camerata musical group, Florence; one of originators of figured-bass (basso continuo) accompaniment. Known esp. for dramatic compositions, as *La rappresentazione di anima e di corpo* (1600), a precursor of opera and oratorio; madrigals, ballos, and lost pastorals.

Cavalieri, Francesco Bonaventura. 1598–1647. Italian mathematician. At early age entered order of Jesuati; professor at Bologna (1629). Originated the method of indivisibles, a precursor of integral calculus, which he published as *Geometria indivisibilibus continuorum nova quadam ratione promota* (1635) and by means of which was able to solve problems proposed by Kepler; improved method in *Exercitationes geometricae sex* (1647); also wrote on trigonometry, conics, etc.

Ca·val·le·ro \ˌkä-väl-ˈler-ō\, Ugo. Conte. 1880–1943. Italian general. Commander of Italian forces in East Africa (1937–40); commander in Albania (1941); successor to Marshal Badoglio as chief of staff, Italian high command (1941–43); marshal of Italy (1942).

Ca·val·li \kä-ˈväl-lē\, Francesco. *Orig.* Pietro Francesco Ca·let·ti di Bru·ni \kä-ˈlāt-tē-dē-ˈbrü-nē\. 1602–1676. Italian composer. Protégé of Federico Cavalli, a Venetian nobleman; pupil of Monteverdi; organist (1665), maestro di cappella (1668–76) in church of San Marco, Venice; aided in development of modern opera by innovations, as introduction of solos and set numbers. His operas included *Didone* (1641), *Egisto* (1643), *Ormindo* (1644), *Rosinda* (1651), *Ciro* (1654), *Erismena* (1655).

Ca·val·li·ni \ˌkä-väl-ˈlē-nē\, Pietro. c.1250–c.1330. Italian painter and mosaicist. Earliest major artist to break with Byzantine style; developed control of light for modeling, illusionist treatment of space; influenced Giotto. Works included frescoes in nave of S. Paolo Fuori le Mora; mosaic scenes from life of the Virgin in Sta. Maria in Trastavere; frescoes in Sta. Cecilia in Trastavere (all Rome); directed pupils in frescoes for convent church of Sta. Maria Donna Regina, Naples.

Ca·val·lot·ti \ˌkä-väl-ˈlòt-tē\, Felice Carlo Emmanuele. 1842–1898. Italian politician and writer. Fought under Garibaldi (1860, 1866); founded antimonarchist journal *Gazzetino rosa* (1866); member of parliament (1873–98); leader of extreme Left (1886 ff.); ardent supporter of Irredentists; bitter opponent of Crispi; killed in his thirty-third duel. His works included lyric poetry and plays.

Cavan, Earl of. See Frederic LAMBART.

Cave \ˈkāv\, Edward. 1691–1754. English printer. Printer and journalist at Norwich; employed in post office, London; supplied country newspapers with London newsletters; founded and edited *Gentleman's Magazine* (1731–54) under pseudonym of "Sylvanus Urban, Gent."; issued reports of debates in House of Commons upon which Samuel Johnson had his first employment.

Cave, George. 1st Viscount Cave. 1856–1928. English jurist. King's counsel (1904); M.P (1906–18); privy councilor (1915); home secretary (1916–18); created viscount, made lord of appeal in ordinary (1918); lord chancellor of England (1922–28).

Cav·ell \ˈkav-əl, kə-ˈvel\, Edith Louisa. 1865–1915. English nurse. First matron of medical institute in Brussels (1907), which became Red Cross hospital (1914); assisted about 200 English, French, and Belgian soldiers to escape to Dutch border (Nov. 1914–July 1915); arrested by Germans, admitted her successful efforts; condemned to death by court-martial; shot along with a Belgian, Phillippe Baucq, who had furnished guides.

Cavendish. See Henry JONES (1831–1899).

Cav·en·dish \ˈkav-ən-(ˌ)dish\. English family, members of which bear titles of marquis of Har·ting·ton \ˈhärt-iŋ-tən\ and duke of Dev·on·shire \ˈdev-ən-ˌshi(ə)r, -shər\; descended from Sir John Cavendish (d. 1381), chief justice of King's Bench (1372–81), who was beheaded by Jack Straw's followers. Other members included ¶Sir William Cavendish (1505?–1557); treasurer of royal chamber under Henry VIII, Edward VI, and Mary; his third wife, Bess of Hardwick (see Elizabeth TALBOT), completed the family seat at Chatsworth. Sir William's brother ¶George (1500–?1562), gentleman usher to Cardinal Wolsey (from 1526); biographer of Wolsey (1557). ¶William (d. 1626), Sir William's second son; M.P. (1586, 1588); active in colonization of Bermuda; created earl of Devonshire (1618).

¶William (1592–1676), Duke of New·cas·tle \ˈn(y)ü-ˌkas-əl, n(y)ü-ˈ\; nephew of 1st Earl of Devonshire; created earl (1628); entertained James I (1619), Charles I (1633) at seat Welbeck; governor to Prince of Wales (1638–41); in Royalist cause invaded Yorkshire (1642), raised siege of Hull (1643); commander of all Royalist forces north of the Tyne; left England after battle of Marston Moor (1644); reduced to poverty; returned at Restoration (1660), restored to lands; created duke (1665). Author of works on horsemanship.

¶William (1640–1707), 1st Duke of Devonshire; son of 3rd earl and great-great-grandson of Sir William; a leader of anticourt and anti-Romanist party in House of Commons (1666–78); aided in raising the north country in favor of William of Orange; argued for James II's deposition (1689); created (1694) duke of Devonshire and marquis of Hartington.

¶William (1720–1764), 4th Duke of Devonshire; great-grandson of 1st duke; M.P. (1741–51); lord lieutenant of Ireland (1755–56); prime minister (1756–57); lord chamberlain (1757–62).

¶Georgiana (1757–1806), daughter of 1st Earl Spencer; m. (1774) 5th Duke of Devonshire (1748–1811); a reigning queen of society; friend of Fox, Sheridan, Selwyn, Dr. Johnson; a beauty whose portrait was painted by Sir Joshua Reynolds and Gainsborough, both as child and as duchess.

¶Spencer Compton (1833–1908), 8th duke; Liberal M.P. (1857–91); war secretary in Lord Russell's government (1866); postmaster general under Gladstone (1868–70); chief secretary for Ireland (1870–74); led Liberal party in House of Commons (1875–80); declined offer of premiership (1880); secretary of state for India under Gladstone (1880–82), war secretary (1882–85); partly responsible for sending Gordon back to Sudan, failed to secure government's support of mission; consistently opposed Gladstone's Irish home rule policy, favoring coercion; with Joseph Chamberlain, founded new party of Liberal Unionists; declined premiership (1886, 1887); joined Salisbury's coalition government as president of council (1895–1902), continued under Balfour (1902–03); opposed to fiscal policy and, as a free trader, opposed to tariff reform; resigned (1903).

¶Lord Frederick Charles (1836–1882), brother of 8th duke; M.P. (1865–82); protégé and (from 1872) private secretary of Gladstone; chief secretary for Ireland (1882); murdered, with Undersecretary Burke, by Irish Invincibles in Phoenix Park, Dublin.

¶Victor Christian William (1868–1938), *known as* Lord Hartington; 9th duke; nephew of 8th duke; M.P. (1891–1908); financial secretary to treasury (1903–05); governor general of Canada (1916–21); secretary of state for colonies (1922–25).

Cavendish, Henry. 1731–1810. English physicist and chemist. Grandson of 2d Duke of Devonshire; lived most of life as virtual recluse. Discovered composition of water (1784–85, simultaneously with James Watt); independently discovered Coulomb's law of electrostatic attraction; developed notion of electrical potential; anticipated Ohm's law; discovered nitric acid; among first to recognize elemental nature of hydrogen; experimented in heat, meteorology, metallurgy; devised Cavendish experiment (1797–98), by which gravitational constant and density of the Earth were determined. Cavendish Laboratory, Cambridge U., endowed by descendants (1871).

Cavendish *or* **Can·dish** \ˈkan-dish\, Thomas. c.1560–1592. English navigator. Imitating Drake, sailed with three ships (1586) to Brazil; discovered Port Desire (Puerto Deseado, Patagonia); passed Strait of Magellan; captured Spanish treasure galleon; returned home via Philippines, Moluccas, Java, Cape of Good Hope, with only one ship, the *Desire,* after 2 years and 50 days; third man to circumnavigate globe. Attempted second voyage with five ships (1591); unable to pass Strait of Magellan; died at sea.

Cavendish, Bentinck. See BENTINCK.

Ca·ven·tou \kȧ-väⁿ-tü\, Joseph-Bienaimé. 1795–1877. French chemist. Taught at École Supérieure de Pharmacie (1826–59); with Pierre-Joseph Pelletier studied and named chlorophyll (1817), studied alkaloids and discovered strychnine (1818), brucine (1819), quinine (1820); discovered caffeine (1821).

Cavour, Conte di. See Camillo BENSO.

Caw·drey \ˈkò-drē\, Robert. 1580–1604. English lexicographer. Published *The Table Alphabetical of Hard Words* (1604).

Caxias, Duque de. See ALVES DE LIMA Y SILVA.

Cax·ton \ˈkak-stən\, William. c.1422–1491. English printer. Apprenticed (1438) to London silk merchant; merchant on his own account at Bruges (1446–70); as governor of English merchants in Low Countries (1463–70), negotiated commercial treaties with dukes of Burgundy. Translated popular medieval romance *Recuyell of the Historyes of Troye* (1469–71), finished at request of Duchess Margaret of Burgundy, sister of Edward IV. Learned printing in Cologne (1471–72); set up press, in partnership with Colard Mansion; printed his *Recuyell* (1475) and another translation, *The Game and Playe of the Chesse* (1476); returned to England (1476); established press at Westminster, first printer in England; issued an indulgence by Abbot Sant (1476), first known piece of printing from Caxton press in England; issued (1477) first dated book printed in England, Earl Rivers's *The Dictes and Sayenges of the Phylosophers* (a translation from the French); printed first English illustrated book, encyclopaedia *The Myrrour of the worlde* (1481), Chaucer's *Canterbury Tales* (1478?, 1484?), Gower's *Confessio amantis* (1483), Malory's *Morte Darthur* (1485), etc.

Cay·ley \ˈkā-lē\, Arthur. 1821–1895. English mathematician. Called to bar (1849); Sadlerian professor of pure mathematics, Cambridge (1863–95). Author of over 900 papers; developed algebraic matrices, founded theory of algebraic invariance, contributed to multidimensional geometry; also contributed to theoretical dynamics and spherical and physical astronomy.

Cayley, Sir George. 1773–1857. English scientist. Pioneer in aerodynamics; built first man-carrying glider (1853); also invented caterpillar tractor, railway devices.

Caylus, Comte de. See TUBIÈRES-GRIMOARD.

Ca·za·lis \kȧ-zȧ-lēs\, Henri. *Pseudonyms* Jean Ca·sel·li \kä-ˈsel-lē, kȧ-zel-ē\ *and* Jean La·hor \lȧ-ȯr\. 1840–1909. French physician and poet. Author of *Chants populaires de l'Italie* (1865), *L'Illusion* (1875–93), etc.

Ca·zin \kȧ-zaⁿ\, Jean-Charles. 1841–1901. French painter and ceramic artist. Director, École des Beaux-Arts, Paris (1868); to England (1871), designed ceramics for Fulham pottery. Best known for his landscapes, as *Souvenir de Fête, The Journey's End, The Marne, The Bathers,* and for religious works, including *Judith, Tobit,* and *Hagar and Ishmael.*

Ca·zotte \kȧ-zȯt\, Jacques. 1719–1792. French writer. Author of *Le Diable amoureux* (1772), and of a continuation of *The Arabian Nights;* joined Illuminati and claimed ability to prophesy, inspiring La Haye's satiric *Vision de Cazotte;* guillotined in Paris as a Royalist.

Cead·da \ˈcha-əd-ə\ *or* **Chad** \ˈchad\. Saint. d. 672. British prelate. An Angle of Northumbria; educated at Lindisfarne by St. Aidan; succeeded brother St. Cedd (*q.v.*) as abbot of Laestingaeu (664); at request of King Oswiu, named bishop of Northumbrians at York (664) despite previous nomination of St. Wilfrid to see; resigned see on return of Wilfrid from France (669); named bishop of Mercia (669), taking Lichfield as seat; founded monasteries; credited with christianization of Mercia.

Ceaw·lin \ˈchau̇-lin\. d. 593. King of West Saxons (560–592). Son of King Cynric; took part in defeat of Britons at Beranbyrg (556); defeated King Aethelberht of Kent (568); defeated Britons at Deorham (577) and seized Gloucester, Cirencester, Bath; defeated by Ceol (592) and exiled.

Ce·bes \ˈsē-bēz\. 5th century B.C. Greek philosopher, of Thebes. Disciple and friend of Socrates; an interlocutor in Plato's *Phaedo.*

Cec·chet·ti \chāk-ˈkāt-tē\, Enrico. 1850–1928. Italian dancer and teacher. Danced in principal cities of Europe; created roles of Bluebird and Carabosse in *Sleeping Beauty* (St. Petersburg, 1887); taught at Imperial Russian Ballet school (1890–1902); instructor of Diaghilev Ballet Russe (1910–18); conducted school in London (1918–25); director of ballet school, La Scala (1925–28). Pupils included Preobrajenska, Karsavina, Nijinsky, Pavlova, Markova, Lifar.

Cecco d'Ascoli. See Francesco STABILI.

Cech \ˈchek\, Svatopluk. 1846–1908. Czech poet and novelist. A leader of nationalist movement in literature; founded (1879) newspaper *Květy.* Author of verse *Ve stínu lípy* (1879), *Hanuman* (1884), *Písně otroka* (1895), epics *Slávie* (1884), *Dagmar* (1885), novels *Humoresky* (1887), *Nový výlet pana Broučka do měsíce* (1888).

Cec·il \ˈses-əl, ˈsis-\. An English family descended from David Cyssell or Sisseld or Cecill, sheriff of Northamptonshire (1532–33) and three time M.P., through his grandson William Cecil, Lord Burghley (see below), whose two sons were founders of two branches of the family, the elder line comprising the earls and marquises of Ex·e·ter \ˈek-sət-ər\, the younger line of earls and marquises (from 1789) of Salis·bur·y \ˈsȯlz-ˌber-ē, -b(ə-)rē\.

¶William Cecil (1520–1598), 1st Baron Burgh·ley, *sometimes* Bur·leigh \ˈbər-lē\. Appointed to Court of Common Pleas (1542); M.P. (1543); member of household and (1548) secretary to lord protector, Somerset; as secretary of state (1550–53), abolished some commerial monopolies; during reign of Queen Mary, conformed to Roman Catholicism and escorted Cardinal Pole from Brussels (1554). As chief secretary of state (1558–72) became the shrewd originator and cautious director of Elizabeth I's policy; worked for Scottish settlement and an appropriate match for Elizabeth; opposed Dudley and Duke of Norfolk; organized a network of spies to detect plots against the queen (1570); created (1571) Baron Burghley of Burghley; lord high treasurer (1572–98); urged cooperation with France to offset Spanish influence; encouraged Protestant Netherlands; assumed responsibility for execution of Mary, Queen of Scots (1587). Succeeded as queen's adviser by his son Robert Cecil (see below).

ELDER LINE:

¶Thomas Cecil (1542–1623), 1st Earl of Exeter and 2d Baron Burghley; son of 1st baron by his first wife, sister of the Greek scholar Sir John Cheke. Soldier; served in Scotland (1573), in Low Countries (1585), against Armada (1588); helped crush rising under Earl of Essex (1601); created earl (1605).

¶Sir Edward (1572–1638), Viscount Wim·ble·don \ˈwim-bəl-dən\; 3d son of 2d baron; held various commands in Low Countries (1596–1610); as deputy to Buckingham, bungled Spanish expedition (1625), letting treasure ships reach Cádiz; avoided censure as favorite of Buckingham and created viscount (1626).

YOUNGER LINE:

¶Robert Cecil (1563–1612), 1st Earl of Salisbury and 1st Viscount Cran·borne \ˈkran-ˌbō(ə)rn, -ˌbȯ(ə)rn\; son of 1st Baron Burghley by his second wife. Entered House of Commons (1584); acting secretary of state from death of Walsingham (1590); conducted foreign affairs as secretary of state (1596–1608); secured accession of James VI of Scotland to English throne (1603) as James I; continued as secretary and chief minister under James I, in charge of administration of national affairs; negotiated end of Spanish war (1604); created viscount (1604), earl (1605); lord treasurer (1608).

¶Robert Arthur Talbot Gas·coyne-Cecil \ˈgas-ˌkȯin-\ (1830–1903), 3d Marquis of Salisbury. M.P. (1853–68); succeeded to marquisate (1868); wrote pungent articles for *Quarterly Review;* secretary for India (1866–67, 1874–78), for foreign affairs (1878); leader of opposition in House of Lords on death of Disraeli (1881); helped defeat Gladstone's home rule bill (1893); opponent of democracy and radical ideas of progress. Prime minister and foreign secretary (1885–86, 1886–92, 1895–1902); followed imperialist but cautiously conciliatory policy; annexed Burma; strengthened hold on Upper Nile and Zanzibar; secured open door in China; reconquered Sudan (1896); retired, after conducting Boer War (1902), in favor of his nephew A.J. Balfour.

¶James Edward Hubert Gascoyne-Cecil (1861–1947), 4th marquis; eldest son of 3d marquis. M.P. (1885–92, 1893–1903); served in Boer War; lord privy seal (1903–05); president of Board of Trade (1905); joined diehards in struggle over Parliament bill (1910–11); critical of coalition government in World War I; lord president of council (1922–23); lord privy seal (1924–29); leader of House of Lords (1925–29).

¶Robert, *in full* Edgar Algernon Robert Gascoyne-Cecil (1864–1958), 1st Viscount Cecil of Chel·wood \ˈchel-ˌwu̇d\; 3d son of 3d marquis. M.P. (1906–23); minister of blockade (1916–18); asst. secretary of state for foreign affairs (1918–19); participated in drafting League of Nations Covenant (1919); representative of South Africa in League Assembly (1920–22). Lord privy seal (1923–24), chancellor of duchy of Lancaster (1924–27), in both offices devoting himself to League affairs; resigned from cabinet because of failure of cabinet to support compromise of cruiser question with U.S. (1927); president of League of Nations Union (1923–45). Awarded Nobel peace prize (1937). Author of *The Way of Peace* (1928), *A Great Experiment* (1941).

¶Hugh Richard Heathcote Gascoyne-Cecil (1869–1956), Baron Quicks·wood \ˈkwik-ˌswu̇d\; 5th son of 3d marquis. M.P. (1895–1906, 1910–37); with Winston Churchill, headed group of independents in House of Commons; resisted tariff reform, limitation of powers of House of Lords, and the Parliament bill; member of Royal Flying Corps (1915); spoke with authority on ecclesiastical questions and Church of England prayer-book proposals; provost of Eton (1936); created baron (1941).

¶Robert Arthur James Gascoyne-Cecil (1893–1972), 5th marquis, son of 4th marquis; M.P. (1929–41); secretary of state for dominion affairs (1940–42, 1943–45); leader of House of Lords (1942–45, 1951–57); lord privy seal (1942–43, 1951–52); lord president of the Council (1952–57).

Ce·cil·ia \si-ˈsil-yə, -ˈsil-ē-ə, -ˈsēl-\. Saint. *Also* Saint Cec·i·ly \ˈses-ə-lē, ˈsis-\. 2d or 3d century A.D. Roman Christian martyr. In spite of vow of celibacy, was compelled to marry young nobleman (later St. Valerian); converted husband to Christianity and with him suffered martyrdom. According to legend, she both sang and played musical instruments; hence, she is patron saint of music.

Cedd \ˈched\ *or* **Ced·da** \ˈched-ə\. Saint. d. 664. English prelate. Brother of St. Ceadda (*q.v.*). Educated by Aidan at Lindisfarne; christianized East Saxons; bishop of East Saxons (654); founded and ruled monastery at Lastingham, Yorkshire; attended council of Whitby (664); died of plague.

Ced·ri·nus \si-ˈdrī-nəs\, George. 11th century. Byzantine historian. Possibly a monk; compiled *Synopsis historiarum,* world history from Creation to 1057.

Ceiriog. See John Ceiriog HUGHES.

Çeiriog, Eos. See Huw MORUS.

Če·la·kov·ský \ˈchel-ȧ-ˌkȯf-skē\, František Ladislav. 1799–1852. Bohemian poet. Professor, Breslau (1842–49), Prague (1849–52). Published collection of Slavic folksongs (1822–27), verse *Ohlas písní ruských* (1829), *Ohlas písní českých* (1839).

Celan, Paul. See Paul ANTSCHEL.

Celano, Thomas of. See THOMAS of Celano.

Celer, Quintus Caecilius Metellus. See METELLUS CELER.

Cel·es·tine \ˈsel-ə-ˌstīn; si-ˈles-tin, -ˌtīn\. Name of five popes:

Celestine I. Saint. d. 432. Pope (422–432). Convoked Council of Ephesus (431) which condemned the Nestorian heresy; sent St. Germanus of Auxerre and St. Lupus of Troyes (429) to England, St. Palladius (431) to Ireland.

Celestine II. *Orig.* Guido di Cit·tà di Cas·tel·lo \dē-ˈchēt-tä-dē-käs-ˈtel-lō\. d. 1144. Pope (1143–44). Cardinal deacon (1127); cardinal priest (c.1134); removed interdict of Innocent II from Louis VII of France (1143).

Celestine III. *Orig.* Giacinto Bo·bo-Or·si·ni \ˈbō-bō-ȯr-ˈsē-nē\. c.1106–1198. Pope (1191–98). Cardinal deacon (1144); crowned Henry VI of Germany emperor (1191); confirmed statutes of the Teutonic Order of Knights (1192), temporized with Henry's hostile acts as invasion of Sicily, imprisonment of Richard I of England.

Celestine IV. *Orig.* Goffredo Cas·ti·glio·ni \ˌkäs-tēl-ˈyō-nē\. d. 1241. Pope (1241). Nephew of Urban III; cardinal priest (1227); cardinal bishop of Sabina (1239); first pope elected in conclave; died within weeks.

Celestine V. Saint. *Orig.* Pietro da Mor·ro·ne \mȯr-ˈrō-nā\. c.1209–1296. Pope (1294). Benedictine monk; lived many years as a hermit; founded order of Celestines, incorporated into Benedictines (1264); elected pope (1294) at age of eighty; resigned after five months, first pope to do so; kept in

confinement by Boniface VIII to prevent a schism.
The original Celestine II, *orig.* ¶Teobaldo Buc·ca·pe·cus \ˌbük-kä-ˈpā-küs\ *or* Buc·ca·por·ci \-ˈpȯr-kē\ *or* Boc·ca·di·pe·co·ra \ˌbȯk-kä-dē-pā-ˈkōr-ä\ was elected pope (1124) by Pierlioni faction in opposition to Frangipani candidate Honorius II; resigned a few days later in favor of Honorius; not counted in official list of popes.

Ce·les·tius \si-ˈles(h)-ch(ē-)əs, -ˈles-tē-əs\. 5th century. Roman theologian. Became disciple of Pelagius in Rome; accompanied him to Sicily (c.409), North Africa (c.410); condemned by Council of Carthage (412) and by several succeeding councils; excommunicated by Pope St. Innocent I (417); received by Pope St. Zosimus but exiled by Emperor Flavius Honorius; again condemned by Council of Ephesus (431).

Céline, Louis-Ferdinand. See Louis DESTOUCHES.

Cel·li·ni \chăl-ˈlē-nē, *Angl* chə-ˈlē-\, Benvenuto. 1500–1571. Florentine goldsmith and sculptor. Banished from Florence as result of duel (1523); employed at Rome; protégé of Clement VII; to France in service of Francis I (1536, 1540–45); returned to Florence as protégé of Cosimo de' Medici (1545); led highly unsettled life, frequently fleeing criminal charges from immorality to murder. Works included bronze relief *Nymph of Fontainebleau,* bronze busts of Cosimo de' Medici and Bindo Altoviti, life-size *Crucifixion* (in the monastery of the Escorial), marble *Hyacinth* and *Narcissus,* bronze *Perseus,* gold saltcellar of Francis I, many decorative works in gold, designs for medals, coins, etc. His *Autobiography* (first printed 1728), invaluable as record of Renaissance life in Italy, is a classic of Italian literature.

Cé·lo·ron de Blain·ville \sā-lō-rōⁿ-də-blaⁿ-vēl\, Pierre-Joseph de. 1693–1759. French explorer, b. Montreal. Commandant of post at Michilimackinac (1734–42); headed expedition (1749) down Ohio River, nailing signs to trees and burying lead plates along riverbanks with inscriptions asserting French sovereignty over region; in command at Detroit (1750–53).

Cel·si·us \ˈsel-sē-ůs, *Angl* -sē-əs, sh(ē-)əs\, Anders. 1701–1744. Swedish astronomer. Professor, Uppsala (1730–44); builder and director of observatory at Uppsala (1740); published collections of observations by himself and others on the Aurora Borealis (1733); on French expedition to measure degree of meridian in polar regions (1736); advocated introduction of Gregorian calendar; first to describe (1742) centigrade thermometer, hence also called Celsius thermometer.

Cel·sus \ˈsel-səs\. 2d century A.D. Roman or Alexandrian philosopher. A Platonist; author of first notable attack on Christianity in his *True Discourse* (c.178 A.D.), answered by Origen (*q.v.*) in his *Contra Celsum.*

Celsus, Aulus Cornelius. 1st century A.D. Roman writer. Compiler of an encyclopedia on agriculture, medicine, military science, law, and philosophy, of which only the portion on medicine is extant and was one of the first medical works to be printed (1478); considered outstanding medical work of Rome.

Celtis *or* **Celtes,** Conradus. See Conrad PICKEL.

Cem \ˈjem\. *Also spelled* Jem \ˈzhem\. 1459–1495. Ottoman prince. Son of Sultan Mehmed II; challenged accession of his brother, Bayezid II (1481); raised revolt of nobles in Anatolia but was defeated; in exile in Rhodes and Rome until death.

Ce·mal Pa·şa \je-ˈmäl-pə-ˈshä\, Ahmed. 1872–1922. Turkish army officer. Took part in Young Turk revolt (1908); governor general of Baghdad (1911); served in Balkan War (1912–13); with Talat Bey and Enver Paşa dominated government during World War I; commanded Fourth Army in Syria (1914–17); minister of marine (1914–18); fled Turkey (1918).

Cen·ci \ˈchen-chē\, Beatrice. 1577–1599. Roman woman. Daughter of Francesco Cenci, a man of great wealth but cruel and vicious nature; suffered much from her father's brutality; conspired with her brother and stepmother to secure father's death (1598); Cenci family arrested and finally confessed the crime; were refused pardon by Pope Clement VIII despite efforts to obtain mercy for them; all executed. Beatrice and her story have been the subject of a number of literary works, including a tragedy by Shelley and a novel by Guerrazzi.

Cendrars, Blaise. See Frédéric SAUSER.

Cen·ni·ni \chān-ˈnē-nē\, Cennino. *Orig.* Cennino di Drea \dē-ˈdrā-ä\. c.1370–c.1440. Florentine painter. Exponent of late Gothic style; none of his paintings survive; known chiefly for his treatise on 14th-century painting *Trattato della pittura* or *Il libro dell'arte* (1437).

Cen·so·ri·nus \ˌsen(t)-sə-ˈrī-nəs\. 3d century A.D. Roman scholar. Only extant work *De die natali* (238 A.D.).

Cent·liv·re \sent-ˈliv-ər, -ˈlē-vər\, Susanna, *nee* Free·man \ˈfrē-mən\ *or* Rawkins \ˈrȯ-kənz\. 1667?–1723. English dramatist and actress, b. probably Ireland. Left a widow at 17, wrote plays, her first a tragedy, *The Perjured Husband* (1700); appeared first in her own comedy *Love at a Venture* (1706); m. (1706) Joseph Centlivre, chief cook to Queen Anne; wrote among her comedies *The Gamester* (1705), *The Busy Body* (1709), *A Bold Stroke for a Wife,* one of the characters in which is Simon Pure (1718), *The Wonder! a Woman Keeps a Secret* (1714).

Cen·wulf \ˈchen-ˌwůlf, ˈken-\. *Also spelled* Coen·wulf \ˈken-\. d. 821. Anglo-Saxon king of Mercia (796–821). During Kentish revolt (c.798) attempted to move chief British see from Canterbury to London; fought war with Northumbria (801–802).

Ce·ol·noth \ˈchā(-ə)l-ˌnȯth\. d. 870. Anglo-Saxon prelate. Archbishop of Canterbury (833?–870); made alliance with Egbert and Aethelwulf of Wessex (838); attempted to conciliate Danes during invasions of Britain (851, 865).

Ceph·i·sod·o·tus \ˌsef-ə-ˈsäd-ət-əs\. fl. c.400 B.C. Greek sculptor. Executed figure of Eirene bearing Plutus, statues for new city of Megalopolis; father of Praxiteles. His grandson ¶Cephisodotus (4th century B.C.), a son of Praxiteles, was also a sculptor.

Ce·rac·chi \chā-ˈräk-kē\, Giuseppe. 1751–1802. Italian sculptor. Worked in Rome, London (1773 ff.), U.S. (1790 ff.), Austria, Paris (1801); allegedly involved in conspiracy against life of Napoléon; executed with fellow conspirators. His works included portrait busts of Sir Joshua Reynolds, Anne Seymour Damer, George Washington, Benjamin Franklin, and Alexander Hamilton.

Ceragno, Il. See Giovanni Battista CRESPI.

Cerceau, du. See DU CERCEAU.

Cer·chi \ˈchār-kē\, Vieri dei. fl. 1300. Florentine noble. A knight in Guelf army of Florence; fought at Campaldino (1289); contested with Corso Donati for leadership of Guelf party, their factions becoming known as Whites and Blacks; exiled after White–Black clash (1300); helped drive out Black faction in Pistoia (1301).

Cer·dic \ˈcher-(ˌ)dich\. d. 534. Saxon leader. Landed in Britain near Southampton (495); defeated Britons (508) and at Charford, Hampshire (519); founded West Saxon kingdom, or Wessex; conquered Isle of Wight (530).

Ce·re·a·lis \ˌsir-ē-ˈā-ləs\, Petillus. 1st century A.D. Roman general. Related to emperor Vespasian; as consul, suppressed revolt of Civilis (70 A.D.); governor of Britain (71), where he defeated the Brigantes.

Ce·re·zo \thā-ˈrā-thō\, Mateo. c.1626–1666. Spanish painter. Leading representative of Madrid school; works included *Ascension of the Virgin, The Magdalene, Betrothal of St. Catharine, Saint Jerome,* and *Christ in Agony* (Burgos cathedral).

Cerf \ˈsərf\, Bennett Alfred. 1898–1971. American publisher and editor, b. New York City. With Donald S. Klopfer acquired (1925) from Boni and Liveright the Modern Library imprint; built it into highly profitable series of reprints of classics; with Klopfer formed Random House publishers (1927), president (1927–65), chairman (1965–70). Wrote syndicated newspaper columns, edited many anthologies of short stories, plays, and of jokes, puns, etc; panelist on television show "What's My Line?" (1952–68).

Ce·rin·thus \si-ˈrin(t)-thəs\. fl. c.100 A.D. Egyptian? heretic. Founded sect of Jewish Christians with Gnostic tendencies, known as Cerinthians.

Cer·mak \ˈsər-ˌmak\, Anton Joseph. 1873–1933. American politician, b. Kladno, Bohemia. To U.S. as infant; in real estate business, Chicago (1908–33); mayor of Chicago (1931–33); fatally wounded in Miami, Fla., by bullet intended for President-elect F. D. Roosevelt.

Cer·ri·to \chār-ˈrē-tō\, Francesca, *known as* Fanny. 1817–1909. Italian dancer. Debut, Naples (1832); gained renown in London performance (1840); performed *Ondine* (London, 1843), created for her by Jules Perrot; appeared with Taglioni, Grisi, Grahn in Perrot's *Pas de quatre* (1845); m. (1845; separated 1851) Arthur Saint-Léon (*q.v.*), who arranged *La Fille de marbre* for her Paris Opéra debut (1847). Noted for brilliance and vivacity of style; undertook choreography with pas de trois for *Alma* (London, 1842); staged *Gemma* (Paris, 1854); retired (1857).

Cerro, Luis M. Sánchez. See SÁNCHEZ CERRO.

Cerularius, Michael. See MICHAEL CERULARIUS.

Cer·van·tes \ther-ˈbän-tās, *Angl* sər-ˈvan-ˌtēz\, Miguel de. *Full surname* Cervantes Saa·ve·dra \-sä-ä-ˈbā-t͟h-rä, *Angl* -ˌsä(-ə)-ˈvā-drə\. 1547–1616. Spanish novelist. Apparently a pupil-teacher in Madrid when he contributed to a volume of exequies (1569) on Elizabeth of Valois; possibly fleeing arrest, went to Naples and then Rome (1569); in service of Cardinal Giulio Acquaviva (c.1570–74); left hand maimed in battle of Lepanto (1571); served also in engagements at Navarino, Corfu, and Tunis; garrisoned at Palermo (1574); captured by Algerian pirates while returning to Spain (1575); enslaved and held for ransom, Algeria (1575–80); discovered or betrayed in numerous escape attempts. To Madrid (1580); essayed play writing (to 1587); naval commissary of Seville (1588–98); imprisoned for three months (1597); suffered poverty and failure to gain official preferment at Valladolid (1604–05); protégé of count of Lemos (1613 ff.). His masterpiece was *Quixote* (in full *El ingenioso hidalgo Don Quijote de la Mancha;* part I, 1605; part II, 1615), novel burlesquing chivalric romances of the day, considered first and one of the greatest of modern novels. His minor works included the pastoral novel *La Galatea* (1585), many early plays (two extant: *El trato de Argel* and *La Numancia*), *Novelas ejemplares* (12 tales, 1613), *Viaje al Parnaso* (rhymed burlesque on contemporary poets, 1614), *Ocho comedias y ocho entremeses nuevos* (1615), *Pérsiles y Sigismunda* (1616), and many poems, esp. sonnets.

Cer·ve·ra y To·pe·te \ther-'bā-rä-ē-tō-'pā-tā\, Pascual. Conde de Je·rez \kā-'rāth\. Marqués de San·ta Ana \'sän-tä-'ä-nä\. 1839–1909. Spanish admiral. Minister of marine (1892); admiral; commander of Spanish squadron in Spanish–American War (1898); defeated and taken prisoner in attempt to break American blockade in harbor of Santiago de Cuba. Vice admiral (1901); chief of staff, Spanish navy (1902); senator (1903 ff.).

Ce·sal·pi·no \,chā-zäl-'pē-nō\, Andrea. *Lat.* Andreas Caes·al·pi·nus \,sez-al-'pi-nəs, ses-\. 1519–1603. Italian physiologist and botanist. Professor of materia medica and director of botanical garden, Pisa (1555–92); physician to Pope Clement VIII and professor, Sapienza, Rome (1592–1603). Wrote first true textbook of botany and created first coherent system of taxonomy in his *De Plantis* (1583), to which Linnaeus acknowledged indebtedness; studied and described heart, heart valves, and pulmonary vessels.

Ce·sa·ri \'chā-zä-rē\, Giuseppe. *Called* Cavaliere d'Ar·pi·no \där-'pē-nō\; *also called* Il Giu·sep·pi·no \ēl-,jü-zāp-'pē-nō\. c.1568–1640. Italian painter, b. Arpino. Representative of Mannerist school. His works included decoration in S. Martino (Naples), unfinished frescoes in Palazzo dei Conservatori, scenes from life of St. John the Baptist in S. Giovannia in Laterano, frescoes in the Capitol and in Borghese chapel of Maria Maggiore (Rome), cartoons for mosaics in dome of St. Peter's.

Ce·sa·ri·ni \,chā-zä-'rē-nē\, Giuliano. *Known as* Cardinal Jul·ian \'jül-yən\. 1398–1444. Italian prelate and diplomat. Counselor to Pope Martin V; cardinal (1426); preached and led unsuccessful crusade against Hussites (1431); president, Council of Basel (1431 ff.); legate to Poland from Pope Eugenius IV to incite crusade against Turks; killed in ensuing battle of Varna.

Cesarion. See PTOLEMY XV.

Ce·sa·rot·ti \chā-zä-'rȯt-tē\, Melchiorre. 1730–1808. Italian poet. Professor of Hebrew and Greek, Padua (1768 ff.); influenced Italian literature toward Romanticism by his translation of Macpherson's *Ossian* (1763). Among his other works were essays *Saggio sulla filosofia del gusto* and *Saggio sulla filosofia delle lingue* (1785); epic poem *Pronea* (1807); and translations, as of Homer's *Iliad.*

Ces·no·la \chāz-'nȯl-ä\, Luigi Palma di. 1832–1904. American army officer and archaeologist, b. Rivarolo, Italy. Officer in Italian army (1849–59); to U.S. (1860); served in Union army through Civil War; naturalized (1865). U.S. consul, Cyprus (1865–76); explored ruins on Cyprus; his large collection of archaeological objects purchased by Metropolitan Museum of Art, New York City. Director, Metropolitan Museum (1879–1904). Author of *Cyprus: Its Ancient Cities, Tombs and Temples* (1877).

Cés·pe·des \'sās-pā-thās\, Carlos Manuel de. 1819–1874. Cuban revolutionist. Finished education in Spain; took part in Prim y Prats' revolution (1843); after return to Cuba led armed revolt (1868), which began Ten Years' War; elected president of revolutionists (1869); deposed (1873). His son ¶Carlos Manuel de Céspedes y Que·sa·da \-ē-kä-'sä-thä\ (1871–1939), lawyer and diplomat; provisional president of Cuba (Aug.–Sept. 1933).

Cés·pe·des \'thās-pā-thās\, Pablo de. 1538–1608. Spanish painter and writer. Prebendary of Córdoba cathedral (c.1577–1608). Author of *Arte de la pintura* (poem, 1649); his paintings included *Last Supper* (in Córdoba cathedral), *Ascension of Christ,* and frescoes in Seville cathedral.

Céspedes y Me·ne·ses \ē-mā-'nā-sās\, Gonzalo de. 1585?–1638. Spanish writer. Author of novels, tales, and romances including *Poema trágico del español Gerardo y desengaño del amor lascivo* (1615–17; source of two plays of John Fletcher), *Historia apologética* (1622), *Historias peregrinas y ejemplares* (1623), *Fortuna varia del soldado Pindaro* (1626); also wrote historical and political works as *Historia de Felipe IV* (1631), *Francia engañada, Francia respondida* (1635).

Ce·sti \'chās-tē\, Antonio, *orig.* Pietro, *sometimes erroneously known as* Marc'Antonio. 1623–1669. Italian composer. Entered Franciscan order (1637); maestro di capella, Volterra cathedral (1645–52); at court of Archduke Ferdinand Karl, Innsbruck (1652–57); member of papal choir (1660–61); director of theatrical music, imperial court of Leopold I, Vienna (1666–69). His works included operas, as *Orontea* (1649), *L'Argia* (1655), *La Dori* (1657), *Le disgrazie d'Amore* (1667), *La Semirami* (1667), *Il pomo d'oro* (1668), and some 68 cantatas.

Ces·ti·us \'sest-ē-əs, 'ses(h)-ch(ē-)əs\, Gaius. 1st century B.C. Roman praetor and tribune of the people. His tomb, known as the Pyramid of Cestius, stands near the gate of St. Paul, Rome. Keats and Shelley were buried nearby.

Cet·e·wayo \kech-'wä-yō, -'wī-ō; *Angl* set-ē-'wā-ō, ket-\. *Also* Cetsh·wa·yo *Angl* kech-\. c.1826–1884. Zulu king (1873–79). Nephew of Shaka; succeeded father Mpande as king (1873); built up military force in response to British annexation of Transvaal (1877); refused ultimatum (1878) and after British invasion of Zululand attacked and destroyed garrison at Isandhlwana (1879); defeated at Ulundi (1879); captured (1879), held prisoner in Cape of Good Hope (1879–82), and taken to England (1882); attempt by British government to reinstate him as king of the Zulus failed (1883).

Ce·the·gus \si-'thē-gəs\, Marcus Cornelius. d. 196 B.C. Roman general and politician. Consul (204); as proconsul in Cisalpine Gaul (203), helped in defeating Hannibal's brother Mago and driving his Carthaginian army from Italy.

Ce·ti·na \thā-'tē-nä\, Gutierre de. 1520?–?1557. Spanish soldier and poet. A leading Spanish Petrarchist; known esp. for his elegant sonnets and his poem "Ojos claros serenos."

Ceu·len \'kœ̄-lən \, Ludolph van. 1540–1610. Dutch mathematician. Professor of fortification at Leiden (1600–10); known for computations of the value of π (sometimes known as Ludolph's number), which he finally carried to 35 decimal places.

Ceva \'chev-ä\, Giovanni. 1647?–1734. Italian mathematician. Taught at U. of Mantua, employed by Duke of Mantua; known for calculations of centers of gravity, areas and volumes of geometric figures, and esp. for Ceva's theorem on intersecting lines drawn through vertices of a triangle. Author of *De lineis rectis* (1678), *Opuscula mathematica* (1682), *Geometria motus* (1692), etc. His brother ¶Tomasso (1648–1737), also a mathematician; entered Jesuit order (1663), taught at Brera Coll., Milan; did work in arithmetic, geometry, higher-order curves. Author of philosophical-theological *De natura gravium* (1669), *Opuscula mathematica* (1699).

Cev·det Pa·şa \jev-'det-pə-'shä\, Ahmed. 1822–1895. Turkish politician and historian. Appointed ecclesiastical judge (1844); adviser to grand vizier Reşid Paşa (1846–58); held various posts in Ottoman government as minister of justice, provincial governor; influential in codification of Ottoman law. Author of volumes of chronicles and observations of events including *Tarih-ı Cevdet, Tezakir-ı Cevdet,* and *Marûzat;* also wrote Turkish grammars as *Kavaid-i Osmaniye,* etc.

Cé·zanne \sā-zȧn\, Paul. 1839–1906. French painter. Friend from boyhood of Zola; associated (c.1862–77) with Impressionists, esp. Pissaro, Monet, Renoir. Developed style using color harmonies to reveal formal structure of objects and compositions; considered a founder of modern painting. Among his notable works were *Joueurs de cartes, La Maison du pendu, Les Baigneurs, Bouquet de fleurs, L'Estaque, Le Lac d'Annecy, La Vielle au chapelet, Scène champêtre, Léda au cygne, La Cour de village.*

Cha·a·da·yev \chə-(,)ə-'dȧ-yiv\, Pyotr Yakovlevich. c.1794–1856. Russian writer. After conversion to mystical Christianity with disposition towards Roman Catholicism, wrote scathing critique of Russian culture and traditions in *Lettres philosophiques* (1827–31); declared insane after first publication of one of the *Lettres* in Russian (1836); became hero to Westernizers among Russian intelligentsia.

Cha·bot \shȧ-bō\, Philippe de. Seigneur de Bri·on \brē-ōⁿ\. Comte de Char·ny \shȧr-nē\. Marquis de Bu·zan·çais \bü̅e̅-zäⁿ-se\. 1480–1543. French soldier. Favored by Francis I; defended Marseilles (1524); governor of Burgundy (from 1526); envoy in Italy (1529) to negotiate ratification of Treaty of Cambrai by Charles V; made admiral of France; commander in chief of troops fighting Duke of Savoy (1535).

Cha·bri·as \'kā-brē-əs\. d. c.357 B.C. Greek mercenary general. For Athens defeated Spartans at Aegina (388 B.C.), and again near Thebes (378); defeated Spartan fleet off Naxos (376); in service of Egyptian king (361); held Athenian naval command at outbreak of Social War (357); killed at siege of Chios.

Cha·bri·er \shȧ-brē-ā\, Emmanuel, *in full* Alexis-Emmanuel. 1841–1894. French composer. In government service (1862–80); associated with d'Indy, Dupare, Fauré in "Le Petit Bayreuth" group. Works included operas *L'Étoile* (1877), *Une Éducation manquée* (1879), *Le Roi malgré lui* (1887); piano works *Dix pièces pittoresques* (1880), *Trois valses romantiques* (1883); orchestral works *España* (1883), *Joyeuse marche* (1888), *Suite pastorale* (1888); songs, etc.

Cha·cón \chä-'kȯn\, Lázaro. 1873–1931. Guatemalan soldier and politician. President of Guatemala (1926–30); settled boundary dispute with Honduras.

Chad, Saint. See CEADDA.

Chad·wick \'chad-(,)wik\, Sir Edwin. 1800–1890. English reformer. Poor-law commissioner (1833); secretary of commission (1834–46); laid foundation of systems of government inspection by experts; commissioner of board of health (1848–54).

Chadwick, George Whitefield. 1854–1931. American conductor and composer, b. Lowell, Mass. Organist in Boston; instructor (from 1880), director (from 1897) of New England Conservatory of Music. Member of New England group of composers; works included theatrical works as *Peer and the Pauper* (1884), *Tabasco* (1894), *Judith* (1901), *The Padrone* (1912); orchestral works as *Rip Van Winkle* (1879), *The Miller's Daughter* (1884), *Symphonic Sketches* (1895–1904), *Tam O'Shanter* (1915), *Elegy* (1921), three symphonies; choral pieces, string quartets, songs, and organ and piano works.

Chadwick, Henry. 1824–1908. American sportswriter, b. Exeter, England. To U.S. (1837); on staff of *New York Times, Brooklyn Eagle, New York Clipper.* Fostered professional baseball; compiled annual handbook (from 1869), later *Spalding's Official Baseball Guide.* Elected to Baseball Hall of Fame (1938).

Chadwick, Sir James. 1891–1974. English physicist. Lecturer and assistant director of research, Cavendish Laboratory, Cambridge (1923–35); professor, U. of Liverpool (1935–43); in U.S. as adviser to atomic bomb program (1943–45); master of Gonville and Caius Coll., Cambridge (1948–58). Discovered the neutron (1932); awarded 1935 Nobel prize for physics.

Chae·rea \ˈkir-ē-ə\, Gaius Cassius. d. 41 A.D. Roman conspirator. Assassin of Emperor Caligula (41 A.D.); executed by order of new emperor, Claudius.

Chae·re·mon \ki-ˈrē-ˌmän\. 4th century B.C. Athenian dramatist. Author of works, extant only in fragments, in florid style.

Chaeremon. 1st century A.D. Alexandrian Stoic philosopher and scholar. Called to Rome (49 A.D.) to assist in education of Nero; author of a *History of Egypt,* and treatises on astrology, comets, hieroglyphics, etc.

Cha·fee \ˈchā-fē\, Zechariah. 1885–1957. American lawyer and educator, b. Providence, R.I. Professor, Harvard (1919–56); authority on equity, negotiable instruments, unfair business competition. Author of *Free Speech in the United States* (1941); also *The Inquiring Mind* (1928), *Government and Mass Communications* (1947), *Blessings of Liberty* (1956).

Chaf·fee \ˈchaf-ē\, Adna Romanza. 1842–1914. American army officer, b. Orwell, Ohio. Served through Civil War, Spanish–American War; as major general of volunteers, commanded American troops in capture of Peking, China, at time of Boxer rebellion (1900); military governor, Philippines (1901–02); lieutenant general and chief of staff, U.S. army (1904–06). His son ¶Adna Romanza (1884–1941), army officer; served in France in World War I; advocate of mechanized army; organized U.S. army's first mechanized brigade; brigadier general (1938); chief of Armored Force (1940–41).

Chaffee, Roger Bruce. 1935–1967. American astronaut, b. Grand Rapids, Mich. Naval pilot (1957–63); chosen to astronaut corps (1963); killed with Virgil Grissom and Edward White in flash fire in Apollo I capsule.

Cha·gall \shä-ˈgäl\, Marc. 1887–1985. French painter, b. Vitebsk, Russia. Considered one of the most original and eminent figures in 20th-century art. Studied painting at Imperial School of Fine Arts, St. Petersburg (1907). To Paris (1910); influenced by Cubism, Fauvism, and Surrealism; created own naive style with subjects drawn from Russian village life, Jewish folklore, and Hasidic mysticism. Returned to Russia (1914), becoming after the revolution district commissar for fine art. To Berlin (1922), then Paris; in U.S. during World War II. To Paris (1948). Created paintings *I and the Village* and *The Rabbi of Vitebsk,* etc. as well as works in stained glass, mosaic, clay, stone, and tapestry. Published *My Life* (1957).

Cha·gas \ˈshä-gəs\, Carlos Ribeiro Justiniano. 1879–1934. Brazilian physician and bacteriologist. Discovered (1909) trypanosome *T. cruzi* and described Chagas' disease caused by it.

Chag·a·tai \ˌchag-ə-ˈtī\. *Also spelled* Tsagadai, Jagatai, Chaghatai. d. 1241. Mongol prince. Second son of Genghis Khan, at whose death (1227) he received Kashgaria and most of Transoxania; founder of the House of the Chagatai; succeeded by grandson Kara Hülegü.

Chaikovski. See Nikolay CHAYKOVSKY; Pyotr TCHAIKOVSKY.

Chail·lé-Long \shä-ˈyā-ˈlȯŋ\, Charles. 1842–1917. American army officer and explorer, b. Somerset Co., Md. Served in Union army through Civil War; appointed officer in Egyptian army (1869); chief of staff under General Gordon (1874); sent by khedive on mission to Uganda, discovered Lake Kyoga (1874). Author of *Naked Truths of Naked People* (1876), *The Three Prophets* (1884), *My Life in Four Continents* (1912).

Chaillu. See DU CHAILLU.

Chain \ˈchān\, Sir Ernst Boris. 1906–1979. British biochemist, b. Germany. Researcher at Charité Hospital, Berlin (1930–33), Cambridge U. (1933–35), Oxford U. (1935–48); director, International Research Center for Chemical Microbiology, Rome (1948–61); professor, Imperial Coll., London (1961–73). Awarded Nobel prize for physiology or medicine (1945) with A. Fleming and H. Florey for their discovery of penicillin.

Chaireddin. See KHAYR AD-DIN.

Chaitanya. See CAITANYA.

Cha·jang Yul·sa \ˈjä-ˈyäŋ-ˈyu̇l-ˈsä\. 7th century. Korean Buddhist monk. Studied Buddhism in China (636–643); chief Buddhist official of Silla state on returning with supposed remains of Buddha; attempted to make Silla first among Korean states, Buddhism official state religion.

Chaka. See SHAKA.

Chak·kri \ˈchäk-ˈkrē\. Dynasty of Siam founded (1782) by Chao Phraya Chakkri, who ruled as Rama I (*q.v.*); subsequent rulers Rama II–VIII (*qq.v.*).

Chal·con·dy·les \kal-ˈkän-də-ˌlēz\ *or* **Chal·co·con·dy·las** \ˌkal-kō-ˈkän-də-ləs\, Demetrius. 1423–1511. Byzantine scholar. To Italy under patronage of Cardinal Bessarion (1447); professor, Padua (1463); called to Florence by Lorenzo de' Medici (1475); taught in Milan (1492). Published editions of Homer, Isocrates, and Suidas; author of important Greek grammar; credited with contributing to revival of letters in Italy. His brother ¶Laonicus (c.1423–?1490) wrote *Historiarum demonstrationes,* history of the Byzantine empire from 1298 to 1463.

Chal·grin \shäl-gra^{n}\, Jean-François-Thérèse. 1739–1811. French architect. Architect to Monsieur (later Louis XVIII); architect of Luxembourg palace, church of Sainte Philippe du Roule, Collège de France, etc.; planned and began (1806) Arc de Triomphe.

Cha·lia·pin \(ˌ)shəl-ˈyäp-yin\, Fyodor Ivanovich. 1873–1938. Russian singer. Sang in Imperial Opera, St. Petersburg (1894–96); member of Bolshoi Opera, Moscow (1899–1914); debut at La Scala (1901), Metropolitan Opera, N.Y. (1907); left Russia (1921); settled in Paris; naturalized. Renowned as a bass of enormous resonance and as inspired actor. His most successful performances included roles in *Faust,* Rimsky-Korsakov's *Maid of Pskov, Sadko,* and *Mozart and Salieri,* Boito's *Mefistofele,* Mussorgsky's *Boris Godunov,* Verdi's *Don Carlos,* Serov's *Judith;* noted also as concert singer.

Chalk·hill \ˈchȯk-ˌhil, ˈchȯ-(ˌ)kil\, John. 17th century. English poet. Reputed author of a pastoral, *Thealma and Clearchus* (1683), published by Izaak Walton; possibly a pseudonym for Walton.

Challe \shäl\, Maurice-Prosper-Félix. 1905–1979. French air force officer. Active in Resistance (1942–44); general in command of French air force in Morocco (1949–51); chief of air ministry staff (1951–53); commandant, École Supérieure de Guerre Aérienne (1953–55); air force chief of staff (1955–58); commander in Algeria (1958–61); led revolt of generals against Pres. De Gaulle over Algerian independence (April 1961); imprisoned (1961–66).

Chal·lis \ˈchal-əs\, James. 1803–1882. English astronomer. Plumian professor of astronomy, Cambridge (1836–82). Using J.C. Adams's (*q.v.*) computations, sought unknown planet indicated by behavior of Uranus and actually observed it (Aug. 4, 1846), but neglected to examine findings until announcement of discovery of Neptune by Berlin Observatory.

Chal·lo·ner \ˈchal-ə-nər\, Richard. 1691–1781. English prelate. Professor of philosophy (1713–20), of divinity (1720–30), Douai; missionary priest in London (1730–41); titular bishop of Debra (1741); vicar apostolic in London (1758). Reedited Douai Bible (1749–50). Author of historical works, *Garden of the Soul,* a manual of devotion (1740), *British Martyrology* (1761), etc.

Chal·mers \ˈchä(l)-mərz\, Alexander. 1759–1834. Scottish journalist and biographer. Editor of works of Shakespeare, Fielding, Johnson, Warton, Pope, Gibbon, Bolingbroke; published *Glossary to Shakespeare* (1797), *Works of the English Poets from Chaucer to Cowper* (1810), *General Biographical Dictionary* (32 vols., 1812–17), *British Essayists* (45 vols., 1817).

Chalmers, James. 1841–1901. Scottish missionary. Ordained Congregationalist minister (1865); for London Missionary Society served on Rarotonga (1867–77), New Guinea (1877–1901); helped establish British rule (1884); killed and eaten by cannibals at Goaribari Island.

Chalmers, Thomas. 1780–1847. Scottish theologian and preacher. Gained wide reputation as preacher at Glasgow (from 1815) and as administrator of poor relief; professor of moral philosophy, St. Andrews (1823–28), of theology, Edinburgh (1828–43). Leader of evangelical section of Church of Scotland; led withdrawal of ministers from general assembly to constitute Free Church of Scotland (1843); chosen first moderator of Free Church and principal of Free Church Coll., Edinburgh (1843–47). Author of *Enquiry into National Resources* (1808), *Christian and Civil Economy* (1821–26).

Chalon, Philibert de. See PHILIBERT.

Chalotais. See LA CHALOTAIS.

Chalukya. See CĀLUKYA.

Cham·ber·lain \ˈchām-bər-lən\, Sir Austen, *in full* Joseph Austen. 1863–1937. British politician. Eldest son of Joseph Chamberlain (*q.v.*) and half-brother of Neville Chamberlain (*q.v.*); M.P. (1892–1937), Conservative leader (1921–22); civil lord of admiralty (1895–1900); financial secretary to treasury (1900–02); postmaster general (1902); chancellor of exchequer (1903–05); supported father's tariff policy of imperial preference. Secretary of state for India (1915–17); resigned after assuming responsibility for Mesopotamia affair; member of war cabinet (1918); chancellor of exchequer (1919–21); lord privy seal (1921–23); cooperated with Lloyd George's administration, made settlement with Sinn Fein, urged creation of Irish Free State (1921). Foreign secretary (1924–29); conducted diplomacy leading to signing of Locarno Pact (1925); awarded Nobel peace prize (jointly with Charles G. Dawes, 1925); facilitated Germany's entry into League of Nations (1926); first lord of admiralty (1931). Author of *Peace in Our Time* (1928).

Chamberlain, Charles Joseph. 1863–1943. American botanist, b. near Sullivan, Ohio. On staff, U. of Chicago (from 1897); professor (1915–29). Known for studies of cycads; postulated evolution of angiosperms from cycads. Author of

Methods in Plant Histology (1901), *The Living Cycads* (1919), *Gymnosperms, Structure and Evolution* (1935), etc.

Chamberlain, George Agnew. 1879–1966. American novelist, b. São Paulo, Brazil, of American parentage. U.S. consul general, Mexico City (1917–19). Author of *Home* (1914), *John Bogardus* (1916), *White Man* (1919), *Cobweb* (1921), *No Ugly Ducklings* (1927), *When Beggars Ride* (1930), *Two on Safari* (1934), *In Defense of Mrs. Maxon* (1938), *Scudda-Hoo! Scudda-Hay!* (1946), *Midnight Boy* (1949), etc.

Chamberlain, Houston Stewart. 1855–1927. British publicist. Resident at Dresden (1885–89), Vienna (1889–1908), Bayreuth (1908–27); naturalized German citizen (1916); m. 2d (1908) Eva Wagner, daughter of Richard Wagner. Author of *Die Grundlagen des Neunzehnten Jahrhunderts* (1899), *Lebenswege meines Denkens* (1919), *Rasse und Persönlichkeit* (1925), and other works postulating superiority of Western Aryan race.

Chamberlain, Joseph. 1836–1914. British politician and reformer. Expanded his cousin's screw-manufacturing business in Birmingham (1854–74), retired with fortune; championed nonconformist opposition to denominationalism; as mayor of Birmingham (1873–76), campaigned to improve municipal housing and sanitation. M.P. (1876–1906); prompted reorganization of Liberal party. President of Board of Trade (1882–85) in second Gladstone cabinet; gained passage of act for reforming laws of bankruptcy (1883), Patent Act (1883), Merchant Shipping Bill (1884); with other left-wing Liberals stumped in favor of "unauthorized program" of tax reform, free schools, etc. Entered third Gladstone cabinet as president of local government board (1886); resigned on introduction of home-rule bill (1886); leader of Liberal Unionists in Parliament. Colonial secretary (1895–1903); instrumental in passing of Workmen's Compensation Act (1897); accused of complicity in Jameson Raid (1896), acquitted by House of Commons committee; supported anti-Boer measures and Boer War; became advocate of federated empire of self-governing colonies; facilitated passage of Commonwealth of Australia Bill (1900). Resigned on refusal of government to adopt his scheme of preferential tariffs favoring colonies and esp. native manufactures; his promotion of scheme led to crushing defeat of Conservatives and Liberal Unionists (1906); withdrew from public life and suffered paralytic stroke (1906). His program of imperial preference adopted in part in 1919, wholly in 1932. Largely instrumental in founding Birmingham U. (1900); its first chancellor (1901).

Chamberlain, Neville, *in full* Arthur Neville. 1869–1940. British politician. Son of Joseph Chamberlain (*q.v.*) and half-brother of Sir Austen Chamberlain (*q.v.*). Managed an estate on Andros Island, Bahamas (1890–97); success in hardware manufacture in Birmingham; as lord mayor (1915–16), established first municipal bank in England. M.P. (1918–40); postmaster general (1922–23); minister of health (1923, 1924–29, 1931); chancellor of exchequer (1923–24, 1931–37). Succeeded Baldwin as prime minister (1937–40); as leader of Conservative party, emphasized urgency of British rearmament (1937); set forth foreign policy calling for avoidance of war by appeasement; sought to keep civil war in Spain from spreading; sought to draw Mussolini away from Hitler by concessions, as recognition of Italian rule in Ethiopia (1938); conferred with Hitler about Sudeten Germans; met with Daladier, Mussolini, and Hitler at Munich (Sept. 1938), agreed to partition of Czechoslovakia; received vote of confidence on return home with Anglo-German amity declaration. Made Anglo–Italian pact by which Italy agreed to retain status quo in Mediterranean, recognize British water rights in Lake Tana, and withdraw from Spanish territory after civil war; recognized Franco government in Spain (Feb. 1939). Pledged armed assistance to Poland (Mar. 1939) and to Rumania and Greece (Apr. 1939); declared war on Germany (Sept. 3, 1939) after German invasion of Poland; following military disaster in Norway, resigned as prime minister (May 1940); lord president of the council in Churchill cabinet.

Chamberlain, Sir Neville Bowles. 1820–1902. British army officer, b. Rio de Janeiro, son of British consul general. Entered Indian army (1837); served through Afghan War (1839–42), Gwalior campaign (1843), Punjab campaign (1848–49); commanded Punjab frontier force (1854–57); distinguished himself during Sepoy Mutiny (1857–58); lieutenant general (1873); commander in chief of Madras army (1876–81); general (1877); field marshal (1900).

Cham·ber·land \shä^n-ber-la^n\, Charles-Édouard. 1851–1908. French bacteriologist. Collaborated with Pasteur (from 1875); contributed to sterilization techniques and development of autoclave; invented an unglazed porcelain filter.

Cham·ber·layne \'chām-bər-ˌlān, -lən\, William. 1619–1689. English poet. Practiced as physician. Author of tragicomedy *Love's Victory* (1658), and *Pharonnida*, a romance in verse (1659), etc.

Cham·ber·len \'chām-bər-lən\, Peter, *called* the Elder. 1560–1631. English midwife. Son of French Huguenot surgeon; to England (1569); became celebrated accoucheur attending wives of James I and Charles I; invented (c.1630) obstetrical forceps, which he kept a family secret. His grandnephew ¶Hugh, *called* the Elder (1630–1720) was midwife to queen of Charles II; translated François Mauriceau's treatise on midwifery (1672); lost in various speculations, fled to Scotland and then Netherlands; sold secret of forceps to Roger van Roonhuysen.

Cham·ber·lin \'chām-bər-lən\, Thomas Chrowder. 1843–1928. American geologist, b. Mattoon, Ill. Professor, Beloit (1873–82); with Wisconsin Geological Survey (1873–82), chief geologist (1876–82); in charge of glacial division, U.S. Geological Survey (1881–1904); president, U. of Wisconsin (1887–92); professor of geology and director of Walker Museum, U. of Chicago (1892–1918). Founded *Journal of Geology* (1893), editor in chief (1893–1922). Formulated, with F. R. Moulton, the planetesimal hypothesis to account for origin of the earth. Author of *The Geology of Wisconsin* (1877–83), *The Origin of the Earth* (1916), *The Two Solar Families* (1928), etc.

Cham·bers \'chām-bərz\, Sir Edmund Kerchever. 1866–1954. English scholar. Member of national education department (1892–1926). Author of *The Medieval Stage* (1903), *The Elizabethan Stage* (1923), *Arthur of Britain* (1927), *William Shakespeare* (1930), *A Sheaf of Studies* (1942), etc.

Chambers, Ephraim. c.1680–1740. English encyclopedist and translator. Published his *Cyclopaedia, or Universal Dictionary of Arts and Sciences* (1728), which inspired *Encyclopédie* of Diderot and d'Alembert. Cf. Robert CHAMBERS.

Chambers, John Graham. 1843–1883. English sportsman. Founded (1866) Amateur Athletic Club; champion walker and oarsman; formulator of definitions of *amateur* and of rules for athletic competitions; drew up Marquis of Queensberry rules for boxing (1867).

Chambers, Raymond Wilson. 1874–1942. English scholar. Librarian, University Coll., London (1901–22), and professor of English language and literature (1922–41). Author of studies of *Widsith* (1912), *Beowulf* (1921), *England before the Norman Conquest* (1926), *Thomas More* (1935), etc

Chambers, Robert. 1802–1871. Scottish publisher and author. Founded (1832), with his brother ¶William (1800–1883), firm of W. & R. Chambers, Ltd., in Edinburgh, which issued multitude of cheap educational works, *Chambers's Cyclopaedia of English Literature* and *Chambers's Encyclopaedia* (1859–68). Cf. Ephraim CHAMBERS. Author of works on biography and Scottish history, geological works, *Popular Rhymes of Scotland* (1826), *Life and Works of Robert Burns* (1848), *Book of Days*, an antiquarian miscellany (1862–64), and *Vestiges of the Natural History of Creation* (1844), proposing a theory of evolution of species and preparing way for Darwin's theories. William, financial expert of the firm, started *Chambers's Edinburgh Journal* (1832); as lord provost of Edinburgh (1865–69), secured reconstruction of old town; restored St. Giles Church; author of notes of travel, tales, etc., and, with Robert, *A Gazetteer of Scotland.*

Chambers, Robert William. 1865–1933. American artist and author, b. Brooklyn, N.Y. Illustrator for *Life, Vogue, Truth,* and other magazines; devoted himself chiefly to writing (from 1893). Author of *A King and a Few Dukes* (1896), *Ashes of Empire* (1898), *Cardigan* (1901), *Tracer of Lost Persons* (1906), *Barbarians* (1917), *The Crimson Tide* (1919), *The Man They Hanged* (1926), *The Rogue's Moon* (1927), etc.

Chambers, Whittaker, *in full* Jay David Whittaker. 1901–1961. American journalist, b. Philadelphia. On staff of *New Masses, Daily Worker, Time* magazine; charged Alger Hiss (1948) with being member of Communist party and with passing State Department documents to Soviet agents, thus opening celebrated round of slander and perjury trials. Author of *Witness* (1952).

Chambers, Sir William. 1726–1796. British architect. Architectural tutor to future George III (1755); a founder of Royal Academy (1768). Works included Somerset House (1776–86), casino at Marino, Ireland (c.1761–80), Duddingston House, Edinburgh (1762–64), pagoda (1757–62) and other ornaments at Kew Palace. Author of *Designs of Chinese Buildings* (1757), *Treatise of Civil Architecture* (1759).

Cham·bon·nières \shä^n-bôn-yer\, Jacques Cham·pion de \shä^n-pyō^n-də-\. c.1602–1672. French musician. First of the classical school of French harpsichordists; musician to Louis XIII and Louis XIV; widely celebrated as performer. Published *Pièces de clavessin* (1670) containing 60 pieces, mainly dances grouped into suites.

Chambord, Comte de. See Henri DIEUDONNÉ D'ARTOIS.

Cham·fort \shä^n-fôr\, Sébastien-Roch Nicolas. 1741–1794. French writer and wit. At outbreak of Revolution, joined Jacobins; later attacked excesses of Terror and National Convention; mortally wounded himself when about to be arrested by order of Convention. Author of comedies *La Jeune indienne* (1764), *Le Marchand de Smyrne* (1770), tragedy *Mustapha et Zéangir* (1776); also of *Éloge de Molière* (1769), *Discours sur les académies* (1791); best known for posthumous *Pensées, maximes et anecdotes* (1795).

Cha·mil·lart \shá-mē-yár\, Michel. 1652–1721. French politician. Intendant of finances (1690–99), controller general of finances (1699–1708), minister of state (1700–09), secretary of state for war (1701–09) under Louis XIV; inept administrator, relied on assistant Nicolas Desmarets; raised funds for War of

Spanish Succession; suffered blame for national financial hardships; reorganized army after defeats of 1704–08; resigned for health.

Chamilly, Comte de. See Noël BOUTON.

Cha·mis·so \shä-'mis-ō\, Adelbert von. *Orig.* Louis-Charles-Adélaïde Cha·mis·so de Bon·court \shȧ-mē-sō-də-bōⁿ-kür\. 1781–1838. German writer and naturalist. Son of French family forced by Revolution to flee from France; served in Prussian army (1798–1807). Founded (1804) Nordsternbund, society of Berlin Romanticists; member of literary coterie near Geneva centering about Mme. de Staël (1811–12). Botanist on the *Rurik* on Otto von Kotzebue's voyage around the world (1815–18), recounted in his *Reise um de Welt* (1821). Editor, *Deutscher Musenalmanach* (1832–35), in which he published much of his verse. Best known work the *Faust*-like prose tale *Peter Schlemihls wundersame Geschichte* (1814); best known verse the cycle of lyrics *Frauenliebe und Frauenleben* (1831; set to music by Schumann).

Cha·mor·ro Var·gas \chä-'mȯr-rō-'b̲är-gäs\, Emiliano. 1871–1966. Nicaraguan general and politician. As ambassador to U.S. (1913–16) negotiated Bryan-Chamorro Treaty (1914); president of Nicaragua (1917–20); again ambassador to U.S. (1921–25); seized power by coup d'état (1925); again elected president (1926); refused recognition by U.S., which ordered gunboats to Nicaragua; resigned (1926) and left country.

Cham·pa·gny \shäⁿ-pȧn-yē\, Jean-Baptiste Nom·père de \nōⁿ-per-də-\. Duc de Ca·do·re \kä-'dō-rā\. 1756–1834. French politician and diplomat. Served in navy (1774–87); elected to Estates General (1789); arrested as former noble (1793); elected to Directory (1795); named to Council of State (1799); ambassador to Austria (1801–04); minister of the interior (1804–07), of foreign affairs (1807–11); negotiated annexation of Papal States (1808), abdication of Charles IV of Spain (1808), Treaty of Schönbrunn (1809); senator (1813); peer of France (1819).

Cham·paigne *or* **Cham·pagne** \shäⁿ-pȧnʸ\, Philippe de. 1602–1674. Belgian painter. To Paris (1621); assisted Poussin in decorating the Luxembourg; commissioned by Richelieu to adorn his palace and paint murals for dome of the Sorbonne; painter royal (1627); known for portraits of Richelieu, Louis XIII, etc., historical and religious works as *Ex Voto de 1662.*

Champeaux. See GUILLAUME DE CHAMPEAUX.

Champfleury. See Jules HUSSON.

Cham·pion·net \shäⁿ-pyȯ-ne\, Jean-Antoine-Étienne. 1762–1800. French general. Served in revolutionary armies; engaged at Fleurus (1794), in Holland (1797); commanded army of Rome (1798), captured Naples, organized Parthenopean Republic; commanded army of Alps (1799) against Austrians; died of plague.

Cham·plain \shäⁿ-plaⁿ, *Angl* sham-'plān\, Samuel de. c.1567–1635. French explorer. As commander of a Spanish vessel (1599–1601), visited West Indies, Mexico, Cartagena, and Panama. Under orders of Henry IV of France, accompanied exploring and fur-trading expedition to Gulf of St. Lawrence (1603); ascended St. Lawrence River to Lachine Rapids. Accompanied expedition of settlers to Port Royal; explored coast from Nova Scotia down as far as Vineyard Haven (1604–07). Headed group of settlers (1608) who founded Quebec; with Quebec as base, explored northern New York, down to lake that bears his name (1609), Ottawa River (1613), Great Lakes (1615); named commandant of New France (1612); organized fur trade, established relations with Indians; held off besieging English (1628–29).

Champ·mes·lé \shäⁿ-mel-ā\, Marie, *nee* Des·mares \dā-mȧr\. 1642–1698. French actress. m. (1666) comedian and playwright Charles Che·vil·et \shə-vē-ye\, *called* Champmeslé (1642–1701); member of Théâtre Marais, Paris (1669–70), Hôtel de Bourgogne (1670–79); long intimate with Racine; created roles of Hermione, Bérénice, Roxane, Iphigénie, Monime, and Phèdre in his plays, Racine himself training her in interpretation of these parts. Joined Molière-Marais company (1679), with Comédie Française (1680–98). La Fontaine dedicated *Belphégor* to her and Boileau immortalized her in his poetry.

Cham·pol·lion \shäⁿ-pȯl-yōⁿ\, *known as* Cham·pol·lion-Fi·geac \-fē-zhȧk\, Jacques-Joseph. 1778–1867. French archaeologist. Librarian and professor at Grenoble; curator of manuscripts, Bibliothèque Royale; dismissed by Republican government (1848), but later appointed librarian at Château of Fontainebleau. Author of *Chartes latines sur papyrus du VIᵉ siècle* (1835), *L'Égypte ancienne* (1839), *Le Palais Roxane, Fontainebleau* (1866), etc. His brother ¶Jean-François Champollion (1790–1832), Egyptologist; professor, Grenoble (1809–16); founded Egyptian museum of the Louvre and was appointed its curator (1826); professor of Egyptian antiquities, Collège de France (1831–32). From study of Rosetta stone, obtained clue for deciphering Egyptian hieroglyphics (1821–22). Author of *Précis du système hiéroglyphique des anciens égyptiens* (1824), *Panthéon égyptien* (1823–25); his Egyptian grammar (1836–41) and dictionary (1841–43) were edited by his brother Jacques.

Chan·cel·lor \'chan(t)-s(ə-)lər\, Richard. d. 1556. English navigator. Pilot general of Sir Hugh Willoughby's expedition (1553–54) into White Sea in search of northeast passage to India; reached Archangel; visited Moscow and laid foundations of English trade with Russia.

Chan·da·ku·ma·ra \'chän-dä-kü-'mär-ä\. *Also called* Ti·an·tha Kou·ma·ne \tē-'än-tä-kü-'mä-nə\ *or* Chan·t'a·ku·man \'chän-tä-'kü-män\ *or* Chan·tha·rad \chän-'tä-räd\. d. c.1869. Laotian ruler. Son of ruler of Luang Prabang; succeeded elder brother (1852); expanded realm and secured relations with Siam and other neighbors; established relations with French (1867).

Chan·dler \'chȧn-(d)lər\, Raymond Thornton. 1888–1959. American novelist, b. Chicago. Creator of fictional detective Philip Marlowe, featured in novels *The Big Sleep* (1939), *Farewell, My Lovely* (1940), *The High Window* (1942), *The Lady in the Lake* (1943), *The Little Sister* (1949), *The Long Goodbye* (1953), *Playback* (1958); also wrote screenplays as *Double Indemnity* (1944), *Blue Dahlia* (1946), *Strangers on a Train* (1951, with C. Ormonde).

Chandler, Richard. 1738–1810. English antiquary. Published *Marmora Oxoniensia* (1763), description of the Arundel marbles, works on antiquities of Ionia and Greece (1769), *Travels in Asia Minor* (1775), etc.

Chandler, Seth Carlo. 1846–1913. American astronomer, b. Boston. With U.S. Coast Survey (1864–70); insurance actuary (1871–81); at Harvard Observatory (1881–85); editor, *Astronomical Journal* (1896–1909). Discovered several variable stars; compiled catalogues of variable stars; invented almucantar and with it demonstrated variation of terrestrial latitude.

Chandos, Barons and dukes of. See BRYDGES family.

Chan·dos \'shan-ˌdäs, 'chan-\, Sir John. d. 1370. English soldier. Fought at siege of Cambrai (1337), at Crécy (1346); at Poitiers (1356) saved life of Black Prince; constable of Guienne (1362); with Black Prince on expedition to restore Pedro the Cruel to throne of Castile, won victory of Navarete (1367); seneschal of Poitiers (1369); mortally wounded near Poitiers.

Chandra, Bankim. See Bankim Chandra CHATTERJEE.

Chandragupta *or* **Chandra Gupta.** See CANDRAGUPTA, CANDRA GUPTA.

Cha·nel \shȧ-nel, *Angl* shə-'nel\, Gabrielle, *called* Co·co \kō-kō\. 1883–1971. French dress designer. Opened millinery shop, Deauville (1913); gained dominant position in Parisian world of haute couture with unorthodox designs based on simplicity and comfort, as jersey dresses and sweaters, turtleneck sweaters, bell bottom trousers, etc.; pioneered look of casual elegance; introduced (1954) classic Chanel suit; also designed accessories as costume jewelry and perfume, esp. (from 1922) Chanel No. 5.

Cha·ney \'chā-nē\, Lon. 1883–1930. American actor, b. Colorado Springs, Colo. Through mastery of pantomime, makeup, and bodily contortion, became known as the "man of a thousand faces" in films. Appeared in *Hell Morgan's Girl* (1917), *The Miracle Man* (1919), *The Penalty* (1920), *Hunchback of Notre Dame* (1923), *Phantom of the Opera* (1925), *Road to Mandalay* (1926), *London After Midnight* (1927), *Mr. Wu* (1927), *Laugh, Clown, Laugh* (1928), *While the City Sleeps* (1928), etc. His son ¶Lon Chaney, Jr., *orig.* Creighton Chaney (1907–1973) also a film actor; appeared in numerous horror films as the Wolf Man, the Mummy, etc., and esp. in *Of Mice and Men* (1939).

Chang \'chaŋ\ and **Eng** \'eŋ\. 1811–1874. The original Siamese twins, b. Meklong, Siam, of Chinese parentage. Joined at the waist; exhibited in U.S. and Great Britain (from 1829); became naturalized American citizens; married (1843) two sisters.

Chan·gar·nier \shäⁿ-gȧrn-yā\, Nicolas-Anne-Théodule. 1793–1877. French soldier. Served in Algeria (1830–48) and was appointed its governor (1848); commanded National Guard in Paris (1848–51); banished (1852) for opposition to Napoléon III; returned after amnesty (1859). In Franco-Prussian War, with Bazaine in Metz at its capitulation (1870). Deputy (1871–75); elected senator for life (1875).

Chang Ch'ien \'jäŋ-chē-'en, -'chen\. d. 114 B.C. Chinese explorer. Minister of Wu Ti of Han dynasty; sent (138 B.C.) to the Yüeh-chih people in Bactria to secure help against the Hsiung-nu; captured by the Hsiung-nu and detained ten years; escaped; lived with the Yüeh-chih one year; returned (126) to China unsuccessful. Negotiated treaties with kingdoms in the west (115–114), opening China to contact with outposts of Hellenistic culture.

Chang Chien \-jē-'en\. 1853–1926. Chinese industrialist and reformer. After career as civil servant retired (1895) to develop industry in Kiangsu Province; built Dah Sun Cotton Mill, flour mill, oil mill, distillery, shipping line, machine works, etc.; built schools, road, parks, clinics, libraries, orphanages, etc.; president of provincial assembly (1909–11); minister of agriculture and commerce in Chinese republican government (1911 ff.).

Chang Chih-tung \-'ji(ə)r-'dùŋ\. *Courtesy name* Hsiao-ta \shē-'aù-'dä\. 1837–1909. Chinese scholar and reformer. Early won renown as literary scholar and educator; governor of Shansi (1882–84); governor general of Kwangtung and Kwangsi (1884–89), Hunan and Hupeh (1889–1907); grand secretary and grand councillor to court of Dowager Empress (1907–09). Planned and supervised construction of Hankow–Peking railroad (completed 1906); encouraged industrialization; proposed (1898) new educational system blending Western techniques and studies with traditional Confucian system; drafted regulations for new national school system (1904); secured abolition of traditional civil service examinations (1905).

Chang Chü-cheng \-'jü-'jəŋ\. d. 1582. Chinese official. Tutor to Lung-ch'ing; became a chief minister to Emperor Lung-ch'ing, retaining post under successor Wan-li; instituted fiscal and tax reforms, restrained party strife and privileges of imperial family, promoted benevolent rule. His period of influence considered zenith of Ming dynasty.

Ch'ang-ch'un \'chäŋ-'chün\. *Monastic name* Chiu Chu-chi \jē-'ü-'jü-'jē\. 1148–1227. Chinese monk, alchemist, and traveler. Member of ascetic Taoist sect; invited to give religious instruction to Emperor Shih Tsung (1188); invited to visit Genghis Khan (1219); journeyed through Gobi Desert, Samarkand, to Genghis's camp in Hindu Kush (1219–22); returned to Peking (1224). Journey recounted in *Hsi Yu Chi* by companion and disciple Li Chih-chang.

Ch'anggang. See Cho Sok.

Chang Heng \'jäŋ-'həŋ\. 78–139 A.D. Chinese scholar and poet. Inventor of an early form of seismograph (132 A.D.).

Chang Heng-ch'ü. See Chang Tsai.

Chang Hsien-chung \-shē-'en-'jüŋ\. *Known as* the Yellow Tiger. c.1605–1647. Chinese rebel. Became leader of gang of freebooters following famine in Shensi province (1628); plundered and raided throughout North China; on fall of Ming dynasty (1644) entered Szechwan province and set up as "king of western kingdom"; established civil government, coined money, etc.; ruled by military power and terror; defeated and executed by Manchu forces.

Chang Ling \-'liŋ\. *In full* Chang Tao-ling \-'daü-'liŋ\. 34?–?156. Chinese religious leader. Originally a faith healer; following revelation from Lao-tzu (142 A.D.) founded organized Taoist religion; considered first patriarch of Taoist religion and with son Chang Heng and grandson Chang Lu one of the Three Changs.

Chang Ping-lin \-'piŋ-'lin\. 1868–1936. Chinese scholar and politician. Imprisoned (1903–06) for journalistic expression of anti-Manchu opinions; in Japan joined (1906) Sun Yat-sen's nationalist T'ung-meng hui party; broke with party after revolution, imprisoned (1911–16); member of Sun's government at Canton (1916–18). Noted esp. as Confucian scholar and opponent of modernization of classical written Chinese.

Chang Sung-ob \-'süŋ-'ōb\. *Also known as* Owon \'ō-'wön\, *i.e.* My Garden. 1843–1897. Korean painter. Self-taught while a servant; remained illiterate and unable to sign paintings; first Korean painter to master working on Chinese fast-reacting paper; considered outstanding Korean painter of his day.

Chang Tao-ling. See Chang Ling.

Chang Ti. See Liu Ta under Liu family.

Chang Tsai \'jäŋ-'dzī\. *Also known as* Chang Heng-ch'ü \-'həŋ-'chü\. 1020–1077. Chinese philosopher. In major work *Cheng-meng* elaborated metaphysical and epistemological foundation for Neo-Confucianism; a great influence on later thinkers, esp. Ch'eng Hao, Ch'eng I, Chu Hsi, and Wang Fu-chih (*qq.v.*).

Chang Tso-lin \-'tsō-'lin\. 1873–1928. Chinese warlord. Common laborer; became (1904) leader of band of Manchurian brigands; joined Chinese army (1905); military governor of Fengtien (1911); with Japanese aid secured control (1918) of three Manchurian provinces; succeeded in occupying northeastern provinces of China (1926); formed cabinet (1927); withdrew from Peking (1928) on advance of Nationalist army; killed on Mukden train by bomb.

Chang Tzu-p'ing \-'dzü-'piŋ\. 1893–?1947. Chinese writer. Exponent of literary Romanticism in novels and stories; a founder of Creation Society, devoted to propagation of Romanticism; tried for collaboration (1947) after assisting Japanese during Sino–Japanese War (1937–45).

Chan·ning \'chan-iŋ\, Edward Perkins. 1856–1931. American historian, b. Dorchester, Mass. Grandson of Walter Channing. Professor, Harvard (1883–1929). Author of 6-volume *History of the United States* (1905–25), of which 6th volume, *War for Southern Independence* (1925) won Pulitzer prize.

Channing, Walter. 1786–1876. American obstetrician, b. Newport, R.I. Brother of William Ellery Channing. Professor (1815–54) and dean (1819–47), Harvard Medical School; a founder of Boston Lying-In Hospital (1832); introduced use of ether to lessen pain of labor (1847).

Channing, William Ellery. 1780–1842. American clergyman, b. Newport, R.I. Pastor, Federal Street Church, Boston (1803–42); liberal Congregationalist; became leader of Unitarian group (from 1819); an organizer of American Unitarian Association (1825), becoming known as the "apostle of Unitarianism." Exercised wide influence by sermons and writings on social and philanthropic issues of his time. Author of *Negro Slavery* (1835), *Self Culture* (1838), etc.

Chan·tal \shä^n-tál\, Jeanne-Françoise de, *nee* Fré·myot \frām-yō\. Saint. 1572–1641. French religious. m. Baron de Chantal (1592; d. 1601); after husband's death devoted herself to prayer and works of charity; met (1607) St. Francis de Sales, under whose guidance she founded (1610) Congregation of the Visitation of Holy Mary; superior (1618–22) of house of the order established in Paris. Canonized (1767).

Chan·trey \'chan-trē\, Sir Francis Legatt. 1781–1841. English sculptor. Works included statues of George III (for Guildhall), George IV (Windsor Castle), George Washington (State House, Boston), William Pitt, Duke of Wellington; busts, as Sir Walter Scott; ideal figures *Plenty, Penelope,* etc.

Cha·nute \shə-'nüt\, Octave. 1832–1910. American civil engineer and aviation pioneer, b. Paris, France. To U.S. (1838); railroad engineer (1853–73); consulting engineer, esp. in bridge building (1873–83). Studied Lilienthal's experiments with gliders; experimented with gliders and scientifically tabulated results (1886–97); designed biplane glider of exceptional stability in flight. Wright Brothers acknowledged value of his experiments and designs. Author of *Aerial Navigation* (1891), *Progress in Flying Machines* (1894).

Chan·zy \shä^n-zē\, Antoine-Eugène-Alfred. 1823–1883. French soldier. Served in Algeria; general (1868); commanded corps, and later 2d Army of the Loire, in Franco–Prussian War; defeated at Le Mans (1871). Governor of Algeria (1873–79); senator (1875); candidate for president of France (1879).

Chao \'jaü\. Name of family providing emperors for the Sung dynasty (960–1279) of China; its rulers, usually known by their reign titles, were:

Chao K'uang-yin \-'kwäŋ-'yin\. *Reign title* T'ai Tsu \'tīd-'zü\. 927–976. 1st emperor (960–76) and founder of dynasty. Son of a military officer; in service (from c.947) of Later Chou dynasty, rising to chief commander of its forces; declared emperor by his troops (960); as emperor reunified much of China except for northern Liao dynasty; created a bureaucracy based on ability rather than birth or favor; reformed legal, fiscal, and civil service examination systems; encouraged innovation and freedom of discussion.

Chao Kuei \-'gü-'ā\. *Orig.* Chao K'uang-i \-'kwäŋ-'ē\. *Reign title* T'ai Tsung \'tīd-'züŋ\. 939–997. 2d emperor (976–97). Succeeded his brother K'uang-yin; continued reunification of China, taking over two remaining independent states in South China; suffered disastrous defeat in attempt to conquer Liao dynasty (986); continued development of civil service examination system; centralized power in his hands; adopted T'ang prefectural system, dividing China into 15 provinces, each with a governor.

Chao Heng \-'həŋ\. *Orig.* Chao Te-ch'ang \-'də-'chäŋ\. *Reign title* Chen Tsung \'jən-'dzüŋ\. 968–1022. 3d emperor (997–1022). Son of Kuei; concluded peace treaty (1004) with Liao dynasty, ceding claims to territory north of Great Wall; created series of new cults resulting in fusion of Buddhist and Taoist religions; increased influence of Confucianism; toward end of reign became insane and his empress assumed power.

Chao Chen \-'jən\. *Orig.* Chao Shou-i \-'shaü-'ē\. *Reign title* Jen Tsung \'zyənd-'züŋ\. 1010–1063. 4th emperor (1022–63). Son of Heng; one of most able and humane of Chinese rulers; under him Sung government reached closest to Confucian ideal of just government; reign troubled by two opposing political and philosophical factions.

Chao Shu \-'shü\. *Orig.* Chao Tsung-shih \-'dzüŋ-'shi(ə)r\. *Reign title* Ying Tsung \'yiŋ-'dzüŋ\. 1032–1067. 5th emperor (1064–67). Great-grandson of Kuei.

Chao Hsü \-'shü\. *Reign title* Shen Tsung \'shən-'dzüŋ\. 1048–1085. 6th emperor (1068–85). Son of Shu; under his administration extensive economic, social, and military reforms carried out (1069–76) by his chief councillor Wang An-shih (*q.v.*); during his reign flourished many intellectual and cultural figures, including Ou-yang Hsiu and Su T'ung-p'o.

Chao Hsü. *Reign title* Che Tsung \'jäd-'züŋ\. 1077–1100. 7th emperor (1086–1100). Son of Hsü; under regency of empress dowager most of Wang An-shih's reforms rescinded; on attaining control (1093) restored Wang's reforms but their effect insignificant.

Chao Chi \-'jē\. *Reign title* Hui Tsung \hü-'ēd-'züŋ\. 1082–1135. 8th emperor (1100–25). Son of the elder Hsü; best remembered as patron of the arts and as painter and calligrapher; sponsored compilation of *Hsüan-ho hua p'u,* a major catalog of artists' biographies and works from 3d century to his time; ineffectual as ruler, unable to resolve political disputes between conservatives and reformers in his court; made alliance with Juchen tribes of Manchuria and destroyed (1125) Liao empire; soon after attacked by the Juchen and lost north territory and his capital of K'ai-feng; abdicated in favor of son; captured (1126) by the Juchen and died in exile in Manchuria.

Chao Huan \-'hwän\. *Orig.* Chao Tan \-'dän\. *Reign title* Ch'in Tsung \'chin-'dzüŋ\. 1100–1160. 9th emperor (1125–26). Ascended throne on abdication of his father Chi; captured with his father during sacking of capital by Juchen tribes (1126); died in exile in Manchuria; last of Northern Sung emperors.

Chao Kou \-'gaü\. *Reign title* Kao Tsung \'gaüd-'züŋ\. 1107–1187. 10th emperor and 1st (1127–62) of Southern Sung dynasty. Fled to South China on capture by Juchen tribes of his father Chi and brother Huan (1126); reestablished there the Sung dynasty with capital at Li-an (modern Hangchow) with himself as emperor (1127); waged long war against the Juchen until conclusion of peace treaty (1141); established strong, centralized bureaucracy with efficient tax system; war with Juchen erupted again but second treaty signed (1162); abdicated (1162) but retained control.

Chao Shen \-'shən\. *Orig.* Chao Po-ts'ung \-'bōt-'su̇ŋ\. *Reign title* Hsiao Tsung \shē-'au̇d-'zu̇ŋ\. 1127–1194. 11th emperor (1163–89). Adopted son of Kou; resumed war with Juchen empire with neither side winning; signed peace treaty (1165); abdicated.

Chao Tun \-'du̇n\. *Reign title* Kuang Tsung \'kwäŋ-'dzu̇ŋ\. 1147–1200. 12th emperor (1190–94). Son of Shen; reign peaceful.

Chao K'uo \-kwō\. *Reign title* Ning Tsung \'niŋ-dzu̇ŋ\. 1168–1224. 13th emperor (1195–1224). Son of Tun; reign noted as period of intellectual and cultural achievements, esp. by philosopher Chu Hsi; government dominated by his chief councillor Han T'o-chou (*q.v.*) who conducted disastrous war against the Juchen and lost much territory; concluded peace treaty with Juchen (1208); control of government later held by Han's successor Shih Mi-yüan.

Chao Yun \-'yu̇n\. *Orig.* Chao Chün \-'chün\. *Reign title* Li Tsung \'lēd-'zu̇ŋ\. 1205–1264. 14th emperor (1225–64). Adopted son of K'uo; led sybaritic life; government controlled by chief councillors Shi Mi-yüan (to 1233) and Chia Ssu-tao.

Chao Ch'i \-'chē\. *Orig.* Chao Meng-ch'i \-'məŋ-'chē\. *Reign title* Tu Tsung \'düd-'zu̇ŋ\. 1240–1274. 15th emperor (1265–74). Nephew of Yun; led life of luxury; government controlled by chief councillor Chia Ssu-tao (*q.v.*).

Chao Hsien \-shē-'en\. *Reign title* Kung Tsung \'gu̇ŋ-'dzu̇ŋ\. 1270–?1276. 16th emperor (1275–76). Son of Ch'i; government still in hands of Chia Ssu-tao.

Chao Shih \-'shi(ə)r\. *Reign title* Tuan Tsung \dwän-'dzu̇ŋ\. 1268–1278. 17th emperor (1276–78). Brother of Hsien.

Chao Ping \-'biŋ\. 1271–79. 18th emperor (1279). Brother of Hsien and Shih; last Sung emperor; dynasty overthrown by Mongol armies of Kublai Khan (1279).

Chao Anou \-'ä-'nō\. *Also* Chao Anu \-'ä-'nü\ *or* Chao Anou·vong \-'ä-'nü-'vȯŋ\. *Also called* Sa·ya-Se·tha·thir·ath III \'sä-yä-,se-tä-'tir-ät\. 1767–1835. Laotian ruler. Fought with Siamese forces against Burma; succeeded brother as king of Lao city-state of Vien Chang (1805); secretly prepared fortifications and launched rebellion against Siam (1826–28), leading Laotian army toward Bangkok; captured and tortured.

Chao-hui \-hwē\. 1708–1764. Chinese general. Led expeditions that pacified tribes of western Mongolia (1755–57), Muslim tribes of Chinese Turkistan, in both instances escaping from prolonged sieges.

Chao Ju-kua \'jau̇z-'yü-'gwä\. 12th century. Chinese official. Superintendent of customs at Ch'üan-chou; author of *Chu fan chih,* widely known account of foreign places, customs, goods.

Chao Kao \'jau̇-'gau̇\. d. 207 B.C. Chinese official and conspirator. Chief eunuch to Emperor Shih Huang Ti; concealed death of emperor (210 B.C.) and with minister Li Ssu forged letter ordering heir apparent to commit suicide and decree naming infant son Hu Hai to succeed; had Li executed, then Hu Hai; assassinated.

Chao Meng-fu \-'məŋ-'fü\. *Literary name* Tzu-ang \'dzü-'äŋ\. 1254–1322. Chinese painter and calligrapher. Served Mongol court of Yüan dynasty (from 1279); early master of literati style; noted for elegantly simplified brushwork and composition in paintings of animal groups, esp. horses, bamboos, landscapes.

Chao Nan \-'nän\. *Also known as* Chao Nan·tha·sen \-nän-'tä-sən\. d. 1795. Laotian ruler. Son of Ong Boun; ruler of principality of Vien Chang (1782–92); conquered neighboring Luang Prabang (1791); deposed and imprisoned by Rama I of Siam.

Cha·pais \shȧ-pe\, Sir Thomas[4], *in full* Joseph Amable Thomas. 1858–1946. Canadian lawyer and politician, b. St.-Denis, Que. Editor, *Le Courrier du Canada* (1884–1901); served in Quebec government; professor of history, Laval U. (1907 ff.). Author of *Cours d'histoire du Canada* (1919–35), and literary and historical studies.

Cha·pe·lain \shȧ-plaⁿ\, Jean. 1595–1674. French poet and critic. An organizer and original member of the Académie Française (1634); acquired great prestige as critic; author of *La Pucelle* (1656), an epic ridiculed by Boileau.

Cha·pin \'chā-pən\, Roy Dikeman. 1880–1936. American industrialist, b. Lansing, Mich. In automobile manufacturing business (from 1901); with Howard E. Coffin organized (1909) Hudson Motor Car Co.; president (1910–23), board chairman (1923–33), again president (1933–36); manufactured Hudson and (from 1919) Essex autos. U.S. secretary of commerce (1932–33).

Cha·pí y Lo·ren·te \chä-'pē-ē-lō-'rān-tā\, Ruperto. 1851–1909. Spanish composer. Composed over 100 zarzuelas beginning with *Abel y Cain* (1870?); also operas, string quartets.

Chap·lin \'chap-lən\, Sir Charles Spencer. 1889–1977. English comedian and actor. With Fred Karno vaudeville troupe (1906–13); while in New York joined Mack Sennett's Keystone film company (1913); achieved huge success in character of "the tramp," a humorous and pathetic character that became world famous; with Mary Pickford, Douglas Fairbanks, D.W. Griffith formed United Artists to produce films (1919); under political attack, left U.S. (1952), settled in Switzerland; knighted (1975). Films included *Kid Auto Races at Venice* (1914), *Tillie's Punctured Romance* (1914), *The Tramp* (1915), *The Floorwalker* (1916), *The Rink* (1916), *Easy Street,* (1917), *Shoulder Arms* (1918), *The Kid* (1921), *The Pilgrim* (1923), *The Gold Rush* (1925), *City Lights* (1931), *Modern Times* (1936), *The Great Dictator* (1940), *Monsieur Verdoux* (1947), *Limelight* (1952), *A King in New York* (1957).

Chap·man \'chap-mən\, Frank Michler. 1864–1945. American ornithologist, b. Englewood, N.J. Curator (1908–42), American Museum of Natural History. Founder (1899) and editor (1899–1935) of *Bird-Lore.* Author of *Handbook of Birds of Eastern North America* (1895), *Guide to the Study of our Common Birds* (1897), *Bird Studies with a Camera* (1900), *Key to North American Birds* (1903), *The Warblers of North America* (1907), *Our Winter Birds* (1918), *What Bird is That?* (1920), *Birds of the Urubamba Valley, Peru* (1921), *Bird Life in Ecuador* (1926), etc.

Chapman, George. 1559?–1634. English poet and dramatist. Playwright in London; wrote poems *The Shadow of Night* (1593), *Ovid's Banquet of Sence* (1595), *Enthymiae Raptus* (1609), and completed Marlowe's *Hero and Leander* (1598); wrote his first play, *The Blind Beggar of Alexandria* (acted 1596); imprisoned with Ben Jonson (1605) for satirizing James I's Scottish followers in play *Eastward Hoe;* aided by Prince Henry, patronized by Robert Carr, Earl of Somerset; published chief tragedies and comedies (1606–12), including *Bussy d'Ambois, The Gentlemen Usher, The Widow's Tears.* Known esp. for his rhyming verse translations of Homer (*Iliad,* 1598–1611; *Odyssey,* 1614–16; the *Hymns,* 1624), for centuries the standard English versions.

Chapman, John. *Nicknamed* Johnny Ap·ple·seed \'ap-əl-,sēd\. 1774–1845. American pioneer, b. Leominster, Mass. Began collecting apple seeds (c.1800) and carried them into Ohio valley, where he ranged widely over the country planting apple seeds and pruning the growing trees. Subject of many legends.

Chapman, John Gadsby. 1808–1889. American painter and etcher, b. Alexandria, Va. His *Baptism of Pocahontas* (c.1847) is in rotunda of Capitol, Washington, D.C.

Chapman, John Jay. 1862–1933. American writer, b. New York City. Practiced law (1888–98); devoted himself to writing (from 1898); best known for his essays. Author of *Emerson and Other Essays* (1898), *Causes and Consequences* (1898), *Practical Agitation* (1900), *Four Plays for Children* (1908), *The Maid's Forgiveness* (play in verse, 1908), *A Sausage from Bologna* (comedy in verse, 1909), *Treason and Death of Benedict Arnold* (play, 1910), *Learning and Other Essays* (1911), *Neptune's Isle* (1912), *William Lloyd Garrison* (1913), *Memories and Milestones* (1915), *Green Genius and Other Essays* (1915), *Songs and Poems* (1919), *Letters and Religion* (1923), *Dante* (1927), *New Horizons in American Life* (1932), etc.

Chapman, Nathaniel. 1780–1853. American physician, b. Summer Hill, Va. Pupil of Dr. Benjamin Rush of Philadelphia (1797); practiced in Philadelphia (from 1804); on staff of U. of Pennsylvania medical school (1810–50). Founder of Medical Institute of Philadelphia, first postgraduate medical school in U.S. (1817); editor, *Journal of Medical and Physical Sciences* (1820); first president of American Medical Association (1848); author of *Elements of Therapeutics and Materia Medica* (1817), etc.

Cha·pone \shə-'pōn\, Hester, *nee* Mul·so \'məl-,sō\. 1727–1801. English essayist. One of the learned women gathered round Mrs. Elizabeth Montagu; known for her *Letters on the Improvement of the Mind* (1772).

Chappe \shȧp\, Claude. 1763–1805. French engineer. Invented an extensively used telegraph employing visual semaphore signals; assisted by his brother ¶Ignace-Urbain-Jean (1760–1829), member of Legislative Assembly, built series of signal towers between Paris and Lille (1794), later Paris and Toulon.

Chap·pell \'chap-əl\, William. 1809–1888. English antiquary. Member of family of music publishers; collected English airs in *Popular Music of the Olden Time* (1855–59); one of founders of Musical Association (1874).

Chap·tal \shȧp-tȧl\. Jean-Antoine. Comte de Chan·te·loup \shäⁿt-lü\. 1756–1832. French chemist. Professor, Montpellier (1780–98); established factory for production of sulfuric, hydrochloric, oxalic and other acids, vitriol, white lead, alum, etc. Suggested addition of sugar to speed fermentation of wine. As minister of interior (1800–04) encouraged industry, technical education; appointed senator and made count by Napoléon; minister of agriculture, commerce, and industry in Hundred Days (1815). Author of *Chimie appliquée aux arts* (1807), *Chimie appliquée à l'agriculture* (1823), etc.

Cha·pu \shȧ-pu̅e̅\, Henri-Michel-Antoine. 1833–1891. French sculptor. Among his works were *Mercure inventant la caducée; Jeanne d'Arc écoutant des voix;*

statue *La Jeunesse* in the École des Beaux-Arts to the memory of Henri Regnault; allegorical figure of Truth as monument to Flaubert; noted also as portrait medallist.

Char·bon·neau \shär-bȯ-nō\, Jean. 1875–1960. French-Canadian poet, b. Montreal. A founder of Montreal Literary School (1895); influenced by Parnassians. Author of verse *Les Blessures* (1912), *Sur la borne pensive* (1952), etc.; also *L'École littéraire de Montreal* (1935).

Char·cot \shär-kō\, Jean-Martin. 1825–1893. French neurologist. Professor of pathological anatomy, Paris (1860–93); physician at the Salpêtrière (from 1862), where he established neurological clinic; renowned as teacher; known for work on hysteria and hypnotism (which influenced his pupil Sigmund Freud), sclerosis, locomotor ataxia, senile diseases, etc.; described Charcot's disease, miliary aneurysms, etc.

His son ¶Jean-Baptiste-Étienne-Auguste (1867–1936), explorer; headed two expeditions to Antarctic (1903–05, 1908–10); mapped Graham Land and its islands, Loubet Coast, etc.; discovered Fallières Coast, Charcot Island; later noted for oceanographic studies; drowned with 38 of his men when the *Pourquoi-Pas?* was wrecked off western Iceland. Author of *Autour du pôle* (1912).

Char·din \shär-da^n, *Angl* 'shärd-^{ə}n\, Jean, *later* Sir John. 1643–1713. French traveler. Made journeys to Persia and India (1665–70, 1671–77), acquiring wealth by trade in jewels; a Protestant, settled in London (1681) and became jeweler to court of Charles II. Author of *Journal du voyage du chevalier Chardin* (1711).

Char·din \shär-da^n\, Jean-Baptiste-Siméon. 1699–1779. French painter. Known for still lifes, family scenes, genre pieces of wholesome simplicity and acute observation. Paintings included *La Raie, Le Buffet, L'Enfant au toton, Le jeune violiniste, Le Bénédicité, Les Tours de carte, La Toilette du matin, La Mère laborieuse, La Serinette.*

Chardin, Pierre Teilhard de. See TEILHARD DE CHARDIN.

Char·don·net \shär-dȯ-ne\, Louis-Marie-Hilaire Ber·ni·gaud de \ber-nē-gō-də-\. Comte. 1839–1924. French chemist. Patented (1884) and demonstrated (1889) artificial fiber later known as rayon; established factories for its manufacture.

Cha·res \'kā-,rēz, 'kar-,ēz\. 4th century B.C. Athenian general. Associate of Chabrias at outbreak of Social War (357 B.C.); after death of Chabrias held joint command with Iphicrates and Timotheus; captured Chersonesus (357); operated against Philip II of Macedon (from 349), and was disastrously defeated at Amphissa (338) and Chaeronea (338); fled Alexander the Great's surrender demand at Thebes (335); entered (332) service of Darius III of Persia.

Chares. 4th century B.C. Greek sculptor. Carved the famous Colossus of Rhodes (about 105 ft. high; considered one of seven wonders of ancient world) to commemorate defense of Rhodes against Demetrius Poliorcetes.

Cha·rette de la Con·trie \shä-ret-də-lä-kō^n-trē\, François-Athanase. 1763–1796. French Royalist. A naval officer; leader in Vendean revolt (1793 ff.) against newly established French Republic; executed at Nantes.

Cha·ri·bert \shä-rē-ber\ *or* **Ca·ri·bert** \kä-\. d. 567. Frankish king. Son of Chlotar I, whom he succeeded as king of West Gaul (561–567) at Paris; variously reputed a patron of learning and a debauchee.

Char·i·de·mus \,kar-ə-'dē-məs\. d. 333 B.C. Greek mercenary. Served under Athenian Iphicrates at Amphipolis (c.367 B.C.); later served Cotys, king of Thebes, against Athens; again with Athens under Timotheus at Amphipolis (c.364–362) and again turned to Cotys; guardian to Cotys's son Cersobleptes; in Social War (357) gained credit for restoring Chersonesus to Athens; commanded Athenian forces against Philip II of Macedon (351); fled to Darius III of Persia when Alexander the Great demanded his surrender following conquest of Thebes (335). Cf. CHARES.

Char·i·ton \'kar-ə-,tän\. 1st or 2d century A.D. Greek writer. Author of *The Loves of Chaereas and Callirrhoë,* earliest fully extant romantic novel in West.

Char·le·magne \shär-lə-mäny, *Angl* 'shär-lə-,mān\, *i.e.* Charles the Great. *Ger.* Karl der Gros·se \'kärl-dər-'grō-sə\. *Lat.* Car·o·lus Mag·nus \'kar-ə-ləs-'mag-nəs\. 742–814. King of the Franks (768–814) and emperor of the West (800–814). Son of Pepin III the Short, at whose death (768) he became king of Neustria (western Franks), Austrasia, etc.; at death of his brother Carloman (771), became king of all the Franks; m. (771) Hildegarde of Swabia. Fought with, subjugated, and converted the Saxons (772–777). Destroyed kingdom of Lombardy (773–774); crowned king of the Lombards (773). Led expedition (778) into northeastern Spain against the amir of Córdoba, a campaign not historically important but which, through death at Roncesvalles of his paladin Roland, gave rise to a great body of medieval literature. Subdued rebellions of Saxons (782, 792–804) by mass executions; deposed Duke Tassilo III of Bavaria (788); united West German tribes under one rule; campaigned against Avars. Established permanent court at Aachen (Aix-la-Chapelle, 794). Crowned Carolus Augustus, Emperor of the Romans (Christmas Day, 800), by Pope Leo III; organized administration of his realm, which at end of his conquests was beginning of Holy Roman Empire; retained its ancient national assemblies, strengthened Christianity, founded schools (see ALCUIN); patron of literature, science, and art. Crowned son Louis of Aquitaine coemperor and successor (813).

Charles. Count of Anjou and Maine. See CHARLES, Count of Valois.

Charles \'chär(-ə)lz\. *Ger.* Karl \'kärl\. Archduke of Austria. 1771–1847. Third son of future Emperor Leopold II; entered Austrian army (1792); distinguished himself at Jemappes, Aldenhoven, Neerwinden (1793); governor general of Austrian Netherlands (1793); field marshal, commander of Austrian army of the Rhine (1796); drove French under Jourdan and Moreau across Rhine (1796); conducted Austrian retreat before Napoléon in Italy (1797); again on Rhine front, defeated Jourdan at Osterach and Stokach (1799), invaded Switzerland and defeated Masséna at Zürich (1799); absent from command at Hohenlinden (1800), unable to halt Moreau's advance on Vienna and forced to make armistice of Steyer (1802). President of Council of War, generalissimo (1801–09); instituted sweeping reorganization of army. In war of 1805 defeated Masséna at Caldiero; in war of 1809 won battle of Aspern-Essling, yielded Pyrrhic victory to French at Wagram. Retired (1809); governor of Mainz (1815). Author of works on strategy.

Charles I. *In full* Charles Francis Joseph. *Ger.* Karl Franz Josef. 1887–1922. Emperor of Austria (1916–18). Son of Archduke Otto; nephew of Francis Ferdinand; grandnephew of Emperor Francis Joseph; m. (1911) Zita, Princess of Bourbon and Parma. Proclaimed himself emperor and, as Charles IV, king of Hungary (1916); failed in secret attempts to take Austria-Hungary out of World War I; failed to quell nationalist movements in empire with plan of federation (1918); renounced participation in government (1918); exiled to Switzerland (1919); formally deposed by Austrian parliament (1919); made two attempts by visits to Hungary to regain throne (1921); deported by Allies to Madeira (1921).

Charles I. King of Bohemia. See CHARLES IV, Holy Roman Emperor.

Charles \shärl, *Angl* 'chär(-ə)lz\. *Called* le Té·mé·raire \lə-tā-mā-rer\, *i.e.* the Bold. 1433–1477. Duke of Burgundy. Son of Duke Philip the Good; styled Count of Charolais until accession as duke of Burgundy (1467); m. 1st Catherine (d. 1446), daughter of Charles VII of France, 2d Isabella, daughter of Charles I de Bourbon (1457; d. 1465), 3d Margaret of York, sister of Edward IV of England (1468). Dedicated himself to winning Burgundian independence from France and establishment as kingdom; extended realm; led League of Public Weal against Louis XI of France; recaptured Burgundian territory taken by Louis (1465), put down rebellions in Dinant (1467), Liège (1467); despite truces (1468, 1472) almost constantly at war with Louis; obtained Alsace, Gelderland, etc.; attempted to gain Cologne and Lorraine; organized government along centralist, monarchical lines; arranged to be crowned king of Burgundy by Emperor Frederick III, who suddenly fled his hospitality (1473); defeated by forces of Lorraine, Swiss cantons, Austria (1474–77); killed in battle near Nancy.

Charles. *Called* le Bon \lə-bō^n\, *i.e.* the Good, *or* the Dane. c.1084–1127. Count of Flanders. Son of St. Canute IV of Denmark; on death of father (1086) taken to Flanders by mother, the daughter of Count Robert of Flanders; succeeded to countship on death of cousin Baldwin VII (1119); refused crown of Jerusalem (1119); renowned for clemency, devotion to Christianity and welfare of subjects; declined to be considered for succession to Emperor Henry V (1125).

Charles. Name of ten or eleven kings of France:

CAROLINGIAN DYNASTY:

Charles the Great (742–814). King of the Franks (768–814). Frequently not included in numbering of kings named Charles. See CHARLEMAGNE.

Charles I *or* **II** (823–877). See CHARLES II, Holy Roman Emperor.

Charles II (839–888). See CHARLES III, Holy Roman Emperor. Often not included among French kings.

Charles III. *Called* le Sim·ple \lə-sa^{n}pl^ə\, *i.e.* the Simple. 879–929. King (893–923). Son of Louis II; because of youth, denied succession on death of half-brother Carloman (844); crowned by Archbishop Fulk of Reims (893) in opposition to Eudes; recognized as king on death of Eudes (898); ceded (911) Normandy to Rollo, but became king of Lorraine; defeated Robert, Count of Paris, at Soissons (923) but captured and imprisoned by Herbert, Count of Vermandois (923).

CAPETIAN DYNASTY:

Charles IV. *Called* le Bel \lə-bel\, *i.e.* the Fair. 1294–1328. King (1322–28), last of direct line of Capetian kings; also, as Charles I, king of Navarre. Son of Philip IV; succeeded brother Philip V (1322); failed in bid for German throne and in attempt to seize Flanders; sought to strengthen royal power by increasing taxes, exacting fines and duties, debasing coinage, confiscations, etc.; renewed war with England; intrigued with sister Isabella, wife of Edward II of England, and secured Agenais from England.

HOUSE OF VALOIS, CAPETIAN BRANCH:

Charles V. *Called* le Sage \lə-säzh\, *i.e.* the Wise. 1337–1380. King

(1364–80). Son of John II; became regent when father made prisoner by English at Poitiers (1356); royal prerogatives strengthened by failure of the Jacquerie, or peasants' revolt (1358), and assassination of Étienne Marcel (*q.v.*); raised ransom for father by ceding territory in treaties of Bretigny and Calais (1360) with England. Regained most of territory held by England (1369–75); greatly aided by Bertrand du Guesclin in suppression of mercenary bands and in wars against Navarre (1365) and England; increased taxes, but rule generally wise and economical; patron of art and literature; collected large and valuable library at the Louvre.

Charles VI. *Called* le Bien-Ai·mé \lə-bya^{n}-ne-mā\, *i.e.* the Well-Beloved; *sometimes called* the Mad. 1368–1422. King (1380–1422). Son of Charles V; during minority (1380–88) under guardianship of four uncles, esp. Louis, Duke of Anjou (regent 1380–82) and Philip the Bold of Burgundy (regent 1382–88); m. Isabeau, or Isabella, of Bavaria (1385); assumed government (1388); ruled well until subject to attacks of insanity (from 1392). Struggle for regency led to civil wars between houses of Orléans and Burgundy; affairs of realm disrupted; at times English aid invited by each party; French severely defeated by Henry V at Agincourt (1415); concluded Treaty of Troyes (1420) providing for marriage of daughter Catherine to Henry V.

Charles VII. 1403–1461. King (1422–61). Son of Charles VI; assumed regency (1418); leader of anti-Burgundian party; excluded from succession by Treaty of Troyes (1420) but assumed title of king on father's death; began reign with all northern France and part in southwest in English possession (1422); raised siege of Orléans with aid of Joan of Arc (1429); crowned at Reims (1429); made peace with Philip of Burgundy (1435); entered Paris (1436) after English had been gradually driven back (1429–36); recovered from English all French lands except Calais (1437–53); reorganized administration, secured financial independence of crown; issued Pragmatic Sanction (1438); put down (1440) Praguerie conspiracy of nobles, including the dauphin; made truce with England (1444–49); regained Normandy (1450), Guyenne (1453). Last part of reign marked by reforms, establishment of a permanent tax, increased power of king, beginning of standing army, etc. For many years influenced by advice of his mistress Agnès Sorel.

Charles VIII. 1470–1498. King (1483–98). Son of Louis XI; first years of reign dominated by regency of sister Anne and her husband Pierre de Bourbon, sire de Beaujeu; assumed power after his marriage to Anne de Bretagne (1491); ambitious to revive rights of house of Anjou to Naples; made concessions to England and the emperor, neglecting France; aided by Sforza in Milan, entered Naples in great pomp (1495); later driven out (1495) by Holy League forces of Ferdinand II of Naples and Gonzalo de Córdoba; died childless, Orléans line succeeding (Louis XII).

HOUSE OF VALOIS, ANGOULÊME BRANCH:

Charles IX. 1550–1574. King (1560–74). Second son of Henry II and Catherine de Médicis; succeeded brother Francis II; during minority, kingdom ruled by his mother; later (1563–74), completely under her domination. Reign marked by fierce civil wars—Catholics (followers of Guise) v. Huguenots (followers of Condé); persuaded by mother to order St. Bartholomew's Day Massacre (Aug. 24, 1572). Had one natural son, Charles, duc d'Angoulême (see Charles de VALOIS).

HOUSE OF BOURBON, RESTORED:

Charles X. 1757–1836. King (1824–30). Grandson of Louis XV; younger brother of Louis XVI and Louis XVIII; known until accession as Charles-Philippe, comte d'Artois; m. Maria Theresa of Savoy (1773). After Revolution became leader of émigrés (1789–95); joined English expedition to Brittany (1795) but abandoned Vendeans; lived in England and Scotland (1795–1814). After Restoration became leader (1815) of ultraroyalists. After accession (1824) attempted to restore absolutism; became increasingly unpopular; dissolved Chamber of Deputies (May 1830); ordered new elections; promulgated "four ordinances" (July 25) terminating freedom of press, decreeing new method of elections, dissolving the chamber; overthrown by ensuing revolution (July 27–29); named Louis-Philippe, duc d'Orléans, lieutenant general of kingdom and then abdicated (Aug. 2); fled to England.

Charles \ˈchär(-ə)lz\. Name of two kings of Great Britain and Ireland, of house of Stuart:

Charles I. 1600–1649. King (1625–49). Second son of James VI of Scotland (James I of England) and Anne of Denmark; created duke of Albany (1600), duke of York (1605), prince of Wales (1616). Went incognito to Madrid with favorite, Duke of Buckingham, to urge his suit with Infanta Maria of Spain (1623); failed, on refusal to turn Roman Catholic. Succeeded James I (1625); m. Henrietta Maria, sister of Louis XIII of France (1625). A tool in hands of prime minister, Buckingham, for whose warlike schemes he demanded supplies of Parliament; dissolved three parliaments in four years for noncompliance; forced to end unsuccessful wars with Spain and France (1629). With Laud and Wentworth as advisers, ruled for eleven years without Parliament, through subservient judges and courts; had recourse to forced loans, poundage, tonnage, and ship money from seaports (1634) and from inland counties (1635) to raise funds, thus arousing John Hampden's resistance; attempted to impose High Church liturgy upon Church of Scotland, which resisted and restored Presbyterianism, adopting National Covenant (1638); invaded Scotland but, lacking funds, had to sign treaty of Berwick (1639). Summoned Short Parliament (Apr. 1640) to obtain money for expedition against Scots; met refusal and demand under leadership of John Pym for redress of grievances. Defied by Long Parliament (Nov. 1640), which impeached Laud and Strafford; sacrificed life of Strafford (1641); yielded pledge that Long Parliament would be dissolved only by its own vote; in Edinburgh endeavored to win Scots by concessions to demands of Scottish Parliament (1641). Attempted (1642) to arrest the Five Members, leaders in passing of Grand Remonstrance in House of Commons, in order to avert impeachment of the queen; declared war on Parliamentarians at Nottingham (1642), beginning civil war that ended in annihilation of royal army at Naseby (1645); took refuge at Oxford (Royalist headquarters from Oct. 1642); surrendered to Scots (1646); was handed over to Parliament (1647). Held by Parliamentary army at Newmarket and then London; escaped to Isle of Wight, where held captive at Carisbrooke Castle; negotiated separately with army, Parliament, Scots; he made secret treaty (the Engagement) with Scots by which he received aid of Scots forces for his consent to establish Presbyterianism in England for three years (1647); removed to London (Jan. 1649) and tried at Westminster, where he refused to plead before court constituted by House of Commons; condemned by court of 67 judges as tyrant and enemy of nation; beheaded at Whitehall.

Charles II. 1630–1685. King (1660–1685). Son of Charles I and Henrietta Maria; present at battle of Edge Hill; withdrew to Scilly, to Jersey, then to Paris; attemped in vain to save his father's life (1649); came to terms with Scots, accepted Covenant, pledged himself to support Presbyterianism in Scotland and England (1650); after defeat of Scots, invaded England but routed by Cromwell at Worcester (1651); escaped (after adventures including concealment in the Royal Oak) to Continent; made futile attempt to unite French and Spanish crowns in expedition against England (1659). After fall of Protectorate, negotiated with General Monck and English Presbyterians; issued Declaration of Breda (1660), promising amnesty and liberty of conscience and providing restoration of parliamentary government; proclaimed king. Entrusted steps of reconstruction (1660–67) to Edward Hyde, Earl of Clarendon; urged lenity in Indemnity bill; m. (1662) Catherine of Braganza (*q.v.*). Endeavored to secure toleration for English Catholics and Puritans by Declaration of Indulgence (1662), thereby provoking strongly Anglican Parliament to severe acts of repression, including Act of Uniformity (1662), Conventicle Act (1664), Five-mile Act (1665). Sold Dunkirk to France (1662); tried by war with Dutch (1665–67) to gain stadholdership for his nephew, William of Orange; forced by naval defeats to conclude Peace of Breda (1667); had to exile Clarendon to appease Parliament. Employed Clifford, Arlington, Buckingham, Ashley, and Lauderdale (making up the Cabal, from which the modern cabinet developed) to conduct affairs but carried on important negotiations himself (1667–74); accepted large subsidies from Louis XIV to favor French queen's claims to Spanish succession and French designs on Netherlands; used Triple Alliance (1668) with Holland and Sweden to gain popularity in England and raise Louis's offers; but reversed policy when he negotiated with Louis secret Treaty of Dover (1670), by which he was to declare himself Roman Catholic and join in war on Dutch; forced by parliamentary agitation to cancel his Declaration of Indulgence in favor of Catholics and to pass Test Act (1673), driving Catholics from office; obliged (1674) to conclude Dutch war (begun 1672); forced by popular feeling to consent to marriage of his niece Princess Mary with William of Orange (1677). Placed Earl of Danby in charge of foreign policy (1674–78) but himself made secret engagements with Louis XIV (1676, 1678); intervened against persecution occasioned by Titus Oates's trumped-up Popish Plot only when queen was accused (1678); dissolved Parliament in attempt to save Danby from impeachment (1679); dissolved Parliament that enacted Habeas Corpus Act (1679) and tried to thwart exclusion of his brother James, Duke of York, from succession by declaring James, Duke of Monmouth illegitimate; ruled without Parliament (1681–85); threatened with assassination by Rye House Plot (1683); suffered apoplectic stroke; made deathbed profession of Catholic faith. Died without legitimate children; had numerous mistresses, including Lucy Walter, the duchesses of Cleveland and Portsmouth, and Nell Gwyn, and many illegitimate children, most of whom he acknowledged and ennobled.

Charles. *Ger.* Karl \ˈkärl\. Name of seven Holy Roman emperors:

Charles I. See CHARLEMAGNE.

Charles II. *Called* le Chauve \lə-shōv\, *i.e.* the Bald. 823–877. King of France (840–877), as Charles I; Holy Roman emperor (875–877). Son of Louis I the Pious; joined his half-brother Louis the German against Lothair, defeating him at Fontenoy (841); by Treaty of Verdun (843), became king of the West Franks (beginning of modern France); in continual strife with Louis the German (after 855); saved from deposition (858) by Archbishop Hincmar of Reims; reign troubled by invading Normans, Bretons. On death of Emperor Louis II (875), invaded Italy; crowned emperor (875) and made king of Italy; failed in attempt to seize kingdom of Louis the German (876).

Charles III. *Called* le Gros \lə-grō\, *i.e.* the Fat. 839–888. King of Swabia (876–887); Holy Roman emperor (881–887). Son of Louis the German; received Italy from brother Carloman (879); gained Saxony on death of brother Louis the Younger (882); on death of West Frankish King Carloman (884) assumed control in place of Carloman's half-brother Charles III the Simple, thus sometimes accounted Charles II of France; made humiliating treaty with Vikings at Paris (886). His deposition by Arnulf (887) marked dismemberment of empire of Charlemagne.

Charles IV. *Known also as* Charles of Luxembourg. 1316–1378. Holy Roman emperor (1355–78). Son of John of Luxembourg, king of Bohemia; elected king of Germany (1346) in opposition to excommunicated Louis IV; succeeded as king of Bohemia (1347); established hereditary monarchy; founded U. of Prague (1348); began building of Karlštejn castle. Led army into Italy (1354), received crown of Lombardy (1355); crowned emperor (1355); extended German holdings, obtained margraviate of Brandenburg for son Wenceslas; issued Golden Bull (1356) regulating election of German king and establishing primacy of Bohemian throne.

Charles V. 1500–1558. Holy Roman emperor (1519–56), and king of Spain as Charles I (1516–56). Son of Philip I of Castile and grandson of Emperor Maximilian I and of Ferdinand and Isabella; inherited Burgundy and Netherlands (1506); succeeded Ferdinand in Spain (1516), Maximilian in Germany (1519); elected over Francis I of France and took title of emperor (1520); m. (1526) Isabella of Portugal. *Religious conflicts:* Summoned Diet of Worms and presided in person over it (1521); Diet of Augsburg (1530) failed to settle religious controversy; Council of Trent (1545–63) and Augsburg Interim (1548) failed to unite Catholics and Protestants. Won Schmalkaldic War (1546–47); faced armed resistance of Lutheran states (1551–52); made Peace of Augsburg (1555) with Protestants. *Wars with France* (1521–44): Defeated Francis I at Pavia (1525) and made him prisoner; Peace of Cambrai (1529); wars renewed; finally terminated by Treaty of Crépy (1544), favorable to Empire; in war (1552–56) with Henry II failed to capture Metz. *Activities in Italy and other countries:* Took Rome and made pope prisoner (1527); last emperor crowned by a pope (1530). Successful in campaign against Turks under Süleyman I but declined all-out battle before Vienna (1532); conquered pirates of Tunis (1535). Succeeded through matrimonial alliances in securing future passage of Portuguese throne to descendants; extended New World possessions through conquests of Mexico by Cortés (1519–21) and of Peru by Pizarro (1531–35), and through expeditions and other conquests in Central and South America. Relinquished kingdom of Naples (1554) and Netherlands (1555) to his son Philip; resigned control of Spain and the Indies to Philip (1556) and imperial crown to his brother Ferdinand (1556; formal abdication, 1558); retired to monastery of Yuste in western Spain (1557).

Charles VI. 1685–1740. Holy Roman emperor (1711–40); and (as Charles III) king of Hungary (1711–40). Son of Leopold I; m. (1708) Elisabeth Christine of Brunswick-Wolfenbüttel. Assigned by his father as heir (as Charles III) to throne of Spain (1700); brought on (1701–14) War of Spanish Succession (see CHARLES II of Spain); recognized as Spanish king by England, Netherlands, Portugal until accession as emperor (1711), whereupon allies switched to Philip V (1713); by Peace of Rastatt (1714) ceded Spanish Netherlands to Austria and gave up all claim of the Empire to Spain. Successful in war against Turks, concluded by Treaty of Passarowitz (1718). Issued Pragmatic Sanction (1713) to secure imperial succession to female heir in absence of a male. Unsuccessful in War of Polish Succession (1733–38), and in second war with Turks, terminated by Treaty of Belgrade (1739).

Charles VII. *In full* Charles Albert. *Ger.* Karl Albrecht \'kärl-'äl-,brekt\. *Known also as* Charles of Bavaria. 1697–1745. Holy Roman emperor (1742–45). Son of Maximilian Emanuel, Elector of Bavaria; succeeded to electorate (1726); acceded to Pragmatic Sanction but nonetheless became claimant of Austrian inheritance; crowned emperor (1742) with aid of France and Prussia and largely as their puppet took part in War of Austrian Succession (1740–48) against Maria Theresa but died before its end.

Charles. Name of four kings of Hungary:

Charles I. *Also* Charles Robert of An·jou \äⁿ-zhü, *Angl* 'an-,jü\ *or* Ca·ro·bert \kȧ-rō-ber\. 1288–1342. King (1308–42). Grandson of Charles II of Naples; claimed Hungarian throne (1301) by right of great-grandfather Stephen V; after deposition of Otto of Bavaria, elected by the diet (1308) and crowned (1310); founder of Anjou line of Hungary; imposed direct taxes, encouraged trade, and increased privileges of towns; secured succession of Polish throne for his son Louis I.

Charles II. See CHARLES III of Naples.

Charles III. See CHARLES VI, Holy Roman emperor.

Charles IV. See CHARLES I, Emperor of Austria and king of Hungary.

Charles \shȧrl, *Angl* 'chär(-ə)lz\. Name of five dukes of Lorraine:

Charles *or* **Charles I.** 953–992. Younger son of Frankish king Louis IV, of Carolingian line; received Lower Lorraine as duchy from Emperor Otto II (977); aided Otto against brother Lothair; defeated by Hugh Capet in attempt to secure Frankish crown (987); died in prison at Orléans.

Charles II (*or* **I**). *Called* le Har·di \lə-hȧr-dē\, *i.e.* the Bold. 1365–1431. Duke of Lorraine (1391–1431). Son of Duke John; allied himself with Burgundian faction; married his daughter Isabella to René I of Anjou, thus uniting duchies of Lorraine and Bar.

Charles III (*or* **II**). *Called* le Grand \lə-gräⁿ\, *i.e.* the Great. 1543–1608. Duke (1545–1608). Son of Duke Francis I; brought up at court of Henry II of France; m. Henry's daughter Claude (1559); took part in religious wars of France (1562–98); member of Holy League.

Charles IV (*or* **III**). 1604–1675. Duke (1624–34, 1641–44, 1659–70). Son of Duke Francis II; perpetually engaged in intrigue against France; provoked Louis XIII into seizing much territory; forced to cede capital Nancy for 4 years (1633); abdicated in favor of brother Francis (1634); fought with Germans at Nordlingen; again duke (1641–44), deposed by Louis; served army of Spain, with Condé in Fronde; again restored (1659); ousted by Créquy (1670), thereafter fought with Germans against France.

Charles V (*or* **IV**). *Also known as* Charles Leopold. 1643–1690. Nephew of Duke Charles IV. Titular duke of Lorraine; kept out of duchy by Louis XIV. Served in Imperial army against Turks and later against French; twice (1668, 1674) unsuccessful candidate for crown of Poland; commanded weak Imperial army at Vienna during siege by Turks; with John III Sobieski defeated Turks (1683); won great victory at Mohács against Turks (1687).

Charles. *Ger.* Karl Alexander. 1712–1780. Prince of Lorraine. Youngest son of Duke Leopold of Lorraine, grandson of Charles V of Lorraine, and brother of Emperor Francis I. Officer in Austrian army; fought against Turks (1737–39); in War of Austrian Succession (1740–48) made field marshal (1744) and governor general of Austrian Netherlands (1744–80) by his sister-in-law Maria Theresa; often in command against Frederick the Great in Silesian Wars; severely defeated at Hohenfriedeberg (1745) and (1746) at Rocourt by Marshal Saxe; again given supreme command of Austrian armies by Maria Theresa at beginning of Seven Years' War (1756–63); victor at Breslau, but completely defeated by Frederick at Leuthen (1757); military adviser at court in Vienna (1757–58).

Charles \'chär(-ə)lz\. Name of four kings of Naples or of Two Sicilies, three of the house of Anjou, one of house of Bourbon:

Charles I. *Also called* Charles of Anjou. 1226–1285. King of Naples and Sicily (1265–85). Son of Louis VIII of France; made count of Anjou and Maine (1232); m. (1246) Beatrice, daughter of Count of Provence, and took possession of that county; accompanied Louis IX on Sixth Crusade (1248–50); accepted crown of Naples and Sicily from Pope Urban IV and undertook to destroy last of Hohenstaufen power; defeated Manfred at Benevento (1266) and Conradin at Tagliacozzo (1268); became one of most powerful rulers in Europe; his harsh rule caused uprising known as Sicilian Vespers (1282); driven from Sicily by Spanish (1284).

Charles II. c.1254–1309. King of Naples (1285–1309). Son of Charles I; held prisoner by Spanish (1284–88); with help of pope attempted to win back Sicily, but was defeated in war with Frederick III (1296–1302).

Charles III. *Known as* Charles of Du·raz·zo \dü-'rät-tsō\. 1345–1386. King of Naples (1381–86) and king of Hungary as Charles II (1385–86). Great-grandson of Charles II, son of Mary of Naples; adopted by Queen Joan I of Naples, but abandoned in favor of Louis I of Anjou; with support of Pope Urban VI seized crown of Naples (1381); caused Joan's death (1382); waged war with Louis I (1382–84); crowned king of Hungary (1385), but assassinated at instance of widow of late King Louis.

Charles IV. See CHARLES III of Spain.

Charles \shȧrl, *Angl* 'chär(-ə)lz\. Name of three kings of Navarre:

Charles I. See CHARLES IV, King of France.

Charles II. *Called* le Mau·vais \lə-mō-ve\, *i.e.* the Bad. 1332–1387. King (1349–87). Son of Juana II of Navarre; m. (1352) Jeanne, daughter of John II of France; in dispute with father-in-law over lands in Angoulême and Normandy; held prisoner by John (1356–57); captain general of Paris (1358); at strife with dauphin (1358–60); spent rest of life making trouble in Spain and France (hence his nickname); made and broke alliances and treaties; accused of other crimes.

Charles III. *Called* le Noble \lə-nȯblᵊ\, *i.e.* the Noble. 1361–1425. King (1387–1425). Son of Charles II; m. (1375) Leonora, daughter of Henry II of Castile; recovered (1393) Cherbourg (given by his father to Richard II of England); long reign of peace and progress; created duke of Nemours; succeeded by his daughter Blanche, mother of Charles, Prince of Viana (*q.v.*).

Charles \'char(-ə)lz\. Name of three dukes of Parma of the Italian line of Bourbons:

Charles I. See CHARLES III, king of Spain.

Charles II. *In full* Charles-Louis-Ferdinand de Bourbon. 1799–1883. Son of Louis, king of Etruria; succeeded father as king (1803–07) under regency of mother, Maria Luisa; deprived of kingdom by Napoléon; succeeded mother as duke of Lucca (1824–47); restored to hereditary duchy of Parma on death of Maria Louisa of Austria (1847) but forced to abdicate following revolution (1848).

Charles III. 1823–54. Duke (1849–54). Son of Charles II; succeeded to duchy on confirmation of father's abdication; severe, dissolute ruler; assassinated.

Charles I. *Port.* Car·los I \'kȧr-lüsh\. 1863–1908. King of Portugal (1889–1908). Son of Louis I; reign troubled by economic distress, dispute with Great Britain (1889–90) over African colonies, political turmoil; appointed João Franco prime minister (1906), allowed him to suspend constitution and rule as dictator; assassinated with son Luís Filipe; succeeded by younger son Manuel II.

Charles. Kings of Romania. See CAROL.

Charles. *Span.* Car·los \'kär-lōs\. Name of four kings of Spain, first two Habsburgs, last two Bourbons:

Charles I. See CHARLES V, Holy Roman Emperor.

Charles II. 1661–1700. King (1665–1700). Son of Philip IV; during minority, under regency of queen mother, Mariana de Austria; assumed government (1675), with kingdom in weak and demoralized condition; took as adviser (1677–79) Don Juan, the younger; m. 1st Marie-Louise d'Orléans (1679); 2d Maria Anna of Bavaria-Neuburg (1689); joined Grand Alliance in war against Louis XIV, terminated by Peace of Rijswijk (1697); having no offspring, was prevailed upon to choose as successor Philip of Anjou, grandson of Louis XIV. His death was signal for beginning of War of Spanish Succession.

Charles III. *In youth known as* Don Carlos de Bor·bón \bōr-'b̲ōn\. 1716–1788. King (1759–88). Son of Philip V and Isabella of Parma; great-grandson of Louis XIV of France. Through mother became duke of Parma (1831–35); in War of Polish Succession conquered Two Sicilies (*i.e.* Naples and Sicily) and became king as Charles IV, first of the Neapolitan Bourbons (1734–59). Became king of Spain (1759) on death of half-brother Ferdinand VI, leaving Two Sicilies to his son Ferdinand I; strengthened kingdom by reforming finances, aiding agriculture and commerce; signed Family Compact (1761) with France against England; suffered losses in Seven Years' War (1756–63); established crown's authority over church; expelled Jesuits (1767).

Charles IV. 1748–1819. King (1788–1808). Second son of Charles III; m. Maria Luisa of Parma, whose complete influence over him caused vacillating policy; made Manuel de Godoy, a favorite of queen, prime minister (1792); long period of trouble with Revolutionary France, subservience to Napoléon, war with Portugal and England; Louisiana retroceded to France (1800); Spanish fleet destroyed at Trafalgar (1805); made secret treaty with Napoléon (1807); Spain invaded by French armies (1807); forced to abdicate (1808); died in Rome.

Charles. *Swed.* Karl \kärl\. Name of 15 kings of Sweden, the first six being of doubtful authenticity:

Charles VII. d. 1167. King (1161–67). Son of Sverker; took title of "king of Swedes and Goths"; fought Russians (1164); assassinated by Knut Eriksson.

Charles VIII. *Known as* Karl Knuts·son \'knüts-sȯn\. c.1408–1470. King of Sweden (1448–57, 1464–65, 1467–70) and of Norway (1449–50). Elected regent by nobles (1438–40); elected king to succeed Christopher of Bavaria (1448); elected by Norway (1449), which was forced to recognize Christian I of Denmark a year later; after war with Christian, deposed in his favor (1457); recalled by nationalist faction of nobility (1464–65, 1467–70).

Charles IX. 1550–1611. Regent of Sweden (1595–1604); king (1604–11). Third son of Gustav I Vasa; a leader of rebellion (1568) against half-brother Erik XIV; emerged as champion of Lutheranism as state religion; called Convention of Uppsala (1593) and secured recognition as regent for absent nephew, King Sigismund (1595); defeated Sigismund in battle at Stangebro (1598); deposed Sigismund and became virtual ruler (1599); formally king (1604); began long war with Poland (1600); began war with Denmark (1611).

Charles X Gustav. 1622–1660. King (1654–60). Son of John Casimir, Count Palatine, and Catherine, daughter of Charles IX; fought in Thirty Years' War (1642–48); became king on abdication of his cousin Christina; invaded and conquered Poland (1655–56); won great battle at Warsaw (1656); made war against Denmark (1657–58); won back lands of south Sweden by Treaty of Roskilde (1658).

Charles XI. 1655–1697. King (1660–97). Son of Charles X Gustav; king under regency of aristocrats (1660–72); assumed control (1672); forced by nobles into Dutch War (1672); defeated by coalition of Holy Roman Empire, Denmark, and Netherlands (1675–76), but more successful during latter part of war (1676–79); won favorable terms at Peace of Nijmegen (1678–79); aided by statesmen Gyllenstierna and Oxenstierna; m. (1680) Danish princess Ulrika Eleonora; began reorganization of Sweden (1680); forced estates of greater nobles to revert to crown; was granted (1693) practically absolute power; improved army and fleet and economic condition.

Charles XII. 1682–1718. King (1697–1718). Son of Charles XI; declared of age at fifteen; confronted by alliance of Poland, Denmark, and Russia (1699); invaded Denmark and forced peace of Travendal (1700); attacked Russians, winning great victory on the Narva (1700); defeated Saxons and Poles at Klissow (1702), dethroned Augustus II and made Stanislas Leszczyński king (1704); forced Peace of Altranstädt (1706). Invaded Russia (1707–08); defeated Peter the Great, but on attempt to reach Moscow met with repeated disasters; with small army, laid siege to Poltava; completely defeated in ensuing battle (1709); fled to Turkish territory; persuaded sultan to declare war on Russia but to no effect; ruled ineffectually from Turkish territory (1709–14); fled back to Sweden (1714); escaped siege at Stralsund; raised another army that kept Russians at bay; made vast plans for recovery; invaded Norway; killed at siege of Fredrikshald.

Charles XIII. 1748–1818. King (1809–18). Second son of Adolf Frederick and younger brother of Gustav III; commanded Swedish fleet against Russia (1788–90); made regent (1792–96) after assassination of Gustav III; again regent on deposition of Gustav IV (1809); made king (1809); signed new constitution, restoring limited monarchy; compelled by peace with Russia (1809) to give up Finland and Åland Islands; made peace with Denmark (1809) and France (1810); during reign, Norway united with Sweden (1814).

Charles XIV John. *Orig.* Jean-Baptiste-Jules Bernadotte. 1763–1844. King of Sweden and Norway (1818–44). French soldier, entered army (1780), served in French Revolution; brigadier general (1794); ambassador to Vienna (1798); minister of war (1799); councillor of state (1800–02); commander of army of the West (1802–03); marshal of empire (1804); named prince of Pon·te·cor·vo \ˌpōn-tā-'kȯr-vō\ (1806); took part in Austrian and Polish campaigns (1805–09). Elected crown prince (1810) of Sweden, taking name of Charles John; allied with Czar Alexander of Russia (1812); commanded an allied army against Napoléon (1813); aided in winning battle of Leipzig; attacked Denmark and by Treaty of Kiel (1814) secured Norway; succeeded Charles XIII as king (1818); his reign peaceful and profitable to both kingdoms, although he was criticized and at times opposed for ultraconservative views.

Charles XV. 1826–1872. King of Sweden and Norway (1859–72). Son of Oscar I; instituted legal reforms, esp. of the estates (1865); promulgated decree (1866) by which two-chamber parliament was established; popular in both kingdoms; writer, poet, and artist of ability.

Charles \shärl, *Angl* 'chär(-ə)lz\. 1270–1325. Count of Valois (1285–1325), of Anjou and Maine (1290–1325). Son of Philip III of France; m. (1290) Margaret, daughter of Charles II of Naples; campaigned in Italy in papal service, capturing Florence (1301); unsuccessfully sought emperor's crown (1308); commanded several French expeditions against Guienne, Flanders; close adviser to brother Philip IV, nephews Louis X, Philip V, Charles IV; father of Philip VI and progenitor of royal house of Valois.

Charles. Prince of Via·na \bē-'än-ä\. 1421–1461. Spanish prince. Son of John II of Aragon and Blanche of Navarre; named by grandfather Charles III and by mother as successor to Navarre, but throne usurped (1441) by father; failed to secure throne by force (1452); governor of Catalonia (1458); recognized as heir by father (1458) but died first. Sometimes called Charles IV of Navarre.

Charles of Anjou. See CHARLES I, King of Naples.

Charles of Bavaria. See CHARLES VII, Holy Roman Emperor.

Charles of Blois \blwä\. *Also called* Charles of Châ·til·lon \shä-tē-yōⁿ\. 1319–1364. Duke of Brittany (1341–64). Son of Guy de Châtillon and nephew of Philip VI of France; engaged in War of Breton Succession (1341–64) with John of Montfort and John IV of Brittany, involving also Philip and Edward III of England; imprisoned in Tower of London (1347–56); killed in battle of Auray with John IV.

Charles of Durazzo. See CHARLES III, King of Naples.

Charles of Hohenzollern-Sigmaringen. See CAROL I.

Charles of Lorraine. See CHARLES, Prince of Lorraine.

Charles of Luxembourg. See CHARLES IV, Holy Roman Emperor.

Charles the Bad. See CHARLES II, King of Navarre.

Charles the Bald. See CHARLES II, Holy Roman Emperor.

Charles the Bold. See CHARLES, Duke of Burgundy; CHARLES, Duke of Lorraine.

Charles the Fair. See CHARLES IV, King of France.

Charles the Fat. See CHARLES III, Holy Roman Emperor.

Charles the Good. See CHARLES, Count of Flanders.

Charles the Great. See CHARLEMAGNE; CHARLES III, Duke of Lorraine.

Charles the Hammer. See CHARLES MARTEL.

Charles the Noble. See CHARLES III, King of Navarre.

Charles the Simple. See CHARLES III, King of France.

Charles the Well-Beloved. See CHARLES VI, King of France.

Charles the Wise. See CHARLES V, King of France.

Charles \'char(-ə)lz\, Ezzard Mack. 1921–1975. American boxer, b. Lawrenceville, Ga. World heavyweight champion (1950–51), winning title from Joe Louis and losing it to "Jersey" Joe Walcott.

Charles \shärl, *Angl* 'chär(-ə)lz\, Jacques-Alexandre-César. 1746–1823. French physicist, chemist, and inventor. Popularized in France Franklin's discoveries concerning electricity; with Nicolas and Anne-Jean Robert, made several balloon ascents, being first to use hydrogen for balloon inflation (1783); developed (c.1787) Charles's law relating temperature to volume of gas. Cf. GAY-LUSSAC.

Charles \'chär(-ə)lz\, Robert Henry. 1855–1931. British clergyman and scholar, b. Ireland. Ordained (1883); professor of biblical Greek, Trinity Coll., Dublin (1898–1906); lecturer at Oxford (1905–14). Canon of Westminster (from 1913) and archdeacon (from 1919). Author of translation of *Book of Enoch* (1893), *Critical and Exegetical Commentary on Daniel* (1929), etc.; general editor of Oxford edition of *Apocrypha and Pseudepigraphia of the Old Testament* (1913).

Charles, Thomas. 1755–1814. Welsh preacher. Joined Methodists (1784); established system of Welsh circulating schools; organized distribution of Bibles; helped found British and Foreign Bible Society (1804); organized Welsh Calvinistic Methodists (1810–11); compiled Welsh biblical dictionary (1805–08).

Charles Albert. See CHARLES VII, Holy Roman Emperor.

Charles Albert. *Ital.* Carlo Alberto. 1798–1849. King of Sardinia-Piedmont (1831–49). Son of Prince Charles Emmanuel of Savoy-Carignan line; succeeded to father's title (1800) as prince of Carignano; at Piedmontese uprising (1821) and abdication of Victor Emmanuel I, made regent for short time; promulgated liberal constitution; arrested by new king, Charles Felix; exiled to Florence. Succeeded to throne (1831) on death of Charles Felix, last of main Savoy line; attempted to introduce order in kingdom; reorganized finances, granted new constitution, and created an army. Strong supporter of Italian unity; declared war against Austria (1848); defeated at Custozza (1848) and Novara (1849); resigned (1849) in favor of his son Victor Emmanuel II; retired to monastery in Portugal.

Charles Anthony. *Ger.* Karl Anton. 1811–1885. Prince of Hohenzollern-Sigmaringen. Relinquished principality to king of Prussia (1849). As Prussian general, prominent in army reorganization dispute (1853–62); Prussian minister president (1858–62); military governor of Rhineland (1863–71); took part (1870) in controversy with France over candidacy of his son Leopold for throne of Spain. His second son became King Carol I of Romania.

Charles Augustus. *Ger.* Karl August. 1757–1828. Duke (1758–1815), Grand Duke (1815–28), of Saxe-Weimar-Eisenach. Under regency of his mother Anna Amalia (1758–75); fought with Prussia against Napoléon (1806, 1813); territories increased, made grand duke by Congress of Vienna (1815); granted first liberal constitution in a German state (1816); forced by reactionary states to curtail liberties (1819). Known for patronage of arts and artists, notably Goethe, Hegel, Herder, Schelling, Schiller.

Charles d'Orléans. See ORLÉANS.

Charles Edward. *In full* Charles Edward Louis Philip Casimir Stuart. *Called* the Young Pretender; *also called* the Young Chevalier *and* Bonnie Prince Charlie. 1720–1788. English prince. Son of James Edward, the Old Pretender; grandson of James II; succeeded as head of Jacobite faction; accompanied abortive French expedition against England (1744); landed in Scotland and raised army of followers among clans (1745); led uprising known as the Forty-five; took Edinburgh and proclaimed James VIII (Sept. 1745); won victory at Prestonpans (Oct.) and briefly invaded England (Nov.–Dec.); completely defeated by Duke of Cumberland at Culloden (April 16, 1746); escaped to France after five months in hiding; expelled from France under terms of Treaty of Aix-la-Chapelle (1748); took title count of Albany; wandered through Europe attempting to plot Stuart restoration but alienating supporters by violent temper and drunken, debauched behavior; settled in Italy (1766).

Charles Emmanuel. *Ital.* Carlo Emanuele. Name of four dukes of Savoy, two of them kings of Sardinia-Piedmont:

Charles Emmanuel I. *Called* the Great. 1562–1630. Duke (1580–1630). Son of Emmanuel Philibert; seized Saluzzo (1588) but forced to abandon territorial ambitions by peace of 1593; sided with Spain against France; failed in attempt to seize and hold Geneva (1602); made French alliance against Spain and Austria (1610); seized Monferrato from Spain (1613) but forced by war to relinquish it (1617); fought French invasion (1628–29). Succeeded by son Victor Amadeus I; his third son Tommaso founded house of Savoy-Carignano.

Charles Emmanuel II. 1634–1675. Duke (1638–75). Son of Victor Amadeus I; reign troubled by civil dissention.

Charles Emmanuel III. 1701–1773. Duke (1730–73) and as Charles Emmanuel I king of Sardinia-Piedmont (1730–73). Son of Victor Amadeus II; as ally of France and Spain in War of Polish Succession, occupied Milan and won victory at Guastella (1734); in Treaty of Vienna (1738) obtained Novara and Tortona; fought Spanish in War of Austrian Succession (1740–48); instituted administrative reforms in kingdom.

Charles Emmanuel IV. 1751–1819. Duke (1796–98) and as Charles Emmanuel II king (1796–1802). Son of Victor Amadeus III; repressed Jacobin disturbances (1797); forced to cede mainland possessions to France (1798); abdicated in favor of brother Victor Emmanuel (1802); entered religious order.

Charles Felix. *Ital.* Carlo Felice. 1756–1831. King of Sardinia-Piedmont (1821–31). Son of Victor Amadeus III; viceroy of Sardinia (1799–1806, 1817–21); became king on abdication of his brother Victor Emmanuel I; last ruler of main Savoy line; secured succession for Charles Albert (*q.v.*).

Charles Frederick. *Ger.* Karl Friedrich. 1728–1811. Ruler of Baden, as margrave (1738–1803), elector (1803–06), grand duke (1806–11). Ruled under regency (1738–46); inherited lands of Baden-Baden line (1771); increased territory and influence of his state, with aid of Austria and later of Napoléon; introduced many liberal reforms, fostered schools, agriculture, industry; introduced Code Napoléon. Grandfather of Grand Duke Charles (*q.v.*).

Charles John. See CHARLES XIV JOHN of Sweden.

Charles Leopold. See CHARLES V, Duke of Lorraine.

Charles Mar·tel \shȧrl-mȧr-tel, *Angl* 'chär(-ə)lz-mär-'tel\. Lat. Mar·tel·lus \mär-'tel-əs\, *i.e.* the Hammer [Fr. *martel*]. c.688–741. Frankish ruler. Illegitimate son of Pepin of Herstal, mayor of the palace of Austrasia; excluded from Pepin's will, but took up arms (714), defeated Chilperic II of Neustria, and became mayor (716); accepted as mayor by Austrasia (719), thus uniting Frankish lands; after Arab invasion of southern France (begun 719), totally defeated caliph's army under 'Abd ar-Raḥmān at Tours, near Poitiers (732), overthrowing Muslim menace to France; subdued Burgundy (733), Frisians (734), campaigned against Saxons. Bequeathed rule to sons Pepin and Carloman; grandfather of Charlemagne.

Charles Robert of Anjou. See CHARLES I of Hungary.

Charles Theodore. *Ger.* Karl Theodor. 1724–1799. Elector of Palatinate branch of house of Wittelsbach (1743–77). Inherited duchy of Bavaria on death (1777) of Elector Maximilian III Joseph; elector of united Palatine lands (1777–99); his dispute with his heir, Charles of Zweibrücken, caused War of Bavarian Succession (1778–79), a war without any battles; his sovereignty recognized by Treaty of Teschen (1779).

Charles William Ferdinand. *Ger.* Karl Wilhelm Ferdinand. 1735–1806. Duke of Brunswick-Lüneburg-Wolfenbüttel (1780–1806). Distinguished himself as soldier in Prussian service, becoming favorite of Frederick II; instituted reforms in duchy; field marshal (1787); defeated Dutch democratic faction and returned William V of Orange to power (1787); commanded Prussian army against France (1792–93), defeated at Valmy (1792) but won several battles on German soil (1793); recalled to command (1806); defeated and mortally wounded at Auerstädt (1806).

Char·let \shȧr-le\, Nicolas-Toussaint. 1792–1845. French artist. Best known for military subjects, as in series of lithographs celebrating glorious events of Napoleonic era, and in paintings, as *Épisode de la retraite de Russie* and *Convoi de blessés faisant halte dans un ravin.*

Char·le·voix \shȧr-lə-vwȧ, *Angl* 'shär-lə-,vȯi\, Pierre-François-Xavier de. 1682–1761. French traveler. Entered Jesuit order; sent by regent of France to find new route from Acadia westward (1719); traveled up St. Lawrence river, through Great Lakes, down Illinois and Mississippi rivers to New Orleans (1720–22); returned to France, and a life of teaching and writing. Author of *Histoire de Saint-Domingue* (1730), *Histoire de description générale de la Nouvelle France* (1744), etc.

Char·lier \shȧr-lyā\, Jean. *Known as* Jean de Ger·son \zher-sōⁿ\. 1363–1429. French theologian, b. Gerson. Chancellor of U. of Paris (1395–1429). Played instrumental role in healing the Great Schism of the Western Church, his ideas on supremacy of conciliar authority prevailing at the Council of Constance (1415–18); spent last 10 years at Lyons. Wrote many theological and moralistic works.

Char·lot \shȧr-lō, *Angl* 'shär-,lō\, André Eugene Maurice. 1882–1956. British theatrical manager and producer, b. France. Manager of Folies-Bergère and other theaters in Paris; to London (1912) as joint manager of Alhambra; known for introducing intimate revue to British stage; produced (1915–35) 36 revues, including *5064 Gerrard* (1915), *Some* (1916), *Buzz-Buzz* (1918), *Pot Luck* (1921), Noel Coward's *London Calling* (1923), *Charlot's Revue* (1924–25); produced "Charlot's Hour" programs for BBC.

Charlotte. Empress of Mexico. See CARLOTA.

Char·lotte So·phi·a \'shär-lət-sə-'fī-ə\. 1744–1818. Queen of George III of England. Niece of Duke of Mecklenburg-Strelitz; m. George III (1761); mother of 15 children including George IV.

Char·mi·des \'kär-mə-,dēz\. 450?–404 B.C. Greek philosopher and politician. Cousin of Critias, disciple of Socrates, and uncle of Plato, who introduced him in one of the dialogues (*Charmides*). One of the Thirty Tyrants; killed in a struggle against Thrasybulus.

Char·nay \shȧr-ne\, Claude-Joseph-Désiré. 1828–1915. French archaeologist. Excavated among ruins of ancient cities of Mexico (1857–61, 1880–82); theorized Asiatic origin of prehistoric Mexicans. Author of *Les anciennes villes du nouveau monde* (1885).

Char·nock \'chär-nək\, Job. d. 1693. English merchant. To India for East India Co. (1656); chief agent at Hooghly (1686); removed company factory from besieged Hooghly to mouth of Ganges (1690), founding what became Calcutta. His tombstone made of charnockite, which was named for him.

Charnwood, 1st Baron. See Godfrey Benson under Frank R. BENSON.

Charolais, Count of. See CHARLES, Duke of Burgundy.

Cha·ron·ton \shȧ-rō^{n}-tō^{n}\, Enguerrand. *Also spelled* Char·ren·ton \-rä^{n}-\ *or* Quar·ton \kȧr-tō^{n}\. fl. 1444–66. French painter. A leading exponent of French Gothic art of Avignon school; known for *Virgin of Mercy* (1452) and *Coronation of the Virgin* (1453–54).

Char·pen·tier \shȧr-pä^{n}-tyā\, Gustave. 1860–1956. French composer. Founded (1902) Conservatoire Populaire Mimi Pinson. Composer of orchestral suite *Impressions d'Italie* (1887–89); dramatic works *Didon* (1887), *La Vie du poète* (1888–89), *Le Couronnement de la muse* (1897); operas *Louise* (1900), *Julien* (1913); and choral works.

Charpentier, Johann von. 1786–1855. German geologist. Mining engineer in Switzerland; director of salt mines at Bex (1813–55). Developed theory of glaciation to account for massive stone blocks strewn through Jura range; largely source of Louis Agassiz's work. Author of *Essai sur les glaciers* (1841).

Charpentier, Marc-Antoine. 1634?–1704. French organist and composer. Composed music for Molière's theatrical company (c.1672–c.1686); music director to Duchess of Guise (1680–88); composer to Dauphin's chapel (from 1679); composition teacher to duc d'Orléans (1692 ff.); music master, Sainte-Chapelle, Paris (from 1698). Composed theatrical music for Molière's *Le Mariage forcé* (1672), *Le Malade imaginaire* (1673), Corneille's *Médée* (1693), etc.; operas, pastorals, cantatas, other stage works; 12 masses, dozens of motets, antiphons, oratorios, and other religious music.

Char·rière \shȧr-yer\, Isabelle Agnès Élizabeth de. *Nee* van Tuyll \'tȯil\. *Pseudonyms* Zé·lide \zā-lēd\ *and* Ab·bé de La Tour \ȧ-bā-də-lȧ-tür\. 1740–1805. Swiss writer, b. Netherlands. Rejected several admirers, including James Boswell; m. her brother's Swiss tutor, St. Hyacinthe de Charrière (1766). Author of *Lettres neuchâteloises* (1784) and *Caliste, ou lettres écrites de Lausanne* (1785–88), *Trois femmes* (1797), etc.

Char·ron \shȧ-rō^{n}\, Pierre. 1541–1603. French theologian and philosopher. Renowned as pulpit orator; friend of Montaigne. Author of *Les trois vérités* (1594), *Traité de la Sagesse* (1601), both expounding a form of skepticism aimed at rationalism in theology.

Char·tier \shȧr-tyā\, Alain. c.1385–after 1433. French writer and diplomat. In service of Charles VI and of dauphin (later Charles VII). His prose works, chiefly written to inspire loyalty among the people to their sovereign, included *Quadrilogue invectif* (1422), *De vita curiali,* and *Traité de l'espérance* (1428). Now remembered chiefly for his poetry, which included *Livre des quatre dames, La Belle Dame sans merci, Le Lay de paix, Bréviaire des nobles.*

Chartier, Émile-Auguste. *Pseudonym* Alain \ȧ-la^{n}\. 1868–1951. French philosopher and essayist. Author of *Les Propos d'Alain* (1908–19), *Mars ou la Guerre jugée* (1921), *Eléments d'une doctrine radicale* (1925), *Propos sur la littérature* (1934), *Propos d'économie* (1935), *Vigiles de l'esprit* (1942), etc.

Chartres, Duc de. See Robert-Philippe-Louis-Eugène-Ferdinand under ORLÉANS family, IV.

Chase \'chās\, Lucia. 1907–1986. American ballet dancer and manager, b. Waterbury, Conn. Made debut as dancer with Mordkin Ballet (1937); principal dancer of Ballet Theatre (later American Ballet Theatre) (1940–60); known for roles in dramatic ballets as *Pillar of Fire* and *Dark Elegies;* with Oliver Smith co-directed American Ballet Theatre (1945–80); offered eclectic fare, introducing works by contemporary choreographers as Antony Tudor, Agnes DeMille, Jerome Robbins, etc.

Chase, Mary, *nee* Coyle \'kȯi(ə)l\. 1907–1981. American playwright, b. Denver, Colo. m. (1928) Robert L. Chase. Author of plays *Me Three* (1937), *Harvey* (1944, Pulitzer prize), *The Next Half Hour* (1945), *Bernardine* (1952), *Mrs. McThing* (1952), *Midgie Purvis* (1961).

Chase, Mary Ellen. 1887–1973. American educator and writer, b. Blue Hill, Me. Professor, Smith Coll. (1926–55). Author of essays, books on writing, novels including *His Birthday* (1915), *Girl from the Bighorn Country* (1916), *Uplands* (1927), *Mary Peters* (1934), *Silas Crockett* (1935), *Dawn in Lyonesse* (1938), *Windswept* (1941), *The Edge of Darkness* (1957); autobiographical *A Goodly Heritage* (1932), *The Goodly Fellowship* (1939), *The White Gate* (1954).

Chase, Philander. 1775–1852. American clergyman, b. Cornish, N.H. Ordained Episcopal priest (1799); missionary in Ohio region (1817–19) organizing parishes; bishop of diocese of Ohio (1819–31); president of Cincinnati Coll. (1821–22); founded Kenyon College (1824). Elected bishop of Illinois (1835); founded (1838) Jubilee Coll. Presiding bishop of Episcopal Church (1843–52).

Chase, Salmon Portland. 1808–1873. American politician and jurist, b. Cornish, N.H. Nephew of Philander Chase. Prominent in defending fugitive slaves; active in free-soil movement (1848); U.S. senator (1849–55, 1860); helped organize Ohio Republican party (1854); governor of Ohio (1855–59). U.S. secretary of the treasury (1861–64); originated national banking system and issued first "greenbacks" (1863). Put forward by a political group as presidential candidate in place of Lincoln; resigned (1864) because of strained relations with the president. Chief justice, U.S. Supreme Court (1864–73).

Chase, Samuel. 1741–1811. American jurist, b. Somerset Co., Md. Member, committee of correspondence (1774); delegate to Continental Congress (1774–78, 1784, 1785); signer of Declaration of Independence; opposed adoption of Constitution. Associate justice, U.S. Supreme Court (1796–1811); impeached (1804) for partisan conduct of circuit court at instance of Pres. Thomas Jefferson; acquitted (1805) in trial that strengthened independence of judiciary.

Chase, William Merritt. 1849–1916. American painter, b. Franklin, Ind. Painter of landscapes, portraits, and still-life subjects in colorful, bravura style.

Chasles \shäl\, Michel. 1793–1880. French mathematician. Professor of geodesy and applied mechanics, École Polytechnique (1841); professor of advanced geometry, Sorbonne (1846). Author of numerous memoirs, many on projective geometry, and textbooks *Traité de géométrie supérieure* (1852), *Traité des sections coniques* (1865), etc.

Chasles, Philarète, *in full* Victor-Euphémien-Philarète. 1798–1873. French scholar and writer. Curator, Bibliothèque Mazarine (1837); professor, Collège de France (1841). Pioneer in field of comparative literature.

Chas·sé \shȧ-sā\, David Hendrik. 1765–1849. Dutch general. Served in Patriot army that deposed William V of Orange (1785); fled to France and entered army (1789); took part in French campaigns in Belgium, Rhineland (1792–94); commander of Batavian Republic army (1795–1805); commanded Dutch division of French army in Spain (1808–13) and against allies in defense of France (1814). Commanded Dutch army on side of allies after abdication of Napoléon (1814); at Waterloo (1815). Governor of Antwerp (1819–32); conducted defense of citadel at Antwerp against Belgians in revolution of 1830 and, later, against French (1832).

Chasse·boeuf \shȧs-bœf, -bœ̄\, Constantin-François. Comte de Vol·ney \vȯl-ne\. 1757–1820. French scholar and politician. Traveled in Egypt and Syria (1782–85); founded republican journal *La Sentinelle du peuple* (1788); member of Estates-General and Constituent Assembly (1789–91); imprisoned during Terror (1793–94); visited U.S. (1795–98), expelled as French agent; created count (1808), peer of France (1814). Author of *Les Ruines, ou méditations sur les révolutions des empires* (1791), etc.

Chasse·loup-Lau·bat \shȧs-lü-lō-bȧ\, François de. 1754–1833. French soldier and military engineer. Entered army (1774); chief of engineers, army of Italy (1799); engineer general to Napoléon (1800); built fortifications of Quadrilateral, northern Italy (1801–05), fortress of Alessandria (1805–06); directed operations at siege of Danzig (1807); raised to peerage by Louis XVIII. His son ¶Justin-Prosper (1805–1873) was minister of marine under Napoléon III (1851, 1859–67), of colonies (1858–59); president of council of state (1869); member of National Assembly (1871); opposed establishment of a republic.

Chasse·pot \shȧs-pō\, Antoine-Alphonse. 1833–1905. French inventor. Invented musket named for him *chassepot,* adopted by French army (1866–74).

Chas·sé·riau \shȧ-sār-yō\, Théodore. 1819–1856. French painter, b. Dominican Republic. Studied under Ingres. Executed decorative murals in Église Saint Merri, Église Saint Roch, and above staircase in Palais d'Orsay. Paintings, often fusing neoclassicism with an exoticism influenced by Delacroix, included *Vénus marine, Suzanne au bain, Les deux soeurs, La Paix, Océanide.*

Chas·te·lard \shȧs-tə-lȧr, shät(ə)-lȧr\, Pierre *or* Piraud de Bos·co·zel de \bȯ-skȯ-zel-də-\. 1540–1564. French poet. Courtier of Francis II; conceived hopeless passion for Mary, Queen of Scots, and followed her to Scotland after death of her husband (1561); arrested after series of indiscretions and executed in Edinburgh.

Chas·tel·lain *or* **Chas·te·lain** \shȧs-tə-le^{n}, shät-la^{n}\, Georges. c.1405 or c.1415–1475. Flemish-born Burgundian chronicler and poet. Soldier in service of Philip the Good (to 1435); historiographer of Burgundian house (1455). Author of *Chronique des ducs de Bourgogne,* covering history of Burgundian house from 1419 to 1474. His poetry included epitaphs, epistles, and panegyrics.

Cha·teau·bri·and \shá-tō-brē-ä^{n}\, François-Auguste-René de. Vicomte. 1768–1848. French writer and statesman. Served in French army (1786); traveled in U.S. (1791–92); returned to France and fought in Royalist army defeated at Thionville (1792); émigré in England (1793–1800). Returned to France (1800); served under Napoléon as minister to Republic of Valais (1803–04); resigned after execution of duc d'Enghien (1804); traveled in Holy Land, Greece, and northern Africa. Supported Bourbon cause (1814); created peer of France (1815); ambassador to Berlin (1821), Great Britain (1822); minister of foreign affairs (1823–24); ambassador at Rome (1828–29). Author of *Essai historique, politique et moral sur les révolutions anciennes et modernes* (1797), *Atala,* unfinished Romantic idyll on American Indian themes (1801), *Génie du christianisme* (1802), *Les Martyrs* (1809), *Itinéraire de Paris à Jérusalem* (1811), *Les Natchez* (1826), *Les Adventures du dernier des Abencérages* (1826), *Mémoires d'outre-tombe* (1849–50).

Cha·teau·bri·ant \shá-tō-brē-ä^{n}\, Alphonse de. 1877–1951. French novelist. Author of *Monsieur des Lourdines* (1911, Prix Goncourt), *La Brière* (1923), *La Réponse du Seigneur* (1933), *La Gerbe des forces* (1937), etc.

Châteauguay, Sieur de. Antoine Lemoyne. See under Charles LE MOYNE.

Châ·teau·re·nault *or* **Châ·teau-Re·nault** \shä-tōr(-ə)-nō\, François-Louis Rous·se·let de \rü-sled-ə-\. Marquis. 1637–1716. French naval officer. Served in army (1658–61), in navy (from 1661); served against Barbary pirates, Dutch; fought English fleet in Bantry Bay (1689); commanded vanguard at Beachy Head (1690); succeeded Tourville as vice admiral of France (1701); during War of Spanish Succession, was disastrously defeated in Bay of Vigo by British and allied fleet under Sir George Rooke (1702); marshal of France (1703).

Châteauroux, Duchesse de. See Marie-Anne de MAILLY-NESLE.

Cha·teil·lon \shá-tā-yō^{n}\, Sébastien. *Lat.* Sebastianus Cas·tel·lio \kas-'tel-yō, -ē-ō\ *or* Cas·tel·li·on \-'tel-yən, -ē-ən\ *or* Cas·ta·li·on \-'tā-lē-ən, -'tāl-yən\. 1515–1563. French theologian. Adopted Protestantism; met Calvin at Strasbourg (1540); to Basel (1545) where he published Latin and French translations of the Bible; professor of Greek, Basel (1553); published essay on tolerance *De haereticis* (1554) after burning of Servet; disputed with Calvin.

Châ·tel \shä-tel\, Jean. 1575?–1594. French fanatic. Attempted to assassinate Henry IV (Dec. 27, 1594); executed at Paris. Because of a belief that his attempt had been inspired by Jesuit influence, the Jesuits were banished from France.

Châ·te·let \shät-le\, Gabrielle-Émilie du. Marquise. *Nee* Le Ton·ne·lier de Bre·teuil \lə-tȯn-əl-yā-də-brə-tœy\. 1706–1749. French writer. m. (1725) marquis du Châtelet-Lomont; mistress of Voltaire (from 1733), residing with him at Montjeu and later at Château de Cirey. Author of *Institutions de physique* (1740), *Réponse à la lettre de Mairan* (1741), *Dissertation sur la nature et la propagation du feu* (1744); translated Newton's *Principia* (pub. 1759).

Chatham, Earl of. See William PITT (1708–1778).

Chatrian, Louis-Alexandre. See under Émile ERCKMANN.

Chat·ter·jee \'chät-ər-(,)jē\, Bankim Chandra. *Also called* Bankim-Chandra Cat·to·pa·dhyay \,kät-tō-'päd-,yī\. 1838–1894. Indian novelist. In civil service (1858–91). Created Indian school of fiction on European model and established Bengali prose as literary language; novels included *Durgesnandini* (1864), *Kapalkundala* (1866), *Mrinalini* (1869), *Bishabriksa* (1873), *Indira* (1873), *Yugalanguriya* (1874), *Radharani* (1875), *Candraskhar* (1875), *Rajani* (1877), *Krishnakanter Vil* (1878), *Rajsimha* (1881), *Ānandamāth* (1882), *Debi Caudhurani* (1884), *Sitaram* (1886).

Chat·ter·ton \'chat-ərt-^{ə}n\, Thomas. 1752–1770. English poet. From early years fascinated by antiquities; began to represent his imitations of ancient authors as antiques (1764) and to fabricate a romance in prose and verse of Thomas Rowley, an imaginary 15th-century monk (1765). Submitted purported transcript of a treatise on painting in England by Rowley to Horace Walpole (1769), who refused it; contributed political diatribes in manner of Junius to London periodicals. Lived abstemiously in London, turning out poems, burlettas, satires, political tirades, assuming style of Junius, Smollet, Churchill, Macpherson's "Ossian," Pope, Gray, Collins; wrote "Excelente Balade of Charitie" as if from parchment of priest Rowley; desperate after rejection of this poem by *Town and Country Magazine,* drank arsenic. His verses subsequently acknowledged to include poetry of a high order of originality, dramatic and imaginative power, and lyric beauty.

Chau·cer \'chȯ-sər\, Geoffrey. c.1342–1400. English poet. Page to wife of Lionel, Duke of Clarence (1357); served in campaign in France (1359), captured, ransomed (1360); employed for ten years on diplomatic missions to Spain, Italy, Flanders, France, Lombardy, meeting Boccaccio and perhaps Petrarch. Comptroller of the customs and subsidy of wools, London (1374); received pensions from Edward III and John of Gaunt (1374); resided (1374–86) above gate of Aldgate, London; comptroller of petty customs, London (1382); elected to Parliament from Kent (1386). Suffered period of misfortune during absence of his patron, John of Gaunt; dismissed from both comptrollerships (1386); sold his pensions to raise money; on John of Gaunt's return, became clerk of works at royal palaces (1389–91) and held small sinecures; fell again into poverty until rescued by pensions from Richard II and Henry IV (1394, 1399); buried in Poets' Corner in Westminster Abbey. His writings fall into three periods: (1) French influence (c.1359–72), marked by use of octosyllabic couplet: translation of *Roman de la Rose, The Book of the Duchess,* a poem in honor of John of Gaunt's first wife (1369). (2) Italian influence (c.1372–86), marked by use of rhyme royal: the poems *Hous of Fame* and *Parlement of Foules;* prose translation of *Consolation* of Boethius; the story of Palamon and Arcite, from Boccaccio's *Teseide,* later incorporated in *Canterbury Tales* as the *Knight's Tale;* the unfinished *Legend of Good Women,* verse prologue and series of verse narratives of women faithful to love; *Troilus and Criseyde,* long narrative poem modeled on Boccaccio's *Filostrato.* (3) English period (1386–1400), marked by use of heroic couplet: *The Canterbury Tales,* representing 23 stories of pilgrims assembled at the Tabard Inn in Southwark; a prose treatise on the astrolabe; and "Complaint of Chaucer to his Purse."

His putative son ¶ Thomas Chaucer (1367?–1434), chief butler to Richard II, Henry IV, Henry V, Henry VI; M.P. (in most parliaments, 1400–31); speaker of House of Commons (1407, 1410, 1411, 1414); fought at Agincourt.

Chau·det \shō-de\, Denis-Antoine. 1763–1810. French sculptor and painter. Sculptures included *Bélisaire, Paul et Virginie, Cyparisse pleurant un faon, La Paix,* and statue of Napoléon I which surmounted Vendôme column in Paris until destroyed at the Restoration.

Chauliac, Guy de. See GUY DE CHAULIAC.

Chaulieu, Abbé de. See Guillaume AMFRYE.

Chau·meix \shō-meks\, André, *in full* Jean-Henri-André. 1874–1955. French journalist. Editor of *Journal des debats* (1905–09); directed *Revue de Paris* (1920–26); editor of *Le Figaro* (1926–30); director of *Revue des Deux Mondes* (from 1937).

Chau·mette \shō-met\, Pierre-Gaspard. 1763–1794. French revolutionary. Member of Cordeliers' Club (1790); contributed to revolutionary journals; extreme radical and leader in Commune of Paris (1792–94); instituted reforms in public administration; one of the founders of the worship of Reason; guillotined by order of Robespierre.

Chaun·cey \'chȯn-sē, 'chän-\, Isaac. 1772–1840. American naval officer, b. Black Rock, Conn. Lieutenant, U.S. navy (1799); served against Tripoli (1802–05); during War of 1812, commander of naval forces on Lakes Ontario and Erie; navy commissioner, Washington (1821–24, 1832–40).

Chaun·cy \'chȯn-sē, 'chän-\, Charles. 1592–1672. American clergyman and educator, b. Herts, England. Held pastorates in England (1626–37); twice summoned before ecclesiastical commissions for investigation and discipline. Fled to America (1638); lived in Plymouth, Mass. (1638–40), Scituate (1641–54), in both places his openly expressed beliefs causing dispute and schism; second president of Harvard College (1654–72), under agreement not to disseminate certain of his doctrinal views.

Chauncy, Charles. 1705–1787. American clergyman, b. Boston. Great grandson of Charles Chauncy (1592–1672). Pastor, First Church, Boston (1727–87); liberal leader; opposed Whitefield revival movement and attempt by English bishops to impose Church of England service and system on the colonies. Author of *Seasonable Thoughts on the State of Religion in New England* (1743), *Salvation for all Men Illustrated and Vindicated* (1782).

Chaussée, Nivelle de La. See LA CHAUSSÉE.

Chaus·son \shō-sō^{n}\, Ernest, *in full* Amédée-Ernest. 1855–1899. French composer. Works, showing influence of Franck and Wagner, included settings of poems by Leconte de Lisle, Verlaine, Maeterlinck, Cros, etc.; a symphony (c.1890); *Concert for Violin, Piano, and String Quartet* (1890–91); *Poème for Violin and Orchestra* (1896); operas including *Le Roi Arthus* (1903); choral and piano works.

Chau·temps \shō-tä^{n}\, Camille. 1885–1963. French politician. Deputy (from 1919); minister of interior (1924) and of justice (1925–26); premier of France (1930); minister of public instruction (1931), of interior (1932–33); again premier (1933–34); minister of public works (1936), of state (1936–37); again premier (1937–38); minister of coordination (1938–39), of state (1939); resident mainly in U.S. (from 1940).

Chau·veau \shō-vō\, Pierre Joseph Olivier. 1820–1890. Canadian politician and novelist, b. Quebec. Member of Legislative Assembly (1844–55), federal House of Commons (1867–73); first premier of Quebec (1867–73). Author of *Charles Guérin, roman de mœurs canadiennes* (1853), etc.

Chauveau-La·garde \-lá-gård\, Claude-François. 1756–1841. French lawyer. Appeared before Revolutionary Tribunal to defend Brissot, Charlotte Corday, Marie Antoinette, and others; imprisoned for a time during Reign of Terror; appointed counselor to the Court of Cassation (1828).

Chau·vel \shō-vel\, Jean. 1897–1979. French diplomat. Entered foreign service (1921); headed department of Far Eastern affairs in Vichy government

(1940–44) while aiding Résistance; joined de Gaulle government in exile (1944); chief French delegate to UN and representative on Security Council (1949–52); ambassador to Switzerland (1952–54); major figure at Geneva Conference on French withdrawal from Indochina (1954); ambassador to Great Britain (1954–63).

Chau·vin \shō-va^{n}\, Nicolas. fl. 1815. Perhaps legendary French soldier. Served in Revolutionary and Napoleonic armies; his enthusiasm for Napoléon and his professions of militant patriotism were so exaggerated that his comrades finally turned him to ridicule. From his name the word chauvinism and its derivatives are said to come. Tale recounted in play *La cocarde tricolor* (1831) by Cogniard brothers.

Chavannes, Puvis de. See PUVIS DE CHAVANNES.

Cha·vez \'chä-väs, *Angl* 'chäv-əs, -ˌez\, Carlos Antonio de Padua. 1899–1978. Mexican orchestra conductor and composer. Director, National Conservatory of Music, Mexico City (1928–34); organized and conducted (1928–48) Mexico Symphony Orchestra. Noted esp. for works utilizing folk melodies and rhythms; works included ballets *El fuego nuevo* (1921), *Los cuatro soles* (1925), *La hija de Cólquide* for Martha Graham (1943); orchestral works *Caballos de vapor [H.P.]* (1926), a piano concerto (1938–40), *Toccata* (1947), violin concerto (1948–50), and 7 symphonies including *Sinfonía Antígona* (No. 1, 1933), *Sinfonía India* (No. 2, 1935–36), *Romantic* (No. 4, 1953); also choral, vocal and other instrumental works.

Chávez, Jorge, *called* Geo \gā-ō\. 1887–1910. Peruvian aviator, b. Paris. In Blériot monoplane made first flight over Alps, crossing through Simplon pass (1910); fatally injured in crash landing.

Cha·yef·sky \chä-'yef-skē, chī-'ef-\, Sidney, *called* Pad·dy \'pad-ē\. 1923–1981. American writer, b. New York City. Author of plays, television dramas, and screenplays including *Marty* (1955, Academy Award), *Bachelor Party* (1957), *Middle of the Night* (1959), *Americanization of Emily* (1964), *Hospital* (1971, Academy Award), *Network* (1976, Academy Award), *Altered States* (1979).

Chay·kov·sky \chī-'kȯf-skəi\, Nikolay Vasilyevich. 1850–1926. Russian Socialist. In St. Petersburg became leader of Narodniki movement; emphasized moral self-improvement, broke with group over extremist and violent tactics; to U.S. (1873); formed Socialist commune in Kansas (1875–77); Socialist propagandist in London (1877–1907); to Russia (1907), becoming leader of cooperative movement; opposed Bolsheviks and coup d'état (1917); head of White provisional government, Archangel (1918–20), which he represented at Versailles Peace Conference (1919); later supported Gen. Deniken; exiled.

Chaykovsky, Pyotr. See TCHAIKOVSKY.

Che·by·shev \chə-bi-'shȯf\, Pafnuty Lvovich. 1821–1894. Russian mathematician. Professor, St. Petersburg (1847–82); founder of Petersburg Mathematical school. Author of treatises on theory of numbers, prime numbers, probability, approximation of functions, theory of integrals, gearings, map making, etc. Devised three-bar mechanical linkage for transforming rotary to rectilinear motion.

Chee·ver \'chē-vər\, John. 1912–1982. American writer, b. Quincy, Mass. Contributed stories to *New Yorker* (from 1930) and other magazines. Author of urbane, ironic, stylistically refined stories of upper-middle-class, suburban America, including novels *The Wapshot Chronicle* (1957), *The Wapshot Scandal* (1964), *Bullet Park* (1969), and *Falconer* (1977), novella *Oh What A Paradise It Seems* (1981), and short-story collections *The Way Some People Live* (1942), *The Enormous Radio* (1954), *The Housebreaker of Shady Hill* (1959), *Some People, Places and Things That Will Not Appear in My Next Novel* (1961), *The Brigadier and the Golf Widow* (1964), *The World of Apples* (1973), *The Stories of John Cheever* (1978, Pulitzer prize).

Che·hab \'kā-häb\, Fuad. 1902–1973. Lebanese soldier and politician. Served with French colonial forces; commander of Lebanese army (1945–58); twice refused to send army to support incumbent presidents against revolts. President of Lebanon (1958–64); noted for integrity and stability of administration; declined second term.

Cheilon. See CHILON.

Cheke \'chēk\, Sir John. 1514–1557. English classical scholar. Adopted principles of Reformation; first regius professor of Greek, Cambridge (1540–51); with Sir Thomas Smith, introduced Erasmian pronunciation of Greek in Cambridge; tutor to Prince of Wales (1544); M.P. (1547); provost of King's Coll., Cambridge (1548); imprisoned (1553–54) by Queen Mary for serving as secretary of state for Lady Jane Grey; taught Greek on Continent; treacherously seized in Belgium (1556), imprisoned in Tower, and forced by Cardinal Pole to make public recantations of Protestantism.

Che·khov \'chā-kȯf; *Angl* 'chek-ˌȯf, -ˌȯv\, Anton Pavlovich. *Surname also spelled* Che·kov *or* Tche·khov. 1860–1904. Russian playwright and writer. Studied medicine but practiced little; resided near Moscow (1891–97), and in the Crimea and abroad (after 1897). Author in early life of hundreds of comic sketches of great popularity; concentrated (from c.1888) on short stories, most vividly portraying physical and psychological realities of Russian life without romantic illusion; best known stories included "The Steppe" (1888), "A Dreary Story" (1889), "The Butterfly" and "Neighbors" (1892), "Anonymous Story" (1893), "Black Monk" (1894), "Murder" and "Ariadne" (1895), "My Life" (1896), "Peasants" (1897), "Gooseberries" (1898), "A Doctor's Visit" (1898), "Lady with the Dog" (1899), "The Bishop" (1902), "The Bethrothed" (1903); author of poignant, deceptively laconic plays of penetrating insight, as *Ivanov* (1887), *Leshy* (*The Wood-Demon,* 1889), *Chayka* (*The Seagull,* 1896; rev. 1898), *Dyadya Vanya* (*Uncle Vanya,* 1897), *Tri sestry* (*Three Sisters,* 1901; rev. 1902), *Vishnyovy sad* (*Cherry Orchard,* 1904).

Che·lard \sh(ə-)lär\, Hippolyte-André-Jean-Baptiste. 1789–1861. French composer. Resided in Munich (1830–40); kapellmeister in Weimar (1840–52). Works included operas *La casa da vendere* (1815), *Macbeth* (1827), *La table et le logement* (1829), *Mitternacht* (1831), *Der Student* (1832), *Die Hermannsschlacht* (1835), *Die Seekadetten* (1844); sacred and secular vocal works, etc.

Chel·čic·ký \'kel-chēdz-kē\, Peter. c.1390–c.1460. Czech theologian and political writer. Joined radical wing of Hussite movement; condemned towns, commerce, war, oaths, all authority; espoused a primitive Christianity that influenced founding of Bohemian Brethren sect. Author of *Šít Víry* ("Net of the Faith," 1440).

Chelmsford, Barons and Viscount. See THESIGER.

Chem·nitz *or* **Kem·nitz** \'kem-nits\, Martin. 1522–1586. German theologian. Librarian to duke of Prussia, Königsberg (1550–53); pastor of St. Aegidi, Wittenberg (1553 ff.); superintendent of churches, Brunswick (from 1567); worked long for Lutheran unity and with Jacob Andreä devised Formula of Concord (1577). Author of *Examen concilii Tridentini* (1565–73), *Loci theologici* (1591), etc. His grandson ¶Bogislaw Philipp von Chemnitz (1605–1678), historian, wrote *Der königliche schwedische in Teutschland geführte Krieg* (1648), and under pseudonym Hip·pol·i·thus a Lap·i·de \hi-'päl-ə-t(h)ə-sā-'lap-ə-(ˌ)dē\, a political treatise on the German system of government (1642–43).

Ch'en \'chən\. A Chinese dynasty (557–589), one of the Six Dynasties, succeeded by the Sui.

Ch'en Ch'eng \-'chəŋ\. 1897–1965. Chinese soldier and politician. Early friend and associate of Chiang Kai-shek, commander under him in northern campaign of 1926; commander of 18th Nationalist army (1930); held various subsequent commands; minister of war (1944–46); chief of staff (1946–48). Premier (1950–54, 1957–63), vice president (1954–65) of the Republic of China.

Ch'en Chiung-ming \-jē-'ůŋ-'miŋ\. 1878–1933. Chinese military leader. In control of Kwangtung (1913); strong supporter (1916–21) of Sun Yat-sen; overthrew Kwangsi militarists (1920); civil governor of Kwangtung (1921); turned against Sun Yat-sen (1922) and drove him out of Canton; himself driven out (1922) and subsequently completely defeated by Chiang Kai-shek (1925).

Chêne·dol·lé \shen-dȯ-lā\, Charles-Julien Lioult de \lyüt-də-\. 1769–1833. French poet. An émigré (1789–99), lived with Klopstock in Germany and Mme. de Stäel in Switzerland. Author of *Le Génie de l'homme* (1807), *L'Esprit de Rivarol* (1810), *Études poétiques* (1820).

Che·ney \'chē-nē\, Charles Edward. 1836–1916. American clergyman, b. Canandaigua, N.Y. Chief pastorate, Christ Church (Episcopal), Chicago (1860–1916); tried for heresy (1869 ff.), convicted, and deposed, but proceedings later (1874) declared legally null and void. Collaborated with Bishop George D. Cummins (*q.v.*) in organizing Reformed Episcopal Church (1873); consecrated bishop of Chicago in the new church (1878).

Cheney, Sheldon Warren. 1886–1980. American critic, b. Berkeley, Calif. Founder (1916) and editor (1916–21), *Theatre Arts Magazine.* Author of *The New Movement in Theatre* (1914), *Art Theatre* (1916), *Primer of Modern Art* (1924), *Stage Decoration* (1928), *The Theatre: 3000 Years of Drama, Acting and Stagecraft* (1929), *New World of Architecture* (1930), *Art and the Machine* (1936), etc.

Cheng \'jəŋ\. *Known as* Shih Huang Ti \'shē-hwäŋ-dē\ *or* Ch'in Shih Huang Ti \'chin-\. c.259–210 B.C. Emperor of China (221–210 B.C.). Ascended throne of state of Ch'in (246); under regency (246–238) of Lü Pu-wei; annexed his six rival states and created (221) the first unified Chinese empire, the Ch'in dynasty; assumed title of Shih Huang Ti, i.e. First Sovereign Emperor. Established a centralized administration; constructed the Great Wall of China and a network of roads and canals; founded capital at Hsien-yang (now Sian); made series of inspection tours of empire (220–210); his quarrels with Confucian scholars culminated (213) in famous Burning of the Books, suggested by his grand councillor Li Ssu.

Cheng Ch'eng-kung \-'chəŋ-'gůŋ\. *Known in West as* Kox·in·ga *or* Cox·in·ga \käk-'siŋ-(g)ə\. 1624–1662. Chinese pirate leader. Son of Cheng Chih-lung; refused to follow father into service of conquering Manchus (1646); gathered remnants of Ming forces on Fukien coast; launched major invasion up Yangtze (1659); ultimately forced back to Amoy; seized Taiwan from Dutch (1661) and made it base of anti-Manchu forces; established civil administration.

Cheng Chen-to \-'jen-'dō\. 1898–1958. Chinese literary historian. Active in Literary Research Society and with magazine *Hsia-shuo yüeh-pao;* chief editor (1926–27); student, collector, and promoter of Chinese vernacular literature; dedicated to creation of new social realist literature in Chinese.

Cheng Ch'iao \-chē-'au̇\. 1108–1166. Chinese historian. Author of *T'ung chih,* celebrated history of Chinese institutions from beginnings through T'ang dynasty (to 907 A.D.).

Cheng Chih-lung \-'ji(ə)r-'lu̇ŋ\. 1604–1661. Chinese pirate leader. After employment by Portuguese at Mação, became pirate; entered service of Ming dynasty (1628), defending coast against pirates and Dutch; on fall of Peking to Manchu tribes (1644) established Chu Yü-chien, prince of T'ang, as Ming pretender in Fukien province; accepted offer of high office in Ch'ing government of Manchus (1646); imprisoned (1655) and executed for resistance led by his son Cheng Ch'eng-kung (*q.v.*).

Ch'eng Hao \'chəŋ-'hau̇\ (1032–1085) and his brother ¶Ch'eng I \'chəŋ-'ē\ (1033–1107). Chinese philosophers. Both studied Confucianism, passed civil service examinations, and briefly held high government posts, Ch'eng I as imperial tutor (1069–70); retired to Ho-nan to develop philosophy. Evolved contrasting systems of Neo-Confucianism: Ch'eng Hao developed a system of introspection and contemplation of *li* (principle) aimed at impartiality of judgment and accord with the universe; influenced later Idealist school; Ch'eng I emphasized active study and participation in affairs as means of discovering *li;* influenced later Rationalist school. Fragments of their writings extant.

Cheng Ho \'jəŋ-'hō\. *Orig.* Ma San-pao \'mä-'sän-'pau̇\. c.1371–c.1433. Chinese admiral. A eunuch; soldier (from c.1381); in service of Emperor Yung Lo of Ming dynasty; sent in command of vast naval expedition (1405–07) to Vietnam, Siam, Malacca, Java, Calicut, Cochin, Ceylon; again (1409–11) as far as Ceylon, whose king was brought back to China as prisoner; third expedition (1411–12) reached Hormuz and Sumatra; fourth (1413–15) to Hormuz, Aden, Egypt, Malindi; later expeditions (1417–19, 1421–22, 1431–33) to Asia, Arabia, Africa, making numerous contacts.

Ch'eng-hua. See Chu Chien-shen under CHU family.

Ch'eng T'ang. See T'ANG.

Cheng-te. See Chu Hou-chao under CHU family.

Ch'eng-tsu. See Chu Ti under CHU family.

Cheng-t'ung. See Chu Ch'i-chen under CHU family.

Ch'en Hung-shou \'chən-'hu̇ŋ-'shō\. 1598–1652. Chinese artist. Fled official post in Ming government during Manchu conquest (1644–46); became Buddhist monk (1646); noted for revival of figure painting, esp. of ancient personalities.

Ch'en I \'chən-'ē\. 1901–1972. Chinese soldier and politician. Joined 4th Red Army of Mao Tse-tung and Chu Teh (1928); guerilla leader in south of China (1934–37); fought Japanese with 4th Army (1937–45); acting commander (1941–46), commander (1946 ff.). Mayor of Shanghai (1949 ff.); member of Politburo, Chinese People's Republic (1956–69); foreign minister (1958–69); stripped of offices following Cultural Revolution.

Ché·nier \shān-yā\, André-Marie de. 1762–1794. French poet. In diplomatic service (1787–89); published during his lifetime only two poetical works, *Le Jeu du paume* and *Hymne aux soldats de Châteauvieux;* protested against excesses of Reign of Terror; guillotined in Paris. Works published by his friends and his family after his death included *La Jeune Captive* (1795), *La Jeune Tarentine* (1801); a complete edition of his works was published (1819); regarded by some as foremost poet in French classic verse since Racine and Boileau. His brother ¶Marie-Joseph-Blaise (1764–1811), politician and poet; member of National Convention, Council of Five Hundred, Committee of Public Safety, and the Tribunat. Author of the tragedies *Charles IX* (1789), *Henry VIII* (1791), *Caius Gracchus* (1792), *Fénelon* (1793), *Cyrus* (1804); also of Revolutionary hymns "Chant du départ" and "Hymne à la liberté."

Chen·nault \shə-'nȯlt\, Claire Lee. 1890–1958. American aviator, b. Commerce, Texas. Joined U.S. Army Air Corps (1917); as commandant of 19th pursuit group, Hawaii (1923–26), began intensive study of aerial tactics; demonstrated use of parachute troops (1926); resigned from U.S. army (1937). Following Japanese invasion of China (1937), became air adviser to Chiang Kai-shek; formed (1941) American Volunteer Group, known as the "Flying Tigers," to aid China; protected Burma Road against Japanese air forces (1941–42). Named brigadier general (1942) commanding U.S. army air forces in China; major general commanding 14th Air Force (1943–45); organized and directed Nationalist Civil Air Transport service (1946–58).

Ch'en Ssu Wang. See Ts'ao Chih under TS'AO TS'AO.

Chen Tsung. See Chao Heng under CHAO family.

Ch'en Tu-hsiu \'chən-'dü-shē-'ü\. *Orig.* Ch'en Ch'ien-sheng \-chē-'ən-'shəŋ\. *Courtesy name* Chung-fu \'ju̇ŋ-'fü\. *Literary name* Shih-an \'shē-'än\. *Pseudonym* Chung-tzu \'ju̇ŋ-'dzü\. 1879–1942. Chinese scholar and Communist leader. Engaged in agitation against Manchu government (from 1901); schoolteacher and journalist; founded (1915) *Youth Magazine* (later *New Youth Magazine*), Shanghai; dean of department of literature, Peking National U. (1917); began movement for adoption of vernacular Chinese as national language. Chief founder of Communist party in China (1920); secretary general (1920–27); directed collaboration with Kuomintang (1924–27); expelled from Communist party (1929); imprisoned (1933–37).

Cheops. See KHUFU.

Chephren. See KHAFRE.

Cher·bu·liez \sher-bu̇̄l-yā\, Victor, *in full* Charles Victor. *Pseudonym* G. Val·bert \väl-ber\. 1829–1899. Swiss novelist and critic. Naturalized French citizen (1880). His novels included *Le comte Kostia* (1863), *Le Prince vitale* (1864), *L'Aventure de Ladislas Bolski* (1869), *L'Idée de Jean Téterol* (1878), *Jacquine Vanesse* (1898); his critical works, *Études de littérature et d'art* (1873), *Profils étrangers* (1889), *L'Art et la nature* (1892), etc.

Cherepnin. See TCHEREPNIN.

Ché·ret \shā-re\, Jules. 1836–1932. French painter and lithographer. Known esp. for contribution to development of advertising poster as artistic medium.

Cherll, Giovanni. See KERLL.

Cher·nen·ko \cher-'nʸeŋ-kō\, Konstantin Ustinovich. 1911–1985. Soviet leader. Protégé of Leonid Brezhnev; rose through ranks of Communist party in 1950s; full member of Central Committee and Politburo (1960–78); upon death of Yuri Andropov, elected general secretary of Communist party and chairman of Presidium of Supreme Soviet (1984). Continued some of Andropov's reforms during brief term in office.

Cher·nov \(,)chər-'nȯf\, Viktor Mikhaylovich. *Pseudonym* Boris Ole·nin \ȯl-'yān-yin\. 1876–1952. Russian journalist and political leader. Joined revolutionary movement (1893); helped found (1902) Social Revolutionary party; took part in Zimmerwald Conference (1915); after Revolution (1917) fought in White army; minister of agriculture (1917); president of All-Russian Constituent Assembly (1918); lived in France (1920–39), U.S. (from 1939).

Cher·nya·yev \(,)chərn-'yä-yif\, Mikhail Grigoryevich. 1828–1898. Russian general. Served in Crimean War (1854–56); captured Tashkent (1865); military governor of Turkistan (1865–66); resigned from army (1867). Edited nationalistic journal *Russky mir* (1871–76); helped rouse pan-Slavic sympathy for anti-Turkish revolt; entered Serbian army as eastern commander (1876); was defeated by Turks. Lieutenant general in Russian army (1881); governor of Turkistan (1882–84).

Cher·ny·shev·sky \chər-ni-'shäf-skē\, Nikolay Gavrilovich. 1828–1889. Russian radical. Became leader of radical groups; imprisoned (1862–64) and exiled for 24 years to Siberia (1864); wrote a classic of the Russian revolutionary movement, *Shto delat?* (*What Is to Be Done?,* 1863).

Cher·si·phron \'kər-sə-,frän\. 6th century B.C. Cretan architect. Traditionally regarded as the architect, with his son Metagenes, of the Artemision (temple of Artemis) at Ephesus.

Che·ru·bi·ni \,kā-rü-'bē-nē\, Luigi Carlo Zenobio Salvadore Maria. 1760–1842. Italian composer. Composer to George III of England (1785); resident (from 1786) in Paris; studied under Sarti in Bologna; music director of royal chapel of Louis XVIII (1816); director of Paris conservatory of music (1821–42). Composed 29 operas (15 Italian, 14 French), contributing greatly to development of that form; operas included *Il Quinto Fabio* (1779), *Armida abbandonata* (1782), *L'Idalide* (1784), *Il Giulio Sabino* (1786), *Ifigenia in Aulide* (1788), *Marguerite d'Anjou* (1790), *Lodoïska* (1791), *Médée* (1797), *Les deux journées* (1800), *Anacréon* (1803); composed 15 masses, esp. the *F Major* (1809) and *Requiem in D Minor* (1836), also much other sacred music; large number of cantatas and ceremonial pieces. A conservative classicist, he nonetheless is considered a forerunner of Romanticism, esp. in musical drama.

Ché·ruel \shā-rwʸel\, Adolphe, *in full* Pierre-Adolphe. 1809–1891. French historian. Rector of academy at Strasbourg, then at Poitiers. His works included *Dictionnaire historique des institutions, mœurs et coutumes de la France* (1885), *Histoire de France pendant la minorité de Louis XIV* (1879–80), and *Histoire de France sous le ministère de Mazarin* (1883); edited memoirs of duc de Saint-Simon (1856–58), letters of Mazarin (1872–91).

Ches·el·den \'chez-əl-dən\, William. 1688–1752. English surgeon. Originated operation of lateral lithotomy and operation of iridectomy for treatment of blindness. Author of *The Anatomy of the Human Body* (1713).

Chesneus, Andreas. See André DUCHESNE.

Ches·ney \'ches-nē, 'chez-\, Charles Cornwallis. 1826–1876. British soldier. Nephew of Francis Rawdon Chesney. Professor of military history, Sandhurst (1858–64), Imperial Staff Coll. (1864 ff.); author of *Waterloo Lectures* (1868), criticizing Wellington's tactics and giving due credit to Prussians for Waterloo victory. His brother ¶Sir George Tomkyns (1830–1895), in Indian army (1848–92); founder and first president (1871–80), Royal Indian Civil Engineering Coll.; general (1892); M.P. (1892–95). Author of article "Battle of Dorking" (1871) on supposed German invasion of England.

Chesney, Francis Rawdon. 1789–1872. British soldier and explorer, b. Ireland, of Scottish ancestry. Surveyed Isthmus of Suez, showing canal feasible (1829); explored Euphrates valley (1831, 1835), proving Euphrates navigable for trade; surveyed and negotiated for railway from Antioch to Euphrates (1856); general (1868).

Ches·nutt \'ches-(,)nət\, Charles Waddell. 1858–1932. American writer, b. Cleveland, Ohio. Principal, State Normal School, Fayetteville, N.C. (1881); practiced law in Cleveland (from 1887). Author of stories collected in *The Conjure Woman* (1899) and *Wife of His Youth* (1899); *Life of Frederick Douglass* (1899); novels *House Behind the Cedars* (1900), *Marrow of Tradition* (1901), *The Colonel's Dream* (1905); noted for subtle treatment of racial themes.

Chess·man \'ches-mən\, Caryl Whittier. 1921–1960. American criminal, b. St. Joseph, Mich. Several times incarcerated for theft, robbery, assault, etc. (from 1937); convicted in Los Angeles for "red-light bandit" series of robberies, kidnappings, and rapes (1948); studied law while awaiting execution at San Quentin prison, initiated numerous legal actions and won several stays of execution; through books *Cell 2455 Death Row* (1954), *Trial by Ordeal* (1955), etc., won support of many prominent persons who made case for his rehabilitation an international cause célèbre; executed.

Ches·ter \'ches-tər\, Earl of. Title in English peerage first held by a Fleming named Gherbod (c.1070), granted with palatine powers to Hugh of Avranches (*q.v.*) and held by members of his family until 1232; see RANULF DE BLUNDEVILLE, RANULF DE GERNONS. Title annexed to English crown (1246), and held since 1254 (when bestowed on Prince Edward, later Edward I) by heirs apparent to English crown.

Chester, George Randolph. 1869–1924. American writer, b. Ohio. Author of *Get-Rich-Quick Wallingford* (1908), *Wallingford and Blackie Daw* (1913), *Wallingford in His Prime* (1913), etc.

Chesterfield, 4th Earl of. See Philip Dormer STANHOPE.

Ches·ter·ton \'ches-tərt-ᵊn\, Gilbert Keith. 1874–1936. English journalist and writer. Began literary work by reviewing art books for *The Bookman;* later contributed regularly to a number of English and American journals, esp. *Speaker, Daily News;* conducted (from 1925) *G.K.'s Weekly.* Became Roman Catholic (1922). Author of verse as *The Wild Knight* (1900), *The Flying Inn* (1914); essays; literary criticism as *Robert Browning* (1903), *Charles Dickens* (1906), *George Bernard Shaw* (1909), *William Blake* (1910), *Victorian Age in Literature* (1913), *William Cobbett* (1925), *Robert Louis Stevenson* (1927); religious works as *St. Francis of Assisi* (1923), *The Everlasting Man* (1925), *The Catholic Church and Conversion* (1926), *St. Thomas Aquinas* (1933), *Avowals and Denials* (1934); plays *Magic* (1913), *Judgment of Dr. Johnson* (1927); journalism and social criticism as *The Defendant* (1901), *Twelve Types* (1902), *Heretics* (1905), *What's Wrong With the World?* (1910); fiction including *Napoleon of Notting Hill* (1904), *The Club of Queer Trades* (1905), *The Man Who Was Thursday* (1908), *The Ball and the Cross* (1910), and series of detective tales featuring "Father Brown," as *The Innocence of Father Brown* (1911), *The Wisdom of Father Brown* (1914), *The Incredulity of Father Brown* (1926), *The Secret of Father Brown* (1927), *The Scandal of Father Brown* (1935).

Che Tsung. See Chao Heng under CHAO family.

Chet·tle \'chet-ᵊl\, Henry. c.1560–c.1607. English dramatist. Author of *The Tragedy of Hoffman* (1602) and collaborator on many plays including *The Blind-Beggar of Bednal-Green* (with John Day, 1600), *Downfall of Robert, Earle of Huntington* and *Death of Robert, Earle of Huntington* (both with Anthony Munday, 1601), *The Pleasant Comodie of Patient Grissill* (with Thomas Dekker and William Haughton, 1603), and some 44 others; also wrote satire *Kind harts dream* (1593), narrative *Piers Plainnes seaven yeres prentiship* (1595), and elegy for Elizabeth I *Englandes mourning garment* (1603).

Chev·a·lier \,shev-ə-'li(ə)r; shə-'val-yər, -(,)yā\, Albert. 1861–1923. English entertainer. Actor (from 1877); made music hall debut at London Pavillion (1891); achieved great popularity through songs of cockney street life as "The Coster's Serenade," "It's the Nasty Way 'E Sez It," "The Future Mrs. 'Awkins," "My old Dutch."

Che·va·lier \shə-val-yā\, Guillaume-Sulpice. *Pseudonym* Paul Ga·var·ni \gä-vär-nē\. 1804–1866. French lithographer and painter. Noted for witty, ironic, observant scenes of everyday life, in later years often imbued with sense of bitterness and the grotesque; published *Journal des gens du monde* (1833); imprisoned for debt (1835–36); traveled in England and Scotland (1847–49). Popular series of lithographs included *Les Lorettes, Les Débardeurs, Les Fourberies de femmes, Masques et visages.*

Chevalier, Jules. 1824–1907. French clergyman and writer. Ordained priest (1851); founded (1854) order of Missionarii Sacratissimi Cordis Jesu, known as Sacred Heart Missionaries; superior general (1854–1901); with Marie-Louise Hartzer founded (1882) Daughters of Our Lady of the Sacred Heart; a chief promoter of cult of Sacred Heart. Author of *Notre-Dame de Sacré-Coeur de Jésus* (1863), etc.

Che·va·lier \shə-vál-yā, *Angl* shə-'val-(,)yā\, Maurice-Auguste. 1888–1972. French entertainer. Achieved success as café singer (from 1901) and music hall entertainer; appeared in American films including *Innocents of Paris* (1929), *Love Parade* (1930), *One Hour with You* (1932), *Love Me Tonight* (1932), *Merry Widow* (1934), *Love in the Afternoon* (1957), *Gigi* (1958), *Can-Can* (1960), *Fanny* (1961); given special Academy Award (1958).

Chevalier, Michel. 1806–1879. French economist. Follower of Saint-Simon; editor of *Le Globe* (1830–32); imprisoned, retracted anti-Christian writings (1832); visited U.S. (1832–33); abandoned socialism; councillor of state (1838); professor, Collège de France (1840); deputy (1845); adopted free trade; with Cobden helped effect treaty with Great Britain (1860).

Chevalier, Ulysse. 1841–1923. French clergyman and scholar. Professor of ecclesiastical history, Lyon (1887). Author of *Répertoire des sources historiques du moyen âge* (1877–1903), *Repertorium hymnologicum* (1892–1912), etc.

Che·ve·rus \shəv-rüs\, Jean-Louis Le·feb·vre de \lə-fev-rə-də-\. 1768–1836. French prelate. Pastor of Notre-Dame, Mayenne; during French Revolution, fled to England (1792), thence to U.S. (1796); consecrated first Roman Catholic bishop of Boston (1810); returned to France as bishop of Montauban (1823); archbishop of Bordeaux (1826); cardinal (1836).

Chev·es \'chiv-əs\, Langdon. 1776–1857. American banker, b. Abbeville District, S.C. Member, U.S. House of Representatives (1810–15); speaker (1814–15); president, United States Bank (1819–22); built up resources and saved bank; known as "the Hercules of the United States Bank."

Che·vreul \shəv-rœl\, Michel-Eugène. 1786–1889. French chemist. Director of dyeworks, Gobelins tapestry works (1824); professor (1830), director (1864–79), Muséum d' Histoire Naturelle. Known esp. for researches on animal fats which led to improvements in the candle and soap industry; isolated oleic, palmitic, stearic acids; with Gay-Lussac developed improved manufacturing process for candles; pioneer in psychology of color, gerontology.

Chevreuse, Duchesse de. See Marie de Rohan-Montbazon under ROHAN family.

Chev·ro·let \,shev-rə-'lā\, Louis. 1879–1941. American automobile racer, designer, and manufacturer, b. La Chaux de Fords, Switzerland. To U.S. (1900); participated in automobile races (from 1905); associate of W.C. Durant in founding Chevrolet Motor Co. (1911), later incorporated into General Motors (1915); designed racers that won Indianapolis 500 (1920, 1921); later worked for Stutz Automobile Co. and Chevrolet (1936).

Cheyne \'chān, 'chēn\, Thomas Kelly. 1841–1915. English scholar. Disciple of Ewald; introduced German critical scholarship in England; member of board of revision of Old Testament (1884); Oriel professor of interpretation of scripture, Oxford (1885–1908). Author of *Prophecies of Isaiah* (1880–81), *Job and Solomon* (1887), *Book of Psalms* (1888), *Founders of Old Testament Criticism* (1893), etc.

Chey·ney \'chā-nē\, Peter. *In full* Reginald Evelyn Peter Sou·thouse-Cheyney \'sau̇th-,(h)au̇s-\. 1896–1951. English writer. Known for detective novels of "hard-boiled" school, including *This Man Is Dangerous* (1936), *You Can't Keep the Change* (1940), *Dance Without Music* (1947).

Ché·zy \shā-zē\, Antoine de. 1718–1798. French engineer and mathematician. Developed Chézy equation, basic formula for calculating velocity of fluid stream; assistant to J.-R. Perronnet; completed Pont de la Concorde, Paris (1795); director of École des Ponts et Chaussées (1798).

Ch'i \'chē\. *Also known as* Southern Ch'i. A Chinese dynasty (479–502 A.D.), one of the Six Dynasties, succeeded by the Liang.

Chia·bre·ra \kyä-'brer-ä\, Gabriello. 1552–1638. Italian poet. Introduced innovations in metrical form adopted by later poets; his work included epics, odes, pastorals, satires, lyrics, eclogues, canzoni inspired by Provençal poetry, and esp. canzonette influenced by Ronsard and other poets of the Pléiade group.

Chia-ching. See Chu Hou-tsung under CHU family.

Chia-ch'ing. See YUNG-YEN.

Chiang Kai-shek \jē-'äŋ-'kī-'shek, *Angl* chaŋ-(,)kī-'shek\. *Pin-yin* Jiang Jie-shī \jē-'äŋ-jē-'esh-'ē\. *Official name* Chiang Chung-cheng \jē-'äŋ-'ju̇ŋ-'jəŋ\. 1887–1975. Chinese general and politician. Trained and served (1909–11) in Japanese army; took part in revolutionary stuggles establishing Chinese Republic (1911–16); associated with Sun Yat-sen in Kuomintang (Nationalist) party (from 1918); visited Russia (1923); developed Kuomintang army (1923–25); head of Whampoa Military Academy (1924). After Sun's death (1925) chosen generalissimo of Kuomintang army; led expedition to north (1926), establishing Kuomintang government at Wuchang; after break with Communists (1927) transferred seat of government to Nanking (1927); resigned all government posts (1927); persuaded to resume command (1928); led Nanking army northward and occupied Peking (1928); president of

Chinese Nationalist government (1928 ff.); chairman of Executive Yuan of National Government (1935–38, 1939–45); adopted policy of civil war against Communists (1927–36); kidnaped on visit to Sian (Dec. 1936) and held prisoner for two weeks; after release, changed policy of appeasement toward Japanese to one of opposition in alliance with Communists. Assumed entire command on outbreak of hostilities with Japan (1937); accepted as one of Big Four in directing Allied war on Axis (1941–45); renewed civil war with Communists (1946); president of National Government (1943–49). Resumed presidency on Taiwan (1950–75) after communists won control of mainland China (1949).

Chia·ri·ni \kyä-'rē-nē\, Giuseppe. 1833–1908. Italian critic, poet, and translator. Known esp. as friend and supporter of Carducci. His works included verse, translations from Heine, and critical studies.

Chia Ssu-tao \jē-'ä-'sü-'daů\. d. 1279. Chinese politician. Achieved power when sister became emperor's concubine; given charge of Mongol affairs; his lenient treatment of Mongol tribes traditionally blamed for inviting their invasion (1279) and overthrow of Sung dynasty.

Chich·e·le *or* **Chich·e·ley** \'chich-ə-lē\, Henry. c.1362–1443. English prelate and diplomat. Envoy to Pope Innocent VII (1405) and Gregory XII (1407); bishop of St. David's (1408); envoy to Pisa (1409), to France (1410); archbishop of Canterbury (1414). Founder of two colleges at Oxford, St. Bernard's (1437, now St. John's) and All Souls' (1437).

Chi·che·rin \chi-'chär-yin\, Georgi Vasilievich. 1872–1936. Russian diplomat. In czarist diplomatic service (1897–1904); resigned and renounced title to estates because of sympathy with revolutionary agitation; member of Menshevik faction; after Revolution (1917), returned to Russia and served as people's commissar for foreign affairs (1918–30); negotiated several trade treaties including secret Treaty of Rapallo with Germany (1922).

Chichester, Earls of. See PELHAM family.

Chi·ches·ter \'chich-əs-tər\, Arthur. Baron Chichester of Bel·fast \'bel-ˌfast, bel-'\. 1563–1625. English administrator in Ireland. Commanded ship against Spanish Armada (1588); took part in Cádiz expedition (1589); sent as general to Ireland to suppress uprising of Hugh O'Neill (1599); lord deputy of Ireland (1604–14); encouraged Scottish colonization in Ulster; obtained relaxation (1607) of repressive measures of James I against Roman Catholics; created baron (1613); recalled (1614).

Chichester, Sir Francis Charles. 1901–1972. English adventurer. Amateur aviator; made solo England–Australia flight (1929–30), first east–west flight over Tasman Sea (1931); later took up sailing; won transatlantic solo race in 40 days (1960); piloted 53-foot yacht *Gipsy Moth IV* around world, 29,617 miles in 226 days (Aug. 1966–May 1967); made solo Atlantic crossing at age 69 (1970–71). Author of *The Lonely Sea and the Sky* (1964), *Gipsy Moth Circles the World* (1967).

Ch'ien-lung. See HUNG-LI.

Chien-wen. See Chu Yün-wen under CHU family.

Chif·ley \'chif-lē\, Joseph Benedict. 1885–1951. Australian politician. Railroad driver and labor unionist; member of federal House of Representatives (1928–31, 1940–51); federal treasurer (1941–49), minister for postwar reconstruction (1942–45); instituted strict wartime economic controls; prime minister (1945–49); failed in attempt to nationalize banks (1947); leader of Labour party in opposition (1950–51).

Chi·gi \'kē-jē\. Italian family of Siena, noted esp. for its protection of the arts. Agostino Chigi (1465?–1520), banker, known as "il Magnifico"; used his great wealth to encourage leading artists, as Peruzzi, Perugino, Sebastiano del Piombo, and esp. Raphael; built (1509–11) the Villa Farnese at Rome, famous for its works of art, esp. frescoes. ¶Fabio Chigi (1599–1677), see Pope ALEXANDER VII.

Chih-i \'ji(ə)r-'ē\. 538–597. Chinese Buddhist monk. Disciple (560–567) of Hui-ssu; established monastery on T'ien-t'ai mountain and developed eclectic T'ien-t'ai sect of Buddhism.

Ch'i Huang. See CH'I PAI-SHIH.

Ch'i Ju-shan \'chēz-'yü-'shän\. 1876–1962. Chinese playwright and scholar. With actor Mei Lan-fang, responsible for restoration of Chinese drama to traditional importance; wrote many dramas based on historical and legendary sources; compiled records and wrote histories of Chinese theater.

Chi·ka·ma·tsu \chē-kä-mät-sů\ Monzaemon. *Orig.* Sug·i·mo·ri \sůg-ē-mō-rē\ Nobumori. 1653–1724. Japanese dramatist. Author of some 160 plays, mainly historical romances and domestic tragedies, most written for the Bunraku, or puppet theater, which he raised to artistic heights. Works included *Sonezaki Shinjū* (1703), *Kokusenya kassen* (1715), *Shinjū ten no Amijima* (1720). Often considered greatest Japanese dramatist.

Chi K'ang. See HSI K'ANG.

Child \'chī(ə)ld\, Charles Manning. 1869–1954. American zoologist, b. Ypsilanti, Mich. On staff (from 1895), professor (1916–34), U. of Chicago. Known for work on reproduction, development, and esp. regeneration; developed axial gradient theory of regeneration. Founded (1928) journal *Physiological Zoology.* Author of *Senescence and Rejuvenescence* (1915), *Individuality in Organisms* (1915), *Physiological Foundations of Behavior* (1924), *Patterns and Problems of Development* (1941), etc.

Child, Francis James. 1825–1896. American philologist, b. Boston. Professor, Harvard (1851–96); authority on the ballad. Edited *Poetical Works of Edmund Spenser* (1855); best known for *English and Scottish Ballads* (1857–58); *English and Scottish Popular Ballads* (1883–98).

Child, Sir John. d. 1690. English colonialist. Joined East India Co. in youth; deputy governor of Bombay (1679–81); president of Surat (1682–90); first person placed in charge of East India Co.'s entire operation in India; harsh and unscrupulous; selected for expulsion by peace terms after war with Aurangzeb. His brother ¶Sir Josiah (1630–1699), merchant and economist; director (from 1677), governor (1681–83, 1686–88) of East India Co.; autocractic and unscrupulous governor. M.P. (1659, 1673–78, 1685–87). A mercantilist, author of *A New Discourse of Trade* (1668, 1690).

Child, Lydia Maria, *nee* Fran·cis \'fran(t)-səs\. 1802–1880. American reformer and author, b. Medford, Mass. m. David L. Child (1828; d. 1874). Founded and edited (1826–34) *Juvenile Miscellany,* first children's monthly in U.S.; edited *National Anti-Slavery Standard* (1841–43); active in abolitionist and woman suffrage causes. Author of novels as *Hobomok* (1824), *The Rebels* (1825), *Philothea* (1836); children's books; reform works as *Appeal in Favor of That Class of Americans Called Africans* (1833), *Progress of Religious Ideas* (1855), *The Freedmen's Book* (1865), *Appeal for the Indians* (1868), etc.

Childe \'chī(ə)ld\, Vere Gordon. 1892–1957. Australian archaeologist and historian. Professor, Edinburgh (1927–46); director, Inst. of Archaeology, U. of London (1946–56). Author of *The Dawn of European Civilization* (1925), *The Danube in Prehistory* (1929), *Man Makes Himself* (1936), *What Happened in History* (1942), etc.

Chil·de·bert \'chil-də-ˌbərt, 'kil-; *Fr* shēl-də-ber; *Ger* 'kil-də-ˌbert\. Name of three Frankish kings of the Merovingian dynasty:

Childebert I. 495?–588. King (511–588). Son of Clovis I; to original kingdom of northwestern France (Paris), added by conquest or intrigue Chartres, Orléans, part of Burgundy, Arles and Marseilles; with brother Clotaire I of Soissons invaded Visigothic Spain (541–542); conquered Pamplona. Built St. Germain-des-Prés, Paris.

Childebert II. 570?–595. King of Austrasia (575–595). Son of Sigebert I; under regency of mother Brunhilda during minority; seized lands on death of uncle Chilperic I of Soissons-Tournai (584), uncle Guntram of Burgundy (592).

Childebert III. c.683–711. King of Neustria and Burgundy (695–711). A puppet ruler, power being held by mayor of the palace Pepin of Herstal.

Chil·der·ic \'chil-də-(ˌ)rik, 'kil-\. *Fr.* Chil·dé·ric \shēl-dā-rēk\. *Ger.* Chil·de·rich \'kil-də-(ˌ)rik\. Name of three Frankish kings:

Childeric I. d. 481 or 482. King of Salian Franks (c.457–482). Helped Aegidius repel Visigoths near Orléans (463); attacked Visigoths (469). Father of Clovis I.

Childeric II. 649–675. King of Austrasia (662–675). Son of Clovis II; proclaimed king of Austrasia in place of rightful heir Dagobert II (662); ruled under guardianship of aunt Himnechildis and of mayor of the palace, Wulfoald; on death of brother Chlotar III (673) seized Neustria and Burgundy, deposing Neustrian mayor Theuderic; last Merovingian to exercise power; assassinated.

Childeric III. d. 754. King (743–751). Placed on throne by Carloman and Pepin the Short, sons of Charles Martel, to clothe their rule in legitimacy; deposed and placed in monastery by Pepin; last Merovingian king.

Chil·ders \'chil-dərz\, Hugh Culling Eardley. 1827–1896. British politician. To Australia (1850); member of Victoria cabinet (1856); agent-general for Victoria in England (1857). M.P. (1860–85, 1886–92); financial secretary to treasury (1865–66); first lord of admiralty (1868–71); as war secretary under Gladstone (1880–82), introduced territorial system and other administrative reforms in army; chancellor of exchequer (1882–85); proposed heavy increase in taxes and duties that caused government's fall; home secretary (1886); supported Gladstone's home rule bill.

Childers, Robert Erskine. 1870–1922. British writer and politician. Cousin of Hugh C.E. Childers. Served in Boer War and as naval intelligence officer in World War I; clerk in House of Commons (1895–1910); devoted himself (from 1910) to cause of home rule for Ireland, and (from 1919) to complete independence as a republic; member of Dáil Éireann (1921); opposed Anglo-Irish treaty of 1921; joined Republican army; captured by Free State soldiers, court-martialed, and shot. Author of a volume of *The Times History of the War in South Africa* (1907), the novel *The Riddle of the Sands* (1903), and *The Framework of Home Rule* (1911).

His son ¶Erskine Hamilton Childers (1905–1974) was member of the Dáil (1938–74); minister for posts and telegraphs (1951–54), for lands (1957–59), for transport and power (1959–66), transport and power and posts and telegraphs (1966–69), of health (1969–73); fourth president of Republic of Ireland (1973–74).

Chi·lem·bwe \chə-'lem-ˌbwā\, John. d. 1915. Nyasaland nationalist. Missionary educated in U.S.; one of first to promote idea of Nyasaland nationality over tribal differences; led abortive but symbolic revolt against British rule (1915); shot by native police.

Chil·ling·worth \'chil-iŋ-ˌwərth\, William. 1602–1644. English theologian and controversialist. Embraced Roman Catholicism and studied at Jesuit college at Douai (1630–31); abjured Catholicism (1634); chancellor of Salisbury (1638); served in Royalist army, invented a siege engine. Author of *The Religion of Protestants a Safe Way to Salvation* (1637).

Chi·lon *or* **Chei·lon** \'kī-ˌlän\ *or* **Chi·lo** \'kī-ˌlō\. 6th century B.C. Spartan ephor (c.550 B.C.). Ranked as one of the Seven Sages, or Seven Wise Men of Greece.

Chil·per·ic \'chil-pə-(ˌ)rik, 'kil-\. *Fr.* Chil·pé·ric \shēl-pā-rēk\. *Ger.* Chil·pe·rich \'kil-pə-ˌrik\. Name of two Frankish kings of the Merovingian line:

Chilperic I. 539–584. King of Neustria (561–584). Son of Chlotar I; received Soissons on death of father (561); seized father's treasure and attempted to assert rule over entire realm; fought unsuccessful war with half-brother Sigebert of Austrasia (562); reign marked by intrigue, civil wars; taxed and otherwise persecuted clergy. Disowned wife to marry (568) Galswintha, sister of Sigebert's wife Brunhilda; had her killed to marry mistress Fredegund. Called by Gregory of Tours the Nero and the Herod of his age.

Chilperic II. c.675–721. King of Neustria (715–721). Supposed son of Childeric II; taken from monastery and proclaimed king by mayor of the palace Ragenfrid as means of throwing off Austrasian control; campaigned against Austrasia; defeated by Charles Martel at Amblève (716); fled to Aquitaine (719); recalled by Charles Martel after death of Chlotar IV (719) and made nominal king of all Frankish lands in order to maintain Merovingian legitimacy.

Chin \'jin\. Name of several Chinese dynasties: (1) Western Chin (265–317), founded by Ssu-ma Yen (*q.v.*); briefly united all China, terminating period of the Three Kingdoms; broken up by civil war known as Revolt of the Eight Kings. (2) Eastern Chin (317–419), one of the Six Dynasties; capital at Nanking; restricted to central and southern regions. (3) Later Chin (936–947), one of the Five Dynasties. (4) Variant name of the JUCHEN dynasty (1122–1234) of Central Asia and North China.

Ch'in \'chin\. Dynasty (221–206 B.C.) from which name China was derived and which established the approximate boundaries and basic administrative system used by subsequent dynasties; founded by Cheng (*q.v.*), ruler of state of Ch'in; succeeded by the Han dynasty.

Ch'in Chiu-shao \-'jü-'shau̇\. *Literary name* Tao-ku \'dau̇-'gü\. c.1202–c.1261. Chinese mathematician. Developed method of successive approximations to solve numerical polynomial equations of any degree, a method not discovered in Europe until 19th century. Chief work *Shu-shu chiu-chang.*

Ch'ing \'chiŋ\ *or* **Man·chu** \'män-'chü\. Last dynasty (1644–1912) of the Chinese Empire, succeeding the Ming dynasty; dynasty first established by Manchus in Manchuria (1636), moved to China after capture of Peking (1644). Under first five emperors Fu-lin, Hsüan-yeh, Yin-chen, Hung-li, and Yung-yen (*qq.v.*), empire increased to three times size of Ming territories, commerce and industries prospered, and arts and letters flourished; dynasty declined severely under last five emperors, Min-ning, I-chu, Tsai-ch'un, Tsai-t'ien, and P'u-i (*qq.v.*); overthrown by founding of Chinese Republic.

Ching Hao \'jiŋ-'hau̇\. *Also known as* Hung-ku-tzu \'hu̇ŋ-'güd-zü\. fl. 910–950. Chinese painter and essayist. Known esp. for landscapes of distinctively northern grandeur.

Chinghiz Khan *or* **Chingiz Khan.** See GENGHIS KHAN.

Ching-t'ai. See Chu Ch'i-yü under CHU family.

Ching Ti. See (1) Liu Ch'i under LIU family; (2) Chu Ch'i-yü under CHU family.

Chini, Eusebio Francisco. See KINO.

Ch'in Kuei \'chin-kü-'ā\. 1090–1155. Chinese politician. Minister of Sung court; argued against war to regain northern territories lost to Jürched tribes; had general Yo Fei executed for supporting war; secured peace treaty (1141); remembered in Chinese history as a traitor.

Ch'in Shih Huang Ti. See CHENG.

Chin T'ai Tsu. See A-KU-TA.

Ch'in Tsung. See Chao Huan under CHAO family.

Chi-nui. See BOJO GUKSA.

Chin Wu Ti. See SSU-MA YEN.

Ch'i Pai-shih \'chē-'pī-'shi(ə)r\. *Also known as* Ch'i Huang \-'hwäŋ\. 1863–1957. Chinese painter. Known for paintings, usually of small subjects, for poetry, and for calligraphy; considered one of the last of great traditional artists.

Chip·pen·dale \'chip-ən-ˌdāl\, Thomas. 1718–1779. English cabinetmaker. Established workshop in London (c.1748); remembered chiefly for collected designs, some by him and some commissioned from others, summarizing the English Rococo style and published as *The Gentleman and Cabinet Maker's Director* (1754). Succeeded by his son ¶Thomas (c.1749–1822).

Chi·ri·co \'kē-rē-(ˌ)kō\, Giorgio De. 1888–1978. Italian painter. Influenced by fantasticality of paintings of Böcklin; developed style marked by bright light and deep shadow, flat, dull color, and eerie juxtapositions of architecture, classical statuary or figures, deserted plazas; with Carlo Carrà founded (1917) *scuola metafisica.* Notable works included *Enigma of an Autumn Afternoon, Soothsayer's Recompense, Mystery and Melancholy of a Street, The Seer, Grand Metaphysical Interior.*

Chi·ri·kov \'chir-yə-kəf\, Aleksey. 1703–1748. Russian explorer. Captain of ship *St. Paul* on second expedition of Vitus Bering; his crew made first sighting of Alaska (July 15, 1741).

Chis·holm \'chiz-əm\, Hugh. 1866–1924. English journalist and editor. Editor, *St. James's Gazette* (1897–99); joint editor (with Sir Donald Wallace and A.T. Hadley) of 10th edition of *Encyclopaedia Britannica* (1902–03); editor in chief of 11th edition (1910–11), 12th edition (1922), *Encyclopaedia Britannica*; city editor, London *Times* (1913–20).

Chisholm, Jesse. 1806?–?1868. American frontiersman. Little known of life; engaged in trade between Mexican border and Abilene, Kansas, establishing route that with the great cattle drives became known as Chisholm Trail.

Chis·um \'chiz-əm\, John Simpson. 1824–1884. American frontiersman, b. Hardeman Co., Tenn. To Texas (1837); engaged in cattle ranching (from 1854), gradually moving operations to New Mexico; at South Spring, near Roswell, N.M., developed largest cattle herd in U.S.; may have engaged in "Lincoln County War" (1878); sometimes said to have engaged Billy the Kid; later led drive for law and order.

Chit·ra·se·na \ˌchi-trə-'sā-nə\. *Also known as* Ma·hen·dra·var·man \mə-ˌhen-drə-'vär-ˌmän\. 6th–7th century. Cambodian soldier and ruler. Brother or cousin of Bhavavarman I; helped conquer Funan (c.550); commanded army of Bhavavarman and conquered much territory; succeeded Bhavavarman as king of Chenla (c.600–c.611), taking reign name Mahendravarman.

Chi-tsang \'jed-'zäŋ\. 549–623. Chinese Buddhist monk. Author of numerous commentaries on and systematizer of teachings of San-lun school of Māhāyana Buddhism, sometimes regarded as its founder; also influenced Neo-Confucian philosophy.

Chiu Chu-chi. See CH'ANG-CH'UN.

Ch'iu Ying \chē-'ü-'yiŋ\. 16th century. Chinese painter. Noted for meticulously rendered paintings of architectural, figural, and still life subjects.

Ch'i-ying \'chē-'yiŋ\. d. 1858. Chinese official. Negotiated Treaty of Nanking (1842) ending first Opium War by granting to British island of Hong Kong and trade through 5 ports; signed British Supplementary Treaty (1843) granting extraterritoriality; signed similar treaties with U.S., France (1844), Sweden, Norway (1847); failed to complete negotiations to end Arrow War with British and ordered by emperor to commit suicide.

Chkhei·dze \'chk̲ād-zā\, Nikolay Semyonovich. 1864–1926. Georgian revolutionist. Helped found and develop Social-Democratic party in Georgia; member of 3d and 4th dumas (1907–11, 1912–17); became leader of Menshevik faction; chairman of Petrograd Soviet (1917), replaced by Trotsky; returned to Georgia, helped form Transcaucasian Federal Republic and then Republic of Georgia (1918); fled to France on Bolshevik overthrow of republic (1921).

Chlad·ni \'kläd-nē\, Ernst Florens Friedrich. 1756–1827. German physicist. Known for studies of acoustics; studied vibration of strings and rods, and of plates, by means of sand figures; measured velocity of sound in gases other than air; invented the euphonium.

Chlo·do·mer \'klō-dō-mər\. d. 524. Frankish prince. Son of Clovis; in division of realm with brothers Theudoric, Childebert, and Chlotar, received Loire and Garonne valleys; attacked Sigismund of Burgundy and captured him; killed by Sigismund's brother Godomer at Vienne; kingdom divided by brothers.

Chlodowech *or* **Chlodwig.** See CLOVIS.

Chło·pic·ki \k̲lȯ-'pēt-skē\, Józef, *in full* Grzegorz Józef. 1771–1854. Polish general. In French service under Napoléon; distinguished himself in Italian campaign (1797–1805), Peninsular War (1808–10); took part in Russian invasion (1812); general of division in Polish army (1814–18). Dictator of Poland (Dec. 1830–Jan. 1831); resigned in face of opposition to his policies and joined Polish army fighting against Russians; wounded and forced into retirement (Feb. 1831).

Chlo·tar \'klō-ˌtär\. *Fr.* Clo·taire \klō-ter\. *Ger.* Chlo·thar \'klō-ˌtär\. Name of four Frankish kings of Merovingian line:

Chlotar I. c.497–561. King of Franks (558–561). Son of Clovis; in division of father's realm with brothers received Soissons-Tournai; added to holdings parts of Orléans (524) and Burgundy (534), Austrasia (555); defeated (531)

Thuringians and m. their princess Radegunda; defeated Saxons (555–556); on death of brother Childebert I (558) acquired rule over all Franks.

Chlotar II. d. 629. King of Franks (613–629). Son of Chilperic I; under regency of mother Fredegund and uncle Guntram of Burgundy; recovered (613) lands lost to cousins Theudebert II and Theuderic II and established rule over all Franks.

Chlotar III. d. 673. King of Neustria (657–673). Son of Clovis II; under regency of mother Bathilda (657–664); later dominated by mayor of the palace Ebroïn.

Chlotar IV. d. 719. King of Austrasia (717–719). Possibly son of Theuderic III; placed on throne by Charles Martel to oppose pretender Chilperic II.

Chlothilde. See CLOTILDA.

Chmielnicki. See KHMELNYTSKY.

Cho \chō\ Sok. *Also known as* Ch'anggang \chäŋ-gäŋ\, *i.e.* Wide River, *or as* Ch'wi Ong \chwē-ōŋ\, *i.e.* Drunken Old Man. Korean painter, of the Yi dynasty (1392–1910). Noted for paintings of birds, esp. magpies.

Cho Sok-chin. *Also known as* Sa·ri·no \sä-rē-nō\, *i.e.* Small Jade. 1853–1920. Korean painter. Member of family of court painters; won favor with court portraits and studies of carp in revived Confucian style; founded academy to train young artists in classic style.

Choate \'chōt\, Joseph Hodges. 1832–1917. American lawyer and diplomat, b. Salem, Mass. Practiced in New York City; counsel in cases of great importance, as the Tweed Ring prosecution, the Tilden will contest, Standard Oil antitrust cases, income tax cases. U.S. ambassador to Britain (1899–1905); head of U.S. delegation to second International Peace Conference at The Hague (1907).

Choate, Rufus. 1799–1859. American lawyer, b. Essex, Mass. Practiced law, Boston (from 1834); eminent jury lawyer and orator. Member, U.S. House of Representatives (1831–34); U.S. senator (1841–45).

Cho·ca·no \chō-'kä-nō\, José Santos. 1875–1934. Peruvian poet. Associate of Pancho Villa and a lifelong revolutionary; considered one of first poets of South American nationalism. Author of *Iras santas* (1895), *En la aldea* (1895), *Azaleares* (1896), *El canto del siglo* (1900), *Fiat Lux* (1908), *Alma América* (1908), *Primicias de oro de las Indias* (1934), etc.

Chō Densu. See KICHIZAN Minchō.

Chod·kie·wicz \kòt-'kyev-ēch\, Jan Karol. 1560–1621. Ruthenian soldier. In Polish service, distinguished himself in campaign (1600) against the Turks; took part in war with Sweden for Lithuania (1601–05); chosen hetman of Lithuania (1602); won battle of Kirchholm on the Dvina against Charles IX of Sweden (1605); relieved Riga from Swedish attack (1609); fought Russia; fought the Turks at Chocim (1621).

Cho·do·wiec·ki \kō-dōv-'yet-skē\, Daniel Nikolaus. 1726–1801. German painter, etcher, and illustrator. Director, Berlin Academy of Art (1797). His works included a set of miniatures *History of the Life of Jesus Christ,* over 2000 vignettes and illustrations for books; known esp. for depictions of middle-class life.

Ch'oe \chœ\ Che-u. 1824–1864. Korean religious leader. Founded (1860) Tonghak sect, religion blending elements of Buddhism, Taoism, Confucianism, Catholicism, and intended to foster Korean nationalism and to resist westernizing influences; rapid spread of sect produced rebellion among peasants (1864) leading to arrest and execution of Ch'oe. See CH'OE Si-hyŏng.

Ch'oe Kyong. *Also known as* Kun·jae \kün-ja\, *i.e.* Prudent Study. 15th century. Korean painter. One of first court painters of Yi dynasty; known esp. for royal portraits.

Ch'oe Si-hyŏng. 1826–1899. Korean religious leader. Assumed leadership of Tonghak sect on death (1864) of Ch'oe Che-u (*q.v.*); built underground organization; published first Tonghak scriptures (1880, 1881), emphasizing service to Heaven and need for Korean national strength to resist West; instigated Tonghak Revolt (1894); executed.

Choe·ri·lus \'kir-ə-ləs, 'ker-\. 6th–5th century B.C. Athenian playwright. Author of tragedies (none extant) said to have been played in competition with works of Aeschylus and Pratinas.

Choerilus of Sa·mos \'sā-,mäs\. 6th–5th century B.C. Greek epic poet. Long resident in court of Archelaus, king of Macedonia. Author of the *Persica,* an epic based on the Greco–Persian wars.

Choi·seul \shwà-zœl \, César de. Duc de Choiseul. Comte du Ples·sis-Pras·lin \plā-sē-prä-laⁿ, ple-, -prà-\. 1598–1675. French soldier. Distinguished himself at siege of La Rochelle (1628); lieutenant general (1642); marshal of France (1645); commanded Royal army before Paris at time of the Fronde; defeated Turenne and Spaniards at Rethel (1650).

Choiseul, Étienne-François de. Duc. *In early life* Comte de Stain·ville \staⁿ-vēl\. 1719–1785. French politician. Fought with distinction in War of Austrian Succession (1740–48); won favor of Mme. de Pompadour in court intrigue (1752); ambassador at Rome (1754–57) and Vienna (1757–58); strengthened Austrian alliance; created duke (1758). Minister of foreign affairs (1758–61), of war and marine (1761–66), of war and foreign affairs (1766–70); directed French policy (1758–63) through Seven Years' War; obtained best possible terms of peace for France at Treaty of Paris (1763); negotiated Family Compact (1761) with Spain; rebuilt army and navy; purchased Corsica (1768); declined to promote domestic reforms; acquiesced in suppression of Jesuits (1762); dismissed (1770) for favoring war with Great Britain.

Chola. See CŌLA.

Cholmon·deley \'chəm-lē\, Hugh. 3d Baron Del·a·mere \'del-ə-,mi(ə)r\. 1870–1931. British colonialist. Settled in British East Africa Protectorate (1903); granted 100,000 acres; experimented in sheep- and cattle-raising, wheat farming; first president (1903) of Farmers' and Planters' Association (from 1904 the Colonists' Association); member of first legislative council (1907); M.P. from renamed Kenya (1920–31); organized intercolonial conferences, headed delegations to London (1923, 1930) aimed at establishing policies of white settlement and supremacy in East Africa.

Chŏng \chəŋ\ Sŏn. *Also known as* Kyŏm·jа \kyòm-jä\, *i.e.* Humble Study. 1676–1759. Korean painter. Known esp. for landscapes, often painted from direct observation; first Korean painter to depart from Chinese academic models.

Chŏng Yak-jong. *Also called* Augustine[1] Chong \'chòng\. 1760–1801. Korean religious leader. Converted to Catholicism; first president of Myongdo-hoe society founded to spread Catholic teachings; wrote first book on Catholicism in Korean; executed.

Cho·ni·a·tes \,kō-nē-'ät-,ēz\, Michael. c.1140–c.1222. Byzantine Humanist and prelate. Metropolitan of Athens (c.1175); amassed library of original and copied manuscripts; helped maintain classical scholarship in period of turmoil and decline; fled to Kéa on fall of Athens to Franks (1204). Author of letters, eulogies, verse including odes to Emperor Isaac II Angelus, etc. His brother ¶Nicetas (c.1140–1213), Byzantine official, historian, and theologian; held numerous civil service posts; wrote 21-volume history, based in part on own eyewitness knowledge, of conquest of Byzantium by Third and Fourth Crusades (1189–1204); compiled authoritative *Thesaurus of Orthodoxy,* anthology of 11th and 12th century Byzantine theological writings.

Cho·pin \'kòp-yin; *Fr* shò-paⁿ; *Angl* 'shō-,pan, 'shō-,paⁿ, 'shäp-ən\, Frédéric-François, *Pol.* Fryderyk Franciszek. 1810–1849. Polish composer and pianist. Son of émigré French father and Polish mother. Professional debut as piano virtuoso, Vienna (1829); settled in Paris (1831). Long the intimate friend of George Sand, who during his illness took him to Majorca, nursed him back to health (1838); center of young artistic and Polish émigré circles in Paris; visited England and Scotland (1848–49). A pianist of delicate, unconventional expressiveness; performed privately, generally for aristocratic drawing-room audiences. Composed mainly for piano in emotionally expressive but economical Romantic manner. Works included polonaises, mazurkas, nocturnes; études as *Twelve Grand Études* (1829–32); sonatas in *C Minor* (1827), *B Flat Minor* (1839), *B Minor* (1844); ballades, scherzos; *Twenty-four preludes* (1836–39); *Fantaisie in F Minor* (1840–41); two piano concertos (1829, 1830); piano trio (1828–29); *Sonata for Piano and Cello* (1845–46); *Seventeen Polish Songs* (pub. 1855).

Cho·pin \'shō-,pan, shō-'; 'shō-pən\, Katherine, *nee* O'Fla·her·ty \ō-'flā-(h)ər-tē\. 1851–1904. American writer, b. St. Louis. m. Oscar Chopin (1870; d.1882); lived with him in New Orleans and on plantation. Author of realistic tales and novels of Creole and Cajun life as *At Fault* (1890), *Bayou Folk* (1894), *A Night in Acadie* (1897), *The Awakening* (1899).

Cho·pi·nel \shò-pē-nel\ *or* **Clo·pi·nel** \klò-\, Jean. *Known as* Jean de Meun \mœⁿ\ *or* Meung \mœⁿ\. c.1240–before 1305. French poet, b. Meung-sur-Loire. Author of continuation of Guillaume de Lorris's *Roman de la rose,* notable for encyclopedic digressions on various topics.

Cho·ri·ci·us \kō-'rish(-ē)-əs\. *Known as* Choricius of Ga·za \'gä-zə, 'gāz-ə\. 6th century. Greek sophist and rhetorician. His extant orations include matter of historical interest, as a defense of actors and a description of churches in Gaza.

Chōshun. See MIYAGAWA Chōshun.

Chosroes. See KHOSROW.

Chou \'jō\. Longest dynasty (c.1122–221 B.C.) in history of China. Founded by Wu Wang (*q.v.*) who overthrew Chou Hsin, last of Shang dynasty. Empire enlarged beyond the Yangtze Valley; during dynasty, China changed from one of more backward areas of the world to one of most advanced; three great philosophers of China, Lao-tzu, Confucius, and Meng-tzu (*qq.v.*), lived during latter part of reign. See also CHOU KUNG and WEN WANG.

An ephemeral dynasty, ¶ Northern Chou (557–581), existed in western China, and the ¶Later Chou (954–960) was one of the Five Dynasties (*q.v.*).

Chouan. See COTTEREAU.

Chouart des Gro·seil·liers \shwàr-dā-grō-ze-yā\, Médard. Seigneur. 1625–1698. French explorer. To Canada (1639 or 1641); m.(1653) Marguerite, sister of Pierre Radisson; explored Northwest with Radisson (1659–60), reputedly reaching upper course of the Mississippi; probably explored to James Bay (1663); led British expedition to Hudson Bay (1668–69), leading to formation of Hudson's Bay Co. (1670); with Radisson led expedition against Hudson's Bay Co. settlement (1682).

Chou En-lai \'jō-'en-'lī\. *Pin-yin* Jou En-lai. 1898–1976. Chinese revolutionary and politician. Joined Chinese Communist party (1921) while a student in France; returned to China, joined Sun Yat-sen's Kuomintang (1924); director of military department of Chinese Communist Central Committee (1927); escaped Chiang Kai-shek's purge of Kuomintang (1927); member of Central Committee and Politburo (1927); briefly replaced Mao Tse-tung as commissar of Red army (1932–34); became chief diplomatic representative and negotiator of Communist party. Premier (1949–76), foreign minister (1949–58) of People's Republic of China; noted for skill in negotiation and in intra-party power struggles.

Chou Fang \-'fäŋ\. 8th century. Chinese painter. Noted for elegant portraits of ladies of the T'ang court.

Chou Hsin \-'shin\. c.1154–c.1122 B.C. Chinese emperor. Last emperor of Shang, or Yin, dynasty (fell 1122 B.C.); according to legend, overthrown because of extreme cruelty and debauchery of reign; taxed populace heavily to build Deer Tower Palace, which he burned and died in on overthrow by Wu Wang.

Chou Kung \-'gu̇g\. *Known as* the Duke of Chou. 12th century B.C. Chinese author and statesman. Brother of Wu Wang; regent during minority of second emperor of Chou dynasty. Supposed author of the much later *Chou li,* code of rules for officials of the state; traditional inventor of the compass; since time of Confucius, revered as paragon.

Chou Shu-jen \-'shü-'jən\. *Pseudonym* Lu Hsün \'lü-'shün\. 1881–1936. Chinese writer. Established reputation with short stories in Western manner, including "Madman's Diary" (1918), "True Story of Ah Q" (1921); published collections *Na-han* (1923), *P'ang-huang* (1926); also published prose essays, translations, etc.; in later years active promoter of Chinese Communist party.

Chou·teau \shü-'tō\. Family of American fur traders and pioneers, including: René Auguste (1749–1829), b. New Orleans, associated with his stepfather Pierre Laclède (*q.v.*) in founding St. Louis, Mo. (1764). His brother ¶Jean Pierre (1758–1849) established (1796) first permanent white settlement in Oklahoma; U.S. agent to all tribes west of Mississippi (1804); with two sons ¶Auguste Pierre (1786–1838) and ¶Pierre (1789–1865) joined Manuel Lisa in forming St. Louis Missouri Fur Co. (1809); held monopoly on Missouri valley fur trade (1809–14).

Chou Tun-i \-'tü-nē\. *Also known as* Chou Lien-hsi \-lē-'en-'shē\. 1017–1073. Chinese philosopher. Held various high governmental posts; developed notion of *T'ai chi* from *I Ching* into Confucian metaphysics, creating basis of Neo-Confucianism.

Chōzaemon. See MIYAGAWA Chōshun.

Chré·tien de Troyes \krā-tyaⁿ-də-trwä\. fl. 1170. French poet. A trouvère, one of first to compose after models established by troubadours of southern France. His Arthurian romances included *Cligès; Erec et Enide; Yvain, ou Le Chevalier au lion; Le Chevalier de la charette;* and *Le Conte du Graal* (or *Perceval*); may also have written non-Arthurian *Guillaume d'Angleterre.*

Christ, Jesus. See JESUS.

Chris·tian \'kris(h)-chən\. Name of ten kings of Denmark, eight of whom were kings of Norway also and two of whom were kings of Sweden:

Christian I. 1426–1481. King of Denmark (1448–81), Norway (1450–81), and Sweden (1457–64). Son of Dietrich, Count of Oldenburg, and Hedvig, heiress of Schleswig and Holstein, and a descendant of Eric V. Elected to succeed Christopher III in Denmark; accepted by Norway over Charles VIII of Sweden (1450); deposed Charles in war and held Swedish throne until overthrown by Swedish nobles (1457–64); lost all claim to Sweden by defeat at Brunkeberg (1471); made duke of Schleswig and count of Holstein (1460). Married daughter Margaret to James III of Scotland (1469); mortgaged Orkney and Shetland Islands to Scotland for dowry. Founded U. of Copenhagen (1479). Founder of house of Oldenburg.

Christian II. 1481–1559. King of Denmark and Norway (1513–23) and of Sweden (1520–23). Son of King John; viceroy in Norway (1502, 1506–12); m. (1515) Elizabeth of Habsburg, sister of Emperor Charles V; conquered Sweden (1520); showed extreme cruelty against Swedes, esp. in massacre of nobility at Stockholm (1520); driven out of Sweden by Gustav Vasa (1523), ending Kalmar Union; deposed and driven out of Denmark (1523); attempted to seize Norway (1531–32) but captured and imprisoned for remainder of life.

Christian III. 1503–1559. King of Denmark and Norway (1534–59). Son of Frederick I; became king at time of civil war (1533–36); ardent Lutheran, arrested Catholic bishops who had opposed his succession and organized Diet of Copenhagen (1536), establishing state Lutheran church; fostered trade, modernized administration, strengthened monarchy.

Christian IV. 1577–1648. King of Denmark and Norway (1588–1648). Son of Frederick II; ruled under regents (1588–96); strengthened Danish navy and army; Kalmar War with Sweden (1611–13) terminated successfully for Denmark by Treaty of Knäred (1613); increased influence along Baltic coast of Germany (1613–21); Christiania in Norway founded (1624) and named after him; joined Protestant cause in Thirty Years' War (1625–29); defeated severely at Lutter am Barenberge by Tilly and Wallenstein (1626); formed alliance with Gustav II Adolphus of Sweden (1628–29); his policies irritated Sweden, which declared war (1643–45), defeating Denmark; forced to yield power to nobles.

Christian V. 1646–1699. King of Denmark and Norway (1670–99). Son of Frederick III; tried to establish new nobility from lower orders; guided (1670–76) by his chancellor, Griffenfeld, who was imprisoned (1676); waged unsuccessful war with Sweden (1676–79); drew up new code for Norway (1683).

Christian VI. 1699–1746. King of Denmark and Norway (1730–46). Son of Frederick IV; conscientious ruler, devoted to pietistic religion; showed much extravagance in new buildings following whims of wife, Sophie Magdalene of Brandenburg-Kulmbach.

Christian VII. 1749–1808. King of Denmark and Norway (1766–1808). Son of Frederick V; brought up by cruel tutor; early became depraved and imbecile; m. (1766) Caroline Matilda, sister of George III of England; appointed as court physician (1769) and privy councillor (1770) Count Johann Struensee (*q.v.*), but had him arrested and beheaded (1772); marriage dissolved (1772); became hopelessly insane and relinquished control to Crown Prince Frederick, who ruled as regent (1784–1808; see FREDERICK VI).

Christian VIII. 1786–1848. King of Denmark (1839–48). Son of Frederick VI; appointed viceroy of Norway (1813); elected king (1814) by Norwegian faction opposed to cession to Sweden; driven out of Norway during brief war (1814); lived in retirement (1815–31); member of council of state (1831–39); as king, opposed liberal projects; restored Iceland's Althing (1843).

Christian IX. 1818–1906. King of Denmark (1863–1906). Son of William, Duke of Schleswig-Holstein-Sonderburg-Beck and (from 1825) of Glücksburg, and Princess Louise of Hesse-Cassel; entered army (1835); m. (1842) Louise of Hesse-Cassel. Since male line became extinct in Frederick VII, confirmed (1852) by council of great powers in London as crown prince; succeeded to throne (1863) on death of Frederick VII. Forced by popular feeling to sign November Constitution (1863), incorporating Schleswig into kingdom; act led to war with Prussia and Austria (1864); Jutland occupied; Denmark forced by Treaty of Vienna to renounce Schleswig, Holstein, and Lauenburg; new constitution promulgated (1866); long struggle of parties of Left and Right for supremacy of Folketing (1872–1905); supported the Conservatives; finally consented to formation of Left ministry (1901). Father of Frederick VIII of Denmark, George, King of the Hellenes (1863–1913), Alexandra (m. Edward VII of Great Britain), Dagmar (Marie Feodorovna; m. heir to Russian throne, later Czar Alexander III).

Christian X. 1870–1947. King of Denmark (1912–47) and Iceland (1918–44). Son of Frederick VIII; during World War I established closer relations with other Scandinavian countries; signed new constitution (1915) enfranchising women; Act of Union (1918) with Iceland, whereby Iceland became independent with connection with Denmark through sovereign; during World War II became symbol of Danish resistance to German occupation; imprisoned (1943–45).

Chris·tian \'kris(h)-chən\. *Known as* der tol·le Christian \der-'tòl-ə-'krist-yän\, *i.e.* Mad Christian. 1599–1626. German soldier. Son of Duke of Brunswick; administrator of bishopric of Halberstadt (1616); fought Spanish in Netherlands (1621); in Thirty Years' War raised and led army for Elector Frederick V of Palatinate; became known for plundering; defeated by Tilly at Höchst (1622), Stadtlohn (1623); in service of Christian IV of Denmark (1625).

Christian, Charles. 1919–1942. American musician, b. Dallas, Tex. Pioneered in use of electrically amplified guitar; with Benny Goodman's band (1939–42); made guitar into a solo jazz instrument with brilliant improvisational technique.

Christian, Fletcher. fl. 1789. English naval mutineer. Master's mate and leader of mutiny against Captain William Bligh (*q.v.*) aboard exploring ship *Bounty* (April 1789); founded colony on Pitcairn Island.

Christian, William. 1608–1663. British soldier, b. Isle of Man. Commandant of Manx militia; revolted against Countess of Derby when she surrendered Man to Parliamentarians in exchange for her hostage husband, the 7th earl (1651); civil governor of Man (1656–58), fled accusations of misappropriating funds; returned, seized by 8th earl, shot. Celebrated as Manx hero Il·liam Dhö·ne \'il-yəm-'t͟hü-nə\, i.e. Brown William, in ballad "Boase Illiam Dhöne."

Christian Augustus. 1798–1869. Duke of Schleswig-Holstein-Sonderburg-Augustenburg (1814–69). On accession (1848) of Frederick VII of Denmark, forced to relinquish his claims under Salic law to Danish throne; renunciation later (on death of Frederick VII, 1863) repudiated by his son Frederick—main cause of war (1866) between Prussia and Austria.

Christianus Democritus. See J. K. DIPPEL.

Chris·tie \'kris-tē\, Dame Agatha Mary Clarissa, *nee* Miller. 1890–1976. English writer. m. 1st, Archibald Christie (1914; div. 1928), 2d, Max Mallowan (1930). Creator of the fictional detectives Hercule Poirot and Jane Marple; Poirot appeared in *Mysterious Affair at Styles* (1920) and some 25 subsequent novels, Marple in *Murder at the Vicarage* (1930) and several others; other works included *Murder of Roger Ackroyd* (1926), plays *The Mousetrap* (1952), *Witness for the Prosecution* (1953); novels sold over 100 million copies.

Christie, James. 1730–1803. English auctioneer. Founder (1766) of line of London auctioneers. His sons ¶James (1773–1831), auctioneer, antiquary, writer on Etruscan and Greek vases, and ¶Samuel Hunter (1784–1865), mathematician, student of magnetism, professor of mathematics at Woolwich (1806–54). S. H. Christie's son ¶Sir William Henry Mahoney (1845–1922), astronomer royal (1881–1910); undertook observations of sunspots; erected 28-inch reflector and 26-inch photographic refractor (1890–98); designed new altazimuth; author of papers on solar eclipses.

Chris·ti·na \kris-'tē-nə\. 1626–1689. Queen of Sweden (1632–54). Daughter of Gustav II Adolphus; ruled (1632–44) under regency of five crown officers, affairs being actually managed by Axel Oxenstierna; came of age and was crowned (1644); reign disturbed by final years of Thirty Years' War, by dissensions in Swedish Diet, by attempted revolts; patron of arts and learning. Proclaimed her cousin Charles X Gustav as successor; abdicated (1654); embraced Roman Catholicism; attempted to gain thrones of Naples (1656), Poland (1667); patroness of Scarlatti, Bernini, Corelli; died in Rome.

Chris·tine de Pi·san \krēs-tēn-də-pē-zäⁿ\. 1364–c.1430. French poet. Daughter of Italian astrologer to Charles V of France. Author of love ballads, rondeaux, lays, verses on courtly love; also wrote biography *Livre des fais et bonnes mœurs du sage roy Charles V* (1404), *Lamentation* (1410) and *Livre de la paix* (1413) inspired by civil wars, several works in defense of women as *Épistre du dieu d'amours* (1399), *Cité des dames* (1405), *Livre des trois vertus* (1406), autobiography *La Vision de Christine* (1405).

Christ·mas Møl·ler \'krēst-mås-'mœl-ər\, Guido Leo John. 1894–1948. Danish politician. Member of Folketing (1920–41, 1945–47); chairman of Conservative party (1932–39); minister of commerce (1940); leader of resistance to German occupation; in London (1942–45); foreign minister (1945–47), party chairman (1945–47).

Chri·stof·fel \kris-'tō-fəl\, Elwin Bruno. 1829–1900. Swiss mathematician. Professor at Zürich, Berlin, and Strassburg (from 1872); known for work in higher analysis, geometry, mathematical physics, and geodesy.

Christoffer. See CHRISTOPHER.

Chris·tophe \krē-stȯf\, Henri. 1767–1820. Haitian revolutionist and ruler. Born a slave in Grenada; able lieutenant to Toussaint L'Ouverture in revolution (1791) against French; fought against Leclerc (1802); joined uprising of Dessalines (1803–04); after death of Dessalines (1806) became provisional chief of northern Haiti; summoned assembly (1806); rejected proposed constitution; defeated by Pétion (1807); established himself as King Henri I (1811) in north; built Citadelle Laferrière; suffered paralytic stroke, shot himself.

Chris·to·pher \'kris-tə-fər\. d. 904. Antipope (903–904). Drove Leo V from papacy; deposed by supporters of Sergius III.

Christopher. Name of three kings of Denmark:

Christopher I. 1219–1259. King (1252–59). Son of Valdemar; made duke of Lolland-Falster; succeeded brother Abel (1252); imprisoned archbishop of Lund; died during ensuing war with Prince of Rügen.

Christopher II. 1276–1332. King (1320–26, 1330–32). Son of Erik Glipping; succeeded brother Erik Menved; forced to accept permanent *hof,* assembly of prelates and secular leaders; driven out by Count Gerhard of Holstein (1326); returned to country in civil upheaval.

Christopher III. *Orig.* Christopher of Bavaria. 1418–1448. King (1440–48). Nephew of Erik of Pomerania; elected king by council (1440), accepted by Sweden (1440) and Norway (1442); made Copenhagen permanent royal residence (1443); restored commercial privileges of Hanseatic League.

Christopher. d. 931. Coruler (921–931) of Eastern Roman Empire with his father, Romanus I Lecapenus.

Chris·toph·er *or* **Chris·tof·fer** \kris-'tō-fər\ of Ol·den·burg \'ōl-dən-ˌbu̇rk\. Count. c.1504–1566. Danish noble and soldier. Engaged as mercenary to lead forces of Copenhagen, Malmö, Lübeck in effort to restore Christian II (1534); war (1534–35) became known as Count's War for him; defeated (1535), surrendered to Christian III (1536).

Chris·tus *or* **Cris·tus** \'kris-tœs\, Petrus. c.1420–1472 or 1473. Flemish painter. Influenced by, perhaps student of, van Eyck; reputedly introduced geometric perspective into Netherlandish art. Works included *Virgin with SS. Jerome and Francis; Portrait of a Carthusian; Virgin with Child, St. Barbara, and a Carthusian; St. Eligius.*

Chris·ty \'kris-tē\, Edwin Pearce. 1815–1862. American actor and singer, b. Philadelphia. Founder and interlocutor of Christy Minstrels (1842; orig. the Virginia Minstrels); developed standard minstrel show routines, as Tambo and Bones comedy, parodies of legitimate plays, etc.; commissioned many songs by Stephen Foster for shows; retired (1855).

Christy, Howard Chandler. 1873–1952. American illustrator and painter, b. Morgan Co., Ohio. Illustrator for New York periodicals esp. (from 1910) *Cosmopolitan* and Hearst magazines; illustrated books, including nine by James Whitcomb Riley and three of his own; developed popular image of the "Christy girl." His paintings included many portraits, as of Will H. Hays, George Harvey, Warren G. Harding, President and Mrs. Calvin Coolidge, Charles E. Hughes, Benito Mussolini, John Nance Garner, Will Rogers, Amelia Earhart, and *Signing the Constitution* (1940) in Capitol building, Washington, D.C.

Chro·de·gang \'krōd-ə-ˌgaŋ\ *or* **Rot·gang** \'rōt-ˌgaŋ\. Saint. d. 766. Frankish prelate. Chancellor under Charles Martel; bishop of Metz (from 742); promulgated regulations for Frankish clergy. Author of *Vita Canonica.*

Chry·san·der \krūē-'zän-dər\, Friedrich, *in full* Karl Franz Friedrich. 1826–1901. German music scholar. Founded Handel Society (1856), and through it published first complete edition of Handel's works (93 vols., 1858–94). Author of a life of Handel (1858–67), left uncompleted at his death.

Chry·sip·pus \krī-'sip-əs, krə-\. c.280–c.206 B.C. Greek Stoic philosopher. Considered with Zeno the founder of Stoa academy at Athens.

Chrys·ler \'krīs-lər\, Walter Percy. 1875–1940. American automobile manufacturer, b. Wamego, Kans. Works manager (1912–16), president and general manager (1916–19), Buick Motor Co.; took over Willys-Overland Co. (1921); reorganized Maxwell Motor Co. (1921), which introduced Chrysler automobile (1924) and became Chrysler Corp. (1925); acquired Dodge Brothers firm (1928); introduced De Soto and Plymouth automobiles; retired as president (1935); chairman (1935–40). Built Chrysler Building, N.Y.C. (completed 1929), then world's tallest.

Chrysologus, Saint Peter. See PETER CHRYSOLOGUS.

Chrys·o·lo·ras \ˌkris-ə-'lōr-əs\, Manuel. c.1353–1415. Greek scholar. To Italy (1394) on mission from Emperor Manuel II Palaeologus to obtain aid against Turks; professor of Greek in Florence (1395–98); translated Plato's *Republic* into Latin. Later, went on mission to Paris (1408) and to Germany (1413). Author of *Erotemata sive quaestiones,* first Greek grammar used in western Europe.

Chrysorrhoas. See JOHN of Damascus.

Chrys·os·tom \'kris-əs-təm, kris-'äs-təm\, John. Saint. c.347–407. Syrian prelate. Called soon after his death Chrysostom, i.e. Golden-mouthed. Became hermit monk; returned to Antioch, gained great reputation as preacher; ordained priest (386); archbishop of Constantinople (398–404); gained popular following by eloquent criticisms of wealthy and powerful; deposed at a synod near Constantinople and banished at instance of Empress Eudoxia and patriarch of Alexandria (403); recalled because of wrath of people, but banished again (404), to Armenia. Author of homilies, commentaries, and letters that had great influence. Later recognized as Doctor of the Church.

Chu \'jü\. Name of family, founded by Chu Yüan-chang, that supplied the emperors of the Ming dynasty (1368–1644) of China. Its sixteen rulers, sometimes known by their temple names and sometimes by their reign titles (era names), were:

Chu Yüan-chang \-'yü-'än-jäŋ\. *Temple name* T'ai Tsu \'tīd-'zü\. *Reign title* Hung-wu \'hu̇ŋ-'wü\, *i.e.* Vastly Martial. 1328–1398. Founder and first emperor (1368–98). Born into peasant family; became a mendicant monk (1344); joined rebel forces of Kuo Tzu-hsing (1352), becoming leader on Kuo's death (1355); brilliant military leader; captured Nanking (1356); conquered (1364) provinces of Hupeh, Hunan, Kiangsi; proclaimed himself Prince of Wu (1364); founded (1368) Ming dynasty with capital at Nanking; captured Peking (1368), ending Yüan dynasty; drove out Mongols and unified all of China (by 1382); ruled despotically; established schools, reformed civil service system; extended his rule to southern Manchuria; gained suzerainty over Korea and Annam.

Chu Yün-wen \-'yün-'wən\. *Temple name* Hui Ti \'hwē-'dē\. *Reign title* Chien-wen \jē-'ən-'wən\. 1377–?1440. Emperor (1398–1402). Grandson of Chu Yüan-chang; attempted to gain control over provinces ruled by his uncles; deposed (1402) in rebellion led by his uncle Chu Ti; may have died during rebellion, but according to legend escaped and lived as an itinerant monk.

Chu Ti \-'dē\. *Temple names* T'ai Tsung \'tīd-'zu̇ŋ\ *and later* Ch'eng-tsu \'chəŋ-dzü\. *Reign title* Yung-lo \'yu̇ŋ-'lō\, *i.e.* Eternal Joy. 1360–1424. Emperor (1402–24). Son of Chu Yüan-chang and uncle of Chu Yün-wen; named Prince of Yen (1370); rebelled (1399) against Chu Yün-wen and deposed him (1402); purged his enemies; annexed Annam (1407); gained suzerainty over Japan; sent naval expeditions throughout Asia and as far as the east coast of Africa; ended Mongol invasions; moved capital to Peking and rebuilt it; rehabilitated the Grand Canal and other waterways; ordered compilation of the *Yung-lo ta-tien,* a compendium of 11,000 volumes on all fields of knowledge. His reign considered pinnacle of Ming dynasty's power.

Chu Kao-chih \-'gau̇-'ji(ə)r\. *Temple name* Jen Tsung \'zhən-'dzu̇ŋ\. *Reign title* Hung-hsi \'hu̇ŋ-shē\. 1378–1425. Emperor (1424–25). Son of Chu Ti; his reign peaceful and prosperous.

Chu Chan-chi \-'jän-'jē\. *Temple name* Hsüan Tsung \'shü-'än-dzu̇ŋ\. *Reign title* Hsüan-te \'shü-'än-'dä\. 1398–1435. Emperor (1425–35). Son of Chu Kao-chih; reign also peaceful.

Chu Ch'i-chen \-'chē-'jən\. *Temple name* Ying Tsung \'yiŋ-'dzu̇ŋ\. *Reign titles* Cheng-t'ung \'jəŋ-'tu̇ŋ\ *for first reign and* T'ien-shun \tē-'ən-shu̇n\ *for second.* 1427–1464. Emperor (1435–49, 1457–64). Son of Chu Chan-chi; during first reign, under dominance of eunuch Wang Chen; captured (1449) while leading expedition against Mongol leader Esen Taiji, imprisoned (1449–50); restored after death of Chu Ch'i-yü (1457); again dominated by eunuchs; first Ming emperor to will that his concubines not be sacrificed after his death.

Chu Ch'i-yü \-'chē-'yü\. *Temple name* Ching Ti \'jiŋ-'dē\. *Reign title* Ching-t'ai \'jiŋ-'tī\. 1428–1457. Emperor (1449–57). Son of Chu Chan-chi; enthroned after capture of his brother Chu Ch'i-chen (1449); attack on Peking by Esen Taiji repelled by his defense minister Yü Ch'ien (1450); caused much resentment by designating his son as heir apparent instead of Chu Ch'i-chen's son; deposed on his deathbed by Chu Ch'i-chen.

Chu Chien-shen \-jē-'ən-'shən\. *Temple name* Hsien Tsung \shē-'ən-'dzu̇ŋ\. *Reign title* Ch'eng-hua \'chəŋ-hwä\. 1447–1487. Emperor (1464–87). Son of Chu Ch'i-chen; indifferent ruler; dominated by his concubine Wan; government controlled by eunuch Wang Chih; reign noted for its enamel pottery.

Chu Yu-t'ang \-'yü-'däŋ\. *Temple name* Hsiao Tsung \shē-'au̇d-'zu̇ŋ\. *Reign title* Hung-chih \'hu̇ŋ-'ji(ə)r\. 1470–1505. Emperor (1487–1505). Son of Chu Chien-shen; reign peaceful.

Chu Hou-chao \-'hō-'jau̇\. *Temple name* Wu Tsung \'wüd-'zu̇ŋ\. *Reign title* Cheng-te \'jəŋ-'dä\. 1491–1521. Emperor (1505–21). Son of Chu Yu-t'ang; devoted himself to pleasure and learning languages; during reign, eunuchs achieved such power that subsequent rulers could not dislodge them; reign also marked by corruption, excessive taxation, and rebellions.

Chu Hou-tsung \-'hōd-'zu̇ŋ\. *Temple name* Shih Tsung \'shi(ə)rd-'zu̇ŋ\. *Reign title* Chia-ching \jē-'ä-'jiŋ\. 1507–1566. Emperor (1521–66). Cousin of Chu Hou-chao; grandson of Chu Chien-shen; notoriously cruel; government controlled by a few favorites; spent much time and money in search of elixir of life; reign marked by lawlessness, persecution of competent officials and deterioration of border defenses.

Chu Tsai-kou \-'dzī-'gō\. *Temple name* Mu Tsung \'müd-'zu̇ŋ\. *Reign title* Lung-ch'ing \'lu̇ŋ-'chiŋ\. 1537–1572. Emperor (1566–72). Son of Chu Hou-tsung; reign saw rise to power of minister Chang Chü-chen, period of stability and prosperity, attempts to erase corruption and limit government spending, and repulsion of attacks of Mongol leader Altan.

Chu I-chün \-'ē-'jün\. *Temple name* Shen Tsung \'shən-dzu̇ŋ\. *Reign title* Wan-li \'wän-'lē\. 1563–1620. Emperor (1572–1620). Son of Chu Tsai-kou; unable to make adequate defenses against Manchu attacks; reign marked by partisan controversies and control of government by eunuchs.

Chu Ch'ang-lo \-'chäŋ-'lō\. *Temple name* Kuang Tsung \'gwäŋ-dzu̇ŋ\. *Reign title* T'ai-ch'ang \'tī-'chäŋ\. 1582–1620. Emperor (1620). Son of Chu I-chün; reigned only one month.

Chu Yu-chiao \-'yü-jē-'au̇\. *Temple name* Hsi Tsung \'shēd-'zu̇ŋ\. *Reign title* T'ien-ch'i \tē-'ən-'chē\. 1605–1627. Emperor (1620–27). Son of Chu Ch'ang-lo; weak and simple-minded, devoted himself to carpentry; government run by eunuch Wei Chung-hsien who let dynasty disintegrate.

Chu Yu-chien \-'yü-chē-ən \. *Temple names* Ssu Tsung \'süd-'zu̇ŋ\, Huai Tsung \'hwīd-'zu̇ŋ\, *and* I Tsung \'ēd-'zu̇ŋ\. *Canonized by Manchus as* Chuang-lieh-ti \'chwäŋ-lē-'ed-'ē\. *Reign title* Ch'ung-chen \'chu̇ŋ-'jən\. 1611–1644. Last emperor of dynasty (1627–44). Brother of Chu Yu-chiao; tried to revive dynastic fortunes; banished Wei Chung-hsien; unable to stop partisan quarreling within government and army; his oppressive taxes caused revolts of populace; committed suicide after Peking captured by rebels.

Two members of the Chu family were claimants to the Ming throne after the downfall of the dynasty:

Chu Yü-chien \-'yü-jē-'ən\. *Reign title* Lung-wu \lu̇ŋ-'wü\. *Also known as* Prince of T'ang \'täŋ\. 1602–1646. Ruler of Fukien Province in southern China; with support of pirate leader Cheng Chih-lung (*q.v.*), proclaimed himself Ming emperor (Aug. 1645); reigned for about 13 months; captured and executed by Ch'ing forces.

Chu Yu-lang \-'yü-'läŋ\. *Reign title* Yung-li \'yu̇ŋ-'lē\. *Also known as* Prince of Kuei \'kwā\. 1623–1662. Grandson of Chu I-chün; after capture of Prince of T'ang (1646), fled to Canton and proclaimed himself emperor; gained nominal control of seven provinces (by 1648); forced by Ch'ing forces to flee to Burma (1659); captured and executed by the Ch'ing.

Chu \chü\ Ki-chol. 1897–1944. Korean clergyman. Ordained Presbyterian minister (1926); leader of opposition to Japanese demand that Korean Christians pay reverence at Shintō shrines; imprisoned several times, then executed.

Chuang-lieh-ti. See Chu Yu-chien under CHU family.

Chuang-tzu \jü-'äŋ-'dzü\. 4th century B.C. Chinese philosopher and teacher. Considered most important of early interpreters of Taoism. Author of *Chuang-tzu,* Taoist work esteemed even above Lao-tzu's *Tao-te Ching.*

Chubb \'chəb\, Thomas. 1679–1747. English deist. Author of *The Supremacy of the Father Asserted* (1715), a defense of William Whiston's argument for Arian view, *Discourse Concerning Reason* (1731), *True Gospel of Jesus Christ Vindicated* (1739), *Discourse on Miracles* (1741).

Ch'ü Ch'iu-pai \'chü-chē-'ü-'pī\. *Also known as* Sung Yang \'su̇ŋ-'yäŋ\. *Orig.* Ch'u Shuang \'chüsh-'wäŋ\. 1899–1935. Chinese politician and writer. Member (from 1922), a leader, and propagandist of Chinese Communist party; head of party (1927, 1934–35); active in enlisting intellectuals. Author of books on Russia, propaganda works, and autobiographical *To-yu te hua* (1935).

Chu Chu'üan-chung. See CHU WEN.

Chu Hsi \'jü-'shē\. *Literary names* Yüan Hui \'yü-'än-hwē\ *and* Chung Hui \'ju̇ŋ-hwē\. *Courtesy names* Hui An \'hwē-'än\, Ch'eng Lang \'chəŋ-'läŋ\, Chi Yen \'jē-'yən\, Hui Weng \'hwē-'wəŋ\, Hsün Weng \'shün-'wəŋ\, *and* Yün Ku Lao-jen \'yün-'gü-'lau̇-'zhən\. *Also known as* Chu-tzu \'jüd-'zü\ *and* Chu-fu-tzu \'jü-'füd-'zü\. 1130–1200. Chinese philosopher. Held various government posts, esp. in administration of public granaries and famine relief; noted also as teacher and public moralist. Developed work of Ch'eng I, Ch'eng Hao, Chang Tsai, Chou Tun-i into system of Neo-Confucianism; compiled and commented on their works, his commentaries on Chinese Classics, known collectively as *Ssu shu,* becoming required reading for civil service applicants.

Chui·kov \chüi-'kȯf\, Vasily Ivanovich. 1900–1982. Russian soldier. Entered Red army (1918); served in Finnish war (1939–40); adviser to Chiang Kai-shek (1940–41); commanded defense of Stalingrad against German troops (1942); led Russian drives into Donets Basin and Crimea, later into Germany; accepted German surrender in Berlin (May 1, 1945); commanded Russian occupation forces (1945–53); later commander of all Russian land forces, deputy minister of defense.

Chü-jan \'jü-'zhän\. 10th century. Chinese painter. Buddhist priest; court painter of Southern T'ang and Sung dynasties; known for evocative landscapes.

Chu-ko Liang \'jü-'gō-lē-'äŋ\. 181–234 A.D. Chinese soldier. Aided in Liu Pei in founding Shu Han dynasty (221–263); chief minister (221–234); known as a strategist and inventor. Subject of many legends and a favorite Chinese hero; made Confucian saint (1724).

Chulalongkorn. See RAMA V of Siam.

Chum·nus \'ku̇m-nəs\, Nicephorus. 1250–1327. Byzantine politician and scholar. Officer and diplomat in imperial service; chief minister of Andronicus II; governor of Thessalonica (1309). Author of letters, orations on philosophical and religious topics.

Chunder Sen, Keshub. See KESHUB CHUNDER SEN.

Ch'ung-chen. See Chu Yu-chien under CHU family.

Chung Ling Soo. See William E. CAMPBELL.

Ch'ung-te. See ABAHAI.

Chung Tsung. See Li Che under LI family.

Chu·quet \shü̅e-ke\, Nicolas. c.1445–c.1500. French mathematician. Author of notable book on mathematics, part of which was published as *Triparty* (1880).

Church \'chərch\, Benjamin. 1734–1778. American physician and spy, b. Newport, R.I. Member of Boston Committee of Correspondence; communicated with Gov. Hutchinson and Gen. Thomas Gage; named director of Continental army hospital at Cambridge, Mass. (1775); detected sending coded letter to British naval commander, court-martialled (1775); deported to West Indies (1778); ship lost at sea.

Church, Frank Forrester. 1924–1984. American politician, b. Boise, Idaho. U.S. senator from Idaho (1956–80); a leading liberal voice and champion of civil rights, environmental legislation, and opposition to Vietnam war.

Church, Frederick Edwin. 1826–1900. American painter, b. Hartford, Conn. Student of Thomas Cole; became known for landscapes, esp. of scenes of grandeur, rendered with striking effects of light; traveled in South America and Middle East. Works included *Falls of Tecemdama, Heart of the Andes, Cotopaxi, Icebergs, Aurora Borealis, Vale of St. Thomas, Horseshoe and American Falls, Niagara.*

Church, Sir Richard. 1784–1873. British soldier, b. Ireland. Disowned by Society of Friends when he enlisted as soldier at age of 16; served in Egypt (1801); advocated British retention of Ionian Islands; formed two Greek training regiments (1809–15); fought in service of King Ferdinand of Naples (1817–20); commander in chief of Greek insurgent army (1827–29) engaged in expelling Turks; took part in Greek revolution (1843); Greek general (1854).

Church, Richard Thomas. 1893–1972. English writer. His books of verse included *Flood of Life* (1917), *Hurricane* (1919), *Portrait of the Abbot* (1926), *Glance Backward* (1930), *Twentieth-Century Psalter* (1943), *Prodigal* (1953), *Burning Bush* (1967); his prose works, *The Prodigal Father* (1933), *The Porch* (1937), *Calling for a Spade* (1939), *Green Tide* (1944), *Dog Toby* (1953), *Bells of Rye* (1960), and three volumes of autobiography: *Over the Bridge* (1955), *The Golden Sovereign* (1957), *The Voyage Home* (1964).

Church, Richard William. 1815–1890. British clergyman. Lifelong friend of Newman, helped allay outcry against Tractarianism; dean of St. Paul's (1871–90); known for literary studies, esp. of Dante.

Church, William. 1778?–1863. American inventor. Devised an early typesetting machine (casting and composing automatically; justification by hand), patented in England (1822).

Chur·chill \ˈchər-ˌchil, ˈchərch-ˌhil\, Arabella. 1648–1730. Mistress of James II of England. Elder sister of John Churchill; entered service of Duchess of York (1665); became (c.1667) mistress of duke, later James II; by enemies often credited with brother's rapid advancement. Mother by James of James Fitzjames, later Duke of Berwick; Henry Fitzjames, later Duke of Albemarle; and two daughters.

Churchill, Charles. 1731–1764. English poet and satirist. Ordained priest (1756); won fame with his *Rosciad* (anonymous, 1761), a satire on London actors and actresses, and the *Apology* (1761), a ruthless attack upon his critics; indulged in dissipation and gave up church offices (1763); became ally of John Wilkes. Author of *The Ghost* (1763), ridiculing Dr. Johnson over his account of the Cock Lane ghost, *The Prophecy of Famine* (1763), attacking Lord Bute and the Scots, *The Duellist* (1764), assailing an unsuccessful assassin of Wilkes, *The Candidate* (1764), exposing "Jemmy Twitcher" (Lord Sandwich).

Churchill, John. 1st Duke of Marl·bor·ough \ˈmärl-bər-ə, ˈmȯl-, -ˌbə-rə, -brə\. 1650–1722. English military commander. Page to Duke of York (1665) and favorite of Duchess of Cleveland; commissioned ensign (1667); attracted attention at Nijmegen (1672); saved life of Duke of Monmouth at Maastricht (1673); close associate of York, by whom, as James II, he was created (1685) Baron Churchill of San·dridge \ˈsan-drij\; second in command in crushing at Sedgemoor Monmouth's rebellion in western counties (1685); lieutenant general (1688). Went over to William of Orange with 5000 troops (1688); privy councilor and earl of Marlborough (1689); sent by William to fight in Netherlands (1689), in Ireland (1690); imprisoned on accusation of plotting restoration of James II (1692); restored to favor (1698). Under Queen Anne, commander in chief over armies of England and Holland in War of Spanish Succession; impeded by jealousy among allies and difference of aims; by brilliant exploits at Kaiserswerth, Venlo, and Liége, drove French out of Spanish Gelderland (1702); created 1st duke of Marlborough. Virtually regent in England, controlling lord treasurer Godolphin, as his wife (see below) controlled Queen Anne. Had to abandon attack on Antwerp (1703) because of Dutch incapacity; thwarted French in attempt to join Bavarians by bloody victory of Blenheim (Aug. 13, 1704); rewarded with manor of Woodstock, where Blenheim Palace was built for him at huge expense; routed French at Ramillies (1706), entered Brussels, Antwerp, Ostend; deserted by emperor and involved in quarrel of Whigs and Tories (1708); defeated French at Oudenarde (1708), keeping Flanders from allegiance to French; captured Lille, Ghent, and Bruges (1708); took Tournai after terrible siege (1709); met Villars in indecisive battle of Malplaquet (1709); took Mons and other French towns. Undermined by political intrigue at home and dismissal of Godolphin and Sunderland, and by Duchess of Marlborough's alienation of Queen Anne and defection to Whig cause; following dismissal of duchess, dismissed from offices on charge of embezzlement of public money (1711); on accession of George I returned to his military post (1714).

His wife (m. 1678) ¶Sarah, *nee* Jennings (1660–1744), Duchess of Marlborough. Entered service of Duke of York (1673) and soon became trusted friend of Princess Anne; lady of the bedchamber (1683); helped Anne to escape (1688); helped effect reconciliation of Anne and William III (1694); gained ascendancy over her on her accession as queen; as mistress of robes and keeper of privy purse, controlled Whig ministry, deducted pension for herself; finally by imperious and tactless behavior alienated Queen Anne and dismissed (1711); succeeded by her cousin Abigail Hill (Mrs. Masham). Her daughter Henrietta m. (1698) Sidney Godolphin, Earl of Godolphin; Anne m. (1700) son of Lord Sunderland.

Churchill, Randolph Frederick Edward Spencer. 1911–1968. British author and journalist. Son of Sir Winston Churchill; foreign correspondent for various journals; M.P. (1940–45); army intelligence officer in Middle East, N. Africa, Yugoslavia during World War II. Author of *They Serve the Queen* (1953), *What I Said About the Press* (1957), *Fight for Tory Leadership* (1964), *Twenty-one Years* (1965); two volumes of biography of father *Winston S. Churchill, Youth* (1966), *The Young Politician* (1967).

Churchill, Randolph Henry Spencer. *Known as* Lord Randolph. 1849–1895. British politician. Third son of 7th Duke of Marlborough (see under SPENCER family); m. (1874) Jennie Jerome of New York; father of Sir Winston Churchill (*q.v.*). As M.P. (from 1874) led a group (nicknamed the "Fourth Party") in aggressive Toryism; assailed both Gladstone and Conservative front bench; favored conciliation in Irish affairs; developed a progressive conservatism, called Tory democracy; promoter and first member of Primrose League; secretary of state for India (1885–86); contested John Bright's seat (1885); chancellor of exchequer and leader of House of Commons (1886); resigned (1886) after rejection of his reduced service budget by prime minister, Marquess of Salisbury; thereafter lost interest in politics; traveled for health and described travels in *Men, Mines, and Animals in South Africa* (1892).

Churchill, Winston. 1871–1947. American novelist, b. St. Louis. Author of historical novels, including *Richard Carvel* (1899), *The Crisis* (1901), *The Crossing* (1904), *Coniston* (1906), *Mr. Crewe's Career* (1908), *A Modern Chronicle* (1910), *The Inside of the Cup* (1913), *A Far Country* (1915), *The Dwelling Place of Light* (1917).

Churchill, Sir Winston Leonard Spencer. 1874–1965. British statesman and author. Elder son of Lord Randolph Churchill; served in Cuba with Spanish forces (1895), in India (1897), in Sudan (1898), present at Khartoum (1898); as war correspondent, captured by Boers but escaped (1899), and engaged in battles up to capture of Pretoria. M.P. (1901–22, 1924–65); joined free traders in opposition to Chamberlain's tariff proposals; undersecretary (1905–08) for colonies under Campbell-Bannerman, whose policy of self-government for Transvaal and Orange River Colony he advanced with skill and vigor. Entered cabinet as president of Board of Trade (1908–10); established state labor exchanges and carried Trade Boards Act providing organization of unorganized trades; by oratory helped carry Parliament Act (1911); home secretary (1910–11); first lord of admiralty (1911–15); built up navy, established naval war staff; directed Antwerp expedition and Dardanelles campaign, after failure of which he was demoted. Served with regiment in France (1916); minister of munitions (1917); secretary for war and air (1919–21), for colonies (1921–22); chancellor of exchequer (1924–29). First lord of admiralty on Britain's entry into World War II (1939–40); prime minister (1940–45). Met at sea with President Roosevelt (Aug. 1941) to draw up the joint statement of international policy known as the Atlantic Charter; conferred on war strategy with Roosevelt at Washington (1942 and 1943), Casablanca (1943), and Quebec (1943 and 1944), with Roosevelt and Chiang Kai-shek at Cairo (1943), with Roosevelt and Stalin at Tehran (1943) and Yalta (1945), with Truman and Stalin at Potsdam (1945). Resigned as prime minister after Labour victory in elections. Gave "iron curtain" speech, Fulton, Mo. (1946). Again prime minister (1951–1955). Author of *Lord Randolph Churchill* (1906), *My African Journey* (1908), *The World Crisis* (1923–29), *Marlborough: His Life and Times* (1933–38); selected speeches, as in *While England Slept* (1938), *Step by Step* (1939), *Into Battle* (1941), *The Unrelenting Struggle* (1942), *The End of the Beginning* (1943), *Victory* (1946), *In the Balance* (1951), *Unwritten Alliance* (1961); *The Second World War* (1948–54), *History of the English-Speaking Peoples* (1956–58). Awarded Nobel prize in literature (1953).

Church·yard \ˈchər-chərd\, Thomas. c.1520–1604. English soldier of fortune and writer. Fought in Scotland, Ireland, Low Countries, in service of England, the emperor, and the prince of Orange. Gave offense to Queen Elizabeth in *Churchyarde's Choise* (1579). Author of poems *Shore's Wife* (1563), *The Worthines of Wales* (1587), etc.

Chur·ri·gue·ra \chür-rē-ˈgā-rä\. Family of Spanish architects prominent in establishing Spanish Rococo style known as *churrigueresque,* including: José Benito (1665–1725), head of family; won competition to design catafalque for tomb of Queen Marie-Louise (1689); given court position under Philip V (1690); architect of Salamanca Cathedral (1690 ff.); other works included church of San Estéban, Salamanca, town of Nuevo Baztán. His brother ¶Joaquín (1674–1720) worked on Salamanca cathedral (1714–24) and Colegio di Calatrava, Salamanca (from 1717). Another brother ¶Alberto (1676–1750) designed Plaza Mayor, Salamanca.

Chu Shih-chieh \ˈjü-ˈshi(ə)r-jē-ˈe\. *Literary name* Han-ch'ing \ˈhän-ˈchiŋ\. fl. c.1280–1303. Chinese mathematician. Known for work on theory of equations, method of finite differences, theory of series. Works included *Ssu-yüan yü-chien* and *Suan-hsüeh ch'i-meng.*

Chu Shun-shui \-ˈshu̇n-shu̇-ˈē\. 1600–1682. Chinese official and historian. Official in Ming government; on overthrow of dynasty (1644) and failure to secure Japanese aid against Manchus, fled to Japan; in service of Tokugawa Mitsukuni, helped organize and compile *Dai Nihon shi,* great national history of Japan.

Chu Ta \-ˈdä\. *Orig.* Pa-ta Shan-jen \ˈbä-ˈdä-ˈshän-ˈzhən\. c.1625–c.1705. Chinese painter. Buddhist monk; painter in Individualist manner, usually in ink monochrome, of birds, fishes, etc.

Chu Teh \-ˈde\. 1886–1976. Chinese soldier. Took part in overthrow of Ch'ing dynasty (1911); joined Chinese Communist party while a student in Germany (1922–26); entered Kuomintang army (1927); took part in Communist Nan-ch'ang uprising (1927), marking foundation of Red army; with Mao

Tse-tung formed (1928) and commanded 4th Red army; commander of Communist forces against Japan (1937–45), in civil war with Nationalists (1946–49); commander of People's Liberation army, People's Republic of China (1949–54); member of Politburo (from 1934); chairman of Standing Committee, National People's Congress (1959–76).

Chu Wen \-'wən\. *Later named* Chu Ch'üan-chung \'chü-'än-'jůŋ\. 854–914. Founder and first emperor (907–914) of the Later Liang dynasty of China. Originally a follower of rebel Huang Ch'ao; surrended his forces to government and rewarded with governorship; defeated Li K'o-yung (*q.v.*) for control of North China; forced last emperor of T'ang dynasty to abdicate to him (907); murdered by his eldest son, who succeeded him on throne.

Chuy·kov \'chwē-kôf\, Vasily Ivanovich. 1900–1982. Soviet army officer. Commanded army corps occupying northeastern Poland (1939); led 62nd Army to victory at Stalingrad (1942–43), turning point in German campaign against U.S.S.R. in World War II; participated in Soviet advance to Berlin; deputy minister of defense and commander in chief of Soviet land forces (1960–64).

Ch'ü Yüan \'chü-'yü-'än\. c.343–c.289 B.C. Chinese poet. Earliest Chinese poet known by name; high official of state of Ch'u; banished to wandering life; drowned himself in Mi-lo river; search for his body gave rise to traditional Dragon Boat Festival. Verse preserved in early anthology *Ch'u tz'u;* work marked by fluency, fanciful imaginativeness.

Chu Yüan-chang. See under CHU family.

Cial·di·ni \chäl-'dē-nē\, Enrico. Duca di Ga·e·ta \gä-'e-tä\. 1811–1892. Italian soldier and diplomat. Commanded regiment of Piedmontese infantry (1848); in Crimean War (1854–56); organized the "Cacciatori delle Alpi" at beginning of Italian War (1859); defeated papal army at Castelfidardo (1860); conquered Gaeta (1861); defeated Garibaldi at Aspromonte (1862). Elected senator (1864); succeeded La Marmora as chief of general staff (1866).

Cia·mi·cian \,chä-mē-'chän\, Giacomo Luigi. 1857–1922. Italian chemist. Professor, Padua (1887–89), Bologna (1889–1922); senator (1910–22). Known for research in organic and photochemistry.

Ciam·pi \'chäm-pē\, Vincenzo Legrenzio. 1719?–1762. Italian composer. Music director of company that introduced Italian comic opera to London (1748). Operas included *La Beatrice* (1740), *La Flaminia* (1743), *Bertoldo, Bertoldino e Cacasenno* (1748), *La clemenza di Tito* (1756–57).

Ciano \'chä-nō\, Galeazzo. Conte di Cor·tel·laz·zo \,kôr-täl-'lät-tsō\. 1903–1944. Italian politician. Entered diplomatic service (1925); m. (1930) Edda, daughter of Benito Mussolini. Secretary of state for press and propaganda (1935); commanded bomber squadron in Ethiopian war (1935–36); minister of foreign affairs (1936–43); member, Fascist Supreme Council; influential in securing Italian entry into World War II (1940); became advocate of separate peace (1942); ambassador to Vatican (1943); helped force Mussolini's resignation (1943); fled Rome, executed by Germans and Mussolini partisans.

Ciar·an \'kyär-ən\. Saint. *Also spelled* Kier·an \'kyer-ən\. *Lat.* Que·ra·nus \kwə-'rā-nəs\. *Called* Ciaran the Younger, *or* of Clon·mac·noise \,klän-mək-'nȯ-shə\. c.516–c.549. Irish religious. Fellow student of SS. Columba and Brendan at Clonard monastery; disciple of Abbot St. Enda on Aranmore; founded abbey at Clonmacnoise (548) and reputedly drew up its severely ascetic rule; renowned for holiness, subject of many legends.

Ciar·di \'chärd-ē\, John Anthony. 1916–1986. American poet and critic, b. Boston. Taught English at Harvard U. (1946–53), Rutgers U. (1953–61). Author of over 40 works of poetry and criticism, including *How Does a Poem Mean?* (1959), long a standard text in poetry courses; translated Dante's *Divine Comedy* (1954–71).

Cib·ber \'sib-ər\ *or* **Cib·ert** \'sib-ərt\, Caius Gabriel. 1630–1700. Danish sculptor. Son of royal cabinetmaker; to England (before 1660); executed *Raving Madness* and *Melancholy Madness* for Bedlam Hospital, tomb (1677) for Sackville family; employed by Duke of Devonshire at Chatsworth, by Sir Christopher Wren on Hampton Court and St. Paul's cathedral.

Cibber, Colley. 1671–1757. English actor and dramatist. Son of Caius Cibber; enrolled in Betterton's company of actors, Theatre Royal, Drury Lane (1690); played Sir Novelty Fashion in first production of his *Love's Last Shift, or the Fool in Fashion* (1696); brought out thirty dramatic pieces including *She Wou'd and She Wou'd Not* (1702), *The Careless Husband* (1704, for himself and Mrs. Oldfield), *The Double Gallant* (1707), and *Nonjuror* (1717); completed Vanbrugh's *The Provoked Husband* (1728). With Wilks and Doggett, took management of Drury Lane (1710–34). Appointed poet laureate (1730). Depreciated by Pope and Johnson; made "hero" of revised version of Pope's *Dunciad* (1743); attacked by Fielding. Author also of *Apology for the Life of Colley Cibber, Comedian* (1740).

His son ¶Theophilus (1703–1758), actor and playwright; appeared first on stage (1721); impersonated Pistol and fine gentlemen with success; wrote *The Lover* (1730), *The Auction* (1757), and other plays; managed Drury Lane (1731–32), Haymarket (1734); involved in intrigues and unsavory practices; abandoned by his wife, Susannah Maria (*q.v.* under Thomas ARNE).

Cicero. See Elyesa BAZNA.

Cic·ero \'sis-ə-,rō\, Marcus Tullius. 106–43 B.C. Roman orator, statesman, and philosopher. To Rome as a youth for study of law, oratory, Greek literature and philosophy; served in army under Pompeius Strabo (89 B.C.); won legal reputation with defense of Sextus Roscius (80–79); quaestor in Sicily (75); obtained impeachment of the governor, Verres, for corruption in office (70). Praetor (66); as consul (63), foiled conspiracy of Catiline, arousing the people to their danger by his famous orations against Catiline, and executed some of the conspirators. Banished (58) through efforts of personal enemy Publius Clodius, but with aid of Pompey recalled (57); found government of First Triumvirate distasteful and retired from politics; proconsul in Cilicia (51–50). Sided with Pompey in Civil War, but became reconciled with Caesar after battle of Pharsalus (48). After assassination of Caesar, attacked Antony in 14 orations known as *Philippics;* proscribed by Second Triumvirate, and slain (43). In addition to his 58 extant orations including *Pro Quinctio, In Caecilium divinatio, Pro Lege Manilia, Contra Rullum, In Catilinam, Pro Sulla, Post Reditum ad Quirites, De domo sua, De provinciis consularibus,* and his more than 900 extant letters, extant works include *Rhetorica, De oratore, De republica, Brutus, De legibus, De finibus bonorum et malorum, Tusculanae disputationes, De natura deorum, De divinatione, De officiis, De amicitia,* etc. Considered one of the great Latin stylists, creator of the periodic style.

His brother ¶Quintus Tullius Cicero (c.102–43 B.C.) distinguished himself as a general in Gaul (54); proscribed and slain (43).

A son of Marcus ¶Marcus Tullius Cicero (65–after 30 B.C.) sided with Brutus after murder of Caesar; fled to Sicily after battle of Philippi (42); returned to Rome on proclamation of amnesty (39); honored by Octavian; consul (30); later a proconsul in Asia (or Syria).

Ci·co·gna·ra \,chē-kōn-'yä-rä\, Leopoldo. Conte. 1767–1834. Italian art historian and diplomat. Accumulated valuable collection of art objects. His works included *Del bello* (1808), *Storia della scultura dal suo risorgimento in Italia* (1813–18), *Le fabbriche piú conspicue de Venezia* (1815–20).

Cid, El. See Rodrigo DÍAZ DE VIVAR.

Cienfuegos, Nicasio Álvarez de. See ÁLVAREZ DE CIENFUEGOS.

Cier·va \'thyer-vä\, Juan de la. *Full surname* Cierva Co·dor·níu \kō-t͟hȯr-'nē-ü\. 1896–1936. Spanish aeronautical engineer. Inventor of autogiro, forerunner of helicopter (first model exhibited and tested, 1928).

Cie·za de Le·ón \'thyā-thä-t͟hā-lā-'ōn\, Pedro de. 1518–1560. Spanish soldier and historian. To America (1534–50) with Spanish armies. Author of monumental *Crónica del Perú* (1553).

Ci·gna·ni \chēn-'yä-nē\, Carlo. 1628–1719. Italian painter. Last important representative of late Bolognese Baroque style; pupil of Francesco Albani; known esp. for his fresco *Assumption of the Virgin* in cathedral of Forlì.

Ci·go·li \'chē-gō-lē\, Lodovico Car·di da \'kär-dē-dä-\. 1559–1613. Italian painter and architect. Forerunner of Baroque painting in Florence. His paintings included *Martyrdom of St. Stephen, St. Francis Receiving the Stigmata, Ecce Homo, Joseph and Potiphar's Wife.*

Ci·lea \'chē-lā-ä\, Francesco. 1866–1950. Italian composer. Director of Naples Conservatory (1916–36). Composed operas including *Gina* (1889), *La tilda* (1892), *L'arlesiana* (1897), *Adriana Lecouvreur* (1902), *Gloria* (1907).

Cilian *or* **Cillíne,** Saint. See KILIAN.

Cil·li \'tsē-lē\, Ulrich II von. c.1406–1456. Austrian noble. Made prince of the empire (1436); regent of Bohemia for Albert II (1438–39); secured coronation of Albert's son Ladislas as Lászlò V, king of Hungary (1446); after defeat of regent János Hunyadi, virtual ruler of Hungary (1453–56).

Ci·ma \'chē-mä\, Giovanni Battista. *Called* Cima da Co·ne·glia·no \,kō-näl-'yä-nō\. c.1459–1517 or 1518. Venetian painter, b. Conegliano. His works included altarpiece for Conegliano cathedral, studies of Madonna with saints, etc.; noted for luminous color, use of landscape.

Cimabue. See BENCIVIENI DI PEPO.

Ci·ma·ro·sa \,chē-mä-'rō-zä\, Domenico. 1749–1801. Neapolitan composer. Called to St. Petersburg by Catherine II as composer and conductor (1787–91); imperial Kapellmeister, Vienna (1791–92); organist of royal chapel, Naples (1796–99); imprisoned (1799–1800) for complicity in revolutionary movement. Works included operas, as *Le stravaganze del conte* (1722), *I tre amanti* (1777), *L'italiana in Londra* (1779), *L'eroe cinese* (1782), *Il credulo* (1786), *Il matrimonio segreto* (1792), *Le astuzie femminili* (1794), *Gli Orazi ed i Curiazi* (1796), oratorios, other sacred music, secular cantatas, keyboard works, etc.

Ci·mon \'sī-mən \. c.510–c.451 B.C. Athenian general and statesman. Son of Miltiades; distinguished himself at Salamis (480 B.C.); elected strategus annually (480–461); helped Aristides secure Athenian leadership and form Delian League (478); commander of Athenian contingent in allied fleet which continued (477) war against Persia; defeated and scattered Persian fleet at mouth of Eurymedon River (c.467). Induced Athens to aid in suppressing revolt of the helots against Sparta (462); after failure of Athenian expedition on this occasion, attacked by democratic faction led by Pericles and ostracized (461–457). After recall, died while leading naval expedition against Persia.

Cimon of Cle·o·nae \klē-'ō-,nā, -(,)nē\. fl. c.525–500 B.C. Greek painter. Said to have invented foreshortened view, introduced folds in drapery, depicted humans in variety of attitudes.

Cin·cin·na·tus \,sin(t)-sə-'nat-əs, -'nāt-\, Lucius Quinctius. b. c.519 B.C. Roman general and statesman. According to legend, consul (c.460 B.C.) and supporter of patricians in struggle with plebeians (462–454). Appointed dictator (458) by Senate when a Roman army was in danger of being destroyed by Aequi; found cultivating small farm when Senate delegation told him of appointment, he gathered troops, attacked and defeated Aequi, and resigned dictatorship, all within 16 days. According to doubtful legend, again appointed dictator (439), defeated and slew traitor Spurius Maelius. In later generations, regarded as model of simplicity, ability, and republican virtue.

Cin·e·as \'sin-ē-əs\. 3d century B.C. Greek politician. Minister of Pyrrhus, king of Epirus; sent to Rome to negotiate a peace after Pyrrhus's defeat of Romans at Heraclea (280 B.C.).

Cin·na \'sin-ə\, Gaius Helvius. d. 44 B.C. Roman poet. Friend of Catullus; killed by the mob at Caesar's funeral when mistaken for Lucius Cornelius Cinna (*q.v.*). Author of epic *Smyrna*.

Cinna, Lucius Cornelius. d. 84 B.C. Roman general and politician. Consul (87 B.C.); with Marius suppressed uprising in Rome and proscribed many leaders of Sulla's party; after Marius's death (86), leader of the popular party; retained consulship (to 84); killed in a mutiny of his troops while preparing to attack Sulla. His daughter ¶Cornelia was lst wife of Julius Caesar. His son ¶Lucius Cornelius, praetor (44 B.C.), sided with the assassins of Caesar.

Cin·na·mus \'sin-ə-məs\, Joannes[1]. 12th century. Byzantine historian. Secretary to Emperor Manuel I Comnenus. Author of a history of period from 1118 to 1176 A.D., continuing *Alexiad* of Anna Comnena.

Cino da Pistoia. See Cino dei SIGHIBULDI.

Cinq-Mars, Marquis de. See Henri COEFFIER-RUZÉ D'EFFIAT.

Cinthio *or* **Cinzio.** See Giambattista GIRALDI.

Cio·ne \'chō-nā\, Andrea di. *Known as* Or·ca·gna \ōr-'kän-yä\. c.1308–c.1368. Florentine painter, sculptor, and architect. Employed as architect on Duomo, Florence (1357, 1364–67), on Orvieto cathedral (1358–60); sculpted tabernacle in guild oratory of Or San Michele (1359); painted altarpieces for Strozzi Chapel of Sta. Maria Novella (1357) and for Arto del Cambio (1367–68). Latter work completed by his brother ¶Jacopo di Cione (d. after 1398). Another brother ¶Nardo (d. 1365 or 1366) was also a noted painter.

Ci·pri·a·ni \,chē-prē-'ä-nē\, Giovanni Battista. 1727–1785. Italian painter and engraver. To London (1755); introduced academic Neoclassicism to England; known for residential decoration as at Somerset House, London, and Buckland House, Berkshire; an original member of Royal Academy (1768).

Ciriaco de' Pizzicolli. *Lat.* Ciriacus Anconitanus. See CYRIACUS of Ancona.

Cisneros, Francisco Jiménez de. See JIMÉNEZ DE CISNEROS.

Cis·sey \sē-sā\, Ernest-Louis-Octave Cour·tot de \kür-tō-də-\. 1810–1882. French soldier and politician. General of division in Franco-Prussian War (1870–71); aided in suppressing Commune of Paris (1871); minister of war four times (between 1871 and 1876); president of the council (1874–75).

Ci·tro·ën \sē-trō-en\, André-Gustave. 1878–1935. French automobile manufacturer. Engaged in making munitions during World War I; after war, devoted his plant to production of low-priced automobiles; introduced American mass-production methods; lost control of firm in bankruptcy (1934). Aided in financing motor caravan expedition over 8000-mile route from Beirut to Peking (1932), and similar expedition through central Africa to open new trade route. Financed lighting of Arc de Triomphe, Place de la Concorde.

Ci·viale \sēv-yȧl\, Jean. 1792–1867. French surgeon. Reputed originator of lithotrity (1823).

Ci·vi·lis \sə-'vī-ləs\, Gaius Julius. 1st century A.D. Germanic chieftain. Commanded cohort of Batavi tribesmen as Roman army auxiliary; induced by supporter of Vespasian to revolt against army and emperor Vitellius (69); enjoyed initial success, but defeated by Petillius Cerealis at Trier (70).

Ci·vi·ta·li \,chē-vē-'tä-lē\, Matteo. 1436–1501. Italian sculptor and architect. Known esp. for his sculptural works in Lucca cathedral.

Cla·del \klȧ-del\, Léon-Alpinien. 1835–1892. French novelist. Author of realistic and later naturalistic novels, including *Les Martyrs ridicules* (1862), *La Fête votive de St.-Bartholomé-Porte-Glaive* (1869–72), *Les Va-nu-pieds* (1874), *N'a qu'un oeil* (1882), *Raca* (1888), *Juive errante* (1897).

Claesz van Haar·lem \'kläs-vän-'här-ləm\, Pieter. 1597 or 1598–1661. Dutch painter. Known for still lifes, esp. monochrome "breakfast pieces" displaying virtuosic handling of light.

Claflin, Victoria and Tennessee. See Victoria C. WOODHULL.

Clai·borne \'klā-,bō(ə)rn, -bərn\, William Charles Coles. 1775–1817. American politician, b. Sussex Co., Va. Member from Tennessee, U.S. House of Representatives (1797–1801); governor of Mississippi Territory (1801–03); with James Wilkinson a commissioner to receive Louisiana from French authorities (1803); governor of Territory of Orleans (1804–12); first governor of Louisiana (1812–16); U.S. senator (1817).

Clair \kler\, René. *Orig.* René Cho·mette \shō-met\. 1898–1981. French film writer and director. Established reputation with avant garde films *Paris qui dort* (1923), *Entr'acte* (1924); gained popularity with comedies of great imagination, verve, artistry, as *Italian Straw Hat* (1927), *Sous les toits de Paris* (1930), *Le Million* (1931), *À nous la Liberté!* (1931), *Le Dernier Milliardaire* (1934), *The Ghost Goes West* (1935); in Hollywood made *Flame of New Orleans* (1940), *I Married a Witch* (1942), *It Happened Tomorrow* (1943), *And Then There Were None* (1945); later films included *La Beauté du diable* (1949), *Les Belles de nuit* (1952), *Les Grandes Manoeuvres* (1955).

Clai·raut \kler-ō\, Alexis-Claude. 1713–1765. French mathematician. Accompanied Maupertuis on expedition to Lapland to measure a degree of the meridian (1736–37); assisted marquise du Châtelet in translation of Newton's *Principia;* developed formula relating terrestrial gravitation to latitude; contributed to lunar theory and three-body problem; predicted perihelion of Halley's Comet (1759). Author of *Théorie de la figure de la terre* (1743), *Théorie de la lune* (1752), *Théorie du mouvement des comètes* (1762), etc.

Clairfait, Graf von. See Charles Joseph de CROIX.

Clai·ron \kler-ōⁿ\, Mlle. *Orig.* Claire-Josèphe-Hippolyte Lé·ris de la Tu·de \lā-rē-də-lȧ-tü̅e-dā\. 1723–1803. French actress. Debut at Comedie-Française (1743) as Phèdre; appeared in plays of Corneille, Marmontel, Savrin, but esp. prominent in a number of Voltaire's tragedies; retired (1766).

Clajus. See KLAJ.

Clanconnel, Earl of. See Turlough O'Neill under O'NEILL family.

Clan·ny \'klan-ē\, William Reid. 1776–1850. British physician and inventor, b. Ireland. Physician with navy and in private practice; wrote on mine safety; invented (1813) one of first safety lamps for use in mines, several features of which were later adopted by Sir Humphry Davy.

Clanricarde, Earls of. See de BURGH family.

Clan·vowe \'klan-,vō\, Sir Thomas. fl. 1400. English courtier and poet. At courts of Richard II and Henry IV. Probable author of poetic dialogue *The Cuckoo and the Nightingale,* long attributed to Chaucer.

Cla·pa·rède \klȧ-pȧ-red\, Édouard. 1873–1940. Swiss psychologist. Lecturer (1898), professor (1908), Geneva; founded (1912) Institut J.J. Rousseau; a leading exponent of functionalism; formulated "law of momentary interest"; known for research in child psychology, concept formation, problem solving, sleep. Author of *L'Association des idées* (1903), *Psychologie de l'enfant* (1909), *L'Education fonctionelle* (1931), *Le Developpement mental* (1947).

Clap·per·ton \'klap-ərt-ᵊn\, Hugh. 1788–1827. Scottish explorer. In Nigeria (1822–27); first European to see Lake Chad (1823) and to report observation of Hausa; died on expedition (1825–27) to discover source of the Niger. Author of *Narrative of Travels and Discoveries* (1828).

Clare \'kla(ə)r, 'kle(ə)r\ of As·si·si \ə-'sis-ē, -'sē-zē, -'sē-sē, -'siz-ē\. Saint. 1194–1253. Italian religious. Took habit from St. Francis (1212), with him founding order of Poor Clares; abbess of San Damiano (1216); known for piety and devotion to eucharist. Canonized (1255).

Clare, Earls of. See (1) de CLARE family; (2) John FITZGIBBON; (3) PELHAM family.

Clare, de \də-'kla(ə)r, -'kle(ə)r\. Name of English family in Suffolk founded by Richard de Clare (d. 1090), 1st Earl of Clare, a Norman known as Richard Fitz-Gil·bert \fits-'gil-bərt\ who followed William the Conqueror to England; granted much land, esp. attached to castle Clare in Suffolk; as chief justiciar helped suppress rebellion (1075). His son ¶Robert (d. 1134) founded baronial house of FitzWalter. Another son ¶Gilbert FitzRich·ard \fits-'rich-ərd\ (d. 1115?), conquered and was granted by Henry I Cardigan in Wales. A third son ¶Walter de Clare (d. 1138) founded Tintern Abbey (1131).

Gilbert FitzRichard's Welsh holdings passed to second son ¶Gilbert FitzGilbert (d. c.1148), created earl of Pembroke (1138). His son ¶Richard de Clare (c.1130–1176), 2d Earl of Pembroke, called Richard Strong·bow \'strȯŋ-,bō\; took strong force to Ireland (1170) to intervene on side of Dermot MacMurrough, dethroned king of Leinster, whose daughter Eva he married; captured Waterford and Dublin but yielded conquests to appease jealousy of Henry II, whom he aided in Normandy (1173); granted all Ireland by Henry, but recognized in Ireland only as ruler of Leinster. See MARSHAL family.

Gilbert FitzRichard's elder son ¶Richard (d. 1136) inherited earldom of Clare, which passed then to his son ¶Gilbert (d. 1152), also created earl of Hertford (1138), and then to a second son ¶Roger (d. 1173). Roger's son ¶Richard (d. 1217) also inherited part of Giffard estates and married heiress of earl of Gloucester. His son ¶Gilbert (d. 1230), 7th Earl of Clare, 5th Earl of Hertford, was recognized (1217) as 6th Earl of Gloucester through his mother; m. daughter of William Marshal, 2d Earl of Pembroke, bringing house to its highest fortunes; one of 25 barons entrusted with carrying out Magna Carta (1215). His son ¶Richard (1222–1262), 8th Earl of Clare, 6th Earl of Hertford,

7th Earl of Gloucester; envoy to Scotland (1255) and to Germany (1256); defeated by Welsh (1244, 1257); joined Simon de Montfort (1258) but quarreled with him. Richard's son ¶Gilbert (1243–1295), 9th Earl of Clare, 7th Earl of Hertford, 8th Earl of Gloucester, known as the "Red Earl"; m. niece of Henry III (1253); joined de Montfort (1263) and contributed to victory at Lewes (1264), but later quarreled with him; joined Prince Edward in repelling de Montfort (1265); took London (1267), but became reconciled to Henry III; obtained restoration of lands to disinherited barons (1271); fought Welsh (1276–83) and built Caerphilly castle; m. Joan, daughter of Edward I (1290). His son ¶Gilbert (1291–1314), 10th Earl of Clare, 8th Earl of Hertford, 9th Earl of Gloucester; mediator between Edward II and Lancaster (1313); killed at Bannockburn; last of male line of Clares. His oldest sister ¶Eleanor married Hugh Despenser the younger. A younger sister ¶Margaret married Piers Gaveston. The third sister ¶Elizabeth (1291?–1360) endowed (1336) and (1359) gave a body of statutes to Clare College, Cambridge.

Clare \ˈkla(ə)r, ˈkle(ə)r\, John. 1793–1864. English poet. Known as the "Northamptonshire peasant poet"; herd boy, gardener, etc. Published *Poems Descriptive of Rural Life and Scenery* (1820); confined in lunatic asylum (1841–64); profited little by other poetical works, *Village Minstrel* (1821), *The Shepherd's Calendar* (1827), *Rural Muse* (1835).

Clar·ence \ˈklar-ən(t)s\, Duke of. Title held several times by younger sons of English monarchs; created first for Lionel of Antwerp (*q.v.*), son of Edward III; subsequently held by Thomas (*q.v.*), son of Henry IV, by George (*q.v.*), brother of Edward IV and Richard III, by William, later William IV (*q.v.*), son of George III; last revived as duke of Clarence and Avondale for Albert Victor (1864–1892), elder son of Edward VII.

Clarendon, Earls of. See Edward HYDE; George William Frederick VILLIERS.

Cla·re·tie \klär(-ə)-tē\, Jules, *orig.* Arsène-Arnaud. 1840–1913. French writer. Director, Comédie-Française (from 1885). Among his novels were *Une Drôlesse* (1862), *Amours d'un interne* (1881); *Le Prince Zilah* (1884), *La Cigarette* (1890), *Brichanteau comédien* (1896); among his plays, *Les Mirabeau* (1879), *Monsieur le Ministre* (1883); also wrote historical, critical, journalistic works as *La Vie moderne au théâtre* (1869–75).

Cla·ret \klä-ˈret\, Antonio María. Saint. 1807–1870. Spanish prelate. Ordained priest (1835); following suppression of monasteries, founded (1849) preaching Congregation of the Missionary Sons of the Immaculate Heart of Mary, commonly called Claretians; bishop of Santiago, Cuba (1850–57); confessor to Queen Isabella II (1857–68). Canonized (1950).

Cla·ri \ˈklä-rē\, Giovanni Carlo Maria. 1677–1754. Italian composer. Maestro di capella at Pistoia cathedral (1703–24), subsequently at Pisa cathedral. Composed an opera *Il savio delirante* (1695), 11 oratorios, 35 masses; known esp. for vocal duets and trios, which influenced Cherubini, Handel, Avison.

Clarín. See Leopoldo ALAS.

Clark. See also CLARKE; CLERK; CLERKE.

Clark \ˈklärk\, Abraham. 1726–1794. American politician, b. near Elizabethtown (now Elizabeth), N.J. Member, Continental Congress (1776–78, 1779–83, 1787–89); member of U.S. Congress (1791–94); signer of the Declaration of Independence.

Clark, Alvan. 1804–1887. American lens maker and astronomer, b. Ashfield, Mass. His firm, Alvan Clark & Sons, made 26-inch telescopes for U.S. Naval Observatory and U. of Virginia, 30-inch telescope for Pulkovo Observatory, Russia, 36-inch for Lick Observatory. His son ¶Alvan Graham (1832–1897) entered firm (1852); discovered 16 double stars including companion of Sirius (1862); made 40-inch lens for the Yerkes telescope (1897).

Clark, Champ, *in full* James Beauchamp. 1850–1921. American politician, b. near Lawrenceburg, Ky. Member from Missouri, U.S. House of Representatives (1893–95, 1897–1921); led revolt against speaker Joseph G. Cannon (1910); speaker (1911–19). Candidate for Democratic presidential nomination (1912); defeated when W.J. Bryan supported Woodrow Wilson. His son ¶Bennett Champ (1890–1954), b. Bowling Green, Mo., practiced law in St. Louis (1919–33); U.S. senator from Missouri (1933–45).

Clark, Charles Edgar. 1843–1922. American naval officer, b. Bradford, Vt. Made celebrated dash (Mar.–May 1898) from San Francisco around Cape Horn to Santiago de Cuba at time of Spanish-American War.

Clark, Francis Edward. 1851–1927. American clergyman, b. Aylmer, Que. Ordained in Congregational ministry (1876); organized (1881) in Portland, Maine, a Young People's Society of Christian Endeavor, incorporated (1885) as United Society of Christian Endeavor; president (1887–1925). Edited *Golden Rule* and made it organ of the movement (1886–97). Organizer and president, World's Christian Endeavor Union (from 1895).

Clark, George Rogers. 1752–1818. American Revolutionary soldier and frontier leader, b. near Charlottesville, Va. Brother of William Clark (*q.v.*). Surveyor in Kentucky; organized and led frontiersmen in defense against Indian raids (1776–77). Gained approval of Patrick Henry, governor of Virginia, for militia expedition to conquer Illinois country (the Northwest); captured key points of Kaskaskia, Cahokia, Vincennes (1778), saving Illinois and Kentucky region for the Colonies; brigadier general (1780); engaged in fighting British and Indians to hold this territory (1779–83).

Clark, James. 1936–1968. British automobile racer, b. Scotland. Began racing (1956); member of Lotus team (from 1960); world driving champion (1963, 1965); compiled record 25 Grand Prix victories; killed in racing accident.

Clark, John Bates. 1847–1938. American economist, b. Providence, R.I. Professor, Carleton Coll. (1877–81), Smith Coll. (1882–92), Amherst (1892–95), Columbia (1895–1923). Known esp. for theory of marginal productivity. Author of *The Philosophy of Wealth* (1885), *The Distribution of Wealth* (1899), *Essentials of Economic Theory* (1907), etc.

Clark, Kenneth Mackenzie. Baron Clark of Salt·wood \ˈsȯlt-,wu̇d\. 1903–1983. British art historian. A leading authority on Italian Renaissance art; director of British National Gallery (1934–45); surveyor of the King's Pictures (1934–44); chairman of the Arts Council (1953–60). Author of *Leonardo da Vinci* (1939); *Landscape Into Art* (1949); *The Nude* (1956), etc. Encouraged popular appreciation of art; created TV series "Civilization" (1969).

Clark, Mark Wayne. 1896–1984. American army officer, b. Madison Barracks, N.Y. Chief of staff of U.S. Army ground forces (1942); as deputy to Gen. Dwight Eisenhower handled assignments relating to invasion of North Africa; put in command of U.S. 5th Army; directed Italian campaign and 1944 capture of Rome; named commander of the 15th Army Group; forced German surrender in Italian Alps (1945). U.N. commander and commander in chief of U.S. Far East command (1952–53); signed Korean armistice; retired (1953).

Clark, Tom Campbell. 1899–1977. American jurist, b. Dallas, Texas. U.S. attorney general (1945–49); associate justice, U.S. Supreme Court (1949–67).

Clark, Walter van Tilburg. 1909–1971. American novelist, b. East Orland, Me. Author of *The Ox-Bow Incident* (1940), *City of Trembling Leaves* (1945), *Track of the Cat* (1949), *The Watchful Gods* (stories, 1950), etc.

Clark, Sir Wilfrid Edward Le Gros. 1895–1971. British anatomist and anthropologist. Professor, Oxford (1934–62); a leading authority on primate evolution. Author of *Early Forerunners of Man* (1934), *History of the Primates* (1949), *Antecedents of Man* (1960), etc.

Clark, William. 1770–1838. American soldier and explorer, b. Caroline Co., Va. Brother of George Rogers Clark. Lieutenant, U.S. army (1792); engaged in frontier service under Gen. Anthony Wayne against Indians (1792–96). Invited (1803) by Capt. Meriwether Lewis to join with him in leading expedition to penetrate Louisiana Purchase and to find route to Pacific Ocean (Lewis and Clark expedition), which left St. Louis (May 14, 1804), crossed continent, reached mouth of Columbia River (Nov. 1805), returned by land, reached St. Louis (Sept. 23, 1806); resigned from army (1807); brigadier general of militia, superintendent of Indian affairs for Louisiana Territory (1807–21); governor of Missouri Territory (1813–21).

Clark, William George. 1821–1878. English scholar. Fellow of Trinity Coll., Cambridge (1844–78); established Cambridge *Journal of Philology* (1868); edited, with John Glover and William Aldis Wright the *Cambridge Shakespeare* (1863–66); edited, with Wright, the *Globe Shakespeare* (1864).

Clark, William Smith. 1826–1888. American educator, b. Ashfield, Mass. Professor, Amherst Coll. (1852–67); president, professor of botany (1867–88), Mass. Agricultural Coll. (now U. of Mass). Helped organize Imperial Coll. of Agriculture, Sapporo, Japan (now Hokkaido U.) (1876–77).

Clarke. See also CLARK; CLERK; CLERKE.

Clarke \ˈklärk\, Alexander Ross. 1828–1914. English geodesist. Entered Royal Engineers (1847); with ordnance survey of Britain (1850–81); published determinations of figure of the earth (1858, 1866), latter the first to approximate modern accepted values. Author of standard text *Geodesy* (1880).

Clarke, Sir Andrew. 1824–1902. British colonial administrator and engineer. Joined Royal Engineers (1844); to New Zealand (1848), where he served in Maori war; surveyor general, Victoria, Australia (1853–57). As governor of Straits Settlements (1873–75) negotiated Pangkor agreement with sultan of Perak (1874); also suppressed piracy. Inspector general of fortifications in British army (1882–90); agent general for Victoria (1891–94, 1897–1902).

Clarke, Austin. 1896–1974. Irish poet. Author of *The Vengeance of Fionn* (1917), *The Fires of Baal* (1920), *The Sword of the West* (1921), *The Cattledrive in Connaught* (1925), *Pilgrimage* (1929), *Night and Morning* (1938), *Echo at Coole* (1968), etc.; verse plays *The Flame* (1930), *Sister Eucharia* (1939), *Black Fast* (1941), *The Moment Next to Nothing* (1953), *Frenzy of Sweeney* (1967), etc.; novels *The Bright Temptation* (1932), *The Singing-Men at Cashel* (1936), *The Sun Dances at Easter* (1952).

Clarke, Charles Cowden. 1787–1877. English critic and scholar. Music publisher in partnership with Alfred Novello, whose sister he married (1828); published lectures (delivered 1834–56) on Shakespeare and European literature; *Shakespeare Characters* (1863), *Molière Characters* (1865), *Shakespeare*

Numskulls, etc.; collaborated with his wife ¶Mary Victoria, *nee* No•vel•lo \nə-'vel-(,)ō\ (1809–1898) on *The Shakespeare Key* (1879) and *Recollections of Writers* (1878). His wife compiled *The Complete Concordance to Shakespeare* (1845).

Clarke, Edward Daniel. 1769–1822. English mineralogist and traveler. Traveled through Asia Minor, Italy, Greece, Scandinavia, Siberia, collected minerals, maps, statues and sarcophagi, manuscripts, coins, etc.; first professor of mineralogy, Cambridge (1808); university librarian (1817).

Clarke, Frank Wigglesworth. 1847–1931. American chemist, b. Boston. Professor, U. of Cincinnati (1874–83); chief chemist, U.S. Geological Survey (1883–1924); known esp. for geochemical research; first calculated average composition of earth's crust. Author of *Elementary Chemistry* (1902) and numerous Geological Survey bulletins.

Clarke, Helen Archibald. 1860–1926. American editor and author, b. Philadelphia. With ¶Charlotte Endymion Porter (1857–1942) founded (1889) and edited (to 1903) journal *Poet Lore.* Together also published editions of Browning, Shakespeare, etc.

Clarke \klȧrk\, Henri-Jacques-Guillaume. Comte d'Hu•ne•bourg \dü̅e-nə-bür\ *and* duc de Fel•tre \feltrᵊ\. 1765–1818. French soldier, of Irish descent. General of brigade (1793); private secretary to Napoléon during Consulate (1799–1804); minister of war (1807–14); after abdication of Napoléon (1814), rallied to Louis XVIII and was appointed minister of war and created marshal of France.

Clarke \'klärk\, James Freeman. 1810–1888. American clergyman, b. Hanover, N.H. Founder and pastor, Unitarian Church of the Disciples, Boston (1841–50, 1854–88). Edited *Western Messenger* (1836–39), *Christian World* (1843–48). Author of *Ten Great Religions* (1871, 1883), *Common Sense in Religion* (1874), *Self-Culture* (1882), etc.

Clarke, Jeremiah. c.1674–1707. English organist and composer. Master of choristers (1703), joint organist with William Croft (1704), of St. Paul's cathedral. Composed liturgical music, anthems, psalms, secular odes and songs for the stage; best known work "Trumpet Voluntary."

Clarke, John. 1609–1676. American clergyman and physician, b. Westhorpe, England. To America (1637); one of founders of Rhode Island (1638); in England (1651–64), upholding the interests of Rhode Island colony; instrumental in maintaining liberal democratic character of Rhode Island.

Clark, John Hessin. 1857–1945. American jurist, b. Lisbon, Ohio. Associate justice, U.S. Supreme Court (1916–22); president, League of Nations Non-Partisan Committee (1922–28).

Clarke, John Mason. 1857–1925. American paleontologist, b. Canandaigua, N.Y. State paleontologist (1898–1925), state geologist (1904–25) of New York; professor, Rensselaer Polytechnical Inst. (1894–1904); authority on Devonian era. Author of *New Devonian Crustacea* (1882), *Early Devonic History of New York and Eastern North America* (1908), etc.

Clarke, Marcus Andrew Hislop. 1846–1881. Australian author, b. London. Emigrated (c.1863); member of staff of Melbourne *Argus.* Author of *For the Term of his Natural Life* (1874), novel of convict life in colonial Australia.

Clarke, Mary Anne, *nee* Thompson. c.1776–1852. English courtier. Mistress (1803–07) of Frederick Augustus, Duke of York and Albany, 2d son of George III of England; received bribes to secure army promotions through duke, then commander in chief, causing his resignation (1809).

Clarke, Mary Cowden. See under Charles Cowden CLARKE.

Clarke, Samuel. 1675–1729. English philosopher. Chaplain to bishop of Norwich (1698), to Queen Anne (1706); disciple of Isaac Newton; expounded Newtonian views in notes to his translation of Jacques Rohault's *Traité de physique* (1697); in Boyle lectures (1704–05), answered Hobbes, Spinoza, and Blount with "mathematical" demonstration of the existence and attributes of God; carried on controversy (1712) over the Trinity with Daniel Waterland. Author of *Demonstration of the Being and Attributes of God* (1705), *Scripture Doctrine of the Trinity* (1712), etc.

Clarke, William Branwhite. 1798–1878. English clergyman and geologist. To New South Wales (1839); discovered gold (1841) in the Blue Mountains; first to determine age of Australian coal measures.

Clark•son \'klärk-sən\, Thomas. 1760–1846. English abolitionist. Led crusade against African slave trade (from 1785); associated with Wilberforce, Granville Sharp, etc.; urged French (1789–90) and czar (1818) to abolish traffic. Author of *Essay on the Slavery and Commerce of the Human Species* (1786), *History of the Abolition of the African Slave-trade* (1808), pamphlets, etc.

Claude \klōd\, Albert. 1898–1983. Belgian biologist. Pioneered use of electron microscope and centrifuge as tools to study cell structure. First (1933) to isolate and chemically analyze a cancer virus and identify it as a ribonucleic acid virus. Published first detailed view of cell anatomy (1945); discovered variety of cell organs and the function of such cell constituents as ribosomes and lysosomes; also discovered mitochondria. Shared Nobel prize for physiology or medicine (1974) with Christian René de Duve and George Emil Palade.

Claude, Georges. 1870–1960. French chemist and physicist. Showed that acetylene dissolved in acetone can be safely transported (1897); produced liquid air by expansion method (1902) and separated from it the various gases of the air; invented neon light (1910); invented new method for synthesis of ammonia (1917); imprisoned (1945–49) as Nazi collaborator.

Claude \klōd\, Georges. 1870–1960. French chemist and physicist. Showed that acetylene dissolved in acetone can be safely transported (1897); produced liquid air by expansion method (1902) and separated from it the various gases of the air; invented neon light (1910); invented new method for synthesis of ammonia (1917); imprisoned (1945–49) as Nazi collaborator.

Claude de France \-də-fräⁿs\. 1499–1524. Queen of Francis I of France. Oldest daughter of Louis XII and Anne de Bretagne; m. (1514) Francis, duc d'Angoulême, later (1515) king of France; through her, duchy of Brittany was joined to French crown.

Clau•del \klō-del\, Paul-Louis-Charles-Marie. 1868–1955. French diplomat, poet, and dramatist. Entered diplomatic service (1892); minister to Denmark (1917); ambassador to Japan (1921), U.S. (1927), Belgium (1933). Author of poetry, as in *Cinq grandes odes* (1910), *Deux poèmes d'été* (1914), *Poèmes de guerre* (1914–15); plays, as *Tête d'or* (1889), *La Ville* (1890), *L'Échange* (1893), *Le Repos du septième jour* (1896), *Partage de midi* (1906), *L'Otage* (1911), *L'Annonce faite à Marie* (1912), *Le Pain dur* (1918), *Le Père humilié* (1920), *Le Soulier de satin* (1924), the lyrical drama *Christophe Colomb* (1928, music by Milhaud), oratorio *Jeanne d'Arc* (1938, music by Honneger).

Claude Lorrain. See Claude GELLÉE.

Clau•di•an \'klȯd-ē-ən\. *Full Latin name* Claudius Clau•di•a•nus \,klȯd-ē-'ā-nəs\. c.370–c.404. Latin poet, b. Alexandria, Egypt. To Rome (c.395); gained recognition by panegyrics celebrating deeds of Theodorus, Honorius, Stilicho, and others; also wrote the *Gigantomachia,* epic *Raptus Proserpinae,* etc.

Clau•di•us \'klȯd-ē-əs\. Name of two Roman emperors:

Claudius I. *Full name* Tiberius Claudius Drusus Nero Ger•man•i•cus \(,)jər-'man-i-kəs\. 10 B.C.–54 A.D. Emperor (41–54 A.D.). Second son of Drusus (Nero Claudius Drusus), nephew of Tiberius, and stepgrandson of Augustus; neglected by Augustus and Tiberius. Proclaimed emperor by soldiers on death of Caligula. Married four times; third wife, at the time of his accession, Valeria Messalina; fourth wife (m. 49 A.D.), his niece Agrippina (*q.v.*), prevailed upon him to set aside his own son Britannicus and adopt her son Nero as heir. Carried on wars in Britain, Germany, Syria, and Mauretania; made the last a province (42 A.D.); also annexed Lycia (43), Thrace (46); founded city of Cologne (orig. Colonia Agrippinensis, 51); built Ostia harbor at mouth of Tiber, and the Claudian aqueduct. Poisoned by Agrippina.

Claudius II. *Full name* Marcus Aurelius Claudius, *surnamed* Goth•i•cus \'gäth-i-kəs\. 214–270. Emperor (268–270). Performed distinguished military service under Decius, Valerian, and Gallienus; as emperor defeated Alamanni in northern Italy (268) and the Goths near Naissus, Moesia (269).

Claudius. Name of a distinguished Roman gens, including: Appius Claudius Sabinus In•reg•il•len•sis \,in-,rej-ə-'len(t)-səs\ *or* Reg•il•len•sis \,rej-\, *orig.* Attus *or* Attius Claudius (6th–5th century B.C.), founder of the Claudian gens; settled in Rome (c.504 B.C.); consul (495); by his enforcement of laws of debt caused secession of the plebeians from Rome (494). ¶Appius Claudius, *surnamed* Cras•sus \'kras-əs\ (5th century B.C.); consul (471 B.C. and 451 B.C.); decemvir (451–450); instituted reign of terror that provoked plebeian revolt and overthrow of the decemvirs; subject of much legend. ¶Appius Claudius, *surnamed* Cae•cus \'sē-kəs\ (4th–3d century B.C.); censor (312–307 B.C.); consul (307); interrex (298); consul (296); praetor (295); famed for many reforms giving more privileges to the plebeians; built Aqua Appia aqueduct and Via Appia highway; as an orator and author, credited with founding Latin prose and oratory. His son ¶Publius Claudius, *surnamed* Pul•cher \'pəl-kər\ (3d century B.C.); consul (249 B.C.); commanded Roman fleet against Carthaginians; disastrously defeated in harbor of Drepanum (Trapani); accused of treason and heavily fined. ¶Appius Claudius, *surnamed* Pulcher (d. 130 B.C.); consul (143 B.C.), censor (136); father-in-law of T. Gracchus and member of Gracchan land commission (133–130); strong senatorial supporter of reform. ¶Appius Claudius, *surnamed* Pulcher (d. 48 B.C.); served under brother-in-law Lucius Lininius Lucullus in war against Pontus (72–70 B.C.); praetor (57); consul (54); governor of Cilicia (53); censor (50); took Pompey's side in Civil War and was appointed to a command in Greece; died before battle of Pharsalus (48).

Clau•di•us \'klau̇-dē-u̇s\, Matthias. *Pseudonym* As•mus \'äs-mu̇s\. 1740–1815. German poet. Edited *Der Wandsbecker Bote* (1771–75); associate of Klopstock, Herder, Lessing; opposed rationalist classical spirit of age. Author of "Der Mond ist aufgegangen" and other poems.

Claudius Nero, Gaius. See Gaius Claudius NERO.

Claudius Tiberius Germanicus. See BRITANNICUS.

Claus \'klau̇s\, Carl Ernst. *Russ.* Karl Karlovich Klaus \'klau̇s\. *Also spelled* Carl Carlovich Claus. 1796–1864. Russian chemist of German descent. Professor at Kazan (1839–52) and Dorpat (1852–64). Known for research on platinum metals; discovered ruthenium (1844).

Clau·se·witz \ˈklau̇-zə-ˌvits\, Carl von. 1780–1831. Prussian army officer. Entered army (1792); captured at Jena (1806); served with Russian army (1812); staff officer with Blücher (1813); chief of staff to Thielmann (1814–18); major general, director of Allgemeine Kriegsschule (1818). Known for writings on the science of war, especially *Vom Kriege* (1833).

Clau·si·us \ˈklau̇-zē-u̇s\, Rudolf Julius Emanuel. 1822–1888. German mathematical physicist. Professor at Zürich (1855–67), Würzburg (1867–69), Bonn (from 1869). Enunciated second law of thermodynamics (1850); credited with making a science of thermodynamics; contributed to kinetic theory of gases and to theory of electrolysis.

Claus·sen \ˈklau̇-sən\, Sophus Niels Christen. 1865–1931. Danish poet. Author of Symbolist verse as *Naturbørn* (1887), *Pilefløjter* (1899), *Djaevlerier* (1904), *Danske Vers* (1912), *Den danske sommer* (1921); also wrote plays as *Frøken Regnvejr* (1894), *Arbejdersken* (1898), stories, travel descriptions, etc.; translated works of Baudelaire, Heine, Shelley.

Clau·zel *or* **Clau·sel** \klō-zel\, Bertrand. Comte. 1772–1842. French soldier. General of division (1802); distinguished himself in Peninsular War (1809–12); defeated royalists in Bordeaux during Hundred Days (1815), made peer of France by Napoléon; fled to U.S. after Restoration (1816–20); deputy (1827); commander in Algeria (1830); again elected deputy (1830); marshal of France (1831); governor of Algeria (1835–37), recalled because of aggressive policy.

Claver, Saint Peter. See PETER CLAVER.

Claverhouse, John Graham of. See John GRAHAM.

Clavers, Mrs. Mary. See Caroline Matilda KIRKLAND.

Cla·vi·jo \klä-ˈb̲ē-k̲ō\, Ruy González de. d. 1412. Spanish diplomat. Ambassador of Henry III of Castile to Timur at Samarkand (1403–06). Author of *Embajada a Tamor Lán.*

Clavijo y Fa·jar·do \-ē-fä-ˈk̲är-t̲h̲ō\, José. 1730–1806. Spanish writer. Edited (1762–67) *El pensador,* Madrid; campaigned successfully against *autos sacramentales* performances; translated Buffon, Racine, Voltaire. Known for his quarrel (1764) with Beaumarchais over his love affair with latter's sister; subject of Goethe's drama *Clavigo.*

Cla·vi·us \ˈklä-vē-u̇s\, Christoph. 1537–1612. Bavarian astronomer and mathematician. Entered Jesuit order (1555); professor, Collegio Romano (1565–1612); contributed to algebraic notation; developed proposal adopted (1582) as Gregorian calendar reform. Author of extended commentary on Euclid's *Elements* (1574), *Algebra* (1608), etc.

Clay \ˈklā\, Cassius Marcellus. 1810–1903. American abolitionist and politician, b. Madison Co., Ky. Published abolitionist paper the *True American* in Lexington, Ky. (1845); served in Mexican War; joined new Republican party and supported Frémont in 1856, Lincoln in 1860; U.S. minister to Russia (1861–62, 1863–69).

Clay, Henry. 1777–1852. American politician, b. Hanover Co., Va. Practiced law, Lexington, Ky. (from 1797). U.S. senator (1806–07, 1810–11); member, U.S. House of Representatives (1811–14, 1815–21, 1823–25); speaker (same years except 1821). Leader of "War Hawk" faction (1812); urged moderately protective tariff together with national bank, internal improvements, in a general policy called the American System; effectively supported Missouri Compromise (1820) from which he gained nickname "Great Pacificator". U.S. secretary of state (1825–29). U.S. senator (1831–42); leader of anti-Jacksonian forces; in nullification crisis, presented compromise of 1833, which prevented conflict. Whig candidate for president (1832, 1844); defeated. U.S. senator (1849–52); reached height of statesmanship by series of resolutions, known as the Compromise of 1850, by which he sought to avoid forever a civil war.

Clay, Lucius DuBignon. 1897–1978. American army officer, b. Marietta, Ga. Served in various engineering assignments; director of matériel, Army Service Forces (1942–44); lieutenant general (1945); deputy military governor (1945–47), military governor (1947–49), U.S. zone, occupied Germany; commander of U.S. forces in Germany (1947–49); oversaw Berlin airlift (1948); general (1950). Chairman of the board, Continental Can Co. (1950–62). Wrote *Decision in Germany* (1950).

Clay·ton \ˈklāt-^{ə}n\, Henry De Lamar. 1857–1929. American politician, b. near Clayton, Ala. Member, U.S. House of Representatives (1897–1914); as chairman of judiciary committee (1911–14) gave name to Clayton Antitrust Act (1914). U.S. district judge (1914–29).

Clayton, John Middleton. 1796–1856. American politician, b. Dagsboro, Del. U.S. senator from Delaware (1829–36); opposed Jackson's United States Bank policy; supported Jackson in nullification crisis. Chief justice of Delaware (1837–39). U.S. senator (1845–49). U.S. secretary of state (1849–50); negotiated Clayton-Bulwer treaty with Great Britain, providing for a neutralized interoceanic canal across the American isthmus (1850). U.S. senator (1853–56).

Cle·an·thes \klē-ˈan-ˌthēz\. 331 or 330–232 or 231 B.C. Greek philosopher. Succeeded Zeno as head of Stoic school (263–232 B.C.); teacher of Chrysippus, Antigonus II of Macedonia; only fragments of his works extant.

Cle·ar·chus \klē-ˈär-kəs\. 5th century B.C. Spartan soldier. Governor of Byzantium (408 B.C.), where his severe administration caused the people during his absence to surrender the city to the Athenians. Commanded contingent of Greek mercenaries in expedition of Cyrus the Younger against Artaxerxes II; handed over to Artaxerxes by Tissaphernes after battle of Cunaxa (401) and executed.

Cleaveland. See also CLEVELAND.

Cleave·land \ˈklēv-lənd\, Moses. 1754–1806. American pioneer, b. Canterbury, Conn. As official of Connecticut Land Company, sent to Western Reserve to survey and settle land bought by company; founded (1796) Cleveland, Ohio, first called Cleaveland.

Clebsch \ˈkläpsh\, Rudolf Friedrich Alfred. 1833–1872. German mathematician. Professor at Giessen (1863), Göttingen (1868); contributed to theory of invariants; made applications of theory of elliptic and Abelian functions to geometry and to the study of rational and elliptic curves.

Cle·burne \ˈklē-(ˌ)bərn\, Patrick Ronayne. 1828–1864. American army officer, b. County Cork, Ireland. Served in British army (1846–49); emigrated to America (1849). In Confederate army in Civil War; major general (1862); led division at Murfreesboro, Chickamauga, Chattanooga, Atlanta; earned nickname of "Stonewall of the West"; framed letter, disapproved by Jefferson Davis, advising slaves be freed and enlisted as soldiers in Confederate army; killed at Franklin, Tenn.

Cleef, Joos van. See CLEVE.

Cleis·the·nes \ˈklīs-thə-ˌnēz\ *or* **Clis·the·nes** \ˈklis-\ of Sic·y·on \ˈsis(h)-ē-ˌän\. 6th century B.C. Greek tyrant of Sicyon (c.600–c.570 B.C.). Emphasized superiority of Ionian over Dorian elements in the people; championed Delphian oracle against city of Crisa in first Sacred War (c.590 B.C.); founded Pythian games at Sicyon and built a Sicyonian treasury at Delphi.

His grandson ¶Cleisthenes of Athens (c.570–after 508 B.C.), Athenian statesman, son of Megacles; banished with rest of Almaeonid family by Peisistratus (546 B.C.); returned and under Hippias became chief archon (525–524); headed a democratic party which, against opposition of great landowners, put into effect reforms of Solon; expelled (507 B.C.) by Isagoras, leader of aristocratic party, but soon recalled; devised new political organization based on locality rather than family and clan. Regarded as founder of Athenian democracy.

Clei·ti·as \ˈklīt-ē-əs\. *Also spelled* Cli·ti·as. fl. c.580–550 B.C. Athenian potter and vase painter. Painter of 5 known vases, with many others attributed to him; known esp. for "François Vase," bearing more than 200 figures from epic themes. Outstanding vase painter of Archaic period.

Clei·to·ma·chus \ˌklīt-ə-ˈmā-kəs\. *Also spelled* Cli·to·ma·chus. *Orig.* Has·dru·bal \ˈhaz-ˌdrü-bəl, haz-ˈ\. 187 or 186–110 or 109 B.C. Greek philosopher, b. Carthage. Head of New Academy, Athens (from 127 or 126 B.C.), succeeding his teacher Carneades; all works lost.

Clei·tus \ˈklīt-əs\. *Also spelled* Cli·tus. d. 329 B.C. Macedonian general. Trusted commander under Alexander the Great; saved Alexander's life at Granicus River (334 B.C.); murdered by Alexander during banquet at Maracanda after he criticized Alexander for adopting oriental ways.

Clel·and \ˈklel-ənd\, John. 1709–1789. English novelist. Consular and commercial agent in Middle East and India; in extreme poverty wrote *Fanny Hill; or, Memoirs of a Woman of Pleasure* (1748–49), pornographic work many times suppressed. Also wrote *Memoirs of a Coxcomb* (1751), *Surprises of Love* (1765), plays *Titus Vespasian* (1755), *Timbo-Chiqui* (1758).

Clémanges, Nicolas de. See NICHOLAS OF CLÉMANGES.

Cle·men·ceau \kle-mä^{n}-sō\, Georges. 1841–1929. French politician. Educated to medicine; in U.S. (1865–69); involved in Paris Commune (1870); mayor and deputy to National Assembly (1870–1871); member of Chamber of Deputies (1876–93); became leader of radical republicans; published newspapers *La Justice* (from 1880), *L'Aurore* (1897), *L'Homme libre* (1913); supported Dreyfus; senator (1902–20). Premier of France (1906–09); carried out law separating church and state; used military force to end a miners' strike; reached accord with Germany over Morocco (1909). Again premier (1917–20); led France through critical days of World War I; headed French delegation to Peace Conference at Paris (1919); retired (1920). Author of *Au pied du Sinaï* (1922), *Démosthène* (1926), *Au soir de la pensée* (1927), *Grandeurs et misères d'une victoire* (1930).

Cle·mens \ˈklem-əns\, Jacobus. *Also called* Clemens non Pa·pa \-nōn-ˈpä-pä\. c.1510–c.1556. Flemish composer. Composed 16 masses, over 200 motets, 90

\ə\ abut \$^{ə}$\ kitten, *Fr.* table \ər\ further \a\ ash \ā\ ace \ä\ cot, cart \au̇\ out \ch\ chin \e\ bet \ē\ easy \g\ go \i\ hit \ī\ ice \j\ job \ŋ\ sing \ō\ go \ȯ\ law \ȯi\ boy \th\ both \t̲h̲\ the \ü\ loot \u̇\ foot \y\ yet \zh\ vision \á, b̲, g̲, k̲, ^{n}, œ, œ̄, ue, ue̅, ^{y}\ *see* Guide to Pronunciation

chansons, and *Souter Liedekens* (1556), almost complete series of metrical psalms.

Clem·ens \'klem-ənz\, Samuel Langhorne. *Pseudonym* Mark Twain \'twān\. 1835–1910. American writer, b. Florida, Mo. Resident, Hannibal, Mo. (1839–53); journeyman printer (1847–55); river pilot on Mississippi (1857–61). In Carson City, Nev., as a prospector (1861); adopted pseudonym Mark Twain as reporter for Virginia City *Territorial Enterprise* (1862); reporter in San Francisco (1864). Published first great success "The Celebrated Jumping Frog of Calaveras County" (1865) and first book *The Celebrated Jumping Frog of Calaveras County, and other Sketches* (1867); successful also on lecture platform. From an excursion to Mediterranean and Holy Land obtained material for *The Innocents Abroad* (1869). At height of powers during next twenty years, wrote: *Roughing It* (1872), *The Gilded Age* (with Charles Dudley Warner, 1873), *The Adventures of Tom Sawyer* (1876), *A Tramp Abroad* (1880), *The Stolen White Elephant* (1882), *The Prince and the Pauper* (1882), *Life on the Mississippi* (1883), *Adventures of Huckleberry Finn* (1884), *A Connecticut Yankee At King Arthur's Court* (1889). Involved in failure of publishing house of Charles L. Webster & Co. (1896), took to lecture stage to clear his obligations, and continued writing. In some of his later works, *What is Man?* (1906), and *The Mysterious Stranger* (1916), showed vein of bitterness not evident theretofore. Other works: *The American Claimant* (1892), *The £1,000,000 Bank Note* (1893), *The Tragedy of Pudd'nhead Wilson* (1894), *Tom Sawyer Abroad* (1894), *Tom Sawyer, Detective* (1896), *Personal Recollections of Joan of Arc* (1896), *Following the Equator* (1897), *The Man That Corrupted Hadleyburg* (1900), *Eve's Diary* (1906), *The $30,000 Bequest* (1906).

Clemens Alexandrinus. See CLEMENT of Alexandria.

Clem·ent \'klem-ənt\. Name of fourteen popes and three antipopes:

Clement I. Saint. *Also* Cle·mens Ro·ma·nus \'klem-ənz-rō-'mā-nəs, 'klē-mənz-\. d. 101? Pope (88–97 or 92–101). First of the Apostolic Fathers; author of *Epistle to the Corinthians* (95 or 96), one of the most valuable works of the early church; said by some to have been martyred.

Clement II. *Orig.* Suid·ger \'swē-jər\. d. 1047. Pope (1046–47). Of noble Saxon origin; bishop of Bamberg; accompanied Henry III to Italy and installed as pope after deposition of rivals Sylvester III, Benedict IX, Gregory VI; crowned Henry emperor; convoked Council of Rome (1047) and began numerous reforms.

Clement III. *Orig.* Paolo Sco·la·ri \skō-'lä-rē\. d. 1191. Pope (1187–91). Cardinal bishop of Palestrina; as pope, preached Third Crusade; made Scottish church dependent on Rome.

Clement IV. *Orig.* Guido Ful·co·di \fül-'kō-dē\, *Fr.* Guy Le Gros Foulques \lə-grō-fülk\. d. 1268. Pope (1265–68). Held office at court of Louis IX; bishop of Le Puy (1257), archbishop of Narbonne (1259), cardinal (1261); papal legate to England when elected pope; favored Charles of Anjou against Manfred in struggle for Naples; befriended Roger Bacon.

Clement V. *Orig.* Bertrand de Got \də-gō\. c.1260–1314. Pope (1305–14). Bishop of Comminges (1295), archbishop of Bordeaux (1299); friend of King Philip the Fair, who secured his election and at whose request papal residence removed from Rome to Avignon (1309); convoked Council of Vienne (1311); suppressed Order of Templars (1312).

Clement VI. *Orig.* Pierre Ro·ger \rō-zhā\. c.1291–1352. Pope (1342–52). Benedictine abbot; archbishop of Sens (1329), Rouen (1330); cardinal (1338); purchased (1348) Avignon for papacy; excommunicated Emperor Louis IV of Bavaria (1346) in favor of Charles IV; centralized and strengthened papal authority.

Clement VII. *Orig.* Giulio de' Me·di·ci \dā-'med-ē-chē, *Angl* -'med-ə-(,)chē\. 1478–1534. Pope (1523–34). Natural son of Giuliano de' Medici (see MEDICI); cousin of Pope Leo X. Cardinal (1513); entered Holy League of Cognac (1526) with France, Venice, and Milan against Charles V; taken prisoner on sack of Rome by Constable Bourbon and imperial troops (1527); fled to Orvieto on release, but returned to Rome (1528); made peace with Charles and crowned him emperor at Bologna (1530); refused (1533) to sanction divorce of Henry VIII from Catherine of Aragon. Patron of Raphael, Michelangelo.

Clement VIII. *Orig.* Ippolito Al·do·bran·di·ni \äl-dō-brän-'dē-nē\. 1536–1605. Pope (1592–1605). Cardinal (1585); as pope recognized Henry IV as king of France; moderated Counter-Reformation; ordered revisions of the Vulgate, breviary, and liturgical books; revision of Vulgate (1592) remained standard Bible text of Roman Catholic church; annexed lands of house of Este to States of the Church (1598); occupied in last years with controversy between Jesuits and Dominicans on question of grace.

Clement IX. *Orig.* Giulio Ro·spi·glio·si \rō-spēl-'yō-sē\. 1600–1669. Pope (1667–69). Papal ambassador to Spain (1644–53); cardinal (1657); mediated (1668) peace of Aix-la-Chapelle between Louis XIV and Spain; secured Peace of Clement (1669) temporarily ending French persecution of Jansenists; failed to gain aid to oppose Ottomans in Crete. Author of verse, libretti, including first comic opera *Chi soffre speri* (1639).

Clement X. *Orig.* Emilio Al·tie·ri \äl-'tyer-ē\. 1590–1676. Pope (1670–76). Served in papal embassy in Poland (1623–27); bishop of Camerino (1627); cardinal (1669); papacy suffered from continuing friction with Louis XIV of France and from Turkish threat in Mediterranean.

Clement XI. *Orig.* Giovanni Francesco Al·ba·ni \äl-'bä-nē\. 1649–1721. Pope (1700–1721). Cardinal (1690); involved (1701–13) in European political disputes in connection with War of Spanish Succession, esp. with Emperor Joseph I, who invaded Papal States and forced him to recognize (1709) Charles VI as king of Spain; in Treaty of Utrecht (1713) lost Sicily to Savoy; published bulls against Jansenist writings, as *Vineam Domini* (1705) and *Unigenitus* (1713), provoking long controversy over Gallicanism in French church; condemned (1704, 1715) Chinese and Malabar rites.

Clement XII. *Orig.* Lorenzo Cor·si·ni \kor-'sē-nē\. 1652–1740. Pope (1730–40). Papal ambassador to Vienna (1691); cardinal (1706); sustained suppression of Jansenism and unsuccessfully opposed Gallicanism; condemned Freemasonry (1738).

Clement XIII. *Orig.* Carlo del·la Tor·re Rez·zo·ni·co \,dāl-lä-'tōr-rā-rād-'dzō-nē-(,)kō\. 1693–1769. Pope (1758–69). Governor of Rieti (1716), Fano (1721); cardinal (1737); bishop of Padua (1743); issued bulls opposing demands of France, Spain, Portugal, Naples for suppression of Society of Jesus.

Clement XIV. *Orig.* Giovanni Vincenzo Antonio Gan·ga·nel·li \,gäŋ-gä-'nel-lē\. 1705–1774. Pope (1769–74). Cardinal (1759); tried to keep peace with Roman Catholic princes; issued (1773) apostolic brief suppressing Jesuit order; founded Clementine Museum at the Vatican.

ANTIPOPES:

Clement III. *Orig.* Gui·bert \'gē-,bert\ *or* Gui·ber·to \gwē-'ber-tō\ *or* Wi·bert \'wē-,bert\ of Ravenna. c.1025–1100. Officer at German court (c.1054–55); imperial chancellor for Italy (1058–63); named archbishop of Ravenna (1073) by King Henry IV; led imperial faction opposing reforms of Gregory VII; excommunicated (1080); elected pope by synod convoked by Henry (1080); crowned Henry emperor (1084); remained antipope in opposition to Victor III, Urban II.

Clement VII. *Orig.* Robert of Geneva. 1342–1394. Bishop of Thérouanne (1361), Cambrai (1368); cardinal (1371); commanded papal army against Florence (1377); elected pope (1378) in opposition to Urban VI by cardinals claiming Urban had been elected through duress; first antipope of Great Western Schism; settled at Avignon; recognized by Charles V of France.

Clement VIII. *Orig.* Gil Sán·chez Mu·ñoz \'sän-chāth-'mün-yōth\. d. 1446. Chosen through influence of Alfonso V of Aragon to succeed antipope Benedict XIII (1423); abdicated (1429) when Alfonso was reconciled with Pope Martin V; had his cardinals acknowledge Martin, thus ending Great Western Schism; made bishop of Majorca.

Clem·ent \'klem-ənt\ of Alexandria. Saint. *Full Latin name* Titus Flavius Cle·mens \'klem-ənz, 'klē-mənz\. c.150–between 211 and 215. Studied in Christian school in Alexandria; succeeded teacher Pantaenus as head of catechetical school in Alexandria (c.180–c.201), which, by his teaching and that of his pupil Origen, became one of famous contemporary centers of learning; left Alexandria during persecutions of Emperor Severus (c.201). Regarded as a founder of the Alexandrian school of theology and greatest of the Christian Apologists of the 2d century; laid groundwork for melding of Christian and Hellenistic thought. His works included the trilogy *Protreptikos, Paidagōgos,* and *Strōmateis*; *Concerning the Salvation of Rich Men, Eclogae Propheticae,* etc.

Clé·ment \klā-mä^{n}\, Jacques. 1564–1589. French assassin. Dominican monk; stabbed Henry III of France (1589).

Cle·men·te \klə-'men-(,)tā\, Roberto Walker. 1934–1972. American baseball player, b. Carolina, P.R. With Pittsburgh Pirates (1954–72); lifetime batting average .317; 11th player to pass 3000 hits; Most Valuable Player in National League (1966), in World Series (1971); noted for ability to hit any type of pitch and for fielding ability in right field.

Cle·men·ti \klā-'men-tē\, Muzio. 1752–1832. Italian pianist and composer. Resident in England (from 1767); gained recognition with keyboard sonatas and duets and own performances; made many concert tours to the Continent; at court of Emperor Joseph II engaged in famous piano contest with Mozart (1781); a leader in modern school of piano technique; major London music publisher (from 1799). Composer of symphonies, sonatas, and a series of piano studies under title *Gradus ad Parnassum* (1817).

Clem·en·tis \'klem-en-tyis\, Vladimír. 1902–1952. Slovak politician. Appointed to Czechoslovak National Council in exile in London (1942); helped organize Communist coup (1948); foreign secretary (1948–50); purged in Stalinist crackdown (1950), executed.

Clem·son \'klem-sən\, Thomas Green. 1807–1888. American mining engineer, b. Philadelphia. m. (1838) Anna Maria, daughter of John C. Calhoun; left fortune to state of South Carolina for founding of college (Clemson College; chartered 1889, opened 1893).

Cle·o·bu·lus \ˌklē-ə-ˈbyü-ləs\. 6th century B.C. Greek sage. Tyrant of Lindus on Rhodes; accounted one of the Seven Wise Men of Greece.

Cle·om·bro·tus I \klē-ˈäm-brət-əs\. d. 371 B.C. King of Sparta (380–371 B.C.). Waged war against Thebes; defeated by Epaminondas and killed at battle of Leuctra.

Cle·om·e·nes \klē-ˈäm-ə-ˌnēz\. Name of three kings of Sparta:

Cleomenes I. d. 490 B.C. King (c.521–490 B.C.). Succeeded father Anaxandridas; attacked Athens and drove out Hippias (510); aided (507) Isagoras and aristocratic party in Athens in expelling Cleisthenes but failed to make Isagoras tyrant of city; defeated Argos (494); forced to flee from Sparta (491 B.C.) when his bribery of Delphian priestesses discovered; committed suicide.

Cleomenes II. d. 309 B.C. King (370–309). Son of Cleombrotus I; succeeded brother Agesipolis II.

Cleomenes III. d. c.219 B.C. King (235–222). Son of Leonidas II; tried to institute social reforms, including redistribution of land, remission of debts, restoration of earlier training system; warred successfully against the Achaeans, but finally defeated at Sellasia (222 B.C.) by an alliance including King Antigonus Doson of Macedonia; fled to Alexandria; committed suicide.

Cle·on \ˈklē-ˌän\. d. 422 B.C. Athenian politician. Became leader of democratic party after death of Pericles (429 B.C.); opposed Nicias, and demanded continuation of Peloponnesian War; led successful expedition against Spartans on Sphacteria; defeated and killed in battle of Amphipolis (422).

Cle·o·pa·tra \ˌklē-ə-ˈpa-trə, -ˈpā-, -ˈpä-\. Name of several queens and princesses of the Ptolemies of Egypt. For Queens Cleopatra I-VI, see PTOLEMY V-XII.

Cleopatra VII. 69–30 B.C. Queen (51–30 B.C.). Daughter of Ptolemy XII; by will of her father, became joint ruler (51) with her brother Ptolemy XIII (who was also her husband); driven out by him (49); supported by Julius Caesar, who defeated Ptolemy (47). Relinquished actual government of kingdom to younger brother, Ptolemy XIV (whom she had married); became Caesar's mistress; lived with him in Rome (46–44). Returned to Egypt (44); murdered Ptolemy XIV to make room for her son Cesarion as her associate on the throne. After Philippi (42), met Mark Antony in Cilicia; won Antony's love; bore him twin children, Alexander Helios and Cleopatra Selene (*q.v.*); deserted by Antony (40) but joined him at Antioch (36–34) where he was in command against the Parthians; celebrated magnificent triumph in Alexandria (34); with him at Actium (31), but withdrew her fleet and fled to Alexandria; could not influence Octavian and killed herself, probably with poison (legend says by an asp), on learning that he intended to exhibit her in his triumph at Rome.

Cleopatra Se·le·ne \-sə-ˈlē-nē\. 1st century B.C. Egyptian queen. Daughter of Cleopatra VII and Antony; m. Juba II, King of Numidia; their son Ptolemy of Mauretania was last of dynastic line; slain by Caligula.

Cleopatra Thea \-ˈthē-ə\. d. 121 B.C. Queen of Syria. Daughter of Ptolemy VI Philometor; m. 1st (150? B.C.) Alexander Balas, by whom she was mother of Antiochus VI; m. 2d Demetrius II Nicator, by whom she was mother of Seleucus V and Antiochus VII Grypus; administered kingdom during campaign of Demetrius in Parthia; after his capture and marriage with Rodogune, daughter of Mithridates I of Parthia, m. as third husband Antiochus VII Euergetes; joint ruler as regent for her son Antiochus VIII (125–121 B.C.), by whom, according to legend, she was poisoned.

Cle·o·phon \ˈklē-ō-ˌfän\. d. 404 B.C. Athenian politican. Leader of democratic party after Cleon, following Cleon's policy of demanding continued prosecution of war against Sparta; executed by Athenian council while Athens was besieged by Lysander.

Cle·oph·ra·des Pain·ter \klē-ˈäf-rə-ˌdēz-ˈpānt-ər\. *Probable name* Epik·te·tos \ˌep-ik-ˈtēt-əs\ *or* Epi·cle·tus \ˌep-i-ˈklēt-əs\. 6th–5th century B.C. Greek vase painter. Son of Amasis, student of Euthymides; known for some 100 painted vessels, most in red-figure, esp. those by Cleophrades Potter (whence name); considered one of finest vase painters of late Archaic period.

Clé·ram·bault \klā-räⁿ-bō\, Louis-Nicholas. 1676–1749. French organist and composer. Organist of Maison Royale de St. Cyr (1714), St. Sulpice, Paris (1714), etc. Known esp. for five volumes of secular cantatas (1710–26); also wrote church music, motets, *Livre d'orgue* (c.1710), etc.

Clerfayt, Count von. See Charles Joseph de CROIX.

Clericus, Johannes. See Jean LECLERC.

Clerk \ˈklärk\, Sir Dugald. 1854–1932. Scottish engineer. Inventor of two-stroke Clerk cycle gas engine (patented 1881). Author of *The Gas, Petrol, and Oil Engine* (1909–13).

Clermont, Count of. Robert de France. See BOURBON.

Cler·mont-Gan·neau \kler-mōⁿ-gä-nō\, Charles. 1846–1923. French archaeologist. In consular service; professor, Collège de France (1890); directed expeditions to Palestine, Syria, Crete, Egypt, etc.; discovered site of Gezer (1873–74); exposed a number of archaeological frauds, including the forgeries of Hebrew texts offered (1883) to British Museum.

Cletus. See Saint ANACLETUS.

Cle·ve \ˈklā-və\ *or* **Cleef** \ˈklāf\, Joos van. *Also* Joos van der Be·ke \ˌvän-dər-ˈbā-kə\. c.1480–1540. Flemish painter. Worked in Antwerp (from c.1511); generally identified with "the Master of the death of the Virgin," painter of two pictures on this subject in Cologne and Munich museums.

Cle·ve \ˈklā-və\, Per Teodor. 1840–1905. Swedish chemist. Professor, Uppsala (1868); known esp. for work on metallic ammonium compounds and rare-earth metals; discovered the elements holmium and thulium (1879).

Cleveland, Duchess of. See Barbara VILLIERS.

Cleve·land \klēv-lənd\, Horace William Shaler. 1814–1900. American landscape architect, b. Lancaster, Mass. Designed municipal park systems for Minneapolis and Omaha, and parks for Chicago and Providence, R.I. Helped establish landscape architecture as profession.

Cleve·land *or* **Cleive·land** \ˈklēv-lənd\, John. 1613–1658. English poet. Author of Royalist and mostly satirical poems valued by contemporaries above Milton's, including "Smectymnuus," "Rupertismus," "The Rebel Scot," "The King's Disguise," "Square Cap."

Cleveland, Grover, *in full* Stephen Grover. 1837–1908. Twenty-second and twenty-fourth president of the United States, b. Caldwell, N.J. Practiced law, Buffalo, N.Y. (from 1859); mayor of Buffalo (1881–82); reformed city administration; governor of New York (1883–85). Democratic president of the United States (1885–89); supported civil service reform and a lower tariff; blocked undeserved Civil War pensions. Defeated for reelection (1888) by Benjamin Harrison. Again president (1893–97); opposed currency inflation and caused repeal of Sherman Silver Purchase Act of 1890; sent U.S. troops to intervene in Pullman strike, Chicago (1894); took strong stand against use of force by British in their boundary dispute with Venezuela.

Cleves, Anne of. See ANNE.

Clif·ford \ˈklif-ərd\. *Orig.* de Clifford. Name of an English family and barony comprising descendants of Walter de Clifford (d. 1190?), who acquired estates in western Herefordshire, taking his surname from Clifford Castle, and whose daughter ¶Rosamund Clifford (d. 1176?), known as "Fair Rosamund," was mistress of Henry II. Walter's grandson ¶Roger de Clifford (d. c. 1285) supported Simon de Montfort (1263) but changed allegiance to Henry III and fought at Lewes (1264), Evesham (1265); granted estates in Westmorland. Other members of the family included:

BARONS OF WEST·MOR·LAND \ˈwes(t)-mər-lənd, *US also* wes(t)-ˈmō(ə)r- *or* -ˈmȯ(ə)r-\:

¶Robert de Clifford (1274–1314), 5th Lord Clifford; 1st Baron of Westmorland; grandson of Roger; soldier and judge; warden of marches (1297); fought Scots, distinguished himself at siege of Caerlaverock Castle (1300); fought against Piers Gaveston; killed at Bannockburn.

¶John de Clifford (1435–1461), 9th baron; called "the Butcher" because of his cruelty in fighting for Henry VI in Wars of the Roses; murdered Edmund, son of 3d Duke of York; killed at Ferrybridge; attainted by Parliament (1461).

¶Henry de Clifford (1454–1523), 10th baron, 1st Baron Ves·ci \ˈves-ē\; called "the Shepherd Lord" from living in disguise as a shepherd before restoration (1485) to titles and estates of his father, 9th baron; subject of Wordsworth's poems "The White Doe of Rylstone" and "Brougham Castle."

EARLS OF CUM·BER·LAND \ˈkəm-bər-lənd\:

¶Henry de Clifford (1493–1542), 11th Baron of Westmorland; son of 10th baron; in constant service against Scots; created earl of Cumberland (1525) by Henry VIII; remained loyal and was besieged by insurgents in Skipton Castle (1536).

¶George de Clifford (1558–1605), 3d earl; grandson of 1st earl; wasted estates in gambling; commanded ship against Spanish Armada (1588); fitted out ten privateering expeditions against Spanish (1586–98). His daughter ¶Anne Clifford (1590–1676), Countess of Dorset, Pembroke, and Montgomery; engaged in lawsuit over estates of her father (to 1617); m. (1609) Richard Sackville, Earl of Dorset; m. (1630) Philip Herbert, Earl of Pembroke and Montgomery (see HERBERT family); restored or rebuilt several castles and churches.

¶ Henry Clifford (1591–1643), 5th earl; supported Charles I through wars with Scots and in Yorkshire in civil war (1642–43); last of male line; through his daughter earldom passed to Boyle and then to Cavendish families.

BARONS CLIFFORD OF CHUD·LEIGH \ˈchəd-lē\ (cadet branch in Devonshire):

¶Thomas Clifford (1630–1673), 1st baron (cr.1672); M.P. (1660–61); commissioner for care of wounded and sick prisoners in Dutch war (1664); confidant of Arlington and member of the Cabal; served with fleet (1665–66); privy councillor (1666); intrigued in France against Triple Alliance; privy to secret Treaty of Dover (1670); as acting principal secretary of state (1672), chiefly responsible for stop of exchequer payments and Declaration of Indulgence (1672); lord treasurer (1672–73).

¶Sir Bede Edmund Hugh Clifford (1890–1969), colonial governor; youngest son of 10th baron; military secretary to governor general of Australia (1919–20) and to governor general of South Africa (1921–24); imperial secretary, Union of South Africa; governor of Bahamas (1932–37), of Mauritius (1937–42), of Trinidad (1942–46).

¶Sir Hugh Charles Clifford (1866–1941), colonial administrator; grandson of 7th baron; entered Malay Straits civil service (1883); resident at Pahang (1896–99, 1901–03); colonial secretary at Trinidad and Tobago (1903–07), Ceylon (1907–12); governor of Gold Coast (1912–19), Nigeria (1919–25), Ceylon (1925–27), Straits Settlements (1927–29). Author of stories of Malayan Peninsula, including *Studies in Brown Humanity* (1898), *Bush Whacking* (1901), *Malayan Monochromes* (1913), *A Prince of Malaya* (1926).

Clifford, John. 1836–1923. English clergyman. Pastor of Praed Street Baptist Church, Paddington, London (from (1858); exercised wide influence in directing church thought toward contemporary social problems. President of Baptist Union (from 1888); first president, Baptist World Alliance (1905–11).

Clifford, Nathan. 1803–1881. American jurist, b. Rumney, N.H. Member, U.S. House of Representatives (1839–43); U.S. attorney general (1846–48); helped negotiate Treaty of Guadeloupe Hidalgo (1848) with Mexico; associate justice, U.S. Supreme Court (1858–81).

Clifford, William Kingdon. 1845–1879. English mathematician and philosopher. Fellow, Trinity Coll., Cambridge (1868); professor, University Coll., London (1871–79); known for theory of biquaternions, research into non-Euclidean space, and topology; developed notions of consciousness and ethics based on terms "mind-stuff" and "tribal self." Author of *Elements of Dynamic* (1878–87), *Seeing and Thinking* (1879), *Common Sense of the Exact Sciences* (completed by Karl Pearson, 1885).

Clin·ton \'klint-ᵊn\, DeWitt. 1769–1828. American politician, b. Little Britain, N.Y. Son of James Clinton; secretary to his uncle, Governor George Clinton (1790–95); member, New York legislature (1798–1802). U.S. senator (1802–03). Mayor of New York City (1803–07, 1808–10, 1811–15); lieutenant governor (1811–13). Candidate for president of the United States (1812); defeated by Madison. Governor of New York (1817–23, 1825–28); principal promoter of Erie Canal (opened 1825).

Clinton, George. 1739–1812. American politician, b. Little Britain, N.Y. Brother of James Clinton, with whom he served in French and Indian War; member of N.Y. Provincial Assembly (1768–75), Continental Congress (1775); brigadier general of militia (1775), in Continental army (1777). Governor of N.Y. (1777–95); opposed ratification of Constitution; again governor (1801–04). Vice president of U.S. (1805–12).

Clinton, Sir Henry. 1738–1795. English soldier, b. Newfoundland. Son of Adm. George Clinton, governor of Newfoundland; entered army (1757); aide-de-camp in Germany in Seven Years' War (1760–62); major general (1772); fought in battles of Bunker Hill and Long Island; succeeded Sir William Howe as commander in chief in North America (1778); captured Charleston (1780); quarreled with Cornwallis, second in command; resigned (1781); general (1793); governor of Gibraltar (1794–95). His elder son ¶Sir William Henry (1769–1846) became a general (1830). His younger son ¶Sir Henry (1771–1829) fought with Prussians in Holland (1789); major general (1810); divisional commander under Wellington in Peninsular War (1811–14) and at Waterloo (1815); lieutenant general (1814).

Clinton, James. 1733–1812. American soldier, b. Little Britain, N.Y. Brother of George Clinton; served in French and Indian War (1757–63); colonel of N.Y. militia (1775); took part in Montgomery's expedition to Quebec (1775); brigadier general in Continental army (1776); driven out of Fort Clinton on Hudson by Sir Henry Clinton (1777); took part in Sullivan's expedition (1779); commanded Northern Dept. (1780–81); led brigade at Yorktown (1781).

Clis·son \klē-sōⁿ\, Olivier de. c.1332–1407. French soldier. Fought for John IV in War of Breton Succession, won battle of Auray (1364); joined French (1365); lieutenant of Guienne (1369); in service of Du Guesclin (from 1370); lieutenant general in Brittany (1374); constable of France (1380); defeated Flemings at Roosebeke (1382); after death (1399) of Duke John IV became protector of the duchy and guardian of the young princes.

Clisthenes, Clitias, Clitomachus, Clitus. See CLEISTHENES, CLEITIAS, CLEITOMACHUS, CLEITUS.

Cli·the·row \'klith-ə-,rō\, Margaret, *nee* Mid·dle·ton \'mid-ᵊl-tən\. Saint. 1556–1586. English religious. m. (1571) John Clitherow; converted to Roman Catholicism (1574); fined and imprisoned several times as recusant; harbored priests in her home; arrested (1586), refused to plead before court; crushed to death. Canonized (1970) with 39 other British martyrs.

Clive \'klīv\, Kitty. *Orig.* Catherine Raf·tor \'raf-tər\. 1711–1785. British actress. Played under manager Colley Cibber at Drury Lane, London (1728–41); m. (1731?) George Clive; won recognition as comedy actress (1731) in *The Devil to Pay;* an original member of Garrick's company, Drury Lane (1747–69); sang in oratorios of her friend Handel.

Clive, Robert. Baron Clive of Plas·sey \'plas-ē\. 1725–1774. British soldier and colonialist. To Madras (1743) in service of East India Company; captured by French, escaped (1746); allowed to make his proposed daring dash to seize Arcot, capital of Chanda Sahib (1751); held citadel eight weeks with small force until relieved; captured other French strongholds; returned to England (1753). Again in India (1755) as governor of Fort St. David; reduced pirate stronghold of Gheriah (1756); sent to avenge atrocity of Black Hole of Calcutta; recovered Calcutta (1757); defeated the Mughal nawab, Sirāj-ud-Dawlah, at Plassey (1757), installed Mīr Ja'far as nawab; virtual ruler of Bengal; repulsed Dutch colonizing attempt (1759). Returned to England (1760); entered Parliament (1760–74); raised to Irish peerage as Baron Clive of Plassey (1762). Sent out (1764) as governor and commander in chief of Bengal to right the disorder and corruption grown up in his absence; reformed civil service; restored military discipline; obtained for East India Company sovereignty over whole province, founding empire of British India. Returned to England (1767) in shattered health to meet storm of obloquy, parliamentary inquiries; committed suicide.

Clo·dia \'klōd-ē-ə\. 1st century B.C. Roman woman. Sister of Publius Clodius; m. Quintus Caecilius Metellus Celer, whom she may have poisoned (59 B.C.); object of great passion of poet Catullus, who addressed her as Lesbia in over 100 poems.

Clodion. See Claude MICHEL.

Clo·di·us \'klōd-ē-əs\, Publius. *Surnamed* Pul·cher \'pəl-kər\. c.93–52 B.C. Roman politician. Brother of Appius Claudius Pulcher (see CLAUDIUS); instigated mutiny while serving in army of brother-in-law L. Lucullus (68–67 B.C.); quaestor in Sicily (61 B.C.); tribune of the people in Rome (58). As bitter opponent of Cicero, had him exiled and his property confiscated; supported Julius Caesar. Rival of T. Annius Milo; their respective gangs kept Rome in turmoil for years. Killed in a street brawl during an election.

Clodius Albinus. See Decimus ALBINUS.

Clodoald, Saint. See CLOUD.

Cloe·te \'klü-tē\, Stuart, *in full* Edward Fairly Stuart Graham. 1897–1976. South African novelist. Author of *The Turning Wheels* (1937), *Watch for the Dawn* (1939), *The Hill of Doves* (1941), *The Third Way* (1946), *The Curve and the Tusk* (1952), *Mamba* (1956), *The Mask* (1957), *Gazella* (1958), *Rags of Glory* (1963), *The Abductors* (1966).

Cloos \'klōs\, Hans. 1885–1951. German geologist. Professor, Breslau (1919–26), Bonn (1926–51); known for studies of rock deformation, faulting mechanisms. Author of *Das Mechanismus tiefvulkanischer Vorgänge* (1921), *Einführung in die Geologie* (1936), *Gespräch mit der Erde* (1947).

Cloots, Baron de. See Jean-Baptiste du VAL-DE-GRÂCE.

Clopinel, Jean. See CHOPINEL.

Close \'klōs\, Maxwell Henry. 1822–1903. Irish geologist. Known for pioneering studies of glaciation in Ireland.

Clo·ster·man \'klō-stər-mən\, John, *orig.* Johann Baptist. 1656–1713. British painter, b. Hanover, Germany. To England (1681); painted portraits of Queen Anne, Dryden, Purcell, and the Blenheim group of Duke of Marlborough and family.

Clotaire. See CHLOTAR.

Clo·til·da \klə-'til-də\. Saint. *Also known as* Chro·te·chil·dis \'krōt-ə-'kil-dəs\ *and* Clotilda of Burgundy. *Fr.* Clo·tilde \klō-tēld\. *Ger.* Chlo·thil·de \klō-'til-də\. c.470–545. Frankish queen. Daughter of Chilperic, king of the Burgundians; educated in Christian faith; m. (c.493) Clovis, whom she converted (c.496); after death of Clovis (511) retired to monastery at Tours. Subject of many later romantic epic narratives.

Cloud \klü\. Saint. *Also* Clo·do·ald \'klō-dō-ält\ *or* Chlo·do·vald \-,vält\. c.522–c.560. Frankish religious. Grandson of Clovis and son of Chlodomer; brought up by his grandmother Clotilda; escaped death from his uncles Chlotar I and Childebert I; lived in solitude as a monk in Provence; returned to neighborhood of Paris where he built abbey at Novigentum (later named Saint-Cloud).

Clou·et \klü-e\. Family of Flemish-French painters, including: Jean *or* Janet *or* Jehannet (c.1485–c.1540); painter in ordinary to King Francis I (from c.1516), chief painter (1523); painter of portraits and miniatures of the king and members of the court; noted for delicacy and power of characterization. His son ¶François (1515 or 1520–1572) succeeded his father as painter to the king (1540); continued under Henry II, Francis II, Charles IX; known for portraits, genre scenes, theatrical settings.

Clough \'kləf\, Anne Jemima. 1820–1892. English educator. Sister of Arthur Hugh Clough; taught in and conducted various schools; a founder (1867), secretary (1867–70), president (1873–74), North of England Council for Promoting the Higher Education of Women; secured admission of women to Manchester and Newcastle colleges; first principal of Newnham Hall (1871; adopted name 1875; became Newnham Coll., Cambridge, 1880); held post until death.

Clough, Arthur Hugh. 1819–1861. English poet. Resigned Oxford fellowship (1848) because of skepticism, and traveled, visiting Emerson (1852); examiner in education office, London (1853); sought recovery from failing health in southern Europe; died in Florence. Subject of Matthew Arnold's elegy

"Thyrsis." Author of a pastoral in hexameters, *The Bothie of Toper-na-Fuosich,* revised to *Tober-na-Vuolich* (1848), "Amours de Voyage," a rhymed novelette (1849), "Dipsychus," a serious satire (1850), *Poems* (1862), and a prose revision of a 17th-century translation of Plutarch's *Lives* (1859).

Clo·vio \'klȯv-yō\, Giulio. 1498–1578. Italian miniaturist, b. Croatia. Known for series of 12 miniatures on victories of Emperor Charles V; book of 26 illustrations of procession of Corpus Domini, Rome, with covers by Cellini; illustrated manuscript life of Federico, Duke of Urbino.

Clo·vis \klȯ-vēs, *Angl* 'klō-vəs\. *Ger.* Chlod·wig \'klōt-vik\. *Also* Chlo·do·wech \'klō-dō-,vek\. c.466–511. King of the Salian Franks (481–511). Son of Childeric I; m. Clotilda (*q.v.*), who converted him to Christianity (496). Overthrew Gallo-Roman colony governed by Syagrius, near Soissons (486); defeated the Alamanni at Tolbiacum (Zülpich) near the Rhine (496); baptized en masse with 3,000 soldiers (498); fixed his court at Paris (507); defeated Visigoths at Vouillé (507); promulgated Lex Salica; succeeded in unifying northern Frankish tribes; just before his death divided his newly organized realm among four sons.

¶Clovis II (c.634–657) and ¶Clovis III (682–695) were descendants of Clovis in the Merovingian dynasty and kings of Neustria and Burgundy (639–657 and 691–695, respectively).

Clu·ett \'klü-ət\, Sanford Lockwood. 1874–1968. American engineer, b. Troy, N.Y. Director of engineering and research (1919–44), vice president (1927–68) in family firm of Cluett, Peabody & Co.; invented Sanforizing process of mechanically preshrinking fabrics.

Clur·man \'klu̇(ə)r-mən\, Harold. 1901–1980. American theatrical director and critic, b. New York City. Helped found Group Theatre (1931). Directed Broadway productions of *Awake and Sing* (1935), *Member of the Wedding* (1950), *Tiger at the Gates* (1955), *Waltz of the Toreadors* (1957), *Touch of the Poet* (1957), *Incident at Vichy* (1965), etc. Drama critic for *New Republic* (1948–52), *The Nation* (from 1953).

Clusius, Carolus. See Charles de L'ÉCLUSE.

Clü·ver \'klu̅e̅-ver\, Philipp. *Lat.* Clu·ve·ri·us \klü-'vir-ē-əs\. *Pol.* Clu·wer \'klü-ver\. 1580–1622. German antiquarian and geographer. Regarded as founder of historical geography; *geographus academicus* in Leipzig (from 1616). Author of *Germaniae antiquae* (1616), *Introductio in universam geographiam* (1624), etc.

Clyde, Baron. See Sir Colin CAMPBELL.

Cly·mer \'klī-mər\, George. 1739–1813. American politician, b. Philadelphia. Merchant in Philadelphia; member, Continental Congress (1776–78, 1780–83); signer of Declaration of Independence. Member of Constitutional Convention; signed Constitution (1787); member, 1st Congress (1789–91).

Clynes \'klīnz\, John Robert. 1869–1949. English labor leader and politician. Textile millworker (1879–91); union organizer and officer (1891 ff.); helped organize Labour party (1899); M.P. (1906–31, 1935–45); food controller (1918–19). Chairman, Parliamentary Labour party (1921–22); lord privy seal and deputy leader of House of Commons (1924) in first British Labour cabinet; home secretary (1929–31).

Cnut. See CANUTE.

Coates \'kōts\, Florence Van Leer, *nee* Earle \'ər(-ə)l\. 1850–1927. American poet, b. Philadelphia. m. (1879) Edward H. Coates. Author of *Poems* (1898), *Mine and Thine* (1904), *Lyrics of Life* (1909), *The Unconquered Air* (1912), *Pro Patria* (1917), etc.

Coates, Joseph Gordon. 1878–1943. New Zealand politician. Member of N.Z. parliament (1911–43); minister of justice (1919–20); postmaster general and minister of telegraphs (1919–25); minister of public works (1920–26), of native affairs (1921–28), of railways (1923–28); prime minister of New Zealand (1925–28); minister of external affairs (1928). Leader of the opposition (1928–31). Minister of public works, employment, and transport (1931–33), of finance, customs, and transport (1933–35); member of N.Z. war cabinet (1940–43).

Cobb \'käb\, Henry Ives. 1859–1931. American architect, b. Brookline, Mass. Designed Newberry Library, City Hall, buildings of the University of Chicago, and Church of the Atonement in Chicago; Pennsylvania State capitol at Harrisburg; American University buildings at Washington, D.C.

Cobb, Howell. 1815–1868. American politician, b. Jefferson Co., Ga. Member, U.S. House of Representatives (1843–51, 1855–57); speaker (1849–51). Governor of Georgia (1851–53). U.S. secretary of the treasury (1857–60). Unionist until Lincoln's election.

Cobb, Irvin Shrewsbury. 1876–1944. American journalist, humorist, and writer, b. Paducah, Ky. Correspondent and columnist, Louisville (Ky.) *Evening Post* (1898–1901); managing editor, Paducah *News Democrat* (1901–04); editor of humor section, New York *Evening Sun* (1904–05); on staff, New York *World* (1905–11), *Saturday Evening Post* (1911–22), *Cosmopolitan Magazine* (1922–32). Among his humorous books and collections of stories were *Back Home* (1912), *Old Judge Priest* (1916), *Speaking of Operations—(1915), J. Poindexter, Colored* (1922), *Stickfuls* (1923), *Alias Ben Alibi* (1925), *Ladies and Gentlemen* (1927), *Red Likker* (1929). Author of and collaborator in many plays, musical comedies, screenplays, etc.

Cobb, John. c.1710–1778. English cabinetmaker. Worked in London in partnership (c.1750–65) with William Vile, afterwards alone; noted for furniture in Neoclassical style; supplied furniture to George III, Horace Walpole, etc.

Cobb, John Rhodes. 1899–1952. Scottish automobile and boat racer. Set world land speed record of 394 mph (1947), which stood for 17 years; killed attempting water speed record.

Cobb, Ty, *in full* Tyrus Raymond. 1886–1961. American baseball player, b. Narrows, Ga. Player (1905–26), manager (1921–26), Detroit Tigers; player (1926–28), Philadelphia Athletics. Considered outstanding offensive player of all time; career batting average a record .367; seasons batted over .300 a record 23; led American League in batting 12 times; career hits a record 4191; career runs scored record 2244; career bases stolen record (to 1977) 892; season bases stolen record 96 (for 156 games). Led all candidates in first balloting for Baseball Hall of Fame (1936). Known as the "Georgia Peach."

Cobbe \'käb\, Frances Power. 1822–1904. British philanthropist and writer. Edited works of Theodore Parker (1863–71); published anonymously *The Theory of Intuitive Morals* (1855); associated with Mary Carpenter in ragged schools (1858); proponent of university education for women; campaigned against vivisection. Author of *Broken Lights* (1864), *Italics* (1864), *Darwinism in Morals* (1872), *The Duties of Women* (1881), etc.

Cob·bett \'käb-ət\, William. *Pseudonym* Peter Por·cu·pine \'pȯr-kyə-,pīn\. 1763–1835. English journalist and essayist. During service in British army (1783–91), taught himself grammar and composition; attempted court martial of his former officers for peculation; fled countercharges to France and then to Philadelphia (1792); published pamphlets attacking French Revolution and any form of radicalism, and vituperative criticism of American democracy; attacked Joseph Priestley as traitor (1794); published newspaper *Porcupine's Gazette;* fined for libelling Dr. Benjamin Rush. Returned to England (1800); edited with aid of John Wright (*q.v.*) works on parliamentary history; edited (from 1802) weekly *Political Register,* at first a Tory journal but (from c.1806) champion of radicalism, demanding parliamentary and social reform; farmed in Hampshire (1805–17); took up cause of dispossessed rural laborers; imprisoned in Newgate (1810–12) for denouncing flogging of militiamen; bankrupt; as leader of discontented working classes after ending of war (1815), had to flee to Long Island (1817–19). Espoused cause of Queen Caroline (1820); developed successful seed farm in Kensington; defended himself against charge of sedition (1831); M.P. (1832–35), leader of handful of extreme radicals. Author of a *Grammar of the English Language* for working-class students (1818), *Cobbett's Cottage Economy* (1822), *The Woodlands* (1825), *The English Gardener* (1829), *Rural Rides* (1830), *Advice to Young Men* (1830), and numerous other works notable for vigorous prose.

Cob·den \'käb-dən\, Richard. 1804–1865. English politician and economist. London calico merchant (1828); as partner in calico-printing factory in Lancashire (1831), gained independent fortune; studied economic and financial systems in U.S., Near East, Germany (1835–38); published pamphlets *England, Ireland, and America,* opposing defense of Turkey against Russia (1835) and *Russia,* attacking doctrine of balance of power (1836). With John Bright, a leader of national Anti-Corn-Law League (1839–46); M.P. (1840–57, 1859–65); converted Peel and succeeded in forcing repeal of corn laws (1846); financially ruined by neglect of his business. Shared unpopularity with John Bright for opposition to Crimean War; published pamphlet *1793 and 1853, in Three Letters* (1853) against war with France; successfully opposed Palmerston's Chinese war policy (1857); declined office in cabinet; negotiated (1859–60) commercial treaty with France providing mutual reduction of tariffs; opposed intervention in favor of Denmark (1864). With John Bright, led the Manchester school; believer in free trade, minimum of government at home, and minimum of intervention abroad.

Cobden-San·der·son \-'san-dər-sən\, Thomas James. 1840–1922. English bookbinder and printer. Under influence of William Morris, withdrew from practice of law (1883) to devote himself to bookbinding; operated the Doves Bindery at Hammersmith (1893–1921); with Emery Walker (1900–09) and alone (1909–16) operated the Doves Press; produced books of outstandingly beautiful design and typography in the Arts and Crafts manner, notably the *Doves Bible* (1903–05).

Co·benzl \'kō-,bent-səl\, Ludwig, *in full* Johann Ludwig Joseph. 1753–1809. Austrian diplomat. Minister to St. Petersburg (1779); took part in Third Partition of Poland (1795) and gained much territory for Austria; lost left bank of Rhine to Napoléon in treaties of Campo Formio (1797), Rastatt (1797–99), Lunéville (1801); foreign minister (1801–05); recognized Napoléon's imperial title (1804) but became embroiled in War of Third Coalition with France (1805); dismissed following defeat at Austerlitz.

Cobenzl, Philipp, *in full* Johann Philipp von. Graf. 1741–1810. Austrian politician. Cousin of Ludwig Cobenzl. Negotiated Treaty of Teschen (1779) renouncing Bavaria; named vice chancellor; sent to pacify Austrian Netherlands (1787); succeeded Kaunitz as chancellor (1792–93); attempted to secure Prussian support for an exchange of Austrian Netherlands for Bavaria; discredited following Austria's exclusion from Second Partition of Poland (1793); ambassador to Paris (1801–05).

Co·ber·gher *or* **Coe·ber·ger** \'kō-ber-gər\, Wenceslas *or* Wensel. 1557 or 1561–1634. Flemish architect, painter, and engraver. Served governors of Spanish Netherlands (from 1605); painted altarpieces; designed St. Augustin, Antwerp, and Church of Notre Dame, Montaigu; one of chief exponents of Flemish Baroque style.

Cobham, Baron. See Sir John OLDCASTLE.

Coccaius, Merlinus *or* Coccaio, Merlino. See Teofilo FOLENGO.

Cocceius *or* **Coccejus,** Johannes. See Johannes KOCH.

Cocceius, Nerva. See NERVA.

Coc·ce·ji \kōk-'tsā-yē\, Heinrich von. Freiherr. 1644–1719. German jurist. Professor, Heidelberg (1671), Utrecht (1688), Frankfurt on the Oder (1690). Author of *Juris publici prudentia* (1695). His son ¶Baron Samuel (1679–1755), jurist; professor, Frankfurt on the Oder (1702); Prussian minister of state and war (1727); chief of Prussian judiciary (1738), which he reformed; chancellor of Prussia (1747).

Co·chin \kȯ-sha^n\. Family of French engravers, including: Charles-Nicolas, *called* the Father (1688–1754), who engraved esp. after painters of French school, as Coypel, Watteau, etc. His son ¶Charles-Nicolas, *called* the Son *or* the Younger (1715–1790), most famous of family; keeper of king's drawings (from 1752); engraved frontispiece of the *Encyclopédie* and vignettes for editions of Ariosto, Tasso, and Boileau; illustrated La Fontaine's *Fables;* also wrote and illustrated *Observations sur les fouilles d'Herculanum* (1754).

Co·chise \kō-'chēs\. 1812?–1874. American Indian leader, b. probably in Arizona. Chief of Chiricahua Apaches; seized by U.S. army authorities on charge of kidnapping white child (1861); escaped, taking hostages, whom he killed in revenge for execution of other Apache prisoners; joined with father-in-law Mangas Coloradas of Mimbreño Apaches in warring on army and white settlers; temporarily routed by Gen. James Carleton's artillery (1862); principal Apache chief on death of Mangas (1862); led band of followers into Dragoon Mountains, evading capture for 10 years; surrendered to Gen. George Crook (1871); fled reservation, returning on establishment of Chiricahua reservation on ancestral lands (1872).

Cochlaeus. See Johannes DOBENECK.

Coch·ran \'käk-rən\, Sir Charles Blake. 1872–1951. English theatrical manager and producer. Secretary and later manager to Richard Mansfield; theatrical agent in London (from c.1900); produced circuses, roller-skating extravaganzas, boxing and wrestling matches, etc.; produced Max Reinhardt's *The Miracle* (1911); produced series of revues beginning with *Odds and Ends* (1914); other productions included Irving Berlin's *Watch Your Step* (1915), Bairnsfather's *The Better 'Ole* (1917), Noel Coward's *This Year of Grace* (1928), *Private Lives* (1930), and *Cavalcade* (1931), and over 120 others; introduced or promoted Bea Lillie, Eleonora Duse, Sacha Guitry, etc.

Cochran, Jacqueline. 1910?–1980. American aviator, b. Pensacola, Fla. Learned to fly (1932); founded and directed (1934–63) cosmetics firm; won Bendix Transcontinental Air Race (1938); trained British women pilots (1941); director of Women's Airforce Service Pilots (1943–45); commissioned lieutenant colonel, U.S. Air Force (1948); first woman to break sound barrier (1953); set numerous altitude and speed records; colonel (1969); retired (1970). First woman president of Fédération Aéronautique Internationale (1959–63).

Coch·rane \'käk-rən\, Thomas. 10th Earl of Dun·don·ald \ˌdən-'dän-əld\. *Called* Lord Cochrane. 1775–1860. British naval commander. Entered navy (1793); as commander of brig *Speedy* took over fifty prizes (1800–01), including a 32-gun Spanish frigate; returned to prize-taking off Azores (1805) and Bay of Biscay (1806); in Parliament (1806–31) exposed naval abuses; on account of jealousy of superiors, only partly successful in burning French fleet in Aix Roads (1809); accused of connivance in speculative fraud, fined, imprisoned, and expelled from navy (1814). In command of Chile's navy (1818–22) in war for freedom by Chile and Peru, neutralized Spanish squadron, took Valdivia, contributed to capture of Lima (1819–22); in command of Brazilian navy (1823–25); commanded Greek navy (1827–28); first to use steam-propelled ships of war; advocated adoption of screw propellers. Received free pardon, reinstated in British navy, and promoted rear admiral (1832); commander in chief on North American station (1848–51); admiral (1851). His uncle ¶Sir Alexander Forrester Inglis Cochrane (1758–1832), admiral; M.P. (1800–06); blockaded Ferrol (1804); held command in West Indies (1805–14) and on American station (1814–15), directing naval operations in unsuccessful attacks on Baltimore and New Orleans.

Cock·burn \'kō-(ˌ)bərn\, Sir Alexander James Edmund. 10th Baronet. 1802–1880. British jurist. Defense counsel in McNaghten's Case (1843), establishing legal test of insanity; M.P. (1847–56); defended Palmerston's foreign policy (1850); attorney general (1851–56); chief justice of common pleas (1856–59); lord chief justice of England (1859; traditional title made official 1874); British representative in arbitration of *Alabama* case at Geneva (1872); presided over trial (1873–74) of Tichborne Claimant.

Cockburn, Alicia *or* Alison, *nee* Ruth·er·ford \'rəth-ə(r)-fərd\. 1713–1794. Scottish poet. Author of Scottish ballad "Flowers of the Forest" (pub. 1765) beginning "I've seen the smiling of Fortune beguiling."

Cockburn, Sir George. 1772–1853. British naval officer. Entered navy (1781); took part in capture of Martinique (1809); served against Spain; rear admiral (1812); in War of 1812 commanded naval forces in battle of Bladensburg and capture of Washington, D.C. (1814); conveyed Napoléon to St. Helena (1815); vice admiral (1819); admiral (1837); admiral of the fleet (1851). M.P. (1818–53); first naval lord (1841–46).

Cockburn, Henry Thomas. *Known as* Lord Cockburn. 1779–1854. Scottish judge. Solicitor general for Scotland (1830); principal author of Scottish Reform Bill (1831); a lord of justiciary (1837). Author of a biography of Lord Jeffrey (1852).

Cock·croft \'käk-ˌ(k)rȯft\, Sir John Douglas. 1897–1967. British physicist. Professor, Cambridge (1939–46); director, Atomic Energy Research Establishment (1946–58); president, Manchester Coll. of Science and Technology (1961–67). With E.T.S. Walton developed Cockcroft-Walton high-voltage generator for use as particle accelerator (1932); used it to split lithium and other atoms; with Walton awarded Nobel prize for physics (1951).

Cock·er \'käk-ər\, Edward. 1631–1675. English engraver and teacher. Published manuals of penmanship, and an *Arithmetick* (1678) that went through a hundred editions—hence the expression "according to Cocker."

Cock·er·am \'käk-ər-əm, 'käk-rəm\, Henry. fl. 1650. English lexicographer. Author of earliest published dictionary of English, *The English Dictionarie, or a New Interpreter of Hard English Words* (1623).

Cock·er·ell \'käk-ər-əl, 'käk-rəl\, Charles Robert. 1788–1863. English architect. Conducted excavations in the Levant; professor of architecture to Royal Academy (1840–57); designed chiefly in classic models, including Ashmolean museum and Taylorian institute, Oxford, Fitzwilliam museum Cambridge, also Gothic chapels at Lampeter and Harrow.

Cock·er·ill \'käk-ər-əl, 'käk-rəl\, William. 1759–1832. English inventor and manufacturer. Constructed (1799) at Verviers, Belgium, first wool-carding and wool-spinning machines on Continent and established (1807) factory at Liège for making these machines. His youngest son ¶John (1790–1840) developed the business and built foundry and machine factory at Seraing, Belgium (1817).

Coco, Vincenzo. See CUOCO.

Coc·teau \kȯk-tō\, Jean. 1889–1963. French poet, novelist, playwright, and artist. Author of verse *Le Cap de Bonne-Espérance* (1919), *L'Ode à Picasso* (1919), *Vocabulaire* (1922), *L'Ange heurtebise* (1925), *Morceaux choisis* (1932), *Allégories* (1941), *Léone* (1945), *Le Chiffre sept* (1952), *Clair-obscur* (1954); novels *Le Potomak* (1919), *Le Grand Écart* (1923), *Thomas l'imposteur* (1923), *Les Enfants terribles* (1929), etc.; plays *Orphée* (1926), *La Voix humaine* (1930), *La Machine infernale* (1934), *Les Parents terribles* (1938), *Les Monstres sacrés* (1940), *La Machine à écrire* (1941), etc.; ballet scenarios *Parade* (1917, music by Satie), *Le Boeuf sur le toit* (1920, music by Milhaud), *Le Gendarme incompris* (1921, with Raymond Radiguet, music by Poulenc), *Les Biches* (1924, Poulenc), *Les Fâcheux* (1924, Auric), *Phèdre* (1950, Auric); wrote and directed films *Le Sang d'un poète* (1932), *La Belle et la bête* (1945), *Ruy Blas* (1947, with Pierre Billon), *La Voix humaine* (1947, with Roberto Rossellini), *Les Parents terribles* (1948), *Orphée* (1950), *Les Enfants terribles* (1950); also noted as graphic artist and designer; considered one of the most creative artists of the 20th century.

Cod·ding·ton \'käd-iŋ-tən\, William. 1601–1678. American colonist, b. Boston, England. To Massachusetts (c.1630); protested the prosecution of Anne Hutchinson (1637); withdrew (1638) to Aquidneck (Rhode Island); a founder of Portsmouth (1638), Newport (1639). Governor of Aquidneck (1640); governor of Rhode Island and Providence Plantations (1674, 1675, 1678).

Codommanus. See DARIUS III.

Co·do·na \kō-'thō-nä\, Alfredo. 1893–1937. Mexican aerialist. With Ringling Brothers Circus (from 1917); famed for triple aerial somersault; considered greatest flying trapeze artist in circus history; m. Lillian Leitzel (1928; *q.v.*).

Co·dre·a·nu \kō-drē-'ä-nü\, Corneliu Zelea. 1899–1938. Romanian political leader. Active in anti-Communist and anti-Semitic organizations, several times arrested; founded (1927) Legion of the Archangel Michael, renamed (1930) Iron Guard and subsequently the All for Fatherland party; scored large electoral success along with terrorist activities; imprisoned on order of King Carol II (1938); killed while in custody.

Cod·ring·ton \'käd-riŋ-tən\, Sir Edward. 1770–1851. British naval officer. Entered navy (1783); commanded ship at Trafalgar (1805); vice admiral (1821); commanded British, French, and Russian fleet in destroying Turkish fleet at Navarino (1827); admiral (1837). His son ¶Sir William John (1804–1884) entered army (1821); major general (1854); commander in chief at Sevastopol (1855–56); governor of Gibraltar (1859–65); general (1863). M.P. (1857–84).

Codrington, Robert Henry. 1830–1922. British clergyman and anthropologist. To New Zealand (1860); headed Melanesian Mission of Anglican church (1871–77); returned to England (1888). Made first systematic study of Melanesian society and culture. Author of *Melanesian Languages* (1865), *The Melanesians* (1891), *Dictionary of the Language of Mota, Sugarloaf Islands, Banks' Islands* (1896, with J. Palmer).

Cod·rus \'käd-rəs\. 11th century B.C. Traditional, perhaps legendary, last king of Athens. According to legend, reigned about 1068 B.C. and sacrificed himself during a Dorian invasion of the Peloponnesus to fulfill a prophecy and insure Athenian success.

Co·duc·ci \kō-'düt-chē\, Mauro. 1440–1504. Venetian architect. Outstanding early Renaissance designer; works included S. Michele in Isola (c.1468), S. Zaccaria (c.1500), S. Giovanni Crisostomo (c.1500), Scuola di S. Marco, and probably the Palazzo Corner-Spinelli (c.1500) and Palazzo Vendramin-Calergi (1501–09).

Co·dy \'kōd-ē\, John Patrick. 1907–1982. American prelate, b. St. Louis. Ordained (1931); auxiliary bishop of St. Louis (1947–54); bishop of St. Joseph (1955–56), of Kansas City-St. Joseph (1956–61); archbishop of New Orleans (1964–65), of Chicago (1965–82); cardinal (1967).

Cody, William Frederick. *Known as* Buf·fa·lo Bill \'bəf-ə-,lō-'bil\. 1846–1917. American scout and showman, b. Scott Co., Iowa. Rider for the Pony Express (1860); scout for Kansas cavalry against Indians (1863); in army (1863–65); furnished buffalo meat for Union Pacific construction crews (1867–68); scout, 5th U.S. Cavalry (1868–72, 1876). On stage as actor (1872–83), at first in *Scouts of the Plains* by E.Z.C. Judson (*q.v.*). Organized and managed Buffalo Bill's Wild West Show (from 1883); toured U.S. and Europe successfully (to 1916).

Coeberger. See Cobergher.

Coef·fier-Ru·zé \kœf-yā-rü̅e-zā\ *or* **Coif·fier-Ruzé** \kwȧ-fyā-\, Antoine. Marquis d'Ef·fiat \dā-fyȧ, de-\. 1581–1632. French soldier and diplomat. Father of Henri Coeffier-Ruzé, marquis de Cinq-Mars. Councillor of state (1616); negotiated marriage of future Charles I to Princess Henrietta Maria (1624); superintendent of finances (1626); marshal of France (1631); killed in siege of Trier.

Coeffier-Ruzé d'Ef·fiat \-dā-fyȧ, -de-\, Henri. Marquis de Cinq-Mars \saⁿ-mȧr\. 1620–1642. French courtier. Son of Antoine, marquis d'Effiat; reared after father's death (1632) by Cardinal Richelieu; became favorite of Louis XIII; notorious for extravagance, arrogance, libertinism; devised conspiracy against Richelieu, signing secret agreement with Philip IV of Spain for armed support of a revolt; plot discovered by Richelieu; arrested, tried, beheaded.

Coe·hoorn \'kü-hōrn\, Menno van. Baron. 1641–1704. Dutch soldier and military engineer. Invented small bronze mortar first used at siege of Grave (1674); took part in capture of Bonn (1689); defeated Vauban at Namur (1695); master general of artillery (1695). Authority on fortification for level terrain; author of *Nieuwe vestingbouw* (1685), etc.

Coelho, José Francisco Trindade. See Trindade Coelho.

Co·e·lho Pe·rei·ra \kü-'āl-yü-pə-'rā-ē-ra\, Duarte. 1485?–1554. Portuguese soldier. Granted captaincy of Pernambuco (1534), which he developed into most flourishing colony in Brazil.

Coello, Alonso Sánchez. See Sánchez Coello.

Co·e·llo \kō-'ā(l)-yō\, Claudio. c.1635–1693. Spanish painter. Pupil of Carreño de Miranda; court painter (1684); painter to cathedral of Toledo (1691); considered last leading painter of Madrid school. Known particularly for his canvas altar panel *La sagrada forma* (1685) for El Escorial; also decorated vestry ceiling, Toledo cathedral (1671); other works included *La sagrada familia, La comunión de santa Teresa, Triunfo de san Agustín.*

Coemgenus, Saint. See Kevin.

Coen \'kün\, Jan Pieterszoon. 1587–1629. Dutch colonial governor. To Indonesia as merchant with Dutch East India Co. (1607); head of post at Bantam (1612); director general of Asian commerce (1614); secured Dutch monopolies of trade in various spices; governor general of Dutch East Indies (1617–29); conquered Jacatra and on its ruins founded Batavia (1619); conquered Banda Islands in bloody campaign (1621); established post on Formosa (1622); largely failed in attempts to attract Dutch settlement and to monopolize inter-Asian trade; died during siege of Batavia by Javanese army.

Coenwulf. See Cenwulf.

Coeur \kœr\, Jacques. c.1395–1456. French merchant. Gained vast wealth through extensive trading and manufacturing activities; became counsellor to King Charles VII; in charge of French royal finances (from c.1436); influence extended from Spain to Levant; eventually creditor of the king and much of nobility; falsely accused of traitorous conduct, condemned, and deprived of his property (1451); in exile in Rome.

Coeur de Lion. See Richard I of England; Louis VIII of France.

Cof·fin \'kȯf-ən, 'käf-\, Henry Sloane. 1877–1954. American clergyman, b. New York City. Ordained in Presbyterian ministry (1900); pastor of Madison Avenue Church, New York City (1905–26); president, Union Theol. Sem. (1926–45); moderator of U.S. Presbyterian General Assembly (1943–44); a leader in Christian approach to social problems. Author of *Meaning of the Cross* (1931), etc.

Coffin, Howard Earle. 1873–1937. American engineer, b. West Milton, Ohio. Engineer with Olds Motor Works (1902–06); vice president and chief engineer, E.R. Thomas Detroit Co. (1906–09, from 1908 Chalmers-Detroit Co.); designed Chalmers automobile; with Roy D. Chapin founded Hudson Motor Car Co. (1909), vice president (1909–30); designed Hudson automobile. Member of Council of National Defense (1916–18) and head of its Aircraft Board (1917–18); helped found (1922) National Aeronautical Association. Founded (1925) National Air Transport, forerunner of United Air Lines; president (1925–28), chairman (1928–30).

Coffin, Levi. 1798–1877. American abolitionist, b. New Garden, N.C. Opened short-lived Quaker Sunday school for slaves (1821); active in Indiana (1826–47) and Cincinnati (1847–60) in organization of "Underground Railroad" for escaped slaves; reputed model for Simon Halliday in *Uncle Tom's Cabin.*

Coffin, Lorenzo S. 1823–1915. American reformer, b. Alton, N.H. Preacher, educator, journalist in Fort Dodge, Iowa (from 1855); as Iowa state railroad commissioner (1883–88) worked tirelessly to secure installation of automatic braking and coupling equipment on freight trains, thus cutting fatal and disabling accidents by more than half.

Coffin, Robert Peter Tristram. 1892–1955. American writer, b. Brunswick, Me. Professor, Wells College, Aurora, N.Y. (1921–34), Bowdoin (from 1934). Author of verse, as *Christchurch* (1924), *Golden Falcon* (1929), *Strange Holiness* (1935, Pulitzer prize), *Saltwater Farm* (1937), *Collected Poems* (1939, 1948); books of essays, as *Book of Crowns and Cottages* (1925), *An Attic Room* (1929); biographies, as *Laud* (1930), *The Dukes of Buckingham* (1931), *Portrait of an American* (1931), *Captain Abby and Captain John* (1939); novels as *Red Sky in the Morning* (1935) and *John Dawn* (1936); and *Kennebec* (1937) in "Rivers of America" series.

Cogălniceanu. See Kogălniceanu.

Coggeshall, Ralph of. See Ralph of Coggeshall.

Cog·hill \'käg-,hil\, George Ellett. 1872–1941. American anatomist, b. Beaucoup, Ill. Professor, U. of Kansas (1913–25), Wistar Institute of Anatomy, Philadelphia (1925–35); known for his researches on the nervous system of amphibia and on the relation of the development of the nervous system to the development of behavior.

Cogh·lan \'käg-lən\, Rose. 1853–1932. American actress, b. Peterborough, England. Stage debut (1865); to U.S. (1872); naturalized (1902). Leading lady in Wallack's company (1877–85); acted Countess Zicka in first American presentation of *Diplomacy* (1878); made great success as Stephanie in *Forget-Me-Not* (1880).

Co·gi·dub·nus \,kō-gə-'dəb-nəs\ *or* **Co·gi·dum·nus** \-'dəm-\. 1st century A.D. British prince. Chief of the Regni; ally of Rome and important figure in Roman government of Britain.

Co·gnacq \kȯn-yȧk\, Ernest, *in full* Théodore-Ernest. 1839–1928. French merchant. Founder (1870) of the Parisian department store À la Samaritaine; widely known for philanthropies.

Cogs·well \'kägz-,wel, -wəl\, Joseph Green. 1786–1871. American librarian and bibliographer, b. Ipswich, Mass. Professor and librarian, Harvard (1820–23); with George Bancroft established Round Hill School, Northampton, Mass. (1823); superintendent and bibliographer of Astor collection (1848–61).

Co·han \'kō-,han\, George Michael. 1878–1942. American actor, playwright, and producer, b. Providence, R.I. On stage from childhood; appeared in *Peck's Bad Boy* (1890); in vaudeville as one of "The Four Cohans". Wrote and starred in *The Governor's Son* (1901), *Little Johnny Jones* (1904, with songs "Give My Regards to Broadway" and "Yankee Doodle Dandy"). Associated with Sam Harris in firm Cohan & Harris (1904–20). Among the many plays that he wrote, produced, and acted in were *Forty-five Minutes from Broadway* (1905, "Mary's a Grand Old Name"), *George Washington, Jr.* (1906, "You're a Grand Old Flag"), *Talk of New York* (1907), *The Man Who Owns Broadway* (1908), *Get-Rich-Quick Wallingford* (1910), *Broadway Jones* (1912), *Seven Keys to Baldpate* (1913), *The Tavern* (1921), *American Born* (1925); also starred in *Ah! Wilderness* (1933), *I'd Rather be Right* (1937). Wrote World War I song "Over There."

Co·hen \kō-ˈhen\, Ernst Julius. 1869–1944. Dutch chemist. Assistant to van't Hoff at U. of Amsterdam (1893); professor of physical chemistry, Utrecht (1902–39); known for studies on the allotropy of metals, esp. tin, and piezochemical phenomena.

Co·hen \ˈkō-ən\, Hermann. 1842–1918. German philosopher. Professor, Marburg (1876–1912); founder of Marburg school of Neo-Kantianism.

Cohen, Morris Raphael. 1880–1947. American philosopher and educator, b. Minsk, Russia. To U.S. (1892); professor of philosophy, C.C.N.Y. (1912–38), and U. of Chicago (1938–41). Author of *Reason and Nature* (1931), *Law and the Social Order* (1933), *Preface to Logic* (1944), *Faith of a Liberal* (1946), *Meaning of Human History* (1948), etc.

Cohen, Octavus Roy. 1891–1959. American writer, b. Charleston, S.C. Author of short stories and novels including *The Crimson Alibi* (1919), *Polished Ebony* (1919), *Come Seven* (1920), *Jim Hanvey, Detective* (1923), *Florian Slappey Goes Abroad* (1928), *Epic Peters, Pullman Porter* (1930), *The Townsend Murder Mystery* (1933), *Child of Evil* (1936), *Kid Tinsel* (1941), *Dangerous Lady* (1946); also plays, screenplays, radio scripts, etc.

Cohn \ˈkōn\, Edwin Joseph. 1892–1953. American chemist, b. New York City. Professor, Harvard (1922–53); known for studies of proteins, amino acids, and esp. for work on fractionating blood into albumin, globulin, fibrin.

Cohn, Ferdinand Julius. 1828–1898. German botanist. Professor, Breslau (from 1859); founder (1866) of Inst. of Plant Physiology and (1870) of journal *Beiträge zur Biologie der Pflanzen.* Worked on morphology and life history of lower algae and fungi; demonstrated that bacteria are plants; proposed first classification system for bacteria; helped disprove notion of spontaneous generation. Author of *Über Bacterien* (1872), *Untersuchungen über Bacterien* in *Beiträge* (1872 ff.); aided Koch in publishing paper on anthrax.

Cohn, Roy Marcus. 1927–1986. American lawyer, b. New York City. Best known as chief counsel for Sen. Joseph McCarthy during U.S. Senate hearings (1953–54) into allegations of Communist infiltration of American government and military.

Cohn·heim \ˈkōn-ˌhīm\, Julius Friedrich. 1839–1884. German pathologist. Professor in Kiel (1868), Breslau (1872), Leipzig (1878). Known esp. for studies of inflammation and pus formation; devised technique of freezing tissue samples before sectioning. Author of *Neue Untersuchungen über die Entzündung* (1873), *Vorlesungen über allgemeine Pathologie* (1877–80).

Coiffier-Ruzé. See COEFFIER-RUZÉ.

Coin·dre \kwa^{n}-drā\, Andre. 1787–1826. French religious. Ordained priest (1812); renowned as preacher; helped Claudine Thévenet found Ladies of the Sacred Hearts of Jesus and Mary (1818); established orphanage and trade school near Lyon (1820) and religious congregation (1821) to serve them; organized group of diocesan missionaries (1822) that became Association of the Sacred Heart of Jesus; opened more schools; congregation became (1824) Fratres a Sacratissimo Corde Jesu, or Brothers of the Sacred Heart; superior general (1824), vicar general (1825).

Coi·ter *or* **Coy·ter** *or* **Koy·ter** \ˈkȯit-ər\, Volcher. 1534–?1590. Dutch anatomist. City physician to Nürnberg (1569); one of the founders of comparative osteology and of pathological anatomy.

Coke \ˈku̇k, ˈkōk\, Sir Edward. *Commonly called* Lord Coke *or* Cooke. 1552–1634. English jurist. Early gained prominence at bar; M.P. (1589); solicitor general (1592); speaker of House of Commons (1593); attorney general (1594), to disappointment of Francis Bacon; m. (1598) Lady Elizabeth Hatton, granddaughter of Burghley, again thwarting Bacon. Began his law reports (1600); prosecuted Essex and Southampton (1600), Raleigh (1603), and Gunpowder Plot conspirators (1605). Chief justice of Court of Common Pleas (1606); implacable adherent of common law, initiated series of conflicts with James I; decided (1610) that king's proclamation cannot change the law; contested church's attempt to have ecclesiastical causes decided by court of high commission; made chief justice of King's Bench and privy councillor (1613); sustained common-law courts in attempt to curtail chancellor's right to interfere in decisions (1615); defied James I's order to stay proceedings in case of commendams (holding of livings in plurality); too zealous to ascertain the truth in Sir Thomas Overbury case (1615); dismissed from judicial functions, partly through Bacon's efforts, on trivial charges (1616). M.P. (1620), leader of popular party; denounced interference with liberties of Parliament; imprisoned nine months (1622). Served on committee to impeach Bacon; instrumental in framing and passing the Petition of Right; opposed Charles I's demand for subsidies; on his death his papers and will seized by Charles I. Made an epoch in the history of the law with his *Reports* (1600–15), compendia of law bearing on cases; now best known for his four *Institutes* (1628–44), the first of which is known as *Coke upon Littleton.*

Coke, Thomas. 1747–1814. British clergyman, b. Wales. Anglican clergyman (1772–76); joined Wesley movement (1777); appointed by John Wesley superintendent of Methodist church in America (1784); assumed title of bishop (1787); visited America (1784–1803); died on mission to India.

Coke, Thomas William. Earl of Leices·ter \ˈles-tər\ of Holk·ham \ˈhäl-kəm, ˈhōl-\. 1752–1842. English agriculturist. M.P. (1776–84, 1790–1806, 1807–32); ardent Whig, protectionist, advocate of parliamentary reform. Bred Southdown sheep, Devon cattle; improved Suffolk breed of pigs; introduced wheat-growing into Norfolk. Created earl (1837).

Cō·la \ˈkō-lə\. Tamil dynasty of South India ruling Coromandel in Cauvery valley; defeated Pallavas (9th century), Pāṇḍyas (10th century); acquired Ceylon, extended rule over most of Deccan; began decline (late 12th century); line extinguished (1279). See RĀJARĀJA I.

Cola di Rienzo. See RIENZO.

Col·bert \kȯl-ber\, Charles. Marquis de Crois·sy \krwá-sē\. 1625–1696. French politician. Brother of J.-B. Colbert. Intendant for Alsace (1656); president of Parlement of Metz (1662–63); ambassador at London (1668–74); helped negotiate Treaty of Nijmegen (1678); secretary of state for foreign affairs (1679–96); devised annexationist policy on eastern frontier for Louis XIV, leading to War of Grand Alliance (1689–97).

Colbert, Jean-Baptiste. 1619–1683. French politician. Entered employ of Cardinal Mazarin (1651); engineered downfall of Fouquet (1661) and succeeded him as intendant (1661) and then controller general of finance (1665); instituted council of finance to purify service; reformed administration and collection of taxes and greatly increased state revenues; developed industry; imposed a protective tariff; built roads and canals; as minister of marine (from 1669) created French navy (1669–72) and mercantile marine; revised civil code; introduced marine code and "code noir" (colonial code); driven to levy oppressive taxes to meet expenses of Louis's wars. Founded Académie des Inscriptions et Belles-Lettres (1663), Académie des Sciences (1666), Académie Royale d'Architecture (1667); as secretary of state for king's household (from 1669) encouraged French arts.

Col·borne \ˈkōl-(ˌ)bərn, ˈkäl-ˌbō(ə)rn, -ˌbȯ(ə)rn\, Sir John. 1st Baron Sea·ton \ˈsēt-^{ə}n\. 1778–1863. British general. Served in Egypt (1801), Sicily (1806); officer in Peninsular War and at Waterloo. Lieutenant governor of Upper Canada (1828–38); crushed revolt of 1838. Created baron (1839). Governor of Ionian Islands (1843–49). General (1854); field marshal (1860).

Col·burn \ˈkōl-(ˌ)bərn\, Irving Wightman. 1861–1917. American inventor and manufacturer, b. Fitchburg, Mass. Perfected (1916) method for continuous production of flat sheet glass, basis of Libby-Owen Sheet Glass Co.

Col·by \ˈkōl-bē\, Frank Moore. 1865–1925. American editor, b. Washington, D.C. Professor, Amherst (1890–91), Columbia U. (1892–95), N.Y.U. (from 1895); editor, *International* (later *New International*) *Year Book* (from 1898), *New International Encyclopaedia* (1900–03 and 1913–15).

Col·den \ˈkōl-dən\, Cadwallader. 1688–1776. American colonialist, b. Ireland, of Scottish parents. To Philadelphia (1710); practiced medicine; moved to New York (1718); lieutenant governor of New York (1761–76); upheld British policy. Noted for scientific interests; classified American plants in his neighborhood according to Linnaean system; submitted work to Linnaeus, who published it (1749). Author of *The History of the Five Indian Nations* (1727).

Cole \ˈkōl\, Fay-Cooper. 1881–1961. American anthropologist, b. Plainwell, Mich. On staff, Field Museum of Natural History, Chicago (1906–23); led expedition to Malay Peninsula, Sumatra, Java, Borneo (1922–23); professor, U. of Chicago (1925–48); authority on anthropology of Malaysia. Author of *The Peoples of Malaysia* (1945), etc.

Cole, George Douglas Howard. 1889–1959. English economist. Active in Socialist and trade-union organizations; proponent of guild socialism; reader in economics, Oxford (1925), professor (1944); chairman, Fabian Society (1939–46, 1948–50), president (1952–59). Author of *The World of Labour* (1913), *Social Theory* (1920), *Organized Labour* (1924), *Gold, Credit and Unemployment* (1930), *What Marx Really Meant* (1934), *Socialism in Evolution* (1938), *British Working Class Politics* (1941), *Socialist Thought* (1953–58), etc.; with wife wrote 29 detective novels.

Cole, Sir Henry. *Pseudonym* Felix Sum·mer·ly \ˈsəm-ər-lē\. 1808–1882. English art critic. Promoted industrial design through Society of Arts; founded (1847) Summerly's Art Manufactures to engage artists in design work; proposed and helped plan and manage Great Exhibition (1851); virtual director (1853–73) of science and art department, Victoria and Albert Museum.

Cole, Nat King. *Orig.* Nathaniel Adams Coles \ˈkōlz\. 1919–1965. American musician, b. Montgomery, Ala. Pianist, leader of Nat Cole Trio (1939–51), successful jazz combo; later achieved international popularity as singer, as of "The Christmas Song," "Unforgettable."

Cole, Thomas. 1801–1848. American painter, b. Bolton-le-Moors, England. To America (1819); settled in Catskill, N.Y. (1826); founder of Hudson River school, a school of painters who found their early inspiration in scenery of the Hudson River Valley. Notable works included *Ox-Bow,* series *Course of Empire,* series *Voyage of Life.*

Cole, Timothy. 1852–1931. American wood engraver, b. London. To U.S. (1858); in employ of *Scribner's* (from 1875) and its successor, *Century Magazine;* sent to Europe to engrave old masters (1883); finished Italian series (1892), Dutch and Flemish series (1896), English series (1900), Spanish series (1907), French series (1910); engaged thereafter in engraving old masters in American public and private collections.

Co·len·so \kə-ˈlen-(ˌ)zō\, John William. 1814–1883. British prelate. Bishop of Natal (1853); compiled grammar and dictionary of Zulu and translated Prayer Book and New Testament into Zulu; provoked controversy (1862) by liberality in not requiring polygamous Zulu converts to divorce their wives, by combating doctrine of eternal punishment, by declaring Pentateuch a post-exile forgery; deposed and excommunicated by bishop of Cape Town (1864); acquitted on appeal (1865) and confirmed in his episcopal income by courts (1866); finally deposed (1869) by autonomous church of South Africa; championed natives against Boer oppression (1875).

Coleoni, Bartolomeo. See COLLEONI.

Colepeper. See also CULPEPER.

Cole·pep·er \ˈkəl-ˌpep-ər\, John. 1st Baron Colepeper. d. 1660. English Royalist leader. Member of Long Parliament (1640); denounced monopolies and Strafford (1641), but defended episcopacy, opposed Grand Remonstrance (1641); chancellor of exchequer (1642–43); master of the rolls (1643); created baron (1644); urged Charles I to make terms, first with Parliament, later with Scots, and Charles II with Scots; accompanied Prince of Wales (later Charles II) in flight and in naval expedition to Thames (1648); accompanied Charles II to southern France (1659) to conclude treaty of the Pyrenees. His eldest son ¶Thomas Colepeper *or* Culpeper (1635–1689), 2d baron, jointly with Lord Arlington received from Charles II grant of all Virginia; commissioned governor (1675); to Virginia (1680); taxed and punished tobacco growers with intolerable severity; dissolved assembly; returned to England (1683).

Cole·ridge \ˈkōl-rij, ˈkō-lə-rij\, Samuel Taylor. 1772–1834. English poet and critic. Notably restless and imaginative from youth; at Cambridge took up with enthusiasm Robert Southey's scheme of pantisocracy and helped form quixotic plan for community in Pennsylvania; wrote act one, Southey acts two and three, of *The Fall of Robespierre* (1794). Published first volume of poems (1796); in Bristol, started the weekly liberal journal *Watchman* (1796); preached in Unitarian chapels. Formed intimate association with William and Dorothy Wordsworth (1797); joined with Wordsworth (*q.v.*) in producing the *Lyrical Ballads* (1798 ff.), contributing "Rime of the Ancient Mariner," "The Nightingale," "Frost at Midnight," "France: An Ode," etc.; during same period wrote fragment "Kubla Khan" (pub. 1816), "Christabel" (pub. 1816); granted annuity by Wedgewood brothers on condition of devoting himself to literature. Visited Germany (1798–99); translated Schiller's *Piccolomini* and *Wallenstein* (1800); became addicted to opium (from 1803); suffered period of despondency, leaving his family dependent on friends. Started *The Friend,* a philosophical magazine, which ran eight months (1809–10); saw play *Osorio* (written c.1797) produced as *Remorse* (1813); published earlier works and *Biographia Literaria* and *Sibylline Leaves* (1817), *Aids to Reflection* (1825), the latter his most popular prose work.

His eldest son ¶Hartley, *in full* David Hartley (1796–1849), poet and man of letters; broght up by Southey; forfeited Oriel fellowship by intemperance; did hack work for a Leeds publisher (1830–36); schoolmaster (1837–38). Author of unfinished lyric drama *Prometheus* and graceful sonnets (pub. 1833, 1851). S.T. Coleridge's daughter ¶Sara (1802–1852) translated Dobrizhoffer's *Account of the Abipones* (1822), *Memoirs of Chevalier Bayard* (1825); for children wrote popular *Pretty Lessons in Verse* (1834) and *Phantasmion* (1837); annotated and edited her father's writings.

Coleridge-Tay·lor \-ˈtā-lər\, Samuel. 1875–1912. English composer. Won reputation with choral works *Hiawatha's Wedding Feast* (1898), *Death of Minnehaha* (1899), and *A Tale of Old Japan* (1911); also composed operas, theatrical music, orchestral pieces, songs, and piano music, notably *24 Negro Melodies* (1905), *Forest Scenes* (1907). Conductor of Handel Society (1904–12).

Col·et \ˈkäl-ət\, John. 1466 or 1467–1519. English scholar and theologian. Studied in Paris and Italy (1493–96); met Budé and Erasmus. Lectured in Oxford (1496–1504) on New Testament, opposing interpretations of scholastic theologians; dean of St. Paul's (1504–19); preached against sale of bishoprics, custom of pluralities, church lawyers; devoted large fortune to founding and endowing (c.1509) St. Paul's School; accused of heresy for liberal opinions but protected by Archbishop William Warham; made Canterbury pilgrimage with Erasmus (1514); preached at Wolsey's installation as cardinal (1515).

Co·let \kȯ-le\, Louise, *nee* Re·voil \rəv-wäl\. 1810–1870. French writer. m. Hippolyte Colet (1834); close friend of Mme. Récamier, Cousin, Alfred de Musset, de Vigny, Flaubert, Villemain. Author of verse, as in *Fleurs du Midi* (1836), *Penserosa* (1840), *Ce qui est dans le coeur des femmes* (1852), *Ce qu'on rêve en amant* (1854), and novels *La Jeunesse de Mirabeau* (1841), *Les Cœurs brisés* (1843), *Lui* (1859), *L'Italie des Italiens* (1862–64).

Co·lette \kȯ-let\. Saint. 1381–1447. Flemish religious. Entered Franciscan order of St. Clare (Poor Clares); instituted reforms in its rules and administration (1408), founding Colettine Poor Clares.

Colette, Sidonie-Gabrielle. 1873–1954. French writer. Wrote four "Claudine" novels published by first husband under his pseudonym "Willy": *Claudine à l'école* (1900), *Claudine à Paris* (1901), *Claudine en ménage* (1902), *Claudine s'en va* (1903); briefly a music hall performer. Subsequently wrote novels of exquisite sensitivity, including *La Retraite sentimentale* (1907), *L'Ingénue libertine* (1909), *La Vagabonde* (1910), *L'Envers du music-hall* (1913), *Mitsou* (1916), *Chéri* (1920), *La Maison de Claudine* (1922), *Le Blé en herbe* (1923), *La Fin de Chéri* (1926), *La Naissance du jour* (1928), *Sido* (1930), *La Chatte* (1933), *Duo* (1934), *Bellavista* (1937), *Le Tontonnier* (1939), *Le Képi* (1943), *Gigi* (1944); wrote volumes of memoirs as *Mes apprentissages* (1936), *L'Étoile vesper* (1947), *Le Fanal bleu* (1949).

Col·fax \ˈkōl-ˌfaks\, Schuyler. 1823–1885. American politician, b. New York City. Member from Indiana, U.S. House of Representatives (1855–69); a leader of Radical Republicans; speaker (1863–69). Vice president of the United States (1869–73). Involved in Crédit Mobilier scandal, and political career terminated.

Col·gate \ˈkōl-ˌgāt\, William. 1783–1857. American manufacturer, b. Hollingbourne, England. To U.S. (1795); founded tallow chandlery and soap manufacturing business (1806), later expanded to include various toilet preparations; firm later became Colgate-Palmolive-Peet Co. Benefactor of Madison U., Hamilton, N.Y., renamed (1890) Colgate U. in his honor.

Co·li·gny \kȯ-lēn-yē\, Gaspard II de. Seigneur de Châ·til·lon \shä-tē-yō^{n}\. 1519–1572. French admiral and religious leader. Son of Gaspard I de Coligny (1470?–1522), marshal of Châtillon; served under duc d'Enghien in Italy (1544); won renown for skill and bravery as a leader; colonel general of infantry (1547); admiral of France (1552); defended St.-Quentin with small force (1557) but defeated and held as prisoner in Spain (1557–59). Converted to Protestantism; became joint leader of Huguenots with Louis I, Prince of Condé (1560); opposed by Guise and Montmorency; aided Huguenots by sending colonies to New World (1562, 1564); at battles of Dreux (1562), Jarnac, and Moncontour (1569), but failed to take Poitiers; joined (1569) by Henry of Navarre as leader of Huguenots. Gained much influence over King Charles IX, thus arousing Guise and Catholics; killed at Massacre of St. Bartholomew (1572).

¶Odet de Coligny (1517–1571), his older brother; cardinal (1533) and archbishop of Toulouse (1534); convert to Calvinism; fled to England (1568). ¶Louise (1555–1620), daughter of Gaspard II, lost first husband in Massacre of St. Bartholomew; fled to Switzerland; m. 2d (1583) William the Silent, Prince of Orange (assassinated 1584).

Co·lijn \kə-ˈlīn\, Hendrikus. 1869–1944. Dutch politician. Soldier and later administrator in Sumatra; member of Dutch parliament (from 1909); minister of war (1911–13); leader of Anti-Revolutionary party (from 1922); finance minister (1923–25); premier (1925–26); member of upper chamber (from 1926); again premier of the Netherlands (1933–39); forced to resign because of his policy of retrenchment; most prominent leader of anti-Fascists; arrested by German occupation forces (1941); died in concentration camp.

Co·lin \kä-ˈlēn\ *or* **Co·lins** *or* **Co·lyns** \kä-ˈlēns\, Alexander. 1527 or 1529–1612. Flemish sculptor. Modeled decorations on castle of Heidelberg, and reliefs on tombs of Maximilian I and Hans Fugger at Innsbruck.

Co·lines \kȯ-lēn\, Simon de. 1480–1546. French printer. First to use italics in France (1528); for edition of St. Augustine's *Sylvius* (1531) designed roman typeface from which Garamond developed.

Co·lin Mu·set \kȯ-la^{n}-mue-ze\. 13th century. French trouvère. Composed verses celebrating wine and good living, courtly verse, etc.

Col·le \kȯ-lā\, Charles. 1709–1783. French playwright and songwriter. Wrote comedies *La Vérité dans le vin* (1747), *La Partie de chasse de Henri Quatre* (1774), genre pieces collected as *Théâtre de Société* (1777), and many songs.

Col·le \ˈkōl-lā\, Raffaello dal. *Known also as* Raf·fa·el·li·no \ˌräf-fä-äl-ˈlē-nō\. c.1495–1566. Tuscan painter. Pupil and associate of Raphael; collaborated with Giulio Romano at Rome and Mantua; founded and directed academy at Borgo San Sepolcro.

Col·le·o·ni \ˌkōl-lā-ˈō-nē\ *or* **Co·le·o·ni** \ˌkō-lā-\, Bartolomeo. 1400–1475. Italian soldier. As condottiere, served Venice and Milan; general in chief for life of armies of Venice (1454); gained reputation as foremost tactician and disciplinarian of 15th century.

Col·les \ˈkä-ləs\, Henry Cope. 1879–1943. English music critic. Music critic, London *Times* (from 1911). Author of *Brahms* (1908), *The Growth of Music* (1912–16), vol. vii of *Oxford History of Music* (1934). Editor of third and fourth editions of *Grove's Dictionary of Music and Musicians* (1927, 1940).

\ə\ abut \ᵊ\ kitten, *Fr.* **table \ər\ further \a\ ash \ā\ ace \ä\ cot, cart \au̇\ out \ch\ chin \e\ bet \ē\ easy \g\ go \i\ hit \ī\ ice \j\ job \ŋ\ sing \ō\ go \ȯ\ law \ȯi\ boy \th\ both \t͟h\ the \ü\ loot \u̇\ foot \y\ yet \zh\ vision \á, b̲, g̃, k̲, ^{n}, œ, œ̄, ue, ue̅, ^{y}** *see* **Guide to Pronunciation**

Col·lett \'köl-ət\, Camilla, *nee* Wer·ge·land \'ver-gə-län\. 1813–1895. Norwegian novelist. Sister of Henrik Wergeland (*q.v.*); m. P. J. Collett (1841). A leader of feminist movement in Norway, reflected in her novels, including *Amtmandens døttre* (1855), *I de lange naetter* (1862), *Sidste blade* (1868–73), *Fra de stummes leir* (1877).

Col·let·ta \kōl-'lāt-tä\, Pietro. 1775–1831. Neapolitan general and historian. Served against the French (1798) but supported the Parthenopean Republic (1799) and later served under Joseph Napoléon and under Murat; general (1812); involved in revolution (1820) and exiled to Florence. Author of *Storia del reame di Napoli* (1834).

Col·lier \'käl-yər, 'käl-ē-ər\, Arthur. 1680–1732. English philosopher. In *Clavis Universalis* (1713) independently arrived at Idealist views of Berkeley on the impossibility of an external world.

Collier, Constance. *Orig.* Laura Constance Har·die \'här-dē\. 1880–1955. English actress. In Beerbohm Tree's company at His Majesty's Theatre (1901–07); New York debut in *Samson* (1908); great success in *Romeo and Juliet, Oliver Twist, Othello, School for Scandal,* and esp. in *Peter Ibbetson* (1915), *Our Betters* (1923), *Hamlet* (with John Barrymore, 1925); also appeared in motion pictures.

Collier, Jeremy. 1650–1726. English clergyman. Refused oath of allegiance to William and Mary; imprisoned for Jacobin sympathies (1688, 1692); outlawed for absolving on the scaffold two would-be assassins of William (1696). Published his famous *Short View of the Immorality and Profaneness of the English Stage* (1698) and defended himself against angry replies by Congreve, Vanbrugh, and others (till 1708). Published (1701–21) his *Historical Dictionary,* founded on Louis Moréri's dictionary, and *Ecclesiastical History of Great Britain* (1708–14). Ordained a nonjuring bishop (1713).

Collier, John. 1884–1968. American sociologist, b. Atlanta, Ga. Social worker and educator; executive secretary, American Indian Defense Assoc. (1923–33); editor, *American Indian Life* (1926–33); U.S. commissioner of Indian affairs (1933–45); secured passage of Indian Reorganization Act (1934) fostering tribal organizations, communal land-holding, traditional culture; director, National Indian Institute (1945–50); professor, CCNY (1947–54); president, Institute of Ethnic Affairs (1947–68). Author of *Indians of the Americas* (1947), *Patterns and Ceremonials of the Indians of the Southwest* (1949).

Collier, John Payne. 1789–1883. English critic. Journalist (1809–47); issued new editions of Dodsley's *Old Plays* (1825–27, 1833, 1851); published *History of English Dramatic Poetry* (1831). In *New Facts, New Particulars,* and *Further Particulars* (1835–39), about Shakespeare, and in *Perkins Folio* (1852), introduced forged marginal corrections in texts; published *Notes and Emendations to Shakespeare* (1852) and brought out texts of Shakespeare based on these forgeries (1853); exposed (1859–61). Edited Spenser's works (1862); compiled critical account of rarest books in English language (1865).

Collier, Peter Fenelon. 1849–1909. American publisher, b. County Carlow, Ireland. To U.S. (1866); in publishing business (from 1877); founded *Collier's Weekly* (1896).

Col·lin \'köl-ēn\, Heinrich Josef von. 1771–1811. Austrian poet and playwright. Author of tragedies *Regulus* (1801), *Polyxena* (1804), *Coriolan* (1804, for which Beethoven composed an overture); composed patriotic songs collected as *Wehrmannsliedern* (1809).

Col·lin d'Har·le·ville \kó-laⁿ-dár-lə-vēl\, Jean-François. 1755–1806. French playwright. Author of *L'Inconstant* (1786), *Le Vieillard et les jeunes hommes* (1804), etc.

Col·lings \'käl-iŋz\, Jesse. 1831–1920. English politician. Mayor of Birmingham (1878–80); M.P. (1880–1918); took part in Joseph Chamberlain's municipal reform from Joseph Arch's land-reform movement; used slogan "Three acres and a cow"; undersecretary to home department (1895–1902).

Col·ling·wood \'käl-iŋ-,wu̇d\, Cuthbert. Baron Collingwood. 1748–1810. English naval commander. Entered navy (1760); served in naval brigade at Bunker Hill (1775); took part in Howe's victory at Brest (1794), Jervis's at St. Vincent (1797); rear admiral (1799), vice admiral (1804); took command on Nelson's death at Trafalgar (1805); Mediterranean commander (1805–10); created baron (1805).

Collingwood, Robin George. 1889–1943. English historian and philosopher. Tutor (1912–34), professor (1934–41), Oxford. Author of works on history and philosophy as *Religion and Philosophy* (1916), *Speculum Mentis* (1924), *Essay on Philosophical Method* (1933), *Principles of Art* (1937), *Essay on Metaphysics* (1940), *The Idea of History* (1946); also authority on Roman Britain, wrote *Archaeology of Roman Britain* (1930), *Roman Britain and the English Settlements* (1936).

Col·lins \'käl-ənz\, Anthony. 1676–1729. English deist. Intimate of John Locke. Author of *Essay Concerning the Use of Reason* (1707), *Discourse of Free-thinking* (1713, which called forth replies from Hoadly, Bentley, Swift), *Inquiry concerning Human Liberty* (1715), defending necessitarianism, *Discourse of the Grounds and Reasons of the Christian Religion* (1724, against William Whiston), and *Scheme of Literal Prophecy considered* (1726).

Collins, Edward Knight. 1802–1878. American shipowner, b. Truro, Mass. Founded (1847) government-subsidized U.S. Mail Steamship Co., known as the Collins Line, to compete with British Cunard Line; operated steamers *Atlantic, Pacific, Arctic, Baltic, Adriatic,* fastest in transatlantic service; line ceased operations (1858).

Collins, Edward Trowbridge. 1887–1951. American baseball player, b. Millertown, N.Y. Member of Connie Mack's "$100,000 infield," Philadelphia Athletics (1907–14); with Chicago White Sox (1915–26), player-manager (1925–26); player-coach, Philadelphia (1927–33). Career batting average .333, total 3310 hits, 743 stolen bases. Vice president (1933–51), general manager (1933–48), Boston Red Sox. Elected to Baseball Hall of Fame (1939).

Collins, Michael. 1890–1922. Irish nationalist leader. Participated in the Easter Rebellion (1916); arrested and held prisoner (1916). Rose to leadership in the Sinn Féin movement and in the military body known as the Irish Volunteers; elected to Dáil Éireann (1918), joined in declaration of independence and adoption of provisional constitution (1919); minister of home affairs (1919), then, after engineering escape of de Valera from Lincoln jail (Feb. 1919), minister of finance in the Sinn Féin ministry (1919–22); with Arthur Griffith negotiated peace treaty with Great Britain (1921); as commander in chief of the military forces of the Irish Free State and, on Griffith's death (1922), head of provisional government, forced to combat republican insurgents; killed in ambush.

Collins, Tom. See Joseph FURPHY.

Collins, Wilkie, *in full* William Wilkie. 1824–1889. English novelist. Son of William Collins (1788–1847). Began literary career with biography of his father (1848); his first novel a historical romance, *Antonina* (1850); published romance *Basil* (1852); contributed two novels to Dickens's *Household Words* (from 1855) and *The Woman in White* (1860) to his *All the Year Round;* collaborated with Dickens in *No Thoroughfare* (1867). Author of novels of mystery with skillful and complex plots (influencing technique of Dickens's later novels), including *No Name* (1862), *Armadale* (1866), *The Moonstone* (1868), *The New Magdalen* (1873). One of the first and greatest mystery writers.

Collins, William. 1721–1759. English poet. At 17, wrote *Persian Eclogues* (1742; 2d. ed. 1757 as *Oriental Eclogues*), his only poems valued by contemporaries; published *Epistle: Addrest to Sir Thomas Hanmer* (1744); composed his memorable *Odes* (12 in number, 1747), including "To Evening," "To Simplicity," etc., which attracted no notice; dedicated "Ode on Popular Superstitions of the Highlands" (written 1750) to John Home. Wrote in Neoclassical forms but a forerunner of Romantics.

Collins, William. 1788–1847. English painter. Known esp. for landscapes, genre scenes, and figure and subject works as *Blackberry Gatherers, Bird Catchers, Cromer Sands.*

Col·lip \'käl-əp\, James Bertram. 1892–1965. Canadian biochemist, b. near Belleville, Ont. Professor, U. of Alberta (1917–28), McGill U. (1928–47); head of the Research Inst. of Endocrinology, McGill (1941–47); dean of medicine, U. of Western Ontario (1947–61). Known for work on endocrine glands and hormones, esp. with F.G. Banting, J.J.R. Macleod (*qq.v.*) on insulin.

Col·li·son \'käl-ə-sən\, Wilson. 1893–1941. American playwright and novelist, b. Glouster, Ohio. Author of the plays *Up in Mabel's Room* (1919, with Otto Harbach), *Getting Gertie's Garter* (1921, with Avery Hopwood), *The Girl with Carmine Lips* (1922), *A Bachelor's Night* (1923), *Desert Sands* (1924), *The Vagabond* (1927), *Red Dust* (1927); author of murder mysteries and novels, as *Murder in the Rain* (1930), *Blonde Baby* (1931), *Red Haired Alibi* (1932), *Dame Dark* (1935).

Col·litz \'köl-its, *Angl* 'käl-əts\, Hermann. 1855–1935. American linguist, b. Bleckede, Germany. To U.S. (1886); professor, Bryn Mawr College (1886–1907), Johns Hopkins (1907–27). Author of *Die neueste Sprachforschung* (1886), *Das schwache Praeteritum und seine Vorgeschichte* (1912).

Collodi, Carlo. See Carlo LORENZINI.

Col·lot d'Her·bois \kó-lō-der-bwá\, Jean-Marie. 1749–1796. French revolutionist. Actor by profession; member of Jacobin Club (from 1791); as member of the Convention (1792), moved abolition of the monarchy; as leading Hébertist, appointed to Committee of Public Safety (1793–95); notorious for his cruelty in hunting down and judging suspected Royalists at Lyon (1793–94); involved in conspiracy against Robespierre (1794); in Thermidorian reaction expelled from the Convention and transported to French Guiana, where he died.

Col·lu·thus *or* **Co·lu·thus** \kəl-'yü-thəs\ of Ly·cop·o·lis \lī-'käp-ə-ləs\. fl. c.500 A.D. Greek poet. Author of several epics, of which only *The Rape of Helen* is extant.

Col·man \'kōl-mən\. Saint. c.605–676. Irish monk. Bishop of Lindisfarne (661); supporter of Celtic usages against the Roman at Whitby (664); withdrew to Iona.

Colman, George, *called* the Elder. 1732–1794. English dramatist. In first play, *Polly Honeycomb* (1760), mocked sentimental novels; won fame with *The*

Jealous Wife (1761), based in part on Fielding's *Tom Jones;* produced *The Clandestine Marriage* jointly with David Garrick (1766); as acting manager of Covent Garden, produced plays of his own and adaptations from Shakespeare (1767–74); manager of Haymarket (1776–89). Edited plays of Beaumont & Fletcher (1778). His son ¶George, *called* the Younger (1762–1836), was also a dramatist; succeeded father as manager of Haymarket (1789–1813); his first play, *The Female Dramatist,* based in part upon *Roderick Random,* produced (1782) at the Haymarket, roundly condemned; wrote or adapted about twenty-five comedies, musical comedies, melodramas, operas, of which best were the comedies *Two to One* (1784), *The Iron Chest* (1796), *Heir at Law* (1797), and *John Bull* (1803); examiner of plays (from 1824).

Colman, Norman Jay. 1827–1911. American agriculturist, b. near Richfield Springs, N.Y. Edited in St. Louis *Colman's Rural World* (1865–1911). U.S. commissioner of agriculture (1885–89); first U.S. secretary of agriculture (1889); instrumental in establishing agricultural experiment stations and in raising bureau to Cabinet level.

Colman, Samuel. 1832–1920. American painter, b. Portland, Me. A founder and first president (1866) of American Water-color Society; known esp. for landscapes.

Co·lo·ma \kō-'lō-mä\, Luis. 1851–1915. Spanish writer. Jesuit (1874 ff.); known esp. for his satirical novel of Madrid society *Pequeñeces* (1890).

Coloman. See KÁLMÁN.

Col·omb \'kä-ləm\, Phillip Howard. 1831–1899. British naval officer and historian, b. Scotland. Entered navy (1846); served in Burmese war (1852); engaged in suppressing slave trade (1868–70); in China (1874–77); retired (1886); rear admiral (1887). Devised new system of night signaling for steam vessels (adopted 1867), a new system of tactics, and new signal book for British navy. Author of *Naval Warfare* (1891), demonstrating prime importance of sea supremacy for military offensive.

Co·lombe \kò-lō^{n}b\ *or* **Co·lomb** \kò-lō^n\, Michel. c.1430–c.1512. French sculptor. Most important work, tomb of Francis II, duc de Bretagne, and his wife Marguerite, in the cathedral at Nantes. Last major Gothic sculptor in France.

Co·lom·bière \kò-lō^n-byer\, Claude de la. 1641–1682. French religious. Entered Jesuit order (1658); professor of rhetoric, Collège de la Trinité, Lyon (1670–73); superior of Jesuit college, Paray-le-Monial (1675–76); court preacher to Mary of Modena, wife of Duke of York (1676); imprisoned following accusations of "Popish Plot"; assisted St. Margaret Mary Alacoque in establishing devotion of Sacred Heart.

Co·lom·bo \kō-'lōm-bō\, Realdo, *perhaps* Matteo Realdo. 1516?–?1559. Italian anatomist. Succeeded Vesalius as professor of anatomy at Padua (1543–45); at Pisa (1545–48), Rome (1548–59); credited with discovery of pulmonary circulation. Author of *De re anatomica* (1559).

Co·lon·na \kō-'lōn-nä\. Noble Roman family descended from counts of Tusculum; first to take name, Piero, who received castle of Colonna (c.1064) on father's death; family held great fiefs in the Campagna; in medieval times, often at feud with the Orsini and Caetani; members included Pope Martin V (*q.v.*), 30 cardinals, Giles of Rome (*q.v.*), and many distinguished generals and senators; most prominent members included:

¶Sciarra (d. 1329), bitter enemy of Pope Boniface VIII; proclaimed caesar by people of Rome during revolt (1290); lost his possessions at Palestrina (1298); excommunicated; returned with French aid and took pope prisoner (1303); supported Louis the Bavarian and crowned him emperor at Rome (1328). ¶Stefano (d. after 1347), Count of Ro·ma·gna \rō-'män-yä\; brother of Sciarra; friend of Petrarch; governor of Bologna (1289); involved in struggle with papacy; defeated by Cola di Rienzo. ¶Vittoria (1492–1547), m. Fernando Francisco de Ávalos (*q.v.*), marqués de Pescara; gradually estranged from him; after his death at Pavia (1525), wrote many poems, esp. Petrarchan sonnets, of which he was the inspiration; friend of Ariosto, Castiglione, Pietro Bembo, and leading literary persons of her time; much admired by Michelangelo, who addressed sonnets to her. ¶Marco Antonio (d. 1584), Duke of Pa·lia·no \päl-'yä-nō\; general and viceroy; exiled from Rome by Pope Paul IV; entered military service of Spain; led Spanish army successfully against Papal States (1557); recalled and commanded papal galleys at Lepanto (1571) against Turks; viceroy of Sicily.

Colonna, Giovanni Paolo. 1637–1695. Italian composer. Composer of church music, oratorios, and secular dramatic works.

Co·lonne \kò-lòn\, Édouard, *orig.* Judas. 1838–1910. French violinist and conductor. Founded (1874), and for many years conducted, the "Concerts Colonne"; brought out for first time in Paris new works of famous composers, as Dubois, Berlioz, Franck, Saint-Saëns, Wagner.

Colonne, Guido delle. See GUIDO DELLE COLONNE.

Colqu·houn \kə-'hün\, Patrick. 1745–1820. Scottish merchant and reformer. Merchant in Virginia and (1766–89) in Glasgow; founded (1783) Glasgow Chamber of Commerce, oldest of its kind in Great Britain; police magistrate in London (1792); advocated reform of police system. Author of numerous pamphlets on economics, reform, etc.

Col·son \kòl-sō^n\, Jean-Claude-Gilles. *Pseudonym* Belle·cour \bel-kür\. 1725–1778. French actor and playwright. Successful actor at Comédie-Française (1750–78), esp. in comedies; wrote successful *Les fausses apparences* (1761). His wife ¶Rose-Perrine le Roy de la Cor·bi·naye \lə-rwà-də-là-kòr-bē-ne\, *known as* Beau·mé·nard \bō-mā-nàr\ *and later as* Mme. Bellecour (1730–1799), was also successful at Comédie-Française (1749–56, 1761–90), esp. in soubrette roles.

Colt \'kōlt\, Samuel. 1814–1862. American inventor, b. Hartford, Conn. Invented revolver (U.S. patent 1836); founded Patent Arms Manufacturing Co. (1836) to produce it; failed (1842); built new firm (1848) on Mexican War orders.

Col·ter \'kōl-tər\, John. c.1775–1813. American explorer, b. near Staunton, Va. Member of Lewis and Clark expedition (1803–06); joined Manuel Lisa in trapping expedition (1807); traveled into Yellowstone country (1807), becoming first white man to see it.

Col·trane \'kōl-ˌtrān\, John William. 1926–1967. American musician, b. Hamlet, N.C. Saxophonist with Eddie Vinson (1947–49), Dizzy Gillespie (1949–51), Miles Davis (1955–57), Thelonius Monk, etc.; later led own quartet; considered one of greatest avant garde jazz musicians of the time, influencing next generation with harmonic and melodic experiments.

Col·um \'käl-əm\, Padraic. 1881–1972. Irish poet and playwright. Author of verse *Wild Earth* (1907), *Dramatic Legends* (1922), *Creatures* (1927), *Poems* (1932), *The Story of Lowry Maen* (1937); plays *Broken Soil* (1903), *The Land* (1905), *Mogu, the Wanderer* (1917), *The Miracle of the Corn* (1917), *The Betrayal* (1920), *Balloon* (1929); juveniles *The King of Ireland's Son* (1916), *The Boy Who Knew What the Bird Said* (1918), *The Girl Who Sat by the Ashes* (1919), *The Children Who Followed the Piper* (1922), *Where the Winds Never Blew and the Cock Never Crew* (1940); volumes of folk tales from Ireland and Hawaii, etc.

Co·lum·ba \kə-'ləm-bə\. Saint. *Irish* Col·um \'kəl-əm\ *or* Col·um·cille \'kəl-əm-ˌkil\. c.521–597. Irish missionary. Ordained priest (c.551); with 12 disciples established (563) monastery on island of Iona; converted northern Picts; gave benediction to Aidan as king of Scots (574); held sway over Columban churches in Ireland and north of England, largely independent of papal supervision; author of three hymns.

Co·lum·ban \kə-'ləm-bən\ *or* **Col·um·ba·nus** \ˌkäl-əm-'bā-nəs\. Saint. c.543–615. Irish missionary. With twelve monks left Ireland and settled in the Vosges (c.590); built abbey of Luxeuil, Haute-Saône, for which he drew up a monastic rule; involved in controversy with French bishops over the tonsure and over keeping Easter according to Celtic usage; expelled through conspiracy in court of Theuderich II (610); founded monastery of Bobbio in the Apennines (c.613).

Co·lum·bus \kə-'ləm-bəs\, Christopher. *Ital.* Cristoforo Co·lom·bo \kō-'lōm-bō\. *Span.* Cristóbal Co·lón \kō-'lòn\. 1451–1506. Spanish explorer, b. Genoa, Italy. To sea at early age; settled in Lisbon, Portugal (1476); gained experience sailing to Iceland, South Atlantic; from Ptolemy, 2d Book of Esdras, Cardinal d'Ailly, concluded that earth is round and conceived idea of reaching Asia by sailing due west; submitted proposals to king of Portugal; meeting with no success, went to Spain (c.1484) and submitted proposals to Ferdinand and Isabella, who, after many refusals, agreed to requests (1492). Fitted out three vessels, *Santa María* (which he commanded, with Juan de la Cosa as his pilot), *Niña* (Vicente Pinzón, captain), and *Pinta* (Martín Pinzón, captain); sailed from Palos (Aug. 3, 1492) and sighted land (Oct. 12, 1492); landed at Guanahaní, renamed by Columbus San Salvador and now called Watlings Island. Continued voyage, sailing along north coast of Cuba and Haiti (Hispaniola); left colony of 40 men on Haitian coast where *Santa María* ran aground, building a fort, La Navidad; started home (Jan. 1493) and reached Palos (March 15, 1493). Named viceroy of the Indies, sailed on 2d voyage (Sept. 25, 1493) with seventeen ships and 1500 men; discovered Dominica, Guadeloupe, Puerto Rico (Nov. 1493); reached La Navidad and found colony destroyed by Indians; made new settlement at Isabella, present Dominican Republic (Dec. 1493), first European town in New World; discovered Jamaica. Returned to Spain (1496) with Juan de Aguado, royal commissioner sent out to investigate his dealings with natives; presented his case to the king, favorably heard, and charges dismissed. Left Spain on 3d voyage (May 1498); discovered Trinidad (July 1498) and mouth of Orinoco River. Further complaints of trouble brought (1500) a new official investigator, Francisco de Bobadilla, who arrested Columbus and his brothers and sent them back to Spain in chains; released in Spain but could not obtain reinstatement in his honors and dignities. Left Spain on 4th voyage (May 1502); discovered Martinique and

Honduras, and coasted down to Isthmus of Panama, believing he was at last near China; after many difficulties, returned to Spain (Nov. 1504). Failed to gain reinstatement in his honors and died in Valladolid in poverty and neglect. His brother ¶Bartholomeo, *Span.* Bartolomé (c.1445–c.1514), captain of Spanish supply fleet to New World (1493); governed Haiti (1496–98) during Christopher's absence; founded Santo Domingo (1496); accompanied Christopher on 4th voyage (1502–04); accompanied his nephew Diego (in 1509) to Haiti and held office in government at Santo Domingo. A second brother ¶Giacomo, *Span.* Diego (1450?–?1515) accompanied Christopher on 2d voyage (1493) and governed at intervals in Isabella and in Santo Domingo; became a priest; again in Santo Domingo (1509).

Christopher's son ¶Diego (1479 or 1480–1526) was created admiral of the Indies and governor of Hispaniola (1508); received father's hereditary title of viceroy of the islands (1511); after much trouble, recalled by Council of the Indies (1523) to defend himself from charges brought against him; failed to obtain redress for grievances. His son ¶Luis (1521?–1572) was granted island of Jamaica in fief, a pension, territories in Veragua, and titles of admiral of the Indies, duke of Ve·ra·gua \bā-'rä-gwä\, and marquis of Ja·mai·ca \jə-'mā-kə\; governed Hispaniola as captain general (1540–51); banished to Oran, Africa (1565), where he died.

Col·u·mel·la \ˌkäl-yə-'mel-ə\, Lucius Junius Moderatus. 1st century A.D. Roman writer. Author of *De re rustica,* on farming, gardening, etc.

Coluthus. See COLLUTHUS.

Col·vin \'käl-vən\, Sir Sidney. 1845–1927. English critic. Slade professor of fine art, Cambridge (1873–85); director, Fitzwilliam Museum (1876–84); keeper of department of prints and drawings, British Museum (1884–1912). Editor of works of R. L. Stevenson; author of lives of Keats, Landor.

Combe \'küm\, George. 1788–1858. Scottish phrenologist. Visited Spurzheim in Paris (1817) and became disciple; founded Phrenological Society (1820) and *Phrenological Journal* (1823); lectured on Continent and in America. Author of *The Constitution of Man* (1828). His brother ¶Andrew (1797–1847), physiologist and phrenologist, became disciple of Spurzheim (1818); practiced medicine in Edinburgh; physician to Queen Victoria (1838). Author of *Principles of Physiology* (1834).

Combe, William. 1741–1823. English adventurer and writer. Nicknamed "Count Combe" for extravagance in spending; private soldier, cook, waiter; made success with a bitter satire, *The Diaboliad* (1776); spent much of life (from 1780) in debtors' prison. Wrote political pamphlets and text for illustrated books; wrote in descriptive and moralizing verse the three *Tours of Dr. Syntax,* in search of the picturesque, in search of consolation, and in search of a wife (1812, 1820, 1821), with illustrations by Thomas Rowlandson; wrote text for Rowlandson's *Dance of Death* (1815–16) and *Dance of Life* (1816).

Combermere, Viscount. See Sir Stapleton COTTON.

Combes \kōⁿb\, Emile, *in full* Justin-Louis-Emile. 1835–1921. French politician. Senator (from 1885); vice president of Senate (1894–95); minister of education (1895–96); premier of France (1902–05); followed strong anticlerical policy in wake of Dreyfus affair; minister without portfolio (1915).

Comenius, John Amos. See Jan KOMENSKÝ.

Comines, Philippe de. See COMMYNES.

Co·mis·key \kə-'mis-kē\, Charles Albert. *Nicknamed* the Old Roman. 1859–1931. American baseball executive, b. Chicago. Professional player (1882–94); manager and player, St. Louis Browns (1883, 1885–89, 1891), Cincinnati (1892–94); founder, owner, and president of Chicago White Sox in American League from its organization (1900); built Comiskey Park (1910). Elected to Baseball Hall of Fame (1939).

Commines. See COMMYNES.

Com·mo·di·a·nus \kə-ˌmō-dē-'ā-nəs\. 3d to 5th century A.D. Christian Latin poet. Author of didactic verses *Instructiones LXXX adversus Gentium Deos* and *Carmen Apologeticum.*

Com·mo·dus \'käm-ə-dəs\, Lucius Aelius Aurelius. 161–192 A.D. Roman emperor (180–192). Son of Marcus Aurelius Antoninus; made co-ruler with father (177); on death of Aurelius made disgraceful peace with German tribes; his reign marked by his violence, prodigality, and unrestrained indulgence; proud of his physical strength which he exhibited in gladiatorial combats; renamed Rome Colonia Commodiana; murdered in conspiracy of mistress, praetorian prefect, and chamberlain.

Com·mons \'käm-ənz\, John Rogers. 1862–1945. American economist, b. Hollandsburg, Ohio. Professor, Oberlin (1892), Indiana U. (1893–95), Syracuse U. (1895–99), Wisconsin (1904–32). Edited *Documentary History of American Industrial Society* (1910–11), *History of Labor in the United States* (1918–35); author of *Legal Foundations of Capitalism* (1924), *Institutional Economics* (1934), etc.

Com·mynes *or* **Com·ines** *or* **Com·mines** \kô-mēn\, Philippe de. c.1447–1511. French politician and chronicler. Reared in court of godfather, Duke Philip the Good of Burgundy; served Charles the Bold in war with France (1465–67) and as counsellor and ambassador to England, Brittany, Spain; negotiated agreement between Charles and Louis XI (1468); entered service of Louis XI as chamberlain and adviser (1472); subsequently served regent Anne of Beaujeu (1483), Charles VIII (from 1489), and Louis XII. Author of *Mémoires* (1524), invaluable chronicle of period.

Comnena, Anna. See ANNA COMNENA.

Com·ne·nus \käm-'nē-nəs\. *Plural* Com·ne·ni \-ˌnī\. Name of a Byzantine noble family, originating in Paphlagonia, that furnished several rulers of the Eastern Roman Empire (1057–1185) and of Trebizond (1204–1461). Manuel Eroticus Comnenus was a general under Emperor Basil II and father of Isaac I, first emperor of the Comneni (1057–59). Isaac's nephew Alexius was emperor (1081–1118), followed by John II, Manuel I, Alexius II, and Andronicus I (d. 1185). See individual biographies; see also ANNA COMNENA. The empire of Trebizond was founded by Alexius I of the younger line (1204) and lasted until conquered by Mehmed II (1461).

Co·mon·fort \kō-môn-'fôrt\, Ignacio. 1812–1863. Mexican politician. A leader with Álvarez in revolution of Ayutla which overthrew Santa Anna (1855); minister of war (1855); provisional president of Mexico (1855–57); elected president (1857); forced to flee to U.S. (1858); returned to fight French invaders (1861–63); killed in ambush.

Com·pa·gni \kōm-'pän-yē\, Dino. c.1255–1324. Florentine historian. Author of *Cronica delle cose occorrenti ne' tempi suoi* (written 1310–12), a chronicle of Florentine history from 1280, with special emphasis on Guelf–Ghibelline and other factional wars.

Com·pa·ret·ti \ˌkōm-pä-'rāt-tē\, Domenico. 1835–1927. Italian philologist. Professor, Pisa, Florence, and Rome; known esp. for his epigraphical, papyrological, and dialect studies. Author of *Virgilio nel medio evo* (1872), etc.

Com·père \kōⁿ-per\, Loyset. c.1445–1518. French composer. Singer in service of Duke of Milan, later of Charles VIII; canon in St. Quentin (from 1491); dean of St. Géry, Cambrai (1498–1500). Composed motets, chansons, masses, magnificats, etc.

Comp·ton \'käm(p)-tən\, Arthur Holly. 1892–1962. American physicist, b. Wooster, Ohio. Brother of K.T. Compton. Professor, Washington U. (1920–23), Chicago (1923–45); discovered change in wavelength of scattered X-rays, known as the Compton effect, for which he was awarded 1927 Nobel prize for physics (jointly with C.T.R. Wilson); discovered total reflection of X-rays; collaborated in the polarization of X-rays and in the production of X-ray spectra by ruled gratings; investigated cosmic rays; director, Metallurgical Project developing first nuclear reactor (1942–45); chancellor (1945–54), professor (1953–61), Washington U.

Comp·ton \'käm(p)-tən, 'kəm(p)-\, Henry. 1632–1713. English prelate. Youngest son of Spencer Compton; bishop of Oxford (1674), of London (1675); religious instructor of James II's daughters Mary and Anne; lost James's favor by close relations with Protestants; suspended (1686); only churchman to vote for declaring throne vacant; crowned William and Mary (1689); one of commissioners for revising the liturgy; one of commissioners for arranging union of Scotland and England.

Comp·ton \'käm(p)-tən\, Karl Taylor. 1887–1954. American physicist, b. Wooster, Ohio. Brother of A.H. Compton. Professor (1915–30), Princeton; president, M.I.T. (1930–48); conducted researches on the structure of crystals by X-ray photography, photoelectric effect, ionization, thermionic emission, etc. Chairman, U.S. Science Advisory Board (1933–35); member, National Defense Research Committee (1940 ff.).

Comp·ton \'käm(p)-tən, 'kəm(p)-\, Spencer. 2d Earl of North·amp·ton \nȯrth-'(h)am(p)-tən\. 1601–1643. English Royalist. Arrayed Warwickshire for king (1642); commanded Royalist forces at Hopton Heath, where he was killed. His grandson ¶Spencer Compton (1673?–1743), Earl of Wil·ming·ton \'wil-miŋ-tən\, was M.P. (1698–1727), speaker of the House of Commons (1715–27); paymaster general (1722–30); created baron (1727), earl (1730); lord privy seal (1730); first lord of treasury (1742–43).

Comp·ton-Bur·nett \'käm(p)-tən-'bər-nət, 'kəm(p)-\, Dame Ivy. 1884–1969. English writer. Author of often grimly comic novels of Victorian or Edwardian families, with melodramatic plots and richly suggestive dialogue, including *Dolores* (1911), *Pastors and Masters* (1925), *Brothers and Sisters* (1929), *Men and Wives* (1931), *More Women than Men* (1933), *A House and Its Head* (1935), *Parents and Children* (1941), *Elders and Betters* (1944), *Manservant and Maidservant* (1947), *Two Worlds and Their Ways* (1949), *A Heritage and Its History* (1950), *Mother and Son* (1955), *A Father and His Fate* (1957), *The Mighty and Their Fall* (1961), *A God and His Gifts* (1965).

Comstock, Anna Botsford. See under John Henry COMSTOCK.

Com·stock \'kəm-ˌstäk\, Anthony. 1844–1915. American reformer, b. New Canaan, Conn. Joined YMCA campaign against pornographic literature, New York City (1872); obtained passage of federal Comstock Law (1873) banning such literature from mails; special agent of U.S. Post Office (1873–1915); founder and secretary, Society for the Suppression of Vice, in New York (1873–1915); conducted spectacular raids on publishers and vendors. Author of *Frauds Exposed* (1880), *Traps for the Young* (1883), *Morals Versus Art* (1888), etc.

Comstock, Henry Tompkins Paige. 1820–1870. American prospector, b. Trenton, Ont. In Nevada (1856–62); prospected the ground where Comstock Lode was discovered (1859), but sold his claim for a small amount.

Com·stock \'käm-ˌstäk\, John Henry. 1849–1931. American entomologist, b. Janesville, Wis. With U.S. Dept. of Agriculture (1879–82); professor, Cornell U. (1882–1914); did pioneering work in classification of scale insects, moths, butterflies. Author of *Introduction to Entomology* (1888), *Manual for the Study of Insects* (1895, illustrated by his wife), *Insect Life* (1897, illustrated by wife), *How to Know the Butterflies* (1904, illustrated by wife), *The Spider Book* (1912), and *The Wings of Insects* (1918). His wife ¶Anna, *nee* Bots·ford \'bäts-fərd\ (1854–1930; m. 1878), was a naturalist and wood engraver, b. Otto, N.Y.; taught nature study at Cornell U. (from 1897; professor from 1920). Author of *Ways of the Six-Footed* (1903), *Handbook of Nature Study* (1911), *The Pet Book* (1914); editor, *Nature Study Review* (1917–23).

Comte \kōⁿt\, Auguste, *in full* Isidore-Auguste-Marie-François-Xavier. 1798–1857. French philosopher. Disciple of Saint-Simon (to 1824); lectured at his home on his philosophical system; conducted free lecture series for workingmen; intensely republican in spirit, stoical and abstemious in habit; on staff, École Polytechnique, Paris (1832–42); subsisted on financial aid secured by J. S. Mill and Littré. Author of *Cours de philosophie positive* (1830–42), *Discours sur l'esprit Positif* (1844), *Ordre et progrés* (1848), *Système de politique positive* (1851–54), *Catéchisme positiviste* (1852), etc. Founder of positivism, conceived by him as a scientific system of thought and knowledge applicable to all spheres of life; also considered founder of sociology as a systematic study.

Com·yn \'kəm-ən\. Name of a Scottish family (from town Comines on Franco-Belgian border), founded by Robert de Comyn, made earl of Northumberland (1068); and including: Alexander Comyn, 2d Earl of Buch·an \'bək-ən, 'bək-\ (d. 1290), constable of Scotland (1270), regent (1286). ¶John the elder (d. 1300?), *called* the Black Comyn, grandnephew of Alexander, one of regents (1286–92), claimant for throne (1291) but supported brother-in-law John de Baliol's claim; submitted to Edward I (1296). ¶John the younger (d. 1306), *called* the Red, son of John the elder, supported Baliol's claim; led resistance to English king; submitted to Edward I (1304); after quarrel with Robert the Bruce, was stabbed to death at Dumfries. ¶John (d. 1308), 3d earl, son of Alexander, was defeated by Bruce (1308) in feud for murder of John Comyn, the younger; fled to England, losing family possessions in Scotland and England to king.

Conan Doyle, Sir Arthur. See DOYLE.

Co·nant \'kō-nənt\, James Bryant. 1893–1978. American educator, b. Dorchester, Mass. Taught chemistry (1917–33, professor 1927), president (1933–53), Harvard; chairman, National Defense Research Committee (1941–46); U.S. high commissioner (1953–55), ambassador (1955–57) to West Germany. Author of *Chemistry of Organic Compounds* (1933), *On Understanding Science* (1947), *Science and Common Sense* (1951), *Education and Liberty* (1953), *The American High School Today* (1959), *Slums and Suburbs* (1961), *Education of American Teachers* (1963), etc.

Con·ca \'kōŋ-kä\, Sebastiano. c.1680–1764. Italian painter. Known esp. for animated, brilliantly colored and executed frescoes as *Crowning of St. Cecilia* for Sta. Cecilia in Trastevere and works in S. Clemente and S. Giovanni in Laterano, Rome; *Solomon and the Queen of Sheba* for Sta. Chiara, Naples.

Con·ci·ni \kōn-'chē-nē\, Concino. Marquis D'Ancre \dänkrᵊ\. *Also known as* Maréchal D'Ancre. d. 1617. Italian adventurer. Member of entourage of Marie de Médicis and a powerful influence on her after her marriage (1600) to Henry IV of France; m. (1601) Eleonora Galigai, the queen's niece and foster sister; became dominant power in government of Louis XIII (from 1610); named lieutenant general of Picardy, then of Normandy; created marquis and (1613) marshal of France; put down rebellion sparked by his unpopularity with great nobles (1616) and arrested their leader, Henry II de Bourbon, prince de Condé; fell to second rebellion planned by Charles d'Albert de Luynes; shot by royal guards at the Louvre. His widow was condemned for sorcery, beheaded, and burned (1617).

Condamine, Charles-Marie de la. See LA CONDAMINE.

Con·dé \kōⁿ-dā\. Name of a great family of French nobility, bearing title Prince de Condé, derived from the town of Condé (-sur-l'Escaut) on the Scheldt, in northeastern France. See also CONTI. The family formed a junior branch of the house of Bourbon (*q.v.*); became extinct (1866); it included:

Louis I de Bour·bon \bür-bōⁿ\. 1530–1569. Youngest son of Charles de Bourbon, duc de Vendôme; first to bear title of prince de Condé; a soldier, active at Metz (1552) and St.-Quentin (1557); joined Huguenots and took part in conspiracy of Amboise (1560); imprisoned, but released on death of Francis II. Made governor of Picardy by Catherine de Médicis (1561). Fought Guise faction (1562), was defeated and made prisoner, but again liberated (1563); led second Huguenot advance on Paris (1567), defeated at Saint-Denis; killed in battle. His son ¶Henry I (1552–1588), 2d prince, joined Huguenot cause, but had to renounce it at the Massacre of St. Bartholomew (1572); fled to Germany and later died of wounds received fighting against the Holy League at Coutras (1587). Henry's son ¶Henry II (1588–1646), 3d prince, posthumous and possibly illegitimate, was brought up a Catholic; spent most of his life in intrigues at court; a partisan of Richelieu.

Henry II's son ¶Louis II (1621–1686), 4th prince, called "the Great Condé," bore title of duc d'En·ghien \däⁿ-gaⁿ\ during his father's life. Entered military service, won battle of Rocroi (1643) against the Spanish, and, partly in cooperation with Turenne, won victories (1643–46) against Imperialists, especially Nördlingen (1645). Became head of Condé family (1646). After victory of Lens (1648), recalled to Paris to put down the Fronde. Arrested by Mazarin (1650), precipitating second War of the Fronde; led rebellion and made alliance with Spain (1651–52); fled to Spain and became generalissimo (1652); defeated at battle of the Dunes by Turenne and the English (1658). Pardoned (1659); commanded attack on Spanish in Franche-Comté (1668); with Turenne commanded armies in Netherlands (1673–75); retired to Chantilly. Friend of Molière, Racine, Boileau, Boussuet, and La Bruyère. His only son ¶Henri-Jules (1643–1709), 5th prince, took part in many campaigns and was a noted eccentric at court of Louis XIV. His son ¶Louis III (1668–1710), duc de Bourbon and 6th prince de Condé, and grandson ¶Louis-Henri (1692–1740), duc de Bourbon and 7th prince, were both known by title "Monsieur le duc."

Louis-Henri's son ¶Louis-Joseph (1736–1818), 8th prince, was distinguished soldier in Seven Years' War; strong supporter of monarchy at time of Revolution; fled (1789) to Germany and organized "army of Condé" (émigrés and Austrians) to fight Revolutionary and Napoleonic armies, but unsuccessful (1792–97); entered Russian service (1797) and English (1801). His son ¶Louis-Henri-Joseph (1756–1830), 9th prince, was known as duc de Bourbon; wounded at Gibraltar (1782); later served under his father against France; supposed to have committed suicide. His son ¶Louis-Antoine-Henri (1772–1804), known as the duc d'Enghien, served in his grandfather's "army of Condé" (1792–97); falsely implicated in plot of Cadoudal and Pichegru (1804); arrested secretly in Baden by French gendarmes by order of Napoléon, tried by court-martial, executed. Deed was widely accounted an atrocity and ended all hope of reconciliation between Napoléon and House of Bourbon. From Louis-Henri-Joseph property of the house passed to a cousin, Henri d'Orléans, duc d'Aumale, whose son ¶Louis (1845–1866) was last to bear title of prince de Condé.

Con·dell \'kən-dᵊl\, Henry. d. 1627. English actor. Member of Lord Chamberlain's company, along with Shakespeare and Burbage; partner with Burbage in Globe Theatre (1599); received mourning ring by will from Shakespeare (1616); with John Heminge edited First Folio of Shakespeare's plays (1623).

Con·dil·lac \kōⁿ-dē-yák\, Étienne Bonnot de \bò-nō-də-\. 1715–1780. French philosopher. Ordained Catholic priest (1640); became associate of Diderot, J.J. Rousseau, and Duclos. Author of works on logic, language, economics, philosophy; follower of Locke; works included *Essai sur l'origine des connaissances humaines* (1746), *Traité des systémes* (1749), *Traité des sensations* (1754), *Traité des animaux* (1755), *Le Commerce et le gouvernement considérés relativement l'un à l'autre* (1776), *La Logique* (1780), *La Langue des calculs* (1798), etc.

Con·don \'kän-dən\, Edward Uhler. 1902–1974. American physicist, b. Alamogordo, N.M. Professor, Princeton (1930–37); associate director, Westinghouse research laboratories (1937–43); involved in atomic bomb project (1943–45); director, U.S. Bureau of Standards (1945–51); director of research, Corning Glass Co. (1951–54); professor, Washington U. (1954–63), U. of Colorado (1963–74); directed Air Force study of unidentified flying objects.

Condorcanqui, José Gabriel. See TUPAC AMARÚ.

Condorcet, Marquis de. See Marie-Jean CARITAT.

Conegliano, Cima da. See CIMA.

Con·fa·lo·nie·ri \ˌkōn-fä-lōn-'yer-ē\, Federico. Conte. 1785–1846. Italian patriot. Ardent nationalist; leader of Milanese *federati;* pleaded cause of Lombard independence in Paris and London; arrested by Austrians after outbreak of Piedmontese revolt (1821); after celebrated trial, sentenced to death; sentence commuted to life imprisonment in fortress of Spielberg (1824); pardoned and exiled to America (1836); returned to Europe (1838) and Milan (1840).

Confucius. See K'UNG CH'IU.

Con·greve \'kän-ˌgrēv, 'käŋ-\, Richard. 1818–1899. English philosopher. Upon meeting Barthélemy St.-Hilaire and Auguste Comte in Paris (1848) adopted Positivism and devoted life to its propagation; founded Church of Humanity in London; claimed leadership of Positivists from Pierre Lafitte (1878). Author of *The New Religion in Its Attitude Toward the Old* (1859), *Essays* (1874–1900), *Human Catholicism* (1876–77), etc.

Congreve, William. 1670–1729. English dramatist. Fellow student at Trinity Coll., Dublin, and thereafter lifelong friend of Jonathan Swift; published a novel of cross-purposes and disguises, *Incognita* (1692); contributed to Dryden's *Juvenal* (1692); won fame with series of brilliant comedies, *Old Bachelour* (1693), *Double-Dealer* (1693), *Love for Love* (1695), *The Way of the World* (1700), remarkable for wit and grace of dialogue; made ambitious attempt at tragedy in blank verse, *The Mourning Bride* (1697); abandoned theater after comparative failure of *The Way of the World* and passed time in series of sinecure posts, writing occasional verses, translations, etc.; defended morality of stage in reply (1698) to Jeremy Collier's *Short View.*

Congreve, Sir William. 2d Baronet. 1772–1828. English artillerist. Invented (1808) Congreve rocket (used as late as 1860); designed new gun for frigates (1813). M.P. (1818–28).

Coningh. See KONINCK.

Con·ing·ham \'kən-iŋ-əm, *esp US* -iŋ-ˌham\, Sir Arthur. 1895–1948. British airman, b. Australia. Entered New Zealand army (1914); joined Royal Flying Corps (1916); air vice marshal (1941); commanded Royal Air Force units in Libya, Tunisia (1940–43); commanded RAF 1st tactical air force, Mediterranean (1943–44), Allied 2d tactical air force, Normandy (1944); demonstrated doctrine of concerted use of air and land power; air marshal (1946).

Co·ninx·loo \'kō-nəŋk-ˌslō\, Gillis van. 1544–1607. Flemish painter. Known for landscapes showing transition from Mannerist to Early Baroque styles.

Conk·lin \'käŋk-lən\, Edwin Grant. 1863–1952. American biologist, b. Waldo, Ohio. Professor, Pennsylvania (1896–1908), Princeton (1908–33); known for studies in embryology, cell division, human evolution. Author of *Heredity and Environment* (1915–21), *Direction of Human Evolution* (1921), etc.

Conk·ling \'käŋk-liŋ\, Roscoe. 1829–1888. American politician, b. Albany, N.Y. Member, U.S. House of Representatives (1859–63, 1865–67); U.S. senator (1867–81); rival of Blaine for Republican presidential nomination (1876); opposed Hayes and Garfield; resigned his Senate seat (1881) in protest against Garfield's interference in his control of patronage in New York; sought but failed of reelection; declined appointment to Supreme Court (1882).

Conn \'kän, 'kȯn\. *In full* Conn Cét·cha·thach \'kȯn-kyed-kə-həḵ\, *i.e.* Conn of the Hundred Battles. 2d century A.D. Irish king. Said to have ruled over northern half of Ireland; subject of numerous legends and sagas; held to be ancestor of Niall and thus of the Uí Néill dynasty.

Connaught, Duke of. See Prince ARTHUR (1850–1942).

Connell, Norreys. See Conal O'RIORDAN.

Con·nel·ly \'kän-əl-ē\, Cornelia Augusta, *nee* Peacock. 1809–1879. American religious, b. Philadelphia. m. Pierce Connelly (1831); signed deed of separation and entered convent (1844) so husband could become Roman Catholic priest; invited to establish teaching order, Society of the Holy Child Jesus (1846); superior (1847–79); founded schools in England, France, U.S.

Connelly, Marc, *in full* Marcus Cook. 1890–1980. American playwright, b. McKeesport, Pa. Coauthor, with George Kaufman, of *Dulcy* (1921), *Merton of the Movies* (1922), *To the Ladies* (1922), *Be Yourself* (1924), *Beggar on Horseback* (1924) and, with Frank Elser, of *The Farmer Takes a Wife* (1934). Sole author of *The Wisdom Tooth* (1926), *The Green Pastures* (based on Roark Bradford's *Old Man Adam an' His Chillun;* awarded Pulitzer prize, 1930).

Con·ner \'kän-ər\, David. 1792–1856. American naval officer, b. Harrisburg, Pa. Served through War of 1812; led attack on Vera Cruz and landed Scott's army (1847).

Conningh. See KONINCK.

Con·nol·ly \'kän-əl-ē\, Cyril Vernon. 1903–1974. English critic and writer. Contributor to various periodicals; founder and editor (1939–50) of *Horizon* magazine. Author of novel *The Rock Pool* (1936), and collections of essays and miscellanea as *Enemies of Promise* (1938), *Unquiet Grave* (1944), *Condemned Playground* (1945), *Previous Convictions* (1963), *Evening Colonnade* (1975).

Connolly, James. 1868–1916. Irish labor leader. Founded Irish Socialist Republican party (1896); in U.S. (1903–10) helped found Industrial Workers of the World; with James Larkin founded Irish Labour party (1912) and Irish National Transport and General Workers' Union (1913); led Dublin transit strike (1913); head of union (1914–16); opposed World War I; chiefly responsible for carrying through of Easter insurrection (1916) in which he was severely wounded; executed.

Connolly, Maureen Catherine. *Known as* Little Mo \'mō\. 1934–1969. American tennis player, b. San Diego, Cal. U.S. singles champion (1951–53), Wimbledon singles champion (1952–54), French champion (1953–54); first woman to win "Grand Slam" of U.S., British, French, Australian championships (1953); retired after injury (1954).

Connor, Ralph. See Charles William GORDON.

Co·non \'kō-ˌnän, -nən\. d. 687. Pope (686–687).

Conon. d. c.390 B.C. Athenian admiral. Admiral of Athenian fleet (406 B.C.); defeated by Spartans (406); in command of a Persian fleet that defeated Spartan fleet off Cnidus (394); restored the long walls and fortifications of the Piraeus, at Athens. Father of Timotheus.

Conon of Sa·mos \'sā-ˌmäs\. fl. c.245 B.C. Greek astronomer and mathematician. Court astronomer to Ptolemy III Euergetes at Alexandria; invented constellation Coma Berenices to flatter Queen Berenice II. Author of a work on astronomy and of a treatise on conic sections later used by Apollonius of Perga.

Conrad. See also KONRAD.

Con·rad \'kän-ˌrad\. *Ger.* Kon·rad \'kōn-ˌrät\. Name of four kings of Germany:

Conrad I. d. 918. King (911–918). Duke of Franconia when elected king (911); not supported by Lotharingian nobles and forced to fight Bavarian and Swabian dukes and esp. Duke Henry of Saxony, who succeeded him.

Conrad II. c.990–1039. King (1024–39) and Holy Roman emperor (1027–39). Son of Count Henry of Speyer and descendent of Otto I; m. (1016) Gisela, widow of Duke of Swabia; exiled by but later reconciled with Emperor Henry II, whom he was elected to succeed as king (1024); crowned emperor by Pope John XIX (1027); subdued numerous revolts in Germany and Italy; acquired Burgundy on death of Rudolf III (1032); campaigned against Milanese uprising (1036–38) led by Archbishop Aribert. Carefully groomed son Henry (later Henry III) for succession. Founder of Salian dynasty.

Conrad III. 1093–1152. King (1138–52); never crowned emperor. Son of Frederick I, Duke of Swabia and grandson of Emperor Henry IV; duke of Franconia (1115); opposed election of Lothair II as king (1125); elected antiking (1127) and crowned king of Italy (1128); finally submitted to Lothair (1135); elected to succeed Lothair (1138); put down rebellion of Duke Henry the Proud of Bavaria and Saxony and his brother Welf (1138–40), but rivalry of Welfs and Hohenstaufens remained; restored brother-in-law Vladislav II as prince of Bohemia (1142); took part in Second Crusade (1147–50); passed over his son to designate Frederick III of Swabia (later Emperor Frederick I Barbarossa) as successor. Founder of Hohenstaufen dynasty.

Conrad IV. 1228–1254. King (1237–54). Son of Emperor Frederick II; duke of Swabia (1235); elected king (1237) in place of half-brother Henry VII; declared deposed, along with father, by Pope Innocent IV (1245); defeated by antiking Henry Raspe (1246); fled to Sicily and assumed throne (1251); captured Naples (1253); died while preparing to invade Germany. Last of Hohenstaufen rulers to claim imperial rule.

Conrad. *Ger.* Konrad. *Called* der Ro·te \dər-'rō-tə\, *i.e.* the Red. d. 955. Duke of Lotharingia (or Lorraine, 944–953). Given Lotharingia by Otto I for help in suppressing a revolt; m. (947) Otto I's daughter Liudgard; joined brother-in-law Liudolf, Duke of Swabia, in revolt (953) against Otto; defeated and deprived of duchy; became reconciled with Otto and fought with him against Magyars at Lechfeld, losing life there. Ancestor of Salian branch of Holy Roman emperors (see CONRAD II).

Conrad. Marquis of Mont·fer·rat \mōⁿ-fer-ȧ\. 1146–1192. Italian crusader. Occupied Tyre and held it (1187) against Saladin; joined by forces of Third Crusade; m. (1190) Isabel, daughter of King Amalric I of Jerusalem; elected king of Jerusalem but slain soon after by an assassin.

Conrad, Con. See Conrad DOBER.

Conrad, Frank. 1874–1941. American electrical engineer and inventor, b. Pittsburgh, Pa. Employed by Westinghouse Co. (1890–1941); made experimental radio broadcasts using phonograph records (1919); chiefly responsible for establishment of pioneer commercial radio station KDKA, Pittsburgh, from which was made (Nov. 2, 1920) the broadcast regarded as the birth of commercial broadcasting.

Conrad, Joseph. *Orig.* Józef Teodor Konrad Kor·ze·niow·ski \kȯ-zhen-'yȯf-skē\. 1857–1924. British novelist, b. Berdichev, Poland (now Ukrainian S.S.R.). Seaman in French merchant marine (1874–78) and in British merchant marine (1878–94); qualified as master (1886); naturalized British subject (1886). Left merchant marine (1894) to devote himself to writing; gained recognition as a master of English prose in a series of brilliant tales, many of them written against the background of his intimate knowledge of the sea. Among his novels were *Almayer's Folly* (1895), *An Outcast of the Islands* (1896), *The Nigger of the 'Narcissus'* (1897), *Lord Jim* (1900), *The Inheritors* (with F. M. Ford, 1901), *Romance* (1903), *Nostromo* (1904), *The Secret Agent* (1907), *Under Western Eyes* (1911), *Chance* (1913), *Victory* (1915), *The Shadow-Line* (1917), *Arrow of Gold* (1919), *The Rescue* (1920), *The Rover* (1923); wrote stories *Tales of Unrest* (1898), *Youth* (1902, including "Heart of Darkness"), *Typhoon* (1903), *Set of Six* (1908), *Twixt Land and Sea* (1912), *Within the Tides* (1915), *Tales of Hearsay* (1925); reminiscences *Mirror of the Sea* (1906), etc.

Con·ra·di \kȯn-'räd-ē\, Hermann. 1862–1890. German writer. Follower of Sturm und Drang school. Author of verse *Brutalitäten* (1886), *Lieder eines Sünders* (1887), novels *Phrasen* (1887), *Adam Mensch* (1889).

Con·ra·din \ˈkän-rə-ˌdēn\. *Ger.* Kon·ra·din \ˈkȯn-rä-ˌdēn\. *Sometimes called* Conrad V. 1252–1268. German prince. Son of Conrad IV; claimed Sicily but lost it to usurper Manfred (1258); duke of Swabia (1262); on death of Manfred (1266), began struggle with Charles of Anjou; defeated and captured (1268); beheaded. Last of the Hohenstaufens.

Con·rad von Höt·zen·dorf \ˈkōn-ˌrät-fȯn-ˈhœt-sən-ˌdȯrf\, Franz Xaver Josef. Graf. 1852–1925. Austrian soldier. Chief of Austro-Hungarian imperial staff (1906–11); dismissed (1911) for aggressive attitude toward Italy but soon reinstated (1912–17); planned Austro-German offensive against Russia (1915), Italian offensive (1916), but hampered by German domination and lack of resources; dismissed by Emperor Charles I (1917); commanded army group on Italian front (1917–18).

Con·rart \kōⁿ-rár\, Valentin. 1603–1675. French man of letters. A founder (1634) of Académie Française; elected (1635) its first secretary for life; known as a chief inaugurator of French literary Classicism.

Con·sal·vi \kōn-ˈsäl-vē\, Ercole. 1757–1824. Italian prelate and diplomat. Chamberlain to Pius VI (1783); auditor of Sacra Romana Rota (1792); secretary of Venice conclave (1799); created cardinal and secretary of state by Pius VII (1800); concluded concordat with France (1801); removed from office through Napoléon (1806); exiled to France (1810–13). Secured restoration of Papal States at Congress of Vienna (1815); again papal secretary of state (1815–23); effected reforms and suppressed administrative abuses.

Con·scien·ce \kȯns-ˈyän-sə\, Hendrik. 1812–1883. Flemish writer. Regarded as creator of Flemish novel and a dominant figure in modern Flemish literature; published over 100 books. Works included *In't wonderjaar* (1837), *De leeuw van Vlaanderen* (1838), *Wat een moeder lijden kan* (1844), *Siska van Roosemael* (1844), *Enige bladzijden uit het boek der natuur* (nature sketches, 1846), *Jacob van Artevelde* (1849), *Baas Gansendonck* (1850), *Houten Clara* (1850), *Blinde Rosa* (1850), *De Loteling* (1850), *De arme edelman* (1851), *Rikke-tikke-tak* (1851), *Het Goudland* (1862), *De Kerels van Vlaanderen* (1871).

Con·si·dé·rant \kōⁿ-sē-dā-räⁿ\, Victor-Prosper. 1809–1893. French reformer. Disciple of Fourier and leader of Fourierists (from 1837); member of Constituent Assembly (1848); moved to Belgium (1849); unsuccessfully tried to establish Fourierist colony near Dallas, Tex. (1855–57). Author of *Destinée sociale* (1834–38), *Débâcle de la politique* (1836), *Le Socialisme devant le vieux monde* (1848), etc.

Con·sta·ble \ˈkən(t)-stə-bəl, ˈkän(t)-\, Archibald. 1774–1827. Scottish publisher. Founded *Edinburgh Review* (1802); published Sir Walter Scott's *Lay of the Last Minstrel* (1805) and *Marmion* (1807); purchased copyright of *Encyclopaedia Britannica* (1810–14) and published supplement (1816–24); purchased copyright of *Waverley* (1814); bankrupt (1826); began (1827) *Constable's Miscellany.*

Constable, Henry. 1562–1613. English poet. Embraced Roman Catholicism; papal envoy to Scotland (1598). Author of *Diana* (volume of sonnets, 1592); contributed four poems to *England's Helicon* (1600).

Constable, John. 1776–1837. English painter. Exhibited regularly at royal Academy (from 1802); produced realistic English landscapes and studies of English rustic life, esp. of native Suffolk; won scant recognition at home; received awards in France (1824, 1825) where his work exerted notable influence upon landscape painting. Notable among his landscapes were *The White Horse, Hay Wain, Bridge of the Stour, Stratford Mill, The Leaping Horse, The Cornfield, Dedham Vale, Salisbury Cathedral, Valley Farm, Arundel Mill and Castle.*

Con·stance \ˈkän-stən(t)s\ of Sicily. *Ger.* Kon·stanz \ˈkȯn-ˌstänts\. 1154–1198. Wife of Holy Roman Emperor Henry VI. Daughter of Roger II of Sicily; m. Henry (1186); crowned empress (1191); claimant of Sicilian throne (from 1189), finally secured it (1194); had her son, Frederick II, crowned (1198).

Con·stans I \ˈkän-ˌstanz\. *Orig.* Flavius Julius Constans. c.323–350. Roman emperor (337–350). Youngest son of Constantine the Great and Fausta; proclaimed caesar (333). On division of empire (337) received Italy, Africa, and Illyricum; in war between the brothers (340) defeated Constantine at Aquileia; slain by soldiers of Magnentius.

Constans II Po·go·na·tus \-ˌpō-gə-ˈnāt-əs\. *Orig.* Flavius Heraclius Constans. 630–668. Byzantine emperor (641–668). Son of Constantine III; lost Egypt (643) to Arabs; defeated by Arab fleet off Asia Minor (655); secured treaty with Arab governor of Syria (659). Issued edict Typos (648) forbidding argument on nature of Christ; arrested and exiled Pope Martin I (653) for condemning edict. Ordered murder of brother Theodosius (660) to remove him from succession; settled in Syracuse (663) intending to make it capital of empire; assassinated.

Constant, Baron d'Estournelles de. See Paul BALLUAT.

Cons·tant de Re·becque \kōⁿ-stäⁿ-də-rə-bek\, Benjamin, *in full* Henri-Benjamin. 1767–1830. French writer and politician. Chamberlain to Duke of Brunswick (1787–94); protégé of Mme. de Staël (from 1794); member of the Tribunat (1799–1802); joined opposition to Napoléon and was banished (1803); returned to France (1814); accepted office under Napoléon during the Hundred Days; banished by Louis XVIII (1815–16); member of Chamber of Deputies (1819–30). Author of the psychological novels *Adolphe* and *Cecile; De l'esprit de conquête et de l'usurpation* (1813) on Napoleonic regime; a historical study, *De la religion* (1824–31); revealing *Journaux intimes,* etc.

Con·stan·tine \ˈkän(t)-stən-ˌtēn, -ˌtīn\. Name of a pope and an antipope:

Constantine. d. 715. Pope (708–715). Received submission of Felix, Archbishop of Ravenna; journeyed to Constantinople (710) on invitation of Justinian II to confirm certain decrees.

Constantine II. d. 769? Antipope (767–768) in opposition to Saint Paul I. Forced to accept pontificate by his brother, duke of bishopric of Nepi; not elected from College of Cardinals; sought Frankish protection, but was deposed and imprisoned by Lombards.

Constantine. 1868–1923. King of Greece (1913–17, 1920–22). Son of King George I of the Hellenes; commanded Greek forces defeated in Turkish War (1897); failed to unite Crete with Greece (1909); restored military reputation as commander in chief in Balkan War (1912–13); succeeded father (1913). Advocated neutrality in World War I; forced by Allies and by Venizelos government to retire in favor of son Alexander (1917); returned to throne by plebiscite (1920); after disastrous losses to Turks in Anatolia and military revolt, abdicated in favor of son George II (1922).

Constantine. Name of two Roman emperors:

Constantine I. *Called* the Great. *Full name* Flavius Valerius Aurelius Con·stan·ti·nus \ˌkän(t)-stən-ˈtī-nəs\. d. 337. Roman emperor (306–337). Eldest son of Constantius Chlorus; accompanied Diocletian in expedition to Egypt (296); proclaimed successor (caesar) by his father at York, Britain (306); at the time one of six claimants to throne of Roman Empire; caused death (310) of Maximian for conspiracy; became sole emperor in the West on defeating Maxentius in three battles, the last at the Milvian Bridge (312) at Rome; on this occasion legend states that a cross and the words *in hoc signo vinces* ("by this sign thou shalt conquer") appeared in the heavens; at that time (or earlier) adopted Christianity; issued with Licinius Edict of Milan (313) extending rights and toleration to Christians; devoted next nine years (314–323) to administration, strengthening of frontiers, and restraining barbarians; built Arch of Constantine (315) at Rome; attempted to suppress schisms in church, esp. that of Donatists. After defeating (324) and executing (325) Licinius, ruled as sole emperor; renamed Byzantium Constantinople (330). Called the great Council of Nicaea (325) at which Nicene Creed was adopted; banished Arius and attempted to suppress Arianism.

Constantine II. *Full name* Flavius Claudius Constantinus. 317–340. Emperor (337–340). Son of Constantine the Great; named caesar (317); on his father's death became joint emperor with his brothers Constantius II and Constans; received Gaul, Britain, Spain; invaded dominions of Constans (340); killed at Aquileia.

Constantine. *Called* Constantine III. *Orig.* Flavius Claudius Constantinus. d. 411. Usurping Roman emperor. Proclaimed emperor (407) by his army in Britain; gained control of eastern Gaul; after fall of Stilicho, recognized as co-ruler by Honorius (409); invaded Italy (411); defeated, executed.

Constantine. Name of nine rulers of the Eastern Roman Empire:

Constantine III He·rac·li·us \ˌher-ə-ˈklī-əs, hə-ˈrak-lē-əs\. 612?–641. Emperor (641). Son of Heraclius; joint emperor with half-brother Heracleonas (641); supposed to have been poisoned.

Constantine IV. *Called* Po·go·na·tus \ˌpō-gə-ˈnāt-əs, ˌpäg-ə-\, *i.e.* the Bearded. d. 685. Emperor (668–685). Son of Constans II; besieged (674–678) in Constantinople by Arabs under Muʿāwiyah I, who were, however, compelled to make peace; Thessalonica saved from attacks of Slavs and Avars, but Bulgars established (679) across the Danube within the empire; summoned ecumenical council at Constantinople (680).

Constantine V. *Called* Cop·ron·y·mus \kə-ˈprän-ə-məs, kä-\. 718–775. Emperor (741–775). Son of Leo III; made co-ruler (720); overcame usurper Artabasdus, his brother-in-law (741–742); won military victories over Arabs, Slavs, and Bulgars; an iconoclast, vigorously suppressed monasticism, convoked council on image worship (754).

Constantine VI. 770–?797. Emperor (780–797). Son of Leo IV; last of the Isaurian emperors; under guardianship of his mother Irene (780–790); quarreled with his mother, who had him put to death, and herself usurped throne.

Constantine VII. *Called* Por·phy·ro·gen·i·tus \ˌpȯr-fə-rō-ˈjen-ət-əs, ˌpȯr-\, *i.e.* born in the purple. 905–959. Emperor (913–959). Son of Leo VI; succeeded uncle Alexander (913); joint ruler with father-in-law, Romanus I Lecapenus (920–944), practically excluded from actual administration of government; banished sons of Romanus (945) and ruled thereafter alone.

Known esp. as patron of arts and literature; author of a life of Basil I and political treatises as *De thematibus, De ceremoniis aulae byzantinae, De administrando imperio;* caused many works to be written that included excerpts from the classics, scientific collections, and collections of laws.

Constantine VIII. c.960–1028. Emperor (976–1028). Son of Romanus II; nominal joint ruler with his brother Basil II (976–1025); sole ruler (1025–28) on Basil's death.

Constantine IX. *Called* Mo·nom·a·chus \mō-'näm-ə-kəs\, *i.e.* who fights in single combat. c.980–1055. Emperor (1042–55). Married Empress Zoë (1042); co-ruler with Zoë and Theodora. During reign, defenses of empire weakened, great sums of money spent on luxuries and public buildings, Italy lost to empire when Normans conquered Benevento (1053), revolts at home, arrival of Seljuq Turks in Armenia.

Constantine X Du·cas \'d(y)ü-kəs\. 1007?–1067. Emperor (1059–67). Able minister under preceding emperors; succeeded Isaac I Comnenus; during reign, army reduced, Armenia conquered (1064) by Seljuq Turks under Alp-Arslan, Belgrade seized by Magyars, Thrace and Macedonia invaded by Turks.

Constantine XI Pa·lae·ol·o·gus \,pā-lē-'äl-ə-gəs\. *Called* Dra·ga·ses \drə-'gä-,sēz\. 1404–1453. Emperor (1449–53). Son of Manuel II; succeeded brother John VIII; last emperor of the Eastern Roman Empire; before accession, general and ruler in the Morea (1441–46); fought Ottomans under Mehmed II, who finally besieged Constantinople (1453); killed in last fighting at one of gates of city.

Constantine. *Russ.* Kon·stan·tin Ni·ko·la·ye·vich \kən-(,)stən-'tyēn-nyik-(,)ə-'lā(-yiv)-,yich\. 1827–1892. Russian grand duke. Son of Czar Nicholas I and brother of Czar Alexander II; commanded Russian fleet in Baltic during Crimean War (1854–55); governor of Poland (1862–63); president of Council of the Empire (1865).

Constantine. *Russ.* Konstantin Pa·vlo·vich \(,)pəv-'lóv-,yich\. 1779–1831. Russian grand duke. Son of Czar Paul I and brother of Alexander I and Nicholas I; served in Napoleonic campaigns (1799–1814); following Congress of Vienna, governor general of Poland (1815–1831), where severity of his administration led to Polish rebellion (1830–31).

Constantine the African. *Lat.* Constantinus Af·ri·ca·nus \-,af-ri-'kā-nəs\. c.1020–1087. Latin scholar, b. Carthage. Spent most of life in Benedictine monastery of Monte Cassino; translated into Latin Arabic works on philosophy, Aristotelian physics, and esp. Greek medicine.

Constantine, Learie Nicholas. Baron Constantine. 1901–1971. Trinidadian sportsman and politician. Outstanding member of West Indian cricket team (1928–40), first West Indian in England to achieve 1,000 runs and 100 wickets in a season (1928); admitted to bar (1955); minister of works and transport, Trinidad (1956–62); high commissioner for Trinidad and Tobago in London (1962–64); member, British Race Relations Board (1966–71). Author of *Colour Bar* (1954), books on cricket. Life peer (1969).

Constantine Manasses. See MANASSES.

Constantine-Sil·va·nus \-sil-'vā-nəs\. *Also called* Constantine of Ma·na·na·li \mä-nä-'näl-ē\. d. c.684. Syrian religious. Probable founder of sect of Paulicians, Christian dualists; founded Paulician community near Colonia, Armenia; arrested on order of Emperor Constantine IV, stoned to death.

Con·stan·ti·us \kən-'stan-chē-əs, -shē-\. Name of three Roman emperors:

Constantius I. *Full name* Aurelius Valerius Constantius. *Surnamed* Chlo·rus \'klōr-əs, 'klór-\, *i.e.* the Pale. d. 306. Emperor (305–306). Son-in-law of Maximian; adopted as caesar by Maximian (293); given government of Gaul; subdued British rebels, Frankish and Saxon pirates, the Alemanni; on abdication of Diocletian and Maximian (305) became senior augustus, or emperor, of the West; died at Eboracum (York) in Britain.

Constantius II. *Full name* Flavius Julius Constantius. 317–361. Emperor (337–361). Second son of Constantine the Great; made caesar (333); appointed ruler in the East (335); at father's death divided empire with brothers Constans I and Constantine II, becoming ruler of Thrace, Macedonia, Greece, Asia, Egypt (337); had many conflicts with Persians; disastrously defeated by them (348); after defeat of Magnentius (351) became sole ruler; appointed Julian as caesar in Gaul (355); died on march to punish Julian, who had been proclaimed emperor by his soldiers.

Constantius III. d. 421. Emperor (421). Roman general; helped overthrow usurper Constantine (411); drove Visigoths from Gaul into Spain (415); m. (417) Galla Placidia, half-sister of Emperor Honorius; made co-emperor of the West by Honorius; died at Ravenna after reign of seven months.

Con·tades \kōⁿ-tád\, Louis-Georges-Érasme de. Marquis. 1704–1795. French soldier. Entered army (1720); field marshal (1740), lieutenant general (1745), marshal of France (1758); commanded army defeated at Minden (1759).

Con·ta·ri·ni \,kōn-tä-'rē-nē\. Noted Venetian family, including: Domenico, doge of Venice (1043–1071). ¶Jacopo, doge (1275–1280). ¶Andrea, doge (1368–1382), during which time Venice gained mastery of the sea over Genoa after victory of Chioggia (1380) and Peace of Turin (1381). ¶Gasparo (1483–1542), cardinal (1535) and diplomat who attempted to effect a reconciliation between Protestants and Catholics at the Diet of Ratisbon (1541). ¶Niccolò, doge (1630–31). ¶Domenico II, doge (1659–1675), signed cession of Candia to the Turks. ¶Alvise, doge (1675–1684).

Con·té \kōⁿ-tā\, Nicolas-Jacques. 1755–1805. French chemist. Invented substitute for plumbago, used by painters and for making Conté crayons or pencils; conducted experiments for inflation of military balloons; chief of Napoléon's balloon corps in Egypt (1798–1802); invented numerous tools, devices, machines.

Con·ti \kōⁿ-tē, *Ital* 'kōn-tē\, House of. Subdivision of House of Condé, junior branch of French Bourbons, whose members bore title Prince de Conti, originally given to younger brothers or cousins of princes de Condé.

François de Bour·bon \bür-bōⁿ\. 1558–1614. Younger brother of Henry I, Prince de Condé; supporter of King Henry IV.

¶Armand de Bourbon. 1629–1666. Brother of the Great Condé; engaged in wars of the Fronde; m. niece of Cardinal Mazarin; engaged in war with Spain and captured Villafranca and Puigcerdá (1654); held command in Italy (1657). His son ¶Louis-Armand (1661–1685) m. Marie-Anne (1680), daughter of Louis XIV and Louise de La Vallière; served in Flanders (1683) and aided Imperialists to defeat Turks (1683) at Gran (Esztergom). Another son ¶François-Louis (1664–1709) also aided Imperialists in Hungary (1683); m. (1688) Marie-Thérèse de Bourbon-Condé, granddaughter of the Great Condé; served with great distinction in battles of Fleurus, Steenkerke, and Neerwinden; elected king of Poland (1697) but on arrival there found Augustus II, Elector of Saxony, already holding crown; succeeded Louis-Armand as prince of Conti (1685); appointed commander of French troops in Italy during War of the Spanish Succession, but died before taking the field. François-Louis's son ¶Louis-Armand II (1695–1727) was infamous for vices.

¶Louis-François de Bourbon. 1717–1776. Son of Louis-Armand II; fought in War of Polish Succession (1733–38) and War of Austrian Succession (1742–46); commanded army in Italy and won battle of Coni (1744); served in Germany (1745) and Netherlands (1746–47); unsuccessful candidate for throne of Poland (1747); became opponent of government of Louis XV (1757). His son ¶Louis-François-Joseph (1734–1814) distinguished himself during Seven Years' War (1756–63); left France as an émigré (1789); returned (1790); arrested as a noble (1793) and tried, but acquitted; banished from France; with his death house of Conti became extinct.

Con·ti \'kōn-tē\, Niccolò de'. c.1395–1469. Venetian traveler and writer. Left Venice (1414); visited Baghdad, thence by water to Cambay on west coast of India; later visited Sumatra, Java, Indochina, and Burma as far north as Ava; traversed Ganges valley; returned to Venice (1444) by way of Aden, Jidda, Cairo. As penance for compulsory renunciation of Christianity, ordered by Pope Eugenius IV to relate to papal secretary Poggio Bracciolini the story of his wanderings, published (1723) as *Historiae de varietate fortunae.*

Con·tuc·ci \kōn-'tüt-chē\, Andrea. *Known as* Andrea San·so·vi·no \,sän-sō-'vē-nō\. c.1467–1529. Italian sculptor and architect. Works reflected transition from early to High Renaissance and included marble Altar of the Sacrament in S. Spirito, Florence (1485–90), marble group *Baptism of Christ* (1502), tombs in Rome of cardinals Ascanio Sforza and Girolamo Basso della Rovere (both 1509), and supervision at Loreto of several buildings and of decoration of the Santa Casa (included marble relief *Annunciation*).

Con·verse \'kän-(,)vərs \, Charles Crozat. 1832–1918. American composer, b. Warren, Mass. Composed cantatas, overtures, songs; best known for hymn "What a Friend We Have in Jesus."

Converse, Frederick Shepherd. 1871–1940. American composer, b. Newton, Mass. Professor, New England Conservatory of Music (1920–31), dean (1931–38). Composed operas as *Pipe of Desire* (1905; first opera by an American performed at Metropolitan Opera, N.Y.C., 1910); orchestral works as *Festival of Pan* (1899), *Mystic Trumpeter* (1904),*Ormazd* (1911), *Flivver Ten Million* (1926), *Haul Away, Jo!* (1939), also vocal and chamber works.

Conway, Francis Seymour-. See SEYMOUR family.

Con·way \'kän-,wā\, Henry Seymour. 1721–1795. English soldier and politician. M.P. (1741–84). At Fontenoy (1745); at Culloden Moor (1746) as aide-de-camp to Duke of Cumberland; major general (1756); discredited by failure of expedition against Rochefort (1757); lieutenant general (1759). Secretary of state in Rockingham and Pitt ministries (1765–68), and leader of House of Commons; carried repeal of Stamp Act (1766); governor of Jersey (1772–95). Opposed Lord North's American policy and brought about his resignation (1782); commander in chief with cabinet seat (1782–83); supported Fox in opposition to Pitt (1784); field marshal (1793).

Conway, Moncure Daniel. 1832–1907. American clergyman, b. Stafford Co., Va. Vigorous abolitionist; edited *The Dial,* Cincinnati (1860–61), *Commonwealth,* Boston (1862); pastor in London, England (1864–84, 1892–97). Author of *Demonology and Devil Lore* (1878), *The Wandering Jew* (1881), *Life of Thomas Paine* (1892), *Autobiography* (1904), etc.

Conway, Thomas. 1735–?1800. Irish soldier of fortune. Served in French army (1749–76); to America (1777); appointed major general, against Washington's recommendation (1777). In apparent conspiracy, known as the Conway Cabal, to supplant Washington by Gen. Horatio Gates (1778); on discovery of conspiracy, resigned his commission. Rejoined French army (1779); served in India (1781–87); governor general, French possessions in India (1787).

Con·well \ˈkän-ˌwel, -wəl\, Russell Herman. 1843–1925. American clergyman, b. South Worthington, Mass. A lawyer (1865–79); Baptist clergyman (from 1879), in Philadelphia (1882–91); founder (1888) and first president, Temple U. His lecture "Acres of Diamonds" delivered over 6000 times.

Con·y·beare \ˈkän-ə-ˌbi(ə)r, ˈkən-\, William Daniel. 1787–1857. English geologist and paleontologist. Vicar in Devonshire (1836–44); dean of Llandaff (1844–57). First to describe *Icthyosaurus* (1821). Author of *On the Origin of a Remarkable Class of Organic Impressions Occurring in Nodules of Flint* (1814) and classic *Outlines of the Geology of England and Wales* (1822, with William Phillips), on Carboniferous stratigraphy of Britain.

Cook \ˈku̇k\, Arthur James. 1885–1931. English labor leader. Coal miner (from 1900); jailed for leading strikes (1918, 1921); secretary of Miners' Federation of Great Britain (1924–31); influential in bringing on the coal miners' strike and the general strike (1926).

Cook, Frederick Albert. 1865–1940. American physician and explorer, b. Hortonville, N.Y. Surgeon in Peary Arctic expedition (1891–92) and Belgian Antarctic expedition (1897–99). Led expeditions to climb Mt. McKinley (1903–06); announced he had succeeded (1906). On Arctic exploration trip (1907–09) in effort to reach North Pole; on his return, announced he had reached the pole April 21, 1908; claim denounced by Peary and rejected, on grounds of insufficient evidence, by scientists at Copenhagen after study of data submitted by Cook. Author of *Through the First Antarctic Night* (1900), *To the Top of the Continent* (1908), *My Attainment of the Pole* (1911).

Cook, George Cram. 1873–1924. American novelist, playwright, and poet, b. Davenport, Iowa. With wife Susan Glaspell (m. 1913; *q.v.*) organized and directed (1915) the Provincetown Players, Provincetown, Mass.; established Playwrights' Theater, New York City (1915). Author of novels *Roderick Taliaferro* (1903), *The Chasm* (1911); plays *Suppressed Desires* (with Glaspell, 1915), *Tickless Time* (with Glaspell, 1920), *The Spring* (1925), *The Athenian Women* (1926); verse *Greek Coins* (1925).

Cook, James. *Known as* Captain Cook. 1728–1779. English mariner and explorer. To sea in merchant service (1746); common seaman in British navy (1755); master (1757); surveyed St. Lawrence Channel (1759), coast of Newfoundland and Labrador (1763–67). Conducted, in the *Endeavour,* expedition (1768) to South Pacific Ocean; at Tahiti observed the transit of Venus (1769); discovered and charted coasts of New Zealand, Australia, and New Guinea; returned by way of Cape of Good Hope (1771). Conducted, with the *Resolution* and the *Adventure,* an expedition (1772–75) in search of the great southern continent then believed to exist; skirted Antarctic ice fields, visited Tahiti, New Hebrides, and discovered New Caledonia; by enforcement of strict hygienic and dietary rules, conquered fever and scurvy and completed three-year voyage with the loss of but one man; awarded Copley gold medal. Conducted, with the *Resolution* and the *Discovery,* his last expedition, to discover a passage round North America from the Pacific (1776); rediscovered Sandwich Islands (1778), charted Pacific coast of North America (1778) as far as Bering Strait; visited Hawaii, where he was killed in scuffle with natives over a stolen boat.

Cook, Sir Joseph. 1860–1947. Australian politician, b. England. To Australia (1885); elected to New South Wales legislature (1891), to federal parliament (1901); leader of Free Trade party (1908); minister for defense (1909–10); prime minister of Australia (1913–14); minister for the navy (1917–20), and Australian representative at the Versailles Peace Conference (1919); commonwealth treasurer (1920–21); high commissioner for Australia in London (1921–27).

Cook, Stanley Arthur. 1873–1949. English Orientalist. On editorial staff of *Encyclopaedia Biblica* (1896–1903), and adviser on Old Testament and Semitic subjects to *Encyclopaedia Britannica.* Professor of Hebrew, Cambridge (1932–38). Joint editor, *Cambridge Ancient History.* Author of *Religion of Ancient Palestine* (1908), *Ethical Monotheism* (1932), *The Old Testament; a Reinterpretation* (1936), *The "Truth" of the Bible* (1938).

Cook, Thomas. 1808–1892. English tourist agent. Woodturner, printer, Baptist missionary (c.1828–29). Arranged special train for temperance meeting (1841), believed to have been first publicly advertised excursion train in England; began arranging excursions on regular basis (1844); organized excursions to the Great Exhibition of 1851, the Paris Exhibition (1855); organized grand tour of Europe (1856); developed business into full tourist agency; organized firm as Thomas Cook and Son (1864).

Cook, Will Marion. 1869–1944. American musician and composer, b. Washington, D.C. Wrote musicals *Clorindy* (with Paul Laurence Dunbar, 1898), *In Dahomey* (with Dunbar, 1903), *Abyssinia* (1906), *Bandana Land* (1908) for Bert Williams and George Walker; toured Europe (1903) with *Dahomey* and later with ragtime and jazz orchestras (1906, 1919).

Cooke \ˈku̇k\, Henry. c.1616–1672. English composer and choirmaster. Chorister of Chapel Royal as child; known as Captain Cooke from Royalist service in Civil War; master of children of Chapel Royal (1660–72); noted esp. for ability to select talented pupils, as John Blow, Henry Purcell, Pelham Humfrey, and to teach them thoroughly; composed anthems, odes, etc.

Cooke, Jay. 1821–1905. American banker, b. Sandusky, Ohio. Founded Jay Cooke & Co. (1861); marketed government bonds for financing Civil War; fiscal agent, U.S. Treasury (1862–64, 1865). After war, financed construction of western railroads, esp. Northern Pacific; failed (1873), precipitating financial panic; recouped fortune by mining investments in Utah.

Cooke, John Esten. 1830–1886. American novelist, b. Winchester, Va. Author of *Leather Stocking and Silk* (1854), *The Virginia Comedians* (1854), *Surry of Eagle's Nest* (1866), *Wearing of the Gray* (1867), *My Lady Pokahontas* (1885), etc.

Cooke, Josiah Parsons. 1827–1894. American chemist, b. Boston. Professor, Harvard (1850–94); investigated atomic weights of elements.

Cooke, Rose, *nee* Ter·ry \ˈter-ē\. 1827–1892. American author, b. near Hartford, Conn. Known esp. for realistic tales of New England collected in *Happy Dodd* (1878), *Somebody's Neighbors* (1881), *The Deacon's Week* (1885), *Root-Bound* (1885), etc.

Cooke, Thomas. 1703–1756. English poet, journalist, and pamphleteer. Known as "Hesiod Cooke" from his translation of Hesiod; translated Terence and other authors; author of a poem, *The Battle of the Poets* (1725), containing criticism of Pope's Greek which won him a place in the *Dunciad.*

Cooke, Sir William Fothergill. 1806–1879. English electrical engineer. Collaborated with Charles Wheatstone in invention of electric telegraphs, the two finally patenting a workable single-needle apparatus (1845); quarreled with Wheatstone, each claiming chief credit for invention.

Cook·wor·thy \ˈku̇k-ˌwər-thē\, William. 1705–1780. English potter. Druggist at Plymouth; discoverer of kaolin and China stone near St. Austell (1756), the foundation of English porcelain and fine earthenware; discovered secret of hard porcelain (patent 1868) and established Plymouth china factory.

Cool·brith \ˈkül-(ˌ)brith\, Ina Donna. *Orig.* Josephine Donna Smith. 1841–1928. American poet, b. Nauvoo, Ill. Associated with Bret Harte in editing the *Overland Monthly* (1868); librarian (1874–1906); crowned poet laureate of California (1915). Author of verse *A Perfect Day* (1881), *Singer of the Sea* (1894), *Songs from the Golden Gate* (1895).

Coo·ley \ˈkü-lē\, Charles Horton. 1864–1929. American sociologist, b. Ann Arbor, Mich. Son of Thomas M. Cooley; taught sociology at U. of Michigan (1895–1929, professor 1904); developed theory of mind as social by nature and that society is a mental construct. Author of *Human Nature and the Social Order* (1902), *Social Organization* (1909), *Social Process* (1918).

Cooley, Thomas McIntyre. 1824–1898. American jurist, b. near Attica, N.Y. Judge, Michigan supreme court (1864–85). Professor of law, U. of Michigan (1859–98). Member, Interstate Commerce Commission (1887–91). Author of *Treatise on Constitutional Limitations* (1868), *Law of Taxation* (1876), *Law of Torts* (1879), *General Principles of Constitutional Law* (1880), etc.

Coo·lidge \ˈkü-lij\, Calvin, *in full* John Calvin. 1872–1933. Thirtieth president of the U.S., b. Plymouth, Vt. Practiced law in Northampton, Mass. (from 1897); lieutenant governor of Massachusetts (1916, 1917, 1918); governor (1919, 1920); attracted nationwide attention by firm stand during Boston police strike (1919). Vice president of the U.S. (1921–23); succeeded to presidency on death of Harding (1923); elected (1924) president of the U.S. and served full term (1925–29).

Coolidge, Charles Allerton. 1858–1936. American architect, b. Boston. Designed quadrangle of Stanford U.; Medical School, Fogg Art Museum, Memorial Chapel for Harvard U.; public library and Art Institute in Chicago; Rockefeller Institute in New York; medical school and hospital group for Vanderbilt U.; medical school for Western Reserve U.

Coolidge, Susan. See Sarah Chauncey WOOLSEY.

Coolidge, William Augustus Brevoort. 1850–1926. American mountaineer and historian, b. New York City. Ordained priest (1883) in the Anglican ministry. Resident chiefly in Switzerland (from 1885), and a student of Swiss geography and history; widely known as mountain climber, making about 1750 ascents among the Alps (1865–1900), including first winter ascent of the Jungfrau (1874). Editor of *Alpine Journal* (1880–89).

Coolidge, William David. 1873–1975. American physical chemist, b. Hudson, Mass. Engaged in research at General Electric Co. (1905–44); director of research laboratory (1932), vice president (1940). Invented (1908) and made applications of ductile tungsten; invented (1916) revolutionary new tube for the production of X-rays; devised portable X-ray units, high-power X-ray units for cancer treatment; with Irving Langmuir developed first submarine detecting device.

Coo·ma·ra·swa·my \kü-'mär-ə-'swäm-ē\, Ananda Kentish. 1877–1947. Indian scholar. Director of mineral survey of Ceylon (1903–06); began study of Indian arts and crafts; instrumental in movement for revival of Indian and Ceylonese culture; research fellow in Indian, Persian, and Muslim art, Museum of Fine Arts in Boston (from 1917). Author of *Indian Drawings* (1910–12), *Buddha and the Gospel of Buddhism* (1916), *Rajput Painting* (1916), *The Dance of Siva* (1918), *History of Indian and Indonesian Art* (1927), *A New Approach to the Vedas* (1933), *Transformation of Nature in Art* (1934), *Elements of Buddhist Iconography* (1935), *Hinduism and Buddhism* (1943), *Figures of Speech or Figures of Thought* (1946), etc.

Coon \'kün\, Carleton Stevens. 1904–1981. American anthropologist, b. Wakefield, Mass. Professor, Harvard (1934–48), U. of Pennsylvania (1948–63); curator, U. Museum of Philadelphia (1948–63); did extensive field work in North Africa, Middle East, South America, India; noted for work in cultural and social anthropology. Author of *Tribes of Rif* (1931), *Reader in General Anthropology* (1948), *Story of Man* (1954), *The Seven Caves* (1957), *Origin of Races* (1962), etc.

Cooper, Alexander. See under Samuel COOPER.

Coo·per \'kü-pər, 'ku̇p-ər\, Alfred Duff. 1st Viscount Nor·wich \'nȯ(ə)r-ˌwich; 'nȯr-ich, 'när-\. 1890–1954. English politician. M.P. (1924–29, 1931–45); financial secretary, War Office (1928–29, 1931–34), Treasury (1934–35); secretary of state for war (1935–37); first lord of the admiralty (1937–38), resigning to protest Munich agreement; minister of information (1940–41); ambassador to France (1944–47). Created viscount (1952). Author of *Talleyrand* (1932), *Haig* (1935–36), novel *Operation Heartbreak* (1950).

Cooper, Anthony Ashley. 1st Earl of Shaftes·bury \'shaf(t)s-ˌber-ē, -b(ə-)rē\. 1621–1683. English politician. Inherited large estates; M.P. in Short Parliament (1640); deserted Royalist cause for Parliamentary side (1644); member of Barebones Parliament (1653); appointed by Cromwell to Council of State (1653–54); M.P. (1654–60); one of 12 commissioners sent by House of Commons to invite Charles II to return (1660); privy councillor (1660); created Baron Ashley (1661), earl of Shaftesbury (1672). Chancellor of exchequer (1661–72); member of "Cabinet Council" and (1667) of the Cabal led by Buckingham; lord chancellor (1672–73), dismissed by Charles for supporting anti-Catholic Test Act; supported Declaration of Indulgence (1672); promoted third Dutch War (1672–74). Became leader of Whig or "Country party" opposition; imprisoned (1677–78) in Tower for opposition to prorogation of Parliament; seized opportunity offered by panic caused by Titus Oates's false revelations of a Popish Plot to consolidate power (1678–80); encouraged anti-Catholic terror, brought about judicial murder of personal enemy William Howard, Lord Stafford; president of Privy Council (1679); secured passage of Habeas Corpus Act (1679); attempted to exclude James from succession in favor of his own puppet, Charles's illegitimate son the Duke of Monmouth; indicted James as recusant (1680); appeared at Oxford Parliament (1681) with armed following; sent to Tower for high treason (1681) but acquitted by grand jury; fled to Holland (1682), where he died. His role in succession dispute savagely satirized by John Dryden in *Absalom and Achitophel* (1681). As president of Council of Trade and Foreign Plantations (1672–74) drew up *Fundamental Constitutions* of Carolina province in America, aided by his protégé John Locke. His grandson ¶Anthony Ashley Cooper (1671–1713), 3rd Earl of Shaftesbury, was tutored by Locke; M.P. (1695–99); succeeded to earldom (1699); prominent and independent member of House of Lords (1699–1702). Wrote numerous philosophical essays influenced by Cambridge Platonists and published as *Characteristicks of Men, Manners, Opinions, Times* (1711), which became chief source of English Deism and influenced Pope, Coleridge, Kant, etc.

¶Anthony Ashley Cooper (1801–1885), 7th Earl of Shaftesbury, was a politician and reformer; known as Lord Ashley (1811–51); M.P. (1826–51); supported Catholic emancipation, repeal of Corn Laws; succeeded Michael Sadler as parliamentary leader of factory reform movement (1833); secured passage of Mines Act (1842), Ten Hour, or Lord Ashley's, Act (1847), factory reform bill (1850). As chairman of lunacy commission (1834–85) secured passage of Lunacy Act (1845). Succeeded to earldom (1851). Member of General Board of Health (1848–54); president of Ragged Schools Union (1843–83); assisted Florence Nightingale in army welfare work.

Cooper, Sir Astley Paston. 1768–1841. English surgeon. Surgeon to Guy's Hospital, London (1800); professor of comparative anatomy, Royal Coll. of Surgeons (1813); surgeon to the king (1828). First to tie the abdominal aorta in treatment of aneurysm (1817). Author of *Anatomy and Surgical Treatment of Hernia* (1804–07), *Dislocations and Fractures* (1822), etc.

Cooper, Gary, *orig.* Frank James. 1901–1961. American actor, b. Helena, Mont. Gained fame for portrayals of strong, taciturn heroes of homespun values; appeared in films *Winning of Barbara Worth* (1926), *Wings* (1927), *The Virginian* (1928), *Morocco* (1930), *Lives of a Bengal Lancer* (1935), *Mr. Deeds Goes to Town* (1936), *The Plainsman* (1937), *Beau Geste* (1939), *The Westerner* (1940), *Meet John Doe* (1941), *Sergeant York* (1941, Academy Award), *Pride of the Yankees* (1942), *For Whom the Bell Tolls* (1943), *The Fountainhead* (1949), *High Noon* (1952, Academy Award), *Friendly Persuasion* (1956), *Ten North Frederick* (1958), etc.

Cooper, Giles Stannus. 1918–1966. British dramatist, b. Ireland. Author of radio and television dramas as "Mathry Beacon" (1956), "Under the Loofah Tree" (1957), "Unman, Wittering and Zigo" (1958), "Loop" (1963), "Carried by Storm" (1964), "The Long House" (1965), "Before the Monday" (1965), etc.

Cooper, James Fenimore. 1789–1851. American novelist, b. Burlington, N.J. Went to sea (1806); midshipman, U.S. navy (1808); resigned (1811). Lived life of a country gentleman (1811–22). Reputedly in response to challenge from his wife, wrote novel *Precaution* (1820); second, *The Spy* (1821), a great success; followed by *The Pioneers* (1823), first of the Leatherstocking series, and *The Pilot* (1823). To New York (1822), and continued his novels: *The Last of the Mohicans* (1826), *The Prairie* (1827), *The Red Rover* (1827), *The Wept of Wish-ton-Wish* (1829), *The Water Witch* (1831). Traveled abroad much of time between 1826 and 1833; returned critical of Americans and their culture; expressed criticism in *The American Democrat* (1838) and novels *Homeward Bound* (1838), *Home as Found* (1838), and suffered sharp loss of popularity. Victorious in several libel suits against newspapers. Completed Leatherstocking series with *The Pathfinder* (1840) and *The Deerslayer* (1841); later works, *History of the Navy of the United States* (1839), *The Wing-and-Wing* (1842), *Satanstoe* (1845), *The Sea Lions* (1849).

Cooper, John Montgomery. 1881–1949. American ethnologist and sociologist, b. Rockville, Md. Ordained Roman Catholic priest (1905); taught at Catholic U. (from 1909; professor, 1923); authority on "marginal" peoples of northern Canada, southern South America, etc. Author of *Analytical and Critical Bibliography of the Tribes of Tierra del Fuego and Adjacent Territory* (1917), *Temporal Sequence and the Marginal Cultures* (1941), *The Gros Ventre* (1957).

Cooper, Merian C. 1895–1973. American writer and motion-picture producer, b. Jacksonville, Fla. Writer, producer of *Four Feathers* (1929), *King Kong* (1933), *Last Days of Pompeii* (1935), *Fort Apache* (1948), *She Wore a Yellow Ribbon* (1949), *The Quiet Man* (1952).

Cooper, Peter. 1791–1883. American manufacturer and philanthropist, b. New York City. Proprietor of ironworks in Baltimore (from 1828); designed and built *Tom Thumb,* first American locomotive, for Baltimore and Ohio Railroad (1830); at Trenton, N.J., factory produced first structural-iron beams for buildings (1854); promoter and financial backer of Cyrus Field in the laying of Atlantic cable; invented washing machine, water-power devices, etc. Founded (1859) Cooper Union, New York City, for the "advancement of science and art," giving free courses in science, chemistry, electricity, engineering, and art.

Cooper, Samuel. 1609–1672. English miniature painter. Painted portraits of Mrs. Pepys, Cromwell, Milton, Prince Rupert, George Monck, as well as portraits of royalty. His brother ¶Alexander (d. 1660) was miniature painter to Queen Christina and King Charles X of Sweden (1647 ff.).

Coo·per *or* **Cou·per** \'kü-pər\, Thomas. c.1517–1594. English prelate. Issued *Thesaurus Linguae Romanae et Britannicae* (1565), known as *Cooper's Dictionary;* bishop of Lincoln (1570), of Winchester (1584).

Coo·per \'kü-pər, 'ku̇p-ər\, Thomas. 1759–1839. American chemist and controversialist, b. London, England. To U.S. (1793); associate of Joseph Priestly; professor, Carlisle (now Dickinson) Coll. (1811–15), U. of Pennsylvania (1816–19), South Carolina Coll. (now U. of S.C., 1820–34); president of S.C. Coll. (1821–33); engaged in frequent disputes with clergy. Author of *Some Information Respecting America* (1794), *Political Essays* (1800), *Discourses on the Connection Between Chemistry and Medicine* (1818), *Elements of Political Economy* (1826), *On the Constitution* (1826), *Treatise on the Law of Libel and the Liberty of the Press* (1830).

Cooper, Thomas. 1805–1892. English Chartist and poet. Apprentice to shoemaker; schoolmaster, journalist; became Chartist and edited Chartist paper, took part in general strike of 1842; imprisoned (1843–45), during which time he wrote *Purgatory of Suicides* (1845).

Coorn·hert \'kōrn-hert\, Dirck Volckertszoon. 1522–1590. Dutch scholar. Secretary of Holland, in service of William of Orange (1572). Author of translations from Cicero, Seneca, Erasmus, and of the *Odyssey* (1561); author of book of songs *Liedekens* (1575), didactic *Comedie van Israël* (1575), moralist tract *De wellevenskunste* (1586). Credited with great influence in establishing the literary language of Holland.

Coote \'ku̇t\, Sir Eyre. 1726–1783. British soldier, b. Ireland. Captain in first British regiment sent to India (1754); associated with Robert Clive; led a division at Plassey (1757); gained victory of Wandiwash (1760); took Pondicherry (1761); commander in Bengal (1761–62). M.P. (1768, 1774–80);

lieutenant general (1777). Commander in chief in India (1777); routed Hyder Ali at Porto Novo (1781).

Coote, Richard. 1st Earl of Bel·la·mont *or* Bel·lo·mont \ˈbel-ə-ˌmänt\. 1636–1701. British colonial administrator. M.P. (1688–95); supporter of William of Orange, who created him earl in Irish peerage (1689). Governor of N.Y., Mass., and N.H. (1697–1701); commissioned to suppress illegal trade and piracy; sent out Captain William Kidd to combat freebooters; had to arrest Kidd for piracy (1699).

Cope \ˈkōp\, Charles West. 1811–1890. English historical and genre painter. Executed frescoes for Houses of Parliament (1843 ff.).

Cope, Edward Drinker. 1840–1897. American paleontologist, b. Philadelphia. Professor, Haverford (1866); with U.S. Geological Survey (1871–79); professor, U. of Pennsylvania (1889–97); owner and editor, *American Naturalist* (1878–97). Known esp. for work on fossil history of horse and of mammalian teeth; discovered some 1000 fossil species; supporter of Lamarckian evolution; engaged in lengthy feud with Othniel C. Marsh.

Co·peau \kȯ-pō\, Jacques. 1879–1949. French actor and theater director. Drama critic for *L'Ermitage* (1904–06), *La Grand Revue* (1907–10); with André Gide and others founded *La Nouvelle Revue* (1909); founded (1913) Théâtre du Vieux-Colombier, where he developed new stage techniques with simplification of setting; developed influential school for actors which he operated separately (1924–30), and which presented dramatic productions under group name Les Copiaux.

Copernicus, Nicolaus. See Mikołaj KOPERNIK.

Cop·land \ˈkäp-lənd, ˈkōp-\, Robert. fl. 1508–1547. English printer. Issued books with his imprint (1515–47). Author of *The hye way to the Spyttel hous, Jyl of Breyntford's Testament* (in verse); translator of French romances.

Cop·ley \ˈkäp-lē\, Sir Godfrey. d. 1709. English philanthropist. Endowed (1709) fund used (since 1736) to sponsor the Copley Medal, awarded annually by the Royal Society to the author of the best work on experimental philosophy.

Copley, John Singleton. 1738–1815. American painter, b. Boston. Painted in Boston until settling (1774) in London; early became outstanding American portraitist of the day. Portrait sitters included Samuel Adams, John Hancock, John Adams, John Q. Adams, Lord Cornwallis; later turned to historical painting with *Death of Lord Chatham, Siege of Gibraltar, Victory of Lord Duncan,* etc. His son ¶John Singleton (1772–1863), Baron Lynd·hurst \ˈlind-ˌhərst\, b. Boston, to England (1775); a jurist; M.P. (1818–27); solicitor general (1819–24), attorney general (1824–26); lord chancellor of England (1827–30, 1834–35, 1841–46).

Cop·pard \ˈkäp-ərd\, Alfred Edgar. 1878–1957. English writer. Author of verse *Hips and Haws* (1922), *Pelagea and Other Poems* (1926), *Cherry Ripe* (1935); best known for stories of English rural life and characters collected in *Adam and Eve and Pinch Me* (1921), *Fishmonger's Fiddle* (1925), *The Field of Mustard* (1926), *Silver Circus* (1928), *Pink Furniture* (1930), *Nixey's Harlequin* (1931), *Crotty Shinkwin* (1932), *Tapster's Tapestry* (1938), *You Never Know, Do You?* (1939), etc.

Cop·pée \kȯ-pā\, Francis-Joachim-Édouard, *called* François. 1842–1908. French writer. Gained repute as one of the Parnassian group with his early poetry, *Le Reliquaire* (1865), *Intimités* (1868), *Les Humbles* (1872), *Le Cahier rouge* (1874); wrote plays including *Le Passant* (1869), *Le Luthier de Crémone* (1876), *Les Jacobites* (1885), *Pour la couronne* (1895); novels including *La Bonne Souffrance* (1898). Active in nationalist and anti-Semitic movements; helped found (1899) Ligue de patrie française.

Coppet, Edward J. de. See DE COPPET.

Co·que·lin \kȯ-klaⁿ\, Benoît-Constant. *Known as* Coquelin Aî·né \ā-nā\. 1841–1909. French actor. With Comédie-Française (1860–92); created roles in *Gringoire, Tabarin, L'Étrangère, Le Monde où l'on s'ennuie,* etc.; actor-manager of the Porte-Saint-Martin theater (1897) where he created his most successful role, Cyrano in *Cyrano de Bergerac* (1897). Author of *L'Art et le comédien* (1880), *Les Comédiens, par un comédien* (1882), *L'Art du comédien* (1894). His brother ¶Ernest-Alexandre-Honoré (1848–1909), known as Coquelin Ca·det \kȧ-de\, comedian, played at the Odéon, Variétés, and Comédie-Française (1868–75, 1879–1909). Author of *Le Monologue moderne* (1881), *Le Rire* (1887), *Pirouettes* (1888), etc.

Coraï. See KORAÏS.

Co·ral·li \kȯ-rȧ-yē\, Jean. *Orig.* Jean Coralli Pe·ra·ci·ni \pā-rȧ-sē-nē\. 1779–1854. French ballet dancer and choreographer. Debut at Paris Académie (now Opéra, 1802); ballet master, Théâtre de la Porte-Saint-Martin (1825–31), Opéra (1831–45); created ballets *L'Orgie* (1831), *La Tempête* (1834), *Le Diable boîteux* (1836), *La Tarentule* (1839), *Giselle* (with Jules Perrot, 1841), *La Péri* (1843), *Ozai* (1847).

Co·ram \ˈkōr-əm, ˈkȯr-\, Thomas. c.1668–1751. English philanthropist. Shipwright by trade; in Massachusetts colony (1693–1704); merchant in London (from 1720); projected and founded Foundling Hospital (chartered 1739).

Co·rax of Syr·a·cuse \ˈkōr-ˌak-səv-ˈsir-ə-ˌkyüs, ˈkȯr-, -ˌkyüz\. 5th century B.C. Greek rhetorician. Believed to have written first Greek treatise on rhetoric; specialist in forensic rhetoric.

Coray. See KORAÏS.

Corbeil, William of. See WILLIAM of Corbeil.

Cor·bet \ˈkȯr-bət\, Richard. 1582–1635. English prelate and poet. Bishop of Oxford (1628), translated to Norwich (1632); friend of Ben Jonson. Author of verses as "Faeries Farewell," "Iter Boreale."

Cor·bett \ˈkȯr-bət\, James John. *Called* Gentleman Jim. 1866–1933. American professional boxer, b. San Francisco, Calif. Won over Joe Choynski (1889); drew 61-round fight with Peter Jackson (1891); won world's championship by knocking out John L. Sullivan in the 21st round (Sept. 7, 1892); lost title to Robert Fitzsimmons in 14th round (Mar. 17, 1897); failed to regain title in fights with James J. Jeffries (1900 and 1903).

Corbett, Sir Julian Stafford. 1854–1922. English naval historian. Author of *Drake and the Tudor Navy* (1898), *The Successors of Drake* (1900), *The Campaign of Trafalgar* (1910), *Naval Operations* (1912–23); also wrote novels.

Cor·bière \kȯr-byer\, Édouard-Joachim, *known as* Tristan. 1845–1875. French poet. Wrote verses notable for use of vernacular and slang and for realistic portrayals esp. of seafaring life. Published *Les Amours jaunes* (1873).

Cor·bin \ˈkȯr-bən\, Margaret, *nee* Coch·ran \ˈkäk-rən\. 1751–1800. American Revolutionary heroine, b. Franklin Co., Pa. m. John Corbin (1772); replaced her husband at his cannon when he was killed at battle of Fort Washington (1776); granted soldier's disability pension by Continental Congress (1779).

Cor·bu·lo \ˈkȯr-byə-ˌlō\, Gnaeus Domitius. d. 67 A.D. Roman general. Conquered Frisii tribe on Rhine (47); legate of Gallatia and Cappadocia (54); led war against Parthians and recovery of Armenia (58–63); recalled by Nero (67), apparently on suspicion of conspiracy; committed suicide.

Corbusier, Le. See Charles-Édouard JEANNERET.

Cor·co·ran \ˈkȯr-kə-rən\, William Wilson. 1798–1888. American financier and philanthropist, b. Baltimore. Founded (1859) Corcoran Art Gallery, Washington, D.C.; gave to it his art collection and financial support.

Cord \ˈkȯ(ə)rd\, Errett Lobban. 1894–1974. American manufacturer, b. Warrensburg, Mo. President, Auburn Automobile Co. (1924); acquired Duesenberg Motor Co. (1926); designed and produced (1929–37) Cord automobiles, first widely sold front-wheel drive cars; ceased production (1937).

Cor·day \kȯr-de\, Charlotte. *In full* Marie-Anne-Charlotte Corday d'Ar·mont \dȧr-mōⁿ\. 1768–1793. French patriot. Believed in principles of French Revolution, but horrified at excesses of Reign of Terror; associated with Girondins; slew Marat, leader among the Terrorists (1793); executed.

Cor·de·moy \kȯr-dem-wȧ\, Géraud de, *in full* Louis-Géraud de. c.1620–1684. French historian and philosopher. Developed an atomistic version of Cartesian physical theory in *Le Discernement du corps et de l'âme* (1666).

Cordière, La Belle. See Louise LABÉ.

Córdoba, Fernández de. See FERNÁNDEZ DE CÓRDOBA.

Cor·do·ve·ro \ˌkȯr-dō-ˈver-ō\, Moses ben Jacob. *Also known as* Rem·ak \ˈrem-äk\. 1522–1570. Galilean rabbi. Known esp. as mystical theologian, contributor to Kabbala.

Cordus, Euricius. See RITZE.

Co·rel·li \kō-ˈrel-lē\, Arcangelo. 1653–1713. Italian violinist and composer. Violinist in orchestra of chapel of San Luigi dei Francesci, Rome (1675–85); music director at Palazzo Pamphili (1687–90); in service of Cardinal Pietro Ottoboni (from 1690). Founded a style of virtuoso playing on violin and created form of concerto grosso; compositions included *12 Trio Sonatas* (1681), *12 Chamber Trio Sonatas* (1685), *12 Church Trio Sonatas* (1689), *12 Chamber Trio Sonatas* (1694), *12 Sonatas for Violin and Violone or Harpsichord* (1700), *Concerti grossi* (1714).

Corelli, Marie. See Mary MACKAY.

Co·ri \ˈkōr-ē, ˈkȯr-ē\, Gerty Theresa, *nee* Rad·nitz \ˈräd-nēts\. 1896–1957. American biochemist, b. Prague, Austria-Hungary (now Czechoslovakia). m. (1920) Carl F. Cori; to U.S. (1922), naturalized (1928); on staff of N.Y. State Institute for Study of Malignant Diseases (1922–31), Washington U. (1931–57, professor 1947); with husband studied carbohydrate metabolism; discovered (1936) phosphated form of glucose, known as the Cori ester; discovered enzyme phosphorylase (1938); synthesized glycogen (1939); shared Nobel prize for physiology or medicine (1947) with husband and B.A. Houssay. Her husband ¶Carl Ferdinand (1896–1984), American biochemist, b. Prague, did research (from 1957) on physicochemical mode of action of enzymes involved in breakdown of glycogen to lactic acid.

Co·rin·na \kə-ˈrin-ə\. 5th? century B.C. Greek poet. Traditionally a contemporary and rival of Pindar. Author of simple lyrics, mainly on Boeotian mythology; only a few fragments of her verse are extant.

Co·rinth \kō-ˈrint\, Lovis. 1858–1925. German painter. A leader in Berlin of Sezession modernist movement in German art; painted landscapes, portraits, religious scenes; disavowed but strongly influenced German Expressionism.

Cor·i·o·la·nus \ˌkȯr-ē-ə-ˈlā-nəs, kə-ˌrī-ə-ˈlan-əs\, Gnaeus Marcius. 6th–5th century B.C. Legendary Roman hero, of uncertain historicity. Gained name Coriolanus because of his courage against the Volsci at the siege of Corioli (493 B.C.). Later exiled from Rome, took refuge among the Volsci, and campaigned successfully as commander of the Volscian army against Rome, retiring finally in answer to pleas from his mother and his wife.

Co·rio·lis \kȯr-yȯ-lēs, *Angl* ˌkȯr-ē-ˈō-ləs\, Gaspard-Gustave de. 1792–1843. French mathematician. Professor, École Polytechnique (1816–38), École des Ponts et Chaussées (1832–43); known for theoretical studies in mechanics; first described Coriolis force (1835). Author of *Du calcul de l'effet des machines* (1829), *Théorie mathématique des effets du jeu de billiard* (1835), *Traité de la mécanique des corps solides* (1844).

Co·rip·pus \kə-ˈrip-əs\, Flavius Cresconius. 6th century A.D. Roman poet. Native of Africa; resident in Constantinople. Author of epics *Johannis,* or *De bellis libycis,* on Byzantine wars with Mauretanians, and *In laudem justini minoris* in praise of Justin II.

Cork, Earls of. See BOYLE family.

Cor·liss \ˈkȯ(ə)r-ləs\, George Henry. 1817–1888. American inventor, b. Easton, N.Y. Developed and manufactured the Corliss steam engine.

Cormenin, Vicomte de. See Louis-Marie de LAHAYE.

Cor·na·ro \kȯr-ˈnär-(ˌ)ō\. Noble Venetian family reputedly descended from the Gracchi, including: Several doges, as Marco (1284?–1367; in office in 1365), ¶Giovanni (in office 1624–29), ¶Giovanni II (1647–1722; in office from 1709). ¶Caterina (1454–1510), queen of Cyprus; succeeded her husband, James II of Lusignan, on throne (1473); forced to abdicate in favor of Venetian republic (1489); set up court at Asolo, Treviso; patroness of art and literature, celebrated in paintings by Veronese, Pordenone, Titian, etc., in operas by Halévy, Lachner, and Donizetti, and in *Gli Asolani* by her cousin Cardinal Pietro Bembo (*q.v.*). ¶Luigi Alvise (1475–1466), architect. ¶Elena Lucrezia Piscopia (1646–1684), writer and scholar; granted doctorate at U. of Padua (1678). ¶Flaminio (1693–1778), historian and statesman.

Cornbury, Viscounts. See 2d and 3d earls of Clarendon, under Edward HYDE.

Cor·neille \kȯr-nāy; *Angl* -ˈnā, -ˈnā(ə)l\, Pierre. 1606–1684. French playwright. Studied law; adm. to bar (1624). Made dramatic debut with a series of comedies: *Mélite* (1629), *Clitandre* (1631), *La Veuve* (1632), *La Galerie du palais* (1632), *La Suivante* (1634), *La Place royale* (1634), *L'Illusion comique* (1635), *Le Menteur* (1643). Made his supreme success with his tragedies, including *Médée* (1635), *Le Cid* (1636 or 1637), *Horace* (1640), *Cinna* (1641), *Polyeucte* (1643), *La Mort de Pompée* (1643), *Rodogune* (1645), *Héraclius* (1647), *Andromède* (1650), *Œdipe* (1659), *Sertorius* (1662), *Sophonisbe* (1663), *Othon* (1664), *Agésilas* (1666), *Attila* (1667), *Pulchérie* (1672), *Suréna* (1674). Regarded as creator of French classical tragedy and one of France's greatest tragic poets.

Corneille, Thomas. 1625–1709. French playwright and miscellaneous writer. Younger brother of Pierre Corneille. Among his plays were *Bertrand de Cigaral* (comedy, 1650), *Timocrate* (tragedy, 1656), *Ariane* (tragedy, 1672), *Circé* (tragicomedy, 1675), *Bellérophon* (opera, 1679).

Cor·ne·jo \kȯr-ˈne-(ˌ)hō\, Mariano Harlan. 1863–1942. Peruvian statesman and jurist. In Chamber of Deputies (1893–1904; pres. 1901–03); senator (1911–20); member, Court of International Justice (1916–42); president of Peruvian constituent assembly (1919–20) and author of constitution adopted by it.

Cor·ne·lia \kȯr-ˈnēl-yə, -ˈnē-lē-ə\. 2nd century B.C. Roman matron. Daughter of Scipio Africanus the elder, and mother of the Gracchi (see Tiberius and Gaius GRACCHUS), leaders of the democratic faction in Rome. Famed for her remark to a visiting lady who wanted to see her jewels, "These [her children] are my jewels." A statue erected to her memory after her death bore the simple inscription, "Cornelia, the mother of the Gracchi."

Cornelia. d. 67? B.C. Roman matron. Daughter of Lucius Cornelius Cinna; m. Julius Caesar (83 B.C.); mother of Julia, wife of Pompey.

Cor·ne·lisz \kȯr-ˈnā-ləs\, Cornelis. *Called* Cornelisz van Haar·lem \vän-ˈhär-ləm\. 1562–1638. Dutch historical and portrait painter. Among his canvases were the *Banquet of the Archer's Guild* (1583), *Massacre of the Innocents* (1590).

Cornelisz, Jakob. *Known also as* Cornelisz van Am·ster·dam \vän-ˌäm(p)-stər-ˈdäm, *Angl* -ˈam(p)-stər-ˌdam\ *or* Jakob van Oost·sa·nen \ōst-ˈsa-nən\. c.1470–1533. Dutch painter. Known esp. for painted and carved altarpieces.

Cor·ne·lius \kȯr-ˈnēl-yəs, -ˈnē-lē-əs\. Saint. d. 253. Pope (251–253). Opposed (251) by antipope Novatian; exiled to Centum Cellae (Civitavecchia); friend of St. Cyprian.

Cor·ne·li·us \kȯr-ˈnā-lē-ùs\, Hans. 1863–1947. German philosopher. Professor, Frankfurt (1910 ff.); advanced an empirical theory of perception; developed psychological interpretation and extension of Neo-Kantianism.

Cornelius, Peter, *in full* Carl August Peter. 1824–1874. German composer. Nephew of Peter von Cornelius. Admirer of Liszt and champion of Wagner; professor, Royal Music School, Munich (1867); composer of many song cycles, choral works, and of the operas *Der Barbier von Bagdad* (1858), *Der Cid* (1865).

Cornelius, Peter von. 1783–1867. German painter. Studied and painted in Rome (1811–19) where he became associated with J. F. Overbeck (*q.v.*), Munich (1819–41), and Berlin (from 1841). His notable works included frescoes in the Glyptothek, Old Pinakothek, and Ludwigskirche in Munich, and cartoons for frescoes to adorn the Campo Santo in Berlin. Credited with inspiring a national German school of painting and reviving interest in murals.

Cornelius Nepos. See NEPOS.

Cor·nell \kȯr-ˈnel\, Ezra. 1807–1874. American financier and philanthropist, b. Westchester Landing, N.Y. Associated with Morse in devising method of insulating wire on poles for telegraph transmission; one of organizers of Magnetic Telegraph Co. to connect New York and Washington. Organized Western Union Telegraph Co. (chartered 1856) to unify competing lines. Founded (with Andrew D. White) and contributed heavily to endowment of Cornell U. (incorporated 1865, opened 1868) in Ithaca, N.Y.

Cornell, Joseph. 1903–1972. American sculptor, b. Nyack, N.Y. Associated with Surrealists; an originator of the assemblage genre of sculpture.

Cornell, Katharine. 1893–1974. American actress, b. Berlin, Germany, of American parentage. m. (1921) Guthrie McClintic. Stage debut with Washington Square Players, New York City (1917). Prominent roles in *Bill of Divorcement, The Green Hat, The Age of Innocence, The Barretts of Wimpole Street, Alien Corn, Romeo and Juliet, Saint Joan, The Wingless Victory, The Constant Wife, Dear Liar.*

Corn·ford \ˈkȯ(ə)rn-fərd\, Frances Crofts, *nee* Dar·win \ˈdär-wən\. 1886–1960. English poet. Granddaughter of Charles Darwin; m. Frances M. Cornford (1908). Author of *Poems* (1910), *Spring Morning* (1915), *Autumn Midnight* (1923), *Mountains and Molehills* (1934), *Collected Poems* (1954), *On a Calm Shore* (1960).

Cornford, Francis Macdonald. 1874–1943. English philosopher. Professor, Cambridge U. Author of *Microcosmographia Academica* (1908), *From Religion to Philosophy* (1912), *Before and After Socrates* (1932), *Plato's Cosmology* (1937), etc.

Cor·ning \ˈkȯr-niŋ\, Erastus. 1794–1872. American businessman, b. Norwich, Conn. President of Utica & Schenectady Railroad (1833–53); first president of New York Central Railroad (1853–64). Democratic congressman from N.Y. (1857–59, 1861–63). Corning, N.Y., was named for him.

Corning, James Leonard. 1855–1923. American neurologist, b. Stamford, Conn. Discovered spinal anesthesia (1885); demonstrated that action of certain medicinal substances is increased while subject remains in compressed air; first to inject liquid paraffin into the tissues and solidify it there.

Corn·plan·ter \ˈkȯ(ə)rn-ˌplant-ər\. *English name* John O'·Bail \ə-ˈbā(ə)l\, O'·Beel \ə-ˈbē(ə)l\, *or* Abeel. c.1732–1836. American Indian leader of partly European ancestry. Led Senecas in attacks on white settlements in western New York and Pennsylvania during Revolution. Ceded Indian lands (1784), advocated nonresistance. Lost leadership to Red Jacket.

Cor·nu \kȯr-nüē\, Marie-Alfred. 1841–1902. French physicist. Professor, École Polytechnique, Paris (from 1867). Known for work in optics and spectroscopy.

Cornu, Paul. 1881–1944. French engineer. Built first helicopter to bear a man in free flight (flown Nov. 13, 1907).

Cor·nu·tus \kȯrn-ˈyüt-əs\, Lucius Annaeus. fl. 54–68 A.D. Roman Stoic philosopher. Teacher and friend of Persius. Author of *Theologiae Graecae compendium.* Banished by Nero.

Cornwall, Duke of. Hereditary title of the Prince of Wales, created for EDWARD (1330–76).

Cornwall, Earls of. See (1) RICHARD (1209–1272); (2) Piers GAVESTON.

Cornwall, Barry. See Bryan Waller PROCTER.

Corn·wal·lis \kȯrn-ˈwäl-əs\, Charles. 1st Marquis Cornwallis. 1738–1805. English soldier. Son of 1st Earl Cornwallis. Commissioned ensign (1756); M.P. (1760); fought in Germany (1761–62). Major general in American War of Independence (1776); drove Washington out of New Jersey (1776); made commander in southern theater (1780); defeated Gates at Camden (1780) and Greene at Guilford Court House (1781), but was besieged at Yorktown by French and American armies, and forced to capitulate (October 19, 1781). Governor general and commander in chief in India (1786–93); interrupted in civil and military reforms by outbreak of third Mysore War under Tippu Sultan, whom he defeated near Seringapatam (1791) and deprived of half his realm. Created marquis (1792); general (1793). Viceroy of Ireland (1798–1801); thwarted threatened rebellion and forced French invasion force to surrender (1798); resigned because of king's refusal to grant Roman Catholic emancipation. Negotiated Treaty of Amiens (1802). Again governor general of India (1805); died at Ghazipur on way to assume command of the troops. His brother ¶Sir William (1744–1819), naval officer, was in constant service

(1755–87) in British West Indies; commodore in East Indies (1789–93); vice admiral (1794); brought off his squadron with small damage in brush with French fleet off Brest (1795); admiral (1799); commander in West Indies (1796) and English Channel (1801–06).

Corn·well \ˈkȯrn-ˌwel, -wəl\, Dean. 1892–1960. American illustrator and painter, b. Louisville, Ky. Mural paintings in Los Angeles Public Library, Rockefeller Center, N.Y.C., many post offices and banks, and General Motors Building at New York's World's Fair (1939).

Cor·nyshe *or* **Cor·nysshe** \ˈkȯr-nish\, William. d. 1523. English actor, dramatist, and composer. Master of the Chapel Royal (from 1509). A favorite court musician of Henry VIII. Wrote many plays, masques, and pageants for the court.

Co·ro·na·do \kō-rō-ˈnäth-ō; *Angl* ˌkȯr-ə-ˈnäd-(ˌ)ō, ˌkär-\, Francisco Vás·quez de \ˈbäs-kāth-th̲ā, -kās-\. c.1510–1554. Spanish explorer. To Mexico (1535); governor of Nueva Galicia (1538–44). Commander of exploring expedition northward (1540) in search of Seven Cities of Cibola, reputed to be fabulously rich. (See Marcos de NIZA.) Found Zuñi pueblos and set out for Gran Quivira, also supposed to be rich. Search ended at Wichita Indian village in Kansas after trek through Texas and Oklahoma. Smaller exploring parties sent out under García Lopéz de Cardenas and Hernando de Alarcón discovered Grand Canyon and mouth of the Colorado River.

Coronado, Juan Vásquez de. 1525?–1565. Spanish conquistador. To Guatemala (1550); active as explorer in various parts of Central America (1550–64); governor of Costa Rica (1562–65); founded Cartago (1563).

Co·ro·nel \kō-rō-ˈnel\, María Fernández. *Religious name* Sor María de Jesús de Agre·da \äg-ˈrā-th̲ä\. 1602–1665. Spanish religious and mystic. Became Franciscan nun (1620); abbess of Franciscan monastery in Agreda (1627–65); adviser to and correspondent with Philip IV (1643–65); encouraged missionary work in North America. On basis of alleged divine revelation wrote a life of Virgin Mary, *Mística ciudad de Diós* (pub. 1670), condemned by Roman Index (1681; ban lifted 1747).

Co·ro·nel·li \ˌkō-rō-ˈnel-lē\, Marco Vincenzo. 1650–1718. Venetian religious and geographer. Founded Accademia Cosmografica degli Argonauti (1684); cosmographer of Venetian republic (from 1685); general of Minorite order (1701–04). His writings included *Atlante veneto* (1690), *Cronologia universale* (1707), and *Roma antica e moderna* (1716).

Co·rot \kȯ-rō\, Jean-Baptiste-Camille. 1796–1875. French painter. Identified with Barbizon school; anticipated later Impressionists. Among his canvases were *La Campagne de Rome, Vue d'Italie, Souvenir des environs de Florence, La Danse des nymphes, Soleil couchant dans le Tyrol, Matin soirée, Orphée, Le Repos.*

Corrado di Suburra. See ANASTASIUS IV.

Cor·rea da Ser·ra \kür-ˈrā-ə-th̲ə-ˈser-rə\, José Francisco. 1750–1823. Portuguese scholar and botanist. A founder of Portuguese Academy of Sciences at Lisbon. Secretary to Portuguese embassy in England; minister at Washington (1816–20); deputy to Portuguese Cortes (after 1820). Known esp. for his *Colecção de livros inéditos da história portuguesa* (1790–1816).

Correia Garção, Pedro Antonio. See Pedro GARÇÃO.

Correggio. See Antonio ALLEGRI.

Correia Botelho, Visconde de. See Camilo CASTELO BRANCO.

Cor·rens \ˈkȯr-ens\, Karl Erich. 1864–1933. German botanist. Professor, Leipzig (1902), Münster (1909); first director, Kaiser Wilhelm Inst. of Biology, Berlin (from 1914); professor of philosophy, Berlin (1920–24). Conducted experiments in genetics that led to his rediscovery of Mendel's law of inheritance (1900; almost simultaneously with De Vries of Holland and Tschermak von Seysenegg of Austria). Author of works on heredity and the determination of sex in plants.

Cor·ry \ˈkȯr-ē, ˈkär-\, Montagu William Lowry. Baron Row·ton \ˈraůt-ᵊn, ˈrōt-\. 1838–1903. English political leader and philanthropist. Private secretary to Disraeli (1866–81); originator of scheme of Rowton houses, hotels with good accommodations at low prices for poor men.

Corse \ˈkȯ(ə)rs\, John Murray. 1835–1893. American army officer, b. Pittsburgh, Pa. Hero of defense of Allatoona Pass (Oct. 5, 1864), which inspired Philip P. Bliss's hymn "Hold the Fort."

Cor·si \ˈkōr-sē\, Jacopo. 1561–1602. Florentine noble and amateur musician. Host to meetings of the Camerata and to first performances of Peri's *Dafne* and *Euridice.*

Cor·si·ni \kōr-ˈsē-nē\. Noble family of Florence and later of Rome, including: Saint Andrea (1302–1373), bishop of Fiesole (1349), canonized by Urban VIII (1629). ¶Filippo (1334–1421), count palatine (from 1371). ¶Filippo (1578–1636), marquess of Sismano. For Lorenzo (1652–1740), see CLEMENT XII.

Cor·son \ˈkȯrs-ᵊn\, Juliet. 1841–1897. American educator, b. Roxbury, Mass. Opened New York Cooking School (1876). Author of *Cooking Manual* (1877), *Miss Corson's Practical American Cookery* (1886), etc.

Cort \ˈkȯrt\, Cornelis. 1533–1578. Dutch engraver and painter. To Venice (1566) and Rome (1571), where he founded a school; engraved after Raphael, Titian, Michelangelo, Zuccaro, Correggio, Michiel van Coxie, Heemskerck, Rogier van der Weyden, and others.

Cort \ˈkō(ə)rt, ˈkȯ(ə)rt\, Henry. 1740–1800. English ironmaster. Invented process for purifying iron by puddling (1783–84) and method of producing iron bars by means of grooved rollers.

Cor·tel·you \ˈkȯrt-ᵊl-ˌyü\, George Bruce. 1862–1940. American politician, b. New York City. Secretary to Pres. McKinley (1900–01) and to Pres. Theodore Roosevelt (1901–03). First secretary, U.S. Department of Commerce and Labor (1903–04); U.S. postmaster general (1905–07); U.S. secretary of the treasury (1907–09). President of Consolidated Gas Co. of N.Y. (1909–35).

Côr·te-Re·al \ˈkōr-tə-rē-ˈäl\, Gaspar. 1450?–?1501. Portuguese navigator. Explored coast of Labrador and Newfoundland (1500); on second voyage (1501) sent back two vessels, but did not return himself. His brother ¶Miguel visited North America (1502) in search for him, but also failed to return.

Côrte-Real, Jerónimo. c.1530–1588. Portuguese epic poet, b. Azores? A soldier and painter in youth. Wrote *Sucesso do segundo cêrco de Dio* (21 cantos, 1574); *Austríada* (15 cantos, in Spanish, 1578); *O Naufrágio de Sousa de Sepúlveda* (17 cantos, 1594).

Cor·tés \kȯr-ˈtās, *Angl* kȯr-ˈtez, ˈkȯr-ˌ\, Hernán *or* Hernando. 1485–1547. Spanish conqueror of Mexico. Sailed to Santo Domingo (1504); officer on expedition of Diego Velásquez to Cuba (1511). Given command on expedition of discovery to mainland (1518–19); coasted along Yucatán and Mexico to San Juan de Ulúa (1519); founded Veracruz; destroyed his fleet. On march inland defeated and made alliance with Tlaxcalans; entered Aztec capital Tenochtitlán, now Mexico City (Nov. 8, 1519); held Montezuma as hostage; made quick march to coast, captured Narváez, who had been sent to arrest him; returned to find Aztecs aroused to revolt (1520). On death of Montezuma, led (June 30, 1520) Spaniards and allies out of city after severe fighting (*la noche triste*); defeated Aztecs in battle of Otumba (July 7, 1520) and retreated to Tlaxcala; captured Mexico City after four-month campaign (August 1521); made governor (1523). Undertook long journey to Honduras (1524–26). Deposed on complaints of political enemies (1526); called back to Spain (1528); granted honors and created marqués del Valle de Oaxaca by Charles V (1529), who confirmed him as captain general of New Spain. Returned to Mexico (1530); discovered Lower California (1536). Went back to Spain (1540); took part in expedition to Algiers (1541); shipwrecked. Died on estate near Seville. See MARINA.

Cortés, Juan Francisco María de la Salud Donoso. See DONOSO CORTÉS.

Cor·tés Cas·tro \kȯr-ˈtā-ˈskäs-trō\, León. 1882–1946. Costa Rican politician. President of Costa Rica (1936–40).

Cor·ti \ˈkȯr-tē\, Alfonso Giacomo Gaspare. 1822–1876. Italian anatomist. Discovered (1850) the complex organ of the ear (organ of Corti) by which sound waves are converted to neural impulses.

Corti, Luigi. Count. 1823–1888. Italian diplomat. Secretary of legation in London (1850–64); various ambassadorial posts (1864–78); minister of foreign affairs (1878) in Cairoli government; Italian representative at Congress of Berlin (1878–79); ambassador to Turkey (1880–86) and Great Britain (1886–87).

Cor·tis·soz \kȯr-ˈtē-səz\, Royal. 1869–1948. American art critic, b. Brooklyn, N.Y. Art editor of New York *Tribune* and its successor, the *Herald-Tribune* (1891–1944). Author of *Augustus St. Gaudens* (1907), *John La Farge* (1911), *Art and Common Sense* (1913), *American Artists* (1923), *The Painter's Craft* (1930), etc. Stout opponent of modernism. His wife ¶Ellen Mackay, *nee* Hutch·in·son \ˈhəch-ə(n)-sən\ (1846?–1933), was a poet and editor; author of *Songs and Lyrics;* editor, with E. C. Stedman, of *The Library of American Literature* (11 vols., 1889–90).

Cortona, Luca da. See Luca SIGNORELLI.

Cortona, Pietro da. See PIETRO DA CORTONA.

Cor·tot \kȯr-tō\, Alfred-Denis. 1877–1962. French pianist and conductor. Outstanding interpreter of Wagner and other late Romantics. Formed trio (1905) with Jacques Thibaud and Pablo Casals; founded (1918) École Normale de Musique, Paris.

Cort van der Lin·den \ˈkȯrt-ˌvän-dər-ˈlin-dən\, Pieter Wilhelm Adriaan. 1846–1935. Dutch statesman. Taught economics until named minister of justice (1897–1901); member of State Council (1901–13, 1918–35); headed extra-parliamentary Liberal cabinet (1913–18) which secured electoral reforms, including universal manhood suffrage, equalized financing for state and denominational schools, and instituted unemployment insurance.

Cor·un·ca·ni·us \ˌkȯr-ən-ˈkā-nē-əs\, Tiberius. d. c.243 B.C. Roman official. First plebeian to hold title of pontifex maximus.

Corvinus, Jakob. See Wilhelm RAABE.

Corvinus, Johannes and Matthias. See MATTHIAS CORVINUS.

Corvinus, Marcus Valerius Messala. See MESSALA CORVINUS.

Cor·vi·sart des Ma·rets \kȯr-vē-zär-dā-mȧ-re\, Jean-Nicolas. Baron. 1755–1821. French physician. Physician to Napoléon (1807). Regarded as a founder of pathological anatomy; developed method of percussion for diagnosing diseases of the chest, esp. heart diseases.

Corvo, Baron. See Frederick ROLFE.

Cor·win \'kȯr-wən\, Edward Samuel. 1878–1963. American political scientist, b. Plymouth, Mich. Taught at Princeton U. (1905–46). Expert on U.S. constitutional law; wrote *Doctrine of Judicial Review* (1914), *President's Removal Power* (1927), *Court over Constitution* (1938), *Liberty Against Government* (1948), etc.

Corwin, Thomas. 1794–1865. American politician, b. Bourbon Co., Ky. Member, U.S. House of Representatives (1831–40, 1859–61). Governor of Ohio (1840–42); U.S. senator (1845–50). U.S. secretary of the treasury (1850–53); minister to Mexico (1861–64). Opposed Mexican War in Senate (1847); chairman of Congressional Committee of Thirty-Three (1861) seeking compromise of secession crisis.

Cory \'kōr-ē, 'kȯr-\, William Johnson. *Orig. surname* Johnson. 1823–1892. English schoolmaster and lyric poet. Taught at Eton (1845–71); assumed name Cory on receipt of an estate (1872). Author of *Ionica* (1858; a volume of verse containing "Mimnermus in Church"), *Lucretilis* (1871; on writing Latin verse), *Iophon* (1873; on Greek iambics), and a *Guide to Modern History from 1815 to 1835* (1882).

Cor·y·ate *or* **Cor·y·at** \'kȯr-ē-ət, 'kȯr-yət, 'kär-\, Thomas. 1577?–1617. English traveler. Became a buffoon at court and entered household of Prince Henry. Traveled mostly on foot to Venice, and back through Switzerland, Germany, and Holland; published narratives of travels, *Coryate's Crudities,* to which at Henry's command was appended *The Odcombian Banquet,* verses of mock praise by Donne, Jonson, Chapman, and others (1611), and *Coryate's Crambe* (1611).

Cor·y·ell \'kȯr-ē-əl, -ˌel; 'kȯr-yəl\, John Russell. 1851–1924. American writer, b. New York City. Author of *The Old Detective's Pupil* (1886), in which the character of Nick Carter was introduced; after several more Dime Novel detective tales he passed the series on to other writers. Wrote other books and magazine serials under numerous pseudonyms including, reputedly, "Bertha M. Clay."

Co·sa \'kō-sä\, Juan de la. 1460?–1510. Spanish navigator and geographer. Master of the *Santa María* on first voyage of Columbus (1492–93) and with him on second voyage (1493). Pilot of expeditions to north coast of South America (1499–1500, 1500–02, 1504–07, 1507–08) with Ojeda, Vespucci, etc.; killed by Indians near Cartagena. Made first large map of New World (1500; now in Madrid), of great value to cartographers.

Co·senz \kō-'zents\, Enrico. 1812–1898. Italian soldier. Colonel in Garibaldi's "Cacciatori delle Alpi" (1859); led third Garibaldian expedition to Sicily (1860); after Garibaldi's seizure of Naples, appointed minister of war; deputy (1860 ff.). Commanded division in Italian army (from 1861); senator (1872 ff.); chief of general staff (1881–93).

Cos·grave \'käz-ˌgrāv\, William Thomas. 1880–1965. Irish politician. Identified with Sinn Féin, took part in Easter uprising (1916). A member of the Dáil Éireann from its beginning (1917). Chairman of the provisional government, and president of Dáil Éireann (1922); first president of the executive council of the Irish Free State (1922–32); leader of Fine Gael party (1922–44).

Cosimo, Agnolo di. See AGNOLO DI COSIMO.

Cosimo, Piero di. See PIERO DI LORENZO.

Cos·in \'kəz-ᵊn\, John. 1594–1672. English clergyman. Named prebendary of Durham (1624). Prepared, by command of Charles I, a *Collection of Private Devotions* (1627); obtained ejection of Peter Smart, Puritan prebendary of Durham (1628). Master of Peterhouse, Cambridge (1634–42) until deprived by Puritan authorities; chaplain to royal household in Paris (1642–60). Bishop of Durham from Restoration (1660); one of revisers of the Book of Common Prayer (1662); patron of revival of Gothic art and architecture.

Cos·mas \'käz-məs\ and **Da·mi·an** \'dā-mē-ən\. Saints. 3rd century. Christian martyrs. Brothers, physicians and missionaries; martyred in Cilicia (c.303) in reign of Diocletian. Justinian I built a church in their honor in Byzantium, and Pope Felix IV one in Rome. Patron saints of physicians and apothecaries.

Cosmas. *Surnamed* In·di·co·pleus·tes \ˌin-də-(ˌ)kō-'plü-(ˌ)stēz\, *i.e.* India Navigator. 6th century. Greek traveler, of Alexandria, Egypt. Traveled and traded as far as western India and Ceylon; later became monk and wrote *Topographia Christiana,* which included one of the earliest world maps, intended to vindicate biblical account of the world.

Cosmas of Prague \'präg\. 1045?–1125. Bohemian chronicler. Wrote earliest Bohemian chronicle, *Chronica Bohemorum,* carrying the history of Bohemia almost up to the year of his death.

Cos·ma·ti \kōz-'mä-tē\. Name of a family of Roman architects, sculptors, and mosaic workers of the 13th century, including: Jacopo (fl. 1205–10), ¶Cosimo (fl. 1210–35), ¶Luca (fl. 1231–35), ¶Jacopo (fl. 1231–93), ¶Adeodato (fl. 1294), ¶Giovanni (fl. 1296–1303); name given to a style of inlay and mosaic work.

Cossa, Baldassare. See Antipope JOHN XXIII.

Cos·sa \'kȯs-sä\, Francesco del. 1436–1478. Italian painter. Regarded as one of the founders of the Bolognese school; best known work the frescoes in Palazzo Schifanoia, Ferrara.

Cossa, Pietro. 1830–1881. Italian playwright. Known as a romantic treating classical subject matter, as in *Nerone* (1871), *I Napolitane nel 1799* (1880).

Cos·sé \ko-sā\, Charles I de. Comte de Bris·sac \brē-sak\. 1505?–1563. French soldier. Engaged in campaigns against the English and Imperialists (1544–46); grand master of the artillery (1547); marshal of France (1550). His brother ¶Artus de Cossé (1512–1582), comte de Se·con·di·gny \sə-gōⁿ-dēn-yē\, soldier, aided in defense of Metz (1552); campaigned against Spanish in Italy (1554); marshal of France (1567).

Cos·su·ti·us \käsh-'ü-sh(ē-)əs, käs(h)-'yü-\. 2d century B.C. Roman architect. Designed most of the temple of Zeus at Athens.

Cos·ta \'kȯs-tȧ\, Cláudio Manuel da. 1729–1789. Brazilian poet. His works, considered classics of Portuguese, included sonnets, songs, and the epic *Villarica* (1773; pub. 1841).

Cos·ta \'kȯs-tä\, Isaäc da. 1798–1860. Dutch poet. A leader of the Réveil movement, a literary revival. Poetic works included *Vijf-en-twintig jaren* (1840), *Hagar* (1847), *De slag bij Nieuwpoort* (1859). A convert to evangelical Calvinism, wrote *Bezwaren tegen den geest der eeuw* (1823) against modern liberalism.

Costa, Lorenzo. c.1460–1535. Italian painter. Painted frescoes in chapel of San Giacomo Maggiore, Bologna; to Mantua (1506), succeeding Mantegna as court painter, and worked under the patronage of Marchese Francesco Gonzaga. His son ¶Ippolito (1506–61) and grandson ¶Lorenzo the Younger (1537–83) were also painters.

Cos·ta \'käs-tə\, Sir Michael Andrew Agnus, *orig.* Michele Andrea Agniello. 1808–1884. British conductor and composer, b. Italy. In England (from 1829). Conducted opera at Her Majesty's Theatre, London (1832–46); conductor of Philharmonic Society (1846–54) and at Covent Garden (from 1846); composed oratorios, operas, and ballets.

Cos·ta \'kȯsh-tə\, Uriel da, *orig.* Gabriel da. *Lat. surname* Acosta. c.1585–1640. Portuguese freethinker. Born of Jewish family forcibly converted to Roman Catholicism; converted to Judaism and fled (c.1617) to Amsterdam, adopting name Uriel; attacked rabbinic ritual and authority (1616); excommunicated (1618); published (1624) refutation of immortality of soul and resurrection; imprisoned by civil authorities; recanted (1633) after 15 years of ostracism; secretly advocated faith based on natural reason; again excommunicated (1633); made humiliating recantation (1640); wrote *Exemplar humanae vitae* (1640); took own life.

Cos·ta Ca·bral \ˌkȯsh-tə-kə-'bräl\, Antonio Bernardo da. Conde de Tho·mar \tü-'mar\. 1803–1889. Portuguese politician. Judge of supreme court, Oporto and Lisbon; radical (later royalist) deputy (1835 ff.); governor of Lisbon (1838); minister of justice (1839–42); fomented insurrection against ruling Septembrist radicals (1842), assuming dictatorial control of government; restored Dom Pedro's constitution of 1826; deposed (1846). Again prime minister (1849–51); deposed by revolution led by Saldanha (April 1851); ambassador to Brazil (1859–61); president, superior administrative court (1862 ff.).

Cos·ta e Sil·va \ˌkȯs-tȧ-ā-'sil-vȧ\, Artur da. 1902–1969. Brazilian general. Led coup that ousted Pres. Goulart (1964). Elected president of Brazil (1966); retired (1969).

Cos·tain \'käs-ˌtān\, Thomas Bertram. 1885–1965. Canadian writer, b. Brantford, Ont. Journalist for various newspapers; an editor (1920–34) of *Saturday Evening Post.* Wrote series of popular historical novels including *For My Great Folly* (1942), *The Black Rose* (1945), *The Silver Chalice* (1952).

Co·stan·zo \kō-'stänt-sō\, Angelo di. Signore di Can·ta·lu·po \ˌkän-tä-'lü-pō\. 1507–1591. Italian poet and historian. Known esp. for his *Rime,* chiefly sonnets, and *Le Istorie del regno di Napoli dal 1250 fino al 1498.*

Cos·ta y Mar·tí·nez \'kōs-tä-ē-mär-'tē-nāth, -nās\, Joaquín. 1846–1911. Spanish jurist and historian. Wrote *El colectivismo agrario* (1898), *Reconstitución y europeización* (1900), *Oligarguía y caciquismo* (1901–02), *Ultimo día del paganismo* (1909).

Cos·tel·lo \'käs-tə-ˌlō; kä-'stel-ō, kə-\, John Aloysius. 1891–1976. Irish politician. Attorney general (1926–32). In Dáil Éireann (1933–59); prime minister (1948–51, 1954–57); leader of Fine Gael in opposition (1951–54, 1957–59). Took Ireland out of British Commonwealth of Nations (1949).

Costello, Louisa Stuart. 1799–1870. Irish miniature painter. Employed at Paris and London; also author of verse, notes of travel, novels, etc.

Cos·ter \'kȯs-tər\, Charles Théodore Henri de. 1827–1879. Belgian writer. Wrote *Légendes flamandes* (in old Flemish, 1857), *Contes brabançons* (in French, 1861), and his nationalistic masterpiece *La Légende et les aventures héroïques, joyeuses, et glorieuses d'Ulenspiegel et de Lamme Goedzak au pays de Flandres et ailleurs* (1866).

Cos·ter *or* **Kos·ter** \ˈkòs-tər\, Laurens Janszoon. c.1370–?1440. Dutch town official of Haarlem. Credited by some scholars with the European invention of the art of printing and by some with the invention of movable type (c.1430). These claims lack contemporary documentation and have been much disputed. Cf. GUTENBERG.

Coster *or* **Koster,** Samuel. 1579–?1665. Dutch physician and playwright. Among his comedies were *Teeuwis de Boer* (1612), *Spel van de Rijcke-Man* (1615), *Tiisken van der Schilden* (1617); among his tragedies, *Ithys* (1615), *Isabella* (1619), *Polyxena* (1619).

Costes \kòst\, Dieudonné. 1892–1973. French aviator. With Maurice Bellonte set distance record of 4913 miles, Paris to Qi-gi-ha-er, China (Sept. 1929); with Bellonte made first nonstop flight from Paris to New York (Sept. 1–2, 1930), 4100 miles in 37 hours, 18 mins.

Cos·tin \ˈkòs-tin\, Miron. 1633–1691. Moldavian poet and chronicler. Chief work *Letopisețul Țării Moldovei de la Aron-Vodă încoace,* a chronicle for the years 1595–1661. Work continued by his son ¶Nicolae (c.1660–1712), who also collected Moldavian folklore.

Cos·way \ˈkäz-ˌwā\, Richard. 1742–1821. English miniature painter. Gained Prince of Wales as patron through clever portraiture of Mrs. Fitzherbert. Elected to Royal Academy (1771). Painted Lady Beechy, Mme. du Barry, members of royal family; made effective use of ivory background in miniatures; m. (1781) ¶Maria Cecilia Louisa Had·field \ˈhad-ˌfēld\ (1759–1838), Irish-Italian painter and musician, subject of one of his finest engravings.

Co·ta de Ma·gua·que \ˈkō-tät͟h-ā-mäg-ˈwäk-ā\, Rodrigo. d. before 1495. Spanish poet. Author of *Diálogo entre el amor y un viejo.*

Cotes \ˈkōts\, Roger. 1682–1716. English mathematician and philosopher. Plumian professor of astronomy and experimental philosophy, Cambridge (1706–16); aided Newton in 1713 edition of *Principia* and wrote the preface; published *Logometria* (1713), treatise on ratios.

Cot·grave \ˈkät-ˌgrāv\, Randle. d. 1634? English lexicographer. Compiled the first French–English dictionary (1611).

Cotignola, Baron von. See G. A. JOCHMUS.

Co·tin \kò-taⁿ\, Charles. 1604–1682. French abbé and poetaster. Councilor and almoner to the king (1630); published works of moral philosophy as *Jérusalem désolée* (1634), *Traité de l'âme immortelle* (1655); known for gallant verses; ridiculed by Boileau, and by Molière, who represented him in the character of Trissotin in *Les Femmes savantes.*

Cot·man \ˈkät-mən\, John Sell. 1782–1842. English landscape painter and etcher. Executed watercolors of Wales and Yorkshire; drawing master, Norwich (1807–12, 1823–34), King's Coll., London (1834–42); best known works included *Greta Bridge, Waterfall,* and *Silver Birches.*

Cots·worth \ˈkäts-(ˌ)wərth\, Moses Bruines. 1859–1943. English advocate of calendar reform. Originator and director of International Fixed Calendar League, organized to promote establishment of a year of 13 months of 28 days each. Appointed expert to League of Nations' committee on calendar reform (1922–31).

Cot·ta \ˈkò-tä\. Name of a family of German publishers, proprietors of J. G. Cottasche Buchhandlung, founded (1659) in Tübingen by Johann Georg Cotta (1631–1692). His great-grandson ¶Johann Friedrich (1764–1832), Freiherr von Cot·ten·dorf \fòn-ˈkò-tən-dòrf\, took over business (1787); with Schiller founded literary journal *Die Horen* (1795); printed works of Schiller, Goethe, Herder, Wieland, Schelling, Hegel, Fichte, and others; founded *Allgemeine Zeitung* (1798); moved firm to Stuttgart (1811), opened branches in Augsburg and Munich. His son ¶Johann Georg (1796–1863), Freiherr von Cottendorf, bought the G. J. Göschen business in Leipzig (1839) and the Vogel business in Landshut (1845), thus greatly extending the scope of the Cotta house. Business sold (1889) to Adolf and Paul Kröner.

Cotta, Heinrich von. 1763–1844. German forester. Founded (1795) near Eisenach, Thuringia, a pioneering school of forestry, later (1811) removed to Tharandt, Saxony, and incorporated (1816) as a state forestry academy.

Cotte \kòt\, de. Family of French architects, including: Fresnin, architect to the king (1630). His son ¶Charles (d. 1662), also architect to the king. Charles's son ¶Robert (1656–1735) built dome of the Invalides, Hôtel de Ville at Lyon, chapel of the château at Versailles, episcopal palace at Verdun, and many châteaux; director of the Gobelins manufactory (1699); premier architect of the king (1708). Robert's son ¶Jules-Robert (1683–1767) completed the church of Saint-Roch, Paris, after his father's plans.

Cot·te·reau \kò-trō\. Family name of four brothers, known as the Chou·an \shwäⁿ\ Brothers, leaders of Royalist insurgents (Chouans) in western France (1794): Pierre (1756–1794), guillotined at Laval. ¶Jean (1757–1794), surprised and killed in flight. ¶François (1762?–1794) died of wounds. ¶René (1764–1846) survived the revolt, awarded small pension at Restoration.

Cot·tet \kò-te\, Charles. 1863–1925. French landscape painter and etcher. Noted for somber, austere views of Brittany.

Cot·ting·ton \ˈkät-iŋ-tən\, Francis. Baron Cottington. c.1579–1652. English diplomat. Ambassador to Spain (1616–17, 1629–31). Leader of pro-Spanish Roman Catholic faction in court of Charles I. Privy councillor (1628); chancellor of exchequer (1629–42); lord treasurer (1643–46). Created Baron Cottington of Hanworth in reward for concluding secret treaty with Spain (1631). Fled from victorious Puritan forces to Continent (1646).

Cot·ti·us \ˈkät-ē-əs\. 1st century A.D. Ligurian chieftain. Established kingdom in the Alps, long independent, but finally subject to Rome. The Cottian Alps derive their name from him.

Cot·tle \ˈkät-ᵊl\, Joseph. 1770–1853. English bookseller and poet. Publisher of some of first works of Southey, Coleridge, and Wordsworth (1796–98). His poems ridiculed by Byron. Author of indiscreet *Recollections* (1837) of the Lake poets.

Cot·to·len·go \ˌkòt-tō-ˈleŋ-gō\, Giuseppe Benedetto. Saint. 1786–1842. Italian religious. Ordained (1811), made a canon in Turin (1818). Founded Piccola Casa della Divina Providenza (Little House of Divine Providence, 1827) and 14 religious congregations to serve it, including Brothers of St. Vincent (1828), Sisters of St. Vincent (1830), Sisters of Thais, Hermits of the Holy Rosary. Canonized (1934).

Cot·ton \kò-tōⁿ\, Aimé-Auguste. 1869–1951. French physicist. Professor and director of laboratory of physical research, Sorbonne (from 1921). Studied anomalous dispersion and dichroism. With H. Mouton, devised simple apparatus for observing ultramicroscopic objects, and discovered double refraction of liquids in a magnetic field. With Pierre Weiss, studied the Zeeman effect, deduced the ratio of the charge of the electron to its mass.

Cot·ton \ˈkät-ᵊn\, Sir Arthur Thomas. 1803–1899. English engineer. Entered Madras engineers (1820), served in First Burmese War (1824–26). Engaged in irrigation work in India (1828–62); built dams on Coleroon, Cauvery, Godavari, and Kistna rivers; transformed drought-stricken Tanjore (now Thanjāvūr) district into richest part of Madras. Founded Indian school of hydraulic engineering.

Cotton, Charles. 1630–1687. English poet. Author of burlesques of Virgil (1664) and Lucian (1675), a humorous *Voyage to Ireland* (1670), the verse *Wonders of the Peake* (1681), a second part to the 5th (1676) edition of Walton's *Compleat Angler,* a standard translation of Montaigne's *Essays* (1685).

Cotton, George Edward Lynch. 1813–1866. English educator. Assistant master at Rugby (1836–51); headmaster of Marlborough College (1852–58). Bishop of Calcutta (1858); founded schools for British and Eurasian children. Figures as the young master in *Tom Brown's School Days.*

Cotton, John. 1585–1652. English Puritan clergyman. Known as "The Patriarch of New England." Ordained in Church of England ministry (1610); pastorate, Boston, Lincolnshire (1612–33). Emigrated to Boston, Massachusetts (1633); teacher of First Church, Boston (1633–52); became head of Congregationalism in America. Engaged in controversies with Roger Williams and Anne Hutchinson; opposed to democratic institutions; upheld authority of the magistrates over religious as well as secular affairs of citizens. Author of *The Keys of the Kingdom of Heaven* (1644), *The Way of the Churches of Christ of New England* (1645), *Spiritual Milk for Babes* (1646), *The Way of the Congregational Churches Cleared* (1648).

Cotton, Nathaniel. 1705–1788. English physician and poet. Treated mental diseases in his asylum at St. Albans. Author of *Visions in Verse* (1751) and short poems still included in anthologies, as "The Fireside" and "To a Child of Five Years Old."

Cotton, Sir Robert Bruce. 1571–1631. English antiquary. Collected ancient records scattered after dissolution of the monasteries, also books, manuscripts, and coins. Probably supervised writings of Camden's *History of Elizabeth,* esp. the account of Mary, Queen of Scots, in James I's interest. Created baronet (1611). M.P. (1604, 1624–28); turned from court to intimacy with Sir John Eliot, John Selden, Pym, and Coke. Wrote tracts against debasement of the currency and criticizing policies of Charles I, notably *The Danger in which the Kingdom now Standeth* (1628), for which he was briefly imprisoned and excluded from his library (1629–31). His son ¶Sir Thomas (1594–1662) greatly increased the Cottonian library, which was presented (1700) to the nation by his great-grandson ¶Sir John (1679–1731). In 1753 it was transferred to the British Museum.

Cotton, Sir Stapleton. 1st Viscount Com·ber·mere \ˈkəm-bər-ˌmi(ə)r\. 1773–1865. English soldier, b. Wales. Commissioned (1790); saw service in Cape Colony (1796), India (1797–1800), Ireland (1800). Major general (1805). Commanded Wellington's cavalry in Peninsular War (1808–12); lieutenant general (1812). Governor of Barbados (1817–20); commander in chief in Ireland (1822–25), and in India (1825–30). Viscount (1827); field marshal (1855).

Cot·trell \'kä-trəl; kä-'trel, kə-,\, Frederick Gardner. 1877–1948. American physical chemist, b. Oakland, Calif. Taught at U. of California (1902–1911); with U.S. Bureau of Mines (1911–20), Dept. of Agriculture (1922–30). Founded (1912) and assigned own patents to nonprofit Research Corporation to support basic research. Inventor of the Cottrell electrostatic precipitation process by which dust and suspended particles are removed from gases.

Co·tu·gno \kō-'tün-yō\, Domenico. *Lat.* Co·tun·ni·us \kə-'tən-ē-əs\. 1736–1822. Italian anatomist and physician. Professor, Naples (from 1766); known for work on the internal ear; described sciatica; eponym of liquor Cotunnii, nerve of Cotunnius, cotunnite.

Co·ty \kȯ-tē\, François. *Orig.* Francesco Giuseppe Spo·tur·no \spō-'tür-nō\. 1874–1934. French industrialist, b. Corsica. Successful manufacturer of perfumes. In order to advance conservative political views, bought *Figaro* (1922); financed royalist journal *Action française;* founded and edited (1928) *Ami du peuple.*

Coty, René-Jules-Gustave. 1882–1962. French politician. In Chamber of Deputies (1923–35, 1945–48); in Senate (1935–40, 1949–53 as vice president); second and last president of the Fourth Republic (1954–59).

Co·tys \'kōt-əs\. Name of several kings of Thrace, esp. Cotys I (d. 359 B.C.), threatened Athenian grain shipping with capture of Sestos (360 B.C.); assassinated.

Cou·ber·tin \kü-ber-ta^n\, Pierre de. Baron. 1863–1937. French educator and sportsman. Revived the Olympic games at 12-nation conference (Paris, 1894); and was president of International Olympic Committee (1894–1925); published treatises on education.

Couch, Sir Arthur Quiller-. See QUILLER-COUCH.

Cou·cy \kü-sē\, Châtelain de. 12th–13th century. French trouvère. Often identified with Guy, castellan of Coucy in 1186–1203. Some 26 songs of notable grace are attributed to him. The legend of his love for the Dame de Fayel dates from a late 13th-century verse romance by Jakemon Sakesep and lacks historical basis. The theme of the romance, a jealous husband forcing his wife to eat the heart of her lover, is common in various literatures.

Cou·der \kü-der\, Louis-Charles-Auguste. 1790–1873. French painter. Known for his historical and religious paintings, esp. *Le Serment du jeu de paume.*

Coué \kwā, *Angl* kü-'ā\, Émile. 1857–1926. French psychotherapist. Pharmacist in Troyes (1882–1910); studied hypnotism and suggestion (from 1901); developed and introduced system of psychotherapy known as Couéism based on autosuggestion, esp. the repetition of the formula "Every day, and in every way, I am becoming better and better."

Coues \'kau̇z\, Elliot. 1842–1899. American ornithologist, b. Portsmouth, N.H. Naturalist and secretary of U.S. Northern Boundary Commission (1873–76); at Columbia U. (1877–86). Author of *Key to North American Birds* (1872), *Birds of the Northwest* (1874), *Field Ornithology* (1874), *Birds of the Colorado Valley* (1878). One of committee which prepared the *Check List of North American Birds* (1886).

Cough·lin \'käg-lən\, Charles Edward. 1891–1979. American clergyman, b. Hamilton, Ont. Ordained Roman Catholic priest (1916); pastor of Shrine of the Little Flower, Royal Oak, Mich. (1926–66). Began regular radio broadcasts (1930), gaining audience of millions. Advocated (from c.1935) increasingly radical social and economic policies. Founded (1935) National Union for Social Justice; published magazine *Social Justice* (1936–42); supported Union party (1936). Later supported pro-Fascist Christian Front. Silenced by church authority (1942).

Cou·le·vain \kül-va^n\, Augustine-Favre de. *Pen name* Pierre de Coulevain. 1838–1913. French novelist. Author of *Noblesse américaine* (1898), *Eve victorieuse* (1901), *Au cœur de la vie* (1908), etc.

Cou·lomb \kü-lō^n; *Angl* 'kü-,läm, -,lōm, kü-'\, Charles-Augustin de. 1736–1806. French physicist. Served as military engineer in early life. Known for work on friction and esp. on electricity and magnetism; invented a torsion balance for measuring force of magnetic and electric attraction; formulated Coulomb's law relating electrical charge and attraction or repulsion; showed that the electrical charge is on the surface of a conductor; established inverse-square law of magnetic attraction and repulsion. The coulomb, unit of electrical charge, is named after him.

Coul·ter \'kōl-tər\, Ernest Kent. 1871?–1952. American lawyer and humanitarian, b. Columbus, Ohio. Practiced law in New York City. One of organizers of Children's Court of New York (1902–12); founder (1904) of Big Brother Movement. General manager and assistant to president, New York Society for the Prevention of Cruelty to Children (1914–36). Author of *The Children in the Shadow* (1913).

Coulter, John Merle. 1851–1928. American botanist, b. Ningpo, China, of missionary parents. Professor, U. of Chicago (1896–1925). Founder and editor, *Botanical Gazette* (1875). Author of *Manual of the Botany of the Rocky Mountain Region* (1885), *Plant Relations* (1899), *Plant Genetics* (1918), etc.

Coul·ton \'kōlt-$^{\partial}$n, 'kōl-tən\, George Gordon. 1858–1947. English historian. Taught at Cambridge, Oxford, Toronto; Rhind lecturer at Edinburgh (1931). Wrote *The Medieval Village* (1925), *Art and the Reformation* (1928), *Life in the Middle Ages* (1928–29), *Reservation and Catholicity* (1930), *St. Bernard and St. Francis* (1932), *Medieval Thought* (1939).

Coup \'küp\, William Cameron. 1837–1895. American circus manager, b. Indiana. Co-organizer and manager (1871–75) of P. T. Barnum's "Greatest Show on Earth." Devised system of rapid loading of circus wagons onto railroad cars.

Couper. See also COOPER and COWPER.

Coup·er \'kü-pər, 'ku̇p-ər\, Archibald Scott. 1831–1892. Scottish chemist. Proposed, independently of R. Kekule, tetravalency of carbon and ability of carbon atoms to bond with one another (1857); devised method of writing structural chemical formulas.

Cou·pe·rin \kü-pra^n\. Family of French musicians, identified with the Church of St. Gervais in Paris, where each served in turn as organist, including: Louis (1626?–1661); to Paris (c.1651); organist at St. Gervais (1653–61); played viol and violin for court ballets; known also as a brillant harpsichordist; composed much keyboard music, including chaconnes and passacaglias, gigues, sarabandes, etc., and several organ pieces. His brother ¶Charles (1638–1679) succeeded as organist at St. Gervais (1661–79). Charles's son ¶François, *called* le Grand (1668–1733), most renowned of the family; organist at St. Gervais (1685 or 1686–1723); an organist of royal chapel (1693–1730); de facto (from c.1701), formally appointed director of court music (1717–30). Leading French composer of his day; works included sacred and secular vocal music; chamber works; much harpsichord music, published in 4 books (1713–30). Other members included ¶Nicolas (1680–1748), nephew of Louis and Charles; organist at St. Gervais (1723–48). His son ¶Armand-Louis (1727–1789), organist at St. Gervais (1748–89). His son ¶Gervais-François (1759–1826) was last of the line at St. Gervais (1789–1826).

Cou·pe·rus \kü-'pā-rœs\, Louis Marie Anne. 1863–1923. Dutch writer. Resided in Batavia (1873–78); novels included *Eline vere* (1889), *Extaze* (1892), *De stille Kracht* (1900), *Babel* (1901), *De Berg van licht* (1906), *De Komedianten* (1917).

Cou·rant \'ku̇r-,änt\, Richard. 1888–1972. American mathematician, b. Lublinitz, Poland. Professor, Göttingen (1920–33); to U.S (1934), naturalized (1940); professor, New York U. (1934–58); founder (1953) and director, Courant Institute of Mathematical Sciences. Author of *Methoden der mathematischen Physik* (with David Hilbert, 1924), *What Is Mathematics?* (1941), etc.

Cou·ray·er \kü-rā-yā\, Pierre-François le. 1681–1776. French theologian. Received (1727) Oxford degree of D.D. for dissertation (1723) demonstrating the apostolic succession of English clergy; forced to spend rest of life in England.

Cour·bet \kür-be\, Amédée-Anatole-Prosper. 1827–1885. French naval officer. In campaign at Tonkin (1883); vice admiral, commander of Far East fleet (1884); after violation by Chinese of the treaty of Tientsin, destroyed Chinese fleet (1884).

Courbet, Jean Désiré Gustave. 1819 –1877. French painter. Leader of the new Realist school, constantly at odds with academic establishment. Associated himself with the Commune (1871). Unjustly imprisoned for six months for alleged role in the destruction of the column in Place Vendôme; fled to Switzerland when condemned (1873) to pay cost of erecting the column again; died in exile in Switzerland. Among his notable canvases were *L'Après-dîner à Ornans, La Vallée de la Loue, Enterrement à Ornans, Casseurs de pierres, Paysans de Flagey, Baigneuses, Fileuse.*

Cour·ci \kür-'sē\, John de. d. 1219? Anglo-Norman conqueror of Ulster (1177). Arrested by younger Hugh de Lacy (1204). Founded many abbeys and priories.

Cour·cil·lon \kür-sē-yō^n\, Philippe de. Marquis de Dan·geau \dä^n-zhō\. 1638–1720. French courtier. Aide-de-camp (1672) and favorite of Louis XIV; his *Mémoires* covering the years 1684–1720 (published 1854) were a valuable source of information on the period, particularly on the life of the court.

Cou·rier \kür-yā\, Paul-Louis. 1772–1825. French writer. In Army of the Rhine (1793–1809). Engaged in political pamphleteering (from 1817) in favor of liberal monarchy. Hellenist; edited pastoral by Longus, *Daphnis and Chloë* (1810).

Cour·not \kür-nō\, Antoine-Augustin. 1801–1877. French economist and mathematician. Professor, Lyons (1834); rector of academies at Grenoble (1835–38), Dijon (1848–62). Conducted researches in the calculus of probabilities; attempted to apply mathematics to solution of economic problems. Published pioneering *Recherches sur les principes mathématiques de la théorie des richesses* (1838).

Court \kür\, Antoine. 1695–1760. French clergyman. Called synod at Monoblet (1715) to begin rebuilding Reformed organization. Founded and directed seminary at Lausanne (1729–60); credited with being leading factor in restoring the Reformed Church in France. Wrote *Histoire des troubles des Cevennes ou de la guerre des Camisars* (1760). His son ¶Antoine Court de Gé·be·lin \də-gā-bla^n\ (1725–1784) was a scholar, resident in Paris (from

1763); author of *Le Monde primitif* (1773–84), *Affaires de l'Angleterre et de l'Amérique* (1776 ff.), etc.

Cour·tauld \'kor-(,)tō, -(,)tōld\, Samuel. 1793–1881. English silk manufacturer. Established business (1816); partnership (1825) with brothers. Under direction of descendants firm became Samuel Courtauld and Co. (1891) and then Courtaulds, Ltd. From 1904 a leading manufacturer of synthetic fabrics.

Courtenay. See also COURTNEY.

Courte·nay \'kō(ə)rt-nē, 'kȯ(ə)rt-\. Name of an illustrious English feudal family that probably sprang from a younger branch of a noble line of Courtenay, France, including descendants from Reinaud de Courtenay, a favorite of Henry II, among them the earls of Dev·on \'dev-ən\ or Dev·on·shire \-shər, -,shi(ə)r\ and the following:

William Courtenay (1342?–1396), prelate. Fourth son of Hugh, 2d Earl of Devon and great-grandson of Edward I. Chancellor of Oxford U. (1367); bishop of Hereford (1370), of London (1375); archbishop of Canterbury (1381–96); briefly chancellor of England (1381). Opposed John of Gaunt, Duke of Lancaster; strove to crush Lollards, prosecuted Wycliffe. ¶Richard (d. 1415), prelate. Grandson of 2d earl; chancellor of Oxford U. (1407, 1411–12), resisted unsuccessfully (1411) attempted intrusion by Archbishop Arundel, supported by Henry IV and Pope John XXIII, upon the independence of the university; bishop of Norwich (1413); treasurer to household of Henry V (1413). ¶Peter (d. 1492), prelate. Grandnephew of Richard; bishop of Exeter (1478), of Winchester (1487); was attainted by Richard III for attempted rebellion (1483); restored by Henry VII.

¶Henry (1496?–1538), Marquis of Ex·e·ter \'ek-sət-ər\ and Earl of Devonshire, courtier and diplomat. Envoy to France (1525); supported his cousin Henry VIII's divorce proceedings (1529–33); commissioner to try Anne Boleyn (1536); commissioned to suppress Pilgrimage of Grace; beheaded as aspirant to crown. His son ¶Edward (1526?–1556), his successor as earl, was released from Tower of London, where imprisoned (1538–53) because of his father's aspiration to crown.

Court·hope \'kō(ə)rt-əp, 'kȯ(ə)rt-, -,(h)ōp\, William John. 1842–1917. English critic and literary historian. Professor of poetry, Oxford (1895–1901); gave promise as poet in *Ludibria Lunae* (1869) and *The Paradise of Birds* (1870); biographer of Addison; author of *History of English Poetry* (1895–1910); editor of concluding five volumes of standard edition of Pope (1871–89) begun by Whitwell Elwin.

Court·ney \'kō(ə)rt-nē, 'kȯ(ə)rt-\, Charles Edward. 1849–1920. American athlete and coach, b. Union Springs, N.Y. Undefeated as an amateur single sculler (1868–77); professional (1877–85). Crew coach, Cornell (1885–1916).

Courtney, Leonard Henry. 1st Baron Courtney of Penwith. 1832–1918. English journalist and politician. m. Catherine, sister of Beatrice Webb. Editorial writer, *The Times* (1865–81); professor of political economy, University Coll., London (1872–75). M.P. (1876–1900); secretary to the treasury (1882–84). Zealous advocate of proportional representation; opponent of British imperialism, and esp. of Boer War. Created baron (1906).

Courtney, William Leonard. 1850–1928. English philosopher and journalist, b. India. On faculty of New College, Oxford (1876–90); literary editor, drama critic for *Daily Telegraph* (1890–1924); editor of *Murray's Magazine* (1891), *Fortnightly Review* (1894). Among his books were *The Metaphysics of John Stuart Mill* (1879), *Studies in Philosophy* (1882), *Constructive Ethics* (1886), *The Idea of Tragedy* (1900), *The Literary Man's Bible* (1907), *The Passing Hour* (1925).

Cour·tois \kür-twä\, Bernard. 1777–1838. French chemist. Employed in father's saltpetre business; discovered iodine in ashes of burnt seaweed (1811).

Courtois, Jacques. *Known as* Le Bour·gui·gnon \lə-bür-gēn-yōⁿ\. *Ital.* Il Bor·go·gno·ne \ēl-,bōr-gōn-'yō-nā\. 1621–1676. French painter. Resided chiefly at Bologna, Italy. Best known for his paintings of cavalry and war scenes. His brother ¶Guillaume (1628–1679) also painted war scenes in Rome.

Cou·sin \kü-zaⁿ\, Jean (1490–1560) and his son Jean (1522–1594). French painters, famous for their work in stained glass and tapestry design and book illustration as well. Jean the Elder's painting *Eva Prima Pandora* is in the Louvre; Jean the Younger's paintings included *Jugement dernier,* also in the Louvre.

Cousin, Victor. 1792–1867. French philosopher. Studied under Royer-Collard and Maine de Biran. Lecturer at the École Normale, U. of Paris (1815–17 and from 1828). Traveled in Germany (1817–18), interesting himself in study of German philosophy, and meeting Hegel, Jacobi, and Schelling. Created (1830) councilor of state, peer of France, director of École Normale, and (1840) minister of public instruction. Retired from public life (1851). Regarded as leader of the Eclectic school, and first to formulate eclecticism as a method. Among his notable works were *Fragments philosophiques* (1826), *Histoire de la philosophie du XVIIIᵉ siècle* (1826), *Cours d'histoire de la philosophie moderne* (1841–46), *Études sur Pascal* (1842), *Philosophie de Kant* (1842), *Du vrai, du bien et du beau* (1858), *Histoire générale de la philosophie* (1863).

Cousin Jacques. See BEFFROY DE REIGNY.

Cou·sin-Mon·tau·ban \kü-zaⁿ-mōⁿ-tō-bäⁿ\, Charles-Guillaume-Marie-Apollinaire-Antoine. Comte de Pa·li·kao \pá-lē-ká-ō\. 1796–1878. French general. Commanded expeditionary force in China and captured Peking (October 1860). Appointed to French Senate (1860) and created count (1862). Headed a 26-day ministry (Aug. 9–Sept. 4, 1870) putting Paris in state of defense during Franco-Prussian War; fled Paris in fall of Second Empire that followed the defeat at Sedan.

Cous·ins \'kəz-ᵊnz\, Samuel. 1801–1887. English mezzotint engraver. Won reputation and great popularity with transcripts of Sir Thomas Lawrence.

Cous·se·ma·ker \küs-má-ker\, Charles-Edmond-Henri de. 1805–1876. French scholar, jurist, and musicologist. A pioneering scholar of the music of the Middle Ages. Author of *Scriptorum de musica medii aevi* (1864–76), etc.

Cousser, Johann Siegmund. See KUSSER.

Cous·tou \kü-stü\. Family of French sculptors, including: Nicholas (1658–1733), whose *Descente de Croix* is at Notre Dame in Paris, *Tritons* and *France* in Versailles, *Les Nymphes* and *Jules César* and bas-relief *La Passage du Rhin* in the Louvre. At Académie Royale (from 1688); chancellor (1733). His brother ¶Guillaume (1677–1746), sculptor of famous *Chevaux de Marly* at the entrance of the Champs Elysées in Paris; *L'Océan et la Méditerranée* at Marly; *Le Rhône* at Lyon; *Mars* and *Minerve* for Hôtel des Invalides; *Hippomène* and *Daphné,* now in Tuileries; *La Mort d'Hercule, Louis XIII,* and *Marie Leczinska* in the Louvre. Director of Académie Royale (from 1735). Guillaume's son ¶Guillaume II (1716–1777), sculptor of statue *Saint Roch,* formerly in the Church of Saint Roch in Paris; bronze bas-relief *Visitation* in the Château at Versailles; the mausoleum of the dauphin, father of Louis XVI, in cathedral at Sens.

Cou·tances \kü-täⁿs\, Walter de. d. 1207. English prelate, diplomat, and administrator. Envoy to Flanders (1177), to France (1186, 1188); bishop of Lincoln (1182), archbishop of Rouen (1184); set out with Richard on Third Crusade (1189); sent back to take over government of England as chief justiciar (1191–93), driving out William Longchamp; managed Richard's release by ransom and became hostage for him in Germany (1194); accepted John on death of Richard.

Cou·tard \kü-tár\, Henri. 1876–1950. French radiologist. Known for work on therapeutic use of radium and radioactive substances, esp. in treatment of cancer.

Cou·thon \kü-tōⁿ\, Georges. 1755–1794. French revolutionist. Member of revolutionary Legislative Assembly (1791) and National Convention (1792); associate and follower of Robespierre; member of ruling Committee of Public Safety (1793–94); director of campaign against Lyons (Aug.–Oct. 1793); secured passage of Law of 22 Prairial that ushered in Reign of Terror; guillotined with Robespierre and Louis de Saint-Just on 10 Thermidor (July 28, 1794).

Coutinho, Manuel de Sousa. See Luís de SOUSA.

Coutts \'küts\, Thomas. 1735–1822. English banker. Founder of London banking firm of Coutts & Co.; banker of George III. His daughter Sophia was mother of the philanthropist Angela Georgina Burdett-Coutts (*q.v.*).

Cou·ture \kü-tuēr\, Thomas. 1815–1879. French painter. Known for portraits (*George Sand, Michelet, Bruyas,* etc.) and historical works as *Les Romains de la décadence.* Teacher of Manet and Puvis de Chavannes.

Couvreur, Adrienne Le. See Adrienne LECOUVREUR.

Couza, Alexandru Ion. See CUZA.

Couz·ens \'kəz-ᵊnz\, James Joseph. 1872–1936. American industrialist and politician, b. Chatham, Ontario. To U.S. (1890). Accumulated fortune by association with Henry Ford; general manager of Ford Motor Co. (1903–15). Mayor of Detroit (1919–22); U.S. senator from Mich. (1922–36).

Co·var·ru·bias \kō-vär-'rüb-yäs\, Miguel. 1904–1957. Mexican artist. Best known for book and magazine illustration. Caricatures collected in *The Prince of Wales and Other Famous Americans* (1925). Wrote and illustrated *Island of Bali* (1937), *Pageant of the Pacific* (1939), *Mexico South* (1946), *The Eagle, the Jaguar, and the Serpent* (1954), showing interest in anthropology.

Cov·en·try \'käv-ən-trē, 'kəv-\, Thomas. 1st Baron Coventry. 1578–1640. English judge. M.P. (1621); attorney general (1621); lord keeper of the seal (1625); moderate in presenting king's policy to Parliament; restrained Star Chamber from tyrannical actions. Created baron (1628).

Coventry, William. 1628?–1686. English political leader. Son of Baron Thomas Coventry. Sought assistance in France for Royalists during Civil War; secretary to Duke of York (1660–67); M.P. (1661–79); commissioner for navy (1662–67) and friend of Samuel Pepys; privy councilor (1665–69); forced Clarendon's resignation (1667); dismissed (1669) to make way for Buckingham and the Cabal. His nephew ¶Sir John Coventry (d. 1682), Royalist, had his nose slit to the bone by Sir Thomas Sandys and his ruffians for a jest in House of

Commons on Charles II's relations with actresses (1670); deed led to "Coventry Act" forbidding mutilations.

Cov·er·dale \ˈkəv-ər-ˌdāl\, Miles. 1488?–1569. English translator of the Bible. Studied at Cambridge; joined Augustinian friars, Cambridge (1514–26), from whose prior, Robert Barnes, he imbibed Lutheran doctrines. Left convent and preached against confession and veneration of images; lived abroad (1528–34); published translations of two theological tracts (1534). Published (1535, Zürich) first translation into English of whole Bible with Apocrypha, using probably the Vulgate, the Latin version of the Italian Hebraist Pagninus (Santes Pagnino), Luther's translation, and the Zürich version, with aid of Tyndale's Pentateuch and New Testament; employed by Thomas Cromwell to superintend printing of the Great Bible (1539), begun at Paris, completed in London, which version was presented to Henry VIII and ordered to be placed in all English churches; edited second Great Bible, called *Cranmer's Bible* (1540); left England on fall of Cromwell. Pastor and schoolmaster in Rhenish Bavaria (1543–47); returned to England (1548), preached against Anabaptists; bishop of Exeter (1551–53); deprived on accession of Mary because of his marriage. Allowed to leave England on intercession of king of Denmark; returned to England (1559); held but resigned living of St. Magnus, London (1564–66), on account of Puritan scruples about the liturgy; continued preaching to large following.

Co·vi·lhã \kü-vēl-ˈyäⁿ\ *or* **Co·vi·lhão** \-ˈyau̇ⁿ\, Pero da. c.1460–after 1526. Portuguese explorer. Sent (1487) by John II to locate land of India, while a companion, Afonso de Paiva, was sent to discover Abyssinia and Prester John; to Aden, Cannanore, Calicut, Goa, Hormuz, Red Sea, Sofala (Madagascar), Cairo; met the king's messenger at Cairo (1490 or 1491) and reported his findings (later reputedly utilized by Vasco da Gama); learned of Paiva's death; visited Mecca, Medina, and Abyssinia where he remained till his death.

Cow·ard \ˈkau̇(-ə)rd\, Sir Noël Peirce. 1899–1973. English actor, playwright, composer. On stage from childhood. Among his productions were *The Vortex* (1924), *Fallen Angels* (1925), *Hay Fever* (1925), *The Marquise* (1927), *Bitter Sweet* (1929), *Private Lives* (1930), *Cavalcade* (1931), *Words and Music* (1932), *Conversation Piece* (1934), *To-Night at Eight-Thirty* (group of one-act plays; 1936), *Blithe Spirit* (1941). His films included *In Which We Serve* (1942) and *Brief Encounter* (1946). Author of *Collected Sketches and Lyrics* (1931), *Present Indicative* (autobiography, 1937), *Future Indefinite* (1954), *Pomp and Circumstance* (novel, 1960), *Bon Voyage* (stories, 1967). Best known songs included "Mad Dogs and Englishmen," "Mad About the Boy," "Some Day I'll Find You," "I'll See You Again."

Cowden Clarke. See Charles Cowden CLARKE.

Cowdray, Viscount. See Weetman PEARSON.

Cow·ell \ˈkau̇(-ə)l\, Edward Byles. 1826–1903. English Sanskrit scholar. Professor of English history, Presidency Coll., Calcutta (1856–64); principal of Sanskrit Coll., Calcutta (1858); edited part of *Black Yajur Veda* (1858–64), edited and translated the *Kusumāñjali* (1864) and other texts; first professor of Sanskrit, Cambridge (1867–1903).

Cowell, Henry Dixon. 1897–1965. American composer, b. Menlo Park, Calif. Taught at New School for Social Research (1928–63) and Columbia U. (1949–65). Developed such innovations as tone clusters and playing directly on piano strings. Compositions included *Tides of Manaunaun* (1912), *The Lilt of Reel* (1925), *Piano Concerto* (1930), *Synchrony* (1931), *Gaelic Symphony* (1942), *Persian Set* (1957), *Ongaku* (1957), *Thirteenth (Madras) Symphony* (1959), *Concerto for Koto and Orchestra* (1964).

Cowell, John. 1554–1611. English jurist. Regius professor of civil law, Cambridge (1594–1610). His law dictionary, *The Interpreter* (1607), upholding king's absolute power, was burned by order of House of Commons.

Cow·en \ˈkau̇-ən\, Sir Frederic Hymen. 1852–1935. English composer and conductor, b. Jamaica. Conductor of Philharmonic concerts (1888–92), the Handel Festival (1903–1923), Cardiff Festival (1902, 1904, 1907, 1910). Among his compositions were cantatas, esp. *The Rose Maiden* (1870), operas, including *Pauline* (1876), *Thorgrim* (1890), and many orchestral works, piano pieces, and songs.

Cowen, Joseph. 1831–1900. English orator and journalist. Supported movements in behalf of democracy and liberty; champion of Kossuth, Mazzini, Garibaldi (1848); Liberal M.P. (1874–85); early advocate of imperial federation and home rule for Ireland; editor of *Newcastle Daily Chronicle.*

Cowen, Joshua Lionel. *Orig. surname* Co·hen \ˈkō-ən\. 1877–1965. American inventor, b. New York City. Invented batteries, electric fuses, and other devices; developed electrified model railroad trains and formed Lionel Corp. (1900) to manufacture and distribute them.

Cowl \ˈkau̇(ə)l\, Jane. *Orig.* Grace Bailey \ˈbā-lē\. 1883–1950. American actress, b. Boston. m. (1906) Adolph Klauber (*q.v.*). Starred in *Within the Law, Common Clay, Lilac Time* (written by her and Jane Murfin, 1917), *Smilin' Through* (by Cowl and Murfin as "Alan Langdon Martin," 1919), *Romeo and Juliet, Easy Virtue, The Road to Rome,* etc.

Cowles \ˈkōlz, ˈkau̇(ə)lz\, Alfred Hutchinson. 1858–1929. American engineer and metallurgist, b. Cleveland. Pioneer with his brother ¶Eugene H. (1855–1892) in electric smelting; with his brother, organized the Electric Smelting and Aluminum Co. (1885); built (1886, Lockport, N.Y.) world's first electric smelting plant.

Cowles, Henry Chandler. 1869–1939. American botanist, b. Kensington, Conn. Taught at U. of Chicago (1902–34); chairman of botany department (1925–34). Pioneer investigator of plant ecology; developed concepts of plant succession and climax community.

Cow·ley \ˈkau̇-lē\, Abraham. 1618–1667. English poet. Joined Royalists; followed queen to Paris (1645); carried on her correspondence in cipher with the king. At Restoration, received through Henry Jermyn, Lord St. Albans, a competency near Chertsey in Surrey, where he devoted himself to botany and experimental science; buried in Westminster Abbey. Author of *Davideis* (1656, unfinished), an epic on life of David; *Pindarique Odes* (1656); *The Mistress* (1647), affected amatory verse; *Verses upon Several Occasions* (1663); and graceful essays with verses interspersed.

Cowley, Hannah, *nee* Park·house \ˈpärk-ˌ(h)au̇s\. 1743–1809. English dramatist. Author of *The Belle's Stratagem* (1782), *A Bold Stroke for a Husband* (1783), *A School for Greybeards* (1786), *A Day in Turkey* (1792), *The Town Before You* (1795), etc.; under pseudonym of "Anna Matilda," contributed sentimental verse to the *World.*

Cow·per \ˈkü-pər, ˈku̇p-ər, ˈkau̇-pər\, William. 1666–1709. English surgeon and anatomist. Author of *The Anatomy of Humane Bodies* (1698), a description (1702) of Cowper's gland (discovered by him), etc.

Cowper, William. 1st Earl Cowper. 1665?–1723. English judge. Gave allegiance to Prince of Orange (1688); parliamentary orator; lord keeper of great seal (1705); conducted negotiations for union with Scotland (1706). Created earl (1706). First lord chancellor of Great Britain (1707–10, 1714–18). Presided at trial of Dr. Sacheverell (1710); presided (1716) as lord high steward at trials of Earl Winton and other peers involved in Jacobite uprising (1715). His brother ¶Spencer (1669–1728), justice of Court of Common Pleas (1727), was grandfather of the poet William Cowper.

Cowper, William. 1731–1800. English poet. Called to bar (1754); began to show symptoms of mental disorder; a commissioner of bankrupts (1759–64). Obsessed with fear of opposition to his appointment to a clerkship in House of Lords, lost his reason temporarily and attempted suicide (1763). Treated at asylum of Dr. Nathaniel Cotton (1763–65, 1773–74). Collaborated with the evangelical curate John Newton on the *Olney Hymns* (1779), composing 67 of them; occupied himself with gardening and writing verses, among them "The Progress of Error," "Truth," "Expostulation," "Hope," "Charity," "Conversation," "Retirement," published in *Poems of William Cowper of the Inner Temple, Esq.* (1782); at suggestion of a neighbor, Lady Austen, turned story of John Gilpin into a famous ballad (1782) and wrote *The Task* (1783; pub. 1785) in blank verse, an immediate success. Began his translation of Homer (1784), which he completed, with help of friends the Throckmortons, at Weston Underwood (1791), despite periods of insanity (1787, 1794); attempted to fight off increasing melancholy by translating Latin and Italian poems and editing Milton; wrote his last poem, *The Castaway,* in 1798. Led the way in freeing English verse of artificiality of Pope's classicism and opening poetry to the consideration of the commonplace. Known also as a letter writer of idiomatic purity.

Cox \ˈkäks\, David. 1783–1859. English landscape painter. By many regarded as greatest English watercolorist. Drawing master in Hereford (1814–26); published *A Treatise on Landscape Painting* (1814). Secured fame in London (1835–40); executed about a hundred works in oil (from 1839), including scenes from his favorite sketching ground, North Wales. Works included *Washing Day, Peace and War, Vale of Clwyd, The Skylark, The Hayfield.* His son ¶David (1809–1885) was also a notable watercolorist.

Cox, George William. 1827–1902. English historical writer, b. India. Ordained (1850). Author of *A Manual of Mythology* (1867), *Mythology of the Aryan Nations* (1870), *The Crusades* (1874), *The Athenian Empire* (1876), *Introduction to the Science of Comparative Mythology* (1881). Styled himself Sir George (from 1877) on claim (later disallowed) of baronetcy from distant relation.

Cox, Jacob Dolson. 1828–1900. American lawyer and army officer, b. Montreal, of American parentage. Active in organizing Ohio Republican party (1855). In Union army through Civil War, rising to major general of volunteers (1864). Governor of Ohio (1866–68); U.S. secretary of the interior (1869–70); in Congress (1877–79). Dean, Cincinnati Law School (1881–97); president, U. of Cincinnati (1885–89).

Cox, James Middleton. 1870–1957. American newspaper publisher and politician, b. Jacksonburg, Ohio. On editorial staff, Cincinnati *Enquirer;* bought Dayton *Daily News* (1898), Springfield (Ohio) *Press-Republic* (1903) and *Sun* (1928). Member, U.S. House of Representatives (1909–13). Governor of Ohio (1913–15, 1917–21). Democratic nominee for president of U.S. (1920).

Cox, Kenyon. 1856–1919. American painter and author, b. Warren, Ohio. Son of Jacob D. Cox. Works included *The Hunting Nymph, Harp Player,* portrait of Saint-Gaudens, murals in Bowdoin College, Library of Congress, Minnesota State Capitol, Iowa State Capitol. Author of *The Fine Arts* (1911), *Concerning Painting* (1917), etc. He married (1892) ¶Louise Howland King (1865–1945), known for murals and paintings of children, including *Lucile, Goldilocks, My Children.*

Cox, Palmer. 1840–1924. American illustrator and author, b. Granby, Que. In California (1863–75); New York City (from 1875). About 1880, began illustrating for *St. Nicholas Magazine.* Wrote and illustrated highly popular series of "Brownie" books for children beginning with *The Brownies, Their Book* (1887).

Cox, Sir Percy Zachariah. 1864–1937. English soldier and administrator. Consul and political agent, Muscat, Arabia (1899–1904); political resident, Persian Gulf (1909); chief political officer, Indian Expeditionary Force (1914–18); acting minister to Persia (1918–20). As British high commissioner in Mesopotamia (1920–23) supervised referendum in which Fayṣal I was elected king of new state of Iraq; assisted in establishing constitution.

Cox, Richard. 1500?–1581. English prelate and promoter of Reformation. In Edward VI's reign became active Protestant of the Reformation; as chancellor of Oxford U. (1547–52), eradicated books, mss., statues savoring of Romanism. Named first dean of Christ Church, Oxford (1547); dean of Westminster Abbey (1549). A refugee in Frankfurt (1555–58) where he led opposition to John Knox and Calvinistic doctrine. Bishop of Norwich (1559), of Ely (1559–80); resigned on intervention of Queen Elizabeth in favor of courtiers coveting episcopal lands. Translated Gospels, Acts, Romans for *Bishops' Bible;* was consulted on compilation of first and second Books of Common Prayer (1549, 1552).

Coxcie, Michiel van. See Coxie.

Coxe \'käks\, Henry Octavius. 1811–1881. English librarian and paleographer. Head librarian of Bodleian library, Oxford (1860–81); sent to Levant to examine monastic libraries (1857); devoted himself to compiling colossal catalogue of Bodleian (1859–80). Published *Rogeri de Wendover Chronica* (1841–44).

Cox·ey \'käk-sē\, Jacob Sechler. 1854–1951. American businessman and politician, b. Selinsgrove, Pa. Employed in silica sandstone quarrying (1881–1929). Led group of unemployed (Coxey's Army) to Washington, D.C. (1894) to protest unemployment and demonstrate in favor of legislation to furnish funds to communities to pay unemployed for work on public improvements. Mayor of Massillon, Ohio (1931–33); several times ran for Congress; Farmer–Labor candidate for president (1932).

Cox·ie *or* **Cox·cie** \'kȯk-sē\, Michiel van. 1499–1592. Flemish painter. Court painter to Philip II of Spain. Works in Ste. Gudule, Brussels, Santa Maria dell' Anima, Rome.

Cox·well \'käks-wəl, -ˌwel\, Henry Tracey. 1819–1900. English aeronaut. Surgeon-dentist in London; made his first balloon ascent (1844); attained (1862), with Dr. James Glaisher, record height of seven miles; managed war balloons for Germans (1870).

Coy·pel \kwȧ-pel\. Family of French painters, including: Noël (1628–1707), director of Académie de France at Rome (1672–76); director of Académie Royale, Paris (from 1695). Produced decorative paintings for the Tuileries, the Louvre, Versailles; also *The Martyrdom of St. James* in Notre Dame. His sons ¶Antoine (1661–1722), who was appointed chief painter to the king (1716), decorated the altar in the château of Meudon for the dauphin, the grand gallery of the Palais Royal for the duc d'Orléans, and the chapel at Versailles, and ¶Noël-Nicolas (1690–1734), who painted esp. mythological scenes. Antoine's son ¶Charles-Antoine (1694–1752), known esp. for genre scenes; painter to the king and director of the Académie Royale (from 1747). Works included *Persée et Andromède, Le Sacrifice d'Iphigénie, La Fuite d'Egypte,* decorations at Versailles and the Trianon.

Coy·se·vox \kwȧz-vȯks\, Antoine. 1640–1720. French sculptor. Sculptor to Louis XIV (1666); employed under Charles LeBrun in carving decorations for Versailles; carved *Chevaux de l'abreuvoir* (now in the Tuileries); best known for his portrait busts of his contemporaries, including Louis XIV, Richelieu, Mazarin, Bossuet, Condé.

Coz·ens \'kəz-ənz\, Alexander. c.1717–1786. English painter, b. Russia. Reputed, incorrectly, to be natural son of Peter the Great. To England (1746), attained wide influence as drawing master and watercolorist. His son ¶John Robert (1752–1797) was also long influential; known for drawings and watercolors of the Alps and the Roman Campagna.

Coz·zens \'kəz-ənz\, Frederick Swartwout. 1818–1869. American humorist, b. New York City. Author of *Sparrowgrass Papers* (1856), *Sayings of Dr. Bushwhacker* (1867), etc.

Cozzens, James Gould. 1903–1978. American novelist, b. Chicago. Author of *Confusion* (1924), *Michael Scarlett* (1925), *Cockpit* (1928), *The Son of Perdition* (1929), *S.S. San Pedro* (1931), *The Last Adam* (1933), *Men and Brethren* (1936), *Ask Me Tomorrow* (1940), *The Just and the Unjust* (1942), *Guard of Honor* (1948, Pulitzer prize), *By Love Possessed* (1957).

C. R. See Chakravarti Rajagopalachari.

Crabbe \'krab\, George. 1754–1832. English poet. Published first poem, *Inebriety,* in Ipswich (1775) while still a practicing surgeon; to London (1780), befriended by Edmund Burke, who helped him with publication of *The Library* (1781) and *The Village* (1783) and in entering church and obtaining livings in Dorsetshire. Published *The Parish Register* (1807), *The Borough* (1810), *Tales in Verse* (1812), *Tales of the Hall* (1819). Noted for simplicity of diction and unromanticized genre portraits.

Cra·beth \krȧ-'bet\, Dirck Pietersz (1501–1577) and his brother Wouter Pietersz (1509–c.1590). Dutch stained-glass painters. Collaborated in painting windows for churches in Belgium, France, and Italy.

Crab·tree \'krab-ˌtrē\, Lotta, *orig.* Charlotte. 1847–1924. American actress, b. New York City. Comedienne, excelling in burlesque; appeared in *Little Nell and the Marchioness, Firefly, Hearts Ease, Topsy, Mam'zelle Nitouche, Zip,* etc.

Craddock, Charles Egbert. See Mary Noailles Murfree.

Crad·ock \'krad-ək\, Sir Christopher George Francis Maurice. 1862–1914. British naval officer. Led vanguard at storming of Taku forts (1900); rear admiral (1910); responsible for keeping South Atlantic free for British trade (1914); defeated in battle with squadron under Admiral von Spee off Coronel, and went down with his flagship, the *Good Hope.* Author of *Whispers from the Fleet* (1907).

Crafts \'kraf(t)s\, James Mason. 1839–1917. American chemist, b. Boston. Professor, M.I.T. (1892–98); president (1898–1900). Co-discoverer (1877, with Charles Friedel) of Friedel-Crafts reaction, in which aluminum chloride acts as a catalytic agent in bringing into existence hundreds of new carbon compounds.

Craggs \'kragz\, James. 1657–1721. English politician. In service to Duke of Norfolk and Duke of Marlborough (1684–95). M.P. (1702–13); joint postmaster general (1715–21). Accepted at least £30,000 in stock of South Sea Company from its directors; deeply implicated in speculation and ultimate bursting of "South Sea Bubble"; died soon after examination by parliamentary committee.

Craig \'krāg\, Edward Gordon. 1872–1966. English actor, stage designer, and producer. Son of Edward William Goodwin and Ellen Terry. Acted in Henry Irving's company (1889–98). Founded *The Mask* (1908), a journal devoted to the art of the theater; founded school in Florence (1913). Among plays produced by him, with sets of his design, were *Dido and Aeneas* (1900), *The Masque of Love* (1901), Handel's *Acis and Galatea* (1902), Housman's *Bethlehem* (1902), Ibsen's *Vikings* (1903), *Much Ado About Nothing* (1903), Ibsen's *Rosmersholm* (in Florence, for Eleonora Duse, 1906), *Hamlet* (with K. Stanislavsky in Moscow, 1912). Author of *The Art of the Theatre* (1905), *Towards a New Theatre* (1913), *Ellen Terry and Her Secret Self* (1931), *Index to the Story of My Days* (1957), several volumes of wood engravings and etchings, etc.

Craig, James. 1744–1795. Scottish architect. Won competition (1767) for plan of new section of Edinburgh, later known as New Town. Designed Physicians Hall (begun 1774).

Craig, James. 1st Viscount Craig·av·on \krā-'gav-ən\. 1871–1940. Irish statesman, b. Belfast. Served in British army in South Africa (1900–02); M.P. (1906–21) as a Unionist. Involved (with Sir Edward Carson) in political and paramilitary opposition to inclusion of Ulster in question of home rule for Ireland. Member of House of Commons of Northern Ireland from its organization (1921) and first prime minister of Northern Ireland (1921–40). Signed tripartite agreement with Great Britain and Irish Free State preserving Irish frontier (1925). Created viscount (1927).

Craig, Sir James Henry. 1748–1812. English soldier, b. Gibraltar. Wounded at Bunker Hill; took part in Burgoyne's campaign, esp. in capturing Ticonderoga (1777); fought in North Carolina (1781). Took part in capture of Cape of Good Hope (1795); served as governor there (1795–97). In India (1797–1802), Italy and Sicily (1805–06). Governor general of Canada (1807–11); general (1812).

Craig, John. 1512?–1600. Scottish reformer. Became a Dominican friar, but his Protestant tenets strengthened on reading Calvin's *Institutes;* sentenced to death by Inquisition in Rome but escaped (1559). Associated with John Knox; minister of Holyrood (1561). Published banns of marriage between Mary and Bothwell. Helped draw up National Covenant (1580); prepared the "King's Confession" (1581).

Craig, Malin. 1875–1945. American army officer, b. Saint Joseph, Mo. Brigadier general (1921); major general (1924); general (1935). Served in Santiago campaign (1898), Boxer Rebellion (1900), and in France (1917–19). Chief of staff, U.S. army (1935–39).

Craig, Sir Thomas. 1538?–1608. Scottish jurist. Justice depute of Scotland; sheriff depute of Edinburgh (1573); commissioner for union with England (1604). Author of an epithalamium on marriage of Mary, Queen of Scots, and Darnley (1565), and other Latin poems, and of *Ius Feudale* (1603) on feudal law of England and Scotland.

Craig, William James. 1843–1906. British scholar, b. Ireland. Professor of English, Aberystwyth (1876–79). Edited *Oxford Shakespeare* (1894), *Little Quarto Shakespeare* (40 vols., 1901–04), the *Arden Shakespeare* (40 vols.).

Craigavon, Viscount. See James Craig (1871–1940).

Crai·gie \'krā-gē\, Pearl Mary Teresa, *nee* Richards. *Pseudonym* John Oliver Hobbes \'häbz\. 1867–1906. English novelist and dramatist, b. Boston. m. (1887) R. W. Craigie (divorced, 1895). Author of novels, including *Some Emotions and a Moral* (1891), *The Sinner's Comedy* (1892), *A Bundle of Life* (1894), *The Herb Moon* (1896), and of plays, including *The Ambassador* (1898), *The Bishop's Move* (1902).

Craigie, Sir William Alexander. 1867–1957. British philologist and lexicographer, b. Scotland. On faculty of St. Andrews (1893–97), Oxford U. (from 1905). On editorial staff of *Oxford English Dictionary* (from 1897), and joint editor (1901–33). Author of *Icelandic Sagas* (1913), *The Pronunciation of English* (1917), *Easy Readings in Anglo-Saxon* (1923), *The Poetry of Iceland* (1925), etc. Editor of *A Dictionary of the Older Scottish Tongue* (1931 ff.), *A Historical Dictionary of American English* (1936–43).

Craik \'kräk\, Dinah Maria, *nee* Mu·lock \'myü-ˌläk\. 1826–1887. English novelist. m. (1864) G.L. Craik. Author of *John Halifax, Gentleman* (1857), *A Life for a Life* (1859), and children's stories, poems, and essays.

Craik, George Lillie. 1798–1866. Scottish man of letters. Studied divinity at St. Andrews; went to London (1824) to pursue literary work. Professor of English literature and history, Belfast (1849–66). Author of *Spenser and His Poetry* (1845), *The History of English Literature and the English Language* (1861).

Craik, Sir Henry. 1846–1927. Scottish educator and politician. Secretary of Scotch Education Department of the Privy Council (1885–1904). Member of Parliament (1906–27). Among his books were *Life of Swift* (1882), *The State and Education* (1883), *A Century of Scottish History* (1901), *Life of Edward, First Earl of Clarendon* (1911).

Craik, James. 1730–1814. American physician, b. near Dumfries, Scotland. Came to Virginia and was commissioned surgeon in the army (1754); chief physician and surgeon of the army (1781–83); physician general (1798–1800). Attended Washington in his last illness (1799).

Cram \'kram\, Ralph Adams. 1863–1942. American architect, b. Hampton Falls, N.H. In practice in Boston with C.F. Wentworth and esp. with Bertram G. Goodhue (from 1890); firm became Cram, Goodhue & Ferguson (1899). Ardent promoter of Gothic Revival. Designed rebuilding of U.S. Military Academy (1903); Rice Institute, Houston (1910); buildings for Wheaton, Williams, and other colleges; new design for Cathedral of St. John the Divine, N.Y.C. (1912); many churches. Supervising architect for Princeton U. (1909–31); professor of architecture, M.I.T. (1914–21). Author of *Church Building* (1901), *The Gothic Quest* (1907), *The Ministry of Art* (1914), *The Great Thousand Years* (1918), *My Life in Architecture* (1936).

Cra·mer \'kräm-ər\, Johann Andreas. 1723–1788. German Protestant theologian and poet. Professor (from 1774) and chancellor, U. of Kiel. Author of odes and hymns, including "Er ist gekommen her," "Der Herr ist Gott und keiner mehr," etc. His son ¶Karl Friedrich (1752–1807), professor of Greek and Oriental languages at Kiel (1775–94); founded publishing house in Paris (1795); wrote two notable studies, on Klopstock and on musical history.

Cramer \'krā-mər, *Ger* 'kräm-ər\, Johann Baptist. 1771–1858. English pianist and composer, b. Germany. To London (1772). Studied under Clementi; foremost professional performer of his time, esteemed by Beethoven; composer of classic *Études.* Founded (1824) Cramer & Co., London music publishers. His brother ¶Franz (1772–1848), violinist, was one of first professors of Royal Academy of Music.

Cramp \'kramp\, William. 1807–1879. American shipbuilder, b. Philadelphia. Established the William Cramp Shipbuilding Co. (1830); president (1830-79). His son ¶Charles Henry (1828–1913), a naval architect of distinction, was president of the company (1879–1903), and developed it into the largest and best known in U.S. Among vessels build by the firm were *New Ironsides, Maine, New York* for the U.S. navy and commercial steamers *St. Louis* and *St. Paul.*

Cram·pel \krä^{n}-pel\, Paul. 1864–1891. French explorer. Explored northern part of French Congo (1888–89); slain on expedition to Lake Chad to unite French Sudan with French Congo.

Cramp·ton \'kram(p)-tən\, Thomas Russell. 1816–1888. English engineer. Designed and patented Crampton locomotive (1843); laid telegraphic cable from Dover to Calais (1851); built Berlin waterworks (1855); constructed Smyrna railway, and Varna railway (in Bulgaria).

Cra·nach \'krän-ˌäk̲\, Lucas, *called* the Elder. *Orig. surname* Mül·ler \'mᵫl-ər\. 1472–1553. German painter, engraver, and woodcut designer. Court painter (1505–50) to Frederick the Wise of Saxony, and his brother in Wittenberg. Court painter in Weimar (1552–53). His works included altarpieces; many portraits of his friends Luther and Melanchthon; a number of biblical paintings; woodcuts; book illustrations; designs for coins, tapestries, dresses, and windows. Called "pictor celerrimus" for the speed with which he worked. One of the most influential of German artists and the originator of Protestant religious painting. His son ¶Lucas Cranach, *called* the Younger (1515–1586) was also a portrait and historical painter.

Cranborne, Viscount. See Cecil family.

Cranbrook, Earl of. See Gathorne Gathorne-Hardy.

Cran·dall \'kran-d^{ə}l\, Prudence. 1803–1890. American schoolteacher, b. Hopkinton, R.I. Opened girls' school (1831) in Canterbury, Conn.; aroused controversy by admitting a Negro pupil (1833); announced plan to open new school for Negro girls and was promptly prosecuted in famous case which intensified the conflict between abolitionists and southern sympathizers in the North.

Crane \'krān\, Charles Richard. 1858–1939. American industrialist and diplomat, b. Chicago. With Crane Co., manufacturers of plumbing supplies; president (1912–14). Member of special diplomatic mission under Elihu Root to Russia (1917). U.S. minister to China (1920–21). Frequent adviser to Pres. Woodrow Wilson. Conducted many private and public philanthropies, including help in developing Marine Biological Laboratory, Woods Hole, Mass. His son ¶Richard (1882–1938), businessman, b. Denver; in employ of Crane Co. (from 1904); first U.S. minister to Czechoslovakia (1919–21).

Crane, Hart, *in full* Harold Hart. 1899–1932. American poet, b. Garrettsville, Ohio. Author of *White Buildings* (1926), *The Bridge* (1930).

Crane, Stephen. 1871–1900. American writer, b. Newark, N.J. First novel, *Maggie: A Girl of the Streets* (1893), a milestone in the development of literary realism; second *The Red Badge of Courage* (1895), a story of the common man under fire in battle, written in an impressionistic style; also published many short stories, notably "The Open Boat" and "The Monster," and *War Is Kind* (1899), a volume of verse. War correspondent in Cuba and Greece (1896–98).

Crane, Walter. 1845–1915. English painter and illustrator. As wood engraver, studied works of Pre-Raphaelites; influenced by Botticelli and by Japanese prints; leader with William Morris in Arts and Crafts movement in British decorative art. Best known for imaginative and humorous illustrations in antique style, esp. of juvenile books; his *Goose Girl,* from illustrations of *Stories from Grimm* (1882), was woven in tapestry by Morris; his finest illustration, Spencer's *Faerie Queene* (1894–96). Founded Arts and Crafts Exhibition Society (1888). Art director of Manchester School of Art (1893–96) and Reading College (1896–98), principal of Royal College of Art (1898–99). Associated with Morris in Socialist movement.

Cran·field \'kran-ˌfēld\, Lionel. 1st Earl of Mid·dle·sex \'mid-^{ə}l-ˌseks\. 1575–1645. English financier. Through Henry Howard, Earl of Northampton, became surveyor general of customs (1613); through George Villiers, Duke of Buckingham, advanced to privy councilor (1620); lord treasurer (1621); created earl (1622); attempted to regulate James I's expenditures and opposed Spanish war on fiscal grounds; impeached and convicted of maladministration by Parliament (1624); imprisoned; pardoned by Charles I (1626).

Cran·ko \'kraŋ-kō\, John. 1927–1973. South African choreographer. Choreographer with Sadler's Wells and Royal ballets, England (1946–61); ballet director, Stuttgart Ballet (1961–68); chief choreographer, Bavarian State Opera, Munich (1968–71). Works included *Pineapple Poll, Lady and the Fool, Prince of The Pagodas, Romeo and Juliet, Jeu de Cartes, Eugene Onegin, Quatre Images, Présence, Ebony Concerto, Traces.*

Cran·mer \'kran-mər\, Thomas. 1489–1556. English prelate and reformer. Fellow of Jesus College, Cambridge (from c.1510); took orders (1523). Gained favor of Henry VIII by suggesting that establishment of Catherine of Aragon's prior marriage to Prince Arthur would nullify her marriage to Henry; dispatched to Rome and to Charles V to argue the case (1530–32). At Nürnberg found Osiander in agreement on the new religious order, and was married to Osiander's niece. Named archbishop of Canterbury (1533); declared Henry's marriage with Catherine null and void; pronounced marriage of Henry and Anne Boleyn; crowned Anne queen; stood godfather to future Queen Elizabeth. Supported the king's claim to supremacy over Church of England, maintaining divine right of kings as against divine right of popes, the joint sovereignty of church and state. Annulled Henry's marriage with Anne Boleyn (1536); was instrument for divorce of Anne of Cleves (1540); informed king of prenuptial frailty of Catherine Howard (1541) and sought to persuade her to confess. Made ineffectual attempt to oppose the Six Articles for abolishing diversity of opinions (1539); took part in persecution of Frith, Lambert, and others. Promoted translation of the Bible into the vernacular;

procured order requiring a copy in each church; repudiated doctrine of transubstantiation (1538); composed litany for reformed Church of England (1545). One of regents during absence of Henry VIII (1541) and on death of Henry (1547); prepared church formularies; edited *Homilies* (1547), four of his own writing; compiled (1548) Edward VI's first Prayer Book (sanctioned 1549) and its revision (1552), the latter of which converted the Mass into the Communion. Sought through Melanchthon to promote union of reformed churches; chief composer of 42 articles of religion (1553; later reduced to 39; hence called the Thirty-nine Articles); gave to Prayer Book its stately and rhythmical language. Perjured himself by signing Edward VI's devise of the crown to Lady Jane Grey, the queen of nine days (1553). On accession of Queen Mary, condemned for treason, convicted by papal commission (1555), excommunicated, degraded from archbishopric (1556), condemned for heresy by Cardinal Pole; signed seven recantations, admitting papal supremacy, but at the last renounced all of them. Burned at the stake, holding his offending right hand in fire to be burned first.

Cran·tor \'kran-ˌtȯr\. 4th century B.C. Greek philosopher. Known as the first commentator on Plato; wrote *On Grief.*

Crap·sey \'krap-sē\, Algernon Sidney. 1847–1927. American Episcopal clergyman, b. Fairmount, Ohio. Rector, St. Andrew's, Rochester, N.Y. (1879–1906). Tried and convicted of heresy (1906); deposed from the ministry. Author of *The Greater Love* (1902, a novel); *Religion and Politics* (1905); *The Last of the Heretics* (1924); etc. His daughter ¶Adelaide (1878–1914) wrote *Verses,* a highly popular volume of poems (publ. 1915), many being in an original verse form called the cinquain.

Crash·aw \'krash-ˌȯ\, Richard. 1613?–1649. English poet. Expelled from fellowship at Peterhouse, Cambridge, for refusal to accept Solemn League and Covenant (1643); embraced Roman Catholicism; while living in France (1644–48); through Queen Henrietta Maria became subcanon at Loreto (1649), where he died soon after. Author of *Epigrammatum Sacrorum Liber* (1634), *Steps to the Temple* (1646), religious poems abounding in conceits in the manner of Herbert and in lyric felicities, *The Delights of the Muses* (1646), secular poems, *Carmen Deo Nostro* (1652).

Cras·sus \'kras-əs\, Lucius Licinius. 140–91 B.C. Roman orator and politician. Consul (95 B.C.); censor (92). Considered one of greatest Roman orators before Cicero; introduced by Cicero as a speaker in his *De oratore.*

Crassus, Marcus Licinius. *Surnamed* Di·ves \'dī-(ˌ)vēz\, *i.e.* the Rich. 115?–53 B.C. Roman financier and politician. Sided with Sulla against Marius in civil war (88–82 B.C.) and laid basis of vast fortune by speculation in confiscated property during the period of Sulla's proscriptions in Rome. Praetor (c.73), crushed revolt led by Spartacus; consul (with Pompey, 70); censor (65). Joined Pompey and Caesar in organizing First Triumvirate, being its financial backer (60); again consul with Pompey (55). Governor of Syria (54); undertook campaign against the Parthians; disastrously defeated at Carrhae (Haran), captured, and executed (53).

Crassus Di·ves Mu·ci·a·nus \-'dī-(ˌ)vēz-ˌm(y)ü-s(h)ē-'ā-nəs\, Publius Licinius. c.180–130 B.C. Roman politician. Brother of Publius Mucius Scaevola, father-in-law of Gaius Gracchus. Supported reforms of Tiberius Gracchus; opposed Scipio Aemilianus. On Gracchan land commission (133 B.C.); pontifex maximus (133); consul (131). Killed in battle with Aristonicus of Pergamum in Asia Minor.

Cra·ter \'krāt-ər\, Joseph Force. 1889–?1937. American jurist, b. Easton, Pa. In legal practice and Democratic politics, N.Y.C. (from 1913); on N.Y. supreme court (1930). Disappeared (Aug. 6, 1930); case received wide publicity owing to hints of political corruption. No trace ever found; declared legally dead (July 1937).

Crat·er·us \'krat-ər-əs\. 370?–321 B.C. Macedonian general in army of Alexander the Great. Played major role in defeat of Porus at Hydaspes (326 B.C.). Associated with Antipater in ruling Macedonia after Alexander's death (323); defeated and killed by Eumenes in Cappadocia.

Cra·tes \'krāt-(ˌ)ēz\. fl. 470–450 B.C. Athenian comedist. Regarded as founder of Greek comedy proper; few fragments of his works extant.

Crates of Athens. 3rd century B.C. Greek Academic philosopher. Succeeded Polemo as scholarch (head of Old Academy, c.270 B.C.).

Crates of Mal·lus \'mal-əs\. 2d century B.C. Greek Stoic philosopher and scholar. Head of library at Pergamum; author of commentary on Homer. Ambassador of Eumenes II to Rome (c.170 B.C.); lectured in Rome and inspired scholarly study among his pupils.

Crates of Tarsus. 2d century B.C. Greek Academic philosopher. Scholarch (head of Old Academy, 131 or 130–127 or 126 B.C.).

Crates of Thebes \'thēbz\. 4th century B.C. Greek cynic philosopher. Disciple of Diogenes; gave up his fortune to devote himself to attaining virtue and self-control. Zeno of Citium was one of his pupils.

Cra·te·uas \krā-'tē-wəs\ *or* **Cra·te·vas** \-vəs\. 1st century B.C. Greek physician. Physician to Mithridates IV of Pontus. Author of multivolume work on pharmacology containing earliest known botanical illustrations.

Cra·ti·nus \krə-'tī-nəs\. d. c.420 B.C. Greek playwright. Author of 21 comedies, and winner of the prize for comedy 9 times, triumphing once (*Putine,* i.e. *The Bottle,* 423 B.C.) over Aristophanes; only fragments of his works extant.

Cra·tip·pus \krə-'tip-əs\. 4th century B.C. Greek historian. Continued the history of Thucydides down to battle of Cnidus (394 B.C.); only fragments of his work extant.

Cratippus of Myt·i·le·ne \ˌmit-ᵊl-'ē-nē\. 1st century B.C. Greek Peripatetic philosopher in Athens. Tutor of Cicero's son; praised by Cicero in his *De Officiis.* Succeeded Andronicus of Rhodes as scholarch (44 B.C.).

Crat·y·lus \'krat-ə-ləs\. 5th–4th century B.C. Greek philosopher. Disciple of Heraclitus; introduced by Plato as chief speaker in one of his dialogues (*Cratylus*).

Crau·furd \'krȯ-fərd\, Quintin. 1743–1819. Scottish author. Served East India Company (till 1780); gathered a library at Paris; friend of Marie-Antoinette and royal family; helped arrange their flight to Varennes. Author of history of the Bastille (1798) and researches on Hindu civilization (1817).

Crauk \krōk\, Gustave-Adolphe-Désiré. 1827–1905. French sculptor. Among his works were monuments to Coligny and Cardinal Lavigerie, many portrait busts, including Niel and MacMahon, *Victory, Twilight,* and *Combat du Centaure.*

Cra·ven \'krā-vən\, Frank, *in full* John Francis. 1875?–1945. American actor and playwright, b. Boston. Appeared on stage in *Bought and Paid For* (1911), *Our Town* (1938); wrote and appeared in *Two Many Cooks* (1914), *This Way Out* (1917), *The First Year* (1920), *Riddle Me This* (1932), etc.; also in motion pictures.

Craven, Pauline. 1808–1891. French author. Daughter of Comte Auguste-Marie de la Ferronays, diplomat; m. (1834) Augustus Craven. Author of *Récit d'une sœur* (1866), a record of the slow passing of her family; *Fleurange* (1869); etc.

Craven, William. Earl of Craven. 1606–1697. English soldier and Royalist. Son of Sir William Craven (1548?–1618), lord mayor of London (1610). Served under princes of Orange (from 1623), under Gustav Adolphus (1631); aided Frederick, exiled king of Bohemia, and his son Charles Louis in attempt to recover the Palatinate (1632, 1637), and afterwards devoted himself to service of Elizabeth of Bohemia; supplied Charles I and II with financial aid; created earl (1665).

Crawford, Earls of. See LINDSAY family.

Craw·ford \'krȯ-fərd\, Francis Marion. 1854–1909. American novelist, b. Bagni di Lucca, Italy. Son of Thomas Crawford. After education in U.S. and Europe, traveled in India (1879–80); returned to New York and wrote his first novel, *Mr. Isaacs* (1882). Settled in Sorrento, Italy (1885) and spent rest of life in writing. Other works: *Dr. Claudius* (1883), *Zoroaster* (1885), *A Cigarette Maker's Romance* (1890), *Don Orsino* (1892), *The Ralstons* (1895), *Via Crucis* (1898), *In the Palace of the King* (1900), *Marietta* (1901), *The Heart of Rome* (1903), *Stradella* (1909), *Wandering Ghosts* (1911), etc.

Crawford, Isabella Valancy. 1850–1887. Canadian poet, b. Dublin, Ireland. To Ontario (1858); journalist in Toronto. Author of *Old Spookses Pass, Malcolm's Katie, and Other Poems* (1884); noted for descriptions of Canadian landscape.

Crawford, Joan. *Orig.* Lucille Le·sueur \lə-'su̇(-ə)r\. 1908–1973. American actress, b. San Antonio, Tex. Portrayed flappers in silent films as *Our Dancing Daughters* (1928); starred in melodramas including *The Women* (1939), *Susan and God* (1940), *Strange Cargo* (1940), *Mildred Pierce* (1945, Academy Award), *Humoresque* (1947), *Sudden Fear* (1952), *Whatever Happened to Baby Jane?* (1962).

Crawford, Thomas. 1814–1857. American sculptor, b. New York City. Studied in Rome, with Thorvaldsen (1835); resident in Rome most of his life. Works in neoclassical style included *Beethoven, Orpheus, Dancing Girl, Dying Indian Maiden, Flora, Peri, Babes in the Woods.* The *Washington* statue in Richmond, Va., and some of the sculptural decorations for the Capitol at Washington, D.C. (notably the Senate pediment, the bronze entry doors, and the armed figure *Freedom* on its dome) were executed from his designs.

Crawford, William Harris. 1772–1834. American lawyer, b. Amherst Co., Va. U.S. senator from Georgia (1807–13); minister to France (1813–15); secretary of war (1815–16); secretary of the treasury (1816–25). One of four candidates for president of the U.S. (1824) in election decided by the House of Representatives.

Craw·furd \'krȯ-fərd\, John. 1783–1868. Scottish Orientalist. East Indian army doctor; envoy to Siam; administrator of Singapore (1823). Author of *History of the Indian Archipelago* (1820) and a Malay grammar and dictionary (1852).

Cra·yer \'krä-yər \, Caspar *or* Gaspard de. 1584–1669. Flemish painter. Known as a historical and portrait painter of Brussels and Ghent.

Crayon, Geoffrey. See Washington IRVING.

Cra·zy Horse \ˈkrā-zē-ˌhȯ(ə)rs\. *Indian name* Ta-sunko-witko *or* Tashunca-Uitco. 1842?–1877. American Indian chief, of the Oglala tribe of the Sioux. Leader in Fetterman Massacre and Wagon-Box Fight in Red Cloud's War (1866–68); principal leader of Sioux uprising (1876–77); defeated Gen. George Crook at Rosebud Creek (June 17, 1876); leader in battle of Little Big Horn, in which Custer was killed (June 25); surrendered (May 1877); killed while resisting imprisonment (Sept. 5, 1877).

Crea·sy \ˈkrē-sē\, Sir Edward Shepherd. 1812–1878. English historian. Barrister; professor, London U. (1840); chief justice of Ceylon (1860–73). Known esp. for his *Fifteen Decisive Battles of the World* (1851).

Crébillon. See Prosper JOLYOT.

Cre·dé \krə-ˈdā\, Karl Siegmund Franz. 1819–1892. German gynecologist. Professor of obstetrics in Leipzig (1856). Developed (1854) the Credé method of expression of the placenta after birth of the child and (1881) use of silver nitrate drops for prevention of ophthalmia neonatorum.

Cre·di \ˈkrā-dē\, Lorenzo di. 1459–1537. Florentine painter. Pupil (with Leonardo da Vinci and Perugino) of Andrea del Verrocchio. His paintings included *Nativity, Adoration of the Shepherds, Annunciation, Venus,* many studies of the Madonna and Child.

Creech \ˈkrēch\, Thomas. 1659–1700. English classical scholar. Translator of Lucretius into rhymed heroic couplets (1682), of Horace (1684), Theocritus (1684), and others.

Creech, William. 1745–1815. Scottish publisher. On withdrawal of his partner Kincaid (1773) became foremost publisher in Scotland; brought out first Edinburgh editions of Burns, Blair, Beattie, Mackenzie, Dugald Stewart; lord provost of Edinburgh (1811–13).

Creel \ˈkrē(ə)l\, George Edward. 1876–1953. American journalist, b. Lafayette Co., Mo. Founder and editor, Kansas City *Independent* (1899–1909); writer for Denver *Post* (1909–10); editor of *Rocky Mountain News* (1911–13). Chairman, U.S. Committee on Public Information (1917–19); chairman, national advisory board, Works Progress Administration (1935). Author of *Quatrains of Christ* (1907), *Wilson and the Issues* (1916), *How We Advertised America* (1920), *The People Next Door* (1926), *Tom Paine—Liberty Bell* (1931), *War Criminals and Punishment* (1944).

Cree·vey \ˈkrē-vē\, Thomas. 1768–1838. English diarist. Whig M.P. (1802); secretary to board of control (1806); treasurer of ordnance (1830); treasurer of Greenwich Hospital. Known for *Creevey Papers* (pub. 1903), consisting of journals and correspondence covering 36 years and depicting political and social life of late Georgian era.

Creigh·ton \ˈkrāt-ᵊn\, Edward (1820–1874) and his brother John Andrew (1831–1907). American businessmen, b. Licking Co., Ohio. Associated with Hiram Sibley in building Pacific telegraph (1861); benefactors of Creighton University (chartered 1879).

Creighton, James Edwin. 1861–1924. American educator, b. Pictou, Nova Scotia. Professor, Cornell (1895–1924). Editor in chief, *Philosophical Review* (1902–24); American editor of *Kantstudien* (1896–1924). First president of American Philosophical Association (1902–03). Leading exponent in America of idealistic or speculative philosophy.

Creigh·ton \ˈkrīt-ᵊn\, Mandell. 1843–1901. English prelate and historian. Professor of ecclesiastical history, Cambridge (1884); first editor of *English Historical Review* (1886–91). Bishop of Peterborough (1891), of London (1897); strove to restore orthodox ritual over protests of extremists on both sides. Author of *Age of Elizabeth* (1876), *History of the Papacy* (1882–97), *Cardinal Wolsey* (1888).

Crell *or* **Krell** \ˈkrel\, Nikolaus. 1551?–1601. Saxon statesman. Councilor of Christian, Elector of Saxony (from 1586); chancellor of Saxony (1589). Endeavored to supplant Lutheranism in Saxony with his own Crypto-Calvinist faith. On death of Christian (1591) deprived of offices and imprisoned; condemned to death and executed.

Crel·le \ˈkrel-ə\, August Leopold. 1780–1855. German engineer. Constructed most of Prussian highroads built 1816–26; planned Berlin–Potsdam railway; publisher of German translations of Legendre's geometry (1822) and Lagrange's mathematical work (1823–24); founder (1826) of the mathematical periodical known today as *Crelle's Journal.*

Cré·ma·zie \krā-mȧ-zē\, Octave, *in full* Joseph Octave. 1827–1879. French-Canadian poet, b. Quebec. Regarded as father of French-Canadian poetry. Founded (1861) monthly *Les Soirées Canadiennes;* best known poem *Chant du vieux soldat canadien* (1855) won for him title as official poet of Canada; resident in France (from 1863).

Cre·mer \ˈkrā-mər\, Jacobus Jan. 1827–1880. Dutch novelist. Author of *De Lelie van's Gravenhage* (1851), *Daniël Sils* (1856), *Doktor Helmond en zijn vrouw* (1870), *Hanna de freule* (1873), *Tooneelspelers* (1875), and short stories.

Cre·mer \ˈkrē-mər\, Sir William Randal. 1838–1908. English pacifist. One of founders of Amalgamated Society of Carpenters and Joiners (1860). Resigned as secretary of British section of First International (1866). As secretary of Workmen's Peace Association (1871–1908), advocated international arbitration in America and Europe; Radical M.P. (1885–95, 1900–08). Edited peace journal *Arbitrator* (from 1889). Awarded Nobel peace prize for 1903.

Cré·mieux \krām-yœ\, Adolphe, *in full* Isaac-Moïsé-Adolphe. 1796–1880. French lawyer and politician. Member of Chamber of Deputies (1842–48, 1849–51, 1869–70, 1871–75); minister of justice (1848, 1870–71); appointed senator for life (1875). A leader of radical left and of the French Jewish community.

Cre·mo·na \krā-ˈmō-nä\, Luigi, *in full* Antonio Luigi Gaudenzio Giuseppe. 1830–1903. Italian mathematician. Professor, Bologna (1860), Milan (1866), and Rome (1873), where he reorganized and directed the engineering college. Senator (1879); minister of education (1898). Known esp. for work in projective geometry and graphical statics.

Cré·qui \krā-kē\, François de Bonne \bȯn\ de. Marquis. *Known as* Maréchal de Créqui. 1624?–1687. French soldier. Member of family long distinguished in military affairs; distinguished himself in fighting in Flanders and Catalonia; marshal of France (1668); refused to serve under Turenne and was disgraced; defeated forces of the Elector of Brandenburg (1679) and had a part in preparing the Peace of Nijmegen.

Cre·rar \ˈkrē-ˌrär\, Henry Duncan Graham. 1888–1965. Canadian soldier, b. Hamilton, Ont. Served in World War I (1914–18); chief of Canadian general staff (1940–41); commander of Canadian Corps (1943), First Army comprising all Canadian forces in Europe (1944).

Crerar, John. 1827–1889. American businessman and philanthropist, b. New York City. Associated with G.M. Pullman in business; endowed John Crerar Library in Chicago.

Cres·cas \ˈkres-käs\, Hasdai ben Abraham. 1340–1410. Spanish philosopher and Talmudist. A member of Aragonese court of John I, became crown rabbi of Aragon. Critic of Christian theology and esp. of application of Aristotelian rationalism to Jewish thought as by Maimonides. Principal work *Or Adonai* ("Light of the Lord").

Cre·scen·ti·us \krə-ˈsen-sh(ē-)əs\. Name of a family of leaders of Roman aristocracy in 10th century, including: Crescentius I, *known also as* the Elder *or* Crescentius de Theodora (d. 984 A.D.); overthrew Pope Benedict VI (974) and installed antipope Boniface VII; later became monk. ¶Crescentius II, *surnamed* No·men·ta·nus \ˌnō-mən-ˈtā-nəs\, *known as* the Younger (d. 998 A.D.); identified variously with John, son of Crescentius I, or with a younger brother of John; assumed title of patrician and dominated Rome and the papacy; may have been involved in murder of John XIV (984); opposed Emperor Otto III and Pope Gregory V and raised John XVI as antipope; defeated by Otto III at castle of Sant' Angelo (April 998) and executed. His son ¶John II Crescentius (d. 1012), Duke of Spoleto, ruled Rome as patrician (1002–12).

Cre·scen·zi \krā-ˈshent-sē\, Pietro de. *Lat.* Petrus de Cre·scen·ti·is \kri-ˈsen-shē-(ˌ)ēs\. 1230?–?1310. Italian writer on agriculture. Author of *Opus ruralium commodorum.*

Cre·scim·be·ni \krā-shēm-ˈben-ē\, Giovanni Mario. 1663–1728. Italian poet and literary historian. One of founders and first secretary (1690–1728) of Academy of Arcadians. His works included *Rime* (1695), *Storia della volgar poesia* (1698), and *Commentario intorno alla volgar poesia* (5 vols., 1702–11).

Cres·i·las \ˈkres-ə-ləs\. 5th century B.C. Greek sculptor. Known for statue of Pericles which inspired a genre of idealized portraiture.

Cres·pi \ˈkrās-pē\, Giovanni Battista. *Known as* il Ce·ra·gno \ēl-chā-ˈrän-yō\. 1575?–1632. Italian painter. Under patronage of Cardinal Federigo Borromeo became leading painter of religious subjects in Milan; director (from 1620) of Milanese academy; supervisor of decorations for cathedral (1629). His nephew ¶Daniele Crespi (c.1595–1630) also a painter of religious subjects, adopted his uncle's starkly realistic style.

Crespi, Giuseppe Maria. *Known as* lo Spa·gno·lo \lō-spän-ˈyō-lō\. 1665–1747. Italian painter. Known for genre and religious paintings and portraits of striking realism and humanity.

Crespi, Juan. 1721–1782. Spanish missionary and explorer. Companion of Fr. Junípero Serra. With Portolá, a discoverer of San Francisco Bay; explored route around the bay (1772).

Cres·po \ˈkrās-pō\, Joaquín. 1845–1898. Venezuelan soldier and political leader. Supporter of Guzmán Blanco, serving as figurehead president under Guzmán Blanco's dominance (1884–86). Led revolution deposing President Andueza Palacio (1892) and set up dictatorship (1892–94); elected president (1894–98).

Cres·sent \kres-äⁿ\, Charles. 1685–1768. French cabinetmaker. Named cabinetmaker to the Regent, the duc d'Orleans (1715). Innovative work in wood and metal made him leading exponent of transitional Regence style; known esp. for marquetry and ormolu work.

Cress·well \ˈkrez-wəl, ˈkres-, -ˌwel\, Sir Cresswell. 1794–1863. English judge. M.P. (1837–42); judge of court of common pleas (1842–58); first judge of probate and divorce court (1858–63).

Cres·sy \'kres-ē\, Hugh Paulinus de. 1605?–1674. English ecclesiastical historian. Converted to Roman Catholicism while visiting Rome (1646); became Benedictine monk as Serenus Cressy; chaplain to Catherine of Braganza in England; described conversion in *Exomologesis* (1647). Chief work *Church-History of Brittany or England* (1668); edited works of Counter-Reformation mystics Walter Hilton, Julian of Norwich, Maurice Chauncey.

Cres·well \'kres-,wel, -wəl\, John Angel James. 1828–1891. American politician, b. Port Deposit, Md. Congressman (1863–65); senator (1865–67); postmaster general (1869–74); instituted great improvements in postal service.

Cret \'krā, *Fr* kre\, Paul Philippe. 1876–1945. American architect, b. Lyon, France. To U.S. as professor of design, U. of Pennsylvania (1903–37). Designed Valley Forge Memorial Arch in Philadelphia; Folger Shakespeare Library and Federal Reserve Board building in Washington, D.C.; battle monuments at Varennes, Château-Thierry, Fismes, etc.; Detroit Institute of Arts; Hall of Science for Century of Progress Exposition, Chicago.

Creutz \'krœits\, Gustav Philip. Count. 1731–1785. Swedish diplomat and poet. Ambassador in Madrid (1763–66) and Paris (1766–83); concluded (Apr. 3, 1783) with Franklin commercial treaty between Sweden and U.S. Poetical works included the idyl *Atis och Camilla* (1762) and the verse narrative *Daphne*, considered among the most graceful writings in Swedish.

Creu·zer \'krȯit-sər\, Georg Friedrich. 1771–1858. German classical philologist. Professor, Marburg (1802) and Heidelberg (1804–45). Chief work, *Symbolik und Mythologie der alten Völker, besonders der Griechen* (1810–12).

Creuziger *or* **Creutzinger,** Caspar. See CRUCIGER.

Crève·coeur \krev-kœr\, Michel-Guillaume-Jean de. *Pseudonym* J. Hector St. John \(,)sānt-'jän, sənt-\. 1735–1813. American writer, b. near Caen, France. In New York (from 1759); naturalized citizen (1765). Returned to France (1780); French consul in New York (1784–90). Fame rests on his *Letters from an American Farmer* (1782), a series of essays giving a farmer's reactions to the life and issues of the times.

Crewe-Milnes \'krü-'milz\, Robert Offley Ashburton. 1st Marquis of Crewe. 1858–1945. English politician and diplomat. Son of Richard Monckton Milnes, whom he succeeded (1885) as Baron Houghton. Lord lieutenant of Ireland (1892–95); lord president of the council (1905–08, 1915–16); lord privy seal (1908, 1912–15); secretary of state for the colonies (1908–10) and for India (1910–15); president, Board of Education (1916). Ambassador to France (1922–28); secretary of state for war (1931). Created marquis (1911). In India was responsible for removal of capital from Calcutta to Delhi and reunion of two Bengals.

Crews \'krüz\, Laura Hope. 1879–1942. American actress, b. San Francisco. Supported Eleanor Robson in *Merely Mary Ann* (1904), Henry Miller in *Joseph Entangled* (1905); played in *The Great Divide* (1906), *Peter Ibbetson* (1917), *Mr. Pim Passes By* (1921), *The Silver Cord* (1926), etc. In motion pictures (from 1929).

Creyton, Paul. See John Townsend TROWBRIDGE.

Cribb \'krib\, Tom. 1781–1848. English pugilist. Defeated Jem Belcher for bareknuckles championship (1807) and again (1809); defeated American Negro boxers Bill Richmond (1805) and Tom Molineaux (1810, 1811).

Crich·ton \'krīt-ᵊn\, James. *Known as* the Admirable Crichton. 1560–1582. Scottish prodigy. M.A., St. Andrews (1575). In Paris (1577) said to have disputed on scientific questions in twelve languages; served in French army two years; in Genoa (1579) made Latin address to doge; in Venice (1580) introduced to learned world by Aldus Manutius and taken up by Humanists; in Padua (1581) disputed with university professors their interpretations of Aristotle and exposed their faulty mathematics. Dubbed "admirable" in John Johnston's *Heroes Scotici* (1603).

Crile \'krī(ə)l\, George Washington. 1864–1943. American surgeon, b. Chilo, Ohio. Professor, Western Reserve (1900–24); a founder and first director (1921–40) of Cleveland Clinic Foundation. Conducted pioneering research into shock, surgical trauma, resuscitation, etc. Author of *Experimental Research into Surgical Shock* (1899), *Blood Pressure in Surgery* (1903), *Hemorrhage and Transfusion* (1909), *Origin and Nature of the Emotions* (1915), *A Bipolar Theory of Living Processes* (1925), *The Phenomena of Life* (1936), etc.

Cril·lon \krē-yōⁿ\. Family of French soldiers, including: Louis des Balbes de Ber·ton de Crillon \dā-bálb-də-ber-tōⁿ-də-\, duc de Ma·hon \má-ōⁿ\ (1718–1796); distinguished himself at Fontenoy (1745) and in the Seven Years' War; lieutenant general (1758); passed into Spanish service (1762) and forced capitulation of Minorca by the English (1782). His son ¶Félix-François-Dorothée des Balbes de Berton de Quiers \kyer\, duc de Crillon (1748–1820), member of Estates-General (1789); a founder of the Feuillants; lieutenant general under Luckner, but later fled to Spain; returned to France under the Directory; appointed to Chamber of Peers (1815). His half-brother ¶Louis-Antoine-François de Paule des Balbes de Berton de Quiers de Crillon, duc de Mahon (1775–1832), lieutenant general in the Spanish army, submitted to Joseph Bonaparte and was appointed viceroy of Navarre; proscribed by Ferdinand VII (1814) and returned to France. Félix's son ¶Marie-Gérard-Louis-Félix-Rodrigue des Balbes de Berton, duc de Crillon (1782–1870), émigré from France, inherited title of duc and dignity of a peer of France; appointed field marshal after the campaign in Spain (1823).

Crillon, Louis Bal·bis de Ber·ton de \bál-bē-də-ber-tōⁿ-də\. *Known as* L'Homme sans Peur \lòm-säⁿ-pœr\. 1543–1615. French soldier. Served against the Huguenots in the French civil wars; engaged as a knight of Malta under Don John of Austria at battle of Lepanto (1571); served in army of Henry III during war against the Holy League (1580–89); fought under Henry IV at Ivry-La-Bataille (1590); with Sully, commanded army of Savoy (1600).

Crip·pen \'krip-ən\, Hawley Harvey. 1862–1910. American murderer, b. Michigan. Businessman in London (from 1900). Questioned on disappearance of wife, he fled with mistress on U.S.S. *Montrose;* apprehended following what is believed to have been first use of wireless telegraphy in criminal investigation. Executed.

Cripps \'krips\, Charles Alfred. 1st Baron Par·moor \'pär-,mu̇(ə)r\. 1852–1941. English lawyer and statesman. Queen's counsel (1890); Conservative M.P. (1895–1900, 1901–06, 1910–14); prominent High Church layman; raised to peerage (1914); staunch peace advocate; joined Labour party, and was lord president of council (1924, 1929–31) in Labour governments, and British representative on council of League of Nations and delegate to assembly. His youngest son ¶Sir Richard Stafford (1889–1952), lawyer and diplomat. King's counsel (1927); solicitor general (1930–31); Labour M.P. (1931–50); champion of united front with left-wing parties (1936); executive officer of Labour party (1937); ambassador to Russia (1940–42); named lord privy seal and leader of House of Commons (1942); conducted Cripps Mission to India (1942); minister of aircraft production (1942–45); president of Board of Trade (1945–47); chancellor of exchequer (1947–50).

Crisp \'krisp\, Charles Frederick. 1845–1896. American lawyer, b. of American parentage at Sheffield, England. Member from Georgia, U.S. House of Representatives (1883–96); speaker (1891–95).

Crisp, Samuel. 1707–1783. English writer. Friend of Charles Burney and mentor of Fanny Burney. Brought from Italy first piano introduced into England. His play *Virginia* produced by Garrick (1754).

Cri·spi \'krēs-pē\, Francesco. 1819–1901. Italian politician. Played prominent role in Sicilian revolutionary government (1848–49); exiled to France and then England for revolutionary acitivity in Milan (1853); became associate of Mazzini in London. Aided Garibaldi in expedition to Sicily (1860); Sicilian representative in Italian parliament (1861–1900); leader of radical Left, later allied with monarchists; president, Chamber of Deputies (1876); minister of interior (1877–78). Premier (1887–91, 1893–96); advocate of Triple Alliance (Germany, Italy, Austria); organized Italy's Red Sea colonies into Eritrea and sought Italian protectorate over Abyssinia; deposed after Italian defeat at Aduwa (1896).

Cris·pin \'kris-pən\ and **Cris·pin·i·an** \kris-'pin-ē-ən, -'pin-yən\. Saints. 3d century. Christian martyrs. Brothers, shoemakers by trade; did missionary work in Gaul; beheaded by order of Emperor Maximian (c.286). Patron saints of shoemakers, saddlers, and tanners.

Cris·pus \'kris-pəs\, Flavius Julius. d. 326 A.D. Roman soldier. Son of Constantine the Great; given title of caesar and made titular ruler of Gaul by father (317). Won naval victory (324) over Licinius in the Hellespont. Executed by his father on charge of high treason.

Cris·tea \'krē-stē-ə\, Miron. 1868–1939. Romanian prelate. Bishop of Caransebeş (1910–19); primate and metropolitan of Walachia (1919–25); first patriarch of Romanian Orthodox church (1925–39). One of three regents during incapacitation of King Ferdinand (1926–30); premier of Romania (1939).

Cri·sto·fo·ri \krē-'stȯ-fō-,rē\, Bartolomeo di Francesco. 1655–1731. Italian instrument maker. A renowned maker of harpsichords; credited with inventing the hammer action characteristic of the modern piano (c.1709–11).

Cris·to·fo·ro Fi·ni \krē-,stȯf-ō-rō-'fē-nē\, Tommaso di. *Known as* Ma·so·li·no \,mä-zō-'lē-nō\. 1383–c.1440 to 1447. Florentine painter. Pupil of Lorenzo Ghiberti (before 1407); teacher and associate of Masaccio. Known for religious paintings in International Gothic style, esp. fresco cycles in S. Clemente church, Rome (c.1428), Church of the Carmine, Florence (1425–28), and Baptistery and Collegiata at Castiglione Olona (1428–35).

Cristus, Petrus. See CHRISTUS.

Cri·ti·as \'krish-(ē-)əs, 'krit-ē-əs\. c.480–403 B.C. Athenian orator and politician. A pupil of Socrates. Aided in overcoming the Four Hundred (411 B.C.); banished (c.407). One of the Thirty Tyrants appointed by the Spartans to govern Athens at end of Peloponnesian War (404). Killed in war against Thrasybulus. Introduced by Plato in one of his dialogues (*Critias*).

Cri·ti·us \'krish-(ē-)əs, 'krit-ē-əs\ and **Nes·i·o·tes** \,nes-ē-'ō-tēz\. 5th century B.C. Greek sculptors. Commissioned to carve duplicates of Antenor's statues of Harmodius and Aristogeiton, the Tyrannicides, when the originals were carried off by Xerxes. The statues were perhaps the first masterpieces of Greek Classical sculpture.

Cri·to \'krīt-ō\. 5th century B.C. Athenian citizen. Friend and disciple of Socrates, whose escape he tried to arrange; introduced by Plato in one of his dialogues (*Crito*).

Cri·to·bu·los \kri-'täb-(y)ə-ləs\ of Imbros. 15th century. Byzantine historian. Wrote *History of Mehmed the Conqueror,* covering years 1451–68 and containing contemporary account of the fall of Constantinople (1453).

Crit·o·la·us \,krit-ə-'lā-əs\. 2nd century B.C. Greek Peripatetic philosopher. Head of Peripatetic school; with Carneades and Diogenes lectured in Rome on philosophy; dismissed from the city by Cato the Elder.

Crit·ten·den \'krit-ᵊn-dən\, John Jordan. 1787–1863. American politician, b. near Versailles, Ky. U.S. senator (1817–19, 1835–41, 1842–48, 1855–61); representative (1861–1863); attorney general (1841, 1850–53). Governor of Kentucky (1848–50). Introduced "Crittenden Compromise" in Senate (Dec. 1860) as measure of conciliation between North and South, but compromise was defeated in committee. His son ¶George Bibb (1812–1880), soldier; major general in Confederate army, was defeated at Mill Springs, Ky. (1862). Another son ¶Thomas Leonidas (1819–1893), a major general in Union army, saw action at Shiloh, Murfreesboro, Chickamauga. A nephew ¶Thomas Theodore Crittenden (1832–1909), also an officer in Union army, was governor of Missouri (1881–85) and consul general in Mexico City (1893–97).

Crit·ten·ton \'krit-ᵊn-tən\, Charles Nelson. 1833–1909. American businessman and philanthropist, b. Henderson, N.Y. In memory of daughter Florence, who died (1882) at age of four, established and endowed Florence Crittenton Homes for unwed mothers, incorporated as National Florence Crittenton Mission (1895).

Cri·vel·li \krē-'vel-lē\, Carlo. 1430?–?1494. Venetian painter. His works included Madonnas, *Pietà, Annunciation, Crucifixion, Coronation of the Virgin, Madonna della Candeletta,* etc., in strongly modeled, exquisitely decorated and detailed Gothic style.

Cro·ce \'krō-chā\, Benedetto. 1866–1952. Italian philosopher, statesman, critic, and historian. Senator (1910 ff.); minister of public instruction (1920–21); minister without portfolio (1944); member of constituent assembly (1946). Founder and president (1943–52) of reconstituted Liberal party. Founded (1947) Istituto Italiano di Studi Storici. Author of *Filosofia dello spirito* comprising four volumes: *Estetica* (1902), *Logica* (1909), *Filosofia della practica* (1909), *Teoria e storia della storiografia* (1917); autobiography *Contributo alla critica di me stesso* (1918); *Ariosto, Shakespeare, e Corneille* (1920); *La poesia di Dante* (1920); *Storia d'Europe nel Seculo decimonono* (1932); *La storia come pensiero e come azione* (1938); *Filosofia, poesia, storia* (1951), etc. Founded (1903) and edited (1903–37) *La Critica.*

Croce, Giovanni. *Called* Chi·oz·zot·to \kē-ȯt-'sȯt-tō\. c.1557–1609. Italian composer. Assistant choirmaster (1593–1603), choirmaster (1603–09) of St. Mark's, Venice. Published several books of madrigals, canzonets, sacred music.

Crock·er \'kräk-ər\, Charles. 1822–1888. American financier, b. Troy, N.Y. In charge of construction, Central Pacific Railroad (1863–69). President, Southern Pacific Railroad of California (from 1871); merged Southern Pacific and Central Pacific railroads (1884).

Crocker, Francis Bacon. 1861–1921. American electrical engineer, b. New York City. Developed, with Charles G. Curtis and Schuyler S. Wheeler, standard electrical motor (1886). As chairman of committees of American Institute of Electrical Engineers was instrumental in establishing American electrical standards.

Crocker, William. 1876–1950. American botanist, b. Medina, Ohio. Taught at Chicago (1906–21); director, Boyce Thompson Inst., Yonkers, N.Y. (from 1921). Known for work on the germination of seeds, on plant hormones, on tropisms, and on the effect of toxic gases on plants.

Crock·ett \'kräk-ət\, David, *known as* Davy. 1786–1836. American frontiersman, b. Greene Co., Tenn. Served under Jackson in Creek War (1813–14). Active on frontier in western Tenn.; known as humorist and expert shot. Member, U.S. House of Representatives, from Tenn. (1827–31, 1833–35). Joined Texan forces (1836); killed at the Alamo (Mar. 6, 1836).

Crockett, Samuel Rutherford. 1860–1914. Scottish novelist. Abandoned Free Church ministry for novel writing; joined kailyard school with *The Stickit Minister* (1893); other works in Scots dialect included *The Raiders* (1894), *The Lilac Sunbonnet* (1894), *Mad Sir Uchtred* (1894), *The Red Axe* (1898), *The Firebrand* (1901), *Kid M'Ghie* (1906), *Man of the Mountain* (1909).

Croe·sus \'krē-səs\. d. c.546 B.C. Last king of Lydia, of house of Mermnadae (c.560–546 B.C.). Conquered regions of western Asia Minor; extended kingdom to the Halys on the east and the Taurus on the south; invaded Cappadocia; surprised at Sardis by Cyrus and overcome (546 B.C.). Acquired great wealth through trade; subject of many legends.

Croft \'krȯft\, Sir Herbert. 1751–1816. English scholar and linguist. Known for his life of poet Edward Young in Johnson's *Lives of the Poets,* and for notorious *Love and Madness* (1780); projected a revision of Johnson's *Dictionary.*

Croft, William. 1678–1727. English composer. Organist of Chapel Royal (1707), Westminster Abbey (1708); published *Musica Sacra* (1724), choral works including his masterly burial service; other works for harpsichord, violin.

Crof·ton \'krȯf-tən\, Sir Walter Frederick. 1815–1897. Irish penologist. Originated the Irish, or Crofton, system of prison administration as commissioner of prisons in Ireland (1853–54, 1869) and in England (1866–68).

Crofts \'krȯf(t)s\, Freeman Wills. 1879–1957. Irish civil engineer and writer. Achieved fame with tightly plotted detective novels including *The Cask* (1920), *Inspector French's Greatest Case* (1925), *Inspector French and the Cheyne Mystery* (1926), *The Box Office Murders* (1929), *Sudden Death* (1932), *Found Floating* (1937), etc.

Cro·ghan \'krō-ən\, George. c.1720–1782. American trader and Indian agent, b. near Dublin, Ireland. To U.S. (1741); won confidence of tribes of Ohio country; negotiated treaties of Lancaster (1748), Logstown (1752); deputy to Sir William Johnson (1756–72); negotiated conclusion of Pontiac's War (1765).

Crois·set \krwä-se\, Francis de. *Orig.* Frantz Wie·ner \'vē-nər\. 1877–1937. French playwright, b. Belgium. Plays included *Qui trop embrasse* (1899), *Chérubin* (1901; set to music by Massenet, 1905), *Le Tour de main* (1906), *Arsène Lupin* (1908), *Le Cœur dispose* (1912), *Le Docteur Miracle* (1926), *Pierre et Jack* (1931), *Le Vol nuptial* (1933).

Croissy, Marquis de. See Charles COLBERT.

Croix \'krwä\, Charles Joseph de. Graf von Cler·fayt *or* Clair·fait \kler-'fe\. 1733–1798. Austrian field marshal. Served in Seven Years' War (1756–63) and Turkish War (1788–91). As commander of Austrian contingent under Charles William Ferdinand, won victories at La Croix-Sous-Bois (1792), Aldenhoven (1793), Neerwinden (1793); as commander of Allied Lower Rhine army defeated Jourdan at Höchst (1795) and Mainz (1795); concluded unpopular armistice.

Cro·ker \'krō-kər\, John Wilson. 1780–1857. British politician and essayist, b. Galway, Ireland. M.P. (1807–32); secretary to admiralty (1810–30), exposed defalcations; determined opponent of Reform Bill, passage of which caused him to give up seat in Commons. Reputedly first to use term "conservative" for Tory party. Author of two widely read satires, *Familiar Epistles ... on the State of the Irish Stage* (1804) and *Intercepted Letter from Canton* (1805); also wrote *The State of Ireland, Past and Present* (1807). Contributor to *Quarterly Review* from its foundation; responsible for scathing *Quarterly* article on Keats's *Endymion;* edited Boswell's *Life of Johnson* (1831); began an annotated edition of Pope's works, completed by Elwin and Courthope. The supposed original of Rigby in Disraeli's *Coningsby.*

Croker, Richard. *Known as* Boss Croker. 1841–1922. American politician, b. County Cork, Ireland. Identified with Tammany Hall (from 1862); joined "Young Democracy" faction opposed to Boss Tweed (1868). Leader of Tammany Hall and dominated Democratic politics in New York City (1886–1902). To England (1903) and later to Ireland, living as a country gentleman.

Croker, Thomas Crofton. 1798–1854. Irish antiquary. Clerk in admiralty, London (1818–50). One of founders of British Archaeological Association. Collected Irish legends, folksongs, etc., which he published in *The Fairy Legends and Traditions of the South of Ireland* (1825), *Legends of the Lakes* (1829), *Popular Songs of Ireland* (1839), etc. Contributed material to Thomas Moore's *Irish Melodies.*

Croll \'krōl\, James. 1821–1890. Scottish geologist and climatologist. Largely self-educated. Keeper of maps and correspondence, Geological Survey of Scotland (1867–80); author of *Climate and Time* (1875), *Philosophic Basis of Evolution* (1890), etc.

Cro·ly \'krō-lē\, David Goodman. 1829–1889. American journalist, b. County Cork, Ireland. Managing editor, New York *World* (1862–72); editor, *Daily Graphic* (1873–78). His wife ¶Jane, *nee* Cun·ning·ham \'kən-iŋ-əm, *esp US* -,ham\, *pseudonym* Jennie June \'jün\ (1829–1901), b. Leicestershire, England, was editor of *Demorest's Illustrated Monthly* (1860–87); founded Sorosis, a woman's club (1868), and the Woman's Press Club, New York (1889).

Croly, George. 1780–1860. Irish author and Anglican clergyman. Settled in London (1810) as journalist. Author of poems, dramas, and novels, including a romance *Salathiel* (1829), founded on the legend of the Wandering Jew.

Croly, Herbert David. 1869–1930. American editor and author, b. New York City. Son of David G. and Jane C. Croly. Edited *Architectural Record* (1900–06); founder and first editor (1914–30) of *The New Republic,* liberal journal. Author of *The Promise of American Life* (1909), *Progressive Democracy* (1914).

Crome \'krōm\, John. *Called* Old Crome. 1768–1821. English painter. Founded (1803) Norwich school of painting; best known for luminous, romanticized scenes from rural Norfolk, notable for fidelity to nature. His son and pupil ¶John Bernay (1794–1842), *called* Young Crome, painted usually coast and river scenes of England and the Continent.

Cromer, 1st Earl of. See BARING family.

Cromp·ton \'krəm(p)-tən, 'kräm(p)-\, Samuel. 1753–1827. English inventor. Invented the spinning mule (1779), the rights to which he sold for about £60 because he was too poor to patent it; finally granted £5000 by House of Commons (1812).

Crompton, William. 1806–1891. American inventor and manufacturer, b. Preston, England. Trained in English textile industry; to U.S. (1836); designed (1837) loom of greatly superior productivity and versatility; pioneered in power-weaving of fancy woollens (1840). His son ¶George (1829–1886), to U.S. (1839); began manufacturing looms at Worcester, Mass. (1851); made numerous improvements in looms.

Crom·well \'kräm-,wel, 'krəm-, -wəl\, Henry. 1628–1674. English ruler of Ireland. Son of Oliver Cromwell. Served under his father in Parliamentary army (1642–51). Irish representative in Little Parliament (1653). Major general of English forces in Ireland and member of Irish council of state (1654); de facto ruler after departure of Charles Fleetwood (1655); moderated religious strife among English settlers while vigorously continuing transplantation of Irish. Named lord deputy (1657); became lieutenant and governor general on accession of brother Richard as Lord Protector (1658); recalled and resigned after Richard's fall (1659).

Cromwell, Oliver. 1599–1658. English soldier and statesman. Great-great-grandson of Morgan Williams, a Welshman who married sister of Thomas Cromwell (*q.v.*), and whose son Richard took the name Cromwell. Left Cambridge to support widowed mother (1617). M.P. (1628–29, 1640–53); moved second reading of bill for annual parliaments (1640); carried resolution putting kingdom in posture of defense (1642). Became known as resolute Puritan and enemy of established church hierarchy. At outbreak of first part of the Civil War, captain of troop of horse at Edgehill (October 23, 1642); formed his unconquerable Ironsides regiment, combining strict discipline and religious enthusiasm; in eastern counties upheld firmly Parliamentary cause which was wavering elsewhere; won battle of Gainsborough (July 28, 1643); persuaded Parliament to create new offensive army under Edward Montagu; named second in command (1644); decided with cavalry charge fortunes of day at Marston Moor (July 2, 1644). Assumed leadership of the Independents, made up largely of religious sects in the army demanding religious toleration and vigorous prosecution of the war, as against the Presbyterians, comprising the aristocratic generals and the majority in Parliament, seeking to make terms with Charles; secured remodeling of the army and passing of Self-denying Ordinance (1645); under Sir Thomas Fairfax, led army to victory at Naseby (June 14, 1645). Probably ordered abduction of king from Holmby (1647). Recognizing grievances of the army against Parliament, marched on London and curtailed growing Presbyterian power; failed to persuade Charles to accept constitutional limitations on monarchy and acquiesced in Parliament's decision to cease further addresses to king (1648). In second part of Civil War, put down Royalist uprising in Wales and then routed Scots under Hamilton at Preston (1648). Active in prosecution of Charles up to execution and abolition of the monarchy. Named chairman of Council of State of proclaimed Commonwealth (1649). As commander in chief and lord lieutenant of Ireland, stormed Drogheda and Wexford, massacred garrisons (1649); left reduction of rest of the island to successors. Commander in chief (1650); defeated one army of Scots at Dunbar (1650) and other in command of Charles II at Worcester (1651). United the three kingdoms; dissolved Rump Parliament (1653); called Puritan convention, nicknamed Barebones Parliament, or Little Parliament, which proved ineffective and was dissolved by the moderates. Installed as "Lord Protector" on adoption of the Instrument of Government, constitution designed to establish balance of power between Parliament and the protector (1653); used power to rule by ordinances until meeting of Parliament, providing judicial administration in Scotland, Irish representation in British Parliament, and reorganization of Church of England (1653–54); forced by attempts of Parliament to perpetuate itself to exclude all who refused to agree not to alter the "four fundamentals" of the Instrument; dissolved Parliament (1655). Placed ten major generals over ten districts of England; called a Parliament (1656) which drafted new constitution, the "Humble Petition and Advice" (1657); refused to take title of king (1657); on renewal of extreme republican agitation dissolved his last Parliament (1658). Brought war against Dutch States-General to successful conclusion (1654); made commercial treaties with Sweden and Denmark; ended war with Portugal by treaty (1653); made treaty with France against Spain in interests of religious liberty and commerce (1655), another (1657) providing for joint attack on Spanish Netherlands; humbled Spanish at Dunkirk (1658); failed in endeavor to form European Protestant league. Buried in Westminster Abbey; attainted (1660) with other regicides; disinterred and hung on gallows (1661). His daughter ¶Bridget married Henry Ireton (*q.v.*).

Cromwell, Richard. 1626–1712. English politician. Son of Oliver Cromwell. Served in Parliamentary army; in Parliament (1654, 1656); member of council of trade (1655); member of Council of State (1657). Named by father to succeed as Lord Protector (1658). Sided with army in its dispute with Parliament, which he dissolved (1659); recalled Rump Parliament of 1653, by which he was dismissed (1659). Lived in France and later Geneva under the name John Clarke; returned to England (1680).

Cromwell, Thomas. Earl of Es·sex \'es-iks\. 1485?–1540. English politician. May have served in French army in Italy (1503); later a trader in Antwerp. Began practice of law in England, became (1520) solicitor to Cardinal Wolsey; M.P. (1523); Wolsey's agent in dissolution of smaller monasteries (1525), and a secretary in arranging for Wolsey's colleges at Oxford and Ipswich; pleaded successfully in House of Commons for quashing bill of attainder against Wolsey (1529). Entered service of Henry VIII (1530) and soon became a favored adviser; privy councilor (1531); master of the jewels (1532); chancellor of exchequer (1533); king's secretary (1534); drafted most of the Reformation acts (1532–39); as vicar general (1535) and king's deputy as head of English church (1536) carried into effect the Act of Supremacy and suppression of monasteries (1536–39) and confiscation of their properties; exerted himself to Protestantize English church, chiefly as a means of supporting absolute monarchy in behalf of Henry VIII; lord privy seal (1536) and Baron Cromwell (1536); lord great chamberlain (1539); rewarded with confiscated lands of monasteries; created earl of Essex (1540). Alienated Henry VIII by negotiating marriage with Anne of Cleves (1539); accused of treason by Norfolk; attainted by Parliament; beheaded.

Cronaca, Il. See Simone del POLLAIUOLO.

Cro·nin \'krō-nən\, Archibald Joseph. 1896–1981. British physician and novelist, b. Scotland. Practiced medicine in Glasgow, Wales, London (to 1930). Author of *Hatter's Castle* (1931), *Three Loves* (1932), *Grand Canary* (1933), *The Stars Look Down* (1935), *The Citadel* (1937), *Keys of the Kingdom* (1942), *The Green Years* (1944), *Shannon's Way* (1948), *The Spanish Gardener* (1950), *Beyond This Place* (1953), *The Northern Light* (1958), *A Song of Sixpence* (1964), *A Pocketful of Rye* (1969), *The Minstrel Boy* (1975); also play *Jupiter Laughs* (1940).

Cron·jé \krȯn-'yā\, Piet Arnoldus. c.1835–1911. Boer leader. Began Transvaal rebellion (1880) as a protest against taxes; distinguished himself in actions at Doornkop and Majuba Hill, captured British garrison at Potchefstroom (1881); forced surrender of Jameson raiders (1896). In Boer War of 1899 commanded western frontier; began siege of Mafeking; by victory over Lord Methuen at Magersfontein checked British column advancing to relief of Kimberley until Lord Roberts's invasion (1900). Surrounded near Paardeberg, forced to surrender; prisoner at St. Helena until end of war (1902).

Cron·stedt \'krün-stət\, Axel Fredrik. Baron. 1722–1765. Swedish mineralogist and chemist. First to isolate nickel in impure condition (1751); introduced use of blowpipe for study of minerals; made chemical composition basis of his classification of minerals. The mineral cronstedtite is named for him.

Crook \'krůk\, George. 1829–1890. American army officer, b. near Dayton, Ohio. Served through Civil War; engaged in Indian fighting in far northwest (1866–71); pacified Apaches under Cochise (1871–73); in Sioux War (1876); defeated by Crazy Horse at Rosebud Creek (June 17, 1876); served against Apaches under Geronimo (1882–85). Promoted major general (1888).

Crookes \'krůks\, Sir William. 1832–1919. English physicist and chemist. On staff of Radcliffe Observatory, Oxford (1854); lecturer in chemistry, Chester Training Coll. (1855); worked in own London laboratory (from 1856). Discovered thallium (1861); invented radiometer (1875); investigated passage of electrical discharge through highly rarefied gases; developed theory of a fourth (radiant) state of matter; invented Crookes tube, a highly exhausted vacuum tube producing X-rays; studied rare earths; produced minute diamonds artificially; studied radium; invented spinthariscope; produced special glass to protect workers from injurious rays emitted by molten glass; also engaged in psychical research. President of Royal Society (1913–15). Founder (1859) and editor of *Chemical News.*

Cros \krō\, Charles, *in full* Émile-Hortensius-Charles. 1842–1888. French inventor and poet. Published (1869) a theory of three-color photography; invented *paléophone,* a phonograph (1877); speculated on means of communication with other planets. Chief poetical work the Symbolist *Le Coffret de santal* (1873).

Cros·by \'krȯz-bē\, Frances Jane, *known as* Fanny. 1820–1915. American hymn writer, b. Southeast, N.Y. Blind from infancy; educated at New York Institution for the Blind; teacher there (1843–58). Composed about 6000 hymns (from 1864) including "Safe in the Arms of Jesus," "Pass me not, O gentle Saviour," "Jesus is Calling." Other works, collections of verse: *The Blind Girl and Other Poems* (1844), *Monterey and Other Poems* (1851), *A Wreath of Columbia's Flowers* (1858), *Bells at Evening and Other Poems* (1897).

Crosby, Harry Lillis, *known as* Bing. 1904–1977. American singer and actor, b. Tacoma, Wash. With Al Rinker and Harry Barris formed (1927) Rhythm Boys with Paul Whiteman's orchestra. Popular in recordings, in films, and on radio from 1930. Appeared in *Big Broadcast of 1932* (1932), *Holiday Inn* (1942), *Going My Way* (1944, Academy Award), *Bells of St. Mary's* (1945), *A Connecticut Yankee* (1949), *White Christmas* (1954), and series of six "Road" comedies (1940–52) with Bob Hope. Best known recordings included "Sweet Leilani," "White Christmas." Generally credited with developing the "crooner" singing style.

Cros·land \ˈkrȯs-lənd\, Anthony, *in full* Charles Anthony Raven. 1918–1977. English politician. Lecturer in economics, Oxford U. (1947–50). Labour M.P. (1950–77); president of Board of Trade (1967–69); minister of environment (1974–76); secretary of state for foreign and Commonwealth affairs (1976–77).

Cros·ley \ˈkrȯz-lē\, Powel. 1886–1961. American manufacturer, b. Cincinnati, Ohio. Developed Crosley Model X radio receiver, first with radio-frequency amplification. Organizer of Crosley Radio Corp. (1921); built radio station WLW, Cincinnati (1921); president of Crosley Corp., manufacturer of radios, refrigerators, washing machines, and a small automobile. President of Cincinnati Reds baseball club (from 1934).

Cross \ˈkrȯs\, Charles Frederick. 1855–1935. English industrial chemist. With collaborators E. J. Bevan and C. Beadle, discovered and patented viscose (1892).

Cross, Hardy. 1885–1959. American engineer, b. Nansemond Co., Va. Taught at Brown U. (1911–18), U. of Illinois (1921–37), Yale U. (1937–51). Developed moment distribution method (1930) whereby moments in complex frameworks could be calculated to any degree of accuracy.

Cross, Mrs. John W. See Mary Ann EVANS.

Cross, Richard Assheton. 1st Viscount Cross. 1823–1914. English political leader. Conservative M.P. (1857–62, 1868–86); home secretary (1874–80, 1885–86); introduced Cross Act (1875), first legislation relating to urban renewal and workers' dwellings, and Factory Act (1875), regulating employment of women and children in textile mills; secretary for India (1886–92); created viscount (1886); lord privy seal (1895–1900).

Cross, Whitman, *in full* Charles Whitman. 1854–1949. American geologist, b. Amherst, Mass. With U.S. Geological Survey (1880–1925). Author (with Iddings, Pirsson, and Washington) of *Quantitative Classification of Igneous Rocks* (1903), introducing the "C.I.P.W." system of petrography. The mineral crossite is named for him.

Cross, Wilbur Lucius. 1862–1948. American educator and politician, b. Mansfield, Conn. Teacher of English at Yale (1894–1930); dean of Yale Graduate School (1916–30). Governor of Connecticut (1931–39). Author of *Development of the English Novel* (1899), *Life and Times of Laurence Sterne* (1909), *History of Henry Fielding* (1918), *Connecticut Yankee, an Autobiography* (1943), etc. Editor of *Yale Review* (1911–40).

Crotch \ˈkräch\, William. 1775–1847. English composer. A musical prodigy, performed in London at age of four; professor of music at Oxford (1797–1806); first principal, Royal Academy of Music (1822–32).

Croth·ers \ˈkrət͟h-ərz\, Rachel. 1878–1958. American playwright, b. Bloomington, Ill. Author of *The Three of Us* (1906), *Myself-Bettina* (1908), *A Man's World* (1909), *The Heart of Paddy-Whack* (1914), *Nice People* (1921), *Expressing Willie* (1924), *A Lady's Virtue* (1925), *Let Us Be Gay* (1929), *Susan and God* (1937), etc.

Crotus Rubianus. See Johann JÄGER.

Crouch \ˈkrau̇ch\, Frederick Nicholls. 1808–1896. English musician and composer. Member of Queen Adelaide's private band (until 1832); lectured on songs and legends of Ireland. To U.S. (1849); settled in Baltimore as teacher of singing. Wrote two operas and many songs; best remembered as composer of "Kathleen Mavourneen" (c.1839).

Crou·saz \krü-zä(s)\, Jean Pierre de. 1663–1750. Swiss philosopher and theologian. Professor at Lausanne (1700–24, 1738–49); tutor to Prince Frederick of Hesse-Kassel (1726–32). Works included *Nouvel essai de logique* (1712), *Traité du beau* (1714), *Traité sur l'education des enfants* (1722), critique of Pope's *Essay on Man* (1737), refutations of Bayle and Leibnitz.

Crouse \ˈkrau̇s\, Russel. 1893–1966. American writer, b. Findlay, Ohio. On staff of Kansas City *Star* (1911–16), New York *Evening Post* (columnist, 1925–31). Author of *Mr. Currier and Mr. Ives* (1930), *It Seems Like Yesterday* (1931), *Murder Won't Out* (1932), etc.; collaborated with Howard Lindsay (*q.v.*) on Broadway shows *Anything Goes* (1934), *Red, Hot, and Blue* (1936), dramatization of Clarence Day's *Life with Father* (1939), *State of the Union* (1946, Pulitzer prize), *Call Me Madam* (1950), *Tall Story* (1959), *Sound of Music* (1959); also author of motion picture screenplays.

Crow·der \ˈkrau̇d-ər\, Enoch Herbert. 1859–1932. American army officer, b. Edinburg, Mo. Judge advocate general (1911–23); as provost marshal general (1917–19) administered Selective Service System in World War I; major general (1917). U.S. ambassador to Cuba (1923–27).

Crowe \ˈkrō\, Catherine, *nee* Stevens. 1800?–1876. English novelist. Author of *Susan Hopley* (1841), *Lilly Dawson* (1847), *Night Side of Nature* (1848).

Crowe, Sir Eyre Alexander Barby Wichart. 1864–1925. English diplomat. Son of Sir Joseph Archer Crowe. In British Foreign Office (from 1885); counsellor of embassy (1907); assistant undersecretary of state (1912). Submitted comprehensive memorandum on German foreign policy (1907); proposed seizure of German ships in English ports (1914). One of six drafters of a convention for League of Nations; participated in Paris Peace Conference (1919); permanent undersecretary for foreign affairs (1920–25).

Crowe, Sir Joseph Archer. 1825–1896. English journalist and art critic. War correspondent in Crimea and during Sepoy Mutiny; held consular posts in Europe (1860–82); collaborator with Italian critic G.B. Cavalcaselle (*q.v.*) on *Early Flemish Painters* (1857), *New History of Painting in Italy* (1864), and other classic histories of art. His brother ¶Eyre (1824–1910) was an artist; Thackeray's secretary (1851–53); inspector under science and art department, South Kensington Museum; known for his *Brick Court, Middle Temple* (1863), *The Queen of the May* (1879).

Crow·ell \ˈkrō-əl\, Luther Childs. 1840–1903. American inventor, b. Cape Cod, Mass. Invented the square-bottomed paper bag and machinery for manufacturing it (1872) and improvements in printing presses.

Crow·foot \ˈkrō-ˌfu̇t\. *Indian name* Sahpo Muxika. c.1836–1890. Canadian Indian leader, b. near Calgary, Alta. Warrior and later head chief of Blackfoot tribe. Firmly opposed warfare against whites; kept tribe out of Northwest Rebellion (1885).

Crow·ley \ˈkrō-lē\, Robert. 1518–1588. English printer and reformer. Set up printing office; as typographer noted for his three impressions of *Vision of Pierce Plowman* (1550) and early printing of Welsh books. Returning from exile on accession of Queen Elizabeth, became archdeacon of Hereford; resisted use of surplice. Author of Christian Socialist tracts, notably *Way to Wealth* (1550), and *A briefe discourse against the outwarde apparell and Ministring garmentes of the popishe church* (1566).

Crowne \ˈkrau̇n\, John. 1640?–?1703. British dramatist, b. Nova Scotia. To England and began career with romance *Pandion and Amphigenia* (1665) and a tragicomedy *Juliana, or the Princess of Poland* (1671); won favor of Charles II with masque *Calisto;* at request of king, adapted Spanish play into *Sir Courtly Nice, or It Cannot Be* (1685); other works, *The Destruction of Jerusalem by Titus Vespasian* (1677), *The English Friar* (1690), *The Married Beau* (1694).

Crown·in·shield \ˈkrau̇n-ən-ˌshēld\, Francis Welch. 1872–1947. American editor, b. Paris, of American parentage. Publisher of *The Bookman* (1895–1900); assistant editor of *Metropolitan Magazine* (1900–02) and *Munsey's Magazine* (1903–07); art editor, *Century Magazine* (1910–13); editor, *Vanity Fair* (1914–36).

Crowquill, Alfred. See Alfred Henry and Charles Robert FORRESTER.

Crow·ther \ˈkrau̇t͟h-ər\, Samuel Adjai. 1809?–1891. African missionary, b. in Yoruba country, West Africa. Rescued from slavery by British (1822); ordained in England (1843); missionary in Yoruba country; prepared schoolbooks and translations of Bible into Yoruba; bishop of Niger territories (1864).

Cro·zet \krō-ze *Angl* -ˈzā\, Claude. 1790–1864. American military engineer, b. Villefranche, France. Artillery officer under Napoléon (1807–15); to U.S. (1816). Taught engineering at West Point (1816–23); state engineer of Virginia (1823–32, 1839–64); supervised construction of first railroad over Blue Ridge (1849–58); first president of Virginia Military Institute (1839–45).

Cro·zier \ˈkrō-zhər\, William. 1855–1942. American army officer, b. Carrollton, Ohio. Coinventor with Gen. Buffington of Buffington-Crozier disappearing gun carriage; inventor of Crozier wire-wound gun. Chief of ordnance, U.S. army (1901–18); member of supreme war council (1917–18); major general (1917).

Cru·cé \krᵫē-sā\, Éméric. c.1590–1648. French writer. May have been a monk. Wrote *Le nouveau Cynée* (1623), proposing permanent assembly of princes or delegates to arbitrate international disputes.

Cru·ci·ger *Lat* ˈkrü-sə-jər, *Ger* ˈkrüt-si-gər\, Caspar. 1504–1548. German Protestant theologian. Professor of theology, Wittenberg (from 1528); collaborated with Luther in translating the Bible.

Cru·den \ˈkrüd-ᵊn\, Alexander. 1701–1770. Scottish bookseller in London. Compiler of a well known biblical concordance (1737). Styled himself "Alexander the Corrector" and dedicated himself to schemes for correcting the nation's morals.

Crü·ger \ˈkrü-gər\, Johann. 1598–1662. German composer. Organist of St. Nicholas Church in Berlin (from 1622); composer of choral music for Protestant churches. His best known tunes included those for "Nun danket alle Gott," "Jesus meine Zuversicht"; author of treatises on musical theory.

Cruik·shank \ˈkru̇k-ˌshaŋk\, George. 1792–1878. English caricaturist and illustrator. Caricaturist of political leaders, enemies of England, court, church, great persons, commoners in *The Scourge* (1811–16) and other satirical magazines. As book illustrator, produced colored etchings for *The Humorist* (1819–21), *Peter Schlemihl* (1823), Grimm's *German Popular Stories* (1824–26), Dickens's *Sketches by Boz* (1836, 1837) and *Oliver Twist* (1838), W. Harrison Ainsworth's *Rookwood* (1836), Charles Lever's *Arthur O'Leary* (1844), and William Hamilton Maxwell's *History of Irish Rebellion in 1798* (1845); started magazine *Table Book* (1845); published own series of *The Comic Almanack* (1835–53). Supported cause of abstinence in his pictures *The Bottle* (series of 8 plates, 1847), and its sequel, *The Drunkard's Children* (1848), and his magnum opus, the cartoon *Worship of Bacchus* (1862). His elder brother ¶Isaac Robert (1789–1856), caricaturist and miniature painter, satirized social extravagances and London life.

Cru·veil·hier \krü̅e-ve-yā\, Jean. 1791–1874. French anatomist. Professor, Paris (from 1836); first to describe multiple sclerosis; gave an account of progressive muscular atrophy (sometimes called Cruveilhier's atrophy or paralysis). Chief work *Anatomie pathologique du corps humain* (1829–42).

Cruz, San Juan de la. See JOHN of the Cross.

Cruz \ˈkrüs\, Juana Inés de la. *Originally* Juana Inés de As·ba·je \äs-ˈb̲ä-kā\. 1651–1695. Mexican nun and poet. An intellectual prodigy, for many years lady in waiting to wife of viceroy of New Spain; entered convent of San Jerónimo (1669). Studied sciences and humanities until 1693, when she sold her large library. Author of many fine lyric poems, published in *Inundación castálida* (1689), *Segundo volumen de las obras de Soror Juana Inés de la Cruz* (1692), *Fama y obras pósthumas de Fénix de México y Dézima Musa* (1700).

Cruz \ˈkrüth\, Ramón de la. *In full* Ramón Francisco de la Cruz Ca·no y Ol·me·dil·la \-ˈkän-ō-ē-ōl-mā-ˈt̲h̲ēl-yä\. 1731–1794. Spanish dramatist. Author of over 500 plays, chiefly *sainetes* (one-act sketches, usually satirical, from everyday life). Author of first Spanish translation of *Hamlet* (1772), and many other translations from French drama.

Cruz e Silva, António Dinis da. See DINIS DA CRUZ E SILVA.

Cruz Go·ye·ne·che \ˈkrüs-gō-yā-ˈnā-chā\, Luis de la. 1768–?1828. Chilean politician. Commanded division in revolutionary army (1810); prisoner of war (1814–1817); acting "supreme director" of Chile in absence of O'Higgins (1817–18), during which time Chilean proclamation of independence was promulgated; minister of war and marine (1827–28).

Cso·ko·nai Vi·téz \ˈchō-kō-ˌnȯi-ˈvi-tāz\, Mihály. 1773–1805. Hungarian poet. Author of a mock-heroic epic *Dorottya* (1804), odes, elegies, etc. in vigorous Enlightenment manner.

Cte·si·as \ˈtē-zē-əs\. 5th century B.C. Greek physician and historian. Physician at court of Darius II and Artaxerxes Mnemon. Author of *Persicha* (only fragments of which are extant), a history of Persia from official Persian sources, intended to discredit the history of Herodotus.

Cte·sib·i·us \tē-ˈsib-ē-əs\ of Alexandria. 2d century B.C. Greek physicist and inventor. Credited with discovering elasticity of air and inventing a clepsydra, a hydraulic organ, and several which operated by air pressure, as an air gun.

Ctes·i·phon \ˈtes-ə-ˌfän, ˈtē-sə-\. 4th century B.C. Athenian citizen. Prosecuted by Aeschines (*q.v.*) for proposing that Demosthenes receive a crown for his distinguished services; his defense was conducted by Demosthenes.

Cua \ˈkwä\, Paulus[3]. *Orig.* Huynh Tinh Cua \ˈhu̇in-ˈtin-\. 1834–1907. Vietnamese scholar. Promoted the use of Quoc-ngu system of romanization to replace Chinese ideographs for written Vietnamese. Author of plays, novels, mathematical texts, a dictionary, etc.

Cuauh·tém·oc \kwau̇-ˈtem-(ˌ)ōk\. *Also spelled* Gua·ti·mo·zin \ˌgwät-ə-ˈmōt-sən\. c.1495–1522. Last emperor of the Aztecs. Nephew and son-in-law of Montezuma II. Succeeded to throne (1520). Captured after Hernán Cortés's siege of Tenochtitlán (1521); resisted torture inflicted to force him to reveal location of Aztec treasury. Hanged by Cortés during march to Honduras.

Cud·a·hy \ˈkəd-ə-hē\, Michael. 1841–1910. American meat packer, b. County Kilkenny, Ireland. Partner, Armour & Co. (1875–90). Formed Cudahy Packing Co. (1890); president (1890–1910). Pioneer in refrigeration of meat.

Cud·worth \ˈkəd-(ˌ)wərth\, Ralph. 1617–1688. English philosopher. Chief of the Cambridge Platonists. Professor of Hebrew (1645–88), master of Christ's Coll. (1654–88), Cambridge. Sought in his magnum opus, *The True Intellectual System of the Universe* (1678), to establish a supreme divine intelligence, to refute determinism, to justify moral ideas, and to establish free will; wrote *Treatise concerning Eternal and Immutable Morality* (1731).

Cuer·vo \ˈkwer-vō\, Rufino José. 1844–1911. Colombian philologist and author. Wrote on evolution of Spanish in the New World; compiled dictionary of Spanish and a Latin grammar for Spanish-speaking people.

Cues·tas \ˈkwā-stäs\, Juan Lindolfo. 1837–1905. Uruguayan political leader. President of Uruguay (1897–1903).

Cue·va \ˈkwā-vä\, Alfonso de la. Marqués de Bed·mar \ˈb̲āt̲h̲-mär\. 1572–1655. Spanish diplomat. Named by Philip II ambassador to Venetian Republic (1607); worked to increase Spanish influence in Italy; expelled for alleged role in fabricated "conspiracy of Venice" (1618); minister to Spanish Netherlands (1618–22); appointed cardinal (1622); later bishop of Málaga and of Oviedo.

Cueva, Beltrán de la. 1440?–1492. Spanish nobleman. Supposed to have been father of Juana la Beltraneja (see JOAN).

Cueva, Juan de la. 1543?–1610. Spanish dramatist and poet. Known esp. for his use of new metrical forms, introduction of historical material, and dramatic adaptation of old romances. Plays included *La muerte del rey don Sancho, Los siete infantes de Lara, El saco de Roma, El infamador;* also wrote epic poem *La conquista de Bética* (1603).

Cu·gnot \kü̅e̅n-yō\, Nicolas-Joseph. 1725–1804. French engineer. Invented (1770) a three-wheeled artillery tractor propelled by a steam engine, believed to be earliest automobile.

Cui *Fr* kü̅e̅-ē, *Russ* kyü-ˈē\, César Antonovich. 1835–1918. Russian military engineer and composer, of French descent. Professor of fortification. Best known as composer of piano works, songs, and operas; associated with Borodin, Balakirev, Mussorgsky, and Rimsky-Korsakov in "the Five"; a fierce nationalist in his musical criticism, as *La Musique en Russie* (1881).

Cu·jas \kü̅e̅-zhäs\ *or* **Cu·jaus** \-zhōs\, Jacques. *Lat.* Jacobus Cu·ja·ci·us \ku̇-ˈyäk-ē-əs\. 1522–1590. French jurist and scholar. Specialist in Roman law; taught at Valence and Bourges; wrote *Paratitla,* summarizing Justinian.

Cu·kor \ˈkyü-kər\, George Dewey. 1899–1983. American motion-picture director, b. New York City. Known for witty, sophisticated films that elicited best performances from actors. Director of *Dinner at Eight* (1933), *Camille* (1936), *The Women* (1939), *The Philadelphia Story* (1940), *Gaslight* (1944), *A Star is Born* (1954), *My Fair Lady* (1964, Academy Award), *The Corn is Green* (1979, TV movie), etc.

Cul·bert·son \ˈkəl-bərt-sən\, Ely. 1891–1955. American authority on contract bridge, b. Romania, of American parentage. Founder (1929) and editor of *Bridge World Magazine;* syndicated newspaper columnist; author of *Contract Bridge Blue Book* (1930), *Contract Bridge Complete* (1954), etc.

Cul·len \ˈkəl-ən\, Countee. 1903–1946. American poet, b. New York City. A leader in the Harlem Renaissance; author of *Color* (1925), *Copper Sun* (1927), *The Ballad of the Brown Girl* (1928), *The Black Christ* (1929), *One Way to Heaven* (1931, a novel), *The Medea and Some Poems* (1935), etc.

Cullen, Paul. 1803–1878. Irish prelate. Archbishop of Armagh (1850–52), of Dublin (from 1852); distrusted national movement and forbade clerical involvement; first Irish cardinal (1866).

Cul·lum \ˈkəl-əm\, George Washington. 1809–1892. American army officer, b. New York City. Served through Civil War; brigadier general (1861). Bequeathed money for erection of Memorial Hall at West Point and to continue his *Biographical Register of the Officers and Graduates of the United States Military Academy* (first ed., 1850).

Cul·mann \ˈkül-ˌmän\, Carl. 1821–1881. German engineer. Professor, Zürich (1855–81). Credited with founding science of graphical statics for determining strength of structures by means of diagrams (Culmann's diagrams, or funicular polygons). Author of *Die graphische Statik* (1865).

Culpeper. See also COLEPEPER.

Cul·pep·er \ˈkəl-ˌpep-ər\, John. 17th century. American colonial political leader, b. England. Surveyor general of Carolina colony (1671); fomented Culpeper's insurrection in protest against British trade laws in Albemarle colony (1677) and, upon deposition of the proprietaries' deputies, aided in formation of popular government, acting as governor (1677–79); tried for treason and acquitted; made plan for city of Charleston (1680).

Cul·ver·wel \ˈkəl-vər-wəl, -ˌwel\, Nathanael. 1618?–?1651. English philosopher and clergyman. One of the Cambridge Platonists; author of *Spiritual Opticks* (1651), *Light of Nature* (1652). Believed to have influenced John Locke.

Cum·ber·land \ˈkəm-bər-lənd\, Duke of. Title of English nobility created five times in favor of the following (*qq.v.*): (1644) Prince Rupert, Count Palatine; (1689) George, Prince of Denmark, husband of Queen Anne; (1726) William Augustus, son of George II; (1766) Henry Frederick, brother of George III; (1799) Ernest Augustus, son of George III and King of Hanover.

Cumberland, Earls of. See CLIFFORD family.

Cumberland, Richard. 1631–1718. English philosopher and theologian. Bishop of Peterborough (1691). Author of *De Legibus Naturae* (1672), written in reply to Hobbes, presenting principle of universal benevolence and setting up the greatest good of universe of rational beings as foundation of ethical theory; hence often regarded as founder of English utilitarianism. Also wrote *Essay Toward the Recovery of the Jewish Measures and Weights* (1686), *Origines Gentium Antiquissimae* (1724).

Cumberland, Richard. 1732–1811. English dramatist. Great-grandson of Bishop Richard Cumberland. Secretary to Earl of Halifax (1761) and to Board of Trade (1776–82). Author of essays, pamphlets, two novels, and plays including *The Brothers* (1769), *The West Indian* (produced by Garrick, 1771), *The Fashionable Lover* (1772), *The Jew* (1794), *The Wheel of Fortune* (1795). Wrote *Memoirs* (1806–07). Ridiculed in Sheridan's *The Critic* as Sir Fretful Plagiary.

Cum·mings \ˈkəm-iŋz\, Bruce Frederick. *Pseudonym* W. N. P. Bar·bel·lion \bär-ˈbel-yən\. 1889–1919. English diarist. Biologist in Natural History Museum, South Kensington (1911–17); published extracts from his diaries as *The Journal of a Disappointed Man* (1919), *Enjoying Life and Other Literary Remains* (1919).

Cummings, Edward Estlin. *Styled by himself* e. e. cummings. 1894–1962. American poet and painter, b. Cambridge, Mass. Writer of poetry distinguished by experimental diction and unorthodox typography and punctuation, including verses in *Tulips and Chimneys* (1923), *XLI Poems* (1925), *&* (1925), *Is 5* (1926), *ViVa* (1931), *No Thanks* (1935), *One Times One* (1944), *95 Poems* (1958, Bollingen prize). Also wrote prose *The Enormous Room* (1922), *Eimi* (1933), *i: Six nonlectures* (1953); play *him* (1927).

Cummings, Homer Stillé. 1870–1956. American lawyer and politician, b. Chicago. Mayor of Stamford, Conn. (1900–02, 1904–05). U.S. attorney general (1933–39); drafted Pres. Roosevelt's "court-packing" plan (1937). Author of *Liberty Under Law and Administration* (1934), *We Can Prevent Crime* (1937).

Cummings, Jonathan. fl. c.1850–60. American religious leader. Follower of William Miller; organized (1860) Advent Christian Church.

Cum·mins \ˈkəm-ənz\, Albert Baird. 1850–1926. American lawyer and politician, b. Carmichaels, Pa. Governor of Iowa (1902–08); U.S. senator (1908–26). Joint author of the Esch-Cummins Transportation Act (1920).

Cummins, George David. 1822–1876. American clergyman, b. near Smyrna, Del. In Protestant Episcopal ministry (1847–74); withdrew because of opposition to emphasis on ritualism. Organized the Reformed Episcopal Church (1873).

Cummins, Maria Susanna. 1827–1866. American novelist, b. Salem, Mass. Author of *The Lamplighter* (1854), a great popular success.

Cu·mont \kūē-mōⁿ\, Franz-Valéry-Marie. 1868–1947. Belgian archaeologist and historian of religion. Professor, Ghent (1892–1910); curator, royal museum, Brussels (1899–1912). Chief works *Textes et monuments figurés relatifs aux mystères de Mithra* (1894–1901), *Les Religions orientales dans le paganisme romain* (1929), *L'Égypte des astrologues* (1937).

Cu·nard \k(y)ů-ˈnärd\, Sir Samuel. 1787–1865. British shipowner, b. Halifax, Nova Scotia. Joined George and James Burns of Glasgow and David MacIver of Liverpool in founding (1839) British and North American Royal Mail Steam Packet Company, known as the Cunard Line; created baronet (1859).

Cu·nedda Wled·ig \kü-ˈneth-ə-ˈwled-ig\. fl. c.450. British chieftain. Led a migration of Britons which displaced Irish settlers and laid foundations of kingdom of Gwynedd in northwest Wales.

Cu·nha \ˈkün-yȧ\, Euclides da. 1866–1909. Brazilian writer. Accompanied government expeditions sent to subdue rebel state in Bahia; described events in *Os sertões* (1902), considered finest prose work in Brazilian literature.

Cu·nha \ˈkün-yə\, Tristão da. 1460–1540. Portuguese navigator. Discovered Tristan da Cunha Islands (1506) while commanding 14-ship fleet, including those of Albuquerque, on voyage to India; later explored Madagascar, Somali coast, Socotra. His son ¶Nuno (1487–1539) consolidated Portuguese possessions in Indies as viceroy (1528).

Cu·ni·bert \kūē-nē-ber\. Saint. c.590–c.663. Frankish prelate. Bishop of Cologne (from 623); took part in synods of Clichy (626–27) and Reims (627–30); counsellor to Pepin I the Elder, Dagobert I, and Sigebert III of Austrasia; founded many monasteries and churches.

Cu·nitz \ˈkü-nits\, Maria. 1610–1664. Silesian astronomer. Published *Urania propitia* (1650) with simplified versions of Kepler's tables of planetary motions.

Cun·ning·ham \ˈkən-iŋ-ˌham, *chiefly Brit* -iŋ-əm\, Alexander. 5th Earl of Glen·cairn \glen-ˈka(ə)rn, -ˈke(ə)rn\. d. 1574. Scottish promoter of Reformation. Signer of invitation to Knox to return from Geneva (1557); stopped queen regent's advance against reformers at Perth with 2500 volunteers (1559), and applied to Queen Elizabeth for aid; demolished monasteries in western Scotland (1561); privy councilor, Scotland (1561); commanded insurgents against Mary, Queen of Scots, and led a division at Langside (1568).

Cunningham, Allan. 1784–1842. Scottish poet and man of letters. Friend of James Hogg; contributed imitations of old Scottish ballads to Cromek's *Remains of Nithsdale and Galloway Song* (1810), which gained him friendship of Scott. Assistant to Sir Francis Chantrey in London (1814–41). Collected and published *Traditional Tales of the English and Scottish Peasantry* (1822), *Songs of Scotland, Ancient and Modern* (1825); edited works of Burns (1834); author of three novels, a life of Sir D. Wilkie (1843), *Lives of the Most Eminent British Painters, Sculptors, and Architects* (1829–33), and many dramatic and lyric poems and songs. Father of: ¶Joseph Davey (1812–1851), who served in Bengal Engineers (from 1831) and wrote *History of the Sikhs* (1849). ¶Sir Alexander (1814–1893), who also served in Bengal Engineers, retired as major general (1861). Conducted excavations at Sārnāth (1837), Sānchi (1850), etc.; studied temple architecture of Kāshmir; was director general of Indian Archaeological Survey (1861–65, 1870–85); wrote *The Bhilsa Topes* (1854), *Ancient Geography of India* (1871), *The Stûpa of Bharhut* (1879), and *Coins of Mediaeval India* (1894). ¶Peter (1816–1869), who wrote *Handbook to London* (1849), *The Life of Drummond of Hawthornden* (1833), and other biographical studies. ¶Francis (1820–1875), field engineer in Indian army, who edited Marlowe (1870), Massinger (1871), Ben Jonson (1871).

Cunningham, Andrew Browne. 1st Viscount Cunningham of Hynd·hope \ˈhīnd-ˌhōp\. 1883–1963. British admiral. Commander in chief of British naval forces in Mediterranean (1939–1943); defeated Italian fleet at Taranto (Nov. 1940) and Ionian Sea (Mar. 1941); commander of Allied naval forces in North Africa and Sicily campaigns (1942, 1943); admiral of the fleet (1943); British first sea lord and chief of naval staff (1943–46); created viscount (1946).

Cunningham, Imogen. 1883–1976. American photographer, b. Portland, Ore. Studio in Seattle, later in San Francisco. Member of Group f.64 (from 1932). Known for portraits and photographs of plants, as *Two Callas* (c.1929).

Cunningham, William. 1805–1861. Scottish churchman and theologian. One of founders of the Free Church (1843); professor in the New College (1843–61).

Cunningham, William. 1849–1919. British economist, b. Edinburgh. Professor of economics, King's Coll., London (1891–97); archdeacon of Ely (1906–19). Author of *The Growth of English Industry and Commerce during the Early and Middle Ages* (1880), *The Growth of English Industry and Commerce in Modern Times* (1882), *The Case Against Free Trade* (1910).

Cun·ning·hame Gra·ham \ˈkən-iŋ-əm-ˈgrā-əm, -ˈgra(-ə)m, *US usu* -iŋ-ˌham-\, Robert Bontine. 1852–1936. Scottish writer. Traveled in South America, Mexico, Spain, Morocco; M.P. (1886–92, 1918). First president of Scottish Labour party (1888) and of Scottish nationalist movement (1928). Among his books were *Mogreb-el-Acksa* (1898), *A Vanished Arcadia* (1901), *Success* (1902), *Progress* (1905), *Faith* (1909), *Hope* (1910), *Charity* (1912), *Life of Bernal Díaz del Castillo* (1915), *A Brazilian Mystic* (1920), *The Conquest of New Granada* (1922), *The Conquest of the River Plate* (1924), *Conqueror of Chile* (1926), *Writ in Sand* (1932), *Portrait of a Dictator* (1933).

Cu·no \ˈkü-(ˌ)nō\, Wilhelm Carl Josef. 1876–1933. German statesman and businessman. Entered government service (1907); during World War I in charge of grain office (1914–16), then assistant to food ministry (1916–17). General director, Hamburg-American Steamship Line (1918–22, 1926–33). Chancellor of republican Germany (1922–23).

Cu·no·be·li·nus \ˌk(y)ü-nə-bə-ˈlī-nəs\ *or* **Cym·be·line** \ˈsim-bə-ˌlēn\. d. c.42 A.D. British king. Chief of Catuvellauni tribe; achieved strong influence over other tribes, leading Suetonius to describe him as "Britannorum rex." Shakespeare's Cymbeline, named for him, is not historical.

Cuo·co \ˈkwō-kō\ *or* **Co·co** \ˈkō-kō\, Vincenzo. 1770–1823. Italian historian. Active in Neapolitan revolution (1799); in exile in France wrote *Saggio storico sulla rivoluzione di Napoli* (1800); editor of *Giornale italiano* in Milan (1800–06); member of royal council of Joseph Bonaparte in Naples (from 1806).

Cuong De \ˈkwȯŋ-ˈdā\. 1882–1951. Vietnamese prince. In exile, principally in Japan (from 1906); a leader of Vietnamese nationalists; ultimately passed over for emperor in favor of Bao Dai.

Cup·py \ˈkəp-ē\, Will, *in full* William Jacob. 1884–1949. American critic and humorist, b. Auburn, Ind. On staff, N.Y. *Herald Tribune*. Author of *How to be a Hermit* (1929), *How to Tell Your Friends from the Apes* (1931), *How to Become Extinct* (1941), *How to Attract the Wombat* (1949), *Decline and Fall of Practically Everybody* (1950).

Curchod, Suzanne. See under Jacques Necker.

Cur·ci \ˈkür-chē\, Carlo Maria. 1810–1891. Italian prelate and writer. Entered Society of Jesus (1826); cofounder (1850) and editor (1850–53, 1856–63) of Jesuit publication *Civiltà Cattolica;* expelled from Jesuit order because of opposition to Vatican political policy (1877); reinstated shortly before death.

Cu·rel \kūē-rel\, François de. Vicomte. 1854–1928. French playwright. Among his dramas were *L'Envers d'une sainte* (1892), *Les Fossiles* (1892), *La Nouvelle Idole* (1899), *La Fille sauvage* (1902), *L'Ivresse du sage* (1922), *Orage mystique* (1927).

Curé of Ars. See Jean-Baptiste-Marie Vianney.

Cure·ton \ˈk(y)ů(ə)rt-ᵊn\, William. 1808–1864. English Syriac scholar. On staff of British Museum; discovered epistles of St. Ignatius among Syriac mss. from the Nitrian monasteries, also the Curetonian Gospels; canon of Westminster (1849–64).

Cu·rie \kūē-rē, *Angl* kyů-ˈrē, ˈkyů(ə)r-(ˌ)ē\, Pierre. 1859–1906. French chemist. Conducted researches on piezoelectricity, the magnetic properties of bodies at various temperatures, relations of magnetism, paramagnetism and diamagnetism, etc.; on faculty of School of Physics and Chemistry at Paris (1882), at the Sorbonne (1904); known esp. for work with his wife on radioactivity, for which they were awarded (with A. H. Becquerel) 1903 Nobel prize for physics; m.

(1895) ¶Manya Skło·dow·ska \sklȯ-ˈdȯf-skȧ\, *known as* Marie (1867–1934), physical chemist, b. Warsaw; began studies at the Sorbonne (1891), receiving doctorate (1904); with husband, investigated radioactivity (a term she coined in 1898), distinguished alpha, beta, and gamma radiation; discovered (1898) polonium and radium. Succeeded husband as professor of general physics at the Sorbonne (1906). Awarded 1911 Nobel prize for chemistry for discovery of polonium and radium and isolation of pure radium. Director of research department of Radium Inst. of U. of Paris (1918–34); organizer of radiological service for hospitals during World War I. Their daughter ¶Irène (1897–1956), physicist, b. Paris; m. (1926) Frédéric Joliot (later Joliot-Curie, *q.v.*); shared with him 1935 Nobel prize for chemistry for their synthesis of new radioactive isotopes of various elements. Contributed also to discovery of the neutron and development of nuclear reactors. Director of Radium Institute (1946–56).

Cu·rio \ˈk(y)u̇r-ē-ˌō\, Gaius Scribonius. d. 53 B.C. Roman politician and soldier. Tribune (90 B.C.); served in Sulla's army in Greece against army of Mithridates, and as Sulla's representative in Asia. Consul (76); governor of Macedonia (75–73), where he defeated the Dardani and extended his conquests to the Danube River; pontifex maximus (57). His son ¶Gaius Scribonius Curio (d. 49 B.C.); tribune (50 B.C.); supported cause of Caesar in Civil War; Caesar's propraetor in Sicily (49); defeated and killed in Africa in battle against Juba I of Numidia.

Curius Dentatus, Manius. See DENTATUS.

Cur·ley \ˈkər-lē\, James Michael. 1874–1958. American politician, b. Boston. In U.S. House of Representatives (1911–14, 1943–47); mayor of Boston (1914–18, 1922–26, 1930–34, 1946–50); governor of Massachusetts (1935–37). Widely considered the type of urban political boss; inspiration for Edwin O'Connor's novel *The Last Hurrah* (1956).

Curll \ˈkər(-ə)l\, Edmund. 1675–1747. English bookseller. Ascribed to Pope authorship of *Court Poems* (1716); lampooned in Pope's *Dunciad;* convicted (1725) of printing obscene books and fined (1728) for publishing *A Nun in her Smock* and *De Usu Flagrorum,* giving rise to term "Curlicism" for literary indecency.

Curme \ˈkərm\, George Oliver. 1860–1948. American philologist and grammarian, b. Richmond, Ind. Professor, Cornell Coll., Iowa (1886–96), Northwestern U. (1896–1934). Author of *A Grammar of the German Language* (1905), *College English Grammar* (1925), *A Grammar of the English Language* (1931–35).

Cur·ran \ˈkər-ən\, John Philpot. 1750–1817. Irish lawyer and politician. Called to Irish bar (1775); king's counsel (1782). A Protestant, gained verdict for Roman Catholic priest against nobleman on charge of assault (1780). Member of Irish parliament (1783–1806); spoke for Catholic emancipation, attacked ministerial bribery. Known chiefly for defense of leaders of insurrection of 1798; acquitted of implication in Robert Emmet's insurrection of 1803. Master of rolls and member of Irish privy council (1806–13).

Cur·rie \ˈkər-ē, ˈkə-rē\, Sir Arthur William. 1875–1933. Canadian soldier and educator, b. Napperton, Ont. Commander of first Canadian division (1915–17); lieutenant general (1917) commanding the Canadian Corps in France (1917–19). Principal and vice chancellor of McGill U. (1920–33).

Currie, Sir Donald. 1825–1909. Scottish shipowner. Joined Cunard Line (1844–62); founded Castle line between Liverpool and Calcutta (1862), line between England and South Africa (1872). Sent by British government to negotiate Kimberley diamond field boundary dispute. M.P. (1880–1900).

Currie, James. 1756–1805. Scottish physician and editor. Wrote *Medical Reports on the Effects of Water, cold and warm, as a Remedy in Fever and Febrile Diseases* (1797); edited collected works of the poet Robert Burns for the benefit of Burns's family (1800).

Cur·ri·er \ˈkər-ē-ər, ˈkə-rē-\, Nathaniel. 1813–1888. American lithographer, b. Roxbury, Mass. Set up business in New York (1834). Issued (1835) lithograph drawn by J. H. Bufford showing the *Ruins of the Merchants' Exchange,* first of series giving vivid picture of manners, picturesque scenes, outstanding events, and persons of the U.S. Admitted to partnership (1857) ¶James Merritt Ives \ˈīvz\ (1824–1895), b. New York City. Firm of Currier & Ives (1857–1907) published thousands of different and individually hand-colored prints that later became collectors' items.

Cur·ry \ˈkər-ē, ˈkə-rē\, Jabez Lamar Monroe. 1825–1903. American educator, b. Lincoln County, Ga. Member, U.S. House of Representatives (1857–61); Confederate congress (1861–63, 1864). In Confederate army (1864–65). President, Howard College, Ala. (1865–68). U.S. minister to Spain (1885–88, 1902). Agent of the Peabody Fund, donated for public education through the South (from 1881); agent of the Slater Fund, for establishment of Negro schools through the South (from 1890). Supervising director, Southern Education Board (from 1901).

Curry, John Steuart. 1897–1946. American painter, b. Dunavant, Kans. Known for works of the Regionalist school, as *Tornado, State Fair, Hogs Killing a Rattlesnake.* Painted murals for U.S. Department of Justice building and U.S. Department of Interior building in Washington, D.C., and for the State Capitol, Topeka, Kans.

Cur·tin \ˈkərt-ᵊn\, John Joseph. 1885–1945. Australian politician. Editor, *Westralian Worker* (1917–28); Australian delegate to International Labor Conference, Geneva (1924); member (1928–31, 1934–45), and leader of opposition (1935–41), Australian Parliament; leader of Australian Labour party (1934–45); prime minister and minister of defense (1941–45).

Cur·tis \ˈkərt-əs\, Benjamin Robbins. 1809–1874. American jurist, b. Watertown, Mass. Brother of George T. Curtis. Associate justice, U.S. Supreme Court (1851–57); resigned in protest of handling of Dred Scott case. Andrew Johnson's chief counsel during impeachment trial (1868).

Curtis, Charles. 1860–1936. Thirty-first vice president of the United States, b. N. Topeka, Kans. Adm. to bar (1881) and practiced in Topeka. Member, U.S. House of Representatives (1893–1907), U.S. Senate (1907–13, 1915–29). Vice president of United States (1929–33).

Curtis, Cyrus Hermann Kotzschmar. 1850–1933. American publisher, b. Portland, Me. In Philadelphia established (1876) *Tribune and Farmer* magazine, from which developed (1883) *Ladies' Home Journal;* head (1890–1933) of Curtis Publishing Co., publishers of *Ladies' Home Journal, The Country Gentleman, Saturday Evening Post;* bought Philadelphia *Public Ledger* (1913), New York *Evening Post* (1924), *Philadelphia Inquirer* (1930), and other newspapers. His daughter ¶Mary Louise (1876–1970), b. Boston; m. 1st Edward Bok (1896; d. 1930), 2d Efrem Zimbalist (1943); founded and endowed (1924) Curtis Inst. of Music, Philadelphia, and served as president (1924–70).

Curtis, Edward Sheriff. 1868–1952. American photographer, b. near Whitewater, Wis. Photographer for Harriman Alaskan expedition (1899); known esp. for photographs of Indians, published in 20 volumes of *North American Indian* (1907–30), *Indian Days of the Long Ago* (1914).

Curtis, George Ticknor. 1812–1894. American lawyer, b. Watertown, Mass. Brother of Benjamin R. Curtis. Appeared before U.S. Supreme Court in Dred Scott case (1857). Author of *Treatise on the Law of Copyright* (1847), *Treatise on the Law of Patents* (1849), *History of the Origin, Formation, and Adoption of the Constitution of the United States* (1854–58), *Life of Daniel Webster* (1870), *Life of James Buchanan* (1833), etc.

Curtis, George William. 1824–1892. American man of letters, b. Providence, R.I. In Brook Farm community (1842–43). As writer of "The Easy Chair" in *Harper's Magazine,* as political editor of *Harper's Weekly* (from 1863), and as lecturer, strongly influenced opinions of his day. Author of *Nile Notes of a Howadji* (1851), *Lotus-Eating* (1852), *Potiphar Papers* (1853), *Prue and I* (1856), *Trumps* (1861). Leader of national movement for civil service reform (from 1871).

Curtis, Heber Doust. 1872–1942. American astrophysicist, b. Muskegon, Mich. Astronomer (1902–20), Lick Observatory; in charge of Lick station in Santiago, Chile (1906–10); director, Allegheny Observatory, U. of Pittsburgh (1920–30); director, U. of Michigan observatories (from 1930). Known for researches on extragalactic nebulae.

Curtis, Lionel George. 1872–1955. English administrator and political writer. Held various posts in government of Transvaal (1900–07); Beit lecturer in colonial history (1912); adviser to colonial office on Ireland (1921–24). Founded quarterly *Round Table* (1910). Author of *Commonwealth of Nations* (1916), *Dyarchy* (1920), *Prevention of War* (1924), *Civitas Dei* (1934–37), *War or Peace?* (1946), *Windows of Freedom* (1952).

Cur·tiss \ˈkərt-əs\, Glenn Hammond. 1878–1930. American inventor and aviator, b. Hammondsport, N.Y. Established motorcyle factory, Hammondsport (1902); set motorcycle speed records (1905, 1907); designed motors for dirigibles (1907–09); director of experimental work of Aerial Experiment Association (from 1907); won trophy for first public airplane flight of a kilometer in U.S. (1908); won New York *World's* $10,000 prize for flight from Albany to New York in 2 hours, 51 minutes (1910); demonstrated first practical seaplane (1911). Expanded his factories to supply U.S., British, and Russian demands in World War I; developed JN-4 "Jenny," Navy-Curtiss (NC) flying boat that made the first Atlantic crossing (1919), and other aircraft, motors, scooters, speedboats, etc.

Cur·ti·us \ˈku̇rt-sē-u̇s\, Ernst. 1814–1896. German archaeologist and historian. In Greece (1836–40); professor, Berlin (1844), Göttingen (1856), again Berlin (1868); directed German excavation of Olympia, Greece (1875–81), unearthing temple of Hera, great altar of Zeus, Olympic stadium, many sculptures; with F. Adler, published *Olympia, die Ergebenisse der...Ausgrabung* (1890–97), official report of work.

Curtius, Ernst Robert. 1886–1956. German historian of literature. Professor of French, Marburg (1920), Heidelberg (1924), Bonn (1929). Author of *Balzac*

(1923), *Französischer Geist im neuen Europa* (1925), *James Joyce* (1929), *Europäische Literatur und lateinisches Mittelalter* (1948), etc.

Curtius, Georg. 1820–1885. German philologist. Brother of Ernst Curtius (1814–96). Professor at Prague (1849–54), Kiel (1854–61), Leipzig (1861–85). Principal works *Die Sprachvergleichung in ihrem Verhältnis zur classischen Philologie* (1845), *Griechische Schulgrammatik* (1852), *Grundzüge der griechischen Etymologie* (1858–62).

Curtius, Julius. 1877–1948. German politician. Member of Reichstag (1920–32) as representative of German People's party; minister of economic affairs (1926–29); invited by von Hindenburg to form a ministry (1927), but failed; succeeded Stresemann as minister of foreign affairs (1929–31) and represented Germany at Hague conference (1929–30). Resigned following rejection of his plan for a German–Austrian customs union by Permanent Court of International Justice.

Curtius, Theodor. 1857–1928. German chemist. Professor, Heidelberg (from 1897); known for organic syntheses from diazo derivatives of the fatty series; discovered hydrazine (1887), hydrazoic acid (1890).

Cur·ti·us Ru·fus \ˈkər-sh(ē-)əs-ˈrü-fəs\, Quintus. 1st century A.D. Roman historian. Author of *De rebus gestis Alexandri magni,* biography of Alexander the Great.

Cur·wen \ˈkər-wən\, John. 1816–1880. English music educator. Adapted work of Sarah Ann Glover (*q.v.*) to develop tonic sol-fa system of music notation. Founded (1853) Tonic Sol-fa Association, publishing house (1863), Tonic Sol-fa College (1879). His son ¶John Spencer (1847–1916), principal of Tonic Sol-Fa Coll., continued to promulgate the system.

Cur·wood \ˈkər-ˌwu̇d\, James Oliver. 1878–1927. American novelist, b. Owosso, Mich. Author esp. of stories of adventure in the American northwest, as *The Courage of Captain Plum* (1908), *The Grizzly King* (1916), *Nomads of the North* (1919), *River's End* (1919), *Valley of Silent Men* (1920), *A Gentleman of Courage* (1924).

Cur·zon \ˈkərz-ᵊn\, George Nathaniel. 1st Baron and 1st Marquis Curzon of Ked·le·ston \ˈked-ᵊl-stən, ˈkəd-\. 1859–1925. English politician. Conservative M.P. (1886–98); traveled widely in Asia; undersecretary of state for India (1891–92), for foreign affairs (1895–98). Viceroy and governor general of India (1898–1905); stabilized financial relations between provinces and the government, reduced salt tax, executed reforms; resigned as result of disagreement with Lord Kitchener. As chancellor of Oxford U. (1907), inaugurated constitutional reforms. Member (from 1908) and leader (1916–24) of House of Lords; created earl (1911), viscount (1911), marquis (1921). Lord privy seal in Asquith's cabinet (1915–16); president of air board (1916); lord president (1916–19); one of four ministers composing the war cabinet. Secretary of state for foreign affairs (1919–24); submitted to dominance of diplomacy by Lloyd George (till 1922); obtained suspension of Russian anti-British action and propaganda in Asia (1923); condemned French expedition into Ruhr (1922–23) and gained approval of advisory committee of experts (later the Dawes committee) to consider German reparations.

Cush·ing \ˈku̇sh-iŋ\, Caleb. 1800–1879. American lawyer and diplomat, b. Salisbury, Mass. Member, U.S. House of Representatives (1835–43). Special U.S. envoy to China (1843–45); negotiated Treaty of Wanghia (1844) opening five Chinese ports to American trade and establishing principle of extraterritoriality. U.S. attorney general (1853–57). Senior counsel for the U.S. before the tribunal of arbitration to settle "Alabama" claims (1871–72). Nominated chief justice, U.S. Supreme Court, but not confirmed by U.S. Senate. U.S. minister to Spain (1874–77).

Cushing, Harvey Williams. 1869–1939. American surgeon, b. Cleveland, Ohio. Eminent as specialist in neurosurgery. Surgeon in chief, Peter Bent Brigham Hosp., Boston, and professor of surgery, Harvard U. (1912–32); professor of neurology, Yale U. (1932–37). Author of *The Pituitary Body and Its Disorders* (1912), *The Life of Sir William Osler* (1925, Pulitzer prize), *Consecratio Medici and other Essays* (1928), *Intracranial Tumours* (1932), *From a Surgeon's Journal, 1915–1918* (1936), etc.

Cushing, Luther Stearns. 1803–1856. American jurist, b. Lunenburg, Mass. Author of *A Manual of Parliamentary Practice* (1844), commonly called *Cushing's Manual.*

Cushing, Richard James. 1895–1970. American Roman Catholic prelate, b. Boston, Mass. Archbishop of Boston (1944–70); cardinal (1958).

Cushing, William. 1732–1810. American jurist, b. Scituate, Mass. Chief justice, Mass. Supreme Court (1777–89). Associate justice, U.S. Supreme Court (1789–1810).

Cushing, William Barker. 1842–1874. American naval officer, b. Delafield, Wis. Noted for daring Civil War exploits, culminating in torpedoing of the Confederate ram *Albemarle* in the Roanoke River (Oct. 27, 1864).

Cush·man \ˈku̇sh-mən\, Allerton Seward. 1867–1930. American chemist. b. Rome, Italy. Founder and director (1910–24), Inst. of Industrial Research, Washington, D.C.

Cushman, Charlotte Saunders. 1816–1876. American actress, b. Boston, Mass. On stage from 1835. Known for powerful emotional portrayals, as in *Guy Mannering* (1837), *Fazio* (London, 1845), and in Shakespearian roles as Lady Macbeth, Bianca, Hamlet, Cardinal Wolsey.

Cushman, Joseph Augustine. 1881–1949. American paleontologist, b. Bridgewater, Mass. With U.S. Geological Survey (1912–21, 1926–49); museum director for Boston Society of Natural History (1913–23); at Harvard U. (1926–40). Founded private Cushman Laboratory for Foraminiferal Research (1923). Author of *Foraminifera: Their Classification and Economic Use* (1928); published 25 volumes of *Contributions from the Cushman Laboratory* (1925–49).

Cust \ˈkəst\, Sir Edward. 1794–1878. English military historian. Fought through Peninsular War; M.P. (1818–32); master of ceremonies to Queen Victoria (1847–76); general (1866); author of *Annals of the Wars of the Eighteenth Century,* and *Lives of the Warriors of the Thirty Years' War.* His nephew ¶Robert Needham Cust (1821–1909), Orientalist and Africanist; Indian civil servant, served in Sikh wars and pacification of Punjab after Sepoy Mutiny of 1858, retiring 1867; author of sixty-odd works, including volumes on philology of the East Indies (1878), of Africa (1882), of Oceania (1887), of the Caucasus (1887), also seven series of linguistic essays (1880–1904). ¶Henry John Cockayne Cust (1861–1917), journalist, nephew of Robert Needham. Unionist M.P. (1890–95, 1900–06); editor of *Pall Mall Gazette* (1892–96); founder of Central Committee for National Patriotic Organizations (1914). ¶Sir Lionel Henry Cust (1859–1929), art critic, first cousin of Henry J. C. Cust. As assistant in department of prints and drawings in British Museum (1884), prepared invaluable indexes; director of National Portrait Gallery (1895–1909); surveyor of king's pictures (1901–27); author of studies of Van Dyck and Dürer, Eton College, and royal collections.

Cus·ter \ˈkəs-tər\, George Armstrong. 1839–1876. American army officer, b. New Rumley, Ohio. Served through Civil War, distinguishing himself as a cavalry commander; brigadier general of volunteers at age 23 (1863); particularly effective against Lee at Richmond (1865). Field commander, 7th Cavalry (1866–76). Engaged on western patrol duty and in Indian fighting (1867–76); led expedition to Black Hills (1874); killed with all his immediate command in battle of Little Bighorn (June 25, 1876).

Cus·tine \kuᵉ-stēn\, Adam-Philippe de. Comte. 1740–1793. French army officer. Quartermaster general of the French troops in America (1780–83). Member of the Estates-General (1789). Commanded one of the Revolutionary armies (1792); captured Speyer, Worms, and Mainz (Oct. 21, 1792); failed in campaign to relieve Mainz (1793) which had been recaptured by Prussian forces. Charged and convicted of conspiring with the enemy to bring about a counterrevolution; guillotined at Paris.

Cus·tis \ˈkəs-təs\. Family name of descendants of Martha Washington (*q.v.*) by her first husband, Daniel Parke Custis; esp. her grandson ¶George Washington Parke Custis (1781–1857), playwright, b. Mount Airy, Md., and his daughter ¶Mary (1806–1873), wife of Robert E. Lee.

Cuth·bert \ˈkəth-bərt\. Saint. 635?–687. English monk. Entered monastery of Melrose (651); prior (661); prior of Lindisfarne (664) following reform of Celtic church in favor of Roman usages; retired (676) to a hermit's cell on island of Inner Farne. Bishop of Hexham (684), of Lindisfarne (685) in exchange; retired again to his cell (687). His body, believed to work miracles, was transferred to Durham cathedral (999?).

Cut·ler \ˈkət-lər\, Manasseh. 1742–1823. American clergyman, botanist, and pioneer, b. Killingly, Conn. Congregational pastor at Ipswich Hamlet (now Hamilton), Mass. (1771–1823). Prepared account of flora of New England, classified by Linnaean method. One of organizers of Ohio Company of Associates for colonizing lands in Ohio River valley (1786); may have assisted in drafting the ordinance of 1787 for government of Northwest Territory; obtained grant of 1.5 million acres on Ohio River. Served in U.S. House of Representatives (1801–05).

Cutpurse, Moll. See Mary FRITH.

Cut·ter \ˈkət-ər\, Charles Ammi. 1837–1903. American librarian, b. Boston. Librarian, Boston Athenaeum (1868–93). Originated system of labeling books by initial letters and numbers to represent authors' names. Published *Catalogue of the Library of the Boston Athenaeum* (1874–82), *Rules for a Printed Dictionary Catalogue* (1875), *Expansive Classification* (1891–1904).

Cutts \ˈkəts\, John. Baron Cutts of Gow·ran \ˈgau̇-rən\. 1661–1707. English soldier. Fought for William III in Revolution of 1688, and distinguished himself at the Boyne (1690); hero of siege of Namur (1695); served under Marlborough in Low Countries (1701–02); third in command at Blenheim (1704); commander in chief in Ireland (1705–07). M.P. (1693–1707).

Cu·vier \kuᵉv-yā; *Angl* ˈk(y)ü-vē-ˌā, -ˌvyā\, Georges, *orig.* Jean-Léopold-Nicolas-Frédéric. Baron. 1769–1832. French naturalist. Called founder of comparative anatomy and of paleontology. Tutor in family of comte d'Héricy (1788–95); assistant at Jardin des Plantes, Museum of Natural History, Paris (1795); lecturer, École Centrale du Panthéon (1796); professor of natural history,

Collège de France (1799); titular professor, Jardin des Plantes (1802). Originated natural system of animal classification (recognizing four distinct branches or phyla), introduced in his *Tableau élémentaire de l'histoire naturelle des animaux* (1797); investigated comparative anatomy of fishes and osteology of mammals; published *Leçons d'anatomie comparée* (1800–05). Studied fossil mammals and reptiles; published works on paleontology, including *Mémoires sur les espèces d'éléphants vivants et fossiles* (1800), *Recherches sur les ossements fossiles de quadrupèdes* (1812), *Discours sur les révolutions de la surface du globe* (1825), attributing fossil succession to series of natural catastrophes rather than to evolution. Inspector of education (1802); appointed to council of Imperial U. by Napoléon (1808); councilor of state (1814); chancellor of U. of Paris; president, committee of the interior (1819).

Cu·vil·liés \kue-vē-yä\, François de. 1695–1768. French architect. Named architect to Elector Maximilian II Emanuel of Bavaria (1725). Chief exponent of Bavarian Rococo style; works included Amalienburg lodge (1734–39), Residenztheater (1750–53). His work was continued by his son ¶François, *called* the Younger (1731–1777).

Cuyp *or* **Cuijp** \'kœip\, Albert. 1620–1691. Dutch landscape painter. Son of Jacob Cuyp. Works included *Herdsman with Cows by a River, Castle by a River Bank, Riders with the Boy and Herdsman, Piper with Cows.* His cousin ¶Benjamin Gerritsz Cuyp (1612–1652), also a painter of landscapes.

Cuyp *or* **Cuijp,** Jacob Gerritsz. 1594–after 1651. Dutch painter. Known esp. for portraits.

Cuy·pers \'kœi-pərs\, Petrus Josephus Hubertus. 1827–1921. Dutch architect. Designed churches in early Gothic style, and the Rijks Museum in Amsterdam; restored Mainz cathedral.

Cu·za \'kü-zä\, Alexandru Ion. 1820–1873. Prince of Romania. Took part in revolution at Jassy (1848); arrested but later made prefect of Galatz (1850). Elected prince of Moldavia and Walachia (1859), effecting personal union of the two; took title of Prince Alexandru Ion I; worked to eradicate feudalism, built schools; forced to abdicate (1866); succeeded by Carol I (*q.v.*).

Cy·ax·a·res \sī-'ak-sə-,rēz\. *Iranian* Uvakh·shtra \ův-äk-'shträ\. d. 585 B.C. King of Media (625–585 B.C.). Son of Phraortes and grandson of Deïoces. Defeated by Scythians and under their rule (653–625 B.C.). United Iranian tribes, reorganized Median army. Captured Ashur (614) and destroyed Nineveh (612); subdued countries of northern Mesopotamia (Armenia); moved boundaries westward to the Halys (Kizil Irmak) after long war with Lydia (590–585). Father of Astyages (*q.v.*).

Cydones, Demetrius and Prochorus. See both at DEMETRIUS CYDONES.

Cyg·nä·us \sueg-'nä-ůs\, Uno. 1810–1888. Finnish clergyman and educator. Chief inspector, Finnish public school system (1861); introduced manual training for first time in a public school system.

Cy·lon \'sī-,län\. 7th century B.C. Athenian statesman. With aid of his father-in-law, Theagenes, tyrant of Megara, attempted to make himself tyrant of Athens, raised a revolt, which was crushed.

Cymbeline. See CUNOBELINUS.

Cyn·ddelw Bryd·ydd Mawr \'kən-,thel-ü-,brəd-ith-'maůr\, *i.e.* Cynddelw the Great Poet. fl. 1155–1200. Welsh poet. Court bard to Madog ap Maredudd, Prince of Powys, and then to Owain Gwynedd, Prince of Gwynedd.

Cyn·e·gils \'kin-ə-,gilz, 'kůn-, 'kuen-\. d. 643. King of West Saxons. Succeeded to throne (611); first West Saxon ruler to convert to Christianity (635).

Cyn·e·wulf \'kin-ə-,wůlf, 'kůn-, 'kuen-\ *or* **Cyn·wulf** \'kin-,wůlf, 'kůn-, 'kuen-\. 9th century. Anglo-Saxon poet. Probably Northumbrian or Mercian. A Latin scholar, familiar with religious literature. Author of four poems preserved in Exeter codex and Vercelli codex (both of 10th century), namely *Juliana, Elene, The Ascension* (known also as *Christ II*), *The Fates of the Apostles,* into the epilogues of which the poet wove "Cynewulf" or "Cynwulf" in runic characters.

Cynewulf. d. 786. King of West Saxons (from 757). Warred against Welsh; defeated by Offa (779); slain by Cyneheard (brother of Sigeberht, whom Cynewulf had deposed).

Cynthius. See Giambattista GIRALDI.

Cyon \syōⁿ\, Élie de. 1843–1912. Russian physiologist. Professor at St. Petersburg Acad. of Medicine (1870); to Paris (1877). Known esp. for work on the vasomotor nerves of the heart.

Cyp·ri·an \'sip-rē-ən\. Saint. *In full* Thascius Caecilius Cyp·ri·a·nus \,sip-rē-'ā-nəs\. 3d century. Christian martyr. Bishop of Carthage (from c.248 A.D.). Following persecutions under emperor Decius, led in establishing principle of church's power to remit deadly sins. Engaged in dispute with Stephen, bishop of Rome, over authority of Rome. During persecutions of Valerian, beheaded at Carthage (258).

Cyp·se·lus \'sip-sə-ləs\. 7th century B.C. Greek ruler. Tyrant of Corinth (c.657–627 B.C.), founder of Cypselid dynasty; succeeded by son Periander (*q.v.*).

Cy·ra·no de Ber·ge·rac \sē-rá-nō-də-ber-zhə-rák\, Savinien de. 1619–1655. French poet and soldier. Served in the army (1637–40); joined the household of the duc d'Arpajon (1653); famous as a duelist. Pupil of Gassendi; influenced by him in direction of free-thinking. Author of *Le Pédant joué* (a comedy, 1654), *La Mort d'Agrippine* (a tragedy, 1654), *Histoire comique des états et empires de la lune* (1656), *Histoire comique des états et empires du soleil* (1662), the last two combining science fantasy with political satire.

Cy·ri·a·cus \sə-'rī-ə-kəs\ of An·co·na \aŋ-'kō-nə\. *Lat.* Ci·ri·a·cus An·co·ni·ta·nus \sə-'rī-ə-kəs-aŋ-,kō-nə-'tā-nəs\. *Ital.* Ci·ri·a·co de' Piz·zi·col·li \chē-'rē-äk-ō-dā-,pēt-sē-'kól-lē\. 1391–1452. Italian Humanist and antiquarian. In guise of itinerant trader, traveled in Egypt, Syria, Aegean Islands, and Greece, collecting manuscripts, coins, works of art, making copies of inscriptions, thus accumulating in diaries and commentaries a vast amount of material on ancient Greece of great value to later scholars.

Cyr·il \'sir-əl\ of Alexandria. Saint. c.375–444 A.D. Christian ecclesiastic. A doctor of the church. Archbishop of Alexandria (412 A.D.). Vigorously defended orthodoxy; persecuted Novatians; expelled Jews from Alexandria; disputed Nestorius over dual nature of Christ; convened Council of Ephesus (431) and had Nestorius condemned as a heretic.

Cyril of Jerusalem. Saint. 315?–?386 A.D. Christian ecclesiastic. A doctor of the church. Bishop of Jerusalem (350 A.D.); opposed Arian heresy, and was exiled from Jerusalem three times. Author of 23 *Catecheses* outlining a eucharistic theology essentially that of transubstantiation.

Cyril. Saint. *Secular name* Constantine. c.827–869 A.D. and his brother Saint Me·tho·di·us \mi-'thō-dē-əs\ c.825–884. *Known as* the apostles of the Slavs. Christian missionaries. Natives of Thessalonica, preached the gospel to the Khazars (860) and later to the Moravians (from 863). Credited with invention of the Cyrillic alphabet whereby they translated the gospels and liturgical books into Old Church Slavonic.

Cy·rus I \'sī-rəs\. *Old Persian* Ku·rash \ků-'räsh\. 7th century B.C. Achaemenian king of Anshan. Son of Teispes, grandfather of Cyrus II the Great.

Cyrus II. *Called* the Great. c.585–c.529 B.C. King of Persia and founder of the Achaemenian dynasty and empire. Son of Cambyses I and father of Cambyses II. Succeeded father as king of Anshan (558); overthrew grandfather, Astyages, king of the Medes (550). Overthrew Croesus and his kingdom of Lydia (547–546); successful in conquest of Babylon (539) and seized its king, Nabonidus (*q.v.*); delivered Jews from their captivity and allowed them to return to Palestine. Created empire extending from Aegean Sea to Indus River. According to Herodotus, killed in fighting the Massagetai, a savage tribe east of the Caspian. See HARPAGUS.

Cyrus. *Called* the Younger. 424?–401 B.C. Persian prince and satrap. Younger son of Darius II and brother of Artaxerxes II. Satrap of Asia Minor (407); conspired (401) against his brother, the king; led great army of Asiatics and about 13,000 Greek mercenaries from Sardis to Babylonia; met at Cunaxa by Artaxerxes, defeated, and killed; battle resulted in famous retreat (401–399) of 10,000 Greeks under Xenophon (*q.v.*), described in Xenophon's *Anabasis.*

Czar·to·rys·ki \chár-tò-'ris-kē\. Polish-Lithuanian noble family, including: Kazimierz (1674–1741), treasurer and later vice chancellor of Grand Duchy of Lithuania. His son ¶Prince Michal Fryderyk (1696–1775), Polish statesman, exercised determining influence on Polish policy during reign of Augustus III of Saxony (1734–63); chancellor of Lithuania (1752). His son ¶Prince Adam Kazimierz (1734–1823) was offered but refused Polish crown at death of Augustus III of Saxony (1763). Served later as minister of education, first such post ever established. Adam's son ¶Prince Adam Jerzy (1770–1861), Polish general and statesman. In Russian foreign ministry under Alexander I (1802–06); secured Alexander's support for campaign to restore Polish sovereignty; Polish representative at Congress of Vienna (1815); member of executive council and senate of Kingdom of Poland (1815–16); at head of November Insurrection (1830–31); president of Polish provisional government (1830) and national government (1831); forced to take refuge in France after Russia crushed Polish state.

Czer·mak \'cher-mák\, Johann Nepomuk. 1828–1873. Bohemian physiologist. Improved upon the laryngoscope; did pioneer work in rhinoscopy.

Czer·nin von und zu Chu·de·nitz \'cher-nēn-fōn-ůnt-tsü-'kü-də-,nits\, Ottokar. Graf. 1872–1932. Austro-Hungarian politician. In foreign service (from 1895); member of Bohemian Landtag (1903) and life member of Austrian upper chamber (from 1912). As Austro-Hungarian minister to Romania (1913–16), endeavored to prevent Romania entering World War I; minister of foreign affairs (1916–18); attempted to extricate Austria-Hungary from World War I; delegate of democratic party to Austrian legislature (1920–23). Author of *Im Weltkriege* (1919).

Czer·ny \'cher-nē, 'chər-nē\, Karl. 1791–1857. Austrian pianist and composer. Noted piano teacher, master of Liszt, Thalberg, Kullak, and others. His best known works were his piano exercises, as in *The School of Fingering, The School of Velocity, The School of Virtuosity.*

Czol·gosz \'chȯl-ˌgȯsh\, Leon F. 1873–1901. American anarchist, b. Detroit. Assassin of William McKinley.

D

Da·blon \dá-blōⁿ\, Claude. 1618–1697. French Jesuit missionary. Superior of Canadian missions (1671–80, 1686–93); named Marquette to accompany Jolliet on his exploration of the Mississippi.

Dą·brow·ska *or* **Dom·brow·ska** \dóⁿm-'bróf-ská\, Maria. 1889–1965. Polish writer and critic. Author of *Ludzie stamtąd* (stories, 1925), *Noce i dnie* (family chronicle novel in 4 parts, 1932–34), *Gwiazda Zaranna* (stories, 1955), *Szkice o Conradzie* (essays on Conrad, 1959), translation of Samuel Pepys's diary.

Dą·brow·ski \dóⁿm-'bróf-skē\, Jan Henryk. 1755–1818. Polish general. In Saxon army (1772–92); served with Poles against Russia (1792); took part in Kościuszko's uprising (1794); formed and led Polish legion in French army in Italy (1797–1801); in Italian service (1802–06); at request of Napoléon, organized and led Polish troops in uprising (1806); in campaign against Austria (1809); commanded Polish division in Napoléon's Russian campaign (1812); at battle of Leipzig (1813); designated by Russian czar to help reorganize Polish army (1814). General of cavalry and senator of Kingdom of Poland (1815).

Dach \'däk\, Simon. 1605–1659. German lyric poet. Member of the Königsberg group of poets, including Heinrich Albert; professor of poetry, U. of Königsberg (1639–59).

Dach·lan \'däk-län\, Kijai Hadji Ahmad. 1868–1923. Indonesian reformer. Founded (1912) Muhammadiyah, popular movement intended to promote Islām and Islāmic education.

Da·cier \dás-yā\, André. 1651–1722. French classical scholar. Keeper of library of Louvre; elected to Académie Française (1695), permanent secretary (from 1713). Translator of Horace, Aristotle, Plato, Epictetus, Plutarch, Sophocles, Festus, Flaccus. His wife (m. 1683) ¶Anne, *nee* Le·feb·vre \lə-fevrᵊ\ (1647–1720), was also a classical scholar; translated the *Iliad* and the *Odyssey*.

da Costa, Uriel. See COSTA.

Da·cres \'dā-kərz\, James Richard. 1788–1853. British naval officer. Surrendered the *Guerrière* after fight with the U.S.S. *Constitution* (1812). See Isaac HULL.

D'Acunha *or* **da Cunha,** Tristão. See Tristão da CUNHA.

Dā·dū \'dä-,dü\. 1544–1603. Hindu religious reformer and poet. Founder of the Dādūpanthīs, a Hindu sect, specially numerous in Rājasthān; author of *Bānī*, anthology of hymns and devotional teachings.

Daen·dels \'dän-dəls\, Herman Willem. 1762–1818. Dutch soldier. Exiled after taking part in revolt of 1787, joined French Revolutionary army (1793). Lieutenant general in Batavian Republic army, opposed Anglo-Russian invasion (1799). Entered service of king of Holland (1806); created marshal (1806) and governor general of Dutch East Indies (1807); governor of Dutch possessions on African Gold Coast (1815).

Da·foe \'dā-(,)fō\, Allan Roy. 1883–1943. Canadian physician. Practiced in Callander, Ontario, where he successfully delivered the Dionne quintuplets (May 28, 1934); author of *Dr. Dafoe's Guide Book for Mothers* (1936).

Dafoe, John Wesley. 1866–1944. Canadian journalist. Editor in chief, Winnipeg *Free Press* (1901–44).

Daft \'daft\, Leo. 1843–1922. American electrical engineer, b. Birmingham, England. To U.S. (1866). Developed electric power generating and transmission equipment and electric traction equipment. Built first complete commercial central power station (Massachusetts, 1884), first urban electric traction system (Baltimore, 1885).

Da·fydd ab Ed·mwnd \'dá-vith-áb-'ed-,münd\. fl. c.1450–1480. Welsh poet. Established and defined the 24 Welsh bardic meters (1451).

Dafydd ap Gruf·fydd \-áp-'grif-ith\. d. 1283. Welsh prince. Brother of Llywelyn ap Gruffydd, whose accession as prince of Gwynedd (1255) he unsuccessfully opposed; also opposed Llywelyn's wars against English, but in response to harsh English rule attacked garrison at Hawarden (1282); succeeded as prince of Gwynedd (1282); betrayed, captured, and executed (1283); last native prince of Wales.

Dafydd ap Gwil·ym \-áp-'gwil-im\. c.1320–c.1380. Welsh poet. Known for odes and lyrics of marked freshness and naturalness that permanently affected the formalistic bardic tradition.

Dafydd ap Llyw·el·yn \-áp-(h)lə-'wel-in\. c.1208–1246. Welsh prince. Son of Llywelyn ap Iorwerth. Imprisoned half-brother Gruffydd (1239); succeeded father as prince of Gwynedd (1240); forced by Henry III of England to cede territory and Gruffydd (1241); declared war on Henry and took title prince of Wales (1244).

Dafydd Nan·mor \-'nán-,mór\. fl. c.1450–1480. Welsh poet. Known for brief odes, love poems, etc.

Da·ger·man \'dág-ər-,mán\, Stig. 1923–1954. Swedish writer. Author of stories, novels, and plays showing influence of Kafka and existentialist thought; books included *Ormen* (1945), *De dömdas ö* (1946), *Nattens lekar* (1947), *Skuggan av Mart* (play, 1948).

Dag·ly \'däg-lē\, Gerhard. c.1653–after 1714? Flemish artist. Learned lacquerwork in Spa; royal chamber artist to Frederick William and Frederick III of Brandenburg (1687–1713). Pioneer in development of chinoiserie decoration and Baroque lacquerwork.

Dag·o·bert \'dag-ə-,bərt\. Name of three Merovingian kings of the Franks:

Dagobert I. 605–639. King of Austrasia (from 623) and of all Franks (from 629). Son of Chlotar II; moved capital to Paris; defeated Bretons (636), Gascons (637); patron of arts; revised Frankish law; last Merovingian to rule united Frankish realm.

Dagobert II. c.650–679. King of Austrasia (656–660, 676–679). Son of Sigebert III; deposed by mayor of the palace Grimoald, who sent him to a monastery in Ireland; located and restored by mother Himnechilde (676) to succeed Childeric II; assassinated.

Dagobert III. 699–715 or 716. King of Neustria and Burgundy (711–715 or 716). Son of Childebert III; dominated by Pepin of Herstal.

Dagobert, Archbishop. See DAIMBERT.

Dagonet. See George Robert SIMS.

Da·guerre \dá-ger\, Louis-Jacques-Mandé. 1789–1851. French painter, inventor of the daguerreotype. Scene painter for the opera. With Bouton, founded the Diorama in Paris (1822); worked on the obtaining of permanent pictures on metal plates by the action of sunlight, collaborating with J.-N. Niepce (*q.v.*) from 1829 until Niepce's death in 1833; continued alone, his work leading to the discovery of the daguerreotype process (1839). Cf. William H. F. TALBOT.

Dahl \'däl\, Anders. 1751–1787. Swedish botanist. A pupil of Linnaeus. The genus *Dahlia* is named for him.

Dahl, Johan Christian Clausen. 1788–1857. Norwegian painter. Best known for Norwegian landscapes.

Dahl, Michael. 1656–1743. Swedish painter. In London (from 1688); became known as portraitist of Princess Anne, Prince George, many naval officers.

Dahl·berg *or* **Dahl·bergh** \'däl-berʸ\, Eric. Count. 1625–1703. Swedish military engineer. Served in Polish campaign (1655–57), wars with Denmark (1657–58, 1675–79); director-general of fortifications (from 1680); gained title of "Vauban of Sweden." Privy counsellor, count, field marshal (1693); governor general of Livonia (1696). Directed defense of Riga (1700).

Dahl·gren \'däl-grān\, Fredrik August. 1816–1895. Swedish poet. Author of dialect songs and ballads and a few plays.

Dahl·gren \'dal-grən\, John Adolphus Bernard. 1809–1870. American naval officer, b. Philadelphia. On ordnance duty, Washington, D.C. (1847–63); reorganized and equipped navy ordnance yard; devised (1851) a new 11-inch gun, known as Dahlgren gun. Chief of Bureau of Ordnance (1862–63, 1868–69); rear admiral in Union navy (1863). On sea duty during Civil War (1863–65).

Dahl·gren \'däl-grān\, Karl Fredrik. 1791–1844. Swedish clergyman and poet. Author of nature lyrics, humorous verse, mock-heroic poems in *Babels Torn* (1825), *Mollbergs Epistlar* (1819–20), *Angbåts-Sånger* (1837), etc.

Dahl·mann \'däl-män\, Friedrich Christoph. 1785–1860. German politician and historian. Professor of history at Kiel (1812–29), Göttingen (1829–37), Bonn (1842–60). Helped draft constitution of Hanover (1833); banished for leading protest of the "Göttingen Seven" against suspension of constitution (1837); member of National Assembly at Frankfurt (1848–49) and of its committee designated to draw up a constitution. Among his works were *Geschichte von Dänemark* (1840–43), *Geschichte der englischen Revolution* (1844), and *Geschichte der französischen Revolution* (1845).

Dahl·stier·na \'däl-sher-nå\, Gunno. *Orig. surname* Eu·re·li·us \eù-'rā-lē-əs\. 1661–1709. Swedish poet. Author of patriotic epic verse, including *Kungaskald* (1697) and *Göta kämpavisa* (1701).

Dahn \'dän\, Felix, *in full* Julius Sophus Felix. 1834–1912. German historian, legal scholar, and poet. Professor of jurisprudence at Würzburg (1863), Königsberg (1872), Breslau (1888). Author of verse, plays, and opera librettos; of novels, as *Ein Kampf um Rom* (1876–78); of legal works and historical works, including his masterpiece *Die Könige der Germanen* (1861–1911) and *Die Urgeschichte der germanischen und romanischen Völker* (1881–90).

Dai·gak Guk·so \'dī-'gäk-'gùk-'sō\. *Secular name* Uich'on \'wē-'chòn\. 1055–1101. Korean Buddhist priest. Studied in China; published some 4750 books of Buddhist scripture; founded (1097) Ch'ont'ae sect, a Korean variant of Son (Zen) Buddhism.

Dai·go \dī-gō\. 885–930. Japanese emperor (897–930). Son of Uda. Continued (until 903) father's policy of ruling without appointing a member of powerful Fujiwara family to post of *kampaku* (chief councillor).

Daigo II. *Jp.* Go-Dai·go \gō-dī-gō\. 1287–1339. Japanese emperor (1318–39). Threw off domination of the court by retired emperors (1322); determined to restore Imperial court's power and end rule by shogunate; plan exposed, leading to civil war (1331–32); captured and exiled (1332–33); escaped and returned to throne; at first supported by Takauji; ruled briefly in the "Kemma restoration" (1333–36); driven out of Kyoto by Takauji in favor of Kōgon (1336); set up rival government south of Nara.

Daim·bert \'dām-(,)bərt\ *or* **Da·go·bert** \'dā-gō-,bərt\. d. 1107. Frankish prelate. Bishop (from 1088) and archbishop (from 1092) of Pisa. Preached First Crusade in France (1095), raised crusading fleet (1098); headed expedition to Holy Land (1100); assumed title of patriarch of Jerusalem after deposing Arnulf of Chocques (1100); driven out by Baldwin I (1102).

Daim·ler \'dīm-lər\, Gottlieb Wilhelm. 1834–1900. German engineer, inventor, and pioneer automobile manufacturer. With Maybach (*q.v.*), established automobile research laboratory at Cannstatt (1882); patented a high-speed internal combustion engine (1885) and later a carburetor to use gasoline as fuel; built perhaps world's first motorcycle (1885); founded Daimler-Motoren-Gesellschaft (1890) which produced the Mercedes automobile (from 1899) and which joined with Firma Benz & Co. to form Daimler-Benz & Co. (1926).

Daing Pa·ra·ni \dīŋ-pär-än-ē\. d. c.1726. Malay leader. As head of Buginese adventurers in Malay peninsula, won dominant role in Kingdom of Johore; successors eventually dominated nearly all of Malaya.

Da·kin \'dā-kən\, Henry Drysdale. 1880–1952. English chemist. With Alexis Carrel developed Dakin's or Carrel-Dakin solution used for treating wounds in World War I; known for researches in biochemistry, esp. on enzymes; awarded Davy medal by Royal Society (1941).

Dal *Russ* 'dälʸ\ *or* **Dahl** \ *Dan* 'dål\, Vladimir Ivanovich. 1801–1872. Russian physician and writer of Danish origin. Author of stories and essays under pseudonym Kosak Luganskij; compiled anthology of Russian proverbs (1862), Russian dictionary (1863–66).

Da·la·dier \då-låd-yā\, Édouard. 1884–1970. French politician. Radical party member, chamber of deputies (1919–40, 1946–58); friend and associate of Édouard Herriot; held several ministerial posts (1924–33); premier of France (1933, 1934, 1938–40); formed Popular Front with Communist party and Leon Blum's Socialist party (1935–38); signed Munich Pact (Sept. 1938). Arrested after fall of France (1940); liberated (1945).

Dalayrac. See ALAYRAC.

Dal·berg \'däl-berk\. Name of an ancient German noble family holding under Holy Roman Empire dignity of First Knight of the Empire, and including: Karl Theodor Anton Maria von Dalberg (1744–1817), last archbishop-elector of Mainz and thereby arch chancellor of the Holy Roman Empire (from 1802); given principalities of Aschaffenburg and Regensburg (1803); sought by alliance with Napoléon to save Germany from dissolution; prince primate of Confederation of the Rhine (1806); on dissolution of empire, made grand duke of Frankfurt with increased territories (1810); on fall of Napoléon, stripped of all but archbishopric of Regensburg; patron of letters; friend of Goethe, Schiller, Wieland. His brother ¶Wolfgang Heribert von Dalberg (1750–1806); while intendant of the national theater at Mannheim (1778–1803) was first to stage Schiller's early plays; wrote plays and adaptations of Shakespeare. The latter's son ¶Emmerich Joseph, duc de Dalberg (1773–1833); envoy from Baden to Paris (1803–09); entered service of Napoléon, who made him duke and councilor of state (1810); member of provisional government (1814); attended Congress of Vienna with Talleyrand; state minister and peer of France (1815); ambassador to Turin (1816).

Dalberg-Acton, J.E.E. See John E.E. Dalberg ACTON.

D'·Al·bert \'dal-(,)bərt, *Ger* 'däl-bert\, Eugen Francis Charles. 1864–1932. German pianist and composer, b. Glasgow of French and Italian descent. Court pianist at Weimar (1885); director of Hochschule, Berlin (from 1907). Composer of operas, as *Tiefland* (1903), *Die toten Augen* (1916), string quartets, piano concertos, a symphony.

Dalcroze, Émile Jaques-. See JAQUES-DALCROZE.

Dale \'dā(ə)l\, David. 1739–1806. Scottish industrialist and philanthropist. Erected mill at New Lanark (1785), at first in partnership with Arkwright; sold mills to Robert Owen (1799), who married his daughter (1799); organized (c.1770) "Old Independents," religious community of which he was chief minister.

Dale, Sir Henry Hallett. 1875–1968. English physiologist. Director, Wellcome Physiological Research Laboratories (1904–14); director, National Institute for Medical Research, London (1928–42). Discovered acetylcholine; awarded, with Otto Loewi, the 1936 Nobel prize for physiology or medicine for work relating to chemical transmission of nerve impulses. Secretary of Royal Society (1925–35), president (1940–45).

Dale, Richard. 1756–1826. American naval officer, b. Norfolk Co., Va. Joined British navy at outbreak of American Revolution, but quickly switched to colonial cause. On the *Bon Homme Richard* under John Paul Jones in battle with the *Serapis.* Captain, U.S. navy (1794); commanded blockading squadron at Tripoli (1801–02).

Dale, Sir Thomas. d. 1619. English naval commander and colonial administrator. Appointed marshal of Virginia (1611); found colonists lazy and insubordinate; placed them under martial law; published rigorous code of laws (*Dale's Code*) and enforced its provisions, causing the years 1611–16 to be known as "five years of slavery"; acting governor of colony (1614–16). Defeated a Dutch fleet near Batavia (1618).

d'Alembert, Jean Le Rond. See ALEMBERT.

Da·lén \då-'lān\, Nils Gustaf. 1869–1937. Swedish inventor. Devised improvements in hot-air turbines, air compressors, and milking machines; invented method of dissolving acetylene in acetone (1909). Invented the Solventil, a sun valve used for regulating gaslights in unmanned beacons, for which he was awarded 1912 Nobel prize for physics. Blinded as the result of an explosion during an experiment (1913).

Da·ley \'dā-lē\, Richard Joseph. 1902–1976. American politician, b. Chicago. Mayor of Chicago (1955–76); known as last of big-city bosses; power in national Democratic party.

Dal·gar·no \dal-'gär-nō\, George. 1626?–1687. Scottish educator. Author of *Ars Signorum* (1661), an attempt at a philosophical language in which letters of the alphabet stand for ideas, and of *Didascalocophus* (1680), presenting the first two-hand deaf-and-dumb alphabet.

Dalhousie, Earls and marquises of. See RAMSAY family.

Da·lin \då-'lēn\, Olof von. 1708–1763. Swedish poet and historian. Published (1732–34) weekly *Then swänska Argus,* Sweden's first literary periodical. Tutor (1751–56) to Crown Prince Gustav, later Gustav III; royal historiographer (1755). Among his works were the verse tragedy *Brynilda* (1738), comedy *Den Afundsjuke* (1738), *Sagan om hästen* (1740), epic *Swenska friheten* (1742), various satires, fables, and lyrics; chief historical work *Svea rikes historia* (1747–62). See Hedvig NORDENFLYCHT.

Dalip Singh. See under RANJIT SINGH.

Dal·lán For·gaill \dä-'län-'fòr-,gīlʸ\. 6th century. Irish poet. Leader of the *filid* (professional bards); probably author of *Amra Choluim Chille,* a eulogy on St. Columba.

Dal·la·pic·co·la \,däl-lä-pēk-'kō-lä\, Luigi. 1904–1975. Italian composer. Known for expressive use of 12-tone serial technique. Works included operas, as *Volo di notte* (1937–39), *Ulisse* (1960–68); choral works, as *Canti di prigionia* (1938–41), *Il prigioniero* (1944–48), *Canti di liberazione* (1952–55); ballets, as *Marsia* (1942–43), etc.

Dal·las \'dal-əs, -is\, Alexander James. 1759–1817. American lawyer and public official, b. Jamaica of Scottish parents. To U.S. (1783); settled in Philadelphia; adm. to bar (1785). U.S. secretary of the treasury (1814–16), at critical period in government finance; restored public credit, advocated a national banking institution (passed 1816), urged protective tariff. Served also as acting secretary of war (1815).

Dallas, George Mifflin. 1792–1864. American diplomat and politician, b. Philadelphia. Son of Alexander J. Dallas. U.S. senator (1831–33); minister to Russia (1837–39); vice president of the U.S. (1845–49); minister to Great Britain (1856–61). Dallas, Texas, was named for him.

Dal·lin \'dal-ən\, Cyrus Edwin. 1861–1944. American sculptor, b. Springville, Utah. Known esp. for naturalistic portrayals of American Indian life and scenes. Among his works were *Signal of Peace,* Lincoln Park, Chicago; *Pioneer*

Monument, Salt Lake City; *Medicine Man,* Fairmount Park, Philadelphia; *The Scout,* Kansas City.

Dalling and Bulwer, Baron. See William Henry Lytton Earle BULWER.

Dall·mey·er \'däl-mī-ər\, John Henry. 1830–1883. British optician, b. Germany. To London (1851); made improvements in portrait and landscape photographic lenses, also in microscope object glasses; made photoheliographs for Harvard observatory (1864), and British government (1873).

Dall'·On·ga·ro \däl-'lōŋ-gä-(,)rō\, Francesco. 1808–1873. Italian writer. Founded revolutionary journal *La Favilla* (Trieste, 1836); organized first Italian legion for Garibaldi (1848); in exile (to 1859); professor of literature, Florence (1859) and Naples (1869). Author esp. of political lyrics, as *Stornelli* (1863).

Dalmatie, Duc de. See SOULT.

Da·lou \dá-lü\, Jules, *in full* Aimé-Jules. 1838–1902. French sculptor. Involved in the Commune (1871); in exile in London (1871–79). Noted for allegorical group compositions and for naturalistic genre works. Among his works were *Le Triomphe de Silène* (1797, Luxembourg Garden), *Victor Moir, Blanqui, Triomphe de la République* (1899, Place de la Nation), and many portrait busts.

Dal·rym·ple \dəl-'rim-pəl, dal-, 'dəl-,, 'dal-,\. Name of a Scottish family descended from one of the Lollards of Kyle summoned before James IV (1494), and possessing the viscountcy and earldom of Stair \'sta(ə)r, 'ste(ə)r\, including:

Sir James Dalrymple (1619–1695), 1st Viscount Stair (cr. 1690), lawyer and judge. Judge of reformed court of session (1657–60) on recommendation of Monck and again (1661–81; president 1670–81); M.P. (1672–74); privy councilor of Scotland (1674); on enforcing of Test Act, retired (1681) to country and worked on *The Institutions of the Law of Scotland* (1681); repaired to Holland on account of hostility of Duke of York and Claverhouse (1682); returned with William of Orange (1688) and was restored to presidency of court of session (1689–95); his daughter Janet's luckless marriage (1669) suggested to Scott the *Bride of Lammermoor.*

His eldest son ¶Sir John Dalrymple (1648–1707), 1st Earl of Stair, lawyer. Imprisoned because of hostility of Claverhouse (1682–84); king's advocate (1686–88); under William III, lord advocate; conciliated Presbyterians; joint secretary of state (1691–95) with chief management of Scottish affairs; culpable, with Breadalbane and king, for the massacre of the Macdonald clan of Glencoe (1692); privy councilor (1702); created earl (1703); supported Act of Union (1707). ¶Sir Hew Dalrymple (1652–1737), Lord North Ber·wick \'ber-ik\, 3d son of 1st viscount. Succeeded his father as president in court of session (1698–1737). ¶Sir David Dalrymple of Hailes \'hā(ə)lz\ (d. 1721); 5th son of 1st viscount. Solicitor general to Queen Anne; Scottish M.P. (1703); commissioner in arranging treaty at Union (1706); British M.P. (1708–21); auditor to Scottish exchequer (1720).

¶John Dalrymple (1673–1747), 2d Earl of Stair, *known as* Marshal Stair. Military leader and diplomat; son of 1st earl. Distinguished himself in Marlborough's campaigns (1701–11), esp. at Oudenarde and Malplaquet; colonel of Royal Scots Greys (1706); general (1712). As ambassador to France (1715–20), counteracted schemes for reinstatement of James Edward, the Old Pretender. Scottish peer in House of Lords (1707–08, 1715–34, 1744–47). Field marshal (1742), commanded army on the Continent until George II's assumption of command; fought at Detingen (1743); general of marines (1746).

¶Sir David Dalrymple (1726–1792), Lord Hailes. Judge and antiquary; grandson of Sir David Dalrymple of Hailes. Judge of court of session (1766–76); judge of the justiciary or criminal court (from 1776), with record of humanitarianism. Author of *Annals of Scotland* (1776); on intimate terms with leading literary men of the day. His younger brother ¶Alexander (1737–1808), hydrographer. In East India Company's service (1752–95); negotiated commercial treaty with sultan of Sulu (1758); first hydrographer to British admiralty (1795–1808); author of accounts of discoveries in South Pacific and vigorous proponent of the existence of a huge continent in South Pacific he called Great South Land.

¶John Dalrymple (1720–89), 5th Earl of Stair; son of 5th son of 1st earl. Opposed in House of Lords measures leading to American Revolution and presented petition in favor of Massachusetts (1774). His son ¶John (1749–1821), 6th earl; served under Sir Henry Clinton in American Revolution; minister to Poland (1782), to Berlin (1785–88).

Dal·ton \'dȯlt-ᵊn\, Hugh, *in full* Edward Hugh John Neale. Baron Dalton. 1887–1962. British politician, b. Wales. M.P (1924–31, 1935–59); minister of economic warfare (1940–42); president of Board of Trade (1942–45); chancellor of the exchequer (1945–47); oversaw nationalization of Bank of England. Life peer (1960).

Dalton, John. 1766–1844. English chemist and physicist. Teacher of mathematics and physics in New Coll., Manchester (1793–1800); lecturer and private teacher. President of Philosophical Society (1817–44). Kept meteorological diary (from 1787); published *Meteorological Observations and Essays,* in which he maintained magnetic origin of Aurora Borealis (1793); gave first detailed description of color blindness, or Daltonism, from which he and his brother suffered (1794); read paper (1803; pub. 1805) on the *Absorption of Gases by Water and Other Liquids* containing statement of Dalton's law, or law of partial pressures; formulated relation of temperature and volume of bodies of gas (known as Charles's law); discovered butylene and determined composition of ether; arranged table of atomic weights (1803); first to give clear statement of atomic theory (1803–07); discovered law of multiple proportions. Published *A New System of Chemical Philosophy* (1808–27).

Dalton, Robert. 1867–1892. American outlaw, b. probably Cass Co., Mo. Deputy U.S. marshal in Indian Terr. (1888–89); with brothers Grattan and Emmet engaged in horse theft, train robbery, and bank robbery in Kansas, Oklahoma, California. Killed during unsuccessful attempt on bank of Coffeyville, Okla. (Oct. 1892).

Da·ly \'dā-lē\, Arnold, *in full* Peter Christopher Arnold. 1875–1927. American actor and producer, b. Brooklyn, N.Y. With *Candida* (1903) began vogue for plays of Bernard Shaw on American stage. *Mrs. Warren's Profession* (1905) was banned by police after one performance; Daly arrested, tried, and acquitted in famous case.

Daly, Augustin, *in full* John Augustin. 1838–1899. American playwright and theatrical manager, b. Plymouth, N.C. Newspaper dramatic critic, New York City (1859–69). After some success in adaptations of French and German plays (as *Leah the Forsaken,* 1862), wrote popular original melodramas, *Under the Gaslight* (1867), *A Flash of Lightning* (1868), and *The Red Scarf* (1869). Leased Fifth Avenue Theater (1869–77) and presented revivals of old English comedies, also his own plays *Divorce* (1871), *Roughing It* (1873), *Pique* (1875), and *The Dark City* (1877). Turned Old Broadway Theater into Daly's Theater (1879); assembled a new company including John Drew, Ada Rehan, and Otis Skinner, and presented again adaptations of French and German dramatic successes. Chosen by Tennyson to adapt *The Foresters* to the stage (1891). Opened theater in London (1893); presented Shakespearean comedies with marked success.

Daly, Marcus. 1841–1900. American mineowner, b. Ireland. To America (1856). In California rose from pick-and-shovel man to one of the wealthiest mineowners of the West. In partnership with George Hearst, James B.A. Haggin, and Lloyd Tevis developed the Anaconda copper mines in Butte, Montana, district; organized Anaconda Mining Company (1891); combined mining, timber, processing, and other holdings in Amalgamated Copper Co., organized (1891) with Henry H. Rogers. Long political feud between Daly and William A. Clark (1888–1900).

Daly, Reginald Aldworth. 1871–1957. American geologist, b. Napanee, Ont. Professor, M.I.T. (1907–12), Harvard (1912–1942). Authority on origin of igneous rocks and glaciers; proposed (1903) theory of magmatic stoping.

Dal·yell \'dal-yəl, dē-'el\ *or* **Dal·zell** \'dal-,zel, dal-'; dē-'el\, Thomas. 1599?–1685. Scottish Royalist soldier. Known as "the Muscovy general." Served in Rochelle military expedition of Duke of Buckingham (1627) and in Ireland. In Civil War, taken prisoner at Worcester (1651); escaped and took part in Highland rebellion (1654); in service of Russian czar, fought against Turks and Tatars; returned to Britain at Restoration; as commander in chief in Scotland subdued Covenanters (1666); privy councilor (1667); M.P. in Scottish parliament (1678–85); commissioned to punish rebels of Bothwell Bridge (1679).

Dal·ziel \'dal-zē-əl, 'dal-yəl, dē-'el\, James Henry. 1st Baron Dalziel of Kirk·cal·dy \kər-'kȯ(l)d-ē, -'kad-, -'käd-\. 1868–1935. British newspaper proprietor. Acquired control of *Pall Mall Gazette;* founded *Sunday Evening Telegram;* also published the *Era* and *Country World.* M.P. (1892–1921); chairman of committee in charge of German prisoners (1914–18).

Dam \'dȧm\, Carl Peter Henrik. 1895–1976. Danish biochemist. Professor, U. of Rochester (1942–45); Polytechnic Inst., Copenhagen (1941–65). For discovery of vitamin K, shared with E. A. Doisy 1943 Nobel prize for physiology or medicine.

Damascene, John. See JOHN of Damascus.

Da·mas·ci·us \də-'mash(-ē)-əs\. c.480-c.550. Greek Neoplatonist philosopher. Last head of Plato's Academy at Athens (422–29); after school was closed by Justinian, went to court of Khosrow I.

Da·mas·ki·nos \dä-mäs-kē-'nȯs\. *Orig.* Dimitrios Pa·pan·dre·ou \,päp-än-'drā-ü\. 1891–1949. Greek prelate and politician. Bishop of Corinth (1922–38); archbishop of Athens (1941–49). In exile for opposition to Metaxas regime (1938–41); regent of Greece (1944–46) for exiled King George II during civil war.

Dam·a·sus \'dam-ə-səs\. Name of two popes:

Damasus I. Saint. 304?–384. Pope (366–384). Election contested, but recognized by Valentinian I; opposed Arianism and other heresies, convening synods (368, 369) which condemned Bishop Macedonius of Constantinople and Bishop Apollinaris of Laodicea; first to proclaim primacy of see of Rome (382); received favor for interest in the tombs of the martyrs, for his inscriptions composed for them, and for restoration of the catacombs; commissioned Jerome to revise the Bible (version later known as the Vulgate).

Damasus II. *Orig.* Poppo. d. 1048. Pope (1048). Bishop of Brixen; nomination as pope contested by Benedict IX; reigned 23 days.

Damian, Saint. See under Saint COSMAS.

Da·mia·ni \däm-'yän-ē\, Pier. Saint. *English* Peter Da·mi·an \'dā-mē-ən\. 1007–1072. Italian ecclesiastic. Entered hermitage of Fonte Avellana near Gubbio, in Umbria (1035); prior (1043). Advocated reforms; denounced vices of clergy, esp. simony; trusted adviser to several popes. Cardinal bishop of Ostia (1057); papal legate to Germany (1069), where he induced Emperor Henry IV to give up idea of divorcing his wife. Declared a doctor of the church (1828).

Damien, Father. See Joseph DE VEUSTER.

Da·miens \dȧm-yaⁿ\, Robert-François. 1715–1757. French servant and criminal. Attempted to assassinate King Louis XV at Versailles (Jan. 5, 1757); tortured and executed. Attempts to link his deranged act to Jansenists or Jesuits failed.

Damīrī, ad- \ˌad-dam-'ē-rē\. *In full* Muḥammad ibn Mūsā Kamāl ad-Dīn ad-Damīrī. 1341–1405. Arab jurist and theologian in Egypt. Known for *Ḥayāt al-ḥayawān* (c.1371), an encyclopedia of animals mentioned in the Qur'ān.

Dam·ja·nich \'dȧm-yȧ-nēch\, János. 1804–1849. Hungarian general and patriot, of Serbian origin. Served in Hungarian war for independence (1848–49); after battle at Világos, surrendered to Russians, was handed over to Austrians and executed.

Dam·o·cles \'dam-ə-ˌklēz\. 4th century B.C. Greek courtier in retinue of Dionysius the Elder of Syracuse. According to story related by Cicero, Damocles, having commented on the good fortune of Dionysius, was invited by Dionysius to a banquet, at which he was seated under a naked sword suspended by a single hair.

Da·mon \'dā-mən\ of Athens. 5th century B.C. Greek musician and philosopher. A teacher of Socrates and Pericles; as a friend of Pericles, accepted ostracism.

Damon and **Phin·ti·as** \'fint-ē-əs\, *usually called* Pyth·i·as \'pith-ē-əs\. 4th century B.C. Pythagorean philosophers. Noted for their mutual devotion. According to the story, when Phintias, condemned to death for plotting against Dionysius of Syracuse, desired time to arrange his affairs, Damon pledged his own life for his friend's return; Phintias returned at the last moment and Dionysius, struck by the strength of their friendship, pardoned him.

Dam·pi·er \'dam-pē-ər, 'damp-yər\, William. 1652–1715. English buccaneer and explorer. With band of buccaneers crossed Isthmus of Darien (1679), plundered Peruvian coast. Engaged (1683) in buccaneering expedition along coasts of Chile, Peru, and Mexico. Made expedition with a Capt. Swan along Mexican coast, to East Indies, Philippines, marooned Swan in Mindanao, was marooned himself in Nicobar Islands (1688), made way back to England (1691). Sent out by admiralty in command of *Roebuck* (1699) on exploration trip along coasts of Australia, New Guinea, New Britain, his second circumnavigation of globe; gave his name to Dampier Archipelago and Dampier Strait. Commanded unsuccessful privateering expedition to South Seas (1703–07); pilot under Capt. Woodes Rogers on privateering expedition (1708–11) which rescued Alexander Selkirk. Author of *A New Voyage round the World* (1697).

Dampierre, Marquis de. See Auguste H. M. PICOT.

Dam·rong Ra·ja·nu·bhab \'dəm-ˌrȯŋ-ˌrəj-ə-'nü-ˌbäb\. 1862–1943. Siamese prince. Son of King Mongkut. Established school for sons of nobility (1880), later the Suankulap school, nation's first training school for civil servants. First director of Siamese department of education (1887–92); developed system of common schools, inspection, etc. As minister of interior (from 1892) reorganized national and local governments, reduced power of feudal princes, reformed system of taxation. A founder of the Siam Society (1904).

Dam·rosch \'däm-ˌrȯsh, *Angl* 'dam-ˌräsh\, Leopold. 1832–1885. American musical conductor, b. Posen, Germany (now Poznań, Poland). Conductor, Breslau Philharmonic Orchestra (1858); founding conductor, Breslau Orchestra Society (1862–71). Accepted invitation to be conductor, Arion Society, New York (1871); organized New York Oratorio Society (1873) and New York Symphony Society (1878); conducted chief Wagnerian operas at Metropolitan Opera House, New York City (1884–85). Introduced many works of Liszt, Berlioz, Brahms, Wagner to U.S.

His son ¶Frank Heino Damrosch (1859–1937), musical director, b. Breslau, Germany. Chorus master, Metropolitan Opera House, New York City (1885–92); conductor, People's Singing Classes (1892–1913), People's Choral Union (1894–1913), Musical Art Society, New York (1893–1920), Orpheus Club, Philadelphia (1897–1905), Symphony Concerts for Young People (1898–1912), Mendelssohn Glee Club (1904–09). Supervisor of music, N.Y.C. public schools (1897–1905); founding director, Institute of Musical Art (1905–26) and dean (1926–33) after Institute's merger with Juilliard Graduate School. A second son ¶Walter Johannes Damrosch (1862–1950), b. Breslau; conductor and composer. Assistant director (1885–91) under Anton Seidl at the Metropolitan Opera Company; succeeded father (1885) as director of the Oratorio and Symphony societies; founded Damrosch Opera Company (1895) and produced U.S. premiere of *Parsifal* (1896); conductor at Metropolitan Opera (1901–02); director, New York Symphony Orchestra (1903–26); musical counsel, National Broadcasting Company (from 1926); founder and conductor of orchestral radio concerts for public schools and colleges (1928–42); composer of *Manila Te Deum,* the operas *Cyrano, The Man Without a Country, The Opera Cloak,* and incidental music. Leopold's daughter Clara married David Mannes (*q.v.*)

Dan \dän\ Takuma. 1858–1932. Japanese businessman. Manager of the Mitsui conglomerate (*zaibatsu*); assassinated by right-wing nationalists.

Da·na \'dā-nə\, Charles Anderson. 1819–1897. American newspaper editor, b. Hinsdale, N.H. At Brook Farm (1841–46). City and later managing editor of Greeley's New York *Tribune* (1847–62). Coeditor with George Ripley of the *New American Cyclopaedia* (1857–63). Assistant secretary of war (1863–65). Owner and editor, New York *Sun* (1868–97), esteemed as the "newspaperman's newspaper."

Dana, Francis. 1743–1811. American diplomat and jurist, b. Charlestown, Mass. Semiofficial representative of Massachusetts in England (1774–76); member of Continental Congress (1776–78, 1784–85); a signer of Articles of Confederation (1778). Secretary to John Adams in France (1780); named minister to Russia but not officially received while there (1780–83). Associate justice, Mass. Supreme Court (1785–91); chief justice (1791–1806).

Dana, James Dwight. 1813–1895. American geologist and naturalist, b. Utica, N.Y. Geologist on Wilkes Exploring Expedition sent by U.S. government into southern Pacific (1838–42); published expedition reports under titles *Zoophytes* (1846), *Geology* (1849), and *Crustacea* (1852–54). Editor, *American Journal of Science* (from 1840). Professor of natural history (1849–64), of geology and mineralogy (1864–90), Yale. Leading American geologist of the day. Other works included *A System of Mineralogy* (1837), *Manual of Geology* (1862), *Textbook of Geology* (1864), *Corals and Coral Islands* (1872), *Characteristics of Volcanoes* (1890). His son ¶Edward Salisbury (1849–1935) was best known as a mineralogist; professor of physics (1890–1917), and curator of mineral collection (1874–1922), Yale; author of *Textbook of Mineralogy* (1877), *Minerals and How to Study Them* (1895), etc.

Dana, John Cotton. 1856–1929. American librarian, b. Woodstock, Vt. Cousin of James D. Dana. Librarian, Denver (Colo.) Public Library (1889–98); Springfield (Mass.) City Library (1898–1902); Newark (N.J.) Public Library (1902–29).

Dana, Richard Henry. 1815–1882. American sailor, author, and lawyer. Grandson of Francis Dana. Sailed on a brig from Boston around Cape Horn to California (1834–36); embodied his experiences in *Two Years Before the Mast* (1840), which became an American classic of sea adventure. Author also of *The Seaman's Friend* (1841) on maritime law. Specialized in admiralty and international law; one of the prosecutors of Jefferson Davis (1867–68).

Danby, Earl of. See Thomas OSBORNE.

Dan·by \'dan-bē\, Francis. 1793–1861. Irish historical and landscape painter. Lived near Lake of Geneva (1829–41), in England (1841–61); known for ideal and poetic landscapes.

Dance \'dȧn(t)s, 'dan(t)s\, George. 1700–1768. English architect. As surveyor to the City of London, designed Mansion House (1739). His son ¶George, *known as* the Younger (1741–1825), architect and artist. Rebuilt Newgate Prison (1770) and designed front of Guildhall. A founder of (1768) and professor of architecture at (1798–1805) the Royal Academy. Another son ¶Sir Nathaniel Dance-Hol·land \-'häl-ənd\ (1735–1811), painter, was associated with his brother in founding the Royal Academy, where he was a frequent exhibitor.

D'·An·co·na \däŋ-'kō-nä\, Alessandro. 1835–1914. Italian critic and historian. Professor at Pisa (from 1860). Pioneer in application of historical and critical methods to study of Italian literature; chief works *Antiche rime volgari* (1875–88), *Origini del teatro in Italia* (1877), *La poesia popolare italiana* (1878), *Ricordi storici del risorgimento italiano* (1914).

Dan·court \däⁿ-kür\, Florent. *Orig. surname* Car·ton \kȧr-tōⁿ\. Sieur d'Ancourt \däⁿ-kür\. 1661–1725. French actor and playwright. Successful as comedian at Comédie-Française (1685–1718). Among his many comedies were *Le Chevalier à la mode* (1687), *La Maison de campagne* (1688), *Les Bourgeoises de qualité* (1724).

Daṇ·ḍin \'dən-din\. 6th–7th century A.D. Sanskrit author and poet. Wrote *Kāvyādarśa,* a manual of poetics, and *Daśakumāracarita* ("Adventures of the Ten Princes"), a collection of stories of love and power.

Dan·do·lo \'dän-dō-(ˌ)lō\. Patrician family of Venice, including: Enrico (1107?–1205), doge (1192–1205). Venetian ambassador in Constantinople (1172), Sicily (1174), Ferrara (1191); vigorously promoted Fourth Crusade;

leader of Venetians and crusaders who captured Constantinople (1203, 1204). His grandson ¶Giovanni Dandolo (d. 1289) was captain-general of the Venetian army (1249) and doge (1280–89); reorganized military forces to meet threat from Genoa. ¶Francesco Dandolo (d. 1339) was doge (1329–39); directed Venetian expansionism toward continental Europe. ¶Andrea Dandolo (1307–1354) was doge (1343–54). Subdued seventh revolt of Zara (1345–46) but provoked debilitating war with Genoa. Friend of Petrarch; compiled valuable annals of Venice.

Dandolo, Vincenzo. 1758–1819. Italian chemist and politician. A leader of the provisional Venetian government (1797); senator of the Cisalpine Republic (1797–1804); general superintendent of Dalmatia (1804–09). Wrote on animal husbandry, viticulture, silkworm culture; author of *Les Hommes nouveaux ou moyens d'opere une regeneration morale* (1799).

Dan·du·rand \dä^n-dᵫ-rä^n\, Raoul. 1861–1942. Canadian politician, b. Montreal. Member of Canadian senate (from 1898), speaker (1905–09); member of privy council (1909). Minister without portfolio in dominion cabinet (1921–26, 1926–30). Government leader in senate (1921–30, 1935–42); Liberal party opposition leader (1930–35). Canadian delegate to League of Nations Assembly (1925, 1927–30); president of assembly (1925).

Dane, Clemence. See Winifred ASHTON.

Dane \ˈdān\, Nathan. 1752–1835. American jurist, b. Ipswich, Mass. Member, Continental Congress (1785–87); shared with Manasseh Cutler the drafting of the ordinance for the government of the Northwest Territory (1787). Author of *General Abridgement and Digest of American Law* (1823; supplementary vol., 1829). The Dane professorship of law in Harvard Law School was named in his honor.

Danei, Paolo Francesco. See PAUL of the Cross.

Dan·en·how·er \ˈdan-ən-ˌhau̇(-ə)r\, John Wilson. 1849–1887. American explorer, b. Chicago. Member of the De Long Arctic exploring expedition (1879–81); was one of George W. Melville's party of survivors; published *Lieutenant Danenhower's Narrative of the Jeannette* (1882).

Da·nev \ˈdän-ef\, Stoyan Petrov. 1858–1949. Bulgarian politician. Minister of foreign affairs (1901) and premier (1902–03); president of Sobranje (1911); again premier for about a month (1913) at outbreak of Second Balkan War; finance minister (1918–19, 1919–21).

Dangeau, Marquis de. See Philippe de COURCILLON.

Dan·ger·field \ˈdān-jər-ˌfē(ə)ld\, Thomas. 1650–1685. English informer. A convicted thief and counterfeiter; imprisoned (1679) for falsely charging Presbyterians with plotting to destroy government; subsequently claimed he had been deceived by Catholics; charged his employer, Mrs. Cellier, had paid him to assassinate Charles II and the Earl of Shaftesbury; "Meal-tub Plot," so called from hiding place of forged papers he had planted to incriminate Mrs. Cellier, finally exposed; convicted of libel (1685).

Da·ni·can \dá-nē-kä^n\. A family of French composers and musicians including: Michel (d. c.1659), who was given the nickname Philidor (after Filidori, eminent Sienese oboist) for his skill by Louis XIII; the family thereafter adopted the name Philidor. ¶Jean Danican (d. 1679), a musician in the Grande Écurie, the king's band. Jean's son ¶André Philidor, *called* L'Aîné (c.1647–1730), chamber and chapel musician to Louis XIV, composer of several opera ballets and instrumental works, and keeper of the royal music library (from 1684), for which he collected hundreds of volumes of music from the time of Henry III on (later known as the Collection Philidor). André's brothers ¶Jacques, *called* le Cadet (d. 1708) and ¶Alexandre (1660–?), both musicians in the Grande Écurie. André's son ¶Anne (1681–1728) played in the Grande Écurie and wrote three pastorales and an exercise book. Another son of André ¶François-André (1726–1795) composed several successful operas, including *Sancho Pança dans son isle* (1762), *Tom Jones* (1765), *La belle esclave* (1787), and other works. Also a noted chess player, devised "Philidor's defense" and "Philidor's legacy," and published *Analyse du jeu des échecs* (1748).

Dan·iel \ˈdan-yəl\. *In full* Da·ni·lo Ro·ma·no·vich \(ˌ)dən-ˈyē-lə-(ˌ)rə-ˈmán(-əv)-ˌyich\. *Known as* Daniel of Galicia. 1202–1264. Russian prince. Inherited rule of principalities of Galicia and Volhynia on death of father (1206); gained full authority after defeating various pretenders in Volhynia (1221) and Galicia (1238). Built cities at Lvov and Chetm. After defeat of Prince Rostislav (1245) was most powerful of eastern European princes. Formed alliances with Hungary, Austria, Lithuania, and papacy. Unsuccessful in attempt to drive out Mongol forces (1256–60).

Daniel *or* **Da·nil** \(ˌ)dən-ˈyēl\. *Known as* Daniel of Kiev. d. 1122. Russian ecclesiastic and traveler. Pilgrim to the Holy Land (c.1106–07); author of *Puteshestvie igumena Daniila,* popular in the Middle Ages.

Da·niel \dán-yel\, Antoine. 1601–1648. French Jesuit missionary in America. Accompanied Samuel de Champlain to Quebec (1633); labored among Huron Indians; slain by hostile Iroquois. Canonized (1930).

Daniel, Arnaut. See ARNAUT DANIEL.

Daniel, Gabriel. 1649–1728. French Jesuit historian. Author of *Histoire de France depuis l'établissement de la monarchie française* (1713), *Histoire de la milice française* (1721), and replies to Pascal and Descartes; named historiographer of France by Louis XIV.

Dan·iel \ˈdan-yəl\, Peter Vivian. 1784–1860. American jurist, b. Stafford Co., Va. Associate justice, U.S. Supreme Court (1841–60).

Daniel, Samuel. 1562?–1619. English poet. Tutor to William Herbert (who became Earl of Pembroke), later, to daughter of Countess of Cumberland. Master of queen's revels (1603); composed pastoral tragicomedies *The Queenes Arcadia* (1606) and *Hymens Triumph* (1615) and masques, as *Tethys Festival* (1610). Author of *Delia* (sonnets, 1592); *The Complaint of Rosamond* (a soliloquy, 1592); *The Tragedie of Cleopatra* (1594); *The Tragedie of Philotus* (1604); verse history of *The Civile Warres* (1595–1609); *Poetical Essayes* (1599); *Defence of Rime* (reply to Thomas Campion, 1603); a prose history of England (1612–18). Official evidence is wanting for the statement that he received, prior to Ben Jonson, the title of poet laureate.

Daniel Aleksandrovich. 1261–1303. Grand prince of Moscow (1276–1303). Son of Aleksander Nevsky. Founder of ruling dynasty of Moscow.

Dan·iell \ˈdan-yəl\, John Frederic. 1790–1845. English chemist and physicist. Invented Daniell's hygrometer (1820); published *Meteorological Essays* (1823); invented improved pyrometer (1832), for which he received Rumford Medal, and the Daniell cell, a great improvement over voltaic cell (1836), for which he received Copley Medal.

Dan·iels \ˈdan-yəlz\, Frank Albert. 1856–1935. American comedian, b. Dayton, Ohio. Achieved fame in Victor Herbert's musical comedies *Wizard of the Nile* (1895), *The Idol's Eye* (1897), *The Tattooed Man* (1907).

Daniels, Josephus. 1862–1948. American journalist and statesman, b. Washington, N.C. Editor of Raleigh (N.C.) *State Chronicle* (1885–92) and *News and Observer* (1894–1933). U.S. secretary of the navy (1913–21); U.S. ambassador to Mexico (1933–41).

Da·ni·els·son \ˈdä-nē-əl-ˌsȯn\, Anders. 1784–1839. Swedish peasant leader. In peasant chamber of Riksdag (from 1809), eventually representing 27 districts. Advocated public education, reduced military spending, occupational freedom, abolition of land tax, and other reforms.

Danielsson, Olof August. 1852–1933. Swedish scholar. Professor of Greek at Uppsala (1890–1917); specialist in comparative grammar of Greek, Venetic, Leponic, Lydian languages; chief work his *Corpus Inscriptionum Etruscarum* (1901–17 and supplements).

Da·ni·lev·sky \(ˌ)dən-yil-ˈyef-skəi\, Nikolay Yakovlevich. 1822–1865. Russian naturalist and philosopher. Propounded a nationalistic view of history emphasizing Russia's uniqueness and urging its development; chief work *Rossiya i Evropa* (1869).

Da·ni·lo \dä-ˈnē-lo\. *In full* Danilo Pe·tro·vić Nje·goš \-ˈpe-tro-vētʸ-ˈnyeg-ósh\. Name of two ruling princes of Montenegro: Danilo (1677–1737); first hereditary prince-bishop (*vladika;* 1711); nearly put to death by Turks (1702); instigated massacre of Muslims (1702); at war with Turks (1711–15). ¶Danilo I (1826–1860); succeeded Peter II as prince-bishop (1851) and reigning prince (1852–60); discontinued hereditary office of bishop; at war with Turkey (1852–53) and again (1856–58); defeated Turks at Grahovo (1858); established independence of Montenegro; succeeded by Nicholas I.

Dan·jon \dä^n-zhō^n\, André-Louis. 1890–1967. French astronomer. Director of Strasbourg Observatory (1930–45), of Paris Observatory (1945–63); professor at Sorbonne (1946–54); director of Institut d'Astrophysique de Paris (1954–63). Developed Danjon astrolabe (1956) and other precision instruments; studied irregularities in Earth's rotation.

Dan·kl \ˈdäŋ-kəl\, Viktor. Graf von Kras·nik \ˈkräs-nik\. 1854–1941. Austrian general. At outbreak of World War I, commanded 1st army; defeated Russians at Krasnik (Aug. 23–24, 1914); commanded Austrian defense in Tirol against Italians (1915–16).

Danks \ˈdaŋks\, Hart Pease. 1834–1903. American composer of hymns and songs, b. New Haven, Conn. Best known song, "Silver Threads Among the Gold".

Dannay, Frederic. See Manfred LEE.

Dan·neck·er \ˈdän-ek-ər\, Johann Heinrich von. 1758–1841. German sculptor. Court sculptor at Württemberg (from 1780); friend of Schiller, Goethe, Herder, Canova. His best known works were busts of Schiller and Gluck and *Ariadne auf dem Panther.*

D'·An·nun·zi·o \dän-ˈnünt-syō\, Gabriele. 1863–1938. Italian author, soldier, and political leader. Journalist on staff of *Tribuna,* Rome; deputy in parliament (1897–1900); in exile in France to escape debts (1910–15); notorious for lavish living and amours, particularly his liaison with Eleonora Duse. Ardent advocate of Italian entry into World War I; served in army, navy, and finally as aviator, winning reputation for sensational exploits, including reconnaissance flight over Vienna (1918); lost eye in aerial combat. During controversy between Italy and Yugoslavia over status of Fiume, headed force of Italian soldiers and, without orders from Italian government, occupied city (Sept. 1919); proclaimed "Italian regency of the Carnaro" and ruled as dictator until Italian government sent force against him (Dec. 1920); lived thereafter in retirement. Strong supporter of Fascist movement; created (1924) Prince of Mon·te Ne·vo·so \'mōn-tā-nā-'vō-sō\ by Mussolini. His works included poetry: *Primo vere* (1879), *Canto novo* (1882), *L'Intermezzo di rime* (1884), *La chimera* (1888), *Il poema paradisiaco* (1891), *Odi navali* (1892–93), *Laudi del cielo, del mare, della terra, e degli eroi* (1899); short stories (written chiefly 1882–86) later collected in *Le novelle della pescara;* dramatic works *Sogno d'un mattino di primavera* (1897), *La città morta* (1898), *La gioconda* (1899), *Francesca da Rimini* (1901), all written for Duse, and *La figlia di Iorio* (1904); novels, many noted for their eroticism and Nietzschean heroes: *Il piacere* (1889), *L'innocente* (1892), *Il trionfo della morte* (1894), *Le vergini delle rocce* (1896), *Il fuoco* (1900), *Forse che sì, forse che no* (1910), *La leda senza cigno* (1916), and *Notturno* (1921); political and patriotic writings and addresses: *Per la più grande Italia* (1915), *Contro uno è contro tutti* (1919), *Per l'Italia degli Italiani* (1923).

Dan·quah \'dän-kwə, 'däŋ-\, Joseph[1] Kwame Kyeretwi Boakye. 1895–1965. Ghanaian politician. A founder of United Gold Coast Convention (1947), moderate nationalist group. Member of Gold Coast legislative assembly (1951–54). Defeated by Kwame Nkrumah for presidency of Ghana (1960); imprisoned (1961–62, 1964–65) for opposition to Nkrumah's dictatorial policies.

Dan·tan \dä^{n}-tä^{n}\, Antoine-Laurent. 1798–1878. French sculptor. Carved statues of Villars, the dauphin of France, the Dauphine Marie Josèphe of Saxony, Duquesne, and portrait busts of Rachel, Baron Mounier, etc. His brother ¶Jean-Pierre (1800–1869), *known as* Dantan the Younger, was also a sculptor, esp. of caricatured figures and grotesques, as of Victor Hugo, Balzac, Rossini; alleged to have originated modern caricature in sculpture.

Dan·te \'dän-tā; *Angl* 'dän-(,)tā, 'dan-, -(,)tē, 'dant-ē, 'dänt-ē\. *In full* Dante *or* Du·ran·te \dü-'rän-tā\ Ali·ghie·ri \,äl-ēg-'ye-rē\. 1265–1321. Italian poet, b. Florence. Spent youth at Florence; met (reputedly c.1273) Beatrice Portinari (*q.v.*); friend of Guido Cavalcanti, who influenced him strongly, Cino da Pistoia, Brunetto Latini, and Giotto; reputed to have studied at Bologna, Padua, Paris, and probably Oxford; fought on side of Guelphs against Ghibellines (Campaldino, 1289) and Pisans (1290); entered political life (c.1295); member of Council to the Captain of the People (1295–96) and the Council of the Hundred (1296); m. Gemma Donati (c.1297); as Guelph partisan and member of the Bianchi (the Whites), entrusted with various diplomatic missions; elected prior of Florence (1300); with victory of Black Guelphs, condemned to death in absentia and thus banished from Florence (1302); led wandering life, living at Verona (1303, 1306), Bologna (1304), Casentino (1308), Pisa (1313), and Ravenna (1318–21). Known esp. for *Commedia,* later called *Divina commedia* (begun c.1308, completed 1321), a philosophico-political poem in terza rima, consisting of 100 cantos, and recounting an imaginary journey of the author through Hell, Purgatory, and Paradise (*Inferno, Purgatorio, Paradiso*), guided through first two by Virgil and through last by Beatrice; considered a masterpiece of world literature. Wrote in Italian *La vita nuova* (c.1293), collection of 31 love poems, chiefly sonnets, in the *dolce stil nuovo* (i.e., sweet new style), with prose commentaries; *Il convivio* (begun c.1304), prose commentary on three canzoni (4 books). Wrote in Latin *De vulgari eloquentia* (begun c.1304), a defense of a hypothetical universalized Italian language as a literary and philosophical medium; *De monarchia; Epistolae* (esp. the *Epistola ad canem grandem*); *Eclogae; Quaestio de aqua et terra.*

Dantin, Louis. See Eugène SEERS.

Dan·tis·cus \dan-'tis-kəs\, Johannes. *Pol.* Jan Dan·ty·szek \dan-'tish-,ek\. *Orig. surname* Flachs·bin·der \'fläks-,bin-dər\. 1485–1548. Polish courtier and Humanist. Attached to court of Sigismund I; bishop of Chełmno (1530), prince bishop of Warmiński (1537). Author of Latin verses, love poems, panegyrics; among first to bring Humanist values to Poland.

Dan·ton \dä^{n}-tō^{n}\, Georges-Jacques. 1759–1794. French revolutionary leader. Practiced law in Paris (1785–91). A founder of the Cordelier (1790); member also of Jacobin Club; advocated extreme action; fled to England (1791). Assumed leadership of revolutionaries and role as tribune of the people; minister of justice following fall of monarchy (1792). In face of foreign dangers, urged action (speech of Sept. 2, 1792: "De l'audace, encore de l'audace, et toujours de l'audace!"). Elected to National Convention (Sept. 1792); voted for death of king (Jan. 1793); elected president of Jacobin Club (Mar. 1793), aim of which was unity of the country and a stable republican government; member of the Committee of Public Safety and effective head of government (April–July, 1793). Gradually identified as leader of moderates opposed to revolutionary excesses; with Desmoulins and followers overcome by more radical Robespierre and leaders of the Reign of Terror; seized and imprisoned; defiant in farcical trial; condemned and guillotined.

Dantzig, Duc de. See Pierre-François-Joseph LEFEBVRE.

d'Anville, Jean-Baptiste Bourguignon. See ANVILLE.

Da Pon·te \dä-'pōn-tā\, Lorenzo. *Orig.* Emanuele Co·ne·glia·no \kō-nāl-'yän-ō\. 1749–1838. Italian poet. Born of Jewish parents, converted to Roman Catholic faith, baptized by bishop of Ceneda, whose name he took. Appointed (c.1780) by Austrian government "Poet to the Italian Theater"; wrote librettos for Mozart's *Le nozze di Figaro* (1786), *Don Giovanni* (1787), *Così fan tutte* (1790). In London (1793–1805), wrote for Drury Lane Theater *La capricciosa correta, L'isola del piacere,* etc. To U.S. (1805); established a class in Italian in New York City; professor of Italian literature, Columbia (from 1825); inspired American interest in Italian culture and esp. in study of Dante.

Da·qī·qī, ad- \åd-då-'kē-kē\. *In full* Abū Manṣūr Muḥammad ibn Aḥmad ad-Daqīqī. d. c.976–981. Persian poet. Wrote panegyrics, lyrics, uncompleted epic on mythical Persian heroes. Contributed to establishment of dominant meter and style of Persian poetry; works of much influence on Ferdowsī.

Da·quin \då-ka^{n}\, Louis-Claude. 1694–1772. French organist and composer. Organist in Chapel Royal (from 1739), Notre Dame (from 1755); composed two masses, organ pieces, carols, motets, and cantatas.

Da·rá·nyi \'där-ån-yē\, Kálmán von. 1886–1939. Hungarian politician. In Congress (1927–39); minister of agriculture (1935–36); pro-Fascist premier (1936–38); president of legislature (1938–39).

Dā·rā Shi·kōh \dä-'rä-shē-'kō\. 1615–1659. Persian prince and scholar. Son of Shāh Jahān. Adherent of Ṣūfī mysticism, attempted synthesis of Ṣūfī and Hindu philosophy; translated Hindu scriptures. Killed by brother Aurangzeb in struggle over succession.

Da·ra·zī \dar-az-'ē\, Muḥammad ibn Ismā'īl ad-. d. 1019/20. Islāmic religious leader. First missionary of the sect of the Druzes (named after him). See al-ḤĀKIM.

d'Arblay, Madame. See Fanny BURNEY.

Dar·boux \dår-bü\, Jean-Gaston. 1842–1917. French mathematician. Author of works on geometry, esp. on orthogonal surfaces and on infinitesimal geometry; also on approximation to functions of large numbers, discontinuous functions, etc. The Darboux integral is named for him.

Dar·boy \dårb-wå\, Georges. 1813–1871. French prelate. Archbishop of Paris (1863–71); chief almoner to Napoléon III, senator, member of privy council and council of regency (1864); arrested and shot by Communards.

Dar·by \'där-bē\, Abraham. 1678?–1717. English ironmaster. Founded Bristol Iron Company (1708); first to use coke to smelt iron ore (1709); produced iron of unprecedented quality. Iron from his works at Coalbrookdale used in Newcomen steam engines (from 1712), world's first iron bridge, built at Coalbrookdale (1759) by Abraham Darby III, and Richard Trevithick's locomotive (1802).

Darby, John Nelson. 1800–1882. English theological writer. Chief founder of the Plymouth Brethren (c.1830) and of an exclusive section of this sect, the Darbyites (1845).

Darc *or* **d'Arc,** Jeanne. See JOAN of Arc.

Dar·cet \dår-se\, Jean. 1725–1801. French chemist and physician. Applied chemistry to art and industry, improving manufacture of coins, tapestries, and porcelain; produced an alloy of bismuth, lead, and tin, fusible in boiling water; investigated the action of fire on diamonds, etc.

Dar·cy \dår-sē\, Henri-Philibert-Gaspard. 1803–1858. French hydraulic engineer. While supervising design and construction of water supply system in Dijon, studied water flow in pipes; discovered importance of surface roughness in retarding flow; derived Darcy's law, describing nonturbulent flow through porous media, the theoretical foundation of ground water hydrology.

Dar·cy \'där-sē\, Thomas. Baron Darcy of Templehurst. c.1467–1537. English nobleman. Led troops in support of Ferdinand and Isabella in Spain (1511) and of Henry VIII in France (1513); broke with Henry and Cardinal Wolsey over papal authority (1529); corresponded with ambassador of Charles V, Holy Roman emperor, on question of European invasion of England to restore Catholic supremacy; suspected of treason after easily yielding castle of Pontefract, Yorkshire, to Catholic rebels (1536); tried and beheaded.

D'·Ar·cy \'där-sē\, William Knox. 1849–1917. English businessman. Made fortune in Mount Morgan goldfield, Queensland (1882–89); secured (1901) 60-year oil concession in Iran; found oil (1908); retired after formation of Anglo-Persian Oil Company (1909).

Dare \'da(ə)r, 'de(ə)r\, Virginia. 1587–? First child born in America of English parents, b. Roanoke Island, Va. (now North Carolina). Granddaughter of Gov. John White, founder and governor of the colony. Nine days after her birth, White sailed to England for supplies. The Spanish war prevented his return. In 1590, aid was sent from England, but all trace of the colony had vanished.

Dar·es Phryg·i·us \'da(ə)r-ēz-'frij-ē-əs, 'de(ə)r-, 'dā-rēz-\. 13–12th century B.C.? Trojan priest. Reputed author of original of the later Latin *De excidio Trojae historia,* purported eyewitness account of Trojan war and a chief source of medieval stories of the Trojan war. Cf. DICTYS CRETENSIS.

Da·reste de la Cha·vanne \dȧ-rest-də-lȧ-shȧ-vän\, Antoine-Élisabeth-Cléophas. 1820–1882. French historian. Author of *Histoire de France* (1865–79), *Histoire de l'administration en France* (1848), etc.

d'Arezzo, Guido and Guittone. See GUIDO of Arezzo and GUITTONE D'AREZZO.

Dar·go·myzh·sky \dər-(ˌ)gə-ˈmish-skyəi\, Aleksandr Sergeyevich. 1813–1869. Russian composer. Known for operas, including *Esmeralda* (1847), *Torzhestvo Vakha* (*Triumph of Bacchus,* 1845; perf. 1867), *Rusalka* (1856); songs; orchestral works as *Kazachok* (1864), *Chukhonskaya fantaziya* (*Finnish Fantasia,* 1869), *Baba-Yaga* (1870). His musical drama *Kamenniy gost* (*The Stone Guest,* after Pushkin) was completed by Cui and Rimsky-Korsakov (1872).

Darío, Rubén. *See* Félix Rubén GARCÍA SARMIENTO.

Da·ri·us \da-ˈrī-əs\. Name of three Achaemenid kings of Persia:

Darius I. *Called* the Great. 550–486 B.C. King (522–486 B.C.). Son of Hystaspes; married Atossa, daughter of Cyrus the Great. Apparently killed Bardiya (522) and assumed throne, although Darius claimed that he had actually killed one Gaumata, who supposedly had usurped throne and impersonated Bardiya. At first troubled by revolts in various parts of empire, esp. in Babylon and Susiana; restored order and reorganized administration; divided land into 20 satrapies; introduced reforms in administration and taxation, built roads, established a postal system, standardized weights and measures and coinage; built Persepolis; liberal in policy toward Jews, allowing them to rebuild temple (519). Conquered eastern Thrace and the Getae but failed in great expedition against Scythians (513); annexed a province of India along the Indus; conquered, through western satraps, Thrace, Macedonia, Lemnos, Imbros; began great struggle with Greece, caused first by revolt of Ionian cities (499–494); raised two expeditions to punish Greece—first (492), under his son-in-law Mardonius, failed when fleet lost in storm—second, under Artaphernes and Datis, defeated at Marathon (490); faced by revolt of Egypt (486); died while preparing third expedition against Greece. Events of reign recorded in many inscriptions, esp. that of Bīsitūn (Behistun). Succeeded by his son Xerxes I.

Darius II Ochus \ˈō-kəs\. *Old Persian* Da·ra·ya·vaush \dä-ˌrī-ä-ˈvau̇sh\. *Surnamed in Greek* No·thus \ˈnō-thəs\, *i.e.* Bastard. d. 404 B.C. King (423–404 B.C.). Natural son of Artaxerxes I. Seized throne from Sogdianus; assumed reign name of Darius; weak sovereign, dominated by his half-sister and wife, Parysatis; reign marked by revolts in Asia Minor and Egypt. Through satraps Pharnabazus and Tissaphernes formed alliance with Sparta (413) against Athens; recaptured most of Ionia; appointed son Cyrus the Younger commander in Asia Minor (407) and rebuilt Spartan fleet. Succeeded by his son Artaxerxes II (*q.v.*).

Darius III. *Old Persian* Darayavaush. *Surnamed* Cod·om·man·us \ˌkäd-ō-ˈman-əs\. d. 330 B.C. Last Achaemenid king (336–330 B.C.). Great-grandson of Darius II. Raised to throne through murder of Artaxerxes III and his son Arses by eunuch Bagoas; his satraps defeated (334) at Granicus by Greeks under Alexander; himself defeated and his family captured at Issus (333); was rebuffed in attempts to ransom family and cede most of empire; overwhelmed (331) at Gaugamela; fled to Ecbatana and Bactria; murdered by his satrap Bessus.

Dar·lan \dar-lä^{n}\, Jean-Louis-Xavier-François. 1881–1942. French naval officer and politician. Chief of naval staff (1936); commander in chief (1939). During Vichy regime, admiral of the fleet, vice premier (1941), foreign minister and minister of defense (1941–42); concluded armistice with Allies following invasion of North Africa (Nov. 1942), ordered cessation of French resistance, and assumed authority as chief of state in French Africa; assassinated.

Dar·ley \ˈdär-lē\, Felix Octavius Carr. 1822–1888. American illustrator, b. Philadelphia. Illustrated Irving's *Rip Van Winkle* (1849) and *Legend of Sleepy Hollow* (1850), Ik Marvel's *Lorgnette* (1851), an edition of the works of James Fenimore Cooper, works of Longfellow, Dickens, etc.

Darley, George. 1795–1846. Irish poet. Author of poems, as *The Errors of Ecstasie* (1822); dramas, as *Sylvia* (verse, 1827), *Thomas à Becket* (1840), *Ethelstan* (1841); unfinished lyrical poem *Nepenthe* (1835), valued for dream imagery and symbolism; also wrote mathematical textbooks.

Dar·ling \ˈdär-liŋ\, Grace Horsley. 1815–1842. English heroine. With her father, keeper of the Longstone lighthouse on Farne Islands, rescued five survivors of the *Forfarshire* (1838).

Darling, Jay Norwood. *Known by his signature* Ding \ˈdiŋ\. 1876–1962. American cartoonist, b. Norwood, Mich. On staff of Des Moines *Register* (1906–11, 1913–49); cartoons syndicated nationally (from 1917); won Pulitzer prizes for editorial cartoons (1923, 1943). Also interested in preservation of wildlife; served as chief of U.S. Biological Survey (1934–36).

Dar·mes·te·ter \dȧr-mes-tə-ter\, Arsène. 1846–1888. French philologist. Professor of Old French at Sorbonne (1881–88); author of *Traité de la formation des mots* (1873), *La Vie des mots* (1887); with Adolphe Hatzfeld and Antoine Thomas, compiled *Dictionnaire général de la langue française* (1890–1900).

Darmesteter, James. 1849–1894. French Orientalist. Brother of Arsène Darmesteter. Taught at École des Hautes Études (1877–85), Collège de France (1885–94). Specialized in ancient Iranian; published *Études iraniennes* (1883) and English (1883–87) and French (1892–93) translations of the Avesta, sacred scripture of Zoroastrianism.

Darnley, Lord. See Henry Stewart under STEWART family.

Dar·racq \dȧ-rȧk\, Alexandre, *in full* Pierre-Alexandre. 1855–1931. French automobile manufacturer. Founded Gladiator Cycle company (1891); later manufactured electric cars and Millet motor bicycles. Began producing Léon Bollée voiturettes (1898), later produced quality automobiles under Darracq, Talbot-Darracq, and Talbot trademarks, notably the Darracq "Flying Fifteen" (1904); built racing cars and operated school for race drivers.

Dar·row \ˈdar-(ˌ)ō\, Clarence Seward. 1857–1938. American lawyer, b. Kinsman, Ohio. Adm. to bar (1878) and practiced in Chicago (from 1887). Prominent as member of counsel for Eugene V. Debs, Socialist leader indicted (1894) for conspiracy in the Railroad Union case; chief counsel for labor interests in anthracite strike arbitration proceedings at Scranton, Pa. (1902–03). Defense counsel in several widely publicized trials, including those of William D. "Big Bill" Haywood, accused of complicity in assassination of Gov. Steunenberg of Idaho (1907), the McNamara brothers, accused of dynamiting the *Los Angeles Times* building (1911), Nathan Leopold and Richard Loeb, charged with killing Bobbie Franks (1924), John T. Scopes of Dayton, Tenn., charged with violating state law forbidding teaching of evolution in public schools (1925). Among his books were *An Eye for an Eye* (novel, 1905), *Crime: Its Cause and Treatment* (1922), and *The Story of My Life* (1932).

d'Arsonval, Arsène. See ARSONVAL.

Dartmouth, Barons and earls of. See LEGGE family.

Da·ru \dȧ-rue̅\, Pierre-Antoine-Noël-Bruno. Comte. 1767–1829. French military administrator and historian. Entered military administration (1784); secretary general of war ministry (1800); successfully reorganized imperial army; councilor of state (1805); intendant general of the Grande Armée in Austria (1805, 1809) and Prussia (1806–07); created count (1809); minister of war (1811); retired (1814) but returned to serve in war ministry during the Hundred Days. Member of Chamber of Peers (from 1819). Translated Horace (1804–05); wrote *Histoire de la République de Venise* (1819) and *Histoire de la Bretagne* (1826).

Dar·win \ˈdär-wən\, Charles Robert. 1809–1882. English naturalist. Grandson of Erasmus Darwin and of Josiah Wedgwood. While a student at Cambridge met John Stevens Henslow, botanist through whom he won appointment as naturalist on the *Beagle* on surveying expedition to southern islands, South American coasts and Andean interior, and Australasia (1831–1836); gathered data on flora, fauna, and geology of many lands and islands, made special study of fossils and species on Galápagos Archipelago; published *Journal of Researches into the Geology and Natural History of the Various Countries Visited by H.M.S. Beagle, 1832–36* (1839), *Structure and Distribution of Coral Reefs* (1842), *Geological Observations on Volcanic Islands* (1844), *Geological Observations on South America* (1846), and edited *Zoology of the Voyage of the Beagle* (1840–43). Secretary of Geological Society (1838–41). Studied variation in living and fossil barnacles (1846–54); Sir Charles Lyell induced him to write out (1856) results of his experiments in inbreeding and his theory of evolution by natural selection (first given written shape, 1842); received (1858) manuscript from Alfred Russel Wallace from the Malay archipelago presenting an abstract of an identical theory of natural selection; published Wallace's essay along with his own 1844 essay (1858). Published *On the Origin of Species by Means of Natural Selection* (1859), arousing a storm of controversy; *The Variation of Animals and Plants under Domestication,* setting up provisional hypothesis of pangenesis (1868); *The Descent of Man and Selection in Relation to Sex,* deriving the human race from an animal of the anthropoid group (1871); *The Expression of the Emotions in Man and Animals* (1872); a series of supplemental treatises on cross-fertilization and self-fertilization, ecology, climbing plants, etc., and a biography of Erasmus Darwin (1879). Buried in Westminster Abbey.

Of his five sons four were prominent scientists: ¶Sir George Howard (1845–1912), mathematician and astronomer; authority on tidal friction, geodesy, and dynamical meteorology; author of *Tides and Kindred Phenomena in the Solar System* (1898), containing hypothesis that the Moon was once part of Earth. ¶Sir Francis (1848–1925), botanist; made researches in vegetable physiology, esp. plant movements and response to stimuli and transpiration through stomata; his father's editor and biographer. ¶Leonard (1850–1943), engineer, economist, and eugenist; author of *Bimetallism* (1898) and *The Need for Eugenic Reform* (1926). ¶Sir Horace (1851–1928), civil engineer.

Darwin, Erasmus. 1731–1802. English physician and poet. Grandfather of Charles Darwin and of Francis Galton. Physician at Lichfield (1757–81), where he cultivated 8-acre botanical garden, and at Derby (from 1781), where he founded a philosophical society (1784). Author of *The Botanic Garden* (verse, 1794–95), *Zoonomia or the Laws of Organic Life* (1794–96), *The Temple of Nature or the Origin of Society* (verse, 1803); anticipated views on evolution later expounded by Lamarck.

Das \'däs\, Chitta Ranjan. 1870–1925. Indian politician. Called to English bar (1894); ardent nationalist; at first (1918) supported Gandhi in non-cooperation movement, but later led modified form of opposition; with M. Nehru organized Swaraj (Independence) party (1922); president of Indian National Congress (1922); elected first mayor of Calcutta (1924). Opposed to Western methods; often advocated measures bordering on violence. Author of volumes of verse and of political speeches, especially *The Way to Swaraj* (1923).

Da·sent \'dās-ᵊnt\, Sir George Webbe. 1817–1896. English Scandinavian scholar. Assistant editor of *Times* (1845–70); professor in King's College, London (from 1853); published popular translations from Norse, including *Popular Tales from the Norse* (1859), *Burnt Njal* (1861), *Gisl, the Outlaw* (1866).

Das·gup·ta \däs-'güp-tə\, Surendranath. 1855–1952. Indian philosopher. Developed philosophy of historical-biological evolution containing elements of western neorealism, Vedantic thought, and mystical Jainism; author of *History of Indian Philosophy* (1922–55).

Dash·ko·va \(,)dəsh-'kò-və\, Yekaterina Romanovna Vorontsova. Princess. 1744–1810. Russian woman of letters. Niece of Mikhail I. Vorontsov. m. Prince Mikhail Dashkov (1759). Took part in coup d'état that placed Catherine I on throne (1762); director, Academy of Arts and Sciences, St. Petersburg (1783–96); suggested establishment and named first president of Russian Academy (1783); planned Russian dictionary to be published by academy, and did some work on it. Author of plays and the memoirs *Mon Histoire* (written in French).

Dash·wood \'dash-,wu̇d\, Elizabeth Monica, *nee* de la Pas·ture \də-'lap-ə-tər\. *Pen name* E. M. Del·a·field \'del-ə-,fēld\. 1890–1943. English novelist. m. Arthur P. Dashwood (1919). Author of *Zella Sees Herself* (1917), *Humbug* (1921), *Messalina of the Suburbs* (1924), *Jill* (1926), and a series beginning with *Diary of a Provincial Lady* (1931).

Dashwood, Francis. 15th Baron le Des·pen·cer \lə-də-'spen(t)-sər\. 1708–1781. English profligate. Member of household of Prince of Wales; a founder of the Dilettanti Society (1736); M.P. (1741–63); founder of "Knights of St. Francis of Wycombe," secret society known also as "Mad Monks of Medmenham" (c.1745), meeting summer nights in ruins of Medmenham Abbey to indulge in obscene parodies upon Roman Catholic ritual, the ringleaders including Lord Sandwich, Earl of Bute, and George Bubb Dodington. Chancellor of exchequer (1762–63); joint postmaster general (1766–81).

Dass \'däs\, Petter. 1647–1707. Norwegian clergyman and poet. Author of lyric, epic, and religious verse notable for freshness of language and broad appeal of everyday subject matter; best known work *Nordlands trompet* (1739).

Das·vant \'däs-,vänt\. 16th century. Mughal artist. Probably a Hindu of humble origin, was patronized by Emperor Akbar; recognized in lifetime as foremost painter of his time and place; only surviving work a miniature in a manuscript of the *Ṭūṭī-nāmeh*.

Da·szyń·ski \dä-'shinʸ-skē\, Ignacy. 1866–1936. Polish politician. A founder of Polish Social Democratic party (1892); Socialist member of Austrian Reichsrat (1897–1918); editor of Socialist newspaper *Naprzód* (from 1912); head of Polish provisional government (1918); member of Sejm, or parliament (1919–31; speaker 1928–30); deputy premier (1920–21); strongly opposed Piłsudski's autocratic rule.

Da·ti \'dä-tē\, Carlo Roberto. 1619–1676. Italian scholar and writer. Crusader for classical linguistic purity in Italian; collaborated in editing *Vocabolario della crusca*.

Da·ti·ni \dä-'tē-nē\, Francesco di Marco da Prato. c.1335–1410. Italian merchant and banker of Prato. Merchant to the exiled papal court in Avignon, France (1350–78); entered cloth manufacturing, banking, insurance with offices in Florence, Bruges, London, Spain, etc.; among first to use double-entry bookkeeping, bills of exchange, written checks.

Da·tis \'dāt-əs\. 5th century B.C. Medean general. Joint commander with Artaphernes of Persian army sent to Greece by Darius I and defeated in battle of Marathon (490 B.C.).

Da·to Ira·dier \'dä-tō-ē-rät͟h-'yer\, Eduardo. 1856–1921. Spanish politician. Member of Cortes (1883–1921); minister of interior (1899–1900), justice (1902–03), foreign affairs (1918); mayor of Madrid (1907 ff.); president, chamber of deputies; premier (1913–15, 1917, 1920–21); leader of Conservative party (1913–21); assassinated by anarchist.

Dat·ta \'dä-tə\ *or* **Dutt** \'du̇t\, Michael[1] Madhusudan. 1824–1873. Bengali poet and dramatist. Foremost poet in modern Bengali; author of *Tilottamasambhab* (1860), *Meghnadbadh* (epic, 1861), *Brajangana* (1861), *Birangana* (1862), and plays *Sarmishtha* (1858), *Krishna Kumari* (1858–61), etc.; introduced sonnet, amitraksar verse form, and other innovations into Bengali.

Dau·ben·ton *or* **d'Au·ben·ton** \dō-bäⁿ-tōⁿ\, Louis-Jean-Marie. 1716–1800. French naturalist. Assistant to Buffon at Jardin des Plantes, Paris (1744); provided anatomical descriptions of mammals for Buffon's *Histoire Naturelle.* Conducted experiments in agriculture; introduced merino sheep into France. Professor of zoology, Collège de France (from 1778); first director, Museum of Natural History (1793–1800); senator (1799).

Dau·ber·val *or* **D'Au·ber·val** \dō-ber-väl\, Jean. 1742–1806. French ballet dancer and choreographer. In companies of Paris Académie (now Opéra) and later Bordeaux; influential teacher; proponent of the *ballet d'action;* best known original work *La Fille mal gardée* (1786), a pioneer comic ballet.

d'Aubignac, Abbé. See François HÉDELIN.

d'Aubigné, Jean-Henri Merle. See MERLE D'AUBIGNÉ.

d'Aubigné, Théodore-Agrippa. See AUBIGNÉ.

Dau·bi·gny \dō-bēn-yē\, Charles-François. 1817–1878. French landscape painter. Concerned, like his friend Corot, with careful observation of nature; portrayal of natural light influenced later Impressionists. Among his notable paintings were *Soleil couché, Les Îles vierges de Bezons, Champs au printemps, Lever de lune, Les Bords de l'Oise.*

Däu·bler \'dȯi-blər\, Theodor. 1876–1934. German poet. Author of the epic *Das Nordlicht* (1910), *Hesperien* (1915), *Das Sternenkind* (1916), *Die Treppe zum Nordlicht* (1920), *Attische Sonette* (1924), *Päan und Dithyrambos* (1924), *L'Africana* (novel, 1928), *Die Göttin mit der Fackel* (novel, 1931), tales, essays, etc.; regarded as a leader of Expressionist school in German literature.

Dau·brée \dō-brā\, Gabriel-Auguste. 1814–1896. French geologist and mineralogist. Professor at Strasbourg (1852), Musée des Sciences Naturelles (1861), École Imperiale des Mines (1862; director 1872); inspector general of mines (1867–86). Studied mineral formation, metamorphosis, fracturing, pebble and sand formation; author of *Études synthétiques de géologie expérimentale* (1879), *Météorites et la constitution géologique du globe* (1886). The minerals daubreeite and daubreelite are named for him.

Dau·det \dō-de\, Alphonse. 1840–1897. French writer. Author of stories, novels, plays often in naturalistic vein. Made first striking success with play *La dernière idole* (1862); later plays included *Le Frère aîné* (1867), *L'Arlésienne* (1872), *L'Obstacle* (1891); novels and story collections included *Le petit chose* (1868), *Lettres de mon moulin* (1869), *Les Aventures prodigieuses de Tartarin de Tarascon* (1872), *Contes du lundi* (1873), *Fromont jeune et Risler aîné* (1874), *Jack* (1876), *Le Nabab* (1877), *Les Rois en exil* (1879), *Numa Roumestan* (1881), *Sapho* (1884), *Tartarin sur les Alpes* (1885), *L'Immortel* (1888), *Port-Tarascon* (1890), *Soutien de famille* (1898).

Daudet, Léon, *in full* Alphonse-Marie-Léon. 1867–1942. French journalist and writer. Son of Alphonse Daudet. On staff of *Figaro, Gaulois, Soleil, La Libre Parole;* founded, with Charles Maurras, *L'Action Française* (1908), a royalist journal. Member of Chamber of Deputies (1919–24). Author of many books, including: novels, *L'Astre noir* (1893), *Les Morticoles* (1894), *Le Voyage de Shakespeare* (1896), etc.; books on psychology and medicine, as *Le Monde des images* (1919); political works, as *Une Campagne d'action française* (1910), *L'Avant-Guerre* (1913), *L'Agonie du régime* (1925); books of literary criticism, as *Le stupide XIXᵉ siècle* (1922); and volumes of reminiscences.

Da·ud Khan \'dä-üd-kän\, Sardar Mohammad. 1909–1978. Afghan politician. Member of royal family; minister of defense (1946–53); prime minister (1953–63); debarred from political activity by new constitution (1964); led coup against King Mohammad Zahir Shah (1973); declared Afghanistan a republic and himself president (1973); killed in leftist military coup.

Daugh·er·ty \'dȯ(-ə)rt-ē\, Harry Micajah. 1860–1941. American politician, b. Washington Court House, Ohio. Managed political career of Warren G. Harding (from 1902); reputedly originated term "smoke-filled room"; U.S. attorney general (1921–24). Tried and acquitted (1927) on charges of conspiracy to defraud U.S. government. Author of *The Inside Story of the Harding Tragedy* (1932, with Thomas Dixon).

Dau·kan·tas \dau̇-'kän-täs\, Simanas. 1793–1864. Lithuanian historian. Author of *Būdas senovės lietuviu, kalnėnu ir žemaičiu* (1845) and *Istorija žemaitiška* (written before 1838; pub. 1891–96), first works of Lithuanian history in Lithuanian language.

Dau·lat \'dau̇-,lät\. 16th–17th century. Mughal painter. Noted for manuscript illuminations, portraits of many noted Mughal artists.

Dau·mer \'dau̇-mər\, Georg Friedrich. 1800–1875. German writer. Author of various anti-Christian works, esp. *Geheimnisse des christlichen Altertums* (1847), but later changed his attitude and adopted the Roman Catholic faith, explaining his act in *Meine Konversion* (1859). For a time guardian of Kaspar

Hauser (*q.v.*), on whom he wrote *Kaspar Hauser, sein Wesen, seine Unschuld* (1873).

Dau·mier \dōm-yā\, Honoré. 1808–1879. French caricaturist. On staff of *La Caricature* (1832) when one of his caricatures of Louis-Philippe caused his arrest and a six months' prison term. Later, joined staff of *Charivari* where he caricatured bourgeois society. Completed some 4,000 lithographs and 4,000 illustrations. Known also as a serious painter in Impressionist manner (from 1848) and skilled sculptor.

Daun *or* **Dhaun** \'daůn\, Leopold Joseph von. Graf. 1705–1766. Austrian soldier. Served in Sicily (1718), Italy and the Rhine (1734–35), against Turkey (1737–39), in War of Austrian Succession (1740–48). Commissioned field marshal (1754); Austrian commander in chief in Seven Years' War (1756–63); defeated Frederick the Great at Kolín (1757) and at Hochkirch (1758); received surrender of General Finck at Maxen (1759); defeated by Frederick the Great at Torgau (1760). President of Imperial War Council (1762–66).

Dau·nou \dō-nü\, Pierre-Claude-François. 1761–1840. French politician and historian. Member of the Convention (1792); imprisoned (1793–94) for moderate views; principal author of the constitution of 1795; member of Council of the Five Hundred (1795); founder of the Institut National (1795); helped write constitution of 1799; member of the Tribunate (1800). Director of national archives (1804–15); professor, Collège de France (from 1819); elected to chamber of deputies (1819), chamber of peers (1839). Author of historical works.

Daurat, Jean. See DORAT.

Dau·then·dey \'daů-tən-ˌdī\, Max. 1867–1918. German poet. Author of works in Impressionist manner, including *Ultraviolett* (1893), *Reliquien* (1899), *Die ewige Hochzeit* (1905), *Singsangbuch* (1907), *Weltspuk* (1910).

Dau·zat \dō-zä\, Albert. 1877–1955. French linguist. On faculty of École Pratique des Hautes Études, Paris (from 1910; director from 1921). Author of *Les Argots franco-provençaux* (1917), *Les Patois* (1927), *Histoire de la langue française* (1931), *Dictionnaire étymologique de la langue française* (1938); founder of journals *Le Français moderne* (1933), *Onomastica* (1947).

Da·vaine \då-ven\, Casimir-Joseph. 1812–1882. French physician. First to produce experimental infection in animals with blood containing the anthrax bacillus and to suggest that the bacillus caused the disease (1863).

Da·vel \då-'vel\, Jean Abraham Daniel. 1670–1723. Swiss patriot. Led uprising in canton of Vaud to overthrow Bernese domination; captured and executed near Lausanne.

Dav·e·nant *or* **D'Av·e·nant** \'dav-ə-nənt\, Sir William. 1606–1668. English poet and dramatist. Reputed by gossip to be godson and possibly natural son of Shakespeare. Entered household of Fulke Greville, on whose death he turned to writing plays and masques, including the tragedy *Albovine, King of the Lombards* (1629), comic masterpiece *The Witts* (1634); became poet laureate following Ben Jonson (1638). Royalist, fought for Charles I; captured on mission to Virginia for Henrietta Maria (1650); while imprisoned in Tower (1650–54), wrote his uncompleted epic *Gondibert;* released through influence of Milton. Presented semiprivate dramatic productions at Rutland House in evasion of Puritan prohibition of plays (from 1656); founded English opera with his *Siege of Rhodes* (1656); opened the Cockpit, a theater in Drury Lane (1658); imprisoned for complicity in insurrection of Sir George Booth (1659). At Restoration, set up company, the Duke of York's Players, at Lincoln's Inn Fields; produced many adaptations of plays by Shakespeare (esp. *The Tempest,* adapted with John Dryden, 1667), Jonson, and Fletcher.

Dav·en·port \'dav-ən-ˌpō(ə)rt, 'dav-ᵊm-, -ˌpȯ(ə)rt\, Charles Benedict. 1866–1944. American zoologist and eugenicist, b. Stamford, Conn. Founding director, Carnegie Institution Station for Experimental Evolution (1904–34) and Eugenics Record Office (1910–34), Cold Spring Harbor, N.Y. Author of *Experimental Morphology* (1897–99), *Heredity in Relation to Eugenics* (1911), *Body Build and Its Inheritance* (1923), *How We Came By Our Bodies* (1936), etc.

Davenport, Christopher. *Name in religion* Fran·cis·cus a Sanc·ta Cla·ra \fran-'sis-kə-sä-ˌsäŋk-tə-'klär-ə, -ˌsaŋk-tə-'klar-ə\. 1598–1680. English cleric and theologian. Entered Franciscan order (1617); chaplain to Queen Henrietta Maria, Queen Catherine of Braganza. Attempted in *Deus, Natura, Gratia* (1634) to reconcile Thirty-nine Articles of Anglican church with Roman Catholic dogma.

Davenport, Edward Loomis. 1815–1877. American actor, b. Boston. In England as leading man to Anna Cora Mowatt (1847–54); leading actor on American stage (1854–74); noted for both tragedies, esp. Shapespeare, and comedies, esp. Massinger's *A New Way to Pay Old Debts.* His daughter ¶Fanny Lily Gypsy (1850–1898), b. London, England, was an actress in Augustin Daly's company (1869–77); starred in *Pique* (1876–77); toured under own management, esp. in plays of V. Sardou (1877–97).

Davenport, George. 1783–1845. American fur trader, b. Lincolnshire, England. To New York (1804); on frontier as settler and trader (1814–26); agent, American Fur Co. (from 1826); one of the founders of Davenport, Iowa, named in his honor (1835).

Davenport, Ira Erastus (1839–1911) and his brother William Henry Harrison (1841–1877). American spiritualistic mediums, b. Buffalo, N.Y.? Prominent in Europe and U.S. (c.1860–77); investigated and exposed as sleight-of-hand experts by Houdini.

Davenport, John. 1597–1670. American clergyman, b. Coventry, England. Pastorates in England (1615–25). Developed Puritan sympathies; fled to Holland (1633); sailed to Boston (1637). Founded New Haven colony (1638); with Theophilus Eaton (*q.v.*) drew up code of laws for the colony. Gave refuge to the regicide judges Whalley and Goffe (1661).

Davenport, Robert. fl. 1623–1639. English dramatist. Author of didactic poems *A Crowne for a Conqueror* and *Too Late to Call Backe Yesterday* (both 1623), comedies *The City Night-cap* (1624) and *A New Tricke to Cheat the Divell* (1639), and a tragedy *King John and Matilda* (1655). Said to have collaborated with Shakespeare.

Davenport, Thomas. 1802–1851. American inventor, b. Williamstown, Vt. Invented an electric motor (1834), which he used to power first electric locomotive (1835); applied motor to other devices but without commercial success; published *Electro-Magnet and Mechanics Intelligencer* newsletter (c.1840–43).

Da·vey \'dā-vē\, John. 1846–1923. American tree surgeon, b. Somersetshire, England. To U.S. (1872); specialized in care of ornamental trees; introduced practice of tree surgery; wrote *The Tree Doctor* (1902), etc. His son ¶Martin Luther (1884–1946) was congressman (1918–21, 1923–29), governor of Ohio (1935–39).

David. In Welsh names see DAFYDD.

Da·vid \'dā-vəd\ *or* **De·wi** \'de-wē\. Saint. c.520–600. Patron saint of Wales. Said to have presided over so-called Synod of Victory at Caerleon-on-Usk; as primate of South Wales, moved seat of ecclesiastical government to Mynyw (now St. David's); founder of churches; canonized (c.1120).

David. d. 962 B.C. Second king of Judah and Israel (c.1000–962 B.C.). Youngest son of Jesse of Bethlehem. Served in Saul's court; m. Michal, Saul's daughter; distinguished himself in war against Philistines; by his successes, became object of Saul's enmity; outlawed for years by Saul; after Saul's death, proclaimed king in Hebron; on death of Ishbaal, surviving son of Saul, became king of all Israel, conquering Jerusalem and making it his capital ("the City of David"); broke power of Philistines and defeated Moab, Ammon, and Edom; reign troubled by revolt and death of Absalom (*q.v.*); m. Bathsheba; succeeded by Solomon, Bathsheba's son, instead of by fourth son, Adonijah; reputed author of many Psalms. See JOAB.

David. Name of two kings of Scotland:

David I. c.1082–1153. King (1124–53). Son of Malcolm III Canmore. Gained by marriage (1113) earldom of Huntingdon; on death of King Edgar (1107), received from brother Alexander I southern Scotland; succeeded (1124) on death of Alexander to whole of Scotland and the crown. Supported claim of Matilda, daughter of Henry I, to English crown as against Stephen, but was defeated at Battle of the Standard (1138); renewed war on behalf of Matilda (1141) and unsuccessfully invaded England (1149); founded bishoprics and monasteries; introduced Norman aristocracy; furthered process of feudalizing Scotland; initiated the chancellery. Succeeded by grandson Malcolm IV.

David II. 1324–1371. King (1329–71). Son of Robert I the Bruce. Succeeded father as king of Scots (1329); supporters under regent Sir Archibald Douglas defeated by Edward III at Halidon Hill (1333); in exile in France (1334–41); captured at Neville's Cross during invasion of England (1346); imprisoned (1346–57); proposed that a son of Edward III succeed to Scottish throne in return for cancellation of ransom for his release; arrangement denounced by nephew (later Robert II) and repudiated by Scottish parliament. Ineffectual reign marked by gain in power by barons and by parliament.

David of **Di·nant** \dē-'nän\. fl. 1200. Belgian Scholastic philosopher. Apparently a materialistic pantheist; his "Notebooks" were burned as heretical in Paris (c.1210).

David, Sir Edgeworth, *in full* Tannatt William Edgeworth. 1858–1934. Australian geologist, b. Wales. Assistant geologist, government survey of New South Wales (1882–91); professor, U. of Sydney (1891–1924); led expedition to Ellice Is. (1897); scientific officer with Shackleton Antarctic expedition (1907–09); led party reaching South Magnetic Pole (Jan. 1909). Author of *The Geology of Australia* (1932).

Da·vid \'däv-ēt\, Eduard Heinrich Rudolph. 1863–1930. German politician. Founded Socialist newspaper *Mitteldeutsche Sonntagszeitung* (1893); member of Reichstag (from 1903); became leader of revisionist wing of Social Democratic party; undersecretary in foreign office (1918); first president of

Weimar National Assembly (1919); minister of interior (1919–20). Author of *Sozialismus und Landwirtschaft* (1903).

Da·vid \dä-vēd\, Félicien-César. 1810–1876. French composer. Member of Saint-Simonian brotherhood (from 1831); traveled in Middle East (1833–35). Composed symphonic ode *Le Désert* (1844), *La Perle du Brésil* (an opera, 1851), *Herculanum* (1859), *Lalla-Roukh* (1862), and *Le Saphir* (1865). His use of exotic Oriental melodies was taken up by other Romantic composers.

Dá·vid \'dáv-id\, Ferenc. *Lat.* Franciscus Da·vid·is \'däv-əd-əs\. 1510–1579. Hungarian cleric and theologian. Adopted Unitarianism (c.1566); court preacher to John Sigismund; secured toleration of Unitarians in Transylvania (1568); later persecuted by Stephen Báthory; broke with his teacher, Giorgius Blandrata, in asserting that Christ should not be worshipped; supporters known as Dávidists, or Old Unitarians; tried and condemned for blasphemy (1579). Author of *De falsa et vera unius Dei Patris, Filii et Spiritus Sancti* (1567).

Da·vid \'dá-vət\, Gerard. c.1460–1523. Dutch painter of religious subjects. Considered last master of the school of Bruges; chief works included *Christ Nailed to the Cross, Madonna Triptych, Enthroned Madonna with Angels, Judgment of Cambyses, Baptism of Christ, Madonna with Angels and Saints.*

Da·vid \dä-vēd\, Jacques-Louis. 1748–1825. French painter. Regarded as founder of French Neoclassical school of painting. Sympathized with principles of the Revolution, and became associate of Robespierre; member of National Convention (1792); abolished Académie Royale after establishment of the Empire, was appointed court painter by Napoléon (1804); at the Restoration (1815), was exiled. Chief works included *Bélisaire demandant l'aumône* (1780), *La douleur d'Andromache* (1783), *Le Serment des Horaces* (1785), *Les Licteurs rapportent à Brutus les corps de ses fils* (1789), *Marat expirant* (1793), *Les Sabines* (1799), *Madame Récamier* (1799).

David d'·An·gers \-dä^{n}-zhā\, Pierre-Jean. 1788–1856. French sculptor. Executed large number of works, as statues of Condé, Cuvier, Talma, and Jean Bart, portrait busts of Goethe, Bentham, Chateaubriand, Lamartine, and Victor Hugo, medallions of Bonaparte, Ney, Jacques-Louis David, Gérard, Rossini, Paganini, Théophile Gautier, Alfred de Vigny, Mme. Récamier, Alfred de Musset, etc.

David de May·re·na \-də-me-rā-na\, Marie-Charles. 1842–1890. French adventurer. Self-styled King Marie I of the Sedang tribe of Vietnam; attempted (1889) to gain German recognition of kingdom.

Da·vi·do·vić \dá-'vē-dò-,vēt^{y}\, Ljubomir. 1863–1940. Yugoslav politician. A founder of Independent Radical party in Serbia (1902; leader 1912–18). Leader of new Yugoslavian Democratic party (from 1919); prime minister of Yugoslavia (1919–20, 1924).

Da·vids \'dā-vədz\, Thomas William Rhys. 1843–1922. English Orientalist. Joined Ceylon civil service (1866); interested himself in study of Pāli and early Buddhism. Professor at University Coll., London (1882–1912), Manchester (1904–15). Among his books were *Buddhism* (1878), *Buddhist Suttas from the Pali* (1881), *Buddhist India* (1903), *Early Buddhism* (1908).

Da·vid·son \'dā-vəd-sən\, Israel. *Orig.* Alter Mov·sho·vitz \mōv-'shō-vits\. 1870–1939. American Hebrew scholar, b. Russia. To U.S. (1888). Professor of medieval Hebrew literature, Jewish Theol. Sem. of America (1917–1939). Compiler of *Thesaurus of Mediaeval Hebrew Poetry* (1924–33).

Davidson, Jo. 1883–1952. American sculptor, b. New York City. Among his notable sculptures were *Woodrow Wilson* and *Anatole France,* in the Luxembourg, Paris; *Robert M. La Follette,* in the rotunda of the Capitol, Washington, D.C.; *Marshal Foch; General Pershing; Will Rogers; Walt Whitman;* and portrait busts *Clemenceau, Tagore, Zangwill, Chaliapin,* etc.

Davidson, John. 1857–1909. Scottish poet and playwright. Plays included *Bruce* (1886), *Smith; a tragic Farce* (1888), *Scaramouch in Naxos* (1889). Gained reputation as gifted, if unconventional, lyric poet with *Fleet Street Eclogues* (1893 and 1895) and several volumes of *Ballads;* expressed pessimistic philosophy in series of *Testaments* (1901–08).

Davidson, Randall Thomas. 1st Baron Davidson of Lambeth. 1848–1930. British prelate, b. Edinburgh. Dean of Windsor (1883), bishop of Rochester (1891) and of Winchester (1895); domestic chaplain to the queen. Consecrated archbishop of Canterbury (1903); resigned on account of ill health (1928). Influential in House of Lords; a leader of ecumenical movement.

Davidson, Thomas. 1817–1885. British paleontologist. Author and illustrator of the exhaustive *Monograph of British Fossil Brachiopoda* (1851–86).

Da·vie \'dā-vē\, William Richardson. 1756–1820. American soldier and lawyer, b. Cumberland, England. To America (1763). Served brilliantly in latter years of Revolutionary War, commanding cavalry troop in victories at Hanging Rock and Charlotte (1780); served under Gen. Nathanael Greene. In North Carolina legislature (1786–98); instrumental in securing cession of Tennessee to the Union, the founding of the U. of North Carolina. Governor of North Carolina (1799).

Da·viel \dáv-yel\, Jacques. 1696–1762. French oculist. Originated surgical treatment of cataract by removal of the lens of the eye. Royal surgeon and oculist (from 1749).

Da·vies \'dā-vēz, *esp Brit* -vis\, Arthur Bowen. 1862–1928. American painter, b. Utica, N.Y. Known for Arcadian pastoral scenes, later for allegorical neo-Romantic compositions; organized show of "The Eight" (1908); experimented in Cubist paintings. Works included *Four o'Clock Ladies, The Girdle of Ares, Leda and the Dioscuri, Maya, Mirror of Illusions, Children of Yesteryear, Dancers.*

Davies, Clara Novello. 1861–1943. British singing instructor and choral conductor, b. Cardiff, Wales. Founder and conductor of Royal Welsh Ladies' Choir. Performed by royal command before Queen Victoria (1894) and George V and Queen Mary (1928). Mother of Ivor Novello (*q.v.*).

Davies, David. 1818–1890. Welsh industrialist. Railway builder in mid-Wales; pioneer exploiter of coal in Rhondda Valley (from 1864); Liberal M.P. (1874–86).

Davies, David. 1st Baron Davies of Llandinam. 1880–1944. Welsh soldier and politician. Grandson of David Davies (1818–1890). Served in Royal Welsh Fusiliers (1914–16); private secretary to Lloyd George; M.P. (1906–29); president of University Coll. of Wales, Aberystwyth. Promoter of League of Nations; founded New Commonwealth Society (1933); author of *The Problem of the Twentieth Century* (1930), *Suicide or Sanity* (1932), *Nearing the Abyss* (1936).

Davies, Emily, *in full* Sarah Emily. 1830–1921. English educator. Active in campaign to secure admission of women to higher education (from 1862); with friends established (1869) a women's college at Hichin that became (1873) Girton College, Cambridge; member of London school board (1870–73); mistress of Girton (1873–75). Author of *The Higher Education of Women* (1866), *Thoughts on Some Questions Relating to Women, 1860–1908* (1910).

Davies, Sir Henry Walford. 1869–1941. English organist, director, and composer. Organist of St. George's Chapel, Windsor (1927–32); master of the king's music (from 1934). Composer of religious music; compiler of songbooks and hymnbooks. Influential music educator, esp. in popular radio talks.

Davies, Hubert Henry. 1876–1917. English playwright. Wrote *Cousin Kate* (1903), *Cynthia* (1904), *The Mollusc* (1907), *Mrs. Gorringe's Necklace* (1910), *Doormats* (1913).

Davies, John. See Sion RHYS.

Davies of Her·e·ford \'her-ə-fərd\, John. 1565?–1618. English poet. Author of *Mirum in Modum* (1602), didactic treatise *Microcosmos* (1603), *Wittes Pilgrimage* containing love sonnets (c.1610), *Scourge of Folly* containing epigrams to literary contemporaries (c.1611), and a popular writing manual *The Writing Schoole-Master.*

Davies, Sir John. 1569–1626. English jurist and poet. Attorney general for Ireland (1606–19); sought to establish Protestantism in Ulster. Speaker of Irish parliament (1613–19); sat in English Parliament (1601, 1621). Appointed lord chief justice (1626) but died before entering office. Known for his poems *Orchestra* (1594), *Nosce Teipsum* (1599), and *Hymnes of Astraea* (1599).

Davies, Joseph Edward. 1876–1958. American lawyer and diplomat, b. Watertown, Wis. U.S. commissioner of corporations (1913–15); first chairman (1915–16) and vice chairman (1916–18), Federal Trade Commission. U.S. ambassador to Russia (1936–38), Belgium (1938–39). Author of *Mission to Moscow* (1941).

Davies, Sir Louis Henry. 1845–1924. Canadian jurist, b. Charlottetown, P.E.I. Premier and attorney general, Prince Edward Island (1876–79). Member of Dominion House of Commons (1882–1901); minister of marine and fisheries (1896–1901). Judge of Supreme Court of Canada (1901–24); chief justice (1918–24).

Davies, Rhys. 1903–1978. Welsh writer. Author of stories and novels, including *Withered Root* (1927), *Arfon* (1931), *Honey and Bread* (1935), *Time to Laugh* (1937), *Jubilee Blues* (1938), *Black Venus* (1944), *A Trip to London* (1946), *Painted King* (1954), *Chosen One* (1967).

Davies, Richard. 1501?–1581. Welsh scholar. Bishop of St. David's (1561); aided in translation of New Testament and Book of Common Prayer into Welsh; revised *Deuteronomy* and *2 Samuel* for Bishops' Bible (1568).

Davies, Samuel. 1723–1761. American educator, b. New Castle County, Del. Ordained in Presbyterian ministry (1747); defended nonconforming Dissenters in Virginia; with Gilbert Tennent, sent to England (1753) to raise funds for The College of New Jersey (Princeton); president of the college (1759–61).

Davies, Thomas. 1712?–1785. Scottish actor and bookseller in London. Introduced Boswell to Dr. Johnson (1763); biographer of Garrick (1780).

Davies, William Henry. 1871–1940. Welsh poet. Lived the life of a tramp in England and U.S. (to c.1905); then devoted himself to writing, esp. verse. Among his books of poetry were *The Soul's Destroyer* (1905), *Nature Poems* (1908), *Forty New Poems* (1918), *The Hour of Magic* (1922), *Song of Love* (1926), *The Loneliest Mountain* (1939). Among his prose works were *The Autobiography of a Super-tramp* (1907), *A Weak Woman* (novel, 1911), *Poet's Pilgrimage* (1918), *Later Days* (1925), *Adventures of Johnny Walker, Tramp* (1926).

Dá·vi·la \'dä-b̲ē-lä\, Carlos Guillermo. 1887–1955. Chilean journalist and politician. Founded *La Nación* (1917), news magazine *Hoy* (1932). Ambassador to U.S. (1927–32); member of junta that overthrew President Montero and for three months provisional president of Chile (1932); secretary general, Organization of American States (1954–55).

Da·vi·la \'dä-vē-(,)lä\, Enrico Caterino. 1576–1631. Italian soldier and historian. Fought in civil wars under Henry IV (1594–98); served Venice as governor of Candia, Friuli, Dalmatia, and Crema; known esp. for his *Historia delle guerre civili di Francia* (1630).

Dávila, Gil González. See Gil GONZÁLEZ DÁVILA.

Dá·vi·la \'dä-b̲ē-lä\, Miguel R. d. 1927. Honduran politician. Provisional president of Honduras (1907–08) placed in power by Zelaya of Nicaragua; elected president (1908); overthrown in U.S. intervention (1911).

Dávila, Pedrarias. See Pedro ARIAS DÁVILA.

Dávila Pa·dil·la \-pä-'t̲h̲ē(l)-yä\, Agustín. 1562–1604. Mexican historian. Called "Chronicler of the Indies". Dominican representative to Rome and Madrid (1596); court preacher at Madrid (1598); bishop of Santo Domingo (1599–1604). His chief work, *Historia de la fundación de la provincia de Santiago de México de la Orden de predicadores* (1596).

Daviot, Gordon. See Elizabeth MACKINTOSH.

Da·vioud \dáv-yü\, Gabriel-Jean-Antoine. 1823–1881. French architect. Collaborated in building Palais du Trocadéro (1878).

Da·vis \'dā-vəs, *esp Brit* -vis\, Alexander Jackson. 1803–1892. American architect, b. New York City. In firm of Town & Davis (1829–44); practicing alone (1843–80). Probably designed New York Custom House (1833), Illinois State Capitol (1837); later known for Gothic and Italianate country houses; illustrated books of Andrew Jackson Downing; wrote *Rural Residences* (1837).

Davis, Andrew Jackson. 1826–1910. American Spiritualist, b. Blooming Grove, N.Y. Practiced as a clairvoyant (from 1843); author of *Principles of Nature, Her Divine Revelations, and a Voice to Mankind* (1847) and other works contributing to the development of organized Spiritualism.

Davis, Arthur Hoey. *Pen name* Steele Rudd \'rəd\. 1868–1935. Australian writer. Founded *Steele Rudd's Magazine* (1904). Known for humorous novels, plays, and sketches depicting farm life in Darling Downs area of Queensland, as *On Our Selection* (1899), *Sandy's Selection* (1904), *Grandpa's Selection* (1916); works often adapted into comic strips, radio programs, and films; also wrote serious novels *The Romance of Runnibede* (1927), *Green Grey Homestead* (1934); championed Australian authors.

Davis, Benjamin Oliver. 1877–1970. American army officer, b. Washington, D.C. Lieutenant of volunteers (1898–99); enlisted in regular army (1899); military attaché in Liberia (1909–12); professor of military science at Wilberforce U. and Tuskegee Inst.; first black general officer in U.S. army (1940); ret. (1948).

Davis, Benny. 1895?–1979. American songwriter, b. New York City? Wrote "Goodbye Broadway, Hello France," "Carolina Moon," "Baby Face," "Margie" (with Conrad Dober), etc.

Davis, Charles Henry. 1807–1877. American naval officer, b. Boston. In Civil War, commanded Union gunboat flotilla on Mississippi (1862); received surrender of Memphis (June 6); rear admiral (1863).

Davis, David. 1815–1886. American jurist, b. Cecil County, Md. Circuit court judge in Illinois (1848–62); active in campaign securing Lincoln's nomination for presidency (1860). Associate justice, U.S. Supreme Court (1862–77). U.S. senator (1877–83; president pro tem 1881–83).

Davis, Dwight Filley. 1879–1945. American public official, b. Saint Louis, Mo. U.S. secretary of war (1925–29); governor general of the Philippines (1929–32). Donor (1900) of the Davis Cup, an international lawn tennis challenge cup now signifying world team championship.

Davis, Edwin Hamilton. 1811–1888. American archaeologist, b. Hillsboro, Ohio. Collaborator with E. G. Squier in study of earthworks of the Mound Builders, and in book *Ancient Monuments of the Mississippi Valley,* first book issued by the Smithsonian Institution (1847).

Davis, Elmer Holmes. 1890–1958. American writer and radio news commentator, b. Aurora, Ind. On staff of *New York Times* (1914–24); radio news commentator (1939–54); head of Office of War Information (1942–45). Author of stories in *Morals for Moderns* (1930), *Love Among the Ruins* (1935); nonfiction *Not to Mention the War* (1940), *But We Were Born Free* (1954).

Davis, Harold Lenoir. 1896–1960. American writer, b. Yoncalla, Ore. Author of *Honey in the Horn* (1935, Pulitzer prize), *Beulah Land* (1945), *Winds of Morning* (1952), *Distant Music* (1957), *Kettle of Fire* (1959).

Davis, Henry Gassett. 1807–1896. American physician, b. Trenton, Me. Pioneer in use of traction in orthopedics (from 1856).

Davis, Henry William Carless. 1874–1928. English historian. Regius professor of modern history, Oxford (1925–28), and curator of the Bodleian Library (1926–28). Director of *Dictionary of National Biography* (from 1902). Among his books were *England under the Normans and Angevins* (1905), *Mediaeval Europe* (1911), *Mediaeval England* (1924).

Davis, Henry Winter. 1817–1865. American politician, b. Annapolis, Md. Member, U.S. House of Representatives (1855–61, 1863–65). Instrumental in preventing Maryland from joining the Confederacy. Opposed Lincoln's reconstruction proposals, wrote Radical plan (Wade-Davis Act) adopted by Congress (1864) but vetoed by Lincoln; with cosponsor Benjamin F. Wade issued "the Wade-Davis Manifesto," ridiculing Lincoln's reconstruction plan and attacking pocket veto.

Davis, Herbert John. 1893–1967. English educator. Professor of English, Cornell (1937–40); president of Smith College (1940–49); professor emeritus, Oxford (from 1960). Authority on Jonathan Swift; editor of *Complete Prose Works of Jonathan Swift* (1938–63), *Complete Poems of Pope* (1966).

Davis, Jefferson. 1808–1889. President of the Confederate States of America, b. present Fairview, Ky. Frontier army service (1828–35); resigned from army (1835). Mississippi planter (1835–45). Member, U.S. House of Representatives (1845–46); resigned to serve in Mexican War; distinguished himself at Buena Vista (Feb. 22, 1847); U.S. senator from Mississippi (1847–51). U.S. secretary of war in Pierce's cabinet (1853–57). U.S. senator (1857–61); conspicuous as defender of South and institution of slavery. Withdrew from senate when Mississippi seceded. Chosen by the provisional congress president of the Confederacy (Feb. 18, 1861); elected by popular vote and inaugurated at Richmond, Va. (Feb. 22, 1862). Conduct of office severely hampered by failure to gain foreign recognition, constant conflict with extreme states' rights advocates, increasing shortage of resources and financial stringency. Fled from Richmond (April 3, 1865), determined to continue struggle from trans-Mississippi territory; captured at Irwinville, Ga. (May 10, 1865). Imprisoned at Fortress Monroe, Va. (1865–67); indicted for treason (May 8, 1866) but never prosecuted. Wrote *The Rise and Fall of the Confederate Government* (1881). His daughter ¶Varina Anne Jefferson Davis (1864–1898), *known as* the Daughter of the Confederacy, was a novelist, author of *The Veiled Doctor* (1895), *A Romance of Summer Seas* (1898), etc.

Davis *or* **Da·vys** \'dā-vis\, John. c.1550–1605. English navigator. Attempted to locate Northwest Passage on three voyages (1585, 1586, 1587), on last of which he discovered Davis Strait and sailed into Baffin Bay. Apparently commanded *Black Dog* against Spanish Armada (1588). With Thomas Cavendish on last voyage (1591); discovered Falkland Is. (1592). Sailed with Sir Walter Raleigh to Cádiz and Azores (1596–97); made three voyages to East Indies (1598, 1601, 1605). Wrote *The Seaman's Secret* (1594), *The World's Hydrographical Description* (1595). Invented a backstaff and the Davis quadrant, long in use.

Davis, John William. 1873–1955. American lawyer and politician, b. Clarksburg, W.Va. Member, U.S. House of Representatives (1911–13). U.S. solicitor general (1913–18). U.S. ambassador to Great Britain (1918–21). Chosen Democratic candidate for president (1924) on 102d ballot as compromise between Alfred E. Smith and William G. McAdoo.

Davis, Joe. 1901–1978. English billiards player. World snooker champion (1927–46) with total of 689 century breaks and record break of 147; world (1928–33) and British (1933–78) billiard champion.

Davis, Nathan Smith. 1817–1904. American physician, b. Greene, N.Y. Instrumental in organization of American Medical Association (1846–47). Professor, Rush Medical College, Chicago (1849–59). Founded Lind U. medical department (1859), later medical department of Northwestern U.; professor and dean (1859–86).

Davis, Norman Hezekiah. 1878–1944. American financier and diplomat, b. Normandy, Tenn. Organized and headed The Trust Company of Cuba (1905–17). In U.S. Treasury Dept. (1917–19); asst. secretary, U.S. treasury (1919–20); undersecretary of state (1920–21). An organizer of Council on Foreign Relations (1921). Member (1932–33) and chairman (1933–34) of U.S. delegation to disarmament conference at Geneva, Switzerland; head of U.S. delegation to London Naval Conference (1935–36), and to Nine-Power Treaty Conference (1937). President of American Red Cross and International Red Cross (1938–44).

Davis, Owen Gould. 1874–1956. American playwright, b. Portland, Me. Began writing popular melodramas, as *Confessions of a Wife, Nellie the Beautiful Cloak Model,* etc. Subsequently wrote *Sinners* (1915), *Forever After* (1918), *The Detour* (1921), *Icebound* (1923, Pulitzer prize), *The Nervous Wreck* (1923), *Lazybones* (1924), *Beware of Widows* (1925) and movie and radio scripts.

Davis, Richard Harding. 1864–1916. American newspaperman and novelist, b. Philadelphia. Joined staff of *New York Sun* (1889). Managing editor, *Harper's Weekly* (1890). War correspondent in six wars; wrote travel books, popular fiction, and plays; fiction, *Gallegher and Other Stories* (1891), *Van Bibber and Others* (1892), *Soldiers of Fortune* (1897), *The King's Jackal* (1898), *Captain Macklin* (1902), *Ranson's Folly* (1902), *The Bar Sinister* (1903), *Vera the Medium* (1908), *The White Mice* (1909); plays, *Ranson's Folly* (1904), *The Dictator* (1904), *Miss Civilization* (1906). His mother ¶Rebecca Blaine, *nee* Harding (1831–1910), b. Washington, Pa., was also a novelist, author of *Margaret Howth* (1862), *A Law unto Herself* (1878), *Dr. Warrick's Daughters* (1896), etc.

Davis, Stuart. 1894–1964. American artist, b. Philadelphia. Exhibited at Armory Show (1913); experimented with Cubism and collage techniques; noted esp. for colorful, rhythmic abstract paintings inspired by urban scenes and life.

Davis, Thomas Osborne. 1814–1845. Irish poet. With John Blake Dillon and Charles Gavan Duffy, founded *The Nation* (1842), to which he contributed lyrics including "A Nation Once Again," "The Battle of Fontenoy," "The Geraldines"; one of leaders of extremist Young Ireland party.

Davis, Varina. See under Jefferson DAVIS.

Davis, William Augustine. 1809–1875. American postal authority, b. Barren Co., Ky. Postmaster at St. Joseph, Mo.; devised system of sorting mail on trains to expedite handling at junction points, thus originating railway post-office service (1862).

Davis, William Morris. 1850–1934. American geographer and geologist, b. Philadelphia. Taught geology at Harvard (1876–1912); developed Davisian system of landscape analysis based on "cycle of erosion". Author of *Elementary Meteorology* (1894), *Geographical Essays* (1909), *Coral Reef Problem* (1928), etc.

Da·vi·son \ˈdā-və-sən\, William. 1541?–1608. Scottish secretary to Queen Elizabeth. Member of Parliament, privy councillor (1586); secretary to Elizabeth I (1586–87); member of commission for trial of Mary, Queen of Scots; imprisoned (1587–89) on Elizabeth's false charge of undue haste in securing her signature to Mary's death warrant.

Da·vis·son \ˈdā-və-sən\, Clinton Joseph. 1881–1958. American physicist, b. Bloomington, Ill. With Bell Telephone Laboratories (1917–46); investigated electron emission and reflection; discovered (with L. H. Germer) the diffraction of electrons by crystals (1927). Shared with George P. Thomson the 1937 Nobel prize for physics.

Dav·itt \ˈdav-ət\, Michael. 1846–1906. Irish nationalist leader. Son of evicted tenant farmer. Joined Fenian brotherhood (1865); secretary of Irish Republican Brotherhood (1868); served seven years penal servitude (1870–77) for attempt to send firearms into Ireland. Met Henry George in America; organized Irish Land League (1879) in order to link up independence movement with agrarian unrest; imprisoned for seditious speeches. Elected M.P. (1882) but disqualified; conducted campaign for land nationalization; repudiated by Parnell. M.P. as anti-Parnellite (1895–99); helped William O'Brien found United Irish League to reconcile factions (1898). Author of *Leaves from a Prison Diary* (1884) and *The Fall of Feudalism in Ireland* (1904).

Da·vout \dȧ-vü\, Louis-Nicolas. Duc d'Au·er·städt \dȧ-wer-stȧt\. Prince d'Eck·mühl \dek-mǖl\. 1770–1823. French soldier. Led regiment in pre-Revolutionary revolt (1790); served in Belgian campaign (1792–93), in Egypt (1798–99); general of division (1800); marshal of France (1804); fought at Austerlitz (1805), Auerstädt (1806), Jena (1806), Eylau (1807), Eckmühl and Wagram (1809), and in Russian campaign (1812). Created duke (1808), prince (1809) by Napoléon; minister of war during Hundred Days (1815).

Da·vy \ˈdā-vē\, Edward. 1806–1885. English physician and chemist. Invented electromagnetic repeater for relaying telegraphic signals (1836), an electrochemical telegraph (1838). Farmer and physician in Australia (from 1839).

Davy, Sir Humphry. 1778–1829. English chemist. Discovered exhilarating effect of nitrous oxide when inhaled (1799); established reputation with *Researches, Chemical and Philosophical* (1800) on physiological effects of various gases; professor of chemistry, Royal Institution, London (1802–12); first prepared potassium (1807), sodium (1807), and calcium (1808), by electrolytic means; discovered boron (1808); showed, contrary to Lavoisier's theory, that some acids are free from oxygen; explained bleaching action of chlorine; showed that diamond is carbon; advanced electrical theory of chemical affinity in *On Some Chemical Agencies of Electricity* (1807); invented miner's safety lamp (1815). President of Royal Society (1820–27). Published *Elements of Chemical Philosophy* (1812), *Elements of Agricultural Chemistry* (1813), *Salmonia, or Days of Fly Fishing* (1827), *Consolations in Travel* (1830).

Davys, John. See John DAVIS (c.1550–1605).

Da·wā·nī \da-ˈwän-ē\. *In full* Muḥammad ibn Jalāl ad-Dīn Dawānī. 1427–1502/03. Iranian jurist and philosopher. Wrote commentaries on Islāmic laws and philosophy and on mysticism of al-Maktul. Wrote *Akhlag-i Jalali* on ideal society and the just ruler.

Dawes \ˈdȯz\, Charles Gates. 1865–1951. American lawyer, financier, and politician, b. Marietta, Ohio. U.S. comptroller of the currency (1897–1902). In Chicago organized (1902) Central Union Trust Co., its president (1902–21) and chairman of board of directors (1921–25); chairman of board of City National Bank and Trust Co., Chicago (from 1932). Served in A.E.F., in France (1917–19; brigadier general). First director, U.S. Bureau of the Budget (1921). President of commission to investigate German budget and payments of war reparations (1923); commission evolved so-called Dawes plan of reorganization and loans (in effect 1924–30). Vice president of the United States (1925–29). U.S. ambassador to Great Britain (1929–32). President, Reconstruction Finance Corp. (1932). Corecipient, with Sir Austen Chamberlain of England, of Nobel prize for peace (1925). Author of *A Journal of the Great War* (1921), *Notes as Vice-President* (1935). His brother ¶Rufus Cutler Dawes (1867–1940), public utility executive, served as adviser to commission that evolved the Dawes plan (1923–24) and as assistant to Owen D. Young, first agent-general of reparations; president, Century of Progress Exposition, Chicago (1933–34).

Dawes, Henry Laurens. 1816–1903. American politician, b. Cummington, Mass. Member, U.S. House of Representatives (1857–75); U.S. Senate (1875–93); author of Dawes Act (1887), dividing Indian lands into individual allotments and ending the status of tribes as "domestic nations."

Dawes, William. 1745–1799. American patriot, b. Boston. Rode with Paul Revere (April 18, 1775) from Lexington toward Concord, warning people of coming of British.

Dawes, William Rutter. 1799–1868. English astronomer. A physician, carried on astronomical work at various private observatories and as head (1839–44) of Bishop Observatory, London. Made measurements of hundreds of double stars; a discoverer of Saturn's "crepe" ring (1850); observed Jupiter's Red Spot (1857); made accurate map of Mars (1864).

Daw·kins \ˈdȯ-kənz\, Sir William Boyd. 1837–1929. British geologist and archaeologist, b. Wales. Curator of Manchester Museum (1870–90); first professor of geology, Owens Coll. (now Victoria U.), Manchester (1872–1908). Author of *Cave-hunting* (1874), *Early Man in Britain* (1880), *British Pleistocene Mammalia* (1866–87).

Daw·son \ˈdȯs-ᵊn\, Bertrand Edward. 1st Viscount Dawson of Penn. 1864–1945. English physician. Physician in ordinary to Edward VII, George V, Edward VIII, George VI, and Queen Mary (1907–45); president, Royal College of Physicians (1931–38), British Medical Association (1943–44); created baron (1920), viscount (1936).

Dawson, Geoffrey, *in full* George Geoffrey. 1874–1944. English journalist. Editor, Johannesburg *Star* (1905–10) and London *Times* (1912–19, 1923–41).

Dawson, Henry. 1811–1878. English landscape painter. Noted for marine and river scenes; praised as colorist by Ruskin.

Dawson, James. 1717?–1746. English Jacobite. Volunteer officer in service of the Young Pretender (1745); hanged, drawn, and quartered on Kensington Green, his betrothed dying of grief in her coach the same day; subject of Shenstone's ballad *Jemmy Dawson.*

Dawson, Sir John William. 1820–1899. Canadian geologist, b. Pictou, N.S. Specialist in natural history and geology of Nova Scotia and New Brunswick. Professor of geology and principal (1855–93), McGill U.; opponent of Darwinian explanation of origin of life forms. Discovered fossil remains of *Psilophyton,* then earliest known land plant, and *Dendrerpeton,* air-breathing reptile. Author of *Acadian Geology* (1855), *Air Breathers of the Coal Period* (1863). His son ¶George Mercer (1849–1901) was also a geologist; member (1875), asst. director (1883), director (1895) of geological survey of Canada; in charge of Yukon expedition (1887); member, Bering Sea Commission (1891). City of Dawson, Yukon Terr., was named for him.

Dawson of Penn, 1st Viscount. See Bertrand DAWSON.

Day \ˈdā\, Arthur Louis. 1869–1960. American geophysicist, b. Brookfield, Mass. With U.S. Geological Survey (1900–07); first director of Geophysical Laboratory, Carnegie Institution of Washington (1907–36). Known for studies of rocks and minerals at very high and very low temperatures, investigations of hot springs and volcanoes.

Day, Benjamin Henry. 1810–1889. American newspaperman, b. West Springfield, Mass. Founded first one-cent daily paper, *New York Sun* (1833). His son ¶Benjamin (1838–1916), New York printer, invented the Ben Day process for shading and color in printing illustrations.

Day, Clarence Shepard, Jr. 1874–1935. American writer, b. New York City. Grandson of Benjamin H. Day. Author of *This Simian World* (1920), *The Crow's Nest* (1921), *Thoughts Without Words* (1928), *God and My Father* (1932), *In the Green Mountain Country* (1934), *Life with Father* (1935; dramatized by Howard Lindsay and Russel Crouse, 1939), *Life with Mother* (1937), *Father and I* (1940).

Day, Dorothy. 1897–1980. American journalist and reformer, b. Brooklyn, N.Y. On staffs of Socialist journals *Call* and *Masses* (1916–18); joined Roman Catholic church (1927); with Peter Maurin founded *Catholic Worker* monthly newspaper (1933) to promote program of communalism, hospices for urban poor, education, etc.; founded hospices in many cities; through *Catholic Worker* promoted social justice, pacifism.

Day, Edmund Ezra. 1883–1951. American economist and educator, b. Manchester, N.H. Professor of economics, U. of Michigan (1923–27), where he organized (1924) and was first dean of school of business administration; with Rockefeller Foundation (1928–37) and General Education Board (1933–37); president, Cornell U. (1937–49).

Day, Holman Francis. 1865–1935. American writer, b. Vassalboro, Me. Author of *Up in Maine* (verse, 1900), *Pine Tree Ballads* (1902), *Squire Phin* (novel, 1905), *King Spruce* (1908), *The Red Lane* (1912), *Leadbetter's Luck* (1923), *Starwagons* (1928), *Ships of Joy* (1932), etc.

Day, John. 1574–?1640. English playwright. Collaborator with Henry Chettle, Thomas Dekker, and others in contributing to Philip Henslowe's theaters. Author of *The Ile of Guls* (1606), *Law Trickes* and *Humour out of Breath* (1608), and *The Parliament of Bees* (a satirically allegorical masque, 1607?).

Day *or* **Daye** \'dā\, Stephen. c.1594–1668. American printer, b. London, England. To America (1638); first printer in English colonies in America, with press in Cambridge, Mass. The *Bay Psalm Book,* printed by him (1640), was (excepting an almanac of 1639) the first book in English printed in America.

Day, Thomas. 1748–1789. English philanthropist and author. Admirer of Rousseau's doctrines; attempted philanthropic schemes of moral and social reform. Author of *The Dying Negro* (poem, 1773) and *History of Sandford and Merton* (1783–89), an attempt in fiction to reconcile Rousseauistic naturalism with conventional morality.

Day, William Rufus. 1849–1923. American diplomat and jurist, b. Ravenna, Ohio. U.S. secretary of state (1898); member of U.S. commission to arrange peace with Spain (1898–99). Judge of U.S. circuit court of appeals (1899–1903); associate justice, U.S. Supreme Court (1903–22).

Da·yan \dī-'än, dä-'yän\, Moshe. 1915–1981. Israeli soldier and politician. Founded Haganah militia force (1939); served in British army during World War II; in Israeli army (from 1948); commander on Jerusalem front (1948); chief of staff (1953–58), credited with success of army in Gaza and Sinai in Suez War (1956); member of Knesset (1958–81); minister of agriculture (1959–64); minister of defense (1967, 1969–74), planned and commanded Six-Day War (1967); foreign minister (1977–79). Author of *Diary of the Sinai Campaign* (1966), *Living with the Bible* (1978).

Da·yan·an·da Sa·ras·va·ti \,dī-(y)ə-'nän-də-,sär-äs-'vä-tē\. *Orig.* Mu·la Sankara \,mü-lə-säŋ-'kär-ə, -sän-\. 1824–1883. Indian Hindu reformer. Wandering ascetic as member of Sarasvati sect (1845–60); founded Arya Samaj (1875), Hindu reform sect devoted to reassertion of authority of the Vedas; program also embraced opposition to child marriage, opening of Vedic study to all castes, education, and Indian nationalism.

Daye, Stephen. See Stephen DAY.

Day-Lewis \'dā-'lü-əs\, Cecil. 1904–1972. English poet, b. Ireland. One of circle of left-wing poets centered on W.H. Auden in 1930s; later turned to traditional lyric forms. Books of verse included *Transitional Poem* (1929), *From Feathers to Iron* (1931), *Magnetic Mountain* (1933), *A Time to Dance* (1935), *Overtures to Death* (1938), *An Italian Visit* (1953), *The Room and Other Poems* (1965), *The Whispering Roots* (1970); also wrote criticism, as *A Hope for Poetry* (1934), *The Poetic Image* (1947); autobiography *The Buried Day* (1960); detective novels under pseudonym Nicholas Blake. Professor of poetry at Oxford (1951–56), Harvard (1964–65). Poet laureate (1968–72).

Day·ton \'dāt-ᵊn\, Elias. 1737–1807. American Revolutionary officer, b. Elizabeth, N.J. Colonel of New Jersey troops (1776–83); promoted brigadier general (1783) on direct recommendation of Washington. Member, U.S. House of Representatives (1787–88). His son ¶Jonathan (1760–1824) was captain in Revolutionary army (1783); member, Continental Congress (1787–89), Constitutional Convention (1787), U.S. House of Representatives (1791–99; speaker, 1795–99); U.S. senator (1799–1805).

Da·za \'dä-sä\, Hilarión. *Orig. surname* Gro·so·lé \grō-sō-'lā\. 1840–1894. Bolivian general. Seized presidency from Tomás Frías (1876); attempted to blunt Chilean territorial incursions by secret treaty with Peru (1873) and by tax on nitrate exports (1878), precipitating War of the Pacific (1878–83); overthrown following military reverses (1880); killed by mob on his return from exile.

Dazai Osamu. See TSUSHIMA Shuji.

d'Azeglio, Marchese. See Massimo TAPARELLI.

Da·zey \'dā-zē\, Charles Turner. 1855–1938. American playwright, b. Lima, Ill. Author of successful melodrama *In Old Kentucky.*

De·ák \'de-äk\, Ferenc. 1803–1876. Hungarian politician. Member of Hungarian Diet (1833–36, 1839–40, 1841); rose to leadership in movement for political emancipation of Hungary. Minister of justice (1848); principal author of "April laws" embodying reforms; opposed Kossuth and radical policies. Became generally acknowledged leader of Hungary (from c.1861); gained from Austrian emperor a "Compromise" including restoration of Hungarian constitution and establishment of the dual monarchy of Austria-Hungary (1867).

Dea·kin \'dē-kən\, Alfred. 1856–1919. Australian politician. In Victoria legislature (1880–1900); drafted constitution bill creating Australian commonwealth and guided it through British Parliament (1900); first attorney general under commonwealth (1901); leader of Liberal party; prime minister (1903–04, 1905–08, 1909–10); promoted legislation on social welfare, immigration restriction.

Deakin, Arthur. 1890–1955. English trade unionist. Assistant general secretary (1935–40) and general secretary (1940–55) of Transport & General Workers Union; chairman of Trades Union Council (1951–52). Led non-Communist unions out of World Federation of Trade Unions (1948) and formed International Confederation of Free Trade Unions.

De Ami·cis \dā-ä-'mē-chēs\, Edmondo. 1846–1908. Italian traveler and writer. Author of *La vita militaire* (1868), *Novelle* (1872), *Poesie* (1880), *Gli amici* (1882), *La carozza di tutti* (1899); known esp. for *Cuore* (1886), children's story widely translated and reprinted.

Dean \'dēn\, James Byron. 1931–1955. American actor, b. Marion, Ind. Brief spectacular film career in *East of Eden* (1955), *Rebel Without a Cause* (1955), *Giant* (1956); personified restless rebellious youth.

Dean, Jay Hanna, *known as* Dizzy. 1911–1974. American baseball player, b. Lucas, Ark. Pitcher with St. Louis Cardinals (1932–37), Chicago Cubs (1938–41); career total 150 wins, 83 losses; led National League in strikeouts (1932–36); won 30 games (1934); with brother Paul won 2 games each in 1934 World Series. Elected to Baseball Hall of Fame (1953). His brother ¶Paul Dee, *sometimes known as* Daffy (1913–1981), also pitched for St. Louis (1933–40), New York Giants (1940–43), St. Louis Browns (1943); won 19 games first season, including a no-hitter.

Dean, Man Mountain. *Orig.* Frank Simmons Lea·vitt \'lē-vət\. 1891–1953. American wrestler, b. New York City. By colorful performances (1926–37) helped make professional wrestling popular; appeared also in motion pictures.

Deane \'dēn\, Richard. 1610–1653. English military and naval commander and regicide. Commander of Parliamentary artillery (1644–47); commander of right wing at Preston (1648); commissioner for trial of Charles I and signed death warrant. Naval commander with title of general at sea (1649); fought as major general at Worcester (1651); as commander in chief in Scotland, pacified Highlands (1652).

Deane, Silas. 1737–1789. American lawyer and diplomat, b. Groton, Conn. Leader of revolutionary agitation in Conn.; member, Continental Congress (1774–76). Sent to France as American confidential agent to secure supplies and aid (1776–78); succeeded in purchasing shiploads of supplies and enlisting the aid of a number of military men, including Lafayette, Steuben, Pulaski. Joined by Benjamin Franklin and Arthur Lee (*q.v.*) to form commission of three; ordered back to America; required to give detailed statement of his transactions in France to meet Lee's charges of embezzlement; failed to satisfy Congress; returned to France for documentary support (1780). From Europe wrote pessimistic letters urging reconciliation with England; died aboard ship bound for America.

Dear·born \'di(ə)r-,bȯ(ə)rn, -bərn\, Henry. 1751–1829. American soldier, b. Hampton, N.H. Served in Revolutionary War (1775–83); colonel on Gen. Washington's staff at Yorktown (1781). Member of Congress (1793–97); secretary of war (1801–09); issued order for erection of fort at "Chikago" (1803); senior major general of army and commander of northern border (1812–13); campaign mismanaged and Dearborn recalled (1813); in command at New York (1813–15). U.S. minister to Portugal (1822–24).

Déat \dā-á\, Marcel. 1894–1955. French politician. Socialist member of Chamber of Deputies (1926–32); helped form Parti Socialiste de France (1933), for which he was a deputy (1933–36); air minister (1936); published pro-Hitler article "Mourir pour Dantzig?" (1939); formed collaborationist Rassemblement National Populaire in occupied France (1940); minister of work and social affairs in Vichy regime of Pierre Laval (1944). Condemned *in absentia* for treason (1945); lived in exile under assumed name.

De Bar·de·le·ben \də-,bär-də-'lā-bən\, Henry Fairchild. 1840–1910. American industrialist, b. Alabama. Developed coal resources and steel industry in Birmingham area.

de Ba·ry \də-bä-'rē\, Heinrich Anton. 1831–1888. German botanist. Founder of science of mycology and of plant pathology. Professor at Freiburg (1855–66), Halle (1867–72), Strasbourg (1872–88). First to work out life histories of many fungi, esp. parasitic fungi; first to demonstrate heteroecism (1865); demonstrated symbiotic nature of lichens (1866); author of *Untersuchungen über die Brandpilze* (1853), *Vergleichende Anatomie der Vegetationsorgane der Phanerogamen und Farne* (1877).

de Ba·sil \də-bá-'zēl\, Colonel W. *Orig.* Vasily Grigoryevich Vos·kre·sen·sky \vòs-kres-'yen-skəi\. 1888–1951. Russian impresario. Assistant to Prince Zeretelli in managing Russian opera company in Europe (1925); with René Blum organized Ballet Russe de Monte Carlo (1932); codirector (1932–38); director of original Ballet Russe (1939–48).

Debayle, Somoza. See SOMOZA.

Debbora. See DEBORAH.

De·be·ney \də-bə-ne\, Marie-Eugène. 1864–1943. French general. Engaged before Verdun and at the Somme (1916); commanded 7th army in Alsace and armies of the north and northeast (1917); commanded 1st army on northeastern front (1918); blunted German offensive at Montdidier (June 1918). Chief of staff of the army (1924–30).

De·bi·dour \də-bē-dür\, Antonin, *in full* Élie-Louis-Marc-Marie-Antoine. 1847–1917. French historian. Chief work *Histoire diplomatique de l'Europe* (1916–17).

De·bierne \dəb-yern\, André-Louis. 1874–1949. French chemist. Discovered element actinium in pitchblende (1899); collaborating with Marie Curie, isolated pure radium (1910); succeeded her as director of research in the Radium Institute (1934).

De Bo·no \dā-'bō-nō\, Emilio. 1866–1944. Italian general and politician. Served with distinction in Italo–Turkish War (1911), World War I (1914–18); retired as major general (1920). An organizer of Fascist party, accompanied Mussolini in March on Rome (1922). Served as chief of police and commander of Fascist militia; governor of Tripolitania (1925). Commander of Italian forces invading Ethiopia (1935) but quickly replaced by Gen. Badoglio; field marshal (1935). Minister of state (1942); voted against Mussolini in Fascist Grand Council (1943); tried and executed for treason.

Deb·o·rah *or* **Deb·bo·ra** \'deb(-ə)-rə\. 12th? century B.C. Hebrew prophetess and heroine. Traditionally the inspiration for the victory of Israelites over Canaanites. Putative author of "Song of Deborah" in biblical book of *Judges,* perhaps oldest section of the Bible.

De Bow \də-'bō\, James Dunwoody Brownson. 1820–1867. American editor, b. Charleston, S.C. Founded and edited *Commercial Review of the South and Southwest* (known as *De Bow's Review*), in New Orleans (from 1846). Superintendent, U.S. census (from 1853); prepared reports of Census of 1850, and *Statistical View of the United States* (1854).

De·brett \də-'bret\, John. d. 1822. English publisher. Compiler of a *Peerage of England, Scotland, and Ireland* (1802) and a *Baronetage of England* (1808).

de Broglie. See BROGLIE.

de Brosses, Charles. See BROSSES.

Debs \'debz\, Eugene Victor. 1855–1926. American Socialist, b. Terre Haute, Ind. Organized local of Brotherhood of Locomotive Firemen (1875); national secretary (1880); a founder and first president of American Railway Union (1893); led successful strike against Great Northern Railway (1894); for his role as a leader in Pullman strike, Chicago (1894), arrested and sentenced to six months' imprisonment for contempt of court. Organized Social Democratic party of America (1897); candidate of Socialists for president of the U.S. (1900, 1904, 1908, 1912, 1920). A founder of Industrial Workers of the World (1905). Indicted for violation of Espionage Act (1918); convicted and sentenced to ten years' imprisonment; released by order of President Harding (1921).

De·bu·court \də-bue̅-kür\, Philibert-Louis. 1755–1832. French painter and engraver. Known for his genre paintings.

De·bu·rau *or* **De·bu·reau** \də-bue̅-rō\, Jean-Baptiste-Gaspard. *Orig.* Jan Kašpar Dvořák. 1796–1846. French mime of Bohemian origin. Created the character of Pierrot and introduced it into traditional Harlequinade.

de Burgh. See BURGH family.

De·bus·sy \də-bue̅-'sē; *Angl* ˌdeb-yü-'sē, ˌdāb-, də-'byü-sē\, Claude, *in full* Achille-Claude. 1862–1918. French composer. Awarded Grand Prix de Rome for *L'Enfant prodigue* (cantata, 1884); greatly influenced by Symbolist poets and Impressionist painters; evolved highly inventive approach to tonal color, harmony, and evocation of atmosphere. Other major works included *La Damoiselle élue* (cantata, 1888), *Deux arabesques* (piano, 1888), *Suite bergamasque* (piano pieces, including "Clair de lune," 1890–1905), *Prélude à l'après-midi d'un faune* (symphonic poem, 1894), *Nocturnes* (1899), *Pelléas et Mélisande* (opera, 1902), *La Mer* (tone poem, 1905), *Douze préludes* (piano, 1910–13 and 1915), *Jeux* (ballet, 1913), and songs, chamber music, etc.

De·bye \də-'bī\, Peter Joseph William. *Orig.* Petrus Josephus Wilhelmus De·bije \də-'bā-ə\. 1884–1966. American physicist, b. Holland. Director, Kaiser Wilhelm Institute for Physics, Berlin (1935–40); professor at Cornell U. (1940–50). Known esp. for studies of molecular structure through investigations on dipole moments and on diffraction of X-rays and electrons in crystals and gases. Awarded 1936 Nobel prize for chemistry.

De·caen \də-kä^{n}\, Charles-Mathieu-Isidore. Comte. 1769–1832. French general in Revolutionary and Napoleonic armies. Sent by Napoléon to command French possessions in East Indies (1803); made headquarters at Mauritius (1803–11) and harassed British trade. Commanded army of Catalonia (1811–13), in Netherlands (1813); commanded division under Louis XVIII; captured at Bordeaux by Clauzel; again sided with Napoléon and made commander in the Pyrénées-Orientales. Imprisoned (1815–17). His son ¶Claude-Théodore (1811–1870) was also a French general; promoted general of division at Magenta (1859); mortally wounded in battle of Borny (Courcelles).

De·caisne \də-ken\, Joseph. 1807–1882. Belgian botanist. Author of *Jardin fruitier du muséum* (1847). His brother ¶Henri (1799–1852), painter, known for historical and genre paintings.

De·camps \də-kä^{n}\, Alexandre-Gabriel. 1803–1860. French painter. Traveled in Italy and Near East (1827–28) and thereafter devoted himself esp. to painting Oriental subjects; a leader in introducing strain of Orientalism in French art.

de Candolle. See CANDOLLE.

De·ca·tur \di-'kāt-ər\, Stephen. 1779–1820. American naval officer, b. Sinepuxent, Md. Commanded schooner *Enterprise* in Tripolitan waters (1803). Led daring exploit in burning *Philadelphia,* which had been captured and held by Tripolitans (Feb. 16, 1804); promoted to captain. In War of 1812, commanded the *United States* in victory over the British ship *Macedonian* (Oct. 25, 1812) and the *President* in victory over *Endymion* (Jan. 15, 1815). Commanded squadron which sailed to Algeria and forced a peace on American terms (1815). At a banquet on his return, he gave the famous toast: "Our country! In her intercourse with foreign nations may she always be in the right; but our country, right or wrong! " Killed by James Barron in a duel.

De·cau·ville \də-kō-vēl\, Paul. 1846–1922. French industrialist. Inventor and manufacturer of equipment for a narrow-gauge railroad (named after him) with demountable and transportable track.

De·cazes \də-käz\, Élie. Duc. *Full surname* Decazes et de Glücks·berg \-ā-də-glue̅ks-berg\. 1780–1860. French politician. Minister of police in Bourbon restoration (1815); in Chamber of Deputies (1815–20) became leader of moderate royalists; recommended dissolution of ultraroyalist-dominated Chamber (1816); as minister of interior (1818–20) was most powerful figure in government; premier (1819–20); resignation forced in aftermath of assassination of duc de Berry. Created duke and peer of France (1820); ambassador to Great Britain (1820–21); in Chamber of Peers (from 1821).

De·ceb·a·lus \di-'seb(-ə)-ləs\. d. 106 A.D. King of the Dacians. On coming to power (85 A.D.) launched war on Rome; reached accommodation with Domitian, acknowledging Roman authority (89); defeated by Trajan in First and Second Dacian wars (101–102, 105–106), after which Dacia became Roman province.

De Celles \də-sel\, Alfred Duclos. 1843–1925. Canadian journalist, librarian, and historian, b. St. Laurent, Que. Librarian of Parliament (1885–1920); author of *Les États Unis* (1898), *A la conquête de la liberté religieuse en France et en Canada* (1898), *Les Constitutions du Canada* (1918), etc.

De·cem·brio \dā-'chem-brē-(ˌ)ō\, Pier Candido. 1392–1477. Italian Humanist. Apostolic secretary to Nicholas V; author of biographies of Visconti and Francesco Sforza; translated Homer, Plato, Caesar and others into Italian.

De Chair \də-'che(ə)r, -'cha(ə)r, -'she(ə)r, -'sha(ə)r\, Sir Dudley Rawson Stratford. 1864–1958. British naval officer. In World War I commanded cruiser squadron in North Sea blockade (1914–16); commanded 3d battle squadron (1917–18); vice admiral (1917); admiral (1920); retired (1923). Governor of New South Wales (1923–30).

Dé·che·lette \dāsh-let\, Joseph. 1862–1914. French archaeologist. Authority on Gallo-Roman and Celtic coins; author of *Manuel d'archéologie préhistorique, celtique, et gallo-romaine* (1908–14).

De·chet \dā-she\, Louis-Alexandre. *Known as* Jen·ne·val \zhen-vál\. 1801–1830. French actor and poet. Popular comedian at Odéon, Comédie-Française, etc. Author of words to "La Brabançonne," Belgian national anthem.

De·ci·us \'dē-sh(ē-)əs\, Gaius Messius Quintus Tra·ja·nus \trə-'jā-nəs\. c.201–251. Roman emperor (249–251). Commanded troops of Emperor Philip on the Danube; his soldiers revolted (249); proclaimed emperor, reputedly against his will; defeated and killed Philip at Verona; conducted first systematic persecution of Christians; killed in Thrace in battle with Goths.

Decius Mus \-'məs\, Publius. Name of three Roman consuls, father, son, and grandson, who sacrificed themselves to assure Roman victory in the Samnite War (340 B.C.), at battle of Sentinum (295 B.C.), and at battle of Ausculum (279 B.C.), respectively.

Deck \dek\, Joseph-Théodore. 1823–1891. French ceramist. Created imitations of Persian and Chinese ware, also new colors for porcelain, including turquoise blue; director of Sèvres factory (1887).

Deck·en \'dek-ən\, Karl Klaus von der. Freiherr. 1833–1865. German explorer. In East Africa (1860–65); explored Lake Nyasa region (1860); first European to attempt Mt. Kilimanjaro (1862); murdered by Somali natives.

Deck·er \'dek-ər\, Sir Matthew. Baronet. 1679–1749. English merchant and economist, of Dutch descent. To London (1702); a director of East India Co.

(1713–43); M.P. (1719–22). Author of *Serious Considerations on the several High Duties which the Nation in general, as well as Trade in particular, labour under* (1743) and *An Essay on the Causes of the Decline of the Foreign Trade* (1744), arguing for tax reform and esp. for free trade, anticipating some arguments of Adam Smith.

Decker, Thomas. See DEKKER.

de Cop·pet \də-(ˌ)kō-ˈpā\, Edward J. 1855–1916. American banker and music patron. Founder of banking and brokerage firm of De Coppet & Doremus. Organizer of the Flonzaley Quartet (1902), a string quartet renowned for its performances of chamber music (disbanded 1927).

de Coster, Charles. See COSTER.

De·cour·celle \də-kür-sel\, Pierre-Henri-Adrien. 1821–1892. French author. Wrote or co-wrote many plays, including the verse comedy *Une Soirée à la Bastille* and the drama *Jenny l'Ouvrière.* His son ¶Pierre (1856–1926) was playwright and novelist; author of *Les Deux Gosses* (1889), plays *L'As de trèfle* (1883) and *Gigolette* (1893), and an adaptation of William Gillette's *Sherlock Holmes* (1907).

De·de·kind \ˈdā-də-kint\, Friedrich. 1525?–1598. German poet and playwright. Author of a satire in Latin verse, *Grobianus* (1549) and dramas *Der christliche Ritter* (1576) and *Papista conversus* (1596).

Dedekind, Julius Wilhelm Richard. 1831–1916. German mathematician. Taught at Zürich Polyteknikum (1858–62), Technische Hochschule of Brunswick (1862–1916); developed arithmetic theory of irrational numbers in *Stetigkeit und irrationale Zahlen* (1872); theory of ideals in *Über die Theorie der ganzen algebraischen Zahlen* (1879).

Dee \ˈdē\, John. 1527–1608. English mathematician and astrologer. Astrologer to Mary Tudor; acquitted by Star Chamber on charge of practicing sorcery against her (1555); enjoyed favor of Queen Elizabeth, for whose coronation he was asked to name a propitious day; drew up hydrographical and geographical accounts of newly discovered territories (1580); advocated adoption of Gregorian calendar in England, and made preparatory calculations (1583); involved in Poland and Bohemia in chicanery of crystal gazing and magic (1583–89). Author of Latin treatises on logic, mathematics, navigation, alchemy, etc., including *Monas Hieroglyphica* (1564).

Deems \ˈdēmz\, Charles Force. 1820–1893. American clergyman, b. Baltimore. Methodist preacher (from 1839); president of Greensboro Women's College, N.C. (1850–54); founded undenominational Church of the Strangers, New York City (1868); served as its pastor (1868–93). Author of *Life of Jesus* (1872), *Scotch Verdict in re Evolution* (1885).

Deep·ing \ˈdēp-iŋ\, Warwick, *in full* George Warwick. 1877–1950. English novelist. Among his many novels were *Unrest* (1916), *Valour* (1918), *Sorrell and Son* (1925), *Old Pybus* (1928), *Old Wine and New* (1932), *Blind Man's Year* (1937), *The Man who went Back* (1940), *Corn in Egypt* (1942), *Reprieve* (1945), *Laughing House* (1947).

Deere \ˈdi(ə)r\, John. 1804–1886. American industrialist, b. Rutland, Vt. Manufacturer of steel plows for use on Great Plains (from c.1838); firm incorporated as Deere & Co. (1868). Cf. John LANE.

Deering, Richard. See DERING.

Deer·ing \ˈdi(ə)r-iŋ\, William. 1826–1913. American industrialist, b. South Paris, Me. Established harvester manufacturing business at Plano, Ill. (1873); perfected and manufactured Appleby twine binder (from 1879); firm incorporated as William Deering & Co. (1883); merged with International Harvester Co., Chicago (1902).

De·fauw \də-faù\, Désiré. 1855–1960. Belgian violinist and orchestra conductor. Musical director of Belgium's Institut National de Radiodiffusion (from 1924); founded Orchestre National de Belgique (1937); controversial conductor of Chicago Symphony (1943–47).

Deffand, Marquise du. See Marie de VICHY-CHAMROND.

De·foe \di-ˈfō\, Daniel. 1660–1731. English journalist and novelist. A London merchant (1683–92); employed by government as writer, produced his *Essay on Projects* (1697), making commercial and social proposals in advance of his time; *The True-Born Englishman* (1701), a satire in verse in defense of William III; fined, imprisoned, pilloried for his "Shortest Way with Dissenters" (1702), and composed "Hymn to the Pillory" (1703). Sent as secret agent of government to Scotland (1706–07) to promote union; showed his skill as a reporter in the *True Relation of the Apparition of one Mrs. Veal* (1706). Edited and largely wrote pro-government *Review* (1704–13). Supported Whig policies of Marlborough and Godolphin (1708–10); on Harley's return to power, supported Tory war policy; shared Harley's downfall; generally discredited, published apologia, *An Appeal to Honour and Justice* (1715); convicted of libel against Lord Annesley but released on condition of serving as government secret agent in subediting the Jacobite *Mist's Journal* (1717–24) and High Church organs; published *The Wars of Charles XII* (1715). Turned to fiction when nearly sixty years old and, with background from Dampier's *Voyage round the World* (1697) and from accounts by Woodes Rogers, Edward Cooke, and Richard Steele, narrated adventures of Alexander Selkirk (*q.v.*) in *Robinson Crusoe* (1719) and sequel, *Serious Reflections* (1720). During next five years, produced prolifically fiction and fictitious histories: *Life of Mr. Duncan Campbell* (1720), *Captain Singleton* (1720), *Moll Flanders* (1722), *The Journal of the Plague Year* (1722), *The History of Colonel Jack* (1722), *John Sheppard* (1724), *Jonathan Wild* (1725); also a three-volume *Tour Thro' the whole Island of Great Britain* (1724–26), *A New Voyage round the World* (1725), and the romance *Roxana* (1724). In closing years, published pamphlets showing social and economic farsightedness, such as *A Plan of the English Commerce* (1728), didactic works, such as *Everybody's Business is Nobody's Business* (1725), and a series of demonological works, including an *Essay on the History of Apparitions* (1728). Lived in hiding from creditors under pseudonym Andrew Moreton.

De' Forciglioni, Antonio. See Saint ANTONINUS.

De For·est \di-ˈfȯr-əst, -ˈfär-\, John William. 1826–1906. American writer, b. Seymour, Conn. Author of novels employing striking realism, including *Miss Ravenel's Conversion* (1867), *Kate Beaumont* (1872), *The Wetherel Affair* (1873), *Honest John Vane* (1875), *Playing the Mischief* (1875), *The Bloody Chasm* (1881), *A Lover's Revolt* (1898); also wrote nonfiction, including *Oriental Acquaintance* (1856), *European Acquaintance* (1858), Civil War memoirs.

De Forest, Lee. 1873–1961. American inventor, b. Council Bluffs, Iowa. Pioneer in wireless telegraphy and radiotelephony in America; sometimes called "the father of radio." Patented over 300 inventions in wireless telegraphy, radio telephony, talking pictures, high-speed facsimile transmission, television, radiotherapy, radar, etc. Devised electrolytic detector (c.1901); formed De Forest Wireless Telegraph Co. (1902); patented (1907) "Audion," first grid-triode vacuum tube, making possible amplification and easier detection of radio waves; broadcast Caruso's voice by radio (1910), first news by radio (1916); invented feedback or regenerative circuit (1912); involved in extensive bankruptcy and patent litigation; established radio station (1916). Invented optical sound recording system and exhibited sound-on-film motion pictures at Rivoli Theater, New York City (1923). Autobiography *Father of Radio* (1950).

De Forest, Robert Weeks. 1848–1931. American lawyer, b. New York City. Helped found N.Y. Charity Organization Society (1882; president 1888–1931); founded School for Social Work (1893); first tenement house commissioner of New York City (1902–03); helped organize Russell Sage Foundation (1907; president 1918–31). Chairman, Municipal Art Commission (1905–29); president, Metropolitan Museum of Art (1913–31).

De·freg·ger \ˈdā-freg-ər\, Franz von. 1835–1921. Austrian painter. Famed for genre pictures of scenes from Tirolese peasant life.

De·gas \də-gä, *Angl* də-ˈgä, ˈdā-ˌgä, dā-ˈgä\, Edgar, *in full* Hilaire-Germain-Edgar. 1834–1917. French painter. Associated with Impressionists; a master draftsman of human and animal figures, esp. in motion. Known for figure groups often in theatrical, orchestral, or race-course settings. Best known works included *La Repasseuse, Bouderie, L'Absinthe, Sur la plage, La Classe de danse, Miss Lola au cirque Fernando, Mlle. Fiocre dans le ballet de "La Source", Le Viol.*

de Gaspé, Philippe Aubert. See GASPÉ.

De Gas·pe·ri \dā-gäs-ˈpā-rē\, Alcide. 1881–1954. Italian politician. Edited journal *Il Nuovo Trentino* (from 1906); member of Austrian parliament (1911–18) seeking annexation of Trentino district by Italy; helped organize Partito Popolare Italiano (1919); PPI representative of Trentino in Italian parliament (1921–27, 1943–54); imprisoned by Fascists (1927–29); minister without portfolio (1944); minister of foreign affairs (1944–46, 1951–53); prime minister (1945–53). Worked for land reform, economic reconstruction, European unity; enacted new constitution (1948); took Italy into NATO (1951). Secretary general of Christian Democratic party (1953–54).

de Gaulle, Charles. See Charles de GAULLE.

de Geer. See GEER.

de' Gianuzzi, Giulio Pippi. See PIPPI DE' GIANUZZI.

de Girardin. See GIRARDIN.

de Goeje. See GOEJE.

De Gol·yer \də-ˈgäl-yər\, Everette Lee. 1886–1956. American geophysicist, b. Greensburg, Kans. Worked with various petroleum companies (from c.1919); president Rycade Oil (1923–41), Amerada Petroleum (1919–26); with own consulting firm (1936–56). Known for applying geophysical methods to petroleum exploration, esp. gravity surveys.

De·goutte \də-güt\, Jean-Marie-Joseph. 1866–1938. French general. Served in World War I; liberated southern Belgium; commanded Allied forces of occupation in the Ruhr region (1923–25).

de Grasse. See GRASSE.

de Grey *or* **de Gray.** See GREY.

de Grey and Ripon, Earl. See George F. S. ROBINSON.

de Groot. See GROOT.

De Hav·il·land \də-'hav-ə-lənd\, Sir Geoffrey. 1882–1965. British aeronautical engineer. Formed De Havilland Aircraft Co. (1920); manufactured Moth, Mosquito, Comet (first commercial jet), Vampire, Venom aircraft.

Deh·mel \'dā-məl\, Richard. 1863–1920. German poet and playwright. A forerunner of Expressionists, concerned with social justice and individual fulfillment; verse published in *Erlösungen* (1891), *Aber die Liebe* (1893), *Lebensblätter* (1895), *Weib und Welt* (1896), *Schöne wilde Welt* (1913); also wrote *Zwei Menschen* (novel, 1903), *Zwischen Volk und Menschheit* (war diary, 1919), and plays.

Dehn \'dān\, Adolf Arthur. 1895–1968. American artist, b. Waterville, Minn. Known as watercolorist and lithographer.

De·ho·dencq \də-ō-dank\, Edme-Alfred-Alexis. 1822–1882. French painter. Known esp. for Spanish and North African scenes.

De·hon \dā-ōn\, Léon-Gustave. *Religious name* John of the Heart of Jesus. 1843–1925. French cleric. Curate (1871) and canon (1876) at Saint-Quentin. Founded (1877) order of Oblates of the Sacred Heart; order dissolved by papacy (1883); reorganized as Congregatio Sacerdotum a Sacro Corde Jesu (1884); first superior general (1886–1925); moved motherhouse to Brussels following suppression by French civil authorities (1906).

de Hondt, Joost. See HONDT.

Deinarchus. See DINARCHUS.

Dein·hard·stein \'dīn-härt-,shtīn\, Johann Ludwig. 1794–1859. Austrian playwright. Vice director, Hofburg theater, Vienna (1832–41); wrote *Hans Sachs* (1829), *Garrick von Bristol* (1832).

Deinocrates. See DINOCRATES.

De·io·ces \'dē-(y)ō-,sēz\. 8th–7th century B.C. Legendary first king of the Medes. According to Herodotus, elected king and ruled (728–675 B.C.); supposed to have united Median tribes and built their capital city of Ecbatana. Historically, probably a tribal chieftain confused by Herodotus with Phraortes.

De·iot·a·rus \di-'(y)ät-ə-rəs\. d. 40 B.C. King of Galatia. An ally of Rome, drove Mithridates VI of Pontus from Phrygia in Third Mithridatic War (74 B.C.); in reward received from Pompey title of king (64); sided with Pompey in civil war and, after Pharsalus (48), fled to Asia; pardoned by Caesar (47); later accused of attempt to assassinate Caesar, his defense being conducted by Cicero (45–44), but trial ended by Caesar's murder; supported cause of Brutus and Cassius but, after Philippi, switched to side of triumvirs and retained his kingdom.

Dé·ja·zet \dā-zhà-ze\, Pauline-Virginie. 1798–1875. French actress. On stage from childhood; excelled as comedienne, esp. in soubrette and "boy" roles in such pieces as *Bonaparte à Brienne, Vert-Vert, Frétillon, Gentil Bernard.* Her son ¶Eugène (1820–1880) was a composer and theater director; author of comic opera *Un Mariage en l'Air;* director (1859–70) of Théâtre des Folies-Nouvelles, renamed Théâtre Déjazet.

De·jean \də-zhän\, Jean-François-Aimé. Comte. 1749–1824. French general in the Revolutionary armies. Sent by Napoléon to organize the Ligurian republic (1800); minister of war (1802–10); peer of France at the Restoration.

Dé·je·rine \dāzh-rēn\, Joseph-Jules. 1849–1917. French neurologist. Coauthor of *Traité des maladies de la moelle épinière,* with A. Thomas, and *Anatomie du système nerveux,* with his wife ¶Augusta, *nee* Klump·ke \'kləm(p)-kē\ (1859–1927), specialist in nervous pathology; first woman to interne at Paris Hospital.

de Kalb, Baron. See Johann KALB.

De·ken \'dā-kən\, Aagje. 1741–1804. Dutch poet and novelist. Collaborated with Elisabeth Wolff-Bekker on *Sara Burgerhart* (1782) and *Willem Leevend* (1784–85), first Dutch novels; also wrote children's and religious poetry.

Dekker, Eduard Douwes. See Eduard DOUWES DEKKER.

Dek·ker \'dek-ər\, Thomas. 1572?–?1632. English dramatist. Engaged (c.1598) by Philip Henslowe to write plays in collaboration with Ben Jonson, John Webster, and others; wrote or contributed to at least 42 plays; published (1600) *Old Fortunatus* and *The Shoemaker's Holiday;* depicted London life and manners of citizens, apprentices, and aristocrats; with Marston held up to ridicule by Jonson in *Poetaster,* retaliated with *Satiro-mastix* (1602); collaborated with Chettle and William Haughton in *Patient Grissel* (1600); collaborated in *The Honest Whore* and *Westward Hoe* (1604); collaborated with Middleton in *The Roaring Girle* (1611), with Massinger in *The Virgin Martyr* (1621), with Ford and Rowley in *The Witch of Edmonton* (pub. 1658); probable sole author of *If it be not Good the Devil is in It* (c.1610) and the tragicomedy *Match Mee in London.* As a pamphleteer, published "The Wonderfull yeare" (1603), "The Guls Horne-booke" (1609).

De Ko·ven \də-'kō-vən\, Reginald, *in full* Henry Louis Reginald. 1859–1920. American composer, b. Middletown, Conn. Organized and led Washington Philharmonic Orchestra (1902–05). Wrote popular light operas *The Begum* (1887), *Robin Hood* (1890), *The Fencing Master* (1892), *Rob Roy* (1894), *The Tzigane* (1895), *Paris Doll* (1897), *The Highwayman* (1897), *The Three Dragoons* (1899), *Happy Land* (1905), *Student King* (1906); grand operas *The Canterbury Pilgrims* (1917), *Rip Van Winkle* (1920), each with libretto by Percy Mackaye; songs as "O Promise Me", musical setting for Kipling's *Recessional;* etc.

de Kruif \də-'krīf\, Paul Henry. 1890–1971. American bacteriologist and writer, b. Zeeland, Mich. Bacteriologist for Rockefeller Institute (1920–22). Author of *Our Medicine Men* (1922), *Microbe Hunters* (1926), *Hunger Fighters* (1928), *Seven Iron Men* (1929), *Men Against Death* (1932), *The Fight for Life* (1939), *Health is Wealth* (1940), *A Man Against Insanity* (1957); collaborated with Sidney Howard on *Yellow Jack!* (1934).

de la Barra. See BARRA.

De la Beche \'del-ə-,besh\, Sir Henry Thomas. 1796–1855. English geologist. Suggested establishment and appointed first director of Geological Survey of Great Britain (1835); influenced establishment of Museum of Practical Geology and Royal School of Mines (1851); wrote *Manual of Geology* (1831), *Researches in Theoretical Geology* (1834), *Geological Observer* (1851).

De·la·borde \də-là-bòrd\, Henri. Vicomte. 1811–1899. French painter and art critic. Author of *La Gravure* (1882), *L'Académie des beaux-arts* (1891), etc. His son ¶Comte Bénigne-Marie-Henri-François (1854–1927), historian, was author of *Jean de Joinville* (1894), *Jean Froissart et son temps* (1895), etc., and editor of medieval texts.

De·la·croix \də-là-krwà, *Angl* ,del-ə-'k(r)wä\, Eugène, *in full* Ferdinand-Victor-Eugène. 1798–1863. French painter. Brilliant colorist and modeler, worked at first in Romantic style in several historical canvases, later developing an innovative style anticipating Impressionists. After 1832 produced many scenes of Moroccan life. Among his notable canvases were *Dante et Virgile aux Enfers, Milton aveugle dictant le "Paradis perdu," Christ en croix, Le Prisonnier de Chillon, Médée, Noce juive dans le Maroc, La Chasse aux lions, Les Femmes d'Alger, La Grèce expirante sur les ruines de Missolonghi.* Also painted great murals in the library of the Chamber of Deputies, in the museum of history at Versailles, in the Galerie d'Apollon in the Louvre, in the library of the Luxembourg, and in the Salon de la Paix of the Hôtel de Ville de Paris.

de Lacy. See LACY.

Delafield, E. M. See E. M. DASHWOOD.

Del·a·field \'del-ə-,fēld\, Edward. 1794–1875. American physician, b. New York City. Specialist in diseases of the eye; cofounder of New York Eye Infirmary (1820); founder and first president (1864) of American Ophthalmological Society. Professor (1825–38) and president (1858–75), College of Physicians and Surgeons. His son ¶Francis (1841–1915), authority in pathology and clinical diagnosis, was founder and first president (1886), Association of American Physicians; professor, College of Physicians and Surgeons (1882–1901); author of *Handbook of Post Mortem Examinations* (1872), *Studies in Pathological Anatomy* (1878–91).

De la Gar·die \də-lä-gàr-'dē\, Jacob Pontusson. Count. 1583–1652. Swedish soldier and statesman. Commander of Swedish forces in Russia (1608–13); captured Moscow (1610); defeated at Klushino (1610); negotiated Peace of Stolbova (1617), winning territory from Finland to Estonia and cutting Russia off from Baltic. Commander of Swedish forces in Livonia (1626–28); a commissioner at Truce of Stuhmsdorf (1635). Member of Swedish state council (from 1613); marshal (1620); one of five regents during minority of Queen Christina (1632–44). His son ¶Count Magnus Gabriel (1622–1686) was a favorite of Queen Christina; ambassador to France (1646); head of Council of Regency during minority of Charles XI (1660–72); chief minister to Charles XI (1672–75); dismissed on failure of foreign policy, later heavily fined on disclosure of financial irregularities during regency.

De·lage \də-làzh\, Yves. 1854–1920. French zoologist. Professor at Sorbonne (from 1886); known esp. for studies of invertebrate anatomy and physiology. Author of *La Structure du protoplasma, les théories sur l'hérédité et les grands problèmes de la biologie générale* (1895), *Traité de zoologie concrète* (1896–1903), etc.

Delaharpe. See LAHARPE.

De la Mare \,del-ə-'ma(ə)r, -'me(ə)r\, Walter John. 1873–1956. English poet and novelist. Among his books were *Songs of Childhood* (1902, under pseudonym Walter Ramal), *Henry Brocken* (novel, 1904), *Poems* (1906), *The Listeners and other Poems* (1912), *Peacock Pie* (1913), *Crossings* (play, 1921), *Memoirs of a Midget* (1921), *The Riddle, and other Stories* (1923), *Broomsticks, and other Tales* (1925), *Stuff and Nonsense* (1927), *Poems for Children* (1930), *The Wind Blows Over* (1936), *Memory, and other Poems* (1938), *Behold, This Dreamer* (1939), *Bells and Grass* (1941), *The Burning Glass* (1945), *The Traveller* (1946), *Collected Stories for Children* (1947), *Inward Companion* (1950), *O Lovely England* (1953).

Del·am·a·ter \də-'lam-ət-ər\, Cornelius Henry. 1821–1889. American mechanical engineer, b. Rhinebeck, N.Y. Built for John Ericsson first iron boats and first steam fire engines used in America, and engines for the *Monitor;* built John P. Holland's first successful submarine (1881).

De·lambre \də-läⁿbrᵊ\, Jean-Baptiste-Joseph. 1749–1822. French astronomer. Computed and published *Tables du Soleil, de Jupiter, de Saturne, d'Uranus et des satellites de Jupiter* (1792); with Méchain, measured arc of the meridian between Dunkirk and Barcelona for French government (1792–99); professor, Collège de France (1807); discovered four formulas (Delambre's analogies) in spherical trigonometry (1807).

Delamere, Barons. See George BOOTH.

de la Motte-Guyon, Jeanne-Marie. See GUYON.

De Lan·cey \də-'lan-sē\, James. 1703–1760. American colonial administrator, b. New York City. Judge, New York supreme court (1731–33); chief justice (1733–60). Opposed Governor Clinton's policies (1744–53). Served as lieutenant governor (1753–55, 1757–60). His brother ¶Oliver (1718–1785) was a Loyalist during the American Revolution, a brigadier general and highest ranking Loyalist in the British army in America. Their nephew ¶James (1746–1804) was a Loyalist during the Revolution, commanded De Lancey's Horse, a raiding cavalry troop operating outside New York City, and fled to Nova Scotia (1782).

De·land \də-'land\, Margaret, *in full* Margaretta Wade, *nee* Campbell. 1857–1945. American novelist, b. Allegheny, Pa. m. Lorin F. Deland (1880). Best known for tales of "Old Chester," grouped about the character "Dr. Lavendar," as in *Old Chester Tales* (1899), *Dr. Lavendar's People* (1903), *Around Old Chester* (1915), *Old Chester Days* (1935); other works included *The Old Garden* (verse, 1886), *John Ward, Preacher* (1888), *The Wisdom of Fools* (1897), *The Awakening of Helena Richie* (1906), *The Iron Woman* (1911), *The Rising Tide* (1916), *The Vehement Flame* (1922), *The Kays* (1926), *If This Be I* (autobiog., 1935).

De·lane \də-'lān\, John Thadeus. 1817–1879. English journalist. Editor of *The Times* (1841–77); attacked government's neglect of commissariat in Crimean War; influenced foreign policy.

Del·a·no \'del-ə-,nō\, Jane Arminda. 1862–1919. American nurse, b. Townsend, N.Y. Superintendent of Bellevue Hospital nursing schools, N.Y.C. (1902–06); chairman of National Committee on Red Cross Nursing Services (1909–19); superintendent, Army Nurse Corps (1909–12); director, Department of Nursing, American Red Cross (1918–19); directed mobilization of some 20,000 nurses for service overseas in World War I.

De·la·ny \də-'lā-nē\, Martin Robinson. 1812–1885. American physician, social reformer, and soldier, b. Charles Town, W. Va. Founded and edited (1847–49) the *North Star* with F. Douglass (*q.v.*). Proponent of colonization as solution to slavery; explored possible sites in South America, Africa; during Civil War helped recruit and served as surgeon to 54th Mass. Volunteers; first black to receive commission in U.S. army (as major, 1865).

Delany, Mary, *nee* Gran·ville \'gran-vil\. 1700–1788. English literary correspondent of Swift. m. (1743) friend of Dean Swift, Patrick Delany (1685?–1768), Irish preacher, dean of Down. She introduced Fanny Burney at court; author of six volumes of autobiography and correspondence.

Delany, Patrick Bernard. 1845–1924. American electrical engineer, b. Kings County, Ireland. Telegraph operator (1863–76). Invented a multiplex telegraph, by which six messages could be sent at the same time over one wire; a rapid machine telegraph system; a telegraph tape perforator; submarine detection devices, etc.

De·la·planche \də-lá-pläⁿsh\, Eugène. 1836–1891. French sculptor. Best known works included *Eve avant le péché, L'Aurore, La Vierge aux lis, Sainte Agnès.*

de la Pole. See POLE.

de la Ramée, Marie Louise. See RAMÉE.

De la Rey \də-lá-rī\, Jacobus Hercules. 1847–1914. Boer general. Distinguished himself at battle of Magersfontein (1899) and in conduct of retreat before Lord Roberts's superior army; made record as brilliant commander in subsequent guerilla warfare; aided in negotiating peace with Great Britain (1902). Member of Transvaal legislative assembly (1907–10); delegate to national convention (1908); in senate of Union of South Africa (1910–14); killed while attempting to foment rebellion in western Transvaal.

de la Rive. See LA RIVE.

de la Roche \də-lə-'rȯsh\, Mazo. 1885–1961. Canadian novelist, b. Newmarket, Ont. After *Explorers of the Dawn* (1922), *Possession* (1923), *Delight* (1926), published *Jalna* (1927), first of a series of 16 novels dealing with Whiteoak family, including *Whiteoaks of Jalna* (1929; dramatized 1936), *The Master of Jalna* (1933), *Young Renny* (1935), *Whiteoak Harvest* (1936), *Whiteoak Heritage* (1940), *Morning at Jalna* (1960); author also of *Portrait of a Dog* (1930), *Growth of a Man* (1938), *Ringing the Changes* (autobiog., 1956).

De·la·roche \də-lá-rósh\, Paul, *in full* Hippolyte-Paul. 1797–1856. French painter. Known esp. as a portrait, historical, and mural painter, combining in his work elements of both classical and romantic schools; best known works included *Les Enfants d'Edouard, L'Assassinat du duc de Guise,* and mural in the École National Supérieure des Beaux-Arts.

De la Rue \del-ə-,rü, ,del-ə-'rü\, Warren. 1815–1889. English astronomer and inventor. Invented envelope-making machine (1851); constructed 13-inch reflecting telescope; took lunar photographs; devised photoheliograph for photographing the sun daily (1858); by photographs of eclipse of the sun proved that the prominences observed during eclipses belong to the sun (1860); made chemical researches on glyceric acid and on electric discharges through gases; invented silver chloride electric cell.

de Launay, Vicomte Charles. See under Émile de GIRARDIN.

De·lau·nay \də-lō-nā\, Charles-Eugène. 1816–1872. French astronomer and mathematician. Taught at École Polytechnique (from 1850); director of Paris Observatory (1870–72). Known for work on lunar theory and on tides; author of *La Theorie de la lune* (1860–67), *Ralentissement de la rotation de la terre* (1866), *Rapport sur les progrès de l'astronomie* (1867).

Delaunay, Jules-Élie. 1828–1891. French painter. Known for historical scenes, as *La Peste à Rome, Le Serment de Brutus,* and murals; executed frescoes for the Paris Opéra, the Panthéon, Hôtel de Ville de Paris, and the Conseil d'État in the Palais Royal.

Delaunay, Robert. 1885–1941. French painter. Founded the "Orphic" movement (c.1910) with introduction of brilliant color into Cubist techniques, as in *La Tour rouge* (1911); painted notable series on *Formes circulaires* (1912) and *Une fenêtre* (1912); work inspired the Blaue Reiter painters in Germany, the Sychromists in America.

Delaunay, Sonia, *nee* Stern. 1885–1979. French artist, b. Russia. m. (1910) Robert Delaunay. Her "Orphic" paintings, developed in conjunction with her husband, strongly affected textile and theatrical design.

De·laune *or* **De·laulne** *or* **De l'Aune** \də-lōn\, Étienne. c.1519–1583. French goldsmith and engraver. Executed several gold portrait medallions for Henry II; engraved coins for La Monnaie (1552–53); engraved after works by Michelangelo and others.

de Laval. See LAVAL.

De·la·vigne \də-lá-vēnʸ\, Jean-François-Casimir. 1793–1843. French poet and playwright. Published three patriotic elegies, *Les Messéniennes* (1818), after Napoléon's fall; ranked with Béranger as a national poet. Among his plays were *Les Vêpres siciliennes* (1819), *Paria* (1821), *École des Vieillards* (1823), *La Princesse Aurélie* (1828), *Marino Faliero* (1829), *La Popularité* (1838), *La Fille du Cid* (1840). Composed song *La Parisienne* (1830). His brother ¶Germain (1790–1868) wrote opera librettos, comedies, and vaudeville sketches.

De La Warr, Baron. See Thomas WEST.

Del·bœuf \del-bœf\, Joseph-Rémy-Léopold. 1831–1896. Belgian philosopher and psychologist. Known for work in logic and on hypnotism; wrote *Essai de logique scientifique* (1865), *La Matière brute et la matière vivante* (1887), *De l'origine des effets curatifs de l'hypnotisme* (1887).

Del·bos \del-bōs\, Yvon. 1885–1956. French politician. In Chamber of Deputies (1924–43, 1945–56); minister of justice and of foreign affairs (1936–38), of education (1939–40); attempted to avert war, later opposed capitulation to Germany.

Del·brück \'del-,brœk\, Berthold. 1842–1922. German linguist. Professor at Jena (1870–1912); considered founder of study of comparative syntax of Indo-European languages; chief work *Grundriss der vergleichenden Grammatik der indogermanischen Sprachen* (1886–93).

Delbrück, Clemens von. 1856–1921. German government official. Prussian minister of commerce (1905); minister of interior (1909–16); directed economic mobilization (1912–16); last chief of William II's civil cabinet (1918).

Delbrück, Hans. 1848–1929. German historian. Professor at Berlin (1883–1919); member of Reichstag (1884–90); author of military histories, including *Geschichte der Kriegskunst im Rahmen der politischen Geschichte* (1900–27), *Krieg und Politik* (1919), *Weltgeschichte* (1923–26), *Vor und nach dem Weltkriege* (1926).

Delbrück, Max. 1906–1981. American biologist, b. Berlin. To U.S. (1937); naturalized (1945); taught at Vanderbilt U. (1940–47); professor, California Inst. of Technology (1947–77). With Salvador Luria and Alfred Hersey conducted genetic researches on bacteriophage viruses and bacteria; discovered (1946) recombination of viral DNA. With Luria and Hershey awarded 1969 Nobel prize for medicine or physiology.

Delbrück, Rudolph, *in full* Martin Friedrich Rudolph von. 1817–1903. Prussian politician. In ministry of commerce (1848); influential in expanding the Zollverein. First president of the chancery of North German Confederation (1867–70); Prussian minister without portfolio (1869–76); president of newly organized imperial chancellery (1871–76).

Del·cas·sé \del-ká-sā\, Théophile. 1852–1923. French politician. Elected to Chamber of Deputies (1885); minister of colonies (1893–95), minister of foreign affairs (1898–1905); negotiated settlement of Fashoda incident with Great Britain preparing ground for Anglo-French agreement (1904) leading to the Entente Cordiale; laid groundwork for Anglo-Russian agreement (1907); minister of marine (1911–13), arranged for Anglo-French naval cooperation in case of war; again minister of foreign affairs in the Ministry of National Defense (1914–15).

De·le·boe *or* **De le Boë** \ˌdā-lā-ˈbō-ā\, Franz. *Name also given as* François Du Bois \dǖ-ˈbō-ä\. *Lat. name* Franciscus Syl·vi·us \ˈsil-vē-əs\. 1614–1672. German physician, anatomist, and chemist. Professor at Leiden (1658–72); based his diagnostic and therapeutic system on analysis of blood acid, alkali, and salts; considered father of iatrochemical school of medicine; one of first to use ward instruction of students; first to conglomerate and conglobate glands; discovered (1641) Sylvian fissure in brain.

De·lé·cluze \də-lā-klǖz\, Étienne-Jean. 1781–1863. French painter and art critic. Wrote studies of Léopold Robert (1838) and Louis David (1855), *Souvenirs de soixante années* (1862).

De·led·da \dā-ˈled-dä\, Grazia. 1875–1936. Italian writer. Known esp. for her stories and novels on Sardinian peasantry; author of *Racconti Sardi* (1893), *Anime oneste* (1899), *Il vecchio della montagna* (1900), *Elias Portolu* (1903), *Cenere* (1904), *L'edera* (1906), *L'ombra del passato* (1908), *Il nonno* (1909), *Nel deserto* (1911), *Canne al vento* (1913), *Le colpe altrui* (1914), *La via del male* (1916), *La madre* (1920), *Il segreto dell'uomo solitario* (1921), *Il dio dei viventi* (1922), *La danza della collana* (1924), *La fuga in Egitto* (1925), *Annalena Bilsini* (1927), and *Cosima* (autobiog., 1937). Awarded Nobel prize for literature (1926).

De Lee \də-ˈlē\, Joseph Bolivar. 1869–1942. American obstetrician, b. Cold Spring, N.Y. Professor, Northwestern U. (1896–1929), U. of Chicago (1929–34); founder, Chicago Lying-in Hospital and Dispensary (1895; from 1932 the Chicago Maternity Center).

De·le·haye \də-lə-ey\, Hippolyte. 1859–1941. Belgian Jesuit scholar. Applied historical methods to study of lives of saints; author of *Les Légendes hagiographiques* (1905), *Les Origines du culte des martyrs* (1912), *Les Passions des martyrs et les genres littéraires* (1921), *Sanctus* (1927); edited *Bibliotheca Hagiographica Graeca* (1895), *Synaxarium* (1902); head of Bollandists (1912–41).

De Le·on \də-lā-ˈōn\, Daniel. 1852–1914. American political radical, b. Curaçao. Taught at Columbia U. (1883–86); national lecturer for Socialist Labor party (from 1890); editor of party journal *The People* (1892); founded Socialist Trade and Labor Alliance (1895); helped found Industrial Workers of the World (1905); expelled and then formed Workers' International Industrial Union (1908).

De·les·cluze \də-lā-klǖz\, Louis-Charles. 1809–1871. French politician. Active in revolutionary agitation (1830, 1848, 1870); member of secret society Amis du Peuple; implicated in plot to assassinate Louis-Philippe (1832); in exile (1832–41, 1849–53); leader of Paris Commune (1871); killed on barricades.

de Lesseps, Ferdinand-Marie. See LESSEPS.

De·les·sert \də-le-ser\, Étienne. 1735–1816. French banker. Founded (1782) first fire-insurance company in France. His son ¶Benjamin, *in full* Jules-Paul-Benjamin (1773–1847), industrialist, financier, and philanthropist, regent of Bank of France; founded first cotton factory (1801), first sugar factory (1802) in France, several learned and philanthropic societies; sat in Chamber of Deputies; created baron of the empire (1812); instrumental in introduction of savings banks into France.

Del·ga·do \del-ˈgä-t͟hō\, José Matías. 1768–1832. Salvadorean cleric and political leader. Headed short-lived revolt against Spanish authorities in San Salvador (1811); took part in Central American declaration of independence (1821); opposed Mexican annexation (1822); elected president of the national constitutional assembly of the United Provinces of Central America (1823); elected by assembly to fill newly created bishopric of San Salvador (1825), but bishopric declared null by Pope Leo XII (1826).

Delgado Chal·baud \-chäl-ˈbō(t͟h)\, Carlos. 1909–1950. Venezuelan soldier. Took part in coup under Gen. Rómulo Betancourt (1945); minister of defense (1945–48); led coup against Pres. Rómulo Gallegos (1948); president of military junta (1948–50); assassinated.

Delharpe. See LA HARPE.

De·libes \də-lēb\, Léo, *in full* Clément-Philibert-Léo. 1836–1891. French composer. Composed operas, including *Le Roi l'a dit* (1873), *Jean de Nivelle* (1880), *Lakmé* (1883); operettas, as *Deux sous de charbon* (1855), *Mon ami Pierrot* (1862), *Le Serpent à plumes* (1864); first to compose seriously for ballets, including *La Source* (with Ludwig Minkus, 1866), *Coppélia* (1870), *Sylvia* (1876).

Deligiánnis *or* **Delijiánnis.** See DHILIYIÁNNIS.

De·lille \də-lēl\, Jacques. 1738–1813. French abbé and poet. Author of a verse translation of Virgil's *Georgics* (1770), the *Aeneid* (1804), *Paradise Lost* (1805); published own verses in *Les Jardins* (1782), *Les trois règnes de la nature* (1809), highly praised in his day.

Delisle *or* **de Lisle** *or* **de l'Isle.** See (1) LECONTE DE LISLE; (2) ROUGET DE LISLE; (3) VILLIERS DE L'ISLE-ADAM.

De·lisle \də-lēl\, Guillaume. 1675–1726. French geographer. Chief geographer to the king (1718); through use of astronomical observations created world and continental maps of a new order of accuracy; published maps showing voyages of discovery and exploration; regarded as a founder of modern cartography.

Delisle, Joseph-Nicolas. 1688–1768. French astronomer. Brother of Guillaume Delisle. In St. Petersburg (1725–47), where he founded school of astronomy; geographical astronomer to French navy (1747). Proposed "diffraction theory" of the corona of the sun (1715); originated method for observing transits of Venus and Mercury, first proposed in letter to J. Cassini (1743); organized worldwide study of Venus transit (1761); proposed first method for determining the heliocentric coordinates of sunspots.

Delisle, Léopold-Victor. 1826–1910. French scholar. Curator (1871) and administrator (1874), Bibliothèque Nationale, Paris. Published papers on French medieval history, esp. on Normandy; responsible for printing of *Catalogue Générale* (begun in 1897) of the Bibliothèque Nationale.

De·li·us \ˈdē-lē-əs, ˈdēl-yəs\, Frederick Theodore Albert. 1862–1934. English composer of German descent. Works included orchestral pieces, including *Legend* (1893), *Over the Hills and Far Away* (1895), *Brigg Fair* (1907), *Dance Rhapsodies* (1908, 1916); choral works, *Paris* (1899), *Appalachia* (1902), *Sea Drift* (1903), *A Mass of Life* (1904–05), *Requiem* (1914–16); operas, *Koanga* (1895–97), *A Village Romeo and Juliet* (1900–01), *Fennimore and Gerda* (1908–10); concerti; sonatas; songs.

De·li·us \ˈdā-lē-ůs\, Nikolaus. 1813–1888. German Shakespearean scholar. Published first critical edition of Shakespeare's works in Germany (1854–61).

Dell \ˈdel\, Ethel Mary. 1881–1939. English writer. Among her many romantic novels were *The Way of an Eagle* (1912), *The Lamp in the Desert* (1919), *The Obstacle Race* (1921), *The Black Knight* (1926), *The Altar of Honour* (1929), *The Prison Wall* (1932), *Sown Among Thorns* (1939).

Dell, Floyd. 1887–1969. American editor and writer, b. Barry, Ill. Associate editor, *The Masses* (1914–17) and *The Liberator* (1918–24). Among his novels were *Moon-Calf* (1920), *The Briary-Bush* (1921), *Runaway* (1925), *Souvenir* (1929), *Diana Stair* (1932), *The Golden Spike* (1934); among his plays, *Little Accident* (with Thomas Mitchell, 1928), *Cloudy with Showers* (with Mitchell, 1931); nonfiction *Intellectual Vagabondage* (1926), *Love in the Machine Age* (1930); autobiog. *Homecoming* (1933).

della Casa, Giovanni. See CASA.

Del·la Rob·bia \ˌdāl-lä-ˈrōb-byä\, Luca, *in full* Luca di Simone di Marco. 1399/1400–1482. Italian sculptor. A pioneer of Florentine Renaissance style; major early work the cantoria for the Florence cathedral. Developed (c.1440) sculptural technique involving polychrome enameling of terra-cotta figures or reliefs; organized family workshop to produce decorative work for Pazzi Chapel, S. Miniato al Monte, S. Domenico at Urbino, Palazzo Vescovile, etc. Succeeded by nephew ¶Andrea Della Robbia, *full given name* Andrea di Marco di Simone (1435–1525); took over workshop (1482); noted esp. for large polychrome decorative reliefs in many churches and series of 10 roundels in form of foundlings for facade of Ospedale degli Innocenti, Florence (c.1463). Andrea's son ¶Giovanni (1469–1529) succeeded to control of family workshop (1525); chief work a frieze for Ospedale del Ceppo, Pistoia (1525–29). A second son ¶Girolamo (1488–1566) trained in workshop, was employed in terra-cotta work for Château de Madrid and at Fontainebleau in France.

della Scala. See SCALA.

Del·la Tor·re \ˌdāl-lä-ˈtōr-rā\, *orig.* Tor·ria·ni \tōr-rē-ˈän-ē\. Name of powerful family of Milan that contested control of the city with the rival Visconti family. Among its members were: Pagano (d. 1241), who rallied the Milanese after their defeat by Frederick II at Cortenuova; his nephew ¶Martino (d. 1263), took the title signore (1256); succeeded by his brother ¶Filippo (ruled 1263–65) and then by nephew ¶Napoleone (ruled 1265–77); Napoleone defeated by Visconti faction at Desio.

Del·len·baugh \ˈdel-ən-ˌbō\, Frederick Samuel. 1853–1935. American painter and writer, b. McConnelsville, Ohio. With Powell expedition down Colorado River (1871–73); with Harriman expedition to Alaska and Siberia (1899). Author of *The North Americans of Yesterday* (1900), *A Canyon Voyage* (1908), *Frémont and '49* (1913), etc.

Del·me·di·go \ˌdel-mā-ˈdē-gō\, Elijah. 1460?–?1497. Cretan philosopher. Known for his *Beḥinat ha-dat,* a criticism of the Kabbala; commentaries on Averroës and Aristotle. His great-grandson ¶Joseph Solomon Delmedigo (1591–1655), a pupil of Galileo, defended the Kabbala in his *Masref le-ḥokha.*

Del·mon·i·co \del-ˈmän-ə-ˌkō\, Loenzo[1]. 1813–1881. American restaurateur, b. Marengo, Switzerland. To U.S. (1832); with uncles John and Peter, established restaurant (Delmonico's) in New York City (about 1834); popularized vegetables, salads, European cuisine.

De·lolme \də-lolm\, Jean Louis. 1740–1806. Swiss jurist. Author of *Constitution de l'Angleterre* (1771), *History of the Flagellants* (1782), etc.

De·lo·ney \də-ˈlō-nē\, Thomas. 1563?–1600. English writer. Composed many ballads, stories, and pamphlets distributed in his travels as itinerant weaver; published *The Garland of Good Will* (1593), *Jack of Newberie* (1597), *The Gentle Craft* (1597–98), *Thomas of Reading* (1599?), *Strange Histories of Kings, Princes, Dukes, Earls, Lords, Ladies, Knights, and Gentlemen* (undated), *Canaan's Calamitie* (undated); many stories and sketches showed striking realism; inspired numerous dramatists, as Thomas Dekker.

De Long \də-ˈlȯŋ\, George Washington. 1844–1881. American naval officer and explorer, b. New York City. Financially aided by James Gordon Bennett, conducted Arctic expedition on ship *Jeannette* (1879–82); ship crushed in ice north of Siberia (June 12, 1881); party set out for Siberia, dividing into three groups. Of the group led by De Long, all died of starvation; bodies found by search party led by George W. Melville (*q.v.*).

De·lorme \də-lȯrm\, Marion. 1613–1650. French courtesan. Mistress of Marquis de Cinq-Mars (beheaded 1642); reputedly mistress thereafter of Saint-Évremond, Buckingham, Gramont, Condé, and others; her salon became a meeting place for rebels during the Fronde uprising (1648–53); found dead by officers sent to arrest her for complicity in the Fronde uprising. Subject of many legends, notably one that she escaped to London and lived to a great age.

Delorme *or* **de l'·Orme** \də-lȯrm\, Philibert. 1515?–1570. French architect. Royal architect to Henri II (1547), overseer of buildings (1548); directed work at Fontainebleau (1548–58) and built châteaux of Anet, Muette, Saint-Germain, Saint-Maur, Meudon, and gallery at the château of Chenonceaux; built Tuileries for Catherine de Médicis.

de Loutherbourg, Philip James. See LOUTHERBOURG.

Del·sarte \del-sȧrt\, François-Alexandre-Nicolas-Chéri. 1811–1871. French singing teacher. Invented system of bodily movements (Delsarte, or Delsarte system) designed to develop coordination, grace, and expressiveness.

De·luc \də-lu̅e̅k\, Jean André. 1727–1817. Swiss geologist and meteorologist. To England (1773). Attempted to reconcile science with the account of creation in *Genesis;* one of first to notice disappearance of heat when ice melts; proved that water is densest at about 39° F.; invented a hygrometer; published first correct rules for determining altitude by the barometer; credited with invention of the dry pile.

Del·vaux \del-vō\, Laurent. 1695–1778. Flemish sculptor. Lived in London (1717–26) where he executed works in bronze and marble for Westminster Abbey; court sculptor to Emperor Charles VI (1734–40), and to Charles, Duke of Lorraine (1750–78).

Del·vigne \del-vēnʸ\, Henri-Gustave. 1799–1876. French soldier and inventor. Devised the Delvigne rifle (1826), a cylindro-conical bullet anticipating the Minié ball, and a chambered-breech rifle (1842) adopted by French army.

De·ma·des \di-ˈmād-ˌēz\. c.380–319 B.C. Athenian orator and politician. Supported cause of Philip II of Macedon and thereby opposed Demosthenes; taken prisoner at battle of Chaeronea (338); on release helped negotiate peace between Athens and Macedonia; secured lenient treatment of Athens by Alexander the Great following revolt (335); deprived of citizenship for accepting bribes (323–322); negotiated with Antipater an end to Lamian War (322); persuaded Athens to pass death sentence on Demosthenes and his followers (322); executed by order of either Antipater or Cassander for having intrigued with regent Perdiccas.

De·man·geon \də-mäⁿ-zhōⁿ\, Albert. 1872–1940. French geographer. Specialist in study of regional and economic geography; author of *Le Déclin de l'Europe* (1920), *L'Empire britannique* (1923), *Les Îles britanniques* (1927), etc.

De·man·tius \dā-ˈmän-sh(ē-)u̇s\, Christoph, *in full* Johann Christoph. 1567–1643. German composer. Cantor at Zittau (1597–1604), Freiburg (1604–43); composed sacred and secular music; works included *Corona Harmonica* (1610), *Deutsche Passion nach Johannes* (1631), *Tympanum Militare;* author of *Isagoge Artis Musicae* (1605).

Dem·a·ra·tus \ˌdem-ə-ˈrā-təs\. 6th–5th century B.C. King of Sparta (c.510–491 B.C.). Colleague of Cleomenes I; quarreled with Cleomenes; deposed (491) by him in favor of Leotychides; fled to Persian court; given Pergamum and other cities to rule; accompanied Xerxes on his expedition to Greece (481–480).

De·mar·çay \də-mȧr-sā\, Eugène-Anatole. 1852–1903. French chemist. Discovered spectroscopically (1896) element europium.

Dem·biń·ski \dem-ˈbēnʸ-skē\, Henryk. 1791–1864. Polish soldier. In Polish Revolution (1830–31), governor of Warsaw (1830); conducted retreat of Polish army through Lithuania (1831). Reorganized army of Muḥammad ʿAlī Pasha of Egypt (1833). Commanded Hungarian army (1849) and was defeated at Temesvár (Timișoara); forced to take refuge in Turkey and, later, in France.

Demetrius. In Russian names see DMITRY.

De·me·tri·us \də-ˈmē-trē-əs\. 2d century B.C. King of Bactria (c.190–167 B.C.). Son and successor of Euthydemus. Invaded India and conquered the Punjab and valley of the Indus; first to strike coins with bilingual Greek and Prakrit inscriptions.

Demetrius. Name of two kings of Macedonia:

Demetrius I Pol·i·or·ce·tes \ˌpäl-ē-ȯr-ˈsēt-(ˌ)ēz\, *i.e.* Besieger. 336–283 B.C. King (c.294–c.288 B.C.). Son of Antigonus I Monophthalmus, whom he aided in wars with generals of Alexander; defeated (312) by Ptolemy (later Ptolemy I) at Gaza; freed Athens (307) from Cassander and Ptolemy; destroyed naval power of Egypt, under Menelaus, in battle at Cyprus (306), a victory commemorated by the statue of Nike of Samothrace; unsuccessfully besieged Rhodes (305); defeated with his father at Ipsus (301) by Seleucus and Lysimachus; lost power for a time, but recovered Athens (294), Aegina, and Salamis; seized throne of Macedonia (294); driven out by Lysimachus and Pyrrhus (288) and taken prisoner by Seleucus I (285). Succeeded by his son Antigonus Gonatas.

Demetrius II. c.276–229 B.C. Son of Antigonus Gonatas. King (239–229 B.C.). Engaged continuously in wars with coalition of Aetolian and Achaean leagues and with wild tribes on northern borders. Succeeded by his cousin Antigonus Doson.

Demetrius. Name of three Seleucid kings of Syria:

Demetrius I So·ter \ˈsōt-ər\, *i.e.* Preserver. c.187–150 B.C. King (162–150 B.C.). Son of Seleucus IV Philopator and father of Demetrius II and Antiochus VII. Lived as hostage at Rome (c.187–162); escaped with aid of Polybius; overthrew his cousin Antiochus V Eupator (162); delivered Babylonians from tyranny of satrap Timarchus (160); fell in battle against usurper Alexander Balas.

Demetrius II Ni·ca·tor \nī-ˈkāt-ȯr, -ər\. 161–125 B.C. King (145–139 and 129–125 B.C.). Son of Demetrius I and brother of Antiochus VII. Aided by Ptolemy VI Philometor, secured throne, defeating and killing Alexander Balas (145); m. (150?) Alexander Balas's widow, Cleopatra Thea (*q.v.*), by whom he was father of Seleucus V and Antiochus VIII; opposed (145–142) by boy king, Antiochus VI, at Antioch; defeated (139) and held prisoner by Parthians; m. Rodogune (*q.v.*), daughter of Mithridates I; regained throne (129); killed in civil war and succeeded by his sons Seleucus V (killed after a very short reign) and Antiochus VIII Grypus.

Demetrius III. *Surnamed* **Eu·kai·ros** \yu̇-ˈkī-rəs\ *and* **Phil·o·me·tor** \ˌfil-ə-ˈmēt-ȯr, -ər\. d. 88? B.C. King (95–88 B.C.). Son of Antiochus VIII Grypus. Seized Damascus (96), ruling in opposition (95–92) to his cousin Antiochus X; ruled jointly (93–88) with his brother Philip, but during part of time engaged in civil war with him; defeated by Arabs and Parthians; died prisoner among Parthians.

Demetrius. 4th century B.C. Greek sculptor. Reputed by ancient commentators to have executed works of great realism, as in portrait of Pellichus.

Demetrius. 1st century A.D. Greek Cynic philosopher. Taught in Rome during reigns of Caligula, Nero, and Vespasian; antimonarchical views caused his exile to Greece (66 A.D.).

Demetrius of **Phar·os** \ˈfar-ˌäs, ˈfer-\. d. 214 B.C. Ruler of Pharos. Defeated by Rome in Second Illyrian War (220–219); fled to Macedonia and incited Philip V to anti-Roman policies.

Demetrius Chal·con·dy·les \-ˌkal-kən-ˈdī-ˌlēz, -ˌchal-\. 1424–1511. Greek teacher. To Italy (1447), taught at Padua, Florence, Milan; renowned as teacher of Greek and Platonic philosophy; published first printed edition of Homer (1488) and Isocrates (1493); wrote *Erotemata,* a Greek grammar.

Demetrius Cy·do·nes \-sī-ˈdō-(ˌ)nēz\ *or* **Demetrios Ky·do·nes** \-kī-\. c.1324–c.1398. Byzantine scholar and statesman. Studied under Latin Scholastic scholars while in Italy, converted to Latin church (c.1365). Conducted Greek academy in Venice (1390–91), helping to spark Italian Renaissance. Prime minister under John V Palaeologus (1369–c.1383) and Manuel II Palaeologus (1391–96). Advocated unity of Latin and Greek churches and of Latin and Byzantine people in face of growing Turkish power. Author of *De contemnenda morte, Symbouleutikoi,* many letters. His brother ¶**Pro·cho·rus Cydones** \prō-ˈkōr-əs, -ˈkȯ-\ *or* **Pro·cho·ros Kydones** (c.1330–c.1369) was an Eastern Orthodox monk; introduced to Latin Scholastic thought by brother; made translations of Aquinas, Boethius, Augustine of Hippo. Wrote *De essentia et operatione Dei* in opposition to Gregory Palamas and the Hesychasts; expelled from priesthood by Synod of Constantinople (1368).

Demetrius Pha·le·reus \-fə-ˈlē-rüs, -ˈlir-ē-əs\. 350?–283 B.C. Athenian orator and statesman. Appointed by Cassander to govern Athens (317–307 B.C.); when democratic government was restored, fled to Alexandria to escape execution and lived at court of Ptolemy I Soter.

Demetrius Triclinius. See TRICLINIUS.

De·metz \də-mets\, Frédéric-Auguste. 1796–1873. French jurist. Interested in prison reform; established farm colony of Mettray (1840) for training juvenile offenders in useful occupations.

De·mi·dov \dyim-ˈyē-dəf\. Distinguished Russian family, descended from Nikita Demidovich Antufyev (1656–1725), who took surname Demidov (1702); ironworker and armorer, built iron foundry at Tula, laying foundation of family fortune; favorite of Peter the Great, by whom he was ennobled. Nikita's son ¶Akinify (1678–1745) discovered and operated gold, silver, and copper mines. Akinify's nephew ¶Pavel Grigoryevich (1738–1821), traveler, patron of scientists, founder of Demidov Yaroslavl Law Lyceum (1805) and botanical garden in Moscow. Pavel's nephew ¶Count Nikolay Nikitich (1773–1828) raised and commanded regiment to fight Napoléon (1812); patron of scientific education in Moscow. Nikolay's son ¶Pavel Nikolayevich (1798–1840), patron of Petersburg Acad. of Science, founded an annual literary award. Nikolay's son ¶Prince Anatoly Nikolayevich (1812–1870), traveler, philanthropist, and art patron; m. (1840) Princess Mathilde Bonaparte, daughter of Jérôme Bonaparte.

De·Mille \də-ˈmil\, Cecil Blount. 1881–1959. American film producer, b. Ashfield, Mass. Son of Henry C. DeMille. An actor, wrote plays in collaboration with brother William (*q.v.*); with Jesse L. Lasky and Samuel Goldwyn formed Lasky Feature Play Co. (1913) to produce motion pictures; produced *The Squaw Man* (1914), *Carmen* (1915), etc.; president (1922–51) Cecil B. DeMille Productions; produced *Ten Commandments* (1923), *King of Kings* (1927), *Cleopatra* (1934), *The Plainsman* (1937), *Union Pacific* (1939), *Samson and Delilah* (1949), *Greatest Show on Earth* (1952, Academy Award), *Ten Commandments* (1956). Noted for spectacular productions.

DeMille, Henry Churchill. 1853–1893. American playwright, b. Washington, N.C. Collaborated with David Belasco in producing *The Wife* (1887), *Lord Chumley* (1888), *The Charity Ball* (1889), *Men and Women* (1890).

De Mille \də-ˈmil\, James. 1836–1880. Canadian writer, b. Saint John, N.B. Taught at Acadia College (1860–64), Dalhousie U. (1864–80). Author of adventure, mystery, historical novels, including *The Dodge Club* (1860), *Martyrs of the Catacombs* (1865), *Cord and Crease* (1869), *The Cryptogram* (1871), *Comedy of Terrors* (1872), *Babes in the Wood* (1875).

de·Mille \də-ˈmil\, William Churchill. 1878–1955. American playwright, b. Washington, N.C. Son of Henry C. DeMille. Wrote *The Genius* (with brother C. B. DeMille, 1904), *Strongheart* (1905), *The Warrens of Virginia* (1907), *Classmates* (1907), *The Royal Mounted* (with brother, 1908), *The Woman* (1911).

Dem·o·ce·des \ˌdem-ə-ˈsēd-(ˌ)ēz\. 6th century B.C. Greek physician. Practiced successively in Aegina, Athens, Samos; captured by Persians and practiced in court of Darius I.

De·moch·a·res \di-ˈmäk-ə-ˌrēz\. c.355–275 B.C. Athenian orator and politician. Nephew of Demosthenes. Orator of anti-Macedonian party (after 322 B.C.) and leader of the popular party after restoration of democratic government by Demetrius Poliorcetes (307).

De·moc·ri·tus \di-ˈmäk-rət-əs\. c.460–c.370 B.C. Greek philosopher. Known as "the Abderite" (because a native of Abdera, in Thrace) and as "the Laughing Philosopher" (because of his amusement at the foibles of man). Regarded as one of most important among Greek physical philosophers, although only fragments of works survive. Extended atomistic theory of Leucippus.

Democritus Junior. See Robert BURTON.

De Moi·vre \dəm-wávrᵊ, *Angl* də-ˈmói-vər\, Abraham. 1667–1754. French mathematician in England (from 1688). Friend of Isaac Newton, Edmund Halley. Author of *The Doctrine of Chances* (1718), which advanced knowledge of probability; *Miscellanea Analytica* (1730), also on probability; works on calculus, annuities, etc. Discovered Stirling's formula, introduced complex numbers in trigonometry. Member of Royal Society (1697).

De·mol·der \də-mòl-der\, Eugène. 1862–1919. Belgian writer. A member of the Jeune Belgique literary renaissance; author of *La Légende d'Yperdamme* (1891), *La Route d'emeraude* (1899), *Les Patins de la reine de Hollande* (1901), *L'Arche de monsieur Cheunus* (1904), *Le Jardinier de la Pompadour* (1904), *L'Espagne en auto* (1906), early narrative of automobile travel.

De·mo·nax \di-ˈmō-naks\. d. c.176 B.C. Greek Cynic philosopher. Taught in Athens.

De Mor·gan \də-ˈmór-gən\, Augustus. 1806–1871. English mathematician and logician. Professor, University Coll., London (1828–31, 1836–66); author of *Essay on Probabilities* (1838), *Formal Logic* (1847), *Trigonometry and Double Algebra* (1849), and treatises on calculus; with George Boole, laid foundation for modern symbolic logic; developed new terminology for logical expression; formulated De Morgan's laws; introduced and rigorously defined term "mathematical induction".

De Morgan, William Frend. 1839–1917. English artist and novelist. Son of Augustus De Morgan. In association with Pre-Raphaelite circle, experimented with stained glass and other decorative arts; devoted himself to ceramics (1871–1905); rediscovered process of making brilliant blue and green glazes; manufactured decorative tiles and other pottery commercially. Wrote novels *Joseph Vance* (1906), *Alice-for-Short* (1907), *Somehow Good* (1908), *It Never Can Happen Again* (1909), *When Ghost Meets Ghost* (1914).

De·mos·the·nes \di-ˈmäs-thə-ˌnēz\. d. 413 B.C. Athenian general. Commander of expedition (426 B.C.) which, after initial setbacks, destroyed power of Corinth over northwestern Greece; defended Pylos (425) against attacks from Sparta and Corcyra (Corfu); unsuccessfully attacked Megara and Boeotia (424); captured in attack on Syracuse (413) and executed.

Demosthenes. 384–322 B.C. Athenian orator and statesman. Regarded as greatest of Greek orators. Leading speaker in Athenian assembly, leader of popular party, and chief spokesman for military preparedness (from 354); attacked Philip of Macedon in a series of orations, the "Philippics" (from 351); denounced Peace of Philocrates and its chief Athenian architect, Aeschines (346–343); caused Athenian fleet to be sent to relief of Byzantium (340), besieged by Philip; advocated Athenian alliance with Thebes against Philip, the allied army being defeated by Philip at Chaeronea (338). Delivered greatest oration, "On the Crown," in own defense against accusations of Aeschines (330). Exiled by pro-Macedonian party (324) but recalled after Alexander's death (323). Fled from Athens when city was threatened by Antipater and Craterus (322); condemned to death; took poison to avoid capture.

Demp·sey \ˈdem(p)-sē\, Jack, *orig.* William Harrison. *Nicknamed* the Manassa Mauler. 1895–1983. American boxer, b. Manassa, Colo. Regarded as one of the greatest boxers of all time; captured world heavyweight championship in 1919; defended title twice in 1920; fought first prizefight to gross over $1 million (1921); knocked out Argentina's Luis Angel Firpo (1923); lost heavyweight crown to Gene Tunney (1926); their rematch (1927) known as the controversial "long count" fight. Folk hero in retirement and renowned proprietor of restaurant in New York City.

Demp·ster \ˈdem(p)-stər\, Arthur Jeffrey. 1886–1950. American physicist, b. Toronto. Taught at U. of Chicago (1919–50); built first mass spectrometer (1918); discovered isotope uranium-235.

De·muth \də-ˈmüth\, Charles. 1883–1935. American painter, b. Lancaster, Pa. A water colorist, noted for literary illustrations and series on flowers, circuses, etc.; later works more abstract and architectural; a leader of the Precisionists.

Denbigh, Earls of. See William FEILDING.

Den·by \ˈden-bē\, Edwin. 1870–1929. American politician, b. Evansville, Ind. Member of U.S. House of Representatives (1905–11); U.S. secretary of the navy (1921–24); criticized for allowing transfer of administration of naval oil reserves from navy department to department of interior (1921); his signature on leases of Teapot Dome oil lands involved him in the scandal, but he was not accused of corruption; resigned from office.

Denck *or* **Denk** \ˈdeŋk\, Hans. c.1495–1527. German theologian. Rector of St. Sebaldus' School, Nürnberg (1523–25); expelled by Lutheran authorities for Anabaptist leanings; formally joined Anabaptists, becoming a leader in Augsburg; wrote *Von der wahren Liebe* (1527), translated Old Testament prophets into German.

Den·fert-Ro·che·reau \däⁿ-fer-ròsh-rō\, Pierre-Marie-Philippe-Aristide. 1823–1878. French soldier. As governor of Belfort in Franco–Prussian War (1870–71), resisted German siege for 104 days; city was retained by France when rest of Alsace-Lorraine ceded.

Dengyō Daishi. See SAICHŌ.

Den·ham \ˈden-əm\, Dixon. 1786–1828. English explorer in Africa. Explored central Sudan with Dr. Walter Oudney and Hugh Clapperton; explored west and south shore of Lake Chad and Waubé, Chari, and Logone rivers (1821–25); governor of Sierra Leone (1827–28).

Denham, Sir John. 1615–1669. English poet, b. Ireland. Made reputation with *The Sophy* (historical tragedy, 1641); published best known poem, *Cooper's Hill* (1642), poetical description of scenery; contributed to popularity of heroic couplets; verses highly regarded by Augustans. Royalist, performed secret service for Charles I in Holland; surveyor general of works (1660).

Den·hardt \ˈden-ˌhärt\, Clemens, *in full* Gustav Clemens Andreas (1852–1928) and his brother Gustav (1856–1917). German explorers. Explored Tana River region in East Africa (1876–77, 1878–79); later acquired possession of Witu, a coastal territory north of mouth of Tana River. Part of the territory was transferred to German colonial society, Deutsche Witu-Gesellschaft, and later (1890) traded to England for Helgoland.

Den·i·fle \ˈden-i-ˌfle\, Heinrich Seuse. 1844–1905. Austrian theologian and historian. Entered Dominican order (1861). Assistant archivist at Vatican (1883); cofounder of *Archiv für Literatur und Kirchengeschichte des Mittelalters* (1885); author of studies of Middle Ages, esp. *Luther und Luthertum* (1904–09).

De·ni·ker \dā-nē-ker\, Joseph. 1852–1918. French anthropologist. Set forth an ethnologic classification of Europeans according to stature, cranial index, and color of hair in *Les races de l'Europe* (1908).

De·ni·kin \dyin-ˈyēk-yin\, Anton Ivanovich. 1872–1947. Russian soldier. Lieutenant general during World War I; after February Revolution (1917), became chief of staff to Mikhail Alekseyev of provisional government; later commander on western front; after October Revolution fled to Caucasus and joined Lavr Kornilov in raising White Russian force to fight the Bolsheviks; succeeded to command after death of Kornilov (1918); set up a South Russian government (1919); defeated by Bolshevik troops under Budenny at Orel (1919). Fled to Constantinople; lived in France (1926–45), U.S. (1945–47).

Den·is *or* **Den·ys** \'den-əs, *Fr* də-nē\ *or* **Di·o·ny·sius** \ˌdī-ə-'nis(h)-ē-əs, -'nish-, -'nī-sē-əs\. Saint. d. 258? The apostle to the Gauls, first bishop of Paris, and patron saint of France. Martyred by decapitation at Paris in the persecutions of Emperor Valerian. He is represented in art as raising himself to carry his severed head. In popular medieval belief identified with Dionysius the Areopagite.

Denis. King of Portugal. See DINIS.

De·nis \də-nē\, Jean-Baptiste. 1643–1704. French physician. Consultant to Louis XIV; one of first to experiment with blood transfusions.

Denis, Maurice. 1870–1943. French painter. Influenced by Gauguin, became a leader of the Symbolists and then of the Nabis group; later returned to representational art and helped revitalize religious art in Europe; best known for his murals, as in the Théâtre des Champs Élysées at Paris, church of Le Vésinet at Geneva.

Denis le Flamand. See Denis CALVAERT.

Den·i·son \'den-ə-sən\, George Taylor. 1839–1925. Canadian soldier and historical writer, b. Toronto. Served in militia, repelling Fenian raids (1866) and suppressing 2d Riel Rebellion (1885); a founder of "Canada First" movement (1868); author of *History of Cavalry* (1877), *The Struggle for Imperial Unity* (1909), etc.

Denk. See DENCK.

Den·man \'den-mən\, Thomas. 1st Baron Denman. 1779–1854. English judge. Solicitor general to Queen Caroline (1820), whose innocence he maintained before bar of House of Lords (1820); attorney general (1830); prosecuted reform rioters (1832); M.P. (1818–26, 1830–32); lord chief justice (1832–50); speaker of House of Lords (1835); condemned Moxon, publisher of Shelley's complete works, for blasphemy (1841). His great-grandson ¶Thomas (1874–1954), 3d baron, served in Boer and World Wars; was governor general of Australia (1911–14); deputy speaker of House of Lords.

Den·ner \'den-ər\, Johann Christoph. 1655–1707. German manufacturer of wood-wind instruments. Highly regarded for his recorders, flutes, oboes, etc.; invented the clarinet (c.1700).

Den·ne·ry \den-rē\, Adolphe-Philippe. *Name legally changed (1858) to* d'En·ne·ry. 1811–1899. French playwright. Author or coauthor of *Gaspard Hauser* (1838), *Don César de Bazan* (1844), *Les deux orphelines* (1874), *Michel Strogoff* (1880), and librettos of *Si j'étais roi* (1852), *Le Tribut de Zamora* (music by Gounod, 1881), *Le Cid* (music by Massenet, 1885).

Den·nett \'den-ət\, Richard Edward. 1857–1921. English writer. Employed by British firm for service in African trade (1875–79). Called attention to atrocities in Congo Free State (1886); his agitation largely responsible for formation of Congo Reform Assoc.

Dennett, Tyler Wilbur. 1883–1949. American historian, b. Spencer, Wis. Author of *The Democratic Movement in Asia* (1918), *Americans in Eastern Asia* (1922), *Biography of John Hay* (1933, Pulitzer prize), etc. State Department official (1924–31); president, Williams Coll. (1934–37).

Den·nie \'den-ē\, Joseph. 1768–1812. American essayist and editor, b. Boston. Contributed series of essays to various periodicals, esp. "Lay Preacher" series to *Farmer's Weekly Museum,* which he edited (1796–99); founded (1801) and edited, as "Oliver Oldschool, Esq.," *The Port Folio,* Philadelphia (1801–12).

Den·nis \'den-əs\, Geoffrey Pomeroy. 1892–1964. English writer. Member of League of Nations staff (1920–37); on UNESCO staff (1949–57). Among his books were *Mary Lee* (1922), *The End of the World* (1930, Hawthornden prize), *Sale by Auction* (1932), *Bloody Mary's* (1934), *Till Seven* (1957).

Dennis, John. 1657–1734. English critic and dramatist. Gained scant success with plays, including *A Plot and No Plot* (1697; a satire on Jacobites), *Rinaldo and Armida* (1699), *Liberty Asserted* (1704), *Appius and Virginia* (1709). Satirized by Pope for bombast, replied in *Reflections, Critical and Satirical* (1711); critical writings, in which he insisted on importance of passion in poetry, included *The Usefulness of the Stage* (1698), *The Advancement and Reformation of Modern Poetry* (1701), *Grounds of Criticism in Poetry* (1704), *Essay on the Genius and Writings of Shakespeare* (1712).

Den·ni·son \'den-ə-sən\, Aaron Lufkin. 1812–1895. American watch manufacturer, b. Freeport, Me. Devised machine-made interchangeable parts in manufacturing watches; established factory (1850), forerunner of American Waltham Watch Co.; known as "the Father of American Watchmaking."

De·non \də-nōⁿ\, Dominique-Vivant. Baron. 1747–1825. French illustrator and government official. Conducted various diplomatic missions to Russia, Italy, Switzerland; accompanied Napoléon on Egyptian campaign (1798); director-general of French museums (from 1804); advised Napoléon on art acquisitions; first administrator to organize the collections in the Louvre.

Dens·more \'denz-ˌmō(ə)r, -ˌmȯ(ə)r\, Frances. 1867–1957. American ethnologist, b. Red Wing, Minn. Specialized in study and recording of American Indian music; published *Teton Sioux Music* (1918), *American Indians and Their Music* (1926), *Seminole Music* (1956), etc., and many monographs; established Smithsonian-Densmore Collection (1943).

Den·su·şia·nu \ˌden-sü-shē-'än-ü\, Ovidiu. 1873–1938. Romanian folklorist and philologist. Professor at Bucharest (from 1901); influential in introducing modernist methods into Romanian literature, esp. through his review *Viața Nouă* (1905–25); published *Histoire de la langue roumaine* (1901–14), *Dicționar general al limbii Române* (1909), *Flori alese din cântecele poporului* (1920), *Literatura română modernă* (1920–33); under pseudonym "Ervin" published *Raze pe lespezi* (poems, 1920).

Dent \'dent\, Joseph Malaby. 1849–1926. English publisher. Opened London bookbinding shop (1872); started publishing business (1888) with issuance of Lamb's *Essays of Elia* and *The Last Essays of Elia,* edited by Augustine Birrell; published pocket-size "Temple" edition of Shakespeare (1893) and "Temple Classics" series (1896 ff.); made great success with "Everyman's Library" series (1904 ff.).

Den·ta·tus \den-'tāt-əs\, Manius Curius. d. 270 B.C. Roman general. Consul (290, 275, 274 B.C.); vanquished Samnites (290, ending a 50-year war), Sabines, Senones (284), Pyrrhus (at battle of Beneventum, 275), Lucanians (274). Served as censor (272); later idealized for simplicity, frugality, and incorruptible patriotism.

Den·ver \'den-vər\, James William. 1817–1892. American politician, b. Winchester, Va. Secretary of state, California (1853); member, U.S. House of Representatives (1855–57); commissioner of Indian affairs (1857–59); governor of Territory of Kansas (1858); restored law and order in the territory. In Civil War, Union brigadier general of volunteers (1861–63). The city of Denver, Colo., is named in his honor.

Denys. See DENIS.

Den·za \'dent-sä\, Luigi. 1846–1922. Italian musician. Settled in London (1887); professor of singing, Royal Acad. of Music, London (1898 ff.); composer of some 600 songs and an opera, *Wallenstein* (1876); known particularly for his Neapolitan song "Funiculì Funiculà" (1880).

Deo van Tri \'dā-ō-'vän-'trē\. *Laotian* Cam Oum \'käm-'ōm\ *or* Kan Oum \'kän-\. c.1849–1908. Tai tribal chief. Named chief of Tai peoples (c.1865) for bravery in repelling Burmese invasion; aided Vietnamese in war with France (1885), but later made separate peace (1888); created semi-autonomous feudal kingdom.

De Pal·ma \də-'päl-mə, -'pal-\, Ralph. 1884–1956. American race driver, b. Troia, Italy. To U.S. (1892); in racing career (1907–34) won 2557 of 2889 races; national champion driver (1912, 1914); won Indianapolis 500 (1915); broke 1-minute mile (1908); world mile speed record (149.8 mph, 1919).

De·par·cieux \də-pȧrs-yœ̄\, Antoine. 1703–1768. French mathematician and statistician. Known esp. for compilation of mortality tables published in *Essai sur les probabilités de la durée de la vie humaine* (1746).

De Pauw \də-'pȯ\, Washington Charles. 1822–1887. American banker and industrialist, b. Salem, Ind. Benefactor of Indiana Asbury U. (est. 1839), which changed its name (1884) to DePauw University.

De·pew \də-'pyü\, Chauncey Mitchell. 1834–1928. American lawyer, b. Peekskill, N.Y. Attorney for Vanderbilt railroad interests (from 1866); president, New York Central Railroad (1885–99); chairman of board (1899–1928). U.S. senator (1899–1911). Renowned after-dinner speaker and wit.

De Peys·ter \də-'pī-ster\, Abraham. 1657–1728. American merchant and shipowner, b. New Amsterdam (New York). Mayor of New Amsterdam (1691–94); member, governor's council (1698–1702, 1709, 1710–22); justice, supreme court (1698–1702); treasurer of the province (1706–21).

Deprés, Josquin. See JOSQUIN DES PREZ.

De·pre·tis \dā-'pre-tēs\, Agostino. 1813–1887. Italian politician. Supporter of Mazzini; founded journal *Il Progresso* (Turin, 1850). Member of Piedmontese parliament (from 1848); premier (1876–78, 1878–79, 1881–87); minister of interior (1879–81); known for political policy of *trasformismo,* i.e., including all parties in his cabinet; his premiership marked by reforms and ameliorations; active in organizing Triple Alliance (1882).

De·prez \də-prā\, Marcel. 1843–1918. French engineer and pioneer electrician. Said to have effected first long-distance transmission of electric power, through a distance of about 35 miles over telegraph wires between Munich and Miesbach (1882); also worked on friction, regulation of speed of electric motors, etc.

De Quin·cey \di-'kwin(t)-sē, -'kwin-zē\, Thomas. 1785–1859. English author. Ran away from school to Wales, then to Bohemian life in London; at Oxford began use of opium, a lifelong addiction; left Oxford (1808); through Coleridge made acquaintance of Wordsworth and Southey at the Lake District and settled (1809) at Grasmere. Wrote voluminously, published little; published

(1821), in *London Magazine,* the *Confessions of an English Opium Eater,* which made him famous. On wife's death (1837), placed children at Lasswade and wandered from lodging to lodging; in magazines issued *Murder considered as one of the Fine Arts* (1827), *Lake Reminiscences* (1834–40), *Suspiria De Profundis* (1845), *The Spanish Military Nun* (1847), *The English Mailcoach, and Vision of Sudden Death* (1849); published two books, *Klosterheim* (1832) and *The Logic of Political Economy* (1844).

De·rain \də-ra^n\, André. 1880–1954. French painter. A leader in the Postimpressionist school, and one of the Fauvists (1905); later work representational and realistic; known also for illustrations and theatrical designs, esp. for Ballets Russes.

Derby, Countess of. See Elizabeth FARREN.

Derby, Earls of. See STANLEY family. The earldom of Derby is one of three existent English earldoms, with Shrewsbury and Huntingdon, created prior to 17th century.

Der·by \'dər-bē\, George Horatio. *Pseudonym* John Phoe·nix \'fē-niks\. *Nickname* Squi·bob \'skwī-ˌbäb\. 1823–1861. American humorist, b. Dedham, Mass. Author of *Phoenixiana* (1856), *The Squibob Papers* (1859), humorous sketches originally published in newspapers, esp. the *San Diego Herald.*

Der·cyl·li·das \dər-'sil-ə-dəs\. 5th–4th century B.C. Spartan general and diplomat. Commander of troops in Asia Minor defending against Persians (399–389?).

De·rennes \də-ren\, Charles. 1882–1930. French novelist and poet. Wrote in French and Provençal; novels included *Le Peuple du pôle* (1907), *La Guenille* (1908), *Les Enfants sages* (1913), *Le Renard bleu* (1921), *Mon gosse* (1923), *Le Pauvre et son chien* (1930).

Derf·fling·er \'der-fliŋ-ər\, Georg von. Baron. 1606–1695. Brandenburg soldier. In Swedish service (1632–48); in Brandenburg service in Thirty Years' War, becoming field marshal (1670); distinguished himself at battles of Warsaw (1656), Fehrbellin (1675); in campaign against Sweden (1678–79).

Der·ing *or* **Deer·ing** \'di(ə)r-iŋ\, Richard. c.1580–1630. English organist and composer. Organist to Henrietta Maria and lutenist and singer to Charles I (1625); known esp. for vocal compositions, motets, madrigals, etc., published in several collections (1617–20).

Der·in·ger \'der-ən-jər\, Henry. 1786–1869. American gun maker, b. Easton, Pa. Supplied military rifles and pistols to U.S. government; invented (c.1852) short-barrelled, large-bore percussion pocket pistol that was widely copied and became known as derringer.

Der Kürenberger. See KÜRENBERGER.

Der·mot Mac·Mur·rough \'dər-mət-mək-'mər-(ˌ)ō\. *Ir. Gael.* Diar·maid Mac·mur·cha·da \'dir-mid-mək-'mu̇r-kə-gə\. d. 1171. Irish ruler. King of Leinster (from 1126); began feud by abducting wife of Tiernan O'Ruark, king of Breifne (1153); driven from Ireland by Tiernan with aid of Leinster rebels (1166); secured permission of Henry II of England to enlist aid of Anglo-Norman nobles; returned to Ireland (1167); joined by Richard de Clare (*q.v.*), 2d Earl of Pembroke (1170), to whom he married his daughter. Anglo-Norman involvement thus begun led to conquest of Ireland.

Dern \'dərn\, George Henry. 1872–1936. American mining executive and politician, b. Dodge County, Neb. Invented, with Theodore P. Holt, Holt-Dern ore roaster. Governor of Utah (1925–32); author of workmen's compensation law, corrupt practices act, and state mineral land leasing law. U.S. secretary of war (1933–36).

De·rosne \də-rōn\, Charles, *in full* Louis-Charles. 1780–1846. French chemist. First to isolate an alkaloid (1803).

Dé·rou·lède \dā-rü-led\, Paul. 1846–1914. French writer and politician. Author of patriotic verse *Chants du soldat* (1872) and *Nouveaux chants du soldat* (1875). One of organizers (1882) of Ligue des Patriotes; supported General Boulanger (1887); involved in intrigues to overturn the government (1899 and 1900), and banished for 10 years; returned to France after amnesty (1905). Other works were *Avant la bataille* (1886), *Chants du paysan* (1894), and the plays *Messire Du Guesclin* (1895), *La Mort de hoche* (1897).

de Ruyter. See RUYTER.

Derwentwater, Earl of. See Sir James RADCLIFFE.

Der·zha·vin \dyir-'zhäv-yin\, Gavrila Romanovich. 1743–1816. Russian lyric poet. Career in army and civil service, including term as minister of justice (1802). Notable poems included *Felitsa,* addressed to Catherine the Great (1783), *Na smert knyazya Meshcherskogo* (1783), *Bog* (1784), *Vodopod* (1791–94); memoirs *Zapiski* (1812). Regarded as greatest Russian poet before Pushkin.

De·sag·u·liers \də-ˌsag-yə-'liərz\, John Theophilus. 1683–1744. English inventor. Popular lecturer and demonstrator in mechanics and optics; devised improvements to Thomas Savery's steam engine; grandmaster of British Freemasons (1719–22).

De·saix de Vey·goux \də-ze-də-vā-gü\, Louis-Charles-Antoine. 1768–1800. French general. Distinguished himself in army of the Rhine (1793–97); commanded advance guard of army in Egypt (1798); took part in battle of the Pyramids (1798) and conquered Upper Egypt (1798–99); commanded reserves and with them decided the issue in the battle of Marengo (June 14, 1800), but was killed in the battle.

De Sanc·tis \dā-'säŋ-tēs\, Francesco. 1817–1883. Italian critic. Minister of education (1861–62); professor, U. of Naples (1871 ff.); known particularly as founder of modern literary criticism in Italy. Author of *Saggi critici* (1866), *Storia della letteratura italiana* (1870), etc.

De·sargues \dā-zärg\, Gérard *or* Girard. 1591–1661. French mathematician. In *Traité de la section perspective* (1636) published Desargues's theorem on the perspective of two triangles, a key step in development of projective geometry; *Brouillon project d'une alleinte aux événemens des rencontres d'une cône avec un plan* (1639) presented further innovations in projective geometry and strongly influenced Pascal.

Dé·sau·giers \dā-zōzh-yā\, Marc-Antoine. 1742–1793. French composer. Wrote light operas, including *Florine* (1780), *La jeune veuve curieuse* (1788), *La Prise de la Bastille* (1790), and a *Requiem* (1786). His son ¶Marc-Antoine-Madeleine (1772–1827), singer and vaudeville actor, émigré (1789–97), director of the Théâtre du Vaudeville, Paris (1815), wrote popular songs and vaudeville sketches.

De·sault \də-sō\, Pierre-Joseph. 1738–1795. French surgeon. Instituted the first clinical school of surgery in France; made improvements in surgical technique and instruments.

Des·barres \dā-'bär\, Joseph Frederick Walsh *or* Wallet. 1722–1824. English military engineer, of Huguenot parentage. Aide to Wolfe at Quebec (1759); made surveys in Nova Scotia and Newfoundland (1763–73); charted North American coast; lieutenant governor of Cape Breton (1784–1805), of Prince Edward Island (1805–13).

Des·bordes-Val·more \dā-bȯrd-väl-mȯr\, Marceline-Félicité-Josèphe, *nee* Desbordes. 1786–1859. French poet. m. Prosper Lanchantin, an actor whose stage name was Valmore (1817). Turned to writing after career on stage; among her books of verse were *Élégies et romances* (1819), *Les Pleurs* (1833), *Pauvres fleurs* (1839), *Bouquets et prières* (1843).

Des·bo·rough *or* **Des·bo·row** \'dez-bər-ə, -brə\ *or* **Dis·browe** \'diz-ˌbrō, -brə\, John. 1608–1680. English soldier. m. (1636) Eltisley, sister of Oliver Cromwell. In Civil War fought on Parliamentary side, becoming major general (1651); nearly captured Charles II after battle of Worcester. Instigated hostility of army against Richard Cromwell's administration; member of council of state and Rump Parliament. Imprisoned (1666–67) for republican intrigue. Caricatured in Butler's *Hudibras.*

Des·cartes \dā-kärt, *Angl* dā-'kärt\, René. *Lat.* Renatus Car·te·si·us \kär-'tē-zh(ē-)əs\. 1596–1650. French mathematician and philosopher. Resident in Holland (1628–49) after many years of travel and study. Fame based on treatise *Discours de la méthode* (1637), in which he attempted to unify all knowledge as the product of clear reasoning from self-evident premises, establishing the ideal of mathematical certitude in all scientific and philosophical thought; considered the foundation of modern philosophical method. Also laid foundation of analytic geometry. Others of his works were *Meditationes de prima philosophia* (1641), *Principia philosophiae* (1644), *Les Passions de l'âme* (1649), and the posthumous publications *De l'homme* (1664) and *Opuscula posthuma, physica et mathematica* (1701).

Des·caves \dā-käv\, Lucien. 1861–1949. French writer. Works included *Le Calvaire d'Heloïse Padajou* (1882), *Une vielle rate* (1883), *Sous-offs* (1889), *Soupes* (1898), *Philémon* (1913), etc.

Des·champs \dā-shä^n\, Émile. *In full* Émile Deschamps de Saint A·mand \-də-sa^n-tä-mä^n\. 1791–1871. French poet. With Victor Hugo, founded (1823) *La Muse française,* journal of the Romanticists; author of *Études françaises et étrangères* (1828), including translations from other languages, and a preface constituting a manifesto of the Romanticists; *Contes physiologiques* (1854); *Réalités fantastiques* (1854); libretto for Berlioz' *Roméo et Juliette* (1839). His brother ¶Antony, *in full* Antoine-François-Marie (1800–1869), also a poet of the Romantic school, translated Dante's *Divina commedia* (1829).

Deschamps, Eustache. c.1346–c.1406. French poet. Author of over a thousand ballades; wrote a long poem *Le Miroir de mariage,* rondeaux, virelays, etc., and *L'Art de dictier* (1392), first French treatise on poetry.

Des·cha·nel \dā-shä-nel\, Émile-Auguste-Étienne-Martin. 1819–1904. French critic and author. Editor, *Journal des Débats* (1859); professor at Collège de France (1876); senator (1881–1904). Works included critical studies of Aristophanes, Racine, Voltaire, Lamartine, and Benjamin Franklin, *Catholicisme et Socialisme* (1850), and *Romantisme des classiques* (1882).

Deschanel, Paul-Eugène-Louis. 1855–1922. French politician. Son of Émile Deschanel. Member of Chamber of Deputies (from 1885), becoming leader of Progressive Republican party; president of chamber (1898–1902, 1912–20); president of France (Feb.–Sept. 1920). Author of *La Question sociale* (1898), *Essai de philosophie politique* (1899), *Gambetta* (1920).

Des·clot \dās-'klȯt\, Bernat. fl. 1285. Catalan historian. Author of a history of James I and Pedro III of Aragon, earliest important composition in Catalan.

de Sélincourt. See SÉLINCOURT.

De Se·ver·sky \dyis-yiv-'yer-skəi, *Angl* də-sə-'ver-skē\, Alexander Procofieff. 1894–1974. American aviator and aeronautical engineer, b. Tiflis, Russia. Russian air ace in World War I. To U.S. (1918); naturalized (1927). President (1931–39), Seversky Aircraft Corp. (forerunner of Republic Aircraft), manufacturing pursuit planes, notably the P-47. Inventor of various airplane devices including a bombsight; interested in air-pollution control; author of *Victory Through Air Power* (1942).

Des·fon·taines \dā-fō^{n}-ten\, René-Louiche. 1750–1833. French botanist. Author of *Flora atlantica* (1798), in which plants collected during his two-year travels in the Barbary States were described.

Des·ga·bets \dā-gȧ-be\, Robert. 1620–1678. French religious. Benedictine; author of works applying Cartesian methods and ideas, esp. mind–body duality, to Christian doctrine.

Des·gar·cins \dā-gȧr-sa^{n}\, Magdeleine-Marie, *orig.* Louise. 1769–1797. French actress. With Comédie-Française (1788–91) and then in own company, became one of great tragediennes of the time.

Des·hayes \dā-ā\, Gérard-Paul. 1795–1875. French naturalist. Authority on fossil conchology; wrote *Traité élémentaire de conchyliologie* (1834–58), *L'Histoire des mollusques terrestres et fluviatiles* (1838–51).

Des·hou·lières \dā-zül-yer\, Antoinette du Li·gier de la Garde \dü̅e-lēzh-yā-də-lȧ-gȧrd\. 1638–1694. French poet. Author of idyls, eclogues, odes, madrigals, elegies, etc., first of which were published in 1672; conducted notable literary salon.

De Si·ca \də-'sē-kə\, Vittorio. 1901–1974. Italian film director. A leader of the post-World War II Neorealist movement; films included *Due dozzine di rose scarlatte* (1940), *Shoeshine* (1946, Academy Award), *The Bicycle Thief* (1948, Academy Award), *Miracle in Milan* (1951), *Umberto D.* (1952), *Yesterday, Today, and Tomorrow* (1964, Academy Award), *The Garden of the Finzi-Continis* (1971, Academy Award).

De·si·de·rio da Set·ti·gna·no \ˌdā-sē-'der-yō-dä-ˌsät-tēn-'yä-nō\. c.1430–1464. Florentine sculptor. One of leading early Renaissance sculptors; chief works included tomb monument of Carlo Marsuppini, frieze in Pazzi Chapel, altar-tabernacle of S. Lorenzo.

Desiderius. See Pope VICTOR III.

Des·i·de·ri·us \ˌdes-i-'dir-ē-əs\. 8th century. Last king of the Lombards (757–774 A.D.). Duke of Tuscany; after succeeding Aistulf as Lombard king, attacked papacy, who sought aid (772) from the Franks; his territory invaded (773) by Charlemagne and his capital, Ticinum (Pavia), captured; taken as prisoner to France.

Dé·si·rée \dā-zē-rā\, Bernardine-Eugénie. 1777–1860. Queen of Sweden (1818–44). m. (1798) Gen. Jean Bernadotte (later King Charles XIV John of Sweden); visited Sweden (1810–11) after Bernadotte's selection as heir to throne, but did not live there until 1823.

de Sitter, Willem. See SITTER.

Des·jar·dins \dā-zhär-da^{n}\, Marie-Catherine. *Pseudonym* Mme. de Ville·dieu \vēl-dyü̅e\. 1640?–1683. French writer. Author of *Les Désordres de l'amour, Les Amours des grands hommes, Annales galantes,* etc.

Desjardins, Martin. *Orig. surname* van den Bo·gaert \vän-dən-'bō-g̅ärt\. 1640–1694. Dutch sculptor. One of the chief decorators of Versailles; statues included *Diane chasseresse, Hercule couronné par la gloire;* director of Académie Royale (1681).

Des·landres \dā-lä^{n}dr^{ə}\, Henri-Alexandre. 1853–1948. French astrophysicist. Director of observatory at Meudon (from 1907), also of observatory at Paris (1927–29). Known esp. for work on spectral analysis of the sun and for invention (simultaneously with G.E. Hale) of spectroheliograph (1891).

Des·ma·rest \dā-mȧ-re\, Nicolas. 1725–1815. French geologist. Discovered volcanic origin of basalt (c.1763).

Des·ma·rets *or* **Des Ma·rets** \da-mȧ-re, -rā\, Nicolas. Sieur de Maille·bois \mȧy-bwä, -bwȧ\. 1648–1721. French financier. Entered government financial service under his uncle, Jean-Baptiste Colbert; director of finances (1703–08) and comptroller general (1708–15) under Louis XIV; renegotiated loans, created royal lottery, devalued coinage, instituted income tax to finance War of Spanish Succession.

Des·ma·rets de Saint-Sor·lin \dā-mȧ-rā-də-sa^{n}-sȯr-la^{n}\, Jean. 1595–1676. French writer. Protégé of Richelieu, and recipient of political preferment from the cardinal; author of verse, plays, Christian polemics; works included *Ariane* (1632), *Les Visionnaires* (1637), *Mirame* (1641), *Clovis ou la France chrétienne* (1657), *Les Délices de l'esprit* (1658); precipitated "quarrel between the ancients and moderns" with *La Comparaison de la langue et de la poésie française avec la grecque et la latine* (1670) and *Défense de la poésie et de la langue française* (1675).

De Smet \də-'smet\, Pierre-Jean. 1801–1873. American Jesuit missionary, b. Termonde, Belgium. To U.S. (1821). Missionary to Indians along western frontier (from 1838), esp. Flatheads and Blackfeet, and frequent mediator of Indian–settler disputes. Called "Blackrobe" by Indians.

Desmond, Earls of. See FITZGERALD family.

Des·mou·lins \dā-mü-la^{n}\, Camille, *in full* Lucie-Simplice-Camille-Benoît. 1760–1794. French journalist and revolutionary leader. Advocate in Paris (1785–88); excited by dismissal of Necker, harangued crowds (July 12, 1789), urging revolt—actual beginning of Revolution, the Bastille being taken two days later. Wrote pamphlets *La France libre* and *Discours de la laterne aux Parisiens* (1789) supporting Revolution; published journals *Les Révolutions de France et de Brabant* (1789) and *Le Vieux Cordelier* (1793); wrote a bitter attack on Girondists; deputy for Paris to National Convention (Sept. 1793). Secretary under Danton in ministry of justice (1792); association with Danton eventually alienated his old friend Robespierre; antagonism with ultra-Jacobins increased; arrested by Robespierre; given only mock trial; executed with Danton. Author also of *La Philosophie du peuple français* (1788), *Histoire des Brissotins* (1793).

Des·nos \des-nōs, -nȯs\, Robert. 1900–1945. French poet. Early works, some composed in hypnotic trance, in Surrealist vein, as *La Liberté ou l'amour!* (1927), *Corps et biens* (1930); later works more traditional in form, as *Fortunes* (1942), *État de veille* (1943), *Contrée* (1944); imprisoned for Resistance activity in World War II.

Desnoyers, Baron. See Auguste BOUCHER.

Des·noy·ers \dān-wȧ-yā\, Louis-Claude-Joseph-Florence. 1802–1868. French writer. Contributor to *Charivari, Journal des enfants;* author of *Mésaventures de Jean-Paul Choppart* (1836), *Adventures de Robert-Robert et de son ami Toussaint-Lavenette* (1840).

de Soto, Hernando. See Hernando de SOTO.

Des·pard \'des-pərd, -ˌpärd\, Edward Marcus. 1751–1803. Irish conspirator. Entered British army (1766); commanded expedition against Spanish possessions in West Indies (1782); governor of Roatán Island and then of Mosquito Coast (1781–84); superintended colony in Yucatán (1784–90); devised plot to assassinate George III; he and six coconspirators were last men sentenced to be hanged, drawn, and quartered in England.

Des·pen·ser \də-'spen(t)-sər\, Le. Family prominent in English politics of the 13th–14th centuries, including: Hugh Le Despenser (d. 1265), last of the justiciaries of England (1260, reappointed 1263). Leader of baronial side in Mad Parliament of Oxford (1258); joined de Montfort party (1264); one of four arbitrators for arranging terms between de Montfort and Earl of Gloucester; killed at Evesham. His son ¶Hugh (1262–1326), Earl of Win·ches·ter \'win-ˌches-tər, -chə-stər\, secured, from Pope Clement V, King Edward I's release from oaths to observe charters (1305); succeeded Piers Gaveston as chief adviser; expelled by barons (1321); restored by Edward II and created earl (1322); with his son, virtually ruled the country; captured by barons under Roger de Mortimer and Queen Isabella (1326), whom he had induced king to outlaw; hanged. His son ¶Hugh (d. 1326) was king's chamberlain (1313); banished with his father (1321) by barons, who hated him for his wealth and rapacity; recalled by king (1322); negotiator of truce with Scotland (1323); taken with king (1326) by barons under Queen Isabella and hanged. ¶Edward (d. 1375), grandson of Hugh the younger, fought at Poitiers and under Pope Urban V in 1369 and was patron of Froissart. ¶Thomas (1373–1400), son of Edward, supported Richard II against Duke of Gloucester and other lords appellant (1397); implicated in Gloucester's death; joined conspiracy against Henry IV and was betrayed; beheaded. ¶Henry (1341?–1406), brother of Edward, became bishop of Norwich (1370); defeated insurgent Norfolk peasants (1381); led crusade in Flanders for Pope Urban VI against antipope adherents but defeated at Ypres (1383); denounced as a fighting prelate by Wycliffe; persecuted the Lollards; imprisoned (1399) for loyalty to Richard II, but reconciled with Henry IV (1401). Cf. SPENCER family.

Des Pé·riers \dā-pā-ryā, de-\, Bonaventure. c.1500–c.1544. French Humanist. Enjoyed patronage of Marguerite d'Angoulême, queen of Navarre; author of *Cymbalum mundi* (1537), sharp attack on Christianity; other works published in posthumous collections *Recueil des oeuvres de feu Bonaventure des Périers* (1544) and *Nouvelles récréations et joyeux devis* (fables and stories, 1558).

Des·piau \des-pyō\, Charles. 1874–1946. French sculptor. Best known for portrait busts in severe Neoclassical style; also carved *Bacchante, Jeune faune, Ève, La Chasse, Athlète au repos, Assia, Monument aux Morts.*

Des·portes \dā-pȯrt\, Alexandre-François. 1661–1743. French painter. Known for portraits and esp. for hunting scenes, many done for Louis XIV and Louis XV; court portraitist for John III Sobieski of Poland (1695–96).

Desportes, Philippe. 1546–1606. French poet. Disciple of Ronsard, whom he replaced (c.1567) as courtier poet to duc d'Anjou (later Henry III); author of elegies, psalms, songs, and collections of love sonnets inspired by Petrarch, Ariosto, Bembo, etc.

des Pres, Josquin. See JOSQUIN DES PREZ.

Des·saix \dā-se\, Joseph-Marie. Comte. 1764–1834. French general. Member of Council of Five Hundred (1798–99); general of brigade (1803); dubbed l'In·tré·pide \laⁿ-trā-pēd\ by Napoléon after battle of Wagram (1809).

Des·sa·lines \dā-sá-lēn\, Jean-Jacques. 1758?–1806. Haitian ruler. Taken as slave from W. Africa to Haiti, took name of French master. Joined insurrection (1791) and aided Toussaint L'Ouverture (1797); helped by British, drove out French (1803) and assumed governor-generalship of Saint-Domingue; established republic of Haiti (1804) with himself as head; declared himself emperor as Jacques I (1804–06); confiscated white-owned lands and instigated massacres of whites; assassinated by Christophe and Pétion.

Des·soir \des-'wär\, Ludwig. 1810–1874. German actor. Known esp. for Shakespearean roles, including Hamlet, Othello, Richard III.

De Ste·fa·ni \dā-'stā-fän-(,)ē, -'stef-än-\, Alberto. 1879–1969. Italian economist. Elected deputy (1921); minister of finance (1922–25); member, Fascist Grand Council.

De·stinn \'des-tən\, Emmy. *Orig.* Ema Kit·tl \'kit-ᵊl\. 1878–1930. Bohemian operatic soprano. Sang title roles in London premiere of Puccini's *Madame Butterfly* (1905) and Berlin and Paris premieres of Richard Strauss's *Salome* (1906); member of Metropolitan Opera Co., New York (1908–16); created lead role in Puccini's *La fanciulla del west* (1910).

Des·touches \dā-tüsh\, André-Cardinal. 1669–1749. French composer. Superintendent of music for king (1718); director of the Opéra Française (1728); among his operas were *Amadis de Grèce* (1699), *Omphale* (1701), *Callirhoé* (1712), *Sémiramis* (1718).

Destouches, Louis-Ferdinand. *Pseudonym* Louis-Ferdinand Cé·line \sā-lēn\. 1894–1961. French physician and novelist. Author of *Voyage au bout de la nuit* (*Journey to the End of Night,* 1932), *Mort à crédit* (*Death on the Installment Plan,* 1936), *Mea Culpa* (1936), *Rigodon* (1969).

Destouches, Philippe. *Orig. surname* Né·ri·cault \nā-rē-kō\. 1680–1754. French playwright. Author of moralizing comedies inspired by English Restoration works, including *Le Médisant* (1715), *Le Philosophe marié* (1727), *Le Glorieux* (1732), *Le Dissipateur* (1736), *L'Ambitieux* (1737).

Des·tutt de Tra·cy \des-tüēt-də-trá-si\, Antoine-Louis-Claude. Comte. 1754–1836. French philosopher. A soldier, and member of Estates-General (1789); member of Académie Française (1808); senator under Napoléon I; peer of France in Restoration; developed sensationalist philosophy of "Idéologie" in *Éléments d'idéologie* (1801–15), *Traité de la volonté et de ses effets* (1805), *Commentaire sur l'Esprit des lois de Montesquieu* (1808).

Des·val·lières \dā-vál-yer\, Georges-Olivier. 1861–1950. French painter. Known for landscape and esp. religious works.

de Tabley, Baron. See John Byrne Leicester WARREN.

De·taille \də-täy\, Édouard, *in full* Jean-Baptiste-Édouard. 1848–1912. French painter. Best known for his battle scenes and paintings of soldiers.

De·ter·ding \'dāt-ər-diŋ\, Sir Henri Wilhelm August. 1866–1939. Dutch oil magnate. Joined Royal Dutch Oil Co. (1896) and became its director general (1902); created by merger the Royal Dutch/Shell Petroleum group and extended firm's interests worldwide.

De Tham \'dā-'täm\. *Also called* Hoang Hoa Tham \'hwäŋ-'hwä-'täm\. *Orig. surname* Truong \trü-'öŋ\. c.1860–1913. Vietnamese nationalist. Became legendary for ferocity of his fight against French colonialists.

Dett \'det\, Robert Nathaniel. 1882–1943. American conductor and composer, b. Drummondsville, Ont. Director of music, Hampton Inst. (1913–32); conductor of Hampton Inst. choir which toured U.S., Canada, and Europe. Composer of much choral music, including *America the Beautiful, The Ordering of Moses, Chariot Jubilee,* instrumental works, including *In the Bottoms Suite, American Sampler,* and songs. Author and editor of *The Dett Collection of Negro Spirituals* (1937).

Deu·cher \'dói-kər\, Adolf. 1831–1912. Swiss politician. President of Swiss Confederation (1886, 1897, 1903, 1909).

De·us·ded·it \,dē-əs-'ded-ət, -'dēd-\. Saint. *Also called* Adeodatus I. d. 618. Pope (615–618).

Deus Ra·mos \'dā-üsh-'ram-üsh\, João de. 1830–1896. Portuguese poet. Journalist; deputy to Cortes (1869). Foremost Portuguese poet of his time; published *Flores do campo* (1868), *Ramode flores* (1875), *Fôlhas Sôltas* (1876), *Campo de flores* (1893).

Deus·sen \'dóis-ən\, Paul. 1845–1919. German philosopher and Sanskrit scholar. Professor at Kiel (from 1889); wrote *Elementen der Metaphysik* (1877), *Das System des Vedânta* (1883), *Die Sûtras des Vedânta* (1887), etc.

Deutsch, Niklaus. See Niklaus MANUEL.

Deutsch·er \'dói-chər\, Isaac. 1907–1967. British historian, b. Poland. Author of *Stalin, a Political Biography* (1949), biography of Trotsky (1954–63), *Russia and the West* (1960).

De·va·dat·ta \,dā-və-'dä-tə\. 6th century B.C. Indian religious leader. Cousin of the Buddha; attempted to displace Buddha as leader of *sangha* monastic community; said to have made three attempts on life of Buddha.

De Va·le·ra \,dev-ə-'ler-ə, -'lir-\, Eamon. 1882–1975. Irish political leader, b. New York City of Spanish father and Irish mother. Led party of insurgents in Irish nationalist uprising (1916); imprisoned (1916–17, 1918–19); president of Sinn Féin (1918–26) and of provisional Republican government (1918–22); leader of opposition to Anglo-Irish treaty (Dec. 1921) and imprisoned by Irish Free State (1923–24); established and presided over Fianna Fáil Republican opposition party (1924); led Fianna Fáil into Free State parliament (1927); president of executive council and minister for external affairs (1932–37); prime minister (1937–48, 1951–54, 1957–59); president of Ireland (1959–73).

De·vant \də-'vant\, David. *Orig. surname* Wight·on \'wīt-ᵊn\. 1868–1941. English magician. Considered one of greatest sleight-of-hand artists; author of *Our Magic* (with J.N. Maskelyne, 1911), *My Magic Life* (1931), *Secrets of My Magic* (1936).

De·vaux \də-vō\, Paul. 1801–1880. Belgian politician. A founder (1824) of opposition journal *Politique,* influential in agitation leading to independence of Belgium from Netherlands. Advocated choice of Leopold of Saxe-Coburg as king (1831); member of Chamber of Deputies (1831–63).

Dé·vay *or* **Dé·vai** \'dā-vói\, Mátyás Biró. 1500?–?1545. Hungarian church reformer. Entered Roman Catholic priesthood; adopted (1529) principles of Reformation and studied at Wittenberg with Luther. Preached Lutheranism, later Calvinism, in Hungary; regarded as founder of Reformed church of Hungary.

De·ven·ter \'dā-vən-tər\, Conrad Theodor van. 1857–1915. Dutch jurist and politician. Formulated "ethical policy" toward East Indian colonies (adopted 1901), including welfare and education; member of parliament (1905–09, 1913–15).

Deventer, Sir Jacob Louis van. 1874–1922. South African soldier. Second in command to Gen. Smuts, Boer War (1899–1902). Served in German South-West Africa (1914–15); as temporary lieutenant general, commanded Allied forces in successful campaign in East Africa (1917).

De Vere \də-'vi(ə)r\, Aubrey Thomas. 1814–1902. Irish poet and critic. Wrote *The Waldenses and Other Poems* (1842), *English Misrule and Irish Misdeeds* (1848), devotional verse and hymns; turned to Irish bardic lore and ecclesiastical medievalism in *Inisfail* (1862), *Legends of St. Patrick* (1872).

Dev·er·eux \'dev-ə-,rü, -,rüks, -,reks, -rə\. Name of an English family bearing the title earl of Essex, including: Walter Devereux (1541–1576), 1st Earl of Es·sex \'es-iks\ of 6th creation (1572) and 2d Viscount of Her·e·ford \'her-ə-fərd\; grandson of Walter Devereux (d. 1558; 1st Viscount and 3d Baron Fer·rers \'fer-ərz\, chief justice of South Wales); aided in suppression of northern rebellion (1569); attempted to subdue rebel O'Neills and Scots under Sorley Boy MacDonnell in Ulster (1573); treacherously captured and executed Irish chief Sir Brian MacPhelim (1574); made earl marshal of Ireland by Queen Elizabeth; defeated Turlough Luineach (1575); massacred hundreds of Irish and followers of Sorley Boy (1575).

His eldest son ¶Robert (1566–1601), 2d earl; distinguished himself at Zutphen (1586); became chief favorite of Elizabeth I on the death of Leicester; joined expedition against Spain (1589); offended Elizabeth by secret marriage with widow of Sir Philip Sidney (1590); commanded fruitless campaign in aid of Henry IV of France (1591–92); gained glory in successful expedition against Cádiz (1596); during quarrel with queen, was counseled and aided by Francis Bacon; on expedition to Azores failed to capture Spanish treasure fleet (1597–98); earl marshal of England (1597); as lord lieutenant and governor general of Ireland, met defeat at Arklow (1599), made truce with Tyrone, left post to vindicate himself before the queen; deprived of his offices and his liberty; induced by Mountjoy, Southampton, and others to form plot for removing queen's counselors (1601), but failed in attempt to raise citizens of London; prosecuted for treason by old friend Bacon and executed; a patron of literature and author of sonnets.

¶Robert (1591–1646), 3d earl, son of 2d earl; restored to his father's titles by Parliament (1604); lived in household with prince of Wales; served in wars of the Palatinate (1620–23); vice admiral in futile expedition to capture Cádiz (1625); supported Petition of Right (1628); second in command of expedition against Scottish Covenanters (1639). Commanded Parliamentary army (1642–45); held the field at Edge Hill (1642), took Reading (1643), relieved Gloucester (1643); lost army in Cornwall, partly because of disease and financial trouble, partly through incompetence (1644); after passing of Self-denying Ordinance, resigned (1645). His first wife Frances Howard m. (1613) Robert Carr (*q.v.*), Earl of Rochester.

¶Penelope (1562?–1607), daughter of 1st Earl of Essex, who intended her to marry her admirer Sir Philip Sidney (*q.v.*); m. (1581) Robert Rich, 3d Baron Rich, afterwards earl of Warwick; dissatisfied with marriage, welcomed attentions and love sonnets of Sir Philip Sidney, collected under title *Astrophel and Stella* (1591); after Sidney's death, became Lord Mountjoy's mistress;

divorced by Lord Rich (1605), m. Mountjoy, Earl of Devonshire (see Charles BLOUNT).

Dev·ers \'dev-ərz\, Jacob Loucks. 1887–1979. American army officer, b. York, Pa. Brigadier general (1940), general (1945); chief of staff, Panama department (1939–40); chief of Armored Force (1941–43); commander, European theater (1943–44), of army forces in North Africa (1944); commander of 6th Army Group in southern France (1944–45).

De Veus·ter \də-'vœs-tər\, Joseph. *Relig. name* Father Damien. 1840–1889. Belgian priest. To Sandwich (Hawaiian) Islands as missionary (1863); volunteered to serve leper colony on Molokai I. (1873); improved housing, water and food supply, public morals, founded two orphanages; worked entirely alone for 10 of his 16 years on Molokai; contracted leprosy (1884), refused cure in order to remain on Molokai. Attack on him by Presbyterian minister elicited R. L. Stevenson's famous *Open Letter to the Rev. Dr. Hyde* (1890).

De·vey \'dē-vē\, George. 1820–1886. English architect. Principally a residential architect; exerted considerable influence on Richard Norman Shaw, C.F.A. Voysey, and others.

De·ville \də-vēl\, Édouard-Gaston. 1849–1924. Canadian surveyor, b. La Charité sur Loire, France. Served in French navy; to Canada (1875); inspector of surveys, Quebec (1875–81); inspector of Dominion land surveys (1881–85); surveyor general (1885–1924). Devised first practical method of photogrammetry.

Deville, Henri-Étienne Sainte-Claire. See SAINTE-CLAIRE DEVILLE.

De Vil·liers \də-'vil-yərz\, John Henry. 1st Baron De Villiers. 1842–1914. South African judge. Attorney general (1872), chief justice (1874) of Cape Colony; president of National Covention (1908); first chief justice of Union of South Africa (1910–14); acting governor general (1912, 1914).

De·vine \də-'vīn\, Edward Thomas. 1867–1948. American social worker, b. Union, Iowa. Secretary of New York Charity Organization Society (1896–1917); editor of *Survey* (1897–1912); professor of social economy at Columbia (1905–19) and American U. in Washington, D.C. (1926–28); director of New York School of Philanthropy (1904–07, 1912–17). Author of *The Practice of Charity* (1901), *Misery and Its Causes* (1909), *Progressive Social Action* (1933), etc.

De Vinne \də-'vin-ē\, Theodore Low. 1828–1914. American printer, b. Stamford, Conn. With Francis Hart's printing shop in New York (1850–58); partner (1858–77); took over business as Theo. L. De Vinne & Co., on Hart's death (1877); incorporated as The De Vinne Press (1908). Brought about great improvements in American typography and fine printing; a founder (1884) and first president of Grolier Club. Author of *The Invention of Printing* (1876), *The Practice of Typography* (1900–1904), etc.

Devizes, Richard of. See RICHARD of Devizes.

Devon *or occasionally* **Devonshire,** Earl of. See (1) Humphrey STAFFORD; (2) COURTENAY family.

Devonshire, Dukes of. See CAVENDISH family.

Devonshire, Earl of. An English title held by Charles BLOUNT and (from 1618) by members of Cavendish family (see William CAVENDISH), the fourth earl being created duke (1694). See also earl of DEVON.

De Vo·to \di-'vōt-(,)ō\, Bernard Augustine. 1897–1955. American writer, b. Ogden, Utah. Taught at Northwestern U. (1922–27), Harvard (1929–36). Editor of "The Easy Chair" in *Harper's Magazine* (1935–55); editor, *Saturday Review of Literature* (1936–38). Author of *The Crooked Mile* (1924), *The Chariot of Fire* (1926), *Mark Twain's America* (1932), *Mark Twain at Work* (1942), *Year of Decision: 1846* (1943), *Across the Wide Missouri* (1947, Pulitzer prize), *The Hour* (1951), *Course of Empire* (1952).

de Vriendt, Cornelis and Frans. See FLORIS.

De·vrient \dəv-rē-'a^{n}, dev-'rēnt\. Family of German actors, including: Ludwig (1784–1832), greatest German actor of the Romantic period, esp. noted in the roles of Shylock, Lear, Richard III, Falstaff, Mercutio. His three nephews ¶Karl August (1797–1872) acted in Dresden (1821–35), Karlsruhe (1835–39), Hanover (1839–72); notable esp. in *Wallenstein, Faust, Lear;* ¶Eduard, *in full* Philipp Eduard (1801–1877), director of Hoftheater, Karlsruhe (1852–77) and author of pioneering *Geschichte der deutschen Schauspielkunst* (1848); and ¶Emil, *in full* Gustav Emil (1803–1872), at court theater, Dresden (1831–68). Eduard's son ¶Otto (1838–1894), active in Karlsruhe and Weimar. Karl's son ¶Max (1857–1929), active in Dresden and Vienna.

De Vries. See also VRIES.

De Vries \dəv-'rēs\, David Pietersen. 1592?–?1655. Dutch colonizer in America, b. La Rochelle, France. Voyaged to America (1631, 1632–33, 1634–36, 1638–44). Established a colony on Staten Island and another near what is now Tappan, both destroyed by Indians (1643). Wrote account of his travels (pub. 1655).

De·wan·to·ro \,de-wän-'tōr-ō, -'tór-\, Ki Hadjar. *Orig.* R. M. Suwardi Surjaningrat \,súr-jän-'ēn-,grät\. 1889–1959. Indonesian educator. Founded Taman Siswa school system to promote Indonesian culture and nationalism and modernization.

Dew·ar \'d(y)ü-ər\, Sir James. 1842–1923. Scottish chemist and physicist. Professor of natural experimental philosophy, Cambridge (1875–1923), and of chemistry, Royal Institution, London (1877–1923). Investigated specific heat of hydrogen and physiological action of light on the eye; made spectroscopic studies; first to produce liquid hydrogen (1898), later (1899) obtaining it as a solid; invented Dewar vessel, forerunner of the vacuum bottle; discovered that the absorbent power of charcoal for gases is increased by cold (1902); studied properties of matter at low temperatures; with Frederick Augustus Abel invented cordite.

Dewar, Thomas Robert. 1st Baron Dewar of Homestall. 1864–1930. British distiller, sportsman, and raconteur, b. Scotland. Became London agent of distillery founded by his father; largely expanded business and succeeded father as head of John Dewar & Sons. M.P. (1900–06). Created baron (1919). Author of *Toasts and Maxims and Wisdom Compressed, A Ramble Around the Globe,* etc.

de Wentworth, Cecile. See Cecile de WENTWORTH.

D'·Ewes \'dyüz\, Sir Simonds. 1602–1650. English antiquarian. Collected and published *Journal of all the Parliaments During the Reign of Queen Elizabeth* (1682); his transcripts from ancient records and his diaries (1621–24, 1643–47) are valuable, often the only, authority for incidents; M.P. (1640–48).

de Wet, Christiaan Rudolph. See WET.

De Wet·te \dā-'vet-ə\, Wilhelm Martin Leberecht. 1780–1849. German Protestant theologian. Professor at Berlin (1810–22), Basel (1822–49); first applied historical criticism to Pentateuch.

Dew·ey \'d(y)ü-ē\, George. 1837–1917. American naval officer, b. Montpelier, Vt. During Civil War, served under Farragut. Commanding officer of Asiatic squadron (1897–99); at Hong Kong received news of declaration of war against Spain; immediately steered for Manila, Philippine Islands; destroyed Spanish squadron in battle of Manila Bay (May 1, 1898) and supported army in capture of city of Manila. Admiral of the navy (from 1899); president, General Board of the navy (1900–17).

Dewey, John. 1859–1952. American philosopher, psychologist, and educator, b. Burlington, Vt. Professor, Minnesota (1888–89), Michigan (1889–94), Chicago (1894–1904), Columbia (from 1904). Principal developer, with C. S. Peirce and William James, of philosophy of Pragmatism; considered leading theorist of progressive education movement. A founder of American Association of University Professors (1915), of New School for Social Research (1919). Among his many books were *School and Society* (1899), *Studies in Logical Theory* (1903), *How We Think* (1910), *Democracy and Education* (1916), *Reconstruction in Philosophy* (1920), *Human Nature and Conduct* (1922), *Experience and Nature* (1925), *The Quest for Certainty* (1929), *Art as Experience* (1934), *Liberalism and Social Action* (1935), *Logic: The Theory of Inquiry* (1938), *Experience and Education* (1938), *Freedom and Culture* (1939).

Dewey, Melvil. 1851–1931. American librarian, b. Adams Center, N.Y. Chief librarian and professor of library economy, Columbia (1883–88); director, New York State Library (1889–1906); founder and director, New York State Library School (1887–1906). A founder of American Library Assoc. (1876), Spelling Reform Assoc.; founder (with R.R. Bowker, F. Leypoldt) and editor, *Library Journal* (1876–81) and *Library Notes* (1886–98). Originated decimal classification system (1876).

Dewey, Thomas Edmund. 1902–1971. American lawyer, b. Owosso, Mich. Assistant U.S. attorney, southern district of N.Y. (1933); special prosecutor in investigation of organized crime, N.Y. (1935–37); district attorney of New York county (1937–38); governor of N.Y. (1943–55). Republican candidate for president of U.S. (1944, 1948).

Dewi, Saint. See Saint DAVID.

Dew·ing \'d(y)ü-iŋ\, Thomas Wilmer. 1851–1938. American painter, b. Boston. Known for figure and portrait work; member (from 1898) of Ten American Artists group of Impressionists.

De Wint \də-'wint\, Peter. 1784–1849. English landscape painter. Chiefly a water-colorist, illustrator of landscape, architecture, and country life of England.

de Winter, Jan Willem. See Jan Willem de WINTER.

de Witt, Johan. See Johan de WITT.

De Wolfe \də-'wúlf\, Ella Anderson, *known as* Elsie. 1865–1950. American decorator, b. New York City. Actress in Charles Frohman's company (1891–1901) and own company (1901–05); became interior decorator; won fame with work at Colony Club, N.Y.C.; established place of women in field; wrote *The House in Good Taste* (1913), *After All* (autobiog. 1935).

Dex·ip·pus \dek-'sip-əs\, Publius Herennius. c.210–after 270 A.D. Greek general and historian. Checked invasion of Greece by the Heruli (c.267 A.D.). Author of a history of Rome's wars with the Goths in 3d century, a history of Alexander the Great's successors, and of a chronicle of world history. Only fragments of his works are extant.

de Young \də-ˈyəŋ\, Michel Harry. 1849–1925. American journalist, b. St. Louis. With his brother Charles (1847–1880) founded (1865) a newspaper that later became the San Francisco *Chronicle;* sole owner and editor in chief (from 1880).

Deyssel, Lodewijk van. See ALBERDINCK THIJM.

Dezh•nyov \ˈdezh-nyòf\, Semyon Ivanov. 1605–1672 or 1673. Russian explorer. Explored Siberia (1640–42); first to sail through Bering Strait (1648), but his report not found until 1736, after Vitus Bering's rediscovery.

Dga'-ldan \də-ˈgä-əl-ˈdän\. 1644?–1697. Mongol leader. Ruler of Dzungar tribes (1676–97); conquered Outer Mongolia, East Turkestan, Tibet; mounted unsuccessful drive on Peking (1690); defeated by Chinese and Khalkha Mongols under emperor K'ang-hsi (1696).

Dhahabī, al-. See AḤMAD AL-MANṢŪR.

Dhar•ma•kir•ti \ˌdär-mə-ˈkir-tē\. 7th century. Indian Buddhist philosopher. Developed Indian system of syllogistic reasoning.

Dhar•ma•vam•sa \ˌdär-mə-ˈväm-sə\. d. 1007. Javanese ruler. King of eastern Java (991–1007); reign noted for literary achievements; compiled legal code; earliest Javanese known in detail to history.

Dhaun, Leopold von. See DAUN.

d'Herelle. See HERELLE.

Dhil•i•yi•án•nis \ˌthil-ē-yē-ˈän-yēs\ *or* **Dil•i•yi•án•nis** *or* **Del•i•gi•án•nis** \ˌthel-\, Theódoros. 1826–1905. Greek politician. Foreign minister (1862, 1877); ambassador to France (1867–68); advocated aggressive, nationalist foreign policy; organized Nationalist party (1880) calling for liberation of Greek territories under Turkish rule; prime minister (1885–86, 1890–92, 1895–97, 1902–03, 1904–05). Prevented from invading Turkish Macedonia by Great Powers (1887); declared war on Turkey on outbreak of revolt on Crete (1897); resigned on defeat of Greek army and imposed cession of strategic territory to Turkey; assassinated.

Dhulip Singh. See under RANJIT SINGH.

Di•a•bel•li \ˌdē-ä-ˈbel-ē\, Anton. 1781–1858. Austrian composer and music publisher. Founded (1818, with P. Cappi) music publishing house that became Diabelli & Co., publishers of Beethoven, Schubert, Czerny, etc. Composer of piano pieces, songs, masses, and an operetta. On one of his waltz themes, Beethoven wrote his *Thirty-Three Variations* (Opus 120).

Di•a•do•chus \ˌdī-ə-ˈdō-kəs\ of Pho•tice \ˈfōt-ˌīs\. 5th century A.D. Greek religious. Bishop of Photice in Epirus; effectively opposed various heresies; author of *Hekaton Kephalaia Gnōstika,* influential work on Christian asceticism.

Dia•ghi•lev \ˈdyág-yil-yif\, Sergey Pavlovich. 1872–1929. Russian art critic and impresario. Founded art journal *Mir Iskusstva* (1899). Joined staff of Imperial Russian Theater, Moscow (1899). To Paris (1906); organized Ballets Russes there (1909); enlisted choreographers M. Fokine, L. Massine, dancers Nijinsky, Pavlova, Karsavina, painters Bonnard, Léger, Picabia, de Chirico, Bakst; produced Stravinsky's *Firebird* (*L'Oiseau de Feu,* 1910), *Petrushka* (1911), *Sacre du printemps* (provoking a famous riot, 1913), Ravel's *Daphnis et Chloë* (1912), Debussy's *L'après-midi d'un faune* (1912), etc.

Di•ag•o•ras \dī-ˈag-ə-rəs\. *Called* the Atheist. 5th century B.C. Greek Sophist and poet. Writer of hymns and dithyrambs; took refuge in Corinth when condemned to death by the Athenians for impiety.

Diagoras of Rhodes \ˈrōdz\. 5th century B.C. Greek athlete. Four times victor in Olympic games; his victory in boxing at 7th Olympian games (464 B.C.) was celebrated in a poem by Pindar.

Dia•man•te \dyä-ˈmän-tā\, Juan Bautista. 1625–1687. Spanish dramatist. Author of *El Honrador de su padre* (1657) based on Corneille's *Le Cid,* etc.

Diane de France \dyán-də-frä^{n}s\. Duchesse de Mont•mo•ren•cy et An•gou•lême \də-mō^{n}-mò-rä^{n}-sē-ā-ä^{n}-gü-lem\. 1538–1619. French noblewoman. Natural daughter (legitimized 1547) of King Henry II of France. m. 1st Orazio Farnese, son of Duke of Parma (1553), 2d François de Montmorency (1559); noted for beauty and culture, politically influential in courts of Henry III and Henry IV of France.

Diane de Poi•tiers \-də-pwà-tyā\. Duchesse de Va•len•ti•nois \də-vá-lä^{n}-tē^{n}-wà\. 1499–1566. Mistress of Henry II of France. m. Comte de Maulevrier, grand seneschal of Normandy (d. 1531). Became mistress of Henry while he was still dauphin (1536); had great influence over him during entire reign (1547–59), supplanting in all but name his queen, Catherine de Médicis.

Dias, Antônio Gonçalves. See GONÇALVES DIAS.

Di•as \ˈdē-əsh\, Bartolomeu. c.1450–1500. Portuguese navigator. Chosen by King John II to lead a voyage around Africa, continuing previous Portuguese discoveries; with two vessels sailed south (1487–88) beyond farthest point reached by Diogo Cão and beyond tip of Africa (1488); reached Algoa Bay; turned back and sighted (May 1488) cape which he may have called Cabo Tormentoso ("Cape of Storms"), either later renamed by King John or, probably, originally named by Dias Cabo da Bõa Esperança ("Cape of Good Hope"); accompanied Vasco da Gama as far as Cape Verde Islands (1497); commanded a ship (1500) in Cabral's fleet to Brazil; perished in a storm.

Dias, Dinís. 15th century. Portuguese navigator. Leader of expedition that discovered Cape Verde (1444).

Di•as \ˈdē-ás\, Henrique. 1600?–1662. Brazilian soldier. Of free Negro ancestry; fought with Portuguese against Dutch (1633); promoted commander in chief of Negro forces; led rebellion against Spaniards (1645); aided in recovery of Recife (1654). His name still given to Brazilian regiment under Negro command.

Di•as de No•vais \ˈdē-əsh-thə-ˈnō-ˌvīsh, -də-\, Paulo. d. 1589. Portuguese official. Grandson of Bartolomeu Dias. Appointed governor of Angola colony (1571); founded (1576) São Paulo de Luanda, first European city in southern Africa.

Diavolo, Fra. See Michele PEZZA.

Dí•az \ˈdē-äs\, Adolfo. 1874–1964. Nicaraguan politician. Provisional president (May–Oct. 1911); suppressed President Luis Mena's revolt; elected president (1913–17); with General Emiliano Chamorro Vargas seized power by coup d'état (1925); again president (1926–28) after Chamorro's resignation and flight; appealed for aid against rebels under Sacasa and Sandino to U.S., which sent marines.

Di•az \ˈdē-äts\, Armando. 1861–1928. Italian general. Served in Italo–Turkish War (1911–12); major general (1914), helped reorganize army; commanded armored corps (1916–17); replaced Luigi Cadorna as chief of staff (1917); organized defense against Austrian offensive; defeated Austrians at Vittorio Veneto (1918); created (1920) marshal of Italy and Du•ca del•la Vit•to•ria \ˈdü-kä-ˌdāl-lä-vēt-ˈtòr-yä\ (1921); minister of war (1922–24).

Dí•az \ˈdē-äs\, Porfirio, *in full* José de la Cruz Porfirio. 1830–1915. Mexican general and politician. Distinguished as soldier in war with U.S. (1846–48), War of the Reform (1857–60) in support of Juárez, and struggle against French (1861–67). Unsuccessful candidate for president against Juárez (1871); overthrew Lerdo de Tejada (1876). Elected president (1877–80); again president (1884–1911); his administrations marked by peace, material prosperity, and foreign investments, but also by dictatorial methods, with little improvement in the condition of the masses; finally forced to resign (1911) in revolt led by Francisco Madero; died in exile in Paris.

Di•az de La Pe•ña \dyàz-də-lá-pān-yà\, Narcisse-Virgile. 1808–1876. French landscape painter. Member of Barbizon school; known esp. for his scenes from forest of Fontainebleau. His son ¶Eugène (1837–1901) was a composer; works included comic opera *Le Roi Candaule* (1865) and lyric drama *Benvenuto Cellini* (1890).

Dí•az del Cas•til•lo \ˈdē-äth-thel-käs-ˈtē(l)-yō\, Bernal. 1492–?1581. Spanish soldier and historian. To Darien (1514) under Pedrarias; to Yucatán with Córdoba (1517); with Cortés during conquest of Mexico (1519–21). Known esp. for *Historia verdadera de la conquista de la Nueva España* (1632), an eyewitness account of the conquest of Mexico and an attack on the history of Francisco López de Gómara, chaplain to Cortés.

Díaz de So•lís \-thā-sō-ˈlēs\, Juan. 1470?–1516. Spanish navigator. Made two voyages with Vicente Yáñez Pinzón along Atlantic coast of South America (1499–1500, 1508–09); named chief pilot of Spain on death of Vespucci (1512); made voyage to South America (1515–16), being one of first explorers to enter Río de la Plata estuary; sailed up the Uruguay River; upon landing was ambushed and killed by Charrúa Indians.

Díaz de Vi•var \-thā-bē-ˈvär\, Rodrigo. *Known as* El Cid \el-ˈthēth\. c.1043–1099. Spanish military leader. Named commander of royal troops on accession of Sancho II of Castile (1065); prominent in Sancho's war on Alfonso VI of León (1067–72); m. (1074) Jimena, daughter of Count of Oviedo and niece of Alfonso; for king of Seville defeated army of Granada under Count Garcia Ordoñez, a favorite of Alfonso (1079); led unauthorized raid on kingdom of Toledo (1081), for which he was banished by Alfonso. Served Muslim kings of Saragossa (1081–90), winning victories over king of Lérida (1082), King Sancho Ramírez of Aragon (1084). Recalled (1087) by Alfonso to help repel Almoravid invasion, but took no part. At culmination of complex political and military maneuvering, besieged Valencia (1093–94) and assumed chief magistracy of Muslim government of Valencia (1094); invited Jerome, a French bishop, to newly Christianized realm (1096) and encouraged Christian colonization. Soon after his death Valencia fell to Almoravids (1102). El Cid became national hero of Castile and subject of many legends, epics, etc., as the 12th century Castilian *El cantar de mío Cid.*

Dí•az Or•daz \ˈdē-äs-òr-thäs\, Gustavo. 1911–1979. Mexican politician. Senator (1946–52); minister of interior (1958–63); president of Mexico (1964–70); ambassador to Spain (1977).

Dib•din \ˈdib-ˌdin\, Charles. 1745–1814. English dramatist, actor, and composer. Produced own operetta *The Shepherd's Artifice* at Covent Garden (1764), followed by *The Padlock* (1768), *The Waterman* (1774), and *The Quaker* (1775); named composer to Covent Garden (1778); managed Royal Circus

(1782–84); staged opera *Liberty Hall* (1785); later produced one-man "table entertainments" for which he wrote many of his sea songs, including "Blow high, blow low," "'Twas in the good ship Rover," "To Bachelors' Hall," "Poor Jack," and "Tom Bowling"; said to have written upwards of 1400 songs and 100 dramatic pieces. His son ¶Charles (1768–1833) was an acting manager of Sadler's Wells Theatre and a dramatist and composer of songs; works included *Goody Two-Shoes, The Farmer's Wife.* Another son ¶Thomas John (1771–1841) had his *Jew and the Doctor* produced at Covent Garden (1798–99); wrote *The British Raft,* containing "The Snug Little Island" (1797); produced his best opera, *The Cabinet* (1801–02); wrote pantomimes, including *Mother Goose* (1807), *The High-Mettled Racer* (1812); said to have written 2000 songs and 200 operas and plays.

Dibdin, Thomas Frognall. 1776–1847. English bibliographer. Nephew of the elder Charles Dibdin. Took orders (1804); with *Introduction to the Knowledge of Rare and Valuable Editions of the Greek and Roman Classics* (1802) gained attention of third Earl of Spencer, who employed him to catalogue library at Althorp; other works included *Bibliomania* (1809), *Bibliotheca Spenceriana* (1814–15), *Bibliographical Decameron* (1817), *A Bibliographical, Antiquarian, and Picturesque Tour* (1821).

Di·be·li·us \di-ˈbā-lē-u̇s\, Martin. 1883–1947. German theologian. Professor, Heidelberg (from 1915); specialized in literature, oral traditions, and history of early Christianity; author of *Die Formgeschichte des Evangeliums* (1919), *Geschichte der urchristlichen Literatur* (1926).

Dibich-Zabalkansky, Ivan. See Hans DIEBITSCH.

Di·cae·ar·chus \ˌdī-sē-ˈär-kəs\. fl. c.320 B.C. Greek Peripatetic philosopher, historian, and geographer. Disciple of Aristotle; wrote *Bios Hellados,* history of Greek civilization; only titles and a few fragments of his works are extant.

Di·cey \ˈdī-sē\, Albert Venn. 1835–1922. English jurist. Taught at Oxford (1882–1909); principal of Working Men's College, London (1899–1912); author of *Lectures Introductory to the Study of the Law of the Constitution* (1885, a standard work now considered part of the British constitution), *England's Case Against Home Rule* (1886), *Digest of the Law of England with Reference to the Conflict of Laws* (1896), *Lectures on the Relation Between Law and Public Opinion* (1905). His brother ¶Edward James Stephen (1832–1911) was a journalist; editor of London *Observer* (1870–89). Author of *England and Egypt* (1884) and *Bulgaria, the Peasant State* (1895).

Dick \ˈdik\, George Frederick. 1881–1967. American physician, b. Fort Wayne, Ind. Professor, Rush Medical Coll. (1918–33), professor and head of department of medicine, U. of Chicago (1933–45). With his wife, isolated (1923) the bacterium of, and originated a serum for, scarlet fever; also devised Dick test to determine susceptibility to scarlet fever. His wife (m. 1914) ¶Gladys, *nee* Hen·ry \ˈhen-rē\ (1881–1963), b. Pawnee City, Neb.; associated with McCormick Institute for Infectious Diseases (1914–36).

Dick·ens \ˈdik-ənz\, Charles John Huffam. 1812–1870. English novelist. Passed childhood of hardships, including work as drudge at a blacking factory (1824), and humiliations, including father's imprisonment for debt (1824); little formal education; shorthand reporter of House of Commons debates for the *True Sun,* the *Mirror of Parliament,* and (1834–36) *Morning Chronicle.* Under pen name Boz \ˈbäz\, contributed to periodicals fictional sketches which were collected and published as *Sketches by Boz* (1836); first editor of *Bentley's Miscellany* (1837). Toured America (1842); advocated international copyright and abolition of slavery; published *American Notes* (1842); lived in Italy (1844–45) and Switzerland (1846); managed theatrical company which toured English provinces (1847–52); started weekly journal *Household Words* (1850), succeeded by *All the Year Round* (1859); began giving extremely popular public readings from his works (1858); reading tour in America (1867–68). Chief works (most serialized before book publication): *Posthumous Papers of the Pickwick Club,* usually called *Pickwick Papers* (1836–37), *Oliver Twist* (1837–39), *Nicholas Nickleby* (1838–39), *Old Curiosity Shop* (1840–41), *Barnaby Rudge* (1841), *Martin Chuzzlewit* (1843–44), *A Christmas Carol* (1843), *The Chimes* (1845), *The Cricket on the Hearth* (1845), *Dombey and Son* (1846–48), *David Copperfield* (1849–50), *Bleak House* (1852–53), *Hard Times* (1854), *Little Dorrit* (1855–57), *A Tale of Two Cities* (1859), *Great Expectations* (1860–61), *Our Mutual Friend* (1864–65), *Mystery of Edwin Drood* (incomplete, 1870). Chief illustrators of his works: George Cruikshank (*Sketches by Boz, Oliver Twist*); Hablot Knight Browne, called "Phiz" (*Pickwick, Chuzzlewit, Copperfield, Bleak House,* and others); John Leech; Marcus Stone (*Great Expectations, Our Mutual Friend*).

Dick·er·son \ˈdik-ər-sən\, Mahlon. 1770–1853. American politician, b. Hanover Neck, N.J. Governor of New Jersey (1815–17); U.S. senator (1817–33); U.S. secretary of the navy (1834–38).

Dick·in·son \ˈdik-ən-sən\, Anna Elizabeth. 1842–1932. American lecturer, b. Philadelphia. Lectured for woman suffrage, labor reform; campaigned for Republican party; noted for vituperation.

Dickinson, Clarence. 1873–1969. American organist and composer, b. Lafayette, Ind. Professor of sacred music, Union Theol. Sem. (1912–45); author of *Sacred Choruses, Sacred Solos,* symphony *Storm King* (1919), comic opera *The Medicine Man* (1895), etc.

Dickinson, Emily Elizabeth. 1830–1886. American poet, b. Amherst, Mass. Passed virtually entire life, increasingly reclusive, in family home; began writing poems in 1850s but published only seven in her lifetime; six volumes of her poems were published after her death, in 1890, 1891, 1896, 1914, 1929, 1935, 1945, establishing her as one of the great American poets.

Dickinson, Goldsworthy Lowes. 1862–1932. English historian and essayist. Lecturer at Cambridge (1896–1920); author of *From King to King* (1891), *The Greek View of Life* (1896), *The Meaning of Good* (1901), *Justice and Liberty* (1908), *Religion and Immortality* (1911), *The European Anarchy* (1916), *War: its Nature, Cause and Cure* (1923), etc.

Dickinson, John. 1732–1808. American politician, b. Talbot Co., Md. Called "the penman of the Revolution." Practiced law, Philadelphia (1757–60). Member, Stamp Act Congress (1765); wrote influential *Letters from a farmer in Pennsylvania, to the Inhabitants of the British Colonies* (1767–68); member, Continental Congress (1774–76); principal author of "Declaration...Setting Forth the Causes and Necessity of Their Taking Up Arms" (1775); helped draft Articles of Confederation (1776); voted against Declaration of Independence, but served for a time in Continental army. Again in Continental Congress (1779, 1780). President of Delaware (1781); delegate from Delaware to Constitutional Convention (1787); published a series of letters, signed "Fabius," urging adoption of Constitution. His brother ¶Philemon (1739–1809) was major general and commander in chief of the New Jersey militia in the Revolutionary War, defeating raiding expedition by Cornwallis's troops (1777), retarding British retreat toward New York before battle of Monmouth (1778), and conducting an attack at battle of Springfield (1780). He was a member, from Delaware, of the Continental Congress (1782–83); U.S. senator (1790–93).

Dickinson, Jonathan. 1688–1747. American clergyman and educator, b. Hatfield, Mass. Leading theologian and moderator of Presbyterianism. Obtained charter for College of New Jersey, now Princeton U. (1746); served as its first president (1747).

Dick·man \ˈdik-mən\, Joseph Theodore. 1857–1927. American army officer, b. Dayton, Ohio. Commanded 3d Infantry Division in France (1917–18), IV Corps and then I Corps (1918), Third Army (in occupied Germany, 1918–19).

Dick-Read \ˈdik-ˈrēd\, Grantly. 1890–1959. British obstetrician. Author of *Natural Childbirth* (1933; called *Childbirth Without Fear* in later editions).

Dick·see \ˈdik-sē\, Sir Francis Bernard, *known as* Frank. 1853–1928. English painter. Known for medieval subjects and portraits; president of Royal Academy (1924–28).

Dick·son \ˈdik-sən\, Leonard Eugene. 1874–1954. American mathematician, b. Independence, Iowa. Taught at U. of Chicago (1900–39); noted for work in theory of numbers and theory of groups. Author of *Linear Algebras* (1914), *History of the Theory of Numbers* (1919–23), *Studies in the Theory of Numbers* (1930), etc.

Dickson, Samuel Henry. 1798–1872. American physician, b. Charleston, S.C. Founder (1833) and professor (1833–47, 1851–58), Medical Coll. of South Carolina; professor, Jefferson Medical Coll., Philadelphia (1858–72).

Dic·tys Cre·ten·sis \ˈdik-təs-kri-ˈten(t)-səs\, *i.e.* the Cretan. Supposed author of a diary of the Trojan War, one of chief sources in medieval times for story of the Trojan War. The diary appears as *Ephemeris belli Trojani,* a 4th-century A.D. Latin version of a supposed Greek original. Cf. DARES PHRYGIUS.

Di·cuil \ˈdē-ˌkyül\. fl. 825. Irish monk and scholar. Author of *De mensura orbis terrae* (825).

Di·de·lot \dēd(-ə)-lō\, Charles-Louis. 1767–1837. French dancer and choreographer. Principal dancer and ballet master, Imperial Theater and School, St. Petersburg (1801–11); created ballets *Flore et Zéphyre* (1796), *Apollon et Daphné* (1802), *Cupidon et Psyché* (1810), *Athis et Galathée* (1816), *Calife de Bagdad* (1818), *Prisonnier du Caucase* (1823); revolutionary teaching methods laid basis of St. Petersburg tradition.

Di·de·rot \dē-drō, *Angl* dē-ˈdrō, ˈdēd-ə-ˌrō\, Denis. *Nicknamed* Pan·to·phile \pän-tō-fēl\ Diderot. 1713–1784. French encyclopedist and philosopher. Worked as teacher and translator; published *Pensées philosophiques* (1746), *Les Bijoux indiscrets* (novel, 1748), *Lettre sur les aveugles* (1749); atheistic materialism of last earned him short prison term. Released to work with d'Alembert on the *Encyclopédie,* originally conceived by publisher as simple translation of Ephraim Chamber's encyclopedia but recast as a grand summation of rational knowledge; with d'Alembert (to 1758) and then alone labored 20 years at this task; aided by Voltaire, Montesquieu, Rousseau, Buffon, Turgot, Quesnay, and others; work published as *Encyclopédie, ou Dictionnaire Raisonné des Sciences, des Arts et des Métiers* (28 volumes,

1751–72), to which he contributed innumerable articles, esp. on philosophy, aesthetics, mechanics; *Encyclopédie* was a major force during the period of the Enlightenment. Other works included *Pensées sur l'interprétation de la nature* (1754), *Le Rêve de d'Alembert* (1769), *Eléments de physiologie* (1774–80); also novels *La Religieuse* (pub. 1796), *Jacques le fataliste* (pub. 1796), *Le Neveu de Rameau* (pub. 1821); stories; essays, including *Plan d'une université pour le gouvernement de Russie* for Catherine the Great (1773), *Essai sur les règnes de Claude et de Néron* (1778); plays *Le Fils naturel* (1757) and *Le Père de famille* (1758).

Did·i·us Ju·li·a·nus \'did-ē-əs-,jü-lē-'ā-nəs\ *or* **Didius Sal·vi·us** \'sal-vē-əs\ **Julianus,** Marcus. c.135–193. Roman emperor (193). Commanded legion at Mogontiacum (Mainz, c.167); later governor in Gaul, Africa, etc.; on death of Emperor Pertinax purchased imperial dignity at auction from Praetorian Guard; killed by invading Danube legions favoring Lucius Septimius Severus.

Di·dot \dē-dō\. Family of French printers and publishers, including: François (1689–1757), founder of family. His two sons ¶François-Ambroise (1730–1804), noted for many improvements in typefounding and printing and invention of a typographic point system, and ¶Pierre-François (1731–1793), founder of paper factory at Essonnes. Two sons of François-Ambroise ¶Pierre (1761–1853) and ¶Firmin (1764–1836), the former publisher of the lavish "Louvre" editions and the latter renowned as printer, engraver, typefounder, and introducer of stereotype in publishing less expensive editions. Pierre-François's son ¶Henri (1765–1852) published editions in microscopic types; a second son ¶Léger (1767–1829) invented a continuous paper-making machine.

Didymus. See THOMAS (the apostle).

Did·y·mus \'did-ə-məs\. *Surnamed* Chal·cen·ter·us \kal-'sen-tər-əs\, *i.e.* of the Brazen Guts. fl. c.80–10 B.C. Greek scholar. Taught in Alexandria and Rome; author of commentaries (only fragments extant) on Greek writers, grammatical and lexicographical works, etc., reputedly 3500 books in all.

Didymus of Alexandria. *Called* the Blind. c.313–c.398. Greek theologian. Blind from age of 4; became head of the catechetical school in Alexandria; extant works include *De Trinitate, De Spiritu Sancto, Adversus Manichaeos.*

Die·bitsch \'dē-,bich\, Hans Karl Friedrich Anton von. Count. *Russ.* Count Ivan Ivanovich Di·bich-Za·bal·kan·sky \'dyē-bich-zə-(,)bəl-'kän-skəi\. 1785–1831. German-born soldier in Russian service. Joined Russian army (1801); rose to major general in Napoleonic war (1805–14); adjutant general to Alexander I; chief of general staff (1824); in Russo–Turkish War (1828–29) commanded Russian forces in Europe; captured Varna (1828) and Silistra (1829); promoted to field marshal (1829); defeated Poles at Grochów and Ostrołenka (1831).

Die·fen·ba·ker \'dē-fən-,bā-kər\, John George. 1895–1979. Canadian politician, b. Grey County, Ont. Member of House of Commons (1940–79); leader of Progressive Conservative party (1956–67); prime minister (1957–63).

Dief·fen·bach \'dē-fən-,bäk\, Johann Friedrich. 1792–1847. German surgeon. Known for improvements in surgical technique, esp. in plastic surgery, tenotomy, and blood transfusion.

Diel·man \'dēl-mən\, Frederick. 1847–1935. American painter and illustrator, b. Hanover, Germany. To U.S. (1856). Designed mosaic panels *Law* and *History* in Library of Congress, Washington, D.C.

Diels \'dēls\, Otto Paul Hermann. 1876–1954. German chemist. Professor at Kiel (1916–45); discovered carbon suboxide (1906); awarded Nobel prize for chemistry (1950) with K. Alder for work on diene synthesis.

Die·men \'dē-mən\, Anthony van. 1593–1645. Dutch colonial. With Dutch East India Co. (from 1618); governor-general of Dutch East Indian colonies (1636–45); conquered Moluccas (1638–43) and thus established spice monopoly; conquered cinnamon-producing areas of Ceylon (1638–44); seized Malacca from Portuguese (1641), Formosa from Spanish (1642); established Dutch as principal power in East Indies; completed construction of Batavia (now Djakarta); dispatched expeditions under Tasman (1642) and Visscher (1644).

Dientz·en·ho·fer \'dēnt-sən-,hō-fər\, Christoph. 1655–1722. German architect. Leading exponent of Bohemian Baroque; works included church of St. Nikolaus (1703–11), Břevnov Monastery (1708–21) in Prague, Klarissinnenkirche (1707–11) in Essen. His brothers ¶Georg (1643–1689), ¶Johann (1663–1726), and ¶Johann Leonhard (1660–1707) were also architects of note. His son ¶Kilian Ignaz (1689–1751) was his student and collaborator; worked on St. Nikolaus (1703–11, 1732–51), St. Thomas (1725–31), St. Johann am Felsen (1730–39) in Prague, St. Maria Magdalena (1733–36) in Karlsbad, etc.

Dierx \dyerks\, Léon. 1838–1912. French poet. One of the Parnassians; published *Aspirations* (1858), *Les Lèvres closes* (1867), *Les Amants* (1879).

Dies \'dīz\, Martin. 1900–1972. American politician, b. Colorado, Texas. Member, U.S. Congress (1931–45, 1953–59). Established (1938) and named chairman of House committee investigating un-American activities.

Dies·bach \'dēs-,bäk\, Niklaus von. 1435–1475. Swiss political leader. Chief magistrate of Bern (1465–66, 1474–75); secured treaties of mutual defense with Louis XI of France (1470, 1474); persuaded Bern Assembly to declare war on Burgundy (1474); led Bernese forces in assault on Pontarlier (1475).

Die·sel \'dē-zəl\, Rudolf. 1858–1913. German mechanical engineer. Trained as refrigeration engineer; began work on pressure-ignited internal combustion engine (1885); received German patents (1892, 1893); in association with the firm of Friedrich Krupp in Essen and the Augsburg-Nürnberg machine factory, built the first successful Diesel engine (1896); license fees on Diesel engine soon made him millionaire; noted also as social theorist.

Dies·kau \'dēs-,kaù\, Ludwig August. 1701–1767. German general in the French service. Commanded French troops against the British in Canada (1755).

Die·ster·weg \'dē-stər-,vāk\, Friedrich Adolf Wilhelm. 1790–1866. German educator. Introduced Pestalozzi's ideas and methods into Germany, revolutionizing its school system; head of Berlin state school seminary (1832–50).

Dietmar. See THIETMAR.

Dietrich *or* **Dietrich von Bern.** See THEODORIC the Great.

Die·trich \'dē-trik\, Albert Hermann. 1829–1908. German composer. Wrote an opera *Robin Hood* (1879), a symphony, chamber music, and choral works.

Dietrich *or* **Die·tri·ci** *or* **Die·tri·cy** \dē-'trit-sē\, Christian Wilhelm Ernst. 1712–1774. German landscape painter and engraver. Court painter to Augustus III in Dresden (from 1741); noted as an imitator of others.

Die·trich·son \'dē-trēk-sòn\, Lorentz Henrik Segelcke. 1834–1917. Norwegian historian of art and literature. Works included *Omrids af den norske poesies historie* (1866–69), *De norske stavkirker* (1892), *Die Holzbaukunst Norwegens* (with Munthe, 1893).

Dietrich von Nie·heim \-fòn-'nē-,hīm\ *or* **Ni·em** \-'nē-əm\ *or* **Ny·em** \-'nē-əm\. 1340–1418. German historian and church official. Officer in papal chancery in Avignon (1370) and later in Rome (1376); bishop of Verden (1395–1401); member of Council of Constance (1414); known as publicist of Western schism. Author of *Nemus Unionis* (1408), *De Scismate libri tres* (1410), *Dialog über Union und Reform der Kirche* (1410), *Avisamenta* (1414).

Dietz \'dēts\, Howard. 1896–1983. American lyricist, b. New York City. Prolific songwriter who wrote the lyrics to more than 500 songs, including "Dancing in the Dark," "That's Entertainment," "You and the Night and the Music." Collaborated with George Gershwin, Jerome Kern, and Arthur Schwartz; with Schwartz created *The Little Show* (1929) and *The Band Wagon* (1931); wrote English adaptations of *Die Fledermaus* (1950) and *La Bohème* (1952).

Dietz, Johann Christian. 1773–1849. German engineer. Invented melodion (1805) and claviharp (1814).

Diet·zen·schmidt \'dēt-sən-,shmit\, Anton Franz. *Orig. surname* Schmidt. 1893–1955. German playwright, novelist, and critic. Dramatic critic, *Berliner Tageblatt.* Author of *Kleine Sklavin* (1918), *Christopher* (1920), *Vom lieben Augustin* (1925), *Hinterhauslegende* (1928), etc.

Dietz·gen \'dēts-gən\, Joseph. 1828–1888. German Socialist. To U.S. following revolution of 1848; visited Russia (1863–69); known as "philosopher of the proletariat" for interpretations of Marxism; author of *Acquisit der Philosophie* (1895), *Die Religion der Sozialdemokratie* (1895).

Dieu·don·né d'Ar·tois \dyœ̄-dò-nā-dàr-twà\, Henri-Charles-Ferdinand-Marie. Comte de Chambord. Duc de Bordeaux. 1820–1883. French nobleman. Son of Charles-Ferdinand, duc de Berry; fled France on assumption of throne by Louis-Philippe (1830); lived in Austria; as last Bourbon heir, proclaimed king of France as Henri V by Legitimist party on death of exiled Charles X (1836); on fall of Napoléon III (1870) issued call for France to unite under Bourbon restoration; motion for restoration defeated in National Assembly (1874).

Dieu·la·foy \dyœ̄-làf-wä\, Marcel-Auguste. 1844–1920. French archaeologist and engineer. Excavated palaces of Darius I and of Artaxerxes II (1885), bringing back architectural specimens now in the Louvre; author of *L'Art antique de la Perse* (1884–89), *L'Acropole de Suse* (1890–92), etc. His wife (m. 1870) ¶Jeanne-Paule-Henriette-Rachel, *nee* Ma·gre \màgrᵊ\ (1851–1916), went on his expeditions; discovered ruins of a 12th-century mosque at Hasan, Morocco; author of works esp. on archaeological expeditions, including *La Perse, la Chaldée et la Susiane* (1887), *Suse, journal des fouilles* (1888).

Diez \'dēts\, Friedrich Christian. 1794–1876. German philologist. Founder of Romance philology; professor, Bonn (from 1823). Notable works included *Die Poesie der Troubadours* (1826), *Grammatik der romanischen Sprachen* (1836–43), *Etymologisches Wörterbuch der romanischen Sprachen* (1853).

Dig·by \'dig-bē\, John. 1st Earl of Bris·tol \'bris-tᵊl\. 1580–1653. English diplomat. Ambassador of James I in negotiations (1611–24) for a Spanish marriage, first for James's son Henry, and after Henry's death, for Charles (later Charles I); offended Prince Charles and Buckingham in Madrid (1623); censured for his conduct of Spanish negotiations; confined in Tower (1626–28); charge against him dismissed; restored to seat in House of Lords; favored acceptance by king of Petition of Right (1628); commissioner to treat with rebellious Scots (1640); distrusted by parliamentary party, dismissed from public office (1643); went into exile at Caen, France (1646). His son ¶George (1612–1677), 2d earl; became adviser to Charles I (1641); fled to Holland after urging arrest of Pym and four fellow members of Parliament (1642); on return became secretary of state (1643); as lieutenant general of king's forces north of Trent, was defeated at Sherburn (1645); fled to Ireland and thence to France; secretary of state to Charles II in exile at Bruges (1657–58) but forced to resign because of turning Catholic; welcomed at court only on expulsion of Clarendon (1667).

Digby, Sir Kenelm. 1603–1665. English courtier, author, naval commander, and diplomat. Joined household of Prince Charles (1623); made privateering expedition, defeating French and Venetian ships in Scanderoon (Iskenderun) harbor (1628); professed Protestantism (from 1630). After his wife's death (1633) retired to Gresham Coll., London, to experiment with chemistry; announced reconversion to Catholicism (1636); one of Queen Henrietta Maria's entourage; solicited money for support of king's Scottish expedition (1640); imprisoned by Parliament (1642–43); in Paris published *Of the Nature of Bodies* and *Of the Nature of Mans soule* (1644); named queen's chancellor (1644); supported king's cause in Civil War and pleaded Charles's cause with Pope Innocent X; banished for a time (1649–54); engaged by Cromwell in diplomatic business (1656). One of first members of Royal Society (1663); after banishment from court (1664) spent time in literary and scientific pursuits; said to have discovered necessity of oxygen to plant life.

His father ¶Sir Everard Digby (1578–1606) came into a large estate (1592), turned Roman Catholic (1599); joining conspirators in the Gunpowder Plot (1605), accepted assignment of inciting a rising in Midlands; deserted his companions in flight; executed.

Digby, Kenelm Henry. 1800–1880. English writer. Author of *The Broadstone of Honour* (1822), a survey of medieval customs, enlarged (1826–27) and published in 4 vols., entitled *Godefridus, Tancredus, Morus,* and *Orlandus; Mores Catholici* (1831–40); *The Lovers Seat* (1856); *Halcyon Hours* (1870); *Ouranogaia* (1871); etc.

Digges \'digz\, Leonard. d. 1571? English mathematician. Experimented with magnifying effects from combinations of lenses, and was said to have anticipated invention of the telescope. His son ¶Thomas (d. 1595) was also a mathematician; M.P. (1582, 1585); mustermaster general of English forces in Netherlands (1586–94); published his father's mathematical treatises; author of works on applied mathematics and military engineering. ¶Sir Dudley (1583–1639), son of Thomas, was a diplomat and judge; M.P. (1610, 1614, 1621, 1624–26, 1628); ambassador in Russia (1618); opened case for impeachment of Buckingham (1626); master of the rolls (1636); joint author with his father of *Four Paradoxes or Politique Discourses* (1604).

Di Gia·co·mo \dē-'jäk-ō-(,)mō\, Salvatore. 1860–1934. Italian writer. Author of novels, dramatic works, poems, and histories of Naples and Neapolitan life; verse included *Sonetti* (1884), *Ariette e sunette* (1898), *Canzoni* (1916).

Dig·nā·ga \dig-'näg-ä\ *or* **Din·nā·ga** \din-\. 5th century. Buddhist philosopher. Noted for contributions to logic; wrote *Pramāṇasamuccaya.*

Dikran. See TIGRANES.

Diliyiánnis. See DHILIYIÁNNIS.

Dilke \'dilk\, Charles Wentworth. 1789–1864. English critic and antiquary. Continued Dodsley's *Old Plays* (6 vols., 1814–16); edited *Athenaeum* (1830–46); manager of *Daily News* (1846–49); wrote many articles on Pope, Burke, Wilkes, the Junius letters, etc. His son ¶Sir Charles Wentworth (1810–1869) was one of proposers and one of executive committee of the (London) International Exhibition of 1851; created baronet (1862). The latter's son ¶Sir Charles Wentworth, 2d Baronet Dilke (1843–1911), wrote of his travels round the world in *Greater Britain* (1868); M.P. (1868–86), saw no incompatibility between his imperialism and extreme radicalism; undersecretary for foreign affairs (1880–82); president of local government board under Gladstone (1882–85); chairman of royal commission on housing of working classes; supported acts legalizing position of trades unions and shortening hours of labor; sought legislation to secure a minimum wage and representation of labor in House of Commons; instrumental in passage of Redistribution bill (1885); career interrupted when he was cited as correspondent in a divorce case; again M.P. (1892–1911).

Dill \'dil\, Sir John Greer. 1881–1944. British soldier. Entered army (1901); promoted through grades to rank of general (1939); served in South Africa (1901–02), in World War I (1914–18); director of military operations and intelligence (1935–36); commander, 1st army corps, France (1939–40); chief of imperial general staff (1940–41); chief British representative on Anglo-American board of strategy (1941–44).

Dil·le·ni·us \di-'lā-nē-ùs, *Angl* di-'lē-nē-əs\, Johann Jakob. 1687–1747. German botanist in England. To England (1721); first professor of botany at Oxford (1728–47); author of *Catalogus Plantarum circa Gissam sponte nascentium* (1718), *Hortus Elthamensis* (1732), *Historia Muscorum* (1741).

Dil·lin·ger \'dil-ən-jər\, John. 1902–1934. American outlaw, b. Indianapolis. Known for bank robberies and daring jail escapes; named "public enemy number one" by FBI (1933); betrayed by "Lady in Red" and ambushed by FBI agents in Chicago.

Dil·ling·ham \'dil-iŋ-,ham, -əm\, Charles Bancroft. 1868–1934. American theatrical manager, b. Hartford, Conn. Manager of Globe Theatre in New York (1910–34), of the Hippodrome (1914–23); partner of A. L. Erlanger in other theaters.

Dillingham, William Paul. 1843–1923. American politician, b. Waterbury, Vt. Governor of Vermont (1888–90); U.S. senator (1900–23); favored quota system in limiting immigration, embodied in Dillingham Bill (enacted May 1921).

Dill·mann \'dil-,män\, August, *in full* Christian Friedrich August. 1823–1894. German theologian and Oriental scholar. Professor at Kiel (1854–64), Giessen (1864–69), Berlin (1869–94); chief work *Lexicon linguae aethiopicae* (1862–63).

Dil·lon \'dil-ən\. Name of an Irish family of royalists and Jacobites that provided a number of military officers in foreign service: Sir James Dillon (c.1580–after 1667), 8th son of Theobald, 1st Viscount Dillon, was M.P. (1639–42); governor of Athlone and Connaught; participant in Leinster revolt (1652); brigadier general in service of Spain and the Fronde. ¶Arthur (1670–1733), son of 7th Viscount Dillon, became colonel (1690) of a Jacobite regiment raised by his father for service under Louis XIV; brigadier (1702), lieutenant general (1707); distinguished himself at Toulon (1707), Briançon (1709), Kaiserslautern (1713), Barcelona (1714); Old Pretender's agent in Paris. His youngest son ¶Arthur Richard (1721–1806) was bishop of Évreux (1753), archbishop of Toulouse (1758), archbishop of Narbonne and primate of the Gauls (1763); member of Assembly of Notables (1787–88); migrated to Coblenz (1790). ¶Arthur Richard (1750–1794), son of 11th Viscount Dillon and grandson of Arthur Dillon (1670–1733), was in service of Louis XV, deputy for Martinique in National Assembly, Jacobin general in Argonne (1792); guillotined.

Dillon, Emile Joseph. 1854–1933. British journalist, b. Ireland. Special correspondent of London *Daily Telegraph,* from Armenia, Spain, Crete, Russia, France, China (1887–1914); noted for linguistic ability and daring journalistic exploits; author of *Maxim Gorky* (1902), *A Scrap of Paper* (1914), *Ourselves and Germany* (1916), *The Peace Conference* (1920), *Russia Today and Yesterday* (1929).

Dillon, George Hill. 1906–1968. American poet, b. Jacksonville, Fla. Editor of magazine *Poetry* (1937–49); author of *Boy in the Wind* (1927), *The Flowering Stone* (1931, Pulitzer prize); with Edna Millay did verse translation of Baudelaire's *Les Fleurs du mal* (1935).

Dillon, John. 1851–1927. Irish Nationalist politician. Supporter of Parnell (1879–c.1890); M.P. (1880–83, 1885–1918); violence of his attacks on government caused his imprisonment on several occasions. Chairman, anti-Parnellite Irish Nationalist Federation (from 1896); associated with Redmond (1900–18) in direction of policies of reunified Irish Nationalist party and, on Redmond's death (1918), succeeded to the chairmanship; vigorously supported government during World War I, aided recruiting, but opposed extension of conscription to Ireland. With rise of Sinn Féin, he was defeated in parliamentary election (1918) by Eamon De Valera. His father ¶John Blake Dillon (1816–1866), also a politician, founded (1842) with T. O. Davis and C. G. Duffy, *The Nation,* organ of the Young Ireland party.

Dillon, Wentworth. 4th Earl of Roscommon. 1633?–1685. British poet, b. Ireland. Made translations of Horace, Virgil; wrote *Essay on Translated Verse* (1684); first critic to praise *Paradise Lost.*

Dil·ly \'dil-ē\, Charles. 1739–1807. English bookseller. Liberal entertainer of writers; publisher of Boswell's *Tour to the Hebrides* (1780), *Life of Johnson* (1791).

Dil·they \'dil-(,)tī\, Wilhelm. 1833–1911. German philosopher. Professor at Basel (1866–68), Kiel (1868–71), Breslau (1871–82), Berlin (1882–1911); noted for attempt to develop methodology for humanities free of influence of natural sciences; works included *Einleitung in die Geisteswissenschaften* (1883), *Das Erlebnis und die Dichtung* (1905), *Der Aufbau der geschichtlichen Welt in den Geisteswissenschaften* (1910).

Dimitri. See DMITRY.

Di·mi·tri·ev \di-'mē-trē-,ef\, Radko. 1859–1918. Bulgarian soldier. Took part in overthrow of Prince Alexander (1886); in Russian service thereafter; served in Balkan wars, World War I.

Di·mi·tri·je·vić \dē-'mē-trē-yev-,ēt^y\, Dragutin. *Known as* Apis \ä-'pēs\ *i.e.* the Bee. 1876–1917. Serbian soldier and intriguer. One of plotters of assassination of King Alexander Obrenović (1903). A founder of secret society Crna Ruka (Black Hand) to strive for union of all southern Slavs; engaged in irregular warfare in Macedonia and in anti-Austrian movement in Bosnia. Chief of intelligence, Serbian general staff (1913); believed to have helped plan murder of Archduke Francis Ferdinand at Sarajevo (1914); later arrested, condemned, and shot.

Di·mi·trov \di-'mē-,tròf\, Georgi Mikhailovich. 1882–1949. Bulgarian Communist leader. Socialist member of parliament (1913–18); helped form

Bulgarian Communist party (1919); elected to executive committee of Comintern (1921); exiled (1923) after leading uprising in Bulgaria; head of European section, Comintern, in Berlin (1929–33); accused with other Communists of plotting Reichstag fire (1933); won worldwide fame for brilliant defense against charge; Comintern secretary general in Moscow (1935–43); directed Bulgarian resistance to Nazi occupation (1944–45); head of Fatherland Front government (1945–46); first prime minister of Bulgarian People's Republic (1946–49).

Dinant, David of. See DAVID of Dinant.

Di·nar·chus *or* **Dei·nar·chus** \dī-'när-kəs\. 360?–after 292 B.C. Greek speech writer. Known esp. for prosecution speeches against Demosthenes, Aristogiton, Philocles (324); works thought to reflect decline of Attic oratory.

Dī·na·wa·rī, ad- \äd-ˌdē-nä-'wär-ē\, *in full* Abū Hanīfah Aḥmad ibn Dā'ūd al-Dīnawarī. c.815–c.895 or c.902. Persian astronomer, botanist, historian. Known for *al-Akhbār aṭ-ṭiwāl* (history of Persia) and fragments of *Kitāb an-nabāt* (on botany) and *Kitāb al-anwā'* (on astronomy).

d'Indy. See INDY.

Dines \'dīnz\, William Henry. 1855–1927. English meteorologist. Known for experimental studies of the upper air, wind force, and solar and terrestrial radiation; developed an anemometer.

Di·ne·sen \'dē-nə-sən, *Angl also* 'din-ə-\, Karen Christence. Baroness Blix·en-Fi·necke \'blēk-sən-'fē-nə-kə\. *Pen name* Isak Dinesen. 1885–1962. Danish writer. m. Baron Bror Blixen-Finecke (1914; div. 1921). Resided on coffee plantation in Kenya (1914–31). Author of *Seven Gothic Tales* (1934), *Out of Africa* (1937), *Winter's Tales* (1942), *Last Tales* (1957), *Shadows in the Grass* (1960).

Ding. See Jay Norwood DARLING.

Din·ga·ne \diŋ-'ä-ne\ *or* **Din·gaan** \'diŋ-gán\. d. 1840. Zulu chieftain. Succeeded his half-brother Shaka as king, having instigated his murder (1828); admitted Boers (1837); entered pact (1838) with Boer colonists in Natal under Piet Retief and treacherously massacred them; defeated by Andries Pretorius (1838); overthrown (1840) by his brother Mpande with help of Boers.

Ding·el·stedt \'diŋ-əl-ˌshtet\, Franz Ferdinand von. Freiherr. 1814–1881. German writer and theater director. Director, Court Opera Theater (1867), Burgtheater (1870), Vienna. Member of the Young Germany literary movement and a master of political satire; author of *Die neuen Argonauten* (1839), *Lieder eines kosmopolitischen Nachtwächters* (1841), *Die Amazone* (1868), *Künstlergeschichten* (1877).

Din·gis·wa·yo \ˌdiŋ-(g)is-'wī-ō, -'wä-yō\. d. 1817. Bantu chieftain. Became chieftain of Mtetwa clan of North Nguni Bantus (1807); conquered some 30 neighboring peoples, creating rudimentary empire; initiated trade with Portuguese in Mozambique; chose Shaka as successor.

Din·gle \'diŋ-gəl\, Herbert. 1890–1978. English astrophysicist. Professor, U. Coll., London (1946–55). Author of *Relativity for All* (1922), *Modern Astrophysics* (1924), *Science and Human Experience* (1931), *Science and Literary Criticism* (1949), *The Scientific Adventure* (1952), etc.

Ding·ley \'diŋ-lē\, Nelson. 1832–1899. American politician, b. Durham, Me. Governor of Maine (1874–75); member, U.S. House of Representatives (1881–99); championed protective tariff; author of Dingley Tariff Act (1897).

Ding·ling·er \'diŋ-liŋ-ər\, Johann Melchior. 1664–1731. German goldsmith. Court goldsmith (1698) to August the Strong of Saxony; outstanding exponent of German Baroque design.

Dinh Bo Linh \'din-'bō-'lin\. *Royal name* Dinh Tien Hoang \-tē-'en-'hwäŋ\. d. 979. Vietnamese emperor. One of 12 chieftains, defeated others and gained control of Nam Viet (968), which he renamed Dai Co Viet; unified nation, created bureaucracy; secured independence from China.

Di·nis \dē-'nēsh\ *or* **Di·niz** \-'nēz(h)\. 1261–1325. King of Portugal (1279–1325). Son of Afonso III and father of Afonso IV; led rebellion against father (1277–79); m. (1283) Saint Elizabeth (*q.v.*), daughter of Peter III of Aragon; encouraged shipbuilding, agriculture, and commerce, earning sobriquet of Ré Lavrador ("farmer, or laborer, king"); founded universities of Lisbon (1290), Coimbra (1307).

Dinis da Cruz e Sil·va \-thə-'krü-zē-'sil-və\, António. 1731–1799. Portuguese poet. One of revivers of poetry of Portugal; associated in founding *Arcádia Lusitana* (1756); known esp. for his heroicomic epic *O hissope* (1770), *O falso heroismo* (1775); author also of lyric poems *Odes Pindáricas* (1801). Called "the Portuguese Pindar."

Din·nyés \'din-yāsh\, Lajos. 1901–1961. Hungarian politician. Member of Smallholders' party; minister of defense (1947); premier (1947–48); began expropriation of banks, religious schools, businesses, leading to Communist-dominated government.

Di·noc·ra·tes *or* **Dei·noc·ra·tes** \dī-'näk-rə-ˌtēz\. 4th century B.C. Greek architect. Designed for Alexander the Great the new city of Alexandria (c.330 B.C.) and built the funeral pyre of Hephaestion.

Din·ter \'din-tər\, Gustav Friedrich. 1760–1831. German theologian and educator. Professor at Königsberg (from 1822); author of *Schullehrerbibel* (1826–30).

Din·wid·die \din-'wid-ē, 'din-ˌ\, Robert. 1693–1770. British administrator in America, b. Scotland. Surveyor general for southern America (1738–51); lieutenant governor of Virginia (1751–58); sent out George Washington with detachment to protect Ohio region from seizure by French (1754); supplied Braddock's force with provisions for its campaign (1755); defended frontier as best he could after Braddock's defeat.

Dio Cas·si·us \'dī-ō-'kash(-ē)-əs, -'kas-ē-əs\ *or* **Di·on Cassius** \'dī-ˌän-\. *Surnamed* Coc·ce·ia·nus \ˌkäk-sē-'(y)ā-nəs\. c.150–235 A.D. Roman politician and historian. Entered Senate (180); consul (c.220, again 229 A.D.), proconsul of Africa (c.222); chief work *Romaika,* a history of Rome written in Greek.

Dio Chry·sos·tom \'dī-ˌō-kris-'äs-təm, -'kris-əs-təm\. *Lat.* Di·on Chry·sos·to·mus \'dī-ˌän-kris-'äs-tə-məs\. c.40–c.112 A.D. Greek rhetorician in Rome. Banished by Diocletian (82–96), during which time he adopted Cynic philosophy; favored by Nerva and Trajan; famed for orations, of which some 80 survive.

Di·o·cles \'dī-ə-ˌklēz\. 5th century B.C. Syracusan democratic statesman. Reputed drafter of new code of laws for Syracuse (411 B.C.).

Diocles. 1st century B.C.? Greek mathematician. Invented the cissoid in order to solve the Delian problem.

Diocles of Ca·rys·tus \kə-'ris-təs\. 4th century B.C. Greek physician. Considered second only to Hippocrates among Greek physicians; author of texts on animal anatomy, dietetics, embryology, medical botany, etc.

Di·o·cle·tian \ˌdī-ə-'klē-shən\. *Full name* Gaius Aurelius Valerius Di·o·cle·ti·a·nus \ˌdī-ə-ˌklē-shē-'ā-nəs\. 245 or 248–313 or 316. Roman emperor (284–305). Served in army; one of the commanders called by Carinus to fight the Persians; proclaimed emperor by the army (284) on death of Numerianus; fought Carinus in Moesia (285) and won full control of empire. Adopted (286) as colleague Maximian and established him in Milan; because of invasions and revolts in the empire, the joint emperors (known as *augusti*) chose (293) subordinate associates, Galerius and Constantius I Chlorus (known as *Caesars*); Diocletian was acknowledged as chief of the four rulers; kept Asia and Egypt as his administrative unit, with Nicomedia as capital. Adopted (287) surname "Jovius," calling Maximian "Herculius." Subdued revolt in Egypt (296); dispatched Galerius to defeat Narses of Persia (297); reformed and centralized civil administration of empire; reorganized and enlarged army; issued edict (301) in attempt to fix wages and prices, especially in interest of soldiers; although previously friendly to Christians, suddenly issued edict (303) against them, beginning terrible persecutions (303–313). Abdicated (305); retired to Salonae, Dalmatia, and engaged in gardening.

Di·o·da·ti \ˌdē-ə-'dät-ē\, Charles. 1608?–1638. English physician and scholar. Nephew of Giovanni Diodati. Known principally as friend of Milton; celebrated by Milton in two Latin elegies and an Italian sonnet, and lamented in *Epitaphium Damonis* (1645).

Diodati, Giovanni. 1576–1649. Swiss Protestant theologian. Published Italian translation of Bible (1607), and French translation (1644).

Di·o·dore \'dī-ə-ˌdōr, -ˌdȯr\ of Tarsus. c.330–c.390. Greek theologian. Bishop of Tarsus (378); leading theologian of Antioch school; declared standard of orthodoxy following Council of Constantinople (381); later condemned for Nestorianism and most writings lost. Teacher of John Chrysostom and Theodore of Mopsuestia.

Di·o·do·rus \ˌdī-ə-'dōr-əs, -'dȯr-\ of Tyre. 2d century B.C. Greek philosopher. Studied under Critolaus and succeeded him as head of Peripatetic school in Athens.

Diodorus Cro·nus \-'krō-nəs\. 4th century B.C. Greek philosopher of Megarian school. Known for work in formal logic.

Diodorus Sic·u·lus \-'sik-(y)ə-ləs\. 1st century B.C. Greek historian. Author of *Bibliotheca historica,* a universal history in 40 books of which only books I–V and XI–XX are extant.

Di·od·o·tus \dī-'äd-ət-əs\. Name of two rulers of Bactria: Diodotus I (d. c.239 B.C.), Seleucid satrap of Bactria; rebelled (c.255) against Antiochus II and took title of king. Succeeded by his son ¶Diodotus II (d. c.235 B.C.); made peace with Parthians but was slain by usurper Euthydemus.

Di·og·e·nes \dī-'äj-ə-ˌnēz\. d. c.320 B.C. Greek philosopher. Studied at Athens under Antisthenes. Rejected social conventions; lived life of voluntary poverty. Founded philosophy of the Cynics, advocating asceticism, self-sufficiency, freedom from convention, moral zeal. Subject of many legends, esp. that he once went through streets holding up a lantern, "looking for an honest man."

Diogenes of Apollonia. 5th century B.C. Greek philosopher. Promulgated cosmology in which air is source of being; cited by Aristotle on physiology; derided by Aristophanes in *Nephelai.*

Diogenes of Babylon. 2nd century B.C. Greek Stoic philosopher. Succeeded Zeno of Tarsus as head of Stoic school in Athens; brought Stoic thought to Rome (156–155 B.C.).

Diogenes La·er·tius \-lā-'ər-sh(ē-)əs\. 3d century A.D. Greek writer. Author of *Peri biōn dogmatōn kai apophthegmatōn tōn en philosophia eudokimēsantōn,* sole source of information about many Greek philosphers.

Di·o·ge·ni·a·nus \ˌdī-ə-ˌjē-nē-'ā-nəs\. 2nd century A.D. Greek grammarian. Author of a lexicon, a collection of proverbs, an anthology of epigrams, etc.

Di·o·me·des \ˌdī-ə-'mēd-ēz\. 4th century A.D. Latin scholar. His *Ars grammatica* (3 books) is extant.

Di·on \'dī-ˌän\. 408?–353 B.C. Syracusan philosopher and politician. Regent for his nephew Dionysius the Younger; made himself master of Syracuse (355 B.C.); assassinated.

Dion Cassius. See DIO CASSIUS.

Dion Chrysostomus. See DIO CHRYSOSTOM.

Dionne \dyȯn, dzyȯn, *Angl* dē-'än, -'ōn\, Cecile, Yvonne, Annette, Émilie (d. 1954), Marie (d. 1970). Canadian quintuplets, b. May 28, 1934, to Elzire, wife of Oliva Dionne, of Callander, Ontario. See Dr. Allan DAFOE.

Dionysius, Saint. See Saint DENIS.

Di·o·ny·si·us \ˌdī-ə-'nis(h)-ē-əs, -'nish-əs, -'nī-sē-əs\. Saint. d. 268. Pope (259–268). Reorganized the church after the persecutions of Decius and Valerian; successfully asserted authority over Dionysius of Alexandria in doctrine of Trinity.

Dionysius. King of Portugal. See DINIS.

Dionysius. Name of two tyrants of Syracuse:

Dionysius. *Called* Elder. c.430–367 B.C. Tyrant (405–367 B.C.). Of humble origin; gained influence by supporting poorer classes; fought with distinction against Carthaginians; usurped power (405); drove citizens from Naxos, Catana, Leontini, and gave cities to mercenaries. Engaged in wars with Carthage (397–396, 392) and made advantageous peace; conducted successful campaign in southern Italy (390–379); captured Rhegium (Reggio di Calabria) after long siege (386); colonized Illyria; his last two wars against Carthage (382–375, 368) disastrous; nonetheless left Syracuse a major power.

Dionysius. *Called* the Younger. Tyrant (367–356 and 354–343 B.C.). Son of Dionysius the Elder. At first ruled under regency of his uncle Dion; made unfavorable peace with Carthage (367); invited Plato to Syracuse as his tutor; driven out (356) by Dion and fled to Locri; returned (354) on assassination of Dion, but his despotic rule caused citizens to invite Timoleon to their assistance; defeated and taken to Corinth (343).

Dionysius of Alexandria. Saint. *Called* the Great. c.200–c.265. Greek theologian. Succeeded Origen as head of catechetical school in Alexandria (231); bishop of Alexandria (247); fled (251) to avoid persecution under Decius; banished (257) in reign of Valerian; returned to his see (260). Engaged in dispute with Sabellians over nature of Trinity; submitted to authority of Pope St. Dionysius on doctrinal question. Only fragments of his works are extant.

Dionysius of Halicarnassus. fl. c.20 B.C. Greek scholar. Settled in Rome (30 B.C.) and devoted himself to writing history of Rome in 20 books, of which 10 are extant; also wrote on rhetoric.

Dionysius the Ar·e·op·a·gite \ˌar-ē-'äp-ə-ˌjīt, -ˌgīt\. An unknown author (c.500 A.D.), probably of Syria, for centuries identified with St. Paul's convert, whose works of mystical and speculative theology (*The Celestial Hierarchy, The Divine Names,* etc.) exercised vast influence on medieval thought. Called also Pseudo-Dionysius and Pseudo-Areopagite. See also Saint DENIS.

Dionysius the Carthusian. *Orig.* Denys van Leeu·wen \-vän-'lā-wən\ *or* van Rijck·el \-vän-'rī-kəl\. 1402 or 1403–1471. Flemish theologian and mystic. Entered Carthusian order (1425); became leader of school of Rhenish spirituality; wrote *De contemplatione.*

Dionysius Ex·ig·u·us \-eg-'zig-yə-wəs\. c.500–c.560. Scythian Christian monk and scholar. In *Cyclus Paschalis* (525) prepared for Pope St. John I, he introduced method of reckoning the Christian era (Dionysian period) which is still used, making the birth of Christ (incorrectly placed in year 753 of Rome) the starting point of modern chronology.

Dionysius Per·i·e·ge·tes \-ˌper-ə-(ˌ)ē-'jēt-ēz\. 2d or 3d century A.D. Greek geographer. Author of *Oikumenes periegesis,* a geographical description of the habitable earth, written in Greek hexameters.

Dionysius Tel·ma·ha·ren·sis \-ˌtel-ˌmä-hə-'ren-sis\ *or* **Dionysius** of Tell Mahre. d. 845. Syrian church patriarch. Chosen patriarch of Syrian Jacobite Church, or Monophysites (818); author of "Chronicles" of Syrian church for the period 582–842, an important source document.

Dionysius Thrax \-'thraks\, *i.e.* of Thrace. fl. 100 B.C. Greek grammarian. Author of the first Greek grammar.

Diop \dyȯp\, David. 1927–1960. Senegalese poet, b. France. Leading writer of Negritude movement; poems collected in *Coups de pilon* (1956).

Di·o·phan·tus \ˌdī-ə-'fant-əs\ of Alexandria. 3d century A.D. Greek mathematician. Chief work, *Arithmetica* (13 books, of which 6 are extant), which introduced symbolism into Greek algebra and treated a variety of types of equations and problems in number theory.

Dior \dyȯr, *Angl* dē-'ȯr, 'dē-ˌȯr\, Christian. 1905–1957. French fashion designer. Founded house of Dior (1947); created "New Look," the "Sack," etc.

Di·os·cor·i·des \ˌdī-əs-'kōr-ə-ˌdēz, -'kȯr-\, Pedanius. c.40–c.90. Greek physician. Author of *De materia medica* which remained for 1500 years the authority in botany and materia medica.

Di·os·co·rus \dī-'äs-kə-rəs\. d. 454 A.D. Greek prelate. Succeeded St. Cyril as patriarch of Alexandria (444); supporter of Eutyches, founder of an extreme form of Monophysitism; presided over "Robber Synod" at Ephesus (449) at which he excommunicated Pope St. Leo I and deposed Patriarch St. Flavian of Constantinople; lost influence with death of Emperor Theodosius II; deposed as patriarch by Council of Chalcedon (451).

Dioscorus. d. 530. Alexandrian prelate. Deacon of Alexandrian church; papal legate of Pope St. Symmachus to Theodoric the Great; head of Roman delegation sent to Constantinople by Pope St. Hormisdas to resolve Acacian schism (519); elected pope by Roman clergy in opposition to Boniface II, designated successor of Felix IV (530); died 23 days later, ending schism.

Diph·i·lus \'dif-(ə-)ləs\. 4th century B.C. Athenian poet. Author of works of the Athenian New Comedy school; only fragments of his works extant.

Dipoenus. See SCYLLIS.

Di·po Ne·go·ro \'dē-pō-neg-'ōr-ō, -'ȯr-\, Pangeran. *Also known as* Ra·den Mas On·to·wir·jo \'räd-en-'mäs-ˌän-tō-'wir-jō\. c.1785–1855. Javanese leader. Eldest son of sultan of Jogjakarta; led anti-Dutch struggle known as Java War (1825–30); arrested at peace negotiations and exiled.

Dip·pel \'dip-əl\, Johann Konrad. 1673–1734. German Pietist theologian, physician, and alchemist. As chemist in Berlin, distilled animal bones in preparing curative mixture known as Dippel's oil; discovered Prussian blue. Published collected writings under title *Eröffneter Weg zum Frieden mit Gott und mit allen kreaturen* (1709) under pseudonym Chri·sti·a·nus De·mo·cri·tus \ˌkris-tē-'än-ůs-dā-'mō-krē-tůs\.

Di·rac \di-'rak\, Paul Adrien Maurice. 1902–1984. British physicist. Creator of the complete theoretical formulation of quantum mechanics; professor of mathematics at U. of Cambridge (1932–1969). Published *The Principles of Quantum Mechanics* (1930); developed the work of Erwin Schrödinger and others by linking it to classical mechanical theory and advancing the theory of positrons, the basis of antimatter. Winner of the Nobel prize for physics (1933).

Dirceu. See Tomás GONZAGA.

Di·ri·chlet \ˌdē-rē-'klā\, Peter Gustav Lejeune. 1805–1859. German mathematician. Professor at Berlin (1828–55), Göttingen (1855–59); known for work on theory of numbers, analysis and mechanics; proposed (1837) modern concept of function; author of *Vorlesungen über Zahlentheorie* (1863).

Dirks \'dərks\, Rudolph. 1877–1968. American cartoonist, b. Heide, Germany. To U.S. (1884); while working for *New York Journal* created (1897) cartoon strip "Katzenjammer Kids," later retitled "The Captain and the Kids."

Dirk·sen \'dərk-sən\, Everett McKinley. 1896–1969. American politician, b. Pekin, Ill. Member of U.S. House of Representatives (1933–48); U.S. senator (1950–69); Senate Republican leader (1959–69); noted for oratory.

Disbrowe, John. See DESBOROUGH.

Dis·ney \'diz-nē\, Walter Elias. 1901–1966. American film producer, b. Chicago. Creator of animated cartoons featuring Oswald the Rabbit, Mickey Mouse, Donald Duck, etc.; produced first animated film with sound, *Steamboat Willie* (1928); produced full-length animated films *Snow White and the Seven Dwarfs* (1937), *Pinocchio* (1940), *Fantasia* (1940), *Dumbo* (1941), *Cinderella* (1950), *Alice in Wonderland* (1951), *Peter Pan* (1953), etc.; built Disneyland amusement park, California, and Disney World, Florida.

Dis·rae·li \diz-'rā-lē\, Benjamin. 1st Earl of Bea·cons·field \'bē-kənz-ˌfēld, 'bek-ənz-\. *Nicknamed* Diz·zy \'diz-ē\. 1804–1881. English politician and author. Son of Isaac D'Israeli. Early career of financial reverses and novel-writing; Tory M.P. (1837–80); first speech a failure; member of Young England group of Tories; supported corn laws; attacked Peel for repealing them (1846), winning acknowledgment as leader of Conservatives in Commons. Chancellor of exchequer under Lord Derby (1852, 1858–59, 1865–68); introduced, but lost, reform bill (1859); carried Reform Act enfranchising all ratepayers (1867). Succeeded Lord Derby as prime minister (1868); resigned after general election (1868); criticized Gladstone's Irish and foreign policy; prime minister (1874–80); established Tory policies of strong foreign policy, consolidation of Empire, social reform; borrowed money and purchased for British government, on own responsibility, khedive's interest in Suez Canal (1875); had Queen Victoria assume title of Empress of India (1876); created earl of Beaconsfield (1876); became intimate friend of Queen Victoria; English plenipotentiary at Congress of Berlin (1878). Author of *Vindication of the British Constitution* (1835), *Letters of Runnymede* (1836), and the novels *Vivian Grey* (1826), *The Young Duke* (1831), *Contarini Fleming* (1832),

Henrietta Temple (1837), *Coningsby* (1844), *Sybil* (1845), *Tancred* (1847), *Lothair* (1870), *Endymion* (1880).

D'·Is·rae·li \diz-'rā-lē\, Isaac. 1766–1848. English man of letters. Son of Benjamin D'Israeli, an Italian Jewish merchant who went to England (1748). Published anonymously *Curiosities of Literature* (1791–1834), a collection of literary and historical anecdotes. Author also of *Calamities of Authors* (1812–13), *Quarrels of Authors* (1814), *Amenities of Literature* (1841), and novels and historical works.

Dithmar. See THIETMAR.

Dit·mars \'dit-,märz\, Raymond Lee. 1876–1942. American naturalist, b. Newark, N.J. Curator of reptiles, New York Zoological Park (from 1899), and of mammals (from 1910). Author of *The Reptile Book* (1907), *Reptiles of the World* (1910), *Strange Animals I Have Known* (1931), *The Book of Insect Oddities* (1938), etc.

Dit·ters von Dit·ters·dorf \'dit-ərs-fōn-'dit-ərs-,dôrf\, Karl. *Orig.* Ditters. 1739–1799. Austrian violin virtuoso and composer. Kapellmeister for bishop of Grosswardein (1765) and for prince-bishop of Breslau (1770–95). Composer of 44 operas, including *Il viaggiatore americano* (1770), *Doktor und Apotheker* (1786), *Hieronymus Knicker* (1789), *Das rote Käppchen* (1790), establishing German *Singspiel* form; oratorios, including *Davidde penitente* (1770), *Esther* (1773), *Giobbe* (1786); over 100 symphonies, including 12 program symphonies on Ovid's *Metamorphoses;* chamber music; and many piano and violin pieces.

Ditz·en \'dit-sən\, Rudolf, *in full* Wilhelm Friedrich Rudolf. *Pen name* Hans Fal·la·da \'fäl-əd-ə\. 1893–1947. German novelist. Author of *Bauern, Bonzen und Bomben* (1931), *Kleiner Mann, was nun?* (1932), *Wir hatten mal ein Kind* (1934), *Wolf unter Wölfen* (1937), *Kleiner Mann, grosser Mann* (1940), *Der Alpdruck* (1947), *Der Trinker* (1950).

Di·vā·ka·ra·paṇ·ḍi·ta \,dē-vä-,kär-ə-pän-'dē-tə\. *Orig.* Di·vā·ka·ra \,dē-vä-'kär-ä\. 1040–c.1120. Cambodian Brahmin. Adviser to four successive kings of Cambodia, esp. Suryavarman II, whom he urged to begin construction of temple at Angkor Wat.

Divine, Father. See George BAKER (1877–1965).

Di·vi·ni \dē-'vē-nē\, Eustachio. 1610–1685. Italian instrument maker. Built clocks, compound microscopes, long-focus telescopes; made astronomical observations and published (1649) copper-engraved map of the moon.

Divino, El. See Fernando de HERRERA; Luis de MORALES.

Dix \'diks\, Dorothea Lynde. 1802–1887. American philanthropist and reformer, b. Hampden, Me. Headed own school for girls, Boston (1821–36). Toured state institutions (1841–43), wrote report for legislature; secured reforms in treatment of the insane in prisons, almshouses, and houses of correction in Mass., and later in other states; served through Civil War as superintendent of women nurses in army.

Dix, Dorothy. See Elizabeth M. GILMER.

Dix, John Adams. 1798–1879. American army officer and politician, b. Boscawen, N.H. Served in War of 1812. Secretary of state of New York (1833–39); U.S. senator (1845–49); U.S. secretary of the treasury (1861). Served as major general during Civil War. U.S. minister to France (1866–69). Governor of New York (1873–75).

Dix, Otto. 1891–1969. German painter. Served in World War I and painted series of scenes of stark realism revealing his abhorrence of war. Moved from Impressionism through Dada to an Expressionism rooted in social despair, called the *Neue Sachlichkeit,* "new realism." Professor at Dresden academy (1927); proscribed by Nazi regime. Later work marked by religious mysticism.

Dixon, Franklin W. See Edward STRATEMEYER.

Dix·on \'dik-sən\, George. 1755?–?1800. English navigator. Sailed with Captain Cook on third expedition (1776–79). Exploring shores of present British Columbia for King George's Sound Co., discovered (1787) Queen Charlotte Islands, Norfolk Sound, Port Mulgrave, Dixon Entrance, Alexander Archipelago; wrote *A Voyage Round the World* (1789).

Dixon, George. 1870–1909. American boxer, b. Halifax, N.S. To Boston (1887); first Negro boxer to win a world title in becoming bantamweight champion (1890); world featherweight champion (1891–97, 1898–1900).

Dixon, Henry Hall. *Pen name* The Druid. 1822–1870. English sporting writer. Author of three novels, *Post and Paddock* (1856), *Silk and Scarlet* (1859), *Scott and Sebright* (1862).

Dixon, Henry Horatio. 1869–1953. Irish botanist. Professor at Trinity Coll., Dublin (1904–49); noted for work on plant transpiration and cell division.

Dixon, Jeremiah. d. 1777. English surveyor. With Charles Mason (*q.v.*), determined boundary between Maryland and Pennsylvania (1763–68) which became known as Mason and Dixon's line and was considered as being in part the boundary between free and slave states before the Civil War.

Dixon, Joseph. 1799–1869. American manufacturer and inventor, b. Marblehead, Mass. Invented method of casting in graphite crucible (patented 1850), a method of printing bank notes in color, a wood-planing machine, process for printing color-fast calico, a galvanic battery.

Dixon, Richard Watson. 1833–1900. English poet. Associated with William Morris and Burne-Jones in Pre-Raphaelite movement; vicar of Warkworth (1883–1900). Author of seven volumes of poetry, including *Historical Odes* (1863) and *Odes and Eclogues* (1884), and *A History of the Church of England* (1877–1900).

Dixon, Roland Burrage. 1875–1934. American anthropologist, b. Worcester, Mass. Professor, Harvard (from 1915) and librarian of the Peabody Museum. Author of *The Northern Maidu* (1905), *Oceanic Mythology* (1916), *Racial History of Man* (1923), *The Building of Cultures* (1928), etc.

Dixon, Thomas. 1864–1946. American clergyman and writer, b. Shelby, N.C. Entered Baptist ministry (1886); chief pastorate in New York City (1889–99). Author of anti-Negro, pro-Ku Klux Klan trilogy comprising *Leopard's Spots* (1902), *The Clansman* (1905) (basis of D.W. Griffith's film *Birth of a Nation,* 1915), and *The Southerner* (1913), other novels critical of socialism, pacifism, feminism; also wrote *The Inside Story of the Harding Tragedy* (1932, with Harry M. Daugherty).

Dixon, William Hepworth. 1821–1879. English journalist and historian. Editor of the *Athenaeum* (1853–69). Author of biographies, including *John Howard and the Prison World of Europe* (1849), *William Penn* (1851, in defense of Penn against Macaulay), *Admiral Blake* (1852), and *Lord Bacon* (1862), travel books, and historical works, including one on Catherine of Aragon and Anne Boleyn, *History of Two Queens* (1873).

Djalski, Ksaver. See BABIĆ.

Djed·ef·re \jed-'ef-,rā\. *Also called* Re·djed·ef \rā-'jed-,ef\. 26th century B.C. Egyptian king. Son of Khufu by a secondary wife; apparently usurped throne on death of Khufu, becoming third king of 4th dynasty; reigned about 8 years; began pyramid at Abū Ruwaysh (not completed); succeeded by Khafre.

Djeserkhepere. See HOREMHEB.

Djo·ser *or* **Zo·ser** \'zhō-sər\. 27th century B.C. King of Egypt. Succeeded brother Sanakht as 2d king of 3d dynasty (in power from c.2686 B.C.); first to make Memphis his sole residence; with his chancellor Imhotep developed administrative system for fully unified Egypt; fostered first great cultural flowering; had built the first great stone pyramid, now known as the Step Pyramid.

Dłu·gosz \'dlü-,gôsh\, Jan. *Lat.* Johannes Lon·gi·nus \län-'jī-nəs\. 1415–1480. Polish historian. Canon of Cracow (1436); protégé of Cardinal Oleśnicki; tutor to children of King Casimir IV (from 1467). Author of *Historia Polonica* (12 vols., completed 1480; pub. in full 1711–12).

Dmi·try \'dmyē-tryə\. *In full* Dmitry Ivanovich. *Known as* Dmitry Don·skoi \(,)dən-'skȯi\. 1350–1389. Russian prince. Son of Ivan II the Meek of Moscow; prince of Moscow (1359–89), grand prince of Vladimir (1362–89); strengthened Kremlin and withstood attacks of Michael of Tver and Algirdas (1368, 1370, 1372); secured obeisance of Michael (1375); enlarged domain of Moscow; defeated Mongol army at Kulikovo Pole (Sept. 8, 1380); independence of Moscow ended with Mongol sacking (1382).

Dmitry *or* **False Dmitry.** Name given to three impostors claiming to be Dmitry, son of Czar Ivan IV: (1) Perhaps Yury Otrepyev, later Gregory, a monk; claimed to be Dmitry (1601); raised army of Lithuanians and Poles and invaded Russia (1604); proclaimed czar by Russian army on death of Boris Godunov (1605); murdered by Vasily Shuysky (1606). (2) Unknown who claimed to have survived Shoysky's coup d'état, raised army of Cossacks, Poles, Lithuanians; won control of southern Russia, raided the north from headquarters in Tushino; driven out by Shuysky (1610). (3) Sidorka, a deacon, appeared at Ivangorod and claimed to be Dmitry (1611); won allegiance of Cossacks (1612); betrayed and executed (1612).

Dmow·ski \'dmȯf-skē\, Roman. 1864–1939. Polish statesman. Helped found Polish National Democratic party (1897); headed Polish representatives in 2d and 3d Russian Dumas (1907, 1907–12), advocating cooperative movement toward autonomy; opposed Piłsudski's revolutionary policy; in Switzerland formed (1917) National Committee, recognized by Allies as official Polish representative; headed Paris committee recognized as temporary government of Poland, and signed Treaty of Versailles (1919); minister of foreign affairs (1923).

Dob·bin \'däb-ən\, James Cochran. 1814–1857. American politician, b. Fayetteville, N.C. In U.S. House of Representatives (1845–47); U.S. secretary of the navy (1853–57); instrumental in enlarging and reorganizing the navy.

Do·bell \dō-'bel\, Bertram. 1842–1914. English bookseller. Befriended James Thomson and arranged publication of *The City of Dreadful Night* (1880); recovered, identified, and edited poetical works of Thomas Traherne.

Dobell, Sydney Thompson. *Pseudonym* Sydney Yen·dys \'yen-dəs\. 1824–1874. English poet and critic. Ardent liberal and advocate of cause of oppressed nationalities and esp. of Italian unity; wrote with Alexander Smith sonnets on Crimean War (1855). Author of the dramatic poem *The Roman* (1850), *Balder* (part I, 1854), *England in Time of War* (1856). Member of the "spasmodic school," so named by W. E. Aytoun, who parodied their style in *Firmilian* (1854). Published *Thoughts on Art, Philosophy and Religion* (1876).

Do·be·neck \'dō-bə-nek\, Johannes. *Lat.* Johannes Coch·lae·us \käk-'lē-əs\. 1479–1552. German Humanist and theologian. Rector, Latin School of St. Lawrence, Nürnberg (1515–20); ordained in Rome (1518 or 1519); dean at Frankfurt (1520–25); court chaplain to Duke George of Saxony (1529–35); canon in Meissen (1535–39), Breslau (1539, 1549). Active critic of Luther at diets of Worms (1521), Nürnberg (1522–23), Speyer (1526), Augsburg (1530); author of *Commentaria de actis et scriptis Lutheri* (1549).

Do·ber \'dō-bər\, Conrad K. *Pen name* Con Conrad \'kän-,rad\. 1893–1938. American songwriter, b. New York City. Songs included "Margie" (with Benny Davis), "Barney Google" (with Billy Rose), "Ma–He's Making Eyes at Me" (with Sidney Clare), "The Continental" (with Herb Magidson; Academy Award 1934).

Dö·be·rei·ner \'dœ-bə-,rī-nər\, Johann Wolfgang. 1780–1849. German chemist. Professor at Jena (from 1810); discovered catalytic action of platinum sponge on hydrogen, an action utilized in Döbereiner's lamp (1823) for instantaneous production of a flame; discovered furfural; recognized (before 1829) relationship between the properties of elements and their atomic weights, upon which the periodic table of elements is based; classed closely related elements in groups of three (known as Döbereiner's triads).

Do·bie \'dō-bē\, James Frank. 1888–1964. American folklorist, b. Live Oak Co., Tex. Professor of English, U. of Texas (1925–47). Author of *A Vaquero of the Brush Country* (1929), *Coronado's Children* (1931), *Apache Gold and Yaqui Silver* (1939), *The Longhorns* (1941), *Voice of the Coyote* (1949), *Up the Trail from Texas* (1955), etc.

Dö·blin \'dœ-(,)blēn\, Alfred. 1878–1957. German physician and writer. Psychiatrist in Berlin (1912–33); in exile in France and U.S. (1933–45). Author of novels including *Die drei Sprünge des Wang-Lun* (1915), *Wallenstein* (1920), *Berge, Meere und Giganten* (1924), *Berlin Alexanderplatz* (1929), *Babylonische Wanderung* (1934), *Pardon wird nicht gegeben* (1935); plays; an epic, *Manas* (1927); and essays including *Deutsche Maskenball* (1921), *Wissen und Verändern* (1931), *Sieger und Besiegte* (1946), *Die Dichtung* (1950).

Do·brée \'dō-brē\, Bonamy. 1891–1974. English literary scholar and editor. Authority on Restoration drama; author of *Restoration Comedy* (1924), *Restoration Tragedy* (1929), *English Revolts* (1937), *The Broken Cistern* (1954); collaborated in *The Victorians and After* (1938).

Do·briz·hof·fer \'dō-brits-,hō-fər\, Martin. 1717–1791. Austrian Jesuit missionary. In Paraguay (1748–67), working seven years among Indians. Author of a valuable ethnological work, *Historia de Abiponibus, Equestri Bellicosaque Paraguariae Natione* (1783).

Do·bro·lyu·bov \də-(,)brəl-'yü-bəf\, Nikolay Aleksandrovich. 1836–1861. Russian journalist and critic. Associated (from 1856) with liberal journal *Sovremennik;* known esp. for essay "What is Oblomovism?" (1859–60); chief among radical critics.

Dob·ro·vol·sky \də-(,)brə-'vòl-skəi\, Georgy Timofeyevich. 1928–1971. Russian astronaut. Commander of Soyuz 11 mission, setting space endurance record of 24 days while docked with Salyut station; killed by decompression during landing along with design engineer Viktor Ivanovich Patsayev (1933–1971) and flight engineer Vladislav Nikolayevich Volkov (1935–1971), who was a veteran of Soyuz 7 flight (1969).

Do·brov·ský \'dò-bròf-skē\, Josef. 1753–1829. Slavic Jesuit and philologist. Regarded as founder of Slavic philology; chief works *Geschichte der böhmischen Sprache und Litteratur* (1792), *Lehrgebäude der böhmischen Sprache* (1809), *Institutiones linguae slavicae dialecti veteris* (1822), first scientific grammar of Old Church Slavonic.

Dob·son \'däb-sən\, Austin, *in full* Henry Austin. 1840–1921. English poet and man of letters. Clerk (from 1856), principal clerk (1884–1901) in marine department of Board of Trade. Author of *Vignettes in Rhyme* (1873), *Proverbs in Porcelain* (1877), and *At the Sign of the Lyre* (1885), and of prose works including critical essays and biographies of Fielding, Steele, Goldsmith, Walpole, Hogarth, Richardson, etc.

Dobson, Frank. 1888–1963. English sculptor. Known for abstract or allegorical figures and portraits; among his notable sculptures were *The Man Child, Susanna, Morning,* bust of Earl of Oxford and Asquith, head of Osbert Sitwell.

Dobson, William. 1610–1646. English portrait painter. Succeeded Van Dyck (1641) as court painter to Charles I; painted portraits of Charles I, Prince of Wales, and Prince Rupert.

Dob·zhan·sky \dəb-'zhän-skəi, *Angl* dəb-'zhan-skē\, Theodosius. 1900–1975. American geneticist, b. Nemirov, Ukraine. To U.S. (1927), naturalized (1937); taught at California Inst. of Technology (1929–40), Columbia U. (1940–62), Rockefeller Inst. (1962–71). Known esp. for work on philosophical implications of evolution; author of *Genetics and the Origin of Species* (1937), *Evolution, Genetics and Man* (1955), *Biological Basis of Human Freedom* (1956), *Mankind Evolving* (1962), *The Biology of Ultimate Concern* (1967), *Genetics of the Evolutionary Process* (1970).

Dock·wra \'däk-rə\ *or* **Dock·wray** \-,rā\, William. d. 1716. London merchant. Established a penny postal system in the London metropolis (1683).

Dodd \'däd\, Frank Howard. 1844–1916. American publisher, b. Bloomfield, N.J. Joined father's publishing business (1860); became head of firm (1870); later took in as partners Edward S. Mead and Bleecker Van Wagenen, forming firm of Dodd, Mead, & Co. In addition to books published *The Bookman* magazine (from 1895), *New International Encyclopaedia* (1st ed. 1902–04).

Dodd, Lee Wilson. 1879–1933. American writer, b. Franklin, Pa. Author of plays *The Return of Eve* (1909), *Speed* (1911), *His Majesty Bunker Bean* (1915), *The Changelings* (1923); novels, *The Book of Susan* (1920) and *The Girl Next Door* (1923); verse, *The Middle Miles* (1915), *The Great Enlightenment* (1928), etc.

Dodd, William. 1729–1777. English cleric and forger. Became fashionable preacher; chaplain to the king (1763); forced to flee England because of wife's attempt to bribe wife of lord chancellor to gain preferment for him (1774); forged a bond in name of Earl of Chesterfield; hanged despite petitions for his pardon, one by Dr. Johnson. Author of *The Beauties of Shakespeare* (1752), *Reflections on Death* (1763), etc.

Dodd, William Edward. 1869–1940. American historian, b. Clayton, N.C. Professor of American history, U. of Chicago (1908–33). U.S. ambassador to Germany (1933–37). Author of *Jefferson Davis* (1907), *Statesmen of the Old South* (1911), *Expansion and Conflict* (1915), *The Cotton Kingdom* (1919), *Woodrow Wilson and His Work* (1920), *The Old South* (1937); joint editor, with Ray Stannard Baker, of *The Public Papers of Woodrow Wilson* (1924–26).

Dodd·ridge \'däd-rij\, Philip. 1702–1751. English nonconformist clergyman and religious writer. Pastor in Northampton (1729–51); author of *On the Rise and Progress of Religion in the Soul* (1745) and several hymns, including "O God of Bethel, by whose hand."

Dodds \dòds\, Alfred-Amédée. 1842–1922. French soldier and colonialist. Served in Franco–Prussian War (1870); commander of marines in Benin (1892); led campaign against King Behanzin of Dahomey (1892–93); won signal victory at Abomey (1892); inspector general of marine infantry (1899); commander of 20th army corps (1903–07).

Dodds \'dädz\, Johnny. 1892–1940. American musician, b. New Orleans. Clarinettist with Kid Ory jazz band (1911–18), King Oliver (1920–24), Louis Armstrong (1926); master of New Orleans emsemble style. His brother ¶Warren, *known as* Baby Dodds (1898–1959) was a jazz drummer.

Dodge, Augustus Caesar. See under Henry DODGE.

Dodge \'däj\, David Low. 1774–1852. American merchant and pacifist, b. Brooklyn, Conn. Founder of New York Peace Society (1815), supposed to have been first such group anywhere. His son ¶William Earl (1805–1883), merchant and philanthropist, formed firm of Phelps, Dodge & Co. (1833) and was an organizer of the Young Men's Christian Association in America.

Dodge, Grace Hoadley. 1856–1914. American social worker, b. New York City. Great-granddaughter of David L. Dodge. Organized a working girls' club from which developed the Working Girls' Association of Clubs (1885); member of New York City Board of Education (1886–89), and prominent in organization (1889) and early activity of Teachers College, Columbia U.; president of national board, YWCA (1906–14); helped found the New York Travelers Aid Society (1907).

Dodge, Grenville Mellen. 1831–1916. American army officer and civil engineer, b. Danvers, Mass. Served through Civil War; major general of volunteers (1864). In U.S. House of Representatives (1867–69). Chief engineer, Union Pacific Railroad (1866–70). Associated with Jay Gould in railroad development in the Southwest (1873–83). Organized and built railroad in Cuba (1899–1903).

Dodge, Henry. 1782–1867. American army officer and politician, b. Vincennes, Ind. Major general of Missouri militia (1814); colonel, U.S. army, in Black Hawk's War (1832–33). Governor of Territory of Wisconsin (1836–41); member, U.S. House of Representatives, as delegate from Territory of Wisconsin (1841–45); again governor (1845–48); U.S. senator (1848–57). His son ¶Augustus Caesar (1812–1883) was first U.S. senator from Iowa (1848–55), and U.S. minister to Spain (1855–59).

Dodge, Mabel. See Mabel LUHAN.

Dodge, Mary Abigail. *Pseudonym* Gail Hamilton. 1833–1896. American writer, b. Hamilton, Mass. Author of *Gala Days* (1863), *A New Atmosphere* (1865), *Woman's Worth and Worthlessness* (1872), *James G. Blaine* (1895), etc.

Dodge, Mary Elizabeth, *nee* Mapes \'māps\. 1831–1905. American writer, b. New York City. m. William Dodge (1851; d. 1858). Editor, *St. Nicholas Magazine* (1873–1905). Successful esp. in books for children, as *Hans Brinker, or the Silver Skates* (1865), *Donald and Dorothy* (1883), *When Life is Young* (poetry, 1894), *The Land of Pluck* (1894).

Dodge, Raymond. 1871–1942. American psychologist, b. Woburn, Mass. Professor at Wesleyan U., Conn. (1898–24), Yale (1924–36); a founder of Yale Institute of Psychology (1924). With Benno Erdmann invented tachistoscope; pioneered in study of eye movements in reading.

Dodge, William Earl. See under David Low DODGE.

Dodg·son \ˈdäj-sən, ˈdäd-\, Charles Lutwidge. *Pseudonym* Lewis Car·roll \ˈkar-əl\. 1832–1898. English mathematician and writer. Mathematical lecturer at Oxford (1855–81); published mathematical treatises. Author of the classics *Alice's Adventures in Wonderland* (1865) and *Through the Looking Glass* (1872), based on stories originally invented for Alice Liddell, second daughter of Henry George Liddell (*q.v.*), and illustrated by Sir John Tenniel (*q.v.*); author also of *Phantasmagoria* (1869), *Hunting of the Snark* (1876), *Rhyme? and Reason?* (1883), *Sylvie and Bruno* (1889).

Dodington, George Bubb. See BUBB DODINGTON.

Do·doens \dō-ˈdüns\, Junius Rembert. *Lat.* Junius Rembertus Do·do·nae·us \ˌdō-də-ˈnē-əs\. 1517–1585. Dutch botanist. Author of *Cruydeboek* (1554 and 1563) on domestic and foreign plants.

Dods·ley \ˈdädz-lē\ Robert. 1703–1764. English poet, playwright, and bookseller. Set up as bookseller (1735); published Dr. Johnson's *London* (1738); helped to finance Johnson's dictionary; founded several literary periodicals, among them the *Annual Register,* with Edmund Burke as editor (1758). Wrote plays including *The Toy-Shop* (1735), *The Blind Beggar of Bethnal Green* (1741). Best known as editor of two collections, *Old Plays* (12 vols., 1744) and *A Collection of Poems. By Several Hands* (3 vols., 1748).

Dod·well \ˈdäd-ˌwel, -wəl\, Henry. 1641–1711. Irish theologian and historian. Camden professor of history, Oxford (1688–91); deprived for refusing oath of allegiance to William and Mary; champion of nonjurors; advanced eccentric theological theories, such as the natural mortality of the soul.

Does \ˈdüs\, Johan van der. *Also called* Janus Dou·sa \ˈdü-sə\. 1545–1604. Dutch political leader and writer. Leader among Dutch nobles in League of the Gueux (Beggars) against Philip II of Spain (1566); commanded citizen resistance to siege of Leiden (1573–74); first curator, U. of Leiden (1575–1604); led delegation to offer sovereignty over Netherlands to Elizabeth I of Great Britain (1584–85). Author of *Odarum Britannicarum liber ad divam Elisabetham* (1586), and esp. *Annales rerum a priscis Hollandiae Comitibus per CCCXLVI annos gestarum* (1599), a verse history of Holland.

Doesburg, Theo van. See KÜPPER.

Dō·gen \dō-gen\. *Also known as* Jōyō Daishi \jō-yō-dī-shē\ *and* Ki·gen Dōgen \kē-gen-\. 1200–1253. Japanese Buddhist. Studied in China (1223–27); introduced Zen to Japan in the form of the Sōtō school. Author of *Fukan zazen gi* and esp. *Shōbōgenzō.*

Dog·gett \ˈdóg-ət\, Thomas. c.1670–1721. Irish actor. Made first London appearance in *Love for Money* (1691); created parts written for him in Congreve's *The Old Batchelour* and *Love for Love* (1693, 1695); author of *The Country Wake* (1696). Founded (1716) a sculling prize, "Doggett's Coat and Badge," for Thames watermen, still rowed for annually on August 1.

Do·he·ny \də-ˈhē-nē\, Edward Laurence. 1856–1935. American businessman, b. Fond du Lac, Wis. Organized Mexican Petroleum Co. (1900), Pan American Petroleum Co. (1916). Involved in Teapot Dome oil scandals; accused of bribing Albert B. Fall (*q.v.*) in order to obtain preferred treatment in distribution of oil leases, esp. of leases of Elk Hills naval oil reserves; indicted (1925) with Fall on charges of conspiracy and bribery; acquitted.

Do·her·ty \ˈdó(-ə)rt-ē, ˈdä(-ə)rt-ē, ˈdō(-ə)rt-ē; ˈdór-ət-ē, ˈdär-, ˈdōr-\, Charles Joseph. 1855–1931. Canadian jurist and diplomat, b. Montreal. Puisne judge, superior court, Quebec (1891–1906); M.P. (1908–21); minister of justice (1911–21); Canadian representative at Versailles Peace Conference (1919), and in Assembly of the League of Nations (1920–21).

Doherty, Henry Latham. 1870–1939. American businessman, b. Columbus, Ohio. Organized Henry L. Doherty & Co., bankers and public utility operators, (1905) and Cities Service Co., utilities and petroleum holding company (1910); president, Cities Service Co. (1910–39).

Doherty, Reginald Frank (1872–1911) and his brother Hugh Lawrence (1875–1919). English lawn-tennis players. All-England singles champions at Wimbledon (Reginald 1897–1900 and Hugh 1902–06), and doubles champions (1897–1901, 1903–1905); Hugh was also American national champion (1903) and was undefeated in Davis Cup play (1902–06). Joint authors of the classic *On Lawn-Tennis* (1903).

Dohm \ˈdōm\, Ernst. 1819–1883. German writer. Coeditor of humorous periodical *Kladderadatsch* (from 1849); translated La Fontaine's *Fables.*

Doh·na \ˈdō-ˌnä\. Distinguished German family, including: Burggraf Fabian von Dohna (1550–1621), soldier in service of John Casimir, count Palatine, whom he accompanied (1587–91) to aid Henry IV of France against Catholic League; and the following, all bearing title Burggraf and Count zu Dohna-Schlo·bit·ten \-ˈshlō-ˌbit-ən\: ¶Alexander (1661–1728), field marshal (1713) in Prussian service. His brother ¶Christoph (1665–1733), colonel of regiment of French émigrés after revocation of Edict of Nantes, ambassador to London (1698–99), general of infantry (1713), ambassador to Vienna (1714–16). ¶Friedrich Ferdinand Alexander (1771–1831), Prussian minister of interior (1808–10), determined opponent of Napoléon, an organizer of Prussian Landwehr (1813). His brother ¶Karl Emil (1784–1859), Prussian general, who resisted French domination in Prussia (1806–11), served in Russian army (1812–15), and returned to Prussians in time for Waterloo (1815).

Doh·ná·nyi \ˈdó-nän-yē\, Ernő. 1877–1960. Hungarian musician and composer. Toured as concert pianist; taught in Berlin (1908–15); conductor of Budapest Philharmonic (1919); in U.S. (from 1949); wrote opera *Der Turm der Woijwoden* (1922), comic opera *Tante Simona* (1912), three symphonies, orchestral rhapsody, piano concerto, violin concerto, string quartets, piano works, and *Variations on a Nursery Song* for piano and orchestra.

Dohrn \ˈdōrn\, Anton. 1840–1909. German zoologist. Founded the zoological laboratory in Naples (1874).

Do·i·ha·ra \dō-ē-hä-rä\ Kenji. 1883–1948. Japanese soldier. In northern China helped engineer "independence" of Manchuria and installation of P'u-i as president (1932); commander in chief of Japanese air force (1942); hanged as war criminal.

Doi·sy \ˈdói-zē\, Edward Adelbert. 1893–1986. American biochemist, b. Hume, Ill. Taught at Washington U. School of Medicine, St. Louis; with embryologist Edgar Allen developed assay techniques that facilitated research on sex hormones. Contributed to the knowledge of vitamins, antibiotics, hormones, and blood buffer systems; isolated sex hormones estrone (1929), estriol (1930), and estradiol (1935); discovered antihemorrhagic vitamin K (1939); isolated K_2, variant form of that vitamin. Shared 1943 Nobel prize for physiology or medicine with Henrik Dam. Writings included *Sex Hormones* (1936) and *Sex and Internal Secretions* (1939).

Do·ku·cha·yev \də-kich-ˈä-yəf\, Vasily Vasilyevich. 1846–1903. Russian geologist. Known for system of classification of soils and introduction (1883) of term chernozem for type of rich black soil.

Dō·kyō \dō-kyō\. d. 772. Japanese Buddhist priest. As preacher at Imperial temple (from 761) won confidence of former empress Kōken; engineered coup against emperor Junnin (764) and installation of Kōken on throne as empress Shōtoku; named prime minster (765); archbishop (766); attempted through an oracle to win recognition as successor to throne; on death of Shōtoku (770) banished by Fujiwara family.

Dol·a·bel·la \ˌdäl-ə-ˈbel-ə\, Publius Cornelius. 70?–43 B.C. Roman general. Son-in-law of Cicero; a notorious profligate. In the civil war, joined Caesar; was engaged at battle of Pharsala (48 B.C.) and accompanied Caesar to Africa and Spain. After assassination of Caesar (44), seized consulship and, by favor of Brutus, was allowed to hold it. Deserted Brutus's cause to accept from Marcus Antonius command of an expedition against the Parthians and governorship of Syria. His extortions and crimes caused him to be declared a public enemy; attacked by Cassius at Laodicea and, to escape capture, ordered one of his soldiers to kill him.

Dol·ce \ˈdōl-chā\, Lodovico. 1508–1568. Italian writer and scholar. Translated Horace, Homer, and Virgil; wrote *Osservazioni nella volgar lingua* (1550) and plays including comedies *Il Ragazzo* (1541), *Il Capitano* (1545), *Il Marito* (1560), *Il Ruffiano* (1560), tragedy *Marianna* (1565).

Dol·ci \ˈdōl-chē\, Carlo *or* Carlino. 1616–1686. Florentine painter. Known chiefly for religious canvases of marked piety and for portraits.

Dole \ˈdōl\, Sanford Ballard. 1844–1926. American lawyer and politician, b. Honolulu. In Hawaiian legislature (1884–87); associate justice, Hawaii supreme court (1887–93). Head of revolutionary provisional government (1893); president, Republic of Hawaii (1894–1900); first governor, Territory of Hawaii (1900–03); judge, U.S. district court for Hawaii (1904–15).

Do·let \dó-le\, Étienne. 1509–1546. French printer and Humanist. Known for his enthusiasm for Renaissance learning, anticlericalism, quarrelsome nature; wrote *Dialogus de imitatione ciceroniana* (1535) against Erasmus; contributed to Latin scholarship with *Commentarii linguae Latinae* (1536–38); established as printer in Lyon, issued *Cato Christianus* (1542), translations of classics, Erasmus, Rabelais, religious works; accused of atheism and imprisoned (1542, 1544, 1546); tortured and burned at stake.

Dol·go·ru·ky \dəl-(ˌ)gə-ˈrü-kē\. Princely Russian family descended from the Rurik prince Yury Dolgoruky (1090–1157) and including notably: Prince Vasily Vladimirovich (1667–1746), soldier; took part in Great Northern War (1700 ff.); suppressed Cossack rebellion (1707–08); exiled for conspiring with other nobles against Peter I (1718–24); field marshal and member of supreme privy council (1728); attempted to impose conditions on accession of Anna Ivanovna and banished by her (1730–39); restored and named president of War College (1741). His distant cousin ¶Vasily Lukich (1670–1739), diplomat; ambassador to Poland (1706–07), Denmark (1707–20), France (1720–22), Sweden (1724–27); became member of supreme privy council (c.1727); attempted to have his niece Yekaterina accepted as successor to Peter II (1730); vainly endeavored to control Empress Anna Ivanovna; convicted of forging a will of Peter II and executed at Novgorod. ¶Vasily Mikhailovich (1722–1782), surnamed Krym·ski \'krim-skəi\ because in 15 days he conquered the Crimea (1771). ¶Yekaterina Mikhailovna (1847–1922), 2d wife (1880) of Czar Alexander II and author of *Alexander II: détails inédits sur sa vie intime et sa mort* (1882).

D'·Olier \'dōl-yā\, Franklin. 1877–1953. American businessman, b. Burlington, N.J. Officer in A.E.F., in France (1917–19); first national commander of American Legion (1919–20); executive in textile and insurance firms; head of U.S. Strategic Bombing Survey (1944–46).

Dol·lar \'däl-ər\, Robert. 1844–1932. American shipping executive, b. Falkirk, Scotland. To U.S. (1882), naturalized (1888). Settled in San Francisco; founder and president, Dollar Steamship Co. (1901), engaged esp. in trade in Orient; introduced round-the-world passenger service with line of "President" steamers (1924).

Doll·fuss \'dòl-(,)füs\, Engelbert. 1892–1934. Austrian politician. Minister of agriculture and forestry (1931–34) and chancellor (1932–34) at head of Christian Social coalition; declined to join German customs union; formed close alliance with Italy and moved toward Fascist regime; dissolved Bundesversammlung (1933); abolished political parties in favor of own Vaterländische Front; promulgated new constitution (1934) embodying dictatorship. Shot and killed by Austrian Nazi rebels, who seized the chancellery.

Dol·ling \'däl-iŋ\, Robert William Radclyffe. *Known as* Father Dolling. 1851–1902. British social reformer, b. Ireland. Engaged in social work, Dublin (1870–78); head of missions in London (1883–85), at Landport (1885–95). Author of *Ten Years in a Portsmouth Slum* (1896).

Döl·ling·er \'dœl-iŋ-ər\, Johann Joseph Ignaz von. 1799–1890. German theologian. Professor at Munich (1826–47, 1849–1890); rector (1871–90). Gradually became leader of antipapal party in German church; excommunicated from Roman Catholic church (1871) for denial of papal infallibility; leader of Old Catholic movement thereafter. Author of *Kirche und Kirchen, Papsttum und Kirchensaat* (1861), *Papstfabeln des Mittelalters* (1863), *Der Papst und des Konzil* (1869), *Geschichte der Moralstreitigkeiten in der römisch-katholischen Kirche seit dem 16. Jahrhundert* (with F. H. Reusch, 1889).

Doll·mann \'dòl-,män\, Georg Carl Heinrich von. 1830–1895. German architect. For Louis II of Bavaria built grandiose follies: Linderhof (1869–78), Neuschwanstein (1869–86), Herrenchiemsee (1878–85; incomplete).

Dol·lond \'däl-ənd\, John. 1706–1761. English optician. Joined his eldest son ¶Peter (1730–1820) in making optical instruments (from 1752); discovered means of constructing achromatic lenses by combination of crown and flint glasses, improving telescopic lenses; invented modern heliometer (1754); Peter invented improved triple achromatic lens (1765). Peter's nephew ¶George (1774–1852) took over family optical business (1819); invented an improved altazimuth and a telescopic micrometer (1821) and an atmospheric recorder.

Dol·metsch \'däl-,mech\, Arnold, *in full* Eugène Arnold. 1858–1940. British musician, b. France. To England (1883); toured with trio performing early music on authentic instruments; founded summer festival (1925), Dolmetsch Foundation (1928) to further study and recovery of early music, instruments, and playing.

Do·lo·mieu \dò-lòm-yœ̄\, Dieudonné *or* Déodat de Gra·tet de \də-grà-ted-ə-\. 1750–1801. French geologist and mineralogist. Studied the Pyrenees and the Alps; described (1791) the mineral named after him "dolomite"; professor, École des Mines (1796). Scientist on Napoléon's expedition to Egypt (1798); captured and imprisoned at Messina for 21 months; while in prison, wrote *Introduction à la philosophie minéralogique* (1801).

Do·magk \'dō-,mäk\, Gerhard. 1895–1964. German bacteriologist and pathologist. Taught at Greifswald and Münster; director of I. G. Farbenindustrie research institute (from 1927). Known for discovery of, and experimental work with, Prontonsil, first of the sulfonamide drugs. Declined 1939 Nobel prize for physiology or medicine in accordance with instructions of German government; later (1947) accepted medal and diploma.

Do·mat \dò-mà\, Jean. 1625–1696. French jurist. Author of *Les Lois civiles dans leur ordre naturel* (1689–94), which introduced methods of Roman law into French jurisprudence.

Dom·basle \dōⁿ-bäl\, Mathieu de, *in full* Christophe-Joseph-Alexandre-Mathieu de. 1777–1843. French agriculturist. Invented a plow; founded school of agriculture near Nancy (1822).

Dombrowska, Dombrowski. See DĄBROWSKA, DĄBROWSKI.

Do·mé·nech y Mon·ta·ner \dü-'mā-nə-chē-mün-'tàn-ər\, Luis. 1850–1923. Catalan architect. Follower of Gaudí in *modernismo* movement; built Museo Zoológico (1888), Palacio de la Música Catalana (1891–1908), Hospital de San Pablo de la Santa Cruz (1902–12) in Barcelona.

Do·me·ni·chi·no \,dō-mā-nē-'kē-nō\. *Also called* Domenico Zam·pie·ri \tsäm-'pyer-ē\. 1581–1641. Bolognese painter. A leader of the Baroque eclectic school after Carracci; chief Vatican architect (1621–23); at Naples (1630–34, 1635–38). Works included *Last Communion of St. Jerome, Diana and Nymphs Hunting, Madonna of the Rosary, Life of St. Januarius, Martyrdom of St. Sebastian;* frescoes at Villa Belvedere in Frascati; S. Andrea della Valle, S. Carlo ai Catinari, Sta. Maria degli Angeli, all in Rome; landscapes and portraits.

Do·me·ni·co di Gio·van·ni \dō-'mā-nē-kō-dē-jō-'vän-nē\. *Called* Il Burchiel·lo \,ēl-bür-'chel-lō\. 1404–1449. Florentine barber. Exiled for political reasons; known for burlesque sonnets and obscure humor.

Domenico di Pace. See BECCAFUMI.

Do·me·ni·co Ve·ne·zi·ano \dō-'mā-nē-kō-və-,net-sē-'än-(,)ō\. *In full* Domenico di Bartolomeo da Ve·ne·zia \-və-'net-sē-ə\. d. 1461. Italian painter. Settled in Florence (c.1439); known for fresco of Virgin and Child, altarpiece for Sta. Lucia dei Magnoli, unsigned portraits, etc.; a founder of Florentine School.

Dom·ett \'däm-ət\, Alfred. 1811–1887. English poet and colonialist. Intimate of Robert Browning; subject of Browning's poem *Waring.* Emigrated to New Zealand (1842), where he was prime minister (1862–63), registrar general of land (1865–71). Author of *Ranolf and Amohia, a South Sea Day Dream* (1872), *Flotsam and Jetsam* (1877).

Do·mey·ko \dò-'me-ē-kò\, Ignacio, *Pol.* Ignacy. 1801–1889. Polish mineralogist. To Chile (1838); founded school of chemistry and mineralogy at Coquimbo; professor (from 1839) and rector (from 1867), U. of Santiago; responsible for speeding development of Chilean resources. Domeyko range of Chilean Andes and mineral domeykite named for him.

Dom·i·nic \'däm-ə-,nik\. Saint. *Orig.* Domingo de Guz·mán \thā-güth-'män\. c.1170–1221. Spanish religious. Canon regular of cathedral at Osma (1196). Began preaching against Albigenses of southern France (1206); developed plan for mendicant preaching order (1215); formed first chapter at Toulouse and received papal approbation for Order of Friars Preachers, known as Dominicans, from Honorius III (1216); established main houses at Paris and Bologna and directed order toward university teaching. Canonized (1234).

Do·mi·nis \'dò-mē-nēs\, Marco Antonio de. 1566–1624. Italian prelate. Bishop of Segnia (1596); archbishop of Spalato (1600) and primate of Dalmatia and Croatia. Involved in quarrel between papacy and Venice, crossed to England (1616); became convert to Anglicanism and dean of Windsor (1619); attacked the papacy in *Consilium profectionis* (1617) and *De republica ecclesiastica* (1617). Returned to Rome (1622) and recanted in *Sui reditus ex Angliae consilium* (1623); imprisoned by the Inquisition.

Do·mi·tian \də-'mish-ən\. *Full name* Titus Flavius Do·mi·ti·a·nus \də-,mish-ē-'ā-nəs\. 51–96 A.D. Emperor of Rome (81–96). Second son of Vespasian and Flavia Domitilla, and brother of Titus. Praetor (70); succeeded Titus as emperor (81). Undertook military expansion in Britain and on the Danube; unsuccessful in campaign against the Dacians under Decebalus (86–90); aroused by jealousy, recalled (84) Agricola from his victories in Britain. Reign noted for severity, esp. in the terror of 93–96, and his personal ostentation; murdered by a freedman, as the result of a conspiracy by the empress Domitia and officers of the court.

Domitius Afer. See AFER.

Domitius Ahenobarbus. See AHENOBARBUS.

Domnus. See DONUS.

Don·ald \'dän-ᵊld\, William Henry. 1875–1946. Australian journalist and economist. On Hong Kong *China Mail* for several years (after 1902); joined Chinese Revolution as adviser to Sun Yat-sen (1911); later, adviser to several governments in China; first revealed Japan's Twenty-one Demands (1915); helped defeat monarchical designs of Yüan Shih-k'ai (1916). Editor of *Far Eastern Review* (from 1911); adviser (1928–33) to Marshal Chang Hsüeh-liang in Manchuria; adviser to Chiang Kai-shek (from 1934); prisoner of Japanese in Philippines (1942–45).

Don·ald·son \'dän-ᵊl(d)-sən\, John William. 1811–1861. English philologist. Attempted in the *New Cratylus* (1839) to apply to Greek scientific principles of comparative philology; in *Varronianus* (1844) applied method to Latin, Umbrian, and Oscan.

Donalitius. See DONELAITIS.

Don·a·tel·lo \,dō-nä-'tel-lō, *Angl* ,dän-ə-'tel-(,)ō\. *Orig.* Donato, *surnamed* de Bet·to di Bar·di \dā-'bāt-tō-dē-'bär-dē\. 1386?–1466. Florentine sculptor. Associate of Ghiberti, Brunelleschi, and Michelozzo; after Brunelleschi, the leading innovator and exponent of new Renaissance style, and the greatest sculptor of his century; strongly influenced by art of classical antiquity. His works in Florence included *St. George, John the Evangelist, David, Poggio, Zuccone, Habakkuk, St. Louis, Magdalen,* and *Judith and Holofernes;* other sculptures by him are in Padua (esp. *Gattamelata*), Naples, and Siena.

Do·na·ti \dō-'nä-tē\, Corso. d. 1308. Florentine political leader. Member of Guelph party; became popular through victory at Campaldino over Arezzo (1289); formed Neri faction against bourgeois Bianchi; exiled (1300);

repatriated (1301) by Charles of Valois; dictator of Florence (1301–08); died attempting to escape popular uprising.

Donati, Giovanni Battista. 1826–1873. Italian astronomer. Director of Florence observatory (1864); discovered six comets, one of which is named after him; by spectroscopic means, discovered (1864) the gaseous composition of comets.

Donato d'Agnolo *or* **d'Angelo.** See BRAMANTE.

Do·na·tus \də-ˈnāt-əs\. 4th century A.D. Name of two figures involved in Donatist schism of North African church who were probably the same person: (1) Bishop of Casae Nigrae; fanatically courted martyrdom during Diocletian persecutions and opposed traditor ecclesiastics who chose to surrender sacred books in order to escape persecution. Apparently leader of opposition to consecration of Caecilian as bishop of Carthage (311); represented rigorist party at Lateran council (313). (2) *Known as* the Great. Leader of Donatist party, which gradually became class and racial party of native Berbers opposed to Roman influences; schismatic bishop of Carthage (313–347); removed by Emperor Constantius II following outrages of Circumcellions, Donatist zealots. Died in exile in Gaul or Spain (c.355).

Donatus, Aelius. 4th century A.D. Roman grammarian. Author of an *Ars grammatica,* comprising *Ars maior* and *Ars minor,* the latter so widely used as an elementary textbook in western Europe into the Middle Ages that the term *donat* or *donet* came to be synonymous with grammar or with any textbook treating elementary principles of a subject.

Don·ders \ˈdȯn-dərs\, Frans Cornelis. 1818–1889. Dutch ophthalmologist and physiologist. Professor at Utrecht (1852–89); investigated physiology and pathology of the eye; discovered physiological bases of farsightedness and astigmatism; introduced use of prismatic and cylindrical lenses for eyeglasses.

Do·ne·lai·tis \ˌdȯn-e-ˈlīt-əs\ *or* **Duo·ne·lai·tis** \ˌdwȯn-\, Kristijonas. 1714–1780. Lithuanian poet. Pastor in Tolmingkehmen (1743–80); wrote *Metai* (pub. 1818) depicting life of Lithuanian peasants in dialect; first use of hexameters in Lithuanian verse; also wrote fables and a verse tale *Pričkaus pasaka apie lietuvišką svodbą* (pub. 1865).

Don·el·son \ˈdän-əl-sən\, Andrew Jackson. 1799–1871. American army officer and diplomat, b. near Nashville, Tenn. Reared by Andrew Jackson; aide-de-camp to Jackson in Seminole War. Secretary to Jackson (1824–37). Negotiated treaty of annexation with Republic of Texas (1844–45); U.S. minister to Prussia (1846–49). Know-Nothing candidate for vice presidency of the United States (1856).

Don·gan \ˈdäŋ-gən\, Thomas. 2nd Earl of Lim·er·ick \ˈlim-(ə-)rik\. 1634–1715. Irish colonial administrator in America. Lieutenant governor of Tangier (1678–80); governor of New York (1682–88); called first representative assembly (1683); issued "Charter of Liberties" (1683).

Dong·en \ˈdȯŋ-ən\, Cornelis Theodorus Maria. *Known as* Kees van Dongen \ˈkās-\. 1877–1968. Dutch painter. Early associated with Fauve and Die Brücke movements; later known esp. for fashionable portraits.

Do·ni \ˈdō-nē\, Anton Francesco. 1513?–1574. Italian writer. Led wandering life as author and editor; founder of Italian bibliography; works included *I Marmi* (1552).

Doni, Giovanni Battista. 1594–1647. Italian scholar. Protégé of Cardinal Barberini; known for researches on ancient music; invented type of double lyre called lyra barberina or Amphichord.

Dö·nitz \ˈdœ-nits\, Karl. 1891–1980. German admiral. Submarine commander in World War I; supervised construction and named commander (1936) of new U-boat fleet; conducted highly destructive "Battle of the Atlantic"; commander of German navy (1943–45); head of northern military and civil command (1945); named by Hitler his successor as head of state (April 1945); executed surrender to Allies (May 1945); tried as war criminal and imprisoned (1946–56).

Don·i·zet·ti \ˌdō-nēd-ˈzāt-tē, *Angl* ˌdän-ə(d)-ˈzet-ē, ˌdōn-\, Gaetano, *in full* Domenico Gaetano Maria. 1797–1848. Italian composer. Wrote 75 operas, enjoying great success in Italy and Paris; influenced Verdi; operas included *Anna Bolena* (1830), *L'elisir d'amore* (1832), *Lucrezia Borgia* (1833), *Lucia di Lammermoor* (1835), *Maria Stuarda* (1835), *Belisario* (1836), *Roberto Devereux* (1837), *La Fille du régiment* (1840), *La Favorite* (1840), *Linda di Chamounix* (1842), *Don Pasquale* (1843), *Dom Sébastien* (1843); also chamber, orchestral, and sacred vocal works.

Don·kin \ˈdäŋ-kən\, Bryan. 1768–1855. English engineer and inventor. Developed first practical working machine for making paper based on Fourdrinier patent (c.1803); subsequently built 191 such machines; invented an early form of rotary printing machine (1813) and composition printing roller; devised (1812) method of processing meat and vegetables in tin.

Don·nan \ˈdän-ən\, Frederick George. 1870–1956. British chemist, b. Ceylon. Professor at Liverpool (1904–13), University Coll., London (1913–37); known for work in membrane equilibrium.

Don·nay \dȯ-nā\, Maurice-Charles. 1859–1945. French playwright. Author of *Eux!* (1889), adaptation of *Lysistrata* (1892), *Amants* (1895), *La Douloureuse* (1897), *L'Affranchie* (1898), *La Clairière* (1900), *La Retour de Jérusalem* (1903), *Oiseaux de passage* (1904), *Les Éclaireuses* (1913), *La Chasse à l'homme* (1919), *La Reprise* (1924), etc.

Donn-Byrne \ˈdän-ˈbərn\, Brian Oswald. *Known as* Donn Byrne. 1889–1928. American writer, b. New York City. Reared in Ireland; to U.S. (1911). Author of *Messer Marco Polo* (1921), *Blind Raftery* (1924), *Hangman's House* (1926), *Crusade* (1928).

Donne \ˈdən, ˈdän\, John. 1572–1631. English poet. Brought up as Roman Catholic; studied law; sailed in Essex's expeditions to Cádiz (1596) and the Azores (1597); private secretary (1598–1602) to Sir Thomas Egerton, lord keeper of the great seal, who sat him in Parliament (1601); dismissed from private secretaryship because of clandestine marriage with his patron's niece. Published extravagant elegies (*Anniversaries*) on daughter of his host Sir Robert Drury, *An Anatomie of the World* (1611), *On the Progres of the Soule* (1612). Again in Parliament (1614); sought in vain for government sinecure. Having won approval of James I with *Pseudo-Martyr* (1610), assuring Roman Catholics of freedom from inconsistency in taking oath of allegiance to James I, followed king's suggestion that he take Anglican holy orders (1615); preached sermons unexcelled in 17th century; executed mission to Bohemia and preached before Princess Elizabeth at Heidelberg (1619); dean of St. Paul's (1621–31); preached often before Charles I. Among his poetical works were sonnets, songs, satires, elegies, and religious verses; first published collections posthumous (1633, 1635); prose works included *Devotions upon Emergent Occasions* (1624), *Foure Sermons* (1625), *Death's Duell* (1630). Verse and prose noted for play of wit and imagery, passion, seriousness; premier among Metaphysical poets.

Don·nel·ly \ˈdän-əl-ē, ˈdän-lē\, Ignatius. 1831–1901. American politician and author, b. Philadelphia. Founded Nininger City, Minnesota (1857); member, U.S. House of Representatives (1863–69). Editor, *Anti-Monopolist* (1874–79), an independent weekly journal. Author of *Atlantis, the Antediluvian World* (1882), *Ragnarok: The Age of Fire and Gravel* (1883), *The Great Cryptogram* (1888; a book intended to prove by a cipher that Francis Bacon was writer of plays attributed to Shakespeare), *Caesar's Column* (1891).

Don·ner \ˈdȯ-nər\, Georg Raphael. 1693–1741. Austrian sculptor. Works included statue of St. Martin in Pressburg (c.1734), fountain on Never Markt, Vienna (1738–39), Perseus and Andromeda fountain, Vienna Rathaus, statue of Emperor Charles VI, Vienna; style considered to mark transition from Baroque to Neoclassical.

Dono, Paolo di. See Paolo UCCELLO.

Do·no·so Cor·tés \dō-ˈnō-sō-kȯr-ˈtās\, Juan Francisco María de la Salud. Marqués de Val·de·ga·mas \väl-dā-ˈgä-mäs\. 1809–1853. Spanish writer and diplomat. Elected to Cortes (1837); supporter of liberal causes until revolutions of 1848 pushed him to the extreme right wing; noted for oratory; ambassador to Berlin (1849–50), Paris (1851); wrote *Ensayo sobre el catolicismo, el liberalismo y el socialismo* (1851).

Don·o·van \ˈdän-ə-vən, ˈdən-\, William Joseph. *Nicknamed* Wild Bill. 1883–1959. American lawyer, b. Buffalo, N.Y. Served in World War I; assistant to U.S. attorney general (1925–29); head of Office of Strategic Services (1942–45); major general (1944); ambassador to Thailand (1953–54).

Do·nus \ˈdō-nəs\ *or* **Dom·nus** \ˈdäm-nəs\. d. 678. Pope (676–678).

Dood·son \ˈdüd-sən, ˈdu̇d-\, Arthur Thomas. 1890–1968. English oceanographer. Associate director (1929–45), director (1946–61), Liverpool Observatory and Tidal Institute; known for application of statistical methods to study of tides.

Dooley, Mr. See Finley Peter DUNNE.

Doo·ley \ˈdü-lē\, Thomas Anthony. 1927–1961. American physician, b. St. Louis. Served in U.S. navy (1953–56); engaged in medical relief among Vietnamese refugees (from 1954); established medical mission at Nam Tha, Northern Laos (1956), followed by hospitals in Cambodia, Laos, Vietnam; established Medico, international medical aid mission (1957); wrote *Deliver Us from Evil* (1956), *Edge of Tomorrow* (1958), *The Night They Burned the Mountain* (1960).

Doo·lit·tle \ˈdü-ˌlit-əl\, Hilda. *Pen name* H. D. 1886–1961. American poet, b. Bethlehem, Pa. m. Richard Aldington (1913; div. 1937). Early poems, in Imagist manner, published by Ezra Pound; poetical works included *Sea Garden* (1916), *Hymen* (1921), *Heliodora* (1924), *Hippolytus Temporizes* (1927), *Red Roses for Bronze* (1931), *The Walls Do Not Fall* (1944), *Tribute to the Angels* (1945), *Flowering of the Rod* (1946); wrote novels *Palimpsest* (1926), *Hedylus* (1928), *Hedgehog* (1936), *Bid Me to Live* (1960).

Door·man \ˈdōr-ˌmän\, Karel Willem Frederik Marie. 1889–1942. Dutch admiral. Entered navy (1910); commander of naval air forces in Dutch East Indies (1937); commander of East Indies fleet (1940); named commander of combined American, British, Dutch, and Australian (ABDA) fleet (Feb. 1942); went down with flagship *De Ruyter* in Battle of Java Sea.

Dopp·ler \ˈdȯ-plər, *Angl* ˈdäp-lər\, Christian Johann. 1803–1853. Austrian physicist. Professor, Vienna, and director of Physical Institute (1850–53); published paper *Über das farbige Licht der Doppelsterne* (1842) in which he enunciated the principle (now known as Doppler effect) that, if an observer and a source of constant vibrations, as of sound or light, are in relative motion, the observed frequency changes.

Dora, Sister. See under Mark PATTISON.

Do·ran \ˈdōr-ən, ˈdȯr-ən; də-ˈran, dō-\, George Henry. 1869–1956. American publisher, b. Toronto. To Chicago (1892); established George H. Doran Co. (in Toronto, 1908; moved to N.Y. 1909); joined with F. N. Doubleday to form Doubleday, Doran & Co. (1927).

Doran, John. 1807–1878. British journalist and writer. Editor of *Athenaeum* (1869), *Notes and Queries* (1870–78). Author of *A History of Court Fools* (1858), *Their Majesties' Servants* (1860), *In and About Drury Lane* (1885), *A Lady of the Last Century* (1873).

Do·rat *or* **Dau·rat** \dȯ-rä\, Jean. 1508–1588. French poet and Humanist. Director, Collège de Coqueret (1547) where Ronsard was his pupil; professor of Greek, Collège de France (1556–67); leader and president of the Pléiade group of poets; prolific writer of Greek and Latin verse, some published in *J. Aurati Lemovicis poetae et interpretis regii poemata* (1586); appointed poet royal by Charles IX.

Dorchester, 1st Baron. See Sir Guy CARLETON.

Do·ré \dȯ-rā, *Angl* dȯ-ˈrā, də-\, Gustave, *in full* Paul-Gustave. 1832–1883. French illustrator. Noted for fantastic imagination; illustrated over 90 books, including *Oeuvres de Rabelais* (1854), Balzac's *Contes drolatiques* (1855), Dante's *Inferno* (1861), *Don Quichotte* (1863), the Bible (1866).

Do·re·mus \də-ˈrē-məs, dȯ-\, Sarah Platt, *nee* Haines \ˈhānz\. 1802–1877. American philanthropist, b. New York City. m. Thomas C. Doremus (1821). Instrumental in founding New York Woman's Hospital (1855), Woman's Union Missionary Society (1861), and shelters and homes for unfortunates.

Dor·gan \ˈdȯr-gən\, Thomas Aloysius. *Pseudonym* Tad \ˈtad\. 1877–1929. American cartoonist and sportswriter, b. San Francisco. On San Francisco *Bulletin* (1892–1902) and New York *Journal* (from 1902).

Dorgelès, Roland. See Roland LÉCAVELÉ.

Dor·gon \ˈdȯr-ˌgän\. 1612–1650. Manchu prince. Son of Nurhachi; named imperial prince by Abahai; led army in breaching Great Wall and subjugating Hopeh and Shantung provinces (1638–39); declined to succeed Abahai (1643) and became co-regent for Fu-lin; drove rebel emperor Li Tzu-ch'eng from Peking (1644) and reorganized government for Fu-lin; extended Manchu rule over outlying provinces (1644–46); named imperial father regent (1648); posthumously declared emperor under temple name Ch'eng Tsung and then declared usurper (1651).

Do·ria \ˈdȯr-yä\, Andrea. 1466–1560. Genoese admiral and statesman. Soldier of fortune in service of Pope Innocent VIII, Ferdinand I and Alfonso II of Naples, etc.; patrolled Mediterranean against Turks and pirates with own fleet of galleys; commanded French fleet against Charles V (1524–28); transferred allegiance from Francis I to Charles V (1528); drove French from Genoa and set up oligarchic form of government (1528); named grand admiral of imperial fleet and prince of Malfi by Charles V (1528); victorious over Turks at Patras (1532); achieved conquest of Tunis (1535); in service of Charles V against Algiers (1541). See Gian Luigi FIESCHI.

Doria, Giacomo. 1840–1913. Italian naturalist and explorer. Made expeditions to Persia (1862), Borneo (1865–66), Tunisia (1879); founded Doria museum, Genoa (1867); senator (1890); director of Società Geografica Italiana (1891–1900).

Do·rion \dȯr-yō^{n}\, Sir Antoine Aimé. 1818–1891. Canadian jurist and politician; b. Sainte-Anne-de-la-Pérade, Que. Member of legislature of United Province (1854–67); leader of liberal faction; joint premier with George Brown (1858) and with J.S. Macdonald (1863–64); in federal parliament (1867–74); minister of justice (1873–74); chief justice of court of Queen's Bench, Quebec (1874–91).

Do·riot \dȯr-yō\, Jacques. 1898–?1945. French politician. Elected deputy as Communist (1924); expelled from party for Trotskyism and participation in "Common Front against Fascism" (1934); organized pro-Fascist Parti Populaire Française (1936); collaborated with German occupation.

Dorn \ˈdȯrn\, Heinrich Ludwig Egmont. 1804–1892. German composer. Founded Cologne Conservatory (1848); conductor of Berlin Royal Opera (1849–68); composed cantatas, symphonies, songs, and ten operas, notably *Die Nibelungen* (1854).

Dorn·berg·er \ˈdȯrn-ˌber-gər\, Walter Robert. 1895–1980. German engineer. Experimented with rockets (from 1930); in charge of army rocket research (from 1932); developed V-2 rocket (1936–44); to U.S. (1947); with Bell Aircraft Corp. (from 1950); wrote *V-2* (1954).

Dor·ner \ˈdȯr-nər\, Isaak August. 1809–1884. German Protestant theologian. Professor, Berlin (from 1861). Author of *Entwicklungsgeschichte der Lehre von der Person Christi* (1839), *System der christlichen Glaubenslehre* (1879–81), etc.

Dor·nier \dȯrn-ˈyā, ˈdȯrn-ˌyā\, Claudius. 1884–1969. German airplane builder. Entered service of Graf von Zeppelin (1910); designed first all-metal airplane (1911); established Dornier factory at Friedrichshafen (1914). Builder of 12-engine "Do-X," largest airplane of its time (1929), fast bombers, reconnaissance flying boats, and torpedo-carrying airplanes.

Do·roth·e·us \də-ˈräth-ē-əs\. 6th century A.D. Roman jurist in Syria. Under emperor Justinian helped compile Digest or Pandects (533) and second edition of the Codex (534); with Tribonian and Theophilus drew up a book of Institutes (533) as an introduction to the Digest.

Dörp·feld \ˈdœrp-ˌfelt\, Wilhelm. 1853–1940. German archaeologist. Worked with Ernst Curtius at Olympia (1877–81), with Schliemann at Troy (1882–83) and Tiryns (1884–85); again at Troy (1893–94); author of *Troja und Ilion* (1902), *Die Heimkehr des Odysseus* (1924), *Alt-Ithaka* (1927), *Alt-Olympia* (1935), *Alt-Athen und seine Agora* (1937–39).

Dorr \ˈdȯ(ə)r\, John Van Nostrand. 1872–1962. American metallurgical engineer, b. Newark, N.J. Inventor of Dorr classifier, Dorr thickener, and Dorr agitator, used in ore dressing.

Dorr, Julia Caroline, *nee* Rip·ley \ˈrip-lē\. 1825–1913. American writer, b. Charleston, S.C. Best known for her poems, of which ten volumes were published between 1872 and 1913.

Dorr, Thomas Wilson. 1805–1854. American lawyer and politician, leader of "Dorr's Rebellion," b. Providence, R.I. Agitator for widening the suffrage in Rhode Island (from 1834); organizer of People's party, which submitted (1841) a new liberal constitution that was almost unanimously approved by electorate. Action declared illegal by state authorities, who submitted (1842) a constitution of their own that failed to gain popular approval. Elected governor (1842) under People's constitution, thus giving Rhode Island two governments; arrested, tried, convicted, and sentenced (1844) to life imprisonment and hard labor but released a year later.

Dor·re·ga·ray \dȯr-rā-gä-ˈrä\, Antonio. 1823–1882. Spanish general. Active in Carlist campaign (1836–39); captain general of Carlist forces (1872–76).

Dor·re·go \dȯr-ˈrā-gō\, Manuel. 1787–1828. Argentine politician. On outbreak of separatist movements (1810), saw military service in Chile, Bolivia, Uruguay, and Argentina; exiled to U.S.; on return (1820) acted as provisional governor of Buenos Aires; prominent in constituent assembly (1826); elected governor of Buenos Aires (1827); terminated war with Brazil (1828); deposed and executed by army rebels favoring Gen. Juan Lavalle.

Dorrien, Sir Horace Smith-. See SMITH-DORRIEN.

d'Orsay. See ORSAY.

Dorset, Countess of. See Anne Clifford, under CLIFFORD family.

Dorset. (1) Earls of: see BEAUFORT and SACKVILLE families, also Thomas SACKVILLE. (2) Dukes of: see SACKVILLE family. (3) Marquises of: see BEAUFORT and GREY families.

Dor·set \ˈdȯr-sət\, Marion. 1872–1935. American chemist, b. Columbia, Tenn. With U.S. Bureau of Animal Industry (1894–1935); known for his work on the chemistry of the tubercle bacillus, codiscoverer of hog-cholera serum.

Dor·sey \ˈdōr-sē, ˈdȯr-\, James (1904–1957) and his brother Thomas (1905–1956). American band leaders, b. Shenandoah, Pa. Began as freelance musicians in jazz and dance bands, Jimmy a clarinettist and saxophonist, Tommy a trombonist; led popular bands together (1933–35, 1953–56) and individually.

Dorsey, James Owen. 1848–1895. American ethnologist, b. Baltimore. Episcopal missionary among Ponca Indians, Dakota Territory (1871–80). Sent by U.S. Bureau of American Ethnology to study Omaha Indians (1880). Author of *Of the Comparative Phonology of Four Siouan Languages* (1883), *Omaha Sociology* (1884), *Osage Traditions* (1888), *Siouan Sociology* (1897); edited *Dakota-English Dictionary* and *Dakota Grammar, Texts, and Ethnography by Stephen Return Riggs* (1893).

Dō·shō \dō-shō\. 629–700. Japanese Buddhist priest. Studied under Hsüan-tsang in China (653–661); introduced Hossō Buddhism to Japan on return.

Do·sith·e·os *or* **Do·sith·e·us** \dō-ˈsith-ē-əs\. 1641–1707. Patriarch of Jerusalem (1669–1707). Called synod at Jerusalem (1672) which adopted so-called Confession of Dositheos, directed against Calvinism, last official statement of doctrine issued by the Orthodox Church.

Dositheus. 3d century B.C. to 1st century A.D.? Name given to one or more Jewish heresiarchs of Samaria whose followers were known as Dositheans.

Dositheus Ma·gis·ter \-mə-ˈjis-tər\. 4th century A.D. Greek grammarian. Teacher in Rome; published Greek translation of Latin grammar, for use as textbook.

Dosoftei. See BARYLOVICZ.

Dos Pas·sos \də-ˈspas-əs\, John Roderigo. 1896–1970. American novelist, b. Chicago. Books included *Three Soldiers* (1921); *A Pushcart at the Curb* (verse, 1922); *Manhattan Transfer* (1925); a trilogy *U.S.A.,* comprising *The 42d Parallel* (1930), *1919* (1932), and *The Big Money* (1936); a *District of*

\ə\ abut \ᵊ\ kitten, *Fr.* table \ər\ further \a\ ash \ā\ ace \ä\ cot, cart \au̇\ out \ch\ chin \e\ bet \ē\ easy \g\ go \i\ hit \ī\ ice \j\ job \ŋ\ sing \ō\ go \ȯ\ law \ȯi\ boy \th\ both \th\ the \ü\ loot \u̇\ foot \y\ yet \zh\ vision \ȧ, b, g, k, ^{n}, œ, ǣ, ue, ue, ʸ\ *see* Guide to Pronunciation

Columbia trilogy comprising *Adventures of a Young Man* (1939), *Number One* (1943), and *The Grand Design* (1949); *Most Likely to Succeed* (1954); *The Great Days* (1958); *Midcentury* (1961).

Dosso Dossi. See Giovanni LUTERO.

Dōst Mo·ham·mad Khān \dōst-mō-'həm-məd-'kän\. 1793–1863. Ruler of Afghanistan. Son of head of Barakzāi clan; took part in revolt against Maḥmūd Shāh (1818–26) and assumed throne (1826), founding Barakzāi dynasty. Caught in rivalry between Britain and Russia; captured (1840) during First Afghan War (1839–42), in which British placed Shāh Shojā' on throne; restored after British driven from Kābul (1843); concluded treaty with India (1855); remained neutral during the Sepoy Mutiny (1857); acquired province of Herāt (1863).

Dos·to·yev·sky \dəs-(,)tə-'yăf-skəi, *Angl* däs-tə-'yef-skē, -'yev-\, Fyodor Mikhaylovich. 1821–1881. Russian novelist. In army (1841–44); resigned to take up writing. Arrested (1849) and tried for conspiracy against the government; convicted and sentenced to be shot; reprieved at last moment and given four years at hard labor at Omsk, Siberia (1849–54) followed by term as soldier (1854–58). Resumed literary work (1858); founded (1860) review *Vremya* (suppressed by government, 1863), and its successor *Epokha* (failed c.1865). Spent some years abroad to escape financial troubles (1864–65, 1867–71); founded review, *An Author's Diary* (1876–77, 1880–1881), which proved successful. His novels, powerful explorations of the lives of ordinary and extraordinary people and their searches for faith, meaning, and truth, included *Bednye lyudi* (*Poor Folk,* 1846), *Netochka Nezvanova* (1849), *Unizhennye i oskorblënnye* (*Insulted and Injured,* 1861), *Zapiski iz podpolya* (*Notes from the Underground,* 1864), *Prestuplenie i nakazanie* (*Crime and Punishment,* 1866), *Igrok* (*The Gambler,* 1866), *Idiot* (1868–69), *Besy* (*The Possessed,* 1871), *Bratya Karamazovy* (*Brothers Karamazov,* 1879–80).

Dou *or* **Douw** \'daů\, Gerrit *or* Gerard. 1613–1675. Dutch painter. Studied under Rembrandt (1628–31); painted portraits of Rembrandt's father and mother; headed school of Leiden after Rembrandt's departure (1631); best known for genre scenes and portraits in highly refined manner.

Dou·ay \dwā\, Charles-Abel. 1809–1870. French general. Distinguished himself at Malakoff (1855) and at Solferino (1859); killed at battle of Wissembourg. His brother ¶Félix-Charles (1816–1879), also a general (from 1863), distinguished himself at Sedan (1870) and in commanding troops entering Paris during Commune of Paris (1871).

Dou·ble·day \'dəb-əl-,dā\, Abner. 1819–1893. American army officer, b. Ballston Spa, N.Y. Served through Mexican War, on routine duty, and through Civil War; major general of volunteers (1862); commanded I Corps at Gettysburg (1863). For many years was credited with the creation and naming, while attending school in Cooperstown, N.Y., of the modern game of baseball, the adoption of the diamond-shaped field and the assignment of definite playing positions being ascribed to him.

Doubleday, Frank Nelson. 1862–1934. American publisher, b. Brooklyn, N.Y. With Charles Scribner's Sons (1877–1895); with S.S. McClure founded firm of Doubleday & McClure Co. (1897–1900); president, Doubleday, Page & Co. in partnership with Walter Hines Page (1900–27); built Country Life Press, Garden City, N.Y. (1910); chairman of board, Doubleday, Doran & Co. (1927–34).

Dou·cet \dü-se\, Charles-Camille. 1812–1895. French playwright. Author of *Un jeune homme* (1841), *Les Ennemis de la maison* (1851), *Le Fruit défendu* (1858), *La Considération* (1860), etc.

Dou·dart de La·grée \dü-dár-də-lá-grā\, Ernest-Marc-Louis de Gon·zague \gōⁿ-zág\. 1823–1868. French diplomat and explorer. In navy (from 1845); served in Crimea (1854), Cambodia (1862); as French diplomatic representative secured treaty of protection from King Norodom of Cambodia (1863), establishing French hegemony in that nation; resident at Phnom Penh (1864). Led geographic expedition up Mekong River to Laos and China (1866).

Douf·fet \dü-'fe\, Gerard. 1594–1660. Dutch painter. Studied under Rubens (1612–14); painter to prince-bishop of Liége (1624); founder of Liége school.

Dough·ty \'daůt-ē\, Charles Montagu. 1843–1926. English poet and traveler. Travels included journey through Arabia disguised as an Arab (1876–78), on which he made valuable geographical, historical, anthropological, and geological observations; wrote *Travels in Arabia Deserta* (1888) in Elizabethan style he considered true English prose style; now recognized as masterpiece of graphic narration and description. Author also of long poems and poetic dramas, including *The Dawn in Britain* (1906), *Adam Cast Forth* (1908), *The Cliffs* (1909), *The Clouds* (1912), *The Titans* (1916), *Mansoul* (1920).

Doughty, Susan Dorothy. 1892–1962. English ceramist. Known for detailed porcelain flowers, esp. those created for Royal Worcester Porcelain Co. (from 1935).

Doughty, Thomas. 1793–1856. American painter, b. Philadelphia. Known esp. for landscapes; member of Hudson River school.

Doughty-Wy·lie \-'wī-lē\, Charles Hotham Montagu. 1868–1915. English soldier and consul. Nephew of Charles Montagu Doughty. Saw active service in India, Egyptian campaign (1898), Boer War, and China (1901); while military consul at Konieh (1906–09) prevented massacre of Armenian Christians (1909); consul general at Addis Ababa (1909–13); killed leading charge at Gallipoli.

Doug·las \'dəg-ləs\. Name of a noble Scottish family having its home in the dale of Douglas in Lanarkshire, represented by the earls of Douglas (created 1358), of Angus (cr. 1389), of Morton (cr. 1458), marquises of Douglas (cr. 1633), dukes of Hamilton (cr. 1660), of Queensberry (cr. 1684), and many lesser dignities. Members of the family included the following:

Sir William of Douglas, *called* the Hardy (d. 1298), 1st Lord of Douglas; swore fealty to Edward I (1291), but commanded Baliol forces at Berwick Castle; surrendered to English (1296); on renewal of homage to Edward I, restored to possessions in seven Scottish counties; joined Wallace's rising (1297).

¶Sir James Douglas, *called* the Good (1286–1330), Lord of Douglas, son of 1st lord; joined revolt of Robert Bruce; escaped with Bruce from battle of Methuen; three times destroyed English garrisons in his castle of Douglas; by raids into England earned dreaded name of "the Black Douglas"; took Teviotdale; commanded left wing at Bannockburn (1314); invaded Yorkshire; defeated army of archbishop of York and bishop of Ely at Mitton (1319); surprised English at Weardale (1327), nearly capturing Edward III; during peace that followed, carrying embalmed heart of Bruce to Holy Land according to dying king's wish; fell fighting Moors in Andalusia. His son ¶William was killed at Halidon Hill (1333), as was his half-brother, the youngest son of Sir William the Hardy, ¶Sir Archibald (1296?–1333), who conquered Edward de Baliol at Annan (1332) and was regent of Scotland (1333).

¶Sir William Douglas (1300?–1353), Knight of Liddes·dale \'lidz-,dāl\; and called the "flower of chivalry"; sided with David II, killing Edward de Baliol's lieutenant in Scotland (1337); commanded division at Neville's Cross, where David II was captured (1346); ambassador to France; killed on hunting trip by his kinsman William, later 1st Earl of Douglas.

EARLS OF DOUGLAS (distinguished as the Black Douglases):

¶William Douglas (1327?–1384), 1st Earl of Douglas (cr. 1358) and, by marriage, Earl of Mar \'mär\; son of Sir Archibald (1296?–1333); returned from training in France (1348) and recovered Douglasdale and Ettrick Forest to Scottish allegiance; present at battle of Poitiers (1356); warden of east marches; rebelled against David II (1363) in consequence of royal misappropriation of funds raised for ransom; reconciled, swore allegiance to Robert II (1371); justiciar of southern Scotland (from 1371).

His son ¶James (1358?–1388), 2d Earl of Douglas and Mar; m. (1373) Isabel, daughter of Robert II; made war on English with aid of French under Jean de Vienne (1385); defeated two sons of Earl of Northumberland in battle of Otterburn, in which he was killed and Hotspur captured (celebrated in Scottish ballad *The Battle of Otterburn* and English ballad *Chevy Chase*).

¶Archibald (1328?–?1400), *called* the Grim; 3d Earl of Douglas, Lord of Gal·lo·way \'gal-ə-,wā\; natural son of Sir James Douglas the Good; nicknamed (like his father) "the Black Douglas"; warden of western marches (1364, 1368); twice sent on missions to French court (1369, 1371); succeeded to earldom of Douglas by rule of entail (1388); invaded England (1389); codified laws of marches; married his daughter Marjory to David, Duke of Rothesay, heir apparent of Scottish crown.

¶Archibald (1370?–1424), 4th Earl of Douglas and 1st Duke of Tou·raine \tü-ren, *Angl* ,tü-'rān\ (cr. 1423), *called* Tine·man \'tīn-mən\, *i.e.* Loser; son of Archibald the Grim; m. (1390) Margaret, eldest daughter of Robert III; made keeper of the castle at Edinburgh (1400); allied himself with ambitious 1st Duke of Albany, with whom he was suspected of complicity in death of David, Duke of Rothesay, the heir apparent (1402); defeated and taken prisoner by George Dunbar, Earl of March, and Hotspur at Homildon Hill (1402); formed personal alliance with John the Fearless, Duke of Burgundy (1412); led Scottish contingent to aid Charles VII of France (1423); defeated and slain at Verneuil.

¶Archibald (1391?–1439), 5th Earl of Douglas and 2d Duke of Touraine; son of 4th earl and 1st duke; fought against English at Beaugé and created count of Longueville (1421); carried James I home from English captivity (1424); his two sons ¶William (1423?–1440), 6th earl and 3d and last Duke of Touraine, and ¶David, were beheaded after mock trial before James II, after which the family's power was broken.

¶William (1425?–1452), 8th Earl of Douglas; son of 7th earl; recovered estates by marriage with Margaret, the Fair Maid of Galloway, sister of 6th earl; stood high in favor of James II (until 1452); on refusal to break up league with Earl of Crawford, was attacked and killed by king and followers.

His brother ¶James (1426–1488), 9th and last Earl of Douglas; forced, by failure of allies, to desist from denunciation of James II as murderer and traitor; married his brother's widow, the Maid of Galloway, and held family estates intact; rebelled again (1455); his forces under his three brothers routed by a kinsman, the Red Douglas, 4th Earl of Angus (see below); his lands forfeited; fled to England; employed by Edward IV to negotiate league with western highlanders; captured during raid with Duke of Albany (1484); died a monk. For restoration of title of Douglas see *marquises of Douglas* below.

EARLS OF AN·GUS \'aŋ-gəs\ (distinguished as the Red Douglases):

¶George Douglas (1380?–1403), 1st Earl of Angus (created by grant of his mother's earldom of Angus, 1389); illegitimate son of William, 1st Earl of Douglas, and his wife's sister-in-law, Margaret Stewart, Countess of Angus (third creation) and of Mar (by marriage); held seat in shire of Forfar (or Angus); m. (1397) Mary, daughter of Robert III; taken prisoner at Homildon Hill (1402); died of plague in England.

¶Archibald (1449?–?1514), 5th Earl of Angus, *known as* the Great Earl; nicknamed "Bell-the-Cat" for his capture of Robert Cochrane, Earl of Mar, hated favorite of James III (1482); warden of east marches (1481); joined Alexander, Duke of Albany, in intrigue with Edward IV (1482); one of leaders in rebellion against James III (1487–88); chancellor of kingdom under James IV (1493–98); lost two sons at Flodden (1513). (For his son Gawin, or Gavin, Douglas, poet and bishop, see separate entry.)

¶Archibald (1489?–1557), 6th Earl of Angus; grandson of 5th earl; m. (1514) queen dowager Margaret Tudor, sister of Henry VIII and widow of James IV of Scotland, thereby arousing jealousy of nobles; made peace (1515) with Duke of Albany, regent and leader of French party in Scotland, who besieged Queen Margaret and took possession of her son, the young king, James V; in absence of Albany, gained supreme power by defeating Arran (1520); charged with high treason by Albany, who was joined, on her return from seeking help in England, by Margaret because of her husband's liaison with daughter of laird of Traquair; sent to France (1520); returning with help of Henry VIII (1521), took charge of his step-son, whose majority he declared (1526); gained as chancellor (1526) supreme power in Scotland; killed his rival Lennox; on divorce (1528) by Margaret and escape of James V to his mother's side, forced to flee to England, while forfeiture was passed against him and his kinsmen (1528) and his sister Janet was burned at the stake by James V (1537); returned (after 1542) to Scotland; forfeiture annulled; joined regent Arran in resisting English; lieutenant general of southern Scotland (1544). His daughter by Margaret Tudor, ¶Lady Margaret Douglas (1515–1578), Countess of Len·nox \'len-əks, -iks\, m. Matthew Stewart, 4th Earl of Lennox, and was mother of Lord Darnley, barred from English succession by Roman Catholicism (1546); grandmother of James VI (James of England).

¶Archibald (1555–1588), 8th Earl of Angus, *called* the Good Earl; son of 7th earl; lieutenant general of southern Scotland (1574); warden of west marches (1577); lieutenant general for all of Scotland (1578); appealed to England for aid to rescue his uncle, 4th Earl of Morton (see below), who was removed from regency (1578) and subsequently executed; welcomed by Queen Elizabeth; joined unsuccessful insurrection of Earl of Mar (see John ERSKINE) and Glamis against government of James Stewart, Earl of Arran (1584); attainted; invaded Scotland and secured restoration of estates from James (1585); warden of marches and lieutenant general (1586).

MARQUISES AND DUKE OF DOUGLAS AND BARONS DOUGLAS OF DOUGLAS:

¶William Douglas (1589–1660), 11th Earl of Angus and 1st Marquis of Douglas (cr. 1633); son of 10th earl; joined Montrose at Philiphaugh (1645); imprisoned, and released only on signing Solemn League and Covenant.

¶Archibald (1694–1761), 3d Marquis and 1st (and only) Duke of Douglas (cr. 1703); son of 2d marquis; a Hanoverian supporter; fought at Sheriffmuir (1715). His sister ¶Lady Jane Douglas (1698–1753) secretly married (1746) Colonel John Stewart, or Steuart, of Grandtully, by whom she had twin sons in Paris, one surviving, ¶Archibald James Edward Stewart, *or* Steuart (1748–1827), 1st Baron Douglas of Douglas (cr. 1790) in British peerage, who won inheritance of Douglas estates in lawsuit (the "Douglas Cause") brought by the Hamiltons (1769); his sons leaving no male issue let estates pass (1857) to earls of Home, representing Douglas line on female side.

MARQUISES AND DUKES OF HAMILTON (from 1660):

¶William Douglas (1635–1694), 3d Duke of Hamilton (cr. 1660); eldest son of 1st Marquis of Douglas; cr. (1646) earl of Selkirk; m. (1656) Anne, Duchess of Hamilton in her own right (see HAMILTON family); on wife's petition created 3d duke (1660); privy councilor of Scotland (1660–76); opposed measures of Duke of Lauderdale; privy councilor in England (1687); president of convention that offered crown of Scotland to William and Mary (1689); royal commissioner (1689, 1693). At his death dukedom reverted to Anne, who resigned it (1698) to her eldest son ¶James (1658–1712), 4th Duke of Hamilton and Duke of Brandon (cr. 1711); commanded regiment of horse against Monmouth's rebellion (1685); in Scottish parliament opposed Act of Union (1707); prevented armed resistance to union; one of 16 Scottish peers elected to British Parliament (1708); killed in duel with Charles Mohun, Baron Mohun, incident narrated in Thackeray's *Henry Esmond.*

EARLS OF MOR·TON \'mȯrt-ᵊn\:

¶Sir James Douglas of Dal·keith \dal-'kēth\, 1st Earl of Morton (cr. 1458), Lord Dalkeith and Ab·er·dour \ˌab-ər-'dau̇r\ (cr. 1458); grandson of Sir James Douglas of Dalkeith, entertainer of Froissart and a nephew of Sir William Douglas (1300?–1353), Knight of Liddesdale (see above); m. daughter of James I. On death of his grandson, 3d earl, without male issue (1553), earldom passed to daughter's husband as 4th earl.

¶James Douglas (1516?–1581), 4th Earl of Morton; son of a younger brother of Archibald, 6th Earl of Angus (see above) and younger brother of David, 7th Earl; m. (1548) Elizabeth, daughter of 3d Earl of Morton; privy councilor on return of Mary, Queen of Scots, to Scotland (1561); lord high chancellor of Scotland (1563); prime mover in assassination of Rizzio, Mary's favorite (1566); lord chancellor and member of council of regency (1567); led army that defeated queen's forces at Langside (1568) and secured her abdication at Lochleven; assisted regent Earl of Moray (1568–69); regent (1572–78); temporarily ousted by Argyll and Atholl, who brought about assumption of government by James VI (Mar.–June 1578); condemned on charge by Esmé Stuart, Earl of Lennox, with connivance of James VI, of complicity in death of Darnley; executed.

¶Sir William Douglas of Loch·le·ven \läk-'lē-vən\ (d. 1606), 6th or 7th Earl of Morton (from 1588); descendant of Sir John of Dalkeith, ancestor of 1st Earl of Morton; implicated in assassination of Rizzio (1566); custodian in charge of Mary, Queen of Scots, after surrender at Carberry Hill (1567); commanded rear guard at Langside (1568); signed bond to support James VI (1582); banished (1583–85); as one of leaders of Presbyterian party, a commissioner for executing acts against Jesuits (1587); influential at court. His grandson ¶William (1582–1650), 7th or 8th Earl of Morton; title contested unsuccessfully by John Maxwell; commanded Scots regiment in Rochelle expedition (1627); lord high treasurer of Scotland (1630–35); privy councilor of England (1635); in return for advances of money to Charles I, received grant to Orkney and Shetland Islands (1643).

EARLS, MARQUISES AND DUKES OF QUEENS·BER·RY \'kwēnz-ˌber-ē, -b(ə-)rē\:

¶Sir William Douglas (d. 1640), 1st Earl of Queensberry; eldest son of Sir James Douglas of Drumlanrig (d. 1616), a descendant of an illegitimate son of James, 2d Earl of Douglas and Mar (see above); created viscount of Drum·lan·rig \(ˌ)drəm-'lan-rig\ (1617) and earl of Queensberry (1633).

¶William (1637–1695), 3d Earl and 1st Marquis (cr. 1682) and 1st Duke (cr. 1684) of Queensberry; son of 2d earl; lord justice general of Scotland (1680–86); lord high treasurer (1682–86); lord high commissioner (1685); president of council (1686); one of lords of privy council of both kingdoms (1687).

¶James (1662–1711), 2d Duke of Queensberry and 1st Duke of Do·ver \'dō-vər\ (cr. 1708); eldest son of 1st duke; lord high treasurer (1693); royal commissioner to famous Scottish parliament of 1700; one of secretaries of state (1702); unintentionally implicated in Jacobite designs of Simon Fraser, Lord Lovat, and temporarily deprived of office (1703–05); as commissioner to Scottish parliament (1706), carried through treaty of union despite Scottish opposition; third secretary of state (1709).

¶Charles (1698–1778), 3d Duke of Queensberry and 2d Duke of Dover; son of 2d duke and 1st duke; created (1706) earl of Sol·way \'säl-ˌwā\; lord justice general of Scotland (1763–78); m. (1720) ¶Catherine Hyde (1703?–1777), daughter of Henry Hyde, 4th Earl of Clarendon, eccentric woman of fashion, friend of wits and writers, including Swift, Congreve, Gay, Pope, Prior, Walpole. Charles took up cause of John Gay over refusal of license for his opera *Polly* (1728); keeper of great seal of Scotland (1760); lord justice general (1763–78). At his death titles passed to second cousin.

¶William (1724–1810), 3d Earl of March \'märch\ and 4th Duke of Queensberry; latterly known as "Old Q"; notorious for his escapades and extravagances; developed horse racing; a representative peer for Scotland (1761–90); vice admiral of Scotland (1766–76); succeeded his second cousin Charles, 3d Duke of Queensberry (1778); lord of bedchamber (1760–89); satirized by Burns, portrayed by Wordsworth, and in Thackeray's *Virginians.* His marquisate passed to Sir Charles Douglas of Kelhead (1777–1837) and his descendants, including 8th marquis (see next name).

¶Sir John Sholto Douglas (1844–1900), 8th Marquis of Queensberry; served in navy (1859–64); a representative peer for Scotland (1872–80); best known as a patron of boxing who supervised formulation by John Graham Chambers (*q.v.*) of Marquis of Queensberry Rules (1867); publicly accused Oscar Wilde of sodomy (1895); sued by Wilde for libel and acquitted.
His third son ¶Lord Alfred Bruce Douglas (1870–1945); editor of *Academy* (1907–10); friend of Oscar Wilde whose *Salomé* he translated into English (1894); author of *The City of the Soul* (1899), *In Excelsis* (1924), *Sonnets and Lyrics* (1935), volumes of light verse, autobiography (1929), *The True History of Shakespeare's Sonnets* (1933), *Without Apology* (1938).

EARLS OF SEL·KIRK \'sel-ˌkərk\: Descendants of William Douglas, 3d Duke of Hamilton (see above), who was created earl of Selkirk (1646), including:

¶Thomas Douglas (1771–1820), 5th Earl of Selkirk; settled 800 emigrants from highlands of Scotland in Prince Edward Island (1803) and about a hundred (1811) in Red River Valley (now Manitoba and Minnesota); latter colonists twice evicted by soldiers of Northwest Fur Co. (1815, 1816); reestablished his colony after leading attack on Fort William, chief post of Northwest Fur Co. (1816).

Douglas, Earls, marquises, and duke of and barons Douglas of. See DOUGLAS family.

Douglas, Lord Alfred Bruce. See under marquises of Queensberry, under DOUGLAS family.

Douglas, Amanda Minnie. 1831–1916. American writer, b. New York City. Author of juvenile stories, esp. of the Kathie series (1868–71), the Little Girl series (1897–1909), and the Helen Grant series (1904–11).

Douglas, Sir Archibald Lucius. 1842–1913. British admiral, b. Quebec. Director of Imperial Japanese Naval College (1873–75) and in large measure creator of modern Japanese navy. Commander in chief in East Indies (1898–99); second sea lord of admiralty (1899–1902); commander in chief (1902–04) in North America and West Indies; admiral (1905).

Douglas, Clifford Hugh. 1879–1952. English engineer and social economist. Developed economic theory of Social Credit, gaining following in England and esp. in Canada; chief reconstruction adviser to government of Alberta, Canada (1935); Social Credit party founded there (1935) and formed government (1935–71). Author of *Economic Democracy* (1920), *Credit-Power and Democracy* (with A. R. Orage, 1920), etc.

Douglas, David. 1798–1834. Scottish botanist. Collector in U.S. for Royal Horticultural Society (1823) and on later expeditions in western America and Canada; discovered the Douglas fir (1825); the Douglas squirrel named for him.

Douglas, Donald Wills. 1892–1981. American engineer and industrialist, b. Brooklyn, N.Y. With Glenn L. Martin aircraft firm (1915–20); formed Davis-Douglas Co. (1920), which became Douglas Aircraft Co. (1928). Produced "Cloudster" biplane for navy (1921), Douglas-Liberty 400 (1924), DC-1 (1932), DC-3 (1936), DC-4 (1938), A-20 Havoc bomber (1939), A-24 Dauntless (1939), B-19 bomber (1941), A-26 Invader (1944), DC-6 (1948), DC-8 (1959), etc. Served as president of firm (1928–57), chairman (1957–67); firm merged into McDonnell Douglas Corp. (1967).

Douglas, Gawin *or* Gavin. 1474–1522. Scottish poet and ecclesiastic. Son of 5th Earl of Angus (see DOUGLAS family). Studied at St. Andrews (1489–94); dean of St. Giles, Edinburgh (1501–14); occupied until battle of Flodden with ecclesiastical duties, classical translation, and writing poetry; ousted by John Hepburn, the prior, from archbishopric of St. Andrews, to which he was appointed after marriage of his nephew, 6th Earl of Angus, to James IV's widowed queen (1514); as member of English party in Scotland, imprisoned by Duke of Albany, leader of French party; ultimately obtained bishopric of Dunkeld (1516–20); deprived of see for appealing to English court on fall of Earl of Angus; died of plague in London. Author of poems *The Palice of Honour* (allegory in tradition of the courts of love), *King Hart* (allegory), *Conscience.* Best known for translation of the *Aeneid* in ten-syllabled meter, earliest translation of a classical work into any English dialect.

Douglas, George. See George Douglas BROWN.

Douglas, Sir Howard. 1776–1861. British soldier and artillery expert. Commissioned in army (1794); commandant of senior department, Military College (1804–20); served in Peninsular War (1808–09, 1812); governor of New Brunswick (1823–31); founder of U. of Fredericton; lord high commissioner of Ionian Islands (1835–40); M.P. (1842–47); general (1851). Author of works on military bridge construction (1816), on Carnot's system of fortification (1819), and a *Treatise on Naval Gunnery* (1820).

Douglas, Sir James. 1803–1877. Canadian businessman and politician, b. Demerara, British Guiana. With Hudson's Bay Co. (1821–58); moved company headquarters to Vancouver Island (1849); governor of Vancouver (1851–63); in Fraser River gold rush (1858) extended authority to mainland to preserve British rule; governor of newly created colony of British Columbia (1858–64).

Douglas, James. 1837–1918. American metallurgist and mining engineer, b. Quebec. Co-inventor of Hunt-Douglas process for copper extraction (1873); for Phelps, Dodge & Co. examined copper ore deposits in Arizona (1881); established mines at Bisbee and Morenci; helped organize Copper Queen Consolidated Mining Co. (1885), president (1908–18); built El Paso and Southwestern Railroad (from 1887); granted numerous patents for ore processing methods and equipment. Author of technical papers and historical books such as *New England and New France* (1913). The town of Douglas, Ariz., is named for him. His grandson ¶Lewis Williams Douglas (1894–1974), b. Bisbee, Ariz., was member of U.S. House of Representatives (1927–33); U.S. director of the budget (1933–34); deputy administrator, war shipping board (1942–44); U.S. ambassador to Great Britain (1947–50).

Douglas, John. 1721–1807. British prelate, b. Scotland. Dean of Windsor (1788); bishop of Salisbury (1791–1807). Author of a defense of Milton (1750), exposing William Lauder's forgeries, and *Letter on the Criterion of Miracles* (1752), attacking Hume.

Douglas, Keith Castellain. 1920–1944. English poet. Served in British army in North Africa; killed in invasion of Normandy; poems, mostly on war and marked by eloquence and fine irony, published posthumously in *Alamein to Zem-Zem* (1946), *Collected Poems* (1951).

Douglas, Lloyd Cassel. 1877–1951. American Congregational clergyman and novelist, b. Columbia City, Ind. Author of *Magnificent Obsession* (1929), *Green Light* (1935), *White Banners* (1936), *Dr. Hudson's Secret Journal* (1939), *Invitation to Live* (1940), *The Robe* (1942), *The Big Fisherman* (1948), etc.

Douglas, Norman, *in full* George Norman. 1868–1952. English writer. In diplomatic service (1893–96); author of *Siren Land* (1911), *Old Calabria* (1915), *South Wind* (1917), *They Went* (1920), *Alone* (1921), *Together* (1923), *Paneros* (1931), *Looking Back* (1933), *Late Harvest* (1946).

Douglas, Stephen Arnold. *Called* Little Giant. 1813–1861. American politician, b. Brandon, Vt. Practiced law in Jacksonville, Ill. (from 1834); judge, Illinois supreme court (1841). Member, U.S. House of Representatives (1843–47); U.S. senator (1847–61). Consistent advocate of national expansion; supported annexation of Texas, Mexican War; drafted Kansas-Nebraska Bill (1854), which repealed Missouri Compromise of 1820 and left decision as to slavery to the territories themselves ("popular sovereignty" doctrine, known also as squatter sovereignty) and thus caused bitter struggles there. Defeated by Buchanan for Democratic nomination to presidency (1856); withdrew support from Buchanan (1858) upon learning he would approve a pro-slavery constitution for Kansas. In senatorial campaign of 1858, engaged with Abraham Lincoln in series of platform debates on slavery, from which Lincoln emerged as a figure of national prominence. Nominated for president by northern wing of Democratic party (1860); defeated by Lincoln; was second in the popular vote; loyally supported Lincoln's administration.

Douglas, William Orville. 1898–1980. American jurist, b. Maine, Minn. Professor of law, Yale (1928–36); member (1936–39) and chairman (1937–39), Securities and Exchange Commission. Associate justice, U.S. Supreme Court (1939–75); known as a consistent liberal, esp. in construing laws bearing on freedom of speech.

Douglas, William Sholto. 1st Baron Douglas of Kir·tle·side \ˈkərt-ᵊl-ˌsīd\. 1893–1969. British air officer. Commanded fighter squadrons in World War I; assistant chief of air staff (1934–40); commander, Fighter Command (1940–42), Middle East Command (1943–44), Coastal Command (1944–45); air marshal, R.A.F. (1946); governor of British zone, Germany (1946–47). Chairman, British European Airways (1949–64). Created baron (1946).

Doug·lass \ˈdəg-ləs\, Andrew Ellicott. 1867–1962. American astronomer, b. Windsor, Vt. On staff of Lowell Observatory (1894–1901); professor at Arizona U. (1906–18); director of Stewart Observatory (1918–38); made first photograph of zodiacal light. Best known for researches in dating prehistoric ruins by tree rings; coined name dendrochronology for such studies.

Douglass, Frederick. *Orig.* Frederick Augustus Washington Bai·ley \ˈbā-lē\. 1817–1895. American abolitionist and writer, b. Tuckahoe, Md. Born a slave; escaped (1838); settled in New Bedford, Mass., changing his name to Frederick Douglass. Addressed antislavery convention, Nantucket (1841); engaged as agent of Massachusetts Anti-Slavery Society; published his autobiography, *Narrative of the Life of Frederick Douglass* (1845). Lectured in Britain and Ireland (1845–47); with proceeds from lectures, bought his freedom; settled at Rochester, N.Y.; founded and edited (1847–60), with M. R. Delany (*q.v.*), the *North Star* (from 1851 called *Frederick Douglass's Paper*), an abolitionist paper. Opposed radical abolitionism as espoused by W.L. Garrison and counselled against John Brown's raid (1859). At outbreak of Civil War, helped recruit Negro regiments; consulted by Lincoln. U.S. marshal for District of Columbia (1877–81); recorder of deeds, District of Columbia (1881–86); U.S. minister to Haiti (1889–91).

Dou·het \dü-ˈe\, Giulio. 1869–1930. Italian general. Commanded Italian army's first air unit (1912–15); court-martialled by military tribunal (1916) for critical analysis of operations of war; with criticisms validated by debacle at Caporetto, recalled to army (1918) as head of aviation service; general (1921); advocate of establishment of independent air unit, and of strategic bombing; wrote *Il dominio dell'aria* (1921).

Doul·ton \ˈdōlt-ᵊn\, Sir Henry. 1820–1897. English potter. Joined father's pottery (1835); introduced (1846) stoneware drainpipes and appliances that made name of Doulton firm famous; began (1870) manufacture of art pottery, a revival in modified form of sgraffito ware of the 17th century.

Dou·mer \dü-mer\, Paul. 1857–1932. French politician. Deputy (1888–96); minister of finance (1895–96); governor general of French Indochina (1896–1902); deputy (1902–12) and president of Chamber of Deputies (1905–06); senator representing Corsica (1912–31); finance minister (1921–

22, 1925–26); president of the Senate (1927–31); 13th president of the Third Republic (1931–32); assassinated by Russian anarchist.

Dou·mergue \dü-merg\, Gaston. 1863–1937. French politician. Colonial judge in Indochina (1885–92) and in Algeria (1893). Deputy (1893–1910); held various cabinet offices (1902–10); senator (1910–14); prime minister (1913–14); colonial minister (1914–17); special agent to Russia (1917); reentered Senate (1917); president of the Senate (1923–24). 12th president of the Third Republic (1924–31); recalled to act as prime minister during Stavisky scandal (Feb.–Nov. 1934).

Dou·mic \dü-mēk\, René. 1860–1937. French writer and critic. Editor of *La Revue des Deux Mondes* (from 1916). Author of *Études sur la littérature française* (1896–1908), etc.

Dou·ris *or* **Du·ris** \'dü-ris\. 5th century B.C. Greek potter and vase painter. Noted for fine draftsmanship in both red- and black-figure styles.

Douris *or* **Duris** of Samos. c.340–c.260 B.C. Greek historian. Author of a history of Greece from battle of Leuctra to death of Lysimachus (371–281 B.C.), annals of Samos, etc.

Dousa, Janus. See Johan van der DOES.

Douw, Gerard. See Gerard DOU.

Dou·wes Dek·ker \'dō-(w)əs-'dek-ər\, Eduard. *Pseudonym* Mul·ta·tu·li \,mùl-tə-'tü-lē\. 1820–1887. Dutch writer. In Dutch colonial service in Java (1838–57); wrote novel *Max Havelaar* (1860) exposing Dutch exploitation of Indonesian natives and satirizing Dutch bourgeois smugness; later books included *Minnebrieven* (1861), *Ideën* (1862–77).

Dove \'dəv\, Arthur Garfield. 1880–1946. American painter, b. Canadaigua, N.Y. Began as magazine illustrator; turned to painting under influence of Alfred Stieglitz; known for nonobjective paintings featuring large masses of muted colors; worked also in collage.

Do·ve \'dō-və\, Heinrich Wilhelm. 1803–1879. German physicist and meteorologist. Professor at Königsberg (1826–29), Berlin (1829–79); formulated meteorological law of gyration, which states that the wind generally shifts in its direction with the sun; investigated climatology. His son ¶Alfred (1844–1916), historian, essayist, and journalist, was professor at Breslau (1874–84), Bonn (1884–97), Freiburg (1897–1916); editor of *Grenzboten* (1870) and of *Allgemeine Zeitung,* Munich (1891–97); published posthumous manuscripts of Ranke (1890). An older son ¶Richard Wilhelm (1833–1907), jurist and politician, helped found (1860) and contributed to *Zeitschrift für Kirchenrecht;* revised Richter's *Lehrbuch ... des Kirchenrechts* (8th ed., 1877–86).

Dover, Dukes of. See dukes of Queensberry, under DOUGLAS family.

Do·ver \'dō-vər\, Thomas. 1660–1742. English physician. Captain of privateer *Duke* on expedition commanded by Captain Woodes Rogers (1708–11); sacked Guayaquil (now in Ecuador, 1709); cured 172 of his sailors of plague (1709); returning on a Spanish prize, rescued Alexander Selkirk *(q.v.)* from one of Juan Fernández Islands (1709). Invented Dover's powder, an anodyne diaphoretic.

Dov·zhen·ko \dȯv-'zheŋ-kō\, Aleksandr. 1894–1956. Ukrainian film director. Known for intensely emotional and symbolic films, including *Yagodki lyubvi* (1929), *Zvenigora* (1928), *Arsenal* (1929), *Zemlya* (1930), *Ivan* (1932), *Aerograd* (1935), *Shors* (1939), *Mitchbourine* (1949).

Dow \'daù\, Charles Henry. 1851–1902. American financial journalist, b. Sterling, Conn. With Edward D. Jones (1856–1920), founded Dow Jones & Co. (1882), publishing financial bulletins and newssheets; began compiling averages of U.S. stock prices (1884), which developed into daily Dow-Jones average; founded *Wall Street Journal* (1889).

Dow, Herbert Henry. 1866–1930. American chemist and manufacturer, b. Belleville, Ont. Discovered electrolytic method for extracting bromine from brine and formed company to exploit it (1889); organized chlorine-extracting firm (1895); founded Dow Chemical Co. (1897). Developed and patented over 100 chemical processes.

Dow, Neal. 1804–1897. American temperance advocate, b. Portland, Me. Mayor of Portland (1851, 1855); drafted prohibition law, known as "Maine law," submitted it to legislature, and saw it passed (1851); cleaned up liquor traffic in Portland and gained nationwide reputation. Candidate of Prohibition party for president of the United States (1880).

Dow·den \'daùd-ᵊn\, Edward. 1843–1913. Irish critic. Professor at Trinity Coll., Dublin (1867–1913); gained wide reputation with *Shakspere, his Mind and Art* (1875); edited *Hamlet* and other plays; author also of *Shakspere Primer* (1877), *Studies in Literature* (1878), *Transcripts and Studies* (1888), *New Studies in Literature* (1895), and a *Life of Shelley* (1886). His brother ¶John (1840–1910), theologian and antiquary, was Episcopal bishop of Edinburgh (1866–1910); author of works on the Book of Common Prayer, the Celtic church, and the medieval church in Scotland.

Dow·ding \'daùd-iŋ\, Sir Hugh Caswall Tremenheere. 1st Baron Dowding. 1882–1970. British soldier. With Royal Flying Corps in World War I; air chief marshal, head of R.A.F. Fighter Command (1936–40, including Battle of Britain period); on special mission in U.S. (1940–42); created baron (1943).

Dow·ie \'daù-ē\, John Alexander. 1847–1907. American religious leader, b. Edinburgh, Scotland. Emigrated to South Australia (1860); ordained Congregational pastor. To U.S. (1888); organized (1896) Christian Catholic Church in Zion. Identified himself (1899) with the messenger of the Covenant; proclaimed himself Elijah the Restorer (1901); built up Zion City, near Chicago, inhabited by his followers but wholly owned and severely ruled by him. Attempted to convert New York City (1903). Deposed from leadership (1906) by revolt of his followers led by Wilbur Voliva.

Dow·land \'daù-lənd, 'dō-\, John. 1563–1626. English composer and lutenist. Traveled widely and played at several European courts; lutenist to Christian IV of Denmark (1596–1606), James I of England (1612–26); composed 88 lute songs, some 90 pieces for solo lute; works marked advances in harmonic and melodic style. His son ¶Robert (c.1591–1641) also a lutenist; musician to Charles I (from 1626).

Downes \'daùnz\, Andrew. 1549?–1628. English classical scholar. One of seven translators of Apocrypha for the Authorized Version of the Bible, and one of six revisers.

Downes, Olin, *in full* Edwin Olin. 1886–1955. American music critic, b. Evanston, Ill. On staff of Boston *Post* (1906–24) and *New York Times* (from 1924); author of *The Lure of Music* (1918), *Symphonic Broadcasts* (1931).

Dow·ning \'daù-niŋ\, Andrew Jackson. 1815–1852. American horticulturist, nurseryman, and landscape architect, b. Newburgh, N.Y. Editor, *The Horticulturist* (1846–52); wrote *Treatise on Landscape Gardening* (1841), widely influential *Architecture of Country Houses* (1850). With his brother ¶Charles (1802–1885), horticulturist and pomologist, wrote *Fruits and Fruit Trees of America* (1845), long a standard work.

Downing, Sir George. 1623–1684. English diplomat, b. Ireland. To America (1638); second graduate of Harvard College (1642). Returned to England (1645); M.P. (1654–56, 1660–84); British resident minister at The Hague (1657). In favor with the Stuarts after the Restoration; his diplomatic activities helped precipitate second Dutch War (1665–67); secretary of treasury commission (1667), introducing reforms; sent to Holland to provoke another war (1671); fled for his life. Created baronet (1663). Downing Street, London, is named in his honor. His grandson ¶Sir George Downing (1684?–1749) left a bequest to found Downing College, Cambridge.

Downing, Major Jack. See Seba SMITH.

Dow·son \'daùs-ᵊn\, Ernest Christopher. 1867–1900. English lyric poet. Member, with Yeats, Beardsley, Arthur Symons, and Lionel Johnson, of Rhymers' Club; with Arthur Moore wrote two novels, *A Comedy of Masks* (1893), *Adrian Rome* (1899); highly polished verse published in *Verses* (1896), *Decorations* (1899); best known for refrain "I have been faithful to thee, Cynara, in my fashion."

Dox·ia·dis \däks-'yä-t͟hēs\, Konstantinos Apostolos. 1913–1975. Greek architect and city planner. Author of *Urban Renewal and the Future of the American City* (1966).

Doy·en \dwá-yaⁿ\, Gabriel-François. 1726–1806. French painter. Decorated chapel of St.-Grégoire in the Invalides; for Catherine II painted murals in the imperial palace at St. Petersburg (1777–84).

Doyle \'dȯi(ə)l\, Alexander. 1857–1922. American sculptor, b. Steubenville, Ohio. Designed scores of public monuments and statues, including *Horace Greeley,* New York City; *National Revolutionary Monument,* Yorktown, Va.; *Thomas H. Benton, Francis P. Blair,* and *John E. Kenna,* Washington, D.C.

Doyle, Sir Arthur Conan. 1859–1930. British physician and writer, b. Edinburgh. Grandson of John Doyle and nephew of Richard Doyle. Practiced medicine, Southsea (1882–90). Among his novels were *Micah Clarke* (1887), *The White Company* (1890), *The Refugees* (1891), *The Great Shadow* (1892), *Rodney Stone* (1896), and *Sir Nigel* (1906). Best known for his detective stories centering about Sherlock Holmes of Baker Street, London, and his friend Dr. Watson, beginning with *A Study in Scarlet* (1887); stories published in *Strand* magazine (from 1891), collected in *Adventures of Sherlock Holmes* (1891), *The Memoirs of Sherlock Holmes* (1893), *The Hound of the Baskervilles* (1902), *Return of Sherlock Holmes* (1905). Author also of *The Great Boer War* (1900) and *History of the British Campaign in France and Flanders* (1916–20). In later years, champion of and writer of books on spiritualism, including *History of Spiritualism* (1926).

Doyle, Sir Francis Hastings Charles. 1810–1888. English poet. Receiver-general of customs (1846–69), commissioner (1869–83). Professor of poetry, Oxford (1867–77); published several volumes of poetry, including *The Return of the Guards* (1866); remembered esp. for ballads "The Loss of the Birkenhead" and "The Private of the Buffs."

Doyle, John. 1797–1868. English painter and caricaturist. Published popular series of lithographed caricatures (1829–51) signed "H.B."; introduced moderate style of caricature in contrast to those of Gillray and Rowlandson.

Doyle, Richard. 1824–1883. English caricaturist and painter. Son of John Doyle. Contributor to *Punch* (1843–50) and designer of cover used by it for more than 30 years. Illustrated three of Dickens's Christmas Books, Thackeray's *Newcomes,* Ruskin's *King of the Golden River,* and Leigh Hunt's *Jar of Honey;* won note as watercolorist.

D'Oyly Carte. See Richard D'Oyly CARTE.

Dó·zsa \'dō-zhä\, György. 1470–1514. Hungarian soldier of fortune and rebel. Raised force from peasantry and rabble for a crusade against Turks; remained their leader when they turned against nobles and government; defeated by János Zápolya at Temesvár (1514); captured and grilled alive upon a throne of red-hot iron.

Do·zy \'dō-zē\, Reinhart Pieter Anne. 1820–1883. Dutch Arabist and historian. Professor, Leiden (from 1850). Author of *Histoire des musulmans d'Espagne, jusqu'à la conquête de l'Andalousie par les Almoravides, 711-1110* (1861), long a standard work, *Essai sur l'histoire de l'islamisme* (1879), etc.

Drach·mann \'dräk-män\, Holger Henrik Herholdt. 1846–1908. Danish writer. Poetry, early concerned with social questions and later more simply lyrical or Romantic, published as *Digte* (1872), *Daempede Melodier* (1875), *Sange ved Havet* (1877), *Venezia* (1877), *Ranker og Roser* (1879), *Östen for Sol og Vesten for Maone* (1880), *Gamle Guder og nye* (1881), *Sangenes Bok* (1889), *Den Hellige Ild* (1899); prose works included *Derovre fra Graensen* (1877), *Med den brede Pensel* (1887), *Forskrevet* (1890); dramatic works included *Der var en gang* (1885), *Völund Smed* (1897), *Brav-Karl* (1897), *Gurre* (1899), *Hallfred Vandraade-skjald* (1900). Foremost modernist poet in Denmark; for a time associated with Georg Brandes.

Dra·co \'drā-kō\ *or* **Dra·con** \'drā-kön\. 7th century B.C. Athenian lawgiver. Prepared probably first comprehensive written code of laws for Athens (c.621 B.C.), prescribing death for nearly all offenses, whence the word draconian; most of code later repealed by Solon.

Dra·con·ti·us \drə-'kän-sh(ē-)əs\, Blossius Aemilius. 5th century A.D. Christian Latin poet. Practiced law in Carthage. Works included *Romulea, Satisfactio, Orestis tragoedia,* and esp. *De laudibus dei.*

Drae·se·ke \'drez-ə-kə\, Felix August Bernhard. 1835–1913. German composer. Wrote operas including *Gudrun* (1884), *Herrat* (1892), *Merlin* (1913), masses and other church music, symphonies, string quartets, a piano quintet, songs, and choral works.

Dra·ga \'drä-gä\, *nee* Lun·je·vi·ca \'lün-yev-ē-kä\. 1867–1903. Queen of Serbia (1900–03). An adventuress, widow of a Czech engineer named Mašín; m. (1900) King Alexander; her doubtful reputation severely weakened regime; both killed in military coup.

Dra·go \'drä-gō\, Luis María. 1859–1921. Argentine jurist. Minister of foreign affairs (1902–03); member, Hague Peace Conference (1907); sat on arbitration tribunal in North Atlantic Fisheries case (1910). Author of Drago Doctrine (proposed in letter to Argentine minister to U.S. in 1902) that public debt could not be used as excuse for armed intervention or territorial occupation in American nations by a European power.

Dra·go·mi·rov \drə-(,)gəm-'yē-rəf\, Mikhail Ivanovich. 1830–1905. Russian soldier. Commanded Russian advance guard against Turks (1877–78); head of Nicholas Academy (1878–89), where he introduced European ideas of training and tactics; governor general of Kiev (1889–1903); general (1891); wrote *Uchebnik taktiki* (1879) and other works.

Drake \'drāk\, Alexander Wilson. 1843–1916. American artist and critic, b. Westfield, N.J. As art director of *Century Magazine* and *St. Nicholas Magazine* (1881–1913), a leading figure in development of American illustrative art.

Drake, Edwin Laurentine. 1819–1880. American pioneer in oil industry, b. Greenville, N.Y. Encouraged by George H. Bissel of Pennsylvania Rock Oil Co., in which he owned stock, he became first to tap petroleum at its source by drilling, at Titusville, Pa. (1859).

Drake, Sir Francis. 1540 or 1543–1596. English admiral. Apprenticed in coastal trade at 13; later entered service of Sir John Hawkins, a kinsman, on whose expedition (1567) to Gulf of Mexico he commanded the *Judith.* Made three expeditions (1570, 1571, 1572) to West Indies, the last with a privateer's commission from Elizabeth I; plundered Spanish towns and shipping; crossed Isthmus of Panama, first English commander to see Pacific (1572); returned and served as volunteer under Earl of Essex in Ireland. Started out (1577) to explore Strait of Magellan and west coast of South America; sailed through straits for 16 days, became separated by storm from other ships; renamed his ship *Golden Hind,* continued to Mocha Islands, plundered coast of Chile and Peru, named California coast New Albion and claimed it for Queen Elizabeth; reached as far north as Vancouver. Failing to find a Northwest Passage into Atlantic, reached Moluccas (1579), Celebes, Java, doubled Cape of Good Hope, touched at Sierra Leone, and returned to Plymouth (1580), having made first circumnavigation of globe by an Englishman. Knighted by queen in face of Spanish protests. Mayor of Plymouth (1581); on reopening of hostilities with Spain, sailed with 25 ships against Spanish Indies, took Santiago (in Cape Verde Islands), Santo Domingo, Cartagena, and St. Augustine; damage to Spanish credit and morale broke Bank of Spain; after great suffering from sickness, returned home (1586), carrying back first colonists of Virginia with potatoes and the material and implements of tobacco smoking. With fleet of 30 destroyed 33 ships in bay of Cádiz and escaped unscathed (1587); seized off Azores (1587) Portuguese carrack said to be worth £100,000. Urged queen to ward off Spanish invasion by attacking Spain; appointed vice admiral under Lord Howard and at approach of Spanish Armada was stationed off Ushant with one of three divisions of fleet; urged use of fireships to drive Armada out of Calais; defeated Armada off Gravelines and pursued it to north of Scotland (1588); captured off Portland the Spanish galleon *Rosario.* Commander of fleet sent with land forces under Sir John Norris (1589) to aid Don Antônio, claimant to Portuguese throne; plundered La Coruña, burned Vigo, but failed in mission. With Sir John Hawkins, commanded an ill-fated expedition to West Indies (1596) on which he died aboard his own ship.

Drake, Joseph Rodman. 1795–1820. American poet, b. New York City. His best known poems, including "The Culprit Fay," "Niagara," and "The American Flag" were published in *The Culprit Fay and Other Poems* (1835). He was eulogized by his friend Fitz-Greene Halleck in poem "Green be the turf above thee."

Dra·per \'drā-pər\, Henry. 1837–1882. American astronomer, b. Prince Edward County, Va. Son of John W. Draper. Professor of natural science (1860–66), and of physiology (1866–73), dean of faculty (1866–82), U. of City of New York. Built for himself an observatory with 15 1/2-inch reflecting telescope, and devised methods for photographing the skies; built and mounted a 28-inch reflector (1869), with which he did pioneering work in stellar spectroscopy; obtained first photograph of stellar spectrum (that of Vega, 1872); first photograph of nebula (Orion, 1880); chosen to organize photographic work of U.S. expedition to observe the transit of Venus (1874). The standard Draper Catalogue (begun 1885, completed 1924) of stellar magnitudes and spectral types was undertaken by the Harvard Observatory as a memorial to him.

Draper, John William. 1811–1882. American scientist and author, b. near Liverpool, Eng. To U.S. (1831); taught chemistry and natural philosophy at Hampden-Sidney Coll. (1836–38); professor of chemistry at U. of City of New York (1838–82) and president of its medical school (1850–73). Made important scientific contributions in fields of radiant energy, photochemistry, photography, and electric telegraphy; anticipated development of spectrum analysis; made first photograph of moon (1840). Made address to British Association for Advancement of Science (1860) that precipitated debate of Huxley and Bishop Wilberforce. Author of *Human Physiology, Statical and Dynamical* containing his researches on carbon dioxide transport by blood and first published photomicrographs (1856), *History of the American Civil War* (1867–70), *History of the Conflict between Religion and Science* (1874), etc.

Draper, Lyman Copeland. 1815–1891. American historical scholar, b. Hamburg (now Evans), N.Y. Secretary, Wisconsin State Historical Society (1854–86); engaged Reuben G. Thwaites as successor; edited first ten volumes of *Wisconsin Historical Collections;* author of *King's Mountain and its Heroes* (1881).

Draper, Ruth. 1884–1956. American monologuist, b. New York City. Began performing professionally (1911); gained fame in such works as "At an English House Party," "French Dressmaker," "Opening a Bazaar," "Italian Lesson."

Dray·ton \'drāt-ᵊn\, Michael. 1563–1631. English poet. His earliest volume of poems, *The Harmonie of the Church* (1591), burned by public order. Published volume of eclogues *Idea, The Shepherd's Garland* (1593); sonnet cycle *Ideas Mirrour* (1594); *Endimion and Phoebe* (1595); three historical poems, *Piers Gaveston* (1593), *Matilda* (1594), *Robert, Duke of Normandy* (1596). His *Mortimeriados* (1596) was recast in ottava rima as *The Barrons Wars* (1603); *Englands Heroicall Epistles* (1597) was popular collection of verse love letters. His *Poems Lyric and Pastoral* (1606) included the spirited "Ballad of Agincourt" and the first English odes in the manner of Horace. Finished his magnum opus, *Polyolbion* (1612, 1622), a topographical description of England in 12-syllabled verse; published collected *Poems* (1619); a miscellaneous volume (1627), including his most graceful poem, *Nymphidia* (an epic of fairyland); his last work, *The Muses' Elizium* (1630), contained pastorals.

Draža. See MIHAJLOVIĆ.

Dreb·bel \'dreb-əl\, Cornelis Jacobszoon. 1572–1633. Dutch inventor. To England (c.1604), where James I became his patron; invented a perpetual motion machine actuated by changes in atmospheric pressure; sometimes credited with invention of the compound microscope, and an improved thermometer; built (1620) first navigable submarine, which successfully negotiated Thames River.

Drei·kurs \'drī-,kùrz\, Rudolf. 1897–1972. American psychiatrist, b. Vienna. To U.S. (1937); professor, Chicago Medical School (1942–66); developed theories of Alfred Adler into practical program for dealing with recalcitrant children; founded several child guidance clinics and Alfred Adler Institutes in Chicago and Tel Aviv.

Drei·ser \'drī-sər, -zər\, Theodore. 1871–1945. American writer, b. Terre Haute, Ind. Editor of various magazines (1906–10). Author of *Sister Carrie* (1900), *Jennie Gerhardt* (1911), *The Financier* (1912), *The Titan* (1914), *The "Genius"* (1915), *Free and Other Stories* (1918), *An American Tragedy* (1925), *Moods* (verse, 1926), *Chains* (1927), *Dreiser Looks at Russia* (1928), *Dawn* (1931), *Tragic America* (1932), *The Bulwark* (1946), *The Stoic* (1947). His brother ¶Paul Dres·ser \'dres-ər\ (1857–1911), songwriter; composed "On the Banks of the Wabash."

Dren·nan \'dren-ən\, William. 1754–1820. Irish poet. Formulator of original prospectus of Society of United Irishmen (1791). Author of patriotic lyrics; supposed to have been first Irish poet to call Ireland "the Emerald Isle."

Drepanius, Latinius Pacatus. See Latinius PACATUS DREPANIUS.

Dres·ser \'dres-ər\, Christopher. 1834–1904. English designer. Pioneer in development of industrial design; author of *Unity in Variety* (1859), *Art of Decorative Design* (1862), *Development of Ornamental Art in the International Exhibition* (1862), *Japan, Its Architecture, Art and Art Manufactures* (1882).

Dress·ler \'dres-lər\, Marie. *Orig.* Leila Marie Koer·ber \'kər-bər\. 1869–1934. American actress, b. Cobourg, Ont. Joined Weber company in New York as leading comedienne (1904); made success as star in *Tillie's Nightmare* (1910); appeared in Mack Sennett's film *Tillie's Punctured Romance* (with Chaplin, 1914); other films included *Min and Bill* (1931, Academy Award), *Emma* (1932), *Tugboat Annie* (1933), *Dinner at Eight* (1933), *The Late Christopher Bean* (1933).

Dre·vet \drə-ve\. Family of French copper engravers, including: Pierre (1663–1738), engraver of portraits of Louis XIV, Louis XV, Prince de Conti, Boileau, Villars, Cardinal de Fleury, Duchesse de Nemours; a son and pupil of Pierre, ¶ Pierre Imbert (1697–1739), also engraver.

Drew \'drü\, Charles Richard. 1904–1950. American physician, b. Washington, D.C. Professor, Howard U. (1945–50); developed efficient way to store blood plasma in blood banks (1940); awarded Spingarn medal (1944).

Drew, Daniel. 1797–1879. American financier, b. Carmel, N.Y. Cattle drover and horse trader (1815–34). In steamboat business, competing with Cornelius Vanderbilt (1834); Wall Street broker (from 1844). Forced himself on board of directors, Erie Railroad (1857); manipulated stock to his own advantage; with Jay Gould and James Fisk victorious in bitter stockmarket fight (the "Erie War") with Vanderbilt (1866–68). Later operations left him bankrupt (1876). His benefactions made possible founding (1866) of Drew Theological Seminary, Madison, N.J.

Drew, John. 1827–1862. American actor, b. Dublin, Ireland. On American stage (from c.1842). Gained success as portrayer of Irish roles in comedies, as Sir Lucius O'Trigger in Sheridan's *Rivals.* His wife ¶Louisa, *nee* Lane \'lān\ (1820–1897), b. London, England; to U.S. (1827); was on the stage from childhood; after her third marriage, to John Drew (1850), concentrated on comedy roles, as Peg Woffington, Lady Teazle, and Mrs. Malaprop; assisted husband in management of Arch Street Theatre, Philadelphia; sole manager of theater and brilliant repertory company as well as leading actress (1861–92). Their son ¶John (1853–1927), b. Philadelphia, was a noted actor; in Augustin Daly's company, New York (1875); supported Jefferson in *Rip Van Winkle;* on barnstorming tour with brother-in-law, Maurice Barrymore; again with Daly's company (1879–92), playing opposite Ada Rehan, one of their chief successes being in *The Taming of the Shrew* (1887); first appeared as a star under Charles Frohman's management (1892), in Clyde Fitch's *Masked Ball,* with Maude Adams; remained under Frohman's management until latter's death (1915); last appearance in revival of Pinero's *Trelawney of the Wells,* shortly before his death. His sister Georgiana Emma married Maurice Barrymore (*q.v.*).

Drew Ali \'drü-ä-'lē, -'äl-ē\, Prophet. *Known as* Noble Drew Ali. *Orig.* Timothy Drew. 1886–1929. American religious leader. Founded (1913) Moorish Science Temple of America in Newark, N.J.; one of first to adopt Islām as instrument of Negro unity. See W.D. FARD.

Drews \'drāvz\, Arthur. 1865–1935. German philosopher. Professor at Karlsruhe (from 1898); works included *Die deutsche Spekulation seit Kant* (1893), *Nietzsches Philosophie* (1904), *Plotin* (1908), *Die Christusmythe* (1909), *Psychologie des Unbewussten* (1924), *Lehrbuch der Logik* (1928).

Drex·el \'drek-səl\, Francis Martin. 1792–1863. American banker, b. Dornbirn, Austria. To U.S. (1817); portrait painter in Philadelphia; established in Philadelphia (1838) a brokerage office, originally for dealing in foreign currencies and securities, which developed into banking house of Drexel & Co. His son ¶Anthony Joseph (1826–1893), b. Philadelphia; became member of the firm (1847) and the dominating influence during its period of expansion (after 1863); founded (1871) Drexel, Morgan and Co., New York City; specialized in government bonds, railroads, mining, real estate. Co-owner, with George W. Childs, of Philadelphia *Public Ledger* (from 1864). Founder (1892) and benefactor of Drexel Institute, Philadelphia.

Drexel, Katharine Mary. 1858–1955. American religious, b. Philadelphia. Granddaughter of Francis M. and niece of Anthony J. Drexel. Founded 63 schools for Indians and Negroes; novice in Sisters of Mercy (1889); founded Sisters of the Blessed Sacrament for Indians and Colored People (1891); superior (1891–1955); founded St. Catherine's School, Santa Fe, N.M. (1894), Xavier U., New Orleans (1915).

Drey·er \'drī(-ə)r\, Carl Theodor. 1889–1968. Danish film director. Known esp. for slow, somber explorations of religious experience and persecution; films included *Praesidenten* (1919), *Blade af satans bog* (1920), *Mikaël* (1924), *Du skal aere din hustru* (1925), *Glomdalsbruden* (1925), *La Passion de Jeanne d'Arc* (1928), *Vampyr* (1930), *Vredens dag* (1943), *Ordet* (1955), *Gertrud* (1964).

Dreyer, Johan Ludwig Emil. 1852–1926. Danish astronomer. Astronomer to Earl of Rosse (1874–82); director of observatory at Armagh (1882–1916). Compiled *New General Catalogue of Nebulae and Clusters of Stars* (1888 and supplements in 1895, 1908), still a standard reference.

Dreyer, Max. 1862–1946. German journalist, playwright, and novelist. Editor, *Täglicher Rundschau* (1888–98). His plays included *Drei* (1892), *Winterschlaf* (1895), *Der Probekandidat* (1899), *Tal des Lebens* (1902), *Die Siebzehnjährigen* (1904), *Der Grünende Zweig* (1913); novels, *Der deutsche Morgen* (1915), *Nachwuchs* (1917), *Tapfere kleine Renate* (1932).

Drey·fus \dre-fǖs, *Angl* 'drī-fəs, 'drā-\, Alfred. 1859–1935. French army officer. Entered army (1882); convicted (1894) of treason and imprisoned (1895) on Devil's Island; later investigation, forced (1898) largely by Émile Zola (*q.v.*), proved that the papers on which he had been convicted were forged by Major Esterhazy and Major Henry (*qq.v.*); defended also by Georges Picquart (*q.v.*); case became center of major political division in France in which anti-Semitism played major part; tried and convicted a second time at Rennes (1899) but pardoned by President Loubet; original conviction set aside by civilian court (1906), and Dreyfus was restored to rank in the army and given the Legion of Honor.

Drey·se \'drī-zə\, Johann Nikolaus von. 1787–1867. German inventor. Invented muzzle-loading (1827) and breech-loading (1836) needle guns, adopted by the Prussian army (1841).

Driesch \'drēsh\, Hans Adolf Eduard. 1867–1941. German biologist and philosopher. Professor, Heidelberg (1911–20), Cologne (1920), Leipzig (1921–33). Pioneer experimenter in embryology; became last important exponent of philosophy of vitalism. Author of *Analytische Theorie der organischen Entwicklung* (1894), *Vitalismus als Geschichte und Lehre* (1905), *Science and Philosophy of the Organism* (1908), *Metaphysik der Natur* (1927), *Parapsychologie* (1932), etc.

Drieu La Ro·chelle \drē-œ̄-là-rò-shel\, Pierre. 1893–1945. French writer. Expressed confusion of values in post-World War I France in novels, including *L'Homme couvert de femmes* (1925), *Le Feu follet* (1931), *Gilles* (1939), *L'Homme à cheval* (1943), and essays, including *Mesure de la France* (1922), *L'Europe contre les patries* (1931), *Socialisme fasciste* (1934); supported Nazi occupation.

Drink·wa·ter \'driŋ-,kwȯt-ər, -,kwät-\, John. 1882–1937. English poet and playwright. A founder and manager of the Pilgrim Players (1907), now the Birmingham Repertory Theatre. His works included *Swords and Ploughshares* (1915), *Collected Poems* (1923), *Mr. Charles, King of England* (1926), *Pepys* (1930), *Shakespeare* (1933), *John Hampden's England* (1933), the autobiographical volumes *Inheritance* (1931) and *Discovery* (1932), and plays including *Rebellion* (1914), *Abraham Lincoln* (1918), *Loyalties* (1919), *Mary Stuart* (1921), *Oliver Cromwell* (1921), *Robert E. Lee* (1923), *Robert Burns* (1925), *Bird-in Hand* (1927), *Midsummer Eve* (1932), *Laying the Devil* (1933), *A Man's House* (1934).

Dri·o·ton \drē-ó-tōⁿ\, Étienne-Marie. 1889–1961. French ecclesiastic and Egyptologist. Director general of antiquities, Egypt (1936–52). Author of *L'Art égyptien* (1930), *L'Égypte* (1938), *L'Égypte pharaonique* (1959), etc.

Dri·ver \'drī-vər\, Samuel Rolles. 1846–1914. English biblical scholar. Regius professor of Hebrew, Oxford, and canon of Christ Church (1882–1914); member of Old Testament revision committee (1875–84). Author of *Notes on Samuel* (1890), *Introduction to the Literature of the Old Testament* (1891). His son ¶Sir Godfrey Rolles (1892–1975), also a biblical scholar; on faculty, Oxford U. (from 1919), professor of Semitic philology (1938–62); joint director with C.H. Dodd of project to develop New English Bible (1965–70).

Dro·bisch \'drō-bish\, Moritz Wilhelm. 1802–1896. German mathematician and philosopher. Professor, Leipzig (1826–96). Author of *Neue Darstellung der Logik* (1836), *Grundlehren der Religionsphilosophie* (1840), etc.

Droes·hout \'drüs-ˌhaüt\, Martin. Flemish engraver, b. London. Known chiefly for his engraved portrait of William Shakespeare prefixed to the First Folio (1623).

Dro·go de Haute·ville \drō-gō-dōt-vēl\. d. 1051. Norman nobleman. Fought Muslims and then Byzantines in Italy (c.1035–42); given Venosa by Prince Gaimar V of Salerno (1042); succeeded older brother Guillaume Iron Arm as count of Apulia (1046); assassinated in anti-Norman conspiracy.

Drop·sie \'dräp-sē\, Moses Aaron. 1821–1905. American lawyer, b. Philadelphia. Bequeathed his estate for founding of Dropsie College for Hebrew and Cognate Learning (opened 1909; now Dropsie U.).

Drost \'dröst\, Aernout. 1810–1834. Dutch writer. First exponent of Romantic movement in Dutch literature; wrote novel *Hermingard van de Eikenterpen* (1832), stories collected in *Schetsen en verhalen* (1835–36); founded journal *De muzen* (1832).

Dro·ste-Hüls·hoff \'drö-stə-'hæls-höf\, Annette Elisabeth von. Freifrau. 1797–1848. German poet. Author of *Gedichte* (1838), *Das geistliche Jahr,* a cycle of religious poems (1851), and a novella, *Die Judenbuche* (1842).

Droste zu Vi·sche·ring \-tsü-'fish-ə-riŋ\, Klemens August von. Freiherr. 1773–1845. German prelate. Archbishop of Cologne (1835–45); imprisoned (1837–39) following dispute with Prussian government over question of mixed marriages.

Drou·ais \drü-e\. Family of French artists, including: Hubert (1699–1767), painter of portraits and miniatures; his son ¶François-Hubert (1727–1775), painter of portraits of Louis XV, Mme. du Barry, Mme. de Pompadour; the latter's son ¶Jean-Germain (1763–1788), historical painter, one of earliest Neoclassicists; works included *La Chananéenne aux pieds de Jésus* and *Marius à Minturnes.*

Drou·et \drü-e\, Jean-Baptiste. 1763–1824. French revolutionist. Recognized Louis XVI at Sainte-Menehould, when the king was attempting to flee France, and caused his arrest at Varennes (1791). Member of National Convention (1792) and Council of Five Hundred (1795); involved in the Babeuf plot (see François-Noël BABEUF) and imprisoned, but escaped.

Drouet, Jean-Baptiste. Comte d'Er·lon \der-lōⁿ\. 1765–1844. French soldier in the Napoleonic armies. General of division (1805); distinguished himself at Jena (1806), Friedland (1807), Waterloo (1815). In exile under sentence of death (1815–30); recalled to France; governor general of Algeria (1834–35); created marshal of France (1843).

Drou·ot \drü-ō\, Antoine. Comte. 1774–1847. French general. General of division and aide-de-camp to Napoléon (1813); accompanied Napoléon to Elba (1814). Called by Napoléon *le Sage de la Grande Armée.*

Drou·yn de Lhu·ys \drü-aⁿ-də-lwʸēs, drwaⁿ-\, Édouard. 1805–1881. French politician. Elected deputy (1842); minister of foreign affairs (1848–49, 1851, 1852–55, 1862–66); worked for Austrian alliance.

Droy·sen \'dröi-zən\, Johann Gustav. 1808–1884. German historian and politician. Professor at Berlin (1835, 1859), Kiel (1840), Jena (1851); ardent advocate of a united Germany under Prussian leadership; member of Frankfurt Parliament (1848); author of *Geschichte des Hellenismus* (1836–43), *Geschichte der preussischen Politik* (1855–86), etc.

Droz \drō\. Family of French artists, of Swiss origin, including: Jean-Pierre (1746–1823), engraver of money and medals; administrator general and conservator of monetary museum (1802). His son ¶Jules-Antoine (1807–1872), a sculptor, created *L'Hiver* and *L'Été* for Luxembourg palace. Jules's son ¶Antoine-Gustave (1832–1895), painter, and author of *Monsieur, Madame et Bébé* (1866), *Entre nous* (1867), *Le Cahier bleu de Mlle. Cibot* (1868), *Autour d'une source* (1869), *Un paquet de lettres* (1870), *Les Étangs* (1875), *L'Enfant* (1885).

Droz, François-Xavier-Joseph. 1773–1850. French moral philosopher and historian. Author of *Philosophie moral* (1823), *Application de la morale à la philosophie et à la politique* (1825), *Histoire du règne de Louis XVI* (1839–42), etc.

Droz, Numa. 1844–1899. Swiss journalist and politician. Editor, *National Suisse* (1864); elected to federal council (1872), federal executive (1875); president of the Swiss Confederation (1881, 1887); as head of federal political department (1887–92) resisted German threats in Wohlgemut affair (1892).

Dru·de \'drü-də\, Paul Karl Ludwig. 1863–1906. German physicist. Professor at Leipzig (1894–1900), Giessen (1900–05), Berlin (1905–06); editor of *Annalen der Physik* (1889–1906). Conducted research in physical optics, electrical and optical properties of matter; developed electronic theory of metals; wrote *Die Physik des Äthers* (1894), *Lehrbuch der Optik* (1900).

Drumcairn, Lord. See Thomas Hamilton under HAMILTON family.

Drum·mond \'drəm-ənd\. Name of an old Scottish family bearing (from 1605 to 1760) the title of earl of Perth \'pərth\, raised by James II to duke of Perth, and including: James Drummond (1648–1716), 4th Earl and 1st titular Duke of Perth; supported Lauderdale in permitting highland raids (1677); joined Scottish nobles in opposition to Lauderdale (1678); associated with William Penn in settlement of New Jersey (1681); justice general (1682), lord chancellor of Scotland (1684); reputed to have introduced use of thumbscrew; converted to Roman Catholic church (1685); retained in office by James II as chief Roman Catholic agent in Scotland; attempted to flee Scotland (1688); imprisoned (1688–93); member of exiled court of James II (1693–1701); created duke of Perth (1701). His brother ¶John Drummond (1649–1714), 1st Earl of Mel·fort \'mel-fərt\, followed him into political power; treasurer-depute of Scotland (1681); secretary of state for Scotland (1684); created earl (1686); declared himself a convert to Roman Catholicism (1685); with brother, virtual ruler of Scotland (1685–88); courtier and diplomat for exiled James II (1688–1701). James's son ¶James (1675–1720), 5th earl and 2d titular duke; took part in the Jacobite uprising of 1715–16, led cavalry at battle of Sheriffmuir, escaped with James Edward, the Old Pretender, to the Continent (1716); father of ¶James (1713–1747), 6th earl and 3d titular duke (self-styled despite the attainting of his father), who commanded Young Pretender's left wing at Culloden Moor (1746), and of ¶John (d. 1747), 4th duke, who was sent from France to join Prince Charles Edward (1745), was instrumental in gaining Jacobite victory at Falkirk (1746), fought at Culloden Moor (1746). ¶Sir James Eric Drummond (1876–1951), 16th Earl of Perth, 12th Viscount Strath·al·lan \strath-'al-ən\; diplomat; entered foreign office (1900); private secretary to prime minister (1912–15), to foreign secretary (1915–18); with Balfour at first months of peace conference in Paris; first secretary general of League of Nations (1919–33); organized secretariat of about 600 persons of forty nationalities on plan of an international civil service; ambassador to Italy (1933–39); succeeded his half-brother, 15th Earl of Perth (1937); representative peer of Scotland in House of Lords (1941–51).

Drummond, Henry. 1786–1860. English banker and religious leader. M.P. (1810–13, 1847–60); under influence of Robert Haldane, became active opponent of Socinian tendencies at Geneva; one of founders (from c.1826) and propagators of the Catholic Apostolic or Irvingite church, of which he was an apostle, evangelist, and prophet.

Drummond, Henry. 1851–1897. Scottish evangelical writer and lecturer. Joined (1873) evangelical movement led by Dwight L. Moody; lecturer on natural science, Free Church School, Glasgow (1877); sought to reconcile evangelical Christianity with evolution in *Natural Law in the Spiritual World* (1883); professor of theology in the New Jerusalem church (1884); emphasized altruistic actions of animals toward each other in scheme of natural selection in *Ascent of Man* (1894); published address *The Greatest Thing in the World* (1890).

Drummond, Thomas. 1797–1840. British engineer and administrator, b. Edinburgh. Entered Royal Engineers (1815); joined ordnance survey of Great Britain (1820), which was facilitated by his limelight apparatus, the Drummond light; devised an improved heliostat. Undersecretary of state for Ireland (1835–40); organized efficient constabulary, disbanded Orange Society.

Drummond of Haw·thorn·den \'hó-ˌthórn-dən\, William. 1585–1649. Scottish poet. Son of John Drummond (1553–1610), 1st Laird of Hawthornden, related to Scottish royal house. Wrote elegy on Prince Henry Frederick (1613); wrote sonnets and songs to memory of Mary Cunningham of Barns, who died on eve of their marriage (1615). Friend and correspondent of Sir William Alexander (from c.1613) and of Michael Drayton; recorded notes of conversations during memorable visit of Ben Jonson (1618–19). Had to subscribe to Solemn League and Covenant but protested in sarcastic verses (1643). Author of *Poems* (1614), *Forth Feasting* (1617), *A Midnight Trance* (1619), *Flowers of Sion* (1623, religious verse), *A Cypresse Grove* (1623, a meditation on death), *History of Scotland 1423–1542* (1655), and many political pamphlets.

Drummond, William. 1st Viscount of Strath·al·lan \strath-'al-ən\. 1617?–1688. Scottish soldier. Royalist commander at battle of Worcester (1651) and in Highlands (1653); held command in Russian service (1655–65). Major general of forces in Scotland (1666); sat in Parliament (1669–74, 1681–82, 1685–86); lieutenant general of Scotland (1685); created viscount (1686); popularly supposed to have introduced torture by thumbscrew from Russia.

Drummond, William Henry. 1854–1907. Canadian poet, b. Ireland. To Canada (c.1864). Portrayed the French-Canadian habitant in numerous poems, mostly in a synthetic patois, collected in *The Habitant* (1897), *Phil-o-Rum's Canoe* (1898), *Johnny Courteau* (1901), *The Voyageur* (1905), *The Great Fight* (1908).

Dru·sil·la \drü-'sil-ə\. 15–38 A.D. Roman noblewoman. Daughter of Germanicus Caesar and Agrippina; sister and mistress of Caligula.

Drusilla. c.38–79 A.D. Judaean princess. Younger daughter of Herod Agrippa I and sister of Herod Agrippa II and Berenice; in defiance of Jewish law, m. as second husband Antonius Felix, Roman procurator of Judea.

Dru·sus \'drü-səs\. Roman plebeian family of the gens Livius, including: Marcus Livius Drusus (d. 109 B.C.), tribune of the people with Gaius Gracchus (122 B.C.); opposed reforms of his colleague; made more extreme democratic proposals (enacted as Leges Livianae) than did Gracchus but refused to carry them out when they were accepted; granted consulship (112) by senatorial party; governor of Macedonia; advanced against Scordisci tribe to the Danube. His son ¶Marcus Livius Drusus (d. 91 B.C.), tribune of the people (91 B.C.); proposed measures to restore judicial functions from equites to senate; to win popular votes proposed also establishment of colonies, lower price of grain, and extension of citizenship to Italians; these measures passed, but aroused senate abrogated them; assassinated at beginning of civil war (Social War). Livia Drusilla (*q.v.*); adopted into this family; third wife of Augustus; by her first husband, Tiberius Claudius Nero, mother of ¶Nero Claudius Drusus Ger·man·icus \jər-'man-i-kəs\ (38 B.C.–9 B.C.), *called* Drusus Senior; Roman general; with his older brother Tiberius (later emperor), subdued Raeti and Vindelici (15 B.C.); governor of Gaul (13–10); made several campaigns from Gaul against German tribes beyond Rhine; consul (9); defeated Frisii, Chauci, Chatti, Suevi, Marcomanni, and others, penetrating as far north as the Elbe (9 B.C.); died after being thrown from his horse. Father by his wife Antonia (daughter of Marcus Antonius, the triumvir) of Germanicus Caesar, the emperor Claudius, and a daughter Livilla or Livia (wife of Drusus Caesar). His nephew ¶Drusus Caesar (13? B.C.–23 A.D.), *called* Drusus Junior; son of Emperor Tiberius and Vipsania Agippina; sent to Pannonia (14 A.D.); consul (15); governor of Illyricum (17); consul with his father (21); incurred enmity of Sejanus (*q.v.*), who supposedly seduced his wife Livilla (daughter of Drusus Senior); allegedly poisoned by Sejanus and Livilla.

Drusus. d. 33 A.D. Roman noble. Son of Germanicus Caesar and Agrippina; kept imprisoned and starved to death by Emperor Tiberius, who was jealous of the favor in which Drusus stood with the populace.

Dryander. See ENZINAS.

Dry·den \'drīd-ᵊn\, Hugh Latimer. 1898–1965. American physicist, b. Pocomoke City, Md. With National Bureau of Standards (1918–47); chief of aerodynamics section (1920–34); chief of mechanics and sound division (1934–46); associate director (1946–47). Director of National Advisory Committee for Aeronautics (1947–58); deputy administrator, National Aeronautics and Space Administration (1958–65). Directed development of Bat radar-homing missile in World War II; helped develop cooperative weather- and communications-satellite programs.

Dryden, John. 1631–1700. English poet. First attracted notice with "Heroic Stanzas" in memorial volume on Oliver Cromwell (pub. with two poems by Thomas Sprat and Edmund Waller, 1659) and *Astrae Redux* (1660) and *To His Sacred Majesty* (1661) on the Restoration; m. (1663) Lady Elizabeth Howard, sister of his patron Sir Robert Howard (*q.v.*). Established reputation with *Annus Mirabilis,* on the Great Fire and the Dutch war (1667), and series of theatrical pieces, including *The Indian Queen* (1664), *The Indian Emperour* (1665), *Secret Love, or the Maiden Queen* (1666), *Sir Martin Mar-all* (1667), *Tyrannick Love* (1669), *Conquest of Granada* (1670), *Marriage A-la-Mode* (his best comedy, 1672), *Aureng-Zebe* (1677), *All for Love* (1677), *The Spanish Fryar* (1681). Poet laureate succeeding Sir William Davenant (1668); historiographer (1670). Partly in retaliation for Buckingham's ridicule of heroic drama in *The Rehearsal,* launched in *Absalom and Achitophel* (1681) a crushing satire upon Monmouth, Shaftesbury, Buckingham, Charles II, Titus Oates, and others involved in "Popish Plot" affair and conspiracy to exclude Duke of York in favor of Monmouth; satirized the ignoramus of grand jury at Shaftesbury's trial in *The Medall* (1682), and Thomas Shadwell in brilliant lampoon *Mac Flecknoe* (1682); defended Anglicanism in *Religio Laici* (1682); eulogized Charles II in *Threnodia Augustalis* (1685); justified his conversion to Roman Catholicism in *The Hind and the Panther* (1687); declining to take oaths at the English Revolution, lost laureateship and pensions (1689). Turned again to playwriting, without much success, in *Don Sebastian* (1690), *Amphitryon* (1690), and *Love Triumphant* (1694); wrote an opera, *King Arthur,* with Henry Purcell (1690). Produced translations in verse of Perseus, satires of Juvenal, and the whole of Virgil (1697); the ode for St. Cecilia's day entitled "Alexander's Feast" (1697) and paraphrases from Chaucer, Boccaccio, and Ovid in *Fables, Ancient and Modern* (1700), his last great work.

Dryden, John Fairfield. 1839–1911. American businessman, b. near Farmington, Me. Established (1875) at Newark, N.J., Prudential Friendly Society, which developed into The Prudential Insurance Co. (so called from 1878); president of the company (from 1881). U.S. senator (1902–07).

Dry·gal·ski \dri-'gäl-skē\, Erich Dagobert von. 1865–1949. German geophysicist, geographer, and explorer. Professor at Munich (1906–34); led scientific expeditions to West Greenland (1891, 1892–93), South Polar region (1901–03); discovered and named Gaussberg volcano, Antarctica; author of *Zum Kontinent des eisigens Südens* (1904); edited 20-vol. *Deutsche Südpolar-Expedition 1901–1903* (1905–31).

Držić \'dər-zhētʸ\, Marin. 1508–1567. Croatian writer. Author of comedies, notably *Dundo Maroje* (c.1551), and pastorals, esp. *Tirena.*

Duane \'dwān, də-'wān\, William. 1760–1835. American journalist, b. near Lake Champlain, N.Y. To Ireland as a child; learned printer's trade; to India (1787); established *Indian World,* Calcutta; deported to England for criticizing authorities. Returned to U.S. (1795); associated with B. F. Bache in editing the *Aurora,* Philadelphia; sole editor (1798–1822) after Bache's death; made the *Aurora* powerful organ of Jeffersonian party; indicted under Sedition Law (1799); charge dismissed when Jefferson became president.

Duane, William. 1872–1935. American physicist, b. Philadelphia. Great-grandson of William Duane (above), descendant of Benjamin Franklin. Professor of physics, U. of Colorado (1897–1907); worked in Curie laboratory, Paris (1907–13); professor of physics (1913–17), of biophysics, (1917–34), Harvard. Developed methods and apparatus for utilizing X-rays and radium in medicine, esp. in the treatment of cancer; investigated the structure of crystals; developed Duane-Hunt law of X-ray frequencies.

Duarte \'dwärt-ē, dü-'ärt-\, Juan Pablo. 1813–1876. Dominican political leader. Organized secret society La Trinitaria (1838) to work for Dominican independence from Haiti; exiled on collapse of uprising (1843); returned on declaration of independence (1844), but again exiled by rival Pedro Santana. Considered father of Dominican independence.

Du·bail \dᵫ-báy\, Auguste-Yvon-Edmond. 1851–1934. French general. Commander of 1st army at Sarrebourg (1914); commander of eastern army group (1915); military governor of Paris (1916); grand chancellor of Legion of Honor (1918–34).

Du·ban \dᵫ-bäⁿ\, Félix-Louis-Jacques. 1797–1870. French architect. Designed reconstruction and enlargement of École des Beaux-Arts (from 1833), restoration of Château de Blois and Sainte-Chapelle, and improvements at Fontainebleau and Chantilly; architect of the Louvre (1848–54).

Du Barry, Comtesse. See Jeanne du BARRY.

du Bartas. See Guillaume de SALLUSTE.

Du·be \'d(y)ü-(,)bā\, John Langalibalele. 1871–1946. South African journalist and educator. Founded schools for African children; helped found (1906) *Illanga Lase-Natal,* first Zulu newspaper; first president general of South African Native National Congress (1912); wrote *Insila ka Shaka,* first novel in Zulu language (1930).

du Bellay. See BELLAY.

Du·bin·sky \dü-'bin-skē\, David. 1892–1982. American labor leader, b. Brest-Litovsk, Russia. To U.S. (1911); became involved in unionizing; president of Local 10 of International Ladies' Garment Workers Union (ILGWU) (1919). President of national ILGWU (1932–66); pioneered initiatives in housing, pension plans, and health centers.

Dub·now \'düb-,nóf\, Simon. 1860–1941. Russian Jewish historian. Lived in Germany (1922–32), Latvia (1932–41). Author of monumental *Weltgeschichte des jüdischen Volkes* (1925–29).

Du·bois \dᵫ-'bwä, -'bwȧ\, Eugène, *in full* Marie Eugène François Thomas. 1858–1940. Dutch anatomist and paleontologist. While serving as military surgeon in the Dutch East Indies (1887–95), discovered in Java the bones of a hominid, apparently intermediate between man and simian ancestors, which he named (1891) *Pithecanthropus erectus* (now *Homo erectus*).

Du Bois, François. See Franz DELEBOE.

Du·bois \dᵫ-bwȧ\, Guillaume. 1656–1723. French prelate and politician. Tutor of Philippe, duc d'Orléans (1687); private secretary of the duke, at that time regent (1715); determined regent's foreign policy; formed Triple Alliance (1717) and Quadruple Alliance (1718) to oppose Spain and claims of Philip V; named secretary of state for foreign affairs (1718); made Franco–Spanish treaty (1721) and arranged betrothal of Louis XV to Spanish infanta. Became archbishop of Cambrai (1720), prime minister (1722).

du·Bois \dᵫ-bwȧ, *Angl* d(y)üb-'wä\, Guy[2] Pène. 1884–1958. American painter, b. Brooklyn, N.Y. Known for genre paintings, illustrations; edited *Arts and Decoration* magazine (1913–16, 1917–22).

Du·bois \dᵫ-bwȧ\, Jean-Antoine. 1765–1848. French Roman Catholic missionary in India. Labored to convert Hindus (1792–1823); superior of Missions Étrangères (1836–39); author of *Mœurs, institutions et cérémonies des peuples de l'Inde* (1817).

Dubois, Paul. 1829–1905. French sculptor. Works included portrait busts of Pasteur, Bonnat, and Gounod, equestrian statues of Constable Anne de Montmorency and Joan of Arc; director of École des Beaux-Arts (1878–1905).

Dubois, Pierre. *Lat.* Petrus a Bos·co \ä-'bäs-(,)kō\. c.1250–c.1320. French lawyer and publicist. Member of Estates-General (1302, 1308); published pamphlets on reform of the monarchy and public administration, on French leadership of Christendom, on the struggle between Philip IV and Pope Boniface VIII, and on recovery of the Holy Land (*De recuperatione Terrae Sanctae,* 1306).

Dubois, Théodore, *in full* François-Clément-Théodore. 1837–1924. French composer and organist. Organist at Sainte-Clotilde (succeeding Franck, 1871) and at the Madeleine, Paris (succeeding Saint-Saëns, 1877); professor (1871–90) and director (1896–1905), Paris Conservatory of Music. Composer of operas, oratorios, notably *Les sept paroles de Christ* (1867), masses, chamber music, organ and piano pieces, and songs.

Du Bois \d(y)ü-'bȯis\, William Edward Burghardt. 1868–1963. American educator, editor, and writer, b. Great Barrington, Mass. Professor of economics and history, Atlanta (1897–1910). Leader of Niagara Movement (1905–09); helped create National Association for the Advancement of Colored People (1909); editor of *Crisis* (1910–34). Professor of sociology, Atlanta (1932–44). Editor of Atlanta U. *Studies of the Negro Problem* (1897–1911). Author of *The Souls of Black Folk* (1903), *John Brown* (1909), *The Negro* (1915), *Darkwater* (1920), *Black Reconstruction* (1935), *Dusk of Dawn* (1940), *Color and Democracy* (1945), *The World and Africa* (1947). Pioneer advocate of Pan-Africanism.

Du·bois-Cran·cé \dü̅-bwȧ-krän-sā\, Edmond-Louis-Alexis. 1747–1814. French revolutionary politician. Member of the Estates-General (1789), the National Convention (1792); voted for execution of Louis XVI; commander of battalion of Paris National Guard (from 1791); largely responsible for capture of rebel Lyons (1793); member of Council of Five Hundred (1795–97); minister of war (1799).

Du Bois-Rey·mond \-rā-mōn\, Emil Heinrich. 1818–1896. German physiologist. Professor at Berlin (1855–96); known esp. for investigations in animal electricity, physiology of muscles and nerves, and metabolic processes. Author of *Untersuchungen über thierische Elektricität* (1848–84).

Du Bos \dü̅-bō\, Charles. 1882–1939. French critic. Wrote studies of Goethe, Shakespeare, Shelley, Flaubert, Byron, Mauriac; published *Le Dialogue avec André Gide* (1929), *Approximations* (1922–37), *Journal intime* (1946–55).

Du·bos \dü̅-bō(s), *Angl* dü-'bōz\, René Jules. 1901–1982. American bacteriologist, b. Saint-Brice, France. To U.S. (1924, naturalized 1938); professor, Rockefeller Institute (1927–42, 1944–57) and its successor Rockefeller U. (1957–70); Harvard (1942–44); State U. of N.Y. (1970 ff.). Discovered (1939) tyrocidine and gramicidin, derived from soil bacteria and effective against pneumococcus; developed (1946) method of culturing tubercle bacilli; studied pollution. Author of *The Bacterial Cell* (1945), *The White Plague—Tuberculosis, Man and Society* (1952), *The Mirage of Health* (1959), *Dreams of Reason* (1961), *Unseen World* (1962), *Torch of Life* (1962), *Health and Disease* (1965), *So Human an Animal* (1968, Pulitzer prize), *A God Within* (1972), *Only One Earth* (with Barbara Ward, 1972), *Celebrations of Life* (1981).

Dubs \'düps\, Jakob. 1822–1879. Swiss politician. Member of national assembly (1861–72); president of Swiss Confederation (1864, 1868, 1870).

Du Bu·at \dü̅-bü̅-ȧ\, Pierre-Louis-Georges. 1734–1809. French hydraulic engineer. Military engineer (1761–91); directed siege of Mappen (1761); fortified Valenciennes (1763–73), Lille (1787–91); derived empirical formulas for calculating discharge of fluids from pipes and channels; wrote *Principes d'hydraulique* (1779).

Du·bufe \dü̅-bü̅f\. Family of French painters, including: Claude-Marie (1789–1864), genre and portrait painter. His son ¶Louis-Édouard (1820–1883), whose works included portraits of Empress Eugénie, Charles Gounod, Dumas fils, Philippe Rousseau. The latter's son ¶Édouard-Marie-Guillaume (1853–1909), painter esp. of murals and allegorical compositions.

Du·buf·fet \dü̅-bü̅-fe\, Jean. 1901–1985. French painter, sculptor, and lithographer. One of the most controversial and influential modern artists; executed paintings in primitive style known as "art brut"; used materials such as glass and sand to enrich texture of paintings; his sculptures included *Quatre Arbres* in New York and *Monument à la Bête debout* in Chicago.

Du·buque \dü̅-bü̅k, *Angl* də-'byük\, Julien. 1762–1810. American pioneer, b. Les Becquets, Que. Negotiated agreement with Fox Indians for right to work lead mines in Iowa region (1788); first white settler near what is now Dubuque.

Du Camp \dü̅-kän\, Maxime. 1822–1894. French journalist and traveler. Contributed to *Revue des Deux Mondes, Journal des débats;* founded *Revue de Paris* (1851) in which he published *Madame Bovary*. Wrote *Souvenirs et paysages d'Orient* (1848), *Égypte, Nobie, Palestine et Syrie* (on one of his trips with Flaubert, 1852), *Le Nil* (1854), *Les Chants modernes* (1855), *Expédition des deux-Siciles* (on his experiences with Garibaldi, 1861), *Paris, ses organes, ses fonctions et sa vie* (1869–75), *Souvenirs littéraires* (1882–83).

Du Cange \dü̅-känzh\, Charles Du Fresne \dü̅-fren\. Sieur. 1610–1688. French scholar. Author of *Histoire de l'empire de Constantinople sous les empereurs français (1657);* compiler of *Glossarium ad Scriptores Mediae et Infimae Latinitatis* (1678), *Glossarium ad Scriptores Mediae et Infimae Graecitatis* (1688); pioneer in historical study of languages.

Du·cange \dü̅-känzh\, Victor-Henri-Joseph Bra·hain \brȧ-an\. 1783–1833. French novelist and playwright. Author of the novels *Agathe* (1820), *Valentine* (1821), *Thélène* (1822), *Léonide* (1823), and the melodramas *Calas* (1819), *Trente ans* (1827), *Le Jésuite* (1830), etc.

Du·cas \'d(y)ü-kəs\. *Also spelled* Dukas *or* Doukas. Name of a noble Byzantine family that furnished rulers of the Eastern Roman Empire: Constantine X, Michael VII, Alexius V, John III, Theodore II, and John IV (*qq.v.*). The last three were also connected with the Lascaris family. ¶Ducas (fl. middle of 15th cent.), probably of this family, was a Byzantine historian; lived at Constantinople and Lesbos; author of a trustworthy history of Eastern Greek Empire for the period 1341–1462, first published in Paris (1649).

Du·casse \dü̅-kȧs\, Isidore-Lucien. *Pseudonym* Le Comte de Lau·tré·a·mont \lō-trā-ȧ-mōn\. 1847–1870. French poet, b. Uruguay of French parents. To France (1860); his prose epic *Les Chants de Maldoror* (1868–70) exerted strong influence on Rimbaud, Baudelaire, and the Surrealists.

Du Casse \dü̅-kȧs\, Pierre-Emmanuel-Albert. Baron. 1813–1893. French army officer and historian. First editor of Napoléon's correspondence; published *Mémoires pour servir à l'histoire de la campagne de 1812 en Russie* (1852), *La Guerre au jour le jour* (1875), *Les Rois frères de Napoléon* (1883), *La Crimée et Sébastopol, de 1853 à 1856* (1892).

Ducasse, Roger. See ROGER-DUCASSE.

Duccio, Agostino di. See AGOSTINO DI DUCCIO.

Duc·cio di Buo·nin·se·gna \'düt-chō-dēb-,wȯ-nēn-'sān-yä\. 1255?–1318. Italian painter. First leading representative of Sienese school; known esp. for *Madonna Rucellai* (for Sta. Maria Novella, Florence, 1285), the *Maesta*, altarpiece (1308–11) for cathedral of Siena.

Du Cer·ceau \dü̅-ser-sō\. Name of a French family of architects and decorators including: Jacques An·drou·et du Cerceau \än-drü-e-\ (c.1520–c.1585). Built residences for several members of royal family, but best known for volumes of architectural and decorative engravings, including *Arcs et monuments antiques* (1549), *Temples* (1550), *Vues d'optique* (1551), *Livre d'architecture* (1559), and esp. *Les plus excellents bastiments de France* (1576–79). His son ¶Baptiste Androuet (1545–1590) continued the father's work on Charles IX's Château Charleval (1572–77), began Pont Neuf (1578), worked on Valois rotunda of Saint-Denis, château of Monceaux, etc.; supervisor of royal office of works (1584–90). Baptiste's brother ¶Jacques II (c.1550–1614) built numerous châteaux and latter portion of the Grand Gallery of the Louvre. Baptiste's son ¶Jean I (1585–1649), architect to the king (1617); built Hôtel de Sully (1624–29), Hôtel de Breton Villieurs (1637–43).

Du·ce·tius \d(y)ü-'sē-sh(ē-)əs, -'kē-\. d. c.440 B.C. Sicilian leader. In aftermath of fall of Syracuse (460 B.C.) welded Sicel communities of eastern Sicily into powerful confederation; established capital at Palice; defeated by alliance of Syracuse and Acragas (450).

Du Chail·lu \dü̅-shȧ-yü̅\, Paul Belloni. 1831–1903. American explorer, b. France. To U.S. (1852); on exploring expedition in Central Africa (1856–59); brought back animal specimens including first gorillas ever seen in America; made second trip to Africa (1863–65). Author of *Explorations and Adventures in Equatorial Africa* (1861), *Stories of the Gorilla Country* (1868), *Wild Life Under the Equator* (1869), *Lost in the Jungle* (1869), *The Country of the Dwarfs* (1871), etc.

Du·champ \dü̅-shän\, Gaston. *Pseudonym* Jacques Vil·lon \vē-yōn, -lōn\. 1875–1963. French artist. Half-brother of Marcel Duchamp and Raymond Duchamp-Villon. Worked in Impressionist, Fauvist, and Cubist manners; known as a painter and esp. as an etcher.

Duchamp, Marcel. 1887–1968. French artist. Created sensation with *Nude Descending a Staircase, No. 2* (1912); spent ten years on *The Large Glass* (1913–23, unfinished); invented medium of "ready mades," e.g. *Bicycle Wheel* (1913), *Mona Lisa* (1919); associated with Dadaists, later Surrealists; experimented in film; settled in U.S. (1942; naturalized 1955); spent much of life working in secret on various projects; largely avoided exhibiting works; rediscovered (c.1960), after years of retirement, as prophet of post-modern art.

Duchamp-Vil·lon \-vē-yōn, -vē-lōn\, Raymond. 1876–1918. French sculptor. Brother of Marcel Duchamp and half-brother of Gaston Duchamp. First major sculptor to employ Cubist principles, as in *Seated Woman* and *Horse*.

Du·chenne \dü̅-shen\, Guillaume-Benjamin-Amand. *Called* Duchenne de Bou·logne \-də-bü-lȯny\. 1806–1875. French physician. Used electricity for diagnosis and treatment of disease; first described locomotor ataxia (1858), progressive muscular paralysis, etc.; invented Duchenne's trocar.

Du·chesne \dü̅-shen\, André. *Lat.* Andreas Ches·ne·us \'kes-nē-əs\ *or* Quer·ce·ta·nus \,kwər-sə-'tā-nəs\ *or* Quer·ne·us \'kwər-nē-əs\. 1584–1640. French historian and geographer. Historiographer to king (c.1602); known as the "father of French history." Author of *Andreae Quernei Egregiarum seu Selectarum Lectionum et Antiquitatum Liber* (1602), *Histoire générale d'Angleterre* (1614), *Histoire des Papes* (1616), *Historiae Normannorum Scriptores Antiqui* (1619), *Historiae Francorum Scriptores* (1636–49).

Duchesne, Louis-Marie-Olivier. 1843–1922. French prelate and scholar. Taught at Institut Catholique (1877–85), École Supérieure des Lettres (1885–95); director of École Française de Rome (1895–1922). Founded (1881) *Bulletin Critique de Littérature, d'Histoire et de Théologie.* Author of *Autonomies ecclésiastiques: églises separées* (1896), *Histoire ancienne de l'église chrétienne* (1905–25).

Duchesne, Père. See Jacques-René HÉBERT.

Du·chesne \dᴂ-shen, *Angl* dü-'shān\, Rose-Philippine. 1769–1852. French religious. Entered Society of Sacred Heart (1804); sent to America (1818) as missionary and teacher; established schools and convents at St. Charles and St. Louis, Missouri, at Grand Coteau, Louisiana, etc.; beatified (1940).

Du·cis \dᴂ-sē(s)\, Jean-François. 1733–1816. French playwright. Best known for his adaptations of Shakespeare's plays for the French stage: *Hamlet* (1769), *Roméo et Juliette* (1772), *Le Roi Lear* (1783), *Macbeth* (1784), etc.

Duck·worth \'dək-(,)wərth\, Sir John Thomas. 1748–1817. English naval commander. Took part in defeat of Brest fleet off Ushant (1794); reduced Swedish and Danish possessions in West Indies (1801); defeated French fleet off Santo Domingo (1806); forced the Dardanelles (1807); admiral (1810); governor of Newfoundland (1810–13); baronet (1813).

Du·claux \dᴂ-klō\, Pierre-Émile. 1840–1904. French biochemist. Professor, Sorbonne (1885); student and associate of Pasteur, whom he succeeded as director, Pasteur Inst. in Paris (1895).

Du·clos \dᴂ-klō\, Charles-Pinot. 1704–1772. French writer. Wrote *Histoire de la baronne de Luz* (novel, 1741), *Essai de grammaire française* (1754), *Mémoires pour servir à l'histoire des mœurs du XVIIIe siècle* (1751), etc.

Du·com·mun \dᴂ-kò-mœⁿ\, Élie. 1833–1906. Swiss journalist. Editor, *Revue de Genève* (1855); contributor to *Progrès, Helvétie, États-Unis d'Europe;* organizer (1891) and honorary general secretary of International Bureau of Peace, Bern. With Charles Albert Gobat, awarded Nobel peace prize (1902).

Du·cos \dᴂ-kō\, Pierre-Roger. 1747–1816. French politician. Member of National Convention (1792) and Council of Five Hundred (1795); Third Consul (with Bonaparte and Sieyès) at the beginning of the Consulate (1799); vice president of the Senate. Exiled after Restoration.

Ducos du Hau·ron \-dᴂ-ō-rōⁿ\, Louis, *in full* Arthur-Louis. 1837–1920. French physicist. Invented (1869) trichrome process for color photography; patented (1891) "anaglyph" for 3-dimensional photography.

Du·crot \dᴂ-krō\, Auguste-Alexandre. 1817–1882. French general. In command of army corps at Wörth and Sedan (1870); captured, but escaped and commanded France's second army in Paris; attempted vainly to break Prussian siege (1870–71). Commanded 8th army corps (1872–78); relieved of his command for demonstrations against the republican regime.

Ducrotay de Blainville. See BLAINVILLE.

Du·crow \d(y)ü-'krō\, Andrew. 1793–1842. English equestrian. Trained in tumbling and horsemanship by father, a Belgian "strong man" performer; developed "Courier of St. Petersburg" act standing on two cantering horses; performed throughout Europe; proprietor and star attraction of Astley's Amphitheatre, London (1824–41).

Dud·dell \də-'del, dyü-\, William du Bois. 1872–1917. English electrical engineer. Invented an oscillograph; discovered the singing arc; designed a high-frequency generator and a thermoammeter.

Du·de·vant \dᴂd(-ə)-vāⁿ\, Amandine-Aurore-Lucile, *nee* Du·pin \dᴂ-paⁿ\. *Pen name* George Sand \säⁿ(d)\. 1804–1876. French novelist. m. (1822) Casimer Dudevant. In Paris (from 1831), formed liaison with Jules Sandeau, with whom she published novel *Rose et Blanche* (1831) under pseudonym Jules Sand; on her own, as George Sand, published *Indiana* (1832), *Valentine* (1832), *Lélia* (1833), *Jacques* (1834), *André* (1835), *Mauprat* (1837), *Spiridion* (1838), *Les sept cordes de la lyre* (1840), *Horace* (1841), *Consuelo* (1842–43), *La Mare au diable* (1846), *François le champi* (1847–48), *La petite Fadette* (1849), *Les Maîtres sonneurs* (1853), etc.; wrote also for the theater and autobiographical works *Histoire de ma vie* (1855) and *Elle et lui* (1859). Noted for liaisons with Prosper Mérimée, Alfred de Musset, Frédéric Chopin, for her unconventionality, and championship of woman.

Dud·ley \'dəd-lē\, Charles Benjamin. 1842–1909. American chemist, b. Oxford, N.Y. Chemist with Pennsylvania Railroad Co. (1875–1909); made revolutionary applications of chemistry in increasing efficiency and safety on railroads; a founder (1898), president (1902–09), American Society for Testing and Materials.

Dudley, Dud. 1599–1684. English ironmaster. First to smelt iron ore with coal, and probably coke, rather than charcoal (1619); author of *Metallum Martis* (1665).

Dudley, Edmund. c.1462–1510. English politician. Adviser to Henry VII (from c.1485); speaker of House of Commons (1504); president of king's council (1506), charged with reestablishing feudal dues and fines; accused of embezzling a fortune but acquitted (1509); convicted of treason after accession of Henry VIII (1509); while imprisoned in Tower, wrote *The Tree of Commonwealth,* political allegory; beheaded.

Dudley, Lady Jane. See Lady Jane Grey, under GREY family.

Dudley, John. Duke of North·um·ber·land \nòr-'thəm-bər-lənd\ and Earl of War·wick \'wär-ik\. 1502–1553. English soldier and politician. Son of Edmund Dudley. Restored in blood on repeal of father's attainder (1512–13); deputy governor of Calais (1538); warden of Scottish marches (1542); raised to peerage as Viscount Lisle (1542); lord high admiral (1542); took part in invasion of Scotland (1544) under Edward Seymour, Earl of Hertford; captured Boulogne (1544); created earl of Warwick (1546); joint regent and high chamberlain of England (1547); defeated Scots at Pinkie (1547); brought about fall (1549) and execution (1552) of Somerset; virtual ruler of England (1549–53); created duke (1551); married his fourth son, Guildford (d. 1554), to Lady Jane Grey and induced Edward VI to sign letters patent altering succession of crown to fall to Lady Jane Grey (see GREY family); proclaimed Lady Jane queen on death of Edward VI, but found no support; executed for resisting Mary's succession (1553). His third son ¶Ambrose (1528?–1590), Earl of Warwick, was pardoned for supporting claim of Lady Jane Grey; aided forces of Philip II of Spain at siege of Saint-Quentin (1557); created Earl of Warwick (1561); besieged in Havre while aiding Protestants there and forced to surrender (1563); took part in trial of Mary, Queen of Scots (1586).

Dudley, Robert. 1st Earl of Leices·ter \'les-tər\ of 4th creation (1564). 1532 or 1533–1588. English courtier. Fifth son of John Dudley, Duke of Northumberland. Sentenced to death with his father for supporting Lady Jane Grey (1554), but pardoned; served in France with his brother Ambrose (1557); advanced, as Queen Elizabeth's favorite, to privy council (1559); rumored to have killed wife (1560) in order to be free to marry Elizabeth, but she refused his suit; intrigued with queen's consent, but unsuccessfully, to gain Spanish and Catholic support for projected marriage with Elizabeth (1561); offended queen and court by presumptuousness (1563); suggested by Elizabeth as husband for Mary, Queen of Scots (1564); created earl (1564); failed to displace Cecil; entertained queen in great magnificence, with masques, at Kenilworth castle (1575); m. (1578) Lettice Knollys, widow of Walter Devereux, 1st Earl of Essex; commanded expedition into Low Countries to aid United Provinces against Spaniards (1585), in which campaign his nephew Sir Philip Sidney was killed; recalled (1587) after an incompetent campaign; restored to favor and appointed lieutenant general in command of armies to resist Spanish Armada. His son by Lady Sheffield, ¶Sir Robert Dudley (1574–1649), titular Duke of Northumberland and Earl of Warwick, engineer, inherited properties of earl of Leicester and of Ambrose Dudley, Earl of Warwick; explored Guiana (1594); took part in expedition to Cádiz (1596); when refused titles of his father and uncle by Star Chamber, deserted family and traveled to Italy (1605), avowing himself a Roman Catholic; employed by Duke of Tuscany draining marshes behind Leghorn; invented scheme of a navy with an added fifth class of war vessel; author of *Dell' Arcano del mare* (1646–47), an omnibus of naval knowledge.

Dudley, Thomas. 1576–1653. English colonial administrator. Steward to the Earl of Lincoln. Emigrated to Massachusetts Bay Colony (1630), where he was governor (1634, 1640, 1645, 1650) and thirteen times deputy governor. Member of committee (1637) considering founding of college at Cambridge; one of first overseers of Harvard. His son ¶Joseph (1647–1720) was president of the council and governor of Massachusetts, New Hampshire, and mainland of Rhode Island west of Narragansett Bay (1686); superseded by Andros (1686); member of Andros's council and chief justice of superior court (1686–89); detested by colonials for his share in Andros's administration; chief of the council of New York (1691–92); deputy governor, Isle of Wight (1693–1701); governor of Massachusetts (1702–15).

Du·do \dü-'dō\ *or* **Du·don** \dü-'dōn\ of Saint-Quentin. c.960–before 1043. Norman historian. Wrote *De moribus et actis primorum Normanniae ducum* (completed c.1015–26), chronicle of dukes of Normandy, historically unreliable but a valuable social record.

Du·dok \'dᴂ-dòk\, Willem Marinus. 1884–1974. Dutch architect. Municipal architect, Hilversum (from 1915); designed city bathhouse (1921), Dr. H. Bravink School (1921), Town Hall (1928); also Bijenkorf store (1929–30), Erasmus Huis (1939–40), Rotterdam.

Duellius, Gaius. See Gaius DUILIUS.

Du·er \'dyü(-ə)r\, William. 1747–1799. American Revolutionary leader, b. Devon, England. To America (1768); settled in province of New York. Delegate to Provincial Congress (1775), New York Constitutional Convention (1776), and Continental Congress (1777–79); a signer of the Articles of Confederation. U.S. assistant secretary of the treasury under Hamilton (1789). Heavily involved in land speculation and government contracts; sued by government for financial irregularities in his official position; arrested for debt and imprisoned, causing financial panic (1792); died in prison.

Due·sen·berg \'düz-ᵊn-,bərg\, Frederick Samuel. 1877–1932. American manufacturer, b. Lippe, Germany. To U.S. (1885); champion bicyclist; designed Mason motor (1903); patented Duesenberg motor (1913); chief engineer, Duesenberg Motors Co. (from 1917); designed racing cars and later luxury autos.

Du·faure \dᵫ-fōr\, Armand, *in full* Jules-Armand-Stanislas. 1798–1881. French politician. Member of Chamber of Deputies (1834–52, 1871–79); minister of public works (1839); vice president of Chamber (1845); supported Republican cause in Legislative Assembly (1848); minister of interior (1848–52); helped form Third Republic (1871); minister of justice (1871–73, 1875–76); prime minister (1876–77, 1877–79); helped force resignation of Marsal Mac-Mahon (1879).

Du Fay \dᵫ-fe\, Charles-François de Cis·ter·nay \də-sē-ster-ne\. 1698–1739. French scientist. Pursued researches on phosphorescence, magnetism, and esp. static electricity; developed theory (1733) of two electricities, positive and negative.

Du·fay \dᵫ-fe\, Guillaume. 1400?–1474. French composer. In service of Carlo Malatesta of Rimini (c.1420–28); member of papal singers (1428); canon of Cambrai (1436), of Mons (1446). Regarded as greatest composer of his time; an early master of counterpoint. Compositions included masses, motets, secular chansons, etc.

Duff \'dəf\, Alexander. 1806–1878. Scottish missionary. Opened mission college in Calcutta (1830) combining religious teaching with western science; changed from Church of Scotland to Free Church (1843) and obliged to give up his college but began building anew; founded *Calcutta Review* (1844); moderator of Free Church (1851, 1873); one of founders of U. of Calcutta.

Duff, Mountstuart Elphinstone Grant. 1829–1906. Scottish administrator in India. M.P. (1857–81); undersecretary of state for India (1868–74), for colonies (1880); governor of Madras (1881–86); author of *Notes from a Diary 1851–1901* (1897–1905), valuable as social history.

Duff Cooper, Alfred. See Alfred Duff COOPER.

Dufferin and Ava, Marquis of. See Frederick BLACKWOOD.

Duff-Gor·don \-'gȯrd-ᵊn\, Lady Lucie, *nee* Austin. 1821–1869. English woman of letters. Daughter of John Austin (*q.v.*); m. (1840) Sir Alexander Duff-Gordon (1811–72). Gathered about her in London a brilliant circle of celebrities; lived in Egypt (from 1862). Known for translations from the German, as well as historical works. Remembered chiefly for her *Letters from the Cape* (1862–63), *Letters from Egypt* (1865), and *Last Letters from Egypt* (1875).

Duf·fy \'dəf-ē\, Sir Charles Gavan. 1816–1903. Irish nationalist and Australian political leader. Journalist in Dublin; a founder with T. O. Davis and John Blake Dillon of *The Nation* (1842), nationalist organ; subsequently organized Young Ireland party; stimulated taste in Ireland for national history and literature. Engaged in nationalist agitation for twelve years; imprisoned (1848–49) for suspected part in abortive insurrection; joined Irish Tenant League for fixed tenure, fair rents, and free sale; M.P. (1852–55); on failure of attempts to unite factions behind aims of Tenant League, retired and emigrated to Australia. Member of Victoria House of Assembly (1856–80); minister of public works, Victoria (1857–59, 1862–65); prime minister (1871–72); speaker of House of Assembly (1877–80). Spend remainder of life in southern Europe in literary work. Author of *Young Ireland 1840–50* (1880–83), *League of North and South, 1850–54* (1886), *My Life in Two Hemispheres* (1898). His son ¶Sir Frank Gavan (1852–1936), Australian jurist, b. Dublin, Ireland; justice of High Court of Australia (1913–31); chief justice (1931–35).

Duffy, Edmund. 1899–1962. American cartoonist, b. Jersey City, N.J. On staff of Baltimore *Sun* (1924–48), *Saturday Evening Post* (1948–56); awarded Pulitzer prize for cartoons (1931, 1934, 1940).

Duffy, Francis Patrick. 1871–1932. American Roman Catholic clergyman, b. Cobourg, Ont. Chaplain of "Fighting" 69th regiment of N.Y. National Guard, which became 165th Infantry in National Army during World War I; accompanied regiment to Mexican border (1916) and overseas (1917–18). Author of *Father Duffy's Story* (1920).

Du·four \dᵫ-für\, Guillaume-Henri, *orig.* William Heinrich. 1787–1875. Swiss soldier. Served in Napoleonic army (1807–14); to Switzerland (1817); helped found military school at Thun (1818); chief of staff of Swiss army (1831); elected general of federal army (1847) to suppress rebellious Roman Catholic cantons in Sonderbund War; again (1849) to maintain Swiss neutrality; again (1856) in conflict with Prussia; again (1859) to prevent French annexation of Savoy. Directed topographical survey of Switzerland (1842–64). Presided over Geneva convention (1864) that led to creation of Red Cross.

du Fresne, Charles. See DU CANGE.

Du·fres·noy \dᵫ-fren-wȧ\, Charles-Alphonse. 1611–1665. French painter. Known esp. for his Latin poem *De arte graphica,* written during his Italian sojourn (1632–56) and influential on later French artists.

Du·fres·ny \dᵫ-frā-nē, -fre-\, Charles-Rivière. 1648–1724. French dramatist. Great-grandson of Henry IV. Author of comedies including *Les Adieux des officiers* (1693), *Le Chevalier joueur* (1697), *L'Esprit de contradiction* (1700), *Le double veuvage* (1702), *La Coquette de village* (1715).

Du·fy \dᵫ-fē\, Raoul. 1877–1953. French painter and designer. Abandoned early Impressionism for Fauvism; bright, colorful paintings did much to popularize the movement; began work in woodcut with illustrations for Apollinaire's *Bestiaire* (1911); operated factories for producing woodblock-printed fabrics (from 1913), pottery (from 1920), tapestries (from 1921); also did theatrical designs and decorations for public works.

du Gard, Roger Martin. See MARTIN DU GARD.

Dug·dale \'dəg-,dāl\, Sir William. 1605–1686. English antiquary. Appointed Rouge Croix pursuivant in ordinary by Charles I (1639); accompanied Charles I to Oxford; collaborated with the antiquary Roger Dodsworth in *Monasticon Anglicanum* (1655, 1664, 1673), an account of English monastic houses; at Restoration (1660) made Norroy King of Arms; garter King of Arms (1677). Author of *Antiquities of Warwickshire* (1656), *History of St. Paul's Cathedral* (1658), *Imbanking and Drayning* (1662), and *Baronage of England* (1675–76).

Dug·gar \'dəg-ər\, Benjamin Minge. 1872–1956. American botanist, b. Gallion, Ala. Professor, U. of Missouri (1902–05), Cornell (1907–12), Missouri Botanical Garden and Washington U. (1912–27), U. of Wisconsin (1927–43). Author of *Fungous Diseases of Plants* (1909), *Plant Physiology* (1911), etc.

Du·ghet \dᵫ-ge\, Gaspard. *Known as* Gas·pard Pous·sin \gȧs-pȧr-pü-saⁿ\. 1615–1675. French painter. Brother-in-law of Nicolas Poussin. Worked in Rome; best known for his landscapes, esp. his topographic views of the Roman Campagna.

Du·go·nics \'dü-gō-nich\, András. 1740–1818. Hungarian novelist. A leader in popular school of Hungarian literature; author of *Etelka* (1788), first Hungarian best seller.

Du·guay-Trou·in \dᵫ-ge-trü-aⁿ\, René. 1673–1736. French sea captain. To sea as a privateer (1689); commissioned in royal navy for exploits (1696); among his naval exploits were capture of a British convoy (1707) and capture and sack of Rio de Janiero (1711); lieutenant general of naval army (1728).

du Guesclin, Bertrand. See GUESCLIN.

Du·guit \dᵫ-gē\, Léon. 1859–1928. French jurist. Professor at Bordeaux (1886–1928); author of *Des Fonctions de l'état moderne* (1894), *Les Transformations générales du droit public* (1913), *Traité de droit constitutionnel* (1921–25), *Le Pragmatisme juridique* (1924), etc.

Du·ha·mel \dᵫ-ȧ-mel\, Georges. 1884–1966. French writer. A physician by profession; a founder, with Jules Romains and others, of the Abbaye community (1906); published volumes of verse *Des Légendes, des batailles* (1907), *L'Homme en tête* (1909), *Selon ma loi* (1910), *Les Compagnons* (1912); plays *La Lumière* (1911), *Dans l'ombre des statues* (1912), *Combat* (1913); novels and tales, including *Vie des martyrs* (1917), *Civilisation 1914–1917* (1918), *Les Plaisirs et les jeux* (1922), *La Possession du monde* (1922), *Le Voyage à Moscou* (1927), *Fables de mon jardin* (1936), *Cri des profondeurs* (1951), etc., and two novel cycles, *Vie et aventures de Salavin* (5 vol., 1920–32), and *Chronique des Pasquier* (10 vol., 1933–44); autobiography *Lumières sur ma vie* (1944–53).

Duhamel du Mon·ceau \-dᵫ-mōⁿ-sō\, Henri-Louis. 1700–1782. French engineer and agriculturist. Experimented in plant and animal physiology and chemistry; author of works on trees and shrubs, naval architecture.

Du·hem \dü-em\, Pierre-Maurice-Marie. 1861–1916. French physicist and philosopher. Taught at Lille (1887–93), Rennes (1893–94), Bordeaux (1894–1916); conducted research in thermodynamics and hydrodynamics; later did much work in philosophy of science and history of medieval science. Wrote *Traité de mécanique chimique* (1897–99), *Thermodynamique et chimie* (1902), *La Théorie physique, son objet et sa structure* (1906), *Études sur Léonard de Vinci* (1906–13), *Traité d'energetique* (1911), *Système du monde* (1913 ff.).

Duhm \'düm\, Bernhard. 1847–1928. German theologian. Professor at Göttingen (1877–88), Basel (1888–1928); author of commentaries on prophetic books of the Old Testament; proposed the Trito-Isaiah theory of authorship of Isaiah lvi-lxvi.

Düh·ring \'dᵫ-riŋ\, Karl Eugen. 1833–1921. German Positivist philosopher and economist. Author of *Capital und Arbeit* (1865), *Natürliche Dialektik* (1865), *Kritische Geschichte der Philosophie* (1869), *Kritische Geschichte der allgemeinen Principien der Mechanik* (1873), *Logik und Wissenschaftstheorie* (1878), autobiography *Sachen, Leben, und Feinde* (1882).

Du·il·i·us \d(y)ə-'wil-ē-əs\, Gaius. 3d century B.C. Roman general. Consul (260 B.C.) with Gnaeus Cornelius Scipio; after defeat of Scipio by Carthaginians off Lipara, took command of Roman fleet; won decisive victory (260) over larger fleet off Mylae; first to use device of grappling irons and boarding bridges; victory of great importance in First Punic War and in establishing beginning of Rome's sea power; in his honor, Duilian Column was erected in Forum at Rome.

Du·jar·din \dᵫ-zhȧr-daⁿ\, Édouard-Émile-Louis. 1861–1949. French journalist and writer. Associated with Symbolists; wrote novels, plays, poetry, essays; works included *Les Lauriers sont coupés,* a novel employing interior monologue device later adopted by James Joyce (1888), *Le Délassement du Guerrier* (verse, 1904), *La Comédie des amours* (verse, 1913), *Le Mystère du Dieu mort et ressuscité* (play, 1923), etc.

Dujardin, Felix. 1801–1860. French biologist. Taught at Tours (1826–39), Toulouse (1839–40), Rennes (1840–60); known for studies of protozoans and invertebrates; distinguished protoplasm, calling it *sarcode* (1835).

Du·jar·din \\ˌdǖ-zhär-ˈda^n\\, Karel. 1622–1678. Dutch painter and etcher. Best known for landscapes, portraits, and genre pictures.

Dukas. See also DUCAS.

Du·kas \\dǖ-käs\\, Paul-Abraham. 1865–1935. French composer. Professor, Paris Conservatory of Music (1910–13, 1928–35); compositions included cantata *Velléda* (1888), *Symphony in C Major* (1892), symphonic poem *L'Apprenti sorcier* (1897), *Sonate* for piano (1901), music for Maeterlinck's lyrical opera *Ariane et Barbe-Bleue* (1907), ballet *La Péri* (1912).

Duke \\ˈd(y)ük\\, Benjamin Newton (1855–1929) and his brother James Buchanan (1856–1925). American industrialists, b. near Durham, N.C. Established their first tobacco factory at Durham (1874), and branch factory in New York (1884); pioneered in introduction of cigarette-making machinery; engaged in "cigarette war" that resulted in joining of rival companies in the American Tobacco Company with J. B. Duke as president (1890); organized American Snuff Co. (1900), American Cigar Co. (1901), later merged into American Tobacco; U.S. Supreme Court ordered dissolution of American Tobacco Co. as a combination in restraint of trade (1911). Both brothers were large benefactors of Trinity College, Durham, which was renamed Duke University (1924) in their honor.

Dukes \\ˈd(y)üks\\, Ashley. 1885–1959. English critic, playwright, and theater manager. Drama critic for *New Age* (1909–12), *Vanity Fair* (1912–14), etc.; m. (1918) Marie Rambert; adapted plays from French and German; wrote plays including *The Man With a Load of Mischief* (1924), *Matchmaker's Arms* (1930); established and managed (from 1933) Mercury Theatre, where he presented T.S. Eliot's *Murder in the Cathedral* (1935), Auden and Isherwood's *Ascent of F.6* (1936), etc.

Du·lac \\dǖ-läk\\, Edmund. 1882–1953. British artist, illustrator, and stage designer, b. France. Naturalized British citizen (1912). Best known for his illustrated editions of classics, including *The Arabian Nights* (1907), *The Tempest* (1908), *The Rubáiyát of Omar Khayyám* (1909), *Sinbad the Sailor* (1914), *Tanglewood Tales* (1918). Designed coronation stamps (1937, 1953) and King George VI's cameo portrait on stamps.

Du·la·ny \\d(y)ə-ˈlā-nē\\, Daniel. 1722–1797. American lawyer and colonial leader, b. Annapolis, Md. Member of Maryland assembly (1751–54, 1756) and of governor's council (1757–76); commissary general of Maryland (1759–61); secretary of Maryland (1761–74). Author (1765) of powerful pamphlet against Stamp Act, *Considerations on the Propriety of Imposing Taxes in the British Colonies, for the Purpose of Raising a Revenue, by Act of Parliament;* he later opposed radical policies of the colonial leaders, disapproved revolution, and had his estates confiscated (1781).

Dul·ce y Ga·ray \\ˈdül-thā-ē-gä-ˈrä-ē; ˈdül-sā-\\, Domingo. Marqués de Cas·tel-flo·ri·te \\käs-tel-flō-ˈrē-tä\\. 1808–1869. Spanish general. Took part in Carlist wars; governor of Catalonia (1858–62); twice governor of Cuba (1862–66 and 1869).

Du·lhut *or* **Du·luth** \\dǖ-lǖt\\, Daniel Grey·so·lon \\gres-ō-ˈlō^n\\. Sieur. 1636–1710. French explorer. To New France (c.1675); explored region around Lake Superior (1678–79); made alliances with Chippewa and Sioux, enabling France to claim the northwest region; rescued Father Hennepin from Sioux (1680); commander of Fort Frontenac (c.1690–95). City of Duluth, Minn., named for him.

Dul·les \\ˈdəl-əs\\, John Foster. 1888–1959. American lawyer and diplomat, b. Washington, D.C. Counsel to American delegation at Versailles peace conference (1918–19); helped prepare United Nations Charter (1944–45); member of U.S. delegation to UN organizing conference, San Francisco (1945); U.S. delegate to UN General Assembly (1946–49); negotiated Japanese peace treaty (1949–51); U.S. senator (1949); U.S. secretary of state (1953–59); considered most powerful secretary of state in U.S. history; chief architect of SEATO pact (1954), Baghdad Pact (1955), Eisenhower Doctrine (1957). His brother ¶Allen Welsh Dulles (1893–1969) served in Foreign Service (1916–26); in law practice (1926–42); chief of Bern office of Office of Strategic Services (1942–45); deputy director (1951–53) and director (1953–61), Central Intelligence Agency; resigned following failure of Cuban invasion. Author of *The Craft of Intelligence* (1963), *Secret Surrender* (1966).

Dul·lin \\dǖ-la^n\\, Charles. 1885–1949. French actor and theatrical producer. Founded (1920) Théâtre de l'Atelier; director (1941–47) of Théâtre Sarah-Bernhardt; produced works by Pirandello, Achard, Salacrou, Sartre, etc.

Du·long \\dǖ-lō^n\\, Pierre-Louis. 1785–1838. French chemist and physicist. Professor (1820–30), director (1830–38), Polytechnical School, Paris. Discovered nitrogen chloride (1813); collaborated with Alexis-Thérèse Petit in research on heat; with Petit, enunciated law of Dulong and Petit, that elements in the solid state have the same gram-atomic heat (1819); investigated fluid densities and water (with Berzelius, 1820), the specific heats of gases, the elasticity of steam at high temperatures (with Arago, 1830); devised empirical formula (Dulong's formula) for calculating the heat value of fuels from their chemical composition.

Duluth. See DULHUT.

Du·mas \\dǖ-mä, *Angl* d(y)ü-ˈmä, ˈd(y)ü-ˌ\\, Alexandre. *Orig.* Thomas-Alexandre Da·vy de La Pail·le·te·rie \\dȧ-vē-də-lȧ-päy-trē\\. 1762–1806. French soldier, b. in Santo Domingo. Natural son of a French marquis and a black colonial. Entered royal army under the name Dumas (1786); served in the Revolutionary and Napoleonic armies; general of division (1793); accompanied Napoléon to Italy (1797); distinguished himself at Bressanone in the Tyrol by his singlehanded defense of a bridge, and was called by Napoléon Ho·ra·ti·us Co·clès du Ty·rol \\ō-rȧs-yǖs-kō-kles-dǖ-tē-rōl\\. Commanded French cavalry in the Egyptian expedition (1798).

Dumas, Alexandre. *Known as* Dumas père \\per\\. 1802–1870. French novelist and playwright. Son of Alexandre Davy de La Pailleterie, called Dumas. Started as clerical worker; obtained post in household of duc d'Orleans (future King Louis-Philippe); soon turned to writing, using many collaborators, esp. Auguste Maquet. Made early success with dramas, including *Henry III et sa cour* (1829), *Christine* (1830), *Napoléon Bonaparte* (1831), *Antony* (1831), *Richard Darlington* (1831), *La Tour de Nesle* (1832), *Kean* (1836); turned to historical novels, including *Les trois mousquetaires* (1844) and its sequel *Vingt ans après* (1845), *Le Comte de Monte Cristo* (1844), *La Reine Margot* (1845), *La Dame de Monsoreau* (1846) and its sequel *Les Quarante-cinq* (1848), *Le Chevalier de Maison Rouge* (1846), *Mémoires d'un médecin* (1848), *Dix ans plus tarde ou le Vicomte de Bragelonne* (1848–50), *La Tulipe noir* (1859), *Ange Pitou* (1853), *La Comtesse de Charny* (1855).

Dumas, Alexandre. *Known as* Dumas fils \\fēs\\. 1824–1895. French playwright and novelist. Natural son of Alexandre Dumas père (*q.v.*). Published volume of verse *Péchés de jeunesse* (1847); achieved first success as novelist but, after successful adaptation of two of his novels for the stage, devoted himself chiefly to playwriting. His works include *La Dame aux camélias* (novel, 1848; play, 1852), *Diane de Lys* (novel, 1851; play, 1853); the novels *Tristan le roux* (1849), *Henri de Navarre* (1850), *La Dame aux perles* (1854), *L'Affaire Clémenceau* (1866); the plays *Le Demi-Monde* (1855), *La Question d'argent* (1857), *Le Fils naturel* (1858), *Un Père prodigue* (1859), *L'Ami des femmes* (1864), *Monsieur Alphonse* (1874), *La Princesse de Bagdad* (1881), *Francillon* (1887).

Dumas, Guillaume-Mathieu. Comte. 1753–1837. French soldier and historian. Aide-de-camp to Rochambeau in America, and to Lafayette (1789); took Louis XVI back to Paris after the king was arrested at Varennes. A moderate during Revolution, was proscribed until establishment of consulate; general of division (1805); minister of war under King Joseph at Naples and later at Madrid. Author of *Essai historique sur les campagnes de 1799 à 1814* (1816–26) and translator of Napier's *History of the Peninsular War.* His brother ¶René-François (1753–1794) was president of the Revolutionary Tribunal during the Reign of Terror; guillotined with Robespierre (1794).

Dumas, Jean-Baptiste-André. 1800–1884. French chemist. Professor, École Centrale des Arts et Manufactures, Paris (which he cofounded in 1829), Sorbonne (1832–68), École Polytechnique (from 1835), École de Médecin (from 1838); minister of agriculture (1850–51); senator (1853). Known for researches on vapor density of the elements, the formulas of alcohols and ethers, atomic weights, the law of substitution in organic compounds, the theory of chemical types, etc.; isolated anthracene (1831), discovered formula for camphor (1832); isolated methyl alcohol (1834). Author of *Traité de chimie appliquée aux arts* (1828–45), etc.

Du Mau·ri·er \\d(y)ù-ˈmȯr-ē-ˌā, *Fr* dǖ-mȯr-yā\\, George Louis Palmella Bus·son \\ˈbǖ-sō^n\\. 1834–1896. British artist and novelist. Illustrated new editions of Thackeray's *Henry Esmond,* Foxe's *Book of Martyrs,* and stories for *Once a Week, Leisure Hour,* and esp. *Cornhill Magazine* (1863–83); successor to John Leech on staff of *Punch* (1864–96), where he gently satirized fashionable upper-class and middle-class life; wrote and illustrated three novels, *Peter Ibbetson* (1891) and *Trilby* (1894), both recording incidents in his own life, and *The Martian* (1897). His elder son ¶Guy Louis Busson du Maurier (1865–1915), lieutenant colonel in Royal Fusiliers, was widely known for military play, *An Englishman's Home* (1909). His younger son, ¶Sir Gerald Hubert Edward Busson du Maurier (1873–1934), was a well known actor-manager; known esp. for his portrayal of J.M. Barrie characters.

Du·mes·nil \\dǖ-mā-nēl, -me-\\, Mlle. *Orig.* Marie-Françoise Mar·chand \\mȧr-shä^n\\. 1713–1803. French tragedienne. At Comédie-Française (1737–75); best known for fiery portrayal of roles in works of Voltaire, Racine, Corneille.

Dum·mer \\ˈdəm-ər\\, Jeremiah. c.1679–1739. English lawyer, b. Boston, Mass. Practiced law in England (from c.1704); agent for Massachusetts (1710–21) and for Connecticut (1712–30); influenced Elihu Yale to contribute for establishment of college in New England, and himself sent (1714) several hundred books to Yale College. Author of *Defence of the New England Charters* (1715).

Dümm·ler \ˈdœm-lər\, Ernst Ludwig. 1830–1902. German historian. Professor at Halle (from 1858); member (from 1875), president (1888) of committee directing the *Monumenta Germaniae historica;* author of *Geschichte des ostfränkischen Reiches* (1862–65).

Du·mon·ceau \dǖ-mō^{n}-sō\, Jean-Baptiste. Comte de Ber·gen·dael \ˈber-gan-dȧl\. 1760–1821. Belgian soldier. Involved in rebellion of Brabant against Austria (1788–89), took refuge in France (1790); distinguished himself in battle of Jemappes (1792) and in conquest of Low Countries by French; lieutenant general of Batavian Republic (1795). Appointed (by Louis Bonaparte, King of Holland) marshal of Holland, councilor of state, and minister to Paris (1806).

Du·mons·tier \dǖ-mō^{n}-tyā\ *or* **Du·mous·tier** *or* **Du·moû·tier** \dǖ-mü-tyā\. Family of French artists including: Geoffroy (1510–1560), miniaturist who apparently worked on Fontainebleau (1537–40). ¶Etienne II (1520–1603), painter and valet for Henry II, François II, Charles IX, Henry III, Henry IV, and diplomatic agent for Catherine de Médicis. His brother ¶Pierre I (c.1524–1604), painter and valet for Catherine de Médicis. Another brother ¶Cosme (d. c.1605), known for decorative work on Paris cathedral. Cosme's son ¶Daniel (1574–1646), painter of startlingly realistic portraits of Prince Charles-Gustave of Sweden, Sully, the duc de Longueville, Malherbe, etc. Daniel's son ¶Nicolas (1612–1667), painter and valet for Louis XIV.

Du·mont \dǖ-mō^{n}\. Family of French sculptors, including: Pierre (1660–1737). His son ¶François (1688–1726) contributed to decoration of Saint-Sulpice, Paris. François's son ¶Edme (1722–1775) designed façade of Hôtel des Monnaies. Edme's son ¶Jacques-Edme (1761–1844) contributed to Saint-Sulpice; sculpted statues on literary themes. Jacques's son ¶Augustin-Alexandre (1801–1884), known for statue of Napoléon on Vendôme column (1863).

Dumont, Alberto Santos-. See SANTOS-DUMONT.

Du Mont \ˈd(y)ü-ˌmänt, d(y)ü-ˈ\, Allen Balcom. 1901–1965. American engineer, b. New York City. For Westinghouse Lamp Co. (1924–28) developed high-speed manufacturing equipment for vacuum tubes; chief engineer, De Forest Radio Co. (1928–31); established Du Mont Laboratories (1931); developed first commercially practical cathode-ray tube and laboratory oscilloscope; began manufacturing commercial television receivers (1937); established Du Mont broadcasting network (1946).

Du·mont \dǖ-mō^{n}\, François. 1751–1831. French miniature painter. Painted portraits of Louis XVI, Marie-Antoinette, Louis XVIII, Charles X, and many other notables.

Du Mont \dǖ-mō^{n}\, Henri. *Orig. surname* de Thier \də-tēr\. 1610–1684. Belgian organist and composer. Organist at St. Paul's Church, Paris (from 1643); music master of the royal chapel (1663); composed masses, motets, etc.

Dumont, Pierre-Étienne-Louis. 1759–1829. Swiss publicist. Ordained in ministry (1781); secretary to Jeremy Bentham and associate of Mirabeau; author of *Souvenirs sur Mirabeau* (1832) and editor of books by Bentham.

Dumont d'Ur·ville \-dǖr-vēl\, Jules-Sébastien-César. 1790–1842. French naval commander and explorer. On expedition to Grecian Archipelago (1819–20) helped secure French possession of newly discovered Venus de Milo; served on voyage around world (1822–25); commanded frigate *Astrolabe* on a voyage to Polynesia in search of remains of La Pérouse (1826–29), returning with botanical and geological specimens and much new geographical information on South Seas; commanded the *Zélée* on a voyage to Antarctica (1837–41), discovering Louis Philippe Land, Joinville Island, Adélie coast; wrote accounts of his expeditions.

Du·mou·lin \dǖ-mü-la^{n}\, Charles. 1500–1566. French jurist. Author of *De Feudis* (1539), *Sommaire du livre analytique des contrats, usures, rentes constituées, intérêts et monnoyes* (1547–1556), *Extricatio labyrinthi dividui et individui,* etc.

Du·mou·riez \dǖ-mür-yā\, Charles-François du Pé·rier \pār-yā\. 1739–1823. French general. Under Louis XVI, commandant of Cherbourg (1778–88); major general (1788). At outbreak of Revolution joined Jacobin Club; minister of foreign affairs (1792); pressed for war with Austria; minister of war (1792); lieutenant general of army of the North (1792); conducted campaign that checked Duke of Brunswick at Valmy (1792); defeated Austrians at Jemappes (1792); was defeated at Neerwinden and Louvain (1793); while planning to use army to overthrow Revolutionary government, was denounced by National Assembly; deserted to Austrians, his defection discrediting his Girondist associates. Wandered through Europe; lived in exile in England.

Dun \ˈdən\, Robert Graham. 1826–1900. American businessman, b. Chillicothe, Ohio. Entered Lewis Tappan's mercantile agency, New York (1850); rose to head concern, reorganized (1859) as R. G. Dun & Co. and merged (1933) with Bradstreet Co. to form Dun & Bradstreet, Inc.; published (from 1893) *Dun's Review,* weekly report of business conditions.

Du·nant \dǖ-nä^{n}\, Jean-Henri. 1828–1910. Swiss philanthropist. Inspired by sight of wounded on battlefield of Solferino (1859), he labored for creation of an organization to aid wounded soldiers; published *Un Souvenir de Solférino* (1862); succeeded in bringing about conference at Geneva (1863) from which came the Geneva Convention (1864) and establishment of International Red Cross. With Frédéric Passy, shared first Nobel prize for peace (1901). Devoted entire fortune to charity.

Du·nash ben Lab·rat \ˈd(y)ü-ˌnäsh-ben-ˈläb-rət\. c.920–c.990. Jewish poet and grammarian. First to adapt Arabic meters to Hebrew verse; helped initiate fruitful period of Hebrew philology with attack on lexicon of Menahem ben Saruq.

Dunash ben Ta·min \-ˈtäm-ˌēn\. c.900–c.960. Jewish physician and scholar. Made one of the first comparative studies of Hebrew and Arabic.

Dun·bar \ˈdən-ˌbär\, Paul Laurence. 1872–1906. American poet, b. Dayton, Ohio. Son of escaped Negro slaves. Published volume of verse *Oak and Ivy* (1893) at own expense; second volume, *Majors and Minors* (1985), received favorable notice by William Dean Howells; *Lyrics of Lowly Life* (1896), with an introduction by Howells, established his reputation. Other works: *Poems of Cabin and Field* (1899), *Lyrics of the Hearthside* (1899), *Candle-Lightin' Time* (1902), *Lyrics of Love and Laughter* (1903), *Lyrics of Sunshine and Shadow* (1905), and four novels, *The Uncalled* (1896), *The Love of Landry* (1900), *The Fanatics* (1901), *The Sport of the Gods* (1902).

Dun·bar \ˈdən-ˌbär, dən-ˈbär\, William. 1460?–?1530. Scottish poet. Traveled over England, perhaps as Franciscan friar; visited England (1501) with embassy to negotiate marriage of James IV and Margaret Tudor. Composed in honor of queen's arrival a political allegory *The Thrissill and the Rois* (1503); described Queen Margaret's visit (1511) to north of Scotland in *The Quenis Progress at Aberdeen;* disappeared altogether after battle of Flodden. Author of satires, including *The Dance of the Sevin Deidly Synnis* (between 1503 and 1508), of an allegorical poem *The Goldyn Targe,* an elegy *The Lament for the Makaris.*

Dun·can I \ˈdəŋ-kən\. d. 1040. King of Scotland. Succeeded his maternal grandfather, Malcolm II, as king (1034); defeated and killed by Macbeth. His grandson ¶Duncan II (d. 1094), son of Malcolm III Canmore, lived for a time as hostage in Normandy; gained English and Norman help to drive out his father's brother Donaldbane (1093); ruled as king for a few months until slain by agents of Donaldbane.

Duncan, Adam. 1st Viscount Duncan of Cam·per·down \ˈkam-pər-ˌdau̇n\. 1731–1804. British naval commander, b. Scotland. Commanded the *Valiant* in reduction of Havana (1762); commanded the *Monarch* at Cape St. Vincent (1780); admiral (1795); commander in chief of North Sea fleet (1795–1801); defeated De Winter, Dutch admiral, off Camperdown (1797), capturing eleven ships.

Duncan, Andrew, *known as* the Elder. 1744–1828. Scottish physician. President of Edinburgh College of Physicians (1790, 1824); professor at U. of Edinburgh (1790–1828); promoted establishment of lunatic asylum (chartered 1807); founded Royal Public Dispensary (chartered 1818); founded Caledonian Horticultural Society (1809).

Duncan, Andrew, *known as* the Younger. 1773–1832. Scottish physician. Son of Andrew Duncan the Elder. Held first chair of medical jurisprudence in Britain, at U. of Edinburgh (1807–19); joint professor of physiology with father (1819–21), of materia medica (1821–32). Leader in rebuilding the university. Published *Edinburgh New Dispensary* (1803 et seq.); edited *Edinburgh Medical and Surgical Journal* (1805–32).

Duncan, Sir Andrew Rae. 1884–1952. British government official. Chairman of British Iron and Steel Federation (1935–40, 1945–52); M.P. (1940–50); president of Board of Trade (1940, 1941–42); minister of supply (1940–41, 1942–45).

Duncan, Isadora. 1878–1927. American dancer, b. San Francisco. Under patronage of Mrs. Patrick Campbell, aroused enthusiasm in London and Paris. Joined Loie Fuller's company (1902) and toured Germany; acclaimed in Vienna and Budapest. Established school of dancing for children at Grünewald, near Berlin (1904). Invited to Russia (1921); opened school in Moscow; m. (1922) Sergey Yesenin (*q.v.*). Wrote autobiography, *My Life* (1926–27). Killed in automobile accident.

Duncan, Sir Patrick. 1870–1943. South African politician. Colonial secretary of the Transvaal (1903–07); acting lieutenant governor (1906–07); member of South African parliament (1910–20, 1921–36); minister of the interior, public health, and education (1921–24); minister of mines (1933–36); governor general, Union of South Africa (1937–43).

Duncan, Thomas. 1807–1845. Scottish portrait, genre, and historical painter. Best known for his *Prince Charles Edward and the Highlanders entering Edinburgh* (1840) and *Charles Edward asleep after Culloden, protected by Flora MacDonald* (1843).

Duncannon, Viscount. See John William PONSONBY.

Dunck·er \'dúŋ-kər\, Max, *in full* Maximilian Wolfgang. 1811–1886. German historian. Professor at Halle (1842–57), Tübingen (1857–59); director of Prussian state archives (1867–74); chief work *Geschichte des Altertums* (1852–86).

Dun·combe \'dən-kəm, 'dəŋ-\, Thomas Slingsby. 1796–1861. English radical leader. M.P. (1826–32, 1834–61); assisted in passing Reform Bill (1832); presented to Parliament (1842) the Chartist petition; took part in letting Prince Louis-Napoléon escape from Ham (1846); member of council of Friends of Italy (1851) at request of Mazzini.

Dun·das \dən-'das, 'dən-,\ of Ar·nis·ton \'är-nəs-tən\. Name of Scottish noble family, including: Sir James Dundas, Lord Arniston (d. 1679); M.P. (1648); lord of session (1662–65); deprived on refusal to renounce Solemn League and Covenant. His grandson ¶Robert Dundas (1685–1753), Lord Arniston the elder; solicitor general for Scotland (1717–20); lord advocate (1720); dean of faculty of advocates (1721); M.P. (1722–37); judge of court of session (1737–48); lord president of session (1748–53); reintroduced "guilty" or "not guilty" as possible findings by juries. The latter's son ¶Robert (1713–1787), Lord Arniston the younger; solicitor general (1742–46); dean of faculty of advocates (1746); lord advocate (1754); M.P. (1754); lord president of session (1760–87); gave his casting vote against Archibald (Stewart) Douglas in Douglas peerage case (1767). His son ¶Robert (1758–1819) was solicitor general for Scotland (1784); lord advocate (1789); M.P. (1790–1801); chief baron of the exchequer in Scotland (1801).

VISCOUNTS MELVILLE: ¶Henry Dundas (1742–1811), 1st Viscount Mel·ville \'mel-,vil\ and Baron Dun·i·ra \də-'ni(ə)r-ə\; 4th son of Robert Dundas, Lord Arniston the elder; solicitor general (1766); M.P. (1774–1802); lord advocate (1775–83); strenuously supported Lord North and war with America; privy councilor and treasurer of navy (1782–83, 1784–1800); initiated movement leading to recall from India and impeachment of Warren Hastings; transferred support to Pitt, becoming home secretary (1791–94), president of board of control (1793–1801), and secretary of war (1794–1801); carried through successful Egyptian campaign (1801) contrary to advice of Pitt and king; raised to peerage (1802); first lord of the admiralty (1804–05); erased from roll of privy council (1805) and impeached (1806) for misuse of funds while treasurer of navy; acquitted of all except negligence (1806); restored to privy council (1807); sometimes called "Starvation Dundas" because of his use of the word in a speech (1775) upholding restrictive trade measures on New England colonies.

¶Robert Saunders Dundas (1771–1851), 2d viscount; son of 1st viscount; M.P. (1796–1811); privy councilor (1807); president of board of control (1807, 1809); Irish secretary (1809); first lord of the admiralty (1812–27); received recognition of his interest in Arctic exploration by naming of Melville Sound. His eldest son, ¶Henry (1801–1876), 3d viscount, officer of Scots guards; M.P. (1826–31); took part in suppression of Canadian rebellion (1837); second in command at capture of Multan (1847); general (1868). The 2d viscount's 2d son ¶Sir Richard Saunders (1802–1861), naval officer; distinguished himself in Opium War (1841); commander in chief of Baltic fleet (1855–61); vice admiral (1858).

Dundas, Sir David. 1735–1820. British army officer, b. Edinburgh. Served in Seven Years' War, Napoleonic campaigns; general (1802); commander in chief (1809–11); devised new system for British army from Prussia code of tactics of Frederick the Great's school.

Dundee, Viscount. See John GRAHAM (of Claverhouse).

Dundonald, Earl of. See Thomas COCHRANE.

Du·nér \dü-'nār\, Nils Christofer. 1839–1914. Swedish astronomer. Senior astronomer, Royal U. Observatory, Lund (1864–88); director of the observatory, Uppsala (1888–1909); investigated double stars, variable stars; pioneered in stellar spectroscopic observations; studied rotation of sun, discovering variability of rotational period by latitude.

Dunfermline, Earls of. See SETON family.

Dun·gli·son \'dəŋ-glis-ᵊn\, Robley. 1798–1869. American physician, b. Keswick, England. To U.S. (1825) on invitation of Thomas Jefferson; professor of medicine, U. of Virginia (1825–33), U. of Maryland (1833–36), Jefferson Medical College, Philadelphia (1836–68). Author of *Human Physiology* (1832), *A New Dictionary of Medical Science and Literature* (1833), etc.

Dun·hill \'dən-,hil\, Thomas Frederick. 1877–1946. English composer. Professor at Royal College of Music (from 1905); founded Dunhill Concerts (1907); known for light operas, esp. *Tantivy Towers* (1931), *Happy Families* (1933), chamber music, songs.

Du·ni \'dü-nē\, Egidio Romualdo. 1708–1775. Italian composer. Resident in Paris (from 1757), where he was one of originators of opéra comique. Works included *Le Peintre amoreux* (1757), *La Fille mal gardée* (1758), *L'Isle des foux* (1760), *La bonne fille* (1761), *Le Milicien* (1762), *La Fée Urgèle* (1765).

Dunk, George Montagu. 2d Earl of Halifax. See under Charles MONTAGU.

Dun·ker·ley \'dəŋ-kər-lē\, William Arthur. *Pseudonym* John Ox·en·ham \'äk-sən-əm, 'äks-nəm\. 1861?–1941. English businessman and writer. Author of several volumes of verse, as *Bees in Amber* (1913), *The Vision Splendid* (1917), and many popular novels, including *God's Candle* (1929), *Anno Domini* (1932), *Christ and the Third Wise Man* (1934).

Dun·lap \'dən-,lap, -ləp\, John. 1747–1812. American printer, b. County Tyrone, Ireland. To America (c.1757). Published (from 1771) *The Pennsylvania Packet, or The General Advertiser,* at first a weekly but from Sept. 21, 1784, a daily, the first daily newspaper published in U.S.

Dunlap, William. 1766–1839. American painter, playwright, and historian, b. Perth Amboy, N.J. Studied painting in London under Benjamin West (1784). Bought (1796) interest in Lewis Hallam's American Company; produced own plays and foreign adaptations at Park Theatre, N.Y.C.; bankrupt (1805). Returned to painting (1816); a founder of National Academy of Design (1826). His plays included *The Father of an Only Child* (1789), *Leicester* (1794), *Fontainville Abbey* (1795), *André* (1798). Other works, *History of the American Theatre* (1832), *History of the Rise and Progress of the Arts of Design in the United States* (1834).

Dun·lop \,dən-'läp, 'dən-,\, John Boyd. 1840–1921. Scottish inventor. Commonly credited with invention of the pneumatic tire; patented pneumatic tire (1888) and began marketing tricycles equipped with pneumatic tires; sold patent to William H. Du Cros, who organized (1889) what became Dunlop Rubber Co. The principle of the pneumatic tire had been patented in 1845 (see Robert William THOMSON) but the company was enabled because of accessory patents to establish rights to the invention.

Dunmore, Earl of. See John MURRAY (1732–1809).

Dunne \'dən\, Finley Peter. 1867–1936. American humorist, b. Chicago. On editorial staff, Chicago *Evening Post* and Chicago *Times-Herald* (1892–97); editor, Chicago *Journal* (1897–1900). Creator of Irish saloonkeeper-philosopher character "Mr. Dooley," as in *Mr. Dooley in Peace and War* (1898), *Mr. Dooley's Philosophy* (1900), *Dissertations by Mr. Dooley* (1906), *Mr. Dooley Says* (1910), etc.

Dunne, John William. 1875–1949. British airplane designer and philosopher. Designed and built first British military airplane (1906–07); published philosophical works including *An Experiment with Time* (1927), *The Serial Universe* (1934), *The New Immortality* (1938), *Nothing Dies* (1940).

Dun·ning \'dən-iŋ\, John. 1st Baron Ash·bur·ton \'ash-,bərt-ᵊn\. 1731–1783. English lawyer. Achieved prominence with memorial in support of East India Co. (1762) and defense of John Wilkes (1763–64); solicitor general (1768–70); M.P. (1768–82); author of famous Parliamentary resolution (April 1780) that "the influence of the crown has increased, is increasing, and ought to be diminished"; raised to peerage (1782).

Dunois, Jean. Comte de. See Branch II of ORLÉANS family.

Du·noy·er de Se·gon·zac \dᵫen-wá-yā-də-sə-gōⁿ-zák\, André. 1884–1974. French painter and engraver. Known for landscapes, figure paintings, portraits.

Dunoyer de Segonzac, Louis-Dominique-Joseph-Armand. 1880–1963. French physicist. Professor at Institut d'Optique (1921–41); invented an induction compass (1907); produced first molecular beam (1912); conducted research on metallic vapors, fluorescence, vacuums.

Dunraven, Earl of. See WYNDHAM-QUIN.

Dunsany, Lord. See Edward J.M.D. PLUNKETT.

Duns Sco·tus \dən(z)-'skōt-əs\, John. *Known as* Doctor Sub·ti·lis \(,)səb-'tī-ləs\. 1266?–1308. Scottish scholastic theologian. Joined Franciscan order; studied at Oxford and Paris; ordained priest (1291); exiled from Paris (1303–04) for support of Pope Boniface VIII against King Philip IV; master in theology, U. of Paris (1305); professor at Cologne (1307–08). Wrote *Ordinatio* or *Opus Oxoniense,* massive commentary on Lombard's *Sententiae, Quaestiones quodlibetales, Tractatus de primo principio,* commentaries on Aristotle, Porphyry, etc. Founder of scholastic system called Scotism; upheld the separability and independence of the rational soul from the body, provoking a long controversy between Scotists and Thomists; argued that faith, upon which theology rests, is not speculative but an act of will; a conceptualist in logic, held that matter, basis of all existences, has some positive entity of its own; zealous defender of the doctrine of the Immaculate Conception. Stubborn opposition of Scotists to classical studies of Renaissance and their obstructionist and caviling practices gave rise to the use of *dunce* for a sophist, pedant, or blockhead.

Dun·sta·ble \'dən(t)-stə-bəl\, John. c.1390–1453. English composer. Master of what became known as the "English manner" of rhythm and harmony; composer of six manuscript volumes of motets, masses, antiphons, and songs including a three-part chanson, *O Rosa bella.*

Dun·stan \'dən(t)-stən\. Saint. 924–988. English prelate. Son of a West Saxon noble; educ. by Irish pilgrims; accused of practicing black arts, expelled from King Athelstan's court; took monastic vows; made abbot of Glastonbury by

King Edmund (c.943). Rebuilt the abbey; introduced stricter Continental form of Benedictine rule, establishing thriving center of religious teaching. As treasurer and chief adviser of King Eadred, virtual ruler of realm; outlawed and driven to Flanders by Eadwig (955–957); recalled by Edgar, created bishop of Worcester and bishop of London (957), archbishop of Canterbury (959); as primate again virtual ruler of kingdom. Sought to make Danes integral part of nation, promoted education and revival of monasticism, urged respect for law, obliged landowners to pay tithes; on death of Edgar secured succession of St. Edward the Martyr; on murder of Edward and accession of Ethelred II, retired to Canterbury (978).

Dun·ster \'dən(t)-stər\, Henry. 1609–1659. American clergyman and educator, b. Lancashire, England. Emigrated to Massachusetts Colony (1640). First president of Harvard College (1640–54), establishing practices that endured for two centuries; forced to resign and subsequently tried and convicted because of his views on infant baptism; pastor in Scituate till his death.

Dünt·zer \'dʊent-sər\, Heinrich, *in full* Johann Heinrich Joseph. 1813–1901. German historian of literature. Librarian in Cologne (from 1846). Published *Erläuterungen zu den deutschen Klassikern* (83 vols., 1855–86), biographies of Goethe, Schiller, Lessing, etc.

Duonelaitis, Kristijonas. See DONELAITIS.

Du·pan·loup \dǖ-pä^n-lü\, Félix-Antoine-Philibert. 1802–1878. French prelate and political leader. Prominent Catholic educator; director of junior seminary of Saint-Nicolas-du-Chardonnet (1837–45); bishop of Orléans (1849); architect of Falloux Law (1850) legally establishing independent secondary schools; leading spokesman of liberal churchmen; member, National Assembly (1871); elected senator for life (1876).

Du·parc \dǖ-pȧrk\, Henri, *in full* Marie-Eugène-Henri. *Orig. surname* Fouques-Duparc \fük-\. 1848–1933. French composer. Compositions included symphonic poem *Lenore,* nocturne for orchestra *Aux Étoiles,* motet for three voices, and many songs on poems of Baudelaire, Gautier, and others.

Du·per·rey \dǖ-pe-rā\, Louis-Isidore. 1786–1865. French naval officer and scientist. Accompanied Freycinet on the *Uranie* around world (1817–20); commanded *Coquille* on trip to Oceania and South America (1822–25); studied ocean currents, terrestrial magnetism; determined positions of the magnetic poles and the magnetic equator.

Duperron, Anquetil-. See ANQUETIL-DUPERRON.

Du Per·ron \dǖ-pe-rō^n\, Jacques Da·vy \de-vē\. 1556–1618. French prelate. In service of Henry III; supported cause of Henry IV and is credited with converting him to the Catholic faith; bishop of Évreux (1591); created cardinal (1604) and archbishop of Sens (1606); member of the Council of Regency (1610).

Du·pe·tit-Thou·ars \dǖp-tē-twȧr\, Louis-Marie Au·bert \ō-ber\. 1758–1831. French botanist. Visited Madagascar and neighboring islands (1792–1802); author of *Histoire des végétaux recueillis dans les îles de France, de Bourbon et de Madagascar.* His nephew ¶Abel Aubert (1793–1864), vice admiral (1846); commanded *Vénus* in voyage around world (1837–39), occupied Tahiti (1841); brought (1842) Marquesas and (1843) Society Islands under French protection.

Dupin, Amandine. See Amandine DUDEVANT.

Du·pin \dǖ-pa^n\, André-Marie-Jean-Jacques. 1783–1865. French lawyer and politician. Elected deputy (1815, 1827); defended Marshal Ney, Béranger, Jouy, and General Alix; took part in Revolution of 1830; procureur général to Court of Cassation; president of Chamber of Deputies (1832–37) and of Legislative Assembly (1849–51).

Dupin, Louis-Ellies. 1657–1719. French Roman Catholic clergyman and historian. Wrote *Nouvelle bibliothèque des auteurs ecclésiastiques* (58 vols., 1686–1704), *Bibliothèque universelle des historiens* (1707), *L'Historie de l'église en abrégé* (1712).

Du·pleix \dǖ-pleks, *Angl* d(y)ü-'pleks\, Joseph-François. Marquis. 1697–1763. French colonial administrator. Governor general of all French possessions in India (1742–54); engaged in long struggle with the British in India; captured Madras (1746) during War of Austrian Succession; intrigued to destroy British East India Co. but, owing largely to work of Robert Clive, failed; recalled (1754), his work unfinished, the value of his services unrecognized, and his fortune swept away.

Du·ples·sis \dǖ-plā-sē, -ple-\, Joseph-Siffred. 1725–1802. French painter. Known for portraits of Louis XVI, Gluck, Franklin, Pius VII, etc.

Duplessis, Maurice Le Noblet. 1890–1959. Canadian politician, b. Trois-Rivières, Que. Member of Quebec legislature (1927–59); head of provincial Conservative party (1933–36); formed Union Nationale party (1936); premier of Quebec (1936–40, 1944–59).

Duplessis-Mornay. See Phillippe de MORNAY.

Du Pont family. See DU PONT DE NEMOURS.

Du·pont de l'Étang \dǖ-pō^n-də-lā-tä^n\, Pierre-Antoine. Comte. 1765–1840. French general. Distinguished himself at Valmy, Marengo, Ulm, Friedland; forced to surrender at Bailén (1808). Appointed minister of war by Louis XVIII (1814), member of privy council (1815).

Dupont de l'Eure \-də-lœr\, Jacques-Charles. 1767–1855. French politician. Member of Council of Five Hundred (1795), Chamber of Deputies (1814). Took part in Revolution of 1830; minister of justice (1830). President of provisional government (1848).

du Pont de Ne·mours \dǖ-pō^n-də-nə-mür, *Angl* d(y)ü-'pänt-də-nə-'mu̇(ə)r, 'd(y)ü-,\, Pierre-Samuel. 1739–1817. French economist. Friend and disciple of François Quesnay; expounded economic doctrines of Quesnay's school (the physiocrats) in his *Physiocratie* (1767). Assisted in negotiating with England treaty to accord independence to United States (1783). Member of Estates-General (1789); his defense of Louis XVI led to his imprisonment (1792) and later (1799) to his emigration to United States. Prepared at Jefferson's request a scheme for national education in U.S., never adopted in U.S. but used in part in French code of education. Returned to France (1802); secretary to provisional government (1814); again emigrated (1815) to U.S., where he died. Other works included *Origines et progrès d'une science nouvelle* (1768), *Du pouvoir législatif et du pouvoir exécutif* (1795). His two sons, Victor Marie and Éleuthère Irénée (see below), founded the two American branches of the family. ¶Victor Marie du Pont (1767–1827), diplomat and industrialist, b. Paris, France, was in U.S. (from 1787) as attaché of French legation (1787–89), aide-de-camp to Lafayette (1789–91), second secretary of French legation (1791–92), and first secretary (1795–96). Settled in U.S. (1800); naturalized. His mercantile importing business in New York (1802–05), V. du Pont de Nemours & Co., failed, as did a land development project (1806–09); became manager of his brother Irénée's woolen mills near Wilmington, Del., but was unsuccessful. Became a director, Bank of the United States, Philadelphia. His son ¶Samuel Francis (1803–1865), b. Bergen Point, N.J., was a naval officer; entered U.S. navy (1815); served through Mexican War; member of board appointed to draw up curriculum and regulations for a naval academy (1850); captain (1855); served through Civil War; in command of South Atlantic Blockading Squadron; captured Port Royal, S.C. (Nov. 1861); rear admiral (1862); captured islands and forts along Georgia and Florida coasts and established 14 blockading stations; repulsed in attack on defenses of Charleston (Apr. 1863); relieved of his command; retired from active duty.

¶Éleuthère Irénée du Pont (1771–1834), industrialist, b. Paris, France, was in father's printing plant, Paris (1791–97), until it was closed by French radicals; to U.S. (1800). Established near Wilmington, Del. (1802), plant for manufacturing gunpowder, the successful beginning of E. I. Du Pont de Nemours & Co. Among his successors were his sons ¶Alfred Victor (1798–1856), president (1834–50), and ¶Henry (1812–1889), president (1850–89). Henry's son ¶Henry Algernon (1838–1926), a U.S. army officer (1861–75) serving through Civil War and winning Medal of Honor for brilliant action at Cedar Creek (1864); a member of the family firm (1878–1902); U.S. senator (1906–17).

Du·port \dǖ-pȯr\, Adrien-Jean-François. 1759–1798. French magistrate. As member of Parlement of Paris, elected to Estates-General (1789); joined Third Estate; for National Assembly created new judicial system; with Antoine Barnave and Alexandre Comte de Lameth known as the Triumvirate; joined royalists in Club of the Feuillants; fled to England after fall of monarchy (1792); returned after fall of Robespierre (1794); fled to Switzerland after coup d'état (1797).

Duport, Louis. 1781–1853. French dancer. Ballet dancer in Paris (1799–1806), St. Petersburg (1808–12), and elsewhere; made notable contributions to classical technique, esp. multiple pirouettes and leaps; director of Kärntnertor Theatre, Vienna (1830–36).

Du·prat \dǖ-prȧ\, Antoine. 1463–1535. French prelate and statesman. Crown attorney for Toulouse (1495); master of requests to Louis XII (1503); president of Parlement of Paris (1508); chancellor of France (1515); negotiated Concordat of Bologna (1516). Consecrated archbishop of Sens (1525); created cardinal (1527); papal legate in France (1530). Chief minister of Louise of Savoy during the second regency (1525). Unsuccessful candidate for the papacy after death of Clement VII.

Du·pré \dǖ-prā\, Giovanni. 1817–1882. Italian sculptor. Among his works were *Abel, Cain, Giotto, Sappho,* and monument to Cavour (Turin).

Dupré, Guillaume. 1574?–1647. French sculptor and medallionist. Designed coinage for Henry IV, Louis XIII; executed statue of Henry IV at Pont-Neuf and his tomb figure.

Dupré, Jules. 1811–1889. French landscape painter. A leader of Barbizon school; regarded as one of founders of modern French school of landscape painting; studied with John Constable in England (1834). Among his works were *L'Étang, La petite charrette, Soleil couchant après l'orage.*

Dupré, Marcel. 1886–1971. French organist and composer. Organist of Saint-Sulpice (from 1934); director of American Conservatory, Fontainebleau (1947–54), Paris Conservatoire (1954–71); virtuoso organist noted for improvisations; wrote preludes and fugues, motets, chorales, *Symphonie-Passion* (1924), *Le Chemin de la croix* (1931–32), etc.

Dupré, Marie-Jules. 1813–1881. French naval officer and colonial administrator. Rear admiral (1867); commanded blockade of Chinese and Japanese ports against German shipping (1870); governor of Cochinchina (southern Vietnam; 1871–74); attempted to extend French influence into Tonkin (northern Vietnam); vice admiral (1875).

Du·puis \dᵫ-pwʸē\, Jean. 1829–1912. French adventurer. Trader in Shanghai and Hankow (1860–64); attempted to force use of Red River through Vietnam as trade route to Yunnan (1872); his detention in Hanoi provided excuse for Gov. Marie-Jules Dupré to send armed force into Tonkin (1873).

Du·puy \dᵫ-pwʸē\, Charles-Alexandre. 1851–1923. French educator and politician. Member of Chamber of Deputies (1885–1900), minister of public instruction (1892–93); premier of France (1893, 1894–95, 1898–99). Tenure in office marred by police repression of student and worker demonstrations, Dreyfus affair; senator (1900–23).

Dupuy, Pierre. 1582–1651. French historian and librarian. Curator (1645), with his brother ¶Jacques (1586–1656), of royal library, Paris, to which they bequeathed valuable collection of books; first to catalog royal archives; author of *Traité des droits et libertés de l'Église gallicane* (1639).

Dupuy de Lôme \-də-lōm\, Stanislas-Charles-Henri-Laurent. 1816–1885. French naval engineer. Designed and built first French screw steamship (*Napoléon,* 1850) and first armored vessels (*Gloire, Invincible, Normandie*). Senator for life (1877).

Du·puy·tren \dᵫ-pwʸē-traⁿ\, Guillaume. Baron. 1777–1835. French surgeon and anatomist. On staff of Hôtel Dieu (from 1802); surgeon in chief (from 1815); surgeon to Louis XVIII and Charles X; devised surgical techniques for cancer of uterine cervix, ligations of subclavian artery, compression of aneurysms, Dupuytren's contracture.

Du·quesne \dᵫ-ken, *Angl* d(y)ü-'kān\, Abraham. Marquis. 1610–1688. French naval commander. Distinguished himself in the Coruña expedition (1639) and in battles at Tarragona (1641), Barcelona (1643), and Cabo-de-Gata. In Swedish service (1644–47), defeated combined Danish and Dutch fleets. Returned to French service; captured Bordeaux, which had revolted and was receiving Spanish aid (1650); lieutenant general of marine (1667); defeated combined fleets of Spain and Holland, under Admiral de Ruyter, near Catania (1676), de Ruyter being mortally wounded; bombarded Algiers (1682–83).

Du·ques·noy \dᵫ-kān-wȧ, -ken-\, François. *Known as* François Fla·mand \flȧ-mäⁿ\. 1597–1643. Flemish sculptor. To Rome (1618); worked with Bernini on St. Peter's (1628); executed *St. Andrew* for St. Peter's, *St. Susanna* for Sta. Maria di Loreto (1629–33).

Du·rán \dü-'rän\, Agustín. 1793–1862. Spanish critic and poet. Author of *Discurso sobre... la decadencia del teatro antiguo* (1828), *Romancero general* (collection of Spanish ballad literature; 1828–32).

Du·ran \dᵫ-räⁿ\, Profiat. *Hebrew* Isaac ben Moses ha-Le·vi \'hä-'lē-ˌvī\. c.1350–c.1415. Jewish philosopher and grammarian, b. southern France. Compelled to profess Christianity (1391); removed to Palestine to resume Judaism; wrote *'Al tehi ka-'avotekha* (c.1396), satirical attack on Christian practices.

Du·ran \dü-'rän\, Simeón ben Zemah. *Known also as* Rash·baz \räsh-'bäth\. 1361–1444. Spanish Jewish rabbi. First rabbi to receive regular salary; wrote commentary *Magen Avot.*

Du·rand \d(y)ủ-'rand\, Asher Brown. 1796–1886. American engraver and painter, b. Jefferson Village, N.J. Established reputation with *The Signing of the Declaration of Independence,* after Trumbull (1823); engraved portraits, gift book illustrations, banknotes. A founder of National Academy of Design (1826); president (1845–61). In 1836 he turned to painting, at first chiefly of portraits and figure pieces; later, turned to landscape painting, drawing inspiration from scenery of Hudson River Valley and New England; regarded as a founder (with Thomas Cole) of Hudson River school of landscape.

Du·rand \dᵫ-räⁿ\, Guillaume. *Known also as* Du·ran·ti \dü-'rän-tē\ the Elder, Gulielmus Du·ran·di \dü-'rän-dē\, Du·ran·tis \-tēs\, *or* Du·ran·dus \d(y)ủ-'ran-dəs\. c.1230–1296. French prelate. Professor of canon law at Bologna; papal auditor (from c.1262); helped draft statutes proclaimed by Pope Gregory X at Council of Lyons (1274); papal commissioner to Bologna and the Romagna (1278); bishop of Mende (1286); published revision of *Pontificale Romanum* that served as basis for Pope Innocent VIII's later (1485) text. Author of *Speculum indiciale* (1271–76) on canon law, *Rationale divinorum officiorum* (c.1285–91) on liturgy.

Du·rand \d(y)ủ-'rand\, William Frederick. 1859–1958. American mechanical engineer, b. Bethany, Conn. In engineering corps, U.S. navy (1880–87); professor, Michigan State (1887–91), Cornell (1891–1904), Stanford (1904–24); member (1914–33, 1941–45), chairman (1916–19), National Advisory Committee for Aeronautics; conducted studies on design of marine and aircraft propellers; consultant on Hoover, Grand Coulee, and other dams. Author of *Fundamental Principles of Mechanics* (1889), *Practical Marine Engineering* (1901), etc.

Du·rand de Saint-Pour·çain \dᵫ-räⁿ-də-saⁿ-pür-saⁿ\, Guillaume. *Lat.* Gulielmus Durandus de Sanc·to Por·cia·no \'saŋk-(ˌ)tō-pȯr-kē-'än-(ˌ)ō\. *Known as* Doc·tor Res·o·lu·tis·si·mus \'däk-tər-ˌrez-ə-l(y)ü-'tis-ə-məs\. c.1270–1334. French Dominican and prelate. Summoned to Avignon by Pope Clement V as lecturer in theology (c.1314); successively, bishop of Limoux (1317), Le Puy (1318), Meaux (1326). Opposed philosophy of Aquinas; author of commentary on Lombard's *Sententiae, De origine potestatum et iurisdictionum,* and *De statu animarum sanctarum.*

Du·ran·do \dü-'rän-dō\, Giacomo. 1807–1894. Italian soldier and politician. Joined Sardinian army as general (1848); checked Austrians at Caffaro; aide-de-camp to Charles Albert at battle of Novara (1849). Senator, minister of war (1855); ambassador to Constantinople (1856–61); minister of foreign affairs under Rattazzi; senate president (1884–87). His brother ¶Giovanni (1804–1869), also a soldier, commissioned by Antonelli to organize troops in Romagna (1848); defeated by Austrians at Vicenza; under Charles Albert, commanded division at battles of Mortara and Novara (1849); took part in Crimean expedition (1854–56); commanded division at battle of Solferino (1859); senator (1860).

Durandus, Gulielmus. See Guillaume DURAND.

Du·rant \d(y)ủ-'rant\, Henry. 1802–1875. American clergyman, b. Acton, Mass. To California (1853); instrumental in securing charter for College of California (1855), succeeded by U. of California (1868); first president, U. of California (1870–72).

Durant, Henry Fowle. *Orig.* Henry Welles Smith. 1822–1881. American lawyer, b. Hanover, N.H. Affected by death of his young son, gave up law, became a lay preacher, and conducted revival meetings in Massachusetts and New Hampshire (1864–75). Founder (1870) and treasurer (1870–81) of Wellesley College.

Durant, Thomas Clark. 1820–1885. American businessman, b. Lee, Mass. An organizer and vice president, Union Pacific Railroad Co. (1863–69); started building of road; secured charter of Crédit Mobilier and became its president (1863–67); during long-drawn factional struggle in Union Pacific directorate for control of road, he personally pushed building of road to completion (May 10, 1869); ousted from directorate two weeks later.

Durant, William Crapo. 1861–1947. American industrialist, b. Boston. Organized Durant-Dort Carriage Co., Flint, Mich. (1886), Buick Motor Car Co. (1905), General Motors Co. (1908), Chevrolet Motor Co. (1915, with Louis Chevrolet, *q.v.*). President of General Motors (1916–20); lost control of General Motors Co. and Chevrolet Motor Co. (1920). Organized Durant Motors, Inc. (1921).

Durant, William James, *known as* Will. 1885–1981. American historian, b. North Adams, Mass. m. (1913) ¶Ida Kaufman, *known as* Ariel Durant (1898–1981), b. Prosurov, Russia. Will taught at Labor Temple School, New York City (1914–27); after success of his *Story of Philosophy* (1926), they collaborated on 11-volume "Story of Civilization" series, comprising *Our Oriental Heritage* (1935), *The Life of Greece* (1939), *Caesar and Christ* (1944), *Age of Faith* (1950), *Renaissance* (1953), *Reformation* (1957), *Age of Reason Begins* (1961), *Age of Louis XIV* (1963), *Age of Voltaire* (1965), *Rousseau and Revolution* (1967, Pulitzer prize), *Age of Napoleon* (1975); also wrote *A Dual Biography* (1977).

Du·ran·te \dü-'rän-tā\, Francesco. 1684–1755. Italian composer. Taught at San Onofrio Conservatory (1710–28); principal teacher (from 1745); head of Conservatorio di Santa Maria di Loreto, Naples (1742–45). Works included masses, motets, oratorios, requiems, and *Lamentations* of Jeremiah.

Du·ran·te \də-'rant-ē\, Jimmy, *orig.* James Francis. 1893–1980. American entertainer, b. New York City. Began as piano player in saloons; achieved vaudeville stardom in team of Clayton, Jackson and Durante; appeared alone in Broadway shows *Strike Me Pink* (1933), *Jumbo* (1935), *Red Hot and Blue* (1936), etc.; appeared in movies, on radio, and (from 1950) on television; noted for gravelly voice, battered hat, nose (whence nickname "Da Schnozz"), themesong "Inka Dinka Doo."

Duranti *or* **Durantis.** See Guillaume DURAND.

Du·ran·ty \d(y)ủ-'rant-ē\, Walter. 1884–1957. American journalist and author, b. Liverpool, England. On staff of *New York Times* (from 1913); its Moscow correspondent (1922–41); awarded Pulitzer prize for reporting (1932). Author of *I Write as I Please* (1935), *One Life, One Kopek* (1937), *The Gold Train* (1938), etc.

Du·rão \t͟hü-'rau̇ⁿ\, José de San·ta Rit·ta \t͟hə-'sȧⁿn-tȧ-'rē-tȧ\. 1737?–1784. Brazilian monk and poet. Entered Augustinian order (1758); to Rome (1763); papal librarian (1763–78); professor of theology, U. of Coimbra, Portugal

(1778–80). Author of *Caramúru* (1781), epic poem on discovery and settlement of Bahia region of Brazil.

Duras, Ducs de. See DURFORT family.

D'·Ur·ban \'dər-bən\, Sir Benjamin. 1777–1849. British general and colonial administrator. Took part in Peninsular War (1808–15); lieutenant general (1837). Governor of Antigua (1820), Demerara and Essequibo (1824); first governor of British Guiana (1831); governor (1834–38) and commander in chief (1834–46) of Cape of Good Hope; attempted to extend eastern boundaries to include Xhosa Kaffirs but was overruled (1835) by colonial secretary, whereupon the great trek of Dutch farmers began (1836); in command of troops in Canada (1847–49). Port Natal was renamed Durban in his honor.

Dü·rer \'dǖr-ər, *Angl* 'd(y)u̇r-ər\, Albrecht. 1471–1528. German painter and engraver. Regarded as foremost German artist of the Renaissance. Worked with equal mastery in painting, woodblock, copper- and iron-engraving. Strongly influenced by Italian sojourns (1494–95, 1505–07), progressing stylistically from Gothic to Renaissance. Court painter for Emperor Maximilian I (1512–19). Woodcuts included *The Apocalypse* (16 subjects), *The Greater Passion* (12 subjects), and *The Lesser Passion* (37 subjects); engravings included *Knight, Death and the Devil, St. Jerome in his Study,* and *Melancholia I;* paintings included *Adoration of the Trinity, Adam and Eve, Four Apostles, Young Jesus with the Doctors,* and portraits, esp. several revealing self-portraits.

Du·rey \dǖ-rā\, Louis-Edmond. 1888–1979. French composer. Member of "The Six" (Honegger, Poulenc, Milhaud, Auric, Taillefere); works included *Pastorale* for orchestra, the choral work *Éloges,* string quartet and string trio, and many songs.

D'·Ur·fey \'dər-fē\, Thomas. *Known as* Tom Dur·fey \'dər-fē\. 1653–1723. English song writer and dramatist. Nephew of Honoré d'Urfé. After his first play, *The Siege of Memphis,* a bombastic tragedy (produced 1676), became successful with comedies, including *The Fond Husband* (1676), *Madame Fickle* (1677), *The Virtuous Wife* (1680), *Sir Barnaby Whig* (1681), *Commonwealth of Women* (1686), *Love for Money* (1691), *The Modern Prophets* (1709); wrote texts to music by Henry Purcell; his songs, noted for wit and mirthful satire, were collected as *Wit and Mirth or Pills to Purge Melancholy* (1719–20).

Dur·fort \dǖr-fȯr\. Name of an old French family taking its name from village of Durfort in southwestern France and tracing descent from Arnaud de Durfort (fl. 1305), who acquired fief of Duras by marriage with niece of Pope Clement V; the family included:

Guy-Aldonce I de Durfort (1605–1665), marquis de Duras; married a sister of Henri de Turenne and had three sons:

¶Jacques-Henri de Durfort (1625–1704), duc de Du·ras \dǖ-rȧs\, governor of Franche-Comté, which he helped to conquer, and marshal of France (1675); at head of English army, took Philippsburg and Mannheim (1688); raised to duke (1689). His brother ¶Guy-Aldonce II de Durfort de Duras (1630–1702), comte de Lorges \-lȯrzh\ and duc de Quin·tin \-kaⁿ-taⁿ\ (1691); became a marshal of France (1676); led an army into Germany and captured Heidelberg (1693). His youngest brother ¶Louis de Durfort de Duras (1641–1709), marquis de Blan·que·fort \bläⁿk-fȯr\ (in French peerage), 2d Earl of Fev·er·sham \'fev-ər-shəm\ (in English peerage), accompanied Duke of York to England and was naturalized (1663); created Baron Duras of Hol·den·by \'hōm-bē\ (1672); succeeded to his father-in-law's title of earl of Feversham (1677); English ambassador to Peace of Nijmegen (1675); enjoyed many preferments under Charles II; under James II was privy councilor; chief commander against rebels under Monmouth at battle of Sedgemoor (1685); commander of James II's army (1686); made peace with William III on intercession of queen dowager.

¶Jean-Baptiste de Durfort (1684–1770), duc de Duras, son of Marshal Jacques-Henri de Durfort, served with distinction in England, Flanders, and Spain, became marshal of France (1741). His son ¶Emmanuel-Félicité (1715–1789), duc de Duras, took part in wars of Louis XV; was ambassador to Spain (1752), marshal of France (1775), without having commanded an army; an academician (1775), having written nothing. ¶Amédée-Bretagne-Malo (1771–1838), duc de Duras, grandson of Emmanuel, was loyal to Louis XVI, made field marshal by Louis XVIII. His wife ¶Claire de Ker·saint \də-ker-saⁿ\ (1777–1828), daughter of Armand Kersaint (*q.v.*), presided over a brilliant salon; author of two novels, *Ourika* (1823) and *Édouard* (1825); an admirer of Chateaubriand.

Durham, Earl of. See John George LAMBTON.

Duris. See DOURIS.

Durk·heim \dǖr-kem\, Émile. 1858–1917. French sociologist. Taught at Bordeaux (1887–1902), U. of Paris (1902–17); pioneered in establishment of methodology and theoretical framework of rigorous social science; author of *De la division du travail social* (1893), *Règles de la méthode sociologique* (1895), *Suicide* (1897), *Les Formes élémentaires de la vie religieuse* (1915).

Du·roc \dǖ-rȯk\, Géraud-Christophe-Michel. Duc de Fri·oul \frē-ül\. 1772–1813. French general. Served as aide to Napoléon in Italian and Egyptian campaigns; general (1799) and grand marshal of the palace (1804); undertook many diplomatic missions; engaged at Austerlitz, Essling, Wagram.

Du·ruy \dǖ-rwʸē\, Victor. 1811–1894. French historian. Professor at Reims, and later at Paris; as minister of education (1863–69), introduced secular secondary education for girls, modern languages and contemporary history studies; attempted to establish free compulsory primary education; author of *Histoire des Romains* (1879–85), etc.

Dur·yea \'du̇(ə)r-ˌyā\, Charles Edgar. 1861–1938. American inventor and manufacturer, b. near Canton, Ill. With brother ¶James Frank (1869–1967) built successful gasoline automobile (1893); organized Duryea Motor Wagon Co., Springfield, Mass. (1895); won (Frank driving) first U.S. auto race, Chicago (1895); sold first commercially-produced American car (1896); brothers separated; Charles organized Duryea Power Co., Reading, Pa., for making automobiles (1900); Frank developed Stevens-Duryea limousine. Cf. Elwood HAYNES and George B. SELDEN.

Dušan, Stefan. See STEPHEN (rulers of Serbia).

Du·se \'dü-zä\, Eleonora. 1858–1924. Italian actress. Began stage career as a child in itinerant companies; established reputation at Naples in Zola's *Thérèse Raquin* (1878); achieved fame in works of Dumas fils, Verga, Ibsen, D'Annunzio (with whom she was closely associated, 1894–99); toured throughout world, from 1886 with own company, Drammatica Compagnia della Città di Roma; American debut, New York (1893); left stage (1909–21).

Dushan, Stephen. See STEPHEN (rulers of Serbia).

Du Som·me·rard \dǖ-sȯm-rȧr\, Alexandre. 1779–1842. French archaeologist. Collected medieval art objects and other relics, which, with his mansion, were bought by the government (1843) to form the Musée de Cluny.

Dus·sek \'du̇-sek\ *or* **Du·šek** \'du̇sh-ek\ *or* **Du·sík** \'du̇-sēk\, Jan Ladislav. 1760–1812. Bohemian pianist and composer. Patronized by Marie-Antoinette, Louis Ferdinand of Prussia, Talleyrand; works included 15 piano concertos, over 60 two-hand and four-hand piano sonatas.

Dus·ton \'dəs-tən\, Hannah, *nee* Emerson. 1657–?1736. American heroine, b. Haverhill, Mass. m. (1677) Thomas Duston (Dustin, Dustan). Captured by Indians (1697); escaped and returned home, after killing and scalping ten of her captors while they slept.

Du Toit \də-'tȯi\, Stephanus Jacobus. 1847–1911. South African cleric and politician. Founded Society of True South Africans (1875), Afrikaner Bond (1879); published books in Afrikaans; made Afrikaans translation of Bible, thus helping establish the language and political identity of Boers; migrated from Cape Colony to Transvaal (1882); superintendent of education there (1882–88). His son ¶Jakob Daniel, *pseudonym* To·ti·us \'tō-ti-œs\ (1877–1953), also a clergyman, was an outstanding poet in Afrikaans; author of *By die Monument* (1908), *Verse van Potgieter's Trek* (1909), *Wilgerboombogies* (1912), *Rachel* (1913), *Trekkerswee* (1915), *Passieblomme* (1934), *Uit donker Afrika* (1936), *Skemering* (1948), and *Afrikaans Psalter* (1936).

Du·tra \'dü-trȧ\, Eurico Gaspar. 1885–1974. Brazilian soldier and politician. Commissioned in cavalry (1910); general (1932); war minister (1936–45); helped write Estado Novo constitution (1937); led coup against Pres. Vargas (1945); president of Brazil (1946–51).

Du·treuil de Rhins \dǖ-trœy-də-raⁿ\, Jules-Léon. 1846–1894. French explorer. Explored region of the Ogooué in equatorial Africa (1883); explored Chinese Turkestan and Tibet (1891–94); published *L'Asie centrale* (1889), etc.

Du·tro·chet \dǖ-trō-she\, René-Joachim-Henri. 1776–1847. French physiologist. Studied development of eggs of birds, respiration in plants, light sensitivity, and geotropism; discovered and named phenomenon of osmosis.

Dutt, Michael Madhusudan. See DATTA.

Duṭ·ṭha·gā·ma·ṇi *or* **Du·tu·gü·mu·nu** \(ˌ)də-tə-'gə-mə-nə\. d. 77 B.C. King of Ceylon (101–77 B.C.). Led rebellion of Buddhist Sinhalese against Indian Tamil Hindus; won battle at Anurādhapura, where he built Brazen Palace.

Dut·ton \'dət-ᵊn\, Clarence Edward. 1841–1912. American geologist, b. Wallingford, Conn. In U.S. army (1862–1901); detailed to U.S. Geological and Geographical Survey (1875–90); made study of plateau region of Utah, Arizona, New Mexico; developed and named principle of isostasy; developed method for determining depth of earthquake focal point (1899). Author of *Report on the Geology of the High Plateau of Utah* (1879–80), *Earthquakes in the Light of the New Seismology* (1940), etc.

Dutton, Edward Payson. 1831–1923. American publisher, b. Keene, N.H. Partner in booksellers Ide & Dutton, Boston (1852); reorganized as E. P. Dutton & Co. with himself as president (1858). Associated with J. M. Dent (*q.v.*), English publisher, in publication and sale of "Everyman's Library".

Duun \'dün\, Olav. 1876–1939. Norwegian writer. Public school teacher (1904–26). Works included series of six novels (1918–23) called *Juvikfolke* (*The People of Juvik*), tracing story of four generations of Norwegian peasant landholders.

Du·val *or* **Du·vall** \dūē-vål\, Claude. 1643–1670. French highwayman in England. Noted for daring and for gallantry to women; originally a domestic servant, accompanied Duke of Richmond to England at Restoration; hanged at Tyburn.

Duval, Paul. *Pseudonym* Jean Lor·rain \lò-raⁿ\. 1855–1906. French writer. Among his books of verse were *Le Sang des dieux* (1882), *Modernités* (1885), *Les Griseries* (1887), *Sensations et souvenirs* (1895); among his plays, *Yanthis* (1894), *Prométhée* (1900), *Une nuit de Grenelle* (1903).

Du·va·lier \dūē-vål-yā\, François. *Called* Papa Doc. 1907–1971. Haitian politician. Trained as physician; active in anti-yaws compaigns; director of National Public Health Service (1946–48); minister of public health and labor (1949–50); leader of opposition to Pres. Magloire; president of Haiti (1957–71); maintained rule through terror campaigns of Tonton Macoutes.

Du·vall \dů-'väl\, Gabriel. 1752–1844. American jurist, b. near Buena Vista, Md. Member of U.S. House of Representatives (1794–96); on Maryland Supreme Court (1796–1802); comptroller of U.S. Treasury (1802–11); associate justice, U.S. Supreme Court (1811–35).

Du·veen \d(y)ů-'vēn\, Joseph. 1st Baron Duveen of Mill·bank \'mil-ˌbaŋk\. 1869–1939. English art connoisseur and dealer. Employed first in father's antique shop; later joined his uncle in U.S. and developed business as art dealer; by 1914 had established virtual monopoly on trade in old masters; built major collections in Europe and America. Benefactor of National Gallery, London, and donor of gallery to house the Elgin marbles; raised to peerage (1933).

Du·ve·neck \'dü-və-ˌnek\, Frank. *Orig.* Frank Deck·er \'dek-ər\. 1848–1919. American painter, sculptor, and teacher, b. Covington, Ky. Studied and painted in Munich (from 1870), where he started (1878) a school; moved his school to Italy (1879); among his students were W.M. Chase, J.W. Alexander, Twachtman; dean of Cincinnati Art Academy (from 1888). On death of his wife (1888), carved magnificent memorial now over her grave in Florence.

Du Ver·gier de Hau·ranne \dūē-ver-zhyā-də-ō-rån\, Jean. *Called* Saint-Cyran. 1581–1643. French theologian. Abbé de Saint Cyran (1620) and director of Port Royal (1636); lifelong friend and associate of Jansen, and with him a critic of contemporary Roman Catholic doctrine and practice, esp. of Jesuits; arrested and imprisoned by Richelieu's orders (1638–42); now regarded, with Jansen, as founder of, and strongest force in spreading doctrines of, Jansenism.

Du·ver·ney \dūē-ver-nā\, Joseph-Guichard. 1648–1730. French anatomist. Known esp. for researches on the eye and ear; wrote *Traité de l'organe de l'ouie* (1683).

Du·vet \dūē-ve\, Jean. 1485–1561. French engraver. Noted for Italianate works, including *Annunciation, Judgment of Solomon, Unicorn* series, *Apocalypse* series.

Du·vey·rier \dūē-ver-yā\, Henri. 1840–1892. French explorer. Explored northern Sahara (1859–61) and later made many journeys to Atlas Mountains, Algeria, Tunisia, Morocco; studied Tuareg people; published *Exploration du Sahara: Les Touâreg du nord* (1864), *La Tunisie* (1881).

Du Vi·gneaud \d(y)ü-'vēn-(ˌ)yō\, Vincent. 1901–1978. American biochemist, b. Chicago. Professor, George Washington U. (1932–38), Cornell U. medical college (1938–67); studied insulin, biotin, biological sulfur compounds; synthesized penicillin (1946); awarded Nobel prize for chemistry (1955) for synthesis of oxytocin and vasopressin (1953).

Duyc·kinck \'dī-ˌkiŋk\, Evert Augustus. 1816–1878. American editor, b. New York City. Editor of influential weekly *Literary World* (1848–53), and a two-volume *Cyclopaedia of American Literature* (1855), in both of which his brother ¶George Long (1823–1863) was an associate.

Duy·se \'dōi-sə\, Prudens van. 1804–1859. Flemish writer. Municipal archivist at Ghent (from 1838); his volumes of verse included *Vaderlandsche Poëzij* (1840) and *Het Klaverblad* (1848).

Duy Tan \'dwē-'tän\. *Orig.* Vinh San \'vin(-yə)-'sän\. 1899–1945. Vietnamese ruler. Son of Emperor Thanh Thai. Proclaimed emperor by French (1907); took reign name Duy Tan; attempted to promote reforms, conspired in nationalist revolt; deposed by French (1916); served heroically with Free French forces in World War II.

Dvo·řák \'dvòr-zhäk, *Angl* (də-)'vòr-ˌzhäk\, Antonín Leopold. 1841–1904. Bohemian composer. First achieved recognition with *Moravian Duets* (1876), *Slavonic Dances* (1878); noted for success in adapting folk materials to serious Romantic music; director, National Conservatory of Music, New York City (1892–95). His operas included *Král a uhlíř* (1874), *Tvrdé palice* (1881), *Dimitrij* (1882), *Jakobín* (1889), *Čert a káča* (1899), *Rusalka* (1901), *Armida* (1904); wrote 9 symphonies, esp. No. 9 *From the New World* (1893), symphonic poems, overtures, rhapsodies, nocturnes, concertos. Choral works included *Stabat Mater* (1876–77), cantata *Svatební košile* (*The Specter's Bride,* 1884), *Svatá Ludmila* (1886), a mass, requiem, and *Te Deum.* Piano music included the well known *Humoresque* (1894).

Dvorsky, Michel. See Josef Casimir HOFMANN.

Dwig·gins \'dwig-ənz\, William Addison. 1880–1956. American type designer, b. Martinsville, Ohio. Associated at various times with Frederic Goudy, Mergenthaler Linotype Co., Yale and Harvard U. presses, A.A. Knopf Co.; designed widely used typefaces Metro (1929), Electra (1935), Caledonia (1939), Eldorado (1953); author of *Layout in Advertising* (1928).

Dwight \'dwīt, də-'wīt\, John. c.1637–1703. English potter. Patentee (1671, 1684) for manufacture of porcelain or china and of Cologne ware; first English potter of note, produced stoneware resembling porcelain; executed statuettes of mythological and contemporary characters in a fine red stoneware later developed by John and David Elers.

Dwight, John Sullivan. 1813–1893. American music critic, b. Boston. Joined Brook Farm community (1841–47). Contributed musical criticism to various periodicals (1847–52); founded and edited the influential *Dwight's Journal of Music* (1852–81). Instrumental in organizing Boston Philharmonic Society (1865), and in establishing professorship of music at Harvard (1876).

Dwight, Timothy. 1752–1817. American clergyman and educator, b. Northampton, Mass. Grandson of Jonathan Edwards. Headmaster, Hopkins Grammar School, New Haven (1769–71); tutor, Yale (1771–77); chaplain in Continental army (1777–79). One of the "Hartford Wits." President, Yale (1795–1817). Author of *The Conquest of Canaan* (1785), *The Triumph of Infidelity, a Poem* (1788), *Greenfield Hill* (1794), *Theology, Explained and Defended* (1818–19), *Travels in New England and New York* (1821–22). A grandson ¶Timothy Dwight (1828–1916), b. Norwich, Conn., was a clergyman and educator; tutor, Yale (1851–55); assistant professor of sacred literature, Yale Divinity School (1858–61); professor (from 1861); ordained (1861); president of Yale (1886–99).

Dwyfor, Earl of. See David LLOYD GEORGE.

Dyce \'dīs\, Alexander. 1798–1869. Scottish editor. Edited Collins's poems (1827), works of Peele (1828, 1839), Webster (1830), Greene (1831), Shirley (1833), Richard Bentley (1836–38), Middleton (1840), John Skelton (1843), Beaumont and Fletcher (1843–46), Marlowe (1850), John Ford (1869); known chiefly for his edition of Shakespeare (1857, 1864–67) and notes on Shakespeare and on Collier's edition of Shakespeare; author of *Recollections of the Table Talk of Samuel Rogers* (1856).

Dyce, William. 1806–1864. Scottish historical and portrait painter. Planned and served as director (1840–43) of government school of design, London; professor of fine arts, King's Coll., London (1844); early paintings largely anticipated Pre-Raphaelite school of painting in England; painted frescoes *Baptism of Ethelbert* (1846), *King Arthur* series (incomplete) for House of Lords.

Dyck, Sir Anthony Van. See VAN DYCK.

Dy·er \'dī(-ə)r\, Alexander Brydie. 1815–1874. American army officer, b. Richmond, Va. Commissioned (1837); served in Seminole War (1837–38), Mexican War (1847–48); commander of National Armory, Springfield, Mass. (1861–64); chief of ordnance, U.S. army (1864–74); brigadier general (1864).

Dyer, Sir Edward. 1543–1607. English courtier and poet. Friend of Sir Philip Sidney, whose books he shared with Fulke Greville under Sidney's will; sent on diplomatic missions to Low Countries (1584), to Denmark (1589); author of small number of identifiable lyrics of notable grace and sweetness, esp. "My Mynd to Me a Kingdom Is."

Dyer, Eliphalet. 1721–1807. American jurist, b. Windham, Conn. Member, governor's council (1762–84); judge, Connecticut Superior Court (1766–93), chief justice (1789–93). In Continental Congress (1774–79, 1780–83). An organizer (1753) of Susquehanna Company, to establish settlement in Wyoming Valley, west of New York province; counsel for Connecticut before board of commissioners that awarded to Connecticut title to the territory (1782).

Dyer, Isadore. 1865–1920. American dermatologist, b. Galveston, Tex. Professor (1905–20), dean (1908–20), Tulane U.; specialized in study of leprosy; founded (1894) Louisiana Leper Home (which became National Leprosarium).

Dyer, Sir James. 1512–1582. English jurist. M.P. (1547, 1553); speaker of House of Commons (1553); judge of common pleas (1556); chief judge (1559–82); first to compile reports of law cases to serve as precedents; reports (published 1585) covered years 1513–82.

Dyer, John. 1699–1757. British poet, b. Wales. Itinerant artist in South Wales; author of "Grongar Hill" (1726), *Ruins of Rome* (1740), *The Fleece* (1757), notable for natural description and precision of phrase.

Dyer, Mary. d. 1660. American Quaker martyr, b. Somersetshire?, England. Emigrated to Massachusetts (c.1635); followed Anne Hutchinson to Rhode Island (1638); to England (1652); became Quaker; to Boston (1657), where she was arrested and banished; after twice (1659, 1660) returning to Boston to visit imprisoned Quakers, condemned for sedition and hanged.

Dyer, Reginald Edward Harry. 1864–1927. British soldier. Served in Burma (1886–87); in World War I commanded operations in southeastern Persia (1916–17). Brigade commander at Jullundur at time of Amritsar Massacre (April 13, 1919) when he marched a detachment to an enclosed square crowded with unarmed native protesters assembled in defiance of his orders and opened fire, killing 379; forced to resign from service (1920). Site of massacre made Indian nationalist shrine.

Dyk \ˈdik\, Viktor. 1877–1931. Czech writer. Author of verse, including *A porta inferi* (1897), *Marnosti* (1900), *Satiry a sarkasmy* (1905), *Milá sedmi loupežníků* (1906), *Giuseppe Moro* (1911); novels, including *Konec Hakkenschmidův* (1904), and plays, including *Zmoudření Dona Quijota* (1913).

Dykes \ˈdīks\, John Bacchus. 1823–1876. English clergyman and composer of hymn tunes. Joint editor of *Hymns Ancient and Modern;* composed "Lead, Kindly Light," "Nearer, my God, to Thee," "Jesus, Lover of my Soul," and other hymn tunes.

Dyk·stra \ˈdik-strə\, Clarence Addison. 1883–1950. American educator, b. Cleveland, Ohio. Professor of political science, Kansas (1909–18). Commissioner of water and power, Los Angeles (1926–30); city manager, Cincinnati, Ohio (1930–37). President, U. of Wisconsin (1937–45); director of selective service (1940–41); provost, UCLA (1945–50).

Dym·oke \ˈdim-ək\. Name of an English family of Lincolnshire holding (since 1377) the office of king's champion, whose function was to challenge all comers to deny the king's title at the coronation banquet. Sir John (d. 1381), lord of Scrivelsby, Lincolnshire, by marriage with Margaret de Ludlow, heiress of the Marmions, was the first to perform the office, at coronation of Richard II. His son ¶Thomas (d. 1422) served as champion at coronations of Henry IV and Henry V. His son ¶Philip (d. 1455) did so for Henry VI. Philip's son ¶Sir Thomas (1428?–1471) joined in a Lancastrian rising (1469); beheaded by Edward IV. His son ¶Sir Robert (d. 1546) was champion at coronations of Richard III, Henry VII, and Henry VIII, fought with distinction at siege of Tournai. Sir Robert's son ¶Sir Edward (?–?) was champion to Edward VI, Mary, and Elizabeth I. His grandson ¶Sir Edward (d. 1625) was champion to James I, and that Sir Edward's grandson ¶Charles (d. 1644) was to Charles I. A nephew of Charles ¶Sir Edward (d. 1664) was champion to Charles II, and his son ¶Sir Charles (?–?) was to James II. The latter's son ¶Charles (d. 1703) was champion to William and Mary and to Anne and also M.P. (1698–1702). His son ¶Lewis (d. 1760) was champion to George I and George II. A nephew ¶John (d. 1784) was champion to George III. His grandson ¶Sir Henry (1801–1865) was champion at coronation of George IV, after which the ceremony was allowed to lapse. Members of a collateral branch of the family bore the standard of England at coronation of Edward VII and George V.

Dy·ott \ˈdī-ˌät, -ət\, Thomas W. 1771–1861. American businessman and reformer, b. England. Dealer in patent medicines, Philadelphia (from 1807); need for bottles led him to buy Kensington Glass Works (1833), which he greatly expanded; built company town, Dyottville, and laid down disciplined, paternalistic regime for employees; factory produced wide range of decorated and portrait glassware.

Dyscolus. See APOLLONIUS.

Dy·son \ˈdīs-ᵊn\, Sir Frank Watson. 1868–1939. British astronomer. Astronomer royal of Scotland (1905–10), of England (1910–33). Studied solar spectra and eclipses, stellar motions; made light-deflection observations (1919) supporting Einstein's prediction.

Dyson, William Henry. 1883–1938. British etcher and cartoonist, b. Australia. On staff of London *Daily Herald* (1913–25, 1931–38); noted for satirical attacks on privileged classes.

Dzer·zhin·ski \dyir-ˈzhēn-skəi\, Feliks Edmundovich. *Pol.* Dzier·zyn·ski \jezh-ˈin-skē\. 1877–1926. Russian politician and administrator, of Polish descent. Banished to Siberia for political agitation (1897); escaped (1899); took part in revolution of 1905; arrested and banished four more times by 1908; in captivity again (1912–17); released after the Russian Revolution (1917) and became organizer and head (1917–21) of the Russian secret police (the Cheka, later known as the OGPU); commissar for internal affairs (from 1919); commissar of transport (1921); reorganized and improved the railway system; head of the supreme economic council (1924); elected to Politburo (1926).

Dzhugashvili, Iosif Vissarionovich. See Joseph STALIN.

Dzier·zon \ˈdzyer-ˌzhȯn\, Johann. 1811–1906. German apiculturist. Discovered parthenogenesis in bees, in which drones develop from unfertilized eggs of queens.

Dzyu·bin \ˈjüb-yin\, Eduard Georgiyevich. *Pseudonym* Edward Bag·rit·sky \(ˌ)bə-ˈgrit-skəi\. 1895–1934. Russian poet. Early follower of Acmeists; best known for Romantic verses celebrating Russian Revolution, esp. the heroic narrative *Duma pro Opanasa* (1925).

E

Ead·bald \ˈed-ˌbȯld, ˈa-əd-ˌbäld\ *or* **Aeth·el·bald** \ˈath-əl-ˌbȯld, -ˌbäld\. d. 640. King of Kent. Son of Aethelberht, whom he succeeded (616); on conversion by Laurentius, archbishop of Canterbury, recalled Christians he had persecuted and built church at Canterbury.

Ead·bert \ˈed-(ˌ)bərt, ˈa-əd-ˌbert\ *or* **Eadberht** \ˈa-əd-ˌberḵt\. d. 768. Anglo-Saxon king. Succeeded cousin Ceolwulf as king of Northumbrians (737); extended realm, fostered church and learning; abdicated in favor of son Oswulf (758); became cleric in York cathedral under his brother Egbert (d. 766), the first archbishop.

Ead·frid \ˈed-frəd, ˈa-əd-frid\ *or* **Ead·frith** \-(ˌ)frith\. d. 721. Anglo-Saxon prelate. Bishop of Lindisfarne, Northumbria (from 698); began compilation of what is known as the *Lindisfarne Book,* containing a text of the Gospels in Latin.

Eadgar, Eadmund, Eadward. See EDGAR, EDMUND, EDWARD.

Ea·die \ˈē-dē\, John. 1810–1876. Scottish Presbyterian theologian and scholar. Published *Biblical Cyclopaedia* (1848), *Ecclesiastical Encyclopaedia* (1861), commentaries on the epistles, critical history of *The English Bible* (1876).

Ead·mer \ˈed-mər, ˈa-əd-ˌmer\ *or* **Ed·mer** \ˈed-mər\. c.1060–c.1128. English monk and historian. Member of Anselm's household (from 1093), probably his secretary and chaplain; author of *Historia novorum in Anglia* (c.1115), accurately detailed chronicle of monastic community at Canterbury, and *Vita Anselmi* (c.1124).

Ead·red \ˈed-rəd, ˈa-ə-ˌdred\ *or* **Ed·red** \ˈed-rəd\. d. 955. English king. Son of Edward the Elder, brother of Edmund I, half-brother of Aethelstan. Succeeded Edmund I as king of the English (946); ravaged Northumbria (948) to put down rebellion of Wulfstan, archbishop of York, who supported Eric Bloodaxe of Norway; after further revolt in which Northumbrians took Olaf Sihtricson and then Eric Bloodaxe as king, Eadred again received allegiance (954); created Northumbria an earldom.

Ead·ric Stre·o·na \ˈed-(ˌ)rik-ˈstrā-ə-nə, ˈa-ə-ˌdrik-\ *or* **Ed·ric Streona** \ˈed-(ˌ)rik-\. d. 1017. Alderman of the Mercians (from 1007). m. (1009) daughter of Aethelred II; said to have acted treacherously to protect Mercia from Danes, allowing them to ravage Wessex; invaded Wales, desolated St. David's (1011); had Sigeferth and Morcar, chief thegns of Danish confederacy, slain through treachery (1015); deserted brother-in-law Edmund Ironside and joined Canute (1015); aided Canute in conquering Wessex and Mercia; reconciled with Edmund, but at battle of Assandun, or Ashington, in Essex, took flight with Mercian troops, perhaps treacherously, and allowed Edmund to be defeated by Canute; may have played part in death of Edmund (1016); restored to earldom by Canute, who nonetheless had him slain as untrustworthy.

Eads \ˈēdz\, James Buchanan. 1820–1887. American engineer and inventor, b. Lawrenceburg, Ind. Invented diving bell; organized partnership to use diving bell for salvaging from steamboats sunk in river and made fortune (1848–57). Suggested fleet of armor-plated gunboats for controlling Mississippi River (1861); contracted to deliver them, ready for armament, in sixty-five days; completed contract on time. Built first bridge (Eads Bridge, 1867–74) across Mississippi at St. Louis. Proposed to Congress (1874) to open a mouth of Mississippi into Gulf of Mexico and keep channel at proper depth for navigation; succeeded by using a jetty system (1879).

Ead·wig \ˈed-wig, -wē; ˈa-əd-wig\ *or* **Ed·wy** \ˈed-wē\. d. 959. King of the English. Son of Edmund I. Succeeded uncle Eadred as king (955); drove Dunstan into exile (955); on revolt of Mercians and Northumbrians (957), who chose his brother Edgar as king, he was left to rule Wessex and Kent (957–959).

Ea·kins \ˈā-kənz\, Thomas. 1844–1916. American painter and sculptor, b. Philadelphia. Instructor at Pennsylvania Academy of Fine Arts (1873–86); noted for mastery of draftsmanship, anatomy; major works included *Max Schmitt in a Single Scull, The Gross Clinic, The Fairman Rogers Four-in-Hand, Swimming Hole, Walt Whitman, Agnew Clinic, Between Rounds;* his sculptures included reliefs on the battle monument in Trenton, N.J.

Eal·dred \ˈel-drəd, ˈa-əl-ˌdred\ *or* **Ald·red** \ˈal-drəd, ˈȯl-\. d. 1069. Anglo-Saxon prelate. Abbot of Tavistock, Devon (c.1027); bishop of Worcester (1046); traveled to Germany to secure release of Edward, son of Edmund Ironside, by Henry III (1054); archbishop of York (1060); probably crowned Harold II (1066); crowned William I at Westminster Abbey (1066).

Ealhwine. See ALCUIN.

Eames \ˈāmz\, Charles. 1907–1978. American designer, b. St. Louis, Mo. Designed molded plywood chair (1940); had first one-man furniture exhibit at Museum of Modern Art, N.Y.C. (1946); later known for work in film, exhibit design, and industrial design.

Ea·nes \ˈyá-nēsh\, Gil. 15th century. Portugese mariner. Under sponsorship of Prince Henry the Navigator, became first to round Cape Bojador (1434), thus dispelling general superstition about the place.

Ear·hart \ˈe(ə)r-ˌhärt, ˈi(ə)r-\, Amelia Mary. 1897–1937. American aviator, b. Atchison, Kans. m. George Palmer Putnam (1931). First woman to cross Atlantic Ocean in airplane, Newfoundland to Wales (1928); first woman to fly Atlantic solo (1932); first Hawaii-to-mainland solo (1935); first Mexico City–New York flight (1935); lost on attempted round-the-world flight (1937). Author of *20 Hrs., 40 Min.* (1928), *The Fun of It* (1932), *Last Flight* (edited by her husband; 1938).

Earle \ˈər(-ə)l\, Alice, *nee* Morse. 1851–1911. American author, b. Worcester, Mass. m. (1874) Henry Earle. Her books included *The Sabbath in Puritan New England* (1891), *Customs and Fashions in Old New England* (1893), *Home Life in Colonial Days* (1898), *Stage Coach and Tavern Days* (1900), *Two Centuries of Costume in America* (1903).

Earle *or* **Earles** \ˈər(-ə)lz\, John. 1601?–1665. English prelate. Tutor (1641) to Prince Charles (later Charles II); chaplain to Charles in France. At Restoration, dean of Westminster (1660); bishop of Worcester (1662–63), of Salisbury (1663–65). Author of *Microcosmographie* (1628), made Latin translation (1649) of the *Eikon Basilike.*

Ear·lom \ˈər-ləm\, Richard. 1743–1822. English mezzotint engraver. Known esp. for engravings of flowers, of plates for Claude Lorraine's *Liber veritatis,* and Hogarth's *Marriage à la Mode.*

Ear·ly \ˈər-lē\, Jubal Anderson. 1816–1894. American Confederate army officer, b. Franklin Co., Va. Opposed secession, but was loyal to Virginia when it seceded, and entered Confederate army; brigadier general (1861); major general (1863); lieutenant general in command of II Corps, sent on great raid (1864) down Shenandoah Valley toward Washington; defeated by Sheridan at Winchester, Fisher's Hill, and Cedar Creek, and his army almost destroyed at Waynesboro (1865). Relieved of command; fled to Mexico, thence to Canada (1866). Returned (1869) to practice law, Lynchburg, Va.

Early, Stephen Tyree. 1889–1951. American journalist, b. Crozet, Va. Assistant secretary to President Roosevelt (1933–37), secretary (1937–45); considered first effective presidential press secretary; deputy secretary of defense (1949–50).

Earn·shaw \ˈərn-ˌshȯ\, Thomas. 1749–1829. English watchmaker. Made improvements to transit clock at Greenwich Observatory; invented bimetallic compensation balance, detached detent escapement; simplified chronometer construction, making them affordable to individuals for the first time.

Earp \ˈərp\, Wyatt Berry Stapp. 1848–1929. American lawman, b. Monmouth, Ill. Assistant marshal, Dodge City, Kans. (1876, 1878–79); deputy marshal, Tombstone, Ariz. (1881) on occasion of "Gunfight at O.K. Corral"; a gambler, subject of many legends.

East \ˈēst\, Sir Alfred. 1849–1913. English landscape painter and etcher. Known esp. for Japanese landscapes.

East, Edward Murray. 1879–1938. American geneticist, b. Du Quoin, Ill. On staff, Harvard (from 1909); contributed to development of hybrid corn; author of *Inbreeding and Outbreeding* (1919), *Mankind at the Crossroads* (1923), *Heredity and Human Affairs* (1927), etc.

East, Thomas. *Surname also spelled* Est, Este, *or* Easte. c.1540–1609. English music printer. Published William Byrd's *Psalmes, Sonets and Songs of Sadnes and Pietie* (1588); edited and published *The Whole Booke of Psalmes, With Their Wonted Tunes* (1592); volumes of madrigals by Thomas Weelkes, John Wilbye, Thomas Morley, etc.

East·lake \ˈēst-ˌlāk\, Sir Charles Lock. 1793–1865. English painter and art critic. From a small boat in Plymouth harbor, made sketches of Napoléon (then a prisoner aboard H.M.S. *Bellerophon*) from which he produced two full-length portraits, on proceeds of which he visited Italy (1816–30); keeper of National Gallery (1843–47), director (1855). Known esp. for "banditti" (Italian genre) pictures, and for *Pilgrims in Sight of Rome, Christ Blessing Little Children, Christ Lamenting over Jerusalem, Byron's Dream.* Author of *Materials for a History of Oil Painting* (1847).

Eastlake, Charles Lock. 1836–1906. English art critic. Nephew of Sir Charles Eastlake. Secretary of Royal Institute of British Architects (1866–77); keeper and secretary of National Gallery (1878–98); known esp. as influential exponent of Gothic and Jacobean revival in architecture and furniture design; author of *Hints on Household Taste in Furniture, Upholstery and Other Details* (1868), *Lectures on Decorative Art and Art Workmanship* (1876); also wrote series of *Notes on the Principal Pictures* on European galleries.

East·land \ˈēst-lənd\, James Oliver. 1904–1986. American politician, b. Doddsville, Miss. U.S. Senator from Mississippi for 38 years (from 1941); powerful chairman of the Senate judiciary committee; a staunch conservative, upholder of states rights, and opponent of desegregation and Communism.

East·man \ˈēst-mən\, George. 1854–1932. American inventor and industrialist, b. Waterville, N.Y. Perfected process for making photographic dry plates (1880) and flexible film (patented 1884), and invented the Kodak box camera (1888); introduced daylight-loading film (1892). Organized business as Eastman Kodak Co. (1892); introduced Brownie camera (1900). Later noted as philanthropist; founder, Eastman School of Music, Rochester, N.Y.

Eastman, John Robie. 1836–1913. American astronomer, b. Andover, N.H. On staff of U.S. Naval Observatory (1862–98); editor of its publications (1872–82); principal work the *Second Washington Catalogue of Stars* (1898).

Eastman, Joseph Bartlett. 1882–1944. American government official, b. Katonah, N.Y. Member, U.S. Interstate Commerce Commission (1919–44); federal co-ordinator of transportation (1933–36); director, Office of Defense Transportation (1941–44).

Eastman, Max Forrester. 1883–1969. American editor and writer, b. Canandaigua, N.Y. Founder and editor of *The Masses* (1913–18) and *The Liberator* (1919–22); roving editor for *Reader's Digest* (from 1941). Author of *Enjoyment of Poetry* (1913), *Colors of Life* (verse, 1918), *Journalism versus Art* (1916), *Since Lenin Died* (1925), *Artists in Uniform* (1934), *Marx and Lenin, the Science of Revolution* (1926), *Enjoyment of Laughter* (1936), *The End of Socialism in Russia* (1937), *Marxism: Is it Science?* (1940), *Heroes I Have Known* (1942), *Enjoyment of Living* (1948), *Love and Revolution* (1965).

Ea·ton \ˈēt-ᵊn\, Amos. 1776–1842. American scientist, b. Chatham, N.Y. Author of *A Manual of Botany for the Northern States* (1817); a lecturer on natural science; professor at Rensselaer School (now Polytechnic Inst.; 1824–42). His grandson ¶Daniel Cady Eaton (1834–1895), professor of botany, Yale (1864–95); author of *The Ferns of North America* (1877–80).

Eaton, Cyrus Stephen. 1883–1979. American businessman, b. Pugwash, N.S. To U.S. (1905), naturalized (1913). Active in gas and electric firms in Cleveland; organized United Light and Power Co. (1923), Continental Shares (1926), Republic Steel Corp. (1930). Later became known for advocacy of improved U.S.–Soviet relations; initiated (1957) annual Pugwash Conferences (named for and originally held at his Nova Scotia lodge) of international scholars and scientists.

Eaton, Dorman Bridgman. 1823–1899. American lawyer and reformer, b. Hardwick, Vt. Chairman, National Civil Service Commission (1873–75); drafted National Civil Service Act (known as Pendleton Act) passed in 1883; head of Civil Service Commission (1883–86). Author of *Government of Municipalities* (1899).

Eaton, Margaret, *nee* O'Neale, *known as* Peggy. 1799–1879. American socialite, b. Washington, D.C. Daughter of a Washington innkeeper; m. 1st John B. Timberlake (1816; d. 1828), 2d (1829) Sen. John H. Eaton, a close friend of Pres. Andrew Jackson. On Eaton's elevation to the cabinet (1829), the wives of the other cabinet members refused to accept her socially, apparently because of gossip concerning her earlier relations with Eaton, and forced her husband to resign (1831), despite President Jackson's intervention; affair sealed break between Jackson and John Calhoun, whose wife had led in snubbing Mrs. Eaton.

Eaton, Theophilus. 1590–1658. American colonist, b. Stony Stratford, England. One of original patentees of Massachusetts Bay Company; emigrated to Massachusetts (1637). Established new colony at New Haven (1638) and was chosen governor; reelected annually till his death. Drew up, with help of John Davenport, code of laws for the colony (printed in London, 1656).

Eaton, Timothy. 1834–1907. Canadian merchant, b. near Ballymena, Ireland. To Canada (c.1854). Founded (1869) at Toronto, T. Eaton Co., Ltd., which developed into one of largest department stores in America, with branches in Winnipeg and Montreal.

Eaton, William. 1764–1811. American army officer and diplomat. Commissioned captain, U.S. army (1792). U.S. consul at Tunis (1798); formed plan to restore exiled pasha Hamet Karamanli to throne of Tripoli usurped by his brother; as "navy agent to the Barbary States" (1804), found Hamet in Upper Egypt, gathered force of Greeks, Italians, and Arabs, and succeeded in bringing Hamet to Derna, a seaport of Tripoli which he captured (Apr. 27, 1805). Ordered to vacate Tripoli because of new negotiations leading to recognition of the usurping pasha.

Eaton, Wyatt. 1849–1896. American painter, b. Phillipsburg, Que. A founder of the Society of American Artists (1877); its first secretary and later its president. Known esp. as a portraitist; subjects included Timothy Cole, William Cullen Bryant, Bishop Horatio Potter, President Garfield, John Burroughs, Mrs. R. W. Gilder.

Eb·bing·haus \ˈeb-iŋ-ˌhau̇s\, Hermann. 1850–1909. German experimental psychologist. Taught at Berlin (1886–94), Breslau (1894–1905), Halle (1905–09); known esp. for study of rote learning and memory; discovered "forgetting curve"; author of *Über das Gedächtnis* (1885), *Grundzüge der Psychologie* (1902), *Abriss der Psychologie* (1908).

Eb·bo \eb-bō\ *or* **Ebo** \ā-bō\ of Reims. c.775–851. Frankish prelate. Friend of Louis I the Pious; archbishop of Reims (816); began construction of cathedral; encouraged arts and letters, esp. the *Evangelarium* or gospel book of Ebbo (c.817–834); apostolic legate (822); led Frankish mission to Denmark (822–823); leader of prelates supporting Lothair I against Louis (833); ordered Louis deposed, imposed penance (833); on Louis's restoration (834) sought refuge near Paris but was seized, deposed, and imprisoned (835); unlawfully reinstated by Lothair (840–841); banished by Charles II the Bald, fled to Rome; made archbishop of Hildesheim (c.846) by Louis the German.

Ebedjesus. See ABHDISHO.

Ebel \ˈā-bəl\, Johann Wilhelm. 1784–1861. German Lutheran clergyman. Pastor in Königsberg (1816), where he founded the mystic and theosophic Mucker society, dissolved (1839) following charges of gross immorality and sectarianism; declared innocent at end of 6 years' trial (1835–41), but removed from office on charge of "neglect."

Eber \ˈā-bər\, Paul. 1511–1569. German Protestant theologian. Professor at Wittenberg (from 1541); at first disciple and secretary of Melanchthon, then follower of Luther. Author of a revision of the Old Testament in the Wittenberg German-Latin edition of the Bible, a postexilic history of the Jews (in Latin), church songs, etc.

Eber·hard \ˈā-bər-ˌhärt\. d. 939. Duke of the Franks. Supported his brother Conrad I against Henry the Fowler of Saxony (915), but after Conrad's death (918) succeeded to duchy of Franconia and conveyed German crown and scepter to Henry. Rebelled (938 and 939) against Henry's successor, Otto I the Great, and was killed in action.

Eberhard. Name of several counts and dukes of Württemberg, including: Eberhard I, *surnamed* der Erlauchte (1265–1325), son of Ulrich I; count (1279–1325). ¶Eberhard II, *surnamed* der Greiner *and* der Rauschebart (1315–1392), count jointly with brother Ulrich IV (1344–66), alone (1366–92). ¶Eberhard III, *surnamed* der Milde (1364–1417), count (1392–1417). ¶Eberhard, *surnamed* im Bart (1445–1496), count (1457–95), duke (1495–96); founded U. of Tübingen (1477); made treaty of Münsingen (1482) whereby Württemberg was reunited; a founder of the Swabian League (1488); created duke by Maximilian I at Diet of Worms (1495).

Eberhard, Johann August. 1739–1809. German philosopher, theologian, and writer. Professor at Halle (from 1778); author of *Neue Apologie des Sokrates,* a criticism of Kantian philosophy in favor of that of Leibnitz (1772–78), *Allgemeine Theorie des Denkens und Empfindens* (1776), *Versuch einer allgemeinen-deutschen Synonymik,* an important dictionary (1795–1802), *Handbuch der Ästhetik* (1803–05), etc.

Eb·er·le \ˈeb-ər-lē\, John. 1787–1838. American physician and medical writer, b. Hagerstown, Md. A founder and first editor (1818–20) of *American Medical Recorder;* proposed founding of Jefferson Medical College (1824), professor there (1825–31); author of textbooks.

Eber·lein \ˈā-bər-ˌlīn\, Gustav. 1847–1926. German sculptor. Professor at Berlin Academy (from 1893); known esp. for statues of William I, Goethe, Wagner, Bismarck.

Ebers \ˈā-bərs\, Georg Moritz. 1837–1898. German Egyptologist and novelist. Taught at Jena (1865–70), Leipzig (1870–89); acquired (1873) the famous 16th-century B.C. Egyptian medical papyrus called *Papyrus Ebers* (pub. 1875). Author of *Ägypten und die Bücher Moses* (1868), and of historical novels of Egypt, as *Eine ägyptische Königstochter* (1864), *Uarda* (1877), *Homo sum* (1878), *Kleopatra* (1894).

Ebert \'ā-bərt\, Friedrich. 1871–1925. German politician. Practiced trade of saddle maker; secretary of Social Democratic party (1905); elected to Reichstag (1912); president of party (1913). Lost left-wing support through support of war appropriations (1914–18); on downfall of government, was appointed chancellor in place of Prince Max of Baden; member of temporary government, the Council of People's Representatives (1918–19); elected first president of German republic by National Assembly at Weimar (1919); suppressed Kapp Putsch (1920) and attempt of Hitler to establish dictatorship in Bavaria (1923); authority undermined by French occupation of Ruhr, inflation, civil war on communists, etc.

Ebert, Friedrich Adolf. 1791–1834. German librarian and bibliographer. Head of royal library, Dresden (1827–34); author of *Allgemeines bibliographisches Lexikon* (1819–30).

Eberth \'ā-bərt\, Karl Joseph. 1835–1926. German anatomist and bacteriologist. Taught at Zürich (1874–81), Halle (1881–95); head of Pathological Institute (1895–1911). Known for work on inflammation, thrombosis, etc., and for identification, simultaneously with Koch, of the bacillus of typhoid fever (1880) named *Eberthella typhosa* (later *Salmonella typhosa*) after him.

Eb·ner-Eschen·bach \'āb-nər-'esh-ən-,bäk\, Marie von. Baroness. *Nee* Countess Dub·sky \'du̇p-skē\. 1830–1916. Austrian novelist and poet. Author of the drama *Maria Stuart von Schottland* (1860), and of humorous and psychological stories and novels chiefly of life in Bohemia and among the Austrian aristocracy, including *Die Prinzessin von Banalien* (1872), *Božena* (1876), *Das Gemeindekind* (1887), *Lotti, die Uhrmacherin* (1889), *Unsühnbar* (1890), *Glaubenslos* (1893), etc.

Ebo of Reims. See EBBO.

Éboli, Princesa de. See Ana MENDOZA DE LA CERDA.

Éboué \āb-wā\, Félix, *in full* Adolphe-Félix-Sylvestre. 1884–1944. French colonial administrator. In colonial service (from 1908); secretary general, acting governor of Martinique (1932); governor of Guadeloupe (1936–39), first black governor in French system; governor of Chad (1938–40); first colonial governor to adhere to Free French cause; governor general of French Equatorial Africa (1940–44).

Ebreo, Leone. See Judah ABRABANEL.

Ebro·in \'ā-brō-ēn\. d. 680 or 681. Neustrian mayor of the palace. Placed puppet Theuderic III on Frankish throne (673, 676); defeated Burgundians and Austrasians (679), establishing himself as sole ruler of Franks.

Eça de Quei·rós *or* **Quei·roz** \'ā-sə-thə-kā-ē-'rōsh\. José Maria de. 1845–1900. Portuguese novelist. Member of "generation of '70" group of intellectuals; lectured on realism in art as part of "Conferências do Casino" series (1871); Portuguese consul in Havana (1872–74), England (1874–88), Paris (1888–1900). Author of novels of satire and, later, rural sentiment, including *O crime do padre Amaro* (1875), *O primo Basílio* (1878), *O Mandarim* (1880), *A relíquia* (1887), *Os Maias* (1888), *A ilustre casa de Ramires* (1900), *A cidade e as serras* (1901).

Ec·card \'ek-ärt\, Johannes. 1553–1611. German composer. Served in chapel of Prince Georg Friedrich, Königsberg (1579–1608); kapellmeister to electors of Brandenburg (1608–11). Composed many vocal and instrumental works, notably his cycle of Lutheran chorales, *Geistliche Lieder auf den Choral* (1597).

Eccard, Johann Georg von. See ECKHARDT.

Eccelino da Romano. See EZZELINO DA ROMANO.

Ecchellensis, Abraham. See IBRĀHĪM AL-ḤAQILĀNĪ.

Ec·cles \'ek-əlz\, Marriner Stoddard. 1890–1977. American banker, b. Logan, Utah. Governor, Federal Reserve Board (1934–36); member (1936–51) and chairman (1936–48), board of governors of Federal Reserve System.

Ecgberht *or* **Ecgbryht.** See EGBERT.

Ecg·frith \'ej-,frith, 'eg-\ *or* **Eg·frith** \'eg-,frith\. d. 685. Anglo-Saxon king. Son of King Oswiu, whom he succeeded as king of Northumbrians (670); defeated Mercian coalition (674) but defeated by Aethelred of Mercia (678); killed in battle with Picts.

Eche·ga·ray y Ei·za·guir·re \ā-chā-gä-'rī-ē-ā-thä-'gēr-rā\, José. 1832–1916. Spanish dramatist and mathematician. Professor of mathematics and physics, Madrid (1854–68); entered government service (1868); minister of finance (1874); established Bank of Spain. His plays included *El libro talonario* (1874), *O locura o santidad* (1877), *El gran Galeoto* (1881), *El estigma* (1895), *La duda* (1898), *El loco Diós* (1900), *La desequilibrada* (1903), and *A fuerza de arrastrarse* (1905). With Frédéric Mistral awarded Nobel prize for literature (1904).

Eche·ver·ría \ā-chā-ver-'rē-ä\, Esteban. 1805–1851. Argentine poet. Credited with introducing into Spanish America the literary conceptions of the European Romantics; banished by the dictator Rosas. Author of *Elvira o la novia del Plata* (1832), *Consuelos* (1834), *Rimas* (1837).

Eck \'ek\, Johann. *Orig. surname* Mai·er \'mī-ər\. 1486–1543. German Roman Catholic theologian. Professor of theology, Ingolstadt (1510); disputed at Leipzig with Karlstadt and Luther (1519), against whom he was influential in procuring the papal bull from Rome (1520); debated Oecolampadius at Baden (1526); attended Augsburg Diet (1530); took part in religious convocations at Worms, where he debated Melanchthon (1540) and Ratisbon (1541).

Eck·e·hart \'ek-ə-,härt\ *or* **Eck·art** \'ek-,ärt\ *or* **Eck·hart** \'ek-,härt\, Johannes. *Called* Meister Eckehart; *also known as* Eckehart von Hoch·heim \-fōn-'hōk-,hīm\. c.1260–?1327. German mystic. Entered Dominican order (c.1275); magister in philosophy, Paris (1302); Dominican provincial for Saxony (1303); vicar of Bohemia (1306); taught in Paris, Strassburg, Cologne; charged with heresy (1327) for mystical doctrine combining elements of scholasticism, neoplatonism, Arabic thought; apparently died before issuance of papal bull (1329) condemning 28 propositions drawn from his writing and preaching. Considered founding spirit of German idealism, Romanticism, Protestantism.

Eck·e·ner \'ek-ə-nər\, Hugo. 1868–1954. German aeronaut. Entered Zeppelin factory (1908); director of German Aerial Navigation Co. (1911); president of the Zeppelin Co. (1924); commanded airship ZR-3 in transatlantic flight (1924); builder of the *Graf Zeppelin* in which he circled the earth (1929) and made polar flight (1931).

Eck·er·mann \'ek-ər-,män\, Johann Peter. 1792–1854. German writer. Became acquainted with Goethe (1822), who helped bring about publication of his *Beiträge zur Poesie mit besonderer Hinweisung auf Goethe* (1823); became Goethe's literary assistant and helped him prepare final edition of his works. Author of *Gespräche mit Goethe in den letzten Jahren seines Lebens, 1823–32* (1836–48); editor of Goethe's *Nachgelassene Schriften* (1832–33) and of *Sämtliche Werke* (with Riemer; 40 vols., 1839–40).

Eck·ers·berg \'ek-ərs-berg\, Kristoffer Vilhelm. 1783–1853. Danish painter. Founder of the national Danish school of painting. Professor (1818–53), director (1827–29), Copenhagen Academy; known for landscapes, seascapes, historical subjects.

Eck·ers·ley \'ek-ərz-lē\, Peter Pendleton. 1892–1963. English radio engineer. Chief engineer, British Broadcasting Corp. (1923–29); first regular broadcaster in Britain (1921–22); proposed BBC's regional broadcast system; author of *The Power Behind the Microphone* (1941).

Eck·ford \'ek-fərd\, Henry. 1775–1832. American shipbuilder, b. Scotland. To New York City (1796). Built the *Robert Fulton,* which made first successful voyage by steam from New York to New Orleans and Havana (1822).

Eck·hardt \'ek-,härt\ *or* **Ec·card** \'ek-,ärt\, Johann Georg von. 1664–1730. German historian. Assisted Leibnitz (1694–1716) and completed the latter's *Annales Imperii* and *Origines Guelficae.* Historiographer, Hanover (1714), and court librarian and historiographer (1716–23); court and university librarian, Würzburg (1724).

Eckhart. See ECKEHART.

Eck·hel \'ek-əl\, Joseph Hilarius. 1737–1798. Austrian numismatist. Founder of modern numismatics; professor, Vienna (from 1775); author of *Doctrina numorum veterum* (1792–98).

Eckhof, Konrad. See EKHOF.

Eckmühl, Prince d'. See Louis-Nicolas DAVOUT.

Eck·stein \'ek-,shtīn\, Ernst. 1845–1900. German humorist. Editor of literary journal *Deutsche Dichterhalle* (1875–82) and comic weekly *Schalk* (1879–82). Author of humorous epics, historical novels, etc., including *Pariser Silhouetten* (1873), *Der Besuch im Karzer* (1875), *Die Mädchen des Pensionats* (1876).

Ed·di \'ed-ē\ *or* **Aed·de** \'ad-de\ *or* **Ed·di·us** \'ed-ē-əs\. fl. 669. Kentish choirmaster. Brought to Northumbria by Wilfrid, Bishop of York, to teach Roman method of chanting (669); his *Life of Wilfrid* possibly earliest extant signed work of an Anglo-Saxon author.

Ed·ding·ton \'ed-iŋ-tən\, Sir Arthur Stanley. 1882–1944. English astronomer. Chief assistant, Royal Observatory, Greenwich (1906–13); professor, Cambridge (from 1913) and director of the observatory (1914). Known esp. for researches on the motion, internal constitution, and evolution of stars, cosmology, and elucidation of the theory of relativity. Author of *Stellar Movements and the Structure of the Universe* (1914), *Space, Time, and Gravitation* (1920), *Mathematical Theory of Relativity* (1923), *Internal Constitution of the Stars* (1925), *The Nature of the Physical World* (1928), *Science and the Unseen World* (1929), *The Expanding Universe* (1933), *New Pathways of Science* (1935), *Relativity Theory of Protons and Electrons* (1936), *The Philosophy of Physical Science* (1939), etc.

Ed·dy \'ed-ē\, Clarence. 1851–1937. American organist and composer, b. Greenfield, Mass. Organist and choirmaster in Chicago (1874–96); widely known as a recitalist.

Eddy, Mary Morse, *nee* Baker. 1821–1910. American founder of the Christian Science Church, b. Bow, N.H. m. (1843) George W. Glover (d. 1844), 2d (1853) Daniel Patterson (div. 1873), 3d Asa G. Eddy (1877; d. 1882). As an invalid, she sought many types of healing; after exhaustive trial of physical methods she investigated mental healing; helped by and became student of Phineas P. Quimby (from 1862); later (c.1866) turned to the Bible during recovery from the effects of a severe fall and discovered the spiritual and metaphysical system known as Christian Science. Completed *Science and Health* (1875) explaining this system; chartered (1879) "Church of Christ, Scientist" and (1881) Massachusetts Metaphysical College; followers multiplied and spread her teachings; founded "Mother Church," Boston (1895). Author of the *Church Manual* (1895). Founded *The Christian Science Journal* (1st issue, 1883) and The Christian Science Publishing Society (1898), publishers of *The Christian Science Quarterly, The Christian Science Monitor* (from 1908), etc.

Edel·felt \ˈā-del-ˌfelt\, Albert. 1854–1905. Finnish painter. Known esp. for landscapes and genre works and for portraits, as of Pasteur.

Ede·linck \ˈā-dəl-iŋk\, Gérard. 1640–1707. Flemish copperplate engraver. In France (from 1666); master of tone, color, and texture; produced over 300 engravings, including portraits of Philippe de Champaigne, Le Brun, Dryden, Descartes, Louis XIV, and *The Holy Family* (after Raphael), etc.

Eden \ˈēd-ᵊn\, Sir Anthony, *in full* Robert Anthony. 1st Earl of Avon \ˈā-vən\. 1897–1977. English politician. Collateral descendant of William Eden, 1st Baron Auckland. Served in World War I; M.P. (1923–57); parliamentary private secretary to foreign secretary Sir Austen Chamberlain (1926–29); undersecretary, foreign office (1931–33); lord privy seal (1934–35); minister without portfolio for League of Nations affairs (1935); secretary of state for foreign affairs (1935–38); concluded "gentlemen's agreement" with Count Ciano concerning Mediterranean (1937); resigned in disagreement with policy of Chamberlain government after the Munich conference; secretary of state for dominions (1939–40); war secretary (1940); as secretary of state for foreign affairs (1940–45, 1951–55) helped settle Anglo-Iranian oil dispute, Italian-Yugoslav dispute over Trieste; prime minister (1955–57); resigned following incomplete success of Anglo-French intervention in Egypt over Suez Canal nationalization (1956). Created Viscount Eden and 1st Earl of Avon (1961). Author of *Full Circle* (1960), *Facing the Dictators* (1962), *The Reckoning* (1965).

Eden, George. Earl of Auck·land \ˈȯk-lənd\. 1784–1849. Son of William Eden. M.P. (1810–12, 1813–14); president of Board of Trade (1830–34), first lord of admiralty (1834) in Lord Grey's reform cabinet; governor general of India (1835–41); in order to strengthen British position, precipitated First Afghan War in driving Dōst Moḥammad Khān from throne in favor of Shāh Shojāʿ (1839–41); recalled following massacre of British troops in Kābul (1841); first lord of the admiralty (1846–49).

Edén \e-ˈdān\, Nils. 1871–1945. Swedish politician and historian. Professor, Uppsala (1903–20); elected to Riksdag (1908); chairman of Liberal party (1915); prime minister of what is considered first parliamentary government in Sweden (1917–20); secured woman suffrage (1919); governor of Stockholm province (1920–38). Author of *1809 års revolution* (1911), *Den svenska riksdagen under fem-hundra år* (1935).

Eden \ˈēd-ᵊn\, William. 1st Baron Auck·land \ˈȯk-lənd\. 1744–1814. English politician. Undersecretary of state (1772); M.P. (1774–89); member of Board of Trade (1776); commissioner to American colonies (1778); chief secretary for Ireland (1780–82); negotiated Pitt's commercial treaty with France (1786–87); ambassador to Spain (1788), Holland (1790–93); president of board of trade under Grenville (1806–07); raised to peerage of Ireland (1789), Britain (1793).

Ed·gar \ˈed-gər\ *or* **Ead·gar** \ˈa-əd-ˌgär\. 944–975. King of the English. Younger son of Edmund I; father of Edward the Martyr. Made king of Northumbria and Mercia (957) by nobles discontented with rule of his elder brother Eadwig, on whose death (959) he succeeded as king of West Saxons and thus of essentially united England; recalled Dunstan from exile and made him chief adviser and archbishop of Canterbury (961); pacified Northumbria (967); allowed northern Danes a degree of self-government; received his deferred coronation (973) and, soon after, homage of eight British princes, including kings of Scotland and Strathclyde; restored monastic houses to Benedictine monks, expelling secular clergy.

Edgar. c.1075–1107. King of Scots. Probably second son of Malcolm III Canmore and Queen Margaret; placed on Scottish throne (1097) to succeed Donaldbane; ceded Hebrides to Magnus III of Norway (1098); succeeded by brother Alexander I.

Edgar *or* **Eadgar.** *Called* the Aethe·ling \ˈath-ə-liŋ, ˈat͟h-\. c.1050–c.1125. Anglo-Saxon prince. Grandson of Edmund II Ironside. After defeat of Harold (1066), chosen king by Morcar and his brother Edwin but forced by defections to submit to William I; led two unsuccessful risings (1068, 1069); fled to Scotland, where his sister Margaret had married Malcolm III Canmore; went to William's Norman court and made peace (1074); led Norman expedition that conquered Apulia (1086); led expedition to Scotland and deposed usurper Donaldbane in favor of nephew Edgar (1097); went on Crusade (c.1102).

Edge \ˈej\, Walter Evans. 1873–1956. American businessman, politician, and diplomat, b. Philadelphia. Proprietor, Atlantic City *Daily Press* and Atlantic City *Evening Union.* Governor of New Jersey (1917–19); U.S. senator from New Jersey (1919–29); U.S. ambassador to France (1929–33); governor of N.J. (1944–47).

Edge·worth \ˈej-(ˌ)wərth\, Francis Ysidro. 1845–1926. British economist. Grandson of Richard Edgeworth. Professor at King's College, London (1888–91), Oxford (1891–1922); author of *Mathematical Psychics* (1881), *Metretike* (1887); first editor of *Economic Journal* (from 1891).

Edgeworth, Maria. 1767–1849. British writer. Daughter of Richard Edgeworth. Accompanied her father to Ireland (1782) and was his inseparable companion and assistant; completed her father's memoirs (pub. 1820) on his death; visited Scott at Abbotsford (1823); rendered practical aid to peasants during Irish famine (1846). Author of twenty-odd volumes, among them novels of Irish life that pioneered regionalism and local color, including *The Parent's Assistant* (children's stories, 1796), *Castle Rackrent* (1800), *Belinda* (1801), *Leonora* (1806), *Tales from Fashionable Life* (1809–12), *The Absentee* (1812), *Ormond* (1817), *Helen* (1834), her last novel.

Edgeworth, Richard Lovell. 1744–1817. British inventor and educator. Invented plan for telegraphic communication between Dublin and Galway and many mechanical inventions, including a semaphore, a velocipede, a pedometer, a new land-measuring machine, various forms of carriage. Formed friendship with Thomas Day, and with Dr. Erasmus Darwin; visited Rousseau, according to whose system he educated his eldest son. Collaborated with his daughter Maria in *Practical Education* (1798) and in *Essay on Irish Bulls* (1802).

Edgeworth de Fir·mont \-də-fēr-mōⁿ\, Henry Essex. 1745–1807. Irish clergyman. Educated in France; took surname de Firmont upon ordination; appointed confessor to Princess Élisabeth, sister of Louis XVI (1791), and to Louis XVI, whom he attended on scaffold (1793); escaped to England (1796) carrying Élisabeth's last message to her brother, future King Charles X; chaplain to Louis XVIII, whom he accompanied to Russia.

Ed·gren \ˈed-gren\, Anne Charlotte, *nee* Leff·ler \ˈlef-lər\. Duchess di Ca·ja·nel·lo \dē-ˌkä-yä-ˈnel-lō\. 1849–1892. Swedish novelist and playwright. m. 1st, G. Edgren (1872; div. 1889); 2d, duca di Cajanello (1890). Ardent feminist; author of short stories, *Ur lifvet* (1882; sketches of upper Swedish society), the comedies *Sanna kvinnor* (1883) and *En Räddande engel* (1883), the dramas *Skådespelerskan* (1873), *Hur man gör godt* (1885), and *Kampen för lyckan* (1887, with Sonya Kovalevski), etc.

Ed·i·son \ˈed-ə-sən\, Thomas Alva. 1847–1931. American inventor, b. Milan, Ohio. At 12, newsboy on Grand Trunk Railway; became telegraph operator in various cities in U.S. and Canada; granted first patent (1869) for vote recording machine; sale of inventions, including telegraphic devices, enabled him to establish own workshop at Newark, N.J., which was removed to Menlo Park, N.J. (1876), and to West Orange, N.J. (1887). His Edison General Electric Co. was merged into new General Electric Co. (1892). Among his inventions, of which he patented over a thousand, were an automatic telegraph repeater, quadruplex telegraph (1874), printing telegraph, electric pen, mimeograph, carbon telephone transmitter, the microphone, the phonograph (1877), the Ediphone, the incandescent electric lamp (1879), the electric valve (1883), a system of telegraphy for communicating with moving trains, kinetoscope (1891), alkaline storage battery (Edison storage battery). Produced talking motion pictures (1913); improved dynamos and motors; worked on magnetic method of concentrating iron ores, and on war problems for the government during World War I. His son ¶Charles (1890–1969) was secretary of the navy (1939–40) and governor of New Jersey (1941–44).

Ed·man \ˈed-mən\, Irwin. 1896–1954. American philosopher, b. New York City. Taught at Columbia (1920–54). Author of *Human Traits and Their Social Significance* (1920), *Adam, the Baby, and the Man from Mars* (1929), *The Contemporary and His Soul* (1932), *The Mind of Paul* (1935), *Four Ways to Philosophy* (1937), *Philosopher's Holiday* (1938), etc.

Edmer. See EADMER.

Ed·mund \ˈed-mənd\ *or* **Ead·mund** \ˈa-əd-ˌmu̇nd\. Saint. *Known as* the Martyr. 841?–870. King of East Anglia. According to tradition, b. Nürnberg, son of King Alkmund; succeeded Offa as king (855); as outcome of Danish invasion of 866–870, defeated at Hoxne (870); although tortured to death, refused to abjure faith. Ultimately interred at Bury St. Edmunds.

Edmund. Saint. *Orig.* Edmund Rich \ˈrich\. *Also called* Edmund of Ab·ing·don \ˈab-iŋ-dən\. 1175?–1240. English scholar and ecclesiastic. Studied and taught (c.1194–1200) at Oxford and Paris; reputedly first to teach Aristotelianism at Oxford; again at Oxford (c.1214–22); canon of Salisbury cathedral (1222); preached the Sixth Crusade in England for Pope Gregory IX (1227); named archbishop of Canterbury (1233). Rebuked Henry III for following advice of foreign favorites; won support of barons through general suspicion of Henry's involvement in murder of Richard Marshal, Earl of Pembroke; by threat of excommunication forced Henry to disavow French advisers, accept English law and customs; authority weakened by presence (from 1237) of Cardinal Otho, papal legate requested by Henry; apparently on route to Rome to seek support of Curia, fell ill and died at Solsy, France; canonized (1247).

Edmund *or* **Eadmund I.** *Called* the Deed-doer *and* the Magnificent. 921–946. King of the English. Son of Edward the Elder. Succeeded his half-brother Athelstan (939), with whom he had fought at Brunanburh. Made truce with Olaf Sihtricson by which the five Danish boroughs were protected from raids by Norwegian kings of Northumbria; on breaking of truce drove Olaf from Northumbria (944); entrusted Cumbria to Malcolm I of Scotland as ally (945); stabbed by an exiled robber at Pucklechurch. Succeeded by his brother Eadred.

Edmund *or* **Eadmund II.** *Called* Ironside. c.993–1016. King of the English. Son of Aethelred the Unready. On invasion of Canute (1015), was deserted by Eadric, his brother-in-law, who was incensed by his marriage to the widow of a Danish earl; earned surname for stout resistance to Canute in Northumbria (1015); on death of father (1016) chosen king by Londoners, while Canute was chosen by witan at Southampton; defeated Canute at Pen and Sherston, gaining Wessex; rejoined by Eadric, who possibly by treachery caused rout of English at Assandun (Ashingdon in Essex); by compromise with Canute received south of England (1016), which at his death was also taken by Canute.

Edmund. Earl of Lancaster. *Called* Crouchback. 1245–1296. Second son of Henry III of England. Granted kingdom of Sicily by Pope Alexander IV (1255); grant annulled (1258); created earl of Lancaster (1267); joined brother Edward in crusade (1271–72). Founder of House of Lancaster.

Edmund of Lang·ley \ˈlaŋ-lē\. 1st Duke of York. 1342–1402. Fourth surviving legitimate son of Edward III of England. Took part in several military campaigns in France and Spain (1359–81); named duke of Brittany jointly with John de Montfort (1374); member of council of regency for nephew Richard II (1377); created duke of York (1385); regent during Richard's absences (1394, 1396, 1399); briefly opposed, then submitted to Henry of Lancaster's usurping crown as Henry IV (1399). Founder of House of York as branch of Plantagenet family.

Ed·munds \ˈed-məndz\, George Franklin. 1828–1919. American lawyer and politician, b. Richmond, Vt. U.S. senator from Vermont (1866–91); regarded as authority on constitutional law. Chairman of Senate Judiciary Committee (1872–79, 1881–91); drafted much of Civil Rights Act of 1875; instrumental in passage of act (1877) providing for appointment of federal electoral commission; name attached to act (1882) aimed at suppressing polygamy in the territories; author of greater part of the Sherman Antitrust Act (1890).

Edred. See EADRED.

Edric. See EADRIC.

Edschmid, Kasimir. See Eduard SCHMID.

Ed·ward \ˈed-wərd\ *or* **Ead·ward** \ˈa-əd-ˌwärd\. Name of three pre-Norman kings of the English:

Edward *or* **Eadward** *or* **Ead·weard** \ˈa-əd-ˌwa(-ə)rd\. *Called* the Elder. d. 924. King of the Angles and Saxons. Son of Aelfred (Alfred the Great) whom he succeeded (899); defeated attempt of his cousin Aethelwald, helped by revolting East Anglian Danes, to take the throne (905); won victories (909–911) over invading Danes; took over from Mercia government of London and Oxford on death of his sister Aethelflaed's husband (911); continued to capture and fortify towns of Essex; received submission of East Anglian Danes (917); annexed Mercia on death of Aethelflaed (918); subdued kings of North Welsh (921), and successively Scottish king, Norwegian king of Northumbria, the Strathclyde Welsh.

Edward *or* **Eadward.** *Called* the Martyr. 963?–978. Son of Edgar, whom he succeeded (975). Following counsels of Dunstan, defended church and monasteries against growing antimonastic reaction; assassinated at Corfe Castle, possibly at instigation of his stepmother Aelfthryth, ambitious for her son Aethelred II.

Edward *or* **Eadward.** *Called* the Confessor. 1003?–1066. Last of Anglo-Saxon line. Son of Aethelred II the Unready; cousin of William the Conqueror. Lived in court of his uncle Richard II, Duke of Normandy, during Danish supremacy; developed ecclesiastical interests; took vow of chastity. Recalled by half-brother Hardecanute (1041) and on his death (1042) placed on throne through influence of the Earl Godwin of Wessex, whose daughter Edith he married (1045). Throughout reign, entrusted more of administration of government to foreign favorites of Norman or court party than to the national party of Godwin and his son Harold; rejected the archbishop-elect (one Aelfric, kinsman of Godwin canonically elected) in favor of Robert of Jumièges for archbishop of Canterbury (1051); quarreled with Godwin over latter's refusal to punish Dover; outlawed Godwin and sons (1051); after flight of foreign favorites before rebellion of the outlawed Godwin, became reconciled and restored Godwin and Harold, whose influence (after 1053) was supreme; fell ill and was unable to attend consecration (1065) of the new Westminster Abbey he had founded and in which he was buried; on his deathbed named Harold his successor. Canonized (1161).

Edward. Name of eight post-Norman English (British) kings:

Edward I. 1239–1307. King of England (1272–1307) of the house of Anjou or Plantagenet. Eldest son of Henry III and Eleanor of Provence. Married Eleanor (1254), half-sister of Alfonso X of Léon and Castile. Granted by his father the duchy of Gascony, earldom of Chester, king's lands in Ireland and Wales; waged ineffective campaign against Llewelyn ap Gruffydd of Gwynedd (1255); dispelled unpopularity by supporting barons in insistence upon reform, cooperating with Simon de Montfort in supporting Provisions of Oxford (1258) curbing Henry's power; also supported Provisions of Westminster (1259) favoring tenants of baronial lands. By rashness in pursuit, contributed to his father's defeat at Lewes (1264); held as hostage, but escaped and with Welsh aid defeated and killed Montfort at Evesham (1265). Joined Eighth Crusade (1270). Succeeded to English crown (1272); received homage of Alexander III of Scotland but had to wage war on Llewelyn to obtain his submission (1277). Carried through legislation (1275–90) enacting major administrative reforms, weakening feudalism and establishing the parliamentary system; summoned (1295) a parliament representing the three estates, later called the Model Parliament. Defeated and killed Llewelyn in Radnorshire (1282); assimilated future administration in Wales to English pattern (1284). Banished 16,000 Jews on charge of extortionate usury (1290). On death of Margaret, Maid of Norway (1290), undertook to arbitrate among claimants for Scottish throne; adjudged throne to John de Baliol (1292), who did homage; put down revolt by Scots, exasperated by claim of jurisdiction over Scotland; accepted Baliol's surrender of crown, and carried Coronation Stone of Scone back to England (1296). Turning to recovery of Gascony, temporarily yielded (1293) to Philip IV of France, met opposition of clergy to fresh subsidies and of barons to proposed campaign in Gascony (1297); made truce with France (1299), married Philip's sister Margaret, gaining restitution of Gascony. Turned to conquest of Scotland; captured Stirling Castle (1304); beheaded Wallace (1305); gave Scotland new constitution and representation in English Parliament. Crushed clerical opposition when Pope Clement V allowed him (1306) to suspend Archbishop Robert de Winchelsey. Died en route to Scotland to crush new revolt by Robert Bruce; buried in Westminster Abbey.

Edward II of Caernarvon. 1284–1327. King of England (1307–27), of the house of Anjou or Plantagenet. 4th son of Edward I and Eleanor of Castile; b. Caernarvon, Wales. Created (1301) prince of Wales, first heir apparent to bear the title; took part in Scottish campaigns (1301, 1303, 1304). On accession to throne (1307), abandoned his father's cherished ambition, subjugation of Scotland, and recalled his Gascon favorite, Piers Gaveston, who had been banished by Edward I, and created him earl of Cornwall; m. Isabella, daughter of Philip IV of France (1308). Forced to consent to government of the realm by baronial committee of 21 lords ordainers (1311); required by barons to banish Gaveston, later recalled, captured by barons, and executed (1312); forced to submit to his kinsman, Thomas, Earl of Lancaster, leader of barons. Led army to relief of Stirling, the only Scottish fortress not occupied by Robert Bruce; defeated by Bruce at Bannockburn (1314). With aid of new favorites, the Despensers, and a faction of the opposition under Aymer de Valence, Earl of Pembroke, overthrew Lancaster at Boroughbridge and had him beheaded (1322). Alienated his wife Isabella by favors heaped upon the Despensers; sent Isabella to king of France, her brother, to do homage for Aquitaine and Ponthieu (1325); forced to flee when Isabella, having formed criminal connection with Roger Mortimer, led a force of baronial exiles in invasion (1326), captured Bristol, executed the Despensers; was captured, imprisoned, forced to resign throne (1327); brutally treated in Berkeley Castle and murdered.

Edward III of Windsor. 1312–1377. King of England (1327–77), of the house of Anjou or Plantagenet. Eldest son of Edward II; b. Windsor. Earl of Chester (1320); Duke of Aquitaine (1325); succeeded to throne on deposing of Edward II by Isabella and Roger Mortimer, who governed in his name for four years; made abortive campaign against Scots (1327); by treaty of Northampton recognized independence of Scotland (1328). m. Philippa of Hainaut (1328). Took government into his own hands (1330), executing Mortimer, invaded Scotland and, assisting Edward de Baliol, claimant to throne of David Bruce, defeated Scots at Halidon Hill (1333); twice vainly restored Baliol to throne. Laid claim (1337, previously made, 1328) to crown of France in right of his mother, Isabella, sister of Charles, and became involved in the Hundred Years' War. Declared war against Philip, and made alliance with Emperor Louis the Bavarian; attempted invasions of France from north (1339, 1340); assumed title of king of France (1340), a pretense maintained by English kings until 1801; won brilliant sea victory over French fleet at Sluis (1340); accompanied by his son Edward, the Black Prince, sacked cities of Normandy, won decisive victory at Crécy (1346), effected reduction of Calais (1347); in want of money made truce, returned to England. Held magnificent tournaments and revels; established Order of the Garter (1349). Renewed war on large scale (1355); despite Black Prince's victory at Poitiers (1356), failed in attempt to assume crown of France at Reims (1359) and in attack on Paris; in Treaty of Calais renounced all claim to French crown in exchange for Aquitaine (1360). Conducted "Burned Candlemas" expedition into Scotland (1356); received surrender of Kingdom of Scotland from Baliol (1356). Passed antipapal and anticlerical legislation, repudiated feudal claims of papacy growing out of King John's submission and promise of tribute thirty years earlier, and forbade payment of Peter's pence (1366). Reign troubled by epidemics of Black Death (1348–49, 1361, 1369). In a second war with France following Charles V's repudiation of Treaty of Calais (1369), lost Aquitaine, lost command of the sea, made truce (1375) retaining little except four posts in France. With public finances ruined and Parliament recalcitrant, gave himself into hands of a greedy mistress, Alice Perrers, letting her and his son, John of Gaunt, dominate the government. Credited with enlightened commercial policy, introduced Flemish weavers to England; devoted himself to naval administration. Father of: Edward, the Black Prince, Lionel of Antwerp (Duke of Clarence), John of Gaunt, Edmund of Langley, and Thomas of Woodstock. Succeeded by his grandson Richard II.

Edward IV. 1442–1483. King of England (1461–70, 1471–83), of the house of York. Son of Richard, Duke of York, and Cecily, daughter of Ralph Neville, 1st Earl of Westmorland; b. Rouen. Driven from England and attainted by Lancastrian king Henry VI, at Ludlow field (1459); with his uncle and cousin, the Nevilles, invaded England, defeated Lancastrians at Northampton (1460); after his father's defeat and death at Wakefield, defeated Lancastrians at Mortimer's Cross (1461), proclaimed himself king, clinched the throne by victory at Towton, and was crowned (1461). Guided by the Nevilles, crushed resistance of Lancastrian queen Margaret, in the north; by privately marrying (1464) Elizabeth, daughter of Richard Woodville, lost his early popularity and offended cousin Richard Neville, Earl of Warwick, who had projected a match with French princess; thwarted Warwick's proposed alliance with France by alliance with Burgundy (1467); by heaping honors on the Woodvilles, provoked Warwick and his own brother George, Duke of Clarence, to unite with Queen Margaret and Lancastrian exiles in driving him from the throne and elevating the helpless Henry VI (1470). Furnished with money by his brother-in-law, Charles of Burgundy, landed with his brother Richard, Duke of Gloucester, at Ravenspur, was rejoined by Duke of Clarence, defeated and slew Warwick at Barnet (1471), captured Queen Margaret at Tewkesbury, and caused murder of her son Prince Edward and probably murder of Henry VI in Tower (1471); reestablished York dynasty (1471); settled rivalry between his brothers for share in Neville estates by judicial murder of Clarence in the Tower (1478). Mounted huge invasion of France (1475), but deserted his ally the Duke of Burgundy in return for an annual subsidy from Louis XI and stipulated marriage of his daughter to the dauphin, secured by treaty of Picquigny (1475); relieved by this subsidy from necessity of heavy taxation and responsibility to Parliament, built up autocratic rule preparing way for absolute monarchy of the Tudors. Patron of the new culture in England; his reign saw introduction of printing and silk manufacture; built up trade and greatly improved public administration. His brother Richard, Duke of Gloucester, deposed his son Edward V and became king as Richard III.

Edward V. 1470–1483. King of England (April–June 1483), of the house of York. Eldest son of Edward IV and Elizabeth Woodville. Created prince of Wales (1471). Seized from his maternal uncle, Earl Rivers, by his paternal uncle Richard, Duke of Gloucester, who had become protector of the realm on death of Edward IV; brought to London, lodged in Tower, along with his brother, the young Duke of York (1483); deposed by an assembly of lords and commons under direction of Gloucester on ground of illegitimacy because of Edward IV's betrothal to lady Eleanor Butler previous to his marriage to Elizabeth Woodville. Generally held to have been murdered, with York, in Tower, probably by command of Gloucester, who had assumed the crown as Richard III.

Edward VI. 1537–1553. King of England and Ireland (1547–53), of the house of Tudor. Only child of Henry VIII by his third wife, Jane Seymour, and his only legitimate son. Succeeded to throne and headship of the church (1547) under regency of his uncle Edward Seymour, Duke of Somerset, who set up project to marry him to Mary, Queen of Scots, as pretext for invading Scotland (1549). Consented (1552) to execution of Somerset on charges of overambition made by John Dudley, Duke of Northumberland, who assumed complete dominion over him and induced him to sign a will excluding his half-sisters Mary and Elizabeth and devising the succession to Lady Jane Grey, to whom Northumberland had married his own son.

Edward VII. *Christened* Albert Edward. 1841–1910. King of Great Britain and Ireland (1901–10), of house of Saxe-Coburg. Eldest son of Queen Victoria; created prince of Wales (1841). Studied at Edinburgh, Oxford, and Cambridge; colonel in army (1858). Paid first visit by a royal prince to a British colony (Canada, 1860); privy councilor and took seat in House of Lords as duke of Cornwall (1863). m. (1863) Alexandra, eldest daughter of Christian IX of Denmark. Created sensation and gave rise to scandalous insinuations on appearing as witness in a divorce suit (1870); known for interest in theater, horse racing, sport; headed many public commissions and institutions; set high standards of dress and deportment; opened International Exhibition at South Kensington (1871); paid official visits to India (1875–76), Ireland (1885); strictly excluded from government by Queen Victoria because of his indiscretion, reluctantly allowed to share in official intelligence in Gladstone's last ministry (1892–94). Carried responsibility for large part of arrangements of queen's jubilees (1887, 1897). Succeeded to throne on death (1901) of Queen Victoria. Instituted Order of Merit (1902); promoted international amity by visits to European capitals (1903–04), and prepared way for treaties of arbitration and Anglo-French and Anglo-Russian ententes; visited Berlin (1909) to dispel suspicions of Anglo-German rivalry. Brought crown into active participation in public life and into touch with all sections of the empire.

Edward VIII. *Full name* Edward Albert Christian George Andrew Patrick David. *After abdication, known as* Duke of Wind·sor \'win-zər\. 1894–1972. King of Great Britain and Ireland (1936) of the house of Windsor. Eldest son of George V and Queen Mary. Created prince of Wales and earl of Chester (1911); at investiture in Caernarvon Castle was first English prince to address Welsh in their own tongue; in World War I served as staff officer in France, Egypt, Italy. Taking up public duties, toured Canada, visited U.S. (1919); paid state visits to Australia and West Indies (1920), India (1921–22), South Africa and South America (1925). Succeeded his father (Jan. 1936), first bachelor king in 176 years; raised storm of official protest by his proposal to marry and elevate as queen Mrs. Wallis Simpson, *nee* Warfield, an American whose second divorce was pending; met by unyielding opposition of his ministers, chose to abdicate (Dec. 1936); created duke of Windsor by his brother and successor, George VI. m. Mrs. Simpson (1937); governor of the Bahama Islands (1940–45); lived thereafter mainly in France.

Edward. Prince of Wales. *Known as* the Black Prince; *called sometimes* Edward IV *or* Edward of Wood·stock \'wůd-ˌstäk\. 1330–1376. Eldest son of Edward III. Created earl of Chester (1333), duke of Cornwall, first duke created in England (1337), prince of Wales (1343). Began career with Edward III's Norman campaign (1346); commanded right wing at Crécy; at siege of Calais and on Calais expedition (1349); one of original Knights of the Garter. As lieutenant in Gascony, led foray through Armagnac and Languedoc and plundered Narbonne (1355); on marauding expedition (1356), routed French and took King John II prisoner at Poitiers; had share in negotiating Treaty of Brétigny (1360). m. (1361) Joan, Fair Maid of Kent. As prince of Aquitaine and Gascony received all English lands in southern France from his father (1362); won favor of towns by fostering trade but was looked on with suspicion by nobles; after peace of six years, restored Peter the Cruel to throne of Castile by expedition into Spain and victory at Nájera (1367). Needing funds badly, obtained hearth tax for five years, which was made pretext by barons for revolt (1368) that spread throughout Aquitaine; captured Limoges and massacred defenders (1370); stricken with mortal disease contracted in Spain, returned to England (1371); resigned his principality in Aquitaine and Gascony (1372).

Edward. Prince of Wales. 1453–1471. Only son of Henry VI. Created prince of Wales (1454); carried for safety by Queen Margaret to Scotland, thence to France and Lorraine, during strife with Yorkists (1461–70). After his father's restoration by Earl of Warwick and Duke of Clarence (1470) returned to England, but was defeated at Tewkesbury and killed by Edward IV.

Edward. *Port.* Duarte. 1391–1438. King of Portugal (1433–38). Son of John I and father of Afonso V. Reformed royal land-grant laws; supported work of his brother, Prince Henry the Navigator; led unsuccessful expedition against Tangier (1437); wrote two prose works: *O Leal conselheiro* ("The Loyal Councilor") and a book of instruction in horsemanship.

Edward. *Known as* Edward of Norwich; *sometimes called* Edward Plantagenet. 2d Duke of York. c.1373–1415. Son of Edmund of Langley, 1st Duke, whom he succeeded (1402). Made admiral of the fleet (1391–98) by Richard II; granted lands and title duke of Albemarle (1398); apparently joined usurping Lancastrians (1399) and after mild persecution enjoyed preferments from Henry IV; briefly imprisoned for part in kidnap of Mortimers (1405); commanded Henry V's right wing at Agincourt, where he was killed (1415).

Edward. Earl of Warwick. 1475–1499. Son of George, Duke of Clarence. After death of father (1478) reared by aunt, Anne, Duchess of Gloucester, wife of Richard, later Richard III. Shut up in Tower by Henry VII (1485); exhibited for one day (1487) to end rumors of his escape, bolstered by impersonation of him by and crowning of Lambert Simnel in Ireland; remained in Tower until execution on false charge of conspiracy with Perkin Warbeck.

Edward Augustus. Duke of Kent and Strath·earn \strath-'ərn\. 1767–1820. 4th son of George III of England. Soldier; commanded Royal Fusiliers,

Gibraltar (1790); major general (1793); took part in capture of Martinique and St. Lucia (1794); created duke of Kent and Strathearn, earl of Dublin (1799); general (1799); commander of British forces in North America (1799–1800); governor of Gibraltar (1802–03); field marshal (1805). m. (1818) Princess Mary Louisa Victoria of Saxe-Coburg-Gotha; father of Queen Victoria. Prince Edward Island (formerly Île Saint-Jean) renamed in his honor (1799).

Ed·wardes \'ed-wərdz\, George. 1852–1915. British theater manager. Business manager of Savoy Theatre (1881–85); co-manager (1885–86), manager (1886–93) of Gaiety Theatre; built (1893) and managed Augustin Daly's London theater; known as inventor and developer of modern musical comedy, beginning with *A Gaiety Girl* (1893).

Edwardes, Sir Herbert Benjamin. 1819–1868. British soldier and official in India. Entered army of East India Co. (1840); aide-de-camp to Gen. Sir Hugh Gough in India through Sikh war. As commissioner of Peshawar (1853–59), during Sepoy Mutiny effected reconciliation with amir of Afghanistan and raised mixed force for use against mutineers at Delhi; commissioner of Ambala (1862); major general (1868).

Ed·wards \'ed-wərdz\, Agustín. 1878–1941. Chilean banker and diplomat. Vice president of Chile (1901–02); minister for foreign affairs (1903, 1905, 1909, 1910); minister to Italy, Spain, and Switzerland (1905–06) and to Great Britain (1910–25); ambassador to Great Britain (1935–38). President, League of Nations Assembly (1922), and of 5th Pan-American conference (1923).

Edwards, Alfred George. 1848–1937. Welsh prelate. Bishop of St. Asaph (1889–1934); first archbishop of Wales (1920–34). Author of books on Welsh church history.

Edwards, Amelia Ann Blandford. 1831–1892. English novelist and Egyptologist. Among her novels were *My Brother's Wife* (1855), *Debenham's Vow* (1870), *Lord Brackenbury* (1880); on Egypt wrote *A Thousand Miles Up the Nile* (1877), *Pharaohs, Fellahs, and Explorers* (1891); helped found Egyptian Exploration Fund (1882).

Edwards, George. 1693–1773. English naturalist. Author of *A History of Birds* (1743–51), the supplementary *Gleanings of Natural History* (1758–64), and *Elements of Fossilology* (1776).

Edwards, Henry Thomas. 1837–1884. Welsh clergyman. Brother of Alfred G. Edwards. Vicar of Caernarvon (1870–76); dean of Bangor (1876–84); leader of movement to separate Church of Wales from that of England; promoted education of Welsh-speaking clergy.

Edwards, John. 1748–1837. American planter, b. Stafford Co., Va. To Kentucky district (1780); prominent in activities leading to Kentucky's becoming a state; one of Kentucky's first two U.S. senators (1792–95). His nephew ¶Ninian Edwards (1775–1833) was chief justice, Kentucky court of appeals (1807); governor of Illinois Territory (1809–18); U.S. senator from Illinois (1818–24); governor of Illinois (1826–30). Ninian's son ¶Ninian Wirt (1809–1889) was first superintendent of public instruction in Illinois (1854–57); secured passage (1855) of law that laid foundation of state's school system; friend of Lincoln; at his house Lincoln first met (1839) Mary Todd, sister of Edward's wife, and in his house they were married.

Edwards, Jonathan. 1703–1758. American Congregational clergyman and theologian, b. East Windsor, Conn. Became colleague and (1729) successor of his grandfather Solomon Stoddard in Northampton, Mass., pastorate; accepted central Calvinistic doctrines of absolute divine sovereignty and predestined eternal salvation or damnation, and ardently opposed Arminian theology; became widely known as powerful preacher. Led a revival (1734–35) that spread through the Connecticut River valley; turned in his sermons to theme of Christian love, as in the series *Charity and Its Fruits* (1738; pub. 1751). Published *A Faithful Narrative of the Surprising Work of God in the Conversion of Many Hundred Souls in Northampton, and the Neighboring Towns and Villages* (1737), which prepared way for "Great Awakening," revivalist response to tour of George Whitefield (1740–42). In defense of revivalism published *Distinguishing Marks of a Work of the Spirit of God* (1741), *Treatise Concerning Religious Affections* (1746). Dismissed (1750) after long dispute with his congregation over his rejection of Halfway Covenant. Accepted (1751) pastorate, as missionary to the Indians, at Stockbridge, Mass., where he wrote and published *Careful and Strict Inquiry into the Modern Prevailing Notions of that Freedom of the Will* (1754); wrote *Great Christian Doctrine of Original Sin Defended* (1758), *Nature of True Virtue* (1765). President (1757–58) of the College of New Jersey (now Princeton U.). Considered the greatest theologian of American Puritanism.

Edwards, Lewis. 1809–1887. Welsh clergyman and educator. Cofounder and principal (1837–87) of Bala Calvinistic Methodist Coll., which became (1867) the theological college of Calvinistic Methodist Church of Wales; lecturer on classics, ethics, metaphysics, and theology; founded periodicals *Yr Esboniwr* (1844), *Y Traethodydd* (1845).

Edwards, Milne. See MILNE-EDWARDS.

Edwards, Ninian and Ninian Wirt. See under John EDWARDS.

Edwards, Sir Owen Morgan. 1858–1920. Welsh writer and educator. Taught history at Oxford (1889–1907); M.P. (1899–1900); founded and edited Welsh nationalist periodicals *Cymru* (1891), *Cymru'r Plant* (1892), *Y Llenor* (1895); published reprints from Welsh literature that helped revive interest in the language; author of *O'r Bala i Geneva* (1889), *Wales* (1901), etc.; chief inspector of Welsh education (1907–20).

Edwards, Richard. 1524–1566. English playwright and composer. Appointed gentleman and master of the children of Chapel Royal (1561). Author of *Palamon and Arcyte,* performed before Queen Elizabeth (1566), and one extant play, *Damon and Pithias* (1564); composed many songs for plays and helped popularize madrigal form.

Edwards, Thomas Charles. 1837–1900. Welsh clergyman and educator. Son of Lewis Edwards. First principal of University College of Wales (1872–91); principal at Bala Calvinistic Methodist College (1891–1900); author of sermons, biblical commentaries.

Edwards, William. 1719–1789. Welsh clergyman and architect. Known for building (1754) Pontypridd Bridge over River Taff, reputed the most beautiful and longest single span bridge of the time.

Ed·wards Bel·lo \āt͟h-'wärt͟hz-'bā(l)-yō\, Joaquín. 1888–1968. Chilean journalist and novelist. Editor of *La nación* (from 1920); author of realistic novels of urban life of poor, including *La cuna de Esmeraldo* (1918), *El roto* (1920), *El chileno de Madrid* (1928), *Criollos en París* (1933), *En el viejo almendral* (1943).

Ed·win \'ed-wən\ *or* **Ead·wi·ne** \'a-əd-'win-ə\. *Lat.* Ae·du·i·nus \ˌēd-yə-'wī-nəs, ˌed-\. 585?–633. King of Northumbria. Son of Aella, King of Deira (559–588). Expelled by Aethelfrith of Bernicia; with help of Raedwald, king of East Anglia, defeated Aethelfrith (616) and formed a united Northumbria extending as far north as Edinburgh; m. (625) Aethelburh, sister of Eadbald of Kent; converted to Christianity by Paulinus, whom he made archbishop of York (627); defeated and slain by Calwallon of North Wales and Penda of Mercia.

Edwy. See EADWIG.

Eeck·hout \'āk-ˌhau̇t\, Gerbrand van den. 1621–1674. Dutch painter. Pupil and imitator of Rembrandt (1635–40); known esp. for genre, biblical paintings, portraits.

Ee·den \'ād-ən\, Frederik Willem van. 1860–1932. Dutch writer and neurologist. Cofounder of the organ of the younger group of writers *De nieuwe gids* (1885); social theorist; founded Walden, agricultural community inspired by Thoreau (1898); author of *De kleine Johannes* (1885), *Het lied van schijn en wezen* (1895), *Van de koele meren des doods* (1900), etc.

Eek·houd \'āk-ˌhau̇t\, Georges. 1854–1927. Belgian novelist and poet. Cofounder of literary journal *La Jeune Belgique* (1881); author of collections of romantic poems, and of realistic and historical novels and short stories of Flemish life, including *Kermesses* (1884), *Nouvelles Kermesses* (1887), *La nouvelle Carthage* (1888).

Ef·fen \'ef-ən\, Justus van. 1684–1735. Dutch writer. Published and edited *Le spectateur français* (1725), *De hollandsche spectator* (1731–35); known for essays on subjects from everyday life.

Effiat, Marquis d'. See Antoine COEFFIER-RUZÉ.

Effingham, Earl of. See Kenneth Alexander Howard, under HOWARD family.

Ef·imo·va \yif-'yēm-əv-ə\, Nina. 1877–1948. Russian puppeteer. Began puppet work (1916); leader of 20th century revival of Russian puppet theater; invented hand-and-rod puppet.

Égalité, Philippe-. See ORLÉANS, IV.

Egan \'ē-gən\, Pierce. 1772–1849. English sportswriter. Wrote *The Mistress of Royalty* (1814), concerning the prince regent and Mary Robinson; author of *Boxiana, or Sketches of Modern Pugilism* (1818–24), *Life in London* (1821), *Book of Sports* (1832); provided slang phrases for Grose's *Dictionary of the Vulgar Tongue* (1823). His son ¶Pierce (1814–1880) executed etchings for his father's *The Pilgrims of the Thames* (1837), and wrote many novels, mostly in serial form, including *Wat Tyler* (1841), *Clifton Grey* (1854–55), *The Waits* (1857), *Love Me, Leave Me Not* (1859–60), *The Poor Girl* (1862–63), and *Eve, or the Angel of Innocence* (1867).

Ega·ña \ā-'gän-yä\, Juan. 1769–1836. Chilean politician and writer. A leader of Chilean revolution (1810); member of governing junta (1813); exiled (1814); helped write constitution (1823); president, constituent congress of Chile (1823). His works included poems, plays, educational textbooks, and essays.

Egas Mo·niz \ā-gäs-'mō-nēzh\, António Caetano de Abreu Frei·re \-dā-'ä-breü-'frā-rā\. 1874–1955. Portuguese neurologist. Professor, Coimbra (1902–11), Lisbon (1911–44); developed (1927–37) cerebral angiography; investigated severe psychoses; developed prefrontal leucotomy as radical treatment (first performed on human, 1936); awarded Nobel prize for physiology or medicine (with Walter Hess, 1949). Deputy in Portuguese parliament (1903–17); Portuguese minister at Madrid (1917–18); foreign minister (1918); headed Portuguese delegation to Paris Peace Conference (1918–19).

Eg·bert \'eg-bərt\ *or* **Ecg·berht** \'ej-ˌberkt\ *or* **Ecg·bryht** \'ej-brækt\. d. 839. King of West Saxons (802–839). Son of an underking of Kent, whose ancestors were early kings of Wessex. Forced into exile by Offa of Mercia and his son-in-law, spent youth at court of Charlemagne; became king (802), regained kingdom of Kent (825), conquered Cornish, gained submission of Mercia (828), was recognized as Bretwalda; first to bring all English peoples under one overlord; lost Mercia to Wiglaf (830); repelled Scandinavian invasion by victory at Hingston Down (837).

Eg·bert \'ek-ˌbert\. d. 993. German prelate. Chancellor under Otto II (976 or 977); archbishop of Trier (from 977); fostered development of Trier as center of book making, gold and enamel work.

Ege·de \'ā-gə-də\, Hans. 1686–1758. Norwegian missionary. First missionary to Eskimos of Danish Greenland (1721–36); to Copenhagen (1736), where he founded a seminary for training missionaries to Greenland, and became superintendent of Greenland mission (1740); published first book in Eskimo language (1742). His son ¶Paul (1708–1789) succeeded him in the Greenland mission, and as director of the seminary; translated New Testament into Eskimo language (1766).

Eg·er·ton \'ej-ərt-ən, -ər-tən\. Name of English family including earls and dukes of Bridgewater, earls of Ellesmere, and their descendants, among them the following: Sir Thomas Egerton (1540?–1617), Baron Elles·mere \'elz-ˌmi(ə)r\ and Viscount Brack·ley \'brak-lē\; statesman and judge; solicitor general (1581); M. P. (1584, 1586); friend of Francis Bacon and Essex; took a leading role in trial of Mary, Queen of Scots (1586); attorney general (1592–94); master of the rolls (1594–1603); lord keeper (1596–1617); adjured Essex to desist from rebellion (1601); lord chancellor (1603–17); gained victory for chancellor's court of equity over Sir Edward Coke, proponent of the common law (1616). His son ¶John (1579–1649), created (1617) 1st Earl of Bridge·wa·ter \'brij-ˌwôt-ər, -ˌwät-\; M. P. (1601); privy councilor (1626); his induction as lord lieutenant of Wales occasion for which Milton's *Comus* was written and first acted at Ludlow Castle (1634), with earl's son ¶John (1622–1686), 2nd earl, as the elder brother. ¶John (1646–1701), 3rd earl; son of 2d earl; first lord of the admiralty (1699); lord justice of the kingdom (1699). ¶Francis (1736–1803), 3d Duke of Bridgewater; pioneer in British inland navigation; employed James Brindley to construct first canal in England entirely independent of a natural stream (1760), from Worsley to Manchester for transport of coal from his collieries; subsequently built Manchester–Liverpool canal (opened 1772). ¶Francis Henry (1756–1829), 8th earl; clergyman and antiquarian; son and grandson of bishops; left £8000 for best work on "Goodness of God as manifested in the Creation," which was allotted eventually to authors of eight separate treatises (Bridgewater Treatises). ¶Francis (1800–1857), 1st Earl of Ellesmere (cr. 1846) and Viscount Brackley; *orig. surname* Leveson-Gower; 2d son of George Granville Leveson-Gower (*q.v.*), 1st Duke of Sutherland; hence, grandnephew of 3d Duke of Bridgewater and second beneficiary of Bridgewater estates; M. P. (1822–46); Irish secretary (1828–30); secretary for war (1830); took name Egerton (1833); author of graceful poems; translator of *Faust* (1823); munificent patron of artists, adding to Bridgewater galleries.

Egestorff, Georg. See Georg von OMPTEDA.

Egfrith. See ECGFRITH.

Egg \'eg\, Augustus Leopold. 1816–1863. English painter. Known for genre works and pictures based on Shakespeare, Scott, Thackeray, etc.; actor in Dickens's company of amateurs.

Eg·ge \'äg-gə\, Peter. 1869–1959. Norwegian writer. Author of realistic novels, including *Almue* (1891), *Gammelholm* (1899), *Hjaertet* (1907), *Hansine Solstad* (1925), *Drømmen* (1927); and plays, including *Idyllen* (1910), *Felen* (1912), *Narren* (1917).

Eg·gen·berg \'eg-ən-ˌberk\, Johann Ulrich von. Fürst. 1568–1634. Austrian statesman. Chancellor to Emperor Ferdinand II, and director of imperial policy during earlier part of Thirty Years' War.

Eg·gle·ston \'eg-əl-stən\, Edward. 1837–1902. American author, b. Vevay, Ind. Bible agent and Methodist pastor in Minnesota (1858–66); editor of *Little Corporal* (1866–67), *National Sunday School Teacher* (1867–73), *Hearth and Home* (1871–72); author of novels, including the regional classic *The Hoosier Schoolmaster* (1871) and *The End of the World* (1872), *The Circuit Rider* (1874), *Roxy* (1878), *The Hoosier Schoolboy* (1881–82), *The Graysons* (1888), *The Faith Doctor* (1891), short stories, and histories. His brother ¶George Cary (1839–1911), b. Vevay, Ind., was a journalist and novelist; author of: boys' books: Big Brother Series (1875–82), *Strange Stories from History* (1886); novels: *A Man of Honor* (1873), *Dorothy South* (1902), *The Master of Warlock* (1903), *Evelyn Byrd* (1904); *A Rebel's Recollections* (1874), *Recollections of a Varied Life* (1910), *The History of the Confederate War* (1910).

Egidio. See Gil ALBORNOZ.

Egill Skall·a·gríms·son \'ā-gid-əl-'skäd-əl-ä-'grēms-sôn\. c.910–990. Icelandic skald and adventurer. Forced to emigrate after Harold Fairhair's victory; fought in service of English king Aethelstan (925 ff.); returned to Norway and sought revenge by killing son of Eric Bloodaxe, successor to Harold (934); taken prisoner, but regained liberty by "Höfudlausn," poem in praise of the king. Author of the sagas "Sonatorrek," on the death of his sons, "Arinbjarnardrápa" and "Skjaldardrápa." His experiences are described in the Icelandic poem *Egils saga*.

Egils·son \'ā-gils-sôn\, Sveinbjörn. 1791–1852. Icelandic philologist and poet. Compiler of the dictionary of Norse poetry *Lexicon poeticum antiquae linguae septentrionalis* (1854–60); translated Homer into Icelandic (1829–55).

Eginhard. See EINHARD.

Eg·lev·sky \ig-'lyef-skəi\, André Yevgenyevich. 1917–1977. American dancer, b. Moscow, Russia. Danced with Ballet Russe de Monte Carlo (1931–35), American Ballet (1937–38), Ballet Theatre (1942–43, 1945), New York City Ballet (1951–58); naturalized American citizen (1939); opened dance school at Massapequa, N.Y. (1958); created roles in ballets by Balanchine, Fokine; considered greatest male classical dancer of his time, noted esp. for noble bearing, technical virtuosity.

Eg·loff \'eg-ˌlôf\, Gustav. 1886–1955. American chemist, b. New York City. Director of research, Universal Oil Products Co. (1917–55); holder of over 800 patents in petroleum chemistry, including multiple-coil process for cracking crude oil, a way of making rubber from butane gas.

Eg·ly \'eg-lē\, Henry. 1824–1890. American Mennonite leader, b. Baden, Germany. To U.S. (1837); ordained Amish-Mennonite minister (1854) and bishop (1858). Withdrew and formed (c.1865) a church known as the "Defenseless Mennonites."

Eg·mond \'ek-mônd\ *or* **Eg·mont** \'ek-mônt\. Name of family prominent in history of the Netherlands during the 15th and 16th centuries, including: John II (1385–1451), created count and prince of the empire (1424) by Emperor Sigismond. His grandson ¶John III (1438–1516), stadholder of Holland, Zeeland, Frisia. His son ¶John IV (d. 1528) was father of Lamoraal van Egmond (*q.v.*). ¶Charles (1467–1538), Duke of Guel·dre \'geldrə\; spent life trying to regain duchy of Gueldre that had been lost to Charles the Bold of Burgundy; at first, leagued with France; later (1537), forced to yield to Emperor Charles V.

Egmond *or* **Egmont,** Lamoraal van. Graaf. Prince of Gavre \gåvrə\. 1522–1568. Flemish general and statesman. Son of John IV of Egmond. Conducted negotiations (1554) for marriage of Philip of Spain with Mary Tudor; served brilliantly in war between Spain and France (1557–59), esp. at battles of St. Quentin and Gravelines. Stadholder of Flanders and Artois (1559–67); member of council of state (1559–65); joined William of Orange in protests to Spain (1561–64); on special mission to Spain (1565) to inform Philip of affairs in Netherlands. Refused to join Orange and other nobles in plans to overthrow Spanish regime; nonetheless arrested by Duke of Alba and condemned to death (1567) by Council of Blood; with Count Horn, executed at Brussels, their deaths leading to revolt of Netherlands; event made theme of Goethe's drama *Egmont* (1788).

Egmont, Earls of. See PERCEVAL.

Eh·ren·berg \'ā-rən-ˌberk\, Christian Gottfried. 1795–1876. German naturalist. Professor at Berlin (1839–76); took part in expeditions to Near East (1820–25), with Humboldt to Asia (1829); made large collection of plants, animals, fossils; demonstrated sexual reproduction in fungi (1819, 1821); studied esp. coral polyps, infusoria, plankton; laid foundation of study of fossil microorganisms; author of *Reisen in Aegypten, Libyen, Nubien und Dongola* (1828), *Die Korallentiere des Roten Meeres* (1834), *Die Infusionsthierchen als vollkommene Organismen* (1838), *Mikrogeologie* (1854).

Eh·ren·burg \'ā-rin-bürk\, Ilya Grigoryevich. 1891–1967. Russian writer. Arrested (1908) for revolutionary activities; escaped to Paris; returned to Russia (1917) after Bolshevik revolution, but later resided in Paris (1921–24); later again in Europe as Soviet journalist; published poems, stories, and novels including *Julio Jurenito* (1921), *Padenie Parizha* (Fall of Paris, 1941), *Burya* (The Storm, 1948), *Devyaty val* (Ninth Wave, 1951).

Ehrencron-Kidde, Astrid. See under Harald KIDDE.

Eh·ren·fels \'ā-rən-ˌfels\, Christian von. Freiherr. 1859–1932. German philosopher. Professor at Prague (1900–29); introduced the term *Gestalt* into psychology (1890); chief work, *System der Werttheorie* (1897–98).

Eh·ren·svärd \'er-əns-verd\. Name of a Swedish family of German origin including: Count Augustin Ehrensvärd (1710–1772), field marshal and military engineer; built fortifications of Sveaborg (1749) and created Swedish coast fleet (1756); commanded briefly in Seven Years' War (1761–62). His son ¶Count Carl August (1745–1800), admiral and art critic; commanded in 1st naval battle of Russian war at Svensksund (1789) and was dismissed following defeat; chief commander of navy (1792–94) following death of Gustav III; resigned to devote life to science and the arts; author of *Philosophie des beaux-arts*

(1787). Augustin's grandson ¶Count Albert Carl August Lars (1821–1901), statesman, champion of free trade and liberalism; foreign minister (1885–89).

Ehr·hard \'ār-,härt\, Albert. 1862–1940. German Roman Catholic theologian. Professor at Würzburg (1892), Vienna (1898), Strassburg (1903), Bonn (1920); author of *Liberaler Katholizismus?* (1902), *Das Mittelalter und seine kirchliche Entwicklung* (1908), etc.

Eh·ricke \'ār-ik\, Krafft A. 1917–1984. American aeronautical engineer and physicist, b. Berlin. Leading rocket specialist who during World War II served as propulsion engineer in Germany's V-2 rocket program. Worked (1947–52) for U.S. Army's missile program; designed and developed Atlas rocket (first U.S. intercontinental ballistic missile) and Centaur (first rocket propelled by liquid hydrogen). Chief scientific adviser to space division of Rockwell International Corp.

Ehr·lich \'ār-,lik\, Eugen. 1862–1922. Austrian legal scholar. Taught at Vienna, Czernowitz (1899–1914); considered founder of sociology of law; author of *Grundlegung der Soziologie des Rechts* (1913).

Ehr·lich \'ār-lik\, Paul. 1854–1915. German chemist and bacteriologist. Conducted researches in histology of the blood that established hematology as a field; developed stains for microscopic studies; proposed the side-chain theory as a chemical explanation of immunity; worked with Emil von Behring on standardization of diphtheria antitoxin; pioneered in chemotherapy; discovered "606" (Salvarsan, or arsphenamine), a remedy for syphilis, yaws, etc. (1909). Awarded, with E. Metchnikoff, 1908 Nobel prize for physiology or medicine.

Ei·chel·ber·ger \'ī-kəl-,bər-gər\, Robert Lawrence. 1886–1961. American soldier, b. Urbana, Ohio. Served in Siberian expedition (1918–19); superintendent at West Point (1940–42); commanded I Corps in New Guinea and New Britain (1942–44); commanded Eighth Army in Philippines (1944–45); developed amphibious tactics; began occupation of Japan (1945).

Ei·chen·dorff \'ī-kən-,dȯrf\, Joseph von. Freiherr. 1788–1857. German poet, novelist, and critic. Served in Prussian army (1813–16); in government service (1816–44). Closely associated with German Romantics; author of lyric poetry published in *Gedichte* (1837) and later collections; epic poetry as *Robert und Guiscard* (1855); novels and other prose works, including *Ahnung und Gegenwart* (1815), *Novellen des Marmorbilds* (1819), *Aus dem Leben eines Taugenichts* (1826), *Der letzte Held von Marienburg* (1830), *Eine Meerfahrt* (1835), *Das Schloss Dürande* (1836), *Die Glückritter* (1841); literary criticism and history, esp. *Geschichte der poetischen Literatur Deutschlands* (1857).

Eich·horn \'ik-,hȯrn\, Hermann von. 1848–1918. German soldier. Took part in campaigns of 1860, 1870–71; inspector general of 7th army (1913); commander of 10th army (1915–16), with which he fought in battle of Masurian lakes (1915) and took Kovno, Grodno, Olita; commanded "Eichhorn," later known as "Kiev," army group (1916–18); general field marshal (1917); commander in chief of German forces on eastern front (1917–18).

Eichhorn, Johann Gottfried. 1752–1827. German Protestant theologian, Orientalist, and historian. Professor at Jena (1775), Göttingen (1788); pioneer in scientific study of biblical literature, sources; author of *Historisch-kritisch Einleitung ins Alte Testament* (1780–83), *Einleitung in das Neue Testament* (1804–12). His son ¶Karl Friedrich (1781–1854) was a jurist, founder of the historical school of German law.

Eich·ler \'ik-lər\, August Wilhelm. 1839–1887. German botanist. Assistant and successor to Karl von Martius in editing *Flora Brasiliensis;* professor at Kiel (1872), Berlin (1878); author of *Blütendiagramme* (1875–78); developed system of classification of plants; known for descriptions of Brazilian plants and for comparative studies of the structure of flowers.

Eich·mann \'ik-,män\, Karl Adolf. 1906–1962. German Nazi leader. Officer of SS; an architect of Jewish extermination program; escaped to Argentina (1945); captured (1960), convicted, and executed in Israel for war crimes.

Eich·rodt \'ik-,rōt\, Ludwig. *Pseudonym* Rudolf Rodt \'rōt\. 1827–1892. German humorous poet. Author, with A. Kussmaul, of satirical works of "Gottlieb Biedermaier," published in *Fliegenden Blättern* (1855–57); term "Biedermeier" style derived from that character.

Eichstätt, Prince of. See Eugène de BEAUHARNAIS.

Ei·el·sen \'ī-əl-sən\, Elling. 1804–1883. American religious leader, b. Voss, Norway. To U.S. (1839); settled at Fox River, Ill. Preached at new settlements in northern Middle West and Texas; organized (1846) the Norwegian Evangelical Lutheran Church of America.

Ei·er·mann \'ī-ər-,män\, Egon. 1904–1970. German architect. Works noted for structural clarity, detailing, elegant proportions and included Blumberg textile mill (1951), West German pavilion at Brussels World Exhibition (1958), Kaiser Wilhelm Memorial Church, Berlin (1956–63), West German embassy, Washington, D.C. (1958–64).

Eif·fel \e-fel, *Angl* 'ī-fəl\, Alexandre-Gustave. 1832–1923. French engineer. Constructed iron bridge over the Garonne (1858), the railway bridge over the Douro at Oporto (1877), the Garabit viaduct (1882), etc.; also, the framework for Bartholdi's Statue of Liberty and the Eiffel tower in Paris (1887–89) for which he is chiefly known. Founded first laboratory of aerodynamics, at Auteuil (1912); investigated effects of air currents on airplanes.

Eijk·man \'īk-,män\, Christiaan. 1858–1930. Dutch physician and pathologist. To Dutch East Indies to investigate beriberi (1886); director of pathological laboratory in Batavia (1888–96); first person to produce a dietary deficiency disease experimentally (1897) when by feeding fowl a diet consisting exclusively of polished rice, he produced a disease resembling beriberi in human beings; recognized that the disease was caused by lack of essential food factor (later shown to be vitamin B_1). Professor at Utrecht (1898–1928). Awarded, with Sir F. G. Hopkins, 1929 Nobel prize for physiology or medicine.

Ei·ke von Rep·gau \'ī-kə-fȯn-'rep-,gau̇\ *or* **Rep·gow** \-,gō\ *or* **Rep·e·gouw** \'rep-ə-,gō\. *Variant spellings* Ei·ko \'ī-(,)kō\, Hei·ko \'hī-(,)kō\. 13th century. Saxon nobleman, jurist, and writer. Author in Latin of *Sachsenspiegel,* a treatise on the law of the Saxons, the beginning of German law writing (1220); reputed author of *Sächsische Weltchronik* (pub. 1877).

Eil·hart von Ober·ge \'īl-härt-fȯn-'ō-ber-gə\. 12th century. German poet. Author (from French sources) of the romantic epic *Tristrant* (c.1170), first German version of *Tristan und Isolde.*

Eil·she·mi·us \(,)ī(ə)l-'shē-mē-əs\, Louis Michel. 1864–1941. American painter, b. North Arlington, N.J. Known for landscapes influenced by Barbizon painters, later works anticipating Expressionists.

Ei·na·u·di \,ā-nä-'ü-dē\, Luigi. 1874–1961. Italian economist and politician. Professor at Turin (1900–43); edited journals *Riforma sociale* (1908–35), *Rivista di storia economica* (1936–42); appointed to senate (1919); in exile in Switzerland (1943–45); governor of Bank of Italy (1945–48); member of Constituent Assembly (1946–48); deputy prime minister and minister of budget (1947); first president of Italian Republic (1948–55).

Ei·nem \'ī-nəm\, Karl Wilhelm von. *Called also* von Roth·ma·ler \'rōt-mäl-ər\. 1853–1934. German soldier. Prussian minister of war (1903–09); commanded VII corps, later 3d army in World War I.

Ein·hard \'īn-,härt\. *Also* Egin·hard \'ā-gin-,härt\. 770?–840. Frankish secretary and biographer of Charlemagne. Trusted adviser to Charlemagne; helped build palace at Aachen; retained favor under Louis the Pious (until 830) and became abbot of various monasteries; wrote (c.829–836) *Vita Caroli Magni.*

Ein·stein \'īn-,shtīn, *Angl* 'īn-,stīn\, Albert. 1879–1955. American physicist, b. Ulm, Germany. Naturalized Swiss at age of 15. Professor, Zürich (1909–11, 1912–14), Deutsche U., Prague (1911–12); invited to Berlin by Prussian Academy of Sciences, adopted German citizenship, and became professor, U. of Berlin (1914). Director, Kaiser Wilhelm Physical Institute, Berlin (1914). To U.S. (1933); member, Institute for Advanced Study, Princeton (1933–55); became naturalized American citizen (1940). Enunciated theory of relativity, publishing account of special theory of relativity (1905) and of general theory (1916), papers on a unified field theory which sought to include in a single mathematical formula the laws of electromagnetism and gravitation (1929); explained Brownian movement and gave formula for it; deduced influence of gravity on propagation of light; discovered and formulated equivalence of mass and energy; developed law of photoelectric effect to explain transformation of light quanta. Awarded 1921 Nobel prize for physics. Author of *The Meaning of Relativity* (1923), *Builders of the Universe* (1932), *Why War?* (with Freud, 1933), *The World As I See It* (1934), *Out of My Later Years* (1950).

Eint·ho·ven \'īnt-,hō-vən\, Willem. 1860–1927. Dutch physiologist. Invented a string galvanometer (1903) that served as the basis for the electrocardiograph; awarded the 1924 Nobel prize for physiology or medicine.

Ei·sai \ā-sī\. *Also called* Yo·sai \yō-sī\. 1141–1215. Japanese priest. Regarded as founder of Rinzai sect of Zen Buddhism.

Eise·ley \'īz-lē\, Loren Corey. 1907–1977. American anthropologist and writer. Professor at Kansas U. (1937–44), Oberlin Coll. (1944–47), U. of Pennsylvania (1947–77); author of *The Immense Journey* (1957), *Darwin's Century* (1958), *Firmament of Time* (1960), *The Unexpected Universe* (1969), *Invisible Pyramid* (1970), *Night Country* (1971), *All the Strange Hours* (1975).

Ei·sen·how·er \'īz-ᵊn-,hau̇(-ə)r\, Dwight David. 1890–1969. Thirty-fourth president of the U.S., b. Denison, Texas. Major general, chief of war plans division, U.S. general staff (1942); lieutenant general, commander in chief of U.S. forces in European theater (1942); commander of allied forces in Northwest Africa (1942); general, supreme allied commander in North Africa (1943) and in western Mediterranean (1943); planned invasions of North Africa, Sicily, Italy; commander in chief of allied forces in western Europe (1943); general of the army (1944); planned and commanded conquest of Germany from D-Day (June 6, 1944) to VE Day (May 2, 1945); U.S. member of Allied Control Commission for Germany; chief of staff of U.S. Army (1945–48); president of Columbia U. (1948–53); supreme commander, NATO forces in Europe (1951–52). President of the U.S. (1953–61); his administrations noted for a truce ending Korean War (1953), dispatch of troops to Little Rock, Ark. to support integration of a high school (1957), sending troops to support government of Lebanon (1958), U-2 affair with Soviet Union (1960), and breaking diplomatic relations with Cuba (1961). Author of *Crusade in Europe* (1948), *Mandate for Change* (1963).

Ei·sen·stein \'īz-ən-,shtīn\, Ferdinand Gottfried Max. 1823–1852. German mathematician. Known esp. for work on theory of functions and theory of numbers.

Ei·sen·stein \'īz-yin-shtəin, *Angl* 'īz-ən-,stīn\, Sergey Mikhaylovich. 1898–1948. Russian theater and motion-picture director. Considered one of the most influential directors in film history and a major contributor to development of cinematic art and criticism; films included *Statschka* (1924), *Potemkin* (1925), *Oktjabr* (1928), *Generalnaja Linija* (1929), *Que viva Mexico!* (1932), *Aleksandr Nevsky* (1938), *Iwan Grosnyj* (*Ivan the Terrible*, 1944–46).

Eis·ner \'īz-nər\, Kurt. 1867–1919. German journalist and politician. On staff of *Frankfurter Zeitung* (1892–93); editor of *Vorwärts*, Berlin (1898); editor in chief of Socialist *Fränkische Tagespost*, Nürnberg (1907–10). In World War I supported government at first, but later (1917) supported Independent Social Democratic party, of which he became leader; organized Munich revolution which overthrew monarchy (1918) and became first prime minister and minister of foreign affairs of Bavarian republic; assassinated.

Ei·tel·ber·ger von Edel·berg \'īt-əl-,ber-gər-fon-'ād-əl-,berk\, Rudolf. 1817–1885. Austrian art historian. Professor, Vienna (from 1852); founder and director, Austrian Museum of Art and Industry (from 1864).

Eit·ner \'īt-nər\, Robert. 1832–1905. German music historian. Published *Biographisch-bibliographisches Quellen-Lexikon für Musikgeschichte* (1900–04).

Ekaterina. In Russian names see CATHERINE.

Eke·berg \'ā-kə-,berʸ\, Anders Gustav. 1767–1813. Swedish chemist. Taught at Uppsala (1794–1813); discovered tantalum, element 73 (1802).

Eke·löf \'ā-kə-,lœf\, Gunnar, *in full* Bengt Gunnar. 1907–1968. Swedish poet and essayist. A leader of modernist "generation of the '40s"; volumes included *Sent på jorden* (1932), *Dedikation* (1934), *Sorgen och stjärnan* (1936), *Färjesång* (1941), *Non serviam* (1945), *Om hösten* (1951), *Strountes* (1955), *En Mölna-elegi* (1960).

Eke·lund \'ā-kə-,lənd\, Vilhelm. 1880–1949. Swedish poet and essayist. Wrote Symbolist and free verse, including *Dithyramber i aftonglans* (1906), and volumes of aphorisms inspired by Nietzsche, including *Veri similia* (1915–16), *Metron* (1918).

Ek·hof *or* **Eck·hof** \'ek-,hōf\, Konrad, *in full* Hans Konrad Dieterich. 1720–1778. German actor and director. A founder of modern German theater and exponent of realistic school of acting; director of new court theater, Gotha (1774–78).

Ek·ke·hard \'ek-ə-,härt\. *Called* the Elder. c.910–973. Frankish monk and poet. Educated and later a teacher in Benedictine monastery of St. Gall; elected dean of St. Gall (957); composed many hymns; traditionally regarded as author of *Waltharius*, Latin heroic poem on life of King Walter of Aquitaine.

Ekkehard IV. 980?–?1069. Frankish monk and historian. Director of cathedral school in Mainz (c.1022–31); member of Benedictine monastery of St. Gall (from 1031); continued compilation of *Casus Sancti Galli;* edited *Waltharius*, which he ascribed to Ekkehard I; wrote *Liber benedictionum*, etc.

Ekkehard von Aura. See under FRUTOLF.

Ek·man \'āk-mån\, Vagn Walfrid. 1874–1954. Swedish oceanographer. On staff of International Laboratory for Oceanographic Research, Oslo (1902–09); professor, Lund (1910–39); made fundamental contributions to hydrodynamic theory of ocean currents; invented Ekman current meter, Ekman reversing water bottle; name given to "Ekman layer," "Ekman spiral," etc.

Ek·rem Bey \ek-'rem-'bā\, Recaizade Mahmud. 1847–1914. Turkish writer. Taught literature and held various government posts; wrote widely influential essays on literature, deriving inspiration from French Parnassian school of poets; published *Talim-i Edebiyyat* (criticism and theory, 1882), *Tefekkür* (verse and prose, 1888); translated from French.

El·a·gab·a·lus \,el-ə-'gab-ə-ləs\. *Corrupt form in Greek* He·lio·gab·a·lus \,hē-lē-ō-'gab-ə-ləs\. *Orig.* Varius Avitus Bas·si·a·nus \,bas-ē-'ā-nəs\. 204–222. Roman emperor. Born in Syria to family of hereditary high priests of Baal, known locally as Elah-Gabal. Proclaimed emperor (218) on fall of Macrinus after his mother had presented him as illegitimate son of Caracalla; imposed Baal worship on Rome; executed several generals; engaged in homosexual debauchery; on urging of grandmother Julia Maesa, adopted cousin Alexander as heir (221); killed by praetorian guard when he attempted to depose Alexander.

Elah \'ē-lə\. d. 876 B.C. King of Israel. Son of Baasha, whom he succeeded (877 B.C.); slain by Zimri, one of his generals.

El·ca·no \el-'kän-ō\, Juan Sebastián de. c.1476–1526. Basque navigator. Sailed in command of *Concepción* in Magellan's fleet (1519); took command of expedition on Magellan's death in Philippines (1521); returned to Spain in *Vittoria* (1522), becoming first sea captain to circumnavigate the Earth. Died while co-commander of expedition sent to claim Moluccas for Charles V of Spain.

El·dad ben Mah·li ha-Da·ni \'el-,däd-ben-'mäk-lē-hä-'dän-ē\. *Also known as* Eldad the Danite. 9th century. Jewish traveler and philologist. Author of *Sefer Eldad*, highly fictionalized account of travels in Africa and Near East in which he supposedly located Ten Lost Tribes of Israel; versions of the work may have given rise to legend of Prester John.

El·der \'el-dər\, John. 1824–1869. Scottish marine engineer and shipbuilder. Inventor of the compound reciprocating steam engine (1854).

Eldon, 1st Earl of. See John SCOTT.

El·ea·nor \'el-ə-nər, -'nò(ə)r\ of Aq·ui·taine \,ak-wə-'tān, 'ak-wə-,\. *Also* Ali·e·nor \á-lē-ā-nòr\. 1122?–1204. Queen of Louis VII of France and of Henry II of England. Succeeded her father, William X, as duchess of Aquitaine (1137); married by her father to Prince Louis, who a month later became Louis VII of France (1137); divorced on pretext of consanguinity (1152) and regained Aquitaine. m. (1152) Henry Plantagenet, Count of Anjou (from 1154 Henry II), bringing Aquitaine to England, thereby setting up strife between England and France lasting some 400 years. Supported her sons in rebellion against her unfaithful husband (1173); held in confinement (1174–89); secured succession of Richard I; administered realm during Richard's crusading; frustrated John's attempted treacherous conspiracy with France during Richard's absence (1193); raised Richard's ransom and escorted him home from Austria (1194); reconciled Richard and John on Richard's return; crushed an uprising in Anjou by partisans of her grandson Arthur against her son King John (1200); arranged marriage of granddaughter Blanche of Castile to future Louis VIII of France (1200).

Eleanor of Cas·tile \kas-'tē(ə)l\. 1246–1290. Queen of Edward I of England. Daughter of Ferdinand III of Castile and Joan of Ponthieu. m. Prince Edward (1254), bringing to English crown her mother's provinces of Ponthieu and Montreuil and a claim on Gascony; accompanied Edward I on crusade (1270–73).

Eleanor of Pro·vence \prò-väⁿs\. 1223–1291. Queen of Henry III of England. Daughter of Raymond Berengar IV, Count of Provence; m. Henry III (1236); accompanied him on expedition to Gascony (1242); joint governor of England with king's brother (1253); collected mercenaries in France to support Henry in Barons' War (1264); her invasion fleet wrecked at Sluis, Flanders (1264); entered nunnery on accession of her son, Edward I (1272).

El·e·a·zar ben Az·a·ri·ah \,el-ē-'ā-zər-ben-,az-ə-'rī-ə\. 1st–2d century A.D. Rabbinic scholar. Author of maxims that constitute some of best known passages of the Talmud.

Eleazar ben Ju·dah \-'jü-də\ of Worms \'wərmz, 'vòrm(p)s\. *In full* Eleazar ben Judah ben Ka·lon·y·mos \-kä-'lòn-ē-mòs\ of Worms. *Known also as* Eleazar Ro·ke·aḥ \rō-'kä-äk\. c.1160–1238. Jewish mystic, Talmudist. Rabbi at Worms, Germany (1201); influential Ḥasidic leader and writer; author of *Rokeaḥ* on ethics, *Te'amin we-sodot ha-tefilla* on Kabbalistic prayers; coauthor of *Sefer Ḥasidim*.

Elena, Princess. See Magda LUPESCU.

El·ers \'el-ərz, *Ger* 'ā-lərs\, John Phillip and his brother David. fl. 1690–1730. English ceramists, of Saxon origin. Produced (from c.1690) in Staffordshire a hard, red, unglazed earthenware (Elers ware).

El·eu·the·ri·us \,el-yə-'thi(ə)r-ē-əs\. Saint. d. 189. Pope (c.175–189). Known for opposition to Montanism.

El·gar \'el-,gär, -gər\, Sir Edward William. 1857–1934. English composer. Organist of St. George's Roman Catholic Church, Worcester (1885–90); professor, Birmingham (1905–08); master of king's music (1924). Notable compositions included *Enigma Variations* (1896); oratorio *Lux Christi* (1896), choral cantata *Caractacus* (1898); oratorios *Dream of Gerontius* (1900), *The Apostles* (1903), and *The Kingdom* (1906); *Cockaigne* overture (1901), *Pomp and Circumstance* marches (1901–07, 1930); two symphonies (1908, 1911); *Violin Concerto* (1910); *Falstaff* (1913); *Cello Concerto* (1919).

Elgin, Earls of. See BRUCE, English family.

El·hu·yar y de Su·vi·sa \ā-lü-'yär-ē-thā-sü-'bē-sä\, Fausto d'. 1755–1833. Spanish chemist and mineralogist. Director general of mines, Mexico (1788–1821); later director general of mines in Spain; with brother Juan José (1754–1804) first to isolate tungsten (1783).

Eli·as \ā-'lē-äs\ of Cor·to·na \kòr-'tō-nä\. c.1180–1253. Italian religious. Disciple and companion of St. Francis of Assisi; first Franciscan minister provincial in Syria (1217); vicar of Franciscan order (from 1221); headed order after death of St. Francis (1226–27); general of order (1232–39); for supporting Emperor Frederick II was excommunicated by Pope Gregory IX (1240) and Pope Innocent IV (1244); later reconciled to church.

Élie de Beaumont. See Élie de BEAUMONT.

Eligius. See ÉLOI.

Eli·jah \i-'lī-jə\. *Hebrew* Eliyyahu. 9th century B.C. Hebrew prophet. Strenuously upheld Yahweh religion against worship of Phoenician god Baal, supported by King Ahab and his wife Jezebel; emphasized morality and salvation.

Elijah ben So·lo·mon \-'säl-ə-mən\ . *Surnamed* Zal·man \'zäl-mən\. *Known also as* Elija Wil·na \'vil-nə\, Elijah Ga·on \'gä-,ōn\, *or by acronym* ha-Gra \'häg-'rä\. 1720–1797. Lithuanian Jewish leader. Became leader of Jewish community of Vilna; known as a scholar, teacher, religious; led exemplary life; vigorous opponent (from 1772) of Ḥasidism; left no written works, but over 40 volumes of his textual notes and his students' notes have been published.

Elijah Levita. See LEVITA.

Elío \ā-'lē-ō\, Francisco Javier. 1767–1822. Spanish soldier. To Plata River (1805) as commander against English; recaptured Montevideo (1807); viceroy of Buenos Aires (1810). To Spain and commanded Catalonian and Valencian army (1812); after restoration of Ferdinand VII (1814) conducted vigorous persecution of Liberals; deposed by Liberal insurgents (1822); executed.

Eliot. See also ELIOTT, ELLIOT, ELLIOTT, ELYOT.

El·iot \'el-ē-ət, 'el-yət\, Sir Charles Norton Edgcumbe. 1862–1931. British diplomat and scholar. Commissioner and consul general (1900–04), East African Protectorate (now Kenya), where he instituted white-supremacy policy and encouraged European settlement; ambassador to Japan (1920–26). Author of *Letters from the Far East* (1907), *Hinduism and Buddhism* (1921), etc.

Eliot, Charles William. 1834–1926. American educator, b. Boston. Taught mathematics and chemistry, Harvard (1858–63); professor of chemistry, M.I.T. (1865–69). President of Harvard (1869–1909); promoted plan to embrace all undergraduate studies in Harvard College and gather about it complete group of graduate and professional schools; established exchange professorships with France and Germany; encouraged "elective system" of undergraduate courses; reformed administration of athletics and helped introduce stricter intercollegiate eligibility rules. Organized graduate school of arts and sciences (1890); made divinity school nonsectarian; raised law school and medical school standards. Cooperated in various steps leading to establishment of Radcliffe College (1894). Author of *The Happy Life* (1896), *Educational Reform* (1898), *The Religion of the Future* (1909), *The Durable Satisfactions of Life* (1910), *A Late Harvest* (posthumous, 1924); editor of the *Harvard Classics* ("five-foot shelf").

Eliot, Edward Granville. 3d Earl of St. Ger·mans \sānt-'jər-mənz\. 1798–1877. British diplomat. M.P. (1824–32, 1837–45); lord of treasury (1827–30); as envoy extraordinary to Spain, induced Carlists and Royalists to adopt Eliot convention providing for better treatment of prisoners of war (1834); chief secretary for Ireland (1841–45); postmaster general (1845–46); lord lieutenant of Ireland (1852–55); confidential adviser of Queen Victoria.

Eliot, George. See Mary Ann EVANS.

Eliot, Sir John. 1592–1632. English Puritan, parliamentary politician, and orator. M.P. (1614, 1624–29); early friend and supporter of George Villiers, Duke of Buckingham, who appointed him vice admiral of Devon (1622); spoke in Parliament for free speech; urged enforcement of laws against Roman Catholics. As leader of House of Commons (1626), was alienated by Buckingham's conduct of war; demanded inquiry into disaster at Cádiz; carried Buckingham's impeachment to House of Lords; imprisoned briefly before Charles I dissolved Parliament (1626); again imprisoned (1627–28) for refusing to pay a forced loan to the crown; insisted on acceptance of the Petition of Right (1628). Presented resolutions in House of Commons against king's right to levy tonnage and poundage and the king's innovations in religion and forcibly held speaker of the House in his seat while resolutions were passed before king arrived to dissolve Parliament (1629); imprisoned in Tower (1629–32) where he died.

Eliot, John. *Called* Apostle to the Indians. 1604–1690. American Puritan clergyman, b. Widford, Hertfordshire, England. Migrated to Massachusetts (1631); teacher of the church at Roxbury (1632–90). Helped prepare *Bay Psalm Book* (1640). Devoted himself also to work among the Indians; many of its results destroyed by King Philip's War. Author of *A Primer or Catechism, in the Massachusetts Indian Language* (1653), Indian translation of Bible (N.T. 1661, O.T. 1663—first Bible printed in North America), *Up-Bookum Psalmes* (1663); also *Christian Commonwealth* (1659), *Harmony of the Gospels* (1678).

Eliot, Thomas Stearns. 1888–1965. British poet and critic, b. St. Louis, Mo. Resident, London (from 1914); naturalized British citizen (1927). Author of *Prufrock and Other Observations* (1917), *Poems* (1919), *Ara Vos Prec* (1920), *The Sacred Wood* (critical essays, 1920), *The Waste Land* (1922), *Homage to John Dryden* (1924), *An Essay of Poetic Drama* (1928), *Dante* (1929), *Ash Wednesday* (short series of poems, 1930), *Selected Essays* (1932), *After Strange Gods* (1934), *The Rock* (verse drama, 1934), *Elizabethan Essays* (1934), *Murder in the Cathedral* (verse drama, 1935), *Essays Ancient and Modern* (1936), *Old Possum's Book of Practical Cats* (1939), *Four Quartets* (1943), *Notes Toward the Definition of Culture* (1948), *The Cocktail Party* (verse drama, 1949), *Poetry and Drama* (1951), *On Poetry and Poets* (1957). Founded and edited *Criterion* (1922–39). Awarded Nobel prize for literature (1948).

El·i·ott \'el-ē-ət, 'el-yət\, George Augustus. 1st Baron Heath·field \'hēth-,fēld\. 1717–1790. Scottish soldier. Entered British army (1739); colonel of 1st Light Horse (1759); served with distinction in Germany (1759–61), Cuba (1762); lieutenant general (1765); governor of Gibraltar (1775), defended it heroically against Spanish (1779–83); raised to peerage (1787).

Eli·pan·do \ā-lē-'pän-dō\. *Lat.* El·i·pan·dus \,el-ə-'pan-dəs\. 717–?808. Spanish prelate. Archbishop of Toledo (from c.783); his doctrine that Christ was son of God not by nature but by adoption (adoptionism) was condemned as heresy at the Council of Frankfurt (794).

Elis·a·beth \i-'liz-ə-bəth\. 1876–1965. Queen of the Belgians (1909–34). Daughter of Duke Charles Theodore of Bavaria; m. (1900) Prince Albert (later Albert I) of Belgium. Devoted to charities; patriotic and of great aid to the king during World War I and, as queen dowager, to her son King Leopold III in World War II.

Elis·a·beth Chris·tine \ā-'lē-zä-bet-kri-'stē-nə\. Name of two German queens: (1) 1691–1750. Empress of Germany as wife (m. 1708) of Emperor Charles VI; mother of Maria Theresa. (2) 1715–1797. Wife (m. 1733) of Frederick the Great of Prussia.

Éli·sa·beth de France \ā-lē-zà-bet-də-fräⁿs\, Madame. *In full* Élisabeth-Philippine-Marie-Hélène. 1764–1794. Sister of King Louis XVI of France. Accompanied Louis XVI on attempted flight from France; captured with him at Varennes (1791); executed.

Eli·sha \i-'lish-ə\. *Gk.* El·i·sai·os \,el-ə-'sī-,ōs\, *Lat.* El·i·se·us \,el-ə-'sē-əs\. 9th century B.C. Hebrew prophet. Disciple and successor of Elijah in opposing Baal worship.

Elisha ben Abu·yah \-,ben-ä-'bü-yä\. fl. c.100 A.D. Jewish freethinker. Trained as scholar of Oral Law; lost faith in rabbinic authority, flouted religious laws; may have been Gnostic or Sadducee, but in later ages considered the type of apostate; referred to in Talmud as "Aḥer" (i.e. "The Other").

Elísio, Filinto. See Francisco Manuel do NASCIMENTO.

Eliz·a·beth \i-'liz-ə-bəth\. Saint. 1207–1231. Daughter of Andrew II, King of Hungary. m. (1221) Louis IV, Landgrave of Thuringia; mother of Sophia of Hesse (d. 1284). Devoted herself to religion and charitable works; on death of Louis driven from Thuringia (1227) by Henry Raspe; found refuge with her uncle the bishop of Bamberg; later lived in Marburg, where she became a lay Franciscan (1228) and built a hospital. Canonized by Pope Gregory IX (1235).

Elizabeth. Saint. c.1271–1336. Daughter of Peter III of Aragon; m. (1282) King Dinis of Portugal. Led devout life despite corruption of Portuguese court; devoted to charitable works; reconciled Dinis and rebelling son Afonso; after death of Dinis (1325) lived near Poor Clare convent she had founded at Coimbra. Canonized (1625) by Pope Urban VIII.

Elizabeth. 1837–1898. Empress of Austria (1854–98). Daughter of Duke Maximilian Joseph of Bavaria; m. (1854) her cousin Emperor Francis Joseph I of Austria; became queen also of Hungary (1867); popular with her people because of her beauty and charm and her philanthropies; assassinated by an Italian anarchist.

Elizabeth. *Also* Elizabeth Stu·art \'st(y)ü-ərt, 'st(y)ů(-ə)rt\. 1596–1662. Queen of Frederick V of Bohemia. Eldest daughter of James VI of Scotland (later I of England); m. (1613) Frederick V, Elector Palatine. Her marriage commemorated in *Epithalamium* by John Donne. Became queen consort (1619); on routing of Frederick V by the Catholic League (1620), took refuge at The Hague; levied (1633) small army in behalf of her son Charles Louis, to whom was restored a portion of the Rhenish Palatinate by the Treaty of Westphalia (1648), and by whom she was deserted and forced to live on the generosity of Holland; returned to England (1661), despite opposition of her nephew Charles II, and was pensioned. Honored as a martyr to Protestantism. Mother of thirteen children, including Sophia, mother of George I, of Great Britain.

Elizabeth. *Sometimes known as* Elizabeth of Bohemia. 1618–1680. Princess palatine. Daughter of Elector Palatine Frederick V and Elizabeth. Abbess of Herford (from 1667). Descartes dedicated his *Principia philosophiae* to her.

Elizabeth. 1437?–1492. Queen of Edward IV of England. Daughter of Sir Richard Woodville, 1st Earl Rivers; m. Sir John Grey (killed 1461); privately m. (1464) to Edward IV; crowned (1465). Withdrew into sanctuary at Westminster on Edward's flight (1470); her sons Edward V and Richard, Duke of York, murdered in the Tower (1483); put in possession of her rights as queen dowager by Henry VII (1486); deprived (1487) and retired to abbey. Her daughter ¶Elizabeth (1465–1503) was queen of Henry VII, marrying him (1486) in pursuance of petition presented to the king by Parliament; subject of an elegy by Sir Thomas More; mother of Henry VIII.

Elizabeth I. 1533–1603. Queen of England and Ireland (1558–1603), of house of Tudor. Only child of Henry VIII and Anne Boleyn; declared illegitimate by Parliament in favor of son of Jane Seymour (1536). Rejected suit of Sir Thomas Seymour; sided with her half-sister Mary against Lady Jane Grey (1553); refused to participate in Wyatt's Rebellion (1554) but nevertheless imprisoned in Tower and at Woodstock. Succeeded Mary on the throne (1558); issued proclamation establishing English litany and proscribing the Catholic (1559); aided Protestants in Scotland and Low Countries; promulgated the Thirty-nine Articles and obtained from Parliament (1563) extension of provisions of the Act of Supremacy, rendering Protestantism and patriotism virtually synonymous in England. Found her rival, the Roman Catholic Mary Stuart, Queen of Scots, in her power after the defeat at Langside (1568); imprisoned her in Carlisle, thus giving rise to plots for liberating her and putting her on English throne. Increased severity of persecution of Roman Catholics; after discovery of Babington Plot (1586), finally yielded to demand of Cecil, Walsingham, and other ministers and to popular outcry for removing Mary, Queen of Scots, as a menace to public safety and peace, and consented to sign the death warrant (1587). By persecutions of Mary's adherents incurred wrath of Roman Catholic powers, among them Philip of Spain, who (1588) sent out the Spanish Armada for invasion of England; prepared to meet the assault, disregarded advice of Walsingham and her council to precipitate an attack on the armada, which was defeated by Howard, Drake, Hawkins, Frobisher, with the aid of a storm. Conducted subtle foreign policy aimed at strengthening Protestant allies and dividing potential enemies; conducted negotiations for marriage to various foreign eligibles and indulged in romances with favorites, esp. Robert Devereux, Earl of Essex, and Robert Dudley, Earl of Leicester, but refused ultimately to marry. Sent Essex, as governor general in Ireland, to quell revolt of Earl of Tyrone (1599), but he failed and lost favor; he attempted a revolt and was executed (1601). Avoided conflict with Parliament and attempted to curb monopolies and curtail expenditures. Called "Good Queen Bess"; reign of 45 years saw England emerge as world power.

Elizabeth. *Nee* Pau·li·ne E·li·sa·beth Ot·ti·lie Lu·i·se \paù-'lē-nə-ä-'lē-zä-bet-ó-'tē-lē-ə-lü-'ē-zə\. Princess of Wied \'vēt\. *Pseudonym* Car·men Syl·va \'kär-men-'sēl-vä, *Ger* -zœl-vä, *Angl* 'kär-mən-'sil-və\. 1843–1916. Queen of Romania. m. (1869) Prince Carol (later Carol I) of Romania, crowned queen (1881). Author of about 20 books including *Pensées d'une reine* (1882), *Pelesch Märchen* (1883), *Astra* (1886), *Defizit* (1890), *The Bard of Dimbovitza* (1891), *Geflüsterte Worte* (1903–10), and several novels in collaboration with Mme. Mite Kremnitz under the pseudonym Di·to und Idem \'dē-tō-ùnt-'ē-dem\.

Elizabeth. *Span.* Isabel. 1602–1644. Queen of Spain. Daughter of Henry IV of France; m. Philip IV of Spain. Mother of Infante Baltasar Carlos and of María Theresa, wife of Louis XIV of France (see MARIE-THÉRÈSE).

Elizabeth of Aragon. Queen of Portugal. See Saint ELIZABETH.

Elizabeth of Bavaria. See ISABEAU.

Elizabeth of Val·lois \vál-wà\. *Fr.* Éli·sa·beth de France \ā-lē-zá-bet-də-fräⁿs\. *Span.* Isabel. 1545–1568. Daughter of Henry II of France and Catherine de Médicis; married (1559) Philip II of Spain. Marriage not a success politically, but queen much beloved.

Elizabeth Farnese. See ISABELLA.

Elizabeth Pe·trov·na \pyi-'tróv-nə\. *Russ.* Yelizaveta Petrovna. 1709–1762. Empress of Russia (1741–62). Younger daughter of Peter the Great and Catherine I. Gained throne by overthrowing government of Anna Leopoldovna, acting regent for Ivan VI. Abolished cabinet council government, reinstituting senate; concluded war with Sweden and annexed portion of Finland (1743); left policy largely to trusted adviser, Bestuzhev-Ryumin; in Seven Years' War allied Russia with Austria and France against Prussia; freed Russia from German dominance. Founded University of Moscow (1755) and Academy of Fine Arts at St. Petersburg (1758); built Winter Palace, St. Petersburg.

Ellenborough, Baron and earl of. See Edward LAW.

El·ler \'el-ər\, Elias. 1690–1750. German religious leader. Founder of Ronsdorfer sect of millenarians (1726).

El·lery \'el(-ə)-rē\, William. 1727–1820. American politician, b. Newport, R.I. Member, Continental Congress (1776–81, 1783–85); a signer of the Declaration of Independence.

Ellesmere, Barons and earls of. See EGERTON family.

El·let \'el-ət\, Charles. 1810–1862. American engineer, b. Bucks County, Pa. Built first wire suspension bridge in America, over Schuylkill R. (1841–42); built Ohio R. bridge at Wheeling, longest single-span bridge in world at the time (1849); designed, built, and commanded fleet of ram boats to clear Mississippi of Confederate vessels (1862); mortally wounded in capture of Memphis (June 6).

El·li·cott \'el-ə-kət\, Andrew. 1754–1820. American surveyor, b. Bucks County, Pa. Member of survey that continued Mason and Dixon's line (1784); on commissions that surveyed western and northern boundaries of Pennsylvania (1785–86), southwestern New York State boundary (1789); surveyed District of Columbia (1791–93); made (1792) redrawing of L'Enfant's plan for City of Washington, known as the Ellicott plan; surveyed boundary between U.S. and Florida (1796–1800), and between Georgia and South Carolina (1811).

Ellicott, Charles John. 1819–1905. English prelate and scholar. Professor of divinity, Cambridge (1860); bishop of Gloucester and Bristol (1863–97), of Gloucester (1897–1905); chairman of New Testament Revision Committee (1870–81); author of numerous biblical commentaries.

El·ling·ton \'el-iŋ-tən\, Edward Kennedy. *Known as* Duke Ellington. 1899–1974. American bandleader and composer, b. Washington, D.C. Composed suites, including *Black, Brown, and Beige* (1943), *Liberian Suite* (1947), *Harlem* (1950); film scores; songs including "Mood Indigo," "Ko Ko," "Sophisticated Lady," "In My Solitude," "Don't Get Around Much Anymore."

Elliot. See also ELLIOTT, ELIOT, ELIOTT.

El·liot \'el-ē-ət, 'el-yət\ of Craig·end \'krā-ˌgend\. Name of a Scottish family of Roxburgh holding the baronetcy, barony, and the earldom of Minto, and including: Sir Gilbert Elliot (1651–1718), Lord Min·to \'min-(ˌ)tō\; writer in Edinburgh; condemned for participation in Earl of Argyll's rising (1685); pardoned; created baronet (1700); judge of session (1705). His son ¶Sir Gilbert (1693–1766), 2d baronet; M.P. (1722–26), lord of justiciary (1733–66). 2d baronet's daughter ¶Jane *or* Jean (1727–1805), author of the ballad *Flowers of the Forest* (1756).

¶Sir Gilbert Elliot (1722–1777), 3d Baronet of Minto; son of 2d baronet. M.P. (1755–77); treasurer of navy (1770–77); brought to bear George III's influence to defeat conciliatory motion to allow American colonies to tax themselves (1775); because of his disapprobation of skeptical philosophy dissuaded Hume from publishing *Dialogues of Natural Religion* during his lifetime; a song writer remembered for his "Amynta," a pastoral, and "Twas at the hour of dark midnight" (1745).

¶Sir Gilbert Elliott-Murray Kyn·yn·mond \-ki-'nin-mənd\ (1751–1814), 1st Earl of Minto; eldest son of 3d baronet. Whig M.P. (1776–84, 1786–94); aided Burke in attack on Warren Hastings; opened case against Sir Elijah Impey (1787); viceroy of Corsica (1794–96); created baron (1798); envoy to Vienna (1799–1801); as governor general of India (1807–13), annexed Amboina (1809), the Molucca Islands and Mauritius (1810), and Java (1811); created earl (1813).

His eldest son ¶Gilbert Elliot-Murray-Kynynmond (1782–1859), 2d earl; M.P. (1806–07, 1812–14); ambassador to Berlin (1832–34); first lord of admiralty (1835–41), lord privy seal (1846–52).

¶Sir George Elliot (1784–1863), British naval commander, 2d son of 1st earl, served at reduction of Java (1811); M.P. (1832–35); commander in chief at Cape of Good Hope (1837–40); in China (1840); admiral (1853).

¶Gilbert John Elliot-Murray-Kynynmond (1845–1914), 4th earl; grandson of 2d earl; served in wars in various parts of world (1870–82); governor general of Canada (1898–1904); viceroy of India (1905–10); worked with John Morely in founding new policy of gradual extension of native representation in Indian government (1909).

El·liot·son \'el-ē-ət-sən, 'el-yət-\, John. 1791–1868. English physician. Professor, U. of London (1831–37); founded a mesmeric hospital (1849); founder and president of the Phrenological Society.

Elliott. See also ELIOT, ELIOTT, ELLIOT.

El·liott \'el-ē-ət, 'el-yət\, Ebenezer. *Called* the Corn-Law Rhymer. 1781–1849. English poet. Despite lack of formal education wrote in youth some Romantic verse, e.g., "Vernal Walk," "The Exile," "Withered Wild Flowers," that won attention; active chartist until chartists dissented from corn-law agitation; attributed all national and personal misfortunes to the "bread tax," which he denounced bitterly in *Corn-Law Rhymes* (1831) and *The Splendid Village* (1833–35).

Elliott, Jesse Duncan. 1782–1845. American naval officer, b. Hagerstown, Md. Captured British brigs *Detroit* and *Caledonia* on Lake Erie (1812); ranking officer under Commodore Perry; his conduct in support of Perry during battle of Lake Erie (Sept. 10, 1813) formed subject of a bitter controversy lasting more than 30 years.

Elliott, Maxine. *Orig.* Jessie Der·mot \'dər-mət\. 1868–1940. American actress, b. Rockland, Me. Member of Augustin Daly's company (1895–96) and appeared in Shakespeare repertory; co-star with Nat Goodwin (1896–1903) and his wife (1898–1908). Owner and manager of Maxine Elliott's Theatre, N.Y. (1908).

Elliott, Sarah Barnwell. 1848–1928. American writer, b. Savannah, Ga. Author of realistic novels of Tennessee mountain people, including *Jerry* (1891), *John Paget* (1893), *The Durket Sperret* (1898), and stories of the South and Southwest.

El·lis \'el-əs\, Alexander John. *Orig. surname* Sharpe \'shärp\. 1814–1890. English philologist and mathematician. Took name Ellis (1825) on receipt of bequest from a relative. First in England to reduce study of phonetics to a science; aided Isaac Pitman in devising system of printing English called phonotypy and in attempts at spelling reform; devised phonetic system (palaeotype, used by Henry Sweet as basis of Romic), and a popular system (glossic); spent large part of his life on *Early English Pronunciation* (1869–89).

Ellis, George. 1753–1815. English author. Son of West Indian planter. Won reputation with *Poetical Tales by Sir Gregory Gander* (1778); edited *Specimens of Early English Poets* (1790), *Specimens of Early English Romances in Metre* (1805); friend of Sir Walter Scott.

Ellis, Harvey. 1852–1904. American architect, b. Rochester, N.Y. Practised in Rochester, in St. Paul, Minn., St. Joseph, Mo.; master of Romanesque style; designed skyscrapers; noted esp. as architectural renderer.

Ellis, Havelock, *in full* Henry Havelock. 1859–1939. English physician and man of letters. Gave up practice to devote himself to scientific and literary work. Editor of Mermaid Series of Old Dramatists (1887), and of Contemporary Science Series (1890); conducted pioneering research leading to monumental 7-volume *Studies in the Psychology of Sex* (1897–1928). Author also of *The Criminal* (1890), *Men and Women* (1894), *The World of Dreams* (1911), *Essays in War-time* (1916), *Little Essays of Love and Virtue* (1922), *The Dance of Life* (1923), *My Confessional* (1934), *My Life* (1940).

Ellis, Robinson. 1834–1913. English classical scholar. Corpus Christi professor of Latin, Oxford (from 1893); chief work, *Commentary on Catullus* (1876).

Ellis, William Webb. 1807–1872. English sportsman. While student at Rugby School (1823), picked up and ran with ball during game of association football (soccer) and thus inspired new game of Rugby football.

El·lis·ton \'el-ə-stən\, Robert William. 1774–1831. English actor and manager. Appeared in Bath, at Haymarket, Drury Lane, which he managed (1819–26), etc. Praised by Charles Lamb and Leigh Hunt; first comedian of his day, esp. in parts of Doricourt, Charles Surface, Rover, and Ranger.

Ells·worth \'elz-(,)wərth\, Lincoln. 1880–1951. American explorer, b. Chicago. Organized, for Johns Hopkins U., expedition to make geological cross section of Andes Mountains (1924); accompanied Roald Amundsen in seaplane flight from Spitsbergen to 87° 44′ N. lat. (1925); with Amundsen and Umberto Nobile made transpolar flight in airship *Norge* from Spitsbergen to Alaska (1926); took part in Sir Hubert Wilkins's transarctic submarine expedition, (1931); made 2300-mile airplane flight across Antarctic (1935), claiming 300,000 sq. miles of new land (Ellsworth Land) for U.S. Author of *The Last Wild Buffalo Hunt* (1915), *Search* (1932), *Beyond Horizons* (1938); collaborated with Amundsen in *Our Polar Flight* (1925) and *First Crossing of the Polar Sea* (1927).

Ellsworth, Oliver. 1745–1807. American politician and jurist, b. Windsor, Conn. Delegate to Continental Congress (1777–84), and Constitutional Convention (1787), where he was instrumental in securing "Connecticut Compromise"; on state superior court (1785–89); U.S. senator from Conn. (1789–96); chairman of committee that drew up Judiciary Act (1789) organizing federal judiciary. Chief justice of the U.S. (1796–1800); submitted to floor first Senate rules and amendments that became Bill of Rights. One of commissioners to France who negotiated agreement with Napoléon (1800). His son ¶Henry Leavitt (1791–1858), b. Windsor, Conn., was first U.S. commissioner of patents (1835–45); helped secure first government appropriation for agriculture, hence sometimes called "father of the Department of Agriculture."

Ell·wood \'el-,wu̇d\, Thomas. 1639–1714. English Quaker. Latin reader to Milton (1662) and friend of the poet thereafter; supposed to have suggested idea of *Paradise Regained* (1665). Author of polemical works on Quakerism, poems, and an autobiography with information about Milton.

El·man \'el-mən\, Mischa. 1891–1967. American violinist, b. Talnoye, Ukraine. Made concert debut (1904), U.S. debut (1908); settled in U.S. (1911, naturalized 1923); noted for virtuoso technique and warmth of tone.

El·men \'el-mən\, Gustav Waldemar. 1876–1957. American electrical engineer, b. Stockholm, Sweden. To U.S. (1893); naturalized (1918). Employed by General Electric Co. (1904–06), Western Electric Co. (1906–25), Bell Telephone Laboratories (1925–41); founder and director (1941–56), magnetism laboratory of U.S. Naval Ordnance Laboratory. Developer of Permalloy (1916) and related metals used in communications equipment.

Elmo, Saint. See Saint ERASMUS.

El·more \'el-,mȯ(ə)r, -,mō(ə)r\, Francis Edward. 1864–1932. English inventor. With his brother Alexander Stanley (1867–1944) developed oil flotation process of ore recovery (1898).

Elm·slie \'elmz-lē\, George Grant. 1871–1952. American architect, b. Huntly, Aberdeenshire, Scotland. To U.S. (1885). Apprentice in office of William Le Baron Jenney (1886); associated with Frank Lloyd Wright in firm of Dankmar Adler and Louis Sullivan (1890–95); Sullivan's assistant (1895–1909); partner in own firm (1910–20), in solo practice thereafter. Considered second only to Wright in influence in developing "prairie school" as principal American architectural style of early 20th century.

Éloi \āl-wä\ *or* **Elig·i·us** \i-'lij-ē-əs\. Saint. 588?–660. French ecclesiastic. Learned goldsmith's trade and, according to legend, gained favor of Chlotar II by skill in making a throne; treasurer and chief councilor to Dagobert I; founded monastery of Solignac (632); bishop of Noyon (641); patron saint of goldsmiths.

Elphege, Saint. See AELFHEAH.

El·phin·stone \'el-fən-,stōn, *chiefly Brit* -stən\. Name of a Scottish family including: Alexander (1522–?1648), 4th Baron Elphinstone; lord high treasurer of Scotland (1599–1601); lord of the articles (1604, 1607); commissioner for the union with England (1604).

BARONS BAL·MER·I·NO \bal-'me(ə)r-ə-(,)nō, -'me(ə)r-nō\: Alexander's brother ¶James (1553?–1612), 1st Baron Balmerino; one of the Octavians (1595); secretary of state in Scotland (1598); commissioner for the union (1604); created baron (1604); disgraced and attainted (1609) for a compromising letter to Pope Clement VIII, to which he had surreptitiously obtained James VI's signature. ¶John (d. 1649), 2d baron; son of 1st baron; restored to blood and peerage (1613); imprisoned (1634) and sentenced to death for handling a petition against Charles I's ecclesiastical measures; pardoned through intercession of poet Drummond of Hawthornden and others (1635); privy councilor and extraordinary lord of session (1641). ¶Arthur (1688–1746), 6th and last baron; joined Jacobites after Sheriffmuir (1715); one of first to join Charles Edward (1745); fought at Falkirk; captured at Culloden Moor and beheaded.

¶George Keith Elphinstone (1746–1823), Viscount Keith \'kēth\ (in peerage of United Kingdom); 5th son of 10th Baron Elphinstone. Entered navy (1761); served on shore at reduction of Charleston (1780); M.P. (1780–90, 1796–1801); helped capture Toulon (1793); rear admiral (1794); helped capture Cape Town (1795); commanded expedition that captured Ceylon (1796); forced Dutch squadron directed at Cape Town to surrender in Saldanha Bay (1796); created baron (1797); helped quell Nore Mutiny (1797); pursued a French fleet from Mediterranean to Brest (1799); took Malta and Genoa (1800); cooperated with Abercromby in operations in Egypt; landed Abercromby's army in Abukir Bay (1801); admiral (1801); commander of North Sea station (1803–07); commander of Channel fleet (1812–15); arranged Napoléon's transfer to St. Helena; created viscount (1814). His wife (m. 1808) ¶Hester Maria (1762–1857), daughter of Henry and Hester Thrale; educated under direction of Dr. Johnson; gave herself to study of Hebrew and mathematics.

¶Mountstuart (1779–1859), 4th son of 11th Baron Elphinstone; appointed to Bengal civil service (1796); diplomatist on Arthur Wellesley's mission to Marāthās; military attaché to Wellesley at battle of Assaye (1803); resident at Nāgpur (1804), Gwalior (1807); envoy to Shāh Shojā at Kabul (1808); resident at Poona (1810–16); put end to Marāthā war (1817) and organized the annexed territory of Poona; as governor of Bombay (1819–27) encouraged indigenous governmental forms, compiled code of laws that lasted forty years, and founded system of state education; twice declined governor-generalship of India; author of *History of India* (1841) and of the incomplete *Rise of the British Power in the East* (1858).

Elphinstone, William. 1431–1514. Scottish prelate and statesman. Bishop of Ross (1481), of Aberdeen (1488–1514); lord high chancellor (1488). Sent by James IV to England, France, and to Emperor Maximilian I; keeper of privy seal (1492–1514); made treaty with Holland (1493); opposed policy of hostility to England. Founded King's Coll. (1494), nucleus of U. of Aberdeen, and rebuilt choir of Aberdeen cathedral. Made possible introduction of first printing press into Scotland (1507), on which he had *Breviarium Aberdonense* (1509–10) printed.

Elsevier. See ELZEVIR.

Els·hei·mer \'els-,hī-mər\, Adam. 1578–1610. German painter and etcher. A founder of modern landscape painting, and strong influence on Rubens, Rembrandt, Claude Lorrain. His works included chiefly biblical and mythological paintings, often on copper, with landscapes.

Els·kamp \'els-,kämp\, Max. 1862–1931. Belgian poet. A leader among the Symbolists, and in the literary and Catholic renaissance in Belgium; volumes included *Dominical* (1892), *Six chansons* (1896), *La Louange de la vie* (1898), *Enluminures* (1898).

Elsschot, Willem. See RIDDER.

Els·sler \'el-slər\, Fanny, *orig.* Franziska. 1810–1884. Austrian dancer. Daughter of copyist and valet to Joseph Haydn. Joined ballet of Kärntnertor Theater, Vienna (1818); won attention by warmth, sensuality, and spontaneity of style; debuts in Berlin (1830), London (1833), Paris in *La Tempête* (1834); cast in rivalry with Marie Taglioni; noted for introducing folk-based character dance into theater, as in *Le Diable boiteux* (1836), *La Gypsy* (1839), *La Tarentule* (1839); earned fortune in U.S. tour (1840–42); retired (1851). Her sister

¶Therese (1808–1878), also a dancer; retired (1850); m. Prince Adalbert of Prussia; was made baroness von Barnim by Frederick William IV.

El·ster \'el-stər\, Julius, *in full* Johann Philipp Ludwig Julius. 1854–1920. German physicist. With ¶Hans Friedrich Gei·tel \'gī-təl\ (1855–1923), credited with constructing the first practical photoelectric cell, first photoelectric photometer, and a Tesla transformer; conducted important researches in atmosphere electricity, radioactivity.

El·tinge \'el-tiŋ\, Julian. *Orig.* William Dalton. 1883–1941. American entertainer, b. Newtonville, Mass. As female impersonator, star of vaudeville (from 1904) and silent films; most successful roles in *Fascinating Widow* (1911), *Crinoline Girl* (1914), *Cousin Lucy* (1915).

El·ton \'elt-ᵊn\, Oliver. 1861–1945. English literary historian. Professor at Liverpool (1901–25). Among his books were *The Augustan Ages* (1899), *Survey of English Literature 1780–1830* (1912), *Survey ... 1830–1880* (1920), *Survey ... 1730–1780* (1928).

Éluard, Paul. See Eugène GRINDEL.

Ely \'ē-lē\, Richard Theodore. 1854–1943. American economist, b. Ripley, N.Y. Professor at Johns Hopkins (1881–92), U. of Wisconsin (1892–1925), Northwestern U. (1925–33); founded Institute for Research in Land Economics (1920); a leader of Progressive movement.

El·yot \'el-yət\, Sir Thomas. 1490?–1546. English diplomat and scholar. On publication of his *Boke Named the Governour* (1531) on education of princes, dedicated to Henry VIII, was appointed ambassador to Emperor Charles V with instructions to gain emperor's consent to Henry VIII's divorce from Catherine of Aragon and to procure arrest of William Tyndale. M.P. (1542). Translator of *The Doctrinal of Princes* (1534, from Isocrates), and of Platonic dialogues. Author of *The Castel of Helth* (a popular medical treatise, 1534), a Latin dictionary (1538; the first complete one in English), and *Defence of Good Women* (1545).

El·ze·vir \'el-zə-vər\ *or* **El·ze·vier** \-ˌvēr\. *Sometimes* El·se·vier \'el-zə-ˌvēr\. Family of Dutch publishers and printers, including: Lodewijk *or* Louis (1546?–1617), who founded the business at Leiden (c.1580). His sons ¶Matthias (1564–1640) and ¶Bonaventura (1583–1652) who instituted a series of literary classics and the series of *Petites Républiques* country guides (1625–49). Matthias's son ¶Abraham (1592–1652); another son of Matthias ¶Isaac (1596–1651); a son of Abraham, ¶Jean (1622–1661); a son of Bonaventura, ¶Daniel (1626?–1680); and a son of Jean, ¶Abraham II (1653–1712), who was university printer at Leiden (1681–1712).

Emants \'ā-ˌmänts\, Marcellus. 1848–1923. Dutch poet, playwright, and novelist. Author of pessimistic and naturalistic works including *Lilith* (1879, verse), *Een nagelaten bekentenis* (1894, novel), *Inwijding* (1901, novel), *Damheidsmacht* (1904, play).

Emb·den \'em-dən\, Gustav Georg. 1874–1933. German chemist. Director of chemistry laboratory, medical clinic of Frankfurt-Sachsenhausen hospital (1904), which became Physiological Institute (1907) and then U. Institute of Vegetative Physiology, U. of Frankfurt (1914); professor there (1914–33). Investigated metabolic processes of liver, laying foundation for understanding diabetes; investigated metabolic processes in muscle, discovering all the steps in breakdown of glycogen to lactic acid.

Emberres, Gil de. See Gil de SILOÉ.

Em·bri·a·co \ˌem-brē-'äk-ō\, Guglielmo. fl. 1099. Genoese noble. Member of powerful Genoese family; joined siege of Jerusalem in First Crusade (1099); led Genoese army in defeat of Egyptians at Ramla (1099); helped capture Arsuf (1101); besieged Caesarea and captured supposed Holy Grail (1101). His son ¶Ugo helped capture and was granted much of Gibilet (1109). Family received remainder of Gibilet (1139) and Genoese quarter of Acre (1154).

Em·bury \'em-ber-ē, -b(ə-)rē\, Philip. 1728–1773. American clergyman, b. prob. in Ballingrane, Ireland. To New York (1760) and began preaching (1766) to first Methodist society in New York; founded (1768) Wesley Chapel (the first John Street Church, New York); established (1770) at Ashgrove, N.Y., the first Methodist congregation north of New York City. Cf. Barbara HECK.

Em·den \'em-dən\, Jacob Israel, *orig.* Jacob ben Zebi \-ˌben-'zā-bē\. *Known as* Yaa·betz \'yä-ˌbets\. 1697–1776. German rabbi and Talmudist. Noted polemicist, engaged in protracted dispute with Rabbi Jonathan Eybeschütz which divided European Jewry over question of ritual and Talmudic authority.

Emden, Robert. 1862–1940. Swiss astrophysicist. Taught in Munich (1889–1934); developed theory of stellar structure; published *Gaskugeln* (1907).

Em·er·son \'em-ər-sən\, Peter Henry. 1856–1936. English photographer. Published volumes of photographs, including *Life and Landscape on the Norfolk Broads* (1886), *Pictures of East Anglia* (1888); in handbook *Naturalistic Photography* (1889) formulated first aesthetic theory of photography as an independent art.

Emerson, Ralph Waldo. 1803–1882. American essayist and poet, b. Boston, Mass. Minister of Second Church of Boston, Unitarian (1829–32). Visited Europe, meeting Wordsworth, Coleridge, and Carlyle, with last of whom he maintained friendship and correspondence for over forty years. Settled in Concord, Mass. (1834); formed circle of friends, including A. B. Alcott, Margaret Fuller, Thoreau, Jones Very, and Hawthorne, and gradually emerged as leader of literary efflorescence in New England (c.1835–65). Preached in various churches during next several years; meantime began delivering public lectures, material for which he drew from the *Journals* he had been keeping for many years. First published work, *Nature* (1836), contained gist of his Transcendental philosophy, which combined strains of European Romanticism, Oriental supernaturalism, American optimism and practicality. His address to the Phi Beta Kappa society of Harvard on "the American scholar" (1837) and another address to the graduating class of the Cambridge Divinity College (1838) applied his doctrine of individuality in quest for truth to the scholar and the clergyman, the second address provoking sharp controversy. Edited Transcendentalist journal *The Dial* (1842–44). His two volumes of *Essays* (1841, 1844) made his reputation international. Lectured in England (1847). Slowly drawn into participation in national issues and delivered many antislavery speeches; welcomed beginning of Civil War. After 1866 did little new writing; gradually declined in mental powers. Other works: *Poems* (1846, but dated 1847), *Representative Men* (1850), *English Traits* (1856), *The Conduct of Life* (1860), *May-Day and Other Pieces* (poems, 1867), *Society and Solitude* (1870), *Letters and Social Aims* (essays, 1876), *Natural History of Intellect* (1893).

Emi·no·vici \em-'ē-nò-vēch\, Mihail. *Pseudonym* Mihail Emi·nes·cu \ˌem-ē-'nes-kü\. 1850–1889. Romanian poet. Between 1870 and 1883 published poems steeped in Romanian folklore and legend and his own pessimism; exerted profound influence on Romanian literature; collected verse in *Poezii* (1883), including best known, "Luceafărul."

Emin Pa·şa \e-'mēn-pä-'shä\, Mehmed. *Orig. name* Eduard Schnit·zer \'shnit-sər\. 1840–1892. German explorer. Became physician in Turkish army (1865); on staff of Ottoman governor of northern Albania (1870–74), during which time he adopted Turkish way of life. To Khartoum (1876), as medical officer in Egyptian service under "Chinese" Gordon (1876). Named governor of equatorial province, with title of bey (1878); added to geographical knowledge of Central Africa, and extended explorations over eastern Sudan; ended slavery in region. Isolated by Mahdi revolt (1883 ff.); made pasha by Egyptian government (1884); isolation broken by arrival of H. M. Stanley (1888) with whom he made his way to eastern coast (1889). Entered service of German government (1890) and undertook expedition to Equatorial Africa; hoisted German flag at Tabora, and founded station of Bukoba (1890); murdered by Arab slave-raiders near Stanley Falls.

Em·lyn \'em-lən\, Thomas. 1663–1741. English clergyman. First to publicly adopt name Unitarian; last English Dissenter to be imprisoned for beliefs (1702–05).

Em·ma \'em-ə, *Ger* 'em-ä, *Du* 'em-å\. *In full* Emma Adel·heid Wil·hel·mi·na The·re·sa *Ger* 'äd-əl-ˌhīt-vil-hel-'mē-nä-tā-'rā-zä\. 1858–1934. Daughter of Prince George Victor of Waldeck-Pyrmont. Queen consort of the Netherlands (1879–90), as second wife (m. 1879) of King William III. As dowager queen, acted as regent (1890–98) until accession of her daughter Wilhelmina.

Em·ma \'em-ə\ of Normandy. d. 1052. Queen of Aethelred the Unready, King of England. Daughter of Richard the Fearless, Duke of the Normans; m. Aethelred (1002) and adopted English name Aelf·gi·fu \'alf-ˌyiv-ü\. After Aethelred's death (1016), married to Canute (1017), on whose death (1035) she made attempt, thwarted by stepson Harold, to set her son Hardecanute on throne; banished by Harold (1037), fled to court of Baldwin V, Count of Flanders; influential during reign of Hardecanute (1040–41); her wealth seized (1043) by Edward the Confessor, who was her son by Aethelred, probably because of her favor to partisans of Danish line.

Em·ma·nuel Phi·li·bert \ā-må-nwʸel-fē-lē-ber\. 1528–1580. Tenth Duke of Savoy (1553–80). Son of Charles III of Savoy. Sided with Emperor Charles V in war with France (1556–59); distinguished himself in capture of Hesdin (1553) and won great victory at Saint-Quentin (1557); results of peace (1559) restored Savoy but on difficult terms; m. (1559) Margaret of France; by diplomacy or purchase regained several former Savoyard territories from Spain and France; restored Turin as captial (1562); lost Geneva and districts in Vaud.

Em·me·rich \'em-ə-rik\ *or* **Em·me·rick** \-rik\, Anna Katharina. *Called* the Nun of Dül·men \'dʉl-mən\. 1774–1824. German religious and visionary. Entered Augustinian order (1802); exhibited stigmata (from 1812); her visions described by the poet Clemens Brentano (*q.v.*).

Em·met \'em-ət\, Robert. 1778–1803. Irish nationalist. Followed older brother Thomas into United Irishmen (c.1799); in exile in Europe (1800–02); returned to Ireland and began preparing for uprising to coincide with expected French invasion of England (1803); forced to begin insurrection early (July 23), soon found that through poor planning and treachery the revolt was hopeless; captured and hanged for treason.

Emmet, Thomas Addis. 1764–1827. Irish lawyer and patriot. Brother of Robert Emmet. Admitted to Irish bar (1790); defended many political prisoners; joined United Irishmen and became a director (1797); arrested following Lord

Edward Fitzgerald's revolt (1798), which he had counseled against, and imprisoned in Scotland till 1802; released on condition he leave British Empire. To U.S. (1804); practiced law in New York till his death; appeared before Supreme Court against Daniel Webster in *Gibbons* v. *Ogden* (1824).

Em•mett \'em-ət\, Daniel Decatur. 1815–1904. American minstrel and song writer, b. Mount Vernon, Ohio. In winter of 1842–43 organized "Virginia Minstrels"; played in New York, Boston, and England. Composed "Dixie," later adopted as war song of the South; other songs, "Old Dan Tucker," "The Road to Richmond," "Blue-Tail Fly," "My Old Aunt Sally."

Em•mich \'em-ik\, Otto von. 1848–1915. German general. Commanded (1909–15) X Army Corps which invaded Belgium (1914).

Empecinado, El. See Juan MARTÍN DÍAZ.

Em•ped•o•cles \em-'ped-ə-,klēz\. c.490–430 B.C. Greek philosopher and statesman. Disciple of Pythagoras and Parmenides; developed theory of four elements governed by Love and Strife to compose physical world; reputed founder of rhetoric; praised as poet. According to tradition, hurled himself into crater of Mt. Etna in order to convince people he was a god.

Emp•son \'em(p)-sən\, Sir Richard. d. 1510. English politican. Speaker of House of Commons (1491); employed in reign of Henry VII in exacting payment of taxes and penalties; his methods popularly accounted tyrannical; convicted of constructive treason and, with Edmund Dudley, beheaded.

Empson, Sir William. 1906–1984. English poet and critic. Taught at universities in Japan (1931–34) and China (1937–39, 1947–52). Professor of English, Sheffield U. (1953–71). Wrote witty, difficult verse in *Poems* (1935). One of the most influential literary critics of his age; *Seven Types of Ambiguity* (1930) stressed multiplicity of meanings in poetry, affected work of school known as "New Critics"; later wrote *Some Versions of Pastoral* (1938), *The Structure of Complex Words* (1951), etc.

Em•re \'em-re\, Yunus. d. c.1321. Turkish poet and mystic. Known as a Ṣūfī mystic and philosopher; author of verse in traditional Anatolian forms on religion and human destiny that had strong influence on later poets.

Em•ser \'em-zər, 'ām-\, Hieronymus. 1478–1527. German theologian. Secretary to Duke George of Saxony (from 1504); at first sided with Reformers, but broke with Luther on doctrine (1519); attacked Luther in 8 polemical tracts (1520–21); engaged in controversy also with Zwingli; helped found reformed Roman Catholic church in Germany; published (1527) translation of New Testament to counter Luther's.

En•ci•na \ān-'thē-nä\, Juan del. *Orig.* Juan de Fer•mo•sel•le \fer-mō-'sā(l)-yā\. 1468–1529 or 1530. Spanish dramatist and composer. In service of Duke of Alba, wrote several plays (*églogas, representaciones,* and *autos*) which mark transition in Spain from religious to secular drama; author also of lyrics.

Encinas. See ENZINAS.

Enciso, Martín Fernández de. See FERNÁNDEZ DE ENCISO.

Encke \'eŋ-kə\, Johann Franz. 1791–1865. German astronomer. On staff (1816–1825), director (1822–25), Seeberg Observatory, Switzerland; professor at Berlin (from 1825). Determined period of the comet (Encke's comet) discovered by Pons (1818) and showed it to be identical with comets of 1786, 1795, and 1805; deduced a solar parallax long accepted as correct.

En•de•cott *or* **En•di•cott** \'en-di-kət, -də-,kät\, John. 1588–1665. American colonist, b. probably Devon, England. One of six persons who, as New England Company, bought patent for territory on Massachusetts Bay; sailed (1628) and settled at Naumkeag (Salem); acted as first governor of colony till arrival of main body of colonists (1630), when John Winthrop took charge; continued in public service of colony, as deputy governor (1641–43, 1650, 1654) and governor (1644, 1649, 1651–53, 1655–64).

En•der \'en-dər\, Otto. 1875–1960. Austrian politican. Governor of Vorarlberg state (1918–34); chancellor of Austria (1930–31); as minister in Dollfuss government (1933–34), supervised drafting of new federal constitution; headed supreme board of accountancy (1934–38); jailed by Nazis (1938–45).

En•ders \'en-dərz\, John Franklin. 1897–1985. American microbiologist, b. West Hartford, Conn. Founded (1946) laboratory for polio research, Children's Medical Center, Boston. Shared with Thomas H. Weller and Frederick C. Robbins 1954 Nobel prize for physiology or medicine for the cultivation of polio viruses in tissue culture; helped develop a measles vaccine.

End•li•cher \'ent-li-k̲ər\, Stephan Ladislaus. 1804–1849. Hungarian botanist. Formulated a system of plant classification that was widely used for a time; author of *Genera Plantarum Secundum Ordines Naturales Disposita* (1836–50) and *Iconographia Generum Plantarum* (1837–40).

Ene•scu \e-'nes-kü\, Gheorghe *or* George. *Fr.* Georges Ene•sco \-kō\. 1881–1955. Romanian violinist and composer. Toured as virtuoso violinist (from 1899); compositions included opera *Oedipe* (1936), piano sonatas, chamber works, three symphonies, etc.; teacher of Yehudi Menuhin.

En•fan•tin \äⁿ-fäⁿ-taⁿ\, Barthélemy-Prosper. *Known as* Le Père Enfantin \lə-per-\. 1796–1864. French Socialist. A leader of Saint-Simonianism (from 1825) with Bazard; broke with those favoring political action (1831); founded model Socialist community at Ménilmontant (1832); arrested and imprisoned for a short time; unsuccessfully projected a Suez canal (1837); helped form (1845) and director of Lyon Railroad Co.; author of *Religion Saint-Simonienne* (1831), *La Vie eternelle* (1861), etc.

Eng. See CHANG.

Eng•el \'eŋ-əl\, Ernst. 1821–1896. German statistician and economist. Formulated generalization (Engel's law) on relation between changes in family income and expenditures for food.

Engel, Johann Jakob. 1741–1802. German writer. Author of works on popular philosophy, art, and aesthetics, and of the novel *Herr Lorenz Starke* (1801).

Eng•el•bert I \'eŋ-əl-,bert\. Saint. 1185?–1225. Archbishop of Cologne (from 1216); reestablished law and order, helped his people. Aroused hatred of Count Frederick of Isenburg, who had him murdered; honored as martyr.

Engelbert I *or* **Engelbrecht I.** See NASSAU.

Eng•el•brecht•sen \'eŋ-əl-,brekt-sən\ *or* **Eng•e•brechtsz** \'eŋ-ə-brekts\, Cornelis. 1468–1533. Dutch religious painter. A pioneer of Dutch Renaissance art and leader of school of Leyden.

En•gel•brekt En•gel•brekts•son \'eŋ-əl-,brekt-'eŋ-əl-,brekt-sȯn\. c.1390–1436. Swedish national hero. Led uprising of Bergslagen region against Erik of Pomerania (1434); rising became nationwide and Erik agreed (1435) to respect Sweden's rights; continued repression by Erik caused Engelbrekt to renew struggle (1436); captured Stockholm (1436); killed by rival.

Eng•el•mann \'eŋ-(g)əl-mən, *Ger* 'eŋ-əl-,män\, George. 1809–1884. American meteorologist, physician, and botanist, b. Frankfurt am Main, Germany. To U.S. (1833); practiced medicine in St. Louis (from 1835). Made meteorological observations and botanical investigations during rest of life; discovered immunity of North American grape to *Phylloxera*.

Eng•els \'eŋ-əls, *Angl* 'eŋ-(g)əlz\, Friedrich. 1820–1895. German Socialist. Early associated with Young Hegelian group (c.1838); in England (1842–44) for family business; helped form Communist League in London (1847); with Karl Marx published *Manifest der kommunistischen Partei* (1848); involved in revolutionary agitation in Baden (1848–49); fled to England, where he was a manufacturer at Manchester (1850–69); largely supported Marx. Associated with Marx in spreading Communist thought; completed volumes 2 and 3 (1885, 1894) of *Das Kapital* after Marx's death; edited and published Marx's works. Author of *Die Lage der arbeitenden Klasse in England* (1845), *Entwicklung des Sozialismus von der Utopie zur Wissenschaft* (1882), etc.

Enghien, Duc d'. A title borne by the eldest son of the Prince of Condé (see CONDÉ).

Eng•land \'iŋ-glənd, *also* 'iŋ-lənd\, John. 1786–1842. American prelate, b. Cork, Ireland. Brought about reforms in transportation of convicts to Australia. To U.S. on being consecrated (1820) bishop of new apostolic see of Charleston (the Carolinas and Georgia); founded *United States Catholic Miscellany* (1822), first Catholic newspaper in U.S.; naturalized (1826); first Catholic cleric to address Congress (1826); apostolic delegate to Haiti (1833).

En•gle•field \'eŋ-(g)əl-,fēld\, Sir Francis. c.1520–1596. English politician. Knighted on accession of Edward VI (1547), but soon at odds with policy of establishment of Protestantism; befriended Mary Tudor, at whose accession (1553) he was made privy councillor; M.P. (1553–58); close adviser to queen on persecution of Protestants; on accession of Elizabeth I (1558) fled to Continent; joined by Catholic exiles in urging intervention by Spain.

Eng•ler \'eŋ-lər\, Adolf, *in full* Gustav Heinrich Adolf. 1844–1930. German botanist. Professor at Kiel (1878–84), Breslau (1884–89); director of Berlin Botanical Garden, Dahlem (1889–1921). Worked out a natural system of classification of plants; also known for work in plant geography. Author of *Versuch einer Entwicklungsgeschichte der Pflanzenwelt* (1879–82), *Die natürlichen Pflanzenfamilien* (1887–1911), *Syllabus der Pflanzennamen* (1892), *Das Pflanzenreich* (1900–37).

Eng•lish \'iŋ-glish, *also* 'iŋ-lish\, Thomas Dunn. 1819–1902. American physician, lawyer, and writer, b. Philadelphia. Author of the song "Ben Bolt" (1843), and novels, plays, and poems; U.S. congressman from New Jersey (1891–95).

Ennery, Adolphe-Philippe d'. See DENNERY.

En•ni•us \'en-ē-əs\, Quintus. 239–169 B.C. Roman poet. Taught Greek and translated Greek plays (esp. Euripides) in Rome (from 204 B.C.); made Roman citizen (184). Regarded as one of founders of Latin literature; author of a number of tragedies, including *Sabinae, Ambrachia, Scipio,* and, notably, of the epic poem *Annales,* the Roman national epic until surpassed by *Aeneid;* credited with invention of Latin shorthand and of double spelling of long consonants. Only fragments of his works are extant.

En•no•di•us \ə-'nōd-ē-əs\, Magnus Felix. 473?–521. Roman churchman and writer. Appointed bishop of Ticinum (c.513); author of *Dictiones* and

Paraenesis didascalica on rhetoric and grammar, biography of Epiphanius, panegyric on Theodorus, *Eucharisticum de vita sua,* etc.

Eno·mo·to \en-ō-mō-tō\ Takeaki. *Also called* Enomoto Buyo. 1836–1908. Japanese naval officer and politician. Last supporter of Tokugawa family to surrender to imperial restoration. With eight ships captured Hokkaido (1868); surrendered to imperial forces (1869); ambassador to Russia (1873–76); concluded Treaty of St. Petersburg (1874) exchanging Sakhalin claim for Kurils; navy minister (1876–82); minister to China (1882–84); created viscount (1887).

Enrique. See HENRY.

En·rí·quez de Ace·ve·do \än-'rē-käth-thā-äth-ā-'vā-thō\, Pedro. Conde de Fuen·tes \-thā-'fwän-tās\. 1525–1610. Spanish soldier. Served in Naples under his uncle, Duke of Alba (1557); captain general in Portugal, defended Lisbon against English (1589); in Flanders in campaign against French (1594); governor general of Netherlands (1595–96); governor of Milan (1600–10).

En·rí·quez Gó·mez \än-'rē-käth-'gō-māth\, Antonio. c.1600–1660. Spanish writer. To France (1636) to escape Inquisition because of Jewish parentage; major domo to Louis XIII. Author of comedies, some collected in *Academias morales de las musas* (1642); a mystic poem *La culpa del primer peregrino* (1644); an epic *El Sansón nazareno* (1656).

Ensenada, Marqués de la. See SOMODEVILLA Y BENGOECHEA.

En·sor \'en-sȯr\, James Sydney. Baron. 1860–1949. Belgian painter and etcher. Known esp. for bizarre fantasies populated by masks, as *Entry of Christ into Brussels, Portrait of the Artist Surrounded by Masks.*

En·tragues \äⁿ-träg\, Catherine-Henriette de Bal·zac \-də-bäl-zäk\ d'. Marquise de Ver·neuil \-də-ver-nœy\. 1579–1633. French courtier. Mistress of Henry IV of France (from 1600) and a central figure in plots and counterplots in the French court.

Entrecasteaux, Chevalier d'. See Antoine-Raymond-Joseph de BRUNI.

En·ver Pa·şa \en-'ver-pä-'shä\. 1881–1922. Turkish soldier and leader of Young Turks. Raised revolt in Macedonia (1908) forcing Sultan Abdülhamid II to restore constitution of 1876; with Mahmud Şevket suppressed reactionary religious uprising (1909); military attaché in Berlin (1909–11); headed Ottoman resistance to Italy in Libya (1911); governor of Bengazi (1912). Led coup of January 1913 which placed revolutionary party in power; chief of staff of Ottoman army in Second Balkan War (1913); minister of war (1914–18) and member of ruling triumvirate with Cemal and Talât. Took Turkey into World War I on side of Germany; pursued largely unsuccessful military schemes; fled Turkey (1918). After abandoning plan to lead Anatolian resistance to Allied occupation, attempted to organize resistance among Central Asian Turkik peoples to Soviet power; killed in battle with Soviets.

En·zi·nas *or* **En·ci·nas** \än-'thē-näs\, Francisco de. *Also known as* Dry·an·der \drē-än-'der\. 1520–1570. Spanish Humanist and scholar. Translated New Testament into Spanish (1542) and dedicated it to Emperor Charles V, who turned him over to the Inquisition; escaped to Wittenberg; wrote account of his imprisonment.

En·zio \'ent-syō\ *or* **En·zo** \'ent-sō\. c.1220–1272. Titular king of Sardinia. Natural son of Emperor Frederick II of Germany; m. (1238) Adelasia, a Sardinian heiress and took (1243) title of king of Sardinia, but never exercised sovereignty; defeated and captured (1249) by Bolognese; imprisoned (1249–72).

Eobanus Hessus. See HESSUS.

Eogh·an *or* **Eog·an** \'ō-ən\. fl. 400–450 A.D. Irish ruler. Son of Niall of the Nine Hostages. With younger brother Conall conquered and colonized northwest Ulster, founding kingdom of Aileach (c.400); ruled areas later known as Tyrone and Inishowen; ancestor of O'Neills of Tyrone.

Éon de Beau·mont \ā-ōⁿ-də-bō-mōⁿ\, Charles-Geneviève-Louis-Auguste-André-Timothée d'. *Known as* Chevalier d'Eon. 1728–1810. French political adventurer. Sent as secret agent to Russia by Louis XV (1755); adopted woman's dress; served as captain of dragoons; agent, then minister plenipotentiary, in London (1762–63) to negotiate Treaty of Paris; returned to London in guise of woman and remained until 1775; by that time claimed to be a woman; in order to receive pension from France, forced by Louis XVI's decree to wear woman's dress to end of his life. Term "eonism" derived from his name.

Eormenric. See ERMANARIC.

Eöt·vös \'œt-vœsh\, József. Baron Vá·sá·ros·ne·mény \vá-shá-rósh-'ne-mänʸ\. 1813–1871. Hungarian statesman and writer. Through novels and essays became a leader of movement for social and political reform in Hungary; minister of education in revolutionary Batthyány cabinet (1848); in Munich (1848–51). Reentered political life in Hungary (1861) and supported Deák in diets of 1861, 1865, 1867; again minister of education (1867–71); established modern system of national education in Hungary. Novels included *A karthausi* (1839–41), *A falu jegyzöje* (1845), *Magyarország 1514-ben* (1847), *Növerėk* (1857); also wrote poetry, political philosophy.

Eötvös, Lóránt, *Eng.* Roland. Baron Vásárosnemény. 1848–1919. Hungarian physicist. Son of Baron József Eötvös. Professor, Budapest (from 1872); minister of education (1894–95). Derived law describing molecular surface tension (1886); studied gravitation and invented a torsion balance that was long unsurpassed for precision; showed equivalence of gravitational and inertial mass.

Epam·i·non·das \i-,pam-ə-'nän-dəs\. c.410–362 B.C. Theban general and statesman. Defeated Spartan army at Leuctra (371 B.C.) with tactical innovations; invaded Peloponnesus (370–369), encouraged revolt of Helots and the founding of Megalopolis by Arcadians, thus containing Spartan power. Saved army sent (367) to rescue Pelopidas in Thessaly. Checked Athenian naval power with new Theban fleet (364–363). Defeated Spartans again at Mantineia (362), but mortally wounded in the battle.

Épée \ā-pā\, Charles-Michel de l'. 1712–1789. French cleric. Perfected one-hand sign alphabet for use of deaf and dumb; founded (1770) institution for deaf and dumb, in Paris.

Épernon, Duc d'. See NOGARET DE LA VALETTE.

Eph·i·al·tes \,ef-ē-'al-tēz\. d. 469 B.C. Greek traitor. Guided Persian detachment up mountain paths to rear of Greek force under Leonidas defending pass of Thermopylae (480 B.C.).

Ephialtes. d. 461 B.C. Athenian general and statesman. Friend of Pericles; elected general (c.464); unsuccessfully opposed Cimon's policy of aid to Sparta (462); sponsor of law curbing power of the Areopagus and instituting democratic government in Athens (462–461); assassinated, probably at instance of oligarchs.

Eph·o·rus \'ef-ə-rəs\. c.405–330 B.C. Greek historian. Author of the first universal history (29 books, down to 340 B.C.) of which fragments remain.

Ephra·em Sy·rus \'ē-frā-em-'sī-rəs, 'ē-frē-əm-\, *i.e.* the Syrian. Saint. *Also* Ephraim *or Syriac* Aphrem. 306?–373. Syrian churchman and writer. Author of historically important commentaries on the scriptures, theological treatises, homilies, and hymns.

Ep·i·char·mus \,ep-i-'kär-məs\. c.530–c.440 B.C. Greek writer of comedies. Works influenced later Attic comedy; only fragments of his plays are extant.

Ep·ic·te·tus \,ep-ik-'tēt-əs\. fl. c.520–c.500 B.C. Greek potter and painter. Worked in Athens; works noted for draftsmanship, vitality.

Epictetus. c.55–c.135 A.D. Greek Stoic philosopher. Originally a slave, he was freed by his master and taught philosophy in Rome until expelled (90 A.D.) with other philosophers by Emperor Domitian. Left no writings; his philosophy known through the *Discourses* and the *Encheiridion* of his pupil Flavius Arrian.

Ep·i·cu·rus \,ep-i-'kyu̇r-əs\. 341–270 B.C. Greek philosopher. Taught in Athens (from 306 B.C.), emphasizing that pleasure is the only good and the end of all morality, but that the genuine life of pleasure must be a life of simplicity, prudence, honor, and justice; in field of physics, he adopted atomistic theory of Democritus; his school endured for several centuries and Epicureanism found adherents in Rome, esp. Lucretius. Only fragments of his many works are extant.

Epimanes. See ANTIOCHUS IV of Syria.

Ep·i·men·i·des \,ep-i-'men-ə-,dēz\. fl. 6th century B.C.? Cretan philosopher, prophet, and poet. Reported author of religious and poetical texts, although none certainly ascribable to him survive; subject of many legends. He sometimes replaces Periander as one of the Seven Wise Men of Greece.

Épi·nay \ā-pē-ne\, Louise-Florence-Pétronille de la Live \də-lá-lēv\ d'. *Nee* Tar·dieu d'Es·cla·velles \tár-dyœ̄-des-klá-vel\. 1726–1783. French author. Friend of Duclos, d'Alembert, Holbach, and esp. of Diderot, Rousseau, and Melchior Grimm; conducted brilliant salon at La Chevrette; visited Geneva where she was guest of Voltaire (1757–59); aided Melchior Grimm with his *Correspondance;* wrote *Les Conversations d'Émilie* (1774), *Mémoires et correspondances* (pub. 1818; genuine letters of Rousseau, Grimm, Diderot, etc., in the form of an autobiographical romance).

Epiphanes. See ANTIOCHUS IV of Syria; PTOLEMY V.

Epiphanes Dionysus. See ANTIOCHUS VI of Syria.

Epiphanes Nicator. See SELEUCUS VI.

Epiphanes Philadelphus. See ANTIOCHUS XI of Syria.

Ep·i·pha·ni·us \,ep-i-'fā-nē-əs\. Saint. 315?–403. Eastern church father and writer. After study in Egypt founded (335) a monastery near Eleutheropolis in native Palestine; bishop of Constantia (formerly Salamis) in Cyprus (from 367). Zealous opponent of Origen. Author of the treatise, directed against 80 heresies, entitled *Panarion* (c.375), and of the anti-Arian work *Ancoratus* (374).

Episcopius, Simon. See Simon BISCOP.

Epp \'ep\, Franz Xaver von. 1868–1947. German general. Formed anti-Communist Bavarian Free Corps following World War I; retired as lieutenant general (1923); joined Nazi party (1925) and helped organize Sturmabteilung army; governor of Bavaria (1933–45).

Épré·mes·nil \ā-prā-me-nēl\, Jean-Jacques Du·val \dūe-vál\ d'. 1746–1794. French jurist and politician. At beginning of French Revolution advocated establishment of constitutional monarchy; defended Parlement of Paris (1788) against royal infringement of its powers; elected to Estates-General (1789) as representative of nobility; defended royal cause; sent to guillotine by Revolutionary Tribunal (1794).

Ep·stein \'ep-ˌstīn\, Sir Jacob. 1880–1959. British sculptor, b. New York City. Settled in London (1905). Created controversy with nude *Strand Statues,* series of 18 symbolical figures decorating British Medical Association Building, London (1907–08), and with tomb of Oscar Wilde (1912); subsequent works included *The Rock Drill* (1913); life-size bronze Christ (1920); several large allegorical works carved from megaliths, as *Genesis* (1930), *Ecce Homo* (1935); large bronzes, as *St. Michael and the Devil* (1958) for Coventry cathedral; and many bronze portraits.

Equi·a·no \ˌek-wē-'än-ō\, Olaudah. *Known as* Gustavus Vas·sa \'väs-ə\. c.1750–1797. African slave and writer. Enslaved and sold in West Indies (c.1762); acquired rudimentary education and eventually freed; became active abolitionist in England; published *The Interesting Narrative of the Life of Olaudah Equiano, or Gustavus Vassa, the African* (1789).

Érard \ā-rȧr\, Sébastien. 1752–1831. French manufacturer of musical instruments. Invented a mechanical harpsichord (c.1775); made first French square piano (1777); invented new piano key mechanism (1809), and a double-action harp (exhibited in London, 1811). His nephew ¶Pierre Érard (1796–1855) succeeded him in the business.

Er·a·sis·tra·tus \ˌer-ə-'sis-trət-əs\ of Ce·os \'sē-ˌäs\. fl. c.250 B.C. Greek physician and anatomist. Founded school of anatomy at Alexandria. Credited with being first to distinguish between motor and sensory nerves; traced veins and arteries to the heart; named trachea and tricuspid valve of heart; first major exponent of theory of pneuma.

Eras·mus \i-'raz-məs\ *or* **El·mo** \'el-(ˌ)mō\. Saint. d. 303? Italian prelate and martyr. Supposed to have been bishop of Formia; subject of many legends; venerated in Italy from 6th century and in medieval Germany as one of Fourteen Holy Helpers; adopted as patron saint by Mediterranean sailors who regarded "St. Elmo's fire" as reassuring sign.

Erasmus, Desiderius. *Father's surname* Gerard *and thus early in life known as* Gerard Ge·rards \'gā-ˌrärts\. 1466?–1536. Dutch Humanist and scholar. Traveled widely; in England (1499–1500), met Colet, Grocyn, Linacre, and More at Oxford; again in England (1509–14), taught Greek at Cambridge; settled in Basel (1521) and Freiburg im Breisgau (1529). At first favored Reformation, but later opposed it and endeavored to promote reform within Roman Catholic church; engaged in dispute with Luther (1524–26). Edited New Testament in Greek, with a Latin translation (1516); author of *Adagia* (1500, 1508), *Enchiridion militis Christiani* (1503), *Encomium moriae* (1509; *The Praise of Folly*), *Novum instrumentum* (1516), *Institutio principis Christiani* (1516), *Colloquia familiaria* (1518), etc.; published editions of Jerome (1516), Cyprian (1520), Hilary (1523), and other church fathers. Regarded as leader in renaissance of learning in northern Europe.

Erastus, Thomas. See Thomas LÜBER.

Er·a·tos·the·nes \ˌer-ə-'täs-thə-ˌnēz\ of Cy·re·ne \sī-'rē-(ˌ)nē\. c.276–c.194 B.C. Greek astronomer and geographer. Called by Ptolemy Euergetes to Alexandria to head the library there (from c.255). Established a system of chronology whereby dates were reckoned from the conquest of Troy; measured the obliquity of the ecliptic; calculated circumference of Earth from angle of sun's rays at separated points; devised method for finding prime numbers called the "sieve of Eratosthenes."

Er·ben \'er-ben\, Karel Jaromír. 1811–1870. Czech scholar, poet, and ethnologist. Author of a volume of ballads (1853); published collections of Czech folk songs (1841–45) and folk tales (1865), editions of old texts, etc.

Erceldoune, Thomas of. See THOMAS of Erceldoune.

Er·cil·la y Zú·ñi·ga \er-'thēl-yä-ē-'thün-yē-gä\, Alonso de. 1533–1594. Spanish epic poet and soldier. To Chile (1554–63) to aid in quelling revolt of Araucanian Indians whose heroic resistance inspired him to write his epic *La Araucana* (1569–1589), the most famous Spanish epic of the Renaissance and the first about America.

Erck·er \'er-kər\, Lazarus. c.1530–c.1594. German metallurgist. Author of *Beschreibung allerfürnemisten mineralischen Ertzt und Berckwercksarten* (1574), probably earliest systematic work on analytical and metallurgical chemistry.

Erck·mann \erk-mȧn\, Émile. 1822–1899. French author. With ¶Louis-Alexandre Chatrian (1826–1890) collaborated on stories and novels on homely regional themes under the joint pen name Erckmann-Chatrian; works included *Contes fantastiques* (1847), *L'Illustre Docteur Mathéus* (1859), *Contes des bords du Rhin* (1862), *Madame Thérèse* (1863), *L'Ami Fritz* (1864), *Histoire d'un conscrit de 1813* (1864), *Waterloo* (1865), *Les Contes populaires* (1866), etc.

Er·dél·yi \'er-dāl-yē\, János. 1814–1868. Hungarian author and scholar. Published *Magyar Népköltési Gyüjtemény, Népdalok és Mondák,* collection of national poems and folk tales (1846–48), etc.

Er·hard \'är-ˌhärt, *Angl* 'e(ə)r-\, Ludwig. 1897–1977. German economist and politician. Economics minister for Bavaria (1945–46); director of economic council for Anglo-U.S. occupation zone (1948–49); federal economics minister (1949–63); chancellor of West Germany (1963–66).

Eric. See ERIK.

Erichsen, Ludvig Mylius-. See MYLIUS-ERICHSEN.

Ericson, Leif. See LEIF ERIKSSON.

Er·ics·son \'er-ik-sən\, John. 1803–1889. American engineer, b. Värmland County, Sweden. Engineer in Swedish army (1816–27); independent engineer in London (1826–39); made improvements in steam engines, experimented with "caloric" engines, built locomotive *Novelty* (1829); devised screw propeller tested successfully in commercial vessel (1837); to New York (1839) on commission from U.S. navy that resulted in *Princeton* (1844), first warship with screw propellers; naturalized (1848); designed and built ironclad *Monitor* (1862) made famous in battle with Confederate *Merrimack;* vessel inaugurated new era in naval warfare; built *Destroyer* (1878) capable of launching underwater torpedoes.

Eri·ge·na \ə-'rē-gə-nə\, John Scotus. *Surname also given as* Er·iu·ge·na \er-'yü-gə-nə\ *or* Scot·ti·ge·na \skä-'tig-ə-nə\. *Also called* John the Scot. c.810–c.877. Irish-born theologian and philosopher. Invited to teach at court of Charles II the Bald near Laon (c.845); to assist Hincmar of Reims in predestination controversy wrote *De predestinatione* (851), later condemned by council of Valencia (855); translated into Latin and provided commentaries on works of Pseudo-Dionysius the Areopagite, St. Maximus the Confessor, St. Gregory of Nyssa, St. Epiphanius (860–865); wrote *De divisione naturae* (862–866), his major work, attempt to reconcile Neoplatonist emanationism and Christian creationism; his doctrine long influential, esp. in its mystical implications, but ultimately condemned (Paris, 1210; Pope Honorius II, 1225) because of pantheistic leaning.

Er·ik \'ir-ēk, *Angl* 'er-ək\. Name of seven kings of Denmark:

Erik I. *Called* Eje·god \'ā-yä-ˌgōd\, *i.e.* Evergood. c.1056–1103. King (1095–1103); fostered church; went on pilgrimage to Palestine; died in Cyprus.

Erik II. *Called* Emu·ne \'ā-mü-nä\, *i.e.* the Memorable. d. 1137. King (1134–37). Son of Erik I; reign marked by civil war; kingdom was divided for 20 years after his death.

Erik III. *Called* Lam \'läm\, *i.e.* the Lamb. d. 1146. King (1137–46) during period of civil war; lost portions of kingdom to rivals; abdicated.

Erik IV. *Called* Plough·pen·ny \'plaů-ˌpen-ē\. 1216–1250. King (1232–50). Son of Valdemar II Sejr; civil war during reign; killed by his brother Abel.

Erik V. *Called* Glip·ping \'glēp-iŋ\. 1249?–1286. King (1259–86). Son of Christopher I; during minority, kingdom under queen mother, Margaret; continued father's struggle with Archbishop Jakob Erlandsen; regained Schleswig (1272); forced by nobles to grant Denmark's first constitution (1282); murdered.

Erik VI. *Called* Men·ved \'men-vith\. 1274–1319. King (1286–1319). Son of Eric V; defeated combined forces of disaffected nobles, Duke Valdemar of Schleswig, and Norwegian king (1295); imprisonment of Archbishop Jens Grand led to papal interdict (1297–1303); won from Emperor Albert I cession of all lands north of Elbe (1304); wars and feuds nearly bankrupted nation, causing renewed trouble with nobles, church.

Erik VII. See ERIK of Pomerania.

Erik \'ā-rēk\. Name of two kings of Norway:

Erik I. d. 1024? Ruler of Norway (1000–15). Earl (jarl) of Lade; took part in battle of Svolder against Olaf Tryggvason (1000) and on Olaf's death became king of parts of Norway not under Danish rule; abdicated (1015) and sailed to England, where he assisted Canute in his conquest.

Erik II Mag·nus·son \'mäŋ-nů-sȯn\. *Called* Pres·ta·ha·ta·re \'prā-stä-ˌhä-tär-ə\, *i.e.* Priesthater. 1268–1299. King (1280–1299). Son of Magnus VI. Much of reign passed under regency of secular magnates; forced to accede to demands of Hanseatic League (1285). By first wife Margaret of Scotland (m. 1282) father of Margaret, the Maid of Norway.

Erik \'ā-rik\. Name of fourteen kings of Sweden, especially:

Erik IX Jed·vards·son \'yed-vȧrd-sȯn\. Saint. d. 1160. King (c.1150–60). Proclaimed king in Svealand during Sverker's reign in Östergötland; according to legend undertook crusade to Finland; patron saint of Sweden.

Erik X Knuts·son \'knüt-sȯn\. d. 1216. King (1210–16). Grandson of Eric IX and son of Knut Eriksson; first Swedish king crowned by archbishop of Uppsala.

Erik XI Eriks·son \'ā-rēks-sȯn\. c.1216–1250. King (1222–50). Son of Erik Knutsson. Appointed Birger to post of jarl (1248).

Erik XII Magnusson. 1339–1359. King (1356–59). Son of Magnus II Eriksson. In rebellion with nobles and Albert of Mecklenburg, forced father to accept him as coregent (1356).

Erik XIII. See ERIK of Pomerania.

Erik XIV. 1533–1577. King (1560–68). Son of Gustav I Vasa. Promulgated new constitution (1562); consolidated power and imprisoned his half-brother John (1563); aggressive pursuit of Baltic ports instigated seven years' war with Denmark (1563–70); unsuccessfully sought marriage with Queen Elizabeth of England; proposed also to Mary, Queen of Scots, and other royal princesses; finally m. (1568) his commoner mistress; became mentally deranged and was deposed in favor of half-brother John (1568); imprisoned and probably finally poisoned (1569–77).

Erik of Pomerania. c.1381–1459. King of Denmark, Norway, and Sweden. Son of Duke Vratislav VII of Pomerania; adopted (1387) by great-aunt Margaret, queen of Denmark, Norway, and Sweden; accepted as king of Norway (1389) and of Denmark and Sweden (1396); crowned (1397) at Kalmar, where union of three realms was formally sealed; gained actual power on death of Margaret (1412); encouraged trade and imposed first toll in the Øresund (1429); angered Norway and Sweden by favoritism toward Denmark; undertook wars (1416–22, 1426–35) to regain Schleswig; friction with Hanseatic League led to Hanseatic blockade (1434); economic hardships spawned rebellions; removed from thrones of Denmark (1438), Sweden (1439), Norway (1442) in favor of Christopher III.

Erik the Red. *Orig. surnamed* Thor·vald·son \'thȯr-väl-sən\. 10th century. Norwegian navigator. Left Iceland (982) and spent three years exploring southwest coast of Greenland (982–985); named new land "Greenland" to make it attractive to colonists; planted colony (986) near present Julianehåb. Subject of Icelandic *Eiríks saga.* See LEIF ERIKSSON.

Erik Bló·døx \'blō-dœks\, *Eng.* **Blood·axe** \'bləd-ˌaks\. d. 954. King of Norway (930–935). Son of Harald I Fairhair, at whose abdication he became king; killed seven of his eight brothers to secure his throne; unpopular because of his cruelty; defeated by his surviving half-brother Haakon who became king (935); fled to England; ruled Northumbria; killed in battle. His son was Harald II Gråfell.

Eriksson, Leif. See LEIF ERIKSSON.

Erin·na \i-'rin-ə\. 4th century B.C.? Greek poet. Known in antiquity for "The Distaff"; only slight fragments of her works are extant.

Eriugena. See ERIGENA.

Er·kel \'er-kel\, Franz *or* Ferencz. 1810–1893. Hungarian conductor and composer. Regarded as creator of Hungarian national opera; composer of Hungarian national hymn (1845) and of 9 operas, including *Bathori Maria* (1840), *Hunyady László* (1845).

Er·lach, d' \der-läk\. Swiss family of soldiers and diplomats, including: Johann Ludwig (1595–1650), who passed into French service and in the Thirty Years' War distinguished himself in campaigns in Germany and at the battle of Lens (1648). ¶Jean (1628–1694), who also entered French service, distinguished himself at Gravelines and Maastricht. ¶Hieronymus (1667–1748), who served in France, and later in Austria, and returned to become chief magistrate at Bern (1721–47). ¶Karl Ludwig (1746–1798), who served France and then was appointed (1798) general in chief of the Bernese army to resist French invasion, was defeated at Fraubrunnen and slain by his own troops. ¶Ludwig Rudolf (1749–1810), who led a rebellion of Bernese against the French (1802).

Erlach, Johann Fischer von. See FISCHER VON ERLACH.

Er·lang·er \'ər-ˌlaŋ-ər\, Abraham Lincoln. 1860–1930. American theatrical manager and producer, b. Buffalo, N.Y. With Marc Klaw formed booking agency (1888); with Charles Frohman and others formed (1896) Theatrical Syndicate which for years had virtual monopoly of American theatrical business.

Erlanger, Joseph. 1874–1965. American physiologist, b. San Francisco. Professor, Washington U. (1910–46); shared with H.S. Gasser 1944 Nobel prize for physiology or medicine, for work on nerve fibers and nerve impulse transmission.

Er·len·mey·er \'er-lən-ˌmī-ər\, Richard August Carl Emil. 1825–1909. German chemist. Helped develop modern structural notation; synthesized numerous organic compounds; proposed the commonly accepted formula for naphthalene (1866); originated (1861) the conical glass flask named after him.

Er·lings·son \'er-liŋs-sȯn\, Thorsteinn. 1858–1914. Icelandic poet. Author of *Thyrnar* (1897), *Eidurinn* (1913).

Erlon, Comte d'. See Jean-Baptiste DROUET.

Ermak. See YERMAK.

Er·man \'er-ˌmän\, Johann Peter Adolf. 1854–1937. German Egyptologist and lexicographer. Founder of modern study of ancient Egyptian language; author of grammar (1894) and dictionary (1926–35) of old Egyptian.

Er·man·a·ric \ər-'man-ə-rik\. d. 370 to 376 A.D. King of the Ostrogoths, first of the Amalings. Built up large empire in eastern Europe on Dnieper River; overthrown by invasion of the Huns. In German legend the type of the cruel tyrant. In Anglo-Saxon poetry appears as Eor·men·ric \'e-ȯr-men-ˌrēch\, in Norse literature as Jör·mun·rekr \'yœr-mün-räk-ər\.

Er·men·gem \er-mäⁿ-gem\, Frédéric van. *Pseudonym* Franz Hel·lens \ā-lens\. 1881–1972. Belgian writer. Author of novels combining realism and fantasy, including *En Ville morte* (1906), *Mélusine* (1921), *Réalités fantastiques* (1923), *Frédéric* (1935), *Moreldieu* (1946), *Entre touts les femmes* (1960), *La Vie seconde* (1963).

Er·mol·dus Ni·gel·lus \ər-'mōl-dəs-nī-'gel-əs\. *Also* Her·mol·dus \hər-\. *Eng.* Er·mold \'ər-ˌmōld\ the Black. 790–838. Frankish poet. Possibly a monk or chaplain at court of Pepin I of Aquitaine; wrote adulatory but historically valuable *De gestis Ludovici* (826–827); may have been Pepin's chancellor (838).

Er·nest \'ər-nəst\. *Ger.* Ernst \'ernst\. *Called* der Be·ken·ner \ˌder-bə-'ken-ər\, *i.e.* the Confessor. 1497–1546. Duke of Brunswick-Lüneburg (1521–46). Introduced Lutheranism into duchy (1527); signed protest against edict of Diet of Spires (1529); signed Augsburg Confession (1530).

Ernest I. *Ger.* Ernst. *Called* der From·me \dər-'frō-mə\, *i.e.* the Pious. 1601–1675. Duke of Saxe-Weimar (1620–40) and of Saxe-Gotha-Altenburg (1640–75). Son of John, Duke of Weimar, of the Ernestine line; founded ducal house which through his sons became houses of Saxe-Coburg-Gotha, Saxe-Meiningen, etc. Fought in Thirty Years' War under Gustav Adolphus and his own younger brother, Bernhard of Saxe-Weimar; signed Peace of Prague (1635); received (1644) half of Eisenach and (1672) the greater part of Altenburg and Coburg.

Ernest. *Ger.* Ernst. Name of two dukes of Saxe-Coburg-Gotha:

Ernest I. 1784–1844. Duke of Saxe-Coburg-Saalfeld (as Ernest III, 1806–26) and of Saxe-Coburg-Gotha (1826–44). Son of Francis Frederick, Duke of Saxe-Coburg-Saalfeld, brother of King Leopold of Belgium. On extinction (1825) of Saxe-Gotha-Altenburg line, exchanged Saalfeld for Gotha and assumed title of Ernest I (1826). His younger son, Albert (*q.v.*), married Queen Victoria of England.

Ernest II. 1818–1893. Duke (1844–93). Older son of Ernest I; by his liberal policies prevented disturbances in duchy during revolutionary crisis (1848–49); favored Austrian leadership and long opposed Bismarck; later sided with Prussia in Seven Weeks' War (1866) and took part in Franco-Prussian War (1870–71).

Ernest. *Ger.* Ernst. 1441–1486. Elector of Saxony. Elder son of Frederick II the Gentle. Founder of the Ernestine line (*q.v.*). Joint ruler of Saxony (1464–85) with his brother Albert III; received central portions of Thuringia in division of dominions (1485).

Ernest Au·gus·tus \-ȯ-'gəs-təs, -ə-\. *Ger.* Ernst Au·gust \-'au̇-gu̇st\. Name of rulers of Hanover:

Ernest Augustus. 1629–1698. First elector (1692–98) of Hanover; m. (1658) Sophia (1630–1714), daughter of Elector Frederick V of the Palatinate and, through mother, granddaughter of James I of England. Their son became king of England as George I, first of the house of Hanover.

Ernest Augustus. 1771–1851. First king (1837–51) of Hanover. Son of George III of England; created (1799) duke of Cum·ber·land \'kəm-bər-lənd\; became king of Hanover on separation (1837) of English and Hanoverian crowns at accession of Victoria as queen of England; crushed revolution of 1848. Succeeded as king by his son George V, who ruled until annexation of Hanover by Prussia (1866).

Ernest Augustus. 1845–1923. Son and successor of George V, and Duke of Cumberland (from 1878) and of Brunswick-Lüneburg (from 1884, at extinction of elder Brunswick line); maintained claim to Hanoverian throne.

Ernest Augustus. 1887–1953. Son of the preceding; m. (1913) Victoria Louise, daughter of William II of Germany; succeeded to duchy of Brunswick (1913–18; abdicated); deprived (1919) of duchy of Cumberland.

Er·nes·tine \'ər-nəs-ˌtēn\ line. Elder line of Wettin family (*q.v.*), established (1485) with division of electoral duchy of Saxony between Ernest and Albert (*qq.v.*), sons of Frederick II the Gentle. At division received central part of region that is now Thuringia but lost (1547) electoral dignity and much territory to Albertine line; remaining lands broken up into Ernestine duchies (see SAXE-ALTENBURG, SAXE-COBURG-GOTHA, SAXE-GOTHA, SAXE-MEININGEN, SAXE-WEIMAR-EISENACH), thus becoming actually the secondary line.

Ernest Louis. *Ger. in full* Ernst Ludwig Karl Albrecht Wilhelm. 1868–1937. Grand duke of Hesse-Darmstadt (1892–1918). Son of Grand Duke Louis IV, whom he succeeded; grandson through mother of Queen Victoria. Founded (1899) Darmstadt Artists' Colony and sponsored much work in design and architecture, esp. in reaction to Jugendstil movement.

Ernst. See also ERNEST.

Ernst \'ernst, *Angl* 'e(ə)rn(t)st, 'ərn(t)st\, Max. 1891–1976. German painter and sculptor. Cofounder with Jean Arp in Cologne of a Dadaist group (1919); experimented in collage and photomontage; to Paris (1929) where he helped found the Surrealist group (1931); experimented in frottage and decalcomania; in U.S. (1939–49), working chiefly in sculpture; returned to France.

Ernst, Otto. See Otto Ernst SCHMIDT.

Ernst, Paul Karl Friedrich. 1866–1933. German writer, dramatist, and critic. Author of dramas of ideas, including *Demetrios* (1905), *Brunhild* (1909), *Ariadne auf Naxos* (1912), *Kassandra* (1915); novels and tales, including *Der* *schmale Weg zum Glück* (1904), *Die selige Insel* (1909), *Der Nobelpreis* (1919), *Spitzbubengeschichten* (1920); an historical epic *Das Kaiserbuch* (1923–28); essays, including *Der Weg zur Form* (1906), *Ein Credo* (1912), *Der Zusammenbruch des Idealismus* (1919), *Der Zusammenbruch des Marxismus* (1919), *Erdachte Gespräche* (1920), *Jugenderinnerungen* (1930), *Tagebuch eines Dichters* (1934).

Er·skine \'ər-skən\, David Steuart. 11th Earl of Buch·an \'bək-ən, 'bək-\. 1742–1829. Scottish nobleman. Called Lord Card·ross \'kär-,dròs, -drəs\ until death of his father, the 10th earl (1767). Instrumental in freeing election of Scottish representative peers of governmental interference; noted antiquarian; presented George Washington (1792) with snuffbox made from tree that sheltered Wallace.

His brother ¶Henry (1746–1817) was lord advocate of Scotland (1783, 1806); dean of Faculty of Advocates (1785–95), not reelected on account of his condemnation of government's sedition and treason bills as unconstitutional; M.P. (1806–07); remembered as eloquent and witty orator at Scottish bar; author of *The Emigrant, an Eclogue* (1773) and other poems.

¶Thomas (1750–1823), 1st Baron Erskine of Res·tor·mel \ri-'stòr-məl\, another brother, was called to bar (1778); won instant success with defense of Captain Baillie of Greenwich Hospital, accused of libel (1778); made successful defenses of Admiral Lord Keppel (1779) and of Lord George Gordon, demolishing the doctrine of constructive treason (1781); M.P. (1783–84, 1790–1806); attorney general to prince of Wales (1783–92); contributed to passing of Fox's Libel Act (1792); particularly effective in blunting harshness of libel prosecutions under Pitt ministry; unsuccessfully defended Thomas Paine (1792); subsequently appeared for Frost, Hardy, and Horne Tooke; attacked current theory of criminal responsibility and established the plea of insanity in defense of Hadfield, charged with shooting at George III (1800); raised to peerage (1806); lord chancellor in Greenville's All the Talents administration (1806–07), despite his ignorance of equity; made last speech in House of Lords (1820), in defense of Queen Caroline.

Erskine, Ebenezer. 1680–1754. Scottish clergyman. Grandson of a cadet of family of Earl of Mar. Refused oath of abjuration (1712); defended heterodox views in the Marrow controversy (1720); censured prevalent doctrinal errors and advocated right of people to choose their pastors (1733); deposed. With his son-in-law James Fisher, William Wilson, and Alexander Moncrieff formed (1733) an Associate Presbytery, setting up the Secession Church of Marrow-kirk, earliest dissenters from the national church; headed (1747) the Burghers in the split of the Seceders into Burghers and Antiburghers. His brother ¶Ralph (1685–1752), clergyman and poet, joined the Associate Presbytery (1737), took side of Burghers; author of *Gospel Sonnets* (1732), *Scripture Songs* (1754), and the odd conceit *Smoking Spiritualized.*

Erskine, John. 6th Baron Erskine, 1st and 18th Earl of Mar \'mär\ of Erskine line. d. 1572. Scottish noble. Son of John, 5th Lord Erskine (d. 1555), who was guardian of King James V, later of Mary, Queen of Scots. Like his father, keeper of Edinburgh Castle (1554); member of council of Mary Stuart (1561) and favored her marriage with Darnley (1565); created (or restored as) earl of Mar (1565); guardian of James, later King James VI, saved young prince from clutches of Bothwell (1567); joined nobles against Mary and Bothwell (1567); regent of Scotland (1571), but under the influence of James Douglas, Earl of Morton.

His only son ¶John (1558?–1634), 2d and 19th Earl of Mar; seized control of Stirling Castle from uncle (1578); named guardian of young King James VI (1578), but a puppet of Earl of Morton; foiled plot to carry off king (1580); took part in seizure of king and carried him off to Ruthven Castle to keep him from Lennox and Arran (1582); on king's escape, fled to England (1584). With support of Elizabeth I conspired (1584) with Sir Thomas Lyon, master of Glamis, captured Stirling, and on flight of Arran became privy councilor of Scotland (1585) and guardian of Prince Henry (1595); helped to thwart Gowrie conspiracy (1600); envoy to London to negotiate James VI's accession to English throne (1601); lord high treasurer of Scotland (1616–30).

¶John (1675–1732), 6th Earl of Mar, Jacobite leader, eldest son of 5th earl, whom he succeeded (1689). One of commissioners for union (1705); elected a representative peer of Scotland (1707, 1708, 1710, 1713); privy councillor (1708); English secretary of state for Scotland (1713); dismissed from office on accession of George I (1714); placed himself at head of adherents of James Edward, the Old Pretender (1715), proclaimed James VIII king (Sept. 6); defeated at Sheriffmuir by John Campbell, Duke of Argyll; escaped with Pretender to France; subsequently intrigued against James and dismissed from his court in exile (1725). Attainted (1716), leaving earldom under forfeiture for 108 years.

Erskine, John. 1879–1951. American educator and writer, b. New York City. Taught English at Columbia (1909–37); president of Juilliard School of Music (1928–37). Author of *The Moral Obligation to be Intelligent* (1915), *Democracy and Ideals* (1920), best selling novel *The Private Life of Helen of Troy* (1925), *Galahad* (1926), *Adam and Eve* (1927), *The Delight of Great Books* (1928), *Tristan and Isolde* (1932), *Brief Hour of François Villon* (1937), *What Is Music?* (1944), *My Life as a Teacher* (1948), etc.

Erskine of Dun \'dən\, John. 1509–1589. Scottish Reformer. Son of 5th Laird of Dun, of branch of Erskine family later honored with earldom of Mar. Brought back from abroad first teacher of Greek in Scotland (c.1534); supported George Wishart and John Knox, Reform preachers, acting as conciliator between Knox and the queen; superintendent of Reformed Church of Scotland for Angus and Mearns (1560–89); one of compilers of *Second Book of Discipline* (1578).

Erskine of Car·nock \'kär-,näk\, John. 1695–1768. Scottish jurist. Professor, Edinburgh (1737–65); presented connected treatment of Scots law in *Principles of the Law of Scotland* (1754); author of *Institutes of the Law of Scotland* (1773). His son ¶John (1721–1803), theologian, friend of Whitefield and Jonathan Edwards, was leader of evangelical party of the church.

Ervin. See Ovidiu DENSUŞIANU.

Er·vine \'ər-vən\, St. John Greer. 1883–1971. Irish playwright and novelist. Manager of Abbey Theatre, Dublin (1915); drama critic, London *Morning Post* and *Observer;* professor, Royal Society of Literature (1933–36). Author of plays, including *Mixed Marriage* (1910), *Jane Clegg* (1911), *John Ferguson* (1914), *The First Mrs. Fraser* (1928), *People of Our Class* (1934), *Robert's Wife* (1937), *The Christies* (1939), *Private Enterprise* (1947), *My Brother Tom* (1952), *Esperanza* (1957); of novels, stories, biographies, etc.

Er·win \'er-vēn\. *After 17th century often called* Erwin von Stein·bach \-fòn-'shtīn-,bäk\. 1244?–1318. German architect. Engaged (from 1277) in construction of Strasbourg cathedral.

Erz·ber·ger \'erts-,ber-gər\, Matthias. 1875–1921. German politician. In Reichstag (from 1903); leader of left wing of Roman Catholic Center party. Made sensational attack on von Bülow's colonial policies (1906); sought to enlist neutral opinion during World War I; advocated negotiated peace without territorial gains (1917); took active part in coalition of Centrists, Progressives, and Social Democrats favoring democratic constitutional reform. Secretary of state without portfolio under Maximilian, Prince of Baden (1918); chairman of armistice commission and signed Compiègne armistice (1918); minister without portfolio under Scheidemann (1919); favored acceptance of Versailles treaty; minister of finance and, briefly, vice chancellor under Bauer (1919); victim of rightist slander campaign; resigned (1920). Shot and killed by nationalist partisans.

Esar·had·don \,ē-sär-'had-ən\. *Assyrian* As·sur-akh-id·di·na \'äs-ür-äk-'id-ē-nä\. d. 669 B.C. Sargonid king of Assyria (680–669 B.C.). Son of Sennacherib. Quelled civil war that broke out as result of murder of Sennacherib by one of his sons; conquered Chaldeans, Medians, other tribes; lost territory in north to Cimmerians; rebuilt Babylon; led two great armies into Egypt (675–669); at first turned back by Taharqa, but later (671) defeated him; plundered Memphis; first Mesopotamian to rule in Egypt. A great builder, erected palace in Nineveh. Father of Shamash-shum-ukin and of Ashurbanipal.

Es·björn \'es-byœrn\, Lars Paul. 1808–1870. American clergyman and educator, b. Delsbo, Sweden. To U.S. (1849). Leader of secession of Swedish Lutherans and of organization of independent Augustana Synod (1860).

Es·ca·lan·te \ā-skä-'län-tā\, Francisco Silvestre Vélez de. fl. 1768–1779. Spanish Franciscan missionary. While seeking route from Santa Fe to Monterey (1776–77) rediscovered Grand Canyon (first seen by Cárdenas, 1540); made first Spanish penetration of Utah (1776).

Esch \'esh\, John Jacob. 1861–1941. American politician, b. near Norwalk, Wis. Member, U.S. House of Representatives (1899–1921). Member of Interstate Commerce Commission (1921–28). Author with Sen. A.B. Cummins of Esch-Cummins Transportation Act (1920).

Eschenbach, Wolfram von. See WOLFRAM VON ESCHENBACH.

Eschen·burg \'esh-ən-,bùrk\, Johann Joachim. 1743–1820. German critic, literary historian, and translator. Translated works of English writers on aesthetics, Italian and English opera and oratorio texts, and first complete dramatic works of Shakespeare (1775–82).

Esch·er \'esh-ər\, Alfred. 1819–1882. Swiss politician. President of Zürich government (1848); member (from 1848), president (1849–50, 1856–57) of national assembly; a founder of the Technische Hochschule (1854); as head of railroad company carried through construction of Gotthard line (1869–78).

Esch·er \'es-kər, *Angl* 'esh-ər\, Maurits Cornelis. 1898–1972. Dutch artist. Known esp. for lithographs and woodcuts incorporating illusions, transformations, geometric distortions, and whimsical but mathematically consistent tricks.

Escher von der Linth \-fòn-dər-'lint\, Hans Konrad. *Orig. surname* Escher. 1767–1823. Swiss politician. Member (1798–1803), president (1798–99) of grand council of Helvetic Republic; devoted himself to canalization of the

Linth River (Escher Canal; 1808–22). Officially granted honorary surname "von der Linth" by grand council of Zürich (1823).

Es·co·bar y Men·do·za \äs-kō-'b̲är-ē-män-'dō-thä\, Antonio. 1589–1669. Spanish Jesuit and theologian. Known esp. for his support of ethical doctrine of probabilism; attacked by Pascal, Molière, La Fontaine, etc.

Es·co·be·do \äs-kō-'b̲ā-t̲h̲ō\, Mariano. 1827–1902. Mexican soldier. As brigadier general, resisted French invasion (1861–63); to San Antonio, Texas; organized Republican army. Reentered Mexico (1865), taking Monterrey; defeated Miramón at San Jacinto (1867); promoted commander in chief of Republican forces; defeated and captured Maximilian at Querétaro (1867); signed order for Maximilian's execution (June 16, 1867).

Es·cof·fier \es-kȯf-yā\, Auguste, *in full* Georges-Auguste. 1846–1935. French chef. Director of kitchen of Grand Hotel, Monte Carlo, later of Savoy and Carlton hotels, London; known for cuisinary innovations and codification; author of *Guide culinaire* (1903), *Ma cuisine* (1934) etc.

Es·cri·vá de Ba·la·guer y Al·bás \es-krē-'b̲ä-t̲h̲ä-'b̲äl-ä-g̲wer-ē-äl-'b̲äs\, José María. 1902–1975. Spanish prelate. Founder (1928) and president general (1946–75) of Opus Dei, Roman Catholic lay order; oversaw establishment of many schools, including U. de Navarra.

Esdras. See EZRA.

Esenin, Sergey. See YESENIN.

Es·en Tai·ji \'es-ən-'tī-jē\. d. 1455. Mongol chief. Became chief of Oyrat Mongols (1439); extended domain to Korea and China; ceased paying tribute to Chinese (1449); defeated Chinese army sent against him and captured Emperor Chen-t'ung (1449); unsuccessfully besieged Peking (1449–50); made peace and resumed tribute (1453).

Eshbaal. See ISHBOSHETH.

Esher, Viscount. See Reginald BRETT.

Esh·kol \esh-'kōl\, Levi. *Orig. surname* Shkol·nik \'shkōl-nēk\. 1895–1969. Israeli politician. To Palestine from native Russia (1914); a founder of Histadrut (1920); minister of finance (1952–63); prime minister (1963–69).

Es·kil \'es-kil\. c.1100–1182. Danish prelate. Bishop of Roskilde (1134); archbishop of Lund (1138); secured from Pope Innocent II full equality of Scandinavian diocese; canonized Canute Lavard (1170) and assisted in establishing hereditary rule of Valdemar dynasty; forced into exile in France (1177). Founded many monasteries.

Es·ko·la \'es-kō-lä\, Pentti Eelis. 1883–1964. Finnish petrologist. Taught at U. of Helsinki (1916–53); known for studies of metamorphism and metasomatism of rocks, theories of origin of Earth's crust and pore magmas.

Es·la·va \ā-'slä-vä\, Miguel Hilarión. 1807–1878. Spanish composer. Director of Royal Chapel, Madrid (1847); professor (from 1854) and director (from 1866), Royal Conservatory, Madrid; works included operas, religious music esp. a Miserere, and *Lira sacrohispana* (1869), a valuable collection of Spanish church music of the 16th–19th centuries.

Es·mā·'īl \is-mä-'ēl\, Name of two rulers of Iran of the Ṣafavid dynasty:

Esmā'īl I. *Also spelled* Ismā'īl. 1487–1524. Shah of Iran (1501–24), founder of Ṣafavid dynasty. Succeeded father as head of Kizilbash group of the Shī'ah sect; conquered Tabriz and proclaimed himself shah (1501); conquered all of Iran; defeated Uzbeks at Marv (1510); proclaimed Shī'ah sect state religion of Iran; defeated by Turkish troops under Selim I (1514), lost Tabriz; continued to battle northern tribes adhering to Sunnī sect. Father of Ṭahmāsp I.

Esmā'īl II. 1551–1577. Shah of Iran (1576–77). Son of Ṭahmāsp I, whom he succeeded.

Esmā'īl ebn Aḥ·mad \-ˌib-ən-'äk̲-ˌmäd\. 9th–10th century. Persian ruler. As governor of Transoxiana under nominal rule of caliph of Baghdad, conquered neighboring territories and came to rule all Persia (892–907) as one of the Sāmānid dynasty.

Es·march \'es-ˌmärk̲\, Johannes Friedrich August von. 1823–1908. German surgeon. Authority on military surgery; inventor of a method for keeping a limb nearly bloodless during amputation; introduced first-aid bandage to battlefield.

Esnambuc, Pierre Belain d'. See BELAIN.

Es·nault-Pel·ter·ie \es-nō-pel-trē, ā-nō-\, Robert-Albert-Charles. 1881–1957. French aviator. Invented ailerons while attempting to duplicate Wright brothers' successful gliders; built one of the first monoplanes (1907) with 7-cylinder radial engine; invented improved fuel pump. Later interested in space exploration; coined term astronautics.

Español, Pedro. See Pedro BERRUGUETE.

Es·par·te·ro \ā-spär-'tā-rō\, Baldomero Fernández. Conde de Lu·cha·na \lü-'chä-nä\. 1793–1879. Spanish general and politician. To South America and fought against colonists (1815–23); supported Isabella II; fought in Carlist war (1833–39); commander in chief of government forces (1836); defeated Carlists notably at Luchana; president of provisional government (1840–41) and regent (virtually dictator) of Spain after resignation of queen regent Maria Christina (1841–43). After Isabella was declared of age, was driven out of Spain by rebels under Narváez (1843); regained honors by royal decree (1848); made triumphal return in revolution (1854); prime minister (1854–56) although real power was held by Leopoldo O'Donnell. Made prince of Ver·ga·ra \ver-'g̲ä-rä\ by King Amadeus.

Esperanto, Dr. See Ludwik ZAMENHOF.

Esperey, Franchet d'. See FRANCHET D'ESPEREY.

Es·pi·na de Ser·na \ā-'spē-nä-t̲h̲ā-'ser-nä\, Concha. 1877–1955. Spanish novelist. Wrote *La niña de Luzmela* (1909), *La esfinge maragata* (1914), *El metal de los muertos* (1920), *Altar mayor* (1926), *El más fuerte* (1947), *Una novela de amor* (1953).

Es·pi·nel \ā-spē-'nel\, Vicente Martínez. 1550–1624. Spanish writer and musician. Revived the *décima* stanza, later called after him the *espinela;* published *Diversas rimas* (1591). Credited by some with having introduced fifth string on the guitar. Known esp. for his picaresque novel *La vida del escudero Marcos de Obregón* (1618), a source for Lesage's *Gil Blas.*

Espi·no·sa \ā-spē-'nō-sä\, Pedro de. 1578–1650. Spanish poet and editor. Compiled *Flores de poetas ilustres de España* (1605), important anthology; best known of his own Baroque verse the *Fábula del Genil.*

Es·poz y Mi·na \ā-'spō-thē-'mē-nä\, Francisco. 1781–1836. Spanish soldier. Conducted guerrilla warfare against the French in Navarre (1808–14); in exile after leading unsuccessful coup against Ferdinand VII (1814–20); led Liberal army in Catalonia against French attempt to restore Ferdinand (1823); defeated and exiled; led Spanish army against the Carlists (1834).

Es·pron·ce·da y Del·ga·do \ā-sprōn-'thā-t̲h̲ä-ē-del-'g̲ä-t̲h̲ō\, José de. 1808–1842. Spanish poet. Involved from early youth in revolutionary struggles and plots, living mostly in exile. A leading exponent of Spanish Romanticism, much influenced by Lord Byron; wrote novel *Sancho Saldaña* (1834); verse *Poesías* (1840), *El estudiante de Salamanca* (1840), unfinished epic *El pelayo.*

Es·py \'es-pē\, James Pollard. 1785–1860. American meteorologist, b. Pa. Called "Storm King" for his convection theory of storms published in *Philosophy of Storms* (1841). As meteorologist to War Dept. (from 1842) and Navy Dept. (from 1848), laid foundation for weather forecasting by system of telegraphic weather bulletins from one locality to another.

Esquilache, Príncipe de. See BORJA Y ARAGÓN.

Es·qui·rol \es-kē-rōl\, Jean-Étienne-Dominique. 1772–1840. French physician. Chief physician, Charenton asylum (1826); effected reforms in treatment of insane; made first attempt to classify mental disorders; author of *Des maladies mentales* (1838), first modern textbook of psychiatry.

Es·sad Pa·şa \e-'sät-pä-'shä\. *Surname* Top·ta·ni \tōp-tän-'ē\. c.1864–1920. Albanian politician. Joined Young Turk revolutionary movement (1908); Albanian deputy in Turkish parliament (1908); in First Balkan War commanded defense of Scutari; attacked by Montenegrins (1912–13), secretly intrigued with them and surrendered city. Instrumental in seating Prince William of Wied on Albanian throne (1914); minister of war and of interior in Albanian cabinet; exiled after discovery of his designs on throne (1914). During World War I headed Albanian delegation in Paris. After war arranged to be proclaimed by so-called National Assembly king of Albania but assassinated by an Albanian in Paris.

Es·sen \'es-sən\, Hans Henrik von. Count. 1755–1824. Swedish soldier. Favorite and aide-de-camp of King Gustav III; governor of Pomerania (1800); defended Stralsund against French (1807); member of council of state (1809); concluded peace between Sweden and France (1810); field marshal (1811). Commanded Swedish army sent against Norway; governor of Norway (1814–16); marshal of Sweden (1816); governor general of Skåne (1817).

Es·sex \'es-iks\, Earl of. An English title borne chiefly by the following: Geoffrey and William de MANDEVILLE; Geoffrey FITZPETER; members of BOHUN family; Thomas CROMWELL; members of DEVEREUX family; Arthur CAPEL and his descendants.

Essling, Prince d'. See André MASSÉNA.

Es·taing \es-taⁿ\, Jean-Baptiste-Charles-Henri-Hector d'. Comte. 1729–1794. French naval commander. Originally a soldier; entered navy (1759); lieutenant general of marine (1763); governor of the Antilles (1763–66); vice admiral (1777); in command of first French squadron sent to aid American Revolution (1778); unsuccessful in attempt to blockade Admiral Howe at New York; wounded at Savannah (1779). Elected to Assembly of Notables (1787); commander of National Guard at Versailles (1789); admiral of France (1792); guillotined in Paris.

Es·tau·nié \es-tōn-yā\, Édouard. 1862–1942. French novelist. Author of *L'Empreinte* (1895), *L'Épave* (1902), *La Vie secrète* (1908), *Les Choses voient* (1913), *L'Ascension de M. Baslèvre* (1920), *L'Appel de la route* (1921), *Madame Clapin* (1932).

Este \'es-tā\. Italian princely family, including: Alberto Azzo II (996–1097), who was invested by Emperor Henry VII with Este, Friuli, Monselice, and other Italian fiefs, and first adopted name Este. His older son ¶Welf IV (d. 1101) became ancestor of the noble houses of Bavaria, Brunswick, and Hanover; through his younger son ¶Folco I (d. c.1136) was descended the Italian branch of the family which played prominent role in medieval and renaissance Italy. Folco's son ¶Obizzo I (d. 1193) was first to bear title of marquis of Este; married into Guelph family of Ferrara. His grandson ¶Azzo VI (1170–1212) became head of Guelph party and (1208) first lord of Ferrara. Azzo's successor ¶Azzo VII (1205–1264) was leagued with Pope Gregory IX against the Ghibellines and succeeded in establishing himself in full control of Ferrara. His son ¶Obizzo II (d. 1293) was created perpetual lord by people of Ferrara (1264); lord of Modena (1288), of Reggio (1289). Among later descendants of note were: ¶Nicolò II, *called* the Lame (1338–1388), who built Este Castle; his brother and successor ¶Alberto V (1347–1393) built U. of Ferrara. Alberto's son ¶Nicolò III (1384–1441) ruled Ferrara, Modena, Parma, Reggio, and nearly got control of Milan. Nicolò III's sons ¶Leonello (1407–1450), his successor, and a patron of arts and learning; ¶Borso (1413–1471), created duke of Modena and Reggio (1452) and of Ferrara (1471); and ¶Ercole I (1433–1505), patron of Boiardo and Ariosto.

Ercole's children included ¶Beatrice d'Este (1475–1497), Duchess of Milan, a noted beauty, patron of learning, and wise politician; m. (1491) Ludovico Sforza. ¶Isabella d'Este (1474–1539), Marchioness of Mantua, was also a beauty, patron of learning, and skilled diplomat; m. (1490) Giovanni Francesco Gonzaga. ¶Ippolito I (1479–1520), Cardinal d'Este and Archbishop of Milan; patron of Ariosto; and his successor ¶Alfonso I (1486–1534), m. (1501) Lucrezia Borgia; successful military commander who contested papal power for Reggio and Modena.

Alfonso I's sons ¶Ercole II (1508–59), patron of arts, husband of Renée, daughter of Louis XII of France; and ¶Ippolito II (1509–72), Cardinal d'Este and Archbishop of Milan, who built Villa d'Este at Tivoli. Ercole II's son ¶Alfonso II (1533–1597), fifth and last Duke of Ferrara, patron of Torquato Tasso. Members of collateral lines included ¶Francesco I (1610–1658), Duke of Modena. ¶Alfonso IV (1634–1662), father of Mary Beatrice, who became wife of King James II of England. Alfonso IV's son ¶Francesco II (1660–1694), who started Este library at Modena and founded the university there; his successor ¶Rinaldo I (1655–1737) who united two branches of the family by marrying Charlotte Felicitas of Brunswick-Lüneburg. Rinaldo was succeeded by his son ¶Francesco III (1698–1780), who married Charlotte, daughter of Philippe II, duc d'Orléans, and was named governor of Lombardy (1754) by Empress Maria Theresa. His son ¶Ercole III (1727–1803) abandoned Modena to French (1796). Ercole's grandson ¶Francesco IV (1779–1846) returned to Modena and ruled as first of Austro-Este line (1814–59) which ended with his son ¶Francesco V (1819–1875).

Es·té·ba·nez Cal·de·rón \ā-'stā-b̲ä-nāth-käl-dā-'rōn\, Serafín. *Pseudonym* El So·li·ta·rio \el-sō-lē-'tär-yō\. 1799–1867. Spanish writer. Author of volume of poetry (1831), *Cristianos y moriscos* (1838), *Escenas andaluzas* (1847), etc.

Estella, Marqués de. See PRIMO DE RIVERA.

Es·ter·há·zy \'es-ter-ˌhá-zē\. *Hung.* Esz·ter·há·zy. Noble Magyar family, including: Ferenc Zer·há·zy \'zer-ˌhá-zē\ (1563–1594), who first took name Esterházy when created baron of Galánta. His son ¶Miklós (1582–1645) founded Fraknó line of family; elected palatine of Hungary (1625); victor over Turks (1623) and strong supporter of plans for consolidating Habsburg dynasty in order to free Hungary from Turkish dominance; Miklós's son ¶Pál (1635–1713), established princely branch of family; elected palatine (1681); fought Turks, aiding in freeing Vienna from siege (1683) and capturing Buda (1686); strong supporter of Habsburg monarchy; created prince of the empire (1687); instrumental in curtailing powers of great Magyar nobles. Later members of family included: ¶Prince Miklós József (1714–1790), grandson of first prince; art patron, rebuilt family castle Esterháza in Renaissance style; employed Haydn for thirty years as his musical director and conductor of his private orchestra. His grandson ¶Prince Miklós (1765–1833) amassed great collection of paintings and engravings, fought Napoléon (1797). His son ¶Prince Pál Antal (1786–1866), Austrian diplomat under Metternich; ambassador to England; Hungarian foreign minister (1848). ¶Count Moritz (1807–1890), Austrian diplomat, minister in Rome (to 1856), where he conducted negotiations for a concordat, and minister without portfolio (1861–66).

Es·ter·ha·zy \es-ter-á-zē\, Marie-Charles-Ferdinand-Walsin. 1847–1923. French army officer. Notorious because of his connection with the Dreyfus case; confessed (1899) that, working as a German spy, he had forged the document which constituted the chief evidence against Dreyfus. Spent rest of his life under an assumed name in exile in England.

Es·tienne *or* **Étienne** \ā-tyen\. *Lat.* Steph·a·nus \'stef-ə-nəs\. French family of scholars, printers, and bookdealers, including: Henri I (c.1470–1520), founder of the business (c.1505); his three sons ¶François I (1502–50), ¶Robert I (1503–1559), who took over business (1526) and adopted its olive tree device; appointed royal printer of Hebrew and Latin works to Francis I (1539); moved to Geneva (c.1552); published many editions of Greek and Latin classics, a *Dictionarium seu linguae latinae thesaurus* (1531), a Latin–French dictionary (1539) and various editions of the Bible, and ¶Charles (1504–1564), who first studied medicine and later succeeded his brother Robert as royal printer (1551) and published a great book on anatomy, *De dissectione partium corporis humani* (1545). Three sons of Robert, ¶Henri II (1528–1598) who succeeded Robert in charge of printing establishment at Geneva (1559) and printed and edited many editions of Greek and Latin classics, most notably a Latin Herodotus (1566), a Greek and Latin Plutarch (1572); compiled *Thesaurus graecae linguae* (1572); ¶Robert II (1530–1570), who remained Roman Catholic when father joined the Reformed Church and succeeded his uncle Charles as royal printer (1564); and ¶François II (1536–?), who founded at Geneva (1562) a studio of typography (1562–82).

Es·ti·gar·ri·bia \ā-stē-gär-'rē-b̲yä\, José Félix. 1888–1940. Paraguayan general. Commander in chief in Chaco war; won victories during early part of contest (1932–35). Minister to U.S. (1938–39); instrumental in arranging peace between Bolivia and Chile (1938); president of Paraguay (1939–40); officially proclaimed himself dictator (1940). Killed in airplane crash.

Estournelles de Constant, Paul d'. See Paul BALLUET D'ESTOURNELLES.

Es·tra·da Ca·bre·ra \ā-'strä-t̲h̲ä-kä-'b̲rā-rä\, Manuel. 1857–1924. Guatemalan politician. Successively judge of the Supreme Court, minister of public instruction, of justice, and of interior; on assassination of President Barrios, made provisional president (1898); constitutional president (1898–1905); ruled as military despot until 1920, using military and secret police to retain power; driven from power by revolution under Carlos Herrera.

Es·tra·da Pal·ma \ā-'strät̲h̲-ä-'päl-mä\, Tomás. 1835–1908. Cuban statesman. Served in Cuban revolution (1868–78); president (1875–77) of provisional government; in exile in Honduras and U.S. (1878–1902); succeeded (1895) Martí as leader of independence movement; first president of Cuba (1902–06); reelected (Mar. 1906) but resigned (Sept. 1906) on charges of electoral fraud.

Es·trades \es-trád\, Godefroi Louis d'. Comte. 1607–1686. French diplomat. Campaigned in Italy (1648), Catalonia (1655), the Low Countries (1672); marshal of France (1675). Ambassador to Holland (1646); negotiated ceding of Dunkerque by Charles II (1662); negotiated Treaty of Breda with Denmark (1667) and Treaty of Nijmegen with Holland (1678).

Es·trées \ā-trā, es-\. Noble French family originally of Picardy, including: Antoine d'Estrées, *called* le Jeune \lə-zhœn\ (d. 1530), founder of the line. His son ¶Jean (1486–1571) and grandson ¶Antoine (?–?) were in turn masters of French artillery. Antoine's daughter ¶Gabrielle (1573–1599) became (probably 1591) mistress of Henry IV; created marquise de Monceaux, duchesse de Beaufort, and duchesse d'Étampes; wielded strong influence on Henry; responsible for his adoption of Catholicism; died before Henry could arrange to marry her. Her son by Henry, ¶César (1594–1665) was founder of the Vendôme branch of the Bourbon family (*q.v.*). Gabrielle's brother ¶Duc François-Annibal d'Estrées (1573–1670), marquis de Coeuvres, while bishop of Noyon strongly influenced the election of Pope Gregory XV (1621); left church for army, rising to lieutenant general; created marshal of France (1626), French ambassador in Rome (1636), governor of Île de France (1654); author of *Mémoires* of the regencies of Marie de Médicis and Anne of Austria. His son ¶Jean d'Estrées (1624–1707); distinguished himself at Gravelines, at the battle of Lens, and during the Fronde; entered naval service and became vice admiral (1669); engaged against the Dutch at Southwold Bay (1672) and Schooneveldt and Texel (1673), and in the Antilles (1677); created marshal of France (1681); appointed viceroy in America (1686). Jean's son ¶Duc Victor-Marie d'Estrées (1660–1737), comte de Coeuvres, served as both lieutenant general and vice admiral; commanded advance guard of the fleet of de Tourville; created marshal of France (1703); distinguished himself in naval campaign ending with battle of Málaga (1704); succeeded father as viceroy in America (1707); appointed minister of state (1715). His grandnephew ¶Louis-Charles-César Le Tel·lier \lə-tel-yā\, marquis de Courtanvaux, Duc d'Estrées (1695–1771), field marshal (1735), lieutenant general (1748); engaged at battle of Fontenoy; created marshal of France (1757) and duc d'Estrées (1763).

Es·trup \'es-trüp\, Jacob Brønnum Scavenius. 1825–1913. Danish politician. Leader of National Landowners' party in Landsting (1864–98, 1900–13); minister of interior (1865); prime minister and finance minister (1875–94).

Étampes, Duchesse d'. See Anne de PISSELEU; Gabrielle d'ESTRÉES.

Etch·e·bas·ter \ich-i-bäsh-'ter\, Pierre. 1894?–1980. French Basque athlete. World champion court-tennis player (1928–54); retired undefeated; 26 undefeated years a world record for any sport.

Etex \ā-teks\, Antoine. 1808–1888. French sculptor, painter, and architect. Known esp. for relief sculptures *La Résistance* and *La Paix* on the Arc de Triomphe de l'Étoile, Paris.

Ethelbald. See AETHELBALD.

Ethelbert. See AETHELBERHT.

Eth·el·dre·da \ˌeth-əl-ˈdrēd-ə\. Saint. 630?–679. Queen of Northumbria. Married (660) Ecgfrith, who became (670) king of Northumbria; disowned marriage duties; founded abbey at Ely; consecrated Abbess of Ely (673).

Ethelfleda. See AETHELFLAED.

Ethelred. See AETHELRED.

Ethelwerd. See AETHELWEARD.

Ethelwold. See AETHELWOLD.

Ethelwulf. See AETHELWULF.

Eth·er·ege \ˈeth-(ə-)rij\, Sir George. 1635?–?1692. English dramatist. Began period of Restoration comedy with *Love in a Tub* (1664), partly in rhymed heroic verse, partly in realistic scenes of lively comedy; continued to picture life of the day in *She wou'd if she cou'd* (1668) and *The Man of Mode* (1676); invented comedy of intrigue; paved way for Congreve and Sheridan.

Étienne. See ESTIENNE; as personal name, see STEPHEN.

Etō \e-tō\ Shimpei. 1835–1874. Japanese politician. Played large role in winning support for imperial restoration (1868); helped influence transfer of new government from Kyōto to Tokyo; helped establish new civil administration; resigned from cabinet (1873) on rejection of his plan to invade Korea; formed dissident group, Aikoku Kōtō, calling for parliamentary government; organized revolt in native Saga region (1874); captured and executed.

Et·ty \ˈet-ē\, William. 1787–1849. English painter. Painted historical and classical works, but best known as a figure painter.

Etzel. See ATTILA.

Eu, Comte d'. See ORLÉANS IV.

Eu·bu·li·des \yü-ˈbyü-lə-ˌdēz\ of Mi·le·tus \mī-ˈlēt-əs, mə-\. 4th century B.C. Greek philosopher. Succeeded Euclid of Megara as head of the Megarian school; by tradition a teacher of Demosthenes; known as inventor of logical paradoxes.

Eu·bu·lus \ˈyüb-yə-ləs\. 4th century B.C. Greek statesman. Ably controlled Athenian finances as chief commissioner (c.355–346 B.C.) of Theoric Fund; improved navy; counseled peace with Philip II of Macedonia and thus opposed faction of Demosthenes; largely responsible for Peace of Philocrates (346), unpopularity of which largely ended his public influence.

Euck·en \ˈȯi-kən\, Rudolf Christoph. 1846–1926. German philosopher. Professor at Basel (1871–74), Jena (1874–1920). Author of works on historical philosophy, esp. on Aristotle, on religion, and on his own philosophy of ethical activism. Works included *Die Grundbegriffe der Gegenwart* (1878), *Die Einheit des Geisteslebens* (1888), *Der Wahrheitsgehalt der Religion* (1901), *Philosophie der Geschichte* (1907), *Der Sinn und Wert des Lebens* (1908), *Können wir noch Christen sein?* (1911), *Mensch und Welt* (1918). Awarded Nobel prize for literature (1908).

Eu·clid \ˈyü-kləd\. fl. c.300 B.C. Greek geometer. Founded a school in Alexandria during reign of Ptolemy I Soter. His chief work *Stoicheia* (*Elements*), drawing on work of earlier thinkers as Theaetetus, Eudoxus, Hippocrates of Chios, remained chief source of geometrical reasoning and methods until 19th century; also wrote *Data, On Divisions, Optics, Phaenomena,* etc.

Euclid *or* **Eu·clei·des** \yü-ˈklīd-ˌēz\ of Meg·a·ra \ˈmeg-ə-rə\. 450?–374 B.C. Greek philosopher. Disciple of Socrates; founder of the Megarian school. Only titles of his works are extant.

Eu·crat·i·des \yü-ˈkrat-ə-ˌdēz\. d. c.159 B.C. King of Bactria (c.170 or 165–c.159 B.C.). Of uncertain origin, possibly related to Seleucid or Bactrian royal house; seized power during absence of King Demetrius in India.

Eu·de·mus *or* **Eu·de·mos** \yü-ˈdē-məs\ of Rhodes \ˈrōdz\. 4th century B.C. Greek philosopher. Pupil and friend of Aristotle; edited or revised *Eudemian Ethics* of Aristotle; wrote *Physics, Analytics,* of which fragments are extant.

Eudes \œ̄d\ *or* **Odo** \ˈōd-ō\. 665–735. Duke of Aquitaine (c.714–735). Sided with Neustrians against Charles Martel (718–720); defeated invading Arabs at Toulouse (721); when threatened later by Arab commander ʽAbd ar-Raḥmān, was aided by Charles Martel, who defeated Arabs at Poitiers (732).

Eudes *or* **Odo.** Name of four dukes of Burgundy, including:

Eudes I Bo·rel \bȯ-rel\. d. 1102. Ruler of Burgundy (1078–1102); helped Raymond IV of Toulouse plan crusade.

Eudes III. 1166–1218. Son of Hugh III; ruler of Burgundy (1192–1218); took part in the Albigensian crusade (1209–18) and commanded part of army at Bouvines (1214).

Eudes IV. d. 1350. Ruled (1315–1350); son of Robert II; inherited Franche-Comté and Artois; fought for Philip of Valois in Flanders.

Eudes *or* **Odo.** Count of Paris. c.860–898. King of West Franks (888–898). Son of Robert the Strong. Defended Paris against siege of Northmen (885–886).

Eudes, Jean. Saint. 1601–1680. French priest. Famed as a preacher; founded (1643) Congregation of Jesus and Mary, whose members became known as Eudist Fathers; also founded, at Caen, Congregation of Our Lady of Charity (1641); originated devotion to Sacred Hearts of Jesus and Mary. Canonized (1925).

Eu·do·cia \yü-ˈdō-sh(ē-)ə\. Name of three empresses of the Eastern Roman Empire:

Eudocia. *Earlier name* Ath·e·na·is \ˌath-ə-ˈnā-əs\. 401?–460. Wife of Theodosius II (m. 421); daughter of Athenian philosopher Leontius; became rival of Pulcheria, sister of the emperor; exiled to Jerusalem (443), where she directed building of many churches and rebuilding of fortifications. Mother of Licinia Eudoxia, wife of Emperor Valentinian III.

Eudocia In·ge·ri·na \-ˌin-jə-ˈrī-nə\. d. 882. Wife of Basil I and mistress of Michael III; mother of Leo VI.

Eudocia Mac·rem·bol·i·tis·sa \-ˌmak-rəm-ˌbäl-ə-ˈtis-ə\. 1021–1096. Wife of Constantine X Ducas; after his death (1067) married Romanus IV Diogenes, making him coregent emperor with her during minority of her son Michael VII Ducas (1067–71); made Michael coruler on capture of Romanus by Turks (1071); relinquished throne to Michael and entered convent (1071).

Eu·dox·ia \yü-ˈdäk-sē-ə, -ˈdäk-shə\. d. 404. Empress of the Eastern Roman Empire. Daughter of Bauto, a Frank. m. Emperor Arcadius (395), whom she completely controlled; designated augusta (400); sent the patriarch John Chrysostom into exile (404) for preaching against her wickedness. Mother of Emperor Theodosius II and of Pulcheria.

Eudoxia. *Russ.* Yvdokiya Fyodorovna Lo·pu·khi·na \(ˌ)lə-ˈpük-yin-ə\. 1669–1731. Czarina of Russia, first wife of Peter I the Great. Daughter of Boyar Fyodor Lopukhin; m. Peter (1689) at command of his mother; bored Peter by her piety; sent to monastery (1698) for refusing divorce; spent most of remaining life in cloisters. Mother of Czarevitch Alexis and grandmother of Czar Peter II, whom she attempted feebly to succeed (1730).

Eu·dox·us \yü-ˈdäk-səs\ of Cni·dus \ˈnīd-əs\. c.400–c.350 B.C. Greek mathematician and astronomer. Studied at Athens under Plato and in Egypt with the priests at Heliopolis; an itinerant teacher before settling in Athens. Demonstrated reality of irrational numbers; developed method of exhaustion for calculating areas and volumes bounded by curves; his work adopted by Euclid. Proposed cosmology of 27 concentric spheres to explain motions of celestial bodies, an approach later perfected by Ptolemy; corrected length of solar year.

Eudoxus of Cyz·i·cus \ˈsiz-ə-kəs\. 2d century B.C. Greek navigator. Commissioned by Ptolemy Euergetes II to explore the Arabian Sea; later made first known attempt to circumnavigate Africa from western Europe.

Euemeros. See EUHEMERUS.

Euergetes. See PTOLEMY III and VIII.

Eu·gène \œ̄-zhen\. Prince of Savoy. *Full name* François-Eugène de Savoie-Carignan. 1663–1736. Austrian general. Son of Eugène-Maurice de Savoie-Carignan, Count of Soissons. Chafing under restrictions laid on him by Louis XIV, renounced his country and entered service of Austrian Emperor Leopold I. Distinguished himself against Turks at Vienna (1683); field marshal (1693); defeated Turks in battle of Zenta (1697). In War of Spanish Succession commanded in Italy (1701–03); president of imperial council of war (1703–14); with Marlborough won battle of Blenheim (1704); saved Turin and expelled French from Italy (1706); with Marlborough victorious at Oudenaarde (1708) and Malplaquet (1709); negotiated peace treaty at Rastadt (1714). Again in command against Turks (1716), won battles of Peterwardein (1716) and Belgrade (1718). Governed Austrian Netherlands (1714–24); again commanded Austrian army against France (1734–35). Considered greatest general of his time and one of greatest in history; noted esp. for tactical brilliance, strategic insight, leadership.

Eugène de Beauharnais. See BEAUHARNAIS.

Eu·gé·nie \œ̄-zhā-nē\. *In full* Eugénia Maria de Mon·ti·jo de Guz·mán \t͟hā-mȯn-ˈtē-kō-t͟hā-güth-ˈmän\. Comtesse de Te·ba \t͟hā-ˈtā-bä\. 1826–1920. Empress of France (1853–71). Daughter of a Spanish grandee, the Count of Montijo; m. Napoléon III (1853) soon after he became emperor. Leader in fashions of Europe, contributed much to brilliancy of French court; had marked influence over Napoléon in many of his policies; strong advocate of church; opposed liberal and democratic ideas; advised sending Maximilian to Mexico (1863); probably urged emperor to enter upon war with Prussia (1870); three times acted as regent during absence of emperor (1859, 1865, 1870). On downfall of Empire fled to England. Her one son, the Prince Napoléon, was killed in Zululand at age of 23.

Eu·gen·i·kos \yü-ˈgen-i-kȯs\, John. fl. 1439–1453. Greek Byzantine scholar and churchman. Deacon and archivist at Hagia Sophia, Constantinople; accompanied Emperor John VIII Palaeologus to Council of Ferrara-Florence (1437), and signed decree of union of Roman and Greek churches (1439); shortly afterward repudiated union; wrote "Oratorio for the Great City" lamenting fall of Constantinople to Turks (1453).

Eugenikos, Markos. c.1392–1445. Greek Orthodox prelate. Entered monastery on Antigone (c.1418); named metropolitan of Ephesus by Emperor John VIII Palaeologus (c.1436); represented patriarchs of Antioch and Alexandria at Council of Ferrara-Florence (1437–39); refused to sign decree of union of Roman and Greek churches (1439) and became leader of anti-union sentiment;

imprisoned (1440–42). Proclaimed saint of Orthodox church (1734).

Eu·ge·ni·us \yü-ˈjē-nē-əs, -ˈjēn-yəs\. Name of four popes:

Eugenius I. Saint. d. 657. Pope (654–657). Elected during exile of Pope St. Martin I; acknowledged by Martin (655).

Eugenius II. d. 827. Pope (824–827). Received Emperor Lothair in Rome (824), accepted reforms in papal elections.

Eugenius III. *Orig.* Bernardo Pa·ga·nel·li \ˌpä-gä-ˈnel-lē\. *Known also as* Bernard of Pisa. d. 1153. Pope (1145–53). Pupil of St. Bernard of Clairvaux. Refused to renounce temporal power; expelled from Rome (1145) by Roman mob following Arnold of Brescia; journeyed to France (1147) where he helped Louis VII make preparations for Second Crusade; returned to Italy and excommunicated Arnold (1148); held synods at Paris, Reims, and Trier; made Treaty of Constance (1153) with Frederick I Barbarossa.

Eugenius IV. *Orig.* Gabriele Con·dul·mer \ˈkän-dəl-mər\. c.1383–1447. Pope (1431–47). Nephew of Gregory XII. Engaged in long struggle (1431–47) with Council of Basel; dissolved council (1431), which refused to dissolve; convened Council of Ferrara (1438); was deposed (1439) by Council of Basel which elected Felix V; Ferrara council, later moved to Florence, effected union with Greek church (1439); success there restored his authority and enabled him to return to Rome (1443).

Eugenius. d. 394 A.D. Roman emperor (392–394). Gallic rhetorician, set up by Arbogast as emperor; held Gaul, Spain, Italy; both defeated in battle near Aquileia by Theodosius I (394).

Eugenius *or* **Eugenius II.** c.1130–c.1202. Sicilian scholar. Financial adviser to rulers of Sicily (from 1174); translated Ptolemy's *Optica* from Arabic to Latin, translated *Prophecy of the Erythraean Sibyl,* and other works; may have written *Historia* and *Epistola ad Petrum* under pseudonym Hugo Falcandus.

Eu·gip·pi·us *or* **Eu·gyp·i·us** \yü-ˈjip-ē-əs\. 455?–?538. Latin scholar and monk. Author of *Vita Sancti Severini* (511; important source for early German church history), and compiler of *Thesaurus Augustinianeus.*

Eu·he·mer·us \yü-ˈhē-mər-əs, -ˈhem-ər-\ *or* **Eu·e·mer·os** \yü-ˈē-mər-əs, -ˈem-ər-\ *or* **Eve·mer·us** \i-ˈvē-mər-əs, i-ˈvem-ər-\. fl. 300 B.C. Greek mythographer. Chief work, *Sacred History,* a philosophical romance in which he rationalized the Greek myths, depicting the gods as originally human heroes and asserting that the myths were distortions of historical events.

Eu·la·lia \yü-ˈlā-lē-ə, -ˈlā(ə)l-yə\ of Barcelona. Saint. d. 304. Spanish religious. Virgin martyred in Barcelona under Diocletian; patroness of Barcelona and of sailors. Often identified with Saint Eulalia of Mé·ri·da \ˈmā-rē-thä\ (c.291–304), also a virgin said to have been martyred under Diocletian, and patroness of Oviedo and Mérida.

Eu·la·li·us \yü-ˈlā-lē-əs, ˈlā(ə)l-yəs\. d. 423. Antipope (418–419). Elected by clerical faction in opposition to Pope St. Boniface I; at first favored but ultimately rejected by Emperor Honorius.

Eu·len·burg \ˈȯi-lən-ˌbu̇rk\, Counts zu. Members of an old noble Prussian family including: Botho Heinrich zu Eulenburg-Wick·en \-ˈvik-ən\ (1804–1879), government official; president, Prussian House of Representatives (1855–58); member of Prussian House of Lords (1864) and of Reichstag (1867–78); headed Prussian national debt administration (1874).

His son ¶Botho Wend August, Graf zu Eulenburg (1831–1912), statesman and administrator; member of Prussian House of Representatives (1863–70) and conservative member of North German Reichstag (1867); chief councilor in ministry of interior (1867); succeeded Friedrich (see below) as minister of interior (1878); formulated Social Democrat law and worked for administrative reforms; resigned following differences with Bismarck (1881); succeeded Caprivi as Prussian prime minister (1892); opposed Caprivi in controversy over liberalization of franchise and legislation against Social Democrats and was dismissed with him (1894); member of House of Lords (from 1899).

¶Friedrich (Fritz) Albrecht, Graf zu Eulenburg (1815–1881), cousin of Botho Heinrich; entered diplomatic service (1852); consul general in Antwerp (1852) and Warsaw (1858); effected trade and maritime agreements with China and Japan (1861); minister of interior (1862); sought to develop town and parish self-administration, was opposed by Bismarck and resigned (1878); member of Prussian Chamber of Deputies (1866–77).

¶Philipp Friedrich Karl Alexander Botho, Fürst zu Eulenburg und Her·te·feld \ˈher-tə-ˌfelt\ (1847–1921), diplomat and writer; intimate friend and adviser of William II; German ambassador at Vienna (1894–1902); raised to rank of prince (1900) and made hereditary member of House of Lords; charged with homosexuality and involved in scandalous but unproved revelations of Maximilian Harden (1906). Author of poems and musical compositions including *Rosenlieder* and *Skaldengesänge* (1892), a volume of reminiscences and letters *Aus 50 Jahren* (1923), etc.

Eu·len·spie·gel \ˈȯi-lən-ˌshpē-gəl\ *or* **Ulen·spe·gel** \ˈü-lən-ˌshpeg-əl\, Till. German traditional figure, hero of a chapbook of early 16th century and much later literature. Supposedly born at Kneitlingen in Brunswick at end of 13th century, died in Mölln (1350); a wily peasant who played jokes on tradespeople, priests, nobles, and esp. innkeepers.

Eu·ler \ˈȯi-lər\, Leonhard. 1707–1783. Swiss mathematician. Called to St. Petersburg by Catherine I (1727) where he became professor of physics (1730) and of mathematics (1733); called to Berlin by Frederick the Great (1741) becoming director of mathematics at the Academy of Science (1744); recalled to St. Petersburg (1766). Lost sight of one eye in 1735 and of the other in 1766 but continued working. Brought integral calculus to full development; in *Introductio in analysin infinitorum* introduced concept of function; devised much modern notation in calculus; published textbooks *Institutiones calculi differentialis* (1755), *Institutiones calculi integralis* (1768–70); developed theories of logarithmic and trigonometric functions and of complex numbers; developed improved theories of lunar motion (1753, 1772); discovered law of quadratic reciprocity (1783).

Eu·ler-Chel·pin \ˈȯi-lər-ˈkel-pin\, Hans Karl August Simon von. 1873–1964. German chemist. Taught at U. of Stockholm (1900–41); director of Institute of Biochemistry there (1929–41); naturalized Swedish citizen (1902). Conducted researches on the fermentation of sugars and coenzyme action. Awarded, jointly with Sir Arthur Harden, 1929 Nobel prize for chemistry.

Euler-Chelpin, Ulf Svante von. 1905–1983. Swedish physiologist. Professor of physiology, Karolinska Institute (1939–71); president of Nobel Foundation (1966–75). Discovered (1946) the compound noradrenaline, the key neurotransmitter in the sympathetic nervous system; confirmed that noradrenaline was stored within nerve fibers themselves; shared 1970 Nobel prize for physiology or medicine with Julius Axelrod and Bernard Katz for discoveries concerning chemistry of nerve transmission.

Eu·me·nes \ˈyü-mə-ˌnēz\. Name of two rulers of Pergamum:

Eumenes I. d. 241 B.C. Ruler (263–241 B.C.); established independence of Pergamum by defeating army of Seleucid king Antiochus I (262).

Eumenes II. d. 160? B.C. King (197–?160 B.C.). Son of Attalus I. An ally of the Romans; took important part (190) in battle of Magnesia (Manisa) in which Antiochus III the Great was defeated; received large part of Asia Minor from Romans for his services; made Pergamum a center of learning; founded great library. Succeeded by his brother Attalus II.

Eumenes. 362–316 B.C. Macedonian general. Secretary on staff of Philip of Macedon and Alexander the Great; at Alexander's death (323 B.C.), allotted Cappadocia and Paphlagonia; supported regent Perdiccas against rebel generals; condemned by rebels after death of Perdiccas (321); defeated (321) Craterus and Neoptolemus, but was betrayed to Antigonus.

Eu·men·i·us \yü-ˈmen-ē-əs\. fl. c.300 A.D. Roman orator. Known for *Oratio pro instaurandis scholis* (delivered 298), source for knowledge of education of the day and a panegyric on Emperor Constantius Chlorus.

Eunan, Saint. See ADAMNAN.

Eu·na·pi·us \yü-ˈnā-pē-əs\. c.345–c.420 A.D. Greek rhetorician. An Eleusinian and opponent of Christianity; wrote *Lives of the Philosophers and Sophists,* an important source; continued *Chronological History* of Publius Herennius Dexippus down to 404 A.D.

Eu·no·mi·us \yü-ˈnō-mē-əs\. c.335–c.394. Cappadocian prelate. Secretary to Aëtius in Alexandria; bishop of Cyzicus (360 or perhaps 366); soon deposed because of extreme Arian views; became with Aëtius recognized leader of the Anomoeans, or Eunomians, extreme followers of Arianism; his views condemned by Council of Constantinople (381). Chief work, *Apologia.*

Eu·nus \ˈyü-nəs\. 2d century B.C. Roman slave. Organized slaves of Enna, Sicily, in revolt (135 B.C.); took control of city and proclaimed himself King Antiochus; revolt suppressed by Lucius Calpurnius Piso and Publius Rupilius (132–131).

Eupator. See ANTIOCHUS V of Syria.

Eu·pho·ri·on \yü-ˈfōr-ē-ən, -ˈfȯr-\. c.275 B.C.–? Greek scholar and poet. Lived in Athens (c.221 B.C.) and then went to Antioch to serve as librarian of royal library. Author of epics about mythological heroes, elegies, and satirical verse.

Eu·phra·nor \yü-ˈfrā-nȯr\. fl. 364 B.C. Greek sculptor and painter. Known for paintings in the Stoa Basileios, Athens; and statues of Paris, Apollo, Philip, etc.

Eu·phro·ni·us \yü-ˈfrō-nē-əs\. fl. 520–470 B.C. Athenian potter and vase painter. Noted for excellence of drawing, innovations in form and design.

Eu·po·lis \ˈyü-pə-ləs\. c.445–c.411 B.C. Greek comic poet. Rival of Aristophanes, with whom he helped create Old Comedy form; 19 titles of his works survive; winner of first prize for comedy seven times.

Eu·pom·pus \yü-ˈpäm-pəs\. 4th century B.C. Greek painter. Founder of the Sicyonian school.

Eu·ric \ˈyü-rik\. d. 484 A.D. King of the Visigoths (466–484). Succeeded his brother Theodoric II, whom he assassinated; held large territory in Gaul and northern Spain, with capital at Toulouse.

Eu·rip·i·des \yü-ˈrip-ə-ˌdēz\. c.484–406 B.C. Greek playwright. Ranked with Aeschylus and Sophocles as greatest of Greek tragic poets; won first prize in four dramatic contests. Lived in Athens (to 408 B.C.) and then at court of

Archelaus of Macedonia. Of 67 (92 were known to ancients) plays attributed to him, 18 (or 19, with disputed *Rhesus*) are extant: *Alcestis, Medea, Hippolytus, Hecuba, Andromache, Ion, The Suppliants, Heracleidae, Mad Heracles, Iphigenia in Tauris, The Trojan Women, Helen, The Phoenician Women, Electra, Orestes, Iphigenia in Aulis, Bacchae, Cyclops.*

Eu·ry·bi·a·des \yůr-i-'bī-ə-,dēz\. 5th century B.C. Spartan fleet commander. Nominal commander of allied Greek fleets in victories against Persians at Artemisium and Salamis (480 B.C.).

Eu·rym·e·don \yů-'rim-ə-,dän\. d. 413 B.C. Athenian general. Commanded Athenian fleet at Corcyra (427 B.C.); in Peloponnesian War slain in attempting to reinforce Athenian troops at Syracuse.

Eus·den \'yüz-dən\, Laurence. 1688–1730. English poet. Made poet laureate (1718) by Duke of Newcastle, whose marriage he had celebrated (1717); remembered as object of Pope's satire and as the "L. E." of Pope and Swift's treatise on bathos.

Eusebes. See ANTIOCHUS X of Syria.

Eu·se·bi·us \yü-'sē-bē-əs\. Saint. d. 309 or 310. Pope (309 or 310); banished by Emperor Maxentius to Sicily, where he died.

Eusebius of Caes·a·rea \,ses-ə-'rē-ə, ,sez-, ,sē-zə-\. *Surnamed* Pam·phi·li \'pam-fə-,lī\. c.260–c.339. Palestinian theologian, church historian, and scholar. Studied under Pamphilus, from whom he took surname; became bishop of Caesarea (c.313) and stood in favor with Emperor Constantine; provisionally excommunicated (325) for mild Arianism of his *Demonstratio evangelica;* reinstated at Council of Nicaea (325) as leader of Origenist middle party of moderates in Arian conflict; attended synods of Antioch (330) and Tyre (335). Author of *Historia ecclesiastica,* history of the church down to 324; *Chronicon,* an epitome of universal history to 303; *Life of Constantine* (c.338), theological works.

Eusebius of Dor·y·lae·um \,dōr-ə-'lē-əm\. d. c.452. Greek theologian. Opposed heresy of Nestorius and provoked his condemnation (431); bishop of Dorylaeum (448); denounced heresy of his friend Eutyches (448); deposed by the synod in Ephesus that restored Eutyches (449); escaped to Rome and was reinstated by Council of Chalcedon (451).

Eusebius of Em·e·sa \'em-is-ə\. c.300–c.359. Greek prelate. Semi-Arian theologian and ecclesiastic writer of the Alexandrian school; favorite of Constantine. Bishop of Emesa (now Homs) in Phoenicia (from c.339).

Eusebius of La·od·i·cea \(,)lā-,äd-ə-'sē-ə\. d. c.269. Egyptian prelate. Pupil of Origen; heroically defended Christians of Alexandria during persecutions of Decius and Valerian; emissary of bishop of Alexandria to synod of Antioch (264); named bishop of Laodicea (265).

Eusebius of Myn·dus \'min-dəs\. 4th century A.D. Greek philosopher. Student of Neoplatonist school of Pergamum, but rejected magic and other excesses of fellow members.

Eusebius of Nic·o·me·dia \,nik-ə-mə-'dī-ə\. d. c.342 Syrian prelate. Held successively sees of Berytus (Beirut) and Nicomedia (c.318); supported Arius before and after his condemnation by synod of Alexandria (323); headed Arian party at Council of Nicaea (325); signed Nicene creed but not the anathema against Arians; exiled to Gaul (325–328); later swayed Emperor Constantine to Arian view; assisted in deposing of St. Athanasius the Great at Tyre (335); favored by Constantius II; bishop of Constantinople (339); presided over synod at Antioch (341).

Eusebius of Sa·mos·a·ta \sə-'mäs-ət-ə\. Saint. d. c.379. Syrian prelate. Bishop of Samosata (361); opponent of Arianism; banished by Valens (374); restored to see (378); killed by Arian woman.

Eusebius of Ver·cel·li \vär-'chel-lē\. Saint. d. 371. Italian prelate. Consecrated first bishop of Vercelli (345); became first western bishop to unite monastic with clerical life; exiled to the East for refusal to condemn St. Athanasius at Council of Milan (355); pardoned by Emperor Julian the Apostate; promulgated decrees on Nicene Creed at Synod of Alexandria (362); a leading opponent of Arianism.

Eus·tace \'yü-stəs\. Name of four counts of Boulogne:

Eustace I. d. c.1049. Count (1023 or 1027–c.1049).

Eustace II. d. c.1093. Count (1049–93). m. Goda, daughter of King Aethelred the Unready; accompanied William the Conqueror to England and fought at Hastings (1066); quarreled with William (1067); his confiscated fiefs later returned to him. Father by second wife of Godfrey of Bouillon, Baldwin I of Jerusalem, and Eustace III.

Eustace III. d. after 1125. Supported Robert II Curthose in attempt to seize English throne from William II Rufus (1088); briefly selected to succeed brother Baldwin I as king of Jerusalem but subsequently replaced by Baldwin II (1118); retired to monastery, leaving county to daughter Matilda and son-in-law Stephen (1125).

Eustace IV. d. 1153. Son of Matilda and Stephen (later king of England), became count (1150); named heir apparent to English throne by father (1152) but not accepted by Theobald, archbishop of Canterbury; his death made possible a peaceful settlement between Stephen and Henry of Anjou.

Eu·sta·chio \äů-'stäk-yō\ *or* **Eu·stac·chi** \-'stäk-kē\, Bartolommeo. *Latin* Eu·sta·chi·us \yů-'stā-kē-əs\. 1520–1574. Italian anatomist. One of the founders of modern anatomy; described the Eustachian tube in the ear and the Eustachian valve of the heart.

Eu·sta·chi·us \yů-'stā-kē-əs\ *or* **Eu·stace** \'yü-stəs\. Saint. 2d century A.D. Roman saint and martyr. By tradition, originally a Roman general named Placidas under Emperor Trajan; miraculously converted; martyred. One of saints called "Fourteen Holy Helpers."

Eustathius. See also EWOSTATEWOS.

Eu·sta·thi·us \yü-'stā-thē-əs\ of An·ti·och \'ant-ē-,äk\. Saint. d. c.337 A.D. Bishop of Antioch. Became (c.320) bishop of Beroea (now Aleppo) and (325) of Antioch in Syria; strongly opposed Arians at Council of Nicaea (325); deposed (326?) and banished through efforts of Eusebius of Caesarea. His deposition resulted in a schism (later known as Melitian Schism, lasting till c.485), the party protesting it being known as Eustathians.

Eustathius of Se·bas·te \si-'bas-tē\. c.300–377 or 380. Bishop of Sebaste in Armenia (c.357). Introduced monasticism; founded the party of ascetics and celibates called Eustathians, condemned by Synod of Gangra (343); later joined semi-Arian Macedonian sect.

Eustathius of Thes·sa·lo·ni·ca \,thes-ə-lə-'nī-kə\. d. c.1194. Byzantine scholar and religious reformer. Metropolitan (from 1175) of Thessalonica. Author of commentaries on Homer, on the geographical epic of Dionysius Periegetes, and on Pindar; of chronicles, esp. of Norman conquest of Thessalonica (1185); and of *Inquiry into the Monastic Life.*

Eus·tis \'yü-stəs\, Dorothy Leib, *nee* Harrison. 1886–1946. American philanthropist, b. Philadelphia. m. (1923) George M. Eustis. Breeder of German shepherd dogs at Fortunate Fields kennel; incorporated (1929) The Seeing Eye to train guide dogs for the blind.

Eu·thar·ic \yü-'thar-ik\. d. 522. Ostrogoth noble. m. Amalasuntha, daughter of Theodoric (515); appointed consul (519); introduced Roman games and circuses, African animals to court at Ravenna.

Eu·thyd·e·mus \yü-'thid-ə-məs\. 3d centruy B.C. King of Bactria. Killed and usurped throne of Diodotus II (perhaps c.235 B.C.); fought lengthy war (from 208) with Antiochus III, whose suzerainty he at length acknowledged.

Eu·thym·i·des \yü-'thim-ə-,dēz\. 6th–5th century B.C. Athenian vase painter. Contemporary of Euphronius; known esp. for stylistic experiments in foreshortening and movement.

Eu·thym·i·us \yü-'thim-ē-əs\. Saint. *Called* the Great. 377–473. Palestinian religious. Established (from c.411) series of cenobitic monasteries in Palestinian desert; converted many Saracens; consulted by Council of Ephesus (431), Council of Chalcedon (451); convinced Empress Eudoxia of error of Monophysitism.

Euthymius I. c.834–917. Byzantine prelate. Abbot of St. Theodora, Constantinople, and confessor to Emperor Leo VI; named patriarch of Constantinople (907) to replace Nicholas I, who had refused to acknowledge Leo's fourth marriage; reluctantly consented to marriage but declined to honor Empress Zoe; deposed in favor of Nicholas by Emperor Alexander (912). Although Euthymius and Nicholas were at last reconciled, their partisans continued the dispute for a century.

Euthymius. *Georgian* Ekv·thi·me Mthatz·mi·de·li \'äkf-tē-mām-tät-'smē-dā-lē\. *Called* the Hagiorite. c.955–1028. Georgian religious and scholar. Abbot of Ivíron monastery, Mt. Athos (998); undertook program to translate biblical and liturgical texts into Georgian, establishing definitive texts still in use; translated also works of Gregory of Nazianzus.

Euthymius of Tŭr·no·vo \'tər-nə-,vō\. c.1317–c.1402. Bulgarian Orthodox prelate and scholar. Successor of Theodosius as leader of Hesychast monasticism; elected patriarch of Tŭrnovo and primate of Bulgarian Orthodox church (1375); forced into exile by Turkish conquest (1393). Revised liturgical and legal codes and translated them into Old Slavonic; promoted Old Slavonic and unifying sacred language to replace decayed Church Slavonic; fostered revival of monasticism and opposed various heresies, notably that of the Bogomils. His work sparked second Slavonic renaissance.

Eu·tro·pi·us \yů-'trō-pē-əs\. d. c.370 A.D. Roman historian. Author of a Roman history, *Breviarium Historiae Romanae,* down to 364; long used as a schoolbook.

Eutropius. d. after 399 A.D. Eastern Roman politician. Arranged marriage of Emperor Arcadius to Eudoxia, Frankish noblewoman; on murder of rival Rufinus became most powerful figure of Eastern empire; repelled invasion of Huns (398); first eunuch to serve as consul (399); overthrown by Gainas, exiled to Cyprus (399), and subsequently beheaded.

Eutropius of Saintes \'saⁿt\. Saint. 3d century. Christian missionary. With St. Denis of Paris and others, sent by Pope St. Fabian to evangelize Gaul (c.250); named first bishop of Saintes but later expelled from see; martyred by Roman governor, whose daughter Eustella he had converted.

Eu·ty·ches \'yüt-i-,kēz\. c.378–c.450. Eastern Orthodox archimandrite. Founder of Eutychianism, an extreme form of Monophysitism, or belief in a single divine nature in Christ. Denounced by Bishop Eusebius of Dorylaeum and condemned for heresy and deposed by Synod of Constantinople under Bishop Flavian (448); reinstated (449) by Council of Ephesus ("Robber Synod"); again condemned by Council of Chalcedon (451), excommunicated, and banished.

Eu·tych·i·a·nus \yü-ˌtik-ē-ˈā-nəs\ *or* **Eu·tych·i·an** \yü-ˈtik-ē-ən\. Saint. d. 283. Pope (275–283).

Eu·tych·i·des \yü-ˈtik-ə-ˌdēz\ of Si·cy·on \ˈsis(h)-ē-ˌän\. 3d century B.C. Greek sculptor. Pupil of Lysippus; known for statue of *Fortune* for city of Antioch.

Evag·o·ras \i-ˈvag-ə-rəs\. d. 374 B.C. King of Salamis in Cyprus (410?–374 B.C.). Pursued policy friendly to Athens and hostile to Persia; awarded Athenian citizenship for his promotion of Hellenic culture; after Peace of Antalcides (386), deserted by Athens; subjugated by Persia following defeat at Citium (381).

Evag·ri·us \i-ˈvag-rē-əs\. *Surnamed* Pon·tic·us \ˈpän-tik-əs\. 364–399. Turkish Christian mystic. Developed Neoplatonic theology of Origen into a doctrine of monastic mysticism that strongly affected Pseudo-Dionysius the Areopagite, John Cassian, and others; wrote *Gnostic Centuries, Monachikos,* biblical commentaries, etc.

Evagrius. *Surnamed* Scho·las·ti·cus \skə-ˈlas-ti-kəs\. 536?–?600. Byzantine church historian. Legal adviser of Gregory, patriarch of Antioch; author of an ecclesiastical history for the period 431–594, a continuation of the work of Eusebius, Socrates, Sozomen, and Theodoret of Cyrrhus.

Ev·ans \ˈev-ənz\, Sir Arthur John. 1851–1941. English archaeologist. Son of Sir John Evans. Curator of Ashmolean Museum, Oxford (1884–1908), professor at Oxford (1909–41); conducted excavations in Crete and discovered pre-Phoenician script (1894 ff.); excavated prehistoric palace of Knossos (1899–1908 and later), seat of early culture he named Minoan. Published *Scripta Minoa* (1909), *The Palace of Minos* (1921–36).

Evans, Charles, *known as* Chick \ˈchik\. 1890–1979. American golfer, b. Indianapolis, Ind. First to win U.S. Amateur and U.S. Open golf tournaments in same year (1916); qualified for every U.S. Amateur from 1907 to 1962; established (1930) Evans Scholars Foundation to offer college scholarships to deserving caddies.

Evans, David. *Pseudonym* Caradoc Evans. 1878–1945. Welsh writer. Known esp. for stories and novels bitterly satirizing the Welsh; author of *My People: Stories of the Peasantry of West Wales* (1915), *Capel Sion* (1916), *My Neighbors: Stories of the London Welsh* (1919), *Nothing to Pay* (1930), *Wasps* (1934), *Pilgrims in a Foreign Land* (1942), *Morgan Bible* (1943).

Evans, Dame Edith Mary. 1888–1976. English actress. Won reputation as one of finest actresses of her day in works of Shakespeare, Shaw, Coward, Wilde; made numerous films, notably *Look Back in Anger* (1959), *The Chalk Garden* (1964), *The Whisperers* (1967).

Evans, Evan. *Pseudonym* Ieu·an Fardd \ˈye-yän-ˈfärth\. 1731–1788. Welsh poet and antiquary. Published *Some Specimens of the Poetry of the Ancient Welsh Bards* (1764), an important scholarly work.

Evans, Frederick Henry. 1853–1943. English photographer. As London bookseller championed work of George Bernard Shaw and Aubrey Beardsley; after retirement (1898) devoted himself to photographing cathedrals of Europe and painstakingly making own prints.

Evans, Sir George de Lacy. 1787–1870. British soldier and politician. Served against French on Iberian Peninsula (1812–14), against Americans at Baltimore, Washington, and New Orleans (1814–15), in Waterloo campaign (1815); commanded British Legion in Carlist insurrection (1835–37); commanded a division in Crimean War, repulsing sortie from Sevastopol (1854); general (1861); M.P. (1831–32, 1833–41, 1846–65).

Evans, George Henry. 1805–1856. American editor and reformer, b. Bromyard, England. To U.S. (1820); founded (1829) and edited (to 1845) *Working Man's Advocate,* first important labor newspaper in U.S.; wrote *History of the Origin and Progress of the Working Men's Party* (1840); agitated for Homestead Act.

Evans, Herbert McLean. 1882–1971. American anatomist, b. Modesto, Cal. Professor at U. of California (1915–52); discovered 48 chromosomes in man (1918) and vitamin E (1922); investigated chemistry and activity of pituitary hormones.

Evans, John. 1814–1897. American businessman and politician, b. Waynesville, Ohio. Helped found Northwestern U. (1851) and city of Evanston, Ill.; territorial governor of Colorado (1862–65); founded Colorado Seminary (1864), forerunner of U. of Denver; active promoter of railroads. Mt. Evans named for him.

Evans, Sir John. 1823–1908. English archaeologist and numismatist. Collected stone and bronze implements, fossils, and British coins; author of *The Coins of the Ancient Britons* (1864), *The Ancient Stone Implements, Weapons, and Ornaments of Great Britain* (1872), *The Ancient Bronze Implements, Weapons, and Ornaments of Great Britain and Ireland* (1881).

Evans, John William. 1857–1930. British geologist. Known for studies of Devonian stratigraphy; introduced term ventifact.

Evans, Mary Ann, *later (from c.1851)* Marian. *Pseudonym* George Eliot. 1819–1880. English novelist. Subeditor of *Westminster Review* (1851–54); formed liaison with George Henry Lewes (1854) and lived with him as in marriage to his death (1878); published translation of Feuerbach's *Essence of Christianity* (1854). Published in *Blackwood's Magazine* (1857) under pseudonym first of sketches collected in *Scenes of Clerical Life* (1858); followed with first of realistic novels *Adam Bede* (1859), *The Mill on the Floss* (1860), *Silas Marner* (1861); wrote historical novels *Romola* (1862–63), *Felix Holt, the Radical* (1866); verse drama *The Spanish Gypsy* (1869); masterpiece novel *Middlemarch* (1871–72); verse *Legend of Jubal* (1874); novel *Daniel Deronda* (1876); essays *Impressions of Theophrastus Such* (1879). Her London home became a center of Victorian intellectual and literary life.

Evans, Oliver. 1755–1819. American inventor, b. Newport, Del. Invented high-speed machine for making textile cards (1777); built fully automated grain mill (1785); constructed first high-pressure steam engine in America (c.1787) and specialized in construction of such engines; applied them to grain mill, boring machine, amphibious dredge that was first powered vehicle to run on roads in America (1802).

Evans, Robley Dunglison. *Known as* Fighting Bob. 1846–1912. American naval officer, b. Floyd Court House, Va. Distinguished himself at Fort Fisher (Jan. 1865); to Chile in charge of gunboat *Yorktown* following Valparaiso Incident (1891); to Bering Sea, in command of flotilla, to stop abuses in seal fisheries (1892); in command of *Iowa,* which fired first gun at Cervera's fleet, at Santiago (1898). Effective proponent of steel navy. Rear admiral (1901); commanding officer, Asiatic fleet (1902–04), Atlantic Fleet (1905–07); appointed commander in chief of U.S. fleet on its voyage round the world (1907), but retired during voyage because of illness. Author of *A Sailor's Log* (1901), *An Admiral's Log* (1910).

Evans, Rudulph. 1878–1960. American sculptor, b. Washington, D.C. Sculptor of statue of Thomas Jefferson in Jefferson Memorial; also did busts of Whittier, Longfellow, George Bancroft, Grover Cleveland in American Hall of Fame, bronze statue of Gen. Robert E. Lee in Virginia state capitol.

Evans, Walker. 1903–1975. American photographer, b. St. Louis, Mo. Known esp. for architectural photographs and for portrayal of Great Depression in rural America, as in *American Photographs* (1938) and *Let Us Now Praise Famous Men* (with James Agee, 1941).

Evans-Pritch·ard \-ˈprich-ərd\, Edward Evan. 1902–1973. English anthropologist. Professor, Oxford (1946–70); noted for studies of Azande and Nuer tribes of Africa and for theoretical work.

Ev·a·ris·tus \ˌev-ə-ˈris-təs\. Saint. d. c.107. Pope (c.99–c.107).

Ev·arts \ˈev-ərts\, William Maxwell. 1818–1901. American lawyer and statesman, b. Boston, Mass. During Civil War undertook diplomatic missions to England (1863–64); chief defense counsel for President Johnson in impeachment proceedings (1868); attorney general of the U.S. (1868–69). Counsel for U.S. before Geneva court of arbitration in *Alabama* claims case (1871–72). As president (1870–80) of Association of the Bar of the City of New York led movements for law reform and against "Tweed Ring." Chief counsel for Republican party in Hayes–Tilden electoral votes dispute before Electoral Commission (1877). U.S. secretary of state (1877–81); U.S. senator from New York (1885–91).

Ev·att \ˈev-ət\, Herbert Vere. 1894–1965. Australian jurist and politician. Justice, federal high court (1930–40); M.P. (1940–60); member, commonwealth advisory war council (1941–45); attorney general and minister for external affairs (1941–49); head of Australian delegation to United Nations (1946–48); president, UN General Assembly (1948); Labour party leader (1951–60); chief justice of New South Wales (1960–62).

Eve·lyn \ˈēv-lən, ˈev-\, John. 1620–1706. English diarist. After Restoration, served in minor offices, such as commissioner of the mint (1663), on council for colonial affairs (1671–74), commissioner for privy seal (1685–87), treasurer of Greenwich Hospital (1695–1703); a founding member of Royal Society (from 1662) and its secretary (1672). Author of over 30 works on numismatics, architecture, landscape gardening, upon which he was an authority; also on painting, engraving, politics, education, commerce, including *Fumifugium* (1661), *Sculptura* (1662), *Sylva,* a book on practical arboriculture (1664). Chronicled his travels and contemporary events in his *Diary* (1640–1706; pub. 1818), a record of historical value.

Evemerus. See EUHEMERUS.

Ever·ding·en \ˈā-vər-ˌdiŋ-ən\, Allart *or* Allaert van. 1621–1675. Dutch painter and engraver. Known esp. for landscapes of northern Scandinavia.

Ev·er·est \ˈev-(ə-)rəst\, Sir George. 1790–1866. British geodesist and engineer. Superintendent of trigonometrical survey of India (1823) and surveyor general of India (1830–43); surveyed great meridional arc from Himalayas to Cape Comorin. Mount Everest was named for him.

Ev·er·ett \ˈev-(ə-)rət\, Alexander Hill. 1790–1847. American editor and diplomat, b. Boston. Brother of Edward Everett. Chargé d'affaires (1818–24) at The Hague; minister to Spain (1825–29); editor of *North American Review* (1830–35); first U.S. commissioner to China under new treaty (1845).

Everett, Edward. 1794–1865. American Unitarian clergyman, orator, and statesman, b. Dorchester, Mass. Pastor of Brattle Street Church, Boston (1814); first professor of Greek, Harvard (1819–25). Member, U.S. House of Representatives (1825–35); governor of Massachusetts (1836–40); U.S. minister to Great Britain (1841–45); president of Harvard (1846–49); U.S. secretary of state (1852–53); U.S. senator (1853–54); candidate of Constitutional Union party for vice president (1860). Renowned as brilliant orator; best known oration delivered at dedication of national cemetery at Gettysburg (Nov. 19, 1863), the occasion on which Lincoln made his celebrated address.

Ev·er·shed \ˈev-ər-ˌshed\, John. 1864–1956. English astronomer. Assistant director (1906–11), director (1911–23), Kodaikanal and Madras observatories, India; made spectrographic studies of sun; discovered horizontal flow of gases outward from centers of sunspots (Evershed effect).

Evil-Merodach. See AWIL-MARDUK.

Ev·in·rude \ˈev-ən-ˌrüd\, Ole. 1877–1934. American inventor, b. Norway. Invented first commercially successful outboard marine engine (1909); founded Evinrude Motors, Milwaukee (1911).

Ev·li·ya Çe·le·bi \ef-liˈyä-chel-eb-ˈē\. *Also known as* Ibn Der·vish Meh·med Zil·li \ˌib-ən-der-ˈvēsh-mem-ˈet-zil-ˈlē\. 1611–c.1684. Turkish traveler. Under patronage of Sultan Murad IV, traveled throughout Ottoman Empire; wrote *Seyahatnâme,* or *Tarihi seyyah,* important source book on Ottoman peoples, history, etc.

Evoe. See Edmund G. V. KNOX.

Évremond, Seigneur de Saint-. See MARGUETEL DE SAINT-DENIS.

Ewald \ˈā-ˌvält\, Heinrich Georg August. 1803–1875. German Orientalist and theologian. Professor, Göttingen (1831–37, 1848–67), Tübingen (1838–48); retired for refusal to take oath of allegiance to king of Prussia. Took active part in movement for Protestant reform in Germany (from 1862). Author of *Kritische Grammatik der hebräischen Sprache* (1827), *Geschichte des Volkes Israel* (1843–59), *Die Dichter des alten Bundes* (1837–63).

Ewald \ˈiv-äl\, Johannes. 1743–1781. Danish poet and dramatist. Works included dramatic poem *Adam og Eva* (1769), historical drama *Rolf Krage* (1770), lyrical ode *Rungsteds Lyksaligheder* (1773), lyric drama *Balders Død* (1774), operetta *Fiskerne* (1779) containing "Kong Kristian stod ved hø jen Mast," Danish national anthem; left uncompleted memoirs *Levnet og Meninger.* One of Denmark's greatest poets, and one of first to draw on national myths and legends.

Ew·art \ˈyü-ərt\, William. 1798–1869. English politician and reformer. M.P. (1828–37, 1839–68); secured legislation abolishing hanging of criminals from chains (1834), capital punishment for cattle stealing, etc. (1837); urged (from 1840) complete abolition of capital punishment.

Ew·ell \ˈyü-əl\, Richard Stoddert. 1817–1872. American soldier, b. Georgetown, D.C. Grandson of Benjamin Stoddert. Resigned from U.S. army to join Confederate cause (1861); major general (1861); led division under "Stonewall" Jackson in Shenandoah Valley campaign; lieutenant general (1863); succeeded to command of Jackson's corps after Chancellorsville; cleared Union forces from the valley; led advance into Pennsylvania; took part in battles of Gettysburg and the Wilderness; in charge of Richmond defenses; captured after evacuation of city.

Ew·ing \ˈyü-iŋ\, Sir Alfred, *in full* James Alfred. 1855–1935. Scottish physicist and engineer. Professor, Tokyo (1878–83), Dundee (1883–90), Cambridge (1890–1903); director of naval education (1903–16); principal and vice chancellor, U. of Edinburgh (1916–29). Investigated magnetic properties of iron, steel, etc.; observed and named the phenomenon of hysteresis.

Ewing, Alfred Cyril. 1899–1973. British philosopher. Taught at U. Coll., Swansea (1927–31), Cambridge (1931–54), Oxford (1954–66); a leader of Neo-Realist school, known esp. for work in normative ethics; author of *Kant's Treatment of Causality* (1924), *Reason and Intuition* (1941), *Fundamental Questions of Philosophy* (1951), *Ethics* (1953), *Non-Linguistic Philosophy* (1968).

Ewing, James. 1866–1943. American pathologist, b. Pittsburgh. First professor of pathology, Cornell (1899–1932); specialist in study of tumors; founded tumor registry, Am. Coll. of Surgeons; established oncology as clinical specialty; author of *Neoplastic Diseases* (1919).

Ewing, Maurice, *in full* William Maurice. 1906–1974. American geophysicist, b. Lockney, Tex. Taught at Columbia U. (1944–74); director, Lamont-Doherty Geological Observatory (1949–74); known for seismic studies of ocean floor, magnetic and gravity surveys, ocean floor photography; author of *Propagation of Sound in the Ocean* (1948), *Elastic Waves in Layered Media* (1957), etc.

Ewing, Thomas. 1789–1871. American lawyer and politician, b. near West Liberty, Va. (now W.Va.). U.S. senator from Ohio (1831–37, 1850–51); U.S. secretary of the treasury (1841); first U.S. secretary of the interior (1849–50); informally adopted William T. Sherman (1829).

Ewos·tat·ewos \yu̇s-ˈtät-yu̇s\. *Lat.* Eu·sta·thi·us \yü-ˈstā-thē-əs\. d. 1369. Ethiopian religious. Founded many monasteries, notably at Kesache and Bizan; considered a saint in Ethiopian church.

Ew·ry \ˈyu̇(ə)r-ē\, Ray C. 1873–1937. American athlete, b. Lafayette, Ind. Despite boyhood poliomyelitis became only person ever to win 8 individual Olympic gold medals: standing broad jump (1900, 1904, 1908), standing high jump (1900, 1904, 1908), standing hop, step, and jump (1900, 1904); won 2 gold medals for standing high and broad jumps at unofficial Olympics (1906).

Ex·ek·ias *or* **Ex·ec·ias** \ek-ˈsek-yəs, -ˈsek-ē-əs\. fl. c.550–525 B.C. Greek potter and painter. Considered, with the Amasis Painter, finest black-figure artist of his time; known from 11 signed works.

Exeter. (1) Dukes of. See John HOLLAND; Sir Thomas BEAUFORT. (2) Earls and marquises of. See CECIL family. (3) Marquis of. See Henry COURTENAY.

Exmouth, 1st Viscount. See Edward PELLEW.

Ex·pert \ek-sper\, Henry, *in full* Norbert-Isidore-Henry. 1863–1952. French musicologist. Cofounder of Société d'Études Musicales (1903); librarian, Paris Conservatory (1909–33); teacher at École des Hautes Études Sociales (from 1902). Edited *Les maîtres musiciens de la Renaissance* (1894–1908), *Monuments de la musique française au temps de la Renaissance* (1924–29), etc.

Ey·be·schütz \ˈī-bə-ˌshœts\, Jonathan. c.1690–1764. Polish-German rabbi and Talmudist. Renowned for Talmudic and Kabbalistic learning; attracted devoted disciples and was reputed to have mystical powers; denounced by Jacob Emden as a heretic for use of amulets containing incantatory prayers to false messiah Shabbetai Tzevi; quarrel divided Polish and German rabbinates and European Jewry generally; free use of excommunication weakened rabbinic authority; effects of dispute felt for generations.

Eyck \ˈīk\, Hubert *or* Huybrecht van (c.1370–1426) and his brother Jan van (before 1395–1441). Flemish painters. Founders of Flemish school of painting; reputed originators of process of oil painting with a drying varnish; studio chiefly at Bruges and Ghent. Only existing known work of Hubert is an altarpiece of cathedral of Saint-Bavon at Ghent, on which he collaborated with Jan (1432). Jan is credited, after Robert Campin, with developing oil techniques of light, texture, etc. to produce a new level of realism in painting; works noted also for religious symbolism in everyday objects. Painter to John of Bavaria, Count of Holland (1422–25), to Philip the Good, Duke of Burgundy (1425–41). His paintings included *Annunciation, Madonna with Canon van der Paele, St. Barbara, Portrait of Young Man, Man in a Turban, Marriage of Giovanni Arnolfini and Giovanna Cenami, The Goldsmith Jan de Leeuwe.*

Ey·me·ric \ā-mā-ˈrēk\ *or* **Ey·me·rich** \-ˈrēch\, Nicolás. *Lat.* Ey·me·ri·cus \ˌī-mə-ˈrī-kəs\. c.1320–1399. Spanish theologian. Entered Dominican order (1334); grand inquisitor (1357–60); removed because of harsh conduct in office; reappointed (1366); his condemnation of writings of Ramon Llull led to clash with King John I of Aragon; author of *Directorium inquisitorum* (1376).

Eyre \ˈa(ə)r, ˈe(ə)r\, Edward John. 1815–1901. English explorer and colonialist. Emigrated to Australia and engaged in sheep farming (1833); explored deserts of interior of Australia and King George Sound; discovered Lake Eyre; published *Discoveries in Central Australia* (1845). Lieutenant governor of New Zealand (1846–53), governor of St. Vincent (1854–60); acting governor (1861–64) and governor (1864–66) of Jamaica; condemned for rigor in suppressing rebellion of Morant Bay natives (1865) and recalled; his conduct subject of great public controversy.

Ey·stein \ˈā-stān\. Name of two kings of Norway:

Eystein I Mag·nus·son \-ˈmäŋ-nü-sȯn\. 1089–1122. King (1103–22). Son of Magnus III Barfot. With his brothers Olaf IV and Sigurd I (*qq.v.*) ruled subdivisions of Norway; brought peace, encouraged building, trade, and the church.

Eystein Ha·ralds·son \-ˈhär-räl-sȯn\. d. 1157. King (1142–57). Son of Harald IV Gille. Brought up in Scotland; his reign a period of civil war; was deserted and assassinated.

Eyth \ˈīth\, Maximilian von, *in full* Edward Friedrich Maximilian. 1836–1906. German engineer and inventor. In association with John Fowler in England did much to improve and speed acceptance of powered machinery for plowing, irrigation, earth moving, etc.; founded German Agricultural Society (1885); travels reflected in his *Wanderbuch eines Ingenieurs* (1871–84).

Ey·vind Finn·sson \ˈā-vēnd-ˈfēn-sȯn\. *Nicknamed* Skal·da·spil·lir \ˈskäl-dä-ˌspēl-lər\. d. c.990. Norwegian skald. Adviser to Haakon the Good, whom he celebrated in his *Hákonarmál;* author of *Haleygjatal,* in praise of Jarl Haakon, and of *Islendingadrapa,* dealing with the Icelanders.

ˈĒzā·nā \ˈā-zä-nä\. 4th century A.D. King of Aksum (ancient Ethiopia). Adopted Christianity and laid foundation of Ethiopian church.

Ezek·iel \i-ˈzēk-yəl\. *Hebrew* Yeḥ·ez·qel \yek-ˈez-kel\. 6th century B.C. One of the major Hebrew prophets. Subject and author, at least in part, of Old Testament book of *Ezekiel.* Priest in Jerusalem (to 597 B.C.) and Babylon; his book prophesies the destruction and eventual rebuilding of Jerusalem.

Ezekiel. fl. c.100 B.C. Jewish dramatist. Resident of Alexandria; wrote in Greek; known esp. for *The Exodus,* showing influence of Euripides.

Ezekiel, Moses Jacob. 1844–1917. American sculptor, b. Richmond, Va. Worked in Rome (from 1872); works included *Virginia Mourning her Dead,* Lexington, Va.; Thomas Jefferson monument, Louisville, Ky.; monument to the Confederate dead, Arlington National Cemetery.

Ez·ra \ˈez-rə\. *Greek* Es·dras \ˈez-drəs\. 5th–4th century B.C. Hebrew scribe and priest. Instituted major reforms in postexilic Judaic practice based on Pentateuchal law. The book of *Ezra* in the Old Testament forms with *Nehemiah* a continuous account of postexilic Jewish history.

Ez·ze·li·no III da Ro·ma·no \ˌad-dzā-ˈlē-nō-dä-rō-ˈmän-ō\. 1194–1259. Italian Ghibelline leader. Feudal mayor (*podesta*) of Verona (1226–30, 1232–59), Vicenza (1236–59), and Padua (1237–56); supported Emperor Frederick II, whose troops in turn enabled him to dominate most of northeastern Italy; ruled with cruelty later noted by Dante in *Inferno;* defeated and captured by Guelphs at Cassano (1259).

F

Fa·ber \ˈfā-bər\, Frederick William. 1814–1863. English clergyman and hymn writer. Orig. Anglican clergyman; joined Roman Catholic church (1845) and formed (1846) Wilfridians, lay community merged (1848) with John Henry Newman's Oratory of St. John Neri; ordained (1847); established London Oratory (1849). Best known for hymns, as "Hark! Hark, my Soul," "My God, how wonderful Thou art"; author of *Lives of Modern Saints* (1847), *All for Jesus* (1853), *At the Foot of the Cross* (1858), etc.

Faber, Sir Geoffrey Cust. 1889–1961. English publisher and writer. Founder (1924) and president (1924–61) of Faber and Faber, Ltd., publishers.

Faber, Jacobus. See LEFÈVRE D'ÉTAPLES.

Fa·ber \ˈfäb-ər\, Johann Lothar von. 1817–1896. German manufacturer. Took over (1839) family pencil-making business (founded 1761 by his great-grandfather Kaspar); established branches and additional manufactories (including mills at Cedar Keys, Fla.) and agencies; added manufacture of other writing, drawing, and painting materials; received patent of nobility (1881); councilor of state for services to German industry. A brother, ¶John Eberhard Faber (1822–1879), representative of firm in U.S. (1848); became naturalized; established in N.Y. independent business, now Eberhard Faber Pencil Co.; built first pencil factory in U.S. (1861); first manufacturer to put rubber tips on pencils.

Faber, Johannes. *Orig. surname* Hei·ger·lin \ˈhī-gər-lin\. *Called* Mal·le·us Hae·ret·i·co·rum \ˈmal-ē-əs-hə-ˌret-ə-ˈkōr-əm\, *i.e.* the Hammer of Heretics. 1478–1541. German bishop and theologian. Vicar general of bishop of Constance and papal prothonotary (1518); friend of Erasmus and sympathizer with Zwingli and Melanchthon; later, strong opponent of Lutherans; court preacher to Emperor Ferdinand (1526); envoy to Spain and England (1527–28); bishop of Vienna (1531). Author of *Opus adversus nova quaedam dogmata Lutheri* (1522), *Malleus in haeresin Lutheranam* (1524).

Fa·ber \ˈfā-bər\, Peter *or Lat.* Petrus. *Orig.* Pierre Fa·vre \fåvr^{ə}\ *or* Le·fè·vre \lə-fevr^{ə}\. 1506–1546. French Jesuit theologian. Tutor and friend of Ignatius Loyola at U. of Paris (1528); said mass at which Loyola and companions took original vows (1534); cofounder of Society of Jesus (1539); professor of theology, Rome (from 1537); attended Diet of Worms (1540), of Regensburg (1541); became effective opponent of Protestantism in Rhineland.

Fa·ber·gé \få-ber-zhā\, Peter Carl, *Russ.* Karl Gustavovich. 1846–1920. Russian goldsmith and jeweler, of Huguenot descent. Followed father's jewelry business; won large patronage among European royalty and nobility with his exquisitely designed and executed decorative objects; noted esp. for imperial Easter eggs, made for Russian rulers (from 1884); business ended by Russian Revolution (1917).

Fa·bert \få-ber\, Abraham de. 1599–1662. French soldier. Distinguished himself as an engineer in sieges of Huguenot strongholds; governor of Sedan (1642); remained loyal during the Fronde; lieutenant general (1651); organized loyalist army in Sedan (1651–52); captured Stenay (1654); marshal of France (1658).

Fa·bi·an \ˈfā-bē-ən, ˈfāb-yən\. Saint. d. 250. Pope (236–250). Martyred in persecutions of Decius.

Fab·i·ola \ˌfab-ē-ˈō-lə\. Saint. d. c.399. Roman noblewoman. After conversion to Christianity became companion of St. Jerome; credited with founding in Rome first public hospital in western Europe.

Fa·bi·us \ˈfā-bē-əs, ˈfāb-yəs\. Name of a number of prominent Romans of one of oldest and most distinguished patrician families, including: Quintus Fabius Vib·u·la·nus \-ˌvib-yů-ˈlā-nəs\, consul for seven successive years (485–479 B.C.), and his brothers ¶Caeso and ¶Marcus. ¶Quintus Fabius, son of Marcus, was consul (467, 465, 459) and member of second decemvirate (450). ¶Marcus Fabius Am·bus·tus \-am-ˈbəs-təs\, pontifex maximus the year that the Gauls captured Rome (390 B.C.), for which, according to tradition, he was largely responsible. ¶Caius Fabius Pic·tor \-ˈpik-tər, -tȯr\ of late 4th century B.C., first Roman patrician to devote himself to painting. Executed (c.304 B.C.) first known Roman painting, in temple of Salus. ¶Quintus Fabius Pictor of late 3d century B.C. wrote a history of Rome (now lost) including Second Punic War, in which he personally served. ¶Quintus Fabius Max·i·mus \ˈmak-sə-məs\, *surnamed* Rul·li·a·nus \ˌrəl-ē-ˈā-nəs\ (d. c.290 B.C.), was six times consul; master of horse in Second Samnite War (326–304); dictator (315 B.C.); defeated Etruscans (310); distinguished himself in Third Samnite War, winning battle of Sentinum (295). His grandson ¶Quintus Fabius Maximus, *surnamed* Ver·ru·co·sus \ˌver-(y)ə-ˈkō-səs\ *and also* Cunc·ta·tor \kəŋk-ˈtāt-ər, -ˈtā-ˌtȯr\, *i.e.* the Delayer (d. 203); consul (233, 228 B.C.); censor (230); emissary to Carthage (218); dictator and army commander (217); again consul (215, 214, 209); in Second Punic War withstood Hannibal's military strength by his strategy (hence termed "Fabian") of conducting harassing operations while avoiding decisive conflicts; following disaster at Cannae (216) his strategy of attrition was resumed; captured Tarentum from Hannibal (209).

Fa·bre \fåbr^{ə}\, Émile. 1869–1955. French playwright. Attained success with social and political satires *Comme ils sont tous* (1894), *L'Argent* (1895), *Le bien d'autrui* (1897), *La Vie publique* (1901), *Les Ventres dorés* (1905), *La Maison d'Argile* (1907), *Les Sauterelles* (1911), *Un grand bourgeois* (1914), *La Maison sous l'orage* (1920); administrator of Comédie-Française (1915–36).

Fabre, Ferdinand. 1827–1898. French novelist. Author of *Les Courbezon* (1862), *Le Chevrier* (1868), *L'Abbé Tigrane* (1873), *Un illuminé* (1881), *Lucifer* (1884), *Toussaint Galabru* (1887); a founder of French regional novel.

Fabre, Jean-Henri. 1823–1915. French entomologist. Taught in lycées in Carpentras, Corsica, and Avignon; devoted himself to direct observational study of habits of insects, esp. Hymenoptera, Coleoptera, and Orthoptera, and spiders; work cited by Darwin; isolated alizarin, coloring agent in madder (1866). Author of *Souvenirs entomologiques* (1879–1907).

Fabre d'É·glan·tine \-dā-glä^{n}-tēn\, Philippe-François-Nazaire. *Orig. surname* Fabre. 1750–1794. French playwright and politician. Wrote poem *Étude de la nature* (1783) and song "Il pleut, il pleut, bergère"; his plays included the comedy *Le Philinte de Molière ou la suite du misanthrope* (1790). Friend of Danton and Desmoulins, and prominent in the Cordeliers; member of National Convention (1792); author of names of months and days in Revolutionary calendar; suspected of moderacy by Robespierre (1794); guillotined same day as Danton and Desmoulins.

Fabriano, Gentile da. See Niccolo di MASSIO.

Fa·brice \ˈfä-brēs\, Georg Friedrich Alfred von. Graf. 1818–1891. German general. Commander of Saxon forces in Bohemia in war against Prussia (1866); after war, Saxon minister of war; commanded German army of occupation in France (1871); again Saxon minister of war (1871); prime minister (1876); minister of foreign affairs (1882).

Fa·bri·ci \fä-ˈbrē-chē\ *or* **Fa·briz·io** \fä-ˈbrēt-syō\, Girolamo *or* Geronimo. *Lat. name* Hieronymus Fa·bri·ci·us ab Aqua·pen·den·te \fə-ˈbrish-(ē-)əs-ab-ˌak-wə-pen-ˈden-tē\. 1537–1619. Italian surgeon and anatomist. Student of Fallopius and his successor as professor at Padua (1562–1613); discovered semilunar valves of the veins, published in *De venarum ostiolis* (1603); conducted studies in embryology of various animals and man, publishing *De formato foetu* (1604) and *De formatione ovi et pulli* (1621); considered founder of comparative embryology; his collected works published posthumously in *Opera omnia anatomica et physiologica* (1625).

Fa·bri·ci·us \fä-ˈbrēt-sē-ůs\, David. 1564–1617. German clergyman and astronomer. His observations utilized by Kepler in researches on planet Mars; discovered variable star Mira in constellation Cetus (1596). His son ¶ Johannes (1587–c.1615), astronomer, is credited with discovery of sunspots (1610) and detection, by means of their movements, of rotation of sun on its axis.

Fa·bri·ci·us \fä-ˈbrē-sē-ůs\, Johann Christian. 1745–1808. Danish entomologist. Studied under Linnaeus; professor at Kiel (from 1775); named and classified some 10,000 species of insects; developed system of classification of insects based on mouth structure; anticipated later ideas of hybridization of species and environmental adaptation; author of *Systema entomologiae* (1775), *Genera insectorum* (1776), *Philosophia entomologica* (1778), *Betrachtungen über die allgemeinen Einrichtungen in der Natur* (1781), *Resultate natur historischer Vorlesungen* (1804).

Fabricius ab Aquapendente, Hieronymus. See Girolamo FABRICI.

Fa·bri·cius Lus·ci·nus \fə-'brish(-ē)-əs-lə-'sī-nəs\, Gaius. d. after 275 B.C. Roman general and statesman. Consul (282, 278 B.C.). After Roman defeat at Heraclea (280), sent to negotiate with Pyrrhus for ransom and exchange of prisoners; established reputation for honesty when he rejected all attempts to bribe him; considered in later ages a model of Roman virtue. Negotiated peace with Pyrrhus (275); censor (275); later defeated Samnites, Lucanians, and Bruttians.

Fa·bri·ti·us \fá-'brēt-sē-ūs\, Barent. *Orig. surname* Pie·terz \'pē-tərs\. 1624–1673. Dutch painter. Brother of Carel Fabritius. Known for biblical, mythological, historical paintings and portraits in the manner of Rembrandt.

Fabritius, Carel. *Orig. surname* Pie·terz \'pē-tərs\. 1622–1654. Dutch painter. Brother of Barent Fabritius; pupil of Rembrandt and probably teacher of Jan Vermeer; worked (from 1650) in Delft; considered a principal figure in school of Delft. Works included portrait of Abraham de Potter, *The Goldfinch, The Sentinel, Raising of Lazarus,* and *Family Group.*

Fa·bri·zi \fä-'brēt-sē\, Nicola. 1804–1885. Italian politician. A leader of Milan uprising against Austria (1831); joined Mazzini's Young Italy group in Marseilles (1832); attempted to instigate revolt in Savoy (1834); fought in Carlist War in Spain; founded secret Italian Legion on Malta; helped organize Sicilian revolutions (1848, 1860); governor of Messina and minister of war in Garibaldi's cabinet (1860); deputy in Italian parliament (1861–85); Garibaldi's chief of staff in war against Austria (1866–67).

Fabrizio, Girolamo. See Girolamo FABRICI.

Fa·bry \fá-brē\, Charles. 1867–1945. French physicist. At U. of Marseilles (1894–1920), Sorbonne (1920–45); known for work in optics, esp. in spectroscopy, photometry, and interferometry; discovered atmospheric ozone layer that screens solar ultraviolet radiation.

Fab·vier \fáv-yā\, Charles-Nicolas. Baron. 1782–1855. French general. Served in Napoleonic armies, notably at Borodino; remained loyal to Louis XVIII during the Hundred Days; later involved in intrigue against Bourbons; aided Greece in struggle with Turkey and gained fame in directing defense of Athens (1827). Returned to France (1830); lieutenant general (1839); peer of France (1845).

Fa·by·an \'fā-bē-ən, 'fāb-yən\, Robert. d. 1513. English chronicler. Author of *The Concordance of Histories,* a chronicle of England to c.1157 and of London to 1485, pub. (1516) under title *The New Chronicles of England and France.*

Fac·cio·la·ti \,fät-chō-'lä-tē\, Jacopo. 1682–1769. Italian philologist and lexicographer. Professor, Padua; collaborated with Forcellini in editing Calepino's *Dictionarium undecim linguarum* (1718); compiled *Totius latinitatis lexicon* (1771).

Fac·ta \'fäk-tä\, Luigi. 1861–1930. Italian politician. Deputy (1892–1924); minister of finance (1911–13), of justice (1919); prime minister (Feb.–July 1922, Aug.–Oct. 1922); temporized in face of Fascist march on Rome, forced to resign to make way for Fascist government.

Fad·den \'fad-ᵊn\, Sir Arthur William. 1895–1973. Australian politician. Leader of Country party; prime minister (1941); treasurer (1940–41, 1949–58); acting prime minister on ten occasions.

Fa·de·yev \(,)fəd-'yā-yif\, Aleksandr Aleksandrovich. *Also called* Aleksandr A. Bul·gya \'bül-gyə\. 1901–1956. Russian novelist. Joined Communist party (1918) and fought in civil war; member of Praesidium, Union of Soviet Writers (from 1932). A leading exponent and theoretician of proletarian literature; works included *Razgrom* (1927), *Posledny iz Udege* (1929–41), and *Molodaya gvardiya* (1946; rev. 1951).

Faes, Pieter Van der. See Sir Peter LELY.

Fag·giu·o·la \,fäd-jü-'ō-lä\, Uguccione della. c.1250–1319. Italian ruler. Ghibelline leader; appointed (1313) podesta of Pisa, becoming captain of war and virtual dictator; captured Lucca (1314); defeated Guelph forces near Florence (1315); overthrown by Castruccio Castracani (1316); podesta of Vicenza (1317–19).

Fa·gniez \fán-yā\, Gustave. 1842–1927. French historian. Author of *Le Père Joseph et Richelieu* (1893–94), *L'Economie sociale de la France sous Henri IV* (1897), etc.

Fa·guet \fá-ge\, Émile. 1847–1916. French literary critic. Professor at the Sorbonne (1890). Author of *La Tragédie française au XVIe siècle* (1883), *Politiques et moralistes du XIXe siècle* (1891–1900), *Histoire de la littérature française* (1900–01), *L'Anticléricalisme* (1906), *Le Féminisme* (1910), *L'Art de lire* (1912), etc.

Fa·gun·wa \fä-'gün-wä\, Daniel O. 1910–1963. Nigerian novelist. A Yoruba chief; first original writer in Yoruba. Author of very popular series of fantastic novels *Igbo Olodumare* (1947), *Ireke Onibudo* (1949), *Ogboju Ode Ninu Igbo Irunmale* (1950), *Irinkerindo Ninu Igbo Elegbeje* (1954), and *Adiitu Olodumare* (1961).

Fah·ren·heit \'far-en-,hīt; *Angl* 'far-, 'fär-\, Daniel Gabriel. 1686–1736. German physicist. Lived most of life in Holland; invented the alcohol thermometer (1709) and the mercury thermometer (1714); introduced Fahrenheit scale commonly used for thermometers in the U.S. and Canada; discovered that water can remain liquid below its freezing point and that the boiling point of liquids varies with atmospheric pressure.

Fa-hsien \'fä-shē-'en\. *Orig.* Sehi. fl. 399–414 A.D. Chinese priest, traveler, and author. Studied Buddhism; journeyed to India (399); spent about ten years (402–412) visiting scenes of Buddha's life, copying Buddhist texts, etc.; in Ceylon (412–414); returned to China; wrote account of travels *Fo Kuo Chi* and translated Buddhist texts.

Fai·dherbe \fe-derb\, Louis-Léon-César. 1818–1889. French soldier and colonial administrator. Assumed his first independent command in Algeria (1849). Governor of Senegal (1854–61, 1863–65); extended French territorial possessions and successfully reorganized administration; drove forces of al-Ḥājj 'Umar Tal off the lower Senegal River; made Senegal dominant military power in that part of West Africa; founded Dakar and Médina. In Franco–Prussian War commanded army of the North; defeated at St.-Quentin (1871). Senator (1879–88).

Fail·ly \fá-yē\, Pierre-Louis-Charles de. 1810–1892. French soldier. Served in Crimea (1854–55); general of division (1855); engaged at Solferino (1859); defeated by Prussians near Beaumont (1870) and replaced by General de Wimpffen.

Fain \faⁿ\, Agathon-Jean-François. Baron. 1778–1837. French historian. Appointed (1806) secretary and archivist to Napoléon's *cabinet particulier* and (1813) Napoléon's private secretary; appointed (1830) first secretary of Louis-Philippe's cabinet and occasional administrator of the civil list. Best remembered for his personal reminiscences of Napoléon's reign, very important as historical sources, including *Manuscrit de 1814* (1823) and memoirs (pub. 1908).

Fair, A. A. See Erle Stanley GARDNER.

Fair·bairn \'fa(ə)r-,ba(ə)rn, 'fe(ə)r-, -,be(ə)rn\, Andrew Martin. 1838–1912. Scottish theologian and Congregational minister. Principal of Mansfield College, Oxford (1886–1909); a leading proponent of the German critico-historical method in liberal theology. Author of *Christ in Modern Theology* (1893), *The Philosophy of the Christian Religion* (1902), *Studies in Religion and Theology* (1910), etc.

Fairbairn, Sir William. 1789–1874. Scottish engineer. Established shipbuilding works in London (1835–49); introduced Lancashire boiler with twin flues (1844); with Robert Stephenson designed (1845) the Britannia and the Conway Tubular railway bridges in Wales; first to use wrought iron for ship hulls, bridges, mill shafting, and structural beams; experimented with strength and manufacture of iron; made baronet (1869). His brother ¶Sir Peter (1799–1861), also an engineer, founded in Leeds an establishment to make textile machinery and machine tools.

Fair·banks \'fa(ə)r-,baŋ(k)s, 'fe(ə)r-\, Charles Warren. 1852–1918. American politician, b. near Unionville, Ohio. Adm. to Indiana bar (1874); U.S. senator from Indiana (1897–1905); vice president of U.S. (1905–09); ran unsuccessfully for vice president on ticket headed by Charles E. Hughes (1916).

Fairbanks, Douglas Elton. *Orig. surname* Ul·man \'əl-mən\. 1883–1939. American actor, b. Denver, Colo. One of first and greatest of the swashbuckling screen heroes, starring in films *The Mark of Zorro* (1920), *The Three Musketeers* (1921), *Robin Hood* (1922), *The Thief of Bagdad* (1924), *The Black Pirate* (1926), *The Iron Mask* (1929), etc.; founded (1917) own producing company; a founder (1919) of United Artists Corp. to produce and distribute films; m. (1920; div. 1935) Mary Pickford (*q.v.*).

Fairbanks, Thaddeus. 1796–1886. American businessman and inventor, b. Brimfield, Mass. Devised first platform scale, obtaining basic patent (1831); thereafter E. & T. Fairbanks & Company (incorporated as Fairbanks Scale Company, 1874) made manufacturing of platform scales for all purposes their chief business. His brother ¶Erastus (1792–1864), b. Brimfield, Mass., was associated with him in business; governor of Vermont (1852–53, 1860–61).

Fair·child \'fa(ə)r-chīld, 'fe(ə)r-\, David Grandison. 1869–1954. American botanist, b. Lansing, Mich. With plant pathology section of U.S. Dept. of Agriculture as botanist (from 1889), agricultural explorer (1898–1903), administrator in charge (1904–28), and, after retirement, collaborator (1928–54). Supervised introduction of thousands of plants into U.S.; published much on plants, as *Exploring for Plants* (1930), and autobiographical *The World Was My Garden* (1938) and *The World Grows Round My Door* (1947).

Fair·fax \'fa(ə)r-,faks, fe(ə)r-\, Thomas. 1st Baron Fairfax of Cam·er·on \'kam(-ə)-rən\. 1560–1640. Scottish soldier and diplomat. Served in Low Countries; used by Queen Elizabeth in communication with James VI of Scotland. His son ¶Edward (c.1575–1635), poet, translated Tasso's *Gerusalemme liberata* as *Godfrey of Bulloigne or the Recoverie of Jerusalem* (1600);

also wrote eclogues. Edward's brother ¶Ferdinando (1584–1648), 2d baron; M.P. (1622, 1624–27, Long Parliament 1640); commanded Parliamentary forces in Yorkshire in Civil War; defended Hull (1643); stationed on right of Parliamentary line in battle of Marston Moor (1644). Ferdinando's son ¶Thomas (1612–1671), 3d baron; commanded Parliamentary forces in his captures of Leeds and Wakefield (1643); secured the north by victories at Winceby (1643) and Marston Moor (1644); commander in chief of the New Model Army (1645) and its organizer and trainer; defeated Charles I at Naseby (1645); crushed Royalist forces at Maidstone and starved Colchester into submission (1647); resigned from military command because of unwillingness to invade Scotland (1650); helped Gen. George Monck restore Parliamentary rule after Cromwell's death (1658); headed commission dispatched to Charles II at The Hague (1660).

¶Thomas (1692–1782), 6th baron; visited maternal estates of the Northern Neck of Virginia (1735–37) and settled there as proprietor (1747); entrusted to George Washington surveying and mapping of the Fairfax estate in Shenandoah Valley (1748); steadfast Loyalist.

Fair·holt \ˈfa(ə)r-ˌhōlt, ˈfe(ə)r-\, Frederick William. 1814–1866. English engraver and antiquarian. Published illustrated antiquarian study *Costume in England* (1846); edited *A Dictionary of Terms in Art* (1854).

Fai·sal \ˈfī-səl\. *Arab.* Fayṣal. Name of two kings of Iraq:

Faisal I. 1885–1933. King of Syria (1920) and Iraq (1921–33). Son of Ḥusayn ibn ʿAli. A leader in Arab revolt against Ottoman rule (1916); took command of Arab rebels at Medina; cooperated with T. E. Lawrence and General Allenby in campaign which captured Jerusalem (1917) and Damascus (1918); proclaimed (Mar. 1920) king of Syria by a Syrian national congress but deposed by French under General Gouraud (July 1920). Placed by British on throne of Iraq (1921); negotiated series of treaties with British, including treaty (1930) giving complete independence to Iraq; succeeded by his son Ghāzī.

Faisal II. 1935–58. King (1939–58). Son of Ghāzī and grandson of Faisal I; under regency of his uncle Amīr ʿAbd al-Ilāh (1939–53); executed during overthrow of the monarchy.

Fai·sal \ˈfī-zəl, -səl\. *Arab. in full* Fayṣal ibn ʿAbd al-ʿAzīz ibn ʿAbd ar-Raḥmān āl-Saʿūd. c.1906–1975. King of Saudi Arabia (1964–75). Son of King Ibn Saʿūd; appointed foreign minister and viceroy of Hejaz (1926); led victorious campaign against Yemen (1934); declared crown prince (1953); prime minister and minister of foreign affairs (1953–60); defense minister (1958–64); became king on deposition of his brother Saud (1964); active in promoting economic and educational programs; assassinated.

Fai·thorne \ˈfā-ˌthȯrn\, William. c.1616–1691. English engraver and portrait draftsman. Pupil of Robert Peake the Elder and John Payne. Engraved map of London (1658) and of Virginia and Maryland; published *The Art of Graving and Etching* (1662). His son ¶William (1656–1710) engraved portraits of Queen Anne, Charles I, Charles II, and John Dryden.

Fa·jans \ˈfā-yäns\, Kasimir. 1887–1975. American physical chemist, b. Warsaw. Professor, Munich (1917–35), U. of Michigan (1936–57); naturalized U.S. citizen (1942). With Otto Gohring discovered protactinium-234*m* (1917); discovered the radioactive displacement law simultaneously with Frederick Soddy. Author of *Radioelements and Isotopes* (1931), *Quanticule Theory of Chemical Binding* (1961), etc.

Fakhr ad-Dīn II \ˈfäk-rəd-ˈdēn\. c.1572–1635. Lebanese ruler (1593–1633). Won struggle for supremacy with Christian Maronite ruler Yūsuf Sayfā (by 1607); united the Druze and Maronite districts of Lebanon mountains under his rule; exiled by Ottomans (1614–18); extended his domain to include most of Syria and Palestine (by 1631); defeated (1633), captured (1634), and executed by the Ottomans. Often regarded as the father of modern Lebanon.

Fakhr ad-Dīn ar-Rāzī \ˈfäk-rəd-ˈdēn-är-rä-ˈzē\. *In full* Abū ʿAbd Allāh Muḥammad ibn ʿUmar ibn al-Ḥusayn Fakhr ad-Dīn ar-Rāzī. 1149–1209. Muslim theologian and scholar. Known as brilliant scholar, debater, and preacher; wrote on medicine, geometry, astrology, grammar, etc.; compiled an encyclopedia. Author of *Mafātīḥ al-ghayb* or *Kitāb at-tafsīr al-kabīr*, one of the principal commentaries on the Qurʾān; *Muḥaṣṣal afkār al-mutaqaddimīn wa-al-mutaʾakhkhirīn*, classic work of Muslim theology; *al-Mabāḥith al-mashriqīyah*, summary of his philosophy and theology.

Fal·cón \fäl-ˈkōn\, Juan Crisóstomo. 1820–1870. Venezuelan soldier and politician. President of Venezuela (1863–68); overthrown by revolution.

Fal·co·ne \fäl-ˈkō-nā\, Aniello. 1600–1665. Italian painter. Pupil of Ribera; known esp. for battle scenes; decorated chapel cupola in San Paolo del Padri Teatini, Naples; painted *Flight Into Egypt* in sacristy of Naples cathedral and frescoes in sacristy at Gesú Nuovo, Naples.

Fal·con·er \ˈfȯk-nər, ˈfȯ(l)-kən-ər\, Hugh. 1808–1865. Scottish paleontologist and botanist. Assistant surgeon on East India Co.'s Bengal establishment (1830); discoverer of fossil mammals and reptiles in Siwalik Hills (1832); made earliest experiments in manufacture of Indian tea; professor of botany, Calcutta Medical Coll. (1848–55).

Falconer, William. 1732–1769. Scottish sailor, lexicographer, and poet. Chief poem, *The Shipwreck* (1762).

Fal·co·net \fàl-kò-ne\, Étienne-Maurice. 1716–1791. French sculptor. Pupil of Lemoyne; patronized by Mme. de Pompadour; director of Sèvres porcelain factory (1757–66); in Russia (1766–78) where he executed bronze equestrian statue of Peter the Great at St. Petersburg. Adapted classical style of French Baroque to Rococo; work considered quintessence of taste in Louis XV period; works included *Milon de Crotone* (1754), *La Baigneuse* (1757), *Pygmalion et Galatée* (1763), and *L'Hiver* (1765).

Fal·co·net·to \ˌfäl-kō-ˈnät-tō\, Giovanni Maria. c.1458–c.1534. Veronese painter and architect. Painted frescoes in S. Nazaro, Verona (1503); decorated doors of S. Giovanni, Padua (1528).

Fal·guière \fàl-gyer\, Jean-Alexandre-Joseph. 1831–1900. French sculptor and painter. Professor at École des Beaux Arts (1882); among his sculptures were *Diane* (1887, 1891), *Femme au paon* (1890), *Danseuse* (1896) and many portrait busts; among his canvases, *Lutteurs, Incendiaire.*

Fa·lier \fäl-ˈyer\ *or* **Fa·lie·ro** \-ˈyer-ō\, Marino. 1274–1355. Doge of Venice. Commanded Venetian army at siege of Zara (1346); led naval squadron against Genoa (1352); elected doge (1354); convicted of conspiracy to murder Venetian patricians and have himself proclaimed prince, executed. Subject of tragedies by Byron and Casimir Delavigne and of novel by Hoffmann.

Falier *or* **Faliero,** Ordelafo. d. 1118. Doge of Venice. Elected doge (1102); sent aid to Baldwin I in capture of Sidon (1104) and to Alexius I in defeat of Bohemond I (1108); conquered Zara from Stephen II of Hungary and assumed title of Duke of Croatia (1115); killed in battle near Zara.

Falk \ˈfälk\, Adalbert, *in full* Paul Ludwig Adalbert. 1827–1900. German politician. Old Liberal member, Prussian House of Representatives (1858); as minister of ecclesiastical affairs and education (1872–79), assisted Bismarck in Kulturkampf and helped work out May laws (1873) aimed at Roman Catholics; member of Prussian House of Representatives and of Reichstag (1873–82), where he opposed modification of his laws; president of Court of Appeals in Hamm (from 1882).

Falk, Johannes Daniel. 1768–1826. German writer. Author of satirical works, as *Der Mensch* (1795), the dramatic poem *Prometheus* (1803), and *Goethe aus näherem persönlichen Umgange dargestellt* (1832).

Falkberget, Johan Petter. See Johan LILLEBAKKEN.

Fal·ke \ˈfäl-kə\, Johannes Friedrich Gottlieb. 1823–1876. German historian. Author of *Geschichte des deutschen Handels* (1859–60), *Die Hansa* (1862), and *Geschichte des deutschen Zollwesens* (1869). His nephew ¶Gustav (1853–1916), lyric poet and novelist, was author of volumes of verse *Mynheer der Tod* (1892), *Hohe Sommertage* (1902), *Frohe Fracht* (1907); volumes of short stories *Geelgösch* (1910) and *Der Spanier* (1910); novels *Der Mann im Nebel* (1899) and *Die Kinder aus Ohlsens Gang* (1908); and the autobiographical *Stadt mit den goldenen Türmen* (1912).

Fal·ken·hau·sen \ˈfäl-kən-ˌhaủz-ᵊn\, Ludwig von. Freiherr. 1844–1936. German soldier. Served in Austro-Prussian War (1866), Franco-Prussian War (1870–71, World War I (1914–18); general governor of Belgium (1917–18).

Fal·ken·hayn \ˈfäl-kən-ˌhīn\, Erich Georg Anton Sebastian von. 1861–1922. Prussian general. Took part in China expedition (1899–1903); general (1913); Prussian war minister (1913–15); chief of general staff of German army (1914–16); active in planning offensives against Russia, Serbia, and Verdun; severely blamed for failure at Verdun; succeeded by von Hindenburg (1916); commanded army in Romania (1916), in Palestine (1917–18), and in Lithuania (1918).

Fal·ken·horst \ˈfäl-kən-ˌhȯrst\, Nikolaus von. 1885–1968. German general. In World War I (1914–18) commanded forces which occupied Norway and Denmark (1940); general governor of Norway (1940–44).

Falkland, 2d Viscount. See Lucius CARY.

Falkland, Samuel. See Herman HEIJERMANS.

Falk·ner \ˈfȯk-nər\, Thomas. 1707–1784. English missionary. Entered Society of Jesus (1732); ordained (1739); missionary in Argentina (1743–68); author of *A Description of Patagonia* (1774) and *Of the Patagonians* (1788).

Falkner, William. See FAULKNER.

Fall \ˈfȯl\, Albert Bacon. 1861–1944. American politician, b. Frankfort, Ky. U.S. senator from New Mexico (1912–21). U.S. secretary of the interior (1921–23); secretly transferred government oil lands (Teapot Dome) to Doheny and Sinclair; convicted (1929) for accepting bribe and imprisoned (1931–32).

Fall \ˈfäl\, Leopold. 1873–1925. Austrian composer. Known for his operettas, as *Der fidele Bauer* (1907), *Die Dollarprinzessin* (1907), *Die geschiedene Frau* (1908), and *Madame Pompadour* (1922).

Fal·la \ˈfäl-yä\, Manuel de. 1876–1946. Spanish composer. Pupil of Felipe Pedrell; in Paris (1907–14), associating with Debussy, Dukas, Ravel; in later years influenced by Stravinsky; lived in Argentina (1939–46). His style at first Romantic and Andalusian, later more Neoclassical and Castilian, but always nationalistic. Works included opera *La vida breve* (1905; rev. 1913), puppet opera *El retablo de Maese Pedro* (1922), ballets *El amor brujo* (1915) and *El sombrero de tres picos* (1919), suite of three impressions for piano and orchestra *Noches en los jardines de España* (1916), *Harpsichord Concerto* (1926), cantata *L'Atlántida* (unfinished), vocal works, and piano pieces.

Fallada, Hans. See DITZEN.

Fallersleben, Hoffmann von. See August HOFFMANN.

Fal·lières \fȧl-yer\, Clément-Armand. 1841–1931. French politician. Member, Chamber of Deputies (1876–80); minister of interior (1882–83, 1887), of public instruction (1883–85, 1889–90), of justice (1887–88, 1890–92); premier (1883); elected to Senate (1890–99), its president (1899–1906). Eighth president of Third Republic of France (1906–13).

Fall·me·ray·er \'fäl-mə-ˌrī-ər\, Jakob Philipp. 1790–1861. German historian. Professor, Munich (1848–49) and member of Frankfurt parliament. Author of a work on Slavic origin of modern Greek people, *Das albanische Elèment in Griechenland* (1857–60), which aroused much controversy.

Fal·lop·pio \fäl-'lȯp-yō\ *or* **Fal·lop·pia** \-'lȯp-yä\, Gabriele. *Lat.* Gabriel Fal·lo·pi·us \fə-'lō-pē-əs\. 1523–1562. Italian anatomist. Professor of surgery and anatomy at Pisa (1548–51) and Padua (1551–62). Discovered function of oviducts (Fallopian tubes); described other anatomical structures, including chorda tympani, sphenoid and ethmoid bones, and opening of oviducts into abdominal cavity; named the vagina, placenta, clitoris, palate, and cochlea; joined Vesalius in assault on Galen's principles; published *Observationes anatomicae* (1561).

Fal·loux \fȧ-lü\, Frédéric-Alfred-Pierre de. Comte. 1811–1886. French politician. Elected to Chamber of Deputies (1846); a leader of monarchist and liberal Catholic causes; minister of public instruction (1848–49); introduced law, known as *Loi Falloux,* providing for freedom of instruction (passed 1850). Author of biography of Louis XVI (1840), *Histoire de saint Pie V* (1844), *Mémoires d'un royaliste* (1888), etc.

Fal·sen \'fäl-sən\, Christian Magnus. 1782–1830. Norwegian politician and jurist. Leader of party desiring complete independence from Sweden; principal author of Norwegian constitution; member of the Storting; president of Supreme Court of Norway (1827).

Fan Chung-yen \'fän-'jůŋ-'yən\. 989–1052. Chinese politician. As chief minister (1043–52) to Emperor Jen Tsung, instituted ten-point reform program, including abolition of corruption, equalization of landholdings, creation of strong local militia system, and reformation of civil service examination system; ardent foe of Buddhism; known as Confucian scholar.

Fane \'fān\, John. 11th Earl of West·mor·land \'wes(t)-mər-lənd, *US also* wes(t)-ˌmō(ə)r-, -ˌmȯ(ə)r-\. 1784–1859. English soldier and diplomat. Served in Peninsular War (1808–10); general (1854). Minister to Florence (1814) and Berlin (1841–51). Founder of Royal Acad. of Music (1823).

Fan·euil \'fan-yəl, 'fan-ᵊl, 'fan-yə-wəl\, Peter. 1700–1743. American merchant, b. New Rochelle, N.Y. Built up large fortune in Boston; gave to city building since known as Faneuil Hall.

Fa Ngum \'fäŋ-'üm\. *Also known as* Fa Ngoun \-'ün\. 1316–1373. Laotian ruler. Son of tribal chieftain of Tai peoples; by military conquests united Laotian territories into state called Lan Xang or Lan Chang (by 1353); took honorific title Phragna Fah La Thorani Sisatana-kanahud; expanded Laos to its largest territory in all its history; introduced Khmer civilization and Theravāda Buddhism; deported by his ministers (1371).

Fa·non \fȧ-nōⁿ\, Frantz Omar. 1925–1961. French West Indian psychoanalyst and social philosopher, b. Martinique. Served in French army during World War II; head of psychiatry department, Blida-Joinville Hospital, Algeria (1953–56); joined (1954) Algerian liberation movement and became (1956) editor of its newspaper *El Moudjahid* in Tunis; appointed ambassador to Ghana by rebel Provisional Government (1960). Developed theory that some neuroses are socially generated. Author of anti-colonial writings *Peau noire, masques blancs* (1952) and *Les Damnés de la terre* (1961) and of *L'An V de la révolution algérienne* (1959), *Pour la révolution africaine* (1964).

Fan·shawe \'fan-ˌshȯ\, Sir Richard. Baronet. 1608–1666. English diplomat. Fought in Royalist army in Civil War; captured at battle of Worcester (1651). Master of requests and Latin secretary to Prince Charles, The Hague (1660). British ambassador to Portugal (1662–63) and Spain (1664–66). Translator of Guarini's *Pastor fido* (1647) and Camões' *Os lusíadas* (1655).

Fan·ti \'fän-tē\, Manfredo. 1808–1865. Italian soldier. In Italian service against Austrians (1849); general of brigade in Crimean War (1854–56); commanded forces of Tuscany, Parma, Modena, and Romagna in war of 1859. Minister of war under Cavour (1860–61); won impressive victories in papal lands; opposed concessions to Garibaldi and followers; commander in chief of military department, Florence (1862).

Fan·tin-La·tour \fäⁿ-taⁿ-lä-tür\, Henri, *in full* Ignace-Henri-Jean-Théodore. 1836–1904. French painter. Studied under Courbet. Best known for still life studies, paintings of intimate familiar scenes, and esp. group compositions of contemporary French celebrities in the arts, as *Hommage à Delacroix* (1864), *Un Atelier des Batignolles* (1870), *Un Coin de table* (1872); in later years devoted himself to lithography and book illustration.

Fan Wen-ch'eng \'fän-'wən-'chəŋ\. 1597–1666. Chinese politician. Captured by the Manchus; trusted adviser to Nurhachi, Dorgan, Abahai, Fu-lin; aided them in developing a Chinese-style government; persuaded Dorgan to seize Peking (1644), initiating Ch'ing dynasty; restored civil service examination system and instituted measures to win loyalty of Chinese subjects; retired (1654).

Fā·rā·bī, al- \al-fä-'rä-ˌbē\. *More fully* Muḥammad ibn Muḥammad ibn Ṭarkhān ibn Uzalagh al-Fārābī. *Known also as* Abū Naṣr al-Fārābī. *Lat.* Al·pha·ra·bi·us \ˌal-fə-'rā-bē-əs\ *or* Aven·na·sar \ˌav-ə-'nā-sər\. c.878–c.950. Muslim philosopher. Wrote commentaries on Aristotle, of whose thought he was an early Muslim master; became known as "second teacher" (after Aristotle); recast philosophy, subsuming ethics, science, etc., under a political theology aimed at defining the good ruler, excellent community; resolved conflict of philosophy and religion by making them analogues.

Far·a·day \'far-ə-ˌdā, -əd-ē\, Michael. 1791–1867. English chemist and physicist. Apprentice to bookbinder; accompanied Sir Humphry Davy on Continental tour (1813–15); director of the laboratory (1825), professor of chemistry (1833), Royal Institution. Discovered two chlorides of carbon (1820) and benzene (1825); first to liquefy chlorine (1823); produced new kinds of optical glass. His discoveries relating to electricity included electromagnetic rotation (1821), electromagnetic induction (1831), laws of electrolysis (1833). Established indentity of electricity generated in different ways; discovered rotation of the plane of polarized light by a magnetic field (1845); described properties of a diamagnetic substance (1845). His publications included *Chemical Manipulation* (1827), *Experimental Researches in Electricity* (1839–55), *Experimental Researches in Chemistry and Physics* (1859), *Lectures on the Chemical History of a Candle* (1861), *On the Various Forces in Nature* (1873).

Fa·raj \'fär-äj\. *In full* al-Malik an-Nāṣir Zayn ad-Dīn Abū as-Saʽādāt Faraj. 1389–1412. 26th Mamlūk ruler of Egypt and Syria. Succeeded his father Barqūq (1399); an ineffectual ruler; lost Damascus and Aleppo to Timur (1400) and became subservient (1400–05) to him; led unsuccessful expeditions to reconquer Syria; defeated and captured in battle at Damascus, killed.

Farazdaq, al-. See TAMMĀM.

Fard \'färd\, Wallace D. *Also called* Walli Far·rad \'fär-əd, -ˌad\, Professor Ford \'fō(ə)rd, 'fȯ(ə)rd\, Farrad Mo·ham·med \mō-'ham-əd, -'häm-\, F. Mohammed Ali *and* Wallace Fard Mu·ham·mad \mü-'ham-əd, -'häm-\. c.1877–?1934. American religious leader, b. Mecca? Founder of the Black Muslim (Nation of Islām) movement (1930); considered by followers to be incarnation of Allāh; disappeared (1934) without a trace.

Fardd, Eben. See Ebenezer THOMAS.

Fa·rel \fȧ-rel\, Guillaume. 1489–1565. French leader in Reformation. Studied under Jacques Lefèvre d'Étaples in Paris; adopted protestant Reformation beliefs (1521); fled to Basel, Switzerland (1523); settled at Geneva (1532) and succeeded in having the Reformation established there by vote of Genevan Great Council (1535). Persuaded Calvin to settle in Geneva (1536); banished with Calvin (1538). Pastor at Neuchâtel (from 1538), from which center he continued to spread Reformation doctrines. Wrote *Summaire et briefve declaration d'aulcuns lieux* (1525), *Du vray usage de la croix de Jesus-Christ* (1560), and sermons.

Far·go \'fär-ˌgō\, William George. 1818–1881. American businessman, b. Pompey, N.Y. With Henry Wells and Daniel Dunning organized (1844) Wells & Company, first express concern west of Buffalo, which merged with two others (1850) to form American Express Company, with Fargo as secretary; president, after larger merger (1868–81). Organized Wells, Fargo & Company to handle express business between New York and California (1852); bought Pony Express (1861) and Overland Mail Co. (1866). Mayor of Buffalo (1862–66).

Fa·ria e Sou·sa \fə-'rē-ə-ē-'sō-zə\, Manuel de. 1590–1649. Portuguese historian and poet. Author of verse *Fuente de Aganipe* (1624–27) and histories *Asia portuguesa* (1666–75), *Europa portuguesa* (1678–80), etc.

Farīd od-Dīn ʽAṭṭār. See ʽAṬṬĀR.

Fa·ri·goule \fȧ-rē-gül\, Louis-Henri-Jean. *Pen name* Jules Ro·mains \rȯ-maⁿ\. 1885–1972. French writer. A founder (c.1908–11) and chief exponent of literary movement *Unanimisme* which emphasized the unifying principles of human groups over individual personalities. Author of novels, including *Mort de quelqu'un* (1911), *Les Copains* (1913), and esp. novel cycle under general title *Les Hommes de bonne volonté* (27 vols., 1932–46); unanimiste dramas as *Cromedeyre-le-Vieil* (1920) and farcical comedies as *Donogoo-Tonka* (1920), *Monsieur Le Trouhadec saisi par la débauche* (1923), *Knock* (1923); verse *La Vie unanime* (1908), *L'Homme blanc* (1937).

Farina, Giuseppe La. See LA FARINA.

Fa·ri·na \fä-'rē-nä\, Salvatore. 1846–1918. Italian novelist. Works included *Mio figlio* (1877), *Il Signor Io* (1882), *Più forte dell' amore* (1890), *I due desideri* (1904).

Fa·ri·nac·ci \,fä-rē-'nät-chē\, Prospero. *Lat.* Fa·ri·nac·ci·us \,far-ə-'näch-ē-əs\. 1544–1618. Italian jurist. Entered papal service under Clement VIII; procurator general to Paul V. His *Praxis et theorica criminalis* (1616) was strongest influence on penology in Roman-law countries until reforms of Cesare Beccaria.

Farinacci, Roberto. 1892–1945. Italian politican. Founded Fascist daily paper *Cremona Nuova;* agitated for Italian intervention in both World Wars. Organized Fascist movement in Cremona; secretary general of Fascist party (1925–26); opposed Mussolini's rapprochement with Vatican; returned to law practice in Cremona (1926); member, Fascist Grand Council (1935–43); captured and executed by partisans.

Farinata degli Uberti. See UBERTI.

Fa·ri·na·ti \,fär-ē-'nä-tē\, Paolo. c.1524–c.1606. Veronese painter, architect, and engraver. Known chiefly for frescoes in Verona churches.

Fa·ri·nel·li \,fär-ē-'nel-lē\. *Orig.* Carlo Bro·schi \'brôs-kē\. 1705–1782. Italian male soprano. Studied under Nicola Porpora; made debut in Rome (1721); famous throughout Europe for extraordinary compass of voice, technical proficiency, and musical expression; outdone in contest only once, by rival castrato Bernacchi. In London with Porpora's Opera of the Nobility (1734–37); at Spanish court (1737–59) under Philip V and Ferdinand VI achieved distinction as impresario and took part in public affairs; retired to villa near Bologna.

Fa·ri·ni \fär-'ē-nē\, Luigi Carlo. 1812–1866. Italian physician, historian, and politician. Deputy in Piedmontese legislature at Turin (1849–65); strong supporter of Cavour; minister of public instruction (1851–52). Dictator of Modena (1859); established league of Modena, Parma, Romagna, and Tuscany and secured its annexation to Piedmont; minister of interior, Cavour cabinet (1860, 1861–62); viceroy of Naples (1860–61); prime minister (1862–63).

Far·jeon \'fär-jən\, Eleanor. 1881–1965. English writer. Granddaughter of Joseph Jefferson; author of books for children, including *Nursery Rhymes of London Town* (1916), *Martin Pippin in the Apple Orchard* (1921), *The Old Nurse's Stocking Basket* (1931), *The Silver Curlew* (1953).

Far·ley \'fär-lē\, James Aloysius. 1888–1976. American politician, b. Grassy Point, N.Y. President, General Building Supply Corp. (1929–33, 1949–58); board chairman, Coca-Cola Export Corp. (1940–73). Chairman, N.Y. State Athletic Commission (1925–33); chairman, Democratic National Committee (1932–40); played key role in F.D. Roosevelt's 1932 and 1936 presidential campaigns; U.S. postmaster general (1933–40).

Far·low \'fär-(,)lō\, William Gilson. 1844–1919. American botanist, b. Boston. Professor at Harvard (from 1874); taught first course in U.S. in plant pathology; pioneered investigations in plant pathology; wrote chiefly on mycology.

Far·man \fär-mäⁿ\, Henri. 1874–1958. French pioneer in aviation and airplane manufacture. With brother Maurice in a Voisin biplane made first airplane flight of one kilometer in a complete circle (1908); flew from Bouy to Reims (1908), first flight from city to city; with Maurice developed the Farman biplane and established (1912) airplane factory at Boulogne-sur-Seine; constructed (1917) first long-distance passenger plane, the *Goliath,* which began regular Paris–London flights (Feb. 8, 1919); held distance, altitude, and duration records for flights. His brother ¶Maurice (1877–1964) was also pioneer in aviation; constructed his first airplane (1909); built modified Voisin biplanes, esp. (1912) the *Longhorn* model; made pioneering experiments in aerial radiotelephony (1911).

Far·mer \'fär-mər\, Fannie Merritt. 1857–1915. American cookery expert, b. Boston. Established Miss Farmer's School of Cookery (1902), with courses designed to train housewives rather than teachers of cookery; also specialized in invalid cookery. Editor of *The Boston Cooking School Cook Book* (1896); author of *Chafing Dish Possibilities* (1898), *A New Book of Cookery* (1912), etc.

Farmer, John. fl. 1591–1601. English composer. Best known for his madrigals.

Farmer, Moses Gerrish. 1820–1893. American inventor, b. Boscawen, N.H. Coinventor (with William F. Channing) of electric fire-alarm system adopted by Boston (1851); discovered means for duplex and quadruplex telegraphy (1855); devised an incandescent electric lamp with platinum filament, supplied by wet-cell battery (1859); patented self-exciting dynamo (1866); installed electric lighting in a Cambridge, Mass., residence, using one of his dynamos and 40 of his lamps arranged in multiple (1868); as electrician at U.S. Torpedo Station, Newport, R.I., effected improvements in torpedo warfare (1872–81).

Far·na·by \'fär-nə-bē\, Giles. c.1563–1640. English composer. Perhaps related to Thomas Farnaby. One of greatest keyboard composers of his day; wrote 52 pieces in the Fitzwilliam Virginal Book; published set of fresh but unimportant canzonets (1598) and several psalm settings. His son ¶Richard (c.1594–?) composed four pieces in the Fitzwilliam Virginal Book.

Farnaby, Thomas. 1575?–1647. English schoolmaster. Founder and a master of a school in London; commissioned by Charles I to prepare new Latin grammar for school use (1641); edited Latin classics.

Farnborough, Baron. See Thomas Erskine MAY.

Far·ne·se \fär-'nā-sā\. Italian family, established as leading Roman aristocratic family by Ranuccio, *called* Il Vec·chio \ēl-'vāk-kyō\, *i.e.* the Elder (d. c.1460), nobleman and condottiere; gained fame, authority, and wealth as defender of Papal States under Pope Eugenius IV; married his sons into the Orsini and Caetani families. His son Alessandro became Pope Paul III (*q.v.*) and established the Farnese family as ducal family of Parma (1545–1731) when he secured consent of sacred college to erect states of Parma and Piacenza into duchy. His natural son ¶Pier Luigi (1503–1547) was first Duke of Parma and of Piacenza (1545–47); organized an effective judicial and administrative system but ruled tyrannically; assassinated by nobles of Piacenza. ¶Ottavio (1524–1586), son of Pier Luigi, recovered duchy from imperialists (1551); sought protection of France (1551–56); subject to Philip II and a Spanish garrison (1556–85); m. (1538) Margaret of Austria, daughter of Emperor Charles V; ruled tyrannically. His son ¶Alessandro (1545–1592), Duke of Parma; general and diplomat; m. Maria of Portugal (1565); brought up in Spain; fought at Lepanto (1571); governor general of the Netherlands (1578–86), ruling as regent for Philip II of Spain; restored peace in southern provinces and secured perpetuation of Catholicism there; besieged and captured Antwerp (1584–85); responsible for maintaining Spanish control in Netherlands; consolidated union of Catholic Netherlands (later Belgium). ¶Ranuccio (1569–1622), son and successor of Alessandro; his large debts led to decline of duchy. ¶Antonio (1679–1731), last of male line. For Isabella or Elizabeth Farnese, see ISABELLA.

Farn·ham \'fär-nəm\, Eliza Wood, *nee* Bur·hans \'bər-ənz\. 1815–1864. American reformer and author, b. Rensselaerville, N.Y. Matron, women's department, Sing Sing prison (1844–48), where she instituted reforms. Author of *Life in Prairie Land* (1846), *Woman and Her Era* (1864), *The Ideal Attained* (1865). Her first husband (m. 1836) ¶Thomas Jefferson Farnham (1804–1848) won fame as Western explorer and author of *Travels in the Great Western Prairies* (1841).

Farns·worth \färnz-(,)wərth\, Philo Taylor. 1906–1971. American engineer, b. Beaver, Utah. Developed (by 1928) a television system employing an "image dissector" camera; unsuccessfully attempted to produce his system commercially; worked as research consultant in electronics, later as researcher in atomic energy.

Fa·ro·ald \fär-'ō-äld\. d. c.591. Duke of Spoleto. A leader in Lombard conquest of Italy; member of Alboin's army that invaded Italy (568); with aid of Lombard chief Zotto founded duchy of Spoleto (570); besieged Rome and conquered Classis (c.579).

Fa·rouk I \fä-'rük, *Angl* fə-'rük\. *Arab.* Fārūq al-Awwal. 1920–1965. King of Egypt (1936–52). Son and successor of Fu'ād I; reign marked by constant disputes with popular-based Wafd party; corrupt and incompetent ruler; lost backing of army after defeat by Israel (1948) and failure to expel British occupying forces; overthrown by Gamal Nasser and forced to abdicate.

Far·quhar \'fär-k(w)ər\, George. 1678–1707. Irish dramatist. Actor in Dublin and (from 1697) London; recruiting officer in army (1704–06). His comedies included *Love and a Bottle* (1699), *The Constant Couple* (1700), *Sir Harry Wildair* (1701), *The Inconstant* (1702), *The Twin Rivals* (1702), *The Stage Coach* (1704), *The Recruiting Officer* (1706), and *The Beaux' Stratagem* (1707).

Far·ra·gut \'far-ə-gət\, David Glasgow, *orig.* James Glasgow (*to 1814*). 1801–1870. American admiral, b. near Knoxville, Tenn. Adopted by David Porter (1808). Midshipman (1810); routine naval duty (1810–47); served in War of 1812; commanded sloop *Saratoga* during Mexican War. Put in command of the West Gulf Blockading Squadron (flagship *Hartford,* 1861), with orders to take New Orleans. Bombarded Fort Jackson (Apr. 18, 1862); ran ships past Forts Jackson and St. Philip (Apr. 24); engaged Confederate flotilla and captured New Orleans without bloodshed; spent rest of 1862 chiefly in blockade duty along Gulf Coast. Ran *Hartford* and one other vessel past Port Hudson defenses (Mar. 1863) and controlled Mississippi between Port Hudson and Vicksburg. Sent against Mobile Bay (1864); attacked (Aug. 5), silencing Fort Morgan, running blockade of "torpedoes" (i.e. mines) across mouth of Bay, dispersing Confederate fleet in the Bay, and obtaining surrender of Forts Gaines and Morgan (Aug. 7 and 23). Vice admiral (1864) and admiral (1866), two grades specially created for him by Congress.

His father ¶George (1755–1817) was a naval and army officer, b. Ciudadela, Minorca (at that time a British possession); joined cause of American colonists, serving at defense of Savannah and siege of Charleston; transferred to army and commanded company of volunteer cavalry against Cornwallis.

Far·rand \'far-ənd\, Livingston. 1867–1939. American psychologist, anthropologist, and educator, b. Newark, N.J. Professor, Columbia U. (1901–14); associated with Franz Boas in study of American Indians; president, U. of

Colorado (1914–19); chairman, American Red Cross (1919–21); president, Cornell U. (1921–37). His brother ¶Max (1869–1945), b. Newark, N.J., was professor of history, Wesleyan U. (1896–1901), Stanford (1901–08), Yale (1908–25); general director (1919–21), director of education (1925–27), Commonwealth Fund; helped plan and served as director of research (1927–41), Huntington Library. Author of *Framing of the Constitution* (1913), *Fathers of the Constitution* (1921); edited *Records of the Federal Convention of 1787* (1911).

Far·rant \ˈfar-ənt\, Richard. c.1525–1580. English composer. Choir master at St. George's Chapel, Windsor (1564–80) and at Chapel Royal (1569–80); wrote plays, none extant; composed church music, including a service in G minor and anthems. Adapted (1576) Blackfriars monastery in London for a theater to present performances by children of the Chapel, the theater used later (from 1596) by Shakespeare's company.

Far·rar \ˈfar-ər\, Frederic William. 1831–1903. English clergyman and writer, b. India. Headmaster of Marlborough (1871–76); canon (1876–83) and archdeacon (1883–95) of Westminster; dean of Canterbury (1895–1903). Author of the school stories *Eric* (1858), *Julian Home* (1859), and *St. Winifred's* (1862); of *An Essay on the Origin of Language* (1860), *The Witness of History to Christ* (1871), *Life of Christ* (1874), *Life of St. Paul* (1879), *Lives of the Fathers* (1889), etc.

Far·rar \fə-ˈrär\, Geraldine. 1882–1967. American singer, b. Melrose, Mass. Member of Metropolitan Opera, New York (1906–22); chief roles included Carmen, Madame Butterfly, Manon, Mignon, Tosca.

Far·rar \ˈfar-ər\, John Chipman. 1896–1974. American publisher and writer, b. Burlington, Vt. With Farrar and Rinehart (1929–44); chairman of board, Farrar, Straus & Giroux (1946–74). Author of *Forgotten Shrines* (1919), *The Magic Sea Shell* (1923), *Songs for Johnny Jump-Up* (1930), *For the Record* (1943).

Far·rell \ˈfar-əl\, James Thomas. 1904–1979. American novelist, b. Chicago. Best known for naturalistic novels of lower middle class Irish life in Chicago, including trilogy *Young Lonigan* (1932), *The Young Manhood of Studs Lonigan* (1934), *Judgment Day* (1935); pentalogy centering on Danny O'Neill *A World I Never Made* (1936), *No Star Is Lost* (1938), *Father and Son* (1940), *My Days of Anger* (1943), *The Face of Time* (1953); and trilogy centering on Bernard Clare (1946–52); other works included *A Note on Literary Criticism* (1936), reminiscences *Reflections at Fifty* (1954), and collections of short stories.

Far·ren \ˈfar-ən\, Elizabeth. Countess of Der·by \ˈdär-bē\. 1759?–1829. English actress. Succeeded Mrs. Abington on stage at Drury Lane (1782–97); m. Edward Stanley, 12th Earl of Derby, and retired from stage (1797).

Far·rer \ˈfar-ər\, William James. 1845–1906. English agronomist. Settled in Australia (1870); surveyor in New South Wales land department (1875–86); working alone, developed several varieties of drought- and rust-resistant wheat that made possible a great expansion of Australia's wheat belt.

Farrère, Claude. See Frédéric BARGONNE.

Far·rukh Beg \fä-ˈrük-ˈbeg\ fl. 1585–1609. Mughal painter. A Kalmyk of Central Asia; in service at Kābul under Mirzā Muḥammad Ḥakīm and (after 1585) of Akbar; paintings generally Persian in character and conservative in style; praised by Jahāngīr as "unrivalled in the age."

Faruk I. See FAROUK.

Far·well \ˈfär-ˌwel, -wəl\, Arthur. 1877–1952. American composer and critic, b. St. Paul, Minn. Best known for American Indian songs and melodies; also composed orchestral works, chamber music, piano pieces, settings for Emily Dickinson poems, songs.

Farwell, John Villiers. 1825–1908. American businessman, b. Steuben Co., N.Y. President, John V. Farwell & Co. (1865–1908), long Chicago's leading wholesale drygoods house; friend of Dwight L. Moody; gave land for first Y.M.C.A. building in U.S., at Chicago.

Fasch \ˈfäsh\, Johann Friedrich. 1688–1758. German composer. Court Kapellmeister in Zerbst (1722–58); composer of orchestral overtures and suites, operas, symphonies, church cantatas, masses, sonata trios, instrumental concertos, etc. His son ¶Carl Friedrich Christian (1736–1800), music teacher in Berlin and (1774–76) Kapellmeister at Royal Opera; founded (1789) and conducted choral society Berliner Singakademie; composed sonatas, a sinfonia, and church music, esp. masses and cantatas.

Fāsī, al-. See LEO AFRICANUS.

Fā·sī, al- \al-fä-ˈsē\. *In full* Yūsuf ibn Muḥammad ibn Yūsuf al-Fāsī. c.1530 or 1531–1604. Moroccan teacher and mystic. Emigrated from Spain, settling in Fās (1580); founded a mystical lodge popular with travelers; noted as teacher and scholar.

Fasi, Isaac. See ALFASI.

Fa·sil·i·des \fə-ˈsil-ə-ˌdēz\ *Also spelled* Fa·sil·i·das \-əd-əs\ *and* Ba·sil·i·de \bə-ˈsil-ə-dē\. d. 1667. Ethiopian emperor (1632–67). Ascended throne on abdication of Susenyos (1632); reestablished close alliance with Egyptian Coptic Christian church; expelled Catholic missionaries and other Europeans; founded new capital at Gonder.

Fass·bin·der \ˈfäs-ˌbin-dər\, Rainer Werner. 1946–1982. German motion-picture director. His films, which examined the problems of contemporary German society, included *Liebe ist kälter als der Tod* (1969), *Katzelmacher* (1969), *Die bitteren Tränen der Petra von Kant* (1972), *Effi Briest* (1974), *Angst isst die Seele auf* (1974), *Faustrecht der Freiheit* (1975), *Mutter Küsters' Fahrt zum Himmel* (1976), *The Marriage of Maria Braun* (1979), *Lili Marleen* (1981), *Lola* (1982).

Fa·sten·rath \ˈfäs-tən-ˌrät\, Johannes. 1839–1908. German writer. Wrote works chiefly on Spain, as *Klänge aus Andalusien* (1866).

Fas·tolf \ˈfas-ˌtä(l)f, -ˌtȯ(l)f\, Sir John. 1378?–1459. English soldier. Distinguished himself in battle of Agincourt (1415); King Henry VI's lieutenant and regent in Normandy (1423); governor of Anjou and Maine (1423–26); defeated French at Verneuil (1424) and Rouvay (1429), but was defeated at Patay (1429); retired from army (c.1440). Friend of John Paston; many of his private papers preserved among Paston letters. A character in Shakespeare's *Henry VI* and supposed by some to be the original of Falstaff in *Henry IV*.

Fa·teh Singh \ˈfä-te-ˈsin(-yə)\, Sant. 1911–1972. Indian Sikh religious. Lifelong campaigner for Sikh rights in India; a leader in movement to secure independence of India from Great Britain (from 1942); an ally, later opponent, of Tara Singh; became leader (1962) of rural Sikh (Jāṭ) population; instrumental in establishment (1966) of Punjabi-speaking state.

Fatḥ ʿA·lī Shāh \ˈfat-ȧ-ˈlē-ˈshȯ\. 1771–1834. Shah of Persia (1797–1834). Nephew and successor of Āghā Moḥammad Khān. Subdued rebellious tribes in Khorāsān; forced to surrender Derbent and other districts to Russia (1797); lost Georgia (1802); involved in other wars with Russia (1811–13, 1826–28), losing Dagestan, Baku, and most of Persian Armenia.

Fā·ṭi·mah \ˈfat-ə-mə\. *Called* az-Zah·rā' \ə-zä-ˈrä\, *i.e.* Shining One. c.616–633. Arab religious figure. Daughter of Muḥammad by his first wife Khadījah; accompanied her father from Mecca to Medina (622); soon after m. ʿAlī, cousin of Muḥammad; clashed with Abū Bakr (632). From her and ʿAlī the Fāṭimid (*q.v.*) dynasty of northern Africa claimed descent.

Fāṭ·i·mid \ˈfat-ə-məd\. A powerful Muslim (Ismāʿīlīyah) dynasty ruling (909–1171) in North Africa and Egypt; claimed descent from Fāṭimah and ʿAlī through Ismāʿīl. Founded by ʿUbayd Allāh with capital at Mahdīyah. Its 14 caliphs included ʿUbayd Allāh (909–934), al-Qāʾim (934–946), al-Manṣūr (946–953), al-Muʿizz (953–975), al-ʿAzīz (975–996), al-Ḥakim (996–1021), al-Mustanṣir (1036–1094), and al-Mustaʿlī (1094–1101). Tried unsuccessfully to oust ʿAbbāsid caliphs as leaders of Islāmic world. In 10th century its boundaries greatly extended, Sicily conquered (c.945), Egypt overrun and new capital established at Cairo (969–973); western part of North Africa gradually lost (after 1000); driven out of Syria by Seljuqs (1076); disappeared when Saladin conquered Egypt (1171).

Fa-tsang \ˈfät-ˈsäŋ\. *Also called* Hsien-shou \shē-ˈen-ˈshau̇\. 643–712. Chinese monk. According to legend, originally associate of Hsüan-tsang in translating sūtras from India; broke with him and mastered the *Hua-yen ching*; served as preceptor to four rulers, esp. favored by empress Wu Chao. Considered founder of Hua-yen school of Buddhism in China.

Fattore, Il. See Gianfrancesco PENNI.

Fau·jas de Saint-Fond \fō-zhȧs-də-saⁿ-fōⁿ\, Barthélemy. 1741–1819. French geologist. Professor at Muséum d'Histoire Naturelle, Paris (1793–1819); made many researches on origin of volcanoes.

Faul·ha·ber \ˈfau̇l-ˌhäb-ər\, Michael von. 1869–1952. German prelate. Ordained (1892); bishop of Speyer (1911–17); archbishop of Munich and Freising (1917–52); cardinal (1921); contributed to failure of Hitler's Munich Putsch (1923) and remained prominent opponent of Nazi regime. Author of *Judentum, Christentum, Germanentum* (1934), *Die Sittenlehre des Evangeliums* (1936), etc.

Faulk·ner \ˈfȯk-nər\, William Cuthbert. *Surname orig.* Falk·ner \ˈfȯk-nər\. 1897–1962. American novelist, b. New Albany, Miss. Lived most of life in Oxford, Miss.; cadet pilot in Canadian R.A.F. (1918); worked at odd jobs, including clerk in New York bookstore (1921) and postmaster at U. of Mississippi (1921–24); later worked on film scripts for Hollywood studios. Author of *The Marble Faun* (1924, poems), *Soldier's Pay* (1926), *Mosquitoes* (1927), *Sartoris* (1929), *The Sound and the Fury* (1929), *As I Lay Dying* (1930), *Sanctuary* (1931), *Light in August* (1932), *Pylon* (1935), *Absalom, Absalom!* (1936), *The Unvanquished* (1938), *The Wild Palms* (1939), *The Hamlet* (1940), *Go Down, Moses and Other Stories* (1942), *Intruder in the Dust* (1948), *Requiem for a Nun* (1951), *A Fable* (1954, Pulitzer prize), *The Town* (1957), *The Mansion* (1959), *The Reivers* (1962, Pulitzer prize). Received Nobel prize for literature (1949).

Faure \fōr\, Élie, *in full* Jacques-Élie-Paul. 1873–1937. French art historian. Author of *Histoire de l'art* (1909–27), *Les Constructeurs* (1914), etc.

Faure, François-Félix. 1841–1899. French politician. Successful industrialist in Le Havre; elected to Chamber of Deputies (1881); cabinet officer in department of commerce and colonies (1882, 1883–85, 1888); minister of marine and colonies (1894–95). Seventh president of the Third Republic (1895–99); term marked by Fashoda conflict with Britain in the Sudan (1898), rapprochement with Russia, and refusal to reopen the Dreyfus case.

Fau·ré \fō-rā\, Gabriel-Urbain. 1845–1924. French composer. Studied piano under Saint-Saëns; professor (1896), director (1905–20), Conservatory of Music, Paris. Composer of piano pieces, esp. 13 nocturnes, 13 barcaroles, 5 impromptus; chamber music, esp. *String Quartet* (1924) and piano quartets (1879, 1886); 2 *Sonatas for Violin and Piano* (1876, 1917); *Ballade* (1881) and *Fantaisie* (1919), both for piano and orchestra; incidental music for plays, as *Pelléas et Mélisande* (1898); lyric dramas *Prométhée* (1900) and *Penélope* (1913); *Masques et bergamasques* (1919); *Messe de requiem* (1887); and over 100 songs, including "Après un rêve" (c.1865) and "Les Roses d'Ispahan" (1884) and song cycles *La Bonne chanson* (1891–92) and *L'Horizon chimérique* (1922). Most advanced composer of his time; his harmonic and melodic innovations greatly influenced later French composers.

Fau·riel \fōr-yel\, Claude-Charles. 1772–1844. French scholar. Professor at the Sorbonne (1830); compiler of *Chants populaires de la Grèce moderne* (1824–25); author of *Histoire de la Gaule méridionale sous la domination des conquérants germains* (1836), *Histoire de la poésie provençale* (1846), *Dante et les origines de la langue et de la littérature italiennes* (1854), and memoirs *Les derniers jours du consulat* (1886).

Faust \'faủst\, Frederick Schiller. *Pseudonym* Max Brand \'brand\. 1892–1944. American writer, b. Seattle. Author of some 100 Western novels as *The Untamed* (1918), *Destry Rides Again* (1930), *Longhorn Feud* (1933), *Dead or Alive* (1938), *The Dude* (1940); wrote scripts for *Dr. Kildare* movie series of 1930s and novelized them as *The Secret of Dr. Kildare* (1940), *Young Dr. Kildare* (1941), etc.; also wrote under other pseudonyms, as Evan Evans, Frank Austin, George Owen Baxter, Walter C. Butler.

Faust \'faủst\, Johann, *orig.* Georg. *Lat.* Johannes Faus·tus \'fō-stəs, 'faủ-\. c.1480–c.1540. German magician, astrologer, and soothsayer. Began to practice magic art (1506); school teacher in university cities; his magical feats considered petty and fraudulent by contemporary scholars but gained prominence and respect. The legend of his performing miracles with help of devil (Mephistopheles) and being carried off by him after death has been frequently treated in literature and music.

Faus·ta \'fō-stə, 'faủ-\. *In full* Flavia Maximiana Fausta. 289–326 A.D. Roman empress. Daughter of m. (307) Maximian; m.(307) Constantine the Great; mother of emperors Constantine II, Constantius II, and Constans.

Faustin I. See SOULOUQUE.

Faus·ti·na \fō-'stī-nə, faủ-\. *In full* Annia Galeria Faustina. Name of two Roman empresses: Faustina the elder (c.104–141 A.D.), wife (m. 138) of Antoninus Pius; supposedly a profligate. Her daughter ¶Faustina the younger (c.125–176 A.D.), cousin and wife (m. 145) of Marcus Aurelius; accompanied him on wars against Danubian tribes (170–174) and against rebel Avidius Cassius (175–176); the accusations that she was unfaithful to Marcus are probably false.

Faus·tus \'fō-stəs, 'faủ-\ of Riez \rē-ez\. Saint. c.400–c.490. French ecclesiastic, b. Roman Britain. Abbot of monastery at Îles de Lérins (c.433); bishop of Riez in Provence (c.458); championed Semi-Pelagian doctrine of free will and divine grace at synods of Arles (471) and Lyons (474); opposed the Arians and was exiled by Euric, king of Visigoths (477–485).

Fa·vart \fà-vàr\, Charles-Simon. 1710–1792. French playwright. Stage manager (1743), director (1758), Opéra Comique, Paris. A creator of French opéra comique; as director made innovation by insisting on historically accurate costuming. Author of librettos for Philidor, Grétry, et al., of plays as *La Chercheuse d'esprit* (1741), *Bastien et Bastienne* (1753; set to music by Mozart, 1768), and *Les trois sultanes* (1761), and of *Mémoires et correspondance littéraires, dramatiques, et anecdotiques* (1808).

Fa·vo·ri·nus \,fav-ə-'rī-nəs, ,fā-və-\. 2d century A.D. Greek Sophist and skeptic philosopher. Eunuch; teacher of Herodes Atticus, Gellius, and Fronto; friend of Plutarch; held high office under Hadrian but later exiled to Chios; returned to Rome after Hadrian's reign and recovered status; wrote philosophical discourses, declamations, a miscellaneous history, and memoirs.

Fa·vo·ry \fà-vȯ-rē\, André. 1889–1937. French painter. Known for landscapes and nudes.

Fav·re \fàvrᵊ\, Claude. Baron de Pé·rouges \pā-rüzh\ *and* Seigneur de Vau·ge·las \vōzh(-ə)-lä\. 1585–1650. French grammarian. Courtier and member of Marquise de Rambouillet's literary salon; original member of Académie Française; his *Remarques sur la langue françoise* (1647) played major role in standardizing the French language of literature and of polite society.

Favre, Jules, *in full* Gabriel-Claude-Jules. 1809–1880. French lawyer and politician. Member of legislative assembly (1848–51); gained fame by defense of Felice Orsini, failed assassin of Napoléon III (1858); leader of opposition to the Second Empire (1863–68); minister of foreign affairs and vice president of the Government of National Defense (1870–71); a negotiator of Treaty of Frankfurt concluding the Franco-Prussian War; member of the Senate (1876–80).

Favre, Louis. 1826–1879. Swiss engineer. Built the St. Gotthard Tunnel (completed 1881).

Favre *or* **Lefèvre,** Pierre. See Peter FABER.

Faw·cett \'fō-sət, 'fäs-\, Henry. 1833–1884. English economist and politician. Accidentally blinded (1858); professor, Cambridge (1863–84). M.P. (1865–84); contributed actively to passage of Reform Act (1867); joined Gladstonian Liberals in opposing Disraeli's Eastern policy; postmaster general (1880–84); introduced parcel post (1882), postal money orders, etc. His wife (m. 1867) ¶Dame Millicent, *nee* Gar·rett \'gar-ət\ (1847–1929), prominent woman-suffrage leader (from 1868); president, National Union of Women's Suffrage Society (1897–1919); a founder of Newnham College, Cambridge (established 1871); wrote report vindicating British concentration camps for Boer civilians during South African War. Author of *Political Economy for Beginners* (1870), *Janet Doncaster* (novel, 1875), *The Women's Victory–and After* (1920), *What I Remember* (1924), etc.

Fawkes \'fȯks\, Guy. 1570–1606. English conspirator. Turned Roman Catholic and enlisted in the Spanish army in Flanders (1593); returned to England (1604) and became involved with Robert Catesby and others in Gunpowder Plot (1604–05) to blow up the Houses of Parliament in revenge for penal laws against Catholics. Plot discovered; Fawkes arrested when entering the gunpowder-filled cellar under the Houses of Parliament (night of Nov. 4–5, 1605); under torture revealed names of fellow conspirators; tried, convicted, and executed.

Fawk·ner \'fȯk-nər\, John Pascoe. 1792–1869. Australian settler, journalist, and politican. Settled on site of Melbourne (1835); founded Melbourne *Advertiser* (1838), Port Phillip *Patriot* (1839); instrumental in effecting separation of Victoria from New South Wales (1850).

Fáy \'fä-ē, 'fī\, András. 1786–1864. Hungarian writer. Author of poems, plays, romances, and tales, including the first Hungarian society novel *A Bélteky-ház* (1832), and more than 600 fables (1820 ff.).

Fay \'fā\, Sidney Bradshaw. 1876–1967. American historian, b. Washington, D.C. Professor, Dartmouth (1902–14), Smith (1914–29), Harvard (1929–46). Author of *Origins of the World War* (1928) in which he proposed thesis of collective responsibility for cause of World War I; also wrote *The Hohenzollern Household and Administration in the Sixteenth Century* (1916), *Rise of Brandenburg-Prussia to 1786* (1937), etc.

Faye \fāy\, Hervé-Auguste-Étienne-Albans. 1814–1902. French astronomer. Discovered the periodic comet named for him (1843); president of the Bureau of Longitudes (1876); minister of public education (1878). Author of works on the parallaxes of stars and planets, on the formation of clouds and hail, on sunspots, the origin of the earth, etc.

Fayn·zil·berg \'fīnz-yil-byirg\, Ilya Arnoldovich. *Pseudonym* Ilya Ilf \'ilf\. 1897–1937. Soviet writer. Collaborated with Yevgeny Katayev (*q.v.*) on satiric short stories for *Pravda* and on humorous adventure novels *Dvenadtsat stulyev* (1928), *Zolotoy telyonok* (1931), and *Odnoetazhnaya Amerika* (1936).

Fayr·fax \'fa(ə)r-,faks, 'fe(ə)r-\, Robert. 1464–1521. English composer. Gentleman of the Chapel Royal (c.1497–1521); in charge of its musicians at Field of Cloth of Gold near Calais (1520). Foremost among early Tudor composers; his extant works include 6 cyclic masses, two Magnificat settings, 10 motets, 8 secular songs, and 3 instrumental pieces.

Fayṣal. See Faisal.

Fazio degli Uberti. See UBERTI.

Fa·zy \fà-zē\, Jean Jacob, *called* James. 1794–1878. Swiss statesman, journalist, and writer. Championed radical republican principles; head of Geneva government (1846–53, 1855–61) and an author of constitution of 1848; completely modernized Geneva; deposed (1862). Fled to Paris; edited journal *La France Nouvelle* (1870); returned to Geneva (1871); became professor of international law.

Fear·ing \'fi(ə)r-iŋ\, Kenneth Flexner. 1902–1961. American writer, b. Oak Park, Ill. Author of books of poetry *Angel Arms* (1929), *Poems* (1935), *Dead Reckoning* (1938), *Afternoon of a Pawnbroker* (1943), *Stranger at Coney Island* (1948), and of novels *The Hospital* (1939), *The Dagger of the Mind* (1941), *The Big Clock* (1946), *The Loneliest Girl in the World* (1951), *The Generous Heart* (1954), *The Crozart Story* (1960).

Feat·ley \'fēt-lē\, Daniel. *Orig.* Daniel Fair·clough \'fa(ə)r-,kləf, 'fe(ə)r-\. 1582–1645. English Anglican priest. Involved in famous debates against Jesuits John Fisher and John Sweet (June 27, 1623) and against four Baptists (Oct. 17, 1642); imprisoned for Royalist sympathies and criticizing Calvinist teaching (1643). Author of collection of sermons *Clavis mystica* (1636) and devotional tracts.

Febronius, Justinus. See Johann von HONTHEIM.

Fech·ner \ˈfek-nər, ˈfek-\, Gustav Theodor. 1801–1887. German physicist, philosopher, and psychologist. A founder of psychophysics; professor of physics, Leipzig (1834–40), where he worked mainly on galvanism, electrochemistry, and theory of color; subsequently devoted himself to psychophysics, natural philosophy, anthropology, and aesthetics; formulated Fechner's law (or the Weber-Fechner law, deduced from Weber's law) that the intensity of sensation increases as the logarithm of the stimulus. Author of *Das Büchlein vom Leben nach dem Tode* (1836), *Zend-Avesta* (1851), *Elemente der Psychophysik* (1860), and *Vorschule der Aesthetik* (1876).

Feck·en·ham \ˈfek-ə-nəm\, John de. *Orig.* John How·man \ˈhau̇-mən\. c.1515–1584. English clergyman. Chaplain and confessor to Queen Mary I (1553); dean of St. Paul's (1554–56); abbot, abbey of St. Peter's, Westminster (1556–59); removed from the abbey (1559) for maintaining his religious faith and complaining of changes inaugurated under Queen Elizabeth's reign; spent most of later years imprisoned.

Fe·der \ˈfād-ər\, Gottfried. 1883–1941. German economist and politician. Civil engineer by profession; became principal economic theorist of Nazi party, esp. with "Manifest zur Brechung der Zinsknechtschaft" (1919) and book *Der deutsche Staat auf nationaler und sozialer Grundlage* (1923); member of Reichstag (1924–36); chairman of party economic council (1931); state secretary of Ministry of Economics (1933); state housing commissioner (1934).

Fe·de·rer \ˈfād-ər-ər\, Heinrich. 1866–1928. Swiss novelist. Ordained Roman Catholic priest (1893); resigned (1899) pastoral duties due to asthma and to desire to write. His novels, emphasizing Christian aspects of Swiss and Italian lives, included *Der heilige Franz von Assisi* (1908), *Lachweiler Geschichten* (1911), *Berge und Menschen* (1911), *Sisto e Sesto* (1913), *Umbrische Reisegeschichtlein* (1921), *Papst und Kaiser im Dorfe* (1925), and *Am Fenster* (1927).

Fe·der·zo·ni \ˌfā-dārt-ˈsō-nē\, Luigi. 1878–1967. Italian journalist and politician. Editor of organ of Nationalist party *Idea Nazionale* (1914–22); leader of Nationalist movement; minister of colonies (1922–24, 1926–28), of interior (1924–26); senator (1928); senate president (1929–34); member, Fascist Grand Council; broke with Mussolini (1943) and sentenced to death in absentia (1945); pardoned (1947).

Fe·din \ˈfyād-yin\, Konstantin Aleksandrovich. 1892–1977. Russian novelist. During 1920s belonged to literary group Serapion Brothers; first secretary (1959), chairman (1971), Union of Soviet Writers. His Socialist Realist novels included *Goroda i gody* (1924), *Bratya* (1928), and trilogy composed of *Pervye radosti* (1945), *Neobyknovennoye leto* (1947–48), *Kostyor* (1961–65).

Fëdor. See FYODOR.

Feh·ren·bach \ˈfā-rən-ˌbäk\, Konstantin. 1852–1926. German politician. Noted criminal lawyer; member (from 1903) and president (1918) of Reichstag; president of Weimar National Assembly (1919–20); chancellor of Weimar Republic (1920–21); chairman of Catholic Center party (from 1923).

Fei·jó \fā(-ē)-ˈzhō\, Diogo Antônio. 1784–1843. Brazilian priest and politician. Ordained Roman Catholic priest (1807); Brazilian deputy to Cortes at Lisbon (1822); deputy to Brazilian Cortes (1823–33); senator (1833 ff.); regent of Brazil (1835–37).

Fei·joo y Mon·te·no·gro \fā-ˈkō-ō-ē-mōn-tā-ˈnā-grō\, Benito Jerónimo. 1676–1764. Spanish Benedictine monk and scholar. Considered one of dominant forces leading to educational reawakening of Spain; taught at U. of Oviedo. Author of encyclopedic works *Teatro crítico universal* (1726–39) and *Cartas eruditas y curiosas* (1742–60).

Feil·ding \ˈfē(ə)l-diŋ\, William. 1st Earl of Den·bigh \ˈden-bē\. d. 1643. English naval and military officer. m. Susan Villiers, sister of George Villiers, future Duke of Buckingham, and rose with the favorite; commanded disastrous attempt to relieve La Rochelle (1628); member of council of Wales (1633); served under Prince Rupert and died of wounds received in attack on Birmingham. His eldest son ¶Basil (1608?–1675), 2d earl, was member of House of Lords (1628); ambassador to Venice (1634–39); commander in chief of Parliamentary forces in Midlands; resigned after passing of Self-denying Ordinance; supported army against Parliament; member of council of state but turned to Royalist side.

Fei·ning·er \ˈfī-niŋ-ər\, Lyonel Charles Adrian. 1871–1956. American painter, b. New York City. Resident in Germany (1887–1936); caricaturist and politicial cartoonist (1895–1910); devoted himself to painting (from 1907) and adopted an individual style influenced by Cubism; taught in Bauhaus workshops at Weimar (1919–24) and Dessau (1925–33); painted architectural subjects, townscapes, seascapes, pictures of sailing ships; titles included *Barfüsserkirche in Erfurt* (1924), *The Glorious Victory of the Sloop Maria* (1926), *Dawn* (1938).

Feisal *or* **Feisul.** See FAISAL.

Feith \ˈfīt\, Rhijnvis. 1753–1824. Dutch writer. Author of sentimental novels of love as *Julia* (1783) and *Ferdinand en Constantia* (1785), poetry, plays, and prose works.

Fe·jér \ˈfe-yār\, Lipót. 1880–1959. Hungarian mathematician. Professor at Budapest (1911–59); worked mainly on harmonic analysis; known for Fejér theorem on summability of trigonometric Fourier series (1900).

Feke \ˈfēk\, Robert. c.1705–c.1750. American painter, b. Oyster Bay, Long Island, N.Y. Known for portraits of leading citizens of his day as *Samuel Waldo* (c.1742), *Isaac Royal and Family* (1741), *The Bowdoin Family* (c.1749).

Fé·li·bien \fā-lēb-yaⁿ\, André. Sieur des Avaux et de Ja·ver·cy \dā-zȧ-vō-ā-də-zhȧ-ver-sē\. 1619–1695. French architect and writer. Author esp. of books on painting, sculpture, and architecture.

Felipe. See PHILIP.

Fe·lix \ˈfē-liks\. Name of three popes and two antipopes:

Felix I. Saint. d. 274. Pope (269–274). Succeeded St. Dionysius; wrote important dogmatic letter on unity of Christ's Person; with aid of Emperor Aurelian settled dispute between anti-Trinitarian Paul of Samosata and orthodox Domnus.

Felix II. d. 365. Antipope (355–358). Chosen by Arian party after Liberius had been banished by Emperor Constantius; deposed (358) when Liberius was reinstated.

Felix III. Saint. d. 492. Pope (483–492). Repudiated the *Henotikon* and excommunicated (484) bishops of Eastern Church; began the 35-year Acacian Schism between Eastern and Western churches.

Felix IV. Saint. d. 530. Pope (526–530). Chosen pope through influence of Theodoric, King of the Ostrogoths; ended controversy over grace by condemning Semi-Pelagianism at 2d Council of Orange (529); converted pagan temple at Rome to Church of SS. Cosmas and Damian.

Felix V. Antipope (1439–49). See AMADEUS VIII of Savoy.

Fé·lix \ˈfā-lēks\ of Ur·gel \ür-ˈgel\. d. 818. Spanish prelate. Bishop of Urgel; champion of Adoptionism with Archbishop Elipando; forced to recant at councils of Ratisbon (792) and Aachen (799).

Félix of Va·lois \vȧl-wä\. Saint. 1127–1212. French religious. Cofounder (1197, with St. John of Matha) of the Order of the Most Holy Trinity for the Redemption of Captives, whose members were known as Trinitarians.

Félix, Élisa. See Mlle RACHEL.

Felix, Lucius Cornelius Sulla. See SULLA.

Felix, Marcus Antonius. 1st century A.D. Roman administrator. Greek freedman of Emperor Claudius; procurator of Judaea (c.52–60 A.D.), under whom St. Paul was tried and kept prisoner.

Felix, Marcus Minucius. See MINUCIUS FELIX.

Fell \ˈfel\, John. 1625–1686. English clergyman. Ordained Anglican priest (1647); fought on Royalist side during Civil War; dean of Christ Church, Oxford, and chaplain to the king (1660); vice chancellor of Oxford (1666–69); bishop of Oxford (1676); restored or built many Oxford structures; installed university press in Sheldonian Theatre, setting up type foundry and designing Fell type for it. Author of *Interest of England Stated* (1659) and *The Vanity of Scoffing* (1674). Subject of Tom Brown's doggerel verse beginning "I do not love thee, Dr. Fell."

Fel·len·berg \ˈfel-ən-ˌberk\, Philipp Emanuel von. 1771–1844. Swiss educator and agriculturist. Bought estate near Bern (1799) where he founded experimental educational institution and sought to advance agriculture and improve Swiss education through training of lower and upper classes. Established several industrial and agricultural schools. Member of cantonal grand council (1820); magistrate, Bern (1833).

Fel·ler \fā-ler\, François-Xavier de. 1735–1802. Belgian priest and writer. Entered Jesuit order (1754); edited *Journal historique et littéraire* (1774–94); compiled *Dictionnaire historique* (1781–84), often reedited under title *Biographie universelle.*

Fel·lows \ˈfel-(ˌ)ōz\, Sir Charles. 1799–1860. English archaeologist. Explored Asia Minor (1838 ff.); discovered ruins of ancient Xanthus and Tlos, and other cities of Lycia; gave archaeological collection to British Museum. Published *A Journal Written During an Excursion in Asia Minor* (1839) and *An Account of Discoveries in Lycia* (1841).

Fell·tham \ˈfel-thəm \, Owen. 1602?–1668. English writer. Steward to the Earl of Thomond (from c.1640). Author of collections of moral essays *Resolves Divine, Morall, and Politicall* (1623) and *Resolves, a Second Centurie* (1628), of *A brief Character of the Low-Countries under the States* (1652), and of poems.

Felt \ˈfelt\, Dorr Eugene. 1862–1930. American inventor, b. Rock Co., Wis. Invented (1886) first multiple-column key-driven adding machine, which he called Comptometer (pat. 1897); president (1889–1930), Felt & Tarrant Co., manufacturers of Comptometer.

Fel·ton \'felt-ən\, Cornelius Conway. 1807–1862. American scholar, b. Newbury, Mass. Professor of Greek (from 1834), president (1860–62), Harvard; edited many classical texts; wrote *Greece, Ancient and Modern* (1867).

Felton, Rebecca Ann, *nee* Lat·i·mer \'lat-ə-mər\. 1835–1930. American politican and writer, b. near Decatur, Ga. m. William H. Felton (1853); regular contributor of political comment to Atlanta *Journal* (1899–1927). Appointed U.S. senator from Georgia (Oct. 1922) and served until her elected successor took his seat (Nov. 1922), becoming first woman to hold senatorial seat.

Felton, William. 1715–1769. English clergyman and composer. Vicar-choral of Hereford cathedral (from 1743); composed harpsichord lessons and 32 organ and harpsichord concertos, the andante of Op. 1, no. 3 achieving popularity as "Felton's Gavotte."

Feltre, Vittorino da. See VITTORINO RAMBOLDINI.

Fé·ne·lon \fān-lōⁿ\, François de Sa·li·gnac de La Mothe- \sá-lēn-yák-də-lá-mōt-\. 1651–1715. French prelate and writer. Ordained priest (1676); director of college for women Nouvelles Catholiques (1678–89); published *Traité de l'education des filles* (1687), arguing for liberalization of women's education. Tutor to Louis, duc de Bourgogne (1689–99); composed for instruction of his pupil *Fables, Les Dialogues des morts* (both 1690), *Les Aventures de Télémaque* (1699). Consecrated archbishop of Cambrai (1695). Involved in development of Semiquietism in France, writing against Bousset *Explication des maximes des saints sur la vie intérieure* (1697), which in part was condemned by the pope; fell into disgrace at the court upon publication of *Télémaque,* which was construed as satirizing the king and his policies.

Fen·es·tel·la \ˌfen-ə-'stel-ə\. 52 B.C.–19 A.D. or 35 B.C.–36 A.D. Roman historian. Author of now-lost *Annales,* history of Rome in some 22 books covering period down to c.59 B.C., used as source by Pliny the Elder, Suetonius, and Diomedes.

Feng Kuei-fen \'fəŋ-'gwā-fən\. 1809–1874. Chinese scholar and official. Urged adoption of Western methods and technology in his *Chiao-pin-lu k'ang-i;* his ideas became basis of Self-Strengthening Movement (1861–95) in China.

Feng Kuo-chang \-'gwō-jäŋ\. 1858–1920. Chinese general and politician. Vice president with Li Yüan-hung (1916–17); acting president (1917–18) of Republic of China; resigned.

Feng Tao \-'daủ\. 881–954 A.D. Chinese administrator. Prime minister under some ten emperors of the Five Dynasties of central China (c.929–954); famed as Confucian scholar; apparently caused the Confucian Classics and their commentaries to be printed (932–953, in 130 volumes, none extant). The printing of this work ushered in the renaissance of the Sung era (960–1127) and demonstrated the practical value of printing.

Feng Yü-hsiang \-'yü-shē-'äŋ\. *Called* the Christian General. 1882–1948. Chinese general. Soldier from age 11; reorganized his soldiers into Kuominchün and seized Peking (1924); defeated by Chang Tso-lin; supported Kuomintang and Chiang Kai-shek (1927); with Yen Hsi-shan reoccupied Peking (1928); declared their independence of Kuomintang (1929) but defeated and driven into exile (1930); made unsuccessful attempt to gain popular support by leading army of volunteers against Japanese invaders (1933); strong opponent of Chiang Kai-shek, denouncing him in visit to U.S. (1947).

Feng Yün-shan \-'yün-'shän\. 1822–1852. Chinese rebel. Schoolmate and early convert of Hung Hsiu-ch'üan; organized (1844) God Worshippers Society (Pai Shang-ti Hui), later (1847) led by Hung; on attack (1850) on Society by government troops became a leader of Taiping Rebellion; given title of Southern King (Nan-wang) by Hung; killed in battle.

Fen·no \'fen-(ˌ)ō\, John. 1751–1798. American editor, b. Boston. Published *Gazette of the United States* (from 1789), a Federalist organ under special favor of Alexander Hamilton.

Fen·ol·lo·sa \ˌfen-əl-'ō-sə\, Ernest Francisco. 1853–1908. American Orientalist, b. Salem, Mass. Taught in U. of Tokyo, Japan (1878–86); manager, Tokyo Fine Arts Academy and Imperial Museum (1888); became Buddhist. Curator, department of Oriental art, Boston Museum of Fine Arts (1890–97); professor, Imperial Normal School, Tokyo (1897–1900) and Columbia U. (1900). Played large part in revival of Japanese school of painting and in movement to preserve ancient shrines and temples and art treasures. Author of *East and West* (1893), *An Outline History of Ukiyo-e* (1901), *Epochs of Chinese and Japanese Art* (1912).

Fen·ton \'fent-ən\, Edward. d. 1603. English mariner. Sailed with Frobisher on his second and third voyages (1577 and 1578) to discover Northwest Passage to China; commanded trading expedition (1582) to Moluccas and China by way of Cape of Good Hope; served against Spanish Armada (1588).

Fenton, Elijah. 1683–1730. English poet. Edited works of Milton and Waller; translated 1st, 4th, 19th, and 20th books of the *Odyssey* for Alexander Pope. Author of *Poems on Several Occasions* (1717), the tragedy *Mariamne* (1723), and *Life of John Milton* (1725).

Fenton, Lavinia. Duchess of Bol·ton \'bōlt-ən\. 1708–1760. English actress. m. (1751) Charles Paulet, 3d Duke of Bolton. Scored immediate success in debut (1726) as Monimia in Otway's *The Orphan;* created role of Polly Peachum in Gay's *Beggar's Opera* (1728).

Fenton, Roger. 1816–1869. English photographer. His pictures of the Crimean War were first extensive photographic coverage of a war.

Feodor. See FYODOR.

Fer·ber \'fər-bər\, Edna. 1887–1968. American author, b. Kalamazoo, Mich. Author of novels and short stories, including *Dawn O'Hara* (1911), *Emma McChesney & Co.* (1915), *Gigolo* (1922), *So Big* (1924, Pulitzer prize), *Show Boat* (1926), *Cimarron* (1929), *Saratoga Trunk* (1941), *Giant* (1952), *Ice Palace* (1958), and autobiographies *Peculiar Treasure* (1939) and *A Kind of Magic* (1963). Coauthor, with George S. Kaufman, of plays *Dinner at Eight* (1932), *Stage Door* (1936), *Bravo!* (1949), etc.

Fer·di·nand \'fərd-ən-ˌand\. *Span.* Fer·nan·do \fer-'nän-dō\. Name of two kings of Aragon:

Ferdinand I. 1379?–1416. King (1412–16). Second son of John I of Castile; co-regent (from 1406) of Castile during minority of his nephew John II; refused suggestion that he usurp John II's throne; captured Granadine fortress of Antequera (1410); achieved throne of Aragon by means of bribes and support of antipope Benedict XIII and St. Vincent Ferrer; his reign ended long Catalan political domination of Aragon.

Ferdinand II. *Called* el Ca·tó·li·co \el-kä-'tō-lē-kō\, *i.e.* the Catholic. 1452–1516. King of Sicily (1468–1516), of Castile (1474–1504) as Ferdinand V (joint ruler with Isabella), of Aragon (1479–1516) as Ferdinand II, and of Naples (1504–16) as Ferdinand III. Son of John II of Aragon. m. (1469) Isabella of Castile; directed her war of succession against Afonso V of Portugal (1474–79); their marriage united kingdoms of Aragon and Castile, basis of modern Spain. Established the Inquisition (1478); conducted war with Moors (1482–92), finally conquering Granada (1492); expelled Jews (1492); aided Columbus's expeditions to the Americas; granted title "the Catholic" by Pope Alexander VI (1496), mainly for interventions in Italy; established foreign policy of expansion. After Isabella's death m. (1505) Germaine de Foix, niece of Louis XII of France; regent of Castile for his daughter Joan because of her insanity (1506–16); conquered Navarre (1512); fought with France for supremacy in Italy (1511–13); succeeded by his grandson Charles I.

Ferdinand I. 1793–1875. Emperor of Austria (1835–48). Son of Francis I. Crowned King of Hungary (1830), of Bohemia (1836), and of Lombardy and Venetia (1838); a weak ruler, government controlled by body of counsellors dominated by Metternich; abdicated (1848) in favor of his nephew Francis Joseph after Revolution of 1848 overthrew Metternich; retired to Prague.

Ferdinand. 1721–1792. Duke of Brunswick and Prussian field marshal. Son of Ferdinand Albert II. Entered Prussian service (1740); fought in Silesian Wars. One of ablest commanders during Seven Years' War; at first campaigned with his brother-in-law Frederick V the Great in Saxony and Bohemia; made head of allied armies in western Germany (1757); defeated the French at Krefeld (1758) and Minden (1759). Became estranged from Frederick and left Prussian service (1766); accepted field marshal rank in Austrian army (1766) but never served actively; refused offer of commander in chief of English army against North American colonies; in later years reconciled with Frederick.

Ferdinand I. 1861–1948. King of Bulgaria (1908–18). Son of Prince Augustus of Saxe-Coburg-Gotha and Clémentine, daughter of Louis-Philippe of France. Elected prince of Bulgaria (1887); first part of reign made difficult by disturbed condition of country and refusal of powers to recognize him; finally recognized by Russia (1896). Declared independence from Ottoman Empire and assumed title of king or czar (1908); joined other Balkan states in First Balkan War (1912–13) against Turkey; badly defeated in Second Balkan War (1913); took Bulgaria into World War I on side of Central Powers (1915); after defeat forced to abdicate (1918) in favor of his son Boris III; retired to Coburg.

Ferdinand. *Span.* Fernando. Name of five kings of Castile and León:

Ferdinand I. *Called* el Mag·no \el-'mäg-nō\, *i.e.* the Great. 1016 or 1018–1065. King of Castile (1035–65) and León (1037–65). Son of Sancho III Garcés of Navarre; m. Sancha, sister and heiress of Bermudo III of León; helped defeat Bermudo at Tamarón and seized Leónese throne (1037); recovered Castilian territory from his brother García IV of Navarre (1054); after his troops killed García (1054) assumed rule of Navarre; won territory back from Moors (1058–65), establishing suzerainty over kings of Toledo, Saragossa, and Seville, thus beginning period of reconquest by Spaniards; on his death divided empire among his sons Sancho, Alfonso, and García.

Ferdinand II. c.1145–1188. King of León (1157–88). Son of Alfonso VII; reign notable for repopulation of Leónese Extremadura and his victories over the Almohads.

Ferdinand III. *Called* el San·to \el-'sän-tō\, *i.e.* the Saint. 1201?–1252. King of Castile (1217–52) and of León (1230–57). Son of Alfonso IX of León and Berenguela, daughter of Alfonso VIII of Castile. His ascension to Leónese throne (1230) permanently united Castile and León; m. (1st) Beatrice of

Swabia (1219), daughter of Holy Roman emperor Philip. Waged successful war against the Moors (1230–48), capturing Córdoba (1236), Jaén (1246), and Seville (1248); held suzerainty over kingdom of Granada; occupied Murcia; began codification of Spanish law, later completed by his son Alfonso X; refounded U. of Salamanca (1242); m. (2d) Joan of Ponthieu (1237), their daughter Eleanor becoming wife of Edward I of England; canonized by Pope Clement X (1671).

Ferdinand IV. *Called* el Em·pla·za·do \el-em-plä-'thä-thō\, *i.e.* the Summoned. 1285–1312. King of Castile and León (1295–1312). Son of Sancho IV; his minority, under regency of his mother María de Molina, a period of anarchy; a weak king; continued wars against the Moors (1305–12), recapturing Gibraltar (1309).

Ferdinand V. King of Castile (1474–1516). See FERDINAND II of Aragon.

Ferdinand. Name of three Holy Roman emperors:

Ferdinand I. 1503–1564. Holy Roman emperor (1558–64). Younger brother of Holy Roman emperor Charles V. Granted Austria, with regency of Habsburg German lands and Württemberg; Charles's deputy in German affairs (1521–58). On death (1526) of father-in-law Louis II of Bohemia and Hungary claimed both domains; took possession of Bohemia without difficulty but waged long war (1526–38) with rival claimant János Zápolya for Hungarian throne and never really took possession of it. Lost Württemberg to landgrave Philip the Magnificent of Hesse (1534); helped Charles defeat the Schmalkaldic League (1546–47); ended religious wars in Germany by concluding Peace of Augsburg (1555). Took over Charles's imperial functions (1555); elected emperor (1558); centralized his administration; had limited success in reviving Roman Catholicism in his lands; after long struggle against Turks negotiated uneasy peace (1562), agreeing to pay tribute to Ottoman sultan for Austria's share of Hungary; succeeded by his son Maximilian.

Ferdinand II. 1578–1637. King of Bohemia (1617–19, 1620–27) and of Hungary (1618–25) and Holy Roman emperor (1619–37). Son of Archduke Charles of Inner Austria, grandson of Ferdinand I, and cousin of emperors Rudolf II and Matthias. Champion of the Catholic Counter-Reformation; deposed by Protestant diet of Bohemia (1619); with aid of Catholic League and Spain overthrew Elector Palatine Frederick V of Bohemia in battle of White Mountain (1620); drove Protestantism out of Bohemia. Issued Edict of Restitution (1629); spent entire reign waging war against Protestants (first part of Thirty Years' War); at first victorious, mainly due to Wallenstein, but final success prevented by intervention of France and Sweden; signed Peace of Prague (1635); succeeded by his son Ferdinand III.

Ferdinand III. 1608–1657. King of Hungary (1625–47) and of Bohemia (1627–56) and Holy Roman emperor (1637–57). Eldest son of Emperor Ferdinand II; conspired in overthrow of Wallenstein and succeeded him (1634) as commander of imperial armies; nominal leader in capture of Regensburg and defeat of Swedes at Nördlingen (both 1634); leader of peace party at imperial court; worked for conclusion of Peace of Prague treaty (1635). Elected king of the Romans (1636); succeeded to the empire (1637); continued struggle against Protestants but signed Peace of Westphalia (1648) which ended Thirty Years' War; created standing army (1649); reformed imperial aulic council (1654). Patron of the arts and an accomplished composer of music, esp. sacred pieces.

Ferdinand. *Ital.* Fer·di·nan·do \ˌfār-dē-'nän-dō\. Name of four kings of Naples:

Ferdinand I. *Also known in Italy as* Don Fer·ran·te \fār-'rän-tā\. 1423–1494. King (1458–94). Natural son of Alfonso V of Aragon; suppressed baronial revolt supporting claim to throne of René of Anjou (1464); faced with Turkish expansionism; recaptured Otranto from Turks (1481); allied with Florence against Venice in War of Ferrara (1482–84); warred against Pope Innocent VIII but concluded peace (1486); suppressed a second baronial revolt (1485–87).

Ferdinand II. *Called* Fer·ran·di·no \ˌfār-rän-'dē-nō\. 1467–1496. King (1495–96). Son of Alfonso II; last of Anjou line in Italy. A gifted Humanist prince, loved by his people; recovered Naples (1495) and most of his kingdom from French invaders.

Ferdinand III. See FERDINAND II of Aragon.

Ferdinand IV. See FERDINAND I of the Two Sicilies.

Ferdinand. 1751–1802. Duke of Parma (1765–1802). Succeeded his father Philip as duke (1765); father of Louis, king of Etruria.

Ferdinand I. *Port.* Fer·nan·do \fər-'nãⁿ(n)-dü\. 1345–1383. King of Portugal (1367–83). Son of Peter I of Portugal; waged two wars (1369–71, 1372–73) in unsuccessful attempt to obtain throne of Castile; waged third unsuccessful war against Castile (1381–82); promulgated laws to encourage development of agriculture, external trade, and the merchant marine and army.

Ferdinand I. 1865–1927. King of Romania (1914–27). Son of Prince Leopold of Hohenzollern-Sigmaringen; adopted as crown prince of Romania by his uncle Carol I (1889); m. (1893) Marie (*q.v.*), daughter of Duke of Edinburgh; commanded Romanian army during Second Balkan War (1913). As king ruled impartially, although a Hohenzollern; entered World War I on side of Allied Powers (1916); defeated by Central Powers (March 1918) but rejoined Allies (Nov. 1918); crowned king of Greater Romania (1922); last years marked by land reforms but also by politicial and domestic difficulties; succeeded by his grandson Michael.

Ferdinand. *Span.* Fer·nan·do \fer-'nän-dō\. Name of two Bourbon kings of Spain, numbered consecutively with those of Castile and León:

Ferdinand VI. 1713–1759. King (1746–59). Son of Philip V; m. (1729) María Bárbara de Bragança, daughter of John V of Portugal. As king kept Spain at peace (from 1748); supported economic, commercial, and military reforms of his able minister Marqués de la Ensenada; treaty with papacy (1753) increased state's power over church; patron of the arts and learning; helped found Academy of Fine Arts (1752), an astronomical observatory, and botanical gardens; became depressed and later mad after death (1758) of his wife; left no issue, succeeded by his half-brother Charles III.

Ferdinand VII. 1784–1833. King (March–May 1808, 1814–33). Became king after forced abdication of his father Charles IV (1808); imprisoned by Napoléon in France (1808–14) and forced to relinquish his crown; restored after Napoléon's fall (1814). Repudiated liberal constitution of 1812; his cruel and repressive policies provoked many rebellions culminating in successful Liberal uprising of 1820; restored by French army (1823); continued tyrannical, absolutist rule; his abolition of Salic Law (1830) led after his death to First Carlist War between supporters of his daughter Isabella and his brother Don Carlos; his reign disastrous to Spain, which not only lost all colonies in the Americas except Cuba but also lost position as European power.

Ferdinand. *Ital.* Ferdinando. Name of four grand dukes of Tuscany:

Ferdinand I de' Me·di·ci \dā-'mā-dē-chē, ***Angl*** də-'med-ə-(ˌ)chē\. 1549–1609. Grand duke (1587–1609). Son of Cosimo I de' Medici; made cardinal (1563); succeeded his brother Francesco I as grand duke; a just ruler; increased strength and prosperity of duchy; by his marriage (1589) to Christine of Lorraine counterbalanced Spanish influence in Italy with French; aided Henry of Navarre to become Henry IV of France; obstructed Spanish designs on Marseilles; patron of the arts.

Ferdinand II de' Medici. 1610–1670. Grand duke (1621–70). Son of Cosimo II de' Medici and grandson of Ferdinand I; patron of arts and sciences; developed scientific instruments, including a thermometer insensitive to barometric presssure (c.1644) and a condensation hygrometer (1655); founded Accademia del Cimento in Florence (1657); pupil and patron of Galileo but acquiesced in his condemnation; attempted to maintain Tuscany's neutrality.

Ferdinand III. 1769–1824. Grand duke (1790–1801, 1814–24). Son of Emperor Leopold II; continued his father's liberal reforms; remained neutral toward French Revolution but recognized (1793) French Republic; forced to side against Napoléon (1793–95); driven from Tuscany by French (1799); by Treaty of Lunéville (1801) ceded Tuscany to France and received principality of Salzburg as compensation; exchanged Salzburg for duchy of Würtzburg (1805); joined Confederation of the Rhine (1806); restored in Tuscany (1814); ruled justly, encouraging development of country and maintaining degree of independence from Austria; succeeded by his son Leopold II.

Ferdinand IV. 1835–1908. Grand duke (1859–60). Succeeded on abdication (1859) of his father Leopold II; never actually reigned, as country run by provisional government; deposed on annexation of Tuscany by Piedmont (1860); retired to Salzburg.

Ferdinand. Name of two kings of the Two Sicilies:

Ferdinand I. 1751–1825. King of Naples (1759–1806, 1815–25) as Ferdinand IV and of the Two Sicilies (1816–25) as Ferdinand I. Third son of Charles III of Spain; under regency of Bernardo Tanucci (1759–67); weak and inept ruler; m. (1768) Maria Carolina of Austria, who influenced him to pursue reactionary policies; joined Austro-English coalition against France (1793); fled to Palermo while France established Parthenopean Republic (1798–99); again fled to Sicily (1806) where he ruled as Ferdinand III while Naples was under French rule (1806–15); under British pressure removed his wife from council of state and granted Sicilians a constitution; restored to Naples (1815). Became king of the Two Sicilies as Ferdinand I (1816); his tyrannical and absolutist rule brought on revolution of 1820; forced to grant a constitution; with aid of Austria overthrew constitutional government (1821); thereafter an era of cruel vengeance and repression.

Ferdinand II. 1810–1859. King (1830–59). Son of Francis I; at first granted amnesty to political prisoners and promised reforms but soon adopted authoritarian policies and severely repressed liberal opinion; entire reign a series of revolts, cruel repressions, and political prosecutions; his heavy bombardment of Sicilian cities (1848–49) to suppress a revolution earned him nickname "King Bomba"; in later years grew even more isolated from his people.

Ferdinand of Portugal. *Port.* Fer·rand \fə-'rä^n(n)d\. 1186–1233. Count of Flanders and Hainaut (1211–33). Son of Sancho I of Portugal; m. (1212) Joan, daughter of Baldwin I of Constantinople; joined anti-French coalition led by Emperor Otto IV and John of England; defeated at Battle of Bouvines (1214); imprisoned in Paris (to c.1227).

Ferdowsī. See FIRDAWSĪ.

Ferenc Rákóczi I. See RÁKÓCZI family.

Fer·en·czi \'fer-ent-sē, *Angl* fə-'ren(t)-sē\, Sándor. 1873–1933. Hungarian psychoanalyst. Friend and collaborator of Sigmund Freud (from 1908); member of Vienna Psychoanalytic Society; accompanied Freud to Clark U., Worcester, Mass. to advance psychoanalysis in U.S. (1909). Made significant contributions to fundamental psychoanalytic theory and techniques of therapy. Author of *Hysterie und Pathoneurosen* (1919), *Versuch einer Genitaltheorie* (1924), *Entwicklungsziele der Psychoanalyse* (1924, with Otto Rank).

Fer·gu·son \'fər-gəs-ən\, Adam. 1723–1816. Scottish philosopher. Professor at Edinburgh (1759–85); member of Scottish "common sense" school of philosophy; traveled to Philadelphia with a British commission to negotiate with American revolutionaries (1778). His works included *The Morality of Stage Plays Seriously Considered* (1757), *Essay on the History of Civil Society* (1767), *Institutes of Moral Philosophy* (1769), *The History of the Progress and Termination of the Roman Republic* (1783), and *Principles of Moral and Political Science* (1792).

Ferguson, Harry George. 1884–1960. Irish industrialist. In airplane of own design and construction made first recorded flight over Ireland (1909); supervised operation of farm machinery in Ireland during World War I; designed and built (1935) the Ferguson tractor, which was manufactured in U.S. (1940–47) by Henry Ford; built plants in Detroit and England to manufacture tractors.

Ferguson, James. 1710–1776. Scottish astronomer. Skilled designer of clocks and planispheres; known esp. as popularizer of science. Wrote *Astronomy Explained Upon Sir Isaac Newton's Principles* (1756), *Young Gentleman's and Lady's Astronomy* (1768), etc.

Ferguson, James Edward. 1871–1944. American politician, b. near Salado, Tex. Governor of Texas (1915–17); impeached and removed from office (1917). His wife (m. 1899) ¶Miriam Amanda, *nee* Wallace (1875–1961), b. Bell Co., Tex., popularly known as "Ma" Ferguson, governor of Texas (1925–27, 1933–35).

Ferguson, Patrick. 1744–1780. Scottish soldier. Entered British army (1759); inventor of first breech-loading rifle used in British army (1776); served in America; killed at battle of King's Mountain.

Ferguson, Sir Samuel. 1810–1886. Irish antiquary and poet. Published *Lays of the Western Gael* (1865), *Congal, an Epic Poem* (1872), and *Deirdre* (1880).

Fer·gus·son \'fər-gə-sən\, Robert. 1750–1774. Scottish poet. Copying clerk in Edinburgh lawyer's office. A leading figure in revival of Scots vernacular writing and chief forerunner of Robert Burns; chief poems included "Auld Reekie," "The Daft Days," "Address to the Tron Kirk Bell," "Leith Races," and "The Farmer's Ingle."

Fe·rid Pa·şa \fer-'ēd-pä-'shä\, Damad. 1853–1923. Turkish politician. Grand vizier (1903); minister of the interior (1909); grand vizier again (1919–20); opposed Mustafa Kemal Atatürk.

Fer·mat \fer-mȧ\, Pierre de. *Orig.* Pierre Fermat. 1601–1665. French mathematician. Served (from 1631) in Toulouse parliament, becoming councillor (1634) and member (1638) of Criminal Court. Founder of modern theory of numbers; inventor of differential calculus and (with Pascal) of the theory of probability; discovered analytic geometry independently of Descartes; discovered Fermat's principle of optics (enunciated 1658), Fermat's principle of least time, Fermat's numbers, Fermat's last theorem (lost and ever since the object of much speculation), and other theorems.

Fer·mi \'fe(ə)r-(,)mē\, Enrico. 1901–1954. American physicist, b. Rome. Taught at Florence (1924–26) and Rome (1927–28); to U.S. (1938, naturalized 1944); professor at Columbia (1939–42) and U. of Chicago (1946–54); with Manhattan Project (1942–45). One of chief architects of the nuclear age. Discovered independently of Dirac a statistical method for predicting atomic structure and behavior (1926); developed theory of beta decay (1933); a discoverer (1935) of slow neutrons and developed (1935–36) theory explaining them. Awarded 1938 Nobel prize for physics for discovery of neutron-induced nuclear reactions (1934–37). Directed the first controlled nuclear chain reaction (1942); worked on atomic bomb project at Los Alamos, N.M.; later studied basic properties of nuclear particles, esp. mesons. Element fermium named, and Fermi Award given, in his honor.

Fer·mor \'fər-(,)mȯ(ə)r, -mər\, William. 1704–1771. Scottish soldier in Russian service. Distinguished himself at Danzig (1734) and against Turks (1736); lieutenant general (1746); commanded Russian army against Prussia at Gross-Jägersdorf (1758); defeated by Frederick the Great at Zorndorf (1758) and relinquished command to Gen. Saltykov (1759); governor general of Smolensk (1762–68).

Fern, Fanny. See Sara PARTON.

Fer·nald \'fərn-^{ə}ld\, Merritt Lyndon. 1873–1950. American botanist, b. Orono, Me. Curator (1915–36), director (from 1937), Gray Herbarium, Harvard; taught at Harvard (1905–49). Enunciated "nunatak" theory in *Persistence of Plants in Unglaciated Areas of Boreal America* (1925) refuting popular theory that a massive ice sheet had destroyed all plant and animal life in much of northeastern America; edited centennial edition of Asa Gray's *Manual of Botany* (1950).

Fer·nan·del \fer-nä^n-del\. *Orig.* Fernand-Joseph-Désiré Con·tan·din \kō^n-tä^n-da^n\. 1903–1971. French actor. Known for comic facial contortions and wide, toothy grin; starred in over 100 films, including *Le Blanc et le noir* (1930), *La Fille du puisatier* (1940), *Le petit monde de Don Camillo* (1952), *Le Mouton à cinq pattes* (1954), *La Vache et le prisonnier* (1959), *Le Voyage du père* (1966); also featured in stage comedies and serious dramatic roles.

Fer·nan·des \fər-'nä^{n}n-dəsh\, Álvaro. 15th century. Portuguese explorer. Sailed (1445) to West Africa; rounded Cape Verde and reached the "Cape of Masts"; returned to West Africa and reached site of present Conakry, Guinea (1447).

Fernandes, António. 16th century. Portuguese explorer. Probably first European to enter Rhodesia when he tried to cross Africa in search of treasure city of empire of Mwene Matapa; reached neighborhood of Que Que.

Fernandes, João. 15th century. Portuguese navigator. Penetrated into interior of Africa by way of Río de Oro (1445); explored parts of West Africa (1446, 1447); made slave-trading agreements with local chiefs.

Fernandes de Quei·rós \-thə-kā-'rōsh\, Pedro. *Sp.* Fer·nán·dez de Qui·rós \fer-'nän-dāth-thā-kē-'rōs\. c.1570–1615. Portuguese navigator in service of Spain. Succeeded Álvaro de Mendaña as commander of Pacific exploring expedition (1595); discovered (1606) Swains Island, part of the Tuamoto Archipelago, the northern Cook Islands, Tikopia, and New Hebrides.

Fernández. See also HERNÁNDEZ.

Fernández, Gregorio. See Gregorio HERNÁNDEZ.

Fer·nán·dez \fer-'nän-dāth, *Angl* fər-'nan-,dez\, Juan. c.1536–c.1604. Spanish navigator. Sailed from Callao, Peru, to Valparaíso, Chile, in 30 days, remarkable feat earning him title brujo, or wizard (1563); discovered (between 1563–74) Juan Fernández Islands off coast of Valparaíso and lived there until 1580; also discovered San Félix and San Ambrosio Islands (1574).

Fernández, Lucas. 1474?–1542. Spanish dramatist and musician. Professor of music at Salamanca (from 1522). Imitator of Encina. Known esp. for his *Farsay y églogas al modo y estilo pastoril y castellano* (1514), a collection of six short plays including his best known piece, *Auto de la pasión,* and first example of a rudimentary zarzuela, *Diálogo para cantar.*

Fernández, Manuel Félix. See Guadalupe VICTORIA.

Fer·nán·dez \fer-'nän-dās\, Próspero. 1834–1885. Costa Rican soldier and politician. President of Costa Rica (1882–85).

Fernández Alon·so \-ä-'lōn-sō\, Severo. 1849–1925. Bolivian politician. Congressman, minister of war, first vice president of Bolivia. President of Bolivia (1896–99); his attempt to name Sucre permanent national capital instigated a civil war; forced from office. Later a justice of supreme court and (from 1921) president of national congress.

Fer·nán·dez Co·ro·nel \fer-'nän-dāth-kȯr-ō-'nel\, María. *Known as* María de Agre·da \äg-'rā-thä\; *religious name* Sor María de Je·sús \kā-'süs\. 1602–1665. Spanish abbess and mystic. Entered Franciscan order (1620); abbess at Agreda (1627); maintained correspondence (1643–65) with Philip IV; encouraged missionaries, esp. to North American Indians, including Junípero Serra; based on visions or revelations, wrote *Mistica ciudad de Dios,* a life of the Virgin Mary (pub. 1670; banned by Roman Index 1681–1747).

Fernández de Avellaneda, Alonso. See AVELLANEDA.

Fernández de Cór·do·ba \-thā-'kȯr-thō-bä\, Diego. Marqués de Gua·dal·cá·zar \thā-gwä-thäl-'kä-thär\ *and* Conde de Po·sa·das \thā-pō-'sä-thäs\. Spanish administrator. Viceroy of Mexico (1612–21); founded Lerma (1613), Córdoba (1618), and Guadalcázar (1620); viceroy of Peru (1622–29).

Fernández de Córdoba, Francisco. 1475?–1525 or 1526. Spanish soldier and explorer. Went with Pedro Arias Dávila to Panama (1514); sent by him to take possession of Nicaragua (1522); founded Granada and León (1523); executed after renouncing allegiance to Arias Dávila.

Fernández de Córdoba, Gonzalo. *Known as* el Gran Ca·pi·tán \el-'grän-kä-pē-'tän\, *i.e.* the Great Captain. 1453–1515. Spanish soldier. Distinguished himself in wars against Moors (from 1474); one of two commissioners who negotiated surrender of Granada (1492); defeated the French at Naples and Ostia (1495–97). Again led Spanish army into Italy (1500); with aid of Venice captured Cephalonia from Turks (1500); defeated French again in Naples (1502–03); recalled from Naples (1507) but given command there again following a French threat after Battle of Ravenna (1512).

Fernández de En·ci·so \-thā-än-'thē-sō, -thā-än-'sē-sō\, Martín. 1470?–?1528. Spanish colonizer. To America (1500); settled as lawyer at Santo Domingo; founded Santa María la Antigua, Darien (1510). Author of *Suma de geografía,* account of discoveries in New World (1519).

Fernández de la Cue·va \-lä-kwä-b̲ä\, Francisco. Duque de Al·bur·quer·que \t̲h̲ä-äl-bür-'ker-kā\. 1617–1676. Spanish administrator. Viceroy of Mexico (1653–60), of Sicily (1660 ff.). His grandson ¶Francisco (d. 1733), duque de Alburquerque, was viceroy of Mexico (1702–11); Albuquerque, New Mexico, founded at this time, was named in his honor.

Fer·nán·dez de Li·zar·di \fer-'nän-däs-t̲h̲ä-lē-'sär-t̲h̲ē\, José Joaquín. 1776–1827. Mexican novelist. A leading literary figure in national liberation movement; founded radical journal *El pensador mexicano* (1812) and other periodicals; known esp. for picaresque novel *El periquillo sarniento* (1816); also wrote *Noches tristes y día alegre* (1818), *La Quijotita y su prima* (1819), *Don Catrín de la Fachenda* (1832).

Fernández de Moratín, Nicolás and Leandro. See MORATÍN.

Fernández de Navarrete, Juan. See NAVARRETE.

Fer·nán·dez de Ovie·do \fer-'nän-däth-t̲h̲ä-ō-'vyä-t̲h̲ō, -däs-\, Gonzalo. 1478–1557. Spanish chronicler and colonial administrator. To America (1514) with Pedro Arias Dávila as inspector general of trade; governor of Cartagena (1526) and Santo Domingo (1535–45). Appointed historiographer of the New World by Charles V (1532); known esp. for *Historia general y natural de las Indias occidentales* (1535).

Fernández de Pa·len·cia \-pä-'län-thyä\, Diego. 1520?–?1581. Spanish soldier and historian. Historiographer of Peru (1555). Known esp. for his *Primera y segunda parte de la historia del Perú,* account of the conquest of Peru, covering period 1544–64 (pub. 1571).

Fernando. See FERDINAND.

Fer·nán Gon·zá·lez \fer-'nän-gón-'thä-läth\. 910–970. 1st Count of Castile (c.930–970). With him began the history of Castile as political entity; secured a measure of autonomy from kings of León; fought Moors.

Fer·nel \fer-nel\, Jean-François. 1497–1558. French physician and astronomer. Known as reformer in medicine, stressing value of observation and condemning magic and astrology. Wrote textbook *Medicina* (1554).

Fer·now \'fer-nō\, Bernhard[2] Eduard[3]. 1851–1923. American forester, b. Inowrazlaw, Germany (now in Poland). To U.S. (1876). Chief, division of forestry, U.S. Department of Agriculture (1886–98); organized (1898) at Cornell U. first forestry school in U.S. and served as dean (1898–1903); head of forestry department, U. of Toronto (1907–19). Founder and editor, *Journal of Forestry* (1902–22); author of *Economics of Forestry* (1902), etc.

Fer·ra·bo·sco \,fär-rä-'bōs-kō, *Angl* ,fer-ə-'bäs-(,)kō\. Family of English musicians of Italian origin, including: Alfonso (1543–1587), settled in England (1562); influential in bringing Italian musical style there; often traveled abroad and may have acted as spy for English government; granted life pension by Queen Elizabeth; returned to Italy (1578) and entered service of Duke of Savoy; composer of madrigals, motets, lamentations, and instrumental music. His illegitimate son ¶Alfonso (c.1575–1628) was educated in music at expense of Elizabeth and remained in royal service until death; collaborated with Ben Jonson and Inigo Jones in producing masques for court of James I; composer of motets, anthems, and esp. music for viol; published *Lessons for 1, 2 and 3 Viols* and *Ayres* for voice and lute (both 1609). His son ¶Alfonso (c.1610–c.1660), violist, was musician in ordinary to Charles I (1628).

Ferrante, Don. See FERDINAND I of Naples.

Fer·rar \'fer-ər\, Nicholas. 1592–1637. English theologian. M.P. (1624); ordained Anglican deacon (1626). Established (1626) at his Little Gidding manor in Huntingdonshire a religious Utopian community largely composed of members of his own family; introduced bookbinding and other crafts as industry of the community. Received from deathbed of friend George Herbert latter's manuscript poems and published them as *The Temple* (1633).

Ferrar, Robert. d. 1555. English prelate. Bishop of St. David's (1548–54); executed for heresy under Mary I; considered martyr for the Reformation in England.

Fer·ra·ri \fär-'rä-rē\, Bartolommeo. 1499–1544. Italian ecclesiastic. A founder (1530) of the Barnabites, or order of Clerics Regular of Saint Paul.

Ferrari, Benedetto. c.1603–1681. Italian poet and composer. Theorbo virtuoso; wrote libretto of and produced *Andromeda,* said to have been first publicly performed opera (Venice, 1637).

Ferrari, Gaudenzio. 1470–1546. Lombard painter. Executed frescoes and altarpieces, as chapel decorations at Varallo.

Ferrari, Giuseppe. 1811–1876. Italian philosopher, historian, and politician. Edited complete works of Vico (1835); wrote *Vico et l'Italie* (1839). Elected deputy (1859); opposed Cavour's single monarchy; professor, Turin, Milan, Rome; senator (1876). Other works included *Filosofia della rivoluzione* (1851), *Histoire des révolutions d'Italie* (1858), *Teoria dei periodi politici* (1874).

Ferrari, Lodovico. *Also* Ludovico Fer·ra·ro \fär-'rä-rō\. 1522–1565. Italian mathematician. Entered service of Gerolamo Cardano (1536) and became his protégé; succeeded him as public mathematics lecturer in Milan (1540); first to find algebraic solution to the bi-quadratic, or quartic, equation and published it in Cardano's *Ars magna* (1545); engaged in famous mathematical controversy with Niccolò Tartaglia; defeated him in public mathematical contest (1548); later in service of Cardinal Ercole Gonzaga, regent of Mantua.

Fer·ra·ris \fär-'rä-rēs\, Galileo. 1847–1897. Italian physicist and electrical engineer. Discovered principle of the rotary magnetic field (1885) which led to the development of polyphase motors and of the hydroelectric industry in Italy; devised transformers for alternating current. Established first electrical engineering school in Italy (1886–87).

Fer·ré \fer-ā\, Charles-Théophile. 1845–1871. French politician. Follower of Auguste Blanqui; a leader of the Commune of Paris (1871); prefect of police (May 14–24, 1871); apparently ordered execution of clerical hostages on failure of Thiers to release Blanqui; captured and shot.

Fer·rei·ra \fər-'rā-rə\, António. 1528–1569. Portuguese poet. Follower of Sá de Miranda, and a founder of Portuguese classicism, imitating Italian and Latin verse forms. Author of the earliest known Portuguese tragedy, *Inês de Castro* (pub. 1587), of the comedies *Bristo* and *O cioso,* and of sonnets, odes, epigrams, and epithalamiums.

Ferreira de Vas·con·ce·los \-dā-vás-kōⁿ(n)-'sā-lüsh\, Jorge. 1515–1585. Portuguese dramatist. Best known for *Comedia Eufrosina* (1555), *Comedia Ulysippo* (1618), and *Comedia Aulegrafia* (1619); also wrote chivalric romance *Memorial das proezas da segunda távola redonda* (1567).

Fer·rel \'fer-əl\, William. 1817–1891. American meteorologist, b. Fulton Co., Pa. With U.S. Coast and Geodetic Survey (1867–1882) and Signal Service (1882–86); made researches on tides, currents, storms; known for his law of the deflection of air currents on the rotating Earth. Wrote *Meteorological Researches* (1877–82), *Popular Essays on the Movements of the Atmosphere* (1882), *Temperature of the Atmosphere and the Earth's Surface* (1884), *A Popular Treatise on the Winds* (1889).

Ferrer, Saint Vincent. See VINCENT FERRER.

Fer·re·ro \fär-'rā-rō\, Guglielmo. 1871–1943. Italian historian. Professor, Geneva (from 1930). Author of *Grandezza e decadenza di Roma* (1902–07), *La ruine de la civilisation antique* (1921), *Bonaparte en Italie* (1936), etc.

Ferrero di Ro·a·sio \-dē-rō-'äs-yō\, Carlo Vincenzo. Marchese d'Or·mea \dór-'mā-ä\. 1680–1745. Piedmontese politician. Minister of finances and interior under Victor Amadeus II, for whom he obtained papal recognition as king of Sardinia (1726); minister of foreign affairs and of interior under Charles Emmanuel III; engineered alliances with France and Austria; negotiated papal concordats (1727, 1741).

Ferrers, 4th Earl. See Laurence SHIRLEY.

Fer·rers \'fer-ərz\, George. 1500?–1579. English politician and poet. One of the authors of the series of historical poems entitled *A Mirror for Magistrates* (1559).

Fer·ri \'fer-rē\, Ciro. 1634–1689. Italian painter and printmaker. Member of Roman school; pupil and successor of Pietro da Cortona; completed Pietro's decorations at Pitti Palace, Florence; painted scriptural frescoes in Sta. Maria Maggiore, Bergamo, and principal altarpiece painting of S. Ambrogio, Rome.

Fer·ri·er \'fer-ē-ər\, Sir David. 1843–1928. Scottish neurologist. Known for research on physiology of the brain, esp. on localization of cerebral functions.

Ferrier, James Frederick. 1808–1864. Scottish philosopher. Professor, Edinburgh (from 1842); known for his theory of agnoiology; introduced term epistemology into English; wrote *Institutes of Metaphysic* (1854).

Ferrier, Kathleen Mary. 1912–1953. English contralto. Established herself as a leading oratorio singer; made stage debut in title role of Britten's *The Rape of Lucretia* (1946); also known for role of Orpheus in Gluck's *Orfeo ed Euridice* and for performances of Mahler's *Das Lied von der Erde;* the contralto parts of Britten's *Spring Symphony* and *Abraham and Isaac* were written for her, as was Bliss's *The Enchantress.*

Ferrier, Susan Edmonstone. 1782–1854. Scottish novelist. Author of *Marriage* (1818), *The Inheritance* (1824), *Destiny* (1831).

Fer·ris \'fer-əs\, George Washington Gale. 1859–1896. American engineer, b. Galesburg, Ill. In railroad and bridge engineering (from 1881); built the Ferris wheel for the World's Columbian Exposition, Chicago (1893).

Fer·ri·zuel \fär-rēth-'wel\ *or* **Fa·ris·sol** \fä-rē-'sōl\, Joseph ha-Nasi. *Called* Ci·de·llus \thē-'da(l)-yüs\. d. c.1145. Spanish Jewish physician. Physician to Alfonso VI of Castile and León; given property by Alfonso in and around Toledo; aided Jews fleeing from Muslim areas of Spain to Christian ones.

Fer·ruc·ci \fär-'rüt-chē\, Andrea. 1465–1526. Tuscan sculptor and architect. Known esp. for statues of apostles at Florence cathedral and for marble baptismal font in cathedral of Pistoia.

Ferrucci *or* **Fer·ruc·cio** \fär-'rüt-chō\, Francesco. 1489–1530. Florentine soldier. Merchant, later city official of Florence; sought to restore the Medicis; defeated and executed at Gavinana in attempt to defend Florence against Pope Clement VII and Emperor Charles V.

Fer·ry \ˈfer-ē\, Jules-François-Camille. 1832–1893. French politician. Mayor of Paris (1870–71), earning nickname "Ferry-Famine"; minister to Greece (1872–73); premier of France (1880–81, 1883–85); pursued vigorous colonial policy extending French possessions in Africa and Asia; enacted anti-clerical measures, including establishment of free compulsory secular education; minister of foreign affairs (1883–85); senator (1891–93).

Fer·sen \ˈfer-sən\, Fredrik Axel von. Count. 1719–1794. Swedish politician and soldier. Entered army (1737); rose to field marshal; served with distinction in Seven Years' War. Elected speaker of noble chamber of Riksdag (1756); leader of the Hat Party; vigorous defender of the rights of the nobility against encroachments by the sovereign. His son ¶Count Hans Axel (1755–1810) was a soldier; aide-de-camp to Rochambeau in American Revolution; resident at French court at Versailles and known as an admirer of Marie-Antoinette; disguised as coachman, aided royal family in attempt to flee from France (1791); named earl marshal of Sweden (1801); adviser to Gustav II during war with France (1805); murdered in a popular uprising.

Fers·man \ˈfyer-smən\, Aleksandr Yevgenyevich. 1883–1945. Russian mineralogist. A founder of geochemistry; taught at Moscow State U. (1907–12); became academician in Academy of Sciences (1919); founded Lomonosov Institute of Geochemistry, Mineralogy, and Crystallography; wrote *Geochemistry* (1933–39).

Fes·ca \ˈfes-kä\, Friedrich Ernst. 1789–1826. German violinist and composer. Wrote chamber music, 3 symphonies, overtures, 2 operas, and sacred music. His son ¶Alexander Ernst (1820–1849) was a pianist; composer of 4 operas, chamber music, and songs.

Fesch \fesh\, Joseph. 1763–1839. French prelate. Half-brother of Napoléon's mother. Ordained priest (1785); archbishop of Lyon (1802); cardinal (1803); Napoléon's ambassador to the Vatican (1803–06); grand almoner at French court and mediator with the pope (1806–12); opposed certain of Napoléon's policies (from 1810). Banished by Bourbons (1815) and retired to Rome (1815–39).

Fes·sen·den \ˈfes-ᵊn-dən\, Reginald Aubrey. 1866–1932. American radio engineer, b. East Bolton, Que., of American parentage. Chief chemist of Edison Laboratory (1887–90); professor, U. of Pittsburgh (1893–1900); headed National Signalling Co. (1902–10). Pioneer in radio; invented the electrolytic detector (1900), high-frequency alternator (1902), and the heterodyne receiver; made first radio broadcast of voice and music (Dec. 24, 1906). Patented some 300 inventions, including radio compass, sonic depth finder, submarine signalling devices, and turbo-electric drive for battleships.

Fessenden, Thomas Green. 1771–1837. American poet and journalist, b. Walpole, N.H. Published *Democracy Unveiled* (1805), a long, bitter poetic attack on Jefferson and other Democratic leaders; in Boston established and edited *New England Farmer* (1822–37).

Fessenden, William Pitt. 1806–1869. American politician, b. Boscawen, N.H. Member, U.S. House of Representatives (1841–43), U.S. Senate (1854–64); opposed Kansas-Nebraska bill (1854); instrumental in founding Republican party (1856); member, Senate Finance Committee (1857–64); opposed Buchanan administration; supported Lincoln's administration. U.S. secretary of the treasury (1864–65); U.S. senator (1865–69).

Fe·sta \ˈfes-tä\, Costanzo. c.1490–1545. Italian singer and composer. Forerunner of Palestrina; composed masses, Magnificats, motets, and many madrigals.

Fes·tus \ˈfes-təs\, Porcius. d. c.62 A.D. Roman administrator. Successor of Felix (*q.v.*) as Roman procurator of Judea (58 or 60–62 A.D.); before him St. Paul made his famous "appeal unto Caesar."

Festus, Sextus Pompeius. 2d or 3d century A.D. Roman grammarian and lexicographer. Compiled an epitome of Marcus Verrius Flaccus's *De significatu verborum*.

Fet \ˈfyāt\, Afanasy Afanasyevich. *Orig. Ger. family name* Foeth \ˈfœt\. *Surname legally changed (1876) to* Shen·shin \shyin-ˈshyēn\. 1820–1892. Russian poet. Friend of Tolstoy and Turgenev. Best known for his nature poetry and love lyrics.

Feti, Domenico. See FETTI.

Fé·tis \fā-tēs\, François-Joseph. 1784–1871. Belgian composer and writer on music. Professor (1821), librarian (1827), Paris Conservatory; founded and edited in Paris (1827–33) *Revue Musicale,* first paper devoted to musical criticism; director of Brussels Conservatory and court Kapellmeister in Brussels (from 1833). Published *Traité du contrepoint et de la fugue* (1825) and *Biographie universelle des musiciens* (1835–44); composed operas, symphonies, church and chamber music, piano and organ pieces, and songs.

Fet·ter·man \ˈfet-ər-mən\, William Judd. 1833?–1866. American army officer, b. New London, Conn.? Served throughout Civil War in Union army; ambushed and killed near Ft. Phil Kearny, Wyo., by Sioux and Cheyenne in "Fetterman massacre" (Dec. 21, 1866).

Fet·ti \ˈfāt-tē\ *or* **Fe·ti** \ˈfā-tē\, Domenico. 1588 or 1589–1623. Italian painter. Pupil of Cigoli; court painter in Mantua (1613–22); known for small representations of biblical parables as scenes from everyday life, as *The Good Samaritan*.

Feucht·wang·er \ˈfoikt-ˌväŋ-ər\, Lion. 1884–1958. German novelist and dramatist. Expatriate (from 1933) in London and France; to U.S. (1940). Author of plays, as *Warren Hastings* (1916) and *Die Petroleuminseln* (1927), a volume of satirical poems, and historical and modern novels, as *Die hässliche Herzogin* (1923), *Jud Süss* (1925), *Josephus-Trilogie* (1932–45), *Die Geschwister Oppenheim* (1933), *Der falsche Nero* (1936), *Goya oder der arge Weg der Erkenntnis* (1951), *Jefta und seine Tochter* (1957).

Feu·er·bach \ˈfoi-ər-ˌbäk\, Paul Johann Anselm von. Ritter. 1775–1833. German jurist. Entered Ministry of Justice at Munich (1805); prepared penal code for Bavaria (effective 1813); first president of appellate court at Ansbach (1817–33). Originated theory of psychological coercion or intimidation in criminal law, secured (1806) abolition of torture, and championed rigorist application of penal law by judges and exemplary rather than vindictive punishment. Wrote authoritative *Lehrbuch des gemeinen in Deutschland gültigen peinlichen Rechts* (1801). His reforms in penal legislation influenced other European states.
His son ¶Anselm (1798–1851), archaeologist; professor of philology at Freiburg (from 1836); author of *Der vatikanische Apollo* (1833). Another son ¶Karl Wilhelm (1800–1834), mathematician and professor at Erlangen (1822–28), after whom the Feuerbach (9-point) circle is named. A third son ¶Ludwig Andreas (1804–1872), philosopher, pupil of Hegel in Berlin; abandoned Hegelian idealism for a naturalistic materialism, subsequently attacked orthodox religion and immortality, concluded that God is the outward projection of man's inward nature; author of *Abälard und Heloise* (1834), *Über Philosophie und Christentum* (1839), *Das Wesen des Christentums* (1841), *Das Wesen der Religion* (1845), *Theogonie* (1857), *Gottheit, Freiheit und Unsterblichkeit* (1866), etc.
Anselm's son ¶Anselm (1829–1880), historical and portrait painter; pupil of Schadow in Düsseldorf (1846) and Rahl in Munich (1848); worked in Paris, Karlsruhe, and (1856–72) Rome; professor at Vienna Academy (1873–76); resident thereafter chiefly in Venice; worked in Romantic Classical style; paintings included *Hafiz at the Well* (1852), *Nanna* (1861), *Iphigenia* (1862, 1871), *Judgment of Paris* (1870).

Feuil·lade \fœ-yád\, Louis. 1873–1925. French film director. Famed for internationally popular screen serials *Fantômas* (1913–14), *Les Vampires* (1915), *Judex* (1916), and *La nouvelle mission de Judex* (1917–18).

Feuil·let \fœ-ye\, Octave. 1821–1890. French writer. Among his novels were *La petite comtesse* (1857), *Le Roman d'un jeune homme pauvre* (1858), *Monsieur de Camors* (1867), *Histoire d'une parisienne* (1881), *La Morte* (1886); among his plays were *La Crise* (1848), *Dalila* (1857), *Le Cheveu blanc* (1860), *Le Sphinx* (1874).

Feuillet, Raoul-Auger. c.1675–c.1730. French dancer and choreographer. Pupil of Pierre Beauchamp; collaborated with André Lorin at Académie Royale de Danse, Paris; published a dance notation system in *Chorégraphie ou l'art de décrire la danse* (1700); described dances performed at Paris Opéra in *Recueil de danses* (1704).

Fé·val \fā-vál\, Paul-Henri-Corentin. 1817–1887. French novelist. Among his works were *Le Club des phoques* (1841), *Les Mystères de Londres* (1844), *Le Bossu* (1858), *Les Habits noirs* (1863).

Feversham, Earl of. See Louis de Durfort de Duras under DURFORT family.

Fewkes \ˈfyüks\, Jesse Walter. 1850–1930. American ethnologist, b. Newton, Mass. With Bureau of American Ethnology of Smithsonian Institution (1895–1918); chief of bureau (1918–28). Noted esp. for investigations of Hopi Indian culture and history.

Fey·deau \fā-dō\, Ernest-Aimé. 1821–1873. French novelist. Author of *Fanny* (1858), *Daniel* (1859), *Le Mari de la danseuse* (1863), *La Comtesse de Chalis* (1867). His son ¶Georges-Léon-Jules-Marie (1862–1921) was a playwright; author of farces *La Dame de chez Maxim* (1899), *La Puce à l'oreille* (1907), *Occupe-toi d'Amélie* (1908), etc.

Fey·der \fed-er\, Jacques. *Orig.* Jacques Fré·dé·rix \frā-dā-rēks\. 1888–1948. French film director, b. Brussels. To Paris (1912, naturalized 1928); in Hollywood (1928–32) filming *The Kiss* (1929), *Daybreak* (1931), *Son of India* (1931). His other films included *Atlantide* (1921), *Crainquebille* (1922), *Thérèse Raquin* (1928), *Les nouveaux messieurs* (1928), *Le grande jeu* (1934), *Pension Mimosas* (1934), *La Kermesse héroïque* (1935).

Ffraid, Saint. See BRIGIT.

Fia·lho de Al·mei·da \ˈfyäl-yü-thē-äl-ˈmā-thə\, José Valentim. 1857–1911. Portuguese writer. Author of *Cuentos* (1881), *A cidade do vicio* (1882), *O pais das uvas* (1893), collections of romantic and realistic stories; known esp. for series of satirical sketches *Os gatos* (1889–94) that contributed to downfall of monarchy.

Fia·lin \fyá-laⁿ\, Jean-Gilbert-Victor. Duc de Per·si·gny \per-sēn-yē\. French politician. Ardent propagandist for succession of Louis-Napoléon to throne; involved in Bonapartist attempts at coups d'état in Strasbourg (1836),

Boulogne (1840), and the final success at Paris (Dec 2, 1851); minister of interior (1852–54, 1860–63); ambassador to Great Britain (1855–58, 1859–60).

Fi·bich \ˈfib-ik\, Zdeněk Antonín Václav. 1850–1900. Czech composer. Composed operas, as *Bukovín* (1874), *Blaník* (1881), *Šárka* (1898), the melodramatic trilogy *Hippodamia* (1890–91), about 400 piano pieces, symphonic poems, overtures, symphonies, chamber music, choral works, songs, etc.

Fi·bi·ger \ˈfē-bē-gər\, Johannes Andreas Grib. 1867–1928. Danish pathologist. Professor, Copenhagen (from 1900); credited with first producing cancer experimentally (in rats); awarded 1926 Nobel prize for physiology or medicine.

Fi·bo·nac·ci \ˌfē-bō-ˈnät-chē, *Angl* ˌfib-ə-ˈnäch-ē\, Leonardo. *Also known as* Leonardo of Pisa. c.1170–after 1240. Italian mathematician. Most distinguished mathematician of the Middle Ages. Studied with an Arab master in North Africa; published *Liber abaci* (1202) by which he introduced Arabic numeral system in Europe; discovered Fibonacci sequence of numbers; also wrote *Practica geometriae* (1220) and *Liber quadratorum* (1225).

Fich·te \ˈfik-tə\, Johann Gottlieb. 1762–1814. German philosopher. Exponent of a system of transcendental idealism emphasizing self-activity of reason and setting forth a perfected Kantian system, or science of knowledge, in which he connected practical reason with pure reason. At first an ardent disciple of Kant; professor at Jena (1794–99); resident in Berlin as member of Romantic circle and private lecturer (1799); delivered his famous patriotic lectures *Reden an die deutsche Nation* (1807–08); professor and first rector of U. of Berlin (1810–14). Author of *Versuch einer Kritik aller Offenbarung* (1792), *Das System der Sittenlehre nach den Principien der Wissenschaftslehre* (1798), *Die Bestimmung des Menschen* (1800), *Die Anweisung zum seligen Leben* (1806), *Die Grundzüge des gegenwärtigen Zeitalters* (1806), etc.
His son ¶Immanuel Hermann von Fichte (1796–1879), philosopher, exponent of an ethical or speculative theism; professor, Bonn (1836) and Tübingen (1842–63); founded (1837) *Zeitschrift für Philosophie und spekulative Theologie*; ennobled (1867). Author of *System der Ethik* (1850–53), *Anthropologie* (1856), *Die theistische Weltanschauung* (1873), etc.

Fi·ci·no \fē-ˈchē-nō\, Marsilio. 1433–1499. Italian philosopher. Known chiefly as Platonist; became head of Platonic Academy of Florence (1462); commissioned by the elder Cosimo de' Medici to translate (into Latin) works of Plato (pub. 1484) and several Neo-Platonists; ordained priest (1473); retired (1494). Author of *Liber de Christiana religione* (1474), *Theologica Platonica* (1482), *De vita libri tres* (1489), and several commentaries on Plato and Plotinus.

Fick \ˈfik\, Adolf Eugen. 1829–1901. German physiologist. Professor at Zürich (1852–68) and Würzburg (1868–99); developed fundamental laws of diffusion in living organisms and published them in *Die medizinische Physik* (1856).

Fick, August. 1833–1916. German philologist. Professor, Göttingen (1876–87) and Breslau (1887–91). Made first comprehensive study of common vocabulary of Indo-European languages and sought to determine its prototype, in *Vergleichendes Wörterbuch der indogermanischen Sprachen* (1868); also wrote *Die griechischen Personennamen nach ihrer Bildung erklärt* (1874).

Fick·er \ˈfik-ər\, Julius von. 1826–1902. German jurist and historian. Professor, Innsbruck (from 1852). Author of *Forschungen zur Reichs- und Rechtsgeschichte Italiens* (1868–74), etc.

Fied·ler \ˈfēd-lər\, Arthur. 1894–1979. American conductor, b. Boston. Viola player with Boston Symphony Orchestra (1915–30); a founder of Boston Sinfonietta (1924); founded free outdoor Esplanade Concerts in Boston (1929); conductor, Boston Pops Orchestra (1930–79).

Field \ˈfē(ə)ld\, Cyrus West. 1819–1892. American financier, b. Stockbridge, Mass. Brother of David D. and Stephen J. Field. Amassed fortune in paper business (1841–53). Chiefly responsible for laying of first submarine telegraph cable between American and Europe (1857–66); owner and president of New York Elevated Railroad Co. (1877–80); with Jay Gould helped develop Wabash Railroad; lost fortune in later years.

Field, David Dudley. 1805–1894. American lawyer, b. Haddam, Conn. Brother of Cyrus W. and Stephen J. Field. Practiced, New York City (from 1828); interested in codification of law; instrumental in preparation and adoption in New York State (1848) of Field Code of Civil Procedure; his code subsequently adopted in many other U.S. states, in federal court system, in England and Ireland (both 1873), and in several British colonies, esp. India; also instrumental in adoption of New York penal code (1865); attempted an international code, collaborating in preparation (1872) of *Draft Outline of an International Code.*

Field, Erastus Salisbury. 1805–1900. American painter, b. Leverett, Mass. His works included portraits, scenes from myth, biblical history, and American history, esp. *Historical Monument of the American Republic* (c.1875).

Field, Eugene. 1850–1895. American poet and journalist, b. St. Louis. With Chicago *Morning News* (later named the *Record*) as editor of column "Sharps and Flats" (1883–95), in which first appeared most of his work, a mixture of whimsical narrative, children's verse, wit and humor. Author of *The Tribune Primer* (1882), *A Little Book of Western Verse* (1889), *With Trumpet and Drum* (1892), *Echoes from the Sabine Farm* (1892), *Lullaby Land* (1894). Best known as a poet of childhood, examples of his children's verse being "Dutch Lullaby" (also known as "Wynken, Blynken, and Nod") and "Little Boy Blue."

Field, Henry. 1902–1986. American anthropologist, b. Chicago. Associated (from 1926) with Chicago Natural History Museum (now Field Museum); research fellow at Harvard U. (1950–69). Authority on Middle Eastern civilizations; discovered what is believed to be earliest known wheel. Author of *The Anthropology of Iraq* (1939–52), *The Track of Man* (1953), etc.

Field, John. 1782–1837. Irish pianist and composer. Protégé of Muzio Clementi; resident chiefly in Russia (from 1803); successful concert pianist throughout Europe, known for his expressive and individualistic style. Composer of 7 piano concertos, piano duets, and much solo piano music, esp. his *Nocturnes* which were used as models by Chopin.

Field, Marshall. 1834–1906. American merchant, b. near Conway, Mass. Clerk in drygoods store, Pittsfield, Mass. (1851–56); to Chicago (1856); became clerk, partner (1862) in drygoods firm Cooley, Wadsworth & Co. Became partner (1865) in drygoods firm Field, Palmer, & Leiter; continued expansion and change of firm names until organization became Marshall Field & Co. (1881); remained head of business as it grew to be largest wholesale and retail drygoods establishment in world. Gave land for U. of Chicago; gave funds for Columbian Museum at Chicago World's Fair (1893), later developed into Field Museum of Natural History. His grandson ¶Marshall Field III (1893–1956), newpaper publisher, b. Chicago; founder (1941) and publisher of *Chicago Sun,* later *Chicago Sun-Times;* consolidated his publishing interests as Field Enterprises (1944); bought *Chicago Daily News* (1947). His son ¶Marshall IV (1916–1965), b. New York City, was editor and publisher of *Chicago Sun-Times* (from 1948) and of *Chicago Daily News* (from 1959); president (1956–64) and chairman of board (from 1964) of Field Enterprises.

Field, Nathan. 1587–?1619. English actor and playwright. Joined Children of the Queen's Revels (c.1600); later (1616–17) a member of King's Men; quit stage after scandal (1619). Author of *A Woman's a Weathercock* (1612) and *Amends for Ladies* (1618); collaborated with Beaumont and Fletcher, and with Philip Massinger in *The Fatal Dowry* (1632).

Field, Stephen Johnson. 1816–1899. American jurist, b. Haddam, Conn. Brother of Cyrus W. and David D. Field. California state supreme court justice (1857–63; chief justice 1859–63). Associate justice, U.S. Supreme Court (1863–97). His decisions important in development of constitutional law.

Fiel·den \ˈfē(ə)l-dən\, John. 1784–1849. English manufacturer and politician. With his brothers inherited family cotton mill at Todmorden (1811); radical M.P. (1833–47); proponent of legislation protecting welfare of factory workers; vigorously opposed poor laws; sponsored successful Ten Hours Act of 1847.

Field·ing \ˈfē(ə)l-diŋ\, Henry. 1707–1754. English novelist and playwright. Half-brother of Sir John Fielding. Called to bar (1740); justice of the peace for Westminster and Middlesex (from 1748). Began literary career with comedies for the stage, including *Love in Several Masques* (1728), *The Temple Beau* (1730), *Tom Thumb* (1730), *The Modern Husband* (1732), *Pasquin* (1736), and adaptations from Molière; edited periodicals *The Champion* (1739–41), *The True Patriot* (1745–46), and *The Jacobite's Journal* (1747–48); reached his height in series of realistic novels including *Joseph Andrews* (1742), *Jonathan Wild* (1743), *Tom Jones* (1749), and *Amelia* (1751); author also of a *Journal of a Voyage to Lisbon* (1755). His sister ¶Sarah (1710–1768), also a writer, wrote romances including *The Adventures of David Simple* (1744), and the first novel in English written for children, *The Governess* (1749).

Fielding, Sir John. 1721–1780. English jurist. Blinded at 19; succeeded his half-brother Henry Fielding as justice of the peace for Westminster and Middlesex; with Henry founded Bow Street Runners, group of detectives; reduced crime and reformed administration of London's criminal justice.

Fielding, William Stevens. 1848–1929. Canadian journalist and politician, b. Halifax, N.S. On staff of Halifax *Morning Chronicle* (1864–84). Prime minister of Nova Scotia (1884–96); dominion finance minister under Laurier (1896–1911) and King (1921–25).

Fields \ˈfē(ə)l(d)z\, Dorothy. 1905–1974. American songwriter, b. Allenhurst, N.J. Daughter of Lew M. Fields. Writer of lyrics for Broadway musicals, as *Let's Face It* (1941), *Mexican Hayride* (1944), *Up in Central Park* (1945), *Annie Get Your Gun* (1946), *Redhead* (1959), *Sweet Charity* (1965), and for motion pictures; wrote lyrics for songs "I Can't Give You Anything But Love, Baby," "On the Sunny Side of the Street," "I'm in the Mood for Love," "A Fine Romance," "The Way You Look Tonight," etc.

Fields, Gracie. *Orig.* Grace Stans·field \ˈstanz-ˌfēld, ˈstan(t)s-\. 1898–1979. English comedienne. Appeared in London with great success in *Mr. Tower of London* (over 4000 performances, 1918–25); later made records and appeared in films, radio, television; gave 10 command performances (from 1928).

Fields, James Thomas. 1817–1881. American author and publisher, b. Portsmouth, N.H. Partner in firm of Ticknor, Reed & Fields (in Boston, 1838–54), which became Ticknor & Fields (1854) and Fields, Osgood & Co. (1868). Succeeded James Russell Lowell as editor, *Atlantic Monthly* (1861–70). Author of *Poems* (1849), *Yesterdays with Authors* (1872), *In and Out of Doors with Charles Dickens* (1876). His 2d wife (m. 1854) ¶Annie, *nee* Adams (1834–1915), author, b. Boston; wrote books of verse, as *Under the Olive* (1881), and biographies of several contemporary writers.

Fields, Lew. See at Joseph M. WEBER.

Fields, W. C. *Orig.* William Claude Du•ken•field \'dü-kən-ˌfēld\. 1880–1946. American entertainer, b. Philadelphia. Vaudeville juggler, esp. (1915–21) with Ziegfield *Follies;* starred in motion pictures *David Copperfield* (1935), *You Can't Cheat an Honest Man* (1939), *The Bank Dick* (1940), *My Little Chickadee* (1940), *Never Give a Sucker an Even Break* (1941), etc.

Fiennes \'fīnz\, William. 1st Viscount Saye and Sele \'sā-ən(d)-'sēl\. 1582–1662. English Parliamentary leader. A leading opponent of James I and Charles I in House of Lords; lord lieutenant of three counties and member of committee of safety (1642); turned scale in favor of Self-denying Ordinance in House of Lords; privy councilor and lord privy seal (1660). His granddaughter ¶Celia Fiennes (1662–1741) traveled throughout England in late 17th century; her journals (pub. 1888) provide comprehensive and invaluable account of all aspects of places she visited.

Fie•schi \'fyā-skē\, Gian Luigi. Conte di La•va•gna \lä-'vän-yä\. 1522–1547. Genoese conspirator. Plotted with Francis I of France, Pope Paul III, and Pier Luigi Farnese, Duke of Parma, the overthrow of Andrea Doria, Doge of Genoa, and Gianettino Doria, his nephew and appointed successor. Popularized by Rousseau, Schiller, and other literary figures.

Fieschi, Giuseppe Maria. 1790–1836. Corsican conspirator. Made unsuccessful attempt on life of Louis-Philippe (July 28, 1835) with "infernal machine" of 25 guns, killing 18 people.

Fiesole, Giovanni da. See GUIDO DI PIETRO.

Fiesole, Mino da. See MINO DA FIESOLE.

Fígaro. See Mariano José de LARRA.

Figg \'fig\, James. c.1695–1734. English pugilist. Won championship (1719); considered first heavyweight champion in boxing history; opened in London Figg's Amphitheatre, prototype of later boxing academies.

Figl \'fig-əl\, Leopold. 1902–1965. Austrian politician. Chancellor of Austria (1945–53); foreign minister (1953–59); president of National Assembly (1959–62); governor of Lower Austria (1962–65).

Fig•ner \'fyēg-nyir\, Vera Nikolayevna. 1852–1942. Russian revolutionist. Involved in Revolutionary Populist movement (from 1873); became a leader in Narodnaya Volya (People's Will party, 1879); involved in assassination of Czar Alexander II (1881); imprisoned in Shlisselburg fortress (1884–1904); exiled abroad (1906–15). Published *Kogda chasy zhizni ostanovalis* (1921) and *Memoirs of a Revolutionist* (1927).

Fi•guei•re•do \fē-gā-'rā-thü\, Antero de. 1866–1953. Portuguese writer. Author of fictionalized historical biographies *D. Pedro e D. Inês* (1913), *Leonor Teles* (1916), *D. Sebastião* (1925), sentimental travel sketches *Recordações e viagens* (1904) and *Jornadas em Portugal* (1918), and romantic novels.

Fi•gue•roa \fē-gā-'rō-ä\, Francisco de. c.1536–c.1620. Spanish poet. Master of blank verse; his works included an eclogue *Tirsi,* sonnets, elegies, and canzoni.

Fig•u•lus \'fig-yə-ləs\, Publius Nigidius. fl. 98–45 B.C. Roman writer. Most learned Roman of his age after Marcus Terentius Varro; supported Cicero during Catilinarian conspiracy; praetor (58); sided with Pompey in Civil War; banished and died in exile. Sought to revive Pythagorean doctrines and combine them with Etruscan and Oriental beliefs. Wrote *De dis,* earliest comprehensive work on Roman religion; also wrote *Commentarii grammatici, De animalibus, De hominum natura, Sphaera graecanica et sphaera barbarica,* etc.

Fi•lan•gie•ri \ˌfē-län-'jer-ē\, Gaetano. 1752–1788. Italian jurist. Author of *La scienza della legislazione* (1780–85). His son ¶Carlo (1784–1867), Principe di Sa•tria•no \sä-trē-'ä-nō\, Neapolitan general, assumed command of army of the Two Sicilies (1831); brutally suppressed Sicilian revolution of 1848; named duke of Taormina (1848); governor of Sicily (1848–55); premier of the Two Sicilies (1859–60).

Fi•la•re•te \ˌfē-lä-'re-tā\. *Orig.* Antonio di Pie•tro Aver•li•no \dēp-'ye-trō-ˌä-vär-'lē-nō\ *or* Ave•ru•li•no \ˌä-vä-rü-'lē-nō\. c.1400–c.1469. Florentine architect and sculptor. Chiefly important for role in disseminating the early Renaissance style in Lombardy; perhaps trained under Lorenzo Ghiberti; employed in Rome (1433–45) on execution of bronze doors of St. Peter's; in service of Francesco Sforza, Duke of Milan (1451–65); designed Ospedale Maggiore (1457–65); began cathedral of Bergamo; wrote (between 1460–64) *Trattato d'architettura* describing a model city called Sforzinda.

Filch•ner \'filk-nər\, Wilhelm. 1877–1957. German explorer and scientist. Explored in Russia, the Balkans, Asia Minor, and (1900) over the Pamir region; explored East Tibet with his wife and Albert Tafel (1903–05); conducted 2d German Antarctic expedition on *Deutschland* into Weddell Sea (1911–12) and discovered southwestern continuation of Coats Land; established many magnetic stations and made maps of region traversed in Central Asiatic expedition (1925–28); made magnetic survey of Nepal (1939–40). Author of *Das Rätsel des Matschu* (1907), *Zum sechsten Erdteil* (1923), *Ein Forscherleben* (1950).

Fi•lel•fo \fē-'lel-fō\, Francesco. *Lat.* Phi•lel•phus \fə-'lel-fəs\. 1398–1481. Italian Humanist. Itinerant teacher of classical languages and literature; in service of dukes of Milan (1440–71); enjoyed enormous prestige; wrote epic and lyrical poetry, erudite classical works, philosophical treatises, and many letters valuable for information on the period.

Fi•lene \fə-'lēn, fī-\, Edward Albert. 1860–1937. American merchant, b. Salem, Mass. Entered father's drygoods and clothing store in Boston; after father's death, became president of company, Wm. Filene & Sons. Successful in applying principles of scientific management in business; active in promoting employees' welfare; helped establish Credit Union National Extension Bureau (1921) and the International Chamber of Commerce.

Fi•li•ca•ia \ˌfē-lē-'kä-yä\, Vincenzo da. 1642–1707. Italian lyric poet. Known for his *Canzoni in occasione dell'assedio e liberazione di Vienna* (1684) and *Poesie toscane* (1707), containing sonnets to Italy.

Fi•li•pe•pi \ˌfē-lē-'pā-pē\, Alessandro di Mariano. *Known as* Sandro Bot•ti•cel•li \ˌbȯt-tē-'chel-lē, *Angl* ˌbät-ə-'chel-ē\. 1445–1510. Italian painter. Apprenticed to Fra Filippo Lippi; patronized esp. by Lorenzo di Pierfrancesco de' Medici and other members of Medici family; assisted in decoration of Sistine Chapel (1481–82), many churches and chapels. Painting known for deep saturated colors, linear rhythms, vividly imagined composition. Works included *Fortitude, The Primavera, Adoration of the Magi, Madonna of the Magnificat, Mars and Venus, Birth of Venus, Madonna of the Pomegranate, Annunciation, Calumny of Apelles, St. Augustine in His Cell, Tragedy of Lucretia, Life of St. Zenobius, Mystic Nativity.* For Lorenzo di Pierfrancesco executed illustrations for Dante's *Divina commedia.*

Fill•more \'fil-ˌmō(ə)r, -mȯ(ə)r\, Charles Sherlock (1854–1948), b. near St. Cloud, Minn., and his wife (m. 1881) Myrtle, *orig.* Mary Caroline, *nee* Page \'pāj\ (1845–1931), b. Pagetown, Ohio. American religious leaders. Cofounders (1888–89) and leaders of the Unity School of Christianity.

Fillmore, Millard. 1800–1874. Thirteenth president of the United States, b. Locke, N.Y. Practiced law, Buffalo (from 1830); member, U.S. House of Representatives (1833–35, 1837–43). Vice president of the United States (1849–50); succeeded to presidency on death of Taylor (1850). Supported compromise policy in slavery issue; signed Fugitive Slave Law, thus alienating abolitionist support; champion of expansion in the Pacific; sent Matthew Perry to Japan (1853). Unsuccessful Whig candidate for president (1852) and National American ("Know-Nothing") candidate (1856).

Fil•mer \'fil-mər\, Sir Robert. c.1588–1653. English political writer. Royalist in sympathy. Author of *Patriarcha* (1680) upholding theory of divine right of kings; attacked by Locke in his *Two Treatises of Government* (1690).

Fil•son \'fil-sən\, John. 1747?–1788. American frontiersman, b. Chester Co., Pa. Pioneer in Kentucky (from 1783); published (1784) *Discovery, Settlement, and Present State of Kentucke,* containing earliest account of adventures of Daniel Boone; to Ohio (1788) where he helped found Losantiville, later Cincinnati.

Fim•bria \'fim-brē-ə\, Gaius Flavius. d. 85 B.C. Roman general. Partisan of Marius; assigned to command in Asia (86 B.C.), where he warred against Mithridates, and persecuted partisans of Sulla; committed suicide when attacked by Sulla.

Finch \'finch\. Name of distinguished English family, including among its members earls of Win•chil•sea \'win-chəl-(ˌ)sē\, Not•ting•ham \'nat-iŋ-əm, *US also* -ˌham\, and Ayles•ford \'ālz-fərd, 'āls-\:

Sir John Finch (1584–1660), Baron Finch of Ford•wich \'fō(ə)r-ˌdwich, 'fȯ(ə)r-\; judge; king's counsel (1626); speaker of House of Commons (1628–29); chief justice of Court of Common Pleas (1634); lord keeper (1640); impeached by Long Parliament (1640). His first cousin once removed ¶Heneage (1621–1682), 1st Earl of Nottingham (cr. 1681); judge; expert on municipal law; solicitor general (1660); attorney general (1670); lord keeper of the seals (1673); Baron Finch and Lord Chancellor (1674); the original of Amri in Dryden's *Absalom and Achitophel.* His son ¶Daniel (1647–1730), 2d Earl of Nottingham; politician; became also 6th Earl of Winchilsea (1729); first lord of admiralty (1681–84); secretary for war (1688–93); secretary of state (1702–04); headed High Church Tories under Queen Anne; carried act forbidding occasional conformance of dissenters; dismissed from presidency of council for leniency to Jacobite peers. His brother ¶Heneage (1647?–1719), 1st Earl of Aylesford (cr. 1714); king's counsel (1677) and solicitor general (1679–86); leading counsel for the Seven Bishops (1688); privy councilor (1703). ¶Ann Finch (1661–1720), Countess of Winchilsea; poet; wife of

Heneage Finch, 4th Earl of Winchilsea; friend of Pope and Rowe; author of occasional verse, including a long poem *The Spleen* (1701).

Finck \'fiŋk\, Heinrich. 1444 or 1445–1527. German composer. Composed masses, part songs, hymns, and motets. His grandnephew ¶Hermann (1527–1558) composed motets and wrote *Practica musica* (1556).

Find·lay \'fin-(d)lē, -(,)(d)lā\, John Ritchie. 1824–1898. Scottish newspaper proprietor and philanthropist. Chief proprietor of the *Scotsman* (from 1870); presented to the nation the Scottish National Portrait Gallery, at Edinburgh (opened 1889).

Fine \fēn\, Oronce. *Latin* Orontius Fi·ne·us \'fi-nē-əs\. 1494–1555. French mathematician. Constructed mathematical and astronomical instruments; drew first map of France printed in that country (1525); published editions of Euclid and other mathematical treatises.

Fi·ni·guer·ra \fē-nē-'gwer-rä\, Maso, *in full* Tommaso di Antonio. 1426–1464. Florentine goldsmith, niellist, and engraver. Believed to have studied under Lorenzo Ghiberti; apparently engraved many of Antonio Pollaiuolo's designs (1459–64); introduced copperplate engraving into Italy; known esp. for his nielli; produced *Seven Planets,* a series of copperplate engravings; often connected with *Florentine Picture-Chronicle* (c.1464), a book of drawings.

Fink \'fiŋk\, Albert. 1827–1897. American engineer, b. Darmstadt, Germany. To U.S. (1849); invented Fink truss and used it (from 1852) in iron railroad bridges. Joined (1857) Louisville & Nashville Railroad and rose to vice president (1869–75); analyzed and standardized freight rates; determined scientifically costs of transportation, thus virtually founding the science of railroad economics.

Fink, Mike. 1770?–1823. American frontiersman, b. Ft. Pitt, Pa. Famed from youth as marksman and Indian scout; became "king of the keelboatmen" on Ohio and Mississippi rivers; with Ashley-Henry trapping expedition to the Rockies (1822); shot and killed. A folk hero, became legendary for his fighting, bragging, and boisterous deeds.

Fin·kel \'fiŋ-kəl\, Nathan Tzevi ben Moses. 1849–1927. Jewish scholar. Mainly responsible for funding of Eastern European yeshivas (1881–1925) and the yeshiva of Hebron, Palestine.

Fin·lay \fēn-'lī\, Carlos Juan. 1833–1915. Cuban physician and epidemiologist. Investigated yellow fever; wrote paper (1881) suggesting mosquito as agent of transmission; his later contention that Stegomyia (later Aëdes) mosquito is agent proved correct by Reed Commission (1900). Chairman, commission on infectious diseases, Havana (1899–1902); chief sanitary officer of Cuba (1902–09). Made notable contributions to etiology and pathology of yellow fever.

Fin·lay \'fin-lē, -(,)lā\, George. 1799–1875. English historian. Joined Byron in Greece and served with him in Greek war for independence (1823); settled on estate in Attica (1825), devoted himself to study of Greek history. Author of *The Hellenic Kingdom and the Greek Nation* (1836), *Greece Under the Romans* (1844), *History of the Byzantine and Greek Empires* (1854), *History of the Greek Revolution* (1861).

Finlay, Robert Bannatyne. 1st Viscount Finlay. 1842–1929. British jurist, b. Scotland. Called to bar (1867); solicitor general (1895–1900); attorney general (1900–06); lord chancellor (1916–18). Member of Hague Tribunal (1920) and one of first judges of Permanent Court of International Justice at The Hague (1921).

Fin·ley \'fin-lē\, Martha. 1828–1909. American writer, b. Chillicothe, Ohio. Author of popular juveniles, including the *Elsie Dinsmore Series* (28 vols., from 1867), the *Mildred Series* (7 vols.), and *Pewit's Nest Series* (12 vols.).

Finley, Robert. 1772–1817. American clergyman, b. Princeton, N.J. Ordained in Presbyterian ministry (1795); organizer of American Colonization Society (1816), formed to plan a colony on African soil to which American Negroes could be sent as a means of solving or ending slavery problem. President, U. of Georgia (1817).

Fin·ney \'fin-ē\, Charles Grandison. 1792–1875. American clergyman and educator, b. Warren, Ohio. Ordained in Presbyterian church (1824); conducted revivalist meetings (1824–32), and continued evangelistic meetings throughout his life. Pastor, the Broadway Tabernacle (Congregational), organized especially for him (1834–37); withdrew from Presbyterian church (1836). Professor, Oberlin College (1837–75), president (1851–66).

Fin·sen \'fin-sən\, Niels Ryberg. 1860–1904. Danish physician. Studied physiological effects of light; developed phototherapy technique for smallpox patients that prevented suppuration and scar formation (1893); discovered therapeutic value of ultraviolet light and developed method of treating skin diseases, esp. lupus vulgaris, by exposure to light. Awarded 1903 Nobel prize for physiology or medicine.

Fio·re \'fyō-rā\, Pasquale. 1837–1914. Italian jurist. Author esp. of treatises on international law.

Fio·rel·li \fyō-'rel-lē\, Giuseppe. 1823–1896. Italian archaeologist. Superintended excavations at Pompeii (1845–49); appointed professor at Naples and resumed directorship of excavations at Pompeii (1860); director general of antiquities and fine arts in museums at Rome (1875–96).

Fio·ril·lo \fyō-'rēl-lō\, Ignazio. 1715–1787. Italian composer. Court conductor in Brunswick (1754–62) and Kassel (1762–80); composed operas, religious music, symphonies, and sonatas. His son ¶Federigo (1755–after 1823), violinist and composer; composed violin concertos and chamber music; known esp. for his 36 études, or caprices, for violin.

Fiorillo, Tiberio. 1608–1694. Italian actor. Creator of the boastful stock character Scaramuccia (Scaramouch) in the commedia dell'arte (c.1640); acted in Paris (1645–47).

Fir·bank \'fər-,baŋk\, Ronald, *in full* Arthur Annesley Ronald. 1886–1926. English writer. Author of comic novels of manners noted for use of dialogue and concise narrative technique, including *Vainglory* (1915), *Inclinations* (1916), *Caprice* (1917), *Valmouth* (1919), *The Flower Beneath the Foot* (1923), *Sorrow in Sunlight* (1924), *Concerning the Eccentricities of Cardinal Pirelli* (1926), etc.

Fir·daw·sī *or* **Fer·dow·sī** \fər-'dau̇-sē\ *or* **Fir·du·si** *or* **Fir·dou·si** \-'dü-sē\. *Orig.* Abū ol-Qāsem Manṣūr. c.935–c.1020 or 1026. Persian poet. Spent about 35 years writing his great epic, *Shāh-nāmeh* (*Book of Kings*); published first edition (1010); its 60,000 rhyming couplets recounted story of Persian kings, legendary and historical, down to Muslim conquest (652), a work highly patriotic and dignified in style, one of the great world epics. Dedicated poem to Maḥmūd of Ghazna; received meager reward; in revenge, wrote bitter satire on Maḥmūd; fled to Herāt, later to Mazanderan and Ṭūs.

Fi·ren·zuo·la \,fē-rānt-'swō-lä\, Agnolo. 1493–1543. Italian writer. Member of Pietro Aretino's literary circle; opposed Giovanni Trissino's spelling reforms in *Discacciamento delle nuove lettere aggiunte* (1524). His works included translations, as Apuleius's *Golden Ass* (1525) and animal fables *La prima veste dei discorsi degli animali* (1548), collection of stories *Ragionamenti di amore* (1523–24), dialogue *I discorsi delle bellezze delle donne* (1540), verse *Liriche* (1549), and comedies *La Trinuzia* and *I Lucidi* (both 1549).

Fire·stone \'fī(ə)r-,stōn\, Harvey Samuel. 1868–1938. American industrialist, b. Columbiana, Ohio. Organized Firestone Tire & Rubber Co. (1900), president (1903–32) and board chairman (1932–38). Pioneered manufacture of nonskid tire treads, low-pressure balloon tires, and other tire innovations; started rubber plantations in Liberia (1924).

Fi·rish·tah \fē-'rish-tä\. *Also known as* Muḥammad Qāsim Hindūshāh. c.1570–c.1620. Muslim Indian historian. Entered service of Ibrāhīm 'Ādil Shāh II, ruler of Bijāpur (1589); wrote history in Persian of Indo-Muslim rulers and saints, known as *Golshan-e Ebrāhīmī* or *Tārīkh-e Fereshteh.*

Fir·mi·cus Ma·ter·nus \'fər-mə-kə-smə-'tər-nəs\, Julius. 4th century A.D. Roman writer. Aristocrat of senatorial rank; converted to Christianity; author of attack upon paganism, *De errore profanarum religionum* (c.346 A.D.), and of *Matheseos libri VIII,* most comprehensive ancient textbook on astrology.

Fī·rūz \fē-'rüz\. d. 484 A.D. King of Persia (457–484), of the Sāsānian dynasty. Son of Yazdegerd II; co-ruler with his brother Hormizd III (457–59); defeated by the Hephthalites; succeeded by his brother Balāsh.

Fī·rū·zā·bā·dī, al- \al-fē-,rü-zä-'bä-dē\. *In full* Abū aṭ-Ṭāhir Majd ad-Dīn al-Fīrūzābādī. 1329–1414. Arab lexicographer. Teacher in Jerusalem (1349–59); traveled in Asia and Egypt; named qāḍī (chief judge) of Yemen (1395). Author of more than 40 works, notably a 60-volume dictionary known esp. in Europe in digest form as *al-Qāmūs.*

Fī·rūz Shāh Tugh·luq \fē-'rüz-'shä-tu̇k-'lüg\. c.1308–1388. Third sultan of Delhi of the Tughluq dynasty (1351–88). Waged wars with Bengal (1353–54, 1360), resulting in Bengal's independence; built several towns, including new capital Fīrūzābād (1354); extended cultivation; failed to check administrative corruption or to reassert control over the Deccan; built Jumna Canal.

Fi·schart \'fish-,ärt\, Johann. *Called* Ment·zer \'ment-sər\. 1546–1590. German jurist and satirist. Advocate to supreme court, Speyer (1580–83); magistrate, Forbach (1583). Author of anti-Catholic polemical writings *Bienenkorb des heiligen römischen Immenschwarms* (1579) and the rhymed *Jesuitenhütlein* (1580); his satires included *Aller Praktik Grossmutter* (1572), *Der Flöhhaz* (1573) against women, *Das glückhafft Schiff von Zürich* (1576), and *Affentheurlich naupengeheurliche Geschichtsklitterung* (1575–90) in imitation of Rabelais's *Gargantua.*

Fischer. See also FISHER.

Fi·scher \'fish-ər\, Emil Hermann. 1852–1919. German chemist. Professor at Würzburg (1885) and Berlin (1892); investigated sugars, purines, proteins, and enzymes; awarded 1902 Nobel prize for chemistry.

Fischer, Hans. 1881–1945. German chemist. Professor at Innsbruck and (from 1921) at Technische Hochschule, Munich. Known for work on the composition of the coloring matter of leaves and of blood; synthesized hemin (1928). Awarded 1930 Nobel prize for chemistry.

Fischer, Johann Michael. 1692–1766. German architect. Most prolific designer of late Baroque and Rococo churches in Bavaria. His churches included St. Anna, Lehel (1727–36), collegiate church, Diessen (1733–39), St. Michael, Berg am Laim (1737–51), Altomünster, Diessen (1763–73), St. Georg, Bogenhausen (1766–68).

Fischer, Kuno, *in full* Ernst Kuno Berthold. 1824–1907. German philosopher. Professor, Jena (1856) and Heidelberg (1872–1906). Founded Neo-Kantian thought with his *System der Logik und Metaphysik* (1852); later subscribed to Hegelian thought. Author of *Geschichte der neueren Philosophie* (1852–93) and studies of Shakespeare, Lessing, Goethe, and Schiller, etc.

Fischer von Er·lach \-fōn-'ər-läk\, Johann Bernhard. 1656–1723. Austrian architect. Inaugurated the Austrian Baroque style; studied in Rome under Bernini. His works included: in Salzburg, the Dreifaltigkeitskirche (1694–1702) and the Kollegienkirche (1696–1707); in Vienna, the Schönbrunn Palace (1696–1711), Winter Palace of Eugene of Savoy (1695–1711), Batthyány Palace (1699–1706); Bohemian Chancellery (1708); Clam-Gallas Palace in Prague (begun 1713). Wrote *Entwurf einer historischen Architektur* (1721), first successful comparative study of architecture. His son and associate ¶Josef Emanuel (1693–1742) completed many of his father's architectural works and plans, esp. Karlskirche (1715–37), imperial stables (1719–23), and imperial library (1723–37), all in Vienna.

Fisch·hof \'fish-ˌ(h)ōf\, Adolf. 1816–1893. Austrian politician. A principal leader in Viennese revolution of 1848; elected president (1848) of Executive Committee of Security; arrested and briefly imprisoned on suppression of revolution (1849); wrote treatises on political theory.

Fish \'fish\, Hamilton. 1808–1893. American politician, b. New York City. Adm. to bar (1830); practiced, New York City. Member, U.S. House of Representatives (1843–45); governor of New York (1849–50); U.S. senator (1851–57). U.S. secretary of state (1869–77); negotiated settlement of "Alabama Claims" with Great Britain (1871) and settlement from Spain for the seizure of ship *Virginius* (1873). His son ¶Hamilton (1849–1936), b. Albany, N.Y., was a lawyer and politician; assistant treasurer of the United States (1903–08); member, U.S. House of Representatives (1909–11). The latter's son ¶Hamilton (1888–1946), b. Garrison, N.Y., politician; member, U.S. House of Representatives (1919–45).

Fish·bein \'fish-ˌbīn\, Morris. 1889–1976. American physician, writer, and editor, b. St. Louis. Assistant editor (1913–24), editor (1924–49), *Journal of the American Medical Association.* Author of *Medical Follies* (1925), *Shattering Health Superstitions* (1930), *Fads and Quackery in Healing* (1933), *Frontiers of Medicine* (1933), *Do You Want to Become a Doctor?* (1939), *Popular Medical Encyclopedia* (1946), *Handy Home Medical Adviser* (1952), etc.

Fisher. See also FISCHER.

Fish·er \'fish-ər\, Andrew. 1862–1928. Australian politician, b. Scotland. To Queensland, Australia (1885); Labourite member of Queensland parliament (1893–96, 1899). Founded Labour newspaper *Gympie Truth.* Member of first Parliament of Commonwealth of Australia (1901–15); minister of trade and customs (1904); prime minister of Australia (1908–09, 1910–13, 1914–15); high commissioner for the Commonwealth of Australia, in London (1916–21).

Fisher, Dorothy, *in full* Dorothea Frances, *nee* Can·field \'kan-ˌfēld\. 1879–1958. American novelist and essayist, b. Lawrence, Kans. m. John Fisher (1907). Author of *The Squirrel-Cage* (1912), *Hillsboro People* (1915), *The Bent Twig* (1915), *Understood Betsy* (1917), *The Day of Glory* (1919), *The Brimming Cup* (1921), *The Deepening Stream* (1930), *Seasoned Timber* (1939), *American Portraits* (1946), *Four Square* (1949), etc.

Fisher, Harry Conway, *known as* Bud. 1885–1954. American cartoonist, b. Chicago. Created (1907) and drew (until death) comic strip "Mutt and Jeff," generally considered first regular comic strip.

Fisher, Herbert Albert Laurens. 1865–1940. English historian. President, Board of Education (1916–22); M.P. (1916–26), instrumental in passage of Fisher Act (1918) reorganizing system of public education in England; warden of New College, Oxford (from 1925). Author of *The Medieval Empire* (1898), *Napoleon Bonaparte* (1913), *The Commonweal* (1924), *History of Europe* (1935), *England and Europe* (1936).

Fisher, Irving. 1867–1947. American economist, b. Saugerties, N.Y. Professor, Yale (1892–1935). Established company (1913) to manufacture his card index file system. Developed concept of relationship between changes in quantity of money and changes in general level of prices; also known as reformer. Author of *The Nature of Capital and Income* (1906), *The Purchasing Power of Money* (1911), *Stabilizing the Dollar* (1920), *The Theory of Interest* (1930), *Booms and Depressions* (1932), *100% Money* (1935), etc.

Fisher, James. See under Ebenezer ERSKINE.

Fisher, John. Saint. *Also known as* John of Rochester. 1469–1535. English prelate and martyr. Professor of divinity (1503), chancellor (1504), president of Queen's Coll. (1505–08), Cambridge; promoted the New Learning. Bishop of Rochester (from 1504). Author of treatises against Luther (1523–25); opponent of church reform (1529); committed to Tower of London (1534) for refusing to recognize validity of Henry's marriage with Anne Boleyn; made cardinal by Pope Paul III (1535); beheaded for refusing to acknowledge the king as supreme head of the church under the Act of Supremacy. Canonized (1935).

Fisher, John Arbuthnot. 1st Baron Fisher of Kil·ver·stone \'kil-vər-stən\. 1841–1920. British admiral. Served at capture of Canton and Pei forts (1859–60); in Egyptian war (1882); a lord of the admiralty (1892–97); commander in chief on North American and West Indies station (1897–99) and Mediterranean station (1899–1902). First sea lord of the admiralty (1904–10, 1914–15); largely responsible for preparing British navy for efficient action in World War I; disapproved Dardanelles enterprise (1915) and resigned in protest against it.

Fisher, Sir Norman Fenwick Warren. 1879–1948. English government official. Permanent secretary to the treasury, and official head of civil service (1919–39). Treasury notes (first issued Oct. 1919) bearing his signature sometimes called *Fishers.*

Fisher, Sir Ronald Aylmer. 1890–1962. English biologist. Professor, University Coll., London (1933–43) and Cambridge (1943–57); contributed to genetics and design of experiments by introducing randomization and statistical procedure known as analysis of variance.

Fisk. See also FISKE.

Fisk \'fisk\, Clinton Bowen. 1828–1890. American army officer and banker, b. Clapp's Corners, N.Y. Served throughout Civil War in Union army; brigadier general (1862); brevetted major general (1865). Founded Fisk U. (chartered 1867). Prohibition candidate for U.S. presidency (1888).

Fisk, James. 1834–1872. American financier, b. Bennington, Vt. Aided by Daniel Drew, founded brokerage house Fisk & Belden, New York (1866); made fortune in stock manipulations that ruined the Erie Railroad; cooperated with Drew and Jay Gould to raise price of gold (1868), reaping a fortune for themselves but causing countrywide depression and loss of millions to others; attempted to corner the gold market (Black Friday, Sept. 24, 1869) and failed when Pres. Grant released government gold.

Fisk, Wilbur. 1792–1839. American clergyman, b. Brattleboro, Vt. Helped change emphasis of New England Methodism from revivalism to intellectual and educational programs; founded and headed Wesleyan Academy, Wilbraham, Mass. (1825–30); first president, Wesleyan U., Middletown, Conn. (1831–39).

Fiske \'fisk\, Bradley Allen. 1854–1942. American naval officer and inventor, b. Lyons, N.Y. Commissioned in navy (1874); rear admiral (1911); retired (1916). Invented system of electric communication for interiors of warships, an electric range finder, an electric ammunition hoist, a naval telescope sight, a system of wireless control of moving vessels, and a torpedoplane.

Fiske, Haley. 1852–1929. American businessman, b. New Brunswick, N.J. Vice president (1891), president (1919–29), Metropolitan Life Insurance Co.; acting on proposal of Lillian D. Wald (*q.v.*), organized (1909) corps of visiting nurses in major industrial centers to provide medical services to families of policyholding workingmen; instrumental in making company largest financial institution in world.

Fiske, John. *Orig.* Edmund Fisk Green. 1842–1901. American philosopher and historian, b. Hartford, Conn. A leading interpreter and supporter of the theory of evolution; applied it to his optimistic theory of inevitable historical progress. Professor, Washington U., St. Louis (from 1884). Author of *Myths and Myth-Makers* (1872), *Outlines of Cosmic Philosophy* (1874), *Darwinism and Other Essays* (1879), *Excursions of an Evolutionist* (1884), *The Critical Period of American History, 1783–1789* (1888), *The Beginnings of New England* (1889), *Civil Government in the United States* (1890), *The American Revolution* (1891), *The Discovery of America* (1892), *A Century of Science and Other Essays* (1899), *Through Nature to God* (1899), *How the United States Became a Nation* (1904), etc.

Fiske, Minnie Maddern, *orig.* Marie Augusta, *nee* Da·vey \'dā-vē\. 1865–1932. American actress, b. New Orleans. Under her husband's management appeared in *Hester Crewe, A Doll's House, Tess of the D'Urbervilles, Frou Frou, Rosmersholm, The Pillars of Society, Ghosts, The School for Scandal,* etc. Did much to popularize Ibsen's plays in America. m. (1890) ¶Harrison Grey Fiske (1861–1942), b. Harrison, N.Y., theatrical manager and director; managed Manhattan Theatre, New York (1901–07); author of plays *Hester Crewe* (1893), *Marie Deloche* (1896), etc.

Fitch \'fich\, Asa. 1809–1879. American entomologist, b. Salem, N.Y. State entomologist of New York (1854–71); published valuable annual reports on effects of insects on agriculture.

Fitch, Clyde, *in full* William Clyde. 1865–1909. American playwright, b. Elmira, N.Y. Wrote large number of plays, excelling in society drama, as *Beau Brummel* (1890), *The Moth and the Flame* (1898), *The Climbers* (1901),

Captain Jinks of the Horse Marines (1901), *The Girl with the Green Eyes* (1902), *The Woman in the Case* (1905), *The Truth* (1907), *The City* (1909).

Fitch, Ebenezer. 1756–1833. American clergyman and educator, b. Norwich, Conn. First president of Williams Coll. (1793–1815).

Fitch, John. 1743–1798. American inventor, b. Windsor, Conn. Served in American Revolution; surveyed land along Ohio River. Became interested in invention of steamboat (1785); obtained from New Jersey (1786) and Pennsylvania, New York, Delaware, and Virginia (1787) exclusive privileges for fourteen years of building and operating steamboats on their waters. Successfully launched his first vessel (Aug. 22, 1787) on Delaware River, a second and larger vessel (1788), and a third and still larger one (in 1790); received U.S. patent (1791). Wrecking of fourth boat by a storm (1792) discouraged financial backers; unable to interest French government in steam navigation (1793).

Fitch, Ralph. c.1550–1611. English merchant and traveler. One of first Englishmen to travel in India and Southeast Asia; sailed to Syria (1583), traveling then to Baghdad and Hormuz; visited court of Akbar near Āgra, India (1584); traveled throughout northern India, then sailed for Burma (1586–87) and Malay Peninsula (1588); returned to London (1591).

Fi·tel·berg \ˈfē-tel-ˌberk\, Grzegorz. 1879–1953. Polish conductor and composer. Champion of a modern national Polish music. Director of Diaghilev's Russian ballet in western Europe (1921–24); conductor of Polish Radio Symphony Orch. (1934–39, 1947–53). Composer of two symphonies, symphonic poems, Polish rhapsodies, songs, and chamber music.

Fit·tig \ˈfit-ik\, Rudolf. 1835–1910. German chemist. Professor, Tübingen (1870), Strasbourg (1876–1902). Discovered phenanthrene in coal tar; effected the synthesis of important aromatic hydrocarbons; introduced the Wurtz-Fittig reaction to prepare toluene from bromobenzene, methyl iodide, and sodium (1864).

Fit·ton \ˈfit-ᵊn\, Mary. 1578–c.1647. English courtier. Maid of honor at court of Queen Elizabeth. Mistress of William Herbert, Earl of Pembroke. Identified by some Shakespearean commentators with the "dark lady" of the sonnets.

Fitz \ˈfits\, Reginald Heber. 1843–1913. American pathologist, b. Chelsea, Mass. Professor, Harvard (from 1878). In his paper *Perforating Inflammation of the Vermiform Appendix* (1886), he named the disease now called appendicitis and proposed surgery for its cure; contributed greatly to scientific pathology in U.S.

Fitz·al·an \fits-ˈal-ən\. Name of Scottish family having common ancestry with Stewart family (*q.v.*), and holding (1267–1580) the earldom of Arundel; members included: Richard Fitzalan (1267–1302), 1st earl; fought for Edward I against Welsh and Scots and in Gascony. His son ¶Edmund (1285–1326), 2d earl; faithful to Edward II; captured and executed by Queen Isabella and Mortimer. His son ¶Richard (1307–1376), 3d earl, and Earl Wa·renne \wä-ˈren\ (or Earl of Surrey); father of Thomas Arundel (*q.v.*); fought at Crécy, siege of Calais, and naval battle off Winchelsea; regent of England (1355). His son ¶Richard (1346–1397), 4th earl, and Earl of Surrey; won naval victory against French and Spanish off Margate (1387); active in Gloucester faction opposing Richard II; imprisoned and beheaded. His son ¶Thomas (1381–1415), 5th earl; restored to title and estates by Henry IV; one of leaders of expedition to help Burgundy (1411); lord treasurer under Henry V. His kinsman ¶John Fitzalan, Lord Mal·trav·ers \mal-ˈtrav-ərz\ (1385–1421), 6th earl; succeeded by his son ¶John (1408–1435), 7th earl, who served Henry VI with distinction in the field. ¶Henry Fitzalan (1511?–1580), 12th earl; opposed passing over of Mary and Elizabeth in royal succession in favor of Lady Jane Grey; under Mary held high appointments; leader of Catholic nobility, twice imprisoned under suspicions of implication in Catholic plots under Elizabeth. On his death title passed through his daughter Mary, wife of Thomas Howard, 4th Duke of Norfolk, into the Howard family (*q.v.*).

Fitzboodle, George Savage. See William Makepeace THACKERAY.

Fitz·ger·ald \fits-ˈjer-əld\. Name of an ancient Irish house descending from Gerald (d. c.1136), steward of Pembroke Castle; m. (c.1095) Nesta, sister of prince of South Wales; maternal grandfather of Gerald de Barri. Members of the family include:

¶Maurice Fitzgerald (d. 1176), 3d son of Gerald and Nesta; invited to Ireland by King Dermot (1169); led English contingent of Dermot's attack on Dublin; founded fortunes of Geraldine family in Ireland with grants of land in Kildare. His son ¶Gerald (d. 1204), Baron of Of·fa·ly \ˈäf-ə-lē, ˈȯf-\; received property from Strongbow in Kildare; built Maynooth. His son ¶Maurice (1194?–1257), 2d baron; justiciar (i.e. viceroy) of Ireland (1232–45); defeated his earl marshal, Earl of Pembroke (1234); fought Irish and Welsh; was ancestor of both earls of Kildare and earls of Desmond.

EARLS OF KIL·DARE \kil-ˈde(ə)r, -ˈda(ə)r\: ¶John Fitz·thom·as \fits-ˈtäm-əs\ (d. 1316), 1st Earl of Kildare and 6th Baron of Offaly: grandson of 2d Baron of Offaly; fought Irish to retain his territories; captured Richard de Burgh, Earl of Ulster (1294), to whose daughter Joan he married his son Thomas; served Edward I in Scotland. ¶Thomas Fitzgerald (d. 1328), 2d earl, son of 1st earl; justiciar of Ireland (1320, 1327); led large army against Edward Bruce (1316). His son ¶Maurice (1318–1390), 4th earl, known as Maurice Fitzthomas, justiciar (1356–57, 1361, 1371, 1376), was great-grandfather of ¶Thomas Fitzgerald (1427–1477), 7th earl, repeatedly in charge of government of Ireland as deputy for dukes of York and Clarence, lord chancellor (1463). ¶Gerald Fitzgerald (d. 1513), 8th earl, called "More \ˈmō(ə)r, ˈmȯ(ə)r\ the Great," son of 7th earl. His son ¶Gerald (1487–1534), 9th earl, and his grandson ¶Thomas (1513–1537), 10th earl, known as "Silken Thomas," were deputy governors of Ireland, fighting the Irish and their hereditary rival, Ormonde, until open revolt against the government (1534) brought death to the survivors, attainder (repealed 1569) and ruin to family. ¶Lady Elizabeth Fitzgerald (1528?–1589), daughter of 9th earl, was the "Fair Geraldine" to whom Henry Howard, Earl of Surrey, addressed famous sonnets published in *Tottel's Miscellany* (1557) and whom Michael Drayton and Sir Walter Scott celebrated in verse.

¶James Fitzgerald (1722–1773), 1st Duke of Lein·ster \ˈlen(t)-stər\, succeeded (1744) as 20th Earl of Kildare, was lord deputy of Ireland (1756). His son ¶Lord Edward Fitzgerald (1763–1798) served in American Revolution, wounded at battle of Eutaw Springs (1781); M.P. in Irish parliament; cashiered for attending revolutionary banquet in Paris, where he repudiated his own title (1792); joined United Irishmen (1796), who were committed to establishment of independent Irish republic; accompanied Arthur O'Connor to the Continent to negotiate for French invasion; seized with other conspirators (1798) and died in prison.

EARLS OF DES·MOND \ˈdez-mənd\: ¶Maurice Fitzthomas *or* Fitzgerald (d. 1356), 1st Earl of Desmond (cr. 1329); great-great-grandson of a younger son of Maurice Fitzgerald (d. 1176); inherited vast estates in Munster; received grant of palatine county of Kerry (1329); took lead of Anglo-Irish party against the English policy of viceroys (1341–46); eventually gained favor of English and ruled as viceroy (1355–56). ¶Thomas (d. 1477), 8th earl; lord deputy of Ireland (1463–67); executed at Drogheda on charge of alliance with Irish. ¶James Fitzgerald (d. 1558), *called* Fitz·john \fits-ˈjän\, 13th earl, played prudent part by submitting to Lord Deputy St. Leger; received by Henry VIII (1542); made lord treasurer of Ireland by Edward VI, continued by Mary; kept Munster quiet and in order. His son ¶Gerald Fitzgerald (c.1538–1583), 14th earl, allied himself with 11th Earl of Kildare in opposition to Thomas Butler, 10th Earl of Ormonde; summoned to London and confined for misdeeds of his clans (1562–64); taken prisoner in open war and imprisoned in Tower (1568–73); after return to Ireland (1573) carried on war in Munster; joined (1579) invading force of his cousin James Fitzgerald; driven into woods by successes of Ormonde and Pelham; finally seized and murdered at Glanaginty in Kerry mountains. His cousin ¶James Fitzgerald (d. 1579), *called* Fitz·mau·rice \fits-ˈmär-əs, -ˈmȯr-\; with aid of Butler family led uprising (1569) against English rule in Munster after arrest (1568) of 14th Earl of Desmond; gave up and accepted pardon (1573); encouraged by Pope Gregory XIII and Philip II of Spain, led small invading force of Spaniards and Italians into Munster against English (1579); soon betrayed and killed but rebellion continued until 1583.

Fitzgerald, Barry. *Orig.* William Joseph Shields \ˈshē(ə)l(d)z\. 1888–1961. Irish actor. With Abbey Theatre Company (from 1915); created part of the "Paycock" in O'Casey's *Juno and the Paycock;* appeared in motion pictures *The Plough and the Stars* (1937), *How Green Was My Valley* (1941), *Going My Way* (1944, Academy Award), *The Quiet Man* (1952), etc.

FitzGerald, Edward. 1809–1883. English poet and translator. Son of John Purcell who assumed wife's maiden name FitzGerald (1818). Best known for his translation in quatrains of the *Rubáiyát of Omar Khayyám* (pub. 1859). Author also of English versions of the *Agamemnon,* two plays of Sophocles, and six dramas of Calderon, and of *Euphranor: a Dialogue on Youth* (1851), and *Polonius: a Collection of Wise Saws and Modern Instances* (1852); known also as a letter writer.

Fitzgerald, Francis Scott Key. 1896–1940. American writer, b. St. Paul, Minn. Officer in World War I; scriptwriter in Hollywood (from 1937). Famed as chronicler of the Jazz Age. Author of novels *This Side of Paradise* (1920), *The Beautiful and Damned* (1922), *The Great Gatsby* (1925), *Tender Is the Night* (1934), *The Last Tycoon* (unfinished, pub. 1941); his short stories published in *Flappers and Philosophers* (1920), *Tales of the Jazz Age* (1922), *All the Sad Young Men (1926), Taps at Reveille* (1935), etc.

FitzGerald, George Francis. 1851–1901. Irish physicist. Professor, Dublin (1881–1901); conducted research in electric waves and electrolysis; developed electromagnetic theory of radiation. Formulated, following the Michelson-

Morley experiment, theory of the change of shape of a body (known as the Lorentz-FitzGerald contraction) due to its motion through the ether.

Fitz·gib·bon \fits-'gib-ən\, John. 1st Earl of Clare \'kla(ə)r, 'kle(ə)r\. 1749–1802. Irish jurist and political administrator. Attorney general (1783); opposed attempts to remove disabilities of Roman Catholics; began policy of repression with stringent measures against Whiteboy raids (1787); lord chancellor of Ireland (1789–1802); kept Irish legislature in subjection to English executive; urged passage of Act of Union (1800), only to find after passage that Pitt and Castlereagh had promised Catholics that union would prepare way for emancipation; thereafter opposed more violently further concessions in Ireland.

Fitz-Gilbert, Richard. See de CLARE family.

Fitz·her·bert \fits-'hər-bə(r)t\, Maria Anne, *nee* Smythe \'smīth, 'smīth\. *Called* Mrs. Fitzherbert. 1756–1837. Wife of King George IV of England. m. 1st, Edward Weld (1775; d. 1775); 2d, Thomas Fitzherbert (1778; d. 1781); 3d, George, Prince of Wales (1785). Marriage to George was illegal under the Royal Marriage Act (1772) and the Act of Settlement, since George was under age at the time and Mrs. Fitzherbert was a Roman Catholic; relations broken at George's marriage (1795) to Caroline of Brunswick, later resumed (to 1803).

Fitz·hugh \fits-'(h)yü\, George. 1806–1881. American lawyer, journalist, and author, b. Prince William Co., Va. Major propagandist of slavery as a beneficent institution and of southern plantation as model for national government. Wrote *Sociology for the South* (1854) and *Cannibals All!* (1857).

Fitz·james \fits-'jāmz\, James. Duke of Ber·wick \'ber-ik\. 1670–1734. English soldier. Illegitimate son of James, Duke of York (later James II); created duke (1687); commanded army of father's supporters in Ireland (1689–91); commissioned lieutenant general by Louis XIV of France (1693); served in Spain (1703–04), against Camisards in Languedoc (1706); captured Nice from Eugene of Savoy (1706); marshal of France (1706). Captured Madrid and defeated English at Almanza (1707), establishing Philip V on Spanish throne; made duc de Fitz-James (1710). Stormed Barcelona for Philip (1714). Commanded invasion of Spain (1719) against Philip. Killed at siege at Philippsburg in War of Polish Succession.

Fitz·neale \fits-'nēl\ *or* **Fitz·ni·gel** \'-nī-jəl\, Richard. *Also known as* Richard of Ely \'ē-lē\. c.1130–1198. English cleric and official. Treasurer of England (c.1169–98); dean of Lincoln (1184) and bishop of London (1189). Wrote *Dialogus de scaccario,* account of procedures used in Exchequer.

Fitz·os·bern \fits-'äz-(ˌ)bərn\, William. Earl of Her·e·ford \'her-ə-fərd\. d. 1071. Anglo-Norman nobleman. Urged William of Normandy to conquest of England and commanded Norman right at battle of Hastings (1066); joint viceroy of England during Williams's absence (1067); as earl of Hereford, defended border against Welsh attacks.

Fitz·pat·rick \fit-'spa-trik\, Thomas. 1799?–1854. American frontiersman, b. County Cavan, Ireland. To U.S. (c.1816); fur trader, trapper, and scout (from 1823); an organizer of Rocky Mountain Fur Co. (1830); guide for first emigrant train bound for Pacific through northwestern Montana (1841); guide for Frémont's second expedition (1843–44) and for Kearny's expeditions (1845 and 1846); Indian agent (1846–50, 1851–54).

Fitz·pe·ter \fit-'spēt-ər\, Geoffrey. Earl of Es·sex \'es-iks\. d. 1213. English politician. During Richard I's absence, one of five justices standing next in authority to Longchamp, the regent; succeeded to earldom of Essex through marriage (1190); aided baronial expulsion of Longchamp; chief justiciar (1198–1213); maintained bureaucracy of Henry I and II.

FitzRichard, Gilbert. See de CLARE family.

Fitz·roy \fits-'rȯi\. Name of descendants of Charles II by Barbara Villiers (*q.v.*), among whom were included dukes of Graf·ton \'graf-tən\:

Henry (1663–1690), 1st Duke of Grafton; 2d son of Charles II by Barbara Villiers; commanded royal troops in Monmouth rebellion; went over to William of Orange; distinguished himself in battle of Beachy Head (1690); mortally wounded at siege of Cork under Marlborough. His grandson ¶Augustus Henry (1735–1811), 3d duke; politician; secretary of state for northern department in Rockingham's first ministry (1765–66); first lord of treasury in Pitt ministry (1766); prime minister (1768–70); opposed American tea duty; resigned under attacks of Junius; privy seal under Lord North (1771–75) and in new Rockingham cabinet (1782–83); favored conciliation of American colonists.

His grandson ¶Robert (1805–1865), naval commander and meteorologist; in command of the *Beagle,* surveyed coasts of Patagonia and Strait of Magellan and circumnavigated globe (1828–36); accompanied by Darwin as naturalist (1831–36); collaborated with Darwin in writing *Narrative of the Surveying Voyages of H.M. Ships Adventure and Beagle* (1839). Governor of New Zealand (1843–45); chief of meteorological department (1854), where he inaugurated a system of storm warnings, the first weather forecasts; invented Fitzroy barometer; published *The Weather Book* (1863).

Fitz·sim·mons \fit(s)-'sim-ənz\, Robert Prometheus, *also called* Bob *or* Ruby Robert. 1862–1917. American pugilist, b. Helston, England. Reared in New Zealand; to U.S. (1890); won world's middleweight championship from Nonpareil Jack Dempsey at New Orleans (Jan. 14, 1891), world's heavyweight championship from James J. Corbett at Carson City, Nev. (Mar. 17, 1897); lost championship to James J. Jeffries at Coney Island (June 9, 1899); won world's light-heavyweight championship from George Gardner at San Francisco (Nov. 25, 1903), lost it to Philadelphia Jack O'Brien at San Francisco (Dec. 20, 1905), retired (1914).

Fitz·ste·phen \fit(s)-'stē-vən\, William. d. c.1190. English cleric. In service of Thomas Becket; wrote first and most valuable biography of Becket.

Fitz·thed·mar \fits-'thed-mər, -ˌmär\, Arnold. 1201–c.1275. English merchant and chronicler. Alderman; custodian of muniments of London (from 1270); compiled chronicle of mayors and sheriffs of London of 1188–1274, chief source on London institutions and politics of that period.

Fitzthomas, John and Maurice. See FITZGERALD family.

Fitz·wal·ter \fit-'swȯl-tər\, Robert. d. 1235. English nobleman. Leader of the barons in their opposition to King John; commanded army which forced John to grant the Magna Carta (1215); went on crusade under King Andrew of Hungary and took part in the siege of Damietta (1219–20).

Fitz·wil·liam \fit-'swil-yəm\, Sir William. 1526–1599. English administrator. Lord deputy of Ireland (1572–75, 1588–94); suppressed several rebellions; took measures to protect Ireland against Spanish Armada (1588); governor of Fotheringhay Castle (1575–88) when Mary Stuart executed there.

Fitzwilliam, William Wentworth. 2d Earl Fitzwilliam. 1748–1833. English politician. Descendant of Sir William Fitzwilliam and nephew of Charles Watson-Wentworth. Associated with Pitt in Old Whig group; president of the council (1794); lord lieutenant of Ireland (1795) but recalled in three months because of expression of sympathy for Catholic emancipation; president of the council in Grenville's administration (1806–07).

Five Dynasties. Name given to five brief dynasties of China (907–960 A.D.) between the T'ang and the Sung dynasties: the Later Liang (907–923), the Later T'ang (923–936), the Later Chin (936–947), the Later Han (947–954), and the Later Chou (954–960).

Fi·zeau \fē-zō\, Armand-Hippolyte-Louis. 1819–1896. French physicist. Made improvements in the daguerreotype; worked with Foucault on heat and light; made determination of the velocity of light (1849); gave correct explanation of Doppler's principle; conducted experiments to detect ether drift.

Flaccus, Gaius Valerius. See VALERIUS FLACCUS.

Flac·cus \'flak-əs\, Lucius Valerius. d. 86 B.C.? Roman politician. Consul (100); censor (96); designated consul after Marius's death (86); opposed Sulla; helped win war against Mithradates VI; murdered by his lieutenant Flavius Fimbria.

Flaccus, Marcus Verrius. See VERRIUS FLACCUS.

Flaccus, Quintus Fulvius. 3d century B.C. Roman politician. Consul (237 B.C.); censor (231); again consul (224); pontifex maximus (216); praetor (215); again consul (212 and 209); defeated Hanno near Beneventum (212) and successfully besieged Capua. His grandnephew ¶Marcus (2d century B.C.), consul (125 B.C.), was supporter of the Gracchi; proposed conferring Roman citizenship on the allies.

Flach \flåsh\, Jacques-Geoffroi. 1846–1919. French jurist and historian. Professor at Collège de France (1879). Author of *Les Origines de l'ancienne France* (1886–1917), etc.

Flachs·bin·der \'fläks-bin-dər\, Jan. *Called* Jan Dan·ty·szek \'dän-tə-shek\. *Lat.* Johannes Dan·tis·cus \dan-'tis-kəs\. 1485–1548. Polish courtier and Humanist, b. Danzig. Attached to court of Sigismund I; bishop of Chetmno (1530); prince bishop of Warmiński (1537). Author, in Latin, of incidental verse, love poems, panegyrics; among first to bring Humanist values to Poland.

Flacius Illyricus, Matthias. See Matija VLAČIC.

Fla·court \flå-kür\, Étienne Bi·zet de \bē-ze-də-\. 1607–1660. French colonizer. Governor of Madagascar (1648–55); author of *Histoire de la grande isle de Madagascar* (1658).

Fla·get \flå-zhe\, Benedict-Joseph. 1763–1850. French clergyman. Entered Sulpician Society (1783); helped establish first Catholic seminary in U.S., at Baltimore (1792); bishop of Bardstown, Ky. (1810–48); founded schools and seminaries.

Flagg \'flag\, Ernest. 1857–1947. American architect, b. Brooklyn, N.Y. Designer of St. Luke's Hospital and Singer building in New York, buildings of U.S.N.A., Annapolis, Md., Corcoran Gallery in Washington, D.C.

Flagg, James Montgomery. 1877–1960. American painter and illustrator, b. Pelham Manor, N.Y. Regular contributor to popular periodicals (from 1892); known for illustrations of buxom girls and esp. for World War I recruiting poster of a pointing Uncle Sam, modeled on himself, with "I Want You" caption. Also known for portraits and book collections of his illustrations.

Flag·ler \'flag-lər\, Henry Morrison. 1830–1913. American financier, b. Hopewell, N.Y. Associated with John D. Rockefeller in development of Standard Oil Co. (from 1867). Organized Florida East Coast Railway (1886); extended line to Miami and built great hotels at shore resorts (1892–96);

extended line to Key West (opened 1913); dredged Miami harbor; established steamship lines to Key West and Nassau.

Flag·stad \'fläg-stä, *Angl* 'flag-ˌstad\, Kirsten Malfrid. 1895–1962. Norwegian operatic soprano. Operatic debut in Oslo (1913); U.S. debut in New York as Sieglinde in *Die Walküre* (1935); best known for interpretation of Wagnerian roles; retired (1953); first director of Royal Norwegian Opera (1958–60).

Fla·haut de la Bil·lar·de·rie \flä-ō-də-lä-bē-yär-drē\, Auguste-Charles-Joseph de. Comte. 1785–1870. French general and diplomat. Almost certainly Talleyrand's son; general of division (1814) under Napoléon; engaged at Leipzig, Hanau, and Waterloo; ambassador to Berlin (1831), Vienna (1841–48), and London (1860–62); successively lover of Napoléon's sister Caroline, the Countess Potocka, and Hortense, queen of Holland.

Fla·her·ty \'flä(-ə)rt-ē, 'fla(-ə)rt-ē\, Robert Joseph. 1884–1951. American explorer, motion picture director, and writer, b. Iron Mountain, Mich. Reared in Canada; explored subarctic eastern Canada (1910–16). Directed motion pictures *Nanook of the North* (1922), *Moana* (1926), *Tabu* (1931), *Man of Aran* (1934), *Elephant Boy* (1937), *The Land* (1941), *Louisiana Story* (1948). Author of novels, and *A Film-Maker's Odyssey* (1939). Considered father of the documentary film.

Flamand, François. See François DUQUESNOY.

Flam·bard \'flam-ˌbärd, -bərd\, Ranulf. d. 1128. Norman ecclesiastic in England. Keeper of the seal for William the Conqueror (c.1083); chief minister of King William II; bishop of Durham (1099); imprisoned by Henry I (1100–01); restored (1101).

Flam·i·ni·nus \ˌflam-ə-'nī-nəs\, Titus Quinctius. c.227–174 B.C. Roman general and statesman. Quaestor (199); consul (198); conducted campaign in Macedonia against Philip V, culminating in victory at Cynoscephalae (197); at Isthmian games in Corinth proclaimed independence of Greek states (196); persuaded Achaean League to declare war on Aetolians and Antiochus III; censor (189). His brother ¶Lucius Quinctius (d. 170 B.C.) commanded Roman fleet during war with Philip V of Macedonia (197); consul (192); proconsul in Gaul (191).

Fla·min·i·us \flə-'min-ē-əs\, Gaius. d. 217 B.C. Roman general and politician. Of plebeian family; tribune of the plebs (232 B.C.); first praetor of Sicily (227); consul (223); censor (220); again consul (217). Pacified the Insubrians (223). While censor built the Circus Flaminius and the Via Flaminia from Rome to Ariminum (Rimini). Defeated by Hannibal and killed at Lago di Trasimeno.

Flam·ma·rion \flä-mär-yōⁿ\, Camille, *in full* Nicolas-Camille. 1842–1925. French astronomer. Studied the moon, Mars, and double stars; founded the French Astronomical Society (1887); popularized study of astronomy in his writings. Author of *Astronomie populaire* (1880), *Le Monde avant la création de l'homme* (1885), *Les Phénomènes de la foudre* (1905), etc.

Flam·steed \'flam-ˌstēd\, John. 1646–1719. English clergyman and astronomer. First astronomer royal (1675); ascertained absolute right ascensions through simultaneous observations of the sun and a star near both equinoxes; furnished data to Sir Isaac Newton; his observations (made 1676–89) of some 3000 stars published as *Historia Coelestis Britannica* (1725).

Flan·a·gan \'flan-i-gən\, Edward Joseph. 1886–1948. American clergyman, b. Roscommon, Ireland. To U.S. (1904; naturalized 1919); ordained Roman Catholic priest (1912). Founded Father Flanagan's Home for Boys, in Omaha (1917); moved (1918) to larger quarters west of Omaha, the farm becoming (1922) an incorporated village known as Boys Town.

Flanders, Henry of. See HENRY, emperor of Constantinople.

Flan·din \fläⁿ-daⁿ\, Gaston-Pierre-Étienne. 1889–1958. French politician. Minister of commerce (1924, 1929–30), of finance (1931–32), of public works (1934); premier of France (Nov. 1934–June 1935); minister without portfolio in Laval's cabinet (1935–36); minister of foreign affairs (1936; 1940–41 in Vichy regime); resisted German demands beyond an armistice. Wrote *Paix et liberté* (1937), *Politique française, 1919–1940* (1947), etc.

Flan·drin \fläⁿ-draⁿ\. Family of French painters, including: René-Auguste (1801–1842), historical painter, as *Prédication de Savonarole.* His brother ¶Hippolyte-Jean (1809–1864), known for portraits, church murals and windows, historical scenes. Another brother ¶Jean-Paul (1811–1902), landscape painter. Hippolyte's son ¶Paul-Hippolyte (1856–1921), painter esp. of religious scenes.

Flan·na·gan \'flan-i-gən\, John Bernard. 1895–1942. American sculptor, b. Fargo, N.D. Trained as painter; encouraged by Arthur B. Davies to take up wood carving (c.1922). Known for small, primitivistic sculptures in fieldstone of animals, birds, fish, and birth themes, as *Dragon Motif* (1933), *Jonah and the Whale* (1937), *Triumph of the Egg* (1937 and 1941).

Flan·ner \'flan-ər\, Janet. *Pseudonym* Ge·nêt \zhe-ne, *Angl* zhə-'nā\. 1892–1978. American journalist, b. Indianapolis. Resident in Paris (from 1922); known for her biweekly "Letter from Paris" in *New Yorker* magazine (1925–75) containing comments on French society and politics; her pieces collected as *An American in Paris* (1940), *Paris Journal, 1944–1965* (1965), etc.

Flat·man \'flat-mən\, Thomas. 1637–1688. English poet and miniature painter. Published devotional verse, pindarics, in *Poems and Songs* (1674).

Flau·bert \flō-ber\, Gustave. 1821–1880. French novelist. Pioneer and master of Realist school of French literature. Studied law but abandoned that to devote himself to writing. His first novel, *Madame Bovary* (1857), brought legal prosecution on the ground of immorality but he was acquitted. Among his works, all characterized by objectivity and distinction of style, were *Salammbô* (1862), *L'Éducation sentimentale* (1869), *La Tentation de Saint Antoine* (1874), *Le Candidat* (play, 1874), *Trois contes* (1877), *Bouvard et Pécuchet* (unfinished, pub. 1881).

Fla·vi·an \'flā-vē-ən\. Saint. d. 449. Patriarch of Constantinople (446–449). Condemned Eutychian heresy at Synod of Constantinople (448); deposed and excommunicated by the Council of Ephesus, or "Robber Synod" (449); beaten to death by theological opponents; canonized as martyr by Council of Chalcedon (451).

Flavian. Name of two bishops of Antioch:

Flavian I. c.320–404. Bishop (381–404). His appointment, since it was not recognized by the bishop of Rome and the bishops of Egypt, continued the Meletian Schism in the orthodox church at Antioch.

Flavian II. d. c.518. Bishop (c.498–512). Accepted decree of union issued (482) by Emperor Zeno; anathematized by patriarch of Constantinople; deposed by Emperor Anastasius.

Flavio Biondo. See BIONDO.

Flavius. Name borne by members of the Roman Flavian gens. The Flavian emperors were Vespasian and his sons Titus and Domitian.

Fla·vi·us \'flā-vē-əs\, Gnaeus. 4th century B.C. Roman legal writer and politician. Secretary to Appius Claudius Caecus; published (c.304 B.C.) *Jus Flavianum,* containing technical rules of legal procedure theretofore kept secret by patricians and pontifices to maintain advantage over plebeians; made curule aedile (304).

Flax·man \'flak-smən\, John. 1755–1826. English sculptor and draftsman. Leading Neoclassical artist in England; designer for Josiah Wedgwood (from 1775); directed Wedgwood studio in Rome and also executed independent commissions there (1787–94). Executed drawings for the *Iliad* and the *Odyssey,* Dante's *Divina commedia,* and tragedies of Aeschylus. First professor of sculpture at Royal Academy of Art (1810); his sculptures included many monuments, as of Earl of Mansfield in Westminster Abbey (1793–1801), of Agnes Cromwell in Chichester cathedral (1800), of Nelson in St. Paul's (1808–18), and statues of Burns and Kemble in Westminster Abbey; also made designs for silversmiths, as *The Shield of Achilles* (1818).

Fleay \'flā\, Frederick Gard. 1831–1909. English scholar. Author of *A Chronicle History of the Life and Work of William Shakespeare* (1886), *A Chronicle History of the London Stage 1559–1642* (1890), *A Biographical Chronicle of the English Drama 1559–1642* (1891).

Fleck·er \'flek-ər\, James Elroy, *orig.* Herman Elroy. 1884–1915. English poet and playwright. In British consular service (1908–15). Author of poetic works *The Bridge of Fire* (1907), *Forty-two Poems* (1911), *The Golden Journey to Samarkand* (1913), and *The Old Ships* (1915); plays *Hassan* (1922) and *Don Juan* (1925).

Fleck·noe \'flek-(ˌ)nō\, Richard. c.1600–c.1678. Irish poet. Possibly a Jesuit; traveled (1640–50) in the Levant, Portugal, Brazil. Published *Relation of Ten Year's Travel* (1654?); author of plays as *Love's Dominion* (1654), poetry as in *Epigrams of all sorts* (1670), and prose sketches *Enigmatical characters* (1658). Lampooned by Marvell in *Fleckno* and by Dryden in *MacFlecknoe.*

Fleet·wood \'flēt-ˌwu̇d\, Charles. d. 1692. English Parliamentarian general. Commanded regiment of horse at Naseby (1645); lieutenant general of horse at Dunbar (1650); commander of English forces before Worcester (1651); m. (1652) Bridget Ireton, eldest daughter of Oliver Cromwell and widow of Henry Ireton; lord deputy and commander in chief in Ireland (1652–55). Helped depose (1659) Richard Cromwell; headed army opposition to Parliament; became commander in chief of army (1659) but soon replaced by Gen. Monck. At Restoration, incapacitated for life from holding public office.

Fleetwood, William. 1656–1723. English prelate. Bishop of St. Asaph (1708–14), of Ely (1714–23). Celebrated preacher; zealous Whig; criticized Tories in *Four Sermons* (1712); his *Chronicon preciosum* (1707) was pioneer work in economic history.

Fle·gel \'flā-gəl\, Edward Robert. 1855–1886. German explorer. Ascended and surveyed Niger and Benue rivers (1879–80); first European to reach the Benue's source (1884); visited present Nigeria several times (1880 ff.), explored Sokoto in northwest and reached Yola and Ngaundéré in east. Author of *Vom Niger-Benue* (1890) and of accounts of his travels.

Fle·gen·hei·mer \'flā-gən-,hī-mər\, Arthur. *Known as* Dutch Schultz \'dəch-'shu̇lts\. 1902–1935. American gangster, b. Bronx, N.Y. Head of crime syndicate in New York and Newark, specializing in bootlegging, extortion, and "numbers" racket (from c.1928); assassinated by a rival gang.

Flei·scher \'flī-shər\, Nathaniel S. 1887–1972. American journalist, b. New York City. Founder (1922) and editor of boxing magazine *The Ring;* frequent judge at championship fights; author of over 50 books on boxing and wrestling.

Fleischer, Oskar. 1856–1933. German musicologist. Professor, Berlin U. (1895–1925); founder and president, Internationale Musikgesellschaft (1899) and coeditor of its publications (until 1904).

Flé·mal *or* **Fle·mael** *or* **Flé·malle** \flā-mȧl\, Bertholet. 1614–1675. Flemish painter. Representative of later Flemish school and pioneer of classicist movement; painted chiefly religious pictures and portraits.

Flémalle, Master of. See Robert CAMPIN.

Flem·ing \'flem-iŋ\, Sir Alexander. 1881–1955. Scottish bacteriologist. Professor, London U. (1928–48); discovered lysozyme (1921); shared with Howard Florey and Ernst B. Chain 1945 Nobel prize for physiology or medicine, for discovery (1928) and development of penicillin.

Fleming, Sir Arthur Percy Morris. 1881–1960. English engineer. Director of research and education, Metropolitan-Vickers Co., Manchester (1931–54); pioneer in development of radio and radar.

Fleming, Ian Lancaster. 1908–1964. English novelist. Author of popular novels of espionage centered around character of British secret service agent James Bond, including *Casino Royale* (1953), *From Russia, with Love* (1957), *Dr. No* (1958), *Goldfinger* (1959), *Thunderball* (1961).

Fleming, Sir John Ambrose. 1849–1945. English electrical engineer. Professor, University College, London (1885–1926); known for many applications of electricity; contributed to development of telephony, electric lighting, and wireless telegraphy; invented the two-electrode radio rectifier (pat. 1904). Author of *The Principles of Electric Wave Telegraphy and Telephony* (1906), *Fifty Years of Electricity* (1921), etc.

Fle·ming \'flā-miŋ\, Paul. 1609–1640. German poet. Disciple of Martin Opitz; with trade mission to Russia and Persia (1633–39). First German to effectively use sonnet form; his love lyrics and religious hymns published in *Teutsche Poemata* (1642) and *Geist- und weltliche Poemata* (1651).

Flem·ing *or* **Flem·ming** *or* **Flem·mynge** \'flem-iŋ\, Richard. d. 1431. English prelate. Bishop of Lincoln (1420–31); represented England at councils of Pavia and Siena (1428–29); founder of Lincoln Coll., Oxford (1427). His nephew ¶Robert (d. 1483) was dean of Lincoln (1451), a benefactor of Lincoln Coll., prothonotary to Pope Sixtus IV, and author of Latin poems.

Fleming, Sir Sandford. 1827–1915. Canadian engineer, b. Kirkcaldy, Scotland. To Canada (1845); chief engineer of Inter-Colonial Railway (1867–76) and Canadian Pacific Railway (1872–80). Devised an internationally accepted scheme for standard time (1884) and a telegraph communication system for British Empire.

Fleming, Williamina Paton, *nee* Stevens. 1857–1911. American astronomer, b. Dundee, Scotland. m. James O. Fleming (1877); to U.S. (1878); on staff, Harvard Observatory (1879–98); noted as discoverer of new stars and variables and as investigator of stellar spectra.

Flem·ming \'flem-iŋ\, Walther. 1843–1905. German anatomist. A founder of cytogenetics. Professor at Kiel (1876–1901); pioneer in use of aniline dyes to discern cell structures; discovered chromatins (1879); first to observe and describe systematically behavior of chromosomes during mitosis (1880); coined term mitosis; published results in *Zell-substanz, Kern und Zelltheilung* (1882).

Fletch·er \'flech-ər\, Alice Cunningham. 1838–1923. American ethnologist, b. Havana, Cuba, of American parentage. Lived among Plains Indians, studying their culture; pioneer in study of Indian music; lobbied successfully for passage of Dawes Act (1887). Wrote *Indian Story and Song from North America* (1900), *The Hako* (1904), *The Omaha Tribe* (1911, with Francis LaFlesche).

Fletcher of Sal·toun \'sȯlt-ᵊn\, Andrew. 1655–1716. Scottish politician. Associate of Monmouth in London and Holland; opposed English rule in Scotland and union of Scotland with England.

Fletcher, Giles, *called* the Elder. c.1548–1611. English diplomat and writer. Uncle of John Fletcher. Envoy to Russia (1588–89); author of *Of the Russe Common Wealth* (1591), Latin poems, and a series of sonnets, *Licia, or Poemes of Love* (1593). His son ¶Giles, *called* the Younger (c.1585–1623), poet, disciple of Spenser; rector of Alderton in Suffolk (1619–23); author of devotional poem *Christ's Victorie and Triumph in Heaven and Earth* (1610). His brother ¶Phineas (1582–1650), poet, also disciple of Spenser; rector of Hilgay, Norfolk (1621–50); author of pastoral play *Sicelides* (1631), poem *Brittain's Ida* (1628), eclogues, and *The Purple Island: or the Isle of Man* (1633), an allegory of the human anatomy.

¶Richard (d. 1596), prelate; brother of Giles the Elder; chaplain to Queen Elizabeth (1581); dean of Peterborough (1583); chaplain at execution of Mary, Queen of Scots; bishop of Bristol (1589), Worcester (1593), London (1594). His son was the playwright John Fletcher.

Fletcher, Harvey. 1884–1981. American physicist, b. Provo, Utah. Professor, Brigham Young U. (1911–16, 1952–81), Columbia U. (1949–52); with Western Electric Co. and later Bell Telephone Laboratories (1916–49), head of physical research (1933–49); developed system of stereophonic sound reproduction (demonstrated 1934).

Fletcher, Horace. 1849–1919. American nutritionist, b. Lawrence, Mass. After active and varied business life, turned attention to researches in field of human nutrition (from 1895); attributed his own health to thorough mastication of his food; wrote and lectured widely on nutrition, popularizing his ideas until *fletcherism* and *to fletcherize* became part of American language.

Fletcher, John. 1579–1625. English dramatist. Son of Richard Fletcher (see under Giles FLETCHER). Collaborated with Francis Beaumont (c.1606–13) on ten comedies and tragedies (see Francis BEAUMONT). Collaborated with Philip Massinger on *The Little French Lawyer* (1619–23), *Sir John van Olden Barnavelt* (1619), *The Custome of the Countrey* (1619), *The False One* (1620), *The Double Marriage* (1621), *The Spanish Curat* (1622), *The Sea Voyage* (1622), *The Prophetesse* (1622), *The Lovers Progress* (1623–24), *The Elder Brother* (1625), *A Very Woman* (1625), with Shakespeare on *Henry VIII* (1613) and *The Two Noble Kinsmen* (1613); also collaborated at times with Middleton, Rowley, Ford, Webster, Jonson, Shirley, etc. Sole author of *The Faithfull Shepheardesse* (1608–09), *Valentinian* (1610–14), *Monsieur Thomas* (1610–16), *The Womans Prize* (1611?), *Bonduca* (1611–14), *The Mad Lover* (1616), *The Chances* (1617?), *The Loyall Subject* (1618), *Women pleas'd* (1619?), *The Island Princesse* (1619–21?), *The Humorous Lieutenant* (1619?), *The Wild-Goose Chase* (1621), *The Pilgrim* (1621), *Rule A Wife And have a Wife* (1624), *A Wife for a Moneth* (1624).

Fletcher, John Gould. 1886–1950. American poet and critic, b. Little Rock, Ark. Identified with the Imagist group of poets (from 1914); later associated with Fugitives. His volumes of verse included *Irradiations: Sand and Spray* (1915), *Goblins and Pagodas* (1916), *Breakers and Granite* (1921), *Parables* (1925), *Branches of Adam* (1926), *The Black Rock* (1928), *XXIV Elegies* (1935), *South Star* (1941), *The Burning Mountain* (1946).

Fletcher, Richard. See under Giles FLETCHER.

Fletcher, Robert. 1823–1912. American surgeon and bibliographer, b. Bristol, England. To U.S. (1847); served in medical corps in Civil War. Assistant to John Shaw Billings in library of surgeon general's office (1876); aided Billings in preparing *Index-Catalogue of the Library of the Surgeon General's Office* (1880–95); on Billings's retirement (1895) continued the work.

Flett·ner \'flet-nər\, Anton. 1885–1961. German engineer. Invented the rotor ship (1924), the Flettner trim-tab control for aircraft, the Flettner marine rudder. Established (1926) in Berlin aircraft company that produced helicopters much used in World War II; to U.S. after war and became president of Flettner Aircraft Co., Queens, N.Y.

Fleury. See Abraham-Joseph BÉNARD.

Fleu·ry \flœ-rē, flœ-\, André-Hercule de. 1653–1743. French cardinal and statesman. Almoner to Queen Marie-Thérèse (1679–83); royal almoner (1683); bishop of Fréjus (1698). Tutor of young Louis XV (1715); had great influence over Louis XV during first part of reign (1715–43); made member of Council of State (1723); cardinal (1726); virtually prime minister (1726–43) after dismissal of Condé; restored economic and political stability; threw French support behind Stanisław Leszczyński in War of Polish Succession; in general minimized French involvement in European conflicts.

Fleury, Claude. 1640–1723. French clergyman and ecclesiastical historian. Abbot of Cistercian abbey of Loc-Dieu (1684–1706); prior of Argenteuil (1706); confessor to Louis XV (1715). His *Histoire ecclésiastique* (1690–1720), covering period down to 1414, was first large history of the Catholic church.

Fle·wel·ling \flə-'wel-iŋ\, Ralph Tyler. 1871–1960. American philosopher, b. De Witt, Mich. Studied under Bordon P. Bowne; professor, U. of Southern Calif. (1917–45). A leading proponent of Personalism; founded review *The Personalist* (1920); wrote *The Person* (1952).

Flex·ner \'flek-snər\, Simon. 1863–1946. American pathologist, b. Louisville, Ky. Professor, U. of Pennsylvania (1899–1903); director of laboratories (1903–35), of the Institute (1920–35), Rockefeller Institute of Medical Research. Isolated dysentery bacillus (1900); developed serum for cerebrospinal meningitis (1907); directed research team that identified poliomyelitis virus; author of treatises on bacteriology and pathology. His brother ¶Abraham (1866–1959), b. Louisville; educator, on staff of Carnegie Foundation for the Advancement of Teaching (1908–12); secretary (1917–25), director of division of studies and medical education (1925–28), General Education Board; founder and first director (1930–39) of Institute for Advanced Study, Princeton. His *Medical Education in the United States and Canada* (1910) caused substantial upgrading of U.S. medical colleges; also wrote *The American College* (1908), *Medical Education in Europe* (1912), *A Modern College* (1923), *Universities—American, English, German* (1930), etc.

Flied·ner \'flēd-nər\, Theodor. 1800–1864. German clergyman and philanthropist. Devoted himself to prison reform and founded first society for prison reform in Germany (1826); opened refuge for discharged female convicts at Kaiserswerth (1833) and first Protestant deaconesses' home devoted to works of religion and charity (1836); opened over 100 more deaconesses' homes; also founded a hospital, infant school (1835), orphanage (1842), asylum for female lunatics (1847), and similar institutions.

Flinck \ˈfliŋk\, Govaert. 1615–1660. Dutch painter. Pupil and imitator of Rembrandt; later influenced by Rubens, developed a more florid and oratorical manner. His portraits, genre, and narrative subjects included *Allegory in Memory of Prince Frederick Henry, Portrait of Rembrandt, A Goldsmith and his Family, Isaac Blessing Jacob, Celebration of the Peace of Westphalia.*

Flin·ders \ˈflin-dərz\, Matthew. 1774–1814. English mariner and hydrographer. With George Bass explored and surveyed coast of New South Wales (1795–1800) and circumnavigated Tasmania (1798); made survey of most of Australian coast and circumnavigated Australia (1801–03). Author of *Voyage to Terra Australis* (1814).

Flint \ˈflint\, Austin. 1812–1886. American physician, b. Petersham, Mass. Helped found Buffalo Med. Coll. (1847) and professor there (1847–61); also professor, U. of Louisville (1852–56) and New Orleans Med. Coll. (1859–61). In New York founded Bellevue Hospital Med. Coll. (1861); professor there (1861–86); also professor, Long Island Coll. Hospital (1861–68). Popularized binaural stethoscope in U.S.; discovered Austin Flint heart murmur (1862); his *Treatise on the Principles and Practice of Medicine* (1866) a medical classic. His son ¶Austin (1836–1915), b. Northampton, Mass., physiologist; professor of physiology, Bellevue Hospital Med. Coll. (1861–98) and Cornell (1898–1906); studied liver function. Wrote *A Textbook of Human Physiology* (1876).

Flint, Frank Stuart. 1885–1960. English poet and translator. High official in Ministry of Labour. Prominent in Imagist movement; author of *In the Net of the Stars* (1909), *Cadences* (1915), *Otherworld* (1925), translations, etc.

Flint, Richard Foster. 1902–1976. American glaciologist, b. Chicago. Taught at Yale (1925–70); made extensive studies of Pleistocene Epoch. Wrote *Glacial and Pleistocene Geology* (1957), *Glacial and Quaternary Geology* (1971), etc.

Flint, Timothy. 1780–1840. American clergyman and author, b. near North Reading, Mass. Congregational minister in Lunenberg, Mass. (1802–14); missionary and farmer in Ohio Valley; edited *Western Monthly Review* in Cincinnati (1827–30). Author of *Recollections of the Last Ten Years* (1826), *Francis Berrian, or The Mexican Patriot* (1826), *Life and Adventures of Arthur Clenning* (1828), *George Mason, the Young Backwoodsman* (1829), *The Shoshonee Valley* (1830), *Daniel Boone* (1833), etc.

Flo·do·ard \flȯ-dȯ-är\ *or* **Fro·do·ard** \frȯ-\. 893 or 894–966. French chronicler. Head of archives at Reims (from 948); author of *Annales,* covering history of France from 919 to 966, and of *Historia ecclesiae Remensis.*

Flood \ˈfləd\, Henry. 1732–1791. Irish politician. Member of Irish Parliament (1759 ff.), leader of opposition; vice treasurer of Ireland (1775–81); cooperated with Grattan in obtaining independence of Irish Parliament (1782), but quarreled with Grattan over later policies. British M.P. (1783 ff.); defeated in attempt to reform Irish Parliament (1784).

Flo·quet \flȯ-ke\, Charles-Thomas. 1828–1896. French politician. Opposed Second Empire and was active in government of national defense (1870); attempted reconciliation between revolutionary leaders and Versailles government during Commune, but was briefly imprisoned at Paris for radical sentiments (1871). Entered Chamber of Deputies (1876); president of Chamber (1885–88); president of council and minister of interior (1888–89); combated Boulangism and wounded Boulanger in duel (1888). Again president of Chamber (1889–93); implicated in Panama scandal (1892–93) and failed of reelection; senator (1894).

Flor \ˈflȯr\, Roger de. 1280–1305. Italian adventurer. Joined Templar order and fought in Palestine; later in service of Frederick of Aragon, King of Sicily; headed Catalan mercenaries in service of Byzantine emperor Andronicus II against Turks in Asia Minor (1303–04); attempted to found his own principality; assassinated by order of emperor.

Flor·ence \ˈflȯr-ən(t)s, ˈflär-\, William Jermyn. *Orig.* Bernard Con·lin \ˈkän-lən\. 1831–1891. American actor, songwriter, and playwright, b. Albany, N.Y. Appearing with his wife (m. 1853) Malvina Pray, enjoyed great success in series of Irish-Yankee comedies, many of which he wrote, as *The Irish Boy and the Yankee Girl, The Ticket-of-Leave Man, No Thoroughfare;* his well known roles included Sir Lucius O'Trigger in Sheridan's *The Rivals,* Zekiel Homespun in *The Heir at Law,* and O'Bryan in John Brougham's *Temptation.*

Flo·res \ˈflō-rās\, Juan José. 1800–1864. Ecuadorian soldier and politician, b. Venezuela. Served under Bolívar in War of Independence; won victory of Tarqui (1829); proclaimed Ecuador independent of Greater Colombia (1830) and became its first president (1830–35); again president (1839–45); deposed by revolution, exiled.

Flo·rey \ˈflōr-ē, ˈflȯr-ē\, Howard Walter. Baron Florey. 1898–1968. British pathologist, b. Australia. Professor, Sheffield U. (1931–35), Oxford (1935–62); provost of Queen's College, Oxford (1962); made life peer (1965). With Ernst B. Chain isolated and purified penicillin for general clinical use (1939); corecipient with Chain and Sir Alexander Fleming of 1945 Nobel prize for physiology or medicine.

Fló·rez de Se·tién y Hui·do·bro \ˈflō-rāth-t͟hā-sā-ˈtyen-ē-wē-ˈt͟hȯ-ḇrō\, Enrique. 1702–1773. Spanish monk and historian. Entered Augustinian order (1718); rector of Colegio de Alcalá (1739). Published (1747–75) 29 volumes of monumental history of church in Spain, *España sagrada* (1754–1879; 22 subsequent volumes written by others). Also wrote *Clave historial* (1743), *Memorias de las reynas católicas* (1761), bibliographical works.

Flo·ri·an \ˈflōr-ē-ən, ˈflȯr-\. *Lat.* Marcus Annius Flo·ri·a·nus \ˌflō-rē-ˈā-nəs\. d. 276 A.D. Roman emperor. Half-brother of Roman emperor Tacitus; proclaimed emperor a few weeks before being killed at Tarsus.

Flo·rian \flȯr-yäⁿ\, Jean-Pierre Cla·ris de \klä-rēs-də-\. 1755–1794. French writer. Author of verse *Fables* (1792), pastoral novels as *Galatée* (1783), plays, songs, memoirs.

Floridablanca, Conde de. See MOÑINO Y REDONDO.

Floridor. See Josias de SOULAS.

Flo·rio \ˈflȯr-ē-ō, *Angl also* ˈflōr-\, John, *also known as* Giovanni. c.1553–c.1625. English lexicographer. Son of an Italian Protestant refugee in London; groom of the privy chamber to Queen Anne (1604–19). Published *Florio His Firste Fruites* (1578) and *Florio's Second Frutes* (1591), series of dialogues; compiled Italian–English dictionary entitled *A Worlde of Wordes* (1598), revised and enlarged under title *Queen Anna's New World of Words* (1611); translated Montaigne's *Essays* (1603, revised 1613).

Flo·ris \ˈflōr-əs\, Cornelis. *Orig.* de Vriendt \dəv-ˈrēnt\. 1514–1575. Flemish architect, sculptor, and medalist. Studied in Rome; issued (1548–57) ornamental engravings of Roman works, introducing Roman grotesque style to Netherlands; headed workshop in Antwerp; designed Antwerp town hall (1561–65), choir screen of Tournai cathedral, and tombs of Danish kings Frederick I (Schleswig, Ger.) and Christian II (Roskilde, Den.). His brother ¶Frans (c.1516–1570), painter, etcher, and designer of woodcuts; studied in Rome with his brother; also headed an Antwerp workshop; works included decorations for receptions of Charles V and Philip II in Antwerp (1549, 1556) and for houses of many Spanish nobles and Antwerp dignitaries.

Flo·rus \ˈflōr-əs, ˈflȯr-\, Publius Annius. 1st–2d century A.D. Roman historian and poet, b. Africa. First of the "new-fashioned" poets of Hadrian's reign. Compiled outline of the history of Rome; wrote dialogue *Vergilius orator an poeta* and perhaps poems *De qualitate vitae* and *De rosis.*

Flo·ry \ˈflōr-ē, ˈflȯr-\, Paul John. 1910–1985. American physical chemist, b. Sterling, Ill. The leading researcher in advancement of macronuclear chemistry; worked for firms as Standard Oil and Goodyear Rubber; associated with Stanford U. (from 1961). Awarded 1974 Nobel prize for chemistry for research on polymers; discovered that polymers could be compared when dissolved in a suitable solvent. Known also as an outspoken champion of human rights.

Flo·tow \ˈflō-(ˌ)tō\, Friedrich Adolf Ferdinand von. Freiherr. 1812–1883. German composer. Composed operas *Alessandro Stradella* (1844), *Martha* (which interpolates Moore's "Last Rose of Summer," 1847), *Sophie Katharina* (1850), *Indra* (1853), *L'Ombre* (1869), etc.; also ballets, two piano concertos, chamber music, and songs.

Flou·rens \flü-raⁿs\, Marie-Jean-Pierre. 1794–1867. French physiologist. Professor in Collège de France (1832). First to demonstrate the general functions of the major portions of the vertebrate brain; first to recognize role of semicircular canals of inner ear in maintaining body equilibrium and coordination. His works included *Recherches expérimentales sur les propriétés et les fonctions du système nerveux dans les animaux vertébrés* (1824) and *De l'instinct et de l'intelligence des animaux* (1858). His son ¶Gustave-Paul (1838–1871) was a revolutionist; as academic wrote *Histoire de l'homme* (1863), *Science de l'homme* (1865); joined Cretan revolt against Turks (1866–68); a leader of the Commune of Paris (1871); killed during skirmish at Chatou. His brother ¶Émile-Léopold (1841–1920) was a politician; councilor of state (1879); minister of foreign affairs (1886–88).

Flow·er \ˈflau̇(-ə)r\, Benjamin Orange. 1858–1918. American editor, b. Albion, Ill. Founded the *American Spectator,* Boston (1886); merged it with the *Arena* (1889); editor of these (1886–96, 1904–09). Founded and edited *Twentieth Century Magazine,* Boston (1909–11).

Flower, Sir William Henry. 1831–1899. English zoologist. Curator of Hunterian Museum, Royal Coll. of Surgeons (1861–84), and Hunterian professor of anatomy and physiology (1870–84); director of Natural History Museum, London (1884–98). President, Zoological Society (1879–99). Author of *An Introduction to the Osteology of the Mammalia* (1870) and, with Richard Lydekker, of *An Introduction to the Study of Mammals* (1891).

\ə\ **abut** \ᵊ\ **kitten,** *Fr.* table \ər\ **further** \a\ **ash** \ā\ **ace** \ä\ **cot, cart** \au̇\ **out** \ch\ **chin** \e\ **bet** \ē\ **easy** \g\ **go** \i\ **hit** \ī\ **ice** \j\ **job** \ŋ\ **sing** \ō\ **go** \ȯ\ **law** \ȯi\ **boy** \th\ **both** \t͟h\ **the** \ü\ **loot** \u̇\ **foot** \y\ **yet** \zh\ **vision** \á, ḇ, g̱, ḵ, ⁿ, œ, œ̄, ue, ue̅, ʸ\ *see* **Guide to Pronunciation**

Floyd \ˈflȯid\, John Buchanan. 1806–1863. American politician, b. Smithfield, Va. Governor of Virginia (1849–52); U.S. secretary of war in Buchanan's cabinet (1857–60); entered Confederate service as brigadier general (1861); removed from his command by Jefferson Davis.

Floyd, William. 1734–1821. American Revolutionary leader, b. Brookhaven, N.Y. Member, Continental Congress (1774–77, 1778–83); a signer of Declaration of Independence. Member, U.S. House of Representatives (1789–91).

Fludd *or* **Flud** \ˈfləd\, Robert. *Lat.* Robertus de Fluc·ti·bus \dā-ˈflək-tə-bəs\. 1574–1637. English physician and Rosicrucian. Practiced in London. Wrote *Apologia Compendiaria Fraternitatem de Rosea Croce* (1616) and other treatises defending the Rosicrucians.

Flüe \ˈflue-ā\, Niklaus von. *Also known as* Bru·der Klaus \ˈbrü-dər-ˈklau̇s\. 1417–1487. Swiss hero. Elected judge and councilor for upper Unterwalden (1448); became hermit (1467); considered folk hero for his intervention in a cantonal conflict which led to the agreement of Stans (1481).

Flü·gel \ˈflue-gəl\, Gustav Lebrecht. 1802–1870. German scholar. Author of editions of the encyclopedic and bibliographical dictionary of Kâtib Çelebî, with Latin translations (1835–58), and of the Qur'ān (1838).

Flügel, Johann Gottfried. 1788–1855. German lexicographer. Compiled *Vollständiges Englisch-Deutsches und Deutsch-Englisches Wörterbuch* (1830).

Flynn \ˈflin\, William James. 1867–1928. American detective, b. New York City. On staff (1897–1917) and chief (1912–16), U.S. Secret Service. Director, bureau of investigation, U.S. Department of Justice (1919–21).

Foch \fȯsh\, Ferdinand. 1851–1929. French soldier. Entered artillery corps (1873); professor of strategy, École Supérieure de la Guerre (1898); general of brigade and commandant of the school (1908). At outbreak of World War I commanded 20th army corps; checked German drive toward Calais; planned strategy by which Joffre defeated Germans on Marne (1914); commanded group of armies of the north (1915), directing spring and autumn offensives in Artois; directed action in battle of the Somme (1916); technical adviser to French government, and president of inter-Allied Council at Versailles (1917); appointed to supreme command of all Allied armies (Mar. 1918); marshal of France (Aug. 1918); carried 1918 offensive to triumphant conclusion.

Fock, Gorch. See Johann KINAU.

Focke \ˈfȯk-ə\, Heinrich Karl Johann. 1890–1979. German aircraft designer. Began building aircraft (1908); built monoplane (1919–20) with Georg Wulf and with him founded (1924) Focke-Wulf Company; designed Fw 61 helicopter (1936), first to be certified airworthy; after firm seized by Nazi government, formed (1937) Focke-Achgelis company to produce Fw 61.

Foerster, Josef Bohuslav. See FÖRSTER.

Foeth, Afanasy. See FET.

Fo·gaz·za·ro \ˌfō-gät-ˈtsä-rō\, Antonio. 1842–1911. Italian novelist. Representative of Liberal Catholic movement in Italian literature; attempted reconciliation of traditional dogma with modern science. His novels included *Malombra* (1881), *Daniele Cortis* (1885), *Il mistero del poeta* (1888), *Piccolo mondo antico* (1896), *Piccolo mondo moderno* (1900–01), *Il santo* (1906), *Leila* (1911); also wrote short stories, plays, and poetry.

Fo·ger·ty \ˈfō-gərt-ē\, Elsie. 1865–1945. English teacher of voice and dramatic diction. Founder and director of Central School of Speech Training and Dramatic Art, London (1906–45); teacher of Sybil Thorndike, John Gielgud, Laurence Olivier, etc. Wrote *The Speaking of English Verse* (1923).

Foix \fwä\. Name of a French family flourishing from 11th to 15th century; the first count was Roger-Bernard I (d. 1035), created comte de Foix (1012–35) by his father, Count Roger of Carcassonne. Other members of family included ¶Gaston III, *surnamed* Phoe·bus \fā-bues\ (1331–1391); became count (1343); named special lieutenant general in southern France (1347); fought Teutonic Knights in Prussia (1356–58); lieutenant general of Languedoc (1380–82); his court famous for luxury; wrote *Livre de chasse.* ¶François-Phoebus (d. 1483), comte de Foix (1473–83); inherited kingdom of Navarre (1479) and passed it on to his sister Catherine. ¶Catherine de Foix (c.1468–1517); queen of Navarre (1483–1517); m. (1484) Jean d'Albret (see ALBRET), the Foix and Albret families becoming merged in Bourbon family. ¶Gaston de Foix (1489–1512), duc de Ne·mours \nə-mür\, soldier, nephew of Louis XII; commanded French army in Italy; noted for the rapidity of his maneuvers; killed at Ravenna. His sister ¶Germaine de Foix (1488–1538); queen of Aragon and Naples; niece of Louis XII of France; m., as 2d wife (1505), her great-uncle Ferdinand II of Aragon; granted by Louis all claims to kingdom of Naples as dowry.

Fo·kine \ˈfȯk-yin, *Fr* fȯ-kēn\, Michel, *orig.* Mikhail Mikhaylovich. 1880–1942. American choreographer, b. St. Petersburg, Russia. A creator of modern ballet; reformed classical ballet by insisting on subservience of ballet elements to overall dramatic expression of theme. Made debut with Imperial Russian Ballet (1898); composed solo *The Dying Swan* for Anna Pavlova (1905). Chief choreographer of Diaghilev's Ballets Russes (1909–14); created *L'Oiseau de feu* (1910) and *Petrushka* (1911); resident in New York (from 1923; naturalized 1932); worked with companies in U.S. and Europe. His 60 or so ballets included *Acis et Galatée, Schéhérazade, Les Sylphides, Cleopâtre, Papillons, Le Coq d'or, Paganini, Bluebeard, L'Épreuve d'amour, Don Juan.*

Fok·ker \ˈfäk-ər\, Anthony Herman Gerard. 1890–1939. American aircraft designer and builder, b. Kediri, Java. Established airplane factory at Johannesthal, Germany (1912), and another at Schwerin (1913); manufactured German pursuit planes during World War I; invented apparatus making it possible to shoot through the field of an airplane propeller. Founded aircraft works at Amsterdam after the war. To U.S. (1922); naturalized; president, Fokker Aircraft Corporation of America, Hasbrouck Heights, N.J.

Fo·lard \fō-lȧr\, Jean-Charles de. Chevalier. 1669–1752. French soldier. Served with French army in War of Spanish Succession, with Knights of Malta against Turks (1713–14), and with Swedish army under Charles XII (from 1714). Wrote *Nouvelles découvertes sur la guerre* (1724) arguing for use of infantry columns instead of battle lines in warfare.

Fo·len·go \fō-ˈleŋ-gō\, Teofilo, *orig.* Girolamo. *Pseudonym* Merlinus Coc·ca·ius \kä-ˈkā-(y)əs\ *or* Merlino Coc·ca·io \kōk-ˈkä-yō\. 1491–1544. Italian poet. Benedictine monk (c.1512–24, 1534–44); known esp. for his mock epic *Baldus* (1517, 1521, 1539–40, 1552) in macaronic verse; also wrote macaronic poems *Epigrammi, Moschaea, Zanitonella,* and *Orlandino.*

Fol·ger \ˈfōl-jər\, Henry Clay. 1857–1930. American businessman, b. New York City. With Standard Oil interests (from 1879); president (1911–23), chairman of board (1923–28), Standard Oil Co. of N.Y. Collected great Shakespearean library, to house which he founded (1928) and endowed Folger Shakespeare Library at Washington, D.C.

Foliot, Gilbert. See GILBERT FOLIOT.

Fol·kung \ˈfōl-ku̇ŋ\. Name of Scandinavian dynastic house, powerful in Sweden (1250–1365) and Norway (1319–1387). It came to Swedish throne through Birger Jarl who ruled as regent (1250–66); succeeded by Valdemar (ruled 1250–75), Magnus I (1275–90), Birger II (1290–1318), and Magnus II Eriksson (1319–65); terminated (1365) with defeat and capture of Magnus by Albert of Mecklenburg. In Norway its rulers were Magnus Eriksson (1319–55), his son Haakon (1355–80), and grandson Olaf (1380–87). See individual biographies.

Fol·len \ˈfōl-ən\, August Adolf Ludwig. *Lat. surname* Fol·le·ni·us \fō-ˈlā-nē-u̇s, *Angl* fäl-ˈē-nē-əs\. 1794–1855. German poet and politician. Led radical student political groups at Giessen and Heidelberg; imprisoned at Berlin for agitation (1819–21); lived thereafter in Switzerland, taught in Aarau (1821–27), and was member of Grand Council at Zürich. His works included songs *Freye Stimmen frischer Jugend* (1819), poems *Harfen-Grüsse aus Deutschland und der Schweiz* (1823), novel *Malagys und Vivian* (1829), and epic poem *Tristans Eltern* (1857). His brother ¶Karl Theodor Christian, *called in U.S.* Charles (1795–1840), poet, clergyman, and reformer; lecturer, U. of Giessen (1818); driven from Germany to France and Switzerland for radical political activities, and finally from Switzerland (1824) to America (naturalized 1830); taught German at Harvard (1825–35); dismissed for abolitionist sympathies. Author of patriotic liberal songs including "Brause, die Freiheitssang."

Fol·mer \ˈfōl-mər\, William Frederic. 1861–1936. American inventor, b. Covington, Ky. Patented over 300 inventions as gas burners, lamps, and esp. photographic equipment; formed Folmer & Schwing firm (1887), which manufactured his Speed Graphic (from 1895) and later his Graflex cameras; firm acquired by Eastman Kodak (1905); formed Folmer Graflex (1927); also developed aerial photography equipment.

Fol·quet de Mar·seille \fōl-ke-də-mȧr-sey\ *or* **Mar·seil·la** \-mȧr-se-yə\. c.1160–1231. Provençal troubadour. Composer of delicate love lyrics; took holy orders (c.1195) and became (c.1205) bishop of Toulouse; persecuted the Albigenses.

Folz \ˈfōlts\, Hans. d. c.1515. German Meistersinger. Worked as barber-surgeon in Nürnberg; author of tales, festival plays, Meistersinger songs, riddles, etc.

Fonck \fōⁿk\, Paul-René. 1894–1953. French aviator. In World War I credited with destruction of 75 enemy planes.

Fon·da \ˈfän-də\, Henry Jaynes. 1905–1982. American actor, b. Grand Island, Neb. Known for portrayals of honest, decent, straightforward men. On Broadway stage (from 1929), achieving success esp. in *The Farmer Takes a Wife* (1934, film 1935), *Mister Roberts* (1948–50; film 1955), and *Clarence Darrow* (1974). Appeared in some 80 movies, including *You Only Live Once* (1937), *Drums Along the Mohawk* (1939), *Young Mr. Lincoln* (1939), *The Grapes of Wrath* (1940), *The Lady Eve* (1941), *The Ox-Bow Incident* (1943), *My Darling Clementine* (1946), *The Fugitive* (1947), *Twelve Angry Men* (1957), *The Best Man* (1964), *In Harm's Way* (1965), *On Golden Pond* (1981, Academy Award).

Fon·se·ca \fōⁿ-ˈsā-kə\, Manuel Deodoro da. 1827–1892. Brazilian general and politician. Active in war with Paraguay (1868–70); governor of Rio Grande do Sul (1887–89); leader in coup that overthrew Dom Pedro and established the Brazilian republic (1889); head of provisional government (1889–91); president of Brazil (Feb.–Nov. 1891; resigned). His nephew ¶Hermes Rodrigues da Fonseca (1855–1923) was president of Brazil (1910–14).

Fonseca Por·tu·gal \-pȯr-tü-'gäl\, Marcos Antônio da. *Also known by Italianized form* Marcantonio Por·to·gal·lo \ˌpȯr-tō-'gäl-lō\. 1762–1830. Portuguese composer. Conductor at Lisbon (1799–1810), Rio de Janeiro (1810–13), Vera Cruz, Mex. (1813–15). Composer of 21 Portuguese and 35 Italian operas, esp. *A Castanheira* (1790), *Demofoonte* (1794), *Le donne cambiate* (1797), *Adrasto* (1800), and of about 100 sacred works.

Fon·tai·nas \fōⁿ-tā-nȧs\, André. 1865–1948. French writer, b. Brussels. Associated with the Symbolists. Author of verse as *Le Sang des fleurs* (1889), *Crépuscules* (1897), *La Nef désemparée* (1908); novels as *L'Indécis* (1903), *Les Étangs noirs* (1912); a comedy, critical studies, essays, translations, etc.

Fon·taine \fōⁿ-ten\, Hippolyte. 1833–1917. French engineer. Discovered that a dynamo can be operated in reverse as an electric motor; first to transmit electric energy (1873). A founder (1870) and editor of *Revue Industrielle.*

Fontaine, Jean de la. See LA FONTAINE.

Fontaine, Pierre-François-Léonard. 1762–1853. French architect. Collaborator with Percier in restoring Malmaison by order of Napoléon and in planning the joining of the Louvre and the Tuileries; chief architect of the emperor (1813); retained favor of Louis XVIII and Louis-Philippe.

Fon·ta·na \fōn-'tä-nä\, Carlo. c.1634 or 1638–1714. Italian architect. Pupil of Bernini; built façade of San Marcello, fountain in Piazza di San Pietro, tombs of Popes Clement XI and Innocent XII and of Queen Christina in St. Peter's, Baptismal Chapel in St. Peter's, church of SS. Apostoli, the Casanatense Library, Cappella Cibo in Sta. Maria del Popolo, Cappella Albani in S. Sebastiano (all in Rome); also built Jesuit church and college at Loyola, Spain; published *Templum Vaticanus* (1694); trained many architects.

Fontana, Domenico. 1543–1607. Italian architect and engineer. Protégé of Pope Sixtus V; chief architect of papacy (1585–92); completed dome and lantern of St. Peter's after Michelangelo's plans, modified by della Porta (1588–90); built Lateran Palace (1586–88), Vatican library (1587–90); became (1592) royal engineer at court of Naples; built Palazzo Reale (1600–02); with his brother ¶Giovanni (1540–1614), also an architect, constructed Acqua Felice aqueduct and Acqua Paola fountain.

Fontana, Prospero. 1512–1597. Italian painter. Worked in Genoa, Florence, Rome, and (after 1540) Bologna; executed many Mannerist paintings as *St. Alessis Distributing Alms* (1576). His daughter and pupil ¶Lavinia (1552–1614) was also a painter; employed at Bologna and by Pope Gregory XIII at Rome; known esp. as fashionable portraitist.

Fon·ta·ne \fōn-'tä-nə\, Theodor. 1819–1898. German writer. Considered first master of modern Realistic fiction in Germany. Editor of *Kreuzzeitung,* Berlin (1860–70); dramatic critic for *Vossische Zeitung* (1870–89). Author of ballad collections *Männer und Helden* (1850) and *Balladen* (1861); books on English life *Ein Sommer in London* (1854) and *Jenseits des Tweed* (1860); and novels as *Vor dem Storm* (1878), *Schach von Wuthenow* (1883), *Frau Jenny Tiebel* (1892), *Effi Briest* (1898), and *Der Stechlin* (1898).

Fon·tanes \fōⁿ-tȧn\, Jean-Pierre-Louis de. Marquis. 1757–1821. French writer and politician. At first wrote in support of French Revolution, later criticized its excesses; founded *Mercure de France* (1799). Member of Corps Législatif (1802) and its president (1804–08); appointed (1808) grand master of U. of Paris by Napoléon; senator (1810); created marquis by Louis XVIII (1817); member of the privy council.

Fon·tanne \fän-'tan, 'fän-ˌ\, Lynn, *orig.* Lillie Louise. 1887–1983. American actress, b. Woodford, England. Debuted as a chorus girl in *Cinderella* (1905); made her U.S. debut in New York City in *The Harp of Life* (1916); scored major success in *Dulcy* (1921); m. (1922) Alfred Lunt (*q.v.*), becoming with him the greatest husband-and-wife team in theater history.

Fon·te·nelle \fōⁿt-nel\, Bernard Le Bo·vier de \lə-bȯv-yā-də-\. Sieur. 1657–1757. French man of letters. Nephew of Pierre and Thomas Corneille. Wrote libretti for operas, including *Psyché* (1678), *Bellérophon* (1679), and *Enée et Lavinie* (1690); published several works of religious skepticism as *Nouveaux dialogues des morts* (after Lucian, 1683–84), *Relation de l'île de Bornéo* (1686), *Histoire des oracles* (1687), and of scientific popularization, esp. *Entretiens sur la pluralité des mondes* (1686). As permanent secretary (1697–1740) of Académie des Sciences issued (1702–40) series of annual volumes under general title *Histoire de l'Académie royal des sciences;* also published *Lettres galantes* (1683), *Poésiès pastorales* (1688), *Histoire du renouvellement de l'Académie* (1708), *De l'origine des fables* (1824), etc.

Fon·vi·zin \(ˌ)fən-'vyēz-yin\, Denis Ivanovich. 1745–1792. Russian playwright. A favorite at court of Catherine the Great (to 1783). Author of comedies satirizing the nobility, as *Brigadir* (1783), *Nedorosl* (1783), etc.

Foote \'fu̇t\, Andrew Hull. *Surname orig.* Foot. 1806–1863. American naval officer, b. New Haven, Conn. Entered navy (1822); active in abolishing the liquor ration throughout navy (put in effect 1862); when in command off African coast, active in capturing slavers and trying to break up slave trade (1849–51). In command of naval operations on upper Mississippi (1861–62); cooperated with army in breaking Confederate defenses along the river in northern Tennessee; rear admiral (1862).

Foote, Arthur William. 1853–1937. American composer, b. Salem, Mass. Organist, First Unitarian Church, Boston (1878–1910); taught at New England Conservatory (1920–37). Composer of church music, songs, organ and piano pieces, overture *In the Mountains* (1886), chamber music, etc.

Foote, Robert Bruce. 1834–1912. English geologist and archaeologist. With geological survey of India (1858–91); often considered founder of study of prehistoric India. Published *Catalogue Raisonné* (1914) and *Indian Prehistoric and Protohistoric Artifacts* (1916).

Foote, Samuel. 1720–1777. English actor and playwright. Played comedy roles at Drury Lane (1745); made success esp. as mimic of prominent persons; made capital of lost leg in *The Devil upon Two Sticks* (1768) and *The Lame Lover* (1770); built and managed (1767–77) new Haymarket Theatre; indicted for libel because of his caricature of the Duchess of Kingston as Kitty Crocodile in *The Trip to Calais* (1776; altered to *The Capuchin*). His plays included *The Knights* (1749), *The Englishman in Paris* (1753), *The Minor* (1760), *The Commissary* (1765), *The Nabob* (1772).

Fop·pa \'fȯp-pä\, Vincenzo. c.1427 or 1430–1515 or 1516. Italian painter. Headed Lombard school; executed fresco *The Martyrdom of St. Sebastian* in Milan (1485) and altarpieces at Pavia (c.1486) and Savona (1489 or 1490); also painted *Three Crosses* (1456) and *Adoration of the Magi* (c.1500).

Fo·rain \fȯ-raⁿ\, Jean-Louis. 1852–1931. French painter and illustrator. Protégé of Degas; succeeded Honoré Daumier as leading illustrator of his day; contributed satirical and humorous drawings to various journals.

For·berg \'fȯr-ˌberk\, Friedrich Karl. 1770–1848. German philosopher. Exponent of Fichte's school of Idealism; wrote *Über die Entwicklung des Begriffs Religion* (1798) and other works in support of atheism.

Forbes \'fȯ(ə)rbz\, Bertie Charles, *orig.* Robert Charles. 1880–1954. American publisher, b. New Deer, Scotland. To U.S. (1904), naturalized (1917). Founder (1916), editor, and publisher of *Forbes Magazine;* author of popular books on finance and business.

Forbes, Edward. 1815–1854. English naturalist. Pioneer in biogeography; professor at King's College, London (1842), Royal School of Mines (1851), Edinburgh (1854); paleontologist to British Geological Survey (1844). Wrote *History of British Starfishes* (1841) and *History of British Mollusca* (1852).

Forbes, George William. 1869–1947. New Zealand politician. M.P. (1908–43); leader of Liberal party (1925–28, 1930–36); prime minister (1930–35).

Forbes \'fȯr-bəs, 'fȯ(ə)rbz\, James David. 1809–1868. Scottish physicist. Professor at Edinburgh (1833–60); principal of St. Andrews College (1860–68). Discovered polarization of radiant heat (1834); published 4 series of "Researches on Heat" (1836–44); also studied structure and movement of glaciers.

Forbes, John. 1710–1759. Scottish officer in British army. In command of expedition that captured French stronghold at Fort Duquesne (Nov. 25, 1758); renamed it Pittsburgh.

Forbes of **Cul·lod·en** \kə-'läd-ᵊn\, Duncan. 1685–1747. Scottish jurist and patriot. Lord advocate (1725); lord president of Court of Session (1737). Aided British government in suppression of Jacobite rebellion (1745–46); fell into disfavor with English for efforts to mitigate punishment of rebels.

Forbes of **Pit·sli·go** \pit-'slī-(ˌ)gō\, Sir William. 1739–1806. Scottish banker. Member of Dr. Johnson's literary club. Author of *Memoirs of a Banking House* (1803).

Forbes-Rob·ert·son \'fȯrbz-'räb-ərt-sən\, Sir Johnston. 1853–1937. English actor. Considered finest Hamlet of his time. Toured with Ellen Terry (1874); member of leading English companies; took over management of Lyceum, London (1895); appeared with Mrs. Patrick Campbell in *The Notorious Mrs. Ebbsmith* and in *Romeo and Juliet* (1895); achieved success in *Othello* and *Hamlet* (1898), Shaw's *Caesar and Cleopatra* (1906), Jerome's *The Passing of the Third Floor Back* (1909–11), etc. His daughter ¶Jean (1905–1962), actress; stage debut in London (1925); appeared in *Romeo and Juliet, Twelfth Night, Peter Pan, The Constant Nymph, St. Joan, As You Desire Me,* etc.

For·bin \fȯr-baⁿ\, Claude de. 1656–1733. French naval commander. Preyed on British, Dutch, and Austrian shipping in Mediterranean and North Sea (1690–1707); commodore in French navy (1702–10); published *Mémoires* (1730).

Force \'fō(ə)rs, 'fȯ(ə)rs\, Peter. 1790–1868. American printer and historian, b. near Paterson, N.J. Printer in Washington, D.C. (from 1815); Whig mayor of city (1836, 1838). Chief historical work, *American Archives,* planned to present original source material of American history (9 vols., pub. 1837–53, covering years 1774–76). His library of Americana bought by government (1867) for Library of Congress.

Forch·hei·mer \'fȯrk-,hī-mər\, Philipp. 1852–1933. Austrian hydraulic engineer. Showed that Laplace's equation was applicable to groundwater flow.

Forck·en·beck \'fŏr-kən-,bek\, Max von, *in full* Maximilian Franz August von. 1821–1892. German politician and jurist. Member (1858) and president (1866–73) of Prussian House of Representatives; cofounder of Progressive (1861) and National Liberal parties (1866). Member (1867) and president (1874–79) of Reichstag; opposed Bismarck's protective tariff policy and, with National Liberal secessionists, founded the Liberal Union (1881), which joined the German Liberal party (1884). Member of Prussian House of Lords (from 1873); chief burgomaster of Berlin (from 1878).

Ford \'fō(ə)rd, 'fȯ(ə)rd\, Ford Madox. *Orig.* Ford Hermann Huef·fer \'hyü-fər\. *Also called* Ford Madox Hueffer. 1873–1939. English writer. Son of Francis Hueffer. Collaborated with Joseph Conrad in novels *The Inheritors* (1901) and *Romance* (1903). Founded *English Review* (1908) and *Transatlantic Review* (1924); served in World War I. Author of novels *The Fifth Queen* (1906), *The Good Soldier* (1915), and tetralogy *Parade's End* comprising *Some Do Not* (1924), *No More Parades* (1925), *A Man Could Stand Up* (1926), and *The Last Post* (1928); also verse and criticism.

Ford, Francis Xavier. 1892–1952. American clergyman, b. Brooklyn, N.Y. Ordained Roman Catholic priest (1917); Maryknoll missionary to China (from 1918); founded seminary (1921); bishop of Mei-hsien (1935); suffered martyrdom under Chinese Communist government.

Ford, Henry. 1863–1947. American automobile manufacturer, b. near Dearborn, Mich. Machinist by trade; chief engineer, Edison Illuminating Co., Detroit (to 1899). An organizer (1899) of Detroit Automobile Co. but soon left it to build racing cars. Organizer and president, Ford Motor Co. (1903–19, 1943–45); employed assembly-line method for production of Model T (1913); introduced the Model A (1928) and the V8 engine (1932). During World War I chartered Peace Ship to Europe in futile attempt to end war (1915–16). Built Henry Ford Hospital, Detroit. His son ¶Edsel Bryant (1893–1943), b. Detroit, president of Ford Motor Co. (1919–43).

Ford, John. 1586–?1639. English playwright. Studied at Middle Temple (1602–06, 1608–c.17); published elegies and prose pamphlets before turning to the theater. His plays included *The Lovers Melancholy* (1629), *'Tis Pity Shee's a Whore* (1633), *The Broken Heart* (1633), *Loves Sacrifice* (1633), *Chronicle Historie of Perkin Warbeck* (1634), *The Ladies Triall* (1638), and *The Fancies, Chast and Noble* (1638); coauthor with Dekker of *The Sun's Darling* (1624) and perhaps of *The Welsh Ambassador* (1623); probably also collaborated with Rowley, Fletcher, Middleton.

Ford, John. *Orig.* Sean Aloysius O'Fee·ney \ō-'fē-nē\. 1895–1973. American motion-picture director, b. Cape Elizabeth, Me. Director of *The Iron Horse* (1924), *The Informer* (1935, Academy Award), *Stagecoach* (1939), *The Grapes of Wrath* (1940, Academy Award), *Tobacco Road* (1941), *How Green Was My Valley* (1941, Academy Award), *My Darling Clementine* (1946), *Wagonmaster* (1950), *Rio Grande* (1950), *The Quiet Man* (1952, Academy Award), *Mister Roberts* (1955), *The Searchers* (1956), *How the West Was Won* (1962), *Cheyenne Autumn* (1964), etc.

Ford, John Thomson. 1829–1894. American theater manager, b. Baltimore. In one of his theaters, known as Ford's Theater, in Washington, D.C., President Lincoln was shot by John Wilkes Booth (1865).

Ford, Paul Leicester. 1865–1902. American historian, b. Brooklyn, N.Y. Edited *The Writings of Thomas Jefferson* (1892–99) and *The Writings of John Dickinson* (1893). Author of *The True George Washington* (1896), *The Many-Sided Franklin* (1899), and the novels *The Honorable Peter Stirling* (1894), *Janice Meredith* (1899).

Fordun, John of. See JOHN of Fordun.

Fo·rel \fō-rel\, Auguste Henri. 1848–1931. Swiss psychiatrist and entomologist. Known for work on the anatomy of the brain and in forensic psychiatry; authority on insects, esp. the psychology of ants; pioneer in sex hygiene. His cousin ¶François Alphonse Forel (1841–1912), naturalist and founder of limnology; conducted limnological investigations on lakes Geneva and Constance; discovered density currents; explained mechanism of seiches; also investigated Swiss glaciers and earthquakes.

Fore·man \'fȯr-mən\, Carl. 1914–1984. American screenwriter, b. Chicago. Wrote or co-wrote scripts for films including *Home of the Brave* (1949), *The Men* (1950), *High Noon* (1952), *The Guns of Navarone* (1961), and *The Bridge on the River Kwai* (1957), the latter anonymously after being blacklisted for being an "uncooperative witness" before the House Committee on Un-American Activities.

Fore·paugh \'fō(ə)r-,pȯ, 'fȯ(ə)r-\, Adam (1831–1890) and his brother Charles (1838–1929). American circus proprietors, b. Philadelphia? Built circus (from 1864) into one of largest in the world and chief competitor of Barnum.

For·es·ter \'fȯr-ə-stər, 'fär-\, Cecil Scott. 1899–1966. English writer, b. Egypt. His novels included *Payment Deferred* (1926), *Brown on Resolution* (1929), *The African Queen* (1935), *The General* (1936), *The Ship* (1943), and esp. series of novels centering about naval commander Horatio Hornblower, as *The Happy Return* (1937), *Ship of the Line* (1938), *Flying Colours* (1939), *Hornblower and the Hotspur* (1962); also wrote biographies, drama, history.

Fo·rey \fō-re\, Élie-Frédéric. 1804–1872. French soldier. Aided coup d'état (1851) of Louis-Napoléon; in Crimean War (1854–55) and war in Italy (1859). Led French force in Mexico (1862–63); created marshal of France (1863).

For·kel \'fȯr-kəl\, Johann Nikolaus. 1749–1818. German musicologist. Director of music, Göttingen (from 1778). Author of *Allgemeine Literatur der Musik* (1792), the first biography of Bach (1802), etc.

For·la·ni·ni \,fȯr-lä-'nē-nē\, Carlo. 1847–1918. Italian medical scholar and educator. His experiments (1882–1906) led to adoption of induced pneumothorax as treatment for pulmonary tuberculosis.

For·man \'fȯr-mən\, Simon. 1552–1611. English astrologer and quack doctor. In London as astrologer and necromancer (from 1583); at death left manuscript of *The Booke of Plaies,* containing earliest account of performances of Shakespeare's *Macbeth, Winter's Tale,* and *Cymbeline.*

For·ment \fȯr-'ment\, Damián. c.1475–c.1541. Spanish sculptor. Apparently trained in Florence; worked at Valencia (1500–09) and Saragossa (from 1509). Influenced by Donatello; his career demonstrated transition from Gothic to Mannerist styles; executed altars of El Pilar, Saragossa (1509–12), Huesca cathedral (1520–24), Santo Domingo de la Calzada (1537–40).

For·mo·sus \fȯr-'mō-səs\. c.816–896. Pope (891–896). Cardinal bishop of Porto (864); sent on an embassy to the Bulgarians (c.866) and later to France; excommunicated by Pope John VIII but restored by Marinus; as pope, crowned Arnulf as emperor (896); his corpse exhumed and in "Cadaver Synod" subjected to posthumous trial by Pope Stephen VI (897).

Form·stech·er \'fȯrm-,stek-ər\, Solomon. 1808–1889. German philosopher. Rabbi at Offenbach (from 1842). Wrote theological and philosophical works, as *Die Religion des Geistes* (1841), and the novel *Buchenstein und Cohnberg* (1863).

For·ner \fȯr-'ner\, Juan Pablo. 1756–1797. Spanish writer. Foremost literary polemicist of 18th-century Spain; attacked verse innovators in *Satira contra los abusos introducidos en la poesía castellana* and dramatist Iriarte in *El asno erudito* (both 1782); defended Spanish and Castilian literature in *Oración apologética por la España y su mérito literario* (1786) and *Exequias de la lengua castellana* (1795).

For·rer \'fȯr-ər\, Ludwig. 1845–1921. Swiss politician. A leader of Zürich radicalism; member of Nationalrat (1873–1900); proponent of legal reform; president of Swiss Confederation (1906, 1912).

For·rest \'fȯr-əst, 'fär-\, Edwin. 1806–1872. American actor, b. Philadelphia. First New York success as Othello (1826); after years of success began a feud with Macready; tragic result (May 10, 1849) when a mob attacked Astor Place Opera House where Macready was appearing and were fired on by the militia with deaths of 22 and wounding of 36 persons. Involved in sensational divorce trial against his wife Catherine Sinclair (1851).

Forrest, John. 1st Baron Forrest of Bun·bury \'bən-b(ə-)rē\. 1847–1918. Australian explorer and politician. Entered survey department of Western Australia (1865); conducted coastal explorations from Perth to Adelaide (1870), Central Australian explorations (1874). First premier of Western Australia (1890–1901); sponsored public works construction and negotiated his state's entry (1901) into Australian Commonwealth. Minister of defense (1901–03) and of treasury in several Liberal ministries. Created baron (1918), first Australian raised to the peerage.

Forrest, Nathan Bedford. 1821–1877. American army officer, b. near Chapel Hill, Tenn. Joined Confederate service at outbreak of Civil War; served at Shiloh and Chickamauga; became head of famous cavalry raiding force; massacred 300 blacks at surrender of Ft. Pillow, Tenn. (Apr. 12, 1864); lieutenant general (1865).

For·res·tal \'fȯr-əs-tᵊl, 'fär-, -,tȯl\, James Vincent. 1892–1949. American public official, b. Beacon, N.Y. Partner (1923), president (1938), New York City investment firm; undersecretary of the navy (1940–44), secretary (1944–47); first secretary of defense (1947–49).

For·res·ter \'fȯr-ə-stər, 'fär-\, Alfred Henry. 1804–1872. English artist. Contributed sketches to *Punch* and *Illustrated London News;* wrote and illustrated humorous and juvenile books. Collaborated as artist with his brother ¶Charles Robert (1803–1850) in novels and *Absurdities in Prose and Verse* (1827) under joint pseudonym Alfred Crow·quill \'krō-,kwil\.

Forsman, George Zachris. See YRJÖ-KOSKINEN.

Forss·mann \'fȯr-,smän\, Werner Theodor Otto. 1904–1979. German physician. Pioneer in heart research, contributing to development of cardiac catheterization. Awarded Nobel prize for physiology or medicine (1956) with A. Cournand and D. Richards.

For·ster \'fȯr-stər\, Edward Morgan. 1879–1970. English novelist. Author of *Where Angels Fear to Tread* (1905), *The Longest Journey* (1907), *A Room with a View* (1908), *Howards End* (1910), *A Passage to India* (1924), *Maurice*

(1971); author also of criticism *Aspects of the Novel* (1927), essay collections *Abinger Harvest* (1936) and *Two Cheers for Democracy* (1951), and libretto for Britten's opera *Billy Budd* (1951).

Forster, Georg, *in full* Johann Georg Adam. 1754–1794. German traveler and writer. Accompanied Captain Cook in his voyage around world (1772–75). Professor at Kassel (1778–84) and Vilna (1784–87); librarian at Mainz (1788). Author of *A Voyage Round the World* (1777), *Ansichten vom Niederrhein* (1791–94). His father ¶Johann Reinhold Forster (1729–1798), clergyman and naturalist, also on the voyage with Cook (1772–75); wrote *Observations Made During Voyage Round the World* (1778).

Forster, John. 1812–1876. English historian and biographer. Close friend of Leigh Hunt and Dickens. Edited *Foreign Quarterly Review* (1842–43), London *Daily News* (1846), London *Examiner* (1847–55). Author of biographies of Goldsmith (1848, expanded 1854), Landor (1869), Dickens (1872–74), and Swift (1876).

För·ster *or* **Foer·ster** \ˈfœr-stər\, Josef Bohuslav. 1859–1951. Czech composer. Professor, music critic in Vienna (1903–18); professor (1919–22), director (1922–31), Prague Conservatory. Composer of 6 operas, esp. *Nepřemožení* (1918), *Srdce* (1923), and *Bloud* (1936), 5 symphonies, symphonic poems, and other orchestral works, a Stabat Mater, choral works with orchestra, chamber music, piano pieces, and songs.

Förster, Max. 1869–1954. German scholar. Professor, Munich (1925–34). Published *Beowulf-Materialien* (1900), *Das Elisabethanische Sprichwort* (1918), *Die Beowulf-Handscrift* (1919), etc.

For·ster \ˈfȯr-stər\, Thomas. c.1675–1738. English Jacobite. M.P. (1708–16); a leader of 1715 rising; proclaimed the Old Pretender as James III at Greenrig, Northumberland (Oct. 6, 1715); inept as general of Jacobite forces; surrendered to government army (1715).

Forster, William Edward. 1818–1886. English politician. Nephew of Sir Thomas Fowell Buxton and brother-in-law of Matthew Arnold. M.P. (1861–86); prepared and secured passage of Education Act of 1870 which established elementary school system in Great Britain; as chief secretary for Ireland (1880–82) acquired nickname "Buckshot Forster" for his repression of radical Land League; avowed opponent of home rule for Ireland.

För·ster-Nietz·sche \ˈfœr-stər-ˈnē-chə\, Elisabeth. 1846–1935. German writer. Acted (1889–1900) as companion, secretary, and nurse to her brother Friedrich Nietzsche; edited his works, unscrupulously changing many passages, and published (1895–1904) his biography. Her husband (m. 1885) ¶Bernhard Förster (1843–1889) was an author and anti-Semitic agitator; attempted to establish a pure Aryan colony (Neuva Germania) in Paraguay with his wife and committed suicide after its failure.

For·syth \fȯr-ˈsīth, fər-\, Alexander John. 1769–1843. Scottish clergyman and inventor. Presbyterian minister at Belhelvie (from 1790); invented the percussion lock for firearms (1805–07).

Forsyth, John. 1780–1841. American politician, b. Fredericksburg, Va. Member, U.S. House of Representatives (1813–18, 1823–27), U.S. Senate (1818–19, 1829–34). U.S. minister to Spain (1819–23); gained Spanish king's ratification of treaty of 1819, ceding Florida to United States. Governor of Georgia (1827–29). U.S. secretary of state (1834–41).

Forsyth, Peter Taylor. 1848–1921. British clergyman, b. Scotland. Served several Congregational churches in England; principal of Hackney Theological College, London (1901–21). His works emphasizing "positive theology" anticipated writings of Karl Barth; author of *Positive Preaching and the Modern Mind* (1907), *The Person and Place of Jesus Christ* (1909), *Christ on Parnassus* (1911), *The Justification of God* (1916), *Lectures on the Church and the Sacraments* (1917), etc.

Fort \fȯr\, Paul. 1872–1960. French poet. A pioneer of Symbolist movement; founded Théâtre des Arts (1890–93); founded and edited magazine *Vers et Prose* (1905–14); published works of Paul Valéry and other Symbolists. Author of plays and *Ballades françaises* (31 vols., 1897–1925).

For·tas \ˈfȯrt-əs\, Abe. 1910–1982. American lawyer and jurist, b. Memphis, Tenn. Assistant professor, Yale law school (1933–37); on staffs of government agencies (1937–46); with Thurman Arnold formed law firm of Arnold, Fortas and Porter, which became one of the most prosperous and influential in Washington, D.C. (1946); argued *Gideon* v. *Wainwright* before Supreme Court (1963); associate justice, U.S. Supreme Court (1965–69); first justice ever to resign owing to public criticism.

For·te·guer·ri \ˌfōr-tā-ˈgwer-rē\, Niccolò. *Pseudonym* Car·te·ro·ma·co \ˌkär-tā-ˈrō-mä-kō\. 1674–1735. Italian prelate and poet. Among his works were a blank verse translation of Terence (1736); *Capitoli; Epistole poetiche;* and a comic epic, *Il Ricciardetto* (1738).

For·ten \ˈfȯrt-ᵊn\, James. 1766–1842. American businessman and reformer, b. Philadelphia. Born of free black parents; served in Revolutionary navy as powder boy; apprenticed to sailmaker in Philadelphia (1786); purchased the business (1798) and made fortune. Prominent supporter of abolitionist cause, esp. of William Lloyd Garrison.

For·tes·cue \ˈfȯrt-ə-ˌskyü\, Chichester Samuel Par·kin·son- \ˈpär-kən-sən-\. Baron Car·ling·ford \ˈkär-liŋ-fərd\. 1823–1898. British political administrator, b. Ireland. Assumed name Parkinson (1862); chief secretary for Ireland (1865–66, 1868–70) under Gladstone; aided with Irish Land Act of 1870; president of Board of Trade (1871–74); lord privy seal (1881–85); ceasing to support Gladstone's Irish policy (1885), rejected home-rule cause.

Fortescue, Sir John. c.1385–c.1479. English jurist. Lord chief justice of the King's Bench (1442–61); attainted (1461) by Edward IV as a Lancastrian, followed Queen Margaret to Flanders (1463); fought and captured at Tewkesbury (1471); pardoned and recognized Edward as rightful king (1471). Known as one of the earliest of English constitutional lawyers; author of *De laudibus legum Angliae* (c.1470), etc.

Forth, Earl of. See Patrick RUTHVEN.

For·tin \fȯr-ta^{n}\, Jean-Nicolas. 1750–1831. French maker of scientific instruments. Devised a precision balance (1788), a cup barometer (Fortin's barometer, c.1800), etc.

For·tis \ˈfȯr-tēs\, Alessandro. 1842–1909. Italian politician. Fought under Garibaldi (1866–67); ardent republican during Risorgimento, later became conservative; elected deputy (1880); minister of agriculture (1898–99); as premier (1905–06), nationalized railways and supported Triple Alliance.

For·tu·na·tus \ˌfȯr-chə-ˈnāt-əs\, Venantius Honorius Clementianus. c.540–c.600 A.D. Italian poet. At court of Sigebert of Austrasia (565); wrote epithalamium on marriage of Sigebert and Brunhilde (566). Protégé and chaplain of Queen Radegunda, wife of Chlotar I, at Poitiers; bishop of Poitiers (599). Among his works were eleven books of short poems, hymns, verse epistles, etc., a poem in four cantos on St. Martin of Tours, and prose lives of saints.

For·tuny y Car·bó \fōr-ˈtün-yē-kär-ˈb̲ō\, Mariano José María Bernardo. 1838–1874. Spanish painter. Dominant influence in Spanish art before rise of Impressionism; resided chiefly in Rome. Known for his historical and genre paintings, as *Battle of Tetuan* and *La vicaria.*

Fo·sca·ri \ˈfōs-kä-rē\, Francesco. c.1373–1457. Doge of Venice (1423–1457). Waged successful wars against Milan extending Venice's power in northern Italy (1426–54). Deposed, partly due to political activities of his son Giacopo (c.1457), who was thrice banished (1445, 1450, 1456). Subject of Byron's tragedy *The Two Foscari* and of opera by Verdi.

Fo·sco·lo \ˈfōs-kō-lō\, Ugo, *orig.* Niccolò. 1778–1827. Italian writer. Served in Napoleonic armies; émigré (1815) to Switzerland, then England (1816); continually involved in romantic intrigues. Author of the epistolary novel *Le ultime lettere di Jacopo Ortis* (1802), tragedies *Tieste* (1797) and *Aiace* (1811), patriotic poem "Dei sepolcri" (1807), sonnets, odes, and critical essays.

Fos·dick \ˈfäz-(ˌ)dik\, Charles Austin. *Pseudonym* Harry Cas·tle·mon \ˈkas-əl-mən\. 1842–1915. American author, b. Randolph, N.Y. Writer of juveniles, including *Frank on the Lower Mississippi* (1869), *The Buried Treasure* (1877), *The Boy Trapper* (1878), *Oscar in Africa* (1894), *Carl the Trailer* (1900), *The Floating Treasure* (1901), *Frank Nelson in the Forecastle* (1904).

Fosdick, Harry Emerson. 1878–1969. American clergyman, b. Buffalo, N.Y. Ordained in Baptist ministry (1903); pastor, Montclair, N.J. (1904–15); professor of practical theology, Union Theol. Sem. (1915–46); pastor, Riverside Church, N.Y. City (1926–46); preacher on National Vespers radio program (1926–46). Championed liberal Protestant theology, pastoral counselling, church cooperation with psychiatry. Author of *The Second Mile* (1908), *The Manhood of the Master* (1913), *As I See Religion* (1932), *The Secret of Victorious Living* (1934), *A Guide to Understanding the Bible* (1938), *On Being a Real Person* (1943), *A Faith for Tough Times* (1952), *The Meaning of Being a Christian* (1964), etc.

Foss \ˈfōs, ˈfäs\, Sam Walter. 1858–1911. American editor and humorist, b. Candia, N.H. Editor, *Yankee Blade,* Boston, and writer for Boston *Globe* (1887–94). Contributor, esp. of light verse, to various magazines. Author of poem "House By the Side of the Road" and verse collections *Back Country Poems* (1892), *Dreams in Homespun* (1897), *Songs of War and Peace* (1899), *Songs of the Average Man* (1907).

Fosse, Charles de La. See Charles de LAFOSSE.

Fos·som·bro·ni \ˌfōs-sȯm-ˈbrō-nē\, Vittorio. Conte. 1754–1844. Italian politician. Minister of foreign affairs in Tuscany (1796–99); to Paris as senator of French empire (1809); as prime minister (1814–44) and chief adviser to Grand Duke Ferdinand III, held real power in Tuscany; pursued liberal policy and responsible for country's peace and prosperity. Also a distinguished mathematician and hydraulic engineer.

Foster, Abby (*or* Abigail) Kelley. See under Stephen Symonds FOSTER.

Fos·ter \ˈfōs-tər, ˈfäs-\, Sir George Eulas. 1847–1931. Canadian politician, b. Carleton Co., N.B. Professor of classics, U. of New Brunswick (1872–79).

Member of House of Commons (1882–1900, 1904–21); minister of marine and fisheries (1885), of finance (1888–96), of trade and commerce (1911–21); senator (1921). Canadian representative at Peace Conference in Paris (1919), and at League of Nations (1921, 1926, 1929).

Foster, Harold Rudolf. 1892–1982. American cartoonist, b. Halifax, N.S. To U.S. (1921, naturalized 1934); drew "Tarzan" cartoon strip (1931–37); created and produced (1937–79) "Prince Valiant" strip.

Foster, John Watson. 1836–1917. American diplomat, b. Pike Co., Ind. U.S. minister to Mexico (1873–80), Russia (1880–81), Spain (1883–85). U.S. secretary of state (1892–93). U.S. agent in arbitration to fix Alaska–Canadian boundary (1903). Author of *A Century of American Diplomacy, 1776–1876* (1900), etc.

Foster, Sir Michael. 1836–1907. English physiologist. Professor (1883–1903), Cambridge U.; with Huxley devised method of practical laboratory work. Founder and editor of *Journal of Physiology* (1878–94); author of *Elements of Embryology* (1874, with F.M. Balfour), *Text-book of Physiology* (1877), *Lectures on the History of Physiology During the Sixteenth, Seventeenth, and Eighteenth Centuries* (1901), etc.

Foster, Stephen Collins. 1826–1864. American songwriter, b. Lawrenceville (later part of Pittsburgh), Pa. Contributed many songs for the then popular Negro minstrel troupes; resident of Pittsburgh (until 1860), New York City (from 1860); improvident, died in charity ward despite large income from his songs. Best known songs "Open thy Lattice, Love," "My Old Kentucky Home," "Massa's in the Cold, Cold Ground," "Old Folks at Home," "Nelly was a Lady," "O Susanna," "Old Dog Tray," "Old Black Joe," "Camptown Races," "Jeanie with the Light Brown Hair," "Beautiful Dreamer."

Foster, Stephen Symonds. 1809–1881. American abolitionist, b. Canterbury, N.H. Antislavery lecturer and agitator, associate of Garrison; later, advocated woman suffrage, temperance, world peace, and reform in conditions of labor. His wife (m. 1845) ¶Abigail, *better known as* Abby, *nee* Kel·ley \ˈkel-ē\ (1810–1887), b. Pelham, Mass., was a pioneer in woman suffrage.

Foster, William Zebulon. 1881–1961. American labor leader and politician, b. Taunton, Mass. Joined Socialist party (1900), I.W.W. (1909); active in organizing steelworkers for the great strike (1919). Secretary general (1921–30), chairman (1945–56), chairman emeritus (1957–61), Communist party of U.S.; Communist party candidate for president of U.S. (1924, 1928, 1932). Author of *Towards Soviet America* (1932), *From Bryan to Stalin* (1937), etc.

Foth·er·gill \ˈfät͟h-ər-ˌgil\, John. 1712–1780. English physician. Practiced in London (from 1740); maintained botanical garden known through Europe. His "Account of the Sore Throat Attended with Ulcers" (1748) contained first recognition of diphtheria in England; first to describe coronary arteriosclerosis. Aided Benjamin Franklin (1774) in drafting scheme of reconciliation between England and American colonies; popularized use of coffee in England.

Fou·cauld \fü-kō\, Charles-Eugène. Vicomte. 1858–1916. French religious. Soldier in Algeria (to 1882); became Trappist monk (1890); hermit in Palestine (1897) and Algeria (1901); worked among the Tuareg tribes, securing their loyalty to the French government.

Fou·cault \fü-kō\, Jean-Bernard-Léon. 1819–1868. French physicist. With Armand Fizeau conducted experiments on light and heat; demonstrated that the velocity of light varies in different media (1850); measured the velocity of light with extreme accuracy (1850); demonstrated the axial rotation of the earth by the apparent clockwise motion of a pendulum's plane of oscillation (1851); invented the gyroscope (1852); appointed physicist at Paris observatory (1855); discovered the eddy, or Foucault, induced electric current; invented the Foucault prism, a variety of Nicol prism (1857); devised method of silvering glass to make mirrors for reflecting telescopes (1857); invented a simple but accurate method of testing telescope mirrors for surface defects (1859).

Foucault, Michel Paul. 1926–1984. French philosopher. Professor of the history of systems of thought, Collège de France (from 1970); a leading French intellectual. Works included *Folie et Déraison* (1961), a study of madness and its treatment in the 17th century; *Surveiller et punir* (1975), on the modern penal system; and a three-volume history of sexuality (1976–84).

Fou·ché \fü-shā\, Joseph. Duc d'O·trante \dō-träⁿt\. 1759–1820. French politician. Member of National Convention (1792–95); minister of police (1799–1802, 1804–10, and 1815). Famous for unfeeling efficiency, his system of spies, and various politicial intrigues designed to save or benefit himself in any contingency. Advised Napoléon to abdicate after Waterloo and assumed leadership of the provisional government; exile at Trieste (1816–20).

Fou·cher \fü-shā\, Simon. 1644–1696. French ecclesiastic and philosopher. Member of Cartesian school; in *Critique de la recherche de la vérité* (1675) was first to criticize philosophy of Nicolas Malebranche.

Foucher de Char·tres \-də-shärtrᵊ\. c.1059–c.1127. French priest and historian. Chaplain (from 1097) of Baldwin, King of Jerusalem. His *Gesta Francorum Jherusalem peregrinantium* (1101, 1106, 1124–27) tells story of First Crusade.

Foucquet. See FOUQUET.

Fould \füld\, Achille-Marcus. 1800–1867. French politician. Minister of finance (1849–52, 1861–67); introduced financial innovations, including direct public loans to government; minister of state (1852–60); directed organization of Paris Exposition of 1855, reorganization of Paris Opéra, completion of new Louvre; exerted great influence in government.

Foulis \ˈfau̇(ə)lz\, Robert (1707–1776) and his brother Andrew (1712–1775). Scottish booksellers and printers. Robert set up press in Glasgow (c.1741); in partnership with Andrew (from 1748); best known for their editions of the classics (over 500) and quarto editions of works of Thomas Gray (1768) and Milton's *Paradise Lost* (1770); founders of Glasgow Academy of Art (1754).

Foulques. See also FULK.

Foulques *or* **Foulque** \fülk\. d. 900. French ecclesiastic. Archbishop of Reims (883); played important political role, esp. in crowning Charles the Simple (893) to contest the claim of Eudes, Count of Paris, to the throne; created chancellor of France (898); assassinated by order of Count Baldwin of Flanders.

Fou·qué \fü-kā\, Ferdinand-André. 1828–1904. French geologist and petrologist. Studied volcanic eruptions and the formation of volcanic craters; introduced into France the use of the microscope for petrographic study; reproduced rocks and minerals artificially.

Fouqué, Friedrich Heinrich Karl de la Motte \də-lä-mȯt\. Freiherr. 1777–1843. German writer, of Huguenot descent. A Romantic; often wrote on chivalric and Old Norse themes; his dramatic trilogy *Der Held des Nordens* (1808–10) was first modern dramatic treatment of Nibelung story; also author of popular fairy tale *Undine* (1811), allegorical novel *Der Zauberring* (1813), lyrics, etc.

Fou·quet \fü-ke\, Jean. c.1420–c.1481. French painter. Apparently trained under the Bedford Master in Paris; in Rome (c.1445–47), where he executed portrait of Pope Eugenius IV; made royal painter (1475). Style combined experiments of Italian painting with characterization and detail of Flemish art. His works included portraits of Charles VII (c.1447) and of his patrons Etienne Chevalier and Jouvenel des Ursins, altarpiece *Pietà* for church of Nouans, and illuminations for manuscripts as Chevalier's *Book of Hours,* Boccaccio's *De Casibus virorum illustrium* and *De claris mulieribus,* Josephus's *Antiquités judaïques;* worked with Michel Colombe on tomb of Louis XI (1474).

Fouquet *or* **Fouc·quet** \fü-ke\, Nicolas. 1615–1680. French government official. Confidential agent of Cardinal Mazarin; appointed superintendent of finance (1653); arrested (1661) and convicted (1664) for embezzlement; imprisoned for rest of life.

Fou·quier-Tin·ville \fü-kyā-taⁿ-vēl\, Antoine-Quentin. 1746–1795. French Revolutionary lawyer. Public prosecutor of the Revolutionary Tribunal (1793–94); claimed to have judged over 2,400 counterrevolutionaries, including Marie-Antoinette, his relative Camille Desmoulins, the Girondins, the Hébertists; guillotined.

Four·croy \für-krwä, -krwȧ\, Antoine-François de. Comte. 1755–1809. French chemist. Professor, Jardin des Plantes (from 1784); one of earliest converts to theories of Lavoisier. Author of *Méthode de nomenclature chimique* (with Lavoisier, Berthollet, and Guyton de Morveau, 1787), etc.

Four·drin·i·er \ˌfōr-drə-ˈni(ə)r, ˌfȯr-; fu̇r-ˈdrin-ē-ər, fōr-, fȯr-\, Henry (1766–1854) and his brother Sealy (d. 1847). English papermakers and inventors. Invented (with aid of Bryan Donkin) and patented (1807) improved papermaking machine capable of producing a continuous sheet of paper of any desired size from the wood pulp.

Fou·rier \für-yā\, Charles, *in full* François-Marie-Charles. 1772–1837. French social theorist. Devoted himself to study of society and methods of improving social and economic conditions; published (1808) *Théorie des quatre mouvements et des destinées générales,* advocating a cooperative organization of society into phalanxes, each one large enough to allow for industrial and social needs of the group. Refined his theories in *Traité de l'association domestique agricole* (1822), *Le nouveau monde industriel et sociétaire* (1829), *La Fausse Industrie morcelée* (1835–36). A number of settlements based on his ideas were started in France and the U.S., esp. Brook Farm at West Roxbury, Mass., and North American Phalanx at Red Bank, N.J.

Fourier, Jean-Baptiste-Joseph. Baron. 1768–1830. French mathematician. Known for researches in the conduction of heat and of numerical equations. Accompanied Napoléon to Egypt (1798) where he became secretary of the Institut d'Égypte at Cairo; returned to France (1801); prefect of Isère (1802–15); created baron by Napoléon (1808); published *Description de l'Égypte* (1808–25); member (from 1817), perpetual secretary (from 1822), Académie des Sciences. His *Théorie analytique de la chaleur* (1822) contained method of analysis of periodic functions (Fourier series) and exerted strong influence on mathematical physics.

Fourier, Pierre. 1565–1640. French cleric. Founder (1597) of the religious order School Sisters of Notre Dame.

Four·net \für-ne\, Louis-René-Marie-Charles Dar·tige du \där-tēg-dü̅-\. 1856–1940. French admiral. Entered navy (1872); served in Indochina; vice admiral (1914); Allied naval commander in Mediterranean (1915–16).

Four·ney·ron \für-ne-rōⁿ\, Benoît. 1802–1867. French hydraulic engineer. Using ideas of Claude Burdin, built first water turbine (1827).

Four·nier \fürn-yā\, Henri-Alban. *Pseudonym* Alain-Four·nier \á-laⁿ-\. 1886–1914. French writer. Published modern classic novel *Le Grand Meaulnes* (1913); killed in first Battle of the Marne. Correspondence and other works published posthumously.

Fournier, Pierre-Simon. 1712–1768. French typefounder and engraver. Set up own typefoundry in Paris (1736); designed many new characters; noted for decorative typographical ornaments in Rococo style. Author of technical treatises, including *Modèles des caractères* (1742) and *Manuel typographique* (1764–66).

Fow·ler \'faù-lər\, Henry Watson. 1858–1933. English lexicographer. Coauthor with his brother Francis George Fowler (d. 1918) of *The King's English* (1906) and *The Concise Oxford Dictionary of Current English* (1911). Alone published *The Pocket Oxford Dictionary* (1924), *A Dictionary of Modern English Usage* (1926), *If Wishes Were Horses* (1929, essays), *Rhymes of Darby to Joan* (1931, verse).

Fowler, Sir John. 1817–1898. English engineer. Designed Pimlico Railway Bridge (1860), Forth Railway Bridge (with his partner, Sir Benjamin Baker, 1882–90). Engineer of London Metropolitan Railway (from 1853), pioneer of underground railways; constructed Victoria Station. Engineering adviser in Egypt to khedive Ismāʽīl (1871–79).

Fowler, John. 1826–1864. English engineer. With Jeremiah Head invented the steam-hauled plow (1858).

Fox. See also FOXE.

Fox \'fäks\, Caroline. 1819–1871. English diarist. Friend of John Stuart Mill, John Sterling, Thomas Carlyle, and other prominent persons. Extracts from her diary (1835–71) published under title *Memories of Old Friends* (1882).

Fox, Sir Charles. 1810–1874. English engineer. Constructing engineer, London and Birmingham railway; introduced the switch into railway use; engaged in railway construction in Ireland, Denmark, France, Canada, India, Cape Colony, Queensland. Designed buildings, including Crystal Palace, for the Great Exhibition (1851), and built the Berlin waterworks.

Fox, Charles James. 1749–1806. English politician and orator. 3d son of Henry Fox (*q.v.*), 1st Baron Holland. Tory M.P. (1768); member of North's cabinet as a lord of admiralty (1770–72) and of treasury (1772–74); dismissed because of independence of action and dislike on part of George III. Went over to Whig opposition and with brilliant oratory led opposition to North's coercive measures against American colonies, including tea duty (1774). Foreign secretary in Rockingham's ministry (1782). Became foreign secretary, with North as home secretary, in coalition ministry of Duke of Portland (1783), which was defeated on Fox's India reform bill through personal influence of king (Dec. 1783). Kept out of office by king (till 1806), joined opposition to Pitt; favored French Revolution; moved impeachment of Warren Hastings (1788); opposed treason and sedition bills (1795–96); carried measure giving juries full powers in libel actions (1792). Remained mostly away from Parliament for five years, engaged in historical and literary work; gave toast "Our Sovereign, the people," for which name erased from privy council (1798). Again foreign secretary in Grenville's ministry (1806); started negotiations for peace with France; moved abolition of slave trade. Author of a *History of Reign of James II,* left incomplete.

Fox, George. 1624–1691. English religious leader. Founder of the Society of Friends (or Quakers). Began preaching in his home neighborhood (1647–48), calling his society the "Friends of Truth"; preached the superiority of God-given inspiration (or inward light) over scriptural authority or creeds; made missionary journeys to Scotland (1657), Ireland (1669), North America and West Indies (1671–72), Holland (1677, 1684); frequently persecuted and imprisoned. His *Journal,* revised by a committee directed by William Penn, appeared in 1694; also wrote *A Collection of ... Epistles* (pub. 1698) and *Gospel-Truth Demonstrated* (pub. 1706).

Fox, Gustavus Vasa. 1821–1883. American government official, b. Saugus, Mass. Naval officer (1841–56); highly efficient as assistant secretary of the navy (1861–66); thereafter in private business.

Fox, Henry. 1st Baron Hol·land \'häl-ənd\. 1705–1774. English politician. Father of Charles James Fox. M.P. (1735–63); secretary at war (1746–54); secretary of state with seat in cabinet and leader of House of Commons (1755–56); amassed fortune as paymaster general (1757–65); again leader of House of Commons (1762–63); carried Treaty of Paris (1763) and rewarded by elevation to peerage.

His grandson ¶Henry Richard Vassall Fox (1773–1840), 3d Baron Holland; a Whig in House of Lords; lord privy seal in Grenville ministry (1806–07); advocated abolition of slave trade and repeal of corn laws; opposed union with Ireland; chancellor of duchy of Lancaster (1830–34, 1835–40).

Fox, John William. *Known as* John Fox, Jr. 1863–1919. American novelist, b. Stony Point, Ky. Author of *A Mountain Europa* (1894), *The Kentuckians* (1897), *The Little Shepherd of Kingdom Come* (1903), *The Trail of the Lonesome Pine* (1908), *The Heart of the Hills* (1913), etc.

Fox, Luke. 1586–1635. English navigator. Commanded expedition seeking the Northwest Passage (1631); wrote an account of his trip.

Fox, Margaret. 1833?–1893. American spiritualist, b. Bath, N.B. To U.S. (1847); claimed by means of spirit rappings to have established communication with supernatural world; with sister ¶Catherine, *known as* Kate (1839?–1892), toured U.S. and Europe as a medium; success responsible for widespread interest in and investigation of spiritualistic phenomena. Confessed imposture (1888); later retracted this confession. Claimed to be common-law wife of Dr. Elisha Kent Kane and assumed his name; published his letters to her, *The Love Life of Dr. Kane* (1866).

Fox, Richard Kyle. 1846–1922. American publisher, b. Belfast, Ireland. To U.S. (1874); proprietor (from 1877) of *National Police Gazette;* developed it into most sensational periodical of the day, stressing sex and crime; later it evolved into a sporting journal.

Fox, Virgil Keel. 1912–1980. American organist, b. Princeton, Ill. Organist at Riverside Church, New York City (1946–65); frequently toured through U.S. and Europe; noted for his dazzling technique, showmanship, and successful attempts to popularize organ music.

Fox, Sir William. 1812–1893. New Zealand politician, b. England. To New Zealand (1842); his work for New Zealand self-government helped shape Constitution Act of 1852; prime minister of New Zealand (1856, 1861–62, 1869–72, 1873); colonial secretary and minister of native affairs (1863–64). Author of *The Six Colonies of New Zealand* (1851) and *The War in New Zealand* (1860).

Fox, William. 1879–1952. American motion picture executive, b. Tulchva, Hungary. To U.S. as a child; organized (1915) Fox Film Corporation, progenitor of 20th Century-Fox studios; controlled large portion of exhibition, distribution, and production of silent films; pioneered in designing theaters for patrons' comfort; introduced organ accompaniment, noiseless projection, and (1927) news series *Movietone Newsreel;* sold controlling interest in firm (1930), declared bankruptcy (1936).

Foxe \'fäks\, John. 1516–1587. English martyrologist. Tutor to children of Henry Howard, Earl of Surrey (1548–53); fled reign of Queen Mary I (1554–59); ordained priest (1560); prebendary in Salisbury cathedral (1563). Author of *Rerum in ecclesia gestarum ... commentarii* (1559), which was translated into English and printed under the title *Actes and Monuments* (1563), or, popularly, *The Book of Martyrs.*

Foxe *or* **Fox,** Richard. c.1448–1528. English prelate and politician. Entered service of Henry, Earl of Richmond, in Paris; appointed by Henry, after his accession to English throne as Henry VII (1485), secretary of state, lord privy seal, and bishop of Exeter (1487), of Bath and Wells (1491–94), of Durham (1494–1501), of Winchester (1501 ff.). Negotiated treaties and executed Henry's financial policies. With accession of Henry VIII, continued as one of chief advisers to the king; gradually lost influence to Thomas Wolsey and retired from politics (1516). Founded Corpus Christi Coll., Oxford (1515–16).

Foxx \'fäks\, James Emory, *called* Jimmie. *Nicknamed* Double X. 1907–1967. American baseball player, b. Sudlersville, Md. Played in American League with Philadelphia Athletics (1925–35), Boston Red Sox (1935–42), in National League with Chicago Cubs (1942–45), Philadelphia Phillies (1945). Most valuable player in American League (1932, 1933, 1938); hit 534 home runs and had .325 career batting average. Elected to Baseball Hall of Fame (1951).

Foy \'fȯi\, Eddie. *Orig.* Edwin Fitzgerald. 1856–1928. American entertainer, b. New York City. Played (1904–13) leading comic roles in series of Broadway musicals, including *Piff! Paff! Pouf!* (1904), *The Earl and the Girl* (1905), *Over the River* (1911–13). Appeared in vaudeville (from 1913) and one motion picture with highly successful act including his children, the "Seven Little Foys."

Foy \fwá\, Maximilien-Sébastien. 1775–1825. French soldier and politician. Served in Napoléon's armies in Rhineland, Near East, Spain; brigadier general (1808); made count of the empire (1815). Member of Chamber of Deputies (1819–25), where he defended freedom of the individual and freedom of the press. Wrote incomplete *Histoire de la guerre de la Péninsule* (pub. 1827).

F.P.A. See Franklin Pierce ADAMS.

Fra·ca·sto·ro \ˌfrä-kä-'stȯ-rō\, Girolamo. *Lat.* Hieronymus Fra·cas·to·ri·us \ˌfrä-kas-'tōr-ē-əs, -'tȯr-\. c.1478–1553. Italian physician, astronomer, and poet. Became (1502) professor of philosophy and colleague of Copernicus at U. of Padua; maintained private medical practice in Verona; studied epidemic diseases; medical consultant for Pope Paul III at Council of Trent (1545 ff.). Gave name to and described syphilis in poem *Syphilis sive morbus Gallicus* (1530); prefigured Copernican model of solar system in *Homocentrica sive de* *stellis liber* (1538); in *De contagione et contagiosis morbis* (1546) made first scientific statement on true nature of contagion and transmission of diseases by germs.

Fra Diavolo. See Michele PEZZA.

Fra·go·nard \frȧ-gō-nȧr\, Jean-Honoré. 1732–1806. French painter and engraver. Studied under Chardin, Van Loo, and Boucher; commissioned (1770) by Mme. du Barry to decorate her Pavillon de Louveciennes, produced four large paintings known as *Progress of Love;* lost patrons in French Revolution and died in obscurity. His style and themes in Rococo manner, in last years turned to Neoclassical idiom; painted landscapes, portraits, *fêtes-galantes,* domestic scenes, most characterized by a delicate hedonism; works included *Landscape with Cowherd* (c.1760–65), *Stolen Kiss* (c.1761–65), *Coresus Sacrifices Himself to Save Callirhoe* (c.1761–65), *Women Bathing* (c.1765), *The Swing* (c.1766), *The Three Graces* (c.1770), *The Happy Family* (c.1773–76), *The Schoolmistress* (c.1778), *The Fountain of Love* (c.1781), *The Beloved Child* (c.1792). His son ¶Alexandre-Évariste (1780–1850) was a historical painter and lithographer.

Framp·ton \'fram(p)-tən\, Sir George James. 1860–1928. English sculptor. His sculptures included *Angel of Death* (1889), *Peter Pan* (1914), portrait busts of King George V and Queen Mary, statue of Edward VI.

France, Anatole. See Jacques THIBAULT.

Fran·ces \'fran(t)-səs\ of Rome. Saint. *Nee* Francesca Bus·so \'büs-sō\. 1384–1440. Roman religious. Famed for her work among the sick and poor; founder (1425), superior (from 1436), of the Oblate Congregation of Tor de' Specchi. Canonized (1608).

Francesca, Piero della. See PIERO DELLA FRANCESCA.

Francesca da Rimini. See under POLENTA family.

Fran·ce·schi·ni \ˌfrän-chā-'skē-nē\, Baldassare. *Called* Il Vol·ter·ra·no \ēl-ˌvōl-ter-'rä-nō\. 1611–1689. Florentine painter, b. Volterra. Studied under his father and Matteo Rosselli. Works included paintings in cupola of Niccolini chapel in S. Croce, Florence (1652–60), *St. John the Evangelist* in S. Chiara, Volterra, and fresco of cupola of the Annunziata, Florence (c.1683).

Franceschini, Marcantonio. 1648–1729. Italian painter. Pupil and associate of Carlo Cignani; last leader of Bolognese school; director, Accademia Clementina, Bologna (1721); known esp. for frescoes and altarpieces.

Francesco. See also FRANCIS.

Fran·ce·sco da Bar·be·ri·no \frän-'chā-skō-dä-ˌbär-bā-'rē-nō\. 1264–1348. Italian poet. Contemporary of Dante and practitioner of *dolce stil nuovo;* works included *Documenti d'amore* (1309–13), *Del reggimento e costumi di donna* (1318–20).

Francesco di Cris·to·fa·no \-dē-ˌkrē-stō-'fä-nō\. *Also known as* Francesco Giu·di·ni \jü-'dē-nē\ *or* Giu·di·ci \'jü-dē-chē\. *Called* Fran·cia·bi·gio \ˌfrän-chä-'bē-jō\. 1482 or 1483–1525. Florentine painter. Associate of Andrea del Sarto, with whom he decorated Medici villa at Poggio a Caiano. His style contained early Renaissance, High Renaissance, and Proto-Mannerist elements; works included *Madonna del Pozzo* (1508), frescoes, and portraits, as *Bath of Bathsheba* (1523).

Francesco di Gior·gio \-dē-'jōr-jō\. *Full name* Francesco Maurizio di Giorgio Mar·ti·ni \mär-'tē-nē\ *or* di Mar·ti·no \-nō\. 1439–1502. Italian engineer, architect, sculptor, and painter. Early works were manuscript illuminations, furniture panels, and altarpieces *Coronation of the Virgin* (1471), *The Nativity* (1475), both for Pinacoteca Nazionale, Siena. Known esp. for his military constructions; military architect under Duke of Urbino (1477 ff.); reputed inventor of mines at siege of Naples (1495); built Maria del Calcinaio church at Cortona, municipal buildings at Ancona and at Iesi; appointed chief architect, cathedral of Siena (1498). Translated Vitruvius; wrote *Trattato di architettura civile e militare.*

Francesco di Ste·fa·no \-dē-stä-'fä-nō\. *Also called* Giu·o·chi \jü-'ō-kē\. *Known as* Il Pe·sel·li·no \ēl-ˌpā-sel-'lē-nō\. 1422–1457. Florentine painter. Pupil of grandfather Giuliano il Pesello and later of Fra Filippo Lippi; partner of Piero di Lorenzo (1453). Known for predelle and for cassone pictures of old legends and tales intended as decorations for marriage chests.

Fran·chet d'Es·pe·rey \frän-she-dā-spā-re, -des-pə-re\, Louis-Félix-Marie-François. 1856–1942. French army commander. General of brigade (1908), of division (1912). In World War I defeated at Aisne (May 1918); commanded Allied army which defeated Bulgars and Germans in Macedonia (Sept. 1918), forcing Bulgaria out of the war; continued drive to the Danube, resulting in surrender of Hungary. Created marshal of France (1921).

Fran·chet·ti \fräŋ-'kāt-tē\, Alberto. Baron. 1860–1942. Italian composer. Composed operas as *Asrael* (1888) and *Germania* (1902), chamber music, overtures, and a symphony in E minor.

Fran·che·ville \fränsh-vēl\ *or* **Fran·que·ville** \frank-vēl\, Pierre de. 1554–1618. French sculptor. Long resident in Italy; recalled to France by Henry IV (1604); executed *Le Temps enlevant la Vérité,* bronze groups *Hercule, Mars et Amour,* portrait busts, etc. Appointed sculptor to King Louis XIII.

Francia. See Francesco RAIBOLINI.

Fran·cia \'frän-syä\, José Gaspar Rodríguez de. *Styled himself* El Su·pre·mo \el-sü-'prā-mō\. 1766–1840. Paraguayan dictator. Active in junta following declaration of Paraguayan independence (1811 ff.); designated by legislature one of two consuls to govern Paraguay (1813) and dictator of Paraguay (1814–17); made dictator for life (1817). Declared (1813) independence from Argentina, thus effectively isolating his country; improved industry, farming, armed forces; abolished aristocratic privileges, the Inquisition, tithes; a frugal and honest ruler but cruel and oppressive as to political liberty.

Franciabigio. See FRANCESCO DI CRISTOFANO.

Francis I. Emperor of Austria. See FRANCIS II, Holy Roman Emperor.

Fran·cis II \'fran(t)-səs\. *Fr.* Fran·çois \frän-swȧ\. 1435–1488. Last duke of Brittany (1458–88). Invaded Normandy (1467) and allied himself with Edward IV of England (1468, 1475, 1480) in attempts to maintain independence from France; finally defeated (1488) and forced to sign Treaty of Verger. His daughter Anne married Charles VIII of France, thus uniting duchy of Brittany with kingdom of France.

Francis. *Fr.* François. Name of two kings of France of Angoulême branch of house of Valois:

Francis I. 1494–1547. King (1515–47). Son of Charles, Count of Angoulême, and Louise of Savoy; brother of Margaret of Navarre; m. Claude de France, daughter of Louis XII (1514). Continued war against Holy League; victorious in Marignano campaign (1515) in northern Italy, gaining possession of Lombardy; made concordat with Pope Leo X (1516); defeated in election to imperial throne (1519), Charles I of Spain becoming emperor as Charles V; entertained Henry VIII of England at Field of Cloth of Gold, near Guînes (1520); by lack of tact drove constable Bourbon to side with enemies (1522–23). Began long series of wars against Empire; in first war (1521–25) defeated and taken prisoner at Pavia (1525); released (Treaty of Madrid, 1526) after giving up Burgundy and making other extreme concessions; broke pledges; waged second war (1527–29), losing Italy by Treaty of Cambrai (1529); conducted third war (1536–38), renewed (1542) with victory over Imperial forces at Ceresole Alba (1544). Possessed a love for letters and arts; his reign marked by Renaissance in France.

Francis II. 1544–1560. King (1559–60). Eldest son of Henry II and Catherine de Médicis; m. Mary Stuart (1558). Sickly and weak-minded; the tool of his uncles François de Lorraine, duc de Guise, and Charles, Cardinal of Lorraine, who actually governed; conspiracy formed by certain nobles against him and the Guises was defeated (1560).

Francis. *Ger.* Franz \'fränts\. Name of two Holy Roman emperors:

Francis I. *Orig.* Francis Ste·phen \'stē-vən\. 1708–1765. Holy Roman emperor (1745–65). Son of Leopold, Duke of Lorraine. Succeeded to duchy (1729), but ceded it (1737) to Stanisław Leszczyński, king of Poland; made grand duke of Tuscany (1737); m. Maria Theresa of Austria (1736), with whom he was coregent as ruler of Austria (1740–45). Chosen emperor (1745); did not concern himself much with wars (1740–48) of Frederick against Maria Theresa nor with Seven Years' War (1756–63).

Francis II. 1768–1835. Last Holy Roman emperor (1792–1806) and emperor of Austria (1804–35) as Francis I. Son of Leopold II. Joined all coalitions against France except fourth and was defeated by Napoléon in all wars resulting from them except last. Proclaimed himself hereditary emperor of Austria (1804) and abdicated crown of Holy Roman Empire (1806); acquired much territory by Congress of Vienna (1814–15); joined Holy Alliance (1815); followed policy of reaction under guidance of Metternich (1815–35); reinstituted power of Roman Catholic church; patron of arts and sciences. His daughter Marie-Louise married Napoléon (1810).

Francis. *Ital.* Fran·ce·sco \frän-'chā-skō\. Name of two kings of the Two Sicilies:

Francis I. 1777–1830. King (1825–30). Son of Ferdinand I; appointed regent of Naples (1812); supported Carbonari uprising of 1820; after ascending throne (1825) abandoned liberal policies for reactionary ones; repressed revolutionary uprising in Cilento (1828).

Francis II. 1836–1894. King (1859–60). Son of Ferdinand II; last of Bourbon kings of Naples; attempted to keep Naples neutral in war with Austria; after capture of Sicily by Garibaldi (1860), unsuccessfully attempted to save monarchy by granting liberal concessions in Naples; driven out of Naples (1860) by revolutionaries under Garibaldi; on capitulation of Gaeta (1861), forced to abdicate; spent rest of life in exile in Rome, France, and Austria.

Francis of As·si·si \ə-'sis-ē, -'sē-zē, -'sē-sē, -'siz-ē\. Saint. *Baptized* Gio·van·ni \jō-'vän-nē\, *renamed* Fran·ce·sco \frän-'chā-skō\, *in full* Francesco di Pie·tro di Ber·nar·do·ne \dē-'pyā-trō-dē-ˌber-när-'dō-nā\. 1181 or 1182–1226. Italian friar, b. Assisi. Founder of the Franciscan orders. Consecrated himself to poverty and religion (1205); began to preach (1208); gathered a group of disciples and drew up for them a rule of life approved by Pope Innocent III (1209); founded Poor Clares, an order for women (1212). Leader of movements to reform the church; acquired thousands of followers; visited the Holy Land (1219); organized a third order for the laity (c.1221); rewrote Franciscan rules (approved 1223); retired to mountain retreat of Alvernia where he received the stigmata (1224). Canonized by Pope Gregory IX (1228).

Francis of Mey·ronnes \me-rôn\. *Also called* Fran·cis·cus de May·ro·nis \fran-'sis-kəs-dē-mā-'rō-nəs\. c.1285–after 1328. French Franciscan monk and Scholastic philosopher. Student of Duns Scotus at Paris; served as legate of Pope John XXII; mediated peace negotiations between Charles IV of France and Edward III of England (1324); preached on sacramental theology before papal court at Avignon (c.1324). Called "prince of the Scotists" for his advocacy of Duns Scotus's subtle system of Realism; opposed Nominalism of William Ockham; his version of Scotism later prompted a Maronitae school of thought. His philosophical works included treatises *De formalitatibus* and *De univocatione entis* and commentaries on Aristotle *In perihemenias* and *Super universalia et praedicamenta;* theological works included commentary on Peter Lombard's *Books of Sentences, Quaestiones quodlibetae,* and collection of tracts on disputed questions and political theories.

Francis of Pao·la \'paù-lä\. Saint. 1416–1507. Italian Franciscan monk. Founder of Order of Minim Friars (c.1435; received papal approval, 1474); in France (from 1483); founded Minim orders for nuns and for laymen. Canonized (1519); named patron of Italian seamen (1943).

Francis of Sales \sål\. Saint. 1567–1622. French prelate. Ordained (1593); successfully completed mission to Chablais, Savoy, to convert Calvinists (1594–98). Bishop of Geneva (1602); aided St. Jane Frances de Chantal in founding Visitation of Holy Mary (1610). His writings included *Introduction to a Devout Life* (1608, definitive ed. 1609) and *Treatise on the Love of God* (1616). Canonized by Pope Alexander VII (1665); declared doctor of the church (1877); named patron of writers (1923).

Francis, James Bicheno. 1815–1892. American hydraulic engineer, b. Southleigh, England. To U.S. (1833); chief engineer (1837–85) of company in Lowell, Mass., engaged in manufacture of locomotives, erection of cotton mills, and management of Lowell's water-power facilities; contributed greatly to Lowell's rise as industrial city; invented the mixed-flow, or Francis, turbine; also known for hydraulic studies, investigations of timber preservation, cast-iron girders, fire protection systems. Author of *Lowell Hydraulic Experiments* (1855).

Francis, Sir Philip. 1740–1818. British government official, b. Dublin. One of commission of four councilors of the governor general of India (1774–81); charged Warren Hastings with official corruption; M.P. (1784–96, 1802–07); aided managers of impeachment of Hastings, esp. with series of anonymous pamphlets (1787–95). Reputed author of the *Letters of Junius* (1769–72), a series of letters attacking public characters of the day connected with the government.

Francis Ferdinand. *Ger.* Franz Fer·di·nand \'fer-dē-,nänt\. 1863–1914. Archduke of Austria. Son of Archduke Charles Louis and nephew of Emperor Francis Joseph; uncle of Charles I of Austria. Inherited title of archduke of Aus·tria-Este \'aù-strē-ə-'es-tā, -tə\ (1875); became heir apparent to crown (1896); m. (1900) Countess Sophie Chotek, Duchess of Hohenberg (1868–1914) but renounced right of succession for their children. Inspector general of army (1913). With his wife, was assassinated (June 28, 1914) by Serbian nationalist Gavrilo Princip at Sarajevo, Bosnia; this assassination was the immediate cause of World War I.

Francis Joseph I. *Ger.* Franz Jo·sef \'yō-zef\. 1830–1916. Emperor of Austria (1848–1916). Son of Archduke Francis Charles and nephew of Emperor Ferdinand I. At accession, empire in state of revolution; pacified Italy (Battle of Novara) and subdued Hungary (1849); defeated in Italian War of Liberation (1859). In alliance with Prussia, waged successful war against Denmark (1864); quarreled with Prussia, bringing on Seven Weeks' War (June–July 1866); overwhelmed at Sadowa; lost Venetia to Italy (1866) and was expelled from the German Confederation. Divided his empire into the Dual Monarchy, with Austria and Hungary as equal partners (1867); became king of Hungary (1867–1916). Adhered to Dreikaiserbund (1872–78); concluded Triple Alliance with Germany and Italy (1882); issued intransigent ultimatum to Serbia (July 1914) that led to World War I. His rule at first entirely absolutist, after 1867 unsympathetically constitutionalist; created a highly efficient civil administration.

Francisque. See Jean-François MILLET (c.1642–1679).

Francis Xavier, Saint. See XAVIER.

Franck \fräⁿk, *Angl* 'fräŋk\, César, *in full* César-Auguste-Jean-Guillaume-Hubert. 1822–1890. French organist and composer, b. Liége, Belgium. Studied at Liége (until 1837) and Paris (until 1842); settled in Paris as teacher (1844); organist at Sainte-Clothilde (from 1858); professor of organ at Paris Conservatory (from 1872); naturalized (1873). His compositions included oratorios *Ruth* (1846), *Rédemption* (1872), *Les Béatitudes* (1880), and *Rébecca* (1881); symphonic poems *Les Éolides* (1876), *Le Chasseur maudit* (1883), *Les Djinns* (1884), and *Psyché* (1888); operas *Hulda* (1894) and *Ghisèle* (1896); *Variations symphoniques* for piano and orchestra (1885), *La Procession* for soprano and orchestra (1888), Symphony in D minor (1889), piano trios and other piano pieces, organ music, a violin sonata (1886), a string quartet (1889), a Mass (1860), and other church music, songs, etc.

Franck \'fräŋk\, James. 1882–1964. American physicist, b. Hamburg, Germany. Professor, Göttingen (1920–33); to Denmark (1933), U.S. (1935); professor, U. of Chicago (1938–49). Known for researches with Gustav Hertz on energy changes that occur when atoms collide with electrons; with Edward Condon formulated Franck-Condon principle in molecular spectroscopy; worked on development of atomic bomb during World War II; also studied photosynthesis. Awarded, jointly with Hertz, 1925 Nobel prize for physics.

Franck, Melchior. c.1579–1639. German composer. Published over 40 collections of motets (1601–36), secular vocal music, dances for instrumental ensemble, etc.

Franck, Sebastian. c.1499–c.1542. German theologian. Roman Catholic priest (c.1524); joined (c.1525) Lutheran church at Nürnberg, becoming a preacher for the Reformation; broke with Lutheranism (1529), rejecting dogmatic beliefs and substituting a mystical attitude, attacking biblical literalism, opposing suppression of Anabaptists by force; friend of Kaspar Schwenckfeld in Strassburg (1529–31); printer and writer in Ulm (1533–39); expelled and settled in Basel. His theological, philosophical, and historical works included *Chronica: Zeitbuch und Geschichtsbibel* (1531), *Paradoxa* (1534), *Die goldene Arche* (1538), *Germaniae chronicon* (1538), and *Kriegsbüchlein* (1539).

Francke \'fräŋ-kə\, August Hermann. 1663–1727. German preacher, educator, and reformer. Taught theology and oriental languages at U. of Halle (1695–1727). Influenced by Philipp Spener, became one of principal promoters of Pietism. Founded at Halle (1695) a charity school, to which were added an orphanage (1698), a training school, a Latin school, a boarding school, etc., later combined into the Francke Institute.

Francke, Kuno. 1855–1930. American historian, b. Kiel, Germany. To U.S. (1884, naturalized 1891); teacher at Harvard (from 1884); professor of German culture (1896–1917); founder and curator, Germanic Museum, Harvard (1903–17). Author of *History of German Literature as Determined by Social Forces* (1901), *A German-American's Confession of Faith* (1915), etc.

Francke, Meister. 15th century. German painter. Executed an altarpiece for a Hamburg church (c.1424); painted representations of *Christ as the Man of Sorrows;* his style marked by realistic details, exaggerated expression of emotions, decorative use of color.

Franck·en \'fräŋ-kən\. Family of Flemish painters, including: Hieronymus *or* Jerom (1540–1610), helped decorate Fountainbleau; court painter to Henry III of France (1574); known for portraits and historical scenes, as *Abdication of Charles V.* His brother ¶Frans (1542–1616) painted religious and historical subjects. Another brother ¶Ambrosius (1544–1618) also helped decorate Fountainbleau; painted *Miracle of the Loaves and Fishes* and *Martyrdom of St. Crispin.* Frans's son ¶Frans (1581–1642), known for *Adoration of the Virgin* (1616), *Woman Taken in Adultery* (1628), *Prodigal Son* (1630).

Fran·co \'fraŋ-(,)kō, 'fräŋ-\ of Cologne. fl. 1250–c.1280. German music theorist. Author of *Ars cantus mensurabilis,* a treatise valuable for its systematization of rules and its exposition of using concords and discords. Commonly identified with an 11th-century Magister Franco of Cologne and sometimes with a Franco of Paris.

Fran·co \'fräŋ-kō\, Battista. *Called* Il Se·mo·lei \ēl-,sā-mō-'le-ē, -'lā-\. c.1498–c.1561. Italian painter. Imitator of Michelangelo; painted a *Last Judgment* in Urbino cathedral.

Fran·co \'fräŋ-kō, *Angl* 'fraŋ-(,)kō, 'fräŋ-\, Francisco. *In full* Francisco Paulino Hermenegildo Teódulo Franco Ba·ha·mon·de \bä-ä-'mòn-dā\. 1892–1975. Spanish soldier and dictator. Commissioned in army (1910); became national hero for role in campaigns (1920–26) against Moroccan rebels; major general (1934); chief of army general staff (1935). Joined insurgents in Spanish Civil War (July 1936); named head (caudillo) of rebel Nationalist government and generalissimo of its forces (Oct. 1936); completely defeated Republican army, capturing Madrid (1939). Kept Spain neutral during World War II; proclaimed (1947) Spain a monarchy, with himself as regent and retaining dictatorial powers; became a strong anti-Communist; ruled authoritatively, responsible for economic progress and political stability of Spain; relaxed his harsh conservatism during 1950s and '60s; designated Prince Juan Carlos as successor (1969); resigned as premier (1973) but retained positions of caudillo and generalissimo.

François. See also FRANCIS.

Fran·çois \fräⁿ-swå\, Jean-Charles. 1717–1769. French engraver. Appointed engraver to King Louis XV of France, and Stanisław of Poland; one of inventors of crayon method of engraving; engraved portraits for Saverien's *Histoire des philosophes modernes* (1761–69).

François, Nicolas-Louis. *Called* François de Neuf·châ·teau \də-nœ̄-shä-tō\. 1750–1828. French politician and writer. Minister of interior (1797); member of the Directory (1797–98); president of the Senate (1804–06); created comte under the Empire. His works included the comedy *Paméla* (1793), *Fables en contes en vers* (1815), translations, and anthologies.

Fran·co·ni \frän-'kō-nā, *Fr* frä-kō-nē\, Antonio. 1738–1836. French impresario, b. Italy. Considered founder of the French circus. To France (c.1756); became associated with Astley's Amphitheater in Paris (1783); leased theater from Astley and renamed it Amphithéâtre Franconi (1793); presented mainly equestrian spectacles; built Cirque Olympique de Franconi in Paris. Transferred (1805) management of circus to his sons ¶Laurent-Antoine (1776–1849) and ¶Jean-Girard-Henri, *called* Mi·nette \mē-net\ (1779–1849), both of whom became notable circus men. Another son ¶Victor-François (1811–1893) established first open-air hippodrome in Paris; developed a flamboyant circus spectacle that influenced American circuses.

Franconian house. See HOHENZOLLERN; SALIAN house.

Fran·gi·pa·ni \,frän-jē-'pän-ē, *Angl* ,fran-jə-'pan-ē\. Noble Roman family influential in affairs of the papacy and the Empire from 11th to 13th centuries, especially Cenzio (fl. early 12th century), head of Imperialist party in Rome; after death of Pope Pascal II (1118) refused to recognize his successor Gelasius II and, with aid of Emperor Henry V, secured election of an antipope, Gregory VIII, thus causing a schism in the church.

Frank \'fräŋk, *Angl* 'fraŋk\, Anne. 1929–1945. German Jewish diarist. To Amsterdam with her parents fleeing Nazi regime (1933); with parents and four other Jews went into hiding (July 9, 1942) from German occupation forces; discovered (Aug. 4, 1944), sent to concentration camps where she died of typhus. Her diary published by her father as *Het Achterhuis* (1947).

Frank \'fraŋk\, Glenn. 1887–1940. American educator, b. Queen City, Mo. Associate editor (1919–21) and editor in chief (1921–25) of *Century Magazine;* president, U. of Wisconsin (1925–37); editor of *Rural Progress Magazine* (from 1937). In early career known as advocate of liberal reforms, later as influential member of Republican party. Author of *The Politics of Industry* (1919), *An American Looks at His World* (1923), *America's Hour of Decision* (1934), etc.

Frank \'fräŋk\, Jacob. *Orig.* Jankiew Lei·bo·wicz \lā-'bȯ-vēch\. 1726–1791. Polish Jewish sectarian and false messiah. Founder of antirabbinical Frankist, or Zoharist, sect among Jews. Proclaimed himself the reincarnation of Shabbetai Tzevi (c.1751); formed (1755) Zoharist sect, abandoning Judaism for a "higher Torah" based on the Kabbalistic *Zohar;* banned as heretic by Polish Jewish community (1756); with hundreds of followers feigned conversion to Roman Catholicism as cover for their activities (1759); imprisoned by the Inquisition (1760–73); settled in Offenbach, styling himself a baron and living in luxury. Succeeded by daughter ¶Eve (d. 1816) as head of sect; spent all Frankist funds and arrested for bankruptcy. The Frankists eventually became real Roman Catholics.

Frank \'fräŋk\, Johann Peter. 1745–1821. German physician. One of chief founders of science of public health; one of first to use international regulation of health problems; favored a "medical police." Physician to Czar Alexander I (1805–08).

Frank, Leonhard. 1882–1961. German novelist. Fled to Switzerland (1914–18) for opposition to World War I; denounced war in *Der Mensch ist gut* (1917); freelance writer (1920–33); again fled to Switzerland (1933) from Nazis; interned in Paris (1940) but escaped to U.S.; returned to Germany (1950). Author of Expressionist novels dealing chiefly with the destruction of the individual spirit by bourgeois society, including *Die Räuberbande* (1914), *Der Burger* (1924), *Im letzten Wagen* (1925; reissued as *Der Absturz*), *Karl und Anna* (1926), *Das ochsenfurter Mannerquartett* (1927), and *Links, wo das Herz ist* (1952).

Frank \'fraŋk\, Waldo David. 1889–1967. American writer, b. Long Branch, N.J. A founder and editor, *The Seven Arts* magazine (1916–17). Author of *Our America* (1919), *Rahab* (1922), *Virgin Spain* (1926), *Death and Birth of David Markand* (1934), *The Bridegroom Cometh* (1938), *Island in the Atlantic* (1946), *Birth of a World* (1951), *Bridgehead* (1957), *Prophetic Island* (1961), etc.

Fran·kau \'fraŋ-(,)kō\, Gilbert. 1884–1952. English novelist. Author of popular novels in an exuberant, colorful style, including *Peter Jackson, Cigar Merchant* (1919), *The Love-Story of Aliette Brunton* (1922), *Christopher Strong* (1932), *Three Englishmen* (1935), *Son of Morning* (1949), *Unborn Tomorrow* (1953).

Fran·kel \'fräŋ-kəl\, Zacharias. 1801–1875. German rabbi, b. Prague. Chief rabbi, Dresden (1836–54); director of Jewish Theol. Sem., Breslau (from 1854). Developed a theology called positive-historical Judaism, which was principal forerunner of Conservative Judaism. Author of *Die Eidesleistung der Juden* (1840), *Vorstudien zur Septuaginta* (1841), *Darke ha-Mishnah* (1859), *Mebo ha-Yerushalmi* (1870).

Frank·fort \'fräŋk-fȯrt, *Angl* 'fraŋk-fərt\, Henri. 1897–1954. Dutch archaeologist. Professor at U. of Chicago and head of Warburg Institute of U. of London (1938–54); directed excavations in Egypt (1922, 1925–29) and Iraq (1929–37). Established relationship between Egypt and Mesopotamia; completed a thoroughly documented reconstruction of ancient Mesopotamian culture and art. Author of *Cylinder Seals* (1939), *Kingship and the Gods* (1948), *Ancient Egyptian Religion* (1948), *The Art and Architecture of the Ancient Orient* (1954), etc.

Frank·furt·er \'fraŋk-fürt-ər\, Felix. 1882–1965. American jurist, b. Vienna, Austria. To U.S. (1894); assistant to Henry L. Stimson (1906–09, 1911–13); professor, Harvard Law School (1914–39); helped found American Civil Liberties Union (1920); adviser to Pres. F. D. Roosevelt. Associate justice, U.S. Supreme Court (1939–1962); leading exponent of doctrine of judicial self-restraint. Author of *The Business of the Supreme Court* (1927, with James Landis), *Mr. Justice Holmes and the Supreme Court* (1938), *Felix Frankfurter Reminisces* (1960), etc.

Frankl \'fräŋ-kəl\, Paul. 1878–1962. German art critic and historian. Professor, Halle (1920–34); member of Institute for Advanced Study, Princeton, N.J. (from 1940). Developed a dialectical theory of art; author of *Das System der Kunstwissenschaft* (1938), *The Gothic* (1960), etc.

Frank·land \'fraŋk-land\, Sir Edward. 1825–1899. English chemist. Professor, Royal Institution (1863–68), Royal Coll. of Chemistry (1865–85); member of Royal Commission on Rivers Pollution (1868–74); founder and first president of Institute of Chemistry (1877–80). Established (1852) a theory of valency which became basis of modern structural chemistry; aided J.N. Lockyer in solar studies (1868). Author of *Experimental Researches in Pure, Applied, and Physical Chemistry* (1877), etc.

Frank·lin \'fraŋ-klən\, Benjamin. 1706–1790. American statesman, scientist, and philosopher, b. Boston. Apprenticed (1718) to his brother James (*q.v.*), printer; wrote (1722) series of 14 satires under pseudonym Silence Dogood; after disagreements with James, left Boston (1723) and settled in Philadelphia as printer. Proprietor of printing business and publisher of *The Pennsylvania Gazette* (1730–48); printer (from 1729) of paper currency for Pennsylvania and later for New Jersey, Delaware, Maryland; gained wide circle of readers by *Poor Richard's Almanack* (1732–57), published under pseudonym of Richard Saunders and containing store of witty aphorisms and moral precepts that influenced the thought of the time; formed discussion club the "Junto" (1727), which (1744) developed into American Philosophical Society; laid foundations of library (1731) for use of public, which developed into Philadelphia Library (chartered 1742); instrumental in improving care and lighting of city streets; clerk of Pennsylvania legislature (1736–51); helped found (1751) Academy of Philadelphia, which became U. of Pennsylvania; deputy postmaster at Philadelphia (1737–53); deputy postmaster general for the colonies (1753–74). Invented Franklin stove (c.1744), bifocal spectacles, and the lightning rod; interested in natural philosophy; became silent partner in his printing house and retired from active business (1748). Began experiments with electricity (c.1746); tried famous kite experiment (1752). In public life from 1754; Pennsylvania's delegate to Albany Congress (1754); to England to represent Pennsylvania Assembly in efforts to enforce taxes on proprietary estates (1757–62); agent in England (1764–75) for Pennsylvania and later for Georgia, New Jersey, Massachusetts. Member, Second Continental Congress (1775); on committee to draft Declaration of Independence, and one of its signers. Sent by Congress as one of committee of three to negotiate treaty with France (1776), becoming immensely popular during his stay (1776–85); after signing (Feb. 6, 1778) of treaties of commerce and of defensive alliance, appointed sole plenipotentiary to France (Sept. 1778); appointed (1781) commissioner, with Jay and Adams, to negotiate peace with Great Britain (preliminary negotiations successfully completed Nov. 1781; final peace signed Sept. 3, 1783). Returned to Philadelphia (1785); president, Pennsylvania executive council (1785–87); member, Constitutional Convention (1787). His *Autobiography* was first published in complete and accurate form in 1868; also published many papers and newspaper articles on political, economic, religious, philosophical, and scientific subjects.

Franklin, Edward Curtis. 1862–1937. American chemist, b. Geary City, Kans. Professor, U. of Kansas (1898–1903), Stanford (1906–29); authority on the ammonia system of compounds and liquid ammonia as an electrolytic solvent.

Franklin, James. 1697–1735. American printer, b. Boston. Brother of Benjamin Franklin. Set up printing business in Boston (1717); printed the *Boston Gazette* (1719–21); founder and publisher of the *New England Courant* (1721–27); established first printing press in Rhode Island (1727); founded (1732) *Rhode Island Gazette,* first newspaper in that state.

Franklin, Sir John. 1786–1847. English explorer. Entered Royal Navy (1801); served at Trafalgar (1805) and New Orleans (1814–15); governor (1836–43) of Van Diemen's Land (now Tasmania). Headed expeditions into Arctic (1818, 1819–22, 1825–27); his last expedition (1845–47), on which all members were lost, proved existence of the Northwest Passage.

Franklin, Rosalind Elsie. 1920–1958. English biophysicist. Her studies on X-ray diffraction important to the discovery (1953) of the molecular structure of DNA.

Franklin, William. 1731–1813. American colonial administrator, b. Philadelphia. Illegitimate son of Benjamin Franklin. Governor of New Jersey (1763–76); upheld royal authority and was in conflict with colonists; arrested as Loyalist (1776), exchanged (1778); returned to England (c.1782).

Franklin, William Buel. 1823–1903. American army officer, b. York, Pa. Commissioned in army (1843); served in Mexican War and in Civil War; fought in Peninsular Campaign and at Antietam (1862); major general (1862); held by Gen. Burnside partly responsible for defeat at Fredericksburg (1862) and relieved of his command; served in Louisiana (1863), in Department of the Gulf (1864); resigned from army (1866).

Frank·lin-Bouil·lon \fräⁿ-klaⁿ-bü-yōⁿ\, Henri. 1872–1937. French journalist and politician. Minister of propaganda (1917); negotiated agreement with Turkey (signed Oct. 20, 1921) recognizing Ankara government and Turko–Syrian frontier.

Fran·ko \'frän-kō\, Ivan Yakovlevich. 1856–1916. Ukrainian writer and journalist. His works included poetry collected in *Vershiny i niziny* (1887–93), stories as "Boa Constrictor" (1878) and novels as *Borislav smeyetsya* (1881–82) of the peasant and working classes, epic *Moysey* (1905), drama, criticism, etc.

Franks \'fraŋks\, Sir Augustus Wollaston. 1826–1897. British curator, b. Switzerland. First curator of British and medieval antiquities and ethnography, British Museum (1866–96); improved its collections, esp. with donation of his own collection.

Franqueville, Pierre de. See FRANCHEVILLE.

Fran·sci·ni \frän-'shē-nē\, Stefano. 1796–1857. Swiss politician. Secretary to the Ticino government (1830–48); instituted liberal reforms, esp. in state education; member of Swiss government (1848–57). Wrote political and social works, including *Statistica della svizzera* (1827), *La svizzera italiana* (1837), etc.

Franz. See FRANCIS.

Franz \'fränts\, Robert. *Orig. surname* Knauth \'knaut\. 1815–1892. German song composer. In Halle as organist of the Ulrichskirche (from 1841), conductor of the Singakademie (from 1842), and director of university music (from 1851); retired (1868). Author of works on Bach and Handel; composed over 350 songs, many set to texts of Heinrich Heine, chorals, a Kyrie, etc.

Fran·zén \frän-'sān\, Frans Mikael. 1772–1847. Swedish poet, b. Finland. Professor, Åbo (1798); clergyman in Sweden (from 1811); bishop of Härnösand (from 1831). Author of *Selma and Fanny* (lyrical cycle, 1824), epic poems as *Christopher Columbus* (1831) and *Gustavus Adolphus in Germany* (unfinished), didactic poems, prose biographies of prominent Swedes, etc.

Frasch \'fräsh\, Herman. 1851–1914. American chemist, b. Gaildorf, Germany. To U.S. (1868); worked as chemist in Philadelphia and Cleveland; to Ontario and organized Empire Oil Co. (1885); devised processes for desulfurizing crude oils, thus making Canadian and Ohio oils commercially valuable; his patents and Empire Oil Co. acquired by Standard Oil Co. (1888). Devised hot-water melting process of extracting sulfur (1891); headed Union Sulphur Co.; founded great American sulfur-mining industry.

Fra·ser \'frā-zər, -zhər\, James Baillie. 1783–1856. Scottish traveler. Traveled in Nepal (1815), Persia (1821–22, 1833–34, 1840). Author of travel books and tales based on Persian life and customs.

Fraser, James Earle. 1876–1953. American sculptor, b. Winona, Minn. Executed portrait busts of Ulysses Grant, Saint-Gaudens, Theodore Roosevelt, and Elihu Root, monuments of John Hay, John Ericsson, Lincoln, equestrian statue *The End of the Trail* (1896), figures of *Justice* and *Law* for Supreme Court Building, Washington, D.C.; designed U.S. buffalo five-cent piece (1913) and World War I Victory Medal (1919).

Fraser, Peter. 1884–1950. New Zealand politician, b. Scotland. To New Zealand (1910); helped found Labour party (1916); M.P. (from 1918); leader of Labour party (from 1919); minister of education, health, marine, and police (1935–40); responsible for legislation revising educational system and creating national health service. Prime minister of New Zealand (1940–49); exerted strong leadership during World War II, increasing New Zealand's international stature; an architect of United Nations (1945).

Fraser, Simon. 1776–1862. Canadian fur trader and explorer, b. Bennington, N.Y. (now in Vt.). To Canada (1784). Clerk (1792), partner (1801), North West Co., fur trading firm; on second expedition (1806–08) to West to establish trading routes discovered the Fraser River and navigated it to its mouth; retired (1818).

Fra·şe·ri \frä-sher-'ē\, Şemseddin Sami. *Also known as* Semseddin Sami Bey Fraseri. 1850–1904. Turkish writer and lexicographer, b. Fraşer, Albania. To Istanbul as journalist; founded newspaper *Sabah* (1875); became associated with new Turkish writers. Author of plays *Besa, Sidi Yahya,* and *Kave;* novels including *Taaşuk-i talât ve fitnet* (1872); and translations from the French; his lexicographical works included French–Turkish, Turkish–French dictionary *Kamus-i Fransevi,* encyclopedia *Kamus-i alam,* and Turkish dictionary *Kamus-i Türki.*

Frauenlob. See HEINRICH VON MEISSEN.

Frau·en·städt \'frau-ən-ˌshtet\, Julius, *in full* Christian Martin Julius. 1813–1879. German philosopher. Disciple and expounder of Schopenhauer; edited Schopenhauer's works (1873–74); author of *Die Freiheit des Menschen und die Persönlichkeit Gottes* (1838), *Studien und Kritiken* (1840), *Briefe über die Schopenhauersche Philosophie* (1854), etc.

Fraunce \'frȯn(t)s, 'frän(t)s\, Abraham. c.1558–c.1633. English poet. Called to bar (1588); apparently practiced in Welsh marches. Author of Latin comedy *Victoria,* critical textbook *Arcadian Rhetorike* (1588), *The Lawiers Logike* (1588), verse *The Countesse of Pembrokes Emanuel* (1591), etc.

Fraun·ho·fer \'fraun-ˌhō-fər\, Joseph von. 1787–1826. Bavarian optician and physicist. Journeyman (1806), director (from 1818), Untzschneider Optical Institute, Benedictbeuern. While investigating refractive index of various kinds of glass, observed (1814) and mapped 576 dark lines in solar spectrum, now called Fraunhofer lines; investigated spectra of planets and fixed stars; invented a heliometer, a micrometer, and a diffraction grating he used to measure wave lengths of light (1814); made improvements in telescopes and other optical instruments.

Fravartish. See PHRAORTES.

Fra·zer \'frā-zər, -zhər\, Sir James George. 1854–1941. Scottish anthropologist. Professor, U. of Liverpool (1907–08), Cambridge U. (from 1908). His great work *The Golden Bough* (2 vols., 1890; expanded to 12 vols., 1907–15), a study of cults, myths, rites, etc., their origins and their importance in the historical development of religions; other works included *Totemism and Exogamy* (1910), *The Belief in Immortality and the Worship of the Dead* (1913–24), *Folk-lore in the Old Testament* (1918), *The Fear of the Dead in Primitive Religion* (1933–36), *Creation and Evolution in Primitive Cosmogonies* (1935), etc.

Fra·zier \'frā-zhər\, Edward Franklin. 1894–1962. American sociologist, b. Baltimore. Professor, Fisk U. (1929–34) and Howard U. (1934–59); authority on racial interactions and the black family. Author of *The Negro Family in the United States* (1939), *Race and Culture Contacts in the Modern World* (1957), *The Negro Church in America* (1963), etc.

Fré·chet \frā-she, -shā\, Maurice-René. 1878–1973. French mathematician. Professor, Poitiers (1910–19), Strasbourg (1920–27); lecturer (1928–33), professor (1933–48), U. of Paris. Proposed first definition and founded theory of abstract spaces; also contributed to topology, statistics, differential and integral calculus. Works included *Les Espaces abstraits* (1928), *Récherches théoriques modernes sur la théorie des probabilités* (1937–38), *Les Probabilités associées à un système d'évenements compatibles et dependants* (1939–43), *Pages choisies d'analyse générale* (1953), *Les Mathématiques et le concret* (1955).

Fré·chette \frā-shet\, Louis-Honoré. 1839–1908. Canadian poet, b. Lévis, Que. Clerk of Quebec Legislative Council (1889–1908). Author of patriotic poems in French, including *Mes loisirs* (1863), *La Voix d'un exilé* (1866–68), *Les Oiseaux de niege* (1879), *Les Fleurs boréales* (1879; with *Les Oiseaux* crowned by French Academy, 1880, first time for work by a Canadian), *La Légende d'un peuple* (1887), *Pêle-Mêle* (1887), *Feuilles volantes* (1891), *Poésies choisies* (1908). Author also of collections of tales *Originaux et détraqués* (1892) and *Le Noël au Canada* (1899), dramas *Félix Poutré* (1871), *Papineau* (1880), *Véronica* (1908), and polemical *Lettres à Brasile* (1872).

Fred·e·gar·i·us \ˌfred-ə-'ga(ə)r-ē-əs, -'ge(ə)r-\. Name assigned (1579) by Claude Fauchet to the 7th-century compiler, or compilers, of the chronicle *Historia Francorum,* a large work in corrupt Latin on general and early Frankish history to the year 642.

Fred·e·gund \'fred-ə-gənd\. *Fr.* Fré·dé·gonde \frā-dā-gōⁿd\. d. 597 A.D. Frankish queen. Wife of Chilperic I of Neustria. Caused assassination (567 or 568) of Galeswintha, previous wife of Chilperic and sister of Brunhilda, wife of Sigebert I, king of Austrasia; after Sigebert's victory in war that followed, had him murdered (575) by her agents; ruled as regent for her son Chlotar II and defeated Brunhilda in war (596).

Fred·er·ic \'fred-(ə-)rik\, Harold. 1856–1898. American novelist, b. Utica, N.Y. In London as correspondent for *New York Times* (1884–98). Author of *The Lawton Girl* (1890), *In the Valley* (1890), *The Copperhead* (1893), *The Damnation of Theron Ware* (1896), *March Hares* (1896), *Gloria Mundi* (1898), *The Market Place* (1899), etc.

Fred·er·ick \'fred-(ə-)rik\. *Ger.* Frie·drich \'frē-ˌdrik\. Name of several dukes and archdukes of Austria, including:

Frederick II. d. 1246. Duke of Austria and Styria (1230–46). Last of the Babenbergs.

Frederick of Austria. Duke (1306–30). See FREDERICK III, king of Germany.

Frederick V. Archduke. See FREDERICK III, Holy Roman emperor.

Frederick. Name of three rulers of Brandenburg:

Frederick I. 1371–1440. Elector and margrave of Brandenburg (1417–40). Son of Frederick V, burgrave of Nürnberg; burgrave of Ansbach (1398); secured election (1410) of Sigismund to German throne; given governorship of Brandenburg as reward (1411); formally made elector (1417); obtained Bayreuth on death of elder brother John (1420). Gave control (1425) of Brandenberg affairs to son John the Alchemist, moved to Franconia, and devoted rest of life to imperial affairs; helped negotiate pacts of Prague (1433) and Iglau (1436); unsuccessful candidate for German throne (1440). Founder of the Brandenburg line of Hohenzollern.

Frederick II. 1413–1471. Elector (1440–70). Son of Frederick I; strict in internal affairs, conciliatory in dealing with neighboring states; waged war with Pomerania; abdicated (1470).

Frederick III. See FREDERICK I of Prussia.

Frederick. *Dan.* Frede·rik \'frith-rik\. Name of nine kings of Denmark, the first six of whom were also kings of Norway:

Frederick I. 1471–1533. King of Denmark (1523–33) and Norway (1524–33). Son of Christian I and brother of John I. Duke of Holstein; chosen king when Christian II dethroned; strengthened nobility; encouraged spread of Lutheranism in Denmark; imprisoned Christian II after latter invaded Norway (1531).

Frederick II. 1534–1588. King (1559–88). Son of Christian III; subdued Dithmarschen (1559); waged war with Sweden (1563–70); made peace at Stettin; rest of reign (1570–88) years of peace; suppressed pirates; built fortress of Kronborg at Elsinore; patron of Tycho Brahe and of arts and science; able and popular ruler.

Frederick III. 1609–1670. King (1648–70). Son of Christian IV; held several positions in the church (1623–34); commanded Danish forces in Schleswig-Holstein against Sweden (1643–45). Engaged in war with Sweden (1657–60); forced by Charles X to sign Treaty of Roskilde (1658); compelled Swedes to raise siege of Copenhagen (1659); finally defeated in war and forced to sign unfavorable peace terms (1660); with aid of commons and clergy, reduced power of nobles; became hereditary monarch (1660) with absolute power; raised Peder Schumacher, his secretary, to high position (1662–70); with aid of adviser Hannibal Sehested, reformed state administration and reorganized government into five departments.

Frederick IV. 1671–1730. King (1699–1730). Son of Christian V; allied himself with Poland and Russia against Sweden (1700) but forced by Charles XII to make peace; freed peasants from serfdom (1702); again declared war on Sweden after Charles's defeat at Poltava (1709) but Danes defeated at Hålsingborg (1710); made peace (1720) by which possessions in Germany were given up.

Frederick V. 1723–1766. King (1746–66). Son of Christian VI; m. (1743) Louisa, daughter of George II of England; took little interest in affairs of state; made Count Bernstorff chief minister (1750–66); maintained neutrality in Seven Years' War (1756–63); saved from Russian attack (1762) by death of Peter III; increased agriculture, commerce, and manufacture, established Asiatic Company; patronized literature, fostered education in Norway.

Frederick VI. 1768–1839. King of Denmark (1808–39) and of Norway (1808–14). Son of Christian VII; called to head of state council (1784) when his father became insane; ruled as regent (1784–1808); greatly assisted by his minister A.P. Bernstorff; aided in abolishing serfdom and slave trade; with his council, caused Denmark to join (1800) armed neutrality of the North; as a result, saw Danish fleet destroyed by British (1801) and Copenhagen bombarded (1807); became ally of Napoléon (1807); lost Norway to Sweden (1814); ruled wisely during period of recovery and reform (1814–39), although somewhat narrow-minded; established (1834) four consultative provincial assemblies, beginning of parliamentary government in Denmark.

Frederick VII. 1808–1863. King of Denmark (1848–63). Son of Christian VIII; promulgated new constitution (1849) which deprived him of absolute power; involved during much of reign in disputes with Germany and Austria over duchies of Schleswig and Holstein; died childless as last of Oldenburg line.

Frederick VIII. 1843–1912. King of Denmark (1906–12). Son of Christian IX; served in war with Germany (1864); m. (1869) Princess Louise of Sweden; a popular ruler with simple style of living; father of Haakon VII of Norway; succeeded by his eldest son Christian X.

Frederick IX. 1899–1972. King of Denmark (1947–72). Son of Christian X; made crown prince (1912); entered navy (1917), rising to rear admiral (1946); m. (1935) Princess Ingrid of Sweden; encouraged Danish resistance movement against German occupation forces; imprisoned (1943–45) by Germans; signed (1953) constitution providing for female succession to throne and reducing parliament to one house; succeeded by his daughter Margrethe.

Frederick. *Ger.* Friedrich. Kings of Germany:

Frederick I, II, IV. See FREDERICK I, II, III, Holy Roman emperors.

Frederick III. *Known also as* Frederick of Austria. *Called* der Schö·ne \'shœ-nə\, *i.e.* the Fair *or* the Handsome. c.1286–1330. Duke of Austria (1308–30); king of Germany (1314–30). Son of Albert I; chosen by a minority of electors (1314); waged long war with Louis of Bavaria (1314–22); defeated at Mühldorf (1322) and imprisoned (1322–25); acknowledged Louis as emperor; joint ruler (1325–30).

Frederick II. *Known as* Prince of Hom·burg \'hōm-,bu̇rk, *Angl* 'häm-,bərg\. 1633–1708. German general and landgrave (1681–1708) of Hesse-Homburg. Son of Landgrave Frederick I; served in Swedish army (1654–59) under Charles X Gustav; general of cavalry (1670–78) under Frederick William, elector of Brandenburg; active in defeat of Swedes at Fehrbellin (1675); succeeded his brother George Christian as landgrave (1681); spent entire rule in improving and beautifying Homburg.

Frederick. *Ger.* Friedrich. Name of two landgraves of Hesse-Kassel:

Frederick I. See FREDERICK I of Sweden.

Frederick II. 1720–1785. Landgrave (1760–85). Fought in war of Austrian Succession and (1745) against the Young Pretender in Scotland; did much to improve Kassel, esp. its fine buildings, but also led a profligate life; to provide funds sold an army of 12,000 Hessians to British to employ in the American Revolution.

Frederick. *Ger.* Friedrich. Name of three Holy Roman emperors:

Frederick I. *Called* Bar·ba·ros·sa \,bär-bə-'räs-ə, -'rōs-\. c.1123–1190. Holy Roman emperor (1152–90; crowned 1155). Son of Frederick II, Duke of Swabia; nephew of Conrad III; duke of Swabia as Frederick III. King of Germany (1152–90) and of Italy (1155–90). Challenged papal authority over the empire; forced Eugenius III to sign Treaty of Constance (1153). Made six expeditions against cities of northern Italy (1154–84); at first successful; after formation of Lombard League (1167) and his defeat at Legnano (1176), Peace of Constance (1183) granted independence to Lombard cities. Opposed by Pope Alexander III in Italian struggle (1159–77). Overcame Guelphs, led by Henry the Lion, in Germany (1180–81). Set out on Third Crusade (1189); drowned while trying to cross the Saleph River in Cilicia. Esteemed by Germans as one of their greatest kings. Empire enlarged, learning advanced, internal peace maintained, and town and city development encouraged.

Frederick II. 1194–1250. King of Sicily as Frederick I (1198–1250). Holy Roman emperor (1212–50; crowned 1220). Son of Henry VI; under guardianship of Pope Innocent III (1198–1208). Elected king of Germany (1212); consolidated his Sicilian holdings by military means and innovations in civil administration; m. (1225), as 2d wife, Isabella of Brienne and through her claimed (1227) kingdom of Jerusalem, assumed crown (1229); excommunicated (1227, 1239, 1245). Led Sixth Crusade (1228–29); captured Jersualem, Bethlehem, and Nazareth. On return, reconquered Sicilian lands from papal troops and issued (1231) new constitutions for Sicily; launched campaign against Lombard League (1235); put down rebellions in Germany (1236–37); died while enjoying some success in Italian campaign. Married (1235), as 3d wife, Isabella, daughter of John of England. Noted for his varied talents and learning; patron of literature and science.

Frederick III. 1415–1493. King of Germany as Frederick IV and Holy Roman emperor (1440–93; crowned 1452). Archduke of Austria as Frederick V. Son of Duke Ernest of Austria; inherited Habsburg possessions of Inner Austria (1424); concordat of Vienna concluded (1448) between emperor and Pope Nicholas V. Sought to increase Empire but in general failed; his reign marked by almost continual conflict, esp. against German princes and Austrian nobles; marriage (1477) of his son Maximilian to Mary of Burgundy resulted in union of Habsburg and Burgundian dynasties.

Frederick. Kings of Norway. See FREDERICK I–VI of Denmark.

Frederick. *Ger.* Friedrich. Name of five electors of the Palatinate:

Frederick I. *Called* der Sieg·rei·che \'zē-,krī-kə\, *i.e.* the Victorious. 1425–1476. Elector (1451–76). Opposed Emperor Frederick III; increased Palatinate territory.

Frederick II. *Called* der Wei·se \'vī-zə\, *i.e.* the Wise. 1482–1556. Elector (1544–56). Commanded Imperial army when Süleyman I besieged Vienna (1529); influenced by Melanchthon, accepted Protestant faith.

Frederick III. *Called* der From·me \'frȯm-ə\, *i.e.* the Pious. 1515–1576. Elector (1559–76). Embraced Lutheranism (1546), Calvinism (1561); had Heidelberg Catechism drawn up (1563); unsuccessful in attempts to unite Protestant princes against the Habsburgs.

Frederick IV. 1574–1610. Elector (1592–1610). Founded Evangelical Union (1608); strongly devoted to Protestant cause.

Frederick V. 1596–1632. Elector (1610–23). Son of Frederick IV; chosen king of Bohemia (1619); completely defeated at battle of White Mountain (1620); deprived of electorate (1623) and in exile until his death. Married (1613) Elizabeth, daughter of James I of England; their daughter Sophia was mother of George I of England.

Frederick. *Ger.* Friedrich. Name of three kings of Prussia:

Frederick I. 1657–1713. King (1701–13). Son of Frederick William, elector of Brandenburg; m. (1684), as 2d wife, Sophia Charlotte (*q.v.*). Elector of Brandenburg (1688–1701) as Frederick III. Member of Grand Alliance against Louis XIV of France (1689–97); for aid to Emperor Leopold I in War of Spanish Succession (1701–14), granted royal title to Prussia; received only small reward at Peace of Utrecht (1713). Freed his kingdom from imperial suzerainty, increased its territory, revenues, industry; patron of scholars, esp. Leibnitz; founder of the U. of Halle (1694).

Frederick II. *Known as* der Gros·se \'grō-sə\, *i.e.* the Great. 1712–1786. King of Prussia (1740–86). Son of King Frederick William I and Sophia Dorothea; grandson of Frederick I; tried to escape from father's control (1730); arrested, tried as deserter, but pardoned; m. (1733) Elisabeth Christine, daughter of Ferdinand Albert II of Brunswick; engaged in literary and social pursuits (1732–40). Became king (1740); on death of Emperor Charles VI (1740) made claims to Silesia for Prussia; began War of Austrian Succession (1740–48); formed alliance with France and Bavaria; won battles at Mollwitz (1741) and Chotusitz (1742), invaded Bohemia (1744), and by Peace of Dresden (1745) secured possession of Silesia; built (1745–47) palace of Sans Souci, near Potsdam, for royal residence. Formed new alliance (1756) with England against Maria Theresa, France, Russia, Sweden, and Saxony, which marked beginning of Seven Years' War (1756–63); displayed great military genius and perseverance in face of great odds; won many battles but was badly defeated in some; emerged after Peace of Hubertusburg (1763) enjoying great military prestige and with Prussia a much strengthened state. Joined Russia in first partition of Poland (1772); took part in War of Bavarian Succession (1778); formed (1785) Fürstenbund, a league of German princes to defend imperial constitution against Austria. Notable patron of literature (esp. 1745–55); invited Voltaire to live at his court (1750–53); favored French culture but indifferent to German writers. Skillful administrator of national economy, encouraging agricultural and industrial improvements; began codification of new Prussian code; instituted many social reforms; liberalized laws of censorship, religion, torture; took special interest in improvement of Prussian army. Voluminous writer; works included *Histoire de mon temps* (1740–45), *Anti-Machiavel* (1740, pub. 1767), *Histoire de la guerre de sept ans* (1763).

Frederick III. *Ger. in full* Friedrich Wilhelm Nikolaus Karl. 1831–1888. King and German emperor (March–June 1888). Son of William I of Prussia; engaged in military duties and travel (1851–58); m. Victoria Adelaide Mary Louise (1858), eldest daughter of Queen Victoria of England. Crown prince of Prussia (1861–88); strongly opposed to Bismarck's policies for strengthening Prussia (1861–66) and to war with Austria (1866), but took part in war, commanding division that secured victory at Königgrätz (1866); in command of armies of southern states in Franco–Prussian War (1870–71); took part in battles of Wörth and Sedan and in siege of Paris. Patron of literature and science. Developed cancer in the throat (1887); reigned only 99 days; dismissed minister of the interior Robert von Puttkamper; succeeded by his son William II.

Frederick. *Ger.* Friedrich. Name of three electors of Saxony:

Frederick I. *Called* der Streit·ba·re \'shtrīt-ˌbär-ə\, *i.e.* the Warlike. 1370–1428. Elector (1423–28). Son of Frederick of Meissen; duke of Saxony (1382–1428); vigorously opposed Hussites (1420–26); made elector of Saxony by Emperor Sigismund (1423), thus securing electorship for House of Wettin. U. of Leipzig founded during his reign.

Frederick II. *Called* der Sanft·mü·ti·ge \'zänft-ˌmue-tē-gə, -tē-yə\, *i.e.* the Gentle. 1411–1464. Elector (1428–64). Son of Frederick I; concluded peace treaty with Hussites (1432); instituted regular diets in his territories; acquired burgravate of Meissen (1439); fought Bruderkrieg (1445–51) with his brother William over partition of lands.

Frederick III. *Called* der Wei·se \'vī-zə\, *i.e.* the Wise. 1463–1525. Elector (1486–1525). Son of Elector Ernest; allied himself with Archbishop Berthold of Henneberg to promote imperial reforms, esp. to increase nobles' power at expense of the emperor; instrumental in securing election of emperor Charles V (1519) after having refused crown. Made his court center of artistic activity; patron of Albrecht Dürer and Lucas Cranach the Elder; founded U. of Wittenberg (1502); called Luther and Melanchthon to its faculty; did not become a follower of Luther but was tolerant of reform; refused (1520) to execute papal ban against Luther and (1521) caused him to be conveyed to the castle of Wartburg under his protection.

Frederick. Name of three kings of Sicily:

Frederick I. See FREDERICK II, Holy Roman emperor; in his minority, king of Sicily (1198–1212).

Frederick II. 1272–1337. King (1296–1337). Son of King Peter III of Aragon; governor of Sicily (1291); supported by Sicilians, refused to give up Sicily to the church (1295); elected king (Dec. 1295) by Sicilian parliament; called himself Frederick III to revive Ghibelline tradition of Holy Roman Emperor Frederick II; waged war with Charles II of Naples (1296–1302), renewed (1313–17) against Charles's successor; island put under interdict by pope (1321–35); war with Angevins continued (1325 ff.).

Frederick III. *Called* el Sim·ple \'sēm-plā\, *i.e.* the Simple. 1341–1377. King (1355–77), last of Aragonese line. Continued war with Naples; held Sicily as fief of Joan I of Naples (1372–77).

Frederick I. 1676–1751. King of Sweden (1720–51), b. Kassel. Fought for England in War of Spanish Succession; as landgrave of Hesse-Kassel, married (1715) Ulrika Eleonora (*q.v.*); elected king on her abdication; deprived of power by new constitution; during rest of reign affairs of state controlled largely by House of Nobles; devoted most of his time to hunting and love affairs; much strife between political parties (Caps and Hats); foreign policy dominated (1720–38) by Count Arvid Horn; war fought (1741–43) with Russia in Finland.

Frederick VII. Count of Tog·gen·burg \'tȯg-ən-ˌbu̇rk\. d. 1436. Swiss noble. Spent most of life adding to his vast land holdings, ruling (by 1436) much of eastern Switzerland; had dynastic aims; died without heir. Conflicts between cantons of Zürich and Schwyz over inheritance to his lands led to first civil war of Swiss Confederation (1439).

Frederick. 1452–1504. King of the Two Sicilies (1496–1501) of the Aragonese line. Son of Ferdinand I of Naples; succeeded his nephew Ferdinand II; forced to yield Naples to Louis XII of France.

Frederick I. *In full* Frederick William Charles. 1754–1816. Duke of Württemberg as Frederick II (1797–1805); king as Frederick I (1806–16). Son of Duke Frederick I Eugene and Sophia Dorothea, niece of Frederick the Great; served in Prussian and Russian armies; as duke, joined second coalition against France; lost some of possessions (1801) but received title of elector (1803); sided with Napoléon, and had his duchy raised to a kingdom (1805); joined Confederation of the Rhine (1806); after defeat of Napoléon at Leipzig (1813), joined Allies. His daughter Catherine married (1807) Jérôme Bonaparte, King of Westphalia.

Frederick Augustus. *Ger.* Friedrich August. (1) Name of three electors of Saxony: see AUGUSTUS II and III of Poland; FREDERICK AUGUSTUS I of Saxony, below. (2) Name of three kings of Saxony:

Frederick Augustus I. *Called* der Ge·rech·te \gə-'rek-tə\, *i.e.* the Just. 1750–1827. Elector of Saxony as Frederick Augustus III (1763–1806); first king (1806–27). As elector brought order and efficiency to country's finances and administration; aided Frederick the Great against Austria (1778–79); joined League of the German Princes (1785) but neutral during Austro–Prussian dispute (1790); refused crown of Poland (1791); fought against France (1792–1806); after defeat of Jena, made peace with Napoléon and by him given duchy of Warsaw (1808); ally of Napoléon (1808–15); deprived of three-fifths of kingdom by Congress of Vienna (1815); spent rest of life in rehabilitation of his kingdom.

Frederick Augustus II. 1797–1854. King (1836–54). Nephew of Frederick Augustus I; joint regent with his uncle Anton (1830–36); at first favored German unification and reforms, reactionary after crushing (1849) insurrection in Dresden; rest of reign tranquil.

Frederick Augustus III. 1865–1932. King (1904–18). Son of King George of Saxony; entered army (1883); general in Prussian service (1902); constitutional struggle continued from preceding reign; abdicated (1918); formed mercantile corporation.

Frederick Augustus. Duke of York and Al·ba·ny \'yȯ(ə)r-kən-'(d)ȯl-bə-nē\. 1763–1827. English soldier. Second son of King George III of England; prince-bishop of Osnabrück (1764–1803). Given command of English army sent to Flanders to aid Austria against France (1793); scored some victories but defeated at Hondschoote (1793) and Tournai (1794); driven in retreat through Belgium; made field marshal (1795), commander in chief (1798); led Anglo-Russian invasion of Holland (1799), defeated, and forced to sign Convention of Alkmaar. Resigned (1809) because of traffic in appointments by his mistress, Mary Anne Clarke; acquitted of wrongdoing and restored (1811). Founded Duke of York's School, London; in later years a leading opponent of Roman Catholic enfranchisement.

Frederick Charles. See FRIEDRICH KARL.

Frederick Christian Augustus. *Ger.* Friedrich Christian August. 1829–1880. Prince of Augustenburg and duke of Schleswig-Holstein-Sonderburg-Augustenburg. After death of father (1863), proclaimed duke as Frederick VIII despite father's renunciation (1852) of family claim to Schleswig-Holstein; proclamation gave Bismarck excuse to send Austro-Prussian army into Danish-held Schleswig, precipitating war.

Frederick Francis. *Ger.* Friedrich Franz. Name of four grand dukes of Mecklenburg-Schwerin, esp.: Frederick Francis II (1823–1883), German general; grand duke (1842–83); in Prussian military service (1842–71); in wars against Denmark (1864) and Austria (1866); took important part in Franco-Prussian War (1870–71).

Frederick Henry. Prince of Orange and Count of Nassau. 1584–1647. Dutch general and politician. Son of William the Silent; joined army under his half-brother Maurice of Nassau (1597); became prince of Orange on death of Maurice (1625). Stadtholder (from 1625) of five of the United Provinces and later (1640) of sixth (Friesland only exception). First of House of Orange to assume semimonarchial powers in foreign and domestic affairs; took many cities from Spaniards including Hertogenbosch (1629), Maastricht (1632), Breda (1637), Hulst (1645); concluded alliances with Denmark, Sweden, and France; negotiated favorable treaty with Spain (concluded 1648).

Frederick Louis. Prince of Wales. 1707–1751. English prince. Eldest son of George II and Queen Caroline; bitter against father for vetoing his marriage to Wilhelmina, Princess Royal of Prussia, and for refusal of adequate allowance; wrote or inspired *Histoire du Prince Titi,* a caricature of his parents (1735); made his home a meeting place for opponents of Walpole; refused permission by father to command British army against Jacobites (1745). His eldest son became George III of England.

Frederick William. *Ger.* Friedrich Wilhelm. *Called* the Great Elector. 1620–1688. Elector of Brandenburg (1640–88). Son of Elector George William; on accession found his dominions devastated by armies of Thirty Years' War, then still in progress; by neutral policy, reorganized finances, restored towns and cities, and built up an army; accorded recognition in Treaty of Westphalia (1648); often changed alliances to gain power and territories; joined Sweden against Poland (1656), granted (1657) suzerainty over duchy of Prussia; entered league against France (1674); at first unsuccessful, Brandenburg being ravaged by Swedes at instigation of Louis XIV; defeated Swedes at Fehrbellin (1675), but forced by Treaty of Saint-Germain (1679) to return conquests made from Sweden; allied himself with France (1679) in unsuccessful attempt to gain western Pomerania; broke alliance and concluded (1685) defense pact with Holland; spent last years in improving condition of electorate; greatly aided education, improved finances and commerce, and developed strong army.

Frederick William. Duke of Brunswick. See BRUNSWICK.

Frederick William I. *Ger.* Friedrich Wilhelm. 1802–1875. Elector of Hesse-Kassel (1847–66). Son of Elector William II; coregent (1831–47); made elector (1847); reactionary during liberal trends of 1848; reinstated (1850) unpopular adviser Hans Hassenpflug (*q.v.*); sided with Austria during Seven Weeks' War (1866); refused to make terms with Prussia; deposed; his territories annexed to Prussia (1866); died at Prague.

Frederick William. *Ger.* Friedrich Wilhelm. Name of four kings of Prussia:

Frederick William I. 1688–1740. King (1713–40). Son of King Frederick I; m. Sophia Dorothea of Hanover (1706). Involved in war with Sweden over Pomerania (1713–20); received greater part of Pomerania by Treaty of Stockholm (1720); most of reign spent in improving kingdom internally; strengthened industry and manufacture; instituted compulsory primary education (1717); centralized his administration (1723); rigidly economical; keenly interested in military matters; left Prussia a strongly established power for his son and successor, Frederick II the Great.

Frederick William II. 1744–1797. King (1786–97). Grandson of Frederick William I; son of Prince Augustus William and nephew of Frederick the Great. In spite of lack of military and politicial skills was able to expand his territories; issued a religious edict (1788) and law code (1794); joined Austria in support of French royalty during French Revolution, which involved him in war (1792–95); compelled by Treaty of Basel (1795) to give up Prussian territories west of Rhine; took part in second and third partitions of Poland (1793, 1795); his court noted for cultural activities.

Frederick William III. 1770–1840. King (1797–1840). Son of Frederick William II; took part in French campaigns (1792–94); m. (1793) Louisa of Mecklenburg-Strelitz, who exerted considerable influence over him. His neutrality in wars of Second and Third Coalition lowered Prussian prestige; unable to strengthen kingdom or solve difficulties of Napoleonic Wars; after complete subjection of Prussia to Napoléon (1801–05), opposed French, resulting in Prussian defeats at Jena and Auerstedt (1806) and dismemberment of kingdom by Treaty of Tilsit (1807); under Stein, Hardenberg, Scharnhorst, and Gneisenau, army reorganized (1807–12); victory at Leipzig (1813) liberated Germany and Blücher's successes in French campaigns and at Waterloo reestablished Prussia's position (1814–15). Acquired Westphalia and most of Saxony at Vienna Congress (1815); Prussia's fortunes declined during last 25 years of his reign.

Frederick William IV. 1795–1861. King (1840–61). Son of Frederick William III; ineffectual ruler; opposed movement toward German national state; failed to carry out promises of liberal reforms; forced by revolution of 1848 to grant a constitution; refused imperial crown offered by Parliament of Frankfurt (1849); soon after, reactionary regime again in control; rendered incompetent to rule by attacks of insanity; government administered by his brother (afterwards William I) as regent (1858–61).

Frederik. See FREDERICK.

Fred·holm \'fred-ˌhōlm\, Erik Ivar. 1866–1927. Swedish mathematician. Professor, Stockholm (from 1906). Founder of modern integral equational theory; in "Sur une nouvelle méthode pour la résolution du problème de Dirichlet" (1900) developed essentials of Fredholm integral equations and solved Fredholm equation of the second type.

Fredrik. See FREDERICK.

Fre·dro \'fre-drō\, Aleksander. Count. 1793–1876. Polish playwright. Fought in Napoleonic Wars. Influenced by Molière and Carlo Goldoni; works noted for brilliant characterization, ingenious construction, skillful use of verse meters. His comedies included *Pan Geldhab* (1821), *Mąż i żona* (1821), *Damy i huzary* (1825), *Śluby panieńskie* (1833), *Zemsta* (1834), *Pan Benet* (1878); also noted for picaresque memoirs *Trzy po trzy* (1877).

Freed·man \'frēd-mən\, Maurice. 1920–1975. English anthropologist. Lecturer (1951–57), reader (1957–65), professor (1965–70), London School of Economics; professor, Oxford (1970 ff.); managing editor, *Jewish Journal of Sociology* (1959–71). Author of *Chinese Family and Marriage in Singapore* (1957), *Chinese Lineage and Society* (1966), *Social and Cultural Anthropology* (1973), etc.

Free·man \'frē-mən\, Douglas Southall. 1886–1953. American editor and historian, b. Lynchburg, Va. Editor, *Richmond News Leader* (1915–49). Author of *Virginia—A Gentle Dominion* (1924), *R. E. Lee* (1934, Pulitzer prize), *The South to Posterity* (1939), *Lee's Lieutenants* (1942–44), *George Washington* (1948–54, Pulitzer prize).

Freeman, Edward Augustus. 1823–1892. English historian. Professor of modern history at Oxford (1884–92). His works included *The History and Conquests of the Saracens* (1856), *The History of the Norman Conquest* (1867–79), *Growth of the English Constitution* (1872), *Chief Periods of European History* (1886), etc.

Freeman, Mary Eleanor, *nee* Wilkins. 1852–1930. American writer, b. Randolph, Mass. m. Charles M. Freeman (1902); lived thereafter in Metuchen, N.J. Her works, chiefly of frustrated lives in New England villages, included novels *Pembroke* (1894) and *The Heart's Highway* (1900), and story collections *A Humble Romance* (1887), *A New England Nun* (1891), *Silence and Other Stories* (1898), *The Wind in the Rose Bush* (1903), *Edgewater People* (1918).

Freeman, Sir Ralph. 1880–1950. English civil engineer. Member (1901 ff.), senior partner (1921), Freeman, Fox & Partners, London; member of Steel Structures Research Committee (1928–36). Works included Sydney (Australia) Harbor Bridge (1932), Victoria Falls Bridge over Zambezi River, Royal Naval Propellant factory, Furness shipbuilding yard in Lancashire, and five major bridges in the Rhodesias.

Freeman, Richard Austin. 1862–1943. English physician and writer. His many detective novels included *The Red Thumb Mark* (1907), which introduced the fictional scientific detective Dr. John Thorndyke, *Dr. Thorndyke's Case Book* (1923), *Pontifex, Son and Thorndyke* (1931), *The Penrose Mystery* (1936), *Mr. Polton Explains* (1940).

Freeman-Thom·as \-'täm-əs\, Freeman. 1st Marquis of Wil·ling·don \'wil-iŋ-dən\. 1866–1941. English administrator. M.P. (1900–10); created baron (1910); governor of Bombay (1913–18), of Madras (1919–24); made viscount (1924); governor general of Canada (1926–31); made earl (1931); viceroy of India (1931–36); raised to marquis (1936).

Freer \'fri(ə)r\, Charles Lang. 1856–1919. American art collector, b. Kingston, N.Y. In railroad and car manufacturing business (1873–99). Great art collection included masterpieces of Whistler, of Chinese and Japanese painters, and of ancient glazed pottery of all regions. Presented collection, with funds for erection of Freer Gallery of Art at Washington, D.C., to the Smithsonian Institution (1906).

Fre·ge \'frā-gə\, Gottlob, *in full* Friedrich Ludwig Gottlob. 1848–1925. German mathematician and philosopher. Taught at Jena (1871–1917; professor from 1879). Founder of modern mathematical logic, presenting his system in *Begriffsschrift* (1879); continued study of philosophy of logic and mathematics in *Grundlagen der Arithmetik* (1884) and *Grundgesetze der Arithmetik* (1893, 1903); abandoned attempt to deduce arithmetic from logic after paradox in his system pointed out (1902) by Bertrand Russell; chief contribution to logic was his theory of quantifiers.

Frei \'frā\, Eduardo. *Full surname* Frei Mon·tal·va \-mōn-'täl-bä\. 1911–1981. Chilean politician. A leader among progressives; minister of roads and public works (1945); head of Christian Democratic party; president of Chile (1964–70); undertook land redistribution, nationalization of industry, and other liberal policies; a leader of opposition to military regime (from 1973).

Frei·dank \'frī-ˌdäŋk\. fl. 1230. German didactic poet. Wandering minstrel of burgher origin; in crusade of Frederick II (1228–29). Wrote *Bescheidenheit,* a collection of proverbs, aphorisms, and satirical observations.

Frei·lig·rath \'frī-lik-,rät\, Ferdinand, *in full* Hermann Ferdinand. 1810–1876. German poet. Won government pension with Romantic *Gedichte* (1838); became radical; exiled after publication of political poems *Glaubens-bekenntnis* (1844); returned (1848) and in Cologne helped friend Karl Marx edit *Neue rheinische Zeitung;* in London (1851–67). Other revolutionary verse included *Ça Ira!* (1846), *Die Toten an die Lebenden* (1848), *Neuere politische und soziale Gedichte* (1849–51); also produced translations from Victor Hugo, Whitman, Longfellow, Burns, Shakespeare, etc.

Frei·re \'frā-rā\, Ramón. 1787–1851. Chilean soldier and politician. Served in Chilean war for independence (1811–20); leader of Liberal party; dictator after fall of O'Higgins (1823); ended Spanish domination of Chile; reelected dictator (1827); forced to resign by accession of Conservative party. Led army revolt against government; defeated by Prieto (1830) and banished to Peru (until 1842).

Fre·ling·huy·sen \'frē-liŋ-,hīz-^{ə}n\, Frederick. 1753–1804. American Revolutionary leader, b. near Somerville, N.J. Practiced law, N.J. (from 1774); identified with colonial cause; served in Continental army. Member, Continental Congress (1778, 1779, 1782, 1783); U.S. senator (1793–96). His son ¶Theodore (1787–1862), b. Franklin Township, N.J., was a politician and educator; attorney general of New Jersey (1817–29); U.S. senator (1829–35); chancellor, N.Y.U. (1839–50); president, Rutgers (1850–62). Theodore's nephew and adopted son ¶Frederick Theodore (1817–1885), b. Millstone, N.J., also a politician; practiced law in Newark; helped found Republican party in N.J.; attorney general of New Jersey (1861–66); U.S. senator (1866–69, 1871–77); U.S. secretary of state (1881–85); obtained Pearl Harbor as naval base.

Fré·miet \frā-mye\, Emmanuel. 1824–1910. French sculptor. Known for his sculptures of animals.

Fré·mont \'frē-,mänt\, John Charles. 1813–1890. American explorer, army officer, and politician, b. Savannah, Ga. Lieutenant, U.S. army (1838); member, Nicollet's expedition to upper Mississippi and Missouri rivers (1838–39). Led expeditions into Oregon territory: on first expedition (summer 1842) mapped Oregon Trail, on second penetrated northern Colorado, Nevada, and crossed Rocky Mountains to California (1843–44), on third reached California (Dec. 1845). Played prominent part in conquering California during Mexican War; appointed by R. F. Stockton military governor of California; became involved in Stockton–Kearny (see Stephen W. KEARNY) quarrel; arrested by Kearny for mutiny and insubordination; court-martialed at Washington and convicted (Jan. 1848); penalty remitted by President Polk; resigned from army. Led winter expeditions to locate passes for southern railway route to California (1848–49, 1853–54). One of first two U.S. senators from California (1850–51); first Republican presidential candidate (1856); defeated by Buchanan. At outbreak of Civil War, appointed major general commanding Department of the West, headquarters at St. Louis (1861); relieved of command and appointed to command mountain department in western Virginia (1862); placed under Pope and asked to be relieved; resigned (1862). Considered for presidential nomination but withdrew to avoid splitting Republican party (1864). Lost fortune in railroad ventures (1870). Saved from dire poverty by wife's writings, by appointment as governor of Territory of Arizona (1878–83), and by restoration of rank as major general, U.S. army, with retired pay (1890).

His wife (m. 1841) ¶Jessie Ann, *nee* Benton (1824–1902), b. near Lexington, Va., daughter of Senator Thomas H. Benton (*q.v.*), was a writer; author of *The Story of the Guard* (1863), *Far-West Sketches* (1890), *The Will and the Way Stories* (1891), etc.

Fré·my \frā-mē\, Edmond. 1814–1894. French chemist. Professor (1850), director (1879–91), Muséum d'Histoire Naturelle, Paris. Studied ferric acid, osmic acid, ozone, cellulose, chlorophyll, the composition of bone and other organic substances, etc.; discovered hydrogen fluoride gas and a series of fluorine salts; contributed to the manufacture of iron and steel, sulfuric acid, etc.; worked on the saponification of fats with sulfuric acid; discovered a process for making artificial rubies. Author of *Traité de chimie générale* (with Pelouze, 1854–57), *Encyclopédie chimique* (with others, 1882–94), etc.

French \'french\, Aaron. 1823–1902. American inventor, b. Wadsworth, Ohio. Invented coil and elliptic railroad-car springs which revolutionized railroad industry.

French, Alice. *Pseudonym* Octave Than·et \'than-ət\. 1850–1934. American writer, b. Andover, Mass. Resident chiefly in Arkansas and Iowa, which supplied the background of her early stories. Among her books were *Knitters in the Sun* (1887), *Stories of a Western Town* (1893), *Man of the Hour* (1905), *The Lion's Share* (1907), *By Inheritance* (1910), *And the Captain Answered* (1917), etc.

French, Daniel Chester. 1850–1931. American sculptor, b. Exeter, N.H. Studio in Washington (1876–78), Boston and Concord, Mass. (1878–87), and New York (from 1888). Among his works were *The Minute Man* at Concord (1873), *John Harvard* in Harvard University yard (1884), *Statue of The Republic* at Chicago Exposition of 1893, equestrian statues of Grant at Philadelphia (1898) and of Washington at Paris (1900), the bronze doors of Boston Public Library (1902), groups representing *Europe, Asia, Africa,* and *America* in front of New York Custom House (1907), *Standing Lincoln* at Lincoln, Neb. (1912), *Alma Mater* at Columbia U. (1915), seated Lincoln in Lincoln Memorial at Washington, D.C. (1922), and portrait busts (in the Hall of Fame) of Poe, Emerson, Hawthorne, and Phillips Brooks.

French, Sir George Arthur. 1841–1921. British soldier, b. Ireland. Entered army (1860); by Canadian government appointed inspector of artillery with rank of lieutenant colonel in militia (1870); organized (1873) North West Mounted Police (now Royal Canadian Mounted Police) and was first commissioner (1873–76); led march from Dufferin, Man., to foothills of Rockies to establish law and order (1874); also head of School of Gunnery, Kingston, Ont.; later (after 1876) served with British army in Australia and India; major general (1900).

French, John Denton Pinkstone. 1st Earl of Ypres \'ēpr^{ə}; 'ē-prə, -,prā\. 1852–1925. English field marshal. Served in navy (1866–70) and army (from 1874). Distinguished himself in Nile expedition (1884–85) and Boer War (1899–1901); general (1907). Chief of imperial general staff (1912–14) and field marshal (1913). Placed in supreme command of British army on Western front in World War I; in battle of Ypres, prevented Germans from reaching Calais; failed to work in harmony with Kitchener and, under criticism for costly advances, resigned (Dec. 1915). Commander in chief in United Kingdom; lord lieutenant of Ireland (1918–21). Author of *1914* (1919).

French, Thomas Valpy. 1825–1891. English clergyman. Accepted by Church Missionary society (1850); to Āgra, India, and founded St. John's College; first Anglican bishop of Lahore (1877–87); died while on pioneering mission to Muscat.

Fre·neau \fri-'nō, 'frē-(,)nō\, Philip Morin. *Known as* the Poet of the American Revolution. 1752–1832. American poet, b. New York City. At outbreak of American Revolution, wrote bitter satires against British. In West Indies (1776–79). Took out privateer; captured by British; held on prison ship until exchanged (1780); wrote verse account of experience in *The British Prison-Ship* (1781). Employed in Philadelphia post office (1781–84); contributor of many poems to *Freeman's Journal.* Again at sea (1784–89). On newspaper editorial work (1789–95); appointed translating clerk in U.S. Department of State by Thomas Jefferson (1791); founded and edited *National Gazette,* a Democratic paper rivaling Fenno's *Gazette of the United States* (1791–93). Retired (1793). Individual poems: "The Indian Burying Ground," "The Wild Honeysuckle," "Eutaw Springs," "The House of Night," "Santa Cruz," "The Jamaica Funeral." Collections of his works: *The Poems of Philip Freneau* (1786), *Poems Written between the Years 1768 and 1794* (1795), *Poems Written and Published During the American Revolutionary War* (1809).

Frens·sen \'fren-sən\, Gustav. 1863–1945. German novelist. Lutheran pastor (1890–1902) but then rejected Christianity. Author of novels chiefly of peasant life in north Germany, including *Die drei Getreuen* (1898), *Jörn Uhl* (1901), *Hilligenlei* (1905), *Peter Moors Fahrt nach Südwest* (1907), *Klaus Heinrich Baas* (1909), *Der Pastor von Poggsee* (1921), and the autobiographical *Otto Babendiek* (1926); also wrote the epic poem *Bismarck* (1914) and plays.

Frep·pel \frā-pel\, Charles-Émile. 1827–1891. French prelate. Bishop of Angers (1869) and founder of the Catholic university there (1875); leader of Clerical party in Chamber of Deputies (from 1881). Author of *Études sur les Pères des trois premiers siècles* (1859–93), *La Révolution française* (1889), etc.

Frere \'fri(ə)r\, John. 1740–1807. English antiquary. Country squire; active member of Royal Society of Antiquaries (from 1771); discovered (1790) Stone Age implements at Hoxne and suggested they dated from earlier than 4004 B.C., then often considered date of creation of Earth; a founder of prehistoric archaeology. His son ¶John Hookham Frere (1769–1846), diplomat and writer; M.P. (1799–1802). British envoy at Lisbon (1800–02), Madrid (1802–04); British minister with the Spanish Junta (1808–09); in retirement at Malta (1820–46). Wrote witty parodies for *The Anti-Jacobin* (1797–98); reintroduced Italian ottava rima into English verse in mock-heroic epic *The Monks and the Giants* (1818); translated Aristophanes (1839–40).

His nephew ¶Sir Henry Bartle Edward Frere (1815–1884), colonial administrator; entered Bombay civil service (1834); chief commissioner of Sind (1850–59); suppressed great Indian Mutiny of 1857 in Sind and the Punjab; governor of Bombay (1862–67); in England as member of the Council of India (1867–77); governor of the Cape and first high commissioner of South Africa (1877); his demands on Cetewayo precipitated the Zulu War (1879), and he was recalled (1880).

Frère-Or·ban \frer-ór-bä^{n}\, Hubert Joseph Walther. 1812–1896. Belgian lawyer and politician. Leading Liberal member of lower house (1847–94); as minister of finance (1848–52, 1857–70), pursued free trade policy, founded Banque Nationale, and abolished newspaper and import taxes. Prime minister (1868–70, 1878–84); established secular primary education (1879), broke diplomatic relations with the Vatican (1880), extended franchise (1883).

Fre·richs \ˈfrā-riks\, Friedrich Theodor von. 1819–1885. German pathologist. Clinical professor and pathologist, Breslau (1851–59); director of Charité Hospital at U. of Berlin (1859–85). A founder of experimental pathology; his emphasis on teaching of pathology and medical biochemistry helped give clinical medicine a scientific foundation; his study of diseased organisms led to improvements in diagnosis and treatment of diabetes and liver diseases.

Fré·ron \frā-rōⁿ\, Élie-Catherine. 1719–1776. French journalist. Founded (1754) and edited (1754–76) *L'Année littéraire,* a journal in which he assailed Voltaire and the Encyclopedists, evoking from Voltaire famous rejoinders, as *Le Pauvre diable* and *L'Écossaise.* His son ¶Louis-Marie-Stanislas (1754–1802), Revolutionary politician, founded (1790) a journal, *L'Orateur du peuple,* in which he attacked the government; sat with the Montagnards in National Convention (1792–95); brutally suppressed counterrevolutionary activities in Marseille and Toulon (1793–94); prominent in conspiracy that overthrew Robespierre (1794); led the *jeunesse dorée* in terrorizing Jacobins during the Thermidorian reaction and led raid on Parisian Jacobin Club (1794); subprefect of Santo Domingo (1801–02).

Fre·sco·bal·di \ˌfrā-skō-ˈbäl-dē\, Girolamo. 1583–1643. Italian organist and composer. Organist at St. Peter's, Rome (1608–28, 1634–43) and at court of Florence (1628–34). Strongly influenced German Baroque school through his pupils J.J. Froberger and Franz Tunder; one of first to develop monothematic writing; his style characterized by dramatic inventiveness, bold use of chromaticism, effective construction. Known for keyboard compositions, including fantasias, canzoni, capricci, toccatas, etc.; also motets, hymns.

Fre·se·ni·us \frā-ˈzā-nē-u̇s\, Carl Remigius. 1818–1897. German chemist. Assistant in Liebig's laboratory, Giessen (1841); professor at the Agricultural Institute (1845) and founder (1848) of a laboratory for teaching and research, Wiesbaden. Known for work in analytical chemistry. Wrote standard textbooks *Anleitung zur qualitativen chemischen Analyse* (1841) and *Anleitung zur quantitativen chemischen Analyse* (1845); founder (1862) and editor (1862–97) of *Zeitschrift für analytische Chemie.*

Fresh·field \ˈfresh-ˌfēld\, Douglas William. 1845–1934. English mountain climber and geographer. Explored mountains of northern India, Uganda, Syria, Algeria, the Caucasus, the Apennines, and the Alpine region; made first ascent of Mt. Elbrus (1868). Secretary (1881–94), president (1914–17), Royal Geographical Society. Author of *The Italian Alps* (1875), *The Exploration of the Caucasus* (1896), *Round Kangchenjunga* (1903), etc.

Fres·nay \fre-ne, -nā\, Pierre. *Orig.* Pierre-Jules-Louis Lau·den·bach \lō-dänbäk\. 1897–1975. French actor. In modern and classical repertory with Comédie-Française (1915–28); leading actor and co-manager of Théâtre de la Michodière, Paris (from 1937), appearing in many modern plays. Appeared (from 1915) in over 100 films, playing leading roles in *Marius* (1931), *Fanny* (1932), *César* (1936), *La grande illusion* (1937), *Le Corbeau* (1943), *Monsieur Vincent* (1947), *Les Aristocrates* (1955).

Fres·nel \frā-nel\, Augustin-Jean. 1788–1827. French physicist. Known for work in optics; by investigations of interference, was instrumental in establishing the wave theory of light; studied double refraction; with Arago investigated polarized light; produced circularly polarized light by means of a rhomb of glass; pioneered in use of compound lenses in lighthouses.

Freud \ˈfrȯit, *Angl* ˈfrȯid\, Anna. 1895–1982. Austrian psychoanalyst. A pioneer in field of child psychoanalysis; daughter of Sigmund Freud (*q.v.*). Taught at Vienna's Cottage Lyceum. To London (1938); founded (1947) Hampstead Child Therapy Clinic, a leading center for the study of child development. Author of *The Ego and the Mechanisms of Defense* (1937), *Young Children in War Time* (1942), *Beyond the Best Interests of the Child* (1973).

Freud, Sigmund. 1856–1939. Austrian neurologist and founder of psychoanalysis. Studied in Vienna under Ernst Brücke (1876–82), in Paris under Charcot (1885–86); on staff of Vienna General Hospital (1882–85); professor of neuropathology (1902–38), U. of Vienna; maintained private psychoanalytic practice; worked with Breuer on the treatment of hysteria by hypnosis; developed (1892–95) method of treatment (which served as basis of his psychoanalysis) in which he replaced hypnosis by free association of ideas; organized (1902) at his home with Alfred Adler and others a weekly discussion meeting which became (1908) the Vienna Psycho-Analytical Society; forced to leave Vienna by Nazi regime (1938), thereafter living in London. Believed that a complex of repressed and forgotten impressions underlies all abnormal mental states and that revelation of these impressions often effects a cure; regarded infantile mental processes, esp. infantile sexuality and the Oedipal complex, of particular importance in later development; developed a theory that dreams are an unconscious representation of repressed desires, especially of sexual desires; considered the mind to be composed of the id, ego, and superego; propounded a genetic origin of motivation for basic drives (instinct theory). Author of *Studien über Hysterie* (with Breuer, 1895), *Die Traumdeutung* (1899), *Zur Psychopathologie des Alltagslebens* (1904), *Über Psychoanalyse* (1910), *Totem und Tabu* (1913), *Vorlesungen zur Einführung in die Psychoanalyse* (1917), *Jenseits des Lustprinzips* (1920), *Das Ich und das Es* (1923), *Die Zukunft einer Illusion* (1927), *Das Unbehagen in der Kultur* (1930), *Neue Folge der Vorlesungen zur Einführung* (1932), *Der Mann Moses und die monotheistische Religion* (1939).

Freu·den·thal \ˈfroi-dən-ˌtäl\, Axel Olof. 1836–1911. Swedish philologist and nationalist, b. Finland. Adherent of Pan-Scandinavian movement (from 1850s); influenced by August Sohlman. Professor of Swedish at U. of Helsinki (1878–1904); became leading ideologist for nationalist movement of Finland's Swedish minority.

Freund \ˈfrȯint\, Wilhelm. 1806–1894. German philologist. Compiled Latin lexicon *Wörterbuch der lateinischen Sprache* (1834–45), on which many Latin–English dictionaries are based.

Freundsberg, George von. See FRUNDSBERG.

Frey \ˈfrī\, Adolf. 1855–1920. Swiss poet and literary historian. Professor of German literature, Zürich (1898–1920). Author of biographies, as *Erinnerungen an G. Keller* (1892), *C.F. Meyer* (1899), *A. Böcklin* (1903), and *Der Tiermaler R. Koller* (1906); lyric and dialect poetry, as in *Duss und underm Rafe* (1891); historical novels, including *Die Jungfer von Wattenwil* (1912).

Frey·berg \ˈfrī-ˌbərg\, Bernard Cyril. 1st Baron Freyberg. 1889–1963. New Zealand general, b. London, England. To N.Z. (1891); served in World War I (1914–18); engaged at Gallipoli; commanded New Zealand Expeditionary Force in World War II (1939–45); engaged in Greece, Crete, North Africa, Italy; lieutenant general (1943); governor general of New Zealand (1946–52).

Frey·ci·net \frā-sē-ne\, Louis-Henri de Saulces de \də-sōls-də-\. 1777–1840. French naval officer. Rear admiral (1826), major general of marine at Toulon (1830), maritime prefect at Rochefort (1834). His brother ¶Louis-Claude (1779–1842) was also a naval officer; with Nicolas Baudin's expedition to Australia and Tasmania (1800–04); published account in *Voyage de découvertes aux terres australes* (1807); directed an expedition around the world (1817–20) studying meteorology and terrestrial magnetism, and published *Voyage autour du monde* (13 vols., 4 maps, 1824–44). His nephew ¶Charles-Louis (1828–1923) was a civil engineer and politician; senator (1876); minister of public works (1877–79); premier of France (1879–80, 1882, 1886, 1890–92); as minister of war (1888–93, 1898–99) instituted many military reforms; minister without portfolio (1915–16).

Freys·si·net \frā-sē-ne\, Eugène, *in full* Marie-Eugène-Léon. 1879–1962. French civil engineer. Bridge and highway engineer at Moulins (1905–14); worked for contracting firm (1919–28); designed and built many reinforced-concrete bridges, esp. Plougastel Bridge over Elorn River at Brest (1930). Developed (1928) pre-stressed concrete, used worldwide after his invention (1938) of a practical tool for applying tension to steel.

Frey·tag \ˈfrī-ˌtäk\, Gustav. 1816–1895. German writer. Coeditor of *Die Grenzboten* at Leipzig (1848–70); champion of German liberalism and German middle classes. Author of plays including the comedies *Die Brautfahrt* (1844) and *Die Journalisten* (1854), of *Soll und Haben* (realistic novel of commercial life, 1855), *Die Verlorene Handschrift* (novel of university life, 1864), and a series of six historical novels entitled *Die Ahnen* (1872–81).

Frí·as \ˈfrē-äs\, Tomás. 1804–1882. Bolivian politician. Acting president of Bolivia (1872–73); president (1874–76); overthrown.

Frick \ˈfrik\, Henry Clay. 1849–1919. American industrialist, b. West Overton, Pa. Organized Frick & Co. to build and operate coke ovens in Connellsville coal district of Pennsylvania (1871); rose to control of two-thirds of capacity of that area (1889). Chairman, Carnegie Steel Co. (1889–1900); managing head of company during Homestead labor strike (1892); played important part in consolidation forming United States Steel Corp. (1901) and later became a director. Bequeathed his home in New York City, with its art treasures and a large endowment, to the public to be used as a museum.

Frick, Wilhelm. 1877–1946. German politician. Participated in Hitler's Munich Putsch (1923); member of Reichstag (from 1924), serving (from 1928) as leader of Nazi members; minister of interior (1933–43); drafted and carried out many anti-Semitic measures, including Nürnberg laws of Sept. 1935; hanged as war criminal.

Frí·da \ˈfrid-ȧ\, Emil. *Pseudonym* Jaroslav Vrch·lic·ký \ˈvərk-lit-skē\. 1853–1912. Czech writer. Author of collections of lyric poetry as *Hudba v duši* (1886) and *Meč Damoklův* (1912); epics as *Mythy* (1879–80) and *Zlomky epopeje* (1886); novels, plays, and translations.

Fri·de·swi·de \ˈfrid-ə-ˌswēd-ə, ˈfrith-ə-ˌswē-thə\. Saint. d. 735. Anglo-Saxon religious. Founder of a monastery at Oxford (c.727); became patron saint of city and university of Oxford.

Fri·do·lin \ˈfrēd-ə-ˌlən\. Saint. 6th century? Irish missionary. Founded a monastery and church on island of Säckingen in the Rhine.

Fried \'frēt\, Alfred Hermann. 1864–1921. Austrian pacifist and publicist. In Berlin founded (1891) and edited pacifist paper *Die Waffen Nieder!* (called *Die Friedenswarte* from 1899); founded German Peace Society (1892); took lead in all international peace movements; with Tobias Asser shared Nobel peace prize (1911). To Switzerland at outbreak of World War I in protest of German policy; edited *Blätter für internationale Verständigung und zwischenstaatliche Organisation* and worked for peace. Author of *Handbuch der Friedensbewegung* (1911–13), *Mein Kriegstagebuch* (1918–20), etc.

Fried, Oskar. 1871–1941. German composer and conductor. Composed lieder and works for chorus and orchestra, as *Das trunkene Lied* (1904).

Frie·del \frē-del\, Charles. 1832–1899. French chemist and mineralogist. Worked on the artificial production of minerals; studied pyroelectric properties of crystals, crystallographic constants, and ketones and aldehydes; with James M. Crafts, prepared various compounds of silicon and discovered (1877) the Friedel-Crafts reaction for producing aromatic homologues; with R. D. da Silva, synthesized glycerine. Chief founder of *Revue Générale de Chemie* (1899). His son ¶Georges (1865–1933), crystallographer; professor (1893), director (1907–19), École des Mines, St.-Étienne; professor, Strasbourg (1919–30); worked on morphology of crystals; proved Bravais's hypothesis of lattice structure of crystals; formulated laws of rational symmetric intercepts (1909) and of mean indices (1908) of crystals; established (1913) Friedel's law that 11 types of crystal symmetry can be distinguished by X-ray diffraction.

Fried·land \'frēt-ˌlänt\, Valentin. *Known as* Valentin Trot·zen·dorf \'trȯt-sən-ˌdȯrf\. 1490–1556. German educator. Rector of a Latin school in Goldberg (from 1523) which gained reputation for efficiency and advanced methods.

Fried·län·der \'frēt-ˌlen-dər\, David. 1750–1834. German writer and Hebrew scholar. Settled in Berlin (1771); devoted himself to emancipation of Jews and improvement of their condition in Berlin.

Friedländer, Ludwig Heinrich. 1824–1909. German classical philologist and archaeologist. Professor, Königsberg (1858–92); chief work, *Darstellungen aus der Sittengeschichte Roms* (1864–71).

Friedländer, Max. 1852–1934. German musicologist. Professor, U. of Berlin (1903). Edited songs of Schubert, Schumann, and Mendelssohn, Beethoven's Scottish songs, Brahms's folksongs, etc.

Fried·mann \'frēt-man\, Alexander Alexandrovich. 1888–1925. Russian mathematician and physical scientist. First to formulate (1922) a model universe in which the average mass density is constant and all fundamental parameters are known except expansion factor; one of first to postulate a "big-bang" model of the universe (1922, 1924); a founder of dynamic meteorology.

Frie·dreich \'frē-ˌdrik̲\, Nikolaus. 1825–1882. German physician. Authority on diseases of the heart and the vascular and nervous systems; described Friedreich's ataxia.

Friedrich. See also FREDERICK.

Frie·drich \'frē-ˌdrik̲\, Caspar David. 1774–1840. German painter. Largely self-taught; taught at Dresden Academy (from 1816). His vast land- and seascapes, marked by sense of isolation and death, did much to establish pessimism and the sublime as concerns of German Romanticism. Works included *The Cross in the Mountains* (1807), *Graveyard in Snow* (1810), *Shipwreck in the Ice* (1822), *Alpine Scenery* (1828), *Rest in a Hayfield* (1835).

Friedrich Karl. Prinz. *Called* the Iron Prince. 1828–1885. Prussian soldier. Nephew of Emperor William I of Prussia; served in Holstein (1848); major general (1854), general of cavalry (1861); fought with distinction against Denmark (1864). Commanded 1st army in Seven Weeks' War against Austria (1866), winning decisive victory at Königgrätz (July 3). Commanded 2d army in Franco–Prussian War (1870–71); made field marshal after capturing Metz (Oct. 1870); also captured Orléans (1870) and Le Mans (1871).

Friedrich Wilhelm. Duke of Brunswick. See BRUNSWICK.

Fries \'frēs\, Elias Magnus. 1794–1878. Swedish botanist. Professor, Uppsala (1835–59). Developed first classification system for fungi, presented it in *Systema mycologicum* (1821–32); published system for classifying lichens in *Lichenographia Europaea reformata* (1831); first to distinguish between lichens with external coverings on fruit and those without. The genus *Freesia* is named for him.

Fries, Jakob Friedrich. 1773–1843. German philosopher. Professor, Heidelberg (1805–16) and Jena (1816–17, 1824–43); attempted to find by psychological method a new basis for critical philosophy of Kant and to reconcile criticism of Kant to Jacobi's religious philosophy. Author of *System der Philosophie als evidente Wissenschaft* (1804), *Neue oder anthropologische Kritik der Vernunft* (1807), *Handbuch der praktischen Philosophie* (1818–32), *System der Metaphysik* (1824), *Die Geschichte der Philosophie* (1837–40), etc.

Friese-Greene \'frēz-'grēn\, William. 1855–1921. English photographer and inventor. Operated photographic studio in London (from mid-1880s). Experimented with motion photography; with Mortimer Evans invented first practical motion-picture camera (pat. 1890); also pioneered in stereoscopic color motion-picture making.

Fri·esz \frē-es\, Othon, *in full* Achille-Émile-Othon. 1879–1949. French painter. Studied under Bonnat; associated with Fauvists. Works included *L'Hiver à Munich* (1909), *Le Port de Dieppe* (1930).

Friet·schie \'frich-ē\, Barbara, *nee* Hau·er \'hau̇(-ə)r\. 1766–1862. American patriot, b. Lancaster, Pa. m. (1806) John C. Frietschie. Heroine of Civil War incident in which she supposedly waved a Union flag above Gen. Thomas J. Jackson's troops as they marched through Frederick, Md. (Sept. 1862). Story elaborated by John G. Whittier into poem "Barbara Frietchie" (1863).

Friis \'frēs\, Johann. 1494–1570. Danish politician. Secretary at court of Frederick I; supporter of Christian III during Count's War (1533–36); as chancellor under Christian, helped establish Lutheran church in Denmark and reform state and local administrations; counseled war against Emperor Charles V; divided Schleswig and Holstein among Christian and his brothers (1544); patron of the arts, esp. of Saxo Grammaticus.

Friml \'frim-əl\, Rudolf, *in full* Charles Rudolf. 1879–1972. American pianist and composer, b. Prague. Studied under Dvořák in Prague; accompanist for Jan Kubelík on tours in U.S. (1901, 1906); settled in U.S. (1906, naturalized 1925). Known for his light operas, including *The Firefly* (1912), *High Jinks* (1913), *Rose Marie* (1924, included song "Indian Love Call") , *The Vagabond King* (1925, included "Only a Rose" and "Some Day"), *The Three Musketeers* (1928), *Bird of Paradise* (1930); composed for motion pictures (from 1934), including song "The Donkey Serenade" for film version of *Firefly* (1937).

Fri·mont \frē-mōⁿ\, Johann Maria Philipp von. Graf. Prince of An·tro·doc·co \ˌän-trō-'dōk-kō\. 1759–1831. Austrian general. Commander in chief of Austrian troops in Italy (1815) and besieged Lyons; suppressed revolution at Naples (1821); received Italian title of prince (1821) and rank of cavalry general. Governor general of Lombardo-Venetian kingdom (1825); suppressed uprisings in Modena, Parma, and the papal territory (1831).

Frioul, Duc de. See DUROC.

Frisch \'frish\, Karl von. 1886–1982. Austrian zoologist. Founded (1932) Munich Zoological Institute, the most advanced research facility of its kind in Europe. Pioneered in study of insect behavior; discovered that fish have exceptionally acute hearing; discovered that bees communicate by means of ritual "dancing" movements to show location of food; wrote *Aus dem Leben der Bienen* (1927). Shared with Nikolaas Tinbergen and Konrad Lorenz 1973 Nobel prize for physiology or medicine. Considered foremost experimental zoologist of his time.

Frisch \'fresh\, Ragnar Anton Kittil. 1895–1973. Norwegian economist. Professor, Oslo (1931–65); a founder of Econometric Society (1931); chief editor of *Econometrica* (1933–55). Developed mathematical models to describe specific economic environments; awarded the first Nobel prize in economic science (1969) with J. Tinbergen.

Frisch·lin \'frish-lēn\, Philipp Nicodemus. 1547–1590. German dramatist. Professor of history and poetry, Tübingen (1568–82); forced to leave for satirical writings on nobility. Author esp. of Latin comedies including *Julius redivivus* (1572), *Priscianus vapulans* (1578), *Phasma* (1580).

Fri·si \'frē-zē\, Paolo. 1728–1784. Italian mathematician, physicist, and astronomer. Professor at Milan; member of Barnabite order. His *Del modo di regolare i fiumi, e i torrenti* (1762) summarized best information in hydraulics; popularized ideas of Galileo and Newton; also author of *Disquisitio mathematica* (on shape and size of the earth, 1751), *Cosmographia physica et mathematica* (1774–75), etc.

Fritchie, Barbara. See FRIETSCHIE.

Frith \'frith\, Mary. *Nickname* Moll Cut·purse \'kət-ˌpərs\. 1584?–1659. English pickpocket. Notorious as bully, pickpocket, forger, and for use of male attire; chief personage in Middleton and Dekker's play *The Roaring Girle.*

Frith, William Powell. 1819–1909. English painter. Known for crowded scenes in style similar to Pre-Raphaelites'. His canvases included *Derby Day* (1858), *The Railway Station* (1862), *The Marriage of the Prince of Wales* (1865).

Fröbel. See FROEBEL.

Fro·ben \'frō-bən\, Johann. *Lat.* Fro·be·ni·us \frō-'bā-nē-u̇s, *Angl* frō-'bē-nē-əs\. c.1460–1527. German printer and publisher. Founded (1491) printing press at Basel famous for accuracy and artistic taste; popularized roman type, introduced italic and Greek fonts, employed such illustrators as Hans Holbein. Published a Latin Bible (1491), works of Tertullian, St. Ambrose, and other Latin church fathers and Roman authors; works written or edited by his friend Erasmus, including the Greek New Testament (1516), etc.

Fro·be·ni·us \frō-'bā-nē-u̇s, *Angl* frō-'bē-nē-əs\, Ferdinand Georg. 1849–1917. German mathematician. Professor at Eidgenössische Polytechnikum, Zürich (1875) and at U. of Berlin (1892). Made major contributions to group theory, esp. concept of abstract groups (with Ludwig Stickleberger) and theory of finite groups of linear substitutions (with Issai Schur); also contributed to means of solving linear homogenous differential equations.

Frobenius, Leo Viktor. 1873–1938. German ethnologist and explorer. Authority on prehistoric art; led 12 expeditions to Africa (1904–35). Propounded theory that culture evolves through stages of youth, maturity, and age. Author of *Probleme der Kultur* (1899–1901), *Und Afrika sprach* (1912–13), *Paideuma* (1921), *Erlebte Erdteile* (1925–29), etc.

Fro·ber·ger \ˈfrō-ˌber-gər\, Johann Jakob. 1616–1667. German organist and composer. Studied in Rome under Frescobaldi (1637–41); court organist at Vienna (1637, 1641–45, 1653–58); toured widely, including London and Paris; in last years in service of Duchess Sybille of Württemburg. Earliest important German harpsichord composer; first German master of keyboard suite; developed style combining German, French, and Italian elements. His keyboard compositions included ricercari, canzonas, toccatas, fantasias, and esp. 30 harpsichord suites.

Fro·bish·er \ˈfrō-bə-shər\, Sir Martin. c.1535–1594. English mariner. Commanded expedition (1576) in search for Northwest Passage and discovered Frobisher Bay; returned to same region in search for gold (1577, 1578). Vice admiral under Drake in West Indian expedition (1586); commanded the *Triumph* against the Spanish Armada (1588); vice admiral under Hawkins (1590); died fighting a Spanish force off French coast.

Frö·ding \ˈfrœ-diŋ\, Gustaf. 1860–1911. Swedish poet. Journalist at Karlstad (1887–94); throughout life suffered attacks of insanity. Considered greatest Swedish lyric poet; his verse, uniting colloquial language with a rich musical form, published as *Guitarr och dragharmonika* (1891), *Nya dikter* (1894), *Stänk och flikar* (1896), *Nytt och Gammalt* (1897), *Gralstänk* (1898), *Efterskörd* (1910), *Reconvalescentia* (1913).

Frodoard. See FLODOARD.

Froe·bel *or* **Frö·bel** \ˈfrœ-bəl\, Friedrich Wilhelm August. 1782–1852. German educator and founder of the kindergarten system. Developed a spiritual philosophy of the unity of the universe, which later influenced his ideas on education. Studied and worked under Pestalozzi at Yverdon, Switz. (1808–10); served during anti-French campaign (1813–14); assistant in mineralogical museum, Berlin (1814–16). Founded school at Griesheim (1816); moved to Keilhau (1817); founded a kindergarten at Blankenburg, Thuringia (1837); established training courses for kindergarten teachers and introduced kindergartens throughout Germany. Author of *Die Menschenerziehung* (1826), *Mutter- und Koselieder* (1844), etc.

Froh·man \ˈfrō-mən\, Charles. 1860–1915. American theatrical manager, b. Sandusky, Ohio. Gradually built up Empire Stock Company (from 1892) with such actors as Maude Adams, Julia Marlowe, Ethel Barrymore, Billie Burke, William Gillette, and Otis Skinner. Produced plays by leading dramatists of the day; leading figure in group of theatrical managers known as The Theatrical Syndicate; died in the *Lusitania* disaster.

Froh·scham·mer \ˈfrō-ˌshäm-ər\, Jakob. 1821–1893. German theologian and philosopher. Roman Catholic priest (1847); professor of philosophy (from 1855), Munich; wrote works on generationism placed on Index; suspended from office (1862). Founded and edited (1862–64) liberal Catholic organ *Athenäum;* excommunicated (1871) for claiming independence of philosophy from church authority. Author of *Über den Ursprung der menschlichen Seelen* (1854), *Einleitung in die Philosophie* (1858), *Der Fels Petri in Rom* (1873), *Die Phantasie als Grundprincip des Weltprocesses* (1877), etc.

Frois·sart \frwà-sàr, *Angl* ˈfrȯi-ˌsärt\, Jean. 1333?–c.1405. French chronicler and poet. Secretary to Queen Philippa of England (1361–69); priest at Estinnes-au-Mont, Belgium (1372–83); canon of Chimay and chaplain to Guy of Blois (1383–97); visited Scotland, England, Italy, France, Spain. His *Chroniques* (4 vols.) covered Hundred Years' War from 1325 to 1400 and is most important document for information on the period. Also wrote chivalric romance *Méliador,* courtly poem *L'Horloge amoureux,* ballades, rondeaux.

Fro·ment \frȯ-mä^{n}\, Nicolas. c.1425–between 1483 and 1486. French painter. With Enguerrand Quarton established school at Avignon (c.1450) and introduced Flemish naturalism into French art; his style crude and unpolished with awkward use of design and color; works included triptychs *Resurrection of Lazarus* (1461) and *Burning Bush* (1475).

Fro·men·tin \frȯ-mä^{n}-ta^{n}\, Eugène-Samuel-Auguste. 1820–1876. French painter and writer. Best known for Algerian landscapes, as *Moisson en Algérie, Diffa, Les Bateleurs nègres, La Lisière d'oasis, Fauconnier arabe, Chasse au héron, La Curée, Centaures et centauresses.* His writings included autobiographical novel *Dominique* (1862), travel books as *Un Été dans le Sahara* (1857) and *Une Année dans le Sahel* (1858), and art criticism as *Les Maîtres d'autrefois* (1876).

Fromm \ˈfrōm, ˈfräm\, Erich. 1900–1980. American psychoanalyst and social philosopher, b. Frankfurt am Main, Germany. To U.S. (1934). On faculties of Columbia U. (1934–41), Bennington Coll. (1941–50), National U. of Mexico (1951–67), Mich. State U. (1957–61), N. Y. U. (1962 ff.). Modified Freudian emphasis on unconscious drives by insisting on influence of economic and social factors on human behavior; advocated application of psychoanalytic principles to social and cultural problems. Author of *Escape from Freedom* (1941), *Man for Himself* (1947), *Psychoanalysis and Religion* (1951), *The Sane Society* (1955), *The Art of Loving* (1956), *Marx's Concept of Man* (1961), *Beyond the Chains of Illusion* (1962), *The Revolution of Hope* (1968), etc.

From·mel \ˈfrȯm-əl\, Gaston. 1862–1906. Swiss Protestant theologian. Professor of theology at Geneva (1894–1906); in opposition to Kant and Schleiermacher, attempted to base theism, religious experience, and moral conscience on objective grounds. Wrote *Études de théologie moderne* (1909) and *Oeuvre systématique* (1910–16).

Fronsberg, Georg von. See FRUNDSBERG.

Frontenac et Palluau, Comte de. See Louis de BUADE.

Fron·ti·nus \frän-ˈtī-nəs\, Sextus Julius. c.35–c.103 A.D. Roman soldier and writer. Governor of Britain (75–78 A.D.); superintendent of the water-supply system at Rome (97). Author of *De aquis urbis Romae* and treatises on military strategy and land surveying.

Fron·to \ˈfrän-(ˌ)tō\, Marcus Cornelius. c.100–c.166 A.D. Roman lawyer and grammarian. Tutor to Marcus Aurelius and Lucius Verus. Consul (143 A.D.). Acquired high reputation for his orations (now lost); strove to revive interest in early Roman literature and to restore the simplicity and force of the old Latin language.

Frosch·au·er \ˈfrȯsh-ˌau̇-ər\, Christoph. d. 1564. Swiss printer. Shop at Zürich; friend and follower of Zwingli, accompanying him to Marburg (1529) to meet Luther. Published works of Zwingli, a complete German Bible (Froschauerbibel), a complete English Bible (1550), and other Reformation works.

Fros·sard \frȯ-sàr\, Charles-Auguste. 1807–1875. French general. Served in Crimean War (1854–55); general of brigade (1855), aide-de-camp to Napoléon III (1857). Commanded 2d corps of army of the Rhine (1870); was defeated, driven back into Metz.

Frost \ˈfrȯst\, Arthur Burdett. 1851–1928. American illustrator, b. Philadelphia. On staff of New York *Graphic* (1875), *Harper's* (1876). Illustrated Joel Chandler Harris's *Uncle Remus* books. Independent collections of humorous sketches: *Stuff and Nonsense* (1884), *The Bull Calf and Other Tales* (1892).

Frost, Edwin Brant. 1866–1935. American astronomer, b. Brattleboro, Vt. Professor, Dartmouth (1895–98), Chicago (1898–1935); director of Yerkes Observatory (1905–32). Made special study of stellar velocities in the line of sight, stellar spectroscopy, sunspots, and solar thermal radiation.

Frost, John. 1784–1877. English reformer. Prosperous draper and tailor, mayor (1836–37) of Newport; leading member of Chartist movement and occasional chairman of its London convention (1839); led Chartist rising in Newport in which about 20 Chartists were killed by troops (Nov. 4, 1839); convicted of high treason and exiled (1840–54) to Tasmania.

Frost, Robert Lee. 1874–1963. American poet, b. San Francisco. Professor of English, Amherst (1916–20, 1923–25, 1926–38); professor of poetry, Harvard (1939–43); on faculty of Dartmouth (1943–49); lecturer at Amherst (1949–63). Awarded Pulitzer prizes for 1924, 1931, 1937, 1943. His poetry characterized by colloquial language, deceptively easy verse forms, and symbols drawn from common experience, esp. from rural New England. Author of *A Boy's Will* (1913), *North of Boston* (1914), *Mountain Interval* (1916), *New Hampshire* (1923), *West-Running Brook* (1928), *A Way Out* (1929), *A Further Range* (1936), *From Snow to Snow* (1936), *A Witness Tree* (1942), *Steeple Bush* (1947), *In the Clearing* (1962), and verse plays *A Masque of Reason* (1945) and *A Masque of Mercy* (1947).

Froth·ing·ham \ˈfrȯth-iŋ-ˌham, -əm\, Octavius Brooks. 1822–1895. American clergyman, b. Boston. Unitarian minister (1847–67); extremely liberal in theology; broke with Unitarianism and helped form (1867) in Boston the Free Religious Association, its president (1867–78); retired from active ministry (1879). Author of *The Religion of Humanity* (1872), *Transcendentalism in New England* (1876), and biographies of Theodore Parker (1874), George Ripley (1882), William Henry Channing (1886).

Froude \ˈfrüd\, James Anthony. 1818–1894. English historian. Edited *Fraser's Magazine* (1860–74); disciple, literary executor, and biographer (1882, 1884) of Thomas Carlyle; professor of modern history at Oxford (1892–94). Among his works were *History of England from the Fall of Wolsey to the Defeat of the Spanish Armada* (1856–70), *The English in Ireland in the Eighteenth Century* (1872–74), *English Seamen in the Sixteenth Century* (1895).

His older brother ¶Richard Hurrell (1803–1836), Anglican clergyman; close friend of John Henry Newman; with Newman and John Keble initiated (1833) the Oxford Movement, writing three of the *Tracts for the Times;* his diaries, when published as *Remains* (1838–39), encouraged development of Anglo-Catholicism and aroused suspicions of Oxford Movement in Protestant circles. Another brother ¶William (1810–1879) was an engineer and naval architect; introduced bilge keels to lessen rolling of ships; conducted scale-model experiments on resistance and propulsion of ships; invented dynamometer to measure power of marine engines.

Fru·e·la \frü-'ā-lä\. Name of two Spanish kings: Fruela I (722–768); king of Asturias (757–768); reign marked by civil rebellions; founded Oviedo. ¶Fruela II (d. 925); king of León (924–925).

Fru·go·ni \frü-'gō-nē\, Carlo Innocenzo. 1692–1768. Italian poet. Took monastic vows (1709) but later obtained remission; founded (1716) an Arcadian society that sought to return ornate verse styles to simple diction and pastoral themes of classical poetry; court poet to Antonio Farnese, Duke of Parma. Wrote immense number of sonnets, lyrical odes, eclogues, librettos, etc.

Fru·men·ti·us \frü-'men-sh(ē-)əs\. Saint. 4th century. Syrian apostle of the Abyssinians and founder of the Abyssinian church. Taken as slave to court of Aksum following shipwreck on Red Sea (c.340); became civil servant; as royal administrator and tutor to crown prince, propagated Christianity throughout kingdom. Consecrated bishop of Aksum by Athanasius in Alexandria (c.347); repudiated Arianism; assumed titles "Abba Salama" (father of peace) and "Abuna" (our father).

Frunds·berg \'frůnts-ˌberk\ *or* **Frons·berg** \'frōns-ˌberk\ *or* **Freunds·berg** \'fröi̇nts-ˌberk\, Georg von. 1473–1528. German general. Called "father of the Landsknechte." Fought for Maximilian I against Swiss (1499); helped Maximilian organize and develop Landsknechte; as its leader, fought against Venetians and French (1509, 1513, 1514); commanded troops of Swabian League against Ulrich von Württemberg (1519); met Luther at Diet of Worms (1521). Received command against French from Charles V; took part in invasion of Picardy, gained victory at La Bicocca (1522), and won distinction at battle of Pavia (1525).

Frun·ze \'frün-zyə\, Mikhail Vasilyevich. 1885–1925. Russian Soviet army commander. Took part in Bolshevik uprising in Moscow (1905); often arrested for revolutionary activities; took part in Bolshevik revolution (1917). Commanded Soviet armies operating against Admiral Kolchak (1919–20) and General Wrangel (1920). People's commissar for war (1925). Developed a "unitary military" doctrine on organization of Red army that was counter to Trotsky's views; considered one of fathers of Red army.

Fru·tolf \'frü-ˌtȯlf\. d. 1103. German chronicler. Prior of Michelsberg Cloister near Bamberg. His history of the world to 1101 was ascribed until 1896 to the Benedictine abbot ¶Ek·ke·hard von Au·ra \'ek-ə-ˌhärt-fȯn-'au̇-rä\ (d. 1125), who revised it several times and brought it down to 1125.

Fry \'frī\, Elizabeth, *nee* Gur·ney \'gər-nē\. 1780–1845. English Quaker philanthropist. m. Joseph Fry (1800). Quaker minister (from 1811); one of chief promoters of prison reform in Europe; also did much to bring about improvements in British hospital system and treatment of the insane.

Fry, Franklin Clark. 1900–1968. American clergyman, b. Bethlehem, Pa. Ordained Lutheran minister (1925); pastorate in Akron, Ohio (1929–44); president of United Lutheran church (1944–62) and, after merger of several Lutheran associations, of Lutheran Church in America (1962–68). Proponent of church-sponsored relief work, a founder and president of Lutheran World Relief. President of Lutheran World Federation (1957–63); active in international ecumenism.

Fry, Roger Eliot. 1866–1934. English painter and critic. Painted landscapes; championed Cézanne and the Post-impressionists. Edited Reynolds's *Discourses* (1905); author of *Vision and Design* (1920), *Transformations* (1926), *Cézanne* (1927), *Henri Matisse* (1930), *Reflections on British Painting* (1934), *Last Lectures* (1939).

Fry, William Henry. 1813–1864. American composer and music critic, b. Philadelphia. His opera *Leonora* (presented 1845 in Philadelphia) was first publicly performed grand opera written by native American; also composed other operas and orchestral works.

Fu'·ād I \fü-'äd\. 1868–1936. Sultan (1917–22) and king (1922–36) of Egypt. Son of Ismā'īl Pasha (1830–1895; *q.v.*); interested in educational matters; founded (1908) Egyptian U. (later known as Fu'ād I University) at Giza; sultan (1917); when native unrest forced British to end protectorate (1922), took title of king; opposed all British attempts at control; throughout reign opposed by ultranationalist Wafd party; promulgated constitution (1923); dissolved parliament twice (1928, 1930), but each time compelled to relinquish autocratic rule; succeeded by his son Farouk I.

Fu·ad Pa·şa \fü-'ät-pä-'shä\, Mehmed. 1815–1869. Turkish politician. Held several diplomatic posts (1840–52). Minister of foreign affairs (1852–53, 55–56); grand vizier and foreign minister (1861–62, 1863–67). Credited with introducing many European methods into Turkey, but blamed for adding to Turkey's financial difficulties by the cost of his reforms. With Ahmed Cevdet wrote *Kavaid-i Osmaniye* (1851), first Turkish work on Turkish grammar and milestone in reform of the language.

Fuchs \'fůks\, Immanuel Lazarus. 1833–1902. German mathematician. Professor at Greifswald, Göttingen, Heidelberg, Berlin. Known for works on the theory of numbers and the theory of functions.

Fuchs, Johann Nepomuk von. 1774–1856. German mineralogist and chemist. Credited with discovery of water glass (1823) and its application in stereochromy.

Fuchs, Johann Neopomuk. 1842–1899. Austrian conductor. Composed opera *Zingara* (1872) and arranged operas of Handel, Gluck, and Schubert. His brother ¶Robert (1847–1927) composed the operas *Die Königsbraut* (1889) and *Die Teufelsglocken* (1893), and symphonies, serenades, masses, chamber music, piano pieces, choruses, and songs.

Fuchs, Leonhard. 1501–1566. German botanist. Professor at Tübingen (1535–66); known for his plant manual *Historia stirpium* (1542), a landmark in development of natural history. The genus *Fuchsia* is named for him.

Füch·sel \'fuek-səl\, Georg Christian. 1722–1773. German physician and geologist. At court of Friedrich Carl of Rudolstadt as curator of natural science collections (1757), physician (1767), librarian (1770). Pioneer in development of stratigraphy; originated idea of stratigraphic formations; made first geological map of Germany and adjacent areas.

Fu·ci·ni \fü-'chē-nē\, Renato. *Anagrammatic pseudonym* Ne·ri Tan·fu·cio \'nä-rē-tän-'fü-chō\. 1843–1921. Italian poet and writer. Known esp. for tales of Tuscan village life, as *Le veglie di Neri* (1884–90), *All'aria aperta* (1887), and *Nella campagna Toscana* (1908).

Fuentes, Conde de. See ENRÍQUEZ DE ACEVEDO.

Fuer·tes \'fyü(ə)rt-(ˌ)ēz\, Louis Agassiz. 1874–1927. American illustrator, b. Ithaca, N.Y. Executed bird illustrations for *Song Birds and Water Fowl* (1897), *The Woodpeckers* (1901), *Birds of the Rockies* (1902), *Handbook of Birds of the Western United States* (1902), *Handbook of Birds of the Eastern United States* (1902), *Waterfowl* (1903), *Birds of New York* (1910).

Fug·ger \'fůg-ər\. Name of a German family of financiers and merchants in Augsburg, descended from the weaver Johannes Fugger (1348–1409), who established himself in Augsburg (1367) and conducted a successful textile trade. His sons ¶Andreas (d. 1457), founder of the Fugger vom Reh branch, and ¶Jakob I (d. 1469), founder of the main branch of the family and of the Fugger firm. Jakob's sons (all ennobled) ¶Ulrich (1441–1510), ¶Georg (1453–1506), and ¶Jakob II, *called* the Rich (1459–1525), carried on and extended the business. Ulrich and Georg leased the Roman mint (1508–15) and handled remittances to papal court for sales of indulgences and church benefices. Jakob II leased mines in Spain, Tirol, Carinthia, and Hungary, traded in spices to India, acted as papal banker, made loans to Maximilian I (who mortgaged to him the county of Kirchberg and the lordship of Weissenhorn, ennobled him as count, 1514, and appointed him imperial adviser), financed election of Charles V (1519), and erected the Fuggerei, a settlement of low-rent dwellings near Augsburg for poor Catholics. His heir, Georg's son ¶Anton (1493–1560), made many loans to Emperor Charles V, esp. for use against Protestants; established trade ties with Peru and Chile, engaged in mining ventures in Sweden and Norway, in slave and spice trades; zealous Roman Catholic supporter of Eck against Luther, patron of art and science; created count by Charles V (1530), admitted to Swabian bench of counts, and given rights of princes, and later (1535) given right to coin gold and silver. His nephew ¶Hans Jakob (1516–1575), made partner (1543), eventually became Bavarian chancellor; art patron and family chronicler.

Fu·ji·ta \fůj-ē-tä\ Tōko. 1806–1855. Japanese scholar and politician. Director (from 1827) of Shōkōkan, historical institute of Miko; in *Kōdōkan kijutsugi* (1849) and other works, argued that Japan could achieve its unique destiny as a united country under imperial rule; his views inspired nationalistic and pro-imperial movement that culminated in Meiji Restoration of 1868.

Fujita Tsuguji. *Also known as* Fujita Tsuguharu. 1886–1968. Japanese painter. Settled in France (1913); applied French oil techniques to Japanese-style paintings; his works, known for blurred black-ink coloring and smooth, milk-white background, included *Self-Portrait with a Cat, The Cat, A Nude,* and *Women on the Beach.*

Fu·ji·wa·ra \fůj-ē-wä-rä\. Japanese noble family, dating from 7th century, that by shrewd intermarriage and diplomacy achieved (858) complete domination over imperial family; thereafter (to c.1156) members ruled as regents while most of emperors were mere puppets; power of family broken in civil wars (1156–60) by Minamoto and Taira leaders, esp. Taira Kiyomori. Its members included:

Fujiwara Kamatari. *Also called* Kamato. *Orig. surname* Na·ka·to·mi \nä-kä-tō-mē\. 614–669. Founder of Fujiwara family. Aided Prince Nakano Ōe (later Emperor Tenchi) murder Soga Iruka and overthrow ruling Soga family (645); as minister of the interior, implemented far-reaching "Reforms of Taika" which strengthened power of central government, including establishment of new capital metropolitan region and division of country into provinces ruled by central government appointees, and transformed the Japanese political and economic system into facsimile of T'ang China; as reward for his services, granted (669) by Tenchi new surname Fujiwara, i.e. "Wisteria Arbor," to commemorate place where they had plotted overthrow of Soga Iruka.

Fujiwara Fuhito. 659–720. Son of Kamatari; wielded great power at imperial court; head of committee that drafted (701) Taihō code of law; two daughters became imperial consorts and all four sons founded branches of the family.

Fujiwara Yoshifusa. 804–872. Courtier. Appointed grand minister of state (857); placed (858) his nine-year-old grandson Seiwa on imperial throne and assigned himself as regent, first time a commoner became regent; this led to practice of emperors retiring at early age, leaving child emperors installed with Fujiwara members as regents wielding actual power.

Fujiwara Mototsune. 836–891. Nephew and adopted son of Yoshifusa; succeeded him as head of family (872); created (880) post of *kampaku* (chief councilor or civil dictator) to exercise complete control over government; regent for emperors Seiwa, Yōzei, Kōkō, and Uta.

Fujiwara Tokihira. 871–909. Succeeded (891) his father Mototsune as head of family; involved in power struggle with emperors Uda and Daigō; made minister of the left (899); caused exile (901) of minister of the right Sugawara Michizane and became virtual dictator of Japan, although never assumed post of *kampaku;* promulgated tax reforms to strengthen government.

Fujiwara Tadahira. 880–949. Succeeded (909) his brother Tokihara as head of family and as de facto ruler of government; assumed post of *kampaku* (941); his dictatorship plagued by provincial rebellions and banditry.

Fujiwara Michinaga. 966–1027. Succeeded as head of family (995); during his reign the imperial capital at Kyōto achieved its greatest splendor and the Fujiwara clan reached zenith of its power; given honorary title of Nairan; married his daughters to four emperors; his palace renowned for its opulence; much great literature produced; conditions in countryside deteriorated and he was troubled by rising power of provincial lords.

Fujiwara Yorimichi. 992–1074. Son of Michinaga; maintained his father's luxurious court style; regent for three emperors (1016–68); deterioration of conditions in countryside greatly accelerated, rebellions and banditry rife, lost much power to provincial lords; established Byōdōin Temple.

Fujiwara Sadaie. *Usually called* Fujiwara Teika. 1162–1241. Japanese poet and critic. Wrote in complex *yōen* ("ethereal beauty") style; in later years advocated the more direct, simpler *ushin* ("conviction of feeling") mode. One of compilers of eighth imperial anthology *Skin kokin-shū* (c.1205); sole compiler of ninth anthology *Shinchoku-senshū* (1232). His poetic treatises and anthologies included *Eiga taigai, Shūka-no-daitai, Kindai shūka* (1209), and *Maigetsushō* (1219). His half-brother ¶Fujiwara Takanobu (1142–1205) was the leading portrait artist of his day; created a simple, realistic style called *nise-e* ("likeness picture"); only three portraits are extant, including that of Minamoto Yoritomo. His son ¶Fujiwara Nobuzane (1176–?1265) was a courtier, poet, and leading Japanese painter of 13th century; carried on his father's *nise-e* style in portraits, as in *The 36 Major Poets.*

Fujiwara Sumitomo. d. 941. Japanese pirate. Originally a government official; sent by court to eliminate pirates on the Inland Sea, but became pirate leader and gained control of area; defeated by government forces.

Fujiwara Yukinari. 972–1027. Japanese calligrapher. Perfected style of writing called *jōdai-yō* ("ancient style"); held several high government offices. Works included *Wakan-Rōei-shū, Hakushi shi-kan* (1020), and his diary *Gon-ki.*

Fu-k'ang-an \'fü-'käŋ-'än\. d. 1796. Chinese soldier. Appointed military governor of Manchuria (1777); governor general of several Chinese provinces (1780–95). A superior military leader; suppressed rebellions in Szechwan and Kansu, pacified Taiwan, and led successful expedition to Tibet and Nepal, making latter a tributary state. Made prince of fourth degree.

Fu·ku·za·wa \fůk-ůz-ä-wä\ Yukichi. 1835–1901. Japanese educator, journalist, and author. Worked tirelessly to introduce Western ideas and methods into Japan; advocated parliamentary government, popular education, and other reforms. Founded at Tokyo (1868) Keiō Gijuku, which became one of Japan's great universities; established (1882) the influential daily paper *Jiji Shimpō.*

Ful·bert de Char·tres \fūel-ber-də-shártr^{ə}\. Saint. c.960–1028. French cleric. Appointed (990) chancellor of Chartres cathedral and developed its school into a center of learning; bishop of Chartres (1006); began rebuilding Chartres cathedral; his *Lettres* are a valuable source for the history of his times.

Fulcher of Chartres. See FOUCHER DE CHARTRES.

Ful·gen·ti·us \fəl-'jen-sh(ē-)əs\ of Rus·pe \'rəs-pē\. Saint. c.467–533. African Christian prelate. Bishop of Ruspe in northern Africa (507); exiled to Sardinia by Thrasimund (508–515, 517–523). Author of works against Arianism and Semi-Pelagianism.

Fulgentius, Fabius Planciades. 5th–6th century A.D. Christian Latin writer, b. Africa. His writings mediocre and fantastic, but his allegorical method of interpreting classical writers greatly influenced medieval scholars. Wrote allegorical interpretations of myths in *Mitologiarum libri iii* and of Virgil in *Expositio Vergilianae continentiae secundum philosophos moralis;* also *Expositio sermonum antiquorum,* on rare words, and *Liber absque litteris de aetatibus mundi et hominis,* an analogy of human life to world history.

Fu-lin \'fü-'lin\. *Reign title* Shun-chih \'shün-'ji(ə)r\. *Temple name* Shih Tsu \'shi(ə)rd-'zü\. *Posthumous name* Chang Huang-ti \'jäŋ-'hwäŋ-'dē\. 1638–1661. Chinese emperor (1644–61), first of the Ch'ing dynasty. Succeeded his father Abahai as leader of Manchu tribes of Manchuria (1643); after overthrow of Ming dynasty, proclaimed at Peking first emperor of Ch'ing dynasty (1644); under regency (1643–50) of his uncle Dorgon, who exercised absolute authority; drove out last Ming remnants from South China (1659); influenced by trusted adviser J.A. Schall von Bell (*q.v.*), eunuch officials, and Buddhist priests; increased number of Chinese serving in Manchu government.

Fulk \'fůlk\. *Fr.* Foulques \fülk\. Name of five counts of Anjou:

Fulk I. *Called* le Roux \lə-rü\, *i.e.* the Red. d. c.942. Count (929–c.942); inherited Anjou from father Ingelger or Enjeuger; enlarged domain, taking part of Touraine; drove out Normans.

Fulk II. *Called* le Bon \lə-bō^{n}\, *i.e.* the Good. d. c.960. Count (c.942–c.960). Son of Fulk I; enjoyed peaceful reign devoted to agricultural progress and arts.

Fulk III. *Called* Ner·ra \ner-rå\ *or* le Noir \lən-wår\, *i.e.* the Black. c.970–1040. Count (987–1040). Son of Geoffrey I Grisegonelle; drove out Bretons; defeated Conan I, Count of Rennes, at Conquereuil (992); defeated Eudes II, Count of Blois, at Pontlevoy (1016); seized Saumur (1026). Founded many abbeys and castles.

Fulk IV. *Called* le Ré·chin \lə-rā-sha^{n}\, *i.e.* the Surly. 1043–1109. Count (1068–1109). Nephew of Geoffrey II Martel; succeeded to countship jointly with brother Geoffrey III le Barbu, whom he defeated (1068); lost lands in disputes with William of Normandy.

Fulk V. See FULK, king of Jerusalem.

Fulk. *Fr.* Foulques. 1092–1143. King of Jerusalem (1131–43). Son of Fulk IV of Anjou; count of Anjou as Fulk V, *called* le Jeune, *i.e.* the Young (1109–31); aided Louis VI against England; obtained countship of Maine by marriage (1110) to Erembourg de Beaugency; m. (1129) Melisend, daughter of Baldwin II of Jerusalem; succeeded to throne (1131); defended Jerusalem against Turks; built fortifications, including Krak of Moab.

Fulk. Archbishop of Reims. See FOULQUES.

Ful·ler \'fůl-ər\, Albert Carl. 1885–1973. American businessman, b. Kings Co., Nova Scotia. To U.S. (1903, naturalized 1948). Organized (1906) in Hartford, Conn., the Capital Brush Co., later (1910) Fuller Brush Co., and served as its president (to 1943); introduced the "Fuller Brush man" to America.

Fuller, Andrew. 1754–1815. English clergyman. Advocated a moderate form of Calvinism; a founder (1792) and first secretary of Baptist Missionary Society.

Fuller, Buckminster, *in full* Richard Buckminster. 1895–1983. American engineer and inventor, b. Milton, Mass. Held patents to over 2,000 inventions, including pole-suspended Dymaxion House (1927), three-wheeled Dymaxion car (1932), Dymaxion Air-ocean World Map (1943), and World Game (1969) that predicted and solved world problems; developed (1947) geodesic dome that was adopted worldwide. Research professor at Southern Illinois U. (1959–68). Famous for asserting that all human needs could be met through technology and planning.

Fuller, George. 1822–1884. American painter, b. Deerfield, Mass. Noted for haunting, dreamlike pictures of figures set in landscape, as *The Tomato Patch, Romany Girl, Winifred Dysart, She Was a Witch, Quadroon, Nydia.*

Fuller, Henry Blake. 1857–1929. American novelist, b. Chicago. On advisory committee of *Poetry* magazine (from 1912). Known esp. for realistic novels set in Chicago: *The Cliff-Dwellers* (1893), *With the Procession* (1895), *Under the Skylights* (short stories, 1901), *On the Stairs* (1918), *Bertram Cope's Year* (1919). Author also of romances set in Europe, as *The Chevalier of Pensieri-Vani* (1890, under pseudonym Stanton Page), *The Chatelaine of La Trinité* (1892), *Waldo Trench and Others* (1908), and *Gardens of This World* (1929), and of *The Puppet Booth: Twelve Plays* (1895) and *Lines Long and Short* (1917, verse biographies).

Fuller, John Frederick Charles. 1878–1966. English soldier. Served in Boer War (1899–1902) and World War I (1914–18); major general (1930). A father of modern armored warfare; his ideas on tactical use of tanks in war greatly influenced German and Soviet armored strategy in World War II. Author of *Tanks in the Great War* (1920), *The Reformation of War* (1923), *On Future Warfare* (1928), *Machine Warfare* (1942), *The Second World War* (1948), *A Military History of the Western World* (1954–56), etc.

Fuller, Loie, *orig.* Marie Louise. 1862–1928. American dancer, b. Fullersburg, Ill. Inventor of serpentine dance (1889); also made innovations in theatrical lighting and costuming; made debut at Folies-Bergère, Paris (1892); toured U.S. and Europe; wrote autobiography *Quinze ans de ma vie* (1908).

Fuller, Margaret, *in full* Sarah Margaret. Marchioness Os·so·li \'ós-sō-lē\. 1810–1850. American critic and social reformer, b. Cambridgeport, Mass. Taught in Bronson Alcott's Temple School in Boston (1836–37) and in Providence (1837–39); conducted "conversations" with a group of ladies in Boston as a means of general cultural education (1839–44); associated with, though not a part of, the Brook Farm experiment; editor of *The Dial,* organ of the Transcendentalists (1840–42). Literary critic, *New York Tribune* (1844–46); established reputation as one of ablest critics in America. Settled in Italy (1847); m. Marquis Giovanni Angelo Ossoli (1847); took part with Ossoli in Revolution of 1848. Lost with husband and child in wreck off Fire Island, N.Y. Author of *Summer on the Lakes, in 1843* (1844), *Woman in the Nineteenth Century* (1845), *Papers on Literature and Art* (1846), *At Home and Abroad* (1856).

Fuller, Melville Weston. 1833–1910. American jurist, b. Augusta, Me. Practiced law in Chicago (from 1856). Chief justice, U.S. Supreme Court (1888–1910); also, member, Court of International Arbitration, The Hague (1900–10).

Fuller, Thomas. 1608–1661. English clergyman. Curate of the Savoy, at London (1641–43); Royalist chaplain during Civil War; rector of Cranford (1658); chaplain in extraordinary to Charles II (1660). Author of *The Holy State and the Profane State* (1642), *History of the Holy Warre* (*i.e.* the Crusades; 1643), *Adronicus* (satire against Cromwell, 1646), *Church-History of Britain* (1655), *History of the Worthies of England* (1662), etc.

Ful·ton \ˈfu̇lt-ᵊn\, Robert. 1765–1815. American engineer and inventor, b. Lancaster Co., Pa. Painted portraits in Philadelphia (1782–86); in England (1786–97); student of Benjamin West until about 1793; devoted himself thereafter to engineering. Patented machines for sawing marble, for spinning flax, for twisting hemp into rope. Interested himself in canals; published *A Treatise on the Improvement of Canal Navigation* (1796). In Paris (1797–1806) invented submarine, but could not interest governments in it. Commissioned by Robert R. Livingston (*q.v.*) to build a steamboat (1801); after successful experiments on the Seine, returned to U.S. (1806); succeeded with the *Clermont,* which steamed from New York to Albany and back (Aug. 17–22, 1807). *Clermont* was not the first steamboat, but was the first one built and operated at a cost which promised fair profits to its owners; it was the first of a line of commercial steamboats. Designed thereafter other steamboats, esp. for Western rivers, and the world's first steam warship (launched 1814).

Ful·via \ˈfəl-vē-ə\. d. 40 B.C. Roman matron. Wife successively of Clodius, Curio, and Mark Antony. Instigated a revolt (41 B.C.) against Octavian in the hope of drawing Antony away from Egypt and Cleopatra.

Fu·nes \ˈfü-nās\, Gregorio. 1749–1830. Argentine priest. Dean, cathedral of Córdoba (1804); rector, U. of Córdoba (1808–13); involved in independence movement (1810–16) and subsequent revolutionary governments. Known esp. for his *Ensayo de la historia civil del Paraguay, Buenos Aires, y Tucumán* (1816–17).

Funj *or* **Fung** \ˈfu̇nj, ˈfənj\. Name of a Muslim dynasty that ruled in the Nilotic Sudan of East Africa from the early 16th century until it was supplanted (1821) by Turkish government of Egypt; from its capital at Sennar (established 1504–05), the Funj expanded northward, conquered the ʽAbdallabi dynasty, and extended its control westward across the southern Gezira region into Kordofan and southward to Fāzūghlī.

Funk \ˈfüŋk, *Angl* ˈfu̇ŋk, ˈfəŋk\, Casimir. 1884–1967. American biochemist, b. Warsaw, Poland. Assistant to Abderhalden in Berlin (1906–10); researcher at Lister Institute, London (1910–13); head of biochemical department, Cancer Hospital Research Institute, London (1913–15); to U.S. (1915, naturalized 1920); researcher at Cornell Medical College (1915–16); head of research department, H. A. Metz and Co., New York (1917–23); biochemist, Columbia (1921–23); head of the department of biochemistry, State School of Hygiene, Warsaw, Poland (1923–27); founded Casa Biochemica, near Paris; research consultant, U.S. Vitamin Corp., New York City (from 1936). Known for researches on vitamins, which he named (1912); isolated thiamine (later vitamin B_1); also made researches on hormones and cancer.

Funk \ˈfəŋk\, Isaac Kauffman. 1839–1912. American publisher, b. Clifton, Ohio. In Lutheran ministry (1861–72). In book business (from 1876); with Adam Wagnalls, formed I. K. Funk & Co. (1877), which became Funk & Wagnalls Co. (1891). Editor, *Literary Digest* (1890), *Standard Dictionary of the English Language* (1890–93); assisted in bringing out *The Jewish Encyclopedia* (1901–06). Interested in prohibition, psychic phenomena, and simplified spelling. His son ¶Wilfred John (1883–1965) was president of Funk & Wagnalls (1925–40).

Fun·ston \ˈfən(t)-stən\, Frederick. 1865–1917. American soldier, b. New Carlisle, Ohio. Served with Cuban insurrectionists in Cuba (1896–98). Appointed to command Kansas regiment in Spanish–American War; sent to Philippines (1898); aided in suppressing rebellion under Aguinaldo and captured him (1901); promoted brigadier general and awarded Medal of Honor. Transferred to regular army as brigadier general; in command at San Francisco at time of earthquake (1906); in command of force that seized Veracruz (1914); major general (1914).

Fu·re·tière \fᵫer(-ə)-tyer\, Antoine. 1619–1688. French writer and lexicographer. Author of comic and satirical verse, fables, *Nouvelle allégorique* on contemporary men of letters (1658), and the pioneering novel *Le Roman bourgeois* dealing realistically with Parisian middle class (1666). Worked some 40 years on his *Dictionnaire universel,* published in Rotterdam (1690) after attempts by French Academy to suppress it.

Fur·man \ˈfər-mən\, Richard. 1755–1825. American clergyman, b. Esopus, N.Y. Pastor of Baptist church, Charleston, S.C. (1787–1822); became leading Baptist personality in the South. Furman U., Greenville, S.C., of which his son ¶James Clement (1809–1891) was president (1852–79), was named in his honor.

Fur·neaux \(ˌ)fər-ˈnō\, Tobias. 1735–1781. English naval officer and explorer. On Samuel Wallis's voyage round the world (1766–68); commanded the *Adventure* in Capt. Cook's second voyage to the Pacific (1771–74); first to circumnavigate the globe in both directions; commanded the *Syren* in British attack on Charleston, S.C. (1776).

Fur·ness \ˈfər-nəs\, Frank Heyling. 1839–1912. American architect, b. Philadelphia. Partner (from 1867) in Philadelphia firm of Furness and Hewitt (later Furness, Evans, & Co.). His Gothic Revival style characterized by polychromatic decoration and massive geometric ornamentation; influenced Louis H. Sullivan. Works included Pennsylvania Academy of Fine Arts (1872–76), Provident Life and Trust Co. Bank (1878–79), and addition to Broad St. Station of Pennsylvania Railroad (1892–94), all in Philadelphia.

Furness, Horace Howard. 1833–1912. American scholar, b. Philadelphia. Adm. to bar (1859); from 1866, devoted himself to preparation and publication of the *Variorum Shakespeare,* the first volume, *Romeo and Juliet,* appearing 1871, and the work being carried to completion by his son ¶Horace Howard (1865–1930). The elder Horace's wife ¶Helen Kate, *nee* Rogers (1837–1883) compiled *A Concordance to Shakespeare's Poems* (1874).

Fur·niss \ˈfər-nəs\, Harry. 1854–1925. British illustrator and caricaturist, b. Ireland. Best known for his political and social lampoons. On staff of *Illustrated London News* (1876–84), *Punch* (1884–94). Illustrated *Sylvie and Bruno* by Lewis Carroll (1889) and editions of Dickens (1910) and Thackeray (1911). Film writer, actor, and producer for Thomas Edison in New York and London (1912–13). Published *Royal Academy Antics* (1890), *Our Lady Cinema* (1914), essays, art instruction manuals, and a novel.

Fur·ni·vall \ˈfər-nə-vəl\, Frederick James. 1825–1910. English philologist. Aided in founding (1854) Working Men's College in London. Member of Philological Society (1847–1910), its secretary (1862–1910); originated concept (1857) and assisted in preparation of the *New English Dictionary.* Founder of Early English Text Society (1864), Chaucer Society (1868), New Shakespeare Society (1873), Wycliffe Society (1881), Browning Society (1881), Shelley Society (1886). Editor of Chaucer's works and (with J. W. Hales) of *Percy Ballads,* and many early English texts.

Fur·phy \ˈfər-fē\, Joseph. *Pseudonym* Tom Col·lins \ˈkäl-ənz\. 1843–1912. Australian novelist. Author of *Such Is Life* (1903), *Rigby's Romance* (1905), and *The Buln Buln and the Brolga* (1948); also wrote *Poems* (1916).

Fur·rer \ˈfu̇r-ər\, Jonas. 1805–1861. Swiss politician. Leader of Zürich liberals (from 1839); member and president (1837, 1846) of grand council; member and president of diet council (1848); first president of Swiss Confederation (1848, 1852, 1855, 1858).

Furse \ˈfərz\, Charles Wellington. 1868–1904. English painter. His paintings included *Return from the Ride, Diana of the Uplands,* and many portraits.

Fur·sey \ˈfər-sē, ˈfu̇r-\ *or* **Fur·sa** \-sə\. Saint. *Lat.* Fur·se·us \ˈfər-sē-əs, ˈfu̇r-\. c.567–c.650. Irish missionary. Founded monastery at Rathmat; to England with his brothers SS. Foillan and Ultán (after 630), where they assisted King Sigebert and St. Felix in christianizing the kingdom; founded monastery of Cnoberesburgh, near Yarmouth (c.640); to France (after 640), where he established (c.644) a monastery at Lagny, near Paris. His visions, as reported by Bede and Aelfric Grammaticus, achieved high popularity and exerted considerable influence on dream literature of the later Middle Ages.

Für·sten·au \ˈfᵫer-stə-ˌnau̇\. Name of a family of German musicians including: Caspar (1772–1819), flutist and composer for the flute; court musician in Oldenburg (from 1794). His son ¶Anton Bernhard (1792–1852), flutist, member of royal chapel in Dresden (from 1820), prolific composer for the flute. ¶Moritz (1824–1889), son of Anton and his successor as flutist of royal chapel at Dresden (1852); custodian of Royal Music Collection (1854) and teacher at Dresden Conservatory (1856).

Für·sten·berg \ˈfᵫer-stən-ˌberk\. Name of two German families of the nobility: (1) *Swabian line:* ruled in a principality of the Black Forest region, with parts of its domain in Baden, Württemberg, and Sigmaringen; named from the ancestral castle (built 1218) in south Baden; its princes were strong supporters of the Habsburgs; has existed in two branches since middle of 19th century. Notable members of the family were: ¶Franz Egon (1625–1682), began (after 1650) ecclesiastical career at Cologne; bishop of Strasbourg (1663–74); deprived of office and fled to France. His brother ¶Wilhelm Egon (1629–1704), soldier in French service; seized and imprisoned at Vienna (1672–79); appointed bishop of Strasbourg (1682) by Louis XIV; cardinal

(1686); deprived of office and retired to France. ¶Karl Egon (1796–1854), inherited Swabian principality (1804); lost much of his estate to Baden (1806); his palace a center of culture.

(2) *Westphalian line:* ruled in Westphalia and the Rhineland; named from the ancestral castle of Fürstenberg on the Ruhr; originated in the 13th century.

Furt·wäng·ler \ˈfu̇rt-ˌveŋ-lər\, Adolf. 1853–1907. German archaeologist. Took part in excavations at Olympia (1878–79); museum director, Berlin Antiquarium (1880–94); professor, Munich (1894); accompanied expeditions to Aegina, Amyclae, and Orchomenus (1901–07). Published *Meisterwerke der griechischen Plastik* (1893) and several catalogues of ancient Greek sculpture, vase painting, and gems. His son ¶Wilhelm, *in full* Gustav Heinrich Ernest Martin Wilhelm (1886–1954) was opera conductor in Lübeck (1911–15), Mannheim (1915–20), and Berlin (1920); succeeded Nikisch as conductor of Leipzig Gewandhaus concerts (1922–28) and of Berlin Philharmonic (1922 ff.); director of Vienna Philharmonic (1930), Bayreuth Festivals (1931–32), and Berlin State Opera (1933–34). Known for his passionate, romantic style and interpretations of romantic music, esp. Beethoven and Wagner; also composer of symphonies, choral works, chamber music, and songs.

Fu·ru·seth \ˈfyü-rə-ˌseth\, Andrew. 1854–1938. American labor leader, b. near Romsdal, Norway. To U.S. (1880). President of International Seamen's Union of America (1908–38); authority on American merchant marine; instrumental in raising standards of employment and working conditions for American seamen.

Fu·ru·ta \fu̇r-u̇t-ä\ Oribe. *Orig.* Furuta Shigenari. 1543–1615. Japanese master of tea ceremony. Soldier; made *daimyo* and placed in command of Fushimi Castle, Kyōto; studied under tea master Sen Rikyū; after Rikyū's death (1591) became foremost tea master in Japan. Influenced elements of tea ceremony, including teahouse architecture, tea-garden landscape, ceremony itself.

Fu·seli \fyü-ˈzel-ē, -ˈsel-\, Henry. *Orig.* Johann Heinrich Füss·li *or* Fuess·li \ˈfu̅e̅s-lē\. 1741–1825. British painter, b. Zürich, Switzerland. To London (1764); studied art in Rome (1770–78); contributed to Boydell's Shakespeare gallery (1786), opened own Milton gallery (1799); member (1790 ff.), professor of painting (1799–1805, 1810–25), keeper (1804–25), Royal Academy. Published *Lectures on Painting* (1801 ff.); edited Pilkington's *Dictionary of Painters* (1805). Painted historical, mythological, and original scenes in an exotic, sensual style; works included *Death of Cardinal Beaufort* (1774), *The Oath of the Rütli* (1778), *Jason Appearing Before Pelias* (1780), *The Nightmare* (1781).

Fust \ˈfüst\, Johann. c.1400–1466. German printer and goldsmith. Made loans (1450, 1452) to Gutenberg for completion of his printing process and printing of the Gutenberg Bible; by lawsuit obtained possession of Gutenberg's apparatus (1455) and established with his future son-in-law Peter Schöffer the first commercially successful printing firm. Published Gutenberg's Bible (1456) and Psalter (1457), Clement V's *Constitutiones* (1460), Cicero's *De officiis* (1465, first classic ever printed), etc.

Fus·tel de Cou·langes \fu̅e̅-stel-də-kü-länzh\, Numa-Denis. 1830–1889. French historian. Professor, Strasbourg (1861–70), Sorbonne (1875–80); director, École Normale Supérieure (1880–83). Authority on ancient and medieval history; wrote *La Cité antique* (1864), *La Gaule romaine* (1891), etc.

Fux \ˈfu̇ks\, Johann Joseph. 1660–1741. Austrian composer and music theorist. Court composer (from 1696) to emperors Leopold I, Joseph I, Charles VI. Author of theoretical work on counterpoint *Gradus ad Parnassum* (in Latin, 1725); composer of 19 operas, 85 masses, 10 oratorios, requiems, psalms and vespers, suites, sonata trios, etc.

Fu·zû·lî \fu̇z-œl-ˈi\. *Arab transliteration* Fu·ḍū·lī \fu̇-dü-ˈlē\. *Orig.* Mehmed ibn Suleyman. c.1495–1556. Turkish poet. Most outstanding figure of Turkish classical school. Resident in Baghdad. Wrote in Turkish, Persian, and Arabic. Author of complaint *Şikâyetname*, allegorical romance *Leylâ ve Mecnun*, and two collections of lyric poems.

Fyffe \ˈfīf\, Will. 1885–1947. Scottish entertainer. Stage actor; famous for his music hall comic sketches of Scottish characters; during 1930s appeared in a number of films, esp. as the Scottish shepherd in *Owd Bob;* noted for entertaining World War II servicemen.

Fyo·dor \ˈfyȯd-ər\. Name of three Russian czars:

Fyodor I Ivan·o·vich \(ˌ)yiv-ˈyän(-əv)-ˌyich\. 1557–1598. Czar (1584–98). Son of Ivan IV the Terrible and Anastasia Romanovna; last of Rurik dynasty; weak and feebleminded, actual government controlled by his brother-in-law Boris Godunov; during reign Russian patriarchate established (1589) and control strengthened over western Siberia and Caucasus; died childless.

Fyodor II Bo·ris·o·vitch \(ˌ)bər-ˈyēs(-əv)-ˌyich\. 1589–1605. Czar (April–June 1605). Succeeded his father Boris Godunov; rule immediately challenged by the first False Dmitry; murdered by boyars after ineffective attempt by his mother to save his throne.

Fyodor III Alek·se·ye·vich \əl-(ˌ)yik-ˈsyā(-yəv)-ˌyich\. 1661–1682. Czar (1676–82). Son and successor of Alexis; government under actual control at first of uncle Ivan B. Miloslavsky, soon after of courtiers I.M. Yazykov and A.T. Likhachev who introduced Western culture, still later (after 1681) of Vasily V. Golitsyn who instituted military reforms; died childless and succeeded by brother Ivan V and half-brother Peter I the Great, both under regency of his sister Sophia Alekseyevna.

Fyt \ˈfīt\, Jan. c.1611–1661. Flemish painter. Known esp. for depictions of animals, with human figures and architectural backgrounds often supplied by others. Works included *Silenus Amongst Fruit and Flowers, Diana and Her Nymphs with the Produce of the Chase, Dead Snipe with Ducks.*

G

Ga·be·lentz \'gäb-ə-,lents\, Hans Conon von der. 1807–1874. German philologist and politician. Held several public offices (from 1830); cabinet president (1848), president (1851), Altenburg diet. Made studies of many languages, including Mongolian, Swahili, Samoyed, Malayo-Polynesian. Author of *Grundzüge der syrjanischen Grammatik* (1841), *Beiträge zur Sprachenkunde* (1852), *Die melanesischen Sprachen* (1860–73), etc.

Ga·bin \gȧ-baⁿ\, Jean. *Orig.* Jean-Alexis Mon·cor·gé \mō-kȯr-zhā\. 1904–1976. French actor. Most popular actor in French cinema of 1930s and '40s; known for portrayals of peasants, working class heroes, and, in later years, criminals and detectives. Appeared in films *Maria Chapdelaine* (1934), *Pépé le Moko* (1937), *Grande Illusion* (1937), *Quai des brumes* (1938), *Le Jour se lève* (1939), *Touchez pas au Grisbi* (1953), *Le Tatoué* (1968), etc.

Ga·bin·i·us \gə-'bin-ē-əs\, Aulus. d. 47 B.C. Roman politician. Partisan of Pompey; tribune (67 B.C.); sponsored Gabinian Law giving Pompey command against pirates together with control over Mediterranean Sea and its coasts. As consul (58), helped Clodius secure Cicero's exile; proconsul in Syria (57–54); entered Caesar's service (49).

Gabirol, Solomon ben Yehuda ibn. See IBN GABIROL.

Ga·ble \'gā-bəl\, Clark, *in full* William Clark. 1901–1960. American actor, b. Cadiz, Ohio. Leading male star in Hollywood films for almost quarter of a century; known for portrayals of rough, masterful, romantic heroes. Appeared (from 1924) in over 70 films, including *Red Dust* (1932), *It Happened One Night* (1934, Academy Award), *Mutiny on the Bounty* (1935), *San Francisco* (1936), *Saratoga* (1937), *Gone With the Wind* (1939), *Boom Town* (1940), *Run Silent, Run Deep* (1958), *The Misfits* (1961).

Ga·bo \'gäb-(,)ō\, Naum. *Orig.* Naum Neemia Pevs·ner \'pyāfs-nyir, *Angl* 'pevz-nər\. 1890–1977. American sculptor, b. Bryansk, Russia. Pioneer and leader of Constructivist school. With his brother Antoine Pevsner (*q.v.*) issued "Realistic Manifesto" of Constructivism (1920); left Russia (1922) for western Europe; settled in U.S. (1946, naturalized 1952). Works included *Spiral Theme, Translucent Variation on Spheric Theme* (1951), sculpture for Byenkorf Building, Rotterdam (1957), *Linear Construction in Space, Number 4* (1957–58), fountain for St. Thomas's Hospital, London (1976).

Ga·bor \'gäb-(,)ȯ(ə)r, gə-'bȯ(ə)r\, Dennis. 1900–1979. British physicist, b. Budapest, Hungary. Reader (1949–58), professor (1958–67), Imperial College of Science and Technology, London; staff scientist, CBS Laboratories, Stamford, Conn. (from 1967). Awarded Nobel prize for physics (1971) for his invention (1947) of holography; also worked on high-speed oscilloscopes, communication theory, physical optics, television.

Ga·bo·riau \gȧ-bȯr-yō\, Émile, *in full* Étienne-Émile. 1832–1873. French novelist. Best known as the father of the *roman policier* (detective novel). His novels, many featuring detective Lecoq, included *L'Affaire Lerouge* (1866), *Le Crime d'Orcival* (1867), *Monsieur Lecoq* (1868), *Les Esclaves de Paris* (1868), *La Vie infernale* (1870), *L'Argent des autres* (1874).

Ga·bri·el \gȧ-brē-el\. Family of French architects, including: Jacques (1630–1686), architect of the king and builder of the Pont Royal and, with Mansart, the Château de Choisy-le-Roi. His son and successor as royal architect ¶Jacques-Jules (1667–1742), designer of hôtels de ville at Rennes and Dijon. His son ¶Jacques-Ange (1698–1782) succeeded him as royal architect and director of Academy of Architecture (1742); designed enlargements of château of Fontainebleau (1749) and the Louvre (1755), École Militaire (1752), Place Louis XV (now Place de la Concorde) in Paris (1755), Petit Trianon at Versailles (1762), and the grand project for Versailles (1763).

Ga·bri·el \'gā-brē-əl\. *Also known by slave name* Gabriel Pros·ser \'präs-ər\. c.1776–1800. American slave insurrectionist, b. near Richmond, Va. Planned (1800) first major slave rebellion in U.S. history, with aim of creating an independent black state in Virginia with himself as king; plot failed when an intense storm scattered his forces (Aug. 30, 1800); arrested, tried, and hanged.

Ga·bri·e·li \,gä-brē-'el-ē\, Andrea. c.1510–1586. Italian organist and composer. Perhaps pupil of Adriaan Willaert; second (1566), then first (1584) organist at St. Mark's, Venice. Master of the divided-choir technique; a pioneer in use of homophony. Equally adept at composing sacred, instrumental, and social music; works included masses, madrigals, canzoni, ricercari, motets, Magnificats, settings of Italian poetry, and large-scale choral and instrumental music for church and state ceremonies. His nephew and pupil ¶Giovanni (c.1556–1612) succeeded Andrea as second organist at St. Mark's (1584–1612); published much music of his uncle, including *Concerti* (1587); famous as a teacher, esp. of Heinrich Schütz. Excelled in divided-choir technique, specifying composition of choirs and which instruments to be used; master of the dialogue- and echo-madrigal. His sacred and secular vocal music and instrumental works included some 85 *sacrae symphoniae* (pub. 1597, 1615), madrigals, masses, motets, Magnificats, canzoni, ricercari, fantasias.

Ga·bri·el·li \,gä-brē-'el-lē\, Cante dei. 14th century. Tuscan nobleman and soldier. Podestà of Florence (1298–1306), Lucca (1312), Perugia (1322); leader of Guelphs, severely suppressing rival Ghibellines and exiling (1304) many of them, including Dante; captured Pistoia (1306).

Ga·bri·el Se·ve·rus \'gā-brē-əl-sə-'vi(ə)r-əs\. 1541–1616. Greek prelate. Ordained Greek Orthodox priest; chosen (1573) head of St. George church in Venice and leader of Greek community in Venice; appointed (1577) metropolitan of Philadelphia (Asia Minor) but continued residence at Venice. Opposed union with Roman church. Author of polemical works against Roman and Protestant doctrines, including *Exposition Against Those Claiming the Eastern Church to be Schismatic* (against Robert Bellarmine's charges of heresy) and *Treatise on the Holy and Sacred Mysteries* (on nature of the Eucharist).

Ga·bri·lo·witsch \gəv-(,)ril-'ȯv-,yich, *Angl* ,gäb-rə-'lō-(,)vich\, Ossip Solomonovich. 1878–1936. Russian pianist and conductor. Studied piano with Anton Rubenstein and Theodor Leschetizky; noted for his elegant and subtle techniques; m. Clara Clemens (1909), daughter of S. L. Clemens. Director, Detroit Symphony Orchestra (1918–36).

Gad·da \'gäd-dä\, Carlo Emilio. 1893–1973. Italian writer. Known for his contorted, complex style employing different dialects, puns, archaisms, technical terms, manufactured words, and classical allusions. Works included novels *Il castello di Udine* (1934), *Quer pasticciaccio brutto de via Merulana* (1957), *La cognizione del dolore* (1963); short-story collections *L'Adalgisa* (1944), *Novelle dal ducato in fiamme* (1953), *I racconti accoppiamenti giudiziosi, 1924–58* (1963); and essays *I viaggi la morte* (1958).

Gaddi, Dario. See Domenico GNOLI.

Gad·di \'gäd-dē\, Taddeo. c.1300–?1366. Florentine painter. Pupil and follower of Giotto; collaborated with him on frescoes in Sta. Croce, Florence (by 1332); other works included triptych of Virgin and Child (1334), further decorations for Sta. Croce of scenes from lives of Christ, St. Francis, St. Bonaventure (1338, 1340s), *Madonna in Glory* for S. Lucchese at Poggibonsi (1355); on commission supervising construction of Florence cathedral (1359–66). His son ¶Agnolo (c.1350–1396) executed series of frescoes illustrating *Legend of the True Cross* for Sta. Croce, Florence (1380s); designed medallions for Loggia dei Lanza, Florence (1383–86); designer or gilder of statues for facade of Florence cathedral (1387–95); painted cycle of scenes from life of Virgin Mary for Prato cathedral (1394–96); at death left unfinished an altar for S. Miniato al Monte.

Ga·de \'gä-thə\, Niels Wilhelm. 1817–1890. Danish composer. Founder of romantic national school in Denmark. Friend of Mendelssohn and Schumann; conducted concerts at Leipzig (1844–48); conductor of Copenhagen Musical Society (1850); director of Copenhagen Academy of Music (1866). Composer of eight symphonies; overtures including *Efterklange af Ossian* (1840), *I højlandene* (1844); cantatas as *Baldurs drøm* (1858), *Zion* (1874), *Psyche* (1882); three ballets, a violin concerto, choral works, chamber music, and songs.

Ga·di·fer de La Salle \gȧ-dē-fer-də-lȧ-sȧl\. Seigneur de Li·gron \lē-grōⁿ\. c.1340–c.1422. French soldier. Distinguished himself in campaigns against English (1368–80); on crusade to Tunis (1390); partner of Jean de Béthencourt in conquest of the Canary Islands (1402); seneschal of Bigorre (from 1414).

Gads·den \'gadz-dən\, Christopher. 1724–1805. American Revolutionary leader, b. Charleston, S.C. Leader of South Carolina radicals. Delegate to Continental Congress (1774–76); brigadier general, Continental army (1776–78); in convention of 1788, voted for ratification of United States Constitution.

Gadsden, James. 1788–1858. American army officer and diplomat, b. Charleston, S.C. Grandson of Christopher Gadsden. In U.S. army (to 1822); U.S. commissioner to move Seminoles to reservations (1823). President of South Carolina Railroad Co. (1840–50); projected southern transcontinental railroad; U.S. minister to Mexico (1853–54); negotiated treaty (ratified 1854) for purchase of strip of land (Gadsden Purchase) in what is now New Mexico and Arizona, total of nearly 30,000 square miles.

Gaeta, Duca di. See Enrico CIALDINI.

Gaetani. See CAETANI.

Gaetano. See CAJETAN.

Ga·fen·cu \gä-'fen-kü\, Grigore. 1892–1957. Romanian journalist and politician. Became editor and publisher of economic journal *Argus* (1924); founded (1930s) *Timul,* leading daily journal of Bucharest. Entered parliament (1928); held several cabinet-level posts; as foreign minister (1938–40) attempted to maintain Romania's neutrality; minister to Soviet Union (1940–41); left Romania (1941), later settling in Paris. Author of *Préliminaires de la guerre à l'Est* (1944) and *Derniers jours de l'Europe* (1946).

Ga·fo·ri \gä-'fōr-ē\ *or* **Ga·fo·rio** \gä-'fōr-yō\ *or* **Gaf·fu·rio** \gäf-'für-yō\, Franchino. 1451–1522. Italian composer and theorist. Maestro di cappella at Milan cathedral (from 1484). His treatises on music theory followed Boethius and other writers, and included *Theorica musicae* (1492), *Practica musicae* (1496), and *De harmonia musicorum instrumentorum opus* (1518). Composer of motets, masses, Magnificats, and hymns.

Ga·ga·rin \(,)gə-'gär-yin\, Yury Alekseyevich. 1934–1968. Soviet cosmonaut. First man to travel in space (Apr. 12, 1961); deputy to Supreme Soviet (from 1962).

Gage \'gāj\, Thomas. 1721–1787. English general and colonial governor. To America under Gen. Braddock (1754); served under Abercrombie in Ticonderoga expedition (1758). Brigadier general under Amherst in conquest of Canada (1760); major general (1761). Commander in chief in North America, headquarters at New York (1763–73). Appointed governor of Massachusetts (1774); used troops to seize military stores; precipitated Battle of Lexington (Apr. 19, 1775) and Battle of Bunker Hill (June 17, 1775); resigned and sailed from Boston (Oct. 1775), the last royal governor of Massachusetts. In England, commissioned general (1782).

Ga·gern \'gäg-ərn\, Hans Christoph Ernst von. Freiherr. 1766–1852. German politician. In Nassau administration (1786–1811), rising to chief minister. Administrator of Orange principalities (1814–15); Luxembourg envoy at German diet (1816–18). Supported restoration of Holy Roman Empire to protect smaller German principalities from Austria and Prussia. Member of lower (1820), upper (1829 ff.), houses of Hesse-Darmstadt.

His sons (all Freiherren): ¶Friedrich Ludwig Balduin Karl Moritz (1794–1848); served in Austrian army (1812–16), wounded at Waterloo; chief of staff to Prince Bernhard of Weimar during Belgian revolt against Dutch rule (1830–31); military governor of North Holland (1842–44) and The Hague (1847–48); killed leading army in Baden against republican revolutionaries. ¶Heinrich, *in full* Wilhelm Heinrich August (1799–1880); fought at Waterloo in Nassau army; took part in liberal nationalist movements, espousing the Kleindeutsch position on German unification; in Landtag (1832–36); first president of German national parliament (1848–49); by 1862 favored Austria-oriented Grossdeutsch solution to unification; Hessian minister to Vienna (1864–72). ¶Maximilian Joseph Ludwig (1810–1889); nationalist and member of Pan-German student Burschenschaft; member of German national parliament (1848); also advocated Kleindeutsch solution to German unification; in service of duchy of Nassau (after 1848) and of Austria (from 1855).

Ga·glia·no \gäl-'yä-nō\, Marco da. 1582–1642. Italian priest and composer. Maestro di capella (1609–42) at S. Lorenzo, court chapel of the Medici in Florence. Composer of operas *Dafne* (1608) and *La flora* (1628), ballets, masques, secular and sacred madrigals, hymns, etc.

Ga·guin \gȧ-gaⁿ\, Robert. c.1433–1501. French priest and scholar. Best known for his chronicle *De origine et gestis Francorum compendium* (1495).

Gahn \'gän\, Johan Gottlieb. 1745–1818. Swedish mineralogist and chemist. Discovered manganese (1774); assisted Carl W. Scheele in discovery of phosphoric acid in bones and in preparation of phosphorus from bones; improved copper-smelting processes; studied technical applications of minerals; appointed assessor of mining college at Stockholm (1784). The mineral gahnite is named after him.

Gail·lard \gəl-'yärd\, David Du Bose. 1859–1913. American army officer and engineer, b. Fulton, S.C. Selected by Gen. Goethals as head of department of dredging and excavating, Panama Canal (1907); later (1908) in charge of excavation at Culebra Cut (renamed Gaillard Cut).

Gai·mar V \'gī-,mär\. *Sometimes called* Gaimar IV. *Also spelled* Guaimar. c.1011–1052. Prince of Salerno. Assumed throne under regency of mother (1027); with aid of Emperor Conrad II, usurped (1038) throne of Capua from Pandulph III, driving him into exile; made alliance with Normans, conquering Apulia and Calabria with their help; stripped of conquered territories by Emperor Henry III (1047), but regained some land in Campania; assassinated.

Gai·nas \'gī-nəs\. d. 400. Visigoth general in Roman army. Caused murder of Rufinus in Constantinople (395); turned traitor and headed revolt (399); his Gothic army defeated; killed by the Huns.

Gaines \'gānz\, Edmund Pendleton. 1777–1849. American army officer, b. Culpeper Co., Va. In War of 1812, commanded defense of Fort Erie; served in Seminole War, Black Hawk War, Florida War, Mexican War.

Gains·bor·ough \'gānz-,bər-ə, -,bə-rə, -b(ə-)rə\, Thomas. 1727–1788. English painter. Studied under Gravelot in London; one of original members of Royal Acad. (1768). Excelled in portraits and landscapes; during last years also painted seascapes and idealized full-size pictures of rustics and country children. Among canvases were *Mr. and Mrs. Andrews* (c.1750), *Painter's Daughters Chasing a Butterfly* (c.1758), *Peasants Returning from Market* (c.1767), *Isabella, Countess of Sefton* (1769), *The Blue Boy* (c.1770), *The Harvest Wagon* (c.1770), *C.F. Abel* (1777), *The Mall in St. James' Park* (1783), *Mrs. Siddons* (c.1783), *The Morning Walk* (1785), *The Market Cart* (1786).

Gaiseric. See GENSERIC.

Gai·tán \gī-'tän\, Jorge Eliécer. 1902–1948. Colombian politician. Mayor of Bogotá (1936); minister of education (1940); his run (1946) for presidency as leader of radical factions of Liberals split his party and gave election to the Conservative candidate; assassinated; revered as martyr.

Gait·skell \'gāt-skəl\, Hugh Todd Naylor. 1906–1963. English politician. M.P. (1945–63); minister of fuel and power (1947–50), of state for economic affairs (1950); chancellor of the Exchequer (1950–51); Labour party leader (1955–63).

Ga·ius \'gā-(y)əs, 'gī-əs\ *or* **Ca·ius** \'kā-, 'kī-\. Saint. d. 296. Pope (283–296). Possibly a Dalmatian; reputedly relative of Diocletian; said to have carried on religious work from concealment in catacombs during last 8 years.

Gaius. fl. 130–180 A.D. Roman jurist. Chief work, *Institutiones* (c.161), an exposition of the elements of Roman law, later used as a basis for the famous Institutes of Justinian.

Gaius Caesar. See CALIGULA.

Gaj \'gī\, Ljudevit. 1809–1872. Croatian writer. Exerted influence in uniting Croats and Serbs in opposition to Magyars in Hungary.

Ga·jah Ma·da \'gäj-ä-'mäd-ä\. d. 1364. Politician of Majapahit empire in Java. Born a commoner; as head of royal bodyguard, recovered throne of King Jayanagara from rebel Kuti by a clever ruse (1319); made member of ruling elite as reward. Prime minister of the empire (c.1331–64) during reigns of Queen Tribhuvana and King Hayam Wuruk; became most powerful figure in the government and came to control most of its affairs and functions; planned and brought about unification of entire Indonesian archipelago, esp. by leading conquests of Bali (1343) and western Java kingdom of Sunda (1351); patron of poet Prapanca and eulogized in his epic *Nāgarakertāgama.* A national hero of Indonesia; first Indonesian university in Jogjakarta named after him (1946).

Gaki. See AKUTAGAWA Ryūnosuke.

Ga·laup \gȧ-lōp\, Jean-François de. Comte de La Pé·rouse \lä-pa-rüz\. 1741–c.1788. French navigator. Commanded expedition to the Pacific (1785–c.88), exploring coasts of Alaska, California, China, Russia, Samoa, southeastern Australia; apparently murdered by natives of Santa Cruz Islands. La Perouse Strait, which he explored, was named after him.

Gal·ba \'gal-bə, 'gȯl-\, Servius Sulpicius. 3 B.C.–69 A.D. Roman emperor (68–69). Of a patrician family; praetor (20 A.D.); consul (33); served as governor under several emperors in Aquitania, Germany, Africa, and Spain (39–68). Joined insurrection of Julius Vindex (68) against Nero; on Nero's death made emperor by Praetorians; executed many who were responsible for his accession; adopted Piso Licinianus as caesar; killed with Piso by Praetorians.

Gal·baio \gäl-'bī-(y)ō\, Giovanni. fl. 800. Doge of Venice (787–803). Opposed pro-Frankish party led by patriarch of Grado, whose death (801) he caused; forced to flee from uprising; replaced (803) by pro-Frankish doge Obelerius.

Galdós, Benito Pérez. See PÉREZ GALDÓS.

Gale \'gā(ə)l\, Zona. 1874–1938. American writer, b. Portage, Wis. Author of *Romance Island* (1906), *The Loves of Pelleas and Etarre* (1907), *Friendship Village* (1908), *Mothers to Men* (1911), *When I Was a Little Girl* (1913), *Heart's Kindred* (1915), *A Daughter of the Morning* (1917), *Birth* (1918), *Miss Lulu Bett* (1920), *Faint Perfume* (1923), *Preface to a Life* (1926), *Papa La Fleur* (1933).

Ga·len \'gä-lən\. 129–c.199 A.D. Greek physician, b. Pergamum, Asia Minor. Chief physician to gladiators in Pergamum (157); to Rome (161) at court of Marcus Aurelius; physician to Commodus (from c.168). Considered founder of experimental physiology; demonstrated that arteries carry blood, not air; believed in theory of four humors of the body; of his many treatises, about 100 are extant. His works were accepted for many centuries as authoritative in Greek, Roman, and Arabic medical practice.

Ga·len \'gä-lən\, Clemens August von. Graf. 1878–1946. German prelate. Ordained Catholic priest (1904); published *Pest des Laizismus und ihre Erscheinungsformen* (1932); as bishop of Münster (from 1933), became a leading critic of Nazi regime, esp. its racial and euthanasic policies; created cardinal (1946).

Ga·le·ri·us \gə-'lir-ē-əs\. *Full name* Gaius Galerius Va·le·ri·us Max·im·i·a·nus \-və-'lir-ē-əs-mak-ˌsim-ē-'ā-nəs\. d. 311. Roman emperor (305–311). Made caesar by Diocletian (293); defeated by Sasanians but later severely defeated them (297); on abdication of Diocletian (305) became emperor (augustus) in the East; made Licinius his successor (308). Probably persuaded Diocletian to issue his edict of persecution of Christians; a ruthless ruler, imposed poll tax on urban population and continued persecutions; issued edict of religious toleration shortly before death.

Gales \'gā(ə)lz\, Joseph. 1786–1860. American journalist, b. Eckington, England. To U.S. (1795). Reporter (1807), owner (1810), co-owner and coeditor (1812–60, with William W. Seaton), *National Intelligencer;* his reports (1807–29) are valuable source material for congressional debates of that period. See William W. SEATON for their joint publications.

Gal·ga·cus \'gal-gə-kəs\ *or* **Cal·ga·cus** \'kal-\. fl. 84 A.D. Caledonian chieftain. Commanded tribes defeated at Mt. Graupius by Agricola.

Ga·lia·ni \gäl-'yä-nē\, Ferdinando. 1728–1787. Italian economist. Secretary in Paris to Neapolitan ambassador (1759–69); thereafter helped formulate and administer economic policy for Neapolitan government. Anticipated modern value theory in treatise *Della moneta* (1750); argued for regulation of commerce, against Physiocrats, in *Dialogues sur le commerce des blés* (1770). His correspondence, much of it with Diderot, Voltaire, Turgot, and Morellet, valuable as source material for life of the day.

Gâlib Dede. See MEHMED ES'AD.

Ga·li·lei \ˌgä-lē-'le-ē, *Angl* ˌgal-ə-'lā(-ē)\, Galileo. *Commonly known as* Galileo. 1564–1642. Italian mathematician, astronomer, and physicist. Discovered isochronism of the pendulum; invented the hydrostatic balance (c.1586); published treatise on center of gravity in solids (1589); proposed law of uniform acceleration for falling bodies; conceived the three laws of motion later formulated by Sir Isaac Newton; demonstrated that the path of a projectile is a parabola. Professor of mathematics at Pisa (1589–91) and at Padua (1592–1610); devised a simple open-air thermometer (1607); constructed (1609) and improved refracting telescope for astronomical use, later making many because of demand for them. First to use telescope to study the skies, making discoveries (all in 1610) that the moon shines with reflected light and that its surface is mountainous, that the Milky Way is made up of countless stars, and that Jupiter has four large satellites; observed phases of Venus; discovered sunspots and noticed that they move across surface of sun; discovered moon's libration (1637). Appointed (1610) philosopher and mathematician extraordinary to grand duke of Tuscany and chief mathematician at U. of Pisa. Denounced for his *Letters on the Solar Spots* (pub. 1613), in which he advocated the Copernican system; attempted to show that there was scriptural confirmation for Copernican system, but the system was condemned and he was admonished by the pope not to defend it (1616); published *Dialogo sopra i due massimi sistemi del mondo* (1632), for which he was again summoned to Rome, tried by the Inquisition, and forced to abjure belief in Copernican system; under house arrest (from 1633) at Arcetri, near Florence; blind after 1637; published *Discorsi e dimostrazioni mathematiche intorno a due nuove scienze attenenti alla meccanica* (1638).

Galilei, Vincenzo. c.1520–1591. Italian composer and theorist. Father of Galileo Galilei. Pupil of Gioseffo Zarlino, whose theories he later attacked, esp. in *Dialogo ... della musica antica, et della moderna* (1581); as a leader of Florentine Camerata, sought to revive monodic singing style and other elements of classical Greek drama and music; published several books of madrigals and instrumental music.

Galitzin. See GOLITSYN.

Gall \'gȯl\. Saint. *Orig.* Cel·lach \'kyel-ə<u>k</u>\ *or* Cail·lech \'kȯil-yə<u>k</u>\. c.550–c.645. Irish missionary. Disciple of Saint Columban, whom he accompanied (c.590) to France; known as apostle to the Suevi and Alamanni; built (612) cell on Steinach River, Switzerland, around which was later developed monastery of Saint Gall.

Gall. *Orig.* Pi·zi \'pē-zē\. 1840?–1894. American Sioux Indian chieftain, b. on Moreau River, S.D. Took part in Red Cloud's War (1865–68); as war chief to Sitting Bull, was a leader in Battle of Little Big Horn (June 25, 1876) where Custer and his command were slain; friendly to the whites (from 1881); a judge at the Indian Agency's Court of Indian Offenses (from 1889).

Gall \'gäl\, Franz Joseph. 1758–1828. German physician and founder of phrenology. Pioneer in ascribing cerebral functions to various areas of the brain (localization); first to identify gray matter of brain with neurons and white matter with ganglia; sought to establish relationship between mental faculties and shape of skull; took up residence in Paris (1807); his phrenological hypothesis developed by Spurzheim and George Combe (*qq.v.*). Chief publication, *Anatomie et physiologie du système nerveux en général* (1810–19).

Gallagher, Ed. See under Al SHEAN.

Gal·land \gȧ-lä^{n}\, Antoine. 1646–1715. French scholar. Accompanied French ambassador to Constantinople (1670–75); made other travels to Middle East; antiquary to Louis XIV (1679); professor of Arabic at Collège de France (1709). Known for *Mille et une nuits* (1704–17), first translation of *Arabian Nights' Entertainment* into a European language; also wrote *Les Paroles remarquables, les bons mots, et les maxims des Orientaux* (1695), *Les Contes et fables indiennes de Bidpai et de Lokman* (1724); translated the Qur'ān.

Galla Placidia. See PLACIDIA.

Gal·las \'gäl-äs\, Matthias. Graf von Cam·po \'käm-pō\ *and* Herzog von Lu·ce·ra \lü-'cher-ə\. 1584–1647. Austrian soldier. Joined army of Catholic League; served in Imperial army in Italy (1628–31) and against Gustav Adolphus (1631–33). Conspired against Wallenstein and succeeded him in command of Imperial army (1634); defeated Swedes at Nördlingen (1634); thereafter his negligence and drunkenness resulted in disastrous campaigns in Thirty Years' War, esp. annihilation of his troops in 1637, 1638, 1644; eventually resigned.

Gal·la·tin \'gal-ət-^{ə}n\, Albert, *in full* Abraham Alfonse Albert. 1761–1849. American politician, b. Geneva, Switzerland. To U.S. (1780) and settled in Pennsylvania; elected U.S. senator (1793) but unseated on ground that he had not been citizen for required nine years (1794). Member, U.S. House of Representatives (1795–1801); leader of Republican minority (from 1797); revealed himself as having genius for finance; helped establish House Committee on Finance (now Ways and Means Committee). U.S. secretary of the treasury (1801–14). A negotiator of peace (1814) with Great Britain after War of 1812; U.S. minister to France (1816–23), to Great Britain (1826–27). President National (later Gallatin) Bank, New York (1832–39). Studied North American Indian tribes and founded (1842) American Ethnological Society of New York.

Gal·lau·det \ˌgal-ə-'det\, Thomas Hopkins. 1787–1851. American educator, b. Philadelphia. Studied in France methods of instructing deaf-mutes (1815–16); established first free American school for the deaf (Connecticut, later American, Asylum), Hartford, Conn. (1817); principal of this school (1817–30). First professor in U.S. of philosophy of education (at N.Y.U., 1832–33); in *Plan of a Seminary for the Education of Instructors* (1825) proposed special schools for training teachers. Gallaudet College, Washington, D.C., is named in his honor. His son ¶Edward Miner (1837–1917) was also a teacher of the deaf and dumb in the American Asylum at Hartford; became head (1857) of Columbia Institution for the Deaf and Dumb, Washington, D.C., the senior department of which became Gallaudet College.

Gal·lé \gȧ-le\, Émile. 1846–1904. French glass and furniture maker. Established workshop at Nancy (1874); made many innovations in manufacture of glassware, esp. development of a deeply colored, thickly layered glass carved or etched with plant motifs in Art Nouveau style and use of special effects such as metallic foils and air bubbles; his works internationally famous and imitated; leading force in establishment (1901) of L'École de Nancy; also known for his furniture designs based on floral and fruit themes, carried out in elaborate marquetry and sometimes employing quotations from Symbolist writers as decorations. Author of *Écrits pour l'art 1884–89* (1908).

Gal·le \'gäl-ə\, Johann Gottfried. 1812–1910. German astronomer. Assistant director, Berlin Observatory (1835–51); director, Breslau Observatory (1851–97). First to observe planet Neptune (Sept. 23, 1846), whose existence had been proved by Le Verrier's calculations; devised method of measuring scale of solar system by observing parallax of asteroids.

Gal·le·go \gäl-'yā-gō\, Juan Nicasio. 1777–1853. Spanish poet. Known esp. for his patriotic ode *Al dos de Mayo,* inspired by the uprising of 1808.

Gal·lén-Kal·le·la \gäl-'lān-'käl-lel-ä\, Akseli Valdemar. 1865–1931. Finnish painter. Best known for his fantastic symbolic paintings interpreting Finnish folk epic *Kalevala;* also portrait and landscape painter.

Gal·li·co \'gal-i-ˌkō\, Paul William. 1897–1976. American journalist and writer, b. New York City. Sportswriter and columnist, *New York Daily News* (1922–36); originator of Golden Gloves boxing competition (1927); freelance writer (from 1936). Author of novels, short stories, children's literature, film scripts, etc., including *The Snow Goose* (1940), *Mrs. 'Arris Goes to Paris* (1958), *The Poseidon Adventure* (1969).

Gal·li-Cur·ci \'gäl-lē-'kür-chē\, Amelita, *nee* Galli. 1889–1963. American operatic soprano, b. Milan, Italy. m. Marquis Luigi Curci (1910; div. 1920). Famed for her florid coloratura singing. Made U.S. debut as Gilda in *Rigoletto* (Chicago, 1916); with Metropolitan Opera Co., New York (1921–30). Roles included Lakmé in *Lakmé,* Violetta in *La Traviata,* Juliette in *Roméo et Juliette,* Lucia in *Lucia de Lammermoor,* Sophie in *Der Rosenkavalier,* Mimi in *La Bohème,* and Elvira in *I Puritani.*

Galli da Bibiena *or* **Bibbiena.** See BIBIENA.

Gal·lie·ni \gȧl-yā-nē\, Joseph-Simon. 1849–1916. French soldier. As governor of French Sudan (1886–88) and governor general of Madagascar (1896–1905), pacified those territories and directed their integration into French Empire. Military governor of Paris (1914–15); led counterattack against Germans at the Marne (Sept. 1914); minister of war (1915–16); created marshal of France posthumously (1921). Author of books on his colonial experiences, as *La Pacification de Madagascar* (1900).

Gal·li·e·nus \ˌgal-ē-'ē-nəs, -'ā-nəs\, Publius Licinius Valerianus Egnatius. d. 268. Roman emperor (253–268). Son of Valerian; made emperor and colleague to his father (253–260); on capture of Valerian by Persians, became sole emperor (260–268). Defeated Alemanni at Milan (258); crushed revolts of Ingenuus and Regalianus in Illyrium (260); lost much territory, finally in control of only Italy and the Balkans.

Gal·lif·fet \gȧ-lē-fe\, Gaston-Alexandre-Auguste de. Marquis. *Also known as* Prince de Mar·tignes \mȧr-tēnʸ\. 1830–1909. French soldier. At siege of Sevastopol (1855), in Napoléon III's wars in Algeria, Italy, and Mexico, and in Franco–Prussian War (1870–71); general of brigade (1870), of division (1875); suppressed revolts of Paris Commune (1871). Became member of Conseil Supérieur de la Guerre (1885); minister of war (1899–1900).

Gal·li·mard \gȧ-lē-mȧr\, Gaston. 1881–1975. French publisher. With André Gide and Jean Schlumberger, founded (1908) periodical *La Nouvelle Revue Française* and established (1911) a publishing house later (1919) known as Librairie Gallimard; served as its president and made it into highly influential publishing firm; started "La Pléiade" editions of French classics.

Gal·lio \'gal-ē-ˌō\, Junius Annaeus. *Orig.* Marcus An·nae·us No·va·tus \ə-'nē-ə-snō-'vā-təs\. c.5 B.C.–65 A.D. Roman politician. Brother of Seneca; consul, senator; as proconsul of Achaea (c.51), refused to try cases arising out of religious disputes and dismissed the Jews' accusation against Paul.

Gallito. See José GOMEZ.

Gal·li·tzin \gə-'lit-sən\, Demetrius Augustine. *Orig. surname* Golitsyn. 1770–1840. American clergyman, b. The Hague, Netherlands. Member of noble Russian family Golitsyn (*q.v.*). Entered Roman Catholic church (1787); to U.S. (1792); ordained priest (1795). Sent to Cambria Co., Pennsylvania, where his missionary efforts gained him epithet "Apostle of the Alleghenies"; founded town of Loretto (1799); became naturalized citizen (1802); vicar general for western Pennsylvania. Author of polemical tracts against Protestant attacks, as *A Defence of Catholic Principles* (1816). Gallitzin, Pa., is named in his honor.

Gal·lo·way \'gal-ə-ˌwā\, Joseph. c.1731–1803. American lawyer and politician, b. West River, Md. Practiced in Philadelphia (from 1747); member, Pennsylvania colonial legislature (1756–64, 1765–75); opposed independence of colonies; as member (1774–75) of Continental Congress, presented a "Plan of a proposed union between Great Britain and the Colonies" which gave ultimate authority to British crown and was rejected by one vote. Joined Howe's British army; fled to England (1778).

Gal·lup \'gal-əp\, George Horace. 1901–1984. American pollster, b. Jefferson, Ia. Research director at Young & Rubicam advertising agency (1932–47); pioneer in scientific sampling of public opinion; founder (1935) and chairman of American Institute of Public Opinion (Gallup Poll). Had a lasting influence on U.S. marketing and political campaign strategy.

Gal·lus \'gal-əs\, Gaius Cornelius. c.70–26 B.C. Roman soldier and poet. Friend of Virgil; supported Augustus and fought at Actium (31). First prefect of Egypt (30); his conduct led to his disgrace and suicide. One of greatest Roman elegiac poets; famous for poems to his mistress "Lycoris"; few works extant.

Gallus, Gaius Vibius Trebonianus. d. 253 A.D. Roman emperor (251–253). Served under Decius in campaign against Goths (251); elected emperor after defeat and death of Decius; killed by his own soldiers.

Gallus, Jacobus. See Jacob HANDL.

Gallus, Udalricus. See Ulrich HAN.

Gallus Cae·sar \-'sē-zər\. *Orig.* Flavius Claudius Constantius. 325 or 326–354 A.D. Roman ruler. Elder half-brother of Julian the Apostate; reared a Christian. Made caesar of Roman eastern provinces by his cousin Constantius II and married Constantius's sister (351); ruled harshly, executing many subjects; suppressed revolts in Palestine and Isauria; repelled Persian attacks; recalled (354) by Constantius and executed.

Ga·lois \gȧl-wȧ\, Évariste. 1811–1832. French mathematician. Failed to gain admission to École Polytechnique (1827, 1829); arrested for republican activities and spent six months in prison (1831); killed in duel. Made important contributions to group theory; discovered essential conditions that an equation must satisfy for it to be solvable by radicals.

Gal·swin·tha \'gal-ˌswin(t)-thə\. c.540–568. Frankish queen. Daughter of Athanagild and sister of Brunhilde; m. (567) Chilperic I, king of Neustria; her murder, at instigation of Chilperic's mistress Fredegund, aroused enmity of Brunhilde and precipitated 40 years of war between Austrasia and Neustria.

Gals·wor·thy \'gȯlz-ˌwər-t͟hē\, John. *Pseudonym in early works* John Sin·john \'sin-jən\. 1867–1933. English novelist and playwright. Called to bar (1890) but did not practice. Known esp. for series of novels dealing with the wealthy Forsyte family, including *The Forsyte Saga* trilogy: *The Man of Property* (1906), *In Chancery* (1920), *To Let* (1921); *A Modern Comedy* trilogy: *The White Monkey* (1924), *The Silver Spoon* (1926), *Swan Song* (1928); and *End of the Chapter* trilogy: *Maid in Waiting* (1931), *Flowering Wilderness* (1932), *Over the River* (1933); other novels included *Jocelyn* (1898), *The Island Pharisees* (1904), *The Country House* (1907), *The Patrician* (1911), *The Freelands* (1915); also *Caravan* (1927, collected short stories). Plays included *The Silver Box* (1906), *Joy* (1907), *Strife* (1909), *Justice* (1910), *The Pigeon* (1912), *The Eldest Son* (1912), *The Fugitive* (1913), *The Mob* (1914), *The Skin Game* (1920), *A Family Man* (1921), *Loyalties* (1922), *Old English* (1924), *Escape* (1926), *Exiled* (1929), and *The Roof* (1929). Awarded Nobel prize for literature (1932).

Galt \'gȯlt\, Sir Alexander Tilloch. 1817–1893. Canadian politician, b. London, England. Son of John Galt; to Canada (1835); clerk (1835), high commissioner (1844–55), British American Land Co., Sherbrooke, Lower Canada. Member of Canadian Legislative Assembly (1849–50, 1853–67), of House of Commons (1867–72); leader of English-speaking minority; as finance minister (1858–62, 1864–67), introduced decimal system of currency and adopted protection policy for Canadian manufacturers; advocated federation. First minister of finance of Dominion of Canada (1867–68); became advocate of Canadian independence; appointed (1875) member of Halifax Fisheries Commission; first Canadian high commissioner in London (1880–83).

Galt, John. 1779–1839. Scottish novelist. Settled in London (1804); trade agent in Europe for British merchant firm (c.1805–14); secretary (c.1823–29) of Canada Land Co., promoting settlement of Canada and founding (1827) Guelph, Ont.; afterwards devoted himself to writing. Author of novels depicting Scottish country and small-town life, including *The Ayrshire Legatees* (1820), *The Annals of the Parish* (1821), *Sir Andrew Wylie* (1822), *The Provost* (1822), *The Entail* (1823), *Lawrie Todd* (1830).

Gal·ton \'gȯlt-ᵊn\, Sir Francis. 1822–1911. English scientist. Nephew of Erasmus Darwin. Independently wealthy, held no scientific or teaching posts. Traveled in Europe, Asia Minor, Holy Land, southwest Africa; made study of meteorology; published *Meteorographica* (1863), basis of modern weather maps. Best known for his work in anthropology and the study of heredity; founder of science of eugenics; devised system of fingerprint identification. Among his works were *Hereditary Genius* (1869), *Inquiries into Human Faculty* (1883), *Natural Inheritance* (1889), *Finger Prints* (1893).

Ga·lup·pi \ga-'lüp-pē\, Baldassare. *Called* Il Bu·ra·nel·lo \ēl-ˌbü-rä-'nel-lō\. 1706–1785. Italian composer, b. Burano. Father of opera buffa. Collaborated on two operas with G. B. Pescetti (1728–29); music director of Ospedale dei Mendicanti, Venice (1740–51); opera composer at King's Theatre, London (1741–42), influencing many English composers; assistant maestro di capella (1748–62), maestro (1762–85), St. Mark's, Venice, and to Catherine II in Russia (1766–68); choirmaster at Ospedale degli Incurabili, Venice (1768–85). Composer of over 30 opere buffe, including *Il filosofo di Campagna* (1754), *L'amante di tutte* (1760), *L'uomo femmina* (1762), and of some 65 opere serie, including *Enrico* (1743), *Idomeneo* (1756), *Ifigenia in Tauride* (1768); also composed cantatas, oratorios, Magnificats, and chamber music.

Gal·va·ni \gäl-'vä-nē\, Luigi. 1737–1798. Italian physician and physicist. Lecturer on anatomy at U. of Bologna (1768–98); professor of obstetrics at Instituto delle Scienze, Bologna (1782–98). Made pioneering researches in electrophysiology (from early 1780s), as causing muscular contractions in a frog's legs by application of static electricity; argued in *De viribus electricitatis in motu musculari commentarius* (1791) that animal tissue contains an innate, vital force which he termed "animal electricity"; his theory partly refuted by Alessandro Volta; announced (1794) experiments which established presence of bioelectric forces in animal tissue.

Gál·vez \'gäl-b̲āth, -b̲ās\, Bernardo de. Conde. 1746–1786. Spanish colonial administrator. Governor of Louisiana (1777); in war against Great Britain captured Baton Rouge and Natchez (1779), Mobile (1780), and Pensacola (1781); made possible Spanish acquisition of Florida in peace settlement (1783). Captain general of Cuba (1784); viceroy of New Spain (1784–86).

Gálvez, José. Marqués de la So·no·ra \t͟hä-lä-sō-'nō-rä\. 1729–1787. Spanish colonial administrator. To Mexico as *visitador general* of New Spain (1765–71); reorganized tax system and frontier defenses, established a government tobacco monopoly; fitted out expeditions (1769) which made first settlements in Upper

California. To Spain (1771); created marqués (1772); president, Council of the Indies; minister of the Indies (1776); effected administrative reforms and expanded commerce. Considered Spain's greatest colonial administrator.

Gál·vez \'gäl-b̠ās\, Manuel. 1882–1962. Argentine novelist. Founded literary magazine *Ideas* (1903); inspector of secondary education in Buenos Aires (1906–31). Author of realistic novels of conflict in Argentine urban society as *La maestra normal* (1914), *El mal metafísico* (1916), *La sombra del convento* (1917), and *Nacha Regules* (1919), historical novels, and biographies.

Gál·vez de Mon·tal·vo \'gäl-b̠āth-t̠h̠ā-mȯn-'täl-b̠ō\, Luis. 1549?–?1591. Spanish writer. Author of the pastoral romance *El pastor de Fílida* (1582).

Galway, Earl of. See Henri de MASSUE.

Ga·ma \'gȧ-mȧ\, José Basílio da. 1740–1795. Brazilian poet. Settled at Lisbon as protégé of Pombal (1760); known esp. for his epic *O Uruguai,* and anti-Jesuit account of Portuguese-Spanish campaign against Guarani Indians (1769).

Ga·ma \'gȧ-mə\, Vasco da. c.1460–1524. Portuguese navigator. Commissioned by King Manuel I to make journey by sea to India; sailed from Lisbon (July 1497) with four vessels; rounded Cape of Good Hope, reached Malindi on east coast of Africa, thence sailed directly across Indian Ocean, arriving at Calicut (May 1498)—the first voyage from western Europe around Africa to the East. On second journey (1502–03), planted Portuguese colonies at Mozambique and Sofala. Viceroy of Portuguese Asia (1524).

Ga·ma·li·el \gə-'mā-lē-əl, -'māl-yəl\. Name of several Palestinian Jewish rabbis, especially: Gamaliel I (fl. c.20–c.50 A.D.); teacher of St. Paul; as member of Sanhedrin, advised against persecuting the apostles; established several lenient ordinances; according to the Talmud, a grandson of Hillel (*q.v.*); first to be given title of rabban (teacher); also given title ha-Zagen (the Elder). His grandson ¶Gamaliel II, of Jabneh (1st–2d century A.D.); as *nasi* (president) of Sanhedrin, was leader of Jewish people in difficult period after destruction of Jerusalem (70); a noted scholar, of liberal views; regulated prayer ritual, esp. establishing final revision of the *'amida;* standardized Jewish calendar and fixed dates of festivals; deposed but later restored. ¶Gamaliel III (3d century A.D.); eldest son of Judah ha-Nasi; became patriarch of Jewish community and *nasi* of Sanhedrin (c.220); directed completion of the Mishna.

Ga·mar·ra \gä-'mär-rä\, Agustín. 1785–1841. Peruvian general and politician. President of Peru (1829–33, 1839–41).

Gam·bet·ta \gäⁿ-bā-tȧ\, Léon-Michel. 1838–1882. French politician. Leader of opposition to government of Napoléon III; elected to Legislative Assembly (1869). During Franco–Prussian War (1870–71), played principal role in proclamation of Third Republic and in formation of provisional government, becoming minister of interior and later minister of war; raised new armies. Member (1871) of the National Assembly and (1876) of the Chamber of Deputies; secured ratification of republic in Assembly (1871); president of the Chamber of Deputies (1879–81); premier of France (1881–82).

Gam·bier \'gam-ˌbi(ə)r\, James. 1st Baron Gambier. 1756–1833. British naval commander, b. Nassau, Bahamas. Admiral (1805); led British fleet in bombardment of Copenhagen and capture of Danish fleet (1807); commander of Channel fleet (1808–11); admiral of the fleet (1830).

Gam·boa \gäm-'b̠ō-ä\, Federico. 1864–1939. Mexican novelist. Author of social novels *Del natural* (1889), *Apariencias* (1892), *Suprema ley* (1896), *Metamorfosis* (1899), *Santa* (1903), *Reconquista* (1908), *La llaga* (1910), plays, and memoirs *Mi diario* (1907–38).

Ga·me·lin \gȧm-laⁿ\, Maurice, *in full* Gustave-Maurice. 1872–1958. French soldier. Promoted general of brigade during World War I (1914–18). Army chief of staff (1931); succeeded Weygand as inspector general of the French army and vice president of the Supreme War Council (1935); chief of staff of national defense (1938). Commander in chief of Allied forces in France (1939); defeated by German attack (May 1940) that led to French collapse that June; dismissed (May 1940), tried, imprisoned (1943–45).

Ga·mow \'gam-ˌȯf\, George. 1904–1968. American physicist, b. Odessa, Russia. Professor, George Washington U. (1934–56), U. of Colorado (1956–68). Developed quantum theory of radioactivity (1928) and liquid drop model of atomic nuclei (1928–29); with Edward Teller, formulated Gamow-Teller theory of beta decay (1936) and a theory of internal structure of red giant stars (1942). Known esp. for applying his studies of nuclear processes to cosmology; postulated that the sun's energy comes from thermonuclear processes; a leading advocate of "big-bang" theory of origin of universe; wrote "The Origin of Chemical Elements" (1948, with Ralph Alpher) hypothesizing that elements were created by neutron capture. Worked (from 1954) on DNA and genetic theory; proposed a genetic code. Author of the "Mr. Tomkins" series (1939–67), *One, Two, Three ... Infinity* (1947), *The Creation of the Universe* (1952), *A Planet Called Earth* (1963), etc.

Gana, Alberto Blest. See BLEST GANA.

Gance \gäⁿs\, Abel. 1889–1981. French film director. Noted esp. for virtuosity and technical innovations of silent films as *J'accuse* (1919), *La Roue* (1923), *Napoléon* (1927); later films included *La Fin du monde* (1931), *Lucrece Borgia* (1935), *Paradis perdu* (1940), *Austerlitz* (1960), *Cyrano et D'Artagnan* (1963).

Gan·dhi \'gän-dē\, Indira Priyadarshini Nehru. 1917–1984. Indian politician. Joined all-India Congress party (1938); m. Feroze Gandhi (1942); served (1947–64) as official hostess for her father Prime Minister Jawaharlal Nehru (*q.v.*); elected president Congress party (1959–60); elected prime minister (1966); instituted major reforms, including strict population control program; supported the Bengalis against West Pakistan (1971); incorporated Sikkim (1974); declared (June 1975) state of emergency and governed by decree; defeated in 1977 elections; imprisoned briefly for abuses while in office; made brilliant comeback as prime minister in 1980 election; met demand for autonomous Sikh state by ordering attack (June 6, 1984) on Golden Temple at Amritsar; assassinated by Sikh extremists among her own bodyguards.

Gandhi, Mohandas Karamchand. *Called* Ma·hat·ma \mə-'hät-mə, *Angl also* -'hat-\ *i.e.* great-souled. 1869–1948. Indian nationalist and spiritual leader. Considered the father of his country. To London to study law (1888–91); practiced in India (1893). To Natal, South Africa (1893); because of mistreatment of Indian immigrants by whites, instituted (1906) Satyagraha ("firmness in truth") campaign of passive resistance and non-cooperation with the government that resulted in some political gains. To India (1914); after passage of Rowlatt Acts (1919), organized a Satyagraha movement against British government; advocated revival of home industries and political independence (swaraj); given title of *Mahatma* by common people (c.1920); his policies went beyond his control and resulted in general boycott of British goods (1920), the Mopla rebellion (1921–22) and other riots and disturbances; imprisoned (1922–24). Resumed control of Swaraj party; president of Indian National Congress (1925). Renewed campaign of civil disobedience (1929–30) which resulted in rioting and a second imprisonment; made truce (1931) and attended Round Table Conference in London. Again urged boycott (1932) and advocated social reforms; began "fast unto death" (1932) in protest against government's treatment of "untouchables"; after six days' fast won pact in their favor; again arrested and again released (1933). Resigned presidency of Indian National Congress (1934); from 1937 less active against government, though still recognized as a leader in struggle for independence; again arrested (1942) for demanding British withdrawal; negotiated for an autonomous Indian state (1947); assassinated by a Hindu fanatic. Author of *Hind Swaraj* (1909), autobiography *The Story of My Experiments with Truth* (1927–29), etc.

Gan·ge·śa \gən-'gā-shə\. *In full* Gangeśa Upādh·yā·ya \ˌu̇p-äd-'yä-yə\. 12th century. Indian philosopher. Founder of Buddhist new school of Nyāya; wrote its basic text, *Tattvacintāmaṇi.*

Ga·nio·da'·yo \ˌgän-yō-'dī-(y)ō\, *i.e.* Handsome Lake. c.1735–1815. American Seneca Indian religious, b. Ganawaugus, N.Y. Received (1799) revelation from the Great Spirit and developed a religion he called Gaiwiio ("good message") which combined Christian and Indian beliefs; as itinerant preacher (from 1800), spread this religion among the Iroquois. Gaiwiio (also known as Handsome Lake Cult) still has adherents today.

Ga·ni·vet \gän-ē-'b̠āt\, Ángel. 1865–1898. Spanish writer. Known esp. for his *Idearium español,* a study of Spanish genius and character (1897); also wrote novels *La conquista del reino de Maya* (1897) and *Los trabajos del infatigable creador Pío Cid* (1898).

Gan·ku \gän-kü\. *Orig.* Sa·eki \sä-ek-ē\ Kishi. 1749–1838. Japanese painter. Court painter of Kyōto; held high rank. Founder of the Kishi school of painting; painted realistic portraits, landscapes, flowers, birds, and esp. tigers.

Gan·nett \'gan-ət\, Henry. 1846–1914. American geographer, b. Bath, Me. Topographer, Hayden Survey (1872–79), mapping in Colorado and Wyoming. Chief geographer, U.S. Geological Survey (from 1882). A founder (1888) and a president, National Geographic Society.

Gans \'gäns\, Eduard. 1798–1839. German jurist. Founder (1819, with Leopold Zunz) of Society for Jewish Culture and Science; converted to Christianity (1825). Disciple of Hegel; professor of law, Berlin (1825–39). Author of *Das Erbrecht in weltgeschichtlicher Entwicklung* (1824–35), *Vorlesungen über die Geschichte der Letzten fünfzig Jahre* (1833–34), etc.

Gans \'gan(t)s\, Joe. *Orig.* Joseph Gaines \'gānz\. *Known as* the Old Master. 1874–1910. American boxer, b. Baltimore. Often considered greatest fighter in lightweight division. Won world lightweight title by knocking out Frank Erne in one round (May 12, 1902); drew with welterweight champion Joe Walcott (Sept. 20, 1904); lost title to Battling Nelson (July 4, 1908).

Gäns·ba·cher \'gens-ˌbäk̠-ər\, Johann Baptist. 1778–1844. Austrian composer. Kapellmeister at St. Stephen's cathedral, Vienna (1824–44). Composer of church music, esp. 35 masses and 8 requiems; also secular choruses and cantatas, a symphony, and chamber music.

Ganse·voort \'ganz-ˌvō(ə)rt, -ˌvȯ(ə)rt\, Peter. 1749–1812. American Revolutionary officer, b. Albany, N.Y. In command of Fort George (1776) and Fort Schuyler (1777), which he defended through a siege by St. Leger at head of

British and Indians. In command at Saratoga (1780); brigadier general, U.S. army (1809).

Ganso. See Hōnen.

Ganz \'gänts\, Rudolph. 1877–1972. American composer and conductor, b. Zürich, Switzerland. Head of piano department (1900–05), vice president (1927), president (1933–54), Chicago Musical College. Conductor of St. Louis Symphony (1921–27) and of Young People's Concerts for New York Philharmonic and San Francisco Symphony (1939–49). Introduced works by contemporary composers; composed a symphony, works for piano and voice, and over 200 songs.

Gar·a·mond *or* **Gar·a·mont** \gȧ-rȧ-mōⁿ\, Claude. c.1480–1561. French type designer and founder. Apprenticed to Antoine Augerau (c.1510); worked with Geoffroy Tory (by 1520). One of first punch cutters to work independently of printers. Perfected design of roman type and introduced it (from 1531) to replace the Gothic then commonly used; by order of King Francis I, designed and cut the three fonts of characters used by Robert Estienne (*q.v.*) in his editions of Greek classics; began (1545) to publish books but apparently unsuccessful.

Gar·and \gə-'rand, 'gar-ənd\, John Cantius. 1888–1974. American inventor, b. St. Rémi, Que. Worked, esp. as toolmaker, chiefly in Providence, R.I. (1907–16), and New York City; naturalized (1920). Designed light machine gun and called to Washington, D.C., to work at U.S. Bureau of Standards (1917). Ordnance engineer, U.S. Armory, Springfield, Mass. (1919–53); invented semiautomatic Garand rifle adopted (1936) by U.S. army as standard shoulder weapon (designated M-1).

Ga·ra·ša·nin \'gȧr-ȧ-shȧ-nēn\, Ilija. *Orig.* Ilija Sa·vić \'sȧ-vētʸ\. 1812–1874. Serbian politician. Played prominent role in election (1842) and in abdication (1858) of Prince Alexander Karageorgević. Prime minister and foreign secretary (1852, 1861–67); introduced enlightened legislation and an efficient bureaucracy; credited with securing guarantee of Serbia's autonomy by Congress of Paris (1856); effected withdrawal of Turkish civil officials and garrisons (by 1867); helped create first Balkan League (1866–68); constantly worked for creation of a Greater Serbia.

Ga·ray \'gär-ˌȯi\, János. 1812–1853. Hungarian poet and playwright. Author of poem *Az obsitos* (1843), whose hero, Háry János, became a national figure and subject of Kodály's opera.

Ga·ray \gä-'rä-ē\, Juan de. c.1527–c.1583. Spanish soldier. To Paraguay (c.1565); founded city of Santa Fe de la Vera Cruz (1573); governor of Paraguay (1576); captain general of La Plata territory, founded Buenos Aires (1580) on site of abandoned (1541) settlement of Mendoza; massacred by Indians.

Gar·bett \'gär-bət\, Cyril Forster. 1875–1955. English clergyman. Bishop of Southwark (1919–32), of Winchester (1932–42); archbishop of York (1942). Author of *In an Age of Revolution* (1952), *The Church of England Today* (1953), etc.

Gar·borg \'gär-bȯrg\, Arne Evenson. 1851–1924. Norwegian writer. Wrote cycle of lyric poems *Haugtussa* (1895); author of novels depicting social and religious problems of the peasant, including *Bondestudentar* (1883), *Hjaa ho mor* (1890), *Fred* (1890), *Den burtkomne Fadern* (1899), *Heimkomin Son* (1908); author also of dramas, literary criticism, translations, etc. Associated with movement for establishing Norwegian literary language based on peasant dialect known as Landsmål.

Gar·ção \gər-'saůⁿ\, Pedro Antônio Correia. 1724–1772. Portuguese poet. A founder (1756) of Arcádia Lusitana, academy devoted to neoclassical reform of poetry; edited *Gazeta de Lisboa* (1760–62). Author of sonnets, odes, epistles, and verse comedies *Teatro novo* (1766) and *Assembléia ou partida*, latter containing celebrated poem "Cantata de Dido."

Gar·cía \gär-'thē-ä, *Angl* -'sē-ə\. Name of five kings of Navarre (Pamplona):

García I Íñi·guez \'ēn-yē-gāth\. d. 870. King (851 or 852–870). Imprisoned by Norman invaders but ransomed (858–859).

García II Sán·chez \'sän-chāth\. d. 970. King (926–970). Son of Sancho I Garcés; under regency of his mother during his minority; paid homage to 'Abd ar-Raḥmān III in Córdoba and secured a his support (958); defeated by Moors and lost some territories (963).

García III Sánchez. d. 1000. King (994–1000). Son of Sancho II Garcés, grandson of García II, and father of Sánchez III Garcés; his capital razed by Almanzor (999).

García IV Sánchez. d. 1054. King (1035–54). Eldest son of Sancho III Garcés, grandson of García III; at Tafallo repelled an attack by his brother Ramiro I of Aragon (1043); invaded by his brother Ferdinand I of Castile to recover annexed territories (1054); killed at Battle of Atapuerca.

García V Ra·mí·rez \rä-'mē-rāth\. *Called* el Res·tau·ra·dor \el-rās-taů-rä-'thōr\, *i.e.* the Restorer. d. 1150. King (1134–50). Son of El Cid's daughter and Ramiro Sánchez, lord of Monzon and great-grandson of García IV; broke union of Aragon and Navarre by declaring vassalage to Alfonso VII of Castile (1134); waged war on Alfonso (1137–40); concluded peace with Alfonso (1140) and helped him capture Almería (1147).

García, Calixto. See García Íñiguez.

García, Carlos Polestico. 1896–1971. Philippine politician. Senator (1941–53); vice president and foreign minister (1953–57); president of the Philippines (1957–61); maintained strong ties to U.S.

García, Manuel del Pópolo Vicente Rodríguez. 1775–1832. Spanish tenor and composer. Created roles in several Rossini operas in Italy (1811–16); sang in Paris and London (from 1816), where he was also famous as singing teacher, introducing methods of instruction recognized as basis of modern teaching. Formed (1825) opera company which included his children. Composer of many operas. His son ¶Manuel Patricio Rodríguez García (1805–1906) was also a singing teacher; professor, Paris Conservatory of Music (1847–50) and Royal Acad. of Music, London (1848–95); inventor of laryngoscope (1855). Author of *Mémoires sur la voix humaine* (1840) and *Traité complet de l'art du chant* (1847).

García Cal·de·rón \-käl-dā-'rȯn\, Francisco. 1834–1905. Peruvian politician. Member of congress (1867); after occupation of Lima by Chilean army and flight of Pres. Piérola, elected provisional president (1881); imprisoned by Chileans; returned to Peru and elected president of Senate (1886). His son ¶Francisco (1883–1953) was Peruvian representative at Paris Peace Conference (1919); minister to Belgium (1918–21), France (from 1930). Author of *Le Pérou contemporaine* (1907), *Hombres y ideas de nuestro tiempo* (1907), *La creación de un continente* (1914), *Testimonios y comentarios* (1934). Another son ¶Ventura (1886–1959) wrote tales and novels as *Frivolamente* (1908), *Dolorosa y desnuda realidad* (1914), *La venganza del cóndor* (1923), and critical studies as *Del romanticismo al modernismo* (1910), *La literatura peruana* (1914), *En la verbena de Madrid* (1920).

García de la Huer·ta y Mu·ñoz \-thā-lä-'wer-tä-ē-mün-'yōth\, Vicente Antonio. 1734–1787. Spanish dramatist. Neoclassicist in style; avowed advocate of national tradition in drama; known esp. for tragedy *Raquel* (1788).

García de Pa·re·des \-thā-pä-'rā-thās\, Diego. 1466–1530. Spanish soldier. Comrade-in-arms of Gonzalo de Córdoba; distinguished himself in Sicily at Cephalonia (1500), Seminara and Cerignola (1503), Pavia (1525). A leading chivalric hero of Spain, popular in Spanish legend.

Gar·cía de Re·sen·de \gər-'sē-ə-thā-rā-'sāⁿ-dā\. c.1470–1536. Portuguese poet and chronicler. In life-long service to Portuguese court, including private secretary to John II. Editor of collection of contemporary verse *Cancioneiro Geral* (1516); author of *Crónica de D. Joao II* (1545) and a supplement, *Miscelânea*, a rhymed chronicle of contemporary events.

Gar·cía Gu·tiér·rez \gär-'thē-ä-gü-'tyer-rāth\, Antonio. 1813–1884. Spanish dramatist. Consul in Bayonne and Genoa (from 1864); director of Archaeological Museum, Madrid (1872 ff.). A foremost representative of Romantic drama in Spain; known esp. for his play *El trovador* (1836), adapted by Verdi as opera *Il trovatore;* other plays included *Simón Bocanegra* (1843, also used by Verdi), *Venganza catalana* (1864), and *Juan Lorenzo* (1865).

Gar·cía Í·ñi·guez \gär-'sē-ä-'ēn-yē-gās\, Calixto. 1839–1898. Cuban lawyer, soldier, and revolutionary. A leader in Ten Years' War (1868–78) against Spain; led Cuban force at El Caney (1898) in Spanish–American War; appointed to represent Cuba in negotiations with U.S. for Cuban independence (1898). Known widely in U.S. through Elbert Hubbard's essay *A Message to Garcia.*

Gar·cía Lor·ca \gär-'thē-ä-'lȯr-kä\, Federico. 1898–1936. Spanish poet and dramatist. Studied music under Manuel de Falla; scored success with Barcelona production of verse drama *Mariana Pineda* (1927, scenery by Salvador Dalí); gained international fame with poems based on gypsy themes *Romancero gitano* (1928); in New York City (1929), which inspired the surrealistic poems of *Poeta en Nueva York* (1940); founder, director, musician for theatrical company La Barraca, which presented Spanish classical drama to rural audiences (1932–35); shot without trial by Nationalists at outbreak of Spanish Civil War. Drew much of his themes and imagery from folk traditions, esp. from his native Andalusia; a constant theme was the cruelty, violence, and death resulting from the frustration of primordial passions by convention. Verse included *Canciones* (1927), *Poema del cante jondo* (1931), *Llanto por Ignacio Sánchez Mejías* (1935), *Diván del Tamarit* (1936); his tragedies included a study of bourgeois life in Granada *Doña Rosita la Soltera* (1935), and esp. a trilogy of folk dramas, *Bodas de sangre* (1933), *Yerma* (1934), *La casa de Bernarda Alba* (1936).

Gar·cía Me·no·cal \gär-'sē-ä-mā-nō-'käl\, Mario. 1866–1941. Cuban soldier and politician. Served in war of independence (1895–98); conservative president of Cuba (1913–21); administration marked by material progress but much repression and corruption; put down liberal revolt (1917).

García Mo·re·no \-mō-'rā-nō\, Gabriel. 1821–1875. Ecuadorian politician. Son-in-law of J. J. Flores. President of Ecuador (1861–65, 1869–75); centralized government and strengthened the economy; established Roman Catholic church as state church; signed concordat with pope (1863); promulgated two conservative constitutions (1861, 1869); assassinated.

García Sar·mien·to \-särm-'yān-tō\, Félix Rubén. *Pseudonym* Rubén Da·río \dä-'rē-ō\. 1867–1916. Nicaraguan poet. Founder, guiding force, and greatest poet of Spanish-American Modernist literary movement. Precocious writer, began publishing poems in 1880; settled in Chile (1886) and thereafter traveled widely. Inaugurated Modernist movement with publication (1888) of *Azul,* a collection of verse and prose influenced by French Parnassian school and marked by exotic themes and simple, direct, and objective language. Colombian consul in Buenos Aires (1893); published (1896) *Prosas profanas,* a collection of verse influenced by French Symbolism and considered high point of "escapist" phase of Modernism. To Europe (1898) as correspondent of Buenos Aires newspaper *La Nación;* began writing on more social, political, and contemporary themes; published verse collection *Cantos de vida y esperanza* (1905), his masterpiece. In Nicaraguan diplomatic service (1906–10); left Europe (1914) for lecture tour in U.S. Other works included verse *El canto errante* (1907), *Poema del otoño* (1910), and *Canto a la Argentina* (1914), short stories, plays, travel books, literary criticism, and journalistic articles.

Gar·ci·la·so de la Ve·ga \gär-thē-'lä-sō-thā-lä-'bā-gä\. 1503–1536. Spanish poet and soldier. Fought at battle of Olías (1521), against French at Navarre (1523), with Charles V's expedition to Tunis (1535); killed in battle at Nice. First major poet of Spanish Golden Age. Friend of Juan Boscán; successfully adapted Italian meters to Spanish poetry. His poems, most on love, included 38 sonnets, 8 songs, 5 canciones, 3 eclogues, 2 elegies, and a blank verse epistle. Often called "the Spanish Petrarch."

Gar·ci·la·so de la Vega \gär-thē-, gär-sē-\. *Called* el In·ca \el-'ēŋ-kä\. 1539–1616. Spanish chronicler, b. Peru. To Spain (1560); served as captain in Spanish army against Moors; settled at Córdoba. Works included an account of Hernando de Soto's expeditions, *La Florida del Ynca* (1605), and a two-part history of Peru: *Comentarios reales que tratan del origen de los Yncas,* history of Incas in Peru (1609) and *Historia general de Peru,* on conquest of Peru (1617). His father ¶Sebastián Garcilaso de la Vega y Var·gas \-ē-'bär-gäs\ (c.1500–1559) served under Cortés in Mexico; to Peru (1535) with Alvarado, joining Pizarro's forces; governor of Cuzco.

Gard, Roger Martin du. See MARTIN DU GARD.

Gar·den \'gärd-ᵊn\, Alexander. c.1730–1791. American naturalist and physician, b. Aberdeenshire, Scotland. Resident in South Carolina (from c.1754). Collected botanical, mineralogical, and zoological specimens; friend of Linnaeus. In American Revolution, remained loyal to British; banished to London (1782). The gardenia is named after him.

Garden, Mary. 1874–1967. American soprano, b. Aberdeen, Scotland. To U.S. (1881). Debut at Opéra Comique, Paris (1900) in title role of Charpentier's *Louise;* chosen by Debussy to create part of Mélisande in his *Pelléas et Melisande* (1902); American debut in *Thaïs* in New York (1907). With Chicago Civic Opera (1910–31). Chief roles Marguerite, Mélisande, Salome, Sappho, Thaïs, Louise.

Gar·den·er \'gärd-nər, 'gärd-ᵊn-ər\, Helen Hamilton. *Orig.* Alice Chen·o·weth \'chen-ə-,weth\. 1853–1925. American woman suffragist and reformer, b. Winchester, Va. Associated with Susan B. Anthony and Elizabeth Cady Stanton in woman suffrage movement. Member, U.S. Civil Service Commission (1920), first woman appointed to that office.

Gardie, de la. See DE LA GARDIE.

Gar·di·ner \'gärd-nər\, James Garfield. 1883–1962. Canadian politician, b. Farquhar, Ont. Liberal member, Saskatchewan Legislative Assembly (1914–35); premier of Saskatchewan (1926–29, 1934–35). Member, dominion House of Commons (1935–58); federal minister of agriculture (1935–58).

Gardiner, Marguerite, *nee* Pow·er \'paù(-ə)r\. Countess of Bles·sing·ton \'bles-iŋ-tən\. 1789–1849. Irish writer. m. 2d, Charles Gardiner, 1st Earl of Blessington (1818); formed brilliant salon in London; lived in Italy and France extravagantly, exhausting earl's fortune; on his death (1829) became companion of Alfred, Comte d'Orsay. Author of novels as *Grace Cassidy* (1833), *The Two Friends* (1835), *Confessions of an Elderly Lady* (1838), *Strathern* (1843), etc.; memoirs *Conversations of Lord Byron* (1834), *The Idler in Italy* (1839–40), *The Idler in France* (1841); edited and contributed to annuals *Book of Beauty* and *Keepsake.*

Gardiner, Samuel Rawson. 1829–1902. English historian. Descendant of Oliver Cromwell. Among his works were *History of England ... 1603–1642* (1883–84), *History of the Great Civil War, 1642–1649* (1886–91), and *History of the Commonwealth and Protectorate, 1649–1660* (1895–1901).

Gardiner, Stephen. c.1482–1555. English prelate and politician. Master of Trinity Hall, Cambridge (1525 ff.); chancellor of Cambridge (1540–47, 1553 ff.). Became secretary to Cardinal Wolsey (1525); employed by Henry VIII in negotiations to obtain divorce from Catherine of Aragon; after fall of Wolsey, acted as secretary to Henry (to 1534). Bishop of Winchester (1531); signer of renunciation of obedience to Roman jurisdiction. After fall of Cromwell, wielded great influence; inspired the Six Articles (1539). Imprisoned in Tower of London during reign of Edward VI, and deprived of his see (1550); reinstated and appointed lord chancellor at accession of Mary (1553); supported persecution of Protestants during Mary's regime, but tried to save Cranmer; supported Mary's severe policy toward Elizabeth.

Gard·ner \'gärd-nər\, Alexander. 1821–1882. American photographer, b. Paisley, Renfrew, Scotland. To U.S. (c.1856); employed (1856–63) by Mathew Brady (*q.v.*), esp. as assistant in photographing Civil War. Opened (1863) own portrait gallery in Washington, D.C.; continued photographing war, published his prints in *Gardner's Photographic Sketch Book of the Civil War* (1866). Offical photographer of Union Pacific Railroad (1867); took valuable photographs of railroad construction and of Great Plains Indians.

Gardner, Erle Stanley. 1889–1970. American lawyer and writer, b. Malden, Mass. Practiced law in Ventura, Calif. (1911–38); founded (1948) Court of Last Resort to aid persons unjustly imprisoned. Author of some 80 detective novels featuring lawyer-detective Perry Mason, including *The Case of the Velvet Claws* (1933), *The Case of the Sulky Girl* (1933), *The Case of the Amorous Aunt* (1963); also author of second series of detective fiction centering about district attorney Doug Selby, as *The D.A. Calls it Murder* (1937) and *The D.A. Goes to Trial* (1940). Under pseudonym A.A. Fair \'fe(ə)r\ wrote third series of books featuring detective Bertha Cool and legalist Donald Lam. Also wrote travel books.

Gardner, Isabella, *nee* Stewart. 1840–1924. American socialite and art collector, b. New York City. m. (1860) John L. Gardner and moved to Boston; made her house a center of intellectual and social life of Boston; aided by Bernard Berenson, assembled an outstanding collection of classical and contemporary paintings and art objects; built a gallery to house this collection (opened 1903) and at her death left it to city of Boston as the Isabella Stewart Gardner Museum.

Gardner, Percy. 1846–1937. English archaeologist. Professor at Cambridge (1880–87) and Oxford (1887–1925). First editor of *Journal of Hellenic Studies* (1880–96). Works included *Samos and Samian Coins* (1882), *Types of Greek Coins* (1883), *A Grammar of Greek Art* (1905), *History of Ancient Coinage* (1918), *New Chapters in Greek Art* (1926). His brother ¶Ernest Arthur (1862–1939) was professor of archaeology at University College, London (1896–1929); author of *Ancient Athens* (1902), *The Art of Greece* (1925), *Greece and the Aegean* (1933).

Gar·field \'gär-,fēld\, James Abram. 1831–1881. Twentieth president of the United States, b. near Orange, Ohio. Teacher and head, Hiram College, Ohio (1857–61). Served (1861–63) in Civil War; fought at Shiloh and Chickamauga; major general of volunteers (1863). Member, U.S. House of Representatives (1863–80); Republican leader (from 1876). Elected to U.S. Senate (1880). Elected (1880) and inaugurated as president (1881). Shot by Charles J. Guiteau in Washington railroad station (July 2, 1881); died two months later.

Gar·ga·llo y Ca·ta·lán \gär-'gä(l)-yō-ē-kä-tä-'län\, Pablo. 1881–1934. Spanish sculptor. Associated with and influenced by Picasso; achieved recognition in 1920s for figurative sculptures constructed of thin leaves of metal; his works, as *Picador* (1928) and *The Prophet* (1933), emphasized the human figure and demonstrated use of Cubist techniques to achieve realism.

Gar·i·bal·di \,gä-rē-'bäl-dē, *Angl* ,gar-ə-'bòl-dē\, Giuseppe. 1807–1882. Italian military and nationalist leader, b. Nice, France. Associated with Mazzini in agitation for Italian freedom; forced to flee from Italy (1834); lived in Uruguay (1836–48), fighting in war against Argentina. Returned to Italy and served in army of the Roman Republic; when that army was defeated (1849), fled to U.S. and later Peru. Returned to Italy (1854); commanded corps known as *Cacciatori delle Alpi* in Sardinian army (1859). Organized expedition of 1000 men (the Redshirts) and attacked Sicily (May 1860); crossed to mainland of Italy and captured Naples (Sept. 7), thus defeating the Kingdom of the Two Sicilies. Retired after union of the Two Sicilies with Sardinia and the proclamation (Mar. 17, 1861) of Victor Emmanuel of Sardinia as king of Italy. Organized another expedition and marched against Rome (1862) but was defeated; again attacked Rome (1867) but was again defeated. Held a command in the French army during the Franco–Prussian War (1870–71).

Gar·is \'gar-əs\, Howard Roger. 1873–1962. American writer, b. Binghamton, N.Y. Best known as author (from 1896) of the "Uncle Wiggley" series of children's stories.

Gar·land \'gär-lənd\, Hamlin, *in full* Hannibal Hamlin. 1860–1940. American writer, b. West Salem, Wis. Author of *Main-Travelled Roads* (1891), *Prairie Folks* (1892), *Rose of Dutcher's Coolly* (1895), *Wayside Courtships* (1897), *Hesper* (1903), *The Long Trail* (1907), *A Son of the Middle Border* (1917), *A Daughter of the Middle Border* (1921, Pulitzer prize), *The Book of the American Indian* (1923), *The Trail-makers* (1926), *Roadside Meetings of a Literary Nomad* (1930), *Mystery of the Buried Crosses* (1939), etc.

Garland, John. *Also known as* Johannes de Gar·lan·dia \gär-ˈlan-dē-ə\. c.1180–c.1272. English grammarian and poet. Teacher in Paris (1202–29), Toulouse (1229–c.32). Author of grammatical works *Compendium grammatice, Liber de constructionibus,* and a Latin vocabulary; poems including *De triumphis ecclesiae* and *Epithalamium beatae Mariae Virginis;* and *Scolarium morale.*

Garland, Judy. *Orig.* Frances Gumm \ˈgəm\. 1922–1969. American singer and actress, b. Grand Rapids, Minn. Appeared in films *Broadway Melody of 1938* (1937), *Love Finds Andy Hardy* (1938), *Babes in Arms* (1939), *The Wizard of Oz* (1939), *For Me and My Gal* (1942), *Meet Me in St. Louis* (1944), *Easter Parade* (1948), *A Star is Born* (1954), *Judgment at Nuremberg* (1961), etc. Also famous as singer in nightclubs and concert halls.

Gar·neau \gär-nō\, François-Xavier. 1809–1866. Canadian historian, b. Quebec, Que. Father of Canadian historiography. Greffier of Quebec (1844–64); author of *Histoire du Canada* (1845–52), etc. His great-grandson ¶Hector de Saint-De·nys \də-saⁿ-də-nē-\ Garneau (1912–1943) was a poet, b. Saint-Catherine de Fossanbault, Que.; cofounder of literary journal *La Relève* (1934); author of introspective poems concerned with death, published in *Regards et jeux dans l'espace* (1937) and *Poésies complètes* (1949); his *Journal* published in 1954.

Gar·ner \ˈgär-nər\, John Nance. *Nicknamed* Cactus Jack. 1868–1967. American politician, b. Red River Co., Tex. Democratic member, U.S. House of Representatives (1903–33), speaker (1931–33); vice president of the U.S. (1933–41).

Gar·ne·rin \gär-nə-raⁿ\, André-Jacques. 1769–1823. French aeronaut. Perfected a parachute in which he made first parachute descent from a balloon (1797); gave parachute jumping exhibitions throughout northern Europe, including (1802) jump of 8,000 feet in England. His brother ¶Jean-Baptiste-Olivier (1766–1849) assisted André in devising improvements in parachutes.

Gar·net \ˈgär-nət\, Henry Highland. 1815–1882. American clergyman, b. a slave in Kent Co., Md. Leader of abolition movement among Negroes; in speech at Buffalo, N.Y., called upon slaves to rise and murder their masters (1843). After various pastorates appointed U.S. minister to Liberia (1881).

Gar·nett \ˈgär-nət\, Edward. 1868–1937. English writer. Son of Richard Garnett. As a publisher's reader and critic, discovered, advised, and tutored many British writers, including Conrad, Galsworthy, F.M. Ford, D.H. Lawrence, W.H. Hudson; author of plays *The Breaking Point* (1907), *The Feud* (1907), and *The Trial of Jeanne d'Arc* (1912). His wife ¶Constance, *nee* Black \ˈblak\ (1862–1946), known under her married name as translator from the Russian of many novels of Turgenev, Tolstoy, Gogol, Chekhov, etc. Their son ¶David (1892–1981), novelist; author of *Lady into Fox* (1922), *A Man in the Zoo* (1924), *The Old Dovecote* (1928), *The Life of Pocahontas* (1931–32), *A Rabbit in the Air* (1932), *Beany-Eye* (1935), and the autobiographical *The Golden Echo* (1953), *The Flowers of the Forest* (1955), *The Familiar Faces* (1962).

Garnett, Henry. 1555–1606. English Jesuit. Superior of the English province (1587–1606); executed on charge of complicity in Gunpowder Plot.

Garnett, Richard. 1835–1906. English librarian and writer. On staff of British Museum (1851–99), keeper of printed books (1890–99); directed (from 1880) and published (1905) a general catalogue of British Museum. Author of *Relics of Shelley* (1862), *The Twilight of the Gods* (1888, fables), *History of Italian Literature* (1897), and several biographies.

Gar·nier \gärn-yā\, Antoine, *known as* Tony. 1869–1948. French architect. Architect of Lyons (1905–19). A pioneer in use of reinforced concrete; exhibited (1904), published (1917) *Cité industrielle,* plan for an industrial city; from this plan were constructed in Lyons the stockyards complex (1908–24), Grange Blanche hospital (1911–27), the stadium (1913–18), and Les États Unis housing project (1920–35).

Garnier, Charles, *in full* Jean-Louis-Charles. 1825–1898. French architect. A leading exponent of Beaux-Arts style. Designed the Paris Opera House (1861–75), Monte Carlo Casino (1878), Nice Conservatory, Hôtel du Cercle de la Librairie in Paris, Exposition des Habitations Humaines for Paris Exposition of 1889, and several villas in Bordighera, including his own. Author of *Le Théâtre* (1871), *Le Nouvel Opéra de Paris* (1876–81), etc.

Garnier, Marie-Joseph-François *called* Francis. 1839–1873. French naval officer and explorer. Took part in French conquest of Cochinchina (1859–62); governor of Saigon (1862). Second in command in Doudart de Lagrée's expedition from Cambodia to Shanghai by way of Yunnan (1866–68), bringing party down Yangtze to coast after Doudart's death.

Garnier, Robert. c.1545–1590. French playwright. *Conseiller du roi* (1569), *lieutenant-général criminel* (1574–86) in his native La Ferté-Bernard district. Author of verse tragedies *Porcie* (1568), *Hippolyte* (1573), *Cornélie* (1574), *Marc-Antoine* (1578), *La Trode* (1579), *Antigone* (1580), *Bradamante* (1582), *Les Juives* (1583).

Garnier-Pa·gès \-pä-zhes\, Louis-Antoine. 1803–1878. French politician. Sat with republican left in Chamber of Deputies (1842–48); a leader of "banquets campaign" against government of Louis-Philippe; minister of finance in provisional government (1848); member of Corps Législatif (1864–70) and of Government of National Defense (1870–71). Author of *Histoire de la révolution de 1848* (1864) and *L'Opposition et l'empire* (1872).

Garn·sey \ˈgärn-sē\, Elmer Ellsworth. 1862–1946. American painter, b. Holmdel, N.J. Best known for murals, as in Boston Public Library, Library of Congress in Washington.

Garofalo, Benvenuto da. See Benvenuto TISI.

Gar·rett \gə-ˈret\, João Baptista da Sil·va Lei·tão de Al·mei·da \thə-ˈsil-və-lā-ˈtaùⁿ-thē-äl-ˈmā-thə\. Visconde de Almeida Garrett. 1799–1854. Portuguese writer and politician. Took part in liberal revolution (1820); forced into exile in Great Britain and France during reaction (1823–32); consul general in Brussels (1834–35); entered parliament (1837); minister of foreign affairs (1852). Founded Portuguese national theater (1836). Foremost Romantic writer in Portuguese; author of verse *O retrato de Venus* (1821), *Adosinda* (1828), *Flores sem fruto* (1845), *Fôlhas caídas* (1853); epic poems *Camões* (1825), *Dona Branca* (1826); dramas *Um auto de Gil Vicente* (1838), *Dona Filipa de Vilhena* (1840), *Mérope* (1841), *Frei Luís de Sousa* (1843).

Gar·rick \ˈgar-ik\, David. 1717–1779. English actor, producer, and dramatist. Pupil of Samuel Johnson at Edial (1736); accompanied Johnson to London (1737). Made reputation by his acting in *Richard III* (1741); continued success in other Shakespearean plays, most of which he rewrote; comanager of Drury Lane Theatre (1747–76); introduced a revolutionary new style of natural, interpretative acting and initiated other reforms in staging. Enjoyed friendship of Johnson and his circle and of other distinguished persons of the day. Regarded as one of the greatest actors in the history of the English stage. Author of some 20 plays, including *Lethe* (1740), *The Enchanter* (1760), *The Clandestine Marriage* (1766, with George Coleman the Elder).

Gar·ri·son \ˈgar-ə-sən\, William Lloyd. 1805–1879. American journalist and reformer, b. Newburyport, Mass. Founder and publisher (1831–65) of *The Liberator,* famous antislavery journal; became leader of radical abolitionists. A founder, American Anti-Slavery Society (1833) and its president (1843–65); opposed Compromise of 1850; urged separation between North and South. After Civil War, campaigned against liquor, prostitution, injustice in treatment of Indians; favored woman suffrage.

Gar·rod \ˈgar-əd\, Sir Archibald Edward. 1857–1936. English physician. Professor at Oxford (1920–28). Conducted research on biochemical genetics of inherited human metabolic diseases, esp. first direct study of alkaptonuria. Author of *Inborn Factors in Disease* (1931). His daughter ¶Dorothy Annie Elizabeth (1892–1968), archaeologist; directed expeditions in Gibraltar (1925–26), Kurdistan (1928), Palestine (1929–34), Lebanon (1958); first woman professor at Cambridge (1939–52); wrote *The Stone Age of Mount Carmel* (1937–39).

Gar·ros \gä-rôs\, Pey de. c.1530–1585. French poet. *Avocat-général* of Pau (1571). Advocated restoration of Gascon dialect to replace French. Author of rhymed Gascon translation of Psalms of David (1565) and *Poesias gasconas* in Gascon (1567).

Garros, Roland. 1888–1918. French aviator. First to fly across the Mediterranean, Saint-Raphaël to Bizerte (Sept. 23, 1913); killed in World War I.

Gar·ro·way \ˈgar-ə-ˌwā\, David Cunningham. 1913–1982. American broadcaster, b. Schenectady, N.Y. Radio announcer in Chicago (1939); host of radio and television news and variety programs, esp. "Today" (1952–61).

Gar·shin \ˈgär-shin\, Vsevolod Mikhaylovich. 1855–1888. Russian author. Fought in Turkish campaign (1876–77), which provided background for his realistic *Chetyre dnya* (1877) that made his reputation; wrote psychological works dealing with madness, war, or moral questions, as *Krasny tsvetok* (1883).

Gar·stang \ˈgär-ˌstaŋ\, John. 1876–1956. English archaeologist. Professor, Liverpool (1907–41); first director of British School of Archaeology in Palestine (1919–26); first director (1948–49), president (1949 ff.), British Institute of Archaeology in Turkey. Conducted excavations (from 1900) in Egypt, Asia Minor, northern Syria, Sudan, and esp. (1930–36) Jericho, Palestine. Author of *The Land of the Hittites* (1910), *Meroë* (1911), *The Foundations of Bible History* (1931), *Prehistoric Mersin* (1953), etc.

Garth \ˈgärth\, Sir Samuel. 1661–1719. English physician. Author of the mock-heroic *The Dispensary* (1699).

Gar·vey \ˈgär-vē\, Marcus Moziah. 1887–1940. Jamaican black-nationalist leader. Founder of Universal Negro Improvement Association (UNIA, 1914); to U.S. (1916); established UNIA branches in Harlem (New York City) and other ghettos in North; in New York City held first UNIA international convention (1920). Sought to achieve dignity and civil rights for black people by preaching pride of race and economic self-sufficiency; projected a "Back-to-Africa" movement to establish a black-governed country in Africa. Founded several businesses; convicted of fraud (1925); sentence commuted by Pres. Coolidge (1927); deported to Jamaica on release.

Gar·vin \ˈgär-vən\, James Louis. 1868–1947. English journalist and editor. Editor of *Outlook* (1905–06), *Observer* (1908–42), *Pall Mall Gazette*

(1912–15); editor in chief, 14th edition of *Encyclopaedia Britannica* (1926–29).

Gary \'ga(ə)r-ē, 'ge(ə)r-ē\, Elbert Henry. 1846–1927. American lawyer and businessman, b. near Wheaton, Ill. Practiced law, Chicago (1871 ff.); judge of DuPage Co., Ill. (1882–90). President, Federal Steel Co. (1898); instrumental in organizing United States Steel Corp.; chairman, executive committee (1901–03), chairman, board of directors (1903–27), U.S. Steel Corp. Improved workers' conditions and wages, but his opposition to unions responsible for steel strike of 1919–20. Gary, Ind., was named in his honor.

Ga·ry \ge-rē\, Romain. *Orig.* Romain Ka·cew \'kät-syif\. 1914–1980. French novelist, b. Vilnius, Russia. In French diplomatic service (1945–60). Author of *Éducation européen* (1945), *Le grand vestiaire* (1948), *Les Couleurs du jour* (1952), *Les Racines du ciel* (1956), *Les Mangeurs d'étoiles* (1966), *La Danse de Genghis Cohn* (1967), *Claire de femme* (1977), *Les Cerfs-volants* (1980).

Gas·coigne \'gas-,kòin\, George. c.1525–1577. English poet. Studied law in London; M.P. (1557–59). Produced (1566) plays *Jocasta,* first translation from Greek tragedy presented on English stage, and *The Supposes,* prose adaptation of Ariosto's *I suppositi.* Published (1573) collection of verse and prose *A Hundreth sundrie Flowres,* containing first original prose narrative of English Renaissance, "The Adventures of Master F.J." Revised *Flowres* and published it (1575) as *The Posies of George Gascoigne,* containing prose essay "Certayne notes of Instruction," regarded as first English critical essay. Continued literary work with didactic play *The Glasse of Government* (1575); verses and masques for Leicester's entertainment of Elizabeth, issued (1576) as *The Princely Pleasures at the Court of Kenilworth;* a blank verse satire *The Steele Glas* (1576); prose account of war in Holland *The Spoyle of Antwerpe* (1576); the serious prose work *The Droomme of Doomesday* (1576).

Gascoigne, William. 1612?–1644. English astronomer. Inventor of the micrometer (c.1640).

Gascoyne-Cecil. See under CECIL family.

Gas·kell \'gas-kəl\, Elizabeth Cleghorn, *nee* Ste·ven·son \'stē-vən-sən\. 1810–1865. English novelist. m. William Gaskell (1832). Author esp. of works depicting life in manufacturing cities of the Midlands, including *Mary Barton* (1848), *Ruth* (1853), *Cranford* (1853), *North and South* (1855), *Sylvia's Lovers* (1863), *Wives and Daughters* (1866). Also wrote *Life of Charlotte Brontë* (1857).

Gaspard Poussin. See Gaspard DUGHET.

Gasparini, Angelo. See Gasparo ANGIOLINI.

Ga·spar·ri \gäs-'pär-rē\, Pietro. 1852–1934. Italian prelate. Ordained Roman Catholic priest (1877); professor of canon law at Catholic Institute, Paris (1880–98); directed (1904–16) new codification of Canon Law (promulgated 1917); created cardinal (1907); papal secretary of state (1914–30); negotiated Lateran Treaty (1929) with Mussolini.

Gas·pé \gás-pā\, Philippe-Joseph Au·bert de \ō-ber-də-\. 1786–1871. Canadian lawyer and writer, b. Quebec. His historical romance *Les Anciens Canadiens* (1863), gave descriptions of life and customs in old Quebec; his *Mémoires* (1866) constitute historical source material for the same period.

Gas·prin·ski \(,)gəs-'pryin-skəi\, Ismail. *Known also as* Ismail Gas·pi·ra·li \gəs-(,)pyir-'äl-yi\. 1851–1914. Russian journalist. Founder and publisher (from 1883) of bilingual Russian-Turkish paper *Terjümān,* chief medium for promotion of pan-Islāmic and pan-Turkic unity in Russia; advocated new methods of teaching Arabic and other subjects.

Gas·quet \gas-'ke, -'kā\, Francis Neil Aidan. 1846–1929. English prelate. Superior of the Benedictine monastery and Coll. of St. Gregory at Downside (1878–85); president of international commission for revision of the Vulgate; cardinal (1914); prefect of the Vatican archives (1917); librarian of Roman church (1919). Author of *Henry VIII and the English Monasteries* (1888–89), *A History of the Catholic Church in England* (1897), etc.

Gas·sen·di \gá-saⁿ-dē\ *or* **Gas·send** \gá-saⁿ\, Pierre. 1592–1655. French scientist, mathematician, and philosopher. Ordained priest (1615); attempted to reconcile mechanistic atomism with Christian dogma; advocate of empirical method; attacked Aristotelian philosophy and opposed Cartesian philosophy; revived and maintained Epicurean doctrines; friend of Galileo and Kepler.

Gas·ser \'gas-ər\, Herbert Spencer. 1888–1963. American physiologist, b. Platteville, Wis. Professor, Washington U., St. Louis (1916–31), and Cornell U. (1931–35); director, Rockefeller Inst. (1935–53); shared with Joseph Erlanger (*q.v.*) 1944 Nobel prize for physiology or medicine for work on nerve fibers.

Gas·ter \'gäs-tər, 'gas-\, Moses. 1856–1939. British scholar, b. Bucharest. Published *Literatura populară română* (1883); expelled from Romania for defending persecuted Jews (1885); to England and became lecturer in Byzantine and Slavonic languages at Oxford (1886, 1891); principal of Montefiore Coll. (1890–96). Chief rabbi of Sephardic communities in England (1887–1918). Active Zionist; chief work, *Chrestomație română* (1890).

Gas·tol·di \gäs-'tòl-dē\, Giovanni Giacomo. d. c.1622. Italian composer. Composed three- and five-voice ballettos, canzones, madrigals, and sacred music.

Gaston de France. Duc d'Orléans. See ORLÉANS, III.

Gates \'gāts\, Frederick Taylor. 1853–1929. American clergyman and philanthropist, b. Maine, N.Y. Baptist minister in Minneapolis (1880–88). Instrumental in raising funds for establishment of U. of Chicago. Called by J.D. Rockefeller to become his chief adviser on philanthropic matters and representative of Rockefeller interests (1893); chairman, General Education Board (1903), and of Rockefeller Institute for Medical Research. Instrumental in establishing Rockefeller Foundation.

Gates, Horatio. c.1728–1806. American Revolutionary officer, b. Maldon, England. Entered British army; on service in America (1755–61). Invited by Washington, took up land in Virginia (1772). Took colonial side at outbreak of Revolutionary War; adjutant general, Continental army (1775); major general (1776); succeeded Gen. Philip Schuyler in northern New York (1777); with assistance from Benedict Arnold, forced Burgoyne to surrender at Saratoga (1777). Made president of Board of War (1777). Friends of Gates sought to put him in Washington's place as commander in chief; Conway Cabal formed for this purpose; failed. Lost disastrous Battle of Camden, S.C. (Aug. 16, 1780). Relieved of his command and asked official inquiry into his conduct at battle of Camden; Congress finally (1782) without inquiry ordered him back into service under Washington; served loyally at Washington's headquarters for remainder of war.

Gates, John Warne. *Nicknamed* Bet-a-million Gates. 1855–1911. American financier, b. Turner Junction, Ill. Made fortune by holding virtual monopoly on manufacture of barbed wire; became notorious for speculations in N.Y. stock market; in market battle with J. P. Morgan over control of Louisville & Nashville Railroad, lost fortune and forced to agree to cease activities on N.Y. stock exchange. Retired to enter oil industry in Texas; one of organizers of Texas Company.

Ga·thorne-Har·dy \'gā-,thórn-'här-dē\, Gathorne. 1st Earl of Cran·brook \'kran-,brùk\. 1814–1906. English politician. Conservative M.P. (1856–78); president of Poor Law Board (1866). As home secretary (1867–68) took resolute measures against Fenian conspirators; secretary for war (1874–78) under Disraeli, whose pro-Turkish policy he supported; secretary for India (1878–80), promoted Lord Lytton's aggressive policy on Afghan frontier; lord president of council (1885–92). Raised to viscount (1878), created earl (1892).

Gat·ling \'gat-liŋ\, Richard Jordan. 1818–1903. American inventor, b. Maney's Neck, N.C. Became wealthy from his agricultural inventions (by 1850s); invented the rapid-fire Gatling gun (patented 1862).

Gat·ti-Ca·saz·za \'gät-tē-kä-'zät-tsä\, Giulio. 1869–1940. Italian operatic manager. Director of La Scala, Milan (1898–1908); general manager of Metropolitan Opera House in New York (1908–35).

Gat·ty \'gat-ē\, Harold Charles. 1903–1957. Austrialian aviator. As navigator, accompanied Wiley Post (*q.v.*) on first fast round-the-world trip, in 8 days, 15 hours (June 1931).

Gau·den \'gòd-ᵊn\, John. 1605–1662. English prelate. Chaplain to Earl of Warwick (1640); bishop of Exeter (1660–62) and Worcester (1662). Claimed, probably justly, authorship of *Eikon Basilike* (1649); edited Hooker's *Laws of Ecclesiastical Polity* (1662).

Gau·dier-Brzes·ka \gōd-yāb-zhes-kå\, Henri. *Surname orig.* Gau·dier \gōd-yā\. 1891–1915. French sculptor. Added name of his companion Sophie Brzeska (1911); protégé of Ezra Pound in London (1912); outstanding exponent of the Vorticist movement in art.

Gau·din \gō-daⁿ\, Martin-Michel-Charles. Duc de Ga·ète \gá-et\. 1756–1841. French politician. Minister of finance (1799–1814); created body of permanent tax officals and instituted tax reforms; founder of the Bank of France (1800) and its governor (1820–34); member of Chamber of Deputies (1815–18).

Gau·di y Cor·net \'gaù-t͟hē-ē-kōr-'nāt\, Antonio. 1852–1926. Spanish architect. A leader in Catalan artistic revival. Developed a Mudéjar style (1880s); experimented with Gothic and Baroque styles (1887–1902); his later work (after 1902) marked by equilibrated structures employing no internal bracing or external buttressing and by highly individualistic organic forms. His designs, all at or near Barcelona, included the church of Sagrada Familia (begun 1883), Casa Vicens (1883–85), Palacio Güell (1886–89), Casa Calvent (1898–1901), Park Güell (1900–14), Casa Batlló (1904–06), Casa Milá (1906–10).

Gau·guin \gō-gaⁿ\, Paul, *in full* Eugène-Henri-Paul. 1848–1903. French painter. Stockbroker in Paris, painting as a hobby (1871–83); associated with Pissarro and Cézanne; devoted himself completely to painting (from 1883). Broke with Impressionism and with Émile Bernard developed (from c.1888)

Synthetism style of painting at Pont-Aven; stressed conceptual method of representation, employing areas of pure color, a few strong lines, and two-dimensional flat patterns. Set up studio in Tahiti (1891–93, 1895–1901) and Marquesas Islands (1901–03) and sent back brilliant, colorful canvases. Considered leading French painter of Post-Impressionist period. Works included *The Vision After the Sermon* (1888), *The Yellow Christ* (1889), *Ia Orana Maria* (1891), *Nafea Faa Ipoipo* (1892), *Holiday* (1896), *Where Do We Come From? What Are We? Where Are We Going?* (1897–98), *The White Horse* (1898), *Golden Bodies* (1901).

Gaulle \gōl, *Angl* 'gōl, 'gȯl\, Charles-André-Marie-Joseph de. 1890–1970. French soldier and statesman. Entered army (1913); served with distinction in World War I; promoted to staff of Supreme War Council (1925); argued for a small but highly mechanized and mobile army, esp. in *Vers l'armée de métier* (1934). Promoted brigadier general (May 1940). On fall of France (June 1940), left for London where he organized and led the Free French Forces; moved headquarters to Algiers (1943); became joint president (June 1943, with Henri Giraud), sole president (Oct. 1943), of shadow government French Committee of National Liberation, thus making him supreme commander of French war effort outside metropolitan France. Returned to France after liberation of Paris (Sept. 1944); headed two successive provisional governments (1945–46); opposed Fourth Republic from retirement (1946–58). Architect and president (1958–69) of French Fifth Republic; strengthened the presidency at expense of National Assembly; granted political independence to 12 African territories; ended Algerian war (1962); formulated international policy independent of Communist and Western powers; restored France to its former rank in world affairs. Author of *Le Fil de l'épée* (1932), *La France et son armée* (1938), *Mémoires de guerre* (consisting of *L'Appel,* 1954; *L'Unité,* 1956; *Le Salut,* 1959), and *Mémoires d'espoir* (*Le Renouveau,* 1970; *L'Effort,* 1971).

Gaul·li \'gau̇l-lē\, Giovanni Battista. *Known as* Ba·cic·cia \bä-'chēt-chä\. 1639–1709. Italian painter. Student and protégé of Bernini; executed frescoes in Sta. Agnese (1668–71), Gesù (to 1683), SS. Apostoli (1707), Rome; exponent of Roman Baroque style. Also did altarpieces, portraits.

Gaul·tier \gō-tyā\, Denys. *Also called* Gaultier Le Jeune \lə-zhœn\. 1603–1672. French composer and lutenist. Celebrated lute virtuoso; his style influenced the French school of harpsichord music; originated the tombeau. His compositions, chiefly dances, published as *La Rhétorique des dieux* (c.1652) and *Pièces de luth* (c.1670).

Gaumata. See under Bardiya and Darius I.

Gaung \'gau̇ŋ\, U. *Official name* Kin·wun Ming·yi \'kin-wu̇n-'miŋ-yē\. 1822–?1908. Burmese politician. Under King Mindon Min held (1853–78) important official posts, including chief minister; conducted foreign affairs; demoted by Queen Supayalat on accession of Thibaw (1878); become adviser to colonial government of Upper Burma (1886).

Gau·ni·lo \gō-nē-lō\. 11th century. French Benedictine monk. Author of *Liber pro insipiente* opposing St. Anselm of Canterbury's ontological argument for God's existence.

Gaunt, John of. See John of Gaunt.

Gauranga. See Caitanya.

Gauss \'gau̇s\, Carl Friedrich, *baptized* Johann Friedrich Carl. 1777–1855. German mathematician and astronomer. Director and professor of astronomy, Göttingen observatory (from 1807). Demonstrated that a circle can be divided into seventeen equal arcs by elementary geometry (1796); published *Disquisitiones arithmeticae* on the theory of numbers (1801); propounded method of least squares; devised solution for binomial equations. Developed new technique for calculating orbits of asteroids (1801); made studies in geodesy; invented the heliotrope (1821); introduced the Gaussian error curve. Contributed to non-Euclidean geometry. Developed the related potential theory and real analysis. Made magnetic and electrical researches; considered founder of mathematical theory of electricity; proposed an absolute system of magnetic units. The gauss, a magnetic unit, is named after him.

Gautama, Siddhārtha. See Siddhārtha Gautama.

Gau·they \gō-te, -tā\, Emiland-Marie. 1732–1806. French civil engineer. Best known for his construction of the Charolais Canal, or Canal du Centre, uniting Loire and Saône rivers (1783–91); also built church at Givry (1773–91) and restored castle of Chagny (1780).

Gau·tier \gō-tyā\, Henri. 1660–1737. French engineer and scientist. Engineer of Languedoc province (1688–1716); national inspector of bridges and highways (1716 ff.). Author of first book on bridge building, *Traité des ponts* (1716).

Gautier, Léon, *in full* Émile-Theodore-Léon. 1832–1897. French literary historian. Keeper of imperial archives at Paris (1859); professor of paleography, École des Chartes (1871); chief of historical section of national archives (1893). Revived interest in early French literature, esp. with *Les Épopées françaises* (1865–68) and his translation and critical discussion of *Chanson de Roland* (1872).

Gautier, Théophile. *Nicknamed* Le Bon Théo \lə-bō^{n}-tā-ō\. 1811–1872. French man of letters. A leader of the Parnassians; advocate of art for art's sake. Weekly contributor to *La Presse* (1836–45) and *Le Moniteur Universel* (1845–55); editor of *Revue de Paris* (1851) and *L'Artiste* (1856). Among his works were books of verse *Albertus* (1832), *La Comédie de la mort* (1838), *España* (1845), *Émaux et camées* (1852); novels *Les Jeunes-France* (1833), *Mademoiselle de Maupin* (1835), *Fortunio* (1837), *Le Roman de la momie* (1858), *Le Capitaine Fracasse* (1863); short stories *La Mort amoureuse, Avatar* (1857); literary criticism *Les Grotesques* (1834–36), *Les Beaux-Arts en Europe* (1855), *Histoire de l'art dramatique en France depuis vingt-cinq ans* (1858–59), *Histoire du romantisme* (1874), *Portraits contemporains* (1874); travel books *Voyage en Espagne* (1845), *Voyage en Italie* (1852), *Constantinople* (1853), *Voyage en Russie* (1866); ballet *Giselle* (1841, with Vernoy de Saint-Georges); and plays.

Gautier d'Ar·ras \-dȧ-räs\. d. 1185. French poet. Official of Philippe d'Alsace, Count of Flanders (c.1160–85). Author of two verse romances, *Eracle* and *Ille et Galeron.*

Gautier de Metz \-də-'mets\. *Also known as* Gauthier de Més en Lo·he·rains \-də-mā-zä^{n}-lō-ə-ra^{n}\. 13th century. French priest and poet. Credited with authorship of octosyllabic verse treatise about the universe *L'Image du monde* (c.1246; also called *Mappemonde*).

Gautier Sans Avoir \-sä^{n}-zȧ-vwȧr\. *Eng.* Walter the Penniless. d. 1097. French knight. A leader, with Peter the Hermit, of the Peasants' Crusade (1096–97); killed in Battle of Nicaea.

Gautsch von Fran·ken·thurn \'gau̇ch-fȯn-'fräŋ-kən-,tu̇rn\, Paul von. Freiherr. 1851–1918. Austrian politician. Minister of education (1885–93, 1895–97); prime minister (1897–98, 1905–06, 1911).

Gavarni, Paul. See Guillaume-Sulpice Chevalier.

Ga·vaz·zi \gä-'vät-tsē\, Alessandro. 1809–1889. Italian religious and social reformer. Ordained Roman Catholic priest; champion of liberal ideas, esp. unity of Italy. Left Italy (1849); joined Evangelical church (1850); organized Italian Protestants in London (1850–60). Chaplain in army of Garibaldi (1860). Organized Free Church of Italy (1870); established theological school, Rome (1875).

Gav·es·ton \'gav-əs-tən\, Piers. Earl of Corn·wall \'kȯrn-wəl, *chiefly US* -,wȯl\. c.1284–1312. English courtier. Companion and favorite of Edward II of England, who created him earl of Cornwall (1307) and, during absence in France (1308), left him regent of kingdom; banished three times, on demand of barons, for insolence and extravagance; secretly returned (1311) and publicly restored to favor by Edward; kidnaped by Earl of Warwick and executed in presence of barons.

Ga·vi·niès \gȧ-vēn-yes\, Pierre. 1726–1800. French violinist and composer. Famed as a violin virtuoso. Composer of a comic opera *Le Prétendu* (1760), six violin concertos, violin sonatas, and a collection of violin studies.

Gav·ri·lo \'gäv-rē-lȯ\. 1881–1950. Serbian prelate. Patriarch of Serbian Orthodox church in Yugoslavia (1938–50); played important part in bringing Yugoslavia into World War II on Allied side.

Gay \ge, gā\, Jean-Baptiste-Sylvère. Vicomte de Mar·ti·gnac \mȧr-tēn-yȧk\. 1778–1832. French politician. Royalist in sympathy; appointed attorney general of Limoges (1819); member of Chamber of Deputies (1821–32); appointed councilor of state (1822); created vicomte (1824). As minister of interior and virtual head of the cabinet (1828–29), superintended final attempt to reconcile monarchy with the people; removed by king for making concessions to the left. Author of *Bordeaux au mois de Mars 1815* (1830) and *Essai sur les révolutions d'Espagne et l'intervention française de 1823* (1832).

Gay \'gā\, John. 1685–1732. English poet and playwright. Member of the Scriblerus Club. Author of verse *Rural Sports* (1713), *Shepherd's Week* (satirical eclogues, 1714), *Trivia, or the Art of Walking the Streets of London* (1716), *Fables* (2 series, 1727, 1738); plays including *The What D'ye Call It* (1715), *Three Hours after Marriage* (1717, with Alexander Pope and John Arbuthnot), *The Beggar's Opera,* his best known work (1728, music by J.C. Pepusch), its sequel *Polly* (1729, with Pepusch), *The Distressed Wife* (1743); libretti for *Acis and Galatea* (1732, music by Handel) and *Achilles* (1733).

Gay·ley \'gā-lē\, James. 1855–1920. American metallurgist, b. Lock Haven, Pa. Managing director, Carnegie Steel Co. (1897); first vice president, U.S. Steel Corporation (1901–09). Invented a bronze cooling plate for the walls of blast furnaces (patented 1891), auxiliary casting stand for Bessemer steel plants (patented 1896), dry-air blast (patented with improvements, 1894–1911).

Gay-Lus·sac \gel-ūē-sȧk\, Joseph-Louis. 1778–1850. French chemist and physicist. Professor of physics, Sorbonne (1808–32), of chemistry, Jardin des Plantes (from 1832). Made balloon ascents to investigate effects of terrestrial magnetism and composition of air at high altitudes (1804); enunciated (1808) the law of volumes (or Gay-Lussac's law) concerning combination of gases; with A. von Humboldt, investigated composition of water (1805); with L.-J. Thénard established properties of potassium (1808), discovered boron (1809), and devised improved methods for analyzing organic compounds; proved that prussic acid contains hydrogen but not oxygen; isolated cyanogen (1815); conducted studies of fermentation (1811–15); showed that iodine is an element (1814); improved processes for manufacturing sulfuric acid, oxalic acid, etc.

G. B. S. See George Bernard SHAW.

gCopaleen, Myles na. See Brian O'NOLAN.

Gea·ry \'gi(ə)r-ē\, John White. 1819–1873. American soldier and politician, b. Westmoreland Co., Pa. Served in Mexican War (1846–47). First postmaster of San Francisco and postal agent for entire Pacific Coast (1849); first mayor of San Francisco (1850). Territorial governor of Kansas (1856–57), then torn by factional strife; firm policy restored peace. Served through Civil War; brigadier general (1862); brevetted major general (1865). Governor of Pennsylvania (1867–73).

Gébelin, Antoine Court de. See COURT.

Ge·ber \gā-'b̲ār\. 14th century. Spanish alchemist. Real name unknown, took name Geber (Latin for Jābir) to trade on reputation of Jābir ibn Ḥayyān (*q.v.*). Author of original works on alchemy *Summa perfectionis magisterii, Liber fornacum, De investigatione perfectionis,* and *De inventione veritatis.* These works were clearest expression of alchemical theory and were immensely influential throughout western Europe in 14th and 15th centuries.

Ged \'ged\, William. 1690–1749. Scottish goldsmith. Inventor of stereotyping (1725).

Ged·des \'ged-əs\, Alexander. 1737–1802. Scottish clergyman. Ordained Roman Catholic priest (1764); planned new translation of Bible for Roman Catholics, issuing the historical books of the Old Testament and the book of Ruth, with *Critical Remarks on the Hebrew Scriptures* (1800), the rationalistic nature of which caused his suspension from ecclesiastical functions.

Ged·des \'ged-,ēz\, James. 1763–1838. American civil engineer, lawyer, and politician, b. near Carlisle, Pa. Elected to N.Y. state assembly (1804). Chiefly responsible for building of the Erie Canal; surveyed its basic route (1808) and was one of four principal engineers (1816–22) during construction. Directed construction of a canal in Ohio (1822) and projected several others.

Geddes, Norman Bel. *Orig.* Norman Geddes. 1893–1958. American stage designer and architect, b. Adrian, Mich. Added wife's middle name Bel to his own (c.1916). Staged 6 of his plays for Los Angeles Little Theater (1916); stage designer for Metropolitan Opera Company (1918) and later for other theaters. Designed, produced, or directed some 200 operas, films, plays, musical comedies; his sets noted for being functional parts of their plays instead of mere ornamentation. Entered industrial designing (1927) and modeled furniture, airplane interiors, radios, skyscrapers, theaters, etc.; largely responsible for popularizing streamlining.

Ged·des \'ged-əs\, Sir Patrick. 1854–1932. Scottish biologist and sociologist. Professor of botany, University Coll., Dundee (1889–1919), professor of sociology and civics, U. of Bombay (1920–23); director of Scots Coll., Montpellier, France (1924–32). Active in city planning in Great Britain, the Continent, and India. Published *City Development* (1904) and *Cities in Evolution* (1915).

Ged·i·min·as \,ged-ī-'min-äs\. *Pol.* Ge·dy·min \ge-'dim-ēn\. c.1275–1341. Grand duke of Lithuania. Inherited territory including Lithuania, Samogitia, Volhynia, northwestern Ukraine, and Belorussia (1316); defended these lands from the Teutonic Knights and the Livonian Knights of the Sword; built chain of forts along his borders; founded Vilnius, capital of Lithuania; protected Roman Catholic and Orthodox clergy. Credited with making Lithuania great power in Europe. Father of Algirdas and grandfather of Władysław II of Poland (*qq.v.*).

Geer \'yār\, Charles de. Baron. 1720–1778. Swedish entomologist. Originated system of insect classification using mouthparts and wings as criteria; published *Mémoires pour servir à l'histoire des insectes* (1752–78).

Geer \'g̲ār\, Dirk Jan de. 1870–1960. Dutch politician. Christian Historical member of parliament (1907–21); minister of finance (1921–23, 1926–33, 1939–40); minister of interior (1925–26); prime minister of the Netherlands (1926–29, 1939–40); resigned in disgrace (1940) for attempting to negotiate peace settlement with Germany.

Geer \'yār\, Louis Gerhard de. Baron. 1818–1896. Swedish politician. Related to Charles de Geer. Prime minister of Sweden (1876–80); introduced numerous reforms, including religious liberty, reform of the penal code, replacement of the four orders of the Diet by two chambers. His son ¶Gerard Jakob de Geer (1858–1943), baron, was a geologist; professor at Stockholm (1897–1924); originator of the varve-counting method in geochronology (1910).

Geert·gen tot Sint Jans \'g̲ārt-g̲ən-tȯt-sint-'yäns\. c.1465–c.1495. Dutch painter. Lived at Haarlem with religious order of Knights of St. John, hence his surname; pupil of Ouwater. Painted religious subjects; noted for harmonious fusion of landscape elements. Chief work a large triptych for high altar of Knights of St. John; paintings ascribed to him include *St. John the Baptist, Virgin and Child, Resurrection of Lazarus, Adoration of the Magi, Man of Sorrows.*

Gef·frard \zhef-rär\, Nicholas-Fabre. 1806–1879. Haitian general and politician. Led insurrection (1858–59) that overthrew Soulouque; declared a republic and became its president (1859–67).

Ge·gen·baur \'gā-gən-,bau̇r\, Karl. 1826–1903. German anatomist. Professor at Jena (1855–73) and Heidelberg (1873–1903); one of first to consider anatomy from evolutionary standpoint; authority on comparative anatomy of vertebrates. Author of *Grundzüge der vergleichenden Anatomie* (1859).

Geh·rig \'ger-ig\, Henry Louis, *called* Lou. *Nicknamed* the Iron Horse. 1903–1941. American baseball player, b. New York City. First baseman, New York Yankees (1925–39); had career batting average of .340, 493 home runs, 1,990 runs batted in (including American League season record of 184 in 1931), and established a record of playing in 2,130 consecutive major league games. Elected to Baseball Hall of Fame (1939).

Geiami. See under NŌAMI.

Gei·bel \'gī-bəl\, Franz Emanuel. 1815–1884. German poet. Head of circle of literary figures at court of Maximilian II in Munich (1852–68); retired on pension. Author of classical lyrics published in *Gedichte* (1840), *Zeitstimmen* (1841), *Junius-Lieder* (1848), *Spätherbstblätter* (1877), etc. Also wrote plays as *Meister Andrea* (1855), and published translations of Romantic and ancient poets, *Spanische Liederbuch* (1852) and *Klassische Liederbuch* (1875).

Gei·ger \'gī-gər\, Abraham. 1810–1874. German theologian. Rabbi at Wiesbaden (1832), Breslau (1838), Frankfurt (1863), Berlin (1870). Leader in early development of Reform Judaism. Helped found (1835) and thereafter edited *Wissenschaftliche Zeitschrift für jüdische Theologie;* chief work *Urschrift und Übersetzungen der Bibel in ihrer Abhängigkeit von der innern Entwicklung des Judentums* (1857).

Geiger, Johannes Hans Wilhelm. 1882–1945. German physicist. Involved esp. in radium research; with Walther Müller, developed (1928) first successful counter (known as Geiger counter) of individual alpha rays.

Geiger, Theodor Julius. 1891–1952. German sociologist. Professor, Brunswick Institute of Technology (1928–33); first professor of sociology in Denmark (1938 ff., at U. of Århus); studied social stratification and social mobility. Works included *Sociologi* (1939), *Vorstudien zu einer Soziologie des Rechts* (1947), *Die Klassengesellschaft im Schmelztiegel* (1949), *Soziale Umschichtungen in einer dänischen Mittelstadt* (1951).

Gei·jer \'yā-ər\, Erik Gustaf. 1783–1847. Swedish historian, poet, philosopher, and composer. Professor, Uppsala (1817–46). A founder (1811) of Gothic Society and an editor of, and contributor to, its journal, *Iduna.* His works included *Geijer i England* (1814), *Svea rikes häfder* (1825), *Svenska folkets historia* (1832–36), and *Människans historia* (1856).

Gei·jer·stam \'yā-ər-,stäm\, Gustaf af. 1858–1909. Swedish writer. Champion of Naturalism in Sweden. Author esp. of novels and tales, including *Fattigt Folk* (1884), *Mina pojkar* (1896), *Boken om lille-bror* (1900), *Kvinnomakt* (1901).

Gei·kie \'gē-kē\, Sir Archibald. 1835–1924. Scottish geologist. Director of Geological Survey of Scotland (1867 ff.); director general of Geological Survey of the United Kingdom and director of the Museum of Practical Geology (1882–1901). Among his books were *The Scenery of Scotland* (1865), *Outlines of Field Geology* (1876), *Textbook of Geology* (1882), *The Ancient Volcanoes of Britain* (1897), *Landscape in History* (1905), and *The Love of Nature Among the Romans* (1912).

Gei·ler von Kay·sers·berg \'gī-lər-fȯn-'kī-zərs-berk\, Johann. 1445–1510. German Roman Catholic priest, b. Switzerland. Preacher at cathedral of Strassburg (1478–1510); known as "the German Savonarola" for his forceful and denunciatory sermons.

Geis·hüs·ler \'gīs-hu̇ēs-lər\, Oswald. *Pseudonym* Oswald My·co·ni·us \mē-'kō-nē-u̇s\. 1488–1552. Swiss reformer. Co-worker of Zwingli and his first biographer (1532); helped draw up Basel Confession of 1543 and First Helvetic Confession of 1536.

Geiss·ler \'gī-slər\, Johann Heinrich Wilhelm. 1815–1879. German glassblower. Founded at Bonn a shop for making scientific apparatus (c.1852); produced the Geissler tube and (c.1855) the Geissler mercury pump.

Geitel, Hans Friedrich. See under Julius ELSTER.

Ge·la·si·us \jə-'lā-shē-əs, -zh(ē-)əs, -zē-əs\. Name of two popes:

Gelasius I. Saint. d. 496. Pope (492–496). Attempted to heal Acacian Schism between Eastern and Western churches; a notable writer of his period, esp. of letters.

Gelasius II. *Orig.* Giovanni da Ga·e·ta \gä-'e-tä\. d. 1119. Pope (1118–19), b. Gaeta. In early life a Benedictine monk at Monte Cassino; as pope, was persecuted by the Frangipani; driven out of Rome by Emperor Henry V, who installed antipope Gregory VIII; fled to France and died in convent of Cluny.

Gel·der \'gel-dər\, Aert *or* Arent de. 1645–1727. Dutch painter. Pupil and imitator of Rembrandt. Painted biblical scenes as *Scenes from the Passion* (c.1715), and portraits as *The Family of Herman Boerhave* (c.1722).

Gel·fond \'gyelʸ-fənd\, Aleksandr Osipovich. 1906–1968. Russian mathematician. Professor, Moscow State U. (1931–68). Profoundly advanced transcendental-number theory, esp. with demonstration (1934) of Gelfond's theorem; also contributed to theory of interpolation and approximation of complex-variable functions. Published *Transtsendentnye i algebraicheskie chisla* and *Ischislenie konechnykh raznostey* (both 1952).

Gel·i·mer \'gel-ə-mər\. 6th century. Last king of the Vandals in Africa (530–534 A.D.). Great-grandson of Gaiseric; deposed his cousin Hilderic (530); captured (534) by Justinian's army under Belisarius.

Gel·lée \zhə-lā\, Claude. *Also spelled* Ge·lée, Gille \zhēl\. *Known as* Claude Lor·rain \lō-raⁿ\. 1600–1682. French painter. To Rome (c.1615); achieved renown as painter of ideal landscapes and seascapes; noted esp. for mastery of light, first use of sun in painting as source of illumination, command of atmospheric effects and recession; known also for drawings, etchings. Considered one of great masters of ideal landscape.

Gel·lert \'gel-ərt\, Christian Fürchtegott. 1715–1769. German poet. Professor, Leipzig (1751 ff.). Best known for *Fabeln und Erzählungen* (1746–48) and religious poems and hymns in *Geistliche Oden und Lieder* (1757); introduced the moralistic family novel into German literature with *Das Leben der schwedische Gräfin von G* (1748); also wrote comedies as *Die Betschwester* (1745) and *Die kranke Frau* (1747).

Gel·li·brand \'gel-ə-ˌbrand\, Henry. 1597–1636. English mathematician and astronomer. Completed Briggs's *Trigonometria Britannica* (1633); wrote *Epitome of Navigation* (pub. 1674).

Gel·li·us \'jel-ē-əs\, Aulus. c.123–c.165 A.D. Roman writer. His *Noctes Atticae* contains notes and miscellaneous information on ancient language and literature, customs, laws, philosophy, and natural science.

Gel·mí·rez \gäl-'mē-rāth\, Diego. c.1068–c.1139. Spanish prelate. Bishop (1101), archbishop (1120), of Santiago de Compostela, which he developed into a pilgrim shrine; competent military commander against the Moors.

Ge·lon \'jē-län\. c.540–478 B.C. Syracusan soldier and politician. Cavalry commander under Hippocrates, tyrant of Gela, whom he succeeded (491) as tyrant. Became tyrant of Syracuse (485) and extended his power in Sicily; noted for beneficence and wisdom of administration; defeated Carthaginians in battle of Himera (480).

Gelt·zer \'gyelt-syir\, Yekaterina Vasilyevna. 1876–1962. Russian dancer. With Moscow Bolshoi Theater (1894–1935), prima ballerina (1901 ff.); danced in Paris with Diaghilev's Ballets Russes (1910); often partnered by her husband Vasily Tikhomirov (*q.v.*). Excelled in dramatic roles and in demi-caractère style of dance; created role of Tao-Hoa in *The Red Poppy* (1927).

Gé·mier \zhā-myā\, Firmin. *Orig.* Firmin Ton·nerre \tō-ner\. 1869–1933. French actor and theater director. Cooperated with André Antoine (from 1892) in effort to introduce realism on French stage; appeared in contemporary plays and revivals of Shakespeare. Director of Théâtre National Populaire at the Trocadero (1920–33) and of the Odéon (1922–30).

Ge·mi·nia·ni \ˌjā-mēn-'yä-nē\, Francesco Xaviero. 1687–1762. Italian violinist and composer. Pupil of Corelli; violin virtuoso and teacher in London (from 1714). Composed violin sonatas, concerti grossi, *Pièces de clavecin* (1743), etc. His treatises, esp. *The Art of Playing on the Violin* (1730), exerted considerable influence.

Ge·mis·tus Ple·thon \jə-'mis-təs-'plē-ˌthän\, George. c.1355–1450 or 1455. Byzantine philosopher and Humanist. Pupil of Eliseus; founded a school of esoteric religious philosophy at Mistra; named consultant to John VIII Palaeologus (1428); lay theologian with Byzantine delegation at Council of Ferrara-Florence (1438–45); persuaded Cosimo de' Medici to found Platonic Academy of Florence. A Neoplatonist; developed a syncretistic system of Platonic philosophy and Oriental religions.

Gem·mei \gem-mā\. 661–721. Japanese empress (708–714). Daughter of Tenchi. Transferred capital to Nara; caused the *Kojiki* (Japanese historical chronicle) to be written; abdicated in favor of her daughter Genshō.

Ge·née \shin-'ē\, Dame Adeline. *Orig.* Anita Jen·sen \'jen-sən\. 1878–1970. Danish dancer. Prima ballerina at Empire Theatre, London (1897–1907); retired (1917) but made occasional appearances. First president of Royal Academy of Dancing (1920–54). Noted for her classic style and precise technique; best known for dancing Swanilda in *Coppélia*.

Ge·ne·si·us \jə-'ne-sh(ē-)əs, -sē-əs, -zē-əs\, Joseph. 10th century Byzantine historian. Under commission from Emperor Constantine VII, wrote *Porphyrogenitus,* history of the Eastern Empire, 813–886.

Genêt. See Janet FLANNER.

Ge·net \zhə-ne\, Edmond-Charles-Édouard. *Surname sometimes* Ge·nest. *Called* Citizen Genet. 1763–1834. French diplomat. Appointed chargé d'affaires to U.S. (1793); hoped to draw U.S. into France's war against Great Britain and Spain; outfitted privateers in American harbors to prey on British commerce and intrigued against Spanish territory; attacked Washington for his neutrality; Washington requested his recall; replaced (1794) but remained in U.S.; m. daughter of George Clinton (*q.v.*) and became U.S. citizen.

Genet, Jean. 1910–1986. French writer. A self-confessed thief, homosexual prostitute, and pimp; dubbed "Black Prince of Letters" by Jean Cocteau; defied bourgeois morality; began writing in prison. Wrote confessional autoerotic poems and novels as *Notre Dame des Fleurs* (1943) and absurdist plays as *Les Bonnes* (1947), *Le Balcon* (1956), *Les Nègres* (1959).

Ge·ne·viève \zhən-vyev; *Angl* 'jen-ə-ˌvēv, ˌjen-ə-'\. Saint. *Ger.* Ge·no·ve·fa \ˌgen-ō-'vā-vä, -'fä-\. c.422–c.500. Patron saint of Paris. Reputed to have saved Paris from the Huns by her prayers (451); supposedly had church built over tomb of Saint-Denis.

Gen·ghis Khan \'geŋ-gə-'skän, 'jeŋ-\. *Also* Chin·gis \'chiŋ-gəs\ *or* Chin·ghiz *or* Chin·giz \'chiŋ-gəz\ Khan. *Original name* Tem·ü·jin \'tem-yə-jən\. c.1162–1227. Mongol conqueror. Became leader of a destitute clan; defeated other clan leaders; proclaimed Genghis Khan (Universal Ruler) of all the Mongols (1206); consolidated his authority among Mongols (1206–12); made his capital at Karakorum. Invaded northern China (1211), capturing Peking (1215); made conquests in west (c.1216–23), overcoming Khwārezm while his generals subdued what is now Iran, Iraq, and part of Russia; died on campaign (1226–27) against Tangut kingdom of Hsi Hsia. A bold leader and military genius. Father of Ögödei (his successor) and Chagatai (*qq.v.*).

Gen·na·di·us \gə-'näd-ē-əs, jə-\. Name of two patriarchs of Constantinople:

Gennadius I of Constantinople. Saint. d. 471. Patriarch (458–71). Champion of Christian orthodoxy; opposed Monophysites, including deposition of Bishop Timotheus Aerulus of Alexandria; charged Cyril of Alexandria with blasphemy; wrote biblical exegeses.

Gennadius II Scho·lar·i·os \skə-'lar-ē-əs, -ˌōs\. c.1405–c.1473. Patriarch (1454–64). Imperial judge and lay preacher at court of John VIII Palaeologus; supported Orthodox independence from Western church; his patriarchate under rule of Sultan Mehmed II; abdicated (1464) and retired to Prodomos monastery at Seres. Author of polemical tracts defending Aristotelian thought, esp. against Gemistus Plethon's Neoplatonism, commentaries on Thomas Aquinas, a treatise favoring Palamism, poetry, etc.

Gennadius of Mar·seilles \mär-sey\. d. between 492 and 505. French priest and theologian. Best known for *De viris illustribus* (written between 467 and 480), which continued St. Jerome's chronicle of same name and constitutes sole biographical and bibliographical source for 91 early Christian authors. Also wrote *Liber ecclesiasticorum dogmatum* in defense of Semi-Pelagian position.

Gennadius of Nov·go·rod \'näv-gə-ˌräd\. d. after 1504. Russian prelate. Archbishop of Novgorod (1485); zealous in suppression of Judaizing Christian sects; commissioned Benjamin of Croatia to produce the first Russian translation of the Bible; translated into Russian Guillaume Durand's *Rationale divinorum officiorum* and wrote studies on calendar reform; forced to resign by government and imprisoned (1504).

Gennaro, San. See JANUARIUS.

Genovefa, Saint. See GENEVIÈVE.

Ge·no·ve·si \ˌjā-nō-'vā-sē\, Antonio. 1712–1769. Italian economist and philosopher. Ordained priest (1737); appointed at Naples professor of metaphysics (1741), of political economy (1754); proposed reforms combining Humanist ideas with a radical Christian metaphysical system. As philosopher, an empiricist influenced by Leibniz; as economist, a mercantilist with a high valuation of labor who attempted to reconcile free competition with protectionist policies. Author of *Disciplinarum metaphysicarum elementa* (1743–52), *Meditazioni filosofiche sulla religione e sulla morale* (1758), *Lettere accademiche* (1764), *Delle lezioni di commercio* (1765), *Universae christianae theologiae elementa* (1771).

Genpachi. See OKUMURA.

Gen·se·ric \'gen-sə-(ˌ)rik, 'jen-\ *or* **Gai·se·ric** \'gī-zə-(ˌ)rik\. d. 477 A.D. King of the Vandals (428–477). Invaded Africa from Spain (429); defeated Roman army sent to oust him; captured Carthage, making it his capital (439). Sacked Rome (455); repelled attacks from Majorian (460) and Basiliscus (468); succeeded by his son Huneric.

Genth \'gent\, Frederick Augustus, *orig.* Friedrich August Ludwig Karl Wilhelm. 1820–1893. American chemist, b. Wächtersbach, Germany. To U.S. (1848); opened chemical laboratory, Philadelphia. Professor, U. of Pennsylvania (1872–88). Specialized in study of minerals; discovered 24 new kinds of minerals, one of which, genthite, is named in his honor.

Gen·til \zhäⁿ-tē\, Émile. 1866–1914. French colonial administrator. Led expedition (1895–97) from French Congo down Shari River to Lake Chad, establishing a French protectorate over Sultanate of Baguirmi; made governor (1900) of Shari region and helped lead campaign against Muslim chieftain Rābaḥ az-Zubayr, whose defeat he described in *La Chute de l'empire de Rabah* (1902); governor of French Congo (1904–08).

Gen·ti·le \jän-'tē-lā\, Giovanni. 1875–1944. Italian philosopher. Professor, Naples (1898–1906), Palermo (1906–14), Pisa (1914–17), Rome (1917–44).

With Benedetto Croce edited *La Critica* (1903–22); founded *Giornale critico della filosofia italiana* (1920). Minister of public instruction (1922–24); reformed Italian educational system; member of Fascist Grand Council (1925–29); president, Supreme Council of Public Education (1926–28). Planned and edited *Enciclopedia Italiana* (1925–43); president of Accademia d'Italia (1943–44). Influenced by Hegel, developed an extreme form of Idealist philosophy which he called "actual Idealism" and which buttressed the Fascist movement. Edited works of Bruno, Campanella, Cuoco, Vico; his works on education and philosophy included *Teoria generale dello spirito como atto puro* (1916), *Le origini della filosofia contemporanea in Italia* (1917–23), *La riforma dell' educazione* (1920), *Che cosa è il fascismo* (1925), *La filosofia dell' arte* (1931), *La mia religione* (1943).

Gentile da Fabriano. See Niccolo di MASSIO.

Gen·ti·le·schi \ˌjän-tē-ˈles-kē\, Orazio Lomi. c.1562–c.1647. Italian painter. Studied under his half-brother Aurelio Lomi; to Rome (c.1580); with Agostino Tassi painted frescoes in Sta. Maria Maggiore, S. Giovanni Laterano, and S. Nicola in Carcave (1590–1600). Dropped Mannerist style and adopted Caravaggio's realism and chiaroscuro style, adding his own lyrical and light-color elements (c.1600). In England (from 1626), esp. as court painter to Charles I. His works included *David and Goliath* (1610?), *St. Cecilia and the Angel* (1610?), *The Annunciation* (1623, his masterpiece), *Rest on the Flight into Egypt* (1626), and series of 9 wall panels for Queen's House, Greenwich (after 1635). His daughter ¶Artemisia (c.1597–after 1651), also a painter; trained by her father and Agostino Tassi; resident chiefly in Naples. Also painted in Caravaggio's style, but added more graceful and colorful aspects; painted many portraits, esp. while visiting her father in London (1638–39), and delighted in gruesome biblical subjects, as *Judith and Holofernes* (c.1618).

Gen·ti·li \jän-ˈtē-lē\, Alberico. *Lat.* Albericus Gen·ti·lis \jen-ˈtī-ləs\. 1552–1608. Italian jurist. To London (1580) because of his Protestantism; professor of civil law at Oxford (1581–1608). Often considered founder of science of international law; said to have been first in western Europe to separate secular law from Catholic theology and canon law. Author of *De jure belli libri tres* (1598), from which Grotius drew extensively, and *Hispanicae advocationis libri duo* (1613).

Gentili, Luigi. *Full name* Aloysius Bonaventura Francesco Camillus Gentili. 1801–1848. Italian Roman Catholic missionary. Joined (1830) Institute of Charity (Rosminians); carried out Rosminian missions in England (from 1835), including aid in founding Roman Catholic college near Bath (1835) and preaching in major cities; died while on mission in slums of Dublin.

Gentz \ˈgents\, Friedrich von. 1764–1832. German political philosopher. Studied under Kant; in Prussian government service (1785–1803); transferred to Austrian service (1803); friend and adviser of Metternich (from c.1812). Chief secretary of important European congresses, including Vienna (1814–15), Aix-la-Chapelle (1818), Carlsbad (1819), Vienna (1819), Troppau (1820), Laibach (1821), Verona (1822). In his writings, attacked French Revolution and, later, Napoléon; at first advocated a united "Free Europe," later turned conservative and counselled Metternich to return to idealized old order of 18th century.

Gé·ny \zhā-nē, zhe-\, François. 1861–1959. French jurist. Professor of civil law (1901), dean of law faculty (1919–25), U. of Nancy. Originator of *libre recherche scientifique* movement in jurisprudence. Author of *Méthode d'interprétation et sources en droit privé positif* (1899) and *Science et technique en droit privé positif* (1915–24).

Geof·frey \ˈjef-rē\. *Fr.* Geof·froi \zhȯf-rwȧ, -rwä\. Name of several counts of Anjou, including:

Geoffrey I Gri·se·go·nelle \grē-zä-gȯ-nel\. d. 987. Count (960–987). Son of Fulk II; extended domain of Anjou; helped Hugh Capet seize Frankish crown.

Geoffrey II Mar·tel \mȧr-tel\. 1006–1060. Count (1040–60). Son of Fulk III Nerra; m. (1032) Agnes, widow of William V, Duke of Aquitaine; in name of her children attacked Duke William the Fat; became involved in civil war with Fulk, a vassal of William; as count, seized Touraine, much of Maine, Vendômois; founded abbeys of La Trinité, Vendôme, L'Esvière in Angers.

Geoffrey III. *Called* le Bar·bu \bȧr-bue̅\, *i.e.* the Bearded. c.1040–?1096. Count (1060–68). Nephew of Geoffrey II Martel; succeeded to countship jointly with brother Fulk IV; defeated by Fulk (1068) and imprisoned for life.

Geoffrey IV Martel II. c.1071–1106. Count (1103–06). Son of Fulk IV, who gave him joint rule in Anjou (1103).

Geoffrey V. *Surnamed* Plan·ta·ge·net \plän-tȧzh-ne, -nā\. 1113–1151. Count of Anjou and Maine (1131–51). Son of Fulk V; m. (1128) Matilda, daughter of Henry I of England; on Henry's death (1135) claimed duchy of Normandy; conquered Normandy (1144), ruled as duke until giving it (1150) to son Henry (later Henry II).

Geoffrey. 1158–1186. Count of Brittany. Fourth son of Henry II of England. Joined his brothers and the French king in invasion of his father's fief of Normandy (1173), but did homage to his father on latter's promise to give him half the revenues of Brittany (1175). Later (1183–84) warred against his brother Richard.

Geoffrey. 1152 or 1153–1212. English prelate. Illegitimate but acknowledged son of Henry II, King of England. Bishop of Lincoln (1173) but never consecrated; resigned (1182); chancellor of England and loyal to father in war with Richard and Philip Augustus (1188–89). Archbishop of York (1189), consecrated (1191); led clergy in refusal to pay tax on church property; fled abroad (1207).

Geoffrey of Mon·mouth \ˈmän-ˌməth\. c.1100–1154. English ecclesiastic and chronicler. Bishop of St. Asaph (1152–54). His mostly fictional *Historia regum Britanniae* (completed c.1135–39) traced descent of British princes from the Trojans and brought the figure of Arthur into European literature.

Geof·frin \zhȯ-fraⁿ\, Marie-Thérèse, *nee* Ro·det \rȯ-de\. 1699–1777. French patroness of literature. Maintained at Hôtel de Rambouillet (1749–77) a famous salon frequented by fashionable, literary, and artistic persons of the period.

Geof·froy \zhȯf-rwȧ, -rwä\, Étienne-François. *Known as* Geoffroy L'Aî·né \len-ā\, *i.e.* the Elder. 1672–1731. French chemist. Professor at Collège de France, Paris (1709–31) and Jardin des Plantes (1712–30). His *Table des différents rapports observés en chimie entre différentes substances* (1718) an authoritative reference for relative affinities of reagents until invalidated by Berthollet.

Geoffroy Saint-Hi·laire \-saⁿ-tē-ler\, Étienne. 1772–1844. French naturalist. Professor, Muséum d'Histoire Naturelle (1793–1841); worked with Georges Cuvier on a zoological classification system (1794–95); accompanied Napoléon's expedition to Egypt to collect specimens (1798–1801); professor, Paris (1809–37). Propounded theory of organic unity which held that a single plan of structure prevails throughout animal kingdom; believed in a form of evolution; violently opposed by Cuvier. Founded teratology with publication of his *Philosophie anatomique* (1818–22). His son ¶Isidore (1805–1861), zoologist, succeeded to his professorships at U. of Paris (1837) and Muséum d'Histoire Naturelle (1841); organized Faculté des Sciences at Bordeaux (1838); founded Société d'Acclimatation to study climatic effects on animals (1854); wrote teratological work *Histoire générale et particulière des anomalies de l'organisation chez l'homme et les animaux* (1832), a scientific biography of his father (1847), and *Histoire naturelle générale des règnes organiques* (1854–62).

Ge·om·et·res \jē-ˈäm-ə-ˌtrēz\, John. *Also called* John Ky·ri·o·tes \ˌkir-ē-ˈōt-(ˌ)ēz\. 10th century. Byzantine poet and ecclesiastic. Officer in command of palace guard; later, ordained priest; made metropolitan of Melitene. Known for short poems in classical meter on contemporary politics and religious subjects; also wrote a prose life of Virgin Mary and sermons for her feast days.

George \ˈjȯ(ə)rj\. Saint. Probably 3d century A.D. Christian martyr. Nothing definite known about his life; adopted in time of Edward III as patron saint of England; among legends developed about him was that of his conquest of the dragon and rescue of the king's daughter Sabra.

George. *Called* George of Po·de·bra·dy \ˈpȯd-yə-ˌbräd-ē\. *Czech.* Jiří z Po·dě·brad \-ˈspȯd-ye-brȧt\. 1420–1471. King of Bohemia (1458–71). Assumed leadership (1444) of Ultraquist faction of Hussite Protestants; captured Prague (1448) and defeated Habsburg faction. Appointed regent of Bohemia (1451) during minority of King Ladislav; following death of Ladislav (1457), elected king (1458). Refused demand of Pope Pius II that he abolish Compactata that legitimized Ultraquists; excommunicated by Pope Paul II (1466), who inspired a crusade against him. Resisted invasion by Matthias Corvinus of Hungary, who had himself crowned king of Bohemia and margrave of Moravia (1469); gained aid of Poland by promising Bohemian succession to Ladislav, son of Polish king Casimir IV; with this aid forced Matthias to come to terms.

George. Name of six kings of England, the first four of the house of Hanover, the last two of the house of Windsor:

George I. *In full* George Louis. 1660–1727. King (1714–1727), 1st king of house of Hanover; also, elector of Hanover, as George I (1698–1727). Son of Sophia, Electress of Hanover, granddaughter of James I of England; m. (1682) Sophia Dorothea (*q.v.*). Fought against French in War of Spanish Succession; as a Protestant, became heir to English throne by virtue of Act of Settlement (passed 1701). Succeeded Queen Anne (1714); regarding Tory party as favorable to Jacobites and Roman Catholic cause, appointed Whig ministry and dissolved the Tory Parliament (1715); left internal policies in hands of his ministers; early years of reign troubled by Jacobite plots; strengthened position of his house by concluding Triple Alliance (1717) with France and Holland; appointed as chief ministers Stanhope (1717) and Sir Robert Walpole (1721).

George II. *In full* George Augustus. 1683–1760. King (1727–1760); also elector of Hanover (1727–1760). Son of George I; m. (1705) Caroline of Ansbach (*q.v.*). Continued father's policy of favoring Whigs for office; retained Sir Robert Walpole as prime minister (to 1742). Became involved in War of Austrian Succession (1740–45); commanded in person and won battle of Dettingen (June 27, 1743); lost popular favor by subordinating British interests to Hanoverian interests. Suppressed Jacobite rebellion in Scotland under the Young Pretender (1745) when his army under his son the Duke of Cumberland won battle of Culloden Moor (Apr. 27, 1746). Attack by the French upon the English colonists in America (1754 ff.) caused him to join alliance with Frederick the Great of Prussia (1756). During last years of his reign, British arms were successful in India, Canada, and on the ocean.

George III. *In full* George William Frederick. 1738–1820. King (1760–1820); also elector (1760–1815), then king (1815–20) of Hanover. Grandson of George II; m. Charlotte Sophia of Mecklenburg-Strelitz (1761). Early part of reign marked by struggles with ministers and attempt to abolish party system; appointed Bute secretary of state (1761) and prime minister (1762), and acted for some time under his advice; suffered first attack of mental illness (1765). Despite opposition, made North prime minister (1770); through patronage system, personally directed government for twelve years; supported policy that led to war with and loss of American colonies; blocked measures for Roman Catholic emancipation. Saved London by his conduct during Gordon Riots (1780); supported Pitt in elections of 1783 and followed his advice as prime minister; suffered second mental attack (1788–89), and third and fourth attacks (1803–04); opened Parliament for last time (1805); took part for last time in forming a ministry, the feeble Perceval ministry (1809–12); became blind and (after 1811) permanently deranged, his son (later George IV) acting as regent till his death (Regency Act, 1811).

George IV. *In full* George Augustus Frederick. 1762–1830. King (1820–30); also king of Hanover. Son of George III; m. (1785) Maria Fitzherbert (*q.v.*) but marriage declared invalid; m. (1795) his cousin Caroline of Brunswick. Gained ill will of his father by his extravagances and dissolute habits, and by his open association with Fox and Sheridan and other leaders of the parliamentary opposition. Prince regent when his father became permanently deranged (1811–20); succeeded as king (1820). Retained Robert Jenkinson as prime minister (to 1827) but intrigued against him; during his reign Catholic Emancipation Act passed (1829). Patron of John Nash and sponsored Wyatville's restoration of Windsor Castle. Succeeded by his brother William IV.

George V. *In full* George Frederick Ernest Albert. 1865–1936. King of England and emperor of India (1910–36), of house of Windsor. Son of Edward VII. Became heir apparent (1892) on death of his elder brother, Albert Victor; created duke of York (1892), prince of Wales (1901); m. Princess Victoria Mary of Teck (1893). Chief events of his reign, World War I (1914–18), agreement with the Irish Free State (1921).

George VI. *In full* Albert Frederick Arthur George. 1895–1952. King of England (1936–52), and emperor of India (1936–48), of house of Windsor. Son of George V; m. (1923) Lady Elizabeth Bowes-Lyon. Served in World War I; created duke of York (1920). Succeeded to the throne (1936) at abdication of his brother Edward VIII; supported Chamberlain's appeasement policy toward Germany and Italy; selected (1940) Winston Churchill as prime minister and supported him completely. His reign saw evolution of British Empire into Commonwealth of Nations and postwar transformation of Great Britain into a welfare state.

George. Duke of Clar·ence \ˈklar-ən(t)s\. 1449–1478. English noble. Son of Richard, Duke of York; created duke of Clarence (1461) by elder brother Edward IV; lord lieutenant of Ireland (1462); m. (1469) Isabel, daughter of Richard Neville, Earl of Warwick; supported Warwick and rebels (1469), fled to France; supported restoration of Henry IV (1470) but soon reconciled with Edward (1471); created (1472) earl of Warwick and Salisbury; imprisoned (1477) and charged with treason and seeking the throne by Edward; attainted by Parliament, executed at Tower of London. His son ¶Edward (1475–99), Earl of Warwick, was imprisoned in Tower by Henry VII (1485–99); beheaded.

George. Prince of Denmark. 1653–1708. Consort of Queen Anne of England. m. Anne (1683); deserted cause of her father James II (1688); naturalized British subject; created duke of Cumberland (1689). At Anne's accession (1702), designated generalissimo and lord high admiral of England.

George. Name of two kings of Greece:

George I. *In full* Christian William Ferdinand Adolphus George. 1845–1913. King (1863–1913). Second son of Christian IX of Denmark. Served some time in Danish navy; after deposition (1862) of Otto I, elected king of the Hellenes (1863) by Greek National Assembly and election approved by Great Powers; m. (1867) Grand Duchess Olga, niece of czar of Russia; during reign, greater part of Thessaly and part of Epirus incorporated (1881) in Greece; Cretan insurrection (1896–97) unsuccessful; involved in First Balkan War (1912–13); assassinated at Salonika; succeeded by son Constantine I.

George II. 1890–1947. King (1922–23, 1935–47). Son of Constantine I and grandson of George I; ruled with no actual authority; unpopular; deposed by military junta (1923); recalled to throne as result of plebiscite (1935); overshadowed by Metaxas, who became dictator (1936); fled (1941) from Nazis to Crete and England; restored to throne by plebiscite (1946); succeeded by his brother Paul I.

George II. 1826–1914. Duke of Saxe-Mei·ning·en \ˈsäk-sə-ˈmī-niŋ-ən\ (1866–1914). Established court theater group, the Meiningen Company, and served as its producer, director, financial backer, and costume and scenery designer; developed many fundamentals of modern stage practice by insisting on realistic speech and stage mechanics and historically accurate costumes and sets.

George. *Surnamed* Syn·cel·lus \sin-ˈsel-əs\, *i.e.* Cellmate. d. after 810. Byzantine historian. Acquired title Syncellus as private secretary to Tarasius, patriarch of Constantinople; after death of Tarasius (806), retired to a monastery. Wrote a chronicle of the world from creation to reign of Diocletian, later continued by Theophanes the Confessor.

George. *Surnamed* Mo·nach·us \mə-ˈnäk-əs\, *i.e.* the Monk, *or* Ha·mar·to·los \ˌhäm-är-ˈtȯl-ȯs\, *i.e.* the Sinner. 9th century. Byzantine historian. Author of a history of the world (from creation to 842) that constitutes prime documentary source for mid-9th-century Byzantine history, esp. of Iconoclast movement.

George of Cap·pa·do·cia \ˌkap-ə-ˈdō-sh(ē-)ə\. d. 361. Greek Orthodox prelate. An extreme Arian; vigorous opponent of St. Athanasius, whom he succeeded (357) as bishop of Alexandria on Athanasius's exile by Constantius II; persecuted his opponents mercilessly; murdered by an Alexandrian mob.

George of La·od·i·cea \(ˌ)lā-ˌäd-ə-ˈsē-ə\. d. c.361. Greek Orthodox prelate. Ordained in Alexandria but excommunicated for advocating Arianism; appointed bishop of Laodicea (c.335); became a principal champion of Homoiousian theology; opponent of St. Athanasius; protected Bishop Eusebius of Emesa during his exile and wrote his biography.

George of Poděbrad. See George, king of Bohemia.

George of Treb·i·zond \ˈtreb-ə-ˌzänd\. 1396–1486. Byzantine scholar. Professor of Greek at Vicenza (1420), Venice (1433); private secretary (to 1453) of popes Eugenius IV and Nicholas V. Ardent Aristotelian; engaged in controversy with Platonists Gemistus Plethon and Cardinal Bessarion; supported Latin church against the Greek. Published (1471) a Latin grammar based on Priscian; produced Latin translations of Aristotle, Plato, Ptolemy, and Greek Church Fathers.

George \zhȯrzh\, Mlle. *Orig.* Marguerite Joséphine Wei·mer \vā-mer\. 1787–1867. French actress. Excelled in tragic roles; rival of Mlle. Duchesnois; member of Théâtre Français company (1802–08). Deserted Paris and played at Vienna, Moscow, and St. Petersburg (1808–13). Rejoined Théâtre Français company (1813–17); played at the Odéon (1821) and at the Porte Saint-Martin (1831); retired (1849). Created many of the roles in plays of Hugo and Dumas père.

George, David Lloyd. See David Lloyd George.

George, Grace. See under William A. Brady.

George \ˈjȯ(ə)rj\, Henry. 1839–1897. American economist, b. Philadelphia. Contributed articles to newspapers in San Francisco (from 1858); an owner of *San Francisco Daily Evening Post* (1871–75); state gas meter inspector (1876). Published pamphlet *Our Land and Land Policy* (1871), containing essence of his single-tax theory, namely, that land values represent monopoly power, that the entire tax burden should be laid on land, freeing industry from taxation and equalizing opportunities by destroying monopoly advantage. Expanded his pamphlet into classic work *Progress and Poverty* (1877–79). Made several lecture tours (to 1890) in U.S., British Isles, Australia; moved to New York (1880); defeated for mayor (1886, 1897). Also published *The Irish Land Question* (1881), *Social Problems* (1883), *Protection or Free Trade* (1886), and *The Science of Political Economy* (1897).

Ge·or·ge \gā-ˈȯr-gə\, Stefan. 1868–1933. German poet. Associated with Baudelaire and Mallarmé in Paris and with Pre-Raphaelite group in London. In Germany founded George-Kreis school of poetry and journal *Blätter für die Kunst* (1892–1919), through which he attempted to revitalize German literary language and to impose a new classicism on poetry; largely dominated German intellectual life by his attacks on materialism and Naturalism and insistence on a new society inspired by humanistic ideals. His lyric poems published in *Hymnen* (1890), *Pilgerfahrten* (1891), *Das Jahr der Seele* (1897), *Der Teppich des Lebens* (1899), *Der siebente Ring* (1907), *Der Stern des Bundes* (1914), *Der neue Reich* (1928).

George Pach·y·me·res \ˈjȯ(ə)rj-ˌpak-ə-ˈmi(ə)r-ˌēz\. 1242–c.1310. Byzantine scholar. Ordained in Greek Orthodox ministry; held ecclesiastic and political offices; taught liberal arts at patriarchal academy of basilica of Hagia Sophia in Constantinople. His chronicle of reigns of Palaeologus emperors Michael VIII and Andronicus II, *Hrōmaikē historia,* is the primary historical source of that period (1261–1308); also wrote *Syntagma tōn tessarōn mathēmatōn,* a handbook on the liberal arts that became a standard academic text.

George Pis·i·des \-ˈpis-ə-ˌdēz\. 7th century. Byzantine poet and cleric. Deacon and archivist of Hagia Sophia in Constantinople. Accompanied Heraclius on campaign against Persians and wrote epic on this subject, *The Expedition of Heraclius Against the Persians* (622); commemorated victory over Parthians in ode *Heracliad* (627). Also wrote *Avarica* on attack by Avars on Constantinople (626), didactic poem *Hexaëmeron* on the creation, moralistic elegy *De vanitate vitae, a Hymn to the Resurrection,* and a metrical polemic *Against Wicked Severus* attacking Bishop Severus of Antioch.

George Sphran·tes \-ˈsfrän-ˌtēz\. *Also spelled* Phran·tzes \-ˈfränt-ˌsēz\. 15th century. Byzantine historian. Held high office in service of Palaeologus rulers; great logothete (chancellor) in Constantinople (1451); on capture of Constantinople by Turks, fled to Corfu and entered a monastery (1468). Author of *Chronicon minus,* a history of Byzantine Empire from 1258 to 1477.

George William. *Ger.* Georg Wilhelm. 1595–1640. Elector of Brandenburg (1619–40). His neutrality in Thirty Years' War earned him hostility of both sides; forced by Gustav II Adolphus to join Protestant side (1631) but defeat of Swedes at Nördlingen (1634) allowed him to resume his neutrality.

George William Frederick Charles. 2d Duke of Cambridge. 1819–1904. British soldier. Son of Adolphus Frederick; served in Hanoverian and (from 1837) British armies; served in Crimean War; general and commander in chief (1856); field marshal (1862); opposed reforms in organization and discipline; resigned (1895).

Ger·ald de Bar·ri \ˈjer-əl(d)-də-ˈbar-ē\. *Best known by his Latin literary name* Gi·ral·dus Cam·bren·sis \jə-ˈrȯl-də-skam-ˈbren-səs, -ˈral-\, *i.e.* Gerald of Wales. c.1146–c.1223. Welsh ecclesiastic and historian. Of noble birth; archdeacon of Brecknock (1175–1204); chaplain to Henry II of England (1184–89). Wrote *Topographia Hiberniae* (c.1188) and *Expugnatio Hibernica* (c.1189) after accompanying Prince John's military expedition (1185–86) to Ireland; described Wales in *Itinerarium Cambriae* (1191) and *Cambriae descriptio* (1194) after assisting (1188) Archbishop Baldwin of Canterbury preach Third Crusade in Wales. Spent much of career in unsuccessful attempt to obtain see of St. David's; opposed Anglo-Norman authority over Welsh church. Also author of autobiography *De rebus a se gestis* (c.1204–05).

Ger·ard *or* **Gi·rard** \ˈjer-ˌärd, -ərd, *also & US usu* jə-ˈrärd\. d. 1108. English prelate. Bishop of Hereford (1096); archbishop of York (1100). At first supported King Henry I against Archbishop Anselm in Investiture Controversy; later (1105) supported Anselm and helped settle the dispute.

Gerard of Cre·mo·na \krā-ˈmō-nä\. c.1114–1187. Italian scholar. Member (from c.1134) of college of translators of Toledo, Spain, established by Archbishop Raymond. Translated many Greek and Arabic texts into Latin, including works by Aristotle, Ptolemy, Euclid, Galen, and Avicenna.

Gerard, Charles. 1st Baron Gerard of Bran·don \ˈbran-dən\. Viscount Brandon. Earl of Mac·cles·field \ˈmak-əlz-ˌfēld\. 1618?–1694. English soldier. Commanded Royalist brigade at Edge Hill (1642); distinguished himself at Newbury (1643) and Newark (1644); commander of Charles I's bodyguard (1645). At Restoration, returned with Charles II from Breda at head of Life Guards; envoy extraordinary to Paris (1662); as adherent of Monmouth, presented by grand jury as disloyal (1684); escaped abroad; returned with William III as commander of bodyguard (1688). His son ¶Charles (1659?–1701), 2d earl, participated in intrigues of Monmouth; sentenced to death (1685) for complicity in Rye House Plot (1683); pardoned (1687); envoy extraordinary to Hanover (1701).

Gé·rard \zhā-rár\, Étienne-Maurice. Comte. 1773–1852. French soldier. Distinguished himself at Austerlitz (1805); general of division in the Russian campaign (1812); engaged at Waterloo (1815). Minister of war under Louis-Philippe (1830, 1834), and created marshal of France; directed siege of Antwerp (1832); senator (1852).

Gérard, François-Pascal-Simon. Baron. 1770–1837. French painter. Pupil of Jacques-Louis David; popular in Napoléon's court; court painter to Louis XVIII; patronized by Charles X. His historical and mythological paintings included *Bélisaire* (1795), *Psyché et l'Amour* (1796), *Bataille d'Austerlitz* (1808), *Entrée d'Henri IV à Paris* (1815); famed esp. for his portraits, including those of Napoléon, Moreau, Mme. de Staël, Talleyrand, Czar Alexander of Russia, Duke of Wellington, Louis XVIII, Charles X, Louis-Philippe.

Gérard, Jean-Ignace-Isidore. *Pseudonym* Grand·ville \gräⁿ-vēl\. 1803–1847. French caricaturist. Achieved fame with satirical lithographs, often of public figures depicted as animal analogies; well known series included "Les Tribulations de la petite propriété," "Les Plaisirs de toute âge," "La Sibylle des salons," "Les Métamorphoses du jour"; contributed to *Le Charivari, Le Caricature,* etc.; illustrated editions of La Fontaine, Swift, etc.

Ge·rard \ˈjer-ˌärd, -ərd, *also & US usu* jə-ˈrärd\, John. 1545–1612. English botanist and barber-surgeon. Became famous for his London garden containing rare plants; superintendent of Burghley's gardens (1577–98). Published a list of plants growing in his own garden (1596) and *The Herball, or generall historie of plantes* (1597). The genus *Gerardia* is named for him.

Ge·rards \zhā-rár\, Balthasar. 1558–1584. French fanatic. Assassinated William I the Silent, Prince of Orange (1584).

Gerardus Magnus. See Gerhard GROOTE.

Gerbert. See Pope SYLVESTER II.

Ger·bert de Mon·treuil \zher-ber-də-mōⁿ-trœy\. 13th century. French poet. Author of *Roman de la Violette* and possibly of a continuation of the *Perceval* of Chrétien de Troyes.

Ger·bert von Hor·nau \ˈger-bərt-fȯn-ˈhȯr-ˌnau̇\, Martin. 1720–1793. German Roman Catholic priest and music historian. Prince-abbot of St. Blaise (1764 ff.). Wrote a history of sacred music *De cantu et musica sacra* (1774) and edited some 40 medieval music treatises in *Scriptores ecclesiastici de musica sacra potissimum* (1784).

Ger·bran·dy \ger-ˈbrän-dē\, Pieter Sjoerds. 1885–1961. Dutch politician. Prime minister of the Netherlands government in exile, London (1940–45); directed war effort of all Dutch forces outside occupied territory; served in lower house of parliament (1948–58).

Ger·gonne \zher-gȯn\, Joseph-Diez. 1771–1859. French mathematician. Founded (1810) *Annales de mathématiques pures et appliquées,* first purely mathematical journal; professor, Montpellier (1816–44). Known for work on principle of geometric duality.

Ger·hard \ˈgār-ˌhärt\, Johann. 1582–1637. German theologian. Leading orthodox Lutheran theologian of his day. Superintendent of churches in Heldburg (1606), later of all churches in duchy of Coburg; professor at Jena (1616–37); chaired every major Lutheran theological assembly of his time. Set forth his strict views in *Loci theologici* (1610–22); also wrote devotional manual *Meditationes sacrae* (1606), *Confessio catholica* (1634–37), etc.

Ger·hardt \zhā-rár\, Charles-Frédéric. 1816–1856. French chemist. Professor at Montpellier (1844) and Strasbourg (1855). Prepared acid anhydrides; experimented on homologous series and on the type theory; with Auguste Laurent, proposed a classification of organic compounds; one of first to use equations to express chemical reactions.

Ger·hardt \ˈgār-ˌhärt\, Elena. 1883–1961. German singer. Best known as a lieder singer, esp. songs of Hugo Wolf; settled in London as teacher (1933).

Gerhardt, Paul. 1607–1676. German Lutheran clergyman and hymn writer. Greatest of German Lutheran hymnists; hymns included "Befiehl du deine Wege," "Ist Gott für mich," "Du, meine Seele, singe," "Geh aus, mein Herz," "O Haupt, voll Blut und Wunden" (from Latin of Bernard of Clairvaux).

Gé·ri·cault \zhā-rē-kō\, Théodore, *in full* Jean-Louis-André-Théodore. 1791–1824. French painter. By his unorthodox coloring and bold designs, broke the classical tradition and had important influence in inaugurating the Romantic movement in French art. Works included *The Charging Chasseur* (1812), *Wounded Cuirassier* (1814), *Raft of the Medusa* (1818–19), series of five paintings of the insane (1822–23), and *Race of the Riderless Horse* (unfinished).

Ge·ring \ˈgā-riŋ\, Ulrich. d. 1510. Swiss printer. Commissioned (c.1470) by Sorbonne professors Heynlin and Fichet to establish a printing press, the first to be set up in France.

Gé·rin-La·joie \zhā-raⁿ-läj-wä\, Antoine. 1824–1882. Canadian editor and writer, b. Yamachiche, Que. Editor of Montreal newspaper *La Minerve* (1845–52); translator to Legislative Assembly of Canada (1852–56); assistant librarian of Parliament (1856–80). A founder of Institut Canadien of Montreal and of literary magazines *Les Soirées canadiennes* (1861–65) and *Le Foyer canadien* (1863–66). Author of poem "Un Canadien errant" (1837), *Catechisme politique* (1851), novels *Jean Rivard, le défricheur* (1862) and *Jean Rivard, l'économiste* (1864), *Le Jeune Latour* (first French-Canadian play, pub. 1884), and history *Dix ans au Canada de 1840 à 1850* (1888).

Ger·lach \ˈger-ˌläk\, Hellmut von. 1866–1935. German journalist and politician. A founder of the National Social Union (1896); member of Reichstag (1903–07); undersecretary in ministry of interior (1918–19). President, League for German Rights. Editor in chief, *Welt am Montag* (1901–31), wherein he presented his pacifist convictions and opposition to German nationalism; editor of radical weekly *Die Weltbühne* (1932–33); exiled from Germany when Hitler gained power (1933).

Gerlach, Leopold von, *in full* Ludwig Friedrich Leopold. 1790–1861. Prussian soldier. Took part in wars against Napoléon; staunch conservative; exerted considerable influence as adjutant general (1850) and political adviser to Frederick William IV; moving spirit of court camarilla which opposed German revolution and attempted to channel 1850 constitution into conservative channels; general of infantry (1859). His brother ¶Ernst Ludwig (1795–1877) was a Prussian jurist and politician; founder (1848) of Conservative party in Prussia, and of its journal, *Kreuzzeitung;* member of Catholic Center party in

Prussian diet (1873–77) and Reichstag (1877); opposed Bismarck, esp. Bismarck's persecutions of Catholics.

Ger·lache \zher-lȧsh\, Étienne-Constantin de. Baron. 1785–1871. Belgian politician. Member of Estates General of United Netherlands (1824); his support of coalition of Belgian Catholic and Liberal parties (1828) helped pave way for Belgian revolution of 1830; as president of National Congress (1831) helped Leopold of Saxe-Coburg become first king of Belgians as Leopold I. President of Cour de Cassation (1832–67). Author of *Histoire de Pays-Bas* (1839), *Essai sur le mouvement des partis en Belgique* (1852), etc.

Gerlache de Go·me·ry \-də-gôm-rē\, Adrien Victor Joseph de. Baron. 1866–1934. Belgian naval officer and explorer. Conducted Antarctic exploration in ship *Belgica* (1897–99); conducted oceanographic studies off Greenland (1905), in Barents and Kara seas (1907), in Barents and Greenland seas (1909); helped Sir Ernest Shackleton plan Trans-Antarctic Expedition of 1914–17.

Ger·main \zher-maⁿ\ of Au·xerre \ō-'se(ə)r\. Saint. *Latin* Ger·ma·nus \jər-'mā-nəs\. c.378–448. French ecclesiastic. Bishop of Auxerre (418). To Britain (429 and 447) and successfully controverted the Pelagian heresy each time.

Germain of Paris. Saint. c.496–576. French ecclesiastic. Bishop of Paris (555); attempted without much success to mediate fratricidal conflicts and civil wars among several Merovingian kings; participated in Councils of Paris (557 and 573) and Council of Tours (566); consecrated Church of Saint Vincent in Paris (558), later dedicated to him under the name of Saint-Germain-des-Prés.

Germain. Family of distinguished silversmiths in France, including: Pierre (1645–1684), admitted as master in guild (1669); given apartments in the Louvre (1679); made ornate portrait frame for Louis XIV (1677), a cross and six chandeliers for Fontainebleau Chapel (1680), and chandeliers for Versailles (1683–84). His son ¶Thomas (1673–1748) was made master of guild (1720) and royal goldsmith (1723); produced elaborate Rococo dishes, candlesticks, sconces, plates, etc., for Louis XV, for Elector of Cologne, and for courts of Spain, Portugal, and Naples; elected (1738, 1741) city councilor and alderman of Paris. His son ¶François-Thomas (1726–1791) took over the family workshop and made royal silversmith (all 1748); produced ornate Rococo tableware, chandeliers, inkstands, etc., for courts of France, Portugal, Russia.

Germain, Lord George and Charles Sackville. See under SACKVILLE family.

Germain, Sophie. 1776–1831. French mathematician. Associate of Lagrange and Gauss; contributed to study of acoustics, elasticity, and theory of numbers; wrote prize treatise on vibration of elastic plates (1816).

Germaine de Foix. See FOIX.

Ger·man \'jər-mən\, Sir Edward. *Orig.* Edward German Jones. 1862–1936. English composer. Became known for his incidental music for plays, esp. *Henry VIII* (1892) and *Nell Gwynn* (1900); completed Sir Arthur Sullivan's *The Emerald Isle* (1901); composer of light operas *Merrie England* (1902), *A Princess of Kensington* (1903), *Tom Jones* (1907), and *Fallen Fairies* (1909, libretto by Sir W.S. Gilbert), and of two symphonies, symphonic poem *Hamlet* (1897), suites, chamber music, songs, etc.

Germanicus. See (1) Nero Claudius DRUSUS; (2) Emperor CLAUDIUS I; (3) Emperor NERO; (4) BRITANNICUS.

Ger·man·i·cus Cae·sar \jər-'man-i-kəs-'sē-zər\. 15 B.C.–19 A.D. Roman general. Son of Nero Claudius Drusus and nephew of Emperor Tiberius. Quaestor (5 A.D.); served under Tiberius in Illyricum (6–9) and on the Rhine (11); as consul (12), commanded Gaul and the two Rhine armies; campaigned against the Germans (14–16) and defeated Arminius (16); received a triumph in Rome (17). Again consul (18); as commander of Eastern provinces, settled Armenian succession, organized Cappadocia and Commagene into provinces, negotiated successfully with Artabanus III of Parthia, engaged in dispute with Gnaeus Calpurnius Piso; died near Antioch, perhaps poisoned by orders of the emperor. By his wife Agrippina, granddaughter of Augustus, was father of nine children, including the emperor Caligula, and Agrippina, mother of Nero.

Ger·ma·nos \yir-'mä-nôs\. *Orig.* Loukas Stre·no·pou·los \strin-'ō-pü-lôs\. 1872–1951. Greek prelate. Archbishop of Thyateira and exarch for Greek Orthodox members in western and central Europe (1922–51); president of World Council of Churches (1948); promoted Christian unity.

Germanus, Saint. See also GERMAIN.

Ger·man·us \(,)jər-'man-əs\. Name of two patriarchs of Constantinople:

Germanus I. Saint. c.634–c.732. Patriarch (715–730). As theological consultant, advised Constantine IV to convoke third Council of Constantinople (680–681). As patriarch, strongly opposed Monothelitism and Iconoclastic heresy and fostered Marian devotion. Author of *De haeresibus et synodis, On the Purpose of Life,* Marian treatises, etc.

Germanus II. c.1175–1240. Patriarch (1222–40). Maintained a conciliatory policy toward Rome; labored with some success to retain unity within Byzantine church; wrote religious tracts and poetry, sermons, many letters.

Germanus of Gran·fel \'grän-fəl\. Saint. c.610–675. German clergyman. Disciple of St. Arnulf; abbot of Granfel (640–675), also of St. Ursitz and of St. Paul zu-Werd; martyred while opposing Duke Cathic's abuse of the poor.

Ger·mer \'gər-mər\, Lester Halbert. 1896–1971. American physicist, b. Chicago. On research staff of Western Electric Co. (1917–53). With Clinton Davisson (*q.v.*) conducted (1927) experiment that first demonstrated the wave properties of the electron, thereby confirming Louis de Broglie's hypothesis; made investigations in thermionics and surface chemistry.

Gerns·back \'gərnz-,bak\, Hugo. 1884–1967. American inventor and publisher, b. Luxembourg. To U.S. (1904); organized (1909) Electro Importing Co. to market his improved dry battery and other radio supplies; patented some 80 radio and electronic inventions; founded *Modern Electronics* magazine (1908). As founder (1926) and publisher of *Amazing Stories* magazine, was largely responsible for the establishment of science fiction as an independent literary form; also founded *Wonder Stories* (1930) and other magazines. The Hugo Award given annually for the best science fiction novel is named after him.

Gé·rôme \zhā-rōm\, Jean-Léon. 1824–1904. French painter. Studied under Paul Delaroche and in Italy (1844–45); professor at École des Beaux-Arts (1863); teacher of Odilon Redon, Thomas Eakins, J.A. Weir. Known for anecdotal, erotic, highly finished paintings, including *Pygmalion and Galatea, The Cockfight,* and *Prayer in the Mosque of 'Amr, Old Cairo.* Executed also a number of sculptures.

Ge·ron·i·mo \jə-'rän-ə-,mō\. *Indian name* Goyathlay, *i.e.* One Who Yawns. 1829–1909. American Apache chieftain, b. site of present Clifton, Ariz. Admitted to warriors' council of Chiricahua Apaches (1846); given nickname Geronimo *(Eng.* Jerome) by Mexicans; led sensational campaign (1885–86) against the whites; finally captured by Gen. Crook; escaped, and surrendered to Gen. Miles, who had relieved Crook. Finally settled as farmer at Fort Sill, Okla. (1894); later worked at expositions; dictated autobiography (1906).

Ger·ry \'ger-ē\, Elbridge. 1744–1814. American politician, b. Marblehead, Mass. Member, Massachusetts Provincial Congress (1774–75), Continental Congress (1776–81, 1783–85); a signer of Declaration of Independence and of Articles of Confederation. Delegate to Constitutional Convention (1787); opposed the Constitution as drafted. Member, U.S. House of Representatives (1789–93). Member, XYZ mission to France (1797–98); recalled for trying to negotiate separate terms with Talleyrand. Governor of Massachusetts (1810, 1811). During second term the redistricting of Massachusetts in a way planned to give Republicans continued control gave rise to term "gerrymander." Vice president of the United States (1813–14).

Gershom, Levi ben. See LEVI BEN GERSHOM.

Ger·shom ben Ju·dah \'gər-shəm-ben-'jüd-ə\. c.960–1028 to 1040. French rabbi. Head of rabbinic academy at Mainz; proposed a series of legal enactments (*taqqanot*) that profoundly molded the social institutions of medieval European Jewry; founder of Talmudic study in France and Germany; revised text of Masora and Talmud, and published biblical exegetical treatises.

Gersh·win \'gərsh-wən\, George. *Orig.* Jacob Gersh·vin \'gersh-vən\. 1898–1937. American composer, b. Brooklyn, N.Y. Scored first success (1919) with song "Swanee," sung by Al Jolson; wrote scores for *George White's Scandals* (1920–24). Composed scores (with lyrics by his brother Ira) for Broadway musical comedies *Lady Be Good* (1924, including "Fascinatin' Rhythm"), *Tip-Toes* (1925), *Oh, Kay* (1926, "Someone To Watch Over Me"), *Funny Face* (1927, "S'Wonderful"), *Strike Up the Band* (1927), *Treasure Girl* (1928), *Show Girl* (1929), *Girl Crazy* (1930, "But Not For Me," "Embraceable You," "I Got Rhythm"), *Of Thee I Sing* (1931, Pulitzer prize), and *Pardon My English* (1933). Wrote scores for films, contributing songs "The Man I Love," "They Can't Take That Away From Me," "Nice Work If You Can Get It," "Let's Call the Whole Thing Off." Also composed orchestral works, many employing elements of jazz, including *Rhapsody in Blue* (1924), *Piano Concerto in F Major* (1925), *Preludes* for piano (1926), tone poem *An American in Paris* (1928), *Second Rhapsody* (1931), and opera *Porgy and Bess* (1935, "Summertime," "I Got Plenty o' Nuttin!," "I Loves You, Porgy").

Gershwin, Ira. 1896–1983. American lyricist, b. New York City. Wrote (from 1920) lyrics for songs composed by his brother George (*q.v.*); composed lyrics for all the Gershwin brothers' stage shows; won first Pulitzer prize awarded to a lyricist for *Of Thee I Sing* (1931); after George's death (1937) completed *The Goldwyn Follies* (1937) with Vernon Duke; collaborated with Kurt Weill on *Lady in the Dark* (1940), with Jerome Kern on *Cover Girl* (1944), and with Harold Arlen on the movie musical *A Star Is Born* (1954).

Gerson, Jean de. See Jean CHARLIER.

Gersonides. See LEVI BEN GERSHOM.

Ger·stäck·er \'ger-,stek-ər\, Friedrich. 1816–1872. German writer. Traveled over much of world, including (1837–52) U.S. Author of many novels and adventure stories, including *Die Regulatoren in Arkansas* (1845), *Die Flusspiraten des Mississippi* (1848), *Germelshausen* (1862).

Ger·sten·berg \'ger-stən-,berk\, Heinrich Wilhelm von. 1737–1823. German poet and critic. Official Danish representative at Lübeck (1775–83); received judicial appointment at Altona (1789). Introduced bardic poetry into German literature with *Gedicht eines Skalden* (1766); also wrote tragedy *Ugolino* (1768); his chief work of literary criticism, *Briefe über die Merkwürdigkeiten* *der Literatur* (1766–67), formulated critical principles of German *Sturm und Drang* movement.

Ger·trude \'gər-ˌtrüd\, *called* the Great. Saint. 1256–1302 or 1311. German mystic. Famed for supernatural visions.

Gertsen, Aleksandr Ivanovich. See Aleksandr I. HERZEN.

Ger·vais \zher-ve\, Paul, *in full* François-Louis-Paul. 1816–1879. French paleontologist and zoologist. Professor at Montpellier (1845–65) and Museum of Natural History, Paris (1868–79); contributed to vertebrate paleontology. Author of *Zoologie et paléontologie françaises* (1848–52), *Zoologie et paléontologie générales* (1867–75), etc.

Ger·vase of Can·ter·bury \'jər-və-səv-'kant-ə(r)-ˌber-ē, -b(ə-)rē\. *Latin* Ger·va-si·us Do·ro·bor·nen·sis \(ˌ)jər-'vā-zh(ē-)əs-ˌdōr-ə-bȯr-'nen(t)-səs\. c.1141–c.1210. English monk and chronicler. Monk at Christ Church, Canterbury (1163 ff.). Author of a history of the archbishops of Canterbury from Augustine to Hubert Walter, a chronicle from the accession of Stephen to the death of Richard I, and a *Gesta regum.*

Gervase of Til·bury \'til-b(ə-)rē\. c.1152–1220. English scholar and courtier. In service of William II of Sicily and (c.1189–c.1218) of Emperor Otto IV; made marshal of kingdom of Arles by Otto. Wrote for Otto his *Otia imperialia,* a medley of medieval legends and superstitions.

Ge·sell \gə-'zel\, Arnold Lucius. 1880–1961. American psychologist and pediatrician, b. Alma, Wis. On teaching staff, Yale (1911–48); founder (1911) and director (1911–48) Yale Clinic of Child Development; consultant, Gesell Institute of Child Development, New Haven (1950–58). Pioneer in study of development of normal infants and children. Author of *An Atlas of Infant Behavior* (1934), *The Child from Five to Ten* (1946, with Frances L. Ilg), *Child Development* (1949), *Youth* (1956, with Ilg and L.B. Ames), etc.

Ge·se·ni·us \gā-'zā-nē-ůs\, Heinrich Friedrich Wilhelm. 1786–1842. German biblical scholar. Professor, Halle (1811 ff.). Inaugurated a modern philological approach in Semitic language studies. Author of a Hebrew and Chaldee dictionary (1810–13), a Hebrew grammar (1813), a commentary on Isaiah (1821–29), etc.

Ges·ner \'ges-nər\, Abraham. 1797–1864. Canadian geologist, b. Cornwallis, N.S. Known for geological mapping and exploration in Nova Scotia; discovered a process for distilling kerosene from petroleum (1852).

Gesner, Conrad. 1516–1565. Swiss physician and naturalist. Published a Greek–Latin dictionary (1537); professor of Greek at Lausanne Academy (1537–40); practiced medicine in Zürich (from 1541), city physician (1554). Provided checklist of 1800 European authors in *Bibliotheca universalis* (1545), first bibliography of its kind; surveyed world knowledge in *Pandectarum sive partitionum universalium* (1548). His compendium of recorded knowledge of animal life, *Historiae animalium* (1551–87), considered basis of modern zoology. Also one of first to write about mountaineering.

Gesner, John Matthias. 1691–1761. German classical philologist. Professor, Göttingen (from 1734); while director of Thomasschule, Leipzig (1730–34), gave much encouragement to J.S. Bach.

Ges·si \'jes-sē\, Romolo. *Also called* Gessi Pa·sha \'päsh-ä\. 1831–1881. Italian soldier and explorer. Fought with British forces in Crimean War (1854–55). Accompanied Charles Gordon to Sudan (1873); explored interior of Sudan (1875); first to circumnavigate and map Lake Albert Nyanza (1876). Named pasha by khedive of Egypt for quelling a revolt of Arab slave traders in southern Sudan.

Gess·ler \'ges-lər\, Otto Karl. 1875–1955. German politician. Minister of reconstruction (1919–20); succeeded Noske as Reichswehr minister (1920); minister of defense (1920–28); collaborated with General von Seeckt in reorganizing Reichswehr.

Gess·ner \'ges-nər\, Salomon. 1730–1788. Swiss poet and artist. As artist, known for landscapes and etchings; as poet, wrote *Daphnis* (1754), pastoral prose *Idyllen* (1756), and epic poem *Der Tod Abels* (1758), translated into most European languages.

Ge·sual·do \jā-'swäl-dō\, Carlo. Prince of Ve·no·sa \vā-'nō-sä\. c.1560–1613. Italian composer. Known esp. for his six books of highly individual madrigals.

Ge·ta \'jēt-ə\, Publius Septimius. 189–212. Roman emperor (209–212). Second son of Septimius Severus, who made him caesar (198) and augustus (209). Joint emperor (211–212) with his brother Caracalla, who caused his murder.

Get·ty \'get-ē\, Jean Paul. 1892–1976. American businessman, b. Minneapolis. Entered oil business (1913); gained control of Pacific Western Oil Corp. (1932; renamed Getty Oil Co., 1956) and other oil interests, amassing fortune valued at over one billion dollars.

Geu·lincx \'gœ̄-liŋks\, Arnold. 1624–1669. Dutch philosopher. Professor at Louvain (1646–58); joined Protestant church and became professor at Leiden (1665). Follower of Descartes; founded metaphysical theory known as occasionalism.

Geyl \'gīl\, Pieter. 1887–1966. Dutch historian. Professor, London U. (1919–36) and Utrecht (1936 ff.). Works included *Willem IV en Engeland tot 1748* (1924), *De Groot-Nederlandsche gedachte* (1925–30), *Geschiedenis van de Nederlandse stam* (1930–37), *Oranje en Stuart* (1939), *Encounters in History* (1962).

Ge·zel·le \gə-'zel-ə\, Guido. 1830–1899. Flemish poet. Ordained (1854); vice rector (1861–65), curate (1865–72), Seminarium Anglo-Belgicum, Bruges; curate at Courtrai (1872–99); chaplain of English convent at Bruges (1899). Founded and edited weeklies *'t Jaer 30* (1864–70), *Rond den Heerd* (1865–70), and *'t Jaer 70* (1870–72), and philological review *Loquela* (1881–95). A leading force in Flemish cultural renaissance of 19th century. His lyric poems published in *Kerkhofblommen* (1858), *Dichtoefeningen* (1858), *Kleengedichtjes* (1860), *Gedichten, gezangen en gebeden* (1862), *Tijdkrans* (1893), *Rijmsnoer* (1897), *Laatste verzen* (1901). Also known as philologist and folklorist.

Ghā·lib \'gä-lēb\, Mīrzā Asadullāh Khān. 1797–1869. Indian poet. Poet laureate of Bahādur Shāh II (1850). Author of love lyrics, parables, and panegyrics in Persian; also known for poetry, prose, and letters in Urdu.

Ghas·sā·nid \ga-'sän-id\. Christianized Arab dynasty originating in a South Arabian tribe and ruling (5th century to 636 A.D.) in Northern Arabia (Palestine, Trans-Jordan and region around Palmyra).

Ghas·sa·niy, al- \al-ga-'sän-ē\, Muyaka bin Haji. 1776–1840. Kenyan poet. Lived in Mombasa. Wrote in Swahili; his verse collected in *Diwani ya Muyaka* (pub. 1962).

Gha·zā·lī, al- \al-ga-'zä-lē\. *In full* Abu Ḥāmid Muḥammad ibn Muḥammad aṭ-Ṭūsī al-Ghazālī. 1058–1111. Islāmic jurist, theologian, philosopher, and educator. Early achieved reputation as theologian; chief professor at Niẓāmīyah college, Baghdad (1091–95); abandoned teaching and became mendicant Ṣūfī mystic; with disciples formed monastic community; returned to college (1106–10). Author of authoritative standard works on jurisprudence, esp. *al-Mustaṣfā;* theology, esp. *al-Iqtiṣād fī al-I'tiqād;* philosophy, esp. *Maqāṣid al-falāsifah,* one of the first books translated from Arabic into Latin (12th century), and *Tahāfut,* critically evaluating Avicenna and others against Islāmic doctrine; theology, esp. *Iḥyā' 'ulūm ad-dīn* relating Ṣūfism to Islāmic doctrine.

Ghā·zān \gä-'zän\, Maḥmūd. 1271–1304. Mongol ruler (Il-khan) of Persia (1295–1304). Son of Arghūn; viceroy of provinces of northeastern Persia (1284–95). As Il-khan, extended dominions and established reforms; friendly to Christians; defeated Muslim sultans of Damascus and Egypt (1299–30); captured Damascus and entered Jerusalem; later defeated, and abandoned Syria (1303); made Islām established religion of Persia.

Ghā·zī I \'gä-zē\. 1912–1939. King of Iraq (1933–39). Son of King Faisal of Iraq; his reign saw much political instability; succeeded by his son, Faisal II.

Ghaz·na·vid \'gœz-nə-vəd\. Name of Turkish dynasty (977–1186) ruling in Khorāsān, Afghanistan, and northern India with its capital at Ghazna (Afghanistan). It was founded (977) by Sebüktigin and its greatest ruler was Maḥmūd of Ghazna (*qq.v.*); overcome by Mu'izz-ud-Dīn Muḥammad of Ghūr (1186).

Ghelderode, Michel de. See Adolphe MARTENS.

Gheor·ghiu-Dej \'gyȯr-gyü-'dā\, Gheorghe. 1901–1965. Romanian politician. Joined Communist party (1930); imprisoned (to 1944) for role in 1933 Griviţa railway strike; minister of communications (1944–46). Secretary general of Communist party (from 1944); instrumental in ouster of Rădescu and establishment of Communist-dominated government (1945); held several economic posts in government (1946–52). Prime minister (1952–55); president of State Council (from 1961); adopted policies which gradually secured independence from Soviet domination.

Ghe·rar·de·sca, del·la \ˌdāl-lä-ˌgā-rär-'dās-kä\. Italian noble family of Tuscan origin, prominent Ghibelline leaders in Pisa and enemies of the Visconti in 13th and 14th centuries. Its members included: Gerardo (d. c.990), who established himself as count of Gherardesca and of Do·no·ra·ti·co \ˌdō-nō-'rāt-ē-kō\. ¶Tedicio, first podestà (feudal mayor) of Pisa (1190). ¶Ugolino, conte di Donoratico (1220?–1289), also known as Ugolino da Pi·sa \dä-'pē-sä\, celebrated by Dante in *Divina commedia;* fought against Genoa (1256) and Sardinia (1267); conspired to seize power in Pisa, imprisoned (1274); escaped and allied himself with Florentine and Luccan Guelphs then at war with Pisa; recalled by Pisa (1276) and distinguished himself against Genoa; reputedly contrived defeat of Pisans by Genoese at battle of Meloria (1284); elected podestà of Pisa (1285); concluded peace with Florence; overthrown by Archbishop Ruggieri degli Ubaldini; imprisoned (1288) with two sons and two grandsons in tower of Gualandi, where they starved to death. ¶Gaddo, conte di Donoratico (d. 1320), overthrew Uguccione della Faggiulola and assumed signoria (lordship) of Pisa (1316); governed justly. ¶Fazzio, conte di Donoratico (d. 1340 or 1341), led insurrection against despot Castruccio Castracani; elected captain of Pisa; maintained good relations with Naples and the Vatican. His son ¶Ranieri (d. 1347) succeeded Fazzio as lord of Pisa; last of his family to play important role in politics.

Gheyn \'gīn\, Matthias van den. 1721–1785. Belgian composer and musician. Organist at Church of St. Peter, Louvain (1741 ff.); carillonneur of Louvain (1745 ff.). Outstanding virtuoso of carillon, known esp. for his brilliant improvisations. Composed for harpsichord, organ, and carillon.

Ghez·zi \'gāt-tsē\, Pier Leone. 1674–1755. Italian artist. Made religious paintings for Roman churches; best known for penned and etched caricatures of citizens and tourists of Rome, making him perhaps first professional caricaturist.

Ghi·ber·ti \gē-'ber-tē\, Lorenzo. c.1378–1455. Florentine sculptor. Constructed bronze doors in International Gothic style for Baptistery of Florence cathedral (1403–24); made three bronze statues for Or San Michele, Florence (1412–28) and reliefs for Siena cathedral (1417–27); his greatest work, a second set of bronze doors (known as *Gates of Paradise*) for Baptistery of Florence cathedral (1425–52) in a Renaissance style. Wrote three treatises on art history and theory.

Ghi·ca *or* **Ghi·ka** *or* **Ghy·ka** \'gē-kä\. Romanian boyar family of Albanian origin that contributed ten princes (hospodars) to the thrones of Moldavia and Walachia, most serving at the pleasure of Turkish suzerains. Members included: Gheorghe (c.1600–1664), designated prince of Moldavia (1658–59) and of Walachia (1659–60). His son ¶Grigore I ruled Walachia (1660–64, 1672–73). His grandson ¶Grigore II (d. 1752) ruled Moldavia (1726–33, 1735–41, 1747–48) and Walachia (1733–35, 1748–52); fought against Russia in Russo-Turkish War (1736–39). His son ¶Matei was prince of Walachia (1752) and Moldavia (1753–56). His brother ¶Scarlat ruled Moldavia (1757–58) and Walachia (1758–61, 1765–66). His son ¶Alexandru I succeeded to Walachia (1766–68). His uncle ¶Grigore III (d. 1777) reigned in Moldavia (1764–67, 1774–77) and Walachia (1768–69). ¶Grigore IV (1765–1834) was prince of Walachia (1822–28). His brother ¶Alexandru II (1795–1862) was last nonelected prince of Walachia (1834–42); unpopular with boyars and nationalist leaders; as deputy prince of Walachia (1856–58), contributed to Romanian unification. ¶Grigore V (1807–1857) was last prince of Moldavia (1849–56); ardent nationalist.

¶Ion Ghica (1816–1897), cousin of Alexandru II; exiled for prominent part in revolution of 1848; prince of Samos (1854–59); returned to Romania (1866) and helped Prince Charles replace Alexandru Cuza; prime minister of Romania (1866, 1870–71); secured Turkish approval of accession of Prince Charles as Carol I; Romanian minister in London (1880–87); also known as man of letters.

Ghil \gēl\, René. 1862–1925. French poet. Advanced (1888) a theory of basing poetry on science and endeavored to create "scientific poetry." Wrote *Dire du mieux* (1889–97), *Dire des sangs* (1889), etc.

Ghirlandajo *or* **Ghirlandaio,** Domenico. See Domenico BIGORDI.

Ghi·yās-ud-Dīn Tugh·luq \gē-'(y)äs-ůd-'dēn-'tůg-lůk\. *Also called* Tughluq Shah. *Orig.* Ghā·zī Ma·lik \gä-'zē-'mä-lēk\. d. 1325. Sultan of Delhi (1320–25). Founder of Tughluq dynasty; extended his domain, capturing Telingara (1323) and bringing Bengal back under sultanate rule; successfully repelled Mongol raids; succeeded by his son Muḥammad ibn Tughluq.

Ghose, Sri Aurobindo. See AUROBINDO.

Ghu·lam Ah·mad \'gü-lam-'ak-mad\, Mirza. c.1839–1908. Indian religious. Founded (1889) a Muslim sect based on his claims of waging a peaceful jihad for Islām and being the reincarnation of both Jesus Christ and Muḥammad.

Ghū·rid \'gü-rid, 'gůr-əd\. Muslim dynasty centered in Ghūr in northwestern Afghanistan from the mid-12th to the early 13th centuries. Its greatest ruler, Mu'izz-ud-Dīn Muḥammad of Ghūr (*q.v.*), extended his domain into northern India.

Ghyka. See GHICA.

Gia·co·met·ti \,jäk-ō-'mät-tē\, Alberto. 1901–1966. Swiss sculptor. Resident chiefly in Paris (from 1922). Produced abstract sculptures influenced by Egyptian and primitive art, Cubism, and Surrealism, as *Torso* (1925), *The Spoon-Woman* (1926), *Observing Head* (1927–28), *Three Figures Outdoors* (1929), *Suspended Ball* (1931), *The Palace at 4 A.M.* (1932–33). Developed (from 1935) a more realistic, ideosyncratic, skeletal style and became noted for his attenuated sculptures of solitary figures, including *City Square* (1948), *Tall Figure* (1949), *The Forest* (1950), *Chariot* (1950), *Walking Man* (1960), *Figure Standing* (1964), *Head of Diego* (1965), *Bust of Elie Lotar* (1965). Also executed paintings, as *The Artist's Mother* (1950) and *Caroline* (1961), and lithographs *Paris sansfin* (1958–65).

Giacomo, Salvatore di. See DI GIACOMO.

Giacomo da Ponte. See Jacopo BASSANO.

Gia·co·sa \jä-'kō-sä\, Giuseppe. 1847–1906. Italian dramatist. His plays included *Una partita a scacchi* (1873), *I tristi amori* (1888), *Come le foglie* (1900). Collaborated with Luigi Illica on librettos of *La Bohème, Madame Butterfly, Tosca.*

Gia Long \gē-'ä-'lòŋ\. *Orig.* Nguyen Phuc Anh \'ŋï-(y)en-'pü-kän, 'nï-\. 1762–1820. Emperor of Vietnam (1802–20). Aided by the French, gained control of Vietnam, winning decisive victories (1802) at Hue and Hanoi; proclaimed himself emperor with title Gia Long and founded the Nguyen dynasty (1802–1945). His reign noted for conservative policies; refused to improve industry and foreign trade and attempted to isolate Vietnam from European influence; repaired old Mandarin Road, built public granaries, established efficient postal system, instituted monetary and legal reforms; secured Cambodia as vassal state; succeeded by his son, Emperor Minh Mang.

Giam·bo·lo·gna \,jäm-bō-'lōn-yä\. *Also called* Giovanni da Bo·lo·gna \bō-'lōn-yä\ *or* Jean Bou·logne \bü-lòn^y\. 1529–1608. Flemish sculptor. To Rome (c.1555), Florence (1557); patronized by Francesco de' Medici; became foremost Mannerist sculptor of the day. Works included bronze *Bacchus, Fountain of Neptune* at Bologna (1563–66), *Samson and a Philistine* (1567), *Rape of the Sabines* (1579–83), *Mercury* fountain at Florence (c.1580), equestrian statue of Cosimo I in Florence (1587–94), altarpieces and reliefs for Lucca cathedral and other churches, garden sculpture, esp. for Medici villas.

Giam·bo·no \jäm-'bō-nō\, Michele. *Orig.* Michele di Tad·deo Bo·no \'täd-dā-ō-'bō-nō\. fl. 1420–1462. Italian painter. Probably student of Jacobello del Fiore; active in Venice; painted in Late Gothic style. Works included *Madonna, St. Crisogono, St. Michael,* and mosaics of Mascoli Chapel in St. Mark's, Venice.

Gi·an·ni·ni \,jē-ə-'nē-nē\, Amadeo Peter. 1870–1949. American banker, b. San Jose, Calif. Established Bank of Italy in San Francisco (1904); opened branch in San Jose (1909) and later in other California cities, thereby creating first system of regional branch banking in U.S. Organized (1928) Transamerica Corporation as holding company for his bank stock; consolidated (1930) his banks into Bank of America National Trust and Savings Association, which grew (by 1948) into largest bank in U.S.

Gian·no·ne \jän-'nō-nā\, Pietro. 1676–1748. Italian historian. Excommunicated for his anti-papal, pro-secular-government *Istoria civile del regno di Napoli* (1723); exile in Vienna, Venice, Geneva; kidnapped (1736) by agents of Sardinian government and imprisoned for rest of life. Also wrote *Il triregno, ossia del regno del cielo, della terra, e del papa* (1895) and *Autobiografia* (1905).

Gianuzzi, Giulio Pippi de'. See PIPPI DE' GIANUZZI.

Giar·di·ni \jär-'dē-nē\, Felice. 1716–1796. Italian violinist and composer. Studied violin under G.B. Somis, becoming a brilliant virtuoso. Successful in London (from 1750) as composer, violinist, concert director, teacher, impresario, and director (1755–95) of Italian Opera at King's Theatre; with colleagues J.C. Bach, K.F. Abel, and J.C. Fischer, a leader of new galant (Rococo) style; to Russia (1793), where he died. Composed operas, concertos, vocal works, chamber music, and keyboard works.

Gi·auque \jē-'ōk\, William Francis. 1895–1982. American chemist, b. Niagara Falls, Ont. Taught at U. of Calif., Berkeley (1922–81, professor from 1934); known for studies in low-temperature chemistry; invented (1933) adiabatic demagnetization method for obtaining temperatures near absolute zero; discovered (1929) isotopes of oxygen; helped experimentally establish quantum statistics and theory of entropy; awarded 1949 Nobel prize for chemistry.

Gib·bon \'gib-ən\, Edward. 1737–1794. English historian. M.P. (1774–80, 1781–83). Chief work, *The History of the Decline and Fall of the Roman Empire* (1776–88); also wrote *Essai sur l'étude de la littérature* (1761), *Memoirs of My Life and Writings* (1789), etc.

Gibbon, Perceval. 1879–1926. British writer, b. Wales. Author of *African Items* (verse, 1903), novels *Souls in Bondage* (1904), *Salvator* (1908), *Margaret Harding* (1911), and many short stories, esp. in collection *The Vrouw Grobelaar's Leading Cases* (1905).

Gib·bons \'gib-ənz\, Grinling. 1648–1721. English woodcarver and sculptor, b. Rotterdam. Employed by Sir Christopher Wren to carve the stalls in St. Paul's and other new London churches; did work for the king at Windsor, Whitehall, and Kensington.

Gibbons, James. 1834–1921. American prelate, b. Baltimore. Ordained Roman Catholic priest (1861). In charge of St. Bridget's Church, near Baltimore, and chaplain at Fort McHenry (1861–65). Consecrated titular bishop of Adramyttium (1868); head of the Vicariate Apostolic of North Carolina. Bishop of Richmond, Va. (1872); bishop of Baltimore (1877). Cardinal (1886). First chancellor (1889) of Catholic U., Washington, D.C. Author of *The Faith of Our Fathers* (1876), *Discourses and Sermons* (1908), *A Retrospect of Fifty Years* (1916).

Gibbons, Orlando. 1583–1625. English organist and composer. Organist of Chapel Royal (1604–25) and Westminster Abbey (1623–25). Composed anthems, keyboard music, madrigals, motets, and fantasies. His brothers ¶Edward (1568–c.1650) and ¶Ellis (1573–1603) and his son ¶Christopher (1615–1676) were all organists and composers.

Gibbs \'gibz\, James. 1682–1754. British architect, b. Scotland. Designed St. Martin-in-the-Fields Church, London (1722–26), Senate house at Cambridge (1722–30), and Radcliffe Camera at Oxford (1737–49).

Gibbs, Josiah Willard. 1839–1903. American physicist, b. New Haven, Conn. Professor of mathematical physics, Yale (1871–1903). Author of "On the Equilibrium of Heterogeneous Substances" (1876, 1878), *Elementary Princi-*

ples in Statistical Mechanics (1902), and papers on mathematical physics. His investigations established the basic theory for physical chemistry.

Gibbs, Oliver Wolcott. 1822–1908. American chemist, b. New York City. Professor at Harvard (1863–87), where he created a modern chemistry laboratory and introduced latest techniques and equipment from Europe; a founder (1863) and president (1895–1900) of National Academy of Sciences. Pioneer in spectroscopy; investigated chemistry of cobalt, platinum, and complex inorganic acids.

Gibbs, William Francis. 1886–1967. American naval architect and marine engineer, b. Philadelphia. Designed (1927) a ship employing numerous watertight compartments that made it extremely safe. In partnership (from 1929) with Daniel Hargate Cox in firm of Gibbs & Cox; with Cox, designed destroyers for U.S. navy (1933); designed (1940) standardized cargo-carrying Liberty ship which could be mass-produced rapidly; directed its production during World War II; after war, continued improvements in ship design and construction for military and civilian use, as in passenger liner *United States* (1952).

Gib·ran *or* **Jibran** \jüb-ˈrän\, Kahlil. *Arab. in full* Jubrān Khalīl Jubrān. 1883–1931. Syrian poet, novelist, essayist, and artist. Resident in New York City (1912 ff.); a founder of Pen League (1920). Influenced by William Blake, Nietzsche, the Bible; wrote in Arabic and English. His works, usually deeply religious and mystical in nature, included *ʻArā'-is al-murūj* (1910, *Nymphs of the Valley*), *Damʻah wa ibtisāmah* (1914, *A Tear and a Smile*), *The Madman* (1918), *The Forerunner* (1920), *al-Arwāḥ al-mutamarridah* (1920, *Spirits Rebellious*), *al-Ajniḥah al-mutakassirah* (1922, *Broken Wings*), *The Prophet* (1923), *al-Awasif* (1923, *The Storms*), *Sand and Foam* (1926), *Jesus, the Son of Man* (1928).

Gib·son \ˈgib-sən\, Charles Dana. 1867–1944. American illustrator, b. Roxbury, Mass. Contributed illustrations to magazines (*Life, Scribner's, Century, Harper's*); master of black-and-white drawing; created "Gibson girl" drawings delineating American ideal of femininity. Illustrated books. His drawings collected in *The Education of Mr. Pipp* (1899), *Americans* (1900), *A Widow and Her Friends* (1901), *The Social Ladder* (1902), *Our Neighbors* (1905).

Gibson, Edward. 1st Baron Ash·bourne \ˈash-ˌbō(ə)rn, -ˈbü(ə)rn, -ˌbərn\. 1837–1913. Irish jurist and politician. M.P. (1875–85); attorney general for Ireland (1877–80); created baron (1885); lord chancellor of Ireland (1885, 1886–92, 1895–1906).

Gibson, John. 1790–1866. English sculptor. Carved in Neoclassical style; his attempt (1847) to revive ancient Greek practice of tinting marble caused much controversy. Works included *Psyche Borne on the Wings of Zephyrus* (1816), *Mars and Cupid* (1819), statues of Queen Victoria for Liverpool (1847) and houses of Parliament (1850–55), and the polychromed *Tinted Venus* (1851–55).

Gibson, Josh. 1911–1947. American baseball player, b. Buena Vista, Ga. Catcher for Pittsburgh Crawfords (1927–29, 1932–36) and Homestead (Pa.) Grays (1930–31, 1937–46); said to have led Negro National League in home runs for 10 consecutive years and compiled career batting average of .347, thus earning him epithet the "Negro Babe Ruth"; barred from major leagues by unwritten rule against black ballplayers. Elected to Baseball Hall of Fame (1972).

Gibson, Thomas Mil·ner- \ˈmil-nər-\. 1806–1884. English politician. Added Milner to original surname Gibson (1839). M.P. (1837–39, 1841–68); president of Board of Trade (1859–66). A leading representative of "Manchester School" of economic and political liberalism; advocated repeal of Corn Laws and taxes on paper and newspapers.

Gibson, Wilfrid Wilson. 1878–1962. English poet. Wrote chiefly of workaday life of ordinary provincial English families; author of *Stonefolds* (1907), *Daily Bread* (1910), *Fires* (1912), *Thoroughfares* (1914), *Borderlands* (1914), *Livelihood* (1917), *Krindlesyke* (1922), *Kestrel Edge* (1924), *Hazards* (1930), *Coming and Going* (1938), *The Outpost* (1944), *Within Four Walls* (1950).

Gibson, William Hamilton. 1850–1896. American illustrator, b. Sandy Hook, Conn. Best known for illustrations of nature articles in *Harper's, Century,* and *Scribner's.* Collected works in *Pastoral Days* (1881), *Sharp Eyes* (1892), *Eye Spy* (1897), *My Studio Neighbors* (1898), *Our Native Orchids* (1905).

Gich·tel \ˈgiḵ-təl\, Johann Georg. 1638–1710. German theosophist. Developed a mystical theology that alienated him from orthodox Lutheran doctrine; disciple of Jakob Böhme and compiled first complete edition of Böhme's works (1682–83); founded a sect that survived in Holland and Germany until recent times; synthesized his doctrine in *Theosophia practica* (1701–22).

Gid·dings \ˈgid-iŋz\, Franklin Henry. 1855–1931. American sociologist, b. Sherman, Conn. Professor, Columbia (1894–1928). From Adam Smith's conception of shared moral reactions developed doctrine of "consciousness of kind." Author of *The Principles of Sociology* (1896), *The Responsible State* (1918), *Studies in the Theory of Human Society* (1922), *The Scientific Study of Human Society* (1924), etc.

Giddings, Joshua Reed. 1795–1864. American politician, b. Tioga Point (now Athens), Pa. Whig member from Ohio, U.S. House of Representatives (1838–42); violent antislavery advocate; censured by House for activities (1842); resigned, but was reelected and served (1842–59); opposed Mexican War and Compromise of 1850; joined Republican party (1854); U.S. consul general to Canada (1861–64).

Gide \zhēd\, André-Paul-Guillaume. 1869–1951. French writer. Works included stories, satires, and fables *Le Prométhée mal enchaîné* (1899), *L'Immoraliste* (1902), *La Porte étroite* (1909), *Les Caves du Vatican* (1914), *La Symphonie pastorale* (1919), *L'École des femmes* (1929), *Thésée* (1946); novel *Les Faux-Monnayeurs* (1926); verse and prose poetry *Le Traité du Narcisse* (1891), *La Tentative amoureuse* (1893), *Les Nourritures terrestres* (1897), *Le Retour de l'enfant prodigue* (1907), *Les Nouvelles nourritures* (1935); plays *Philoctète* (1899), *Le Roi Candaule* (1901), *Bethsabé* (1912), *Oedipe* (1931), *Perséphone* (1934), *Le Retour* (1946); criticism *Prétextes* (1903), *Incidences* (1924), *Interviews imaginaires* (1943), *Préfaces* (1948), *Rencontres* (1948), *Éloges* (1948); travel books; *Journal, 1889–1939* (1939) and *Journal, 1939–49* (1954); and other works, as *Si le grain ne meurt* (1926), *L'Affaire Redureau* (1930), *La Séquestrée de Poitiers* (1930), Jeunesse (1945), *Et Nunc Manet in Te* (1947–51), *Feuillets d'automne* (1949), *Littérature engagée* (1950). Awarded Nobel prize for literature (1947).

Gié, Seigneur de. See Pierre de Rohan under ROHAN family.

Gie·di·on \ˈgē-dē-ōn\, Sigfried. 1888–1968. Swiss art historian. One of first to successfully apply scholarly methods of analysis to 20th-century architecture. Author of *Space, Time and Architecture* (1941), *Mechanization Takes Command* (1948), etc.

Gier·ke \ˈgēr-kə\, Otto Friedrich von. 1841–1921. German legal scholar. Professor, Breslau (1871–84), Heidelberg (1884–87), Berlin (1887–1921). Leader of Germanist school of historical jurisprudence in opposition to Romanist theoreticians of German law. Author of *Das deutsche Genossenschaftsrecht* (1868–1913) and *Deutsches Privatrecht* (1895–1917). His son ¶Julius Karl Otto von Gierke (1875–1960), also a legal scholar; professor, Königsberg (1903), Halle (1919), Göttingen (1925); authority on commercial, insurance, and admiralty law.

Giers \ˈgyērs\, Nikolay Karlovich. 1820–1895. Russian politician. Minister to Teheran (1863), Bern (1869), and Stockholm (1872); married into family of Prince Gorchakov, whom he succeeded (1882–95) as minister of foreign affairs; concluded alliance with France (1891).

Gie·se·brecht \ˈgē-zə-ˌbreḵt\, Friedrich Wilhelm Benjamin von. 1814–1889. German historian. Student of Leopold von Ranke; professor at Königsberg (1857–62) and Munich (1862–89). Author of *Geschichte der deutschen Kaiserzeit* (1855–95, completed by B. von Simson), first general history of medieval Germany based on modern critical methods; also published *Jahrbücher des deutschen Reichs unter Otto II* (1840) and *Annales Altahenses* (1841).

Gie·se·king \ˈgē-zə-kiŋ\, Walter Wilhelm. 1895–1956. German pianist, b. France. On tours as concert pianist in Europe and America (from 1923); master of pedal technique; known for interpretations of Debussy, Ravel, Beethoven, Prokofiev, Domenico Scarlatti. Composed a set of variations and a sonata for flute and piano.

Gie·se·ler \ˈgē-zə-lər\, Johann Karl Ludwig. 1792–1854. German Protestant church historian. Professor of theology at Bonn (1819–31) and Göttingen (1831–54); wrote *Lehrbuch der Kirchengeschichte* (1824–57).

Gif·fard \ˈjif-ərd\, Hardinge Stanley. 1st Earl of Hals·bury \ˈhȯlz-b(ə-)rē\. 1823–1921. English politician. Solicitor general (1875); lord chancellor (1885–86, 1886–92, 1895–1905). Led diehards in House of Lords against Parliament Act (1911). Presided over preparation of digest of *Laws of England* (1905–16).

Gif·ford \ˈgif-ərd\, Edward Winslow. 1887–1959. American anthropologist, b. Oakland, Calif. With U. of Calif. Museum of Anthropology, Berkeley (1912–56; curator, 1925–47; director, 1947–56); developed it into a major U.S. collection. Taught at U. of Calif., Berkeley (1920–54; professor, 1947–54). Led anthropological expedition to Tonga Islands (1921) and archaeological expeditions to New Caledonia, Fiji, Yap. Author of *California Kinship Terminologies* (1922), *California Anthropometry* (1926), *Tongan Society* (1929), *World Renewal* (1949, with A.L. Kroeber), *Archaeological Excavations in Fiji* (1951).

Gifford, William. 1756–1826. English critic and poet. In *Baviad* (1794) and *Maeviad* (1795), ridiculed the Della Cruscans and the minor playwrights. First editor (1809–24) of *Quarterly Review;* credited with writing the magazine's attack on Keats's *Endymion* (1818). Edited Juvenal; translated Persius; edited plays of Massinger, Ben Jonson, and Ford.

Gi·gli \'jēl-yē\, Beniamino. 1890–1957. Italian operatic tenor. Member, Metropolitan Opera Co., New York City (1920–32); appeared in concert performances in Europe and South America (from 1932); made numerous films in Germany and Italy (1935–51); gave last concert (1955).

Gi·gnoux \zhēn-yü\, Maurice-Irénée-Marie. 1881–1955. French geologist. Professor at Grenoble (1925 ff.); known for studies on stratigraphy of the Mediterranean.

Gi·ka·ti·lla \ge-kä-'tē(l)-yä\, Joseph. 1248–c.1305. Spanish Kabbalist. Pupil of Abraham Abulafia; turned to mysticism and attempted to reconcile philosophy with the Kabbala. His *Ginnat 'egoz* greatly influenced Moses de León's *Zohar;* also wrote *Sha'are 'ora.*

Gil·bert \'gil-bərt\ of Sem·pring·ham \'sem-priŋ-əm\. Saint. *Also spelled* Guilbert. c.1083–1189. English religious. Ordained priest (1123); became parson of his native Sempringham. Founder (1131) of Ordo Gilbertinorum Canonicorum, commonly called Gilbertines; order approved by Pope Eugenius III and Gilbert confirmed as its first master general (1148). Supported Thomas Becket against Henry II. Canonized (1202).

Gilbert, Sir Alfred. 1854–1934. English sculptor and goldsmith. Among his works were a seated statue of Queen Victoria for Winchester (1887), memorial fountain (known as *Eros*) for Earl of Shaftesbury in Piccadilly Circus, London (1893), the tomb of Duke of Clarence in Albert Chapel at Windsor Castle (1926), and a memorial to Queen Alexandra in Marlborough House (1932).

Gilbert, Alfred Charles. 1884–1961. American businessman, b. Salem, Ore. Co-winner of gold medal in pole vault at Olympic Games in London (1908). Established (c.1909) Mysto Manufacturing Co., New Haven, Conn. (from 1916, A.C. Gilbert Co.); invented (1912) Erector Set toy kits; expanded toy line to include chemistry sets, radio kits, etc., for adolescents. Bought (1938) American Flyer Co., Chicago, and made its toy electric trains into one of leading lines in nation.

Gilbert, Cass. 1859–1934. American architect, b. Zanesville, Ohio. Among his works were the Minnesota capitol in St. Paul (1896–1903), the U.S. Custom House (1899–1905) and the Woolworth Building (1908–13) in New York City, the St. Louis (1912) and Detroit (1921) public libraries, the U.S. Treasury Annex (1918–19) and U.S. Supreme Court Building (completed 1935) in Washington, D.C., the West Virginia capitol in Charleston (1924–31), and the campuses of the universities of Minnesota (Minneapolis) and Texas (Austin).

Gilbert, Grove Karl. 1843–1918. American geologist, b. Rochester, N.Y. On surveys of George M. Wheeler to the Colorado River basin (1871–74) and of John Wesley Powell to Utah (1874–79); senior geologist (1879–89), chief geologist (1889–92), U.S. Geological Survey. First to apply concept of dynamic equilibrium to landform configuration and evolution; a founder of modern geomorphology. Author of *Report on the Geology of the Henry Mountains* (1877), *The Bonneville Monograph* (1890), *History of the Niagara River* (1890), and *Introduction to Physical Geography* (1902).

Gilbert, Henry Franklin Belknap. 1868–1928. American composer, b. Somerville, Mass. Studied under Edward A. MacDowell (1888–92); first composer to rely primarily on American folk music. His compositions included *Negro Episodes* (1903), *Comedy Overture* (1905), ballet *Dance in Place Congo* (1906), *Negro Rhapsody* (1912), *Indian Sketches* (1914), *American Dances in Rag-Time Rhythm* (1915), *Jazz Study* (1924), *Symphonic Piece* (1925), *Nocturne, after Whitman* (1925), chamber music, and songs.

Gilbert, Sir Humphrey. c.1539–1583. English navigator and soldier. Half-brother of Sir Walter Raleigh. Served under Sir Henry Sidney in Ireland (1566–70); served in Netherlands but failed to capture Goes (1572). Undertook expedition for exploration and colonization in New World (1578), but failed in first attempt (1579); in second attempt (1583) established first British colony in North America at St. John's, Newfoundland.

Gilbert, Sir John. 1817–1897. English painter and book illustrator. Painted romantic and historical subjects, as *Sir Lancelot du Lake* (1887); contributed drawings to *The Illustrated London News* (1842–72); illustrated many literary classics, esp. works of Scott (1857) and Shakespeare (1859–60).

Gilbert, Sir Joseph Henry. 1817–1901. English chemist. Collaborated with John Bennet Lawes in experiments at Rothamsted (1843–1900); professor of rural economy at Oxford (1884–90). Known for studies of nitrogen fertilizers and their effects on crops.

Gilbert, Marie Dolores Eliza Rosanna. See Lola MONTEZ.

Gil·bert \zhēl-ber\, Nicolas-Joseph-Laurent. 1751–1780. French poet. Known for satirical poems *Le Dix-huitième siècle* (1775) and *Mon apologie* (1778).

Gil·bert \'gil-bərt\, Rufus Henry. 1832–1885. American physician and inventor, b. Guilford, N.Y. Patented (1870) elevated railway system; incorporated Gilbert Elevated Railway Co. (1872); railway built in New York City (1876–78).

Gilbert *or* **Gyl·berde** \'gil-bərd\, William. 1544–1603. English physician and physicist. Practiced medicine in London (1573 ff.); physician to Elizabeth I (1601) and James I (1603). His experiments in magnetism, and his use for the first time of terms *electric force, electric attraction,* and *magnetic pole* gained him title of "father of electricity." His treatise *De magnete, magneticisque corporibus, et de magno magnete tellure* (1600) was the first great scientific work published in England; also left manuscript published (1651) as *De mundo nostro sublunari philosophia nova,* which held modern views on structure of universe.

Gil·bert \'gil-bərt\, Sir William Schwenck. 1836–1911. English playwright. First literary work, *Bab Ballads* (1869, 1873). Began collaboration with Arthur Sullivan (Gilbert writing the librettos, Sullivan the music) with the burlesque *Thespis* (1871), and continued with highly popular comic operas, performed by D'Oyly Carte's opera company, *Trial by Jury* (1875), *The Sorcerer* (1877), *H.M.S. Pinafore* (1878), *The Pirates of Penzance* (1879), *Patience* (1881), *Iolanthe* (1882), *Princess Ida* (1884), *The Mikado* (1885), *Ruddigore* (1887), *The Yeomen of the Guard* (1888), *The Gondoliers* (1889), *Utopia, Limited* (1893), *The Grand Duke* (1896). Also wrote independently *The Palace of Truth* (1870), *Pygmalion and Galatea* (1871), *The Wicked World* (1873), *The Happy Land* (1873), *Charity* (1874), *Broken Hearts* (1875), *Dan'l Druce* (1876).

Gilbert Cris·pin \-'kris-pən\. d. c.1117. Anglo-Norman cleric. Benedictine monk at Bec, Normandy; abbot of Westminster (from c.1085). Deeply influenced by his friend St. Anselm of Canterbury. His historical and doctrinal works included *Disputatio Iudaei et Christiani, De simoniacis, De Spirito Sancto,* and *Disputatio Christiani cum gentili.*

Gil·bert de La Por·rée \zhēl-ber-də-lá-pòr-ā\. 1076–1154. French scholastic theologian. Chancellor of Chartres cathedral (1126–36); bishop of Poiters (1142); accused of trinitarian heresy by St. Bernard (1147) but exonerated; considered influential in introducing Aristotelian philosophy in France.

Gil·bert Fo·liot \'gil-bərt-'fōl-yō\. c.1110–1187. Anglo-Norman cleric. Abbot of Gloucester (1139); bishop of Hereford (1148); unsuccessful rival of Thomas Becket for archbishopric of Canterbury; bishop of London (1163) but refused to profess obedience to Becket; confessor to Henry II and strongly supported Henry against Becket.

Gil·breth \'gil-breth\, Frank Bunker. 1868–1924. American engineer and efficiency expert, b. Fairfield, Me. General contractor in Boston (1895–1904) and New York (1904–11); consulting engineer (from 1911). With his wife, developed method of time-and-motion study as applied to work habits of industrial workers. Author of *Primer of Scientific Management* (1911). His wife (m. 1904) ¶Lillian Evelyn, *nee* Mol·ler \'mäl-ər\ (1878–1972), also an engineer, took over her husband's efficiency-engineering projects at his death. Professor of management, U. of Wisconsin (1955). Author of *Psychology of Management* (1912), *The Home-Maker and Her Job* (1927). Collaborated with husband in *Motion Study* (1911), *Fatigue Study* (1919), *Time Study* (1920), etc.

Gilchrist. See HAROLD GILLE.

Gilchrist, Percy Carlyle. See Sidney G. THOMAS.

Gil·das \'gil-dəs\. *Called* the Wise. d. 570. British monk and historian. Founded St. Gildas de Rhuys monastery in Brittany. Author of *De excidio et conquestu Britanniae,* a history of Britain from earliest times.

Gil de Hon·ta·ñón \'kēl-dā-ōn-tän-'yōn\, Juan. c.1480–1526. Spanish architect. Worked in Burgos with Simon of Cologne. Official architect of Segovia cathedral, designing it in late medieval style and laying cornerstone (1525). His son ¶Rodrigo (c.1500–1577) succeeded (1526) as official architect of Segovia cathedral and completed the project; his style a mixture of late medieval and second Plateresque; also designed Monterrey Palace in Salamanca (1539), University of Alcalá de Henares (completed 1553), cathedral of Astorga (1559), church of Las Bernardas, Salamanca (1563); also worked on Salamanca cathedral (after 1538).

Gil·der \'gil-dər\, Richard Watson. 1844–1909. American poet and editor, b. Bordentown, N.J. Assistant editor, *Scribner's Monthly* (1870–81); editor, *Century* (1881–1909). Published volumes of verse as *The New Day* (1876), *Two Worlds* (1891), *The Fire Divine* (1907).

Gil·der·sleeve \'gil-dər-,slēv\, Basil Lanneau. 1831–1924. American philologist, b. Charleston, S.C. Professor of Greek, U. of Virginia (1856–76), Johns Hopkins (1876–1915). Founded (1880) and edited (1880–1920) *American Journal of Philology.* Author of *A Latin Grammar* (1867), *Syntax of Classical Greek from Homer to Demosthenes* (Part I, 1900; Part II, with C.W.E. Miller, 1911).

Gil·do \'gil-(,)dō\. d. 398 A.D. Moorish ruler in northern Africa. Helped Romans defeat his brother Firmus (375); as reward, given command of army and appointed count of Africa; his revolt against Rome (397–398) crushed by Roman army headed by his brother Mascezel.

Gil Eanes. See EANES.

Giles \'jī(ə)lz\ of As·si·si \ə-'sis-ē, -'sē-zē, -'sē-sē, -'siz-ē\. *Lat.* Ae·gid·i·us \i-'gid-ē-əs\. c.1190–1262. Italian religious. Third companion of St. Francis of Assisi; became widely famous for mystical raptures and for pithy sayings collected in *Dicta* or *Golden Sayings.*

Giles of Rome. *Lat.* Aegidius Ro·ma·nus \rō-'män-əs\. *Honorific name* Doctor Fun·da·tis·si·mus \,fən-də-'tis-ə-məs\, *i.e.* best-grounded teacher. *Orig.* Egidio Co·lon·na \kō-'lōn-nä\. c.1245–1316. Italian theologian and prelate. Member of Colonna family (*q.v.*); joined Augustinian Hermits (c.1257); studied in Paris (1260–72), perhaps under Thomas Aquinas; provincial (1283), vicar general (1285), general (1292–95), of Augustinian Hermits; taught theology at U. of Paris (1285–91). Archbishop of Bourges (1295); supported Pope Boniface VIII against Philip IV of France, esp. with *De ecclesiastica potestate* (1301). Scholastic theologian, basing his philosophy on Augustinian and Thomistic doctrines; wrote theological treatises and commentaries on Aristotle and the Bible.

Giles, Herbert Allen. 1845–1935. English Oriental scholar. Member of China consular service (1867–93); professor of Chinese, Cambridge U. (1897–1932). Compiler of a *Chinese-English Dictionary* (1892) and a *Chinese Biographical Dictionary* (1897); author of *Chinese Sketches* (1876), *Confucianism and its Rivals* (1915), *Chaos in China* (1924), etc. Modified Sir Thomas F. Wade's Chinese transcription system, now known as Wade-Giles system.

Gilianes. See Gil EANES.

Gil·kin \zhēl-kaⁿ\, Iwan. 1858–1923. Belgian writer. A founder of *La Jeune Belgique* (1881). Author of verse *La Nuit* (1897) and *Le Cerisier fleuri* (1899), and plays *Savonarole* (1906), *Étudiants russes* (1906), and *Le Roi Cophétua* (1919).

Gill, André. See GOSSET DE GUINES.

Gill \'gil\, Sir David. 1843–1914. Scottish astronomer. Director of James L. Lindsay's private observatory near Aberdeen (1872–76); astronomer royal at Cape of Good Hope (1879–1907). A pioneer in applying photography to astronomy; known for measurements of solar and stellar parallax; made photographic survey of southern heavens (1885–98).

Gill, Eric, *in full* Arthur Eric Rowton. 1882–1940. English sculptor, engraver, and typographic designer. As sculptor, inspired English revival of direct carving in stone; carved *Mother and Child* (1912), stations of the cross for Westminster cathedral (1914–18), *Mankind* (1928), relief *Prospero and Ariel* over entrance of Broadcasting House, London (1931), and three bas-reliefs of *The Creation of Adam* in Palace of Nations, Geneva (1935–38). With Douglas Pepler, founded (1915) St. Dominic's Press and contributed wood engravings and lettering to it; remembered esp. for his hundreds of engravings for Golden Cockerel Press (from 1924), esp. for *Four Gospels* (1931). Designed typefaces Perpetua (1925), Gill Sans Serif (1927), Joanna (1930), Bunyan (1934; renamed Pilgrim, 1953). Author of *Christianity and Art* (1927), *Work and Property* (1937), *Autobiography* (1940), etc.

Gill, Irving John. 1870–1936. American architect, b. Lakeside, Calif. Draftsman with architectural firm of Adler & Sullivan, Chicago; practiced in San Diego (from 1892). Introduced a severe, geometrical style in California; among first to eliminate ornamentation from his buildings and to construct slab-tilt walls. Works included Wilson Acton Hotel (1908; now Hotel Cabrillo) and Women's Club (1913), both in La Jolla, Calif., and Dodge House in Los Angeles (1916).

Gill, Theodore Nicholas. 1837–1914. American zoologist, b. New York City. Member of staff, Smithsonian Institution, Washington, D.C. (from 1861); senior assistant librarian, Library of Congress (1866–74). Taught at Columbian College (1860–1910). Specialist in ichthyology.

Gil·lam \'gil-əm\, Bernhard. 1856–1896. American political cartoonist, b. Banbury, England. To U.S. (1866). Noted for his cartoons influential in presidential campaigns. Worked with Thomas Nast on *Harper's Weekly* (1880); with *Puck* (1881); part owner and director in chief of comic weekly *Judge* (1886–96).

Gille \zhēl\, Philippe-Émile-François. 1831–1901. French playwright and literary critic. Author of, or collaborator in writing, the librettos of *Vent du soir* (1857) and *Les Bergers* (1865), both with music by Offenbach, *Le Bœuf apis* (1865), *Jean de Nivelle* (1880), *Lakmé* (1883), the last three with music by Delibes.

Gil·len \'gil-ən\, Francis James. 1856–1912. Australian anthropologist. Collaborated with Sir Baldwin Spencer on first major studies of Australian Aborigines; with him published *The Native Tribes of Central Australia* (1899) and *The Northern Tribes of Central Australia* (1904).

Gilles li Mui·sis \zhēl-lē-mwʸē-zē\. *Also called* Le Mui·set \lə-mwʸē-ze\. 1272–1352. French chronicler. Prior (1329), abbot (1331), of Benedictine abbey of Saint-Martin in Tournai. Wrote in Latin *Chronicon majus* and *Chronicon minus,* important sources for history of France; also author of moralistic poems in Tournaisien dialect.

Gil·les·pie \gə-'les-pē\, Eliza Maria. *Known as* Mother Angela. 1824–1887. American religious, b. Brownsville, Pa. Entered (1853) sole American convent of French order of Sisters of Holy Cross; superior of the order in America (1854–69); on establishment (1869) of order as independent branch in America, was made its provincial superior and is considered its founder. Known as educator; as director (1855) of St. Mary's College, South Bend, Ind., greatly improved its curriculum; directed her order's establishment (1855–82) of 45 institutions, including St. Mary's Academy, Austin, Tex. (1874), St. Catherine's Normal Institute, Baltimore (1875), and Holy Cross Academy, Washington, D.C. (1878).

Gillespie, George. 1613–1648. Scottish clergyman. A leader of Church of Scotland; negotiated with Church of England so his church could diverge from Anglican worship and doctrine (1640); represented Church of Scotland in Westminster Assembly (1643); drafted legislation sanctioning Presbyterian directory of public worship and confession of faith (1645).

Gillespie, Thomas. 1708–1774. Scottish clergyman. Deposed by general assembly of Scottish Presbyterian church (1752); with his followers formed a presbytery and founded the Relief Church in Scotland (1761).

Gil·lett \jə-'let\, Frederick Huntington. 1851–1935. American politician, b. Westfield, Mass. Member, U.S. House of Representatives (1893–1925), and speaker (1919–25); member, U.S. Senate (1925–31).

Gil·lette \jə-'let\, King Camp. 1855–1932. American inventor and businessman, b. Fond du Lac, Wis. Invented the safety razor (1895–1901); organized and headed Gillette Safety Razor Co. (1901–32). Author of *Human Drift* (1894), *Gillette's Industrial Solution* (1900), *The People's Corporation* (1924).

Gillette, William Hooker. 1855–1937. American actor, b. Hartford, Conn. Best known for his dramatization and portrayal (1899) of Conan Doyle's *Sherlock Holmes;* his other plays included *Esmeralda* (1881), *Held by the Enemy* (1886), *Secret Service* (1895).

Gil·liss \'gil-əs\, James Melville. 1811–1865. American naval officer and astronomer, b. Georgetown (now in Washington, D.C.). In U.S. navy (1827–55). Instrumental in obtaining appropriation for new Naval Observatory in Washington (1841–44). In charge, expedition to Santiago, Chile, to study Venus and Mars and determine solar parallax (1849–52); observed solar eclipse in Peru (1858) and in Washington Territory (1860). Director, Naval Observatory, Washington, D.C. (1861–65).

Gil·lot \zhē-lō\, Claude. 1673–1722. French painter, engraver, and theatrical designer. Best known as master of Watteau and Lancret. Painted sportive, mythological subjects, as *Feast of Pan* and *Feast of Bacchus;* engraved popular scenes and courtly comic adventures.

Gill·ray \'gil-,rā\, James. 1756–1815. English caricaturist. Known esp. for his political caricatures, many satirizing the royal family.

Gil·ly \'gil-ē\, Friedrich. 1772–1800. German architect. Teacher of Leo von Klenze and Karl Schinkel; designed influential but unrealized plans for a monument to Frederick the Great of Prussia (1796–97) and for Prussian National Theater (1798).

Gil·man \'gil-mən\, Charlotte Anna, *nee* Per·kins \'pər-kənz\. 1860–1935. American feminist and writer, b. Hartford, Conn. m. 2d George H. Gilman (1900). Lecturer on feminism and Socialism; published and edited monthly *Forerunner* (1909–16). Author of stories, notably "The Yellow Wall-Paper" (1892), verse *In This Our World* (1893), and nonfiction *Women and Economics* (1898), *Concerning Children* (1900), *The Home* (1903), *Human Work* (1904), *The Man-Made World* (1911), etc.

Gilman, Daniel Coit. 1831–1908. American educator, b. Norwich, Conn. Drew up plans for a scientific school at Yale (1856); librarian, secretary, and professor of geography, Sheffield Scientific School, Yale (1861–72). President, U. of California (1872–75); first president, Johns Hopkins (1875–1901); first president, Carnegie Institution of Washington, D.C. (1901–04). President, National Civil Service Reform League (1901–07).

Gil·mer \'gil-mər\, Elizabeth, *nee* Mer·i·weth·er \'mer-ē-,weth-ər\. *Pseudonym* Dorothy Dix \'diks\. 1870–1951. American journalist, b. near Woodstock, Tenn. m. George O. Gilmer (1888). Editor of woman's department, New Orleans *Picayune* (1896–1901); began writing her famous column of advice to the lovelorn. Joined staff of New York *Journal* (1901), Wheeler Syndicate (1917), Ledger Syndicate (1923), and Bell Syndicate (1933). Author of *Mirandy* (1914), *Hearts à la Mode* (1915), *How to Win and Hold a Husband* (1939), etc.

Gil·more \'gil-,mō(ə)r, -,mȯ(ə)r\, Patrick Sarsfield. 1829–1892. American bandmaster, b. near Dublin, Ireland. To U.S. (1848). Director of Boston Brigade Band (1859) and New York 22d Regiment Band (1872–92; each also called Gilmore's Band). Noted for flamboyant showmanship and innovations in instrumentation; organized in Boston (1869, 1872) concerts with over 10,000 performers. Composer (1863), under pseudonym Louis Lambert, of "When Johnny Comes Marching Home Again."

Gil·pin \'gil-pən\, Bernard. 1517–1583. English clergyman. Rector at Houghton-le-Spring (1558–83); after some hesitation, supported royal supremacy over Anglican church; his annual journeys through neglected sections of Northumberland and Yorkshire, where he preached and ministered to the poor, gained him the title "Apostle of the North."

Gilpin, Charles Sidney. 1878–1930. American actor, b. Richmond, Va. One of first black actors to gain wide following on American stage. Broadway debut as William Custis in Drinkwater's *Abraham Lincoln* (1919); great success as Brutus Jones in O'Neill's *Emperor Jones* (1920–24).

Gilpin, William. 1724–1804. English writer. His poetical accounts of his travels throughout British Isles set a fashion for picturesque travel books.

Gil Po·lo \k̲ēl-'pō-lō\, Gaspar. c.1530–1591. Spanish poet. Author of the romance *La Diana enamorada,* a continuation of Montemayor's *Diana* (1564).

Gil Ro·bles y Qui·ño·nes \k̲ēl-'rō-blā-sē-kēn-'yō-nās\, José María. 1898–1980. Spanish politician. Editor of Catholic newspaper *El Debate* (1922); leader of Catholic faction Acción Popular (1931); organized (1933) right-wing coalition Confederación Española de Derechos Autónomos, a major force in Spanish politics of 1930s; minister of war (1934–35); fled to Portugal (1936). Returned to Spain (1953); leader of Christian Democratic movement.

Gil·son \zhēl-sōⁿ\, Étienne-Henry. 1884–1978. French philosopher. Professor at the Sorbonne (1921–32) and Collège de France (1932–51); helped found Pontifical Institute of Medieval Studies at U. of Toronto (1929). Authority on history of philosophy and a leading exponent of Thomism. Author of *Le Thomisme* (1922), *La Philosophie au Moyen-Age* (1922), *L'Esprit de la philosophie médiévale* (1932), *Christianisme et philosophie* (1936), etc.

Gil y Zá·ra·te \'k̲ē-lē-'thä-rä-tā\, Antonio. 1793–1861. Spanish dramatist. Works included *Un año después de la boda* (1826), *Blanca de Borbón* (1829), *Carlos II el Hechizado* (1837), *Guzmán el Bueno* (1842), *Un amigo en el candelero* (1842).

Gim·bel \'gim-bəl\. Family of American merchants, owners of a chain of department stores whose members came from Vincennes, Ind., including: Jacob (1850–1922) and his brother ¶Isaac (1856–1931), sons of a Bavarian immigrant; entered father's Palace of Trade store, Vincennes; opened branches in Milwaukee (1889), Philadelphia (1894), New York City (1910); organized Gimbel Bros., Inc. (1922), of which Isaac was president (1922–27), chairman (1927–31); by 1930 largest department store chain in the world. Other brothers associated in the firm were ¶Charles (1861–1932) and ¶Ellis A. (1865–1950). Isaac's son ¶Bernard Feustmann (1885–1966) joined the firm (1907).

Gim·son \'gim-sən, 'jim-\, Ernest. 1864–1920. English furniture designer. One of Cotswold school of designers who sought to combine rural craftsmanship with ideas of William Morris; worked at Daneway House, Sapperton (from 1902); known esp. for his set of pews and kneeling benches in St. Andrews Chapel of Westminster cathedral (c.1912).

Gi·na·ste·ra \ˌk̲ē-nə-'ster-ə\, Alberto Evaristo. 1916–1983. Argentine composer. Classified his own artistic evolution into three segments: objective nationalism (1936–48), subjective nationalism (1948–54), and neoexpressionism (1958–83). Composed his first recognized work, ballet *Panambí* (1936), as an imaginary re-creation of primitive Indian rites; in later compositions used rhythms and motifs of music of pampas; used a variety of techniques, including the integration of microtones, serial procedures, and chance music as well as traditional forms. Composed operas *Don Rodrigo* (1964), *Bomarzo* (1967), *Beatrix Cenci* (1971), and *Barabbas* (1977); also composed concerti, vocal and chamber music, and film scores.

Gi·ner de los Rí·os \k̲ē-'nār-t̲h̲ā-lōs-'rē-ōs\, Francisco. 1839–1915. Spanish educator. Professor of philosophy of law at Madrid (1866 ff.), but often dismissed (1867, 1875–81) for liberal ideas. Founded Institución Libre de Enseñazana, Madrid (1876); most influential exponent of *krausismo,* a liberal educational and philosophical movement based on teachings of Karl Krause. Works included *Estudios de literatura y arte* (1876), *Estudios sobre educación* (1886), *Filosofía y sociología* (1904), *Resumen de filosofía del derecho* (1912).

Gin·kel \'giŋ-kəl\, Godard van Ree·de- \vän-'rā-də-\. 1st Earl of Ath·lone \ath-'lōn\. 1644–1703. Dutch general in British service. Accompanied William of Orange to England (1688); in command of English forces in Ireland (from July 1690); captured Athlone, won victory of Aughrim, took Limerick (all 1691), thus completing conquest of Ireland for William. Created earl of Athlone and Baron Aughrim (1692).

Ginn \'gin\, Edwin. 1838–1914. American publisher, b. near Orland, Me. Opened publishing house, Boston (1867), known as Ginn & Co. (from 1885); esp. successful in textbook field.

Gins·burg \'ginz-ˌbərg\, Christian David. 1831–1914. British Hebrew and biblical scholar, b. Poland. Adopted Christian faith (1846); to England, naturalized (1858); an original member of Old Testament revision group. Works included translations with commentaries of Song of Solomon, Ecclesiastes, and Leviticus, treatises on the Karaites, the Essenes, and the Kabbalah, an edition of the Masorah (1880–86), and *Introduction to the Massoretico-Critical Edition of the Hebrew Bible* (1897).

Ginz·berg \'gyins-byirg\, Asher. *Pseudonym* Aḥad Ha·'am *or* Achad Ha-am \á-'k̲ád-há-'ám\. 1856–1927. Russian Zionist leader. Member of Ḥovevei Ẕiyyon movement; published several collections of essays, including *'Al parashat derakhim* (1895), in which he urged Hebrew cultural and spiritual rebirth; emphasized rational and moral aspects of Judaism; supported creation of homeland in Palestine.

Ginz·berg \'ginz-ˌbərg\, Louis. 1873–1953. American Judaic scholar, b. Kovno, Lithuania. To U.S. (1899); professor of Talmud at Jewish Theol. Sem., New York (1902–53). Wrote *Legends of the Jews* (1909–38) and *Commentary on the Palestinian Talmud* (1941, in Hebrew).

Gio·ber·ti \jō-'ber-tē\, Vincenzo. 1801–1852. Italian philosopher and politician. Ordained Roman Catholic priest (1825); imprisoned (1833) for advocating a united Italy; premier of Sardinia (1848–49); ambassador at Paris (1849–51). Attacked Cartesianism and developed a philosophy called ontologism. Author of *Introduzione allo studio della filosofia* (1839–40), *Del primato morale e civile degli italiani* (1843), *Del rinnovamento civile d'Italia* (1851).

Gio·con·do \jō-'kōn-dō\, Lisa di Anton Maria del, *nee* Ghe·rar·di·ni \ˌgā-rär-'dē-nē\. *Called* La Gio·con·da \lä-jō-'kōn-dä\. fl. 1500. Florentine noblewoman. Wife of Francesco del Giocondo; subject of Leonardo da Vinci's masterpiece portrait *Mona Lisa.*

Gio·lit·ti \jō-'lēt-tē\, Giovanni. 1842–1928. Italian politician. In civil service (1862–82); deputy in parliament (1882–1928); minister of the treasury (1889–90). Prime minister of Italy (1892–93, 1903–05, 1906–09, 1911–14, 1920–21). Opposed Italy's entry into World War I.

Gio·no \zhyó-nō\, Jean. 1895–1970. French novelist. Author of novels depicting esp. peasant life in remote districts of the Basses-Alpes; works included *Un de Baumugnes* (1929), *Regain* (1930), *Le Chante du monde* (1934), *Que ma joie demeure* (1935), *Les Grands Chemins* (1951), *Le Hussard sur le toit* (1952), *Le Moulin de Pologne* (1952), *Le Bonheur fou* (1957), *Deux cavaliers de l'orage* (1965), *Ennemonde et autres caractères* (1967).

Gior·da·ni \jōr-'dä-nē\, Pietro. 1774–1848. Italian patriot and writer. His works included critical essays, eulogies as *Panegirico a Napoleone,* pamphlets, addresses, and *Epistolario* in *Opere complete* (14 vols., 1854–65).

Gior·da·no \jōr-'dä-nō\, Luca. *Nicknamed* Luca fa pre·sto \fä-'pres-tō\. 1632–1705. Neapolitan painter. Influenced at first by José de Ribera, later by Pietro da Cortona; court painter to Charles II of Spain (1692–1702). Painted oils and frescoes chiefly on religious and mythological themes. Executed frescoes in Palazzo Medici-Riccardi (1682–83) and Corsini Chapel of Sta. Maria del Carmine (1682), both Florence; S. Felippo Neri, Naples (1684), El Escorial, Spain, and Cappella del Tesoro in S. Martino, Naples (1702–04).

Giordano, Umberto. 1867–1948. Italian composer. Known for his operas in verismo style, including *Mala vita* (1892), *Andrea Chénier* (1896), *Fedora* (1898), *Siberia* (1903), *Madame Sans-Gêne* (1915), *La cena della beffe* (1924).

Giorgio, Francesco di. See FRANCESCO DI GIORGIO.

Gior·gio·ne \jōr-'jō-nā\. *Also* Giorgione da Ca·stel·fran·co \dä-ˌkäs-täl-'fräŋ-kō\. c.1477–1511. Italian painter. Chief master of Venetian school in his day. To Venice (c.1490); studied under Giovanni Bellini; influenced contemporaries, including Titian; commissioned to decorate Ducal Palace (1507) and façade of Fondaco dei Tedeschi (1508), both Venice. Works generally considered his include *Madonna and Child with SS. Francis and Liberale* (c.1504), *Boy with an Arrow* (c.1505), *The Tempest* (c.1505), *Adoration of the Shepherds* (c.1508), *Holy Family* (c.1508), *Self Portrait as David* (c.1510), *Sleeping Venus* (c.1510), *The Three Philosophers* (c.1510), *La vecchia* (c.1510).

Giot·ti·no \jōt-'tē-nō\. *Also known as* Giot·to di Maes·tro di Ste·fa·no \'jót-tō-dē-'mī-strō-de-stā-'fä-nō\. 14th century. Florentine painter. Employed at Vatican (1369). Works included frescoes in lower church of Assisi representing *Coronation of the Virgin* and two scenes from legend of St. Nicholas and frescoes in Bardi family chapel in Sta. Croce, Florence, representing miracles of Pope St. Silvester.

Giot·to \'jót-tō\. *In full* Giotto di Bon·do·ne \dē-bōn-'dō-nā\. 1266/67 or 1276–1337. Florentine painter, architect, and sculptor. Chief Italian pre-Renaissance painter; pupil of Cimabue. Works attributed to him include series of frescoes depicting life of St. Francis and life of Christ (both in Church of St. Francis at Assisi), altarpiece for St. Peter's, fresco fragment entitled *Boniface VIII Proclaiming the Jubilee* (St. John Lateran, Rome), decorative frescoes *Life of Christ, Life of the Virgin, Last Judgment, Allegories,* etc. (Arena chapel, Padua), allegorical frescoes *Marriage of St. Francis with Poverty, Triumph of Charity, Triumph of Obedience, Glorification of St. Francis* (all in St. Francis lower church, Assisi), fresco series depicting life of John the Evangelist and life of John the Baptist (both in Peruzzi Chapel, Church of Santa Croce, Florence), and *Ognissanti Madonna.* As architect of the Duomo in Florence (from 1334), designed the campanile and façade.

Giovane, Palma. See under Jacopo PALMA.

Giovanna. See JOAN (of Naples).

Giovanni. See also JOHN.

Gio·van·ni \jō-'vän-nē\. *Surnamed* San·ti \'sän-tē\. d. 1494. Italian painter and poet. Father of Raphael; court painter to duke of Urbino; works included *Annunciation* and several *Madonnas;* wrote a rhymed chronicle of art.

Giovanni, Agostino di. See AGOSTINO DI GIOVANNI.

Giovanni da Mon·te·cor·vi·no \-dä-,mōn-tā-kòr-'vē-nō\. 1247–1328. Italian prelate. Franciscan; emissary of Emperor Michael VIII Palaeologus to Pope Gregory X to negotiate church union (1272); missionary in Armenia and Persia (c.1280); papal emissary to Il-Khan of Persia (1289); founded first Catholic missions in India and China; reached Peking (1294); first archbishop of Peking and patriarch of the Orient (1307).

Giovanni di Pao·lo di Gra·zia \-dē-'paù-lō-dē-'grät-sē-ä\. c.1403–1482. Italian painter. Worked in his native Siena; probably pupil of Taddeo di Bartolo, later influenced by Gentile da Fabriano. One of last practitioners of medieval painting; his religious paintings maintained mystical intensity and conservative style of Gothic decorative painting. Works included *Madonna and Child with Angels* (1426), *Madonna* (1427), altarpieces *Presentation of Christ in the Temple* (1447–49) and *Madonna* (1463, Pienza cathedral), and polyptych *Assumption* (1475).

Gio·vio \'jòv-yō\, Paolo. *Latin* Paulus Jo·vi·us \'jō-vē-əs\. 1483–1552. Italian biographer and historian. Distinguished as Latin stylist; chief work, *Historiarum sui temporis* (1550–52) covering period 1494–1547.

Gippius. See MEREZHKOVSKY.

Gipps \'gips\, Sir George. 1791–1847. English colonial administrator. Governor of New South Wales (1838–46), where he did much to open up the country and prevent exploitation of the native population.

Gi·ral·di \jē-'räl-dē\, Giambattista. *Known also as* Cin·thio \'chēn-thyō\ *or* Cin·zio \'chēnt-syō\, *Ital. forms of his Lat. academic name* Cyn·thi·us \'sin(t)-thē-əs\. 1504–1573. Italian writer. Succeeded his teacher Celio Calcagnini in chair of rhetoric at Ferrara (1541); later taught at Turin and Pavia. Advocated reform of theater along Aristotelian lines; created tragicomedy by providing a happy ending to his Senecan models; wrote *Orbecche* (1541), the first modern tragedy on classical principles to appear on Italian stage. Other works included tragedies *Didone* (1542), *Altile* (1543), *Cleopatra* (1543), *Antivalomeni* (1549), *Epitia* (1583; source for Shakespeare's *Measure for Measure*); pastoral drama *Egle* (1545); poem *Ercole* (1557); prose treatises *Discorso delle comedie e delle tragedie* (1543) and *Discorso intorno al comporre de' romanzi* (1549); and *Ecatommiti* (1565), a collection of some 130 moralistic tales patterned on Boccaccio's *Decameron,* translated and imitated in France, Spain, and England, and source for Shakespeare's *Othello* and some plays of Beaumont and Fletcher.

Giraldus Cambrensis. See GERALD DE BARRI.

Gi·rard \zhē-rár\, Jean-Baptiste. *Known as* Père Girard *and (in Franciscan order)* Père Gré·goire \grā-gwár\. 1765–1850. Swiss educator. Entered Franciscan order (1782); professor of philosophy at Fribourg seminary (1790–99); first Catholic pastor at Berne (1800–04). Principal of primary school at Fribourg (1804–23) and of free school at Lucerne (1827–34); retired (1834) to devote himself to writing on theory of education. In Switzerland, regarded as an educator second only to Pestalozzi; emphasized moral and religious aspects of education. Wrote *De l'enseignement régulier de la langue maternelle* (1834), *Cours éducatif* (1844–46), etc.

Girard, Marc-Antoine. Sieur de Saint-Amant \sa^{n}-tá-mä^{n}\. 1594–1661. French poet. One of first members of Académie Française; traveled in America, Africa, Europe. His *Rome ridicule* (1649) started a fashion for burlesque poems; also known for mock-heroic poem *Albion* (1643) and biblical epic *Moïse sauvé* (1653). His work neglected for two centuries after being ridiculed by critic Nicolas Boileau.

Gi·rard \zhē-rár, *Angl* jə-'rärd\, Stephen. 1750–1831. American businessman and philanthropist, b. Bordeaux, France. Merchant in Philadelphia (from 1777). Founded (1812) of Bank of Stephen Girard to take over business of Bank of United States. Aided government in financing the War of 1812; aided in establishing the Second Bank of the United States (1816). Bequeathed funds used to build Girard College, Philadelphia, for education of "poor, white, male orphans."

Gi·rar·din \zhē-rár-da^{n}\, Émile de. 1806–1881. French journalist. Published autobiographical novel *Émile* (1827); founded periodical *Le Voleur* (1828); inaugurated low-priced journalism in France with *La Presse* (1836–56, 1862–66); edited *La Liberté* (1866), *Le Petit Journal* (1872), *La France* (1874); member of Chamber of Deputies (1834–51, 1877–81). His wife (m. 1831) ¶Delphine, *nee* Gay \ge\ (1804–1855), *pseudonym* Vicomte Charles de Lau·nay \lō-ne\, was a writer of novels, comedies, verse, and a series of *Lettres parisiennes.*

Gi·rar·don \zhē-rár-dō^{n}\, François. 1628–1715. French sculptor. Employed under direction of Le Brun in decoration of Versailles and the Louvre. Works at Versailles included *Apollon servi par les nymphes* (1666), *Bain des nymphes* (1668–70), *Enlèvement de Proserpine* (1677–79); also executed tomb of Cardinal Richelieu in the Sorbonne (begun 1675) and an equestrian statue of Louis XIV in Palace Vendôme, Paris (1683–92).

Giraud, Albert. See KAYENBERGH.

Gi·raud \zhē-rō\, Henri-Honoré. 1879–1949. French general. Served through World War I; served in Morocco against Riffs (1922–26). Commanded allied defenses in northern France (1940); to Algeria (Nov. 1942) to organize French colonial army; commander of French forces in North Africa; co-president with Charles de Gaulle of French Committee of National Liberation (June–Oct. 1943); retired from Committee (Apr. 1944). Vice president of Supreme War Council (1948–49).

Gi·rau·doux \zhē-rō-dü\, Jean, *in full* Hyppolyte-Jean. 1882–1944. French writer. Commissioner of information (1939–40). Created an impressionistic form of drama by emphasizing dialogue and style, as in *Amphitryon 38* (1929), *Judith* (1931), *Intermezzo* (1933), *La Guerre de Troie n'aura pas lieu* (1935), *Ondine* (1939), *Sodome et Gomorrhe* (1943), *La Folle de Chaillot* (1946), *L'Apollon de Bellac* (1946), *Pour Lucrèce* (1953). Author of novels *Suzanne et le Pacifique* (1921), *Siegfried et le Limousin* (1922), *Bella* (1926), *Combat avec l'ange* (1934), *Le Cantique des cantiques* (1938), etc.; also essays and scripts of films *La Duchesse de Langeais* (1942) and *Les Anges du péché* (1944).

Gi·ro·det de Rou·cy \zhē-rō-ded-ə-rü-sē\, Anne-Louis. *Known as* Gi·ro·det-Tri·o·son \zhē-rō-de-trē-ō-sō^{n}\. 1767–1824. French painter. Pupil of Jacques-Louis David. His Romantic paintings included *Joseph Recognized by His Brothers* (1789), *Sleep of Endymion* (1792), *Ossian Receiving the Generals of Napoléon at the Palace of Odin* (1801), *Deluge* (1806), *Entombment of Atala* (1808), portrait of Chateaubriand (1809), landscape sketches, and book illustrations.

Gir·tin \'gərt-ᵊn\, Thomas. 1775–1802. English painter. Regarded as founder of art of modern watercolor painting. Among his works were *The Chelsea White House* (1800), *Bolton Bridge* (1801), series of sketches of Paris (1802), and *Eidometropolis,* a gigantic panorama of London (1802).

Gi·ry \zhē-rē\, Arthur, *in full* Jean-Marie-Joseph-Arthur. 1848–1899. French historian. Author of *Histoire de la ville de Saint-Omer et des ses institutions jusqu'au XIVe siècle* (1877), *Les Établissements de Rouen* (1883–85), *Documents sur les relations de la royauté avec les villes de France de 1180 à 1314* (1885), *Études sur les origines de la commune de Saint-Quentin* (1887), *Manuel de diplomatique* (1894).

Gisander. See Johann Gottfried SCHNABEL.

Gi·se·la \'gē-zə-lä\. c.990–1043. Holy Roman empress. m. Conrad II (1016) and was crowned with him in Rome (1027); mother of Emperor Henry III.

Gish \'gish\, Dorothy. 1898–1968. American actress, b. Massillon, Ohio. On stage (from 1903); under contract to D.W. Griffith (1912–22). Appeared with her sister Lillian in *Hearts of the World* (1918), *Broken Blossoms* (1919), *Orphans of the Storm* (1922), *Romola* (1924); primarily on stage (from 1928), esp. in *The Inspector General* (1930), *Brittle Heaven* (1934), *The Magnificent Yankee* (1946), *The Chalk Garden* (1956); other films included *Nell Gwyn* (1926), *Our Hearts Were Young and Gay* (1944), *The Cardinal* (1964).

Gis·le·ber·tus \,gēz-lə-'ber-tüs\. 12th century. French sculptor. Contributed to decoration of abbeys of Cluny (to c.1115) and Vézelay (c.1120–25); for cathedral of St. Lazarus at Autun, executed (1125–35) a Romanesque tympanum of the Last Judgment for the west doorway, a nude *Eve* sculpture for north doorway, and some 60 capitals illustrating biblical stories.

Gisors, Duc de. See BELLE-ISLE.

Gis·sing \'gis-iŋ\, George Robert. 1857–1903. English novelist. Became prominent for realistic depiction of middle-class life in England, and esp. for portrayals of degrading effect of poverty on character. His novels included *Workers in the Dawn* (1880), *The Unclassed* (1884), *Demos* (1886), *The Nether World* (1889), *New Grub Street* (1891), *The Town Traveller* (1898), *The Private Papers of Henry Ryecroft* (1903).

Gist \'gist\, Christopher. 1706?–1759. American frontiersman, b. probably near Baltimore. For Ohio Company of Virginia, explored its lands in Pennsylvania, Ohio, and Kentucky (1750–51); explored region between Monongahela and Little Kanawha rivers (1751–52); guide for George Washington (1753–54) and for Braddock's expedition (1755).

Gi·sulph II \'jē-süլf\. c.1040–after 1089. Prince of Salerno. Succeeded to throne on assassination of his father Gaimar V (1052); lifelong opponent of Normans in Italy, in spite of his being brother-in-law of Robert Guiscard; besieged at Salerno by Guiscard and Richard of Aversa (1076–77), his defeat marking end of effective resistance of Lombards to Norman conquest of southern Italy; doge of Amalfi (1088–89).

Giudici *or* **Giudini,** Francesco. See FRANCESCO DI CRISTOFANO.

Giulio Romano. See (1) Giulio CACCINI; (2) Giulio PIPPI DE' GIANUZZI.

Giun·ta Pi·sa·no \ˈjün-tä-pē-ˈsä-nō\. d. c.1260. Italian painter, b. Pisa. To Assisi, where he influenced development of Umbrian art. Credited with executing 3 large Crucifixions for churches at Pisa and Assisi.

Giuseppino, Il. See Giuseppe CESARI.

Giu·sti \ˈjüs-tē\, Giuseppe. 1809–1850. Italian poet. Known for his political and social satires, including *La guigliottina a vapore* (1833), *Il dies irae* (1835), *Lo stivale* (1836), *Il gingillino* (1845), *Sant' Ambrogio* (c.1846); also prose works, esp. *Epistolario* (1904).

Giu·sti·nia·ni \ˌjüs-tēn-ˈyä-nē\. Italian family, including: Leonardo (1388–1446), Venetian poet and politician; member (1428), head (1443), of Council of Ten, ruling body of Venice; procurator of St. Mark's (1443); advocated revival of classical studies; translated Petrarch and composed original works in Latin and Greek; with *Canzoni o strambotti d'amore* and other verse, developed a genre of amorous poetry called *giustiniane* after him. ¶Giovanni (d. 1453), governor of Genoese colony of Caffa in the Crimea; mortally wounded while defending Constantinople against successful Turkish attack. ¶Agostino (1479–1536), Genoese prelate and scholar; joined Dominicans (1487); bishop of Nebbio, Corsica (1514); attended fifth Lateran Council (1516–17); authority on Eastern studies; first professor of Hebrew at U. of Paris (1517); friend of Pico della Mirandola, Erasmus, Thomas More; first in Europe to publish a Polyglot Bible (1516); also wrote a history of Genoa and translated classical authors. ¶Pompeo (1569–1616), soldier; known as Brac·cio di Fer·ro \ˈbrät-chō-de-ˈfer-rō\, *i.e.* Iron Arm, because of mechanical arm worn to replace one lost in battle; in service of Alessandro Farnese in Low Countries; helped defend Crete against the Turks; killed while fighting against Austrians in northeastern Italy; wrote *Bellum Belgicum* (1609), account of his military experiences in Flanders.

Gjel·le·rup \ˈgil-lā-rüp\, Karl Adolph. 1857–1919. Danish writer. Resident in Germany (from 1892); wrote many of his later works in German. Among his works were novels *En Idealist* (1878), *Germanernes laerling* (1882), *Minna* (1889), *Pilgrimen Kamanita* (1906), *Den gyldne Gren* (1917); plays *Brynhild* (1884), *Wuthhorn* (1893), *Hans Excellence* (1895); and verse *Aander og Tider* (1882), *Fra Vaar til Høst* (1895). Recipient, jointly with Henrik Pontoppidan, of Nobel prize for literature (1917).

Gla·ber \glȧ-ber\, Radulfus. c.985–c.1047. French chronicler. Itinerant monk; his *Historiae* (written 1030–35) in five books covers the period from 900.

Glack·ens \ˈglak-ənz\, William James. 1870–1938. American painter, b. Philadelphia. Settled (1896) in New York as newspaper illustrator and magazine reporter; devoted himself to painting (from c.1905). Pupil of Robert Henri and member of artistic group known as The Eight or Ashcan School. Known for realistic portrayals of street scenes and middle-class urban life, esp. *Hammerstein's Roof Garden* (1901) and *Chez Mouquin* (1905); in later years, an imitator of Renoir.

Glad·den \ˈglad-ᵊn\, Washington, *orig.* Solomon Washington. 1836–1918. American clergyman, b. Pottsgrove, Pa. Ordained Congregational minister (1860); religious editor of *New York Independent* (1871–75); pastorate at Springfield, Mass. (1875–82), and Columbus, Ohio (1882–1918). An early advocate of Social Gospel movement, preached the practical application of the principles of religion to current social problems. Author of *Plain Thoughts on the Art of Living* (1868), *Applied Christianity* (1887), *Social Salvation* (1901), *Ultima Veritas and Other Verses* (1912), etc.

Glad·kov \(ˌ)glət-ˈkȯf\, Fyodor Vasilyevich. 1883–1958. Russian novelist. Author of *Tsement* (1925), *Energiya* (1932–38), reminiscences *Povest o detstve* (1949), etc.

Glad·stone \ˈglad-ˌstōn, *chiefly Brit* -stən\, Herbert John. Viscount Gladstone. 1854–1930. English politician. Son of W. E. Gladstone; M.P. (1880–1910); chief Liberal whip (1899); secretary of state for home affairs (1905–10); created viscount (1910). First governor general and high commissioner of Union of South Africa (1910–14).

Gladstone, John Hall. 1827–1902. English chemist. Professor, Royal Institution (1874–77); known for work on optical refractivity; used copper-zinc couple to prepare organic compounds; made spectroscopic studies of sun.

Gladstone, William Ewart. 1809–1898. English politician. M.P. (1832–95, except 1846–47). President of Board of Trade in Peel's cabinet (1843–45), and secretary of state for colonies (1845–46). Chancellor of the exchequer in cabinets of Aberdeen (1852–55), Palmerston (1855), and Lord Russell (1859–66). Succeeded Lord Russell as leader of the Liberal party (1867). Prime minister (1868–74, 1880–85, 1886, 1892–94). Among his important measures and policies were the disestablishment of the Irish church (1869), an Irish land bill (1870), denunciation of Turkish atrocities in Bulgaria (1875–76), reform of Irish government by a new land bill (1881) and a home-rule bill (presented to Parliament, but defeated, 1886 and again 1893). Author of *The State in its Relations to the Church* (1838), *Studies on Homer and the Homeric Age* (1858), *Juventus Mundi* (1869), *Homeric Synchronism* (1876), *Gleanings of Past Years* (1879).

Glan·vill \ˈglan-vəl\, Joseph. 1636–1680. English clergyman and philosopher. Rector of Abbey Church at Bath (1666–80); chaplain to Charles II (1672); prebend of Worcester (1678). Attacked scholastic philosophy in *The Vanity of Dogmatizing* (1661); defended preexistence of souls in *Lux Orientalis* (1662), belief in witchcraft in *Witches and Witchcraft* (1666), and experimental method of Royal Society in *Plus Ultra* (1668).

Glan·ville *or* **Glan·vill** *or* **Glan·vil** \ˈglan-vəl\, Ranulf de. d.1190. English jurist. Justiciar of England (1180–89), and influential adviser of King Henry II. Reputed author of *Tractatus de legibus et consuetudinibus regni Angliae* (c.1188), first authoritative text on English common law.

Glan-y-gors, Jac. See John JONES.

Glap·thorne \ˈglap-ˌthȯrn\, Henry. 1610–c.1643. English playwright. Works included *Poems* (1639), pastoral tragedy *Argalus and Parthenia* (1639), historical tragedy *Albertus Wallenstein* (1639), comedies *The Hollander* and *Wit in a Constable* (both 1640).

Glareanus, Henricus. See Heinrich LORIS.

Glas, John. See John GLASS.

Gla·ser \ˈglä-zər\, Christopher. 1615–1672. Swiss chemist. Opened apothecary shop in Paris (c.1662); apothecary to Louis XIV of France; credited with discovery of potassium sulfate. Wrote popular textbook *Traité de la chymie* (1663).

Glas·gow \ˈglas-(ˌ)gō\, Ellen Anderson Gholson. 1873–1945. American novelist, b. Richmond, Va. Author of *The Descendant* (1897), *The Voice of the People* (1900), *The Battle-Ground* (1902), *The Wheel of Life* (1906), *Virginia* (1913), *The Builders* (1919), *Barren Ground* (1925), *The Romantic Comedians* (1926), *They Stooped to Folly* (1929), *The Sheltered Life* (1932), *Vein of Iron* (1935), *In This Our Life* (1941, Pulitzer prize).

Glas·pell \ˈglas-(ˌ)pel, -pəl\, Susan. 1882–1948. American writer, b. Davenport, Iowa. m. (1913) George Cram Cook (*q.v.*), with whom she founded (1915) Provincetown Playhouse. Author of novels *The Glory of the Conquered* (1909), *The Visioning* (1911), *Brook Evans* (1928), *The Fugitive's Return* (1929), *The Morning Is Near Us* (1940), *Norma Ashe* (1942); plays *Trifles* (1917), *Suppressed Desires* (with George Cram Cook, 1917), *Bernice* (1920), *Inheritors* (1921), *Verge* (1922), *The Comic Artist* (with Norman H. Matson, 1927), *Alison's House* (1930).

Glass \ˈglas\, Carter. 1858–1946. American politician, b. Lynchburg, Va. Proprietor (from 1888) of Lynchburg newspapers *Daily News* and *Daily Advance*. Member of U.S. House of Representatives (1902–19); patron and floor manager in the House of Federal Reserve Bank Act (passed 1918). U.S. secretary of the treasury (1918–20). U.S. senator from Virginia (1920–46); opposed Pres. F.D. Roosevelt's New Deal program.

Glass, Hugh. d. 1833. American frontiersman. Joined William Ashley's trapping expedition to upper Missouri country (1823); mauled by a bear and left for dead by his companions, including Jim Bridger (*q.v.*); crawled a hundred miles to Fort Kiowa, where he recovered; later found and forgave Bridger. Became subject of legends for this exploit and for later fur-trapping adventures.

Glass *or* **Glas,** John. 1695–1773. Scottish clergyman. Became Presbyterian minister of Tealing Church, Dundee (1719); expounded his opposition to a national church in *The Testimony of the King of Martyrs* (1727); organized a sect of independent Presbyterians; moved to Perth (1733) and was joined by Robert Sandeman. Members of the sect were known as Glasites or Sandemanians.

Glass·bren·ner \ˈgläs-ˌbren-ər\, Adolf. *Pseudonym* Adolf Brenn·glas \ˈbren-ˌgläs\. 1810–1876. German writer. Best known for humorous and satirical sketches of Berlin life as *Berlin, wie es ist und—trinkt* (1832–49) and *Buntes Berlin* (1837–53).

Gla·ti·gny \glȧ-tēn-yē\, Joseph-Albert-Alexander. 1839–1873. French poet. Member of Parnassian school; best known for his satirical poems and peripatetic life as strolling actor and improvisationalist. Author of verse collections *Les Vignes folles* (1860), *Les Flèches d'or* (1864), *Gilles et Pasquins* (1872), and of plays *La Singe* (1872), *Les Folies-Marigny* (1872), *L'Illustre Brizacier* (1873).

Glau·ber \ˈglau̇-bər\, Johann Rudolf. 1604–1668. German chemist. Resident in Amsterdam (from 1655). Probably first to distill coal and obtain benzene and phenol; investigated decomposition of common salt through action of acids and bases. Glauber's salt is named after him.

Gla·zu·nov \glə-zü-ˈnȯf\, Aleksandr Konstantinovich. 1865–1936. Russian composer. Studied under Rimsky-Korsakov (1880–82); his *First Symphony* premiered by Balakirev (1882); visited Liszt at Weimar (1884); professor (1899–1905), director (1905–28), St. Petersburg Conservatory; left Soviet Union (1928), settling (1932) in Paris. Compositions included 8 symphonies, ballets *Raymonda* (1896–97), *Ruses d'amour* (1898), and *Les Saisons* (1899), a violin concerto (1904), 2 piano concertos (1911, 1917), *Concerto-Ballata for Cello and Orchestra* (1931), *Concerto for Saxophone, Flute, and Strings* (1934), symphonic poem *Stenka Razin* (1885), serenades, fantasies, and other orchestral works, choral works, chamber music, piano pieces, and songs.

Gleim \'glīm\, Johann Wilhelm Ludwig. 1719–1803. German poet. Member of Anacreontic poets at Halle who employed a Rococo literary style during 1740s. Best known for verse collections *Versuch in scherzhaften Gedichten* (1744) and *Preussiche Kriegslieder von einem Grenadier* (1758).

Glencairn, Earl of. See Alexander CUNNINGHAM.

Glen·dow·er \glen-'daü-ər\, Owen. *Welsh* Owain Glyn·dwr \glin-'dür\ *or* Owain ap Gruf·fydd \äp-'grif-ith\. c.1359–c.1416. Welsh rebel. Studied law in London; served in forces of Henry Bolingbroke (later Henry IV). Head of Welsh rebellion against Henry IV (from 1400); proclaimed himself prince of Wales; gained control of most of Wales (by 1404); established an independent Welsh parliament; twice defeated (1405) by Prince Henry (later Henry V), who later (1408–09) captured his strongholds of Aberystwyth and Harlech; still active as late as 1412, but his rebellion effectively crushed by then.

Glidden, Carlos. See under Christopher Latham SHOLES.

Glid·den \'glid-ᵊn\, Charles Jasper. 1857–1927. American pioneer in telephone industry, b. Lowell, Mass. Organized first telephone exchange, Lowell, Mass. (1877); developed system rapidly through country under New England Telephone & Telegraph Co. and Erie Telephone & Telegraph Co.; sold out interests to Bell organization (c.1901).

Glidden, Joseph Farwell. 1813–1906. American inventor, b. Charlestown, N.H. Farmer in Illinois (from 1844); invented first commercially successful barbed wire (pat. 1874); with Isaac L. Ellwood established (1874) Barb Fence Co. of De Kalb, Ill.; sold interest in company (1876).

Glin·ka \'glyēn-kə\, Mikhail Ivanovich. 1804–1857. Russian composer. Composed *Zhizn'za tsarya* (*A Life for The Czar,* first Russian national opera, 1836), and a second opera, *Ruslan and Lyudmila,* based on a poem of Pushkin (1842); lived in Spain (1845–47) and wrote *Capriccio brillante* (1845) and *Souvenir d'une nuit d'été à Madrid* (1851) on Spanish themes; other works included symphonies, songs, and orchestral suites as *Kamarinskaya* (1848). Considered founder of Russian national school of composers.

Gloucester, Dukes of. See THOMAS of Woodstock; HUMPHREY; RICHARD III; Prince HENRY (1900–1974).

Gloucester, Earls of. See ROBERT (d. 1147), Earl of Gloucester; de CLARE family.

Gloux \glü\, Olivier. *Pseudonym* Gustave Ai·mard \em-är\. 1818–1883. French adventurer and writer. Author of *Les Trappeurs de l'Arkansas* (1858), *Le Chercheur de pistes* (1858), *Les Pirates des prairies* (1859), *Les Bohèmes de la mer* (1865), *La Forêt vierge* (1870), *Par mer et par terre* (1879), *Les Bandits de l'Arizona* (1882), etc.

Glov·er \'gləv-ər\, John. 1732–1797. American Revolutionary officer, b. Salem, Mass. Colonel of Massachusetts militia regiment (1775); joined Continental army (1776); commanded vessels that transported American troops from Long Island; manned boats and led advance on Trenton (Dec. 25, 1776). Brigadier general (1777); in campaign against Burgoyne; on court that sentenced André.

Glover, Julia, *nee* Bet·ter·ton \'bet-ərt-ᵊn\. 1779–1850. Irish actress. m. Samuel Glover (1800); excelled in comedy.

Glover, Sarah Ann. 1786–1867. English music teacher. Invented (c.1812) tonic sol-fa system of notation. Cf. John CURWEN.

Gło·wac·ki \glo-'väts-kē\, Aleksander. *Pseudonym* Bolesław Prus \'prüs\. 1847–1912. Polish writer. A leading figure in positivist period after revolt of 1863; contributed "chronicles" to periodicals. His novels included *Placówka* (1885), *Lalka* (1890), *Emancypantki* (1891–3), *Faraon* (1897); tales included *Z legend dawnego Egiptu, Kamizelka,* and *Katarynka.*

Gluck \'glük\, Alma. *Orig.* Reba Fier·sohn \'fir-,zōn\. 1884–1938. American singer, b. Iaşi, Romania. To U.S. (1890); m. 1st (1902) Bernard Gluck, 2d (1914) Efrem Zimbalist. Operatic debut at Metropolitan Opera, N.Y.C. (1909); known esp. as concert and recording artist; retired (1925).

Gluck, Christoph Willibald. 1714–1787. German composer. Worked in Milan (1737–45), London (1745–46); traveled widely in Italy, Germany, Austria; settled in Vienna (1752), in service of Prince of Saxe-Hildburghausen and of imperial court; frequently visited Paris. Early achieved fame as composer of Italian operas as *Artaserse* (1741), *Arsace* (1743), *Sofonisba* (1744), *La caduta de' giganti* (1746), *Le nozze d'Ercole e d'Ebe* (1747), *Semiramide riconosciuta* (to open Burgtheater, Vienna, 1748), *La clemenza di Tito* (1752), *Le Cinesi* (1754), *Il rè pastore* (1756), *Le cadi dupé* (1761). With librettist Raniero Calzabigi produced series of operas *Orfeo ed Euridice* (1762), *Alceste* (1767), *Paride ed Elena* (1770), which achieved a revolution in opera by placing music at service of drama through expressiveness and simplicity. Carried reform to Paris with *Iphigénie en Aulide* (1772), *Armide* (1777), *Iphigénie en Tauride* (1779), *Écho et Narcisse* (1779), precipitating "opera war" between his adherents and those of Piccinni. Also composed ballets and pantomimes as *Don Juan ou le festin de pierre* (1761), *Semiramide* (1765); a *De profundis* (1785?); trio sonatas, etc.

Gluck·man \'glək-mən\, Max, *in full* Herman Max. 1911–1975. South African anthropologist. On staff (1939–47), director (1941–47), Rhodes-Livingston Institute of Northern Rhodesia; professor, Oxford (1947–49), Manchester (1949–71); known for studies of Ila, Tonga, Lamba and other tribes. Author of *Rituals of Rebellion in South-East Africa* (1954), *Custom and Conflict in Africa* (1955), *Politics, Law and Ritual in Tribal Society* (1965), *The Ideas in Barotse Jurisprudence* (1965), etc.

Glueck \'glük\, Sheldon, *in full* Sol Sheldon. 1896–1980. American criminologist, b. Warsaw, Poland. To U.S. (1903); on staff, Harvard U. (from 1925), professor in law school (from 1929); with wife (m. 1922) ¶Eleanor, *nee* Tou·roff \'tü(ə)r-,óf, -,äf\ (1898–1972), b. Brooklyn, N.Y., and on staff, Harvard (from 1925), studied criminals, juvenile delinquents, rehabilitation, recidivism. Joint authors of *Five Hundred Criminal Careers* (1930), *Five Hundred Delinquent Women* (1934), *One Thousand Juvenile Delinquents* (1934), *Later Criminal Careers* (1937), *Juvenile Delinquents Grown Up* (1940), *Unraveling Juvenile Delinquency* (1950), *Predicting Delinquency and Crime* (1959), etc.

Gly·cas \'glī-kəs\. Michael. 12th century. Byzantine historian, theologian, and poet. Author of popular *Biblos Chronike* covering world history from creation to 1118; also wrote commentaries on Bible, etc.; blinded by order of Emperor Manuel I (1159).

Gly·ce·ri·us \glī-'sir-ē-əs\. 5th century A.D. Western Roman emperor (473–474). Enthroned by Gundobad to succeed Olybrius; not recognized by Eastern emperor Leo I; surrendered to Julius Nepos and became bishop of Salona (474); helped arrange assassination of Nepos (480).

Glyn \'glin\, Elinor, *nee* Suth·er·land \'səth-ər-lənd\. 1864–1943. British novelist, b. Island of Jersey. m. Clayton Glyn (1892; d. 1915). Author of *The Visits of Elizabeth* (1900), *Three Weeks* (1907), *Halcyone* (1912), *Man and Maid* (1922), *It* (1927), *Did She?* (1934); author also of motion-picture scenarios.

Gme·lin \'gmā-lēn\, Johann Georg. 1709–1755. German botanist. Explored Siberia as far as the Lena (1733–43); professor at St. Petersburg Academy of Sciences (1731–47), Tübingen (1749–55). Author of *Flora sibirica* (1747–69). A nephew ¶Leopold (1788–1853), professor of medicine and chemistry in Heidelberg (1817–51); discovered potassium ferricyanide (also called Gmelin's salt). Author of long-standard text *Handbuch der Chemie* (1817–19).

Gnei·se·nau \'gnī-zə-,naü\, August Wilhelm Anton Neit·hardt von \'nīt-,härt-fón-\. Graf. 1760–1831. Prussian field marshal. With British mercenary force in America (1782–83); in Prussian army (from 1786); fought against Napoléon (1806–07); defended Kolberg (1807); after Peace of Tilsit (1807), engaged with Scharnhorst in military reorganization of Prussia (1807–09); served under Blücher in War of Liberation (1813–14); Blücher's chief of staff (1813–16); governor of Berlin (1818); field marshal general (1825).

Gneist \'gnīst\, Rudolf von. 1816–1895. German jurist and politician. Professor, Berlin (1844); member, Berlin high court (1847–49); member of Prussian Diet (1858–93) and of German Reichstag (1868–84). Author of *Verwaltung, Justiz, Rechtsweg, Staatsverwaltung, und Selbstverwaltung nach englischen und deutschen Verhältnissen* (1869), *Englische Verfassungsgeschichte* (1882).

Gno·li \'nyò-lē\, Domenico. *Pseudonyms* Giulio Or·si·ni \ór-'sē-nē\ *and* Dario Gad·di \'gäd-dē\. 1838–1915. Italian scholar and poet. Director, Vittorio Emanuele National Library, Rome (1882–1907). Author of verse *Odi Tiberine* (1879), *Fra terra ed astri* (1903), *Poesie edite ed inedite* (1907), *Have Roma* (1909), etc.

Go·bat \gò-bà\, Charles Albert. 1834–1914. Swiss politician and philanthropist. Member of Nationalrat (1890–1914); active in Inter-Parliamentary Union (from 1888) and prominent advocate of international peace; awarded, jointly with Élie Ducommun, Nobel prize for peace (1902); president, Bureau International Permanent de la Paix, Bern (1906–14).

Gobat, Samuel. 1799–1879. Swiss prelate. Anglican missionary, esp. in Ethiopia; nominated (1845) by Frederick William IV of Prussia as second bishop to head joint Anglican-Lutheran mission to Jerusalem; bishop of mission (1846–79).

Gobbo. See Cristoforo SOLARI.

Go·bel \gò-bel\, Jean-Baptiste-Joseph. 1727–1794. French prelate. Member of Estates-General (1789); constitutional archbishop of Paris (1791); accepted principles of the Revolution, and favored the worship of reason and marriage of the clergy; resigned see (1793); joined Hébertists and was guillotined with them.

Gob·e·lin \gò-blaⁿ\. Family of 15th-century French dyers, including Gilles and Jehan (fl. 1450), who established near Paris a factory, later famous for its tapestry, which was made a royal establishment by Louis XIV and is now the Manufacture Nationale des Gobelins.

Go·bind Singh \'gō-,bind-'sin(-hə)\. *Orig.* Gobind Rāi \-'rī\. 1666–1708. Tenth and last Sikh Gurū. Military leader; created Khālsā brotherhood (1699);

author of body of martial poetry; led Sikh armies against Mughals and hill tribes; declared himself last of personal Gurūs.

Go·bi·neau \gō-bē-nō\, Joseph-Arthur de. Comte. 1816–1882. French diplomat, Orientalist, and writer. Secretary to de Tocqueville (1849); in diplomatic service (1849–77). Author of romances *Pléiades* (1874), *Les nouvelles asiatiques* (1876); *Histoire des Perses* (1869), *La Renaissance* (1877); best known for *Essai sur l'inégalité des races humaines* (1854–55), in which he advanced the theory that the dolichocephalic Aryan, or Teuton, is the superior among the races of men.

Go·blet \gō-ble\, René. 1828–1905. French politician. Deputy (1871–76, 1877–89, 1893–98); minister of interior (1879–80), of public instruction (1885–86); premier of France (1886–87); brought Gen. Boulanger into cabinet, precipitating crisis.

Go·brecht \ˈgō-brekt\, Christian. 1785–1844. American engraver, b. Hanover, Pa. Engraver, U.S. Mint, Philadelphia (from 1836); his name appears on some of the specimens of U.S. pattern coins, known as Gobrecht dollars, of series struck in 1836, 1838, and 1839.

Go-Daigo. See DAIGO II.

Go·dard \gō-dȧr\, Benjamin-Louis-Paul. 1849–1895. French composer. Composed symphonic and chamber music, piano pieces and songs, and operas including *Jocelyn* (1881, containing "Berceuse"), *Pédro de Zalaméa* (1884), *La Vivandière* (1895).

God·dard \ˈgäd-ərd\. Family of American cabinetmakers including: John (1724–1785), b. Dartmouth, Mass.; settled in Newport, R.I., as apprentice to Job Townsend, whose daughter he married; founded own workshop and became leading cabinetmaker of Newport; developed block, or tub, front designs for Queen Anne style furniture. His sons ¶Stephen (d. 1804) and ¶Thomas (1765–1858) carried on workshop, creating elegant adaptations of Hepplewhite and Sheraton styles. Stephen's son ¶John Goddard II (1789–1843) was also a cabinetmaker.

Goddard, Henry Herbert. 1866–1957. American psychologist, b. Vassalboro, Me. Professor, Ohio State U. (1922–38). Author of *The Kallikak Family* (1912), *Feeble-mindedness* (1914), *The Criminal Imbecile* (1915), etc.

Goddard, Rayner. Baron Goddard. 1877–1971. English jurist. Recorder of Poole, Bath, Plymouth (1917–32); judge of High Court, King's Bench division (1932–38); lord justice of appeal (1938–44); created life peer (1944); lord of appeal in ordinary (1944–46); lord chief justice (1946–58); notable for firmness in administration of traditional punishments.

Goddard, Robert Hutchings. 1882–1945. American physicist, b. Worcester, Mass. Professor, Clark U. (1914–43); pioneer experimenter with rockets (from 1908); made first demonstration that rockets can operate in vacuum (1908); tested first successful liquid-fueled rocket (1926), first with instrument package (1929), first to exceed speed of sound (1935); granted over 200 patents in rocketry, including those for step-rockets and for basic guidance mechanisms, fuel pumps, etc.

Go·de·froid de Claire \gōd-frwä-də-kler\. *Also called* Godefroid de Huy \wyē\. fl. 1130–1150. Flemish goldsmith and enamellist. Outstanding exponent of Mosan school; apparently did most work in service of abbot of Stavelot.

Go·de·froy \gōd-frwä\. *Lat.* Goth·o·fre·dus \ˌgäth-ə-ˈfrēd-əs\. French family of jurists and historians, including: Denis, *called* the elder (1549–1621); author of *Corpus juris civilis* (1583). His son ¶Théodore (1580–1649), historian, was historiographer of France (1617). Another son ¶Jacques (1587–1652); professor, Geneva (1619); edited *Codex Theodosianus* (1665). Théodore's son ¶Denis, *called* the younger (1615–1681), succeeded as historiographer of France (1649); author of *Histoire des connétables* (1658).

Godehard. See GOTTHARD.

Gö·del \ˈgœd-əl, *Angl* ˈgə(r)d-əl\, Kurt. 1906–1978. American mathematician, b. Brünn, Austria (now Brno, Czechoslovakia). Professor, Vienna (1930–38); to U.S. (1940); member (from 1938), professor (1953–76), Institute for Advanced Study, Princeton, N.J. Discovered (1931) Gödel's proof of impossibility of rigorously self-consistent mathematical systems; author of *Consistency of the Axiom of Choice* (1940).

Goderich, Viscount. See Frederick John ROBINSON.

Go·dey \ˈgō-dē\, Louis Antoine. 1804–1878. American publisher, b. New York City. With Charles Alexander, established in Philadelphia the *Lady's Book* (1830), later known as *Godey's Lady's Book,* the first and long most popular woman's periodical in the U.S.

God·fred \ˈgōth-frəth\. *Also known as* Gud·fred \ˈgüth-frəth\. d. 810. Danish king. Ruled southern Jutland from Hedeby; warred with Carolingians and allies; destroyed Wendish port of Reric (now Lübeck, 804); built the Danevirke earthwork (804); killed while campaigning in Frisia.

God·frey II \ˈgäd-frē\. *Du.* God·fried \ˈgōt-frēt\. *Called* Godfried met de Baard \-ˌmet-də-ˈbȧrd\, *i.e.* the Bearded. d. 1069. Duke of Upper Lorraine (1044–47) and Lower Lorraine (1065–69). Son of Duke Gozelo the Great, on whose death he received Upper Lorraine; attempted to seize Lower Lorraine on death of brother Gozelo II the Little; deprived by Emperor Henry III (1047); m. (1054) Beatrice, widow of Margrave Boniface of Tuscany, becoming margrave of Tuscany and duke of Spoleto; finally submitted to Henry (1056); gained influence with election of brother Frederick as Pope Stephen IX (1057); with Archbishop Anno of Cologne, regent for Emperor Henry IV in his minority (1062–66); granted Lower Lorraine (1065).

Godfrey of Bouil·lon \bü-yō^{n}\. c.1060–1100. Duke of Lower Lorraine (1082–1100). Son of Count Eustace II of Boulogne and grandson of Duke Godfrey II of Lower Lorraine; barred from succession to Lower Lorraine by Emperor Henry IV, but granted it (1082) in reward for services in Saxon war; joined First Crusade (1096); accepted crown and title of "protector of the Holy Sepulchre" (1099); defeated Egyptian attack (1099). Idealized in later legends as perfect Christian knight.

Godfrey of Fon·taines \fō^{n}-ten\. before 1250–after 1305. French philosopher. Taught at U. of Paris (1285–1304), regent of faculty (1291–1304); proponent of Aristotelianism, often controverting Christian interpretations of Aristotle by Thomas Aquinas and Duns Scotus. Author of 15 *Quodlibeta,* several *Scholia* on Aquinas's *Summa theologiae.*

Godfrey of Saint-Vic·tor \sa^{n}-vēk-tȯr\. c.1125–1194. French religious, theologian, and poet. Entered Augustinian abbey of Saint-Victor (c.1160); sought solitude in rural priory (c.1180–c.1190), returning to Saint-Victor. Author of *Microcosmus* on man's natural and spiritual natures and of verse *Fons philosophiae* on knowledge.

Godfrey of Strassburg. See GOTTFRIED VON STRASSBURG.

Godfrey of Vi·ter·bo \vē-ˈter-bō\. 1125–c.1200. Italian or German chronicler. Chaplain and notary in service of Emperor Frederick I Barbarossa. Author of *Gesta Friderici I,* chronicle of period 1155–81, verse *Speculum regum,* and universal history *Memoria seculorum.*

Godfrey, Sir Edmund Berry. 1621–1678. English jurist. Justice of the peace, city of Westminster; received first depositions of Titus Oates (1678); found murdered shortly thereafter; perjured anti-Catholic testimony led to execution of 3 men (1679), but Godfrey was possibly assassinated by agents of Oates.

Godfrey, Thomas. 1704–1749. American mathematician and inventor, b. Philadelphia. Friend of Benjamin Franklin; invented (1730) the improved quadrant known as Hadley's quadrant. His son ¶Thomas (1736–1763) was a poet and playwright; author of lyric and narrative verse and the *Prince of Parthia,* first drama by a native American to be produced on professional stage (Philadelphia, 1767).

Go·din \gō-da^{n}\, Jean-Baptiste-André. 1817–1888. French industrialist and reformer. Head of ironworks at Guise; influenced by Fourierism, established a *familistère* among his operatives. Author of *Solutions sociales* (1871), *La Politique du travail et la politique des privilèges* (1875), etc.

Go·di·va \gə-ˈdī-və\ *or* **God·gi·fu** \ˈgäd-yə-vü\. fl. c.1140–1180. Wife of Leofric, Earl of Mercia. According to legend, rode naked through Coventry to win from her husband relief for the people of the town from burdensome taxation. Built and endowed monasteries at Stow and Coventry.

God·kin \ˈgäd-kən\, Edwin Lawrence. 1831–1902. American editor and author, b. Moyne, County Wicklow, Ireland. To U.S. (1856); founder and editor, the *Nation,* a weekly periodical (1865; merged into New York *Evening Post,* 1881); editor in chief, N.Y. *Evening Post* (1883–99).

God·lee \ˈgäd-lē\, Sir Rickman John. 1849–1925. English surgeon. Surgeon (1885–1914), professor (1892–1914), U. Coll. Hospital, London; performed first operation for removal of a tumor from the brain (1884). Author of biography (1917) of Joseph Lister, his uncle.

Go·dol·phin \gə-ˈdäl-fən\, Sidney. 1610–1643. English poet. Friend of Ben Jonson and Thomas Hobbes; M.P. (1628–40); killed in Royalist service in Civil War. Author of *The Passion of Dido for Aeneas,* translated from *Aeneid* and completed by Edmund Waller (pub. 1658).

Godolphin, Sidney. 1st Earl of Godolphin. 1645–1712. English politician. Royal page (1662); M.P. (1668–81); lord of the treasury (1679); secretary of state and head of treasury (1684); chamberlain to Queen Mary (1685); loyal to James II, with whom he kept up secret correspondence after James left England (1688). Lord high treasurer of England (1700–01, 1702–10); ally of Marlborough and Harley; secured ejection of Tories from Queen Anne's ministry; helped negotiate union with Scotland (1706–07); created earl (1706); dismissed from office by Queen Anne (1710), but allowed a pension for life. Noted breeder of racing horses.

Go·dow·sky \gə-ˈdȯf-skē\, Leopold. 1870–1938. American piano virtuoso and composer, b. Soshly, Lithuania. To U.S. (1890, naturalized 1891); taught in New York City, Chicago, Philadelphia, Vienna (1909–14), etc.; known for advanced piano techniques.

Go·doy \gō-ˈthȯi\, Manuel de. *In full* Manuel de Godoy Ál·va·rez de Fa·ria Rí·os Sán·chez Zar·zo·sa \-ˈäl-vä-räth-thā-ˈfär-yä-ˈrē-ōs-ˈsän-chāth-thär-ˈthō-sä\. 1767–1851. Spanish politician. Gained favor of King Charles IV and Queen Maria Luisa; prime minister (1792–98); declared war against France (1793–95); defeated; negotiated Treaty of Basel (1795), for which he was granted title of "Prince of the Peace"; negotiated Treaty of San Ildefonso against England (1797); forced to resign (1798) after Spanish naval defeats. Returned to power (1801); compelled by French to lead Spain in attack on Portugal (1801); aided France in war with England (1801–05) but made very unpopular by arbitrary acts and by defeat of Spanish fleet at Trafalgar (1805); attempted to flee with Charles from French invasion (1807); arrested by Ferdinand and given over (1808) to custody of Napoléon; in exile (1808–47).

Godoy Al·ca·ya·ga \-äl-kä-'yä-gä\, Lucila. *Pseudonym* Gabriela Mis·tral \mē-'sträl\. 1889–1957. Chilean poet. Schoolteacher, college professor, public official, diplomat. Author of lyrics collected in *Desolación* (1922), *Ternura* (1925), *Tala* (1938), *Lager* (1954), etc. Awarded 1945 Nobel prize for literature.

Go·du·nov \gə-dü-'nȯf\, Boris Fyodorovich. c.1551–1605. Czar of Russia (1598–1605). A favorite of Ivan IV; chief member of regency during reign (1584–98) of his brother-in-law, Czar Fyodor I; said to have caused death (1591) of Czarevitch Dmitri; defeated the Crimean Tatars (1591), recovered territory from Sweden (1595), and recolonized Siberia. On Fyodor's death (1598), elected to throne; reformed legal system, encouraged education; died in struggle with false Dmitri and boyars.

God·win \'gäd-wən\ *or* **God·wi·ne** \'gäd-,win-ə\. d. 1053. Earl of Wessex. Favorite of Canute II, who made him earl (c.1018); instrumental in placing Edward the Confessor on the throne (1042); arranged marriage of his daughter Edith (Eadgyth) to the king; outlawed by Edward (1051), but returned in force (1052) and recovered possessions. Father of Harold II.

God·win \'gäd-wən\, Edward William. 1833–1886. English architect and designer. With decoration of own house in Japanese style (c.1861) helped initiate Aesthetic movement; designed Northampton town hall (1861), Dromore and Glenbegh castles, Ireland (1867–71), White House, London, for J.A.M. Whistler (1877), etc.; designed furniture, textiles, wallpaper, theatrical sets and costumes. Companion of Ellen Terry and father of Edward Gordon Craig (*qq.v.*).

Godwin, Francis. 1562–1633. English prelate and historian. Bishop of Llandaff (1601), of Hereford (1617). From his romance *Man in the Moone* (pub. 1638), John Wilkins and Cyrano de Bergerac are supposed to have borrowed their sketches of life in the moon; also wrote *Catalogue of the Bishops of England* (1601) and *Rerum Anglicarum* (1616).

Godwin, Mary, *nee* Woll·stone·craft \'wu̇l-stən-,kraft\. 1759–1797. English author. Formed connection in Paris with Gilbert Imlay (1793–95) and on his desertion of her and their daughter Fanny, attempted suicide; m. William Godwin (1797) and died on birth of daughter Mary (see Mary Wollstonecraft SHELLEY). Author of novel *Mary* (1788), stories, *Historical and Moral View of the Origin and Progress of the French Revolution* (1794), and esp. *Vindication of the Rights of Woman* (1792), influential attack on conventions.

Godwin, William. 1756–1836. English philosopher and writer. Dissenting minister (1777–82); became atheist and devoted himself to study and writing. Married (1797) Mary Wollstonecraft, who died same year. Bookseller and publisher (1805–25); published Lamb's *Tales from Shakespeare* and some children's books of his own (under pseudonym Edward Bald·win \'bȯl-dwən\). Author of *Enquiry Concerning Political Justice* (1793), which gained him a reputation as philosophical representative of English radicalism; novels *Adventures of Caleb Williams* (1794) and *St. Leon* (1799); *Life of Chaucer* (1803); essays *The Enquirer* (1797) and *Of Population* (1820, in answer to Malthus); *History of the Commonwealth* (1824–28); *Thoughts on Man* (1831); etc. See Mary Wollstonecraft GODWIN and Mary Wollstonecraft SHELLEY.

Godwin-Aus·ten \-'ȯs-tən, -'äs-\, Henry Haversham. 1834–1923. English explorer and geologist. Attached to Great Trigonometrical Survey of India (1856); carried on survey work in northern India, Assam, Tibet, Bhutan, etc., regions not theretofore visited by Europeans (1856–77). K2, second highest mountain in the world, often called Mount Godwin Austen after him.

Goeb·bels \'gœb-əls\, Joseph, *in full* Paul Joseph. 1897–1945. German politician. District leader of Nazi party in Berlin (1926); organized party membership in northern Germany; founder (1927) and editor of the Nazi journal *Der Angriff;* Nazi party propaganda director (1928); minister for propaganda and national enlightenment (1933–45); master of modern propaganda techniques in retaining support of German people for war effort; named by Hitler his successor as chancellor; took own life in Hitler's bunker, Berlin.

Goe·bel \'gœ̄-bəl\, Karl Immanuel Eberhard von. 1855–1932. German botanist. Professor, Rostock (1881–87), Marburg (1887–91), Munich (1891–1931). Principal work *Organographie der Pflanzen* (1898–1901).

Goe·ben \'gœ̄-bən\, August Karl von. 1816–1880. Prussian soldier. Distinguished himself in Danish war (1864), Seven Weeks' War (1866), and against France in battles of Spichern and Gravelotte (1870); succeeded Manteuffel in command of 1st army and won decisive battle of St.-Quentin (1871).

Goe·de·ke \'gœ̄-də-kə\, Karl. 1814–1887. German scholar. Professor, Göttingen (1873). Author of *Grundriss zur Geschichte der deutschen Dichtung* (1859–81).

Goe·je \'gü-yə\, Jan de, *in full* Michael Jan de. 1836–1909. Dutch scholar. Professor at Leiden (1866–1906); edited and translated many Arabic works, esp. *Description de l'Afrique et de l'Espagne* (with R.P. Dozy, 1866) after Idrīsī; also wrote *Mémoires d'histoire et de géographie orientales* (1866).

Goer·de·ler \'gœr-də-lər\, Carl-Friedrich. 1884–1945. German politician. Second mayor of Königsberg (1922–30); mayor of Leipzig (1930–37); federal commissioner for price control (1931–32, 1934–35); dismissed from Leipzig post by Nazi party; joined resistance; active in planning attempt to assassinate Hitler (1944), to be followed by coup; arrested (1944), executed by Gestapo.

Goering. See GÖRING.

Go·es *or* **Gó·is** \'gō-ish\, Damião de. 1502–1574. Portuguese Humanist, historian, and diplomat. Engaged in diplomatic missions in Flanders, Poland, Denmark, and Sweden; historiographer and archivist, Lisbon (1546); arrested by Inquisition on charges of Lutheranism (1571). Known esp. for *Chrónica do felicíssimo rei Dom Manuel* (1566–67).

Goes \'güs\, Hugo van der. c.1440–1482. Flemish painter. Painted great "Portinari Altarpiece," containing *The Adoration of the Shepherds,* for chapel in hospital of Santa Maria Nuova, Florence, Italy, now preserved in Ufizzi Gallery in Florence; other works included *Lamentation, Adoration of the Magi, Holy Trinity Adored by Sir Edward Bonkil, Death of the Virgin;* noted for ability to convey emotion and profound spirituality.

Goe·thals \'gō-thəlz\, George Washington. 1858–1928. American army officer and engineer, b. Brooklyn, N.Y. Appointed by President Theodore Roosevelt as chief engineer and chairman of Panama Canal Commission (1907); carried canal construction through to completion (1914); major general (1915); governor of Canal Zone (1914–17). During World War I returned to active duty as acting quartermaster general and director of purchase, storage, and traffic.

Goe·the \'gœ̄-tə, *Angl* 'gə(r)-tə, *also* 'gə(r)-tē\, Johann Wolfgang von. 1749–1832. German poet. Licensed to practice law (1771); strongly influenced by Herder; contributed to *Sturm und Drang* movement with tragedy *Götz von Berlichingen* (1773), whose success established Shakespearean form of drama on German stage; published *Die Leiden des jungen Werthers* (1774), a romantic love story inspired by a chaste affair. On invitation from Duke Charles Augustus of Saxe-Weimar, settled in Weimar (1775), then the literary and intellectual center of Germany; became a leader in the life at Weimar and an associate of Wieland, Herder, and later of Schiller; formed romantic attachment for Charlotte von Stein, wife of a Weimar official. Was ennobled, created a privy councilor, and appointed to administrative posts, where he acquitted himself with credit. Visited Italy (1786–88, 1790) and received new inspiration; published the verse dramas *Iphigenie auf Tauris* (1787), *Egmont* (1788), *Torquato Tasso* (1790). Firm literary friendship (from 1794) with Schiller stimulated Goethe; published *Wilhelm Meisters Lehrjahre* (1795–96), the epic idyll *Hermann und Dorothea* (1798). m. Christiane Vulpius (1806), who had been a member of his household (from 1788), but continued to form romantic and often inspiring attachments. In later years celebrated as a sage as well as poet; visited by luminaries from around the world; presiding spirit of German literature, with affinities for schools of Romanticism, sentimentality, modernism. Other works included verse *Das Buch Annette* (1767), *Neue Lieder* (1770), *Römische Elegien* (1793), *Venezianische Epigramme* (1795), *Epilog zu Schillers Glocke* (1805); dramatic works *Clavigo* (1774), *Die Geschwister* (1776), *Der Gross-Cophta* (1792), *Der Bürgergeneral* (1793), *Die natürliche Tochter* (1804), *Pandoras Wiederkunft* (1808), *Des Epimenides Erwachen* (1815), and his masterpiece *Faust* (1808–32); novels *Achilleis* (1808), *Die Wahlverwandtschaften* (1809), *Wilhelm Meisters Wanderjahre* (1821–29). Also wrote extensively on botany, optics, and other scientific topics; published autobiography under the title *Aus meinem Leben, Dichtung und Wahrheit* (1811–22) and travel book *Italienische Reise* (1816–17).

Goetz. See GÖTZ.

Goe·ze \'gœt-sə\, Johann Melchior. 1717–1786. German theologian. Lutheran preacher in Magdeburg, Hamburg; known esp. for long controversy with Lessing because of publication of Reimarus's *Fragmente eines Ungenannten* in Lessing's "Wolfenbüttel Fragments."

Goffe *or* **Gough** \'gäf, 'gȯf\, William. c.1605–1679. English regicide. One of judges at trial of Charles I; held military command under Cromwell at Dunbar (1650), Worcester (1651); major general for Sussex, Berkshire, and Hampshire (1655). At Restoration, fled to America.

Go·ga \'gō-gä\, Octavian. 1881–1938. Rumanian writer and politican. Member of Rumanian delegation at Peace Conference in Paris (1919); minister of religion (1920), of interior (1926); prime minister (1937–38). Author of verse *Ne cheamă pămîntul* (1909), *Cîntece fără ţară* (1916), etc.

Go·gar·ty \'gō-gərt-ē\, Oliver Joseph St. John. 1878–1957. Irish physician and writer. Senator (1922–36), Irish Free State. Author of *Poems and Plays* (1920), *An Offering of Swans* (1923), *As I Was Going Down Sackville Street* (1937), *Tumbling in the Hay* (1939), *It Isn't This Time of Year at All* (1954).

Gogh \'gōg; *Angl* 'gō, 'gäk, 'kòk\, Vincent Willem van. 1853–1890. Dutch painter. Took up painting (1880) after failing as art dealer, evangelist; evolved wholly individual style of broad expressive brushwork, heightened colors and contours in depicting peasant, rural, domestic scenes; developed elements of Expressionism and Symbolism that deeply influenced both schools; beset by mental disturbances in last years; took own life. Notable works included *In the Field, The Loom, Potato Eaters, Boots, La Mousmé, Chair and Pipe, Night Cafe, Self-Portrait with Pipe and Bandaged Ear, L'Arlésienne, Bedroom at Arles, Starry Night, Church at Auvers.*

Go·gol \'gò-gəlʸ, *Angl* 'gò-gəl, 'gō-ˌgòl\, Nikolay Vasilyevich. 1809–1852. Russian writer. His first works two series of Ukrainian sketches, *Vechera na khutore bliz Dikanki* (*Evenings on a Farm Near Dikanka,* 1831) and *Mirgorod* (1835), including "Taras Bulba" (rewritten and enlarged, 1842), a tale of Cossack struggles with Poles and Tartars in 16th century; other notable stories included "Nos," "Kolyaska," "Nevsky prospekt," "Shinel" ("The Overcoat"). Published masterpiece novel *Myortvye dushi* (*Dead Souls,* 1842), comedy *Revizor* (*The Inspector General,* 1836); called father of realism in Russian literature.

Goijen, Jan van. See Jan van GOYEN.

Góis, Damião de. See GOES.

Gökalp, Ziya. See Mehmed ZIYA.

Go·kha·le \'gō-kə-ˌlāⁿ\, Gopāl Krishna. 1866–1915. Indian educator and politician. Professor, Fergusson Coll., Poona (1884–1902); became identified with Indian National Congress movement, president (1905); founded Servants of India Society (1905); member of Indian Public Services Commission (1912–15); a leader of the moderate Nationalists.

Golaw, Salomon von. See Friedrich von LOGAU.

Gold·bach \'gōld-ˌbäk\, Christian. 1690–1764. Prussian mathematician. Professor, St. Petersburg (1725–28); tutor to Czarevitch Peter II (1728–42); in Russian ministry of foreign affairs (1742–64); made contributions to number theory, differential equations, etc.; best known for "Goldbach conjecture" that every even natural number is sum of two prime numbers.

Gold·berg \'gōl(d)-ˌbərg\, Reuben Lucius, *known* as Rube \'rüb\. 1883–1970. American cartoonist, b. San Francisco. On staff of *San Francisco Chronicle* (1904–05) and *Bulletin* (1905–07), New York *Evening Mail* (1907–21); syndicated cartoonist (1921–64); known esp. for cartoons depicting inventions of Prof. Lucifer Gorgonzola Butts, which achieved simple ends by means of mechanical contrivances of absurdly unnecessary complexity; also creator of comic characters "Boob McNutt," "Lala Palooza," etc.

Gold·ber·ger \'gōl(d)-bər-gər\, Joseph. 1874–1929. American physician, b. Austria. To U.S. (1880); with U.S. Public Health Service (from 1899); at Hygienic Laboratory, Washington, D.C. (from 1904); discoverer of nature of and remedy for pellagra (1913–25).

Gol·den \'gōl-dən\, Harry Lewis. *Orig.* Gold·hirsch \'gōld-ˌhərsh\. 1903–1981. American editor and writer, b. New York City. Settled in Charlotte, N.C. (1941); founder and editor (1941–68), *Carolina Israelite* newspaper; leader in campaign against racial segregation. Author of *Only in America* (1958), *For 2 Cents Plain* (1959), *Enjoy, Enjoy* (1960), *You're Entitle'* (1962), *So What Else Is New* (1965), *The Lynching of Leo Frank* (1966), *So Long as You're Healthy* (1969), *The Israelis* (1970), etc.

Gol·den·wei·ser \'gōl-dən-ˌwī-zər\, Alexander Alexandrovich. 1880–1940. American anthropologist, b. Kiev, Russia. To U.S. (1900). Lecturer, Columbia (1910–19), New School for Social Research, New York (1919–26), Rand School of Social Science (1915–29); professor, U. of Oregon Extension (from 1930). Author of *Totemism* (1910), *Early Civilization* (1922), *Sex in Civilization* (1929), *Robots or Gods* (1932), *History, Psychology and Culture* (1933), *Anthropology, An Introduction to Primitive Culture* (1937).

Gold·fa·den \'gōl(d)-ˌfäd-ᵊn\, Abraham. *Orig.* Gol·den·fad·en \'gōl-dən-ˌfäd-ᵊn\. 1840–1908. American poet and playwright, b. Old Constantine, Russia. Teacher in Russia; to Poland (1875), founded two Yiddish newspapers; to Romania (1876), founded at Iaşi first Yiddish theater; moved to Warsaw (1883), to U.S. (1887). Author of some 400 plays and operas in Yiddish, as *Shulamit* (1880), *Bar Kochba* (1882), *David at War* (1904).

Gol·die \'gōl-dē\, Sir George Dashwood Taubman. *Orig.* Goldie-Taub·man \-'tòb-mən\. 1846–1925. English colonial administrator, b. Isle of Man. Formed (1876) Central African Trading Co.; visited Niger region (1877) and set out to add this region to the British Empire; merged commercial companies trading in the Niger region into Royal Niger Co. (1879); received charter (1886) establishing British rule through company; government organized with Lord Aberdare as governor (1886–95), succeeded by Goldie (1895–1900). The Royal Niger Co. transferred its territories to the British government (1900) and they were organized into the protectorates of Northern Nigeria and Southern Nigeria.

Gol·ding \'gōl-diŋ\, Louis. 1895–1958. English writer. Author of verse, stories, and novels as *Forward from Babylon* (1920), *Store of Ladies* (1927), *Give up Your Lovers* (1930), *Magnolia Street* (1932), *The Camberwell Beauty* (1935), *Mr. Emmanuel* (1939), etc.

Gold·man \'gōl(d)-mən\, Edwin Franko. 1878–1956. American composer and bandmaster, b. Louisville, Ky. Formed (1911) New York Military Band, later known as Goldman Band; conducted annual concert series in Central Park Mall (1922–55). Author of band books and composer of "On the Mall" and other pieces. His son ¶Richard Franko (1910–1980) succeeded as leader of Goldman Band; director of Peabody Conservatory, Baltimore (1968–77).

Goldman, Emma. 1869–1940. American anarchist, b. Kovno (now Kaunas), Lithuania. To U.S. (1885) and soon after identified herself with anarchist and Socialist groups; associated with Alexander Berkman (*q.v.*); for agitation in New York, arrested and jailed (1893); founded and edited (1906–17) *Mother Earth;* jailed (1917–19) for anti-conscription agitation; deported (1919). Author of *Anarchism and Other Essays* (1910), *My Disillusionment in Russia* (1923), *Living My Life,* autobiography (1931).

Gold·mann \'gòlt-ˌmän\, Nahum. 1895–1982. German Zionist, b. Lithuania. Creditor and publisher of *Encyclopedia Judaica* (1922 ff.); on staff of Jewish Agency for Palestine (from 1934); forced to flee Germany (1934); helped organize World Jewish Congress (1936; president 1951–78); in U.S. (1940–45); negotiated reparations payments by West Germany to victims of Nazi persecution (1951).

Gold·mark \'gòlt-ˌmärk, *Angl* 'gōl(d)-ˌmärk\, Karl. 1830–1915. Hungarian composer. Composed operas as *Die Königin von Saba* (1875), *Merlin* (1886), *Das Heimchen am Herd* (1896), *Götz von Berlichingen* (1902), *Ein Wintermärchen* (1908); orchestral works as overture *Sakuntala* (1865), symphonies; choral, chamber, piano works; noted as teacher. His nephew ¶Rubin Goldmark (1872–1936), b. New York City, was a noted teacher; head of composition department, Juilliard School (1924–36); pupils included Aaron Copland, George Gershwin.

Gold·mark \'gōl(d)-ˌmärk\, Peter Carl. 1906–1977. American engineer, b. Budapest, Hungary. To U.S. (1933); with Columbia Broadcasting System Laboratories (1936–72); vice president, CBS (1950); president, CBS Labs (1972); demonstrated first color television system (1940); developed 33 1/3-rpm phonograph record (1948).

Gol·do·ni \gōl-'dō-nē\, Carlo. 1707–1793. Italian playwright. Wrote for Teatro Sant'Angelo (1748–52) and Teatro San Luca (1753–62) in Venice; to France (1762). Created modern Italian comedy in style of Molière, superseding conventional buffoonery of commedia dell'arte. Among his comedies, about 150 in all, were *La putta onorata* (1759), *La Pamela* (1750), *I pettegolezzi delle donne* (1750), *Il bugiardo* (1750), *Il vero amico* (1750), *La locandiera* (1753), *I rusteghi* (1760), *Le baruffe chiozzote* (1762); also published *Mémoires* (1787).

Golds·bor·ough \'gōl(d)z-ˌbər-ə, -ˌbə-rə, -brə\, Louis Malesherbes. 1805–1877. American naval officer, b. Washington, D.C. Served in Mexican War; explored California and Oregon (1849–50); superintendent, U.S. Naval Academy (1853–57); commander, North Atlantic Blockading Squadron (1861–62); commanded fleet that captured Roanoke Island and destroyed Confederate fleet (Feb. 7–9, 1862); rear admiral (1862).

Gold·schmidt \'gòlt-ˌshmit\, Hans. 1861–1923. German chemist. Invented the aluminothermic, or Goldschmidt's, process for reducing certain metals from their oxides and for obtaining molten iron for welding.

Gold·schmidt \'gōl-shmit\, Meïr Aron. 1819–1887. Danish journalist, writer, and politician. Founded (1840) satirical weekly *Corsaren* (discontinued 1846); later published journal *Nord og Syd.* Author of novels *En Jøde* (1845), *Hjemløs* (1853–57), *Ravnen* (1867), short stories, and an autobiography *Livserindringer* (1877).

Gold·schmidt \'gòlt-ˌshmit\, Richard Benedikt. 1878–1958. German zoologist. Director of genetics department, Kaiser-Wilhelm-Institut for Biology, Berlin (1913–35); professor, U. of California (1936–58); known for genetic studies of geographic variation, intersexuality, etc. Author of *Physiological Genetics* (1938), *The Material Basis of Evolution* (1940), etc.

Goldschmidt, Victor Mordechai. 1853–1933. German mineralogist. Professor, Heidelberg (1893); a founder of modern crystallography. Author of *Index der Kristallformen der Mineralien* (1886–91), *Kristallographische Winkeltabellen* (1897), *Atlas der Kristallformen* (1913–23).

Goldschmidt, Victor Moritz. 1888–1947. German mineralogist and petrologist. Professor and director of mineralogical institute, U. of Kristiania (now Oslo; 1914–29), Göttingen (1929–35), Oslo (1935–42); a founder of geochemistry and inorganic crystal chemistry. Author of *Die Kontaktmetamorphose im Kristiania-gebiete* (1911), *Die Injektionsmetamorphose im Stavanger-gebiete* (1921), *Geochemische Verteilungsgesetze der Elemente* (1923–38).

Gold·schmied \'gólt-shmēt\, Johannes. *Lat.* Johann Au·ri·fa·ber \'aù-ri-ˌfäb-ər, 'ór-ə-ˌfā-bər\. 1519–1575. German theologian. Assistant to Luther (1545); court preacher in Weimar (1550–61); editor of Jena edition of Luther's works (1555–58) and of his letters (1556, 1565) and other writings.

Gold·smid \'gōl(d)-sməd\. Prominent English Jewish family, including: Benjamin (1755–1808) and his brother ¶Abraham (1756–1810), financiers; both b. Amsterdam; to England (c.1763); became brokers (1777); negotiated several large government loans, helping finance Pitt's wars with France (1792–99). Abraham's nephew ¶Sir Isaac Lyon Goldsmid (1778–1859), financier and philanthropist; England's first Jewish baronet (1841); helped secure passage of Jewish Disabilities Bill (1759). Isaac's son ¶Sir Francis Henry (1808–1878), first English Jewish barrister (1833); M.P. (from 1860). Benjamin's grandson ¶Sir Frederick John (1818–1908), army officer in China (1840), Crimean War (1855), and Sepoy Mutiny; negotiated (1861–64) and superintended construction (1864–65) of Indo-European telegraph; director general (1865–70); helped negotiate Iran–Baluchistan border dispute (1871), Iran–Afghanistan dispute (1872); retired as major general (1875). See also C.J. Goldsmid-MONTEFIORE.

Goldsmid-Montefiore, Claude Joseph. See C. J. Goldsmid-MONTEFIORE.

Gold·smith \'gōl(d)-ˌsmith\, Oliver. 1730–1774. British poet, playwright, and novelist, b. Ireland. Studied medicine in Edinburgh; devoted himself to literary work (from 1756); became acquainted with Dr. Johnson (1761) and a member of the famous club centered around Johnson. Author of *Enquiry into the Present State of Polite Learning in Europe* (1759), *The Citizen of the World* (1762, orig. contributed as "Chinese Letters" to *Public Ledger), The Traveller* (didactic poem, 1764), *The Vicar of Wakefield* (novel, 1766), *The Good Natur'd Man* (comedy, 1768), *The Deserted Village* (poem, 1770), *She Stoops to Conquer* (comedy, 1773), *Retaliation* (poem, 1774), *An History of the Earth, and Animated Nature* (1774).

Gold·stein \'gólt-ˌshtīn\, Eugen. 1850–1930. German physicist. Investigated electrical phenomena in gases; studied and named cathode rays; credited with discovery of canal rays (1886).

Gold·wyn \'gōl-dwən\, Samuel. *Orig. surname* Gold·fish \'gōl(d)-ˌfish\. 1882–1974. American motion picture producer, b. Warsaw, Poland. To U.S. (1896); glovemaker and salesman; with brother-in-law Jesse Lasky and C.B. DeMille formed Lasky Feature Play Co. (1913); director and chairman, Famous Players-Lasky (1917); organized Goldwyn Pictures Corp. (1917), merging with L.B. Mayer's Metro Pictures to form (1925) Metro-Goldwyn-Mayer; later an independent producer. Helped establish practice of employing well known authors and actors for films; noted for malapropisms. Produced films including *Squaw Man* (1913), *All Quiet on the Western Front* (1930), *Arrowsmith* (1931), *Stella Dallas* (1937), *Wuthering Heights* (1939), *Little Foxes* (1941), *Best Years of Our Lives* (1946, Academy Award), *Secret Life of Walter Mitty* (1947), *Guys and Dolls* (1955), *Porgy and Bess* (1959).

Gol·gi \'gól-jē\, Camillo. 1843 or 1844–1926. Italian physician. Professor, Pavia (1876–1918); senator (1900). First to use silver nitrate to stain nerve tissue for study (1873); discovered dendritic nerve cells called Golgi cells; discovered Golgi tendon spindle (1880), Golgi apparatus or complex (1883); studied malaria (1885–93) and discovered two forms of malarial parasite. Shared with Santiago Ramón y Cajal 1906 Nobel prize for physiology or medicine.

Go·li·tsyn \(ˌ)gəl-'yēt-sin\. Noble Russian family, descended from the boyar Mikhail Ivanovich Bul·ga·kov \bül-'gä-kəv\, *called* Golitsa (d. 1558), and including: ¶Prince Vasily Vasilyevich Golitsyn (1643–1714), general and politician; created boyar by Czar Alexis (1676); under Czar Fyodor reorganized Russian army; head of foreign office (1682–89) and virtual prime minister during regency of Sophia Alekseyevna; negotiated Polish alliance (1686); led disastrous campaigns against Crimean Tartars (1687, 1689); exiled to Siberia. His cousin ¶Prince Mikhail Mikhaylovich (1674–1730), general; served under Peter the Great in defeating Charles XII of Sweden at Poltava (1709). Mikhail's brother ¶Prince Dmitry Mikhaylovich (1655–1737), diplomat and politician; governor general of Kiev (1715–19), senator (from 1719); president of finance ministry (1719–22); deprived (1724); member of Supreme Privy Council (1726–30), and supporter of charter forced upon Anna Ivanovna at her elevation to throne (1730); imprisoned by Empress Anna when she repudiated charter (1731). ¶Prince Boris Alekseyevich (1654–1713), minister under Peter the Great; made boyar (1690); member of regency council in Peter's absence (1697–98). ¶Prince Aleksandr Nikolayevich (1773–1844); close adviser to Czar Alexander I; super-procurator of Holy Synod (1802–17); minister of public education (1816–17); chief of ministry of spiritual affairs and public education (1817–24). ¶Nikolay Borisovich (1794–1866), patron of Beethoven, commissioned three quartets and an overture. ¶Prince Boris Borisovich (1862–1916), physicist, known for his work in seismography; invented (1906) electromagnetic seismograph. See also D.A. GALLITZIN.

Gol·lancz \gə-'lan(t)s\, Sir Hermann. 1852–1930. British rabbi and Semitic scholar, b. Germany. Preacher at the Bayswater Synagogue (1892–1923); professor of Hebrew, University Coll., London (1902–23); knighted (1923), first British rabbi so honored. His brother ¶Sir Israel (1864–1930) was lecturer at Cambridge (1896–1906); professor, University Coll., London (1905–30); a founder (1902) and first secretary (1902–30) of British Academy. Edited and published *Cynewulf's Christ* (1892), *Exeter Book of Anglo-Saxon Poetry* (1895), *Temple Shakespeare* (1894–96), and *The Sources of Hamlet* (1926); edited also *The Temple Classics,* and *The Caedmon Manuscript of Anglo-Saxon Biblical Poetry.*

Gollancz, Sir Victor. 1893–1967. British publisher and writer. Managing director, Ernest Benn Ltd. (1920–28); founded Victor Gollancz Ltd. (1928), Left Book club (1936); directed campaigns to rescue Jews from Nazi Germany, to relieve starvation in postwar Germany, to relieve Arab refugees from Palestine, to abolish capital punishment, for nuclear disarmament, etc.

Go·lo·vin \gə-(ˌ)ləv-'yin\, Fyodor Alekseyevich. Count. 1650–1706. Russian diplomat and politician. In service of Sophia Alekseyevna; sent by Vasily Golitsyn to negotiate Treaty of Nerchinsk (1685–89) with China; made boyar (1689) by Peter the Great; took part in Azov campaigns (1695, 1696); accompanied Peter on European tour (1697–98); admiral general in charge of new navy (1699); also head of foreign affairs, concluding treaty with Turks (1700) and negotiating alliance with Poland against Sweden.

Go·lov·kin \(ˌ)gə-'lóf-kyin\, Gavriil Ivanovich. Count. 1660–1734. Russian diplomat and politician. Supporter of Peter the Great; director of treasury (1689); accompanied Peter on European tour (1697–98); succeeded Golovin in charge of foreign affairs (1706); state chancellor (1709); made count (1710); member of Supreme Privy Council (1725); supporter and guardian of Peter II; promoted succession of Anna Ivanovna (1730) and made cabinet member and senator (1731).

Go·lov·nin \gə-(ˌ)ləv-'nyēn\, Vasily Mikhaylovich. 1776–1831. Russian navigator. Served in British navy (1801–06); surveyed Kamchatka and Russian America (1807–10); prisoner in Japan (1810–13); circumnavigated globe (1817–19). Author of *Narrative of My Captivity in Japan* (1816), *Journey to Kamchatka* (1819).

Goltz \'gólts\, Colmar von der, *in full* Wilhelm Leopold Colmar von der. Freiherr. *Called* Goltz Pa·sha \-pə-'shä\. 1843–1916. German general. In Turkey (1883–96), reorganized Turkish army; in Germany, general of infantry (1900), colonel general (1908), field marshal (1911). Military governor of Belgium after its conquest (1914); commander of Turkish First army in Mesopotamia (1914–16); successfully invested Gen. Sir Charles Townshend's Anglo-Indian army at Kut (1915–16).

Goltz, Friedrich Leopold. 1834–1902. German physiologist. Professor, Halle (1870), Strassburg (1872); known esp. for studies of nervous system and reflex actions.

Goltz, Rüdiger von der, *in full* Gustav Adolf Joachim Rüdiger von der. Graf. 1865–1946. German general. Commanded a division in battle of the Masurian Lakes (1915); led division to aid Finnish national army against Finnish-Russian Red army (1918); occupied Helsinki (1918); named governor of Libau, Latvia (1919); led German-Latvian corps against Russians; occupied Riga (1919); defeated by Estonian-Latvian force; returned to Germany (1919).

Gol·tzi·us \'gōl-tsē-œs\, Hendrik. 1558–1617. Dutch engraver, etcher, and painter. Founded engraving school at Haarlem (1582); executed portraits, miniatures, mythological and historical scenes; outstanding engraver and woodcut artist of the day.

Go·łu·chow·ski \gól-ü-'kóf-skē\, Agenor. Graf. 1812–1875. Polish nobleman. In Austrian service; governor of Galicia (1849–59, 1866–68, 1871–75); Austrian minister of the interior (1859–61); a principal author of "October diploma" (1860), granting federal status and diets to Habsburg lands. His son ¶Agenor (1849–1921) was Austro-Hungarian minister of foreign affairs (1895–1906); negotiated Austro-Russian agreement (1897); mediated Moroccan crisis between France and Germany (1905).

Go·ma·rus \gə-'mä-rəs\, Franciscus. *Orig. surname* Gom·mer \'gōm-ər\. 1563–1641. Dutch theologian. Professor, Leiden (1594); conservative Calvinist, leader of the opponents of Arminius; debated Arminius (1608); later professor at Saumur, Groningen; took part in Synod of Dort (1618) which condemned Arminianism.

Gom·berg \'gäm-ˌbərg\, Moses. 1866–1947. American chemist, b. Elisavetgrad (now Kirovograd), Ukraine. To U.S. (1884); professor, U. of Michigan (1899–1936); first to prepare a free radical, triphenylmethyl (1900); founded study of free radicals.

Gom·bert \gōⁿ-ber\, Nicolas. c.1490–c.1556. Flemish composer. Singer and later master of choirboys in chapel of Emperor Charles V; later connected with cathedrals of Courtrai, Tournai. Composed motets, chansons, masses, Magnificats, in free style linking those of Josquin des Prez and Palestrina; helped spread influential Franco-Netherlandish style.

Gom·ber·ville \gōⁿ-ber-vēl\, Marin Le Roy de \lə-rwä-də-\. 1600–1674. French writer. Author of romances *Polexandre* (1637), *La Cythérée* (1639).

Göm·bös \'gœm-bœsh\, Gyula. 1886–1936. Hungarian general and politician. Organized (1919) network of counterrevolutionary, nationalistic, anti-Semitic societies to oppose Communist government; minister of defense in émigré Szeged government; associate of Horthy; organized military opposition to King Charles's return (1921); minister of defense (1929–31); prime minister (1932–36); failed to achieve rightist program.

Gom·bro·wicz \gòm-'brò-vēch\, Witold. 1904–1969. Polish writer. Lived in Argentina (1939–60), West Germany. Author of novels *Ferdydurke* (1938), *Trans-Atlantyk* (1953), *Pornografia* (1960), *Kosmos* (1964); plays *Iwona* (1938), *Ślub* (1953); memoirs *Dziennik* (1957–62).

Go·mes \'gō-mis\, Antônio Carlos. 1836–1896. Brazilian composer. Composed operas including *A noite do castelo* (1861), *Joana de Flandres* (1863), *Il Guarany* (1870), *Fosca* (1873, 1878), *Lo schiavo* (1889), *Condor* (1891).

Go·mes \'gō-mish\, Diogo. fl. 1440–84. Portuguese navigator. Sent by Prince Henry the Navigator to explore West African coast (1456); ascended Gambia River and learned of Tombouctou; landed at Cape Verde Islands (1460).

Gomes, Manuel Teixeira. See TEIXEIRA GOMES.

Gomes Coe·lho \-'kòil-yü\, Joaquim Guilherme. *Pseudonym* Júlio Di·nis \dē-'nēsh\. 1839–1871. Portuguese writer. Author of popular realistic novels of middle class life as *As pupilas do Sr. Reitor* (1867), *Uma família inglêsa* (1868), *A morgadinha dos Canaviais* (1868), *Os fidalgos da casa maurisca* (1871).

Gó·mez \'gō-māth\, José. *Known as* Jo·se·li·to el Ga·llo \kō-sā-'lē-tō-el-'gä(l)-yō\ *or* Ga·lli·to \gä(l)-'yē-tō\. 1895–1920. Spanish matador. Youngest man ever to receive title matador (1912); with Belmonte revolutionized bullfighting with new grace and daring; killed in ring.

Gó·mez \'gō-mās\, José Miguel. 1858–1921. Cuban general and politician. President of Cuba (1909–13); led insurrection against Menocal (1917); exiled.

Gómez, Juan Vincente. 1864–1935. Venezuelan soldier and politician. Joined private army of Cipriano Castro (1899); vice president and commander of army (1902–08); in Castro's absence, seized government (1908); supreme dictator (1908–35): provisional president of Venezuela (1908–10); elected president (1910–15, 1922–29, 1931–35); ruled through terror and efficient army; eliminated foreign debt; developed oil industry (from 1918).

Gómez, Laureano Eleuterio. *Full surname* Gómez Ca·stro \-'käs-trō\. 1889–1965. Colombian politician. Entered parliament (1911); minister of public works (1925–26), foreign affairs (1947–48); ambassador to Argentina (1923–25), Germany (1931); leader of Conservative party (1932); president of Colombia (1950–53); instituted harsh rule, censored press, conducted anti-Protestant campaign; deposed (1953), fled to Spain; returned (1957) to form national front with Liberals to oust Pres. Rojas Pinilla.

Gó·mez de Ave·lla·ne·da \'gō-mās-thā-ä-vā(l)-yä-'nā-thä, 'gō-māth-\, Gertrudis. *Pseudonym* La Pe·re·gri·na \lä-pā-rāg-'rē-nä\. 1814–1873. Cuban writer. To Spain (1836). Considered a leading exponent of Spanish Romantic literature. Works included verse *Poesías liricas* (1841); plays, including *Alfonso Munio* (1844), *Saúl* (1849), *Flavio Recaredo* (1851), *La hija de las flores* (1852), *Baltasar* (1858); novels, including *Sab* (1841), *Espatolino* (1844), *Guatimozín* (1847), *El artista barquero* (1861).

Gó·mez de la Ser·na \'gō-māth-thā-läs-'ər-nä\, Ramón. *Known as* Ra·món \rä-'mōn\. 1888–1963. Spanish writer. Leading exponent of Expressionism in Spain; known esp. for *Greguerías*, metaphoric maxims or aphorisms in prose and verse (1917); founded important avant garde journal *Prometeo.* Books included *El doctor inverosímil* (1921), *Gollerías* (1926), *Efigies* (1929), *Ismos* (1931), *El hombre perdido* (1946), *Automoribundia* (1948).

Gó·mez Fa·rí·as \'gō-mās-fä-'rē-äs\, Valentín. 1781–1858. Mexican politician. Physician, liberal reformer; vice president under Santa Anna (1833–34); in Santa Anna's absence obtained legislation reducing army, forming civil militia, reducing powers of church, ending tithes, reforming finances; forced to flee reaction (1835); president briefly (1846) until ousted by Santa Anna; reforms adopted by Benito Juárez (1857).

Gómez Pe·dra·za \-pāth-'räs-ä\, Manuel. 1789–1851. Mexican general and politician. Elected president (1829) but election annulled; took part in revolts (1832); president of Mexico (1832–33); senator (1844).

Gómez y Bá·ez \-ē-'bä-äs\, Máximo. 1836–1905. Cuban patriot and general, b. Dominican Republic. Served in Dominican army against Haiti and Spain; settled in Cuba as farmer; joined insurgents during revolution of 1868–78, becoming commander in chief (1870); general in chief of Cuban forces of second Cuban revolution (1895); on American intervention, placed troops at disposal of U.S. army; declined to be considered for presidency (1902).

Gom·pers \'gäm-pərz\, Samuel. 1850–1924. American labor leader, b. London, England. To America (1863); journeyman cigarmaker (1863); in reorganization of Cigarmakers' Union (1877), became president of his local. Helped found Federation of Organized Trades and Labor Unions (1881), which was reorganized as American Federation of Labor (1886); president, A.F. of L. (1886–1924, except 1895); chiefly responsible for determining its nature and development. Member, Council of National Defense (1917), Commission on International Labor Legislation at Versailles peace conference (1919).

Gom·perz \'gòm-pərts\, Theodor. 1832–1912. German philologist and philosopher. Professor, Vienna (1873–1901). Author of *Griechische Denker* (1896–1909).

Go·mul·ka \gō-'mùl-kə\, Wladyslaw. 1905–1982. Polish leader. Joined secret Communist party in Poland (1926); acted as Communist organizer during World War II; elected first secretary of Polish Workers' (Communist) Party; as deputy head of Soviet-sponsored provisional government, fell into Stalin's disfavor and was dismissed from government and party and arrested (July 1951); rehabilitated after Stalin's death; served as head of Polish United Workers' Party (1956–70); ousted after ordering security forces to fire upon striking workers.

Gon·çal·ves \gōⁿ-'säl-vish\, Nuno. fl. 1450–72. Portuguese painter. Court painter to Afonso V (1450); considered founder of Portuguese school of painting; lost to history until discovery (1882) of only extant work, altarpiece for convent of São Vincente.

Gon·çal·ves de Ma·ga·lhães \gōⁿ-'säl-vis-thā-mä-gäl-'yīⁿs\, Domingos José. 1811–1882. Brazilian poet. In diplomatic service; founded (1836) review *Niterói* in Paris. Author of verse *Suspiros poéticos e saudades* (1836), considered earliest work of Brazilian Romanticism.

Gonçalves Di·as \-'thē-äs\, Antônio. 1823–1864. Brazilian poet. Generally considered national poet of Brazil. His works included collections of lyric poems, as *Primeiros cantos* (1846), *Segundos cantos* (1848), and *Últimos cantos* (1851), an unfinished Indian epic *Os Tambiras* (1857), a dictionary of Tupi (1858), and historical and ethnographical studies.

Gon·cha·rov \gən-(,)chə-'ráf\, Ivan Aleksandrovich. 1812–1891. Russian novelist. Author of *Obyknovennaya istoriya* (1847), *Oblomov* (1859), *Obryv* (1869).

Goncharova, Natalya. See under Mikhail LARIONOV.

Gon·court \gōⁿ-kür\, Edmond-Louis-Antoine Hu·ot de \ue-ō-də-\ (1822–1896) and his brother Jules-Alfred Huot de (1830–1870). French novelists. Collaborated on social histories, art criticism as *L'Art du dix-huitième siècle* (1859–75), and novels in Naturalistic manner as *Charles Demailly* (1860), *Sœur Philomène* (1861), *Renée Mauperin* (1864), *Germinie Lacerteux* (1864), *Madame Gervaisais* (1869); kept *Journal* (1851–96). Edmond endowed the Académie des Goncourt (officially constituted 1903), which awards each year the Prix Goncourt to the author of a prose work of high merit.

Gondebaud. See GUNDOBAD.

Gondemar. See GUNDIMAR.

Gondéric *or* **Gondioc**. See GUNDERIC.

Gon·di \gōⁿ-dē\, Jean-François-Paul de. Cardinal de Retz \re(s)\. 1613–1679. French prelate and politician. Led riotous life as young man; deeply involved in the Fronde (1648–52), at first on side of court, later on rebels' side; determined opponent of Mazarin; created cardinal (1651); imprisoned (1652) but escaped; archbishop of Paris (1654–62); resigned archbishopric (1662) in return for rich benefices. Retired to private life in Lorraine, where he wrote his *Mémoires,* valuable as source of information on contemporary life.

Gondicaire. See GUNDICAR.

Gondomar, Conde de. See Diego SARMIENTO DE ACUÑA.

Gon·do·pher·nes \,gän-dō-'fər-,nēz\ *or* **Gon·do·pha·res** \-'far-,ēz, -'fär-\. 1st century A.D. Indo-Parthian king. Ruled areas of present Afghanistan and Pakistan; subject of various legends; identified by some scholars with Gaspar, one of Three Wise Men of Christian gospels.

Gón·go·ra y Ar·go·te \'gòŋ-gō-rä-ē-är-'gō-tā\, Luis de. 1561–1627. Spanish poet. Wrote fine lyrical poems and several dramas in early years; later, originator of intensely difficult and complex style known since as *gongorismo;* works in this style included *Fábula de Polifemo y Galatea* (1612), *Soledades* (1613), *Fábula de Píramo y Tisbe* (1617).

Gonne \'gän, 'gən\, Maud. 1866–1953. Irish actress and patriot. A founder of Sinn Féin; active in movements to release Irish political prisoners. Early member of W.B. Yeats's theater movement; loved by Yeats and heroine of many of his lyrics and plays. Wrote memoirs *A Servant of the Queen* (1938).

Gon·taut \gōⁿ-tō\, Armand de. Baron de Bi·ron \bē-rōⁿ\. 1524–1592. French soldier. Named grand master of artillery (1569) by Charles IX; named marshal of France (1577) by Henry III; commander in chief under Henry IV (1589–92). His son ¶Charles (1562–1602), companion of Henry IV; brilliant soldier; marshal of France (1594); created duc de Biron (1598); conspired with Spain and later Savoy against Henry; beheaded for treason. His grandnephew ¶Charles-Armand (1663–1756) was created duc de Biron (1723); marshal of France (1734). His son ¶Louis-Antoine (1700–1788) succeeded as duke (1756); marshal (1757). Louis-Antoine's nephew ¶Armand-Louis (1747–1793), duc de Lauzun, succeeded to duchy of Biron; served in army in America under Rochambeau; lieutenant general (1792); commanded armies of the Rhine, in Italy (1792), army of the West (1793); guillotined.

Gon·ville *or* **Gon·vile** \'gän-vəl\, Edmund. d. 1351. English cleric. Founded (1349) what became (1557) Gonville and Caius Coll., Cambridge.

Gon·za·ga \gōn-'dzä-gä\. Italian princely family, descended from Luigi Gonzaga (c.1268–1360), who drove out Bonacolsi family and gained control of Mantua (1328) with title of captain general; subsequently gained control also of Cremona, Reggio, Asolo; eventually forced to recognize suzerainty of Visconti of Milan. Successors ruled Mantua as marquises (1403–07, 1433–1530), then as dukes (to 1707). Among notable members of the family were: ¶Gianfrancesco (1394 or 1395–1444); captain general of Mantua (1407), marquis (1433); commanded troops of antipope John XXIII against King Ladislas of Naples (1411); supported school of Vittorino da Feltre and patronized arts. ¶Francesco II (1466–1519) m. (1490) Isabella d'Este, who greatly beautified Mantua; led Italian forces opposing invasion of Charles VIII of France (1494); opposed Louis XII at Milan and defended Faenza against Cesare Borgia; joined coalition of France, Spain, and Holy Roman Empire against Venice; captured by Venetians (1509); in reward for services, ducal title granted by Emperor Charles V to his son ¶Federigo II (1500–1540), who also became marquis of Montferrat. Federigo's brother ¶Ferrante (1507–1557) was soldier in Habsburg service; administered duchy of Mantua for emperor (1546–54); obtained county of Guastalla (1539). A third brother ¶Ercole (1505–1563), bishop of Mantua (1521), cardinal (1527); regent of duchy (1540–46); presided over Council of Trent (1561–63). ¶Vincenzo (1562–1612), Duke of Mantua; friend and patron of Tasso and Rubens. Extinction of direct male line (1627) led to War of Mantuan Succession (1628–31), a phase of Thirty Years' War.

Gon·za·ga \gōn-'dzä-gä; *Angl* gən-'zäg-ə, gän-, -'zag-\, Aloysius. Saint. 1568–1591. Italian religious. Of noble family; entered Jesuit order (1585); died while ministering to those stricken by famine and pestilence in Rome. Canonized by Pope Benedict XIII (1726); declared patron saint of Christian youth by Pius XI (1926).

Gon·za·ga \gōⁿ-'zá-gə\, Tomás Antônio. *Pseudonym* Dir·ceu \dir-'sāù\. 1744–1810. Portuguese poet. To Brazil (1768); exiled to Mozambique (1792) for alleged complicity in conspiracy. Known esp. for his *Marília de Dirceu* (1792), collection of love poems.

Gon·zá·lez \gòn-'thäl-āth\, José Victoriano. *Pseudonym* Juan Gris \'grēs\. 1887–1927. Spanish artist. To Paris (1906); associated with Picasso and Braque, evolved their intuitive Cubism into more disciplined, severely classical Synthetic Cubism; created still lifes, paper collages, etc.

González, Julio. 1876–1942. Spanish sculptor and painter. Known esp. for abstract welded iron sculptures as *El sueño, Mujer peinándose, Mujer con un cesto, Beso,* series of *Hombres-cactos, La Montserrat.*

Gon·zá·lez \gòn-'säl-ās\, Manuel. 1833–1893. Mexican general and politician. Supporter of Porfirio Díaz; president of Mexico (1880–84).

Gon·zá·lez Bra·vo \gòn-'thäl-āth-'bräv-ò\, Luis. 1811–1871. Spanish politician. Deputy (1841); prime minister (1843–44); ambassador to Lisbon (1844–47, 1854 ff.); minister of interior (1864–65, 1866–68); prime minister (1868); forced to resign at deposition of Queen Isabella II (1868).

González Dá·vi·la \-'t͟hä-vē-lä\, Gil. c.1570–1658. Spanish historian. Author of ecclesiastical histories as *Teatro eclesiástico de las ciudades e iglesias catedrales de España* (1618–1700), *Teatro eclesiástico de la primitiva iglesia de las Indias Occidentales* (1649–55).

González de Clavijo, Ruy. See CLAVIJO.

González de Mendoza, Pedro. See MENDOZA.

Gon·zá·lez Mar·tí·nez \gōn-'säl-ā-smär-'tē-nās\, Enrique. 1871–1952. Mexican physician, poet, and diplomat. Minister to Chile (1920–22), Argentina (1922–24), Spain and Portugal (1924–31). Author of verse *Preludios* (1903), *Lirismos* (1907), *Silenter* (1909), *Los senderos ocultos* (1911), *Parábolas* (1918), *La palabra del viento* (1921), *El romero alucinado* (1923), *Poemas truncos* (1935), *Ausencia y canto* (1937), *Bajo el signo mortal* (1942), *Babel* (1949), *El nuevo Narciso* (1952). Best known poem "La muerte del cisne" (1915), attack on modernist followers of Rubén Darío.

González Na·ve·ro \-näb̲-'ā-rō\, Emiliano. 1861–1938. Paraguayan politician. Vice president of Paraguay (1908, 1930); president (1908–10); provisional president (1912, 1931–32).

Gon·za·lo de Ber·ceo \gòn-'thäl-ō-t͟hā-ber-'thā-ō\. c.1195–c.1264. Spanish poet, b. Berceo. Earliest name known in history of Castilian poetry; author of about 13,000 verses dealing principally with lives of saints, miracles of the Virgin, and other devotional subjects.

Gonzalo de Córdoba. See Gonzalo FERNÁNDEZ DE CÓRDOBA.

Gooch \'güch\, Sir Daniel. 1st Baronet. 1816–1889. English engineer. Locomotive superintendent, Great Western Railway (1837–64); made great improvements in locomotive construction; superintended laying of first 2 telegraph cables from England to U.S. (1865–66); M.P. (1865–85).

Gooch, George Peabody. 1873–1968. English historian. M.P. (1906–10, 1913); editor, *Contemporary Review* (1911–60). Author of *Germany and the French Revolution* (1920), *Franco-German Relations 1871–1914* (1923), *English Democratic Ideas in the 17th Century* (1927), *Courts and Cabinets* (1944), *Maria Theresa and Other Studies* (1951), *Second Empire* (1960), etc.

Goode \'gùd\, George Brown. 1851–1896. American ichthyologist. With Smithsonian Institution, Washington, D.C. (from 1877); assistant secretary in charge of National Museum (1887–96); reorganized and recatalogued collection of museum, developing new methods of display for educational purposes. U.S. Fish Commissioner (1887–88). Author of *American Fishes* (1888), *Oceanic Ichthyology* (with T. H. Bean, 1895), etc.

Good·hue \'gùd-(,)(h)yü\, Bertram Grosvenor. 1869–1924. American architect, b. Pomfret, Conn. Head draftsman with Cram & Wentworth, Boston (1889); admitted as partner (1891) in Cram, Goodhue, & Ferguson. In competition, designed successful plans for buildings of United States Military Academy, West Point; other works included St. Thomas's Church and St. Bartholomew's Church in New York; Trinity Church, Havana, Cuba; Academy of Sciences, Washington, D.C.; Nebraska State Capitol; Cathedral of Maryland, Baltimore; Rockefeller Chapel, U. of Chicago.

Good·man \'gùd-mən\, Benjamin David, *known as* Benny. 1909–1986. American bandleader and clarinetist, b. Chicago. Founded Benny Goodman orchestra (1935); gave first jazz concert in New York's Carnegie Hall (1938); first major white bandleader to integrate black and white musicians; toured widely; as a clarinetist performed classical music with symphony orchestras; dubbed "King of Swing."

Goodman, Paul. 1911–1972. American writer, b. New York City. Wrote criticism, fiction, poetry, and works on city planning and psychotherapy, including *Communitas: Means of Livelihood and Ways of Life* (with his brother Percival, 1947), *Growing Up Absurd* (1960).

Good·night \'gùd-,nīt\, Charles. 1836–1929. American cattleman, b. Macoupin Co., Ill. To Texas (1846); established cattle operations in Texas, New Mexico, Colorado; established Goodnight Trail (Belknap, Tex., to Fort Sumner, N.M.) and with Oliver Loving the Goodnight-Loving Trail north to Wyoming; with J.G. Adair established (1877) JA Ranch, Texas; bred superior beef cattle, protected buffalo herd; produced cattalo cross.

Good·now \'gùd-,nō\, Frank Johnson. 1859–1939. American educator, b. Brooklyn, N.Y. Professor of administrative law, Columbia U. (1883–1914); president, Johns Hopkins U. (1914–29). Author of *Politics and Administration* (1900), *Social Reform and the Constitution* (1911), *Principles of Constitutional Government* (1916), etc.

Good·pas·ture \'gùd-,pas-chər\, Ernest William. 1886–1960. American pathologist, b. Montgomery Co., Tenn. Professor, Harvard (1915–22), Vanderbilt U. (1924–55); developed (1931) method of cultivating viruses and rickettsia in fertile chicken eggs, making many vaccines possible.

Good·rich \'gùd-(,) rich\, Benjamin Franklin. 1841–1888. American industrialist, b. Ripley, N.Y. Formed (1870) firm to manufacture rubber goods in Akron, Ohio; reorganized as B.F. Goodrich Co. (1880).

Goodrich, Samuel Griswold. *Pen name* Peter Par·ley \'pär-lē\. 1793–1860. American writer, b. Ridgefield, Conn. In publishing business (from 1816); issued gift books as the *Token* (annually 1828–42), textbooks, juveniles; inaugurated series of "Peter Parley" books with *The Tales of Peter Parley about America* (1827), followed by over a hundred others of the series, written under Goodrich's direction by members of a staff assembled for the purpose; gained enormous popularity in their day. Founded and edited *Robert Merry's Museum* (1841–54). U.S. consul, Paris (1851–53).

Good·rich \'gùd-(,)rich\ *or* **Good·ricke** \-(,)rik\, Thomas. 1480?–1554. English prelate. Bishop of Ely (1534); advised Henry VIII on divorce from Catherine of Aragon; supported his reform of English church. Helped write *Institution of a Christian Man,* known as the *Bishop's Book* (1537).

Good·ricke \'gùd-(,)rik\, John. 1764–1786. English astronomer. Deaf and mute from early age; discovered (1782–83) variability in brightness of star Algol and established its period; awarded Copley Medal of Royal Society (1783); suggested variation due to interposition of revolving companion body (confirmed 1889); discovered two other variable stars (1785–86), founding new branch of astronomy.

Good·sir \'gùd-sər\, John. 1814–1867. Scottish anatomist. Conservator of anatomy, U. of Edinburgh museum (1840), of museum of Royal Coll. of Surgeons, Edinburgh (1841–43); curator, University museum (1843 ff.); professor, Edinburgh (1846–67); known for studies of cells, whose importance in metabolism and growth he recognized in advance of Virchow.

Good·speed \'gùd-,spēd\, Edgar Johnson. 1871–1962. American scholar, b. Quincy, Ill. Professor, U. of Chicago (1902–37), chairman of New Testament department (1923–37). Author of *Formation of the New Testament* (1926), *The Meaning of Ephesians* (1933), *History of Early Christian Literature* (1942), *How to Read the Bible* (1946), *Life of Jesus* (1950); translator of *New Testament: An American Translation* (1923), *Apocrypha* (1938), *Complete*

Bible (with J.M.P. Smith, 1939); helped prepare Revised Standard Version (1946).

Good·win \'gu̇d-wən\, Hannibal Williston. 1822–1900. American clergyman and inventor, b. Taughannock, N.Y. Invented flexible photographic film (1887; patent issued, after long litigation with Eastman Co., 1898).

Goodwin, Thomas. 1600–1680. English clergyman. Vicar of Trinity Church, Cambridge (1632–34); fled persecution of Puritans to Holland; returned and embraced Congregationalism (1640); head of Magdalen Coll., Oxford, and chaplain to Oliver Cromwell (1649–58); helped draft Savoy Declaration (1658), confession of faith for Congregational churches.

Goodwin, William Watson. 1831–1912. American scholar, b. Concord, Mass. Teacher and professor of Greek, Harvard (1856–1901). Author of *Syntax of the Moods and Tenses of the Greek Verb* (1860), *Elementary Greek Grammar* (1870), *Greek Reader* (1871).

Good·year \'gu̇d-ˌyi(ə)r, 'gu̇j-ˌi(ə)r\, Charles. 1800–1860. American inventor, b. New Haven, Conn. Began experiments in treatment of rubber (c.1830); purchased patent rights of N. M. Hayward to a sulfur treatment process (1838); developed vulcanization process (1839, patented 1844), the basic patent of rubber manufacturing industry; engaged in patent litigation with rivals (to 1852); lost patents in England and France to technicalities, suffered heavy infringement in U.S.; died in debt.

Googe \'gu̇j, 'güj\, Barnabe. 1540–1594. English poet. Author of *Eglogs, Epytaphes, and Sonnetes* (1563), etc.

Goo·kin \'gü-kən\, Daniel. 1612–1687. English colonist in America. Settled in Virginia (1641); to Massachusetts (1644); assistant on the governor's council (1652–75, 1677–87); major general of militia (1681); superintendent of Indians in Massachusetts (1656–87); with John Eliot worked to protect Indians from exploitation.

Goos·sens \'güs-ᵊnz\, Eugene, *in full* Aynsley Eugene. 1893–1962. British conductor and composer. Member of Philharmonic String Quartet (1912 ff.), Queen's Hall Orchestra (1912–15); conductor of Handel Society (1921 ff.), Rochester, N.Y., Symphony (1923–31), Cincinnati Symphony (1931–46), Sydney, Australia, Symphony (1947–55); director, New South Wales Conservatorium (1947–55). Composed operas *Judith* (1929), *Don Juan de Mañara* (1937); chamber and orchestral works, etc.

Gor. See BAHRAM V of Persia.

Go·rakh·nāth \ˌgȯr-ək-'nät\. *Also called* Go·rak·ṣa·nā·tha \ˌgȯr-ək-shə-'nä-tə\. 10th–11th century. Indian religious. Hindu master yogi; regarded as founder of Kānphaṭa Yogis. Author of *Gorakṣaśataka,* a fundamental yogi text.

Gor·cha·kov \gər-(ˌ)chə-'kȯf\, Aleksandr Mikhailovich. Prince. 1798–1883. Russian politician and diplomat. Member of noble family; entered diplomatic service (1817); ambassador at Vienna (1854–56); succeeded Nesselrode as foreign minister (1856–82); chancellor (1866–82). Succeeded in maintaining generally good relations with France and Prussia, esp. during suppression of Polish insurrection (1863); renounced ban on Russian naval use of Black Sea (1870); formed Dreikaiserbund alliance with Germany and Austria-Hungary (1873); failed to prevent imposition of harsh Treaty of San Stefano on Turks after Russo–Turkish War (1877–78) and thus to forestall unfavorable Treaty of Berlin that replaced it (1878).

Gorchakov, Mikhail Dmitriyevich. 1793–1861. Russian soldier and politician. Cousin of A.M. Gorchakov; served in Persian campaign (1810), Napoleonic invasion (1812–14), Russo–Turkish War (1828–29); general (1830); took part in suppression of Polish insurrection (1830–31), distinguishing himself at capture of Warsaw (1831); military governor of Warsaw (1846); chief of staff of Russian forces aiding suppression of Hungarian uprising (1848). Chief of staff, Russian army (1853); commanded occupation of Moldavia (1853); commander in chief in Moldavia and Walachia (1853–55), in Crimea (1855–56); defeated at Chernaya River (1855), withdrew from and burned Sevastopol (1855). Governor general of Poland (1856–61).

Gor·di·a·nus \ˌgōr-dē-'ā-nəs, ˌgȯr-\. *Eng.* Gor·di·an \'gōr-dē-ən, 'gȯr-\. Name of three Roman emperors:

Gordianus I. *In full* Marcus Antonius Gordianus. *Surnamed* Af·ri·ca·nus \ˌaf-ri-'kā-nəs\. c.157–238. Emperor (238). Twice chosen consul; appointed proconsul of Africa by Alexander Severus (237); elected emperor by insurgents in his province against Emperor Maximinus (238); recognized by Senate; after a reign of three weeks committed suicide in grief for death of his son Gordianus II.

Gordianus II. *In full* Marcus Antonius Gordianus. d. 238. Emperor (238). Son of and co-ruler with Gordianus I; killed in battle with Capellianus, governor of Numidia.

Gordianus III. *In full* Marcus Antonius Gordianus. *Usually known as* Gordianus Pi·us \'pī-əs\. 225–244. Emperor (238–244). Grandson of Gordianus I; on death of uncle and grandfather, proclaimed caesar by populace at Rome along with Pupienus Maximus and Balbinus, chosen by the Senate; made sole emperor (238–244) by the Praetorian Guard; aided by Timesitheus, his father-in-law, raised army and defeated Goths, forced Antioch, and won several victories (242) over Sāsānians; during further campaign in Persia, slain by troops favoring Philip the Arabian, an officer in the guard who had succeeded Timesitheus.

Gor·din \'gȯrd-ən\, Jacob. 1853–1909. American playwright, b. Mirgorod, Russia. To U.S. (1891); became leading Yiddish playwright of New York City; produced over thirty original plays, including *Siberia* (1892), *The Jewish King Lear* (1892), *Mirele Efros* (1898), *God, Man and Devil* (1900), *Kreutzer Sonata* (1907).

Gor·don \'gȯrd-ᵊn\. Name of Scottish family having, according to genealogists, 157 main branches, taking its name from the village Gordon in Berwickshire, where a younger son of an Anglo-Norman nobleman settled in time of David I as Adam de Gordon. His great-grandson ¶Sir Adam de Gordon (d. 1333) sided with Edward I in latter's struggle for Scottish throne (1305); justiciar of Scotland (1310–14); after Bannockburn, attached himself to Robert Bruce, who granted him lordship of Strathbogie in Aberdeenshire, which he renamed Huntly; killed at Halidon Hill. From him descended almost all of Gordons of eminence in Scotland. Sir Adam's great-grandson ¶Sir Adam Gordon (d. 1402) was ancestor through his daughter Elizabeth, who married Alexander Seton (d. 1470), of Seton-Gordons holding earldom of Huntly (see below) and of dukes of Gordon and Sutherland.

EARLS AND MARQUISES OF HUNT·LY \'hənt-lē\ AND DUKES OF GORDON: ¶Alexander Se·ton-Gordon \'sēt-ᵊn-\ (d. 1470), 1st Earl of Huntly (created 1449), son of Elizabeth Gordon and Alexander Seton; accompanied Margaret of Scotland to France on marriage with Dauphin Louis (1436); held command at siege of Roxburgh Castle (1460). His son ¶George Gordon (d. 1502?), 2d earl, was lord high chancellor of Scotland (1498–1501); m. Princess Annabella, daughter of James I of Scotland; from their second son descended the earls of Sutherland; from their third son were descended the Gordons of Gight, maternal ancestors of Lord Byron. The eldest son ¶Alexander Gordon (d. 1524), 3d earl, led Scots vanguard at Flodden (1513); twice member of council of regency (1517, 1523). His grandson ¶George Gordon (1514–1562), 4th earl, a regent (1536–37), supported Cardinal Beaton against Arran (1543); as lieutenant of north, crushed Camerons and Macdonalds (1544); lord chancellor (1546); received earldom of Moray (1548) but, when stripped of it through queen's jealousy of his power, joined lords of the congregation (1560) and died in revolt against royal authority. His second son ¶George Gordon (d. 1576), 5th earl, restored to his father's lands and dignities (nominally, 1565; actually, 1567), allied himself with Bothwell and Queen Mary (1566); lord chancellor; aided in murder of Darnley, divorce of his sister from Bothwell, and Mary's marriage with Bothwell; conspired for Queen Mary's deliverance from Loch Leven Castle (1567), but seceded from her cause (1572). His son ¶George Gordon (1562–1636), 6th earl, was head of Roman Catholics of Scotland; took part in plot leading to execution of Morton (1581) and in conspiracy that delivered King James VI from Ruthven raiders (1583); raised rebellion in north (1589) but had to submit to king; conducted private war against earl of Moray and killed him (1592); after destruction of his castle Strathbogie by the king, had to leave Scotland (1595), charged with treason; pardoned, received into kirk, created marquis of Huntly and joint lieutenant of the north (1599). His son ¶George Gordon (d. 1649), 2d marquis, was created (1632) Viscount Aboyne \ə-'bȯin\; refused to subscribe covenant (1638); as lieutenant of the north, driven from Strathbogie by Montrose; in civil war, took king's side, stormed Aberdeen (1645); excepted from general pardon (1647); beheaded by order of Scots Parliament. His grandson ¶George Gordon (1643–1716), 4th marquis, was restored to family titles and estates (1661); created duke of Gordon (1684); held Edinburgh Castle for James II in Revolution of 1688. His son ¶Alexander Gordon (1678?–1728), 2d duke, also a Jacobite, as marquis of Huntly led 2300 men to Old Pretender at Perth (1715).

¶Lord George Gordon (1751–1793), agitator, 3d son of 3d duke of Gordon, rose to rank of lieutenant in navy (1772); M.P. (1774–81); headed Protestant associations organized to secure repeal of act relieving Roman Catholics of certain disabilities (1778); headed mob of about 50,000 in march from St. George's Fields to houses of Parliament with repeal petition, precipitating so-called No-Popery, or Gordon, Riots (June 2–8, 1780); acquitted of treason through Erskine's skillful defense; excommunicated, converted to Judaism (1786); convicted of libel on Marie-Antoinette (1787); lived at ease in Newgate, giving dinners and dances, until his death. ¶George Gordon (1770–1836), 5th and last duke, raised (1794) Gordon Highlanders regiment and commanded it in Spain, Corsica, Ireland, Holland; general (1819); commanded division in Walcheren expedition (1809); left dukedom extinct at death.

EARLS OF SUTH·ER·LAND \'sə<u>th</u>-ər-lənd\: ¶Adam Gordon of Aboyne (d. 1538), 2d son of George Gordon, 2d Earl of Huntly, took title earl of Sutherland in right of his wife Elizabeth, Countess of Sutherland, sister of 9th earl. ¶John Gordon (1609–1663), 14th earl, active and popular Covenanter, was one of leaders at battle of Auldearn (1645); lord privy seal in Scotland (1649–51); raised force against Cromwell (1650). His grandson ¶John Gordon

(1661–1733), 16th earl, served under William III in Flanders; privy councilor to Queen Anne (1704); commissioner for union of Scotland and England (1706); Scottish representative peer; lord lieutenant for northern counties (1715); put down Jacobite uprising (1715). His great-great-granddaughter ¶Elizabeth (1765–1839), sole heir of 18th earl, was recognized (1771) as countess of Sutherland; m. (1785) George Granville Leveson-Gower (*q.v.*).

VISCOUNTS KEN·MURE \'ken-ˌmyü(ə)r\: ¶Sir John Gordon of Loch·in·var \ˌläk-ən-'vär, ˌläk-\ (1599?–1634), 1st Viscount Kenmure (created 1633) and Baron Lochinvar, descendant of younger son of Sir Adam de Gordon (d. 1333); puritan Presbyterian. ¶William Gordon (d. 1716), 6th viscount; Jacobite; in rising of 1715 commanded in southern Scotland; proclaimed James VIII at Lochmaben; captured at Preston and beheaded.

EARLS AND MARQUIS OF AB·ER·DEEN \ˌab-ər-'dēn, 'ab-ər-ˌ\: ¶George Gordon (1637–1720), 1st Earl of Aberdeen (created (1682); Scottish statesman; according to tradition descended from Sir John (d. 1394), illegitimate brother of Sir Adam Gordon (d. 1402); member of Scots Parliament; chancellor of Scotland under James, Duke of York (1682–84); dismissed for leniency to nonconformists; supported treaty of union (1705–06). ¶George Ham·il-·ton-Gordon \'ham-əl-tən-, -əlt-ən-\ (1784–1860), 4th earl; succeeded grandfather as earl (1801); as special ambassador to Austria negotiated and signed Treaty of Töplitz (1813) creating alliance against Napoléon; signed Treaty of Paris (1814). British foreign secretary under Wellington (1828–30) and Peel (1841–46); established friendly relations with France, and with U.S. by Webster-Ashburton and Oregon treaties (1842, 1846). Headed coalition ministry (1852) which was forced into Crimean War; resigned (1855) upon vote of censure on mismanagement of war. His grandson ¶John Campbell Gordon (1847–1934), 7th earl, was lord lieutenant of Ireland (1886, 1906–1915); governor general of Canada (1893–98); created marquis of Aberdeen and Te·mair \tə-'ma(ə)r, -'me(ə)r\ (1915).

Gordon, Dukes of. See GORDON family.

Gordon, Aaron David. 1856–1922. Palestinian leader, b. Ukraine. To Palestine (1904); advocated return of Jews to working soil; inspired formation (1909) of Deganya, first kibbutz; ideologist of Hapoel Hatzair (Younger Worker) party.

Gordon, Adam Lindsay. 1883–1870. Australian poet, b. Azores. Sent to South Australia (1853), where he joined mounted police; member, House of Assembly (1865); moved to Victoria (1867). Author of *Sea Spray and Smoke Drift* (1867), *Ashtaroth* (1867), *Bush Ballads and Galloping Rhymes* (1870).

Gordon, Charles George. *Called* Chinese Gordon *and* Gordon Pa·sha \'pä-shä\. 1833–1885. British soldier. Entered army (1852); distinguished himself at Sevastopol (1855–56); took part in capture of Peking and destruction of Summer Palace (1860); commander of "Ever Victorious Army," a Chinese force, suppressed Taiping rebellion (1863–64). Employed by Ismāʿīl Pasha, khedive of Egypt, in opening up equatorial provinces of Africa (1874–76); resigned because thwarted in suppression of slave trade; returned as governor general of Sudan, equatorial provinces, and Red Sea littoral (1877–80); established communications, developed natural resources, and suppressed slave trade. On overwhelming disaster to Hicks Pasha's army at hands of the Mahdī, sent to rescue Egyptian garrisons in Sudan preparatory to its abandonment (1884); reappointed governor general; by intention or not, failed to evacuate Khartoum before it came under siege by forces of the Mahdī (Feb. 1884); killed in fall of Khartoum (Jan. 1885), becoming in popular view a hero and martyr.

Gordon, Charles William. *Pseudonym* Ralph Con·nor \'kän-ər\. 1860–1937. Canadian clergyman and novelist, b. Glengarry, Ont. To Canadian Northwest as missionary among miners and lumberjacks (1890–94); pastor in Winnipeg (1894–1936); moderator, general assembly of Presbyterian Church of Canada (1922). His novels included *Black Rock* (1898), *The Sky Pilot* (1899), *The Man from Glengarry* (1901), *The Foreigner* (1909), *To Him That Hath* (1921), *The Rock and the River* (1931), *The Girl from Glengarry* (1933).

Gordon, Lady Duff-. See DUFF-GORDON.

Gordon, Lord George. See under GORDON family.

Gordon, John Brown. 1832–1904. American soldier and politician, b. Upson Co., Ga. In Confederate army through Civil War, ending as lieutenant general (1865); led last charge at Appomattox. U.S. senator from Georgia (1873–80, 1891–97). Governor of Georgia (1886–90).

Gordon, Sir John Wat·son- \'wät-sən-\. 1788–1864. Scottish painter. Succeeded to practice of portraitist Henry Raeburn; assumed name of Gordon (1826); exhibited at Royal Academy, London (from 1827). Portraits included Macaulay, De Quincey, Sir Walter Scott.

Gor·don \'gör-dōn\, Judah Leib. *Also called* Leon Gordon. *Orig.* Judah Leib ben Asher \'äsh-ər\. 1830–1892. Lithuanian writer. Teacher of Hebrew; to St. Petersburg (1872); co-editor of Hebrew review *Ha-melitz* (1879–88). Author of poems and stories that strongly influenced development of modern Hebrew; considered leading poet of the Haskalah, or Hebrew Enlightenment. Verses collected in *Kol Shire Yehuda* (1883–84), stories in *Kol Kithbe Yehuda* (1889).

Gor·don \'gȯrd-ən\, Patrick. 1635–1699. Scottish soldier of fortune. Fought in Polish–Swedish war (1655–60); took service in Russian army (1661); suppressed Moscow riots (1663); fought Turks and Tatars, establishing reputation with defense of Chigirin (1678); major general (1678); governor of Kiev (1679); lieutenant general (1683); on diplomatic mission to England (1686–87); general (1687); quartermaster general in expedition against Tatars (1687, 1689); provided decisive aid to Czar Peter I in overthrow of Sophia Alekseyevna (1689); close friend of Peter; made admiral (1694); crushed revolt of army musketeer regiments (1698).

Gordon, Ruth. 1896–1985. American actress and writer, b. Quincy, Mass. Debuted on Broadway in *Peter Pan* (1915). Stage appearances included *Ethan Frome* (1936), *A Doll's House* (1937), *The Matchmaker* (1954). Film roles included *Abe Lincoln in Illinois* (1940), *Rosemary's Baby* (1968, Academy Award), *Where's Poppa?* (1970), and *Harold and Maude* (1971); m. (1942) Garson Kanin; with him wrote screenplays for *A Double Life* (1948), *Adam's Rib* (1949), *Pat and Mike* (1952), etc.

Gordon-Lennox. See under LENNOX family.

Gore \'gō(ə)r, 'gȯ(ə)r\, Charles. 1853–1932. English prelate. Canon of Westminster (1894–1902); bishop of Worcester (1902–05), Birmingham (1905–11), Oxford (1911–19); dean of theological faculty, London U. (1924–28); regarded as a leader of the Anglo-Catholic movement. Author of *Ministry of the Christian Church* (1888), *Roman Catholic Claims* (1888), *Incarnation of the Son of God* (1891), *Reconstruction of Belief* (1921–24), *Christ and Society* (1928); edited *Lux Mundi* (1889).

Go·re·my·kin \gər-yi-'mik-yin\, Ivan Logginovich. 1839–1917. Russian politician. Minister of interior (1895–99); succeeded Witte as prime minister (1906); again prime minister during World War I (1914–16); arrested after revolution (1917); imprisoned and murdered in Caucasus by Bolsheviks.

Go·ren·ko \(ˌ)gər-'yän-kə\, Anna Andreyevna. *Pseudonym* Anna Akh·ma·to·va \(ˌ)ak-'mä-tə-və\. 1889–1966. Russian poet. Member of neoclassical Akmeist group (c.1910–17); poetry noted for lyrical beauty, integrity. Published *Vecher* (1912), *Chyotki* (1914), *U samogo morya* (1914), *Belaya Staya* (1917), *Podorozhnik* (1921), *Anno Domini MCMXXI* (1922), *Iz shesti knig* (1940), *Iva* (1940). Banned by Soviet government (1921–40, 1946–59). Considered greatest woman poet in Russian literature.

Gor·gas \'gȯr-gəs\, Josiah. 1818–1883. American army officer, b. Dauphin Co., Pa. Served in army (from 1841); in Mexican War; entered Confederate army (1861); chief of ordnance for the Confederacy through Civil War; efficient in producing munitions under heavy handicaps; brigadier general (1864). Professor, U. of the South (1870–78); president, U. of Alabama (1878–79).

Gorgas, William Crawford. 1854–1920. American army officer and physician, b. Mobile, Ala. Son of Josiah Gorgas; officer, medical corps, U.S. army (1880). In charge, yellow fever camp in Cuba (1898); chief sanitary officer, Havana, Cuba (1898–1902); following discoveries of Walter Reed board that mosquitoes were carriers of yellow fever, applied strict measures to destroy mosquitoes; succeeded in freeing Havana from yellow fever. Chief sanitary officer, Panama Canal Commission (1904–13); did notable work again in suppressing yellow fever and malaria and thus making digging of the canal possible; member of Isthmian Canal Commission (1907–14). Surgeon general, U.S. army, with rank of brigadier general (1914); major general (1915); retired (1918).

Gorgeous George. See George R. WAGNER.

Gor·ges \'gȯr-jəz\, Sir Ferdinando. c.1566–1647. English proprietor in America. Devoted himself (from 1605) to colonization of New England; received charter (1620) for Council of New England to distribute lands in fiefs and manors to gentry; scheme made worthless by charters granted Plymouth and Massachusetts Bay companies; granted (1639) province of Maine.

Gör·gey *or* **Gör·gei** \'gœr-ge-ē\, Artúr. 1818–1916. Hungarian general. Served in national army in uprising of 1848–49; appointed commander in chief (Feb. 1849) and won a series of victories over Austrians, culminating in capture of Buda (May 1849). Succeeded Kossuth as governor of Hungary; overwhelmed by Russian armies intervening to restore Austrian power; surrendered at Világos to the Russians (Aug. 1849). Interned (1849–67) by the Austrians.

Gor·gi·as \'gȯr-jē-əs\ of Le·on·ti·ni \ˌlē-ən-'tī-nī\. c.483–c.376 B.C. Greek Sophist and rhetorician. Settled in Athens and taught oratory and rhetoric; immortalized by Plato in his dialogue *Gorgias*.

Gor·ham \'gȯr-əm\, Jabez. 1792–1869. American silversmith, b. Providence, R.I. Founder of Gorham Manufacturing Co. (1842; incorporated 1865).

Gorham, Nathaniel. 1738–1796. American politician, b. Charlestown, Mass. Member of Massachusetts board of war (1778–81) and of Continental Congress (1782, 1783, 1785–87; president 1786); as delegate to Federal Convention (1787), signed the Constitution.

Go·ring \'gō-riŋ, 'gȯ-\, George. Earl of Nor·wich \'när-ij, -ich\. 1585–1663. English Royalist. Negotiated marriage between Prince Charles and Henrietta

\ə\ abut \ᵊ\ kitten, *Fr.* table \ər\ further \a\ ash \ā\ ace \ä\ cot, cart \aü\ out \ch\ chin \e\ bet \ē\ easy \g\ go \i\ hit \ī\ ice \j\ job \ŋ\ sing \ō\ go \ȯ\ law \ȯi\ boy \th\ both \t͟h\ the \ü\ loot \u̇\ foot \y\ yet \zh\ vision \à, ḇ, ḡ, ḵ, ⁿ, œ, œ̄, ue, ue̅, ʸ\ *see* Guide to Pronunciation

Maria of France; helped raise funds for Charles; created earl (1644); ineffectual Royalist commander; after capitulation at Colchester (1648), sentenced to death, but respited; with Charles II on Continent (1649); pensioned (1661). His son ¶George (1608–1657), Baron Goring, also fought for Charles I; defeated Fairfax at Seacroft Moor (1643); lieutenant general of horse (1644); commanded left wing at Marston Moor (1644); helped relieve Oxford (1645); retired to Spain (1645) and commanded English regiments in Spanish service.

Gö·ring \ˈgœ-riŋ\, Hermann. 1893–1946. German politician. Served in German air force in World War I (1914–18); joined National Socialist party (1922) and took command of SA, or Storm Troopers; took part in Munich putsch (1923); exiled in Austria (1923–27); member of the Reichstag (from 1928) and its president (1932 ff.). In Hitler's government became (1933) minister for air forces, Prussian minister of the interior, and general of infantry; built up new Luftwaffe (air force); succeeded Schacht as economic dictator of Germany (1937) and given charge of war economy; field marshal (1938); declared successor by Hitler (1939); named Reichsmarschall (1940); enriched himself, amassed vast art collection at baronial estate Carinhall. Convicted of war crimes by Nürnberg tribunal (1946); committed suicide in jail.

Gor·ky \ˈgȯr-kē\, Arshile. *Orig.* Vosdanig Adoi·an \ä-ˈdȯi-ən\. 1905–1948. American painter, b. Khorkom Vari, Armenia. To U.S. (1920); influenced by Surrealism, developed style that in turn helped produce school of Abstract Expressionism. Works included *The Liver Is the Cock's Comb, How My Mother's Embroidered Apron Unfolds in My Life, Diary of a Seducer.*

Gorky, Maksim. See Aleksey M. Peshkov.

Gorm \ˈgȯrm\. *Called* the Old. d. c.935. Danish ruler. Founder of dynasty centered at Jelling that succeeded in uniting Denmark; father of Harold Bluetooth.

Gor·man \ˈgȯr-mən\, Arthur Pue. 1839–1906. American politician, b. Woodstock, Md. U.S. senator from Maryland (1881–99, 1903–06). Advocated moderate protective tariff; co-author of the Wilson-Gorman Act (1894).

Gör·res \ˈgœr-əs\, Joseph von, *in full* Johann Joseph von. 1776–1848. German writer and journalist. Associated with Heidelberg Romantics; with Arnim and Brentano edited journal *Zeitung für Einsiedler* (later *Tröst Einsamkeit,* 1806–08); published *Die teutschen Volksbücher* (1807), *Mythengeschichte der asiatischen Welt* (1810). After Napoléon's fall, opposed Prussian reactionary measures; founded and edited (1814–16) *Der rheinische Merkur* (suppressed 1816); in exile in Switzerland (1819–24); joined Catholic church (1824); professor of history at Munich (1827). Author also of *Christliche Mystik* (1836–42).

Gorria, Tobio. See Arrigo Boito.

Gor·rie \ˈgȯ(ə)r-ē, ˈgō(ə)r-ē\, John. 1803–1855. American physician and inventor, b. Charleston, S.C. Took out patent (1851) on expansion cycle refrigeration process containing basic principle of present-day mechanical refrigerators.

Gorst \ˈgȯ(ə)rst\, Sir John Eldon. 1835–1916. English politician. M.P. (1866–68, 1875–1906); traveled widely (1868–75) reorganizing Conservative party at local level; member of Randolph Churchill's "Fourth Party" (1880–85); solicitor general (1885–86); undersecretary of state for India (1886).

Gort, Viscount. See John S.S.P. Vereker.

Gor·ter \ˈgȯrt-ər\, Herman. 1864–1927. Dutch poet. Achieved reputation with poem "Mei" (1889); became chief representative of aesthetics of 1880 revival. Published *Verzen* (1890). Later became Socialist and Marxist publicist; published journals *De Jonge Gids* (1898), *De Nieuwe Tijd* (1899), verse collections *Een klein heldendicht* (1906), *Pan* (1912).

Gor·ton \ˈgȯrt-ᵊn\, Samuel. 1592–1677. English religious leader. Emigrated to Massachusetts Colony (1637); tried for heresy and banished (1637–38); had similar difficulties in other settlements until he obtained a safe conduct from the earl of Warwick (1648); settled in Rhode Island; named town Warwick; inspired sect called Gortonites.

Görtz \ˈgœrts\, Georg Heinrich von. Freiherr. 1668–1719. German politician. In service of dukes of Holstein-Gottorp (from 1698); instrumental in preserving independence of Holstein and Schleswig from Denmark (1713); entered service of Charles XII of Sweden (1714) as chief financial adviser and diplomatic agent; secured financing for Great Northern War and negotiated with Jacobites, Prussia, Russia; represented Sweden at Åland congress (1718); arrested after death of Charles XII by Frederick of Hesse-Kassel (later Frederick I); used as scapegoat by anti-absolutist forces in Sweden to undo policies of Charles XII without damaging his name; tried and convicted of having alienated Charles from Swedish people; executed.

Go·schen \ˈgō-shən\, George Joachim. 1st Viscount Goschen. 1831–1907. British politician. Entered father's banking firm; attracted favorable attention by his *Theory of the Foreign Exchanges* (1861). M.P. (1863–1900); member of various ministries (from 1865); first lord of admiralty (1871–74); chancellor of the exchequer (1886–92); first lord of admiralty (1895–1900); created viscount (1900). Vigorous supporter of Lord Hartington in forming Liberal Unionist party (1886); aided in defeating Gladstone's home-rule bill (1886); had a share in building huge British navy.

Gos·cin·ny \gȯ-skē-nē\, René. 1926–1977. French cartoon author. Creator of characters Astérix the Gaul and his friend Obélix; author of 23 Astérix stories, illustrated by Albert Uderzo, published in books (from 1959).

Gosford, Earl of. See Archibald Acheson.

Goś·lic·ki \gȯsh-ˈlē-kyē\, Wawrzyniec. *Lat.* Laurentius Gri·ma·lus \grə-ˈmā-ləs\. c.1530–1607. Polish prelate and diplomat. Served in Polish chancery under Sigismund II Augustus and Stephen Báthory (from 1569); bishop of Kamieniec Podolski (1586), Chelm (1590), Przemysl (1591), Poznań (1601); only prelate to sign Compact of Warsaw (1587) granting equal rights to Poles of all religions. Author of *De optimo senatore* (1568), anticipating Catholic liberalism.

Gos·nold \ˈgäz-ˌnōld\, Bartholomew. d. 1607. English navigator. In command of expedition that touched southern Maine shore and coasted southward as far as Narragansett Bay (1602); second in command of expedition that carried settlers to Jamestown, Va. (1606–07).

Gos·saert \ˈgȯs-ärt\, Jan. *Also spelled* Jenni Gossart. *Called* Jan Ma·bu·se \mä-ˈbüe-zə\. *Lat.* Mal·bo·di·us \mal-ˈbōd-ē-əs\. c.1478–c.1532. Flemish painter. In early works in Antwerp followed ornate Antwerp style, as in *Adoration of the Kings, Agony in the Garden, Jesus, the Virgin, and the Baptist;* following journey to Rome (1508–09) in service of Philip of Burgundy, introduced Italian High Renaissance to Netherlands; produced such Italianate works as *Neptune and Amphitrite, Danae, Hercules and Deianira;* noted also as portraitist, as of Charles of Burgundy, Eleanor of Austria, Jean Carondelet.

Gosse \ˈgäs\, Sir Edmund William. 1849–1928. English poet and man of letters. Son of Philip H. Gosse; on staff of British Museum (1865–75); translator for Board of Trade (1875–1904); lecturer in English literature at Cambridge (1885–90); librarian to House of Lords (1904–14); noted for sound literary criticisms and for introducing Scandinavian literature to the English reading public. Author of verse as *Collected Poems* (1911); autobiographical works, esp. *Father and Son* (1907); and literary criticism, surveys, and biographies, including *Seventeenth Century Studies* (1883), *History of Eighteenth Century Literature* (1889), studies of Fielding (1898), Donne (1899), Jeremy Taylor (1904), Ibsen (1907), Swinburne (1917), etc., and essays in *Gossip in a Library* (1891), *Inter Arma* (1916), *Books on the Table* (1921), *Leaves and Fruit* (1927).

Gosse, Philip Henry. 1810–1888. English naturalist. Built first aquarium for long-term housing and display of marine life (1854); known also for study of rotifers. Author of *Manual of Marine Zoology* (1855–56), *Actinologia Britannica* (1858–60), *Evenings at the Microscope* (1859), *Romance of Natural History* (1860–62), *Year at the Shore* (1865), etc.

Gos·sec \gȯ-sek\, François-Joseph. 1734–1829. French composer. In Paris (from 1751) associated with Rameau and Stamitz; director of private theater of Prince de Condé (1762–70); founded and directed (1769–73) Concert des Amateurs; a director of Concert Spirituel (1773–77); master of music (1775–80), sub-director (1780–89), Opéra-Comique; director of École Royale de Chant (1784); musical director of revolutionary Garde Nationale (1789); inspector and professor at Conservatoire from its founding (1795–1816). Composed stage works as *Le Périgourdin* (1761), *Les Pêcheurs* (1766), *Toinon et Toinette* (1767), *Sabinus* (1773), *La Nativité* (1774); ballets as *Mirza* (1779), *Le Premier Navigateur* (1785), *Le Pied de boeuf* (1787); 30 symphonies, a form he helped establish, along with other classical forms as string quartet; Revolutionary hymns and chants as "Chant du 14 juillet," "Hymne à l'Etre suprême," "Le Triomphe de la République," "Hymne à la liberté," "Hymne à l'humanité." Experimented with new instrumentations, massed choruses and bands; introduced horns and clarinets to French orchestras.

Gos·set de Guines \gȯ-se-də-gēn\, Louis-André. *Pseudonym* André Gill \zhēl\. 1840–1885. French caricaturist. Introduced style of enlarged heads dwarfing undersized bodies; famous for his portrait caricatures of illustrious people of his day, as Sarah Bernhardt, Richard Wagner, Balzac.

Gotama, Siddhattha. See Siddhārtha Gautama.

Go·tar·zes \gō-ˈtär-ˌzēz\ *or* **Go·darz** \ˈgō-ˌdärz\. Name of two kings of Parthia:

Gotarzes I. 1st century B.C. King (91–87 or 80 B.C.). A satrap under Mithradates II, on whose death he remained as sole ruler in Parthia; displaced by Orodes I.

Gotarzes II. d. 51 A.D. King (c.38–51). Killed brother Artabanus III for throne; fought third brother and Roman-sponsored rival.

Gotch \ˈgäch\, Frank. 1878–1917. American wrestler, b. Humboldt, Iowa. World champion freestyle wrestler (1905–06, 1906–13); retired (1913); won 154 of 160 matches; sometimes considered greatest freestyle wrestler of all time.

Got·hardt \ˈgȯt-ˌhärt\, Matthias. *Known from 17th century as* Matthias Grü·ne·wald \ˈgrüe-nə-ˌvält\. d. 1528. German painter. Court painter to archbishop of Mainz (c.1509–26); known through few works as one of greatest painters of the day. Works included altarpieces for Lindenhardt, Antonite monastery of Isenheim, Mariaschnee Chapel of SS. Peter and Alexander in Aschaffenburg; paintings *Mocking of Christ, Crucifixion, SS. Erasmus and Mauritius, Mourning Over the Body of Christ;* also executed some 35 extant drawings.

Gothicus. See CLAUDIUS II.

Gothofredus. See GODEFROY.

Gotoku Shinran. See SHINRAN.

Go·tō \gō-tō\ Shimpei. 1857–1929. Japanese politician and administrator. Director of civil administration, Taiwan (1901–06); reorganized island's economy and helped it achieve economic independence; minister of communications (1908–1913), of foreign affairs (1916–18); mayor of Tokyo (1920–22); home minister (1923). Created viscount (1922) and count (1926).

Gotō Shōjirō. 1838–1897. Japanese politician. Chief councilor to feudal lord of Tosa; an instigator and leader of rebellion against shogunate (1867) and restoration of emperor (1868); served briefly in Meiji government; cofounder (1881) of Jiyūtō (Liberal) party, first political party in Japan.

Got·ter \'gȯt-ər\, Friedrich Wilhelm. 1746–1797. German poet. With H.C. Boie founded (1770) *Göttinger Musenalmanach;* member of Goethe's circle (1770–72). Author of verse and stage pieces as *Die Geisterinsel* (1797).

Gott·fried von Strass·burg \'gȯt-ˌfrēt-fȯn-'shträs-ˌbu̇rk\. fl. 1210. German poet. Author of courtly epic *Tristan und Isolde* (Celtic in origin), which influenced later literature and furnished Wagner the title for his opera.

Gott·hard \'gȯt-ˌhärt\ *or* **Go·de·hard** \'gōd-ə-ˌhärt\. Saint. c.960–1038. German religious and prelate. Became Benedictine (990); provost and abbot (996 or 997) of Niederaltaich; bishop of Hildesheim (1022–38); completed cathedral, built many churches, founded schools and a hospice, reformed education and Bavarian church. Canonized (1131) by Pope Innocent II.

Gotthelf, Jeremias. See Albert BITZIUS.

Gottorp. See OLDENBURG, 3.

Gott·schalk \'gȯt-ˌshälk\. *Also spelled* Got·te·scalc \'gȯt-ə-ˌshälk\ *or* Go·de·scal·chus \ˌgōd-ə-'shäl-kəs\. *Called* Gottschalk of Or·bais \ȯr-be\. c.803–c.868. German religious and theologian. Benedictine monk at Fulda and (from c.829) Orbais; caused great controversy with teachings on predestination of elect; condemned for heresy by Synod of Mainz (848).

Gotts·chalk \'gäch-ˌȯk, 'gät-ˌshȯk\, Louis Moreau. 1829–1869. American pianist and composer, b. New Orleans, La. Toured successfully in Europe, U.S., South America; first American musician and composer to achieve critical and popular success in Europe. Composed piano pieces as *Polka de salon* (1844), *Bamboula* (1844), *La Savane* (1845), *Le Bananier* (1845), *Le Mancenillier* (1851), *Souvenirs d'Andalousie* (1854), *Tournament Galop* (1854), *Last Hope* (1854), *Le Banjo* (1854), *Souvenir de Porto Rico* (1859), *Ojos criollos* (1859), *Réponds-moi* (1859), *Berceuse* (1860), *Suis-moi!* (1861), *The Dying Poet* (1864); also songs and instrumental and orchestral works.

Gott·schall \'gȯt-ˌshäl\, Rudolf von. 1823–1909. German writer. Editor of *Blätter für literarische Unterhaltung* (1865–88) and the review *Unsere Zeit.* Author of verse *Lieder der Gegenwart* (1842), *Gedichte* (1849), etc.; dramatic works *Robespierre* (1845), *Lord Byron in Italien* (1847), *Pitt und Fox* (1854), *Mazeppa* (1859); novels *Das goldene Kalb* (1880), *Verschollene Grössen* (1886), *Moderne Streber* (1896); critical works.

Gott·sched \'gȯt-ˌshāt\, Johann Christoph. 1700–1766. German critic and writer. Professor, Leipzig (1734–66); influenced esp. by Boileau, introduced French classical standards into German literary and dramatic criticism; made strong impression on German theater, founding with Caroline Neuber the Leipzig school of acting and criticism. Author of *Die vernunftigen Tadlerinnen* (1725–26), *Der Biedermann* (1727–29), *Versuch einer critischen Dichtkunst vor die Deutschen* (1730), *Ausführliche Redekunst* (1836), *Grundlegung einer deutschen Sprachkunst* (1848); also published translations from French stage, *Deutsche Schaubühne* (1741–45) and his own plays, esp. *Der sterbende Cato.*

Gott·wald \'gȯt-ˌväld\, Klement. 1896–1953. Czech politician. Active in Czech Communist party (from 1921); general secretary (from 1929); opposed peaceful cession of Sudetenland to Germany (1938); in Soviet Union (1939–45). Deputy premier (1945–46); premier (1946–48); president of Czechoslovakia (1948–53).

Götz \'gœts\, Hermann. 1840–1876. German composer. Known esp. for opera *Der widerspenstigen Zähmung* (1874, after Shakespeare's *Taming of the Shrew*); also wrote choral works, lieder, piano and instrumental works.

Gou·cher \'gau̇-chər\, John Franklin. 1845–1922. American clergyman and educator, b. Waynesburg, Pa. Benefactor of Woman's College of Baltimore (renamed Goucher College, 1910), and president of the college (1890–1908).

Gou·di·mel \gü-dē-mel\, Claude. c.1510–1572. French composer. Published (1551–66) several books of vernacular settings of Psalms, including complete cycles (1564, 1565); also wrote masses, chansons, etc.

Gou·dy \'gau̇d-ē\, Frederic William. 1865–1947. American printer and type designer, b. Bloomington, Ill. Established the Village Press in Park Ridge, Ill. (1905); designer of over 90 type faces, including Goudy, Goudy Old Style, Deepdene, Forum, Kennerly, Village. Author of *The Alphabet* (1918), *Elements of Lettering* (1922), *Typologia* (1949).

Gough \'gäf\, Sir Hubert de la Poer. 1870–1963. English soldier. Served in Boer War (1899–1902); in World War I commanded brigades and divisions (1914–16), and from its formation the 5th army in France and Flanders (1916–18); bore brunt of and blunted German offensive (March 1918); retired with rank of general (1922).

Gough, Hugh. 1st Viscount Gough. 1779–1869. British soldier, b. Ireland. Entered army (1793); served in West Indies (1797–1800); commanded battalion at Talavera de la Reina (1809); distinguished himself at Barrosa and Tarifa (1811) and Vitoria (1813); major general (1830). In command in Opium War (1839–42); commander in chief in India at defeat of the Marāthās (1843) and Sikhs (1845, 1848–49). General (1854); field marshal (1862).

Gough, William. See GOFFE.

Gou·in \ˌgü-'a^n, 'gwa^n\, Sir Lomer. 1861–1929. Canadian politician, b. Grondines, Que. Member of Quebec legislature (1897–1921); minister of public works (1900–04); prime minister and attorney general of Province of Quebec (1905–20). Member of federal parliament (1921–25); minister of justice (1921–24); Canadian representative at League of Nations (1924).

Gou·jon \gü-zhō^n\, Jean. 1510?–1568. French sculptor. Engaged (1541) in Paris with Pierre Lescot in decorating Saint-Germain l'Auxerrois, later (1544–47) in decorating Château d'Écouen for Constable Anne de Montmorency, and (c.1549–53) in work on the Louvre; created set of six relief figures of nymphs (1547–49) for Fontaine des Innocents, Paris.

Gould \'güld\, Augustus Addison. 1805–1866. American naturalist, b. New Ipswich, N.H. Physician in Boston; specialized in study of mollusks. Author of *Report on the Invertebrata of Massachusetts* (1841), *Principles of Zoology* (with Louis Agassiz, 1848), etc.

Gould, Benjamin Apthorp. 1824–1896. American astronomer, b. Boston. Founded *Astronomical Journal* (1849); edited it (1849–61, 1886–96); director, longitude determinations, U.S. Coast Survey (1852–67); pioneer in use of telegraph in longitude determination; director, Dudley Observatory, Albany, N.Y. (1855–59); interested in study of southern celestial hemisphere (from 1865); instrumental in establishing Argentine National Observatory at Córdoba (1870) and meteorological stations south to Tierra del Fuego (1872); determined magnitudes of southern stars, published in *Uranometria Argentina* (1879); prepared zone catalogues of the southern stars, published in *Resultados del Observatorio Nacional Argentino* (15 vols., 1879–96).

Gould, Chester. 1900–1985. American cartoonist, b. Pawnee, Okla. Introduced crime and violence into the comics with creation (1931) of "Dick Tracy," the first nonhumorous comic strip; created a rogues' gallery of bizarre criminals; masterminded strip until retirement (1977).

Gould, Glenn Herbert. 1932–1982. Canadian pianist, b. Toronto. Debuted as concert pianist (1946). Toured in Canada (early 1950s), worldwide (1955–64). Began (1955) recording career with Bach's *Goldberg Variations;* pioneered the highly engineered recording; stretched technological possibilities of recorded music; made 65 albums. Created commentaries and documentaries for Canadian radio and television.

Gould, Helen Miller. See Helen Miller Gould SHEPARD.

Gould, Jay, *orig.* Jason. 1836–1892. American financier, b. Roxbury, N.Y. In early years a clerk, surveyor, leather merchant (1859–60); engaged in stock market manipulation of railroad securities (from c.1860); associated with James Fisk and Daniel Drew in struggle against Cornelius Vanderbilt for control of Erie Railroad (1867–68); looted the Erie's treasury; president of Erie (1868–72). With Fisk, attempted to corner gold, causing panic of Black Friday (Sept. 24, 1869). Extended railroad control to western roads, to include Missouri Pacific, Texas & Pacific, St. Louis Southwestern, International & Great Northern (by 1890). Also owned New York *World* (1879–83), New York Elevated Railways (1886), and controlled Western Union Telegraph Co. His son ¶George Jay (1864–1923), b. New York City, inherited vast railway interests but by overextending resources in seeking outlets to both coasts he lost them one by one to opposition financiers led by Kuhn, Loeb & Co., and Edward H. Harriman. Another son ¶Edwin (1866–1933) was president (1898–1912), St. Louis Southwestern Railroad; organizer (1894) of Continental Match Co., consolidated (1899) with Diamond Match Co.; president (1900–09) of Bowling Green Trust Co., New York, later merged with Equitable Trust Co.; noted as philanthropist. See Helen Miller SHEPARD.

Gould, John. 1804–1881. English ornithologist. Taxidermist to Zoological Society of London (1827). Author of lavishly illustrated *Birds of Europe* (1832–37), *Monograph of the Ramphastidae* (1834), *Birds of Australia* (1840–48; with supplement, 1851–69), *Birds of Asia* (1850–80), *Birds of Great Britain* (1862–73).

\ə\ abut \ᵊ\ kitten, *Fr.* **table \ər\ further \a\ ash \ā\ ace \ä\ cot, cart \au̇\ out \ch\ chin \e\ bet \ē\ easy \g\ go \i\ hit \ī\ ice \j\ job \ŋ\ sing \ō\ go \ȯ\ law \ȯi\ boy \th\ both \th\ the \ü\ loot \u̇\ foot \y\ yet \zh\ vision \à, b, g̅, k, ^{n}, œ, œ̅, ue, ue̅, ^{y}** *see* Guide to Pronunciation

Gou·nod \gü-nō, *Angl* 'gü-ˌnō\, Charles-François. 1818–1893. French composer. Conductor of Orphéon in Paris (1852–60). Composed operas including *Sapho* (1851), *La Nonne sanglante* (1854), *Le Médecin malgré lui* (1858), *Faust* (1859), *La Colombe* (1860), *Philémon et Baucis* (1860), *La Reine de Saba* (1862), *Mireille* (1864), *Roméo et Juliette* (1867), and *Cinq-Mars* (1877); also composed church music as *Messe de Sainte Cécile* (1885) and oratorios *La Rédemption* (1882) and *Mors et Vita* (1885). Among his songs was the famous *Ave Maria,* based on Bach's Prelude in C Major.

Gou·raud \gü-rō\, Henri-Joseph-Eugène. 1867–1946. French army officer. Served in Sudan, Morocco; general of division (1914), commanded colonial army in France (1915); led French expeditionary force at Dardanelles (1915) and lost an arm there; commanded 4th army in Champagne (1917–18). French high commissioner in Syria (1919–23); governor of Paris, and member of the supreme war council (1923–37).

Gour·gaud \gür-gō\, Gaspard. 1783–1852. French army officer. Served in Napoleonic armies; voluntarily accompanied Napoléon into exile at St. Helena (1815). At Napoléon's dictation he wrote *Mémoires pour servir à l'histoire de France sous Napoléon* (1822–23); also wrote *Campagne de dix-huit cent quinze* (1818), *Napoléon et la grande armée en Russie* (1824), *Sainte-Hélène; journal inédit de 1815 à 1818.* Returned to France (1821); promoted lieutenant general (1835); member of Legislative Assembly (1849).

Gour·mont \gür-mōⁿ\, Rémy de. 1858–1915. French writer. A founder of (1889) and contributor to *Mercure de France;* helped found (1894) review *L'Ymagier.* Among his novels and prose works were *Sixtine* (1890), *Les Histoires magiques* (1893), *Les Chevaux de Diomède* (1897), *Le Songe d'une femme* (1899), *Un Coeur virginal* (1907); among his critical and philosophical works *Le Latin mystique* (1892), *Épilogues, reflexions sur la vie* (1895–1912), *Livres des masques* (1896, 1898), *Esthétique de la langue française* (1899), *La Culture des idées* (1901), *Le Problème du style* (1902), *Promenades littéraires* (1904–13), *Promenades philosophiques* (1905–09); also wrote verse and plays. Played major role in disseminating Symbolist aesthetic.

Gour·nay \gür-ne\, Jean-Claude-Marie-Vincent de. Seigneur. 1712–1759. French economist. Reputed author of the phrase *laissez-faire,* or in full, *laissez faire, laissez passer.*

Gour·sat \gür-sȧ\, Édouard-Jean-Baptiste. 1858–1936. French mathematician. Professor, Toulouse (1881–85), École Normale Supérieure (1885–97), U. of Paris (1897 ff.); known for contributions to analysis. Author of *Cours d'analyse mathématique* (1902–05).

Gou·thière \güt-yer\, Pierre. 1732–1813 or 1814. French metalworker. Executed pieces for Marie-Antoinette, duc d'Aumont, duchesse de Mazarin, and Madame du Barry.

Gou·vion-Saint-Cyr \güv-yōⁿ-saⁿ-sēr\, Laurent de. Marquis. 1764–1830. French soldier. Joined army (1792); made general for performance in battles of Mainz and Mannheim (1795); served in Egypt and Italy; appointed ambassador to Spain (1801); created marshal for victory at battle of Polotsk (1812) in Russian campaign; commanded unsuccessful defense of Dresden (1813). As minister of war (1815, 1817–19) responsible for reorganizing recruitment procedures in French army. Author of *Mémoires sur les campagnes des armées du Rhin et de Rhin-et-Moselle* (1829) and *Mémoires pour servir à l'histoire militaire sous le Directoire, le Consulat, et l'Empire* (1831).

Go·vard·han \ˌgō-värd-'hän\. 17th century. Mughal painter. Known for portraits, illustrations in *Bābur-nāmeh,* etc.

Gove \'gōv\, Philip Babcock. 1902–1972. American lexicographer, b. Concord, N.H. Editor in chief, *Webster's Third New International Dictionary* (1961).

Govind Singh. See GOBIND SINGH.

Gow \'gaü\, Niel. 1727–1807. Scottish fiddler and composer. Composed esp. strathspey reels, for some of which Burns wrote words; published collections (1784, 1788, 1792). His son ¶Nathaniel (1766–1831) was also a musician but best known as collector and publisher of Scottish music; published 3 more collections of strathspey reels (1808–22) and *Complete Repository of the Original Scotch Slow Tunes* (1799–1817), to which he contributed pieces of his own.

Gow·er \'gaü(ə)r, 'gō(-ə)r, 'gȯ(-ə)r\, John. 1330?–1408. English poet. Friend of Chaucer, who referred to him as "moral Gower." Chief works, *Speculum meditantis* (written in French), *Vox clamantis* (in Latin elegiacs), *Confessio amantis* (in English).

Gowrie, Baron and earls of. See RUTHVEN family.

Go·ya y Lu·cien·tes \'gō-yä-ē-lüth-'yān-tās \, Francisco José de. 1746–1828. Spanish painter, etcher, and lithographer. Executed frescoes for Saragossa cathedral (1771 ff.); employed by Raphael Mengs to design cartoons for tapestries, Madrid (intermittently, 1775–92); member (1780) and deputy director (1785), director (1795–97), Acad. of San Fernando, Madrid; painter to king (1786), chief painter (1799). Painter to Bonaparte court during French occupation (1808–13); on accession of Ferdinand VII (1814), reinstated as royal painter; left Spain because of political views (1824), settling at Bordeaux, France. Works included many portraits, often showing influence of Velázquez, religious scenes, historical and allegorical works, including *Adoration of the Name of God, Queen of Martyrs, Family of Charles IV, Naked Maja, The Colossus, The 3d of May 1808;* also series of engravings, frequently satirical or pessimistic, as *Los caprichos* (1797–98), *Los desastres de la guerra* (1810–14), *La tauromaquia* (1815–16), *Los disparates* or *Los proverbios* (c.1820–24).

Go·yen *or* **Go·i·jen** \'gō-ē-yən\, Jan Josephszoon van. 1596–1656. Dutch painter. Best known for landscapes and river scenes, often rendered in muted atmospheric tones; also made etchings.

Goz·zi \'gōt-tsē\, Carlo. Conte. 1720–1806. Italian writer. Member of purist and rationalist Accademia dei Granelleschi; attacked dramatic innovations of Carlo Goldoni in poem *La tartana degl'influssi* (1747) and in commedia dell' arte play *L'amore delle tre melarance* (1761); continued attempt to revive commedia with *Il re cervo* (1762), *Turandot* (1762), *La donna serpente* (1762), *L'augellino belverde* (1765), etc. Also wrote memoirs *Memorie inutili* (1797).

Gozzi, Gasparo. Conte. 1713–1786. Italian writer. Brother of Carlo Gozzi; founded and edited *La Gazzetta Veneta* (1760–61) and *L'Osservatore* (1761–62) on the model of the English *Spectator.* Author of *Lettere famigliari* (1755), *Difesa di Dante* (1758), etc.

Gozzoli, Benozzo. See Benozzo di LESE.

Gqo·ba \'kō-bə\, William Wellington. 1840–1888. Bantu writer. Worked as teacher, translator, clerk, etc.; edited Xhosa-language *Isigidimi samaxosa* (1884–88). Known esp. for didactic poems "Discussion between the Christian and the Pagan" and "Great Discussion on Education."

Graaf \grȧf\, Reinier de. 1641–1673. Dutch physician and anatomist. Author of works on the pancreatic juice and on the generative organs; discovered the Graafian follicles in the ovary.

Graaff \'grȧf\, Simon de. 1861–1948. Dutch politician. In service of Dutch East Indies government; member of Council of the Indies (1913); as colonial minister (1919–25) reorganized administration of Dutch East Indies and revised constitution in conservative direction.

Gra·bau \'grä-bō\, Amadeus William. 1870–1946. American paleontologist, b. Cedarburg, Wis. Professor, Rensselaer Polytechnic (1899–1901), Columbia (1901–19), and National U., Peking, China (1919–46); known for work on stratigraphic deposits, invertebrate evolution, etc. Author of *Principles of Stratigraphy* (1913), *Text Book of Geology* (1920–21), *Silurian Fossils of Yunnan* (1920), *Stratigraphy of China* (1924–25), *Early Permian Fossils of China* (1934), etc.

Grab·be \'gräb-ə\, Christian Dietrich. 1801–1836. German dramatist. Author of verse plays anticipating Expressionism, including *Scherz, satire, ironie und tiefere bedeutung* (1827), *Don Juan und Faust* (1829), *Friedrich Barbarossa* (1829), *Heinrich VI* (1830), *Napoleon oder die Hundert Tage* (1831).

Grab·ski \'gräp-skē\, Władysław. 1874–1938. Polish economist and politician. Member of Russian Duma (1906–12); member of Polish Assembly (1919); minister of agriculture (1919–20), of finance (1920, 1923); prime minister of Poland (1920, 1923–25); stabilized economy, created new currency, the zloty (1924).

Gra·ça Ara·nha \'grä-sə-ə-'rán-yə\, José Pe·rei·ra da \pə-'rā-rə-t͟hə\. 1868–1931. Brazilian diplomat and novelist. Known esp. for novel *Canaã* (1902).

Grac·chus \'grak-əs\. Name of a plebeian family of ancient Rome, including notably: Tiberius Sempronius Gracchus (210?–?151 B.C.), husband of Cornelia (*q.v.*) and father of "the Gracchi"; tribune (185); praetor in Hither Spain (181); censor (169); consul (163).

¶Tiberius Sempronius Gracchus (163–133) and his brother ¶Gaius Sempronius Gracchus (153–121), *known as* the Grac·chi \'grak-ˌī\, Roman statesmen; Tiberius, as tribune of the people (133), sponsored proposals to restore the class of peasant farmers by restricting amount of public land a citizen might occupy and by instituting greater subdivision of lands; at end of his term of office, tried (unconstitutionally) to be reelected and was killed in a riot. Gaius served on land commission established by Tiberius's law (132); quaestor (126); as tribune of the people (123–122), renewed agrarian law sponsored by his brother and proposed measures circumscribing powers of Senate and courts and limiting corruption; in second tribunate (122–121) advocated extension of citizenship to the Latins; committed suicide during riots between opposing factions.

Grace \'grās\, William Gilbert. 1848–1915. English cricketer. Physician by profession, practicing at Bristol (1879–99). Regarded as one of greatest of cricketers and the best batsman of his day; played for England in test matches against Australia (1880, 1882); in first-class cricket (1865–1908) scored 54, 896 runs, 126 centuries, took 2,876 wickets; for M.C.C. scored 344 runs in one innings (1876).

Grace, William Russell. 1832–1904. American merchant and shipowner, b. Queenstown, Ireland. Established chandlery business, Peru; in New York (from 1865); organized W. R. Grace & Co. to engage in South American trade (1865); secured control of virtually all of Peru's resources (1890); organized New York and Pacific Steamship Co. (1891) and Grace Steamship Co. Mayor of New York (1880–82, 1884–86).

Gra·cián y Mo·ra·les \gräth-'yän-ē-mō-'rä-lās\, Baltasar. 1601–1658. Spanish writer. Entered Jesuit order (1619); rector of Jesuit college at Tarragona. Chief representative of conceptism in Spanish literature. Author of *El héroe* (1637), *Agudeza y arte de ingenio* (1642), *El discreto* (1646), *El oráculo manual* (1647), and *El criticón,* a philosophical novel analyzing civilization through its effects on a savage (1651, 1653, 1657).

Gra·dy \'grā-dē\, Henry Woodfin. 1850–1889. American journalist and orator, b. Athens, Ga. Editor and part owner, Atlanta *Constitution* (1879–89); prominent as public speaker on questions involving the South; best known speech "The New South" (1886).

Grae·be \'greb-ə\, Carl. 1841–1927. German chemist. Professor, Königsberg (1870–78), Geneva (1878–1906); with Liebermann, produced first synthetic alizarin (1869).

Graeb·ner \'greb-nər\, Fritz, *in full* Robert Fritz. 1877–1934. German ethnologist. On staff of Royal Museum of Ethnology, Berlin (1899–1906), Rautenstrauch-Joest Museum, Cologne (1906–28); developed theory of Kulturkreise, diffusion of culture complexes. Author of *Methode der Ethnologie* (1911), *Das Weltbild der Primitiven* (1924), etc.

Grae·fe \'gref-ə\, Karl Ferdinand von. 1787–1840. German surgeon. Superintended military hospitals (1800–15); professor, Berlin (1810–40); pioneer in plastic surgery; also known as oculist. His son ¶Albrecht Friedrich Wilhelm Ernst (1828–1870), oculist; considered founder of modern ophthalmology; founded eye clinic, Berlin (1850); professor, Berlin (1857–70); introduced use of Helmholtz's ophthalmoscope in diagnosis; treated glaucoma successfully by iridectomy; treated cataract by extraction of lens; described (1864) Graefe's sign of exophthalmic goiter.

Graetz \'grets\, Heinrich. 1817–1891. German historian. Professor, Breslau (1869–91); chief work *Geschichte der Juden von den ältesten Zeiten* (1853–76).

Graf \'gräf\, Urs. c.1485–1527. Swiss artist, engraver, goldsmith. Known for drawings, woodcuts, engravings, nielli in style influenced by Dürer; also executed gold reliquary of St. Bernard for monastery of St. Urban (1514; lost).

Grafton, Dukes of. See FITZROY family.

Graf·ton \'graf-tən\, Richard. c.1513–1573. English printer and chronicler. With Edward Whitchurch, had Thomas Matthews's Bible printed in Antwerp (1537); published Coverdale New Testament (1538); printed Great Bible in London (1539); received exclusive patents for church service books and primers (1545); issued Book of Common Prayer, 1st edition (1549); printed Lady Jane Grey's proclamation (1553). Compiled two sets of English historical chronicles (1562, 1568).

Graham, Ennis. See Mary Louisa MOLESWORTH.

Gra·ham \'grā-əm, 'gra(-ə)m\, Ernest Robert. 1868–1936. American architect, b. Lowell, Mich. Partner in D. H. Burnham & Co., Chicago (1904–12); senior partner in Graham, Burnham & Co. (1912–17) and Graham, Anderson, Probst & White (1917–36). Involved in design of Equitable Building, Flatiron Building, Gimbel Brothers store, and Chase National Bank in New York City; Union Station and General Post Office in Washington, D.C.; Field Museum of Natural History, Continental Illinois Bank, Civic Opera house, Shedd Aquarium, Merchandise Mart, Marshall Field & Co. stores, Wrigley Building in Chicago; Pennsylvania Station and Wanamaker Store in Philadelphia; Filene's store in Boston; Selfridge & Co. store in London, England.

Graham, George. 1673–1751. English mechanician. Partner and successor (1713) of Thomas Tompion; invented the mercurial pendulum, the deadbeat escapement; with Tompion built first orrery; produced quadrants, zenith sectors, and other astronomical instruments for Halley, Bradley, and the French Academy.

Graham, George Rex. 1813–1894. American journalist, b. Philadelphia. Assistant editor, *Saturday Evening Post* (1839); established *Graham's Magazine* (1841) and edited it (1841–53).

Graham, Hugh. Baron Ath·ol·stan \'ath-əl-ˌstan\. 1848–1938. Canadian publisher, b. Atholstan, Que. Founded (1869) *Montreal Star;* later founded *Family Herald, Weekly Star, Montreal Standard;* acquired *Montreal Herald.* Created baron (1917).

Graham, James. 5th Earl and 1st Marquis of Mont·rose \män-'trōz, mən-\. 1612–1650. Scottish general. Succeeded to earldom (1626); one of four nobles who drew up National Covenant (1638); pacified Aberdeen; disaffected by ambition of Argyll, but led Covenanting army in forcing River Tyne (1640); imprisoned (1640) on charge of conspiring against Argyll; on outbreak of English Civil War (1644) created marquis and named lieutenant general of Scotland; raised force of Highlanders and Irish, won victories over pro-Parliamentary Scottish forces at Tippermuir, Aberdeen, Inverlochy, Auldearn, Alford, Kilsyth (1644–45); defeated with reduced army by David Leslie at Philiphaugh (1645); in exile (1646–50); landed with small force in Orkneys (1650), defeated, captured, hanged.

Graham, Sir James Robert George. 2d baronet. 1792–1861. English politician. M.P. (1818–20, 1826–37, 1838–61); first lord of the admiralty (1830–34, 1852–55); home secretary (1841–46); strong supporter of Peel and successor as leader of Peelites (1850).

Graham, *called* Graham of Clav·er·house \'klā-vər-ˌhau̇s\, John. 1st Viscount Dun·dee \ˌdən-'dē\. *Known as* Bloody Clav·erse \'klav-ərz, 'klā-vərz\ *and* Bonnie Dundee. 1648–1689. Scottish Royalist and Jacobite. Served in William of Orange's horse guards (1672); under marquis of Montrose, employed (1677–79) in repression of conventicles and in rigorous persecution of Covenanters; defeated at Drumclog (1679) but victorious over Covenanters at Bothwell bridge (1679); sheriff of Wigtown (1682); major general (1686); second in command of Scottish forces marching to stem revolution (1688); created viscount (1688); permitted by William III to return to Scotland with troopers; collected three thousand Highlanders, met attack of Scottish commander in chief at Killiecrankie (July 27) in bloody victory but fell mortally wounded.

Graham, Robert Bontine Cunninghame. See CUNNINGHAME GRAHAM.

Graham, Sylvester. 1794–1851. American reformer, b. West Suffield, Conn. Promoted temperance, vegetarianism, and esp. the use of the whole of wheat unbolted and coarsely ground in making flour (hence graham flour).

Graham, Thomas. Baron Lyne·doch \'lin-ˌdäk\. 1748–1843. British soldier, b. Scotland. Raised infantry battalion (1794); distinguished himself at capture of Minorca (1798); brigadier general (1799); commanded force blockading Malta (1799–1800); aide-de-camp to Sir John Moore in La Coruña campaign (1808); commanded brigade in Walcheren expedition (1809); lieutenant general (1810). Division commander under Wellington (1812–13); commanded left wing at Vittoria (1813); captured Tolosa (1813). Commanded British contingent in Holland (1814); created baron (1814); general (1821).

Graham, Thomas. 1805–1869. Scottish chemist. Professor, Andersonian U., Edinburgh (1803–37), U. Coll., London (1837–55); master of the mint (1855–69). Formulated Graham's law of diffusion of gases (1833); discovered and named the process of dialysis used for separating crystalloids from colloids; made study of the three forms of phosphoric acid that led to concept of polybasic acids; investigated water of hydration and alcoholates.

Gra·hame \'grā-əm, 'gra(-ə)m\, James. 1765–1811. Scottish poet. Author of *Mary Queen of Scots* (1801), *The Sabbath* (1804), *Birds of Scotland* (1806), etc.

Grahame, Kenneth. 1859–1932. Scottish writer. On staff of Bank of England (from 1879), secretary (1898–1908). Wrote *Pagan Papers* (1893), *The Golden Age* (1895), *Dream Days* (1898), and classic children's story *The Wind in the Willows* (1908).

Gra·hame-White \-'hwīt, -'wīt\, Claude. 1879–1959. English aviator and engineer. First Englishman to gain aviator's certificate of proficiency (1910); founded at Pau, France, first British school of aviation (1909); helped establish (1911) London Aerodrome, Hendon; established Grahame-White Aviation Co. (1911).

Grahn \'grän\, Lucile. 1819–1907. Danish dancer and choreographer. Made debut (1829) in Bournonville's Royal Danish Ballet; danced title roles in *Waldemar* (1835), *La Sylphide* (1836), both created for her; left Denmark (1839), achieved fame in Paris, St. Petersburg, London; appeared with Grisi, Taglioni, Cerrito in *Pas de Quatre* (London, 1845); retired as dancer (1856); ballet mistress, Leipzig State Theater (1858–61), Munich Opera (1869–75).

Grail·ly \grȧ-yē\, Jean III de. Captal de Buch \bu̅e̅sh, bük\. 1321–1376. French knight. Leader of Gascon nobility; headed delegation to Edward III of England asking for appointment of a royal ruler (1355); distinguished himself against French at Poitiers (1356); later fought for Navarre against France and (1366–70) for English against Spanish; captured by French (1371); refused to serve Charles V of France and imprisoned. Extolled by Froissart as ideal of chivalric valor, courage, loyalty.

Grain·ger \'grān-jər\, Percy Aldridge, *orig.* George Percy. 1882–1961. American pianist and composer, b. Melbourne, Australia. Settled in London (1901); to U.S. (1914); taught in Chicago, New York; collected and notated English, Danish folk songs. Composed experimental "free music" with novel rhythms and harmonies; works included several *Hill Songs, Mock Morris, Children's March, To a Nordic Princess,* etc., scored for keyboard or orchestra or chorus, etc.

Gram \'gräm, *Angl* 'gram\, Hans Christian Joachim. 1853–1938. Danish physician. Professor, U. of Copenhagen (1891–1900); in bacteriological research developed Gram's stain (1884).

Gramme \gräm\, Zénobe Théophile. 1826–1901. Belgian electrical engineer. Invented (1869) first direct-current dynamo; opened factory (1871) to produce dynamos, Gramme rings, Gramme armatures, etc.

Gra·mont \grȧ-mōⁿ\, Antoine-Agénor-Alfred de. Duc. 1819–1880. French diplomat and statesman. Ambassador to Rome (1857), Vienna (1861); minister of foreign affairs (May–Aug. 1870); largely responsible for precipitating Franco–Prussian War.

Gram·sci \'gräm-shē\, Antonio. 1891–1937. Italian politician. Joined (1914) and became leading theoretician of Socialist party; founded newspaper *L'Ordine Nuovo* (1919); led leftist walkout from Socialists (1921); took part in founding Italian Communist party (1921); head of party (1924); deputy (1924–26); imprisoned (1926–37) by Fascist authorities.

Gra·na·da \grä-'nä-thä\, Luis de. c.1504–1588. Spanish prelate. Entered Dominican order (1524); gained fame as preacher; prior at Córdoba (1544), Badajoz (1554); provincial of Portugal (1555–60). Author of vernacular works on spirituality and mysticism as *Libro de la oración y meditación* (1554), *Guía de pecadores* (1556), *Memorial de la vida christiana* (1566).

Gra·na·dos \grä-'nä-thōs\, Enrique. *Full surname* Granados y Cam·pi·na \-ē-käm-'pē-nä\. 1867–1916. Spanish pianist and composer. Composed zarzuelas as *Maria del Carmen* (1898), *Picarol* (1901), *Follet* (1903); piano works as *Danzas españolas* (1892–1900) and very successful *Goyescas* (1911), latter made into opera (1916); a leader of nationalist movement in Spanish music.

Granby, Marquises of. See MANNERS family.

Grand·gent \'gran-jənt\, Charles Hall. 1862–1939. American linguist, b. Dorchester, Mass. Professor of Romance languages, Harvard (1896–1932); authority on Vulgate Latin. Author of *Introduction to Vulgar Latin* (1907), *From Latin to Italian* (1927); edited Dante's *Divina commedia* (1909).

Gran·di \'grän-dē\, Alessandro. d. 1630. Italian composer. Worked in Ferrara (1597–1617); singer, St. Mark's, Venice (1617); assistant to Monteverdi (1620); music director, Sta. Maria Maggiore, Bergamo (1627–30). Composed secular songs published as *Cantade et arie a voce sola* (1620–29); first to use "cantata" in modern sense; published several books of sacred motets (1610–30).

Grandi, Guido, *orig.* Francesco Lodovico. 1671–1742. Italian mathematician. Professor, Pisa (from 1700); known for studies of conchoid, cissoid, and other curves; developed versiera, later known as "witch of Agnesi."

Grand·jean \grän-zhän\, Philippe. 1666–1714. French type engraver. Known for cutting series of roman and italic typefaces called Romain du Roi for Imprimerie Royale of King Louis XIV.

Grandville. See Jean-I.-I. GÉRARD.

Gra·net \grá-ne\, François-Marius. 1775–1849. French painter. Curator of museum at Versailles (1826–48). Known for landscapes in Neoclassical style, scenes of religious life as *Choeur de l'Église des Capucins.*

Gran·ger \'grān-jər\, James. 1723–1776. English biographer. Collected 14,000 engraved portraits and used them for illustrations in his *Biographical History of England...adapted to a Methodical Catalogue of Engraved British Heads* (1769), including blank leaves for readers to paste other illustrations onto.

Gran·jon \grän-zhōn\, Robert. 1513–1589. French type founder and engraver. Printer in Paris (1551) and Lyon (1559). Known esp. for his *caractères de civilité,* based on French Gothic handwriting.

Grant \'grant\, Cary. *Orig.* Archibald Alexander Leach. 1904–1986. American actor, b. Bristol, Gloucestershire, Eng. Film actor noted for his roles as debonair, witty sophisticate. Made film debut in *This Is the Night* (1932). Also starred in *She Done Him Wrong* (1933), *Bringing Up Baby* (1938), *Holiday* (1938), *His Girl Friday* (1940), *The Philadelphia Story* (1940), *Notorious* (1946), *To Catch a Thief* (1955), *North by Northwest* (1959), *Charade* (1963), etc. Received special Academy Award (1970).

Grant, Duncan James Corrowr. 1885–1978. Scottish painter. Known for bold, bright paintings in Post-Impressionist style; known also for designs for furniture, fabrics, stage sets, interiors; associated with Bloomsbury group.

Grant, Heber Jedediah. 1856–1945. American religious leader, b. Salt Lake City. Elected member, Council of Twelve, Church of Latter-Day Saints (1882), and president of the church (1918–45).

Grant, James Augustus. 1827–1892. British soldier and explorer, b. Scotland. Entered army (1846); accompanied Speke (*q.v.*) in search for source of Nile (1860–62). Published journal of expedition as *A Walk Across Africa* (1864).

Grant, Sir James Hope. 1808–1875. British soldier, b. Scotland. Entered army (1826); distinguished himself in China (1842), Sikh War (1845–46), Sepoy Mutiny (1857); commanded final pacification of India; commanded British contingent in Chinese expedition (1859–60); lieutenant general commanding Madras army (1861–65); general (1872).

Grant, Ulysses S., *orig.* Hiram Ulysses. 1822–1885. Eighteenth president of the United States, b. Point Pleasant, Ohio. Entered U.S.M.A., West Point, as Ulysses S. through congressman's error. Served through Mexican War; resigned from army (1854); in various business occupations without marked success (1854–61). Reentered service at outbreak of Civil War as colonel of Illinois volunteer regiment; appointed brigadier general of volunteers (Aug. 1861); led expedition which captured Fort Henry, Fort Donelson, and a Confederate force of 15,000 under Gen. S.B. Buckner (Feb. 1862); at once appointed major general. In command at battle of Shiloh, or Pittsburg Landing (Apr. 6–7, 1862); broke Confederate control of Mississippi by capturing Vicksburg with 30,000 Confederate troops under Pemberton (July 4, 1863); commissioned regular army major general (1863). Undertook operations against Gen. Bragg at Chattanooga; stormed Lookout Mountain (Nov. 24) and Missionary Ridge (Nov. 25, 1863). Promoted to lieutenant general (March 1864) with command of all the armies of the United States; made headquarters with Army of the Potomac; in spite of heavy losses in the battle of the Wilderness and at Spotsylvania (May 1864), continued attack and wore the Confederates down. Received Lee's surrender at Appomattox Court House (Apr. 9, 1865). Promoted to new rank of general of the army (1866); interim secretary of war (1867–68). Elected president of the United States (1868); reelected (1872). Though he was personally absolutely honest, his administration was marked by serious scandals, as the Crédit Mobilier, the Whisky Ring, and the attempt of speculators to corner the gold market. On retiring from presidency, made tour of the world; settled in Galena, Ill. (1877) and then New York City (1881). Wrote *Personal Memoirs of U.S. Grant* (1885–86).

Gran·velle \grän-vel\, Antoine Per·re·not de \per-nō-də-\. 1517–1586. French prelate and politician in Spain. Bishop of Arras (1540); secretary of state under Charles V (1550); drew up Treaty of Passau (1552); negotiated (1553) marriage of Mary of England and Philip II of Spain; archbishop of Malines (1560); at appointment of Philip II, prime minister to Margaret of Austria, regent of the Netherlands (1560–64); cardinal (1561). Viceroy of Naples (1571–75); secretary of state for Spain (1579–86); negotiated union of Spanish and Portuguese crowns (1580); archbishop of Besançon (1584).

Granville, Earls. See (1) John CARTERET; (2) Granville George LEVESON-GOWER.

Gran·ville-Bar·ker \ˌgran-ˌvil-'bär-kər\, Harley Granville. 1877–1946. English actor, manager, and playwright. Made stage debut (1891); with Ben Greet Co. (1895); later, appeared in productions of William Poel's Elizabethan Stage Society and acted in support of Mrs. Patrick Campbell. Manager with J.E. Vedrenne of Court Theatre (1904–07); later associated with Savoy, Duke of York's, Little, Kingsway, and other theaters; chairman, British Drama League (1919–32); director, British Institute in Paris (1930–39). Noted for stress on natural acting, ensemble work, esp. in Shakespeare. Among his plays were *The Marrying of Ann Leete* (1901), *The Voysey Inheritance* (1905), *Prunella* (1906), *Waste* (1907), *The Madras House* (1910), *Vote by Ballot* (1917), and adaptations of Schnitzler, Guitry, and Romains; author also of *A National Theater* (with William Archer, 1907), *The Exemplary Theatre* (1922), *Prefaces to Shakespeare* (1927–48), *The Study of Drama* (1934), etc.

Gras \grä\, Félix. 1844–1901. French writer. A leader among the Félibristes; (1891) became head of Félibrige. Author of *Li Carbounié* (1876), *Toloza* (1882), *Li Papalino* (1891), *Li Rouge dou Mie jour* (1896).

Grasse \gräs\, François-Joseph-Paul de. Comte de Grasse and Marquis de Grasse-Til·ly \-tē-yē\. 1722–1788. French naval officer. Fought English in West Indies (1779–80); commanded French fleet in Chesapeake Bay which prevented English fleet from giving aid to Cornwallis at Yorktown (1781); captured St. Kitts, but defeated by Admiral Rodney in the West Indies (1782).

Gras·si \'gräs-sē\, Giovanni Battista. 1854–1925. Italian zoologist. Professor, Catania (1883–95), Rome (1895–1925); senator (1908). Known for studies in entomology and esp. in parasitology; determined vectors and pathogens of malaria, organized campaign to eliminate malaria in Italy (1898 ff.).

Grass·mann \'gräs-ˌmän\, Hermann Günther. 1809–1877. German mathematician and Sanskritist. Teacher in Stettin (1831–34, 1836–77); in *De lineale Ausdehnungslehre* (1844) laid foundation of modern vector analysis; published Sanskrit dictionary and concordance (1875) and translation of Rigveda (1876–77).

Gras·so \'gras-(ˌ)ō\, Ella Rosa Giovanna Oliva, *nee* **Tam·bus·si** \tam-'b(y)ü-sē\. 1919–1981. American politician, b. Windsor Locks, Conn. m. T.A. Grasso (1942); member of Democratic National Committee (1956–58); Conn. secretary of state (1958–70); member, U.S. House of Representatives (1971–75); governor of Conn. (1975–81), first woman to hold a U.S. state governorship in her own right.

Gra·ti·an \'grā-sh(ē-)ən\. *Lat.* Flavius Gra·ti·a·nus \ˌgrā-shē-'ā-nəs\. 359–383. Roman emperor (367–383). Son of Valentinian I; made augustus with a share in the government (367); succeeded as emperor in the West (375) with a brother, Valentinian II, as joint augustus; after defeat of Valens at Adrianople (378) chose Theodosius to rule in East (379); fought several campaigns against Goths, Alamanni, and others (379–381); killed at Lugdunum by rebels under usurper Maximus.

Gratian. *Full Latin name* Franciscus Gratianus. *Called* Magister Gratianus. d. before 1159. Italian ecclesiastic and jurist. Compiler of *Concordia discordantium canorum* or *Decretum Gratiani* (c.1140) and founder of the science of canon law.

Grat·tan \'grat-ən\, Henry. 1746–1820. Irish politician. Called to Irish bar (1772); member of Irish Parliament (1775–97, 1800) and of British Parliament (1805–20); by brilliant oratory succeeded Flood as leader of patriot party; secured lifting of restrictions on Irish trade (1779); called Convention of Dungannon (1782) to demand legislative independence (granted 1782); failed in campaigns against parliamentary corruption and for Catholic emancipation; opposed union with England (1800).

Grau \ˈgrau̇\, Maurice. 1849–1907. American impresario, b. Brünn, Austria. To U.S. (1854); organized Clara Louise Kellogg English Opera Co. (1873); managed appearances of Tommaso Salvini in U.S. Business manager, under Abbey, Metropolitan Opera House, N.Y. (1883–84, 1891–96); later (1898–1903) its managing director as head of Maurice Grau Opera Co.

Grau·man \ˈgrau̇-mən\, Sidney Patrick. 1879–1950. American theater owner, b. Indianapolis. In Los Angeles built series of opulent theaters, including Grauman's Chinese Theater.

Graun \ˈgrau̇n\, Karl Heinrich. 1704–1759. German composer. Singer at Dresden Opera (1721–25), Brunswick Opera (1725–35); Kapellmeister to Frederick the Great (1735–59). Composed operas in Italian manner, including *Lo specchio della fedeltà* (1733), *Rodelinda* (1741), *Cesare e Cleopatra* (which opened new Royal Berlin Opera House, 1742), *Montezuma* (1755), *La Merope* (1756); also composed church music including Passion oratorio *Der Tod Jesu* (1755), *Te Deum* celebrating Frederick's victory at Prague (1757).

Graunt \ˈgrant\, John. 1620–1674. English statistician. Prepared original mortality table in his *Natural and Political Observations...made upon the Bills of Mortality* (1662); an original member of the Royal Society.

Graup·ner \ˈgrau̇p-nər\, Christoph, *in full* Johann Christoph. 1683–1760. German composer. Harpsichordist at Hamburg opera (1707–09); assistant (1709–12), Kapellmeister (1712–60), to landgrave of Hesse-Darmstadt; offered but declined (1723) post of cantor of St. Thomas, Leipzig, that went instead to J.S. Bach. Composed operas, over 1400 cantatas in early Rococo style, 113 symphonies, about 50 concertos, over 80 suites, 36 trio sonatas, keyboard works.

Graupner, Johann Christian Gottlieb. 1767–1836. American musician, b. in Verden, Prussia. To Charleston, S.C. (1795) and Boston (1796); organized Philharmonic Society in Boston (c.1810), first symphony orchestra in America; an organizer of Handel and Haydn Society (1815); gave first oratorio performance in U.S.

Grau San Mar·tín \ˈgrau̇-sän-mär-ˈtēn\, Ramón. 1887–1969. Cuban physician and politician. Head of provisional junta and provisional president of Cuba (1933–34); president (1944–48).

Graves \ˈgrāvz\, Richard. 1715–1804. English poet and novelist. Author of *The Spiritual Quixote* (1772), *The Reveries of Solitude* (1793), etc.

Graves, Robert Ranke. 1895–1985. British poet, novelist, and critic. Professor of poetry at U. of Oxford (1961–66). Wrote romantic poetry in traditional meters and with precise, clear diction; recognized as one of the finest contemporary lyric poets; published several collections of his poetry (1948–75). Nonfiction included *Lawrence and the Arabs* (1927), autobiographical *Goodbye to All That* (1929), *King Jesus* (1946), and *The White Goddess* (1948). Best known for historical novels *I, Claudius* and *Claudius the God* (both 1934), etc. Also wrote critical essays and translated Greek and Latin works.

Graves, Thomas. 1st Baron Graves. 1725?–1802. British admiral. Commanded British fleet operating against American colonies (1781), and was defeated at Chesapeake Bay by the French fleet (Sept. 5, 1781); commanded Channel fleet in war with France (1793–94); admiral, baron (1794).

Graves, William Sidney. 1865–1940. American army officer, b. Mount Calm, Tex. Commanded American expeditionary force in Siberia (1918–20).

Gra·ve·san·de \ˌgrā-və-ˈsän-də\, Willem Jakob 's. 1688–1742. Dutch mathematician and philosopher. Professor, Leiden (1717–42); friend of Sir Isaac Newton. Introduced Newtonian philosophy into Leiden with *Physices elementa mathematica, experimentis confirmata* (1720–21).

Gra·vi·na \grä-ˈb̲ē-nä\, Federico Carlos de. Duque. 1756–1806. Spanish admiral. Took part in defense of Toulon (1794), actions at Brest and Cádiz (1797); commanded Santo Domingo expedition (1801–02); ambassador to Paris (1804–05); commander of Spanish fleet at Trafalgar (1805); mortally wounded in action.

Gra·vi·na \grä-ˈvē-nä\, Gian Vincenzo. 1664–1718. Italian jurist and writer. Professor, Sapienza, Rome (from 1699); a founder (1695) of academy of Arcadia. Author of *Originum juris civilis* (1708–13) and of a theory of poetics in *Ragion poetica* (1708).

Gray. See also GREY.

Gray \ˈgrā\, Asa. 1810–1888. American botanist, b. Sauquoit, N.Y. Assistant to John Torrey (1834); collaborator with him in preparing *Flora of North America* (1838–43). Professor of natural history, Harvard (1842–73); assembled large botanical library, herbarium; correspondent of and chief American supporter of Charles Darwin. Author of *Elements of Botany* (1836), *Botanical Text-Book* (1842; renamed *Structural Botany*, 1879), *Manual of the Botany of the Northern United States* (known as *Gray's Manual*, 1848), *First Lessons in Botany and Vegetable Physiology* (1857), *How Plants Grow* (1858), *How Plants Behave* (1872), *Synoptical Flora of North America* (1878), etc.

Gray, David. 1838–1861. Scottish poet. Author of lyrical verse including a group of sonnets published posthumously as *The Luggie and Other Poems* (1862).

Gray, Elisha. 1835–1901. American inventor, b. Barnesville, Ohio. With E. M. Barton (1844–1916), organized manufacturing concern Gray and Barton (1872) from which developed the Western Electric Co.; made numerous inventions in telegraphy; filed caveat on telephone on same day Alexander Graham Bell filed for patent (1876); long and bitter patent infringement battle was decided by U.S. Supreme Court in favor of Bell; patented telautograph (1888 and 1891); professor, Oberlin Coll. (1880–1901).

Gray, Harold Lincoln. 1894–1968. American cartoonist, b. Kankakee, Ill. On staff of *Chicago Tribune* (1917–19); assistant on comic strip "Andy Gump" (1919–24); creator and author-illustrator (1924–68) of comic strip "Little Orphan Annie."

Gray, Henry. 1825 or 1827–1861. English anatomist. Lecturer in anatomy, St. George's Hospital, London (from 1853); noted for studies of development of endocrine glands, spleen. Author of *Anatomy, Descriptive and Surgical* (1858), widely known as *Gray's Anatomy*.

Gray, Horace. 1828–1902. American jurist, b. Boston. Associate justice, Mass. supreme judicial court (1864–73); chief justice (1873–81). Associate justice, U.S. Supreme Court (1882–1902).

Gray, Sir James. 1891–1975. English zoologist. Professor, Cambridge (1937–59); known for studies in cytology and animal movement and esp. for influential editorship (1925–54) of *Journal of Experimental Biology*. Author of *Ciliary Movement* (1928), *Text-book of Experimental Cytology* (1931), *How Animals Move* (1953), *Animal Locomotion* (1968), etc.

Gray, Robert. 1755–1806. American shipmaster and explorer, b. Tiverton, R.I. Served in American navy in American Revolution; master of sloop *Lady Washington* which sailed from Boston (1787) around Cape Horn to load furs on the northwest coast; transferred to the *Columbia* and completed first voyage of an American captain around the world (1790). Commanding *Columbia*, left Boston (1790), arrived Vancouver Island (1791); discovered Grays Harbor and Columbia River (named in honor of his vessel). His trip and discoveries were foundation of American claim to Oregon country.

Gray, Robert. 1809–1872. English prelate. First Anglican bishop (1847) and metropolitan (1853) of Cape Town; established independence of South African church; deposed Bishop Colenso (1863).

Gray, Stephen. 1666–1736. English scientist. Experimented in microscopy; noted amateur astronomer; in late years experimented in static electricity; first to divide substances into electrics and nonelectrics, according as they can or can not be electrified by friction; discovered (1729–32) conduction of electrical charge and distinction between conductors and insulators.

Gray, Thomas. 1716–1771. English poet. Accompanied Horace Walpole on Continental tour (1739–41); Professor of modern history at Cambridge (1768). Author of several striking lyrics, including "Ode on the Spring," "Sonnet on the Death of Mr. Richard West," "Hymn to Adversity," Ode on a Distant Prospect of Eton College," "Progress of Poesy," "The Bard," and esp. "Elegy Written in a Country Churchyard."

Grayson, David. See Ray Stannard BAKER.

Gra·zia·ni \gräts-ˈyä-nē\, Rodolfo. Marchese di Ne·ghel·li \dē-nā-ˈgel-lē\. 1882–1955. Italian marshal and administrator. Commander of Italian forces in Libya (1930–34); governor of Italian Somaliland (1935–36); viceroy of Ethiopia (1936–37); commander in Libya (1940–41); defeated in Egypt by British under Wavell; minister of defense (1943–45); surrendered Ligurian army (1945); tried for war crimes, sentenced (1950) but released same year; leader of neo-Fascist movement.

Graz·zi·ni \grät-ˈtsē-nē\, Anton Francesco. *Known as* Il La·sca \ēl-ˈläs-kä\. 1503–1584. Italian writer. A founder (1540) of Accademia degli Umidi and (1582) of Accademia della Crusca, a literary society whose purpose was purification of the Italian language. Author of burlesque verses, stories collected in *Cene,* and comedies as *La spiritata, La gelosia, La strega, La sibilla, La pinzochera.*

Great·head \ˈgrāt-ˌhed\, Henry. 1757–1816. English boatbuilder. Inventor of the lifeboat (1789); received grant of £1200 for his invention.

Greathead, James Henry. 1844–1896. British engineer, b. South Africa. To England (1859); designed improved version of Brunel's tunnelling shield; constructed subway under the Thames near the Tower of London (1869) and the City and South London railroad tunnels (1886); pioneered in use of compressed air with shield.

Greb \ˈgreb\, Harry, *in full* Edward Henry. 1894–1926. American boxer. Career (1913–26) record 283 wins, 9 losses; world middleweight champion (1923–26).

Gré·ban \grā-bäⁿ\, Arnoul. 1420–1471. French poet. Organist and choirmaster of Notre-Dame, Paris (1455); later canon at Le Mans. Author of drama *Mystère de la Passion* (1453 or 1454).

Gre·bel \'grā-bəl\, Konrad. c.1498–1526. Swiss religious leader. Originally a supporter, broke with Zwingli (1524); organized Swiss Brethren (1524), branch of Anabaptist church; disobeyed order of Zürich city council and performed first modern adult baptism (1525); proselytized in Swiss cities; twice imprisoned.

Gre·cha·ni·nov \gryə-(,)chən-'yē-nəf\, Aleksandr Tikhonovich. 1864–1956. Russian composer. Teacher of piano, St. Petersburg and Moscow; fled to Europe (1925), U.S. (1939). Known for opera *Dobrinya Nikitich* (1903), religious music, five symphonies, songs, children's music.

Grechetto, Il. See Giovanni Benedetto CASTIGLIONE.

Greco, El. See Doménikos THEOTOKÓPOULOS.

Gré·court \grā-kür\, Jean-Baptiste-Joseph Wil·lart de \vē-lår-də-\. 1683–1743. French poet. Minor churchman; expressed epicurean leanings in *Le Solitaire et la fortune;* composed also elegies, songs, fables in verse, etc.

Gree·ley \'grē-lē\, Horace. 1811–1872. American journalist and political leader, b. Amherst, N.H. To New York (1831); with Jonas Winchester, founded and edited (1834–41) weekly *The New Yorker.* Founded New York *Tribune* (1841), a Whig newspaper of high journalistic standards that became important influence in molding thought of the people of the North. Supported Free Soil movement, abolitionism, free common-school education, dress and diet reforms, etc. Opposed Mexican War, Kansas-Nebraska Act; joined Republican party (1854). After Civil War, advocated universal amnesty and universal suffrage; defied public opinion in the North by signing a bail bond for Jefferson Davis. Accepted nomination for presidency by Liberal Republicans and was endorsed by Democrats (1872); badly beaten in election.

Gree·ly \'grē-lē\, Adolphus Washington. 1844–1935. American army officer and explorer, b. Newburyport, Mass. Entered army (1861). Commanded U.S. expedition (1881) to establish Arctic meteorological station; established Fort Conger on Ellesmere Island; attained the most northerly point reached up to that time, 83° 24′ N.; explored Ellesmere, northern Greenland; lost 19 of 25 men when relief ships failed to appear (1883–84). Promoted chief signal officer with rank of brigadier general (1887) and major general (1906); in charge of building and operation of telegraph lines in Cuba, China, Philippine Islands, Alaska; in charge of relief operations in San Francisco after the fire and earthquake (1906); retired (1908). Author of *Three Years of Arctic Service* (1886), *Handbook of Polar Discoveries* (1909), *True Tales of Arctic Heroism* (1912), etc.

Green \'grēn\, Alice Sophia Amelia, *nee* Stop·ford \'stäp-fə(r)d\. *Known as* Mrs. Stopford Green. 1847–1929. Irish historian. To England (1874); m. (1877) John Richard Green (*q.v.*). Became zealous advocate of home rule for Ireland; to Dublin (1917); Irish senator (1922). Author of *Henry II* (1888), *Town Life in the Fifteenth Century* (1894), *The Making of Ireland and its Undoing* (1908), *A History of the Irish State to 1014* (1925).

Green, Anna Katharine. 1846–1935. American writer, b. Brooklyn, N.Y. m. Charles Rohlfs (1884). One of the chief creators of detective fiction in novels as *The Leavenworth Case* (1878), *A Strange Disappearance* (1880), *Behind Closed Doors* (1888), *Marked "Personal"* (1893), *The Circular Study* (1900), *The Filigree Ball* (1903), *Initials Only* (1911), *Step on the Stair* (1923).

Green, Charles. 1785–1870. English aeronaut. Began experimenting in balloon ascensions (1821); introduced use of coal gas in place of hydrogen (1821); with two companions made flight from London to Weilburg, Germany (480 miles, 1836); reached altitude over 27,000 feet (1838).

Green, Duff. 1791–1875. American journalist and politician, b. Woodford Co., Ky. To Missouri (1816); bought St. Louis *Enquirer* and supported Jackson (1824); to Washington (1825); founded (1825) Jacksonian *United States Telegraph;* attacked Adams's administration in his paper; printer to Congress (1829–33) and influential leader of Democratic party; broke with Jackson and supported Clay for presidency (1832). In Baltimore published *Reformer* (1837–38), *Pilot* (1840); supported Harrison and Tyler (1840); in England as unofficial representative of United States (1840–44). U.S. consul, Galveston, Texas (1844); failed in attempt to negotiate for U.S. purchase of Texas, New Mexico, and California; acquired extensive railroad interests later lost to Crédit Mobilier.

Green, George. 1793–1841. English mathematician. Self-taught as mathematician; known for studies of attraction in *n*-dimensional space, fluid motion, and esp. for first attempt to formulate mathematical theory of electricity and magnetism (1828).

Green, Henrietta Howland, *nee* Robinson. *Known as* Hetty Green. 1834–1916. American financier, b. New Bedford, Mass. m. Edward Henry Green (1867; d. 1902). Inherited fortune from father and aunt and greatly increased it by shrewd investment and manipulation; reputed to have been the richest woman in America, called sometimes the "witch of Wall Street"; subject of many anecdotes based on her personal frugality.

Green, Henry. See Henry V. YORKE.

Green, John Richard. 1837–1883. English historian. Ordained (1860); vicar of Saint Philip's, Stepney (1866); librarian at Lambeth (1869). Author of a standard *Short History of the English People* (1874), *The Making of England* (1881), *Conquest of England* (1883), the last completed by his wife Alice Stopford GREEN.

Green, Matthew. 1696–1737. English poet. Known for *The Grotto* (1733) and esp. for *The Spleen* (1737), gently satirical verse epistle.

Green, Paul Eliot. 1894–1981. American playwright, b. Lillington, N.C. Professor, U. of North Carolina (1923–44); president, American Folk Festival (1934–45). Author of plays including *The No 'Count Boy* (1924), *The Lord's Will* (1925), *In Abraham's Bosom* (1926, Pulitzer prize), *The Field God* (1927), *In the Valley* (1928), *Potter's Field* (1929), *House of Connelly* (1931), *Johnny Johnson* (1936, music by Kurt Weill), *Native Son* (1941, with Richard Wright); created "symphonic dramas" as *Lost Colony* (1937), *Highland Call* (1941), *Faith of Our Fathers* (1950), *Wilderness Road* (1956), *The Founders* (1957), *Cross and Sword* (1964), *Trumpet in the Land* (1970); wrote also novels, screenplays, radio plays.

Green, Mrs. Stopford. See Alice Sophia Amelia Stopford GREEN.

Green, Thomas. 1735–1812. American printer, b. New London, Conn. Founded *Connecticut Courant* (now *Hartford Courant*) (1764), *Connecticut Journal and New Haven Post Boy* (1767, now *New Haven Journal Courier).*

Green, Thomas Hill. 1836–1882. English philosopher. Professor, Oxford (1878–82). Developed an Idealist philosophy of the Neo-Kantian school; known esp. for lectures on ethics and politics. Author of *Prolegomena to Ethics,* left incomplete at his death and edited by A.C. Bradley (1883), and *Lectures on the Principles of Political Obligation* (1885).

Green, William. 1873–1952. American labor leader, b. Coshocton, Ohio. Employed in mines in Ohio; subdistrict president (1896–1906), district president (1906–10), secretary-treasurer (1912–24), United Mine Workers; council member (from 1913), president (1924–52), American Federation of Labor; on governing council, International Labor Organization (1935–37); expelled CIO unions from AFL (1936).

Green·a·way \'grē-nə-,wā\, Catherine, *known as* Kate. 1846–1901. English painter and illustrator. Published *Under the Window* (1879), *Kate Greenaway's Birthday Book* (1880), *Mother Goose* (1881), *Little Ann* (1883), *Language of Flowers* (1884), *A Apple Pie* (1886), and other children's books; issued *Kate Greenaway's Almanacs* (1883–95, 1897).

Greene \'grēn\, Charles Sumner (1868–1957), b. St. Louis, and his brother Henry Mather (1870–1954), b. Cincinnati. American architects. Established partnership in Pasadena, Cal. (1894); developed distinctive bungalow style emphasizing interpenetration of interior and exterior spaces, local materials, high craftsmanship; best known work the Gamble house (1908), now the Greene and Greene Library, Pasadena.

Greene, Maurice. 1696–1755. English organist and composer. Organist, St. Paul's, London (1718–55), and Chapel Royal (1727–55); master of king's music (1735–55). Composed much sacred and secular vocal music including 103 anthems as *O clap your hands together* and *Lord, let me know mine end;* 7 *Te Deums;* oratorios as *Song of Deborah and Barak* (1732), *Jephtha* (1737); settings of Pope's *Ode for St. Cecilia's Day* (1730), Spenser's *Amoretti* (1739), Addison's *The Spacious Firmament* (c.1740), etc.

Greene, Nathanael. 1742–1786. American Revolutionary officer, b. Potowomut, Warwick, R.I. Commissioned brigadier general in Continental army (June 1775); major general (1776); led left wing of American force at Trenton (Dec. 26, 1776); quartermaster general of the army (1778–80); president of court-martial that tried Major André (1780). Succeeded Gates in command of the army in the South (1780); conducted strategic retreat (1781) and finally turned and forced British out of Georgia and the Carolinas in battles of Cowpens (Jan. 17, 1781), Guilford Courthouse (Mar. 15), Hobkirk's Hill (April 25), Eutaw Springs (Sept. 8); besieged Charleston (1781–82).

Greene, Robert. 1558?–1592. English poet and playwright. Chief dramatic work, *The Honorable Historie of frier Bacon and frier Bongay* (acted 1594); perhaps also author of *Comicall Historie of Alphonsus King of Aragon* (c.1588); noted for songs and eclogues found scattered through his works, as in the romances *Perimedes the Blacke-Smith* (1588) and *Menaphon* (1589). Author of prose works as *Euphues, his Censure to Philautus* (a continuation of Lyly's *Euphues,* 1587), *Pandosto* (1588; source of plot of Shakespeare's *Winter's Tale*), *Greene's Mourning Garment* (1590), *Farewell to Folly* (1591), *Groatsworth of witte bought with a million of Repentance,* which attacked Marlowe and Peele and referred to Shakespeare as an "upstart crow."

Green·er \'grē-nər\, William. 1806–1869. English gunmaker and inventor. Developed (1836) self-expanding bullet for muzzle-loading rifles, anticipating Minié ball; received settlement from British government when it made large award to Capt. Minié after rejecting Greener's bullet.

Green·how \'grēn-,haü\, Rose, *nee* O'·Neal \ō-'nēl\. 1815?–1864. American Confederate spy, b. Maryland. m. Dr. Robert Greenhow (1835; d. 1854); prominent social figure in Washington, D.C. (1856 ff.); secured and forwarded information on Union troop movements and plans (1861–62); imprisoned in Old Capitol Prison (1862), exiled to Confederacy (1862); unofficial Confederate agent in Great Britain (1863–64); drowned attempting to run blockade of Wilmington, N.C. Author of *My Imprisonment and the First Year of Abolition Rule at Washington* (1863).

Green·leaf \'grēn-,lēf\, Ralph. c.1899–1950. American billiard player, b. Monmouth, Ill. World pocket billiard champion (1919–24, intermittently 1926–37); achieved record runs of 126 (1929, on a 10 by 5 table) and 269 (exhibition).

Greenleaf, Simon. 1783–1853. American jurist, b. Newburyport, Mass. Professor of law, Harvard Law School (1833–48); associated with Story in developing efficiency of this school. Chief work, *A Treatise on the Law of Evidence* (1842–53).

Greenock, Lord. See Charles Murray CATHCART.

Gree·nough \'grē-,nō\, George Bellas. 1778–1855. English geographer and geologist. M.P. (1807–12); founder (1811) and first president of the Geological Society, London; an original member (from 1830), president (1839–40) of the Royal Geographical Society; produced important geological map of England and Wales (1820).

Greenough, Horatio. 1805–1852. American sculptor, b. Boston. To Italy as student (1825); leading member of American artist colony in Italy (1828–51). Works included *Washington,* colossal statue in classical style, commissioned (1832) by Congress for Capitol rotunda and now in Smithsonian Institution; *The Rescue* (1851), group on portico of the Capitol, Washington, D.C.; *Angel and Child; Cupid Bound;* busts of Alexander Hamilton, Lafayette, John Quincy Adams. His brother ¶Richard Saltonstall (1819–1904) was also a sculptor. Works included *Shepherd Boy and Eagle,* colossal statue of Benjamin Franklin in front of Boston City Hall, *Carthaginian Maiden.*

Greenwich, Duke of. See John Campbell under CAMPBELL family.

Green·wood \'grēn-,wu̇d\, Arthur. 1880–1954. British politician. M.P. (from 1922); secretary to minister of health (1924); minister of health (1929–31); deputy leader of Labour party (1935–45); minister without portfolio (1940–42); lord privy seal (1945–47); paymaster general (1946–47); national chairman, Labour party (1953–54).

Greenwood, Frederick. 1830–1909. English journalist. Succeeded Thackeray as editor of *Cornhill Magazine* (1862–68); founded (with George Smith) and edited *Pall Mall Gazette* (1865–80); founded and edited *St. James's Gazette* (1880–88); highly influential supporter of Conservative party and esp. of Disraeli.

Greenwood, John. d. 1593. English Puritan clergyman. Imprisoned (1586–92) for nonconformist activities; helped found (1592) Separatist church with Robert Brown; arrested, hanged at Tyburn.

Greenwood, John. 1760–1819. American dentist, b. Boston. Reputed inventor of footpower drill, springs holding artificial plates in position, and use of porcelain for artificial teeth; made sets of artificial teeth for George Washington.

Greenwood, Walter. 1903–1974. English novelist and playwright. Author of highly successful proletarian novel *Love on the Dole* (1933, dramatized 1934), followed by *Standing Room Only* (1936), *Only Mugs Work* (1938, dramatized 1938), *What Everybody Wants* (1953), etc.; collection of stories *The Cleft Stick* (1937); plays, *My Son's My Son* (1935), *Give Us This Day* (1936), *The Cure for Love* (1945), *Saturday Night at the Crown* (1953), *Happy Days* (1959), etc., also screenplays.

Greet \'grēt\, Sir Ben, *in full* Phillip Barling Ben. 1857–1936. English actor and manager. Debut (1879); acted in support of Lawrence Barrett (1884), Mary Anderson, and others. Undertook management of summer open-air performances (1886 ff.); toured with own company (1890–1902) in such plays as *The Little Minister, Diplomacy, The Belle of New York;* with William Poel revived *Everyman* (1902); specialized in Shakespearean productions in U.S. (1902–14); with Lilian Baylis formed Old Vic company (1914).

Greg \'greg\, Sir Walter Wilson. 1875–1959. English bibliographer. President of Bibliographical Society (1930–32); general editor of Malone Society (1906–39). Editor of Henslowe's diary (1904–08), and Elizabethan plays and Chester plays. Author of *A List of English Plays* (1900), *Dramatic Documents from the Elizabethan Playhouses* (1931), etc.

Gregg \'greg\, John Robert. 1867–1948. American inventor and publisher, b. Shantonagh, Ireland. Invented and published new shorthand system in *Light Line Phonography* (1888); to U.S. (1893); established Gregg Publishing Co., Gregg Schools; edited *Gregg Writer* (from 1899), *American Shorthand Teacher* (from 1920; renamed *Business Education World,* 1933). Author of *Gregg Shorthand Manual* (1888), *Gregg Phrase Book* (1901), *Gregg Speed Studies* (1917), etc.

Gregg, Josiah. 1806–1850. American frontiersman, b. Overton Co., Tenn. Trader, army agent and translator in Southwest. Author of influential *Commerce of the Prairies* (1844).

Gregg, William. 1800–1867. American industrialist, b. near Carmichaels, Va. (now W.Va.). Amassed fortune with cotton and watch factories; settled in Charleston, S.C. (1838), and published influential *Essays on Domestic Industry* (1845) urging industrialization; built textile mill and factory town at Graniteville (1846) which he operated to his death.

Gregh \greg\, Fernand. 1873–1960. French poet. Author of *La Maison de l'enfance* (1896), *Les Clartés humaines* (1904), *La Chaîne eternelle* (1910), *Couleur de la vie* (1927), *La Gloire du coeur* (1932), *La Couronne perdue et retrouvée* (1945), etc.

Grégoire, Père. See Jean-Baptiste GIRARD.

Gré·goire \grā-gwȧr\, Henri. 1750–1831. French prelate and revolutionary. Member of the Estates-General and Constituent Assembly (1789); accepted Constitutional church and became bishop of Loir-et-Cher (1790); member of the National Convention (1792), the Council of Five Hundred (1795), the Senate (1801); opposed Napoléon's coup (1799), Concordat (1800), proclamation of empire (1804); proposed deposition of Napoléon (1814).

Greg·or \'greg-ər\, William. 1761–1817. English clergyman, chemist, and mineralogist. Discovered titanium (1791).

Greg·o·ras \'greg-ə-rəs\, Nicephorus. 1295–1360. Byzantine scholar and historian. Diplomat in service of Andronicus II Palaeologus; opponent of Aristotelianism and hesychasm. Chief work, a history of the Eastern Empire in the years 1204 to 1354.

Gregorios Akindynos. See AKINDYNOS.

Gre·go·ro·vi·us \grā-gō-'rō-vyu̇s\, Ferdinand. 1821–1891. German historian. Author of *Geschichte der Stadt Rom im Mittelalter* (1859–72), *Geschichte der Stadt Athen im Mittelalter* (1889), etc.

Greg·o·ry \'greg-(ə-)rē\. Saint. *Called* the Illuminator. 240–332. Armenian apostle of Christianity. Said to have been Parthian prince; converted Tiridates III (c.300); patriarch of Armenia (302 ff.); founder and patron saint of Armenian church.

Gregory. Name of 16 popes and two antipopes:

Gregory I. Saint. *Called* the Great. c.540–604. Pope (590–604). Prefect of Rome (c.572–574); established several monasteries; papal nuncio to Constantinople (579–584). As pope, restored monastic discipline, enforced celibacy of clergy, and was zealous in propagating Christianity; sent Augustine as missionary to England (597); worked with Theodolinda, wife of Agilulf, and with Brunhilda of Merovingians to extend influence of western church; sought peace with Lombards. Transformed patriarchate of Rome into the papal system that endured through the Middle Ages; supposed to have arranged the Gregorian chant; author of dialogues, letters, homilies, and esp. the *Moralia* (morals from the Book of Job). Canonized by popular acclaim; fourth doctor of the church.

Gregory II. Saint. 669–731. Pope (715–731). Although a supporter of Eastern Empire, opposed iconoclastic edicts of Leo III the Isaurian; sent (719) Boniface as missionary to the Germans.

Gregory III. Saint. d. 741. Pope (731–741). Convoked a council in Rome (731) to condemn iconoclasm; supported St. Boniface and made him metropolitan of Germany (732).

Gregory IV. d. 844. Pope (827–844). Cardinal priest of St. Mark's at election; attempted to mediate revolt (833–834) of Lothair I against emperor Louis the Pious; gave St. Ansgar metropolitan jurisdiction over Scandinavia (831–832); promulgated (835) observance of All Saints' Day.

Gregory V. *Orig.* Bru·no·ne di Ca·rin·zia \brü-'nō-nā-dē-kä-'rint-sē-ä\ *or* Bru·no \'brü-nō\ of Carinthia. 972–999. Pope (996–999). First German pope; named by cousin Otto III, whom he in turn crowned emperor; forced to flee (996) during Otto's absence; pontificate contested by antipope John XVI; restored by Otto (998); had dispute with French king Robert II, whom he excommunicated.

Gregory VI. *Orig.* Giovanni Gra·zi·a·no \,grät-sē-'ä-nō\. d. 1048. Pope (1045–46). Paid Pope Benedict IX to resign in order to prevent scandal (1045); elected to succeed Benedict; accused of simony, deposed and banished to Germany (1046).

Gregory VII. Saint. *Orig.* Hil·de·brand \'hil-də-,brand\. c.1020–1085. Pope (1073–85). Benedictine monk; as chaplain of Gregory VI (1045–47), accompanied him on exile to Germany; recalled by Leo IX (1049); influential adviser to Leo and succeeding popes; created cardinal archdeacon; presided as papal legate over synod of Tours (1054). As pope, aimed to establish supremacy of papacy within the church and of the church over the state; took strong measures against simony and nicolaitanism. Issued decree (1075) against lay investitures which aroused Henry IV of Germany to anger; summoned Henry to Rome to answer charges; on his refusal, excommunicated him (1076); received Henry in penance at Canossa (1077) and granted him absolution; attempted to mediate between Henry and Rudolf of Swabia in struggle for German throne (1078–80); again resisted by Henry in continuation of quarrel (1080), and again excommunicated him; driven from Rome by Henry and displaced by Guibert as Clement III (1084); retired to Salerno, under protection of Robert Guiscard; died in exile.

Gregory VIII. *Orig.* Alberto de Mor·ra \'mȯr-rä\. d. 1187. Pope (1187). Cardinal (1155 or 1156); began preparation for Third Crusade; died after two months on throne.

Gregory IX. *Orig.* Ugo \'ü-gō\ *or* Ugo·li·no \ˌü-gō-'lē-nō\. Count of Se·gni \'sān-yē\. before 1170–1241. Pope (1227–41). Nephew of Innocent III; cardinal deacon (1198); cardinal bishop of Ostia (1206). Excommunicated Emperor Frederick II (1227) because he refused to keep his promise to go on crusade; waged struggle against Frederick (1228–41); again excommunicated Frederick for invasion of Sardinia (1239). Encouraged mendicant orders; helped to develop the Holy Office of the Inquisition (from c.1232); promulgated Decretals (1234), code of canon law.

Gregory X. *Orig.* Teobaldo Vis·con·ti \vē-'skōn-tē\. 1210–1276. Pope (1271–76). Accompanied Edward I of England to Holy Land (1270); elected to papacy three years' vacant; promoted election of Emperor Rudolf I (1273); convoked Council of Lyon (1274), which effected temporary union between Eastern and Western churches and regularized papal elections by conclave.

Gregory XI. *Orig.* Pierre-Roger de Beau·fort \də-bō-fȯr\. 1329–1378. Pope (1370–78). Ended Babylonian captivity of popes by removing from Avignon to Rome (1377); issued bulls against Wycliffe's doctrines.

Gregory XII. *Orig.* Angelo Cor·rer \'kär-ər\. c.1325–1417. Pope (1406–15). Bishop of Castello (1380); cardinal (1405); elected in opposition to antipope at Avignon, Benedict XIII; deposed, along with antipope, by Council of Pisa (1409); refused to yield to new pope, Alexander V, until Council of Constance (1415); there resigned.

Gregory XIII. *Orig.* Ugo Buon·com·pa·gni \bwȯn-kōm-'pän-yē\. 1502–1585. Pope (1572–85). Professor of jurisprudence, Bologna (1531–39); held papal offices (1539–72); bishop of Viesti (1558); attended Council of Trent (1561–63); cardinal (1565); as pope, vigorous in propaganda against Protestantism; established many colleges and seminaries and placed them under direction of Jesuits; established *Index Librorum Prohibitorum;* aided Philip II in Netherlands and Catholic League in France; aided Irish Catholic rebels against Elizabeth I of England; commissioned reform that produced (1582) the Gregorian calendar still in use.

Gregory XIV. *Orig.* Niccolò Sfon·dra·to \sfȯn-'drä-tō\. 1535–1591. Pope (1590–91). Bishop of Cremona (1560); cardinal (1583); continued reforms and struggle against Protestant Henry IV of France begun by predecessor Pope Sixtus V.

Gregory XV. *Orig.* Alessandro Lu·do·vi·si \lü-dō-'vē-zē\. 1554–1623. Pope (1621–23). Archbishop of Bologna (1612); cardinal (1616); reformed papal elections by introducing secret ballot; founded (1622) Congregation of Propaganda.

Gregory XVI. *Orig.* Bartolomeo Alberto Cap·pel·la·ri \ˌkäp-pāl-'lä-rē\. 1765–1846. Pope (1831–46). Camaldolese monk; procurator general (1807), vicar general (1823); cardinal (1826). With aid of Austria, suppressed revolution in Papal States (1831–32); his rule disturbed by French occupation (1832–38); opponent of liberalism; concerned with spiritual reform of clergy, orders, fostering of missions. Author of *Il trionfo della santa sede contro gli assalti dei novatori* (1799).

ANTIPOPES:

Gregory VI. 11th century. Antipope (1012). Installed in Lateran by powerful Crescenti family to succeed Sergius IV; driven from Rome by Benedict VIII, candidate of rival Tusculani family; lost appeal to Henry II of Germany.

Gregory VIII. *Orig.* Maurice Bour·din \bür-daⁿ\. d. c.1137. Antipope (1118–21). Benedictine monk; bishop of Coimbra (1098); archbishop of Braga (1111); envoy of Paschal II to Henry V of Germany, to whose cause he defected; set up as antipope in opposition to Gelasius II by Henry; excommunicated by Gelasius (1118) and Calixtus II (1119); died in exile.

Gregory of Na·zi·an·zus \ˌnā-zē-'an-zəs\. Saint. c.330–c.389. Greek prelate of Asia Minor. Early friend of St. Basil the Great; entered Cappadocian order (c.356); with Basil edited *Philocalia,* anthology of Origen's works; ordained (362); bishop of Sasima (372); after Basil's death (379), chief spokesman of Nicene party; as head of Anastasia Chapel, Constantinople (379), became famous for scriptural exposition and esp. for trinitarian theology; barred from election as bishop of Constantinople (381), but his trinitarian doctrine accepted. Father of the Church; with Basil and St. Gregory of Nyssa one of the Cappadocian Fathers.

Gregory of Nys·sa \'nis-ə\. Saint. c.335–c.394. Greek prelate of Asia Minor. Brother of St. Basil the Great; bishop of Nyssa (372); deposed by civil governor (376), restored (378); attended Council at Constantinople (381) and succeeded Gregory of Nazianzus as chief theologian of orthodoxy in Asia Minor. Author of numerous works against Arianism, of *Creation of Man* (continuation of Basil's *Hexaëmeron*), of the *Great Cathechesis,* of *On Not Three Gods, Life of Macrinus, Life of Moses,* etc. With Basil and Gregory of Nazianzus, one of three Cappadocian Fathers of the Church.

Gregory of Ri·mi·ni \'rim-ə-(ˌ)nē, 'rē-mə-\. d. 1358. Italian philosopher and theologian. Augustinian monk; superior general (1357); taught a moderate Nominalism combined with Augustinian doctrine of man's moral depravity and utter dependence on divine grace. Author of *Lectura in librum I et II sententiarum.*

Gregory of Si·nai \'sī-ˌnī *also* -nē-ˌī\. *Also called* Gregory Si·nai·tes \sī-'nīt-ˌēz, -nē-'īt-ˌēz\. d. 1346. Greek religious. Monk on Cyprus, later Mt. Sinai, then on Mt. Athos; chief medieval advocate of hesychasm, of which Mt. Athos became a chief center; fled Ottoman Turks, established hesychast monastery of Mt. Paroria, Bulgaria (c.1325). Author of hymns, tracts on asceticism, and esp. *137 Chapters; or Spiritual Meditations,* widely influential exposition of hesychasm.

Gregory of Tours \'tu̇(ə)r\. *Orig.* Georgius Flo·ren·tius \flōr-'en-ch(ē-)əs, flȯr-\. 538–594. Frankish prelate. Bishop of Tours (573); engaged in dispute (575–584) with Chilperic; restored church of St. Martin. Author of *Historia Francorum,* history of Merovingian kingdom to 591; also of lives of saints and books of miracles.

Gregory the Great. See Pope St. GREGORY I.

Gregory the Illuminator. See St. GREGORY.

Gregory, David. 1659–1708. Scottish mathematician and astronomer. Nephew of James Gregory; professor, Edinburgh (1683–91), Oxford (1691–1708); expositor of Newtonian mechanics. Author of *Treatise of Practical Geometry* (1695), *Catoptricae et dioptricae sphaericae elementa* (1695), *Astronomiae physicae & geometricae elementa* (1702), etc.

Gregory, Lady Isabella Augusta, *nee* Persse \'pərs\. 1852–1932. Irish playwright. m. Sir William Gregory (1880; d. 1892). With W. B. Yeats and others, aided in founding (1899) Irish Literary Theatre; became (1904) a director of the Abbey Theatre, Dublin. Author of plays, many on Irish peasant themes, including *Seven Short Plays* (1909), *The Image* (1910), *Damer's Gold* (1913), *The Golden Apple* (1916), *The Dragon* (1920), *Aristotle's Bellows* (1923), *Sancho's Master* (1928); also translated and arranged Irish legends and sagas as *Cuchulain of Muirthemne* (1902), *Gods and Fighting Men* (1904); also wrote *Poets and Dreamers* (1903), *Book of Saints and Wonders* (1907), etc.

Gregory *or* **Greg·o·rie** \'greg-(ə-)rē\, James. 1638–1675. Scottish mathematician and inventor. Professor, U. of St. Andrews (1669–74), Edinburgh (1674–75); perfected earliest form of reflecting telescope, the Gregorian telescope, described in his *Optica promota* (1663); published *Vera circuli et hyperbolae quadratura* (1667) and *Geometriae pars universalis* (1668), demonstrating method of determining areas and volumes of geometrical figures; anticipated later discoveries in number theory and calculus.

Gregory II Cyp·ri·us \-'sip-rē-əs\. *Orig.* George \'jȯ(ə)rj\. 1241–1290. Greek prelate. Chaplain at Byzantine court; supported Emperor Andronicus II in opposition to conciliation with Western church; succeeded deposed proconciliation John XI Beccus as patriarch of Constantinople (1283–89); forced to resign owing to criticism of his theology, as in *Tomos pisteos,* as speculative and unorthodox.

Gregory Na·re·kat·zi \ˌnär-ə-kät-'sē\. Saint. *Also known as* St. Gregory Na·rek \'när-ək\. 951–1001. Armenian poet and theologian. Author of mystical poems and hymns, sacred elegies, biblical commentaries; leading figure in Armenian literature of the time.

Gregory Thau·ma·tur·gus \ˌthȯ-mə-'tər-gəs\. Saint. *Also known as* Saint Gregory of Neo·caes·a·rea \ˌnē-ō-ˌses-ə-'rē-ə, -ˌsez-ə-, -ˌsē-zə-\. 213?–?270 A.D. Greek prelate. Bishop of his native city, Neocaesarea (c.240 A.D.); attended first synod of Antioch (c.264); became champion of orthodoxy and trinitarian doctrine. Author of *Exposition of Faith, Canonical Epistle, Panegyric to Origen,* etc.

Greif \'grīf\, Andreas. *Lat.* Gry·phi·us \'grue-fē-ůs, 'grif-ē-əs\. 1616–1664. German poet. Traveled widely; syndic of Glosgan (1650–64). Author of lyric verse, much of it pessimistic and melancholy, as *Sonette* (1637, 1643), *Sonn- und Feiertags-Sonette* (1639), *Oden* (1643, 1650, 1657), *Epigrammata* (1643, 1663); tragedies, often on themes of Christian stoicism, as *Leo Armenius* (1650), *Catharina von Georgien* (1657), *Cardenio und Celinde* (1657), *Ermordete Majestät Carolus Stuardus* (1657), *Grossmütiger Rechts-Gelehrter,* or *Papinanus* (1659); comedies *Die geliebte Dornrose* (1661), *Absurda Comica oder Herr Peter Squentz* (1663), *Horribilicribrifax* (1663).

Greig \'greg\, Sir Samuel. 1735–1788. Scottish naval officer. Served in Russian navy (from 1764); commanded division of Russian fleet under Orlov which defeated Turks at Çeşme (1770). Rear admiral (1770); vice admiral (1773); commanded Russian fleet against Swedes in Gulf of Finland (1788); helped create modern Russian navy.

Grein \'grīn\, Jacob Thomas, *known as* Jack. 1862–1935. English dramatic critic, b. Amsterdam. To England as a young man; on staff of *Life* (1888–93), *Sunday Times* (1897–1918), *Illustrated London News* (1920–35). Founded Independent Theatre (1891) and People's Theatre (1923). Published volumes of collected criticism.

Gren·fell \ˈgren-ˌfel, -fəl\, Bernard Pyne. 1869–1926. English papyrologist. Professor, Oxford (1908–26). With Arthur Surridge Hunt (*q.v.*) discovered, edited, and published many Greek papyri, including collections known as the Oxyrhynchus papyri (published 1898–1927), the Amherst papyri (1900–01), Tebtunis papyri (1902–07), and the Greek papyri in the Cairo Museum.

Grenfell, George. 1849–1906. English missionary and explorer. Baptist missionary to Cameroons (1874); surveyed Congo basin as far as the equator (1884), and affluents of the Congo (1885). As representative of Belgium, negotiated settlement with Portugal of boundary between Congo Free State and Angola (1891). Explored Aruwimi River (1900–02).

Grenfell, Julian Henry Francis. 1888–1915. British soldier and poet. Killed in France in World War I; remembered for poem "Into Battle" (1915).

Grenfell, Sir Wilfred Thomason. 1865–1940. English physician and missionary. Fitted out first hospital ship to serve fishermen in the North Sea; to Labrador (1892) for missionary work, and built hospitals, schools, industrial centers, cooperatives, etc.; supported mission with books, speaking tours, and (from 1912) through International Grenfell Association. Author of *Vikings of To-day* (1895), etc.

Gren·ville \ˈgren-vəl\ *or* **Greyn·ville** \ˈgrān-vəl, ˈgren-\, Sir Richard. 1542–1591. British naval commander. M.P. (1571, 1584); commanded (1585) fleet for colonization of Virginia, for his cousin Sir Walter Raleigh; pillaged Azores (1586); organized defenses of west of England against Armada (1586–88); second in command (1591) under Lord Thomas Howard of Azores fleet sent to intercept Spanish treasure ships; mortally wounded and captured in celebrated battle when his ship, the *Revenge,* was isolated from rest of fleet off Flores.

His grandson ¶Sir Bevil Grenville (1596–1643), Royalist soldier; supported Sir John Eliot, but shifted to king's side and under Sir Ralph Hopton defeated Parliamentarians at Bradock Down (1643); killed at head of Cornish infantry at Lansdowne.

Grenville, Richard Temple. 1st Earl Tem·ple \ˈtem-pəl\. 1711–1779. English politician. Eldest son of Richard Grenville and Hester Temple, afterward Countess Temple; succeeded to mother's peerage (1752) and took name Grenville-Temple. M.P. (1734–52); first lord of admiralty (1756–57); lord privy seal (1757–61) under elder Pitt; opposed Bute; refused treasury and quarreled with Pitt over Stamp Act (1766); opposed conciliation of American colonies; paid Wilkes's law expenses; known to contemporaries as Squire Gaw·key \ˈgȯ-kē\; credited by some with authorship of *Letters of Junius* (cf. Sir Philip FRANCIS).

His brother ¶George Grenville (1712–1770); M.P. (1741–70); treasurer of the navy (1754–55, 1756–57, 1757–62); carried bill improving system of paying seamen's wages; leader of House of Commons and member of cabinet (1761); first lord of admiralty (1762–63); first lord of treasury, chancellor of exchequer, and prime minister (1763–65); resisted Bute's influence with George III, but best known for enactment of Stamp Act (1765) and early proceedings against Wilkes (1763). The eldest of George's sons ¶George Nu·gent-Temple-Grenville \ˈn(y)ü-jənt-\ (1753–1813), M.P. (1774–79); succeeded uncle as 2d Earl Temple (1779); lord lieutenant of Ireland (1782–83, 1787–89); instituted order of St. Patrick (1783); instrument of George III in defeating Fox's East India bill in House of Lords (1783); created marquis of Buckingham (1784). The youngest son ¶William Wyndham Grenville (1759–1834), Baron Grenville; M.P. (1782–90); chief secretary for Ireland (1782–83); speaker of House of Commons (1789); home secretary (1789–90); president of board of control (1790); created baron (1790); foreign secretary (1791–1801), not always in agreement with Pitt; resigned because of George III's refusal of consent to any measure of Roman Catholic relief; refused office without his ally, Fox (1804); after Pitt's death, nominal head of coalition government, so-called All-the-Talents Administration (1806–07), which abolished slave trade; resigned on Catholic question.

Grenville-Temple, Richard. See Richard Temple GRENVILLE.

Gresh·am \ˈgresh-əm\, Sir Thomas. 1519–1579. English financier. As adviser to government, raised exchange value of pound sterling and discharged royal debts (1551–53); ambassador to Netherlands (1559–61); crown financial agent (to 1574). Built (1566–68) Royal Exchange and Gresham College, in London. Traditionally but mistakenly credited with "Gresham's law," observation that when two coins are equal in nominal value but unequal in intrinsic value, the one having the less intrinsic value tends to remain in circulation and the other tends to be hoarded.

Gresham, Walter Quintin. 1832–1895. American politician and jurist, b. near Lanesville, Ind. Served through Civil War; brevetted major general (1865). U.S. district judge, Indiana (1869–83). U.S. postmaster general (1883–84); secretary of the treasury (1884). U.S. circuit judge, 7th judicial district (1884–93). U.S. secretary of state (1893–95).

Gres·set \grā-se\, Jean-Baptiste-Louis. 1709–1777. French poet and playwright. Entered Jesuit order (1726); expelled. Author of witty satire *Ver-Vert* (1734), *Édouard III* (tragedy, 1740), and the comedies *Sidney* (1745), *Le Méchant* (1747), *Les Parvenus* (1748).

Gres·sly \ˈgres-lē\, Amanz. 1814–1865. Swiss geologist. Noted for studies of stratigraphy; introduced (1838) term "facies" to describe differences in aspect of terrain.

Gress·mann \ˈgres-ˌmä^n\, Hugo. 1877–1927. German theologian. Professor, Kiel (1902–06), Berlin (1907–27); prominent exponent of religio-historical method of biblical criticism. Author of *Der Ursprung der israelitisch-jüdischen Eschatologie* (1905), *Altorientalische Texte und Bilder* (1909), *Moses und seine Zeit* (1913), *Die Anfänge Israels* (1914), *Der Messias* (1929).

Gré·try \grā-trē\, André-Ernest-Modeste. 1741–1813. French composer. Contributed greatly to evolution of opéra comique with *Le Huron* (1768), *Lucile* (1769), *Le Tableau parlant* (1769), *Silvain* (1770), *Zémire et Azor* (1771), *Le Magnifique* (1773), *Le Jugement de Midas* (1778), *Les Fausses apparences* (1778), *Les Événements imprévus* (1779), *Colinette à la cour* (1782), *La Caravane du Caire* (1783), *Richard Coeur-de-lion* (1784), etc.

Greuze \grœ̄z\, Jean-Baptiste. 1725–1805. French painter. Gained great popularity with moralistic or sentimental genre works as *L'Accordée de village, Le Fils ingrat, Le Fils puni,* etc.; also painted portraits.

Grev·ille \ˈgrev-əl\, Charles Cavendish Fulke. 1794–1865. English diarist. Clerk to the privy council (1821–59). For 40 years kept a diary in which he recorded his impressions and close knowledge of English politics and politicians, published as *Memoirs* (1875, 1885, 1887).

Greville, Fulke. 1st Baron Brooke \ˈbru̇k\. 1554–1628. English poet and courtier. Friend of Sir Philip Sidney; favorite of Queen Elizabeth. Secretary for principality of Wales (1583–1628); M.P. (1592, 1597, 1601, 1620); chancellor of the exchequer (1614–21); created baron (1621). Works included sonnets collected as *Caelica* (1633), tragedy *Mustapha* (1609), a life of Sidney (1652), songs, etc.

Gré·vin \grā-va^n\, Jacques. 1538–1570. French physician, poet, and playwright. Credited with writing first original French dramas to follow classical models, as *La Trésorière* (1559), *La Mort de César* (1561); author also of sonnets in *L'Olympe* (1560), *La Gélodacrye* (1560).

Gré·vy \grā-vē\, Jules, *in full* François-Paul-Jules. 1807–1891. French politician. Republican deputy from Jura to Constituent Assembly (1848–49); withdrew from politics (1851). Returned to politics (1868), holding prominent place in Republican party; president of National Assembly (1871–73), of Chamber of Deputies (1876–79). President of Third Republic (1879–87); forced to resign by scandals affecting son-in-law.

Grew \ˈgrü\, Joseph Clark. 1880–1965. American diplomat, b. Boston. Joined Foreign Service (1904); chief of Division of Western European Affairs (1918); U.S. minister to Denmark (1920), Switzerland (1921); negotiated treaty with Turkey (1923). Undersecretary of state (1924–27); ambassador to Turkey (1927–32), Japan (1932–41); undersecretary of state (1944–45). Author of *Report from Tokyo* (1942), *Ten Years in Japan* (1944).

Grew, Nehemiah. 1641–1712. English botanist. A founder of plant anatomy; pioneer microscopist; first to hypothesize in print on sex in plants. Author of *Anatomy of Vegetables Begun* (1672), *The Anatomy of Plants* (1682).

Grey. See also GRAY.

Grey \ˈgrā\. Name of English family including Greys de Wilt·on \ˈwilt-^{ə}n\, Greys de Ru·thin \ˈrith-ən, ˈrüth-\, Greys of Gro·by \ˈgrü-bē\, and present earls of Stam·ford \ˈstam(p)-fərd\ and earls Grey:

GREY DE WILTON. John de Grey (1268–1323), 2d Baron Grey de Wilton; judge; lord ordainer (1310); justice of North Wales (1315). From a younger son of his were descended barons Grey de Ruthin. From his eldest son were descended barons Grey de Wilton, including ¶William Grey (d. 1562), 13th baron, who distinguished himself in French war in reign of Henry VIII and as a leader of English army at Pinkie (1547); suppressed rebellion in Oxfordshire (1549); imprisoned as supporter of Duke of Somerset (1551); involved in Northumberland's attempt to set Lady Jane Grey on throne (1553); pardoned, put in charge of defense of Guînes, which he was forced to surrender (1558). His elder son ¶Arthur (1536–1593), 14th baron, helped defend Guînes; lord deputy of Ireland (1580–82), having Edmund Spenser as secretary; one of commissioners who tried Mary, Queen of Scots. Arthur's son ¶Thomas (d. 1614), 15th and last baron, served against Spanish Armada (1588); general of horse against Essex and Southampton (1601).

GREY DE RUTHIN. ¶Roger de Grey (d. 1353), 1st Baron Grey de Ruthin, soldier, younger son of 2d Baron Grey de Wilton (see above); M.P. (1324); served in Scottish campaigns (1318, 1327, 1341). His grandson ¶Reginald de Grey (1362?–1440), 3rd baron, won famous lawsuit (1401–10) for right to bear Hastings arms and title earl of Pembroke, from Edward Hastings, to whom title did not belong; governor of Ireland (1398); warred on Owen Glendower

(1402); continued Welsh war (1409); member of council of regency (1415). From him descended earls and dukes of Kent, earls de Grey, barons and earls Grey of Groby, and marquises of Dorset.

¶Sir George Grey (1812–1898), colonial administrator; member of Grey of Groby branch; served in army (1829–37); explored in Western Australia (1837–39); governor of South Australia (1841–45). Governor of New Zealand (1845–53); pacified Maoris, pioneered in study of Maori culture. Governor of Cape Colony (1854–59); again governor of New Zealand (1861–68); again pacified Maoris; elected to New Zealand legislature (1874–94); prime minister (1877–79). Author of vocabularies of Australian aboriginal language, of *Polynesian Mythology* (1855), etc.

MARQUISES OF DOR·SET \'dȯr-sət\. ¶Thomas Grey (1451–1501), son of John Grey (1432–1461), 7th Baron Fer·rers \'fer-ərz\ of Groby, a Lancastrian killed at St. Albans, and of Elizabeth Woodville, later queen of Edward IV (see ELIZABETH); as stepson of Edward IV, fought at Tewkesbury (1471); created marquis of Dorset (1475); had to flee from Richard, Duke of Gloucester, after supporting his half-brother Edward V; one of leaders of Buckingham insurrection (1484); imprisoned on suspicion (1487); pardoned, helped quell Cornish uprising (1497). His grandson ¶Henry Grey (d. 1554), 3d marquis; lord high constable for coronation of Edward VI (1547); attached himself (from 1548) to John Dudley, Duke of Northumberland; created duke of Suffolk (1551) by right of his wife; married his daughter, Lady Jane Grey, to Northumberland's son (1553); pardoned for support in Lady Jane Grey's cause; executed for taking part in Wyatt's rising against Mary Tudor's Spanish marriage.

Henry's daughter ¶Lady Jane Grey (1537–1554), a great-granddaughter of Henry VII, gained mastery of several languages; married against her wish to Lord Guildford Dudley (1553) as part of plot to alter succession to her favor on death of Edward VI; proclaimed queen (July 9, 1553); on dispersal of her father-in-law's troops, imprisoned (July 19); pleaded guilty to charge of high treason; death sentence suspended; beheaded, with her husband, after her father's participation in Wyatt's Rebellion.

EARLS GREY. ¶Charles Grey (1729–1807), 1st earl; soldier; served in Germany, West Indies; to America (1776); defeated Anthony Wayne near Paoli (1777); commanded brigade at Germantown (1777); defeated Virginia dragoons at Old Tappan, N.J. (1778); major general (1778) and commander in chief in America (1782); lieutenant general (1782); cooperated with Jervis in capture of French West Indies (1794); appointed general and privy councilor (1795); created Baron Grey (1801), and Earl Grey and Viscount Ho·wick \'hō-ik\ (1806).

His son ¶Charles (1764–1845), 2d earl; M.P. (1786–1807); helped form Society of Friends of the People (1792); as lieutenant of Fox, moved impeachment of Pitt; on failure of his parliamentary reform bill, promoted Whig secession (1797) from House of Commons in protest; first lord of the admiralty in All-the-Talents ministry (1806) and, on Fox's death, foreign secretary (1806–07); entered House of Lords (1807). On Napoléon's return from Elba (1815), followed former policy of Fox, maintaining right of France and other nations to choose own governors; opposed renewal of war and suspension of Habeas Corpus Act (1817); opposed bill for Queen Caroline's divorce (1820); denounced Canning ministry (1827), losing thereby most of following. On issue of reform regained leadership; prime minister of Great Britain (1830–34); by gaining William IV's reluctant promise to create sufficient new peers to swamp opposition in House of Lords, carried Reform Bill (1832) providing reform of electoral system and suffrage, and bill abolishing slavery throughout British Empire.

His son ¶Henry George (1802–1894), 3d earl; M.P. (1826–45); secretary at war (1835–39); Whig leader in House of Lords (1845); secretary for colonies (1846–52); first minister to proclaim government of colonies for their own benefit, first to accord self-government in accordance with capacity for it, first to introduce free trade between Great Britain and Ireland.

Henry's nephew ¶Albert Henry George (1851–1917), 4th earl; M.P. (1880–86); a director (from 1889) of British South Africa Co., and a supporter of Cecil Rhodes; administrator of Rhodesia (1896–97); governor general of Canada (1904–11).

¶Sir George Grey (1799–1882), 2d Baronet Grey; grandson of 1st earl and nephew of 2d earl; M.P. (1832–52, 1853–74); judge advocate general (1839–41); home secretary (1846–52, 1855–58, 1861–66); outmaneuvered Chartists' leaders and kept them in order (1848); by further suspension of Habeas Corpus Act, repressed Irish discontent (1849); colonial secretary (1854–55); carried convict discipline bill (1846), which ended transportation of convicts and laid foundation for modern British prison system.

¶Sir Edward Grey (1862–1933), 3d baronet and Viscount Grey of Fal·lo·don \'fal-əd-ᵊn\; grandson of 2d baronet; M.P. (1884–1916); undersecretary of state for foreign affairs (1892–95); secretary of state for foreign affairs (1905–16); shaped careful policy of support for France against Germany; won over divided cabinet to declaration of war (1914); negotiated secret treaty (1915) that brought Italy into war on Allied side; resigned because of ill health (1916); created viscount (1916). Author of *Twenty-Five Years, 1892–1916* (1925) and *Fallodon Papers* (1926).

Grey, Maria Georgina. See SHIRREFF.

Grey *or* **Gray** \'grā\, Walter de. d. 1255. English prelate and politician. Chancellor of England under King John (1205–14); bishop of Worcester (1214–15); archbishop of York (1215–55); attested reissue of Magna Carta (1217) and Charter of the Forest (1217); helped restore order in north following barons' revolt; built south transept of York Minster.

Grey, Zane. 1875–1939. American novelist, b. Zanesville, Ohio. Practiced dentistry in New York (1898–1904); devoted himself to writing (from 1904). Author of *Betty Zane* (1904), *Spirit of the Border* (1905); best known for adventure stories of American West, including *Riders of the Purple Sage* (1912), *The Lone Star Ranger* (1915), *The U.P. Trail* (1918), *The Mysterious Rider* (1921), *Call of the Canyon* (1924), *The Thundering Herd* (1925), *Wild Horse Mesa* (1928), *Code of the West* (1934), *West of the Pecos* (1937).

Gri·beau·val \grē-bō-väl\, Jean-Baptiste Va·quette de \vá-ket-də\. 1715–1789. French general. General of artillery on loan to Austrian army in Seven Years' War (1756–63); inspector general of artillery, French army (1776); introduced reforms which made French artillery the best in Europe.

Gri·bo·ye·dov \gryi-(ˌ)bə-'yā-dəf\, Aleksandr Sergeyevich. 1795–1829. Russian poet and diplomat. Minister at Teheran (1828–29); murdered with members of embassy staff by a mob. Author of several plays, esp. *Gore ot uma* (1822–24), a satirical comedy in rhymed verse.

Grid·ley \'grid-lē\, Charles Vernon. 1844–1898. American naval officer, b. Logansport, Ind. Commanded *Olympia,* flagship of Asiatic squadron (1897–98); to him Dewey gave famous command: "You may fire when you are ready, Gridley."

Gridley, Richard. 1711–1796. American military engineer, b. Boston. Artillery officer in expedition against Louisbourg, Cape Breton Island (1745); at Crown Point (1755), capture of Quebec (1759). Joined Massachusetts provincial forces at outbreak of American Revolution; chief engineer of Continental army (1775–76); built breastworks on Breed's Hill; wounded in battle of Bunker Hill; fortified Dorchester heights (1776). Engineer general, eastern department (1777–80).

Grieg \'grig\, Edvard Hagerup. 1843–1907. Norwegian composer. Considered founder of Norwegian national school of composition; toured frequently as pianist. Works included music for Bjørnson's *Sigurd Jorsalfar* (1872) and Ibsen's *Peer Gynt* (1876); orchestral works as two piano concertos, suite *Fra Holbergs tid* (1884); choral works; many songs based on Norwegian folk melodies; piano works as ten collections of *Lyriske smaastykker* (1867–1901), *Norske folkeviser og dandse* (1869), *Ballade* (1876), *Slåtter* (arrangements of folk dances, 1902–03); chamber works including two string quartets (1877–78, 1891), violin sonatas.

Grieg, Johan Nordahl Brun. 1902–1943. Norwegian poet, novelist, and playwright. A hero of Norwegian resistance to German occupation (1940–43). Author of often nationalistic verse *Rundt Kap det Gode Haab* (1922), *Norge i våre hjerter* (1929), novel *Skibet gaar videre* (1924), social dramas *Vår aere og vår makt* (1935), *Nederlaget* (1937).

Grien, Hans. See Hans BALDUNG.

Grier \'gri(ə)r\, Robert Cooper. 1794–1870. American jurist, b. Cumberland Co., Pa. Associate justice, U.S. Supreme Court (1846–70).

Grier·son \'gri(ə)rs-ᵊn\, Benjamin Henry. 1826–1911. American army officer, b. Pittsburgh, Pa. Led cavalry raid from La Grange, Tenn., to Baton Rouge, La., through heart of Confederacy (April–May 1863), contributing to Grant's capture of Vicksburg; brigadier general of volunteers (1863); brigadier general, U.S. army (1890).

Grierson, Sir George Abraham. 1851–1941. Irish philologist. In Indian civil service (1873–96); during that time studied Indian languages and dialects, publishing many papers and books; director of Linguistic Survey of India (1898–1928). Works included *Seven Grammars of the Dialects and Subdialects of the Bihārī Language* (1883–87), *Bihar Peasant Life* (1885), *Dictionary of the Kashmīrī Language* (1916–32), numerous translations of ancient texts and inscriptions.

Grierson, John. 1898–1972. British film maker. Initiated documentary film-making in Britain with *Drifters* (1929); helped organize National Film Board of Canada (1939); director of mass communications, UNESCO (1946–48); film controller, British Central Office of Information (1948–50).

Gries·bach \'grēs-ˌbäk\, Johann Jakob. 1745–1812. German theologian. Professor, Jena (1775–1812); pioneer in systematic literary analysis of Gospels; coined term "synoptic" for first three Gospels and held that Mark derived from Matthew and Luke.

Grieve \'grēv\, Christopher Murray. *Pseudonym* Hugh Mac·Diar·mid \mək-'dər-məd, -mət\. 1892–1978. Scottish poet. Founded (1922) monthly *Scottish Chapbook* in which he advocated a Scottish literary revival; later embraced Marxism and often wrote in English. Among his books of verse were

Sangschaw (1925), *Penny Wheep* (1926), *A Drunk Man Looks at the Thistle* (1926), *To Circumjack Cencrastus* (1930), *Scots Unbound* (1932), *Stony Limits* (1934), *Second Hymn to Lenin* (1935), *A Kist of Whistles* (1947), *In Memoriam James Joyce* (1955), *A Clyack Sheaf* (1969); also prose works *Scottish Scene* (with Lewis Gibbon, 1934), *Scottish Eccentrics* (1936), *The Islands of Scotland* (1939), and autobiographies *Lucky Poet* (1943), *The Company I've Kept* (1966).

Griffenfeld, Count Peder Schumacher. See SCHUMACHER.

Grif·fes \'grif-əs\, Charles Tomlinson. 1884–1920. American pianist and composer, b. Elmira, N.Y. Composed in generally Impressionistic style, often adopting Oriental or Russian themes. Works included dance dramas *Kairn of Koridwen* (1917), *Sho-jo* (1917); piano pieces as *Three Tone-Pictures* (1911–12), *The Pleasure-Dome of Kubla Khan* (1912), *Roman Sketches* (1915–16, esp. *The White Peacock*); *Poem* (1918) for flute and orchestra; songs and chamber works.

Grif·fin \'grif-ən\, Cyrus. 1748–1810. American jurist, b. Richmond Co., Va. Member, Continental Congress (1778–81, 1787, 1788); president of the Congress (1788). U.S. district judge, Virginia (1789–1810).

Griffin, Gerald. 1803–1840. Irish playwright, novelist, and poet. His novels included *Holland Tide* (1827) and *The Collegians* (1829), on which Dion Boucicault based his play *The Colleen Bawn.*

Griffin, Walter Burley. 1876–1937. American architect, b. Maywood, Ill. Began career in office of Frank Lloyd Wright; awarded first prize by government of Australia in international competition for designs for a federal capital at Canberra (1912); in charge of construction there (1915–20); also designed Newman Coll., U. of Melbourne (1915), etc.

Grif·fith \'grif-əth\, Arthur. 1872–1922. Irish political leader. Joined Irish Republican Brotherhood; a founder (1899) and editor (1901) of journal *The United Irishman.* Withdrew from Irish Republican Brotherhood to move for establishment of an Irish parliament linked by the crown to the English Parliament; organized group (1902) to forward this movement, which became known as Sinn Féin; changed name of his journal to *Sinn Féin* (1906), later *Eire* and (1917) *Nationality.* Supported (1912) organization of Irish Volunteers to oppose the Ulster Volunteers, but took no part in the Easter Rebellion (1916); held in concentration camp (1916–17); newspaper suppressed (1918); again imprisoned (1918). While in prison, was elected vice president of the "Irish Republic"; acting head of "Irish Republic" in absence of de Valera (1919–20). Leader of delegation which negotiated (1921) treaty with England involving recognition of the Irish Free State; elected president (1922).

Griffith, David Lewelyn Wark. 1875–1948. American motion picture director and producer, b. Floydsfork (later Crestwood), Ky. Actor in touring companies (1897 ff.); wrote screenplays and acted in films for Edison Film Co. and Biograph Studios; director at Biograph (1908–13), making *Adventures of Dollie* (1908), *Judith of Bethulia* (1913), etc.; with G.W. Bitzer (*q.v.*) pioneered film techniques as close-up, cross-cutting, fade-in and fade-out, pan shots, soft focus, special framing, etc.; introduced actors as Mary Pickford, Dorothy and Lillian Gish, Mae Marsh, Lionel Barrymore, Mack Sennett. Produced epic film dramas that revolutionized cinema, including *Birth of a Nation* (1915), *Intolerance* (1916); smaller-scale films as *Broken Blossoms* (1919), *Way Down East* (1920), *Orphans of the Storm* (1921), *White Rose* (1923), *America* (1924), *Sorrows of Satan* (1927), *Abraham Lincoln* (1930). With Mary Pickford, Douglas Fairbanks, Charlie Chaplin formed (1919) United Artists Co.; awarded special Academy Award (1935).

Griffith, Sir Samuel Walker. 1845–1920. Australian politician and jurist. First chief justice of Australia (1903–19).

Grif·fiths \'grif-ə(th)s\, Ann, *nee* Thomas. 1776–1805. Welsh hymnist. Convert to Calvinistic Methodism; composed hymns of great emotional intensity and piety, few of which she wrote down; hymns collected posthumously from correspondence and from servant girl to whom she had recited them.

Griffiths, John Willis. 1809–1882. American naval architect, b. New York City. Designed "extreme" clipper ships *Rainbow* (1845), *Sea Witch* (1846); steamships; armored gunboat *Pawnee* (1858); developed iron keelson, bilge keel, twin- and triple-screws, etc. Author of *A Treatise on Marine and Naval Architecture* (1850), etc.

Griggs \'grigz\, John William. 1849–1927. American politician and jurist, b. near Newton, N.J. Governor of New Jersey (1895–98). U.S. attorney general (1898–1901). Judge, Permanent Court of Arbitration, The Hague (1901–12).

Gri·gnard \grēn-yär\, Victor, *in full* François-Auguste-Victor. 1871–1935. French chemist. Professor, Nancy (1910–19), Lyons (1919–35); discovered (1900) Grignard reagent, an organo-magnesium compound, opening new field of study; shared (with Paul Sabatier) 1912 Nobel prize for chemistry.

Grignion de Montfort, St. Louis-Marie. See MONTFORT.

Gri·go·ro·vich \gryi-(,)gə-'rō-vyich\, Dmitry Vasilyevich. 1822–1900. Russian novelist. Author of naturalistic novels of peasant life, esp. *The Village* (1846), *Anton Goremyka* (1847).

Gri·gor·yev \gri-'gȯr-yəf\, Apollon Aleksandrovich. 1822–1864. Russian poet and critic. Edited journal *Moskvityanin* (1850–56); contributed to St. Petersburg journals *Vremya* (1861–63), *Epokh* (1864); developed nationalistic critical view of art as organically rooted in national soil; followers became known as *pochvenniki* (from *pochva,* soil).

Gri·jal·ba *or* **Gri·jal·va** \grē-'häl-bä\, Juan de. 1489?–1527. Spanish explorer. Nephew of Diego Velásquez; sent to follow up Córdoba's discovery of Yucatán (1518); sailed along east coast of Mexico; learned of rich Aztec empire in interior; first to give region the name of New Spain.

Grill·par·zer \'gril-,pärt-sər\, Franz. 1791–1872. Austrian playwright. In Austrian government service (1813–56). His notable works included *Die Ahnfrau* (1817); *Sappho* (1818); a trilogy, *Das goldene Vlies* (1818–22), comprising *Der Gastfreund, Die Argonauten,* and *Medea; König Ottokars Glück und Ende* (1825); *Des Meeres und der liebe Wellen* (1831); *Der Traum ein Leben* (1834); *Weh dem, der lügt* (1838); *Die Jüdin von Toledo, Libussa,* and *Ein Bruderzwist in Habsburg* (all published posthumously, 1872).

Grim·ald *or* **Grim·alde** \'grim-əld\ *or* **Grim·oald** \'grim-wəld\, Nicholas. 1519–1562. English poet. Contributor of verses to first edition (1557) of Tottel's poetical anthology, *Songes and Sonettes;* author of Latin tragedies *Christus Redivivus* and *Archipropheta;* also translator of parts of Virgil and Cicero.

Gri·mal·di \grē-'mäl-dē\. A family of nobility of Genoa, prominent for several centuries (esp. 14th to 18th) in Italian history; leaders of Guelph party. Monaco was under their rule (from 1419); took title of princes of Monaco (1659); direct male line became extinct with death of Antoine I (1661–1731); his daughter, Louise Hippolyte, married (1715) Jacques de Goyon-Matignon, Count of Thorigny, who took the name Grimaldi and whose family held Monaco until driven out (1792) by the French Revolution; restored (1814). See ALBERT I of Monaco.

Grimaldi, Francesco Maria. 1618–1663. Italian physicist. Entered Jesuit order (1632); taught at Coll. of Santa Lucia, Bologna (from 1638); known for studies in optics, esp. in diffraction of light, and for theories of light and color.

Gri·mal·di \grə-'mäl-dē, -'mȯl-\, Joseph. 1779–1837. English comic actor and pantomimist. Debut as baby clown (1781); became renowned in clown character "Joey"; enjoyed great success esp. in pantomime *Mother Goose* (1806); contributed greatly to development of modern clown.

Grimes \'grīmz\, James Wilson. 1816–1872. American politician, b. Deering, N.H. Governor of Iowa (1854–58); U.S. senator (1859–69). Stricken by apoplexy during impeachment trial of President Johnson (1868); carried into Senate to vote for acquittal when his vote was required to prevent conviction.

Grim·ké \'grim-kē\, Sarah Moore (1792–1873) and her sister Angelina Emily (1805–1879). American reformers, b. Charleston, S.C. Became Quakers, and thence involved in abolitionist movement (from c.1835); lecturers for American Anti-Slavery Society; took up women's rights campaign. Angelina author of *Appeal to the Christian Women of the South* (1836), *Appeal to the Women of the Nominally Free States* (1837); Sarah of *Epistle to the Clergy of the Southern States* (1836), *Letters on the Equality of the Sexes* (1838); collaborated with Theodore D. Weld (m. Angelina, 1838) on *Slavery As It Is* (1839).

Grimm \'grim\, Friedrich Melchior von. Baron. 1723–1807. German critic. While student at Leipzig contributed tragedy *Banise* to Gottsched's *Deutsche Schaubühne* (1743); to Paris (1748) as tutor; in service of duc d'Orléans (1755); developed associations with Diderot, Madame d'Épinay, J.J. Rousseau; produced (1753–73) fortnightly private newsletter on Parisian life for noble subscribers, frank and witty compounds of criticism and chronicle of great historical value, collected as *Correspondance littéraire* (1812).

Grimm, Hans. 1875–1959. German writer. Merchant in Cape Colony, South Africa (1901–10). Author of novels and stories expressing Pan-Germanic viewpoint, including *Südafrikanische Novellen* (1913), *Der Gang durch den Sand* (1916), *Volk ohne Raum* (1928–30), *Der Richter in der Karu* (1930).

Grimm, Jacob Ludwig Carl (1785–1863) and his brother Wilhelm Carl (1786–1859). German philologists and folklorists. Came under influence of Clemens Brentano and Herder while students at Marburg; Jacob became librarian to Jérôme Bonaparte, King of Westphalia (1808); Wilhelm was employed in library of elector of Kassel (1814–30), joined by Jacob there (1816); both were professors and librarians at Göttingen (1830–37); accepted invitation of Frederick William IV of Prussia to settle in Berlin (1841). Encouraged by Brentano and Achim von Arnim, collected German folk tales and published them as *Kinder- und Hausmärchen* (1812–15, known in English as *Grimm's Fairy Tales*), *Deutsche Sagen* (1816–18). In Berlin undertook work on their massive *Deutsches Wörterbuch* (first volume 1852; completed 1961). Jacob was author of *Deutsche Grammatik* (1819–37), generally regarded as the foundation of Germanic philology, containing his formulation of the philological law known as Grimm's law; *Über den Altdeutschen Meistergesang* (1811), *Rechtsaltertümer* (study of old Teutonic laws, 1828), *Deutsche Mythologie* (1835), *Geschichte der Deutschen Sprache* (1848). Wilhelm was author of *Altdänische Heldenlieder, Balladen und Märchen* (1811), *Die deutsche Heldensage* (1828), etc.

Grim·mels·hau·sen \'grim-əls-ˌhaù-zən\, Hans Jacob Christoph von *or* Hans Jakob Christoffel von. 1622?–1676. German writer. Served in Thirty Years' War; steward to Schauenburg barons (1648–60); later a tavernkeeper, then bailiff at Renchen. His masterpiece was *Der Abentheuerliche Simplicissimus* (1669), commonly referred to as *Simplicissimus,* a picaresque novel, satirical and partly autobiographical, telling the adventures of a simple youth who becomes successively soldier, jester, bourgeois, robber, pilgrim, slave, and hermit; continued in sequels *Die Lanstörtzerin Courage* (1669), *Das wunderbarliche Vogelnest* (1672).

Grimoald. See also GRIMALD.

Grim·oald \'grim-wəld\. Name of several rulers of Benevento including:

Grimoald I. d. 671. Duke of Benevento (from 647). Seized Lombard crown from co-regents (662); defeated Byzantine invasion, revolt of Duke of Friuli, rebellion of his own allies, Avar troops from Hungary; assassinated.

Grimoald III. d. c.806. Prince of Benevento (788–806). Hostage of Charlemagne (787–788); allowed to assume throne of Benevento only as Frankish vassal; defeated Byzantines in south; threw off vassalage (792), defeated armies of Pepin (792, 800).

Gri·mod de La Rey·nière \grē-mōd(-ə)-lä-ren-yer\, Alexandre-Balthasar-Laurent. 1758–1838. French gastronome and writer. Author of *Almanach des gourmands* (1803–12), *Manuel des Amphitryons* (1808), etc.

Grim·shaw \'grim-ˌshó\, Beatrice Ethel. 1871–1953. British traveler and writer, b. Ireland. While on world tour as correspondent of London *Daily Graphic* settled in Papua (1907); traveled through Pacific islands and East Indies. Author of travel books as *From the Fiji to the Cannibal Islands* (1907), *The New New Guinea* (1910); novels as *The Red Gods Call* (1910), *Coral Queen* (1919), *Sands of Oro* (1923), *Dream Islands* (1930), *Victorian Family Robinson* (1934).

Grimthorpe, 1st Baron. See Edmund BECKETT.

Grin·dal \'grin-dᵊl\, Edmund. 1519?–1583. English prelate. Bishop of London (1559); archbishop of York (1570); archbishop of Canterbury (1576), but under suspension (1577) for refusing to carry out Elizabeth's mandate suppressing Puritan activities.

Grin·del \graⁿ-del\, Eugène. *Pseudonym* Paul Éluard \ā-lwʸär\. 1895–1952. French poet. A founder of the Surrealist movement, with which he later broke (1938); early verse experiments gave way to poetry of political militance; active in Resistance and (from 1942) in Communist party. Volumes included *Le Devoir et l'inquiétude* (1917), *Mourir de ne pas mourir* (1924), *Capital de la douleur* (1926), *Défense de savoir* (1928), *L'amour, la poésie* (1929), *La Rose publique* (1934), *Les Yeux fertiles* (1936), *Donner à voir* (1939), *Poésie et vérité* (1942), *Au rendez-vous allemande* (1944), *Dignes de vivre* (1944), *Poèmes politiques* (1948), *Le Phénix* (1951).

Gri·nev·sky \gryin-'yef-skəi\, Aleksandr Stepanovich. *Pseudonym* Aleksandr Grin \'grēn\. 1880–1932. Russian writer, of Polish descent. Author of exotic tales of adventure and mystery; works condemned as decadent, antisocial, etc. (1950), but later rehabilitated.

Grin·gore \graⁿ-gór\ *or* **Grin·goire** \-gwär\, Pierre. 1475?–?1538. French poet. Created spectacles and dramatic entertainments for court of Louis XII, esp. with band of comic actors known as *sots;* mouthpiece for political satire. Author of *Folles entreprises, Jeu du prince des sots,* etc.

Grin·i·us \'grin-ē-ùs\, Kazys. 1866–1950. Lithuanian politician. A leader in liberal democratic circles; leader of Peasant Populist party in Lithuanian assembly; prime minister of Lithuania (1920–22); president (June–Dec. 1926), ousted by coup; opposed German occupation (1941); fled Soviet occupation (1944); to U.S. (1947).

Grin·nell \gri-'nel\, George Bird. 1849–1938. American naturalist and writer, b. Brooklyn, N.Y. Took part in O.C. Marsh's paleontological expedition (1870), Gen. Custer's Black Hills expedition (1874), William Ludlow's expedition to Yellowstone Park (1875), and Harriman Alaska expedition (1899); editor, *Forest and Stream* magazine (1880–1911); helped found Audubon Society (1886), Boone and Crockett Club (1887); instrumental in establishment of Glacier National Park (1910); known for studies of Plains Indians. Author of *Pawnee Hero Stories* (1889), *Blackfoot Lodge Tales* (1892), *The Indians of Today* (1911), *The Cheyenne Indians* (1923), etc.

Grinnell, Henry. 1799–1874. American merchant, b. New Bedford, Mass. In shipping business, New York City (1818–50). Financed expedition under Lt. E. J. De Haven to find Franklin in the Arctic (1850) and E. K. Kane's expedition for same purpose (1853); aided in financing other Arctic expeditions. Grinnell Land named in his honor.

Grinnell, Josiah Bushnell. 1821–1891. American clergyman and pioneer, b. New Haven, Vt. It was he whom Horace Greeley advised "Go west, young man, go west"; moved to Iowa (1854); founded town of Grinnell; a founder of college that became part of present Grinnell Coll. Member, U.S. House of Representatives (1863–67).

Gri·pen·berg \'grē-pən-ˌberʸ\, Bertel Johan Sebastian. Baron. 1878–1947. Finnish poet. Author of poems, esp. sonnets, in Swedish collected in *Dikter* (1903), *Gallergrinden* (1905), *Svarta sonetter* (1908), *Drivsnö* (1909), *Aftnar i Tavastland* (1911), *Skuggspel* (1912), *Spillror* (1917), *Vid gränsen* (1930), *Livets eko* (1932), *Sista ronden* (1941), etc.

Gri·pen·stedt \'grē-pən-ˌstet\, Johan August. Baron. 1813–1874. Swedish politician. Member of upper house of Riksdag; minister without portfolio (1848–50, 1852–55); finance minister (1851, 1856–66); leading advocate of economic liberalism and free trade; influential in keeping Sweden from defense alliance with Denmark (1863) and out of Pan-Scandinavian movement.

Gris, Juan. See José V. GONZÁLEZ.

Gri·si \'grē-zē\, Carlotta, *orig.* Caronne Adele Josephine Marie. 1819–1899. Italian dancer. Cousin of Giulia and Giuditta Grisi; debut at La Scala, Milan (1827); enjoyed great success in Vienna, London, Paris; associated with Jules Perrot, later with Lucien Petipa; created title role in *Giselle* (1841) at Paris Opéra; created roles in *La Péri* (1843), *Esmeralda* (1844), *Pas de quatre* (1845) with Taglioni, Cerrito, and Grahn, and *Paquita* (1846).

Grisi, Giulia. 1811–1869. Italian singer. Debut (1828) in Bologna; appeared regularly in Paris (from 1832) and London (from 1834); created roles, many written especially for her, in Bellini's *I Capuleti ed i Montecchi* (1830), *Norma* (1831), *I puritani* (1835), Donizetti's *Maria Faliero* (1835), *Don Pasquale* (1843), etc.; one of the reigning dramatic sopranos of the day. Her sister ¶Giuditta (1805–1840), a mezzo-soprano, made debut (1826); created role of Romeo in *Capuleti ed i Montecchi* (1830).

Gris·som \'gris-əm\, Virgil Ivan, *called* Gus. 1926–1967. American astronaut, b. Mitchell, Ind. Air Force pilot (1951–59); chosen to original Project Mercury astronaut corps (1959); flew suborbital Mercury flight (1961), 3-orbit Gemini 3 flight (1965); killed in flash fire in Apollo 1 capsule, along with Edward H. White and Roger B. Chaffee.

Gris·wold \'griz-wəld, -ˌwōld, -ˌwóld\, Rufus Wilmot. 1815–1857. American critic and anthologist, b. Benson, Vt. Literary editor of *Graham's Magazine* (1842–43); named literary executor of Edgar Allan Poe, whom he slandered. Edited *Poets and Poetry of America* (1842), *Female Poets of America* (1848), etc.; author of *The Republican Court* (1855).

Gri·vas \'grē-väs\, Georgios Theodoros. 1898–1974. Cypriot political leader. Served in Greek army (from 1920); organized resistance to German occupation of Athens (1944–45); returned to Cyprus (1951), joined campaign of Archbishop Makarios for independence from Great Britain and union with Greece; leader of secret terrorist group EOKA (Ethnikí Orgánosis Kipriakoú Agónos, from 1955); general (1959); commander, Greek Cypriot National Guard (1964–67); founded EOKA B (1971) to continue terrorist campaign for union.

Grock. See Charles A. WETTACH.

Gro·cyn \'grōs-ᵊn\, William. c.1446–1519. English scholar. Reputedly the first to lecture in Greek at Oxford (1491); helped prepare ground for Humanism; friend of Linacre, More, Colet, and Erasmus.

Groe·ner \'grœ̄-nər\, Wilhelm, *in full* Karl Eduard Wilhelm. 1867–1939. German soldier and politician. General (1915); served under von Mackensen in conquest of Romania (1916); in War Office (1916–17); on Eastern front (1917–18); replaced Ludendorff as first quartermaster general (1918); with Hindenburg helped bring about abdication of William II (1918); with army, assisted Ebert in suppressing Communist uprising (1918); minister of transport (1920–23); minister of defense (1928–32); minister of interior (1931–32).

Groen van Prin·ste·rer \'grün-vän-'prin-stər-ər\, Guillaume. 1801–1876. Dutch journalist, politician, and historian. Converted from liberalism (c.1830) to strict orthodoxy; a leader of the Reveil anti-modernist movement; laid groundwork for later Anti-Revolutionary and Christian Historical Union parties; member of Second Chamber of government (1849–57, 1862–65). Edited *Archives ou correspondance inédite de la maison d'Orange-Nassau* (1835–61); author of influential *Ongeloof en Revolutie* (1847).

Groete, Geert. See Gerhard GROOTE.

Gro·fé \grō-'fā, 'grō-ˌ\, Ferde. *Orig.* Ferdinand Rudolf von Grofé. 1892–1972. American composer, b. New York City. Violinist with Los Angeles Symphony (1909–19); later pianist and arranger for Paul Whiteman, for whom he orchestrated Gershwin's *Rhapsody in Blue* (1924). Compositions included *Mississippi Suite* (1924), *Metropolis* (1927), *Grand Canyon Suite* (1931), *Symphony in Steel* (1935), *Café Society* (1938), *Wheels* (1939), and other works generally of program music.

Gro·lier de Ser·vières \gról-yā-də-serv-yer\, Jean. Vicomte d'Agui·sy \dá-gē-zœ̄\. 1479–1565. French bibliophile. Treasurer general of France (1547);

famous for his love of books excellent in subject matter, paper, printing, and binding; his library of some 3,000 volumes was one of finest of the time.

Grol·man \'grōl-ˌmän\, Karl von. 1777–1843. Prussian soldier. Quartermaster general on Blücher's staff (1814); engaged at Waterloo, where he persuaded Gneisenau to go to Wellington's aid.

Gron·lund \'grœn-lůn, *Angl* 'grän-lənd\, Laurence. 1846–1899. American political writer, b. Copenhagen, Denmark. To U.S. (1867); practiced law, Chicago; gave up practice to write and lecture on Socialism (c.1875). Author of *The Coming Revolution* (1878), *Cooperative Commonwealth* (1884), etc.

Groom·bridge \'grüm-(ˌ)brij\, Stephen. 1755–1832. English merchant and astronomer. From observation compiled *Catalogue of Circumpolar Stars* (1838), listing 4,243 stars of magnitude greater than 9; a founder of the Astronomical Society (1820).

Groot \'grōt\, Huigh *or* Hugeianus de. *Lat.* Hugo Gro·tius \'grō-sh(ē-)əs\. 1583–1645. Dutch scholar, Humanist, and politician. Precocious student of Latin and law; published *Pontifex romanus* (1598); Latin historiographer to states of Holland (1601); began that year his *Annales et historiae de rebus belgicis;* edited works of Martianus Capella (1598), Aratus of Soli (1598), Theocritus (with Daniel Heinsius, 1599), Lucanus (1614). For Dutch government wrote (1604) *De jure praedae,* containing separately published essay on freedom of seas *Mare liberum* (1609). Attorney general, province of Holland (1607); led trade embassy to court of James I of England (1613); for province published *Ordinum hollandiae et westfrisae pietas* (1613) on politico-religious controversy over Arminianism; imprisoned by Prince Maurice (1618); in prison wrote *Bewijs van den waren Godsdienst,* published in Latin as *De veritate religionis christianae* (1627) and widely translated; escaped prison in trunk of books (1621); lived in Paris (1621–31). Swedish ambassador to Paris (1634–44). Other works included dramas as *Adamus Exul* (1601), *Christus Patiens* (1608); Latin verse *Sacra* (1601); *Inleydinghe tot de hollandsche Rechts-geleerdheyt* (1631), on jurisprudence of Holland; *De jure belli ac Pacis* (1625), fundamental work on international law; *Historia gotthorum, vandalorum, et langobardorum* (1637); edited Tacitus (1640).

Groo·te \'grō-tə\, Gerhard. *Also known as* Geert Groe·te \'grü-tə\. *Lat.* Gerardus Mag·nus \'mag-nəs\. 1340–1384. Dutch religious reformer. Under influence of mystic Jan van Ruysbroeck, gave up wealth and entered Carthusian monastery (c.1375); became itinerant preacher (1380), opponent of scholastic theologians and lax clergy; founder of Brothers of the Common Life, from which sprang also Windesheim Congregation of Canons Regular, both exponents of Groote's *devotio moderna* theology.

Gro·pi·us \'grō-pē-ůs, -əs\, Walter Adolph. 1883–1969. American architect, b. Berlin. In office of Peter Behrens, Berlin (1907–10); own practice (1910–14, 1928–34); founded (1919) in Weimar, Bauhaus school having program of cooperation of art, science, and technology, and celebrated for achievement in abstract art, functionalism in architecture, and experimentation in glass, metals, and textiles as materials; directed school (until 1928), which was removed (1925) to buildings in Dessau designed by him. To England (1934), U.S. (1937); professor and chairman, School of Architecture, Harvard (1938–52); practiced in partnership with Marcel Breuer (*q.v.*); formed The Architects Collaborative (1946). Works included Fagus Works, Alfeld, Germany (1911); model factory and office, Cologne (1914); Harvard Graduate Center (1949–50); U.S. Embassy, Athens (1960).

Grop·per \'gräp-ər\, William. 1897–1977. American painter and illustrator, b. New York City. Editorial cartoonist for N.Y. *Tribune* (1920); dismissed for radical political sympathies; published *The Golden Land* (1927), *Fifty-six Drawings of the U.S.S.R.* (1928); turned to painting, in social protest manner; executed mural for U.S. Department of the Interior building in Washington, D.C.

Gros \grō\, Antoine-Jean. Baron. 1771–1835. French painter. Painted esp. Romantic canvases celebrating Napoléon's career; accompanied Napoléon on several campaigns; helped create Napoleonic myth with dramatic works as *Napoléon on the Bridge at Arcole* (1796), *Napoléon Visiting the Pesthouse at Jaffa* (1804), *Napoléon at Eylau* (1808); after Bourbon restoration, succeeded to head of J.-L. David's studio, adopted more Neoclassical style; painted ceiling of Egyptian room, Louvre (c.1824).

Grose \'grōs, 'grōz\, Francis. c.1731–1791. English antiquary. Author of *Antiquities of England and Wales* (1773–87), *Antiquities of Scotland* (1789–91), etc.

Groseilliers, Sieur de. See CHOUART DES GROSEILLIERS.

Gross \'grōs\, Samuel David. 1805–1884. American surgeon, b. near Easton, Pa. Professor, Cincinnati Medical Coll. (1835–40), U. of Louisville (1840–50, 1851–56), Jefferson Medical Coll., Philadelphia (1856–82). Author of *Elements of Pathological Anatomy* (1839), *A System of Surgery* (1859), *A Manual of Military Surgery* (1861).

Grosse·teste \'grō-ˌstest\, Robert. c.1175–1253. English theologian and prelate. Chancellor of Oxford (probably c.1215–21); first rector of Franciscans at Oxford (1229 or 1230–35); resigned all ecclesiastical preferments (1232); bishop of Lincoln (1235–53); vigorously upheld mission of church to cure souls and opposed use of church power and offices to political ends, whether by King Henry III or even by pope. Author of commentaries on and translations of Aristotle.

Gros·si \'grȯs-sē\, Tommaso. 1790–1853. Italian poet and novelist. Author of satirical dialect poems *La Prineide* (1815); verse novels *La fuggitiva* (1816), *Ildegonda* (1820), *Ulrico e Lida* (1837); epic poem *I Lombardi alla prima crociata* (1826); historical novel *Marco Visconti* (1834).

Gross·mith \'grō(s)-ˌsmith\, George. 1847–1912. English comedian and singer. Created roles in many Gilbert and Sullivan operas (1877–89); composed over 600 humorous songs and sketches. Author of *Diary of a Nobody* (with brother Weedon Grossmith, 1892). His son ¶George (1874–1935) achieved success in many musical comedies; entered motion-picture field (1932); reputed to have introduced the revue in England.

Gros·ve·nor \'grōv-nər\, Gilbert Hovey. 1875–1966. American geographer, b. Constantinople. Director (from 1899), president (1920–54), chairman (1954–66), National Geographic Society; editor (1899–1954), *National Geographic Magazine;* built circulation from 900 to 1.9 million; sponsored numerous expeditions and scientific projects as Mt. Palomar Sky Survey (1949–56).

Grosz \'grōs\, George. 1893–1959. American artist, b. Berlin, Germany. Following World War I developed style of caricature and painting expressing hatred of bourgeoisie, militarism, and capitalism; associated with Dada movement, later with school of German Expressionism known as New Objectivity; to U.S. (1932).

Grote \'grōt\, George. 1794–1871. English historian. In family banking business (to 1843); member of circle of Bentham and Mill; M.P. (1832–41). Author of *Essentials of Parliamentary Reform* (1831); best known for *History of Greece* (1846–56).

Gro·te·fend \'grō-tə-ˌfent\, Georg Friedrich. 1775–1853. German scholar. Schoolteacher in Göttingen (1797–1803), Frankfurt (1803–21), Hanover (1821–49); on a bet, deciphered 13 symbols (9 correctly) in thitherto wholly undecipherable Persian cuneiform inscriptions (1802). Author of *Neue Beiträge zur Erläuterung der persepolitanischen Keilschrift* (1837).

Groth \'grōt\, Klaus. 1819–1899. German writer. Schoolteacher, later professor at Kiel (1866). Author of *Quickborn* (poems in Low German, 1853; 2d part 1871), *Hundert Blätter* (poems in High German, 1854), *Voer de Goern* (children's rhymes, 1858), *Vertelln* (prose tales, 1855–59), *Rothgeter Meister Lamp un sin Dochder* (an epic, 1862), etc.

Grotius, Hugo. See Huigh de GROOT.

Grou·chy \grü-shē\, Emmanuel de. Marquis. 1766–1847. French soldier. General of brigade (1792) and of division (1795); served in Ireland expedition (1796), against Russians and Austrians; commanded cavalry in Russia and Poland (1806–07), Italy (1809), France (1814); made marshal and peer of France (1815). Commanded cavalry reserve in Waterloo campaign; failed to prevent Blücher's main force from joining Wellington and to aid Napoléon at Waterloo; in exile in U.S. (1815–21).

Groulx \grü\, Lionel-Adolphe. 1878–1967. Canadian historian. Professor, Valleyfield Coll. (1901–06, 1909–15), U. of Montreal (from 1915); spokesman for Quebec nationalist group L'Action Française; founded Institut d'Histoire de l'Amérique française (1946). Author of *La Confédération canadienne* (1918), *Vers l'emancipation* (1921), *Notre maître, le passé* (1924–44), *Le Français au Canada* (1931), *Histoire du Canada française* (1950–52), etc.; also novels.

Grove \'grōv\, Frederick Philip. 1871–1948. Canadian novelist, b. Russia. To Canada (1892); itinerant farm worker, teacher, editor. Author of series of naturalistic novels of Canadian pioneer life including *Our Daily Bread* (1928), *Yoke of Life* (1930), *Fruits of the Earth* (1933).

Grove, Sir George. 1820–1900. English engineer and writer. Superintended construction of lighthouses in Jamaica (1842) and Bermuda (1846). Editor, *Macmillan's Magazine* (1873–83). Noted amateur musicologist; with Sir Arthur Sullivan discovered Schubert's music for *Rosamunde* (1867). Edited a standard *Dictionary of Music and Musicians* (1878–89), subsequently revised and continued. First director, Royal College of Music, Kensington (1882–94).

Grove, Sir William Robert. 1811–1896. British jurist and physicist, b. Wales. Professor, London Institution (1841–46); invented improved voltaic cell known as the Grove cell; devised "gas battery," the earliest fuel cell (1839); demonstrated thermal dissociation of water. Author of *Correlation of Physical Forces* (1846). Judge of the Court of Common Pleas (1871), of the Queen's Bench (1880); privy councilor (1887).

Groves \'grōvz\, Leslie Richard. 1896–1970. American army officer, b. Albany, N.Y. Commanded Manhattan Engineer District, the atomic bomb project (1942–47); major general (1944), lieutenant general (1948).

Grow \'grō\, Galusha Aaron. 1822–1907. American politician, b. Ashford, Conn. Member from Pennsylvania, U.S. House of Representatives (1851–63, 1894–1903), speaker (1861–63).

Gru·ben·mann \'grü-bən-,män\, Hans Ulrich (1709–1783) and his brother Johannes (1707–1771). Swiss carpenters. Built (1758) 200-foot bridge over Limmat River at Wettingen, believed to have been first timber bridge to employ true arch design.

Gru·ber \'grü-bər\, Franz Xaver. 1787–1863. Austrian organist and choral director. Composer (1818) of "Stille Nacht, heilige Nacht."

Gruber, Johann Gottfried. 1774–1851. German scholar. Collaborator with J. S. Ersch in editing *Allgemeine Enzyklopädie der Wissenschaften und Künste.*

Gruber, Max von. 1853–1927. Austrian bacteriologist. Professor, Graz (1884–87), Vienna (1887–1902); director, Institute for Hygiene, Munich (1902–23). Discovered specific agglutination of bacteria by the serum of an organism immune to a certain disease, such as typhoid fever, cholera, or cerebrospinal meningitis; this reaction was first utilized by Fernand Widal in his test for diagnosis of typhoid fever.

Gru·elle \grü-'el\, John Barton. 1880–1938. American cartoonist and writer, b. Arcola, Ill. Author of many juveniles, including *Raggedy Ann* (1918 ff.) and *Raggedy Andy* series.

Gru·en \'grü-ən\, Victor. *Orig.* Victor David Gru·en·baum \'grü-ən-,baủm\. 1903–1980. American architect, b. Vienna. To U.S. (1933); established Victor Gruen Associates design and planning firm (1950); designed first regional shopping center, Northland in Detroit (1952); also designed Southdale in Minneapolis, etc.; worked also in city planning, as for Teheran, Vienna.

Gru·en·berg \'grü-ən-,bərg\, Louis. 1884–1964. American composer, b. near Brest-Litovsk, Poland. To U.S. (c.1886). Composed operas as *Jack and the Beanstalk* (1929), *The Emperor Jones* (1931), *Green Mansions* (1937); orchestral works as *Jazz Suite* (1925), *American Suite* (1945), 4 symphonies; piano pieces as *Jazzberries* (1925); wrote motion picture scores.

Grue·ning \'grē-niŋ\, Ernest. 1887–1974. American politician, b. New York City. Journalist (1914–34); in U.S. Department of the Interior (1934–39); governor of Alaska (1939–53); U.S. senator (1957–69). Author of *Mexico and Its Heritage* (1928), *The Public Pays* (1931), *The State of Alaska* (1954), etc.

Gruf·fydd \'grif-ith\, William John. 1881–1954. Welsh poet and scholar. Professor, U. Coll., Cardiff (1906–46); M.P. (1943–50). Founded and edited review *Y Llenor* (1922–51). Author of verse *Telynegion* (with R.S. Roberts, 1900), *Caneuon a Cherddi* (1906), *Yns yr Hud* (1923), *Caniadau* (1932), etc.; also *Llenyddiaeth Cymru o 1450 hyd 1600* (History of Welsh Literature, 1922), *Math vab Mathonwy* (1928), *Rhiannon* (1953).

Grum·bach \grüⁿ-bàsh\, Jean-Pierre. *Pseudonym* Jean-Pierre Mel·ville \mel-vēl\. 1917–1973. French motion picture director. Strongly influenced *nouvelle vague* directors with camera techniques of early films as *Le Silence de la mer* (1947), *Les Enfants terribles* (1949), *Bob le flambeur* (1955), *Deux hommes dans Manhattan* (1959); later films included *Léon Morin, prêtre* (1961), *Le Doulos* (1962), *L'Aîné des ferchaux* (1962), *Le Deuxième Souffle* (1966).

Grum·bach \'grủm-,bäk\, Wilhelm von. 1503–1567. German knight. In service of Margrave Albert II Alcibiades of Brandenburg (c.1540–57), of Duke John Frederick II of Saxe-Weimar (1557–67); sought ownership of lands held in fief from bishop of Würzburg; lands confiscated (1553) after series of plundering raids into Franconia; organized assassination of bishop (1558), precipitating "Grumbach feuds"; captured Würzburg and lands (1563); attempted to enlist imperial knights in campaign to restore John Frederick to electorship; executed after capture of John Frederick's seat Gotha by Elector Augustus I of Saxony.

Grum·man \'grəm-ən\, Leroy Randle. 1895–1982. American industrialist, b. Huntington, N.Y. President (1929–46) and board chairman (1946–66) of Grumman Aircraft Engineering Corporation; developed company into major defense contractor; during World War II produced Wildcat and Hellcat fighter planes and Avenger torpedo bomber; innovations included wing retraction system and retractable landing gear.

Grün, Anastasius. See A. A. von AUERSPERG.

Grün, Hans. See Hans BALDUNG.

Grundt·vig \'grủnt-vig\, Nikolai Frederik Severin. 1783–1872. Danish theologian and poet. Long embroiled in controversy for his criticisms of rationalist tendencies in Danish church; inspired Grundtvigian movement to revitalize church; received titular rank of bishop (1861). Author of verse as *Roskilde-riim* (1814) and hymns in *Sang-vaerk til den danske kirke* (1837–81); theological and controversial works as *Kirkens gienmaele* (1825), *Christelige praedikener* (1827–30), *Nordens mytologi* (1832), *Haandbog i verdenshistorien* (1833–43).

Grünewald, Matthias. See Matthias GOTHARDT.

Gru·son \'grü-,zỏn\, Hermann August Jacques. 1821–1895. German industrialist. Founded shipyard at Buckau (1855) which became Gruson Works (1869) and later (1893) was bought by Krupp. Developed chill-casting process; manufactured railway equipment, armor plate, armored turrets, shells, etc.

Gryphius, Andreas. See Andreas GREIF.

Grypus. See ANTIOCHUS VIII of Syria.

Gua *or* **Guast** \gà, gwà\, Pierre du. Sieur de Monts \mōⁿ\. c.1568–c.1630. French colonizer. Obtained from Henry IV (1603) letters patent as vice admiral and lieutenant general of Acadia (French America); with Champlain founded (1604) Port Royal (now Annapolis Royal, N.S.), first French establishment in America; returned to France and continued to send out expeditions, including Champlain's of 1608, by which Quebec was founded.

Gua·da·gni·ni \,gwä-dän-'yē-nē\. Family of Italian violin makers orig. of Piacenza, including: Lorenzo (before 1690–1748) and esp. his son ¶Giovanni Baptista, *known as* J.B. Guadagnini (c.1711–1786), who worked in Piacenza, Milan, Cremona, etc. and produced violins and violas of high quality. Descendants continued to make violins into the 20th century.

Gua·det \gà-de\, Marguerite-Élie. 1758–1794. French politician. Member of Legislative Assembly (1791), National Convention (1792); leader among the Girondists in opposing the Jacobins; guillotined.

Guar·di \'gwär-dē\, Giovanni Antonio, *called* Gianantonio (1699–1760), and his brother Francesco (1712–1793). Venetian painters. Collaborators in studio (from c.1731) with third brother ¶Nicolò (1715–1786), specializing in original works and copies. From mid-1750s Francesco specialized in veduta, paintings of rural and city views, patterned on those of Canaletto.

Guar·dia \'gwär-thyä\, Tomás. 1832–1882. Costa Rican politician. Elected president (1870–76); dictator (1876–82).

Guar·dio·la \gwär-'thyō-lä\, Santos. 1812?–1862. Honduran politician and general. Commanded Honduran and Salvadoran forces against Nicaragua (1844); led revolt that drove out president of Honduras (1855); president of Honduras (1856–62); assassinated.

Gua·ri·ni \gwä-'rē-nē\, Giovanni Battista. 1538–1612. Italian poet. Professor, Ferrara (1558–67); in service of Duke Alfonso II of Ferrara (1567–82); succeeded Tasso as court poet (1579–82). Credited with Tasso with development of pastoral drama; chief work, *Il pastor fido* (1590).

Guarini, Guarino, *orig.* Camillo. 1624–1683. Italian architect. Built or designed in Turin six churches and chapels, including S. Lorenzo (1668–87) and SS. Sindone (1667–90), five palaces including Palazzo Carignano (1679), etc.; also supplied designs for Sta. Maria della Divina Providenza, Lisbon, and palaces for Bavaria and Baden; published books on astronomy, mathematics, architecture; works were major source for later Baroque designers.

Gua·ri·no da Ve·ro·na \gwä-'rē-nō-dä-vā-'rō-nä\. *Also called* Guarino Ve·ro·ne·se \,vā-rō-'nā-sā\. 1370 or 1374–1460. Italian Humanist. Professor of classics in Florence (1402), Venice (1415), Verona (1422); tutor in house of Este, Ferrara (1436). Works included editions of Plautus, Livy, Pliny the Elder, and Catullus; translations of Strabo and Plutarch.

Guar·ne·ri \gwär-'nye-rē\. *Lat.* Guar·ne·ri·us \gwär-'nir-ē-əs\. Family of Italian violin makers in Cremona, including: Andrea (c.1626–1698); studied under Nicolò Amati. Andrea's sons ¶Pietro (1655–c.1728) and ¶Giuseppe (1666–c.1739). Giuseppe's son ¶Pietro II (1695–1762). Andrea's nephew ¶Giuseppe, *known as* Giuseppe del Ge·sù \-del-'jā-sü\ (1687–1745) became most noted of the family; produced variety of instruments of markedly robust tone.

Guarnerius. See IRNERIUS.

Guas \'gwäs\, Juan. d. 1497. Spanish architect. Assisted on Puerta de los Leones of Toledo cathedral (1459–69); architect of cathedral (1494); other works included San Juan de los Reyes, Toledo (1479–80), Infantado palace, Guadalajara (1480–83), chapel of S. Gregorio, Valladolid (1488); chief figure among architects of Isabelline style.

Guatemotzin. See CUAUHTÉMOC.

Guch·kov \güch-'kóf\, Aleksandr Ivanovich. 1862–1936. Russian politican. Member of First Duma; leader of Octobrists in Third Duma (1907–12) and elected its president (1910). In revolution (1917), was delegated to make formal demand of Czar Nicholas II for his abdication; minister of war and navy (1917) under Kerensky; emigrated to Paris after Bolshevik takeover.

Gu·dea \gü-'dä-ä\. fl. c.2144–c.2124 B.C. Ruler of Lagash, a Sumerian city-state. A temple builder and patron of arts; greatly influenced religion of Sumer; deified by later generations.

Gu·de·ri·an \gü-'dā-rē-än\, Heinz Wilhelm. 1888–1954. German general. A leading tactical theorist of mobile armored warfare before World War II; commanded blitzkrieg strikes against Poland (1939), France (1940), Russia (1941); recalled for failure at Moscow; inspector general of armored troops (1943–44); acting chief of staff (1944–45). Author of *Achtung! Panzer!* (1937).

Gudfred. See GODFRED.

Guébriant, Comte de. See Jean-Baptiste BUDES.

Gue·dal·la \gwi-'dal-ə\, Philip. 1889–1944. English writer. Among his books were *Ignes Fatui* (verse, 1911), *Supers and Supermen* (1920), *The Second Empire* (1922), *Palmerston* (1926), *The Duke* (biography of Wellington, 1931), *The Queen and Mr. Gladstone* (1933), *The Hundred Days* (1934), *The Hundred Years* (1936), *1936: The Hundredth Year* (1940), *The Two Marshals* (1943).

Gueldre, Duke of. See EGMONT.

Güe·mes de Hor·ca·si·tas \'gwā-māth-thā-ōr-kä-'sē-täs\, Juan Francisco. Conde de Re·vil·la·gi·ge·do \thā-rā-'bēl-yä-gē-'gā-thō\. 1682–1768. Spanish soldier. Captain general of Cuba (1734–1746); viceroy of Mexico (1746–1755). To Spain (1756); president, council of war. His son ¶Juan Vicente Güemes-Pa·che·co de Pa·dil·la y Horcasitas \pä-'chā-kō-thā-pä-'thēl-yä-ē-\, conde de Revillagigedo (1740–1799), was captain of viceregal guard, Mexico; viceroy of Mexico (1789–94); on return to Spain was appointed director general of artillery.

Gué·ran·ger \gā-rä^n-zhā\, Prosper-Louis-Pascal. 1805–1875. French religious and liturgist. Ordained (1827); acquired ancient monastery of Solesmes (1832), accepted as Benedictine abbey (1837); head of Benedictine Congregation in France (1837); worked to restore unity of Roman liturgy. Author of *Institutions liturgiques* (1840–51).

Guercino. See Giovanni BARBIERI.

Gue·ricke \'gā-rik-ə\, Otto von. 1602–1686. German physicist. Engineer in army of Gustav II Adolphus (1631–35); mayor of Magdeburg (1646–81). Invented air pump (1650); devised Magdeburg hemispheres to illustrate pressure of the air (1657); devised (1663) first electrical generating machine, a ball of sulfur on a crank-turned shaft, the friction of the hand held against the turning ball generating static electricity; discovered (1672) electroluminescence.

Gué·rin \gā-ra^n\, Charles. 1873–1907. French poet. Author of *Fleurs de neige* (1893), *Joies grises* (1894), *L'Eros funèbre* (1900), *Le Semeur de cendres* (1901), etc.

Gue·rin \'ger-ən\, Jules. 1866–1946. American painter, b. St. Louis. Best known for his murals in Lincoln Memorial in Washington, D.C., Pennsylvania Railroad Station in New York City, Civic Opera Building in Chicago.

Gué·rin \gā-ra^n\, Maurice de, *in full* Georges-Maurice de. 1810–1839. French poet. Member of Abbé de Lamennais's radical community (1831), experience recorded in *Le Cahier vert* (1861). Author of Romantic verse *Le Centaure,* printed (1840) by George Sand in *Revue des Deux Mondes; La Bacchante* (1861); *Méditation sur la mort de Marie* (1861). Subject of a cultish following. His sister ¶Eugénie (1805–1848) wrote mystical verse; known esp. for her *Journal* (1862) and *Lettres* (1865).

Guérin, Pierre-Narcisse. Baron. 1774–1833. French painter. Professor at École des Beaux-Arts, Paris (1814); best known as teacher of Delacroix and Géricault; director of Académie de France at Rome (1822–28). Paintings included *Retour de Marcus Sextus, Phèdre et Hippolyte, Andromache et Pyrrhus, Enée racontant à Didon les malheurs de la ville de Troie.*

Guernes \gern\ *or* **Gar·nier** \gär-nyā\. *Called* Guernes de Pont-Sainte-Max·ence \pō^n-sa^{n}t-mák-sä^{n}s\. 12th century. French scholar. Author of *Vie de Saint Thomas Becket* (c.1174).

Guernieri. See WERNER, Duke of Urslingen.

Guer·raz·zi \gwär-'rät-tsē\, Francesco Domenico. 1804–1873. Italian political leader and writer. With Mazzini and Carlo Bini founded journal *Indicatore livornese* (1829); premier of Tuscany (1848); triumvir and dictator of Florentine republic (1849); imprisoned (1849–1853); banished to Corsica (1853–1861); member of parliament (1862). Author of historical novels as *La battaglia di Benevento* (1827), *L'assedio di Firenze* (1836), humorous allegory *L'asino* (1857), etc.

Guer·re·ro \ger-'rer-ō\, Francisco. 1528–1599. Spanish composer. Chapelmaster at Jaén cathedral (1546–49); singer (1549), assistant (1551–74), chapelmaster (1574–99) at Seville cathedral. Composed 18 masses, some 150 motets and other liturgical pieces, many secular songs.

Guerrero, Manuel Amador. See AMADOR GUERRERO.

Guerrero, María. 1867–1928. Spanish actress. Director (from 1895) of Teatro Español, Madrid, where she presented and appeared in Spanish classics and the best modern plays.

Guerrero, Vicente. 1783–1831. Mexican soldier and politician. Joined in war for independence under Morelos (1810); became leader of guerrilla forces; joined Itúrbide (1821) but later turned against him; under Guadalupe Victoria, vice president of Mexico (1824–28); chosen president by Congress (1829); overthrown in revolt (1829) led by Bustamante; captured and shot.

Guer·ri·ni \gwär-'rē-nē\, Olindo. *Pseudonym* Lorenzo Stec·chet·ti \stak-'kät-tē\. 1845–1916. Italian poet. Chief representative of verism. Author of *Postuma* (1877), *Polemica* (1878), *Rime di Argia Sbolenfi* (1897), *Rime* (1903), etc.

Gues·clin \gā-kla^n, ge-\, Bertrand du. c.1320–1380. French soldier. In service of Charles de Blois, Duke of Brittany, distinguished himself at siege of Vannes (1342); to England to ransom Charles (1354); fought celebrated duel with Sir Thomas Canterbury (1356); defended Rennes against English siege (1356–57); almost constantly in the field (1359–63) in service of house of Valois; won major victory at Cocherel (1364) against Charles II of Navarre, but defeated and captured at Auray (1364). Led mercenaries in support of Henry of Trastámara against Peter I of Castile (1366, 1369); installed Henry on throne of Castile after winning battle of Montiel (1369). Recalled to France by Charles V and made constable of France (1370); recovered from English provinces of Poitou, Guienne, Auvergne; seized duchy of Brittany (1373); died at siege of Châteauneuf-de-Randon.

Guesde \ged\, Jules. *Orig.* Mathieu Ba·sile \bá-zēl\. 1845–1922. French Socialist. Editor, *Les Droits de l'homme* (1870); defended the Commune of Paris (1871) and had to flee to Switzerland. Returned (1876), founded weekly *L'Égalité* (1877). Collaborated with Marx and Lafargue in preparing program adopted by national congress of the Labor party (1880); caused split among Socialist groups by rejecting all tactical compromise with capitalistic government. Deputy (from 1893); minister without portfolio (1914–15).

Guest \'gest\, Lady Charlotte Elizabeth, *nee* Ber·tie \'bärt-ē\. 1812–1895. Welsh writer. m. Sir Josiah Guest (1833; d. 1852). Published *Mabinogion* (1838–49) from old Welsh manuscripts with translations.

Guest, Edgar Albert. 1881–1959. American journalist and poet, b. Birmingham, England. To U.S. (1891); on staff of Detroit *Free Press* (from 1895); conductor of column of verse and humorous sketches. Author of many volumes of popular verse as *A Heap o' Livin'* (1916), *Just Folks* (1917), *When Day is Done* (1921), etc.

Guet·tard \ge-tár\, Jean-Étienne. 1715–1786. French geologist and botanist. In service of the duc d'Orléans (from 1747); discovered volcanic origin of the Auvergne (1751); created a mineralogical map of France (1746) and worked with Lavoisier on a geological survey of France (1766–77).

Gue·va·ra \gā-'bä-rä\, Antonio de. c.1481–1545. Spanish religious and writer. Entered Franciscan order; court preacher to Charles V; bishop of Guadix (1528), of Mondoñedo (1537). Author of *Reloj de príncipes o libro aureo del emperador Marco Aurelio* (1529), widely translated and influential model for rulers; also wrote *La década de Césares* (1539), *Epístolas familiares* (1539–42), etc.

Gue·va·ra \gā-'bä-rä, *Angl* gə-'vär-ə, g(w)ə-'ver-ə\, Ernesto. *Known as* Che Guevara. *Full surname* Guevara de la Ser·na \'ser-nä\. 1928–1967. Argentinian revolutionary leader. Doctor of medicine (1953); aide to Fidel Castro in Cuban revolution (1956–59); active in leftist guerilla movements in Congo and Latin America (1965–67); killed in Bolivia. Author of *Guerrilla Warfare* (1961), *Episodes of the Revolutionary War* (1963), etc.

Guevara, Luis Vélez de. See VÉLEZ DE GUEVARA.

Guè·vre·mont \gev-rə-mō^n, gāv-\, Germaine, *nee* Gri·gnon \grēn-yō^n\. 1900–1968. Canadian novelist, b. Que. m. Hyacinthe Guèvremont. Author of poetic novels of Quebec peasant life as *En pleine terre* (1942), *Le Survenant* (1945), *Marie-Didace* (1947).

Guè·ye \ge-yā, gā-\, Lamine. 1891–1968. Senegalese politician. Active in nationalist and Socialist movements; judge in Réunion Island; Senegalese deputy in French National Assembly (1945–51); mayor of Dakar (1945–61); joined Union Progressiste Sénégalaise party of former protégé Léopold Senghor (1958); president of Senegalese Legislative Assembly (1959–68).

Gug·gen·heim \'gu̇g-ən-ˌhīm, 'gü-gən-\, Meyer. 1828–1905. American industrialist, b. Langnau, Switzerland. To U.S. (1847); formed firm to import Swiss embroidery (1872); interested himself in copper industry; formed Philadelphia Smelting and Refining Co. (1888); with aid of his seven sons, gained dominant place in industry; controlled American Smelting and Refining Co. (from 1901). His son ¶Daniel (1856–1930), b. Philadelphia, joined father in copper industry; established himself as leading figure in copper industry; extended his interests to gold mines in Alaska, rubber plantations in Africa, tin mines in Bolivia, and nitrate deposits in Chile; head of firm (to 1919). Noted also for philanthropy, as in establishing (1924) Daniel and Florence Guggenheim Foundation to promote "the well-being of mankind," and (1926) the Daniel Guggenheim Foundation for the Promotion of Aeronautics. Another son ¶Simon (1867–1941), b. Philadelphia, was U.S. senator from Colorado (1907–13); established (1925) as memorial to his son the John Simon Guggenheim Memorial Foundation to award fellowships to artists and scholars for study abroad. A granddaughter of Meyer, ¶Marguerite Guggenheim, *known as* Peggy (1898–1979) was a noted patron of artists and collector of modern art; financed galleries Guggenhiem Jeune, London (1938–39), Art of This Century, New York (1943–47), Museo Palazzo Venier dei Leoni, Venice (1951– 79); noted esp. for patronage of Pollock, Motherwell, Baziotes, Tanguy. Author of *Out of This Century* (1946), *Confessions of an Art Addict* (1960).

Gu·gliel·mi \gül-'yel-mē\, Pietro Alessandro. 1728–1804. Italian composer. Active in Naples, Rome, London (1767–72), Venice, etc.; maestro di capella, St. Peter's, Rome (1793–97), S. Lorenzo Lucina (1797–1804). Composed over 90 comic and serious operas, including *Il ratto della sposa* (1765), *La sposa fedele* (1767), *La villanella ingentilita* (1779), *Le vicende d'amore* (1784), *L'inganno amoroso* (1786), *La pastorella nobile* (1788), *La bella pescatrice* (1789); also sacred oratorios, cantatas, masses and other liturgical works.

Gu·gliel·mi·ni \ˌgül-yel-ˈmē-nē\, Domenico, *in full* Giovanni Domenico. 1655–1710. Italian mathematician and hydrologist. Professor, Bologna; known for studies of stream flow and resistance; founder of Italian school of hydraulics.

Gu·gliel·mo da Sa·li·ce·to \gül-ˈyel-mō-dä-ˌsä-lē-ˈchā-tō\. *Fr.* Guil·laume de Sa·li·cet \gē-yōm-də-sál-ē-se\. *Eng.* William of Saliceto. c.1210–c.1277. Italian physician and cleric. Considered foremost European surgeon of 13th century. Practiced in Lombardy (to 1270); taught at Bologna (1270–74); city physician of Verona (1274 ff.). Author of *Cyrugia* (1275) which advocated a union between medicine and surgery.

Gui \gē\, Bernard. *Lat.* Bernardus Gui·do·nis \g(w)ē-ˈdō-nəs\. c.1261–1331. French prelate. Dominican; bishop of Túy, Spain, and later Lodève, France (1324); inquisitor of Toulouse (1307–23). Author of a valuable chronicle and of *Manuel de l'inquisiteur.*

Gui·bert \gē-ber\, François-Apollini de. Comte. 1744–1790. French soldier and writer. Served in Seven Years' War, later in Corsica (1767); field marshal (1788). Author of *Essai de tactique générale* (1773), *Défense du système de guerre moderne* (1779).

Guibert de No·gent \-də-nó-zhä^{n}\. 1053–c.1124. French theologian and historian. Benedictine abbot of Nogent-sous-Coucy (from 1104). Author of a history of the Crusades, regarded as best of contemporary accounts.

Guic·ciar·di·ni \ˌgwēt-chär-ˈdē-nē\, Francesco. 1483–1540. Florentine historian and politician. Florentine ambassador to Aragon (1512–14); papal governor of Modena and Reggio (1516–21, 1522–24); governor of Romagna under Clement VII (1524 ff.); instrumental in creation of League of Cognac (1526); papal lieutenant general (1526); worked for restoration of Medici (1529–31); governor of Bologna (1531–34). Author of *Storia d'Italia,* principal historical work of 16th century (1561–64); also of *Storie fiorentine,* etc.

Guic·cio·li \ˈgwēt-chō-lē\, Teresa. Countess. *Nee* Gam·ba-Ghi·sel·li \ˈgäm-bä-gē-ˈsel-lē\. 1800–1873. Italian noblewoman. m. Count Alessandro Guiccioli (1818). Known for her liaison with Lord Byron, who through her family was inducted into Carbonari society. Author of *Lord Byron jugé par les temoins de sa vie* (1868).

Gui·di \ˈgwē-dē\, Alessandro. 1650–1712. Italian poet. A founder of Accademia dell'Arcadia (1690); introduced canzone with free strophes, later developed by Leopardi. Author of *Rime* (1681), melodrama *Amalasunta in Italia* (1681), mythological drama *Endimione* (1692), etc.

Guidi, Tommaso. See TOMMASO DI GIOVANNI DI SIMONE GUIDI.

Guido. See also GUY.

Gui·do \ˈgwē-dō\ of Arez·zo \ə-ˈret-(ˌ)sō, ä-\. *Ital.* Guido d'·Arez·zo \dä-ˈrät-tsō\ *or* Guido Are·ti·nus \ä-rā-ˈtē-nəs\. *Also called* Fra Guit·to·ne \gwēt-ˈtō-nā\. c.991–1050. Italian monk and music theorist. Benedictine monk in monastery of Pomposa near Ferrara; later settled at Arezzo (c.1025); prior of Camaldolese monastery near Avellano (1047). Devised four-line staff that made possible precise notation of pitch, and solmization syllables as aid in teaching singers. Among his works on musical theory were *Micrologus, Regulae de ignoto cantu, Aliae regulae.*

Guido da Sie·na \-dä-ˈsyā-nä\. fl. 1250–1275. Italian painter. Among earliest painters to break with rigid Byzantine formality and introduce use of spontaneous gesture and posture into paintings.

Guido del·le Co·lon·ne \-ˌdāl-lā-kō-ˈlōn-nā\ *or* **da Co·lon·na** \-dä-kō-ˈlōn-nä\. c.1215–c.1290. Sicilian poet. Chief work, *Historia destructionis Troiae* in Latin (1287), possibly based on *Roman de Troie* by Benoît de Sainte-Maure (*q.v.*), was used as source by Boccaccio, Chaucer, Shakespeare; Caxton's English version of it (1475) was first printed English book.

Guido di Pie·tro \-dē-ˈpyā-trō\. *Known as* Fra An·ge·li·co \än-ˈjā-lē-kō\. c.1400–1455. Florentine painter. Early attained reputation as painter under orig. name; entered Dominican order (c.1420) as Fra Giovanni da Fiesole; resident of monastery of S. Marco, Florence (1439–45); in Rome (1445–50); prior of S. Domenico, Fiesole (1450–52). Outstanding painter of early Renaissance. Chief works included altarpieces *Madonna della Stella, Deposition* for Sta. Trinità, Florence; *Linainuoli Altarpiece, Lamentation* for Sta. Maria della Croce al Tempio; *Annalena Altarpiece,* believed to be first *sacra conversazione* composition; known esp. for altarpiece and murals at S. Marco, murals for chapel of Pope Nicholas V, series of 35 scenes from life of Christ for silver chest in SS. Annunziata, Florence.

Guido Reni. See RENI.

Guil·bert \gēl-ber\, Yvette. 1867–1944. French singer. Famed as singer of topical songs, often in argot, with subjects drawn from Latin Quarter or from lower-class Parisian life.

Guilbert of Sempringham. See GILBERT.

Guilford, Baron and earl of. See NORTH family.

Guil·lau·mat \gē-yō-mà\, Louis, *in full* Marie-Louis-Adolphe. 1863–1940. French soldier. Commanded 2d army in defense of Verdun (1916–17); commander in chief of allied armies in the East (1918); commanded 5th army in forcing passage of the Aisne River (Oct.–Nov. 1918); commander of French army on Rhine (1924–30); minister of war (1925).

Guillaume. See also WILLIAM.

Guil·laume \gē-yōm\, Charles Édouard. 1861–1938. Swiss physicist. Assistant (1883), director (1915), International Bureau of Weights and Measures at Sèvres. Known esp. for invention of nickel-steel alloys invar and elinvar that, because of very slight expansion or contraction or slight change in elasticity with changes in temperature, is used for standard measures and precision instruments; awarded 1920 Nobel prize for physics.

Guillaume de Cham·peaux \shä^{n}-pō\. *Lat.* Guglielmus de Cam·pel·lis \kam-ˈpel-əs\. c.1070–1121. French philosopher. Taught at cathedral school, Notre Dame, Paris, with Abelard among pupils; head of school, archdeacon (c.1100); retired to abbey of Saint-Victor (1108); bishop of Châlons-sur-Marne (1113); became champion of reform and orthodoxy; ordained Bernard of Clairvaux (1115). Known for controversy, esp. with Abelard, over nature of universals.

Guillaume de Haute·ville \ōt-vēl\. *Called* Bras de fer \brá-də-fer\, *i.e.* Iron Arm. d. 1046. Norman soldier. With brothers Drogo (*q.v.*) and Humphrey joined Rainulf of Aversa in conquest of southern Italy (c.1035); earned sobriquet by killing Muslim āmir of Syracuse; made count of Apulia (1042).

Guillaume de Lor·ris \lò-rēs\. d. c.1240. French poet. Author of the first part of *Roman de la Rose.* See Jean CHOPINEL.

Guillaume de Ma·chaut *or* **Ma·chault** \má-shō\. c.1300–1377. French poet and composer. In service of John of Luxembourg, king of Bohemia (1323–46); canon of Reims cathedral (from 1337). Author of dits, lais, and other verse, of which best known is *Voir-dit.* Considered chief exponent in music of Ars Nova style; composed settings for own poems, a polyphonic mass, motets, virelais, rondeaux, ballades, etc.; his music circulated widely through Europe in his day.

Guillaume de Poi·tiers \pwá-tyā\. 1020–between 1087 and 1101. Norman chronicler. Chronicler of William the Conqueror. Author of *Gesta Guillelmi Ducis.*

Guillaume de Salicet. See GUGLIELMO DA SALICETO.

Guil·lau·min \gē-yō-ma^{n}\, Armand, *in full* Jean-Baptiste-Armand. 1841–1927. French painter. Member of Impressionist group; known esp. for Parisian cityscapes, seascapes, etc.

Guil·lo·tin \gē-yó-ta^{n}\, Joseph-Ignace. 1738–1814. French physician. Deputy to Estates-General (1789); first to demand doubling of representatives of Third Estate. Defended capital punishment and proposed use of beheading machine (1789), called guillotine after him.

Guil·mant \gēl-mä^{n}\, Félix-Alexandre. 1837–1911. French organist and composer. Organist of Trinité, Paris (1871–1901); professor, Conservatoire (1896 ff.); with Bordes and d'Indy founded (1894) Schola Cantorum. Composer of organ works, esp. 8 sonatas, and choral works.

Gui·ma·rães \gē-má-ˈrä^{n}s\, Bernardo Joaquim da Sil·va \dá-ˈsēl-vá\. 1825–1884. Brazilian poet and novelist. Author of verse *Cantos da solidão* (1852), *Poesias* (1865), *Fôlhas de Outono* (1883); novels *O seminarista* (1872), *A escrava Isaura* (1875), *Maurício* (1877).

Guimarães Ro·sa \-ˈrō-sá\, João. 1908–1967. Brazilian writer. Physician and diplomat. Author of stories collected as *Sagarana* (1946), *Corpo de baile* (1956), *Primeiras estórias* (1962), *Tutaméia* (1967); novel *Grande sertão: Veredas* (1956).

Gui·mard \gē-már, -mär\, Hector-Germain. 1867–1942. French architect and designer. Leading French exponent of Art Nouveau in architecture. Works included Castel Béranger apartments, Paris (1894–98); several cast iron entrance structures for Paris Métro (1898–1901); Castel Henriette, Sèvres (1903).

Guimard, Marie-Madeleine. 1743–1816. French dancer. Debut at Comédie-Française (1759); at Opéra (1762–89); featured in ballets of Noverre and Gardel, esp. *Les Caprices de Galatée, Médée et Jason;* notorious for licentiousness and for exhibition of legally prohibited plays in her private theater.

Gui·me·rà \ˌgē-mā-ˈrà\, Ángel. 1847–1924. Catalan dramatist and poet. Fervent supporter of Renaixensa movement in Catalan literature. Author of tragedies as *Judit de Welp* (1883), *Mar i Cel* (1888), *Rei i Monjo* (1890), *Terra Baixa* (1896), *La filla del mar* (1899), *La pecadora* (1902), etc.

Gui·nan \ˈgī-nən\, Mary Louise Cecilia. *Known as* Texas Guinan. 1884–1933. American actress and hostess, b. Waco, Tex. Actress on tour, on Broadway, in silent films; achieved fame as hostess of speakeasies in New York City as El Fay Club, Del Fay Club, Texas Guinan Club, Club Intime, etc. (1924–28); produced Broadway revue *Padlocks of 1927,* appeared in films *Queen of the Night Clubs* (1929), *Broadway Thru a Keyhole* (1933).

Gui·ney \ˈgī-nē\, Louise Imogen. 1861–1920. American poet and essayist, b. Boston. Her volumes of verse included *Songs at the Start* (1884), *The White Sail and Other Poems* (1887), *A Roadside Harp* (1893), *Happy Ending* (1909); her essays, *Goose Quill Papers* (1885), *A Little English Gallery* (1894), *Patrins* (1897).

Gui·ni·zel·li \ˌgwē-nēt-ˈsel-lē\, Guido. between 1230 and 1240–?1276. Bolognese poet. Forerunner of the *dolce stil nuovo;* held by Dante as father of Italian love poetry.

Guin·ness \ˈgin-əs, gə-ˈnes\. Name of a family of brewers in Ireland, including: Sir Benjamin Lee Guinness (1798–1868); manager (from 1825), sole proprietor (1855) of brewing business founded by his father; first lord mayor of Dublin (1851); M.P. (1865–68); restored St. Patrick's Cathedral in Dublin (1860–65); created baronet (1867). His sons ¶Sir Arthur Edward (1840–1915), 1st Baron Ar·di·laun \ˌär-di-ˈlȯn\, head of the business (1868–77), benefactor of Dublin and Church of Ireland, and ¶Edward Cecil (1847–1927), 1st Earl of Iveagh \ˈī-vā\, chairman of Guinness brewery at Dublin (1886–89), erected workmen's dwellings in London and Dublin, destroyed Dublin slums, endowed Lister Inst. for bacteriological research. Edward Cecil's son ¶Walter Edward (1880–1944), 1st Baron Moyne \ˈmȯin\, M.P. (1907–31); minister of agriculture (1925–29, 1940–41); colonial secretary (1941–42); leader of House of Lords (1941–42); deputy minister of state, Cairo (1942–44); assassinated.

Gui·on \ˈgī-ən\, David Wendel Fentress. 1895–1981. American songwriter, b. Ballinger, Tex. Transcribed many folk melodies into fiddle tunes, as "Turkey in the Straw," "Arkansas Traveler," "Short'nin' Bread." Best known song "Home on the Range."

Güi·ral·des \gē-ˈräl-dās\, Ricardo. 1886–1927. Argentinian writer. Author of *El cencerro de cristal* (1915), *Cuentos de muerte y de sangre* (1915), *Xamaica* (1923); best known for *Don Segundo Sombra,* an epic of gaucho life on the Argentinian pampas (1926).

Gui·raut de Bor·neil \gē-rō-də-bȯr-ney\ *or* **de Bor·nelh** \-bȯr-ney\. 12th century. French troubadour. Reputed in his day the master of troubadours; mentioned with Arnaut Daniel and Bertran de Born in Dante's *Divina commedia.*

Gui·san \gē-zäⁿ\, Henri. 1874–1960. Swiss soldier. General and commander in chief during World War II (1939–45); devised defensive strategy of holding mountain fortress core of nation, the *réduit.*

Guiscard, Robert. See ROBERT GUISCARD.

Gui·teau \gə-ˈtō\, Charles Julius. 1840?–1882. American lawyer and assassin. Disappointed office seeker who shot President Garfield in Washington, D.C. (July 2, 1881); hanged in Washington.

Gui·te·ras \gē-ˈtā-räs\, Juan. 1852–1925. Cuban physician. Member of Havana Yellow Fever Commission (1879); entered U.S. Marine Hospital service (1880–89); professor of pathology, U. of Pennsylvania (1889–99). Served with American army in Cuba (1898). Study of yellow fever brought him into association with Major Gorgas and Major Reed; verified Reed's findings by independent experiments. Professor, U. of Havana (1900–20); director of public health in Cuba (1909–21).

Gui·try \gē-trē\, Lucien-Germain. 1860–1925. French actor. Debut (1878); acted at the Odéon (1891), the Théâtre de la Renaissance (1895), the Vaudeville (1898), Comédie-Française (1902); manager of the Renaissance (1902–09); noted for unfashionable economy of gesture and expression; in his later years, appeared in a number of plays written by his son ¶Sacha (1885–1957), actor and dramatist; author of *Nono* (1905), *Chez les Zoaques* (1906), *Petite Hollande* (1908), *Le Scandale de Monte Carlo* (1908), *Le Veilleur de nuit* (1911), *Un Beau Mariage* (1911), *Debureau* (1918), *Pasteur,* in which the elder Guitry enjoyed great success (1919), *Béranger* (1920), *Françoise* (1932), *Le Mot de Cambronne* (1936), etc.; also wrote operettas and films as *Le Roman d'un tricheur* (1935), *Les Perles de la couronne* (1937).

Guit·to·ne d'·Arez·zo \gwēt-ˈtō-nā-dä-ˈrāt-tsō\. c.1235–1294. Italian poet. Author of love lyrics of the troubadour type and, later, of poems on moral, religious, and political subjects; known also as writer of earliest extant letters in the Italian language.

Gui·zot \gē-zō\, François-Pierre-Guillaume. 1787–1874. French historian and politician. Professor, Paris (1812); proponent of constitutional monarchy; elected deputy (1830); minister of interior (1830), education (1832–37); foreign minister (1840–47); premier of France (1847–48); forced into retirement by Revolution of 1848. Author of *Histoire de la civilisation en Europe* (1828) and *Histoire...en France* (1829–32), *Histoire des origines du gouvernement représentatif* (1851), *Mémoires pour servir à l'histoire de mon temps* (1858–67), etc.

Gul·ben·ki·an \gu̇l-ˈbeŋ-kē-ən\, Calouste Sarkis. 1869–1955. British financier, b. Turkey of Armenian descent. In petroleum business (from 1888); British subject (1902); involved in organization of Royal Dutch Shell, Turkish Petroleum, Iraq Petroleum firms; negotiated Saudi Arabian oil concessions to U.S. firms (1948 ff.); amassed fortune and notable art collection.

Gul·brans·son \ˈgu̇l-brän-sȯn\, Olaf. 1873–1958. Norwegian illustrator. On staff of *Simplicissimus* in Munich (from 1902); a leader among modern caricaturists.

Guld·berg \ˈgu̇l-ber(g)\, Cato Maximilian. 1836–1902. Norwegian chemist and mathematician. Professor, U. of Christiania (now Oslo, 1869); with Peter Waage, established (1864) law of mass action; formulated (1890) Guldberg's law of boiling points.

Guld·berg \ˈgu̇l-berḡ\, Ove Høegh- \ˈhœḡ-\. 1731–1808. Danish scholar and politician. Professor, Sorø Academy (1761); tutor (1764), secretary (1771) to Prince Frederick; took part in conspiracy against Struensee (1772); effective head of government of incompetent Christian VII (1772–84); retired to provincial office in coup d'état of Frederick.

Gul·din \ˈgu̇l-dən\, Paul, *orig.* Habakkuk. 1577–1643. Swiss mathematician. Entered Jesuit order (1597); taught in Jesuit colleges in Rome, Graz; professor, Vienna. Author of treatises defending Gregorian calendar, on centers of gravity, etc.; chief work *Centrobaryca* (1635–41), on centers of gravity, volumes and areas of figures.

Gu·lick \ˈgyü-lək\, Luther Halsey. 1865–1918. American educator, b. Honolulu. Staff member and then director, physical training course, YMCA College, Springfield, Mass. (1886–1903); cooperated there with James Naismith in inventing game of basketball; director of physical education, New York City public schools (1903–06); director, child hygiene department, Russell Sage Foundation (1907–13); an organizer of The Camp Fire Girls of America (1910).

Gull·strand \ˈgəl-strȧnd\, Allvar. 1862–1930. Swedish ophthalmologist. Professor in Uppsala (from 1894); investigated dioptrics of the eye; developed new theory of optical images; devised Gullstrand slit lamp and Gullstrand ophthalmoscope; awarded 1911 Nobel prize for physiology or medicine.

Gul·ly \ˈgəl-ē\, John. 1783–1863. English sportsman and politician. Succeeded Henry Pearce as heavyweight champion boxer (1806–08); took up horse racing and fielded winners of the Derby (1832, 1846, 1854), St. Leger (1832), Two Thousand Guineas (1844, 1854), Oaks (1846); M.P. (1832–37); later invested in coal mines.

Gum·me·re \ˈgəm-ə-rē\, Samuel René. 1849–1920. American diplomat, b. Trenton, N.J. Consul general for Morocco (1898–1905) at time Perdicaris was kidnaped by Raisuli for ransom; transmitted John Hay's famous dispatch, "Perdicaris alive or Raisuli dead"; U.S. minister to Morocco (1905–09).

Gum·plo·wicz \güm-ˈplȯ-vēch\, Ludwig *or Pol.* Ludwik. 1838–1909. Polish economist and sociologist. Professor, Graz (from 1875); known for theory that society originates in conflict. Author of *Der Rassenkampf* (1883), *Grundriss der Soziologie* (1885), *Die sociologische Staatsidee* (1892), etc.

Gun·de·ric \ˈgən-də-rik\. *Fr.* Gon·dioc \gōⁿ-dyȯk\ *or* Gon·dé·ric \gōⁿ-dā-rēk\. d. c.470. Second king of Burgundy (436–c.470). Son of Gundicar; widened boundaries of kingdom; left four sons who disputed for the throne.

Gun·di·car \ˈgən-di-ˌkär\. *Also known as* Gun·ther \ˈgən(t)-thər\. *Fr.* Gon·di·caire \gōⁿ-dē-ker\. c.385–437 A.D. First king of Burgundy (413–437). Crossed Rhine (c.413) and established new kingdom; ally of Romans (435); killed in war against Attila. Figured in numerous medieval legends.

Gun·di·mar II \ˈgən-də-ˌmär\. *Fr.* Gon·de·mar \gōⁿd-(ə-)mȧr\. d. 534. King of Burgundy (523–532). Son of Gundobad; succeeded his brother Sigismund; defeated Franks (524); made peace with Theodoric, king of the Ostrogoths; besieged at Autun and driven from throne by sons of Clovis.

Gun·di·sal·vo \gün-dē-ˈsäl-b̲ō\, Domingo. *Lat.* Dominicus Gun·dis·sa·li·nus \ˌgən-dis-ə-ˈlī-nəs\. 12th century. Spanish cleric, philosopher, and linguist. Member of cathedral chapters at Toledo (c.1150), Segovia (c.1190); aided by Jewish scholars, produced Latin translations of many Greco-Arabic philosophical works; instrumental in introducing Neoplatonism to western scholars as Bonaventure and Albert the Great.

Gun·do·bad \ˈgən-dō-ˌbad\. *Fr.* Gon·de·baud \gōⁿd-(ə-)bō\ *or* Gon·do·bald \ˈgän-dō-ˌbȯld\. 474–516. King of Burgundy (c.480–516). Son of Gunderic and nephew of Ricimer; at first shared kingdom with three brothers; later became sole ruler with capital at Vienne; briefly placed puppet Glycerius on Western throne at Ravenna; defeated by Clovis (500); issued (c.500) codification of Burgundian law (*Lex Gundobada,* Fr. *Loi Gombette*); made alliance with Clovis (506). His niece Clotilda became wife of Clovis.

Gun·du·lić \ˈgün-dü-lētʸ\, Ivan Franov. *Ital.* Giovanni Gon·do·la \ˈgōn-dō-lä\. 1589–1638. Croatian poet. Author of lyric and dramatic poems; of epic *Osman* (1626; published 1826), inspired by Tasso; and of dramas *Cleopatra, Dubravka, Proserpina,* which laid foundation of Slavic drama at Ragusa.

Gungl \ˈgu̇ŋ-gəl\, Joseph. 1810–1889. Hungarian bandmaster and composer. Bandmaster in Austrian army (1828–43); formed orchestra, Berlin (1843); toured U.S. (1849); director of music to king of Prussia (1849–64); toured widely with second orchestra (1864 ff.). Composed over 300 popular dances and marches, as "Ungarischer Marsch" (1836), "Träume auf dem Ozean" (1849), "Klänge von Delaware" (1849), "Amorettentänze" (1860), "Themselieder" (1873).

Gun·gun·ha·na \ˌgüŋ-(g)ün-ˈhän-ə\. *Also spelled* Gun·gun·ya·na \-ˈyän-ə\. c.1850–c.1896. Bantu ruler. King of Gaza, or Shangane, last independent Bantu kingdom (1885–95); attempted to preserve independence through European alliances; conquered by Portugal (1895); exiled to Canary Islands.

Gun·kel \ˈgu̇ŋ-kəl\, Hermann. 1862–1932. German scholar. Professor, Berlin (1894–1907), Giessen (1907–20), Halle (1920–27); leading exponent of "history of religion" school of biblical criticism. Author of *Schöpfung und Chaos in Urzeit und Endzeit* (1895), *Genesis* (1901), *Die israelitische Literatur* (1906), *Die Urgeschichte und die Patriarchen* (1911), *Psalmen* (1926), etc.

Gunn \ˈgən\, Neil Miller. 1891–1973. Scottish novelist. Author of *Grey Coast* (1926), *Morning Tide* (1931), *Highland River* (1937), *Wild Geese Overhead* (1939), *The Silver Darlings* (1941), *Green Isle of the Great Deep* (1944), *The White Hour* (1950), etc.

Gunn·laugr Orms·tunga \ˈgœn-ˌlœi-gər-ˈórm-ˌstüŋ-ä\. 10th–11th century. Icelandic skald. Author of *Gunnlaugssaga*, etc.

Gun·sau·lus \(ˌ)gən-ˈsȯ-ləs, -ˈsäl-əs\, Frank Wakeley. 1856–1921. American clergyman, b. Chesterville, Ohio. Ordained (1875) in Methodist ministry; Congregational minister (from 1879). Pastor, Plymouth Church, Chicago (1887–99); Central Church, Chicago (1899–1919). With Philip D. Armour, established Armour Institute (opened 1893); president of the Institute (1893–1921).

Gün·te·kin \ˌgu̅en-tä-ˈkēn\, Reşat Nuri. 1892–1956. Turkish novelist. Known esp. for *Çalıkuşu* (1922).

Gun·ter \ˈgən-tər\, Edmund. 1581–1626. English mathematician. Professor of astronomy, Gresham Coll., London (1619–26); invented the chain, line, quadrant, and scale known by his name; introduced terms cosine and cotangent in his *Canon triangulorum* (1620).

Gunther. See also GUNDICAR.

Gün·ther \ˈgu̅en-tər\. Graf von Schwarz·burg-Blan·ken·burg \ˈshfärts-ˌbu̇rk-ˈbläŋ-kən-ˌbu̇rk\. 1304–1349. German noble. Diplomat and military commander under Emperor Louis IV (1334–39); elected king of Germany (1348) after Louis's death, in opposition to Charles of Luxembourg, who had been proclaimed Charles IV (1346); defeated by Charles at Eltville (1349); signed treaty relinquishing claim to throne shortly before death.

Günther, Ignaz. 1725–1775. German sculptor. A leading Rococo artist in Germany; his statues typically of carved wood and polychromed, noted for elegance and esp. treatment of drapery or clothing; works created for numerous Bavarian churches.

Günther, Johann Christian. 1695–1723. German poet. Chief German lyric poet of the day, expressing personal sorrows in classical style. Works included *Lieder* and *Leonorenlieder;* collected *Gedichte* published posthumously (1724).

Gun·ther \ˈgən(t)-thər\, John. 1901–1970. American journalist, b. Chicago. European correspondent for various American newspapers (from 1924). Author of *Inside Europe* (1936), *Inside Asia* (1939), *Inside Latin America* (1941), *Inside U.S.A.* (1947), *Inside Africa* (1955), *Inside Russia Today* (1958), etc.

Gun·tram \gün-tràm\. d. 592. King of Burgundy (561–592). Son of Chlotar I; after death of eldest brother Charibert (567), held balance of power between brothers Sigebert I and Chilperic I in contest for Charibert's kingdom; after many wars and broken alliances, made pact (587) with Childebert and Brunhilda, son and widow of Sigebert.

Günz·burg \ˈgu̅ents-ˌbu̇rk\, Joseph. 1812–1878. Russian financier and philanthropist. Amassed fortune as contractor, banker, railroad financier; created baron. Helped found (1863) Society for the Promotion of Culture among the Jews, first president (1863–78); sponsored translations of Bible and other works into Russian; worked to reduce discrimination against Jews. His son ¶Horace (1833–1909) continued his work; president of Society (1878 ff.); major contributor to Stock Exchange Hospital, St. Petersburg. His son ¶David (1857–1910) was a noted Orientalist and bibliophile; translated *Tarshish* of Moses ibn Ezra (1887); author of *L'Ornement Hebrew* (1903).

Gur·ko \ˈgu̇r-kə\, Iosif Vladimirovich. 1828–1901. Russian general. Served in Crimean War (1854–56) and in Poland (1863). Commanded army of the Danube in Russo–Turkish War (1877–78); defended Shipka Pass (1877); forced surrender of Pleven (1877) and occupied Sofia, Plovdiv, Edirne (1878). Governor general of St. Petersburg (1879–80), Odessa (1882–83), Poland (1883–94); retired as field marshal. His son ¶Vasily Iosifovich (1864–1937) served in Russo–Japanese War (1904–05), World War I; last imperial Russian chief of staff (1916–17); commander on Romanian front (1917); emigrated after Revolution.

Gur·ley \ˈgər-lē\, Ralph Randolph. 1797–1872. American philanthropist. b. Lebanon, Conn. Agent and later director, American Colonization Society, formed to colonize Liberia with American Negroes (1822–72); drew up plan of government, coined names Liberia and Monrovia (1824).

Gur·ney \ˈgər-nē\, Sir Goldsworthy. 1793–1875. English inventor. Invented oxyhydrogen blowpipe, a high-pressure steam jet, an improved limelight generally known as the Drummond light, and a steam carriage that traveled from London to Bath and back at rate of 15 miles per hour (1829).

Gurney, Joseph John. 1788–1847. English religious leader and philanthropist. Quaker minister (1818); visited U.S., Canada, and West Indies (1837–40); active in movements for prison reform, abolition of capital punishment, Negro emancipation; inspired Gurneyite, or Friends United Meeting branch of Quakers.

Gus·tav \ˈgəs-ˌtäv\ *or* **Gus·ta·vus** \gə-ˈstā-vəs, -ˈstäv-əs\. Name of six kings of Sweden, the first four of the Vasa dynasty:

Gustav I Va·sa \ˈvä-sȧ\. *Orig.* Gustav Eriks·son \ˈā-rik-ˌsȯn\. 1496?–1560. King (1523–60). Descended on mother's side from ancient house of Sture; entered service of Regent Sten Sture; fought against Christian II of Denmark; held hostage in Denmark (1518–19); escaped and returned to Dalarna province; sought by Christian (1520), who beheaded many Swedish nobles, among them his father and brother-in-law; with aid from Lübeck, led successful revolt (1521–23) against Danes; elected king (1523), first of house of Vasa. Supported establishment of state Lutheranism; acquired vast holdings by confiscation and taxation, establishing power of monarchy and house of Vasa; had throne declared hereditary (1544); established national standing army, Swedish navy.

Gustavus II Adolph \ˈäd-ˌȯlf\ *or* **Adol·phus** \ə-ˈdäl-fəs, -ˈdȯl-\. 1594–1632. King (1611–32). Son of Charles IX and grandson of Gustav Vasa. Inherited domestic troubles and wars with Denmark, Poland, and Russia; supported by his chancellor, Count Oxenstierna, changed policy of repressing nobility and sought cooperation of all classes; reorganized internal government and instituted major reforms; fostered education; won back districts in southern Sweden from Denmark (1611–13); victorious in war with Russia (1613–17) at peace of Stolbova; fought long defensive war (1621–29) against Sigismund of Poland, who claimed throne of Sweden. Led by religious interest and fear of Habsburg domination to support Protestant cause in Thirty Years' War; showed brilliant generalship in devising and directing tactical innovations; secured aid of France against Holy Roman Empire (1631); left Oxenstierna in control in Sweden; defeated Tilly at Breitenfield (1631) and again at the Lech (1632); in march toward Vienna, confronted by Wallenstein, whom Emperor Ferdinand II had reinstated, at Lützen (1632); won the battle, but mortally wounded.

Gustav III. 1746–1792. King (1771–92). Son of Adolph Frederick; became king when royal power was low and party strife intense; arrested council in a body (1772); regained power and introduced many enlightened reforms; waged unpopular war against Russia (1788–90); received new powers from Diet (1789); assassinated by J. J. Anckarström (*q.v.*), one of a conspiracy of nobles. Author of dramatic works and poems of merit.

Gustav IV Adolph. 1778–1837. King (1792–1809). Son of Gustav III; king under regency of his uncle Charles, Duke of Södermanland (1792–96); crowned (1800); actuated by hatred of Napoléon, entered (1805) into coalition against him; lost Swedish Pomerania and last German possessions; threatened by Denmark (1807); received help of English, but lost Finland to Russia (1808); dethroned (1809).

Gustav V. 1858–1950. King (1907–50), of the Bernadotte dynasty. Son of Oscar II; m. (1881) Victoria, daughter of Frederick William Louis, Grand Duke of Baden; lieutenant general (1892); favored Allies in World Wars I and II but kept Sweden neutral; reigned as popular constitutional monarch.

Gustav VI. 1882–1973. King (1950–73). Son of Gustav V; m. 1st (1905) Princess Margaret of Great Britain (1882–1920), daughter of Duke of Connaught, 2d (1923) Princess Louise of Battenberg (1889–1965). Entered army (1902); general (1932); noted amateur archaeologist; last Swedish monarch with real political power, following constitutional reforms (1971).

Gus·ton \ˈgəs-tən\, Philip. 1913–1980. American painter, b. Montreal, Que. Employed in Federal Art Project (1935–40); taught at various universities. With Pollock, de Kooning, Kline, etc., developed school of Abstract Expressionism in 1950s; works characterized by brushwork, muted colors tending later to sombre. Well known works included series of "White Paintings" as *Dial* (1956), *The Clock* (1957), *The Tale* (1961).

Gu·ten·berg \ˈgüt-ᵊn-ˌbərg, ˈgu̇t-\, Beno. 1889–1960. American seismologist, b. Darmstadt, Germany. Professor, Frankfurt (1926–30); to U.S. (1930); professor, Calif. Inst. of Technology (1930–57); known for studies of earthquake waves and energies.

Gu·ten·berg \ˈgü-tən-ˌberk; *Angl* ˈgüt-ᵊn-ˌbərg, ˈgu̇t-\, Johannes. *Orig.* Johannes Gens·fleisch zur La·den \ˈgens-ˌflīsh-tsu̇r-ˈläd-ən\. between 1390 and 1400–1468. German inventor. Assumed alternative family name from an estate; possibly a goldsmith, also a gem cutter. Began experiments in printing before 1438; invented printing by movable type, including use of molds and type-metal, special press, and oil-based inks; settled in Mainz (c.1446) and formed partnership with a goldsmith, Johann Fust, of that city to exploit his invention; Fust's demand for repayment of money advanced (1455) caused a settlement whereby Gutenberg abandoned his claims to his invention and surrendered his stock including type and work to date on the famed 42-line Bible, to Fust, who continued the business, printing Gutenberg's Psalter (1457) with help from Peter Schöffer. Aided later by one Conrad Humery, Gutenberg again established himself in the printing business; printed works attributed, not unanimously, to him include indulgences, school grammars, a *Missale speciale constantiense,* and a *Catholicon* (1460). Archbishop Adolph of Nassau, Elector of Mainz, gave recognition to his works (1465) by presenting him with a benefice yielding him an income and various privileges.

Guth·rie \'gəth-rē\, Thomas. 1803–1873. Scottish clergyman and philanthropist. Noted orator and fund-raiser for Free Church, ragged schools, compulsory education, temperance. Author of *Plea for Ragged Schools* (1847).

Guthrie, Thomas Anstey. *Pseudonym* F. An·stey \'an-stē\. 1856–1934. English novelist. On staff of *Punch* (from 1887). Author of *Vice Versa* (1882), *Brass Bottle* (1900), *Only Toys!* (1903), *In Brief Authority* (1915), etc., and of plays.

Guthrie, Tyrone, *in full* William Tyrone. 1900–1971. British theatrical director. Actor and assistant manager, Oxford Repertory Co. (1923); director, Scottish National Theatre (1926–27), Festival Theatre, Cambridge (1929–30); made reputation as creative director of modern drama with *The Anatomist* (1931), *Six Characters in Search of an Author* (1932); director, Shakespeare Repertory Co. (1933–34, 1936–45); manager, Old Vic and Sadler's Well theaters (1939–45); noted also as director of operas as *Peter Grimes* (1946), *Carmen* (1949); produced own play *Top of the Ladder* (1950). Author of *Theatre Prospect* (1932), *A Life in the Theatre* (1960).

Guthrie, Woodrow Wilson, *called* Woody. 1912–1967. American folksinger and composer, b. Okemah, Okla. Traveled widely, often in support of labor unions and populist causes. Composed over 1000 songs, including "So Long (It's Been Good to Know Yuh)," "Union Maid," "Hard Traveling," "This Land Is Your Land."

Guth·rum \'gu̇th-ru̇m\. *Also* God·rum \'go̅th-ru̇m\ *or* Gut·horm *or* Gut·torm \'gu̇t-ȯrm\. d. 890. Danish king of East Anglia. Led large Danish invasion of Anglo-Saxon England (878); defeated by Alfred at Edington in Wiltshire (878); adopted Christianity (878); reigned in peace (880–890).

Gutiérrez, Antonio García. See Antonio GARCÍA GUTIÉRREZ.

Gu·tiér·rez Ná·je·ra \gü-'tyer-rā-'snä-kā-rä\, Manuel. 1859–1895. Mexican writer. Contributor of influential articles and prose sketches to *La Iberia* (from 1872); founded *Revista Azul* (1894) to promote modernist poetry. Author of modernist verse, tales and sketches collected as *Cuentos frágiles* (1883), *Cuentos de color de humo* (1898).

Gu·tiér·rez So·la·na \gü-'tyer-rāth-sō-'lä-nä\, José. 1886–1947. Spanish painter. Influenced by Goya, created sombre, energetic pictures often depicting scenes of grief or horror or seemingly banal everyday life; notable works included *La vuelta de la pesca, La tertulia de Pombo, Las vitrinas, Las coristas, La reunión en la botica, Los ermitaños, La procesión de la muerte.* Also author of sharply satirical sketches in *Madrid, escenas y costumbres* (1912, 1918).

Guttorm. See GUTHRUM.

Gutz·kow \'gu̇t-skō\, Karl Ferdinand. 1811–1878. German journalist, novelist, and playwright. Emerged as a leader of Young Germany movement with satirical skeptical novels *Maha Guru, Geschichte eines Gottes* (1833) and *Wally, die Zweiflerin* (1835); imprisoned briefly. Literary adviser to court theater, Dresden (1846–49). Others of his novels were *Die Ritter vom Geiste* (regarded as beginning the modern German social novel; 9 vols., 1850–51), *Der Zauberer von Rom* (9 vols., 1858–61), *Hohenschwangau* (1867–69). Among his plays were *Richard Savage* (1839), *Zopf und Schwert* (1844), *Das Urbild des Tartüffe* (1844), *Uriel Acosta* (1846), *Der Königsleutnant* (1849).

Gütz·laff \'gu̇et-släf\, Karl Friedrich August. 1803–1851. German missionary. Lutheran missionary in China (from 1831); organized (1847) society of Chinese Christian teachers who evangelized in 12 of 18 provinces of China; translated Bible into Chinese. Author of *Journal of Three Voyages Along the Coast of China* (1834).

Guy \'gē\ of Dam·pierre \däⁿ-pyer\. *Fr.* Gui \gē\. 1225–1305. Count of Flanders. Succeeded to rule of Flanders (1278); engaged in long struggle to maintain Flemish independence of France; captured by Philip IV (1300), died in captivity.

Guy of Spo·le·to \spō-'lā-tō\. d. 894. Holy Roman emperor (891–894) and king of Italy (889–894). Duke of Spoleto (from 882); rebelled against Emperor Charles the Fat (883–885); proposed as king of France by Archbishop Fulk of Reims (887) but blocked by Count Odo of Paris; defeated Berengar and took throne of Italy (889); forced Pope Stephen V to crown him emperor (891); made son Lambert co-emperor (892).

Guy, Thomas. 1644 or 1645–1724. English bookdealer and philanthropist. One of Oxford U. printers (1769–92); M.P. (1695–1707). Founder of Guy's Hospital, London (1722).

Guy de Chau·liac \gē-də-shōl-yák\. *Ital.* Gui·do de Cau·lia·co \'gwē-dō-dā-kau̇l-'yä-kō\. c.1300–1368. French physician. Physician to popes Clement VI, Innocent VI, Urban V at Avignon. Author of *Inventorium sive collectorium in parte chirurgiciali medicine,* known as *Chirurgia magna* (1363), long a standard text on surgery.

Guy de Lu·si·gnan \'gē-də-lu̅e̅-zēn-yäⁿ\. *Fr.* Gui. 1129–1194. King of Jerusalem (1186–87) and of Cyprus (1192–94). Member of Lusignan family (*q.v.*); brother of Amalric II; m.(1180; d.1190) Sibylla, daughter of Amalric I, King of Jerusalem; succeeded Baldwin V (1186); was defeated (1187) and taken prisoner by Saladin; released (1188) on renouncing his claim to throne; laid siege to Acre (1189); supported by Richard I of England; in exchange for his claim to throne of Jerusalem was granted Cyprus by Richard I (1192).

Guy·ne·mer \gēn-mer\, Georges-Marie. 1894–1917. French military aviator. In World War I, was credited with destruction of 53 enemy planes; first and most celebrated of French aces.

Guy·on \gwʸē-yōⁿ\, Jeanne-Marie de la Motte \də-lá-mȯt\, *nee* Bou·vier \bü-vyā\. *Known as* Mme. Guyon du Chesnoy \du̅e̅-shen-wä\. 1648–1717. French mystic. m. Jacques de la Motte Guyon (1664; d. 1676); preached and practiced quietism; introduced to French court (1688); influenced Abbé de Fénelon, who defended her at Issy (1695); imprisoned (1695–1703), later banished to Blois. Author of *Moyen court et très facile de faire oraison* (1685).

Guy·on \'gī-ən\, Richard Debaufre. 1803–1856. English soldier of fortune. Distinguished himself in command of Hungarian forces at battles of Tyrnau and Schwechat (1848). Joined Turkish service; appointed by the sultan lieutenant general (1852) with title Kurshid Pasha; served against Russians in Anatolia (1853–55).

Guy·ot \'gē-()(y)ō\, Arnold Henry. 1807–1884. American geographer and geologist, b. Boudevilliers, Switzerland. Professor, Neuchâtel (1839–48); with Agassiz studied glaciers of Switzerland; to U.S. (1848); professor, Princeton (1854–84); influential lecturer on geological education, author of pedagogic materials; helped establish system of meteorological observatories that led to founding of U.S. Weather Bureau; developed topographical maps of Catskill and Appalachian mountains. Author of *Earth and Man* (1849), *Creation* (1884), etc.

Guys \'gœis, *Fr* gwʸē(s), *Angl* 'gȯis\, Constantin, *in full* Ernest-Adolphe-Hyacinthe-Constantin. 1802–1892. French illustrator, b. Holland. Correspondent for *Illustrated London News* during Crimean War; settled in Paris (c.1865) and sketched the life and manners of the Second Empire.

Guy·ton de Mor·veau \gē-tōⁿ-də-mȯr-vō\, Louis-Bernard. Baron. 1737–1816. French chemist. Member of Parlement of Burgundy (1762–82). Published *Digressions académiques* setting forth his ideas on phlogiston and crystallization (1772); collaborated with Lavoisier, Berthollet, and Fourcroy in devising system of chemical nomenclature (1787).

Gü·yük \gü-'yük\. *Also spelled* Ku·yuk \kü-\. 1206–1248. Mongol leader. Grandson of Genghis Khan; son and successor (1246) of Ögödei as great khan; supporter of Nestorianism.

Guzmán, Alonso Pérez de. See PÉREZ DE GUZMÁN.

Guzmán, Jacobo Arbenz. See ARBENZ GUZMÁN.

Guz·mán Blan·co \güs-'män-'bläŋ-kō\, Antonio. 1829–1899. Venezuelan soldier and politician. Vice president of Venezuela (1863–68); following overthrow of Falcón (1868), led successful revolution of Regeneración movement; de facto dictator (1870–89) and constitutional president part of the time; fostered education, public works, economic growth; diminished power of church; ousted in coup d'état (1889), exile in Paris.

Guz·mán y Pi·men·tal \güth-'män-ē-pē-män-'täl\, Gaspar de. Conde-duque de Oli·va·res \ō-lē-'bä-räs\. 1587–1645. Spanish politician. Prime minister to Philip IV (1621–43); attempted to unify Spanish kingdoms into a nation; introduced unsuccessful economic reforms; renewed war with Netherlands (1621); caused Spain to enter Thirty Years' War against France (1636); levied taxes that stirred Catalonia and Portugal to revolt (1640–43); dismissed and exiled through influence of queen.

Gwalch·mai ap Mei·lyr \'gwälk-ˌmī-äp-'mī-lir\. c.1140–1180. Welsh poet. Court poet to Owain Gwynedd; extant works include eulogies to Owain and to Madog ap Maredudd and *Gorhoffedd Gwalchmai.*

Gwilym, Dafydd ap. See DAFYDD.

Gwin·nett \gwin-'et\, Button. c.1735–1777. American Revolutionary leader, b. Gloucester, England. To America (before 1765); resident, Savannah, Ga.; member, Continental Congress (1776, 1777); a signer of Declaration of Independence. President of State of Georgia (1777). Best known for rarity and consequent high value of his autograph.

Gwyn *or* **Gwynn** *or* **Gwynne** \'gwin\, Eleanor, *known as* Nell. 1650–1687. English actress. Debut at king's theater (1665); as leading comedienne (1666–69), excelled in gay and sprightly roles; became mistress of Charles II (1667); retained affection of the king until his death; bore him two sons,

Charles Beauclerk (1670–1726, later duke of St. Albans) and James, Lord Beauclerk (1671–79).

Gwynn \'gwin\, Stephen Lucius. 1864–1950. Irish novelist and poet. London journalist (1896–1904); Irish M.P. (1906–18); member of Irish Convention (1917–18). His many works included *The Decay of Sensibility* (1900), *The Queen's Chronicler* (verse, 1901), *The Fair Hills of Ireland* (1906), *Duffer's Luck* (1924), *Irish Literature and Drama* (1936), *Fond Opinions* (essays, 1938).

Gwynne-Vaughan \'gwin-'vȯn\, Dame Helen Charlotte Isabella, *nee* Fra•ser \'frā-zər\. 1879–1967. English botanist. m. D. T. Gwynne-Vaughan (1911; d. 1915). Head of department of botany, Birkbeck Coll., London (1909–17, 1921–39, 1941–44). Organizer (1917) and chief controller, Women's Army Auxiliary Corps (WAAC) in France (1917–18); commandant, Women's Royal Air Force (1918–19); director (1939–41), Women's Auxiliary Territorial Service (WATS).

Gy•ges \'jī-ˌjēz, 'gī-\. d. c.648 B.C. King of Lydia (c.680–c.648 B.C.). Gained throne by killing King Candaules; founder of Mermnad dynasty; menaced by Cimmerians; aided by Ashurbanipal; made war upon Greek Ionian cities; defeated and slain by Cimmerians.

Gy•lip•pus \jə-'lip-əs\. 5th century B.C. Spartan general. Sent to aid in defense of Syracuse (414–413 B.C.); defeated Athenians under Demosthenes and Nicias. Later, embezzled money entrusted to him by Lysander and fled into exile.

Gyl•len•borg \'yu̅e̅l-ən-ˌbȯrʸ\, Carl. Count. 1679–1746. Swedish politician. President of the chancellery (1739); his policies, esp. an alliance with Turkey (1739), led to war with Russia (1741–43) wherein Sweden lost the province of Viborg.

Gyllenborg, Gustaf Fredrik. Count. 1731–1808. Swedish poet. Nephew of Count Carl Gyllenborg. Author of satirical and pessimistic verse; best known poems included "Verldsföraktaren," "Menniskjans Elände"; verse published as *Vitterhetsarbeten af Creutz och Gyllenborg* (1795).

Gyl•len•stier•na \'yu̅e̅l-ən-ˌsher-nȧ\, Johan. Count. 1636–1680. Swedish politician. Entered Riksdag (1660), president (1668); councilor of state; chief counselor to the young King Charles XI; after fall of De la Gardie (1675), principal power in government; at peace congress of Lund (1679), negotiated an alliance with Denmark.

Gyön•gyö•si \'dyœn-dyœsh-ē\, István. 1620–1704. Hungarian poet. Author of epics and epithalamia, as *Murányi Venus* (1664), *Rózsa-Koszorú* (1690), *Kemény-Janos* (1693), *Cupidó* (1659), and *Chariklia* (1700).

György Rákóczi. See RÁKÓCZI.

Gyp. See Sibylle de RIQUETI DE MIRABEAU.

Gy•ro•wetz \'gē-rō-ˌvets\, Adalbert. 1763–1850. Bohemian composer. To Vienna (1784), where he remained except for a period in London (1789–92); composer and conductor of Vienna Court Theater (1804–31). Composed operas as *Selico* (1804), *Agnes Sorel* (1806), *Der Augenarzt* (1811), *Robert* (1815), *Hans Sachs* (1834); some 40 symphonies, some misattributed to Haydn, chamber works, vocal music including a set of 6 Czech songs.

Gyu•lai \'dyu̇l-ȯi\, Franz. Count von Ma•ros-Né•meth und Ná•das•ka \fōn-'mä-rȯsh-'nā-met-u̇nt-'näd-äsh-kä\. 1798–1868. Hungarian soldier. Major general (1846) and commandant in Trieste; at outbreak of revolution (1848), assumed command of Austrian naval vessels in the Adriatic and maintained strict coast defense; minister of war (1849); commander in chief of Austrian army in war with French and Sardinians (1859); retired after defeat in battle of Magenta.

H

Haa·kon \'hä-kȯn\. Name of eight rulers of Norway, seven of them numbered as kings:

Haakon I. *Called* the Good. d. c.961. King (935–c.960). Youngest son of Harold I Fairhair; reared at court of Aethelstan in England; returned to Norway and deposed half-brother Erik Blódøx (935); brought Christian missionaries from England and built churches; killed in battle with Erik's sons including Harold II Graycloak.

Haakon. *Called* the Great. d. 995. Chief ruler of Norway (c.970–995). Son of jarl of Lade; exiled to Denmark after murder of his father by Harold II Graycloak; returned and with aid of Harold Bluetooth overthrew Harold II (c.970); ruled west of Norway; opposed Harold Bluetooth's attempt to christianize Norway.

Haakon II. *Called* the Broad-Shouldered. c.1147–1162. King (1157–62). On death of uncle, King Eystein (1157), proclaimed king by Eystein's partisans in opposition to rival Ingi I; sole ruler on death of Ingi (1161); defeated and killed by forces of usurper Magnus Erlingsson.

Haakon III. d. 1204. King (1202–04). Illegitimate son of King Sverre Sigurdsson, whom he succeeded; attempted to reconcile church and crown.

Haakon IV Haa·kons·son \'hä-kȯns-ˌsȯn\. *Called* the Old. 1204–1263. King (1217–63). Illegitimate posthumous son of Haakon III; reared at court of Ingi II; consolidated authority of crown, improved administration, gained new wealth for crown; made commercial treaty with Henry III of England (1217), earliest such treaty by either nation; crowned by papal legate (1247); gained sovereignty over Iceland and Greenland (1261–62); built Haakonshallen palace in Bergen; patron of arts; died on expedition to defend Hebrides and Isle of Man from Scottish invasion.

Haakon V Mag·nus·son \'män-yu̇s-ˌsȯn\. 1270–1319. King (1299–1319). Son of Magnus VI Lawmender; succeeded elder brother Erik II Magnusson; attempted to curb power of nobles and clergy; pursued policy hostile to England while allowing Hanseatic merchants to gain great power; fought wars with Denmark and Sweden; revised law of succession to allow succession of Magnus VII Eriksson, son of daughter Ingeborg.

Haakon VI. 1340–1380. King (1355–80). Younger son of Magnus VII Eriksson; named successor in Norway (1343); intervened in Swedish civil war on side of father against nobles led by brother Erik (1361–62); joint king of Sweden with father (1362–64); m. (1363) Margaret, daughter of King Valdemar IV of Denmark; again intervened on behalf of father (1364) but defeated; rescued father from captivity (1371); conceded extensive trading rights to Hanseatic League (1376); secured succession of son to Danish throne (as Olaf II) and Norwegian throne (as Olaf V).

Haakon VII. *Orig.* Prince Charles of Denmark. 1872–1957. King (1905–57). Son of Frederick VIII of Denmark; m. (1896) Princess Maud, daughter of Edward VII of England; offered crown of Norway on dissolution of Swedish-Norwegian union (1905); ratified by national plebiscite; in exile in England (1940–45); heartened resistance to German occupation by refusal to abdicate.

Haas \'häs\, Joseph. 1879–1960. German composer. Teacher (1921–50), president (1945–50), Akademie der Tonkunst, Munich. Composed operas as *Tobias Wunderlich* (1937), folk oratorios, 6 masses, lieder, piano pieces, etc.

Haa·se \'hä-zə\, Hugo. 1863–1919. German politician. Succeeded Bebel as president, German Social Democratic party; member of Reichstag (1897–1906, 1912–18); organized (1917) and led Independent Social Democratic party, hostile to the government; spread propaganda credited with inspiring the naval mutiny (Aug. 1918); member of ruling Council of People's Representatives (Nov.–Dec. 1918); assassinated.

Haast \'häst\, Sir John Francis Julius von. 1824–1887. British geologist and explorer, b. Germany. To New Zealand (1858); discovered coal and gold deposits (1859); professor of geology, New Zealand U., and founder of Canterbury Museum (1866).

Há·ba \'hä-bä\, Alois. 1893–1972. Czech composer. Taught at Prague Conservatory (1923–51); pioneer in microtonal music; compositions noted also for use of Moravian folk themes and harmonies; designed microtonal instruments as pianos, harmoniums, clarinets, trumpets. Works included operas *Matka* (1927–29), *Přijd Království Tvé* (1932–42); 16 string quartets and other chamber music; orchestral suite *Mládí* (1913), *Valašská* suite (1951–52); much piano and vocal music.

Ha·bak·kuk \hə-'bak-ək, 'hab-ə-ˌku̇k\. 7th? century B.C. Hebrew prophet. Author of biblical book of Habakkuk.

Habbema, Koos. See Herman HEIJERMANS.

Ha·be·neck \äb-nek\, François-Antoine. 1781–1849. French conductor. Violinist (1804–17), principal violin (1817–21), director (1821–24), chief musical director (1824–46) of Paris Opéra; raised standards of Opéra orchestra; taught at Paris Conservatoire (1808–16, 1825–48); introduced music of Beethoven into France; organized Société des Concerts du Conservatoire (1828).

Ha·ber \'häb-ər\, Fritz. 1868–1934. German chemist. Professor, Karlsruhe (1898); director, Kaiser-Wilhelm Inst. for Physical Chemistry, Berlin (1911–33). Worked in electrochemistry and on thermodynamic gas reactions; produced ammonia synthetically (1908–09); with Carl Bosch, invented Haber-Bosch process for industrial production of ammonia from atmospheric nitrogen; during World War I helped develop poison gas for army; attempted to extract gold from seawater. Awarded 1918 Nobel prize for chemistry for synthesis of ammonia.

Ha·berl \'häb-ərl\, Franz Xaver. 1840–1910. German clergyman and musician. Kapellmeister, Passau cathedral (1862–67); choirmaster (1871–82) at Regensburg, where he founded (1874) school of ecclesiastical music. Completed (1879–94) volumes 10–33 of complete edition of Palestrina's works (begun 1862); began edition of Lasso's works (1894–1927, completed by A. Sandberger). Author of *Magister choralis* (1864) on Gregorian chant, etc.

Ha·ber·landt \'häb-ər-ˌlänt\, Gottlieb. 1854–1945. Austrian botanist. Professor, Graz (1888–1910), Berlin (1910–23); pioneer in physiological approach to plant anatomy and in study of plant tissue cultures. Author of *Physiologische Pflanzenanatomie* (1884).

Hä·ber·lin \'heb-ər-ˌlēn\, Paul. 1878–1960. Swiss philosopher. Professor, Bern (1914–22) and Basel (from 1922). Author of *Wissenschaft und Philosophie* (1910–12), *Der Leib und die Seele* (1923), *Der Charakter* (1925), *Das Gute* (1926), *Das Wunderbare* (1930), *Ethik im Grundriss* (1946), *Logik im Grundriss* (1947), and pedagogical works.

Ḥa·bīb·ol·lāh Khān \hə-'bē-bu̇l-'lä-'k̲än\. 1872–1919. Amīr of Afghanistan (1901–19). Son of ʿAbdor Raḥmān; maintained friendly relations with British in India; kept kingdom neutral in Anglo–Russian affairs and during World War I; assassinated.

Hab·ing·ton \'hab-iŋ-tən\, William. 1605–1654. English poet. Author of love poems *Castara* (1634) and tragicomedy *The Queene of Arragon* (1640).

Habs·burg \'häps-ˌbu̇rk, *Angl* 'haps-ˌbərg\. German noble, later royal, house that supplied rulers to Austria, Germany, the Holy Roman Empire, Hungary and Bohemia, Spain, and other states. House took its name from castle of Habsburg, or Habichtsburg, i.e. Hawk's Castle, on the Aar River in present Switzerland, built by Werner, bishop of Strasbourg, and his brother Count Radbot. Radbot's son ¶Werner I (d. 1096) was first to bear title count of Habsburg. His descendant Count Rudolf IV was elected (1273) king of Germany as Rudolf I (*q.v.*). Ruling Habsburgs included the following:

GERMANY: Rudolph I, Albert I, Frederick III, Albert II; Holy Roman emperors from Frederick III through Charles VI (1440–1740), and thereafter (to 1806) those of the Habsburg-Lorraine line (see below).

AUSTRIA: Generally under rule of German kings or sons, later of emperors (1282–1918).

HOLY ROMAN EMPIRE: Rudolf I, Frederick III, Maximilian I, Charles V, Ferdinand I, Maximilian II, Rudolf II, Matthias, Ferdinand II, Ferdinand III,

Leopold I, Joseph I, Charles VI, Charles VII, followed by Habsburg-Lorraine line (see below).

HUNGARY AND BOHEMIA: Ruled by Holy Roman or Austrian emperors as separate crowns (1526–1918).

SPAIN: Philip I (king of Castile), Charles I (Emperor Charles V), Philip II, Philip III, Philip IV, Charles II.

Habsburg-Lor·raine \-lȯ-'ren, *Angl* -lō-'rān\. Direct male succession of Habsburg emperors ended with death of Charles VI (1740); his daughter Maria Theresa m. (1736) Francis Stephen, Duke of Lorraine, who was recognized (1745) as Emperor Francis I; followed by Joseph II, Leopold II, Francis II (to 1806); Francis II became Emperor Francis I of Austria (1804), followed by Ferdinand I, Francis Joseph, Charles I.

Há·cha \'hä-k̲ȧ\, Emil. 1872–1945. Czech jurist and politician. Second president (1919–25), first president (1925–38) of high court of Czechoslovakia. Third president of Czechoslovakia (1938–39); president of the German protectorate of Bohemia and Moravia (1939–45); died in jail awaiting trial as war criminal.

Ha·chette \ȧ-shet\, Louis-Christophe-François. 1800–1864. French editor and publisher. Founder of publishing house Hachette et Cie. (1826).

Hack·en·schmidt \'häk-ən-ˌshmit, *Angl* 'hak-\, George. 1877–1968. Estonian wrestler. World amateur Greco-Roman wrestling champion (1898–1900); undefeated as professional freestyle wrestler (1900–08), finally beaten by Frank Gotch; later naturalized French citizen and (1950) British subject.

Hack·ert \'häk-ərt\, Jacob Philipp. 1737–1807. German painter. Court painter in Naples (1786); known for landscapes, redute, etc.; friend of Goethe, who wrote his biography (1811).

Hack·ett \'hak-ət\, James Henry. 1800–1871. American actor, b. New York City. Debut (1826); succeeded as character impersonator; chief roles included Falstaff, Rip Van Winkle, Nimrod Wildfire, Melodious Migrate. His son ¶James Keteltas (1869–1926), b. Wolfe Island, Ont., was also an actor; m. Mary Mannering (1897; div. 1910); member of Frohman's Lyceum stock company (1895–98); excelled in romantic hero roles, as in *Prisoner of Zenda, Rupert of Hentzau, The Princess and the Butterfly, The Fortunes of the King,* etc.

Ha·da·mard \ȧ-dȧ-mȧr\, Jacques-Salomon. 1865–1963. French mathematician. Professor, Collège de France (1897–1935), École Polytechnique (1912–35), École Centrale des Arts et Manufactures (1920–35); known for contributions to theory of functions, functional analysis; proved (1896) important prime number theorem.

Haddington, Earl of. See Thomas Hamilton (1563–1637) under HAMILTON family.

Haddington, Viscount. See Sir John RAMSAY.

Haddock, Albert. See Alan Patrick HERBERT.

Had·don \'had-ᵊn\, Alfred Cort. 1855–1940. English anthropologist. Professor, Royal Coll. of Science, Dublin (1880–1901); lecturer (1900–09), reader (1909–25), Cambridge; considered a founder of modern observational anthropology. Author of *Evolution in Art* (1895), *Head-Hunters, Black, White and Brown* (1901), *Wanderings of Peoples* (1911), etc.

Ha·den \'hād-ᵊn\, Sir Francis Seymour. 1818–1910. English surgeon and etcher. Noted for such works as *Breaking Up of the Agamemnon, Thames Fishermen, Sub Tegmine, By-Road in Tipperary, Combe Bottom, Shere Mill Pond.*

Had·field \'had-ˌfēld\, Sir Robert Abbott. 1858–1940. English metallurgist. Entered father's steel firm and became its head (1888); inventor of manganese steel (1883), silicon steel, and other alloy steels. Author of *Metallurgy and Its Influence on Modern Progress* (1925).

Hā·dī, al- \al-'häd-ē\. 8th century. Islāmic caliph (785–786). Fourth caliph of ʿAbbāsid dynasty; by persecution of ʿAlid sect, provoked rebellion in Mecca; unable to secure succession to son, succeeded by Hārūn ar-Rashīd.

Ha·dik \'häd-ik\, Andreas. Count Hadik von Fu·tak \-fōn-'fü-ˌtäk\. 1710–1790. Austrian general. Distinguished himself in Seven Years' War; commanded Austrian army in campaign against Turkey (1789).

Had·ley \'had-lē\, Arthur Twining. 1856–1930. American economist and educator, b. New Haven, Conn. Teacher (from 1879), professor (1886–99), president (1899–1921), Yale. Author of *Railroad Transportation* (1885), *Economics* (1896), *Standards of Political Morality* (1907), *Conflict Between Liberty and Equality* (1925).

Hadley, George. 1685–1768. English physicist and meteorologist. Directed meteorological observations for Royal Society; formulated (1735) first accurate theory of trade winds and circulation pattern later named Hadley cell.

Hadley, Henry Kimball. 1871–1937. American composer, b. Somerville, Mass. Conductor, Seattle Symphony (1909–11), San Francisco Symphony (1911–15), Manhattan Symphony in New York (1929–32); associate conductor, N.Y. Philharmonic (1920–27). Composed Romantic works including operas *Azora* (1917), *Bianca* (1918), *Cleopatra's Night* (1920); symphonies including *The Four Seasons* (1902); symphonic suites and poems, chamber music, choral works, songs.

Hadley, John. 1682–1744. English mathematician and inventor. Built first serviceable reflecting telescope (1719–20); invented (1731, simultaneously with Thomas Godfrey, *q.v.*) improved quadrant known as Hadley's quadrant.

Had·ow \'had-(ˌ)ō\, Sir William Henry. 1859–1937. English writer on music. Compiler, with G.E. Hadow, of *Oxford Treasury of English Literature* (1906–08); author of *Studies in Modern Music* (1892–95) and *English Music* (1931); editor of *Oxford History of Music* (1901–06).

Hadrian. See also ADRIAN.

Ha·dri·an \'hā-drē-ən\. *Lat.* Publius Aelius Ha·dri·a·nus \ˌhā-drē-'ā-nəs\. 76–138 A.D. Roman emperor (117–138). Cousin of Trajan; m. (100) Sabina, grandniece of Trajan; accompanied Trajan on many of his expeditions; quaestor (101), tribune of the plebs (105), praetor (106), consul (108); adopted as successor by Trajan shortly before death (117). On becoming emperor, established the river Euphrates as eastern boundary of Roman empire; traveled throughout all parts of the empire (121–125); visited Britain (122) and caused construction of Hadrian's Wall from Solway Firth to mouth of Tyne; made second tour (128–?132), lingering in Athens; created Panhellenion league; avid promoter of hellenic culture; suppressed revolt of Jews under Bar Kokhba (132–135). Rebuilt and named Hadrianopolis (modern Adrianople) and erected many fine edifices in Rome, including Tivoli villa, the mausoleum (now Castel Sant'Angelo), temple to Venus and Roma, the Aelian bridge, etc.

Haeck·el \'hek-əl\, Ernst Heinrich Philipp August. 1834–1919. German biologist and philosopher. Professor of zoology, Jena (1865–1909); on scientific expeditions to the Canary Islands (1866–67), Red Sea (1873), Ceylon (1881–82), Java (1900–01), etc. First German advocate of Darwin's theory of evolution; formulated dictum "ontogeny recapitulates phylogeny"; first to draw up a genealogical tree relating all the various orders of animals; proposed that all nature is a unity, with life originating in crystals and evolving to man. Author of *Die Radiolarien* (1862), *Generelle Morphologie der Organismen* (1866), *Natürliche Schöpfungsgeschichte* (1868), *Anthropogenie oder Entwicklungsgeschichte des Menschen* (1874), *Monismus als Band zwischen Religion und Wissenschaft* (1892), *Systematische Phylogenie* (1894–96), *Welträtsel* (1899), etc.

Haetzer. See HETZER.

Ḥā·fez \'k̲ä-fez\. *More completely* Moḥammad Shams od-Dīn Ḥāfez. 1325 or 1326–1389 or 1390. Persian poet. Court poet to rulers of Shīrāz before and after a period out of favor (c.1368–88); adherent of Ṣūfism; perfected the *ghazal* form of lyric, and first to use it in panegyrics; master of simple musical language conveying levels of meaning; considered greatest of Persian lyric poets.

Haff·kine \'haf-kən\, Waldemar Mordecai Wolfe. 1860–1930. Russian bacteriologist. Librarian and assistant at Pasteur Inst., Paris (1889–93); discovered and in India used method of inoculation against cholera (1893–94), by which 45,000 persons were treated in 28 months; introduced into India a successful method of inoculation against plague (1897); became British subject (1899); again in India fighting epidemics (1902, 1907–15).

Hā·fiz-i Ab·rū \'hä-fē-zē-ab-'rü\. *In full* ʿAbd Allāh ibn Lutf Allāh ibn ʿAbd ar-Rashīd al-Bihdādīnī Hāfiz-i Abrū. d. 1430. Persian historian. Traveled widely, accompanying Timur on various campaigns; court historian in Herāt. Author of *Majmūʿa*, based on older works, and compendious history *Majmaʿ al-tavārīkh.*

Ḥā·fiẓ Ib·rā·hīm \'k̲ä-fē-zē-brä-'hēm\, Muḥammad. 1872–1932. Egyptian poet. Lawyer and army officer; director of literature at national library, Cairo (1911–31). Author of widely circulated anti-imperialist and nationalist verse.

Haf·sid \'haf-səd\ *or* **Haf·site** \-ˌsīt\. Name of Berber dynasty ruling in Tunis and eastern Algeria (c.1229–1574) until overthrown by Turks.

Haf·stein \'häv-ˌstān\, Hannes. 1861–1922. Icelandic politician and poet. Leader of home rule party in Iceland; first Icelander to serve as minister of state to Danish crown (1904–07, 1912–14). Author of lyric verse as *Ýmisleg ljóthmaeli* (1893), *Ljóthabók* (1916).

Ha·ge·dorn \'häg-ə-ˌdȯrn\, Friedrich von. 1708–1754. German poet. Author of light and graceful verse as *Fabeln und Erzählungen* (1738), *Oden und Lieder* (1742–52), *Moralische Gedichte* (1750), etc.

Hageladas. See AGELADAS.

Ha·gen \'häg-ən\, Gotthilf Heinrich Ludwig. 1797–1884. German engineer. Hydraulic engineer in Prussian state service; known for studies of laminar and turbulent flow and for discovery of Hagen-Poiseville law of laminar flow in circular pipes.

Hagen, Johann Georg. 1847–1930. Austrian astronomer. Entered Jesuit order; director, Georgetown U. observatory, Washington, D.C. (1888–1906), Vatican observatory, Rome (from 1906). Investigated and classified variable stars, publishing *Atlas Stellarum Variabilium* (1890–1908); also examined the dark nebulae and claimed to have observed dark interstellar matter, called Hagen's clouds.

Ha·gen \ˈhā-gən\, Walter Charles. 1892–1969. American golfer, b. Rochester, N.Y. Winner of British Open championship (1922, 1924, 1928, 1929), U.S. Open (1914, 1919), PGA tournament (1921, 1924, 1925, 1926, 1927); playing captain of U.S. Ryder Cup team (biennially 1927–37).

Ha·gen·beck \ˈhäg-ən-ˌbek\, Karl. 1844–1913. German animal trainer and circus director. Toured Europe and U.S. (from 1866) with exhibition of animals trained by friendship; established (1907) zoological garden near Hamburg, pioneering venture in open-air exhibit.

Hag·gai \ˈhag-ē-ˌī, ˈhag-ˌī\. 6th century B.C. Hebrew prophet. Presumed author of biblical book of *Haggai.*

Hag·gard \ˈhag-ərd\, Sir Henry Rider. 1856–1925. English novelist. Best known for romantic novels written against a South African background, as *King Solomon's Mines* (1885), *Allan Quatermain* (1887), *She* (1887), *Ayesha* (1905).

Hag·gin \ˈhag-ən\, James Ben Ali. 1827–1914. American businessman, b. Harrodsburg, Ky. In law partnership with Lloyd Tevis, Sacramento, Cal. (1850–99); partner with George Hearst in Anaconda Copper Co.; owned and developed huge ranch and farm acreage, San Joaquin and Sacramento valleys; noted horse breeder.

Ha·gi·wa·ra \hä-gē-wä-rä\ Sakutarō. 1886–1942. Japanese poet. Inaugurated new style in Japanese poetry through use of concrete, often harsh, imagery. Published collections *Tsuki ni hoeru* (1917), *Atarashiki yokujo* (1922).

ha-Gra. See ELIJAH BEN SOLOMON.

Hague \ˈhāg, ˈheg\, Frank. 1876–1956. American politician, b. Jersey City, N.J. Mayor of Jersey City (1917–47); member of Democratic National Committee (1922–52); head of a major Democratic political "machine."

Hahn \ˈhän\, Hermann. 1868–1945. German sculptor. Among his sculptures were the Liszt monument, Weimar (1902), Luther monument, Speyer (1905), Goethe monument, Chicago (1914), and portrait busts.

Hahn, Otto. 1879–1968. German chemist. Member (from 1912), director (1928–46), president (1946–60), Kaiser-Wilhelm Institute, subsequently the Max Planck Institute, Berlin; with Lise Meitner discovered (1917) protactinium; with Meitner and then Fritz Strassmann discovered (1938) nuclear fission. Awarded with Strassmann 1944 Nobel prize for chemistry; with Meitner and Strassmann 1966 Fermi award.

Hahn, Reynaldo. 1875–1947. Venezuelan composer. To Paris (1878); music critic for *Le Figaro* (from 1934); director of Paris Opéra (1945–47). Composer of song cycles as *Chansons grises* (1893), *D'une prison* (1899), *Études latines* (1900); operas as *L'Île du rêve* (1898), *La Carmélite* (1902), *Le Marchand de Venise* (1935); operettas as *Ciboulette* (1923), *Brummel* (1931); ballets as *Le Dieu bleu* (1912).

Hah·ne·mann \ˈhän-ə-ˌmän\, Samuel, *in full* Christian Friedrich Samuel. 1755–1843. German physician. While translating Cullen's *Materia medica* into German, noticed similarity between effects of quinine on a healthy person and the symptoms of malaria, for which it was the cure; announced homeopathic principle that a disease could be cured by a drug that would produce in a healthy person symptoms similar to those of disease (1796). Expounded homeopathic system in *Organon der rationellen Heilkunde* (1810), *Reine Arzneimittellehre* (1811).

Hahn-Hahn \ˈhän-ˈhän\, Ida von. Gräfin. *Nee* Hahn. 1805–1880. German writer. m. Graf Friedrich W.A. von Hahn (1826; soon separated). Adopted Roman Catholic faith (1850) and entered convent (1852). Author of lyric verse and novels including *Gräfin Faustine* (1841), *Aus der Gesellschaft* (1835–46).

Hai ben She·ri·ra \ˈhī-ben-shä-ˈrir-ä\. 939–1038. Talmudist. Last great *gaon,* or head, of Talmudic academy in Baghdad (998–1038). Author of nearly a thousand extant *responsa,* or authoritative pronouncements on Talmudic law.

Haidar Ali. See HYDER ALI.

Haig \ˈhāg, ˈheg\, Douglas. 1st Earl Haig. 1861–1928. British soldier. Engaged in Sudan (1898), Boer War (1899–1902), India (1903–06); major general (1904), lieutenant general (1910), general (1914), field marshal (1916). In World War I commanded 1st army (1914–15); commander in chief of British Expeditionary Force in France and Flanders (1915–19), devised controversial strategy of attrition (1916–17); criticized for heavy casualties in battles of Somme (1916), Ypres (1917). Commander in chief (1919–21) of the Home Forces in Great Britain. Created earl (1919).

Hailes, Lord. See David Dalrymple (1726–1792), under DALRYMPLE family.

Hai·le Se·las·sie \ˈhī-lə-sə-lä-ˈsē, *Angl* ˈhī-lē-sə-ˈlas-ē\. *Also known as* Ras (Prince) Ta·fa·ri \ˈräs-tə-fä-ˈrē\. *Orig.* Lij Tafari \ˈlēj-\. 1892–1975. Emperor of Ethiopia (1930–74). Governor of Harar province (1906–16) under Emperor Menelik II; elected regent and heir to Empress Zaudita (1916); assumed title of king (1928); succeeded Zaudita (1930) as Haile Selassie, *i.e.* Might of the Trinity; fostered education, modernization; driven from Ethiopia by Italian occupation (1936–41); lived in England; restored to throne (1941) after successful British campaign in East Africa; deposed (Sept. 1974).

Hailsham, 1st Viscount. See Douglas HOGG.

Haines \ˈhānz\, Jackson. 1840–1876. American dancer and iceskater, b. New York City. Trained as ballet dancer; adapted ballet techniques to figure skating; known as father of modern figure skating; U.S. men's champion (1865); to Europe, where he enjoyed success esp. in Vienna; founded or inspired many skating schools.

Hai·nisch \ˈhī-nəsh\, Michael Arthur Josef Jakob. 1858–1940. German economist and politician. First president of the Austrian Republic (1920–28); minister of commerce (1929–30).

Ḥaj·jāj, al- \al-ka-ˈjäj\. *In full* al-Hajjāj ibn Yūsuf ath-Thaqafī. 661–714. Arab ruler. General of Eastern caliphate during reigns of ʻAbd al-Malik (692–705) and al-Walīd (705–715); crushed rebellion in Mecca (692); governor of surrounding provinces; made governor of Iraq (694), put down revolt with great cruelty (703); promoted irrigation and agriculture; instrumental in consolidating power and efficiency of Umayyad dynasty.

Ḥājjī Khalīfa. See KĀTIB ÇELEBİ.

Ḥājj ʻUmar, al- \al-ˈkäj-ˈü-mär\. *Also known as* ʻUmar ibn Saʻid Tal \ˈü-mär-ˌib-ən-sä-ˈēd-ˈtäl\ *or* ʻUmar Tal. c.1797–1864. West African ruler. Member of Tukulor tribe of Senegal Valley; early gained reputation as Muslim mystic; m. daughter of amīr of Sokoto; named caliph for black Africa; gathered army of followers, conquered and forcefully converted several tribes of western Sudan; established empire of Masina (1848–97); defeated Fulani and captured Timbuktu (1863); defeated by Tuaregs, Fulani, Moors (1864).

Ḥa·kam, al- \al-ka-ˈkam\. Name of two Umayyad rulers of Córdoba:

Ḥakam I. 770–822. Amīr of Córdoba (796–822). Son of Hishām I.

Ḥakam II. d. 976. Caliph of Córdoba (961–976). Son of ʻAbd ar-Raḥman III; took title of al-Mustanṣir; defeated Norman attacks (966, 971); continued wars against Christian Spain, Fāṭimid dynasty in Morocco.

Hake \ˈhāk\, Edward. fl. 1579. English Puritan. Known for satire *Newes out of Powles Churcheyarde* (1567 or 1579), attacking corruption of judges, clergy, physicians, apothecaries, sumptuary laws, Sunday sports, etc.

Ḥā·kim, al- \al-ˈkä-kim\. *In full* Abū ʻAli al-Manṣūr al-Ḥākim bi-Amrih Allāh. 985–?1021. Fāṭimid caliph of Egypt (996–?1021). Reign marked by persecutions of Christians and Jews, often arbitrary laws; founded mosques, encouraged Shīʻī missionaries who proclaimed his divinity. Subsequently held divine by Druze religion.

Hak·luyt \ˈhak-ˌlüt\, Richard. c.1552–1616. English geographer. Lectured on geography at Oxford (from 1580); became publicist of exploration and colonization; promoter of Virginia Company, Northwest Passage Company. Author of *Divers voyages touching the discouerie of America* (1582), *Discourse on the Western Planting* (1584), *Principall Navigations, Voiages, and Discoveries of the English Nation* (1589; enlarged edition, 1598–1600).

Håkon. See HAAKON.

Ha·ku·in \hä-kü-ēn\. 1685–1768. Japanese religious, artist, and writer. Joined Rinzai Zen sect (1708); by personal humility, spirituality, poverty, attracted great following, thus reviving Zen Buddhism in Japan. Author of Zen tracts as *Keisō dokozui, Orate-gama, Hogo-roku, Yasen kanna;* noted also as artist and calligrapher.

Ḥalabī, al-. See IBN ABĪ ʻASRŪN.

Ḥa·la·bī, al- \al-ˌkal-ab-ˈē\. *More completely* Burhān ad-Dīn Ibrāhīm ibn Muḥammad ibn Ibrāhīm al-Ḥalabī. c.1460–1549. Islāmic jurist. Imam of mosque of Mehmed II, Istanbul. Author of theological works and of *Multaka al-abhur* (1517), major study of and source for Hanafi legal doctrines.

Hal·be \ˈhäl-bə\, Max. 1865–1944. German playwright and novelist. Author of plays *Jugend* (1893), *Mutter Erde* (1897), *Der Eroberer* (1899), *Der Strom* (1904); novels *Die Tat des Dietrich Stobäus* (1911), *Jo* (1917), *Die Friedeninsel* (1945).

Hal·dane \ˈhȯl-ˌdān\. Name of distinguished Scottish family including: James Alexander (1768–1851), clergyman; became (1799) first Congregational minister in Scotland. His brother ¶Robert (1764–1842), evangelist and writer; founded Society for Propagating the Gospel at Home (1797); carried on evangelistic work in Geneva and southern France (1816–19).

¶Richard Burdon Haldane (1856–1928), Viscount Haldane of Cloan \ˈklōn\; grandson of James A. Haldane; called to bar (1879); queen's counsel (1890); M.P. (1885–1911); secretary of state for war (1905–12); reorganized British army, instituted national (1904) and imperial (1909) general staffs, and formed the Territorial Force (1908); lord chancellor (1912–15, 1924). Created viscount (1911); head of Labour party opposition in House of Lords (1925–28). Author of *The Pathway to Reality* (1903), *The Reign of Relativity* (1921), *The Philosophy of Humanism* (1922), *Human Experience* (1926).

¶John Scott Haldane (1860–1936), brother of Richard B.; demonstrator and reader in medicine, Oxford (1887–1913); studied mechanics and physics of respiration, including studies of mining and industrial diseases caused by poor ventilation; discovered that regulation of breathing is determined by blood partial pressure of carbon dioxide in respiratory center of brain; discovered basis of toxicity of carbon monoxide; developed decompression technique to prevent caisson disease; served as director of a mining research laboratory (from 1912; affiliated with Birmingham U. from 1921). Author of *Causes of Death in Colliery Explosions* (1896), *Mechanism, Life and Personality* (1913), *Respiration* (1922), *Materialism* (1932), *The Philosophy of a Biologist* (1935), etc. ¶Elizabeth Sanderson Haldane (1862–1937), sister of Richard and John; promoted slum reconstruction, Edinburgh (from 1884); helped save Sadler's Wells Theatre, London; vice chairman of territorial nursing service; first woman justice of the peace in Scotland (1920). Author of *British Nurse in Peace and War* (1923), *George Eliot and her Times* (1927), *Mrs. Gaskell and her Friends* (1930), *From One Century to Another* (1937), etc.

¶John Burdon Sanderson Haldane (1892–1964), son of John Scott Haldane; reader, Cambridge (1922–32); professor of genetics, London U. (1933–37); professor of biometry, University Coll., London (1937–1957); emigrated and took Indian citizenship (1957). Noted as Marxist, researcher, popularizer of science. Author of *Possible Worlds* (1927), *Animal Biology* (with J. S. Huxley, 1927), *Science and Ethics* (1928), *Enzymes* (1930), *The Inequality of Man* (1932), *Causes of Evolution* (1933), *Fact and Faith* (1934), *Heredity and Politics* (1938), *The Marxist Philosophy and the Sciences* (1939), *Science and Everyday Life* (1939), *New Paths in Genetics* (1941), *Biochemistry of Genetics* (1954), etc.

Hal·de·man-Jul·ius \'hȯl-də-mən-'jül-yəs\, Emanuel. *Orig. surname* Julius. 1889–1951. American publisher and writer, b. Philadelphia. m. (1916) Marcet Haldeman (d. 1941), prefixed her family name to his own. Founder and head of Haldeman-Julius Publishing Co., publishers of popular ten-cent reprint series Little Blue Books (from 1919) and the journals *American Freeman, Agnostic,* and *Critic and Guide.* Author of *The Color of Life* (1920), *The Art of Reading* (1922), *An Agnostic Looks at Life* (1926), *Myths and Myth-Makers* (1927), *The Big American Parade* (1929), etc.

Hal·der \'häl-dər\, Franz. 1884–1972. German army officer. Quartermaster general (1938); colonel general, and chief of the German general staff (1938–42); dismissed for opposing Hitler's Russian strategy; in concentration camp (1944–45).

Hal·di·mand \'hȯl-də-mənd\, Sir Frederick. 1718–1791. British general, b. Switzerland. Entered British service in Royal American Regiment (1756); served at Ticonderoga (1758) and Oswego (1759), with Amherst's expedition against Montreal (1760); lieutenant governor of Trois Rivières (1762); commander in Florida (1767–73); commander of British army in North American at Boston (1773–74); governor and commander in chief in Quebec (1778–84).

Hale \'hā(ə)l\, Edward Everett. 1822–1909. American clergyman and author, b. Boston. Pastor, Church of the Unity, Worcester, Mass. (1846–56), South Congregational Church, Boston (1856–1901); chaplain, U.S. Senate (1903–09). Author of stories and novels as *If, Yes, and Perhaps* (1868, containing tale "Man Without a Country," orig. pub. 1863), *The Ingham Papers* (1869), *Ten Times One Is Ten* (1871), *In His Name* (1873); also *A New England Boyhood* (1893), *James Russell Lowell and His Friends* (1899), *Memories of a Hundred Years* (1902), etc.

Hale, George Ellery. 1868–1938. American astronomer, b. Chicago. Professor, U. of Chicago (1892–1904); organizer and director of Yerkes Observatory (1895–1904); organizer and director of Mount Wilson Observatory under Carnegie Institution of Washington (1904–23); began planning and fund-raising for Mount Palomar Observatory (opened 1948); performed important research work in solar and stellar spectroscopy; invented the spectroheliograph (1891); founded (1895) *Astrophysical Journal.* Author of *Ten Years' Work of a Mountain Observatory* (1915), *Beyond the Milky Way* (1926), *Signals from the Stars* (1931).

Hale, Horatio Emmons. 1817–1896. American anthropologist, b. Newport, N.H. Son of Sarah Josepha Hale; member of Wilkes naval exploring expedition (1838–42), studying languages of Polynesia and American Northwest; later made pioneering studies of Iroquoian languages and collected Iroquoian literature; influenced Franz Boas. Author of *Ethnology and Philology* (1846), *Iroquois Book of Rites* (1883), etc.

Hale, John Parker. 1806–1873. American politician, b. Rochester, N.H. Member, U.S. House of Representatives (1843–45); U.S. senator (1847–53), first antislavery man elected to the Senate; Free-Soil candidate for president (1852); again senator (1855–65). U.S. minister to Spain (1865–69).

Hale, Lucretia Peabody. 1820–1900. American writer, b. Boston. Sister of Edward Everett Hale; noted for two children's books, *The Peterkin Papers* (1880) and *The Last of the Peterkins* (1886).

Hale, Sir Matthew. 1609–1676. English jurist. Called to bar (1637); defended Archbishop Laud and other Royalists; justice of common pleas (1654–58); M. P. (1654–60); took leading part in reform of legal system; promoted Restoration; lord chief baron of exchequer (1660); lord chief justice of King's Bench (1671–76); renowned for integrity, sagacity; one of the greatest scholars of English common law. Author of *History of the Pleas of the Crown* (pub. 1736), etc.

Hale, Nathan. 1755–1776. American Revolutionary hero, b. Coventry, Conn. Taught school (1773–75); joined Continental army (1775); captain (1776). Volunteered for hazardous spy duty behind British lines on Long Island (1776); captured by British, hanged the following morning. His last words are said to have been, "I only regret that I have but one life to lose for my country."

Hale, Sarah Josepha, *nee* Bu·ell \'byü(-ə)l\. 1788–1879. American writer and editor, b. Newport, N.H. m. David Hale (1813; d. 1822). Editor, *Ladies' Magazine,* Boston (1828–37), *Godey's Lady's Book,* Philadelphia (1837–77). Author of *Northwood* (novel, 1827), *Poems for Our Children* (1830, containing "Mary Had a Little Lamb"), *Woman's Record, or Sketches of Distinguished Women from the Creation to the Present Day* (1853–76).

Há·lek \'häl-ek\, Vítězslav. 1835–1874. Czech poet. Best known as lyricist and founder (with Neruda) of modern school of Czech poetry. Author of *Večerní písně* (1859), *Děuče z Tater* (1871), *V přírodě* (1872–74), etc.

Hales \hā(ə)lz\, John. 1584–1656. English clergyman. Lecturer in Greek, Oxford (1612); canon of Windsor and chaplain to Laud (1639–42); in retirement during Commonwealth period. Author of anonymously published tract *Schism and Schismaticks* (1636), *Golden Remains* (pub. 1659).

Hales, Stephen. 1677–1761. English clergyman and physiologist. First measured transpiration, sap flow in plants; measured growth rates; investigated role of gases in plant metabolism; first to measure blood pressure, heart capacity; invented artificial ventilator for ships, prisons, etc. Author of *Vegetable Staticks* (1727), credited with inaugurating the science of plant physiology, *Haemastaticks* (1733).

ha-Levi, Isaac. See Profiat DURAN.

ha-Levi *or* **Halevi,** Judah. See JUDAH HA-LEVI.

Ha·lé·vy \à-lā-vē\, Fromental, *in full* Jacques-François-Fromental-Élie. *Orig.* Élie Lé·vy \lā-vē\. 1799–1862. French composer. Professor, Paris Conservatory (from 1827), had among his pupils Gounod and Bizet; director of singing, Théâtre-Italien (1826–29), Paris Opéra (1829–45). Composer of many operas, including *Clari* (1828), *La Juive* (1835), *L'Éclair* (1835), *La Reine de Chypre* (1841), *La Tempestà* (1850), *Le Juif errant* (1852), *La Magicienne* (1858).

Halévy, Ludovic. 1834–1908. French dramatist. Nephew of Fromental Halévy. In collaboration with Henri Meilhac wrote libretti for Offenbach's operas *La Belle Hélène* (1864), *Barbe-bleu* (1866), *La Vie parisienne* (1866), *Le Château à Toto* (1868), *La Périchole* (1868), *La Diva* (1869), *Les Brigands* (1869), etc., and for Bizet's *Carmen* (1875); wrote comedies *Fanny Lear* (1868), *Froufrou* (1869), *Tricoche et Cacolet* (1872), *La Boule* (1874); novels *Un mariage d'amour* (1881), *L'Abbeé Constantin* (1882). His son ¶Élie (1870–1937) was a historian. Author of *La Formation du radicalisme philosophique* (1901–04) and esp. *Histoire du peuple anglais au XIXe siècle* (1913–23).

Ha·ley \'hā-lē\, William John Clifton, *known as* Bill. 1925–1981. American musician, b. Highland Park, Mich. An originator of "rockabilly," precursor of "rock 'n roll" music; known for recordings "Crazy Man Crazy" (1953), "Rock Around the Clock" (1954), "Shake Rattle and Roll" (1954), etc. with band the Comets.

Hal·i·bur·ton \'hal-ə-ˌbərt-ᵊn\, Thomas Chandler. *Pseudonym* Sam Slick \'slik\. 1796–1865. Canadian jurist and humorist, b. Windsor, N.S. Judge of supreme court, Nova Scotia (1841–54); to England (1856); M.P. (1859–65). Created character of Sam Slick in newspaper serials, later in books *The Clockmaker, or Sayings and Doings of Samuel Slick of Slickville* (1836, 1838, 1840), *The Attaché, or Sam Slick in England* (1843–44), *Sam Slick's Wise Saws and Modern Instances* (1853), etc.; also wrote *The Old Judge, or Life in a Colony* (1843).

Ha·li·de Edib Adı·var \hä-lē-'dā-ed-'ēb-äd-ə-'vär\. 1883–1964. Turkish reformer and writer. Active in nationalist movement; labored for educational reforms, women's rights, etc.; in political exile (1925–38); professor, Istanbul (from 1939); member of parliament (1950–54). Author of novels *Yeni Turan* (1912), *Handan* (1912), *Ateşten Gömlek* (1922), *Zeyno'nun Oğlu* (1928), *Sinekli Bakkal* (1936); also *Turkey Faces West* (1930), etc.

Ha·lid Zi·ya Uşak·lig·il \hä-'lēd-zē-yä-ü-shäk-lē-'yēl\. 1865–1945. Turkish writer. First major exponent of novel in European manner in Turkish. Author of *Bir Muhtıranın Son Yaprakları* (1888), *Bir Olünün Defteri* (1889), *Mai ve Siyah* (1897), *Aşk-ı Memnu* (1900); stories collected as *Bir Yazın Tarihi* (1900), *Solgun Demet* (1901), *Bir Şür-i Hayâl* (1914), *Onu Beklerken* (1935), *Kadın Pençesi* (1939), etc.

Halifax. (1) Earls of. See Charles MONTAGU and Edward F. L. WOOD. (2) Marquis of. See Sir George SAVILE.

Halifax, John of. See Johannes de SACROBOSCO.

Ha·lil \hä-'lēl\ *or* **Kha·lil** \kä-'lēl\, Patrona. d. 1730. Turkish revolutionist. Led mob uprising (1730) following Turkish defeat by Persia, leading to replacement of Sultan Ahmed III by Mahmud I; only Turkish uprising not originating in army; assassinated.

Ha·lim Pa·şa \hä-'lēm-pä-'shä\, Said. 1863–1921. Ottoman politician. Grandson of Muḥammad 'Alī Pasha; foreign minister (1911–13); grand vizier (1913–16); signed treaty of alliance with Germany (1914); senator (1916–18); banished to Malta by British (1918); assassinated.

Hal·kett \'häl-kət, 'hal-; 'hak-ət\, Hugh. Baron von Halkett. 1783–1863. Hanoverian general, b. Scotland. Distinguished himself in British service at Copenhagen (1807), La Albuera (1811), Salamanca (1812), and during the Burgos retreat (1812); commanded two brigades of Hanoverian militia at Waterloo (1815).

Hall \'hȯl\, Abraham Oakey. 1826–1898. American politician, b. Albany, N.Y. District attorney, New York City (1855–58, 1862–68); joined Tammany Hall organization (1864); mayor of New York (1868–72) when Tweed Ring was looting the city; tried for corruption, but acquitted (1872).

Hall, Asaph. 1829–1907. American astronomer, b. Goshen, Conn. Obtained post at Harvard Observatory (1858); joined staff (1862), professor of mathematics (1863–91), U.S. Naval Observatory, Washington, D.C.; lectured at Harvard (1895–1901). Discovered (1877) the two satellites of planet Mars, which he named Deimos and Phobos.

Hall, Basil. 1788–1844. British naval officer and writer. Son of Sir James Hall; served in navy (1802–23); explored in Orient. Author of *Account of a Voyage of Discovery to the West Coast of Corea* (1818), *Extracts from a Journal Written on the Coasts of Chile, Peru and Mexico* (1824), *Travels in North America* (1829), etc.

Hall \'hal\, Carl Christian. 1812–1888. Danish politician. Leader of National Liberal party (from 1848); minister of public worship (1854–57, 1870–74); prime minister (1857–63) and foreign minister (1858–63); pursued policy leading to incorporation of Schleswig (1863) and thus war with Prussia (1863).

Hall \'hȯl\, Charles Francis. 1821–1871. American explorer, b. Rochester, N.H. Led expeditions to Arctic (1860–62, 1864–69, and 1871); on first expedition discovered remains of Martin Frobisher's expedition of 1578; on second expedition, learned from Eskimos fate of part of Franklin expedition. Author of *Arctic Researches, and Life among the Esquimaux* (1865).

Hall, Charles Martin. 1863–1914. American chemist and manufacturer. Invented (1886), simultaneously with Paul Héroult, electrolytic process of making aluminum inexpensively; with aid of Mellon interests, formed (1888) Pittsburgh Reduction Co., which developed into Aluminum Company of America; vice president (from 1890).

Hall, Chester Moor. 1703–1771. English scientist. Inventor of achromatic lens (1729); built achromatic telescope (1733).

Hall *or* **Halle** \'hȯl\, Edward. c.1498–1547. English historian. Author of *Union of the Noble and Illustre Famelies of Lancastre and York,* commonly called *Hall's Chronicle* (1542), used as a source by Shakespeare in some of his historical plays.

Hall, Edwin Herbert. 1855–1938. American physicist, b. Great Falls, now North Gorham, Me. Professor, Harvard (1888–1921); discovered (1879) Hall effect, the production of a transverse electrical field in a current-carrying conductor in a magnetic field.

Hall, Granville Stanley. 1844–1924. American psychologist and educator, b. Ashfield, Mass. Professor, Antioch Coll. (1872–76); lecturer at Harvard (1876–81); professor, Johns Hopkins (1883–88); president, Clark U. (1889–1920). Founded and edited *American Journal of Psychology* (1887), *Journal of Applied Psychology* (1915); first president, American Psychological Association (1891). Considered the founder of child psychology, educational psychology, and of scientific psychology generally in U.S. Author of *The Contents of Children's Minds* (1883), *Adolescence* (1904), *Youth* (1906), *Educational Problems* (1911), *Senescence, the Last Half of Life* (1922), *Life and Confessions of a Psychologist* (1923).

Hall, Sir James. 1761–1832. Scottish geologist and chemist. His series of experiments (1798–1805) made to test Huttonian theories of igneous rock is credited with inaugurating science of experimental geology.

Hall, James. 1793–1868. American author, b. Philadelphia. Circuit judge (1825–28), treasurer (1828–31) in Illinois; later a banker in Cincinnati. Edited first western literary annual, the *Western Souvenir* (1828); edited *Illinois Monthly Magazine* (1830–32) and successor *Western Monthly* (1832–36); wrote *Letters from the West* (1828), *Romance of Western History* (1857), and fiction as *The Harpe's Head* (1833), *Tales of the Border* (1835).

Hall, James. 1811–1898. American geologist and paleontologist, b. Hingham, Mass. Professor, Rensselaer Polytechnic (1832–36); directed portion of N.Y. state geological survey (1837–43); state geologist of Iowa (1855–58), Wisconsin (1857–60), New York (1893); director, N.Y. Museum of Natural History (1871–98). Contributed to development of geosynclinal theory of mountain building. Author of *Geology of New York* (Part IV, 1843), *Paleontology of New York* (1847–94).

Hall, James Norman. 1887–1951. American writer, b. Colfax, Iowa. Resident in Tahiti (from 1920). Coauthor with Charles B. Nordhoff (*q.v.*) of *Falcons of France* (1929); a trilogy on the ship *Bounty* including *Mutiny on the Bounty* (1932), *Men Against the Sea* (1934), *Pitcairn's Island* (1934); *The Hurricane* (1936); *Botany Bay* (1941); *Men Without Country* (1942); etc.

Hall, Joseph. 1574–1656. English prelate and writer. Chaplain to Prince Henry; dean of Worcester (1616); bishop of Exeter (1627–41), Norwich (1641–47); impeached and imprisoned (1643); expelled from his palace (c.1647). Author of satires as *Virgidemiarum* (1597–1602), *Mundus alter et idem* (c.1605); *Characters of Vertues and Vices* (1608) modelled on Theophrastus; philosophical works as *Heaven upon Earth* (1606), *Contemplations* (1612–26) that won him epithet the "Christian Seneca" or "English Seneca."

Hall, Lyman. 1724–1790. American Revolutionary leader, b. Wallingford, Conn. To Georgia; one of founders of town of Sunbury (1758); member, Continental Congress (1775–78, 1780); a signer of Declaration of Independence. Governor of Georgia (1783).

Hall, Marshall. 1790–1857. English physician and physiologist. Studied reflex action (from 1832) and developed theory of reflex arc mediated by spinal cord; maintained theory in face of denunciation by colleagues. Author of *Observations on Blood-Letting* (1830), *Circulation of the Blood* (1831), etc.

Hall, Radclyffe, *in full* Marguerite Radclyffe. 1886–1943. English writer. Author of novels *The Forge* (1924), *The Unlit Lamp* (1924), *Adam's Breed* (1926), *The Well of Loneliness* (1928), *The Sixth Beatitude* (1936).

Hall, Robert. 1764–1831. English clergyman. Popular Baptist preacher; noted supporter of liberal causes, esp. freedom of the press, religious liberty.

Hall, Samuel. 1781–1863. English engineer and inventor. Invented (1838) surface condenser for steam boilers which enabled steamships to recycle fresh water rather than use seawater in boilers.

Hall, Samuel Carter. 1800–1889. Irish editor and writer. To London (1822); founded and edited *The Amulet* (1826–36), *Art Union Monthly,* later *Art Journal* (1839–80); author of many books in collaboration with his wife ¶Anna Maria, *nee* Fiel·ding \fē(ə)l-diŋ\ (1800–1881), who also wrote independently stories and novels, including *The Buccaneer* (1832), *Marian, or a Young Maid's Fortunes* (1839), *Tales of the Irish Peasantry* (1840), *Midsummer Eve, a Fairy Tale of Love* (1848).

Hall, Samuel Read. 1795–1877. American clergyman and educator. Established training school for teachers, Concord, Vt. (1823), first American normal school. Writer of textbooks in geology, arithmetic, grammar, history, and geography.

Ḥal·lāj, al- \al-ka̱l-'aj\. *In full* Abū al-Mughīth al-Ḥusayn ibn Manṣūr al-Ḥallāj. c.858–922. Islāmic mystic. Studied under noted Ṣūfi masters; traveled widely to proselytize; incurred suspicion of radicalism or subversion; after lengthy imprisonment (c.911–922), crucified and tortured to death in Baghdad.

Hal·lam \'hal-əm\, Henry. 1777–1859. English historian. Chief works *Europe during the Middle Ages* (1818), *Constitutional History of England from Henry VII's Accession to the Death of George II* (1827), *Introduction to the Literature of Europe* (1837–39). His son ¶Arthur Henry (1811–1833), friend of Tennyson, was subject of Tennyson's poem *In Memoriam.*

Hallam, Lewis. 1714–1756. English actor. Brought family and theatrical company to America (1752); gave first professional dramatic production in America, *Merchant of Venice,* at Williamsburg, Va. (1752); built first theater in New York City (1753); toured Colonies and West Indies. His son ¶Lewis, *called* the Younger (c.1740–1808) acted in family company under father and stepfather David Douglass; appeared in Philadelphia in Thomas Godfrey's *Prince of Parthia,* first professional production of an American play (1767); instrumental in founding professional theater in U.S.

Halle, Adam de la. See ADAM DE LA HALLE.

Hal·lé \'hal-ə, -ē\, Sir Charles. *Orig.* Carl Hal·le \'häl-ə\. 1819–1895. British pianist and conductor, b. Germany. To England (1848); established Hallé Orchestra and conducted (1858–95) Hallé Concerts, Manchester; first principal, Royal Coll. of Music at Manchester (1893).

Hal·leck \'hal-ək\, Charles Abraham. 1900–1986. American politician, b. Demotte, Ind. Republican congressman from Indiana (1935–69); majority leader of U.S. House of Representatives (1947–48; 1953-54); minority leader of House (1959–64); held celebrated joint news conferences with Sen. Everett Dirksen; aided in passage (1963) of major civil-rights bill.

Halleck, Fitz-Greene. 1790–1867. American poet, b. Guilford, Conn. Member of Knickerbocker group, New York City. Author of *Alnwick Castle, with Other Poems* (1827), *Poetical Works* (1847). Best known poems "Green be the turf above thee" (commemorating the death of his friend Joseph Rodman Drake), "Burns," "Marco Bozzaris," "Red Jacket," "Young America."

Halleck, Henry Wager. 1815–1872. American army officer, b. Westerville, N.Y. At outbreak of Civil War (1861), commissioned major general; commanded Department of Missouri (1861–62); called to Washington as general in chief (1862–64); effective in organizing training and mobilization but not in tactics or strategy; with appointment of Grant as lieutenant general, became chief of staff (1864–65). After the war, commanded military division of the Pacific (1865–69) and division of the South (1869–72).

Hal·ler \'häl-ər\, Albrecht von, *in full* Victor Albrecht. 1708–1777. Swiss biologist. Professor of medicine, anatomy, and surgery, Göttingen (1736–53); practiced medicine, Bern (1753–77); elucidated mechanism of respiration; discovered function of bile; first to distinguish and relate muscle irritability and nerve sensibility and show transmission of nervous impulse; contributed to anatomy, embryology; devised botanical taxonomic system. Author of *Elementa Physiologiae Corporis Humani* (1757–66) and other scientific works; compiled *Bibliothecae Medicinae Practicae* (1776–88); also wrote philosophical romances as *Usong* (1771), *Alfred* (1773), *Fabius and Cato* (1774), verse including "Die Alpen" (1732).

Haller, Bertold. 1492–1536. Swiss clergyman. Pastor at Bern (from 1513); accepted principles of Reformation (from 1522) and was influential in securing their acceptance at Bern.

Haller de Hal·len·burg \-dā-'häl-ən-,bu̇rk\, Józef. 1873–1960. Polish soldier. With Piłsudski organized Polish legion at outbreak of World War I (1914) to oppose Russians; after treaty of Brest Litovsk (1918), entered the Ukraine, but was defeated by the Germans (1918); made his way to Paris and organized "Blue Army" of Polish troops fighting with the Allies; fought the Bolsheviks in Poland (1919); organized volunteer army in Poland (1920); retired for opposition to Piłsudski (1926).

Hal·let \á-le\, Étienne Sulpice. *Also known as* Stephen Hal·lette *Angl* ha-'let\. 1755–1825. American architect, b. France. To U.S. (c.1788); submitted designs (1792) for the National Capitol at Washington, and was awarded second prize; commissioned to revise structurally impractical plans of William Thornton, winner in the competition; dismissed in dispute over plans.

Hal·ley \'hal-ē, 'hā-lē\, Edmond *or* Edmund. 1656–1742. English astronomer. Made first complete observation of a transit of Mercury (1677) while compiling catalog of southern stars; by his suggestions, encouraged Newton to write his *Principia,* which Halley published (1687) at his own expense. Conducted researches in navigation, published first magnetic sea charts (1701); professor, Oxford (1704); astronomer royal succeeding Flamsteed (1720). Editor, Royal Society's *Transactions* (1685–93). Best known for his study of comets; predicted accurately the return in 1758 of comet previously observed in 1531, 1607, and 1682 (subsequently known as Halley's comet). Also credited with originating the science of life statistics by his *Breslau Table of Mortality* (1693).

Hall·gríms·son \'häd-ᵊl-,grēms-sȯn\, Jónas. 1807–1845. Icelandic poet. Chief Romantic lyric poet of Iceland; a founder of Copenhagen journal *Fjölnir* (1835). Verse collected in *Ljóthmaeli* (1847), etc.

Hal·li·bur·ton \'hal-ə-,bərt-ᵊn\, Richard. 1900–1939. American explorer and writer, b. Brownsville, Tenn. Traveled in South and Central America, Asia, etc.; lost at sea in typhoon while sailing in a Chinese junk from Hong Kong to San Francisco. Among his books were *The Royal Road to Romance* (1925), *The Glorious Adventure* (1927), *New Worlds to Conquer* (1929), etc.

Hal·li·die \'hal-ə-dē\, Andrew Smith. *Orig.* Andrew Smith. 1836–1900. American engineer and inventor, b. London, England. To California (1853); built wire suspension bridges; invented cable street railway, first introduced in San Francisco (1873).

Hal·li·well-Phil·lipps \'hal-ə-wəl-'fil-əps, -ə-,wel-\, James Orchard. *Orig.* James Halliwell. 1820–1889. English scholar. Librarian, Jesus Coll., Cambridge (1838); after earlier antiquarian studies, concentrated upon Shakespeare's life and editions of his works. Author of *Nursery Rhymes and Tales of England* (1845), *Dictionary of Archaic and Provincial Words* (1847), *Outlines of Life of Shakespeare* (1848), folio edition of Shakespeare (1853–65).

Halloy, Jean-Baptiste-Julien Omalius d'. See OMALIUS D'HALLOY.

Hall·stein \'häl-,shtīn\, Walter. 1901–1982. West German jurist and diplomat. Headed German delegation at Messina Conference (1955), which led directly to formation (1958) of European Economic Community (the Common Market); served as first president (1958–67) of executive commission of the Common Market; a firm believer in European unity; sparred with French Pres. Charles de Gaulle over issue of supranationality in the Common Market; president of the European Movement (1968–74).

Hall·wachs \'häl-,väks\, Wilhelm Ludwig Franz. 1859–1922. German physicist. Professor, Technische Hochschule, Dresden (1893 ff.); discovered (1888) Hallwachs effect, now known as photoelectric effect.

Halm, Friedrich. See MÜNCH-BELLINGHAUSEN.

Hals \'häls\, Frans. between 1581 and 1585–1666. Dutch painter. One of the greatest of portraitists; master of character depiction, of subtle color, of expressive brushwork; remarkable joviality of many early portraits replaced later by sense of discouragement, even tragedy. Among his notable canvases were *Banquet of the Officers of the Civic Guard of St. George, Laughing Cavalier, Portrait of a Lady, Jolly Trio, Herring Vender, Merry Toper, Daniel van Aken Playing the Violin, Governors of the Old Men's Home in Haarlem.*

Halsbury, 1st Earl of. See Hardinge Stanley GIFFARD.

Hal·sey \'hȯl-sē, -zē\, William Frederick, Jr. 1882–1959. American naval officer, b. Elizabeth, N.J. Commanded destroyer patrol force in World War I; qualified as naval aviator (1935); rear admiral (1938); vice admiral (1940); led task force attack on Marshall and Gilbert islands (1942); commander of Allied naval forces in South Pacific (1942–44); defeated Japanese in 3-day battle off Solomon Islands (Nov. 1942); admiral (1942); commander of U.S. Third fleet (1944–45); commanded Battle of Leyte Gulf (Oct. 1944); admiral of the fleet (1945).

Hals·man \'hȯl-smən\, Philippe. 1906–1979. American photographer, b. Riga, Latvia. Fashion photographer in Paris; to U.S. (1940); became a leading portrait photographer; produced 101 cover photographs for *Life* magazine. Author of *Piccoli* (1953), *Dali's Mustache* (1954), *Jump Book* (1959).

Hal·sted \'hȯl-stəd, -,sted\, William Stewart. 1852–1922. American surgeon, b. New York City. Administered (1881) perhaps first blood transfusion in U.S.; discovered (1885) technique of block anaesthesia by injection of cocaine into certain nerves; professor of surgery, Johns Hopkins (from 1890); established first school of surgery in U.S.; emphasized aseptic procedures, introduced rubber gloves; developed new surgical techniques for hernia, goiter, aneurysms, gall bladder, intestines, etc.

Ha·ma·dā·nī \,há-má-dá-'nē\. *More completely* 'Alī ibn Shihāb ad-Dīn ibn Muḥammad Hamadānī. 1314–1385. Persian mystic. Traveled widely as itinerant holy man; responsible for wide propagation of Kubrāwīyah order of Ṣūfis, esp. in Kashmir.

Ha·ma·dhā·nī, al- \al-,ham-ə-tha-,nē\. *In full* Badī' az-Zamān Abū al-Faḍl Aḥmad ibn al-Ḥusayn al-Hamadhānī. 969–1008. Arab writer. Known for devising *maqāmah* form, combining prose, rhymed prose, and poetry; credited with writing 400 *maqāmahs,* of which some 52 are extant; also compiled a *Dīwān,* collection of poetry, and *Rasā'il,* collection of letters.

Ha·ma·gu·chi \hä-mä-gü-chē\ Osachi *or* Yuko. *Orig. surname* Ta·ne·hi·ra \tä-nä-hē-rä\. 1870–1931. Japanese politician. Elected to Diet (1914); finance minister (1924–25); minister of home affairs (1927–29); prime minister (1929–30) and head of the Minseitō party; instituted program of economic austerity and rebuilding, including a return to the gold standard to combat inflation; supported Japan's acquiescence in London Naval Conference program (1930), arousing opposition; shot by assassin.

Ha·mann \'hä-män\, Johann Georg. 1730–1788. German philosopher. In government service at Königsberg (1767–77); in mercantile house (1777–84); friend of Kant; impatient with rationalism and abstraction, developed a form of fideism expressed in cryptic style. Author of *Gedanken über meinen Lebenslauf* (1758–59), *Sokratische Denkwürdigkeiten* (1759), *Kreuzzüge eines Philologen* (1762), *Golgatha und Scheblimini* (1784), etc.

Ham·bro \'häm-brō\, Carl Joachim. 1885–1964. Norwegian politician. Member of Norwegian Storting (1919–57); president of the Storting (from 1926); Norwegian delegate to the League of Nations and president of the League Assembly (1939–46); delegate to United Nations (1945–57).

Ham·dā·nī, al- \al-,ham-'da-,nē\. *More fully* Abū Muḥammad al-Hasan ibn Aḥmad al-Hamdānī. 893?–c.945. Arab geographer, poet, scholar. Influential scholar and writer, known as the "tongue of South Arabia"; works included an encyclopedia *al-Iklīl.*

Ha·me·lin \åm(-ə)-laⁿ\, Ferdinand-Alphonse. 1796–1864. French naval officer. Commanded Black Sea squadron during Crimean War (1853–55); admiral (1854); minister of navy (1855–60); leader in developing naval armor; oversaw construction of *Gloire* (launched 1859), prototype of seagoing ironclads.

Ha·me·rik \'há-mə-rēk\, Asger. *Orig. surname* Ham·me·rich \'há-mə-rēk\. 1843–1923. Danish composer. Director of conservatory of Peabody Inst., Baltimore (1871–98). Composer of operas as *Tovelille* (1863–65), *Hjalmar och Ingeborg* (1868), *Den rejsende* (1871); orchestral works including 8 symphonies, 5 *Nordische Suiten* (1872–77); choral works.

Hamerling, Robert. See Rupert HAMMERLING.

Ham·er·ton \'ham-ərt-ᵊn, -ər-tən\, Philip Gilbert. 1834–1894. English artist and essayist. A founder (1869) and editor (1869–94) of art periodical *The Portfolio.* Author of *Thoughts about Art* (1862), *Etching and Etchers* (1866), *The Intellectual Life* (1873), *The Graphic Arts* (1882), etc.

Ha·mil·car \hə-'mil-,kär, 'ham-əl-\. d. 480 B.C. Carthaginian general. Commanded expedition against Sicily; defeated by Gelon (*q.v.*) and died in battle.

Hamilcar Bar·ca \'bär-kə\ *or* **Bar·cas** \'bär-kəs\. 270?–229 or 228 B.C. Carthaginian general. Commanded in Sicily (247–241); forced to make peace with Rome (241) after naval defeat at hands of G. Lutatius Catullus; crushed revolt of troops in Carthage (241–238); led campaign to conquer Spain (237–228); killed in action. Father of Hannibal.

Ham·il·ton \'ham-əl-tən, -əlt-ᵊn\. Name of noble Scottish family of English origin descended from Walter Fitz-Gil·bert \fits-'gil-bərt\ of Hamilton, who swore fealty as overlord of Scotland to Edward I of England but surrendered fortress of Bothwell to Robert Bruce after Bannockburn. Surname Hamilton first assumed by his grandson ¶Sir David of Hamilton of Cad·zow \'kad-(,)zō, -(,)yü\ (d. before 1392). Among titles held by branches of family were baron, marquis, and duke of Hamilton; earl of Arran; earl, marquis, and duke of Abercorn.

BARONS, MARQUISES, DUKES OF HAMILTON; EARLS OF AR·RAN \ˈar-ən\.

¶Sir James Hamilton of Cadzow (d. 1479), 1st Baron Hamilton; great-grandson of Sir David; allied himself by marriage to Douglases; joined them in renunciation of allegiance to crown (1453), but deserted them (1454) in their struggle with crown and married (1469) Mary Stewart, eldest daughter of James II of Scotland.

His son ¶James Hamilton (1477?–1529), 2d Baron Hamilton and 1st Earl of Arran; favorite of James IV, by whom he was created earl (1503); during minority of James V plotted against regent Albany and became president of council of regency (1517–20); again a member (1522); engaged in long feud with Douglases; joined Margaret, queen dowager, in ousting Albany and proclaiming James V (1524); rewarded on James V's escape from Angus and assumption of government.

¶Patrick Hamilton (1498?–1528); grandson of 1st baron; early advocate of doctrines of Reformation; saw Luther and Melanchthon at Wittenberg; on return sentenced for heresy and burned at St. Andrews.

¶James Hamilton (1515?–1575), 2d Earl of Arran and Duke of Châ·tel·he·rault \shä-tel-rō\; eldest son of 1st earl; on death of James V (1542), governor of Scotland and second person in realm; regent and tutor to Princess Mary (till 1554); created duke (1548) by Henry II of France; went over to English party (1559); banished for opposition to Darnley marriage (1566).

¶James Hamilton (1530–1609), 3d Earl of Arran; eldest son of 2d earl; proposed by Henry VIII as husband of Princess Elizabeth but reserved by his father as possible husband for Mary, Queen of Scots; with Lord James Stuart supported Protestant cause and stymied French invasion (1559–60); became insane (1562). The title Earl of Arran was granted (1581) to his cousin, Capt. James Stewart (d. 1595), but later recovered by his nephew James, 4th earl.

¶John Hamilton (1532?–1604), 1st Marquis of Hamilton; 2d son of 2d earl; head of house on death (1575) of his father and heir after James VI to Scottish throne; with his brother Claud, became devoted partisan of Queen Mary; aided in her delivery from Lochleven and reestablishment on throne (1568) and, forfeited by Parliament, in revenge took part in assassination of Moray (1570); in danger of his life from Sir William Douglas, escaped to France (1579); reconciled (1585) with James VI; sent to negotiate marriage of James and Danish Princess Anne (1588); one of jurors that found Huntly guilty of high treason; created marquis (1599).

¶Claud Hamilton (1543?–1622), Baron Pais·ley \ˈpāz-lē\; 4th son of 2d earl; fled (1579) after implication, along with brother John, in series of plots in behalf of Mary, Queen of Scots; aided Ruthven lords (1584) in Gowrie conspiracy to gain possession of person of James VI; recalled from Paris by James VI and shared with Huntly leadership of Scottish Catholics; in communication with Spain, urged invasion of England by Armada; created baron (1587). One of his grandsons ¶Gustavus Hamilton (1639–1723), Viscount Boyne \ˈbȯin\ in Irish peerage, commanded regiment at the Boyne (1690) and in Spain (1702); major general (1703); privy councilor under William III, Anne, and George I; created viscount (1717). A great-grandson of Baron Paisley, ¶Anthony Hamilton (c.1645–1720), known as "Count Anthony"; a grandson of 1st earl of Abercorn; served with Scottish regiment in French service (1674–76); returned to Ireland; governor of Limerick (1685); commanded Jacobite dragoons at Enniskillen and Newtown Butler (1689), and engaged at Battle of the Boyne (1690); spent rest of life in France; known esp. for witty memoirs of his brother-in-law comte de Gramont; also wrote some French verse and tales.

¶James Hamilton (1589?–1625), 2d Marquis of Hamilton, 4th Earl of Arran, Earl of Cam·bridge \ˈkām-brij\ in English peerage (cr. 1619); son of 1st marquis; secured enactment of Five Articles of Perth in Scottish Parliament (1621) and negotiated (1623) for marriage of Prince Charles to Spanish Infanta.

¶James Hamilton (1606–1649), 3d Marquis and 1st Duke of Hamilton, 2d Earl of Cambridge; son of 2d marquis; commanded British force (1631–33) under Gustav Adolphus; an advocate of compromise, persuaded Charles I (1638) to consent to election of a Scottish parliament; failed to mollify Covenanters; refused Covenant (1643) and joined king; created duke (1643); attempted mediation between Charles and Scots (1646); led Scottish army; defeated at Preston (1648); condemned and executed.

¶William Hamilton (1616–1651), 2d Duke of Hamilton; brother and successor of 1st duke; secretary of state for Scotland (1640–43, 1646); signed at Carisbrooke Castle (1647) for Scots a treaty by which King Charles granted consent to Presbyterianism in England; aided in organizing second civil war; died of wounds received at Worcester. On his death title devolved on his daughter ¶Anne (1636–1716), duchess in her own right; m. (1656) William Douglas, Earl of Selkirk, for whom and subsequent dukes of Hamilton see DOUGLAS family.

EARLS, MARQUISES, AND DUKES OF AB·ER·CORN \ˈab-ər-ˌkȯ(ə)rn\.

¶James Hamilton (1575?–1618), eldest son of Claud Hamilton, Lord Paisley; favorite of James VI; privy councilor (1598); created baron (1603), earl (1606) of Abercorn for services as commissioner of union with England. His son ¶James (fl. 1617–51), 2d earl, was created Baron Stra·bane \strə-ˈban\ in Irish peerage but resigned title (1633) in favor of his brother Claud; on death of 2d Duke of Hamilton (1651) became male representative of house.

¶James Hamilton (1656–1734), 6th Earl of Abercorn, aided in defense of Derry (1689); created viscount Strabane (1701).

¶James Hamilton (1712–1789), 8th earl, renewed family connection with Scotland by purchase of estates; Scottish representative peer (1761–86); created Viscount Hamilton in English peerage (1786).

¶James Hamilton (1811–1885), 10th earl; lord lieutenant of Ireland (1866–68, 1874–76); created duke of Abercorn (1868). His son ¶Lord George Francis Hamilton (1845–1927) was M.P. (1868–1906); undersecretary for India (1874–78); first lord of the admiralty (1885–86, 1886–92), where he instituted reforms and increases in armament and readiness; ceded Heligoland to Germany (1890); secretary of state for India (1895–1903).

¶James Hamilton (1869–1953), 3d duke, was M.P. (1900–13); governor of Northern Ireland (1922–45).

Among other titles of nobility borne by descendants in different branches of Hamilton family are: (1) Barons Bel·ha·ven \bel-ˈhā-vən\, including ¶John Hamilton (1656–1708), 2d baron, who aided settling of Scottish crown on William, became privy councilor, and strongly opposed union of England and Scotland in famous speech called "Belhaven's Vision" (1706). (2) Earls of Had·ding·ton \ˈhad-iŋ-tən\, including ¶Thomas Hamilton (1563–1637), lord of session (1592); one of 8 "Octavians" appointed to manage Scottish finances (1596); secretary of state for Scotland (1612–26); lord president of court of session (1616–26); lord privy seal (1627); a favorite of James VI; created Lord Drumcairn (1592), Lord Binning (1613), Earl of Melrose (1619), Earl of Haddington (1627). (3) Earls of Orkney, including ¶Lord George Hamilton (1666–1737), brother of 4th duke of Hamilton; served at Battle of the Boyne (1690) under William of Orange; created earl of Orkney (1696); major general (1702); lieutenant general (1704); distinguished himself at Blenheim (1704), capturing 13,000 men and officers; led pursuit after Ramillies (1706); prominent at Oudenard (1707); opened attack at Malplaquet (1709); representative peer of Scotland (from 1707); governor of Virginia (1714); field marshal (1736).

Hamilton, Alexander. 1755–1804. American politician, b. island of Nevis, Leeward Islands. To New York (1772); wrote several pamphlets for patriot cause while student at King's Coll. (now Columbia U.); secretary and aide-de-camp to Washington (1777–81). Member, Continental Congress (1782, 1783, 1787, 1788). Practiced law, New York City (from 1783). Represented New York in Annapolis Convention (1786) and Constitutional Convention (1787); supported new constitution by contributions (with Madison and Jay) to *Federalist* (1787–88). First U.S. secretary of the treasury (1789–95); planned and initiated policies establishing a national fiscal system, strengthening central government, stimulating trade and enterprise, developing national resources, and placing public credit on sound basis; opposition to policies led to factional divisions, from which developed political parties, Hamilton emerging as leader of Federalists. Appointed inspector general of army, rank of major general (1798–1800). Instrumental in defeating Aaron Burr for presidency (1800–01) and for governorship of New York (1804); mortally wounded in a duel with Burr.

Hamilton, Alice. 1869–1970. American toxicologist, b. New York City. Sister of Edith Hamilton; director of Ill. survey of industrial poisons (1910–11); investigator of occupational poisons, U.S. Bureau of Labor (1911–21); professor, Harvard medical school (1919–35). Author of *Industrial Poisons in the United States* (1925), *Exploring the Dangerous Trades* (1943), etc.

Hamilton, Andrew. *Orig. surname* Trent \ˈtrent\. 1676–1741. American lawyer, b. Scotland. To U.S. (1697). Successfully defended John Peter Zenger, publisher of *New York Weekly Journal,* against charge of seditious libel (1735).

Hamilton, Anthony. See under HAMILTON family.

Hamilton, Edith. 1867–1963. American scholar, b. Dresden, Germany. Sister of Alice Hamilton; headmistress, Bryn Mawr School, Baltimore (1896–1922). Author of *The Greek Way* (1930), *The Roman Way* (1932), *Prophets of Israel* (1936), *Mythology* (1942), *Witness to the Truth* (1949), *The Echo of Greece* (1957), etc.

Hamilton, Lady Emma. *Nee* Amy Ly·on \ˈlī-ən\. 1765–1815. Mistress of Lord Nelson. As Emma Hart, accepted protection (1781–84) of Charles Greville; mistress (from 1786), second wife (from 1791) of Greville's uncle Sir William Hamilton (*q.v.*); intimate with Queen Maria Carolina at Naples; accompanied her husband and Lord Nelson to Palermo (1800); gave birth (1801) to Horatia, later acknowledged by Lord Nelson as his daughter.

Hamilton, Gail. See Mary Abigail DODGE.

Hamilton, Gavin. 1723–1798. Scottish painter. Resident in Rome (1742–52, 1754–98); a fashionable portraitist in London (1752–54); a pioneer of Neoclassicism, esp. in series of paintings from the *Iliad;* also noted as a Roman archaeologist.

Hamilton, Lord George. See under HAMILTON family.

Hamilton, Sir Ian Standish Monteith. 1853–1947. British soldier. Served in Second Afghan War (1878–80), South African revolt (1881), Nile expedition (1884–85), Third Burmese War (1886–87), Tirah campaign (1897–98), Boer War (1899–1901); chief of staff to Kitchener (1901–02). Commander in chief, Mediterranean (1910–15); commanded expeditionary force (1915) in vain attempt to land troops in force at Gallipoli; relieved of command.

Hamilton, James. 1769–1829. British educator. Devised (1815) method of teaching foreign languages by use of texts with interlinear translations, which he used with success in U.S. and Great Britain. Published numerous such texts, as Gospels, *Aesop's Fables, Robinson Crusoe,* etc., and *History, Principles, Practice and Results of the Hamiltonian System* (1829).

Hamilton, Patrick, *in full* Anthony Walter Patrick. 1904–1962. English playwright and novelist. Author of plays including *Rope* (1929), *Gaslight* (1938), *The Governess* (1945); novels including *Craven House* (1926), *Midnight Bell* (1929), *Plains of Cement* (1934).

Hamilton, William. *Known as* Hamilton of Gil·bert·field \ˈgil-bərt-ˌfēld\. c.1665–1751. Scottish poet. Exchanged with Allan Ramsay a series of "Familiar Epistles" on which Burns later modelled poetic letters; produced modernized version (1722) of Blind Harry's *Wallace.*

Hamilton, William. 1704–1754. Scottish poet. Contributed lyrics to Allan Ramsay's *Tea-Table Miscellany* (1724); composed esp. ballads, including "The Braes of Yarrow."

Hamilton, Sir William. 1730–1803. British diplomat and archaeologist. Grandson of 3d duke of Hamilton (see marquises and dukes of HAMILTON). British envoy to court of Naples (1764–1800); studied activities of Vesuvius and Etna and Calabrian earthquakes; collector of antiquities, sold to British Museum (1772); took active part in excavations of Herculaneum and Pompeii; privy councilor (1791); m. (1791) Emma Hart, who became Lord Nelson's mistress (see Emma HAMILTON).

Hamilton, Sir William. 1788–1856. Scottish philosopher. Professor of civil history (1821), of logic and metaphysics (1836), Edinburgh. Made contributions to logic; helped introduce Kantian thought to Britain.

Hamilton, William Gerard. 1729–1796. English politician. M.P. (1755 ff.); gained nickname "Single-speech Hamilton" because his 15-hour maiden speech so far excelled his later efforts. Chief secretary for Ireland (1761–64); chancellor of Irish exchequer (1763–84).

Hamilton, Sir William Rowan. 1805–1865. Irish mathematician. Professor of astronomy, Trinity Coll., Dublin, and astronomer royal of Ireland (1827–65); developed comprehensive theory of geometrical optics (1827); predicted conical refraction (1832); discovered (1835) quaternions and developed applications.

Hamilton-Gordon. See Earls of Aberdeen under GORDON family.

Ham·lin \ˈham-lən\, Cyrus. 1811–1900. American clergyman, b. Waterford, Me. Congregational missionary in Turkey (1839–60); with funds supplied by C. R. Robert of New York, established Robert College, first at Bebek (1863) and then at Constantinople (1871); served as its head until 1877; president, Middlebury Coll., Vt. (1881–85).

Hamlin, Hannibal. 1809–1891. American politician, b. Paris Hill, Me. Member, U.S. House of Representatives (1843–47), U.S. Senate (1848–57). Governor of Maine (1857); again U.S. senator (1857–61); prominent as antislavery advocate. Vice president of the United States (1861–65). U.S. senator (1869–81); minister to Spain (1881–82).

Ḥam·mād ar-Rā·wi·yah \kam-ˈmäd-ar-ˈrä-wē-(y)äh\. *Known also as* Ḥammād the Transmitter *or* Reciter. c.694–c.772. Persian-Arabic anthologist and scholar. Renowned for vast store of memorized Arabic verse and associated lore of battles, genealogies, etc.; credited with collecting the 7 early odes known as *al-Mu'allaqāt.*

Ham·mar·skjöld \ˈhȧm-ər-ˌshœld; *Angl* ˈham-ər-ˌshəld, ˈhäm-, -ˌshu̇ld, -ˌshēld\, Dag Hjalmar Agne Carl. 1905–1961. Swedish statesman. Son of Hjalmar Hammarskjöld; professor of economics, Stockholm (1933–36); in ministry of finance (1936–47), of foreign affairs (1947–53); vice chairman (1951–52), chairman (1952–53), Swedish delegation to United Nations; secretary general of UN (1953–61); took part in settling crises in Suez, Lebanon; sent UN force to keep peace in Congo (1960); killed in airplane crash over Congo.

Hammarskjöld, Hjalmar, *in full* Knut Hjalmar Leonard. 1862–1953. Swedish politician. Professor of law, Uppsala (1891–95); acting head of ministry of justice (1901–02); member of Permanent Court of Arbitration, The Hague (1904–46); minister in Copenhagen (1905–07); governor of Uppsala province (1907–30); chief delegate to Hague Peace Conference (1907); prime minister (1914–17); kept Sweden neutral in World War I; chairman of Nobel Prize foundation (1929–47).

Ham·mer \ˈham-ər\, William Joseph. 1858–1934. American electrical engineer, b. Cressona, Pa. Assistant in laboratory of Thomas A. Edison (1879); chief engineer, Edison Lamp Works (1880–81). To England (1881), chief engineer for English Edison Co.; established in London first central station in the world for incandescent electric lighting. Chief engineer, German Edison Co. (1883–84). Consulting engineer in U.S. (from 1890).

Ham·mer·ling \ˈhäm-ər-liŋ\, Rupert. *Pseudonym* Robert Ha·mer·ling \ˈhäm-ər-liŋ\. 1830–1889. Austrian poet. Schoolteacher in Vienna, Graz, Trieste. Best known for epics *Ahasverus in Rom* (1865), *Der König von Sion* (1869), *Homunculus* (1888); also wrote lyrics as *Sangesgruss* (1857), *Venus in Exil* (1858), *Schwanenlied der Romantik* (1862), novel *Aspasia* (1876), dramas, etc.

Ham·mer·schmidt \ˈhäm-ər-ˌshmit\, Andreas. 1611 or 1612–1675. German organist and composer. Organist to Count von Bünau (1633–34), of St. Petri, Freiberg (1634–39), of St. Johannis, Zittau (1639–75). Composed over 400 sacred vocal works including motets, hymns, concertos, arias; influential in development of Lutheran liturgical music.

Ham·mer·stein \ˈham-ər-ˌstīn\, Oscar. 1846–1919. American theatrical manager, b. Stettin, Germany. To U.S. (c.1863); worked in cigar factory; invented machine for spreading tobacco leaves; founded and edited *United States Tobacco Journal* (until 1885). Leased Stadt Theater, New York City (1870); built Harlem Opera House (1880), Columbus Theater, Olympia Music Hall (1895), Victoria Music Hall (1899), Republic Theater (1900), Manhattan Opera House (1906), Lexington Theater (1912); also opened theaters in Philadelphia and London. His grandson ¶Oscar II (1895–1960) became one of the greatest lyricists in the American musical theater; wrote lyrics for Youmans's *Wildflower* (1923, with Otto Harbach), Friml's *Rose Marie* (1924), Kern's *Sunny* (1925), Romberg's *Desert Song* (1926, with Harbach), Kern's *Show Boat* (1927), Romberg's *New Moon* (1928), Kern's *Sweet Adeline* (1929), *Music in the Air* (1932), *Very Warm for May* (1939); with Richard Rodgers wrote hit shows *Oklahoma!* (1943, special Pulitzer prize), *Carousel* (1945), *South Pacific* (1949), *The King and I* (1951), *Me and Juliet* (1953), *Flower Drum Song* (1958), *Sound of Music* (1959), and score for motion picture *State Fair* (1945, Academy Award for "It Might As Well Be Spring"); won Academy Award for song "The Last Time I Saw Paris" (with Kern, in *Lady, Be Good!,* 1941).

Ham·mett \ˈham-et\, Dashiell, *in full* Samuel Dashiell. 1894–1961. American writer, b. St. Marys Co., Md. Creater of "hard-boiled" school of detective fiction in novels *Red Harvest* (1929), *The Dain Curse* (1929), *The Maltese Falcon* (1930), *The Glass Key* (1931), *The Thin Man* (1932), etc.

Ham·mond \ˈham-ənd\, Henry. 1605–1660. English clergyman. Archdeacon of Chichester (1643); chaplain to royal commissioners at Uxbridge (1645) and to Charles I (1647); deprived of subdeanship of Christ Church, Oxford, by Parliamentary visitors and imprisoned (1648). Author of *Paraphrase and Annotations on the New Testament* (1653).

Hammond, James Henry. 1807–1864. American politician, b. Newberry District, S.C. Advocated secession from beginning of nullification issue; member, U.S. House of Representatives (1835–36); governor of South Carolina (1842–44); member, U.S. Senate (1857–60). In speech (Mar. 4, 1858) he taunted northern sympathizers with: "You dare not make war on cotton—no power on earth dares make war upon it. Cotton is king."

Hammond, John Hays. 1855–1936. American mining engineer, b. San Francisco. On staff, U.S. Geological Survey, in California goldfields (1880); associated with Cecil Rhodes in development of South African resources; a leader in Transvaal reform movement (1895–96); arrested after Jameson Raid and sentenced to death; sentence commuted to imprisonment; freed finally on payment of fine. Consulting engineer, esp. to Guggenheim Exploration Co. (1900–07). His son ¶John Hays, Jr. (1888–1965), electrical and radio engineer and inventor; established (1911) Hammond Radio Research Laboratory; developed radio remote control devices; invented radio-controlled torpedo for coast defense, variable pitch ship propeller, various devices relating to telephony and telegraphy.

Hammond, John Lawrence Le Breton. 1872–1949. English journalist and historian. Author of *Charles James Fox* (1903), *Gladstone and the Irish Nation* (1938); m. (1901) ¶Lucy Barbara, *nee* Brad·by \ˈbrad-bē\ (1873–1961), with whom he collaborated on *The Village Labourer 1760–1832* (1911), *The Town Labourer 1760–1832* (1917), *The Skilled Labourer 1760–1832* (1919), *The Rise of Modern Industry* (1925), *The Bleak Age* (1934).

Hammond, Laurens. 1895–1973. American inventor, b. Evanston, Ill. Developed (1933) an electric organ known as the Hammond electronic organ, and an electrical musical instrument, producing tones similar to orchestral instruments, known as the Hammond Novachord. Brother of Eunice Tietjens (*q.v.*).

Ham·mu·ra·bi \ˌham-ə-ˈräb-ē, häm-\ *or* **Ham·mu·ra·pi** \-ˈrä-pē\. d. 1750 B.C. King of the first dynasty of Babylon (1792–50 B.C.). Conducted lengthy rivalry and war with Rim-Sin of Larsa, finally conquering Larsa and southern Babylonia (1762); best known for code of laws, once thought to be oldest extant.

Ham Nghi \ˈhäm-əŋ-ˈhē\. *Orig.* Ung Lich \ˈu̇ŋ-ˈlēsh\. 1870–c.1940. Vietnamese emperor (1884–86). Nephew of Emperor Tu Duc; through intrigue succeeded over numerous claimants to throne; at instigation of regents, led insurrection against French (1885); forced to flee, deposed, exiled to Algeria.

Hamp·den \ˈham(p)-dən\, John. 1594–1643. English politican. M.P. (1621 ff.); imprisoned (1627) for refusing to pay forced loan of 1626; resisted second ship-money writ (1636), and was defendant in case of the king vs. John Hampden (1637–38). Popular member in Short and Long parliaments (1640), where he led opposition to king's demand for subsidies in exchange for giving up ship money. Impeached by attorney general (1642) as one of Five Members in opposition to king, but escaped arrest. At outbreak of war, raised regiment of foot for Parliamentary army; mortally wounded in action.

Hamp·den \ˈham-dən\, Walter. *Orig.* Walter Hampden Dough·er·ty \ˈdäk-ər-tē\. 1879–1955. American actor, b. Brooklyn, N.Y. First appeared in London (1901); on American stage (from 1907); formed own company (1919); known esp. for his work in Shakespearean roles and in *The Servant in the House, Cyrano de Bergerac, Richelieu, The Admirable Crichton.*

Hampole, Richard Rolle de. See ROLLE DE HAMPOLE.

Hamp·son \ˈham(p)-sən\, William. 1854–1926. English inventor. Invented (1895) device for producing liquid air in quantity by "cascade" effect.

Hamp·ton \ˈham(p)-tən\, Wade. 1751?–1835. American politician and soldier, b. Halifax Co., Va. Served in American Revolution; colonel (1782); member, U.S. House of Representatives (1795–97, 1803–05). Reentered army (1808); brigadier general (1809); major general (1813); held responsible by Gen. James Wilkinson for failure of expedition against Montreal (1813); resigned (1814).

Hampton, Wade. 1818–1902. American politician and Confederate officer, b. Charleston, S.C. Grandson of Wade Hampton (1751?–1835); at outbreak of Civil War (1861) raised "Hampton's Legion" and was engaged at Bull Run; brigadier general (1862); as second in command under J. E. B. Stuart in cavalry, engaged at Gettysburg and in the Wilderness; led raids in upper Shenandoah Valley. Major general (1863) and commander of Confederate cavalry after Stuart's death (1864); lieutenant general (1865). Governor of South Carolina (1876–79); senator (1879–91).

Hamsun, Knut. See Knut PEDERSEN.

Ḥam·zah ibn ʿAlī \ˈḵam-zä-ˌib-ən-al-ˈē\. *More completely* Ḥamzah ibn ʿAlī ibn Aḥmad. *Also known as* az-Zūzānī. 11th century. Arab religious leader. Entered Egypt (1017) and became spokesman and then imām to Caliph al-Ḥakīm, encouraging his claim to be divine incarnation; instrumental in organizing Druze religion.

Han \ˈhän\. Name of several Chinese dynasties:

(1) A dynasty divided into two periods: Former, or Western, Han (206 B.C.–8 A.D.), founded by Liu Pang with its capital at Ch'ang-an, and the Later, or Eastern, Han (23–220 A.D.), founded by Liu Hsiu with its capital at Lo-yang. The two dynasties, interrupted by the reign of the usurper Wang Mang (*q.v.*), were marked by a highly centralized administrative structure, Confucian ideology, establishment of literary civil service examination system, revival of letters, introduction of Buddhism (in reign of Liu Chuang), and extension of territory; succeeded by breakup of empire into the Three Kingdoms (*q.v.*). For its more prominent emperors, see the LIU family.

(2) Minor Han. Usually called Shu Han \ˈshü-ˈhän\. A dynasty (221–263 A.D.), founded by Liu Pei (*q.v.*), a descendant of the house of Han, ruling in the west of China, one of the Three Kingdoms following the downfall of the Later Han dynasty; annexed by the Wei dynasty.

(3) Later Han. One of the Five Dynasties (*q.v.*).

Han \ˈhän\, Ulrich. *Lat.* Udalricus Gal·lus \ˈgal-əs\. *Also called* Bar·ba·tus \bär-ˈbāt-əs\. d. 1478. Austrian printer. Set up printing press in Rome, his first publication (1467) being Juan de Torquemada's *Meditationes de Vita Christi,* first illustrated book published in Italy.

Han \hän\ Yong-un. *Also called* Man-hae \män-ha\. 1879–1944. Korean religious leader and poet. Took part in Tonghak Revolt (1894); entered Buddhist priesthood (1905); leader in movement to rationalize Korean Buddhism; imprisoned (1919–22) for role in drafting and signing anti-Japanese declaration of independence (1919); led in establishing Singanhoe society (1927), national independence front. Author of *Pulgyo-yusin-ron* (1909) and much patriotic verse.

Ha·na·bu·sa \hä-nä-bu̇s-ä\ Itchō. *Orig.* Fu·ji·wa·ra \fu̇j-ē-wä-rä\ Nobuka. 1652–1724. Japanese artist. Made reputation with depictions of humorous subjects from everyday life, influencing the *Ukiyo-e* school; exiled (1698–1709) for caricaturing the shogun; on return to Edo (now Tokyo), changed name and opened painting school.

Han·cock \ˈhan-ˌkäk\, John. 1737–1793. American Revolutionary politician, b. Braintree (now Quincy), Mass. In mercantile business (from 1754); identified himself with colonial cause in pre-Revolutionary agitation; elected to Massachusetts legislature (1769–74). Member, Continental Congress (1775–80, 1785, 1786); president of congress (1775–77); first signer of Declaration of Independence. First governor of State of Massachusetts (1780–85); again governor (1787–93).

Hancock, Thomas. 1786–1865. English inventor and manufacturer. Invented (1821) "masticator" by which rubber scraps were worked into a shredded mass capable of being molded into blocks or rolled into sheets; formed partnership with Charles Mackintosh to produced waterproof fabrics and articles as raincoats, known as mackintoshes.

Hancock, Winfield Scott. 1824–1886. American army officer, b. Montgomery Co., Pa. Served in Mexican War, in West; brigadier general (1861); major general (1862); commander of II Corps, Army of the Potomac (1863–65); defended key position on Cemetery Ridge in Battle of Gettysburg (July 2–3, 1863). Later again engaged in Indian wars. Democratic candidate for president of the United States (1880); defeated by Garfield.

Hand \ˈhand\, Learned, *in full* Billings Learned. 1872–1961. American jurist, b. Albany, N.Y. U.S. district judge (1909–24); judge of U.S. Court of Appeals, 2d Circuit (1924–51); continued to hear special cases (1951–61), compiling record tenure on federal bench; considered one of the greatest jurists of his day. Author of *The Spirit of Liberty* (1952), *The Bill of Rights* (1958).

Han·del \ˈhan-dᵊl\, George Frideric. *Ger.* Georg Friedrich Hän·del \ˈhen-dəl\. 1685–1759. British composer, b. Germany. Composed first opera, *Almira* (1705); to Italy (1707); presented his opera *Rodrigo* at Florence (1707), cantatas and oratorio *La Resurrezione* in Rome (1708), and opera *Agrippina* at Venice (1708). Musical director to prince of Hanover (1710); enjoyed great success in London visit with opera *Rinaldo* (1711); remained in England (from 1712); naturalized (1726). Musical director for Duke of Chandos at Cannons (1718–20); director of Royal Academy of Music (1720–28); director (with Heidegger) of the King's Theatre, Covent Garden (1728–34); director of Rich's new theater in Covent Garden (1735–37). Other operas included *Il pastor fido* (1712), *Radamisto* (1720), *Tamerlano* (1724), *Scipione* (1726), *Sosarme* (1732), *Serse* (1738); instrumental in shaping English popularity of oratorio with *Esther* (1732, orig. *Haman and Mordecai,* 1720), *Alexander's Feast* (1736), *Saul* (1739), *Israel in Egypt* (1739), *The Messiah* (1742), *Samson* (1743), *Semele* (1744), *Hercules* (1745), *Belshazzar* (1745), *Judas Maccabaeus* (1746), *Jephthah* (1752); other works included 6 concerti for oboe, 21 organ concerti, orchestral *Water Music* (1717) and *Fireworks Music* (1749), many overtures, chamber works, harpsichord works.

Han·del-Maz·zet·ti \ˈhan-dəl-mät-ˈset-ē\, Enrika von. Baroness. 1871–1955. Austrian novelist. Author of *Jesse und Maria* (1906), *Die arme Margaret* (1910), *Stefana Schwertner* (1912–14), *Frau Maria* (1929–31), *Die Waxenbergerin* (1934), etc.

Han·dl \ˈhan-dᵊl\ *or* **Hän·dl** \ˈhen-dᵊl\ *or* **Häh·nel** \ˈhen-əl\, Jakob. *Orig. surname perhaps* Pe·tel·in \pə-ˈtel-ēn\. *Known as* Jacobus Gal·lus \ˈgäl-əs\. 1550–1591. Slovenian composer. Cistercian monk; singer in imperial chapel (1574); choirmaster to bishop of Olmütz (now Olomouc, 1579–85). Composed 19 masses and many motets, esp. the cycle *Opus musicum* (1586–91).

Handley Page, Frederick. See Frederick Handley PAGE.

Han·dy \ˈhan-dē\, William Christopher. 1873–1958. American musician and composer, b. Florence, Ala. First to codify and publish songs in the mode known as blues; best known songs included "Memphis Blues" (1911), "St. Louis Blues" (1914), "Beale Street Blues," "Yellow Dog Blues," "Careless Love," etc. Autobiography *Father of the Blues* (1941).

Han-fei-tzu \ˈhan-ˈfā-ˈdzü\. d. 233 B.C. Chinese philosopher. Considered greatest of the Legalist philosophers; evolved doctrine based on authority of rulers, duty of citizens, military power of state; strongly influenced King Cheng of Ch'in, founder of Ch'in dynasty; imprisoned through jealousy of a rival official; committed suicide.

Han Kan \ˈhän-ˈgän\. 8th century A.D. Chinese painter. A leading artist of the T'ang dynasty, known for his paintings of horses.

Han·kel \ˈhäŋ-kəl\, Wilhelm Gottlieb. 1814–1899. German physicist. Professor, Halle (1847–49), Leipzig (1849–87); known for studies of piezoelectricity, thermoelectricity, atmospheric electricity. His son ¶Hermann (1839–1873), mathematician; professor, Leipzig (1867), Erlangen (1867–69), Tübingen (1869–73); known for studies in complex numbers, theory of functions. Author of *Theorie der complexen Zahlensysteme* (1867), etc.

Han·key \ˈhaŋ-kē\, Maurice Pascal Alers. 1st Baron Hankey. 1877–1963. British army officer and public official. Served in Royal Marine artillery (1895–1901), naval intelligence (1902–06). Secretary of Committee of

Imperial Defense (1912–38), of Imperial War Cabinet (1917–19), of the Cabinet (1919–38); clerk of Privy Council (1923–38). British secretary at various international conferences (1919–32). In Cabinet as minister without portfolio (1939–40), chancellor of duchy of Lancaster (1940–41), paymaster general (1941–42); created baron (1939).

Hanks \'hanks\, Nancy. 1783–1818. American woman. m. (1806) Thomas Lincoln; mother of Abraham Lincoln.

Hann \'hän\, Julius Ferdinand von. 1839–1921. Austrian meteorologist. Professor, Vienna (1874–97, 1900–10), Graz (1897–1900); director, Zentralanstalt für Meteorologie und Erdmagnetismus, Vienna (1877–97); known for studies of cyclones, atmospheric dynamics, etc.

Han·na \'han-ə\, Marcus Alonzo, *known as* Mark. 1837–1904. American businessman and politician, b. New Lisbon, Ohio. In father's grocery and commission business (1853–62); partner (from 1862); acquired interests in coal, iron, banking, etc. Sponsored John Sherman in convention of 1888; supported McKinley for governor of Ohio (1891 and 1893) and for president of the United States (1896 and 1900); influential presidential adviser, instrumental in forging alliance of Republican party and business; U.S. senator (1897–1904).

Han·nay \'han-(,)ā\, James. 1827–1873. Scottish novelist. Author of the naval stories *Singleton Fontenoy* (1850) and *Eustace Conyers* (1855), also of *Satire and Satirists* (1854) and *Studies on Thackeray* (1869).

Hannay, James Owen. *Pseudonym* George A. Bir·ming·ham \'bər-miŋ-əm\. 1865–1950. Irish clergyman and novelist. Rector of Westport, County Mayo (1892–1913), and canon of St. Patrick's Cathedral (1912–21); rector of Mells, Frome (1924–34); vicar of Holy Trinity, Kensington Gore (from 1934). Author of *The Seething Pot* (1905), *Spanish Gold* (1908), *Lalage's Lovers* (1911), *The Island of Mystery* (1918), *Lady Bountiful* (1921), *The Grand Duchess* (1924), *Wild Justice* (1930), *The Search for Susie* (1941), etc.

Han·ni·bal \'han-ə-bəl\. 247–183 B.C. Carthaginian general. Son of Hamilcar Barca; trained under father's command in Spain and sworn to eternal enmity to Rome; after father's death (228 B.C.), served under his brother-in-law Hasdrubal (*q.v.*). After Hasdrubal's assassination (221), became commander in chief of Carthaginian army in Spain; provoked Second Punic War by attacking and capturing Roman-allied city of Sagunto in Spain (218); crossed Alps, defeating various Gallic and Celtic tribes, and carried war into Italy, defeating Romans under P. Cornelius Scipio at Ticino River and Trebbia River (218), army of Gaius Flaminius at Lago di Trasimeno (217), and Quintus Fabius Cunctator at Cannae (216). Wintered at Capua (216–215) and captured Tarentum (212); marched against Rome (211), but Romans held successfully to fortified positions. Defeat of Carthaginian reinforcements at Metaurus River (207) and Roman successes under Scipio Africanus in North Africa forced his recall to Carthage (203) after he had maintained campaign in Italy for fifteen years. In North Africa, he was defeated by Scipio Africanus in great battle of Zama (202). Headed Carthaginian government (c.202–195), but was accused by Romans of conspiring to break the peace; fled Carthage (195) and joined Antiochus III of Syria; military career ended when Antiochus, defeated (190) at Magnesia (Manisa), was forced to promise to surrender him to Rome. Escaped to Bithynia and there, with no further hope of escape, committed suicide.

Han·ning·ton \'han-iŋ-tən\, James. 1847–1885. British prelate. Anglican missionary to Uganda (1882); first Anglican bishop of East Equatorial Africa (1884–85); attempted to open new route to Lake Victoria (1885); killed by natives.

Hanno, Saint. See ANNO.

Han·no \'han-(,)ō\. 5th century B.C. Carthaginian navigator. Made exploring and colonizing voyage down African west coast, reaching Gambia, Sierra Leone, or perhaps Cameroon.

Hanno. *Called* the Great. 3d century B.C. Carthaginian politician. Opponent of Hamilcar Barca and Hannibal; as representative of landed aristocracy, advocated peace with Rome during Second Punic War (218–201 B.C.); after battle of Zama (202), was one of ambassadors sent to Scipio Africanus to sue for peace.

Ha·no·taux \á-nȯ-tō\, Gabriel, *in full* Albert-Auguste-Gabriel. 1853–1944. French historian and politician. On faculty, École des Hautes Études (from 1880); entered foreign ministry (1880); deputy (1886–89); minister of foreign affairs (1894–98); directed colonial expansion in Africa. Author of *Histoire de Richelieu* (1893–1947), *Histoire de France contemporaine* (1903–08), *Histoire illustrée de la guerre de 1914* (1915–26).

Han·o·ver \'han-,ō-vər, 'han-ə-vər\. *Ger.* Han·no·ver \hän-'ō-vər, -fər\. An electoral house of Germany and a royal family of England. The electoral house was directly descended from the Welf family (see WELF), which acquired Bavaria (1070) and Lüneburg, etc. (1120); name Hanover gradually became interchangeable with that of duchy of Lüneburg-Calenberg and (from 1692) with that of electorate of Brunswick-Lüneburg. Duke Ernest Augustus (*q.v.*) was first elector (1692); his son, the second elector, succeeded (as George I) to English crown, establishing English royal house of Hanover (1714–1901), whose other rulers were George II, III, IV, William IV, and Victoria. Electorate was made a kingdom by Congress of Vienna (1815). Separated from English ruling house at accession of Victoria (1837); its first independent king was Ernest Augustus (*q.v.*), Duke of Cumberland, son of George III.

Han·riot \äⁿr-yō\, François. 1759–1794. French Revolutionary leader. Leader of sans-culotte section of Paris national guard (1792–93); commander in chief of Paris national guard (1793–94); instrumental in overthrow of Girondins (1793); supporter of Robespierre and guillotined with him.

Hans. King of Denmark. See JOHN I.

Han·sard \'han-,särd, 'han(t)-sərd\, Luke. 1752–1828. English printer. Printed the House of Commons's journals (from 1774). Official reports of parliamentary proceedings in England are still known as *Hansards.* His eldest son ¶Thomas Curson (1776–1833), also a printer, printed parliamentary debates (from 1803); patented improved hand press; published a treatise on printing, *Typographia* (1825).

Hans·ber·ry \'hanz-,ber-ē, -b(ə-)rē\, Lorraine. 1930–1965. American playwright, b. Chicago. Author of *Raisin in the Sun* (1959), first play by a black woman to be produced on Broadway, and *The Sign in Sidney Brustein's Window* (1964).

Han·sen \'han(t)-sən\, Alvin Harvey. 1887–1975. American economist, b. Viborg, S.D. Professor, U. of Minnesota (1919–37), Harvard (1937–75); one of the chief American exponents of Keynesian economics and an adviser to many governmental boards. Author of *Economic Stabilization in an Unbalanced World* (1932), *New Plan for Unemployment Reserves* (1933), *Fiscal Policy and Business Cycles* (1941), *Guide to Keynes* (1953), *The American Economy* (1957), etc.

Han·sen \'hän-zen\, Anton. *Pseudonym* Anton H. Tamm·saa·re \'täm-sär-e\. 1878–1940. Estonian writer. Author of psychological novels, including *Kõrboja peremees* (1922), his masterpiece *Tõde ja õigus* (1926–33), and *Elu ja armastus* (1934); also of plays, as *Juudit* (1921) and *Kuningal on Külm* (1936), short stories, essays, etc.

Han·sen \'hȧn-sən\, Emil Christian. 1842–1909. Danish botanist. Superintendent of laboratory, Carlsberg brewery, Copenhagen (from 1879); investigated fungi and alcoholic fermenting yeasts; proved that there are different species of yeast; developed technique of growing one-cell cultures; collaborated in inventing ferment used in European breweries.

Han·sen \'hän-sən\, Gerhard Henrik Armauer. 1841–1912. Norwegian physician. Discovered (1869) bacillus of leprosy, known also as Hansen's disease.

Han·sen \'hȧn-sən\, Hans Christian Svane. 1906–1960. Danish politician. Secretary (1929–33), chairman (1933–37), Social Democratic youth organization; elected to parliament (1936); active in resistance during German occupation; finance minister (1947–50); minister of foreign affairs (1953–60); prime minister (1955–60); achieved economic stability, led Denmark into NATO.

Hansen, Jens Andersen. 1806–1877. Danish journalist and politician. Co-editor (1842–43), editor (1843–56), peasant newspaper *Almuevennen;* member of Constituent Assembly (1849), parliament (1849–77); a leader of peasant party (to 1865).

Han·sen \'han(t)-sən\, Marcus Lee. 1892–1938. American historian, b. Neenah, Wis. Professor, U. of Ill. (1928–38); pioneer student of history of immigration. Author of *Atlantic Migration, 1607–1860* (1940), *Mingling of the Canadian and American Peoples* (1940), etc.

Han·sen \'hȧn-sən\, Martin Jens Alfred. 1909–1955. Danish writer. Author of novels *Nu opgiver han* (1935), *Kolonien* (1937), *Jonatans rejse* (1941), *Lykkelige Kristoffer* (1945), *Løgneren* (1950); also critical works as *Leviathan* (1950), *Orm og tyr* (1952).

Hansen, Peter Andreas. 1795–1874. Danish astronomer. Assistant at Altona observatory in measuring arc of meridian (1821); director of Seeberg observatory (from 1825) which was removed to Gotha (1857). Known for work in celestial mechanics, esp. theories of motion for comets, minor planets, moon; lunar tables (1857) long in use; published lunar theory in *Fundamenta* (1838), *Darlegung* (1862–64).

Hansi. See Jean-Jacques WALTZ.

Hans·lick \'häns-lik\, Eduard. 1825–1904. Austrian music critic. Music critic or editor for *Wiener Zeitung* (1846–50), *Die Presse* (1855, from 1864 the *Neue Freie Presse*); lecturer (1856), professor (1870), U. of Vienna; noted for elegant reviews, championship of musical formalism, esp. in works of Schumann, Brahms. Author of *Vom Musikalisch-Schönen* (1854), *Die moderne Oper* (1875–1900), etc.

Han·som \'han(t)-səm\, Joseph Aloysius. 1803–1882. English architect. Designed the Birmingham town hall (1833); invented (1834) a patent safety cab named after him, the predecessor of later hansoms.

Han·son \'han(t)-sən\, Howard Harold. 1896–1981. American composer, b. Wahoo, Neb. Professor (1916), dean (1919–21), conservatory of Coll. of the Pacific; director, Eastman School of Music, Rochester, N.Y. (1924–64); established annual festival to promote American composers; founded (1958)

Eastman Philharmonia, with which he toured widely. Compositions included symphonies including No. 1 *Nordic* (1923), No. 2 *Romantic* (1930), No. 4 *Requiem* (1943, Pulitzer prize), No. 5 *Sinfonia Sacra* (1955), No. 7 *Sea* (1977); symphonic poems *Lux aeterna* (1923), *Pan and the Priest* (1926); other orchestral works *Mosaics* (1958), *Bold Island Suite* (1961), *Dies natalis I* (1967); choral works *Lament for Beowulf* (1925), *Songs from Drum Taps* (1935, after Whitman), *Song of Democracy* (1957), *Song of Human Rights* (1963), *Mystic Trumpeter* (1970), *New Land, New Covenant* (1976); opera *Merry Mount* (1934).

Hanson, John. 1721–1783. American Revolutionary politician, b. Charles Co., Md. Active in colonial cause (from 1765); member, Continental Congress (1780); first president (1781–82) of the Congress under Articles of Confederation.

Hans·son \'hän-sōn\, Ola. 1860–1925. Swedish writer. Established reputation with lyrics in *Dikter* (1884), *Notturno* (1885); left Sweden owing to shocked response to his morbidly erotic sketches in *Sensitiva amorosa* (1887); published verse *Ung Ofegs visor* (1889) showing influence of Nietzsche, *Nya visor* (1907), tales *Parias* (1890), novel *Risan hem* (1895), etc.

Hansson, Per Albin. 1885–1946. Swedish politician. Joined Social Democratic party (1903); editor of party organ *Social-Demokraten* (1917–24); elected to Riksdag (1918); minister of defense (1920–23, 1924–26); became party leader at death of Hjalmar Branting (1925); prime minister (1932–46); secured much welfare legislation, maintained Swedish neutrality in World War II.

Han·steen \'hän-stān\, Christopher. 1784–1873. Norwegian astronomer and physicist. Professor, Christiania (now Oslo, 1816–61); known for researches in terrestrial magnetism.

Han T'o-chou \'hän-'tō-'jō\. d. 1207. Chinese politician. Minister to Sung emperor Ning Tsung; provoked war in attempting to regain northern lands lost to Juchen tribes; on attempting to prolong disastrous war, executed by own people; his head was offered to Juchen in conciliation.

Hantzsch \'hänch\, Arthur Rudolf. 1857–1935. German chemist. Professor, Zürich (1885–93), Würzburg (1893–1903), Leipzig (1903–27); discovered (1881) methods for synthesizing pyridines; established stereochemistry of nitrogen (1890, with A. Werner); conducted studies in spectrophotometry, absorption spectra, dissociation of acids.

Han Yü \'hän-'yü̅\. *Also called* Han Wen-kung \'hän-'wən-'gůŋ\. 768–824 A.D. Chinese poet, essayist, and philosopher. An official at the court under T'ang dynasty; for his criticism of the emperor's policy, was banished for a year. Resurrected neglected works of Confucius and laid foundation of Neo-Confucianism in opposition to dominant Taoism and Buddhism; championed simple, unmannered prose style and unorthodox poetic forms, earning epithet "Prince of Letters."

Hap·good \'hap-ˌgůd\, Norman. 1868–1937. American editor and writer, b. Chicago. Editor, *Collier's Weekly* (1903–12), *Harper's Weekly* (1913–16), *Hearst's International Magazine* (1923–25). U.S. minister to Denmark (1919). Author of *Daniel Webster* (1899), *Abraham Lincoln* (1899), *George Washington* (1901), *Industry and Progress* (1911), *Up from the City Streets* (with Henry Moskowitz, 1927), *The Changing Years* (1930), etc. His brother ¶Hutchins (1869–1944), journalist, wrote *Spirit of the Ghetto* (1902), *Autobiography of a Thief* (1903), *Types from the City Streets* (1910), *The Story of a Lover* (1919).

Hapsburg. See HABSBURG.

Hāqilāni, Ibrāhīm al-. See IBRĀHĪM AL-HĀQILĀNI.

Ha·ra \hä-rä\ Kei. *Also called* Hara Takashi. 1856–1921. Japanese politician. Entered foreign service (1892); ambassador to Korea (1897); an organizer (1900) of Rikken-Seiyūkai party; elected to Diet (1902); prime minister (1918–21), first Japanese commoner to receive this honor; built party into patronage machine; expanded electorate; his ministry criticized for attitude toward "Twenty-one Demands" on China and for Siberian policy; assassinated.

Harald. See HAROLD.

Ha·rasz·thy de Mok·csa \'här-äs-tē-də-'mòk-chä\, Agoston. 1812?–1869. American viticulturist, b. Futtak, Hungary. To U.S. (1840); founded town now known as Sauk City, Wis. (c.1841); to California (1849); introduced Tokay, Zinfandel, and Shiras grapes into California (from 1852) and created grape-growing industry.

Har·bach \'här-ˌbäk\, Otto Abels. 1873–1963. American playwright and librettist, b. Salt Lake City. Author of plays *Madame Sherry* (1909), *Girl of My Dreams* (1910), *The Firefly* (1912), *High Jinks* (1913), *The Silent Witness* (1915). Lyricist or librettist for Broadway shows including *Up in Mabel's Room* (1919), *Kid Boots* (1923), *Wildflower* (1923), *No! No! Nanette* (1924), *Rose Marie* (1924), *Sunny* (1925), *The Desert Song* (1926), *Cat and the Fiddle* (1931), *Roberta* (1933), *Meet Miss April* (1945), etc.

Har·bord \'här-bərd\, James Guthrie. 1866–1947. American army officer and businessman, b. Bloomington, Ill. Enlisted in U.S. army (1889); rose through grades to brigadier general (1918) and major general (1919). Chief of staff, American Expeditionary Force in France (1917–18); commanded 4th Marine Brigade, 2d Division in combat (1918); chief of service of supply (1918–19); again chief of staff, A.E.F. (1919). Deputy chief of staff, U.S. army (1921–22); retired; lieutenant general (1942). President (1922–30), chairman (1930–47), Radio Corp. of America.

Har·burg \'här-ˌbərg\, Edgar Yipsel, *known as* E.Y. *or* Yip \'yip\. 1896–1981. American lyricist, b. New York City. Wrote lyrics for songs including "Brother, Can You Spare a Dime?" "It's Only a Paper Moon," "April in Paris," "Over the Rainbow," "How Are Things in Glocca Morra?"; libretto and lyrics for musical *Finian's Rainbow* (1947, with Fred Saidy).

Harcourt, Henri de Lorraine, comte de. See LORRAINE.

Har·court \år-kür\, Henri I d'. Duc. 1654–1718. French soldier and diplomat. Son of marquis of Thury; conducted brilliant defense of Luxembourg (1692); engaged at Neerwinden (1693); ambassador at Madrid (1697–1701); created duc (1700), marshal of France (1703), and peer (1709).

Har·court \'här-kərt, -ˌkō(ə)rt, -ˌkò(ə)rt\, Sir William George Granville Venables Vernon. 1827–1904. English politician. M.P. (from 1868); solicitor general (1873–74); home secretary (1880–85); chancellor of exchequer (1886, 1892–94, 1894–95); leader of Liberal opposition in Commons (1895–98). Noted for introduction (1894) of graduated estate tax. His son ¶Lewis (1863–1922) was M.P. (1904–17); first commissioner of works (1905–10, again 1915–16); secretary of state for colonies (1910–15); created Viscount Harcourt (1917).

Har Day·al \'här-'dī-äl\. 1884–1939. Indian revolutionary and scholar. Lived in U.S., Switzerland, Germany, Sweden, England; active in anti-imperialist and anarchist circles; attempted to foment anti-British uprisings in India, Afghanistan; later worked for creation of secular world state.

Har·de·ca·nute *or* **Har·di·ca·nute** \ˌhard-i-kə-'n(y)üt\. c.1019–1042. King of Denmark (1028–42) and of England (1040–42). Son of Canute II and Emma of Normandy; made king of Denmark (1028) by father; barred from succeeding to English throne (1035) by Leofric of Mercia and others favorable to his illegitimate half-brother Harold; arrived in England with large fleet (1040); crowned king (1040); unpopular with English subjects.

Har·dee \'hard-ē\, William Joseph. 1815–1873. American army officer, b. Camden Co., Ga. Entered Confederate service (1861); major general (1861); lieutenant general (1862); engaged at Shiloh, Perryville, Murfreesboro, Missionary Ridge, Atlanta, etc. His *Rifle and Light Infantry Tactics* (1855) was used as an army textbook.

Har·den \'härd-ᵊn\, Sir Arthur. 1865–1940. English chemist. Lecturer and demonstrator, Owens Coll. (1888–97); head of chemistry department (1897–1907), of biochemistry (1907–30), British Institute of Preventive Medicine (from 1898 the Jenner Institute; from 1903 the Lister Institute); professor of biochemistry, London (1912 ff.). Known esp. for researches in alcoholic fermentation and the enzymatic action involved. Shared the 1929 Nobel prize for chemistry with Hans von Euler-Chelpin.

Har·den \'här-dən\, Maximilian. *Orig.* Felix Ernst Wit·kow·ski \vit-'kòf-skē\. 1861–1927. German journalist. Founded and edited (1892–1922) political weekly *Die Zukunft,* in which he attacked, often tastelessly, government policies and ministers; accused several of homosexuality; attacks finally brought charge of criminal libel, but he was exonerated, and some of the leading figures in the court were driven from public life (1906–07). Advocate of war as nationalist campaign, but became pacifist during World War I and later professed radical socialism. Author of *Apostata* (1892), *Literatur und Theater* (1896), *Köpfe* (1910–24), *Krieg und Friede* (1918), and *Deutschland, Frankreich, England* (1923).

Har·den·berg \'här-dən-ˌberk\, Friedrich Leopold von. Freiherr. *Pseudonym* No·va·lis \nō-'väl-əs\. 1772–1801. German poet. A leader of early romanticists in Germany. Best known as author of *Hymnen an die Nacht* (1800, prose lyrics inspired by death of his fiancée), *Geistliche Lieder* (1799); unfinished novels *Die Lehrlinge zu Sais* (1798), *Heinrich von Ofterdingen* (1802); and essays on Christian history *Die Christenheit oder Europa* (1799).

Hardenberg, Karl August von. Fürst. 1750–1822. Prussian politician. Councilor of Hanover (1773–82); in service of duke of Brunswick (1787–90); administrator of Prussian principalities of Ansbach and Bayreuth (1790–95); signed treaty of peace between Prussia and France at Basel (1795). In Prussian cabinet of Frederick William III (1798–1804); foreign minister of Prussia (1804–06); tried to preserve neutrality; kept out of office by hostility of Napoléon (1806–10). Chancellor of Prussia (1810–22); made prince in recognition of part in War of Liberation (1813–14); took part in Congress of Vienna (1815) and in conferences at Paris; reorganized Council of State (1817); advocate of constitutionalism; considered chief architect of Prussian independence.

Hardicanute. See HARDECANUTE.

Har·die \'härd-ē\, Keir, *in full* James Keir. 1856–1915. British labor leader and politician, b. Scotland. Worked as a miner (1866–78); organized labor union among miners, and became secretary of Scottish Miners' Federation (1886); published newspapers *The Miner* (1887–89), *Labour Leader* (from 1889); organized Scottish Labour party (1888); helped found Independent Labour party (1893), Labour party (1900); M.P. (1892–95, 1900–15); first leader of Labour party in Parliament (1906–07).

Har·ding \'här-diŋ\, Chester. 1792–1866. American painter, b. Conway, Mass. Cabinetmaker, house painter, tavern keeper, sign painter, and finally self-taught portrait painter; successful in London (1823–26); studio in Springfield, Mass. (from c.1830). Portrait subjects included Daniel Webster, John Randolph, Amos Lawrence, Daniel Boone, Robert Owen, John Marshall, John C. Calhoun.

Harding, Karl Ludwig. 1765–1834. German astronomer. Professor, Göttingen (1805–34); discovered (1804) minor planet Juno, three comets (1813, 1824, 1832).

Harding, Stephen. Saint. c.1060–1134. English religious. Joined Cluniac abbey, Molesmes, France; cofounder (1098, with St. Robert de Molesmes) of the monastery of Cîteaux, south of Dijon, France, first abbey of the Cistercian order, and its abbot (from 1109); founded also various branches of the Cîteaux monastery, including that at Clairvaux, where he installed St. Bernard as abbot.

Harding, Warren Gamaliel. 1865–1923. Twenty-ninth president of the United States, b. Caledonia (now Blooming Grove), Ohio. Bought Marion (Ohio) *Star* and edited it (from 1884); lieutenant governor (1903–04); U.S. senator (1915–21). With aid of Harry M. Daugherty (*q.v.*), won Republican presidential nomination (1920); called for "return to normalcy," favored protective tariffs; opposed League of Nations, high taxes on war profits. President (1921–23); administration suffered from the corruption of officials appointed by Harding, notably Daugherty, Edwin N. Denby, and Albert B. Fall. Died at San Francisco while on speaking tour.

Har·dinge \'här-diŋ\, Charles. 1st Baron Hardinge of Pens·hurst \'penz-ˌhərst\. 1858–1944. British diplomat. Grandson of Henry Hardinge; entered foreign service (1880); ambassador to St. Petersburg (1904–06); permanent under-secretary (1906–10); created baron (1910); viceroy of India (1910–16); reversed Lord Curzon's partition of Bengal; moved Indian capital from Calcutta to Delhi (1911); fostered good relations with nationalists; again permanent undersecretary for foreign affairs (1916–20); ambassador to Paris (1920–22).

Hardinge, Henry. 1st Viscount Hardinge of La·hore \lə-'hō(ə)r, -'hȯ(ə)r\. 1785–1856. British soldier. Entered army (1799); served in Peninsular War, lost arm at Ligny (1815); M.P. (1820–44); secretary at war (1828–30, 1841–44); secretary for Ireland (1830, 1834–35). Lieutenant general (1841); general (1854). Governor general of India (1844–48); fostered social reform, economic development; negotiated Treaty of Lahore (1846) ending First Sikh War; created viscount (1846). British commander in chief (1852); blamed for poor state of preparedness at outbreak of Crimean War (1854); demoted to field marshal (1855).

Har·douin \år-dwaⁿ\, Jean. 1646–1729. French cleric and scholar. Entered Jesuit order (1666); professor at Jesuit college, Paris (1683–1718); edited Pliny's *Historia naturalis;* conspicuous for maintaining certain remarkable theories, as that most books attributed to the ancients were actually written by 13th-century monks under the direction of one Severus Archontius, and that the coins and medals supposed to be of antiquity were actually made by relatively modern artists; attacked authenticity of Roman Catholic church councils anterior to the Council of Trent. Author of *Nummi antiqui* (1684) and other works on numismatics, and of *Conciliorum collectio regia maxima* (1714–15).

Hardouin-Mansart. See MANSART.

Hardt \'härt\, Ernst. 1876–1947. German poet, novelist, and playwright. Director, National Theater, Weimar (1919–24), State Theater, Cologne (1925), and West German Broadcasting Co. (1926–33). Author of stories *Priester des Todes* (1898), *Bunt ist das Leben* (1902), *An den Toren des Lebens* (1904); plays *Der Kampf ums Rosenrote* (1903), *Nipon von Lenclos* (1905), *Tantris der Narr* (1907), *Gudrun* (1911), *König Salomo* (1915).

Harduin. See ARDUIN.

Hardwicke, Earls of. See Philip YORKE.

Hard·wicke \'här-(ˌ)dwik\, Sir Cedric Webster. 1893–1964. English actor. London debut (1912); member of F. R. Benson's company; with Birmingham Repertory Co. (1922–24); in London appeared in Shaw's *Back to Methuselah* and *Caesar and Cleopatra, Show Boat, The Barretts of Wimpole Street, Heartbreak House, The Late Christopher Bean, Tovarich;* Broadway debut in *Promise* (1936); later appeared in *Shadow and Substance, Antigone, Don Juan in Hell, Majority of One,* numerous motion pictures.

Har·dy \år-dē\, Alexandre. 1572?–?1632. French playwright. Hired poet for various troupes of actors in Paris and the provinces; first Frenchman known to have made living as dramatist; claimed authorship of some 600 plays, of which c.34 survive; works introduced a freedom from classical strictures for which he was later criticized; works ceased to be produced on his death.

Har·dy \'här-dē\, Godfrey Harold. 1877–1947. English mathematician. Lecturer, Cambridge (1906–19); professor, Oxford (1919–31), Cambridge (1931–47). Concurrently with Wilhelm Weinberg developed Hardy-Weinberg law (1908) describing genetic distribution and equilibrium in large populations; known also for contributions to complex analysis, Diophantine analysis, Fourier series, distribution of prime numbers, etc.

Hardy, Oliver. See under Stanley LAUREL.

Hardy, Thomas. 1840–1928. English novelist and poet. Early practiced architecture, but devoted himself to literature (from 1867). Among his novels were *Desperate Remedies* (1871), *Under the Greenwood Tree* (1872), *A Pair of Blue Eyes* (1873), *Far from the Madding Crowd* (1874), *The Return of the Native* (1878), *The Trumpet-Major* (1880), *Mayor of Casterbridge* (1886), *Tess of the d'Urbervilles* (1891), *Jude the Obscure* (1895); among his poetical works were *Wessex Poems* (1898), *Poems of the Past and Present* (1901), *The Dynasts* (poetic drama in 3 parts, 1903–08). Works noted for philosophy of stoical pessimism, echoes of Greek tragic themes, mastery of regional dialect and folkways.

Hardy, Sir Thomas Masterman. Baronet. 1769–1839. British naval officer. Entered navy (1781); flag captain under Nelson (1799–1805), commanding *Vanguard* and *Victory;* baronet (1806); first sea lord of the admiralty (1830); vice admiral (1837).

Har·dyng \'härd-iŋ\, John. 1378–?1465. English chronicler. In service of Sir Henry Percy and later of Sir Robert de Umfraville. Composed metrical chronicle of England that came down originally to 1436, for Edward IV was extended to 1461.

Hare \'ha(ə)r, 'he(ə)r\, James H. 1856–1946. American photographer, b. London, England. Early experimenter with hand-held cameras; to U.S. (1889); covered Cuban revolution and Spanish–American War (1898), Russo–Japanese War (1904–05), Balkan War (1912) for *Collier's Weekly,* and World War I for *Leslie's Weekly;* a pioneer in aerial photography.

Hare, Sir John. *Orig.* John Fairs \'fa(ə)rz, 'fe(ə)rz\. 1844–1921. English actor and theater manager. Member of Prince of Wales's company in London (1865–74); co-manager of Court Theatre (1874–79) and St. James's Theatre (1879–88); actor-manager of Garrick Theatre (1889–95); considered one of finest character actors of the day.

Hare, Robert. 1781–1858. American chemist, b. Philadelphia. Professor, U. of Pennsylvania (1810–12, 1818–47). Invented oxyhydrogen blowpipe (1801).

Hare, Thomas. 1806–1891. English reformer. Best known for his proposed election system, giving each class of voters in the electorate representation in proportion to its numerical strength.

Hare, William. See William BURKE.

Har·go·bind \'här-gō-ˌbind\. 1595–1644. 6th Sikh Gurū. Son of Gurū Arjun, whom he succeeded (1606); devoted much time to martial training, building up Sikh army and stamping Sikh religion permanently with military character; built Akāl Takht temple and hall (1609); jailed for 12 years by Emperor Jahāngīr; led Sikh army to four victories over armies of Emperor Shāh Jahān.

Har·grave \'här-ˌgrāv\, Lawrence. 1850–1915. Australian aeronautical pioneer, b. England. To Australia (1866); experimented with monoplane models propelled by clockwork, rubber bands in tension, compressed air, and steam (1883–1903); invented a model rotary airplane engine (1889); invented the box kite (c.1893) and with 4 of them made an ascent (1894); abandoned experiments because of illness.

Har·graves \'här-ˌgrāvz\, Edward Hammond. 1816–1891. Australian gold prospector, b. England. To Australia (1832); managed sheep ranch (1834–49); discovered gold deposits near Bathurst (1851).

Har·greaves \'här-'grēvz\, James. d. 1778. English inventor. Weaver and mechanic near Blackburn; inventor of the spinning jenny (c.1764; patented 1770).

Ha·ri·bha·dra \ˌhə-ri-'bä-drə\ *or* **Haribhadra Sū·rī** \-sü-'rē\. 8th century. Indian writer. Adopted Jaina faith, entered monastery. Best known for treatises on Jaina doctrine and ethics and for commentaries, esp. *Ṣaḍdarśanasmuccaya.*

Ha·ri Krish·en \'här-ē-'krish-ən\. 1656–1664. 8th Sikh Gurū. Installed as Gurū at age five; said to have demonstrated great wisdom, percipience, healing power, and other attributes; died in cholera epidemic after being summoned to Delhi by Emperor Aurangzeb.

Hä·ring \'her-iŋ\, Georg Wilhelm. *Pseudonym* Willibald Alex·is \ä-'lek-səs\. 1798–1871. German journalist and novelist. Author of *Walladmor* (1824) and *Schloss Avalon* (1827), at first purported to be written by Sir Walter Scott; other works included *Cabanis* (1832), *Der falsche Waldemar* (1842), *Isegrimm* (1854), *Dorothee* (1856), etc.

Harington. See also HARRINGTON.

Har·ing·ton \'har-iŋ-tən\, Sir Charles Harington. 1872–1940. British soldier. Served in Boer War (1899–1900), World War I (1914–18); lieutenant general (1920); commanded Black Sea army (1920–21); commanded Allied forces of occupation in Turkey (1921–23); general (1927); commanded in India (1927–31); governor and commander in chief at Gibraltar (1933–37).

Harington *or* **Har·ring·ton** \'har-iŋ-tən\, Sir John. 1561–1612. English courtier and writer. Godson of Queen Elizabeth; translated Ariosto's *Orlando Furioso* (1591) by command of Elizabeth; banished from court because of certain satires, including *Metamorphosis of Ajax* (1596) on his invention of the flush toilet. Accompanied Essex to Ireland (1599). Author of numerous barbed epigrams, an account of Elizabeth's last days, a *Tract on the Succession to the Crown,* and an appendix to Godwin's *De Praesulibus Angliae.*

Harington, John. 1st Baron Harington of Ex·ton \'eks-tən\. d. 1613. English nobleman. Cousin of Sir John Harington; entrusted by James I at his coronation (1603) with guardianship of Princess Elizabeth at Combe Abbey; saved Elizabeth from Gunpowder Plot conspirators (1605); accompanied her to Germany on her marriage to elector palatine (1613); died on return journey.

Hariot, Thomas. See Thomas HARRIOT.

Ḥa·rī·rī, al- \al-ka-'rē-rē\. *In full* Abū Muḥammad al-Qāsim ibn 'Alī al-Ḥarīrī. 1054–1122. Arab scholar. Author of works on grammar and composition; known esp. for *Maqāmāt,* collection of humorous tales in refined style.

Ha·rish·chan·dra \,hə-rish-'chən-drə\. *Also known as* Bha·ra·ten·du \,bə-rə-'ten-dü\. 1850–1885. Indian writer. Established (1867) first Hindi literary magazine *Kavivachana-sudha* and (1872) its successor *Harishchandra Magazine* (later *Harishchandra Chandrika*); by own verse, dramas, etc., and those of writers patronized by magazines, helped usher in modern era of Hindi writing and helped establish Hindi as a chief language of official India.

Ha·ri·zi \hä-'rē-thē\, Judah ben Solomon. c.1170–c.1235. Spanish man of letters. Translated works from Arabic into Hebrew, including Maimonides's *Guide of the Perplexed* and al-Ḥarīrī's *Maqāmāt.* Author of collection of maqāmahs entitled *Tahkemoni.*

Har·khuf \'här-,küf\. fl. c.2290–2270 B.C. Egyptian official. Governor of southern Upper Egypt and overseer of caravans under Merenre and Pepi II of 6th dynasty; encouraged trade with Nubia and traveled widely through region.

Har·kins \'här-kənz\, William Draper. 1873–1951. American chemist, b. Titusville, Pa. Professor, U. of Montana (1900–12), U. of Chicago (1912–51); consultant to U.S. Bureau of Mines (1920–22), Chemical Warfare Service (from 1927). Known esp. for work on surface tension, isotopic weights, and atomic structure; first theorized hydrogen fusion reaction, predicted existence of heavy hydrogen.

Hark·ness \'härk-nəs\, Anna M., *nee* Richardson. 1837–1926. American philanthropist, b. Dalton, Ohio. m. Stephen V. Harkness (1854; d. 1888), who amassed fortune in oil business; at his death turned to philanthropy; gave $3 million to build Harkness Memorial Quadrangle (completed 1921) at Yale in memory of her son; with $20 million endowed (1920) Commonwealth Fund, to which she left additional $22 million in her will.

Har·lan \'här-lən\, John Marshall. 1833–1911. American jurist, b. Boyle County, Ky. Served in Union army in Civil War (1861–63); attorney general of Kentucky (1863–67). Associate justice, U.S. Supreme Court (1877–1911); noted esp. for forceful dissents as in civil rights cases; dissenting in *Plessy v. Ferguson* (1896) declared Constitution "color-blind." His grandson ¶John Marshall Harlan (1899–1971), jurist, b. Chicago; associate justice, U.S. Supreme Court (1955–71).

Har·land \'har-lənd\, Henry. 1861–1905. American writer, b. St. Petersburg, Russia, of American parents. Lived in London, England (from c.1890); associated with Aubrey Beardsley in publishing the *Yellow Book* (1894–97). Best known novels *The Cardinal's Snuff Box* (1900), *The Lady Paramount* (1902), *My Friend Prospero* (1904).

Har·lay de Champ·val·lon \àr-le-də-shäⁿ-và-lōⁿ\, François de. 1625–1695. French prelate. Archbishop of Rouen (1651) and of Paris (1671); strong supporter of Louis XIV and his policies, and one of the three witnesses to the secret marriage (1684) of Louis XIV and Mme. de Maintenon.

Har·ley \'här-lē\, Robert. 1st Earl of Ox·ford \'äks-fərd\. 1661–1724. English politician. M.P. (1689–1711) as moderate Tory; speaker (1701–05), a principal secretary of state (1704–08) through influence of Marlborough; employed Defoe and Swift as political writers; forced out of secretaryship by Godolphin and Marlborough for intriguing against them through behind-the-scenes influence with the queen; joined Tories. Chancellor of exchequer and head of ministry (1710) but unable to organize a government; created earl and made lord treasurer (1711), continuing as head of ministry (1711–14); negotiated separate peace, independently of Allies, and by dismissal of Marlborough and creation of new peers, carried treaty of Utrecht (1713). Superseded in queen's favor by his former friend St. John, Viscount Bolingbroke, and dismissed from office; imprisoned (1715–17).

Har·low \'här-(,)lō\, Jean. *Orig.* Harlean Car·pen·ter \'kär-pən-tər, 'kärp-ᵊm-tər\. 1911–1937. American actress, b. Kansas City, Mo. Achieved stardom through appeal of her languorous beauty, frankly sensual manner, and wisecracking humor; appeared in motion pictures including *Double Whoopee* (1928, with Laurel and Hardy), *Hell's Angels* (1930), *Platinum Blonde* (1931), *Public Enemy* (1931), *Red Dust* (1932), *Red-Headed Woman* (1932), *Dinner at Eight* (1933), *Bombshell* (1933), *Reckless* (1934), *China Seas* (1935), *Saratoga* (1937).

Har·man \'här-mən\, Martin Coles. 1885–1954. British ruler. Financier in London; bankrupt (1932) and imprisoned for fraud (1933–34). Purchased (1925) island of Lundy in Bristol Channel, of which he made himself absolute ruler; issued private postage stamps and, contrary to British law, private coinage (1929) bearing his likeness.

Har·men·sen \'här-mən-sən\ *or* **Her·mansz** \'her-,mänts\, Jacob. *Lat.* Jacobus Ar·min·ius \är-'min-ē-əs\. 1560–1609. Dutch clergyman and theologian. Professor at Leiden (1603–09); gradually turned against Calvinist doctrine of predestination and asserted conditional election, emphasizing free will and God's grace; drawn into numerous controversies, esp. with Gomarus. His followers signed a *Remonstrance* (1610) and were later expelled from Dutch Reformed church and persecuted; works published (1629); Arminianism and Remonstrant Brotherhood granted toleration (1630).

Harmhab. See HOREMHEB.

Har·mo·di·us \här-'mō-dē-əs\ and **Aris·to·gi·ton** \ə-,ris-tō-'jī-,tän, ,ar-əs-tō-\. d. 514 B.C. Athenian tyrannicides. Assassinated Hipparchus, tyrant of Athens, Harmodius being killed by guard and Aristogiton captured, tortured, and executed. In later age honored as heroes by Athenian people, although their act, contrary to popular legend, did not end Peisistratid tyranny.

Har·mon \'här-mən\, Millard Fillmore. 1888–1945. American army officer, b. San Francisco. Pilot in World War I; brigadier general (1940), major general (1941); commander, 2d air force (1941–42); chief of air staff (1942); lieutenant general (1943); commander, army ground and air forces in South Pacific (1942–44); commander, army air forces in Pacific (1944–45); lost in flight.

Harms·worth \'härmz-(,)wərth\. Family of British publishers and politicians, including:

Alfred Charles William (1865–1922), Viscount North·cliffe \'nȯrth-,klif\, b. Ireland; with his brother Harold, set up general publishing business in London (1887); started (1888) *Answers to Correspondents,* later called *Answers;* acquired (1894) and reorganized *Evening News,* Conservative party organ; founded (1896) *Daily Mail,* half-penny morning newspaper with innovative features and lively, condensed style; founded (1903) *Daily Mirror;* through newspapers sponsored scientific expeditions, aeronautical competitions, etc.; created baron (1905); controlled the *Observer* (1905–12); acquired *The Times* (1908); in World War I, advocate of vigorous conduct of war; criticized Lord Kitchener; engaged in controversies with Lloyd George; director of propaganda in enemy countries (1918).

¶Harold Sidney (1868–1940), 1st Viscount Roth·er·mere \'rät͟h-ər-,mi(ə)r\, joined Alfred in publishing periodicals and building up Amalgamated Press; bought Alfred's *Daily Mirror* (1914); created baron (1914); director general of royal army clothing dept. (1916–17); air minister (1917–18); viscount (1919); succeeded Alfred at head of Associated Newspapers (1922). Endowed King Edward VII chair of English literature and Vere Harmsworth chair of naval history at Cambridge, and Harold Vyvyan chair of American history at Oxford.

¶Cecil Bisshopp (1869–1948), 1st Baron Harmsworth; Liberal M.P. (1906–10, 1911–22); undersecretary for home affairs (1915) and foreign affairs (1919–22); acting minister of blockade (1919); member of supreme economic council; member of Council, League of Nations (1922); created baron (1939).

Har·nack \'här-,näk\, Adolf Karl Gustav von. 1851–1930. German theologian. Son of Theodosius Harnack; professor, Leipzig (1876–79), Giessen (1879–86), Marburg (1886–88), Berlin (1888–1921); became authority on church fathers, dogma and institutions of ancient church; recognized as historian of the first rank; general director of Prussian State Library (1905–21) and president of Kaiser-Wilhelm-Institut (1911–30). Author of *Lehrbuch der Dogmengeschichte* (1886–90), *Das apostolische Glaubensbekenntnis* (1892), *Geschichte der altchristliche Literatur* (1893–1904), *Vorlesungen über das Wesen des Christentums* (1900), *Die Mission und Ausbreitung des Christentums in den ersten drei Jahrhunderten* (1902), etc.

Harnack, Theodosius. 1817–1889. German theologian. Professor, Dorpat (1847–53, 1866–75), Erlangen (1853–66). Author of authoritative *Luthers Theologie* (1862–86); also *Die Kirche, ihr Amt, ihr Regiment* (1862), *Die freie lutheranische Volkskirche* (1870), *Praktische Theologie* (1877–78).

Har·nett \'här-nət\, William Michael. 1848–1892. American painter, b. County Cork, Ireland. To U.S. as child; became known as master of trompe l'oeil still lifes. Works included *After the Hunt, The Faithful Colt, The Old Violin, Artist's Card Pack.*

Har·ney \'här-nē\, George Julian. 1817–1897. English political leader. Advocate of Chartism and twice unsuccessful Chartist candidate for Parliament;

took up Socialism; edited Socialist *Northern Star* (1845–50); associated with Marx and Engels in Communist International.

Ha·ro \'ä-rō\, Luis de. *Full surname* Mén·dez de Ha·ro y Guz·mán \'mān-dāth-thā-'ä-rō-ē-güth-'män\. Duque de Car·pio \thā-'kärp-yō\. 1598–1661. Spanish politician. Nephew of Duke of Olivares; succeeded his uncle as chief minister of Philip IV (1623); negotiated peace of Pyrenees with France (1659).

Har·old \'har-əld\. *Dan.* Ha·rald \'här-äl\. Name of four kings of Den-mark:

Harold I. d. c.863. Warred with sons of Godfred for power; while exiled under protection of Emperor Louis I the Pious, adopted Christianity (826); on return to Denmark, aided missionary Ansgar.

Harold II. *Known as* Harald Blå·tand \'blō-,tän\, *i.e.* Bluetooth. c.910–c.985. King (c.950–c.985). Son of Gorm; claimed to have unified Denmark; conquered Norway, but could not retain it; converted to Christianity (c.960).

Harold. d. 1018. King (1014–18). Son of Sweyn I and brother of Canute the Great.

Harold. *Known as* Harald Hén \'hīn\, *i.e.* the Gentle. d. 1080. King (1074–80). Son and successor of Sweyn II.

Harold. Name of two kings of the English:

Harold I. *Called* Harold Hare·foot \'ha(ə)r-,fůt, 'he(ə)r-\. d. 1040. King (1035–1040). Illegitimate son of Canute; on death of Canute (1035), named regent for absent half-brother Hardecanute; claimed crown (1037) and banished Hardecanute's mother; elected king (1037) by the witan.

Harold II. c.1022–1066. King (1066). Son of Godwine, Earl of Wessex; served as chief minister of his brother-in-law, Edward the Confessor (1053–66); subjugated Wales (1063); on Edward's death, secured his own election as king; defeated his brother Tostig and Harold III Hardraade of Norway, Tostig's ally, at Stamford Bridge (Sept. 25, 1066); hastened south to meet William, Duke of Normandy, who had just landed in England; killed in battle of Hastings or Senlac (Oct. 14, 1066).

Harold. *Norw.* Harald. Name of three kings of Norway:

Harold I. *Called* Hår·fa·ger \'hòr-,fäg-ər\. *Old Norse* Hár·fag·ri \'hòr-,fäg-rē\, *i.e.* Fairhair. d. c.940. Son of Halvdan the Black, whom he succeeded to rule in southeastern Norway; waged continual war, culminating in battle of Hafrsfjord (traditionally 872, probably 10 to 20 years later), gaining control of western Norway; conquests and taxation compelled many Norsemen to settle elsewhere; established strong kingdom but power lost by dissension of sons; abdicated (930) in favor of Eric Bloodaxe.

Harold II. *Called* Grå·fell \'grò-,fel\. *Old Norse* Grá·feldr \'grò-,fel-dər\, *i.e.* Graycloak. d. c.970. King (961–970). Son of Eric Bloodaxe; with aid of brothers and uncle Harold Bluetooth, invaded Norway from Danish exile, overthrew and killed Haakon I (c.961); ruled harshly; overcome by Haakon the Great.

Harold III. *Called* Hard·raa·de \'hòr-,ròd-ə\, *i.e.* Hard Ruler. 1015–1066. King (1045–66). Son of Sigurd and a descendant of Harold I; present at battle of Stiklestad (1030) when his half-brother King Olaf was killed; visited courts of Novgorod, Kiev, and later (1033) Constantinople; many adventures attributed to him in Norse sagas; returned to Russia (1044) and to Norway (1045), becoming co-ruler with Magnus I Olafsson and sole king at death of Magnus (1047; fought long war with Danes (1047–62); requested by Tostig, brother of English king, Harold II, to aid in conquest of England (1066); sailed with large fleet; killed at battle of Stamford Bridge (Sept. 25).

Harold Gille \-'gil\. *Known as* Harold IV. *Also called* Gil·christ \'gil-(,)krist\. c.1103–1136. Norwegian pretender, b. Ireland. Claimed to be son of Magnus III Barefoot; appeared in Norway (1128); at death of Sigurd I (1130), chosen by one faction as king opposed to Magnus IV; civil war (1134–35); captured and blinded Magnus (1135); slain by pretender Sigurd Slembi.

Haroun-al-Raschid. See HĀRŪN AR-RASHĪD.

Har·pa·gus \'här-pə-gəs\. 6th century B.C. Median general. Sent by King Astyages to subdue rebel Cyrus II; instead joined Cyrus and became one of Cyrus's most trusted generals in conquest of Asia Minor.

Har·pa·lus \'här-pə-ləs\. c.355–323 B.C. Macedonian aristocrat. Associate of Alexander the Great; entrusted by Alexander with government of conquered Babylonia and guardianship of the royal treasure; stole the treasure and fled, first to Athens and then to Crete, where he was assassinated.

Har·per \'här-pər\, James. 1795–1869. American publisher, b. Newtown, Long Island, N.Y. With brother ¶John (1797–1875) set up printing office, New York (1817); began publishing books (1818); admitted brothers ¶Joseph Wesley (1801–1870) in 1823, and ¶Fletcher (1806–1877) in 1825; adopted firm name Harper & Bros. (1833); firm introduced *Harper's New Monthly* (1850), *Harper's Weekly* (1857), *Harper's Bazar* (1867, later *Bazaar*); James served as reform mayor of New York City (1844).

Harper, Jesse. 1884–1961. American athletic coach. Football coach at Wabash Coll. (1910–13), Notre Dame (1913–18); with players Knute Rockne and Gus Dorais, developed forward pass as a principal offensive weapon.

Harper, Robert Almer. 1862–1946. American biologist, b. Le Claire, Iowa. Professor, Lake Forest Coll. (1891–98), U. of Wisconsin (1898–1911), Columbia U. (1911–30); known for studies of cytology and esp. spore formation in Ascomycetes fungi.

Harper, Robert Goodloe. 1765–1825. American politician, b. near Fredericksburg, Va. U.S. representative from Maryland (1795–1801); served in War of 1812 as major general. U.S. senator (1816); an original member of American Colonization Society (1817). Known for toast proposed in aftermath of XYZ Affair (1798): "Millions for defense, but not a cent for tribute."

Harper, William Rainey. 1856–1906. American educator, b. New Concord, Ohio. Professor, Baptist Union Theological Seminary, Chicago (1879–86), Yale (1886–91); first president of U. of Chicago (1891–1906). Noted as Hebraic scholar. Author of *Religion and the Higher Life* (1904), *The Trend in Higher Education* (1905), etc.

Har·pi·gnies \ár-pēn-yē\, Henri-Joseph. 1819–1916. French painter. Known for landscapes, much in the manner of Corot.

Har·po·cra·ti·on \,här-pō-'krā-shē-ən\, Valerius. 2d century A.D. Greek scholar of Alexandria. Compiled valuable lexicon of works of Attic orators.

Har·pur \'har-pər\, Charles. 1813–1868. Australian poet. Author of sonnet series *Thoughts* (1845), verse drama *The Bushrangers* (1853), etc.

Har·ra·den \'har-ə-dən\, Beatrice. 1864–1936. English novelist. Author of *Ships that Pass in the Night* (1893), *Katharine Frensham* (1903), *The Scholar's Daughter* (1906), *Rachel* (1926), *Search Will Find It Out* (1928), etc.

Har Rāi \'här-'rī\. 1630–1661. 7th Sikh Gurū. Grandson and successor of Hargobind; Gurū (from 1644); contemplative, unmartial, reclusive; reign weakened Sikh power versus Mughal empire.

Har·ri·gan \'har-ə-gən\, Edward, *called* Ned. 1845–1911. American actor, b. New York City. Member of comedy team Harrigan and Hart (1872–85); with Hart co-manager of Theatre Comique, N.Y. (1876–81) and new Theatre Comique (1881–84); managed Harrigan's Park Theatre (from 1884).

Har·ri·man \'har-ə-mən\, Edward Henry. 1848–1909. American financier, b. Hempstead, N.Y. Office boy in Wall Street (1862–70); member, stock exchange (1870); acquired Lake Ontario Southern Railroad (1881); director (1883), vice president (1887), Illinois Central; reorganized Union Pacific (from 1898); acquired (1901) Southern Pacific and Central Pacific, dominating western traffic; lost battle with James J. Hill for Chicago, Burlington & Quincy (1901–04); investigated by Interstate Commerce Commission (1906–07). Sponsored scientific expedition to Alaska (1899).

Harriman, Florence Jaffray, *nee* Hurst \'hərst\. 1870–1967. American diplomat, b. New York City. m. J. Borden Harriman (1889; d. 1914). On board of managers, New York State Reformatory for Women (1906–18); member of Federal Industrial Relations Commission (1913–16); served in France with Red Cross Women's Motor Corps (1918). U.S. minister to Norway (1937–40). Author of *From Pinafores to Politics* (1923), *Mission to the North* (1941).

Harriman, William Averell. 1891–1986. American statesman, b. New York City. Leading U.S. diplomat in dealings with U.S.S.R. during Cold War. Served as U.S. diplomat to Britain and Soviet Union to expedite lend-lease aid; U.S. ambassador to Soviet Union (1943–46); ambassador to Great Britain (1946); assistant secretary of state for Far Eastern affairs (1961–63); chief U.S. negotiator in the Nuclear Test-Ban Treaty (1963); U.S. representative to Paris talks about peace in Vietnam. Also served as U.S. secretary of commerce (1946–48) and governor of New York (1955–59). Writings included *America and Russia in a Changing World* (1971).

Harrington. See also HARINGTON.

Har·ring·ton *or* **Har·ing·ton** \'har-iŋ-tən\, James. 1611–1677. English political theorist. Author of *The Commonwealth of Oceana* (1656), said to have influenced U.S. Founding Fathers, and several tracts supporting his Utopian state.

Har·ri·ot *or* **Har·i·ot** \'har-ē-ət\, Thomas. 1560–1621. English mathematician. Accompanied Raleigh's expedition to Roanoke Island (1585–86); described observations in *Briefe and True Report of the New Found Land of Virginia* (1588). His posthumously published *Artis analyticae praxis ad aequationes algebraicas resolvendas* (1631) contained inventions which gave algebra its modern form. Built telescope contemporaneously with Galileo, independently discovered sunspots and Jovian satellites; discovered law of refraction before Snell but did not publish.

Har·ris \'har-əs\, Alexander. 1805–1874. British writer. To Australia (1826); returned to England (1842); later a missionary and schoolteacher in Canada. Author of *Settlers and Convicts; or, Recollections of Sixteen Years' Labour in the Australian Backwoods* (1847).

Harris, Benjamin. fl. 1673–1716. English publisher and journalist. To America and opened bookshop in Boston (1686); published short-lived *Publick Occurrences Both Forreign and Domestick,* first newspaper printed in America (Sept. 25, 1690); published the famous *New England Primer* (c.1690). Returned to London (1695); published *London Post* (1699–1706).

Harris, Chapin Aaron. 1806–1860. American dentist, b. Pompey, N.Y. Founder with Horace H. Hayden of world's first dental college, Baltimore College of

Dental Surgery (chartered 1840); founded (1839) *American Journal of Dental Science.*

Harris, Charles Kassell. 1865–1930. American songwriter, b. Poughkeepsie, N.Y. Writer of "After the Ball" (1892), "Break the News to Mother" (1897), "Hello, Central, Give Me Heaven" (1901), etc.

Harris, Frank, *orig.* James Thomas. 1856–1931. Irish journalist and writer. To U.S. (1870); editor, London *Evening News* (1884–86) and *Fortnightly Review* (1886–94); acquired control of *Saturday Review,* London (1894–98); failed in attempt to enter politics; edited *Pearson's Magazine* in U.S. (1914–18). His biography *Oscar Wilde* (1916) and the autobiographical *My Life and Loves* (1923) excited hostile criticism because of their sexual frankness. Other works included *The Man Shakespeare* (1909), *Contemporary Portraits* (1915–30); short stories *Elder Conklin* (1894), *Montes the Matador* (1900), *The Veils of Isis* (1915); novels *The Bomb* (1908), *Great Days* (1914), and *Love in Youth* (1916); plays *Mr. and Mrs. Daventry* (1900), *Shakespeare and His Love* (1910), and *Joan la Romée* (1926).

Harris, George. 1st Baron Harris. 1746–1829. English soldier. Wounded at Bunker Hill (1775); served against Tippu Sultan in India (1790–92), commanded troops in Madras (1796–1800), and captured Seringapatam and conquered Mysore (1799); general (1812); baron (1815).

Harris, George Washington. 1814–1869. American humorist, b. Allegheny City, Pa. Contributed sketches to *Spirit of the Times* and other newspapers; known esp. for comic tales of the old Southwest featuring the character Sut Lovingood. Published collection as *Yarns* (1867).

Harris, Howel. 1714–1773. Welsh clergyman. Methodist preacher (from 1735); a founder of Welsh Calvinistic Methodism.

Harris, James. 1st Earl of Malmes·bury \ˈmämz-bər-ē, -brē\. 1746–1820. English diplomat. M.P. (1770–74, 1780–88); minister, Berlin (1772–76); ambassador at St. Petersburg (1777–82); minister at The Hague (1784–88); instrumental in overthrow of republican party in Holland in favor of house of Orange. Sent on futile mission to hold Prussia to first coalition against France (1793); negotiated match between Prince of Wales and Princess Caroline of Brunswick; failed in last missions to negotiate peace with French Republic (1796, 1797). Created earl (1800).

Harris, Joel Chandler. 1848–1908. American writer, b. Eatonton, Ga. On staff, Atlanta *Constitution* (1876–1900). Fame rests on his creation of Uncle Remus, Brer Rabbit, Brer Fox, and other characters as in *Uncle Remus, His Songs and His Sayings* (1880), *Nights with Uncle Remus* (1883), *Uncle Remus and His Friends* (1892), *The Tar Baby* (1904), *Uncle Remus and Brer Rabbit* (1906); edited *Uncle Remus's Magazine* (1907–08). Other works included *Mingo, and Other Sketches in Black and White* (1884), *Free Joe and Other Georgia Sketches* (1887), *Gabriel Tolliver* (1902).

Harris, John. c.1666–1719. English theologian and scientist. Compiled *Lexicon Technicum,* first dictionary in English of the arts and sciences (1704).

Harris, John Wyndham Parkes Lucas Beynon. *Pseudonym* John Wynd·ham \ˈwin-dəm\. 1903–1969. English writer. Author of science fiction novels *The Day of the Triffids* (1951), *The Kraken Wakes* (1953; U.S. title *Out of the Deeps*), *The Chrysalids* (1955; U.S. title *Rebirth*), *The Midwych Cuckoos* (1957), *Trouble with Lichen* (1960), *Chocky* (1968), *Web* (1979), etc., and science fiction stories collected in *Jizzle* (1954), *The Seeds of Time* (1956), *Consider Her Ways* (1961).

Harris, Paul Percy. 1868–1947. American lawyer, b. Racine, Wis. In Chicago founded (1905) first Rotary club for young businessmen; organized National Association of Rotary Clubs and served as first president (1910–12).

Harris, Renatus *or* René. c.1652–1724. English organ builder, b. France. Son and grandson of organ builders; built some 39 instruments; one of finest builders of the day and a bitter rival of Bernard Smith.

Harris, Roy Ellsworth. 1898–1979. American composer, b. Lincoln Co., Okla. Taught at Juilliard School (1932–40), Cornell U. (1940–42), Colorado Coll. (1942–48), Utah State Coll. (1948–49), Peabody Coll. (1949–51), Pennsylvania Women's Coll. (1951–56), Indiana U. (1957–60), UCLA (1961–79). Compositions included 14 symphonies, notably No. 3 (1937) and choral *Folksong Symphony* (No. 4, 1940); other orchestral works as *When Johnny Comes Marching Home* (1935), *American Creed* (1940), *Kentucky Spring* (1949), *Salute to Youth* (1965); choral works as *Song for Occupations* (1934), *Symphony for Voices* (1935), *Railroad Man's Ballad* (1941), *Year that Trembled* (1941), *Walt Whitman Suite* (1944), *Folk Fantasy for Festivals* (1956); chamber and vocal pieces.

Harris, Sam Henry. 1872–1941. American theatrical producer, b. New York City. Associated with George M. Cohan (*q.v.*) in firm Cohan & Harris (1904–20); in business alone (from 1920), produced *Rain* (1922), *The Jazz Singer* (1925), *The Cocoanuts* (1925), *Animal Crackers* (1928), *Dinner at Eight* (1932), *Of Thee I Sing* (1932), *As Thousands Cheer* (1933), *Night Must Fall* (1936), *You Can't Take It With You* (1937), *I'd Rather Be Right* (1937), *Of Mice and Men* (1938), *The Man Who Came to Dinner* (1939), *Lady in the Dark* (1941).

Harris, Thomas Lake. 1823–1906. American spiritualist, b. Fenny Stratford, England. To U.S. as a child; became Universalist minister (1843); interested in spiritualism (from 1847); became medium (about 1850). Established brotherhood communities, notably at Amenia, N.Y. (about 1863), near Dunkirk, N.Y. (about 1866), and Santa Rosa, Calif. (about 1875).

Harris, Townsend. 1804–1878. American diplomat, b. Sandy Hill, N.Y. Merchant in New York City; instrumental in founding (1847) of Free Academy (later Coll. of the City of New York). Entered consular service after meeting Matthew C. Perry in Shanghai (1853); first U.S. consul general to Japan (1855–60); overcame Japanese antipathy and negotiated commercial treaty (1858).

Harris, William Torrey. 1835–1909. American philosopher and educator, b. North Killingly, Conn. Taught school, St. Louis, Mo. (1857–80); superintendent of schools (from 1868). Founded and edited *Journal of Speculative Philosophy* (1867–93). Associated with Bronson Alcott in Concord School of Philosophy (1880–89). U.S. commissioner of education (1889–1906). Became leading American interpreter of German philosophical thought, esp. that of Hegel. Editor in chief, *Webster's New International Dictionary,* first edition (1909). Author of *Introduction to the Study of Philosophy* (1889), *The Spiritual Sense of Dante's Divina Commedia* (1889), *The Psychologic Foundations of Education* (1898).

Harrison, Alexander. See Thomas Alexander HARRISON.

Har·ri·son \ˈhar-ə-sən\, Benjamin. 1726?–1791. American Revolutionary leader, b. Charles City Co., Va. Member, Virginia legislature (1749–75). Member, Continental Congress (1774–78); a signer of Declaration of Independence. Governor of Virginia (1782–84).

Harrison, Benjamin. 1833–1901. Twenty-third president of the United States, b. North Bend, Ohio. Grandson of William Henry Harrison; served through Civil War; brevetted brigadier general (1865); after war, resumed law practice at Indianapolis; unsuccessful candidate for governor (1876). U.S. senator (1881–87). President of the United States (1889–93); defeated by Cleveland (1892).

Harrison, Frederic. 1831–1923. English writer and philosopher. Called to bar (1858); professor in Lincoln's Inn (1877–89). Interested himself in positivism and the Church of Humanity (from c.1856); regarded as one of the leaders in the movement in England; with his associates opened a meeting place in London (1881); founded the *Positivist Review* (1893). Author of *The Meaning of History* (1862), *Order and Progress* (1874), *The Choice of Books* (1886), *Oliver Cromwell* (1888), *Positivism* (1901), *Ruskin* (1902), *The Positive Evolution of Religion* (1913), *De Senectute* (1923).

Harrison, Jane Ellen. 1850–1928. English scholar. Lecturer in classical archaeology, Newnham College, Cambridge (1898–1922). Author of *The Mythology and Monuments of Ancient Athens* (1890), *Prolegomena to the Study of Greek Religion* (1903), *Themis* (1912), etc.

Harrison, John. 1693–1776. English horologist and inventor. Invented gridiron pendulum (1726); developed (1730–63) marine chronometer for use in determining longitude at sea, winning government prize (1773).

Harrison, Peter. 1716–1775. American architect, b. York, England. To America (1740); settled in Newport, R.I. Designer of buildings in pure Palladian style, as Redwood Library, Newport, King's Chapel, Boston, and Christ Church, Cambridge, Mass.

Harrison, Ross Granville. 1870–1959. American biologist, b. Germantown, Pa. Professor, Johns Hopkins (1899–1907), Yale (1907–38); devised techniques for tissue culture, tissue transplants; studied embryonic development. Chairman, National Research Council (1938–46). Managing editor, *Journal of Experimental Zoology* (1903–46).

Harrison, Thomas. 1606–1660. English Parliamentary soldier and regicide. In action at Edgehill, Marston Moor, Naseby; elected to Parliament (1646); member of Fifth Monarchy group; advocated trial of Charles I, and escorted him from Hurst to London; signed king's death warrant; held chief command in England during Cromwell's absence (1650–51); member of Council of State (1651); refused to acknowledge Protectorate (1653); imprisoned (1655–56, 1658–59). At Restoration (1660), refused to flee or compromise; executed.

Harrison, Thomas Alexander, *known as* Alexander. 1853–1930. American painter, b. Philadelphia. Resided in France; noted esp. for marines.

Harrison, Wallace Kirkman. 1895–1981. American architect, b. Worcester, Mass. Trained in offices of McKim, Mead & White and Bertram G. Goodhue; as partner of Harvey W. Corbett, worked with Raymond Hood on design of Rockefeller Center and designed 1939 New York World's Fair, including the Trylon and Perisphere symbols. As partner in Harrison & Abramovitz (1940–79) designed United Nations complex; Time & Life, McGraw-Hill,

Exxon, Celanese buildings; and Lincoln Center, all in New York City; Empire State Plaza, Albany.

Harrison, William. 1534–1593. English topographer and clergyman. Rector of Radwinter (1559–93); canon of Windsor (1586). Author of valuable *Description of England* (1577).

Harrison, William Henry. 1773–1841. Ninth president of the United States, b. Charles City Co., Va. Son of Benjamin Harrison (1726?–1791); served in army (1791–98); secretary, Northwest Territory (1798); governor, Territory of Indiana (1800–12); negotiated large purchases of Indian lands; led military campaign against Indians culminating in Battle of Tippecanoe Creek (Nov. 7, 1811). Appointed to command army of the northwest, with rank of brigadier general, U.S. army (1812); occupied Detroit, won Battle of the Thames (1813) over Tecumseh and the British; major general (1813). Member, U.S. House of Representatives from Ohio (1816–19), U.S. Senate (1825–28). U.S. minister to Colombia (1828–29). Unsuccessful Whig candidate for president (1836). Elected president after boisterous campaign that featured slogan "Tippecanoe and Tyler too" (1840); died of pneumonia after one month in office.

Har•ry \ˈhər-ē\ *or* **Hen•ry** \ˈhen-rē\ the Minstrel. *Also called* Blind Harry. fl. 1470–92. Scottish poet. Traditionally, a blind wandering minstrel; collected legends of Sir William Wallace and evolved them into verse novel *Acts and Deeds of the Illustrious and Valiant Champion Sir William Wallace, Knight of Elderslie* (1488), immensely popular work of Scottish patriotism.

Har•ṣa \ˈhər-shə\. *Also spelled* Har•sha. *Called* Har•ṣa•var•dhana \ˈhər-shə-ˈvər-də-nə\. c.590–c.647. King of northern India (606-647). Reduced anarchy in the north (606-612) and established strong kingdom, with Kanauj as capital; failed to conquer the Deccan (c.620). Convert to Buddhism; a patron of art and literature, and himself a poet and author, esp. of three Sanskrit plays *Ratnāvalī, Nāgānanda,* and *Priyadarśikā;* his court made famous by the Brahman author Bāṇa and events of his reign described by the Chinese pilgrim Hsüan-tsang.

Hars•dör•fer \ˈhärs-ˌdər-fər\, Georg Philipp. 1607–1658. German poet. Town official, Nürnberg (from 1632); with Johann Klag founded (1644) Pegnitzer Hirtengesellschaft, chief of the German Baroque literary societies; a leading theorist of Baroque style. Author of *Frawenzimmer Gesprech-Spiele* (1641–49), *Poetischer Trichter, die Teutsche Dicht und Reimkunst, ohne Behuf der Lateinischen Sprache, in sechs Stunden einzugiessen* (1647–53).

Hart \ˈhärt\, Albert Bushnell. 1854–1943. American historian, b. Clarksville, Pa. Teacher, Harvard (from 1883), professor (1897–1926). Author of *Formation of the Union* (1892), *Guide to the Study of American History* (1896, with Edward Channing), *Foundations of American Foreign Policy* (1901), *Essentials of American History* (1905), *The Monroe Doctrine* (1917), *We and Our History* (1923), etc. Editor of several series of histories, as *Epochs of American History* (1891–1926) and *The American Nation* (1903–18).

Hart, Basil Henry Liddell. See LIDDELL HART.

Hart, Charles. d. 1683. English actor. Grandson of Shakespeare's sister Joan; popular in private theatricals during Commonwealth; became one of leading actors on Restoration stage; member of Thomas Killigrew's company at Theatre Royal (1663–82); said to have trained Nell Gwyn.

Hart, Heinrich (1855–1906) and his brother Julius (1859–1930). German writers and critics. Collaborators in editing *Kritische Waffengänge* (1882–84), through which they were instrumental in introducing Naturalism into German theater; founded Freie Bühne theater group (1889). Heinrich published verse *Weltpfingsten* (1872), unfinished epic *Lied der Menschheit* (1888–96); Julius, the verse *Sansara* (1879), *Homo Sum* (1890), dramas *Don Juan Tenorio* (1881), *Der Rächer* (1883), *Der Sumpf* (1886).

Hart, John. 1711?–1779. American Revolutionary leader, b. Stonington, Conn. Member, N.J. provincial assembly (1761–71) and congress (1775–76), Continental Congress (1776). A signer of Declaration of Independence. Chairman, N.J. council of safety (1777–78).

Hart, Liddell. See LIDDELL HART.

Hart, Lorenz Milton. 1895–1943. American lyricist, b. New York City. With Richard Rodgers wrote songs for Broadway shows *The Little Ritz Girl* (1920), *Garrick Gaieties* (1925), *Dearest Enemy* (1925), *A Connecticut Yankee* (1927), *Present Arms* (1928), *America's Sweetheart* (1931), *Jumbo* (1935), *I'd Rather Be Right* (1937), *Babes in Arms* (1937), *The Boys from Syracuse* (1938), *I Married an Angel* (1938), *Pal Joey* (1940), *By Jupiter* (1942). Songs included "Sentimental Me," "Thou Swell," "You Took Advantage of Me," "Where or When," "The Lady is a Tramp," "My Funny Valentine," "Bewitched, Bothered, and Bewildered," "Blue Moon."

Hart, Marvin. 1876–1931. American boxer. Held disputed world heavyweight title (1905–06) from resignation of James J. Jeffries to defeat by Tommy Burns.

Hart, Moss. 1904–1961. American playwright, b. New York City. Collaborator with Irving Berlin in *Face the Music* (1932) and *As Thousands Cheer* (1933), with Cole Porter in *Jubilee* (1935), and with George S. Kaufman in *Once in a Lifetime* (1930), *You Can't Take It With You* (1936, Pulitzer prize), *I'd Rather be Right* (1937), *The Man Who Came to Dinner* (1939), *George Washington Slept Here* (1940). Alone wrote *Lady in the Dark* (1941), *Winged Victory* (1943), *Light Up the Sky* (1948), and movie scripts *Broadway Melody of 1936* (1935), *Gentlemen's Agreement* (1947, Academy Award), *Hans Christian Anderson* (1952); noted also as Broadway director as of *Miss Liberty* (1949), *My Fair Lady* (1956), *Camelot* (1960).

Hart, Sir Robert. 1835–1911. British diplomat, b. Ireland. Entered Chinese consular service (1854); became inspector general of maritime customs (1863–1908), and practically creator of Chinese imperial customs.

Hart, Thomas Charles. 1877–1971. American naval officer, b. Davidson, Mich. Submarine officer in World War I; rear admiral (1929); admiral and commander in chief, Asiatic fleet (1939–42); commander, Allied naval forces in Far East (1942); U.S. senator from Conn. (1945–46).

Hart, William Surrey. 1872–1946. American actor, b. Newburgh, N.Y. On legitimate stage (1889–1914) starred in *Ben Hur, The Squaw Man, The Virginian, The Barrier, The Trail of the Lonesome Pine,* etc.; in motion pictures achieved worldwide fame as western hero; films included *The Passing of Two-Gun Hicks* (1914), *Hell's Hinges* (1916), *Captive God* (1916), *Dawnmaker* (1916), *Truthful Tulliver* (1917), *Gunfighter* (1917), *Wild Bill Hickok* (1923), *Singer Jim McKee* (1924), *Tumbleweeds* (1925).

Harte \ˈhärt\, Francis Brett, *known as* Bret \ˈbret\. 1836–1902. American writer, b. Albany, N.Y. Went to California, via Nicaragua (1854); in San Francisco, typesetter on *Golden Era;* began contribution of poems and sketches to this journal (1860); contributor to the *Californian* (1864–66). Editor, *Overland Monthly* (1868–70). Tales of California mining camps as "The Luck of Roaring Camp," "Outcasts of Poker Flat," won him adulation in East and in England; also wrote poem "Plain Language from Truthful James" (1870, also known as "The Heathen Chinee"); books included *The Luck of Roaring Camp and Other Sketches* (1870), *Mrs. Skagg's Husbands* (1873), *Tales of the Argonauts* (1875).

Harthacnut. See HARDECANUTE.

Hartington, Marquises of. See CAVENDISH family.

Hart•le•ben \ˈhärt-ˌlā-bən\, Otto Erich. 1864–1905. German writer. Author of verse; tales as *Vom gastfreien Pastor* (1895), *Das Ehefest* (1906); comedies *Angele* (1890), *Hanna Jagert* (1893); naturalistic dramas *Der Frosch* (1889), *Rosenmontag* (1900).

Hart•ley \ˈhärt-lē\, David. 1705–1757. English psychologist and philosopher. Practicing physician; attempted to ground psychology in physiology and expounded his doctrine of associationism in *Observations on Man, his Frame, his Duty, and his Expectations* (1749). His son ¶David (1731–1813) was M.P. (1774–80, 1782–84); with Benjamin Franklin, drafted and signed Treaty of Paris between U.S. and Great Britain (1783); invented method of fireproofing houses. Published *Letters on the American War* (1778–79).

Hartley, Leslie Poles. 1895–1972. English writer. Author of tales of the fantastic or the macabre, as *Night Fears* (1924), *The Killing Bottle* (1932); novels *The Shrimp and the Anemone* (1944), *The Sixth Heaven* (1946), *Eustace and Hilda* (1947), *The Boat* (1949), *The Go-Between* (1953), *A Perfect Woman* (1955), *The Hireling* (1957), *My Sister's Keeper* (1970).

Hartley, Marsden. 1877–1943. American painter, b. Lewiston, Me. Experimented in various abstract styles marked by bold forms and color contrasts; evolved a personal style of Expressionism; painted harsh landscapes.

Hart•lib \ˈhärt-(ˌ)lib\, Samuel. c.1600–1662. English reformer, b. Prussia of Polish father and English mother. Friend of Milton; introduced Comenius's works in England. Published pamphlets on universal education and husbandry and utopian essay *Macaria* (1641).

Hart•line \ˈhärt-ˌlīn\, Halden Keffer. 1903–1983. American biophysicist, b. Bloomsburg, Pa. Professor of biophysics at Cornell U. Medical College (1936–49) and at Johns Hopkins U. (1949–53); researcher in electrophysiology of the retina at Rockefeller U. (1953–74). Shared 1967 Nobel prize for physiology or medicine with George Wald and Ragnar Granit for discoveries about chemical and physiological processes of vision. His discoveries paved the way for advances in the neurophysiology of vision.

Hart•mann \ˈhärt-mən\, Carl Sadakichi. 1869–1944. American writer, b. Nagasaki, Japan, of a German father and a Japanese mother. To U.S. (1882); became notable bohemian. Author of privately published plays *Christ* (1893), *Buddha* (1897), *Confucius* (1923), *Moses* (1934); poetry, *Drifting Flowers of the Sea* (1906), *My Rubaiyat* (1913), *Tanka and Haikai* (1913); and books on art as *Shakespeare in Art* (1900), *Japanese Art* (1904), etc.

Hart•mann \ˈhärt-ˌmän\, Eduard von, *in full* Karl Robert Eduard. 1842–1906. German philosopher. Synthesized views of Schopenhauer, Kant, Hegel into doctrine of evolutionary history based on conflict of unconscious will with unconscious reason; generally considered a pessimist. Author of *Philosophie des Unbewussten* (1869), *Die Phänomenologie des sittlichen Bewusstseins* (1879), *Die Religion des Geistes* (1882), etc.

Hart•mann \ˈhärt-mán\, Johann Peter Emilius. 1805–1900. Danish composer. Organist of Garnisonkirke (1824–43), Vor Frue Kirke (1843–1900), Copenhagen; a director of Copenhagen Conservatory (1867–1900). Composed operas *Ravnen* (1832), *Korsarerne* (1835), *Liden Kirsten* (1846); ballets for August

Bournonville and other theatrical music, as for plays of Oehlenschlaeger; a chief exponent of Danish Romanticism.

Hart·mann \'härt-ˌmän\, Johannes Franz. 1865–1936. German astronomer. On staff of Potsdam observatory (1896–1909); professor and director of observatory, Göttingen (1909–21), La Plata, Argentina (1921–35). Known esp. for work in spectroscopy; established existence of interstellar matter; invented a microphotometer and a spectrocomparator.

Hartmann, Karl Amadeus. 1905–1963. German composer. Founded (1945) Musica Viva concerts, Munich. Works included symphonies as *Miserae* (1933–34), *L'Oeuvre* (1938), *Klagegesang* (1944), *Adagio* (1946); *Concerto funebre* (1939), overture *China kämpft* (1942); vocal works as *Simplicius Simplicissimus* (1934–35), *Friede–Anno 48* (1936), *Lamento* (1956), *Gesangsszene* (1963); chamber works, etc.

Hartmann, Moritz. 1821–1872. German writer. His collected patriotic verse, *Kelch und Schwert* (1845), caused imprisonment by Austrian authorities; member of the Frankfurt parliament (1848); on suppression of the revolution, fled abroad. Returned to Vienna (1868) and served on staff of *Neue Freie Presse.* Author also of satire *Reimchronik des Pfaffen Maurizius* (1849), *Der Krieg um den Wald* (1850), etc. His son ¶Ludo Moritz (1865–1924) was a historian; professor, Vienna (1918–24); Austrian minister to Berlin (1918–21); chief work, *Geschichte Italiens im Mittelalter* (1897–1915).

Hartmann, Nicolai. 1882–1950. German philosopher. Professor, Marburg (1920–25), Cologne (1925–31), Berlin (1931–46), Göttingen (1946–50). Influenced by Plato and early by Kant, evolved an ontological view of world as orderly, alien, partly knowable; rejected system-building in philosophy and developed aporetic approach to problems. Author of *Platos Logik des Seins* (1909), *Die Philosophie des deutschen Idealismus* (1923–29), *Ethik* (1926), *Neue Wege der Ontologie* (1942), *Philosophie der Natur* (1950), *Ästhetik* (1953), etc.

Hartmann von Aue \-fōn-'au̇-ə\. fl. 1190–1210. Middle High German poet. Chiefly notable for Arthurian romances *Erek* and *Iwein,* both being free versions of work of Chrétien de Troyes (*q.v.*); through his *Erek,* Arthurian legend entered German literature. Others were poems *Gregorius auf dem Steine* and *Der Arme Heinrich.*

Hart·ness \'härt-nəs\, James. 1861–1934. American engineer and inventor, b. Schenectady, N.Y. Superintendent, manager, president of Jones & Lamson Machine Co., Springfield, Vt.; invented the flat turret lathe, automatic die, Hartness chuck, turret equatorial telescope, and an optical screw thread comparator. Governor of Vermont (1921–23).

Har·tog \'här-tȯk\ *or* **Har·togs·zoon** \'här-tȯk-sən, -sȯn, -sōn\, Dirck. fl. 1616. Dutch navigator. First sighted and explored western coast of Australia (1616).

Har·ty \'härt-ē\, Sir Hamilton, *in full* Herbert Hamilton. 1880–1941. British conductor and composer, b. Ireland. Conductor of Hallé Orchestra (1920–33). Composer of *An Irish Symphony,* tone poem *With the Wild Geese,* cantata *Mystic Trumpeter,* etc.

Hart·zen·busch \'härt-säm-ˌbüch, *Ger* 'härt-sən-ˌbu̇sh\, Juan Eugenio. 1806–1880. Spanish playwright. A leader in Romantic movement in Spanish literature. Author of *Los amantes de Teruel* (1837), *Doña Mencía* (1839), *Los polvos de la madre Celestina* (1840), *La madre de Pelayo* (1846), *La luz de la raza* (1852), etc.

Hā·rūn ar-Ra·shīd \hä-'rü-nar-ash-'ēd\. *In full* Hārūn ar-Rashīd ibn Muḥammad al-Mahdī ibn al-Manṣūr al-'Abbāsī. 763 or 766–809. Fifth caliph (786–809). Son of al-Mahdī; nominal leader of military expeditions against Byzantine Empire (780, 782); succeeded his brother Musa al-Hādī (caliph 785–786). Under him, Eastern caliphate attained its greatest power and covered all southwestern Asia and northern Africa; made Baghdad center of Arabic culture. Engaged in war (791–809) with Byzantines; led armies in person against Emperor Nicephorus I, who had broken peace treaty (805), defeating him at Heraclea Pontica (Eregli) and Tyana (806) and exacting extra tribute. Became jealous of Barmakids and destroyed their head (c.803), Vizier Yaḥyā and his sons; faced many insurrections and toward end of reign had only nominal allegiance of much of North Africa because of rise (788) of Idrisid dynasty; died on expedition to suppress uprising in Khorāsān. Much of the splendor associated with his name is the result of legends and of his idealization among Arabs as the caliph of *Thousand and One Nights.*

Ha·ru·no·bu \här-ü-nō-bü\ Suzuki. 1724–1770. Japanese painter and printer. As a painter, much influenced by Masanobu; said to have invented color printing in Japan; known esp. for portrayals of mothers and children.

Har·vard \'här-vərd\, John. 1607–1638. American colonial clergyman, b. London, England. To America (1637); settled at Charlestown, Mass. Left his library and half his estate, valued at about £800, to the newly founded college at "New Towne" (later Cambridge). The Massachusetts General Court named the college in his honor (1639).

Har·vey \'här-vē\, Edmund Newton. 1887–1959. American physiologist, b. Philadelphia. Professor, Princeton (1911–56); known for studies of bioluminescence, cell permeability, nerve conduction, brain potentials, etc.

Harvey, Frederick Henry. 1835–1901. American restaurateur, b. London, England. To U.S. (c.1850); opened restaurant at depot of Atchison, Topeka & Santa Fe railroad, Topeka, Kans. (1876); created chain of restaurants along AT & SF and other Western lines, staffed by trained "Harvey Girl" waitresses; expanded to hotels and started (1890) fleet of dining cars.

Harvey, Gabriel. 1545?–?1630. English poet and controversialist. Friend of Spenser, as celebrated in latter's *Shepheardes Calender* (1579); champion of classical prosody, claimed to be the father of English hexameter. His satirical verse gave offense at court (1579); attacked Robert Greene and Thomas Nash, creating a literary scandal finally quashed by the archbishop of Canterbury (1599). Author of elegies as *Smithus: vel Musarum lachrymae* (1578), and other verse.

Harvey, George Brinton McClellan. 1864–1928. American journalist, b. Peacham, Vt. Owner and editor, *North American Review* (1899–1926); president, Harper & Bros. (1900–15); editor, *Harper's Weekly* (1901–13), *Harvey's Weekly* (1918–21). Instrumental in bringing about Wilson's nomination for governor of New Jersey (1910); supported Wilson for presidency (1912); influential in selection of Harding as Republican candidate (1920). U.S. ambassador to Great Britain (1921–23).

Harvey, Hayward Augustus. 1824–1893. American steel manufacturer and inventor, b. Jamestown, N.Y. Founded (1886) Harvey Steel Co.; invented a hay cutter, peripheral grip bolt, and the carburizing or cementing process for hardening the surface of steel, esp. for use in armor plate for battleships.

Harvey, Sir John Martin. *Known also as* Martin-Harvey. 1863–1944. English actor and theater manager. Member of Sir Henry Irving's company (1882–96); manager of various London theaters. Achieved great success in *The Only Way* (1899) and Max Reinhardt's production of *Oedipus Rex* (1912).

Harvey, William. 1578–1657. English physician and anatomist. Studied medicine under Fabricius and Galileo at Padua (1597–1602); practiced in London; physician of St. Bartholomew's Hospital (1609–43); Lumleian lecturer at Coll. of Physicians (1615–56); physician extraordinary to James I (1618) and Charles I (1625). Royalist in sympathy during Civil War; present at battle of Edgehill; accompanied Charles I to Oxford. First expounded theory of circulation of the blood in *Exercitatio de Motu Cordis et Sanguinis in Animalibus* (1628), including explanations of heart valves, arterial pulse, pulmonary circulation, venous valves; also wrote *Exercitationes de Generatione Animalium* (1651) on animal reproduction.

Harvey, William Hope. *Known as* Coin Harvey. 1851–1936. American economist, b. Buffalo, Va. (now W.Va.). Vigorous advocate of bimetallism (from 1893); founded Coin Publishing Co., Chicago, to promote the cause. Author of *Coin's Financial School* (1894), *Coin on Money, Trusts and Imperialism* (1899), *Common Sense* (1920), etc.

Har·wood \'här-wu̇d\, Sir Henry Harwood. 1888–1950. British naval officer. Commander of South America division (1936–40); commanded British naval forces in action against German pocket battleship *Admiral Graf Spee* off the Plate River (Dec. 1939); rear admiral (1939); commander of British Mediterranean fleet (1942–43); admiral (1945).

Ḥa·san \ka-'san\. *In full* Ḥasan ibn 'Alī ibn Abī Ṭālib. 624–680. Islāmic caliph (661). Grandson of Muḥammad, son of 'Alī and Fatima; sent by father to secure allegiance of Kūfah to 'Alī's caliphate; proclaimed caliph by most of 'Alī's followers on his assassination (661); at first resisted but then bowed to Mu'āwiyah I and abdicated; retired to Medina. His brother ¶Ḥusayn, *in full* Ḥusayn ibn 'Alī (c.629–680), revolted against Mu'āwiyah's successor Yazīd and attempted to claim caliphate (680); assassinated. Became object of devotion among Shī'ite Muslims.

Ha·san \ha-'san\, Moulay. *Arab.* Mawlāy Abū 'Alī al-Ḥasan. *Also known as* Ḥasan ibn Muḥammad. 1857–1894. Sultan of Morocco (1873–94). By careful diplomacy reduced European threats to Moroccan sovereignty; instituted reforms; created standing army.

Ḥa·san \ka-'san\, Sayyid Muḥammad ibn 'Abd Allāh. 1864–1920. Somali religious leader. Joined (1894) Ṣaliḥīyah Order, militant fundamentalist Islāmic sect; began to agitate for expulsion of British infidels from Somaliland; declared holy war on European colonialists (1899); followers became known as Dervishes and he as the "Mad Mullah"; forced to conclude truce (1904); resumed holy war (1908); finally conquered (1920).

Ḥasan al-Ban·nā' \-ab-ban-'nä\. 1906–1949. Egyptian political and religious leader. Founded (1928) al-Ikhwān al-Muslimūn, known as the Muslim Brotherhood, aimed at spiritual regeneration of Islām and increasingly at Egyptian nationalism; assassinated with connivance of Egyptian government.

Ḥa·san al-Baṣ·rī, al- \al-'ka-san-al-ˌbäs-'rē\. *In full* Abū Sa'īd ibn Abī al-Ḥasan Yasār al-Baṣrī. 642–728. Islāmic leader. Took part in conquest of eastern Iran; became a leading figure of Basra; noted preacher, renowned for piety and asceticism; considered a founder by both Mu'tazilah and Ash'arīyah schools; his letter to caliph 'Abd al-Malik on free will is oldest extant theological treatise in Islām.

Ḥa·san-e Ṣab·bāḥ \ka-'san-a-shab-'bä\. d. 1124. Iranian religious leader. Convert to Ismā'īlī faith; in Egypt (1076–79); Ismā'īlī proselytizer; seized (1090) strong mountain fortress of Alamūt, near Kazvin; became leader of Nizārī sect of Ismā'īlīs and commanded corps of fanatic terrorists known as Assassins.

Hasdai Crescas. See CRESCAS.

Hasdai ibn Shaprut. See ḤISDAI IBN SHAPRUT.

Haş·deu \häsh-'dyü\, Bogdan Petriceicu. 1836–1907. Romanian archivist and philologist. Director of state archives (1876); professor, Bucharest (1878). Compiled *Arhiva istorică României* (1865–68), in which many ancient Slavonic and Romanian documents were first published; wrote *Cuvente den Bătrâni* (1878–81).

Has·dru·bal \'haz-ˌdrü-bəl, haz-'\. Name of several Carthaginian generals: Hasdrubal. d. 221 B.C. Son-in-law of Hamilcar Barca, whom he succeeded as commander in Spain (228); founded Cartagena; assassinated.

¶Hasdrubal. d. 207 B.C. Son of Hamilcar Barca and brother of Hannibal; commanded Carthaginian army in Spain after Hannibal left for Italy (218); operated successfully against Romans under Publius and Gnaeus Scipio; crossed Alps (207) in effort to take reinforcements to Hannibal; defeated at Metaurus and fell in battle.

¶Hasdrubal. d. c.202 B.C. Son of Gisco; associated with Mago (*q.v.*) in command of Carthaginian armies in Spain (214–206); recalled to Carthage (204); decisively defeated by Scipio Africanus near Utica (204).

¶Hasdrubal. 3d century B.C. Cavalry commander in Hannibal's army; defeated Roman cavalry and charged rear of Roman infantry in battle of Cannae (216 B.C.).

¶Hasdrubal. 2d century B.C. Commanded Carthaginian army against Masinissa (150); defeated and exiled; recalled at outbreak of Third Punic War (149); entrusted with defense of Carthage; forced to surrender city (146) and appear in triumph of Scipio Aemilianus.

Ha·se·ga·wa \häs-e-gä-wä\ Tatsunosuke. *Pseudonym* Fut·a·ba·tei \füt-ä-bä-tā\ Shimei. 1864–1909. Japanese novelist. Journalist, Russian teacher, government official. Introduced modern Realism to the Japanese novel with *Ukigumo* (1887–89), which was also one of first attempts to replace classical literary language with modern colloquial idiom; also published novels *Sono Omokage* (1906) and *Heibon* (1907), translations of Russian authors, and articles on Esperanto, literary criticism, and social conditions.

Hasegawa Tōhaku. 1539–1610. Japanese painter. Founder of Hasegawa school of painters; known esp. for screen and wall paintings for Buddhist temples; worked equally in robust, candid style and in style of elegant simplicity.

Ha·šek \'há-shek\, Jaroslav. 1883–1923. Czech writer. Author of verse *Májove výkřiky* (1903), volumes of stories as *Když člověk spadne v Tatrách* (1912), *Tři muži se žralokem* (1920); best known for series of 4 novels (of 6 planned) titled *Osudy dobrého vojáka Švejka za světové války* (1920–23, *Good Soldier Schweik*), masterpiece of satire.

Haselrig, Sir Arthur. See HESILRIGE.

Ha·sel·wan·der \'häz-əl-ˌvän-dər\, Friedrich August. 1859–1932. German engineer. Inventor of the three-phase dynamo (1887) and of the compressorless diesel motor (1897).

Ha·sen·au·er \'häz-ə-ˌnaù-ər\, Karl von. Freiherr. 1833–1894. Austrian architect. Built Hofmuseen (1872–81), Burgtheater (1880–88), Neue Hofburg (1881–1907) in Vienna.

Ha·sen·cle·ver \'häz-ən-ˌklā-vər\, Walter. 1890–1940. German writer. Author of verse *Der Jüngling* (1913), *Tod und Auferstehung* (1916), *Gedichte an Frauen* (1922); Expressionist dramas *Der Sohn* (1914), *Der Retter* (1915), *Antigone* (1917), *Die Menschen* (1919), *Jenseits* (1920), *Gobseck* (1921), *Mord* (1926); comedies *Ein besserer Herr* (1927), *Napoleon greift ein* (1930).

Hā·shim ibn Hā·kim \'ha-shim-ˌib-ən-'ha-kim\. *Called* al-Mu·qan·na' \ùl-mù-'kän-nä\, *i.e.* The Veiled One. d. 779. Muslim religious leader. Preaching doctrine combination of Islām and Zoroastrianism, led in Khorāsān a revolt against 'Abbāsid caliph al-Mahdī; committed suicide after fall of his fortress Sanam. Villian of Thomas Moore's *Lalla Rookh* (1817).

Has·kins \'has-kənz\, Charles Homer. 1870–1937. American educator, b. Meadville, Pa. Professor of European history, U. of Wisconsin (1892–1902), Harvard (1902–31); dean of Harvard Graduate School (1908–24). Chief of division of western Europe, American commission to negotiate peace (1918–19); author of solution to Saar question. Noted as leader in graduate education and as medievalist. Author of *Norman Institutions* (1918), *The Renaissance of the Twelfth Century* (1927), *Studies in Mediaeval Culture* (1929), etc.

Hasler, Hans Leo. See HASSLER.

Has·mo·nae·an *or* **Has·mo·ne·an** \ˌhaz-mə-'nē-ən\. Family name of the Maccabees (*q.v.*) and name given to the Judaean dynasty descended from them; name derived from their ancestor Hassmoneus (Hasmon) or Asmonaios. Simon Maccabreus (see at MACCABEES) was the first of the dynasty; later rulers (*qq.v.*) were Alexander Jannaeus, Antigonus I and II, John Hyrcanus I and II, Salome Alexandra.

Has·ner \'häs-nər\, Leopold. Ritter von Ar·tha \'är-tä\. 1818–1891. Austrian economist and politician. Professor, Prague (1849), Vienna (1865); member of Bohemian assembly (1861), imperial Reichsrat (1861–67), Herrenhaus (1867 ff.); minister of education (1807–70); prime minister (1870).

Ha·sping·er \'häs-piŋ-ər\, Joachim. 1776–1858. Tyrolese patriot. Fought for freedom of his country, against French (1796, 1797, 1799–1801, 1809) and Bavarians (1810).

Has·sall \'has-əl\, Christopher Vernon. 1912–1963. English writer. Author of *Poems of Two Years* (1935), *Devil's Dyke* (play, 1936), *Christ's Comet* (play, 1937), *Penthesperon* (verse, 1938), biographies as of Rupert Brooke (1964); best known as librettist for Ivor Novello and of William Walton's *Troilus and Cressida* (1954), Arthur Bliss's *Tobias and the Angel* (1960).

Has·sam \'has-əm\, Childe, *in full* Frederick Childe. 1859–1935. American painter and etcher, b. Boston. Regarded as one of foremost exponents of Impressionism in America, member of The Ten. Known for scenes of New England, New York City, seascapes, emphasizing light and atmosphere.

Ḥas·sān ibn Thā·bit \ka-'san-ˌib-ən-'tha-bit\. c.563–c.674. Arab poet. Adopted Islām at Medina and became first poetic defender of Islām and Muḥammad.

Has·se \'häs-ə\, Ernst. 1846–1908. German political leader. Professor, Leipzig; converted Allgemeiner Deutscher Verband into militant and anti-Semitic Alldeutscher Verband (1894); member of Reichstag (1893–1903); chief theorist of Pan-Germanism. Author of *Deutsche Politik* (1905–07).

Hasse, Johann Adolf. 1699–1783. German composer. In service of elector of Saxony (from 1730); presented operas in Dresden, Naples, Venice, Vienna, etc. One of leading German exponents of Italian opera; composed over 60 operas, including *Antioco* (1721), *Sesostrate* (1726), *Attalo* (1728), *Dalisa* (1730), *Issipile* (1732), *Numa Pompilio* (1741), and *Ruggiero* (c.1771), oratorios, intermezzos, cantatas, and church music.

Has·sel·blad \'häs-səl-ˌbläd\, Victor. 1906–1978. Swedish inventor. For Swedish air force developed (1941) camera marketed commercially (from 1948) as the Hasselblad, first 2 1/4" single-lens reflex with interchangeable lenses and magazines; president, Hasselblad Photography, Inc. (1944–66).

Has·selt \'häs-əlt\, André-Henri-Constant van. 1806–1874. Belgian poet. A chief figure in Belgian Romanticism. Author of *Primevères* (1834), *La Belgique* (1842), *Poésies* (1852), *Poémes* (1862), *Les Quatre Incarnations du Christ* (1863).

Has·sen·pflug \'häs-ən-ˌpflük\, Hans Daniel Ludwig Friedrich. 1794–1862. German politician. In civil service of Hesse-Kassel; minister of interior and of justice (1831–37); attempted to thwart constitution of 1831; civil governor of Luxembourg (1839–40); in Prussian service (1841–50); again chief minister to Friedrich Wilhelm I of Hesse-Kassel (1850–55); took Hesse out of Erfurt Union; called on Austria to intervene against Hesse liberals, nearly precipitating war between Austria and Prussia.

Hass·ler \'häs-lər\, Ferdinand Rudolph. 1770–1843. American geodesist, b. Aarau, Switzerland. To. U.S. (1805); while professor at West Point (1807–09) devised plan for survey of U.S. coastline; superintendent, U.S. Coast Survey (1816–18, 1832–43); superintendent of weights and measures (1830–32).

Hass·ler *or* **Has·ler** \'häs-lər\, Hans Leo. 1562–1612. German composer. Organist to banking house of Fugger, Augsburg (1586–1600); director of town music, Augsburg (1600–01), Nürnberg (1601–05); organist and later Kapellmeister to elector of Saxony (1608–12). Composed much church music, as *Cantiones sacrae* (1591), *Madrigali* (1596), *Psalmen und christliche Gesänge* (1607), and secular songs as *Lustgarten* (1601). Two brothers, ¶Kaspar (1562?–1618) and ¶Jakob (1569–1622), were also organists.

Has·tie \'hā-stē\, William Henry. 1904–1976. American jurist, b. Knoxville, Tenn. Admitted to bar, District of Columbia (1931); judge of district court, U.S. Virgin Islands (1937–39); dean, Howard U. Law School (1939–46); governor of Virgin Islands (1946–49); first black judge of U.S. Circuit Court of Appeals (1949–71).

Has·tings \'hās-tiŋz\. Name of an English family including among its members barons Hastings, earls of Pem·broke \'pem-(ˌ)brùk, *US also* -ˌbrōk\, and earls of Hunt·ing·don \'hənt-iŋ-dən\.

Sir Henry de Hastings (d. 1269), 1st Baron Hastings (1264); baronial leader in command of Londoners at Lewes (1264) and in last stand of "disinherited" barons in island of Ely; made submission to Henry (1267). His son ¶John Hastings (1262–1313), 2d baron; m. Isabella, daughter of William de Valence (1275); served against Scots and Welsh; laid claim to vacant Scottish throne (1290) on ground of descent through paternal grandmother from brother of William the Lion; fought almost continuously in France or in Scotland; signed baronial letter to Pope Boniface VIII repudiating papal interference in Scotland (1301).

¶Laurence Hastings (1318?–1348), 1st Earl of Pembroke; soldier; grandson of 2d Baron Hastings; created earl palatine (1339), inheriting estates of Valence earls of Pembroke; fought in Gascon campaigns (1345–46). ¶John (1347–1375), 2d earl, son of 1st earl; soldier; served with Black Prince in France; defeated by Spanish fleet at La Rochelle (1372) and imprisoned; m. Margaret Plantagenet, daughter of King Edward III.

¶William (1430?–1483), Baron Hastings; Yorkist adherent; ambassador and deputy for Edward IV; commander of forces in France (1475); encouraged by Jane Shore to contest succession of Richard, Duke of Gloucester (1483); beheaded by Richard III. His grandson ¶George (1488?–1545), 1st Earl of Huntingdon and 3d Baron Hastings; created earl (1529); one of royalist leaders during suppression of insurrection known as Pilgrimage of Grace (1536). ¶Henry (1535–1595), 3d Earl of Huntingdon; m. (1553) Catherine, daughter of Duke of Northumberland; heir presumptive to throne through his mother (Catherine Pole, great-granddaughter of Duke of Clarence, brother of Edward IV); a custodian of Mary, Queen of Scots (1569); president of council of north (1572) and engaged in north until he became active in defense against Spanish Armada (1588).

¶Selina, *nee* Shirley (1707–1791), Countess of Huntingdon; m. Theophilus Hastings (1728; d. 1746); joined Methodist society in London (1739); joined Wesleys (1746); had Whitefield preach in her house before Chesterfield, Walpole, Bolingbroke, and bishops; supported itinerant preachers, built many chapels and Trevecca House seminary in South Wales (1768); assisted in founding of Dartmouth Coll. and Coll. of New Jersey (Princeton); compelled to become dissenter and register her chapels as dissenting meeting houses (1779); supported Whitefield against Wesley in Calvinist controversy. Chapels subsequently became known as Countess of Huntingdon's Connexion.

Hastings, Francis Rawdon-. 1st Marquis of Hastings. See RAWDON-HASTINGS.

Hastings, Frank Abney. 1794–1828. British naval officer. Cashiered from British navy (1820); joined Greek war of independence; with financial aid of Lord Byron and others, ordered six steam warships for Greek patriot navy (1824); with ship *Karteria* sank 7 Turkish vessels in Bay of Salona; successes led to defeat and withdrawal of Egyptian fleet and expansion of Greek-controlled territory; died of wounds.

Hastings, James. 1852–1922. Scottish clergyman and editor. Compiled *Dictionary of the Bible* (1898–1904), *Dictionary of Christ and the Gospels* (1906–07), *Dictionary of the Apostolic Church* (1915, 1918), *Encyclopaedia of Religion and Ethics* (1908–21).

Hastings, Warren. 1732–1818. English colonial administrator. To Calcutta in East India Company's service (1750); member of Calcutta council (1761–64); resigned in dispute. Returned as second in council at Madras (1769); governor of Bengal (1772); created governor general of India (1773); began numerous reforms, regularized British control of government. Opposed by members of his council, esp. Philip Francis; accused of various misdeeds; lodged accusation of forgery against one of his accusers, Maharaja Nandakumar, who was hanged (1775). Regained control of council after duel with and departure of Francis (1777); fought bitter Marāthā War (1778–82), requiring extraordinary measures for fund-raising; demanded subsidy from and then deposed Chait Singh, zamindar of Benares (1781); confiscated (1782) part of lands and treasure of the begum of Oudh. Returned to England (1785); impeached (1788) for corruption and cruelty in his administration of India; acquitted (1795) after famous trial in which Burke and Sheridan were among the prosecuting counsel. Credited with establishing political and judicial organization in India, and the method of governmental administration.

Ha·ta \hä-tä\ Shunroku. 1879–1962. Japanese general. General (1937); commander, Japanese forces in Shanghai (1938); minister of war (1939); commander in chief of Japanese forces in China (1941); field marshal (1944); in charge of defense of home islands against anticipated Allied invasion (1945).

Hata Sukehachiro. 1873–1938. Japanese bacteriologist. Aided Dr. Paul Ehrlich in experiments leading to discovery of Salvarsan; professor, Keiō U.; department chief at Keiō Hospital, Tokyo (from 1911).

Ha·ta·no \hä-tä-nō\ Seiichi. 1877–1950. Japanese scholar. Professor, Tokyo Semmon Gakkō (now Waseda U., 1899–1904), Tokyo U. (1904 ff.), and Kyōto U.; known as interpreter of Western philosophy and Christianity. Author of *Seiyō Tetsugakushi Yō* (1907), *Kiristokyo no Kigen* (1909), *Seiyō Shukyo Shisoshi* (1921), *Shukyo Tetsugāku* (1935), *Toki to Eien* (1943), etc.

Hatasu. See HATSHEPSUT.

Hatch \'hach\, Carl Atwood. 1889–1963. American jurist and politician, b. Kirwin, Kans. New Mexico state district judge (1923–29); U.S. senator (1933–49); U.S. district judge for New Mexico (1949–62). Sponsor of the Hatch Act, or Political Activity Act (1939), restricting political activities of federal officials.

Hatch, Edwin. 1835–1889. English theologian. Vice principal, St. Mary Hall, Oxford (1867–85). Author of *Organisation of Early Christian Churches* (1881), *Growth of Church Institutions* (1887), etc.

Hatch, William Henry. 1833–1896. American politician, b. Scott Co., Ky. Member from Missouri, U.S. House of Representatives (1879–95); instrumental in passing Hatch Act (1887), granting federal aid to agricultural experiment stations in states and territories.

Hatch·ett \'hach-ət\, Charles. 1765–1847. English chemist. Discovered (1801) the metallic element niobium, which he called columbium.

Hathaway, Anne. See William SHAKESPEARE.

Hat·lo \'hat-(,)lō\, James Cecil. 1898–1963. American cartoonist, b. Providence, R.I. Cartoonist for *Los Angeles Times, San Francisco Call;* created (1928) series "They'll Do It Every Time" and comic strip "Little Iodine."

Ha·to·ya·ma \hä-tō-yä-mä\ Ichirō. 1883–1959. Japanese politician. Member of Diet (1915–37, 1952–59); minister of education (1931); helped reorganize Liberal party (1946); forbidden office by American occupation authorities (1946–52); prime minister (1954–59); helped organize merged Liberal-Democratic party (1955), president (1955–59).

Hat·shep·sut \hat-'shep-süt\. *Also* Ha·ta·su \hə-'tä-sü\, Hat·shop·si·tu \,hat-,shäp-'sē-,tü\, Ha·shep·sowe \hə-'shep-(,)sō\. 16th–15th century B.C. Queen of Egypt (1503–1482 B.C.). Daughter and heiress of Thutmose I, who early proclaimed her his successor; m. her half-brother Thutmose II (*q.v.*); after his death (c.1504) regent for his son Thutmose III (1504–03); proclaimed herself pharaoh, adopted traditional pharaonic regalia. Fostered trade and building; renovated portions of Karnak; built magnificent temple Dayr al-Baḥrī on west side of Nile near Thebes, which contained pictorial representations on its walls of expedition to land of Punt.

Hat·to I \'hät-ō, *Angl* 'hat-(,)ō\. c.850–913. German prelate. Abbot of Reichena (888) and Ellwangen (889); trusted adviser to King Arnulf of Bavaria; archbishop of Mainz (891–913); regent of Germany during minority of King Louis III the Child (900–911); influential in securing election of Conrad of Franconia as king (911).

Hat·ton \'hat-ᵊn\, Sir Christopher. 1540–1591. English courtier and politician. M.P. (from 1571); captain of queen's bodyguard (1572); attracted attention of Queen Elizabeth by his graceful dancing at a court masque; commissioner in trial of Mary, Queen of Scots (1586); lord chancellor (1587–91).

Hatton, John Liptrot. 1808–1886. English composer. Composed operas *Queen of the Thames* (1842), *Pasqual Bruno* (1844), cantata *Robin Hood* (1856), much theatrical music, and English songs and partsongs as *Songs by Herrick, Ben Jonson and Sedley* (1850), *Songs for Sailors* (1878).

Hat·tu·si·lis \,hat-ə-'sil-əs\. *Also spelled* Khat·tu·shi·lish \,kät-ü-'shē-lish\. Name of several Hittite kings, including:

Hattusilis I. *Also called* La·bar·nas II \lə-'bär-nəs\. 17th century B.C. King of Hittite Old Kingdom (c.1650–c.1620 B.C.). Son of Labarnas I; assumed new name on transferring capital to Hattusas; expanded kingdom into northern Syria. Author of an important "Farewell Address" in Hittite cuneiform.

Hattusilis III. 13th century B.C. King of Hittite New Kingdom (c.1275–c.1250 B.C.). Overthrew nephew Urhi-Teshub (Mursilis III); restored capital Hattusas; made treaty (c.1269) with Egypt which included marriage of his daughter to Ramses II.

Hatza *or* **Hätzer.** See Ludwig HETZER.

Hatz·feld \át-sfeld\, Adolphe. 1824–1900. French linguist. Professor, Grenoble; with Arsène Darmesteter and Antoine Thomas compiled *Dictionnaire général de la langue française* (1890–1900).

Hatz·feldt \'häts-,felt\, Melchior. Graf von Glei·chen \'glī-kən\ und Hatzfeldt. 1593–1658. German general. Served under Wallenstein (1625–32); took part in conspiracy against Wallenstein (1634) and created count by Emperor Ferdinand III (1635); campaigned in Westphalia (1639–43); defeated and captured by Torstenson at Jankov (1643). Led imperial army to defend Poland against Swedish army (1657); captured Kraków; forced by illness to retire.

Hat·zi·da·kis \,hät-sē-'dä-kēs\ *or* **Khat·zi·da·kis** \,kät-\, George N. 1848–1941. Greek linguist. Professor, National and Capodistrian U. (1885–1923), Aristotelian U., Salonika (1926–28); noted for studies of ancient, medieval, and modern Greek. Author of *Einleitung in die neugriechische Grammatik* (1892), *Mesaionikón kaí neón Hellinikón* (1905–07); initiated *Historical Lexicon of the Greek Language.*

Hauch \'hauk\, Johannes Carsten. 1790–1872. Danish poet, playwright, and novelist. Lecturer in natural sciences, Sorø (1827–46); professor of Scandinavian languages, Kiel (1846–48), of aesthetics, Copenhagen (1848–72). Author of historical tragedies; verse, esp. ballad cycle *Valdemar Atterdag* (1861); historical novels as *Vilhelm Zabern* (1834), *Guldmageren* (1836), *En polsk Familie* (1839), *Robert Fulton* (1853).

Hauck \'hau̇k\, Albert. 1845–1918. German theologian. Professor, Erlangen (1878–89), Leipzig (1889 ff.). Author of classic *Kirchengeschichte Deutschlands* (1887–1920).

Hau·er \'hau̇-ər\, Franz von. Ritter. 1822–1899. Austrian geologist. Known for geological map of Austria-Hungary (1867–71) and works on geology and paleontology of Austria. The mineral hauerite is named for him.

Hauff \'hau̇f\, Wilhelm. 1802–1827. German novelist and poet. Author of novels *Lichtenstein* (1826), *Mitteilungen aus den Memoiren des Satans* (1826–27), and *Phantasien im Bremer Ratskeller* (1827); wrote also a few lyrics, some of which attained the status of folksongs, as "Steh ich in finstrer Mitternacht" and "Morgenrot, Morgenrot."

Haug \ōg\, Émile, *in full* Gustave-Émile. 1861–1927. French geologist and paleontologist. Professor, U. of Paris (from 1900); known for theory of geosynclines, mountain building. Author of *Traité de géologie* (1907–11).

Hau·ge \'hau̇-gə\, Hans Nielsen. 1771–1824. Norwegian religious leader. Lutheran lay preacher and revivalist; founded pietist brotherhood in reaction to rationalist state church; imprisoned (1804–11, 1814–16).

Haugh·ton \'hȯt-ᵊn\, Percy Duncan. 1876–1924. American football coach, b. Staten Island, N.Y. Coached at Cornell (1899–1900), Harvard (1908–16); at Harvard compiled 71–7–5 record with strict coordination and such innovations as hidden ball, lateral pass, and other deceptions.

Haughton, William. c.1575–1605. English playwright. Collaborator with Thomas Dekker on plays for Admiral's Men, London (1597–1602); credited with sole authorship of *English-men For my Money* (1616).

Haug·witz \'hau̇k-vits\, Christian August Heinrich Kurt von. Graf. 1752–1832. Prussian politician. Minister to Vienna (1791); minister of foreign affairs (1792–1804, 1805–06); negotiated second partition of Poland (1793), Treaty of Basel (1795), and punitive Treaty of Schönbrunn (1805), which led him to join disastrous war of Fourth Coalition against France (1806).

Hauk \'hau̇k\, Minnie. 1851?–1929. American singer, b. New York City. Operatic debut (1866); sang lead in American premiere of Gounod's *Roméo et Juliette* (1867); Paris debut (1869); enjoyed great success in Europe; *prima donna assoluta* at Komische Oper, Vienna (1874); with Berlin Royal Opera (1874–77); sang title role in British and American premiers of *Carmen* (1878); retired (1895).

Hauks·bee *or* **Hawks·bee** \'hȯks-(,)bē\, Francis. c.1666–1713. English physicist. Studied surface tension and capillary action; invented (1706) electrostatic generator; constructed two-cylinder vacuum pump.

Haupt \'hau̇pt\, Herman. 1817–1905. American engineer, b. Philadelphia. Chief engineer, Pennsylvania Railroad (1853–56); in charge of construction of Hoosac tunnel (1856–62). In Civil War, chief of construction and transportation on military railroads (1862–63).

Haupt, Moritz. 1808–1874. German philologist. Professor, Leipzig (1841–50), Berlin (1853–74); secretary, Academy of Sciences (1861). Published *Altdeutschen Blätter* (1836–40); edited Middle High German texts as *Erec* (1839), *Der arme Heinrich* (1842), *Der gute Gerhard* (1840), etc.

Haupt·mann \'hau̇pt-,män\, Gerhart. 1862–1946. German writer. Earliest published work was the epic *Das Promethidenlos* (1885), followed by collected verse in *Das bunte Buch* (1888). Established dramatic reputation with Naturalistic drama *Vor Sonnenaufgang* (1889), followed by a mixture of realist, proletarian, neoromantic, and neoclassical plays including *Das Friedensfest* (1890), *Einsame Menschen* (1891), *Die Weber* (1892), *Der Biberpelz* (1893), *Hannele* (1894), *Florian Geyer* (1896), *Die versunkene Glocke* (1897), *Fuhrmann Henschel* (1898), *Michael Kramer* (1900), *Der rote Hahn* (1901), *Und Pippa tanzt!* (1906), *Kaiser Karls Geisel* (1908), *Die Ratten* (1911), *Gabriel Schillings Flucht* (1912), *Festspiel* (1913), *Der weisse Heiland* (1920), *Veland* (1925), *Hamlet in Wittenberg* (1935), and "Die Atridentetralogie" comprising *Iphigenie in Delphi* (1941), *Iphigenie in Aulis* (1944), *Agamemnons Tod* (1948), *Elektra* (1948). Also wrote novels as *Der Narr in Christo, Emanuel Quint* (1910), *Atlantis* (1912), *Der Ketzer von Soana* (1918), *Phantom* (1922), *Die Insel der grossen Mutter* (1924), *Wanda* (1928), and verse and stories. Awarded Nobel prize in literature (1912).

Hauptmann, Moritz. 1792–1868. German composer and writer. Cantor, Thomasschule, Leipzig (1842–68); professor, Leipzig Conservatory (1843–68). Composed much church music, an opera *Mathilde* (1826), and instrumental pieces. Author of *Die Natur der Harmonik und der Metrik* (1853).

Hau·ser \'hau̇-zər\, Kaspar. 1812–1833. German foundling. Picked up by Nürnberg police (1828); popular belief spread that he was of noble birth; accepted by some to be prince of Baden. Placed in custody of G.F. Daumer and later adopted by Lord Stanhope, who sent him to Ansbach. Died from stab wounds which he said he had received when called to a rendezvous with the promise of information regarding his parentage. Subject of various literary works.

Haus·ho·fer \'hau̇s-,hō-fər\, Karl Ernst. 1869–1946. German army officer and geographer. Served in World War I; retired as major general (1919). Professor, Munich (1921–39); evolved theory and discipline of geopolitics. Founder and editor, *Zeitschrift für Geopolitik* (1924 ff.); author of *Japan und die Japaner* (1923), *Geopolitik des Pazifischen Ozeans* (1924), *Macht und Erde* (1934), *Weltpolitik von Heute* (1936), *Weltmeere und Weltmachte* (1937), etc.

Haus·mann \'hau̇s-,män\, Raoul. 1886–1971. Austrian painter and photographer. An early leader of Dadaism; editor of *Dada,* Berlin (1919–20); known esp. as an originator of photomontage technique.

Häus·ser \'hȯis-ər\, Ludwig. 1818–1867. German historian and journalist. Professor, Heidelberg (1850–67); active supporter of German unification under Prussian leadership. Founded newspapers *Deutsche Zeitung* (1847), *Suddeutsche Zeitung* (1862). Author of *Deutsche Geschichte vom Tode Friedrichs der Grosse bis zur Gründung des deutschen Bundes* (1854–57).

Hauss·mann \ōs-mán\, Georges-Eugène. Baron. 1809–1891. French administrator. Prefect of the Seine (1853–70); inaugurated and carried through huge municipal improvements in Paris, including new water supply and sewage system, the creation of new wide boulevards (one of which was named Boulevard Haussmann in his honor), the landscape gardening of the Bois de Boulogne, the parks of Vincennes, Luxembourg, etc., Les Halles market, Paris Opéra. Created baron (1857); deputy (1877–81).

Haute·feuille \ōt-fœy\, Jean de. 1647–1724. French physicist. Invented the spiral spring for the movement of watches, later patented by Huygens, and an internal combustion engine using the explosions of gunpower as motive power.

Ha·üy \á-wʸē\, René-Just. 1743–1822. French mineralogist. Professor, Collège Cardinal Lemoine (1770–84), École des Mines (1795–1802), Muséum d'Histoire Naturelle (1802 ff.), Sorbonne (1809 ff.). A founder of crystallography, elucidated geometrical properties of various crystals and laid theoretical basis for further work; also studied pyroelectricity. Author of *Essai d'une théorie sur la structure des cristaux* (1784), *Traité de mineralogie* (1801), *Traité de cristallographie* (1822). His brother ¶Valentin (1745–1822), a teacher of the blind, invented characters embossed on paper as a means of reading for the blind; established an institute for teaching the blind at Paris (1784) and, later, one at St. Petersburg.

Ha·vas \á-väs\, Charles. 1785–1858. French journalist. Authorized by Napoléon to gather and forward news from armies in the field to Paris; organized news distributing agency (1832), converted into the company Havas Agency (1879), the oldest news agency in Europe.

Hav·ell \'hav-əl\, Robert, Jr. 1793–1878. American engraver and painter, b. Reading, England. Made most of plates for Audubon's *Birds of America* (1827–38); resident of U.S. (from 1839); as a painter counted among Hudson River school.

Have·lock \'hav-,läk, -lək\, Sir Henry. 1795–1857. British soldier. Entered army (1815); seved in First Anglo–Burma war (1824–26), First Afghan War (1839–42); distinguished himself during Sepoy Mutiny (1857); major general (1857); relieved Lucknow and held it against native siege until arrival of Sir Colin Campbell (1857). His son ¶Sir Henry Marshman Havelock-Al·lan \-'al-ən\ (1830–1897) distinguished himself in Sepoy Mutiny (1857–59); given baronetcy created for his father (1858); M.P. (1874–81, 1885–92, 1895–97); lieutenant general (1881); killed on Afghan frontier.

Ha·vers \'hā-vərz, 'hav-ərz\, Clopton. c.1655–1702. English physician and anatomist. Author of *Osteologia Nova* (1691), giving first minute account of the microscopic structure of bone. Haversian canals and the Haversian system derive their names from him.

Ha·ver·schmidt \'há-vər-shmət\, François. *Pseudonym* Piet Paalt·jens \'pält-yəns\. 1835–1894. Dutch preacher and poet. Author of popular *Snikken en grimlachjes* (1867), ironically Romantic verse in style of Heine and Byron.

Havilland, Geoffrey De. See De Havilland.

Ha·vlí·ček \'há-vlē-chek\, Karel. *Pseudonym* Havel Bo·rov·ský \'bó-rôf-skē\. 1821–1856. Czech journalist. Imprisoned and exiled because of his liberal articles (1851). Considered a master prose stylist, influenced modern Czech. Author also of satirical verse as *Tyrolské elegie* (1852), *Král Lávra* (1854).

Hawes \'hȯz\, Harriet Ann, *nee* Boyd \'bȯid\. 1871–1945. American archaeologist, b. Boston. m. (1906) Charles H. Hawes. Instructor (1900–06), lecturer (1920–36), Smith Coll.; conducted excavations in Crete (from 1900); discovered Early Bronze age Minoan site at Gournia (1901). Author of *Gournia, Vasiliki and Other Prehistoric Sites* (1908), *Crete: The Forerunner of Greece* (with her husband, 1909).

Hawes, Josiah J. See Albert S. Southworth.

Hawes, Stephen. fl. 1502–1521. English poet. Groom of the chamber to Henry VII (from 1502). Author of the allegorical poem *Passetyme of Pleasure, or History of Graunde Amoure and la Bel Pucel* (printed 1509).

Hawke \'hȯk\, Edward. 1st Baron Hawke. 1705–1781. English naval commander. Entered navy (1720); rear admiral of the white (1747); defeated and captured great part of French squadron protecting convoy from La Rochelle (1747); commanded western fleet (1755–56); admiral (1757). Defeated French in Quiberon Bay (1759), capturing five ships and running others ashore, thus preventing invasion of England. First lord of the admiralty (1766–71); admiral of the fleet (1768); created baron (1776).

Haw·ker \'hȯk-ər\, Robert Stephen. 1803–1875. English poet. Vicar of Morwenstow (1834), Wellcombe (1851). Author of *Tendrils* (1821), *Reeds Shaken with the Wind* (1843), *Quest of the Sangraal* (1864), *Cornish Ballads* (1869), etc.

Hawkesbury, Baron. See Robert Banks JENKINSON.

Hawkes·worth \'hȯks-(,)wərth\, John. 1715?–1773. English writer. Early friend and imitator of Dr. Johnson; succeeded Johnson as compiler of parliamentary debates for *Gentleman's Magazine* (1744); collaborated in continuing the *Adventurer* (1752–54). Author of a play *Edgar and Emmeline* (1761), and *Account of the Voyages Undertaken in the Southern Hemisphere* (1773).

Haw·kins \'hȯk-ənz\, Sir Anthony Hope. *Pseudonym* Anthony Hope \'hōp\. 1863–1933. English novelist and playwright. Author of novels *The Prisoner of Zenda* (1894), *The Dolly Dialogues* (1894), *Rupert of Hentzau* (1898), *The King's Mirror* (1899), *The Intrusions of Peggy* (1902), *Double Harness* (1904), *Mrs. Maxon Protests* (1911), *Little Tiger* (1925); and plays *The Adventure of Lady Ursula* (1898), *English Nell* (1900), *Pilkerton's Peerage* (1903), etc.

Hawkins, Benjamin. 1754–1816. American politician and Indian agent, b. Warren Co., N.C. On Gen. George Washington's staff (1778–79); member of Congress of Confederation (1781–84, 1786–87); one of first U.S. senators from North Carolina (1789–95). Negotiated Treaty of Coleraine (1796) with Creek Confederacy; U.S. agent to Creeks and general superintendent for southern tribes (1796–1816); maintained peace, fostered agriculture until outbreak of Creek War (1813–14).

Hawkins, Coleman. 1904–1969. American musician, b. St. Joseph, Mo. Tenor saxophonist in jazz bands (from 1921); with Fletcher Henderson (1924–34); toured Europe (1934–39); led various ensembles (from 1939). First major jazz saxophonist, master of improvisation, tonal beauty; best known recording "Body and Soul" (1939).

Hawkins, Henry. 1st Baron Bramp·ton \'bram(p)-tən\. 1817–1907. English judge. Counsel in several famous cases (1852–76) including that of Tichborne Claimant (1871–74); raised to bench (1876); gained in murder cases nickname of "Hanging Hawkins."

Hawkins *or* **Haw·kyns** \'hȯk-ənz\, Sir John. 1532–1595. English naval commander. Engaged in slave trade, carrying Negroes from Africa to West Indies and Spanish Main (1562–67); exposed Ridolfi plot by Spain to depose Elizabeth (1571); as treasurer of the navy (from 1573) rebuilt much of fleet; controller of navy (1589). Rear admiral in command of rear squadron in defeat of Spanish Armada (1588), and in command of center of Howard's division at Gravelines (1588). Joint commander with Frobisher of squadron on Portuguese coast (1590); second in command to Drake on expedition to West Indies (1595), dying at sea off Puerto Rico.

Hawkins, Sir John. 1719–1789. English magistrate and writer. Friend of Dr. Johnson and member of Johnson's club; drafted Johnson's will and served as one of his executors. Edited Johnson's works and wrote a biography of him (1787–89); author also of invaluable and pioneering *General History of the Science and Practice of Music* (1776).

Hawkins *or* **Hawkyns,** Sir Richard. c.1560–1622. English naval officer. Son of Sir John Hawkins; served against Spanish Armada (1588) and in expedition to Portugal (1590). Started (1593) on voyage around world; sailed up west coast of South America; plundered Valparaiso; captured in San Mateo Bay, Peru (1594); prisoner in Spain (1597–1602). Vice admiral of Devon (1604); vice admiral on unsuccessful expedition against Algerian pirates (1620–21). Author of *Observations in His Voyage into the South Sea* (1622).

Hawks \'hȯks\, Howard Winchester. 1896–1977. American film director, b. Goshen, Ind. Noted for consistent personal style in wide range of film genres. Major films included *A Girl in Every Port* (1928), *Dawn Patrol* (1930), *Scarface* (1932), *Twentieth Century* (1934), *Bringing Up Baby* (1938), *Only Angels Have Wings* (1939), *His Girl Friday* (1940), *Sergeant York* (1941), *To Have and Have Not* (1944), *The Big Sleep* (1946), *Red River* (1948), *The Big Sky* (1952), *Gentlemen Prefer Blondes* (1953), *Rio Bravo* (1959), *Hatari!* (1962), *El Dorado* (1967), *Rio Lobo* (1971).

Hawksbee, Francis. See HAUKSBEE.

Hawk·shaw \'hȯk-shȯ\, Sir John. 1811–1891. English civil engineer. Chief engineer, Manchester and Leeds Railway (1845–50); consulting engineer (from 1850). With Sir John Wolfe-Barry, built inner District line of London underground railroad; designed Charing Cross and Cannon Street railways and their Thames bridges; built East London Railway through Thames tunnel of Brunel; built Severn tunnel for Great Western Railway; designed nearly mile-long bridge over Narmada River, India; engineer of Amsterdam ship canal.

Hawks·moor \'hȯk-,smu̇(ə)r\, Nicholas. c.1661–1736. English architect. Assisted Sir Christopher Wren on St. Paul's Cathedral, Sir John Vanbrugh on Castle Howard and Blenheim Palace; succeeded Wren (1723) as surveyor general of Westminster Abbey, to which he added west towers (1734–45); designed and erected library and south quadrangle of Queen's College, Oxford, and section of north quadrangle of All Souls' College; numerous Baroque churches as St. Anne, Limehouse, St. George-in-the-East, Christ Church, Spitalfields, all in London.

Hawk·wood \'hȯk-,wu̇d\, Sir John de. *Also known as* Giovanni Acu·to \ä-'kü-tō\. c.1320–1394. English soldier of fortune. Joined mercenary White Company in Italy (1363) in service of Pisa; captain general (1364); made company renowned for mobility, tactics, longbow; in service alternately of Pope and Duke of Milan (1372–78); captain general of Florence (1378–94).

Hawkyns. See HAWKINS.

Haw·ley \'hȯ-lē\, Willis Chatman. 1864–1941. American politician, b. near Monroe, Ore. Professor (1891–1907), president (1893–1902), Willamette U.; member, U.S. House of Representatives (1907–33); chairman of joint committee of Senate and House on Internal Revenue taxation; cosponsor of the Hawley-Smoot Tariff Act (1930).

Ha·worth \'hȯ(-ə)rth, 'hȯ-(,)wərth, 'hau̇(-ə)rth\, Sir Walter Norman. 1883–1950. English chemist. Professor, Durham (1920–25), U. of Birmingham (from 1925); engaged in research on carbohydrates and vitamin C; accomplished first synthesis of a vitamin (1933); shared with Paul Karrer (*q.v.*) the 1937 Nobel prize for chemistry.

Haw·thorn \'hȯ-,thȯ(ə)rn\, John Michael. 1929–1959. British racing driver. Raced for Ferrari (1953, 1957–58); won French Grand Prix (1953), Le Mans (1955); first British world champion driver (1958).

Haw·thorne \'hȯ-,thȯ(ə)rn\, Nathaniel. *Surname orig.* Ha·thorne \'hȯ-,thȯ(ə)rn\. 1804–1864. American writer, b. Salem, Mass. Lived at Salem, devoting himself to writing (1825–37). Published stories in *Token* and *New England Magazine* (1828–42). Literary success established by *Twice-Told Tales* (1st series, 1837; 2d series, 1842), *Mosses from an Old Manse* (1846), *The Scarlet Letter* (1850), *The House of the Seven Gables* (1851), *The Blithedale Romance* (1852), *A Wonder-Book for Girls and Boys* (1852), *Tanglewood Tales for Girls and Boys* (1853). Best known stories included "Young Goodman Brown," "Roger Malvin's Burial," "Dr. Heidegger's Experiment." Worked in Boston customhouse (1839–41); lived at Brook Farm for a year; resident of Concord (1842–45); surveyor of the port, Salem (1846–49). U.S. consul, Liverpool, England (1853–58). Resident in Italy (1858–59) and in London (1859–60); returned to Concord, Mass. (1860). Latest works, *The Marble Faun* (1860), *Our Old Home* (1863).

Hawthorne, Rose. See Mary Alphonsa LATHROP.

Haw·trey \'hȯ-trē\, Sir Charles Henry. 1858–1923. English actor. First success in *The Private Secretary* (1884), which he adapted from a German farce; best known as interpreter of comedy roles. Also known as theater manager (at the Globe, to 1887, and the Comedy, 1887–93, 1896–98) and producer.

Haxo \ák-sō\, François-Nicolas-Benoît. 1774–1838. French military engineer. Served in Napoleonic armies; inspector general of fortifications under the Restoration; directed siege of the citadel of Antwerp (1832) in the Belgian revolution.

Hay \'hā\, Sir Gilbert. *Also called* Sir Gilbert of the Haye \'hā\. fl. 1456. Scottish translator. In service of Charles VII of France and (from c.1456) of Earl of Orkney and Caithness. For earl produced translations *Buke of the Law of Armys,* or *Buke of Bataillis* (from Bonet's *L'Arbre des batailles*), *Buke of the Order of Knyghthood* (from French version of Llull's *Libre de cavayleria*), *Buke of the Governaunce of Princes* (from *Le Gouvernement des Princes*); also translated verse *Buik of Alexander the Conqueror* (from *Roman d'Alexandre*). Works are earliest extant samples of literary Scots prose.

Hay, Ian. See John Hay BEITH.

Hay, Lucy. Countess of Car·lisle \kär-'lī(ə)l, 'kär-,\. 1599–1660. English courtier. Daughter of Henry Percy, 9th Earl of Northumberland; m. James Hay, later Duke of Carlisle (1617; d. 1636); celebrated for her wit and beauty, and commemorated in verse by Carew, Herrick, Suckling, Waller, D'Avenant; befriended Strafford; disclosed king's intended arrest of the Five Members of the House of Commons (1642); attached herself to Presbyterian party; in second Civil War was zealous in royal cause; betrayed secrets of both sides; imprisoned in Tower (1649–50).

Hay, John Milton. 1838–1905. American diplomat and writer, b. Salem, Ind. Private secretary to Abraham Lincoln (1861–65); served at legations in Paris, Vienna, Madrid (1865–70); assistant secretary of state (1879–81). Achieved literary reputation with *Pike County Ballads* (1871), *Castilian Days* (1871), *The Bread-Winners* (1883), *Poems* (1890), and, with John Nicolay, *Abraham Lincoln, a History* (10 vols., 1890). U.S. ambassador to Great Britain (1897–98); U.S. secretary of state (1898–1905); promulgated Open Door policy toward China (1899–1900); negotiated Hay-Pauncefote treaty (1901) providing for construction of Panama Canal and superseding Clayton-Bulwer treaty.

Hay, Oliver Perry. 1846–1930. American paleontologist, b. Saluda, Ind. Professor, Butler U., Indianapolis (1879–92); associate curator, American Museum of Natural History, New York City (1901–07); research associate, Carnegie Institution of Washington (1912–26). Author of standard *Bibliography and Catalogue of the Fossil Vertebrata of North America* (1902) and *Second Bibliography* (1929); also of *Fossil Turtles of North America* (1908), *Pleistocene of North America* (1923–27).

Ha·ya de la Tor·re \'ä-yä-thā-lä-'tȯr-rā\, Víctor Raúl. 1895–1979. Peruvian political leader. Exiled for agitation against regime of Augusto Leguía (1923–31); founded (1924) Alianza Popular Revolucionaria Americana, known as Aprista movement; defeated in presidential contest and jailed (1931–33); power behind victory of renamed People's party and regime of Pres. Bustamante (1945–47); cause célèbre in asylum in Colombian embassy in Lima (1949–54); returned to Peru (1957); leading presidential candidate (1962) until army coup; defeated by army candidate Gen. Belaúnde in new election (1963).

Ha·yam Wu·ruk \'hī-,(y)äm-'wü(ə)r-ək\. *Known as* Ra·ja·sa·na·ga·ra \,räj-ə-sä-'näg-ə-rə\. 1334–1389. Javan ruler. Succeeded to throne of Hindu state of Majapahit (1350); with prime minister Gajah Mada extended influence throughout Indonesia; maintained monopoly of trade through sea power; at death divided realm among sons, leading to rapid decline of Majapahit and of Hindu civilization in Java.

Ha·ya·shi \hä-yä-shē\ Fumiko. *Orig.* Mi·ya·ta \mē-yä-tä\ Fumiko. 1904–1951. Japanese novelist. Author of realistic novels of women's lives in Japan as *Hōrōki* (1930), *Seihin-no-sho* (1931), *Shitamachi* (1948), *Ukigumo* (1949).

Hayashi Razan. *Orig.* Hayashi Nobukatsu. *Buddhist name* Dō·shun \dō-shün\. 1583–1657. Japanese scholar. Turned against Buddhism and took up study of Confucianism (1604); in service of Tokugawa shogunate (from 1607); developed Neo-Confucianism of Chu Hsi and secured its adoption as official doctrine in Japan; opened academy in Edo (Tokyo, 1630). His son ¶Gahō, *also called* Harukatsu (17th century), succeeded him as chief official scholar; with a brother collected Razan's works as *Hayashi Razan bunshū*.

Hayashi Senjūrō. 1876–1943. Japanese general and politician. As commander of Japanese forces in China ordered march into Manchuria (1931); general (1932); minister of war (1934–35); prime minister (1937).

Hayashi Shihei. 1738–1793. Japanese scholar. Student of western military affairs; attempted to rouse opinion in favor of greater military preparedness in face of Russian and other threats; arrested for agitation (1792). Main work *Kaikoku hei dan* (1787).

Hayashi Tadasu. Count. 1850–1913. Japanese diplomat. Minister to China (1896–98), Russia (1898–99), Great Britain (1899–1906); responsible for treaties of Anglo-Japanese alliance (1902, 1905); created count (1907).

Hay·den \'hād-ᵊn\, Carl Trumbull. 1877–1972. American politician, b. Tempe, Ariz. Member of U.S. House of Representatives (1912–27), U.S. Senate (1927–69); president pro tem (1957–69); his 56 years in Congress was record length service.

Hayden, Charles. 1870–1937. American banker and philanthropist, b. Boston. Founded firm of Hayden, Stone & Co., bankers and brokers (1892). Gave (1934) $150,000 for apparatus of the planetarium in New York, named Hayden Planetarium in his honor; established Hayden Foundation.

Hayden, Ferdinand Vandeveer. 1829–1887. American geologist, b. Westfield, Mass. Explored Dakotas, Montana, etc. (from 1853); professor, U. of Pennsylvania (1865–72); head of U.S. Geological and Geographic Survey (1869–79); with reorganized U.S. Geological Survey (1879–87); instrumental in creation of Yellowstone National Park (1872).

Hayden, Horace H. 1769–1844. American dentist, b. Windsor, Conn. With Chapin A. Harris, a founder of Baltimore Coll. of Dental Surgery, first dental college in the world (chartered 1840).

Hay·dn \'hīd-ᵊn, *Angl also* 'hād-ᵊn\, Joseph, *in full* Franz Joseph. 1732–1809. Austrian composer. Sang in cathedral choir of St. Stephen's, Vienna (1740–49); assistant and then musical director in the service of the Esterházy family (1761–90), during which period he wrote some of his greatest music, operas, masses, piano sonatas, symphonies, overtures, etc. Long friendship with Mozart (beginning 1781–82) aided in developing a fuller mastery of orchestral effects in his later symphonies. In England (1791–92) wrote and conducted six symphonies, and again (1794–95) another six symphonies. Resident in Vienna and again in Esterházy service (from 1795), where he wrote his last masses, his finest chamber music, the Austrian national anthem, the two great oratorios *Die Schöpfung* (The Creation, 1798) and *Die Jahreszeiten* (The Seasons, 1801). Regarded as first great master of the symphony and the quartet. Works included 106 symphonies, some 79 quartets, 54 piano sonatas, various concerti, 13 masses and other church music, operas as *La canterina* (1767), *Lo speziale* (1768), *La fedeltà premiata* (1780), *Orlando paladino* (1782). A brother ¶Johann Michael, *known as* Michael (1737–1806), was Kapellmeister at Salzburg (1762–1806); composed over 360 works for the church, including masses and a set of graduals, also some 40 symphonies, a string quartet in C major, and instrumental music; teacher of C.M. von Weber.

Hay·don \'hād-ᵊn\, Benjamin Robert. 1786–1846. English painter. Known for historical and biblical canvases as *Dentatus, Judgment of Solomon, Raising of Lazarus, Mock Election, Reform Banquet,* and for *Autobiography* (1847).

Hayes \'hāz\, Isaac Israel. 1832–1881. American explorer, b. Chester Co., Pa. Surgeon on Kane's second Arctic expedition (1853–55); led Arctic expedition, financed largely by Henry Grinnell, aimed at proving existence of open seas around North Pole (1860–61); on third Arctic expedition, with the painter William Bradford (1869). Author of *An Arctic Boat Journey* (1860), *The Open Polar Sea* (1867), *Land of Desolation* (1871).

Hayes, Patrick Joseph. 1867–1938. American prelate, b. New York City. Chancellor of New York (1903); auxiliary bishop of New York (1914); bishop of U.S. armed forces in World War I; archbishop (1919); cardinal (1924). Founded Catholic Charities (1920).

Hayes, Roland. 1887–1977. American singer, b. Curryville, Ga. Member of Fisk Jubilee Singers (1911); gave solo concert, Boston Symphony Hall (1917); made successful European tour (1921–22); gained great international reputation with renditions of spirituals and of classical works.

Hayes, Rutherford Birchard. 1822–1893. Nineteenth president of the United States, b. Delaware, Ohio. Practiced law, Cincinnati (from 1850); in Union army through Civil War; brigadier general (1864); brevetted major general (1865). Member, U.S. House of Representatives (1865–67); governor of Ohio (1868–72, 1876–77). Opposed Democrat Samuel J. Tilden in presidential election (1876); contest decided by Electoral Commission after Republicans challenged votes of South Carolina, Florida, Louisiana, Oregon; awarded votes and kept peace with Southern Democrats by agreeing to end military Reconstruction; after single term (1877–81) retired to Ohio.

Hayes, Woody, *in full* Wayne Woodrow. 1913–1987. American football coach, b. Clifton, Ohio. Coached football at Denison U. (1946–48), Miami U. (1949–50), and Ohio State U. (1951–78). Won 238 games in his coaching career; developed 58 All-American players; won 13 Big Ten championships and four Rose Bowl victories. Known as a stern taskmaster with an explosive temper that ultimately led to his dismissal.

Hay·ford \'hā-fərd\, John Fillmore. 1868–1925. American civil engineer and geodesist, b. Rouses Point, N.Y. With U.S. Coast and Geodetic Survey (1889–95, 1898–1909); professor, Cornell (1895–98); director, Coll. of Engineering, Northwestern U. (1909–25). Known for work establishing theory of isostasy and in calculating figure of Earth; derived figure adopted (1924) as international spheroid of reference.

Hay·ley \'hā-lē\, William. 1745–1820. English poet. Friend of Cowper and Southey; patron of William Blake and George Romney. Author of *Triumphs of Temper* (1781), a life of Cowper (1803–04), *Triumphs of Music* (1804), *Ballads Founded on Anecdotes of Animals* (1805).

Haym \'hīm\, Rudolf. 1821–1901. German philosopher and literary historian. Professor, Halle (from 1860); member of Prussian assembly (1866–67). Founded and published *Preussischen Jahrbuch* (1858–64). Author of *Die Krisis unserer religiösen Bewegung* (1847), *Hegel und seine Zeit* (1857), *Die romantische Schule* (1870), etc.

Hay·mer·le \'hī-mər-lə\, Heinrich Karl von. Freiherr. 1828–1881. Austrian diplomat. Entered diplomatic service (1850); ambassador to Copenhagen (1864), Constantinople (1868), Athens (1870), The Hague (1872), Rome (1877); represented Austria in the Berlin Congress (1878); foreign minister (1879–81); concluded Dreikaiserbund with Germany and Russia (1881), Serbian compact (1881).

Hay·nau \'hī-,naù\, Julius Jacob von. Freiherr. 1786–1853. Austrian general. While campaigning in Italy (1848–49) gained reputation for brutality in repressing uprising in Brescia; as commander (1849) and military governor (1849–50) in Hungary again employed undue violence.

Hayne \'hān\, Paul Hamilton. 1830–1886. American poet, b. Charleston, S.C. Nephew of Robert Y. Hayne. Published *Poems* (1855), *Sonnets and Other Poems* (1857), *Avolio* (1860), *Legends and Lyrics* (1872), *The Mountain of the Lovers* (1875), *The Broken Battalions* (1885).

Hayne, Robert Young. 1791–1839. American politician, b. Collection District, S.C. Practiced law, Charleston (from 1812); U.S. senator (1823–32); noted for brilliant debate with Daniel Webster on principles of the Constitution, authority of the federal government, and states' rights (1830). A leader of nullification movement (1832); governor of South Carolina (1832–34).

Haynes \'hānz\, Elwood. 1857–1925. American inventor, b. Portland, Ind. Built horseless carriage (1893–94), one of first in U.S.; claimed to have received first traffic ticket (Chicago, 1895); formed Haynes-Apperson Co., Kokomo, Ind. (1898), which continued as Haynes Automobile Co. (1902–25). Discoverer of various alloys, as tungsten chrome steel (1881), alloy of chromium and nickel (1897), alloy of cobalt and chromium (1900), stainless steel (1911).

Hays \'hāz\, Arthur Garfield. 1881–1954. American lawyer, b. Rochester, N.Y. Practiced, New York City (from 1905); general counsel, American Civil Liberties Union (from 1912); involved in many celebrated cases, as Scopes trial (1925), Sweet trial (1926), Sacco-Vanzetti trial (1927), Scottsboro trials (1932), labor union cases. Author of *Let Freedom Ring* (1928), *Trial by Prejudice* (1933), *Democracy Works* (1939).

Hays, John Coffee. 1817–1883. American soldier, b. Wilson Co., Tenn. To Texas (1836); scout with Texas army (1836–40); captain of Texas Rangers (1840–48); reputed to have introduced Colt revolver to Texas; led Ranger force in Mexican War; to California (1849); sheriff of San Francisco County (1850–53).

Hays, Will H., *in full* William Harrison. 1879–1954. American lawyer and politician, b. Sullivan, Ind. Chairman, Republican National Committee (1918–21); U.S. postmaster general (1921–22). President, Motion Picture Producers and Distributors of America (1922–45); instituted Production Code for motion pictures (1930); efforts on behalf of film censorship caused the MPPDA to be known popularly as the Hays Office.

Hay·ton \ˈhāt-ᵊn\. *Also known as* Hai·thon \ˈhā-thən\ *or* He·thum \ˈhā-thəm\. d. 1271. King of Little Armenia (1224–69). Made journey to Mongol capital of Karakorum (1251–54), the record of which by one of his courtiers was one of the earliest written accounts of Mongolian geography and ethnology.

Hay·ward \ˈhā-wərd\, Abraham. 1801–1884. English essayist. Author of *The Art of Dining* (1852), *Juridical Tracts* (1856), *Biographical and Critical Essays* (1858), *Sketches of Eminent Statesmen and Writers* (1880), etc.

Hayward, Sir John. c.1564–1627. English historian. Author of *First Part of the Life and Raigne of Henrie the IIII* (1599–1601), *Lives of the III Normans, Kings of England* (1613), *Life and Raigne of King Edward the Sixt* (1630).

Hay·wood \ˈhā-wu̇d\, Eliza, *nee* Fowler. 1693?–1756. English novelist and playwright. Author of popular scandalous romances as *Memoirs of a Certain Island* (1725), *Secret History of the Present Intrigues of the Court of Caramania* (1727); satirized in Pope's *Dunciad,* to which she replied in *Female Dunciad* (1729); issued *Female Spectator* (1744–46); also wrote realistic novel *History of Jemmy and Jenny Jessamy* (1753).

Haywood, William Dudley, *orig.* William Richard, *called* Big Bill. 1869–1928. American labor leader, b. Salt Lake City. A miner from age of fifteen; joined Western Federation of Miners (1896); member of Socialist party (1901–12); a founder of Industrial Workers of the World (1905). Tried on charge of having a part in murder of Frank R. Steunenberg, former governor of Idaho (1907); acquitted. His advocacy of violence by workers in industrial disputes led to his ejection from Socialist executive board (1912). Arrested for sedition on entrance of U.S. into World War I (1917); sentenced to 20 years (1918); fled to Soviet Union while free on bail (1921); died there.

Haz·a·el \ˈhaz-ā-el, ˈhā-zā-el, hə-ˈzā-el\. 9th century B.C. King of Damascus. Killed Ben-hadad II and succeeded to throne; fought and oppressed Israel, seizing part of it; ravaged Judah; defeated by Shalmanesar III.

Ha·zard \á-zár\, Paul-Gustave-Marie-Camille. 1878–1944. French literary historian. Professor, Lyon (1911–13), Sorbonne (1913–26), Collège de France (1926–44). Author of *La Crise de la conscience européenne, 1680–1715* (1935), *La Pensée européenne* (1946).

Ha·ze·li·us \hä-ˈzā-lē-u̇s\, Arthur Immanuel. 1833–1901. Swedish philologist and ethnographer. Founded (1873) ethnographic museum that became Nordiska Museet, Stockholm; founded (1891) open-air museum Skanset; influential in reform of Swedish orthography.

Ha·zel·tine \ˈhā-zəl-ˌtin\, Louis Alan. 1886–1964. American electrical engineer, b. Morristown, N.J. Professor, Stevens Inst. of Technology (1907–24, 1933–60); consultant to U.S. navy in World War I, to Office of Scientific Research and Development in World War II. Invented neutrodyne circuit which made possible commerical broadcasting by suppressing noise inherent in receivers; organized (1924) Hazeltine Corp.

Ha·zen \ˈhā-zən\, William Babcock. 1830–1887. American army officer, b. West Hartford, Vt. Served through Civil War; major general (1864). Chief signal officer, U.S. army, rank of brigadier general (1880); in charge of organizing Greely expedition into Arctic (1881); objected to secretary of war's delay in sending relief expedition (1883). Court-martialed for criticism of his superior officer (1885).

Haz·litt \ˈhaz-lət, ˈhāz-\, William. 1778–1830. English writer. Encouraged in early study of painting by Lamb, Wordsworth, Coleridge; drama critic on *Morning Chronicle* (1814); contributed to Leigh Hunt's *Examiner;* wrote for *Edinburgh Review* (from 1814), *London Magazine,* and *Colburn's New Monthly.* Lectured widely, esp. on Shakespeare and the English drama. Author of *The Characters of Shakespeare's Plays* (1817), *Lectures on English Poets* (1818), *View of the English Stage* (1818), *Lectures on the English Comic Writers* (1819), *Lectures on the Dramatic Literature of the Age of Elizabeth* (1821), *Table Talk* (1821), *Liber Amoris* (1823), *Spirit of the Age* (1825), *Plain Speaker* (1826), *Life of Napoleon* (1828–30), etc.

H.D. See Hilda DOOLITTLE.

Head \ˈhed\, Edith. 1898?–1981. American costume designer, b. San Bernardino, Cal. Chief costume designer, Paramount Studios (1938–67), Universal Studios (1967–81); won Academy Awards for costume design for films *The Heiress* (1949), *All About Eve* (1950), *Samson and Delilah* (1950), *A Place in the Sun* (1951), *Roman Holiday* (1953), *Sabrina* (1954), *The Facts of Life* (1960), *The Sting* (1973); nominated for 27 others; costumed over 1000 films.

Head, Sir Edmund Walker. 8th Baronet. 1805–1868. British colonial governor. Governor of New Brunswick (1847–54); governor general of Canada (1854–61).

Head·lam \ˈhed-ləm\, Arthur Cayley. 1862–1947. English prelate. Principal of King's Coll., London (1903–12); regius professor of divinity, Oxford, and canon of Christ Church at Oxford (1918–23); bishop of Gloucester (1923–45). Author of *Doctrine of the Church and Christian Reunion* (1920), etc.

Hea·ly \ˈhē-lē\, George Peter Alexander. 1813–1894. American painter, b. Boston. Worked in Chicago, Paris, Rome. Paintings included *Webster Replying to Hayne* and many portraits, as of Louis-Philippe, Pius IX, Calhoun, Clay, Longfellow, Taney, and a series of U.S. presidents.

Healy, Timothy Michael. 1855–1931. Irish nationalist and politician. M.P. (1880–1918); broke with Parnell (1886), turned to Gladstone and vigorously advocated home rule; authority on land law and effective advocate of agrarian reform; opposed violence and supported Sinn Féin (from 1917). First governor general of Irish Free State (1922–28).

Hearn \ˈhərn\, Lafcadio, *in full* Patricio Lafcadio Tessima Carlos. 1850–1904. American writer, b. Levkás, Greek Ionian Islands, of Greek and British parents. To U.S. (1869); on staff, Cincinnati (Ohio) *Enquirer,* Cincinnati *Commercial* (1873–77), New Orleans *Item* (c.1878–79), New Orleans *Times-Democrat* (1881–87). In island of Martinique on commission from *Harper's* (1887–89). Went to Japan (1890); taught English in Japanese schools (1890–1903); became Japanese citizen (1895) under name of Ko·i·zu·mi \kō-ē-zu̇m-ē\ Yakumo. Author of *One of Cleopatra's Nights* (1882), *Stray Leaves from Strange Literatures* (1884), *Gombo Zhèbes* (1885), *Chita* (1889), *Two Years in the French West Indies* (1890), *Glimpses of Unfamiliar Japan* (1894), *Gleanings in Buddha-Fields* (1897), *Exotics and Retrospectives* (1898), *In Ghostly Japan* (1899), *Shadowings* (1900), *Japan, An Attempt at Interpretation* (1904).

Hearne \ˈhərn\, Samuel. 1745–1792. English explorer. Joined Hudson's Bay Co.; to Canada (1769); explored inland from Fort Prince of Wales, Manitoba (1770–72), becoming first European to make overland trip to Arctic Ocean; founded (1774) Cumberland House, first permanent settlement in present Saskatchewan; captured and held by French (1782–83). Author of *A Journey from Prince of Wales' Fort to the Northern Ocean* (1795).

Hearne, Thomas. 1678–1735. English historian and antiquarian. Assistant in Bodleian Library, Oxford (1699–1716). Issued editions of Camden's *Annals* (1717), Fordun's *Scotichronicon* (1722), etc.; author of *Ductus historicus* (1698), *Reliquiae Bodleianae* (1703), and numerous histories.

Hearst \ˈhərst\, George. 1820–1891. American mining magnate, b. Franklin Co., Mo. To California (1850); in partnership at various times with James B.A. Haggin, Lloyd Tevis, Marcus Daly, acquired mines in western Nevada, Utah, Montana, South Dakota, and Mexico, including the Ophir and Comstock silver mines, Homestake gold mine, Anaconda copper mine. Proprietor, *San Francisco Daily Examiner* (from 1880). U.S. senator (1886–91). His wife ¶Phoebe, *nee* Ap·per·son \ˈap-ər-sən\ (1842–1919), m. Hearst (1862), was noted for her philanthropies, esp. educational philanthropies in California and in Washington, D.C., including several buildings for U. of California at Berkeley, National Cathedral.

Hearst, William Randolph. 1863–1951. American newspaper publisher, b. San Francisco. Son of George Hearst; took over father's *San Francisco Examiner* (1887); acquired *New York Morning Journal* (1895) and began *Evening Journal* (1896); built circulation with sensational reportage, color comics and other features; circulation war with Joseph Pulitzer's *New York World* gave rise to era of "yellow journalism"; built national chain of papers including *Chicago American, Boston American, Chicago Examiner, New York Mirror;* acquired magazines *Cosmopolitan, Harper's Bazaar, Good Housekeeping,* etc.; established newspaper and motion picture syndicate. Pursued editorial policy of bellicose nationalism and anti-British isolationism; credited with stirring up public opinion in favor of war with Spain (1898); opposed U.S. entry into World War I. Member of U.S. House of Representatives (1903–07). Defeated for New York City mayoralty (1905, 1909) and for New York governorship (1906). Built sumptuous residence San Simeon in California, furnished with antiques and artifacts from around the world.

Heath \ˈhēth\, Nicholas. c.1501–1578. English prelate and politician. Bishop of Rochester (1539), Worcester (1543); archbishop of York (1555–59). Lord chancellor (1556–58). Opposed acts of supremacy and uniformity; deprived of his archbishopric (1559) and temporarily confined in Tower of London.

Heath, William. 1737–1814. American Revolutionary officer, b. Roxbury, Mass. Major general in Continental army (from 1776); reprimanded by

Washington for his handling of attack on Fort Independence (1777); commanded Eastern Department (1777–79), in Hudson Valley (1779–81).

Heath·coat \'hēth-,kōt\, John. 1783–1861. English inventor. Invented lace-making machine (c.1808–09); factory destroyed by Luddites (1816); also invented net- and ribbon-making machines and a rotary self-narrowing stocking frame. M.P. (1832–59).

Heat·ter \'hēt-ər\, Gabriel. 1890–1972. American journalist, b. New York City. Reporter for New York City papers, writer for *Forest and Stream* magazine, etc.; radio news broadcaster (from 1932); gained national attention with coverage of trial of Bruno Hauptmann for kidnap of Lindbergh baby (1935); highly popular as nightly news broadcaster; also conducted program "We, the People" (1935–41) and later "Brighter Tomorrow" commentaries; retired (1965).

Heav·i·side \'hev-ē-,sīd\, Oliver. 1850–1925. English physicist. Telegrapher (1870–74); made suggestions for rendering duplex telegraphy practicable; suggested a new system of magnetic and electrical units; introduced operational calculus (now known as Laplace transforms) for studying transient currents in networks; worked on the propagation of waves in telegraphy; predicted (1902) existence of region of ionized air affecting radio-wave propagation, first called the Heaviside, or Kennelly-Heaviside, layer or region (cf. A.E. KENNELLY), now known as ionosphere.

Heav·y·sege \'hev-ē-,sej, -,sēj\, Charles. 1816–1876. Canadian poet, b. Liverpool, England. To Montreal (1853); woodcarver and later journalist. Author of ambitiously Shakespearian verse dramas including *Saul* (1857), *Count Filippo* (1860), *Jephthah's Daughter* (1865); also wrote a novel *The Advocate* (1865).

Heb·bel \'heb-əl\, Friedrich, *in full* Christian Friedrich. 1813–1863. German poet and playwright. Author of realistic, psychological tragedies involving Hegelian concepts of history and moral values, including *Judith* (1840), *Genoveva* (1841), *Maria Magdalena* (1844), *Julia* (1847), *Herodes und Mariamne* (1850), *Agnes Bernauer* (1852), *Gyges und sein Ring* (1854), and *Die Niebelungen Trilogie* (1862) comprising *Der Gehörtte Siegfried, Sigfrieds Tod, Kriemhilds Rache;* also wrote stories, verse tales as *Mutter und Kind* (1859).

He·bel \'hā-bəl\, Johann Peter. 1760–1826. German poet. Known for *Allemannischen Gedichte* (1803), a collection of poems in the Alamannic dialect.

He·ber \'hē-bər\, Reginald. 1783–1826. English prelate and hymn writer. Bishop of Calcutta (1823–26). Among his best known hymns were "From Greenland's Icy Mountains," "Holy, Holy, Holy."

Heb·er·den \'heb-ərd-ən, -ər-dən\, William. 1710–1801. English physician. Practiced in London (from 1748); first described angina pectoris; distinguished chickenpox; attended Johnson, Cowper, Warburton.

Hé·bert \ā-ber\, Jacques-René. *Called* Père Du·chesne \per-dü̅e̅-shen\. 1757–1794. French journalist and politician. In Paris (from 1780), published radical Republican papers, esp. *Le Père Duchesne* (from 1790); influential member of Cordeliers; helped plan overthrow of monarchy (1792); procurator of the Commune of Paris; joined Jacobins and advocated overthrow of Girondists (1792); leader of sans-culottes, forced expulsion of Girondists from Convention (1793), and pressured Jacobin regime into radical measures; with Chaumette instituted the worship of the Goddess of Reason; arrested by Committee of Public Safety (1794); guillotined with many of his adherents.

He·bra \'hā-brä\, Ferdinand von. 1816–1880. Austrian dermatologist. Founder of New Vienna School, basis of modern dermatology; attributed most diseases of skin to local irritation instead of to morbid condition of fluids of the body in accordance with the previously held humoral pathology. Author of *Atlas der Hautkrankheiten* (1856–76).

Hebreo, León. See Judah ABRABANEL.

He·ca·tae·us \,hek-ə-'tē-əs\ of Mi·le·tus \mī-'lēt-əs, mə-\. 6th–5th century B.C. Greek traveler and historian. Opposed Ionian revolt (500 B.C.) against Persia and, after Ionians were defeated (494), was Ionian ambassador to negotiate terms of peace with Artaphernes. Author of *Genealogia,* or *Historiai,* largely lost account of Greek traditions and mythology, and of *Ges periodos,* or *Periegesis* (Tour Round the World), widely used by Herodotus and other writers.

Hecht \'hekt\, Ben. 1894–1964. American writer, b. New York City. On staff of Chicago *Journal* (1910–14), *Daily News* (1914–23); founder and publisher, Chicago *Literary Times* (1923–25). Author of *Erik Dorn* (1921), *Gargoyles* (1922), *Fantazius Mallare* (1922), *The Florentine Dagger* (1923), *1001 Afternoons in Chicago* (1923), *The Egoist* (1923), *Humpty Dumpty* (1924), *Count Bruga* (1926), *A Jew in Love* (1930), *1001 Nights in New York* (1941), *Collected Stories* (1945), *The Sensualists* (1959); frequent collaborator with Charles MacArthur (*q.v.*), as in the plays *The Front Page* (1928), *Twentieth Century* (1933), *Ladies and Gentlemen* (1939), and the motion pictures *The Scoundrel* (1935), *Wuthering Heights* (1939); alone wrote screenplays for *Gunga Din* (1938), *Spellbound* (1945), *Notorious* (1946); memoirs *Child of the Century* (1954), *Gaily, Gaily* (1963); also *Guide for the Bedevilled* (1944), *Perfidy* (1961).

Heck \'hek\, Barbara, *nee* Ruck·le \'rük-əl\. 1734–1804. American religious leader, b. Ballingrane, County Limerick, Ireland. m. (1760) Paul Heck; to New York (1760); with Philip Embury (*q.v.*), organized (1766) first Methodist society in New York City, regarded as beginning of Wesleyan movement in America; instrumental in opening of first Methodist chapel in America (1768); as Loyalist, fled to Canada (1774).

Heck·el \'hek-əl\, Erich. 1883–1970. German painter. A founder, with Schmidt-Rottluff, Kirchner, and Bleyl of Die Brücke (1905); influenced esp. by primitive art, Van Gogh, German woodcut tradition; denounced as decadent by Nazi regime (1937); professor, Karlsruhe (1949–55).

Heck·er \'hek-ər\, Friedrich Karl Franz. 1811–1881. German political agitator. Elected to Baden assembly (1842); led radical republican wing with Gustave Struve; failed to carry resolution abolishing monarchy (1848); tried to lead revolt to establish German republic (1848); uprising suppressed; fled to Switzerland and later to America (1848); served in Union army through Civil War.

Hecker, Isaac Thomas. 1819–1888. American clergyman, b. New York City. Converted to Catholicism (1844); joined Redemptorists (1845), serving as missionary priest in New York City (1851–57). Founded (1858), with four associates, the Congregation of the Missionary Priests of St. Paul the Apostle (known as Paulist Fathers, or Paulists), and was its first superior (1858–88); founded the *Catholic World* (1865) and the *Young Catholic* (1870), and organized (1866) Catholic Publication Society. Author of *Questions of the Soul* (1855), *Aspirations of Nature* (1857), *The Church and the Age* (1887).

He·da \'hā-dä\, Willem Claesz. c.1594–between 1680 and 1682. Dutch painter. Best known for his still-life paintings, displaying mastery of texture and surface of glass and metal vessels, foods, etc.

He·dā·yat \hā-'dä-yat\, Ṣādeq *or* Ṣādeq-e. 1903–1951. Iranian writer. Translated works of Kafka, Sartre, Chekhov, etc. into Persian; began influential studies of Persian folk literature, songs, history. Works included stories *Zendeh be gūr* (1930), *Sē qaṭreh-khūn* (1932); play *Parvīn dokhtar-e Sāsān* (1930); novel *Būf-A Kūr* (1937); folk collections *Osāneh* (1931), *Neyrangestān* (1932).

Hé·de·lin \ād(-ə)-laⁿ\, François. Abbé d'·Au·bi·gnac \dō-bēn-yak\. 1604–1676. French playwright and critic. Entered church (1628); tutor to nephew of Richelieu. Author of prose tragedies *Cyminde* (1642), *La Pucelle d'Orléans* (1642), *Zénobie* (1647); wrote critical essays on Corneille and others and *La Pratique du théâtre* (1657), commissioned by Richelieu and influential in development of French classical drama.

He·din \he-'dēn\, Sven Anders. 1865–1952. Swedish geographer and explorer. Traveled through Persia and Mesopotamia (1885–86); attached to King Oscar's embassy to the shah of Persia (1890); traveled through Khurāsān and Turkistan (1890–91), Asia from Orenburg to Peking (1893–97), Gobi Desert and Tibet (1899–1902), Persia to India, through Tibet (1905–08); on Sino-Swedish expedition (1927–33). Author of *Through Asia* (1898), *Central Asia and Tibet* (1903), *Overland to India* (1910), *Från pol till pol* (1911), *Southern Tibet* (1916–22), *Bagdad, Babylon, Ninive* (1917), *Tsangpo Lamas vallfärd* (1920–22), *Mount Everest* (1922), *Across the Gobi Desert* (1931), *The Silk Road* (1938), *The Wandering Lake* (1940), etc.

Hed·ley \'hed-lē\, William. 1779–1843. English coal mine operator and inventor. Built "Puffing Billy" (1813), probably first commercially employed steam locomotive of adhesion type, used to pull coal trucks from Northumberland mine to dockside.

Hed·toft \'heth-,tōft\, Hans Christian. *Surname in full* Hedtoft-Han·sen \-'hän-sən\. 1903–1955. Danish politician. Social Democratic member of parliament (1935–40, 1945–55); minister of social affairs (1945); prime minister (1947–50, 1953–55); led Denmark into NATO (1949), initiated closer ties with Norway and Sweden.

Hedwig. See also JADWIGA.

Hed·wig \'hāt-,vik\. Saint. 1174–1243. German religious. Daughter of Count of Andechs; m. (1186) Duke Henry I of Silesia; endowed many religious houses including Cistercian convent at Trebnitz, to which she retired at husband's death (1238). Canonized (1267); patron saint of Silesia.

Hedwig, Johann. 1730–1799. German botanist. Professor, Leipzig (1786–99); founder of modern study of mosses. Author of *Fundamentum historiae naturalis muscorum frondosorum* (1782–83), *Specieis muscorum frondosorum* (1801).

Heem \'hām\, Jan Davidsz de. 1606–1683 or 1684. Dutch painter. Considered perhaps the finest of Dutch still life painters; painted flower arrangements, compositions of fruits, metal dishes, wine glasses, or of books and musical instruments. His son ¶Cornelis de Heem (1631–1695) was also a still life painter of note.

Heems·kerck \'hāms-kərk\, Jacob van. 1567–1607. Dutch explorer and admiral. Captain of vessel that, under Willem Barents's direction, explored Barents Sea in search of Arctic passage to India (1596–97); vice admiral in

Dutch navy (1598); established trade relations with various kingdoms of Indonesia (1599); admiral (1600); commander of fleet of United Provinces (1607); killed during victory over Spanish fleet off Gibraltar.

Heemskerck, Johan van. 1597–1656. Dutch poet. In his *Batavische Arcadia* (1637) introduced the Italian pastoral romance into Dutch literature.

Heemskerck, Maerten van. 1498–1574. Dutch painter. A leading Mannerist painter, noted for religious works and portraits. Works included portrait *Anna Codde* (1529), *Crucifixion* altarpiece, Linköping cathedral, Sweden (1538–43), a *Crucifixion* for Ghent (1543).

Hee·nan \'hē-nən\, John Carmel. 1835–1873. American boxer, b. West Troy, N.Y. Declared American heavyweight bare-knuckles champion on retirement of John Morrissey (1858); fought celebrated world championship bout in England with Tom Sayers, declared a draw after 42 rounds (1860); defeated by British Tom King (1863), retired.

Heer \'hār\, Oswald. 1809–1883. Swiss botanist and paleontologist. Professor, Zürich (1835 ff.); known for studies in paleobotany, botany of high altitudes and Arctic region. Author of *Flora tertiaria Helvetiae* (1855–59), *Flora fossilis arctica* (1868–83), *Flora fossilis Helvetiae* (1876), *Über die nivale Flora der Schweiz* (1883).

Hee·ren \'hā-rən\, Arnold Hermann Ludwig. 1760–1842. German historian. Professor, Göttingen (from 1787). Author of *Ideen über Politik* (1793–96), etc.

He·fe·le \'hā-fə-lə\, Karl Joseph von. 1809–1893. German prelate and historian. Professor, Tübingen (1837); bishop of Rottenburg (1869). Author of history of church councils *Conciliengeschichte* (1855–74), continued by J. Hergenröther (1887–90).

Hef·fel·fin·ger \'hef-əl-ˌfiŋ-gər\, William Walter, *known as* Pudge \'pəj\. 1867–1954. American football player, b. Minneapolis. Star guard on Walter Camp's Yale teams (1888–91); All-American (1889–91); helped develop tactics of pulling guard and running interference; known as powerful blocker and tackler.

Hef·ner-Al·te·neck \'hāf-nər-'äl-tə-nek\, Friedrich Franz von. 1845–1904. German electrical engineer. Employed by Siemens firm (1867–90); invented the drum armature (1872), the Hefner lamp, producing standard Hefner candle (1884), signaling and telemetering devices.

He·gel \'hā-gəl\, Georg Wilhelm Friedrich. 1770–1831. German philosopher. Tutor at Bern, Switzerland (1793–96) and Frankfurt am Main (1797–1800); lecturer at Jena (1801) and professor there (1806); rector of the Gymnasium at Nürnberg (1808–16); professor, Heidelberg (1816–18), Berlin (1818–31). Last of the great German Idealist system-building philosophers; broke dominance of Kant to create philosophy celebrating reason as spirit of man, capable of absolute knowledge; created monistic system reconciling opposites by means of dialectic process; viewed history as similar process, dialectic of thesis and its implied antithesis leading to synthesis. Exerted great influence on Kierkegaard and Existentialists, on Marx, and on the Positivists. His works included *Die Phänomenologie des Geistes* (1807), *Wissenschaft der Logik* (1812–16), *Enzyklopädie der philosophischen Wissenschaften im Grundrisse* (1817), *Naturrecht und Staatswissenschaft im Grundrisse* (1821).

He·ge·si·as \hē-'jē-zē-əs\ of Mag·ne·sia \mag-'nē-zhē-ə, -zhə\. 3d century B.C. Greek rhetorician and historian. Said to have introduced mannered "Asianic" style of historiography, modeled on Gorgias, in opposition to classic "Atticist" style modeled on Isocrates.

Heg·e·sip·pus \ˌhej-ə-'sip-əs\. Saint. 2d century A.D. Greek historian. Jewish convert to Christianity; traveled widely in support of orthodoxy against Gnosticism. Author of *The Memoirs,* a history of the Christian church down to his own time, only fragments of which are extant.

Hegesippus. 4th century A.D. or later. Latin writer. Author of *De bello Judaico et excidio urbis Hierosolymitanae,* free adaptation of Josephus's *Jewish War;* sometimes identified with St. Ambrose of Milan.

He·gi·us \'hā-gē-u̇s\, Alexander. c.1433–1498. German Humanist. Influential schoolmaster in Wessel, Emmerich, Deventer; among his pupils were Erasmus, future Pope Adrian VI, and Hermann von dem Busche.

Hei·berg \'hā-ber\, Gunnar. 1857–1929. Norwegian playwright. Author of Expressionist plays, many subject of scandal, including *Tante Ulrikke* (1884), *Kong Midas* (1890), *Balkonen* (1894), *Det store Lod* (1895), *Folderådet* (1897), *Harald Svans Mor* (1899), *Kjaerlighetens Tragedie* (1904), *Jeg vil vaerge mit land* (1912).

Heiberg, Peter Andreas. 1758–1841. Danish writer. In comedies, songs, pamphlets, and periodical *Rigsdalersedlens haendelser* (1787–93) satirized social conventions and the government until he was exiled (1799). To Paris; in department of foreign affairs; accompanied Talleyrand on various diplomatic journeys. Works included *De Vonner og de Vanner* (1792), *Heckingborn* (1794), *Sproggranskning* (1798). His son ¶Johan Ludvig (1791–1860) was director of the Theater Royal, Copenhagen (1849–56); creator of vaudeville in Denmark. Author of vaudevilles, including *Aprilsnarrene* (1826), *De Uadskillelige* (1827), *De Danske i Paris* (1832), *Nej* (1836); other stage works as *Elverhøj* (1828), *Fatamorgana* (1838), *Syvsoverdag* (1840), *En sjael efter døden* (1841); and philosophical works expounding Hegelianism.

Hei·deg·ger \'hī-ˌdeg-ər, *Angl* 'hīd-ə-gər\, Johann Heinrich, *also called* Hans Heinrich. 1633–1698. Swiss theologian. Chief author of the *Formula Consensus Helvetica* (1675), which failed in its purpose of uniting the Swiss Reformed churches.

Heidegger, Martin. 1889–1976. German philosopher. Professor, Marburg (1923–27), Freiburg (1927–44); an original thinker on the topic of the meaning and modes of Being; strongly influenced Sartre and Existentialists. Author of *Sein und Zeit* (1927), *Vom Wesen des Grundes* (1929), *Was ist Metaphysik?* (1929), *Vom Wesen der Wahrheit Einführung in die Metaphysik* (1953), *Identität und Differenz* (1957), *Die Frage nach dem Ding* (1962), etc.

Hei·den·berg \'hī-dən-ˌberk\, Johannes. *Known as* Johannes Trit·heim \'trit-ˌhīm\ *or Lat.* Trit·he·mi·us \trit-'hā-mē-əs\. 1462–1516. German abbot and historian. Abbot of Sponheim (1485–1503) and of Scottish monastery of St. Jakob at Würzburg (from 1506); author of *De viris illustribus Germaniae* (1495), *Annales Hirsaugienses* (1514), etc.

Hei·den·hain \'hī-dən-hīn\, Rudolf Peter Heinrich. 1834–1897. German physiologist. Professor, Breslau (1859–97); known for studies of the mechanics, metabolism, and production of heat in muscles, and of physiology of secretion in glands.

Hei·den·stam \'hā-dən-stám\, Verner von, *in full* Carl Gustaf Verner von. 1859–1940. Swedish writer. His first volume of verse, *Vallfart och Vandringsår* (1888), reflected his life in the Orient; its contrast to the Naturalism characteristic of Swedish literature at that period marked the beginning of a literary renaissance in Sweden. Other work included verse *Dikter* (1895), *Ett folk* (1899), *Nya dikter* (1915); *Endymion* (1889), the epic *Hans Alienus* (1892); historical fiction *Karolinerna* (1897–98), *Folkungaträdet* (1905–07). Awarded Nobel prize for literature (1916).

Heijden, Jan van der. See HEYDEN.

Hei·jer·mans \'hī-yər-mäns\, Herman. 1864–1924. Dutch writer. Edited (from 1897) Socialist literary journal *De Jonge Gids,* Amsterdam. Author of fiction, including *Trinette* (1893), *Intérieurs* (1897), *Diamantstad* (1904), *Droomkoninkje* (1924); under pseudonym Koos Hab·be·ma \'häb-ä-má\, of a realistic novel of Jewish life *Kamertjeszonde* (1897); of plays including *Ghetto* (1899), *Op hoop van zegen* (1900), *Allerzielen* (1905), *Uitkomst* (1907), *Glück auf* (1911), *Eva Bonheur* (1919), *De Dageraad* (1921); and under pseudonym Samuel Falk·land \'fäl-ˌklänt\, of a collection of sketches of Dutch small-town life, *Schetsen* (1896–1915).

Heike. See TAIRA family.

Hei·ler \'hī-lər\, Friedrich, *in full* Johann Friedrich. 1892–1967. German theologian. Converted from Catholic to Lutheran church (1919); professor, Marburg (from 1920); leader of German High Church Union (from 1929); editor of the *Hochkirche* (from 1930). Author of *Das Gebet* (1918), *Evangelische Katholizität* (1926), *Im Ringen um die Kirche* (1931), etc.

Heim \'hīm\, Albert. 1849–1937. Swiss geologist. Professor, Federal Polytechnic School, Zürich (1873–1911), U. of Zürich (1875–1911); president, Swiss Geological Commission (1894–1926); known for studies on mountain-forming processes and glaciation in the Alps. Author of *Mechanismus der Gebirgsbildung* (1878), *Handbuch der Gletscherkunde* (1885), *Geologie der Schweiz* (1916–22).

Hein *or* **Heyn** \'hīn\, Piet. *Orig.* Pieter Pie·ter·szoon \'pēt-ər-sōn\. 1577–1629. Dutch admiral. Held as a galley rower by Spanish (1597–1601); became wealthy merchant captain; a director of Dutch West Indies Co. (1621); vice admiral of Dutch fleet (1624); captured 22 Portuguese ships in Cuba (1627); captured Spanish treasure fleet and huge treasure that financed Dutch war with Spain (1628); lieutenant admiral (1629); killed in battle with Dunkirk pirates.

Hei·ne \'hī-nə\, Heinrich, *orig.* Harry. 1797–1856. German poet and critic. Resident in Paris (from 1831); afflicted with an incurable disease of the spine which confined him to bed (from 1848). Author of verse that transcended Romanticism to begin expressing modern temperament, of political and social criticism notable for sardonic wit and arrogant radicalism. His volumes of verse were *Gedichte* (1821), *Buch der Lieder* (1827), *Neue Gedichte* (1844), *Romanzero* (1851); they contain some of the best-loved German lyrics, many of them set to music by Schumann, Schubert, and others. His prose works included *Reisebilder* (1826–31), *Französische Zustand* (1832), *Geschichte der neueren schönen Literatur in Deutschland* (1833), *Der Salon* (1834–40), *Deutschland. Ein Wintermärchen* (1844), *Atta Troll* (1847), *Lutezia* (1854), *Vermischte Schriften* (1854).

Hei·ne·mann \'hī-nə-mən\, William. 1863–1920. British publisher. Established business in London (1890) and published works of Hall Caine, Whistler,

Stevenson, Kipling, Galsworthy, Wells, Conrad, Pinero, Maugham, and others; had translations made of works of Dostoyevsky, Turgenev, Tolstoy, Ibsen, Bjørnson, Rolland; published Loeb Classical Library of translations.

Hei·nicke \'hī-ni-kə\, Samuel. 1727–1790. German educator. Founded at Leipzig (1778) first school for the deaf and mute in Germany.

Hein·kel \'hiŋ-kəl\, Ernst Heinrich. 1888–1958. German airplane builder. Founded (1922) Heinkel-Flugzeugwerke, in Warnemünde; built several speed-record setting aircraft, esp. the He 100; built He 111 and He 162 bombers widely used in World War II; first rocket-powered aircraft He 176 (1939), first turbojet aircraft He 178 (1939).

Heinrich. See also Henry.

Hein·rich der Glî·che·sae·re \'hīn-rik-dər-'glē-kə-,ser-ə\. 12th century. Middle High German poet. Wrote (c.1180) the famous beast epic *Reinecke Fuchs,* earliest German version of *Reynard the Fox.*

Heinrich von dem Tür·lin \-fón-dəm-'tu̇er-lēn\. fl. c.1215. Middle High German poet. Author of *Die Krone,* collection of Arthurian adventures.

Heinrich von Frei·burg \-'frī-bu̇rk\. fl. c.1300. Middle High German poet. Author of *Vom Heiligen Kreuz, Ritterfahrt des Johann von Michelsberg,* and a continuation of Gottfried von Strassburg's *Tristan.*

Heinrich von Meis·sen \-'mī-sən\. *Called* Frau·en·lob \'frau̇-ən-,lōp\. between 1250 and 1260–1318. German poet. One of 12 masters of the Meistersingers; exercised great influence on German poetic diction.

Heinrich von Melk \-'melk\. fl. 1150. Middle High German poet. Benedictine lay brother; regarded as first satirist in German literature. Author of *Von des Tôdes gehugede, Vom Priesterleben.*

Heinrich von Mo·rung·en \-'mōr-u̇ŋ-ən\. d. 1222. German Minnesinger. Author of highly regarded love lyrics.

Heinrich von Mü·geln \-'mu̇e-gəln\. d. 1369. Middle High German poet. Court poet to John of Bohemia, Ludwig I of Hungary, Charles IV of Bohemia. Translator of Valerius Maximus and of Nicholas of Lyra's *Commentary on the Psalms;* author of an allegorical poem *Der Meide Kranz,* fables, and songs.

Heinrich von Vel·de·ke \-'fel-də-kə\. between 1140 and 1150–before 1210. German poet. Author of a version of the legend of St. Servatius, of an *Eneide* in Flemish, based on a French version of the *Aeneid,* and of lyrics; considered one of founders of German court epic poetry.

Hein·se \'hīn-zə\, Johan Jakob Wilhelm. 1746–1803. German writer. Friend of the poet Wieland (*q.v.*); librarian to Elector Karl Joseph (from 1787). Among his works were novels *Ardinghello und die glückseligen Inseln* (1787), *Hildegard von Hohenthal* (1795–96), and *Anastasia und das Schachspiel* (1803); critical works. A leading exponent of *Sturm und Drang* Romanticism.

Hein·si·us \'hīn-sē-əs\, Anthonie. 1641–1720. Dutch politician. On William III's accession to English throne (1688), became grand pensionary of Holland and determined his country's foreign policy; rose to leadership in European combinations against Louis XIV of France; finally accepted terms of peace in Treaty of Utrecht (1713).

Heinsius, Daniël. 1580–1655. Dutch philologist and poet. Professor, Leiden (from 1605); prepared editions of classical works, esp. of Aristotle. Author of drama *Herodes Infanticida* (1632), critical tract *De tragoediae constitutione* (1611), verse *Nederduytsche Poemata* (1616), etc. His son ¶Nicolaas (1620–1681) was also a classical philologist; author of poem *Breda expugnata* (1637). A son of Nicolaas, ¶Nicolaas (1656–1718), was physician in ordinary to Queen Christina of Sweden (c.1687) and, later, to princes of the Brandenburg house. Author of medical books and of the satirical picaresque novels *Den vermakelyken avanturier* (1695) and *Don Clarazel de Gontarnos* (1697).

Heinz \'hīnz\, Henry John. 1844–1919. American businessman, b. Pittsburgh. With brother and cousin, founded firm F. & J. Heinz to make and sell pickles and other prepared foods (1876); firm reorganized as H.J. Heinz Co. (1888); incorporated (1905); president of company (1905–19). Introduced advertising slogan "57 Varieties" (1896).

Hei·sen·berg \'hī-zən-,berk\, Werner Karl. 1901–1976. German physicist. Professor, Leipzig (1927–41); director, Kaiser Wilhelm Institut (1941–45) and of Max Planck Institut (1945–76). Known esp. for development of quantum mechanics and principle of indeterminacy (1927); awarded 1932 Nobel prize for physics.

Heis·man \'hīs-mən \, John William. 1869–1936. American football coach. Coached at Oberlin (1892), Akron (1893–94), Auburn (1895–1903), Georgia Tech. (1904–19), Pennsylvania (1920–22), Rice Inst. (1924–27); inaugurated center snap; instrumental in legalization of forward pass (1906); reputed inventor of scoreboard; ran up highest score in football history, against Cumberland Coll. (222–0, 1916). Heisman Trophy named for him (1935).

Heiter, Amalie. See Amalie Friederike Marie Auguste.

Hek·to·ro·vić \hek-'tôr-ô-vich\, Petar. 1487–1572. Dalmatian poet. Author of Latin and Italian verse; important as figure in Dalmatian literature as author of lyrics and philosophical poem *Ribanje i ribarsko prigovaranje* (1555).

Held \'held\, Anna. 1865?–1918. American entertainer, b. Warsaw, Poland. To Paris (c.1871); with Yiddish Theatre company (1885–90); became star of French stage; to U.S. (1896) under management of Florenz Ziegfeld; m. Ziegfeld (1897); starred in comedies and vaudeville.

Held, John, Jr. 1889–1958. American cartoonist, b. Salt Lake City. Contributor to *Life, Judge, College Humor, New Yorker;* created image of "flaming youth" and "flappers" of the Jazz Age. Author of *Grim Youth* (1930), *Saga of Frankie and Johnny* (1931), *The Flesh is Weak* (1932), *Crosstown* (1934), etc.

Hel·e·na \'hel-ə-nə\. Saint. c.248–c.328. Roman empress. Wife of Constantius I Chlorus and mother of Constantine the Great; divorced by Constantius when he became caesar (292); influenced Constantine to adopt Christianity; made pilgrimage to Jerusalem (326) and there built Church of the Holy Sepulcher and Church of the Nativity; in legend credited with discovery of Christ's cross.

Helf·fe·rich \'hel-fə-rik\, Karl. 1872–1924. German economist, banker, and politician. Director, Deutsche Bank (1908–15); minister of finance (1915–16) and of the interior (1916–18). Aided in reorganizing German trade and industry after World War I; instrumental in securing the Rentenmark currency (1923); opposed fulfillment of provisions of Treaty of Versailles.

Hel·frich \'hel-frik\, Conrad Emil Lambert. 1886–1962. Dutch naval officer. In Netherlands East Indies (from 1907); chief of staff (1939–42), Netherlands East Indies forces; commander of Allied naval forces in southwest Pacific (1942); oversaw withdrawal from Java to Australia; commander of Netherlands armed forces in Far East (1942–44); Dutch delegate to UN (1945); head of naval ministry (1945–49).

Hel·gaud \el-gō(d)\ *or* **Hel·gal·dus** \hel-'gȯl-dəs, -'gäl-\. d. 1048. French religious. Benedictine monk at Fleury-sur-Loire. Author of history of Fleury abbey and of *Epitoma vitae Roberti regis,* unreliable but interesting history of reign of King Robert II the Pious.

Hel·ge·sen \'hel-gə-sən\, Paul. *Lat.* Paulus Hel·ie \'hel-(,)yā\ *or* El·i·ae \'el-ē-,ī\ *or* El·ie·sen \el-'yā-sən\. c.1485–c.1535. Danish Humanist. Carmelite monk; professor, Copenhagen (1519–22); Scandinavian provincial of Carmelites (1522–34); opponent of Luther and other reformers. Translated Erasmus into Danish.

He·li·o·do·rus \,hē-lē-ō-'dōr-əs\ of Eme·sa \i-'mā-sə\. 3d century A.D. Greek writer. Author of *Ethiopica,* earliest of extant Greek romances.

Heliogabalus. See Elagabalus.

Hel·land-Han·sen \'häl-län-'hän-sən\, Bjørn. 1877–1957. Norwegian oceanographer. Professor, Bergen (1914); director, Geophysical Inst. (1917 ff.); member of exploring expeditions in northern seas; known esp. for studies of oceanic dynamics.

Hel·la·ni·cus \,hel-ə-'nī-kəs\ of Les·bos \'lez-,bäs, -bəs\. 5th century B.C. Greek historian. Author of histories of Persia, Media, Assyria, and the Aeolians. Only fragments extant.

Hellens, Franz. See Frédéric van Ermengem.

Hel·ler \'hel-ər\, Hermann. 1891–1933. German political scientist. Professor, Berlin (1928–32), Frankfurt (1932–33); developed eclectic, sociological approach to political theory; opposed Nazi party and fled Germany (1933). Author of *Sozialismus und Nation* (1925), *Die Souveränität* (1927), *Europa und der Faschismus* (1929), *Staatslehre* (1934).

Heller, Robert. *Orig.* William Henry Palmer. c.1830–1878. American magician, b. England. Took up conjuring under influence of Robert-Houdin; to U.S. (c.1848); popularized conjuring in U.S.

Heller, Stephen. 1813–1888. Hungarian pianist and composer. To Paris (1838); friend of Chopin, Liszt, and Berlioz; best known for his piano studies.

Heller, Yom Tov Lipmann ben Nathan ha-Levi ben Wallerstein. 1579–1654. German rabbi. Rabbi of Vienna (1625–27), Prague (1627–29), Kraków (1643–54); noted Talmudist and commentator on the Mishna. Author of *Megillat eva,* description of massacres of Jewish communities of Prague and the Ukraine.

Hell·man \'hel-mən\, Lillian Florence. 1905–1984. American playwright, b. New Orleans. Wrote well-crafted plays that explored unprincipled characters and the workings of evil. Plays included *The Children's Hour* (1934), *The Little Foxes* (1939), *Watch on the Rhine* (1941), *Another Part of the Forest* (1946), and *Toys in the Attic* (1960); also wrote adaptations of Anouilh's *The Lark* (1955) and Voltaire's *Candide* (1956). Wrote three volumes of memoirs: *An Unfinished Woman* (1969), *Pentimento* (1973), and *Scoundrel Time* (1976). Prominent for her leftist politics; had 30-yr. relationship with writer Dashiell Hammett.

Hel·lo \ä-lō, e-\, Ernest. 1828–1885. French writer. Exponent of Catholic mysticism; founded journal *Le Monde catholique.* Author of *Les Physionomies des Saints* (1858), *L'Homme* (1872), *Contes extraordinaires* (1879), etc.

Hell·rie·gel \'hel-,rē-gəl\, Hermann. 1831–1895. German agricultural chemist. Discovered (1886) that leguminous plants are able by means of the bacteria living in nodules on their roots to fix the free nitrogen of the air.

Hell·ström \'hel-strœm\, Gustaf, *in full* Erik Gustaf. 1882–1953. Swedish novelist. Correspondent for newspaper *Dagens Nyheter* in London, Paris, New York (1907–35). Author of realistic novels as *Kuskar* (1910), *Kring en kvinna*

(1914), *Snörmakare Lekholm får en idé* (1927), *Carl Heribert Malmros* (1931), *Storm över Tjurö* (1935).

Hel·mers \ˈhel-mərs\, Jan Frederik. 1767–1813. Dutch poet. Author esp. of intensely patriotic verse, as *De Hollandsche Natie* (1812).

Helm·holtz \ˈhelm-ˌhōlts\, Hermann Ludwig Ferdinand von. 1821–1894. German physicist, anatomist, and physiologist. Military physician at Potsdam (1843–48); professor of physiology, Königsberg (1849), Bonn (1855), Heidelberg (1858), of physics, Berlin (1871); director of physicotechnical institute at Charlottenburg (1888). One of the founders of the principle of the conservation of energy, by virtue of his paper *Über die Erhaltung der Kraft* (1847); known for numerous other contributions to science, including determination of the velocity of nerve impulses (1850), invention of the ophthalmoscope (1851), investigation of the mechanisms of sight and hearing, development of a theory of color vision, study of the vortex motion of fluids, application of the principle of least action to electrodynamics, development of the theory of electricity, investigation of the motion of electricity in conductors. Published works included *Tonempfindungen als physiologische Grundlage für die Theorie der Musik* (1863), *Zur Thermodynamik chemischer Vorgänge* (1882–83).

Hel·mold \ˈhel-ˌmōlt\ of Bo·sau \ˈbō-ˌzau̇\. c.1120–after 1177. German historian. Author of *Chronica Slavorum* (c.1172).

Hel·mont \ˈhel-ˌmȯnt\, Jan Baptista van. 1579–1644. Flemish physician and chemist. Invented the word *gas* (suggested by Latin and Greek *chaos*) to designate aeriform fluids; first to distinguish gases distinct from air, as carbon dioxide; regarded water as prime element; believed digestion and nutrition due to action of ferments which convert food into living flesh; suggested use of alkalies to correct undue acidity of the digestive juices. His works were published (1648) as *Ortus Medicinae, vel Opera et Opuscula Omnia* by his son ¶Franciscus Mercurius (1614?–1699), naturalist and philosopher, who developed a monistic doctrine before Leibnitz, and concerned himself with the physiology of speech and the instruction of the deaf and dumb.

Hé·lo·ïse \ā-lȯ-ēz, *Angl* ˈel-ə-ˌwēz\. c.1098–1164. French religious. Niece of Fulbert, canon of Notre-Dame, who entrusted her to Peter Abelard (*q.v.*) for instruction (c.1118); m. Abelard secretly; after relevation of marriage and mutilation of Abelard, entered convent of Argenteuil; abbess of Le Paraclet, founded by Abelard.

Hel·per \ˈhel-pər\, Hinton Rowan. 1829–1909. American writer, b. Rowan (now Davie) Co., N.C. Published (1857) *The Impending Crisis of the South, and How to Meet It,* a book attacking slaveholding on economic grounds; book was banned by several Southern states; 100,000 copies were circulated in North during campaign of 1860; U.S. consul, Buenos Aires, Argentina (1861–66).

Help·mann \ˈhelp-mən\, Sir Robert. 1909–1986. Australian dancer, choreographer, actor, and director. Principal male dancer with Sadler's Wells Ballet (later Royal Ballet) (1933–50); producer and director of ballets, operas, and plays during 1940s and 1950s; acted in films, including *The Red Shoes* (1948); served as co-director (1965–74) and director (1974–76) of Australian Ballet.

Helst \ˈhelst\, Bartholomeus van der. c.1613–1670. Dutch painter. Among his notable canvases were *Kompagnie des Hauptmanns Bicker, Friedensmahl der Schützen, Guitarist;* a leading portraitist of Amsterdam.

Hel·tai \ˈhel-tȯi\, Gáspár. c.1520–1574. Hungarian Humanist, printer, and reformer. Published Hungarian translation of Bible (1551–61) and also *Chronicon Hungariae* (1575).

Hel·vé·tius \el-vās-yu̅e̅s\, Claude-Adrien. 1715–1771. French philosopher. Appointed farmer general (1738); retired to his country estate to devote himself to study (1751); noted as host to Philosophes; evolved sensationalist philosophy. Author of *De l'esprit* (1758), condemned by Sorbonne and publicly burned (1759), leading to attacks on other Philosophes, notably Voltaire.

Hel·vid·i·us Pris·cus \hel-ˈvid-ē-ə-ˈspris-kəs\. d. between 70 and 79 A.D. Roman philosopher. Senator under Nero; praetor (70); incurred enmity of Vespasian by outspokenness and belief in nearly coordinate authority of Senate; executed; a strong influence on Epictetus and the Stoics.

Hel·wys \ˈhel-(ˌ)wis\, Thomas. c.1550–c.1616. English religious leader. Member of Separatist group that emigrated to Amsterdam (1608); returned, established first General Baptist congregation in London (1612); imprisoned for advocating universal tolerance, independence of churches from state control.

Hé·lyot \āl-yō\, Pierre. *Known as* Le Père Hip·po·lyte \lə-per-ē-pȯ-lēt\. 1660–1716. French religious and historian. Franciscan monk (from 1683). Best known for his *Histoire des ordres monastiques, religieux et militaires* (1714–19, finished by P. Maximilien Bullot).

Hem·a·can·dra \ˌhem-ə-ˈkän-drə\. *Also called* Hemacandra Sū·ri \-ˈsü-rē\, So·ma·can·dra \ˌsō-mə-ˈkän-drə\ *or* Can·ga·de·va \ˈkäŋ-gə-ˈdā-və\. *Orig.* Can·dra·de·va \ˌkän-drə-ˈdā-və\. 1088–1172. Indian religious. Ordained Jain priest (1110); by learning and eloquence won concessions for Jain religion from King Siddharaja Jayasimha of Gujarāt; converted succeeding King Kumārapāla. Author of Sanskrit and Prākrit grammars, philosophical works, political tract *Arhanniti,* verse works.

Hem·ans \ˈhem-ənz\, Felicia Dorothea, *nee* Browne. 1793–1835. English poet. m. Alfred Hemans (1812; separated 1818). Known for light Romantic lyrics, including "Casabianca," "Homes of England," "Dirge," "Lost Pleiad," "Vespers of Palermo," "Landing of the Pilgrims."

Hem·by·ze \ˈhem-bē-zə\ *or* **Im·bi·ze** \ˈēm-bē-zə\, Jan van. 1513–1584. Dutch religious leader. Led troops and Calvinist townspeople in overthrow of Catholic government of Ghent (1577); assumed office of mayor; countenanced anti-Catholic pillaging and violence; attempted to suppress Catholicism entirely (1578, 1579); opposed by Prince William I of Orange, who invaded Ghent (1579) to restore toleration; fled to Palatinate (1579–83); returned to and elected mayor of Ghent (1583); apparently conspired to surrender Ghent to Spanish; executed for treason.

Hem·inge \ˈhem-iŋ\, John. *Also spelled* Hem·ing, Hem·ming, Hem·minge. c.1556–1630. English actor and editor. Member of King's Men company; closely associated with Henry Condell, Richard Burbage, and Shakespeare; known to have acted in Shakespeare's *Henry IV, Part I* and several of Ben Jonson's plays; a chief proprietor of Globe Theatre. Chiefly known as editor, with Condell, of the First Folio of Shakespeare (1623).

Hem·ing·way \ˈhem-iŋ-ˌwā\, Ernest Miller. 1899–1961. American writer, b. Oak Park, Ill. Served in World War I as volunteer in American ambulance unit in France and later with the Italian Arditi; European correspondent for Toronto *Star,* and later Paris correspondent for Hearst's Syndicated News Service. Awarded Nobel prize for literature (1954). Author of stories *Three Stories and Ten Poems* (1923), *In Our Time* (1925), *Men Without Women* (1927), *Death in the Afternoon* (1932), *Winner Take Nothing* (1933), *The Green Hills of Africa* (1935), *The Fifth Column* (1938), *A Moveable Feast* (1964); novels *The Torrents of Spring* (1926), *The Sun Also Rises* (1926), *A Farewell to Arms* (1929), *To Have and Have Not* (1937), *For Whom the Bell Tolls* (1940), *The Old Man and the Sea* (1952), *Islands in the Stream* (1970).

Hemming *or* **Hemminge,** John. See John HEMINGE.

Hé·mon \ā-mō^{n}\, Louis. 1880–1913. French novelist. Resident in Canada (from 1911). Author of *Maria Chapdelaine* (1914), widely translated story of Canadian pioneer life, *Colin-maillard* (1924), *Battling Malone* (1926), etc.

Hem·ster·huis \ˈhem-stər-ˌhœis\, Tiberius. 1685–1766. Dutch philologist. Professor, Amsterdam (1704–17), Franeker (1717–50), Leiden (1750–66). Published editions of Pollux's *Onomasticon,* Lucian's *Dialogues,* and Aristophanes's *Plutus.* His son ¶Franz (1721–1790) was a philosopher and writer on art; influenced Herder, Hölderlin. Author of *Sophyle ou de la philosophie* (1778), *Aristée ou de la divinité* (1779), *Simon ou des facultés de l'âme* (1790).

Hé·nault \ā-nō\, Charles-Jean-François. 1685–1770. French jurist and writer. Counselor to the parlement of Paris (1705); president of the Chamber (1710–31). A leader of salon of Mme. du Deffand; host of the Entresol club (1720–31). Author of tragedies, comedies, ballets, *Abrégé chronologique de l'histoire de France* (1744), and *François II, scènes historiques* (1747).

Hench \ˈhench\, Philip Showalter. 1896–1965. American physician, b. Pittsburgh. With Mayo Clinic (1923–57). Awarded Nobel prize for physiology or medicine (1950) with E. C. Kendall and T. Reichstein for research on adrenal hormones, esp. cortisone, and application to treatment of rheumatoid arthritis.

Hen·cke \ˈheŋ-kə\, Karl Ludwig. 1793–1866. German astronomer. An amateur observer; discovered minor planets Astraea (1845), Hebe (1847).

Henck·ell \ˈheŋ-kəl\, Karl. 1864–1929. German writer. Works included *Umsonst* (1884), *Strophen* (1887), *Amselrufe* (1888), *Trutznachtigall* (1891), *Zwischenspiel* (1894), *Neues Leben* (1900), *Gipfel und Gründe* (1904), *Ein Lebenslied* (1911), *Weltmusik* (1918), etc.

Hen·der·son \ˈhen-dər-sən\, Alexander. 1583?–1646. Scottish clergyman and diplomat. Held parish of Leuchars, Fife (1612–37); refused imposition of new books of canons and worship (1636–37); prepared and read in Edinburgh the National Covenant (1638); drafted Solemn League and Covenant adopted by Westminster Assembly (1643). Rector, Edinburgh U. (1640–46); introduced teaching of Hebrew there. Moderator of Glasgow Assembly (1638), St. Andrews Assembly (1641). Author of *Bishop's Doom* (1638).

Henderson, Arthur. 1863–1935. British labor leader and politician, b. Glasgow. Iron molder in Newcastle; elected Labour member in Parliament (1903 ff.); Labour party chairman (1908–10, 1914–17), secretary (1911–34); party whip in Commons (1914, 1921–23, 1925–27); at outbreak of World War I, instrumental in influencing most of party to support government's war policy. In Asquith's cabinet (1915), president of board of trade; in Lloyd George's cabinet (1916), minister without portfolio; in first Labour ministry under MacDonald (1924), became home secretary; in second ministry, secretary for foreign affairs (1929–31). Vigorous advocate of international peace; chairman of International Disarmament Conference summoned by League of Nations (1932); awarded Nobel peace prize (1934).

Henderson, David Bremner. 1840–1906. American politician, b. Old Deer, Scotland. To U.S. (1846); practiced law, Dubuque, Iowa (from 1866). Member, U.S. House of Representatives (1883–1903) and speaker (1899–1903).

Henderson, Fletcher, *in full* James Fletcher. 1898–1952. American pianist and bandleader, b. Cuthbert, Ga. To New York City (1920); organized band to accompany recording blues singers; developed jazz band notable for use of written arrangements, paving the way for great success of disciplined bands of the 1930s; disbanded group (1934); contributed arrangements to Benny Goodman's band (1934–36, 1939 ff.).

Henderson, Lawrence Joseph. 1878–1942. American biochemist, b. Lynn, Mass. Professor, Harvard (from 1919); known for study of buffer solutions, esp. in physiological systems, and contribution to Henderson-Hasselbach equation describing them. Author of *The Fitness of the Environment* (1913), *The Order of Nature* (1917), *Blood* (1928), and *Pareto's Sociology: A Physiologist's Interpretation* (1935).

Henderson, Sir Nevile Meyrick. 1882–1942. British diplomat. Entered diplomatic service (1905); minister to Egypt (1924–28), France (1928–29), Yugoslavia (1929–35); ambassador to Argentina (1935–37), Germany (1937–39). Author of *Failure of a Mission* (1940).

Henderson, Richard. 1735–1785. American colonizer, b. Hanover Co., Va. Judge of North Carolina superior court (1768–73); sent Daniel Boone to explore beyond Cumberland Gap (1769); organized Transylvania Company to settle colony in Kentucky (1774); acquired Indian lands in Treaty of Sycamore Shoals (1775); sent Boone to found Boonesborough (1775); outbreak of Revolution caused collapse of enterprise; later helped settle Nashville, Tenn. (1780).

Henderson, Thomas. 1798–1844. Scottish astronomer. Astronomer royal at Cape of Good Hope (1831–33); observed transit of Mercury (1832) and Encke's and Biela's comets. First astronomer royal of Scotland and professor, Edinburgh (1834–44).

Henderson, Yandell. 1873–1944. American physiologist, b. La Jolla, Cal. Professor, Yale (1911–1938); consulting physiologist, U.S. Bureau of Mines (1913–25). Known for work on circulation, respiration, pharmacology of gases, etc.; discovered usefulness of carbon dioxide-oxygen mixture in resuscitation.

Hen·drick \'hen-drik\, Burton Jesse. 1870–1949. American writer, b. New Haven, Conn. Coauthor, with Adm. William S. Sims, of *The Victory at Sea* (1920, Pulitzer prize); author of *Age of Big Business* (1919), *Life and Letters of Walter H. Page* (1922, Pulitzer prize), *The Training of an American* (1928, Pulitzer prize), *Andrew Carnegie* (1932), *The Lees of Virginia* (1935), *Bulwark of the Republic, a Biography of the Constitution* (1937), *Statesmen of the Lost Cause* (1939), *Lincoln's War Cabinet* (1946).

Hen·dricks \'hen-driks\, Thomas Andrews. 1819–1885. American politician, b. near Zanesville, Ohio. Member from Indiana, U.S. House of Representatives (1851–55); U.S. senator (1863–69); governor of Indiana (1872). Vice presidential candidate with S.J. Tilden on Democratic ballot (1876); vice president of the U.S. (1885).

Hen·gist *or* **Hen·gest** \'heŋ-gəst, -,gist\ and **Hor·sa** \'hȯr-sə\. 5th century A.D. British settlers. Brothers who led the band of Jutes who (c.449 A.D.) invaded southern Britain; Hengist was reputed founder of line of kings of Kent.

Heng·sten·berg \'heŋ-stən-,berk\, Ernst Wilhelm. 1802–1869. German theologian. Professor, Berlin (1826–69); founded (1827) and edited *Evangelische Kirchen-Zeitung;* champion of Lutheran orthodoxy; opponent of modern Bible criticism, rationalism. Author of *Christologie des Alten Testaments* (1829–35).

Hen·ie \'hen-ē\, Sonja. 1912–1969. Norwegian ice skater. Won world women's amateur figure skating championship 10 times (1927–36); Olympic gold medallist (1928, 1932, 1936); noted for introducing ballet movements into figure skating, tranforming it into dramatic exhibition; starred in touring ice shows and appeared in motion pictures.

Hen·le \'hen-lə\, Friedrich Gustav Jacob. 1809–1885. German pathologist and anatomist. Professor, Zürich (1840–44), Heidelberg (1844–52), Göttingen (1852–85); pioneer in histology, investigated the anatomical structure of the hair, blood and lacteal vessels, kidney, nails, central nervous system, etc. Author of *Allgemeine Anatomie* (1841) and *Handbuch der rationellen Pathologie* (1846–53), in which physiology and pathology were treated for the first time as branches of one science.

Hen·lein \'hen-,līn\, Konrad. 1898–1945. Sudeten-German politician. Founded (1933) Sudetendeutsche Heimatfront, subsequently known as Sudetendeutsche Partei, which gained ascendancy in Czechoslovak election (1935); Reichskommissar for Sudeten areas after German occupation (Oct. 1938); Gauleiter of Sudetenland (1938–39); suicide.

Hen·ley \'hen-lē\, John. 1692–1756. English clergyman. Known as "Orator Henley" from claim to have restored church oratory in England; widely known for his eccentricities; caricatured by Hogarth, and ridiculed by Pope in his *Dunciad*.

Henley, William Ernest. 1849–1903. English man of letters. Cripple from childhood; editor of *Magazine of Art* (1882–86), *Scots Observer* (1889; renamed *National Observer,* 1891), *New Review* (1894–98). Author of volumes of verse as *Book of Verses* (1888), *London Voluntaries* (1893), *For England's Sake* (1900), *Hawthorn and Lavender* (1901), *In Hospital* (1903); his best known poem, "Invictus." Collaborated with Robert Louis Stevenson in four plays, *Deacon Brodie, Beau Austin, Admiral Guinea, Macaire* (1880–85); with T.F. Henderson edited centenary edition of Robert Burns (1896–97).

Hen·ne am Rhyn \'hen-ə-äm-'rēn\, Otto. 1828–1914. Swiss historian. Teacher and archivist, Sankt Gallen (1857–72); editor of *Freimaurerzeitung,* Leipzig (1872–79), *Neue Zürcher Zeitung,* Zürich (1879 ff.). Author of *Allgemeine Kulturgeschichte* (1877–1908), *Kulturgeschichte des deutschen Volkes* (1903).

Hen·ne·bique \en-bēk\, François. 1842–1921. French engineer. Devised methods of reinforcing concrete and a complete system of construction from reinforced elements.

Hen·ne·pin \en-pa^n, *Angl* 'hen-ə-pən, ,en-ə-'pa^n\, Louis, *baptized* Johannes. 1626–after 1701. French missionary and explorer. Joined Recollect Order of Friars Minor; to Canada (1675); accompanied La Salle through Great Lakes (1679); with exploring party in upper Mississippi region (1680); while captive of Sioux, taken to and named Falls of St. Anthony; rescued by Dulhut; returned to France (1682). Published *Description de la Louisiane* (1683), *Nouvelle découverte d'un très grand pays situé dans l'Amérique* (1697).

Hen·ne·quin \en-ka^n\, Philippe-Augustin. 1762–1833. French painter. Student and successor of David; noted for historical works.

Hen·ner \ā-ner, *also* e-ner, en-\, Jean-Jacques. 1829–1905. French painter. Gained considerable success as painter esp. of nymphs, naiads, idealized young women, as *La Liseuse, Suzanne au bain, Idylle.*

Henri. See HENRY.

Hen·ri \'hen-rē\, Robert. 1865–1929. American painter, b. Cincinnati. Taught at Women's School of Design, Philadelphia (1891–96), Art Students League, New York City (1915–23); with Sloan, Glackens, Luks, A.B. Davies, Prendergast, Shinn, formed The Eight, also called Ashcan School (1908); championed realism; noted also as portraitist. Author of *The Art Spirit* (1923). His canvases included *Willie Gee, Himself, Herself, The Equestrian, Laughing Girl, Spanish Gypsy, Snow.*

Hen·ri·ci \hen-'rēt-sē\, Christian Friedrich. *Pseudonym* Pi·can·der \pē-'kän-dər\. 1700–1764. German poet, satirist, and playwright. Best known as author of text of J.S. Bach's *St. Matthew Passion.*

Hen·ri·et·ta Anne \,hen-rē-'et-ə-'an\. Duchesse d'Or·lé·ans \dȯr-lā-ä^n\. 1644–1670. English princess. Fifth daughter of Charles I of England and his queen, Henrietta Maria; taken to France (1646); brought up a Roman Catholic; returned to England at Restoration (1660); m. Philippe, duc d'Orléans and brother of Louis XIV (1661); became a favorite of Louis XIV and an intermediary between him and Charles II.

Henrietta Ma·ria \-mə-'rī-ə\. 1609–1669. Queen of Charles I of England. Daughter of Henry IV of France and sister of Louis XIII; m. Charles (1625); attempted to influence king to aid Roman Catholics as he had promised; to the Continent to raise money and troops to aid Royalist cause (1642); led force to Oxford to join Charles (1643); forced to take refuge in France (1644); continued to plot for aid to Charles until she learned of his execution (1649); continued to live mainly in France after Restoration of her son Charles II (1660).

Henriot, Émile. See Émile MAIGROT.

Henrique. See HENRY.

Henry II \'hen-rē\. *Ger.* Hein·rich \'hīn-rik\. *Called* Henry Ja·so·mir·gott \,yäz-ō-'mir-,gȯt\. c.1114–1177. Duke of Austria (1156–77). Son of Leopold III of Austria; made count palatine (1140) by half-brother King Conrad III; succeeded brother Leopold IV as margrave of Austria (1141); granted duchy of Bavaria (1143); refused to give up Bavaria after its award (1154) by Emperor Frederick I Barbarossa to Henry the Lion of Saxony; agreed to compromise, giving up Bavaria in exchange for raising of Austria to duchy (1156) and certain privileges, including succession in male or female line.

Henry. *Ger.* Heinrich. Name of ten dukes of Bavaria including:

Henry I. c.920–955. Duke (947–955). Son of King Henry I of Germany and brother of Otto I the Great; engaged in conspiracies against Otto (939, 941) but forgiven and granted duchy (947).

Henry III. See Holy Roman emperor HENRY II.

Henry X. *Called* der Stol·ze \der-'shtȯlt-sə\, *i.e.* the Proud. c.1100–1139. Duke (1126–39). Son and successor of Henry IX the Black; m. (1127) Gertrud, daughter of Emperor Lothair II; strong supporter of Lothair against Hohenstaufens; opposed Conrad III as Lothair's successor; inherited duchy of Saxony (1137); lost Bavaria to Leopold IV of Austria.

Henry. *Ger.* Heinrich. *Called* der Jüng·e·re \der-ˈyuœŋ-ə-rə\, *i.e.* the Younger. 1489–1568. Duke of Brunswick-Wolfenbüttel (1514–68). Served Emperor Charles V in Spain and Italy; vigorous opponent of Reformation, attacked by Luther; driven from Brunswick by Schmalkaldic League (1542), restored (1547) after defeat of League by Charles V; defeated Albert II Alcibiades of Kulmbach-Bayreuth at Sievershausen (1553).

Henry. *Sp.* En·ri·que \än-ˈrē-kä\. Name of four kings of Castile:

Henry I. 1203–1217. King (1214–17). Son of Alfonso VIII and Eleanor of Aquitaine; killed accidentally before his marriage to a daughter of Alfonso IX of León which would have united the two lands; succeeded by his sister Berenguela.

Henry II. *Known as* Henry of Tra·stá·ma·ra \trä-ˈstä-mä-rä\. 1333–1379. King (1369–79). Illegitimate son of Alfonso XI; made count of Trastámara; fled to France on accession of half-brother Peter the Cruel (1356); invaded Castile with French aid, defeated by English army under Edward the Black Prince at Nájera (1367); murdered Peter and assumed throne (1369); gave support to France in war with England.

Henry III. *Called* el Do·lien·te \el-dōl-ˈyān-tā\, *i.e.* the Sufferer. 1379–1406. King (1390–1406). Son of John I; m. Catherine of Lancaster, gaining thereby province of Vizcaya; under regency (1390–93), period marked by violent anti-Semitic outbreaks; reasserted crown authority over nobility; took strong measures against Moroccan pirates; dispatched expedition (1402) under Jean de Bethencourt that conquered Canary Islands.

Henry IV. 1425–1474. King (1454–74). Son of John II; weak and dissolute ruler, reign marked by lawlessness, corruption; m. 2d (1462) Joana, sister of Portuguese king; paternity of her daughter Joana disputed, succession passed to Henry's sister Isabella I.

Henry. *Known as* Henry of Flan·ders \ˈflan-dərz\. c.1174–1216. Emperor of Constantinople (1206–16). Son of Baldwin V, Count of Flanders and Hainaut, younger brother of King Baldwin I; fought against Theodore I Lascaris in Asia Minor (1204–05); regent of Romania, the Latin kingdom of Constantinople, on capture of Baldwin (1205); named emperor (1206); fought Bulgars and Theodore, settled disputes by diplomacy; attempted to secure Latin rule.

Henry. Name of two kings of Cyprus:

Henry I de Lu·si·gnan \lue-zēn-yä^{n}\. 1217–1253. King (1218–53). Under regency of uncles Philippe and Jean d'Ibelin; assumed power (1233); refused to recognize suzerainty of Emperor Frederick II; accompanied Louis IX of France on crusade (1249).

Henry II de Lusignan. 1271–1324. King (1285–1324). Son of Hugh III; succeeded brother John I as king; chosen king of Jerusalem (1285) to succeed Charles of Anjou; weak ruler; lost Acre to Mamlūks (1291); exiled to Cilicia (1310) by his brother Amalric; restored by barons.

Henry. Name of eight kings of England:

Henry I. *Called* Henry Beau·clerc \ˈbō-kler\. 1068–1135. King of England (1100–35). Fourth son of William the Conqueror and Matilda; bought duchy of Côtentin (1187) but driven from it by brothers Robert Curthose and William Rufus (1091); in service of William Rufus (1096–1100); took advantage of Robert's absence from England at time of William's death (1100) to have himself elected king by the witan; consolidated position by issuing charter restoring laws of Edward the Confessor, by recalling Anselm, and by marrying (1100) Edith, later called Matilda, daughter of Malcolm III of Scotland. Conquered Normandy (1106) and captured and imprisoned Robert; defended Normandy in wars (1113, 1116–20, 1124) with Louis VI of France; married daughter Matilda to Geoffrey Plantagenet, Count of Anjou (1126). Succeeded as king by Stephen.

Henry II. *Sometimes known as* Curt·man·tle \ˈkərt-ˌmant-ᵊl\. 1133–1189. King (1154–89), first king of house of Anjou or Plantagenet. Son of Geoffrey Plantagenet, Count of Anjou, and Matilda, daughter of Henry I of England; became duke of Normandy (1150), count of Anjou (1151); defeated in attempts to seize English crown from Stephen; m. (1152) Eleanor of Aquitaine; adopted as successor by Stephen (1153) and acceded on Stephen's death (1154). Obtained from Malcolm of Scotland restoration of northern English counties (1157); conquered the Welsh (1158, 1163, 1165) and southeastern Ireland (1171); carried on struggle with Louis VII for provinces in France (1157–80); greatly increased crown authority over barons; instituted internal reforms in judicial and financial systems; had son Henry crowned (1170) to ensure succession. Carried on bitter controversy with Thomas Becket, archbishop of Canterbury, who refused to be subservient to king; after murder of Becket by four of Henry's knights (1170), did penance at archbishop's shrine (1174). Suppressed rebellion of sons (1173–74); died while preparing to suppress another rebellion headed by his sons Richard and John aided by Philip of France. Succeeded by his son Richard I.

Henry III. 1207–1272. King (1216–72). Son of John of England and Isabella of Angoulême; during minority, under regency of William Marshal, Earl of Pembroke (1216–19), and (1219–32) of the justiciary Hubert de Burgh, with the support of Stephen Langton, archbishop of Canterbury; finally seized power from de Burgh (1232); countenanced ruthless civil administration of Peter des Roches and Peter of Rivaux until forced by barons to expel them (1234); m. Eleanor of Provence (1236). Showed great favor toward foreigners, esp. his Lusignan half-brothers, and attempted European adventures beyond his means, thus provoking rebellion of barons, who compelled him to accept (1258) Provisions of Oxford, a series of reforms to be carried out by a commission of barons; repudiated this agreement, causing rebellion (Barons' War) under Simon de Montfort, who defeated and took him prisoner at Lewes (May 14, 1264); rescued by his son Edward, who defeated Montfort at Evesham (Aug. 4, 1265); took little part in government thereafter. Succeeded by his son Edward I.

Henry IV. *Surnamed* Bol·ing·broke \ˈbäl-iŋ-ˌbrůk, ˈbůl-, *US also* ˈbō-liŋ-ˌbrōk\. *Often called by contemporaries* Henry of Lan·cas·ter \ˈlaŋ-kəs-tər, *US also* ˈlan-ˌkas-tər, ˈlaŋ-\. 1366–1413. King (1399–1413). Son of John of Gaunt and Blanche of Lancaster; distinguished himself in knightly prowess, military adventure, and travels in Prussia, Lithuania, Venice, Cyprus, and Jerusalem. Created earl of Derby (1377?) and duke of Hereford (1397). Banished from England by his cousin Richard II (1398), who confiscated estates of Lancaster on John of Gaunt's death (1399); raised army, invaded England, and defeated and captured Richard, who forthwith abdicated. Formally acclaimed king by Parliament (1399); suppressed rebellions of Richard's sympathizers (1400), of Welsh under Owen Glendower (1399 ff.), of powerful Percy family led by Henry Percy (Hotspur) in battle of Shrewsbury (July 21, 1403), and of earl marshal Mowbray supported by Archbishop Scrope of York (1405). Succeeded by his son Henry V.

Henry V. 1387–1422. King (1413–22). Son of Henry IV; created earl of Chester, duke of Cornwall, prince of Wales (1399); directed war on Welsh rebels (1402–08); planned French war and commanded English army which invaded France and won battle of Agincourt (Oct. 25, 1415); influential in election of Pope Martin V (1417); m. (1420) Catherine of Valois, daughter of Charles VI of France; recognized by French in treaty of Troyes (1420) as regent and heir to French throne; died while planning to secure his position against further French opposition. Succeeded by his son Henry VI.

Henry VI. 1421–1471. King (1422–61 and 1470–71). Son of Henry V and Catherine of Valois; succeeded to throne in infancy, under protectorship (1422–29) of his uncle Humphrey, Duke of Gloucester; proclaimed king of France (1422) under regency of uncle John, Duke of Bedford; crowned king of France (1431), but military successes of Joan of Arc and Charles VII expelled English forces from all of France except Calais (by 1453). Latter part of reign marked by periods of mental derangement (1453 ff.), by economic unrest culminating in Cade's Rebellion (1450), and by struggle for power between houses of Lancaster and York leading to Wars of the Roses (1455–85); captured by Yorkists at Northampton (1460), released on recognizing Duke of York as heir; after defeat at 2d battle of St. Albans (Feb. 17, 1461), Yorkists successful; Henry deposed (Mar. 4, 1461) and Duke of York proclaimed king as Edward IV; imprisoned (1465–70); rescued and restored as king during uprising headed by Earl of Warwick (1470), but soon recaptured and imprisoned in Tower of London, where he was murdered.

Henry VII. *Often referred to as* Henry Tu·dor \ˈtü-dər\. 1457–1509. King (1485–1509), first of house of Tudor. Son of Edmund Tudor, Earl of Richmond, and Margaret Beaufort, direct descendant of John of Gaunt; during supremacy of house of York (1471–85), lived as an exile, chiefly in Brittany; encouraged by unrest under Richard III, invaded England; defeated and killed Richard III at Bosworth Field (Aug. 22, 1485); immediately acknowledged as king. m. (1486) Elizabeth, eldest daughter of Edward IV, thus uniting houses of Lancaster and York. Defeated impostors Lambert Simnel (who pretended to be Earl of Warwick) and Perkin Warbeck (who pretended to be Duke of York); suppressed Cornish insurrection (1497). Instituted Star Chamber, by means of which he was able to restrict power of nobles; greatly increased royal power during reign; accumulated vast fortune. Succeeded by his son Henry VIII.

Henry VIII. 1491–1547. King (1509–47). Son of Henry VII and Elizabeth of York; thoroughly educated in spirit of Renaissance; m. (1509) Catherine of Aragon (*q.v.*), widow of his brother Arthur. Engaged in war on Continent, joining Holy League against France (1511); personally commanded English troops in victory of battle of the Spurs (Aug. 16, 1513); in England, his troops defeated and killed James IV of Scotland at Flodden (Sept. 9, 1513). Held interview with Francis I of France at Field of Cloth of Gold (1520). Appointed Cardinal Wolsey lord chancellor (1515); for his treatise *Assertio Septem Sacramentorum,* received from Pope Leo X (1521) title Fi·dei De·fen·sor \ˈfīd-e-ˌē-dā-ˈfān-ˌsȯr\, i.e. Defender of the Faith. Involved in conflict with papal power, originating in his wish to divorce Catherine, who had failed to produce a male heir; dismissed Wolsey for failure to procure from pope a decree of divorce, appointing Sir Thomas More chancellor in his stead (1529); on advice of Cranmer, secured opinions declaring marriage with Catherine invalid (because she was his deceased brother's wife); thereupon secretly married Anne Boleyn (1533), by whom he became the father of Elizabeth I. Because of continued conflict with papal power, obtained from Parliament the Act of Supremacy, creating a national church separate from Roman Catholic church and appointing the king protector and sole supreme head of church and clergy of England; executed Sir Thomas More (1535) for refusal to acknowledge royal supremacy; suppressed monasteries in England and confiscated their properties. Beheaded Anne Boleyn on charge of adultery (1536); m. Jane Seymour (1536; mother of Edward VI); m. Anne of Cleves (1540; divorced 1540); m. Catherine Howard (1540; beheaded on charge of adultery, 1542); m. Catherine Parr (1543; survived him). During reign, unified and centralized administrative power, increased scope of parliamentary powers, and improved English naval defenses; brought Wales into union with England (1434–36); pacified Ireland; attempted to subdue Scotland. Succeeded by his son Edward VI.

Henry. *Orig.* Henry Fitz·hen·ry \fits-'hen-rē\. *Known as* the Young King. 1155–1183. English prince. Son of King Henry II; on death of elder brother William (1156) became heir apparent; m. (1160) Margaret, daughter of Louis VII of France; crowned at Westminster (1170) by Archbishop Roger of York in attempt by father to secure succession; again crowned (1172); revolted with brothers Richard and Geoffrey (1173); at war with Richard over Poitou (1182–83); died while preparing to renew war.

Henry. Duke of Lan·cas·ter \'laŋ-kə-stər, *US also* 'lan-ˌkas-tər, 'laŋ-\. c.1300–1361. English soldier. Son of Henry, Earl of Lancaster; great-grandson of King Henry III; created earl of Derby (1337); succeeded to earldoms of Lancaster and Leicester (1345); made earl of Lincoln (1349), duke palatine of Lancaster (1351); trusted adviser of King Edward III. Took part in naval battles of Sluis (1340), Winchelsea (1350); king's lieutenant in southwestern France (1345–47); won victory at Auberoche (1345), sacked Poitiers (1346). Captain and viceregent for Gascony and Poitou (1349–61); negotiated treaty of Brétigny (1360). His estates passed to daughter Blanche and her husband, John of Gaunt.

Henry. *In full* Henry William Frederick Albert. Duke of Glouces·ter \'gläs-tər, 'glȯs-\. 1900–1974. English prince. Son of George V; served in army (1919–36); created duke (1928); governor general of Australia (1945–47); field marshal (1955).

Henry. *Fr.* Hen·ri \äⁿ-rē\. Name of four kings of France:

Henry I. c.1008–1060. King (1031–60). Son of Robert II; spent first years in putting down rebellions, esp. that of younger brother Robert, whom he gave Burgundy (1032); aided Duke William of Normandy in subduing nobles (1035–47); later (1054, 1058) involved in war with William and defeated. Succeeded by son Philip I.

Henry II. 1519–1559. King (1547–59). Second son of Francis I; with his brother the dauphin Francis, hostage in Spain (1526–30); m. Catherine de Médicis (1533); became heir apparent at death of dauphin (1536). Largely under influence of his mistress, Diane de Poitiers, and of Anne de Montmorency, constable of France. Signed treaty of Chambord (1552) allying France with German Protestant princes against Emperor Charles V; seized three bishoprics (Toul, Metz, Verdun) from emperor (1552); in wars with England, took Boulogne (1550) and recovered Calais (1558); unsuccessful in later wars (1556–59); beaten in Italy and defeated by Spaniards in Low Countries; accepted Peace of Cateau-Cambrésis (1559). Laid groundwork for continuing systematic persecution of Protestants in France. Died of wound received in a tournament. Of his seven children three became kings of France.

Henry III. 1551–1589. King (1574–89). Third son of Henry II and Catherine de Médicis; as duke of An·jou \äⁿ-zhü\, credited with winning battles of Jarnac and Moncontour over Condé and Coligny (1569); aided mother in plotting Massacre of St. Bartholomew (1572); with mother's aid elected king of Poland (1573). On death of brother Charles IX (1574) became king of France; his reign marked by continuous civil conflicts between Catholics (Holy League) and Huguenots (1574–89). After death (1584) of his brother François, duc d'Alençon, forced to take sides with Huguenots; fled Paris on Day of Barricades (1588); had Henry, duc de Guise, and his brother Cardinal Louis II of Lorraine murdered (1588). After Catherine's death (1589), murdered by a monk, Jacques Clément; with his death Valois male line extinct.

Henry IV. *Often called* Henry of Na·varre \nə-'vär\. *Fr.* Henri de Navarre. 1553–1610. King of Navarre as Henry III (1572–89); king of France (1589–1610), first of Bourbon line. Son of Antoine de Bourbon, duc de Vendôme, and Jeanne d'Albret, queen of Navarre; early known as prince of Bé·arn \bā-ärn\; reared a Protestant; joined Huguenots in religious war (1568–70); after death of Condé at Jarnac (1569) proclaimed leader, though Coligny in actual command (1569–70). m. Margaret of Valois, sister of Charles IX (1572); virtual prisoner at court (1572–76); became heir presumptive on death of François, duc d'Alençon (1584); concluded War of Three Henrys (1585–87) by victory over Henry III at Coutras. Became king at death of Henry III (1589); won battles of Arques (1589) and Ivry (1590) over Charles, duc de Mayenne, of the Holy League; formally renounced Protestantism (1593) for Catholic faith; entered Paris (1594) and terminated war with Holy League (1596); signed Edict of Nantes (1598) establishing rights of Protestants; concluded peace of Vervins with Phillip II of Spain (1598). m. (1600), as second wife, Marie de Médicis (*q.v.*). His final years (1600–10) a period of recovery from wars and of prosperity for France; finances reorganized and agriculture and industry encouraged under guidance of Maximilien de Béthune, duc de Sully. Conducted successful foreign policy; helped achieve Twelve Years' Truce (1609) between Spain and Netherlands; about to declare war on Austria (1610) but assassinated by a religious fanatic, Ravaillac.

Henry. *Ger.* Heinrich. Name of eight kings of Germany:

Henry I. *Called* der Vo·gel·fäng·er \'fō-gəl-ˌfeŋ-ər\, *i.e.* the Fowler. c.876–936. King (919–936). Duke of Saxony (912–936); son of Otto, Duke of Saxony; elected king (919) to succeed Conrad I; first of the Saxon line of kings of Germany; brought Swabia (919) and Bavaria (921) into German confederation; regained Lotharingia (925); fortified and strengthened the cities; reorganized the army; defeated the Wends (929), Magyars (933), and Danes (934).

Henry II–VI. See Holy Roman emperors HENRY II–VI.

Henry. *Sometimes known as* Henry VII. 1211–1242. King (1220–35). Son of future Emperor Frederick II; crowned king of Sicily (1212); made duke of Swabia (1216 or 1217); elected king by diet of Frankfurt (1220); under regency of Archbishop Engelbert I of Cologne (1220–25), of Louis I, Duke of Bavaria (1225–28); m. (1225) Margaret, daughter of Leopold VI of Austria; asserted rule (1228), supporting towns against bishops and princes; forced to submit, issued *Statutum in favorem principum* (1231); rebelled against emperor (1234), submitted (1235), deposed, held captive in Sicily to death.

Henry VII. See Holy Roman emperor HENRY VII.

Henry. *Ger.* Hein·rich \'hīn-rik\. *Called* das Kind \dä-'skint\, *i.e.* the Child. 1244–1308. Landgrave of Hesse (1265–1308). Grandson of St. Elizabeth of Hungary; son of Henry II, Duke of Brabant; founder of the line of landgraves of Hesse.

Henry. *Ger.* Heinrich. Name of six Holy Roman emperors, numbered as kings of Germany:

Henry II. *Called* der Hei·li·ge \der-'hī-lig-ə\, *i.e.* the Saint. 973–1024. Duke of Bavaria (995–1024); king of Germany (1002–24) and Holy Roman emperor (1014–24). Son of Henry II, Duke of Bavaria, and great-grandson of Henry I; elected king to succeed Otto III; forced to fight various princes, esp. Bolesław I of Poland; opposed by antiking Arduin of Ivrea; made alliance with Rudolf III of Burgundy (1006); to Rome (1013), recognized as pope Benedict VIII, who crowned him emperor; again in Italy (1020) to fight Greeks and Lombards. Made two expeditions to Italy (1004, 1013); energetic in church reform; founded monasteries and schools; secured establishment of bishopric of Bamberg (1007); canonized (1146).

Henry III. 1017–1056. Holy Roman emperor and king of Germany (1039–56; crowned 1046). Son of Conrad II; m. (1036; d. 1038) Gunhilda, or Kunigunde, daughter of King Canute of England; m. (1043) Agnes of Poitou. Subdued Bohemians (1041) and Moravians (1043–45); made expedition to Rome and deposed three rival popes, appointing Clement II (1046), by whom he was crowned emperor; devoted to church reform; appointed three more popes in succession; later years marked by revolts in Germany. Patron of learning; founded schools and completed cathedrals.

Henry IV. 1050–1106. King of Germany (1056–1106) and Holy Roman emperor (1056–1106; crowned 1084). Son of Henry III; during minority (1056–66) empire under regency of his mother, Agnes of Poitou. Engaged in war (1073–88) with Saxon nobles that became entangled with his struggle with Hildebrand (Pope Gregory VII) on question of lay investiture; excommunicated (1076); absolved after humiliating himself at Canossa (1077); defeated by Rudolf, Duke of Swabia (1078–80); again excommunicated (1080); deposed Gregory (1084) and set up antipope Clement III, by whom he was crowned emperor (1084); invaded Italy (1090). Last years marked by rebellion of sons (1093–1105); dethroned and imprisoned by younger son Henry (1105), but escaped.

Henry V. 1081–1125. King of Germany and Holy Roman emperor (1106–25; crowned 1111), last of Franconian dynasty. Son of Henry IV; restored peace at home; generally successful in wars against Flanders, Bohemia, Hungary, and Poland; continued controversy with papacy over lay investiture; twice invaded Italy (1110 and 1116); m. Matilda, daughter of Henry I of England (1114); accepted Concordat of Worms from Calixtus II (1122).

Henry VI. 1165–1197. King of Germany (1190–97) and of Sicily (1194–97); Holy Roman emperor (1190–97; crowned 1191). Son of Frederick I; m. Constance of Sicily (1186). Endeavored to secure control of inheritances in Sicily and southern Italy, but failed in siege of Naples (1191); kept Richard I of England a prisoner (1193–94); subdued the Two Sicilies in two expeditions (1194, 1197); attempted to transform German crown into a hereditary one

(1195–96); died as he was about to set off on a crusade to the Holy Land.

Henry VII. *Known also as* Henry of Lux·em·bourg \'lük-səm-ˌbürk, *Angl* 'lək-səm-ˌbərg\. 1275?–1313. Count of Luxembourg (as Henry IV); king of Germany and Holy Roman emperor (1308–13; crowned 1312). Elected king on death of Albert I; confirmed charters to Swiss cantons (1300); made expedition into Italy (1310–13); opposed in southern Italy by Robert, king of Naples (1312–13).

Henry. *Ger.* Heinrich. *Called* der Er·lauch·te \der-er-'lau̇k-tə\, *i.e.* the Illustrious. c.1215–1288. Margrave of Meissen (1221–88). Supported Emperor Frederick II against pope; on death of uncle Henry Raspe (1247) received Thuringia; created lasting family feuds through division of lands among sons.

Henry. *Fr.* Henri. Name of three kings of Navarre:

Henry I. c.1210–1274. King (1270–74). Son of Theobald I of Navarre; succeeded brother Theobald II as king and as count of Champagne (1270); died without male issue. Daughter Joan married (1284) future Philip IV of France.

Henry II. 1503–1555. King (1517–55). Son of Catherine de Foix-Grailly, queen of Navarre, and Jean d'Albret; succeeded to nominal kingship, Navarre having been lost to Ferdinand II of Aragon (1512); invaded Navarre with French aid but defeated (1521); in Italy with Francis I of France (1525); captured at Pavia but escaped; m. (1527) Margaret of Angoulême, sister of Francis I; ceded northern portion of Navarre by Emperor Charles V (1530); given government of Guienne by Francis.

Henry III. See HENRY IV of France.

Henry. *Port.* Hen·ri·que \ãⁿ-'rē-kə\. 1512–1580. King of Portugal (1578–80). Fifth son of Manuel I; entered church; archbishop of Braga (1534), Evora (1540), Lisbon (1564); made cardinal (1545); increased power of Inquisition in Portugal. Regent during minority of grandnephew Sebastian (1562–68); succeeded Sebastian; as king weak and helpless; last of house of Aviz; after his death, throne seized by Philip II, Portugal becoming a dependency of Spain (1580–1640).

Henry. *Port.* Henrique. *Called* o Na·ve·ga·dor \ü-nȧ-veg-ȧ-'thōr\, *i.e.* the Navigator. 1394–1460. Prince of Portugal. Third son of John I; at conquest of Ceuta (1415); governor of Ceuta (1415–18); as governor of the Algarve (from 1419) took up residence at Sagres, Cape St. Vincent; made grand master of Order of Christ (1420); established observatory and school of navigation; made no voyage himself, but spent life directing voyages of discovery along African coast; collected accounts of journeys to Africa and Asia; improved compass and shipbuilding. His pupils and captains (including Gil Eanes, Dinís Dias, Nuno Tristão, Diogo Gomes, Alvise Ca' da Mosto) reached Madeiras (1420), doubled Cape Bojador (1434), reached Cape Blanco (1441) and Cape Verde (1445) and the mouth of the Gambia about 15° north of the equator (1446), these voyages leading later to circumnavigation of Africa and establishment of Portuguese colonial empire.

Henry. *Ger.* Heinrich. Name of princes of Prussia:

Henry. 1726–1802. Son of Frederick William I and brother of Frederick the Great; served with distinction in Seven Years' War (1756–63), esp. at Prague (1757) and Freiberg (1762); served as diplomat at St. Petersburg (1770), at Paris (1784), and in negotiating Treaty of Basel (1795).

Henry. 1862–1929. Son of Frederick III of Germany and brother of William II; entered navy (1878); rear admiral (1895), admiral (1901), grand admiral (1909); general inspector of marine (1909); in command of fleet in Baltic during World War I (1914–18).

Henry. *Ger.* Heinrich. *Called* der Lö·we \der-'lœ-və\, *i.e.* the Lion. c.1130–1195. Duke of Saxony (1142–80) and Bavaria (1156–80). Son of Henry X the Proud of Bavaria; recovered Saxony (1142), which his father had lost; laid claim to Bavaria and recognized in it by Emperor Frederick I Barbarossa (1154); supported Frederick in Poland and Italy (1157–61); refounded Lübeck (1159); laid foundation of Munich (1156); expanded rule over Mecklenburg; established court in Brunswick; opposed by Saxon nobles led by Albert I the Bear of Brandenburg; m., as 2d wife (1168), Matilda, daughter of Henry II of England; made pilgrimage to Jerusalem (1172–73). Quarrel with the emperor (1175–76) led to imperial ban and loss of possessions (1180); exiled twice (1182, 1189); spent most of time in England; in conflict with Emperor Henry VI, settled by Peace of Fulda (1190).

Henry of Blois \blwȧ, blwä, *Angl* blə-'wä\. c.1099–1171. English prelate. Younger brother of King Stephen; abbot of Glastonbury (from 1126); bishop of Winchester (from 1129); papal legate in England; except briefly (1141), supported Stephen against Empress Matilda; to France after Stephen's death (1154); reorganized and contributed liberally to finances of abbey of Cluny; returned to England (1162).

Henry of Flanders. See HENRY, emperor of Constantinople.

Henry of Ghent \'gent\. *Known as* Doctor So·lem·nis \sə-'lem-nəs\, *i.e.* Exalted Teacher. c.1217–1293. Belgian philosopher and theologian. Canon of Tournai (1267); archdeacon of Brugge (1276), of Tournai (1278); lecturer at U. of Paris (1276–92). Served on commission that condemned Averroism (1277). Evolved an eclectic philosophy, disagreeing in part with Aristotelians and Thomists; influenced Duns Scotus. Author of a *Summa theologica*, a *Quodlibeta;* other works doubtfully attributed to him.

Henry of Hun·ting·ton \'hənt-iŋ-tən\. between 1080 and 1090–c.1155. English chronicler. In service of bishop of Lincoln; archdeacon of Hertford and Huntington (1110). Author of *Historia anglorum,* chronicle of period 55 B.C. to 1154 A.D.; also of *Epistola ad Walterum de contemptu mundi* (c.1135), etc.

Henry of Lancaster. See HENRY IV of England; HENRY, Duke of Lancaster.

Henry of Luxembourg. See Holy Roman emperor HENRY VII.

Henry of Navarre. See HENRY IV of France.

Henry of Trastámara. See HENRY II of Castile.

Henry the Child. See HENRY, Landgrave of Hesse.

Henry the Fowler. See HENRY I of Germany.

Henry the Illustrious. See HENRY, Margrave of Meissen.

Henry the Lion. See HENRY, Duke of Saxony.

Henry the Minstrel. See HARRY the Minstrel.

Henry the Navigator. See HENRY, prince of Portugal.

Henry the Proud. See HENRY X, Duke of Bavaria.

Henry the Saint. See Holy Roman emperor HENRY II.

Henry the Sufferer. See HENRY III of Castile.

Henry the Younger. See HENRY, Duke of Brunswick-Wolfenbüttel.

Hen·ry \'hen-rē\, Andrew. 1775?–1833. American explorer and fur trader, b. York Co., Pa. To Missouri (c.1800); engaged in lead mining; with Manuel Lisa, A. and P. Chouteau, William Clark, etc., organized (1809) St. Louis Missouri Fur Co.; led trapping party up Missouri River to Three Forks (1809–10), thence to mouth of Snake River and built Henry's Post, first American outpost in Rockies; with William H. Ashley formed new fur operation (1822); led expedition to mouth of Yellowstone (1822); crossed South Pass into Green River valley (1824); retired (1824).

Hen·ry \äⁿ-rē\, Hubert-Joseph. 1846–1898. French army officer. Chief of intelligence department, War Office (1896); forged papers to prove Dreyfus's guilt; finally confessed his forgery and was arrested; suicide in prison.

Hen·ry \'hen-rē\, Joseph. 1797–1878. American physicist, b. Albany, N.Y. While a schoolteacher in Albany, conducted experiments in electromagnetism; developed improved electromagnet; built first electric motor (1829); ahead of Faraday, observed electrical induction (1830). Professor, Princeton (1832–48); discovered principle underlying transformers; invented low-resistance and high-resistance galvanometers; discovered oscillatory nature of electric discharge; investigated solar radiation and sunspots. Became first secretary and director, Smithsonian Institution, Washington, D.C. (1846); initiated weather report system. Unit of electrical inductance named henry in his honor (1893).

Henry, O. See William Sydney PORTER.

Henry, Patrick. 1736–1799. American Revolutionary leader and orator, b. Hanover Co., Va. Storekeeper (1751–60); adm. to bar (1760), practiced in Virginia; won celebrated case known as the Parson's Cause (1763). In Virginia House of Burgesses (1765); introduced radical resolutions opposing Stamp Act, ending his speech with "Caesar had his Brutus; Charles the First, his Cromwell; and George the Third—may profit by their example"; sprang into leadership of radical group in Virginia (from 1765). With Thomas Jefferson and Richard Henry Lee initiated intercolonial committee of correspondence (1773). Member, Continental Congress (1774–76); in provincial convention (Mar. 1775), pressed resolutions for putting colonies in state of defense with speech containing famous words "Give me liberty, or give me death." Governor of Virginia (1776–79, 1784–86); dispatched western expedition of George Rogers Clark (1778). Member, Virginia constitutional ratification convention (1788); opposed ratification; instrumental in causing adoption of first ten amendments to U.S. Constitution.

Hen·ry \äⁿ-rē\, Paul-Pierre. 1848–1905. French astronomer. On staff of Paris observatory (from 1865); with his brother ¶Prosper-Mathieu (1849–1903) undertook preparation of ecliptic atlas of the sky; discovered 14 minor planets and observed (1882) the transit of Venus; greatly improved process of astronomical photography; built (1885) photographic equatorial telescope adopted as international standard for Carte du Ciel survey.

Hen·ry \'hen-rē\, William. 1774–1836. English chemist. Formulated (1803) Henry's law, that the weight of a gas dissolved by a liquid is proportional to the pressure of the gas. Author of popular text *Elements of Experimental Chemistry* (1810).

Henry de Lusignan. See HENRY, king of Cyprus.

Henry Fitzhenry. See HENRY, prince of England.

Hen·ry Fred·er·ick \'hen-rē-'fred(-ə)-rik\. 1745–1790. English prince. Fourth son of Frederick, Prince of Wales, and brother of George III; created duke of

Cumberland and Strathearn and earl of Dublin (1766); a scapegrace long out of favor at court.

Henry Jasomirgott. See HENRY II of Austria.

Henry Ju·lius \-'jü-lē-əs, -'jül-yəs\. *Ger.* Hein·rich Ju·lius \'hīn-rik-'yül-yůs\. 1564–1613. Duke of Brunswick. Bishop of Halberstadt (1578); succeeded to duchy (1589); established English theatrical company in castle at Wolfenbüttel (1592). Author of Baroque dramas and comedies including *Von einem Wirthe* (1593), *Von einem Buler und einer Bulerin* (1593), *Von einer Ehebrecherin* (1594), *Von einem ungeratnen Sohn* (1594), *Von Vincentio Ladislao* (1594).

Henry Ra·spe \-'räs-pə\. c.1202–1247. Landgrave of Thuringia (1227–47). Seized government of Thuringia on death of brother Louis IV (1227), expelling brother's widow, St. Elizabeth of Hungary, and her son Hermann; supported Emperor Frederick II against Frederick II of Austria (1236–37); excommunicated (1240) for continued support of emperor; appointed vice regent for Germany (1242); deserted emperor (1244); at behest of Pope Innocent IV, elected antiking (1246) in opposition to Conrad IV.

Hen·ry·son \'hen-rē-sən\ *or* **Hen·der·son** \'hen-dər-sən\, Robert. c.1425–c.1508. Scottish poet. Chief works, *Tale of Orpheus, Testament of Cresseid* continuing Chaucer's *Troilus and Criseyde*, and *The Morall Fabillis of Esope the Phrygian.*

Hen·ry Stu·art \'hen-rē-'st(y)ü-ərt, -'st(y)ů(-ə)rt\. *In full* Henry Benedict Maria Clement Stuart. Cardinal duke of York \'yȯ(ə)rk\. 1725–1807. Claimant to British throne. Second son of James Edward, the Old Pretender, and last direct male descendant of Stuart (*q.v.*) royal line. Named duke of York by his father (1725); raised forces in France (1745) to aid Forty-five Rebellion of his elder brother Charles Edward, but uprising was crushed before he could sail; to Rome (1746); created cardinal of York (1747); ordained priest (1748); made archbishop of St. Peter's (1751), titular archbishop of Corinth (1758), bishop of Frascati (1761), vice chancellor of Roman church (1763). Upon death of Charles Edward (1788), proclaimed himself Henry IX, king of Great Britain. Stripped of his fortune by French invasion of Rome; fled to Venice (1800); granted pension by George III of England; made dean of College of Cardinals (1803).

Hen·schel \'hen-shəl\, Georg Christian Carl. 1759–1835. German manufacturer. Founded (1810) manufacturing firm of Henschel & Sohn, at Kassel; developed into largest European locomotive manufactory.

Henschel, Sir George, *in full* Isidor George. 1850–1934. British singer, conductor, and composer, b. Germany. Conductor of Boston Symphony (1881–83); to London (1884); organized and conducted London Symphony Orchestra (1886–97); founded and conducted Scottish Symphony Orchestra, Glasgow (1893–95). His compositions included operas *A Sea Change* (1887) and *Nubia* (1899).

Hensch·ke \'hench-kə\, Alfred. *Pseudonym* Kla·bund \'klä-,bůnt\. 1890–1928. German writer. Influenced German Expressionist movement with free adaptations from Chinese, Japanese, Persian literatures. Author of verse *Morgenrot!* (1913), *Soldatenlieder* (1914), *Die Himmelsleiter* (1916), *Die Geisha O-sen* (1918), *Montezuma* (1919), *Der himmlische Vagant* (1919), *Dreiklang* (1920), *Totenklage* (1928), etc.; plays *Li-tai-pe* (1916), *Lao-tse* (1921), *Die Kreidekreis* (1924); novels *Moreau* (1916), *Mohammad* (1917), *Bracke* (1918), *Franziskus* (1921), *Pjotr* (1923), *Rasputins Ende* (1928), *Borgia* (1928), etc.

Hen·sen \'hen-zən\, Viktor, *in full* Christian Andreas Viktor. 1835–1924. German physiologist. Professor, Kiel (1868–1911); known for work in embryology, in the anatomy and physiology of the organs of sense, and for studies on plankton, which he named. The cells and canal or duct of Hensen in the ear are named for him.

Hens·low \'henz-(,)lō\, John Stevens. 1796–1861. English botanist. Professor, Cambridge (1822–61); introduced new methods of teaching botany; pupils included Charles Darwin. Compiled *Catalogue of British Plants* (1829) and *Dictionary of Botanical Terms* (1857).

Hens·lowe \'henz-(,)lō\, Philip. c.1550–1616. English theater manager. Built (1587) and managed (to 1603) the Rose Theatre on the Bankside, London; associated with Edward Alleyn in management of other theaters; bought plays from Dekker, Drayton, Chapman, and others, for presentation in his theaters; his Admiral's Men company long chief rival of Shakespeare's company. Kept (from c.1592) an account of his theatrical ventures which was edited and published by the Shakespeare Society (1845) and provides valuable source material for study of the drama of that period.

Hen·son \'hen(t)-sən\, Herbert Hensley. 1863–1947. English prelate. Canon of Westminster (1900); bishop of Hereford (1918–20), of Durham (1920–39); opponent of Anglo-Catholic tendencies, advocate of disestablishment. Author of *Ad Clerum* (1937), *Bishoprick Papers* (1946).

Hen·ty \'hent-ē\, George Alfred. 1832–1902. English writer. Author of some 80 books for boys, including *Out in the Pampas* (1868), *The Young Franc-Tireurs* (1872), *Under Drake's Flag* (1883), *With Clive in India* (1884), *The Cat of Bubastes* (1889), *Redskin and Cowboy* (1892), *With Frederick the Great* (1898), *With Roberts to Pretoria* (1902).

Hen·zi *or* **Hent·zi** \'hent-sē\, Samuel. 1701–1749. Swiss revolutionist. Joined group (1744) petitioning the Council of Bern for a revision of the constitution, and was banished (1744–48); conspired to abolish existing constitution, and was discovered and executed.

Hep·burn \'hep-(,)bərn\, James. 4th Earl of Both·well \'bäth-wəl, 'bäth-,wel\. 1535?–1578. Scottish nobleman. Although Protestant, member of French party supporting Mary of Lorraine, regent for young Queen Mary; member of Privy Council (1561); accused by Earl of Arran of plotting kidnap of queen, imprisoned (1562); to France (1564). Recalled (1565) to help suppress rebellion of Earl of Moray; became Mary's chief adviser and protector after murder of secretary Rizzio (1566); evidently engineered murder of Lord Darnley (1567) but acquitted in rigged trial; created duke of Orkney and Shetland and the next day became Mary's third husband (1567). Forced to flee by revolt of nobles; in exile in Orkney, Shetland, Denmark; imprisoned after collapse of Mary's cause (1573); died insane.

Hepburn, William Peters. 1833–1916. American politician, b. Wellsville, Ohio. Member from Iowa, U.S. House of Representatives (1881–87, 1893–1909); U.S. solicitor of the treasury (1889–93); author of Hepburn Act (1906) giving Interstate Commerce Commission power to regulate railroad rates; instrumental also in writing and passing Pure Food and Drug Act (1906).

He·phaes·ti·on \hi-'fest-ē-ən\. d. 324 B.C. Macedonian general. Intimate friend of Alexander the Great, who charged him with establishment of Greek colonies in conquered lands and with building of fleet for descending Indus River; married sister of Alexander's wife Barsine. On his sudden death at Ecbatana, Alexander ordered erection of a vast funeral pyre and construction of temples in his honor.

Hephaestion. 2d century A.D. Greek scholar. Author of treatise on Greek meter that, in condensed manual form, was long popular as schoolbook and is only complete ancient text on meter extant.

Hep·ple·white \'hep-əl-,(h)wīt\, George. d. 1786. English cabinetmaker. Worked in London, but not known to have been fashionable; fame secured by publication of *Cabinet-Maker and Upholsterer's Guide* (1788), containing his delicate, elegant Neoclassical designs.

Hep·worth \'hep-(,)wərth\, Dame Barbara, *in full* Jocelyn Barbara. 1903–1975. English sculptor. Abandoned early naturalistic manner for abstract, formal approach; works noted for mastery of texture, interplay of mass and interior space through use of voids, perforations, painted hollows; notable pieces included *Reclining Figure* (1932), *Wave* (1943–44), *Groups* series, *Winged Figure* (1962), *Single Form* for United Nations (1962–63).

Her·a·clei·des Pon·ti·cus \,her-ə-'klīd-,ēz-'pänt-i-kəs\. *Also spelled* Her·a·cli·des. c.390–after 322 B.C. Greek philosopher and astronomer. Pupil of Plato; attributed apparent motions of Mercury and Venus to revolution about Sun; first to suggest rotation of Earth.

Her·a·clei·tus \,her-ə-'klīt-əs\. *Also spelled* Her·a·cli·tus. c.540–c.480 B.C. Greek philosopher. Evolved cosmology in which fire is principal element, all things are in state of dynamic equilibrium, apparent opposites are actually bound by underlying connection, and the whole is manifestation of logos; later interpreted by Plato to have claimed all things are in constant flux. Writings extant only in fragments notable for difficulty; in later ages known as "weeping philosopher."

He·rac·le·on \hə-'rak-lē-ən\. 2d century A.D. Italian Gnostic Christian. Orginally a disciple of Valentinus (*q.v.*); developed more conservative form of Gnosticism. Author of earliest exegesis of Gospel of John; only fragments of his works are extant.

Heracleonas. See HERACLONAS.

He·rac·li·an \hə-'rak-lē-ən, ,her-ə-'klī-ən\. d. 413 A.D. Roman general. Commissioned by Emperor Honorius to assassinate Stilicho (408 A.D.); given government of Africa; revolted (413) and was assassinated at Carthage by agents of emperor.

He·ra·cli·us \,her-ə-'klī-əs, hə-'rak-lē-əs\. c.575–641. Emperor of the Eastern Roman Empire (610–641). Son of Heraclius, a general and exarch of Africa under Emperor Mauricius; with aid of father, dethroned Phocas (610); proclaimed emperor. Threatened by Slavs, Avars; defeated by Persians under Khosrow II, who conquered Syria (613–614), Palestine (615), and Egypt (619), and besieged Constantinople. First campaign (622) fought to stalemate; in second completely defeated Persians at Nineveh (628); took treasure from Persian capital Dastagird, recovered Holy Cross (628) and restored it to Jerusalem (630); held off Avars in the north (619, 626). Opposed by nobles and church in reforms. Faced new threat of Muslim invasions; lost Damascus (635) and suffered great defeat in the Yarmuk valley, Palestine (636); lost (635–641) Syria, Palestine, Mesopotamia, and Egypt. Instituted theme system of defense by armed peasantry.

Her·a·clo·nas \,her-ə-'klō-nəs\. *Also spelled* He·rac·le·o·nas \hə-,rak-lē-'ō-nəs\. 615–?641. Byzantine emperor (641). Son of Emperor Heraclius, half-brother of Constantine III; augustus (638); joint emperor with Constantine III (641); sole ruler on death of brother (641); rumored, probably falsely, to have murdered Constantine; deposed, mutilated, banished to Rhodes.

Hé·rault de Sé·chelles \ā-rō-də-sā-shel\, Marie-Jean. 1759–1794. French lawyer and politician. Attorney to Louis XVI (1777); attorney general to the parlement of Paris (1785); member of the Legislative Assembly (1791), the National Convention (1792); member of Jacobin club; member of Committee of Public Safety (1793); ordered arrest of Girondins (1793); led in drafting new constitution (1793); accused of plotting with Hébertists, guillotined at Paris.

Her·bart \'her-,bärt\, Johann Friedrich. 1776–1841. German philosopher and educator. Tutor in Switzerland (1797–1800), where he became interested in Pestalozzi's pedagogical methods; professor, Göttingen (1805–08, 1833–41), Königsberg (1808–33); developed general metaphysical theory of pluralistic realism, important esp. for its psychology, which rejected notions of faculties and innate ideas and constructed full theory on which to ground a pedagogy similar to that of Pestalozzi. Major works included *Aesthetische Darstellung der Welt* (1804), *Allgemeine Pädagogik* (1806), *Hauptpunkte der Metaphysik* (1806), *Lehrbuch zur Psychologie* (1816), *Psychologie als Wissenschaft, neu gegründet auf Erfahrung, Metaphysik und Mathematik* (1824–25), *Allgemeine Metaphysik* (1828–29).

Her·bert \'hər-bərt\. Name of an English family, including holders of marquisate of Powis, earldoms of Powis, Pembroke, Montgomery, Torrington, Carnarvon, and barony of Herbert of Cherbury.

EARLS OF PEM·BROKE \'pem-,bru̇k\ AND MONT·GOM·ERY \mənt-'gəm-rē\: Sir William Herbert (d. 1469), 1st Earl of Pembroke (of 1st creation, 1468); Yorkist leader; possessor of castle, town, and lordship of Pembroke; in Wars of the Roses, effective against Jasper Tudor; chief justice of South Wales (1461), North Wales (1467); taken by northern Lancastrians and beheaded. His son ¶William (1460–1491) surrendered earldom of Pembroke to crown for earldom of Huntingdon (1479).

¶Sir William Herbert (1501?–1570), 1st Earl of Pembroke (creation of 1551); courtier, soldier, and diplomat; son of an illegitimate son of Sir William (d. 1469); m. Anne Parr, sister of Henry VIII's 6th wife; one of Henry VIII's executors; member of Edward VI's council; president of Wales (1550); supported Mary Tudor against claims of Lady Jane Grey (1553); commanded forces putting down insurrection of Sir Thomas Wyatt (1554) in protest against marrying Mary to Philip of Spain; envoy to France (1555); supported Protestant party in Elizabeth's reign; lord steward (1568). His son ¶Henry (1534?–1601), 2d earl; president of Wales (1586); prominent in trial of Mary, Queen of Scots (1586); m. (1553) Lady Catherine Grey, sister of Lady Jane Grey; m. (1577) Mary Sidney.

¶Mary Herbert, *nee* Sidney (1561–1621); sister of Sir Philip Sidney; m. (1577) 2d earl, taking title of countess of Pembroke; patroness of Michael Drayton, Samuel Daniel, John Davies, etc.; dedicatee of her brother's *Arcadia*, of Edmund Spenser's *Ruines of Time*, of Nicholas Breton's *Pilgrimage to Paradise*, of Thomas Morley's *Canzonets*. Completed brother's verse translation of Psalms and made translations of Robert Garnier's *Marc-Antoine*, Duplessis-Mornay's *Discours de la vie et de la mort*, Petrarch's *Trionfo della morte*.

¶William (1580–1630), 3d earl; son of 2d earl and Mary; banished from court for illicit connection with Mary Fitton (*q.v.*) and imprisoned (1601); patron of Ben Jonson, Philip Massinger, Inigo Jones, and William Browne; interested in Virginia, Northwest Passage, Bermuda, Guiana, and East India companies; lord chamberlain of royal household (1615–26); lord steward (1626–30); chancellor of Oxford (from 1617), having Pembroke Coll. named after him (1624). Identified by some Shakespearean commentators with subject of Shakespeare's sonnets and with "Mr. W.H." in the dedication (1609). Object, with his brother Philip Herbert, of inscription in First Folio of Shakespeare to the "incomparable pair of brothers."

¶Philip (1584–1650), 4th Earl of Pembroke and 1st Earl of Montgomery; brother of 3d earl; favorite of James I; created earl of Montgomery (1605); lord chamberlain (1626–41); m. (1630) Anne Clifford (*q.v.*); strove to promote peace between Charles I and Scots (1639–40); deserted king for Parliamentary side (1641); Parliamentary governor of Isle of Wight (1642); commissioner at Oxford (1643), at Uxbridge (1645); received Charles I from the Scots (1647); vice chancellor of Oxford (1641–50).

¶Thomas (1656–1733), 8th earl; grandson of 4th earl; first lord of admiralty (1690); lord privy seal (1692); first plenipotentiary at Treaty of Rijswijk (1697); lord high admiral (1702, 1708); lord lieutenant of Ireland (1707); a lord justice (1714–15). His son ¶Henry (1693–1751), 9th Earl of Pembroke and 6th Earl of Montgomery, known as "the Architect Earl," was responsible for erection of first Westminster bridge (1739–50).

¶Sidney (1810–1861), 1st Baron Herbert of Lea \'lē\; 2d son of 11th earl; M.P. (1832–60); war secretary under Peel (1845–46), during Crimean War (1852–55), and under Palmerston (1859–60); his administration remarkable for invitation to Florence Nightingale to take nurses to Crimea, improvement of army sanitation and education, amalgamation of Indian forces with imperial army, and organization of volunteer movement; created baron (1860).

EARLS, MARQUISES, DUKES OF POW·IS \'pō-əs\:

¶William (1617–1696), 1st Marquis of Powis and titular Duke of Powis; head of Roman Catholic aristocracy in England; arrested on suspicion of complicity in Popish Plot (1678), imprisoned five years; privy councilor (1686); created marquis (1687); fled with James II; became James II's lord steward and chamberlain of household; created duke of Powis by dethroned king (1689). His eldest son ¶William (d. 1745), 2d marquis; Jacobite, imprisoned (1696–97) on suspicion of complicity in Sir J. Fenwick's plot to assassinate William III; called Viscount Montgomery until restoration of title and estates (1722).

¶Edward Herbert (1785–1848), 2d Earl of Powis; son of 1st earl and grandson of Baron Clive of Plassey; assumed mother's surname, Herbert (1807); M.P. (1806–39); active in suppression of Chartist riots (1839); brought about defeat of scheme for creating bishopric of Manchester, thereby winning gratitude of clergy and universities.

EARLS OF CAR·NAR·VON \kə(r)-'när-vən\, *descendants of Thomas Herbert, 8th Earl of Pembroke:*

¶Henry Howard Molyneux (1831–1890), 4th Earl of Carnarvon; son of 3d earl; undersecretary for colonies (1858–59); as colonial secretary (1866–67, 1874–78), brought in bill for federation of North American provinces (1867) which created federal dominion of Canada; abolished slavery on Gold Coast (1874), introduced permissive federation bill for South Africa (1877); resigned in opposition to breach of neutrality in Russo-Turkish conflict (1878); as lord lieutenant of Ireland (1885–86), favored limited self-government; opposed Gladstone's home rule and land purchase bills.

¶George Edward Stanhope Molyneux (1866–1923), 5th Earl of Carnarvon; son of 4th earl; indulged fondness for travel and horse racing; collaborated (1907–12, 1919–23) with Howard Carter in excavation near Thebes; discovered tombs of Egyptian 12th and 18th dynasties, including (1922) tomb of Tutankhamen, in Valley of the Kings; died as result of infection of mosquito bite.

BARONS HERBERT OF CHER·BURY \'chər-b(ə-)rē\:

¶Edward Herbert (1583–1648), 1st Baron Herbert of Cherbury; philosopher and diplomat; served in prince of Orange's army (1614); ambassador to France (1619–24); created baron (1629); attended Charles I on Scottish expedition (1639–40); after attempt at neutrality, submitted to Parliament (1645). Author of *Autobiography* (to 1624; pub. 1764), and of *De Veritate* (1624), his chief philosophical work; advanced an antiempirical theory of knowledge like that of the Cambridge Platonists and maintained that the common articles of all religions, apprehended by instinct, include existence of God, duty of worship and repentance, future rewards and punishment (whence often called "Father of English Deism"); author of *Life of Henry VIII* (1649) and poems in Latin and English, representing the metaphysical school.

His brother ¶George (1593–1633); fellow of Trinity Coll., Oxford (1614); public orator of Oxford (1620–28); ordained priest (1630). Author of 160 religious poems, marked by ingenious imagery and metrical inventiveness, collected in *The Temple* (1633), and of prose works, including the fervently pious *A Priest to the Temple* (1652), rules for the country parson; accounted one of the Metaphysical poets.

Another brother ¶Sir Henry (1595–1673); as master of the revels (1623–42 and again after Restoration), claimed right of licensing every kind of public entertainment throughout England, even books, a right often contested by theatrical producers, including Davenant.

¶Sir Edward (1591?–1657), judge; cousin of 1st Baron Herbert of Cherbury; M.P. (1620–29, 1640–41); solicitor general (1640); attorney general (1641); under instructions by Charles I, exhibited articles of impeachment against Pym, Hampden, and four other members of Parliament for subversion of fundamental laws; impeached by House of Commons and barred from office; went to sea with Prince Rupert (1648).

¶Arthur (1647–1716), Earl of Torrington (cr. 1689); 2d son of Sir Edward (1591?–1657); served as naval officer against the Dutch (1666) and Algerian corsairs (1669–71, 1678–83); as admiral, relieved Tangier (1680); cashiered for refusing to support repeal of Test Act (1687); commanded fleet conducting William of Orange to England (1688); 1st lord of admiralty (1689); obliged by queen's order to engage whole French fleet of Beachy Head (1690); charged before court martial with holding back, acquitted.

Herbert, Sir Alan Patrick. *Pseudonym* Albert Had·dock \'had-ək\. 1890–1971. English journalist and writer. Joined staff of *Punch* (1924). M.P. for Oxford U. (1935–1950). Author of theatrical revues, musicals, and operettas as *Riverside Nights* (1926), *La Vie Parisienne* (1929), *Tantivy Towers* (1930), *Helen* (1932), *Derby Day* (1932), *Big Ben* (1946), *Bless the Bride* (1947);

novels including *The Secret Battle* (1919), *The Water Gipsies* (1930), *Holy Deadlock* (1934).

Herbert, George. See under Barons Herbert of Cherbury in HERBERT family.

Herbert, Victor. 1859–1924. American conductor and composer, b. Dublin, Ireland. To U.S. (1886); conducted 22d N.Y. Regiment band (1893–98), Pittsburgh Symphony (1898–1904); organized and conducted his own orchestra in New York (from 1904). Success of his light opera *Prince Ananias* (1894) led to other works in this field: *The Wizard of the Nile* (1895), *The Fortune Teller* (1898), *Babes in Toyland* (1903), *Mlle. Modiste* (1905), *The Red Mill* (1906), *Little Nemo* (1908), *Naughty Marietta* (1910), *Sweethearts* (1913), *Hearts of Erin* (1917, later called *Eileen*). Also wrote two grand operas, *Natoma* (1911) and *Madeleine* (1914), musical scores for Ziegfeld Follies (1917, 1921–24), and many nondramatic compositions.

Herbert of Cherbury, Barons. See HERBERT family.

Herbert of Lea, Baron. See Sidney Herbert, under HERBERT family.

Herbois, Jean-Marie Collot d'. See COLLOT D'HERBOIS.

Her·cu·la·no de Car·va·lho e Ara·ú·jo \ēr-kü-'lä-nü-t͟hə-kər-'väl-yü-ē-ə-rə-'ü-zhü\, Alexandre. 1810–1877. Portuguese poet and historian. A liberal, opponent of Dom Miguel; political exile at Paris (1828–30), London (1830–32); editor of *O Panorama,* Lisbon (1837–39); member of Cortes (1840–41); director, royal library at Ajuda (1839–56). His works included verse *A voz do propheta* (1836), novels *Enrico o presbytero* (1843), *O monge de Cister* (1848), tales *Lendas e narrativas* (1851), major historical works *História de Portugal* (1846–53), *Da origem e estabelecimento da Inquisicão em Portugal* (1854–59).

Her·czeg \'hert-seg\, Ferenc. 1863–1954. Hungarian writer. Founded (1895) literary magazine *Új Idők;* a leader of conservative nationalist opinion in Hungary. Author of novels *A Gyurkovics lányok* (1893), *A Gyurkovics fiuk* (1895), *Pogányok* (1902), *Az élet kapuja* (1919); plays *A három testőr* (1894), *Bizánc* (1904), *Kék róka* (1917), *A híd* (1925).

Her·der \'her-dər\, Johann Gottfried von. 1744–1803. German philosopher and theologian. Teacher and preacher in Riga (1764–69); court preacher at Bückeburg (1771–76); called to Weimar (upon Geothe's recommendation) as general superintendent of the church district there (1776–1803). Out of profound criticisms of Enlightenment rationalism, helped lay basis of German Romanticism; developed an organic philosophy of mind, art, history. Works included *Über die neuere deutsche Literatur: Fragmente* (1766–67), *Kritische Wälder* (1769), *Abhandlung über den Ursprung der Sprache* (1772), *Auch eine Philosophie der Geschichte* (1774), *An Prediger* (1774), various collections of German folksongs (the first pub. 1778; in later editions under title *Stimmen der Völker in Liedern*), *Ideen zur Philosophie der Geschichte der Menschheit* (1784–91), *Zerstreute Blätter* (1785–97), *Briefe zur Beförderung der Humanität* (1793–97).

Herd·man \'hərd-mən\, Sir William Abbott. 1858–1924. Scottish naturalist. Professor, Liverpool (1881–1920); founded Liverpool Marine Biology Committee (1885), which opened (1887) a research laboratory at Puffin Island, later (1892) moved to the Isle of Man; organized a marine research laboratory in U. of Liverpool (1891); aided in establishing a fish hatchery in Barrow Strait (1897). Author of *The Founders of Oceanography* (1923), etc.

He·re·dia \ā-'rät͟h-yä\, José María de. 1803–1839. Cuban poet. Cousin of French poet José María de Heredia; banished from Cuba (1823) as insurrectionary; wandered in U.S. (1823–25), later settling in Mexico. Known for patriotic lyrics; considered by many Cuba's foremost lyricist. His works included the widely translated *Al Niágara,* his best known poem; verse translations of dramas by Voltaire, Alfieri, Chénier, etc.; and *Lecciones de historia universal* (1830–31).

He·re·dia \ā-rād-yȧ, *Sp* ā-'rät͟h-yä\, José María de. 1842–1905. French poet, b. Cuba. To Paris (1859); one of leading representatives of French Parnassians; friend and disciple of Leconte de Lisle; one of foremost masters of the French sonnet; known esp. for *Les Trophées* (1893); notable also for his translation (1877–87) of Bernal Díaz del Castillo's *Historia verdadera de la conquista de la Nueva España* and for the prose romance *La Nonne Alferez* (1894).

Hereford, Earls of. See William FITZOSBERN; BOHUN.

Hé·relle \ā-rel\, Felix d'. 1873–1949. Canadian microbiologist, b. Montreal. Conducted field studies in Guatemala, Mexico (1901–09); assistant at Pasteur Institute, Paris (1909–21); professor, Leiden (1921–23); director, Bacteriological Service, Egypt (1923–27); professor, Yale (1928–34); discovered and named bacteriophage (1916–17). Author of *Le Bactériophage* (1921).

Herennius Byblius. See PHILO BYBLIUS.

Her·e·ward \'her-ə-wərd\. *Called* Hereward the Wake \'wāk\. fl. 1070–1071. Anglo-Saxon rebel and outlaw. Headed English rebellion at Ely (1070) against William the Conqueror; plundered Peterborough (1070); escaped when his allies surrendered to William; established on Isle of Ely a refuge that sheltered Morcar of Northumbria and other Anglo-Saxons. Subject of many legends and of Charles Kingsley's prose romance *Hereward the Wake.*

Her·ford \'hər-fərd\, Oliver. 1863–1935. American writer and illustrator, b. Sheffield, England. To U.S. (1875); contributor to magazines. Author of volumes of humorous verse and prose, illustrated by himself, including *Artful Anticks* (1888), *Overheard in a Garden* (1900), *Rubaiyat of a Persian Kitten* (1904), *Little Book of Bores* (1906), *Simple Jography* (1908), *Jingle Jungles* (1915), *Cynic's Calendar* (1917), *The Herford Aesop* (1921), *Excuse It Please* (1930), *The Deb's Dictionary* (1931).

Her·ges·hei·mer \'hər-gəs-ˌhī-mər, -gə-ˌshī-\, Joseph. 1880–1954. American novelist, b. Philadelphia. Author of lushly descriptive, psychologically penetrating novels of manners as *The Lay Anthony* (1914), *Mountain Blood* (1915), *The Three Black Pennys* (1917), *Gold and Iron* (1918), *Java Head* (1919), *Linda Condon* (1919), *Cytherea* (1922), *The Bright Shawl* (1922), *Balisand* (1924), *Tampico* (1926), *Swords and Roses* (1929), *The Party Dress* (1929), *The Limestone Tree* (1931), *Tropical Winter* (1933), *The Foolscap Rose* (1934), etc.

Her·i·bert \'her-i-ˌbert\. c.970–1021. German prelate. Son of Hugo, Count of Worms; companion and adviser to Emperor Otto III; chancellor of Italy (994), of Germany (998); archbishop of Cologne (999); assisted Emperor Henry II in founding bishopric of Bamberg (1012).

Her·i·hor \'her-i-ˌhȯ(ə)r\. 11th century B.C. Egyptian priest and ruler. Possibly originally a soldier under Ramses XI; probably expelled viceroy of Nubia from Thebes; moving to assume power during dissolution of 20th dynasty, took titles of high priest of Amon and general; built temple in Thebes; ignoring Ramses, took full pharaonic title, established domain in southern Egypt; founded dynasty of priest-kings.

Her·ing \'hā-riŋ, *Angl* 'her-iŋ\, Constantine. 1800–1880. American physician, b. Oschatz, Saxony, Germany. To U.S. (1833); practiced in Philadelphia; organized first homeopathic school in the world, North American Academy of the Homeopathic Healing Art (chartered 1836); founded Homeopathic Medical Coll. of Pa. (1848) and Hahnemann Medical Coll. of Philadelphia (1867).

He·ring \'hā-riŋ\, Ewald, *in full* Carl Ewald Constantin. 1834–1918. German physiologist and psychologist. Professor, Military Medico-Surgical Academy, Vienna (1865–70), U. of Prague (1870–95), Leipzig (from 1895). Investigated respiration and visual space perception and opposed a nativistic theory to Helmholtz's empiristic one; advanced a theory of color vision; demonstrated (1868, with Josef Breuer) role of vagus nerve in regulating respiration.

Her·i·ot \'her-ē-ət\, George. 1563–1624. Scottish goldsmith and philanthropist. Jeweler to James VI (James I of England); endowed Heriot's Hospital at Edinburgh (opened 1659). Original of Geordic in Scott's *Fortunes of Nigel.*

Her·ki·mer \'hər-kə-mər\, Nicholas. 1728–1777. American Revolutionary officer, b. near present Herkimer, N.Y. Brigadier general of militia (1776); led force against Sir John Johnson (1776); mortally wounded at Oriskany, N.Y. (Aug. 1777) when, attempting to relieve Fort Stanwix, his troops were ambushed and defeated.

Her·ko·mer \'hər-kə-mər\, Sir Hubert von. 1849–1914. British painter, b. Germany. To England (1857); professor of fine art, Oxford (1885–94). His paintings included portraits of Wagner, Ruskin, Lord Kelvin, the Marquis of Salisbury.

Her·lin \'her-lēn\ *or* **Her·lein** \'her-ˌlīn\, Friedrich. d. 1491. German painter. Works included altarpieces and other church decoration in Nördlingen, Rothenburg, etc.; a chief figure of Swabian school.

Her·mag·o·ras \hər-'mag-ə-rəs\. 1st century B.C. Greek rhetorician. Founded school in Rome for teaching of oratory.

Her·man de Va·len·ciennes \er-mäⁿ-də-vȧ-läⁿ-syen\. 12th century. French cleric and poet. Author of scriptural poem *Histoire de la Bible* (after 1189), also known as *Le Roman de sapience.*

Hermann. See ARMIN.

Her·mann I \'her-ˌmän\. c.1156–1217. Landgrave of Thuringia and count palatine of Saxony. Seized Saxony from brother Louis III (c.1180); granted Thuringia (1190) by Emperor Henry VI at behest of German princes; instrumental in preventing Henry from making German throne hereditary (1196); frequently changed sides in conflict between Otto IV and Hohenstaufen rivals. Patron of Walther von der Vogelweide and other Minnesingers; promoted singing contest at the Wartburg, for which he is celebrated in opera and story.

Hermann V. *Also known as* Hermann of Wied \'vēt\. 1477–1552. Count of Wied. Elector and archbishop of Cologne (1515–47); converted to Protestantism, instituted reforms in his diocese, and invited Martin Bucer and Melanchthon to aid him in carrying them out. Failed in reforms; deposed as elector, and excommunicated by Pope Paul III (1546); resigned his office (1547) and retired to Wied.

Hermann, Eduard. 1869–1950. German scholar. Professor at Kiel, Frankfurt, Göttingen. Author of *Sprachwissenschaftlicher Kommentar zu ausgewählten Stücken aus Homer* (1914), *Herkunft unserer Fragefürwörter* (1943).

Hermann, Gottfried, *in full* Johann Gottfried Jakob. 1772–1848. German scholar. Professor, Leipzig (1798–1848); championed importance of linguistic over historical or antiquarian research. Author of *De emendanda ratione Graecae grammaticae* (1801), *Elementa doctrinae metricae* (1816).

Hermann von Rei·che·nau \-fōn-'rī-k̲ə-naů\. *Called* der Lah·me \dər-'lä-mə\, *i.e.* the Lame. *Known also as* Her·man·nus Con·trac·tus \hər-'man-əs-kən-'trak-təs\. 1013–1054. German monk, historian, and poet. Benedictine monk in abbey of Reichenau; author of a world history *Chronicon*, down to the year 1054, continued by a pupil Berthold down to 1066; also wrote astronomical, musical, and mathematical treatises, etc.

Hermenegild. See under Leovigild.

Her·mes \'her-mes\, Georg. 1775–1831. German theologian and philosopher. Professor, Münster (1807–19), Bonn (1819–31); evolved philosophic doctrine known as Hermesianism, attempting to fix rational necessity of tenets of Christian dogma. Works, including *Einleitung in die christkatholische Theologie* (1819–29) and *Christkatholische Dogmatik* (1834–35), condemned by Pope Gregory XVI (1835).

Her·me·si·a·nax \ˌhər-mə-'sī-ə-ˌnaks\. fl. c.300–250 B.C. Greek poet. One of first poets of Alexandrian school; known chiefly as elegist; only fragments of his works are extant.

Hermiae, Ammonius. See Ammonius Hermiae.

Her·mip·pus \hər-'mip-əs\. *Known as* the One-Eyed. 5th century B.C. Athenian dramatist. Writer of some 40 works in Old Comedy manner; political opponent of Pericles; said to have prosecuted Aspasia for impiety and immorality. Only fragments of his works are extant.

Her·mite \er-mēt\, Charles. 1822–1901. French mathematician. Professor, École Polytechnique (1869–76), Faculté des Sciences (1869–97); known for work on elliptic functions, the theory of numbers, continued fractions, algebraic forms, etc.; first to solve general equation of the fifth degree; showed that *e*, the base of natural logarithms, is a transcendental number.

Her·moc·ra·tes \(ˌ)hər-'mäk-rə-ˌtēz\. d. 408 or 407 B.C. Syracusan general and politician. Persuaded other cities of Sicily to make peace with Syracuse (424 B.C.), forcing withdrawal of Athenian forces; commanded defense against new Athenian invasion (415–413); led Syracusan naval force in support of Sparta (412–410); killed attempting to reenter Syracuse, then under control of radical democrat Diocles.

Her·mog·e·nes \(ˌ)hər-'mäj-ə-ˌnēz\. 2d century A.D. Greek rhetorician. Teacher in Rome; his rhetorical treatises widely used as textbooks.

Hermoldus Nigellus. See Ermoldus.

Hernándarias. See Arias de Saavedra.

Hernández. See also Fernández.

Her·nán·dez \er-'nän-dāth\ *or* **Fer·nán·dez** \fer-\, Gregorio. c.1576–1636. Spanish sculptor. Known for polychromed wood sculptures, esp. statues as *St. Veronica* and *Pietà*, and altarpieces, notable for realism, Baroque expressiveness.

Her·nán·dez \er-'nän-dās\, José. 1834–1886. Argentinian poet. Took part in revolt against Sarmiento regime (1870), fled to Brazil (1871–72). Author of epic *El gaucho Martín Fierro* (1872) and sequel *La vuelta de Martín Fierro* (1879), considered finest examples of gaucho poetry.

Hernández Mar·tí·nez \-mär-'tē-nās\, Maximiliano. 1882–1966. Salvadoran general and politician. While vice president, took part in military coup against Pres. Araujo (1931); president of El Salvador (1931–44), winning elections (1935, 1939); resigned.

Hern·don \'hərn-dən\, William Henry. 1818–1891. American lawyer, b. Greensburg, Ky. Law partner of Abraham Lincoln (from 1844). Author of unreliable *Herndon's Lincoln; the True Story of a Great Life* (with Jesse W. Weik, 1889). His letters and papers relating to Lincoln were edited as *The Hidden Lincoln* (1938).

Herne \'hərn\, James A. *Orig.* James Ahern \ə-'hərn\. 1839–1901. American actor and playwright, b. Cohoes, N.Y. With David Belasco wrote *Hearts of Oak* (orig. *Chums*; produced 1879), and toured in it (1879–86); other successes included *Shore Acres* (1892), *The Reverend Griffith Davenport* (1899), *Sag Harbor* (1899). Two daughters ¶Julie (1881–1955) and ¶Chrystal Katharine (1882–1950) were also on the stage.

He·ro \'hē-(ˌ)rō, hi(ə)r-(ˌ)ō\ *or* **He·ron** \'hi(ə)r-ˌän\ of Alexandria. 1st century A.D. Greek scientist. Derived Hero's formula for area of a triangle; invented aeolipile, first steam-powered engine. Author of numerous works in mathematics, physics, and mechanics including *Pneumatica, Belopoeica, Mechanica, Geometria, Geodaesia, Mensurae, Catoptrica, Cheirobalistra.*

Her·od \'her-əd\. *Latin* **He·ro·des** \her-'ō-dēz\. Name of several rulers over Palestine, forming a dynasty:

Herod I. *Called* the Great. 73–4 B.C. King of Judea (37–4 B.C.). Son of Antipater, of an Edomite family; converted to Judaism; made governor (47) and tetrarch (41) of Galilee; after murder of his father (43) and death (40) of Phasael, his elder brother, forced by disturbed conditions in Palestine to flee to Rome (40); there made king of Judea (39) by Antony, Octavian, and the Senate; took possession (37). Early years of reign (37–25) marked by revolts; his position strengthened by battle of Actium (31); next period (25–13) of rule prosperous, marked by building of cities Caesarea Palaestinae and Sebaste, many fortresses, theaters, hippodromes, and other public buildings; began rebuilding Great Temple at Jerusalem (20 B.C.; not completed until 64 A.D.); his last years marred by political and family intrigues and his increasing mental instability.

Herod Ar·che·la·us \-ˌär-kə-'lā-əs\. *Orig.* Archelaus. 22 B.C.–c.18 A.D. Son of Herod the Great; on father's death (4 B.C.) became ethnarch of Judea, Idumaea, and Samaria; deposed (6 A.D.) by Augustus on complaints of the Jews and banished to Vienne in Gaul.

Herod An·ti·pas \-'ant-ə-ˌpas, -pəs\. *Orig.* Antipas. 21 B.C.–39 A.D. Tetrarch of Galilee (4 B.C.–39 A.D.). Son of Herod I and brother of Herod Archelaus; on father's death (4 B.C.) invested with tetrarchy of Galilee and Perea; m. daughter of Aretas, king of Nabataeans; divorced her to marry his niece Herodias, daughter of Aristobulus (who was then wife of his brother Herod Philip), thus bringing on war with Nabataeans and making him many enemies; reproved by John the Baptist; tricked into killing John by Herodias and her daughter, Salome; declined to pass judgment on Jesus of Nazareth, returning him to Roman procurator, Pontius Pilate; driven to his ruin by ambitions of Herodias; attempted to denounce nephew Herod Agrippa I to Caligula; lost favor, banished to Gaul.

Herod Philip. *Orig.* Philip. d. 34 A.D. Son of Herod I; first husband of Herodias. Often confused with Philip the Tetrarch (*q.v.*).

Herod Agrip·pa I \-ə-'grip-ə\. *Orig.* Marcus Julius Agrippa. c.10 B.C.–44 A.D. King of Judea (41–44 A.D.). Son of Aristobulus and grandson of Herod I; educated at Rome with Claudius and Drusus; thrown into prison for an offense against Tiberius; released by Caligula (37) and made ruler of Batanaea, Trachonitis, etc.; after banishment of Herod Antipas (39) received tetrarchy of Galilee; for services to Claudius rewarded (41) with annexation of Judea and Samaria to his dominions; strongly pro-Jewish; caused death of Apostle James and imprisonment of Peter.

Herod Agrippa II. *Orig.* Marcus Julius Agrippa. 27?–c.93 A.D. Son and successor of Herod Agrippa I. Educated at Rome at court of Claudius; given Chalcis (50) with title of king after death (48) of his uncle Herod of Chalcis; his domains increased (53) by what had been the tetrarchy of Philip; with Roman procurator Festus, heard defense of Paul (60); when Zealot Revolt (66–70) against Rome began, tried to dissuade Jews; sided with Romans; after capture of Jerusalem (70) retired to Rome with his sister Berenice (75); granted dignity of praetor; spent remainder of life at Rome.

Herod of Chal·cis \'kal-səs\. d. 48 A.D. Brother of Herod Agrippa I; by Emperor Claudius made king of Chalcis (41), a small district (former tetrarchy) of Coele-Syria, north of Galilee.

He·ro·das \hə-'rō-dəs\ *or* **He·ron·das** \hə-'rän-dəs\. 3d century B.C. Greek poet. Author of short humorous dramatic genre sketches in choliambic verse.

He·ro·des At·ti·cus \hə-'rō-(ˌ)dē-'zat-ə-kəs\, Lucius Vibullius Hipparchus Tiberius Claudius. c.101–177. Greek scholar. Friend of Emperor Hadrian; consul (143); entrusted by Emperor Antoninus Pius with education of Marcus Aurelius and Lucius Verus. Famed for public works, including Odeum at Athens, theater at Corinth, stadium at Delphi, aqueduct at Canusium, and restoration of many ruined cities in Greece. Known as brilliant orator and a leader of the Second Sophistic movement.

He·ro·di·an \hə-'rō-dē-ən\. *Latin* He·ro·di·a·nus \hə-ˌrō-dē-'ā-nəs\. 3d century A.D. Greek historian. Author of history of Rome for years 180 to 238 A.D.

He·ro·di·a·nus \hə-ˌrō-dē-'ā-nəs\, Aelius. *Also called* Herodianus Tech·ni·cus \-'tek-ni-kəs\. 2nd century A.D. Greek scholar of Alexandria. Son of Apollonius Dyscolus; taught in Rome under patronage of Marcus Aurelius. Author of works on prosody, etc.

He·ro·di·as \hə-'rō-dē-əs\. d. after 39 A.D. Consort of Herod Antipas of Galilee. Daughter of Aristobulus and sister of Herod Agrippa I; m. her uncle Herod Philip, whom she left to marry his brother Herod Antipas as second wife; mother of Salome; goaded Antipas into rivalry with her brother Herod Agrippa I, resulting in banishment to Gaul (39).

He·rod·o·tus \hi-'räd-ə-təs\. c.484–between 430 and 420 B.C. Greek historian. During course of his studies, traveled over most of known world of his time; lived for a while in Samos, later in Athens, and finally settled as a colonist in Thurii in Italy. His great work was a history of Greco–Persian wars from 500 to 479 B.C. His systematic treatment and mastery of style gained for him the title "Father of History."

Hé·ro·ët \ā-rô-e\, Antoine. *Called* la Mai·son·neuve \mez-ōⁿ-nœv\. 1492?–1568. French ecclesiastic and poet. Member of court of Margaret of

Angoulême until becoming bishop of Digne (1552). Author of poems on courtly and mystical love as *La Parfaicte Amye* (1542).

Hé·rold \ā-rōld\, Louis-Joseph-Ferdinand. 1791–1833. French composer. Known esp. for his comic operas, including *La Gioventu di Enrico quinto* (1815), *Charles de France* (1816, with Boieldieu), *Les Rosières* (1817), *La Clochette* (1817), *Le Muletier* (1823), *Vendôme en Espagne* (1823, with Auber), *Marie* (1826), *Zampa* (1831), *Le Pré aux clercs* (1832); wrote ballets *La Fille mal gardée* (1828), *La Belle au bois dormant* (1829); also piano and chamber works.

Heron. See HERO.

Herondas. See HERODAS.

He·roph·i·lus \hə-'räf-ə-ləs\. c.335–c.280 B.C. Greek anatomist and surgeon. Founder of school of anatomy in Alexandria. One of first to conduct post-mortem examinations, to describe the ventricles of the brain, the liver, the spleen, and genital organs, to distinguish nerves as sensory or motor in function, to time the pulse.

Hé·roult \ā-rü\, Paul-Louis-Toussaint. 1863–1914. French metallurgist. Invented (1886) Héroult process for producing aluminum by electrolysis of alumina in cryolite (called Hall process in America, where it was invented contemporaneously by C. M. Hall); also invented electric-arc Héroult furnace for production of electric steel.

Herr \'her\, Herbert Thacker. 1876–1933. American engineer, b. Denver, Colo. General superintendent, Norfolk & Western Railroad (1906–08); vice president and general manager (1908–13), director (1913–17), Westinghouse Machine Co.; vice president (1917–33), Westinghouse Electric and Manufacturing Co. Invented locomotive air-brake equipment, a doubleheading device for two or more locomotives, a remote control for marine steam turbines, improvements in turbines and oil and gas engines, etc.

Herr, John. 1781–1850. American clergyman, b. West Lampeter, Pa. One of founders of Reformed Mennonite church (1812).

Her·rán \er-'rän\, Pedro Alcántara. 1800–1872. Colombian general and politician. Served in republican army under Sucre in Ecuador, Peru, and Bolivia (1824–26); distinguished himself at Ayacucho (1824); president (1841–45) of New Granada (Colombia); promulgated constitution (1843).

Her·re·ra \er-'rer-ä\, Dionisio. 1783–1850. Central American politician, b. Nicaragua. Under the Central American federation, president of Honduras (1824–27) and of Nicaragua (1830–33); retired (1833) to live in El Salvador.

Herrera, Fernando de. *Called* el Di·vi·no \el-dē-'vē-nō\. 1534?–1597. Spanish poet. Head of neoclassical Sevillian school of lyric poetry; friend of Cervantes; disciple of Garcilaso de la Vega; known esp. for poems in the Italian style, particularly for his *canciones* and *sonetos;* began fashion for *culteranismo,* an affectedly ornate style.

Herrera, Francisco de. *Called* el Vie·jo \el-'b̲ye-hō\, *i.e.* the Elder. 1576–?1656. Spanish painter. Often regarded as founder of national style of Spain; works marked transition from Mannerism to the Baroque; said to have been first teacher of Velázquez. Works included *Pentecost, Apotheosis of St. Hermenegild, Miracle of Loaves and Fishes.* His son ¶Francisco (1622–1685), *called* el Mo·zo \el-'mō-sō, -thō\, *i.e.* the Younger, also a painter; fled his father to Italy; called by the Italians lo Spa·gnuo·lo de·gli Pe·sci \lō-,spän-yə-'wō-lō-,dā-lē-'pā-shē\ because of his popular still lifes with fish; to Seville (1656); one of founders of Seville Academy (1660); to Madrid (1661); court painter to Philip IV (1672); master of royal works under Charles II; notable also as an architect. Paintings included *Triumph of St. Hermenegild, Ecstasy of St. Francis.*

Herrera, José Joaquín. 1792–1854. Mexican general and politician. Supported Iturbide in revolution (1821); later opposed Iturbide as emperor; minister of war (1823–24). Opposed war with U.S. (1846–47) but was second in command under Santa Anna; twice acting president of Mexico (1844, 1844–45); president (1848–51); his attempts to establish more liberal government generally unsuccessful.

Herrera, Juan de. c.1530–1597. Spanish architect. Courtier of Philip II; assistant (1563) to Juan Bautista de Toledo, whom he succeeded (1572) as chief architect of El Escorial; also built Exchange in Seville and cathedral of Valladolid.

Herrera y Reis·sig \-ē-'rā-sēg\, Julio. 1875–1910. Uruguayan poet. Leader of a group of youthful, rebellious poets; wrote much experimental verse, controversial for its innovative forms and language, but also master of traditional forms, esp. the sonnet. Volumes included *Wagnerianas* (1900), *Las pascuas del tiempo* (1900), *Los maitines de la noche* (1902), *Los éxtasis de la montaña* (1904–07), *Poemas violetas* (1906), *Sonetos vascos* (1906), *Los parques abandonados* (1908), *Pianos crepusculares* (1910).

Herrera y Tor·de·sil·las \-ē-tōr-th̲ā-'sē(l)-yäs\, Antonio de. 1559–1625. Spanish historian. Historiographer of Castile and chronicler of the Indies. Known esp. for his *Historia general de los hechos de los Castellanos en las islas y tierra firme del Mar Océano* (1601, a history of America from 1492 to 1554) and *Descripción de las Indias Occidentales* (1601).

Herreros, Manuel Bretón de los. See BRETÓN DE LOS HERREROS.

Her·res·hoff \'her-ə-,sóf, -əs-,hóf\, James Brown. 1834–1930. American inventor, b. near Bristol, R.I. Invented (1860) sliding seat for rowboats (later used in racing shells); improved process for making nitric and hydrochloric acids; built gasoline-motor bicycle (1872); improved marine steam boilers. His brother ¶John Brown (1841–1915) was yacht designer; blind from age of fourteen; organized (1878) with another brother ¶Nathanael Greene (1848–1938) the Herreshoff Manufacturing Co. (1878), later famed for designing yachts to defend America's Cup, including *Vigilant* (1892), *Defender* (1895), *Columbia* (1899, 1901), *Reliance* (1903), *Resolute* (1920). Nathanael was superintendent of Herreshoff Manufacturing Co. (1881–1915) and president (1915–24); built first seagoing torpedo boat for U.S. navy; made the first practicable application of the principle of the fin keel (1891), and was first to propose (1903) the "univeral rule" of measurement for the racing of yachts.

Her·rick \'her-ik\, Myron Timothy. 1854–1929. American politician and diplomat, b. Huntington, Ohio. Active in nomination and election of McKinley as president (1896); governor of Ohio (1903–05). U.S. ambassador to France (1912–14, 1921–29); active in relief work early in World War I.

Herrick, Robert. 1591–1674. English poet. Vicar of Dean Prior, Devonshire (1629–47, 1662–74); ejected for Royalist sympathies (1647); restored (1662). Author of epigrams and classically elegant lyrics as "Corinna's Gone a-Maying," "To Daffodils"; published collected verse as *Hesperides, or the Works both Human and Divine of Robert Herrick, Esq.* (1648).

Herrick, Robert Welch. 1868–1938. American novelist, b. Cambridge, Mass. Teacher of English, U. of Chicago (1893–1923; professor from 1905). His novels included *The Gospel of Freedom* (1898), *The Web of Life* (1900), *The Real World* (1901), *The Common Lot* (1904), *The Master of the Inn* (1908), *Together* (1908), *The Healer* (1911), *One Woman's Life* (1913), *The World Decision* (1916), *Homely Lilla* (1923), *Waste* (1924), *The End of Desire* (1931), *Sometime* (1933), etc.

Herries, Baron. See MAXWELL family.

Her·ri·man \'her-ə-mən\, George Joseph. 1880–1944. American cartoonist, b. New Orleans. Newspaper artist (from 1897); created comic strip *Lariat Pete* for *San Francisco Chronicle* (1903); later created strips *Major Ozone, The Family Upstairs, Professor Otto and his Auto, The Dingbat Family;* created *Krazy Kat* (1910) and conducted it until his death, attracting wide readership with highly original language, abstract scenes, and theme of impossible and unrequited love.

Her·ring \'her-iŋ\, John Frederick. 1795–1865. English painter. Known esp. for pictures of race horses and sporting subjects.

Her·ri·ot \e-ryō\, Édouard. 1872–1957. French politician and writer. Mayor of Lyons (1905–42, 1945–57); senator (1912–19), member of Chamber of Deputies (from 1919), and a leader of the Radical party (from 1919); minister of public works (1916–17); premier of France and foreign minister (1924–25); minister of public instruction (1926–28); again premier (1932); minister of state (1934–36); president of Chamber of Deputies (1936–40); Nazi prisoner (1942–45); president, National Assembly (1947–54). Author of *Philon le Juif* (1898), *Madame Récamier et ses amis* (1904), *La Russie nouvelle* (1922), *La Vie de Beethoven* (1929), *Les États unis d'Europe* (1930), etc.

Her·schel \'hər-shəl\, Clemens. 1842–1930. American hydraulic engineer, b. Vienna, Austria. To U.S. as a child; inventor of Venturi tube (pat. 1888) for measuring the flow of water in pipes.

Her·schel \'her-shəl, *Angl* 'hər-shəl\, Sir William, *orig.* Friedrich Wilhelm. 1738–1822. British astronomer, b. Hanover, Germany. To England (1757), where he first taught music in Leeds, Halifax, and Bath. Devoted himself to study of mathematics and astronomy; built reflecting telescope of superior quality (c.1773) and with it discovered planet Uranus (Mar. 13, 1781), which he named Georgium Sidus in honor of George III; appointed court astronomer (1782). Discovered (1787) two satellites of Uranus (Oberon and Titania), and (1789) sixth and seventh satellites of Saturn. Regarded as virtual founder of sidereal science; discovered period of rotation of Saturn, existence of motion of binary stars; studied nebulae, showing that most are star clusters; first to theorize on stellar evolution and evolutionary cosmology. Aided in observations by his sister ¶Caroline Lucretia (1750–1848), who independently discovered 8 comets. Sir William's son ¶Sir John Frederick William (1792–1871) continued Sir William's studies on double stars and nebulae; led expedition to take observations at Cape of Good Hope (1834–38); contributed further to knowledge of Milky Way, brightness and color of stars, variable stars, and Magellanic Clouds; also known for researches in light, sound, and celestial physics; discovered (1819) solvent power of sodium hyposulphite on silver salts (important for its use in photography) and was first to apply terms "positive" and "negative" to photographic images. A founder (1820) of Royal Astronomical Society. Author of *Outlines of Astronomy* (1849). Two of Sir John Frederick's sons ¶Alexander Stewart (1836–1907) and ¶John (1837–1921) also achieved renown as astronomers.

Her·sent \er-säⁿ\, Louis. 1777–1860. French painter and lithographer. Fashionable portraitist following Restoration (1815); professor, École des Beaux-Arts (1825).

Her·shey \'hər-shē\, Lewis Blaine. 1893–1977. American army officer, b. near Angola, Ind. In army service (1917–73); brigadier general (1940), lieutenant general (1956), general (1969). Director, Selective Service System (1941–70).

Hershey, Milton Snavely. 1857–1945. American industrialist, b. Dauphin Co., Pa. Worked as confectioner, candy manufacturer; established (1903) Hershey Chocolate Co.; built town of Hershey, Pa.; founded (1909) Hershey Industrial School for orphan boys.

Her·sholt \'her-shōld, *Angl* 'hər-,shōlt\, Jean. 1886–1956. American actor, b. Copenhagen, Denmark. Stage debut (1905); to Canada (1909), U.S. (1914); appeared in films *Tess of the Storm Country* (1922), *Greed* (1923), *Don Q* (1925), *The Country Doctor* (1936), *Heidi* (1937), etc.; on radio as "Dr. Christian" (1937–54); noted for philanthropic work as president of Motion Picture Relief Fund (1938–56), American-Denmark Relief (1940–46), etc.; given special Academy Award (1949). Jean Hersholt Humanitarian Academy Award instituted in his honor.

Her·sko·vits \'her-skō-vəts\, Melville Jean. 1895–1963. American anthropologist, b. Bellefontaine, Ohio. Professor, Northwestern U. (1927–63); organized (1951) first U.S. program of African studies; known for studies on the Negro in Africa and America, folklore, primitive economics, etc. Author of *American Negro* (1928), *Dahomey* (1938), *Myth of the Negro Past* (1941), *Man and His Works* (1948), *Economic Anthropology* (1952), *Cultural Dynamics* (1964).

Her·ter \'hərt-ər\, Christian Archibald. 1895–1966. American politician, b. Paris, France, of American parents. Member of U.S. House of Representatives (1943–53); governor of Massachusetts (1953–57); U.S. secretary of state (1959–61); chief U.S. trade negotiator (1962–66).

Hertford, Earls and marquises. See family de CLARE; SEYMOUR family.

Hert·ling \'hert-,liŋ\, Georg Friedrich von. Graf. 1843–1919. German politician and philosopher. Professor, Bonn (1880–82), Munich (1882 ff.); a founder and head (1876) of Görres-Gesellschaft; member of Reichstag (1875–90, 1896–1912); parliamentary leader of Catholic Center party (1909–12); prime minister and foreign minister to Ludwig III of Bavaria (1912–17); chancellor of Germany (1917–18). Wrote *Naturrecht und Sozialpolitik* (1893), *Recht, Staat und Gesellschaft* (1906).

Hert·wig \'hert-vik̲\, Oskar Wilhelm August. 1849–1922. German embryologist. Professor, Jena (1881–88), Berlin (1888–1921); founder and director (1888–1921), Anatomisch-Biologische Inst., Berlin; showed that fertilization is the fusion of the nuclei of sperm and ovum; investigated malformations of vertebrate embryos, etc. His brother ¶Richard Carl Wilhelm Theodor von Hertwig (1850–1937), zoologist, was professor, Königsberg (1881–83), Bonn (1883–85), Munich (1885–1924); with Oskar, investigated formation of the coelom and developed the germ-layer theory; accomplished artificial fertilization of sea urchin's egg with strychnine; investigated sex differentiation in frogs, etc.

Hertz \'herts\, Gustav Ludwig. 1887–1975. German physicist. Nephew of Heinrich Hertz. Professor, Halle (1925–28); director, Physical Inst., Berlin Technische Hochschule (1928–45); in U.S.S.R. (1945–54); professor, Leipzig (1954–61). Known for researches with James Franck on ionization potentials of atoms by means of electron bombardment; results confirmed Bohr's prediction in quantum theory; awarded, with Franck, 1925 Nobel prize for physics.

Hertz, Heinrich Rudolph. 1857–1894. German physicist. Professor, Karlsruhe Technische Hochschule (1885–89), Bonn (1889–94). Investigated Maxwell's electromagnetic theory of light; demonstrated (c.1886) existence of electric or electromagnetic waves, measured their length and velocity, and showed that they could be reflected, refracted, and polarized as light is; studied the discharge of electricity in rarefied gases. His discoveries led to the development of wireless telegraphy.

Hertz, Henrik, *orig.* Heyman. 1797–1870. Danish writer. Associated with J.L. Heiberg in opposition to Romanticism. Author of plays as *Herr Burchardt og hans Familie* (1827), *Kaerlighed og Politi* (1828), *Sparekassen* (1836), *Svend Dyrings hus* (1837), *Kong Renés datter* (1845); novel *Stemninger og Tilstande* (1839); collection of satirical letters *Gjenganger-breve* (1830); etc.

Hertz \'hərts\, Joseph Herman. 1872–1946. British rabbi, b. Hungary. To U.S. in childhood; rabbi in Johannesburg, South Africa (1898–1911); expelled temporarily during Boer War because of his pro-British sympathies. Chosen chief rabbi of the United Hebrew Congregations of the British Empire, succeeding Hermann Adler (1913–46).

Hertz·berg \'herts-,berk\, Ewald Friedrich von. Graf. 1725–1795. Prussian statesman. In Prussian state service (from 1745); prominent as publicist and diplomat during the Seven Years' War (1756–63); negotiated treaty of Hubertusburg (1763), and became minister of foreign affairs (1763–91) and adviser to Frederick the Great and Frederick William II; failed in attempts to make Prussia political arbiter of Europe.

Hertzen. See HERZEN.

Her·tzog \'hert-sȯk̲\, James Barry Munnik. 1866–1942. South African soldier and politician. A Boer general and guerilla leader in the Boer War (1899–1902); voted against peace at Vereeniging (1902) and encouraged hostility to the British. Attorney general and minister of education, Orange Free State (1907–10); minister of justice, Union of South Africa (1910–12). Organized (1914) Afrikaner Nationalist party, demanding complete independence from Great Britain; opposed Botha-Smuts policy of South African development within the British Empire. Prime minister of South Africa (1924–39); formed coalition with Smuts (1933) and merged party into United party (1934); advocated neutrality in World War II and was forced out of office.

Hertz·sprung \'hert-sprůŋ\, Ejnar. 1873–1967. Danish astronomer. Professor, Göttingen (1909); on staff of Potsdam observatory (1909–19), U. of Leiden observatory (1919–45, director from 1935); investigated applications of photography to astronomy; demonstrated relationship of colors (spectral type) of stars to luminosity (1905–07) and demonstrated existence of giant and dwarf stars; established (1913) luminosity scale for Cepheid variables; evolved what is now known as Hertzsprung-Russell diagram (see Henry N. RUSSELL).

Her·vé \er-vā\, Aimé-Marie-Édouard. *Pseudonym* Raoul Val·nay \vál-nā\. 1835–1899. French journalist. Founded *Le Soleil* (1873), a journal supporting principle of constitutional monarchy in France, and the authorized organ of Orléanist party (after 1879).

Her·vey \'här-vē, 'hər-\, John. Baron Hervey of Ick·worth \'ik-(,)wərth\. 1696–1743. English politician and writer. Son of 1st Earl of Bristol; M.P. (1725–33); created baron (1733); lord privy seal (1740–42). Author of *Memoirs of the Reign of George the Second,* important source for study of the period.

Her·vieu \er-vyœ̄\, Paul-Ernest. 1857–1915. French novelist and playwright. Among his novels were *L'Inconnu* (1886), *Flirt* (1890), *Peints par eux-mêmes* (1893), *Amitié* (1900); among his plays, *Les Paroles restent* (1892), *Les Tenailles* (1895), *La Loi de l'homme* (1897), *La Course au flambeau* (1901), *L'Énigme* (1901), *Théroigne de Méricourt* (1902), *Le Dédale* (1903), *Le Réveil* (1905), *Connais-toi* (1909), *Bagatelles* (1912), etc.

Her·wegh \'her-veg\, Georg. 1817–1875. German poet. Fled military discipline to Switzerland (1839); published *Gedichte eines Lebendigen* (1841), youthful revolutionary poems that gained great popularity; returned to Germany (1842) but soon expelled for insulting King Frederick William IV; again returned during Revolution (1848), led disastrous uprising in Baden; exiled in Switzerland and France (1848–66). Also wrote *Neue Gedichte* (1877).

Herz \'herts\, Henri, *orig.* Heinrich. 1803–1888. Austrian pianist, composer, and teacher. Toured successfully as virtuoso pianist in Europe, U.S., South America; professor, Paris Conservatoire (1842–74); founded firm (1851) that manufactured prize-winning pianos. Composed piano works and widely used finger exercises.

Herz, Marcus. 1747–1803. German physician and philosopher. Friend of Kant and Moses Mendelssohn. His wife ¶Henriette, *nee* de Le·mos \də-'lā-mōs\ (1764–1847), was a famous beauty and society leader; conducted brilliant salon frequented by Humboldt, Fichte, Schadow, Schleiermacher, etc.; adopted the Christian faith (1817).

Her·zen \'hert-sən\, Aleksandr Ivanovich. *Russ. surname* Gert·sen \'gyärt-syin\ *from mother; father's name* Ya·ko·vlev \'yá-kəv-lyif\. *Pseudonym* Iskander \i-(,)skən-'dyär\. 1812–1870. Russian writer and political agitator. Illegitimate son of nobleman; arrested, exiled to provinces (1834–42) for membership in university circle of idealist revolutionaries; evolved philosophy of "Left-Hegelianism," allied with Westernizers against Slavophiles; left Russia (1847) and lived chiefly in Paris and London; became disenchanted with West, esp. in aftermath of revolutions of 1848; evolved new philosophical view of Socialist revolution inspired by Russian communalism; published newspaper *Kolokol* (The Bell, 1857–67), leading journal of Russian reformers and revolutionaries. Author of novels, esp. *Kto vinovat?* (Who Is to Blame? 1847), memoirs *My Past and Thoughts* (1852–55).

Herzl \'hert-səl\, Theodor. 1860–1904. Hungarian Zionist leader. Paris correspondent of *Neue Freie Presse,* Vienna (1891–95), and its literary editor (from 1896). Wrote *Der Judenstaat* (1896), advocating founding of a Jewish state in Palestine; organized Zionist World Congress, Basel (1897); president, Zionist Organization (1897–1904). Considered founder of organized Zionist movement.

Her·zog \er-zȯg\, Émile-Salomon-Wilhelm. *Pseudonym* André Mau·rois \mōr-wá, -wä\. 1885–1967. French writer. Author of novels as *Les Silences du Colonel Bramble* (1918), *Les Discours du docteur O'Grady* (1921), *Bernard Quesnay* (1926), *Climats* (1928), *Le Peseur d'âmes* (1931), *La Machine à lire les pensées* (1937); histories *Histoire de l'Angleterre* (1937), *Histoire des*

États-Unis (1943), *Histoire de France* (1947), *Les Deux Géants* (1962); best known for biographies including *Ariel* (of Shelley, 1923), *Disraeli* (1927), *Byron* (1930), *Edward VII* (1937), *Chateaubriand* (1938), *À la recherche de Marcel Proust* (1949), *Lélia* (George Sand, 1952), *Olympio* (Victor Hugo, 1954), *Les Trois Dumas* (1957), *Robert et Elizabeth Browning* (1957), *Prométhée* (Balzac, 1965).

Her·zog \ˈhərt-ˌsäg\, Isaac Halevi. 1888–1959. Polish rabbi. Chief rabbi, Dublin (1919); chief rabbi, Irish Free State (1925–36); chief rabbi, Palestine, later of Israel (from 1936).

Her·zog \ˈhert-ˌsōk\, Johann Jakob. 1805–1882. German theologian. Professor, Halle (1847–54), Erlangen (1854–77); founder and editor, *Real-Enzyklopädie für protestantische Theologie und Kirche* (1854–66; American edition by Philip Schaff, 1882–84, known as *The Schaff-Herzog Encyclopedia of Religious Knowledge).*

Hesch·el \ˈhesh-əl\, Abraham Joshua. 1907–1972. American theologian, b. Warsaw, Poland. Teacher in centers of Jewish studies, Berlin and Frankfurt (1932–38), London (1938–40); taught at Hebrew Union Coll. (1940–45), Jewish Theological Seminary of America (1945–72). Author of *Analysis of Piety* (1942), *Faith* (1944), *The Earth Is the Lord's* (1950), *Man Is Not Alone* (1952), *The Sabbath* (1951), *Man's Quest for God* (1954), *God in Search of Man* (1956), *The Prophets* (1962), *Who Is Man?* (1965), etc.

Hes·el·tine \ˈhez-əl-ˌtīn\, Philip Arnold. *Pseudonym* Peter War·lock \ˈwȯ(ə)r-ˌläk\. 1894–1930. English composer and writer. Founded (1920) musical journal *The Sackbut;* produced exemplary editions of works of Dowland, Purcell, Ravenscroft, and other Elizabethan composers. Known as composer esp. of songs as in cycles *Lilligay* (1923), *The Curlew* (1924), *Candlelight* (1924).

He·sil·rige \ˈhez-əl-ˌrij\ *or* **Ha·sel·rig** \ˈhā-zəl-ˌrig\, Sir Arthur. d. 1661. English Parliamentarian soldier and politician. One of Five Members of Parliament impeached by Charles I (1642). Engaged at Edge Hill (1642), Lansdown and Roundway Down (1643), Cheriton (1644); accompanied Cromwell to Scotland (1648) and commanded his reserve army. Opposed Cromwell's government after dissolution of Long Parliament (1653), and intrigued with army leaders against Richard Cromwell (1658). Arrested at Restoration.

He·si·od \ˈhē-sē-əd, ˈhes-ē-\. fl. c.800 B.C. Greek poet. His epic poem *Works and Days* included experiences of his daily life and work in the field, intermingled with precepts, fables, allegories; his earlier epic *Theogony* was an account of the beginnings of the world and birth of the gods.

Hess \ˈhes\, Germain Henri. 1802–1850. Russian chemist, b. Switzerland. Professor, St. Petersburg (1830–50); promulgated (1840) Hess's law of constant heat summation.

Hess, Harry Hammond. 1906–1969. American geophysicist, b. New York City. Professor, Princeton (1937–69); known for studies of Pacific Ocean seamounts, island arcs, orogeny, theory of sea-floor spreading.

Hess, Moses, *orig.* Moritz. 1812–1875. German Socialist. As journalist, associated with Engels and Marx; broke with Marx after 1848 and adopted more pragmatic views; later a champion of Zionism. Author of *Heilige Geschichte der Menschheit* (1837), *Europäischen Tetrarchie* (1841), *Rom und Jerusalem* (1862), etc.

Hess, Dame Myra. 1890–1965. English pianist. Known esp. as interpreter of Bach, Beethoven, Mozart, Schumann.

Hess, Victor Franz. 1883–1964. American physicist, b. Schloss Waldstein, Austria. Director of research, U.S. Radium Corp. (1921–23); consultant, U.S. Bureau of Mines (1922–23); professor, Graz (1922–31, 1937–38), Innsbruck (1931–37), Fordham (1938–56); naturalized U.S. citizen (1944). Pioneer investigator of cosmic rays, which he demonstrated were of extraterrestrial origin; shared with Carl D. Anderson the 1936 Nobel prize for physics.

Hess, Walter Rudolf. 1881–1973. Swiss physiologist. At U. of Zürich (1917–51); known for studies of autonomic nervous system, topology of brain functions; awarded Nobel prize for physiology or medicine (1949) with A. E. Moniz.

Hes·se \ˈhes-ə, *Angl* ˈhes\. *Ger.* Hes·sen \ˈhes-ən\. A German landgraviate, later grand duchy, in Prussia, and its ruling house, which originated with Sophia (d.1284), niece of Henry Raspe, and her son and successor, Henry I the Child (1263–1308). Philip the Magnanimous (*q.v.*) divided his lands among four sons; lands later consolidated in two parts: see HESSE-KASSEL and HESSE-DARMSTADT.

Hes·se \ˈhes-ə\, Hermann. 1877–1962. German author. To Switzerland as pacifist (1914), becoming citizen (1923). Author of novels and stories of man in search of spiritual fulfillment, often with Oriental and mystical themes, including *Peter Camenzind* (1904), *Unterm Rad* (1906), *Gertrud* (1910), *Rosshalde* (1914), *Knulp* (1915), *Demian* (1919), *Siddharta* (1922), *Der Steppenwolf* (1927), *Narziss und Goldmund* (1930), *Die Morgenlandfahrt* (1932), *Das Glasperlenspiel* (1943); awarded 1946 Nobel prize for literature.

Hesse-Darm·stadt \ˈhes-ˈdärm-ˌstat\. *Ger.* Hes·sen-Darm·stadt \ˈhes-ən-ˈdärm-ˌshtät\. Younger line of the house of Hesse (*q.v.*), founded (1567) by George I (landgrave 1567–96), fourth son of Philip the Magnanimous; made a grand duchy (1806); forced to yield territory to Prussia (1866); became part of new German Empire (1871), since which time generally known as Hesse. Chief rulers were: *Landgraves:* Louis V (1596–1626), George II (1626–61), Louis VI (1661–78), Ernest Louis (1678–1739), Louis VIII (1739–68), Louis IX (1768–90), Louis X (1790–1806); *Grand Dukes:* Louis X as Louis I (1806–30), Louis II (1830–48), Louis III (1848–77), Louis IV (1877–92), Louis Ernest (1892–1918; abdicated).

Hesse-Kas·sel \ˈhes-ˈkas-əl\. *Ger.* Hes·sen-Kas·sel \ˈhes-ən-ˈkäs-əl\. Elder line of the house of Hesse (*q.v.*), founded (1567) by William IV the Wise (landgrave 1567–92), eldest son of Philip the Magnanimous; made an electorate (1803); incorporated in Napoleonic Kingdom of Westphalia (1807–15); incorporated with Prussia (1866). Rulers were: *Landgraves:* Maurice (1592–1627), William V (1627–37), William VI (1637–63), William VII (1663–70), Charles I (1670–1730), Frederick I (1730–51; also king of Sweden, 1720–51), William VIII (1751–60), Frederick II (1760–85; sent Hessian troops as mercenaries to fight with British against American Revolutionists), William IX (1785–1803); *Electors:* William IX, as William I (1803–21), William II (1821–47), Frederick William (1847–66; last ruler; deposed).

Hes·sus \ˈhes-ůs, *Angl* ˈhes-əs\, Helius Eobanus. *Orig. surname* Koch \ˈkōk\. 1488–1540. German Humanist and poet. Professor, Erfurt (1517–26), Nürnberg (1526–33), Marburg (1536–40); took part in political, religious, and literary quarrels of his day and favored Luther and the Reformation. Considered foremost Latin poet of his day; author of the poetry collection *Sylvae* (1539), of pastoral poems as *Bucolicon* (1509), of *Heroides Christianae* in imitation of Ovid (1514), of translations into Latin of the Psalms (1538) and the *Iliad* (1540); one of authors of the *Epistolae Obscurorum Virorum.*

He·sych·i·us \hə-ˈsik-ē-əs\ of Alexandria. 5th century A.D. Greek grammarian. Compiled Greek lexicon of unusual words, forms, and phrases. His lexicon was derived from a similar, but larger, work by Diogenianus, which in turn was derived from the dictionary compiled by Pamphilus and Zopyrion (*qq.v.*).

Hesychius of Jerusalem. d. c.450 A.D. Greek theologian. Priest and monk of church in Jerusalem; gained renown as teacher and exegete. Author of biblical commentaries, earliest known liturgical addresses on Virgin Mary, and a church history controverting Nestorianism and other heresies that was adopted by second Council of Constantinople (553).

Hesychius of Mi·le·tus \mī-ˈlēt-əs, mə-\. *Also called* the Illustrious. 6th century A.D. Greek historian and biographer. Author of *Historia Romaike te kai pantodape,* chronicle of world history invaluable for information on early Byzantine times; also compiled biographical directory of learned Greeks.

He·teph·e·res \hə-ˈtef-ə-ˌrēz\. 27–26th century B.C. Egyptian queen. Daughter of Huni; married by Sneferu, probably to establish his claim to succession; mother of Khufu.

Hett·ner \ˈhet-nər\, Alfred. 1859–1941. German geographer. Conducted exploring expeditions to the Andes Mountains (1882–84, 1888–90) and to East Asia and India (1913–14); professor, Leipzig (1894–97), Tübingen (1897–99), Heidelberg (1899–1928); developed a philosophical foundation for geography. Author of *Grundzüge der Länderkunde* (1907–24), *Die Geographie* (1927), *Vergleichende Länderkunde* (1933–35).

Het·zel \et-sel\, Pierre-Jules. 1814–1886. French publisher. Established publishing house in Paris (1862), specializing in literature for young people; published books of Jules Verne. Author of books for children.

Het·zer *or* **Hät·zer** \ˈhet-sər\ *or* **Hat·za** \ˈhät-sä\, Ludwig. c.1500–1529. Swiss religious leader. Iconoclast and Anabaptist; expelled from Zürich, Augsburg; wrote *Judicium Dei* (1523), *Ein Beweis* (1524); with collaboration of Johannes Denk, translated into German the Hebrew prophets, first Protestant version of the prophets in German (1527). Imprisoned for heresy (1528); beheaded.

Heug·lin \ˈhȯik-lən\, Theodor von. 1824–1876. German traveler. Traveled in northeast Africa (1850–65) and in Spitsbergen and Novaya Zemlya (1870–71); wrote on his travels and on ornithology.

Heu·reaux \œ-rō\, Ulises *or* Ulysse. 1845–1899. Dominican soldier and politician. Took part in revolts against Spain; president (1882–83 and 1887–99) and in power during intervening period (1883–87); assassinated; bankruptcy of nation at his death led to U.S. intervention.

Heus·ler \ˈhȯis-lər\, Andreas. 1865–1940. German scholar. Professor, Berlin (1894–1919), Basel (1919–40); known for studies of old German and Nordic literatures. Author of *Lied und Epos in germanischen Sagendichtung* (1905), *Das Strafrecht der Isländersagas* (1911), *Deutscher und antiker Vers* (1917), *Die altgermanische Dichtung* (1924), etc.

Heuss \ˈhȯis\, Theodor. 1884–1963. German politician. Political journalist and writer; German Democratic party representative in Reichstag (1924–28, 1930–33); returned to journalism, writing under pseudonym during Nazi period; helped form (1946), headed (1949–63) Free Democratic party; first president of German Federal Republic (1949–59). Author of *Kriegssozialismus* (1915), *Die neue Demokratie* (1920), *Staat und Volk* (1926), *Brüderlichkeit* (1953), etc.

Heussgen, Johannes. See HUSZGEN.

Heutsz \'hœts\, Johannes Benedictus van. 1851–1924. Dutch soldier and colonialist. To Dutch East Indies (1873); advocated subjugation of kingdom of Acheh on Sumatra; civil and military governor of Atjeh (1899); governor general of East Indies (1904–09); conquered Acheh, took over Tapanoeli, Jambi, central Borneo, Celebes, Bali, Sunda Islands, etc., consolidating Dutch rule over entire Indonesian archipelago.

He·vel \'hā-vəl\, Johannes. *Surname also spelled* He·wel \'hā-vəl\, He·welcke \'hā-vəl-kə\, He·we·liu·sza \,hā-vel-'yüt-sä\. *Known by Lat.* He·ve·li·us \hā-'vā-lē-ùs\. 1611–1687. German-Polish astronomer, b. Danzig. Built observatory in his residence (1641) and constructed the instruments for it; charted the lunar surface, catalogued many stars, observed sunspots, discovered four comets; one of first to observe transit of Mercury; studied phases of Saturn. Published *Selenographia* (1647), *Cometographia* (1668), *Machina coelestis* (1679).

He·ve·sy \'he-vesh-ē\, Georg Karl von, *orig.* György. 1885–1966. Hungarian chemist. Professor, Freiburg (1926–33), Copenhagen (1933–42), Stockholm (1942 ff.); codiscoverer (with Dirk Coster) of the element hafnium (1923); developed use of radioactive isotopes as tracers in chemistry and biology, etc. Awarded 1943 Nobel prize for chemistry.

Hew·art \'hyü-ərt\, Gordon. 1st Viscount Hewart of Bury \'ber-ē\. 1870–1943. English jurist. M.P. (1913–22); solicitor general (1916–19) and attorney general (1919–22). Lord chief justice of England (1922–40).

Hewes \'hyüz\, Joseph. 1730–1779. American Revolutionary leader, b. Kingston, N.J. Member, Continental Congress (1774–77, 1779); signer of Declaration of Independence.

Hew·itt \'hyü-ət\, Abram Stevens. 1822–1903. American industrialist and politician, b. Haverstraw, N.Y. With Edward Cooper (son of Peter Cooper, *q.v.*) formed (1845) Cooper, Hewitt and Co., iron-manufacturing business; introduced first American open-hearth furnace (1862) and made first American-made steel (1870). Active in establishment and management of Cooper Union; aided in overthrowing Tweed Ring. Member, U.S. House of Representatives (1875–79, 1881–86). Mayor of New York (1887–88). His son ¶Peter Cooper (1861–1921) was an electrical engineer; invented mercury vapor electric lamp and a mercury vapor rectifier; discovered fundamental principle of vacuum-tube amplifier; experimented with hydro-airplanes and helicopters.

Hewitt, Henry Kent. 1887–1972. American naval officer, b. Hackensack, N.J. Entered navy (1908); rear admiral (1940); commander, Amphibious Force, Atlantic Fleet (1942–43); directed landings in North Africa (Nov. 1942); vice admiral (1942); directed landings in Sicily (July 1943), Italy (Sept. 1943), southern France (Aug. 1944); admiral (1945).

Hew·lett \'hyü-lət\, Maurice Henry. 1861–1923. English essayist, novelist, and poet. Among his books were *The Forest Lovers* (1898), *Little Novels of Italy* (1899), *Richard Yea-and-Nay* (1900), *New Canterbury Tales* (1901), *The Queen's Quair* (1904), *The Fool Errant* (1905), *Rest Harrow* (1910), *Mrs. Lancelot* (1912), *A Lovers' Tale* (1915), *The Song of the Plow* (1916), *Wiltshire Essays* (1921).

Hew·son \'hyü-sən\, William. 1739–1774. English physician. First to fully describe coagulation of blood (1770); isolated fibrinogen (1770); studied lymphatic system.

Hext, Harrington. See Eden PHILLPOTTS.

Ḥey·dar \'kā-dȧr\, Sheykh. d. 1488. Persian religious leader. Head of Ṣafavid order; formed ties with Ak Koyunlu dynasty that laid foundation for establishment of Ṣafavid dynasty (1501); led raids against Christian Circassians (1483, 1487, 1488).

Hey·de·brand und der La·sa \'hī-də-,bränt-ùnt-dər-'lä-zä\, Ernst von. 1851–1924. German jurist and politician. Leader of ultraconservatives in Prussian assembly (1888–1918) and in Reichstag (1903–18).

Hey·den *or* **Heij·den** \'hī-dən\, Jan van der. 1637–1712. Dutch painter. Known esp. for technically brilliant cityscapes of Amsterdam.

Hey·drich \'hī-drik\, Reinhard Tristan Eugen. *Known as* der Hen·ker \dər-'heŋ-kər\, *i.e.* the hangman. 1904–1942. German politician. Joined SS (1931); chief deputy to Heinrich Himmler; head of security police (1936); German "protector" of Bohemia and Moravia (1941–42); assassinated. In reprisal for his assassination, the Nazis demolished the village of Lidice, Czechoslovakia, and executed the male population.

Hey·er \'hā-ər, 'ha(ə)r, 'he(ə)r\, Georgette. 1902–1974. English novelist. Author of popular Regency romances as *The Black Moth* (1921), *Beauvallet* (1929), *Devil's Cub* (1932), *Regency Buck* (1935), *Beau Wyndham* (1941), *Penhallow* (1943), *The Grand Sophie* (1950).

Hey·lyn *or* **Hey·lin** \'hā-lən, 'hī-\, Peter. 1600–1662. English clergyman and historian. Royalist during Civil War. Author of *Ecclesia Restaurata: the History of the Reformation of the Church of England* (1661) and a life of Laud.

Heym \'hīm\, Georg. 1887–1912. German poet. A leader in Expressionist movement; author of *Der ewige Tag* (1911), *Umbra vitae* (1912).

Hey·mans \'hī-,mäns\, Corneille-Jean-François. 1892–1968. Belgian physiologist. Professor, U. of Ghent (1930–68); awarded 1938 Nobel prize for physiology or medicine for discovery of pressoreceptors and chemoreceptors in carotid sinus and sinus aorta that regulate respiration.

Heyn, Piet. See Piet HEIN.

Hey·rov·ský \'hā-rȯf-skē\, Jaroslav. 1890–1967. Czech physical chemist. Professor, Prague (from 1922); awarded Nobel prize for chemistry (1959) for his discovery and development of polarographic analysis.

Hey·se \'hī-zə\, Paul Johann Ludwig von. 1830–1914. German writer. Leader of traditionalist Munich circle. Author of carefully wrought stories collected in *Gesammelte Novellen in Versen* (1864), *Meraner Novellen* (1867), *Deutscher Novellenschatz* (1870–76), *Novellen vom Gardasee* (1902), etc.; also wrote novels as *Kinder der Welt* (1873), *Im Paradiese* (1875), *Merlin* (1892), and dramatic works. Awarded Nobel prize for literature (1910).

Hey·ward \'hā-wərd\, DuBose, *in full* Edwin DuBose. 1885–1940. American author, b. Charleston, S.C. Author of verse *Carolina Chansons* (1922, with Hervey Allen), *Skylines and Horizons* (1924), *Jasbo Brown* (1931); novels *Porgy* (1925), *Angel* (1926), *Mamba's Daughters* (1929), *Peter Ashley* (1932), *Lost Morning* (1936); play *Brass Ankle* (1931); etc. Produced dramatized version of *Porgy* (1927) which became the basis for the operatic work *Porgy and Bess* by George Gershwin.

Heyward, Thomas. 1746–1809. American Revolutionary politician, b. St. Luke's Parish, S.C. Member, Council of Safety (1775, 1776) and Continental Congress (1776–78); signer of Declaration of Independence.

Hey·wood \'hā-,wùd\, John. 1497?–?1580. English playwright and epigrammatist. At court of Henry VIII (from 1519); a favorite with Queen Mary; retired to Malines at accession of Elizabeth (1558). Wrote interludes, including *The Foure P's, The Play of the Wether, The Play of Love, Wytty and Wytless,* which in the personal representation of characters were the predecessors of English comedy. Wrote also *Dialogue on Wit and Folly,* verse allegory *The Spider and the Flie* (1556), proverbs, epigrams, ballads, etc. His son ¶Jasper (1535–1598) entered the Jesuit order (1562); superior of English Jesuit mission (1581–85); deported to France (1585). Author of influential translations of Seneca, including *Troades* (1559), *Thyestes* (1560), *Hercules furens* (1561).

Heywood, Thomas. 1574?–1641. English playwright. Actor on London stage; member of Queen's company (1619). Claimed to have written or collaborated on 220 plays; those believed to be chiefly his included *If you know not me, You know no bodie* (1605–06), *A Woman Kilde with Kindnesse* (1607), *The Rape of Lucrece* (1608), *Four Prentices of London* (1615), *Fair Maid of the West* (1631), *The Captives* (1634), *A Challenge for Beauty* (1636), *Love's Maistresse* (1636), *The Royall King and the Loyall Subject* (1637). Also wrote *An Apology for Actors* (1612), and verse, including *Hierarchy of the Blessed Angels* (1635).

Hez·e·ki·ah \,hez-ə-'kī-ə\. *Hebrew* Ḥiz·qiy·ya \kēz-'kē-yä\. *Greek* Eze·ki·as \,ā-zä-'kē-äs\. d. c.686 B.C. King of Judah (c.715–c.686 B.C.). Son and successor of Ahaz. Possibly joined revolt against Sargon II of Assyria (710); defeated again in revolt against Sennacherib (701); thereafter paid tribute to Sennacherib; his reign marked by prophecy of Isaiah; succeeded by his son Manasseh.

H. H. See Helen Hunt JACKSON.

Hi·a·wa·tha \,hī-ə-'wȯ-thə, ,hē-ə-, -'wäth-ə\. *Orig.* Haionhwat'ha, *i.e.* He Makes Rivers. fl. c.1570. American Indian leader. Perhaps purely legendary figure of Onondaga tribe; credited, with Dekanawidah, with forging Iroquois League of Onondaga, Mohawk, Oneida, Cayuga, and Seneca tribes (c.1570).

Hib·bert \'hib-ərt\, Robert. 1770–1849. British merchant and philanthropist, b. Jamaica. Merchant and slaveowner in Jamaica (1791–1836); to England (c.1836). Created Hibbert trust (1847), originally designed for the elevation of the Unitarian ministry, also used to support Hibbert lectures, the *Hibbert Journal* (1902–70), etc.

Hich·ens \'hich-ənz\, Robert Smythe. 1864–1950. English novelist. Author of *The Green Carnation* (1894), *The Londoners* (1898), *The Garden of Allah* (1904), *Bella Donna* (1909), *Mrs. Marden* (1919), *Doctor Artz* (1929), *The Paradine Case* (1933), *The Journey Up* (1938), *The Million* (1940), *A New Way of Life* (1942).

Hickes \'hiks\, George. 1642–1715. English nonjuring clergyman and scholar. Dean of Worcester (1683); deprived of his living for refusing to take oath of allegiance to William and Mary (1690); remained in hiding (1690–99); consecrated suffragan bishop of Thetford (1694).

Hick·ok \'hik-,äk\, James Butler. *Known as* Wild Bill Hickok. 1837–1876. American frontiersman, b. Troy Grove, Ill. Stage driver, first on Santa Fe Trail, later on Oregon Trail; fought McCanles gang, Rock Creek Station, Neb. (1861); scout in Union army in Civil War. Deputy U.S. marshal, Fort Riley, Kans. (1866–67); U.S. marshal, Hays City (1869–71) and Abilene, Kans.

(1871); reputation as fighter and crack shot inspired many dime novels. On tour with Buffalo Bill's Wild West Show (1872–73). Murdered in Deadwood, Dakota Territory.

Hicks \'hiks\, Edward. 1780–1849. American painter, b. Attleboro (now Langhorne), Pa. Coach and sign painter, itinerant Quaker preacher; took up easel painting in middle life; known for naive scenes of rural Pennsylvania and New York and for many versions of allegorical *The Peaceable Kingdom.*

Hicks, Elias. 1748–1830. American religious leader, b. Hempstead, Long Island, N.Y. Carpenter by trade; Quaker preacher (from c.1775); identified with liberal thought and esp. with opposition to slavery; opposed Evangelicalism and adoption of set creed; by many held responsible for separations in Quaker communities (1827–28), following which his followers were dubbed Hicksites.

Hicks, Granville. 1901–1982. American writer and literary critic, b. Exeter, N.H. Member of Communist party (1934–39); literary editor, *New Masses* magazine (1934–39); a leader of proletarian literary movement of 1930s; contributing editor, *Saturday Review* (1958–69) . Best known for *The Great Tradition* (1933), a Marxist critical interpretation of American literature; also wrote *John Reed* (1936), *Figures of Transition* (1939), *Only One Storm* (novel, 1942), *Small Town* (1946), *Literary Horizons* (1970), etc.

Hicks, William. *Known as* Hicks Pa·sha \'päsh-ə, 'pash-ə\. 1830–1883. British soldier. Served in India (1849–80); in command of Egyptian army in Sudan (1883); undertook expedition against al-Mahdī; ambushed and killed along with most of army at Kashgil.

Hi·dal·go y Cos·ti·lla \ē-'thäl-gō-ē-kȯs-'tē-yä\, Miguel. 1753–1811. Mexican priest and revolutionist. In attempt to improve condition of peasants, rang church bell of Dolores to proclaim revolt (Sept. 16, 1810) against Spanish government; seized Guanajuato and Guadalajara. With army of 80,000 marched on Mexico City (Oct. 1810); won first battle but forced to fall back when defeated by Spanish force under Félix Calleja (Nov. 1810); completely defeated by Calleja at Calderón (Jan. 1811); captured and shot. His campaign the beginning of war for Mexican independence.

Hidetada. See under TOKUGAWA family.

Hideyori. See under TOYOTOMI family.

Hideyoshi. See under TOYOTOMI family.

Hiel \'hēl\. 9th century B.C. Palestinian ruler or priest. Supposed founder of Jericho.

Hiel \'hēl\, Emanuel. 1834–1899. Flemish poet. A leader in the revival of Flemish language and literature; best known for cantatas and oratorios, as *De Schelde* (1866).

Hielm \'hyelm\, Jonas Anton. 1782–1848. Norwegian politician. Member of Storting, or parliament (1830 ff.); attempted unsuccessfully to forge peasant-liberal coalition; succeeded in obtaining improved status of Norway in union with Sweden; secured right of Norwegian ships to fly Norwegian, rather than union, flag.

Hi·en Vu·ong \hē-'en-vü-'ȯŋ\. *Also known as* Nguy·en Phuoc Tan \'nī-en-pü-'ōk-'tän\ *and* Thai Ton \'tī-'tȯn\. d. 1687. Nguyen ruler of southern Vietnam (1648–87). Expanded territory at expense of Chams in the south, Cambodians, and, less successfully, Trinh dynasty in the north; persecuted European missionaries and converts.

Hierax, Antiochus. See ANTIOCHUS HIERAX.

Hi·ero \'hī-ə-(,)rō\ *or* **Hi·er·on** \'hī-ə-,rän\. Name of two tyrants of Syracuse:

Hiero I. d. 467 or 466 B.C. Tyrant (478–467 or 466 B.C.). Brother of Gelon; distinguished himself at battle of Himera (480); succeeded Gelon; founded city of Aetna (475); won naval victory over Etruscans at Cumae (474); by defeat (472) of Thrasydaeus of Aeragas (modern Agrigento), gained supreme control of Sicily; noted for his patronage of poets and philosophers (Pindar, Aeschylus, Simonides, Bacchylides).

Hiero II. 308?–216 or 215 B.C. Tyrant (c.270–216 or 215 B.C.). Fought under Pyrrhus in Sicilian campaigns (278–276); succeeded Pyrrhus as commander of Syracusan forces (276); successful against Mamertini at Messina (270); chosen king (270); aided Carthaginians under Hanno against Mamertini but defeated by Romans under Appius Claudius (264); concluded treaty with Romans (263); furnished support to Rome in both First and Second Punic wars. A kinsman of Archimedes.

Hi·er·o·cles \hī-'er-ə-,klēz\. fl. c.535 A.D. Byzantine grammarian. Compiled *Synekdemos,* valuable list of eparchies and cities in realm of Justinian I.

Hierocles of Alexandria. fl. c.430 A.D. Greek Neoplatonic philosopher. Author of *Peri pronoias* and of a commentary on the *Chrysa epe* attributed to Pythagoras.

Hi·eron·y·mus \,hī-ə-'rän-ə-məs, hir-'än-\ of Car·dia \'kär-dē-ə\. 4th–3d century B.C. Greek general and historian. Served under Alexander the Great, Eumenes, Antigonus, and Antigonus Gonatas, successively. Author of a history of the Diadochi down to 272 B.C..

Hieronymus of Prague. See JEROME of Prague.

Hieronymus, Saint Eusebius. See Saint JEROME.

Hierta, Hans. See JÄRTA.

Hier·ta \'hyer-tä\, Lars Johan. 1801–1872. Swedish journalist and politician. Established and edited (1830–51) *Aftonbladet,* daily newspaper and liberal organ; member of third chamber of Riksdag (1859–65); instrumental in creation of bicameral Riksdag (1865); president of lower chamber (1866–72).

Hig·den *or* **Hig·don** \'hig-dən\, Ranulf. c.1280–1364. English monk and chronicler. Entered Benedictine order (1299); author of *Polychronicon,* a general history (in Latin; trans. into English by John Trevisa, *q.v.*) down to 1340 (continued by others into reign of Richard II).

Hig·gins \'hig-ənz\, Alexander Pearce. 1865–1935. English lawyer. Adviser to British government on prize and international law during World War I; professor, U. of London (1919–23), Cambridge (1920–35); member of Permanent Court of Arbitration, The Hague (1930–35); president, Institut de Droit International (1929–31). Author of *The Binding Force of International Law* (1910), *War and the Private Citizen* (1912), *Armed Merchant Ships* (1914), etc.

Higgins, Edward John. 1864–1947. English Salvation Army leader. Chief of staff in England (1918–29); general, succeeding W. Bramwell Booth (1929–34).

Hig·gin·son \'hig-ən-sᵊn\, Thomas Wentworth Storrow. 1823–1911. American clergyman, army officer, and writer, b. Cambridge, Mass. In Unitarian ministry (1847–61); active in antislavery and women's rights movements. Served in Civil War; colonel of first Negro regiment in Union army (1862–64). Author of biographies, including *Francis Higginson* (1891), *Henry Wadsworth Longfellow* (1902), *John Greenleaf Whittier* (1902); of *A Ride Through Kansas* (1856), *Malbone* (novel, 1869), *Army Life in a Black Regiment* (1870), *Young Folks' History of the United States* (1875), etc.; long a correspondent of Emily Dickinson and an editor of her poems.

High·more \'hī-,mō(ə)r, -,mȯ(ə)r\, Joseph. 1692–1780. English painter. Known for portraits and for illustrations, as for Richardson's *Pamela* (1744), in which field he was a more restrained rival of Hogarth.

Hi·guchi \hē-gu̇ch-ē\ Ichiyō, *orig.* Natsuko. 1872–1896. Japanese poet and novelist. Best known for novels of life in and around Tokyo's pleasure district, as *Ōtsugomori* (1894), *Takekurabe* (1895); her diary published as *Wakabakage* (1896).

Hik·met \hik-'met\, Nazım. *Also called* Nazım Hikmet Ran \'rän\. 1902–1963. Turkish poet. Communist journalist and propagandist (1924–51), frequently jailed; lived in U.S.S.R. and eastern Europe (from 1951). Author of epics *Şeyh Bedreddin destanı* and *Memleketimden insan manzaraları,* influential in freedom of language and prosody, and other verse.

Hikotarō. See MAEBARA Issei.

Hi·lar·i·on \hə-'lar-ē-ən\. Saint. c.291–371 A.D. Palestinian hermit. Converted to Christian faith in Alexandria; influenced by ascetic Anthony of Egypt, established himself in Gaza desert (306); introduced monasticism into Palestine (329).

Hilarion of Kiev. 11th century. Russian prelate. Second archbishop of Kiev; delivered (c.1050) panegyric on St. Vladimir important in defining Russian Orthodoxy; first native metropolitan of Kiev (1051–54).

Hi·lar·i·us \hə-'lar-ē-əs\ *or* **Hil·a·rus** \'hil-ə-rəs\ *or* **Hil·a·ry** \'hil-(ə-)rē\. Saint. d. 468. Pope (461–468). Legate of Leo I to Council of Ephesus (449), where he opposed deposition of Patriarch Flavian of Constantinople; continued vigorous policy of Leo I, esp. in Gaul and Spain.

Hilarius. fl. 1125. French poet and scholar. Pupil of Peter Abelard; author of light verses in Latin and of three Latin religious plays.

Hil·a·ry \'hil-(ə-)rē\. Saint. *Latin* Hi·lar·i·us \hə-'lar-ē-əs\. c.315–c.367. French prelate. One of the Doctors of the Church; bishop of Poitiers (c.353); vigorously opposed Arianism. Author of *De trinitate,* first Latin work on Trinitarian controversy, *De synodis,* book of hymns, etc.

Hilary. Saint. *Latin* Hilarius. 401–449. French prelate. Bishop of Arles (429–449). Endeavored to establish primacy over church in southern Gaul; deposed bishop of Besançon for claiming metropolitan dignity for his see; deprived of his rights as metropolitan by Pope Leo I (444).

Hil·ber·sei·mer \'hil-bər-,sī-mər\, Ludwig. 1885–1967. American city planner, b. Karlsruhe, Germany. Founder and director (1928–38), department of city planning of Bauhaus School; to U.S. (1938); professor, Illinois Inst. of Technology (1938 ff.); pioneered in urban decentralization and regional planning. Author of *The New City* (1944), *The New Regional Pattern* (1949), *The Nature of Cities* (1955), etc.

Hil·bert \'hil-bərt\, David. 1862–1943. German mathematician. Professor, Königsberg (1886–95), Göttingen (1895–1930); worked on the theory of invariants, on the theory of numbers, and on integral equations; produced definitive set of axioms for Euclidean geometry; investigated multidimensional space; contributed to kinetic theory of gases and theory of radiation. Author of *Zahlbericht* (1897), *Grundlagen der Geometrie* (1899), *Methoden der Mathematischen Physik* (with R. Courant, 1924).

Hil·da \ˈhil-də\ *or* **Hild** \ˈhild\. Saint. 614–680. Anglo-Saxon abbess. Abbess of Hartlepool (649); founded monastery of Streaneshalch, later called Whitby (657), and ruled it (657–680); known as Abbess of Whitby.

Hil·de·bert \ēl-də-ber, *Angl* ˈhil-də-(ˌ)bərt\. c.1055–1133. French prelate. Bishop of Mans (1097) and archbishop of Tours (1125); engaged in struggle with Louis VI the Fat of France, ended by intervention of a papal legate.

Hildebrand. See Pope GREGORY VII.

Hildebrand. See Nicolaas BEETS.

Hil·de·brand \ˈhil-də-ˌbränt\, Adolf von. 1847–1921. German sculptor. Studio in Florence (1872–97); a leading theorist of aesthetics of modern sculpture; carved portrait busts of Clara Schumann, Ludwig of Bavaria; among his other sculptures were *Adam, Nackter Jüngling,* the Wittelsbach Fountain in Munich.

Hil·de·brandt \ˈhil-də-ˌbränt\, Johann Lukas von. 1668–1745. Austrian architect. Fortifications engineer in Austrian army (1695–1701); court engineer, Vienna (from 1701); developed highly decorative Baroque style that was widely imitated. Works included Piaristenkirche (1698), St. Peter (1702), palaces Schönborn (1706–11), Daun-Kinsky (1713–16), Belvedere (1714), the Chancellery (1717–19), all in Vienna; Göttweig monastery (1719), Schlosshof Castle, Ráckeve Castle in Hungary; rebuilt Mirabell Palace (1721–27) in Salzburg; built great hall and staircase of Pommersfelden Castle (1711–14), Bamberg.

Hil·de·gard \ˈhil-də-ˌgärt, *Angl* -ˌgärd\. Saint. *Also called* Hildegard von Bing·en \-fön-ˈbiŋ-ən\. 1098–1179. German religious. Founder (c.1147–50) and abbess of convent of Rupertsberg; famed for visions and prophecies, recorded in *Scivias.*

Hil·fer·ding \ˈhil-fər-ˌdiŋ\, Rudolf. 1877–1941. German statesman, b. Vienna. Instructor in Berlin training school of Social Democratic party (1906); financial editor of *Vorwärts* (1907–15); naturalized German citizen (c.1920); editor of *Die Freiheit* (1918–22). Minister of finance (1923, 1928–29); deputy in Reichstag (1924–33). Author of Marxist works *Böhm-Bawerks Marx-Kritik* (1904), *Das Finanzkapital* (1910).

Hil·gard \ˈhil-ˌgärd\, Eugene Woldemar. 1833–1916. American geologist, b. Zweibrücken, Germany. To U.S. (1836); director, Mississippi state geological survey (1858–60, 1870–73); professor, U. of Mississippi (1866–73), U. of Michigan (1873–75), U. of California (1875–1904); director, Agricultural Experiment Station, Berkeley, Cal. (1875–1904). Known for studies of soil; first to relate soil types to climate; contributed to scientific cultivation of cotton.

Hill \ˈhil\, Aaron. 1685–1750. English poet and playwright. Wrote scenario for and helped stage Handel's opera *Rinaldo* (1711); wrote or adapted numerous plays; enjoyed considerable success with *Zaïre* (1736) and *Mérope* (1749), adapted from Voltaire; satirized by Pope in the *Dunciad,* to which he replied in *Progress of Wit* (1730).

Hill, Ambrose Powell. 1825–1865. American army officer, b. Culpeper, Va. Entered Confederate service (1861); brigadier general (1862); major general (1862); led "Light Division" through Seven Days' Battles, Second Bull Run, Antietam; lieutenant general (1863); initiated attack that began battle of Gettysburg (July 1, 1863). Killed in action before Petersburg.

Hill, Archibald Vivian. 1886–1977. English physiologist. Professor, Manchester (1920–23), University Coll., London (1923–25), Royal Society (1926–51); secretary of Royal Society (1935–1945). Investigated the liberation of energy in muscles, discovering anaerobic nature of contraction; shared with Otto Meyerhof the 1922 Nobel prize for physiology or medicine.

Hill, Daniel Harvey. 1821–1889. American army officer, b. York District, S.C. In U.S. army (1842–49); professor, Washington Coll. (now Washington and Lee U., 1849–54), Davidson Coll. (1854–59); entered Confederate service (1861); brigadier general (1861); major general (1862); held South Mountain against McClellan (1862); lieutenant general (1863). President, U. of Arkansas (1877–84) and Georgia Military College (1885–89).

Hill, David Octavius. 1802–1870. Scottish painter and photographer. With commission to portray founders of Scottish Free church (1843) sought aid of chemist ¶Robert Adamson (1821–1848); together first to apply photography to portraiture, using the calotype process; produced some 1500 photographs (1843–48), including also landscapes, views of towns, villages.

Hill, George Birkbeck Norman. 1835–1903. English educator. Nephew of Sir Rowland Hill (1795–1879). Schoolmaster (1858–75); known chiefly as authority on life and works of Dr. Johnson. Edited Boswell's *Life of Johnson* (1887), *Johnson's Letters* (1892), *Johnsonian Miscellanies* (1897), *Johnson's Lives of the English Poets* (1905), etc.

Hill, George Washington. 1884–1946. American businessman, b. Philadelphia. Joined American Tobacco Co. (1904), vice president (1911–25), president (1925–46); pioneer in aggressive marketing of cigarettes; introduced Lucky Strike brand (1917), devised slogans "It's toasted," "Reach for a Lucky instead of a sweet," "Lucky Strike Green has gone to war," "LS/MFT"; sponsored "Your Hit Parade" radio show (from 1935).

Hill, George William. 1838–1914. American astronomer, b. New York City. On staff of *American Ephemeris and Nautical Almanac* (1861–98); professor, Columbia (1898–1901); known for his work in celestial mechanics and mathematics, esp. in refinement of lunar theory.

Hill, Graham, *in full* Norman Graham. 1929–1975. English automobile race driver. Team driver for British Racing Motors (1960–66); drove in record 176 Grand Prix events, winning over 20; won Indianapolis 500 (1966), Le Mans 24-hour (1972); world champion driver (1962, 1968).

Hill, James Jerome. 1838–1916. American financier, b. near Guelph, Ont. To U.S. (1856); settled in St. Paul, Minn. With associates, bought St. Paul and Pacific Railroad (1878); reorganized and extended line; created Great Northern Railway Co. to merge all properties into one unit (1890); president of road (1882–1907), chairman of board (1907–12). Engaged in stock market battle, J.P. Morgan and Hill against Harriman and Schiff, to control Northern Pacific Railroad, causing panic of 1901. Attempted to insure stability of control by organization of Northern Securities Co., a holding company for all his properties; defeated by U.S. Supreme Court decision (1904). Interests widened to include Canadian railroads, steamship lines to Orient, Mesabi iron ore range, and banks.

Hill, Joe. *Orig.* Joel Häg·glund \ˈheg-lünd\. *Also known as* Joseph Hill·strom \ˈhil-strəm\. 1879–1915. American labor leader and songwriter, b. Sweden. To U.S. (c.1901); became active in Industrial Workers of the World (c.1910); worked in strike organization, contributed to IWW journals *Industrial Worker* and *Solidarity;* his songs as "The Preacher and the Slave," "Coffee An'," "There is Power in a Union," "The Rebel Girl" became widely popular; arrested (1914), convicted on circumstantial evidence (1914), and after numerous appeals executed for murder. Became hero of radical labor movement.

Hill, John. 1707?–1775. English botanist. Apothecary and contributor to periodicals; edited monthly *British Magazine* (1746–50). Author of *General Natural History* (1748–52), *British Herbal* (1756), 26-vol. *Vegetable System* (1759–75), which introduced Linnaean taxonomic system to England.

Hill, Matthew Davenport. 1792–1872. English lawyer and penologist. M.P. (1832–35); judge in Birmingham (1839–65); advocate of reforms in treatment of criminals as release on good behavior, life terms without hope of parole for incorrigibles; ideas incorporated into Penal Servitude Acts (1853, 1864). Author of *Suggestions for the Repression of Crime* (1857), etc.

Hill, Octavia. 1838–1912. English reformer. Leader in promoting improvements in housing conditions in poorer districts of London and active manager of housing projects (from 1864); with Edward Denison founded (1869) Charity Organization Society; a leader in open-air movement and a founder (1895) of National Trust for Places of Historic Interest or Natural Beauty.

Hill, Patty Smith. 1868–1946. American educator, b. Anchorage, Ky. Kindergarten teacher (from 1889); introduced new methods and materials as alternative to doctrinaire Froebelian system; lecturer (1904–05), professor (1906–35), Columbia U. Teachers Coll.; president, International Kindergarten Union (1908); advocate of nursery school movement; invented Patty Hill blocks. Author of *Song Stories for the Kindergarten* (with sister Mildred J. Hill, 1893; contained original version of "Happy Birthday to You"), *Conduct Curriculum for the Kindergarten and First Grade* (1923), etc.

Hill, Rowland. 1744–1833. English evangelist. Ordained (1773) but denied priestly orders in Anglican church owing to his irregular preaching; built Surrey Chapel, London (1783) and attracted large audiences; helped found Religious Tract Society, British and Foreign Bible Society, London Missionary Society. Author of popular *Village Dialogues* (1801).

Hill, Rowland. 1st Viscount Hill. 1772–1842. British soldier. Distinguished himself in Peninsular campaign, esp. at Arroyomolinos de Montánchez (1811) and Almaraz (1812), and at Waterloo (1815); general (1825); commander in chief in England (1828–42); created viscount (1842).

Hill, Sir Rowland. 1795–1879. English postal reformer. Schoolmaster for many years; a founder of Society for Diffusion of Useful Knowledge (1826). Began advocacy of postal reform with pamphlet submitted to Lord Melbourne, *Post Office Reform; its Importance and Practicability* (1837); advocated uniform low rates, prepayment by means of postage stamps; secured adoption of penny postage in the budget (1839); on post office staff (1840–42); secretary to postmaster general (1846); secretary to the post office (1854–64).

Hil·le·brand \ˈhil-ə-ˌbränt\, Joseph. 1788–1871. German philosopher and historian. Professor, Heidelberg (1817–22), Giessen (1822–50). Author of *Die Anthropologie als Wissenschaft* (1822–23), *Philosophie des Geistes* (1835), *Die deutsche Nationalliteratur seit dem Anfang des 18. Jahrhunderts* (1845). His son ¶Karl (1829–1884) was a journalist and historian; fled to Paris after taking part in Baden uprising (1849). Author of *Zeiten, Völker und Menschen*

(1874–85), *Geschichte Frankreichs von der Thronbesteigung Ludwig Philipps bis zum Fall Napoleons III* (1877–79).

Hil·le·brand \ˈhil-ə-ˌbrand\, William Francis. 1853–1925. American chemist, b. Honolulu. Chemist, U.S. Geological Survey (1880–1908); chief chemist, Bureau of Standards (1908–25).

Hil·le·gas \ˈhil-ə-gəs\, Michael. 1729–1804. American merchant, b. Philadelphia. Made fortune in sugar refining and iron manufacturing. First treasurer of the U.S. (1777–89).

Hil·lel \ˈhil-əl, -ˌel\. 1st century B.C.–1st century A.D. Jewish sage. Entered Palestine from Babylonia and gained recognition as an authority on interpretation of biblical law; first teacher to formulate definite hermeneutic principles; a leader of exemplary virtue who strongly affected Jewish life and outlook.

Hillel ben Sam·uel \-ben-ˈsam-y(ə-w)əl\. *Also called* El-Al ben Sha·char \el-ˈal-ben-ˈshäk-är\. c.1220–c.1295. Italian? Talmudist and physician. Staunch defender of Maimonides against Averroists. Criticized Averroës and upheld immortality of soul in *Tagmule ha-nefesh.*

Hil·ler \ˈhil-ər\, Ferdinand. 1811–1885. German pianist and composer. Conductor, Gewandhaus concerts, Leipzig (1843–44), Düsseldorf Orchestra (1847–50); organizer and director of the Conservatory of Music, Cologne (1850–84). Composer of operas, symphonies, oratorios, cantatas, etc.; author of *Aus dem Tonleben unserer Zeit* (1867–76).

Hiller, Johann Adam. 1728–1804. German composer. Founder and director (1781–85) of the Gewandhaus concerts, Leipzig. Composer of operettas, a symphony, orchestral music, choral works, and songs. Influential in establishing the *Singspiel* and the *Lied* as opposed to the Italian operatic aria.

Ḥil·lī, al- \al-kil-ˈē\. *More completely* Jamāl ad-Dīn Ḥasan ibn Yūsuf ibn ʿAlī ibn Muṭhahhar al-Ḥillī. 1250–1325. Iraqi theologian. A leading theologian of Shiʿite doctrine; emigrated to Iran (1305); converted (1305) Öljeytü, eighth ruler of Il-Khan dynasty, to Shiʿism, which was then proclaimed state religion. Author of *al-Bāb al-ḥādī ʿashar* and *Sharḥ tajrīd al-iʿtiqād.*

Hil·liard \ˈhil-yərd\, Nicholas. 1547–1619. English goldsmith and painter. Goldsmith, carver, and limner to Queen Elizabeth (from c.1570); founder of English school of miniature painting. Author of *Treatise on the Arte of Limning* (c.1600). His son ¶Laurence (c.1582–1640) was also a miniaturist; succeeded father as limner to James I (from 1619).

Hill·man \ˈhil-mən\, Sidney. 1887–1946. American labor leader, b. Žagarė, Lithuania. To U.S. (1907); organizer among textile workers; president, Amalgamated Clothing Workers of America (from 1914); vice president of CIO; chairman of executive council, Textile Workers' Union of America (from 1939); codirector (with William S. Knudsen), Office of Production Management (1941); head of labor division, War Production Board (1942); vice chairman, World Federation of Trade Unions (1945–46).

Hill·quit \ˈhil-(ˌ)kwit\, Morris. 1869–1933. American lawyer and Socialist leader, b. Riga, Latvia. To U.S. (1866); practiced law in New York (from 1893). Joined Socialist party (1888); Socialist candidate for mayor of New York (1917, 1932). Author of *History of Socialism in the United States* (1903), etc.

Hil·ton \ˈhilt-ᵊn\, Conrad Nicholson. 1887–1979. American hotelier, b. San Antonio, N.M. Bought hotel in Cisco, Tex. (1919), later adding others in Dallas, Fort Worth, Waco; built or acquired hotels in major U.S. cities; formed Hilton Hotels Corp. (1946), Hilton International (1949); acquired Statler chain (1954); retired (1966). Author of autobiography *Be My Guest* (1957).

Hilton, James. 1900–1954. English novelist. Author of *Lost Horizon* (1933), *Goodbye, Mr. Chips* (1934), *We Are Not Alone* (1937), *To You, Mr. Chips* (1938), *Random Harvest* (1941).

Hilton, Walter. c.1340–1396. English religious and mystic. Augustinian prior; author of long-popular treatise on asceticism and contemplation, *The Scale* (or *Ladder*) *of Perfection.*

Hi·me·ri·us \hi-ˈmi(ə)r-ē-əs, hī-\. c.315–c.386. Greek Sophist and rhetorician. Called to Antioch (362 A.D.) to be secretary to Emperor Julian. Established school of rhetoric in Athens; teacher and practitioner of florid style.

Hi·mi·ko \hē-mē-kō\. *Also known as* Pi·mi·ko \pē-mē-kō\, Pi·mi·ku \-kü\ *or* Ya·ma·to-Hi·me-Mi·ko·to \yä-mä-tō-hē-mem-ē-kō-tō\. 1st century B.C. Japanese ruler. By tradition, daughter of Emperor Suinin; earliest Japanese ruler known certainly to history; supposed to have built Great Shrine of Ise.

Hi·mil·co \hə-ˈmil-(ˌ)kō\. fl. c.450 B.C. Carthaginian navigator. Explored coast of Europe north from Gades (Cádiz) as far as Britain and Ireland, perhaps in search of Cornish tin mines; believed by some to have sailed as far as the Sargasso Sea.

Himilco. 5th–4th century B.C. Carthaginian general. Son of Hanno. Commanded expedition against Sicily (406 B.C.); led second expedition (396) and, after initial successes, was forced to capitulate by Dionysius; committed suicide.

Himm·ler \ˈhim-lər\, Heinrich. 1900–1945. German politician. Took part in Munich Putsch (1923); joined Nazi party (1925); Reich director of propaganda (1926–30); leader of Schutzstaffel (1929–45); chief of the Gestapo (1936–45); in charge of establishment of concentration camps and internment of Jews and others; directed extermination campaign (1941–45); minister of interior (1943); second only to Hitler in power; chief of home front and of Wehrmacht inside Germany (1944–45); attempted to negotiate surrender of Germany (Apr. 1945); captured by British; committed suicide.

Hincks \ˈhiŋks\, Sir Francis. 1807–1885. Canadian journalist and politician, b. Cork, Ireland. To Canada (1831); worked in bank; founded (1837) Toronto *Examiner,* merged (1855) with *Toronto Globe;* M.P. (1841–54); receiver general (1842–43), inspector general (1848–51); prime minister of Canada (1851–54); governor of Barbados and Windward Islands (1855–62), and of British Guiana (1862–69); again Canadian M.P. (1869–74); finance minister (1869–73).

Hinc·mar \aⁿk-mȧr, *Angl* ˈhiŋk-ˌmär\ of Reims \raⁿs\. c.806–882. French prelate. Archbishop of Reims (845); prominent in political and religious issues of his period; at various times opposed emperor and pope over jurisdictional questions; opposed Gottschalk's predestinarian doctrines. Author of controversial treatises, as *Ad reclusos et simplices, De predestinatione Dei et libero arbitrio,* and of a continuation (from 861) of *Annales Bertiniani.*

Hind \ˈhīnd\, Henry Youle. 1823–1908. Canadian geologist and explorer, b. Nottingham, England. To Canada (1846); professor, Trinity Coll., Toronto (1853–64); geologist on government expeditions to Red River (1858), Labrador (1861); surveyed New Brunswick (1864), Nova Scotia goldfields (1869–71).

Hin·de·mith \ˈhin-də-(ˌ)mit\, Paul. 1895–1963. German composer. Concertmeister, Frankfurt (1915–23); professor, Berlin (1927–35); forced by Nazi condemnation to leave Germany; taught at Ankara, Turkey (1935–37), Yale U. (1940–53), Zürich (1951–58). A leading musical theorist; sought in criticism, teaching, and composition to revive tonality; developed idea of *Gebrauchmusik,* pieces composed for everyday practical occasions in a workmanlike manner. Compositions included operas *Sancta Susanna* (1921), *Cardillac* (1926), *Neues vom Tage* (1928–29), *Mathis der Maler* (1934), *Die Harmonie der Welt* (1956–57), *The Long Christmas Dinner* (1960); vocal music as song cycles *Die junge Magd* (1922), *Das Marienleben* (1923), *Nine English Songs* (1942–44); orchestral works as *Kammermusik* series (1922–27); chamber works, esp. series of sonatas for various instruments (1917–55). Author of *Unterweisung im Tonsatz* (1937–39), etc.

Hin·den·burg \ˈhin-dən-ˌbu̇rk, *Angl* ˈhin-dən-ˌbərg\, Karl Friedrich. 1741–1808. German mathematician. Professor, Leipzig (1781–1808); credited with being originator of combinatorial analysis.

Hindenburg, Paul von. *Full name* Paul Ludwig Hans Anton von Be·neck-en-dorff \ˈben-ə-kən-ˌdȯrf\ und von Hindenburg. 1847–1934. German general and politician. Fought in Seven Weeks' War (1866), Franco–Prussian War (1870–71); member of general staff (1877); commanding general of 4th army corps (1903); retired (1911). Summoned at beginning of World War I (1914) to command army in East Prussian campaign; won complete victory over Russians at Tannenberg (1914); made field marshal general (1914). In command in successful campaign against Russia in Poland (1915); promoted to chief of staff (1916) to succeed von Falkenhayn; with Ludendorff, directed all German strategy for remainder of war (1917–18); retired (1919). Wrote autobiography *Aus meinem Leben* (1920); took no part in politics of the Reich (1919–25). Elected second president of Weimar Republic (1925–32); sought unity of German nation; approved Treaty of Locarno and Germany's admission to League of Nations; reelected president (1932–34), defeating Adolf Hitler at the polls; forced to yield to Nazis by appointing Hitler as chancellor (1933).

Hine \ˈhīn\, Lewis Wickes. 1874–1940. American photographer, b. Oshkosh, Wis. Photographer in New York City (from 1905); made photographic study of Ellis Island immigrants (1905); made study of children in industry (1907–09); on staff of *Charities and the Commons* (later *Survey*) magazine (1909–18), in which appeared many of his pioneering picture stories; recorded American Red Cross relief work in World War I; recorded progress of construction of Empire State Building in *Men At Work* (1932).

Hines \ˈhīnz\, Duncan. 1880–1959. American food critic and writer, b. Bowling Green, Ky. Worked as traveling salesman for various firms; as hobby kept notebook of notable restaurants encountered across U.S.; compiled and published *Adventures in Good Eating* (1936 and regularly updated thereafter). Also wrote *Lodging for a Night* (1938), *Adventures in Good Cooking* (1939), *Duncan Hines' Vacation Guide* (1948).

Hines, Earl Kenneth. *Known as* Fatha Hines. 1905–1983. American pianist, b. Duquesne, Pa. Performed in 1920s with big bands of Lois B. Deppe and Louis Armstrong; led his own band (1928–47); rejoined briefly (1948) Armstrong's All Stars but formed (1951) his own sextet; toured from 1950s throughout Europe, U.S. and Japan. A seminal figure in jazz; originated "trumpet style" of piano playing in which he produced hornlike solo lines in octaves with his right hand while stating the harmony with his left; recordings included "Rosetta," "My Monday Date," "Fifty-Seven Varieties."

Hines, Frank Thomas. 1879–1960. American army officer and administrator, b. Salt Lake City. Served in army (1898–99, 1901–20); chief of embarkation service (1918–19), responsible for transporting over 2,000,000 soldiers to Europe and bringing them home again; brigadier general (1920). Head of U.S. Veterans Bureau (1923–30) and of reorganized Veterans Administration (1930–45); ambassador to Panama (1945–48).

Hines, Walker Downer. 1870–1934. American lawyer and administrator, b. Russellville, Ky. On staff of Louisville & Nashville Railroad (1890–1904), Atchison, Topeka & Santa Fe (1906–18); U.S. director general of railroads (1919–20). Author of *War History of American Railroads* (1928).

Hin·kle \'hiŋ-kəl\, Beatrice, *nee* Moses. 1874–1953. American psychiatrist, b. San Francisco. m. Walter Scott Hinkle (1892; d. 1899). To New York (1905); with Dr. Charles R. Dana, opened first psychotherapeutic clinic in America, at Cornell Medical College, New York City (1908). Author of *The Recreating of the Individual* (1923).

Hinkmar. See HINCMAR.

Hinkson, Katharine Tynan. See TYNAN.

Hin·schi·us \'hin-shē-u̇s\, Paul. 1835–1898. German jurist. Professor, Halle (1863–65), Berlin (1865–68), Kiel (1868–72), Berlin (1872–98); member of Reichstag (1872–78, 1880–81). Author of *Decretales Pseudo-Isidorianae et Capitula Angilramni* (1863), *Das Kirchenrecht der Katholiken und Protestanten in Deutschland* (1869–97), etc.

Hin·shel·wood \'hin-shəl-,wu̇d\, Sir Cyril Norman. 1897–1967. English chemist. Professor, Oxford (1937–64); awarded Nobel prize for chemistry (1956) with N. Semyonov for research on reaction rates and mechanisms, esp. of the oxygen–hydrogen reaction.

Hins·ley \'hinz-lē\, Arthur. 1865–1943. English prelate. Rector of the English College at Rome (1917–28); archbishop of Westminster (from 1935); created cardinal (1937); outspoken leader of opposition to fascist powers.

Hint·ze \'hint-sə\, Paul von. 1864–1941. German naval officer and diplomat. Ambassador to Mexico (1911–14), Peking (1914–15), Oslo (1915–18); foreign secretary (1918) until fall of the empire.

Hip·par·chus \hə-'pär-kəs\. d. 514 B.C. Tyrant of Athens (527–514 B.C.). Son of Pisistratus and brother of Hippias, with whom he ruled jointly; assassinated by Harmodius and Aristogiton (*qq.v.* at HARMODIUS).

Hipparchus. *Also spelled* Hipparchos. fl. 146–127 B.C. Greek astronomer. Discovered precession of the equinoxes; compiled first catalogue of stars, containing some 850; developed trigonometry; devised method of locating geographical positions on the earth by giving their latitude and longitude. Considered greatest astronomer of antiquity.

Hip·pa·sus \'hip-ə-səs\ of Met·a·pon·tum \,met-ə-'pän-təm\. fl. c.500 B.C. Greek philosopher. Follower of Pythagoras; held that fire is chief element; supposed to have been drowned for revealing a mathematical secret of Pythagorean brotherhood.

Hip·pel \'hip-əl\, Theodor Gottlieb von. 1741–1796. German writer. Mayor of Königsberg (1780 ff.); friend of Kant. Author of novels *Lebensläufe nach aufsteigender Linie* (1778–81), *Kreuz- und Querzüge des Ritters A bis Z* (1793–94), essays *Über die Ehe* (1774), *Über die bürgerliche Verbesserung der Weiber* (1792), etc.

Hip·pi·as \'hip-ē-əs\. d. 490 B.C. Tyrant of Athens (528 or 527–510 B.C.). Son of Pisistratus and brother of Hipparchus (*q.v.*), with whom he shared the administration; ruled with great severity after assassination of Hipparchus (514); forced into exile by Spartans under Cleomenes I (510).

Hippias of Elis \ē-ləs\. 5th century B.C. Greek Sophist. Lectured in Athens on mathematics, music, astronomy, and politics; invented a curve (later termed "quadratrix of Dinostratus") used in connection with the problem of subdivision of an angle.

Hippius. See MEREZHKOVSKY.

Hip·poc·ra·tes \hip-'äk-rə-,tēz\. c.460–c.377 B.C. Greek physician, b. Cos. Known as "Father of Medicine." Little is known of his life; highly regarded by contemporaries; probably taught medicine at Cos; traditionally but incorrectly credited with Hippocratic oath administered to graduate physicians; author perhaps of some of the 60 or 70 treatises of the Hippocratic Collection, brought together and edited at Alexandria (2d–3d century A.D.).

Hippocrates of Chi·os \'kē-,äs, -əs\. fl. c.460 B.C. Greek geometer. Author of earliest known work on elements of geometry (not extant), perhaps used by Euclid.

Hip·pod·a·mus \hip-'äd-ə-məs\. 5th century B.C. Greek architect. Commissioned by Pericles to lay out the Piraeus; later, planned colonial town of Thurii and laid out city of Rhodes.

Hippolithus a Lapide. See Bogislaw von CHEMNITZ.

Hip·pol·y·tus \hip-'äl-ət-əs\. Saint. c.170–c.235. Christian martyr and antipope. Leader of Roman church; advocate of Logos doctrine; attacked Pope St. Zephyrinus as modalist and was elected antipope by followers (217 or 218) in first schism of Roman church; finally reconciled with Pope Pontianus (235) while both exiled to mines of Sardinia by Emperor Maximinus. Author of *Philosophumena* on pagan origin of heresies and probably of *Apostolic Tradition,* a liturgical order.

Hip·pon \'hip-,än, -ən\. *Also known as* Hip·po \'hip-(,)ō\ *or* Hip·po·nax \hə-'pō-,naks\. fl. c.450 B.C. Greek philosopher. Revived theory of Thales that water is principal element; ascribed disease and death to drying up of natural moisture of body.

Hip·po·nax \hə-'pō-,naks\. 6th century B.C. Greek poet. Famous for scurrilous and vituperative verse; reputed inventor of the choliamb.

Hi·ram \'hī-rəm\ *or* **Hu·ram** \'hyü-rəm\ *or* **Ahir·am** \ə-'hir-,äm\. 989?–936 B.C. King of Tyre (969–936 B.C.). Improved port of Tyre; friend of Solomon and David; furnished cedar timber and skilled workmen for building of Solomon's temple and David's palace.

Hi·ra·ta \hē-rä-tä\ Atsutane. *Orig. surname* Ōwa·da \ō-wä-dä\. *Also known as* Han·be-e \hän-be-e\, Ma·su·ge-no-ya \mä-su̇g-en-ō-yä\, Ibu·ki-no-ya \ē-bu̇k-ē-nō-yä\. 1776–1843. Japanese scholar. Strongly influenced by Moto-ori Norinaga; works contributed to strengthening of Restoration Shintō and of national sentiment and prepared way for abolition of shogunate.

Hires \'hī(ə)rz\, Charles Elmer. 1851–1937. American businessman, b. near Bridgeton, N.J. Introduced soft drink named root beer at Centennial Exposition, Philadelphia (1876); incorporated Charles E. Hires Co. (1890), president (1890–1937).

Hirn \ērn\, Gustave-Adolphe. 1815–1890. French physicist. Known for researches in thermodynamics, esp. on the mechanical equivalent of heat, and for improvements in steam engine design.

Hi·ro·shi·ge \hē-rō-shē-ge\. *Full name* An·dō \än-dō\ Hiroshige. *Professional names* Ut·a·ga·wa \u̇t-ä-gä-wä\ Hiroshige *and* Ichi·yū·sai \ē-chē-yu̇s-ī\ Hiroshige. 1797–1858. Japanese artist. Last great master of *Ukiyo-e* color woodblock print; known for landscapes in such series as *Fifty-three Stages of the Tōkaidō, Views of Kyōto, Sixty-nine Stations of the Kiso Highway.*

Hirsau *or* **Hirschau.** See WILHELM VON HIRSAU.

Hirsch \'hirsh\, Moritz von. Freiherr von Hirsch auf Ge·reuth \,au̇f-gə-'ròit\. *Fr.* Maurice de Hirsch \də-ērsh\. 1831–1896. German businessman and philanthropist. Amassed fortune in banking and in building Balkan railroad to Constantinople. Interested himself in improving conditions of Jews, esp. those of Middle East and Russia; founded and financed Jewish Colonization Assoc. "to assist and promote the emigration of Jews from any part of Europe or Asia... to any part of the world"; initiated the Baron de Hirsch Fund (incorporated in New York, 1891) to assist Jewish immigrants in U.S. to find employment and homes, learn mechanical trades, etc.

Hirsch, Samson Raphael. 1808–1888. German theologian. Rabbi at Oldenburg, Emden, Nikolsburg, Frankfurt; evolved Separatist or Neo-Orthodox position in response to Reform Judaism. Author of *Neunzehn Briefe über Judenthum* (1836), biblical commentaries, etc.

Hirsch \'hərsh\, Samuel. 1815–1889. American clergyman and theologian, b. Thalfang, Germany. Rabbi at Dessau (1838–41); chief rabbi of Luxembourg (1843–66); to U.S. (1866); rabbi of Congregation Keneseth Israel, Philadelphia (1866–88); a chief formulator and leader of Reform Judaism. Author of *Religionsphilosophie der Juden* (1842).

Hirsh·horn \'hərsh-,(h)ò(ə)rn\, Joseph Herman. 1899–1981. American financier and art collector, b. Mitau, Latvia. To U.S. (1905); became office boy on Wall street (1913); built fortune in mining and petroleum stocks; largely created uranium-mining industry in Canada. Amassed large collection of mainly modern paintings and sculptures; donated collection to U.S. (1965) and built Hirshhorn Museum (opened 1974) in Washington, D.C., to house it.

Hirt \'hirt\, Hermann. 1865–1936. German philologist. Professor, Giessen (1912–36); studied Germanic and Celtic languages and esp. Indo-European. Author of *Die Indogermanen* (1905–07), *Indogermanische Grammatik* (1921–37).

Hir·ti·us \'hər-shē-əs\, Aulus. c.90–43 B.C. Roman historian and politician. Friend of Julius Caesar and Cicero; served under Caesar in Gaul; praetor (46 B.C.); governor of transalpine Gaul (45); consul (43); supported senatorial party after Caesar's assassination and was killed in action at Mutina. Reputed author of parts of the continuations of Caesar's *Commentaries,* notably the 8th book of the Gallic War and the history of the Alexandrian War.

His \'his\, Wilhelm. 1831–1904. German anatomist. Professor, Basel (1857–72), Leipzig (1872–1904); invented (1865) microtome; known for researches on the embryological development of various tissues, esp. nervous system. Author of *Anatomie menschlicher Embryonen* (1880–85). His son ¶Wilhelm (1863–1934), physician, was director of the first medical clinic and professor of internal medicine, U. of Berlin (1907–26); investigated the nervous system of the vertebrate heart; discovered (1893) His's bundle, composed of nerve fibers connecting the auricles with the ventricles.

Ḥis·dai ibn Sha·prut \ḵis-'dī-,ib-ən-shäp-'rüt\. *Also spelled* Ḥas·dai \ḵäs-'dī\. *In full* Ḥisdai Abu Yusuf ben Isaac ben Ezra ibn Shaprut. c.915–?975. Spanish physician. Court physician and de facto vizier to Caliph 'Abd ar-Raḥmān III; undertook numerous diplomatic missions; helped translate into Arabic pharmacological text of Dioscorides given to caliph by Byzantine emperor; patronized Hebrew scholars and literary figures, fostered Talmudic studies, and helped inaugurate golden age of Hebrew letters in Spain.

Hi·shām \hē-'shäm\. Name of three Umayyad rulers of Córdoba:

Hishām I. 757–796. Emir (788–796). Son of 'Abd ar-Raḥmān I; led expeditions against Franks; completed Great Mosque of Córdoba.

Hishām II. 965–1013. Caliph (976–1013). Dominated by al-Manṣūr (to 1002) and his son; driven from throne (1009–10) by Muḥammad II but restored.

Hishām III. 975–1036. Caliph (1027–31). Last Umayyad caliph of Córdoba.

Hishām ibn 'Abd al-Ma·lik \-ˌib-ən-əb-'dụl-mä-'lēk\. 691–743. Tenth caliph of Islām (724–743). Worked to consolidate empire and esp. to reconcile northern and southern Arabs; reign marked last of period of peace and prosperity of Umayyad dynasty.

Hishām ibn al-Kal·bi \-ˌib-ən-ək-kal-'bē\ *or* **Hishām ibn Mu·ḥam·mad al-Kalbī** \-mụ-'kam-məd-\. *Also called* Abū al-Mun·dhir \-al-mụ̇nd-'hir\. before 747–819 or 821. Arab scholar. Followed father in collecting and studying oral traditions; author of works on early customs, battles, etc., and notably *al-Khayl* on famous horses, *Jamharat an-nasab* on pre-Islāmic and early Muslim politics, literature, etc., and *Kitāb al-aṣnām* on pre-Islāmic idolatry.

Hi·shi·da \hē-shē-dä\ Shunsō. 1874–1911. Japanese painter. With Yokoyama Taikan helped revitalize traditional Japanese painting; influenced by Western Impressionism.

Hi·shi·ka·wa \hē-shē-kä-wä\ Moronobu. *Known as* Ki·chi·bē \kē-chē-bē\. 1618–c.1694. Japanese artist. First great master of *Ukiyo-e* art, both in painting and in woodblock prints; noted esp. for pictures of courtesans and of Kabuki theater.

Hi·sing·er \'hē-siŋ-ər\, Wilhelm. 1766–1852. Swedish chemist, geologist, and mineralogist. With Berzelius, discovered (1803) element cerium.

His·ti·ae·us \ˌhis-tə-'ē-əs\. d. 494 B.C. Tyrant of Miletus, under the Persian king Darius I. Recalled to Susa by Darius in alarm at his power in Ionia; allowed to leave Susa on mission to suppress a rebellion in Ionia. Established himself, perhaps as a pirate, at Byzantium; captured by Harpagus and crucified at Sardis by Artaphernes.

Hita, Ginés Pérez de. See Ginés PÉREZ DE HITA.

Hitch·cock \'hich-ˌkäk\, Sir Alfred Joseph. 1899–1980. English film director. First film *The Pleasure Garden* (1925), followed by *The Lodger* (1926), *Blackmail* (1929; first successful British talking picture), *The Skin Game* (1932), *The 39 Steps* (1935), *The Lady Vanishes* (1938); worked in Hollywood (from 1939); became known as master of suspense and film technique with *Rebecca* (1940, Academy Award), *Suspicion* (1941), *Spellbound* (1944), *Notorious* (1946), *Strangers on a Train* (1951), *Dial M for Murder* (1954), *Rear Window* (1954), *Vertigo* (1958), *North by Northwest* (1959), *Psycho* (1960), *The Birds* (1963), *Torn Curtain* (1966), *Topaz* (1969), *Frenzy* (1972), *Family Plot* (1976). Host of television mystery program (1955–65); edited anthologies of mystery stories.

Hitchcock, Edward. 1793–1864. American geologist, b. Deerfield, Mass. Professor, Amherst (1825–45, 1854–64); president (1845–54). Conducted geological survey of Massachusetts (1830–33, 1837–41); investigated dinosaur tracks in Connecticut Valley sandstone; state geologist of Vermont (1856–61). Author of *Fossil Footsteps* (1848), *Religion of Geology* (1851), *Illustrations of Surface Geology* (1857).

Hitchcock, Frank Harris. 1869–1935. American politician, b. Amherst, Ohio. Campaign manager for William H. Taft (1908); U.S. postmaster general (1909–13); instituted economies, eliminated deficit; established postal savings banks and parcel post, and started first air mail service (Garden City–Mineola, N.Y., 1911).

Hitchcock, Lambert. 1795–1852. American cabinetmaker, b. Cheshire, Conn. Established furniture factory in Barkhamsted (1818); best known for his design and manufacture of Hitchcock chairs.

Hitchcock, Thomas, Jr. 1900–1944. American sportsman, b. Aiken, S.C. Generally regarded as greatest polo player of all time; achieved 10-goal rating (1922–34, 1936–40); member of U.S. National Open championship team (1923, 1927, 1935, 1936), of U. S. Westchester Cup-winning teams (1921, 1924, 1927, 1930, 1939). Served in Lafayette Escadrille in World War I; commander of fighter group in England (1942–44); killed in crash.

Hit·ler \'hit-lər\, Adolf. 1889–1945. German politician and Führer (leader), b. Upper Austria. Frustrated in efforts to become an artist; to Munich (1913); served in World War I in Bavarian regiment and received Iron Cross. Joined (1919) German Workers' party, which was renamed (1920) Nationalsozialistische Deutsche Arbeiterpartei (National Socialist German Workers' party, known as the Nazi party); party president (from 1921); editor of party organ *Der völkische Beobachter;* with Ernst Röhm organized private army Sturmabteilung (SA, 1921). With Gen. Ludendorff organized unsuccessful revolt in Munich (Nov. 8–9, 1923) known as "Beer Hall Putsch"; sentenced to five years' imprisonment but paroled after nine months (1924). In prison, dictated to his secretary, Rudolf Hess, *Mein Kampf* (1925–27). Rebuilt party, secured financial backing of several industrialists, and achieved mass popularity; defeated by Hindenburg in presidential election (1932); displayed great political skill; swept into power (1933) on rising tide of German nationalism and economic discontent; named chancellor by Hindenburg (Jan. 1933); gained control of Reichstag in new election; granted by it (Mar. 1933) dictatorial powers for four years by constitutional amendments; gained support of army by executing Röhm and dissolving SA; on death of Hindenburg (Aug. 1934), united presidential office and chancellorship, assuming title Der Führer. With associates Göring, Goebbels, Himmler, Streicher, etc., established regime of terror based on philosophy of superiority of Aryan (German) race and infallibility of Führer; inaugurated violent anti-Semitic policy; established new economic program; undertook rearmament program under cover of various peace proposals; broke conditions of Versailles Treaty; reoccupied Rhineland zone (Mar. 1936); established Berlin–Rome Axis with Mussolini regime (1936), formed pact with Japan (1936); annexed Austria (Mar. 1938), the Sudetenland (Oct. 1938), all of Czechoslovakia (Mar. 1939); made nonaggression pact with Russia (Aug. 1939). By invading Poland (Sept. 1, 1939) brought on general war; conquered Denmark, Norway, the Netherlands, Belgium, France (1940), Greece (1941); failed to conquer Britain in air war (1940); undertook campaigns in North Africa, Balkans; invaded Russia (June 1941); declared war on U.S. (Dec. 1941). Ordered creation of system of concentration and extermination camps to hold and murder millions of Jews, political enemies, etc. Early military successes followed by failures in Russia, Africa, Italy; became increasingly reclusive; survived several assassination attempts; when inevitability of defeat finally borne in on him, committed suicide in chancellery bunker on eve of Russian occupation of Berlin.

Hitotsubashi. See under TOKUGAWA family.

Hit·ti \'hit-ē\, Philip Khuri. 1886–1978. American Orientalist, b. Shimlan, Lebanon. To U.S. (1913, naturalized 1919); taught at Columbia (1915–19), Beirut (1919–26), Princeton (1926–54). Author of *The Origins of the Islamic State* (1916), *Syria and the Syrians* (1926), *History of the Arabs* (1937), *Lebanon in History* (1957), *The Near East in History* (1961), *History of the Arabs* (1967), etc.

Hit·torf \'hit-ˌȯrf\, Johann Wilhelm. 1824–1914. German physicist. Professor, Münster (1852–90); pioneer in electrochemical research; investigated the migration of ions during electrolysis, developed expressions for and measured transport numbers; studied electrical phenomena in rarefied gases, the Hittorf tube being named for him; determined a number of properties of cathode rays, including (before Crookes) the deflection of the rays by a magnet.

Hit·torff \ē-tȯrf\, Jacques-Ignace. 1792–1867. French architect. Government architect in Paris (from 1830); built church of Saint Vincent de Paul (1832) and various public and private buildings; designed embellishments for the Place de la Concorde, Champs-Élysées, and Avenue de l'Étoile.

Hit·zig \'hit-ˌsik\, Eduard, *in full* Julius Eduard. 1838–1907. German physiologist. Professor and director of psychiatric clinic, Zürich (1875–79), Halle (1879–1903); demonstrated conclusively (1870) localization of functions of cerebral cortex; founder of electrophysiology.

Ḥi·wi al-Bal·khī \'kē-vē-ab-bal-'kē\. *Also spelled* Hivi. 9th century. Jewish theologian of Persia. Author of 200 criticisms of the Hebrew Bible, known now only through refutation, as by Sa'adia ben Joseph.

Hjär·ne \'yer-nə\, Harold Gabriel. 1848–1922. Swedish historian. Professor, Uppsala (1885–1913); member of Riksdag (1902–08, 1909–18).

Hjelm \'yelm\, Peter Jacob. 1746–1813. Swedish chemist. Master of assaying, Royal Mint (1782); director of chemical laboratories, bureau of mines (1794); discovered (1782) element molybdenum.

Hjort \'jȯrt\, Johan. 1869–1948. Norwegian biologist. Founder and director (1900–16), Norwegian government fisheries; professor, Oslo (1921–39); known for studies of fish populations and migration, esp. of Atlantic herring.

Hlin·ka \'hliŋ-kä\, Andrej. 1864–1938. Slovak clergyman and patriot. Roman Catholic priest; imprisoned (1906–10) for Slovak nationalist activities; founder and leader of the Slovakian People's party and founder of its journal *Slovák;* opposed policy of unification with Bohemia, and presented a memorandum to the Versailles Peace Conference (1919) demanding a plebiscite in Slovakia; desisted (1926) from continued opposition to unification, but pressed for autonomy in the new Czechoslovak state; became tool of German and Magyar opposition.

Hlo·the·re \'(h)lō-thə-rə\. d. 685. Anglo-Saxon king of Kent (673–685). Succeeded brother Egbert; may have ruled jointly with Egbert's son Eadric; with Eadric issued important code of laws; quarreled with Eadric, and mortally wounded in battle with him.

Ho \hō\ Ryong. *Also known as* So·ch'i \sō-chē\, *i.e.* Little Fool. 1809–1892. Korean painter and calligrapher. Executed highly popular renditions of flowers and trees in style drawn from traditional Chinese academic style; resisted Japanese influences; master of traditional Korean *ch'usa* calligraphy.

Hoar \'hō(ə)r, 'hȯ(ə)r\, Samuel. 1778–1856. American lawyer and politician, b. Lincoln, Mass. Practiced, Concord, Mass.; member, U.S. House of Representatives (1835–37). Sent by Massachusetts to South Carolina to test constitutionality of certain South Carolina laws prohibiting free Negroes (as seamen of Massachusetts vessels) from entering state (1844); forcibly expelled from South Carolina in accordance with vote of South Carolina legislature; helped found Republican party in Massachusetts (1855). His son ¶Ebenezer Rockwood (1816–1895), b. Concord, Mass., was a jurist; on Massachusetts Supreme Court (1859–69); U.S. attorney general (1869–70); member, U.S. House of Representatives (1873–75). Another son ¶George Frisbie (1826–1904), b. Concord, served in U.S. House of Representatives (1869–77), U.S. Senate (1877–1904); championed civil service reform. Wrote *Autobiography of Seventy Years* (1903).

Hoard \'hō(ə)rd, 'hȯ(ə)rd\, William Dempster. 1836–1918. American publisher and agriculturist, b. Munnsville, N.Y. Founded (1870) *Jefferson County Union,* Wisconsin; promoted dairy farming, scientific methods in agriculture, opening new markets for Wisconsin products; founded and edited (1885–1918) *Hoard's Dairyman;* governor of Wisconsin (1889–90).

Hoare \'hō(ə)r, 'hȯ(ə)r\, Sir Samuel John Gurney. 1st Viscount Tem·ple·wood \'tem-pəl-,wu̇d\. 1880–1959. English politician. M.P. (1910–44); secretary of state for air (1922–24, 1924–29, 1940), for India (1931–35), for foreign affairs (1935); attempted to settle Italian claims in Ethiopia with Hoare-Laval plan (1935); first lord of the admiralty (1936–37); secretary of state for home affairs (1937–39); lord privy seal (1939–40); ambassador to Spain (1940–44); created viscount (1944).

Ho·ban \'hō-bən\, James. c.1762–1831. American architect, b. County Kilkenny, Ireland. To America (c.1785); designed South Carolina capitol (1791); designed and supervised construction of the White House, Washington, D.C. (1793–1801; destroyed by the British 1814), and the new White House (1815–29) replacing it.

Ho·bart \'hō-,bärt\, Alice Tisdale. *Nee* Alice Nourse \'nō(ə)rs, 'nȯ(ə)rs\. 1882–1967. American novelist, b. Lockport, N.Y. m. Earle Tisdale Hobart (1914); author of *Pidgin Cargo* (1929), *Oil for the Lamps of China* (1933), *Their Own Country* (1940), *The Cup and the Sword* (1942), *The Cleft Rock* (1948), *Innocent Dreamers* (1964), etc.

Ho·bart \'hō-,bärt, -bərt\, Garret Augustus. 1844–1899. American politician, b. Long Branch, N.J. Vice president of the U.S. (1897–99).

Hobart, John Henry. 1775–1830. American prelate, b. Philadelphia. In New York City founded (1806) Protestant Episcopal Theological Society, forerunner of General Theological Seminary; professor (from 1821); founded Protestant Episcopal Tract Society (1810), Protestant Episcopal Press (1817). Rector, Trinity Church, New York (from 1816); bishop of New York diocese (from 1816).

Hobart-Hamp·den \-'ham(p)-dən\, Augustus Charles. *Known as* Hobart Pa·şa \-'päsh-ə, -'pash-ə\. 1822–1886. English naval officer and adventurer. Son of 6th Earl of Buckinghamshire; in British navy (1835–63); entered Ottoman service (c.1867); given rank of rear admiral and command of fleet; given title paşa for actions in suppressing Cretan insurrection; commanded blockade of Russian ports and mouths of the Danube in Russo–Turkish war (1877–78); apppointed *müşir* (marshal, 1881), first Christian to hold that office.

Hob·be·ma \'hȯb-ə-må\, Meindert *or* Meyndert. 1638–1709. Dutch painter. Studied under Jacob van Ruisdael; became one of leading Baroque landscape painters of day. Among his notable pictures were *The Hermitage, St. Petersburg, Avenue at Middelharnis, Ruins of Brederode Castle, Entrance to a Village, Water Mill.*

Hobbes, John Oliver. See Pearl CRAIGIE.

Hobbes \'häbz\, Thomas. 1588–1679. English philosopher. Associated (from 1608) as tutor and companion with family of dukes of Devonshire; visited Continent several times; an exile in France because of his political convictions (1641–51); tutor to Prince of Wales in Paris (1646). In his travels on Continent, met Galileo, Gassendi, Mersenne; in England was friendly with Bacon, Harvey, Ben Jonson, Cowley, Sidney Godolphin, Selden. Evolved materialist philosophy in which all was conceived of as body in motion; propounded an ethical theory that laid foundation of Utilitarianism; best known for political philosophy, based on idea of social contract, for purpose of security of each individual, and absolute authority of sovereigns. Works included trilogy in Latin *Elementorum philosophiae,* comprising *De cive* (1642), *De corpore* (1655), *De homine* (1658); *Human Nature* (1650), *De corpore politico* (1650), *Leviathan; or the Matter, Forme, and Power of a Commonwealth, Ecclesiasticall and Civil* (1651), *The Questions Concerning Liberty, Necessity, and Chance* (1656); also wrote on geometry and numerous controversial works.

Hobbs \'häbz\, Sir John Berry, *known as* Jack. 1882–1963. English sportsman. Professional cricketer in first-class competition (1905–34); scored 197 centuries and record total of 61,237 runs; played in 61 test matches; first cricketer to be knighted (1953).

Hobertus, Jakob. See OBRECHT.

Hob·house \'häb-,hau̇s\, Emily. 1860–1926. English reformer and social worker. Criticized Boer War and traveled to South Africa (1900, 1901) to investigate mortality rate of Boer women and children in concentration camps; roused public indignation leading to institutional improvements; organized educational programs for women in Orange Free State (1903–08); engaged in relief work in Central Europe during and after World War I.

Hobhouse, John Cam. Baron Brough·ton de Gyf·ford \'brȯt-ᵊn-də-'gif-ərd\. 1786–1869. British politician. Radical M.P. (1820–33, 1835–47, 1848–51); secretary at war (1832–33); chief secretary for Ireland (1833); president, Board of Control (1835–41, 1846–52); created baron (1851). Supposed to have coined phrase "His Majesty's Opposition." Friend and traveling companion of Lord Byron in Spain, Portugal, Greece, and Turkey (1809–10, 1816–17); visited Byron in Switzerland and Italy; as Byron's executor, advised destruction of his memoirs (1824). Author of *Journey through Albania with Lord Byron* (1813); from personal observation, wrote Bonapartist account of the Hundred Days (1816); author also of *Recollections of a Long Life* (1865).

Hobhouse, Leonard Trelawney. 1864–1929. English journalist and philosopher. Taught at Oxford (1887–97); first professor of sociology, London U. (1907–1929); editor of *Sociological Review* (1903 ff.); secretary of Free Trade Union (1903–05). Author of *The Labour Movement* (1893), *The Theory of Knowledge* (1896), *Mind in Evolution* (1901), *Morals in Evolution* (1906), *Development and Purpose* (1913), *Metaphysical Theory of the State* (1918), *The Rational Good* (1921), *The Elements of Social Justice* (1922), *Social Development* (1924).

Hobrecht, Jakob. See OBRECHT.

Hob·son \'häb-sən\, John Atkinson. 1858–1940. English economist. Formulated theory of underconsumption. Author of *Physiology of Industry* (1889), *Evolution of Modern Capitalism* (1894), *The Economics of Distribution* (1900), *Imperialism* (1902), *The Industrial System* (1909), *Work and Wealth* (1914), *Problems of a New World* (1921), *Wealth and Life* (1929), *God and Mammon* (1931), *Democracy* (1934), *Confessions of an Economic Heretic* (1938), etc.

Hobson, Thomas. 1544–1630. English liveryman at Cambridge. His practice of requiring every customer to take the horse which stood nearest the door gave rise to the expression "Hobson's choice."

Ho·by \'hō-bē\, Sir Thomas. 1530–1566. English diplomat and translator. Known for *The Courtyer of Count Baldesser Castilio* (1561), translation of Castiglione's *Il cortegiano* that was highly influential on contemporary manners and language.

Hoc·cleve \'häk-,lēv\ *or* **Oc·cleve** \'äk-\, Thomas. 1368 or 1369–c.1450. English poet. Clerk in the privy seal office. Author of mediocre verse of considerable historical value, including *La Mâle règle* (1406) and *De regimine principum* or *The Regement of Princes* (1411), culled from Aegidius Romanus.

Hoche \ȯsh\, Louis-Lazare. 1768–1797. French Revolutionary soldier. Promoted from corporal (1789) to general of brigade and general of division, commanding the army of the Moselle (1793); raised seige of Landau and drove Austro-Prussian armies from Alsace (1793); imprisoned on charges lodged by rival Gen. Pichegru (1794); as commander of army of Brest, suppressed Vendée uprising (1794–96); commanded army on Rhine, defeating Austrians at Neuwied (1797).

Ho Chi Minh \'hō-'chē-'min, -'shē- \. *Orig.* Nguy·en That Thanh \'nī-ən-'tät-'tän\. 1890–1969. Vietnamese political leader. Lived in London (1915–17), France (1917–23); early an active Vietnamese nationalist; joined French Communist party (1920); in U.S.S.R. (1923–24); organized Vietnamese nationalists in Canton, China (1924–27); founded Indochinese Communist party (1930); in exile in U.S.S.R., Shanghai, Siam (1930–41); adopted name Ho Chi Minh, i.e. He who Enlightens (c.1940); returned to Vietnam, formed Viet Minh (1941); occupied Hanoi and declared Vietnamese independence (1945); president (1945–69). Presided over successful war against French colonial forces (1946–54); chose policy of reuniting North and South Vietnam (1959); presided over war with South and with U.S. (1959–69).

Hock·ing \'häk-iŋ\, Silas Kitto. 1850–1935. English clergyman and novelist. Minister of United Methodist Free church. Novels included *Alec Green* (1878), *Sea Waif* (1882), *Cricket* (1885), *God's Outcast* (1898), *Pioneers* (1905), *Nancy* (1919), *The Mystery Man* (1930), *Gerry Storm* (1934). His brother ¶Joseph (1860–1937), also a clergyman, wrote novels *Jabez Easterbrook* (1891), *Ishmaël Pengelly* (1894), *The Scarlet Woman* (1899), *Woman of Babylon* (1906), *The Trampled Cross* (1907), *The Jesuit* (1911), *Prodigal Daughters* (1922), *Prodigal Parents* (1923), *The Man Who Found Out* (1933).

Hocking, William Ernest. 1873–1966. American philosopher, b. Cleveland, Ohio. Professor, U. of California (1906–08), Yale (1908–14), Harvard (1914–43). Author of *The Meaning of God in Human Experience* (1912), *Man and the State* (1926), *Spirit of World Politics* (1932), *Lasting Elements of Individualism* (1937), *Living Religions and a World Faith* (1940), *The Coming World Civilization* (1956), *Strength of Men and Nations* (1958).

Hodge \ˈhäj\, Charles. 1797–1878. American scholar and theologian, b. Philadelphia. Presbyterian clergyman; professor, Princeton (1822–77); moderator of "Old School" Presbyterian church (1846); a leading figure in Calvinist, or Reformed, theology and conservative wing of church; founded and edited (1825–71) *Biblical Repertory and Princeton Review.* Author of *Systematic Theology* (1871–73).

Hodg·kin \ˈhäj-kin\, Thomas. 1798–1866. English physician. First to describe (1832) Hodgkin's disease.

Hodg·son \ˈhäj-sən\, Brian Houghton. 1800–1894. British Orientalist. Joined East India Co. (1816); served in India (1818–20), Nepal (1820–43). Collected valuable manuscripts on northern Buddhism, thousands of zoological specimens. Author of *Illustrations of Literature and Religion of the Buddhists* (1841), *Essays on Language, Literature, and Religion of Nepal and Tibet* (1874).

Hodgson, Ralph. 1871–1962. English poet. One of the "Georgian" poets, known esp. for lyrics in celebration of nature. Volumes included *The Last Blackbird* (1907), *Eve* (1913), *Poems* (1917), *The Skylark* (1958).

Ho·dler \ˈhō-dlər\, Ferdinand. 1853–1918. Swiss painter and illustrator. Known for landscapes in both Symbolist and Expressionist manners.

Hod·son \ˈhäd-sən\, William Stephen Raikes. 1821–1858. British cavalry officer. Served in Indian army in First Sikh War (1845–46); adjutant (1846–52), commandant (1852–55) of the Guides corps; dismissed on charges. Restored (1857); raised troop of "Hodson's Horse," which served through Sepoy Mutiny (1857–58); after capture of Delhi (Sept. 1857), seized Emperor Bahādur Shāh II and shot the princes of Delhi when their rescue was attempted; killed in attack on Lucknow.

Ho·dža \ˈhò-jä\, Milan. 1878–1944. Czechoslovak politician. Member of Hungarian parliament (1905–18), Czechoslovakian parliament (1918–38); prime minister (1935–38); went into exile following Munich Agreement.

Hoe \ˈhō\, Robert. 1784–1833. American industrialist, b. Hoes, Leicestershire, England. To U.S. (1803); manufacturer of printing presses (from 1805); firm organized as R. Hoe & Co. (from 1823); manufactured Samuel Rust's iron-framed press as "Washington" press (from 1827). His son ¶Richard March (1812–1886) succeeded him in management of R. Hoe & Co. (1833); invented rotary, or "lightning," press (1847), web press (c.1847), and web perfecting press (1871); improvements made possible the modern large-circulation daily newspaper. Richard's nephew ¶Robert (1839–1909) succeeded him as head of R. Hoe & Co. (1886); devised improvements increasing speed of newspaper press; perfected rotary art press (1890); developed color presses.

Hoef·na·gel \ˈhüf-ˌnä-gəl\ *or* **Huf·na·gel** \ˈhüf-ˌnä-gəl\, Joris. 1542–1600. Dutch miniature painter and illustrator. His masterpiece the *Missale Romanum,* preserved in the National Library at Vienna.

Høegh-Guldberg. See GULDBERG.

Ho·el \ˈhü-əl\, Halvor Nielsen. 1766–1852. Norwegian political leader. Spokesman for peasant interests; agitated for abolition of urban-dominated parliament in favor of direct royal rule; denied seat in parliament (1815); arrested, sentenced to prison following peasant demonstrations at coronation of Charles XIV (1818); pardoned by king.

Hoel, Sigurd. 1890–1960. Norwegian novelist. Author of *Syndere i sommersol* (1927), *En dag i oktober* (1931), *Sesam, Sesam* (1938), *Møte ved milepaelen* (1947), *Jeg er blitt glad i en annen* (1951), *Trollringen* (1958); also wrote essays, criticism, and popular autobiography *Veien til verdens ende* (1933).

Ho·ë·vell \ˈhō-ə-vəl\, Wolter Robert van. Baron. 1812–1879. Dutch politician. Clergyman in Dutch East Indies (1836–48); founded newspaper *Het Tijdschrift* in Batavia; became critic of colonial government; as member of Dutch parliament (1848 ff.) brought about end of extractive and exploitive "culture system" of colonial agriculture.

Hof·bau·er \ˈhōf-ˌbaù-ər\, Klemens Maria. Saint. 1751–1820. German religious. Ordained (1785); from Warsaw traveled through Switzerland and Germany (1788–1808) establishing Redemptorist monasteries; exiled on closing of Warsaw Redemptorist community by Napoléon (1808); to Vienna, where he established a monastery and worked to rebuild Redemptorists. Canonized and named patron saint of Vienna by Pope St. Pius X (1909).

Ho·fer \ˈhō-fər\, Andreas. 1767–1810. Tyrolese patriot. At first with Austrian aid and then alone led rebellion (1808–09) against Bavarian government of the Tyrol, and defeated Bavarian army at Berg Insel (1809); established independent administration in Tyrol with Austrian acquiescence; after Austrian cession of Tyrol to France, he was defeated by combined French and Bavarian army. Forced into hiding, but was captured and executed.

Hofer, Karl. 1878–1955. German painter. Teacher (1920–34), director (1945–55), Berlin Hochschule; strongly influenced by Cézanne; known esp. for landscapes, figure studies.

Hoff, Jacobus Hendricus van't. See VAN'T HOFF.

Hof·fa \ˈhò-fə, ˈhäf-ə\, James Riddle. 1913–?1975. American labor leader, b. Brazil, Ind. Began labor organizing (1930); president of Detroit local, Teamsters union (1935–71); vice president (1952–57), president (1957–71), International Brotherhood of Teamsters; accused of corruption on various occasions; convicted of mail fraud and mishandling funds (1964); imprisoned (1967–71); sentence commuted by Pres. Richard Nixon; disappeared and presumed murdered.

Höff·ding \ˈhœf-diŋ\, Harald. 1843–1931. Danish philosopher. Professor, Copenhagen (from 1883). Author of *History of Modern Philosophy* (1894–95), *Philosophy of Religion* (1901), etc.

Hof·fen·stein \ˈhòf-ən-ˌstīn\, Samuel Goodman. 1890–1947. American humorist, b. Lithuania. To U.S. in his youth; worked as drama critic, press agent, newspaper columnist, motion picture scenario writer (from 1927). Author of *Life Sings a Song* (1916), *Poems in Praise of Practically Nothing* (1928), etc.

Hoffman. See also HOFFMANN and HOFMANN.

Hoff·man \òf-màn\, François-Benoît. 1760–1828. French writer. Author of verse, dramas, criticism, and opera libretti as for Lemoyne's *Phèdre* (1786) and *Nepthté* (1789), Méhul's *Euphrosine* (1790), *Adrien* (1799), and *Ariodant* (1799), Cherubini's *Médée* (1797).

Hoff·man \ˈhäf-mən, ˈhòf-\, Malvina. 1887–1966. American sculptor, b. New York City. Executed bronzes of 110 racial types for Field Museum in Chicago (1930–33); other works included *Russian Dancers, The Sacrifice* (Harvard U. war memorial), portrait busts of Paderewski, Pavlova, John Muir, etc. Author of *Heads and Tales* (1930), *Sculpture Inside and Out* (1939).

Hoffman, Paul Gray. 1891–1974. American businessman, b. Chicago. Joined Studebaker Corp. (1911); vice president (1925–35), president (1935–53), chairman (1953–54); chairman, Studebaker-Packard Corp. (1954–56). Head of U.S. Economic Cooperation Administration directing Marshall Plan in Europe (1948–50); president, Ford Foundation (1951–53); U.S. delegate to UN General Assembly (1956–57); director, Special UN Fund for Economic Development (1959–66); administrator of UN Development Program (1966–72).

Hoff·mann \ˈhòf-män\, August Heinrich. *Known as* Hoffmann von Fal·lers·le·ben \ˈfäl-ər-ˌslā-bən\. 1798–1874. German poet, philologist, and historian of literature. Librarian (1823–38) and professor of German (1830–42), Breslau U. Author of lyric and generally patriotic verse, as *Lieder und Romanzen* (1821), *Unpolitische Lieder* (1840–41), *Kinderlieder* (1843–47), *Liebeslieder* (1851), *Soldatenlieder* (1851–52), *Vaterlandslieder* (1871); best known poem, "Deutschland, Deutschland über Alles" (1841), used as a national hymn (from 1922). Other works included *Fundgruben für Geschichte deutscher Sprache und Literatur* (1830–37), *Geschichte des deutschen Kirchenliedes bis auf Luther* (1832), *Die deutsche Philologie im Grundriss* (1836).

Hoffmann, Ernst Theodor Wilhelm. *As composer, known as* Ernst Theodor Amadeus Hoffmann, *in honor of Mozart.* 1776–1822. German composer, music critic, writer, and illustrator. Composed operas *Aurora* (c.1811) and *Undine* (1816, libretto by La Motte-Fouqué); wrote tales of supernatural collected as *Die Serapionsbrüder* (1819–21), *Die Lebensansichten des Katers Murr* (1820–22), which were inspiration for Offenbach's *Les Contes d'Hoffmann,* Delibes's *Coppelia,* Hindemith's *Cardillac,* etc. Other works included *Ritter Gluck* (1809), *Don Juan* (1813), *Die Elixiere des Teufels* (1816), *Nachtstücke* (1817), *Prinzessin Brambilla* (1821), *Meister Floh* (1822).

Hoffmann, Friedrich. 1660–1742. German physician. Experimented with various remedies, Hoffmann's anodyne and Hoffmann's drops being named after him; adherent of the iatrophysical school of medicine; an influential theorist and systematizer of medicine.

Hoffmann *or* **Hoff·mann-Don·ner** \-ˈdòn-ər\, Heinrich. 1809–1894. German physician and poet. Widely known for his children's books, illustrated by himself, including *Struwwelpeter* (1847), *König Nussknacker* (1851), *Im Himmel und auf der Erde* (1858), *Prinz Grünewald* (1871), etc.

Hoffmann, Josef. 1870–1956. Austrian architect. A founder (1899) of Wiener Sezession group and (1903) of Wiener Werkstätte, which he directed (1903–33); city architect of Vienna (1920 ff.). Works included sanatorium at Purkersdorf (1903), Stoclet House in Brussels (1905), Austrian pavilions for Deutscher Werkbund exhibition (1914) and Venice Biennale (1934).

Hoffmann, Max. 1869–1927. German general. Served on the eastern front in World War I; succeeded Ludendorff as chief of the general staff under Prince Leopold of Bavaria (1916); negotiated armistice of Brest-Litovsk with the Soviets (1917–18); opposed annexation of Poland by Germany.

Hof·hai·mer \ˈhōf-ˌhī-mər\, Paul von. 1459–1537. German organist and composer. Organist to Maximilian I of Germany (1489–1519), to archbishop and cathedral of Salzburg (1519–37); considered greatest organist of the time;

influential teacher. Composed organ music, now mostly lost, songs, etc.; among surviving works is *Harmoniae poeticae,* settings of odes of Horace (1539).

Hofmann. See also HOFFMAN and HOFFMANN.

Hof·mann \'hōf-,män, 'hòf-\, August Wilhelm von. 1818–1892. German chemist. Professor and first director of Royal Coll. of Chemistry, London (1845–64); professor, Berlin (1865–92); founder of German Chemical Society (1868). Known for researches in organic chemistry, esp. on coal-tar products; discovered methods for preparation of coloring substances from aniline; discovered formaldehyde, hydrazobenzene, etc.; discovered Hofmann reaction for converting an amide into an amine and a method for determining molecular weights of liquids by means of vapor densities.

Hofmann, Hans. 1880–1966. American painter, b. Weissenberg, Germany. Taught painting in Munich (1915–31); to U.S. (1931); directed Hans Hofmann School of Fine Arts, New York City and Provincetown, Mass. (1932–58). A founder and leading exponent of Abstract Expressionism; works noted for formal experiments and improvisation in bold colors.

Hofmann, Johann Christian Konrad von. 1810–1877. German theologian. Professor, Rostock (1842–45), Erlangen (from 1845); founder of Protestant Erlangen school of theologians.

Hof·mann \'hòf-,män, *Angl* häf-mən\, Josef Casimir. 1876–1957. American piano virtuoso, b. Kraków, Poland. Child prodigy; studied with Anton Rubinstein; first U.S. tour (1887); lived chiefly in U.S. (from 1898); director, dean, and teacher, Curtis Institute of Music, Philadelphia (1926–38). Composer, under pseudonym Michel Dvor·sky \'dvòr-skē\, of 5 concertos, a symphony, an orchestral suite, and piano pieces.

Hof·mann \'hōf-,män, 'hòf-\, Ludwig von. 1861–1945. German painter. Known esp. for historical and allegorical canvases and for murals.

Hofmann *or* **Hoffmann,** Melchior. c.1495–1543 or 1544. German preacher and mystic. Lutheran lay missionary in Livonia, Sweden, northern Germany; preached in Stockholm (1526–28); appointed preacher at Kiel by Frederick I of Denmark; banned from Denmark for disagreeing with Luther on Eucharist (1529); converted to Anabaptist beliefs; developed eschatology calling for end of the world in 1533; won many converts; arrested in Strassburg (1533) and imprisoned for life. Melchiorite groups soon died out.

Hof·manns·thal \'hōf-män-,stäl\, Hugo von. 1874–1929. Austrian poet and playwright. Author of short verse plays as *Gestern* (1891), *Der Tod des Tizian* (1892), *Der Tor und der Tod* (1893), *Das kleine Welttheater* (1897), *Der weisse Fächer* (1898), *Die Frau im Fenster* (1898), *Der Abenteurer und die Sängerin* (1899), *Die Hochzeit der Sobeide* (1899); larger theatrical works *Elektra* (1903, later set to music by Richard Strauss), *Christina's Heimreise* (1910), *Jedermann* (1911), *Der Schwierige* (1921), *Das Salzburger grosse Welttheater* (1922), *Der Unbestechliche* (1923), *Der Turm* (1925); wrote libretti for Strauss's operas *Der Rosenkavalier* (1911), *Ariadne auf Naxos* (1912), *Die Frau ohne Schatten* (1919), *Die ägyptische Helena* (1928), *Arabella* (1933); also wrote novel *Andreas* (1932), much lyric poetry.

Hof·manns·wal·dau \,hōf-mäns-'väl-,daù\, Christian Hofmann von. 1617–1679. German poet. Traveled widely in youth; civic official of Breslau (1646–79). Chief representative of Baroque "Second Silesian school" of German verse; translated Guarini's *Il pastor fido;* wrote *Grabschriften* (1643), *Heldenbriefe* (1663), etc.

Hof·meis·ter \'hōf-,mī-stər\, Sebastian. *Called* Oe·co·no·mus \œ̄-'kō-nō-mùs\. 1476–1533. Swiss religious leader. Entered Franciscan order, became lecturer in theology at Zürich and Constance; accepted Zwingli's Reform views and began to preach the Gospels (1522); driven from Lucerne (1522), Schaffhausen (1525); took part in Zürich disputations (1523), Bern disputation (1528).

Hofmeister, Wilhelm Friedrich Benedikt. 1824–1877. German botanist. Entirely self-taught; from careful experiment and microscopic observation described cell division, explicated role of sexuality in all higher plants; explained and named alternation of generations; considered a founder of modern botany; professor at Heidelberg (1863–72), Tübingen (1872–76). Chief work *Vergleichende Untersuchungen* (1851).

Hof·meyr \'hòf-,mār\, Jan Hendrik. 1845–1909. South African politician. Editor, *Volksvriend* (1861–83, from 1871 united with *Zuid-Afrikaan*); formed Farmers' Protection Association (1878); member of Cape Parliament (1879–95); negotiated for Great Britain with President Kruger and arranged Swaziland convention (1890); supported Cecil Rhodes until Jameson Raid (1895). Initiated Bloemfontein conference between Milner and Kruger (1899). Advocated conciliation after the Boer War (1903); favored federation in South Africa.

Hof·stadt·er \'hōf-,stat-ər\, Richard. 1916–1970. American historian, b. Buffalo, N.Y. Professor, U. of Maryland (1942–46), Columbia (1946–70). Author of *Social Darwinism in American Thought* (1944), *American Political Tradition* (1948), *Age of Reform* (1955, Pulitzer prize), *Development of Academic Freedom in the United States* (with W.P. Metzger, 1955), *Anti-Intellectualism in American Life* (1963, Pulitzer prize), *The Paranoid Style in American Politics* (1965), *The Idea of a Party System* (1969), etc.

Hof·ste·de de Groot \'hòf-,stā-də-də-'grōt\, Cornelis. 1863–1930. Dutch art scholar. Compiled catalogue of 17th-century Dutch painters (with Wilhelm Valentiner, 1907–28); wrote esp. on Rembrandt and his works.

Hof·zins·er \'hōft-,sin-sər\, Johann Nepomuk. 1806–1875. Austrian magician. An amateur conjurer, master and inventor of many manipulative tricks, esp. with playing cards.

Ho·garth \'hō-,gärth\, David George. 1862–1927. English archaeologist. Assisted in excavations at Paphos in Cyprus (1888), in Egypt with Egypt Exploration Fund (1894–96), at Naucratis (1899, 1903), Knossos (1900), Ephesus (1904–05), Carchemish (1911); keeper of Ashmolean Museum, Oxford (1909–27). Sent to help organize Arab revolt against Turks (1915); later associated with T.E. Lawrence. Author of *Hittite Seals* (1920), *Kings of the Hittites* (1926), etc.

Hogarth, William. 1697–1764. English painter and engraver. Apprenticed to a silversmith; opened own engraver's shop (1718). Produced first notable work, plates for Butler's *Hudibras* (1726); followed this with *The Harlot's Progress* (1732) and *A Rake's Progress* (1735). Secured legislation (Hogarth's Act, 1735) protecting designers from piracy. Painted historical pictures at St. Bartholomew's Hospital (1736), and published the prints and *The Distrest Poet, Company of Undertakers,* and *Sleeping Congregation.* Others of his engravings were *Strolling Actresses Dressing in a Barn* (1738), *Marriage à la Mode* (1745), *Industry and Idleness* and *Stage Coach* (1747), *Election* (1755–58), *Cockpit* (1759), *Five Orders of Periwigs* (1761), *The Bathos* (1764). Paintings included *The Beggar's Opera* (1728), *The Conquest of Mexico* (1731), *Southwark Fair* (1733), *The Distressed Poet* (c.1735), portraits of Thomas Coram, David Garrick, a *Self-Portrait* (1745), etc. A revolutionary in painting, but chiefly remembered as creator of satirical narrative pictures.

Hog·ben \'hòg-bən, 'häg-, -,ben\, Lancelot. 1895–1975. English scientist, educator, and writer. Professor of social biology, London (1930–37); professor, Aberdeen (1937–41), Birmingham (1941–61). Author of *Nature and Nurture* (1933), *Mathematics for the Million* (1936), *Science for the Citizen* (1938), *Dangerous Thoughts* (1939), *Chance and Choice* (1950–55), *The Mother Tongue* (1964), etc.

Ho·gen·dorp \'hō-gən-,dòrp\, Dirk van. 1761–1822. Dutch colonialist. Agent of Dutch East Indies Co. (1786–98); criticized exploitive colonial administration and imprisoned (1798); escaped to Netherlands and roused controversy with report on colonial conditions; member of governmental commission empowered to formulate new policy but ineffective; aide to Napoléon (1810–15) after annexation of Netherlands.

Hogg \'hòg, 'häg\, Douglas McGarel. 1st Viscount Hail·sham \'hā(ə)l-shəm\. 1872–1950. English politician. Son of Quintin Hogg. Barrister (1902); attorney general to Prince of Wales (1920); M.P. (1922–28); attorney general (1922–28); created baron (1928), viscount (1929); lord chancellor (1928–29, 1935–38); leader of Conservative opposition in House of Lords (1929–31); secretary of state for war (1931–35); lord president of the Council (1938).

Hogg, James. *Known as* the Ett·rick Shepherd \'e-trik\. 1770–1835. Scottish poet. Friend of Scott, Byron, John Wilson, Wordsworth, Southey. Settled in Edinburgh (1810) and at Eltrive Lake in Yarrow (1816). Among his works were *Donald M'Donald* (1800), *Scottish Pastorals* (1801), *The Mountain Bard* (1807), *Forest Minstrel* (1810), *The Queen's Wake* (1813), *Pilgrims of the Sun* (1815), *The Poetic Mirror* (1816), *Private Memoirs and Confessions of a Justified Sinner* (1824, novel), *Queen Hynde* (1826).

Hogg, Quintin. 1845–1903. English philanthropist and reformer. Founded a ragged school (1864–65) in Of Alley, Charing Cross, London; established Working Lads' Institute (1878) and the Regent Street Polytechnic (1882), which became model for educational centers for underprivileged youth.

Hogg, Thomas Jefferson. 1792–1862. English lawyer and writer. Friend of Shelley; contributed reminiscences of Shelley at Oxford to Bulwer-Lytton's *New Monthly Magazine* (1832), and published valuable *Life of Shelley* (1858).

Hohenberg, Duchess of. See under FRANCIS FERDINAND.

Ho·hen·lo·he \,hō-ən-'lō-ə\. A district in Franconia and a German princely family named from it, originating as a countship in early part of 12th century with Henry I (d. 1183), Count of Hohenlohe, whose grandsons, supporters of Frederick II, founded (1230) two lines, which soon through marriages and inheritances (such as Langenburg, Ohringen, Neuenstein, Waldenburg, etc.) became divided and subdivided many times, most branches being now extinct; independence of principality lost (1806); lands now parts of Bavaria and Württemberg. Many members of family held important military or political posts during 19th and 20th centuries. Among prominent members were:

¶Friedrich Ludwig. Fürst zu Hohenlohe-In·gel·fin·gen \-'iŋ-əl-,fiŋ-ən\. 1746–1818. Prussian general. Served with distinction in war of Bavarian Succession (1778–79); governor of Berlin (1791); prominent at Weissenburg (1793) and

Kaiserslautern (1794); commanded one of two armies defeated by Napoléon at Jena (1806); capitulated at Prenzlau (1806); retired (1809).

¶Kraft Karl August Eduard Friedrich. Prinz zu Hohenlohe-Ingelfingen. 1827–1892. Prussian general. Grandson of Friedrich Ludwig. Served in Crimean War; in Seven Weeks' War distinguished himself at Königgrätz (1866); major general (1868); improved tactical training of Prussian artillery; prominent in Franco–Prussian War, esp. at the siege of Paris (1870–71); wrote several works on military science.

¶Hermann. Fürst zu Hohenlohe-Lang·en·burg \-'läŋ-ən-,bůrk\. 1832–1913. German soldier. Served in armies of Württemberg, Austria (1854–60), Baden (1862–71), and Prussia; member of Imperial Reichstag (1871–80); governor of Alsace-Lorraine (1894–1907); founder and president (1887–94) of Deutsche Kolonialgesellschaft.

¶Chlodwig Karl Viktor. Fürst zu Hohenlohe-Schil·lings·fürst \-'shil-iŋs-,fuerst\ and Prinz von Ra·ti·bor und Cor·vey \'rä-tē-bòr-ůnt-'kòr-vē, -tē-bōr-\. 1819–1901. German politician. Active in Bavarian politics (1846–70); minister president and minister of foreign affairs (1866–70); labored for a united Germany. German ambassador at Paris (1874–78); a representative of Germany at the Congress of Berlin (1878); governor of Alsace-Lorraine (1885–94). Succeeded Caprivi as Prussian minister president and imperial German chancellor (1894–1900); attempted but failed to restrain William II's impetuous policies.

Ho·hen·stau·fen \,hō-ən-'shtaů-fən\. *Also called* Stau·fer \'shtaů-fər\. A German princely family which furnished sovereigns of Germany (1138–1208, 1215–54) and of Sicily (1194–1268). It derived its name from the ancestral castle at Staufen in Swabia and originated with Conrad III, King of Germany, who was the son of Agnes, daughter of Emperor Henry IV, and Frederick of Hohenstaufen, Duke of Swabia (d. 1105). It included the Holy Roman emperors Frederick I, Henry VI, Otto IV, and Frederick II, the German kings Philip of Swabia and Conrad IV, and the kings of Sicily Henry VI, Frederick II, Conrad IV, Manfred, and Conradin (*qq.v.*).

Ho·hen·wart \'hō-ən-,värt\, Karl Siegmund von. Graf. 1824–1899. Austrian politician. Governor of Upper Austria (1868–71); prime minister and minister of interior (1871); failed to secure agreement of German majority in Reichsrat to measures to pacify Czech nationalists; leader of opposition in Reichsrat (1871–79); leader of government forces (1879–99); founded Hohenwart Club (1891).

Ho·hen·zol·lern \,hō-ənt-sòl-ərn\. A German royal family, deriving its name from the ancestral castle Zollern, later Hohenzollern, in Swabia, with counts dating from Burchard I in the 11th century. Two branches, Swabian and Franconian, established (1227): (1) Swabian branch existed in two petty principalities, Hohenzollern-Hech·ing·en \-'hek-iŋ-ən\ (became extinct 1869) and Hohenzollern-Sig·ma·ring·en \-'zēk-mä-,riŋ-ən\ (until 1849). See CAROL I and II and FERDINAND I, kings of Romania, and CHARLES ANTHONY and LEOPOLD, princes of Hohenzollern-Sigmaringen. (2) Franconian branch gave support (12th to 15th centuries) to Hohenstaufens and Habsburgs. From Conrad III (d. 1261) to Frederick VI (1417–40), territory and influence increased. Frederick VI became first elector and margrave of Brandenburg as Frederick I (*q.v.*) and was followed by eleven electors of Brandenburg (1440–1701); the last, Frederick III (1688–1713), became first king of Prussia as Frederick I (1701–13), being succeeded by the Hohenzollern kings of Prussia (1713–1871): Frederick William I, Frederick II the Great, Frederick William II, Frederick William III and IV, and William I (*qq.v.*). Last kings of Prussia (1871–1918) were also German emperors: William I, Frederick III, and William II (*qq.v.*).

Hō·jō \hō-jō\. Japanese family that obtained and held as hereditary right (1219–1333) office of *shikken,* or regent for shoguns; during that period held real power in Japan. Members included:

¶Hōjō Tokimasa. *Orig. surname* Tai·ra \tī-rä\. 1138–1215. Warrior in service of kinsman Taira Kiyomori; on death of Minamoto Yoshitomo (1160), given Yoshitomo's son Yoritomo to guard; assisted Yoritomo in revolt against Kiyomori (1180–81); made warden of Kyōto (1189); guardian of Yoritomo's son and heir Yoriie (1199) and effective ruler of Japan through nominal regency of daughter Masako (see below); ordered assassination of Yoriie (1204); named *shikken* for Yoriie's younger brother and successor Sanetomo; prevented by Masako from assassinating Sanetomo; forced to resign office to son Yoshitoke (1205); retired to monastery.

¶Hōjō Masako. 1157–1225. Daughter of Tokimasa; m. Minamoto Yoritomo and assisted him in gaining control of Japan as first shogun; on his death (1199) became regent for son Yoriie; regent for second son Sanetomo (1204–19); forced replacement of father as *shikken* by brother Yoshitoke (1205); on murder of Sanetomo (1219) installed puppet shogun to succeed him; continued to wield great influence.

¶Hōjō Yoshitoki. 1162–1224. Son of Tokimasa; assumed office of *shikken* from father (1205); on murder of shogun Sanetomo (1219) installed as puppet an infant of Fujiwara line; defeated revolt against his power by Emperor Toba II (1221) and consolidated power of Kamakura shogunate over imperial government and of Hōjō family over shogunate; assassinated.

¶Hōjō Yasutoki. 1183–1242. Son of Yoshitoki; commanded military forces of shogunate in defeating Emperor Toba II (1221); established military headquarters in imperial city of Kyōto to control court; succeeded father as *shikken* (1224); further strengthened power of his office and family; issued (1232) Jōei Shikimoku, code of laws regulating samurai class and administration and establishing new land system and standards for fair trials.

Succeeding *shikken* were ¶Tsunetoki (1214–46), grandson of Yasutoki; regent (1242–46). ¶Tokiyori (1227–1263), brother of Tsunetoki; regent (1246–56); resigned office to son Tokimune and became priest.

¶Hōjō Tokimune. 1215–1284. Son of Tokiyore; assumed regency (1256); rejected a demand for tribute from Kublai Khan (1268); aided by typhoon, defeated Mongol invasion (1274); built up defenses and again defeated invasion in two-months' battle (1281), again aided by typhoon (*kamikaze,* or divine wind); cost of defenses and maintaining large army greatly weakened Hōjō family and shogunate. Succeeded by his son ¶Sadatoki (1270–1311); *shikken* (1284–1303); retired and became Buddhist priest.

¶Hōjō Takatori. 1303–1333. Last Hōjō regent; weak and dissolute; entered long-standing dispute over imperial succession; exiled Emperor Daigo II (1331); betrayed by own general, Ashikaga Takauji; committed suicide while besieged in Kamakura by Yoshisada Nitta.

Ho·kin·son \'hō-kən-sən\, Helen Elna. 1893–1949. American cartoonist, b. Mendota, Ill. Contributed over 1700 cartoons to *New Yorker* magazine (from 1925), usually gently lampooning the American matron or clubwoman. Cartoons collected in *So You're Going to Buy a Book!* (1931), *My Best Girls* (1941), *When Were You Built?* (1948), *The Ladies, God Bless 'Em* (1950), *There Are Ladies Present* (1952).

Ho·ku·sai \hō-kůs-ī\. *Surname* Ka·tsu·shi·ka \kät-sůsh-ē-kä\. 1760–1849. Japanese artist. Trained in wood block printing; began publishing prints of Kabuki actors (1779); produced book illustrations, special occasion prints, etc., becoming leading exponent of *Ukiyo-e* school; developed landscape art to new level of simple grandeur. Exerted considerable influence on European artists. Works included *Festivals for the Twelve Months* (c.1790), *Fifty Fanciful Poets* (1802), *Fifty-three Stations on the Tōkaidō* (1804), *Thirty-six Views of Mt. Fuji* (c.1826–33).

Hol·a·bird \'häl-ə-bərd\, William. 1854–1923. American architect, b. Amenia Union, N.Y. Draftsman in Chicago office of William L. Jenney (1875); founded own firm (1880) which became (1881) Holabird and Roche; with Martin Roche helped develop Chicago School of commercial architecture; designed Tacoma Building (1886–89), first total steel skeleton; other works included Marquette Building (1894), Gage Building (1898), Republic Building (1905), City Hall (1910), Crerar Library (1919).

Hol·bach \òl-bák, *Ger* 'hòl-,bäk\, Paul-Henri-Dietrich d'. Baron. 1723–1789. French philosopher. Leading atheist and materialist; contributed 376 articles to the *Encyclopédie.* Author, often under pseudonyms, of such works as *Le Christianisme dévoilé* (1761), *Système de la nature* (1770), *Système social* (1773).

Hol·bein \'hòl-,bīn, *Angl* 'hōl-\, Hans. *Called* the Elder. 1465?–1524. German painter. Worked chiefly in native Augsburg; known for religious works including altarpieces for Augsburg cathedral (1493), St. Afra (c.1495), St. Catherine (1512), St. Sebastian (1516) in Augsburg and Dominican monastery, Frankfurt (1501); other works included *Basilica of St. Mary* (1499), *Presentation of Christ* (1502), *Basilica of St. Paul* (1503–04), *Fountain of Life* (1519). His son ¶Hans, *called* the Younger (1497?–1543) was a portrait and historical painter; worked in Basel (1515–26); in England, employed by Sir Thomas More (1526–28); again in Basel (1528–32); again in England (from 1532); court painter to Henry VIII of England (c.1536); as designer and artist, shaped taste of court. Known as exquisite draftsman and one of greatest portraitists in history, with a style of objective realism. Among his works were portraits of Erasmus, Sir Thomas More, Anne of Cleves, Henry VIII, and numerous courtiers, a famous series of woodcuts entitled *The Dance of Death* (c.1523–26, pub. 1538), and a number of religious paintings.

Hol·berg \'hòl-berg\, Ludvig. Baron. 1684–1754. Norwegian man of letters. Regarded as founder of both Norwegian and Danish literature. Traveled throughout Europe, largely on foot (1714–16); professor, Copenhagen (from 1717). Author of *Introduction til de fornemste europaeiske rigers historie* (1711) on history of Europe, *Introduction til natur-og folkeretten* (1716) on natural history; wrote classic seriocomic epic *Peder Paars* (1719); series of comedies for Danish theater (1722–27) including *Den politiske kandestøber, Jeppe påa bjerget, Ulysses von Ithacia,* and *Erasmus Montanus;* romance *Niels Klims underjordiske reise* (1741).

Hol·brook \'hōl-,brůk\, Josiah. 1788–1854. American educator, b. Derby, Conn. Conducted experimental schools; itinerant lecturer; organized "lyceum" for adult education in Millbury, Mass. (1826); inspired some 3000 similar groups by 1834; published *Family Lyceum* (1832) and other periodicals for lyceum use; secretary of lyceum lecturers bureau (1842–49).

Hol·brooke \'hōl-ˌbru̇k\, Josef. 1878–1958. English pianist, conductor, and composer. Composed orchestral works as *The Raven* (1900), *Queen Mab* (chorus and orchestra, 1902), *The Bells* (1903), *Apollo and the Seaman* (1907), 4 symphonies, concertos, etc.; operas, esp. trilogy *The Cauldron of Annwyn,* comprising *The Children of Don* (1912), *Dylan* (1914), *Bronwen* (1929).

Hol·croft \'hōl-ˌkrȯft\, Thomas. 1745–1809. English playwright and writer. Successively stableboy, shoemaker, and tutor in family of Granville Sharp; later an actor. Among his plays were *Duplicity* (1781), *Follies of a Day* (1784, adopted from Beaumarchais), *The Road To Ruin* (1792); published also comic operas, novels, and translations.

Hol·de·man \'hōl-də-mən\, John. 1832–1900. American religious leader, b. New Pittsburg, Ohio. Founder (1859) of a group now known as the Church of God in Christ, Mennonite.

Hol·den \'hōl-dən\, Edward Singleton. 1846–1914. American astronomer, b. St. Louis. Assistant to Simon Newcomb at Naval Observatory, Washington, D.C. (1873–79); director, Washburn Observatory, U. of Wisconsin (1881). President, U. of California (1885–88); planned, designed, and served as first director of Lick Observatory (1888–97). Librarian, U.S.M.A., West Point (from 1901).

Holden, Sir Isaac. 1807–1897. British inventor. Obtained patent (1847, jointly with Samuel Lister) for new method of carding, combing, and preparing genappe yarns; established factory near Paris (1848), later moved to Bradford, England (1864). M.P. (1865–68, 1882–95).

Hol·der \'hōl-dər\, Alfred Theophil. 1840–1916. Austrian philologist. Chief librarian of court and national library, Karlsruhe (1870–1916). Edited works of Horace (1864–69, with Otto Keller), Ekkehard (1874), Tacitus (1882), Caesar (1882, 1898), Saxo Grammaticus (1886), Avienus (1887), Bede (1890), and the *Beowulf* (1882–84); produced part two of Holtzmann's *Altdeutsche Grammatik* (1870–75) and *Germanische Alterthümer* (1873); compiled *Altceltischer Sprachschatz* (1891–1913) and *Die Reichenauer Handschriften* (1906–18).

Höl·der·lin \'hœl-dər-ˌlēn\, Friedrich, *in full* Johann Christian Friedrich. 1770–1843. German poet. Befriended in youth by Schiller; worked as tutor; except for brief periods, insane from 1802. Author of lyric verse on classical themes exhibiting profound expressiveness and passionate intensity; works included *Hyperion* (1797–99), "Tod des Empedokles," "Menons Klagen um Diotima," "Brot und Wein," "An die Hoffnung," "Der blinde Sänger," "Der Einzige," "Patmos"; translated *Antigone* and *Oedipus Tyrannus* (both 1804) of Sophocles.

Holderness, Earls of. See Sir John RAMSAY; Prince RUPERT.

Hold·heim \'hōlt-ˌhīm\, Samuel. 1806–1860. German theologian. Rabbi at Frankfurt an der Oder (1836–40); rabbi of Mecklenburg-Schwerin (1840–47); preacher of the Jewish Reform movement in Berlin (from 1847). Author of *Gottesdienstliche Vorträge* (1839), *Über die Autonomie der Rabbinen* (1843).

Ho·le·ček \'hȯ-lə-ˌchek\, Josef. 1853–1929. Czech writer. Author of travel books as *Zájezd na Rus* (1896–1903), verse as *Kanteletar* (1905) and *Sokolovič* (1922), and the chronicle romance *Naši* (1898–1901), depicting life in southern Bohemia.

Hol·i·day \'häl-ə-ˌdā\, Eleanora, *called* Billie. *Also known as* Lady Day. 1915–1959. American singer, b. Baltimore. Made recordings with Benny Goodman, Teddy Wilson, Count Basie (1933–36); toured with Basie and Artie Shaw bands (1937–38); cabaret and concert performer (from 1940); considered supreme jazz singer of her day, with an intensely dramatic style of phrasing and diction.

Hol·ins·hed \'häl-ən-ˌshed, -ənz-ˌhed\ *or* **Hol·lings·head** \-iŋz-ˌhed\, Raphael. d. c.1580. English chronicler. Employed by Reginald Wolfe, printer, to do translating and to continue a chronicle of universal history which Wolfe had begun; published *Chronicles of England, Scotlande, and Irelande* (1577), source from which Shakespeare took much of his data for his historical plays, and for parts of *Macbeth, King Lear,* and *Cymbeline.*

Hol·kar \'hōl-kər\. Name of the Marāthā dynasty of the rulers of Indore, one of the native states of Central India. Its founder, Malhār Rāo Holkar (1693–1766), gained favor of the peshwa, obtained western half of Mālwa with Indore as his capital; joined (1761) league of Hindu princes to oppose Aḥmad Shāh, the Afghan king; was at Panipat (1761) but fled before the battle and great defeat of Hindus began; suspected of treason. His son's widow ¶Ahalyābāi (d. 1795) succeeded to rule; reign became proverbial for peace and prosperity. She was succeeded by ¶Tukōji (d. 1797), a distant relative. On his death throne seized by ¶Jaswant Rāo Holkar (d. 1811), illegitimate son of Tukōji; neutral at beginning of Second Marāthā War (1803); attacked British and besieged Delhi but defeated (1804); died insane. Family continued to rule Indore until after Indian independence (1947).

Holl \'hȯl\, Elias. 1573–1646. German architect. Leading exponent of German Early Baroque; architect of city of Augsburg (1602–35); designed Augsburg Zeughaus (1602–07), Wertachbrugger Tor (1615), and city hall (1615–20) with its famous "Goldner Saal."

Hol·la·day \'häl-ə-ˌdā\, Ben. 1819–1887. American businessman, b. Carlisle Co., Ky. Engaged in Indian trade, army contract supply business, etc.; acquired bankrupt firm of Russell, Majors and Waddell (1862) and its government mail contract to Far West; organized system of stagecoach mail and freight lines among mining districts of Colorado, Montana, Idaho; earned fortune and nickname "Napoleon of the Plains"; sold out to Wells, Fargo (1866); operated coastal steamship line (1867–73), controlled Oregon Central Railroad (1868–73); ruined in Panic of 1873.

Holland, Barons. See Henry FOX.

Holland, Earl of. See Sir Henry RICH.

Hol·land \'häl-ənd\, Clifford Milburn. 1883–1924. American civil engineer, b. Somerset, Mass. Engineer, Public Service Commission of New York, in charge of the double subway tunnels under the East River (1914–19); chief engineer, New York State and New Jersey Interstate Bridge and Tunnel commissions, building vehicular tunnel subsequently named Holland Tunnel under Hudson River (1919–24).

Holland, Sir Erskine, *in full* Thomas Erskine. 1835–1926. English jurist. Professor of international law and diplomacy, Oxford (1874–1910); a founder of *Law Quarterly Review* (1885); British plenipotentiary at Geneva Conference (1906). Author of *Elements of Jurisprudence* (1880), *Admiralty Manual of Naval Prize Law* (1888), *Law and Customs of War on Land* (1904), *Laws of War on Land* (1908).

Holland, Henry. 1745–1806. English architect. Assistant, later partner and son-in-law of Lancelot Brown; exponent of an elegant Neoclassicism. Works included Brooks's Club (1776–78), remodeling of Carlton House (1787) and of Theatre Royal or Drury Lane Theatre (1791–94), and development of Sloane Street, Cadogan Place, and other streets in London (from 1790); also built Marine Pavilion, Brighton (1786–87) for prince regent (later George IV).

Holland, Henry Edmund. 1868–1933. New Zealand politician, b. Australia. Labor leader in Australia (1892–1912); to New Zealand (1912); editor of *Maoriland Worker* (1913–18); imprisoned for sedition (1913–14); helped found Labour party (1916); M.P. (1918–33), leader of Labour party (1919–33).

Holland, Henry Scott. 1847–1918. English clergyman and theologian. Canon of Truro (1882), St. Paul's (1884), Christ Church (1910); professor, Oxford (1910–18); leader of High Church *Lux Mundi* group of theologians devoted to social reform.

Holland, John. Duke of Ex·e·ter \'ek-sət-ər\ *and* Earl of Hun·ting·don \'hənt-iŋ-dən\. 1352?–1400. 3d son of Sir Thomas Holland, 1st Earl of Kent, and half-brother to Richard II. Distinguished himself under John of Gaunt in Spain (1386); chamberlain for life of England (1389); aided Richard II against Gloucester and Arundel (1397), rewarded with dukedom; executed for conspiracy against Henry IV. His second son ¶John (1395–1447), Duke of Exeter (restored 1443) and Earl of Huntingdon (restored 1416), distinguished himself at Agincourt (1415), commanded fleet off Harfleur (1417), won victory of Fresney (1420), and commanded expedition for relief of Guînes (1438).

Holland, John Philip. 1840–1914. American inventor, b. Liscannor, County Clare, Ireland. Taught school, Ireland (1858–72); to U.S. (1873); settled in Paterson, N.J., as teacher. Offered submarine design to U.S. navy (1875); navy rejected it as impracticable. Fenian Society financed further experiments; launched first submarine, *Fenian Ram,* in Hudson River (1881); continued experiments with aid of naval officers; at Elizabeth, N.J. (1898) launched the *Holland* which had internal-combustion engines for surface power and electric motor for submerged cruising, being the first submarine thus equipped; U.S. government purchased *Holland* (1900) and ordered additional submarines. Last years clouded by litigation with financiers who had supported his company (which later became Electric Boat Co.).

Holland, Josiah Gilbert. 1819–1881. American editor and writer, b. Belchertown, Mass. Associate editor, Springfield (Mass.) *Republican* (1850–57); editor, *Scribner's Monthly* and its successor *Century Magazine* (from 1870). Author of *Titcomb's Letters to Young People, Single and Married* under pseudonym Timothy Tit·comb \'tit-kəm\ (1858), *Lessons in Life* (1861), *Every-Day Topics* (1876, 1882), *The Marble Prophecy and Other Poems* (1872); novels including *Miss Gilbert's Career* (1860), *Sevenoaks* (1875), *Nicholas Minturn* (1877).

Holland, Philemon. 1552–1637. English scholar. Known as "Translator General." Chief translations, *Livy* (1600), Pliny's *Natural History* (1601), Plutarch's *Moralia* (1603), *Suetonius* (1606), Camden's *Britannia* (1610).

Holland, Sir Sidney George. 1893–1961. New Zealand politician. Engaged in engineering and business; entered Parliament (1935), becoming leader of

National party (1940–57); prime minister (1949–57), finance minister (1949–54); secured abolition of Legislative Council (1950); retired (1957).

Holland, Vyvyan Oscar Beresford. 1886–1967. English writer and translator. Son of Oscar Wilde; name changed after father's imprisonment (1895). Author of *Son of Oscar Wilde* (1954), *Time Remembered, after Père Lachaise* (1966).

Hol·lar \'hōl-ər, *Angl* 'häl-,är, -ər\, Wenzel. *Czech* Václav Ho·lar \'hȯl-är\. 1607–1677. Bohemian engraver. Worked in Germany, England, Amsterdam. Engraved *Ornatus Muliebris Anglicanus* (1640), *Charles I and his Queen* (after Vandyke, 1641); illustrated Dugdale's *History of St. Paul's Cathedral,* Ogilby's *Vergil.* Executed panoramic view of London after the great fire (1666).

Hol·le·rith \'häl-ə-(,)rith\, Herman. 1860–1929. American inventor, b. Buffalo, N.Y. Statistician with U.S. Census (1880); in U.S. Patent Office (1884–90); invented system of recording information on punched cards and reading it electrically by tabulating machines; system employed in censuses of 1890, 1900; organized (1896) Tabulating Machine Co.; consulting engineer with successor firm Computing-Tabulating-Recording Co. (1911–21). Firm became International Business Machines (1924).

Hol·les \häl-əs\, Denzil. 1st Baron Holles of Ifield \'ī-vəl\. 1599?–?1680. English politician. M.P. (1624 ff.); one of three members who held speaker in his chair when he tried to adjourn House of Commons at king's order (1629); imprisoned and heavily fined, but compensated by Long Parliament. Impeached as one of Five Members (Jan. 1642). Fought in Parliamentary army at Edgehill and Brentford; later advocated peace with king; impeached by Parliamentary army (1647); fled to France. After Restoration, admitted to Privy Council and created baron (1661); ambassador to France (1663–66).

Holles, Thomas Pelham-. See PELHAM-HOLLES.

Hol·ley \'häl-ē\, Alexander Lyman. 1832–1882. American engineer, b. Lakeville, Conn. Published *Holley's Railroad Advocate* (1855–57); bought American rights to Bessemer process for making steel (1863); built plant and began steel production, first in U.S. by Bessemer process, Troy, N.Y. (1865); built numerous other steel plants. Obtained patents for improvements in Bessemer process.

Holley, Marietta. *Pseudonym* Josiah Allen's Wife. 1836–1926. American humorist, b. near Pierrepont Manor, N.Y. Author of *Samantha at the Centennial* (1876), *Samantha at Saratoga* (1887), *Samantha at the World's Fair* (1893), *Josiah Allen on the Woman Question* (1914), etc.

Hol·lings·head \'häl-iŋz-,hed\, John. 1827–1904. English journalist and theater manager. Contributor to *Household Words, Cornhill, Punch,* etc.; first manager of Gaiety Theatre (1866–88), where he produced burlesque, operas, and serious drama, and introduced Ibsen to England by presenting *Pillars of Society* (1880).

Hollingshead, Raphael. See HOLINSHED.

Hol·lins \'häl-ənz\, George Nichols. 1799–1878. American naval officer, b. Baltimore. Served in War of 1812, Algerine War (1815); bombarded Grey Town, Nicaragua, in reprisal for outrages on American citizens (1854). Entered Confederate service (1861); in command of naval forces in upper Mississippi (1862).

Hol·lo·way \'häl-ə-,wā\, Thomas. 1800–1883. English businessman and philanthropist. Successful in manufacture and sale of patent medicines (from 1837), esp. an ointment bearing his name. Endowed asylum for insane (1885), woman's college at Egham (1886).

Hol·low Horn Bear \'häl-ō-'hȯ(ə)rn-'ba(ə)r, 'häl-ə-, -'be(ə)r\. 1850–1913. American Sioux Indian chief, b. Sheridan Co., Neb. His portrait appears on the 14-cent stamp of the 1922 series of United States postage stamps.

Hollweg, Theobald von Bethmann. See BETHMANN HOLLWEG.

Hol·ly \'häl-ē\, James Theodore. 1829–1911. American prelate, b. Washington, D.C. Ordained deacon (1855), priest (1856) of Episcopal church; encouraged emigration of American Negroes to Haiti; bishop and resident of Haiti (from 1874).

Holm \'hōlm\, Gustav Frederik. 1849–1940. Danish naval officer and explorer. On expeditions to south Greenland (1876, 1880–81); explored east coast of Greenland to Angmagssalik (1883–85); discovered Eskimo communities and five ice fjords.

Hol·man \'hōl-mən\, James. *Known as* the Blind Traveler. 1786–1857. English traveler. In British navy (1798–1810); became totally blind; traveled through France, Italy, the Rhineland (1819–21); attempted round the world journey, but was turned back in Siberia as suspected spy (1822); completed round the world journey (1827–32). Author of *Voyage round the World* (1834–35), etc.

Holmes \'hō(l)mz\, Arthur. 1890–1965. English geologist. Professor, Durham (1924–43), Edinburgh (1943–65); pioneer in rock dating by radioactivity and geothermal methods. Author of *The Age of the Earth* (1913), *Principles of Physical Geology* (1944), etc.

Hol·mès \ȯl-mes\, Augusta Mary Anne. 1847–1903. French composer, of Irish parents. Studied under César Franck. Works included symphonic pieces as *Orlando furioso* (1877), *Lutèce* (1878), *Irlande* (1882), *Pologne* (1883), *Andromède* (1901); opera *La Montagne noire* (1895); choral works and songs.

Holmes \'hō(l)mz\, Sir Charles John. 1868–1936. English painter and art critic. Professor of fine art, Oxford (1904–10); director, keeper, and secretary, National Portrait Gallery (1909–16); director of the National Gallery (1916–28). Author of *Leonardo da Vinci* (1919), *Constable, Gainsborough, and Lucas* (1922), *Grammar of the Arts* (1931), etc.

Holmes, Joseph Austin. 1859–1915. American geologist and mining engineer, b. Laurens, S.C. Professor, U. of North Carolina (1882–92); head, testing laboratories (1904–07), technological branch (1907–10), U.S. Geological Survey; worked for organization of U.S. Bureau of Mines, of which he became first director (1910–15). A pioneer in accident-prevention practice in coal mines; popularized slogan "safety first."

Holmes, Mary Jane, *nee* Hawes. 1825–1907. American novelist, b. Brookfield, Mass. m. Daniel Holmes (1849). Wrote many novels, popular in latter half of 19th century, including *Tempest and Sunshine* (1854), *Lena Rivers* (1856), *Hugh Worthington* (1865), *Gretchen* (1887), *Dr. Hathern's Daughters* (1895), *The Abandoned Farm* (1905).

Holmes, Oliver Wendell. 1809–1894. American man of letters, b. Cambridge, Mass. Practiced medicine, Boston (from 1836); professor of anatomy, Dartmouth (1838–40) and Harvard Med. School (1847–82). Wrote *The Contagiousness of Puerperal Fever* (1842). Sprang into literary fame with "The Autocrat of the Breakfast-Table," a series of light, witty talks in the first numbers of the *Atlantic Monthly* (1857, pub. in book form 1858); followed by series *The Professor at the Breakfast-Table* (in book form, 1860) and *The Poet at the Breakfast-Table* (book, 1872). Other works: poetry *Songs in Many Keys* (1862), *Songs of Many Seasons* (1875), *The Iron Gate* (1880), *Before the Curfew* (1887); novels *Elsie Venner* (1861), *The Guardian Angel* (1867), *A Mortal Antipathy* (1885); essays *Soundings from the Atlantic* (1864), *Pages from an Old Volume of Life* (1883), *Our Hundred Days in Europe* (1887); biography *John Lothrop Motley* (1879), *Ralph Waldo Emerson* (1885). Among his best known poems were "Old Ironsides," "The Chambered Nautilus," "The Wonderful One-Hoss Shay," "The Last Leaf."

Holmes, Oliver Wendell. 1841–1935. American jurist, b. Boston. Son of Oliver Wendell Holmes (1809–1894). Served in Union army in Civil War, wounded at Ball's Bluff, Antietam, Fredericksburg; practiced law in Boston (from 1867); coeditor, *American Law Review* (1870–73); professor of law, Harvard Law School (1882). Associate justice (1882–99) and chief justice (1899–1902), supreme court of Massachusetts. Associate justice, U.S. Supreme Court (1902–32); became known for vigorous, lucid opinions, often in dissent; a narrow constructionist and believer in legislative prerogative; promulgated "clear and present danger" test for freedom of speech (*Schenck* v. *U.S.,* 1919). Author of *The Common Law* (1881).

Holmes, William Henry. 1846–1933. American anthropologist and archaeologist, b. near Cadiz, Ohio. Archaeologist, Bureau of American Ethnology (1889–98); chief, Bureau of American Ethnology (1902–09); curator of anthropology, U.S. National Museum (1897–1902, 1910–20); curator (1910–20) and director (from 1920), National Gallery of Art. Author of *Art in Shell of the Ancient Americans* (1883), *Pottery of the Ancient Pueblos* (1886), *Archaeological Studies among the Ancient Cities of Mexico* (1895–97), *Handbook of Aboriginal American Antiquities* (1919), etc.

Holm·gren \'hōlm-,grān\, Alarik Frithiof. 1831–1897. Swedish physiologist. Professor, Uppsala (1864–97); discovered (1864–65) electrical response of retina to light; studied color blindness and secured adoption (1876) of color blindness tests for railroad engineers, etc.

Hol·royd \'häl-,rȯid\, Sir Charles. 1861–1917. English painter and etcher. First keeper of Tate Gallery, London (1897–1906); director of National Gallery, London (1906–16). Etcher of figure subjects, landscapes, and portraits.

Holst \'hōlst\, Gustav Theodore. *Orig.* Gustavus von Holst. 1874–1934. English composer and teacher. Music master, St. Paul's Girls School, London (1905–34); director of music, Morley Coll. (1907–34). Influenced by English folk music, Hindu literature, Stravinsky, etc.; works included operas as *The Revoke* (1895), *Sāvitri* (1908), *The Perfect Fool* (1918–22), *At the Boar's Head* (1924); choral and orchestral works as *Choral Hymns from the Rig Veda* (1908–12), *Hymn of Jesus* (1917), *Ode to Death* (1919), *Choral Symphony* (1923–24), *Choral Fantasia* (1930); orchestral works as *Winter Idyll* (1897), *Indra* (1903), *St. Paul's Suite* (1912–13), *The Planets* (1918), *Fugal Overture* (1922), *Egdon Heath* (1927); many songs and choral pieces.

Hol·ste \'hōl-stə\, Luc. *Lat.* Lucas Hol·ste·ni·us \hōl-'stē-nē-əs\. 1596–1661. German scholar. Employed in Vatican Library (from 1629); librarian (from 1641). Produced annotated editions of Porphyry (1630), Clüver's *Italia antiqua* (pub. 1666), Stephanus Byzantinus's *Ethnica* (1684), etc.

Hol·stein \'hōl-,shtīn\, Friedrich von. 1837–1909. German diplomat. Entered Prussian diplomatic service (1860); protégé of Bismarck, later becoming his critic esp. over policy of alliance with Russia; after dismissal of Bismarck (1890), wielded powerful influence in shaping German foreign policy; declined offer to head foreign ministry (1900); dismissed (1906) in aftermath of damaging Moroccan crisis.

Holstein-Gottorp. See OLDENBURG, 3.

Holstein-Sönderborg. See OLDENBURG, 4.

Holt \'hōlt\, Edwin Bissell. 1873–1946. American psychologist and philosopher, b. Winchester, Mass. Professor, Harvard (1901–18), Princeton (1926–36); a leading advocate of behaviorist approach to psychology. Author of *The Concept of Consciousness* (1914), *The Freudian Wish* (1915), *Animal Drive and the Learning Process* (1931).

Holt, Harold Edward. 1908–1967. Australian politician. M.P. (1935–67); minister of labor and national service (1941, 1949–58), of immigration (1949–56); federal treasurer (1958–66). Deputy leader, Liberal party (1956–66); prime minister of Australia (1966–67).

Holt, Henry. 1840–1926. American publisher and author, b. Baltimore. In publishing business (from 1866); organized firm of Henry Holt & Co. (1873). Author of the novels *Calmire, Man and Nature* (1892) and *Sturmsee, Man and Man* (1905), and of *Talks on Civics* (1901), *On the Cosmic Relations* (1914), *Garrulities of an Octogenarian Editor* (1923).

Holt, Sir John. 1642–1710. English jurist. Lord chief justice of King's Bench (1689–1710). Known for discouraging prosecutions for witchcraft, for liberal construction of statute compelling church attendance, and for strict views of treason and seditious libel.

Holt, Joseph. 1807–1894. American politican, b. Breckinridge Co., Ky. U.S. commissioner of patents (1857); postmaster general (1859–61); secretary of war (1861); first judge advocate general, U.S. army (1862–75). As judge advocate general, prosecuted those charged with having conspired with John Wilkes Booth in assassination of Lincoln; accused of suppressing evidence and keeping from President Johnson the military commission's recommendation of clemency for Mrs. Surratt.

Holt, Luther Emmett. 1855–1924. American physician, b. Webster, N.Y. Director, Babies Hospital, N.Y.C. (1888 ff.); professor, New York Polyclinic Hospital (1890), College of Physicians and Surgeons (1901); a founder (1898) and first president, American Pediatric Society. Author of *The Care and Feeding of Children* (1894), *Diseases of Infancy and Childhood* (1896).

Holt, Winifred. 1870–1945. American welfare worker, b. New York City. Daughter of Henry Holt; an accomplished amateur sculptor. Founder, New York Association for the Blind (1905); organized classes and workshops for the blind; established (1913) headquarters known as "The Lighthouse" in New York City; extended work to France during World War I and then to Poland, Italy, and other countries. Author of *The Light Which Cannot Fail* (1922).

Holt·by \'hōlt-bē\, Winifred. 1898–1935. English novelist. Author of *Mandoa! Mandoa!* (1933), *South Riding* (1936), etc.

Hol·tei \'hòl-ˌtī\, Karl von. 1798–1880. German actor and writer. Actor, theatrical manager in various cities. Noted esp. for his vaudevilles, including *Der alte Freiherr* (1825), *Lenore* (1829), *Theater* (1845); also wrote verse *Schlesischen Gedichte* (1830), novels *Die Vagabunden* (1852), *Der letzte Komödiant* (1863), autobiography *Vierzig Jahre* (1843–50).

Höl·ty \'hœl-tē\, Ludwig Heinrich Christoph. 1748–1776. German poet. Member of the Göttingen "Hain" group; wrote verse celebrating nature, friendship. Best known for *Elegie auf einen Dorfkirchhof* (1771), *Elegie auf einen Stadtkirchhof* (1771).

Ho·lub \'hò-lüp\, Emil. 1847–1902. Bohemian explorer and naturalist. Surgeon in diamond fields of South Africa (1872–73); made three exploring trips in southern Africa, reaching the Zambezi and the Victoria Falls (1873–75); on third trip, accompanied by his wife, intended to traverse Africa from Cape Town to Egypt, but was prevented by hostile tribesmen from going more than a third of the distance (1883–87). Collected thousands of specimens; author of *Sieben Jahre in Südafrika* (1880–81), etc.

Ho·ly·oake \'hō-lē-ˌōk, 'hōl-ˌyōk\, George Jacob. 1817–1906. English reformer. A Chartist (1832); an Owenite (1838) and minister to Owenites at Worcester (1840); turned rationalist, and edited *Oracle of Reason* (1841). Imprisoned on charge of blasphemy (1842). To London (1843); edited *Reasoner* (1846) and *Leader* (1850). Author of *A History of Co-operation* (1875–77), *Sixty Years of an Agitator's Life* (1892), *Bygones Worth Remembering* (1905).

Holywood, John of. See Johannes de SACROBOSCO.

Holz \'hòlts\, Arno. 1863–1929. German writer. Author of verse *Buch der Zeit* (1886), *Phantasus* (1898–99), *Die Blechschmiede* (1902); dramatic works *Die Familie Selicke* (1890, with J. Schlaf), *Sozialaristokraten* (1896, with P. Ernst), *Traumulus* (1904, with O. Jerschke), *Sonnenfinsternis* (1908), *Ignorabimus* (1913); as critic considered a founder and leader of Naturalism, as in *Die Kunst, ihr Wesen und ihre Gesetze* (1891–92).

Holz·bau·er \'hòlts-ˌbaù-ər\, Ignaz Jakob. 1711–1783. Austrian composer. Kapellmeister to Elector Karl Theodor in Mannheim (1753–78). Composed operas *Il figlio delle selve* (1753), *I cinesi* (1756), *Nitteti* (1758), *Günther von Schwarzburg* (1776); symphonies, concertos, chamber music, oratorios, masses.

Hom·berg \'hòm-ˌberk\, Wilhelm. 1652–1715. Dutch naturalist and chemist, b. Batavia, Java. Practiced medicine at Paris (1682–85, and after 1691) and Rome (1685–90); helped establish analytical chemical techniques in studies of acid-alkali reactions, etc.; discovered boric acid (1702).

Home. See also HUME.

Home \'hyüm\, Daniel Dunglas. 1833–1886. Scottish spiritualist medium. To U.S. (c.1842); adopted by an aunt, but turned out of her home because of mysterious rappings; held séances attended by prominent persons, including William Cullen Bryant. To England (1855); his séances there attended by prominent persons, including the Brownings; subject of Robert Browning's poem *Sludge the Medium* (1864). Held séances before French, Prussian, and Dutch sovereigns (1857–58); expelled from Rome as sorcerer (1864); convinced scientist Sir William Crookes by submitting to tests in full light (1871).

Home, Henry. Lord Kames \'kāmz\. 1696–1782. Scottish jurist and philosopher. Lord of justiciary (1763–82). Author of *Essays on the Principles of Morality and Natural Religion* (1751), *Introduction to the Art of Thinking* (1761), *Elements of Criticism* (1762), etc.

Home, John. 1722–1808. Scottish clergyman and playwright. Fought on Hanoverian side against Jacobite rebellion of 1745; minister at Athelstaneford (1747–57); private secretary to Bute, and tutor to prince of Wales; pensioned by George III. His plays included *Douglas* (1756), *Agis* (1758), *Alonzo* (1773).

Ho·mer \'hō-mər\. 9th–8th? century B.C. Greek poet. Traditional name of presumed single author of the *Iliad* and the *Odyssey,* epics on the Trojan War and the wanderings of Odysseus (Ulysses), and as such one of the greatest poets of human history. Some critical schools have held that the poems are composites and no single author can be credited with them. A historical Homer would probably have been an Ionian and an oral poet, reciter of verse to accompaniment of a lyre. The so-called "Homeric Hymns," once attributed to Homer, are probably the work of rhapsodists.

Homer the Younger. 3d century B.C. Greek tragic poet. Ranked as a member of the Pleiad of Alexandria.

Homer, Louise Dilworth, *nee* Beat·ty \'bēt-ē\. 1871–1947. American singer, b. Pittsburgh. Operatic debut in *La Favorita* at Vichy, France (1898); leading contralto at Metropolitan Opera, New York (1900–19); with Chicago Opera (1922–26); chief roles in *Aïda, Tristan und Isolde, Orfeo ed Euridice, Hänsel und Gretel, Samson et Dalilah* (opposite Caruso); extremely popular recording artist (from 1902). m. (1895) ¶Sidney Homer (1864–1953), American composer of songs and ballads.

Homer, Winslow. 1836–1910. American painter, b. Boston. Apprenticed to lithographer (1855–57); contributed drawings to *Harper's Weekly* (1859–67), esp. from Civil War battlefields. Produced paintings of American genre scenes, seascapes, landscapes, etc.; esp. noted as watercolorist, in which medium he achieved remarkable effects of light, atmosphere, color. Works included *Prisoners from the Front, Snap the Whip, Breezing Up, Fog Warning, Eight Bells, Northeaster, The Gulf Stream, Huntsman and Dogs, West Point Prouts Neck, After the Hurricane.*

Hom·ma \hōm-mä\ Masaharu. 1887–1946. Japanese soldier. Commanded invasion of Philippines (1941); convicted (1946) of ordering "Bataan Death March" and other atrocities; executed.

Ho·molle \ò-mòl\, Théophile. 1848–1925. French archaeologist. Professor, Collège de France (1884); director (1890–1904, 1912–13), French school at Athens and its excavations at Delphi (1892–1903); director, national museums in France (1904–11); director, French National Library (1913–24).

Ho·na·mi \hō-nä-mē\ Kōetsu. 1558–1637. Japanese calligrapher and painter. Noted as connoisseur of swords and the tea ceremony, as teacher of painting, as innovator in lacquer-work.

Hon·da \'hōn-dä\ Toshiaki. 1744–1821. Japanese scholar. Studied Dutch, mathematics, astronomy, economics, etc.; one of earliest Japanese scholars to investigate Western thought and to urge Westernization of Japanese institutions.

Hon·de·coe·ter \'hòn-də-ˌkü-tər\, Melchior d'. 1636–1695. Dutch painter. Son of the painter Gijsbrecht d'Hondecoeter (1604–1653) and grandson of Gilles (d. 1638); noted as a painter of animals, esp. birds.

Hondt \'hònt\, Joost de. *Lat.* Jodocus Hon·di·us \'hän-dē-əs\. 1563–1611. Flemish engraver. Worked in England (c.1584–93), Amsterdam; produced globes, maps, notably of voyages of Drake, Cavendish; engraved works of John Speed; published successful new edition of Mercator's atlas (1605).

Hone \'hōn\, Philip. 1780–1851. American businessman and diarist, b. New York City. Mayor of New York (1825). His *Diary,* kept from 1828 to 1851 (pub. in part 1889), gives valuable impressions of life in New York and of the beginnings of the Whig party.

Hone, William. 1780–1842. English satirist and bookdealer. Published radical newspapers *The Traveller* (1814–15), *Reformist's Register* (1816–17); won landmark freedom of press cases (1817); wrote political satires illustrated by

Cruikshank including *Political House that Jack Built* (1819), *Man in the Moon* (1820), *Political Showman* (1821), etc.; other writings included *Every-day Book* (1826), *Table-book* (1827–28).

Ho·neg·ger \ô-ne-ger, *Angl* ˈhō-ˌneg-ər\, Arthur. 1892–1955. French composer, of Swiss descent. Member of group known as "Les Six" (Honegger, Auric, Durey, Milhaud, Poulenc, Tailleferre). Among his compositions were operas *Antigone* (1924–27), *Judith* (1926), *L'Aiglon* (1935), *Charles le téméraire* (1943–44); other dramatic works *Le Roi David* (1921), *Jeanne d'Arc au bûcher* (1934–35), *Nicolas de Flue* (1939); ballets as *Skating Rink* (1921), *Sémiramis* (1931); orchestral works as *Pacific 231* (1923), *Rugby* (1928), 5 symphonies, concertos, etc.; vocal and chamber works; radio and film scores, esp. for Abel Gance's *La Roue* (1923) and *Napoléon* (1927), and *Pygmalion* (1938), *Cavalcade d'amour* (1939, with Milhaud), *La Village perdu* (1947).

Hō·nen \hō-nen\. *Orig.* Gen·kū \gen-ku̇\. *Also known as* Seishi-Mara, Hōnenbō Genkū, Urushima, Fujii Motohiko, Enkō Daishi, Ganso. 1133–1212. Japanese religious. Entered Tendai Buddhist monastery (1148); became convinced of essential sinfulness of man and consequent impossibility of following Shōdō (Sacred Way) of Buddha; proclaimed Jōdo (Pure Land) doctrine in *Senchaku hongan nembutsu-shu* (1198); gathered disciples in Kyōto; by simple teachings of faith and by exemplary life helped establish pietistic Jōdo sect as one of principal forms of Japanese Buddhism; banished from Kyōto (1207–11).

Honnecourt, Villard de. See VILLARD DE HONNECOURT.

Ho·no·ria \hō-ˈnōr-ē-ə\, Justa Grata. 5th century A.D. Roman princess. Daughter of Emperor Constantius III; brought up in the court of Theodosius II at Constantinople. Reputed to have sought marriage with Attila the Hun, who through her claimed (c.450) a portion of the Roman Empire and, his demands being rejected, invaded Gaul.

Ho·no·ri·us \hō-ˈnōr-ē-əs\. Name of four popes and one antipope:

Honorius I. d. 638. Pope (625–638). Took great interest in affairs of the church in England; promoted restoration of Roman Christian antiquities; wrote letters (634) to Sergius, Patriarch of Constantinople, favoring the Monothelite doctrine; condemned for this by Council of Constantinople (680).

Honorius II. *Orig.* Lamberto Scan·na·bec·chi \ˌskän-nä-ˈbak-kē\. d. 1130. Pope (1124–30). Cardinal bishop of Ostia (1117); helped conclude Concordat of Worms (1122) with Henry V, settling the question of investiture; supported by the Frangipani; recognized Lothair III of Saxony as emperor (1125); opposed but defeated by Roger II of Sicily (1128); confirmed order of Knights Templars.

Honorius III. *Orig.* Cencio Sa·vel·li \sä-ˈvel-lē\. d. 1227. Pope (1216–27). Treasurer of Holy See (1188); made cardinal priest by Innocent III; urged crusades against the Albigenses and to the Holy Land; engaged in protracted dispute with Emperor Frederick II over Frederick's frequent postponements of promised crusade; succeeded in keeping peace in several European countries; confirmed orders of Dominicans (1216), Franciscans (1223), Carmelites (1226); author of many ecclesiastical works and letters.

Honorius IV. *Orig.* Giacomo *or* Jacobus Savelli. 1210?–1287. Pope (1285–87). Grandnephew of Honorius III; cardinal (1261); elected to succeed Martin IV; sought to restore Sicily to papal vassalage.

Honorius II. *Orig.* Peter Ca·da·lus \kə-ˈdā-ləs\. d. 1072. Antipope (1061–72). Bishop of Parma (c.1045); opposed reform movement of Cardinal Hildebrand (later Gregory VII); supported by Lombard and German bishops and Empress Agnes, elected pope in opposition to Hildebrand's choice, Alexander II; installed in Rome by armed force (1062); maintained claim despite contrary decisions of church councils (1062, 1064).

Honorius, Flavius. 384–423. Roman emperor of the West (395–423). Second son of Theodosius the Great; named augustus (393); on death of his father received western half of empire under guardianship of Stilicho; resided at Milan and later, for most of his reign, at Ravenna; m. daughter of Stilicho; caused death of Stilicho (408); lived in ease at Ravenna while Alaric ravaged Italy and sacked Rome (410); several provinces lost to empire, Roman power greatly declined; made Constantius III coemperor of the West (421).

Hontañón, Juan and Rodrigo Gil de. See GIL DE HONTAÑÓN.

Hont·heim \ˈhònt-ˌhīm\, Johann Nikolaus von. 1701–1790. German prelate and theologian. Professor, Trier (1734–39); auxiliary bishop and vicar general of Trier (1748); opponent of ultramontanism. Best known for his *De Statu Ecclesiae et Legitima Potestate Romani Pontificis* (1763), published under pseudonym Justinus Fe·bro·ni·us \fā-ˈbrō-nē-u̇s\, origin of the Febronian doctrine.

Hont·horst \ˈhònt-ˌhòrst\, Gerrit van. 1590–1656. Dutch painter. Influenced by Caravaggio; best known as a portrait and figure painter, often of night scenes, as *Beheading of St. John, Christ Before the High Priest, Supper Party, A Concert.*

Hooch *or* **Hoogh** \ˈhōk\, Pieter de. 1629–after 1684. Dutch painter. Member of Delft Baroque school; known for genre paintings, esp. of interiors, marked by use of light; works included *The Pantry, Backgammon Players, A Mother Beside a Cradle, At the Linen Closet.*

Hood \ˈhu̇d\. Name of an English family several members of which were high-ranking British naval officers, including: Samuel (1724–1816), 1st Viscount Hood; British admiral; entered navy (1741); in command of the *Vestal,* captured French frigate *Bellona* (1759); commander in chief on North American station (1767–70); rear admiral (1780); second in command under Adm. Lord Rodney in West Indies (1781–83); fought de Grasse (1781) and outmaneuvered him off St. Kitts (1782); commanded rear under Rodney in defeat of De Grasse off Dominica (1782). Commander in Mediterranean (1793–94); took possession of Toulon (1793) and Corsica (1794); admiral (1794); created viscount (1796). His younger brother ¶Alexander (1727–1814), 1st Viscount Brid·port \ˈbrid-ˌpō(ə)rt, -ˌpȯ(ə)rt\; entered navy (1741); recaptured *Warwick* from French (1761); commanded the *Robust* at Ushant (1778); rear admiral (1780) and one of Howe's flag officers at relief of Gibraltar (1782); vice admiral (1787); had full share in operations culminating in action of "the Glorious First of June" off Ushant (1794); captured three French ships (1795); as commander in chief of Channel fleet directed blockade of Brest (1797–1800); vice admiral of England (1796).

A cousin ¶Sir Alexander (1758–1798) entered navy (1767), accompanied Capt. Cook in the *Resolution* on second circumnavigation (1772); commanded one of Rodney's frigates in victory off Dominica (1782); in command of the *Mars,* mortally wounded in victory over French *Hercule* (1798). His brother ¶Sir Samuel (1762–1814) entered navy (1776), served in actions in West Indies leading to Rodney's victory off Dominica (1782); resourcefully extricated his frigate from Toulon (1794); participated in Nelson's attack on Santa Cruz de Tenerife (1797) and in battle of the Nile (1798); commodore at Leeward station (1803–04); lost an arm blockading Rochefort (1805); rear admiral (1807); captured Russian *Sevolod* in Baltic (1808); vice admiral (1811); commander in chief in East Indies (1811–14).

¶Arthur William Acland (1824–1901), 1st Baron Hood of Av·a·lon \ˈav-ə-ˌlän, -lən\; grandson of Sir Alexander Hood (1758–98); entered navy (1836), served before Sevastopol; participated in capture of Canton, China (1857); director of naval ordnance (1869–74); rear admiral (1876); vice admiral (1880); commanded Channel fleet (1880–82); first sea lord of admiralty (1885–89) and admiral (1885); known for his antagonism to innovation. ¶Sir Horace Lambert Alexander (1870–1916), son of 4th Viscount Hood; entered navy (1883), served on the Nile (1897–98) and Somaliland expedition (1903–04); commander of naval college at Osborne (1910–13); rear admiral (1913); commanded 3d battle cruiser squadron at Jutland (1916) and went down with his flagship *Invincible.*

Hood, John Bell. 1831–1879. American army officer, b. Owingsville, Ky. In U.S. army (1853–61); entered Confederate army (1861); brigadier general (1862) in command of "Texas Brigade" which won reputation at Gaines's Mill, Second Manassas, and Antietam; major general (1862); under Longstreet at Gettysburg; lost right leg at Chickamauga; lieutenant general (1864); transferred to J.E. Johnston's army; replaced Johnston and conducted defense of Atlanta against Sherman; after unsuccessful engagements against Thomas and Schofield, relieved at own request (Jan. 1865).

Hood, Raymond Mathewson. 1881–1934. American architect, b. Pawtucket, R.I. Collaborated with John Mead Howells in submitting successful designs in competition for Tribune Tower in Chicago (1922); with J. A. Fouilhoux designed Daily News Building (1930), McGraw-Hill Building (1930–31), N.Y.C.; one of three firms collaborating on design of Rockefeller Center (1929–40).

Hood, Thomas. 1799–1845. English poet. Learned engraving; subeditor, *London Magazine* (1821–23); wrote, with his brother-in-law J. H. Reynolds, *Odes and Addresses to Great People* (1825); won reputation with series of *Comic Annuals* (1830–42), treating current events with caricature; showed poetical powers as editor (1829) of the *Gem,* an annual in which appeared *Eugene Aram's Dream* (1829); other serious verse included *The Plea of the Midsummer Fairies* (1827), "The Bridge of Sighs" (1844); began *Hood's Magazine* (1844); his "Song of the Shirt" appeared in *Punch* (1843); other works, *Whims and Oddities* (1826, 1827), *Tylney Hall,* a novel (1834), *Miss Kilmansegg,* comic poem, and *Whimsicalities* (1844). His son ¶Thomas, *known as* Tom (1835–1874), humorist and journalist, served in the war office five years; became editor of *Fun* (1865), and began series of *Tom Hood's Comic Annuals* (1867).

Hooft \ˈhōft\, Pieter Corneliszoon. 1581–1647. Dutch historian, poet, and playwright. Center of a group of artists, poets, and men of letters identified with the Dutch renaissance. Writings included verse *Stich-rijmen* (1618 or 1619); dramatic works *Grandida* (1605), *Geeraert van Velsen* (1613), *Baeto* (1617); and *Nederlandse historiën* (1642–54).

Hoogh. See HOOCH.

Hoog·strae·ten \ˈhōk̲-ˌsträ-tən\, Jakob van. c.1460–1527. Belgian Dominican monk. Papal inquisitor for Cologne, Mainz, and Trier; involved in controversy with Reuchlin (*q.v.*); ridiculed in *Epistolae obscurorum virorum.*

Hoog·stra·ten \ˈhōk̲-ˌsträ-tən\, Samuel van. 1627–1678. Dutch painter. Studied under his father Dirck van Hoogstraten (1596–1640) and under Rembrandt; painter of genre pictures, portraits, and still life.

Hook \ˈhu̇k\, James. 1746–1827. English organist and composer. Organist at Vauxhall Gardens, London (1774–1820). Composed comic operas as *Dido* (1771), *Lady of the Manor* (1778), *Double Disguise* (1784), and much other theatrical music; keyboard and orchestral works; and more than 2000 songs.

Hook, Theodore Edward. 1788–1841. English humorist and novelist. Son of James Hook; wrote many comic librettos for his father; accountant general of Mauritius (1813–17); held liable for large loss of public money and imprisoned (1823–25); edited *John Bull* (1820) and *New Monthly Magazine* (1836–41). Author (under several pseudonyms, as Richard Jones, Mrs. Ramsbottom, Vicesimus Blenkinsop) of *Exchange no Robbery* (farce), *Tentamen* (satire on Queen Caroline), a collection of *Sayings and Doings* (1824), and popular novels of fashionable society as *Maxwell* (1830), *Gilbert Gurney* (1836), *Jack Brag* (1836), *Births, Marriages, and Deaths* (1839).

Hook, Walter Farquhar. 1798–1875. English clergyman. Grandson of James Hook. Vicar of Leeds (1837–59), dean of Chichester (1859–75); compiled *Church Dictionary* (1842) and *Dictionary of Ecclesiastical Biography* (1845–52), and wrote *Lives of the Archbishops of Canterbury* (1860–76).

Hooke \ˈhu̇k\, Robert. 1635–1703. English scientist. Assistant to Thomas Willis in chemistry researches and to Robert Boyle with his air pump; propounded (1660) Hooke's law of elasticity; curator of experiments to Royal Society (1662); Gresham professor of geometry, Oxford (1665); surveyor of London and designer of Montague House, Bethlehem Hospital, and Coll. of Physicians. Author of *Micrographia* (1665), in which he published results of his microscopic investigations; first used term cell to designate individual cavities observed in cork; discussed crystalline structure of snowflakes. Proved experimentally that center of gravity of earth and moon is the point describing an ellipse around sun; discovered fifth star in Orion; inferred rotation of Jupiter; discovered phenomenon of diffraction (1672) and propounded wave theory of light; suggested a kinetic hypothesis of gases (1678); anticipated Newton in formulation of law of inverse squares (1678); constructed first Gregorian telescope; invented a marine barometer.

Hook·er \ˈhu̇k-ər\, Joseph. 1814–1879. American army officer, b. Hadley, Mass. In army (1837–53); at outbreak of Civil War, appointed brigadier general of volunteers (May 1861); distinguished himself at Williamsburg (May 5, 1862), winning sobriquet of "Fighting Joe"; wounded at Antietam; brigadier general, U.S. army (1862); commanded Center Grand Division at Fredericksburg. Succeeded Burnside in command of army of the Potomac (Jan. 1863); failed to defeat Lee at Chancellorsville (May 2–4, 1863); at own request, relieved of command and succeeded by Meade (June 1863); served under Thomas and Sherman. Retired as major general (1868).

Hooker, Richard. 1553 or 1554–1600. English theologian. Widely read in Renaissance literature; fellow (1577), master of Temple Church (1585), Corpus Christi Coll., Oxford; staunch Anglican, opposed to Calvinist tendencies. Established Anglican position versus Roman Catholics and Puritans in masterly work *Of the Lawes of ecclesiasticall politie* (1594–97).

Hooker, Thomas. 1586?–1647. American colonial clergyman, b. Markfield, Leicestershire, England. Pastorates in England (1620–30); Puritan sympathies caused him to be cited to appear before Court of High Commission (1630); fled to Holland (1630) and to America, with John Cotton and Samuel Stone (1633). Pastor, Newtown, Mass. (1633–36); migrated with his congregation to Connecticut and settled Hartford (1636). Active in framing and securing adoption of the "Fundamental Orders" which served as constitution for Connecticut (1639). Author of *Survey of the Summe of Church Discipline* (1648).

Hooker, Sir William Jackson. 1785–1865. English botanist. Professor, Glasgow (1820–41); first director of Royal Botanic Gardens, Kew, London (1841–65); founded Museum of Economic Botany at Kew (1847). Author of *Journal of a Tour in Iceland* (1811), *British Jungermanniae* (1816), *Musci Exotici* (1818–20), *Flora Scotica* (1821), *Icones Filicum* (1829–31), *British Flora* (1830), etc. His son ¶Sir Joseph Dalton (1817–1911), also a botanist; member of Ross's Antarctic expedition (1839–43), publishing botanical results in six volumes (1844–60); collaborated with Darwin in researches on origin of species; explored eastern Nepal (1848–49) and eastern Bengal (1850–51); assistant director of Kew Gardens (1855) and director (1865–85); extended travels in North Africa and in Rocky Mountains in U.S. in search of botanical specimens. Author also of monumental *Genera plantarum* (1862–83, with George Bentham), *New Zealand Flora* (1864), and *Flora of British India* (1872–97).

Hoo·per \ˈhü-pər, hu̇p-ər\, Ellen, *nee* Stur·gis \ˈstər-jəs\. 1862–1848. American poet. m. (1837) Robert W. Hooper. Author of hymns and lyrical verse, including the poem "Beauty and Duty" (beginning "I slept, and dreamed that life was beauty").

Hooper, Franklin Henry. 1862–1940. American editor, b. Worcester, Mass. On staff of Century Co., New York (1883–96), and an editor of *Century Dictionary;* on staff of *Encyclopaedia Britannica* (from 1899); managing editor (1910–11), U.S. editor (1921–29), and editor in chief (1932–38). His brother ¶Horace Everett (1859–1922) was stationery and book salesman; directed sales for *Century Dictionary;* with partners and in collaboration with *Times* of London, produced highly successful inexpensive reprint of 9th edition of *Encyclopaedia Britannica* (1897 ff.); planned and published 10th edition (1902–03); with W. M. Jackson acquired ownership of *Britannica;* advertising manager of the *Times* (1905–08); published 11th (1910–11), 12th (1922) editions of *Britannica.*

Hooper, John. d. 1555. English prelate and martyr. Entered Cistercian monastery (1518); turned Protestant; fled from England (1539) to escape persecution. Returned to England (1549); bishop of Gloucester (1550), Worcester (1552). Deprived of his see by Queen Mary; condemned for heresy; burned at the stake at Gloucester.

Hooper, Johnson Jones. 1815–1862. American humorist, b. Wilmington, N.C. Author of backwoods tales collected in *Some Adventures of Captain Simon Suggs, Late of the Tallapoosa Volunteers* (1846) and *The Widow Rugby's Husband* (1851).

Hooper, William. 1742–1790. American Revolutionary leader, b. Boston. Member, Continental Congress (1774–77); signer of Declaration of Independence.

Hoorn, Count of. See Filips van MONTMORENCY.

Hoo·ton \ˈhüt-ᵊn\, Earnest Albert. 1887–1954. American anthropologist, b. Clemansville, Wis. On Harvard faculty (1913–54, professor from 1930); curator of Peabody Museum, Harvard (from 1914); known for studies of human evolution, racial types, somatotypes, criminality. Author of *Up from the Ape* (1931), *Apes, Men and Morons* (1937), *Crime and the Man* (1939), *Twilight of Man* (1939), *Why Men Behave Like Apes, and Vice Versa* (1940), *Man's Poor Relations* (1942), etc.

Hoo·ver \ˈhü-vər\, Herbert Clark. 1874–1964. Thirty-first president of the United States, b. West Branch, Iowa. Mining engineer in many parts of world (1895–1913), with headquarters in London (from 1902). Chairman of American Relief Commission in London (1914–15) and of Commission for Relief in Belgium (1915–19); U.S. food administrator (1917–19). U.S. secretary of commerce (1921–29); laid foundation for federal regulation of radio broadcasting, commercial aviation. Directed relief following Mississippi flood (1927). President of the U.S. (1929–33); in response to financial distress secured creation of Federal Farm Board (1929), Reconstruction Finance Corp. (1932); overwhelmingly defeated for reelection (1932). Headed panels investigating government waste and inefficiency (1947–49, 1953). Author of *American Individualism* (1922).

Hoover, John Edgar. 1895–1972. American lawyer and public official, b. Washington, D.C. On staff of Department of Justice (1917); director, Federal Bureau of Investigation, Department of Justice (1924–1972). Author of *Persons in Hiding* (1938), *Masters of Deceit* (1958).

Hoover, William Henry. 1849–1932. American industrialist, b. near North Canton, Ohio. Proprietor of tannery and harness business (from 1870); purchased patent of James Murray Spangler (1907) on electric cleaning machine and formed Electric Suction Sweeper Co. (1908), called Hoover Suction Sweeper Co. (from 1910); president (1908–22); chairman of successor Hoover Co. (1922–32); noted as philanthropist.

Hope, Anthony. See Sir Anthony Hope HAWKINS.

Hope \ˈhōp\, John. 1868–1936. American educator, b. Augusta, Ga. Professor, Atlanta Baptist Coll. (1898–1906); president of renamed Morehouse College (1906–31), and of Atlanta University (1929–36); opponent of Booker T. Washington's accommodationist tactics and advocate of full social equality for Negroes.

Hope, John Adrian Louis. 7th Earl Hope·toun \ˈhōp-tən, -ˌtau̇n\ *and* 1st Marquis of Lin·lith·gow \lin-ˈlith-(ˌ)gō\. 1860–1908. British statesman. Governor of Victoria, Australia (1889–95); paymaster general (1895–98); lord chamberlain (1898–1900). First governor general, Commonwealth of Australia (1900–02). Secretary of state for Scotland (1905). His son ¶Victor Alexander John (1887–1952), 8th earl and 2d marquis, soldier and administrator, served in World War I; chairman of joint select committee on Indian constitutional reform, which prepared the so-called Linlithgow Report (1934); viceroy and governor general of India (1936–43).

Hope, Thomas. 1769–1831. English antiquarian and writer. Collector of marbles and sculptures; a major exponent of Neoclassical Regency style in architecture and decoration, exemplified esp. at his country seat Deepdene (from 1807); patron of Canova, Thorvaldsen, and Flaxman. Author of influential *Household Furniture and Interior Decoration* (1807), *Designs of Modern Costume* (1812), novel *Anastasius* (1819).

Hope-Jones \'hōp-'jōnz\, Robert. 1859–1914. American organ builder, b. Cheshire, England. Engineer with National Telephone Co.; invented numerous improvements in electrified organs and headed Hope-Jones Organ Co. (1891–97); to U.S. (1903); headed new Hope-Jones Organ Co., Elmira, N.Y. (1907–10), selling out to and thereafter employed by Wurlitzer Co.

Hophra. See APRIES.

Hop·kins \'häp-kənz\, Edward John. 1818–1901. English organist. Organist of Temple Church, London (1843–98); author of *The Organ; its History and Construction* (1855).

Hopkins, Esek. 1718–1802. American naval officer, b. in what is now Scituate, R.I. Merchant sea captain; appointed commodore of the Continental navy (Dec. 1775); captured British post at New Providence, Bahamas (Mar. 1776); after lengthy period of inactivity, censured by Congress (Oct. 1776); suspended from command (Mar. 1777); dismissed (Jan. 1778).

Hopkins, Sir Frederick Gowland. 1861–1947. English biochemist. At Cambridge U. (1898–1943, professor from 1914); with S. W. Cole, isolated tryptophan (1901); codiscoverer (1907, with Sir Walter Fletcher) of the connection between lactic acid and muscular contraction; isolated glutathione from living tissue (1922); demonstrated the existence of essential amino acids and of accessory food factors later called vitamins. Shared (with Christiaan Eijkman) the 1929 Nobel prize for physiology or medicine.

Hopkins, Gerard Manley. 1844–1889. English poet. Ordained Jesuit priest (1877); professor, U. Coll., Dublin (1884–89). Author of poems, all published posthumously, including "Wreck of the Deutschland," "The Windhover," "Carrion Comfort," "Pied Beauty," notable for extraordinary prosodic and technical innovations, such as sprung rhythm and outrides.

Hopkins, Harry Lloyd. 1890–1946. American administrator and politician, b. Sioux City, Iowa. In social welfare work in New Orleans and New York (1912–33); appointed head of Federal Emergency Relief Administration (1933) and Works Progress (later Projects) Administration (1935–38), overseeing distribution of $8.5 billion for unemployment relief; secretary of commerce (1938–40); head of Lend-Lease Administration (1941); President Roosevelt's personal envoy to Russia and Britain (1941); member of War Production Board (1942); special assistant to President Roosevelt (1942–45).

Hopkins, John. See Thomas STERNHOLD.

Hopkins, Johns. 1795–1873. American financier, b. Anne Arundel Co., Md. Made fortune as grocer, commission merchant, banker, investor in Baltimore & Ohio Railroad; left $7 million to found hospital and university, now located in Baltimore, and named in his honor The Johns Hopkins Hospital and The Johns Hopkins University.

Hopkins, Mark. 1802–1887. American educator, b. Stockbridge, Mass. Professor of moral philosophy and rhetoric, Williams Coll. (1830–87); president (1836–72); known as inspired teacher and lecturer. Author of many books on moral and religious subjects.

Hopkins, Matthew. d. 1647. English witch hunter. Established himself as "Witch Finder Generall" (1644) and caused scores to be tried and hanged for witchcraft in Norfolk, Suffolk, Essex, Huntingdonshire; because of his success, eventually suspected of witchcraft; tried by own methods and hanged.

Hopkins, Sam, *known as* Lightnin'. 1912–1982. American musician, b. Centerville, Tex. Considered one of the greatest exponents of country blues music and esp. an innovative guitarist.

Hopkins, Samuel. 1721–1803. American theologian, b. Waterbury, Conn. Intimate friend of Jonathan Edwards; evolved Hopkinsianism, a systematic theology long a major school of Congregational doctrine, in his book *System of Doctrines Contained in Divine Revelation, Explained and Defended* (1793).

Hopkins, Stephen. 1707–1785. American colonial administrator, b. Providence, R.I. Governor of Rhode Island (1755, 1756, 1758–61, 1763, 1764, 1767). Member, Continental Congress (1774–80); signer of Declaration of Independence.

Hop·kin·son \'häp-kən-sən\, Francis. 1737–1791. American political leader and writer, b. Philadelphia. Adm. to bar (1761); practiced, Philadelphia, and Bordentown, N.J. (from 1773). Active in pre-Revolutionary agitation; began publishing political satires (1774). Member, Continental Congress (1776); signer of Declaration of Independence; had important part in designing American flag (1777). U.S. district judge, eastern district of Pennsylvania (1789–91). Among his satires were *The Battle of the Kegs* (verse, 1778), *Date Obolum Bellesario* (allegory, 1778), *Modern Learning Exemplified* (1784), *A Letter from a Gentleman in America on White-washing* (1785).

Hopkinson, John. 1849–1898. English electrical engineer. Consultant engineer (from 1878); professor, King's Coll., London (1890–98); worked out theory of alternating current and patented three-wire system of distributing electricity (1882).

Hopkinson, Joseph. 1770–1842. American politician, b. Philadelphia. Son of Francis Hopkinson. Member, U.S. House of Representatives (1815–19). Judge, U.S. district court, eastern district of Pennsylvania (1828–42). Author of the patriotic song "Hail Columbia" (1798), first sung by Gilbert Fox in Philadelphia.

Hop·pe \'häp-ē\, William Frederick, *known as* Willie. 1887–1959. American billiard player, b. Cornwall-on-the-Hudson, N.Y. World's champion at the 18.1 balkline game (1906, 1907, 1909–11, 1914–27), the 18.2 balkline game (1907, 1910–20, 1923–24, 1927), and the three-cushion game (1936, 1940–44, 1947–52); retired.

Hop·per \'häp-ər\, DeWolf, *orig.* William D'Wolf. 1858–1935. American actor, b. New York City. With own company (1878 ff.) starred in *Hazel Kirke, Castles in the Air, Wang,* etc.; appeared (1900–01) with Weber and Fields; later a great success in Gilbert and Sullivan productions; popularized poem "Casey at the Bat."

Hopper, Edward. 1882–1967. American painter, b. Nyack, N.Y. Known for starkly realistic scenes of contemporary life, often imbued with sense of isolation and loneliness, and marked by mastery of light. Works included urban scenes as *Nighthawks, Early Sunday Morning, Sunlight in a Cafeteria, House by the Railroad,* and scenes of rural and coastal New England.

Hopper, Hedda. *Orig.* Elda Fur·ry \'fər-ē, 'fə-rē\. 1890–1966. American newspaper columnist, b. Hollidaysburg, Pa. Stage and film actress (1908–c.1920); m. DeWolf Hopper (1913; div. 1922); began radio gossip program, Hollywood (1936); conducted syndicated gossip column (1938–66) in rivalry with Louella Parsons; known for exotic hats. Author of *From Under My Hat* (1952), *The Whole Truth and Nothing But* (1963).

Hop·pe-Sey·ler \'hóp-ə-'zī-lər\, Felix, *in full* Ernst Felix Immanuel. 1825–1895. German physiologist and chemist. Professor, Tübingen (1861–72), Strassburg (1872–95); a founder of physiological chemistry; studied properties of hemoglobin, chlorophyll, and protein, activation of oxygen, fermentation, etc. Founded and edited (1877–95) *Zeitschrift für physiologische Chemie.*

Hopp·ner \'häp-nər\, John. 1758–1810. English painter. Rival of Thomas Lawrence as fashionable portraitist; sitters included Prince of Wales, Lord Nelson, Wellington, Sir Walter Scott, Countess of Oxford.

Hop·ton \'häp-tən\, Ralph. 1st Baron Hopton. 1596–1652. English Royalist commander. M.P. (1624 ff.); orig. of Puritan leanings, but later, as Royalist sympathizer, expelled from House of Commons (1642). Made lieutenant general for western England (1642); won victories at Stratton, Lansdowne (1643); created baron (1643); commander of Royalist army (1646); forced to surrender at Truro (1646); left England with Prince Charles (1648).

Hop·wood \'häp-,wu̇d\, Avery, *in full* James Avery. 1882–1928. American playwright, b. Cleveland, Ohio. First play, *Clothes* (with Channing Pollock, 1906). Best known for mystery melodramas as *The Bat* (with Mary Roberts Rinehart, 1920) and for clever, often somewhat risqué, farce comedies as *Our Little Wife* (1916), *The Gold Diggers* (1919), *Getting Gertie's Garter* (1921), *The Demi-Virgin* (1921), *Why Men Leave Home* (1922), *Little Miss Bluebeard* (1923).

Hor·ace \'hór-əs, 'här-\. *In full* Quintus Ho·ra·tius Flac·cus \hə-'rā-sh(ē-)əs-'flak-əs\. 65–8 B.C. Roman poet and satirist. Educated in Rome and Athens; commanded legion in republican army at Philippi (42). On return to Rome, enjoyed patronage of Maecenas and received from him gift of a villa in the Sabine Hills; also enjoyed favor of Emperor Augustus. Among his works were two books of *Satires,* four of lyrical *Odes,* two of verse *Epistles,* one of *Epodes,* and the treatise *Ars poetica.*

Hor·a·pol·lon \,hō-rə-'päl-ən, ,här-\ *or* **Hor·a·pol·lo** \-(,)ō\. 4th–5th century A.D. Greek grammarian of Egypt. Author of treatises on hieroglyphics.

Hore-Be·li·sha \'hō(ə)r-bə-'lē-shə, 'hȯ(ə)r-\, Leslie, *in full* Isaac Leslie. 1st Baron Hore-Belisha. 1893–1957. English politician. M.P. (1923–45); financial secretary to treasury (1932–34); minister of transport (1934–37) and originator of Belisha beacons used at pedestrian crossings; as secretary for war (1937–40) instituted conscription (1939); minister of national insurance (1945); created baron (1954).

Ho·rem·heb \'hór-əm-,heb, 'hōr-\. *Also spelled* Harmhab, Haremhab. *Also called* Djeserkhepere. 14th century B.C. Egyptian king (c.1348–c.1320 B.C.). Commander of army in northern Egypt and powerful figure in court of Tutankhamen and Ay; succeeded Ay and secured claim to throne by marrying sister of Nefertiti; ruled as last of 18th dynasty; eradicated vestiges of Aton religion, restoring traditional Amon religion; began great hypostyle hall at Karnak; restored foreign trade.

Hor·lick \'hȯ(ə)r-lik\, William. 1846–1936. American industrialist, b. Ruardean, Gloucestershire, England. To U.S. (1869); settled in Racine, Wis. (1876). With brother ¶James, *later* Sir James (1844–1921), organized J. & W. Horlick Co. (1873), manufacturers of foods for infants, invalids, etc.; originated malted milk (1887), dry extract of malt, etc. James returned to England to establish branch firm (1890); he served as president of Horlick's Food Co.

(1876–1906), Horlick's Malted Milk Co. (1906–21); succeeded by William (1921–36).

Hor·mayr \'hȯr-ˌmīr\, Joseph von. Freiherr. 1782–1848. Austrian historian. Director of archives, Vienna (1803); imperial historiographer (1816). To Munich (1828) and became Bavarian minister to Hanover (1832) and Bremen (1839); director, Munich royal archives (1846).

Hor·mis·das \hor-'miz-dəs\. Saint. d. 523. Pope (514–523). Effected union of Eastern and Western churches (519), ending Acacian schism.

Hor·mizd \'hȯr-mizd\. *Also spelled* Ormazd, Ormizd. Name of four kings of the Sāsānian Empire of Persia:

Hormizd I. *Called* the Brave. 3d century. King (272–273). Son and successor of Shāpūr I; successful military leader under his father.

Hormizd II. d. 309. King (302–309). Son and successor of Narses; at his death a rebellion of nobles led to death of his son Adhur-Narses and imprisonment of second son.

Hormizd III. d. 459. King (457–459). Son and successor of Yazdegerd II; overthrown and slain by brother Fīrūz.

Hormizd IV. d. 590. King (578 or 579–590). Son and successor of Khosrow I; carried on father's wars against Byzantine Empire and Turks; deposed and killed in insurrection of general, Bahrām Chubīn.

Horn, Count of. See Filips van MONTMORENCY.

Horn \'hürn\, Arvid Bernhard. Count. 1664–1742. Swedish soldier and politician. General in army of Charles XII (1700); active in deposition of Augustus II of Poland (1704); count and counselor to the king (1705); on death of Charles XII (1718), persuaded Ulrika Eleonora to be elected queen and then to abdicate in favor of her husband Frederick of Hesse (1720); speaker of chamber of nobles in Riksdag (1720–38).

Horn \'hȯ(ə)rn\, Charles Edward. 1786–1849. English singer and composer. Composer of operas and oratorios, glees and piano pieces, and many popular airs, including "On the banks of Allen Water," "The deep, deep sea," "Cherry ripe," "I know a bank."

Horn \'hürn\, Gustaf Karlsson. Count till Björ·ne·borg \til-ˌbyœr-nə-'bȯrʸ\. 1592–1657. Swedish soldier. Field marshal (1628); served in Thirty Years' War under Gustav Adolphus and with Baner and Bernhard of Saxe-Weimar.

Hor·na·day \'hȯr-nə-ˌdā\, William Temple. 1854–1937. American zoologist, b. Plainfield, Ind. Chief taxidermist, U.S National Museum (1882–90); director, New York Zoological Park (1896–1926). Promoted game preserves and laws for the protection of wildlife.

Horn·blow·er \'hȯ(ə)rn-ˌblō-ər\, Jonathan (1717–1780) and his son Jonathan Carter (1753–1815). English engineers. Employees of James Watt; designed a reciprocating compound steam engine (patented 1781) utilizing an application of the expansion principle which was judged by the courts (1799) an infringement on Watt's patent.

Horn·bos·tel \'hȯrn-bȯs-tᵊl\, Erich Moritz von. 1877–1935. Austrian musicologist. Director, Berlin Phonogrammearchiv (1906–33); professor, Berlin (1917–33); fled to U.S. (1933), England (1934). Pioneer in study of primitive and non-European music; made special studies in Japan, Madagascar, Turkey; studied Pawnee Indian music.

Horn·by \'hȯ(ə)rn-bē\, Sir Geoffrey Thomas Phipps. 1825–1895. English naval officer. Son of admiral; entered navy (1837); rear admiral (1869), vice admiral (1875); lord of the admiralty (1875–77); commander in Mediterranean (1877–80); took fleet through Dardanelles to Constantinople in Russo-Turkish war (1878); admiral (1879); admiral of the fleet (1888).

Horne \'hȯ(ə)rn\, Henry Sinclair. 1st Baron Horne of Stir·koke \'stər-kək\. 1861–1929. English soldier. Entered army (1880); served in Boer War (1899–1902); brigadier general (1912); in World War I successively artillery commander of 1st corps in France, commander (1915) of 2d division, commander (1916) of 15th corps, general and commander (1916) of 1st army; captured Vimy Ridge (April 1917); broke through Hindenburg Line (Sept. 1918), occupied Mons. Created baron (1919); commander in chief in the East (1919–23).

Horne, Richard Henry *or* Richard Hengist. 1803–1884. English writer. Served in Mexican navy; commissioner for crown lands, and magistrate, in Australia (1852–69). Author of tragedies *Cosmo de' Medici* (1837), *Death of Marlowe* (1837), epic poem *Orion* (1843), *Ballad Romances* (1846), *Australian Facts and Prospects* (1859), etc.

Hor·ne·mann \'hȯr-nə-ˌmän\, Friedrich Konrad. 1772–1801. German explorer. In employ of African Association of London, became first European to cross northeastern Sahara, making trek from Cairo to Marzūq (1798) disguised as Muslim merchant in a caravan; died at Nupe on journey south to country of the Hausa.

Hor·ner \'hȯr-nər\, Francis. 1778–1817. British politician. M.P. (1806 ff.). As chairman of the bullion committee, recommended in his Bullion Report resumption of specie payments (1810). A founder of *Edinburgh Review* (1802).

Horner, William George. 1786–1837. English mathematician. Schoolmaster in Bristol (1790–1809), Bath (1809–37); discovered (1819) Horner's method for deriving roots of algebraic equations by successive approximations.

Hor·ney \'hȯr-ˌnī\, Karen, *nee* Danielsen. 1885–1952. American psychoanalyst, b. Hamburg, of Norwegian father and Dutch mother. m. Oscar Horney (1909; div. 1937). Teacher and practitioner of psychoanalysis at Berlin Psychoanalytic Institute (1920–32). To U.S. (1932); associate director, Inst. for Psychoanalysis, Chicago (1932–34); in practice and teacher at New School for Social Research, N.Y.C. (1934–52); expelled (1941) from N.Y. Psychoanalytic Inst. for critique of Freudian practices in *New Ways in Psychoanalysis* (1939); founded Association for the Advancement of Psychoanalysis and American Inst. for Psychoanalysis. Author also of *Neurotic Personality of Our Time* (1937), *Self-Analysis* (1942), *Our Inner Conflicts* (1945), *Neurosis and Human Growth* (1950).

Hor·ni·man \'hȯr-nə-mən\, Annie Elizabeth Fredericka. 1860–1937. English theater manager. Secretly sponsored theatrical season (1894–95) that included *Arms and the Man,* G. B. Shaw's first publicly produced play; built and managed Abbey Theatre in Dublin for the Irish National Theatre Society (1904); bought and managed Gaiety Theatre in Manchester (1908–21), where she built a pioneering and widely influential repertory company.

Horns·by \'hȯrnz-bē\, Rogers. 1896–1963. American baseball player, b. Winters, Tex. Player (1915–26), player-manager (1925–26), St. Louis Cardinals; player, N.Y. Giants (1927); player-manager, Boston Braves (1928); player (1929), player-manager (1930–32), Chicago Cubs; player, Cardinals (1932); manager, occasional player, St. Louis Browns (1933–37); thereafter managed major and minor league teams. Considered greatest right-handed batter of all time; lifetime batting average .358 (second to Ty Cobb); led National League in batting (1920–25, 1928), including highest season average in modern baseball, .424 (1924); won triple crown (1922, 1925); led Cardinals to World Series victory (1926). Elected to Baseball Hall of Fame (1942).

Hor·nung \'hȯr-nəŋ\, Ernest William. 1866–1921. English writer. Brother-in-law of Arthur Conan Doyle. Creator of Raffles, gentleman burglar, featured in novels *The Amateur Cracksman* (1899), *Raffles* (1901), *Thief in the Night* (1905), *Mr. Justice Raffles* (1909); also wrote *At Large* (1902), *Stingaree* (1905), *The Crime Doctor* (1914), etc.

Ho·ro·witz \'hȯr-ō-ˌvits\, Isaiah ben Abraham ha-Levi. *Called* ha-She·lah ha-Ka·dosh \hä-'shel-ä-hä-'kä-dōsh\. c.1565–1630. Jewish clergyman and mystic. Ashkenazik rabbi in Jerusalem; author of *Shene luḥot ha-berit* (1649), influential in disseminating teachings of Isaac ben Solomon Luria.

Hor·rocks *or* **Hor·rox** \'här-əks, 'hȯr-\, Jeremiah. c.1617–1641. English astronomer. After correcting Kepler's *Rudolphine Tables,* made first observation of a transit of Venus (1639); assigned to the Moon an elliptical orbit with the earth at one of the foci, a discovery accepted by Newton; improved lunar theory; calculated long unsurpassed value for solar parallax; studied planetary perturbations.

Horsa. See HENGIST.

Hor·sley \'hȯrz-lē, 'hȯrs-\, John. c.1685–1732. English antiquary. Author of *Britannia Romana, or the Roman Antiquities of Britain* (1732), long unsurpassed in the field.

Horsley, Samuel. 1733–1806. English prelate. Bishop of St. Davids (1788), of Rochester (1793), of St. Asaph (1802). Carried on long controversy with Joseph Priestley on the divinity of Christ, the Trinity, and necessity; edited Newton's works (1779–85).

Horsley, Sir Victor Alexander Haden. 1857–1916. English physiologist. Son of John Callcott Horsley. Professor, U. of London (1882–1906); surgeon, U. Coll. Hospital (from 1885), National Hospital for the Paralysed and Epileptic (from 1886); conducted research on thyroid gland in relation to myxedema and cretinism; confirmed Pasteur's work on rabies prevention; pioneer in surgery of brain and spinal cord.

Horsley, William. 1774–1858. English organist and composer. Published five collections of glees (between 1801 and 1827), anthems, psalm settings, songs and airs. His son ¶John Callcott (1817–1903) was a painter, esp. of genre scenes and portraits; noted for refusal to paint nudes; works included *L'Allegro* and *Il Penseroso* for Prince Albert; for Sir Henry Cole created (1843) first Christmas card. Another son ¶Charles Edward (1822–1876) was an organist and composer, notably of oratorios *David* (1850), *Joseph* (1853), and *Gideon* (1860), ode *Euterpe* (1870), and music for Milton's *Comus* (1874).

Horst \'hȯ(ə)rst\, Louis. 1884–1964. American pianist, composer, and choreographer, b. Kansas City, Mo. Musical director of Denishawn Dancers (1915–25); musical director of Martha Graham dance company (1926–48); composed scores for Graham works including *Primitive Mysteries* (1931), *Frontier* (1935), *El Penitente* (1940); accompanist also to Doris Humphrey,

\ə\ abut \ᵊ\ kitten, *Fr.* table **\ər\ further \a\ ash \ā\ ace \ä\ cot, cart \au̇\ out \ch\ chin \e\ bet \ē\ easy \g\ go \i\ hit \ī\ ice \j\ job \ŋ\ sing \ō\ go \ȯ\ law \ȯi\ boy \th\ both \th\ the \ü\ loot \u̇\ foot \y\ yet \zh\ vision** \á, b, ḡ, k, ⁿ, œ, œ̄, ue, ue̅, ʸ\ *see* Guide to Pronunciation

Helen Tamiris, etc.; pioneer in formal teaching of choreography at Neighborhood Playhouse School, N.Y.C. (1928–64), Bennington Coll. (1934–45), Connecticut Coll. (1948–63), Juilliard School (1951–64). Founded and edited (1933–64) *Dance Observer;* author of *Pre-classic Dance Forms* (1937), *Modern Dance Forms* (1961).

Hort \'hȯrt\, Fenton John Anthony. 1828–1892. English theologian and scholar. Produced a critical edition of Greek New Testament (1881, with Brooke Foss Westcott) that served as basis for English Revised Version of Bible (1881).

Hor·ta \'hȯr-tə\, Victor. Baron. 1861–1947. Belgian architect. A leading exponent of Art Nouveau style; designed Hôtel Tassel (1892–93), Hôtel Winssingers (1895–96), Hôtel Solvay (1895–1900), Maison du Peuple (1896–99), all in Brussels; director of Academy des Beaux-Arts, Brussels (from 1912); designed Palais des Beaux-Arts (1922–28) in severe neoclassical style.

Hortense de Beauharnais. See BEAUHARNAIS.

Hor·ten·sia \hȯr-'ten(t)-sē-ə, -'ten-sh(ē-)ə\. 1st century B.C. Roman noblewoman. Daughter of Quintus Hortensius (114–50 B.C.); remembered for oration (43 B.C.) against proposal of triumvirs to tax wealthy women to support war against assassins of Julius Caesar.

Hor·ten·si·us \hȯr-'ten(t)-sē-əs, -'ten-ch(ē-)əs\, Quintus. 3d century B.C. Dictator of Rome (287 B.C.). Decreed in Lex Hortensia that resolutions adopted by the mass (plebiscita) of Roman citizens should be binding on all citizens without necessity of Senate approval.

Hortensius, Quintus. 114–50 B.C. Roman lawyer and orator. A leader of the aristocratic party; quaestor (81); aedile (75); praetor (72); consul (69); best known as opponent of Cicero in trial of Verres (70).

Hor·thy de Nagy·bá·nya \'hȯr-tē-də-'nȯdʸ-bän-yä\, Miklós. 1868–1957. Hungarian admiral and politican. Aide-de-camp to Emperor Francis Joseph (1909–14); at outbreak of World War I, commanded cruiser *Novara,* operating in Adriatic; distinguished himself in action at Otranto (1917); appointed admiral and commander in chief of Austro-Hungarian fleet (1918). After war, returned to Hungary to combat Communist regime of Béla Kun; commander in chief of national army (1919); occupied Budapest (1919). Regent of Hungary (1920–1944), consistently thwarting efforts of Charles IV to recover throne; abducted by Nazi forces (1944); lived in Portugal (1945–57).

Hor·ton \'hȯrt-ᵊn\, Robert Elmer. 1875–1945. American hydraulic engineer, b. Parma, Mich. Consulting engineer (from 1911); devised Horton's laws, system of empirical rules for analysis of natural drainage networks; invented a water level gauge, a joint for wood stove pipe. Author of *Weir Experiments* (1905), *Water Wheels* (1907), *Surface Runoff Phenomena* (1935), etc.

Hø·rup \'hœ̄-rüp\, Viggo Lauritz Bentheim. 1841–1902. Danish journalist and politician. Leader of radical left opposition in parliament (1876–92); later a leader of Left Reform party; minister of transportation (1901–02). Editor of *Morgenbladet* (1881–83), editor and publisher of *Politiken* (1884–1901); a chief advocate of parliamentary government.

Hor·váth \'hȯr-ˌvät\, Mihály. 1809–1878. Hungarian prelate and politician. Bishop of Csanád (1848); involved in revolution, becoming minister of public education and worship (1849); after crushing of revolution, lived abroad (1849–66); entered lower house of Diet (1876).

Hor·váth \'hȯr-ˌvät\, Ödön von. 1901–1938. German writer. Author of plays as *Revolte auf Côte 3018* (1927), *Sladek* (1929), *Italienische Nacht* (1931), *Hin und Her* (1934), *Der jüngste Tag* (1937); novels *Der ewige Spiesser* (1930), *Ein Kind unserer Zeit* (1938), *Jugend ohne Gott* (1938).

Ho·sea \hō-'zā-ə, -'zē-\. 8th century B.C. Hebrew prophet. Active in reign of Jeroboam II; his reproofs and prophecies for apostate Israel, symbolized by marriage to faithless wife, were recorded in the Old Testament book of *Hosea.*

Ḥo·seyn I \k̲ō-'sīn\. *Also known as* Shāh Solṭān Ḥoseyn. *Orig.* Solṭān Ḥoseyn Mīr·zā \mir-'zä\. 1668–1726. Shāh of Iran (1694–1722). Ineffectual ruler; lost territory to Turkey and Russia; depleted treasury; after seven-month siege, surrendered Isfahan and abdicated in favor of Maḥmūd, leader of invading Afghans (1722); last independent ruler of Ṣafavid dynasty.

Ho·shea \hō-'shē-ə\. *Also spelled* Osee \'ō-(ˌ)zē, -(ˌ)sē\. d. 724? B.C. Last king of Israel (c.732–724 B.C.). Son of Elah. Murdered Pekah and with aid of Tiglath-pileser III ascended throne; withheld tribute from Shalmaneser V, king of Assyria; his kingdom invaded; taken captive; Samaria besieged (727–724) and captured by Sargon, who took leading inhabitants away as captives to Media.

Ho-shen \'hō-'shən\. 1750–1799. Chinese courtier. Gained favor of Ch'ien-lung emperor and secured several high posts in government; while in charge of suppression of Pai-lien chiao (White Lotus Society) revolt (1774), embezzled huge sums from treasury, leaving soldiers to loot populace; on death of emperor, deprived of office and forced to commit suicide.

Ho·si·us \'hō-zhē-əs\ *or* **Os·si·us** \'ō-zhē-əs\ of Córdoba. c.256–357 or 358. Spanish prelate. Bishop of Córdoba (c.295); ecclesiastical adviser to Emperor Constantine; convoked synods at Alexandria and Antioch at which Arianism was condemned (324); one of presiding bishops at Council of Nicaea (325). For refusing to condemn Athanasius (355), banished by Emperor Constantius II; at Council of Sirmium (357); signed under pressure a document favoring Arianism, but still refused to condemn Athanasius; restored to his see.

Hosius, Stanislaus. *Pol.* Stanisław Ho·zjusz \'kō-zyüsh\. 1504–1579. Polish prelate. Bishop of Chełmno (1549), of Ermeland (1551); cardinal (1561). Actively opposed Protestant Reformation; wrote *Confessio Catholicae Fidei Christiana* adopted by Synod of Piotrków (1557).

Hos·kyns \'häs-kənz\, Sir Edwyn Clement. 1884–1937. English theologian. Fellow of Corpus Christi Coll., Cambridge (1919–37); opposed liberal interpretation of "historical Jesus," emphasizing complexity of religious mystery unaffected by textual criticisms. Author of *Riddle of the New Testament* (1931, with F.N. Davey), *The Fourth Gospel* (1940).

Hos·mer \'häz-mər\, Harriet Goodhue. 1830–1908. American sculptor, b. Watertown, Mass. In Rome and England (1852–1900). Notable works included *Puck, Zenobia, Sleeping Faun, Heroine of Gaeta, Beatrice Cenci, Thomas H. Benton* in Lafayette Park, St. Louis, *Oenone.*

Ho·so·ka·wa \hō-sō-kä-wä\ Katsumoto. 1430–1473. Japanese warrior. Head of a principal supporting family of Ashikaga shogunate; named *kanrei,* or shogunal prime minister (1452–64); engaged in lengthy feud with emerging Yamana family led by Yamana Mochitoyo; feud developed into Ōnin War (1467–77).

Hos·til·ian \häs-'til-ē-ən, -'til-yən\. *Lat. in full* Gaius Valens Hostilianus Messius Quintus. d. 251 A.D. Roman emperor (251). Younger son of Decius; made caesar (250); on death of Decius (251), adopted by Vibius Trebonianus Gallus and made augustus.

Hos·tos \'ō-stōs\, Eugenio María de. 1839–1903. Puerto Rican writer. Lawyer in Madrid, where he frequented liberal intellectual circles; became a leading advocate of independence and federation of Spanish West Indian colonies; in Santo Domingo (1879–88) founded first normal school; considered a leader in movement for liberal education. Author of novel *La peregrinación de Bayoán* (1863), critical and philosophical works *Sociología* (1883–1901), *Moral social* (1888), *Meditando* (1909).

Hotch·kiss \'häch-(ˌ)kis\, Benjamin Berkeley. 1826–1885. American inventor, b. Watertown, Conn. Invented Hotchkiss machine gun (1872) and Hotchkiss magazine rifle (1875).

Hot·man \ȯt-män\, François. Sieur de Vil·liers Saint-Paul \də-vēl-yā-saⁿ-pȯl\. *Lat.* Hot·man·nus \hät-'man-əs\. 1524–1590. French jurist. Professor at Paris, Lyon, Geneva, Lausanne, Strasbourg, Valence, Bourges; as a Protestant, fled to Switzerland after the Massacre of Saint Bartholomew (1572). Among his many works were *De statu primitivae Ecclesiae* (1553), *Jurisconsultus* (1559), *L'Antitribonien* (1567), *Franco-Gallia* (1573).

Hotspur. See Sir Henry Percy (1364–1403) under PERCY family.

Hot·ta \hȯt-tä\ Masatoshi. 1634–1684. Japanese politican. Adviser to Tokugawa shogun Ietsuna; prevented transfer of shogunate to imperial family on Ietsuna's death (1680) and secured succession of Tsunayoshi.

Hotta Masayoshi. 1810–1864. Japanese diplomat. Minister in shogunal government (from 1837); in charge of foreign affairs (1856); advocate of Western trade and contacts; negotiated trade treaty with U.S. minister Townsend Harris (1857); emperor refused to sanction treaty, further weakening deteriorating shogunate; dismissed from office (1862).

Hotte·terre \ȯt-ter\. Family of French musicians and instrument makers including: Jean (c.1605–between 1690 and 1692); to Paris (1632); woodwind virtuoso; often credited with invention of the oboe. His son ¶Martin (c.1640–1712) improved the musette; played and composed for musette. His son ¶Jacques-Martin, *known as* Le Ro·main \lə-rō-maⁿ\ (1674–1763) was bassoonist in the Grands Hautbois and a flutist of note; composed works for flute and devised influential teaching methods published in *Principes de la flûte transversière* (1707), etc.

Hötzendorf, Franz Conrad von. See CONRAD VON HÖTZENDORF.

Hou·bra·ken \'hau̇-ˌbrä-kən\, Arnold. 1660–1719. Dutch painter. Known for scenes from Dutch history; author of a biography of Dutch painters. His son ¶Jakob (1698–1780) was a painter and engraver known for portraits.

Hou·chard \ü-shär\, Jean-Nicolas. 1740–1793. French Revolutionary soldier. Commander of army of the North; defeated the British at Hondschoote (1793), but failed to follow up his advantage; accused of conspiracy, guillotined.

Hou·dar de La Motte \ü-där-də-lä-mȯt\, Antoine. *Known as* La Motte-Houdar \lä-mȯ-tü-där\. 1672–1731. French writer. Author of verse *Odes* (1709), *Fables* (1719); plays *Les Machabées* (1721), *Romulus* (1722), *Inès de Castro* (1723), *Le Magnifique* (1731); best known for French verse translation of *Iliad* (1713), which reopened quarrel of Ancients and Moderns.

Houdenc, Raoul de. See RAOUL DE HOUDENC.

Houdin, Jean-Eugène Robert. See ROBERT-HOUDIN.

Hou·di·ni \hü-'dē-nē\, Harry. *Orig.* Ehrich Weiss \'vīs, 'wīs\. 1874–1926. American magician, b. Budapest, Hungary. To America (1874) and settled in Appleton, Wis. Joined circus, orig. as trapeze artist (1882); developed conjuring act and took name Houdini after French magician Robert-Houdin. Known for his ability to extricate himself from handcuffs and locked and sealed containers of all kinds. Campaigned against mind readers, mediums, and other charlatans. Author of *The Unmasking of Robert Houdin* (1908), *Miracle Mongers and their Methods* (1920), *A Magician Among the Spirits* (1924).

Hou·don \ü-dōⁿ, *Angl* 'hü-dän\, Jean-Antoine. 1741–1828. French sculptor. Leading exponent of Rococo style in sculpture. Among his figures were *Saint Bruno, Morphée, Vestale, Minerve, Écorché, Diane, Apollon.* Noted esp. as perceptive portraitist; executed busts of George Washington, Diderot, Voltaire, Catherine II, Turgot, Molière, J. J. Rousseau, Buffon, d'Alembert, Franklin, LaFayette, Louis XVI, Mirabeau.

Hough \'həf\, Emerson. 1857–1923. American writer, b. Newton, Iowa. Known as advocate of the preservation of wildlife and national parks. Author of *Story of the Cowboy* (1897), *The Mississippi Bubble* (1902), *The Way to the West* (1903), *Story of the Outlaw* (1907), *The Sowing* (1909), *The Passing of the Frontier,* in Chronicles of America series (1918), *The Covered Wagon* (1922).

Houghton, Baron. See Richard Monckton MILNES.

Hough·ton \'hōt-ᵊn\, Amory. 1837–1909. American industrialist. Founded the Corning Glass Works at Corning, N.Y. (1875). His son ¶Alanson Bigelow (1863–1941), b. Cambridge, Mass., entered Corning Glass Works (1889); president (1910–18) and chairman (from 1918). Member, U.S. House of Representatives (1919–22). U.S. ambassador to Germany (1922–25), to Great Britain (1925–29).

Houghton, George Hendric. 1820–1897. American clergyman, b. Deerfield, Mass. Ordained priest (1846) in Protestant Episcopal church; founder and pastor (1849–97) of the Church of the Transfiguration, New York City (better known as The Little Church Around the Corner).

Houghton, Henry Oscar. 1823–1895. American publisher, b. Sutton, Vt. Opened printing office, Cambridge, Mass.; incorporated as H. O. Houghton & Co. (1852), known as The Riverside Press. Joined partnership in publishing business (1864) which eventually developed into Houghton Mifflin Co. (after 1880).

Hough·ton \'hȯt-ᵊn\, Stanley, *in full* William Stanley. 1881–1913. English playwright. Author of *The Dear Departed* (1908), *The Younger Generation* (1910), *Hindle Wakes* (1912), etc.

House \'hau̇s\, Edward Mandell. *Known as* Colonel House. 1858–1938. American diplomat, b. Houston, Tex. Friend and confidant of President Wilson (from 1912); personal representative of the president to European nations (1914, 1915, 1916); chief presidential liaison with Allies during World War I; appointed to act for U.S. in negotiating armistice with Central Powers (1918); secured Allied acceptance of Fourteen Points, which he had helped to draft. Member of American commission to negotiate peace (1918–19); member of commission to frame the covenant of the League of Nations.

House, Royal Earl. 1814–1895. American inventor, b. Rockland, Vt. Invented a printing telegraph (1844; pat. 1846) and other telegraphic devices as a glass insulator.

House·book \'hau̇s-ˌbu̇k\, Master of the. *Ger.* Haus·buch·meis·ter \'hau̇s-ˌbük-ˌmī-stər\. *Also known as* Meis·ter des Am·ster·da·mer Ka·bi·netts \'mī-stər-des-ˌäm-stər-'däm-ər-ˌkäb-ē-'nets\. fl. 1450–70. German painter and engraver. Unknown master of late Gothic art, known from 91 extant prints depicting satirically scenes of contemporary life, and from a Hausbuch, or sketchbook, done for the Wolfegg family.

Hous·man \'hau̇-smən\, Alfred Edward. 1859–1936. English scholar and poet. Clerk in Patent Office (1882–92); professor of Latin, University Coll., London (1892–1911) and Cambridge (1911–36). Edited works of Manilius, Juvenal, and Lucan. Published volumes of Romantic, yet impeccably classical verse *A Shropshire Lad* (1896) and *Last Poems* (1922). Another volume, *More Poems,* was published posthumously (1936), as was the definitive *Collected Poems of A. E. Housman* (1940). His brother ¶Laurence (1865–1959), writer and illustrator; author of *The Writings of William Blake* (1893), *The House of Joy* (1895), *Gods and their Makers* (1897), *Rue* (1899), *Bethlehem, a Nativity Play* (1902), *Mendicant Rhymes* (1906), *The Chinese Lantern* (1908), *The Sheepfold* (1918), *Angels and Ministers* (1921), *Little Plays of St. Francis* (1922, 1931), *Trimblerigg* (1924), *Nunc Dimittis* (1933), *Victoria Regina* (play, 1934), *A. E. H.* (a memoir of his brother, 1937), etc.

Hous·say \ü-'sī\, Bernardo Alberto. 1887–1971. Argentine physiologist. Professor, U. of Buenos Aires (1910–43, 1945–46); founder and director (1946–71), Institute of Biology and Experimental Medicine; known for research on pituitary and pancreatic hormones; awarded Nobel prize for physiology or medicine (1947) with C. and G. Cori.

Hous·saye \ü-se\, Arsène. *Orig.* Arsène Hous·set \ü-se\. 1815–1896. French writer. Manager of the Comédie-Française (1849–56). Author of *Histoire de la peinture flamande et hollandaise* (1847), *Galerie de portraits du XVIIIᵉ siècle* (1848); novels as *La Pantoufle de Cendrillon* (1852), *Les Femmes du Diable* (1876); plays as *Les Caprices de la marquise* (1844), *Mademoiselle de Trente-Six Vertus* (1873). His son ¶Henry (1848–1911) was a historian and literary critic; on staff of *Revue des Deux Mondes* and *Journal des débats;* author of *Athènes, Rome, Paris* (1878), *1814* (1888), *1815* (1893–1905).

Hous·ton \'(h)yü-stən\, Samuel. 1793–1863. American soldier and politician, b. Lexington, Va. Entered army (1813); wounded at Horseshoe Bend; agent helping oversee removal of Cherokees to Arkansas; resigned (1818). Studied law; practiced, Lebanon, Tenn. Member, U.S. House of Representatives (1823–27). Governor of Tennessee (1827–29); resigned and moved to the Indian country of Cherokee Nation, now Oklahoma (1829); adopted by Cherokee tribe; traveled to Washington, D.C., to secure improved treatment of Indians; sent by Pres. Jackson to negotiate with tribes in Texas (1832); settled there (1833). As trouble developed with Mexico, Houston was chosen commander in chief of the forces of Texan provisional government (1835); met and defeated Mexican troops under Santa Anna at San Jacinto (Apr. 21, 1836). First president of Republic of Texas (1836–38) and again president (1841–44). On admission of Texas to Union, U.S. senator (1846–59); strong believer in maintenance of the Union. Governor of Texas (1859–61); deposed for refusal to take oath of allegiance to Confederacy.

Hout \'hau̇t\, Jan van. 1542–1609. Dutch Humanist, historian, poet. Perceptive literary theorist and promoter of study of national tradition in literature.

Hout·man \'hau̇t-ˌmän\, Cornelis de. c.1540–1599. Dutch navigator. Commanded first Dutch trading expedition to the East Indies (1595–96), establishing relations with Java, Sumatra, Bali; on second expedition (1598–99), visited Madagascar, Cochin China, and Sumatra; murdered by order of the sultan of Acheh. His brother ¶Frederik (1570–1627), who also went on this expedition, was arrested by the sultan of Acheh but released; governor of Amboina (1605–11), of Moluccas (1621–23); discovered (1619) shoals known as Houtman's Abrolhos. Published first dictionary of the language of the Malays (1603).

Hoveden *or* **Howden,** Roger of. See ROGER of Hoveden.

Hoven, J. See VESQUE VON PÜTTLINGEN.

Hov·ey \'həv-ē\, Richard. 1864–1900. American poet, b. Normal, Ill. Author of poetic drama *Launcelot and Guenevere* (1891), *Seaward* (elegy, 1893), *Songs from Vagabondia* (with Bliss Carman, 1894, 1896, 1900), *Along the Trail* (1898), *To the End of the Trail* (1908).

Hov·gaard \'hau̇-gȯr, *Angl* 'hōv-ˌgärd\, William. 1857–1950. American naval architect, b. Aarhus, Denmark. To U.S. (1901, naturalized 1919). Professor of naval design and construction, M.I.T. (1901–33); consulting naval architect for U.S. navy department (1909–26, 1935–38). Author of *Structural Design of Warships* (1915), *General Design of Warships* (1920), *Modern History of Warships* (1920), etc.

Hov·land \'hōv-lənd\, Carl Iver. 1912–1961. American psychologist, b. Chicago. On faculty, Yale (1936–42, 1945–61; professor from 1945); associated with Information and Education Division, U.S. War Dept. (1942–45); known for pioneering studies of social communication, modification of attitudes and beliefs. Co-author of *Experiments on Mass Communication* (1949), *Communication and Persuasion* (1953), *Personality and Persuasibility* (1960).

How·ard \'hau̇-ərd\. Name of an old English house standing at head of English Catholic nobility; in various branches, family has held earldoms of Norfolk, Nottingham, Carlisle, Suffolk, Berkshire, Northampton, Arundel, Wicklow, Norwich, Effingham. Family founded by Sir William Howard *or* Ha·ward \'hā-wərd, 'hō(-ə)rd\ (d. 1308), of Norfolk; summoned to Parliament (1295); justice of common pleas (1297). His grandson ¶Sir John Howard was admiral of the king's navy in the north. ¶Sir Robert Howard (d. before 1436), great-grandson of Sir John, married Margaret, daughter of 1st duke of Norfolk and coheiress of house of Mowbray.

DUKES OF NOR·FOLK \'nȯr-fək\ AND OF NOT·TING·HAM \'nät-iŋ-əm, *US also* -ˌham\: Their son ¶Sir John Howard (1430?–1485), *known as* Jack of Norfolk; 1st Duke of Norfolk (of Howard line, 1483); fought with Edward IV in France (1475); created by Richard III (1483) earl marshal of England, a distinction still borne by his male heirs; served against Lancastrians and in Brittany; envoy to France and Flanders; lord admiral of England, Ireland, and Aquitaine (1483); led archer vanguard at Bosworth Field; slain there in battle.

His son ¶Thomas I (1443–1524), 2d Duke of Norfolk, Earl of Sur·rey \'sər-ē, 'sə-rē\ (created 1483); wounded and captured at Bosworth Field (1485); imprisoned three years in Tower by Henry VII, then obtained reversal of his own and his father's attainder; as lieutenant general of the north, defeated Scots at Flodden Field (1513); quelled rioting apprentices (1517).

¶Thomas II (1473–1554), 3d Duke of Norfolk, Earl of Surrey; son of 2d duke; m. (1495) Edward IV's daughter Anne (1475–1512), thus becoming brother-in-law of Henry VII; m. (1513) Elizabeth (d. 1558), daughter of Edward Stafford, Duke of Buckingham; lord high admiral (1513); led vanguard of English at Flodden; lord lieutenant of Ireland (1520–21); raided Boulogne (1522) and south of Scotland; Roman Catholic; headed party hostile to

Wolsey; president of privy council (1529); as lord steward presided at trial of Anne Boleyn, his niece; punished rebels of Pilgrimage of Grace (1536); arrested Thomas Cromwell (1540); led English army in Scotland (1542–44); lost court influence upon execution of Catherine Howard (*q.v.*), the second niece of his to be wife of Henry VIII; imprisoned throughout reign of Edward VI under condemnation as accessory to treason of his son Henry, Earl of Surrey (see below); released and restored on accession of Queen Mary (1553).

Thomas II's brother ¶William (1510?–1573); a favorite of Henry VIII, who sent him on various diplomatic missions; convicted of misprision of treason in concealing offenses of his niece Queen Catherine, but pardoned; lord high admiral (1554–73); created Baron Howard of Effingham (1554) for his defense of London against Sir Thomas Wyatt; lord chamberlain (1558); lord privy seal (1572). His son ¶Charles (1536–1624), 2d Baron Howard of Effingham, 1st Earl of Nottingham (in Howard line), was ambassador to France (1559); lord chamberlain (1574–85); as lord high admiral (1585–1618), held chief command against Armada (1588); colleague of Essex in Cádiz expedition (1596); created earl (1596); commissioner for trials of Mary, Queen of Scots (1586), of Essex (1601), for union with Scotland (1604), and for trial of Gunpowder Plotters (1606).

¶Henry (1517?–1547), Earl of Surrey; son of Thomas II; m. (1532) Frances de Vere, daughter of 15th Earl of Oxford; accompanied father in suppression of Pilgrimage of Grace (1536); distinguished himself as marshal of the army besieging Montreuil (1544); commander at Boulogne and Guisnes (1545–46); defeated in skirmish with French and superseded in command by rival, the Earl of Hertford (1546); accused of treasonable ambition by Hertford faction, convicted on flimsy evidence, and beheaded. Author of sonnets, elegies, lyrics in the courtly manner; with Wyatt, helped introduce sonnet into English; produced blank verse translation of two books of *Aeneid;* verses first published in Tottel's *Miscellany* (1557).

¶Thomas III (1536–1572), 4th Duke of Norfolk; son of Henry Howard, Earl of Surrey; succeeded his grandfather as duke and earl marshal (1554), and in absence of princes of the blood became first subject of England under Elizabeth; lieutenant of north country (1559); one of commissioners to inquire into Scottish affairs (1568); imprisoned (1569–70) for project to marry Mary, Queen of Scots; communicated with Philip of Spain regarding planned Spanish invasion of England to free Mary, Queen of Scots; beheaded on failure of plot. His 3d son ¶Lord William (1563–1640) was a scholar; known to contemporaries as "Bauld Willie" and in Scott's "Lay of the Last Minstrel" as "Belted Will"; m. (1577) Elizabeth Dacre, one of three heirs of Thomas, Lord Dacre of Gilsland; became Roman Catholic (1584); imprisoned on suspicion of treason (1583, 1585, 1589). Assembled notable collection of books, manuscripts, Roman antiquities.

¶Henry (1628–1684), 6th Duke of Norfolk; 3d son of Henry Frederick Howard, 3d Earl of Arundel (see below); succeeded (1677) his brother Thomas, duke by reversal (1660) of attainder of 1572; presented Arundel marbles to Oxford (1667); envoy to Morocco (1669).

EARLS OF CAR·LISLE \kär-ˈlī(ə)l, kər-, ˈkär-,\: ¶Charles Howard (1629–1685), 1st Earl of Carlisle (in Howard line); great-grandson of Lord William Howard (1563–1640); became Protestant (1645); supported Commonwealth; distinguished himself at battle of Worcester (1651); member of council of state (1653) and of Cromwell's House of Lords (1657); lord lieutenant of Cumberland and Westmorland (1660); created Baron Da·cre of Gils·land \ˈdā-k(ə-)rəv-ˈgilz-lənd\, Viscount Howard of Mor·peth \ˈmȯr-ˌpeth, -pəth\, Earl of Carlisle (1661); ambassador to Russia, Sweden, and Denmark (1663–64); governor of Jamaica (1677–81); lieutenant general (1667).

¶Frederick (1748–1825), 5th earl; headed commission sent by Lord North to attempt reconciliation with American colonies (1778); viceroy of Ireland (1780–82); on regency question took part on side of Prince of Wales in opposition to Pitt (1789); appointed (1798) guardian of his cousin Lord Byron, the poet, who attacked him in *English Bards and Scottish Reviewers.* Author of two tragedies, *The Father's Revenge* (1783) and *The Stepmother* (1800), and some poems. Frederick's son ¶George (1773–1848), 6th earl; commissioner for affairs of India in All-the-Talents Administration (1806–07); lord privy seal (1827–28, 1834).

¶George William Frederick (1802–1864), 7th earl; M.P. (1826–41, 1846–48) as Viscount Morpeth; as Irish secretary under Lord Melbourne (1835–41), carried Irish reform bills; carried Public Health Bill (1848); chancellor of duchy of Lancaster (1850–52); viceroy of Ireland (1855–58, 1859–64); established on his estate a reformatory for juvenile criminals; author of poems and travel books.

¶George James (1843–1911), 9th earl; nephew of 7th earl; M.P. (1879–89); succeeded his uncle in peerage (1889); trustee for 30 years of National Gallery, to which he transferred his Mabuse's *Adoration of the Kings;* connoisseur of art and skilled painter of landscapes; lifelong temperance advocate.

EARLS OF SUF·FOLK \ˈsəf-ək\ AND BERK·SHIRE \ˈbärk-shər, *US also* ˈberk-\: ¶Lord Thomas Howard (1561–1626), 1st Earl of Suffolk and 1st Baron Howard de Wal·den \-də-ˈwȯl-dən\; second son of 4th Duke of Norfolk; distinguished himself against Armada (1588); vice admiral of fleet sent to capture Spanish ships in Cádiz harbor (1596); created baron (1597), earl (1603); lord chamberlain (1603–14); lord high treasurer (1614–18); with his wife, imprisoned for embezzlement (1619) but released after ten days and finally restored to favor; later urged investigation of Lord Bacon's offenses. His 2d son ¶Thomas was created (1626) earl of Berkshire, a title merged (1645) with that of earl of Suffolk. ¶Theophilus (1584–1640), 2d Earl of Suffolk and 2d Baron Howard de Walden; eldest son of 1st earl; governor of Jersey (1610); lord lieutenant of Cambridgeshire, Suffolk, and Dorset (1626); warden of Cinque Ports (1628).

EARLS OF SURREY: see Thomas (I) Howard (2d Duke of Norfolk), above, and descendants; Thomas Howard (2d Earl of Arundel), below.

EARL OF NORTH·HAMP·TON \nȯrth-ˈ(h)am(p)-tən\: ¶Henry Howard (1540–1614), 1st Earl of Northampton (cr. 1604; only one in Howard line); 2d son of Henry Howard (*q.v.*), Earl of Surrey; younger brother of 4th Duke of Norfolk; tutored, with his brother and sisters, by John Foxe; long under suspicion of Elizabeth for mysterious relations with Mary, Queen of Scots; imprisoned for a time after publishing (1583) an attack on judicial astrology suspected of treasonable intent; on accession of James I, created Earl of Northampton (1604); lord privy seal (1604); commissioner at trials of Raleigh (1603), Guy Fawkes (1605), Garnet (1606); a commissioner of treasury (1612). Roman Catholic; founder of hospitals; framer of James I's edict against duelling; author of three apothegms in Bacon's collection; builder of Northumberland House.

EARLS OF AR·UN·DEL \ˈar-ən-dᵊl\: ¶Philip Howard (1557–1595), 13th Earl of Arundel (1st in Howard line); eldest son of 4th Duke of Norfolk and Lady Mary, daughter and heiress of Henry Fitzalan, 12th Earl of Arundel; succeeded to title (1580); suspected of being involved in conspiracy headed by Francis Throckmorton (1583); became Roman Catholic through influence of his wife (1584); imprisoned for attempt to escape from England; died in Tower of London.

His son ¶Thomas (1585?–1646), 14th earl (2d in Howard line), Earl of Surrey and of Norfolk (titles restored on accession of James I, 1604); patron of arts and learning; became Protestant (1615); privy councilor (1616); president of committee of peers on Bacon's case (1621; general of army against Scots (1639); as lord high steward presided at trial of Strafford (1641); escorted Queen Henrietta Maria to Continent (1642) and took residence at Padua. One of first large-scale collectors of art in England; collected statues, pictures, guns, coins, manuscripts, books, and the marbles, known as Arundel marbles, presented by his grandson, 6th Duke of Norfolk, to Oxford (1667).

EARL OF NOTTINGHAM. See Charles Howard (1536–1624) under Dukes of Norfolk above.

EARL OF EF·FING·HAM \ˈef-iŋ-əm, *US also* -ˌham\: ¶Kenneth Alexander Howard (1767–1845), 1st Earl of Effingham (2d creation); descendant of William Howard (1510?–1573); entered army (1786); served in Flanders (1793–95), Ireland, and Holland (1799); brigade and division commander in Peninsular War (from 1811); headed first division of army of occupation after Waterloo; general (1837). Succeeded a kinsman as Baron Howard of Effingham (1817); raised to earl (1837).

Howard, Ada Lydia. 1829–1907. American educator, b. Temple, N.H. First president, Wellesley Coll. (1875–81).

Howard, Blanche Willis. 1847–1898. American novelist, b. Bangor, Me. Author of *One Summer* (1875), *Aunt Serena* (1881), *Guenn* (1884), *The Open Door* (1889), etc.

Howard, Bronson Crocker. 1842–1908. American playwright, b. Detroit. In newspaper work until he gained success with play *Saratoga* (produced by Augustin Daly in New York, 1870). Other notable plays included *Moorcroft* (1874), *Hurricanes* (1878), *Wives* (1879), *Young Mrs. Winthrop* (1882), *One of Our Girls* (1885), *The Henrietta* (1887), *Shenandoah* (1889), *Aristocracy* (1892), and *Peter Stuyvesant* (with Brander Matthews, 1899).

Howard, Catherine. 1520?–1542. Fifth queen of Henry VIII of England. Granddaughter of Thomas Howard, 2d Duke of Norfolk, and niece of Thomas (II), 3d duke (see HOWARD family); a dependent in her grandmother's house; entertained lovers, including her music master Henry Mannock or Manox, her cousin Thomas Culpepper, and Francis Dereham, a retainer of Duchess of Norfolk; m. (1540) to King Henry after his divorce from Anne of Cleves; clandestinely met Dereham and Culpepper, who were executed upon Catherine's confession of prenuptial unchastity; attainted by Parliament and beheaded on conviction for adultery.

Howard, Sir Ebenezer. 1850–1928. English reformer. Shorthand reporter in London law courts; remembered as originator of the garden city movement, aimed at establishing limited-size cities surrounded by agricultural greenbelts; influenced founding of prototype garden cities Letchworth (1903) and Welwyn Garden City (1920). Author of *Tomorrow: A Peaceful Path to Social Reform* (1898), reissued as *Garden Cities of Tomorrow* (1902).

Howard, H. L. See Charles J. WELLS.

Howard, John. 1726–1790. English prison reformer. As high sheriff of Bedfordshire (1773), inspected county jails; secured passage of bills by Parliament (1774) providing for standards of cleanliness in jails and for jailers' salaries to replace fees paid by prisoners; made several tours of British and European jails. Author of *State of Prisons in England and Wales* (1777), *Account of the Principal Lazarettos in Europe* (1780), etc.

Howard, Leslie. *Orig.* Leslie Stei·ner \'stī-nər\. 1893–1943. English actor. Stage debut in *Peg o' My Heart* (1917); London debut in *The Freaks* (1918); New York debut in *Just Suppose* (1920); notable appearances in *Her Cardboard Lover* (1928), *Berkeley Square* (1929), *This Side Idolatry* (1933), *Petrified Forest* (1935), *Hamlet* (1936); in films *Outward Bound* (1930), *Of Human Bondage* (1934), *Petrified Forest* (1935), *Scarlet Pimpernel* (1935), *Gone With the Wind* (1939), etc.

Howard, Luke. 1772–1864. English pioneer in meteorology. Published *Climate of London* (1818–20, enlarged 1830).

Howard, Oliver Otis. 1830–1909. American army officer, b. Leeds, Me. Entered army (1854); instructor at West Point (1855–61); served through Civil War; brigadier general (1861) and major general of volunteers (1862); lost right arm at Fair Oaks; engaged at Chancellorsville and Gettysburg; commanded Army of the Tennessee in Sherman's march to the sea. Commissioner, Bureau of Refugees, Freedmen, and Abandoned Lands (1865–74). Founder (1867) and president (1869–74), Howard U. Commander in Chief Joseph's War (1877). Superintendent of West Point (1881–82); major general (1886); retired (1894).

Howard, Sir Robert. 1626–1698. English dramatist. 6th son of Thomas Howard, 1st Earl of Berkshire (see under HOWARD family). Distinguished himself on Royalist side at second battle of Newbury (1644); imprisoned during Commonwealth; at Restoration, made auditor of exchequer; privy councilor (1689). Author of a comedy, *The Committee, or the Faithful Irishman* (1663). Patron of Dryden, who married his sister Lady Elizabeth and who assisted him in the *Indian Queen* (1664), a tragedy in heroic verse. Opposed Dryden's contention that rhyme was more suitable to heroic tragedy than blank verse. His brother ¶Edward wrote tragedies, including *The Usurper* (1668), and comedies, including *The Women's Conquest* (1671); ridiculed by George Villiers in *The Rehearsal.* Another brother ¶James wrote the comedies *All Mistaken, or the Mad Couple* (1667) and *The English Mounsieur* (1666), the latter a success through the acting of Nell Gwyn.

Howard, Roy Wilson. 1883–1964. American journalist, b. Gano, Ohio. On staff of Indianapolis *News* (1902); New York manager of United Press Association (1907), its president and general manager (1912) and chairman of the board (1921–36, 1953–64); president (1936–53). Business director of Scripps-McRae, later Scripps-Howard, newspapers (1921), and editorial director of these papers, with Robert P. Scripps (from 1925); chairman (1921–36), president (1936–53). Bought *New York Telegram* (1927); merged it with *World* (1931) and *Sun* (1950); editor (1950–60), *World-Telegram and Sun.*

Howard, Sidney Coe. 1891–1939. American playwright, b. Oakland, Calif. Author of *They Knew What They Wanted* (1924, Pulitzer prize), *The Silver Cord* (1926), *Salvation* (with Charles MacArthur, 1928), *The Late Christopher Bean* (1932, adapted from the French), *Alien Corn* (1933), *Yellow Jack* (1934, with Paul de Kruif), *Dodsworth* (1934), *The Ghost of Yankee Doodle* (1937); also wrote screenplays as for *Arrowsmith* (1932), *Dodsworth* (1936), *Gone With the Wind* (1939).

Howe \'haù\, Ed, *in full* Edgar Watson. 1853–1937. American journalist and author, b. Wabash Co., Ind. Trained in father's printing office; editor and proprietor, Atchison (Kans.) *Daily Globe* (1877–1911), *E. W. Howe's Monthly* (1911–33); gained reputation for homely wisdom and nickname "Sage of Potato Hill." Author of *The Story of a Country Town* (1883), *Country Town Sayings* (1911), *Ventures in Common Sense* (1919), *Plain People* (autobiography, 1929), etc.

Howe, Elias. 1819–1867. American inventor, b. Spencer, Mass. Nephew of William Howe. Apprentice in textile machinery works (1835–37), in watchmaking shop (1837). Worked on design for a sewing machine (from 1843); patent issued (1846). First machine marketed in England. Established his rights by patent-infringement suits (1849–54). A perfected sewing machine of Howe's design won gold medal, Paris Exhibition (1867). Cf. Isaac M. SINGER, Barthélemy THIMONNIER, Walter HUNT.

Howe, John. 1630–1705. English clergyman. Domestic chaplain to Oliver Cromwell and his son Richard Cromwell (1656); ejected from living by Act of Uniformity (1662); chaplain at Antrim Castle, Ireland (1671–76); pastor in London (1676–85). Author of *The Good Man the Living Temple of God* (1676–1702).

Howe, Joseph. 1804–1873. Canadian journalist and politician, b. Halifax, N.S. Edited the *Nova Scotian* (from 1828); member of provincial assembly (1836–63), of executive council (1840–43); instrumental in securing responsible government for Nova Scotia; premier (1860–63); opposed federation; member of federal Parliament (1867–73); lieutenant governor of Nova Scotia (1873).

Howe, Julia, *nee* Ward. 1819–1910. American writer and reformer. m. (1843) Samuel Gridley Howe. Active in abolitionist, peace, and woman suffrage campaigns; a founder and first president (1868–77, 1893–1910), New England Woman Suffrage Association; a founder (1868) and president (from 1871), New England Women's Club. Author of verse *Passion Flowers* (1854), *Words for the Hour* (1857), "Battle Hymn of the Republic" (published in *Atlantic Monthly,* 1862); essays *From the Oak to the Olive* (1868), *Modern Society* (1880), *Is Polite Society Polite?* (1895), etc. Edited *Woman's Journal* (1870–90). First woman elected to American Academy of Arts and Letters (1908).

Howe, Mark Antony DeWolfe. 1864–1960. American editor and writer, b. Bristol, R.I. Associate editor of *Youth's Companion* (1888–93, 1899–1913), of *Atlantic Monthly* (1893–95). Author of *Shadows* (1897), *Boston, the Place and the People* (1903), and biographies of George Bancroft (1908), Barrett Wendell (1924, Pulitzer prize), James F. Rhodes (1929), John Jay Chapman (1937), O. W. Holmes (1939), etc.

Howe, Richard. Earl Howe. 1726–1799. English naval officer. Entered navy (1739); M.P. (1757–82); succeeded as 4th Viscount Howe (1758); rear admiral (1770) and vice admiral (1775); engaged in the American Revolution (1776–78); admiral (1782); raised to viscount (1782); first lord of admiralty (1783–88); earl (1788); commanded Channel fleet in great victory over the French (June 1, 1794); named admiral of the fleet, and general of marines (1796). His brother ¶Sir William (1729–1814), 5th Viscount Howe, an army officer; entered army (1746); commanded regiment at capture of Louisbourg and defense of Quebec (1759–60); M.P. (1758–80); major general (1772); lieutenant general (1775); commanded British at battle of Bunker Hill (1775) and succeeded Gage as commander in chief in America; defeated Americans on Long Island (1776); captured New York City and defeated Americans at White Plains and Brandywine (1776); occupied Philadelphia (1777); resigned command (1778); appointed general (1793); succeeded to viscountcy (1799).

Howe, Samuel Gridley. 1801–1876. American educator and reformer, b. Boston. Served as soldier and surgeon in Greek war for independence from Turkey (1824–30). Head of Perkins School for the Blind (1832–76); excited widespread interest by successful work with Laura Bridgman (*q.v.*); interested in care of the feebleminded, prison reform, abolishment of imprisonment for debt, and antislavery movement; edited *The Commonwealth;* chairman, Mass. Board of State Charities (1865–74). m. (1843) Julia Ward Howe (*q.v.*).

Howe, William. 1803–1852. American inventor, b. Spencer, Mass. Uncle of Elias Howe; received contract (1838) to construct bridge for Boston and Albany Railroad at Warren, Mass.; invented improved Howe truss bridge (pat. 1840); built bridge over Connecticut River at Springfield, Mass., and many others.

Höwelcke, Johannes. See HEVEL.

Howel Dda. See HYWEL DDA.

How·ell \'haù-əl\, James. c.1594–1666. English author. Royalist sympathizer in Civil War; imprisoned (1643–51). At Restoration, named historiographer royal (1661). Chief work *Epistolae Ho-Elianae* (1645–55), letters mostly written while in prison and chiefly to imaginary correspondents; revised Cotgrave's *French and English Dictionary* (1650), and compiled an English–French–Italian–Spanish dictionary (1659–60).

Howell, John Adams. 1840–1918. American naval officer and inventor, b. Bath, N.Y. Commissioned (1858); taught at Naval Academy (1867–71, 1874–79); rear admiral (1898); retired (1902). Invented flywheel-driven and guided Howell torpedo (pat. 1885), disappearing gun carriage, and high-explosive shells.

How·ells \'haù-əlz\, John Mead. 1868–1959. American architect, b. Cambridge, Mass. Son of Dean Howells. Designed Title Guarantee and Trust building in New York City; collaborated with Raymond M. Hood (*q.v.*) in design of Daily News building in New York and Tribune Tower in Chicago.

Howells, William Dean. 1837–1920. American man of letters, b. Martin's Ferry, Ohio. Compositor in printing office (to 1856); on staff, *Ohio State Journal,* Columbus, Ohio (1856–61); contributor of poems to *Atlantic Monthly.* Published (1860) a campaign *Life of Lincoln;* U.S. consul, Venice, Italy (1861–65). Assistant editor, *Atlantic Monthly* (1866–71); editor (1871–81). On editorial staff, *Harper's Magazine* (1886–91) and *Cosmopolitan Magazine* (1891–92); conducted "Easy Chair" column in *Harper's* (1900–20). In later years considered the dean of American letters; instrumental in forwarding the careers of such diverse writers as Mark Twain, Henry James, Bret Harte, Stephen Crane, Hamlin Garland, Frank Norris. Author of *Poems of Two Friends* (with John J. Piatt, 1860), *Venetian Life* (1866), *Their*

Wedding Journey (1872), *A Chance Acquaintance* (1873), *A Foregone Conclusion* (1875), *The Lady of the Aroostook* (1879), *A Fearful Responsibility* (1881), *A Modern Instance* (1882), *A Woman's Reason* (1883), *The Rise of Silas Lapham* (1885), *Indian Summer* (1886), *The Minister's Charge* (1887), *Annie Kilburn* (1889), *A Hazard of New Fortunes* (1890), *The Quality of Mercy* (1892), *The World of Chance* (1883), *A Traveler from Altruria* (1894), *The Landlord at Lion's Head* (1897), *Story of a Play* (1898), *The Kentons* (1902), *The Son of Royal Langbrith* (1904), *The Leatherwood God* (1916). Also wrote criticism, as *Criticism and Fiction* (1891), dramas, travel sketches, etc.

Hox·ie \ˈhäk-sē\, Vinnie, *nee* Ream \ˈrēm\. 1847–1914. American sculptor, b. Madison, Wis. m. Richard L. Hoxie (1878). Her full-length marble statue of Lincoln (unveiled 1871) is in the rotunda of the Capitol, Washington, D.C.; executed statues of Samuel Kirkwood and Sequoya for Statuary Hall; executed statue of Adm. Farragut for Farragut Square, Washington, D.C.; did busts of Grant, McClellan, Frémont, Custer, Sherman, etc., ideal figures *Miriam, Sappho, The West, America,* etc.

Ho Yen \ˈhō-ˈyən\. d. 249 A.D. Chinese philosopher. Reared in family of Ts'ao P'ei, founder of Wei dynasty; official at court; evolved a synthesis of Taoist and Confucian thought and helped found *ch'ing-t'an* ("pure conversation") movement.

Hoyle \ˈhȯi(ə)l\, Edmond. 1671 or 1672–1769. English writer on card games. Author of *Short Treatise on the Game of Whist* (1742); established code of laws of whist that was in effect over a hundred years (1760–1864); codified laws of backgammon (1743), wrote on chess, etc.

Hoy·sa·la \hȯi-ˈsä-lə\. Name of an Indian dynasty ruling (c.1006–c.1346) in southern Deccan and for a time in Cauvery Valley; expanded at expense of Cōlas, Cālukyas, Pāṇḍyas; notable members included: Viṣṇuvardhana (reigned c.1110–41), gained territory from Kadambas, Cōlas. His grandson ¶Ballāla II (reigned 1173–1220) gained territory from Cālukyas, Cōlas, Yādavas; made Hoysala kingdom dominant in southern India. His great-grandson ¶Rāmanātha (reigned 1254–95) was evicted from the Cauvery by Pāṇḍya emperor; attempted to wrest plateau kingdom from brother Narasimha III. Dynasty succeeded by the Vijayanagar.

Hoyt \ˈhȯit\, Charles Hale. 1860–1900. American playwright, b. Concord, N.H. In newspaper work (from 1878). Made success in writing farces, including *A Bunch of Keys* (1882), *A Hole in the Ground* (1887), *A Texas Steer* (1890), *A Trip to Chinatown* (1891), *A Milk White Flag* (1893), *A Stranger in New York* (1897), *A Day and a Night in New York* (1898).

Hrabanus. See RABANUS MAURUS.

Hr·dlič·ka \ˈhərd-lich-ˌkä\, Aleš. 1869–1943. American anthropologist, b. Humpolec, Bohemia. To U.S. (1882); trained as physician; with expeditions under sponsorship of American Museum of Natural History (1899–1902). On staff of U.S. National Museum, Washington, D.C. (from 1903), curator (1910–42). Founder and editor (from 1918), *American Journal of Physical Anthropology.* Known for studies of early man in America; supporter of theory that American Indians are of Asian origin. Author of *Ancient Man in North America* (1907), *Physical Anthropology* (1919), *Old Americans* (1925), *Practical Anthropometry* (1939).

Hrólfr Kra·ki \ˈhrōl-fər-ˈkrä-kē\. *Eng.* Hrolf Pole-stick \ˈrōlf-ˈpōl-ˌstik\. fl. 6th? century. Danish king. Largely known through legends, as of his battle with brother-in-law Hjörvarthr, recounted in 10th-century poem *Bjarkamál;* life recounted in Icelandic *Hrólfs saga Kraka;* often identified with Hrothulf mentioned in *Beowulf.*

Hros·vi·tha \rōs-ˈvē-tä\. *Also spelled* Hrots·vi·tha \rōts-\ *and* Ros·wi·tha \rōs-ˈvē-\. c.935–1000. German poet. Of noble birth; spent most of life as Benedictine nun at Gandersheim; regarded as first German woman poet. To counteract pagan morality of classical works wrote (c.960) six Latin comedies based on Terence but embodying Christian themes; manuscripts of plays rediscovered by Conradus Celtis (c.1500). Other works included narrative poems based on Christian legends and two verse chronicles on Otto the Great and the history of the Gandersheim convent.

Hroz·ný \ˈhrȯz-nē\, Bedřich, *known in Ger. as* Friedrich. 1879–1952. Czech archaeologist and Orientalist. Professor, Vienna (1905–19), Prague (1919–52). Renowned as decipherer of the Hittite language; excavated Assyrian sites of Kültepe (1925), Kanes. Author of *Sprache der Hethiter* (1915), *Hethitische Keilschrifttexte aus Boghazköi* (1919).

Hsia \shē-ˈä\. Traditionally, the first Chinese dynasty (c.2205–1766 B.C.); mentioned in legends but of undetermined historicity; purportedly founded by the Emperor Yü (*q.v.*); succeeded by the Shang dynasty.

Hsia Kuei \shē-ˈä-ˈkwā\. fl. 1195–1224. Chinese painter. Painter to Southern Sung court at Hangchow; with fellow academician Ma Yüan inspired Ma-Hsia school of painting; known for highly individual style of landscape painting marked by lyric expressiveness, bold brushwork.

Hsiang Yü \shē-ˈäŋ-yü̅\. *Orig.* Hsiang Chi \-ˈjē\. 233–202 B.C. Chinese rebel. Member of prominent family of state of Ch'u; became leader of Ch'u rebellion against Ch'in dynasty; captured capital and executed emperor (206); attempted to restore system of many feudal kingdoms with himself, as king of Ch'u, foremost among kings; engaged in contest for supremacy with Liu Pang; defeated in battle and took own life.

Hsiao Tsung. See Chu Yu-t'ang under CHU family.

Hsiao Wen Ti \shē-ˈau̇-ˈwən-ˈdē\. d. 499 A.D. Chinese emperor (471–499) of Northern Wei dynasty. Converted state of nomadic tribesmen into Chinese-style dynasty, adopting Chinese dress, customs, names into court usage and making Chinese official language; instituted land reforms that retarded formation of large holdings.

Hsiao Yen \-ˈyən\. *Reign title* Wu Ti \ˈwü-ˈdē\. 464–549. Founder and first emperor (502–549) of the Liang dynasty of China. Led successful revolt against his relative, the emperor of the Southern Ch'i dynasty, and proclaimed himself emperor of Liang dynasty (502); his reign longer and more stable than any other southern emperor of this period; helped establish Buddhism in South China; prepared first Chinese collection of all Buddhist scripts; twice (527, 529) renounced world and entered monastery, but each time persuaded to resume throne; captured by barbarian general (549) and died of starvation in a monastery.

Hsieh Ho \she-ˈe-ˈhō\. 5th century A.D. Chinese painter and critic. Formulated "Six Principles" of painting, the basis for art criticism in the Far East for centuries.

Hsien-feng. See I-CHU.

Hsien Ti. See under LIU family.

Hsien Tsung. See Chu Chien-shen under CHU family.

Hsi K'ang \ˈshā-ˈkäŋ\. *Also known as* Chi K'ang \ˈjē-\. 223–262. Chinese philosopher and poet. High official at court; one of the iconoclastic Seven Sages of the Bamboo Grove; author of poems and essays combining Taoist philosophy with humorous accounts of his own free-spirited doings; became metalworker and alchemist; executed on suspicion of sedition.

Hsin \ˈshin\. Dynastic name given to the reign (8–23 A.D.) of Wang Mang (*q.v.*), who usurped the throne of the Han dynasty.

Hsin·byu·shin \ˈshin-ˈbyü-ˈshin\. d. 1776. King of Burma (1763–76) of Konbaung or Alaungpaya dynasty. Conquered Siam and sacked capital Ayutthaya (1767); invaded Manipur 3 times; repelled 4 Chinese attacks (1765–69); ruthlessly suppressed Mon revolt (1773).

Hsin Ch'i-chi \ˈshin-ˈchē-ˈjē\. 1140–1207. Chinese poet and soldier. Soldier in service of Southern Sung dynasty; known for 623 poems of the *tz'u* form, considered finest Chinese verse of the day.

Hsi Tsung. See Chu Yu-chiao under CHU family.

Hsiung Fo-hsi \shē-ˈu̇ŋ-ˈfō-ˈshē\ *or* **Fu-hsi** \-ˈfü-ˈshē\. 1900–1965. Chinese playwright. Influenced by Western drama, helped create problem-centered "popular drama" aimed at education and entertainment of peasantry.

Hsüan-te. See Chu Chan-chi under CHU family.

Hsüan Ti. See Liu Ping-i under LIU family.

Hsüan-tsang \shü̅-ˈänd-ˈzäŋ\. *Orig.* Ch'en I \ˈchən-ˈē\. *Also known as* San-tsang \ˈsänd-ˈzäŋ\, Mu-ch'a T'i-p'o \ˈmä-ˈchä-ˈtē-ˈpō\, Yüan-tsang \yü̅-ˈänd-ˈzäŋ\, *and in Skt.* Mok·ṣa·de·va \mōk-ˈshäd-ə-və\. 602–664 A.D. Chinese Buddhist traveler. Ordained as Buddhist monk (620); set out (629) on pilgrimage from Ch'ang-an to India via Tien Shan and Hindu Kush mountains to Peshawar, thence (633) to Kanauj on the Ganges; visited famous Buddhist sites; mastered Sanskrit and Buddhist philosophy; greatly impressed King Harṣa; returned (645) in time of T'ang dynasty via the Pamirs and Kashgar with 657 sacred Buddhist books and 150 relics of Buddha; given warm welcome by emperor. Translated some 73 of the books from Sanskrit; wrote treatise *Ch'eng-wei-shih-lun,* which inspired Ideation Only school of Buddhism, and a vivid account of his travels.

Hsüan Tsung. See (1) Chu Chan-chi under CHU family; (2) Li Lung-chi under LI family; (3) MIN-NING.

Hsüan-t'ung. See P'U-I.

Hsüan-yeh \shü̅-ˈän-ˈyə\. *Reign title* K'ang-hsi \ˈkäŋ-ˈshē\. *Temple name* Sheng-tsu \ˈshəŋd-zü\. *Posthumous name* Jen Huang-ti \ˈzyən-ˈhwäŋ-ˈdē\. 1654–1722. Chinese emperor (1661–1722), second of the Ch'ing dynasty. Third son of Fu-lin; at first dominated by advisers (1661–69); defeated Wu San-kuei (1678) and suppressed his Revolt of the Three Feudatories (1681); conquered Taiwan (1683); concluded Treaty of Nerchinsk with Peter the Great on boundaries (1689); annexed Outer Mongolia (1697) and Tibet (1720). His reign largely one of internal peace; constructed many public works, including embankment of Huang Ho River and dredging of Grand Canal; traveled over empire; kept taxes low; opened four ports for foreign trade. Patron of arts and letters and himself very learned; ordered compilation of many books of the Chinese classics; encouraged introduction of Western arts and education; for many years friendly to Jesuits and other Roman Catholic missionaries until decree (1717) denying them right to propagate Christian religion; gave many Jesuits, as Ferdinand Verbiest, important scientific posts at court.

Hsü Chih-mo \'shü̅e̅-'ji(ə)r-'mō\. *Pen names* Nan-hu \'nän-'hü\ *and* Shih-che \'shi(ə)r-'jə\. 1896–1931. Chinese poet. University teacher and literary editor; helped organize (1928) Crescent Moon Book Co., which disseminated Western literature. Author of verse and essays, influenced by Western models, that helped shape modern vernacular Chinese literature.

Hsü Kuang-ch'i \-'kwäŋ-'chē\. 1562–1633. Chinese official. Attained highest level of civil service; converted to Christianity; studied with Matteo Ricci and with him made first translations of Western books into Chinese, including Euclid's *Elements*; obtained high post at court through successful use of Western methods to predict solar eclipse precisely; last influential Chinese Catholic before 20th century.

Hsün-tzu \'shü̅e̅nd-'zü\. *Orig.* Hsün K'uang \-'kwäŋ\. *Also known as* Hsün-ch'ing \-'chiŋ\. c.298–c.230 B.C. Chinese philosopher. For a time an official of Ch'u; a teacher of renown, his pupils including Han-fei-tzu and Li Ssu. Chief work *Hsün-tzu,* 32 essays on Confucian philosophy, ethics, music, etc.; developed philosophical essay to high level of rigor; developed doctrine that tradition and ritual are fundamental to society. Considered third of the great philosophers of Classical period, after Confucius and Mencius.

Hsü Ta \'shü̅e̅-'dä\. 1329–1383. Chinese general. Joined rebel band of Hung-wu (1353); became leader of rebellion against Mongol dynasty; captured Peking; helped establish Ming dynasty (1368); pursued Mongols northward, decimating armies and burning Karakorum.

Hsü Wei \-'wā\. 1521–1593. Chinese painter. Considered variously a member of conservative Che school and one of Eight Eccentrics of Yang-chou; at times a drunkard and a (perhaps pretended) madman.

Huai-nan-tzu. See LIU AN.

Huai Tsung. See Chu Yu-chien under CHU family.

Huang Ch'ao \'hwäŋ-'chau̇\. d. 884. Chinese rebel. Salt smuggler; formed rebel band; captured Canton (879); captured capital Ch'ang-an (880) and proclaimed himself emperor of Ta Ch'i dynasty; driven out (883); captured and executed. His activities helped accelerate fall of T'ang dynasty.

Huang Hsing \-'shiŋ\. 1871–1916. Chinese general. Founded Hua hsing hui revolutionary group dedicated to overthrow of Ch'ing dynasty; forced to flee to Japan; became second in command of revolutionary alliance under Sun Yat-sen (1905); commander on the scene in revolution (1911); declined office of generalissimo of republic (1911); with Sun led revolt against Yüan Shih-k'ai (1913); fled to Japan but returned (1916).

Huang Kung-wang \-'gu̇ŋ-'wäŋ\. 1269–1354. Chinese painter. Known both for landscapes, many from the Fu-ch'un Mountains, and for literary accomplishments; one of Four Masters of the Yüan dynasty.

Huang T'ing-chien \-'tiŋ-jē-'än\. 1045–1105. Chinese painter and calligrapher. One of Four Masters of the Sung dynasty.

Huang Tsung-hsi \-'dzu̇ŋ-'shē\. *Also called* Huang Li-chou \-'lē-'jō\. 1610–1695. Chinese scholar and reformer. Among last Ming resisters of Ch'ing dynasty; retired to scholarly pursuits; founder of objective eastern Chekiang school of history; advocated legal and administrative reforms. Author of *Ming-tai-fang lu* on reform of political system (1662), *Ming-ju hsüeh-an,* considered first systematic history of Chinese philosophy (1676).

Huang Tsun-hsien \-'dzün-shē-'än\. 1848–1905. Chinese diplomat and poet. Broke new ground in Chinese poetry through use of vernacular and development of folk-ballad style.

Huás·car \'wäs-ˌkär\. *In full* Inti Cusi Huallpa Huáscar, *i.e.* Sun of Joy. d. 1532. Inca ruler. Son of Huayna Capac; succeeded father (1525) but forced to divide realm with younger half-brother Atahualpa; defeated in attempts to subdue Atahualpa's rebellion and captured; ordered assassinated by Atahualpa to prevent his being returned to power by Pizarro.

Huay·na Ca·pac *or* **Way·na Qha·paq** \'wī-nä-'kä-ˌpäk\. d. 1535. Inca ruler (1493–1525). Divided realm between his sons Atahualpa and Huáscar.

Hubald. See HUCBALD.

Hub·bard \'həb-ərd\, Elbert Green. 1856–1915. American writer, editor, and printer, b. Bloomington, Ill. Freelance newspaper writer, Chicago (1872–76). Influenced by William Morris, founded (1895) at East Aurora, N.Y., Roycroft Shop, so called from 17th-century English printer Roycroft, to revive old handicrafts, esp. artistic printing; founded, edited, and wrote the material in *The Philistine,* a monthly magazine (1895–1915); founded and edited *The Fra* (1908–17). Published *Little Journeys,* sketches, chiefly biographical, ultimately filling fourteen volumes. Works included widely reprinted tale "A Message to Garcia" (1899), *Time and Chance* (1899), *So Here Cometh White Hyacinths* (1907), *Man of Sorrows* (1908). Went down with the *Lusitania.*

Hubbard, Frank McKinney, *known as* Kin \'kin\. 1868–1930. American humorist, b. Bellefontaine, Ohio. On staff of Indianapolis *News* (1891–94, 1901–30); author of homely, humorous sketches of rustic life, folk, philosophy, for which he created character Abe Martin.

Hubbard, Gardiner Greene. 1822–1897. American lawyer, b. Boston. A founder of Clarke Institution for the Deaf and first president (1867–77); chief backer of commercial development of telephone invented by son-in-law A.G. Bell (from 1876); founder of *Science* (1883); founder and first president, National Geographic Society (1888–97).

Hubbard, Robert Calvin, *known as* Cal. 1900–1977. American sportsman, b. Keytesville, Mo. Outstanding football player at Centenary Coll. and Geneva Coll.; tackle, New York Giants (1927–28, 1936), Green Bay Packers (1929–35); umpire (1935–51), supervisor (1951–69), American Baseball League; only man elected to both Football Hall of Fame (1963), Baseball Hall of Fame (1976).

Hub·ble \'həb-əl\, Edwin Powell. 1889–1953. American astronomer, b. Marshfield, Mo. Astronomer, Mt. Wilson Observatory, Pasadena, Calif. (from 1919) and Mt. Palomar (from 1948); known for studies of nebulae; demonstrated that some nebulae are independent galaxies (1923); classified extragalactic nebulae by shapes; discovered "red-shift" of light and determined that galaxies are receding from ours (1929); deduced Hubble constant for expansion of visible universe.

Hu·ber \'hü-bər\, Eugen. 1849–1923. Swiss jurist. Professor, Basel (1880–88), Halle (1888–92), Bern (1892–1923); developed Swiss civil code (completed 1904, adopted 1912); member of Nationalrat (1903–11). Author of *Geschichte des schweizerischen Privatrechtes* (1886–93), *Die Bedeutung der Gewere in deutschen Sachenrecht* (1894), etc.

Huber, Hans. 1852–1921. Swiss composer. Teacher of piano and composition (1889–1918), director (1896–1918), Basel school of music; composed Romantic works including operas, oratorios, symphonies, piano concertos, chamber music, choral works, piano pieces, and songs.

Huber, Ludwig Ferdinand. 1764–1804. German writer. Editor, *Allgemeine Zeitung,* Stuttgart (1798–1803); known for plays and stories, many of the latter actually written by his wife (m. 1794), ¶Maria Therese, *nee* Hey·ne \'hī-nə\ (1764–1829); one of earliest woman journalists in Germany, editor (1817–23) of *Morgenblatts für gebildete Stände.* Their son ¶Victor Aimé (1800–1869) was a historian of literature; professor, Rostock (1832–36), Marburg (1836–43), Berlin (1843–51); specialized in study of Spanish language and literature; leader of conservative opinion; published journal *Janus* (1845–48). Author of *Skizzen aus Spanien* (1828–33), *Die Geschichte des Cid* (1829), *Spanisches Lesebuch* (1832), etc.

Huber, Max, *in full* Hans Max. 1874–1960. Swiss jurist. Professor, Zürich (1902–21); judge of the Permanent Court of International Justice (1921–30); president of the court (1925–28).

Huber, Wolf. 1485–1553. German painter and printmaker. Court painter to prince-bishop of Passau (from 1515); one of leading masters of the Danube school. Known esp. for altarpiece of St. Nikolaus in Feldkirch (1515–21), and for landscape drawings of Danube valley.

Hu·ber·man \'hü-bər-ˌmän\, Bronisław. 1882–1947. Polish violin virtuoso. Child prodigy; toured Europe (from 1893); played for Adelina Patti's farewell performance (1895); frequently toured U.S. (from 1896); organized (1936) Palestine Symphony (from 1948 the Israel Philharmonic).

Hu·bert \ue-ber, *Angl* 'hyü-bərt\. Saint. c.655–727. Frankish prelate. Bishop of Maestricht (c.705); according to legend, converted while hunting by the sight of a stag bearing a luminous cross on his head; hence, patron saint of hunters.

Hubert, Henri. 1872–1927. French sociologist. Professor, École du Louvre (1902–27); a leading disciple of Émile Durkheim. Author of *Étude sommaire de la représentation du temps dans la religion et la magie* (1905), *Mélanges d'histoire des religions* (1909, with Marcel Mauss).

Hubert Walter. See Hubert WALTER.

Hub·mai·er \'hüp-ˌmī-ər\, Balthasar. 1485–1528. German religious leader. Cathedral preacher at Regensburg (1516); to Switzerland (1521), where he became a leader of Anabaptists; arrested in Zürich (1525) and forced to recant; resumed Anabaptist preaching, traveling as far as Moravia; captured, burned at the stake in Vienna.

Huc \ü̅e̅k\, Régis-Evariste. 1813–1860. French missionary. Member of Vincentian (Lazarist) order; to China (1839); labored in Mongolia (1839–44); journeyed to Tibet (1844–46), becoming first European to enter Lhasa. Author of *Souvenirs d'un voyage dans la Tartarie, le Tibet et le Chine* (1850).

Huc·bald \'hək-ˌbȯld\ *or* **Hug·bal·dus** \(ˌ)həg-'bal-dəs, -'bȯl-\ *or* **Hu·bald** \'hyü-ˌbȯld\. c.840–930. Frankish religious. Benedictine monk; author of *De harmonica institutione,* one of the earliest treatises on polyphonic music.

Huch \'hük\, Ricarda. 1864–1947. German writer. Author of verse as *Gedichte* (1891–94), *Herbstfeuer* (1944); novels as *Erinnerungen von Ludolf Ursleu dem Jüngeren* (1893), *Fra Celeste* (1899), and volumes of tales; historical works as *Das Risorgimento* (1908), *Der grosse Krieg in Deutschland* (1912–14), *Urphänomene* (1946); criticism as *Die Romantik* (1899, 1902); memoirs as *Aus der Triumphgasse* (1902).

Hud·de \'hœd-ə\, Johan van Waveren. 1628–1704. Dutch mathematician. Burgomaster of Amsterdam (for 21 years in period 1672–1704). Contributed to general solutions of higher-degree equations; anticipated power series expansion. Author of papers as *De reductione aequationum* and *De maximis et minimis.*

Hud·son \'həd-sən\, George. 1800–1871. English financier. Invested inheritance in North Midland Railway (1827); helped organize and served as chairman (1837 ff.) of York and North Midland Railway; eventually controlled over 1,000 miles of railroad; lost everything in exposure of financial irregularities (1847–48). M.P. (1845–59).

Hudson, Henry, *sometimes known incorrectly as* Hendrick. d. 1611. English navigator. Conducted expedition in the *Hopewell* for English Muscovy Company to discover northeast passage to Far East (1607); followed Svalbard archipelago eastward; on second voyage for same company, reached Novaya Zemlya (1608). Third voyage, in the *Halve Maen* or *Half Moon,* for Dutch East India Company, discovered Hudson River and sailed up it as far as Albany (1609). Fourth voyage, in the *Discovery,* for group of English enterprisers, reached Hudson Bay (1610–11); after a hard winter, mutineers seized Hudson and eight others and set them adrift in a small boat (June 1611); no record of their fate.

Hudson, Jeffery. 1619–1682. English dwarf. Page to Queen Henrietta Maria; captain of horse in Royalist army at beginning of Civil War; imprisoned for a time (1679) for supposed connection with Popish plot. His portrait painted by Vandyke.

Hudson, Manley Ottmer. 1886–1960. American jurist, b. St. Peters, Mo. Professor, U. of Missouri (1910–19), Harvard (1919–54); director of research in international law, Harvard Law School (1927–38). Member of American commission at Paris Peace Conference (1919); member of legal section, secretariat of the League of Nations (1919–23). Judge, Permanent Court of Arbitration (1933–45), Permanent Court of International Justice (1936–45). Author of *The Permanent Court of International Justice* (1925), *Progress in International Organization* (1932), *By Pacific Means* (1935), etc.

Hudson, Thomas. 1701–1779. English painter. Pupil and son-in-law of Jonathan Richardson; achieved renown as portraitist; teacher of Joshua Reynolds.

Hudson, William Henry. 1841–1922. British naturalist and author, b. Argentina, of American parentage. Spent youth in Argentina; to England (1869), naturalized (1900). Author of *The Purple Land that England Lost* (1885), *The Naturalist in La Plata* (1892), *British Birds* (1895), *El Ombú* (1902), *Green Mansions* (romance, 1904), *Adventures among Birds* (1913), *Far Away and Long Ago* (1918), *The Book of a Naturalist* (1919), etc.

Hueffer, Ford Madox. See Ford Madox FORD.

Huef·fer \'hef-ər, 'hyü-fər\, Francis. *Orig.* Franz Hüf·fer \'hœf-ər\. 1845–1889. British music critic, b. Germany. To London (1869); naturalized (1882). Music critic on *The Times* (1878–89); edited *Musical World* (1886). Author of *Richard Wagner and the Music of the Future* (1874), *The Troubadours* (1878).

Huer·ta \'wer-tä\, Adolfo de la. 1883?–1955. Mexican politician. Joined Obregón and Calles in revolution (1920) against government; after death of Carranza, made provisional president (June–Nov. 1920); minister of finance under Obregón (1920–23); revolted against Obregón and Calles (1923–24); defeated (1924) and lived in exile in U.S. (1924–35).

Huerta, Victoriano. 1854–1916. Mexican soldier and politician. Took part in revolution that raised Díaz to power; brigadier general (1902). Served Madero (1911–13) but then turned against him, deposed and arrested him; provisional president of Mexico (1913–14); failed of recognition by U.S.; faced with revolts of Carranza, Obregón, Villa, Zapata; involved in difficulties with U.S. in Tampico and Veracruz; resigned. In exile in Europe and U.S. (1914–16); arrested twice in U.S. on Mexican border for conspiracy to incite revolution; died in custody of U.S. government.

Huerta y Muñoz, Vicente Antonio García de la. See GARCÍA DE LA HUERTA Y MUÑOZ.

Huet, Conrad Busken. See Conrad BUSKEN HUET.

Huet \wᵞe, wᵞā\, Paul. 1804–1869. French painter. Noted for Romantic landscapes as *Intérieur de forêt, Le Bois de La Haye.*

Huet, Pierre-Daniel. *Lat.* Hue·tius \'(h)wē-sh(ē-)əs\. 1630–1721. French prelate and scholar. Renowned as mathematician, Hellenist, and Hebraist; bishop of Avranches (1689–99). Editor of Origen's *Commentaria in Sacram Scripturam* (1668); author of *Censura Philosophiae Cartesianae* (1689), a critique on the philosophy of Descartes, and *Nouveaux memoires pour servir a l'histoire* (1692).

Hu·fe·land \'hü-fə-ˌlänt\, Christoph Wilhelm. 1762–1836. German physician. Professor, Jena (1793–1801), Berlin (from 1801); wrote on Wieland, Herder, Goethe, and Schiller as well as on scientific subjects.

Hufnagel. See HOEFNAGEL.

Hugbaldus. See HUCBALD.

Hü·gel \'hue-gəl\, Friedrich von. Baron. 1852–1925. British theologian, b. Florence, Italy. Son of Baron Karl von Hügel; to England (1873). Founder (1905) of London Society for the Study of Religion; became center of modernist group. Wrote *Mystical Element of Religion* (1908), *Eternal Life* (1912), *The Reality of God* (1931), etc.

Hügel, Karl von. Baron. 1795–1870. Austrian explorer, horticulturist, and diplomat. Served as a soldier; then took up the study of horticulture and natural history; traveled in the East Indies (1830–36) and to New Zealand; ambassador in Florence and Brussels (1850–69).

Hu·gen·berg \'hü-gən-ˌberk\, Alfred. 1865–1951. German industrialist and politician. Chairman of Krupp industries (1909–18); built industrial concern including newspapers, a major film company, etc.; member of Reichstag (1919–45); chairman, German National People's party (1928–33); used propaganda apparatus at his disposal to campaign against Socialists and Communists; formed (1931) Harzburg Front with Nazi party, aiding Hitler gain influence and power; failed to manipulate Hitler; minister of national economy, food, and agriculture in Hitler cabinet (1933); retired, his party dissolved (1933).

Hugensz, Lucas. See LUCAS VAN LEYDEN.

Hug·gins \'həg-ənz\, Sir William. 1824–1910. English astronomer. With W. A. Miller, invented stellar spectroscope (c.1860); demonstrated (1863) that stars resemble the sun in composition; deduced emission of hydrogen shell by nova (1866); determined nature of gaseous nebulae; studied comets; determined velocity of stars from spectral Doppler shift (1868). Published *An Atlas of Representative Stellar Spectra* (1900).

Hugh \'hyü\. *Fr.* Hugues \ueg\. Name of five dukes of Burgundy:

Hugh. *Called* le Noir \lə-'nwär\, *i.e.* the Black. d. 952. Duke (936–952). Son of Richard the Justiciar and nephew of King Rudolph.

Hugh I. c.1040–1093. Duke (1076–78). Abdicated in favor of brother Eudes I and entered monastery.

Hugh II. *Surnamed* Bo·rel \bȯ-rel\. *Called* le Pa·ci·fique \lə-pȧ-sē-fēk\, *i.e.* the Peaceful. d. 1143. Duke (1102–43). Son of Eudes I; first to organize a ducal court.

Hugh III. c.1148–1192. Duke (1162–92). Son of Eudes II; took part in Third Crusade and died at Tyre.

Hugh IV. 1213–1272. Duke (1218–72). Son of Eudes III; to Egypt with Saint Louis (1248) and imprisoned with him (1251–54); granted hereditary title of king of Thessalonika (1265) by Baldwin II.

Hugh. *Fr.* Hugues. Name of four kings of Cyprus:

Hugh I. c.1195–1218. King (1205–18). Son of Amalric II.

Hugh II. 1252–1267. King (1253–67). Son of Henry I; last of direct Lusignan line.

Hugh III. d. 1284. King (1267–84). Succeeded cousin Hugh II, founding house of Antioch-Lusignan; king of Jerusalem (1269–84), but crown disputed by Charles I of Sicily.

Hugh IV. 1299–1359. King of Cyprus and Jerusalem (1324–59). Succeeded uncle Henry II; allied with Venice and the pope in conquest of Smyrna (1343).

Hugh. *Fr.* Hugues \ueg\. *Ger.* Hu·go \'hü-gō\. d. 947. King of Italy (926–947). Count of Arles (from 898) and of Provence (from 911); defeated Rudolph II of Burgundy (925) and secured Lombard crown; attempted to win imperial power but opposed by stepson Alberich; crowned son Lothair II co-king (931); lost control of Italy to Berengar II of Ivrea (945).

Hugh of Avranches \ȧ-vräⁿsh\. 1st Earl of Ches·ter \'ches-tər\. d. 1101. Norman viscount of Avranches; contributed 60 ships to invasion of England by William the Conqueror (1066); created earl and chief noble of the land (1071); fought prolonged war with Welsh; a principal adviser and supporter of Henry I.

Hugh of Clu·ny \klue-nē\. Saint. 1024–1109. French religious. Abbot of Benedictine monastery of Cluny (1049–1109); served several popes in diplomatic missions and in cause of ecclesiastical reforms; took active part in councils of Lateran (1050, 1059, 1080), etc.

Hugh of Lin·coln \'liŋ-kən\. Saint. c.1140–1200. English prelate, b. Avalon, France. Carthusian monk in La Grande Chartreuse (from c.1165); called to England by Henry II (c.1179) and became his adviser; bishop of Lincoln (1186–1200); excommunicated John (1194); took lead (1198) in first refusal of a money grant. Canonized (1220).

Hugh of Lincoln. Saint. *Known also as* Little St. Hugh. 1245–1255. English martyr. According to legend, ritually crucified by a Jew at Lincoln; subject of Chaucer's *Prioress's Tale* in *Canterbury Tales;* legend also used in Marlowe's *Jew of Malta.*

Hugh of St. Cher \saⁿ-sher\. *Fr.* Hugues de Saint-Cher. 1200?–1263. French ecclesiastic. Entered Dominican order (1225); cardinal (1244); regarded as first compiler of a concordance to the Bible (1240).

Hugh of St. Vic·tor \(ˌ)sānt-'vik-tər\. *Fr.* Hugues de Saint-Vic·tor \-də-saⁿ-vēk-tȯr\. 1096–1141. Saxon or Flemish theologian and mystic. Spent most of his adult life (from c.1115) in abbey of St. Victor, Paris; directed school of St.

Victor (from 1133). Author of *De sacramentis Christianae fidei,* the encyclopaedic *Didascalion,* spiritual works *De unione corporis et spiritus, De arca Noe morali, De arca Noe mystica, De vanitate mundi,* etc.

Hugh the Great. *Fr.* Hugues le Grand \-lə-gräⁿ\. *Called also* le Blanc \lə-bläⁿ\, *i.e.* the White. d. 956. Duke of the Franks and count of Paris. Son of Robert, Count of Paris; ruler of large regions in northern France (923–956); prevented by rivalries from succeeding father as king (923); styled himself duke of the Franks (from 937); in conflict with Louis IV until forced by pope to submit (950); virtual ruler of France after death of Louis (954).

Hugh Ca·pet \-kȧ-pe, -pā, *Angl* -'kā-pət, -'kap-ət, -ka-'pā\. c.938–996. King of France (987–996) and founder of Capetian line. Son of Hugh the Great, duke of the Franks; succeeded as duke (956); gained influence at expense of King Lothair, against whom he intrigued; aided by Archbishop Adalberon, elected to succeed Louis V (987) over Carolingian claimant, Charles of Lower Lorraine; imprisoned Charles (991) and forced Adalberon's successor, Arnulf, to resign (991) for intriguing against him; faced continued opposition from Blois, Anjou, etc.

Hugh de Pui·set \-də-pwʸe-ze, *Angl* -pwē-'zā\. c.1125–1195. English prelate. Bishop of Durham (1153); bought earldom of Northumberland and was appointed justiciar of England (1189) by Richard I; deprived by William Longchamp; helped bring about Longchamp's fall (1191).

Hughes \'hyüz, *also* 'yüz\, Charles Evans. 1862–1948. American jurist, b. Glens Falls, N.Y. Adm. to bar (1884) and practiced in New York City; counsel for New York State legislative commission investigating financial methods of life insurance companies (1905–06). Governor of New York (1907–10). Associate justice, U.S. Supreme Court (1910–16). Unsuccessful candidate for president of United States, defeated by Wilson (1916). U.S. secretary of state (1921–25); planned and chaired Washington Arms Limitation Conference (1921–22). Member of Hague Tribunal (1926–30) and judge on Permanent Court of International Justice (1928–30). Chief justice, U.S. Supreme Court (1930–41).

Hughes, David Edward. 1831–1900. English inventor. To U.S. as a boy. Began experiments with printing telegraph (about 1852); devised improvement over Royal E. House machine (pat. 1855); succeeded in having machine adopted for use in foreign countries. Invented carbon microphone (1878), induction balance, and Hughes electromagnet.

Hughes, Howard Robard. 1905–1976. American industrialist and aviator, b. Houston, Tex. Assumed control of Hughes Tool Co. (1923); to Hollywood (1926); produced films including *Two Arabian Nights* (1928), *Hell's Angels* (1930), *Scarface* (1932), *The Outlaw* (1941); controlled RKO studios (1948–55). Formed Hughes Aircraft Co.; in airplane of his own design, set speed record of 352 mph (1935) and transcontinental flight time record of 7 hrs. 28 mins. (1937); set round-the-world record of 91 hrs. 14 mins. (1938); designed, built, and flew (1947) eight-engine wooden flying boat, known as the "Spruce Goose." Held controlling share in Trans World Airlines until forced by legal action to sell out (1966); in later years bought land and casinos in and around Las Vegas. Complete recluse (from 1950), attracting much publicity to supposed eccentricities.

Hughes, Hugh Price. 1847–1902. English clergyman. Founded *Methodist Times* (1885); established West London mission (1886); renowned as pulpit orator; first president of National Council of the Evangelical Free Churches (1896).

Hughes, John. 1797–1864. American prelate, b. County Tyrone, Ireland. To U.S. (1817); ordained (1826); coadjutor bishop of New York (1838); founded (1841) St. John's Coll. (now Fordham U.); led campaign for parochial schools; consecrated bishop of New York (1842); first archbishop of New York (1850); laid cornerstone of St. Patrick's Cathedral, N.Y. City (1858).

Hughes, John Ceiriog. *Pen names* Cei·riog \'kär-yȯg\ *and* Syr Meu·rig Gryn·swth \ˌsər-'mī-rig-'grən-ˌsüth\. 1832–1887. Welsh poet. Author of volumes of verse including *Oriau'r Hwyr* (1860); known as ardent collector of Welsh folk tunes, to many of which he wrote new lyrics; published *Canto Ganeuon* (1863), one of planned four volumes of such tunes.

Hughes, Langston, *in full* James Langston. 1902–1967. American writer, b. Joplin, Mo. Variously employed as seaman, waiter, laundry sorter, garden worker, bus boy, etc. Gained recognition with poem "The Negro Speaks of Rivers" (1921); author of *Weary Blues* (1926), *Not Without Laughter* (1930), *The Dream Keeper* (1932), *The Ways of White Folks* (stories, 1934), *The Big Sea* (autobiographical, 1940), *Shakespeare in Harlem* (1942), *Fields of Wonder* (1947), *Simple Speaks His Mind* (1950), *Simple Stakes a Claim* (1957); wrote lyrics for opera *Street Scene* (1947, with Kurt Weill).

Hughes, Richard Arthur Warren. 1900–1976. English writer. Author of *Gipsy-Night and Other Poems* (1922), *The Sister's Tragedy and Other Plays* (1924), *A Moment of Time* (stories, 1926), *Confessio Juvenis* (verse, 1926), *A High Wind in Jamaica* (1929), *The Spider's Palace* (children's stories, 1931), *In Hazard* (1938), *Fox in the Attic* (1961), *Wooden Shepherdess* (1973).

Hughes, Sir Samuel. 1853–1921. Canadian soldier and politician, b. Darlington, Ont. Member of Dominion Parliament (1892–1921); entered Canadian militia and served in Boer War (1899–1902); major general (1914); minister of militia and defense (1911–16), and organizer of Canadian Expeditionary Force in World War I; lieutenant general (1916).

Hughes, Thomas. 1822–1896. English jurist, reformer, and writer. Associated with Frederick Denison Maurice (*q.v.*) in work of Christian Socialism; active in founding (1854) Working Men's College; its principal (1872–83); M.P. (1865–74); founded model community in Tennessee, U.S.A. (1879), which failed. Served as county court judge (1882–96). Best known as author of *Tom Brown's School Days* (1857) and *Tom Brown at Oxford* (1861); also wrote biographies of Daniel Macmillan, Livingstone, and Alfred the Great.

Hughes, William Morris. 1864–1952. Australian politician, b. Wales. To Australia (1884); Labour member of New South Wales legislature (1894–1901), federal Parliament (1901–52); minister for external affairs (1904); attorney general (1908–09, 1910–13, 1914–21); prime minister of Australia (1915–23); formed Nationalist party (1916); minister for external affairs (1921–23); Australian representative at League of Nations Assembly (1932). Minister for health and repatriation (1934–37); minister in charge of territories (1937–38); minister for external affairs (1937–39); attorney general (1939–41); minister for industry (1939–40), for the navy (1940–41). Member of War Advisory Council (1941–44).

Hugo. See also HUGH.

Hu·go \ɯ̄-gō\, Joseph-Léopold-Sigisbert. Comte. 1773–1828. French general and writer. Served in the Revolutionary and Napoleonic armies; well known for his defense of Thionville (1813–14).

Hu·go \ɯ̄-go *Angl* '(h)yü-(ˌ)gō\, Victor-Marie. 1802–1885. French writer. Son of Comte J.-L.-S. Hugo. Published *Odes et poésies diverses* (1822), and was granted a pension by Louis XVIII. Then followed the romantic novel *Han d'Islande* (1823), *Nouvelles odes et ballades* (1824), the dramas *Cromwell* with its famous *Préface* (1827) and *Marion de Lorme* (1829), and *Les Orientales* (verse, 1829), establishing his position as leader of the Romantic movement in French literature. The presentation of his *Hernani* (1830) at the Théâtre Français was marked by clashes between the Classicists and Romanticists for nearly 100 nights. Other works of this period were novels *Le dernier jour d'un condamné* (1829), *Notre-Dame de Paris* (1831), *Claude Gueux* (1834); plays *Le Roi s'amuse* (1832), *Lucrèce Borgia* (1833), *Marie Tudor* (1833), *Ruy Blas* (1838), *Les Burgraves* (1843); and verse collections *Feuilles d'automne* (1831), *Chants du crépuscule* (1835), *Voix intérieures* (1837), *Les Rayons et les ombres* (1840). Elected to Académie Française (1841); created a peer of France (1845) and elected member of Constituent Assembly (1848); banished from France by Napoléon III (1851) and resided on island of Guernsey (to 1870). During this period wrote satirical *Napoléon le Petit* (1852); verse *Les Châtiments* (1853), *Les Contemplations* (1856), *La Légende des siècles* (vol. 1, 1859), *Chansons des rues et des bois* (1865); novels *Les Misérables* (1862), *Les Travailleurs de la mer* (1866), *L'Homme qui rit* (1869). Returned to France (1870) and was member of the National Assembly at Bordeaux (1871); resigned after the Commune and fled to Brussels and Luxembourg; wrote *L'Année terrible* (1872), *Quatre vingt-treize* (1874), *L'Art d'être grandpère* (1877), and published (1877) his *Histoire d'un crime* (written 1852). Thereafter he added other parts to his *La Légende des siècles* (1877, 1883), wrote a few philosophical poems, and published the drama *Torquemada* (1882).

Hugues. See also HUGH.

Hugues \ɯ̄g\, Bezanson. c.1491–1532 or 1533. Swiss leader. Appointed syndic of Geneva (1518); a leader of Eidguenot (anti-Savoyard) faction; fled to Fribourg (1525); created first alliance of Geneva with Swiss cantons (1526), leading to eventual Genevese independence.

Hugues de Pa·yens \-də-pȧ-yaⁿs\ *or* **de Payns** *or* **Pains** \-paⁿs\. 1070?–1136. Burgundian knight. With Geoffroi de Saint-Omer, founded (1119) at Jerusalem the religious and military order whose members were known as Knights Templars; first grand master of order.

Hu·guet \üg-'wāt\, Jaime. c.1415–1492. Spanish painter. Worked in Barcelona; considered last master of Catalan Gothic style; noted esp. for altarpieces.

Hu Han-min \'hü-'han-'min\. 1879–1936. Chinese politician. Aided Sun Yat-sen in organizing revolutionary party; military governor of Canton (1911–13); forced to flee government of Yüan Shih-k'ai (1913); aided Sun in establishing Kuomintang (1924); chairman of Nationalist government at Nanking (1927–28); president of Legislative Yüan (1928–31); with Chiang Kai-shek and Wang Ching-wei formed a triumvirate (1932–35).

Hui·do·bro \wē-'thō-brō\, Vicente. 1893–1948. Chilean poet. To Paris (1916), Madrid (1918); a leading figure of experimental avant garde, in particular the chief spokesman for and exponent of *creacionismo* and its later Spanish offshoot *ultraísmo.* Verse collections included *Las pagodas ocultas* (1914), *Adán* (1916), *Poemas árticos* (1918), *Saisons choisies* (1921), *El pasajero de su* *destino* (1930), *Altazor* (1931); also wrote novels *Mio Cid Campeador* (1929), *Sátiro o El poder de las palabras* (1939).

Hui-neng \'hwē-'nəŋ\. 638–713. Chinese religious leader. Made pilgrimage to seat of Hung-jen, 5th Ch'an (Zen) patriarch; according to tradition, recognized in poetry contest as sixth patriarch (661); preached doctrines of originally pure Buddha-nature of all persons and of search for tranquillity through detached calm, but not meditation, leading to sudden enlightenment; founder of eventually dominant Southern school of Ch'an.

Hui Shih \'hwē-'shi(ə)r\. b. 380 B.C. Chinese philosopher. A chief representative of Dialectician school of logicians; prolific writer, but only extant work the "Ten Paradoxes" quoted in Taoist *Chuang-tzu;* for a time a minister of the state of Liang.

Hui Ti. See Chu Yün-wen under CHU family.

Hui Tsung. See Chao Chi under CHAO family.

Hui-yü·an \'hwē-yü-'än\. 333–416. Chinese religious. Convert to Buddhism; formed devotional society of monks and lay worshippers of Buddha Amitābha that inspired later widely popular Ch'ing-t'u (Pure Land) cult.

Hui·zinga \'hœi-ziŋ-ȧ\, Johan. 1872–1945. Dutch historian. Professor, Groningen (1905–15), Leiden (1915–42). Author of *Herfsttij der middeleeuwen* (1919; *The Waning of the Middle Ages*), *Erasmus* (1924), *In de schaduwan van Morgen* (1935), *Homo Ludens* (1938).

Hü·le·gü \hü-'lā-ˌgü, ˌhü-lā-'\. c.1217–1265. Mongol ruler. Grandson of Genghis Khan and brother of Mangu Khan and Kublai Khan; sent (1252) by Mangu Khan to quell uprising in Persia; destroyed sect of the Assassins (1256); laid siege to Baghdad; seized and sacked the city (1258), overthrowing 'Abbāsid caliphate; broke Seljuq power in Persia. Invaded Syria (1260) and captured Aleppo and Damascus; on hearing of Mangu Khan's death assumed title of Il-khan as ruler of conquered provinces; his armies defeated at Ain Jalut (1260) by Mamlūk sultan of Egypt.

Hu·lin \ue̅-laⁿ\, Pierre-Augustin. Comte. 1758–1841. French general. Took part in the capture of the Bastille (1789); served in Italian campaign; aided in defense of Genoa, under Masséna (1800); presided at court-martial which condemned the Duc d'Enghien (1804). Distinguished himself at Jena (1806); general of division (1807); comte (1808); governor of Paris; suppressed Malet's conspiracy to overthrow Empire (1812).

Hull \'həl\, Albert Wallace. 1880–1966. American physicist, b. Southington, Conn. On research staff, General Electric Co. (1914–50); discovered (1917), independently of Debye and Scherrer, powder method of X-ray crystallography; invented thyratron and magnetron electron tubes.

Hull, Clark Leonard. 1884–1952. American psychologist, b. Akron, N.Y. Taught at U. of Wisconsin (1918–29); member of Institute of Human Relations, Yale U. (1929–52); known for behavioral studies emphasizing analysis of empirical data and rigorous, formalistic approach to theory construction. Author of *Aptitude Testing* (1928), *Hypnosis and Suggestibility* (1933), *Mathematico-Deductive Theory of Rote Learning* (1940), *Principles of Behavior* (1943), *A Behavior System* (1952).

Hull, Cordell. 1871–1955. American statesman, b. Overton (now Pickett) Co., Tenn. Tennessee circuit court judge (1903–07); member, U.S. House of Representatives (1907–21, 1923–31), U.S. Senate (1931–33); author of federal income tax law of 1913 and its revision in 1916, also of the federal inheritance act of 1916. U.S. secretary of state (1933–44); negotiated reciprocal trade agreements, esp. with Latin American countries; chief architect of Good Neighbor policy; began early in World War II to plan postwar international organization that became United Nations; awarded Nobel peace prize for 1945.

Hull, Isaac. 1773–1843. American naval officer, b. Derby, Conn. Nephew of William Hull; entered navy (1798); served in war with Tripoli (1803–04). In command of the *Constitution* (popularly called "Old Ironsides") in its defeat of British frigate *Guerrière* (Aug. 19, 1812). In command of Pacific squadron (1824–27), Washington Navy Yard (1829–35), Mediterranean squadron (1838–41).

Hull, William. 1753–1825. American army officer, b. Derby, Conn. Served through Revolution; governor, Michigan Territory (1805–12). Appointed brigadier general (1812); led American attack from Detroit into Canada (July 1812); outmaneuvered and defeated by British; surrendered Detroit without resistance (Aug. 1812). Court-martialed; convicted of cowardice and neglect of duty and sentenced to be shot (1814); sentence stayed by Pres. Madison because of Hull's Revolutionary service.

Hul·lah \'həl-ə\, John Pyke. 1812–1884. English organist, composer, and singing teacher. Inaugurated singing classes for schoolteachers at Exeter Hall, London (1841); professor, King's Coll. (1844–74); government inspector of music (1872–82); opposed tonic sol-fa method of Curwen. Composed an opera, *Village Coquettes* (1836; words by Charles Dickens), motets, duets, and songs.

Hulls \'həlz\, Jonathan. 1699–1758. English inventor. Patented (1736) and published pamphlet (1737) on a tugboat to be powered by a Newcomen steam engine; believed to be first detailed plan for steam-driven vessel, although never built.

Hulme \'hyüm\, Thomas Ernest. 1883–1917. English philosopher and poet. With Ezra Pound, a founder and theoretician of Imagist movement; translated works of Bergson, Sorel; killed in action in World War I. Poems, notes, and essays collected and published posthumously as *Speculations* (1924, edited by Herbert Read), *Notes on Language and Style* (1929, edited by Read).

Hulse \'həls\, John. 1708–1790. English clergyman. Bequeathed property to Cambridge U. for advancement of religious learning; his bequest endowed the Hulsean professorship of divinity, Hulsean lectures, and certain Hulsean prizes.

Hul·ton \'həlt-ᵊn\, Sir Edward. 1869–1925. English newspaper proprietor. Entered (1885) business of his father, owner of Manchester *Sunday Chronicle* and *Sporting Chronicle;* introduced Manchester *Evening Chronicle* (1897), *Daily Dispatch* (1900), London *Daily Sketch* (1909), *Illustrated Sunday Herald* (1915); acquired (1915) London *Evening Standard;* sold newspaper properties (1923) to lords Rothermere and Beaverbrook.

Hu·mann \'hü-ˌmän\, Carl. 1839–1896. German railway engineer and archaeologist. While in charge of building railways for Ottoman government, became interested in archaeology of Asia Minor; excavated Pergamum (1878–86) and discovered much choice sculpture; excavated Magnesia (1891–94) and Priene (1895–96).

Hu·mā·yūn \hu̇-'mä-ˌyu̇n\. *Also known as* Nā-ṣin-ud-Dīn Mu·ḥam·mad \'nä-shē-nu̇d-'dēn-mu̇-'k̲am-ad\. 1508–1556. Second Mughal emperor of India (1530–40, 1555–56). Son of Bābur; faced unrest throughout realm; occupied Gujarāt (1535); defeated (1539, 1540) by Shēr Shāh of Bengal. Driven from India, found shelter in court of Persia (1542–1555); recovered Qandahar and Kabul (1545–47); spent next nine years (1547–55) in Afghan kingdom; returned to India (1555) and seized Delhi from Afghan ruler; died six months later.

Humbert. See also UMBERTO.

Hum·bert \œⁿ-ber, *Angl* 'həm-bərt\ of Sil·va Can·di·da \'sil-və-kan-'dēd-ə\. *Also known as* Humbert de Moy·en·mou·tier \mwȧ-yaⁿ-mü-tyā\. c.1000–1061. French prelate. Benedictine monk at Moyenmoutier; became expert in Greek, Latin, and Christological doctrine; associated with Bruno of Toul, who, as Pope Leo IX, called him to Rome (1049); archbishop of Sicily and later cardinal (1050); instrument of ecclesiastical reform under Leo; an intransigent defender of orthodoxy; condemned heresiarch Berengar of Tours; sent by Leo to Constantinople (1054); failed to secure submission of Greek church to Rome and excommunicated Patriarch Michael Cerularius. Continued as adviser to Victor II; made papal chancellor and librarian by Stephen IX (1057); under Nicholas II helped effect Norman-papal alliance (1059); attacked simony.

Hum·boldt \'hu̇m-ˌbōlt, *Angl* 'həm-ˌbōlt\, Alexander von, *in full* Friedrich Wilhelm Karl Heinrich Alexander von. Freiherr. 1769–1859. German naturalist, traveler, and statesman. After training at Freiburg school of mines, appointed by Prussian government to post in Ansbach-Bayreuth (1792); resigned (1797) to continue private studies of geodesy, etc. Accompanied by French botanist Aimé Bonpland, undertook scientific journey to South America, Cuba, and Mexico (1799–1804); covered over 6000 miles on foot, horseback, by canoe; settled in Paris (1804), worked on the description of his American travels, published as *Voyage de Humboldt et Bonpland aux Regions Équinoxiales* (23 vols., 1805–34). Resided in Berlin (after 1827); on scientific expedition to Russian Asia (1829); on several diplomatic missions for Prussian government. Scientific contributions included founding of comparative climatology by his delineation of isothermal and isobaric lines; studied rate of decrease in mean temperature with increase of elevation, the origin of tropical storms; wrote on plant distribution; discovered decrease in intensity of the earth's magnetic field from the poles to the equator; studied volcanoes, demonstrated igneous origin of certain rocks. Greatly important as patron of younger scientists as Liebig and Agassiz. Contributed to popularization of science with *Kosmos* (1845–62).

Humboldt, Wilhelm von, *in full* Karl Wilhelm von. Freiherr. 1767–1835. German philologist and diplomat. Brother of Alexander von Humboldt. Prussian resident minister in Rome (1801–08), Vienna (1810), London (1817); signatory of Treaty of Paris (1815). As minister of education (1809) chiefly responsible for founding of Friedrich-Wilhelm (now Humboldt) U., Berlin. Pioneer in ethnolinguistics; made notable study of Basque language. Author of *Die baskischen Sprache* (1821), *Über die Aufgabe des Geschichtsschreibers* (1822), and esp. *Über die Kawisprache auf der Insel Jawa,* published posthumously (1836–40).

Hume \'hyüm\, Alexander. c.1560–1609. Scottish poet. Minister at Logie (from 1590); author of *Hymnes, or Sacred Songs* (1599) in Scottish dialect, containing "Of the Day Estival" and "Epistle to Maister Gilbert Mont-Crief."

Hume, Allan Octavian. 1829–1912. British colonialist, b. Scotland. Son of Joseph Hume; entered Indian civil service, Bengal (1849); retired (1882); helped convene first Indian National Congress, Bombay (1885); returned to England (1894) and involved himself in liberal politics.

Hume, David. 1711–1776. Scottish philosopher and historian. Led unsettled early life; keeper of Advocates' Library, Edinburgh (1752–63); on staff of British embassy in Paris (1763–66); undersecretary of state (1767–68). As a philosopher, known esp. for his philosophical skepticism, restricting human knowledge to experience of ideas and impressions and denying the possibility of obtaining any ultimate verification of their truth; deeply influenced subsequent metaphysical thought. Author of *A Treatise of Human Nature* (1739–40), *Essays Moral and Political* (1741–42), *Philosophical Essays Concerning Human Understanding* (1748; revised as *Enquiry Concerning Human Understanding,* 1758), *Political Discourses* (1752), *History of England* (1754–62), *Four Dissertations* (1757), *Dialogues Concerning Natural Religion* (1779).

Hume, Fergus. 1859–1932. British writer. Member of New Zealand bar; returned to England (1888). Author of detective novels as *Mystery of a Hansom Cab* (1887), *The Bishop's Secret* (1900), *Jonah's Luck* (1906), *The Other Person* (1920), and *The Caravan Mystery* (1926).

Hume, Joseph. 1777–1855. British physician and politician, b. Scotland. In medical service in India (1797–1807). M.P. (1812, 1818–41, 1842–55); identified with radical group; known for his repeated predictions of national disaster; instrumental in obtaining repeal of corn laws (1834) and laws prohibiting emigration and export of machinery.

Hume *or* **Home** \ˈhyüm\, Sir Patrick. 1st Earl of March·mont \ˈmärch-mənt\ *and* Baron Pol·warth \ˈpōl-(ˌ)wərth\. 1641–1724. Scottish politician. Member of Argylle's expedition (1684); involved in Rye House Plot, and outlawed (1685); escaped to Utrecht. Became adviser to William of Orange; accompanied him to England (1688); sheriff of Berwickshire (1692–1710) and lord chancellor of Scotland (1696–1702); created earl (1697). Passed act for security of Presbyterianism; supported union with England.

Hume-Roth·e·ry \-ˈrät͟h-ə-rē\, William. 1899–1968. English metallurgist. Taught at Oxford (1926–68), professor (from 1957); known for studies of alloys and intermetallic compounds.

Hum·frey \ˈhəm(p)-frē\, Pelham. 1647–1674. English lutenist and composer. Chorister of Chapel Royal; royal lutenist (1666); master of children of the Chapel Royal (1672). Composed songs and anthems that rank him among masters of English Baroque monodic style; also wrote music for theatrical works of Dryden, Wycherly.

Hum·mel \ˈhu̇m-əl\, Johann Nepomuk. 1778–1837. German pianist and composer. Pupil of Mozart; toured Europe as child prodigy piano virtuoso; concertmaster to Prince Esterházy (1804–11); Kapellmeister at Weimar (1819–37); continued to tour as pianist. Known principally as composer of piano works in a variety of forms and styles; also wrote chamber and orchestral works, cantatas, 3 masses, 9 operas.

Hum·per·dinck \ˈhu̇m-pər-ˌdiŋk, *Angl* ˈhəm-\, Engelbert. 1854–1921. German composer. Teacher in Barcelona (1885–87), Cologne (1887–88), Frankfurt (1890–96). Best known as composer of the fairy operas *Hänsel und Gretel* (1893) and *Die Königskinder* (1910); composed also incidental music for Shakespeare's *Merchant of Venice, The Tempest, As You Like It, Winter's Tale,* and Maeterlinck's *Blue Bird.*

Hum·phrey \ˈhəm-frē\. Duke of Glouces·ter \ˈgläs-tər, ˈglȯs-\ *and* Earl of Pem·broke \ˈpem-ˌbru̇k\. 1391–1447. English prince. Youngest son of Henry IV. Called "the Good Duke Humphrey" because of patronage of men of letters, including Lydgate and Capgrave. Created duke and earl (1414); fought in France (1415–20); wounded at Agincourt (1415); took Cherbourg (1418). Regent of England (1420–21); named in Henry V's will protector during Henry VI's minority, but functioned (1422–29) merely as deputy to his brother John, Duke of Bedford. Made vain attempt to deprive his uncle Henry Beaufort as cardinal of his English see (1432); denounced Beaufort's peace policy in French relations and led short campaign in Flanders (1436); as popular leader of war party, advocated violation of truce with France (1445); suspected of designs on king's life, died in custody. Collector of books; gave first books for library at Oxford; his first library later formed part of Bodleian.

Humphrey, Doris. 1895–1958. American dancer and choreographer, b. Oak Park, Ill. Soloist with Denishawn Company (1918 ff.); director of Denishawn House, N.Y.C. (1927–28); with Charles E. Weidman (*q.v.*), formed dance group and opened studio (1928). Taught at Bennington Coll. (1934 ff.), at Juilliard School (from 1952). Known esp. for her exploration of imbalance, fall and recovery; works included *Color Harmony* (1928), *Drama of Motion* (1930), *The Shakers* (1930), *Race of Life* (1937), *Song of the West* (1940), *El Salon Mexico* (1944); for Jose Limón created *Day on Earth* (1947), *Story of Mankind* (1947), *Deep Rhythm* (1953), *Theatre Piece No. 2* (1956), etc.

Humphrey, Hubert Horatio. 1911–1978. American politician, b. Wallace, S.D. Helped forge Democratic-Farmer-Labor alliance in Minnesota (1944); mayor of Minneapolis (1945–48); U.S. senator from Minnesota (1949–64, 1970–78); U.S. vice president (1965–69); Democratic candidate for president of the U.S. (1968).

Humphrey *or* **Hum·frey** \ˈhəm(p)-frē\, Laurence. c.1527–1590. English clergyman. President, Magdalen Coll., Oxford (1561–90), and vice chancellor, Oxford (1571–76); helped make Oxford a Puritan stronghold; central figure in vestiarian controversy (1564 ff.). Dean of Gloucester (1571) and of Winchester (1580–90).

Hum·phrey de Haute·ville \œm-fred-ōt-vēl\. d. 1057. Norman soldier of fortune. Joined Norman conquest of southern Italy (c.1035); count of Lavello (1045); succeeded brothers William and Drogo as count of Apulia (1051); played major role in defeat of Byzantines at Salerno (1052) and of papal army at Civitate (1053); designated half brother Robert Guiscard as guardian of infant son Abelard.

Hum·phreys \ˈhəm(p)-frēz\, Joshua. 1751–1838. American naval constructor, b. Delaware Co., Pa. Commissioned to outfit Continental ships under Esek Hopkins (1775). Appointed first U.S. naval constructor (1794–1801); designed and supervised building of frigates *Constitution, President, United States, Chesapeake, Constellation, Congress,* which formed nucleus of U.S. navy for War of 1812.

Humphreys, West Hughes. 1806–1882. American jurist, b. Montgomery Co., Tenn. Tennessee attorney general, reporter of cases (1839–51); U.S. district judge (1853–62); accepted appointment as district judge by Confederate States of America (1862); impeached by U.S. House of Representatives, convicted by Senate (1862), only U.S. official so handled in Civil War.

Hu·nald \ue̅-nȧld\. 8th century. Duke of Aquitaine (735–745). Followed father's policy of opposition to Carolingian power; lost Bordeaux, Auvergne to Charles Martel (735–740); conducted raids against Carolingian territories of Pepin and Carloman (742–744); forced to abdicate in favor of Waifer, his brother or son.

Ḥun·ayn ibn Isḥ·āq al-Ibā·dī \ˈku̇n-ˌī-ˌnib-ə-nish-ˈäk-al-ib-ä-ˈdē\. *Known in West as* Jo·han·ni·tius \ˌyō-(h)ə-ˈnish(-ē)-əs\. 808–873. Arab scholar. Known for his translations into Arabic of works of Plato, Aristotle, Galen, and neo-Platonists.

Hun·e·ker \ˈhən-ə-kər\, James Gibbons. 1860–1921. American musician and critic, b. Philadelphia. Taught in National Conservatory of Music (1886–98); edited weekly column of musical comment, *Musical Courier* (1887–1902); dramatic and literary critic, New York *Sun* (1902–17); music critic, New York *World* (1919–21). Author of *Mezzotints in Modern Music* (1899), *Melomaniacs* (1902), *Overtones* (1904), *Iconoclasts* (1905), *Egoists* (1909), *Franz Liszt* (1911), *Ivory Apes and Peacocks* (1915), *Unicorns* (1917), *Steeplejack* (1920), etc.

Huneric. See HUNNERIC.

Hung Ch'eng-ch'ou \ˈhu̇ŋ-ˈchəŋ-ˈchō\. 1593–1665. Chinese official. Official of Ming dynasty; captured and made grand secretary of Ch'ing (Mongol) dynasty (1644); helped persuade Chinese gentry to accept new dynasty; raised funds to support Ch'ing armies stamping out Ming resistance in South China; commanded forces that drove Ming claimant to throne into Burma (1659); retired as grand secretary (1660).

Hung-chih. See Chu Yu-t'ang under CHU family.

Hun·ger·ford \ˈhəŋ-gər-fərd\, Sir Thomas. d. 1398. Summoned to 16 parliaments from Wiltshire and Somerset; first person formally mentioned in rolls of Parliament as speaker of House of Commons (1377).

Hung-hsi. See Chu Kao-chih under CHU family.

Hung Hsiu-ch'üan \ˈhu̇ŋ-shē-ˈü-chue̅-ˈän\. 1814–1864. Chinese religious leader and rebel, of Hakka ancestry. Failed Confucian civil service exam three times and suffered breakdown; experienced religious visions that he interpreted in quasi-Christian terms; concluded he was second son of God, commissioned to destroy evil demons among mankind; became leader in a mystic society in Kwangsi; taught and made converts in his district (c.1840–48), using certain forms from Protestant doctrine. His teachings aroused his disciples to some violence (1848–50) and (1850) into open rebellion, actually a revolt against the Manchus, known as Taiping rebellion; styled himself T'ien-wang \ˈtyən-ˈwäŋ\, i.e. Heavenly Prince, and proclaimed (1851) the T'ai-p'ing T'ien-kuo, i.e. Heavenly Kingdom of Great Peace, dynasty; captured and made Nanking headquarters (1853), where he issued edicts and directed his generals; at first everywhere successful, later his armies became lawless and destructive; defeated (1860–62) by Frederick Ward and his Ever-Victorious army and completely overcome (1862–64) by forces of General Gordon and Li Hung-chang; seeing collapse of rebellion, poisoned himself.

Hung-jen \ˈhu̇ŋ-zhən\. *Orig.* Chiang T'ao \jē-ˈäŋ-ˈtau̇\. 1610–1663. Chinese painter. Foremost representative of Anhwei, or Hsin-an, school of landscape painting.

Hung Jen-kan \ˈhu̇ŋ-ˈzhən-ˈkän\. *Also called* Hung Jin \-zhēn\. 1822–1864. Chinese rebel. Cousin of Hung Hsiu-ch'üan; fled to Hong Kong at outbreak of Taiping rebellion (1850); educated by Western missionaries; made his way to rebel capital Taiping (Nanking) intending to teach correct version of Protestant Christianity (1859); made prime minister by cousin; attempted to introduce Western administrative methods and a program of railroad, telegraph, hospital, and bank construction; opposed by other leaders, demoted; executed after fall of Nanking to government troops.

Hung-li \'hùŋ-'lē\. *Reign title* Ch'ien-lung \chē-'ən-'lùŋ\. *Temple name* Kao Tsung \'gaùd-'zùŋ\. *Posthumous name* Ch'un Huang-ti \'chùn-'hwäŋ-dē\. 1711–1799. Chinese emperor (1735–96), fourth of the Ch'ing dynasty. Son of Yin-chien; one of ablest of Manchu rulers; during his reign Chinese empire reached its widest limit; eliminated Turk and Mongol threats to northeastern China (1755–60); created the New Province (modern Sinkiang); suppressed revolts in Tibet (1752), Yünnan (1776), and Taiwan (1787). Enjoyed friendly relations with Western powers; sanctioned establishment of trade relations with U.S. at Canton (1784). Patron of literature and art, esp. of pottery; ordered (1772) compilation of the "Complete Library in the Four Branches of Literature." In later years his administration weakened by great cost of military expenditures and excessive reliance on the unscrupulous minister Ho-shen; abdicated in favor of his son Yung-yen.

Hung Shen \'hùŋ-'shən\. 1893–1955. Chinese dramatist and film maker. Teacher at various universities; associated with Shanghai Dramatic Society (1923–30), helped introduce modern drama; wrote plays and translated Western works; joined Star Motion Picture Corp. (1930) and produced highly successful films.

Hung Vuong \'hùŋ-'vwòŋ\. 29th? century B.C. Vietnamese ruler. Legendary founder of Vietnamese state, traditionally dated 2879 B.C., although archaeological evidence suggests period 1000–500 B.C.

Hung-wu. See Chu Yüan-chang under CHU family.

Hun·ley \'hən-lē\, Horace Lawson. 1823–1863. American inventor, b. Sumner Co., Tenn. Experimented with submarine vessels (from 1861); built submarine commissioned as *H.L. Hunley* in Confederate navy (1863); tested it successfully but went down with it while attempting to attack blockading federal ships at Charleston, S.C. *Hunley* was raised and sank sloop *Housatonic* (Feb. 1864), first sinking of a warship by submarine.

Hun·ne·ric \'hən-ə-rik\ *or* **Hu·ne·ric** \'hyü-nə-rik\. d. 484. King of Vandals in Africa (477–484). Son of Genseric; sent to Italy as hostage (435); on return to Carthage married daughter of Theodoric I, king of Visigoths. An Arian; persecuted orthodox Christians in his kingdom.

Hunsdon, Baron. See Henry CAREY (1524?–1596).

Hunt \'hənt\, Arthur Surridge. 1871–1934. English paleographer. Engaged in research in Egypt (1896–1907); professor of papyrology at Oxford (1913–34); best known for collaboration with Bernard Pyne Grenfell (*q.v.*).

Hunt, Haroldson Lafayette. 1889–1974. American businessman, b. near Vandalia, Ill. Built fortune dealing in cotton land, then oil leases in Arkansas, Louisiana, Texas, Oklahoma; organized Hunt Oil Co. (1936), which became largest of independent oil and gas producers in the country. Founded Facts Forum (1951), Life Line (1958) to promote his conservative political views; distributed newspaper column and radio talks; at his death left estimated $2 or $3 billion.

Hunt, Henry. *Called* Orator Hunt. 1773–1835. English radical politician. Presided at a reform meeting in Manchester (Aug. 16, 1819) which was broken up forcibly by the yeomanry in what became known as the Peterloo Massacre; sentenced to two years' imprisonment. M.P. (1831–33).

Hunt, Holman, *in full* William Holman. 1827–1910. English painter. With Millais and D. G. Rossetti founded (1848) Pre-Raphaelite Brotherhood, joined later by Woolner, W.M. Rossetti, James Collinson, and F. G. Stephens. His notable paintings included *Rienzi, The Hireling Shepherd, Claudio and Isabella, The Light of the World, The Scapegoat, Isabella and the Pot of Basil, The Shadow of Death, Nazareth, The Triumph of the Innocents.* Author of *Pre-Raphaelitism and the Pre-Raphaelite Brotherhood* (1905).

Hunt, Leigh, *in full* James Henry Leigh. 1784–1859. English essayist and poet. Editor of *The Examiner* (1808 ff.) and *The Reflector* (1810–11); sentenced to two years' imprisonment (1813) for articles reflecting on the Prince Regent; published and defended verse of Shelley, Keats, etc., and championed Romanticism against attacks of *Blackwood's* magazine. Founded and edited *The Indicator* (1819–21); associated with Byron in editing *The Liberal* (1822–23). His many works included *The Story of Rimini* (poem, 1816), *Foliage* (verse, 1818), *Hero and Leander* (1819), *Lord Byron and Some of his Contemporaries* (1828), *Captain Sword and Captain Pen* (1835), *A Legend of Florence* (play, 1840), *Imagination and Fancy* (1844), *Wit and Humour* (1846), *Men, Women, and Books* (1847), *A Jar of Honey from Mount Hybla* (1848), *Autobiography* (1850).

Hunt, Richard Morris. 1827–1895. American architect, b. Brattleboro, Vt. Brother of William M. Hunt. In Paris engaged in work on Louvre, Tuileries, Pavillon de la Bibliothèque (1854–55); employed on extension of U.S. Capitol (1855); offices in New York (from 1858). Works included Administration Building, Chicago World's Fair (1893); main section of Metropolitan Museum of Art, Lenox Library, and Tribune Building, New York; National Observatory, Washington, D.C.; Fogg Museum, Harvard; theological library and Marquand Chapel, Princeton U.; Yorktown Monument, Virginia; residences for W.K. Vanderbilt, G.W. Vanderbilt ("Biltmore"), J.J. Astor, etc.

Hunt, Walter. 1796–1859. American inventor, b. Martinsburg, N.Y. Invented a sewing machine incorporating an eye-pointed needle and double lock stitch (1834, but never patented; cf. Elias HOWE), Globe stove, iron alarm gong, safety pin (pat. 1849), paper collar (1854), etc.; failed to profit from any of them.

Hunt, Ward. 1810–1886. American jurist, b. Utica, N.Y. Associate justice, U.S. Supreme Court (1873–82).

Hunt, William Henry. 1790–1864. English painter. Known esp. for humorous and still-life watercolors.

Hunt, William Holman. See Holman HUNT.

Hunt, William Morris. 1824–1879. American painter, b. Brattleboro, Vt. Brother of Richard M. Hunt. Studied with Millet in France; introduced work of Millet, Corot, and Barbizon school to U.S. Works included *Girl Reading, Peasant Girl at Barbizon, Hurdy-Gurdy Boy, Landscape, Girl at a Fountain, The Bathers.*

Hun·ter \'hənt-ər\, David. 1802–1886. American army officer, b. Washington, D.C. Entered army (1822); served through Civil War; brigadier general, major general of volunteers (1861); commanded Department of the South (1862) and issued order (May 9, 1862; annulled by Lincoln, May 19, 1862) freeing the slaves in his department; organized first regiment of Negro troops (1862) and declared felon by Confederacy. President, military commission that tried conspirators for assassination of Lincoln.

Hunter, John. 1728–1793. British anatomist and surgeon, b. Scotland. Assistant to his brother William (1748–59); surgeon at St. George's, London (1756); staff surgeon with English army (1760–63); practiced in London (1763); took house pupils, among whom was Edward Jenner (*q.v.*); began to lecture on surgery (1773); surgeon extraordinary to George III (1776); surgeon general to army (1790). His investigations included work relating to the descent of the testes in the fetus, course of the olfactory nerves, formation of pus, placental circulation, function of lymphatics, coagulation of blood, digestion in hibernating snakes and lizards, recovery of people apparently drowned, the structure of whales, bees, growth of deer's antlers; discovered that smaller arteries increase in size to compensate when circulation is arrested in larger ones; first to ligate artery for aneurysm (1785). Author of *Natural History of the Human Teeth* (1771), *Treatise on the Venereal Disease* (1786), *Animal Oeconomy* (1786). His brother ¶William (1718–1783) was a physiologist and anatomist; surgeon-accoucheur, Middlesex Hospital (1748), British Lying-in Hospital (1749); physician extraordinary to Queen Charlotte Sophia (1764); first professor of anatomy, Royal Academy (1768). Began teaching (1746); devoted practice to obstetrics (from 1756). Author of *Anatomy of the Human Gravid Uterus* (1774).

Hunter, Robert Mercer Taliaferro. 1809–1887. American politician, b. Essex Co., Va. Member, U.S. House of Representatives (1837–43, 1845–47; speaker 1839–41); U.S. Senate (1847–61). Secretary of state of the Confederacy (1861–62); member, Confederate senate (1862–65); one of Confederate negotiators at Hampton Roads conference (1865). Treasurer of Virginia (1874–80).

Hunter, Sir William Wilson. 1840–1900. British civil servant, b. Scotland. Entered Indian civil service (1862); organized and directed statistical survey of Indian Empire (1871–87), whose reports filled 128 volumes, later condensed in *The Imperial Gazetteer of India* (9 vols., 1881); member of governor-general's council (1881–87).

Huntingdon, Countess of. See Selina Hastings under HASTINGS family.

Huntingdon, Earl of. Title of one of three oldest English earldoms still existent, held from just before the Conquest by Scottish kings beginning with David I; by William Herbert (see HERBERT family); by John HOLLAND (1352?–1400) and his son; from 1529 by HASTINGS family.

Hun·ting·ton \'hənt-iŋ-tən\, Archer Milton. 1870–1955. American writer and Hispanic scholar, b. New York City. Son of Collis P. Huntington. Founded Hispanic Society of America (1904) and gave it a building, an endowment, and a valuable collection. Author of *A Note Book in Northern Spain* (1898) and verse collections as *Lace Maker of Segovia* (1928), *The Ladies of Vallbona* (1931), *Alfonso the Eighth Rides By* (1934), *Vela Venenosa, Rimas* (1936). m. 2d (1923) Anna Vaughn Hyatt (*q.v.*).

Huntington, Collis Potter. 1821–1900. American railroad builder, b. Harwinton, Conn. Itinerant peddler (1836–42); storekeeper, Oneonta, N.Y. (1842–49). To California (1849). Interested in building of transcontinental railroad (from 1861), completed when Central Pacific Railroad joined Union Pacific (1869). Southern Pacific Railroad organized (1884); president of this road (from 1890). Served as active lobbyist in Washington for favorable railroad legislation (1870–80). Also interested in Chesapeake and Ohio Railroad (from

1869), Pacific Mail Steamship Co., United States and Brazil Steamship Co., Old Dominion Steamship Co. See Henry Edwards HUNTINGTON.

Huntington, Ellsworth. 1876–1947. American geographer and explorer, b. Galesburg, Ill. On teaching staff, Euphrates College, Turkey (1897–1901); explored canyons of Euphrates River (1901). On Pumpelly expedition to Russian Turkestan (1903–04) and R. L. Barrett expedition to Chinese Turkestan (1905–06). Teacher of geography (1907–15) and research associate (from 1917), Yale. Author of *The Pulse of Asia* (1907), *Civilization and Climate* (1915), *World Power and Evolution* (1919), *Earth and Sun* (1923), *The Pulse of Progress* (1926), *The Human Habitat* (1927), *Season of Birth* (1938), *Mainsprings of Civilization* (1945), etc.

Huntington, Henry Edwards. 1850–1927. American railway executive, b. Oneonta, N.Y. Nephew of Collis P. Huntington. Installed by uncle in executive positions on Huntington railroads (1881–1900); built urban and interurban transit systems in San Francisco, Los Angeles; inherited from uncle large railroad interests; sold control of Southern Pacific Railroad to E. H. Harriman. From about 1903, collected book and art treasures for his library at San Marino, which he left to trustees to be maintained for public benefit.

Huntington, Samuel. 1731–1796. American Revolutionary politician, b. Windham, Conn. Member, Continental Congress (1776–84) and its president (1779–81, 1783); signer of Declaration of Independence. Governor of Connecticut (1786–96).

Huntly, Earls and marquises of. See GORDON family.

Hunts·man \'hənt-smən\, Benjamin. 1704–1776. English inventor. Clockmaker and instrument maker; at Sheffield opened steel foundry for producing spring steel (c.1740); invented and under extreme secrecy produced crucible, or cast, steel, more uniformly pure than any other available.

Hun·tzi·ger \œⁿt-sē-zher\, Charles-Léon-Clément. 1880–1941. French army officer. Distinguished himself in World War I; major general (1934). During German invasion (1940), commanded 2d army and 4th army group; headed delegation that signed peace terms with Germany at Compiègne Forest (July 22, 1940). In Pétain regime, commander in chief of land forces and minister of war (1940–41).

Hu·nya·di \'hu̇n-yȯd-ē\, János. 1407?–1456. Hungarian national hero. Son of a knight of King Sigismund; saw first military service under Sigismund (1410–38); learned military arts from Francesco Sforza; successful against Turks (1437–38); won many honors, including post of governor of Transylvania; after death of King Albert (1439), successfully supported Władysław III (*q.v.*) of Poland for throne of Hungary; won several victories over Turks (1441–43), broke Ottoman hold on Bosnia, Hercegovina, Serbia, Bulgaria, Albania, and secured treaty advantageous to Hungary; with failure of Venetian fleet to support him, suffered overwhelming defeat at Varna (1444); regent (1446–52) for young king, László V; fought two years (1446–48) against Frederick III and again against Turks, but defeated at Kosovo (1448); defended (1456) Belgrade against Turkish army of Mehmed II.

Huram. See HIRAM.

Hur·ban \'hu̇r-bȧn\, Jozef Miloslav. 1817–1888. Slovak patriot and writer. Influential in establishment of Czech as literary language of Slovaks; established journal *Slovenské pohľady* (1846). Author of verse *Svatba krále velko-moravského* (1842), novels *Gottšalk* (1861), *Olejkár* (1889). His son ¶Svetozar Hurban-Va·jan·ský \-'vȧ-yȧn-skē\ (1847–1916), author of fiction and patriotic verse and founder (1881) of *Národnie Noviny*.

Hurd \'hərd\, Peter. 1904–1984. American artist, b. Roswell, N.M. Studied under N.C. Wyeth; war artist for *Life* magazine during World War II. Noted for sun-drenched landscapes of the American Southwest and portraits of its inhabitants, including *Portrait of José Herrera* (1938); official portrait of Pres. Lyndon B. Johnson (1967) was rejected by its subject; also illustrated books and painted murals in public buildings.

Hurd, Richard. 1720–1808. English prelate. Bishop of Lichfield and Coventry (1774–81), of Worcester (1781–1808). Author of *Moral and Political Dialogues* (1759), *Letters on Chivalry and Romance* (1762), etc.

Hur·ley \'hər-lē\, Patrick Jay. 1883–1963. American diplomat, b. Indian Territory (now Oklahoma). Practiced law in Tulsa (from 1908); U.S. secretary of war (1929–33); U.S. minister to New Zealand (1942–43); appointed by President Roosevelt his personal representative in Near and Middle East (1943) and on missions to Afghanistan and China (1944); temporary major general (1944); U.S. ambassador to China (1944–45) with special mission of reconciling Kuomintang and Communists.

Hu·rok \'(h)yu̇(ə)r-,äk\, Solomon. 1888–1974. American impresario, b. Pogar, Russia. To U.S. (1906); began arranging musical entertainments for local clubs; began popular weekly concert series at New York Hippodrome (1915); undertook management of U.S. appearances of Comédie-Française, Isadora Duncan, Richard Strauss, Ballet Russe de Monte Carlo, Azuma Kabuki Dancers, Bolshoi Ballet, etc.; became leading impresario in U.S. Author of memoirs *Impresario* (1946), *S. Hurok Presents* (1953).

Hurst \'hərst\, Sir Cecil James Barrington. 1870–1963. English jurist. Legal adviser to British foreign office (1918–29); judge of the Permanent Court of International Justice at The Hague (1929–46), and president (1934–36).

Hurst, Fannie. 1889–1968. American writer, b. Hamilton, Ohio. Author of novels, including *Stardust* (1919), *Lummox* (1923), *Appassionata* (1925), *A President is Born* (1928), *Five and Ten* (1929), *Imitation of Life* (1933), *Anitra's Dance* (1934), *Lonely Parade* (1942), *Anywoman* (1950), *Family!* (1960), *Fool—Be Still* (1964); collections of stories as *Just Around the Corner* (1914), *Gaslight Sonatas* (1918), *Song of Life* (1927), *We Are Ten* (1937); also plays, screenplays.

Hurs·ton \'hər-stən\, Zora Neale. 1903–1960. American writer, b. Eatonville, Fla. Studied anthropology under Franz Boas; private secretary to Fannie Hurst. Author of novels *Jonah's Gourd Vine* (1934), *Their Eyes Were Watching God* (1937), *Moses, Man of the Mountain* (1939), *Seraph on the Suwanee* (1948); *Mules and Men,* a study of Negro folkways in Florida (1935); *Tell My Horse,* on Haiti (1938); and autobiography *Dust Tracks on a Road* (1942).

Hur·ta·do de Men·do·za \u̇r-'tä-t͟hō-t͟hä-män-'dō-thä\, Andrés. 2d marqués de Ca·ñe·te \kän-'yā-tā\. c.1490–1561. Spanish colonialist. Viceroy of Peru (1555–61); concluded treaty with Inca king Sayri Tupac. His son ¶Garcia (1535–1609), 4th marqués, was appointed by his father to govern Chile (1556–61); viceroy of Peru (1589–97); dispatched expedition that discovered Marquesas Islands (1595), named for him.

Hurtado de Mendoza, Diego. 1503–1575. Spanish diplomat and writer. Ambassador to England (1537), Venice (1539); representative of Charles V at Council of Trent (1545); governor and captain general of Siena (1547); imperial representative in Rome (1549). Later exiled to Granada, where he wrote firsthand account of Morisco uprising as *Guerra de Granada* (pub. 1627); also wrote verse; reputed author of novel *Lazarillo de Tormes.*

Hus \'hu̇s\, Jan. 1372 or 1373–1415. Czech religious leader. Teacher at U. of Prague (1396 ff.); rector and preacher, Bethlehem Chapel, Prague (1402 ff.); influenced by works of John Wycliffe, became leader of movement for church reform in Bohemia; rector of university after departure of German majority of faculty (1409); recognized Pope Alexander V (1409), but at instance of archbishop of Prague prohibited from preaching and, on refusal to obey or to appear before Roman Curia, excommunicated (1411); defended by King Wenceslas IV; denounced Pope John XXII's sale of indulgences and lost support of king (1411); placed under major excommunication and Prague placed under interdict (1412); left Prague; conducted literary controversy with enemies (1412–14). Invited to attend Council of Constance (1414); seized, despite safe-conduct guarantee, and placed on trial for heresy; convicted despite his denials, burned at the stake. Written works included *De ecclesia, Postilla,* and treatises in Czech.

Hu·sain \hu̇s-'ān\, Zakir. 1897–1969. Indian politician. Vice chancellor of Muslim National U. (1926–48), Alīgarh Muslim U. (1948–52); in parliament (1952–57); governor of Bihar (1957–62); vice president (1962–67), president of India (1967–69).

Ḥusayn. See under ḤASAN.

Ḥusayn. See SHAH SULTAN HUSAYN.

Ḥu·say·nī \k̲u̇s-,ī-'nē\, Amīn al-. *Called* Haj Āmīn \'haj-ä-'mēn\. 1893–1974. Arab leader, b. Jerusalem. Served in Ottoman army (1910–18); permanent president and mufti of Supreme Muslim Council, Palestine (1921–36); staunch opponent of Zionist attempt to settle Palestine; led developing resistance to British authority and was removed as head of Council; fled to Lebanon (1937), reconstituted Arab High Committee, and continued to oppose British rule, esp. concessions of 1939; in Germany (1939–45).

Ḥu·sayn ibn 'Alī \k̲u̇s-'ī-,nib-ə-nal-'ē\. c.1854–1931. King of the Hejaz (1916–24). Amīr of Mecca (1908–16) as result of Young Turk movement; in World War I allied himself with Great Britain against Turks; rendered valuable service in Arabia; on proclamation of Arabian independence chosen (1916) first king of the Hejaz; refused to sign Versailles Treaty (1919) and treaty with Great Britain (1924) because not satisfied with settlement of Arab problems in Near East. Proclaimed himself head of new caliphate (1924); defeated and forced to abdicate by Wahhabiyah attack led by Ibn Saud (1924); in exile in Cyprus (1924–30). Succeeded by son ¶'Alī ibn Ḥusayn (1878–1935), king of the Hejaz (1924–25); other sons were King Abdullah of Jordan and King Faisal I of Iraq (*qq.v.*).

Ḥu·sayn Shāh 'Alā' ad-Dīn \k̲u̇s-'īn-'shä-al-'ä-u̇d-'dēn\. d. 1519. Ruler of Bengal (1493–1519). Officer at court of Muẓaffar Shāh; led rebellion and proclaimed himself king (1493); established new capital at Ikdālā; replaced Abyssinian officers with Muslims and Hindus; conquered Kamrup and Assam (1498), annexed Orissa (1516). Founder of Ḥusayn Shāhī dynasty.

Hü·sey·in Rah·mi Gür·pi·nar \hue̅-sä-'ēn-rä-'mē-gue̅r-pē-'när\. 1864–1944. Turkish novelist. Author of *Mürebbiye* (1895), *Iffet* (1897), *Mutallaka* (1898),

Metres (1900), *Son arzu* (1918), *Ben deli miyim?* (1925) and other novels noted esp. for depiction of life in Istanbul; also wrote plays, stories, translated novels from French.

Hu Shih \'hü-'shi(ə)r\. 1891–1962. Chinese philosopher. Professor of philosophy, later dean (1917–26) at Peking National U.; championed *pai-hua,* modern Chinese literary language based on vernacular and wrote poems in it collected in *Ch'ang-shih chi* (1920); professor of philosophy (1927–31) at Kuang Hua U., Shanghai. One of leading liberals in China, opponent of Communists; Nationalist ambassador to the United States (1938–42), to UN (1957); president of Academia Sinica, Taiwan (1958–62). Author of *Outline of Chinese Philosophy* (1919), *Chinese Renaissance* (1934).

Hus·kis·son \'həs-(,)kis-ən\, William. 1770–1830. English financier and politician. M.P. (1796–1802, 1804–30); secretary to treasury (1804–05, 1807–09); treasurer of navy and president of Board of Trade (1823–27); colonial secretary, and leader of House of Commons (1827–28); advocate of free trade.

Huss, Jan. See Hus.

Hus·sa·rek von Hein·lein \'hùs-ä-,rek-fòn-'hīn-,līn\, Max. Freiherr. 1865–1935. Austrian politician. Professor, Vienna (1895 ff.); minister of justice (1911–17); Austro-Hungarian chancellor during last days of the monarchy (July–Oct. 1918).

Hussein. See Husain, Husayn.

Hus·serl \'hùs-ərl\, Edmund. 1859–1938. German philosopher, b. Moravia. Student of Brentano (1883–86); lecturer at Halle (1886–1901); professor, Göttingen (1901–16), Freiburg (1916–28); attempted to establish an analysis of consciousness on rigorously logical and scientific basis; developed phenomenological method. Author of *Philosophie der Arithmetik* (1891), *Logische Untersuchungen* (1900–01), *Ideen zu einer reinen Phänomenologie* (1913), *Erste Philosophie* (1923–24), *Formale und transzendentale Logik* (1929), *Die Krisis der europäischen Wissenschaften* (1936).

Hus·sey \'həs-ē\, Obed. 1792–1860. American inventor, b. Maine. Invented a reaper (patented 1833; improved model, 1847), which he manufactured (1834–58) in competition with the McCormick reaper.

Hus·son \ü̅e̅-sōⁿ\, Jules-François-Félix. *Pseudonym* Champ·fleu·ry \shäⁿ-flœ-rē, -flü̅e̅-\. 1821–1889. French novelist. Theorist of a style of Realism inspired by newly invented daguerreotype and discussed in *Le Réalisme* (1857). Author of novels *Chien-Caillou* (1847), *Les Oies de Noël* (1853), *Les Bourgeois de Molinchart* (1855), *Le Violon de faïence* (1862), *Fanny Minoret* (1882), etc. Helped popularize painting of Courbet.

Hus·ton \'(h)yü-stən\, Walter. 1884–1950. American actor, b. Toronto. On legitimate stage and in vaudeville in U.S. (1909–29); notable performances in *Mr. Pitt* (1924), *The Fountain* (1925), *Elmer the Great* (1928), *Dodsworth* (1934), *Knickerbocker Holiday* (1938); appeared in films *Abraham Lincoln* (1930), *Dodsworth* (1936), *All that Money Can Buy* (1941), *Treasure of the Sierra Madre* (1948, Academy Award).

Hu·szár \'hù-sár\, Károly. 1882–1941. Hungarian journalist and politician. Head of Christian Social party, and editor of its journals *Népujsag* and *Alkotmány;* imprisoned for Catholic activity during Communist dictatorship in Hungary (1919); prime minister of coalition cabinet (1919–20) which made Admiral Horthy regent of Hungary; member of upper house of Diet (from 1929).

Husz·gen \'hùs-gən\, Johannes. *Also spelled* Huss·chyn \'hùs-k̲ən\, Hüss·gen \'hu̅e̅s-gən\, Heuss·gen \'hu̅e̅s-gən\. *Lat.* John Oec·o·lam·pa·di·us \,ek-ō-läm-'päd-ē-ùs\. 1482–1531. German clergyman, scholar, and Humanist. Tutor to sons of elector palatine (1506); preacher at Weinsberg (1510–13); to Basel (1515); assisted Erasmus on Greek New Testament; produced translations of several Greek Church Fathers; preacher at Augsburg cathedral (1518–20); in Brigittine monastery, Altomünster (1520–22); growing attraction to church reform movement drew him back to Basel (1522), where he became close associate of Zwingli; professor, U. of Basel (1523); took part in disputations at Baden (1526), Bern (1528); debated Luther in defense of Zwingli at Marburg (1529); died soon after Zwingli.

Hutch·e·son \'həch-ə-sən\, Francis. 1694–1746. Scottish philosopher. Professor, Glasgow (1729–46); popular preacher; known for ethical theory of innate moral sense. Author of *Inquiry into the Original of Our Ideas of Beauty and Virtue* (1725), *Essay on the Nature and Conduct of the Passions and Affections* (1728), *System of Moral Philosophy* (1755).

Hutch·ins \'həch-ənz\, Robert Maynard. 1899–1977. American educator, b. Brooklyn, N.Y. Professor (1925–29), dean (1927–29), Yale Law School. President (1929–45), chancellor (1945–51), U. of Chicago; introduced "Great Books" undergraduate program, abolished intercollegiate football. Associate director, Ford Foundation (1951–54); president, Fund for the Republic (1954–59); founder and president (1959–69), chairman (1969–77), Center for the Study of Democratic Institutions. Author of *The Higher Learning in America* (1936), *No Friendly Voice* (1936), *Education for Freedom* (1943), *University of Utopia* (1953), *Education: The Learning Society* (1968).

Hutchins, Thomas. 1730–1789. American cartographer, b. Monmouth Co., N.J. Appointed by Congress "geographer to the United States" (1781); in charge of survey of lands in the Northwest Territory as provided by the Ordinance of 1785; on western expeditions (1785, 1786–87, 1788–89) ran Geographer's Line and began platting the Seven Ranges basic to all subsequent surveying in the West.

Hutch·in·son \'həch-ən-sən\, Alfred. 1924–1972. South African writer. Teacher in South Africa, England, Nigeria; in South Africa an opponent of apartheid; imprisoned (1952–56), escaped. Author of essays, stories, plays including *The Rain-Killers* (1964); best known for autobiography *Road to Ghana* (1960).

Hutchinson, Anne, *nee* Mar·bury \'mär-b(ə-)rē\. 1591–1643. American religious leader, b. Alford, England. m. William Hutchinson (1612, d. 1642); to America (1634); settled in Boston. Preached salvation by individual intuition of God's grace and love without regard for obedience to the specific laws of church and state; tried for "traducing the ministers and their ministry"; convicted (1637) and banished from Massachusetts Bay Colony. Emigrated (1638) to Aquidneck (Rhode Island); moved (1642) to home near what is now Pelham Bay, N.Y. She and her family were massacred by Indians.

Hutchinson, John. 1615–1664. English Puritan soldier and regicide. Governor of Nottingham, and M.P. (1646 ff.); signed death warrant of Charles I; imprisoned after the Restoration.

Hutchinson, John. 1674–1737. English theologian. Author of *Moses's Principia* (1724), attacking Newton, and works of religious symbolism; taught that Hebrew scriptures contain a complete system of natural science and theology, and gained many followers (known as Hutchinsonians).

Hutchinson, Sir Jonathan. 1828–1913. English surgeon. Surgeon, London Hospital (1859–83); Hunterian professor at Royal Coll. of Surgeons (1879–83); specialist in ophthalmology, dermatology, and congenital syphilis.

Hutchinson, Thomas. 1711–1780. American colonial administrator, b. Boston. Merchant, Boston (from 1727). In Massachusetts legislature (1737–49); member, governor's council (1749–66); lieutenant governor (1758–71); as chief justice (1760–69) upheld legality of Stamp Act and hence had his house destroyed by mob (1765). Royal governor of Massachusetts (1771–74); upheld British authority and by his policies brought nearer the Revolution. To England (1774); in exile there until his death.

Hut·ten \'hùt-ᵊn\, Philipp von. 1511?–1546. German adventurer. Nephew of Ulrich von Hutten. One of a contingent sent to conquer Venezuela in behalf of Augsburg family of Welser, to whom province had been granted by Emperor Charles V; in Venezuela (1535–46; captain general from 1540); after years of exploration in interior, returned to coast to find in power a Spanish governor who had him seized and executed.

Hutten, Ulrich von. 1488–1523. German nobleman and Humanist. Joined imperial army (1513); under patronage of elector of Mainz (1514, 1518). The murder of his uncle by the duke of Württemberg caused him to join the Swabian League against the duke (1519); joined Franz von Sickingen in the struggle of the nobility of the Upper Rhine against the ecclesiastical principalities (1522). Engaged vigorously in defense of Luther, and by his writings appealed to the sympathies and patriotism of the nobility, thus supplementing Luther's appeal to the common folk. Had dispute with Erasmus (1522–23); died in care of Zwingli. Known in literature chiefly as a bitter satirist; author of a large share of the second part of *Epistolae obscurorum virorum* (1515–17) and of Latin pamphlets on Luther's behalf, published in German as *Gesprächbuchlein* (1522).

Hut·ter \'hùt-ər\ *or* **Hüt·ter** \'hu̅e̅t-ər\, Leonhard. 1563–1616. German theologian. A champion of Lutheran orthodoxy; influenced the Confessio Augustana. Author of *Compendium locorum theologicorum* (1610).

Hut·ton \'hət-ᵊn\, James. 1726–1797. Scottish geologist. With James Davie, developed method of producing sal ammoniac from coal soot; member of Edinburgh scientific circle; in two papers (1785) formulated uniformitarian principle of geologic evolution; published *Theory of the Earth* (1795). See John Playfair.

Hux·ley \'hək-slē\, Thomas Henry. 1825–1895. English biologist. Entered Royal Navy medical service (1846); assistant surgeon, H.M.S. *Rattlesnake* in exploration of southern seas (1846–50); established reputation with collection specimens and subsequent studies of them. Lecturer, Royal School of Mines (1854–85; in later years the Normal School of Science); Hunterian professor, Royal College of Surgeons (1863–69), and Fullerian professor, Royal Institution (1863–67); president, Royal Society (1883–85). Foremost advocate in England of Darwin's theory of evolution; engaged Bishop Wilberforce in famous exchange at Oxford (1860). Influential member of first London school board (1870–72). In late years studied and wrote on philosophy. Author of *Evidence as to Man's Place in Nature* (1863), *Introduction to the Classification of Animals* (1869), *Lay Sermons* (1870), *Manual of the Comparative Anatomy of Vertebrated Animals* (1871), *Critiques and Addresses* (1873), *Physiography* (1877), *The Crayfish* (1880), *Science and Culture* (1881), *Evolution and Ethics* (1893).

His son ¶Leonard (1860–1933), editor and author, taught in Charterhouse (1884–1901); assistant editor (1901–16), editor (1916–33) of *Cornhill Magazine.* Wrote *Life of Huxley* (1900), *Anniversaries and other Poems* (1920); edited letters of Jane Carlyle, Elizabeth Browning.

¶Sir Julian Sorell (1887–1975), biologist, son of Leonard Huxley; professor, Rice Institute, Texas (1913–16); senior demonstrator in zoology, Oxford (1919–25); professor (1925–27), King's College, London; Fullerian professor, Royal Institution (1926–29); director general, UNESCO (1946–48). Author of *The Individual in the Animal Kingdom* (1912), *Essays of a Biologist* (1923), *Religion without Revelation* (1927), *The Science of Life* (with H. G. and G. P. Wells, 1931), *The Captive Shrew and other Poems* (1932), *At the Zoo* (1936), *Evolution: The Modern Synthesis* (1942), *Toward a New Humanism* (1957), etc.

His brother ¶Aldous Leonard (1894–1963), novelist and critic; author of *Limbo* (1920), *Crome Yellow* (1921), *Mortal Coils* (1922), *Antic Hay* (1923), *Those Barren Leaves* (1925), *Jesting Pilate* (1926), *Point Counter Point* (1928), *Brief Candles* (1930), *Brave New World* (1932), *Eyeless in Gaza* (1936), *After Many a Summer* (1939), *The Perennial Philosophy* (1945), *Ape and Essence* (1948), *Themes and Variations* (1950), *Doors of Perception* (1954), etc.

Huy·gens \'hœi-kəns *Angl* 'hī-gənz, 'hȯi-\, Christiaan. 1629–1695. Dutch mathematician, physicist, and astronomer. Son of Constantijn Huygens. With his brother, discovered improved method of grinding and polishing lenses (1655); discovered a satellite of Saturn (1655), stars in the Orion nebula (1656), true shape of Saturn's rings (1659); devised negative eyepiece and micrometer for use in telescopes; first to use pendulum to regulate movement of clocks (1656) and to determine acceleration due to gravity. In Paris (1666–81); a founder of French Academy of Sciences (1666). Published *Horologium oscillatorium* (1673) solving problems involving rotation of bodies, centrifugal force, pendulums, etc. Enunciated laws governing the impact of elastic bodies (1669); developed wave theory of light (first stated in 1678); enunciated Huygen's principle according to which the surface constituting a wave front is determined; investigated polarization of light. Author also of *Discours de la cause de la pesanteur* (1690), *Traité de la lumière* (1690), etc.

Huygens, Constantijn. 1596–1687. Dutch diplomat and writer. Several times to England on diplomatic missions, meeting Donne and Bacon. Author of verse in variety of styles, collected in *Korenbloemen* (1658, 1672); prose works as satirical *Costelyck Mal* (1622), earthy *Scheepspraet* (1625) and *Trijntje Cornelis* (1653), patriotic *'t Voorhout van 's-Gravenhage* (1621) and *De uitlandighe Herder* (1622), autobiographical *Dagwerck* (1639), *Hofwijck* (1651), *Cluyswerck* (1683).

Huynh Phu So \'hü-yən-'pü-'sō\. *Also spelled* Huyen. *Known also as* Dao Khung \'dau̇-ku̇ŋ\, *i.e.* Mad Monk, *and* Phat Song \'pät-'sȯŋ\. 1919–1947. Vietnamese religious leader. As itinerant Buddhist preacher, advocated Theravāda over Mahāyāna Buddhism; evolved new religion, called Phat Giao Hoa Hao, or simply Hoa Hao, stressing austerity and simple worship and combining elements of Buddhism, Confucianism, sorcery, animism; gained following as healer and successful prophet; persecuted and exiled by French authorities; Japanese prisoner during World War II; executed by Communist Viet Minh authorities.

Huys·man \'hœi-smän\ *or* **Huus·man** \'hü̅e-\, Roelof. *Lat.* Rodolphus Agric·o·la \ə-'grik-ə-lə\. 1443 or 1444–1485. Dutch Humanist. Early exponent of Renaissance ideas in northern Europe; lectured at Heidelberg (1484). Author of an oration in praise of philosophy (1476), a life of Petrarch (1477), *De inventione dialectica* (1479), *De formando studio* (1484). Strongly influenced Erasmus.

Huys·mans \'hœi-smäns\, Camille. 1871–1968. Belgian writer and politician. Professor, Université Nouvelle, Brussels; secretary of Second International (1905–22); in House of Representatives (1910–65); minister of education (1925–27); helped form Socialist party (1933); president of House (1936–39); vice chairman, Belgian Parliamentary Consultative Committee, London (1939–45); prime minister (1946–47); minister of education (1947–49). Author of *Soixante-quinze années de domination bourgeoise* (1905), *La Révolution de 1830* (1905), *L'Affiliation des syndicats* (1907), *Études sur les assurances sociales* (1913), *Quatre Types* (1937).

Huysmans, Cornelius. 1648–1727. Flemish painter. Best known for his landscapes and a few large religious pictures. His brother ¶Jan Baptist (1654–1716) was also noted as a landscape artist.

Huysmans, Jacob. 1636?–1696. Flemish painter. Worked in England; known as fashionable portraitist, esp. of Catherine of Braganza, Izaak Walton.

Huys·mans \'hœi-smäns, *Fr* w^{y}ēs-mä^{n}s\, Joris-Karl, *orig.* Georges-Charles. 1848–1907. French novelist, of Dutch descent. Author of a series of realistic novels, including *Marthe, histoire d'une fille* (1876), *Les Sœurs Vatard* (1879), *En ménage* (1881), *À vau-l'eau* (1882), *À rebours* (1884), *En rade* (1887), followed by novels showing a reaction from materialism, as *Là-bas* (1891), *En route* (1895), *La Cathédrale* (1898), *L'Oblat* (1903); also wrote perceptive art criticism as *L'Art moderne* (1883), *Certains* (1889).

Huy·sum *or* **Huij·sum, van** \vän-'hœi-sœm\. Name of a family of Dutch painters, including: Justus (1659–1716), noted esp. for still lifes of flowers, seascapes, etc. His son ¶Jan (1682–1749), noted for paintings of flowers and fruit, in oils and water colors. Another son ¶Justus (1685–1707), painter esp. of battle scenes.

Hviezdoslav. See Pavol ORSZÁGH.

Hy·a·cinth \'hī-ə-(,)sin(t)th, -sən(t)th\. Saint. *Orig.* Jacek Od·ra·waż \ȯ-'drá-vázh\. before 1200–1257. Polish missionary. Entered Dominican order (1217 or 1218); traditionally credited with founding many convents, as at Kraków and Danzig, and with walking vast distances to proselytize in Poland, Bohemia, Prussia, Pomerania, Lithuania, the Scandinavian countries, Russia, Tartary, etc.; canonized (1594).

Hyacinthe, Père. See Charles LOYSON.

Hy·att \'hī-ət\, Alpheus. 1838–1902. American zoologist and paleontologist, b. Washington, D.C. Custodian, Boston Society of Natural History (1870–81) and curator (1881–1902). A founder and editor (1867–71) of *American Naturalist;* established marine laboratory at Annisquam, Mass. (1879), later moved to Woods Hole, Mass. Taught zoology and paleontology, M.I.T. (1870–88) and Boston U. (1877–1902); paleontologist to U.S. Geological Survey (1889–1902). Founded new school of invertebrate paleontology; studied esp. evolution of cephalopoda. Author of *Genesis of the Arietidae* (1889), *Phylogeny of an Acquired Characteristic* (1894).

Hyatt, Anna Vaugh. 1876–1973. American sculptor, b. Cambridge, Mass. Daughter of Alpheus Hyatt. Exhibited at Paris Salon (from 1907); early gained notice with animal figures; later works included equestrian *Joan of Arc, Diana and the Chase, El Cid Campeador* for Seville (1927), *Bulls Fighting, Don Quixote* (1942), *Boabdil* (1944), figures of Martí, Lincoln, Andrew Jackson. m. (1923) Archer M. Huntington.

Hyatt, John Wesley. 1837–1920. American inventor. b. Starkey, N.Y. Invented composition billiard ball (1869); discovered principle of making celluloid (pat. 1870); invented water filter and purifier, a type of roller bearing, a lock-stitch sewing machine with fifty needles, and a process of solidifying hard woods.

Hyde, Catherine. See under dukes of Queensberry, under DOUGLAS family.

Hyde \'hīd\, Charles Cheney. 1873–1952. American jurist, b. Chicago. Professor of international law, Northwestern U. (1907–25), Columbia U. (1925–45); solicitor for U.S. Dept. of State (1923–25); member, Permanent Court of Arbitration, the Hague (1951–52). Author of influential *International Law, Chiefly as Interpreted and Applied by the United States* (1922).

Hyde, Douglas. *Ir. Gael.* Dubhigh·las de Hi·de \'du̇v-läs-də-'ē-t͟hə\. *Pen name* An Craoi·bhín Aoi·bhinn \ən-'krē-vēn-'ē-vən\, *i.e.* the Fair Branch. 1860–1949. Irish writer and politician. Identified with Irish nationalist movement from its inception; first president of Gaelic League (1893–1915); professor of modern Irish, U. Coll., Dublin (1909–32). President of Ireland (1938–45). Among his many works, including verse, plays, histories, essays, were *Love Songs of Connacht* (1893), *Story of Early Irish Literature* (1897), *Literary History of Ireland* (1899), *Legends of Saints and Sinners* (1915), *An Leath-rann* (1922), *Mise Agus an Connradh* (1938).

Hyde, Edward. 1st Earl of Clar·en·don \'klar-ən-dən\. 1609–1674. English statesman and historian. Slighted study of law for literature and the company of Lord Falkland, Ben Jonson, Edmund Waller and others. Member of Short and Long Parliaments (1640), favoring popular party (till 1641); influential in suppressing earl marshal's court; supported Strafford's impeachment; supporter of Church of England and old constitution; opposed Grand Remonstrance and wrote king's reply; counseled moderation on king's part; openly joined Royalist cause (1642); composed king's manifestoes and, by his legalistic justification, won half the nation to Charles. Expelled from House of Commons (1642); followed king, as privy councilor and chancellor of exchequer (1643); followed Prince Charles (1646) to Scilly and Jersey, where he began his *History;* engaged in fruitless embassy to Spain for aid in money and for recovery of Ireland (1649–50). Chief adviser to Charles, later Charles II (1651), who appointed him lord chancellor (1658); composed Declaration of Breda (1660) and succeeded in making Restoration a national, not a factional, restoration of king and monarchy. Confirmed as lord chancellor (1660), created earl (1661); became virtual head of government in control of all departments of state; adopted religious policy of comprehension but not of toleration; vigorously enforced Act of Uniformity and other repressive measures; endeavored to restore episcopacy in Scotland; supported Ormonde's enlightened Irish administration; one of lord proprietors of colony of Carolina (1663), but supported navigation laws; pursuing feeble foreign policy, initiated disgraceful system of pensions from Louis XIV and dependence on France; became unpopular because of sale of Dunkirk and of Dutch War. Fell victim to court cabal, and to king's resentment at his disapproval of royal mistresses; dismissed (1667). Fled to France under impeachment by House of Lords; banished, lived in exile compiling his *History* and writing autobiography; died after assault by disgruntled English seamen. Author of *History of the Great Rebellion* (printed 1702–04 from transcript, 1826 from original ms.), *History of Civil War in Ireland* (1721), *Life of Edward, Earl of Clarendon* (1759), and *Contemplations on the Psalms.* Grandfather of Queen Mary, wife of William III, and Queen Anne, through secret marriage (1660) of his daughter Anne (1637–1671) to James II when Duke of York.

¶Henry (1638–1709), 2d earl, eldest son of 1st earl; M.P. as Viscount Corn·bury \'kȯrn-bə-re\ (1661–74); privy councilor through influence of Duke of York (1680); lord privy seal (1685); viceroy of Ireland (1685–87); opposed settlement of crown on William and Mary; imprisoned (1690, 1691); succeeded in title by his son ¶Edward (1661–1723), 3d earl; M.P. (1685–1701); governor of New York as Viscount Cornbury (1702–08).

¶Lawrence (1641–1711), 1st Earl of Roch·es·ter \'räch-ə-stər, *US also* -ˌes-tər\; 2d son by 2d wife of 1st Earl of Clarendon; M.P. (1660–79); with his elder brother Henry, warmly defended his father on impeachment charge in Parliament (1667); first lord of treasury (1679–85); created Viscount Hyde and then earl (1681); forced to take part in negotiation of Charles II's infamous subsidy treaty with Louis XIV (1681); lord president of the council (1684, 1710–11); lord high treasurer to James II (1685–87), dismissed because of resistance to Roman Catholicism. Accepted regime of William III; viceroy of Ireland (1700–03). His only son ¶Henry (1672–1753), 2d earl, inherited (1724) earldom of Clarendon as well; with his death both titles became extinct.

Hyde, Henry Baldwin. 1834–1899. American businessman, b. Catskill, N.Y. Founder of Equitable Life Assurance Society of the United States (1859), president (from 1874); introduced Tontine plan (1868).

Hyde de Neu·ville \ed-də-nœ-vēl\, Jean-Guillaume. Baron. 1776–1857. French diplomat. Agent of Louis XVI from outbreak of Revolution; took part in royalist insurrection at Berry (1796); attempted to persuade Napoléon to restore Bourbon monarchy; left France (1804); in U.S. (1806–14); undertook mission to Italy for Louis XVIII (1814); deputy (1815–30); ambassador to U.S. (1816–21), Portugal (1823–24); named count of Bemposta for role in saving John VI from coup d'état (1824); minister of navy (1828); cast sole vote against exclusion of duc de Bordeaux from succession (1830).

Hy·der Ali \'hī-dər-al-'ē\. *Also spelled* Hai·dar Ali \'hī-ˌdär-\. 1722–1782. Indian ruler and soldier. Helped form first corps of sepoys with European arms and artillery for Mysore army; gained army command; displaced prime minister and raja and made himself ruler of Mysore (c.1761); conquered several petty states; faced with British-Marāthā alliance (1766), captured Mangalore and defeated Bombay army; suffered Marāthā attack (1771) without promised British aid; increased army with French aid. Attacked Carnatic (1780); defeated by Sir Eyre Coote at Porto Novo and other battles (1781); died suddenly, leaving campaign to son Tippu Sahib.

Hy·gi·nus \hə-'jī-nəs\. Saint. d. c.140 A.D. Pope (136?–?140). Traditionally credited with organizing clerical hierarchy.

Hyginus, Gaius Julius. 1st century B.C. Latin author. According to Suetonius, appointed by Augustus superintendent of the Palatine library. Author of biographical and topographical works, literary commentaries, a collection of mythological legends, an elementary work on astronomy, etc., none extant.

Hyk·sos \'hik-ˌsōs, -ˌsäs\. Egyptian kings, often called the "Shepherd Kings," of 15th and 16th dynasties, reigning about 1674–1567 B.C. Very little known about them; probably a nomadic, possibly Semitic, people from the east. See SALITIS.

Hylacomylus. See Martin WALDSEEMÜLLER.

Hy·man \'hī-mən\, Libbie Henrietta. 1888–1969. American zoologist, b. Des Moines, Iowa. Conducted research at U. of Chicago (1916–31), American Museum of Natural History, N.Y.C. (1937–69). Known for reference and textbooks in zoology as *Laboratory Manual for Elementary Zoology* (1919), *Laboratory Manual for Comparative Vertebrate Zoology* (1922), *Comparative Vertebrate Anatomy* (1942), and esp. *The Invertebrates* (1931–68).

Hy·mans \'hī-mäns\, Paul. 1865–1941. Belgian politician and diplomat. Professor of history, Free U. of Brussels (1898–1914); member of Chamber of Deputies (from 1900) and a leader of the Liberal party; Belgian ambassador to Great Britain (1915–17); minister of economic affairs (1917), of foreign affairs (1918–20). Represented Belgium at the Paris Peace Conference (1919) and at the League of Nations, where he was the first presiding officer (Jan. 1920). Helped form Belgium–Luxembourg customs union (1921); helped negotiate Dawes Plan (1924). Minister of justice (1926–27), of foreign affairs (1927–35); member of council of ministers (1935–36).

Hynd·man \'hīnd-mən\, Henry Mayers. 1842–1921. English Socialist. Adopted Marxist Socialism (1880); founded Democratic Federation (1881; from 1884 called Social Democratic Federation); exerted influence on William Morris, George Lansbury, etc.; opposed Boer War (1899–1902); expelled from British Socialist party for supporting World War I and organized National Socialist party (1916); carried on agitation for social improvement. Author of *Economics of Socialism* (1896), *Evolution of Revolution* (1920).

Hyne \'hīn\, Charles John Cutcliffe Wright. 1865–1944. English traveler and writer. Best known as creator of fictional character Captain Kettle, as in *Adventures of Captain Kettle* (1898), *Captain Kettle on the Warpath* (1916), etc.

Hy·pa·tia \hī-'pā-sh(ē-)ə\. c.370–415. Greek philosopher. Taught at Alexandria and became recognized head of Neoplatonist school there; renowned for learning, eloquence, beauty; wrote esp. on mathematics; murdered by a mob incited by Cyril, then archbishop of Alexandria.

Hy·per·bo·lus \hī-'pər-bə-ləs\. d. 411 B.C. Athenian politician. Succeeded Cleon (422 B.C.) as head of democratic party; assassinated in Samos by the oligarchy.

Hy·pe·ri·des *or* **Hy·pe·rei·des** \ˌhī-pə-'rī-ˌdēz\. c.390–322 B.C. Athenian statesman and orator. Probably a pupil of Plato and Isocrates; supported anti-Macedonian policy advocated by Demosthenes; promoted Lamian War and, after Athenian defeat at Cranon, was condemned to death; fled to Aegina, but was captured and executed.

Hypselantes *or* **Hypsilantis.** See YPSILANTIS.

Hyrcanus, John. See JOHN HYRCANUS.

Hyrtl \'hirt-ᵊl\, Joseph. 1810–1894. Austrian anatomist. Professor at Prague (1837–45), Vienna (1845–74); influential teacher; widely known for technical excellence of his anatomical preparations; known also for work on the anatomy of the ear. Author of *Lehrbuch der Anatomie des Menschen* (1846), *Handbuch der topographischen Anatomie* (1847).

Hys·tas·pes \his-'tas-pēz\. *Old Persian* Vish·tas·pa \vish-'tas-pə\. 7th–6th century B.C. Persian ruler. Ruler of a Persian land known in the Avesta as Aryana Vaejah; remembered as a follower and the protector of Zoroaster.

Hystaspes. *Old Persian* Vishtaspa. fl. 521 B.C. Persian noble. One of the Achaemenidae of the younger line, kinsman of Cyrus the Great and father of Darius I Hystaspis and Artaphernes. Satrap of Parthia and Hyrcania.

Hy·wel ab Owain Gwyn·edd \'hə-wel-ȧb-'ō-ˌwīn-'gwin-eth\. d. 1170. Welsh prince and poet. Son of Owain Gwynedd; took leading part in occupation of Ceredigion by house of Gwynedd; ruled southern Ceredigion (1139–53); in constant struggle with kinsmen in northern Ceredigion; attacked Norman strongholds; killed in battle with half-brothers. Remembered chiefly as author of lyric poems celebrating love and natural beauty of Gwynedd.

Hywel Dda \-'thȧ\, *i.e.* Hywel the Good. d. 950. Welsh ruler. Succeeded father Cadell as ruler of Seisyllwg jointly with brother Clydog (c.910–920) and then alone (920–950); through wife gained control of Dyfed; extended rule to Gwynedd and (942) Powys, creating larger Welsh realm than any previous ruler; only Welsh ruler to issue own coinage; reign peaceful, marked by subservience to English throne; codified Welsh laws.

I

Iam·bli·chus \ī-ˈam-bli-kəs\. 2d century A.D. Greek romancer of Syria. Author of *Babyloniaca,* a story of the adventures of two lovers, Rhodanes and Sinonis.

Iamblichus. c.250–c.330. Greek philosopher, b. Syria. Traditionally credited with transformation of Neoplatonism of Plotinus into a theology of magic and mystery.

Iaroslav. See YAROSLAV.

Ibá·ñez \ē-ˈbän-yās\, Carlos. *Full surname* Ibáñez del Cam·po \-thel-ˈkäm-pō\. 1877–1960. Chilean soldier and politician. Took part in military overthrow of Pres. Alessandri Palma (1924); minister of war, later of interior, and effective ruler of Chile (1925–27); president of Chile (1927–31; forced to resign); in exile (1931–37); attempted military coups with Nazi aid (1937, 1939); unsuccessful candidate for president (1938, 1942); president of Chile (1952–58).

Ibáñez, Vicente Blasco. See BLASCO IBÁÑEZ.

Ibert \ē-ber\, Jacques-François-Antoine. 1890–1962. French composer. Director of Académie de France (1937–60). Composed operas as *Persée et Andromède* (1921), *Angélique* (1926), *Le Roi d'Yvetot* (1928); ballets; film scores and theatrical music; orchestral works including *La Ballade de la geôle de Reading* (1920); vocal and chamber works.

Iberville, Sieur d'. See Pierre Le Moyne under Charles LE MOYNE.

Ibn ʿAb·bād \ˌib-ən-ab-ˈbäd\. *In full* Abū ʿAbd Allāh Muḥammad ibn Abī Isḥāq Ibrāhīm an-Nafzī al-Ḥimyarī ar-Rundī. 1333–1390. Islāmic theologian. Emigrated from Spain to Morocco at early age; joined (1359) Shādhilīyah order of Ṣūfī mystics; by teachings and writings helped spread order; *imām* of Morocco (from 1375).

Ibn ʿAbd al-Wahhāb. See ʿABD AL-WAHHĀB.

Ibn Abī ar-Ri·jāl \-a-ˈbē-ər-rē-ˈjäl\, Aḥmad ibn Ṣāliḥ. 1620–1681. Yemeni scholar and theologian. Secretary and orator at temporal-spiritual court of Yemen. Author of *Maṭlaʿ al-budūr wa-majmaʿ al-buḥūr,* standard commentary on esoteric Zaydī sect, and of a biographical dictionary of Zaydī leaders.

Ibn Abī ʿAṣ·rūn \-as-ˈrün\. *In full* Sharaf ad-Dīn Abū Saʿd ʿAbd Allāh ibn Muḥammad ibn Hibat Allāh ibn Muṭahhar at-Tamīmī al-Mawṣilī ibn Abī ʿAṣrūn. *Also known as* al-Ḥa·la·bī \ül-ˌkal-a-ˈbē\ *and as* ad-Di·mash·qī \üd-ˌdē-mash-ˈkē\. 1099 or 1100–1189. Islāmic theologian and jurist. Held numerous administrative and judicial posts in native Iraq, Turkey, Syria; appointed *qāḍī* of Syria by Saladin (1177/78–1179/80); leading theologian of Shāfiʿī school.

Ibn al-Ab·bār \ˌib-nül-ab-ˈbär\. *In full* Abū ʿAbd Allāh Muḥammad al-Qudāʿī. 1199–1260. Muslim historian, theologian, and humorist. Secretary to Muslim governor of Valencia; on fall of Valencia to Christian forces (1238), settled in Tunisia. Known for humorous and satirical works and esp. for *Tuḥfat al-qadīm,* scholarly study of Islāmic poets of Muslim Spain; executed perhaps for satiric poem on Tunisian ruler al-Mustanṣir.

Ibn al-ʿAra·bī \ˌib-nül-ar-a-ˈbē\. *In full* Muḥyi ad-Dīn Abū ʿAbd Allāh Muḥammad ibn ʿAlī ibn Muḥammad ibn al-ʿArabī al-Ḥātimī aṭ-Ṭāʾī ibn al-ʿArabī. *Known in Islām as* ash-Shaykh al-Ak·bar \üsh-ˈshīk-ül-ak-ˈbär\ *and in Turkish as* Muḥ·yi ad-Dīn ʿAra·bī \mük-ˈyē-üd-ˈdēn-ar-a-ˈbē\. *Literary name* Abū Bakr \ə-ˌbü-ˈbak-ər\. *Called also* Abū Bakr al-Ḥatīmī aṭ-Ṭāʾī al-Andalusī. 1165–1240. Islāmic mystic and philosopher. Studied Islāmic thought in Seville, Spain; sought out Ṣūfī masters in Spain and North Africa; in youth had celebrated meeting with Ibn Rushd; set out (1198) on pilgrimage that took him to Mecca (1201), Egypt, Anatolia, Baghdad, Aleppo, Damascus (1223), where he remained. From own visions and those of earlier mystics evolved systematic theosophical system expressing for the first time the full esoteric aspect of Islām. Author of *al-Futūḥāt al-Makkīyah,* major work on esoteric sciences and own experiences; *Fuṣūṣ al-ḥikam,* most mature expression of his thought; *Tarjumān al-ashwāq,* love poems.

Ibn al-Athīr \ˌib-nül-a-ˈthir\. *In full* Abū al-Ḥasan ʿAlī ʿIzz ad-Dīn ibn al-Athīr. 1160–1233. Arab historian. Author of history of the world from creation of Adam, *al-Kāmil fī at-tārīkh;* account of local Seljuq rulers of Mosul, *al-Bāhir;* biographical and genealogical compilations, etc. His brother ¶Majd ad-Dīn ibn al-Athīr (1149–1210) was also a scholar; compiled collection of sayings and acts of Muḥammad and a dictionary of obscure theological terms.

Ibn al-ʿAw·wām \ˌib-nül-aü-ˈwäm\. 12th century. Muslim agriculturist. Native of Spain; author of *Kitāb al-filāḥah,* most extensive and valuable medieval work on agriculture.

Ibn al-Baw·wāb \ˌib-nül-baü-ˈwäb\. *In full* Abū al-Ḥasan ʿAlī ibn Hilāl ibn al-Bawwāb. *Known also as* Ibn as-Sit·rī \ˌib-nüs-si-ˈtrē\. d. 1022 or 1031. Arab calligrapher. Reputedly invented cursive *rayḥānī* and *muḥaqqaq* scripts; refined scripts of Ibn Muqlah; reputedly produced 64 copies of the Qurʾān by hand.

Ibn al-Fā·riḍ \ˌib-nül-ˈfär-ēd\. *More completely* Sharaf ad-Dīn Abū Ḥafṣ ʿUmar ibn al-Fāriḍ. 1181 or 1182–1235. Arab poet. Abandoned law for solitary religious life near Cairo; came to be regarded even in his lifetime as Ṣūfī saint. Author of odes considered finest poetic expression of Ṣūfī mysticism.

Ibn al-Haytham. See ABŪ ʿALĪ AL-ḤASAN IBN AL-HAYTHAM.

Ibn al-ʿIbrī. See BAR HEBRAEUS.

Ibn al-Jaw·zī \ˌib-nül-jaü-ˈzē\. *In full* ʿAbd ar-Raḥmān ibn ʿAlī ibn Muḥammad Abū al-Farash ibn al-Jawzī. 1126–1200. Islāmic theologian. Gained favor of caliph through strong support of Islāmic orthodoxy; headed several religious colleges in Baghdad; chief spokesman of Ḥanbalī school; noted preacher; instigated persecution of non-orthodox Muslims, esp. Ṣūfīs and Shīʿites. Fell from favor (1194) with his patron Ibn Yūnus and was banished; later allowed to return to Baghdad.

Ibn al-Mu·qaf·faʿ \ˌib-nül-mü-ˈkaf-fa\. *More completely* Abū Muḥammad ibn al-Muqaffaʿ. d. c.756. Arab translator. Author of *Kalīlah wa Dimnah,* translation of Persian fables of Bidpai.

Ibn an-Na·fīs \ˌib-nün-na-ˈfēs\. *More completely* ʿAlāʾ ad-Dīn Abū al-ʿAlāʾ ʿAlī ibn Abī al-Ḥaram al-Qurayshī ad-Dimashqī ibn an-Nafīs. d. 1288. Muslim physician. Head of Nāṣirī Hospital, Cairo; discovered pulmonary circulation of blood; wrote treatises on eye diseases, diet.

Ibn ʿAqīl \ˌib-ən-a-ˈkēl\. *In full* Abū al-Wafāʾ ʿAlī ibn ʿAqīl ibn Muḥammad ibn ʿAqīl ibn Aḥmad al-Baghdādī aẓ-Ẓafarī. 1040–1119. Islāmic theologian. Instructed in orthodox Ḥanbalī school of Islāmic law; attempted to broaden Ḥanbalī thought to encompass such ideas as logical inquiry and Ṣūfī mysticism; incurred resentment of conservative Ḥanbalī leaders, esp. when named professor at mosque of al-Manṣūr (1066); forced to live in partial retirement (1067 or 1068–72) and to publicly retract liberal ideas (1072). Author of *Kitāb al-funūn,* an encyclopaedia of the sciences.

Ibn Bā·baw·ayh \-ˈbä-baü-ˌwī\. *In full* Abū Jaʿfar Muḥammad ibn Abū al-Ḥasan ʿAlī ibn Ḥusayn ibn Mūsā al-Qummī. *Also known as* aṣ-Ṣadūq \əs-sa-ˈdük\. c.923–991. Islāmic theologian. Left native Iran for Baghdad; became acknowledged spokesman for Ithā ʿAsharī (Twelver) branch of Shīʿism; formulated much of doctrinal basis of Iranian Shīʿism.

Ibn Bājjah. See ABŪ BAKR MUḤAMMAD IBN YAḤYĀ.

Ibn Baṭ·ṭū·ṭah \-bat-ˈtü-tä\. *In full* Abū ʿAbd Allāh Muḥammad ibn ʿAbd Allāh al-Lawātī aṭ-Ṭanjī ibn Baṭṭūṭah. 1304–1368 or 1369. Arab traveler and author. Armed with reputation as scholar, traveled to Tunis, Tripoli, Egypt, Syria, Mecca (1325–26); Iraq, Iran, Baghdad (1326–27); Yemen, Aden, east coast of Africa (1330–32); planned great journey to Delhi, where he arrived (c.1333) via Anatolia, lower Volga region, Constantinople, Samarkand, Khorāsān, Afghanistan; enjoyed status of favorite at court of Muḥammad ibn Tughluq in Delhi, and was named his envoy to Chinese emperor (1342); en route to Peking visited Maldive Islands, Ceylon, Assam; returned to Syria (1348); visited Granada (1350), Sudan (1352), completing round of all Muslim nations. Dictated memoirs *Riḥlah* to Ibn Juzayy, relating political, social, cultural observations.

Ibn Da·ud \-ˈda-üd\, Abraham. *Known also as* Rab·ad I \ˈrab-ad\. c.1110–c.1180. Spanish Jewish physician and historian. Author of *Sefer ha-Kabbala,* chronology down to 1161 demonstrating chain of rabbinic authority from Moses; first Jewish philosopher to draw systematically on Aristotelian thought in *Emuna rama.*

Ibn Dervish Mehmed Zilli. See EVLIYA ÇELEBI.

Ibn Du·rayd \-'dur-,īd\. *More completely* Abū Bakr Muḥammad ibn al-Ḥasan ibn Durayd al-Azdī. 837 or 838–933. Arab philologist. Lived in Basra, Oman, Fārs, Baghdad (from 920); pensioned by caliph. Compiled *Jamharat al-lughah,* major dictionary of Arabic, and other works.

Ibn Ez·ra \,ib-ən-'ez-rə\, Abraham ben Meir. c.1090–1164. Jewish scholar, b. Toledo, Spain. A foremost scholar of medieval Spain; traveled to North Africa, Italy, France, England. Author of works on the sciences and philosophy and of poems of high quality; best known for biblical exegeses, esp. his commentaries on the Pentateuch.

Ibn Ezra, Moses ben Jacob ha-Sallaḥ. c.1060–c.1139. Jewish poet and critic, b. Granada. One of the first Jewish poets to write secular verse; author of unsurpassed verses celebrating love, wine, nature; in later years wrote penitential verse; author also of Arabic treatise on poesy, *Kitāb al-muḥādarah wa al-mudhākarah.*

Ibn Fa·la·que·ra \'ib-ən-fä-lä-'kā-rä\. *Also called* Shemtob ben Joseph ibn Falaquera *or* Pal·que·ra \päl-'kā-rä\. c.1225–c.1295. Jewish philosopher and translator, b. Spain. Author of numerous works attempting to reconcile Jewish orthodoxy and philosophy and esp. defending works of Maimonides, as *More ha-more.*

Ibn Ga·bi·rol \'ib-ən-gä-'bē-rōl\. *In full* Solomon ben Yehuda ibn Gabirol. *Lat.* Avi·ce·bron \,av-ə-'seb-rən\. c.1022–c.1070. Jewish poet and philosopher, b. Spain. One of outstanding figures of Jewish "Golden Age" in Spain; a prodigy, celebrated in youth for the mastery of his verse; poet at court of Samuel ha-Nagid, vizier of Granada; involved in numerous disputes arising from his interest in Neoplatonism, his unorthodox opinions, and his habit of self-aggrandizement. Works included religious verse; secular verse on joys of love, wine, nature, etc.; *Mukhtār al-jawāhir,* a collection of proverbs; a philosophical treatise surviving only in Latin translation as *Fons vitae* (Fountain of Life); influenced Spinoza, the Kabbalists, Scholastics.

Ibn Ḥanbal. See AḤMAD IBN ḤANBAL.

Ibn Ḥayyān, Jābir. See JĀBIR IBN ḤAYYĀN.

Ibn Ḥazm \,ib-ən-'kaz-əm\. *In full* Abū Muḥammad 'Alī ibn Aḥmad ibn Sa'īd ibn Ḥazm. 994–1064. Muslim scholar and writer, b. Córdoba, Spain. Author of controversial works on theology, jurisprudence, ethics, history, etc.; a leader of Ẓāhirī school of jurisprudence; known esp. for *Ṭawq al-ḥamāmah* (Ring of the Dove) on art of love.

Ibn Isḥāq \-ē-'shäk\. *More completely* Muḥammad ibn Isḥāq ibn Yasār ibn Khiyār. c.704–767. Muslim writer. Became authority on life and campaigns of the Prophet Muḥammad; composed a *Sīrah,* or life of Muḥammad that, in later recension by Ibn Hishām, remained one of most important sources on Muḥammad.

Ibn Ja·nāḥ \-jan-'äk\. *In full* Abū al-Walīd Marwān ibn Janāḥ. *Known also as* Rabbi Jonah. c.990–1050. Spanish Hebrew grammarian. In such works as *al-Mustalha* and *Kitāb at-tanqiḥ,* written in Arabic, established Hebrew syntax and lexicon and set forth rules for biblical exegesis; his work of permanent value.

Ibn Ju·bayr \-jü-'bīr\. *More completely* Abū al-Ḥusayn Muḥammad ibn Aḥmad ibn Jubayr. 1145–1217. Muslim writer. Secretary to governor of Granada; undertook pilgrimage (1183–85) to Mecca recounted in lively and historically valuable account *Riḥlah.*

Ibn Ka·thīr \-ka-'thir\. *In full* 'Imād ad-Dīn Ismā'īl ibn 'Umar ibn Kathīr. c.1300–1373. Islāmic theologian and historian. Held various official posts in Damascus; professor at Great Mosque (from 1366). Author of still-valuable history of Islām *al-Bidāyah wa an-nihāyah;* also wrote *Kitāb al-jāmi'* on the Ḥadīth.

Ibn Kemal Paşa. See KEMALPAŞAZÂDE.

Ibn Khal·dūn \-kal-'dün\. *More completely* Abū Zayd 'Abd ar-Raḥmān ibn Khaldūn. 1332–1406. Arab philosopher, historian, and sociologist. In service at various times of Tunis, Fez, Granada; retired from politics (1375) and wrote *Muqaddimah,* a masterly theory of history and pioneering work in sociology, and *Kitāb al-'ibar,* definitive history of Muslim North Africa. To Cairo (1382), where he became professor at al-Azhar and at Qamḥīyah colleges and chief judge of Mālikī rite. Caught in Timur's siege of Damascus (1400); negotiated freedom of civilians before sack of the city.

Ibn Khal·li·kān \-,kal-lē-'kän\. *More completely* Shams ad-Dīn Abū al-'Abbās Aḥmad ibn Muḥammad ibn Khallikān. 1211–1282. Muslim jurist. *Qāḍī* (chief judge) of Damascus (1261–71, 1278–82); best known for *Wafayāt al-a'yān wa-anbā' abnā' az-zamān,* classic Arabic biographical dictionary.

Ibn Mis·ka·wayh \-,mis-ka-'wī\. *More completely* Abū 'Alī Aḥmad ibn Muḥammad ibn Ya'qūb Miskawayh. c.930–1030. Muslim scientist, philosopher, and historian. Best known for ethical treatise *Tahdhīb al-akhlāq,* which influenced Naṣīr ad-Dīn, and for universal history *Kitāb tajarīb al-umam wa ta'aqub al-ḥimam,* also influential on subsequent historians.

Ibn Muq·lah \-'mük-la\. *In full* Abū 'Alī Muḥammad ibn 'Alī ibn Muqlah. 886–940. Arab calligrapher. Reputed inventor of the first cursive style of Arabic lettering, the *naskhī* script; three times vizier of 'Abbāsid court.

Ibn Paquda. See BAHYA BEN JOSEPH IBN PAKUDA.

Ibn Qu·tay·bah \-kü-'tī-bə\. *In full* Abū Muḥammad 'Abd Allāh ibn Muslim al-Dīnawarī ibn Qutaybah. 828–889. Arab writer. Religious judge of Dinawar (c.851–870); teacher in Baghdad (from c.871). Author of various works including *Kitāb adab al-kātib,* compendium of Arabic usage and vocabulary; *Kitāb al-'Arab* on Arabic culture; an anthology of early Arabic poetry. Introduced a prose style notable for its simplicity.

Ibn Rushd \-'rüsht\. *In full* Abū al-Walīd Muḥammad ibn Aḥmad ibn Muḥammad ibn Rushd. *Known in West as* Aver·ro·ës \ə-'vēr-ə-,wēz, ,av-ə-'rō-,ēz\. 1126–1198. Islāmic philosopher. Trained in medicine; became chief *qāḍī* (religious judge) in native Córdoba; succeeded Ibn Ṭufayl as physician to caliph Abū Yūsuf (1184–95); banished briefly (1195). Author of treatise *Kulliyāt* (General Medicine, c.1169); philosophical works *Faṣl* (c.1179, on religious law and philosophy), *Manāhij* (c.1179, on logic and religion), *Tahāfut at-tahāfut* (c.1180); and esp. commentaries on Aristotle and on Plato's *Republic.* A principal interpreter of Aristotle, influencing later Jewish and Christian writers, and chief reconciler of Islāmic and Greek thought.

Ibn Sa'ūd \-sa-'üd\. *In full* 'Abd al-'Azīz ibn 'Abd ar-Raḥmān ibn Fayṣal ibn Turkī 'Abd Allāh ibn Muḥammad Āl Sa'ūd. c.1880–1953. Muslim leader and founder of Saudi Arabia. Scion of family that had ruled much of Arabia from capital Riyadh since 1780; during infancy driven with family into exile in Kuwait by rival Rashīd family; with small band of followers seized Riyadh (1902); gradually conquered Najd and other areas of central Arabia; fostered puritanical Wahhābi form of Islām and gained allegiance of religious leaders and nomadic tribesmen; accepted British protectorate status (1915) and with British subsidies gradually undertook campaign against Turkish-allied Ibn Rashīd; eliminated Rashīd rule (1920–22); attacked rival Sharīf Ḥusayn of the Hejaz, captured Mecca (1924); proclaimed king of the Hejaz (1926) and of Najd (1927); defeated fanatic Wahhābite Ikhwān warriors (1929). Unified domains as Saudi Arabia (1932); granted first oil concession to a U.S. company (1933); took first steps toward development with oil wealth that flowed in after World War II.

Ibn Shad·dād \-shad-'däd\. *In full* Abū al-Maḥāsin Yūsuf ibn Rāfi' ibn Shaddād Bahā' ad-Dīn. 1145–1234. Arab writer. Teacher at Baghdad, Mosul; entered service of Saladin (1187); judge of army and of Jerusalem; made judge of Aleppo by Malik aẓ-Ẓāhir; headed regency for Malik al-'Azīz. Author of biography *Sirat Salāḥ ad-Dīn.*

Ibn Shem Tov \-'shem-'tōb, -'tōv\, Shem Tov. c.1380–c.1441. Spanish Kabbalist. Vociferous opponent of Aristotelian and rationalist strain in Jewish thought; opposed esp. Maimonides in principal work *Sefer ha-Emunot.* His son ¶Joseph ben Shem Tov ibn Shem Tov (c.1400–c.1460) was a physician at court of Castile; strove in many writings to mediate between Jewish religious thought and rationalist philosophy. Author of commentaries on Aristotle, Porphyry, Averroës, etc., and of *Kevod Elohim,* a comparison of ethical teachings of Aristotle and the Torah. His son ¶Shem Tov ben Joseph ben shem Tov ibn Shem Tov (fl. 1461–89) was a leading champion of Maimonides; wrote commentaries on Averroës.

Ibn Sī·nā \-'sē-nä\. *In full* Abū 'Alī al-Ḥusayn ibn 'Abd Allāh ibn Sīnā. *Known in West as* Av·i·cen·na \,av-ə-'sen-ə\. 980–1037. Islāmic scientist and philosopher. Enjoyed patronage of Sāmānid court in native Bukhara; after Turkish conquest (999) wandered through Persia, becoming court physician and twice vizier to Būyid prince Shams ad-Dawlah in Hamadan; passed last years (1022–37) in Isfahan. Renowned for learning and medical skill. Author of nearly 200 works on science, language, religion, philosophy, etc. Major works included *Kitāb ash-shifā',* a huge philosophical-scientific encyclopaedia; *Qānūn fī aṭ-ṭibb,* known in the West as *Canon of Medicine; Kitāb al-ishārāt wa at-tanbīhāt* on mystical religion. A chief Islāmic interpreter of Aristotle.

Ibn Tay·mī·yah \-tī-'mē-(y)ä\. *In full* Taqī ad-Dīn Abū al-'Abbās Aḥmad ibn 'Abd as-Salām ibn 'Abd Allāh ibn Muḥammad ibn Taymīyah. 1263–1328. Islāmic theologian. Trained in juridical school of Ibn Ḥanbal; became outspoken critic of contemporary theology and political practice; several times imprisoned for controversial writings or pronouncements; leader of resistance to Mongol occupation of Damascus (1299–1303); under watch or imprisoned in Cairo and Alexandria (1306–13); teacher in Damascus (from 1313); died during another imprisonment. Expounded a fundamentalist form of Islām based solely on the Qur'ān and the *sunnah* prophetic tradition; his views gained in influence over the years and inspired 'Abd al-Wahhāb among others. Works included *As-Siyā-sat ash-shar'īyay* on juridical politics, *Minhāj as-sunnah* on comparative theology.

Ibn Tib·bon \-'tib-ən\, Judah ben Saul. 1120–c.1190. Jewish physician and translator. Fled persecutions in native Granada to southern France (1150);

practiced medicine. Translated into Hebrew works of Arabic-speaking Jewish writers including Sa'adia ben Joseph, Bahya ben Joseph ibn Pakuda, Judah ha-Levi, Ibn Janāḥ; thus helped disseminate both Arabic and Greek culture in western Europe. His son ¶Samuel ben Judah ibn Tibbon (c.1150–c.1230), also a physician and translator; published (c.1190) Hebrew translation of Maimonides' *Guide of the Perplexed* as *More nevukhim*. His son ¶Moses ben Samuel ibn Tibbon (fl. 1240–83), also a physician in southern France; wrote commentaries on the Pentateuch, the Song of Songs, and parts of the Talmud; translated into Hebrew works of Maimonides, Averroës, Avicenna, al-Fārābī. A grandson of Samuel ¶Jacob ben Macheir ibn Tibbon, *known in Spain as* Don Pro·fiat \dōn-prōf-'yät\ (c.1236–c.1312), was a physician, regent of the medical faculty of U. of Montpellier; noted as astronomer, invented a quadrant that was widely adopted by mariners and became known as the "Quadrans Judaicus"; published book of astronomical tables; supporter of Maimonides and rationalist tradition against anti-rationalist strictures of Solomon ben Adret. Translated into Hebrew works of al-Ghazālī and Averroës and Arabic versions of Euclid's *Elements* and Ptolemy's *Almagest*.

Ibn Ṭu·fayl \-tü-'fīl\. *In full* Muḥammad ibn 'Abd al-Malik ibn Muḥammad ibn Muḥammad ibn Ṭufayl al-Qaysī. *Also called* Abū Bakr Muḥammad ibn 'Abd al-Malik ibn Muḥammad ibn Muḥammad ibn Ṭufayl al-Qaysī. d. 1185 or 1186. Moorish philosopher and physician. Physician at Almohad court (1163–84). Author of medical treatises and esp. a philosophical romance *Risālat Ḥayy ibn Yaqẓān* (c.1175).

Ibn Tū·mart \-'tü-märt\. *In full* Abū 'Abd Allāh Muḥammad ibn Tūmart. c.1080–1130. Berber religious leader. Evolved doctrine calling for juridical and moral reform of Islām; proclaimed himself mahdi and founded al-Muwaḥḥidūn (Almohad) movement among tribesmen of Anti-Atlas and Great Atlas mountains; conducted unsuccessful campaign against Almoravid regime; established Muslim Berber state with capital at Tinmel; designated as his successor 'Abd al-Mu'min (*q.v.*).

Ibn Waḥ·shī·yah \-wäk-'shē-(y)ä\. fl. c.900. Muslim agriculturist. Reputed author of *al-Fillāḥah an-Nabaṭīyah,* agricultural treatise, largely based on Greek originals, that was a major source for Ibn al-'Awwām.

Ibn Zuhr \-'zü-hər, *Angl* -'zůr\. *In full* Abū Marwān 'Abd al-Malik ibn Abī al-'Ala' Zuhr. *Lat.* Av·en·zoar \ˌav-ən-'zō(-ə)r, -zə-'wär\ *or* Abu·me·ron \ə-ˌbü-mə-'rän\. c.1090–1162. Muslim physician, b. Seville. Greatest clinician of Western caliphate; described pericarditis, mediastinal abscesses, surgery for cataracts, kidney stones; major written work *at-Taysīr fī al-mudāwāt wa at-tadbīr* was influential throughout Europe in Latin and Hebrew translations.

İb·ra·him \əb-rə-'him\. 1615–1648. Ottoman sultan (1640–48). Son of Ahmed I; succeeded brother Murad IV; a weak, unstable ruler who benefitted from able guidance of grand vizier Kemankeş Kara Mustafa Paşa early in reign; recovered Sea of Azov from Cossacks; had Kara Mustafa executed (1644) and came under influence of harem and of inferior ministers; sent expedition against Crete (1645), beginning 24-year war with Venice; deposed by Janissary uprising and executed.

Ib·rā·hīm I \ib-rä-'hēm\. *In full* Ibrāhīm ibn-al-Aghlab. 756–812. North African ruler. Seized Tunis (800); given government of province of Ifrīqīyah (Tunisia) by caliph Hārūn ar-Rashīd; secured right to appoint son to succeed him, thus establishing Aghlabite dynasty (800–909).

Ibrāhīm al-Ḥā·qi·la·nī \-ül-ˌkä-kē-la-'nē\. *Lat.* Abraham Ec·chel·len·sis \ˌek-ə-'len(t)-səs\. 1605–1664. Maronite Catholic scholar. Taught Arabic and Syriac in Pisa, Rome; professor at Collège de France (1646–52). Author of Syriac grammar (1628), history of patriarch of Alexandria (1653), translations of several books for Arabic Bible (pub. 1671).

Ibrāhīm ibn 'Abd Allāh. See Johann BURCKHARDT.

Ibrāhīm Lo·dī \-lō-'dē\. 16th century. Last Afghan sultan of Delhi (1517–26). A tyrant who alienated own nobles; defeated and killed by Mughal king Bābur at Pānīpat.

İb·ra·him Mü·te·fer·ri·ka \əb-rə-'him-ˌmu̅e-tä-ˌfer-ē-'kä\. c.1670–1745. Ottoman diplomat, b. Transylvania. Fled Habsburg rule to Ottoman empire, converted to Islām, entered diplomatic service; promoted Ottoman–French alliance (1737–39); served on staff of Ferenc Rákóczi. Best known for establishment of first printing press in Ottoman empire (1727); published western works in support of military and administrative reforms.

İbrahim Pa·şa \-pə-'shä\. c.1493–1536. Ottoman politician and soldier. Appointed grand vizier by Süleyman I (1523); commanded expedition to restore order in Egypt (1524); commanded Danube campaigns (1526, 1529, 1532); as plenipotentiary negotiated Ottoman suzerainty over Hungary with Emperor Charles V (1533). Suppressed Ṣafavid revolt in Iran; occupied Tabriz (1534), Baghdad (1535). Conducted negotiations with French (1536). Executed by Süleyman for fear of further usurpation of power.

Ib·rā·hīm Pa·sha \ib-rä-'hēm-'pash-ä\. 1789–1848. Ottoman general and ruler of Egypt (1848). Son or adopted son of Muḥammad 'Alī, viceroy (*wālī*) of Egypt; governor of Cairo (1805), controller of land revenue (1810); commanded army against Wahhābī rebels in Arabia (1816–18); helped train new Egyptian army on European model (1822 ff.); commanded expedition in support of Sultan Mahmud II against Greek rebels (1824) and subdued the Morea. In father's revolt against sultanate, led Egyptian army into Palestine, captured Acre, defeated Ottoman army at Homs, forced Bailan Pass, took Iskenderun, won victory at Konya (1832); governor general of Syria and Adana from their cession to Egypt (1833); reformed administration and suppressed several revolts; won greatest victory in defeating invading Ottoman army at Nizip (June 24, 1839); forced by European powers to abandon Syria and Adana (1840–41). Appointed viceroy of Egypt in place of senile father (1848) but died 40 days later.

İbrahim Şinasi Efendi. See İbrahim ŞINASI.

Ib·sen \'ip-sən, *Angl* 'ib-sən\, Henrik Johan. 1828–1906. Norwegian poet and dramatist. Studied medicine and was chemist's assistant at Grimstad (1844–50); helped edit weekly journal *Andhrimner* (1851). Stage director and dramatist at Ole Bull's National Theater, Bergen (1851–57); director of Norwegian Theater, Oslo (1857–62); received traveling scholarship (1863) and government pension (1866). Left Norway (1863) to live chiefly in Italy and Germany (until 1891); returned to Oslo (1891). His early and less successful works included *Catilina* (1850; under the pseudonym Brynjolf Bjar·me \'byär-mə\), *Kjaempehøjen* (1850), *Sankthansnatten* (1853), *Gildet paa Solhoug* (1856), *Haermaendene paa Helgeland* (1858), *Kongsemnerne* (1863); achieved success with *Brand* (1866) and developed rapidly the form of bleakly poetic, realistic drama that G.B. Shaw later termed "Ibsenism"; subsequent works included *Peer Gynt* (1867), *De unges forbund* (1869), *Kejser og Galilaeer* (1873), *Samfundets støtter* (*Pillars of Society,* 1877), *En dukkehjem* (*A Doll's House,* 1879), *Gengangere* (*Ghosts,* 1881), *En folkefiende* (*An Enemy of the People,* 1882), *Vildanden* (*The Wild Duck,* 1884), *Rosmersholm* (1886), *Fruen fra havet* (*The Lady from the Sea,* 1888), *Hedda Gabler* (1890), *Bygmester Solness* (*The Master Builder,* 1892), *Lille Eyolf* (1894), *John Gabriel Borkman* (1896), *Naar vi døde vaagner* (*When We Dead Awaken,* 1899). Plays noted esp. for psychological insight, symbolism, and social criticism. Also published verse, as *Digte* (1871).

Ib·y·cus \'ib-i-kəs\. 6th century B.C. Greek poet. Patronized by Polycrates, tyrant of Samos; wrote anacreontic and amatory verse, fragments of which are extant; one of nine lyric poets recognized by later Greek criticism.

Ichi·jō \ē-chē-jō\ Kaneyoshi. *Also known as* Ichijō Kanera. 1402–1481. Japanese philosopher and official. Prime minister (1446), adviser to the emperor (1447). Best known as scholar and philosopher of Shintō, which he attempted to reconstruct on basis of an idealistic monism.

Ichi·ka·wa \ē-chē-kä-wä\. Name of a Japanese family that supplied outstanding actors to the Kabuki stage from the 17th century. The leading members of the family have borne the personal name Danjūrō and include:

Ichikawa Danjūro I. 1660–1704. Most famous actor of the Genroku period; originated the *aragato* ("rough business") style of heroic drama. His son ¶Danjūrō II (1688–1758) was also a notable success in heroic roles.

¶Danjūrō VII. 1791–1859. Greatest actor of the Edo period; established the *Kabuki Jūhachiban,* special repertoire of 18 plays of the Ichikawa family.

¶Danjūrō IX. 1838–1903. Greatest Kabuki actor of the Meiji era; largely responsible for revitalization of Japanese theater; performed in first Kabuki play witnessed by an emperor (1891).

Lesser honorific names borne by members of the family include Ebizō (of whom there have been 10), Danzō (7), and Ebijūrō (6).

I-chu \ē-'jü\. *Reign title* Hsien-feng \shē-'ən-'fəŋ\. *Temple name* Wen Tsung \'wənd-'zůŋ\. *Posthumous name* Hsien Huang-ti \shē-'ən-hwäŋ-'dē\. 1831–1861. Chinese emperor (1851–61), seventh of the Ch'ing dynasty. Son of Min-ning; during his reign occurred several rebellions, esp. the Taiping Rebellion (1850–64), as well as the Treaty of Tientsin (1858), war with England (1859–60); fled to Jehol after Western allied force captured Peking (1860); government run by his brother Prince Kung (see I-HSIN); his consort was Tz'u-hsi (*q.v.*).

Ick·es \'ik-əs\, Harold LeClair. 1874–1952. American administrator and politician, b. Frankstown Township, Pa. Practiced law in Chicago (from 1907); prominent in Republican politics (to c.1926); worked for Roosevelt-Garner ticket (1932); U.S. secretary of the interior (1933–46); petroleum administrator; head of Public Works Administration (1933–39), controlling spending of some $5 billion. Author of *Autobiography of a Curmudgeon* (1943); his *Secret Diaries* published posthumously (1953–54).

Ic·ti·nus *or* **Ik·ti·nos** \ik-'tī-nəs\. 5th century B.C. Greek architect. Chief designer (with Callicrates) of Parthenon at Athens, temple to Demeter and Persephone at Eleusis, temple of Apollo Epicurius at Bassae.

Ida \'ē-ˌdä, 'ī-də\. d. 559. Chieftain of the Angles. First king (547 ff.) of Bernicia (northern Northumbria).

Iddesleigh, Earl of. See Sir Stafford Henry NORTHCOTE.

Id·dings \ˈid-iŋz\, Joseph Paxson. 1857–1920. American geologist, b. Baltimore. Professor, U. of Chicago (1895–1908). Co-author, with Cross, Pirsson, and Washington, of *Quantitative Classification of Igneous Rocks* (1903); author of *Rock Minerals* (1906), *Igneous Rocks* (1909–13), *The Problem of Volcanism* (1914).

Idel·sohn \ˈēd-ᵊl-ˌzōn\, Abraham Zevi. 1882–1938. Jewish music scholar, b. Kurland (now Latvia). To Jerusalem (1905); founded Institute for Jewish Music (1910); a pioneer in ethnomusicology; collected and recorded music of various Jewish groups. In U.S. (1922–30); professor, Hebrew Union College, Cincinnati (1924–30). Author of *Thesaurus of Hebrew Oriental Melodies* (1914–32), *Jewish Liturgy* (1932), etc. Composed first Hebrew opera *Yiftaḥ* (1922) and song "Hava nagila."

Idrī·sī, al- \əl-i-ˈdrē-sē\. *In full* Abū ʽAbd Allāh Muḥammad ibn Muḥammad ibn ʽAbd Allāh ibn Idrīs al-Ḥammūdī al-Ḥasanī al-Idrīsī. *Known as* ash-Sharīf al-Idrīsī. 1100–1165. Arab geographer and cartographer, b. Morocco. Traveled widely from youth; lived in Sicily under patronage of King Roger II (from c.1145); devised a silver planisphere of the world, a great map consisting of 70 sections, and a work of descriptive geography *Kitāb nuzhat al-mushtāq fī ikhtirāq al-āfāq,* called also *Kitāb Rujār* or *al-Kitāb ar-Rujārī* (Book of Roger), valued for revealing extent of Arab knowledge of geography in 12th century.

Id·rī·sid \ˈid-ri-(ˌ)sid\. Name of Muslim dynasty in Morocco (789–926). Founded by Idrīs I (d. 791), a sharif (noble by descent from Muḥammad) who fled to Morocco to escape ʽAbbāsid persecution. His son ¶Idrīs II (d. 828), ruled (791–828); founded capital city of Fās (Fez or Fès).

Ieharu. Also Iemitsu, Iemochi, Ienari, Ienobu, Iesada, Ieshige, Ietsuga, Ietsuna, Ieyasu, Ieyoshi. See TOKUGAWA family.

Iff·land \ˈif-ˌlänt\, August Wilhelm. 1759–1814. German actor, director, and dramatist. Member of Gotha court theater (1777–79); member and virtual manager of Mannheim court theater (1779–98); guest artist at Weimar on invitation of Goethe (1796); manager, Berlin National Theater (1798); director general of Prussian royal theaters (1811). Created role of Franz Moor in Schiller's *Die Räuber* (1782). Author of over 60 dramas, mainly domestic and sentimental comedies.

Igle·sias \ē-ˈglās-yäs\, José María. 1823–1891. Mexican politician. Minister of justice (1857); held ministries in government of Juárez; president of supreme court of Mexico (1873); when Lerdo de Tejada was overthrown (1876), assumed presidency of Mexico until Díaz took power.

Iglesias, Miguel. 1830–1909. Peruvian general and politician. Civil and military chief in the north during War of the Pacific (1879–83) with Chile; advocate of peace; negotiated treaty of Ancón (1883). Elected provisional president by constituent assembly (1883); forced to resign by revolution led by Cáceres (1886).

Iglesias Pos·se \-ˈpȯs-sā\, Pablo. 1850–1925. Spanish political leader. A founder of Spanish Socialist party (1879); president of party central committee (1885 ff.); editor of *El Socialista,* official Socialist organ (1886 ff.); first Socialist deputy in the Cortes (1910 ff.); president, Unión General de Trabajadores.

Ig·na·ti·us \ig-ˈnā-sh(ē-)əs\. Saint. *Surnamed* The·oph·o·rus \thē-ˈäf-ə-rəs\. *Called* Ignatius of Antioch. d. c.110 A.D. Christian prelate. Bishop of Antioch and one of the fathers of the church; arrested, taken to Rome, and martyred under Trajan. Seven of his *Epistles* are extant, written during his journey from Antioch to Rome.

Ignatius of Constantinople. Saint. *Called* Ni·ce·tas \ˌnī-ˈsēt-əs, nə-\. c.799–877. Byzantine prelate. Son of Emperor Michael I; patriarch of Constantinople (846–858 and 867–877). Excommunicated Bardas, regent for Michael III; for this was deposed and exiled (858). Replaced by Photius (*q.v.*). Restored by Basil I (867); innocence confirmed by Council of Constantinople (869).

Ignatius of Loy·o·la \lȯi-ˈō-lə\. Saint. *Orig.* Iñigo de Oñaz y Loyola \ōn-ˈyä-thē-lȯi-ˈō-lä\. 1491–1556. Spanish religious. Member of noble family; knight in service of duke of Nájera, a kinsman (1517–21); severely wounded at French siege of Pamplona (1521); passed period (1522–23) in ascetic retreat at Manresa, resolved upon religious life; began composition of his *Spiritual Exercises* (approved by Pope Paul III, 1548); made pilgrimage to Jerusalem (1523–24); gained following of disciples as he studied at Barcelona, Alcalá, and (1528–35) Paris; with group of followers including Francis Xavier took vows (1534); ordained in Venice (1537); with companions founded Society of Jesus (1539; approved by Paul III, 1540); general of the order (1540–56). Founded Roman Coll. (later Gregorian U.), the Germanicum. Created Jesuit *Constitutions* and directed order toward worldwide apostolate and the education of youth. Canonized by Gregory XV (1622); declared patron of all spiritual retreats by Pius XI (1922).

Ig·nat·yev \yig-ˈnät-yif\, Nikolay Pavlovich. Count. 1832–1908. Russian politician and diplomat. Officer in Russian Guard (1849 ff.); attended Congress of Paris (1856); concluded treaty with khan of Bukhara (1858); negotiated Treaty of Peking (1860), settling Sino–Russian border and gaining considerable territory. Ambassador to Constantinople (1864–77); as proponent of pan-Slavism, encouraged Serbs and Bulgarians in their unsuccessful revolts against Turkish rule (1876–77); at conclusion of Russo–Turkish War (1877–78) negotiated Treaty of San Stefano, which created independent states of Serbia and Bulgaria; forced to retire on failure to prevent imposition of Treaty of Berlin (1878). Minister of interior (1881–82) under Alexander III; carried out emancipation of serfs and other liberal reforms but failed to check pogroms and continued to promote pan-Slavism.

Igor \ˈē-gȯr^{y}, *Angl* ˈē-ˌgȯ(ə)r\. c.877–945. Russian ruler. Presumed son of Rurik; succeeded Oleg as grand prince of Kiev (912); led disastrous campaign into Transcaucasia (913–914); led unsuccessful expeditions against Byzantium (941, 944); killed while attempting to extort extraordinary tribute from Drevlyane Slavs.

Igor Svya·to·sla·vich \-sfyi-(ˌ)tə-ˈslȧv-ˌyich\. 1151–1202. Russian ruler. Prince of Novgorod-Seversky (1178–1202) and of Chernigovsky (1198–1202); led unsuccessful expedition against Polovtsy nomads and was captured (1185); escaped (1186). His campaign the subject of *Slovo o polku Igoreve,* major work of old Russian literature.

Iha·ra \ē-här-ä\ *or* **Iba·ra** \-bär-\ Saikaku. *Orig. probably* Tō-go \tō-gō\ Hirayama. 1642–1693. Japanese poet and novelist. Early renowned for amazing speed in composing haiku and linked verses, once composing 23,500 haiku in one day (1684); better known for novels of manners of merchant class and the demimonde, as *Kōshoku ichidai otoko* (1682), *Kōshoku gonin onna* (1686), *Nihon Eitaigura* (1688).

Ihering, Rudolf von. See JHERING.

I-hsin \ˈē-ˈshin\. *Known as* Prince Kung \ˈgu̇ŋ\. 1833–1898. Chinese statesman. Son of Emperor Min-ning and brother of Emperor I-chu. Left in charge in war with British and French (1859–60) when emperor fled; made best terms possible under Treaty of Peking (1860); first president of foreign affairs office Tsungli Yamen (1861). Coregent (1862–73) with the empress dowager Tz'u-hsi for Tsai-ch'un during his minority and for his successor Tsai-t'ien (1875–84); also prime minister during this period; finally suppressed Taiping Rebellion (1864); advocated government reforms and adoption of Western methods, esp. military techniques and arms; gradually lost power to T'zu-hsi until dismissed (1884) from court.

Ii \ē-ē\ Naosuke. *Also known as* Ii Kamon-no-kami. 1815–1860. Japanese politician. After Commodore Perry's visit (1853), sought in best interests of Japan to accept limited foreign contact; became chief councilor to shogun Iyesada (1858); opposed baronial candidate Hitotsubashi for shogunate; secured election of 12-year-old Iyemochi as shogun (1858). Without emperor's approval, signed treaties of friendship with U.S., England, Russia, etc., arousing great hostility, esp. among the nobility; assassinated.

Iio \ē-ē-ō\ Sōgi. 1421–1502. Japanese poet. A Buddhist monk; celebrated in his day as greatest master of *renga,* or linked verse. Composed *renga* sequences *Minase Sangin Hyakuin* (1486), *Yuyama Sangin Hyakuin* (1491).

Ike \ē-ke\ Taiga. *Also known as* Ike·no \ē-ken-ō\ Taiga. 1723–1776. Japanese painter. A master of calligraphy, from which he turned to painting; followed *Nan-ga* style of Chinese painting and, with Yosa Buson, developed Japanese *bunjin-ga,* or literati, style; works included landscapes, portraits.

Ike·da \ē-kä-dä\ Hayato. 1899–1965. Japanese politician. In ministry of finance (1925–49); member of House of Representatives (1949–65); minister of finance (1949–52, 1956–57), of trade and industry (1952–53, 1959–60); a chief architect of Japan's economic growth and development in postwar period. Prime minister (1960–64).

Ikhnaton. See AKHENATON.

Ilacomilus. See Martin WALDSEEMÜLLER.

Ilf, Ilya. See Ilya FAYNZILBERG.

Il-Khan \ēl-ˈkän\. Mongol dynasty (1256–1353) in Persia, founded by Hülegü (*q.v.*); its real power terminated (1335); divided between five petty dynasties (1335–53).

Il·tut·mish \il-ˈtu̇t-məsh\. *Also written* Al·tamsh \əl-ˈtəmsh\. d. 1236. Third Delhi sultan of the Slave Dynasty (1211–36). Son-in-law and successor of Quṭb-ud-Dīn Aybak; consolidated and expanded domain, capturing eastern Punjab and some Rājput territory; moved capital to Delhi; considered founder of independent Muslim sultanate of Delhi; built (1231–32) tower of Quṭb Mīnār in Delhi.

Il·yu·shin \yil-ˈyü-shin\, Sergey Vladimirovich. 1894–1977. Russian aircraft designer. Entered Red army (1919), rising to lieutenant general; professor at Zhukovsky Air Force Engineering Academy. Designed Il-2 Stormovik armored attack aircraft (1939), Il-12 twin-engine passenger craft (1946), Il-18 Moskva 4-engine turboprop, Il-62 turbojet, Il-86 airbus (1977).

ʽIm·ād ad-Daw·lah \im-ˈäd-üd-ˈdau̇-lä\. *Orig.* ʽAlī ebn Būyeh \ä-ˈlē-ˌib-ən-ˈbü-ye\. 892–949. Iranian ruler. Appointed governor of Karaj (c.930); revolted against Zeyārid rule, seized Fars and Isfahan (934); with establishment of Būyid rule in Baghdad (946) by brother Aḥmad (see MUʽIZZ AD-DAWLAH), assumed dynastic name.

Im·am Bon·djol \im-ˈäm-bän-ˈjōl\, Tuanku. 1772–1864. Indonesian religious leader. Converted to puritanical Wahhābī form of Islam (c.1803); became leader of religious Padri faction in civil war of Minangkabau people of Sumatra; finally defeated by intervening Dutch forces (1831–37).

Im·ber \ˈim-bər\, Naphtali Herz. 1856–1909. Hebrew scholar and poet, b. Poland. Associated with Israel Zangwill in London (1889–92); in U.S. (from 1892); his hymn "ha-Tiqwa" (The Hope) became anthem of the Zionist movement (1933) and unofficial national anthem of Israel (1948). Published collection of verse *Barkai* (1886).

Im·bert \aⁿ-ber\, Barthélemy. 1747–1790. French writer. Author of the poem *Le Jugement de Pâris* (1772) and a volume of *Fables* (1773).

Im·hoff \ˈim-hȯf\, Gustaaf Willem van. Baron. 1705–1750. Dutch colonialist. Entered Dutch East India Co. (1725); member of Council of the Indies (1732); governor of Ceylon (1736–40); governor general of Dutch East Indies (1743–50); began but failed to complete numerous reforms; intervened tactlessly in Indonesian disputes, precipitating esp. the Third Javanese War of Succession (1749–57).

Im·ho·tep \im-ˈhō-ˌtep\. *Gr.* Imou·thes \i-ˈmü-ˌthēz\. 27th century B.C. Egyptian physician and sage. Counselor of King Djoser of 3d dynasty; architect and probable builder of Djoser's pyramid; skilled in medicine and priestly magic. Later regarded by Egyptians as a deity; identified by Greeks with Asclepius.

Im·man·u·el ben Sol·o·mon \i-ˈman-yə-wəl-ben-ˈsäl-ə-mən\. c.1260–c.1328. Hebrew poet. Probably an itinerant teacher, lived mainly in Rome. Author of sacred and secular Hebrew verse, later collected in *Maḥbarot Immanuel,* and of Italian verse under pseudonym Manoello Giu·deo \jü-ˈdā-ō\; introduced sonnet form into Hebrew verse.

Im·mel·mann \ˈim-əl-ˌmän, *Angl* -mən\, Max. 1890–1916. German aviator. World War I ace; regarded, with Boelcke, as founder of the German technique of air combat; the maneuver known as the "Immelmann turn" was developed by him; killed in action.

Im·mer·mann \ˈim-ər-ˌmän\, Karl Leberecht. 1796–1840. German poet, dramatist, and novelist. Civil servant and jurist, Münster, Magdeburg, Düsseldorf. Author of lyric poems; dramatic works *Trauerspiel in Tyrol* (1828), satire *Tulifäntchen* (1830), triology *Alexis* (1830–31), *Merlin* (1831–32); novels *Die Epigonen* (1836) and *Münchhausen* (1838–39, continuing the village idyl *Der Oberhof*); critical works, etc.

Imouthes. See IMHOTEP.

Im·pey \ˈim-pē\, Sir Elijah. 1732–1809. English jurist. Chief justice of Bengal, India (1774–89); cooperated with Warren Hastings. Impeached (1783) by House of Commons for his conduct in India; successfully defended himself; acquitted (1788). M.P. (1790–96).

Im·rédy \ˈim-rādʸ\, Béla. 1891–1946. Hungarian politician. Director of National Bank (1928–32); minister of finance (1932–35); president of National Bank (1935–38). Premier of Hungary (1938–39); followed generally pro-German, right-wing, and anti-Semitic policies; forced to resign on publication of his Jewish ancestry; minister of economy (1944–45); executed for war crimes.

Im·ru' al-Qays \ˈim-rü-ül-ˈkīs\. *In full* Imru' al-Qays ibn Ḥujr. d. c.550 A.D. Arab poet. Son of last king of Kindah; expelled from court for writing erotic poetry; devoted much of life to seeking revenge for murder of father by Bedouins, receiving aid at one time from Byzantine Emperor Justinian I. Author of finest ode in anthology *al-Mu'allaqāt;* credited with inventing form of classical ode, *qaṣīdah;* regarded as preeminent Arab poet of pre-Islāmic times.

Ina. See INE.

Inca, El. See GARCILASO DE LA VEGA (1539–1616).

Ince \ˈin(t)s\, Thomas Harper. 1882–1924. American film director and producer, b. Newport, R.I. Actor in Daniel Frohman's company; actor and director at Biograph Studios (1910–15), becoming famous as director of Civil War films and films of William S. Hart; with D.W. Griffith and Mack Sennett formed (1915) Triangle Pictures; credited with development of production units and other organizational techniques of film-making.

Inch·bald \ˈinch-ˌbȯld\, Elizabeth, *nee* Simp·son \ˈsim(p)-sən\. 1753–1821. English actress and author. m. Joseph Inchbald (1772); wrote comedies and farces, chiefly adaptations from French; best known for two tales, *A Simple Story* (1791) and *Nature and Art* (1796).

Inchiquin, Barons and earls of. Titles borne by O'Brien family (*q.v.*).

Inclán, Ramón del Valle. See VALLE-INCLÁN.

Ind·ra·var·man I \ˌin-drə-ˈvər-mən\. 9th century. Cambodian ruler. King of Khmer kingdom of Angkor (877–889); created vast system of reservoirs, canals, and irrigation channels to open new ricelands.

In·dy \aⁿ-dē\, Vincent d', *in full* Paul-Marie-Théodore-Vincent. 1851–1931. French composer. Studied under César Franck; a leader of radical modern French school. A founder (1894) and director of the Schola Cantorum, in Paris; author of *Cours de composition musicale* (1902–09); helped revive interest in Gregorian plainchant. Works included operas as *Le Chant de la cloche* (1879–83), *Fervaal* (1889–93), *L'Étranger* (1898–1901); orchestral works as *Wallenstein* overtures (1873, 1879–81), *Symphonie sur un chant montagnard française* (1886), *Istar* (1896); religious, vocal, keyboard, chamber pieces.

Ine *or* **Ini** \ˈin-ə\ *or* **Ina** *Lat* ˈī-nə\. d. after 726. West Saxon king (688–726). Established power over England south of the Thames; promulgated laws (690–693), earliest extant West Saxon legislation; abdicated (726) and died on pilgrimage to Rome.

Infarinato. See Leonardo SALVIATI.

In·feld \ˈēn-felt\, Leopold. 1898–1968. Polish physicist. Worked with Einstein at Princeton (1936–38); professor, Toronto (1938–50), Warsaw (1950–68); known for work in relativity and quantum theory. Author of *Evolution of Physics* (with Einstein, 1938), *Albert Einstein* (1950).

Inge \ˈiŋ\, William Ralph. 1860–1954. English prelate. Fellow and tutor, Hertford Coll., Oxford (1888–1904); professor of divinity, Cambridge (1907–11). Dean of St. Paul's, London (1911–34); sometimes referred to as "the gloomy Dean." Among his books were *Christian Mysticism* (1899), *Faith and Knowledge* (1904), *Outspoken Essays* (1919, 1922), *Lay Thoughts of a Dean* (1926), *Christian Ethics and Modern Problems* (1930), *Vale* (1934), *Our Present Discontents* (1938).

Ing·e·borg \ˈiŋ-ə-ˌbȯ(ə)rg\ *or* **In·ge·burge** \aⁿzh-bu̅e̅rzh\. *Fr.* Isam·bour \ē-zäⁿ-bür\. 1176?–?1236. Queen of France. Daughter of Valdemar I of Denmark and sister of Canute VI; m. (1193) Philip Augustus. Immediately became object of Philip's dislike; her marriage repudiated but Philip's attempt to secure separation opposed by Popes Celestine III and Innocent III; kept in prison, but finally (1213) regained her rights.

In·ge·gne·ri *or* **In·ge·gnie·ri** \ˌēn-jān-ˈyā-rē\ *or* **In·gi·gnie·ri** \-jēn-\, Marc'Antonio. c.1547–1592. Italian composer. Prefect (c.1576), maestro di capella (1581), Cremona cathedral. Composed madrigals, masses, etc., in polyphonic style.

In·ge·low \ˈin-jə-(ˌ)lō\, Jean. 1820–1897. English writer. Her verse included three series of *Poems* (1871, 1876, 1885) and her best known piece, "High Tide on the Coast of Lincolnshire, 1571"; novels included *Off the Skelligs* (1872) and *John Jerome* (1886).

Ing·e·mann \ˈēŋ-ə-män\, Bernhard Severin. 1789–1862. Danish poet and novelist. Helped spread German Romanticism in Denmark. Author of the romantic tragedy *Blanca* (1815); the historical novels *Valdemar Seier* (1826), *Erik Menveds Barndom* (1828), and *Kong Erik* (1833); the lyrics *Holger Danske* (1837) and *Morgen og aftensange* (1837–39), etc.

Ing·en·housz \ˈiŋ-ən-ˌhau̇s\, Jan. 1730–1799. Dutch physician and plant physiologist. Practiced as physician in England (1765–68, 1779 ff.); physician to Maria Theresa in Vienna (1772–79). Discovered (1779) photosynthesis by green plants in sunlight. Author of *Experiments on Vegetables* (1779), etc.

In·ger·soll \ˈiŋ-gər-ˌsȯl, -səl\, Robert Green. 1833–1899. American lawyer and orator, b. Dresden, N.Y. Commanded Illinois volunteer cavalry regiment in Civil War; attorney general of Illinois (1867–69). Became noted agnostic lecturer, attacking popular Christian beliefs. Author of *The Gods, and Other Lectures* (1876), *Some Mistakes of Moses* (1879), *Why I Am an Agnostic* (1896), *Superstition* (1898).

Ingersoll, Robert Hawley. 1859–1928. American industrialist, b. Delta, Mich. Developed mail-order business and chain-store system; introduced (1892) Ingersoll one-dollar watch, "the watch that made the dollar famous." Insolvent (1921); sold assets to Waterbury Clock Co. (1922).

Ingersoll, Royal Eason. 1883–1976. American naval officer, b. Washington, D.C. Vice admiral, admiral (1942); commander of U.S. Atlantic fleet (1942–44); commander, Western Sea Frontier (1944–46).

Ingi I \ˈiŋ-ē\. 1135–1161. King of Norway (1136–61). Son of Harold IV; succeeded to throne jointly with illegitimate half-brother Sigurd II; defeated pretenders Sigurd Slembi and Magnus IV; joined in rule by Eystein, another illegitimate son of Harold (1142); emerged as most powerful of the three; sole ruler after deaths of Sigurd and Eystein at hands of his supporters (1155–57); fought (1157–61), defeated by Haakon II.

In·gle·by \ˈiŋ-gəl-bē\, Clement Mansfield. 1823–1886. English philosopher and critic. Among his works were *Introduction to Metaphysic* (1864–69), *Shakespeare Hermeneutics* (1875), and *Shakespeare; the Man and the Book* (1877–81).

In·glis \ˈiŋ-gəlz, -gləs\, Charles. 1743–1816. Canadian prelate, b. Glencolumbkille, Co. Donegal, Ireland. To America (1757); missionary among Mohawk Indians in Delaware (1758 ff.); assistant rector, Trinity Church, N.Y.C. (1765–83); driven out as Loyalist; to Nova Scotia (1783); first Anglican bishop of Nova Scotia (1787); founded (1788) church academy that became U. of King's Coll.; retired (1796).

Inglis, Sir John Eardley Wilmot. 1814–1862. British soldier, b. Nova Scotia. Grandson of Charles Inglis; entered British army (1833); served in Canada (1837) and in the Punjab (1848–49); famed for his gallant defense of Lucknow (1857) during Sepoy Mutiny; major general (1857).

Ingoldsby, Thomas. See R.H. BARHAM.

In·gra·ham \ˈiŋ-grə-həm, -ˌham; ˈiŋ-grəm\, Duncan Nathaniel. 1802–1891. American naval officer, b. Charleston, S.C. In command of sloop *St. Louis* at Smyrna and by show of force obtained release of a Hungarian-American from Austrian imprisonment (1853). Entered Confederate service (1861); commanded rams which tried to break Union blockade off Charleston (1863).

Ingraham, Joseph Holt. 1809–1860. American clergyman and novelist, b. Portland, Me. Began writing sensational fiction as a young man: *Pirate of the Gulf* (1836), *Burton, or, The Sieges* (1838), *The Quadroone* (1841), *Scarlet Feather* (1845), etc. Ordained priest in Protestant Episcopal church (1852); wrote religious romances: *The Prince of the House of David* (1855), *The Pillar of Fire* (1859), *The Throne of David* (1860). His son ¶Prentiss (1843–1904) was a soldier of fortune, serving the Confederacy, under Juarez in Mexico, in Africa, Cuba, etc.; settled in New York and became writer of Dime Novels and adventure novels numbering some 700.

In·gram \ˈiŋ-grəm\, Herbert. 1811–1860. English publisher. Founded (1842) and made great success of *London Illustrated News.*

Ingram, John Kells. 1823–1907. British scholar and writer, b. Ireland. Professor of oratory (1852–66) and Greek (1866–77), librarian (1879–87), and vice provost (1898–99), Trinity Coll., Dublin. Author of *History of Political Economy* (1888), *Outlines of the History of Religion* (1900), *Sonnets and other Poems* (1900), *Practical Morals* (1904), etc.

In·gras·sia \ēŋ-ˈgräs-syä\, Giovanni Filippo. c.1510–1580. Sicilian anatomist and physician. In practice in Palermo (from 1556); contributed to management of epidemics and other public health matters. Skilled anatomist esp. in field of osteology.

In·gres \a^{n}gr^{ə}\, Jean-Auguste-Dominique. 1780–1867. French painter. Studied under David and in Italy; director of Académie de France in Rome (1835–41); in Paris (after 1841); senator (1862); recognized as a leader among the Classicists. Works included *Envoys from Agamemnon, Bonaparte as First Consul, Napoléon I on the Imperial Throne, Oedipus and the Sphinx, Romulus Victorious over Acron, Virgil Reading the Aeneid, Paolo and Francesca, Vow of Louis XIII, Apotheosis of Homer, Odalisque with Slave, La Source, Turkish Bath;* executed many portraits; his drawings also highly valued.

Ini. See INE.

In·man \ˈin-mən\, Henry. 1801–1846. American painter, b. Utica, N.Y. Apprenticed to John Wesley Jarvis (1815–22); helped found National Academy of Design (1826). Leading portraitist of his day; sitters included Van Buren, W. C. Macready, Fitz-Green Halleck, W. H. Seward, Audubon, Clara Barton, Hawthorne, and in England (1844–45) Macaulay, Thomas Chalmers, Wordsworth.

In·nes \ˈin-əs\, Cosmo. 1798–1874. Scottish antiquary. Professor of constitutional law, Edinburgh (1846–74). Published *Scotland in the Middle Ages* (1860), *Facsimiles of National Manuscripts of Scotland* (1867), etc.

In·ness \ˈin-əs\, George. 1825–1894. American painter, b. near Newburgh, N.Y. Influenced early by Hudson River school and later by Dutch landscapists and by Barbizon school. Works included *Millpond, Florida Pines, Threatening, Rainbow after a Storm, Peace and Plenty, Delaware Water Gap, Delaware Valley, Autumn Oaks, Spring Blossoms, September Afternoon, Georgia Pines, Niagara, Evening at Medfield.* His son ¶George (1854–1926), b. Paris, France, was also an artist; studied with his father (1870–74); followed father in rejecting Impressionism; works included *Shepherd and Sheep* and *First Snow at Cragsmoor.*

In·nit·zer \ˈin-ət-sər\, Theodor. 1875–1955. Austrian prelate, b. Bohemia. Professor (1911), head of theological faculty (1918), rector (1928), U. of Vienna; archbishop of Vienna (1932); cardinal (1933). Endorsed affirmative Roman Catholic vote in Austria prior to Anschluss plebiscite of 1938; early a supporter of Nazi occupation regime until rebuked by Pope Pius XI; later preached and wrote pastoral letters against Nazi regime and provoked demonstrations; provided refuge for many Jews.

In·no·cent \ˈin-ə-sənt\. Name of thirteen popes and one antipope:

Innocent I. Saint. d. 417. Pope (401–417). Possibly son of Pope St. Anastasius I, whom he succeeded; during his pontificate, Rome was sacked (410) by Alaric; ended Meletian schism (414); condemned Pelagianism and excommunicated Pelagius (417).

Innocent II. *Orig.* Gregorio Pa·pa·re·schi dei Gui·do·ne \ˌpä-pä-ˈrā-skē-dā(-ē)-gwē-ˈdō-nā\. d. 1143. Pope (1130–43). Cardinal (by 1116); helped draft Concordat of Worms (1122); on death of Honorius II, irregularly elected to succeed by a minority; fled to France when Anacletus II was elected as antipope (1130); championed by Bernard of Clairvaux and Norbert of Magdeburg; installed at Rome by Emperor Lothair (1133) but again forced to leave; fully recognized after death of Anacletus (1138). Excommunicated Roger II of Sicily for support of Anacletus (1139); forced to acknowledge Roger (1139); condemned Peter Abélard and Arnold of Brescia (1140).

Innocent III. *Orig.* Lo·thar \ˈlō-tär\ of Se·gni \ˈsān-yē\. 1160 or 1161–1216. Pope (1198–1216). Son of Count Trasimund, a Roman noble; cardinal deacon (1190); succeeded Celestine III. Tried to continue policy of Gregory VII to make papacy supreme over the state; restored authority in Papal States; brought papal power to its highest point; urged Fourth Crusade (1202–04), which resulted in capture of Constantinople and establishment of the Latin Empire; promoted a crusade against the Albigenses (1208); asserted papal rights against King John of England in controversy over Stephen Langton (1206), placed England under an interdict (1208), deposed John (1212), and compelled his submission (1213); supported election of Otto IV as king of Germany (1207) but on Otto's invasion of Sicily excommunicated him (1210); deposed Otto and crowned Frederick II of Sicily as emperor (1215); presided at fourth Lateran Council (1215).

Innocent IV. *Orig.* Sinibaldo Fie·schi \ˈfyes-kē\. d. 1254. Pope (1243–54). Master of canon law; bishop of Albenga (1225); cardinal priest (1227). Carried on struggle with Emperor Frederick II, taking refuge in Lyons (1244–53); declared Frederick deposed (1245); continued contest of civil and spiritual power with Frederick's sons Conrad IV and Manfred; just before his death, suffered severe defeat (1254) by Manfred at Foggia.

Innocent V. *Orig.* Peter of Ta·ren·taise \tȧ-rä^{n}-tez\. c.1224–1276. Pope (1276). Entered Dominican order (c.1240); professor, Paris (1259–64, 1267–69); provincial for France (c.1264–67, 1269–72); archbishop of Lyons (1272); cardinal bishop of Ostia (c.1273). As pope continued Gregory X's efforts to initiate a crusade.

Innocent VI. *Orig.* Étienne Au·bert \ō-ber\. d. 1362. Pope (1352–62). Professor of civil law, Toulouse; bishop of Noyon (1338), Clermont (1340); cardinal priest (1342), cardinal bishop of Ostia (1352). As pope, reformed Curia at Avignon; caused Charles IV of Bohemia to be crowned emperor (1355); arranged Anglo-French Treaty of Brétigny (1360).

Innocent VII. *Orig.* Cosimo Gentile de' Mi·glio·ra·ti \dā-ˌmēl-yō-ˈrä-tē\. 1336–1406. Pope (1404–06). Archbishop of Ravenna (1387); bishop of Bologna (1389); cardinal (1389). Pope of the Western Schism; resided at Rome while antipope Benedict XIII held court at Avignon.

Innocent VIII. *Orig.* Giovanni Battista Ci·bò \ˈchē-bō\. 1432–1492. Pope (1484–92). Bishop of Savona (1467); cardinal (1473). Appointed (1487) Torquemada as grand inquisitor of Spain; condemned witchcraft and fostered persecution of those accused; condemned Pico della Mirandola (1486); made treaty (1489) with Sultan Bayezid II; deposed (1489) Ferdinand of Naples but later (1492) restored him.

Innocent IX. *Orig.* Giovanni Antonio Fac·chi·net·ti \ˌfäk-kē-ˈnet-tē\. 1519–1591. Pope (1591). Bishop of Nicastro (1560); active in Council of Trent (1562); papal nuncio to Venice (1566–75); patriarch of Jerusalem (1576); cardinal (1583); conducted much of papal administration for infirm Gregory XIV; died two months after succeeding Gregory.

Innocent X. *Orig.* Giovanni *or* Gian Battista Pam·phi·li \päm-ˈfē-lē\. 1574–1655. Pope (1644–55). Nuncio to Spain and cardinal (1526). Succeeded Urban VIII; changed papal sympathies from France to Habsburgs; aided in putting down insurrection in Naples and helped Venice against Turks; protested against Treaty of Westphalia (1648); condemned Jansenism (1653).

Innocent XI. *Orig.* Benedetto Ode·scal·chi \ˌō-dā-ˈskäl-kē\. 1611–1689. Pope (1676–89). Cardinal (1645); bishop of Novara (1650–56); member of Curia (1656–76). Engaged in long struggle with Louis XIV and Gallicanism; joined Holy League (1684) against Turks; approved League of Augsburg (1686).

Innocent XII. *Orig.* Antonio Pi·gna·tel·li \ˌpēn-yä-ˈtel-lē\. 1615–1700. Pope (1691–1700). Nuncio to Tuscany (1652), Poland (1660), Vienna (1668); cardinal (1681). Active in various church reforms; improved relations with France and induced Louis XIV to revoke Gallican articles; condemned Quietism of Fénelon (1699).

Innocent XIII. *Orig.* Michelangelo *or* Michelangiolo Con·ti \ˈkōn-tē\. 1655–1724. Pope (1721–24). Nuncio to Switzerland (1695), Lisbon (1698); cardinal (1706); bishop of Osimo (1709), Viterbo (1712–19). Granted Naples (1722) to Emperor Charles VI; supported James the Old Pretender as king of England.

Innocent III. *Orig.* Lando of Sez·ze \ˈsät-tsē\. 1160 or 1161–? Antipope (1179–80) in opposition to Alexander III.

İnö·nü \i-nœ-ˈnü\, İsmet. 1884–1973. Turkish soldier and politician. In World War I fought in Syria and against Russians in eastern Turkey; Kemal Atatürk's chief of staff in war against Greeks (1919–22); defeated Greeks twice at village of İnönü, which he adopted as his last name; Turkish representative in negotiating Treaty of Lausanne (1922–23). First prime minister of new republic (1923–37); in large measure responsible for transformation of Turkey into modern state, introducing many reforms; on Atatürk's death unanimously elected president (1938–50); made several important treaties with object of keeping Turkey neutral; leader of opposition (1950–60); premier (1961–65).

In·oue \in-ō-(w)e\ Enryō. 1859–1919. Japanese philosopher and educator. Opposed excessive Westernization of Japan; founded (1887) Tetsugaku kan (Philosophical Inst.) to promote study of Buddhism, and nationalistic magazine *Nihonjin;* reinterpreted Buddhism to make it more relevant to modern, Western-influenced culture.

Inoue Kaoru. *Orig.* Mon·ta \mōn-tä\ Shidō. 1835–1915. Japanese politician. Of a samurai family; during disturbed period made way to England (1863) with his friend Itō Hirobumi; sought unsuccessfully (1864) to prevent clash between Choshu clan and foreign war vessels; severely wounded by reactionary samurai. After Restoration (1868) made vice minister of finance in new government (1870–73); held other important cabinet offices (1878–98), esp. minister for foreign affairs (1881–88); created count (1885), marquis (1907). Special commissioner to Korea (1895); one of five elder statesmen of Meiji period; adviser to emperor during Russo–Japanese War (1904–05).

Inoue Tetsujirō. 1855–1944. Japanese philosopher. Professor, Tokyo Imperial U. (1882–84, 1890–1923); influential as a historian of Oriental and esp. Japanese philosophy; member of House of Peers (1925–26). Author of *Teishitsu to shukyo no kankei* (1890), *Nippon yōmei gakuha no tetsugako* (1900), *Shakamuni-den* (biography of Buddha, 1902), *Nihon kogaku-ha no tetsugaku* (1902), etc.

In·skip \ˈin-(ˌ)skip\, Thomas Walker Hobart. 1st Viscount Cal·de·cote \ˈkȯl-də-kət\. 1876–1947. British politician and jurist. With intelligence and law divisions of Admiralty (1915–18); M.P. (1918–29, 1931–39); solicitor general (1922–24, 1924–28, 1931–32), attorney general (1928–29, 1932–36); minister for coordination of defense (1936–39); created viscount (1939); lord chancellor (1939–40); lord chief justice (1940–46).

In·sull \ˈin(t)-səl\, Samuel. 1859–1938. American financier, b. London, England. To U.S. (1881); private secretary to Thomas A. Edison; on consolidation of Edison interests, became vice president of Edison General Electric Co. (1889); president, Chicago Edison Co. (1892) and of Commonwealth Electric Co. of Chicago (1898), which he merged as Commonwealth Edison; also president of Peoples' Gas Light and Coke Co., Chicago, and various other companies. Overexpansion caused financial difficulties for a pyramid of holding companies he created and three of his largest companies went into receivership (1932); indicted (1932), fled to Europe; returned (1934), three times acquitted of fraud, embezzlement, etc.

In·tef II \ˈin-ˌtef\. *Also called* Wa·hankh Intef \ˈwä-ˌhäŋk-\. 22d–21st century B.C. King of Egypt (2117–2067 B.C.) of 11th dynasty. Expanded domain to include Abydos and the Thinite nome; made peace with Heracleopolitan dynasty of Lower and Middle Egypt.

Intrépide, l'. See Joseph-Marie DESSAIX.

Inu·kai \ē-nü-kī\ Tsuyoshi. 1855–1932. Japanese journalist and politician. War correspondent for *Hōchi Shimbun* during Satsuma rebellion (1877) and later its editor (until 1890). Member (1890–1932) of first House of Representatives in Imperial Diet; minister of education (1898); successfully opposed Katsura government (1913); founded (1922) Kakushin Kurabu (Reformation party); minister of communication (1923); joined Rikken Seiyūkai party (1924), president (1929–32); prime minister (1931–32); opposed army's autonomous authority in Manchuria; assassinated by ultranationalist army officers.

Io·ne·scu \yō-ˈnes-kü\, Dumitru, *known as* Take. 1858–1922. Romanian politician. Member of parliament (1884–1922); minister of justice and finance (1891–1900); founded Conservative-Democratic party (1908); foreign minister (1912, 1916–17, 1920); in World War I, favored Romanian intervention on Allied side; after the war, leader in formation of Little Entente; prime minister of Romania (1921–22).

Io·phon \ˈī-ə-ˌfän\. 5th–4th century B.C. Greek tragic author. Son of Sophocles; only scattered fragments of his works are extant. According to tradition, he accused his father of insanity in order that he might gain control of his fortune; Sophocles proved his sanity by reciting to the judges the chorus from his *Oedipus at Colonus.*

Ior·ga \ˈyär-gä\, Nicolae. 1871–1940. Romanian historian and politician. Professor, Bucharest (1895 ff.); founder of Institute for the Study of Southeastern Europe (1913). Member of parliament (1907–40); founder of National Democratic party (1910); prime minister and foreign minister (1931–32); assassinated by members of Iron Guard. Author of *Geschichte des rumänischen Volkes* (1905), *Geschichte des osmanischen Reiches* (1908–12), etc.

Ipa·tieff \i-ˈpät-yəf\, Vladimir Nikolayevich. 1867–1952. American chemist, b. Moscow, Russia. Professor, Artillery Academy, St. Petersburg (1898–1906), U. of St. Petersburg (1906–15); to U.S. (1931); professor, Northwestern U. (1931–35). Authority on high-pressure catalytic reactions, many of which are important in the refining of petroleum and the synthesis of hydrocarbons; synthesized isoprene (1892–96); developed a polymerization process of making high-octane gasoline and a method of making olefins from alcohols.

Iphic·ra·tes \i-ˈfik-rə-ˌtēz\. c.410–353 B.C. Athenian general. Improved armor and discipline of Athenian troops; developed lightly armed *peltast* troops; commanded peltasts in defeating Spartans near Corinth (390) and in Thrace (389), and in relieving Corcyra (Corfu) when besieged by Sparta (373). Commanded fleet off Macedonian coast (369) and aided in keeping family of Amyntas on Macedonian throne.

Ip·pi·tsus·ai \ēp-pēt-sü̇s-ī\ Bunchō. d. 1791. Japanese artist. Worked in *Ukiyo-e* manner, producing paintings of actors, theatrical scenes, and other aspects of everyday life; noted esp. as a colorist.

Ip·po·li·tov-I·va·nov \ip-(ˌ)pəl-ˈyē-təfʸ-yi-ˈvä-nəf\, Mikhail Mikhaylovich. 1859–1935. Russian composer. Professor (1893–1906), director (1906–22), Moscow Conservatory; conductor, Mamontova Opera (1899–1906); reorganized Georgian State Conservatory (1924–1925); conductor, Bolshoi Theater (1925–35). Compositions, influenced by Caucasian and Georgian folk songs, included operas as *Ruf'* (1887), *Izmena* (1910); orchestral works *Kavkazskiye eskizï* (Caucasian Sketches, 1894), *Armyanskaya rapsodiya* (1895), *Mtsïri* (1929); choral and chamber works.

Iq·bāl \ik-ˈbäl\, Sir Muḥammad. 1877–1938. Indian poet and philosopher. In verse and speeches called for regeneration and revitalization of Islām, abandonment of quietism, and undertaking of creative and progressive work in the world; associated with Muslim League; called for separate Muslim state (1930) that eventuated in creation of Pakistan. Verse in Persian included *Asrār-e khūdī* (1915), *Rumūz-e bīkhūdī* (1918), *Payām-e Mashriq* (1923), *Zabūr-e ʿAjam* (1927), *Jāvīd-nāmeh* (1932); verse in Urdu included *Bāng-e darā* (1924), *Bāl-e Jibrīl* (1935), *Zarb-e kalīm* (1937), *Armaghān-e Hijāz* (1938); also wrote *Reconstruction of Religious Thought in Islam* (1934).

Irala, Domingo Martínez de. See MARTÍNEZ DE IRALA.

Iradier, Eduardo Dato. See DATO IRADIER.

ʿIrā·qī \ir-ˈä-kē\. *More completely* Fakhr ad-Dīn Ibrāhīm ʿIrāqī Hamadānī. c.1211–1289. Persian poet. Known esp. for mystical verse as *Kitāb al-lamaʿāt,* inspired by Ibn al-ʿArabī, and *ʿUshshāq-nāmeh.*

Ire·dell \ˈī(ə)r-ˌdel\, James. 1751–1799. American jurist, b. Lewes, England. To America as comptroller of customs, Edenton, N.C. (1768); collector of the port (1774–76). Attorney general of North Carolina (1779–81). Member, Council of State (1787). In constitutional ratification convention, supported adoption of Constitution (1788). Associate justice, U.S. Supreme Court (1790–99).

Ire·land \ˈī(ə)r-lənd\, John. *Also called* Johannes de Ir·lan·dia \i(ə)r-ˈlan-dē-ə\. c.1435–c.1500. Scottish writer. Undertook diplomatic missions for Louis XI while a student in Paris; chaplain to James III (1483–88) and James IV; member of Scottish parliament. Author of *The Meroure of Wyssdome* (1490), earliest extant example of original Scots prose.

Ireland, John. 1838–1918. American prelate, b. Burnchurch, Co. Kilkenny, Ireland. To U.S. (1849); ordained priest (1861); chaplain in Union army (1862–63). Rector of the cathedral, St. Paul (1867); bishop of St. Paul (1884); first archbishop (1888). Encouraged Catholic settlement of western Minnesota; leading spokesman for Catholic integration, liberal theology. Influential in founding Catholic U., Washington, D.C. (1889).

Ireland, John Nicholson. 1879–1962. English composer. Organist and choirmaster, St. Luke's, Chelsea (1904–26); professor, Royal College of Music (1923–39). Works included orchestral pieces *Forgotten Rite* (1913), *London Overture* (1936), *Satyricon* (1946); *London Pieces* (1917–20), *Sarnia* suite (1940–41), etc. for piano; and esp. songs to poems by Hardy, Symons, Masefield, Housman, and others.

Ireland, William Henry. 1777–1835. English forger. Produced numerous false Shakespearean manuscripts, including a transcript of *King Lear* and extracts from Hamlet, and the pseudo-Shakespearean plays *Vortigern and Rowena* and *Henry II;* confessed the forgeries (1796) after their authenticity was challenged by Malone. Author also of original romances, ballads, and narrative verse.

Ire·nae·us \ˌī-rē-ˈnē-əs\. Saint. c.120 to 140–c.200 to 203. Greek prelate. Apostle of the Gauls; bishop of Lugdunum (modern Lyons, 177); reputed to have been martyred under Emperor Septimius Severus. Known esp. for writings against Gnosticism.

Ire·ne \ī-ˈrē-nē\. Name of three rulers of the Eastern Roman Empire:

Irene. Saint. c.752–803. Ruled (780–802). m. Leo IV (769); on his death (780) became regent during minority of son Constantine VI; reestablished image worship; summoned Second Nicene Council (787) which defined veneration due to images; abdicated and banished (790) as Constantine took power; returned as co-ruler (792); plotted continuously for return to power; arrested and imprisoned Constantine (797); sole ruler (797–802); finally turned against by patricians; dethroned (802) and exiled to Lesbos.

Irene Du·cas \ˈdyü-kəs\. c.1066–1120. Wife of Alexius I Comnenus; with her daughter Anna Comnena (*q.v.*), plotted against her son John II Comnenus in favor of Nicephorus Bryennius; retired to a monastery (1118) following crowning of John.

Irene. d. 1161. First wife (m. 1146) of Emperor Manuel I Comnenus and sister-in-law of Conrad III of Germany.

Ire·ton \'ī(ə)rt-ᵊn\, Henry. 1611–1651. English soldier and politician. Joined Parliamentary army (1642); commanded cavalry at Edgehill (1642); took part in battles of Marston Moor (1644), Naseby (1645). m. (1646) Bridget, daughter of Oliver Cromwell. M.P. (1645 ff.); presented "Heads of Proposals" scheme calling for constitutional monarchy (1647); signed warrant for execution of Charles I. Second in command under Cromwell in Irish campaign (1649); captured Carlow, Waterford, and Duncannon (1650), and Limerick (1651).

Iriar·te \ēr-'yär-tā\, Tomás de. 1750–1791. Spanish poet. Known esp. for *Fábulas literarias* (1782); author also of didactic poem *La música* (1779), comedies and numerous translations, as of Horace's *Ars poetica*.

Iri·go·yen \ē-rē-'gō-yān\, Hipólito. 1852–1933. Argentine politician. Took part in revolution of 1890; leader of Radicals (from 1896). President of Argentina (1916–22, 1928–30); forced out by military coup (1930).

Ir·ne·ri·us \ir-'nir-ē-əs\ *or* **War·ne·ri·us** \wär-'nir-ē-əs\ *or* **Guar·ne·ri·us** \gwär-\. c.1055–1125 or after. Italian jurist. Professor, Bologna; reviver of Roman law in Middle Ages; authority on Justinian Code; author of *Summa Codicis,* first systematic treatise on Roman law, and prob. of *Authentica,* an epitome of Justinian's *Novellae.*

Iron, Ralph. See Olive SCHREINER.

Iron·side \'ī(-ə)rn-,sīd\, William Edmund. 1st Baron Ironside. 1880–1959. British army officer, b. Scotland. Served in Boer War (1899–1902) and World War I; commanded Allied forces at Archangel (1918–19); major general (1919); commanded Allied contingent in north Persia (1920); commanded Meerut District, India (1928–31); lieutenant general (1931); general (1935); commander of Middle East forces and governor general of Gibraltar (1938). Chief of imperial general staff (1939–40); commander of Home Defense forces (1940); field marshal (1940); created baron (1941).

Ir·ving \'ər-viŋ\, Edward. 1792–1834. Scottish clergyman. To London (1822) as minister of Hatton Garden Chapel; built new church in Regent Square; acquired fame as preacher. Compelled to retire from Regent Square church because of his acceptance of pentecostal phenomena (1832); condemned by presbytery of Annan on charge of heresy (1833). His followers, known as Irvingites, assumed title of Catholic Apostolic church.

Irving, Sir Henry. *Orig.* John Henry Brod·ribb \'brä-drib\. 1838–1905. English actor. Played in provincial stock companies (1856–66); first London successes in *Hunted Down* (1866), *Two Roses* (1870), and *The Bells,* produced by H.L. Bateman (1871); followed by successes as Hamlet (1874), Macbeth (1875), Othello (1876). Lessee and manager of Lyceum Theatre, London (1878–1902); professionally associated with Ellen Terry (1878–1902); acted with her in *Hamlet, Merchant of Venice, Romeo and Juliet, Much Ado About Nothing, Twelfth Night, King Lear,* etc.; triumphed in Tennyson's *Becket* (1893); noted for sumptuous, meticulously detailed productions, which contributed to eventual bankruptcy (1902). Made eight American tours (first, 1883–84; last, 1903–04). Knighted (1895), first actor to be so honored; buried in Westminster Abbey. His son ¶Lawrence Sidney Irving (1871–1914) was also an actor and theater manager; briefly played in Frank Benson's Shakespearean company; after several failures, succeeded as playwright and naturalistic actor in *The Unwritten Law* (1910, from Dostoyevesky's *Crime and Punishment*); appeared successfully in Ibsen's *The Pretenders* (1913); died in *Empress of Ireland* disaster. Another son ¶Henry Brodribb (1870–1919) acted in Ben Greet's and other repertory companies; attempted to revive father's Lyceum Theatre successes. Best known as author of *French Criminals of the Nineteenth Century* (1901), *Book of Remarkable Criminals* (1918), *Last Studies in Criminology* (1921).

Irving, Washington. *Pseudonyms* Geoffrey Cray·on \'krā-ən, -,än\, Jonathan Old·style \'ōl(d)-,stīl\, Launcelot Wag·staffe \'wag-,staf\, Friar Antonio Aga·pi·da \,ä-gä-'pē-thä\. 1783–1859. American author, b. New York City. While engaged in desultory study of law, contributed whimsical letters to brother Peter's *Morning Chronicle;* in Europe on trip for health (1804–06); leading figure in group (brother William, James K. Paulding, etc.) that published *Salmagundi* (1807–08), a series of whimsical essays somewhat in style of Addison's *Spectator,* in which the name Gotham was first applied to New York City. Established reputation with genially satirical *History of New York ... by Diedrich Knickerbocker* (1809). To Liverpool, representing his brothers' hardware firm of P. and E. Irving (1815); when firm failed (1818), turned seriously to writing to bring in money. Remained in England; under pseudonym Geoffrey Crayon wrote the essays that appeared in *The Sketch Book* (1819–20), which included "Rip Van Winkle," "Legend of Sleepy Hollow," "Spectre Bridegroom"; published *Bracebridge Hall* (1822). Traveled in Germany and France (1822–25). On staff of U.S. embassy, Madrid (1826–29); published *History of ... Christopher Columbus* (1828), *A Chronicle of the Conquest of Granada* (1829), *Companions of Columbus* (1831). Secretary of U.S. legation, London (1829–32); U.S. minister to Spain (1842–46). Resided (from 1846) at "Sunnyside," country home near Tarrytown, N.Y. Published also *The Alhambra* (1832), *A Tour on the Prairies* (1835), *Adventures of Captain Bonneville, U.S.A.* (1837), *Oliver Goldsmith* (1849), *Mahomet and His Successors* (1849–50), *Life of Washington* (1855–59).

Irwin, Baron. See Edward F. L. WOOD.

Ir·win \'ər-wən\, May. *Orig.* Ada Campbell. 1862–1938. American actress, b. Whitby, Ont. Entered vaudeville with sister Georgia as the "Irwin Sisters" (1875); member of Tony Pastor's company (1877–83) and Augustin Daly's company (1883–87); excelled in farce comedy, as *The Widow Jones* (1895), *Courted into Court* (1896), *Mrs. Peckham's Carouse* (1907), *The Mollusc* (1908), *Getting a Polish* (1910). Introduced songs "After the Ball," "A Hot Time in the Old Town Tonight."

Irwin, Will, *in full* William Henry. 1873–1948. American journalist and writer, b. Oneida, N.Y. On staff of San Francisco *Wave* (1899–1900), San Francisco *Chronicle* (1901–04), New York *Sun* (1904–06), *McClure's Magazine* (1906–07), *Collier's Weekly* (1907–08); war correspondent for *Saturday Evening Post* (1916–18). Author of *The Hamadryads* (verse, 1904), *The City That Was* (1907), *The Confessions of a Con Man* (1909), *The House of Mystery* (1910), *The Red Button* (1912), *Men, Women, and War* (1915), *The House That Shadows Built* (1929), *Propaganda and the News* (1936), etc.

Isaac \'ī-zək\. Saint. *Armenian* Sa·hak \sä-'häk\. *Called* the Great. c.345–439. Armenian prelate. Monk; named head of Armenian church (c.388); instituted reforms and encouraged monasticism; firmly established independence of Armenian church; with Mesrop Mastots began development of Armenian alphabet (c.391); directed first translation of Bible into Armenian (completed c.435); briefly removed from office (428–432) by intrigue.

Isaac. Name of two rulers of the Eastern Roman Empire:

Isaac I Com·ne·nus \käm-'nē-nəs\. c.1005–1061. Emperor (1057–59), first of the Comneni. Son of Manuel Comnenus; reared by Emperor Basil II; deposed Michael VI; instituted stringent fiscal policies; quarreled with Patriarch Michael I Cerularius and had him imprisoned (1058); repelled Hungarians (1059); abdicated because of severe illness; author of several works on Homer.

Isaac II An·ge·lus \'an-jə-ləs\. c.1135–1204. Emperor (1185–95 and 1203–04), first of the Angeli. Raised to throne by a revolution, succeeding cousin Andronicus I Comnenus; defeated Normans, but failed to suppress revolts of Walachians and Bulgarians (1185–87); dethroned, blinded, and imprisoned by his brother Alexius III (1195); restored by crusaders who took Constantinople (1203) but again deposed by Alexius V Ducas.

Isaac of An·ti·och \'ant-ē-,äk\. *Also called* Isaac the Great. d. c.460. Syrian writer. Probably a priest of Syrian Jacobite church. Credited with verse descriptions of Roman festivals and of capture of Rome by Alaric (410), of destruction of Antioch by earthquake (459). Formerly credited with two collections of poetic discourses on theological subjects, now believed the work of two or more other writers.

Isaac of Nin·e·veh \'nin-ə-və\. *Also called* Isaac the Syrian. d. c.700. Syrian prelate. Monk; bishop of Nineveh (c.670) of East Syrian Nestorian church; resigned shortly thereafter and resumed solitary monastic life. Wrote numerous treatises, dialogues, etc., on monastic and ascetic themes that were widely translated and influential.

Isaac of Stel·la \'stel-ə\. c.1100–c.1169. English religious and philosopher. Entered abbey of Cîteaux; abbot of Cistercian abbey of Étoile (1147). Author of treatises on monasticism, mysticism, theory of atonement, and esp. of *Epistola de anima ad Alcherum* (1162), synthesizing Aristotelian and Neoplatonic psychologies with Christian mysticism.

Isaac ben Jo·seph \-ben-'jō-zəf *also* -səf\ of Cor·beil \kòr-bey\. *Also known as* Se·mak \sā-màk\. d. 1280. French religious writer. Author of popular *Sefer mitzwot qaṭan* (1277).

Isaac ben Mo·ses \-ben-'mō-zəz\ of Vi·en·na \vē-'en-ə\. *Also known as* Isaac Or Za·ru'a \ē-'zäk-òr-,zär-ü-'ä\. c.1180–c.1250. German Talmudist. Author of popular ritualistic work *Or zaru'a,* containing biblical and Talmudic commentary in vernacular and still a valuable picture of Middle European Jewish culture of the day.

Isaac ben She·shet Per·fet \-ben-shā-'shāt-per-'fāt\. *Also known as* Ri·bash \rē-bäsh\. 1326–1408. Spanish Talmudist. Outstanding authority on Halakha; rabbi of Saragossa; rabbi of Algiers (1391). Opponent of both rationalist philosophy and Kabbala; author of 417 *responsa,* or legal opinions and commentaries.

Isaac *or* **Isaak** \ē-'zä(-ä)k\, Heinrich. c.1450–1517. Flemish composer. In service of Lorenzo de' Medici (c.1484–92), Emperor Maximilian I (1496–1517); court composer, Vienna (from 1497). With Jakob Obrecht and Josquin Després a leader of Flemish school; compositions included polyphonic settings of nearly 40 Ordinary masses and 99 Propers, as well as motets and some 40 secular songs.

Isaacs \'ī-zəks\, Sir Isaac Alfred. 1855–1948. Australian jurist and statesman. Member of Federal Convention (1897); member of Parliament (1901–06); attorney general (1905–06). Justice of high court of Australia (1906–30); chief justice of Australia (1930–31). Governor general of Australia (1931–36).

Isaacs \ē-'säks, ē-'sä-äks\, Jorge. 1837–1895. Colombian writer. Author of *Poesías* (1864) and the widely read novel *María* (1867).

Isaacs \'ī-zəks\, Rufus Daniel. 1st Marquis of Read·ing \'red-iŋ\. 1860–1935. British politician. Liberal M.P. (1904–13); attorney general (1910–13), first attorney general to be member of cabinet (1912); lord chief justice of England (1913–21); ambassador to U.S. (1918–19); created Viscount Er·leigh \'ər-lē\ (1917); viceroy of India (1921–26); created marquis (1926); foreign secretary (1931).

Isa·beau \ē-zä-bō\ *or* **Is·a·bel·la** \ˌiz-ə-'bel-ə\ of Bavaria. 1371–1435. Consort of Charles VI of France. Daughter of Stephen II, Duke of Bavaria; m. (1385) Charles VI of France; crowned (1389); after king became insane (1392), consorted with duc d'Orléans until his death (1407). Sided sometimes with Armagnacs, sometimes with Burgundians. Later (1419–20) went over to the English; instigated the Treaty of Troyes (1420). Her daughter Catherine married Henry V of England (1420).

Isabel of Portugal, Saint. See St. ELIZABETH.

Is·a·bel·la \ˌiz-ə-'bel-ə\. *Span.* Isa·bel \ē-sä-'bel\. Name of two queens of Spain:

Isabella I. *Called* la Ca·tó·li·ca \lä-kä-'tō-lē-kä\, *i.e.* the Catholic. 1451–1504. Queen of Castile (1474–1504). Daughter of John II. m. (1469) Ferdinand II of Aragon (*q.v.*); joint sovereign with him as Ferdinand V of Castile and Aragon (1479–1504); took close interest in conquest of Granada (1482–92); approved proposal of and gave much aid to Columbus; took deep interest in reform of secular clergy and religious orders, esp. Poor Clares; granted title "the Catholic" by Pope Alexander VI.

Isabella II. *In full* Ma·ria Isabella Lou·i·sa \mə-'rē-ə- ... -lü-'ē-zə\. 1830–1904. Queen of Spain (1833–68). Daughter of Ferdinand VII; became heiress apparent by decree of the Cortes (1830) setting aside Salic law; became queen (1833) on death of her father, with her mother as queen regent; civil war waged by Don Carlos, her uncle (1833–39), resulted in court triumph, followed by reactionary policy against religious orders and the church; queen regent resigned (1840) in favor of Gen. Espartero, who was overthrown (1843) by an insurrection; declared of age by the Cortes (1843); last 25 years of reign a period of continuous strife, political intrigues, attempted insurrections, frequent changes in ministries; overthrown by revolution (1868); abdicated in favor of her son Alfonso XII (1870).

Isabella. *Also* Eliz·a·beth \i-'liz-ə-bəth\. 1692–1766. Queen consort of Philip V of Spain. Daughter of Odoardo II Farnese, Duke of Parma; second wife (m. 1714) of Philip V; from beginning exerted great influence over her weak husband; spent much of reign attempting to secure Italian possessions for her children, eventually succeeding in getting lands and titles for sons Charles (later Charles III of Spain) and Philip; chose able and devoted ministers who instituted beneficial internal reforms and improved Spain's economy.

Isabella of An·gou·lême \äⁿ-gü-lem\. d. 1246. Consort of King John of England. Daughter of Aymer, Count of Angoulême; m. John (1200); mother of Henry III. Imprisoned by John in Gloucester (1214–16); returned to France (1217); m. Hugh, Count of La Marche (1220). Her daughter by John, Isabella (1214–41), married (1235) Emperor Frederick II.

Isabella of France. Name of two queens consort of England:

Isabella. 1292–1358. Daughter of Philip IV of France; m. (1308) Edward II, who treated her with great unkindness; returned to France (1325); raised army with Roger de Mortimer, Earl of March, landed at Harwich (1326), and routed forces of Edward and his favorites, the Despensers; installed her son as Edward III and ruled with Mortimer (1327–30) as coregent for him; arrested with Mortimer (1330) by Edward III and Henry of Lancaster.

Isabella. 1389–1409. Second daughter of Charles VI of France; m. (1396) Richard II of England; after Richard's death returned to France (1401); m. the poet Charles d'Orléans, Count of Angoulême.

Isabella of Hai·naut \en-ō\. 1170–1190. Queen consort of France. Daughter of Baldwin V, Count of Hainaut; m. (1180) Philip II Augustus of France; brought to king as dowry the province of Artois; mother of Louis VIII.

Isa·bey \ē-zä-be\, Jean-Baptiste. 1767–1855. French miniaturist. Patronized by Louis XVI, Marie-Antoinette, Napoléon and Joséphine, Louis XVIII, Louis-Philippe; remembered esp. for *Bonaparte dans les jardins de Malmaison.* His son ¶Eugène-Louis-Gabriel (1804–1886) was a painter; esp. of marines.

Isae·us \ī-'sē-əs, -'zē-\. c.420–c.350 B.C. Athenian orator and rhetorician. Composed forensic speeches for others, esp. for use in inheritance cases; speeches noted for careful logical construction.

Isag·o·ras \ī-'sag-ə-rəs\. 6th century B.C. Athenian politican. Archon (508 B.C.); on resistance of Cleisthenes and mass of people to his administration, asked help from Spartans, who occupied city; fled into exile when Athenians successfully revolted.

Isa·iah \ī-'zā-ə, -'zī-ə\ *or* **Isa·ias** \-əs\. *Hebrew* Ye·sha·'ya·hu \yə-'shä-yə-ˌhü\. 8th century B.C. Hebrew prophet. Called by a vision to prophesy (c.742 B.C.); ministered in kingdom of Judah, attacking corruption and warning of God's wrath and of imminent destruction (by the Assyrians). Considered author of first 39 chapters of the Old Testament book of *Isaiah.*

ʽIsā ibn Mū·sā \'ē-ˌsä-ˌib-ən-'mü-ˌsä\. fl. 754–784. Islāmic leader. Helped secure caliphate of al-Manṣūr by putting down Shīʽite revolt in Medina (762); nominated to succeed al-Manṣūr but forced by intimidation to step aside in favor of al-Manṣūr's son al-Mahdī.

Īśā·na·var·man \ē-'shän-ə-ˌvər-mən\. fl. 554 A.D. Indian ruler. Chief of Maukhari family; revolted against suzerain Gupta dynasty and established kingdom in the Ganges valley. Kingdom passed later under control of Harṣa.

Ish·bo·sheth \ish-'bō-shet(h)\. *Orig.* Ish·baal *or* Esh·baal \ish-'bā(-ə)l\. 11th century B.C. King of Israel. Fourth son of King Saul; proclaimed king by Abner, commander of the army; soon at war with Judah, which had proclaimed David; rebuked Abner, who defected to David; murdered by soldiers. Last of family of Saul to rule.

Ish·er·wood \'ish-ər-ˌwu̇d\, Benjamin Franklin. 1822–1915. American naval engineer, b. New York City. Entered navy (1844); engineer in chief of the navy (1861–84); responsible for design and building of engines for expansion of U.S. navy during Civil War. Author of *Engineering Precedents* (1859), *Experimental Researches in Steam Engineering* (1863–65).

Isherwood, Christopher William Bradshaw, 1904–1986. American writer, b. Cheshire, England. Screenwriter for various film studios (from 1939). Author of autobiographical and quasi-autobiographical works including short-story collection *Goodbye to Berlin* (1939), the novels *The World in the Evening* (1954), *Down There On A Visit* (1962), *A Meeting by the River* (1967), and *Christopher and His Kind* (1976). As a convert, wrote, edited, and translated works on Vedantism.

Ishi·da \ē-shē-dä\ Baigan. 1685–1744. Japanese scholar. Founded (1729) Shingaku ("Heart Learning") movement, aimed at teaching to common people an ethical doctrine compounded from Confucian, Taoist, Buddhist, and Shintō elements. Author of *Tohi mondo* (1739), *Seika ron* (1774).

Ishida Mitsunari. 1563–1600. Japanese warrior. Valued supporter of Toyotomi Hideyoshi; plotted against Tokugawa Ieyasu; unsupported by allies, attacked forces of Ieyasu and was defeated in battle of Sekigahara (1600); captured and executed. Thereafter Tokugawa family assumed hereditary shogunate.

Ishii \ē-shē-ē\ Kikujirō. 1866–1945. Japanese diplomat. Attaché at legation in Paris (1891–96); consul in Korea (1896–1900); investigated anti-Japanese riots in California and British Columbia (1907). Ambassador to France (1912–15); minister of foreign affairs (1914–16); created viscount (1916). Negotiated Lansing-Ishii Agreement (1917) by which U.S. recognized Japan's special interests in China. Again ambassador to France (1920–27); president of council and assembly of League of Nations (1923, 1926).

Ishi·ka·wa \ē-shē-kä-wä\ Takuboku. *Orig.* Ishikawa Hajime. 1885–1912. Japanese poet. On staff of newspaper *Asahi Shimbun* in Tokyo. Author of verse collections *Akogare* (1905), *Ichiaku-no-suna* (1910) in which he showed himself a master of the *tanka* form, and *Yobuko no fue* (1912).

Ish·mael ben Eli·sha \'ish-ˌmā(-ə)l-ˌben-i-'lī-shə\. 2d century A.D. Jewish teacher of Galilee. Outstanding *tanna* (Talmudic teacher); compiled the thirteen hermeneutical rules for interpreting the Torah; founded a school which produced the legal commentary *Mekhilta.*

Is·i·dore \'iz-ə-ˌdō(ə)r, -ˌdo̊(ə)r \ of Ki·ev \'kē-ˌ(y)ef, -ˌ(y)ev, -(y)əf\. c.1385–1463. Greek prelate. Abbot of St. Demetrius monastery, Constantinople; envoy of Emperor John VIII Palaeologus to Council of Basel (1434), failed to arrange for a new council to unite Roman and Greek churches; patriarch of Kiev and all Russia (1436); one of six Greek representatives at council of Ferrara-Florence (1438–39) and helped draw up document of unification (1439); made cardinal of Roman church (1439); as legate of Pope Eugenius IV, instituted unification in Kiev but was opposed in Moscow by Grand Duke Vasily II; convicted of apostasy to Orthodox church, imprisoned; escaped (1444); to Constantinople (1452) for Pope Nicholas V, proclaimed unification in Hagia Sophia basilica; joined in defense of city against Turks, fled fall of Constantinople; resigned offices, named Greek patriarch of Constantinople (1459).

Isidore of Se·ville \sə-'vil, 'sev-əl\. Saint. *Lat.* Is·i·do·rus His·pa·len·sis \ˌiz-ə-'dō-rəs-ˌhis-pə-'len-səs\. c.560–636. Spanish prelate and scholar. Archbishop of Seville (c.600); considered most learned man of his time; last of the Latin fathers of the Western church. Known particularly for his vast encyclopedia *Etymologiae,* which remained a popular reference work through the Middle

Ages; also wrote *Differentiarum libri, De natura rerum, De ortu et obitu patrum,* etc.

Is·i·do·rus \ˌiz-ə-ˈdōr-əs, -ˈdȯr-\ of Mi·le·tus \mī-ˈlēt-əs, mə-\. 6th century A.D. Byzantine architect. Collaborated with Anthemius of Tralles in designing Church of Hagia Sophia in Constantinople.

Is·kan·dar Mu·da \i-ˈskän-där-ˈmüd-ä\. 1590–1636. Sultan of Acheh (1607–36). Expanded domain to include much of eastern and western coastal Sumatra, Kehah and Pahang; his attempt to monopolize pepper trade finally blocked by naval defeat by Portuguese of Malacca, Johore and Patani (1629); patronized writers and made Acheh a center of Islāmic learning.

Iskander. See Aleksandr HERZEN; George KASTRIOTI.

Is·la \ˈēs-lä\, José Francisco de. *Full surname* Isla y Ro·jo \-ē-ˈrō-kō\. 1703–1781. Spanish satirist. Jesuit; taught sacred literature in various schools (1727–54). Known esp. for his satire on bombastic pulpit oratory *Historia del famoso predicador Fray Gerundio de Campaszas alias Zotes* (1758; banned by Inquisition, 1760).

Islebius, Magister. See Johann SCHNEIDER.

Is·lip \ˈiz-lip\, Simon. d. 1366. English prelate. Archbishop of Canterbury (1349–66).

Is·mā·ʽīl \is-ˈmä-ˌēl\. d. 760. Islāmic leader. Son of sixth imam, Jaʽfar ibn Muḥammad; designated as successor by his father; died five years before Jaʽfar, but his followers proclaimed him and formed Ismāʽīlīyah sect of Shīʽah; sect claimed imamate and by developing an effective religio-political doctrine threatened the caliphate and gave rise to other powerful sects, as the Fāṭimids, Qarmaṭians, Assassins.

Ismāʽīl. *In full* Mawlāy Ismāʽīl ibn Sharīf. 1645 or 1646–1727. Ruler of Morocco (1672–1727). Half-brother of Mawlāy ar-Rashīd, founder of ʽAlawid dynasty; on death of ar-Rashīd seized throne; defeated other claimants in series of wars; built large black army, trained and armed by Europeans (esp. French); conducted expeditions against Ottoman Algiers (1679, 1682, 1695–96); seized Spanish settlements, expelled English from Tangier (1684).

Ismāʽīl. Shahs of Iran. See ESMĀʽĪL.

Ismāʽīl Pa·sha \-pə-ˈshä\. d. 1822. Ottoman soldier. Son of ʽAlī Pasha, viceroy of Egypt; led expedition against Mamlūks of Sudan; captured Dongola (1820), occupied Sennar (1821).

Ismāʽīl Pasha. 1830–1895. Viceroy of Egypt (1863–79). Proclaimed Ottoman viceroy (1863) on death of uncle Saʽīd Pasha; received title of khedive (1867) from sultan; rebuilt Cairo and improved Alexandria; encouraged Suez Canal project as advantageous to Egypt; annexed Darfur (1874); becoming involved financially, sold his canal shares to Great Britain (1875); dismissed (1879) in favor of son Tawfīq Pasha.

Is·may \ˈiz-ˌmā\, Hastings Lionel. 1st Baron Ismay. 1887–1965. British soldier, b. India. Entered army (1905); served in India, Somaliland; assistant secretary (1926–30), secretary (1938–40), Committee of Imperial Defense; chief of staff to Winston Churchill (1940–46); secretary of state for Commonwealth relations (1951–52); secretary general of NATO (1952–57). Created baron (1947).

Isoc·ra·tes \ī-ˈsäk-rə-ˌtēz\. 436–338 B.C. Athenian orator and rhetorician. Founder (392 B.C.) and head of school in Athens; pupils included Timotheus, Ephorus, Theopompus of Chios, Isaeus, Lycurgus, and Hyperides; a leader of conservative, Panhellenic opinion, expressed in his orations written mainly for others.

Isouard \ēz-wȧr\, Nicolas. *Known as* Nicolò *or* Nicolò de Malte \ˈmȧlt\. 1775–1818. French composer, b. Malta. Composer chiefly of operas, becoming (from 1802) one of the chief composers for the Opéra-Comique, Paris; with Cherubini, Méhul, Boieldieu, etc., formed publishing firm Le Magasin de Musique (1802–11). Operas included *Artaserse* (1794), *Le Petit Page* (1800), *Michel-Ange* (1802), *Le Baiser et la quittance* (1803), *Cendrillon* (1810), *Jeannot et Colin* (1814), *Joconde* (1814).

Is·ra·el ben El·i·e·zer \ˈiz-rē-əl-ˌben-ˌel-ē-ˈā-zər\. *Known as* Baʽal Shem Tov \ˈbā(-ə)l-ˈshem-ˈtȯv\, *i.e.* Master of the Good Name, *and called by acronym* Besht \ˈbesht\. c.1700–1760. Polish Jewish religious, b. Ukraine. Employed in schools, as lime digger, innkeeper, ritual slaughterer in various places; settled (1736) in Medzhibozh, Podolia; gained reputation as healer, clairvoyant, mystic; taught the holiness of everyday life and acts, opposed rigid asceticism and traditional rituals; gained large following. Founder of Ḥasidism, emphasizing joyful spirituality.

Is·rae·li \iz-ˈrā-lē\, Isaac ben Solomon. *Arab.* Abū Ya·ʽqūb ibn Sulaymān al-Isrāʼīlī. *Called* Isaac Israeli *or* Isaac the Elder. c.832 to 855–c.932 to 955. Jewish physician and philosopher, b. Egypt. Court physician in al-Qayrawān. Regarded as father of medieval Jewish Neoplatonism; author of scientific and philosophical treatises, including *Kitāb al-ḥudūd,* renowned among Latin scholastics; also wrote 8 medical works that were translated from Arabic into Latin and claimed by Carthaginian monk Constantine (1087).

Is·ra·ëls \ˈiz-rȧ-els\, Jozef. 1824–1911. Dutch painter. Leader of Hague school of peasant genre painting; known esp. for scenes of fisherfolk; also produced portraits, watercolors, historical pictures, and etchings.

Issa. See KOBAYASHI.

Is·ser·les \ē-ˈser-les\, Moses ben Israel. *Also known as* RMA. c.1525–1572. Polish rabbi. Head of a leading yeshiva in Kraków. Author of *Mappa* (1571), commentary on and additions to Joseph Karo's *Shulḥan ʽarukh* that made it acceptable to Ashkenazic Jews.

Istria, Vincentello d'. See VINCENTELLO.

István. See STEPHEN.

Ita·ga·ki \ē-tä-gä-kē\ Taisuke. 1837–1919. Japanese politican. Military commander in Tosa; took part in Meiji Restoration (1868); government official (1868–73); resigned over government's refusal to go to war against Korea; founded (1881) Jiyūtō (Liberal) party, first political party in Japan; made count (1887); head of party (1890–1900).

Italicus, Tiberius Catius Silius. See SILIUS ITALICUS.

Italus, John. See JOHN ITALUS.

Itard \ē-tȧr\, Jean-Marc-Gaspard. 1775–1838. French physician. Military surgeon; specialist in diseases of the ear; pioneer in education of deaf-mutes and the mentally retarded. Described attempts to educate a boy found living wild in the forest in *Rapports sur le sauvage de l'Aveyron* (1801).

Ita·ya \ē-tä-yä\ Hazan. 1872–1963. Japanese potter. Known for depictions in ceramics of noble figures and as a colorist.

Itō \ē-tō\ Hirobumi. 1841–1909. Japanese politician. Made early visit to Europe as student; strong supporter of Western ideas; visited U.S. (1871) and reported a system of coinage for Japan; minister of interior (1878–82); premier (1885–88, 1892–96, 1898, 1900–01); drafted Meiji Constitution (adopted 1889) and largely responsible for establishment of National Diet (1890); founder and head (1900–03) of Rikken Seiyūkai party. Created prince (1895) after successful conduct of Chinese–Japanese War (1894–95); special adviser to emperor during Russo–Japanese War (1904–05); resident general of Korea (1905–09); assassinated by Korean nationalist.

Itō Jakuchū. *Orig.* Shun·kyō \shün-kyō\. 1716–1800. Japanese painter. Known for realistic pictures of flowers, fish, and birds, esp. fowl.

Itō Jinsai. 1627–1705. Japanese scholar and educator. Founded Kogaku school of studies, based on classical Confucianism, to oppose official Neo-Confucianism of Tokugawa regime; through students of his Kyōto school Kogidō, exerted powerful and lasting influence. Chief written work *Gōmōjigi* (1683).

I Tsung. See Chu Yu-chien under CHU family.

Itur·bi \ē-ˈtür-bē\, José. 1895–1980. Spanish pianist and conductor. Concert debut at 7; taught at Geneva Conservatory (1919–23); toured Europe, South America; to U.S. (1929) on concert tour; took up residence in U.S.; musical director, Rochester Philharmonic Orchestra (1936–44); appeared in several motion pictures.

Itur·bi·de \ē-tür-ˈbē-thā\, Agustín de. 1783–1824. Mexican soldier and emperor. Defended Valladolid (now Morelia) against revolutionary forces of Morelos (1810); took command of pro-independence army (1820) and formed alliance with rebel Guerrero; formulated Plan of Iguala (1821); forced Spanish government to capitulate in Treaty of Córdoba (1821), assuring Mexican independence. Head of provisional government; emperor, as Agustín I (1822–23); his harsh measures of repression led to revolution by Santa Anna, Guerrero, etc. Abdicated (1823); exile in Europe. Returned, and was captured and shot.

Ivan \i-ˈvȧn, *Angl* ˈī-vən\. Name of several grand princes and czars of Russia:

Ivan I. *Russ.* Ivan Danilovich. *Called* Ivan Ka·li·ta \kəl-yi-ˈtȧ\, *i.e.* Moneybag. 1304?–1341. Grand prince of Moscow (1328–41) and of Vladimir (1331–41). Son of Prince Daniel of Moscow; succeeded brother Yury; vassal of Tatars; made collector of taxes by Tatar Khan; extended boundaries of domain and increased importance of Moscow, laying foundation of Muscovite kingdom; caused metropolitan see to be transferred to Moscow (1326).

Ivan II. *Called* Ivan Kras·ny \ˈkrȧs-nəi\, *i.e.* the Red. 1326–1359. Grand prince of Moscow (1353–59). Son of Ivan I; succeeded brother Semyon; father of Dmitry Donskoy.

Ivan III Vasilyevich. *Called* Ivan the Great. 1440–1505. Grand prince (1462–1505). Son of Vasily II; continued policy of former rulers to strengthen leadership of Moscow; conquered Novgorod (1471–78) and Tver (1485) and annexed them; threw off yoke of Tatars (1480); gained further territory by conquest or by voluntary allegiance of princes; m. (1472) Sophia (Zoë), niece of last Byzantine emperor; this marriage important in establishing claim of Russian rulers as protectors of Orthodox Christianity; added two-headed eagle of Byzantine empire to arms of Muscovy; vacillated in choice of successor between son Vasily and nephew Dmitry; at length (1502) chose Vasily; twice invaded (1492, 1501) Lithuania and acquired part of it by treaty (1503).

Ivan IV Vasilyevich. *Called* Ivan the Terrible. 1530–1584. Ruler (1533–84). Son of Vasily III and grandson of Ivan III. Ruled under regency of mother (1533–38) and then of powerful boyars (1538–46); assumed control (1546) and had himself crowned czar (1547), first Russian ruler to use the title formally; m. (1547) Anastasiya Romanovna (see ROMANOV); formed advisory council of boyars (1547); convoked (1549) first national assembly (*zemski sobor*); reformed administration and sponsored new legal code (1550). Conquered Kazan and Astrakhan (1552–56); began long war (1558–82) over Livonia, at first successful but later defeated by Poland and Sweden; created inner circle of advisers, instituted campaign of terror against disfavored boyars, exacerbated by military reverses and defections; ravaged Novgorod (1570); defeated by Swedes (1578) and lost Polotsk (1579); beaten in Livonia by Stephen Báthory (1581); acquired Siberia (1581) through conquest by Cossacks under Yermak Timofeyevich; in a fit of anger killed his son Ivan (1581).

Ivan V Alekseyevich. 1666–1696. Czar (1682–96). Son of Czar Alexis I; physically and mentally weak; affairs administered by his half-sister Sophia; associated in rule with half-brother Peter, son of Alexis's second wife; became purely a figurehead (1689) when Sophia was overthrown.

Ivan VI Antonovich. 1740–1764. Czar (1740–41). Son of Anna Leopoldovna and Prince Anton Ulrich; although only eight weeks old on death of Anna Ivanovna, proclaimed emperor under regency of Biron (*q.v.*); forced to abdicate soon after Biron's overthrow; succeeded by Elizabeth; kept in prison for rest of life.

Ivan Asen. See ASEN.

Iva·nov \i-vȧ-nôf\, Lev Ivanovich. 1834–1901. Russian dancer and choreographer. Member of Imperial Ballet, St. Petersburg (from 1852); premier danseur (1869); régisseur or stage manager (1882); assistant ballet master under Petipa (1885); noted for ability to choreograph for emotional effect, esp. for corps de ballet; contributed to *Nutcracker* (1892), *Cinderella* (1893), *Swan Lake* (1895), etc.; with Cecchetti rechoreographed *Coppélia.*

Ivanov, Vsevolod Vyacheslavovich. 1895–1963. Russian writer. Served in Red army in Revolution (1917); in Petrograd associated with Romanticists of Serapion Brethren; wrote naturalistic novels later much revised to comport with Soviet critical canons. Best known novel *Armored Train 14-69* (1922).

Ivanov, Vyacheslav Ivanovich. 1866–1949. Russian poet. Published first volume of poems *Kormchiye zvyozdy* (1903), which made him chief Russian Symbolist; followed with *Cor ardens* (1911), etc.; professor, Baku (1921–24); exile in Italy (from 1924).

Iveagh, Earl of. See GUINNESS family.

Ives \ˈīvz\, Charles Edward. 1874–1954. American composer, b. Danbury, Conn. In insurance business in New York (1898–1930). As composer, known for innovative use of dissonance, polytonal harmonies, and unusual rhythms. Works, many frequently revised and many not performed for decades, included symphonies, esp. Second (1900–02), Third (1904–11; Pulitzer prize 1947), *New England Holidays* (1904–13); other orchestral or band pieces as *The Unanswered Question* (1906), *Central Park in the Dark* (1906), *First Orchestral Set* or *Three Places in New England* (1903–14); chamber works including string quartets, violin sonatas; piano works, esp. Second Piano Sonata *Concord* (1909–15); choral works including settings of poems by Whitman, Tennyson, Longfellow, Whittier, Emerson, Vachel Lindsay; songs including collection *114 Songs* (1919–24).

Ives, Frederic Eugene. 1856–1937. American inventor, b. Litchfield, Conn. Invented (1881) halftone photoengraving process; perfected optical screen process for producing halftone printing plates (1885); pioneered in color photography, making the first trichromatic halftone process printing plates (1881) and developing a process for motion pictures in natural colors (1914); invented halftone photogravure process (anticipating rotogravure), the short-tube single-objective binocular microscope, and the photochromoscope.

Ives, James Merritt. See Nathaniel CURRIER.

Ives *or* **Ivo** of Chartres. See YVES DE CHARTRES.

Iwa·ku·ra \ē-wäk-u̇r-ä\ Tomomi. Prince. *Orig. surname* Ya·su·chi·ka \yäs-u̇ch-ē-kä\. 1825–1883. Japanese politician. After adoption into Iwakura family gained position of influence at court; opposed opening of ports to foreigners and influenced emperor to veto U.S.–Japanese commerce treaty (1858); sided with imperial party and was instrumental in carrying out palace revolution that accomplished Meiji Restoration (1868); head of mission sent (1871–73) to Western countries to seek revision of treaties and to study Western administrative methods; opposed war with Korea (1873); chief councilor of emperor (1873–83).

Iwa·sa \ē-wäs-ä\ Matabei. *Orig. surname* Ara·ki \är-äk-ē\. 1578–1650. Japanese painter. Developed individual style from both Japanese and Chinese models. Noted for paintings based on Japanese literature, esp. *Tale of Genji,* and on Chinese legends; best known work a series of portraits of the Sanjūrokkasen (Thirty-Six Poets) for Tōshōgū shrine in Kawagoe.

Iwa·sa·ki \ē-wäs-äk-ē\ Yatarō. 1834–1885. Japanese businessman. Financial manager of fief of Tosa; developed shipping line (1868); expanded business, founding (1873) Mitsubishi, a finance and trading company specializing in banking, shipping, and insurance that became Japan's second largest industrial combine. His brother ¶Yanosuke (1851–1908) succeeded him as head of Mitsubishi; created baron (1896); founded Seikadō library.

Ix·tlil·xo·chitl \ˌisht-ləl-ˈshō-chit-ᵊl\. 1500?–1550. Aztec leader. Chief of Texcoco; rival of Montezuma; at war with his brother (1516) for kingdom of Texcoco; aided by Cortés (c.1520) in securing leadership of Texcoco; aided Cortés in siege of Tenochtitlán.

Iyemitsu, Iyemochi, Iyenari, Iyesada, Iyeyasu, Iyeyoshi. See TOKUGAWA family.

Iz·ard \ˈiz-ərd\, Ralph. 1742–1804. American Revolutionary leader, b. near Charleston, S.C. Lived in London (1771–76); while in Paris (1777) named commissioner to Tuscany by Congress but not received there; engaged in disputes with Benjamin Franklin, recalled (1779); member, Continental Congress (1782–83), U.S. Senate (1789–95).

Izu·mi \ē-zu̇m-ē\ Kyōka, *orig.* Kyotaro. 1873–1939. Japanese writer. Disciple of Ozaki Kōyō (1891–94). Author of stories in highly individual style, including *Yakō juhsa* (1895), *Gekashitsu* (1895), *Kōya hijiri* (1900), *Onna keizu* (1907), *Shirasagi* (1909), *Uta andon* (1910).

Izu·mo \ē-zu̇m-ō\ Okuni. 16th century. Japanese dancer. Perhaps a maid attached to the shrine at Izumo; said to have begun performing (1586) dances parodying Buddhist prayers; gathered troupe of men and women dancers; considered the founder of Kabuki art.

Iz·vol·sky \iz-ˈvȯlʸ-skəi\, Aleksandr Petrovich. Count. 1856–1919. Russian diplomat. Minister to Vatican (1890), Belgrade (1896), Munich (1897), Tokyo (1900), Copenhagen (1903); minister of foreign affairs (1906–10); negotiated treaty with Great Britain (1907) settling disputes in Persia, Tibet, Afghanistan; attempted to secure right of passage of Russian warships through Dardanelles Strait in agreement with Austria-Hungary (1908) in which he undertook to support Austrian annexation of Bosnia and Hercegovina; supported annexation, which precipitated crisis in Balkans, but blocked by Great Britain from passage right; attempted to offset Austrian influence in Balkans with Racconigi Agreement (1909) with Italy but to little effect; dismissed (1910); ambassador to France (1910–17).

J

Jā·bir ibn Ḥay·yān \\'jab-ˌir-ˌib-ən-hī-'(y)an\\, Abū Mūsā. c.721–c.815. Arab alchemist and mystic. Court physician to caliph Hārūn ar-Rashīd; author of large number of works on alchemy and metaphysics that enjoyed extremely high reputation with later alchemists; his theory of mercury and sulfur as fundamental substances contributed to later theory of phlogiston.

Ja·blo·now·ski \\yȧ-blȯ-'nȯf-skē\\, Josef Aleksander. Prince. 1711–1777. Polish patron of arts and letters. To Leipzig (1768) and established (1774) Jablonowski Scientific Foundation, which published studies on Polish history, economics, mathematics, physics, etc. (to 1939).

Ja·blon·ski \\yä-'blȯn-skē\\, Daniel Ernst. 1660–1741. German theologian. Bishop of Moravian church (1699); worked with Leibnitz for union between Lutherans and Reformed Protestants.

Ja·bo·tin·sky \\yə-(ˌ)bət-'yēn-skəi, *Angl* ˌyab-ə-'tin-skē\\, Vladimir. 1880–1940. Zionist leader. Foreign correspondent and editorial writer for Odessa newspapers (1898 ff.); adopted Zionist cause (1903); persuaded British authorities to employ Jewish volunteers in Palestine during World War I, and served in a battalion there; organized Haganah self-defense force in Palestine (1920); presided over World Union of Zionist Revisionists (1925), New Zionist Organization (1935).

Jach·mann \\'yäk-män\\, Eduard Karl Emanuel von. 1822–1887. German admiral. Commanded Prussians against Danes in naval victory near Jasmund (1864); commander in chief in North Sea (1870–74).

Jack \\'jak\\ the Ripper. Sobriquet of an unknown criminal, to whom is attributed a series of gruesome murders in the East End of London (Aug.–Nov. 1888).

Jack·ling \\'jak-liŋ, -lən\\, Daniel Cowan. 1869–1956. American mining engineer and metallurgist, b. Appleton City, Mo. Chemist and metallurgist in Colorado, Utah (1894 ff.); issued report on prospects for copper mining in Bingham Canyon, Utah, that led to formation (1905) of Utah Copper Co.; devised methods for profitable processing of low-grade porphyry copper ores.

Jacks \\'jaks\\, Lawrence Pearsall. 1860–1955. English clergyman, philosopher, and writer. Unitarian minister (from 1887); professor of philosophy (1903–31) and principal (1915–31), Manchester Coll., Oxford. Editor of *Hibbert Journal* (1902–43). Author of *Alchemy of Thought* (1910), the *Smokeover* series of allegorical stories, *My Neighbour the Universe* (1928), *Education through Recreation* (1932), *The Revolt against Mechanism* (1934), etc.

Jack·son \\'jak-sən\\, Abraham Valentine Williams. 1862–1937. American linguist, b. New York City. Professor of Indo-Iranian languages, Columbia (1895–1935). Author of *An Avesta Grammar* (1892), *Avesta Reader* (1893), *Zoroaster* (1899), *Persia Past and Present* (1906), *From Constantinople to the Home of Omar Khayyam* (1911).

Jackson, Andrew. *Called* Old Hickory. 1767–1845. Seventh president of the United States, b. Waxhaw, S.C. Adm. to N.C. bar (1787); opened law office in Nashville, Tenn. (1788); member, U.S. House of Representatives (1796–97) and U.S. Senate (1797–98). Judge, Tennessee Supreme Court (1798–1804). Major general of Tennessee militia (1802); defeated Creek Indians at Horseshoe Bend (1814); commissioned major general, U.S. army (1814); captured Pensacola, Fla. (1814); sent to defend New Orleans (1814); succeeded and became national hero (Jan. 1815); added to fame by operations against Seminole Indians (1818); involved federal government by pursuing Indians into Spanish territory and hanging two English troublemakers. Governor of Florida territory (1821). U.S. senator (1823–25). Unsuccessful Democratic candidate for president (1824); elected (1828) and reelected (1832). Outstanding features of his administration: introduction of spoils system; social scandal caused by Peggy O'Neale (see Margaret EATON) incident, which broke up Jackson's cabinet; overthrow of United States Bank by veto of its charter renewal (1832); the South Carolina nullification issue (1832–33); encouragement of Western expansion; the complete paying off of the national debt.

Jackson, Charles Thomas. 1805–1880. American chemist and geologist, b. Plymouth, Mass. Practiced medicine, Boston (1832–36); abandoned medicine for work in chemistry and mineralogy (1836). Claimed to have pointed out to S. F. B. Morse the basic principles of the electric telegraph; also claimed priority in discovery of guncotton; suggested to W. T. G. Morton (*q.v.*) the use of ether as anesthetic for extracting a tooth.

Jackson, Cyril. 1746–1819. English clergyman and scholar. Preacher at Lincoln's Inn (1779–83); dean of Christ Church, Oxford (1783–1809); noted as an educator, with George Canning and Robert Peel among his pupils.

Jackson, Frederick George. 1860–1938. British explorer. Served in Boer War and World War I. Explored various parts of the world, including the Australian deserts, Lapland and the Arctic tundra, and Africa; commanded polar expedition sent out by Alfred Harmsworth to Franz Josef Land (1894–97). Author of *The Great Frozen Land* (1895), *A Thousand Days in the Arctic* (1899), *Lure of the Unknown Lands* (1935).

Jackson, Helen Maria Hunt, *nee* Fiske. 1830–1885. American writer, b. Amherst, Mass. m. Edward Hunt (1852; d. 1863), William S. Jackson (1875). Began contributing to magazines (1865) over signatures H. H. *or* Saxe Holm \\'saks-'hō(l)m\\. Author of *Verses* (1870), *Sonnets and Lyrics* (1886), the novels *Mercy Philbrick's Choice* (1876), *Hetty's Strange History* (1877), and *Ramona* (1884); also of *A Century of Dishonor* (1881), recording government wrongs in dealing with Indians; appointed (1882) as special commissioner to investigate conditions among the Mission Indians of California.

Jackson, Henry Martin. *Called* Scoop \\'sküp\\. 1912–1983. American politician, b. Everett, Wash. Member U.S. House of Representatives (1941–53); U.S. senator from Washington (1953–83); staunch supporter of organized labor, civil rights, military spending, Vietnam War, Israel, emigration of Soviet Jewry; leader of Democratic neoconservatives; unsuccessful for Democratic Presidential nomination (1972, 1976).

Jackson, Howell Edmunds. 1832–1895. American jurist, b. Paris, Tenn. Practiced law (from 1856); U.S. senator (1881–86). Federal circuit judge (1886–91); presiding judge, U.S. Court of Appeal, Cincinnati (1891–93); associate justice, U.S. Supreme Court (1893–95).

Jackson, John. *Known as* Gentleman Jackson. 1769–1845. English boxer. Defeated Daniel Mendoza (1795) for English heavyweight championship; retired (1803); established school of self-defense in London; introduced "scientific" principles of boxing as countering, agile footwork.

Jackson, John Hughlings. 1835–1911. English neurologist. Physician to National Hospital for Paralyzed and Epileptic (1862–1906), London Hospital (1859–94); studied speech defects in brain disease; associated abnormal mental states with brain damage; identified (1863) Jacksonian epilepsy and located causative lesions in cerebral cortex (1875); confirmed Broca's location of speech center of brain (1864).

Jackson, Mahalia. 1911–1972. American singer, b. New Orleans. To Chicago (1927); sang in church choirs; began recording (1934); achieved wide attention with recording of "Move On Up a Little Higher" (1945); in recordings, radio, television, and concert appearances, won acknowledgment as finest gospel singer of her day, helping popularize gospel music among new audiences.

Jackson, Peter. 1861–1901. West Indian boxer, b. St. Croix. Won Australian heavyweight championship (1886), British Empire title (1892); because of his color, denied opportunity to box J.L. Sullivan, J.J. Corbett, or R. Fitzsimmons for world title; knocked out by J.J. Jeffries (1898).

Jackson, Robert Houghwout. 1892–1954. American jurist, b. Spring Creek, Pa. General counsel for U.S. Bureau of Internal Revenue (1934); solicitor general of the U.S. (1938–39); attorney general of the U.S. (1940–41); associate justice, U.S. Supreme Court (1941–54); chief prosecutor for U.S. at Nürnberg war crimes tribunal (1945–46).

Jackson, Sheldon. 1834–1909. American missionary and educator, b. Minaville, N.Y. Presbyterian missionary to Choctaw Indians in Indian Territory (1858–59); missionary superintendent (1859–83); to Alaska (1884); U.S. superintendent of public instruction there (1885–1908); edited *Sitka North Star* (1887–97); introduced Siberian reindeer (1891); moderator of Presbyterian General Assembly (1897).

Jackson, Shirley. 1919–1965. American writer, b. San Francisco. Author of tales involving often psychological disturbance or the supernatural, as "The Lottery"

(1948); wrote novels *The Bird's Nest* (1954), *The Haunting of Hill House* (1959), *We Have Always Lived in the Castle* (1962), etc., children's books including *Witchcraft of Salem Village* (1956), fictionalized memoirs *Life Among the Savages* (1953), *Raising Demons* (1957).

Jackson, Sir Thomas Graham. 1835–1924. English architect. Among buildings of his design were new Examination Schools and new buildings for Lincoln, Trinity, Brasenose, and Hertford colleges at Oxford; restoration of Bodleian Library; new law library and law school at Cambridge; new buildings for Eton, Rugby, Harrow, and for the Inner Temple at London; many churches.

Jackson, Thomas Jonathan. *Known as* Stone·wall \'stōn-,wȯl\ Jackson. 1824–1863. American Confederate general, b. Clarksburg, Va., now W. Va. In U.S. army (1846–52); entered Confederate service at outbreak of Civil War; brigadier general (June 1861); gained sobriquet "Stonewall" by his stand at Bull Run (July 1861); major general (Oct. 1861). Led Confederates in brilliant Shenandoah Valley campaign, gave invaluable aid to Lee in Seven Days' Battles, 2d Bull Run, Maryland campaign (1862). Mortally wounded accidentally by fire from his own troops just after routing the federal right wing at Chancellorsville (1863).

Jackson, William. *Known as* Jackson of Ex·e·ter \'ek-sət-ər\. 1730–1803. English composer. Organist and lay vicar, Exeter cathedral (1777–1803). Composed the operas *The Lord of the Manor* (1780) and *Metamorphosis* (1783); musical settings for Milton's *Lycidas,* Warton's *Ode to Fancy,* and Pope's *Dying Christian to his Soul; Twelve Songs* (1755), *Twelve Canzonets* (1770, c.1782), and other vocal music; much church music.

Jackson, William. 1737?–1795. English clergyman. Active as editor of radical daily *Public Ledger,* London; to France in support of Revolution; sent by Committee of Public Safety to Dublin (1794) to arrange cooperation of United Irishmen Society in French invasion of England; arrested, convicted of treason; suicide.

Jackson, William Henry. 1843–1942. American photographer, b. Keesville, N.Y. Photographer for U.S. Geological and Geographical Survey of the Territories (1870–78); operated studio in Denver (1879 ff.); known for photographs of Indians, Union Pacific Railroad route, landscapes esp. of Yellowstone country, Grand Tetons, Mesa Verde cliff dwellings.

Ja·cob \zhȧ-kȯb\. Family of French furniture makers including: Georges (1739–1814); among first to make extensive use of mahogany; noted for carved furniture, esp. chairs, made for Marie-Antoinette and others; made furniture for Committee of Public Safety (1793 ff.) and for Bonapartes. His son ¶François-Honoré (1770–1841) worked in firm, which became known as Jacob-Desmalter; produced furniture for Empire and for Louis XVIII. François-Honoré's son ¶Georges-Alphonse (1799–1870) headed the firm (1841–47).

Ja·cob \'jā-kəb\ of Edes·sa \i-'des-ə\. c.640–708. Syrian theologian and prelate. Bishop of Edessa (from c.684); author of biblical commentaries, Syriac homilies, canons, liturgies, etc.; revised Peshitta Old Testament; produced earliest extant Syriac grammar and introduced Greek vowels into written Syriac.

Jacob of Ser·ugh \'ser-u̇k\ *or* Sa·rug \'sär-u̇k\. 451–521. Syriac writer and prelate. Bishop of Batnan (519); author of homilies, letters (some betraying a Monophysite leaning), 760 homiletic poems on apostles, saints, martyrs, Old and New Testament incidents.

Ja·cob \zhä-kȯb\, Max. 1876–1944. French writer. Associated with Cubists and Surrealists; converted to Christianity (1909) and Roman Catholicism (1915); in semimonastic retirement (from 1921); died in concentration camp. Author of *Oeuvres mystiques et burlesques de Frère Matorel* (novel, 1911), *La Côte* (1913), *Le Cornet à dés* (Surrealist prose poems, 1917), *La Défense de Tartuffe* (1919), *Le Laboratoire central* (1920), *Les Pénitents en maillot rose* (1925), *Le Sacrifice impérial* (1929), *Le Bal masqué* (1932), *Ballades* (1938), etc.

Ja·cob \'jā-kəb\, Violet, *nee* Ken·ne·dy-Er·skine \'ken-ə-dē-'ər-skən\. 1863–1946. Scottish novelist and poet. m. A.O. Jacob. Author of novels *The Interloper* (1904), *Flemington* (1911); verse *Songs of Angus* (1915), *Bonnie Joann* (1921), *Northern Lights* (1927).

Ja·co·ba \yä-kō-bä\. *Known also as* Jacqueline of Hai·naut \en-ō\. 1401–1436. Countess of Holland, Zeeland, and Hainaut. Daughter of William, Count of Zeeland and Holland and of Hainaut and Duke of Bavaria; m. John of Touraine, dauphin of France (1415; d. 1417); with popular support fought against John of Bavaria, who was recognized by King Sigismund of Germany as her father's successor (1417–18); m. Duke John IV of Brabant (1418), who mortgaged Holland and Zeeland to John of Bavaria (1420); repudiated husband, went to England (1421); m. Humphrey, Duke of Gloucester (1422; marriage declared illegal by pope, 1428); with Humphrey and an army invaded Hainaut (1424) but, deserted soon after by Humphrey, captured and held by Philip the Good of Burgundy; escaped (1425); made treaty (1428) with Philip in which she retained title of countess but relinquished actual sovereignty to him; forced to abdicate title (1433) after marrying a Zeeland noble against Philip's wish; later duchess in Bavaria and Countess of Ostrevant.

Ja·cob ben Ash·er \'jā-kəb-ben-'ash-ər\. 1269?–?1340. Jewish scholar, b. Germany. Son of Asher ben Jehiel; to Spain (1303); best known for *Arba'a turim* (printed 1475), code of post-Talmudic Jewish law that remained a standard authority for over two centuries.

Ja·co·bi \jə-'kō-bē\, Abraham. 1830–1919. American physician, b. Hartum, Westphalia. To U.S. (1853); professor, N.Y. Medical Coll. (1860–65), U. of City of N.Y. (1865–70), Coll. of Physicians and Surgeons (1870–1902); established first children's clinic in U.S. (1860); helped found (1862) *American Journal of Obstetrics;* considered founder of pediatrics in U.S. His wife (m. 1873) ¶Mary Corinna Put·nam \'pət-nəm\ (1842–1906), daughter of George Palmer Putnam, was also a physician; associate of Elizabeth Blackwell at Woman's Med. Coll., N.Y. (1871–89). Author of *The Value of Life* (1879), *Essays on Hysteria, Brain-Tumor, etc.* (1888), *"Common Sense" Applied to Woman Suffrage* (1894).

Ja·co·bi \yä-'kō-bē\, Carl Gustav Jacob. 1804–1851. German mathematician. Professor, Königsberg (1827–44), Berlin (1844–51); developed, independently of N.H. Abel, theory of elliptic functions (1829); contributed also to differential equations, dynamics, theory of determinants. Author of *Fundamenta Nova Theoriae Functionum Ellipticarum* (1829), *De Formatione et Proprietatibus Determinantium* (1841), *Vorlesungen über Dynamik* (1866).

Jacobi, Friedrich Heinrich. 1743–1819. German philosopher and writer. Member of council of duchies of Jülich and Berg (1772 ff.); privy councilor in Munich (1779); professor (from 1805), president of Bavarian Academy of Science (1807–12), Munich. With Wieland founded (1773) periodical *Der teutsche Mercur;* evolved, in reaction to rationalism of Spinoza and Kant, philosophy of immediately conveyed truths, known as *Gefühlsphilosophie* (philosophy of feeling). Author of philosophical novels *Eduard Allwills Briefsammlung* (1776), *Woldemar* (1777); treatises *Über die Lehre des Spinoza* (1785), *David Hume über den Glauben* (1787), *Jacobi an Fichte* (1799), *Über das Unternehmen des Kritizismus* (1802). His brother ¶Johann Georg (1740–1814), lyric poet; professor at Halle (1766–68) and Freiburg (1784); coeditor of *Iris* (1774–76), to which Gleim, Goethe, and others contributed.

Ja·cobs \'jā-kəbz\, Joseph. 1854–1916. British scholar and writer, b. Sydney, Australia. Devoted himself to writing and editorial work in England and in U.S. (from 1900). Author of *Earliest English Version of the Fables of Bidpai* (1888), *Fables of Aesop* (1889), *English Fairy Tales* (1890), *The Jews of Angevin England* (1893), *Studies in Biblical Archaeology* (1894), etc. Revising editor, *Jewish Encyclopedia,* in New York (from 1900).

Jacobs, William Wymark. 1863–1943. English writer. Author esp. of sea stories, as *Many Cargoes* (1896), *The Skipper's Wooing* (1897), *Sea Urchins* (1898), *A Master of Craft* (1900), *Captains All* (1905), *Night Watches* (1914), *Deep Waters* (1919); best known for story "The Monkey's Paw" (1902; dramatized with L.N. Parker, 1903).

Ja·cob·sen \'yȧ-kȯp-sən\, Arne. 1902–1971. Danish architect and designer. Leading exponent of severe modernist style. Buildings included Bellavista housing development near Copenhagen (1933), group of houses at Søholm (1950–55), Jesperson Building, Copenhagen (1955), Rødovre town hall (1954–56), SAS skyscraper, Copenhagen (1959), St. Catherine's Coll., Oxford (1964); known also for furniture designs as three-legged stacking chair (1952), "egg" chair (1959).

Jacobsen, Jens Peter. 1847–1885. Danish novelist and poet. Introduced and led Naturalist movement in Denmark; influenced by Darwin and Brandes. Works included story "Mogens" (1872), novels *Fru Marie Grubbe* (1876), *Niels Lyhne* (1880).

Jacobsz, Lucas. See LUCAS VAN LEYDEN.

Ja·co·bus de Vo·rag·i·ne \jə-'kō-bəs-də-vō-'raj-ə-nē\. 1228 or 1230–1298. Italian prelate and writer. Entered Dominican order (1244); provincial of Lombardy (1267–78, 1281–86); archbishop of Genoa (1292–98). Author of a chronicle of Genoa to 1296 and of the celebrated *Legenda aurea* (*Golden Legend*).

Jacopo da Ponte. See Jacopo BASSANO.

Ja·co·po del·la Quer·cia \'yäk-ō-pō-dāl-lä-'kwer-chä\. *In full* Jacopo di Pie·tro d'Agno·lo della Quercia \-'pyā-trō-dän-'yō-lō-\. c.1374–1438. Sienese sculptor. Chief master of Quattrocento Sienese sculpture; works included tomb of Ilaria del Caretto in Lucca cathedral, *Fonte Gaia* in Siena, bronze relief *Zacharias in the Temple* in baptistery of Siena cathedral, portal of S. Petronio, Bologna.

Ja·co·po·ne da To·di \,yäk-ō-'pō-nā-dä-'tō-dē\. *Orig.* Ja·co·po dei Be·ne·det·ti \'yä-kō-pō-,dā-ē-,bā-nā-'dāt-tē\. *Lat.* Ja·co·bus de Ben·e·dic·tis \jə-'kō-bəs-dē-,ben-ē-'dik-tēs\. c.1230–1306. Italian religious and poet, b. Todi. Of noble birth; practiced law until sudden adoption of ascetic life (1268); became Franciscan lay brother (1278); excommunicated and imprisoned (1298–1303) for criticisms of Pope Boniface VIII; released by Benedict XI. Author of over 100 mystical poems, mostly in vernacular; probable author of *Stabat mater dolorosa.*

Ja·co·tot \zhá-kó-tō\, Jean-Joseph. 1770–1840. French educator. Subdirector and professor, École Polytechnique, Dijon (1795 ff.); served in Napoleonic armies; deputy (1815); lecturer at Louvain (1818). Developed an egalitarian "universal" method of education in *Enseignement universel* (1823).

Jac·quard \zhá-kár\, Joseph-Marie. 1752–1834. French inventor. Invented (1801) Jacquard loom, first to include all weaving motions and first to weave figured patterns, using punched cards to control weaving; awarded patent and medal by Napoléon (1804); loom declared public property, with a pension and royalty going to Jacquard (1806).

Jacque \zhák\, Charles-Émile. 1813–1894. French painter and engraver. Member of the Barbizon school; well known for his paintings of sheep, and for his etchings of scenes from rural life.

Jacqueline of Hainaut. See JACOBA.

Jac·que·mart \zhák-már\, Nélie. 1840–1912. French painter. m. Édouard André (1881). Excelled in genre paintings; established by bequest in her will the Musée Jacquemart-André in Paris.

Jac·que·mont \zhák-mōⁿ\, Victor. 1801–1832. French botanist and traveler. In India (1828–32), collecting specimens of plants new to Europe; remembered for his *Correspondance* (1834) and his *Voyage dans l'Inde* (edited by Guizot, 1836–44).

Jacques \zhák\, Jules Marie Alphonse. Baron de Dix·mude \də-dēks-mü̅d\. 1858–1928. Belgian soldier and explorer. In Belgian Congo (1887–1905), founded Albertville; in World War I commanded 12th brigade in its defense of Dixmude (1914) and 3d division, called the Iron Division, which repulsed the German assault at Merckem (1918).

Jacques de Vi·try \-də-vē-tre\. c.1170–1240. French prelate and historian. Preached against the Albigensians; bishop of Acre (1216), and prominent in the Fifth Crusade; cardinal bishop of Tusculum (1228). Author of sermons, letters constituting a principal source for knowledge of the Fifth Crusade, and *Historia orientalis et occidentalis,* valuable source book of 13th-century history and customs.

Jad·wi·ga \yád-'vē-gá\. *Ger.* Hed·wig \'hāt-vik\. 1373 or 1374–1399. Queen of Poland (1384–99). Daughter of Louis the Great of Hungary and Poland; married (1386) Władysław II.

Jae·ger \'yeg-ər\, Hans Henrik. 1854–1910. Norwegian writer. A leader of "Bohème" group of urban, unconventional artists. Author of highly naturalistic novels, esp. *Fra Kristiania-Bohêmen* (1885), which was suppressed for advocacy of free love and became cause célèbre; after brief jail terms, to Paris.

Ja'far. See BARMAKIDS; MĪR JA'FAR.

Ja·'far al-'As·ka·rī \'jaf-ar-ül-as-kar-'ē\. 1887–1936. Arab soldier, b. Baghdad. Served in Ottoman army; captured in Egypt in World War I; joined Ḥusayn ibn 'Alī of Mecca; organized Ḥusayn's Arab army and led it in revolt against Ottoman rule; first minister of defense of Iraq (1920–22, 1930, 1931–32); prime minister (1923, 1926–28); minister of foreign affairs (1926–28, 1931–32).

Ja'far ibn Mu·ham·mad \-mü-'kam-mad\. *Also known as* Ja'far aṣ-Ṣā·diq \-əs-'säd-ēk\. 699/700 or 702/703–765. Islāmic leader. Great-grandson of the fourth caliph, 'Alī, founder of Shī'ism; recognized as sixth imām of Shī'ite Muslims and last imām to be acknowledged by all Shī'ite sects; reputed a teacher of great wisdom, his pupils including Abū Ḥanīfah, Mālik ibn Anas, Wāṣil ibn 'Ata'.

Jagatai. See CHAGATAI.

Jä·ger \'yeg-ər\, Johann. *Known by Lat. name* Cro·tus Ru·bi·a·nus \'krōt-əs-,rü-bē-'ā-nəs\. 1480?–c.1539. German Humanist. Head of monastery school at Fulda (1510); visited Bologna and Rome (1517–20). Accepted principles of Reformation; received Luther at Erfurt (1521), where he was rector of the university. Reentered Roman Catholic church (c.1530); canon in Halle. Described return to Catholicism in *Apologia* (1531); contributed satirical letters on scholasticism and monasticism to first part of *Epistolae obscurorum virorum* (1515).

Ja·giel·lon \yäg-'yel-ón\. Name of second Polish dynasty (1386–1572), succeeding the Piast; so called from Jogaila (*Pol.* Jagiełło), Duke of Lithuania who married (1386) Jadwiga, queen of Poland, and ruled as Władysław II. Subsequent rulers were Władysław III, Casimir IV, John I Albert, Alexander I, Sigismund I and II (*qq.v.*). See also ULÁSZLÓ II of Hungary. Succeeded by Vasa dynasty, formed from union of John III Vasa of Sweden and Catherine, daughter of Sigismund I.

Jahān, Shāh. See SHĀH JAHĀN.

Ja·hān·gīr \jə-'hän-gēr\, *i.e.* Conqueror of the World. *Orig.* Sa·līm \sä-'lēm\. 1569–1627. Emperor of India (1605–27), fourth of the Mughal dynasty. Son of Akbar the Great; rebelled against his father (1599), but reconciled; after accession carried on long wars in Deccan; added little territory to empire; visited by first English envoys, Capt. William Hawkins (1609–11) and ambassador Sir Thomas Roe (1615–18); much influenced by his empress (m. 1611; d. 1645) ¶Mihr-un-Ni·sā' \'mir-ún-nē-'sä\, *known as* Nūr Ja·hān \'nür-jə-'hän\, *i.e.* Light of the World *or* Nūr Ma·hāl \-mə-'häl\, *i.e.* Light of the Palace; faced with frequent rebellions (1622–26) by his son Shāh Jahān; held captive (1626).

Ja·hān Shāh *or* **Ji·hān Shāh** \jə-'hän-'shä, -'shó\. d. 1467. Turkic ruler. Leader of Kara Koyunlu federation of Turkmen tribes in Azerbaijan (c.1438–67); extended rule over Iraq, Fārs, Isfahan (1453); seized Herāt (1458); defeated and killed by Uzun Hasan and the Ak Koyunlu.

Jā·hiẓ, al- \əl-'jäk-iz\. *In full* Abū 'Uthmān 'Amr ibn Baḥr ibn Maḥbūb al-Jāḥiẓ. c.776–868 or 869. Muslim theologian and writer. Author of works on theology, politics, of *Kitāb al-Bayān we al-tabyīn* on composition and style, of *Kitāb al-bukhalā'* collecting tales of avarice, and of other works celebrated for masterful prose style.

Jahn \'yän\, Friedrich Ludwig. 1778–1852. German educator. Ardent nationalist; opened in Berlin (1811) a *Turnplatz,* or athletic field, first of many throughout Germany; used his system of training to inspire patriotism in youth and a spirit of resistance to Napoleonic domination; led Lützow Corps in Napoleonic war (1813–15); imprisoned in reaction (1819–25); member of Frankfurt assembly (1848). Known as *Turnvater,* father of gymnastics.

Jahn, Otto. 1813–1869. German philologist, archaeologist, and critic. Professor, Greifswald, Leipzig, Bonn; pioneer in introducing the scientific philological method into classical archaeology and opponent of the genealogical and symbolical schools of interpretation. Author of archaeological and philological works and a biography of Mozart (1856–59).

Jaime. See JAMES.

Ja·kob·son \'yäk-əb-sən\, Roman. 1896–1982. American linguist, b. Moscow, Russia. Professor at Higher Dramatic School, Moscow (1920–33), Masarykova U., Brno, Czechoslovakia (1933–39); to U.S. (1941); professor at Columbia U. (1943–49), Harvard (1950–67), M.I.T. (1957–67). A leading authority on Slavic languages; principal founder of Prague school of structural linguistics and of phonology. Author of *Remarques sur l'évolution phonologique du russe* (1929), *Kharakteristichke yevrazi-yskogo yazykovogo soyuza* (1931), *Kindersprache* (1941), *Aphasie und allgemeine Lautgesetze* (1941), *Preliminaries to Speech Analysis* (with G. Fant and M. Halle, 1952), *Fundamentals of Language* (1956), etc.

Ja·lāl ad-Dīn ar-Rū·mī \jə-'läl-üd-'dēn-ər-'rü-mē\. *Sometimes called* Maw·lā·nā \maú-'lä-nä\. c.1207–1273. Persian poet. Teacher in Konya; profoundly influenced by the mystic Shams ad-Dīn of Tabriz; on death of Shams began writing poetry; notably influenced by music, natural rhythms; often danced while reciting verses to disciples or amanuenses; acknowledged as greatest Ṣūfī poet; after his death his disciples were organized by Sulṭān Walad into fraternity of Mawlawīyah, known in West as Whirling Dervishes. Principal verse works the *Dīvān-e Shams* on mystical love and *Masnavī-ye Ma'navī* on aspects of Ṣūfism.

Jalāl ad-Dīn Ming·bur·nu \-miŋ-'bür-nü\. d. 1231. Last of Khwārezm-Shāhs (1220–31). Son of 'Alā' ad-Dīn; defeated Mongols at Parwandarah but driven into India by Genghis Khan (1221); failed to regain former territories; defeated and lands taken by Mongols (1231).

Jalāl-ud-Dīn Fī·rūz Khal·jī \-üd-'dēn-fir-'üz-kal-'jē\. d. 1296. Indian ruler. Established as sultan in Delhi (1290) on collapse of Slave dynasty; founded Khaljī dynasty (1290–1320); murdered by his son-in-law Jūnā Khān, who succeeded as 'Alā'-ud-Dīn.

Jalāl ud-Dīn Muḥammad. See AKBAR.

Ja·loux \zhá-lü\, Edmond. 1878–1949. French novelist and critic. Novels included *L'Agonie de l'amour* (1902), *Le Reste est silence* (1909), *Fumées dans la campagne* (1918), *Les Profondeurs de la mer* (1922), *O toi que j'eusse aimée* (1927), *La Grenade mordue* (1934); criticism *L'Esprit des livres* (1923–31), *Du rêve à la réalité* (1932), *Visages français* (1954).

Ja·māl ad-Dīn al-Af·ghā·nī \jə-'mäl-üd-'dēn-ül-af-'gä-nē\. *In full* Jamāl ad-Dīn al-Afghānī as-Sayyid Muḥammad ibn Ṣafdar al-Ḥusayn. 1838–1897. Muslim political agitator and journalist. Traveled widely in Islāmic world; confidential adviser to Moḥammad A'ẓam Khān in Kābul (1866–68), ousted by Shīr 'Alī; deported from Istanbul on suspicion of heresy (1871); in Egypt (1871–79) became center of loose group of radicals and nationalists; deported; in Paris (1883 ff.) helped publish anti-British newspaper; visited Russia several times; to Iran (c.1889); deported (1892), in revenge for which he instigated murder of Nāser od-Dīn Shāh (1896); died in Istanbul. One of leading contributors to Pan-Islāmism.

James \'jāmz\. Saint. *Known also as* James the Great *and* James, son of Zeb·e·dee \'zeb-ə-(,)dē\. d. c.44 A.D. One of the twelve Christian apostles. After preaching Christianity in Spain, he returned to Judea where he was put to death at order of Herod Agrippa I; according to Spanish tradition, his body was miraculously translated to Spain, eventually to Compostela (Santiago de Compostela), which became a famous center of pilgrimage; hence, sometimes known as St. James of Com·pos·te·la \,käm-pə-'stā-lə, -'stel-ə\.

James. Saint. *Known also as* James, son of Al·phae·us \'al-fē-əs\. 1st century A.D. One of the twelve Christian apostles. Brother or father of St. Judas.

James. Saint. d. c.62 A.D. Christian leader. Regarded by St. Paul as an apostle, although not one of original 12; believed variously to have been brother, stepbrother, or cousin of Jesus, after a biblical passage that calls him "the Lord's brother"; sometimes identified with St. James, son of Alphaeus. Leader of Christians in Jerusalem; gained sobriquet "the Just" for pious observance of Jewish law; put to death at instance of high priest Ananus. Reputed author of New Testament Epistle of James.

James. *Span.* Jai·me \'kī-mā\. Name of two kings of Aragon:

James I. *Called* el Con·quis·ta·dor \el-kōn-kē-stä-'thōr\, *i.e.* the Conqueror. 1208–1276. King of Aragon and Catalonia (1214–76). Son of Peter II; assumed throne under protection of Knights Templars; under regency (1214–27); conquered Balearic Islands (1229–35); conquered Saracen kingdom of Valencia (1233–38) and made treaty (1244) with Alfonso X of Castile dividing new territory; by Treaty of Corbeil (1258) abandoned claims to southern France; in later years suppressed rebellious Moors of Murcia, undertook unsuccessful crusade (1269).

James II. 1264–1327. King of Aragon (1291–1327). Son of Peter III; made king of Sicily (1285); succeeded brother Alfonso III in Aragon (1291); exchanged Sicily for Corsica and Sardinia (1295).

James. Name of three kings of Cyprus:

James I. 1334–1398. King of Cyprus and Jerusalem (1382–98) and of Armenia (1393–98). Succeeded nephew Peter II.

James II. *Called* the Bastard. 1440–1473. King of Cyprus, Jerusalem, and Armenia (1460–73). Natural son of John II; regained Famagusta from Genoa (1464); m. (1472) Caterina Cornaro (*q.v*), who succeeded him.

James III. 1473–1474. King (1473–74). Posthumous son of James II; titular king only.

James. Name of two kings of Great Britain, of house of Stuart:

James I. 1566–1625. King of Scotland as James VI (1567–1625) and of Great Britain as James I (1603–25). Son of Mary, Queen of Scots, and Henry Stewart, Lord Darnley; great-great-grandson of Henry VII of England through Henry's daughter Margaret, queen of James IV of Scotland. After succession of regents (Moray, Lennox, Mar, Morton), ruled Scotland (from 1581) with aid of two favorites, James Stewart, Earl of Arran, and Duke of Lennox; seized by Protestant nobles in Raid of Ruthven (1582) and forced to give up his favorites; escaped (1583) but compelled by Protestant nobles to make treaty of Berwick with England (1586). m. Anne, daughter of king of Denmark (1589). Succeeded (1594) in curbing powers of great Roman Catholic nobles of Scotland and centralizing power in monarchy. Succeeded to English throne at death of Queen Elizabeth (1603); sought to assert divine right of kings; alienated Scottish Presbyterian sentiment by instituting episcopacy (1612) and ritualism, and English nonconformist sentiment by severity and rudeness to Puritan divines at Hampton Court conference (1604); his severity toward Roman Catholics engendered Gunpowder Plot (1605); disputed frequently with Parliament, esp. over revenues, and in period 1612–21 summoned only the Addled Parliament (1614), financing lavish court by sale of monopolies; in foreign policy much under influence of Spanish ambassador Gondomar. Aspired to literary fame; published works in verse and prose, including famous *Counterblaste to Tobacco* (1604). During reign, a group of scholars prepared new version of Bible called in his honor King James Bible (1611).

James II. 1633–1701. King of England, Scotland, and Ireland (1685–88). Son of Charles I and Henrietta Maria; created duke of York (1634); in exile (1648–60) served in French army under Turenne. At Restoration, became lord high admiral of England (1660) till forced by Test Act to resign (1673); received grant of New Netherland (1664); won victory over de Ruyter (1672); accepted Roman Catholic faith (1668 or 1669) but continued friendly to Anglican church; retired to Continent during national furor over Popish Plot; object of attempt by House of Commons to exclude him from succession to throne (1678–81); as high commissioner in Scotland inflicted cruelties upon Covenanters (1679–80); resumed direction of naval affairs (1684). Succeeded to throne on death of his brother Charles II (1685); began almost at once to show special favor to Roman Catholics; by appointments, gave evidence of intention to restore powers to this church; published Declaration of Indulgence, providing for liberty of conscience for all denominations (1687); aroused public fear of Roman Catholic tyranny, resulting in English nobles offering throne to his son-in-law William of Orange; escaped to France (Dec. 1688) after William had landed in England; landed in Ireland (1689), but was decisively defeated by William at battle of the Boyne (July 1, 1690).

James. Name of six kings of Scotland:

James I. 1394–1437. King (1406–37). Son of Robert III. Sent by father to France for safety (1406), captured on way by English seamen and held prisoner by Henry IV; lodged at Windsor and well treated, after accession of Henry V to English throne (1413); accompanied Henry on French campaign (1420–22). Released (1423) after negotiations by Scottish leaders; crowned king of Scotland at Scone (1424); attempt to suppress great feudal lords of Scotland led to plots against his life; murdered at Perth by Sir Robert Graham at instigation of Walter Stewart, Earl of Atholl. Gained reputation as poet by *The Kingis Quair,* allegorical poem of courtly love.

James II. 1430–1460. King (1437–60). Son of James I. Minority marked by bitter conflicts between great Scottish families; assumed control of government (1449); executed his guardian Sir Alexander Livingstone (1450) for having expelled queen mother from joint guardianship; continued father's policy of suppressing great feudal lords; stabbed to death 8th Earl of Douglas, who conspired against him (1452), and attainted James, 9th earl, and confiscated his properties, along with those of Earl of Moray; killed by accidental bursting of a cannon during siege of Roxburgh Castle.

James III. 1452–1488. King (1460–88). Son of James II. During minority, government in hands of Mary of Gueldres, then James Kennedy, then the unscrupulous Lord Boyd of Kilmarnock, high justiciar (d. 1469?); assumed control (1469); continued policy designed to break power of great nobles; arrested his brothers Alexander, Duke of Albany, and John, Earl of Mar (1479); held in custody by Scottish nobles at outbreak of war following Alexander's escape to England and recognition (1482) by Edward IV as king of Scotland; after Alexander, with aid of English troops, had captured Berwick and marched to Edinburgh, favored peace with English; in resultant rebellion among his nobles, defeated in battle near Stirling and murdered shortly afterward.

James IV. 1473–1513. King (1488–1513). Son of James III; m. (1503) Margaret, daughter of Henry VII of England, a union which led ultimately to succession of member of Stuart house to English throne. After disputes with Henry VIII, gathered army and invaded England; defeated and killed at Flodden Hill (Sept. 9).

James V. 1512–1542. King (1513–42). Son of James IV and Margaret. During minority, regency exercised by mother and, later, by Duke of Albany; proclaimed by queen mother and Parliament competent to rule (1524) on retirement of Albany; held prisoner by Archibald Douglas, Earl of Angus, in turn with other nobles (1525–28); assumed control (1528); introduced reforms designed to protect people from oppression by nobles; waged war on England; defeated at Solway Moss (Nov. 24, 1542) and died soon thereafter. Succeeded by Mary, Queen of Scots (*q.v.*), his week-old daughter by second wife (m. 1538), Mary of Guise.

James VI. See JAMES I of Great Britain.

James, Daniel, Jr., *nicknamed* Chap·pie \'chap-ē\. 1920–1978. American air force officer, b. Pensacola, Fla. Entered Army Air Corps (1943); fighter pilot and instructor; combat service in Korea and Vietnam; brigadier general (1969); general, commander of North American Air Defense Command (1975–78). First black 4-star officer in U.S. military service.

James, George Payne Rainsford. 1799–1860. English novelist and historical writer. Prolific author of historical romances including *Richelieu* (1829), *Philip Augustus* (1831), *Henry Masterton* (1832), *The Gypsy* (1835), *Attila* (1837), *Agincourt* (1844).

James, Henry. 1811–1882. American philosopher and author, b. Albany, N.Y. Influenced by Swedenborgianism and Fourierism. Author of *Christianity the Logic of Creation* (1857), *Relation to Life* (1863), *The Secret of Swedenborg* (1869), *Society the Redeemed Form of Man* (1879), etc.

James, Henry. 1843–1916. American writer, b. New York City. Son of Henry James (1811–1882). Devoted himself to writing from about 1865; contributor to *Nation, Atlantic, Galaxy* (1865–69). Resident of London, England (from 1876); naturalized British citizen (1915). Author of novels *Roderick Hudson* (1876), *The American* (1877), *The Europeans* (1878), *Daisy Miller* (1879), *An International Episode* (1879), *The Portrait of a Lady* (1881), *Washington Square* (1881), *The Bostonians* (1886), *The Princess Casamassima* (1886), *The Reverberator* (1888), *The Tragic Muse* (1890), *The Spoils of Poynton* (1897), *What Maisie Knew* (1897), *In the Cage* (1898), *The Awkward Age* (1899), *The Sacred Fount* (1901), *The Wings of the Dove* (1902), *The Ambassadors* (1903), *The Golden Bowl* (1904); shorter fiction *A Passionate Pilgrim* (1875), *The Madonna of the Future* (1879), *Siege of London* (1883), *The Author of Beltraffio* (1885), *The Aspern Papers* (1888), *The Real Thing* (1893), *The Private Life* (1893), *Embarrassments* (1896), *The Two Magics* (containing *The Turn of The Screw,* 1898), *The Better Sort* (1903), *The Finer Grain* (1910); essays and criticism, as *Transatlantic Sketches* (1875), *French Poets and Novelists* (1878), *Portraits of Places* (1883), *The Art of Fiction* (1884), *English Hours* (1905), *The American Scene* (1907), *Italian Hours* (1909); biography, as *Life of Hawthorne* (1880), *William Wetmore Story* (1903); and autobiographical *A Small Boy and Others* (1913), *Notes of a Son and Brother* (1914).

James, Jesse Woodson. 1847–1882. American outlaw, b. near Kearney, Mo. Member of pro-Confederate guerilla band in Civil War; led (from c.1867) gang comprising brother Frank, Younger brothers, and others, in career of train and bank robbing; nearly captured in disastrous attempt on bank at Northfield, Minn. (1876); treacherously murdered for reward by one of his band at St. Joseph, Mo.

James, Marquis. 1891–1955. American journalist and author, b. Springfield, Mo. On staff of various newspapers, *American Legion Monthly, New Yorker;* writer of much pulp fiction. Author of *The Raven, a Biography of Sam Houston* (1929, Pulitzer prize), and a biography of Andrew Jackson comprising *The Border Captain* (1933), *Portrait of a President* (1937, Pulitzer prize).

James, Montague Rhodes. 1862–1936. British scholar. Provost of King's Coll., Cambridge (1905–18); provost of Eton (from 1918). Among his works were commentaries on biblical texts, catalogues of manuscripts in several libraries, lectures on antiquarian subjects, and *Ghost Stories of an Antiquary* (1905–11), *Twelve Medieval Ghost Stories* (1922), etc.

James, William. 1842–1910. American psychologist and philosopher, b. New York City. Son of Henry James (1811–1882) and brother of Henry James (1843–1916). Taught anatomy, physiology, and hygiene, Harvard (from 1872); professor of philosophy (from 1881). Known esp. as one of the founders of pragmatism. Author of *The Principles of Psychology* (1890), *The Will to Believe and Other Essays* (1897), *The Varieties of Religious Experience* (1902), *Pragmatism* (1907), *The Meaning of Truth* (1909), *A Pluralistic Universe* (1909), *Some Problems in Philosophy* (1911), *Essays in Radical Empiricism* (1912).

James Edward. *In full* James Francis Edward Stu·art \ˈst(y)ü-ərt, ˈst(y)u̇(-ə)rt \. *Known as* the Old Pretender. 1688–1766. Claimant to British throne. Son of James II and Mary of Modena; reared in French exile; proclaimed James III (VIII of Scotland) by Louis XIV and Jacobite followers on death of father (1701); attainted by Parliament (1701); failed in attempt to land in Scotland (1708); fought with French in War of Spanish Succession; landed at Peterhead, Aberdeen, during Earl of Mar's Jacobite uprising (1715) but was driven out by Duke of Argyll (1716); passed remainder of life in or near Rome under patronage of the pope.

Jame·son \ˈjām-sən\, Anna Brownell, *nee* Mur·phy \ˈmər-fē\. 1794–1860. Irish writer. m. Robert Jameson (1825). Published *Diary of an Ennuyée* (1826), *Characteristics of Shakespeare's Women* (1832), *Poetry of Sacred and Legendary Art* (1848), *Legends of the Monastic Orders* (1850), etc.

Jameson, John Franklin. 1859–1937. American historian, b. near Boston. Professor, Brown U. (1888–1901), U. of Chicago (1901–05); director, department of historical research, Carnegie Institution of Washington, D.C. (1905–28); chief, division of manuscripts, Library of Congress (1928–37). A founder of American Historical Association (1884). Author of *Dictionary of United States History* (1894), *The American Revolution Considered as a Social Movement* (1926), etc.

Jameson, Sir Leander Starr. *Known as* Doctor Jameson. 1853–1917. South African physician and statesman, b. Edinburgh. To Kimberley, South Africa (1878) and practiced medicine; became friend of Cecil Rhodes, and was employed by Rhodes in various negotiations with natives, notably with the Matabele (Ndebele) chief Lobengula; explored Mashonaland (1891) and was made its administrator; authority extended to Matabele territory (1893). Led Jameson Raid (Dec. 1895), abortive attempt to overthrow Boer government of Transvaal; forced to surrender to General Cronjé (Jan. 1896); sent to England and imprisoned for a short time. Returned to South Africa and entered Cape legislature (1900); prime minister of Cape Colony (1904–08); founded Unionist party (1910) and led it in opposition (1910–12).

Ja·met \zhȧ-me\, Marie. *Known as* Marie-Augustine de la Com·pas·sion \də-lȧ-kō^{n}-päs-yō^{n}\. 1820–1893. French religious. A founder of the Little Sisters of the Poor, and superior of the order (from 1843).

Jā·mī \ˈjä-mē\. *In full* Mowlanā Nūr od-Dīn ʼAbd or-Raḥmān ebn Aḥmad. 1414–1492. Persian poet and mystic. Despite numerous offers of court positions, passed most of life in Herāt; gained great reputation as scholar and mystic. Prose works included commentaries and mystical treatise *Lavāyeh;* verse included philosophical and Ṣūfī expositions, as compendium *Haft Owrang.*

Ja·mie·son \ˈjā-mə-sən, ˈjam-ə-, ˈjem-ə-, ˈjim-ə-\, John. 1759–1838. Scottish clergyman, antiquary, and lexicographer. Compiled *Etymological Dictionary of the Scottish Language* (1808).

Jam·i·son \ˈjam-ə-sən\, Cecilia Viets, *nee* Da·kin \ˈdā-kən\. 1837–1909. American painter and author, b. Yarmouth, N.S. To Boston as a young girl; m. 2d Samuel Jamison (1878; d. 1902). Author of romances and juveniles including *Something To Do* (1871), *Woven of Many Threads* (1872), *My Bonnie Lass* (1877), *Lady Jane* (1891), *Thistledown* (1903), *The Penhallow Family* (1905); painted portraits of Longfellow, Agassiz, etc.

Jammes \zhȧm\, Francis. 1868–1938. French poet and novelist. Among his books of verse in manner of Naturism, a reaction against Symbolism, were *De l'Angélus de l'aube à l'Angélus du soir* (1898), *Le Deuil des primevères* (1901), *Le Triomphe de la vie* (1902), *Les Géorgiques chrétiennes* (1911–12), *Quatre livres de quatrains* (1923–25); prose works included *Clara d'Ellébeuse* (1899), *Le Roman du lièvre* (1903), *Pomme d'anis* (1904), *Cloches pour deux mariages* (1924), etc.

Jam·nit·zer \ˈyäm-nit-sər\, Wenzel. 1508–1585. German goldsmith. Conducted a workshop with his brother Albrecht (until 1550) and later with his sons and sons-in-law; court goldsmith to Charles V, Ferdinand I, Maximilian II (from 1564), and Rudolf II. His grandson ¶Christoph (1563–1618) designed ornamental works and published *Neuw Grotteszken Buch* (1610) containing 63 fantastic engravings.

Jan. See JOHN.

Jan of Leiden. See Jan BEUCKELSON.

Ja·ná·ček \ˈyä-nä-chek, *Angl* ˈyän-ə-ˌchek\, Leoš. 1854–1928. Czech composer. Choir director in Brno (1873–74, 1875–79); founded and directed (1881–1920) organ school in Brno; professor, Prague Conservatory (1919–25). A leading exponent of musical nationalism; deeply influenced by Moravian folk music. Composed operas *Šárka* (1887–88, performed 1925), *Jenůfa* (1904; orig. title *Její pastorkyňa*), *Výlet pana Broučka do měsíce* (1908–17), *Výlet pana Broučka do XV století* (1917), *Příhody Lišky Bystroušky* (1924), *Věc Makropulos* (1926), *Z mrtvého domu* (1930); ballet *Rákos Rákoczy* (1891); choral works as *Kačena divoká* (c.1885), *Zápisník zmizelého* (1917–19), *Říkadla* (1925–27), *Glagolská mše* (1926); orchestral works, notably *Taras Bulba* (1918); keyboard and chamber works. Collected and arranged much folk music.

Jane \ˈjān\, Frederick Thomas. 1870–1916. British writer. Founder and first editor of the annuals *Jane's Fighting Ships* (1898 ff.), an authoritative description of the world's navies, and *All the World's Aircraft* (1910 ff.); author of novels and non-fiction works on naval matters.

Ja·ne·quin \zhȧn-ka^{n}\, Clément. c.1485–1558. French composer. In service of bishops of Luçon, Bordeaux, and (from c.1555) of King Henry II. Composed much sacred music but best known for 286 chansons, many narrative and programmatic as "La Bataille de Marignan," "Voulez ouir les crises de Paris," "Le Chant des oiseaux."

Jane Seymour. See under SEYMOUR family.

Ja·net \zhȧ-ne\, Pierre-Marie-Félix. 1859–1947. French psychologist and neurologist. Director of psychological laboratory, Salpêtrière hospital, Paris (1889 ff.); professor, Collège de France (1902–36); known for studies of disorganized and schizophrenic personalities, hysteria, hypnosis; pioneer in attempt to relate psychology to clinical work; anticipated (1889) Freud's notion of an unconscious. Author of *Les Accidents mentaux des hystériques* (1893), *Néuroses et idées fixes* (1898), *L'État mental des hystériques* (1911), *La Médecine psychologique* (1923), etc.

Ja·nin \zhȧ-na^{n}\, Jules-Gabriel. 1804–1874. French writer. Journalist in Paris; drama critic for *Journal des Débats* (1830–74). Author of novels *L'Âne mort et la femme guillotinée* (1829), *Barnave* (1831), *La Fin d'un monde et du neveu de Rameau* (1861); also of *Histoire de la littérature dramatique* (1858).

Jan·is \ˈjan-əs\, Elsie. *Orig.* Elsie Jane Bier·bow·er \ˈbi(ə)r-ˌbau̇(-ə)r\. 1889–1956. American actress, b. Columbus, Ohio. Appeared in vaudeville (1898–1903); starred in *The Belle of New York* (1904), *The Fortune Teller, The Vanderbilt Cup* (1906), *The Fair Co-ed* (1909), etc.; entertained troops in France in World War I; starred in *Elsie Janis and Her Gang* (1919) in New York, London, Paris; noted for devastating impressions of celebrities.

Jan·kó \ˈyän-kō\, Paul von. 1856–1919. Hungarian pianist. Inventor (1882) of the Jankó keyboard, a pianoforte keyboard of six rows of keys.

Jan·nings \ˈyän-iŋs, *Angl* ˈjan-iŋz\, Emil. 1886–1950. German actor, b. Brooklyn, N.Y. To Germany in infancy; joined Max Reinhardt's company, Berlin (1906); entered films (1916); won renown for portrayals in *Der letzte Mann* (1924), *Varieté* (1925), *Tartuffe* (1925), *Faust* (1926); in U.S. appeared in *The Way of All Flesh* (1927, Academy Award), *The Last Command* (1928); in Germany played in *Der blaue Engel* (1930), *Traumulus* (1936), *Robert Koch* (1939), *Die Entlassung* (1942), etc.

Jan·sen \ˈyän-sən, *Angl* ˈjan(t)-sən\, Cornelis Otto. *Lat.* Cornelius Jan·se·ni·us \jan-ˈsē-nē-əs, -ˈsēn-yəs\. 1585–1638. Dutch theologian. Head of Dutch theological college of St. Pulchérie, Louvain (1617); professor at Louvain (1630); bishop of Ypres (1636). Author of *Mars Gallicus* (an anti-French, anti-Richelieu attack, 1635), and of *Augustinus* (pub. posthumously, 1640; condemned by Urban VIII, 1642), in which he maintained that the teaching of St. Augustine on grace, free will, and predestination was opposed to the teaching of the Jesuit schools. In the religious controversies that it provoked, his view was championed by Pascal, Arnauld, Nicole, and the Port-Royalists. See also Jean DU VERGIER DE HAURANNE.

Jan·sky \ˈjan-skē\, Karl Guthe. 1905–1950. American electrical engineer, b. Norman, Okla. With Bell Telephone Laboratories (from 1928); while studying sources of interference in telephone calls discovered (1931) extraterrestrial origin of certain radio waves and located their source in the direction of the center of the galaxy.

Jan·son \'yän-sòn\, Anton. 1620–1687. Dutch type founder. Designed Janson type.

Janson, Kristofer Nagel. 1841–1917. Norwegian novelist. To America (1879); Unitarian missionary in Minnesota and Wisconsin region (1881–93); resident of Norway (from 1893). Novels included *Han og ho* (1868), *Fraa Dansketidi* (1875), *Vore Bedsteforaeldre* (1882), *Nordmaend i Amerika* (1887), *Hjördis* (1909).

Jans·sen \'yän-sən\ *or* **Janssen van Ceu·len** \-vän-'kœ̄-lən\, Cornelis. *Angl.* Cornelius John·son \'jän-sən\. 1593–1661. English painter of Dutch ancestry. Fashionable portraitist, patronized by James I and Charles I; apparently lost popularity to Van Dyck (from 1632); left England for Holland (1643).

Janssen, Geraert *or* Gerard. fl. 1616. English sculptor. Son of immigrant Dutch sculptor; known for his portrait bust of Shakespeare at Stratford-upon-Avon.

Janssen, Johannes. 1829–1891. German clergyman and historian. Ordained priest (1860). Author of controversial history of German Reformation *Geschichte des deutschen Volkes seit dem Ausgang des Mittelalters* (1876–94); contributed to development of Kulturgeschichte school of historiography.

Jans·sen \zhäⁿ-sen\, Pierre-Jules-César. 1824–1907. French astronomer. Traveled widely to study solar eclipses, terrestrial magnetism, etc.; director of Meudon Observatory (1876 ff.); demonstrated that "telluric rays" in solar spectrum arise from water vapor in Earth's atmosphere (1862–64); devised means of observing solar prominences in absence of an eclipse (1868); established observatory on Mont Blanc (1893) and demonstrated that oxygen lines in solar spectrum are of terrestrial origin; a pioneer in celestial photography, compiled *Atlas de photographies solaries* (1904).

Jans·sen *or* **Jan·sen** \'yän-sən\, Zacharias. 1580–c.1638. Dutch spectacles maker. Invented the compound microscope (1590); with Hans Lippershey made first telescope (1608).

Jans·sens \'yän-səns\, Abraham. *Called* Janssens van Nuys·sen \-vän-'nœi-sən\. c.1575–1632. Flemish painter. Leading Flemish exponent of classical Baroque style, influenced by Caravaggio, Domenichino; painted chiefly religious, mythological, and allegorical pictures, and portraits.

Jans·son \'yän-sòn\, Hans. 1792–1854. Swedish politician. Member of Riksdag (from 1828; speaker 1844–45, 1847–48); leading spokesman of peasant interests.

Jan·u·ar·i·us \ˌjan-yə-'wer-ē-əs\. Saint. *Ital.* Gen·na·ro \jän-'nä-rō\. 272?–?305. Italian prelate. Bishop of Beneventum; martyred, according to legend. Patron saint of Naples, where a phial said to contain his blood is preserved; the substance in the phial turns from solid to liquid 18 times a year.

Jan z Ro·ky·can \'yänz-'rò-kit-sán\. c.1390–1471. Bohemian religious leader. To Prague (1410); succeeded Jakoubek of Stříbro as chief organizer of the Hussites; minister of largest church in Prague (1423); became leader of left-wing Hussite group, the Orphans (1432); Hussite spokesman at Council of Basel (1433) and signed (1436) resulting Prague Compactata; archbishop of Hussite church (1435); driven from Prague by Sigismund (1437–48); on return secured acceptance of Hussite church with aid of George of Poděbrady; helped George repel Roman Catholic crusade against Hussites (1467–71).

Jaques-Dal·croze \zhák-dál-krōz\, Émile. 1865–1950. Swiss composer and teacher. Professor, Geneva Conservatory (1892–1910); founder and director (from 1914) of Institut Jaques-Dalcroze, Geneva, where he pursued the teaching of eurythmics, a system of rhythmic training of the whole body.

Ja·rīr \ja-'rēr\. *In full* Jarīr ibn 'Aṭiyah ibn al-Khaṭafā. c.650–c.729. Patronized by al-Ḥajjāj, governor of Iraq; briefly at Umayyad court in Damascus. Known esp. for satirical verse and poems insulting rivals or enemies of his patrons; engaged in celebrated poetic duels with al-Farazdaq and al-Akhṭal.

Jar·nac \zhár-nák\, Guy Cha·bot de \shá-bō-də-\. Baron. 1509–1572. French soldier. Known for his duel (1547) with La Châteigneraie before King Henri II and his court, when Jarnac by a sudden and unexpected blow (whence the expression "coup de Jarnac") won the decision.

Jär·ne·felt \'yer-nə-felt\, Edvard Armas. 1869–1958. Swedish composer and conductor, b. Finland. Introduced Wagner's operas to Finland; conductor, Swedish Royal Opera (1907–32); court composer and Swedish citizen (1923); director, Finnish National Opera (1932–36); conductor, Helsinki Philharmonic (1942–43). Composed orchestral works, notably *Berceuse* and *Praeludium,* and choral works.

Jar·ratt \'jar-ət\, Devereux. 1733–1801. American clergyman, b. Kent Co., Va. Anglican minister; initiated religious revival in southern Virginia and North Carolina (1763) in emulation of John Wesley, but opposed formation of separate Methodist denomination.

Jar·rell \jə-'rel, ja-\, Randall. 1914–1965. American writer, b. Nashville, Tenn. Taught at Kenyon Coll. (1937–39), U. of Texas (1939–42), Sarah Lawrence Coll. (1946–47), U. of North Carolina (1947–51, 1953–54, 1961–65). Author of verse *Blood for a Stranger* (1942), *Little Friend, Little Friend* (1945), *Losses* (1948), *Seven-League Crutches* (1951), *The Woman at the Washington Zoo* (1960), *The Lost World* (1965); novel *Pictures from an Institution* (1954); criticism *Poetry and the Age* (1953), *Sad Heart at the Supermarket* (1962).

Jar·ry \zhá-rē\, Alfred. 1873–1907. French writer. Led bohemian career in Paris ending in alcoholism and destitution. Author of Symbolist verse *Minutes de sable mémorial* (1894), *Les Jours et les nuits* (1897); novels *L'Amour en visites* (1898), *Le Surmâle* (1902); best known for play *Ubu roi* (1896), which caused riot at its production and which inspired Theater of the Absurd, and sequels *Ubu enchaîné* (1900), *Ubu sur la butte* (1901).

Jär·ta \'yer-tá\, Hans. *Orig. surname* Hier·ta \'hyer-tá\. 1774–1847. Swedish politician. Member of noble family; elected to Riksdag as leftist; changed name and renounced title (1800); helped plan and execute coup d'état that overthrew Gustav IV (1809); helped draft new constitution. Governor of Kopparberg (1812–22).

Jar·ves \'jär-vəs\, James Jackson. 1818–1888. American art collector and critic, b. Boston. Founded and edited *Polynesian* in Honolulu, first newspaper published in Hawaiian Islands (1840); settled in Florence, Italy (after 1851), and collected works of art, later (1871) sold to Yale Art School and known as the Jarves Collection; presented collection of Venetian glass to Metropolitan Museum of Art, New York City (1881). Author of *Scenes and Scenery in the Sandwich Islands* (1843), *Parisian Sights* (1852), *Italian Sights* (1856), *Art Studies* (1861), *The Art Idea* (1864).

Jar·vis \'jär-vəs\, Anna M. 1864–1948. American promoter, b. Grafton, W. Va. Conducted campaign (1907–14) culminating in national observance of Mothers Day.

Jarvis, John Wesley. 1780–1840. American painter, b. England. To U.S. as child; traveled widely from base in New York City; noted as a portraitist and as a bohemian dandy. Works included oversize portraits of O.H. Perry and others under commission of New York City Common Council.

Jasmin, Jacques. See Jacques BOÉ.

Jasomirgott, Henry II. See HENRY II, duke of Austria.

Ja·son \'jā-sən\. *Hebrew* Josh·ua \'jäsh(-ə)-wə\. 2d century B.C. Jewish high priest of Jerusalem. Made high priest by Antiochus IV Epiphanes; promoted Greek culture and religion; on retreat of Antiochus from Egypt to Jerusalem, displaced by Menelaus, another Hellenizer; fled to Asia on failure to capture city and regain position (c.170 B.C.).

Jason of Cy·re·ne \sī-'rē-nē\. fl. c.100 B.C. Jewish writer in Egypt. Author of a history in Greek of the Maccabean revolt, the basis of the present *II Maccabees* of the biblical Apocrypha.

Jas·par \zhás-pár\, Henri. 1870–1939. Belgian politician and diplomat. Minister of economic affairs (1918); foreign minister (1920–24), advocate of close cooperation with France and membership in League of Nations; helped form customs union with Luxembourg (1921); prime minister (1926–31); finance minister in Broqueville's cabinet (1932–34).

Jas·pers \'yäs-pərs\, Karl Theodor. 1883–1969. German psychiatrist and philosopher. Conducted research psychiatric clinic, U. of Heidelberg (1910–15); contributed to establishment of psychopathology on a rigorous, scientifically descriptive basis; professor of psychology (1916–20), of philosophy (1920–37); barred from teaching or publishing by Nazi regime (1938–45); joined U. of Basel (1948), becoming Swiss citizen (1967). From psychological reflection evolved a philosophy concerned with the modes of man's being and freedom; in postwar era strove to develop a "world philosophy." Works included *Allgemeine Psychopathologie* (1913; rev. 1946), *Psychologie der Weltanschauungen* (1919), *Die geistige Situation der Zeit* (1931), *Philosophie* (1932), *Vernunft und Existenz* (1935), *Existenzphilosophie* (1938), *Die Schuldfrage* (1946), *Von der Wahrheit* (1947), *Der philosophische Glaube* (1948), *Vom Ursprung und Zeit der Geschichte* (1949), *Die grossen Philosophen* (1957), etc.

Jas·trow \'yás-trō, *Angl* 'jas-(ˌ)trō\, Morris. 1861–1921. American scholar, b. Warsaw, Poland. To U.S. (1866). Professor, U. of Pennsylvania (from 1892) and librarian (from 1898). Author of *The Study of Religion* (1901), *Aspects of Religious Belief and Practice in Babylonia and Assyria* (1911), *Hebrew and Babylonian Traditions* (1914), *Zionism and the Future of Palestine* (1919), *The Book of Job* (1920), *The Song of Songs* (1921). His brother ¶Joseph (1863–1944), b. Warsaw; to U.S. (1866); professor of psychology, U. of Wisconsin (1888–1927); known for studies of sensation, perception, association, etc. Author of *The Subconscious* (1906), *Character and Temperament* (1915), *Psychology of Conviction* (1918), *Piloting your Life* (1930), *Effective Thinking* (1931), *The House that Freud Built* (1932), *The Life of the Mind* (1938), etc.

Jaswant Rāo Holkar. See HOLKAR.

Ja·tho \'yä-tō\, Karl. 1873–1933. German aviator. Claimed first successful flight in mechanical airplane (August 1903), four months before flight by Wright brothers at Kitty Hawk, N.C. Established airplane works at Hanover (1913); founded one of first aviation schools in Germany.

Jau·fré Ru·del \zhō-frā-rü̅-del\. Prince of Blaye \blāy\. fl. 1130–50. French troubadour. Accounted second only to William IX of Poitiers. Subject of popular legend of a "far-away love," possibly the Countess of Tripoli.

Jauregg, Julius Wagner von. See WAGNER VON JAUREGG.

Jáu·re·gui y A·gui·lar \'kaủ-rā-gē-ē-ä-gē-'lär\, Juan Martínez de. 1583–1641. Spanish poet. Once believed to be painter of Cervantes's portrait now in Real Academia Española, Madrid. Known esp. for verse translation of Tasso's *Aminta* (1607) and Lucan's *Pharsalia* (1684); author of verse *Rimas* (1618), critical *Discurso poético* (1624).

Jau·rès \zhō-res, zhō-\, Jean-Joseph-Marie-Auguste. 1859–1914. French Socialist and politician. Deputy (1885–89); retired to teaching and writing philosophy (1889); again deputy (1893–98, 1902–14); leader of moderate Socialists and a founder of Parti Socialiste Français; helped found coalition Section Française de L'Internationale Ouvrière (1905); leader of Socialists in the Chamber of Deputies; founder (with Briand, 1904) and editor of *L'Humanité* (1904–14). Fought militaristic legislation on eve of outbreak of World War I. Author of *Histoire socialiste de la Révolution française* (1901–07), *La Guerre franco-allemande* (1908), *L'Armée nouvelle* (1910), etc.

Jav·its \'jav-its\, Jacob Koppel. 1904–1986. American politician, b. New York City. U.S. senator from New York (1957–80). One of the most influential senators and a leader of Republican liberals; helped to shape landmark legislation in foreign affairs, social welfare, urban redevelopment, and civil rights.

Javier, Francisco. See Saint Francis XAVIER.

Jaw·len·sky \(,)yəv-'lyān-skəi\, Alexey von. 1864–1941. Russian painter. Left Imperial Guard to take up painting (1889); to Munich (1896), associated with Kandinsky; with Kandinsky, Klee, Feininger formed (1924) Der Blaue Vier. Known for colorful Expressionist works of high emotional content, later for abstract, mystical portraits of faces.

Jay \'jā\, John. 1745–1829. American jurist and statesman, b. New York City. Member, Continental Congress (1774–77, 1778, 1779; president 1778–79); drafted New York's first constitution (1777); chief justice of state supreme court (1777–78); American minister to Spain (1779); called to Paris by Franklin to join commission for negotiating peace with Great Britain (1782); returned to New York (1784). U.S. secretary of foreign affairs (1784–89). Joined with Hamilton and Madison in writing the *Federalist,* explaining new Constitution (1787–88). Chief justice, U.S. Supreme Court (1789–95); negotiated Jay's Treaty with Great Britain settling outstanding disputes (1794–95). Governor of New York (1795–1801).

Ja·ya·de·va \jə-yə-'dā-və\. 12th century. Indian poet. Author of a lyric drama in Sanskrit in varied meters, *Gītagovinda* ("Song of the Cowherd") recounting the love of Kṛṣṇa for the milkmaid Rādhā.

Ja·ya·var·man \,jä-yä-'vär-män\. Name of several Cambodian rulers, esp.:

Jayavarman I. 7th century. King of Chenla. Last of line of rulers of unified Chenla-Funan.

Jayavarman II. *Posthumous name* Pa·ra·mes·va·ra \,pär-ä-'mes-və-rä\, *i.e.* Supreme Lord. c.770–850. King (c.790–850). Of Khmer descent but lived in exile or captivity in Java; returned to Cambodia as Javanese puppet ruler (c.790 or 800); asserted Cambodian independence (802); established idea of unified Cambodian state, deification of rulers, Hindu Brahminism as state religion; founded Khmer Empire; first ruler of so-called Angkor Period.

Jayavarman VII. c.1120–1215 or 1219. King (1181–1215 or 1219). Son of King Dharanindravarman II; conducted military campaigns in Champa; failed to prevent overthrow of brother Yasovarman II by usurper Tribhuvanadityavarman; organized Khmer resistance to Cham invasion (1176–77), reestablished state, and was crowned (1181); conquered Champa, southern Laos, parts of Burma and Malay Peninsula; instituted vast program of building Buddhist temples, hospitals, rest houses, etc.; rebuilt city of Angkor.

Jaz·zār \jaz-'zär\, Aḥmad al-. *Also known as* Jazzār Pa·sha \-pə-'shä\. *Called* the Butcher. c.1734–1804. Ottoman governor of Syria (1775–1804). With aid of a British fleet, forced Napoléon to raise siege of Acre (1799).

Jean. See also JOHN.

Jean d'Ar·ras \zhäⁿ-dà-rás, -räs\. 15th century. French trouvère. With Antoine du Val and Fouquart de Cambri wrote *Évangile des quenouilles,* compilation of tales, sayings, and miscellanea of great historical value.

Jean de France \-də-fräⁿs\. Duc de Ber·ry \ber-i\. 1340–1416. French prince. Third son of John II the Good; made count of Poitiers (1356); lieutenant for Auvergne, Languedoc, Périgord, Poitou (1358), thus controlling a third of France; duke of newly created duchies of Berry and Auvergne (1360). His burdensome taxes led to peasant revolt (1381–84). Regent for brother Charles (1380); sought reconciliation with England; attempted to mediate feud between houses of Orléans and Burgundy; allied with Orléanists (1410); arranged peace of Auxerre (1412) and of Pontoise (1413). Patron of arts.

Jean de Ma·tha \-də-má-tà\. Saint. 1160–1213. French priest. Consecrated himself to redemption of Christian captives in the hands of the Turks; founded order of Trinitarians (rule approved, 1198). Canonized (1679).

Jean de Meun. See Jean CHOPINEL.

Jean de Mire·court \-də-mēr-kür\. 14th century. French religious and theologian. Entered Cistercian order; became known as *monachus albus,* "the white monk"; wrote commentary (1345) on Peter Lombard's *Sentences,* several propositions from which were condemned (1347). A chief theorist of skeptical nominalism, denying possibility of rational certitude, and of voluntarism, basing belief on faith and love rather than knowledge.

Jean de Pa·ris \-də-pá-rē\. *Also known as* Jean Qui·dort \kē-dȯr\ *or* Jean le Sourd \-lə-sür\. *Lat.* Johannes de Soar·dis \-dā-'swär-dəs\. c.1255–1306. French religious and theologian. Dominican monk; disciple of St. Thomas Aquinas. Author of *De potestate regia et papali* (c.1302) on separate powers of church and state and esp. limits of papal authority, and *Determinatio* (1304) on consubstantiation doctrine of eucharist that was condemned.

Jean de Ve·nette \-də-vä-net\. c.1308–c.1369. French chronicler. Entered Carmelite order; prior of Carmelite convent, Paris (1339); provincial of France (1342); taught at U. of Paris. Author of a history of Carmelites and esp. of Latin chronicle of period 1340–68, continuing that of Guillaume de Nangis.

Jean le Bel \-lə-bel\. c.1290–1370. Belgian soldier and chronicler. Companion of Jean, comte de Beaumont; compiled in French *Vrayes chroniques,* valuable eyewitness record of his time.

Jeanne d'Albret. See ALBRET.

Jeanne d'Arc. See JOAN of Arc.

Jean·ne·ret \zhán-re\, Charles-Édouard. *Known as* Le Cor·bu·sier \lə-kȯr-bü̅z-yā\. 1887–1965. Swiss architect and city planner. Largely self-taught during travels in Greece, Italy, France, Germany; associated for periods with Josef Hoffmann, Auguste Perret, Peter Behrens; settled in Paris (1917); with Amédée Ozenfant developed Purist aesthetic and issued manifesto *Après le cubisme* (1918); with Ozenfant and Paul Dermée founded review *L'Esprit Nouveau* (1920); published *Vers une architecture* (1923). Opened architectural studio in Paris, with cousin Pierre Jeanneret (1922); developed personal version of International style, utilizing pillar supports, roof terraces, unornamented facades, strip windows; developed ideas of high-rise residential complexes surrounded by green spaces. Realized works included numerous private residences as Savoye House, Poissy (1929–30); Unité d'habitation community, Marseilles (1946–52); Villa Shodan, Ahmādābād (1955–56), and government buildings, Chandigarh (1952–56), India; developed plans for Algiers, Buenos Aires, Saint-Dié, etc. Author of *Urbanisme* (1925), *La Ville radieure* (1935), *Le Modulor I* (1948), etc.

Jean·nin \zhá-naⁿ\, Pierre. c.1540–1622. French lawyer and diplomat. Advocate (1569), councilor (1579), president (1580) of Parlement of Burgundy; Catholic League emissary to Spain (1591); opposed, then supported (from (1595) Henry IV; member of Council of State; negotiated Treaty of Lyons (1601) with Savoy; French ambassador to Holland (1607–09); controller general of finances (1610–16).

Jean Re·nart \zhäⁿ-rə-nár\. fl. 1200–1222. French poet. Author of romances noted for realistic settings and brilliant depictions of chivalric society, *L'Escoufle* (c.1200), *Guillaume de Dôle* (c.1212), and *Lai de l'ombre* (c.1222).

Jeans \'jēnz\, Sir James Hopwood. 1877–1946. English physicist, astronomer, and author. Professor of applied mathematics, Princeton (1905–09); lecturer in applied mathematics, Cambridge (1910–12); secretary, Royal Society (1919–29); research associate, Mt. Wilson Observatory, Cal. (1923–44). Worked esp. on kinetic theory of gases, radiation, multiple star systems, stellar evolution, etc. Author of *The Dynamical Theory of Gases* (1904), *Theoretical Mechanics* (1906), *The Mathematical Theory of Electricity and Magnetism* (1908), *Radiation and Quantum Theory* (1914), *Problems of Cosmogony and Stellar Dynamics* (1919), etc., and books popularizing science, including *The Universe Around Us* (1929), *The Stars in their Courses* (1931), *Through Space and Time* (1934), *Science and Music* (1937).

Jeau·rat \zhō-rá, zhō-\, Étienne. 1699–1789. French painter. Known for historical scenes, Parisian scenes, etc.

Je·ba·vý \'yeb-á-vē\, Václav Ignác. *Pseudonym* Otakar Bře·zi·na \'brzhez-i-ná\. 1868–1929. Czech poet. Schoolmaster in Moravia. Author of cycle of lyric verse epitomizing his spiritual development from pessimism to encompassing love of man, comprising *Tajemné dálky* (1895), *Svitani na zapade* (1896), *Vrěty od pólů* (1897), *Stavitelé chramu* (1899), *Ruce* (1901); influenced development of modern Czech poetry.

Jebb \'jeb\, Sir Richard Claverhouse. 1841–1905. Scottish scholar. Professor, Glasgow (1875–89), Cambridge (1889–1905). M.P. for Cambridge U. (1891–1905). Author of *Attic Orators* (1876), *The Growth and Influence of Greek Poetry* (1893), etc. Edited and translated works of Sophocles.

Jef·feries \'jef-rēz\, Richard, *in full* John Richard. 1848–1887. English naturalist and writer. Best known for the descriptions of nature and Wiltshire countrymen in his stories *The Gamekeeper at Home* (1878), *Hodge and His Masters* (1880), *Bevis* (1882), *Life of the Fields* (1884), *The Open Air* (1885),

Amaryllis at the Fair (1887), *Field and Hedgerow* (1889); autobiography *Story of My Heart* (1883), etc.

Jef·fers \'jef-ərz\, Robinson, *in full* John Robinson. 1887–1962. American poet, b. Pittsburgh, Pa. Author of lyrics expressing bitter contempt of humanity and love of the harsh eternal beauties of nature; works included *Californians* (1916), *Tamar* (1924), *The Roan Stallion* (1925), *The Woman at Point Sur* (1927), *Cawdor* (1928), *Dear Judas* (1929), *Thurso's Landing* (1932), *Solstice* (1935), *Be Angry at the Sun* (1941), *The Double Axe* (1948), *Hungerfeld* (1954); plays including *The Tower Beyond Tragedy* (produced 1950) based on Euripides.

Jef·fer·son \'jef-ər-sən\, Joseph. 1829–1905. American actor, b. Philadelphia. On stage from age of 3; made success in Laura Keene's company, New York, in *Our American Cousin, The Cricket on the Hearth, The Rivals,* etc. Most famous role, Rip Van Winkle in Dion Boucicault's play of that name (from 1865).

Jefferson, Thomas. 1743–1826. Third president of the United States, b. Goochland, now Albemarle Co., Va. Member, Virginia House of Burgesses (1769–75); with R. H. Lee and Patrick Henry initiated intercolonial committee of correspondence (1773); wrote widely circulated *Summary View of the Rights of British America* (1774). Member, Continental Congress (1775, 1776); chairman of committee that prepared Declaration of Independence; wrote and presented first draft of declaration to Congress (July 2, 1776); signed Declaration of Independence. Governor of Virginia (1779–81). Again member, Continental Congress (1783–85); proposed decimal coinage, series of provisions later embodied in Ordinance of 1787. U.S. minister to France (1785–89). U.S. secretary of state (1790–93); differing policies caused bitter antagonism with Alexander Hamilton, secretary of treasury; emerged as leader of Democratic Republican party. Vice president of the U.S. (1797–1801); drafted Kentucky Resolves (1798) against Alien and Sedition acts. President of the U.S. (1801–09), elected by House of Representatives after tie in electoral vote (with Aaron Burr, *q.v.*). Features of administration: purchase of Louisiana from France (1803) and dispatch of Lewis and Clark to explore it; war against Algerian pirates (1801–05); diplomatic trouble with Great Britain over impressment of American seamen (Embargo Act of 1807); prohibition of the importation of slaves. On retirement from presidency, lived on plantation at "Monticello," near Charlottesville, Va. Instrumental in founding U. of Virginia (1819). Noted naturalist, scholar, architect. Author of *Notes on the State of Virginia* (1785).

Jef·frey \'jef-rē\, Francis. Lord Jeffrey. 1773–1850. Scottish critic and jurist. One of founders of *Edinburgh Review* (1802) and its editor (1803–29). M.P. (1830–34); lord advocate (1830–34); judge of Court of Session (1834–50). Highly influential although occasionally inflexible critic; noted for attacks on Romantics.

Jef·freys \'jef-rēz\, George. 1st Baron Jeffreys of Wem \'wem\. 1645–1689. British jurist, b. Wales. Solicitor general to Duke of York (1677). Lord chief justice and privy councilor (1683); baron and lord chancellor (1685). On overthrow of James II, attempted to flee from England but was captured and imprisoned in Tower of London (1688), where he died. As chief justice and chancellor, made himself notorious by injustice and brutality. The assizes conducted by him (1685) at which those involved in Monmouth's rebellion against James II were tried became known as the Bloody Assizes because of the number of executions decreed.

Jef·fries \'jef-rēz\, James Jackson. 1875–1953. American boxer, b. Carroll, Ohio. World heavyweight champion from 1899 (winning title from Bob Fitzsimmons) until he retired in 1905; returned to ring for match with Jack Johnson (1910), in which he was defeated.

Jeffries, John. 1745–1819. American physician and balloonist, b. Boston. Loyalist during American Revolution; resident in England after the war. Interested himself in use of balloons for scientific observations and experiments; with François Blanchard, French aeronaut, crossed English Channel from Dover to forest of Guînes, France, in balloon (Jan. 7, 1785), first crossing of English Channel by air.

Je·han des Murs \zə-ä^{n}-dā-mu̅e̅r\. *Lat.* Johannes de Mu·ris \-də-'myůr-əs\. c.1300–c.1350. French mathematician, astronomer and music theorist. Worked in Paris, Evreux, and elsewhere; perhaps in service (1338–42) of Philippe d'Evreux, king of Navarre; consulted by Pope Clement VI at Avignon on calendar reform. Known for musical treatises *Notitia artis musice,* known as *Ars nove musice* (1321), *Compendium musice practice* (c.1322), *Musica speculativa secundum Boetium* (1323), and perhaps others, supporting Ars nova style and practices.

Jehoahaz. See Ahaz.

Je·hoi·a·chin \jə-'hȯi-ə-kən\ *or* **Jo·a·chin** \'jō-ə-kən\. 615?–?560 B.C. King of Judah (598 or 597 B.C.). Son of Jehoiakim; reigned few months only; with Judean leaders, carried away as prisoner to Babylon by Nebuchadrezzar; held captive 37 years.

Je·hoi·a·kim \jə-'hȯi-ə-kim\ *or* **Jo·a·kim** \'jō-ə-kim\. d. 598? B.C. King of Judah (c.609–598 B.C.). Son of Josiah; placed on throne by Necho, who had deposed Jehoahaz; revolted against Babylon after hegemony over Palestine passed (605) from Necho to Nebuchadrezzar at battle of Carchemish; died at siege of Jerusalem just before city was taken.

Je·ho·ram \jə-'hō-rəm\ *or* **Jo·ram** \'jō-rəm\. d. c.842 B.C. King of Israel (c.849–c.842 B.C.). Son of Ahab; succeeded older brother Ahaziah as king; with Jehoshaphat of Judah, put down revolt in Moab; in revolt against him by Elisha and his party, slain by Jehu, who seized throne.

Jehoram *or* **Joram.** d. c.842 B.C. King of Judah (c.849–c.842 B.C.). Son and successor of Jehoshaphat; m. Athaliah, daughter of Ahab and Jezebel; during his reign Edom rebelled; succeeded by his son Ahaziah.

Je·hosh·a·phat \jə-'häsh-ə-fat\ *or* **Jos·a·phat** \'jäs-ə-fat\. d. c.849 B.C. King of Judah (c.873–c.849 B.C.). Son of Asa; ruled righteously and introduced reforms; made alliance with Israel and joined Ahab in battle at Ramoth-gilead against Syrians; practically vassal of Israel; succeeded by son Jehoram.

Je·hu \'jē-hyü\. d. 815 B.C. King of Israel (c.842–815 B.C.). Founder of new dynasty; soldier under King Ahab; led revolt against him; anointed king by Elisha; killed kings Jehoram and Ahaziah; seized throne of Israel and controlled Judah by destroying royal family; paid tribute to Shalmaneser III; at war with Hazael of Damascus.

Je·jee·bhoy \jə-'jē-bȯi\, Sir Jamsetjee. 1783–1859. Indian merchant and philanthropist. From great fortune amassed in trade, built schools, hospitals, public works in Bombay; first Indian to be knighted (1842), created baronet (1857).

Jek·yll \'jek-əl\, Gertrude. 1843–1932. English landscape architect. Associated with William Robinson and later Sir Edwin Lutyens in developing a modern, informal style of garden marked by rhythmic use of color and form. Author of *Wood and Garden* (1899), *Home and Garden* (1900), *Wall and Water Gardens* (1901), *Colour in the Flower Garden* (1908), *Garden Ornament* (1918), etc.

Je·la·čić \'yel-á-chet^{y}\ *or* **Je·la·čić od Bu·ži·ma** \'yel-á-,chēt-yȯd-'bü-zhē-má\, Josip. Count. 1801–1859. Croatian general and politician. Lieutenant general and ban (governor) of Croatia (1848); incited by Austria, had Croatian diet declare independence from Hungary and led army against Hungarian nationalists (1848); defeated Görgey at Schwechat (1848). Returned to Zagreb as ban of Croatia and Slavonia; created count (1855).

Jel·li·coe \'jel-i-,kō\, John Rushworth. 1st Earl Jellicoe. 1859–1935. British naval commander. Entered navy (1874); served in Egypt (1882); commanded land force that relieved Peking in Boxer Rebellion (1900); director of naval ordnance (1905–07); rear admiral (1907); third sea lord (1908–10); vice admiral (1910); second sea lord (1912–14). During World War I, commander of the Grand Fleet (1914–16) and chief of the naval staff (1917); admiral (1915); commanded the Grand Fleet in battle of Jutland (May 31, 1916); first sea lord (1916–17). Admiral of the fleet (1919). Governor general of New Zealand (1920–24); created earl (1925).

Jel·li·nek \'yel-i-nek\, Adolf. 1821–1893. Moravian theologian, scholar, and orator. Rabbi and preacher, Leipzig (1845–56) and Vienna; forceful and popular preacher; noted student of Kabbala. A son ¶Georg (1851–1911) was a jurist; professor at Vienna (1883), Basel (1889), Heidelberg (1891); opposed legal positivists with theory of social origin of law. Author of *Die sozialethische Bedeutung von Recht, Unrecht und Strafe* (1878), *Die rechtliche Natur der Staatenverträge* (1880), *Die Erklärung der Menschen- und Bürgerrechte* (1895), *Allgemeine Staatslehre* (1900), etc.

Jem. See Cem.

Je·natsch \'yā-näch\, Georg *or* Jürg. 1596–1639. Swiss soldier and political leader. Vicar of Scharans (1617); became leader of anti-Catholic, anti-Spanish sentiment in Grisons (Graubünden) canton; established "penal court" that executed 150 Spaniards; murdered Pompeius Planta, head of Spanish party (1621), and fled; in alliance with France, expelled Spanish and Austrians from Grisons (1624); in Venetian service (1629–31); returned to Grisons (1631) with the duc de Rohan; adopted Catholicism (1635), becoming dictator of Grisons; assassinated.

Jen·kin \'jeŋ-kən\, Fleeming, *in full* Henry Charles Fleeming. 1833–1885. British electrician. Collaborator with Lord Kelvin in work on insulation and resistance of submarine telegraphy cables; as reporter for Committee on Electrical Standards, influential in establishing absolute electrical units as ohm.

Jen·kins \'jeŋ-kənz\, John. 1592–1678. English musician and composer. String player and lutenist to Charles I and II and various noble patrons; known for his string fantasias or fancies, rounds, songs, anthems.

Jenkins, Robert. fl. 1731–1738. English mariner. While trading in West Indies, had his ear cut off by the Spanish coastal guards (1731). His display of what was allegedly the ear before the House of Commons (1738) was the immediate cause of the war between England and Spain that became known as "the War of Jenkins's Ear" (1739).

Jen·kin·son \'jeŋ-kən-sən\, Charles. 1st Earl of Liv·er·pool \'liv-ər-,pül\. 1727–1808. English politician. Private secretary to Earl of Bute (1760); M.P. (1761–86); vice treasurer for Ireland and privy councilor (1773); master of the mint (1775–78); secretary at war (1778–82); popularly credited with great influence at court of George III and with controlling relations of prime minister, Lord North, with king. Created Baron Hawkesbury (1786); president of Board of Trade (1786–96); created earl (1796). His son ¶Robert Banks (1770–1828) was M.P. (1790–1803); master of the mint (1799–1801); foreign secretary (1801–04); home secretary (1804–06, 1807–09); secretary for war and colonies (1809–12); Baron Hawkesbury (1803), succeeded to earldom (1808). Prime minister (1812–27); conducted largely sound, unimaginative administration in which he was outshone by Canning and Castlereagh.

Jen·ner \'jen-ər\, Edward. 1749–1823. English physician. Apprenticed to surgeon near Bristol; pupil of John Hunter in London (1770–72); began practice in Berkeley (1773). Observed that dairymaids who had had cowpox did not get smallpox; vaccinated James Phipps, a boy of eight, with matter from cowpox vesicles on hands of a milkmaid (1796); several weeks later the boy was inoculated with smallpox but did not contract the disease; published *Inquiry into the Cause and Effects of the Variolae Vaccinae* in which he announced his discovery of vaccination (1798).

Jenner, Sir William. 1815–1898. English physician and anatomist. Established separate identities of typhus and typhoid fevers (1847); professor, U. Coll., London (from 1849); physician-in-ordinary to Queen Victoria (1862).

Jenneval. See Louis-Alexandre DECHET.

Jen·ney \'jen-ē\, William Le Baron. 1832–1907. American architect, b. Fairhaven, Mass. Designed Home Insurance Co. Building, Chicago (1884–85), with type of steel skeleton construction, making it the forerunner of modern skyscrapers; also build Leiter Building (1879), Manhattan Building (1889–90), Fair store (1891–92), etc.

Jen·nings \'jen-iŋz\, Herbert Spencer. 1868–1947. American zoologist, b. Tonica, Ill. Professor, Johns Hopkins (1906–38); known for studies of behavior and physiology of lower organisms and of genetics.

Jennings, Sarah. See under John CHURCHILL.

Jen·sen \'yen-sən\, Gerrit. *Eng.* Gerrard John·son \'jän(t)-sən\. fl. 1680–1715. English cabinetmaker, b. Netherlands? Settled in London (before 1680); became fashionable cabinetmaker, serving Charles II, William and Mary, Anne, and nobility; foremost furniture designer in England, apparently first to win individual fame in that field; known esp. for metal inlay work similar to that of A.-C. Boulle, lacquer-work.

Jen·sen \'yen-zən\, Hans, *in full* Johannes Hans Daniel. 1907–1973. German physicist. Professor, Hamburg (1936–41), Hanover (1941–49), Heidelberg (from 1949). Awarded Nobel prize for physics (1963) with M.G. Mayer and E.P. Wigner for research on nuclear shell structure.

Jen·sen \'yen-sən, *Angl* 'jen-sən\, Jens. 1860–1951. American landscape architect, b. Dybbøl, Denmark. To U.S. (1884); in Chicago redesigned Humboldt Park, designed Columbus Park, chiefly responsible for establishment of Cook County Forest Preserve system; laid out parks for Racine, Wis., and Springfield, Ill., and numerous private clients, often working in association with Frank Lloyd Wright, Louis Sullivan, etc.

Jensen, Johannes Vilhelm. 1873–1950. Danish poet and novelist. Author of tales in *Himmerlandsfolk* (1898), *Intermezzo* (1899), *Skovene* (1904), *Nye Himmerlandshistorier* (1904), *Tordenkalven* (1905), *Eksotiske Noveller* (1907–17), *Jørgine* (1926), etc.; novels as *Danskere* (1896), *Einar Elkœr* (1898), *Kongens Fald* (1900–01), *Madame d'Ora* (1904), *Hjulet* (1905), *Den lange Rejse* (6 vols., 1908–22), *Gudrun* (1936); 9 volumes of "myths," *Myter* (1907–44); critical works and essays. Awarded 1944 Nobel prize for literature.

Jen·son \zhäⁿ-sōn, *Angl* 'jen-sən\, Nicolas. c.1420–1480. French engraver and printer. Sent by Charles VII to Mainz to learn art of printing (1458); worked three years under Gutenberg; set up printing establishment in Venice (1470) and perfected roman type.

Jen Tsung. See (1) Chao Chen under CHAO family; (2) Chu Kao-chih under CHU family; (3) YUNG-YEN.

Jep·sen \'jep-sən\, Glenn Lowell. 1903–1974. American paleontologist, b. Lead, S.D. Professor, Princeton U. (1934–74); curator of vertebrate paleontology, Princeton Natural History Museum (1935–74); known for studies of Tertiary stratigraphy, primates, genetics, etc.

Jer·e·mi·ah \,jer-ə-'mī-ə\ *or* **Jer·e·mi·as** \-əs\. 650?–c.570 B.C. Hebrew prophet. Began to prophesy (627 or 626) in reign of King Josiah, condemning false worship and warning of imminent conquest; denounced Jehoiakim; counseled submission to Babylon. Author of Old Testament book of Jeremiah; sometimes held to be author also of Lamentations.

Jer·e·mi·as II \,jer-ə-'mī-əs\. c.1530–1595. Greek prelate. Patriarch of Constantinople (1572–79, 1580–84, 1586–95); a reformer, prosecuted simony; restored to post by popular acclaim after being deposed twice; noted also as a scholar, encouraged learning and reorganized Patriarchal Academy of Constantinople (1593). Consecrated Job, metropolitan of Moscow, as first Russian patriarch (1589) and proclaimed Moscow the "third Rome"; rejected Western influences, including Gregorian calendar (1582). Engaged in notable theological exchange with Lutheran theologians of Tübingen (1572–81).

Je·ri·tza \'yer-it-sȧ\, Maria. *Orig.* Mizzi Jed·lič·ka \'yed-lich-kȧ\. 1887–1982. Czech singer. Operatic debut at Olomouc (1910); sang in Vienna (from 1911) and at Metropolitan Opera, New York City (1921–32); achieved international fame as prima donna soprano; created roles in *Ariadne auf Naxos* (1912), *Die Frau ohne Schatten* (1919), *Die tote Stadt* (1921); acclaimed esp. in title role of *Tosca;* lived in U.S. (from 1935).

Jer·myn \'jər-mən\, Henry. 1st Earl of St. Al·bans \sənt-'ȯl-bənz\. c.1604–1684. English courtier. Entered Parliament (1625); vice chamberlain to Queen Henrietta Maria (1628) and her master of the horse (1639). Fought in Royalist army; accompanied queen to France (1644). After execution of Charles I (1649), remained in France with Charles II; rumored to have married the queen; after Restoration was created earl (1660) and lord chamberlain (1674).

Jer·o·bo·am \,jer-ə-'bō-əm\. Name of two kings of Israel:

Jeroboam I. d. 901 B.C. First king of northern kingdom of Israel (922–901 B.C.). An Ephraimite, leader in plot against Solomon; fled to Egypt on failure of plot, but returned on accession of Rehoboam; chosen king of ten northern tribes; made Shechem his capital; according to Bible account, favored idolatry.

Jeroboam II. d. 741 B.C. King (783–741 B.C.). Son and successor of Joash; reconquered lost provinces, seizing Damascus; ruled Israel at height of its power; during his reign, Amos and Hosea prophesied doom of Israel.

Je·rome \jə-'rōm\. Saint. *Lat.* Eusebius Hieronymus. *Literary name* So·phro·ni·us \sə-'frō-nē-əs\. c.347–419 or 420. Latin Church Father, b. Pannonia. One of the four Doctors of the Church recognized as such during the Middle Ages. Studied in Rome; traveled widely; lived as a hermit in the desert of Chalcis (375–377); ordained by Paulinus (378); secretary to Pope Damasus (382–385). Went to Bethlehem in Palestine (386) and in a monastery there devoted himself to study and writing. Published a Latin version of the Bible, known as the Vulgate; wrote also a large number of works of ecclesiastical history, biblical exegesis, and controversial works; translated many of Origen's works into Latin.

Jerome of Prague. c.1365–1416. Czech theologian. Adopted views of Jan Hus and, while a student at Oxford, of John Wycliffe; professor, Charles U., Prague (1401–04), Sorbonne (1405), Heidelberg and Cologne (1406); rejoined Hus in Prague (1407) and held public debates critical of church and esp. papal practices; with Hus denounced sale of indulgences by antipope John XXIII (1412); condemned by Council of Constance and burned at the stake.

Je·rome \jə-'rōm, 'jer-əm\, Chauncey. 1793–1868. American inventor, b. Canaan, Conn. Carpenter and later clockmaker; designed a popular bronze looking-glass clock (1824); formed successful manufactory for clocks; devised a one-day brass movement (1838), making possible mass production of cheap clocks; exported clocks to Europe.

Je·rome \jə-'rōm\, Jerome Klapka. 1859–1927. English humorist, novelist, and playwright. Variously a railroad clerk, schoolmaster, actor, journalist. Among his works were *The Idle Thoughts of an Idle Fellow* (1889), *Three Men in a Boat* (1889), *Three Men on the Bummel* (1900), and the plays *Barbara* (1886), *Miss Hobbs* (1899), *Fanny and the Servant Problem* (1908), *The Passing of the Third Floor Back* (1908), *The Great Gamble* (1914).

Jérôme Bonaparte. See BONAPARTE.

Jer·rold \'jer-əld\, Douglas William. 1803–1857. English playwright and humorist. Started magazine (1845) and newspaper (1846) bearing his name; contributed to *Punch;* editor of *Lloyd's Weekly Newspaper* (from 1852). His most successful plays were *Black-eyed Susan* (1829), *Mutiny at the Nore* (1830), *Bride of Ludgate* (1831), *Time Works Wonders* (1845). Among his contributions to *Punch,* the best known were *Mrs. Caudle's Curtain Lectures* (1845). His son ¶William Blanchard (1826–1884) wrote the play *Cool as a Cucumber* (1851); also *Life of Napoleon III* (1874–82), and a number of novels.

Jer·vas \'jär-vəs, 'jər-\ *or* **Jar·vis** \'jär-\, Charles. 1675?–1739. Irish painter and translator. Court painter to George I and George II; painted portraits of Pope and Swift; translated *Don Quixote,* perhaps using Thomas Skelton's translation; his version (pub. 1742) enjoyed wide popularity.

Jer·vis \'jär-vəs, 'jər-\, John. Earl of St. Vin·cent \sānt-'vin(t)-sənt, sənt-\. 1735–1823. English naval commander. Entered navy (1749); commanded the *Foudroyant* in battle of Ushant (1778); captured French *Pégase* (1782); vice admiral (1793); with Sir Charles Grey captured Martinique and Guadeloupe (1794); commanded Mediterranean fleet (1795); with 15 sail, defeated Spanish fleet of 27 sail off Cape St. Vincent (1797), for which he was created earl. Through foresight and severe discipline, averted mutiny (1798) and subdued spirit of sedition in Channel fleet (1799–1801); first lord of admiralty (1801–04), eliminated corruption in dockyards and brought about impeachment of Melville and reform of naval administration; resumed command in Channel (1806–07).

Jer·vis \'jər-vəs\, John Bloomfield. 1795–1885. American engineer, b. Huntington, N.Y. Chief engineer on Erie Canal (1821–25), Delaware and Hudson Canal (1827–30), Mohawk & Hudson Railway (1830–33), for which he invented the swiveling truck; chief engineer of Croton Aqueduct (1836–46), building dams, bridges, etc.; oversaw redesign of Boston water supply system (1846–48).

Jes·per·sen \'yes-pər-sən\, Otto, *in full* Jens Otto Harry. 1860–1943. Danish philologist. Professor of English language and literature, Copenhagen (1893–1925); rector of the university (1920–21). Helped revolutionize teaching of languages in Europe and wrote numerous texts; contributed to phonetics and other areas of linguistics; proposed an international language, Novial (1928), for which he prepared a grammar and lexicon. Among his notable works were *Progress in Language* (1894), *Fonetik* (1897–99; later translated into German as two separate books, *Lehrbuch der Phonetik* and *Phonetische Grundfragen*), *Sprogundervisning* (1901), *Growth and Structure of the English Language* (1905), *A Modern English Grammar on Historical Principles* (1909–49), *Language: Its Nature, Development, and Origin* (1922), *Philosophy of Grammar* (1924), *Analytic Syntax* (1937).

Jes·se \'jes-ē\, Friniwyd Tennyson. 1889–1958. English writer. Grandniece of Lord Tennyson; collaborated with husband, H.M. Harwood, on plays and books; best known for novels including *The White Riband* (1921), *Tom Fool* (1926), *Moonraker* (1927), *The Lacquer Lady* (1929), *A Pin to See the Peepshow* (1934).

Jes·sel \'jes-əl\, Sir George. 1824–1883. English jurist. Queen's counsel (1865); M.P. (1868–73); solicitor general (1871–73); master of the rolls (from 1873); oversaw fusion of law and equity courts (1873, 1875); renowned for clarity and soundness of equity judgments.

Jessel, George Albert. 1898–1981. American entertainer, b. New York City. Entered vaudeville as a child; played in various acts with Walter Winchell, Eddie Cantor, etc.; starred in *The Jazz Singer* on Broadway (1925); appeared in motion pictures. Writer and producer of films (from 1943); best known for benefit performances, appearances as master of ceremonies and after-dinner speaker, becoming known as the "toastmaster general." Wrote autobiography *Hello Momma* (1946).

Jess·ner \'yes-nər\, Leopold. 1878–1945. German theatrical producer and director. Director of theaters in Hamburg (1904–15), Königsberg (1915–19), of State Theater, Berlin (1919–28); general director of state theaters (1928–30); closely associated with Expressionist movement, produced notable performances of *Wilhelm Tell, Richard III, Hamlet,* and plays of Wedekind, esp. *Marquis von Keith.* Fled (1933) to Palestine and thence to U.S.

Jes·up \'jes-əp\, Morris Ketchum. 1830–1908. American merchant and banker, b. Westport, Conn. An incorporator (1868) and benefactor of American Museum of Natural History; sponsored several expeditions to the Arctic.

Je·sus \'jē-zəs, -zəz\. *Hebrew* Josh·ua \'jäsh-(ə-)wə\. *Called* Jesus Christ \'krīst\ *or* Christ Jesus *from Greek* Christos, *translation of Hebrew* Messiah. *Called also* Jesus of Naz·a·reth \'naz-ə-rəth\. c.6 B.C.–c.30 A.D. Founder of Christianity. Legally son of Joseph, carpenter of Nazareth, but believed by his followers to have been miraculously conceived by his mother, Mary; born at Bethlehem of line of David; lived as child at Nazareth; as young man followed carpenter's trade. Lifetime a period of distress in Palestine under rule of three sons of Herod (see HEROD ARCHELAUS, HEROD ANTIPAS, and PHILIP the Tetrarch) and oppressive Roman procurators. Baptized by John the Baptist (*q.v.*); gathered twelve disciples; preached in Galilee; received with enthusiasm by common people because of extraordinary healing powers, effective teaching by parables, message of redeeming love of God for every person; strongly opposed by Pharisees and privileged classes because of attacks on hypocrisy and interest in the poor. Regarded by some as long-expected Messiah, hence suspected by rulers of revolutionary aims. After brief ministry in Galilee went with disciples to Jerusalem to observe Passover; taught in Temple and drove out money changers, arousing hostility of priestly class. After Last Supper with disciples, betrayed by one of them, Judas Iscariot; seized by Roman soldiers; examined by high priest and Sanhedrin and condemned as blasphemer deserving death; sent to Roman procurator, Pontius Pilate, and by him to Herod Antipas, who sent him back to Pilate; turned over by him to the Jewish authorities. Crucified on Golgotha and buried in tomb of Joseph of Arimathea; believed by his followers to have risen from the dead and ascended to heaven. Christian religion grew out of his disciples' proclamation of him as the Messiah and savior of mankind.

Jev·ons \'jev-ənz\, William Stanley. 1835–1882. English economist and logician. Assayer at the mint, Sydney, Australia (1854–59). Professor of logic, political economy, and philosophy, Owens Coll., Manchester (1866–79); professor of political economy, University Coll., London (1876–80). Developed marginal utility theory of value. Author of *Pure Logic* (1864), *The Coal Question* (1865), *Theory of Political Economy* (1871), *Principles of Science* (1874), *The State in Relation to Labour* (1882), etc.

Jew·el \'jü-əl\, John. 1522–1571. English prelate. Absented himself in Europe during reign of Mary (1553–59); named by Queen Elizabeth bishop of Salisbury (1560–71). Author of *Apologia pro Ecclesia Anglicana* (1562), first methodical statement of the Anglican church's position against the Roman Catholic church.

Jew·ett \'jü-ət\, Milo Parker. 1808–1882. American educator, b. St. Johnsbury, Vt. Founded Judson Female Institute, Marion, Ala. (1838–55). Induced Matthew Vassar to endow a women's college, chartered (1861) as Vassar College, with Jewett as first president (1862–64).

Jewett, Sarah Orne, *in full* Theodora Sarah Orne. 1849–1909. American writer, b. South Berwick, Me. Author of sketches and tales of New England important in the "local color" school, including *Deephaven* (1877), *A Country Doctor* (1884), *A Marsh Island* (1885), *A White Heron* (1886), *Tales of New England* (1890), *The Country of the Pointed Firs* (1896), etc.

Jews·bury \'jüz-bər-ē, -brē\, Maria Jane. 1800–1833. English writer. Wrote *Phantasmagoria* (1824), *The Three Histories* (1830). Her sister ¶Geraldine Endsor (1812–1880) wrote *Zoe* (1846), *Marian Withers* (1851), *Right or Wrong* (1859).

Jex-Blake \'jeks-'blāk\, Sophia Louisa. 1840–1912. English physician. Founded London School of Medicine for Women (1874); gained legal right to practice in Great Britain (1877); practiced in Edinburgh (1878–99), where she also founded (1886) a school of medicine for women. Her brother ¶Thomas William (1832–1915) was a clergyman and educator; headmaster of Rugby School (1874–87); dean of Wells (1891–1910).

Jez·e·bel \'jez-ə-bel, -bəl\. d. c.843 B.C. Phoenician princess. Daughter of Ethbaal, king of Tyre and Sidon, and wife of Ahab, king of Israel; mother of Ahaziah, Jehoram, and Athaliah. Introduced worship of Baal into Israel and persecuted prophets of Jehovah, esp. Elijah.

Jhe·ring *or* **Ihe·ring** \'yā-riŋ\, Rudolf von. 1818–1892. German legal scholar and writer. Professor, Basel, Rostock, Kiel, Giessen (1852–68), Vienna (1868–72), Göttingen (1872–92); considered father of sociological jurisprudence. Author of *Geist des römischen Rechts* (1852–65), *Der Zweck im Recht* (1877–83), etc.

Jibran, Khalil. See GIBRAN.

Ji·en \jē-en\. *Orig.* Fu·ji·wa·ra \fü̇j-ē-wä-rä\ Dokai. 1145–1225. Japanese religious and historian. Member of highest circle of powerful Fujiwara family; entered Tendai Buddhist monastery; became first great historian of Japan. Chief work *Gukanshō* (c.1220).

Jī·lī, al- \əl-jē-'lē\. *In full* 'Abd al-Karīm Quṭb ad-Dīn ibn Ibrāhīm al-Jīlī. 1365–c.1424. Islāmic mystic. Evolved doctrine of the "perfect man," who can achieve unity with the Divine Being. Chief work *al-Insān al-kāmil fī ma'rifat al-awākhir wa al-awā'il.*

Ji·mé·nez \hē-'mā-nāth\, Juan Ramón. 1881–1958. Spanish poet. Works included *Almas de violeta* (1900), *Ninfeas* (1900), *Jardines lejanos* (1905), *Elegías puras* (1908), *Pastorales* (1911), *Sonetos espirituales* (1917), *Diario de un poeta recién casado* (1917), *Eternidades* (1918), *Piedra y cielo* (1919), *La estación total* (1946), *Animal de fondo* (1949); also wrote widely translated prose work *Platero y yo* (1914). Awarded Nobel prize for literature (1956).

Jiménez de Cis·ne·ros \-thā-thēs-'nā-rōs\, Francisco. 1436–1517. Spanish prelate and statesman. In Rome (1459–66); imprisoned by archbishop of Toledo (1473–79); vicar general of Sigüenza (1482); entered Franciscan order (1484); named confessor to Queen Isabella (1492); provincial of Franciscan order of Castile (1494); archbishop of Toledo and primate of Spain (1495). Instigated forced mass conversions of Moors of Granada, leading to revolt (1499–1500). Cardinal (1507), and inquisitor general of Castile and León; in expedition to Africa, captured Oran (1509). Regent of Castile for Charles I (1516).

Jiménez de Que·sa·da \-thā-kā-'sä-thä\, Gonzalo. c.1495–1579. Spanish conquistador. To New World (1535) as chief magistrate of Santa Marta colony; led expedition up Magdalena River and reached interior plain of Colombia (1536); drove out Chibcha Indians; challenged by rival conquistadors for honor of having conquered New Granada; became most influential citizen of New Granada; led expedition in search of El Dorado (1569–71).

Jiménez de Ra·da \-thā-'rä-thä\, Rodrigo. 1170–1247. Spanish prelate and historian. Bishop of Osma (1208); archbishop of Toledo (1209); exercised considerable influence over Alfonso VIII and Ferdinand II; encouraged crusades; asserted authority over Valencia (1238). Author of *De rebus Hispaniae,* also known as *Historia gótica* or *Crónica del toledano.*

Ji·mé·nez Ore·a·mu·no \hē-'mā-nās-ō-rā-ä-'mü-nō\, Ricardo. 1859–1945. Costa Rican politician. President of Costa Rica (1910–14, 1924–28, 1932–36).

Jim·mu Ten·nō \jēm-mu̇-ten-nō\. *Orig.* Kamu-yamato-ihare-biko. 7th? century B.C. First emperor of Japan in legendary period. Regarded by Japanese as founder of present dynasty and believed to be direct descendant of sun goddess. Traditionally held to have reigned (660–585 B.C.). Japanese Era dated from beginning of his reign (Feb. 11, 660 B.C.).

Jin·gō \jin-gō\. *Also known as* Jin-gu Kō·gō \jin-gu̇-kō-gō\. 169?–269 A.D. Japanese empress. According to tradition, wife of Chūai, 14th emperor, and regent for son Ōjin; credited with conquest of Korea (200–203).

Jin·nah \'jin-(,)ä, 'jin-ə\, Mohammed Ali. 1876–1948. Indian politician. Educated in London; became a leading member of bar in Bombay; a leading moderate in Indian National Congress; president of Muslim League (1913); negotiated Lucknow Pact (1916) with Congress, providing political safeguards for Muslim community; opposed Hindu ideology and methods of Gandhi and gradually abandoned goal of Hindu–Muslim unity for separate Muslim statehood; head of reconstituted Muslim League (1934 ff.); formally adopted separation as goal (1940); first governor general of Pakistan (1947–48).

Ji·rá·sek \'yi-rä-sek\, Alois. 1851–1930. Czech novelist. Author of novels on Czech national themes including trilogy on the age of Jan Hus *Mezi proudy* (1891), *Proti všem* (1894), *Bratrstvo* (1899–1908); also *Psohlavci* (1886), *F.L. Věk* (1888–1906), *Temno* (1915); also wrote historical dramas.

Jñā·na·de·va \jə-,nän-ə-'dev-ə\ *or* **Jñā·neś·va·ra** \jə-,nän-əsh-'vär-ə\. 1275–1296. Indian poet. Foremost of the Mahārāshtrian mystical poets, a founder of the Vārakarī school of mysticism. Chief work the *Jñanesvarī,* celebrated commentary in Marathi verse on the *Bhagavadgītā.*

Jo·ab \'jō-ab\. fl. 1000 B.C. Hebrew soldier. Son of Zeruiah, David's half-sister. Led capture of Jerusalem and thereupon made commander of David's army; defeated and killed Abner; victorious in wars against Ammonites; put down conspiracy of Absalom; deposed by David for killing Absalom; killed his rival Amasa but was executed by Solomon after David's death.

Jo·a·chim \'yō-ä-ḵim, yō-'ä-\. Name of three electors of Brandenburg:

Joachim I Nes·tor \'nes-tȯr\. 1484–1535. Elector (1499–1535). Staunch foe of the Reformation; improved administration of justice, settled unruly nobles; founded university at Frankfurt an der Oder (1506).

Joachim II Hek·tor \'hek-tȯr\. 1505–1571. Elector (1535–71). Son of Joachim I; tolerated Protestantism in Brandenburg and attempted to mediate between emperor and Protestant nobles; supported Charles V against Schmalkaldic League and helped mediate its end; helped negotiate Peace of Augsburg (1555).

Joachim Friedrich. 1546–1608. Elector (1598–1608). Grandson of Joachim II. Promulgated Gera Bond (1598), formally confirming practice of primogeniture in family.

Jo·a·chim \yō-'ä-kēm\ of Fio·re \'fyō-rā\. *Also* of Flo·ra \'flōr-ə, 'flȯr-\ *or* Flo·ris \-əs\. c.1130 or 1135–1201 or 1202. Italian religious. Entered Cistercian order (c.1160); abbot at Corazzo (1177–78); retired to San Giovanni in Fiore (1191) and founded community of hermits that became Florensian order (rule approved 1196). In opposition to Peter Lombard developed view of Trinity that was condemned by Fourth Lateran Council (1215) as tritheistic; developed theory of history as comprising three ages, those of the Father, the Son, and (to commence c.1260) the Holy Spirit. Author of *Concordia novi et veteris testamenti, Expositio in Apocalypsim, Psalterium decem chordarum,* and other tracts.

Joachim, George. See RHÄTICUS.

Joachim, Joseph. 1831–1907. Hungarian violinist and composer. Public debut at 7; great success in London under sponsorship of Mendelssohn (1844); concert conductor and violinist to the king at Hanover (1853–66); director of the musical Hochschule at Berlin (from 1868), where he founded (1869) and directed the Joachim Quartet. Known esp. for interpretations of Bach, Mozart, Beethoven, subordinating technical brilliance to aesthetic considerations. Composed violin concertos, including *Hungarian Concerto in D minor,* variations, overtures, etc.

Joachin. See JEHOIACHIN.

Joad \'jōd\, Cyril Edwin Mitchinson. 1891–1953. British philosopher. In civil service (1914–30); professor, U. of London (1930–53). Works included *Common Sense Ethics* (1921), *Common Sense Theology* (1922), *The Present and Future of Religion* (1930), *Guide to Philosophy* (1936), *Guide to the Philosophy of Morals and Politics* (1938), *Good and Evil* (1943), *Recovery of Belief* (1952), etc.

Joakim. See JEHOIAKIM.

Joan \'jōn, 'jō-ən, jō-'an\. *Span.* Jua·na \'ḵwä-nä\. Name of several queens, queens consort, and princesses of Castile, including:

Joan. 1439–1475. Queen of Henry IV of Castile (1455–74). Daughter of King Edward of Portugal; m. Henry (1455); secured from Henry and the Cortes recognition of her daughter Joan (b. 1462) as heir apparent; on death of Henry (1474) failed to secure succession of daughter.

Joan. *Called* la Bel·tra·ne·ja \lä-ḇel-trä-'nā-ḵä\. 1462–1530. Princess of Castile. Daughter of Henry IV and Joan; declared father's heir (1462, 1470) but opposed by court faction who circulated rumor that she was actually the daughter of Beltrán de la Cueva; at father's death (1474) blocked from succession by faction favoring Isabella I (*q.v.*), who secured throne after five years' civil war; retired to monastery in Portugal.

Joan I. *Called* la Lo·ca \lä-'lō-kä\, *i.e.* the Mad. 1479–1555. Queen of Castile (1504–55) and Aragon (1516–55). Daughter of Isabella I and Ferdinand II; m. (1496) Philip of Burgundy; by deaths of other heirs, became heir apparent to Aragon and Castile (1500); began to exhibit instability (1502); completely lost her reason at death of Philip (1506); lived under guard at Tordesillas. Mother of emperors Charles V and Ferdinand I.

Joan *or* **Jo·anne** \jō-'an\. *Ital.* Gio·van·na \jō-'vän-nä\. Name of two queens of Naples:

Joan I. 1326–1382. Queen (1343–82). Daughter of Charles, Duke of Calabria; succeeded grandfather Robert on throne; participant in plotting of assassination (1345) of her husband Andrew, brother of Louis I of Hungary; m. (1347) Louis of Taranto; driven from Naples by invasion of Louis I of Hungary (1348); sold Avignon to papacy and with aid of Pope Innocent VI returned to Naples (1352); after death of 2d husband (1362) m. James III of Majorca (d. 1375); m. (1376) Otto of Brunswick; recognized as heir Louis I, duc d'Anjou, displacing previously recognized Charles of Durazzo (see CHARLES III); captured and imprisoned by Charles (1382) and put to death.

Joan II. 1371–1435. Queen (1414–35). Daughter of Charles III; succeeded brother Ladislas; reign marked by power struggles of her various paramours and adoptive heirs; chief figures in kingdom included Muzio Sforza, Pandolfello Alopo, Giovanni Caracciolo; adopted Alfonso V of Aragon and Louis III of Anjou alternately, finally settling succession on Louis's son René.

Joan I. *Span.* Jua·na \'ḵwä-nä\. 1273–1305. Queen of Navarre (1274–1305) and of France (1285–1305). Daughter of Henry I of Navarre; m. (1284) future Philip IV the Fair of France; union brought to French crown Navarre and counties of Brie and Champagne. Mother of Louis X, Philip V, and Charles IV of France.

Joan. *Called* Joan of the Tower. 1321–1362. Queen of Scotland. Youngest child of Edward II of England and Isabella, b. in Tower of London. m. (1328) Robert Bruce's son and heir David, who became king (1329). Shared husband's exile in France (1334–41). After David's defeat and capture in England (1346), made repeated efforts to obtain his release from prison (1346–57).

Joan of Arc \,jō-nə-'värk *also* jō-ə-nə-, jō-,an-ə-\. Saint. *Fr.* Jeanne d'Arc \zhän-dȧrk\. *Called* La Pu·celle d'Or·lé·ans \lȧ-pu̅e̅-sel-dȯr-lā-äⁿ\, *i.e.* the Maid of Orleans. c.1412–1431. French national heroine, b. Domremy-la-Pucell. At age of twelve, believed she heard voices from angels or from God, at first giving her advice to help her lead a holy life and, later, directions to aid the dauphin in the then troubled times of France (see CHARLES VII). Visited military commandant at Vaucouleurs (1428) and finally persuaded him to guide her to the dauphin, holding court at Bourges; counseled by the voices to raise the siege of Orléans (1428) by the English; obtained consent of Charles; clad in armor, with small army forced English to withdraw (May 4–8, 1429) and brought relief to Dunois and the besieged, arousing enthusiasm throughout France and changing trend of war. Persuaded dauphin to be conducted to Reims and crowned (July 17, 1429); took part in many conflicts (1429–30), some successful. Captured by Burgundians at Compiègne (May 23, 1430); sold six months later to the English; charged with witchcraft and heresy; subject to long, disgraceful, and unfair trial at Rouen by tribunal of French ecclesiastics; condemned and burned at the stake (May 30, 1431). Revision of her trial obtained and her innocence proclaimed (1456); beatified by Pope Pius X (1909); canonized by Pope Benedict XV (1920).

Joan *or* **Jo·an·na** \jō-'an-ə\ of Na·varre \nȧ-vȧr, *Angl* nə-'vär\. 1370–1437. Queen of Henry IV of England. Daughter of Charles d'Albret of Navarre; m. 1st (1386) John V, Duke of Brittany, by whom she had eight children; after his death (1399), regent of Brittany for her son John; m. 2d (1402) Henry IV of England; on friendly relations with her stepson King Henry V (1413–22); accused and imprisoned (1419–22) on vague charges of witchcraft probably actuated by anti-French sentiment in England.

Joannes. See JOHN.

João. See JOHN.

Jobst \'yōpst\. *Also called* Jost \'yōst\ *and* Jo·docks \'yō-dōks\. 1351–1411. Margrave of Moravia (1376–1411). Member of Luxembourg dynasty; general vicar of Italy (1383, 1389); gained control of Luxembourg and Brandenburg (1388); captured cousin Wenceslas, king of Germany, and forced him to yield regency of Bohemia (1394); received two Lusatias (1397); prince of the empire (1397); elected by a faction of Frankfurt assembly to succeed King Rupert (1410); reigned only 15 weeks.

Joce·lin de Brake·lond \'jäs-lən-də-'brak-lənd\. fl. 1173–1215. English monk and chronicler. Entered Benedictine abbey at Bury St. Edmunds (1173); author of *Cronica,* relating history of abbey under abbot Samson of Tottington (*q.v.*).

Jochanan ben Zakkai. See JOHANAN BEN ZAKKAI.

Jo·chel·son \'yȯk-yil-sən\, Vladimir Ilich. 1855–1937. Russian ethnographer and linguist. Sent to Siberia for revolutionary activities, began studying Siberian peoples, esp. the Koryaks; took part in Jesup North Pacific Expedition of American Museum of Natural History (1900–01); associate curator, Anthropological and Ethnographical Museum, Petrograd (1912–22); to U.S. (1922). Author of *The Koryak* (1908), *The Yukaghir* (1926), *Peoples of Asiatic Russia* (1928).

Joch·mus \'yȯk-mu̇s\, Giacomo August. Baron von Co·ti·gno·la \kō-tēn-'yō-lä\. 1808–1881. German soldier of fortune. Fought in Greek war of independence (1827); general in British foreign legion during Spanish Civil War (1835–38); general chief of staff of combined Turkish, British, and Austrian forces in Syrian campaign (1840–41); in Turkish war ministry (1848). Returned to Germany (1848) and served as minister of foreign affairs and of the navy (1849); named lieutenant field marshal (1859).

Jō·chō \jō-chō\. d. 1057. Japanese sculptor. Developed and perfected joined-wood techniques; accorded unprecedented honors as Buddhist sculptor; organized "Bussho" guild of Buddhist sculptors.

Jo·chums·son \'yäk-kœms-sȯn\, Matthías. 1835–1920. Icelandic poet. Lutheran clergyman; drew on Iceland's history for subjects, as in *Grettisljóth* (1897), verse series dealing with exploits of Grettir, famous outlaw; also wrote lyrical dramas, hymns, and funeral poems; translated works of Shakespeare, Byron, Ibsen, etc.

Jo·delle \zhȯ-del\, Étienne. 1532–1573. French poet. Member of the Pléiade; regarded as founder of French tragedy for his *Cléopâtre captive* (1553); also helped shape French comedy with *Eugène* (1552).

Jodl \'yōd-ᵊl\, Alfred. 1890–1946. German army officer. Chief of German operations staff (1939–45) and a principal adviser of Hitler; signed act of military surrender (May 7, 1945); hanged as war criminal.

Jo·el \'jō-əl\. A minor Hebrew prophet of uncertain date, but considered to have lived in period of the Second Temple (after 516 B.C.), whose predictions of judgment on Judah, with exhortation to repentance and promise of final blessing, the Old Testament book of Joel records.

Joest van Kal·kar \'yōst-vän-ˌkäl-kär\, Jan. c.1460–1519. Dutch painter. Known for altarpieces as *Altar der sieben Schmerzen* in Palencia, Spain (1505), altar in Nicolaikirche, Kalkar (1505–08).

Jof·fre \zhȯfrᵊ\, Joseph-Jacques-Césaire. 1852–1931. French soldier. Took part in defense of Paris (1870); engaged in engineering duties; general of brigade (1902) and of division (1905). At outbreak of World War I (1914), became commander in chief of the French armies, and later of the allied armies in France; planned and directed the victory in the battle of the Marne (Sept. 1914), which stopped the German advance upon Paris; created field marshal; following Verdun, resigned as commander in chief and made marshal of France (1916).

Jogues \zhȯg\, Isaac. Saint. 1607–1646. French missionary. Entered Jesuit order (1624); stationed among Indians south of Lake Huron (1636–39); accompanied Indians to strait which he named Sault de Ste. Marie (1641). Captured by Iroquois, tortured, hands mutilated (1642); rescued by the Dutch and taken (1643) to New Amsterdam (New York). Again on mission to Iroquois (1646). Undertook mission to Mohawks; tomahawked on site of what is now Auriesville, N.Y. Canonized (1930).

Johan. See JOHN.

Jo·han·an ben Zak·kai \jō-'han-ən-ben-'zak-ā-ˌī, jō-'kan-\. 1st century A.D. Jewish sage. A Pharisee; taught in Jerusalem; escaped into Roman camp during siege of Jerusalem; founded (with Vespasian's permission) and became first head of the school at Jamnia (Jabneh); headed the Jewish community after destruction of Jerusalem and the Second Temple by the Romans, and helped restore and regenerate Jewish national life.

Johann and **Johannes.** See also JOHN.

Jo·han·na \yō-ȧ-nȧ\. d. 1406. Duchess of Brabant. On occasion of a ceremonial visit to Brabant (1356) issued Joyeuse Entrée, a constitution embodying extraordinarily broad liberties.

Johannes à Lasco. See Jan ŁASKI.

Johannes de Anglicus. See John BACONTHORPE.

Johannes de Garlandia. See John GARLAND.

Johannes Erigena. See ERIGENA.

Johannes Scotus. See ERIGENA.

Jo·han·not \zhȯ-ȧ-nō\, Charles (1798–1825) and his brothers Alfred (1800–1837) and Tony (1803–1852). French engravers and illustrators. Works illustrated by them included Byron's *Don Juan, Don Quixote,* Goethe's *Faust* and *Werther,* works of George Sand, Sir Walter Scott, Lamartine, etc.

Jo·hann·sen \yō-'hȧn-sən\, Wilhelm Ludvig. 1857–1927. Danish botanist and geneticist. Professor, Copenhagen Agricultural Coll. (1903–05), U. of Copenhagen (1905 ff.; rector 1917). Pioneer in modern experimental genetics; known for experiments with beans leading to his development of the pure-line theory; originated distinction of genotype and phenotype, coined term "gene" (1909) for unit of heredity.

Jo·hann von Neu·markt \yō-'hän-fȯn-'nȯi-ˌmärkt\. *Lat.* Johannes No·vi·fo·ren·sis \nō-və-fə-'ren(t)-səs\. c.1310–1380. German prelate. Preacher in Neumarkt (1344); chancellor to Emperor Charles IV (1353–74); bishop of Naumburg (1352), Leitomischl (1353), Olmütz (1364), Breslau (1380); emissary to Italy (1354–55, 1367–69); associated with Petrarch and Cola di Rienzo; influenced development of medieval Latin and German literary languages.

Johann von Tepl \-fȯn-'tep-əl\. *Also* Johann von Saaz \-'zäts\. c.1350–c.1415. Bohemian educator and writer. Headmaster of a grammar school in Saaz (Žatec); notary there and later in Prague. Author of *Der Ackermann aus Böhmen* (c.1400), dialogue of a plowman and Death that is regarded as first important prose work in German.

Jo·han·sen \yō-'hän-sən\, Frederic Hjalmar. 1867–1923. Norwegian explorer. Accompanied Nansen toward North Pole (1895), and Amundsen to South Pole (1911).

Jo·hans·son \yō-'hȧn-sən\, Christian, *in full* Per Christian. 1817–1903. Danish dancer and teacher. Student of Bournonville; premier danseur at Imperial Ballet, St. Petersburg (1841–69); began teaching (1860); contributed greatly to development of Russian ballet style, esp. in evolving male techniques and roles.

Jo·hans·son \yō-'hän-sən\, Lars. *Pseudonym* Las·se Lu·ci·dor \'lȧs-sə-'lü-sə-dȯr\. 1638–1674. Swedish poet. One of outstanding writers of Swedish Baroque verse; wrote epithalamia, drinking songs, funeral elegies, etc., including his best known "Skulle jag sörja så vore jag tokot."

John, Saint. See JOHN the Apostle; JOHN the Baptist.

John \'jän\. Name of twenty-one popes (owing to a scribal error, there is no John XX), and three antipopes:

John I. Saint. d. 526. Pope (523–526). Sent (525) by Theodoric, king of the Ostrogoths, to Constantinople to urge Emperor Justin I to show toleration to Arians; mission only partly successful; on return was imprisoned at Ravenna, where he died.

John II. *Orig.* Mer·cu·ri·us \(ˌ)mər-'kyu̇r-ē-əs\. d. 535. Pope (533–535). First pope to change his name on election; much occupied with opposing Nestorianism; excommunicated the Acoemeti monks of Constantinople (534) for Nestorianism; cooperated with Emperor Justinian I, who paid him notable deference.

John III. *Orig. probably* Ca·te·li·nus \ˌkät-ᵊl-'ī-nəs\. d. 574. Pope (561–574). Invited Byzantine general Narses to defend Rome against Lombards (571), but because of unpopularity of Narses among Romans was forced to retire to catacombs until death of Narses (c.573).

John IV. d. 642. Pope (640–642). Redeemed Christian captives taken in Slavic invasions of the Balkans; condemned Pelagianism and Monothelitism and defended orthodoxy of Pope Honorius I; censured Celtic date for celebrating Easter.

John V. d. 686. Pope (685–686). As a deacon, legate of Pope St. Agatho to 6th ecumenical council at Constantinople (680–681); reigned briefly.

John VI. d. 705. Pope (701–705). Quelled militia revolt against exarch Theophylactus; negotiated release of captives and withdrawal from Campania of Gisulfo, Duke of Benevento; ordered restoration of St. Wilfrid to see of York.

John VII. d. 707. Pope (705–707). Restored many Roman churches; declined to recognize canons drawn up by Quinisext Synod (or Council of Trullo, 692) and submitted to him by Emperor Justinian II.

John VIII. d. 882. Pope (872–882). Approved use of Slavonic liturgy by St. Methodius; recognized Photius as patriarch of Constantinople (879); struggled against Saracen invasions of Italy, allying himself with Emperor Louis II; crowned succeeding emperors Charles II the Bald (875) and Charles III the Fat (881); deposed and excommunicated Formosus (876); founded papal navy.

John IX. d. 900. Pope (898–900). Excommunicated rival Sergius; held councils in Rome and Ravenna to exculpate Pope Formosus; restored clergy deposed by Pope Stephen and negated acts of Stephen's synod.

John X. d. 928. Pope (914–928). Archbishop of Ravenna (c.905); crowned Berengar emperor (915); defeated Saracens (915) on the banks of the Garigliano; approved rule of Cluniac order; formed alliance with King Hugh, which enraged Marozia, powerful senator of Crescentii family who had him imprisoned and killed.

John XI. 910?–935 or 936. Pope (931–935 or 936). Son of Marozia and reputed son of Pope Sergius III. Made pope through influence of mother; held prisoner in Lateran palace by (probably half-) brother Alberic II.

John XII. *Orig.* Oc·ta·vian \äk-'tāv-yən\. 937?–964. Pope (955–964). Son of Alberic II; called Otto I of Germany to his aid against King Berengar II of Italy (961); crowned Otto emperor (962); conspired against Otto and deposed (963) in favor of Leo VIII; recaptured Rome (964) and deposed Leo, but died suddenly.

John XIII. d. 972. Pope (965–972). Subservient to Emperor Otto I; driven out by Roman nobles but restored (966); crowned Otto II as joint emperor (967); established metropolitan see of Magdeburg (968).

John XIV. *Orig.* Pietro Ca·ne·pa·no·va \kä-ˌnā-pä-ˈnō-vä\. d. 984. Pope (983–984). Bishop of Pavia before election; made pope at instance of Otto II, who died immediately afterward; imprisoned and murdered by Crescentii faction in favor of antipope Boniface VII.

John XV. d. 996. Pope (985–996). Candidate of Crescentius II and largely dominated by Crescentii; performed first formal canonization by papal decree (St. Ulric of Augsburg, 993).

John XVII. *Orig.* Giovanni Sic·co·ne \sēk-ˈkō-nā\. d. 1003. Pope (1003). A puppet of Crescentii, reigned 6 months.

John XVIII. *Orig.* Giovanni Fa·sa·no \fä-ˈsä-nō\. d. 1009. Pope (1004–09). Elected by but somewhat independent of Crescentii; abdicated.

John XIX. *Orig.* Ro·ma·no \rō-ˈmä-nō\ *or* Ro·ma·nus \rō-ˈmā-nəs\. d. 1032. Pope (1024–32). Member of powerful Tusculani family; assumed papacy as an inheritance on death of brother, Benedict VIII; crowned Emperor Conrad II (1027); notorious for sale of hierarchical appointments.

John XXI. *Orig.* Petrus Ju·lia·ni \jül-ˈyä-nē\. *Also called* Petrus His·pa·nus \his-ˈpā-nəs\, *i.e.* Peter of Spain. d. 1277. Pope (1276–77), b. Lisbon. Archbishop of Braga (1272); cardinal bishop of Tusculum (1273); as pope sought to unify Eastern and Western churches. Author of commentaries on Aristotle, a popular treatise on logic *Summulae logicales,* and several books on medicine.

John XXII. *Orig.* Jacques Du·è·se \dü-ˈā-sā\. *Also spelled* d'Euse \dœz\, Deuze, Dueza, de Osa, *etc.* c.1245–1334. Pope (1316–34). Chancellor of Charles II of Naples (1309); cardinal (1312); as pope resided at Avignon, under French influence; had long conflict with the emperor, Louis of Bavaria; opposed by antipope Nicholas V, installed (1328) by Louis; engaged in controversy with Franciscan Spirituals.

John XXIII. *Orig.* Angelo Giuseppe Ron·cal·li \rȯŋ-ˈkäl-lē\. 1881–1963. Pope (1958–1963). Ordained (1904); on staff of Society for Propagation of the Faith (1921); titular archbishop of and apostolic visitor to Bulgaria (from 1925); apostolic delegate to Turkey and Greece (1934–44); nuncio to France (1944–53); cardinal and patriarch of Venice (1953). Convoked 2d Vatican Council (1962); notably interested in ecumenism; issued encyclical *Pacem in terris* (1963).

ANTIPOPES:

John. 9th century. Antipope (844). Archdeacon of Rome; elected by populace in opposition to candidate of the nobility, Sergius II; spared but imprisoned by Sergius.

John XVI. *Orig.* Giovanni Fi·la·ga·to \ˌfē-lä-ˈgä-tō\. *Lat.* Joannes Phil·a·ga·thus \ˌfil-ə-ˈgā-thəs\. d. c.1013. Antipope (997–998). Monk; named abbot of Nonantola by Emperor Otto II; influential at court of Otto's widow Theodora; bishop of Piacenza (988), later archbishop; godfather to Otto III; Otto III's emissary to Constantinople (995); named pope by Crescentius II in opposition to Otto's choice, Gregory V; captured with Crescentius by Otto, blinded, mutilated, imprisoned or confined to a monastery.

John XXIII. *Orig.* Baldassare Cos·sa \ˈkōs-sä\. d. 1419. Antipope (1410–15). Entered Roman Curia during Great Western Schism; made cardinal (1402) by Boniface IX; papal representative in Bologna (1403–08); deserted Pope Gregory XII and took leading role at Council of Pisa (1409) and in council's election of antipope Alexander V; elected by schismatic cardinals to succeed Alexander (1410); made alliance with Louis II of Anjou and with him entered Rome (1411); later attempted alliance with Ladislas of Naples; forced to flee Rome (1413); called Council of Constance (1414) and at its request agreed to abdicate if Gregory XII and Benedict XIII would also; fled Constance (1415) and was thereupon deposed by council, which elected Martin V; captured, held by King Sigismund (1415–18); cardinal bishop of Tusculum (1419).

John. *Span.* Juan \ˈk̲wän\. Name of two kings of Aragon and Navarre:

John I. 1350–1395. King of Aragon (1387–95). Son of Peter IV; suppressed revolt of Sardinia (1391); patron of learning and, with his wife Yolande de Bar, of troubadours.

John II. 1397–1479. King of Aragon (1458–79) and of Navarre (1425–79). Son of Ferdinand I of Aragon; m. (1425; d. 1441) Blanche of Navarre; succeeded brother Alphonso as king of Aragon; m. 2d (1447) Juana Enriquez of Castile; involved in civil war with son Charles, prince of Viana, over throne of Navarre (1441–62); faced revolt in Catalonia (1462–72); arranged marriage (1469) of his son Ferdinand to Isabella of Castile.

John. *Ger.* Jo·hann \yō-ˈhän, ˈyō-ˌ\. 1782–1859. Archduke of Austria. Son of Leopold II; commanded Austrian army in French wars; defeated at Hohenlinden (1800), Raab (1809); retired to private study (1815); chosen regent of Germany by National Assembly at Frankfurt (1848–49).

John. King of Bohemia. See JOHN of Luxembourg.

John I. *Fr.* Jean \zhäⁿ\. *Called* the Victorious. d. 1294. Duke of Brabant and Lower Lorraine (1261–94). Son of Duke Henry III; by purchase (1283) and in War of Limburg Succession (1283–88), culminating in victory over Limburg and Luxembourg forces at Worringen (1288), united Limburg with Brabant and prevented southward expansion of Dutch Guelders.

John. *Ger.* Johann. 1513–1571. Margrave of Brandenburg-Küstrin (1535–71). Son of Elector Joachim I, who divided his lands between John and elder brother Joachim II; received eastern Neumark portion; fought with Schmalkaldic League but defected to Emperor Charles V (1545) and helped defeat League (1547); at his death left no sons, lands reverting to nephew John George.

John. *Fr.* Jean. Name of five dukes of Brittany:

John I. *Called* le Roux \lə-rü\, *i.e.* the Red. 1217–1286. Duke (1237–86). Son of Peter I Mauclerc; patron and practitioner of arts; accompanied St. Louis IX on crusade (1270).

John II. d. 1305. Duke (1286–97). Son of John I; m. (1259) Béatrix, daughter of Henry III of England.

John III. *Called* le Bon \lə-bōⁿ\, *i.e.* the Good. 1286–1341. Duke (1312–41). Son of Arthur II; left no male heirs, named as successor his niece Jeanne de Penthièvre, thus fomenting long War of Breton Succession (see CHARLES of Blois; JOHN of Montfort).

John IV. *Called* le Vail·lant \lə-vȧ-yäⁿ(t)\, *i.e.* the Valiant, *or* le Con·qué·reur \lə-kōⁿ-kā-rœr\, *i.e.* the Conqueror. 1341–1399. Duke (1365–99). Son of John of Montfort; educated at court of Edward III of England; defeated Charles of Blois at Auray (1364), ending War of Breton Succession; recognized by Charles V of France in Treaty of Guérande (1365); aided Edward in war with France and granted earldom of Richmond (1372); forced to flee to England on French conquest of Brittany (1373); property confiscated by Charles V (1378); made alliance with Richard II of England (1380); regained duchy in second Treaty of Guérande (1381).

John V. *Called* le Sage \lə-sȧzh\, *i.e.* the Wise. 1389–1442. Duke (1399–1442). Son of John IV; maintained relationships with Henry V of England and Charles VII of France during their war; in French civil war gradually came to favor Armagnac faction over Burgundian but took no part; upheld Treaty of Troyes (1420) but maintained relationship with disowned dauphin; took part in revolts of the Praguerie (1440), League of Nevers (1442).

John. Duke of Burgundy. See JOHN the Fearless.

John. *Span.* Juan \ˈk̲wän\. Name of two kings of Castile and León:

John I. 1358–1390. King (1379–90). Son of Henry II; m. 2d (1383) Beatriz, daughter of Ferdinand of Portugal; on Ferdinand's death (1383), invaded Portugal and proclaimed himself king (1384); resisted by John of Aviz (see JOHN I of Portugal) and defeated at Aljubarrota (1385); faced invasion of Anglo-Portuguese army (1386–88) under John of Gaunt; made Treaty of Bayonne (1388), in which in return for heavy indemnity, John of Gaunt renounced claim to Castilian throne.

John II. 1405–1454. King (1406–54). Son of Henry III; under regency (1406–19) of uncle, Don Fernando, and his mother, Catherine of Lancaster; for much of reign virtually abandoned government to favorite, Alvaro de Luna; Luna achieved victories over Moors (1431), rebellious nobles (1445); m. 2d (1447) Isabella of Portugal, who persuaded him to arrest and execute Luna (1453); died reputedly of remorse.

John. Name of several patriarchs of Constantinople, esp.:

John III. *Surnamed* Scho·las·ti·cus \skə-ˈlas-ti-kəs\. *Also called* John of An·ti·och \ˈant-ē-ˌäk\. c.503–577. Lawyer and priest; legate of patriarch of Antioch at Constantinople; named patriarch of Constantinople by Emperor Justinian (565); attempted to mediate factional disputes of Monophysites and tritheists; later agent of Emperor Justin II in harsh persecution of Monophysites and other heretics. Compiled (c.545) earliest extant catalogue of canons of the Byzantine church, collating laws of Basil of Cappadocia with imperial ecclesiastical statutes. Author of controversial works, a catechetical treatise *Mystagogia,* etc.

John IV. *Called* the Faster. d. 595. Ordained deacon of Hagia Sophia by John III; given charge of care of the poor; famed for asceticism; named patriarch by Tiberius II (582); at a synod (588) adopted title "ecumenical patriarch," leading to controversy with popes Pelagius II and Gregory I. Canonized in Orthodox church.

John XI. *Surnamed* Bec·chus \ˈbek-əs\. c.1235–1297. Patriarch (1275–82). In service of Patriarch Arsenius; gradually adopted views of Emperor Michael VIII Palaeologus favoring reunion of Eastern and Western churches; accepted primacy of pope, Latin doctrine of Trinity, etc.; at Council of Lyons (1274) effected union; named by Michael to succeed abdicated Arsenius; unable to persuade Orthodox clergy and laity to accept union; excommunicated anti-unionists in Orthodox monasteries; position rendered untenable by demand for absolute submission by Pope Nicholas III; resigned on death of Michael.

John. *Dan.* Hans \'häns\. 1455–1513. King of Denmark and Norway (often called John I, 1483–1513) and of Sweden (as John II, 1497–1501). Son of Christian I of Denmark and Norway; allowed to succeed only by accepting stringent charter imposed by nobles; coronation in Sweden delayed by regent Sten Sture the Elder; offset power of nobles by making alliance with merchant class, which he supported against Hanseatic League; with aid of Grand Prince Ivan III of Moscow forced Sten Sture to resign (1497) and secured crown, but forced out by peasant and noble rebellions (1500–01); trade alliance with England (1490) led to war with Sweden and Lübeck (1510–12), in which new Danish navy was successful.

John. Name of eight rulers of the Eastern Roman Empire:

John I Tzim·is·ces \zə-'mis-,ēz\. 925–976. Emperor (969–976). With Nicephorus II Phocas in imperial army; helped Nicephorus gain throne; intrigued with Empress Theophano in assassination of Nicephorus (969) and assumed throne; m. (970) Theodora, sister of Constantine VII Porphyrogenitus; defeated Bulgars (971); drove Russians out of Bulgaria (971–973); recovered Syria (974–976).

John II Com·ne·nus \käm-'nē-nəs\. 1088–1143. Emperor (1118–43). Son of Alexius I Comnenus; at war in Balkans, with Hungary (1128), etc.; allied with German kings Lothair II, Conrad III; defeated Danismends (1135), forced Raymond of Poitiers to acknowledge his suzerainty over Antioch (1137), conquered Cilicia (1137).

John III Du·cas Va·tat·zes \'dyü-kəs-və-'tat-sēz\. 1193–1254. Emperor at Nicaea (1222–54). Son-in-law of Theodore I Lascaris; conquered most of Asia Minor; with Bulgarian help, defeated Theodore Ducas of Epirus (1230); attempted to isolate Latin Constantinople; unsuccessful in siege of Constantinople (1235).

John IV Las·ca·ris \'las-kə-rəs\. 1250–?1261. Emperor (1258–61) in Nicaea. Son of Theodore II Lascaris; under control of Michael Palaeologus, who seized regency; blinded and imprisoned by Michael (1261).

John V Pa·lae·ol·o·gus \,pā-lē-'äl-ə-gəs, ,pal-ə-\. 1332–1391. Emperor (1341–91). Son of Andronicus III; for two periods virtually superseded by John VI Cantacuzenus (1347–54) and by Andronicus IV (1376–79); reign marked by gradual weakening of imperial power and by encroachments of Ottoman Turks.

John VI Can·ta·cu·ze·nus \,kan-tə-kyü-'zē-nəs\. 1292–1383. Emperor (1347–54). Chief adviser to Andronicus III; made guardian for John V (1341); disputed regency with John's mother, Anna of Savoy; set himself up as emperor in Thrace (1341); civil war with John's supporters followed (1341–47); gained victory with Turkish aid; ruler in Constantinople, nominally jointly with John V (1347–54); period of successful attacks on empire by outsiders (Serbians, Turks, Genoese); driven out, retired to monastery; wrote a history of years 1320–56.

John VII Palaeologus. 1360–c.1410. Emperor (1390). Grandson of John V; seized power for short time (1390); regent for uncle, Emperor Manuel II (1399–1402); governor of Thessalonica (from 1403).

John VIII Palaeologus. 1390–1448. Emperor (1425–48). Son of Manuel II; offered no military opposition to Turks, who encircled the capital; appeared (1438–39) at councils of Ferrara and Florence and offered union of Eastern and Western churches as inducement for Western help against Turks; union rejected by Byzantine people.

John. *Often called* John Lack·land \'lak-,land\. 1167–1216. King of England (1199–1216), of house of Anjou or Plantagenet. Son of Henry II; made earl of Cornwall (1175); granted lordship of Ireland (1177); excluded from regency appointed by brother Richard I; succeeded to throne on death of Richard (1199); inherited also French duchies of Normandy, Anjou, Maine, and Touraine, but lost them (by 1206). Refused to recognize Stephen Langton as archbishop of Canterbury (after Pope Innocent III, to whom dispute had been referred, ordered his election, 1206), provoking papal interdict against England (1208) and excommunication (1209); made peace by accepting his kingdom in fief from pope (1213) and by paying annual tribute. Invaded France, but was defeated (1214). On return to England, met barons at Runnymede, where he was forced to sign (June 15, 1215) Magna Carta, laying foundation for security of English political and personal liberty; immediately appealed to pope and obtained from him bull annulling charter; thereupon imported foreign mercenaries to fight against barons; died before war was decided.

John. *Also* Jo·han·nes *or* Yo·han·nes \yō-'han-əs, -'hän-\. Name of four emperors of Ethiopia, esp.:

John I. *Called* the Just. d. 1682. Emperor (1667–82). Son and successor of Fasilides; championed Ethiopian Orthodox church; continued construction of capital city Gonder.

John IV. *Orig.* Kas·sa \'käs-sä\. 1831–1889. Emperor (1872–89). Prince of Tigre; defeated Menelik II in contest to succeed Tewodros II; aroused Muslim opposition by attempt to impose Ethiopian church; defeated Egyptians (1870s), Italy (1887), and preserved Ethiopian territory; suffered invasion of Mahdist forces from Sudan (1887); invaded Sudan, killed at battle of Metemma.

John. *Fr.* Jean \zhä^{n}\. Name of two kings of France:

John I. *Called* le Pos·thume \lə-pò-stüēm\, *i.e.* the Posthumous. 1316. King (1316). Posthumous son of Louis X, born five and one half months after his father's death, during which period Louis's brother Philip (afterwards Philip V) was regent; lived five days only.

John II. *Called* le Bon \lə-bō^{n}\, *i.e.* the Good. 1319–1364. King (1350–64). Son of Philip VI; rule of first years unwise and tyrannical; defeated by Edward, the Black Prince, at Poitiers (1356) and taken prisoner; detained in England (1356–60) while his son Charles V (*q.v.*) acted as regent; released for ransom by Treaty of Brétigny (1360); secured duchy of Burgundy (1363) for his son Philip (*q.v.*); failing to secure all of his own ransom, returned to England (1364), where he died.

John II. *Fr.* Jean \zhä^{n}\. *Du.* Jo·hann \yō-'hän\. *Also called* John of Avesnes \á-ven\. c.1247–1304. Count of Hainaut (1257–1304) and of Holland and Zeeland (1299–1304). Son and successor of John of Avesnes; friend of Philip IV of France; persuaded Floris, Count of Holland, to transfer alliance from England to France, an act that led to assassination of Floris (1296); guardian of Floris's son, at whose death (1299) he became count of Holland and Zeeland; stopped northward expansion of Flemish house of Dampierre.

John. *Hung.* Já·nos \'yä-nòsh\. Name of two kings of Hungary:

John. *Surnamed* Zá·pol·ya \zá-'pòl-yä\ *or* Szá·pol·yai \sá-'pòl-yòi\. 1487–1540. King (1526–40). Son of palatine Stephen Zápolya; at Diet of Rákos proposed successful motion that no foreign prince would ever again be elected king of Hungary after death of Ulászló II; governor of Transylvania (1511–16), brutally suppressed peasant uprising (1514); named governor of infant king Louis II (1516); disappointed by appointment of István Báthory as palatine (1519), his dissention enabling Turks to capture Belgrade (1521); failed to arrive in time to relieve king at battle of Mohács (1526) against Süleyman I; nonetheless elected by diets of Tokaj and Székesfehérvár to succeed as king.

John. *In full* John Sig·is·mund \'shig-is-mùnd\. 1540–1571. King (1540–71). Son of John Zápolya; ruled under Turkish protection; lost Transylvania; ruled over devastated realm.

John. *Pol.* Jan \'yän\. Name of three kings of Poland:

John I Albert. *Pol.* Jan I Ol·bracht \'òl-bräkt\. 1459–1501. King (1492–1501). Son of Casimir IV; defeated Tatars at Kopystryzn (1487) and Zaslaw (1491); called first national Sejm (parliament, 1493), granting extensive legislative power; invited to help repel Turks by Stephen, hospodar of Moldavia, but, his ambition for annexing Moldavia suspected, defeated by Stephen at Suceava (1497).

John II Cas·i·mir Va·sa \'kaz-ə-,mi(ə)r-'väs-ə\. *Pol.* Jan II Ka·zi·mierz Wa·za \ká-'zēm-yesh-'vá-zá\. 1609–1672. King (1648–68). Second son of Sigismund III Vasa; fought on Habsburg side against France in Thirty Years' War; imprisoned in France (1638–40); briefly a Jesuit novice (1646–47); elected to succeed brother Władysław IV (1648); temporarily suppressed revolt of Ukrainian Cossacks by victory at Beresteczko (1651); while fighting in east, lost most of Poland to sudden Swedish invasion (1655); fled but returned (1656); at conclusion of war (1666) forced to renounce claim to Swedish throne and to cede northern Livonia; signed treaty (1667) with Russia ceding Ukraine and Kiev; facing internal rebellion, abdicated (1668); became titular abbot of Saint-Germain-des-Prés, France.

John III So·bie·ski \sób-'yā-skē\. 1629–1696. King (1674–96). Son of castellan of Kraków; served against Cossacks (1651–52); sided with Swedes in invasion (1655) but returned to Polish service (1656) and again served against Cossacks and Tatars; commander in chief of Polish army (1668); engaged in conspiracies, with French backing, to gain throne; inflicted several defeats on invading Turks, esp. at Khotin (1673), but abandoned war to attend diet, which he virtually forced to elect him king (1674); concluded war with Turks and Tatars, recovering much of Ukraine. Concluded treaty with Emperor Leopold (1683), in observance of which he relieved siege of Vienna, personally leading charge of Polish cavalry; lifting of siege led to ejection of Ottomans from Hungary. Last years of reign marked by rebellion, conspiracy, failed campaigns.

John. *Port.* João \'zhwaù^{n}\. Name of six kings of Portugal, the first three of the House of Aviz, the others of the House of Bragança:

John I. *Called* o Grande \ü-'grä^{n}(n)d\, *i.e.* the Great. 1357–1433. King (1385–1433). Natural son of Peter I; grand master of Order of Aviz (1364); on death of half-brother Ferdinand, became regent and defender of the kingdom (1383–85); throne claimed by John I of Castile, resulting in war and siege of Lisbon; defeated Spaniards; chosen king (1385) and with aid of English won victory of Aljubarrota over Castilians (1385); made treaty of friendship and alliance with England (1386); married (1387) Philippa of Lancaster, daughter of John of Gaunt. Took Ceuta from Moors (1415), setting off great age of exploration, conquest, colonization. His six sons included Edward, his successor, and Prince Henry the Navigator.

John II. *Called* o Per·fec·to \ü-per-'fe-tü\, *i.e.* the Perfect. 1455–1495. King (1481–95). Son of Afonso V and great-grandson of John I; acted ably as regent during absences of father; fought against and, with help of Cortes and common people, overcame feudal nobility; had leaders, notably Duke of Bragança, put to death; refrained from conflict with Spain; encouraged explorations, sending out Diogo Cão and Bartolomeu Dias, who discovered mouth of the Congo (1484) and Cape of Good Hope (1488) respectively; concluded Treaty of Tordesillas (1494) with Spain, by which possessions in New World were delimited; fostered trade in Africa.

John III. *Called* o Pie·do·so \ü-pyā-'thō-sü\, *i.e.* the Pious. 1502–1557. King (1521–57). Son of Manuel I; m. (1525) Catherine, sister of Emperor Charles V; introduced Inquisition (1531); placed U. of Coimbra under Jesuits (1555); during his reign power of Portugal began to decline, although colonial expansion continued, especially in East Indies; title to Brazil confirmed by Congress of Badajoz (1524).

John IV. *Called* o Afor·tu·na·do \ü-å-fôr-tü-'nä-thü\, *i.e.* the Fortunate. 1604–1656. King (1640–56), founder of Bragança dynasty. Son of Teodosio, Duke of Bragança (d. 1630); m. (1633) Luisa de Guzmán, daughter of the Duke of Medina Sidonia; offered crown after conspiracy and bloodless revolution had expelled Spanish usurpers (1640), proclaimed king (1640); choice confirmed by Cortes (1641); Spaniards defeated at Montijo (1644); Dutch driven out of Brazil (1654) and Angola (1656); Portugal restored to respected position among European nations.

John V. *Called* o Ma·gna·ni·mo \ü-mán-yá-nē-mü\, *i.e.* the Generous. 1689–1750. King (1706–50). Son of Peter II and grandson of John IV; came to throne in midst of War of Spanish Succession (1701–14); involved as ally of England; by Treaty of Utrecht (1713) Portugal confirmed in possession of Amazon region. Devoted much attention to ecclesiastical matters, but his court was profligate and extravagant; church strengthened, but army and navy neglected; granted title (1741) of "Most Faithful King" by Pope Benedict XIV; patron of arts, sciences, scholarship.

John VI. *Called* o Cle·men·te \ü-klā-'mān(n)-tā\, *i.e.* the Merciful. 1767–1826. King (1816–26). Son of Peter III and María I; m. (1790) Carlota, daughter of Charles IV of Spain; took over government (1792) because of his mother's insanity; formally declared prince regent (1799); driven out of Portugal by French army under Junot (1807); sailed to Brazil with court (1807), remaining there till 1821; elevated Brazil to kingdom united with Portugal (1815); declared king of Portugal on death of his mother (1816); returned to Portugal (1821) and declared for the new constitution, Brazil becoming independent (1822) with his son Dom Pedro I its first ruler; last years troubled with reactionary disturbances and attempted rebellion of Queen Carlota and younger son, Dom Miguel.

John. *Ger.* Jo·hann \yō-'hän, 'yō-,\. *Called* der Bes·tän·dige \dər-besh-'ten-dig-ə\, *i.e.* the Constant *or* Steadfast. 1468–1532. Elector of Saxony (1525–32). Son of Elector Ernest; ruled Ernestine lands jointly with brother Frederick III the Wise (1486–1525), thereafter alone. Devout Lutheran; formed League of Gotha (1525) with Philip the Magnanimous of Hesse, Torgau League (1526) with northern German princes, creating first German Lutheran alliance; led reform party at Diet of Speyer (1526); protested (1529) retraction of concessions won at Speyer; a leader in formation of Schmalkaldic League (1530–31).

John. *Ger.* Johann. 1801–1873. King of Saxony (1854–73). Succeeded brother Friedrich Augustus; took part in war with Denmark (1864); entered North German Confederation (1867); took part in Franco-Prussian War (1870–71). Under pseudonym Phil·a·le·thes \'fil-ə-'lē-,thēz\ published (1839–49) translation of Dante's *Divina commedia.*

John. *Swed.* Jo·han \'yü-,hån\. Name of three kings of Sweden:

John I. 1201?–1222. King (1216–22). Son of Sverker Karlsson; succeeded Erik X Knutsson.

John II. See JOHN, king of Denmark and Norway.

John III. 1537–1592. King (1568–92). Second son of Gustav I Vasa; duke of Finland (1556); seized and imprisoned (1563–67) by his brother King Erik XIV; with brother Charles (later Charles IX) conspired against and deposed Erik (1568); signed Treaty of Stettin (1570), ending war with Denmark and relinquishing Estonian territories. Theological student; held synods (1574–75); failed in attempt to impose on Sweden his own synthesis of Lutheranism and Catholicism and his "Red Book" liturgy. Concluded alliance with Poland in war against Russia (1578–83); m. (1562) Catherine, sister of Sigismund II Augustus of Poland; had Sigismund, their son, crowned king of Poland (1587).

John of Antioch. See JOHN III, patriarch of Constantinople.

John of Asia. See JOHN of Ephesus.

John of Austria. *Span.* Juan de Aus·tria \'kwän-dā-'aùs-trē-ä\. *Commonly known as* Don John; *Span.* Don Juan. 1547–1578. Spanish general. Natural son of Emperor Charles V and Barbara Blomberg; reared in concealment in Spain; recognized as his son by Charles in his will (1558); granted rank of prince by half-brother Philip II. Given command (1568) of squadron against Barbary pirates; suppressed Morisco rebellion in Andalusia (1569–70); held supreme command of fleet of Holy League that defeated Turks at Lepanto (Oct. 7, 1571); took Tunis from Turks (1573). Appointed governor general of the Netherlands (1576); Pacification of Ghent (1576) united Dutch provinces against Spain; compelled by it to issue "Perpetual Edict" (1577); entered Brussels (1577) but forced to promise to remove Spanish soldiers from Netherlands; deposed by the Estates-General; defeated Dutch in battle of Gembloux (1578) but failed in campaign because of lack of support from Philip; died suddenly in camp at Namur.

John of Austria. *Called* Don John the Younger. 1629–1679. Spanish general. Natural son of Philip IV of Spain; recognized by king as his son, educated, and granted princely rank. Sent to Naples to help in suppressing revolt of Masaniello (1647); made viceroy of Sicily (1647–51); terminated revolt in Catalonia (1651–53); governor of the Netherlands (1656–58); defeated by Turenne at the Dunes (1658); led campaign against Portugal (1661–63); defeated at Estremoz (1663); removed from power by queen regent (1665–69); led military uprising that forced dismissal of Father John Nithard, favorite of queen regent (1669); led successful revolution (1677) that drove queen regent from court and established himself as chief minister to half-brother Charles II.

John of Avesnes. See JOHN II, Count of Hainaut.

John of Avi·la \ə-'vē-lə\. Saint. *Span.* Juan de Ávi·la \-dā-'ä-bē-lä\. 1499 or 1500–1569. Spanish cleric and reformer. Ordained (1525); missionary in Andalusia (1529–38); gained fame as preacher and evangelist; champion of clerical reform, esp. of celibacy; supported Jesuits; helped found U. of Granada (1537). Influenced Francis Borgia, John of God, Theresa of Avila, Luís of Granada, etc.; author of *Audi filia* on Christian perfection. Canonized (1970).

John of Bev·er·ley \'bev-ər-lē\. Saint. d. 721. English prelate. In Whitby Abbey; bishop of Hexham (687–705), of York (705–c.717 or 720); founded thereafter monastery at Inderawood (later Beverly). Credited by King Henry V with victory at Agincourt (1415).

John of Bri·enne \brē-en\. c.1148–1237. King of Jerusalem (1210–25). Impoverished younger son of Count Erard II of Brienne; by arrangement of Philip II Augustus of France, m. (1210) Marie de Montferrat, Queen of Jerusalem; on her death (1212) became regent for daughter Isabella; led part of Fifth Crusade (1218–21) against Egypt. Left Jerusalem, living in various parts of western Europe (1223–29). Lost throne to Emperor Frederick II, who married Isabella (1225). Elected regent and co-emperor of Constantinople (1228–37) until Baldwin II came of age. Repelled attacks (1235) by Greeks and Bulgars.

John of Ca·pi·stra·no \,kä-pē-'strä-nō\. Saint. *Ital.* Giovanni da Capistrano. *Lat.* Johannes Cap·is·tra·nus \,kap-ə-'strā-nəs\. 1386–1456. Italian religious. Civil magistrate of Perugia (1412); imprisoned (1412–16); entered Franciscan order (1416); ordained (1426); renowned as preacher; a leader in founding ascetic Franciscan Observants; papal delegate to Austria to preach against Hussites (1451); led army of crusaders against Turks besieging Belgrade (1456). Author of *Speculum conscientiae.* Canonized by Alexander VIII (1690).

John of Da·mas·cus \də-'mas-kəs\ *or* John Dam·a·scene \'dam-ə-,sēn\. Saint. *Lat.* Johannes Dam·a·sce·nus \,dam-ə-'sē-nəs\. *Called* Chry·sor·rho·as \krə-'sär-ō-əs\, *i.e.* stream of gold, *for his eloquence.* c.675–749. Greek religious and theologian, b. Damascus. A doctor of the Eastern church. Served as financial officer under caliph of Damascus; became monk at Mar Saba near Jerusalem (shortly after 730), where he was ordained priest. Author of the standard textbook of dogmatic theology in the Greek church *Pēgē gnōseōs,* or *Source of Knowledge;* also wrote 3 *Discourses on Sacred Images* against Emperor Leo III and the Iconoclasts, *Sacra parallela* anthologizing moral exhortations; revised Eastern hymnal *Octoēchos.*

John of Eph·e·sus \'ef-ə-səs\. *Also called* John of Asia \'ā-zhə, -shə\. c.507–c.586. Syrian prelate. Monk; deacon at Amida (529); persecuted as Monophysite; gained support of Empress Theodora; named titular bishop of Ephesus (c.542); renowned as evangelist in Asia Minor, built many churches and monasteries; imprisoned (572), later banished by Emperor Justin II. Author of an *Ecclesiastical History* of period 44 B.C.–585 A.D., *Lives of the Eastern Saints.*

John of For·dun \'fȯrd-ən, 'fôr-dən\. d. after 1384. Scottish chronicler. Perhaps a minor cleric in Aberdeen. Author of 7-part chronicle of Scotland, first attempted continuous history of Scotland; work later adapted, expanded, continued by Walter Bowers in *Scotichronicon.*

John of Gaunt \'gȯnt, 'gänt\. Duke of Lan·cas·ter \'laŋ-kəs-tər\. 1340–1399. English prince. 4th son of Edward III and brother of Black Prince; b. Ghent, hence his name; m. his cousin Blanche (1359; d. 1369), daughter of Henry, 1st Duke of Lancaster. Leading first division of Black Prince's army in Spain, fought in van at Nájera (1367); with Black Prince at sack of Limoges (1370) and his lieutenant in Aquitaine (1371). Assumed by marriage (1369) with Constance of Castile kingship of Castile and León (1372); led futile expedition from Calais to Bordeaux (1373). Forced into domestic leadership by Black Prince's illness; reversed proceedings of Good Parliament of 1376; supported John Wycliffe, despite disbelief in his religious opinions, as means of resisting opposition of prelates, and incurred anger of Londoners, who rioted; on accession of Richard II, his nephew, retired from government; after disastrous failure in attack on St.-Malo (1378), accepted command of Scottish border; unsuccessful in Scottish campaign (1384) and accompanied Richard's expedition (1385); subject of several court intrigues (1381–85). In attempt to win his Spanish throne, conquered Galicia (1386) and formed alliance with Portugal, but failing in invasion of Castile, surrendered his Castilian claims to his daughter Catherine on her marriage with the son of John I of Castile (1388). Lieutenant of Aquitaine (1388–89); duke of Aquitaine (1390); exerted influence in support of Richard II (1390–94) and effected truce with France (1394); failed to establish rule over his duchy of Aquitaine; m. (1396) Catherine Swynford, his mistress, and obtained from Richard legitimation of her sons under surname Beaufort (from eldest of whom descended Henry VII); presided at trial of Arundel (1397); broken in spirit by exile of his son Henry.

John of God \'gäd, 'gȯd\. Saint. *Span.* Juan de Dios \'kwän-thā-'thyōs\. *Orig.* Juan Ciu·dad \thyü-'thäth\. 1495–1550. Spanish religious, b. Portugal. Shepherd in Castile; fought under Charles V against Turks. Influenced by John of Avila, devoted himself to care of poor and sick (from 1537); founded hospital at Granada (1537) and attracted followers who were given habit by bishop of Tuy; after his death, followers formally organized as Hospitaller Order of St. John of God (Brothers Hospitallers). Canonized (1690) by Alexander VIII.

John of Jan·dun \zhan-'dən\. *Fr.* Jean de Jan·dun \zhäⁿ-də-zhäⁿ-dœⁿ\. c.1286–1328. French philosopher. Lecturer at Collège de Navarre, Paris; associated with Marsilius of Padua and to some extent collaborated on *Defensor pacis,* for which both were excommunicated (1327). Author of influential commentaries on Aristotle and Averroës.

John of Je·ru·sa·lem \jə-'rü-s(ə-)ləm, -'rüz(-ə)-ləm\. c.356–417. Palestinian prelate and theologian. Monk; succeeded Cyril as bishop of Jerusalem (c.387); attacked by Jerome and by Epiphanius of Salamis for Origenism; feud culminated in virulent attack by Jerome (396); reconciled (397); received Pelagius in Jerusalem and presided over synod that found his views acceptable (415); reproved by Pope Innocent I for permitting sack of anti-Pelagian monastery in Bethlehem. Author of at least part of *Catecheses* formerly attributed solely to Cyril of Jerusalem.

John of Kron·stadt \'krōn-,shtät\. *Orig.* Ivan Ilich Ser·ge·yev \syir-'gyā-yəf\. 1829–1909. Russian cleric. Priest in Kronstadt (from 1855); gained fame for charitable and educational work among the poor; credited by many with wonders and miracles; influential in revitalizing spirituality of Russian Orthodoxy. Author of *My Life in Christ.*

John of Lan·cas·ter \'laŋ-kəs-tər\. Duke of Bed·ford \'bed-fərd\. 1389–1435. English prince. 3d son of Henry IV; warden of Scottish marches till Henry IV's death; created duke by brother Henry V (1414); lieutenant of England during Henry V's French campaigns; defeated French fleet at mouth of the Seine (1416); marched on Scotland and raised seige of Berwick (1417); regent in France (1422); made alliances with Philip the Good of Burgundy and John VI of Brittany; prosecuted war with Charles, dauphin of France, gaining victory at Verneuil (1424) and other successes up to siege of Orléans (1429); allowed Joan of Arc, bought from Burgundians, to be burnt as a witch (1431); secured Henry VI's coronation as king of France (1431); his cause in France ruined by separate peace made by Philip of Burgundy with Charles VII (1435).

John of Leiden. See Jan BEUCKELSON.

John of Lux·em·bourg \'lu̇k-səm-,bu̇rk, *Angl* 'lək-səm-,bərg\. *Also called* John of Bo·he·mia \bō-'hē-mē-ə\. 1296–1346. King of Bohemia (1310–46). Son of future emperor Henry VII; made count of Luxembourg (1310); as king, supported Emperor Louis IV; conducted numerous campaigns against Lithuanians, Russians, Hungary, Austria, in Italy and the Tirol, etc.; acquired parts of Upper Lusatia (1320–29), Silesia (1327–30), Lombardy; turned against Louis and secured his deposition by Pope Clement VI (1346); had son elected King Charles IV of the Romans; killed fighting on French side at Crécy.

John of Matha. See JEAN DE MATHA.

John of Mirecourt. See JEAN DE MIRECOURT.

John of Mont·fort \'mänt-fərt\. *Fr.* Jean de Mont·fort \zhäⁿ-də-mōⁿ-fȯr\. 1293–1345. French nobleman. Son of Arthur II, Duke of Brittany; on death of his half-brother John III of Brittany (1341), claimed duchy of Brittany and briefly held it until forced out by King Philip VI; fought War of Breton Succession against rival claimant Charles of Blois (1341–45); died at siege of Hennobant; his son Duke John IV eventually defeated Charles (1364).

John of Ne·po·muk \'ne-pō-mu̇k\ *or* Po·muk \'pō-mu̇k\. Saint. *Orig.* Johannes Wölf·lin \'vœl-flin\. c.1345–1393. Bohemian cleric, b. Pomuk. Pastor (1380) and student, Prague, where he later became cathedral canon and (1390) vicar general to the archbishop; as agent and defender of archbishop in actions contrary to wishes of King Wenceslas IV, tortured personally by the king and drowned in the Vltava River. Canonized by Benedict XIII (1729); patron saint of Czechs.

John of Od·zun \'äd-,zün\. *Also called* Hov·han·nes IV Otz·ne·tzi \hō-'vän-əs-ōt-snet-'sē\. 650–729. Armenian prelate. Catholicos (supreme head) of Armenian Orthodox church (718–729); called synods at Dvin (718), Manzikert (726) to reform Armenian liturgy; at latter considered union with Monophysite Syrian Jacobite church, eliciting notable letter from Patriarch Germanus I of Constantinople. Author of theological works as *Contra phantasticos* on the Incarnation, Christological works generally consonant with decrees of Council of Chalcedon, revisions of Armenian psalter and prayer book; credited with *Kanonagirk',* first collection of Armenian canon law.

John of Ox·ford \'äks-fərd\. d. 1200. English prelate. In service of Henry II as envoy to European courts (from 1163); opponent of Becket; bishop of Norwich (from 1175).

John of Paris. See JEAN DE PARIS.

John of Rochester. See St. John FISHER.

John of St. Thom·as \sānt-'täm-əs, sənt-\. *Lat.* Jo·han·nes a Sanc·to Tho·ma \yō-'han-ə-sä-'säŋk-tō-'tō-mə\. *Orig.* John Poin·sot \'pōⁿ(n)-sōt\. 1589–1644. Portuguese religious and philosopher. Entered Dominican order (1610); taught at Madrid, Piacenza, Alcalá (1641–43); adviser and confessor to Philip IV (1643–44). Author of *Cursus philosophicus* (1632–36) and *Cursus theologicus* (1637–44) explicating and commenting on Thomas Aquinas's *Summa theologiae;* also of *De domis Spiritus Sancti* (c.1644).

John of Salis·bury \'sȯlz-,ber-ē, -b(ə-)rē\. 1115 or 1120–1180. English prelate and scholar. Studied at Paris under Abelard (1136–38); attended Pope Eugenius III and served in Curia; secretary to Archbishop Theobald at Canterbury, by whom he was sent on missions; in disfavor with Henry II after denouncing exactions on church for Toulouse expedition (1159) and supporting Becket's cause; retired to Reims (1163) and wrote *Historia pontificalis;* returned to England, and was present at murder of Becket at Canterbury (1170). Bishop of Chartres (1176–80); present at peace made between England and France at Ivry (1177). Author of the *Policraticus* (1159) on court vanities and diplomacy, *Metalogicon* (1159), and biographies of Becket and Anselm.

John of Scy·thop·o·lis \skə-'thäp-ə-ləs\. 6th century. Byzantine prelate and theologian. Orig. a learned lawyer; bishop of Scythopolis (c.536–550). Author of treatises developing neo-Chalcedonian Christology in opposition to Monophysites, esp. Severus of Antioch and Eutyches of Constantinople; also wrote one of earliest commentaries on and defenses of orthodoxy of Pseudo-Dionysius the Areopagite.

John of Tella. See JOHN BAR QURSOS.

John of the Cross. Saint. *Span.* Juan de la Cruz \'kwän-dā-lä-'krüth\. *Orig.* Juan de Ye·pes y Ál·va·rez \-dā-'yā-pā-sē-'äl-vä-rāth\. 1542–1591. Spanish mystic and poet. Entered Carmelite order (1563); ordained (1567); met Theresa of Ávila (1567) and with her founded ascetic order of Discalced Carmelites (1568); established monastery at Durnelo (1569); confessor to Theresa's convent (1571); imprisoned (1577) by opponents of monastic reform; vicar provincial of Andalusia (1585–87). In poems, esp. intensely lyrical "Cántico espiritual" (Spiritual Canticle), "Noche obscura del alma" (Dark Night of the Soul), and "Llama de amor viva" (Living Flame of Love), schematized steps of mystical ascent toward union of soul and God. Canonized (1726) by Benedict XIII; declared doctor of the church (1926) by Pius XI.

John the Apostle. Saint. 1st century A.D. Christian apostle. With brother James a member of the original 12 disciples of Jesus; with James and Simon Peter formed inner circle of disciples; a pillar of the church in Jerusalem; said to have been buried at Ephesus. Traditionally held to have written the fourth Gospel, three epistles, and the book of Revelation in the New Testament.

John the Baptist. Saint. 1st century A.D. Jewish prophet. Son of Judaean priest; became ascetic; preached imminence of God's judgment and the messiah; baptized followers as token of repentance; baptized Jesus; executed by Herod Antipas (before 35–36 A.D. and by tradition before crucifixion of Jesus). Considered by Christians the last Jewish prophet and the forerunner of Christ.

John the Conqueror. See JOHN IV, Duke of Brittany.

John the Constant. See JOHN, Elector of Saxony.

John the Faster. See JOHN IV, patriarch of Constantinople.

John the Fearless. *Fr.* Jean sans Peur \zhäⁿ-säⁿ-pœr\. 1371–1419. Duke of Burgundy (1404–19). Son of Philip the Bold; succeeded maternal grandfather as count of Nevers (1384); m. (1385) Margaret, daughter of Duke Albert of Bavaria; fought for Hungary against Turks (1396), captured at Nicopolis; ransomed (1397); engaged in struggle for influence over King Charles VI with cousin Louis, duc d'Orléans (1404–07), culminating in assassination of Louis on John's order; put down revolt in Liège (1408); absolved of murder by royal decree and made guardian of the dauphin (1409); dispute between his followers

(Burgundians) and opponents led by Bernard, Count of Armagnac, escalated into civil war (from 1411); forced from Paris by popular opposition (1413) and denounced by University and John Gerson; took no part at Agincourt (1415); reentered Paris (1418), causing dauphin to flee; accepted proposed reconciliation with dauphin, but assassinated by his companions.

John the Fortunate. See JOHN IV, king of Portugal.

John the Generous. See JOHN V, king of Portugal.

John the Good. See JOHN III, Duke of Brittany; JOHN II, king of France.

John the Grammarian. See JOHN PHILOPONUS.

John the Great. See JOHN I, king of Portugal.

John the Just. See JOHN I, king of Ethiopia.

John the Merciful. See JOHN VI, king of Portugal.

John the Parricide. 1290–1313. German prince. Grandson of Rudolph I; demanded portion of Habsburg domain from uncle, King Albert I, who refused in order to keep family lands unified; murdered Albert (1308), fled to Italy; arrested and executed in Pisa.

John the Perfect. See JOHN II, king of Portugal.

John the Pious. See JOHN III, king of Portugal.

John the Posthumous. See JOHN I, king of France.

John the Red. See JOHN I, Duke of Brittany.

John the Scot. See ERIGENA.

John the Steadfast. See JOHN, Elector of Saxony.

John the Valiant. See JOHN IV, Duke of Brittany.

John the Victorious. See JOHN I, Duke of Brabant.

John the Wise. See JOHN V, Duke of Brittany.

John, Augustus Edwin. 1878–1961. British painter and etcher, b. Wales. Known esp. for portraits, for landscapes often showing affinities with Symbolists, for vigorous brushwork and superb draftsmanship. Works included *Encampment on Dartmoor, Lyric Fantasy,* large mural cartoon *Canadians Opposite Lens, Spanish Flower Girl, Mother and Child,* and *Seraphita;* portraits of Lloyd George, George Bernard Shaw, Lord Fisher, Princess Bibesco, Madame Suggia, Dylan Thomas.

John, Sir William Goscombe. 1860–1952. British sculptor, b. Wales. Among his works were statues of Edward VII at Cape Town, George V and Queen Mary at Liverpool, David Lloyd George at Carnarvon. Designed George V Silver Jubilee Medal (1935), Great Seal of Edward VIII (1936).

John Albert. See JOHN I, king of Poland.

John bar Qur·sos \-bär-'kü(ə)r-,sōs\. *Also known as* John of Tel·la \'tel-ə\. 483–538. Syrian prelate and theologian. Soldier and later monk; bishop of Tella (519); developed a moderate form of Monophysitism, rejecting extreme view and also the formulation of Chalcedon; persecuted and killed in violent orthodox reaction in Syria under Emperor Justinian.

John Becchus. See JOHN XI, patriarch of Constantinople.

John Casimir. See also JOHN II, king of Poland.

John Cas·i·mir \'kaz-ə-,mir\. 1543–1592. Count Palatine of the Rhine. Son of Elector Palatine Frederick III; joined Reformation; led troops to help French Huguenots and Dutch (1575–78), but with small success; as regent of the Palatinate (1583–92), compelled return of Protestants to Calvinism.

John Chrysostom, Saint. See CHRYSOSTOM.

John Cli·ma·cus \-klī-'mā-kəs\. Saint. c.579–c.649. Byzantine religious. Monk at St. Catherine on Mt. Sinai (from c.600); lived apart as hermit; abbot (c.639–c.649). Author of *Climax tou paradeisou* (Ladder of Divine Ascent, or Heavenly Ladder), handbook of ascetic and mystical devotion.

John Frederick. *Ger.* Johann Friedrich. *Called* der Gross·mü·ti·ge \-dər-grōs-'mœ-tig-ə\, *i.e.* the Magnanimous. 1503–1554. Elector of Saxony (1532–47) of the Ernestine line (*q.v.*). Son of John the Constant; a leader of League of Schmalkalden; at war (1546–47) with his cousin Maurice of the Albertine line (*q.v.*); defeated and made prisoner by Charles V (1547) at Mühlberg; forced to renounce his electorate; set free by Maurice (1552), but unsuccessful in attempt to regain title. His son ¶John Frederick II, *called* der Mitt·le·re \-dər-'mit-lər-ə\, *i.e.* the Middle One (1529–1595), was duke of Saxony, ruling (1547–66) small part granted him by emperor after division (1547) of his father's lands; founded (1558) U. of Jena; conspired with Wilhelm von Grumbach to regain father's electorate; deposed (1566) and imprisoned (1567–95).

John George. *Ger.* Johann Georg. 1525–1598. Elector of Brandenburg (1571–98). Son of Joachim II; by public economies earned epithet Oeko·nom \œ-kō-'nōm\, i.e. Steward; succeeded in reuniting divided electorate.

John George. *Ger.* Johann Georg. Name of four electors of Saxony of the Albertine line (*q.v.*):

John George I. 1585–1656. Elector (1611–56). Son of Elector Christian I; as ruler of Saxony during Thirty Years' War, held position of great importance; policy during entire reign changeable; at first, fought against Protestants; later (1631) made alliance with Gustav II Adolphus; his troops fought at Breitenfeld (1631) but were routed; after Lützen (1632), negotiated for peace; concluded Treaty of Prague (1635) with Emperor Ferdinand II and received Lusatia; by indolence failed to capitalize opportunities to acquire Bohemian crown, archbishopric of Magdeburg; declared war on Sweden (1636) but was beaten at Wittstock; forced to make peace with Swedes (1645); confirmed in possessions by Treaty of Westphalia (1648). By end of his reign Saxony had yielded to Brandenburg position of chief among German states.

John George II. 1613–1680. Elector (1656–80). Son of John George I; friendly to France, under influence and subsidy of Louis XIV; much interested in music and art; spent enormous sums in beautifying Dresden and making it musical center of Germany.

John George III. 1647–1691. Elector (1680–91). Son of John George II; joined alliance against France (1683); aided Emperor Leopold I against Turks (1682–85); took part (1688) in war of League of Augsburg against France and made commander in chief of Imperial army (1690).

John George IV. 1668–1694. Elector (1691–94). Son of John George III; quarreled with emperor; m. Eleonore of Brandenburg-Anspach; celebrated for romantic attachment for Magdalene Sibylle von Neitschütz (created countess of Rochlitz, 1693).

John Hyr·ca·nus \-hir-'kā-nəs\. Name of two high priests and rulers of Judaea, of the Hasmonean dynasty:

John Hyrcanus I. c.175–104 B.C. High priest and ruler (135–104 B.C.). Son of Simon Maccabeus; with brother Judas commanded force that repelled Cendebeus and Syrian army of Antiochus VII Sidetes (137); succeeded to rule on assassination of father and brothers (135); brought Judaea to last bloom of power and prosperity; conquered Samaria and Idumaea (Edom), repelled Syrian incursions.

John Hyrcanus II. d. 30 B.C. High priest (72–40 B.C.) and ruler (67). Son of Alexander Jannaeus and Salome Alexandra; made high priest on father's death; succeeded mother as ruler but driven from throne after three months by brother Aristobulus; restored to priesthood on appeal to Roman general Pompey; a tool in hands of Romans; rendered powerless by Mark Antony (42); had ears cut off (rendering him unfit for priesthood) by invading Parthians (40); exiled to Babylon (40–36); executed by Herod.

John Ita·lus \-ə-'tā-ləs\. 11th century. Byzantine philosopher, b. Calabria. Favored at court of Michael VII Ducas; succeeded Michael Psellus as first philosopher of Constantinople; an eclectic, attempted to synthesize Aristotelian logic and Platonic metaphysics; accused of heresy in attempting to rationalize Christian mysteries.

John Lackland. See JOHN, king of England.

John Mau·rice \-'mȯr-əs, -mȯ-'rēs\. *Du.* Jo·han Mau·rits \yō-'hän-'mau̇-rits\. *Called* the Brazilian. Count of Nassau-Siegen. 1604–1679. Dutch soldier and colonialist. Son of John, Count of Nassau-Siegen-Dillenburg; fought under cousin Frederick Henry, Prince of Orange, against Spain (1621 ff.); governor general of Dutch colony in Brazil (1636–44); consolidated Dutch rule over vast territory; defeated Spanish fleet (1640); sponsored seizure of Angola (1641) and several West African ports to secure slave trade; fostered scientific studies of region; built up capital of Mauritsstad (Recife); failed to reconcile Portuguese landowners to Dutch rule; resigned (1644). Stadholder of Cleves, Mark, and Ravensberg (1647); commanded Dutch army against bishop of Münster in second Anglo-Dutch War (1665); commanded forces in Friesland and Groningen (1672–75) in war with France. Built Mauritshuis (designed by Pieter Post) in The Hague.

John Paul I \-'pȯl\. *Orig.* Albino Lu·cia·ni \lü-'chä-nē\. 1912–1978. Pope (1978). Ordained (1935); bishop of Vittorio Veneto (1958); patriarch of Venice (1969); cardinal (1973); first pope to assume a double name; reigned only 34 days.

John Peck·ham \-'pek-əm\ *or* **Pech·am** \-'pech-əm\. d. 1292. English prelate. Entered Franciscan order (c.1250); provincial in England (1275). Taught in Oxford (c.1271–75) and Rome (1277); elected archbishop of Canterbury (1279); defended Augustinianism; insisted on discipline and rights of the church. Author of treatises on science, scriptural and moral subjects, and of hymns and lyrical poems, esp. *Philomena praevia.*

John Phi·lo·po·nus \-,fi-lə-'pō-nəs\. *Also known as* John the Grammarian. 6th century A.D. Greek Christian theologian, b. Alexandria, Egypt. Pupil of Ammonius Hermiae. Author of two treatises on grammar, Christianizing commentaries on Aristotle, and, his chief work, *Diaitētēs,* an attempted reconciliation of Monophysite and Orthodox teachings.

John Scholasticus. See JOHN III, patriarch of Constantinople.

John Scotus Erigena. See ERIGENA.

John Scy·lit·zes \-skī-'lit-,sēz\. 11th century. Byzantine historian. High officeholder at Byzantine court; his *Synopsis historiarum,* covering years 811–1057, is known through George Cedrenus's almost verbatim use of it.

John Sigismund. See also JOHN, king of Hungary.

John Sig·is·mund \'sij-əs-mənd, 'sig-\. *Ger.* Johann Si·gis·mund \'zē-gis-,mu̇nt\. 1572–1619. Elector of Brandenburg (1608–19). m. (1594) Anne of Prussia; through that connection acquired Cleves, Mark, and Ravensburg in

Treaty of Xanten (1614) and became duke of Prussia (1618), thus extending Hohenzollern power eastward; espoused Calvinism (1613).

John Sobieski. See JOHN III, king of Poland.

John·son \'jän(t)-sən\, Alvin Saunders. 1874–1971. American economist, b. near Homer, Neb. Taught at several universities (1901–16); editor, *The New Republic* (1917–23); a founder (1919), director (1923–45), New School for Social Research, New York City.

Johnson, Amy. 1903–1941. British aviator. m. (1932) James A. Mollison (*q.v.*; div. 1938). First woman to make solo flight from London to Australia (1930), part of which was a record solo flight from England to India in 6 days; established records on flight to Japan and back (1931), and to Cape Town and back (1932); with husband made flight from England to U.S.A. (39 hours, 1933), from England to India (22 hours, 1934); made record solo flight from London to Cape Town and return (1936). Drowned after bailing out over Thames estuary.

Johnson, Andrew. 1808–1875. Seventeenth president of the United States, b. Raleigh, N.C. Apprenticed to a tailor; moved to Tennessee, settled at Greeneville (1826); engaged in tailoring business. Wholly self-educated. Member, U.S. House of Representatives (1843–53). Governor of Tennessee (1853–57). U.S. senator (1857–62). Loyal to Union during Civil War; military governor of Tennessee, rank of brigadier general (1862–64). Vice president of the U.S. (Mar. 4–Apr. 15, 1865); succeeded to presidency on death of Lincoln and served 1865–69. Differences between Congress and the president with regard to Reconstruction policies led to impeachment proceedings (1868); acquitted. Again U.S. senator (1875). See E. M. STANTON.

Johnson, Byron Bancroft, *called* Ban \'ban\. 1864–1931. American baseball organizer, b. Norwalk, Ohio. President, Western League (1893–1900); organized American League (1900) and was its president (to 1927). Proposed and inaugurated "World's Series" at the close of each baseball season between the pennant-winning clubs of the two major leagues (National and American). Elected to Baseball Hall of Fame (1937).

Johnson, Charles Spurgeon. 1893–1956. American sociologist, b. Bristol, Va. For Chicago Commission on Race Relations produced study *The Negro in Chicago* (1922); research director, New York City Urban League (1922–28); professor (1928–47), first black president (1946–56), Fisk U. Also wrote *The Negro in American Civilization* (1930), *Growing Up in the Black Belt* (1941), *Patterns of Negro Segregation* (1943).

Johnson, Cornelius. See Cornelis JANSSEN.

Johnson, Douglas Wilson. 1878–1944. American geologist, b. Parkersburg, W. Va. Professor, Harvard (1907–12), Columbia U. (1912–44); known for studies of coastal erosion. Author of *Topography and Strategy in the War* (1917), *Shore Processes and Shoreline Development* (1919), *New England–Acadian Shoreline* (1925), *Stream Sculpture on the Atlantic Slope* (1931), *Origin of Submarine Canyons* (1939).

Johnson, Eastman, *in full* Jonathan Eastman. 1824–1906. American painter, b. Lovell, Me. Known for genre scenes as *Old Kentucky Home, Husking Bee, Cranberry Pickers,* and portraits of J.Q. Adams, Daniel Webster, Longfellow, Emerson, Chester A. Arthur, Grover Cleveland, Benjamin Harrison, etc.

Johnson, Esther. 1681–1728. English woman. Fellow member with Jonathan Swift of Sir William Temple's household, to whom Swift addressed the *Journal to Stella.*

John·son \'yün-sȯn\, Eyvind. 1900–1976. Swedish writer. Author of novels including *De fyra främlingarna* (1924), *Stad i ljus* (1928), *Bobinack* (1932), *Romanen om Olof* (1934–37), *Grupp Krilon* (1941), *Krilons resa* (1942), *Krilon själv* (1943), *Strändernas svall* (1946), *Hans nådes tid* (1960), *Favel ensam* (1968); stories *Sju liv* (1944). Awarded 1974 Nobel prize for literature with Harry Martinson.

John·son \'jän(t)-sən\, Hall. 1888–1970. American choral conductor, b. Athens, Ga. Organized (1925) and directed Hall Johnson Negro choir, which became widely known in concert and later in motion picture appearances; wrote folk drama *Run Little Chillun* (1933), cantata *Son of Man* (1946), etc.

Johnson, Hiram Warren. 1866–1945. American politician, b. Sacramento, Calif. Practiced law in Sacramento (1888–1902) and San Francisco (from 1902); succeeded Francis Heney in prosecuting and securing conviction of political boss Abe Ruef on charges of corruption (1908). Governor of California (1911–17). Theodore Roosevelt's running mate on "Bull Moose" Progressive ticket (1912). U.S. senator (1917–45); staunch isolationist.

Johnson, Howard Deering. 1896?–1972. American businessman, b. Boston. Entered drug store business (1924); built up ice cream business; licensed name of restaurant supplied by his food-supply house (1929); established franchised "Howard Johnson" restaurants on major highways in Massachusetts, spreading to New York, New Jersey, and eventually across the country; became largest commercial food supplier in U.S.

Johnson, Hugh Samuel. 1882–1942. American army officer and politician, b. Ft. Scott, Kans. Entered army (1903); served in World War I; originated, planned, directed selective service conscription (1917–18); brigadier general (1918); retired (1919). National Recovery Administration administrator (1933–34). Works Progress Administration administrator in New York City (1935). Lecturer, radio publicist, and editorial writer for Scripps-Howard newspapers (from 1934). Wrote *The Blue Eagle from Egg to Earth* (1935).

Johnson, James Weldon. 1871–1938. American author, b. Jacksonville, Fla. Practiced law in Jacksonville (1897–1901). U.S. consul, Puerto Cabello, Venezuela (1906–09) and Corinto, Nicaragua (1909–12). Joined staff (1916), executive secretary (1920–30), National Association for Advancement of Colored People. Awarded Spingarn medal (1925). Professor of creative literature, Fisk U. (from 1930). Author of *The Autobiography of an Ex-Colored Man* (1912), *Fifty Years and Other Poems* (1917), *The Book of American Negro Poetry* (1922), *The Book of American Negro Spirituals* (1925, 1926), *God's Trombones* (1927), *Black Manhattan* (1930), *Negro Americans, What Now* (1934), etc. With brother John Rosamond Johnson wrote numerous songs, including "Lift Every Voice and Sing" (1899).

Johnson, Sir John. See under Sir William JOHNSON (1715–1774).

Johnson, John Arthur, *known as* Jack. 1878–1946. American boxer, b. Galveston, Tex. Became first Negro world heavyweight champion by knocking out Tommy Burns (Dec. 1908); defeated James J. Jeffries (1910); lost title to Jess Willard (1915).

Johnson, Lionel Pigot. 1867–1902. British poet and critic. Published *Poems* (1895), *Ireland and Other Poems* (1897), wistful and melancholy lyrics; also known for critical essays for periodicals and a notable study of Thomas Hardy.

Johnson, Lyndon Baines. 1908–1973. Thirty-sixth president of the United States, b. near Stonewall, Tex. Member, U.S. House of Representatives (1937–49), Senate (1949–61; Democratic whip 1951; minority leader 1953–55; majority leader 1955–61); noted as a persuasive and effective legislator. U.S. vice president (1961–63); president (1963–69); secured adoption of several "Great Society" social welfare proposals; administration bogged down in escalating U.S. involvement in war in Vietnam; declined renomination for president (1968).

Johnson, Martin Elmer. 1884–1937. American explorer and naturalist, b. Rockford, Ill. Accompanied Jack London in cruise of *Snark* (1907); made expeditions to Solomon and New Hebrides islands (1914), Borneo (1917–19, 1935), Africa (several times from 1921 to 1934), photographing native tribes and wildlife; produced motion pictures including *Jungle Adventures* (1921), *Head Hunters of The South Seas* (1922), *Simba, the King of the Beasts* (1928), *Congorilla* (1932), *Baboona* (1935), *Borneo* (1937). Author with wife of *Cannibal-Land* (1922), *Camera Trails in Africa* (1924), *Lion* (1929), etc. His wife (m. 1910) ¶Osa Helen, *nee* Leigh·ty \'lāt-ē\ (1894–1953), b. Chanute, Kans., accompanied him on all expeditions as hunter and pilot; led expedition to Africa (1937); produced films *Jungle Calling* (1937), *I Married Adventure* (1940), *African Paradise* (1941), *Tulagi* (1943). Wrote *Jungle Babies* (1930), *Osa Johnson's Jungle Friends* (1939), *I Married Adventure* (1940), *Bride in the Solomons* (1944), etc.

Johnson, Pamela Hansford. *In private life* Lady Snow \'snō\. 1912–1981. English novelist. Gained critical and popular success with first novel *This Bed Thy Centre* (1935); m. 2d (1950) C.P. Snow (*q.v.*). Author of some 25 novels dealing with contemporary social issues, including *Too Dear for My Possessing* (1940), *An Evening of Stone* (1947), *A Summer to Decide* (1948), *The Unspeakable Skipton* (1959), *Cork Street, Next to the Hatter's* (1965), *The Good Husband* (1978), *A Bonfire* (1981); also wrote *Corinth House* (1948, play), *On Iniquity* (1967, social criticism), essays, and literary criticism.

Johnson, Pauline, *in full* Emily Pauline. *Mohawk name* Tekahionwake. 1862–1913. Canadian poet, b. Brant Co., Ont. Daughter of Mohawk chief. Among her volumes of verse celebrating Indian heritage were *The White Wampum* (1894), *Canadian Born* (1903), and *Flint and Feathers* (1912); also wrote tales collected in *Legends of Vancouver* (1911), *The Shagganappi* (1913), *Moccasin Maker* (1913).

Johnson, Reverdy. 1796–1876. American politician, b. Annapolis, Md. Noted lawyer; represented defense in Dred Scott case. U.S. senator (1845–49). U.S. attorney general (1849–50). Aided in keeping Maryland in Union (1861). Again U.S. senator (1863–68); activities as mediator and compromiser won him sobriquet of "the Trimmer." U.S. minister to Great Britain (1868–69).

Johnson, Richard. 1573–?1659. English writer. Author of popular romances as *Nine Worthies of London* (1592) and esp. *The Most famous History of the Seaven Champions of Christendome* (1596–97); also wrote ballad collection *A Crowne-Garland of Goulden Roses* (1612).

Johnson, Richard Mentor. 1780–1850. Vice president of the United States, b. near Louisville, Ky. Member, U.S. House of Representatives (1807–19, 1829–37), U.S. Senate (1819–29). Served under Gen. W. H. Harrison in War of 1812, and at battle of the Thames (Oct. 5, 1813) reputedly killed Tecumseh.

In electoral vote for vice president (1837), no candidate gained majority in electoral college; election thereupon thrown into U.S. Senate; only vice president ever thus elected; served 1837–41.

Johnson, Robert Underwood. 1853–1937. American editor and writer, b. Washington, D.C. On staff of *Century Magazine* (1873–1913), editor (1909–13); U.S. ambassador to Italy (1920–21). Active in conservation movement. Edited (with C.C. Buel) *Battles and Leaders of the Civil War* (1887). Author of *The Winter Hour and Other Poems* (1891), *Songs of Liberty* (1897), *Poems of War and Peace* (1916), *Aftermath* (1933), etc. His son ¶Owen McMahon (1878–1952), b. New York City, wrote novels and stories including *Arrows of the Almighty* (1901), *In the Name of Liberty* (1905), *The Salamander* (1913), *The Wasted Generation* (1921), *Children of Divorce* (1927); best known for tales of Lawrenceville School, as *The Eternal Boy* (1909), *The Humming Bird* (1910), *The Varmint* (1910), *The Tennessee Shad* (1911), and a sequel *Stover at Yale* (1911).

Johnson, Samuel. *Known as* Dr. Johnson. 1709–1784. English writer, lexicographer, critic, and conversationalist. Beset by poverty and ungainly appearance; educated by omnivorous reading and a year at Oxford; married a widow, Elizabeth Porter, of Birmingham (1735; d. 1752), and opened a school at Edial, near Lichfield, in which David Garrick was one of his first pupils. To London (1737), accompanied by Garrick; became a contributor to Edward Cave's *Gentleman's Magazine.* Published a poem, *London* (1738), in imitation of a satire of Juvenal, and a prose *Life of Savage* (1744). Issued a prospectus of his English dictionary (1747) and worked on it until its publication (1755). Also published poem *The Vanity of Human Wishes* (1749), produced *Irene* at Drury Lane Theatre (1749), edited the *Rambler* (1750–52), and in a famous letter repulsed Lord Chesterfield's tardy offer of patronage for his dictionary (1755). Publication of the dictionary (1755) brought fame and a degree from Oxford. Contributed book reviews to *Literary Magazine* (1756–58); wrote the *Idler* papers for Newbery's *Universal Chronicle* (1758–60) and the prose romance *Rasselas, Prince of Abyssinia* (1759). Aided in exposing the Cock Lane ghost (1762). Received pension of £300 from Lord Bute and degrees of LL.D. from Dublin and Oxford. Made acquaintance of James Boswell (May 1763) and soon after founded his Literary Club, including Reynolds, Garrick, Goldsmith, Boswell, Burke, and others. Published critical edition of Shakespeare (1765); wrote *Lives of the Poets* (10 vols., 1779–81). Traveled in Scotland with Boswell (1773) and wrote *Journey to the Western Isles of Scotland* (1775). Frequently enjoyed hospitality of the Thrales (from 1764) and was Mr. Thrale's executor (1781). See James BOSWELL.

Johnson, Thomas. 1732–1819. American Revolutionary leader, b. Calvert Co., Md. Member, Continental Congress (1774–77); nominated George Washington for commander in chief, Continental army (1775). Raised troops in Maryland for Continental army (1777). First governor of Maryland (1777–79). Associate justice, U.S. Supreme Court (1791–93).

Johnson, Tom Loftin. 1854–1911. American politician, b. near Georgetown, Ky. Acquired street-railway interests in Indianapolis, Ind., and then in Cleveland, Ohio; made many inventions, including a streetcar farebox; became follower of Henry George. Member, U.S. House of Representatives (1891–95). Mayor of Cleveland (1901–1909); administration noted for efficiency and municipal reforms, marked by long bitter fight with street-railway interests.

Johnson, Walter Perry. *Nicknamed* Big Train. 1887–1946. American baseball player, b. Humboldt, Kans. Pitcher for Washington Senators (1907–27); managed Senators (1929–32), Cleveland Indians (1933–35). Won 414 games out of 802; pitched record 113 shutouts, 3497 strikeouts, 5923 total innings; his record of 56 consecutive scoreless innings (1913) stood until 1968. Among first 5 elected to Baseball Hall of Fame (1936).

Johnson, Sir William. 1715–1774. British colonial official, b. Ireland. To America and settled in Mohawk Valley (c.1738); successful in dealing with Indians, esp. those of the Six Nations; member of Council of New York (from 1750); commissioned major general and sent against Crown Point (1755); created baronet for victory over French under Dieskau (1755); superintendent of Indian affairs (1756–74); captured Niagara (1759); with Amherst at Montreal (1760); negotiated Treaty of Ft. Stanwix (1768). His son ¶Sir John (1742–1830) organized Tories and Indians and inspired raids against colonials in the Mohawk and Schoharie valleys (1777–81); superintendent of Indian affairs (from 1782); granted estate in Canada after the Revolution.

Johnson, William. 1771–1834. American jurist, b. Charleston, S.C. Associate justice, U.S. Supreme Court (1804–34); frequent dissenter from opinions of Chief Justice Marshall.

Johnson, William Eugene. 1862–1945. American reformer, b. Coventry, N.Y. Journalist (1884–1905); active in temperance movement; chief special officer in U.S. Indian service (1908–11); became known as Pussyfoot Johnson because of his methods in pursuing lawbreakers in Indian Territory. Managing editor, publications of Anti-Saloon League (1912–16); publicity director of the league (1916–18); temperance lecturer.

Johnson, William Samuel. 1727–1819. American politician and educator, b. Stratford, Conn. Son of Samuel Johnson (1696–1772), clergyman and first president of King's Coll. (Columbia U.); member of Conn. legislature (1761–66, 1771–75); Conn. agent in London (1767–71); declined election to Continental Congress (1774); member of Congress of Confederation (1784–87); delegate to Constitutional Convention (1787) and signer of the Constitution; U.S. senator (1789–91). First president of Columbia Coll. (1787–1800).

John·ston \ˈjän(t)-stən, -sən\, Albert Sidney. 1803–1862. American army officer, b. Washington, Ky. In U.S. army (1826–34); served in Texas army (1835–38), as commanding brigadier general (1837); secretary of war, Texas (1838–40). Reentered U.S. army (1849); commanded expedition to pacify Mormons in Utah (1857–58); resigned to enter Confederate service as general (1861). In battle at Shiloh, surprised and defeated Union army under Grant, but was killed in action (Apr. 6, 1862).

Johnston, Alexander Keith. 1804–1871. Scottish geographer. Organized, with his brother ¶Sir William (1802–1888), map publishing firm of W. & A. K. Johnston at Edinburgh (1826); chief works the *National Atlas* (1843), the first English atlas of physical geography (1848, prepared at Humboldt's suggestion), a *Dictionary of Geography* (1850), and the *Royal Atlas* (1861).

Johnston, Annie, *nee* Fel·lows \ˈfel-(ˌ)ōz, -əz\. 1863–1931. American writer, b. Evansville, Ind. m. William L. Johnston (1888; d. 1892). Author of *The Little Colonel* (1896) and 11 popular sequels, and a second series of juveniles beginning with *Mary Ware* (1908).

Johnston, Archibald. Lord War·ris·ton *or* War·is·ton \ˈwȯr-ə-stən\. 1611–1663. Scottish political leader. A leading author of the National Covenant (1638); made lord of session by Charles I (1641); helped direct operations of Covenanting and Parliamentary armies (1644–46); lord advocate (1646); led anti-Royalist Covenanters (1647); supported cause of Charles II (from 1649); removed from offices by Cromwell (1651) but later (1657) made lord clerk register, a commissioner of justice, member of House of Peers; condemned at Restoration, fled to France (1661) but was captured, returned, and executed.

Johnston *or* **Jon·ston** \ˈjän(t)-stən\, Arthur. 1587–1641. Scottish poet. Practiced medicine in France, Germany, Italy; physician to Charles I (c.1625); rector of King's Coll., Aberdeen (1637). Renowned for Latin verse, including translation of Psalms (1637); contributed to and helped publish anthology *Deliciae Poetarum Scotorum* (1637).

Johnston, David Claypoole. 1799–1865. American cartoonist, b. Philadelphia. Achieved fame as caricaturist and lithographer; issued annual (1830–49) series titled *Scraps,* containing humorous etchings that earned him title of "The American Cruikshank."

Johnston, Edward. 1872–1944. British calligrapher, b. Uruguay. Taught writing at London Central School of Arts and Crafts (1899–1912), Royal Coll. of Art (1901–44). For London Underground Railway designed (1916) new sans serif typeface that was widely influential. Author of *Writing and Illuminating, and Lettering* (1906), *Manuscript and Inscription Letters* (1909).

Johnston, Sir Harry Hamilton. 1858–1927. British explorer and writer. To Tunis (1879); explored Portugese West Africa and Congo River (1882–83); led Royal Society expedition to Mt. Kilimanjaro (1884) and made first British treaties with tribes of the region; joined Consular Service (1885); led expedition (1889) which founded British Central Africa Protectorate; commissioner for South Central Africa (1891–96); consul general, Tunis (1897–99); special commissioner in Uganda Protectorate (1899–1901). Author of books on Africa including *British Central Africa* (1897), *Uganda Protectorate* (1902), and novels *The Gay Dombeys* (1919), *Mrs. Warren's Daughter* (1920), and *The Veneerings* (1922).

Johnston, Joseph Eggleston. 1807–1891. American army officer, b. near Farmville, Va. Entered army (1829); on frontier duty; served through Mexican War. Resigned (1861) to enter Confederate service; brigadier general (May 1861); general (July 1861); commanded army of Northern Virginia (1861–62). In command on Mississippi (1863); lost Vicksburg to Grant. With army of the Tennessee (1864); outmaneuvered by Sherman; relieved of command (July 1864); restored (Feb. 1865); surrendered to Sherman (Apr. 26, 1865). Member, U.S. House of Representatives (1879–81).

Johnston, Mary. 1870–1936. American author, b. Buchanan, Va. Author of historical romances including *Prisoners of Hope* (1898), *To Have and to Hold* (1900), *Audrey* (1902), *Cease Firing* (1912), *Hagar* (1913), *Foes* (1918), *Silver Cross* (1922), *The Great Valley* (1926), *Miss Delicia Allen* (1933), etc.

Johnston, Sir William. See under Alexander Keith JOHNSTON.

John Ta·laia \-tä-ˈlī-ə\. 5th century. Greek prelate and theologian, b. Alexandria, Egypt. Named bishop of Alexandria by Emperor Zeno (482); denounced as Eutychian heretic by Patriarch Acacius of Constantinople and forced to step down; sought redress from Pope Felix III, who responded by excommunicating Acacius (485) for imposing heterodox doctrine of his *Henoticon;* schism thus created allowed establishment of separate Byzantine church. Named bishop of Nola (484).

John William Fri·so \-'frē-(,)zō\. *Du.* Jo·han Wil·lem Fri·so \yō-'hän-'vil-əm-'frē-sō\. 1687–1711. Prince of Nassau-Dietz and Orange. Son of Henry Casimir II; succeeded as stadholder of Friesland and Groningen (1696); named successor (1695) as stadholder general by William, Prince of Orange (William III of England), but rejected as stadholder general by Estates General (1702), beginning stadholderless period (1702–47); distinguished himself in War of Spanish Succession.

John Zápolya. See JOHN, king of Hungary.

Joinville, Prince de. See under LOUIS-PHILIPPE.

Join·ville \zhwaⁿ-vēl\, Jean de. Sire. c.1224–1317. French chronicler. Accompanied Saint Louis (Louis IX) to Egypt on the Seventh Crusade (1248–54); made seneschal of Champagne. Author of invaluable record of the Seventh Crusade, commissioned by Jeanne, wife of Philip IV, and called *Histoire de Saint-Louis.*

Jó·kai \'yō-,kȯi\, Mór. 1825–1904. Hungarian novelist. Author of popular novels including *Erdély aranykora* (1852), *Egy magyar nábob* (1853–54), *Az új földesúr* (1863), *A kőszívű ember fiai* (1869), *Fekete gyémántok* (1873), *Az aranyember* (1873), *Sárga rózsa* (1893); also wrote verse and plays.

Jokl \'yȯk-əl\, Norbert. 1877–1942. Czech linguist. Librarian (1908–23), professor (1923–42), U. of Vienna; known for studies of linguistic history of Balkans and esp. of Albanian. Author of *Linguistisch-kulturhistorische Untersuchungen aus dem Bereiche des Albanischen* (1923).

Jo·liot-Cu·rie \zhȯl-yō-kū̅-rē\, Frédéric, *in full* Jean-Frédéric. *Orig. surname* Joliot. 1900–1958. French physicist. Assistant to Marie Curie (1925); m. (1926) Irène Curie (*q.v.*); professor, Radium Inst., Paris; artificially produced radioactive isotopes; first observed production of electron-positron pair (1932); professor, Collège de France (from 1937); director, Centre National de la Recherche Scientifique (1944); French high commissioner for atomic energy (1946–50). With wife shared 1935 Nobel prize for physics.

Jo·li·vet \yō-lē-ve\, André. 1905–1974. French composer. Student of Varèse; helped form La Spirale (1935) to promote contemporary music; musical director, Comédie-Française (1943–59); taught composition, Paris Conservatoire (1966–70). Composed works notable for tonal and rhythmic experiments, use of primitive themes; works included orchestral *Andante* (1935), *Cinq danses rituelles* (1939), *Concerto for Ondes Martenot* (1947), *Percussion Concerto* (1958), symphonies, etc.; ballets *Les quatre vérités* (1941), *Guignol et Pandore* (1943), *L'Inconnue* (1950), *Ariadne* (1964); comic opera *Dolorès* (1942); solo works *Mana* (piano, 1935), *Hymne à l'universe* (organ, 1962), *Mandala* (organ, 1969); choral and chamber works.

Jol·li·et *or* **Jo·li·et** \zhȯl-ye; *Angl* jäl-ē-'et, jō-lē-\, Louis. 1645–1700. French explorer, b. prob. Beaupré, Canada. Sent west (1669) with supplies for expedition looking for copper in Lake Superior region; with Jacques Marquette led expedition to discover the great river reported by Indians; followed Fox and Wisconsin rivers westward; sighted Mississippi (June 1673) and floated down as far as what is now Arkansas; reported discovery in Quebec (1674). Given island of Anticosti; made further explorations in Gulf of St. Lawrence and Hudson Bay region. Canadian royal hydrographer (1697).

Jol·ly \'jäl-ē\, George. d. 1673? English actor and manager. Led troupe of strolling players in Germany (1648–60), influencing German theatrical work; managed Cockpit theater, London (1660–63); pioneered in use of elaborate sets and stage machinery in England.

Jol·ly \'yȯl-ē *Angl* 'jäl-ē\, Philipp Johann Gustav von. 1809–1884. German physicist. Professor, Heidelberg (from 1839); invented an air thermometer and a spring balance (Jolly balance) for determining specific gravity; determined the mass and density of the earth and the coefficient of expansion of air and other gases; studied osmosis.

Jol·son \'jōl-sən\, Al. *Orig.* Asa Yoel·son \'yœl-sən\. 1886–1950. American entertainer, b. Srednike, Russia. To U.S. (1893); in vaudeville, Lew Dockstader's minstrel troupe; gained fame as blackface singer; appeared on Broadway in *La Belle Paree* (1911), *Honeymoon Express* (1913), *Sinbad* (1918), *Bombo* (1921), *Big Boy* (1925), etc.; appeared in films *The Jazz Singer* (1927; first feature with full soundtrack), *Singing Fool* (1928), *Mammy* (1930), *Hallelujah, I'm a Bum* (1933), *Swanee River* (1940), etc.; collaborated on songs as "Back in Your Own Back Yard," "California, Here I Come," "Me and My Shadow," "Sonny Boy."

Joly \'jäl-ē\, John. 1857–1933. Irish physicist. Professor, Trinity Coll., Dublin (1897–1933); devised a photometer, meldometer, and a method of color photography; invented a steam calorimeter; perfected (with Walter Stevenson) the "Dublin method" of radio therapy; conducted researches on the crust formation of the earth; determined role of radioactive decay in geologic processes; determined (1899) age of earth as 100 million years.

Jo·lyot \zhȯl-yō\, Prosper. Sieur de Crais-Bil·lon \kre-bē-yōⁿ\. *Pen name* Cré·bil·lon \krā-bē-yōⁿ\. 1674–1762. French tragic poet. Considered in his time the rival of Voltaire. Works included *Idoménée* (1705), *Atrée et Thyeste* (1707), *Électre* (1708), *Rhadamiste et Zénobie* (1711), *Xerxès* (1714), *Sémiramis* (1717), *Pyrrhus* (1726), *Catilina* (1748), *Le Triumvirat* (1754). His son ¶Claude-Prosper Jolyot de Crébillon, *known as* Crébillon fils (1707–1777), was a novelist; depicted satirically the licentiousness of French high society in *L'Écumoire* (1733), *Les Égarements du coeur et de l'esprit* (1736), *Le Sopha, conte moral* (1742), *Les Heureux orphelins* (1754), etc.

Jo·mi·ni \zhȯ-mē-nē\, Henri de, *in full* Antoine-Henri. 1779–1869. Swiss soldier and writer on military affairs. In French army (1798–1800, 1804–13); made staff colonel by Napoléon (1805), with Ney at Ulm (1805); Jena and Eylau (1806), in Spain (1808); general of brigade (1810); Ney's chief of staff (1813); joined Russian army as lieutenant general and aide-de-camp to Alexander I (1813); general in chief (1826) and military tutor to czarevich Nicholas; organized Russian staff college (1830); retired to Brussels; recalled to Russia to advise Czar Nicholas on Crimean War (1854); consulted by Napoléon III on Italian campaign (1859). Author of greatly influential works on conduct of war including *Traité des grandes opérations militaires* (1805), *Principes de la stratégie* (1818), *Précis de l'art de la guerre* (1838).

Jom·mel·li \yōm-'mel-lē\ *or* **Jo·mel·li** \yō-'mel-lē\, Niccolò. 1714–1774. Italian composer. Musical director for ducal court, Stuttgart (1753–69); in service of Portuguese court (1769–74). Composed operas, including *Merope* (1741), *Achille in Sciro* (1749), *Ifigenia in Aulide* (1751), *Fetonte* (1768), and *Armida* (1770); also wrote oratorios, cantatas, psalms, a Requiem, a Miserere, and other church music.

Jon \'yȯn\, François du. *Lat.* Fran·cis·cus Ju·ni·us \fran(t)-'sis-kəs-'jü-nē-əs\. 1589–1677. Dutch scholar. Pastor in Netherlands (1617–20); to England as tutor in household of Thomas Howard, Earl of Arundel (1620); collected and edited large collection of manuscripts later bequeathed to Bodleian Library; work greatly stimulated interest in Anglo-Saxon and other old Germanic languages; returned to Netherlands (1650). Edited works of Caedmon (1655), the Gothic codex of Ulphilas (1665), etc.

Jonah, Rabbi. See IBN JANĀH.

Jo·nas \'yō-näs\, Justus. *Also called* Jodocus Koch \'kȯk\. 1493–1555. German reformer. Friend of Luther; professor of theology, Wittenberg (1521–41); court preacher, Coburg (1550); helped draft Augsburg Confession (1530). Important esp. as translator of Latin works of Luther and Melanchthon.

Jones \'jōnz\, Alfred Gilpin. 1824–1906. Canadian politician, b. Weymouth, N.S. Headed importing firm; opposed Confederation; member of federal House of Commons (1867–72, 1874–78, 1887–91); minister of militia (1878); lieutenant governor of Nova Scotia (1900–06).

Jones, Anson. 1798–1858. American politician, b. Great Barrington, Mass. Practiced medicine in Philadelphia and in Brazoria, Texas (from 1833). Served in Sam Houston's army; Texas minister to U.S. (1835); Texas secretary of state (1841); president of Texas (1844–46); turned over government to J.P. Henderson, first governor under Constitution of the United States.

Jones, Casey. See John Luther JONES.

Jones, Catesby ap Roger. 1821–1877. American naval officer, b. Fairfield, Va. Nephew of Thomas ap Catesby Jones; entered navy (1836); entered Confederate service (1861); executive officer of the *Merrimac* (1862); in command during battle with *Monitor* (March 9, 1862).

Jones, Charles Jesse. *Known as* Buffalo Jones. 1844–1918. American hunter, b. Illinois. Renowned buffalo hunter (to 1872); began breeding experiments (1886) leading to buffalo–cattle cross called cattalo; game warden, Yellowstone National Park (from 1902).

Jones, Daniel. 1881–1967. English phonetician. Teacher of phonetics, University Coll., London (from 1907; professor 1921–49). Assistant secretary (1907–27), secretary (1927–49), president (1950–67), International Phonetic Assoc. Among his works were *Outline of English Phonetics* (1916) and *English Pronouncing Dictionary,* based on Southern British speech (1917).

Jones, David Michael. 1895–1974. British artist and writer. Known as water color painter of landscapes, seascapes, animal figures. Author of novel *In Parenthesis* (1937, Hawthornden prize), religious verse *The Anathemata* (1952).

Jones, Donald Forsha. 1890–1963. American geneticist, b. Hutchinson, Kans. Geneticist with Connecticut Agricultural Experiment Station (1915–60); developed (1917) a double-cross hybrid corn of great yield that made hybrid corn a commercially practical crop; developed method of genetically transmitting pollen sterility, eliminating need for detasselling of corn in the field; developed first hybrid sweet corn (1924).

Jones, Ebenezer. 1820–1860. English poet. Remembered esp. for three poems, "Winter Hymn to the Snow," "When the World is Burning," "To Death," written near the close of his life.

Jones, Edward D. See under Charles H. DOW.

Jones, Ernest, *in full* Alfred Ernest. 1879–1958. British psychoanalyst, b. Wales. Professor, Toronto (1909–12); in private practice, London (from 1913);

founder, president (1919–40), British Psycho-Analytical Society; president (1920–24, 1932–49), International Psycho-Analytical Association; established (1924) Institute of Psycho-Analysis; founded and edited (1920–39) *International Journal of Psycho-Analysis.* Close associate of Freud; played key role in securing release of Freud and his family from occupied Austria (1938). Author of *Hamlet and Oedipus* (1949), *Sigmund Freud* (1953–57).

Jones, Ernest Charles. 1819–1869. English Chartist reformer and poet. Leader of Chartist movement (1845); imprisoned (1848–50). Author of *The Battleday* (1855), *The Emperor's Vigil* (1856), *Corayda* (1860), etc.

Jones, Harold Spencer. 1890–1960. English astronomer. Astronomer at Cape of Good Hope (1923–33); astronomer royal (1933–55); known for work in determining solar parallax. Author of *Worlds Without End* (1935), *Life on Other Worlds* (1940), *Picture of the Universe* (1947).

Jones, Henry. *Pseudonym* Cav·en·dish \ˈkav-ən-(ˌ)dish\. 1831–1899. English physician and writer. Authority on whist and other games.

Jones, Henry Arthur. 1851–1929. English playwright. First stage success *The Silver King* (with Henry Herman, 1882); other plays included *Saints and Sinners* (1884), *Judah* (1890), *The Tempter* (1893), *The Masqueraders* (1894), *Rebellious Susan* (1894), *Michael and his Lost Angel* (1896), *The Liars* (1897), *Mrs. Dane's Defence* (1900), *The Hypocrites* (1906), *Mary Goes First* (1913), *Cock o' the Walk* (1915), and *The Pacifists* (1917).

Jones, Howard Mumford. 1892–1980. American educator and writer, b. Saginaw, Mich. Professor, U. of Texas (1916–25), U. of North Carolina (1925–30), U. of Mich. (1930–36), Harvard (1936–60). Author of *Gargoyles* (verse, 1918), *A Bibliography of Byron* (1924), *America and French Culture, 1750–1848* (1927), *The Harp that Once* (1937), *Ideas in America* (1944), *Theory of American Literature* (1948), *American Humanism* (1957), *O Strange New World* (1964, Pulitzer prize), *Age of Energy* (1971), etc.

Jones, Inigo. 1573–1652. English architect. Designed stage sets, etc., for court masques written by Ben Jonson, Heywood, Davenant, and others. The king's surveyor general of works (1615–42); designed the queen's house at Greenwich, Lincoln's Inn Chapel, Queen's Chapel at St. James's, banqueting hall at Whitehall (1619–22), reconstruction of St. Paul's Cathedral, Covent Garden piazza, Ashburnham House in Westminster. Influenced by Palladio; considered founder of English classical architecture.

Jones, Jacob. 1768–1850. American naval officer, b. near Smyrna, Del. Entered navy (1799); commanded sloop *Wasp* when it fought and captured British brig *Frolic* (Oct. 18, 1812); commanded captured frigate *Macedonian* in Decatur's squadron operating against Algiers (1815).

Jones, James. 1921–1977. American novelist, b. Robinson, Ill. Author of naturalistic novels as *From Here to Eternity* (1951), *Some Came Running* (1957), *The Pistol* (1959), *The Thin Red Line* (1962), *Go to the Widow-Maker* (1967), *Merry Month of May* (1971), *Whistle* (1978, completed by Willie Morris).

Jones, John. *Pseudonym* Jac Glan-y-Gors \ˈjäk-ˌglän-ə-ˈgörs\. 1766–1821. Welsh poet and political writer. Influenced by Thomas Paine and French Revolution, wrote pamphlets *Seren Tan Gwmmwl* (1795), *Toriad y Dydd* (1797); known esp. for satiric verse including "Sessiwn yng Nghymru," "Dic Shon Dafydd," "Offeiriad yn Sir Aberteifi."

Jones, John Beauchamp. 1810–1866. American writer, b. Baltimore. Magazine editor in Baltimore, Washington, D.C., Philadelphia; during Civil War employed in Confederate War Department. Author of novels including *Wild Western Scenes* (1841) and of valuable *Rebel War Clerk's Diary* (1866).

Jones, John Luther, *known as* Casey. 1864–1900. American railroad engineer, b. near Cayce, Ky. Engineer for Illinois Central R.R. (1890–1900); engineer on run of "Cannonball Express" that was wrecked near Vaughan, Miss. (April 30, 1900), an event memorialized in ballad "Casey Jones" by Wallace Saunders.

Jones, Sir John Morris-. See MORRIS-JONES.

Jones, John Paul. *Orig. full name* John Paul. 1747–1792. American naval officer, b. Kirkcudbrightshire, Scotland. In British mercantile marine (from c.1759). Settled in Fredericksburg, Va. (c.1773), and added Jones to his name. Entered American navy at outbreak of Revolution; commissioned senior lieutenant (Dec. 1775); promoted captain (1776); successful cruise as commander of *Ranger* in waters around British Isles (1778). With aid of France, organized fleet to attack British; commanded flagship *Bonhomme Richard* (1779); in celebrated battle (during which he is supposed to have said "I have not yet begun to fight!"), defeated British ship *Serapis* (Sept. 23, 1779) but *Bonhomme Richard* sank two days later. Awarded gold medal by Congress (1787). Served in Russian navy on Black Sea (1788–89); in Paris (1790–92). Remains brought to U.S. (1905).

Jones, John Winston. 1791–1848. American politician, b. near Amelia Courthouse, Va. Member, U.S. House of Representatives (1835–45), speaker (1843–45).

Jones, Joseph Stevens. 1809–1877. American physician, actor, and playwright, b. Boston. Successful actor in Boston; managed Tremont Theatre (1839–41). Author of over 150 plays, notably *The Liberty Tree* (1832), *The People's Lawyer* introducing popular Yankee character Solon Shingle (1839), *The Silver Spoon* (1852).

Jones, Lewis Ralph. 1864–1945. American botanist, b. Brandon, Wis. Professor, Vermont (1893–1910), Wisconsin (from 1910); known for researches in plant pathology and success in controlling diseases of crop plants as potato blight, pear and apple scab, soft rot.

Jones, Mary, *nee* Harris. *Known as* Mother Jones. 1830–1930. American labor leader, b. Cork, Ireland. To U.S. as a child. Interested herself in labor movement after death of husband (1867). Became agitator, prominent speaker, and organizer in labor circles; active in Pennsylvania, West Virginia, Colorado miners' strikes, New York City garment workers' strike, etc.; helped found Industrial Workers of the World (1905).

Jones, Owen. 1809–1874. English architect. Superintendent of the London Exhibition (1851); joint director of decoration of Crystal Palace; designed St. James's Hall, London. Author of *Plans, Elevations, Sections and Details of the Alhambra* (1842–45) and standard *Grammar of Ornament* (1856).

Jones, Robert. fl. 1600–11. English lutenist and composer. Published five books of airs and songs and a collection of madrigals (1607).

Jones, Robert Edmond. 1887–1954. American scene designer, b. Milton, N.H. Designed sets for many plays, including *The Man Who Married a Dumb Wife, The Jest, Richard III, Macbeth, Green Pastures,* and for films *La Cucaracha, Becky Sharp,* etc.; initiated reaction against realism in sets. A director of Greenwich Village Playhouse, N.Y.C. (from 1925). Author of *Continental Stagecraft* (1922), *Dramatic Imagination* (1941).

Jones, Robert Tyre, *known as* Bobby. 1902–1971. American golfer, b. Atlanta, Ga. Adm. to bar (1928) and practiced at Atlanta, Ga. Won U.S. Amateur championship (1924, 1925, 1927, 1928, 1930), U.S. Open (1923, 1926, 1929, 1930), British Open (1926, 1927, 1930), British amateur (1930); first player to win the "Grand Slam," the amateur and open championships of Great Britain and U.S. in the same year (1930). Leader in initiating Masters Tournament (1934).

Jones, Rufus Matthew. 1863–1948. American educator and religious leader, b. South China, Me. Edited *Friends' Review* (1893 ff.); taught at Haverford Coll. (1893–1934); helped found (1917) American Friends Service Committee, chairman (1917–28, 1935–44). Author of series of works on history of Quakers: *Studies in Mystical Religion* (1909), *The Quakers in the American Colonies* (with others, 1911), *Spiritual Reformers in the 16th and 17th Centuries* (1914), *Later Periods of Quakerism* (1921); also wrote *Practical Christianity* (1899), *Story of George Fox* (1919), *Preface to Christian Faith* (1932), *Spirit in Man* (1941), *The Radiant Life* (1944), autobiographical *Small-Town Boy* (1941).

Jones, Samuel Milton. *Known as* "Golden Rule" Jones. 1846–1904. American industrialist, politician, and reformer, b. Ty Mawr, Wales. To U.S. (1849); worked in the oil fields; later established manufacturing plant at Toledo, Ohio; advocated Golden Rule policy in all his dealings. Mayor of Toledo (1897–1904); led crusade to wipe out dishonesty and political corruption.

Jones, Thomas ap Catesby. 1790–1858. American naval officer, b. Westmoreland Co., Va. Entered navy (1805); commanded gunboat flotilla that held up superior British force on Lake Borgne, La. (Dec. 1814); commanded Pacific Squadron (1825–31); made first U.S. naval call at Tahiti (1826); signed treaty with Kamehameha III of Hawaii (1826); believing war had broken out, seized Monterey, Calif. (Oct. 1842); commanded Pacific Squadron (1844–48) during Mexican War.

Jones, Thomas Gwynn. 1871–1949. Welsh poet and scholar. With National Library, Aberystwyth (1909–13); lecturer, later professor of Welsh literature, U. Coll. of Wales (1913–37). Translated Goethe's *Faust* into Welsh (1922) and published *Blodau o Hen Ardd* (1927), collection of Greek poems and Latin epigrams. Known for narrative poems "Broseliawnd," "Anatiomaros," "Argoed," "Cynddilig," etc., verse play *Tir na n-Og.*

Jones, Thomas Hudson. 1892–1969. American sculptor, b. Buffalo, N.Y. Among his works were the Tomb of the Unknown Soldier (1931) in Arlington National Cemetery, the bust of Ulysses S. Grant in the Hall of Fame.

Jones, Sir William. 1746–1794. English Orientalist and jurist. Judge of the high court at Calcutta (1783–94). Founded Bengal Asiatic Society (1784). His notable works included *Persian Grammar* (1772), *Essay on the Law of Bailments* (1781), a version of the Arabic *Mu'allaqāt* (1783), translations of *Hitopadesa* and *Sakuntala,* etc.

Jonescu. See IONESCU.

Jong·en \ˈyȯŋ-ən\, Joseph Marie Alphonse Nicolas. 1873–1953. Belgian composer. Taught at Liège Conservatory (1902–14), Brussels Conservatory (1920–53, director 1925–39). Composed string quartets, sonatas, and other pieces for violin and violoncello; piano trios and quartets; cantatas; orchestral works including the symphonic poem *Lalla Roukh* (1904), *Symphonie concertante* (1926), *Trois mouvements symphoniques* (1951); choruses, and songs.

Jong·kind \ˈyȯŋ-kint\, Johan Barthold. 1819–1891. Dutch painter and etcher. Known for landscapes exhibiting mastery of atmospheric rendering and effects of light; influenced Monet.

Jon·nart \zhȯ-när\, Célestin-Auguste-Charles. 1857–1927. French politician. Member of Chamber of Deputies (1889–1914) and of the Senate (from 1914); governor of Algeria (1900–11, 1918); founded (1909) U. of Algiers. Minister of foreign affairs (1913). During World War I, served as French high commissioner in Greece; instrumental in forcing King Constantine's abdication and in securing Greece's participation in the war on the side of the Allies. Ambassador to the Vatican (1921–24).

Jon·son \ˈjän(t)-sən\, Ben, *in full* Benjamin. 1572–1637. English playwright and poet. Apprenticed to his stepfather, a bricklayer; served briefly with English army in Flanders; returned to London (c.1592) and became associated with the stage as both actor and playwright. His plays included *The Case is Altered* (1597?), *Every Man in his Humour* (1598), *Every Man out of his Humour* (1599), *Cynthia's Revels* (1600), *The Poetaster* (1601), *Sejanus* (1603), *Volpone* (1605), *Epicoene* (1609), *The Alchemist* (1610), *Catiline* (1611), *Bartholomew Fair* (1614), *The Devil is an Ass* (1616), *The Staple of News* (1625), *The New Inn* (1629), *Tale of a Tub* (1633), and a number of court masques. Among his poems (pub. 1616) were epigrams, epistles, and songs, including the famous "Drink to me only with thine eyes." Noted also as a wit and a critic. Generally regarded as first poet laureate, although William Davenant (*q.v.*) was first to receive official title.

Jóns·son \ˈyōns-sȯn\, Arngrímur. *Called* the Learned. 1568–1648. Icelandic scholar. Head of Latin school at Hólar; collected Icelandic manuscripts; revolutionized Icelandic and Scandinavian historiography. Author of *Crymogaea* (1609), *Specimen Islandiae Historicum et Magna ex Parte Chorographicum* (1643).

Jónsson, Finnur. 1704–1789. Icelandic bishop and historian. Author of *Historia Ecclesiastica Islandiae* (1772–78), used as a source of Icelandic history and literature.

Jónsson, Hjálmar. *Known also as* Bó·lu-Hjál·mar \ˈbō-lœ-ˈyäl-mär\. 1796–1875. Icelandic poet. Author of rough, satirical folk poetry critical of church, bureaucracy, etc.; much of his verse circulated orally, collected posthumously in *Ljóthmaeli* (1879), *Rímur af Göngu-Hrólfi* (1884), *Kvaethi og kvithlingar* (1888), *Tvennar rímur* (1905).

Jooss \ˈyōs\, Kurt. 1901–1979. German dancer and choreographer. A founder of Neue Tanzbühne, Münster (1924); established school (1927) and company (1928), Essen; ballet master, Essen Opera (1930–33); fled Nazi regime to England (1933); toured widely with Ballet Jooss (1933–47); reestablished school and company in Essen (1949); ballet master, Düsseldorf Opera (1954–56). In choreography extended classic technique, adopting Laban's eukinetics, to create dances of modern temper, often on topical themes; works included *The Green Table* (1932), *Big City* (1932), *Seven Heroes* (1933), *Prodigal Son* (1933), *The Mirror* (1935), *Chronica* (1939), *Pandora* (1944), *Colombinade* (1951), *Castor and Pollux* (1962), *Dido and Aeneas* (1966).

Joos van Wassenhove. See JUSTUS of Ghent.

Jop·lin \ˈjäp-lən\, Janis. 1943–1970. American singer, b. Port Arthur, Tex. Achieved fame as singer, in expressive blues tradition of Bessie Smith and Billie Holiday, with rock bands Big Brother and the Holding Company and Full Tilt Boogie Band.

Joplin, Scott. 1868–1917. American composer, b. Texarkana, Ark. Enjoyed success with "Maple Leaf Rag" (1899), published while living in Sedalia, Mo.; later lived in St. Louis and New York City. Other works included "The Entertainer" (1902), "The Sycamore" (1904), "Gladiolus Rag" (1907), "Sugar Cane Rag" (1908), "Wall Street Rag" (1909), ragtime opera *Treemonisha* (1911; first full performance 1972).

Joram. See JEHORAM.

Jor·daens \ˈyȯr-däns\, Jacob. 1593–1678. Flemish painter. Known for vigorous, colorful scenes of Flemish life, historical, religious, and mythological subjects, murals, portraits, designs for tapestries, etc.

Jor·dan \ˈjȯrd-ᵊn\, Archibald C. 1906–1968. South African writer. Taught Bantu languages and African studies at U. of Cape Town, UCLA (1962), U. of Wisconsin (1963–68). Author of novel *Ingqumbo Yeminyanya* (1940, in Xhosa), critical studies.

Jor·dan \zhȯr-däⁿ\, Camille, *in full* Marie-Ennemond-Camille. 1838–1922. French mathematician. Professor, École Polytechnique and Collège de France (1873–1912); known for work on substitution groups, Abelian functions, the symmetry of polyhedrons, topology, etc. Author of widely used *Cours d'analyse* (1882).

Jor·dan \ˈjȯrd-ᵊn\, David Starr. 1851–1931. American biologist and educator, b. near Gainesville, N.Y. Professor of natural history, Lombard U. (1872–73), of biology, Butler U. (1875–79), of zoology, Indiana U. (1879–85); president, Indiana U. (1885–91); first president (1891–1913), chancellor (1913–16), Stanford U. Author of *Manual of Vertebrates of Northern United States* (1876–1929), *The Fishes of North and Middle America* (with B.W. Evermann, 1896–1900), *Footnotes to Evolution* (1898), *American Food and Game Fishes* (with Evermann, 1902), *Fishes* (1907), *The Genera of Fishes* (1918–20), *Fossil Fishes of Southern California* (1919–26), of books on world peace, war, and related topics, such as *The Care and Culture of Men* (1896), *Imperial Democracy* (1899), *Human Harvest* (1907), *War and Waste* (1914), *Democracy and World Relations* (1918).

Jordan, Dorothea *or* Dorothy. *Orig.* Dorothea Bland \ˈbland\. 1762–1816. Irish actress. Dublin debut (1777); London debut at Drury Lane as Peggy in *The Country Girl* (1785); last part that of Lady Teazle at Covent Garden (1814). Leading comedy actress of her day; praised by Hazlitt, Lamb, Leigh Hunt; mistress of Duke of Clarence, later William IV (c.1790–1811, her 10 children by him being ennobled under surname FitzClarence).

Jor·dan \jȯr-ˈdan\, Elizabeth Garver. 1865–1947. American writer, b. Milwaukee. Reporter for New York *World* (1890–1900); editor, *Harper's Bazar* (1900–13). Author of *Tales of the City Room* (1895), *May Iverson, Her Book* (1904), *The Lady from Oklahoma* (comedy, produced 1913), *Wings of Youth* (1917), *Red Riding Hood* (1924), *The Fourflusher* (1930), *The Life of the Party* (1935), *Three Rousing Cheers* (autobiography, 1938), etc.

Jor·dan \ˈjȯrd-ᵊn\, Thomas. 1612?–?1685. English writer. Prolific author of verse, esp. of panegyrics on lord mayors of London (as poet laureate of London, 1671–85), of plays, etc. Books included *A Royal Arbour of Loyall Poesie* (1664), *Nursery of Novelties in Variety of Poetry.*

Jor·dan \ˈyȯr-ˌdän\, Wilhelm. 1819–1904. German writer and politician. Journalist in Leipzig (1844); member of Frankfurt parliament (1848). Author of verse *Schaum* (1846), dramatic epic *Demiurgos* (1852–54), the epic *Die Nibelunge* (1867–74), novel *Die Sebalds* (1885), translations of Shakespeare, Sophocles, Homer, and the Edda, etc.

Jor·da·nes \jȯr-ˈdā-nēz\ *or* **Jor·da·nis** \jȯr-ˈdā-nəs\. 6th century. Gothic historian. Author of *De origine actibusque Getarum* (551), condensed from Cassiodorus, Priscus, and others, and of chronicle *De summa temporum vel origine actibusque gentis Romanorum* (551).

Jør·gen·sen \ˈyœ̄r-gən-sən\, Johannes, *in full* Jens Johannes. 1866–1956. Danish poet, journalist, and novelist. Favored realism and, later, French Symbolism; embraced Roman Catholicism (1896). Author of verse *Digte* (1898), *Blomster og Frugter* (1907), *Af det Dybe* (1909), *Der er en Brønd, som rinder* (1920), *Isblomster* (1926), *Vers fra Vadstena* (1941); travel sketches *Rejsebogen* (1895), *Romersk Mosaik* (1901), *Pilgrimsbogen* (1903); biographies of St. Francis of Assisi (1907), St. Catherine of Siena (1915), St. Bridget of Sweden (1941–43); autobiography *Mit livs legende* (1916–28).

Jo·ris \ˈyō-ris\ *or* **Jo·ris·zoon** \ˈyō-ri-sən, -sän, -sōn\, David, *orig.* Jan. c.1501–1556. Dutch Anabaptist leader. Joined Anabaptists (1533); founded new sect known as Davidists or Jorists (1536); assumed role of messianic prophet, the "third David"; retired incognito to Basel as Jan van Brug·ge \vän-ˈbrœ̄g-ə\ (1543–56). Identified after death, denounced for heresy; remains exhumed and burned (1559).

Jorn \ˈyȯrn\, Asger Oluf. *Orig. surname* Jørgensen. 1914–1973. Danish painter. Influenced by Expressionists James Ensor, Paul Klee; a founder of Cobra group (1948–51); works noted for strong color, distorted forms, creating dramatic and emotional impact.

Josaphat. See JEHOSHAPHAT.

Jo·sa·phat Kun·ce·vyč \yȯ-ˈsä-fät-kůnt-ˈsav-ēch\ *or Pol.* **Kun·ce·wicz** \kůnt-ˈsev-ēch\. Saint. 1580?–1623. Lithuanian clergyman. Ordained priest (1609); labored for the Brest union of Lithuanian Orthodox and Roman churches; bishop of Vitebsk (1617); murdered by opponents of unification. Canonized (1867).

José. See JOSEPH.

Jo·sel \ˈyō-zəl, -səl\ *or* **Jo·se·lin** \ˈyōs(-ə)-lən\ *or* **Jo·sel·mann** \ˈyō-zəl-ˌmän\ of Ros·heim \ˈrōs-ˌhīm\. *Also known as* Joseph ben Ger·shon Lo·ans \-ben-ˈger-shȯn-ˈlō-əns\. c.1478–1554. German Jewish leader. *Shtadlan,* or advocate of Jewish interests; gained influence at imperial courts of Maximilian I, Charles V; succeeded in diverting or suppressing much anti-Semitic activity and legislation.

Joselito el Gallo. See José GÓMEZ.

Jo·seph \ˈjō-zəf *also* -səf\. Saint. 1st century B.C.–1st century A.D. Husband of Mary, mother of Jesus.

Joseph. Name of two Holy Roman emperors:

Joseph I. 1678–1711. King of Hungary (1687–1711), king of the Romans (1690–1711), and Holy Roman emperor (1705–11). Son of Leopold I; War of the Spanish Succession continued throughout his reign; imperial armies campaigned in Italy, Germany, and Flanders under Prince Eugene of Savoy; attacked Papal States (1708) to regain papal support for Habsburg claim on Spanish throne; his death ended any hope of realizing claim.

Joseph II. 1741–1790. King of Germany (1764–90) and Holy Roman emperor (1765–90). Son of Francis I and Maria Theresa; coregent with his mother in Austria (1765–80); acquired territory at first partition of Poland (1772). In full control of Austria on mother's death (1780); undertook policy of paternal despotism; prohibited publication of any new papal bulls, suppressed convents, and reduced clergy; published Edict of Toleration (1781); attempted administrative reforms; settled German colonists in Slavic and Hungarian territory; had many schemes for territorial aggrandizement, but succeeded only in alienating other nations and his own ministers.

Joseph I. *Port.* Jo·sé \zhü-ˈze\. *Called* o Re·for·ma·dor \ü-rā-fȯr-mȧ-ˈthȯr\, *i.e.* the Reformer. 1714–1777. King of Portugal (1750–77). Son of John V; indolent, benevolent ruler; relied (from 1755) on chief minister, the Marquês de Pombal (see CARVALHO E MELLO).

Joseph, Father. See TREMBLAY.

Joseph. *Indian name* In-mut-too-yah-lat-lat. c.1840–1904. American Indian chief of the Nez Percé tribe, b. Wallowa Valley, Ore. Succeeded to leadership (1871); led resistance to white encroachment; led people in Nez Percé War (1877), defeating U.S. army at several engagements while conducting masterly retreat toward Canada; at last surrendered to Gen. Nelson A. Miles (Oct. 5, 1877).

Joseph of Ar·i·ma·thea \ˌar-ə-mə-ˈthē-ə\. 1st century A.D. Samaritan Christian. A rich merchant; secretly a disciple of Jesus, whom he buried in his own tomb. In medieval legend, entrusted with Holy Grail; said to have brought Christianity to Britain and founded a monastery at Glastonbury.

Joseph of Vo·lo·ko·lamsk \ˌvəl-ə-ˈkō-ləm(p)sk\. Saint. *Orig.* Joseph Pa·nin \(ˌ)pən-ˈyēn\. 1439–1515. Russian religious and theologian. Entered monastery of Abbot Pafnutius at Borovsk; abbot (1477); instituted ascetical reforms but clashed with royal patrons, esp. Prince Ivan III Vasilyevich, and resigned; established monastery at Volokolamsk, which became center of monastic reform, social action, popular devotion; opposed as heretics Judaizing Christian sects; opposed Westernizing influences. Author of *Prosvetitel.*

Joseph ben Abra·ham ha-Co·hen \-ben-ˈā-brə-ˌham-hä-ˈkō-ən\. *Arab.* Abū Ya'qub al-Basir. 11th century. Jewish philosopher. A leading thinker of Karaite sect.

Joseph Bonaparte. See BONAPARTE.

Joseph Calasanctius. See José CALASANZ.

Joséphine de Beauharnais. See BEAUHARNAIS.

Jo·se·phus \jō-ˈsē-fəs\, Flavius. *Orig.* Jo·seph ben Mat·thi·as \ˈjō-zəf-ˌben-mə-ˈthī-əs, *also* ˈjō-səf-\. c.37–c.100. Jewish historian and general, b. Jerusalem. Studied Hebrew and Greek literature, and spent 3 years in desert with a hermit; joined Pharisee sect; served as delegate to Nero and won favor with Poppaea. Chosen governor of Galilee by Sanhedrin in Jerusalem; took part in Jewish revolt against Romans (66); resisted siege of Jotapata for 47 days (67); surrendered finally to Vespasian, who he predicted would become emperor; won his favor and accompanied him to Alexandria. Subsequently freed, and adopted name of Flavius; remained under patronage of Vespasian and his successors Titus (whom he accompanied to Rome after fall of Jerusalem, 70) and Domitian; received tracts of land in Judea and a pension. His works included a *History of the Jewish War* (in Aramaic, later in Greek), *Antiquities of the Jews* (a history of the Jews from the Creation to 66 A.D.), an *Autobiography,* and *Against Apion* (an apology of the Jews).

Josh·ua \ˈjäsh-(ə-)wə\ the Stylite. 5th–6th century. Syriac religious and chronicler. Monk in convent of Zuknin; under commission of Sergius, abbot at Edessa, wrote chronicle of period 495–506, including Byzantine–Persian war (502–506).

Jo·si·ah \jō-ˈsī-ə\ *or* **Jo·si·as** \-əs\. d. 609 B.C. King of Judah (c.640–609 B.C.). Son and successor of Amon; during his reign, book of the law (Deuteronomy?) found in temple; began reform movement; beginning of Jeremiah's prophesying; opposed Necho II of Egypt and killed in battle at Megiddo.

Josiah Allen's Wife. See Marietta HOLLEY.

Jó·si·ka \ˈyō-shi-kä\, Miklós. Baron. 1794–1865. Hungarian novelist. Introduced the romantic-historical novel into Hungary. Works included *Abafi* (1836), *A csehek Magyarországon* (1839), *Jő a tatár!* (1856).

Jos·quin des Prez *or* **Des·prez** \zhȯ-skaⁿ-dā-prā\. *Lat.* Jodocus Pra·ten·sis \prə-ˈten(t)-səs\ *or* Jodocus a Pra·to \ä-ˈprä-tō\. c.1440–1521. French composer. Singer at Milan cathedral (1459–72); in service of Duke Galeazzo Sforza (c.1474–76), later of Cardinal Ascanio Sforza; member of papal chapel (1486–?93); returned to France (c.1493); patronized by Louis XII; in service of Duke Ercole I of Ferrara (1503); canon and provost of Notre Dame, Condé (1504–21). Considered greatest composer of the Renaissance, breaking new ground in formal structure and in deep expressiveness; composed masses (20 extant in full), motets (c.100), and many secular chansons.

Jost. See also JOBST.

Jost \ˈyōst\, Isaak Markus. 1793–1860. German historian. Author of *Geschichte der Israeliten* (1820–29), a translation into German of the *Mishnah* with commentary (1832–34), etc.

Jou·bert \zhü-ber\, Barthélemy-Catherine. 1769–1799. French soldier. Served with distinction in Italy (1793–99); chief of the army in Italy (1798–99); served under Moreau (1799), killed at Novi.

Joubert, Joseph. 1754–1824. French moralist. Associate of Chateaubriand and Bonald; selections from his *Pensées* were edited by Chateaubriand (1838).

Joubert, Petrus Jacobus, *known as* Piet. 1834–1900. Boer soldier and statesman, b. Cape Colony. Migrated to the Transvaal (1840) and made living as a farmer; studied law. Elected to Volksraad (1860); attorney general of South African Republic (1870) and acting president (1875). Opposed British annexation of the Transvaal and was commandant general of Boer forces in the war (1880–81); won victories at Laing's Nek, Ingogo, and Majuba Hill. Remained prominent in political life, opposing Kruger in presidential elections (1883, 1888, 1893, 1898). Held command at outbreak of Boer War (1899) but retired because of ill health.

Jouf·froy \zhüf-rwä, -rwȧ\, Théodore-Simon. 1796–1842. French philosopher. Professor, Collège de France (1833–35), U. of Paris (1835–42); translated works of Scottish school, esp. Thomas Reid. Author of *Mélanges philosophiques* (1833), *Cours d'esthétique* (1843), etc.

Jouffroy d'Ab·bans \-dȧ-bäⁿs\, Claude-François-Dorothée de. Marquis. 1751–1832. French engineer. Made successful attempt to propel a boat by a steam engine with his *Pyroscaphe,* launched on the Saône (1783).

Jou·haux \zhü-ō\, Léon. 1879–1954. French labor leader and politician. Rose in matchworkers' union; secretary general of Confédération Générale du Travail (1909–40, 1945–47); member of the administrative council, International Labor Office, and French delegate to the League of Nations on economic and disarmament questions (1925–28). In German concentration camp (1943–45). President, Economic Council of France (1947–54). A founder of Force Ouvrière (1948), International Confederation of Free Trade Unions (1949). Awarded Nobel prize for peace (1951).

Joule \ˈjül, ˈjau̇(ə)l, ˈjōl\, James Prescott. 1818–1889. English physicist. In paper *On the Production of Heat by Voltaic Electricity* announced Joule's law describing the rate at which heat is produced by an electric current (1840); published paper *On the Heat Evolved during the Electrolysis of Water* (1843), determined the mechanical equivalence of heat in several ways (1843–47). The joule, a unit of work or energy, is named after him.

Jour·dan \zhür-däⁿ\, Jean-Baptiste. Comte. 1762–1833. French soldier. Served in West Indies (1778–84); retired; joined Revolutionary army; general of division (1793); commanded army of the North and defeated Austrians at Wattignies (Oct. 16, 1793); made commander of army of the Moselle (1794), defeated Austrians at Fleurus (June 26, 1794); occupied Belgium; defeated at Höchst (1795) and Würzburg (1796). Member of Council of Five Hundred (1797–98), sponsored military conscription (1798). Commanded army of the Danube and was defeated at Ostrach and Stockach (1799). Again member of Five Hundred (1799). Governor of Piedmont (1800). Created marshal of France (1804). Commander in chief in Italy until replaced by Masséna (1805); governor of Naples (1806); chief of staff to Joseph Bonaparte in Spain (1808); defeated at Vittoria (1813). Gave support to Louis XVIII, given command of army of the Rhine, made count (1816), peer of France (1819).

Jou·ve·net \zhüv-ne\, Jean. 1644–1717. French painter. Known for religious paintings, decoration of ceilings of chapels of Versailles and the Invalides.

Jou·vet \zhü-ve\, Louis. 1887–1951. French actor, director, and designer. Paris debut (1910); joined Comédie des Champs-Élysées (1922), director (1924–34); director, Athénée (1934–51); greatly influenced acting techniques, stage and lighting design, etc.; introduced work of Giraudoux; notable productions included *Monsieur Le Trouhadec* (1923), *Knock* (1923), *La Guerre de Troie* (1935), *Electre* (1937), *La Folle de Chaillot* (1945); appeared in motion pictures.

Jo·va·no·vić \yȯ-ˈvȧ-nȯ-ˌvētʸ, *Angl* -vich\, Jovan. *Pseudonym* Zmaj \ˈzmī\. 1833–1904. Serbian journalist and author. Edited humorous journal *Zmaj,* children's paper *Neven.* Author of humorous, satirical, and didactic verse as *Djulići* (1864), *Djulići uveoci* (1883), *Snohvatice* (1895).

Jo·va·no·vić \ˈyō-vän-ō-vēch\, Slobodan. 1869–1958. Serbian jurist and politician. Professor, Belgrade (1897–1939); leading authority on constitutional law; prime minister of Yugoslav government in exile, London (1942–43); president, Yugoslav National Committee in exile (from 1946). Considered a master of Serbian prose; author of *O totalitarizmu* (1952), *Moji savremenici* (1961–62).

Jo·ve·lla·nos \kō-väl-ˈyä-nōs\, Gaspar Melchor de. 1744–1811. Spanish politician and writer. Chief justice of king's court, Seville (1767), Madrid (1778); banished to Asturias (1790–97); minister of justice (1797). As enemy of Godoy, exiled in Gijón (1797–1801); imprisoned (1801–08). Member of Central Junta; aided in reorganization of the Cortes. Author of plays, notably comedy *El delincuente honrado* (1787); verse; works on government and reform including *Informe de la sociedad economica* (1795), *Defensa de la Junta Central* (1811); critical works as *Elogio de las Bellas Artes* (1782).

Jo·vel·lar \kō-vä(l)-ˈyär\, Joaquín. 1819–1892. Spanish general. Served in Cuba (1842–51); lieutenant general (1871); governor of Cuba (1873–74, 1876–78);

in Spain (1874–76), commanded army against Carlists and assumed ministry of war in new government under Alfonso XII; second administration in Cuba saw end of war for independence with Convention of Zanjón (1878); governor general of Philippines (1883–85).

Jo·vey·nī \jō-vā-'nē\, 'Āṭā Malek. *More completely* 'Alā' od-Dīn 'Āṭā Malek Joveynī. 1226–1283. Persian historian. Visited Mongol court (1249–51, 1251–53); in service of Hülegü (from 1256); governor of Iraq and Khūzistān (1258–83). Author of *Tārīkh-i jehān-gushā,* history of conquests of Genghis Khan and his successors down to 1256.

Jo·vi·an \'jō-vē-ən\. *Lat.* Flavius Jo·vi·a·nus \,jō-vē-'ā-nəs\. c.331–364. Roman emperor (363–364). Son of Veronianus of Moesia; general in army of Emperor Julian; on Julian's death in Persia, was chosen his successor by soldiers. To save the army, made peace with Persians by giving up all Roman provinces beyond the Tigris; promulgated edict restoring privileges to Christians; supported Nicene Creed against Arians.

Jovius, Paulus. See Paolo GIOVIO.

Jow·ett \'jō-ət, 'jaù-\, Benjamin. 1817–1893. English scholar. Professor, Oxford (1855); master of Balliol (1870–93); vice chancellor of Oxford (1882–86). Best known for his translations of *The Dialogues of Plato* (1871), *Thucydides* (1881), Aristotle's *Politics* (1885), Plato's *Republic* (1894). Considered one of the greatest teachers of the century.

Joy \'jȯi\, James Frederick. 1810–1896. American financier, b. Durham, New Hampshire. Attorney for Michigan Central Railroad (from 1837); gained interests in many lines; created Chicago, Burlington & Quincy and extended it westward; created "Joy system," first large western railroad combination; later sold properties; president, *Detroit Post and Tribune* (1881–84).

Joyce \'jȯis\, James Augustine. 1882–1941. Irish writer. Left Ireland (1904), lived in Italy, Switzerland, France (from 1920). Published *Chamber Music* (verse, 1907), *Dubliners* (stories, 1914), *Portrait of the Artist as a Young Man* (novel, 1916); developed techniques of interior monologue and stream-of-consciousness narrative in masterpiece *Ulysses* (novel, 1922) and displayed linguistic virtuosity in *Finnegan's Wake* (1939); also wrote *Exiles* (play, 1918), *Pomes Penyeach* (1927).

Joyce, William. *Called* Lord Haw-Haw \'hȯ-'hȯ\. 1906–1946. British traitor, b. New York City. Son of Irish immigrant parents; lived in England (from (1922); member of pro-Fascist groups; to Germany (1939); made English-language broadcasts for Josef Goebbels's Nazi propaganda ministry (1939–45); convicted of treason and hanged.

Jó·zsef \'yō-zhef\, Attila. 1905–1937. Hungarian poet. Founded literary journal *Valóság* (1932); helped found review *Szép Szó* (1936); combined Marxian and Freudian ideas in powerfully proletarian verse expressed in unique style.

Juan. See also JOHN.

Juana. See JOAN.

Juan de Ávila. See JOHN of Avila.

Juan Ma·nuel \'kwän-män-'wel\. Don. 1282–1349. Spanish soldier, politician, and writer. Grandson of King Ferdinand III of León and Castile and nephew of Alfonso X. In youth fought against Moors in Granada; regent for his cousin Alfonso XI (1320–25); engaged in long civil war with king (1325–38); secured aid of Portugal and alliance with Granada (1328); in exile (1336–38); made peace with Alfonso and later again fought against Moors. Wrote many works of a didactic, religious, or historical nature, the most important being *Libro del caballero y del escudero* (1326) and *El conde Lucanor* (1328–35), a collection of 49 romantic tales of an Oriental character, with moral lessons, and a model or source for Boccaccio, Chaucer, Lope de Vega, Calderón, and possibly Shakespeare's *Taming of the Shrew.*

Juan y San·ta·cil·ia \-ē-sän-tä-'thēl-yä\, Jorge. 1713–1773. Spanish explorer and writer. Accompanied Antonio de Ulloa to America (1735–44) and with him wrote *Relación histórica del viaje a la América meridional* (1748) and *Noticias secretas de América* (1826); founded observatory of Cádiz (1753). Also wrote *Compendio de navegación* (1757), *Examen marítimo teórico-práctico* (1771).

Juan Yüan \zhü-'än-yüē-'än\. 1764–1849. Chinese scholar. Official of Ch'ing dynasty; governor general of Kwangtung (1817–26) and thus chief Chinese official in contact with British; noted as traditionalist scholar and bibliophile.

Juanes, Juan de. See Juan Vicente MASIP.

Juá·rez \'kwä-räs\, Benito Pablo. 1806–1872. Mexican revolutionary and statesman. Lawyer in his native state, Oaxaca (1834–46), and elected its governor (1847). Exiled by Santa Anna (1853), returned (1855) and joined Álvarez in revolution against Santa Anna; as minister of justice (1855) under Álvarez wrote "Ley Juárez," law abolishing special courts and reducing power of army and church; minister of interior under Comonfort (1857). On fleeing of Comonfort (1858), proclaimed himself de jure president and established capital at Veracruz in opposition to Zuloaga; obtained U.S. recognition (1859); issued Reform Laws (1859) completing nationalization and secularization of church; after three years of civil war entered Mexico City (1861); elected president (1861–65); self-proclaimed president (1865–67; elections impossible because of French invasion); continued warfare against Maximilian (proclaimed emperor of Mexico, 1864) and French; Maximilian captured and shot (June 1867). Elected president (two terms, 1867–72); administration marked by many reforms, but last years troubled with attempted revolutions; died in office.

Ju·ba \'jü-bə\ *or* **Iu·ba** \'yü-bə\. Name of two kings of Numidia:

Juba I. c.85–46 B.C. King (between 63 and 50–46 B.C.). Son and successor of Hiempsal; in civil war, sided with Pompey; defeated (49) G. Scribonius Curio, Caesar's general; joined Pompey's force which was defeated at Thapsus (46); committed suicide.

Juba II. c.50 B.C.–c.24 A.D. King (29–25 B.C.). Son of Juba I; carried as a child to Rome by Caesar; reinstated in Numidia (29) by Octavian; m. (29) Cleopatra Selene, daughter of Antony and Cleopatra; transferred (25) from Numidia to Mauretania, which he ruled until his death.

Jubainville, Marie-Henri d'Arbois de. See ARBOIS DE JUBAINVILLE.

Ju·chen \'zhü-'jen\ *or* **Chin** \'jin\. Dynasty of Central Asia and North China (1122–1234) formed by nomadic Juchen tribes; threw off rule of Liao and established state; drove Sung dynasty south of Huai River and established capital at Yen-ching (present Peking); adopted Chinese model for bureaucracy but maintained tribal speech, customs, etc.; destroyed by Sung-Mongol alliance.

Jud \'yüt\, Jakob. 1882–1952. Swiss linguist. Taught at Zürich lyceum (1906–22); professor, U. of Zürich (1922–52); known for studies of Rhaeto-Romance dialects, French, Provençal, Italian, and use of subtle linguistic analyses to illuminate cultural history. Works included *Sprach- und Sachatlas Italiens und der Südschweiz* (1928–40, with Karl Jaberg).

Jud, Leo. *Known as* Mei·ster Leu \,mī-stər-'lōi\. 1482–1542. Swiss clergyman. Colleague of Zwingli at Zürich and with Heinrich Bullinger succeeded him (1531) as head of Reform in Zürich; helped draft First Helvetic Confession (1536); aided in translating the Zürich Bible and made a Latin translation of the Old Testament.

Ju·dah \'jü-də\. *Called* ha-Na·si \,hä-nä-'sē\, *i.e.* the Prince. 135?–?220. Jewish scholar in Palestine. Succeeded his father, Simeon ben Gamaliel II, as patriarch and head of the Sanhedrin; one of the last *tannaim,* masters of Jewish Oral Law; devoted some 50 years to reducing Oral Law to authoritative written form, known as the Mishna.

Judah ben Sam·u·el \-ben-'sam-y(ə-w)əl\. *Also known as* Yehuda the Ḥasid *and* the Ḥasid of Regensburg. d. 1217. German Jewish mystic. Member of Kalonymos family; established yeshiva at Regensburg (c.1195); among followers founded a fervently pious movement (German Ḥasidism). Author of ethical treatise *Sefer Ḥasidim.*

Judah ha-Le·vi \-hä-'lē-,vī\. *Hebrew* Yehuda ben Shemuel ha-Levi. *Arabic surname* Abū al-Ḥasan. c.1075–1141. Hebrew poet and philosopher. Native of northern Spain; early companion of Ibn Ezra in Granada; became prominent physician in Christian Toledo until anti-Semitism forced him to return to Muslim Spain; died in Egypt en route to Jerusalem. Known for poems celebrating Jerusalem and Land of Zion, including "Zionide"; collected verse as *Dīwān;* also wrote Arabic prose work on nature of Judaism, known in Hebrew translation as *Sefer ha-Kuzari.*

Ju·das \'jü-dəs\. *Also known as* Jude \'jüd\, Thad·dae·us \'thad-ē-əs, thə-'dē-\, *and* Leb·bae·us \'leb-ē-əs, lə-'bē-\. 1st century A.D. Christian apostle. One of original 12 Apostles; by some authorities not identified with the Thaddaeus of Gospels of Matthew and Mark.

Judas. *Called* Is·car·i·ot \is-'kar-ē-ət\. d. c.30 A.D. Christian apostle. One of original 12 Apostles; notorious for having betrayed Jesus into hands of Jewish elders; traditionally held to have committed suicide.

Judas Maccabaeus. See MACCABEES.

Judd \'jəd\, Charles Hubbard. 1873–1946. American psychologist and educator, b. Bareilly, British India. To U.S. (1879); professor and head of psychological laboratory, Yale (1907–09); head of department of education, U. of Chicago (1900–38). Author of *Genetic Psychology for Teachers* (1903), *Psychology: General Introduction* (1907), *Psychology of High School Subjects* (1915), *Psychology of Social Institutions* (1926), *Psychology of Secondary Education* (1927), *Problems of Education in the United States* (1933), *Education and Social Progress* (1934), etc.

Jude. See JUDAS.

Judge \'jəj\, Jack. 1878–1938. British vaudeville performer. Composer of song "It's a Long, Long Way to Tipperary" (1912).

Jud·son \'jəds-ᵊn\, Adoniram. 1788–1850. American missionary, b. Malden, Mass. Helped establish (1810) American Board of Commissioners for Foreign Missions; under its auspices, to Burma (1812); became Baptist (1812); remained there, working from Ava and (from 1829) Moulmein; translated

Bible into Burmese (1834); compiled *Dictionary, English and Burmese* (1849). His first wife (m. 1812) ¶Ann, *nee* Has·sel·tine \'has-əl-ˌtīn\ (1789–1826), accompanied him to Burma; first American woman in foreign mission; wrote tracts in Burmese, began evangelistic work among Burmese women; during husband's imprisonment (1824–26) in Anglo–Burmese War, exhibited great heroism in caring for him; subject of many literary works.

Judson, Arthur Leon. 1881–1975. American impresario, b. Dayton, Ohio. Gave up violin to become manager of Philadelphia Orchestra (1915–35); manager, Philharmonic Society of New York (1922); organized first concert radio broadcasts (1926) and organized network of stations (1927) to carry them, forerunner of Columbia Broadcasting System (1928); formed Columbia Concerts Corp. (1930), which became Columbia Artists Management and Columbia Records; president (1930–48).

Judson, Edward Zane Carroll. *Pseudonym* Ned Bunt·line \'bənt-lən, -ˌlīn\. 1823–1886. American adventurer and writer, b. Stamford, N.Y. Served in navy; journalist in Cincinnati; established *Ned Buntline's Own* magazine, Nashville, Tenn. (1845); helped precipitate Actor Place Opera House riot (1849); helped create "dime novel" genre of cheap fiction; met William F. Cody (1869), dubbed him "Buffalo Bill" in series of dime novels; wrote play *Scouts of the Plains* for Cody.

Juel \'yül\, Jens. 1745–1802. Danish painter. Known for landscapes, still lifes, and esp. for portraits.

Juel, Niels. 1629–1697. Danish admiral. Served in Anglo–Dutch War (1652–54); distinguished himself in wars with Sweden (1658–60, 1676–79), notably as commander at Jasmund, off Rügen (1676), and at naval victory in Køge Bay (1677).

Ju·gur·tha \jü-'gər-thə\ *or* **Iu·gur·tha** \yü-\. c.160–104 B.C. King of Numidia (118–105 B.C.). Natural son of Mastanabal and grandson of Masinissa. Sent by his uncle Micipsa to Spain (134) to aid Romans; on death of Micipsa (118), shared rule with cousins Adherbal and Hiempsal; murdered Hiempsal, drove out Adherbal; obtained division of realm, taking richer western half; attacked Adherbal in eastern Numidia (112), provoking war (111–106) with Rome (Jugurthine War); defeated by Quintus Metellus; captured by Bocchus I of Mauretania (105) and turned over to Romans; imprisoned in Rome, executed.

Juil·li·ard \'jül-ē-ˌärd, 'jül-ˌyärd\, Augustus D. 1840–1919. American merchant and patron of music, b. Canton, Ohio. Bequeathed bulk of fortune to establish Julliard Musical Foundation (1920) for providing musical education for promising students; became (1926) Juilliard School of Music.

Juin \zhw^{y}a^{n}\, Alphonse-Pierre. 1888–1967. French soldier. Served in World War I, Morocco; commander of motorized division in Belgium when captured by Germans (1940); released to Vichy government (1941); as commander of Vichy forces in North Africa, compelled to oppose Allied landings (Nov. 1942) but subsequently joined Allies; led Free French forces in Italy and entered Rome (1944); French resident in Morocco (1947–51); commander of Allied land forces in Central Europe (1951–56); marshal of France (1952); broke with De Gaulle over Algerian policy (1960); retired (1962).

Jui Tsung. See Li Tan under LI family.

Jukes \'jüks\, Joseph Beete. 1811–1869. English geologist. Director of Irish survey (1850–69); known for studies of river action.

Jul·ia \'jül-yə\. 39 B.C.–14 A.D. Roman noblewoman. Only child of Augustus Caesar and Scribonia; m. 1st Marcellus (25; d. 23 B.C.), 2d Marcus Vipsanius Agrippa (23; d. 12 B.C.), 3d Tiberius (11 B.C.). Mother of Gaius and Lucius Caesar, Agrippa Posthumus, Julia, and Agrippina. Notorious for vice, she was banished by her father. Her daughter ¶Julia (d. 28 A.D.) married Lucius Aemilius Paulus and was mother of Aemilia (1st wife of Emperor Claudius); notorious for profligacy; banished (9 A.D.) by her grandfather Augustus.

Julia Augusta. See LIVIA DRUSILLA.

Julia Dom·na \-'däm-nə\. 167?–217 A.D. Roman empress, b. Syria. m. Septimius Severus (187 A.D.). Mother of Caracalla and Geta; had intellectual power and literary taste; exerted much influence over husband; committed suicide soon after Caracalla was put to death.

Julia Mae·sa \-'mī-sə\. d. c.226 A.D. Roman noblewoman, b. Syria. Sister of Julia Domna; on murder of nephew Caracalla (217) induced Syrian legions to proclaim her grandson Elagabalus emperor; exerted great influence over him and his successor Alexander Severus. Her daughter ¶Julia Mamaea (d. 235) was mother of Alexander Severus; dominated regency (222–235) and government; accompanied Persian expedition (232) whose failure is generally ascribed to her meddling; murdered along with Alexander by soldiers.

Jul·ian \'jül-yən\. *Called* the Apostate. *Lat.* Flavius Claudius Ju·li·a·nus \ˌjül-ē-'ā-nəs\. c.331–363. Roman emperor (361–363). Youngest son of Julius Constantius, who was half-brother to Constantine the Great. Escaped general massacre of Flavian family (337); studied in philosophical schools at Athens. m. Helena, sister of Constantius II, and was created caesar (355) with government of Gaul, Spain, and Britain; defeated Alamanni (357) in great battle near Strasbourg; won popularity with army; proclaimed emperor by his troops (361) and became master of empire on death of Constantius; made expedition against Persians; slain in battle in desert beyond Ctesiphon. Persistent enemy of Christianity; publicly announced his adherence to paganism (361) and made it state religion while maintaining toleration of Christianity.

Julian, Cardinal. See Giuliano CESARINI.

Julian of Ecla·num \i-'klā-nəm\. 380–c.455. Italian prelate. Bishop of Eclanum (c.417); adherent of Pelagius; refused to sign *Epistola tractoria* (418) of Pope St. Zosimus, excommunicating Pelagius; deposed and banished (421); settled in Sicily as teacher. Considered principal systematizer of Pelagianism; main target of St. Augustine's refutations.

Julian *or* **Ju·li·ana** \ˌjü-lē-'an-ə\ of Nor·wich \'när-ij, -ich\. 1342–after 1416. English mystic. Experienced healing and visions of Christ and Blessed Virgin (1373) recounted in *Revelations of Divine Love,* a mystical and theological work of clarity, beauty, and profundity unequalled in English.

Julian, Percy Lavon. 1899–1975. American chemist, b. Montgomery, Ala. Taught at West Va. State Coll. (1926–27), Howard U. (1927–29); professor, head of chemistry dept., Howard (1931–32); research fellow, DePauw U. (1932–35); synthesis of physostigmine (1935) led to post of director of research for Glidden Co., Chicago (1935–53); founder and president (1953–64), Julian Laboratories, Inc.; president (1964–75), Julian Associates; developed numerous derivatives of soya protein, including indoles, steroids, phosphatides. Awarded Spingarn medal (1947).

Julianus. See DIDIUS JULIANUS.

Ju·lien \zhü̅-ē-ya^{n}\, Pierre. 1731–1804. French sculptor. Collaborated with Guillaume II Coustou on monument of the dauphin; other works included *Gladiateur mourant, La Chèvre Amalthée.*

Jul·ius \'jül-yəs, 'jü-lē-əs\. Name of three popes:

Julius I. Saint. d. 352. Pope (337–352). Firmly supported Athanasius after his deposition by the Arians (339); convoked Council of Sardica (342 or 343) and secured acknowledgment of papal authority; restored Athanasius to see.

Julius II. *Orig.* Giuliano del·la Ro·ve·re \ˌdāl-lä-'rō-vā-rā\. 1443–1513. Pope (1503–13). Nephew of Sixtus IV; bishop of Carpentras (1471); held 8 bishoprics, archbishopric of Avignon from uncle; legate in France (1480–82); opponent of Borgias; elected by simony. Sought to extend papal territory and enlarge temporal power; formed League of Cambrai (1508) against Venice; formed Holy League (1511) against France; convened 5th Lateran Council (1512); commenced to rebuild St. Peter's; patronized arts and aided Raphael, Michelangelo, Bramante, and others.

Julius III. *Orig.* Giovanni Maria Cioc·chi del Mon·te \'chȯk-kē-dāl-'mōn-tā\. 1487–1555. Pope (1550–55). Archbishop of Seponto (1511); bishop of Pavia (1520); cardinal (1536); cardinal bishop of Palestrina (1543); co-president of Council of Trent (1545). Instituted reforms; promoted Jesuits; founded (1552) Collegium Germanicum.

Julius. See Gaius Julius HYGINUS.

Julius Africanus, Sextus. See AFRICANUS.

Julius Caesar. See Gaius Julius CAESAR.

Jul·lien \zhü̅-ē-ya^{n}\, Louis-Antoine. 1812–1860. French conductor. Conducted highly popular concerts of serious and light music in Great Britain (1840–59).

Ju·nayd \jü-'nīd\. 14th century. Arab painter. An outstanding exponent of Baghdad School, influenced later Persian art.

Junayd, Shaykh. c.1430–1460. Persian religious leader. Succeeded father (1447) as head of Ṣafavid order of Ardabīl; ambition for temporal power produced schism in order; expelled from Ardabīl (1448), from Aleppo; led followers to Black Sea area; unsuccessfully attacked Trebizond (1456); blocked by Jahān Shāh from reoccupying Ardabīl (1459); killed in attack on Circassians.

June, Jennie. See Jane Croly under David CROLY.

Ju·neau *Fr* zhü̅-nō, *Angl* 'jü-(ˌ)nō, jü-'nō\, Solomon Laurent. 1793–1856. American fur trader, b. near Montreal. First permanent settler in what is now Milwaukee, Wis. (1818); naturalized American citizen (1831); helped plot and organize Milwaukee (1835); first mayor of Milwaukee (1846).

Jung \'yu̇ŋ\, Carl Gustav. 1875–1961. Swiss psychologist and psychiatrist. On staff of Berghölzli Asylum, Zürich (1902 ff.); lecturer, U. of Zürich (1905–13). Conducted experiments in mental association which led him to develop the theory of complexes and brought him into association (1907–12) with Freud, with whose earlier views his were in harmony; founded analytic psychology; president (1911–12), International Psychoanalytic Society. Differed from Freud in regarding the libido as a will to live rather than a manifestation of the sex instinct, and denied sexual basis of neuroses. Developed classification scheme dividing personalities into extroverted and introverted and mental functions into thinking, feeling, sensation, intuition; developed theory of collective unconscious and archetypes. Professor, Zürich (1933–41), Basel (1944–61). Author of *Diagnostische Assoziationsstudien* (1906–10), *Über die Psychologie der Dementia Praecox* (1907), *Wandlungen und Symbole der Libido* (1911–12), *Versuch einer Darstellung der psychoanalytischen Theorie* (1913), *Psychologische Typen* (1921), *Psychologie und Religion* (1939),

Psychologie und Alchemie (1944), *Aufsätze zur Zeitgeschichte* (1946), *Aion* (1951), *Antwort auf Hiob* (1952), *Erinnerungen, Träume, Gedanken* (1962).

Jung, Johann Heinrich. *Pseudonym* Jung-Stil·ling \'yůŋ-'shtil-iŋ\. 1740–1817. German writer. School teacher, tailor; overcame poverty to become physician; while a student at Strassburg met Goethe, who encouraged him; achieved renown as physician at Elberfeld, esp. for cataract operations; lectured on economics at Kaiserslautern (1778), Marburg (1787). Best known for 5-vol. autobiography *Heinrich Stillings Leben* (1777–1804), including the volume *Heinrich Stillings Jugend* (pub. by Goethe, 1777), which gave a moving picture of a German Pietist family; also wrote novels, pietistic works as *Das Heimweh* (1794–96) and *Scenen aus dem Geisterreich* (1795–1801), medical works, etc.

Jung Ba·ha·dur \'jəŋ-bə-'hä-důr\. 1816–1877. Nepalese politician. Prime minister (1846–77), virtual ruler; established office as hereditary (remained in his family to 1951); maintained Nepalese independence, instituted reforms; as friend of British, sent Gurkha troops to aid of British during Sepoy Mutiny (1857–58).

Jun·ge \'yůŋ-ə\, Joachim. *Lat.* Jung·i·us \'yůŋ-ē-ůs\. 1587–1657. German philosopher and scientist. Professor of mathematics, Giessen (1609–14); physician in Lübeck, Brunswick, Wolfenbüttel (1619–25); professor, Rostock (1624–25, 1626–28), Hamburg (1629–57). Author of *Logica Hamburgensis* (1638); opponent of scholastic philosophy; emphasized value of study of mathematics; set forth a classification of plants in his *Isagoge Phytoscopica* (1678) reputed to have served as a basis for Linnaeus's classification.

Jung-lu \'zhůŋ-'lü\. 1836–1903. Chinese general. Head of army under Empress Tz'u Hsi; quashed conspiracy of emperor to turn army against empress (1898); acquiesced in but did not press empress's order to kill all foreigners (1899) and in subsequent siege of legations in Peking.

Jung·mann \'yůŋ-,män\, Josef. 1773–1847. Czech writer and philologist. Champion of a revival of Czech national sentiment; credited largely with creation of modern Czech literary language; translated works of Milton, Goethe, Schiller, Voltaire, Chateaubriand. Compiled *Slovník českoněmecký,* Czech–German dictionary (1835–39).

Jung-Stilling, Johann Heinrich. See Johann H. JUNG.

Junípero, Father. See Junípero SERRA.

Jun·ius \'jün-yəs, 'jü-nē-əs\. Pseudonym of the author of a series of letters appearing in London *Public Advertiser* (1769–72) attacking the British ministry, often attributed to Sir Philip Francis (*q.v.*).

Junius, Franciscus. See François du JON.

Jun·ker \'yůŋ-kər\, Wilhelm, *in full* Johann Wilhelm. 1840–1892. German explorer, b. Moscow. Traveled to Iceland (1869), Tunisia (1873–74), Egypt and Sudan (1875); explored Nile region (1876–78), reaching Emin Paşa at Lado on the upper White Nile (1883); isolated there by Mahdi revolt but finally reached Zanzibar (1886). Author of *Reisen in Afrika 1875–86* (1889–91).

Jun·kers \'yůŋ-kərs\, Hugo. 1859–1935. German airplane engineer and builder. Established at Dessau an airplane factory (1919), a motor works (1924). Credited with designing a flying wing (1910), first all-metal airplane to fly successfully (J.1, 1915); instrumental in establishing one of first regular mail and passenger air lines, operating in several European countries.

Ju·nod \zhue-nō\, Henri Alexandre. 1863–1934. Swiss missionary and anthropologist. During tours as missionary in southern Africa (1889–96, 1899–1903, 1904–09, 1913–20) made close studies of Thonga tribes, esp. the Ronga. Published Ronga grammar (1896), anthology of folksongs and tales (1897), ethnography (1898); best known for *Life of a South African Tribe* (1912–13).

Ju·not \zhue-nō\, Andoche. Duc d'A·bran·tès \dȧ-brä^n-tēs, *Port* də-'brä^n(n)-tēsh\. 1771–1813. French soldier. Entered Revolutionary army (1792); secretary (1793), aide-de-camp (1794) to Napoléon; general of brigade (1797), of division (1801); served in Italian and Egyptian campaigns; distinguished himself in victory over Turks at Nazareth (1799). Governor of Paris (1806). Commanded army invading Portugal and capturing Lisbon (1807); created duke; defeated by Wellesley (afterward Duke of Wellington) at Vimeiro (1808) and forced to evacuate Portugal. Defeated at Smolensk (1812); governor of Illyrian Provinces (1813).

Junot, Laure, *nee* Per·mon \per-mō^n\. Duchesse d'Abrantès. 1784–1838. French writer. Met Napoléon at mother's Paris salon; m. (1800) Andoche Junot; accompanied him to Portugal; ordered by Napoléon to leave Paris (1813); returned, but again forced to leave at Restoration (1815). Known for witty, caustic, inaccurate *Mémoires sur Napoléon, la Révolution, le Consulat, l'Empire et la Restauration* (1831–35).

Jun·quei·ro \zhü^{n}ŋ-'kā-rü\, Abílio Manuel Guer·ra \'ger-ə\. 1850–1923. Portuguese poet. Member of "Generation of Coimbra" and a leader in overthrow of Romanticism in Portugal; politically a republican; deputy (1878 ff.); on establishment of republic (1910) made envoy to Bern. Works included *A morte de D. João* (1874), *A musa em férias* (1879), *A velhice do Padre Eterno* (1885), *A Inglaterra* (1890), *Os simples* (1892), *Pátria* (1896), *Oração ao pão* (1902), *Oração á luz* (1904).

Ju·rien de la Gra·vière \zhuer-ya^n-də-lȧ-grȧv-yer\, Jean-Pierre-Edmond. 1812–1892. French naval officer. Commanded French forces sent to Mexico (1861); vice admiral (1862) and aide-de-camp to the emperor (1864); protected flight of the empress (1870).

Jur·jā·nī, al- \ůl-,jur-jä-'nē\. *In full* Abū Bakr ʻAbd al-Qāhir ibn ʻAbd ar-Raḥmān al-Jurjānī. d. 1078. Arab philologist. Author of compendium of Arabic grammar called *Kitāb al-ʻawāmil al-miʼah* or *Miʼat ʻāmil,* a study of literary criticism and style called *Asrār al-balāghah,* etc.

Jurjānī, al-. *In full* ʻAlī ibn Muḥammad al-Jurjānī. *Also known as* as-Sayyid ash-Sharīf. 1339–1413. Islāmic theologian. Teacher in Shīrāz (1377–87); his fame was such that after fall of Shīrāz he was taken by Timur to Samarkand (1387–1405). Leading traditionalist theologian of 15th century Persia; best known work the *Kitāb at-taʻrīfāt,* a dictionary of technical terms from theology, philosophy, philology.

Jus·se·rand \zhues-rä^n\, Jean-Jules, *in full* Jean-Adrien-Antoine-Jules. 1855–1932. French writer and diplomat. French minister at Copenhagen (1898) and Washington, D.C. (1902–25). Student of English literature and history. Among his books were *Le Théâtre en Angleterre depuis la conquête jusqu'aux prédécesseurs immédiats de Shakespeare* (1878), *Les Anglais au moyen âge* (1884), *Le Roman au temps de Shakespeare* (1887), *Histoire littéraire du peuple anglais* (1895–1909), *En Amérique jadis et maintenant* (1916, Pulitzer prize).

Jus·sieu, de \də-zhues-yœ\. Family of French botanists including: Antoine (1686–1758), physician; professor, Jardin du Roi, Paris (1710–58); first to describe coffee plant (1715); studied lichens, fern fossils, etc.; editor of Tournefort's *Institutiones Rei Herbariae* (1719). His brother ¶Bernard (1699–1777), demonstrator at the Jardin du Roi (1722); established (1759) a botanical garden at Trianon at request of Louis XV; renowned as a teacher; laid foundation for a natural system of plant classification. Another brother ¶Joseph (1704–1779) collected plants in South America (1735–71); introduced various ornamental plants into Europe. Their nephew ¶Antoine-Laurent (1748–1836) studied under his uncle Bernard; demonstrator, Jardin du Roi; elaborated in his *Genera Plantarum* (1789) the system of classification founded by Bernard, which served as basis of modern natural classification; helped reorganize Jardin as Muséum National d'Histoire Naturelle (1793), professor (1793–1826), director (1802–26). Antoine-Laurent's son ¶Adrien-Henri-Laurent (1797–1853), professor of botany at Muséum (1826–53); brilliant teacher; author of long-used textbook *Botanique* (1842).

Jus·tin \'jəs-tən\. *Called* Justin Mar·tyr \'märt-ər\. Saint. c.100–c.165. Greek theologian, b. modern Nablus. One of the Fathers of the Church; student of philosophy and a teacher of Platonic doctrines; converted to Christianity probably at Ephesus; in two *Apologies* and *Dialogue with Trypho* developed historical view of Christianity as fulfillment; adapted notion of *logos* to Christ; opened first Christian school at Rome; scourged and martyred at Rome.

Justin. *Lat.* Jus·ti·nus \(,)jə-'stī-nəs\. Name of two rulers of the Eastern Roman Empire:

Justin I. c.450–527. Emperor (518–527). An uneducated soldier of Gothic parentage; commander of guards under Anastasius I; secured throne on death of Anastasius; entrusted administration to Proclus and to his nephew Justinian; helped end Acacian Schism (519); issued decrees against Arians.

Justin II. d. 578. Emperor (565–578). Nephew of Justinian I; married Sophia, niece of Empress Theodora; after period of toleration, began persecution of Monophysites (571); dismissal of Narses as exarch of Ravenna allowed Lombard armies to overrun northern and central Italy (568–574); lost territory to Persians, Avars; subject to fits of insanity; turned over administration to Sophia and, at her urging, to Tiberius, one of his generals (574).

Justin. *Full Latin name* Marcus Junianus Justinus. 3d century A.D. Roman historian. Author of *Historiarum Philippicarum,* an epitome of a lost history by Trogus.

Jus·tin·i·an \(,)jə-'stin-ē-ən\. Name of two rulers of the Eastern Roman Empire:

Justinian I. *In full* Flavius Petrus Sabbatius Jus·tin·i·a·nus \(,)jəs-,tin-ē-'ā-nəs\. *Called* the Great. 483–565. Emperor (527–565). Nephew of Justin I; m. (525) Theodora (*q.v.*); made co-emperor by Justin shortly before death (527). Reign most brilliant of Eastern Empire. Had no military capacity, but chose able generals, as Belisarius and Narses. Military events of reign: treaty with Khosrow I (532) ending long Persian war; Nika riot (532) of Greens and Blues factions in the Hippodrome, Belisarius and others with barbarian mercenaries killing 30,000 people; Vandal kingdom of North Africa conquered by Belisarius and reannexed to empire (533–534); imperial authority in Rome restored; Rome occupied (536) but besieged by Goths for a year (537–538); northern

Italy, including Ravenna, reconquered (538–540), but after recall of Belisarius (549), Goths again victorious and nearly all Italy overcome; southern Spain conquered by imperial armies (554); practically all of Western Empire again in hands of barbarians, but after 20 years of warfare Goths and Franks finally defeated (552–555); war fought with Persia (540–545); Huns, Bulgars, and Slavs repeatedly invaded Balkan region. A great builder, causing erection throughout the empire of many forts, public buildings, monasteries, and churches, esp. Sant' Apollinare in Classe and San Vitale, both in Ravenna, and Hagia Sophia (532–562) in Constantinople. Issued edict (543) against Nestorians in fruitless attempt to placate Monophysites; alienated Roman church. Preserved Roman law for future generations; appointed commissions, with Tribonian in charge, which collected all imperial statutes as *Codex constitutionum* (528–529), and issued a digest of all writings of Roman jurists as *Digesta* or *Pandectae* (533), a revised *Code* (534), and a textbook for students *Institutiones* (533), all of which with the new laws in *Novellae* (534–565) formed the *Corpus juris civilis,* the foundation of actual law in most of continental Europe today.

Justinian II. *Called* Rhi·no·tme·tus \ˌrī-nōt-ˈmēt-əs\, *i.e.* with the nose cut off. c.669–711. Emperor (685–695, 705–711). Son and successor of Constantine IV; successfully attacked Slavs in Thrace and Macedonia (688–689); defeated by Arabs in Armenia (692). Caused dissensions in the church and persecuted Manichaeans. Overcome by his general, Leontius (695), who cut off his nose; banished to Cherson in the Crimea (695). Escaped and at head of Bulgarian army captured Constantinople (705); vengeance and atrocities stirred up revolt; killed Leontius (705); seized by Philippicus and put to death.

Jus·tus \ˈjəs-təs\. Saint. d. 627. English prelate, b. Rome. Sent (601) by Pope St. Gregory I to assist St. Augustine in conversion of Britain; first bishop of Rochester (604); fled to Gaul (616–617) in anti-Christian reaction following death of King Aethelberht; archbishop of Canterbury (624); oversaw conversion of Northumbria by St. Paulinus.

Justus *or* **Jod·o·cus** \ˈjäd-ə-kəs\ of Ghent \ˈgent, *Angl* ˈgent\. *Also called* Joos van Was·sen·ho·ve \ˈyōs-vän-ˈväs-ən-ˌhō-və\. c.1435 or 1440–c.1480. Flemish painter. Influenced by Dirck Bouts; introduced Flemish style into Italy; chief and only completely authenticated work the *Communion of the Apostles* for Duke of Urbino.

Ju·var·ra \yü-ˈvär-rä\ *or* **Ju·va·ra** \yü-ˈvär-ä\, Filippo. 1678–1736. Italian architect and stage designer. Designed stage scenes for Cardinal Ottoboni, Maria Casimira of Poland, Emperor Joseph I of Austria; architect to king of Sicily in Turin (1714 ff.). Designed S. Filippo Neri (1715), Church of the Carmine (1732), Palazzo Madama (1718), all in Turin; palace at Mafra, Portugal (1719–20); hunting lodge at Stupinigi (1729). Considered one of finest Rococo designers.

Ju·ve·nal \ˈjü-vən-ᵊl\. Saint. d. 458. Palestinian prelate. Bishop of Jerusalem (422–458); at Council of Ephesus (431) failed but at Chalcedon (451) succeeded in separating Palestine and Arabia from patriarchate of Caesarea; patriarch of Palestine (451–458).

Juvenal. *Full Latin name* Decimus Junius Ju·ve·na·lis \ˌjü-və-ˈnā-ləs\. c.55 or 60–in or after 127 A.D. Roman satirist. Served in army but failed to secure civil office or promotion; banished by Domitian for satirical attack; in late years attained comfortable living. In 16 satiric poems, issued in 5 books, attacked with brutal frankness vices of Rome under the empire.

Jux·on \ˈjək-sən\, William. 1582–1663. English prelate. President of St. John's Coll., Oxford (1621–33); bishop of London (1633–49) and lord high treasurer (1636–41). Attended Charles I during his trial and on the scaffold. Archbishop of Canterbury (1660–63).

K

Ka·a·hu·ma·nu \ˌkä-ä-hü-ˈmä-nü\. c.1772–1832. Hawaiian queen. Wife of Kamehameha I; *kuhina nui* (premier) to his successor Kamehameha II (1819–24); acting regent during minority of Kamehameha III (1824–32); started reforms; welcomed Christian missionaries and was herself baptized.

Kaa·lund \ˈkȯ-lün\, Hans Vilhelm. 1818–1885. Danish poet. Author of collections of lyrics and children's fables, including *Fabler for Børn* (1845), *Et Foraar* (1858), *En Eftervaar* (1877).

Kaʻb ibn Zu·hayr \ˈkab-ˌib-ən-zu̇-ˈhīr\. 7th century A.D. Arab poet. Son of Zuhayr; contemporary of Muḥammad, whom at first he ridiculed; on decree of death wrote a eulogy which became famous.

Ka·bīr \kə-ˈbēr\. 1440–1518. Indian mystic and poet. Born a Muslim; influenced by Hindu ascetic Rāmānanda; preached and wrote in Hindi, expounding essential unity of all religions and attempted to unite Hindu and Muslim thought; rejected idolatry, asceticism, and caste system, accepted idea of one God and the equality of men before God; his followers known as Kabīrpanthīs; his teachings a forerunner of Sikhism, which was established by his disciple Nānak.

Ka·bu·ra·gi \kä-bu̇r-ä-gē\ Kiyokata. *Orig.* Ke·ni·chi \ken-ē-chē\. 1878–1972. Japanese painter. Studied under Mizuno Toshikata; well known illustrator for newspapers (from c.1895); organized (1900) group Ugōkai, aimed at improving art of *Ukiyo-e* painting. Known for *Ukiyo-e* paintings depicting Tokyo daily life, including *Ichiyō joshi-no-haka, Hareyuku murasame,* and *Tsukiji Akashichō*.

Ka·čić-Mio·šić \ˈkȧch-etʸ-ˈmyȯ-shētʸ\, Andrija. 1704–1760. Croatian poet. Author of *Razgovor ugodni naroda slovinskoga* (1756), a popular chronicle in verse and prose of the South Slav peoples.

Ka·den-Ban·drow·ski \ˈkȧ-den-bȧn-ˈdrȯf-skē\, Juliusz. 1885–1944. Polish writer. Author of realistic and satirical stories dealing esp. with Polish everyday life, including short-story collection *Miasto mojej matki* (1925) and novels *Czarne skrzydła* (1928–29) and *Mateusz Bigda* (1933).

Kaf·ka \ˈkäf-kä\, Franz. 1883–1924. Austrian writer, b. Prague. Worked for insurance company in Prague (1908–22). His visionary, metaphorical, and psychological fiction expressed the anxiety and alienation of 20th-century Western society. Author of novels *Der Prozess* (1925), *Das Schloss* (1926), *Amerika* (1927); story collections *Betrachtung* (1913), *Ein Landarzt* (1919), *Ein Hungerkünstler* (1924); and stories *Das Urteil* (1916), *Die Verwandlung* (1916), *In der Strafkolonie* (1919), *Beim Bau der chinesischen Mauer* (1931).

Kā·fūr \ˈka-für\, Abū al-Misk. 10th century. Egyptian ruler. Originally a slave; as vizier in Ikhshīdid dynasty, was de facto ruler during reign of Ūnūjūr (946–961) and de jure ruler during reign of ʻAlī (961–966).

Ka·ga·no·vich \kə-(ˌ)gə-ˈnȯ-ˌvyich\, Lazar Moiseyevich. 1893–after 1957. Soviet politician. Joined Communist party (1911); head (1920) of Tashkent government, consolidating Soviet rule in Turkistan; as head (c.1921) of party personnel, placed Stalin supporters in critical positions, thus being instrumental in Stalin's rise to supreme power. Full member of Central Committee and secretariat (from 1924) and of Politburo (from 1930); headed (1930–35) Moscow regional party organization and directed construction of Moscow subway; commissar for transportation (1935), for heavy industry (1937), for fuel and petroleum industries (1939). Deputy premier of Soviet Union (1938); member of State Defense Committee (1942–43); personally controlled all Soviet transportation during World War II. Minister of construction materials industry (1946); vice chairman of Council of Ministers (1947); member of Presidium of Council of Ministers and of party Presidium (1953). Chairman of State Committee on Labor and Wages (1955); minister of building materials industry (1956); member of group that failed to depose Khrushchev (1957); lost all government and party offices and expelled from party.

Ka·ga·wa \kä-gä-wä\ Toyohiko. 1888–1960. Japanese reformer. Converted to Christianity; became a leader in labor movement and social welfare work; helped found Federation of Labor (1918) and Farmers' Union (1921); organized many cooperatives; conducted great evangelistic campaigns throughout country; a pacificist, founded National Anti-War League (1928) and member of group that went to U.S. in attempt to avert war (1941); after World War II, a leader in woman suffrage movement and in attempt to adapt democratic institutions to Japan. Wrote over 150 books, including novels *Across the Death Line* (1920) and *Before the Dawn* (1924).

Kag·gwa *or* **Ka·gwa** \ˈkäg-ˌwä\, Sir Apolo. d. 1927. Bugandan politician. A leader of Protestant faction in civil wars of Ganda people (1888–92); *katikiro* (prime minister) of Buganda (1890–1926) and regent during minority of king (1897–1914); won degree of autonomy from British protectorate by supporting British against a Sudanese rebellion; reorganized central bureaucracy.

Ka·han·a·mo·ku \kä-ˌhän-ä-ˈmō-kü\, Duke Paoa. 1890–1968. Hawaiian swimmer. In 100-yard freestyle, won U.S. indoor (1913) and outdoor (1916–17, 1920) titles and gold medals at Olympic Games (1912, 1920); also won gold medal in 800-meter relay in 1920 Olympics; developed the flutter kick. Sheriff of city and county of Honolulu (1932–61); official greeter of Hawaii (1961–68).

Ka·ha·ne·man \kä-ˈhän-ā-män\, Joseph Solomon. 1888–1969. Israeli rabbi, b. Lithuania. Founder of "City of Torah" yeshiva at Bene Berak, Israel (1944).

Kahn \kȧn\, Gustave. 1859–1936. French poet. Identified with Symbolist school; a founder of *Le Symboliste* (1886) and other literary reviews; invented vers libre almost simultaneously with his friend Jules Laforgue. Among his books were verse collections *Les Palais nomades* (1887), *Chansons d'amant* (1891), *Domaine de fée* (1895), *Le Livre d'images* (1897), *Images bibliques* (1929); novels *Les petites âmes pressées* (1898), *L'Adultère sentimental* (1902), *L'Aube enamourée* (1925); and *Symbolistes et décadents* (criticism, 1902).

Kahn \ˈkän\, Herman, 1922–1983. American social theorist, b. Bayonne, N.J. Founded (1961) Hudson Institute, a think tank devoted to solving problems of national security and international order. Works included *On Thermonuclear Warfare* (1960) and *Thinking About the Unthinkable* (1962), which predicted the probability and survivability of nuclear war; *The Year 2000* (1967); *The Emerging Japanese Superstate* (1970), which predicted Japanese economic ascendancy over the U.S.; and *The Coming Boom* (1982), which prophesied a bright U.S. future.

Kahn, Louis Isadore. 1901–1974. American architect, b. Osel (now Saaremaa), Estonia. To U.S. (1905, naturalized 1917). In private practice (1947–74); professor, Yale (1947–57) and U. of Pa. (1957–74). Broke with International style by designing buildings with powerful massive forms. Works included Yale U. Art Gallery; Jewish Community Center; Richards Medical Research Building, U. of Pa.; Salk Institute, La Jolla, Calif.; First Unitarian Church, Rochester, N.Y.; Kimbell Art Museum, Ft. Worth, Tex.; capitol buildings at Dacca, Bangladesh; Indian Institute of Management, Ahmadābād; and Theater for Performing Arts, Ft. Wayne, Ind.

Kahn, Otto Hermann. 1867–1934. American banker and philanthropist, b. Mannheim, Germany. To U.S. (1893, naturalized 1917). Partner in banking firm of Kuhn, Loeb & Co., New York (from 1897). Main stockholder (from 1908), chairman (1911–18), president (1918–31), Metropolitan Opera Company, New York; contributed generously to many cultural and educational institutions, perhaps greatest patron of arts in U.S. history.

Kahr \ˈkär\, Gustav von. Ritter. 1862–1934. German politician. Prime minister of Bavaria (1920–21); state commissioner general of Bavaria (1923–24) with virtually dictatorial powers; in defiance of Reich government, fostered plans for a Bavarian secession and restoration of monarchy; suppressed Hitler's Beer Hall Putsch in Munich (Nov. 1923); president of Bavarian court administration (1924–30); killed in Nazi party purge.

Kai·ba·ra \kī-bär-ä\ Ekiken, *orig.* Atsunobu. 1630–1714. Japanese philosopher. Wrote some 100 philosophical works based on Neo-Confucian philosophy of Chu Hsi (*q.v.*); itinerant and popular teacher, his detailed accounts of journeys used by later preachers as travel guides; first to apply Confucian ethics to women (in *Onna daigaku*) and children (in *Dōji-kun*). Considered father of botany in Japan; wrote *Yamato honzō* (Study of Japanese Plants).

\ə\ **abut** \ᵊ\ **kitten,** *Fr.* table \ər\ **further** \a\ **ash** \ā\ **ace** \ä\ **cot, cart** \au̇\ **out** \ch\ **chin** \e\ **bet** \ē\ **easy** \g\ **go** \i\ **hit** \ī\ **ice** \j\ **job** \ŋ\ **sing** \ō\ **go** \ȯ\ **law** \ȯi\ **boy** \th\ **both** \t͟h\ **the** \ü\ **loot** \u̇\ **foot** \y\ **yet** \zh\ **vision** \ȧ, b̲, g̲, k̲, ⁿ, œ, œ̄, ue, ue̅, ʸ\ *see* Guide to Pronunciation

Kai·du \'kī-dü\. d. 1301. Grand khan of Mongolia and Turkistan (1269–1301). Great-grandson of Genghis Khan; upheld traditional Mongol customs against newer Chinese ones; long at enmity with Kublai Khan.

Kai·ge·tsu·dō \kī-get-sů-d-ō\ Ando. *Commonly known as* Oka·za·ki \ō-kä-zä-kē\ Genshichi. 1671–1743. Japanese painter. Founded Kaigetsudō school of *Ukiyo-e* painting. Known esp. for paintings of courtesans, including *Courtesan and a Young Girl in Attendance, Standing Beauty,* and *Beauty in the Breeze.*

Kai·hō \kī-hō\ Yūshō. 1533–1615. Japanese painter. Studied under a Kanō artist, probably Eitoku; founded own independent school of painting; adept in using Eitoku's rich, colorful style and also subdued monochromatic ink style of Zen priest-painters. Known for screen paintings as *Pine Tree and Myna Birds, Plum Tree,* and *Fishing Nets.*

Kai·kei \kī-kā\. *Later* Ana·mi·da \än-äm-ē-dä\. fl. 1183–1236. Japanese sculptor. Did much to establish traditional pattern of Buddhist sculpture; style (often called Anamida) known for gentleness and grace; later became a monk and assumed name Anamida. Works included statues of Japanese gods for temples of Kōfuku-ji and Tōdai-ji at Nara.

Kai·ser \'kī-zər\, Georg. 1878–1945. German playwright. A leader of Expressionist movement; to Switzerland (1938) after plays banned by Nazis. Author of chiefly farcical, and social and ethical problem plays including *Die jüdische Witwe* (1911), *Die Bürger von Calais* (1914), *Von Morgens bis Mitternachts* (1916), *Die Koralle* (1917), *Gas I* (1918), *Hölle, Weg, Erde* (1919), *Gas II* (1920), *Nebeneinander* (1923), *Zweimal Oliver* (1926), *Der Silbersee* (1933, music by Kurt Weill), *Der Gärtner von Toulouse* (1938), and a mythological trilogy (pub. 1948) consisting of *Zweimal Amphitryon, Pygmalion,* and *Bellerophon.*

Kaiser, Henry John. 1882–1967. American industrialist, b. near Canajoharie, N.Y. Engaged in highway construction in British Columbia, Washington, California (1914–29), and Cuba (1930); chairman (1933) of committee of companies constructing Boulder and Parker dams; president of companies which constructed Oakland–San Francisco Bay Bridge (1936), Grand Coulee Dam (1942), Bonneville Dam (1943); formed company to produce cement for Shasta Dam (1939). Acquired (1940–42) shipbuilding yards in California and Oregon, and developed methods of extremely rapid prefabrication and assembly, esp. for Liberty cargo ships. Established (1942) Kaiser Foundation to provide health services to his workers and later to public. Expanded his empire (from 1945) to steel, aluminum, and automobiles (esp. Jeeps and Henry J. cars).

Ka·ja·nus \kä-'yä-nůs\, Robert. 1856–1933. Finnish composer and conductor. Champion of a national Finnish music. Founded in Helsinki (1882) and conducted first Finnish symphonic orchestral association. Director of music (1897–1926) and professor, U. of Helsinki. Composer of symphonies, symphonic poems *Kullervo* (1881) and *Aino* (1885), two Finnish rhapsodies, piano works, orchestral suites, cantatas, choruses, and songs.

Kajar. See QĀJĀR.

Ka·ji·ka·wa \käj-ē-kä-wä\. Family of Japanese lacquerware artists flourishing in Edo (now Tokyo) from the late 16th to early 19th centuries. Its founder and inaugurator of its traditions was Kyūjirō, *also called* Kijirō (d. c.1700), who specialized in lacquer *inrō* (portable medicine cases) and netsuke; long in service of Tokugawa family.

Kakiemon. See SAKAIDA.

Ka·ki·no·mo·to \kä-kē-nō-mō-tō\ Hitomaro. fl. c.680–710. Japanese poet. In court service; later a provincial official. First great Japanese literary figure; wrote in *tanka, chōka,* and *sedōka* poetic forms. His poems, covering a wide field of subjects from personal emotions to descriptions of scenery to an elegy on his regal master, are found in *Manyō-shū,* first Japanese anthology of native poetry.

Ka·la·ka·ua \kä-'lä-'kä-ů-ä\. 1836–1891. King of Hawaii (1874–91). By his ideas of reform aroused political opposition culminating in revolution (1887); his powers restricted by new constitution (1887).

Kalb \'kälp, *Angl* 'kalb\, Johann. *Known as* Baron de Kalb \də-'kalb\. 1721–1780. German soldier. In French army (1743–?64). On confidential mission to America to ascertain American colonies' attitude towards Britain (1768); commissioned major general in Continental army (1777); served in American Revolution (1777–80); mortally wounded at Camden, S.C.

Kalck·reuth \'kälk-rȯit\, Friedrich Adolf von. Graf. 1737–1818. Prussian soldier. Adjutant to Prince Henry in Seven Years' War; distinguished himself at siege of Mainz (1793); commander in chief of Pomerania (1795); served with distinction in unsuccessful defense of Danzig and made field marshal (1807); negotiated truce of Tilsit (1807); governor of Königsberg, Berlin (1809, 1814), Breslau (1812).

Ka·le·din \(,)kəl-'yā-dyin\, Aleksey Maksimovich. 1861–1918. Russian soldier. In World War I led cavalry division in successful campaign in Galicia; commanded (1915–16) 12th corps, then 8th army, carrying out Lutsk offensive; resigned after Revolution; led Don Cossacks against Bolsheviks (1917–18); on failure of campaign shot himself.

Kalff \'kälf\, Willem. 1619–1693. Dutch painter. Influenced by Rembrandt and Vermeer. Painted chiefly still lifes, esp. popular banquet pieces and lavish representations of fine objects as *Still Life with a Nautilus Cup* and *Still Life with a Silver Decanter and Fruit.*

Kā·li·dā·sa \'käl-ē-'däs-ə\. 5th century A.D. Indian dramatist and poet. Probably resident at court of Candra Gupta II of Ujjain. Master of Sanskrit; considered greatest Indian writer. His masterpiece was drama *Abhijñānaśakuntala,* a love story of King Duṣyanta and the nymph Śakuntalā; other works included dramas *Vikramorvaśī* and *Mālavikāgnimitra,* epic poems *Raghuvamśa* and *Kumārasambhava,* and lyric "Meghadūta."

Ka·li·man \kä-'lē-män\. Name of two czars of Bulgarian Empire of Asen dynasty:

Kaliman I. d. 1246. Czar (1241–46). Son of Ivan Asen II; lost large portions of empire to Greeks.

Kaliman II. d. 1257. Czar (1257). Ruled only three months; last of direct Asen line.

Ka·li·nin \(,)kəl-'yēn-yin\, Mikhail Ivanovich. 1875–1946. Russian politician. Factory worker (1893); joined Social Democratic party (1898); early supporter of Lenin's Bolshevik faction; active in revolutionary planning; candidate member of Bolshevik Central Committee and cofounder of newspaper *Pravda* (1912); took prominent part in Revolution (1917); full member of Politburo (1925). Formal head of Soviet state (1919–46) under titles chairman of All-Union Central Executive Committee (1924–38) and chairman of presidium of Supreme Soviet (1938 ff.).

Ka·lin·ni·kov \(,)kəl-'yēn-nyik-əf\, Vasily Sergeyevich. 1866–1901. Russian composer. Works included two symphonies, two symphonic poems, two intermezzi, an orchestra suite, piano pieces, and vocal music.

Ka·lir \kä-'lēr\, Eleazar. Between 4th and 8th centuries. Palestinian Hebrew poet. Author of *piyyutim* (synagogal poetry), festival prayers, and hymns.

Kal·las \'käl-läs\, Aino Julia Maria, *nee* Krohn \'krůn\. 1878–1956. Finnish author. Known esp. for prose ballads *Barbara von Tisenhusen* (1923), *Reigin pappi* (1926), and *Sudenmorsian* (1928).

Kál·lay \'käl-lȯi\, Miklós. 1887–1967. Hungarian politician. Minister of agriculture (1932–35); as prime minister (1942–44), pursued liberal policies and unsuccessfully attemped to extricate Hungary from German alliance; imprisoned by Nazis (1944–45); left Hungary (1946), settling in U.S. (1951).

Kállay von Nagy-Kál·ló \-vȯn-nädʸ-'käl-lō\, Benjamin. 1839–1903. Austro-Hungarian politician. Reichsminister of finance and administrator of Bosnia and Herzegovina (from 1882); instituted vigorous program of public works and improved medical and civil services. Author of a *History of the Serbs* (1877), etc.

Kal·lér·gis \käl-'ler-gēs\, Dimítrios. 1803–1967. Greek army officer and politician. Led revolt that forced Otto I to dismiss his Bavarian advisers and adopt a more liberal constitution (1844); exiled (1845–48); minister of war (1854–55); after deposition of Otto (1862), took part in negotiations leading to accession (1863) of Prince George of Denmark to Greek throne.

Kal·lio \'kal-lyȯ\, Kyösti. 1873–1940. Finnish politician. Leader of Agrarian party; prime minister (1922–24); president of Finland (1937–40); resisted Russian demands (1939) but compelled to yield (1940).

Kal·li·wo·da \'kä-lə-,vȯ-dä, *Ger* ,kä-lē-'vō-dä\, Johann Wenzel. 1801–1866. Czech composer and violinist. Composed 10 masses, a Requiem, and other church music, 7 symphonies, 2 operas, overtures, violin concertos and solos, chamber music, piano pieces, male choruses and songs.

Kalm \'kälm\, Pehr. 1716–1779. Swedish botanist. Traveled in North America on natural history survey (1748–51), writing an account of his travels, etc., in three volumes (1753–61).

Kál·mán \'käl-män\. *Called* Köny·ves Kálmán \'kœnʸ-ves-\, *i.e.* Kálmán the Possessor of Books. *Eng.* Co·lo·man \'kō-lə-mən\. c.1070–1116. King of Hungary (1095–1116). Natural son of Géza I; exiled to Poland; returned, seized throne on death of uncle, King László; allowed Godfrey of Bouillon and crusaders to cross Hungary; seized Croatia (1097), Dalmatia (1102); instituted new code of laws, just administration; renowned for learning and statesmanship.

Kál·no·ky von Kö·rös·pa·tak \'käl-nȯ-kē-vȯn-'kœr-œs-pä-täk\, Gusztav Siegmund. Graf. 1832–1898. Austro-Hungarian politician. Professional soldier, rising to general (1879); entered Austrian diplomatic service (1854). Succeeded Haymerle as minister of foreign affairs of Austria-Hungary (1881); his policies conservative, sought to strengthen friendly relations with Russian, brought Italy into Triple Alliance with Germany and Austria (1882), and negotiated secret agreements with Serbia (1881) and Romania (1883); his pro-papal views mainly responsible for his resignation (1895).

Kalonymos, Eleazar ben. See ELEAZAR BEN JUDAH.

Ka·lo·yan \'kä-lȯ-yän\. d. 1297. Czar of Bulgaria, third ruler (1197–1207) of Asen dynasty. Brother of Ivan I and Peter Asen. Completed conquest of North Bulgaria (1201); opened negotiations with Pope Innocent III and carried on correspondence with him; quarreled with crusaders, completely defeated their emperor, Baldwin, at Adrianople (1205), and captured and probably murdered him; ravaged Thrace.

Kal·ten·born \'költ-ᵊn-ˌbörn, 'kalt-\, Hans von, *known as* H.V. 1878–1965. American news commentator, b. Milwaukee. Reporter and editor for *Brooklyn Eagle* (1910–30). Began radio commentary (1922); chief news commentator for CBS (1929–40) and NBC (1940 ff.); famed for his almost nonstop broadcasts during Munich crisis of 1938, reports from European and Pacific fronts in World War II, and coverage of presidential campaigns from 1932.

Kál·vos \'käl-vös\, Andréas Ioannídis. 1792–1869. Greek poet. Spent most of life in Italy and England; secretary (1812–17) to Ugo Foscolo, who greatly influenced him. Published *Líra* (1824) and *Néas Odás* (1826), patriotic odes in an Italian Neoclassical style.

Kal·witz \'käl-vits\, Seth. *Lat.* Sethus Cal·vi·sius \kal-'vē-sh(ē-)əs, -sē-əs\. 1556–1615. German composer and music writer. Cantor in Schulpforta (1582–94), Leipzig (1594–1615). Author of works on music theory including *Melopoeia* (1592), *Compendium musicae* (1594), *Exercitationes musicae* (1600–11); composed hymns and other sacred vocal music.

Kamakaeha, Liliu. See LILIUOKALANI.

Ka·ma·ku·ra \kä-mä-kůr-ä\. A shogunate of Japan (1192–1333) founded by Minamoto Yoritomo after defeat of Taira clan (1185); its capital the village of Kamakura. See MINAMOTO family for its shoguns.

Kamatari. See under FUJIWARA family.

Kam·ban \'käm-bän\, Guðmundur Jónsson. 1888–1945. Icelandic writer. His novels included *Ragnar Finnsson* (1922), *Skálholt* (1930–32), *Jeg ser et stort skønt Land* (1936); plays included *Hadda-Padda* (1914), *Vi Mordere* (1920), *Ørkenens Stjerner* (1925), *Komplekser* (1941), *Grandezza* (1941).

Ka·me·ha·me·ha \kä-'mā-hä-'mā-hä\. Name of five rulers of Hawaii:

Kamehameha I. *Surnamed* Nui \'nü-ē\, *i.e.* the Great. *Orig.* Pai·ea \pī-'ā-ə\. 1758?–1819. King (1795–1819). Directed negotiations between his uncle King Kalaniopuu and Capt. James Cook (1779); m. Kaahumanu (*q.v.*); gained control of northern Hawaii (1782); conquered other islands (1785–1810); organized government, allowed foreign traders to settle, ended human sacrifice; his rule autocratic but humane.

Kamehameha II. *Orig.* Li·ho·li·ho \'lē-hō-'lē-hō\. 1797–1824. King (1819–24). Son of Kamehameha I; overthrew taboo system and ancient religion of Hawaiians; received first American missionaries (1820); with his queen visited England (1823–24), both dying suddenly there.

Kamehameha III. *Orig.* Kau·i·ke·ao·u·li \'kaů-ē-kā-'aů-ü-lē\. 1813–1854. King (1825–54). Brother of Kamehameha II; two constitutions adopted (1840, 1852) during his reign; had difficulties with foreign governments; finally secured, from U.S. (1842) and from Great Britain and France (1843), recognition of independence of Hawaii; extended organization of government and established courts; sought closer relations with U.S.

Kamehameha IV. *Christened* Alexander Liholiho. 1834–1863. King (1854–63). Nephew of Kamehameha III; took steps to establish independence of his kingdom; curbed political power of American Protestant missionaries and ousted Americans from cabinet; established political and commercial relations with many nations; promulgated improvements in commerce, agriculture, and whaling industry; sponsored social and medical programs for his people; an extremely popular, benevolent, and efficient monarch.

Kamehameha V. *Orig.* Lot \'lät\. 1830–1872. King (1863–72). Brother of Kamehameha IV; promulgated his own constitution (1864) to supersede that of 1852; in his reign Molokai Leper Settlement established (1864); last of direct line.

Ka·me·nev \'käm-yin-yif\, Lev Borisovich. *Orig. surname* Ro·sen·feld \'röz-yin-fyilʸt\. 1883–1936. Russian Communist leader. Joined Social Democratic party (1901); associated with Lenin in western Europe (1908–14); banished to Siberia (1915–17) for antiwar propaganda; after Revolution took part in establishing Bolshevik government; elected to Politburo (1917); chairman of Moscow Soviet (1919–25); with Stalin and Zinovyev, member of triumvirate ruling Russia after Lenin's death (1924); held high positions in Soviet government (1924–32) but eventually lost power and positions because of Stalin's opposition; m. Trotsky's sister and at times accused of Trotskyite sympathies; sentenced to imprisonment (1934) during purge of party after murder of Kirov; executed with Zinovyev.

Ka·mer·lingh On·nes \'kä-mər-liŋ-'ön-əs\, Heike. 1853–1926. Dutch physicist. Professor, U. of Leiden (1882–1923); founded (1894) Cryogenic Laboratory, now named after him. Liquefied helium (1908); attained low temperature, within one degree of absolute zero, in his work on helium; discovered that the electrical resistance of certain metals practically disappears at temperatures close to absolute zero. Awarded 1913 Nobel prize for physics.

Kames, Lord. See Henry HOME.

Ka·mień·ski \kä-'myenʸ-skē\, Maciej. 1734–1821. Polish composer. Wrote Polish and German operas, including *Nędza uszczęśliwiona* (first Polish opera, 1778), church music, etc.

Kā·mil \'kä-mēl\, al-Malik al-. 1180–1238. Sultan of Egypt, Palestine, and Syria (1218–38). Last of Ayyūbid line; fought armies of Fifth Crusade (1218–21), negotiating their withdrawal from Egypt (1221); resisted proselytizing of St. Francis of Assisi; ceded (1229) Jerusalem and other Palestinian towns to Frederick II, leader of Sixth Crusade.

Kāmil, Muṣṭafa. 1874–1908. Egyptian nationalist. Founded (1907) Ummah party which advocated withdrawal of British troops from Egypt.

Kâ·mil Pa·şa \kä-'mēl-pə-'shä\. 1832–1913. Turkish soldier and politician. Grand vizier of Turkey (1884–87, 1896); governor of Izmir (1896–1908); again grand vizier (1908–09, 1912–13); supported parliament and opposed anti-British policies of Committee of Union and Progress.

Ka·min·ska \kå-'mēn-skå\, Ida. 1899–1980. Polish actress and theatrical producer, b. Odessa, Ukraine. Organizer of Warsaw Jewish Art Theater (1923–31) and own drama company (1932–39). Manager, director, and star of Jewish State Theater of Poland (1946–68); considered leading Yiddish actress of the day; scored international success in film *The Shop on Main Street* (1966); to U.S. (1968) and unsuccessfully attempted to establish a permanent Yiddish theater.

Ka·min·ski \kä-'min-skē\, Heinrich. 1886–1946. German composer. Advocate of revival of polyphonic music in modern spirit; composer of a concerto grosso for double orchestra and piano (1922), two operas, religious music, motets, choruses, chamber music, etc.

Kam·mer·er \'käm-ər-ər\, Paul. 1880–1926. Austrian biologist. Caused controversy by claiming to have produced experimental evidence that acquired traits in animals could be inherited (1918); his evidence was proven (1926) by G.K. Noble and Hans Przibram to have been doctored.

Kam·mu \käm-mü\. *Orig.* Ya·ma·be \yä-mäb-e\. 737–806. Emperor of Japan (781–806). A strong ruler; curbed power of local officials and of Buddhist church; subdued Ainu tribes on northern frontier; built great city of Heian (later Kyōto) and established his capital there (794).

Ka·mo \kä-mō\ Chōmei. 1155?–1216. Japanese writer. Held court office; took Buddhist orders and became hermit (1204). Chief work *Hōjō-ki* (1212), prose essay on his life in seclusion; also wrote poetry, literary criticism *Mumyō shō* (c.1208), and collection of Buddhist tales *Hosshin shū* (1214 or 1215).

Kamo Mabuchi. 1697–1769. Japanese scholar. Made study of earliest collection of Japanese poems (the *Manyō-shū*) and of collection of Shintō rituals (*Norito*); insisted they were free of foreign influence and represented the pure Japanese spirit, thereby helping foster a revival of early poetic style; considered one of earliest representatives of Kokugako (National Learning) school. Chief work *Kokuikō*, a rejection of Chinese thought and literature.

Ka·mose \'kä-ˌmōs\. d. c.1570 B.C. Egyptian king (c.1575–c.1570 B.C.), last of 17th dynasty. Son and successor of Seqenenre II; inherited southernmost third of Egypt; began (c.1572) expulsion of the Hyksos, a task successfully completed by his brother Ahmose I.

Kämp·fer \'kemp-fər\, Engelbert. 1651–1716. German physician and traveler. Member of trade missions (1683–94) to Russia, Persia, Batavia, Java, and esp. (1690–92) Japan. Author of *History of Japan and Siam* (1728).

Ka·na·ga·ki \kän-äg-äk-ē\ Robun. *Orig.* Bun·zō \bün-zō\ Nozaki. 1829–1874. Japanese writer. Disciple of Hanagasa Bunkyō. Author of humorous, satirical, light fiction *(gesaku)* as *Kokkei Fuji mōde* (1860–61) and *Aguranabe* (1871).

Kan-ami \kän-äm-ē\. *Orig.* Sa·bu·ro-Ki·yo·tsu·gu \säb-ůr-ō-kē-yōt-sůg-ü\. 1334–1385. Japanese poet. Credited with beginning transformation of primitive song-and-dance playlets into present Nō drama, a process continued by his son Zeami Motokiyo (*q.v.*); acted in and wrote many Nō plays.

Ka·ná·ris \kä-'nä-rēs\, Konstantínos. 1790–1877. Greek naval commander and politician. Renowned for daring exploits against Turkish naval units (1822 ff.); prime minister of Greece (1848–49); took part in revolution that overthrew Otto I (1862) and seated Prince George of Denmark on Greek throne; again prime minister (1864–65, 1877).

Kan·din·sky \(ˌ)kən-'dyēn-skəi *Angl* kan-'din(t)-skē\, Wassily. 1866–1944. Russian painter. One of founders of nonfigurative painting; usually credited with executing first pure abstraction *First Abstract Watercolor* (1910). To Munich (1896); associated with avant-garde groups, including Phalanx and Die Brücke; with Franz Marc, founded in Munich the group Der Blaue Reiter (1911–14), whose members included Paul Klee and August Macke; in Moscow (1914–22) as professor, director of Moscow Museum for Pictorial Culture (1919) and founder (1921) of Russian Academy of Artistic Sciences; instructor with Bauhaus school at Weimar (1922–25) and Dresden (1925–33); settled in Paris (1933), naturalized (1939). Author of *Über das Geistige in der Kunst* (1922), pioneering treatise on theory of abstract art; also wrote *Rückblicke* (1913) and second treatise on art *Punkt und Linie zu Fläche* (1926). His canvases, marked by bright colors and geometrical abstractions, included *With* *the Black Arch* (1912), *Black Lines* (1913), *Autumn* (1914), *One Center* (1924), *Three Sounds* (1926), *Affirmed Pink* (1932), *Violet Dominant* (1934).

Känd·ler \'ken-dlər\, Johann Joachim. 1706–1775. German sculptor. Head of modeling department of porcelain factory at Meissen (1731–75). Helped design and model figurines, dinner sets, vases, and other Meissen porcelain.

Kane \'kān\, Elisha Kent. 1820–1857. American explorer, b. Philadelphia. Senior medical officer with first Grinnell Expedition, searching Arctic for Sir John Franklin (1850–51). Headed second Grinnell Expedition into Arctic (1853–55); reached territory not previously discovered. Works included *The U.S. Grinnell Expedition in Search of Sir John Franklin* (1853), *Arctic Explorations: The Second Grinnell Expedition* (1856).

Kane, John. *Surname orig.* Cain \'kān\. 1860–1934. American painter, b. West Calder, Scotland. To U.S. (1879). Known for primitivist landscapes of Pennsylvania and Scotland, cityscapes of Pittsburgh, and a self-portrait (1929). Wrote autobiography *Sky Hooks* (1938).

Kane, Paul. 1810–1871. Canadian painter, b. Mallow, Ireland. To Canada (c.1818). Known for paintings depicting life of Indians of North West.

K'ang-hsi. See HSÜAN-YEH.

K'ang-te. See P'U-I.

K'ang Yu-wei \'käŋ-'yō-'wā\. 1858–1927. Chinese scholar and reformer. Studied Western history and philosophy and became leader of a reform party; adviser of Emperor Tsai-t'ien; suggested famous reform decrees (1898); proscribed by Empress Dowager Tz'u-hsi but escaped; in exile in Hong Kong, Singapore, Europe, etc. (1898–1914); worked for reform and active in Revolution (1911–12), although living outside China; an ardent monarchist, took part in attempted restoration (1917) of P'u-i; opponent of Sun Yat-sen. Author of *The Forged Classics* (1891), *Confucius as a Reformer* (1897), etc.

Ka·niṣ·ka *or* **Ka·nish·ka** \kə-'nish-kə\. fl. 78?–?103 A.D. King of India (78?–?103, but dates very uncertain) of the Kushan dynasty. Ruled over northern part of Indian subcontinent from capital at Peshāwar, with realm extending to Madura in southern India, to Kabul, and to Bokhara in the north; might have crossed the Pamirs and conquered city-states in present Chinese Turkistan; founded Sirsukh. Adopted Buddhism; his reign of great importance in its effect on Buddhism and because of ideas introduced from the West.

Kan·krin \(,)kən-'krēn\, Yegor Frantsevich. Count. *Ger.* Georg von Can·crin \'kän-,krēn\. 1774–1845. German administrator. Entered Russian service (1797); administrator of army (1813–20); minister of finance (1823–44); exercised considerable influence on Nicholas I; made count (1829).

Ka·nō \kä-nō\. Name of a family or school of Japanese painters from village of Kanō, Shizuoka prefecture, birthplace of Masanobu (1453–1490), founder of family; chief painter to shogun Ashikaga Yoshimasa; influenced by Shūbun; painted landscapes, birds, and figure compositions, chiefly in ink. His son ¶Motonobu (1477–1559), one of foremost artists of Japan; most famous painter of the school and its actual founder; gave school its distinctive characteristic of subordinating color to design; painted landscapes, screens, murals, blending native and Chinese style; master of technique; employed exquisite color harmonies. His grandson ¶Eitoku, *orig.* Kuninobu (1543–1590), official painter of court and shogunate; departed somewhat from earlier classicism of school; painted screens and landscapes and decorated interiors of royal palaces; displayed energy and inventiveness, introducing gold and brilliant colors. His son-in-law and disciple ¶Sanraku, *orig.* Ki·mu·ra \kim-ůr-ä\ Mitsuyori (1559–1635), excelled in large-scale decorative designs in gold and brilliant colors; introduced subject of historical figures from Chinese book *Illustrations of Exemplary Emperors;* painted screens and sliding panels used to decorate palaces and temples. ¶Tanyū, *orig.* Morinobu (1602–1674), grandson of Eitoku; most influential painter of Tokugawa era; appointed painter to shogun Tokugawa Ieyasu and given estate at Kajibashi (1619); his conservative subject matter and return to subdued tones and designs of early Kanō painters set standards for later Kanō artists; painted scrolls illustrating life of Ieyasu and decorated porticoes of his mausoleum at Nikkō; also painted screens and decorated walls of Nijō Castle at Kyotō, shogun's castle at Nagoya, and Kyotō Imperial Palace; with Eitoku and Motonobu considered one of "three famous brushes" of Kanō family. His brother ¶Naonobu (1607–1650), painter to shogun Tokugawa Iemitsu and founder of Kobikichō branch of family; known for his "grass" (*sō*) or "running" style of brushwork combining broad, free strokes with simple ink wash to create impression of brevity and freshness; painted screens of landscapes and historical figures.

Kant \'känt *Angl* 'kant\, Immanuel. 1724–1804. German philosopher. Privatdozent (1755–70), professor of logic and metaphysics (1770–97), Königsberg; came into conflict with Prussian government as consequence of liberal religious views (1792–94). Began as Leibnitz-Wolffian disciple; later influenced by David Hume and English empiricists; gradually developed his own critical philosophy in which he sought to determine the nature and limits of human knowledge, the necessary categories of consciousness, and their ethical and aesthetic consequences. His works included *Allgemeine Naturgeschichte und Theorie des Himmels* (1755), *Der einzig mögliche Beweisgrund zu einer Demonstration des Daseyns Gottes* (1763), *Beobachtungen über das Gefühl des Schönen und Erhabenen* (1764), *De mundi sensibilis atque intelligibilis forma et principiis* (1770), *Critik der reinen Vernunft* (1781, rev. 1787, *Critique of Pure Reason*), *Prolegomena zur einer jeden künftigen Metaphysik die als Wissenschaft wird auftreten können* (1783), *Grundlegung zur Metaphysik der Sitten* (1785), *Metaphysische Anfangsgründe der Naturwissenschaft* (1786), *Critik der practischen Vernunft* (1788, *Critique of Practical Reason*), *Critik der Urtheilskraft* (1790, *Critique of Judgment*), *Die Religion innerhalb der Grenzen der blossen Vernunft* (1793), *Zum ewigen Frieden* (1795), *Die Metaphysik der Sitten* (1797).

Kan·te·mir \kən-tyi-'myir\, Antiokh Dmitriyevich. *Also spelled* Antioch Cantemir. 1708–1744. Russian diplomat and writer. Son of Dmitry Kantemir; ambassador to England (1732–36), minister in Paris (1836–44). Author of satirical verse, first secular poems in Russian; also of philosophical works, etc.

Kantemir, Dmitry Konstantinovich. *Rom.* Dimitrie Cantemir. 1673–1723. Romanian-Russian prince and scholar. Son of Prince Constantin Cantemir; succeeded as prince of Moldavia (1710–11); fled Turkish overlords to Russia; made prince of empire by Peter the Great. Wrote on linguistics and history, including *Istoria ieroglifică* (1705), *Historia incrementorum atque decrementorum aulae othomanicae* (1715–16), *Descriptio Moldaviae* (1718).

Kan·tor \'kan-tər\, MacKinlay. 1904–1977. American writer, b. Webster City, Ia. Author of *Long Remember* (1934), *Gentle Annie* (1942), *Glory For Me* (1945), *Andersonville* (1956, Pulitzer prize), etc.

Kan·to·ro·vich \,kän-tō-'rō-vich\, Leonid Vitaljevich. 1912–1986. Soviet economist and mathematician. Shared with Tjalling C. Koopmans 1975 Nobel prize for economics for "linear programming" that aided policymakers in maximizing the output of limited resources.

Kan·to·ro·wicz \kän-'tō-rō-vich\, Hermann. 1877–1940. German jurist. Professor, Freiburg (1908–29), Kiel (1929–33); lecturer, All Souls College, Oxford (1936–40). Known for his doctrine of free law (*Freirechtslehre*) proclaimed in *Der Kampf um die Rechtswissenschaft* (1906); also wrote *Der Geist der englischen Politik* (1929), *Studies in the Glossators of the Roman Law* (1938, with W. Buckland), *The Definition of Law* (1958), etc.

Kaō \kaů\ Ninga. d. 1345. Japanese painter. One of founders of Chinese-inspired *suiboku* school of monochromatic ink painting; known esp. for his portrait of Kanzan. Very little known about his life.

Kao Ch'i-p'ei \'gaů-'chē-'pā\. 1672–1734. Chinese painter. Served in official capacity. Painted landscapes in orthodox manner; also known for paintings executed with his palms, fingers, and nails instead of a brush.

Kao Huang-ti. See NURHACHI.

Kao Kang \'gaů-'gäŋ\. c.1902–c.1955. Chinese Communist leader. Helped establish Communist guerrilla base on Shensi–Kansu border (early 1930s); became a close associate of Mao Tse-tung; made full Politburo member and head of Northeast region (by early 1950s); his purge in 1954–55 was biggest scandal in Communist China before the late 1960s; committed suicide.

Kao Tsu. See (1) Li Yüan under LI family; (2) Liu Pang under LIU family.

Kao Tsung. See (1) Chao Kou under CHAO family; (2) Li Chih under LI family; (3) HUNG-LI.

Ka·pi·la \'kəp-ə-lə\. fl. 550 B.C.? Indian philosopher. Reputed founder of the Sāmkhya system of Hindu philosophy; his teaching entirely dualistic.

Ka·pit·sa \'käp-yit-sə\, Pyotr Leonidovich. 1894–1984. Soviet physicist. In Britain (1921–34) studied under atomic physicist Lord Rutherford; named (1934) director of the U.S.S.R.'s Institute of Physical Problems but dismissed (1946) for refusal to work on atomic bomb; reinstated (1955) as director, serving till his death. Developed pioneering methods for liquefying helium, intensifying magnetic fields, and liquefying air in industry at low cost. Awarded 1978 Nobel prize for physics.

Kap·lan \'käp-län\, Viktor. 1876–1934. Austrian inventor. Invented the variable propeller Kaplan turbine (pat. 1920).

Kap·nist \(,)kəp-'nyēst\, Vasily Vasilyevich. 1757–1823. Russian dramatist and poet. Produced sensation with his comedy *Yabeda* (1798), dealing with bribery and corruption in Russian judicial circles.

Ka·po·dí·stri·as \,kä-pō-'thē-strē-äs\, Ioánnis Antónios. Count. *Ital.* Giovanni Antonio Ca·po d'Istria \,kä-pō-'dēs-trē-ä\. 1776–1831. Greek politician. Entered Russian service (1809); represented Russia at congresses of Vienna (1814–15) and Troppau (1820); given equal responsibility with Karl Nesselrode to conduct Russian foreign policy (1816); gained political enmity of Metternich, who undermined his power; left Russian service (1822). Devoted himself to cause of Greek independence; elected provisional president of Greece (1827); assassinated. His brother ¶Avgoustinos *or* Augustinus (1778–1857) was provisional president of Greece (1831–32).

Kapp \'käp\, Friedrich. 1824–1884. German politician. Took part in German revolution (1849). To U.S. (1850); lawyer and editor in New York (1850–70); influential among German-Americans. Lived in Berlin (from 1870); National Liberal deputy in Reichstag (1871–78, 1881–84). Author of lives of Baron von Steuben (1858; pub. 1884) and Johann Kalb (1862), and *Aus und über Amerika*

(1876). His son ¶Wolfgang (1858–1922), German revolutionist, b. New York; in Prussian government service (1886–1906); director general of East Prussian agricultural credit banks (1906–20); opposed Bethmann-Hollweg's policy; with von Tirpitz founded German Fatherland party (1917); member of Reichstag (1918); led monarchist revolt (Kapp Putsch) against republican government (Mar. 1920); seized Berlin and declared himself imperial chancellor; failed in revolt because of general strike; fled to Sweden (1920); returned to Germany (1922) but died while awaiting trial.

Kap·teyn \käp-ˈtīn\, Jacobus Cornelis. 1851–1922. Dutch astronomer. Professor, Groningen (1878–1921), where he established an observatory. Measured and computed the positions of the stars on David Gill's photographic plates of the southern sky, producing (1896–1900) catalog *Cape Photographic Durchmusterung;* devised method of determining structure of galaxy by counting stars in a selected area; investigated the structure of fixed-star systems; discovered two streams of stars moving in opposite direction in the plane of the Milky Way.

Ka·ra·đor·đe \kȧ-rȧ-ˈdyȯr-dyə\. *Eng.* Kar·a·george \ˈkar-ə-ˌjȯ(ə)rj\, *i.e.* Black George. *Orig.* Đorđe Pe·tro·vić \ˈpe-trȯ-vēt^y^ *Angl* -ˌvich\. 1762–1817. Serbian hero. Leader in struggle for independence from Turkish sovereignty; founder of Karađorđević dynasty. Son of peasant; served as sergeant in Austrian army against Turkey (1788–91); settled in Topola (1791); engaged in irregular fighting against Turks (between 1791 and 1804). Elected supreme leader at outbreak of Serb rebellion against Turks (1804); conducted operations with great success until (after treaty of Bucharest, 1812) Turkey was free to throw whole strength against Serbs; decisively defeated (1813) and took refuge in Austria. Suddenly reappeared in Serbia (1817), prepared to head new rebellion, but was murdered on orders from Miloš Obrenović.

Ka·ra·đor·đe·vić \kȧ-rȧ-ˈdyȯr-dyə-vēt^y^\ *or* **Kar·a·geor·ge·vić** \ˌkar-ə-ˈjȯr-jə-ˌvich\. Name of a Serbian dynasty founded (1808) by Karađorđe. Its ruling members: Prince Alexander, Alexander I, Peter I, and Peter II (*qq.v.*). Cf. OBRENOVIĆ.

Ka·ra·džić \kä-ˈrä-jēt^y^, *Angl* -jich\, Vuk Stefanović. 1787–1864. Serbian scholar. Reformed Cyrillic alphabet as used in Serbia; advocated use of vernacular Serbian as the literary language. Published anthology of Serbian folk songs (1814), Serbian–German–Latin dictionary *Srpski Rječnik* (1818, rev. 1852), collection of Serbian folk literature *Srpske Narodne Pjesme* (1823–33), collection of Serbian proverbs (1837), Serbian translation of New Testament (1847).

Ka·ra·ï·ska·kis \ˌkä-rä-ē-ˈskäk-yēs\, Georgios. c.1780–1827. Greek klepht. Served in bodyguard of Turkish pasha of Ioannina (1808–20); joined war of independence on Greek side (1821), but often capitulated to Turks; attempted to relieve second siege of Missolonghi (1826); killed in action.

Ka·ra·khan \kə-(ˌ)rə-ˈk̲än\, Lev Mikhaylovich. 1889–1937. Russian diplomat. Member of foreign ministry (1917); issued (1919) Karakhan Manifesto offering to relinquish Soviet privileges won by Russian czarist government in China; ambassador to China (1924–27); vice commissar of foreign affairs (1928–34); ambassador to Turkey (1934–37); executed on charge of espionage.

Ka·ra Mus·ta·fa Pa·şa \kä-ˈrä-mu̇s-tä-ˈfä-pä-ˈshä\, Merzifonlu. 1634–1683. Turkish grand vizier (1676–83). Brother-in-law of Ahmed Köprülü, whom he succeeded as vizier; sent by sultan to take Vienna; delayed attack and finally (1683) met complete defeat at hands of John III Sobieski and Charles of Lorraine; beheaded by sultan.

Ka·ram·zin \kə-(ˌ)rəm-ˈzyēn\, Nikolay Mikhaylovich. 1766–1826. Russian historian and novelist. Described travels (1789–90) in western Europe in *Pisma russkogo puteshestvennika* (1791–92); became leading exponent of sentimentalist school in Russia; wrote several novels, esp. *Bednaya Liza* (1792); appointed court historian (1803); composed *Istoriya gosudarstva rossiyskogo* (*History of Russia;* 1819–29), down to accession of Romanovs (1613). Reformed the literary language, introducing many Gallicisms to supplant Slavonic words and idioms; had great influence on development of Russian language and literature.

Ka·ra·ve·lov \kȧ-ˈrȧ-vä-lȯf\, Lyuben Stoychev. 1834–1879. Bulgarian writer. Journalist in Moscow (1857–67); long supported Bulgarian revolutionary cause; in Bucharest edited revolutionary journals *Svoboda* (1869–72) and *Nevavisimost* (1873–74). Author of novels *Bălgare ot staro vreme* (1867) and *Maminoto detentse* (1878) and of many short stories.

Kar·bū·qah \kär-bü-ˈkä\ of Mo·sul \mȯ-ˈsül\. *Also spelled* Ker·bo·gha \ker-bō-ˈgä\. d. 1102. Turkish ruler. *Atabeg* (regent) of Mosul under ʿAbbāsid caliph of Baghdad; formed coalition of Muslim princes of Syria and unsuccessfully attempted to raise Christian siege of Antioch (1098).

Karg-Elert \ˈkärk-ˈā-lərt\, Sigfrid. 1877–1933. German composer. Added mother's maiden name to his original Karg; virtuoso organist; professor, Leipzig conservatory (1919). Composed works for harmonium and for organ, many piano pieces, chamber music, chorals, etc.

Ka·rīm Khān Zand Mo·ḥam·mad \kȧ-ˈrēm-k̲än-ˈzänd-mō-ˈk̲äm-mȧd\. c.1705–1779. Persian sovereign (1750–79), first of Zand dynasty. General under Nāder Shāh; placed (1750) Shāh Esmāʿīl III on throne as figurehead king, retaining actual power; took title *vakīl* (regent) but never claimed that of shāh; controlled all of Persia except for Khorāsān; made Shīrāz his capital, erecting many buildings in it; restored peace to country; reorganized fiscal system; patron of the arts; allowed English East India Company to establish trading post at Bushire (1763); captured Basra (1776).

Kar·io·tá·kis *or* **Kar·yo·tá·kis** \kar-yō-ˈtä-kēs\, Kóstas. 1896–1928. Greek poet. Government clerk in Athens, Patras, Prevesa; friend of Maria Polidoúri. Influenced by French Symbolist poets and by New School of Poetry of Athens; published two volumes of poems (1919, 1927).

Kar·ka·vít·sas \kär-kä-ˈvēt-säs\, Andréas. 1860–1922. Greek writer. Army doctor; worked for acceptance of Demotic Greek as literary language. Author of realistic novels and short stories depicting village life, esp. novel *O zitiános* (1899).

Karl. See also CHARLES.

Karl I and **II.** Dukes of Brunswick. See BRUNSWICK.

Karl·feldt \ˈkärl-felt\, Erik Axel. 1864–1931. Swedish poet. Author of volumes of poems dealing chiefly with nature and with peasant life of Dalecarlia, including *Vildmarks-och kärleksvisor* (1895), *Fridolins visor* (1898), *Fridolins lustgård* (1901), *Flora och Pomona* (1906), *Flora och Bellona* (1918), *Hösthorn* (1927); awarded Nobel prize for literature posthumously (1931) after earlier (1918) refusing it.

Karlmann. See CARLOMAN.

Kar·loff \ˈkär-(ˌ)lȯf, -ləf\, Boris. *Orig.* William Henry Pratt \ˈprat\. 1887–1969. American actor, b. London, England. To Canada (1909), U.S. (1917). Gained international fame as the monster in films *Frankenstein* (1931), *The Bride of Frankenstein* (1935), *The Son of Frankenstein* (1939); appeared in some 130 films, mainly in horror or villainous roles, as *The Mummy* (1932), *The Old Dark House* (1932), *The Mask of Fu Manchu* (1932), *The Raven* (1935), *Black Friday* (1940); on stage in *Arsenic and Old Lace* (1941) and as Capt. Hook in *Peter Pan* (1950); also on television and radio.

Karlstadt, Andreas Rudolf Bodenstein von. See BODENSTEIN.

Karl Wil·helm Fer·di·nand \ˈkärl-ˈvil-helm-ˈfer-dē-ˌnänt\. 1735–1806. Duke of Brunswick (1780–1806). Son of Karl I (1713–1780) and nephew of Frederick the Great. General in Prussian army (1773); commanded invasion of Holland (1787); commanded Allied army against French (1792); defeated at Valmy (1792); resigned command (1794); resumed command (1806), defeated and mortally wounded at Auerstedt.

Kár·mán \ˈkär-män\, József. 1769–1795. Hungarian novelist. Author of *Fanni hagyományai* (1794), first sentimental novel in Hungary.

Kármán, Theodor von. 1881–1963. American physicist and aeronautical engineer, b. Budapest, Hungary. Director of Aeronautical Institute at Aachen, Germany (1912–30). To U.S. (1930, naturalized 1936); professor of aeronautics and director of Guggenheim Aeronautics Laboratory, Calif. Inst. of Tech. (1930–49). A founder of Applied Mechanics Congress Committee (1922); co-founder of Jet Propulsion Laboratory (1944); a founder (1951) and chairman (1951–63) of Advisory Group for Aeronautical Research and Development, NATO. Pioneered in use of mathematics and the basic sciences in aeronautics and astronautics; made analysis (1911) of alternating double row of vortices behind a bluff body in a fluid stream (Kármán's vortex street); helped develop (from 1938) JATO rocket for conventional aircraft; instrumental in development of rocket technology.

Ka·ro *or* **Ca·ro** *or* **Qa·ro** \ˈkär-ō\, Joseph ben Ephraim. *Called* Ma·ran \ˈmär-än\, *i.e.* our master. 1488–1575. Spanish Talmudist. Settled in Turkey after expulsion of Jews from Spain (1492); to Safad, Palestine (c.1536). Author of authoritative codification of and commentary on Jewish law *Bet Yosef* (1550–59), based on Jacob ben Asher's *Arbaʿa turim* and on works of Maimonides, Alfasi, and Asher ben Jehiel; also wrote condensed version *Shulḥan ʿarukh* (1565); wrote mystical diary *Maggid mesharim* (pub. 1646).

Karoline. See CAROLINE.

Ká·ro·lyi \ˈkä-rȯl-yē\, Mihály. Count. 1875–1955. Hungarian politician. Entered parliament (1910); held extreme liberal views; prime minister (1918–19) and president (1919) of the Hungarian Democratic Republic; lost much land to Allies in postwar peace treaty; replaced by Béla Kun and the Hungarian Soviet Republic; fled abroad (1919–46); ambassador to Paris (1947–49); resigned in protest over trial of Lászlo Rajk and again went into exile.

Karr \kȧr\, Alphonse, *in full* Jean-Baptiste-Alphonse. 1808–1890. French journalist and novelist. Editor of *Figaro* and founder of the satirical review *Les Guêpes.* Author of *Une heure trop tard* (1833), *Voyage autour de mon jardin* (1845), *Histoire d'un pion* (1854), etc.

Kar·rer \'kär-ər\, Paul. 1889–1971. Swiss chemist. Professor, Zürich (1918–59). Determined constitution of vitamin A (1931); awarded (jointly with Walter N. Haworth) the 1937 Nobel prize for chemistry for work on carotenoids, flavins, and vitamins A and B_2.

Kar·sa·vi·na \(,)kər-'säv-yi-nə\, Tamara Platonovna. 1885–1978. British dancer, b. Russia. Danced with Maryinsky Theater, St. Petersburg (1902–18); leading ballerina (1909–22) and partner of Nijinsky (1909–13) with Diaghilev's Ballets Russes; created roles in Michel Fokine's *Les Sylphides* (1909), *Firebird* (1910), *Carnaval* (1910), *Le Spectre de la Rose* (1911), *Petrouchka* (1911), *Thamar* (1912), etc., and in Massine's *The Three-Cornered Hat* (1919) and *Pulcinella* (1920). Lived in London (from 1918); helped found Royal Academy of Dancing, London (1920), for which she organized Teachers' Training Course and Camargo Society (1930); revived some of her roles for Ballet Rambert (1930–31) and created new ones for Frederick Ashton. Wrote autobiography *Theatre Street* (1930) and text *Classical Ballet* (1962).

Kar·tēr *or* **Kar·tir** \kär-'tēr\. 3d century A.D. Persian priest. High priest of Zoroastrianism; *magaput* (chief) of Magi of Hormizd; attempted to purge Persia of all religions except Zoroastrianism; persuaded King Bahrām I to imprison Kartēr's archrival Mani.

Kar·ti·ni \kär-'tē-nē\, Raden Adjeng. 1879–1904. Javanese noblewoman. Early proponent of emancipation for Javanese women; her letters to Dutch friends, published as *Door duisternis tot licht* (1911), made her an important symbol for Indonesian independence movement and for Indonesian feminists.

Kar·ve \'kär-və\, Maharishi Dhondo Keshav. 1858–1962. Indian reformer. Instructor in mathematics at Fergusson College, Poona (1891–1914). Worked for education for women and elimination of Hindu restrictions on remarriage of widows; established Widow Marriage Association (1893); founded Shreemati Nathibai Damodar Thackersey Women's University (1916).

Karyotákis, Kostas. See KARIOTÁKIS.

Ka·sa·vu·bu \kä-sä-'vü-bü\, Joseph[3]. 1910?–1969. Zairian politician. Entered civil service (1942); early leader in independence movement for Belgian Congo; president (1955) of cultural-political association Abako. First president (1960–65) of independent Congo republic (now Zaire); ousted (1960) his bitter rival, Patrice Lumumba; deposed in military coup.

Kasimir. See CASIMIR.

Kas·pro·wicz \käs-'prò-vēch\, Jan. 1860–1926. Polish poet. Journalist (1898–1909); professor of comparative literature (1909 ff.), Lwów. His verse included *Krzak dzikiej róży* (1898), *Ginącemu światu* (1901), *Księga ubogich* (1916); translated works of Aeschylus, Euripides, Shakespeare, Browning, etc.

Kas·sák \'käs-säk\, Lajos. 1887–1967. Hungarian writer. First important working-class writer of Hungary. Author of verse, novels *Misilló királysága* (1916), *Angyalföld* (1929), and *Akik eltévedtek* (1936), and esp. his 8-volume autobiography *Egy ember élete* (1928–39).

Kas·sem \kä-'säm\, Abdul Karim. *Also spelled* Quas·sim \kä-'sēm\. 1914–1963. Iraqi soldier and politician. Career soldier; brigadier general (1955); led military coup that overthrew King Faisal II (1958). Prime minister and head of Republic of Iraq (1958–63); opposed Pan-Arab movement; suppressed political opposition and ruled autocratically; unsuccessfully attempted to crush Kurdish rebellion (1961–63); overthrown and killed in military coup.

Kast·ler \käst-ler\, Alfred. 1902–1984. French physicist. Professor at École Normale Supérieure, Paris (1941–68); director of research, Centre National de la Recherche Scientifique (1968–72). Awarded 1966 Nobel prize for physics for discovery and development of optical methods for studying Hertzian resonance in atoms, which led to development of the laser. A leading activist against nuclear weapons.

Kast·ner \'käst-nər\, Johann Georg. 1810–1867. German composer. Settled in Paris (1835). Wrote textbooks on music theory and treatises on instrumentation and vocalization; composer of operas, choral and instrumental works, symphonic tone poems, etc. His son ¶Georg Friedrich Eugen (1852–1882), physicist, invented the pyrophone, a heat-powered organ; wrote on the theory of vibration and oscillation, and on the pyrophone.

Kas·tri·o·ti \,käs-trē-'ōt-ē\, George. *Known as* Skan·der·beg \'skän-dər-,beg\. *Turk.* Is·kan·der \ə-skän-'der\. 1405–1468. National hero of Albania. Son of John Kastrioti, prince of Emathia; as youth given as hostage to Turkish sultan; converted to Islām; served in Turkish army; given name Iskander and rank of Bey (hence Skanderbeg). Abandoned Turkish service (1443) and became Christian; organized (1444) a league of Albanian princes and elected commander in chief; repulsed 13 Turkish invasions (1444–66); his defeat of Murad II's armies (1450) made him a hero throughout Western world. After his death Albania soon became a part of the Ottoman Empire.

Ka·tay Don Sa·so·rith \kä-'tī-'dōn-sä-'sō-rēt\. *Also* Don Sasorith Katay. *Pen name* William Rab·bit \'rab-ət\. 1904–1959. Laotian politician. Civil servant in French administration of Laos (1926 ff.); chief spokesman for national resistance movement during World War II; minister of finance in provisional government (1945–46); from exile in Thailand (1946–49) exhorted expulsion of French, esp. in *Contribution à l'histoire du mouvement d'independence national Lao* (1948) written under his pen name. Elected to National Assembly (1951); premier of Laos (1954–56); zealous opponent of the Pathet Lao.

Ka·ta·yev \(,)kə-'tä-yəf\, Yevgeny Petrovich. *Pseudonym* Yevgeny Pe·trov \'pyä-trəf\. 1903–1942. Soviet writer. Collaborated with Ilya Faynzilberg (*q.v.*) on satiric short stories for *Pravda* and on humorous adventure novels *Dvenadtsat stulyev* (1928), *Zolotoy telyonok* (1931), and *Odnoetazhnaya Amerika* (1936); war correspondent (1941–42).

Kâ·tib Çe·le·bî \kä-'təb-chā-lā-'bē\. *Arab.* Kha·tīb Che·le·bī \kä-'tēb-\. *Also known as* Haci Ha·li·fa \hä-lē-'fä\ *and* Ḥājjī Kha·lī·fa \kä-'lē-fä\. 1609–1657. Turkish historian, geographer, and scholar. Close observer of Ottoman decline. Author of bibliographical encyclopedia of Arabic, Persian, Turkish books *Kashf al-ẓunūn'an;* first Turkish geographical work to make use of European atlases, *Jihannuma;* Ottoman naval history *Tuhfat al-Kibar fi Asfar il-Bahar;* treatise on economic reform *Dustūr al-amal li islah al-khalal;* etc.

Katharine *or* **Katharina.** See CATHERINE.

Kat·kov \(,)kət-'kòf\, Mikhail Nikiforovich. 1818–1887. Russian journalist. Editor of Moscow *News* (1851–87); a leader of Slavophile movement but a reactionary; personal adviser of Alexander III.

Ka·tō \kä-tō\ Hiroyuki. 1836–1916. Japanese educator and political theorist. Entered government office for study of foreign documents (1860); after Meiji Restoration (1868), appointed private tutor to the emperor and held high government posts in education and foreign affairs. Advocated adoption of European models of government, democracy, and human rights, esp. in books *Shinsei Taii* (1870) and *Kokutai Shinron* (1874); later (c.1880) became more reactionary. First president of Tokyo Imperial U. (1890–1900); created baron (1900); made member of Privy Council (1906).

Katō Kiyomasa. 1562–1611. Japanese soldier. In service of his relative Toyotomi Hideyoshi (to 1598); led Toyotomi's campaign in Korea (1592); aided regent Tokugawa Ieyasu's attempt to unify Japan (from 1598) but remained loyal to rightful heir Toyotomi Hideyori.

Katō Takaakira. *Known also as* Katō Kōmei. 1860–1926. Japanese politician. Ambassador to London (1894–99, 1908–13); foreign minister (1900, 1906, 1913, 1914–15); organized the Kenseikai or Constitutionalist party (1913); premier of coalition cabinet (1924–26); instituted democratic policies as universal male suffrage, reduction of army and of power of House of Peers, and moderate social legislation.

Ka·to·na \kä-'tò-nä\, József. 1791–1830. Hungarian lawyer and playwright. Author of several dramas, esp. *Bánk bán* (1815), often considered greatest Hungarian tragedy.

Ka·tsu \kät-sü\ Awa. *Also called* Katsu Yasuyoshi *and* Kai·shū \kī-shü\. 1823–1899. Japanese naval officer. Commanded first Japanese ship to sail to the West (1860); helped strengthen coastal defenses and modernize navy; commander in chief of armed forces (c.1867); peacefully surrendered shogunal forces during Meiji Restoration (1868); made minister of the navy (1872) and member of privy council (1873).

Ka·tsu·ka·wa \kät-sùk-ä-wä\ Shunshō. *Professional name* Tsu·bo \tsùb-ō\ Shunshō. 1726–1792. Japanese painter. Known for portrayals of actors and of scenes from the theater.

Ka·tsu·ra \kät-sùr-ä\ Tarō. Prince. 1847–1913. Japanese soldier and politician. Premier (1901–06, 1908–11, 1912–13); concluded alliance with Great Britain (1902), successfully conducted Russo–Japanese War (1904–05); annexed Korea (1910); founded (1913) Rikken Dōshi-kai party.

Kauff·man \'kaùf-män\, Nikolaus. *Lat.* Nicolaus Mer·ca·tor \(,)mər-'kāt-ər\. c.1619–1687. German mathematician and astronomer. Resident in London (from c.1660); commissioned to construct Versailles fountains (1683). Known for work in trigonometry, spherical geometry, astronomy, theory of numbers.

Kauff·mann \'kaùf-män\, Angelica, *in full* Maria Anna Angelica. 1741–1807. Swiss painter. In London (1766–81); friend of Sir Joshua Reynolds, who influenced her and whose portrait she painted (1766); an original member of Royal Academy (1769); helped decorate St. Paul's, London (1773); resident in Rome (from 1781), where she befriended Goethe and J.G. von Herder. Her Neoclassical paintings included pastoral, mythological, and historical subjects and portraits and self-portraits; also known for her decorative wall paintings for residences designed by Robert Adam (during 1770s).

Kauf·man \'kaùf-mən\, Denis. *Pseudonym* Dzi·ga Ver·tov \'dzyē-gəv-'yer-təf\. 1895–1954. Soviet film director. Newsreel cameraman during Russian Civil War; developed film-eye (kino-eye) theory that had international influence on development of documentaries and cinema realism during 1920s; organized (1919) Kinoki (Film-Eye Group) to disseminate his theory; later, a director in Central Documentary Film Studio. His pictures included *Shagay, Sovet* (1925), *Shestaya chast mira* (1926), *Odinnadsaty* (1928), *Chelovek skinoapparatom* (1929), *Simfoniya Donbassa* (1930), *Tri pesni o Lenine* (1934).

Kauf·man \'kòf-mən\, George Simon. 1889–1961. American playwright, b. Pittsburgh. Wrote for drama department of *New York Times* (1917–30). Author of *The Butter and Egg Man* (1925); coauthor of *Dulcy* (1921), *Merton* *of the Movies* (1922), and *Beggar on Horseback* (1924), with Marc Connelly; of *Minick* (1924), *The Royal Family* (1927), *Dinner at Eight* (1932), *Stage Door* (1936), *The Land Is Bright* (1941), with Edna Ferber; of *June Moon* (1929) with Ring Lardner; of *Once in a Lifetime* (1930), *You Can't Take It with You* (1936, Pulitzer prize), *I'd Rather Be Right* (1937), *The Man Who Came to Dinner* (1939), with Moss Hart; of *The Solid Gold Cadillac* (1953) with Howard Teichmann; of *Silk Stockings* (1955) with Abe Burrows; coauthor also of the musical comedies *Cocoanuts* (1925), *Animal Crackers* (1928), *The Band Wagon* (1931), *Of Thee I Sing* (1932), etc.

Kauf·mann \'kaůf-mən\, Konstantin Petrovich. 1818–1882. Russian general. Governor general of Turkistan (1867–82); took Samarkand (1868); subjugated khanates of Bokhara, Khiva, and Kokand, bringing Russian domain to Afghan border (1868–75).

Kauikeaouli. See KAMEHAMEHA III.

Kaul·bach \'kaůl-bä<u>k</u>\. Family of German painters, including: Wilhelm von Kaulbach (1805–1874), historical painter and illustrator; pupil of Peter von Cornelius; settled in Berlin (1847–65), where he and his pupils decorated the grand staircase of the Neues Museum with 6 historic murals illustrating the evolution of civilization; director of Munich Academy (1849–74). His works included many ceiling and mural paintings and illustrations to *Reynard the Fox* (1841) and poetry books. His son ¶Hermann (1846–1909) was illustrator and painter chiefly of historical genre scenes. ¶Friedrich Kaulbach (1822–1903), nephew and pupil of Wilhelm, was historical and portrait painter; court painter in Hanover. ¶Friedrich August von Kaulbach (1850–1920), son of Friedrich, was genre and portrait painter; director, Munich Art Academy (1886–91).

Kaun \'kaun\, Hugo. 1863–1932. German composer. His works included operas *Sappho* (1917), *Der Fremde* (1920), and *Menandra* (1925), three symphonies, overtures, piano pieces, a Requiem, male choruses, chamber music, songs, etc.

Kau·nitz \'kaů-nits\, Wenzel Anton von. Prince von Kaunitz-Riet·berg \-'rēt-berk\. 1711–1794. Austrian statesman. Entered foreign service (1740); ambassador at Turin (1742–44); negotiator in interests of Maria Theresa at Peace Congress in Aachen (1748); ambassador at Paris (1750–53). State chancellor and director of foreign policy (1753–92); effected Austro-Russo-French coalition against Frederick the Great during Seven Years' War (1756–63); negotiated Peace of Paris (1763); created prince (1764); represented Austria in first partition of Poland (1772); acquired Bucovina from Turks (1775); organized and centralized administration of many Habsburg domains; influenced domestic policies of Maria Theresa, Joseph II, and Leopold II.

Kau·pert \'kaů-pərt\, Gustav. 1819–1897. German sculptor. Executed, after Thomas Crawford's designs, reliefs and figures for a monument in Richmond, Va., and the colossal bronze statue on dome of Capitol in Washington; original works included *Sleeping Lion* on Hessian memorial at Kassel (1874) and *Christ and the Evangelists* at Trier (c.1880–87).

Kau·ṭil·ya \kaů-'til-yə\. fl. 300 B.C. Indian philosopher and politician. Adviser to Candragupta, king of the Mauryan Empire. Author of *Artha-śāstra, a* classic treatise on polity much used by Candragupta. Kauṭilya is believed by some to have been a pen name used by the Hindu philosopher Cāṇakya.

Kaut·sky \'kaůt-skē\, Karl Johann. 1854–1938. German Marxist theorist, b. Prague. Joined Social Democratic party in Vienna (1875); private secretary to Friedrich Engels in London (1881); founded in Stuttgart (1883) and edited in London and Stuttgart (until 1917) Marxist review *Die neue Zeit*. Chief creator of the Erfurt program (1891); opposed Bernstein's reform Marxist policy. Co-organizer (with Haase) and member of Independent Socialist Democratic party (1917–22); opposed Bolshevism and Russian Revolution, and refused to join United German Communist party. Settled in Vienna and rejoined Socialist Democratic party (1917); edited German Foreign Office documents on origins of World War I (1919); became naturalized citizen of Czechoslovakia (1934). Author of *Karl Marx' ökonomische Lehren* (1887), *Thomas More und seine Utopie* (1888), *Die soziale Revolution* (1903), *Die Diktatur des Proletariats* (1918), etc.

Ka·vadh \ka-'väd\. *Arab.* Qo·bād \kȯ-'bäd\. Name of two Sāsānid kings of Persia:

Kavadh I. d. 531. King (488–96, 499–531). Son of Fīrūz; succeeded his uncle Balāsh; at first favored Mazdakites; deposed by his brother Jāmāsp (496); lived with Hephtalites, who restored him to throne; made war against Romans (503–505, 524–531); withdrew support of Mazdakites and ordered great massacre (523) of them; invaded Syria and defeated Belisarius (531). Succeeded by his son Khosrow I.

Kavadh II. d. 628. King (628). Son of Khosrow II, whom he deposed and slew.

Ka·vá·fis \kä-'vä-fēs\, Konstantínos Pétrou. *Pseudonym* Constantine Ca·va·fy \kä-'vä-fē\. 1863–1933. Greek poet. Known for small body of work, some 200 poems in intimate, realistic, lyrical style, viewing the world from a consciously nonconformist point of view.

Kav·a·nagh \'kav-ə-nə, -ˌnä\, Patrick. 1905–1967. Irish writer. Journalist in Dublin. Known esp. for long poem *The Great Hunger* (1942) and novel *Tarry Flynn* (1948), both depicting Irish country life; also wrote autobiography *A Green Fool* (1939) and volumes of verse *A Soul for Sale* (1947) and *Come Dance with Kitty Stobling* (1960).

Ka·wa·ba·ta \kä-wä-bä-tä\ Yasunari. 1899–1972. Japanese novelist. Author of *Izu no Odoriko* (1925), *Yukiguni* (1947, *Snow Country*), *Yama no oto* (1949–54), *Sembazuru* (1959, *Thousand Cranes*), etc. First Japanese to win Nobel prize for literature (1968).

Ka·wai \kä-wī\ Gyokudō. *Orig.* Kawai Yoshisaburō. 1873–1957. Japanese painter. Studied under Kōno Bairyū and Hashimoto Gahō; developed a highly personal style, esp. in his landscapes. Works included *The New Moon, The Departing Springs, Evening at the Mountain Top, Snow in the Evening.*

Kawai Kanjirō. 1890–1963. Japanese potter. Set up kiln in Kyōto (1920); with Yanagi Sōetsu and Hamada Shōji, founded (1925) folk art movement, developing ceramic ware for daily use employing traditional Japanese and English designs; after World War II, involved in mass production of pottery with handicraft characteristics. Works included celadon porcelain flower vase with blood-red figure (1924), pot with grass and flowers colored in copper-red and iron-black (1937), and flat pot with *uchi-gusuri* glazing (1962).

Ka·wa·ka·mi \kä-wä-kä-mē\ Hajime. 1879–1946. Japanese economist. One of first Marxist theoreticians in Japan. Instructor (1908), professor of economics (1915–28), Kyōto Imperial U.; imprisoned (1932–37) for engaging in Communist political activities. Translated E.R.A. Seligman's *Economic Interpretation of History,* first analysis of dialectical materialism to appear in Japanese; expounded Marxist economics in his magazine *Shakai mondai kenkyū*. Author of *Keizagaku taikō* (1928) and an introduction to Japanese edition of *Das Kapital.*

Kawakami Otojirō. 1864–1911. Japanese actor and playwright. Founder of *Soshi* drama; wrote first Japanese plays based on Western models; introduced to Japan productions of Shakespeare, Maurice Maeterlinck, and Victorien Sardou.

Ka·wa·na·be \kä-wä-näb-ē\ Gyōsai. *Also used pseudonym* Shō·jō \shō-jō\ (*i.e.* Drunken) Gyōsai. 1831–1889. Japanese painter and caricaturist. Studied under Utagawa Kuniyoshi and Kanō Tōhaku; later embraced popular school and was influenced by Hokusai; often imprisoned for his caricatures published during and after political revolution of 1867. Known for sketches of goblins and animals, esp. birds, fish, and reptiles.

Kay *or* **Kaye,** John. 1510–1573. See John CAIUS.

Kay \'kā\, John. 1704–1764. English inventor. Invented flying shuttle (patented 1733) used in weaving.

Ka·yen·bergh \'kä-yəm-ˌber<u>k</u>\, Marie-Émile-Albert. *Pseudonym* Albert Giraud \zhē-rō\. 1860–1929. Belgian poet. A founder of *La Jeune Belgique* (1881); editor of *Étoile Belge*. Author of *Pierrot lunaire* (1884), *Pierrot narcisse* (1891), *Dernières fêtes* (1891), *Guirlande des dieux* (1910), *La Frise empourpée* (1912).

Kaye-Smith \'kā-'smith\, Emily Sheila. 1887–1956. English novelist. Known esp. for tales laid in Sussex; among her novels were *Sussex Gorse* (1916), *Tamarisk Town* (1919), *Green Apple Harvest* (1921), *Joanna Godden* (1921), *The Village Doctor* (1929), *The Valiant Woman* (1938), *Ember Lane* (1940).

Kay·ser \'kī-zər\, Heinrich Gustav Johannes. 1853–1940. German physicist. Professor at Bonn (1894–1920). Collaborated with Carl Runge in mapping of large number of spectra of specific elements, in discovery of spectral series, and in development (1883) of mathematical formula showing relationship of series; discovered helium in Earth's atmosphere (1895). Wrote *Lehrbuch der Spectralanalyse* (1883), *Handbuch der Spectroskopie* (1900–34), etc.

Kay-Shut·tle·worth \'kā-'shət-əl-ˌwərth\, Sir James Phillips. Baronet. *Surname orig.* Kay. 1804–1877. English physician and public health reformer. Chief founder of English system of publicly financed elementary education; with E. Carleton Tufnell founded (1839–40) St. John's College, London, one of first normal schools in England.

Ka·zant·za·kis \kä-zänt-'zä-kēs\, Nikos. 1885–1957. Greek writer. Best known for epic *Odysseia* (1938) and novels *Víos kai politía tou Aléxi Zormpá* (1946, *Zorba the Greek*), *Kapetan Mikhalis* (1948), *Christos xanastavronetai* (1948), *Televtaio peirasmo* (1951); also published philosophic essays, lyric poetry, tragedies, travel books, and translations of Dante's *Divine Comedy* and Goethe's *Faust.*

Kazimierz. See CASIMIR.

Ka·zin·czy \'kä-zin-tsē\, Ferenc. 1759–1831. Hungarian writer and linguistic reformer. Sought to promote contemporary Hungarian literary activity; as leader of the neologists, championed a modern Hungarian language. Author of translations into Magyar from German, French, English, and the classical languages, and of plays, poems, and prose works.

Kean \'kēn\, Edmund. 1789–1833. English actor. Made striking success at Drury Lane as Shylock (1814), and followed this with Hamlet, Othello, Iago, Macbeth, Lear, and Richard III; reintroduced a naturalistic style of acting; last stage appearance (1833). Unrivaled in his day as a tragedian. His son ¶Charles John (1811–1868) acted in his company (1827–33) and independently; leased Princess's Theatre (1850) and directed series of revivals of great plays; toured in Australia, America, and Jamaica (1863–66); m. (1842) ¶Ellen Tree \'trē\ (1805–1880), actress at Drury Lane (1826–29), Covent Garden (1829–36, 39–42), and in America (1836–39, 1845–47), who played opposite him (1842–68); excelled as Gertrude in *Hamlet* and Viola in *Twelfth Night*.

Kear·ny \'kär-nē\, Stephen Watts. 1794–1848. American army officer, b. Newark, N.J. Promoted to captain during War of 1812; on frontier duty thereafter. Brigadier general in Mexican War; conquered New Mexico; moved westward to California; fought inconclusive action at San Pascual (Dec. 6, 1846); aided by Robert F. Stockton (*q.v.*), occupied Los Angeles (Jan. 10, 1847); after later conflict of authority with Stockton, arrested Lieut. J.C. Frémont (*q.v.*) for refusing to carry out his orders; military governor of Vera Cruz and later Mexico City (1848); major general. His nephew ¶Philip Kearny (1814–1862), b. New York City, was also an army officer (1837–51), serving in Mexican War; served with French army in Italy (1859); awarded cross of the French Legion of Honor; brigadier general of volunteers, Union army (1861), major general (1862); killed on reconnoitering expedition.

Kea·ton \'kēt-ᵊn\, Joseph Francis, *known as* Buster. 1895–1966. American comedian, b. Piqua, Kans. On vaudeville stage from childhood; made first film *The Butcher Boy* (1917); writer, director, and star of silent film comedies including *The Navigator* (1924), *Seven Chances* (1925), *The General* (1926), *Steamboat Bill Jr.* (1928), *The Cameraman* (1928); famed for deadpan character in conflict with machines; revived career in *Sunset Boulevard* (1950), *Limelight* (1952), *It's a Mad Mad Mad Mad World* (1963), etc.

Keats \'kēts\, John. 1795–1821. English poet. Studied medicine but never practiced. First published verse was sonnet "O Solitude" in Leigh Hunt's *Examiner* (May 5, 1816), followed by sonnet "On First Looking into Chapman's Homer" (Dec. 1816) and other sonnets (1817); published *Poems* (1817) and long mythological poem *Endymion* (1818). In spring of 1819 wrote narrative poem "The Eve of St. Agnes," lyrical poem "La Belle Dame sans Merci," and odes "On Melancholy," "To a Nightingale," "On a Grecian Urn," "To Psyche." Fell in love with Fanny Brawne. Published *Lamia and other Poems* (1820). Health failing, went to Italy; died in Rome. His *Hyperion* (begun 1818) remained unfinished at death. His poetry marked by vivid imagery, sensuous appeal, and use of classical themes.

Ke·ble \'kē-bəl\, John. 1792–1866. English clergyman and poet. Professor of poetry, Oxford (1831–41); vicar of Hursley, Hampshire (1836–66). By his sermon "National Apostasy" (1833), initiated Oxford Movement. Published collection of his hymns in *Christian Year* (1827); wrote number of *Tracts for the Times* in support of Oxford Movement; edited Richard Hooker (1836). Keble College, Oxford, founded in his honor (1869).

Keck \'kek\, Charles. 1875–1951. American sculptor, b. New York City. Among his works were equestrian monuments of Stonewall Jackson at Charlottesville, Va., and Andrew Jackson at Kansas City, Mo.; monuments of Booker T. Washington at Tuskegee, Ala., and James B. Duke at Durham, N.C.; and portrait busts of James Madison, Patrick Henry, and Elias Howe for the American Hall of Fame, New York.

Kee·ler \'kē-lər\, James Edward. 1857–1900. American astronomer, b. LaSalle, Ill. Director, Allegheny Observatory (1891–98) and Lick Observatory (1898–1900). Specialist in spectroscopy; determined wave length of the fundamental green line of the nebular spectrum; demonstrated truth of Maxwell's theory regarding meteoric constitution of rings of Saturn.

Keeler, William Henry, *known as* Wee Willie. 1872–1923. American baseball player, b. Brooklyn, N.Y. In major leagues (1892–1910), esp. with National League Baltimore Orioles (1894–98); career batting average .341 or .345; batting champion (1897, 1898). Elected to Baseball Hall of Fame (1939).

Kee·ly \'kē-lē\, John Ernst Worrell. 1827–1898. American fraud. Claimed invention of a perpetual-motion system (1873); organized Keely Motor Co., Philadelphia, to sell stock in this system, proven a fraud after his death.

Keen \'kēn\, William Williams. 1837–1932. American surgeon, b. Philadelphia. Surgeon, U.S. army, in Civil War; practiced at Philadelphia (from 1866); professor at Jefferson Medical College, Philadelphia (1889–1907). Pioneer in brain surgery. Edited *Surgery: Its Principles and Practice* (1906–13).

Keene, Carolyn. See Edward STRATEMEYER.

Keene \'kēn\, Charles Samuel. 1823–1891. English artist. On staff of *Punch* (from 1851); known for gentle satires of lower- and middle-class subjects; published collection of *Punch* drawing as *Our People* (1881).

Keene, Laura. *Orig.* Mary Moss \'mȯs\. c.1826–1873. American actress, b. London, England. On American stage (from 1852); excelled in light comedy; operated own theater in New York (1855–63), first important woman theater manager in U.S.; was acting in *Our American Cousin* at Ford's Theatre, Washington, D.C., the night President Lincoln was assassinated there.

Kees, John. See John CAIUS.

Ke·fau·ver \'kē-ˌfȯ-vər\, Estes, *in full* Carey Estes. 1903–1963. American politician, b. near Madisonville, Tenn. Practiced law in Chattanooga (1927–39); Democratic member, U.S. House of Representatives (1939–49), U.S. Senate (1949–63); conducted televised Senate investigation of organized crime (1950–51); unsuccessful candidate for vice president of U.S. (1956).

Kei·fer \'kī-fər\, Joseph Warren. 1836–1932. American lawyer, soldier, and politician, b. near Springfield, Ohio. Practiced law (from 1858). In Civil War; brigadier general (1864) and major general (1865). Member, U.S. House of Representatives (1877–85, 1905–11; speaker 1881–83).

Keig·win \'keg-wən, 'kāg-\, Richard. d. 1690. English naval commander. Led attack on Dutch-held island of St. Helena in South Atlantic (1673); in Bombay in service of East India Company (1676–80, 1681–84); led "Keigwin's Rebellion" in capture of Bombay from company (Dec. 1683); ruled Bombay; surrendered to company and pardoned (Nov. 1684); killed while leading assault on Basseterre, St. Kitts, Leeward Islands.

Keiki. See under TOKUGAWA family.

Kei·ser \'kī-zər\, Reinhard. 1674–1739. German composer. Composed some 120 Baroque operas, including *Octavia* (1705), *Der angenehme Betrug* (1707), *Croesus* (1710), *Der lächerliche Printz Jodelet* (1726), *Circe* (1734); also oratorios, cantatas, motets, psalms, etc.

Kei·ta \'kā-tä\, Modibo. 1915–1977. Mali politician. A founder and leader of anticolonial Union Soudanaise party (1945) and multi-national Rassemblement Démocratique Africain (1946); member of territorial assembly of French Sudan (1948–58); deputy (1956–58) and first African vice president (1956–57) of French National Assembly; held two cabinet posts in French government (1957–58). President of Council of Sudanese Republic (1959–60); campaigned for a West African federation of former French territories; president of Mali Federation (1959–60). First president of Mali (1960–68); ousted by military coup because of pro-Communist policies.

Kei·tel \'kīt-ᵊl\, Wilhelm. 1882–1946. German field marshal. Entered army (1901); captain in World War I; major general (1934); chief of staff of armed forces office (1935–38). On army reorganization (1938), Hitler assumed personal and direct command of Germany's armed forces, exercising his authority through a supreme command headed by Keitel; read terms of armistice to French representatives (June 1940); in command on Russian front (1941); signed act of military surrender (May 9, 1945); hanged as war criminal.

Keith, Viscount. See George Keith Elphinstone under ELPHINSTONE family.

Keith \'kēth\, Sir Arthur. 1866–1955. Scottish anthropologist. Professor, Royal Institution, London (1918–23); rector, U. of Aberdeen (1930–33); master of research institute at Downe, Kent (1933–55). Specialized in study of fossil man. Author of *Ancient Types of Man* (1911), *The Antiquity of Man* (1915), *Concerning Man's Origin* (1927), *Darwinism and its Critics* (1935), *A New Theory of Human Evolution* (1948), etc.

Keith, Benjamin Franklin. 1846–1914. American theatrical manager, b. Hillsboro, N.H. Associated with E. F. Albee (*q.v.*) in establishing Boston Bijou Theatre (1885) and in operating Keith-Albee theater circuit, eventually controlling some 400 vaudeville theaters across U.S.

Keith, James Francis Edward. 1696–1758. Scottish soldier. Forced into exile after participating in Alberoni's futile Jacobite expedition (1719); colonel in Spanish army (1719–28); in Russian army (1728–47), distinguishing himself in War of Polish Succession (1733–35) and in campaigns against Turkey (1737) and Sweden (1741–43). In Prussian service (1747 ff.); created field marshal by Frederick the Great and served as his close adviser; during Seven Years' War commanded Prussian forces at siege of Prague (1757) and successfully defended Leipzig against the Austrians; killed at Battle of Hochkirch.

Keith, William. 1839–1911. American painter, b. Old Meldrum, Scotland. To U.S. as a boy; settled in California (1859). Known for his California landscapes.

Kei·zan \kā-zän\. *Posthumous name* Jō-sai \jō-sī\ Daishi. *Also called* Tai·so \tī-sō\, *i.e.* Great Master. 1267–1325. Japanese priest. Member of Sōtō sect of Buddhism; founded many temples, esp. Sōji-ji (1321) in modern Ishikawa Prefecture; popularized teachings of Sōtō founder Dōgen and now worshipped as restorer of the Sōtō sect.

Kek·ko·nen \'kek-ə-nən, -ˌnen\, Urho Kaleva. 1900–1986. Finnish politician. President of Finland (1956–81). Carefully steered foreign policy course, known as "Finlandization," that allowed Finland to trade with the West and keep good relations with the U.S.S.R.

Ke·ku·le von Stra·do·nitz \'kā-kü-lā-fȯn-'shträ-dō-nits\, Friedrich August. *Surname orig.* Kekulé. 1829–1896. German chemist. Known esp. for work on constitution of organic compounds; set forth doctrine of the linking of carbon atoms; showed that carbon is tetravalent (1858); originated the ring, or closed-chain, theory of the constitution of the benzene molecule (1865). Author of *Lehrbuch der organischen Chemie* (1861–87).

Kel·lar \'kel-ər\, Harry. *Surname orig.* Keller. 1849–1922. American magician, b. Erie, Pa. First great magician native to U.S. Opened his first full evening show (1884); reigned supreme (1896–1908); called "dean of magic".

Kel·ler \'kel-ər\, Ferdinand. 1800–1881. Swiss archaeologist. A founder of Zürich Antiquarian Society (1832); pioneer in European prehistoric archaeology. Discovered lake dwellings of Obermeilen on Lake Zürich (1854); organized researches on Swiss lake dwellings.

Keller, Gottfried. 1819–1890. Swiss writer. Most representative national author of the German-speaking Swiss. Author of collections of verse, novels *Der grüne Heinrich* (autobiographical, 1854–55, rev. 1879–80) and *Martin Salander* (1886), and short stories of Swiss provincial life, some collected in *Die Leute von Seldwyla* (1856–74) and *Sieben Legenden* (1872).

Keller, Helen Adams. 1880–1968. American author and lecturer, b. Tuscumbia, Ala. Left blind, deaf, and mute by illness at age of 19 months. Educated (1887–1936) by Anne Sullivan Macy (*q.v.*). Lecturer in U.S. and abroad on behalf of the blind. Author of *The Story of My Life* (1902), *The World I Live In* (1908), *Out of the Dark* (1913), *My Religion* (1927), *Helen Keller's Journal* (1938), *The Open Door* (1957), etc.

Kel·ler·mann \'kel-ər-ˌmän\, Bernard. 1879–1951. German novelist. Author of *Yester und Li* (1904), *Ingeborg* (1906), *Der Tor* (1909), *Das Meer* (1910), *Der Tunnel* (1913), *Der Krieg im Westen* (1915), *Krieg in Argonnerwald* (1916), *Der Neunte November* (1920), *Die Brüder Schellenberg* (1925), *Das blaue Band* (1938); also of works on his travels in Japan and the East.

Kel·ler·mann \kā-ler-mȧn\, François-Christophe. Duc de Val·my \də-vȧl-mē\. 1735–1820. French soldier. Entered army (1752); fought with distinction in Seven Years' War (1756–63); promoted field marshal (1788), lieutenant general (1792). Commanded army of the Moselle (1792) and cooperated with Dumouriez in defeating the Prussians at Valmy (Sept. 20, 1792). Commanded army of the Alps (1792–93, 1795–97); recaptured Savoy (1793); appointed senator (1804); created marshal of France (1804), duc de Valmy (1808), and a peer (1814). His son ¶François-Étienne (1770–1835) was one of Napoléon's generals; brigadier general (1797); led decisive charge at Marengo (1800) and was promoted general of division; prominent at Austerlitz and Waterloo.

Kel·ley \'kel-ē\, Florence. 1859–1932. American reformer, b. Philadelphia. Resident at Hull-House, Chicago (1891–99); helped create and first holder of post of Illinois state factory inspector (1895–97); general secretary, National Consumers' League, New York City (1899–1932); founded National Child Labor Committee (1902); helped found National Association for the Advancement of Colored People (1909). Author of *Some Ethical Gains through Legislation* (1905), *Modern Industry* (1913).

Kelley, Oliver Hudson. 1826–1913. American agricultural organizer, b. Boston. An organizer (1868) and secretary (1868–78) of National Grange of the Patrons of Husbandry; zealous in promoting its growth; wrote *Origin and Progress of the Patrons of Husbandry* (1875).

Kell·gren \'ḵel-grān\, Johan Henrik. 1751–1795. Swedish poet. Cofounder and critic (1778), then owner and editor (from 1788) of the journal *Stockholmsposten;* championed rationalism. Librarian (1780), private secretary (from 1785), and literary adviser to Gustav III. Author of satirical, lyrical, and patriotic verse, esp. *Mina löjen* (1778) and *Den Nya Skapelsen eller Ibillningens värld* (1789); also wrote verse dramas and collaborated with Gustav on opera *Gustaf Wasa* (1786).

Kel·logg \'kel-ˌȯg, -ˌäg\, Frank Billings. 1856–1937. American lawyer, politician, and diplomat, b. Potsdam, N.Y. Practiced law in Minnesota; special counsel for government in successful antitrust suits against Standard Oil (1906) and Union Pacific Railroad (1907). U.S. senator (1917–23); U.S. ambassador to Great Britain (1923–25); U.S. secretary of state (1925–29). With Aristide Briand negotiated Kellogg-Briand Pact to outlaw war as an instrument of national policy (1928). Awarded Nobel peace prize for 1929. Judge, Permanent Court of International Justice (1930–35).

Kellogg, John Harvey. 1852–1943. American physician, b. Tyrone, Mich. Superintendent, Battle Creek (Mich.) Sanitarium (from 1876); founder and president (1923–26), Battle Creek College; founder (1931) and medical director, Miami-Battle Creek Sanitarium, Miami Springs, Florida. Aided by his brother Will, developed dry breakfast cereals for use in his sanitarium; wrote numerous medical books. His brother ¶Will Keith (1860–1951), b. Battle Creek, Mich., took position at Battle Creek Sanitarium (1880) and helped John in his nutritional experiments. Founder (1906), president (1906–29), board chairman (1929–46), W.K. Kellogg Co., which became a leading manufacturer of cornflakes and other prepared breakfast foods; established major philanthropic institution, W.K. Kellogg Foundation (1930).

Kel·ly \'kel-ē\, Alvin Anthony. *Known as* Shipwreck Kelly. 1893–1952. American stunt man. Famous during 1920s for spending long periods of time on high perches; sat atop a flagpole at Atlantic City for 1177 hours (1930).

Kelly, Colin P. 1915–1941. American army officer, b. Madison, Fla. Pilot of bomber that destroyed Japanese battleship *Haruna* (Dec. 9, 1941) following attack on Pearl Harbor; when his airplane was damaged by enemy fire, ordered crew to bail out; died in crash.

Kelly, Emmett Lee. 1898–1979. American clown, b. Sedan, Kans. Created (1923) role of "Weary Willie," a mournful tramp dressed in tattered business suit with a growth of beard and a bulbous nose; appeared in this role with English and American circuses, esp. Ringling Bros. and Barnum & Bailey Circus (1942–57), in films as *The Greatest Show on Earth* (1952).

Kelly, George. 1887–1974. American actor and playwright, b. Philadelphia. Author of *The Torchbearers* (1922), *The Show-Off* (1924), *Craig's Wife* (1925, Pulitzer prize), *Maggie the Magnificent* (1929), *Philip Goes Forth* (1931), *Reflected Glory* (1936), *The Fatal Weakness* (1946).

Kelly, George. *Known as* Machine Gun Kelly. *Orig.* George Kelly Barnes \'bärnz\, Jr. 1895–1954. American gangster, b. Memphis, Tenn. Gained notoriety (by 1933) for series of robberies and slayings in Midwest; kidnapped Oklahoma millionaire Charles F. Urschel (July 1933); arrested (Sept. 1933), convicted, and spent rest of life in prison.

Kelly, Grace. Princess Grace of Monaco. 1929–1982. American actress, b. Philadelphia. Known as a leading lady of patrician beauty and cool reserve. Niece of playwright George Kelly. Made film debut in *Fourteen Hours* (1951). Other films included *High Noon* (1952), *The Country Girl* (1954, Academy Award), *Dial M for Murder* (1954), *Rear Window* (1954), and *To Catch a Thief* (1955). m. (1956) Prince Rainier of Monaco and retired from films.

Kelly, Howard Atwood. 1858–1943. American physician, b. Camden, N.J. Professor of gynecology, Johns Hopkins, and chief gynecologist, Johns Hopkins Hospital (1899–1919). Devised operations to correct retroposition of the uterus; among first to use radium in cancer treatment; invented a rectal and vesical speculum. Author of *Operative Gynecology* (1898, 1906), *Cyclopedia of American Medical Biography* (1912), etc.

Kelly, Hugh. 1739–1777. Irish playwright. Author of comedies *False Delicacy* (1768), *A Word to the Wise* (1770), *The School for Wives* (1773), *The Romance of an Hour* (1774), *The Man of Reason* (1776); also of *Thespis* (1766–67, literary criticism) and *Memoirs of a Magdalen* (1767, novel).

Kelly, Ned, *in full* Edward. 1855–1880. Australian outlaw. Last and most famous bushranger (Australian rural outlaw); led gang in series of daring robberies on Victoria–New South Wales borderland (1878–80); captured and hanged; became symbol of protest against arbitrary authority and rich landowners.

Kelly, Walter Crawford, *known as* Walt. 1913–1973. American cartoonist and illustrator, b. Philadelphia. Worked as animator for Walt Disney Productions, Hollywood (1935–41); commercial artist in New York City (1941 ff.). Created (1948) comic strip "Pogo," eventually syndicated in over 450 newspapers; also illustrated children's books and published collections of "Pogo" strips.

Kelly, William. 1811–1888. American inventor, b. Pittsburgh. Invented (c.1850) converter (later known as Bessemer converter, from Sir Henry Bessemer's similar process) for the making of steel, utilizing an air blast on molten iron to obtain greater heat for the process; patent issued (1857).

Kel·sey \'kel-sē\, Henry. d. 1729. English explorer. Entered service of Hudson's Bay Company (1687); on expedition to Manitoba, Canada, to find new sources of fur (1690–92); possibly first European to explore central Canada.

Kelvin, Baron. See William THOMSON.

Ke·mal \ke-'mäl\, Namık, *in full* Mehmed Namık. 1840–1888. Turkish writer, journalist, and patriot. Became disciple of İbrahim Şinasi; edited (1865–67) Şinasi's newspaper *Tasvir-i Efkâr* after Şinasi fled to Paris; member of secret revolutionary society Young Ottomans; fled to London (1867), publishing newspaper *Hürriyet* there (1868) and continuing revolutionary novels in Paris and Vienna. Returned to Turkey (1871), becoming editor of newspaper *İbret;* enthusiastic reception of performance of his patriotic play *Vatan yahnut Silistre* (1872) caused his imprisonment (1873–76); governor of Sakız (1888). His ideas of *vatan* (fatherland) and *hürriyet* (freedom) helped establish a Turkish national consciousness and greatly influenced the Young Turk and other Turkish nationalist movements. Championed rejection of classical Ottoman literary forms and adoption of European models. Works included verse, plays *Zavallı çocuk* (1873) and *Akif Bey* (1874), historical novels *İntibah* (1874) and *Cezmi* (1887/88), political essays as *Rüya* (1907), historical works, and translations of Hugo, Rousseau, Montesquieu, and others.

Kemal Atatürk. See ATATÜRK.

Ke·mal·pa·şa·zâ·de \kā-ˌmäl-pä-ˌshä-zä-'de\. *Known also as* Ibn Ke·mal \ˌib-ən-kā-'mäl\ *and* Ibn Kemal Pa·şa \-pä-'shä\. *In full* Şemseddin Ahmet ibn Süleyman ibn Kemal Paşa. c.1468–1534. Turkish scholar, poet, and historian. Taught at religious colleges; commissioned by Sultan Bayezid II to write *Tevarih-i Al-i Osman,* a chronicle covering Ottoman history of 1481–1526. Military judge of Anatolia (1516–17); appointed Shaykh al-Islām by Sultan

Süleyman I, thus heading religious institutions of Ottoman Empire. His works included commentaries on the Qur'ān, treatises on jurisprudence and on Muslim theology and philosophy, philological work *Daqa'iq al-Haqa'iq,* and much verse, as *Nigaristan, Yusuf ü Züleyha,* and collection of lyrics *Divān.*

Kem·ble \'kem-bəl\. Name of English family of actors, including:
Roger Kemble (1721–1802); formed traveling company in which his children acted; acted Falstaff at the Haymarket, London (1788).
His children: See Sarah SIDDONS. ¶John Philip (1757–1823); with Drury Lane Theatre (1783–1802, its manager from 1788); introduced live animals and aquatic effects on stage for first time and made reforms in costumes, scenery, management; manager of Covent Garden (1803–17); played many Shakespearean roles; regarded as chief founder of declamatory school of acting. ¶Stephen, *in full* George Stephen (1758–1822), Shakespearean actor; managed Edinburgh Theatre (1792–1800); played Falstaff at Covent Garden (1806) and Drury Lane (1816). ¶Elizabeth (1761–1836), m. (1785) Charles E. Whitlock; accompanied him to America and acted there; appeared before President Washington. ¶Charles (1775–1854), actor at Drury Lane and Covent Garden; manager of Covent Garden (1822–36); first to use detailed historical sets and costumes on English stage; toured U.S. with his daughter Fanny (1832, 1834); excelled in comic roles; examiner of plays for government (1836–40); m. (1806) Maria Theresa De Camp \də-'kamp, ˌdē-\ (1774–1838), who acted (1786–1819) at Haymarket, Drury Lane, and Covent Garden theaters, esp. in Gay's *Beggar's Opera* (1792) and in her own plays *The Day After the Wedding* (1808) and *Smiles and Tears* (1815), as well as Shakespearean roles.
Charles's daughter ¶Frances Anne, *called* Fanny (1809–1893), acted (1829–34) in her father's company at Covent Garden; successful as Lady Teazle in *School for Scandal* and in Shakespearean roles; created role of Julia in James S. Knowles's *The Hunchback* (1832); toured U.S. (1832–34); retired (1834–47); again on stage 1847–68); gave dramatic readings in England and U.S.; resided in U.S. (1849–68, 1873–78). Author of poems, plays, and esp. her *Journal* (1835, 1863), valuable for stage and social information.

Kemble, Gouverneur. 1786–1875. American manufacturer, b. New York City. Established (1818) West Point Foundry, Cold Spring, N.Y., and produced the finest cannon of his day; known esp. for cannon designed by J.A.B. Dahlgren and his brother-in-law Robert P. Parrott (*qq.v.*); succeeded as head of foundry by Parrott (1839). Member, U.S. House of Representatives (1837–41). Friend of Washington Irving and appeared as "Cockloft" in his *Salmagundi* papers.

Ke·mény \'ke-mānʸ\, Zsigmond. Baron. 1814–1875. Hungarian novelist and journalist. Editor in Pest of *Pesti Napló* (1855–68), making it most influential newspaper in Hungarian politics; supporter of Ferenc Deák; by journalistic campaign prepared way for compromise (1867) between Hungary and the Habsburgs. Author of historical novels as *Gyulai Pál* (1847), *Özvegy és leánya* (1855), *A rajongók* (1858–59), *Zord idő* (1862), and of social novels as *Férj és nő* (1852).

Kem·mer·er \'kem-ər-ər\, Edwin Walter. 1875–1945. American economist, b. Scranton, Pa. Professor, Princeton (1912–43). Financial adviser to governments of 14 underdeveloped nations. Author of *The ABC of the Federal Reserve System* (1918).

Kemnitz, Martin. See CHEMNITZ.

Kemp *or* **Kempe** \'kemp\, John. c.1380–1454. English prelate. Chancellor of Normandy and keeper of privy seal (1418–22); bishop of Rochester (1419), of London (1421); on diplomatic missions for Henry V. Archbishop of York (1426–52) and chancellor of England (1426–32, 1450); strong supporter of Henry Beaufort against Humphrey, Duke of Gloucester; became leader of Lancastrian party of Henry VI; archbishop of Canterbury (1452). Created cardinal priest by Pope Eugenius IV (1439) and cardinal bishop by Pope Nicholas (1452).

Kemp, William. fl. 1600. English comedian and dancer. Played comic roles with Lord Strange's company (1588–94) and Chamberlain's Men (1594–1600), including original Dogberry in Shakespeare's *Much Ado About Nothing;* famous for jigs and for dancing a morris-dance from London to Norwich (1600).

Kempe \'kemp\, Margery, *nee* Brun·ham \'brün-əm\. c.1373–c.1440. English mystic. m. (1393) John Kempe, burgess of Lynn; made pilgrimages (1414–25) to Jerusalem, Rome, Germany, Spain. Described her travels and religious ecstasies in *The Book of Margery Kempe* (written c.1432–36), one of earliest autobiographies in English literature.

Kem·pe·neer \'kem-pə-när\, Pieter de. *Called in Spain* Pedro de Cam·pa·ña \thä-käm-'pän-yä\. 1503–1580. Flemish painter and tapestry designer. Lived in Seville (1537–62); director of tapestry factory in Brussels (1563 ff.). Painted *Descent from the Cross* (1547) and altarpiece *Purification of the Virgin* (1555), both in Seville cathedral.

Kem·pen·felt \'kem-pən-ˌfelt\, Richard. 1718–1782. English naval commander. Rear admiral (1780); gained brilliant victory over French fleet off Ushant (1781). Introduced French tactics and signaling system into British navy.

Kempis, Thomas à. See THOMAS À KEMPIS.

Ken *or* **Kenn** \'ken\, Thomas. 1637–1711. English prelate and hymn writer. Clergyman of Winchester cathedral (1669); appointed (1680) royal chaplain to Charles II and attended him on his deathbed. Bishop of Bath and Wells (1684–91). One of the "seven bishops" (see William SANCROFT) who petitioned against James II's Declaration of Indulgence (1688) but were acquitted of seditious libel; refused to take oath of allegiance to William and Mary (1689). Author of *Manual of Prayers* (1674) and of hymns, including "Praise God, From Whom All Blessings Flow," "Awake, My Soul, and With The Sun," and "Glory to Thee, My God, This Night."

Ken·dal \'ken-dᵊl\, Dame Madge. *Nee* Margaret Shafto Rob·ert·son \'räb-ərt-sən\. 1849–1935. English actress. Sister of T. W. Robertson; made London debut as Ophelia in *Hamlet* (1865); m. (1869) William Hunter Grim·ston \'grim-stən\ (1843–1917), *professional name* Kendal. With her husband acted in Shakespearean revivals and old English comedies, made annual tours of the provinces (1874–1908), and managed St. James's Theatre, London (1879–88). They brought social respectability to the acting profession by their personal and professional example and trained many performers.

Ken·dall \'ken-dᵊl\, Amos. 1789–1869. American politician, b. Dunstable, Mass. Editor in Frankfort, Ky., of influential newspaper *Argus of Western America* (1816–26); auditor in U.S. Treasury (1829–35); U.S. postmaster general (1835–40); supporter, speechwriter, and adviser of Andrew Jackson. Business agent (from 1845) of Samuel F.B. Morse, organizing several telegraph companies.

Kendall, Edward Calvin. 1886–1972. American biochemist, b. S. Norwalk, Conn. Head of biochemistry section, Mayo Clinic, Rochester, Minn. (1914–51); professor of physiological chemistry, Mayo Foundation (1921–51). Isolated thyroxine; crystallized and established chemical nature of glutathione; isolated cortisone (1935) and, with Philip S. Hench, successfully applied it in treatment of rheumatoid arthritis (1948). For this and other work on hormones of the adrenal cortex, awarded (with Hench and Tadeus Reichstein) 1950 Nobel prize for physiology or medicine.

Kendall, George Wilkins. 1809–1867. American journalist, b. Mount Vernon, N.H. Founder and editor, New Orleans *Picayune* (1837).

Kendall, Thomas Henry. 1839–1882. Australian poet. Published his lyrical poems in *Poems and Songs* (1864), *Leaves from Australian Forests* (1869), and *Songs from the Mountains* (1880).

Keng Ching-chung \'gəŋ-'jiŋ-'jəŋ\. d. 1682. Chinese general. Ruler of Fukien fief in South China; became a leader (1674) in Revolt of Three Kingdoms against Manchu suzerains; eventually surrendered and pardoned, but later executed.

Kenmure, Viscounts. See GORDON family.

Ken·ne·dy \'ken-əd-ē\, John Fitzgerald. 1917–1963. Thirty-fifth president of the United States, b. Brookline, Mass. Son of Joseph P. Kennedy; naval officer in World War II; member, U.S. House of Representatives (1947–53), Senate (1953–60). First Roman Catholic to be elected president (1960); approved disastrous Bay of Pigs invasion of Cuba (1961); forced Soviet Union not to sign separate peace treaty with East Germany (1961) and to remove their missiles from Cuba (1962); with Great Britain and Soviet Union signed Nuclear Test-Ban Treaty (1963); launched Alliance for Progress in Latin America and the Peace Corps; assassinated at Dallas, Texas (Nov. 22, 1963). Author of *Why England Slept* (1940) and *Profiles in Courage* (1956, Pulitzer prize).

Kennedy, John Pendleton. *Pseudonym* Mark Lit·tle·ton \'lit-ᵊl-tən\. 1795–1870. American novelist and politician, b. Baltimore. Member, U.S. House of Representatives (1838–39, 1841–45); U.S. secretary of the navy (1852–53). Author of *Swallow Barn* (1832), *Horse-Shoe Robinson* (1835), *Rob of the Bowl* (1838), *Quodlibet* (1840), *Memoirs of the Life of William Wirt* (1842).

Kennedy, Joseph Patrick. 1888–1969. American businessman and diplomat, b. East Boston, Mass. Acquired large fortune in banking, stock market, shipbuilding, motion pictures; retired from business (1929). Chairman of Securities and Exchange Commission (1934–35) and of U.S. Maritime Commission (1937); ambassador to Great Britain (1937–40).

Kennedy, Margaret. 1896–1967. English novelist. Author of *The Constant Nymph* (1924), *Red Sky at Morning* (1927), *The Midas Touch* (1938), *The Mechanized Muse* (1942, critical study), *Jane Austen* (1950, biography), *The Outlaws on Parnassus* (1958), *The Forgotten Smile* (1961), etc.

Kennedy, Robert Francis. 1925–1968. American politician, b. Brookline, Mass. Son of Joseph P. Kennedy. Chief counsel of U.S. Senate Select Committee on Improper Activities in Labor or Management Field (1957–60); successfully managed presidential campaign of his brother John F. Kennedy (1960). U.S. attorney general (1961–64); promoted civil rights and litigation against trusts and rackets; member from New York, U.S. Senate (1964–68); assassinated in Los Angeles while campaigning for Democratic presidential nomination. Author of *The Enemy Within* (1960) and *Pursuit of Justice* (1964).

Kennedy, Walter. c.1460–c.1508. Scottish poet. Poetic rival of William Dunbar with whom he carried on a flyting, published in *The Flyting of Dunbar and Kennedie;* also author of *The Praise of Age, The Passion of Christ,* etc.

Ken·nel·ly \'ken-ᵊl-ē\, Arthur Edwin. 1861–1939. American electrical engineer, b. Colaba, India. To U.S. (1887); assistant to Thomas A. Edison (1887–94); professor, Harvard (1902–30), M.I.T. (1913–24). Developed analytic methods in electronics, esp. application of complex-number theory to alternating-current circuits. Announced in same year (1902) as Oliver Heaviside the probable existence of region of ionized air favorable to radio-wave propagation (Kennelly-Heaviside layer, now called ionosphere).

Ken·neth \'ken-əth\. Saint. *Also called* Can·ice \'kan-əs\ *or* Ken·ny \'ken-ē\. *Gael.* Chain·nech \'k̲öin-yək̲\. *Lat.* Ca·ni·cus \ka-'nī-kəs\. 515/16 or 521/27–599/600. Irish religious. Studied under SS. Finian, Mobhi, and Cadog; ordained priest (545); in Scotland as missionary (c.565–c.577); founded a chapel and monastery at Inchkenneth; said to have established eccelesiastical settlement that later developed into burgh of St. Andrews, Fife; associated with St. Columba of Iona in converting the Picts. To Ireland (c.577); founded monasteries at Aghaboe and at Kilkenny. Author of poems and *Glas-Chainnigh,* a commentary on the Gospels. Patron saint of diocese of Ossory; one of most popular saints in Scotland and Ireland.

Kenneth. Name of two kings of Scotland:

Kenneth I Mac·Al·pin \mə-'kal-pən, -'köl-\. d. 858 A.D. Traditional founder of Scottish kingdom; succeeded his father Alpin as king of Scots of Dalriada (c.834); subdued the Picts (841–846); united them with Gaelic Scots in kingdom first called Scotland; established his capital at Scone.

Kenneth II. d. 995 A.D. King (971–995). Son of Malcolm I; consolidated his lands; at war almost continually with English; according to some sources, submitted to King Edgar and from him received Lothian, first instance of the Tweed River as recognized English–Scottish border.

Ken·ny \'ken-ē\, Elizabeth. *Known as* Sister Kenny. 1880–1952. Australian nurse. Began practicing as nurse in back-country of New South Wales (1912); with Australian army nursing corps (1915–19); developed technique of rehabilitating victims of paralytic diseases, esp. poliomyelitis, by stimulation and reeducation of muscles; established clinic at Townsville (1933); opened clinics in England (1937), Minneapolis (1940), traveled to other countries to demonstrate methods.

Ken·sett \'ken-sət\, John Frederick. 1816–1872. American painter, b. Cheshire, Conn. Studio in New York (from 1847). Leader of second generation of the Hudson River school. Known for landscapes as *High Bank, Genesee River* (1857) and *Storm Over Lake George* (1870).

Kent and Strathern, Duke of. See EDWARD AUGUSTUS.

Kent, Earls of. Title held by ODO; Hubert de BURGH; members of Holland family (1360–1408); Grey de Ruthin branch of GREY family (1465–1740).

Kent \'kent\, James. 1763–1847. American jurist, b. Fredericksburgh, N.Y. Practiced law, Poughkeepsie, N.Y. (1785–93); professor of law, Columbia (1793–98, 1823–26). Judge, New York Supreme Court (1798–1823) and chief judge (1804–23); chancellor, New York Court of Chancery (1814–23). His decisions and writings did much to create American system of equity jurisdiction based on principles established in English chancery practice. Author of *Commentaries on American Law* (1826–30).

Kent, Rockwell. 1882–1971. American artist, b. Tarrytown Heights, N.Y. Known for landscape and figure painting characterized by rhythmic use of silhouetted shapes and symbolic treatment of nature, as in *The Road Roller* (1909) and *North Wind* (1919), and for wood engraving and lithography. Illustrated works of Shakespeare, Melville, Chaucer, Whitman, etc. His books, most of which he illustrated, included *Wilderness* (1920), *Voyaging* (1924), *N by E* (1930), *This Is My Own* (1940), autobiography *It's Me, O Lord* (1955), *Greenland Journal* (1963).

Kent, William. c.1686–1748. English artist and architect. Studied painting in Rome (1709–19); under patronage (from 1719) of Richard Boyle, 3d Earl of Burlington (see under BOYLE family); portrait painter to the king (1739). Edited (1727) *Designs of Inigo Jones,* which included designs by himself and Boyle. As architect, attempted to restore English Palladian style; designed in this style many public buildings in London as Royal Mews, Trafalgar Square (1732), treasury buildings in Whitehall (1734–36), Horse Guards Building, Whitehall (1750–58), and also residences Holkham Hall, Norfolk (1734), No. 44, Berkeley Square, London (1742–44), etc.; also one of first to work in Gothic Revival, as his alterations and additions to Esher Place, Surrey (c.1730) and Rousham Hall, Oxfordshire (1738–41). Decorated Burlington House, Cupola Room at Kensington Palace, Chiswick House (all in London). As landscape gardener, freed English garden from formality, introducing romantic designs, as in his gardens at Rousham Hall and at Stowe House, Buckinghamshire. Also designed monuments, Gothic screens at Westminster Hall (1739) and Gloucester cathedral (1741), stage scenery, a royal barge, and illustrations for Spenser's *Faerie Queene* and Gay's *Fables.*

Ken·ti·gern \'ken-tə-ˌgərn\ *or* **Mun·go** \'məŋ-gō\. Saint. d. c.612. Celtic ecclesiastic. To Glasgow (c.550), where he converted the Strathclyde Britons and established see; first bishop of Glasgow; driven by persecution to take refuge in Wales (c.553), where he founded monastery at Llanelwy (now St. Asaph's) and served as its first abbot; returned (c.573) to reclaim Picts of Galloway from idolatry.

Ken·yat·ta \ken-'yät-ə\, Jomo. *Orig.* Ka·mau \'kä-ˌmau̇\. c.1894–1978. Kenyan politician. Clerk in Public Works Dept., Nairobi (1922–28); involved (from 1922) in nationalist movement; general secretary of political protest group Kikuyu Central Association (1928); worked and studied intermittently in London (1929–46); published (1938) *Facing Mount Kenya,* anthropological study of the Kikuyu culture. An organizer of Pan-African Congress, Manchester, England (1945); returned to Kenya (1946); president of nationalist Kenya African Union (1947); imprisoned (1953–61) by British on charge of leading Mau Mau terrorist organization. At London Conference (1962) negotiated terms leading to independence of Kenya; first prime minister of Kenya (1963–64). President of Kenya (1964–78).

Ken·yon \'ken-yən\, John Samuel. 1874–1959. American phonetician, b. Medina, Ohio. Professor of English, Hiram Coll., Ohio (1916–44). Author of *American Pronunciation—a Textbook of Phonetics* (1924); coauthor (with Thomas A. Knott) of *A Pronouncing Dictionary of American English* (1944).

Kenzan. See OGATA.

Ke·o·kuk \'kē-ə-ˌkək\. 1788–?1848. American Indian chief, b. near present Rock Island, Ill. A war chief of Sauk tribe and rival of Black Hawk; aided Americans at time of Black Hawk War (1832); in Washington, arranged peace between Sauks and Sioux (1837). Keokuk, Iowa, is named in his honor.

Kep·ler \'kep-lər\, Johannes. 1571–1630. German astronomer. Studied at Tübingen under Michael Mästlin, who imparted to him Copernican principles. Professor, Graz (1594); assistant to Tycho Brahe at observatory near Prague (1600); succeeded Brahe at observatory and as imperial mathematician and court astronomer (1601). Mathematician to the states of Upper Austria at Linz (1612); moved to Ulm (1626); completed and published Brahe's *Tabulae Rudolphinae* (1627); moved to Sagan in Silesia (1628). Discovered Kepler's laws of planetary motion, announcing the first two in his *Astronomia nova* (1609) and the third in *Harmonice mundi* (1619). Also published *Mysterium cosmographicum* (1596), *De stella nova* (1606), *Epitome astronomiae Copernicanae* (1618–21), *Somnium seu astronomia lunari* (1634). Considered founder of modern optics by his postulation of the ray theory of light to explain vision. Did pioneer work that led to invention of calculus.

Kep·pel \'kep-əl\, Arnold Joost van. 1st Earl of Al·be·marle \'al-bə-ˌmärl\. 1669–1718. Dutch soldier. Devoted follower of William III in England, after whose death he returned to Holland; fought at Ramillies and Oudenarde. His son ¶William Anne Keppel (1702–1754), 2d earl, British soldier, was governor of Virginia (1737); general on staff at Dettingen (1743); wounded at Fontenoy (1745); fought at Culloden Moor (1746); commander in chief in North Britain (1748); privy councilor (1750). His son ¶George (1724–1772), 3d earl, was aide to Duke of Cumberland at Fontenoy and Culloden Moor; M.P. (1746–54); general (1759); governor of Jersey (1761); commanded land forces in capture of Havana (1762–63).

¶Augustus (1725–1786), 1st Viscount Keppel, British naval officer; 2d son of 2d earl; served through Seven Years' War (1756–63); captured French settlement of Gorée (1758); commanded leading ship in battle of Quiberon Bay (1759); second in command at capture of Havana (1762). Whig M.P. (1761–80); vice admiral (1770); commander in chief of grand fleet (1778–79); met French in indecisive action off Ushant, allowed French to escape (1778); acquitted by court-martial of neglect of duty; first lord of admiralty (1782–83). ¶George Thomas (1799–1891), 6th earl, grandson of 3d earl, fought at Waterloo (1815); served at Cape of Good Hope and in India; Whig M.P. (1832); general (1874). ¶Sir Henry (1809–1904), naval officer, son of 4th earl; served in Opium War (1841–42), in campaign against Borneo pirates (1843–44), in Baltic campaign (1854); commanded naval brigade ashore at Sevastopol (1855); admiral (1869); author of *A Sailor's Life under Four Sovereigns* (1899). His son ¶Sir Colin Richard (1862–1947), naval officer, served in Egyptian War (1882), in Sudan (1884–85), on Nile (1897–98), in battle of Omdurman (1898); commanded Atlantic fleet as rear admiral (1909–10); admiral, retired (1917).

Kepp·ler \'kep-lər\, Joseph. 1838–1894. American cartoonist, b. Vienna, Austria. To U.S. (1867); in New York City founded and edited *Puck,* first successful American humorous weekly (from 1876, first in German; English edition inaugurated 1877).

Ker. See also CARR and KERR.

Ker \'ke(ə)r, 'kər, 'kär\, William Paton. 1855–1923. British scholar, b. Glasgow. Professor, University College, London (1889–22), Oxford (1920–23); author of *Epic and Romance* (1897), *The Dark Ages* (1904), *Essays on Medieval Literature* (1905).

Ke·ren·sky \ˈkye-ren-skē *Angl* ker-ˈen-skē\, Aleksandr Fyodorovich. 1881–1970. Russian revolutionary leader. Joined Socialist Revolutionary party (c.1905); Labor Group delegate to 4th Duma (1912). After February Revolution (1917) made minister of justice in provisional government; minister of war and of the navy (May–July 1917); prime minister (July 1917); overthrown by Bolshevik Revolution (Nov. 1917) because of moderate policies and indecision; fled to Paris (1918); in U.S. (from 1940). Author of *Prelude to Bolshevism* (1919), *The Crucifixion of Liberty* (1934), *Russia and History's Turning Point* (1965), *The Kerensky Memoirs* (1966).

Ker·én·yi \ker-ˈān-yi\, Károly. 1897–1973. Hungarian philologist. Resident in Switzerland (from 1943); member of Carl Jung Institut, Zürich. Authority on comparative religions and primitive mythology; formulated a theory of the "Humanism of integral man." Wrote *Die antike Religion* (1940), *Die Mythologie der Griechen* (1951–58), etc.

Ker·gué·len-Tré·ma·rec \ker-gā-lən-trā-ma-rek\, Yves-Joseph de. 1734–1797. French navigator. Discovered the subantarctic Kerguelen, or Desolation, Island while searching for new southern continent in southern Indian Ocean (1772).

Ker·le \ˈker-lə\, Jacobus de. 1531?–1591. Flemish composer. Published (1562) *Preces speciales,* polyphonic settings of Latin poems; also composed hymns, vesper psalms, masses, motets, etc.

Kerll \ˈkerl\, Johann Kaspar von. *Surname also* Kerl *or* Kherl. *Ital.* Giovanni Gasparo Cherll \ˈkerl\. 1627–1693. German organist and composer. Sent by Ferdinand III to study in Rome under Carissimi and Frescobaldi (1645); court Kapellmeister at Munich (1656–74); produced there his first opera *L'Oronte* (1657) and ten others, all now lost; organist at Vienna for St. Stephen's Cathedral (1674–84) and imperial court (1677–84); produced there his sacred play *Pia et Fortis Mielier* (1677); returned to Munich (1684). Introduced operatic, dramatic devices into his church music; helped establish concertato style in Germany; influential teacher. Composed masses, Magnificats, requiems; also, for organ and harpsichord, toccatas, canzonas, and versets.

Kern \ˈkərn\, Jerome David. 1885–1945. American composer, b. New York City. Best known for his scores in musical comedies as *The Red Petticoat* (1912), *Very Good, Eddie* (1915), *Have a Heart* (1916), *Oh Boy!* (1917), *Sally* (1920), *Sunny* (1925), *Show Boat* (1927), *Sweet Adeline* (1929), *The Cat and the Fiddle* (1931), *Music in the Air* (1932), *Roberta* (1933), etc.; also composed film scores. His songs included "The Song is You," "Smoke Gets in Your Eyes," "Ol' Man River," "A Fine Romance," "The Last Time I Saw Paris."

Kern \ˈkern\, Johann Conrad. 1808–1888. Swiss politician. Member of Swiss Diet (1833–48); led Swiss opposition to French demand for expulsion of Prince Louis-Napoléon (1838); helped overthrow the Sonderbund (1847); with Henry Druey drew up new federal constitution (1848). President of Federal Supreme Court (1850); Swiss minister to France (1857–83).

Ker·ner \ˈker-nər\, Justinus Andreas Christian. 1786–1862. German poet and physician. Formed Swabian School of poetry with his friends Uhland, Gustav Schwab, and others; at Weinsberg (1819–51) his home became a literary mecca. Wrote lyrical verse, satirical humorous novel *Reiseschatten* (1811), a study of somnambulist and clairvoyant Friederike Hauffe *Die Seherin von Prevorst* (1829), a study of Franz Mesmer and animal magnetism (1856), etc.

Ker·ou·ac \ˈker-ə-ˌwak\, Jean-Louis, *called* Jack. 1922–1969. American novelist, b. Lowell, Mass. Roamed (1943–50) through U.S. and Mexico, working at odd jobs; published conventional novel *The Town and the City* (1950). With publication of *On the Road* (1957), became leader and representative spokesman of the Beat generation of 1950s and '60s; wrote in a spontaneous, unedited, nonconformist style. Other novels included *The Dharma Bums* (1958), *The Subterraneans* (1958), *Doctor Sax* (1959), etc.

Ké·roualle \kār-wȧl\, Louise-Renée de. Duchess of Ports·mouth \ˈpōrt-smath, ˈpȯrt-\. 1649–1734. Mistress (from 1671) of King Charles II of England, b. France. To England (1670); made Duchess of Portsmouth (1673); rewarded by Louis XIV with fief of Aubigny (1674), for her service in keeping Charles dependent upon France.

Kerr *or* **Ker** \ˈke(ə)r, ˈkər, ˈkär\. Name of Scottish family having two chief branches, the Cess·ford \ˈses-fərd\ and the Fer·nie·hirst \ˈfər-nē-ˌhərst\ (in Roxburghshire), to latter of which belonged Robert Carr (*q.v.*), Earl of Somerset.

EARLS AND MARQUISES OF LO·THI·AN \ˈlō-thē-ən\:
Mark Kerr *or* Ker (d. 1609), 1st Earl of Lothian; master of requests (1577–1606); extraordinary lord of session under King James VI; made baron, Lord Newbattle (1587); interim chancellor (1604). ¶William Kerr *or* Ker (1605?–1675); created 3d Earl of Lothian (1631); governor of Newcastle (1641); secretary of state (1648–52). His son ¶Robert (1636–1703), 4th Earl and 1st Marquis of Lothian; privy councilor to William III; justice general (1688); united his grandfather Robert's title of earl of An·crum \ˈaŋ-krəm\ to his own (1690).

EARLS AND DUKES OF ROX·BURGH *or* ROX·BURGHE \ˈräks-brə\:
¶Robert Ker (1570?–1650), 1st Earl of Roxburgh; supported James VI against Bothwell (1594–99); created Baron Roxburgh (1600); accompanied James to London (1603); created earl (1616); lord privy seal of Scotland (1637–49); Royalist in Civil War. ¶John Ker (d. 1741), 5th Earl and 1st Duke of Roxburgh; secretary of state for Scotland (1704); promoted union of Scotland with England and Protestant succession, rewarded with dukedom (1707); keeper of privy seal of Scotland (1714); accompanied rebels under Duke of Argyll and distinguished himself at Sheriffmuir (1715); one of lords justices during George I's absence from England (1716, 1720, 1723, 1725). His grandson ¶John Ker (1740–1804), 3d duke; bibliophile; lord of the bedchamber (1767), groom of the stole, and privy councilor (1796); amassed private library containing remarkable collection of books from Caxton's press.

Kerr, John. 1824–1907. Scottish physicist. Discovered the Kerr electro-optic effect (announced 1876). Author of *An Elementary Treatise on Rational Mechanics* (1867).

Kerr, Sir John Graham. 1869–1957. English zoologist. On two expeditions to Paraguay (1889–91, 1896–97); professor, Glasgow (1902–35); M.P. for Scottish universities (1935–50). Best known for studies of embryology of lungfishes. Author of *A Textbook of Embryology with the Exception of Mammalia* (1914–19), *Zoology for Medical Students* (1921), *Evolution* (1926), *A Naturalist in the Gran Chaco* (1950), etc.

Kerr, Michael Crawford. 1827–1876. American politician, b. Titusville, Pa. Practiced law in New Albany, Ind. (1852 ff.); member, U.S. House of Representatives (1865–73, 1875–76; speaker, 1875–76); known for aggressive stands against the tariff, monopolies, and Reconstruction.

Ker·saint \ker-saⁿ\, Armand-Guy-Simon de Coet·nem·pren de \də-kwet-nem-pren-də-\. 1742–1793. French naval officer and politician. Girondist member of Constituent Assembly and Legislative Assembly; promoted vice admiral (1793), but resigned after execution of Louis XVI; guillotined. For his daughter Claire, see under DURFORT family.

Ker·ta·na·ga·ra \ˌker-tə-ˈnä-gə-rə\. d. 1292. Last king (1268–92) of Tumapel (or Singhasāri) in Java. Zealous follower of Tantric Buddhism; united Java; took Bali (1284); extended his influence to Sumatra; refused to pay tribute to Kublai Khan (1287). Venerated by Javanese as one of their greatest leaders.

Ker·tész \ker-ˈtesh\, André. 1894–1985. American photographer, b. Budapest. Photographed scenes of World War I while in Hungarian army. To Paris (1925) to work as free-lance photographer for European magazines; to U.S. (1936) to work for commercial studio. Began (1937) doing work for general-interest and fashion magazines; pioneered and refined use of hand-held 35-millimeter camera. Turned (1963) to personal creative photography; created lyrical portraits, still lifes, nudes, and records of urban street life; helped public accept photography as an art form.

Ke·shub Chun·der Sen \ˈkā-shȯb-ˈchȯn-drȯ-ˈsān\. 1838–1884. Indian reformer. Joined Brahmo Samaj (1857); became active leader in samaj (1859); wrote *The Brahma Samaj Vindicated* (1863); caused division in the society (1865), founding (1866) separate organization Brahmo Samaj of India; made his samaj more cosmopolitan and Christian than Hindu; lost many followers (1878), renamed his church Nava Vidham (New Dispensation) and declared himself prophet of a new universal religion; wrote *The New Samhita* (1883).

Kes·sel \kes-el\, Joseph. 1898–1979. French journalist and writer, b. Argentina. Traveled throughout world as reporter (1920 ff.); served during World War II in French Resistance and wrote lyrics (1942) for its "Chant des Partisans." Author of travel books, essays, and esp. novels as *Belle de jour* (1929), *Le Tour de malheur* (1950), *Le Lion* (1958), *Les Cavaliers* (1967).

Kes·sel·ring \ˈkes-əl-riŋ\, Albert. 1885–1960. German field marshal. Served in World War I; chief of air staff (1936); air commander, invasion of Poland (1939) and France (1940), attacks on England (1940–41) and Russia (1941); commander in chief, south (late 1941); with Rommel directed Axis campaign in North Africa; conducted brilliant defensive action in Italy against Allied attack (1943–44); commander in chief, west (March 1945); surrendered southern half of German forces (May 1945); imprisoned for war crimes (1947–52). Wrote memoir *Soldat bis zum letzten Tag* (1953).

Kęs·tu·tis \kas-ˈtü-tis\. c.1300–1382. Grand duke of Lithuania (1381–82). Ruled southern and western Lithuania for his father Gediminas; overthrew his brother Jaunutis and installed another brother, Algirdas (*q.v.*), on throne; retained control of southern and western Lithuania; waged long defensive campaigns against Teutonic Knights; with Algirdas, defeated them at Rudava (1370); after death of Algirdas (1377), involved in dynastic intrigues; overthrew his nephew Jagiełło (later King Władysław II of Poland) and became grand duke (1381); arrested and executed by Jagiełło.

Ket *or* **Kett** \ˈket\, Robert. d. 1549. English rebel. Leader of uprising at Norfolk against enclosures of common land (1549); defeated and executed.

Ketch \ˈkech\, John, *known as* Jack. d. 1686. English executioner. Public hangman (from c.1663); executed Monmouth (1685); notorious for barbarity; his name a synonym for hangman.

Ketch·el \ˈkech-əl\, Stanley. *Orig.* Stanislaus Kie·cal \ˈkyet-səl\. *Sometimes called* the Michigan Assassin. 1886–1910. American boxer, b. Grand Rapids, Mich. Began professional career (1903); defeated Mike Sullivan at Colma,

Calif., for world middleweight championship (Feb. 22, 1908); lost title to Billy Papke (Sept. 7, 1908) but regained it from him (Nov. 26, 1908); lost to Jack Johnson for world heavyweight title (Oct. 16, 1909); still middleweight champion when shot to death.

Ket·te·ler \'ket-ə-lər\, Wilhelm Emmanuel von. Freiherr. 1811–1877. German ecclesiastic. Member, Frankfurt National Assembly (1848–49); consecrated bishop of Mainz (1850) and became Catholic leader in Germany. At first opposed papal infallibility at Vatican Council (1870), but subsequently supported it; represented Center party in Reichstag (1871–72) and became ultramontane leader and strong opponent of Bismarck in Prussian Kulturkampf; championed Christian socialism and social and economic reforms. Author of *Die Arbeiterfrage und das Christentum* (1864), etc.

Ket·ter·ing \'ket-ə-riŋ\, Charles Franklin. 1876–1958. American electrical engineer, b. near Loudonville, Ohio. With National Cash Register Co., Dayton (1904–09); devised first electric cash register. With Edward A. Deeds founded (1909) Delco (Dayton Engineering Laboratories Company); invented the automotive electric self-starter (introduced on 1912 Cadillacs) and developed lighting and ignition systems for automobiles. Organized Dayton-Wright Airplane Co. (1914). Vice president and director of research for General Motors Corp. (1920–47); developed the high-speed two-cycle diesel engine and (1951) a revolutionary high-compression automobile engine; also helped develop quick-drying lacquer finishes for automobiles, anti-knock fuels and leaded gasoline, variable-speed transmissions, etc. Established at Antioch College the C.F. Kettering Foundation for the Study of Chlorophyll and Photosynthesis; cofounder of Sloan-Kettering Institute for Cancer Research, New York City.

Keuss·ler \'kȯis-lər\, Gerhard von. 1874–1949. German composer and conductor. Composer of symphonic dramas with original texts as *Gefängnisse* (1914) and *Die Geisselfahrt* (1923), oratorios as *Jesus aus Nazareth* (1917), symphonies, songs with original words, etc.

Kev·in \'kev-ən\. Saint. *Ir. Gael.* Caem·gen \'kev-gən\. *Lat.* Coem·ge·nus \kȯim-'gā-nəs\. d. 618. Irish religious. Founded (c.570) monastery at Glendalough and became its abbot; made it one of leading Irish monastic centers. A patron saint of Dublin.

Key \'kē\, Sir Astley Cooper. 1821–1888. English naval commander. Admiral (1878); first naval lord of the admiralty (1879–85). Organized Royal Naval Coll. at Greenwich (1872) and became its president (1873).

Key \'ke-ē\, Ellen Karolina Sofia. 1849–1926. Swedish educationalist and writer. Teacher in Stockholm (1880–99) and lecturer at the Workers' Institute (1884–1903) and elsewhere; her liberal opinions aroused much controversy. Author of works on the feminist movement, child welfare, pacifism, sex, love and marriage, etc., esp. *Barnets århundrade* (1900) and *Lifslinjer* (1903–06).

Key \'kē\, Francis Scott. 1779–1843. American lawyer and poet, b. Frederick (now Carroll) Co., Md. Practiced law, Georgetown and Washington, D.C. (from 1802); U.S. attorney for District of Columbia (1833–41). On mission to obtain exchange of an American held by British fleet, was detained while British bombarded Fort McHenry, key to Baltimore defenses (night of Sept. 13–14, 1814); at sight of U.S. flag still flying over fort (morning of Sept. 14), wrote poem "Defence of Fort M'Henry," published in *Baltimore Patriot* (Sept. 20, 1814); poem later set to John Stafford Smith's song "To Anacreon in Heaven" and became known as "The Star-Spangled Banner"; it was adopted as U.S. national anthem in 1931.

Key, Valdimer Orlando, Jr. 1908–1963. American political scientist, b. Austin, Tex. Taught at Johns Hopkins (1938–49), Yale (1949–51), Harvard (1951 ff.); on staff of Bureau of Budget (1942–45). Author of *Politics, Parties, and Pressure Groups* (1942), *Southern Politics in State and Nation* (1949), *A Primer of Statistics for Political Scientists* (1954), *Public Opinion and American Democracy* (1961), *The Responsible Electorate* (1966).

Keyes \'kīz\, Frances Parkinson, *nee* Whee·ler \'hwē-lər, 'wē-\. 1885–1970. American novelist, b. Charlottesville, Va. m. Henry W. Keyes (1904; d. 1938). Among her novels were *The Old Gray Homestead* (1919), *Written in Heaven* (1937), *All That Glitters* (1941), *Came a Cavalier* (1947), *Joy Street* (1950), *The Heritage* (1968).

Keyes \'kēz\, Roger John Brownlow. 1st Baron Keyes. 1872–1945. British naval commander, b. India. Entered navy (1885); served in Boxer Rebellion in China (1900); in charge of submarine service (1910–14); chief of staff, Eastern Mediterranean squadron (1915); grand-fleet captain (1916–17); rear admiral (1917); director of plans at the Admiralty (1917); commanded operations against Zeebrugge and Ostend (Apr. 1918); admiral (1926); commander in chief, Mediterranean station (1925–28), Portsmouth station (1929–31); admiral of the fleet (1930); retired (1935); recalled for organization of commando units (1940–41). M.P. (1934–43); created baron (1943).

Keynes \'kānz\, John Maynard. 1st Baron Keynes of Tilton. 1883–1946. English economist. Son of John Neville Keynes. On staff of the Treasury (1915–19) and its principal representative at the Paris Peace Conference (1919); published *The Economic Consequences of the Peace* (1919) arguing against the excessive reparations required of Germany; between world wars, financial adviser in London and teacher at Cambridge; played a central role in British war finance during World War II; chief British representative at Bretton Woods Conference (1944) that established International Monetary Fund. Known for his revolutionary economic theory that recovery from a recession is best achieved by a government-sponsored policy of full employment, elucidated esp. in *The General Theory of Employment, Interest and Money* (1935). Co-editor, *Economic Journal* (1912–45). Author also of *A Revision of the Treaty* (1922), *A Tract on Monetary Reform* (1923), *The End of Laissez-Faire* (1926), *A Treatise on Money* (1930), *How to Pay for the War* (1940), etc.

Keynes, John Neville. 1852–1949. English educator. University lecturer in moral science, Cambridge (1884–1911); registrary, Cambridge (1910–25). Author of *Formal Logic* (1884) and *Scope and Method of Political Economy* (1891).

Keys, John. See CAIUS.

Key·ser \'kī-sər\, Hendrik de. 1565–1621. Dutch architect and sculptor. Settled in Amsterdam (1591); city sculptor (1594); city architect (1612). Designed, mostly in Dutch Renaissance style, the Zuiderkerk (1603–14), the East India House (1606), the exchange (1608–17), the Westerkerk (1620), all in Amsterdam; the town hall (1620), the monument of William I of Orange at Delft (1614); and the bronze statue of Erasmus at Rotterdam (1621). His son ¶Thomas (1596–1667) was a painter and architect; executed historical and mythological pictures as *Theseus* and *Ariadne;* excelled in portraits distinguished by rich colors and Rembrandtesque chiaroscuro as *Anatomy of Dr. Vrij* (1619), *Constantin Huygens and His Secretary* (1627), *Group of Amsterdam Burgomasters* (1638); designed tower of Amsterdam Town Hall.

Key·ser·ling \'kī-zər-liŋ\, Hermann Alexander. Graf. 1880–1946. German social philosopher. His philosophy centered on theme of spiritual regeneration. Author of *Unsterblichkeit* (1907), *Reisetagebuch eines Philosophen* (1919), *Schöpferische Erkenntnis* (1922), *Wiedergeburt* (1927), *Südamerikanische Meditationen* (1932), etc.

Kgama III. See KHAMA.

Kha·cha·tu·ri·an \ˌkäch-ä-'tu̇r-yən; *Angl* ˌkäch-ə-'tu̇r-ē-ən, ˌkach-\, Aram Ilich. 1903–1978. Armenian composer. Professor at Gnesiny Institute, Moscow, and at Moscow Conservatory (both from 1951). Composer of three symphonies (1934, 1943, 1947), ballets *Happiness* (1939), *Gayane* (1942, included "Sabre Dance"), and *Spartak* (1954), symphonic suite *Masquerade* (1944), concertos for piano (1936), violin (1940), and cello (1946), choral works, chamber music, some 25 film scores, and music for the Armenian national anthem.

Kha·dī·jah \ka-'dē-jä\. d. 619. First wife of the prophet Muḥammad. Twice married and widow of a wealthy merchant when she hired Muḥammad as a business agent; according to most sources, was about 40 to his 25 years of age at time of their marriage; provided constant support and encouragement to his mission.

Khaf·re \'kaf-rā\ *or* **Khaf·ra** \-rä\. *Gr.* Cheph·ren \'kef-ren\ *or* Sou·phis \'sü-fēs\. 26th century B.C. Fourth king of 4th dynasty of Egypt (reigned c.2540–c.2514 B.C.). Son of Khufu; succeeded Djedefre, probably his elder brother; builder of second pyramid at Giza; possibly also builder of the Sphinx, which is supposed to be his image and a symbol of the god Harmachis.

Khai Dinh \'kī-'din\. *Orig.* Nguy·en Bun Dao \'nī-ən-'bu̇n-'dau̇\. d. 1925. Emperor of Vietnam (1916–25). Son of Dong Khanh; sought support and protection of French government.

Khā·lid \'kä-lēd\. *In full* Khālid ibn 'Abd al-'Azīz ibn 'Abd ar-Raḥmān āl Sa'ūd. 1913–1982. King of Saudi Arabia (1975–82). Son of King Ibn Sa'ūd; succeeded to throne on assassination of his half-brother Faisal; fostered improvements in education, medical care, housing, roads, etc.

Khā·lid al-Qas·rī \'kä-lē-du̇l-kas-'rē\. *In full* Khālid ibn 'Abd Allāh al-Qasrī. d. 743. Governor of Iraq (724–738) under Umayyad caliph. Governor of Mecca (710–715). As governor of Iraq established an efficient administration by ruthless means; increased arable land and maintained peace.

Khā·lid ibn al-Wa·līd \'kä-lē-ˌdib-ə-nu̇l-wa-'lēd\. d. 642 A.D. Arab general. Given command of expedition against Syria by Abū Bakr (633); defeated Byzantine armies of Heraclius south of Damascus (634–635), took Damascus (635), and won final great battle of the Yarmuk (636).

Kha·līl \ka-'lēl\, al-Ashraf Ṣalāḥ ad-Dīn. d. 1293. Mamlūk sultan of Egypt (1290–93). Completed his father Qalā'ūn's campaign to drive the Franks from Syria (1291); murdered by his emirs.

Khalīl ibn Aḥ·mad, al- \u̇l-kä-'lē-ˌlib-ə-'nak-mad\. *In full* Abū 'Abd ar-Raḥman al-Khalīl ibn Aḥmad ibn 'Amr ibn Tamīm al-Farāhīdī al-Azdī al-Yuḥmadī. c.718–between 786 and 791. Arab philologist. Lived and taught in Basra; teacher of Sībawayh. His *Kitāb al-'ayn* was first Arabic dictionary;

reputed first to have classified meters of Arabic prosody and determined its rules.

Khal·jī \k̲al-'jē\. A Muslim dynasty ruling in India (1290–1320) with Delhi as its capital; founded by Jalāl-ud-Dīn (*q.v.*); its other two rulers were 'Alā'-ud-Dīn (*q.v.*) and Quṭb-ud-Dīn (ruled 1316–20); succeeded by the Tughluq dynasty.

Kha·ma III \'k̲ä-ma\. *Also spelled* Kga·ma \'kä-ma\. *Called* the Great. c.1837–1923. African king in northern Bechuanaland. Converted to Christianity (1860); became king (1875); had Bechuanaland declared a British protectorate (1885); aided British in defeating the Matabeles (1893).

Khan·sā', al- \,al-k̲an-'sä\. *Orig.* Tumāḍir bint 'Amr ibn al-Ḥārith ibn ash-Sharīd. d. after 630. Arab poet. Wrote elegies on her father and brothers killed in battle.

Khā·qā·nī \k̲ä-kä-'nē\. *In full* Afzal od-Dīn Bādel Ebrāhim ebn 'Alī Khāqānī Shīrvānī. *Early pen name* Ḥaqā'iqī \k̲ä-'kä-ē-'kē\. c.1106–c.1185. Persian poet. Established reputation as lyric poet under name Ḥaqā'iqī; at court of Manūchehr of Shīrvān; later at court of Tabriz. Wrote long poem *Tohfeh ol-'Erāqeyn* describing his pilgrimage (1156 or 1157) to Mecca; also composed laudatory poems, satires, epigrams; one of few Persian poets to use Christian imagery.

Kha·se·khe·mui \,käs-ek-'em-wē\. *Also spelled* Khasekhemwy *or* Khe·se·khem \,kes-ek-'em\. d. c.2686 B.C. King of Egypt, sixth and last of 2d dynasty. Ended internal struggles and reunited Egypt; raided Nubia; his reign a period of technological and cultural advances.

Khatīb Chelebī. See KÂTIB ÇELEBÎ.

Khatzidakis, George N. See HATZIDAKIS.

Khayr ad-Dīn \'k̲ī-rüd-'dēn\. *Orig. name* Khiḍr \'k̲id-ər\. *Known to Europeans as* Bar·ba·ros·sa \,bär-bə-'rö-sə, -'rō-\, *i.e.* Redbeard. d. 1546. Barbary pirate and Ottoman admiral. With brothers, esp. ¶'Arūj (d. 1518), took up piracy in Mediterranean, attacking Spanish and Portuguese shipping; encouraged Turkish and Muslim immigration into North Africa; established stronghold on Algerian coast (1516) but driven out by Spanish (1518). On death of 'Arūj (1518), Khiḍr assumed leadership and title Khayr ad-Dīn; made homage to sultan of Istanbul and received military aid and title *beylerbey;* captured Algiers (1529) and created strong base for piracy; made admiral of Ottoman fleet (1533); conquered Tunisia (1534) and made Tunis base for piracy against Italy; lost Tunis to Emperor Charles V (1535) but defeated his fleet at Preveza (1538).

Khayyám, Omar. See OMAR KHAYYÁM.

Khaz·'al Khan \'k̲ä-zäl-'k̲än\. 1861–1936. Persian ruler. Became (1897) shaykh of Moḥammarah (now Khorramshahr); secured British support; attempted to create an independent state in Khuzistan; opposed Reza Khan; defeated by government forces (1924); under house arrest in Teheran (from 1925).

Khe·ra·skov \k̲yi-'rä-skəf\, Mikhail Matveyevich. 1733–1807. Russian poet. Composed tragedies, novels, and miscellaneous poems, but esp. the two epic poems *Rossiyada* (1771–79) describing invasion of Kazan by Ivan the Terrible, and *Vladimir vozrozhdyonny* (1785) portraying St. Vladimir's introduction of Christianity into Russia.

Khe·ven·hül·ler \'kā-fən-,hue-lər\, Ludwig Andreas. 1683–1744. Austrian soldier. Served under Prince Eugene in War of Spanish Succession; fought in War of Polish Succession (1734); field marshal (1737); participated in Turkish War; commanded with distinction against France and Bavaria in Austrian War of Succession, overrunning Bavaria and capturing Munich (1742); wrote military manuals.

Khleb·ni·kov \'k̲lyep-nyi-kəf\, Velemir Vladimirovich, *orig.* Viktor Vladimirovich. 1885–1922. Russian poet. Founder (c.1910) of Russian Futurism; known for esoteric and experimental verse.

Khlesl *or* **Kle·sel** *or* **Klesl** \'klā-səl\, Melchior. 1552–1630. Austrian cardinal and statesman. Bishop of Vienna (1598); chancellor to Archduke (later Emperor) Matthias (from 1599) and virtual head of imperial politics after latter's succession (1612); cardinal (1615). Came into conflict with Ferdinand II (then archduke) for attempts to achieve reconciliation with Protestant princes; imprisoned for recommending concessions to rebelling Bohemian Protestants (1618); brought to trial before Curia in Rome (1622) and acquitted (1623).

Khmel·nyt·sky \k̲myel-'nyit-skəi\, Bohdan. *Also spelled* Bogdan Chmiel·nic·ki \-'nyit-skē\. *Orig. surname* Zi·no·vy \zyin-'ȯv-yē\. c.1595–1657. Cossack leader. Hetman of Zaporozhian Cossacks (1648–57); led revolt against Polish rule (1648) that quickly became general Ukrainian uprising; after several victories and capture of Lvov made Compact of Zborów (1649) with Polish king John Casimir, establishing virtually independent Cossack principality; renewed revolt (1651), defeated at Beresteczko; sought Russian aid, took oath of allegiance to Czar Alexis (1654). After his death Russia gradually asserted rule over Cossacks and the Ukraine.

Kho·mya·kov \k̲əm-yi-'kȯf\, Aleksey Stepanovich. 1804–1860. Russian poet. Leader of Slavophiles against Westernizing movement; influential lay theologian of Russian Orthodox church; developed system based on *sobornost* ("togetherness-symphony," roughly corresponding to "catholic") that taught that true progress depended on cooperation, not competition. Wrote poetry, verse tragedies, and works on philosophy, history, politics, economics, sociology, theology, etc.

Khoriv. See under KIY.

Khos·row \k̲ȯs-'rau̇\. *Arab.* Kis·rā \kis-'rä\. *Gr.* Chos·ro·es \'käz-rə-,ēz, 'käs-\. Name of two kings of the Sāsānian Empire of Persia:

Khosrow I. *Called* Anū·shīr·van \an-,ü-shēr-'vän\, *i.e.* Immortal Soul. d. 579. King (531–579). Son of Kavadh I. At war (531–532, 540–545) with Justinian, Byzantine emperor; sacked Antioch (540); extended power to Black Sea and Caucasus; failed to take Edessa (544); granted a truce (545), forcing Justinian to pay tribute; after nine years of peace (562–571), engaged again in war against Justin II; took fortress of Dara (573); defeated (576). One of the greatest Persian kings; reformed imperial taxation, restored Zoroastrianism in full; reorganized Sāsānian bureaucracy and initiated system of ministries; a great patron of culture; his reign the golden age of Pahlavi literature.

Khosrow II. *Called* Par·vīz \par-'väz\, *i.e.* the Victorious. d. 628. King (590–628). Son of Hormizd IV; grandson of Khosrow I. Aided by Byzantine emperor Maurice in securing his throne; after murder of Maurice (602) made war on Eastern Roman Empire; occupied Egypt (616) and reached (617) Chalcedon opposite Constantinople; defeated by Heraclius (623–628). Under him Sāsānian Empire reached its greatest extent; patron of the arts. Celebrated in poetry for his love for his wife Shīrīn.

Khrapovitshy, Antony. See ANTONY KHRAPOVITSHY.

Khru·shchev \krüsh-'chȯf; *Angl* krüsh-'(ch)ȯf, -'(ch)ȯv, -'(ch)ef, -'(ch)ev, 'krüsh-,\, Nikita Sergeyevich. 1894–1971. Soviet politician. Joined Communist party (1918), began full-time party work (1925); elected full member of Central Committee (1934) and of Politburo (1939); served Stalin loyally during Great Purge of 1930s; lieutenant general during World War II. Returned to Moscow as first secretary of All-Union Central Committee (1949); victorious in power struggle with Georgy Malenkov after death of Stalin (1953). First secretary of Communist party (1953–64); premier of Soviet Union (1958–64); launched destalinization campaign (1956); crushed Hungarian Revolution (1956); forced by Pres. Kennedy to remove missiles from Cuba (1962); removed from offices (1964) chiefly due to antagonistic policy toward China and repeated failures of his agricultural programs.

Khu·ang Aphai·wong *or* **Apai·wong** \'kü-äŋ-ä-'pī-wȯŋ\. 1902–1968. Thai politician. Took part in coup that overthrew King Prajadhipok and established a constitutional government (1932); prime minister of Thailand (1944–46); founded (1946) pro-monarchial conservative Democratic party; thrice more prime minister (1946–48); ousted by Pibul Songgram (1948); thereafter a vociferous opponent of military regime.

Khubilai Khan. See KUBLAI KHAN.

Khu·en-Hé·der·vá·ry \'kü-en-'hā-der-,vär-ē\, Károly. 1849–1918. Hungarian politician. As *ban* of Croatia and Slavonia (1883–1903), founded pro-Hungarian Croatian Nationalist party and effected administrative reforms; minister president of Hungary (1903); minister in Tisza's cabinet (1904–05); again Hungarian minister president (1910–12); founder and head of National Workers' party (1913).

Khu·fu \'kü-,fü\. *Also spelled* Khu·fwey \'küf-,wā\ *or* Khnom-Khuf·wey \kə-'näm-\. *Gr.* Che·ops \'kē-äps\. 26th century B.C. Second king of 4th dynasty of Egypt. Son and successor of Snefru; erected Great Pyramid at Giza; succeeded in turn by his sons Djedefre and Khafre.

Khu·ri \'k̲ür-ē\, Bishara al-. 1890–1964. Lebanese politician. Minister of the interior (1926); prime minister (1926–29); bitter rival of fellow Christian leader Émile Eddé. President of Lebanon (1943–52).

Khwān·da·mīr \,k̲wän-dä-'mēr\, Ghiyās ad-Dīn Muḥammad. c.1475–1534 or 1537. Persian historian. Grandson of Mirkhwānd; lived in Herāt; to India (1528); there in service of Bābur and later Humāyūn. Works included *Khulāsat al-Akhbār* (written 1499–1500), general history *Habīb al-Siyar* (1524), *Humāyūnnāme* on the Mughal Empire, and the 7th and final volume of Mirkhwānd's *Rowzat al-Safā'.*

Khwā·riz·mī, al- \al-'k̲wär-iz-,mē\. *In full* Muḥammad ibn Mūsā al-Khwārizmī. c.780–c.850. Arab mathematician. Lived at Baghdad; one of the greatest scientific minds of Islām, markedly influencing mathematical thought. Compiled set of astronomical tables; wrote a treatise on algebra *Kitab al-jabr wa al-muqābalah,* introducing the name (al-jabr) and greatly advancing knowledge of the science; in its Latin translation (by Gerard of Cremona) this treatise was source of much of mathematical knowledge of medieval Europe; wrote also a work on algorism (a term deriving from his name), which introduced Arabic numerals and the art of calculating by decimal notation.

Ki Tsurayuki. See KINO Tsurayuki.

Ki·bi \kē-bē\ Mabi *or* Makibi. 693–775. Japanese diplomat. To China as student (717) and later as special envoy of Japanese government; did much to introduce Chinese culture to Japan; later adviser to Empress Kōken; appointed minister of the right (766).

Kichibē. See Hishikawa Moronobu.

Ki·chi·zan \kē-chē-zän\ Minchō. *Also called* Chō \chō\ Densu. 1352–1431. Japanese painter. Zen Buddhist priest; known esp. for works of Buddhist iconography, as portrait of Shōichi; believed to have executed *Hut in the Valley* (1413), oldest extant Japanese ink landscape.

Kick·ham \'kik-əm\, Charles Joseph. 1826–1882. Irish writer. Joined (1860) Fenians, quickly rising to leadership; imprisoned (1865–69) for Fenian activities. Author of extremely popular nationalistic works, including *Poems, Sketches, and Narratives Illustrative of Irish Life* (1870), and novels *Sally Cavanagh* (1869), *Knocknagow* (1879), and *For the Old Land* (1886).

Kidd \'kid\, William. *Known as* Captain Kidd. c.1645–1701. British pirate, b. Scotland. Shipowner and sea captain, New York City (1690); in British colonial service against French (1690–95). Commissioned head of expedition against pirates in Indian Ocean; sailed from England (1696), reaching Madagascar a year later; began to sanction attacks on merchantmen; captured (Jan. 1698) *Quedagh Merchant,* richly laden Armenian vessel, took her for his own ship, and captured other prizes; sailed to West Indies, learned he had been proclaimed a pirate, returned to New England and surrendered on promise of a pardon (1699). Sent as prisoner to London (1700); convicted for murder and piracy; hanged. After his death, rumors spread that he had buried his plunder in places along the American coast.

Kid·de \'kēth-ə\, Harald Henrik Sager. 1878–1918. Danish novelist. Author of social and psychological novels as *Aage og Else* (1902–03), *Helten* (1912), *Jaernet* (1918); m. (1907) ¶Astrid Eh·ren·cron \'ē-rən-,krōn\ (1871–1960), author of mystery novels and stories laid chiefly in parsonages and small Swedish towns.

Kid·der \'kid-ər\, Alfred Vincent. 1885–1963. American archaeologist, b. Marquette, Mich. Director (1915–29) of excavations for Phillips Academy, Andover, Mass., at large pueblo at Pecos, N.M.; member of Carnegie Institution, Washington, D.C. (1927–50); on faculty of Peabody Museum, Harvard U. (1939–50). Proposed Pecos archaeological classification system (1927); also conducted excavations at Mayan sites in Mexico and Central America. Author of standard work *Introduction to the Study of Southwestern Archaeology* (1924).

Ki·der·len–Wäch·ter \'kēd-ər-lən-'vek-tər\, Alfred von. 1852–1912. German diplomat. Prussian minister at Hamburg (1894); German minister at Copenhagen (1895), Bucharest (1900), and Constantinople (at various times); foreign secretary under Bethmann Hollweg (1910). Pursued belligerent foreign policy; worked to establish Germany as leader of Triple Alliance; his aggressive response to France's acquisition of Morocco helped bring about Agadir incident (1911); ultimately signed agreement with France on Moroccan–Congo question (1911), but his inept handling of the situation helped divide Europe into two armed camps before outbreak of World War I.

Kid·in·nu \'kid-ə-,nü\. *Also spelled* Kid·e·nas *or* Cid·e·nas \'kid-ə-nəs\. fl. c.379 B.C. Babylonian astronomer and mathematician. Head of astronomical school at Sippar; discovered precession of the equinoxes; incorporated the 19-year cycle into Babylonian calendar (383); developed System B describing more clearly motions of Sun and planets; calculated length of synodic month to less than one second from actual value.

Ki·do \kē-dō\ Kōin. *Also called* Kido Takayoshi. *Orig.* Ka·tsu·ra \kät-sůr-ä\ Kogorō. 1833–1877. Japanese politician. Took prominent part in overthrow of Tokugawa shogunate and restoration of emperor (1868); became powerful member of new administration; responsible for transfer of capital from Kyōto to Tokyo, restoration of feudal domains to emperor, and establishment of prefectural system; worked for establishment of Western-style constitution.

Kid·ston \'kid-stən\, Robert. 1852–1924. English paleobotanist. With W.H. Lang made study (1917–21) of silicified plants of Rhynie Chert bed of the Devonian Period, discovering a new class of vascular cryptogams and three new genera. Wrote *The Fossil Plants of the Carboniferous Rocks of Great Britain* (1923–25).

Ki·el \kē-el\ Sun-chu. 1869–1935. Korean clergyman. Converted to Christianity (1897); first Korean minister to work in pastoral ministry; perhaps most effective evangelist of revival of 1907; vice chairman of Presbyterian General Assembly in Korea (1912). One of first two signers of Korean Declaration of Independence (1919).

Kiel·land \'kel-län\, Alexander Lange. 1849–1906. Norwegian novelist and playwright. Foremost stylist of his day. Author of works criticizing social institutions and injustices, including novels *Garman og Worse* (1880), *Arbeidsfolk* (1881), *Skipper Worse* (1882), *Gift* (1883), *Fortuna* (1884), *Sankt Hans Fest* (1887); plays *Tre Par* (1886), *Betty's Formynder* (1887), *Professoren* (1888); and short stories.

Kier·an \'kir-ən\, John Francis. 1892–1981. American journalist, b. New York City. Sports writer, *New York Times* (1915–43); columnist, *New York Sun* (1943–44). Regular panelist on "Information Please" radio program (1938–48).

Kier·ke·gaard \'kir-kə-,gȯr\, Søren Aabye. 1813–1855. Danish philosopher. Regarded as founder of Existentialist philosophy. Opposed Hegel's objective philosophy; held that each person must make a conscious, responsible choice among the aesthetic, ethical, and religious "stages" (alternatives) of life, but that only the religious, which necessarily involves suffering, can lead to the highest freedom for the self; in later years attacked the Church of Denmark for its secularization. His works, most published under pseudonyms, included *Enten-Eller* (*Either/Or,* 1843), *Frygt og Baevan* (1843), *Gjentagelsen* (1843), *Philosophiske Smuler* (1844), *Begrebet Angst* (1844), *Stadier paa Livets vei* (1845), *Afsluttende uvidenskabelig Efterskrift* (1846), *Kjerlighedens Gjerninger* (1847), *Sygdommen till Døden* (1849), *Indøvelse i Christendom* (1850).

Kies·ler \'kēs-lər\, Frederick John. 1896–1965. American architect, sculptor, and stage designer, b. Vienna. Associated with de Stijl group (c.1923) and later (late 1930s–early 1940s) with Surrealists; developed own theory, called Correalism, which attempted to express infinity and the environmental context of a work of art. Designed stage sets, esp. for Berlin production (1922) of Čapek's *R.U.R.;* designed first theater-in-the-round while architect and director of International Music Theater Festival, Vienna (1924); created a "floating city" model based on suspension principle for 1925 Paris International Exposition of Decorative Arts. To U.S. (1926); scenic director for Juilliard School of Music, New York (1933–57); director of design laboratory of Columbia U. School of Architecture (1936–42). Other architectural designs included womblike, free-form "Endless House" model (1923) and Shrine of the Book (1959–65) for Dead Sea Scrolls in Israel. Also executed Correalistic sculpture as *Galaxy* (c.1950) and *Marriage of Heaven and Earth* (1961–64).

Kigen Dōgen. See Dōgen.

Kiheiji. See Miyagawa Chōsun.

Ki·ku·chi \kē-ku̇ch-ē\ Kan. *Also called* Kikuchi Hiroshi. 1888–1948. Japanese writer and publisher. Established reputation with short stories *Mumei sakka no nikki* and *Tadanao gyōjō ki* (both 1918); founded (1923) *Bungei shunjū,* a popular literary magazine that eventually developed into a major publishing house. Also wrote plays *Okujō no kyōjin* (1916) and *Chichi kaeru* (1917) and novel *Shinju Fujin* (1920).

Kildare, Earls of. See Fitzgerald family.

Kil·ham \'kil-əm\, Alexander. 1762–1798. English clergyman. Expelled from Methodist Connexion (1796); organized Methodist New Connexion church (1797); followers known as Kilhamites.

Kil·i·an \'kīl-ē-ən\. Saint. c.640–c.689. Irish bishop. Missionary in Thuringia and eastern Franconia; beheaded, with companions SS. Colman and Totnan, at Würzburg on orders of Duke Gozbert.

Kil·li·grew \'kil-ə-grü\, Thomas. 1612–1683. English playwright. Followed Prince Charles into exile (1647); after Restoration given several court appointments; formed (1662) company of players, the King's Servants; built original Theatre Royal in Drury Lane (1663); made master of the revels (1673). Best known works, a coarse comedy *The Parson's Wedding* and tragicomedies including *The Prisoners* and *Claracilla.* His niece ¶Anne Killigrew (1660–1685) was a poet and painter; subject of one of Dryden's odes.

Kil·mer \'kil-mər\, Joyce, *in full* Alfred Joyce. 1886–1918. American poet, b. New Brunswick, N.J. On staff of *Standard Dictionary* (1909–12); contributed verse to various periodicals, including "Trees" to *Poetry* magazine (1913). Killed in action in World War I. Author of *Summer of Love* (1911), *Trees and Other Poems* (1914), *Main Street* (1917). m. (1908) ¶Aline Murray (1888–1941), b. Norfolk, Va., author of *Candles That Burn* (1919), *Vigils* (1921), *A Buttonwood Summer* (1929), and other verse.

Kil·pi \'kil-pē\, Volter. 1874–1939. Finnish novelist. Known esp. for experimental novel *Alastalon salissa* (1933).

Kil·vert \'kil-vərt\, Robert Francis. 1840–1879. English clergyman and diarist. His diary (discovered 1937, published 1938–40) gives detailed and valuable information on English country life of 1870s.

Kim \'kim\, Andrew. *Orig.* Kim Dae-gon. 1821–1846. Korean priest. Ordained in Shanghai (1845), first Korean Catholic priest; arrested and executed by Korean government while attempting to discover sea route for surreptitious entry of missionaries into Korea.

Kim Chŏng-hi. *Known also as* Ch'u-sa \chü-sä\ *or* Wan-dang \wän-däŋ\. 1786–1856. Korean calligrapher. Held several high government positions; exiled (1840) for anti-monarchical activities. Developed *ch'usa* style which remains one of major calligraphic styles.

Kim Dae-gon. See Andrew Kim.

Kim Hong-do. *Known also as* Tan·wŏn \tän-wən\, *i.e.* Sandalwood Garden. 1745?–? Korean painter. Master of many styles; used ancient linear style in his genre paintings, except for *Sennin* (Immortals) done in heroic style; known esp. for landscapes and depictions of common people in natural settings.

Kim·ban·gu \kim-'bäŋ-gü\, Simon[2]. 1889?–1951. Congolese religious leader. Proclaimed himself the *Gounza* (Swahili for Messiah) and founded (1921) a separatist Christian church whose religion is called Gounzism or Kimbanguism; preached against Belgian colonial regime;- arrested by Belgian authorities (1921) and spent rest of life in prison. The church Église de Jésus-Christ sur la Terre par le Prophet Simon Kimbangu admitted to World Council of Churches (1969).

Kim·hi *or* **Kim·ḥi** *or* **Kim·chi** *or* **Qim·ḥi** \ˈkim-k̲ē\. Medieval Jewish family of Hebrew grammarians and biblical scholars in Narbonne, Provence, including: Joseph (1105?–?1170), first to indicate 8 verb classes and to divide Hebrew vowels into 5 short and 5 long vowels; helped introduce Hebraic studies into Europe by his Hebrew translations of Arabic works by Spanish Jews; wrote grammar *Sefer ha-zikkaron, Sefer ha-galui* on lexicography and exegesis, and commentaries on Old Testament. His son ¶Moses (d. c.1190), first to introduce the verb *paqad* as a model for conjugation and to introduce the sequence now usual in enumerating stem forms; wrote first methodical manual of Hebrew grammar, *Mahalakh shevile ha-da'at.* His brother and pupil ¶David (c.1160–c.1235), *called* Ra·dak \rä-ˈdäk\ (from initials of Rabbi David Kimhi), author of *Sefer ha-shorashim* (a grammar much used by Christian Hebraists), *'Eṭ sofer* (a guide to punctuation of biblical manuscripts), *Sefer mikol* (a popular lexicon), and biblical commentaries.

Ki·mi·ta·ke \kē-mē-tä-ke\ Hiraoka. *Pseudonym* Mi·shi·ma \mē-shē-mä\ Yukio. 1925–1970. Japanese writer. Author of novels and stories exploring cultural dislocations of postwar Japan and psychological disturbances caused thereby, including *Kamen no kokuhaku* (1948), *Kinkakuji* (*Temple of the Golden Pavilion,* 1950), "Yūkoku" (story, "Patriotism," 1956; made into film), *Taiyō to tetsu* (nonfiction *Sun and Steel,* 1968), *Hōjō no umi* (*Sea of Fertility,* 1965–70); committed public hara-kiri to protest Westernization and military weakness of Japan.

Kim·mei \kēm-mā\. 509–571 A.D. Emperor of Japan (539–571). At war with Korea; during his reign (562) Buddhism was introduced in Japan.

Kim·mel \ˈkim-əl\, Husband Edward. 1882–1968. American naval officer, b. Henderson, Ky. Admiral (1941); commander of U.S. Pacific fleet (1941), commander in chief of combined U.S. fleet; relieved of command (Dec. 1941) after Japanese attack on Pearl Harbor.

Ki·nau \ˈkē-ˌnau̇\, Johann. *Pseudonym* Gorch Fock \ˈgȯrk̲-ˈfōk\. 1880–1916. German writer. Author of novels *Hein Godenwind* (1912) and *Seefahrt ist not* (1912), plays *Doggerbank* (1911) and *Cili Cohrs* (1914), and short stories.

Kinck \ˈkiŋk\, Hans Ernst. 1865–1926. Norwegian novelist and dramatist. Neoromanticist; his works often explored the national psychology or "mystery of the people." Best known for short-story collections *Flaggermusvinger* (1895) and *Fra hav til hei* (1897), verse play *Driftekaren* (1908), and novel *Sneskavlen brast* (1918–19).

Kind \ˈkint\, Johann Friedrich. 1768–1843. German novelist and dramatist. Author of librettos for Weber's *Freischütz* and K. Kreutzer's *Nachtlager von Granada.*

Kin·dī, al- \al-ˈkin-dē\. *In full* Ya·qūb ibn Isḥāq aṣ-Ṣabah al-Kindī. *Called* the Philosopher of the Arabs. d. c.870 A.D. Arab philosopher. Flourished in Iraq under caliphs al-Ma'mūn and al-Mu'taṣim; one of first Arab students of Greek philosophers; tried to formulate system combining views of Plato and Aristotle; translated Greek works into Arabic and wrote over 270 treatises on scientific subjects.

King \ˈkiŋ\, Clarence. 1842–1901. American geologist, b. Newport, R.I. With Josiah Whitney's Geological Survey of California (1863–66); discovered Mt. Whitney and explored desert regions of southern California and Arizona. Organized and directed (1867–77) U.S. Geological Survey of land along the 40th parallel; discovered first glaciers in U.S.; his report "Systematic Geology" (1878) a classic. First head of U.S. Geological Survey (1878–81); mining engineer (from 1881). Author of *Mountaineering in the Sierra Nevada* (1872).

King, Edward. 1612–1637. English poet. Friend of John Milton; subject of Milton's elegy *Lycidas.*

King, Ernest Joseph. 1878–1956. American naval officer, b. Lorain, Ohio. Commissioned in navy (1903); commander in chief, U.S. Atlantic fleet (1940), combined fleet (Dec. 1941); admiral (1941); chief of naval operations (1942–45); admiral of the fleet (1944).

King, Frank O. 1883–1969. American cartoonist, b. Cashton, Wis. On staff of *Chicago Tribune* (from 1909); created (1919) and drew (to 1951) comic strip "Gasoline Alley."

King, Franklin Hiram. 1848–1911. American agricultural scientist, b. near Whitewater, Wis. Taught at U. of Wisconsin (1888–1901); with U.S. Bureau of Soils (1901–04). Inventor of the cylindrical tower silo for silage storage (1889).

King, Gregory. 1648–1712. English genealogist, herald, and engraver. His *Natural and Political Observations and Conclusions upon the State and Condition of England, 1696* (pub. 1801) gives best information on 17th-century English population and wealth.

King, Henry. 1592–1669. English prelate and poet. Friend of Ben Jonson, Izaak Walton, John Donne; bishop of Chichester (1642–69). Published (1657) *Poems, Elegies, Paradoxes, and Sonets* which included his great elegy on his wife, "Exequy to his Matchless never to be forgotten Friend."

King, Martin Luther, Jr. 1929–1968. American clergyman and reformer, b. Atlanta, Ga. Ordained Baptist minister (1954); led boycott of Montgomery, Ala., transit system to force desegregation of city's buses (1956); founder (1957) and president of Southern Christian Leadership Conference; advocate of nonviolence and racial brotherhood; copastor with his father of Ebenezer Baptist Church, Atlanta (1960 ff.); major organizer of massive March on Washington where he delivered famous "I Have a Dream" speech (Aug. 1963); awarded Nobel peace prize (1964); assassinated at Memphis, Tenn.

King, Richard. 1825–1885. American rancher, b. Orange Co., N.Y. Operated steamboats on Rio Grande River; purchased (1852) 15,500 acres in southern Texas and built his King Ranch into largest ranch in U.S., controlling some 600,000 acres at time of death; his heirs increased ranch to almost a million acres.

King, Rufus. 1755–1827. American politician, b. Scarborough, Mass. (now part of Maine). Member, Continental Congress (1784–87), Constitutional Convention (1787); helped frame federal Constitution and instrumental in securing its ratification in Massachusetts. To New York City (1788); U.S. senator (1789–96, 1813–25); U.S. minister to Great Britain (1796–1803, 1825–26). Unsuccessful candidate for vice president of the U.S. (1804 and 1808), and for president (1816).

King, William. 1663–1712. English poet, wit, and miscellaneous writer. Engaged in most literary controversies of the day on Tory and High Church side; attacked Richard Bentley in *Dialogues of the Dead* (1699); wrote poem *The Art of Cookery* (1708), burlesque of contemporary science *Useful Transactions in Philosophy* (1709), and contributed to the *Tatler* and the *Examiner.*

King, William. c.1795–1882. See Wiremu KINGI.

King, William Lyon Mackenzie. 1874–1950. Canadian politician, b. Berlin (now Kitchener), Ont. Member of Dominion parliament (1908–11, 1919–48); minister of labor (1909–11); leader of Liberal party (1919–48). Prime minister of Canada (1921–26, 1926–30, 1935–48); helped preserve unity of English and French populations in Canada; championed Canadian independence in international affairs. Author of *Industry and Humanity* (1918).

King, William Rufus de Vane. 1786–1853. American politician, b. Sampson Co., N.C. Settled in Alabama (1818); U.S. senator (1819–44, 1848–53). U.S. minister to France (1844–46). Vice president of the U.S. (1853).

King-Hall \-ˈhȯl\, William Stephen Richard. Baron. 1893–1966. English author and commentator. Founder (1936) and editor (1936–59) of *King-Hall News-letter Service* (later *National News-letter*); Independent National M.P. (1939–44); founded Hansard Society of Parliamentary Government (1944). Author of *Our Own Times, 1913–34* (1935), *Defence in the Nuclear Age* (1958), etc.

Kin·gi \ˈkiŋ-(g)ē\, Wiremu. *Called also* Te Ran·gi·ta·ke \ˈtä-ˌräŋ-(g)ē-ˈtä-ke\ *or* William King. c.1795–1882. Maori chief. Converted to Christianity and at first supported British; resisted Sir George Grey's attempt to take over tribal lands in Taranaki province of North Island (1847); joined Maori King Movement and fought in First Taranaki War (1860–61); continued resistance to colonial usurpation of tribal lands by participation in Waikato War (1863–64) and other actions; finally submitted to authorities (1872).

Kingo \ˈkēŋ-ō\, Thomas Hansen. 1634–1703. Danish poet and prelate. Bishop of Fyn (1677). Greatest Danish Baroque poet; author of collections of hymns *Aandeligt sjungekor* (1674, 1681) and religious and secular poems and pastoral allegories.

Kings·ford \ˈkiŋz-fərd\, Anna, *nee* Bo·nus \ˈbō-nəs\. 1846–1888. English religious writer. m. (1867) Algernon G. Kingsford; collaborated with Edward Maitland in founding (1884) Hermetic Society to reconcile Christianity with Eastern religions.

Kingsford-Smith \-ˈsmith\, Sir Charles Edward. 1897–1935. Australian aviator. Served in Royal Flying Corps in World War I; in commercial aviation in Australia (from 1919). Made record flight around Australia, 7539 miles in 10 days (with Charles T. P. Ulm, 1927); flew from Oakland, Calif., to Brisbane, Australia (with Ulm, 1928; flying time 3 days, 11 hours, 19 min.). Set world's record for flight from Australia to England (with Ulm, 1929); flew from Portmarnock, Ire., to Harbour Grace, Nfd. (with others, 1930); made record-breaking solo flight, England to Australia, in 7 days, 4 hours, 43 min. (1933); lost en route to Singapore in attempted flight from England to Australia.

Kings·ley \ˈkiŋz-lē\, Charles. 1819–1875. English clergyman and novelist. A founding member of Christian Socialist movement; in novels *Yeast* (1848) and *Alton Locke* (1850) showed sympathy with the Chartists. Rector at Eversley, Hampshire; chaplain to Queen Victoria (1859); professor of modern history, Cambridge (1860–69); canon of Westminster (1873). Involved in controversy with Cardinal Newman, who wrote his *Apologia pro Vita Sua* (1864) in reply to a Kingsley attack. Author also of historical novels *Hypatia* (1853), *Westward*

Ho! (1855), *Hereward the Wake* (1866), and children's books *The Heroes* (1856) and *Water Babies* (1863).

His brother ¶Henry (1830–1876), novelist; left Oxford for unsuccessful undertaking in Australian goldfields (1853–58); war correspondent in Franco-Prussian War; editor, *Edinburgh Daily Review* (1869–70); wrote *Recollections of Geoffrey Hamlyn* (a picture of Australian life, 1859), *Ravenshoe* (1861), *Austin Elliott* (1863), *The Hillyars and the Burtons* (1865).

Another brother ¶George Henry (1827–1892), physician; traveled in most countries of the world; wrote books of sport and travel, including *South Sea Bubbles* (with G.R.C. Herbert, 1872). His daughter ¶Mary Henrietta (1862–1900), traveler and ethnologist; traveled extensively in West Africa, keeping careful record of her experiences and observations; died of typhoid fever while nursing wounded soldiers in Boer War; author of *Travels in West Africa* (1897), *West African Studies* (1899), *The Story of West Africa* (1899).

King·ston \'kiŋ-stən\, William Henry Giles. 1814–1880. English writer. Known for boys' books of adventure as *Peter the Whaler* (1851), *The Three Midshipmen* (1873), *Mungo Park's Travels* (1886).

Kin·kaid \kin-'kād, kiŋ-\, Thomas Cassin. 1888–1972. American naval officer, b. Hanover, N.H. Entered navy (1908); rear admiral (1941); commanded carrier *Enterprise* in Pacific (1941–43); commander of naval forces, North Pacific (1943); vice admiral (1943); commander, Seventh Fleet and Allied naval forces, Southwest Pacific (1943–45); directed naval support and landings in New Guinea, Philippines, Korea; fought battle of Philippine Sea or Leyte Gulf (Oct. 24–26, 1944); admiral (1945); retired (1950).

Kin·kel \'kiŋ-kəl\, Gottfried. 1815–1882. German poet and art historian. Published *Gedichte* (1843) and Romantic epic *Otto der Schütz* (1846); professor of art, Bonn (1845); founded newspaper *Demokratische Verein* (1848); actively supported German Revolution of 1848; imprisoned but escaped (1850) to London; professor of archaeology and art history, Zürich (1866).

Kin·ners·ley \'kin-ərz-lē\, Ebenezer. 1711–1778. American educator and scientist, b. Gloucester, England. To America (1714); chief master (1753–73) and professor of English and oratory (1755–73), College of Philadelphia. Known for investigations of electricity; invented an electrical air thermometer (c.1755).

Ki·no \'kē-nō\, Eusebio Francisco. *Orig.* Eusebio Francesco Chi·no \'kē-nō\ *or* Chi·ni \'kē-nē\. 1645–1711. Spanish missionary, b. Italy. Entered Society of Jesus (1665); to Mexico (1681) and Lower California (1682); missionary to Indians in Pimería Alta region (now northern Mexico and southern Arizona; 1687–1711); founded several missions; said to have explored sources of Rio Grande, Colorado, and Gila rivers; discovered and described Casa Grande ruins; prepared and published map of Lower California; wrote autobiographical *Favores celestiales* (1708).

Ki·no \kē-nō\ Tsurayuki. *Sometimes spelled* Ki \kē\ Tsurayuki. d. c.945 A.D. Japanese politician and man of letters. While chief of Imperial Documents Division helped compile first Imperial anthology of poetry *Kokin-shū* (905), writing for it a prose introduction regarded as first serious attempt at literary criticism in Japan. Governor of Tosa province (930–934); wrote (935) *Tosa nikki,* account of return trip from Tosa to capital. A prolific and proficient writer of Japanese verse (*uta*). His son ¶Tokibumi *or* Tokifumi (d. c.950) was one of five poets (later called the Five Men of the Pear-Jar Room) who compiled (951) the *Gosenshū,* second Imperial poetic anthology.

Kin·sey \'kin-zē\, Alfred Charles. 1894–1956. American zoologist and sexologist, b. Hoboken, N.J. Professor of zoology (1920 ff.), Indiana U.; began scientific study of human sexual behavior (1938); founder (1942) and director (1942–56) of Institute for Sex Research at Indiana U. His extensive surveys of sexual behavior and opinions of Americans published in *Sexual Behavior in the Human Male* (1948) and *Sexual Behavior in the Human Female* (1953).

Kinwun Mingyi. See GAUNG.

Kip·ling \'kip-liŋ\, Rudyard, *in full* Joseph Rudyard. 1865–1936. English writer, b. India. Reared in England; returned to India (1882); on editorial staff of *Civil & Military Gazette and Pioneer,* Lahore (1882–89); began writing verse and tales while in India and continued in England (from 1889). Awarded Nobel prize for literature (1907). Among his works were *Departmental Ditties* (1886), *Plain Tales from the Hills* (1888), *Soldiers Three* (1888), *Wee Willie Winkie* (1888), *The Light That Failed* (1890), *Life's Handicap* (1891), *Barrack-Room Ballads* (1892), *Many Inventions* (1893), *The Jungle Book* (1894), *Second Jungle Book* (1895), *The Seven Seas* (1896), *Captains Courageous* (1897), *The Day's Work* (1898), *Stalky and Co.* (1899), *Kim* (1901), *Just So Stories for Little Children* (1902), *Traffics and Discoveries* (1904), *Puck of Pook's Hill* (1906), *Actions and Reactions* (1909), *Rewards and Fairies* (1910), *The Harbour Watch* (play, 1913), *A Diversity of Creatures* (1917), *The Years Between* (1918), *Inclusive Verse* (1919), *Debits and Credits* (1926), *A Book of Words* (1928), *Limits and Renewals* (1932), and *Something of Myself* (autobiography, 1937).

Kip·ping \'kip-iŋ\, Frederic Stanley. 1863–1949. English chemist. Professor at University College, Nottingham (1897–1936); pioneered in study of silicones.

Kir·by \'kər-bē\, Rollin. 1875–1952. American cartoonist, b. Galva, Ill. Cartoonist for *New York World* (1913–31), *New York World-Telegram* (1931–39), *New York Post* (1939–42); freelance cartoonist (from 1942). Known for cartoons criticizing Wall Street, New York's political machine, imperialism, fascism, etc.; created "Mr. Dry," symbol of Prohibition; awarded Pulitzer prizes for cartoons "On the Road to Moscow" (1921), "News from the Outside World" (1924), and "Tammany" (1928).

Kirby, William. 1817–1906. Canadian writer, b. Kingston-upon-Hull, Yorkshire, England. Settled in Niagara, Canada (1839); editor of Niagara *Mail* (1850–71); collector of customs (1871–95). His works included epic poem *The U.E.* (1859), historical novel *The Golden Dog* (1877), and history *Annals of Niagara* (1896).

Kir·by-Smith \ˌkər-bē-'smith\, Edmund. *Orig.* Edmund Kirby Smith; *hyphenated form adopted by his family after his death.* 1824–1893. American army officer, b. St. Augustine, Fla. In U.S. army (1845–61). Entered Confederate service (1861); major general (Oct. 1861), lieutenant general (Oct. 1862), general (Feb. 1864); led advance in Kentucky campaign, defeated Union forces at Richmond, Ky., and fought at Perryville, Ky., and Stones River, Tenn. (all 1862). In command of Trans-Mississippi Department (from 1863); defeated Federal Red River expedition (Apr. 1864); last Confederate commander to surrender (May 26, 1865). President, U. of Nashville (1870–75); professor of mathematics, U. of the South (from 1875).

Kir·cher \'kir-k̲ər\, Athanasius. 1601–1680. German Jesuit and scholar. Taught mathematics and Hebrew at the College of Rome (from c.1638); gave up teaching to study hieroglyphics and archaeology (1643). Credited with invention of the magic lantern.

Kirch·hoff \'kirk̲-hȯf\, Gustav Robert. 1824–1887. German physicist. Professor at Heidelberg (1854–75) and Berlin (1875–86). Enunciated (1845) Kirchhoff's laws which allow calculation of currents, voltages, and resistances of electrical networks; discovered, jointly with R. W. Bunsen, method of spectrum analysis (1859) which led to their discovery of cesium (1860) and rubidium (1861). Studied composition of the Sun, including explanation of Fraunhofer's lines; announced (1859) Kirchhoff's radiation law relating emission and absorption spectral lines of any body at a definite temperature. Published *Vorlesungen über mathematische Physik* (1876–94), *Chemische Analyse durch Spectralbeobachtungen* (with R. Bunsen, 1895), etc.

Kirchman, Jacob. See KIRKMAN.

Kirch·ner \'kirk̲-nər\, Ernst Ludwig. 1880–1938. German painter and printmaker. Cofounder in Dresden (with Erich Heckel and Karl Schmidt-Rottluff) of Expressionist group Die Brücke (1905; disbanded 1913). Influenced by Dürer, African and Polynesian art, Cubism; his style highly personal, notable for its psychological tension, eroticism, sharp colors. Works included canvases as *Girl Under Japanese Umbrella* (1906), *Artist and His Model* (1907), *Street, Berlin* (1907 and 1913), *Bathers at Moritzburg* (1908), *Amselfluh* (1923); lithographs as *Head of a Man with a Nude* (1908); woodcuts for periodical *Der Sturm;* and illustrations as for Chamisso's *Peter Schlemihls wundersame Geschichte* (1915) and Heym's poem "Umbra Vitae" (1924).

Kirch·wey \'kərch-ˌwā\, Freda. 1893–1976. American editor and publisher, b. Lake Placid, N.Y. Joined editorial staff of liberal journal *The Nation* (1918); rose to editor (1933); purchased (1937) *Nation* and continued as editor (to 1955); known for support of liberal government policies, disarmament, civil rights, etc.

Kir·dorf \'kir-ˌdȯrf\, Emil. 1847–1938. German industrialist. A founder (1920) of the Rhine-Elbe Union, later merged (1926) into the gigantic Vereinigte Stahlwerke. Criticized the Weimar Republic; championed a nationalistic policy and was an early supporter of Hitler.

Ki·re·yev·sky \kyir-yi-'yef-skəi\, Ivan Vasilyevich. 1806–1856. Russian critic and editor. Founded (1832) literary journal *Yevropeyets* to advocate introduction of European culture; for same purpose founded (1852) *Moskovsky sbornik,* for which he wrote his best known article "About the Character of European Education and Its Bearing on Education in Russia."

Kirk \'kərk\, Alan Goodrich. 1888–1963. American naval officer and diplomat, b. Philadelphia. Commissioned in navy (1909); rear admiral (1941); commander of Amphibious Force, Atlantic fleet (Feb. 1943); supervised landing of Gen. Patton's 7th army on Sicily (June 1943); commanded Western Naval Task Force that landed American troops and supplies at Omaha and Utah beaches of Normandy on D-Day (June 6, 1944); commander of U.S. naval forces in France (Oct. 1944); retired as admiral (1946). Ambassador to Belgium (1946–49), Moscow (1949–52), Taiwan (1962).

Kirk, Sir John. 1832–1922. Scottish naturalist and colonial administrator. Physician and naturalist with David Livingstone's expedition in Africa (1858–63). Vice consul of Zanzibar (1867–73) and consul general (1873–87).

Kirk, Norman Eric. 1923–1974. New Zealand politician. M.P. (1957–74); leader of Labour party (from 1964); prime minister and minister of foreign affairs (1972–74).

Kirk·cal·dy *or* **Kir·kal·dy** \kər-ˈkȯ(l)-dē\ of Grange \ˈgrānj\, Sir William. d. 1573. Scottish soldier and politician. Involved in murder of Cardinal Beaton (1546); opposed marriage of Mary, Queen of Scots, to Darnley (1565); participated in murder of Riccio (1566); held Edinburgh for Mary (1568–73), but forced to surrender it; executed.

Kirke \ˈkərk\, Edward. 1553–1613. English clergyman. Rector of Risby, Suffolk (1580–1613). Usually identified with "E.K.," author of preface, arguments, and commentary to Edmund Spenser's *Shepheardes Calender* (1579).

Kirk·land \ˈkərk-lənd\, Caroline Matilda, *nee* Stans·bury \ˈstanz-ˌber-ē, -bər-ē\. *Pseudonym* Mrs. Mary Clav·ers \ˈklav-ərz \. 1801–1864. American author, b. New York City. m. (1828) William Kirkland (d. 1846). Author of *A New Home—Who'll Follow* (1839), *Forest Life* (1842), *Western Clearings* (1845). Her son ¶Joseph (1830–1894), b. Chicago; lawyer and novelist; author of trilogy of Midwestern pioneer life *Zury* (1885), *The McVeys* (1888), *The Captain of Company K* (1891); also wrote *The Story of Chicago* (1892–94).

Kirkland, Samuel. 1741–1808. American clergyman, b. Norwich, Conn. Congregational missionary to the Iroquois Indians (from 1764); influential in securing declaration of neutrality from the Six Nations at outbreak of American Revolution (1775); chaplain to colonial troops during Revolution; founded Hamilton Oneida Academy (1793), later (1812) chartered as Hamilton College. His son ¶John Thornton (1770–1840), b. near Little Falls, N.Y., was president of Harvard (1810–28).

Kirk·man *or* **Kirck·man** *or* **Kirch·mann** \ˈkərk-mən\, Jacob. 1710–1792. British harpsichord maker, b. Lower Alsatia. To London (early 1730s), naturalized (1755); harpsichord maker to the queen (1763); gained wide reputation for the excellence of his instruments; rival of Burkat Shudi. Entered partnership (c.1770) with his nephew ¶Abraham Kirkman (1737–1794).

Ki·rov \ˈkyē-rəf\, Sergey Mironovich. *Surname orig.* Kos·tri·kov \ˈkȯs-tryi-kəf\. 1886–1934. Soviet politician. Engaged in revolutionary activities (from 1905); after revolution (1917), took part in wars against counterrevolutionists (1917–20). Secretary of Communist party in Azerbaijan (1921–26) and in Leningrad (1926–34); one of Stalin's chief aides; elected to party's Central Committee (1922), Politburo (1930), Central Committee's Secretariat (1934). His assassination instigated Stalin's Great Purge (1934–38).

Kir·wan \ˈkər-wən\, Richard. 1733–1812. Irish chemist. Author of *Elements of Mineralogy* (1784), first English systematic treatise on this subject.

Ki·sel·yov \kyis-yil-ˈyȯf\, Pavel Dmitriyevich. 1788–1872. Russian general and politician. As chief administrator of Russian occupation of Walachia and Moldavia (1829–34), supervised formulation of the *Règlement organique;* minister of state domains (1837–56); ambassador to France (from 1856).

Kis·fa·ludy \ˈkish-fäl-u̇d-ē\, Sándor. 1772–1844. Hungarian writer. Author of song cycle *Kesergő szerelem* (1801), three poetic romances published as *Regék a magyar előidőkből* (1807), and plays. His brother ¶Károly (1788–1830) was a poet and dramatist of the Romantic school, founder of modern national drama of Hungary; cofounder, with Sándor, and editor (from 1822) of *Aurora,* organ of the Romantics; author of historical dramas of Hungary as *A tatárok Magyarországon* (1819), of comedies as *A kérők* (1817), and of tragedies as *Iréne* (1820) of contemporary Hungarian life.

Kisrā. See KHOSROW.

Kiss \ˈkis\, August. 1802–1865. German sculptor. His works included *Mounted Amazon Attacked by a Tiger,* an equestrian statue of Frederick the Great, statues of Frederick William III, and *St. George and the Dragon.*

Ki·ta·ba·ta·ke \kē-tä-bä-täk-e\ Chikafusa. 1292–1354. Japanese warrior, politician, and writer. Chief military and administrative official of Emperor Daigo II (from 1333). Author of politico-historical treatise *Jinnō shōtōki* (written 1339, published 1369) which originated mystic and nationalist doctrine that Japan had unique superiority among nations because of its unbroken succession of divine rulers.

Ki·ta·ga·wa \kē-tä-gä-wä\ Utamaro. *Also known as* Uta·ma·ro \u̇t-ä-mä-rō\. 1753–1806. Japanese artist. At first designed prints for books and published illustrated books on nature, as *Gahon chūsen* (1788); specialized (from c.1791) in making half-length single portraits of sensuous female beauties in *Ukiyo-e* style. Works included *Ten Physiognomies of Women, Twelve Hours at the Gay Quarters, Seven Beauties of the Gay Quarters, Women in Love.*

Ki·ta·sa·to \kē-tä-zä-tō\ Shibasaburo. 1852–1931. Japanese bacteriologist. Studied under Koch in Berlin (1885–91); isolated bacilli of tetanus and of symptomatic anthrax (1889) and of dysentery (1898). Prepared a diphtheria antitoxin (1890). Discovered etiological agent of bubonic plague *Bacillus pestis* (1894).

Kitch·e·ner \ˈkich(-ə)-nər\, Horatio Herbert. 1st Earl Kitchener of Khar·toum \kär-ˈtüm\ and of Broome \ˈbrüm\. 1850–1916. British soldier, b. Ireland. Commissioned in Royal Engineers (1871); served (from 1874) in the Middle East, including Wolseley's expedition for relief of General Gordon (1884–85). Governor general of Eastern Sudan (1886). Sirdar of Egyptian army (1892); invaded Sudan, annihilated al-Mahdī's army at Omdurman, and reoccupied Khartoum (1898); governor general of Sudan (1899). Chief of staff to Lord Roberts in South Africa (1899); succeeded Roberts as commander in chief and organized forces to combat guerrilla warfare of Boers (1900–02). Created viscount (1902), earl (1914). Commander in chief in India (1902–09). Proconsul of Egypt (1911–14). Secretary of state for war (1914); promoted to field marshal (1914); engaged in organizing British forces for war (1914–16).

Kit·tel \ˈkit-əl\, Rudolf. 1853–1929. German scholar. Professor at Breslau (1888–98) and Leipzig (1898–1924). One of first to use archaeological evidence in studying Palestinian and Israelite history; his edition of the Hebrew Bible (1905–06) superseded all previous ones; also wrote *Geschichte des Volkes Israel* (1909–29) and *Die Religion des Volkes Israel* (1921).

Kittl, Ema. See Emmy DESTINN.

Kit·tredge \ˈki-trij\, George Lyman. 1860–1941. American educator, b. Boston. Teacher of English, Harvard (1888–1936; professor from 1894). Authority on Shakespeare and medieval English literature. Author of *The Language of Chaucer's Troilus* (1894), *Words and Their Ways in English Speech* (with J. B. Greenough, 1901), *English Witchcraft and James I* (1912), *Advanced English Grammar* (with F. E. Farley, 1913), *Chaucer and His Poetry* (1915), *Gawain and the Green Knight* (1916), *Shakespeare* (1916), *Sir Thomas Malory* (1925), *Witchcraft in Old and New England* (1929), etc. Edited *Albion Series of Anglo-Saxon and Middle English Poetry* (with J. W. Bright, 1900–07), *Complete Works of Shakespeare* (1936).

Kivi, Aleksis. See Aleksis STENVALL.

Kiy \ˈkē\ and his brothers **Kho·riv** \ˈkȯr-ēv\ and **Shchek** \ˈshchek\. 6th–7th century A.D. Slavic chiefs. According to 12th-century *Russian Primary Chronicle,* leaders of the Polyane tribe of East Slavs and founders of present-day Ukrainian city of Kiev, named for Kiy.

Kiyomori. See under TAIRA family.

Kjel·dahl \ˈkel-däl\, Johan Gustav Christoffer Thorsager. 1849–1900. Danish chemist. Director of Carlsberg Laboratory, Copenhagen (1876–1900). Known for devising Kjeldahl method for estimation of nitrogen in organic substances (1883).

Kjel·len \ˈkyel-ən\, Johan Rudolf. 1864–1922. Swedish political scientist. Expounded theory that the state is an organism with qualities of growth and decay in *Staten som lifs-form* (1918–19); coined term geopolitics.

Kje·rulf \ˈke-ru̇lf\, Halfdan. 1815–1868. Norwegian composer. Representative of national Norwegian music. Composed lyric piano pieces, choruses, and songs.

Klabund. See Alfred HENSCHKE.

Klacz·ko \ˈkläch-kō\, Julian. 1825–1906. Polish political commentator and literary critic. Settled in Paris (1849); co-editor of Polish review *Wiadomosci Polskie* (1857–61); writer for *Revue des Deux Mondes* (1862–93); his articles collected in *Études de diplomatie contemporaine* (1866) and *Les Deux Chanceliers* (1876). Privy councilor to court of Vienna (1870); member of Galician Sejm and of Austrian Reichsrat (1870–73).

Klaf·sky \ˈkläf-skē\, Katharina. 1855–1896. Hungarian soprano. Sang Brangäne in first Leipzig performance of Wagner's *Tristan und Isolde* (1882); principal star of Hamburg Opera (from 1886); sang with Damrosch Opera Co. in U.S. (1895–96); known for Wagnerian roles and as Donna Anna in *Don Giovanni,* Leonora in *Fidelio,* Bellini's Norma.

Klaj \ˈklī\, Johann. *Lat.* Cla·jus \ˈklä-yu̇s\. 1616–1656. German poet. In Nürnberg founded, with Harsdörfer, literary group Pegnitzer Hirtengesellschaft (1644); author of mystery plays in verse, religious oratorios, pastoral poetry, a satirical novel *Royaume de la Cocqueterie* (1659).

Klap·ka \ˈkläp-kä\, György. 1820–1892. Hungarian soldier and nationalist. Entered Austrian army (1838); joined Hungarian national army (1848); general (1849); led Northern Hungarian army (1849); served in battle of Kápolna and with distinction under Görgey at Komárno and elsewhere; defended Komárno, capitulating on honorable terms (1849). In exile (1849–67); organized Hungarian legion with Kossuth in Italy (1859) and with Bismarck in Upper Silesia (1866). Returned to Hungary following amnesty (1867) and supported Deák party as member of Hungarian parliament.

Klap·roth \ˈkläp-ˌrōt\, Martin Heinrich. 1743–1817. German chemist. With Prussian medical bureaucracy (1782–1817); taught chemistry at Berlin Mining School (1784–1817); professor at Berlin U. (1810–17). Helped improve and systematize analytical chemistry and mineralogy; discovered uranium (1789), zirconium (1789), and cerium (1803). His son ¶Heinrich Julius (1783–1835), Orientalist; taught at St. Petersburg Academy (1804–12); made extensive ethnographic and linguistic exploration of the Caucasus (1807–08); published *Reise in den Kaukasus* (1814) and *Asia polyglotta nebst Sprachatlas* (1823), latter being sole source of information of several extinct Caucasian languages; lived in Paris (from 1815), becoming (1816) professor of Asiatic languages and literature in pay of king of Prussia.

Klau·ber \ˈklō-bər\, Adolph. 1869–1933. American theatrical producer, b. Louisville, Ky. m. (1906) Jane Cowl (*q.v.*). Produced Eugene O'Neill's *Emperor Jones* (1920) and, with his wife, *Lilac Time, Smilin' Through, Romeo and Juliet, Pelleas and Melisande, Antony and Cleopatra.*

Klaus, Bruder. See Niklaus von FLÜE.

Klaus, Karl Karlovich. See Carl Ernst CLAUS.

Klaw \ˈklō\, Marc. 1858–1936. American theatrical manager, b. Paducah, Ky. With Abraham L. Erlanger formed booking agency in New York (1888); partner (1896–1916) with Erlanger, Charles Frohman, and others in Theatrical Syndicate which controlled majority of American theatrical bookings.

Klé·ber \klā-ber\, Jean-Baptiste. 1753–1800. French soldier. Officer in Austrian army (1776–82); joined French national guard (1789); defended Mainz (1793); general (1793); crushed counter-revolutionary uprising in the Vendée (Oct.–Dec. 1793); engaged at Fleurus (1794); commanded army of the Rhine and Moselle (1795); commanded a division in Napoléon's army in Egypt and Syria (1798–1800) and was left as commander in chief when Napoléon returned (1799) to France; recaptured Cairo from Turks (Apr. 1800); assassinated by an Egyptian fanatic.

Klebs \ˈklāps\, Edwin. 1834–1913. German pathologist. Assistant to Virchow at Berlin (1861–66). To U.S.; professor, Rush Medical College, Chicago (1896); later returned to Germany. Described (1883) the bacillus causing diphtheria, later isolated by Friedrich Löffler and known as the Klebs-Löffler bacillus; also investigated the bacteriology of malaria, anthrax, tuberculosis, etc.

Klee \ˈklā\, Paul. 1879–1940. Swiss painter. Lived in Munich (1906–20); cofounder (with Kandinsky and Marc) of the German abstract group Blaue Reiter (1912); taught at the Bauhaus at Weimar (1921–26) and Dessau (1926–31); cofounder (with Feininger, Kandinsky, and Jawlensky) of Die Blaue Vier (1924); published *Pädagogisches Skizzenabuch* (1925); on faculty of Düsseldorf Academy (1931–33); lived in Switzerland (from 1933). Developed own highly inventive pictorial language and private symbolism to express the subconscious mind and fantasy in art. His abstract canvases included *A Young Lady's Adventure* (1922), *Around the Fish* (1926), *The Mocker Mocked* (1930), *Child Consecrated to Suffering* (1935), *Rich Harbor* (1938), *Demonry* (1939), *Death and Fire* (1940); also executed etchings, drawings, lithographs.

Klei·ber \ˈklī-bər\, Erich. 1890–1956. Austrian conductor. General music director of Berlin State Opera (1923–34); conducted German opera at Buenos Aires (1936–49); chief conductor of Berlin State Opera (1954–56). Known for interpretations of Mozart, Beethoven, Wagner, Strauss, and for fidelity to composers' intentions. Composed concertos for piano and for violin, orchestral and chamber works, and songs.

Klein \ˈklīn\, Abraham Moses. 1909–1972. Canadian lawyer and poet, b. Montreal. Practiced law in Montreal (1933–54). Author of works on Jewish themes as volumes of poetry *Hath Not a Jew* (1940), *Poems* (1944), *The Hitleriad* (1944), and novel *The Second Scroll* (1951); also *The Rocking Chair and Other Poems* (1948) on changes wrought by industrialization on Quebec.

Klein, Bernhard Joseph. 1793–1832. German composer. His works included oratorios *Job* (1820), *David* (1830), and *Jephthah* (1828); operas *Dido* (1823) and *Ariadne* (1823); church music, songs, etc.

Klein, Christian Felix. 1849–1925. German mathematician. Professor at Erlangen (1872–75), Leipzig (1880–86), Göttingen (1886–1913); founded (1895) and supervised (until death) *Enzyklopädie der mathematischen Wissenschaften.* Known esp. for his *Erlanger Programm* (1872), a synthesis of geometry as the study of the properties of a space that are invariant under a given group of transformations; collaborated with Sophus Lie on discovery (1870) of fundamental properties of asymptotic lines of the Kummer surface and was first to systematize Lie's contact transformations; also worked on theory of functions, hyperbolic geometry, and application of mathematics to physics. Published *Vorlesungen über das Ikosaeder* (1884), *Vorlesungen über die Theorie der automorphen Functionen* (1897–1912), *Elementarmathematik vom höheren Standpunkt* (1911), etc.

Klein, Melanie, *nee* Rei·zes \ˈrīt-səs\. 1882–1960. British psychoanalyst, b. Vienna. m. Arthur S. Klein (div. 1923). Resident in Berlin (1921–26) and London (from 1926, naturalized 1934). Influenced chiefly by Karl Abraham; developed (1921–34) technique of "play therapy" for psychoanalysis of children. Author of *The Psychoanalysis of Children* (1932), *Envy and Gratitude* (1957), *Narrative of a Child Analysis* (1961).

Kleist \ˈklīst\, Ewald Christian von. 1715–1759. German poet and soldier. Officer in Danish army (1736) and in Prussian army (from 1740); mortally wounded at battle of Kunersdorf. Author of the descriptive nature poem *Der Frühling* (1749), the *Ode an die preussische Armee* (1757), the short epic poem *Cissides und Paches* (1759), and other lyrics, odes, idyls, hymns, etc.

Kleist, Ewald Georg von. 1700–1748. German ecclesiastic and scientist. Dean of cathedral of Kamin, Pomerania. Discovered (1745) principle of the Leyden jar, later described more fully by Pieter van Musschenbroek.

Kleist, Heinrich von, *in full* Bernd Heinrich Wilhelm von. 1777–1811. German dramatist, poet, and prose writer. Officer in Prussian army (1792–99); founded in Dresden (with Adam Müller) the journal *Phöbus* (1808); pamphleteer and journalist on Austro-French war front (1809) and in Prague against Napoléon; edited and contributed to *Berliner Abendblätter* (1810–11, suppressed for attacks on Hardenberg); poverty-stricken and despondent, killed his friend Henriette Vogel and himself by mutual agreement. Considered first great German dramatist of 19th century. Author of the tragedies *Die Familie Schroffenstein* (1803), *Robert Guiskard* (1808, unfinished), and *Penthesilea* (1808), the Romantic chivalric drama *Das Käthchen von Heilbronn* (1810), the psychological drama *Prinz Friedrich von Hamburg* (1810; pub. 1821), the patriotic drama *Die Hermannschlacht* (1810; pub. 1821), the comedy *Der zerbrochene Krug* (1812), eight novellas collected in *Erzählungen* (1810–11, including *Michael Kohlhaus* and *Die Marquise von O...*), essays, lyric poetry, etc.

Kleist, Paul Ludwig Ewald von. 1881–1954. German general. In command against France (1940), in Yugoslavia (1941), and on southern Russian front (Aug. 1941); advanced through Ukraine into Caucasus (1941–42) until defeats and withdrawals forced by Russian winter offensive (1942–43).

Klemm \ˈklem\, Gustav Friedrich. 1802–1867. German anthropologist. Director of royal library at Dresden (from 1831). Developed concept of three stages of cultural evolution; thought to have influenced Sir Edward Burnett Tylor. Author of *Allgemeine Kulturgeschichte der Menschheit* (1843–52), *Allgemeine Kulturwissenschaft* (1854–55), etc.

Klem·pe·rer \ˈklem-pər-ər\, Otto. 1885–1973. German conductor. Conductor, German National Theater at Prague (1907–10), Hamburg (1910–12), Barmen (1913–14), Cologne (1917–24), Wiesbaden (1924–27), Kroll Opera at Berlin 1927–31), Los Angeles Philharmonic (1933–39), Budapest Opera (1947–50), Philharmonia Orchestra of London (1955–72). Known especially for readings of German Romantic composers.

Kle·nau \ˈklā-ˌnaü\, Paul August von. 1883–1946. Danish composer and conductor. Composed operas as *Sulamith* (1913), *Kjarten und Gudrun* (1918), and *Elisabeth von England* (1939), seven symphonies, ballet *Klein Idas Blumen* (1916), choral works, piano pieces, etc.

Klen·gel \ˈkleŋ-əl\, Paul. 1854–1935. German violinist, pianist, and composer. Teacher at Leipzig Conservatory (1907–31); composed songs, piano pieces, etc. His brother ¶Julius (1859–1933), cellist and composer; teacher at Leipzig Conservatory (from 1881); composed four cello concertos, suites, sonatas, concert pieces and studies, chamber music, and a *Hymnus* for 12 cellos.

Klen·ze \ˈklent-sə\, Franz Karl Leo von. 1784–1864. German architect. Court architect in Munich (from 1816). Author of works chiefly on Greek architecture. Designed, mainly in Italian Renaissance and Greek Revival styles, the Glyptothek (1816), the war department building (1824–30), the palace of Duke Maximilian (1826–30), the Alte Pinakothek (1826–36), the king's residence (1826–32) and banquet building (1831–42), and the Propylaea (1846–63), all in Munich.

Klerk \ˈklerk\, Michel de. 1884–1923. Dutch architect. Leader of Amsterdam school which stressed individualism, fantasy, and picturesqueness. Designed Hille Building (1911) and De Dagenaad (1920–22) and Eigen Haard (1921) apartment blocks, all in Amsterdam.

Klesel *or* **Klesl,** Melchior. See KHLESL.

Klič *or* **Klietsch** \ˈklēch\, Karl. 1841–1926. Bohemian artist and printer. Invented most precise and commercially successful method of photogravure printing (1878); later associated with Samuel Fawcett; established (1895) first rotogravure firm, the Rembrandt Intaglio Printing Co., Lancaster, England.

Klie·gl \ˈklē-gəl\, John H. (1869–1959) and his brother Anton T. (1872–1927). American businessmen, b. Bad Kissingen, Germany. Pioneers in development of lighting equipment (including klieg light, 1911) and scenic effects for the stage and for motion pictures. John emigrated to U.S. in 1888, Anton in 1892; formed partnership (1896) of Kliegl Brothers Universal Electric Stage Lighting Co., New York City.

Klimt \ˈklimt\, Gustav. 1862–1918. Austrian painter. Founder (1897) of Vienna Sezession school of painting marked by a highly decorative style; his allegorical murals (1900–03) for U. of Vienna rejected for their erotic symbolism and pessimism. Works included *The Kiss* (1908), portraits *Frau Fritza Riedler* (1906) and *Frau Adele Block-Bauer* (1907), *Beethoven Frieze* mural (1902), and murals in Stoclet House, Brussels (1909–11).

Kline \ˈklīn\, Franz Joseph. 1910–1962. American painter, b. Wilkes-Barre, Pa. His early style merged Cubism and social realism, as in *Chinatown* (1948). Became (from 1949) a leading member of "action painting" branch of Abstract

Expressionism, developing highly personal style often employing graphic networks of rough but controlled bars of black paint on white backgrounds, as in *Mahoning* (1956); later introduced color into paintings, as in *Orange and Black Wall* (1959). Other works included *Nijinsky* (c.1950), *Riverbed* (1961), *Caboose* (1961).

Kling·er \'kliŋ-ər\, Friedrich Maximilian von. 1752–1831. German dramatist and novelist. Joined Russian army (1780), rising to lieutenant general (1811); ennobled (1780). Curator of Dorpat U. (1803–17). Author of dramatic works, including *Der Wirrwarr, oder Sturm und Drang* (1776), which gave its name to the Sturm und Drang period of German literature, *Die Zwillinge* (1776), *Simsone Grisaldo* (1776), and *Die neue Arria* (1776); philosophical and realistic novels, as *Fausts Leben, Taten, und Höllenfahrt* (1791), *Geschichte eines Teutschen der neuesten Zeit* (1798), and *Der Weltmann und der Dichter* (1798).

Klinger, Max. 1857–1920. German engraver, painter, and sculptor. His works included series of pen-and-ink drawings and cycles of etchings, as *Fantasies upon the Finding of a Glove, Eve and the Future, A Love, Of Death, Brahms Fantasy;* engraved self-portraits and bookplates; paintings, as the *Judgment of Paris, Crucifixion, Pietà, Christ on Olympus,* and frescoes for Leipzig U.; polychromatic marble figures of Salome and of Cassandra; polychromatic statue of Beethoven; busts of Nietzsche, Liszt, and others; a colossal bronze *Athlete.*

Klint \'klint\, Kaare. 1888–1954. Danish furniture designer. Worked first as architect; founded (1924) Danish Academy of Art and became its first professor of furniture department. Originator of modern Scandinavian style; his designs noted for functionalism and beautiful wood finishes, as in collapsible teak deck chair with wicker seat (1933).

Klo·no·wic \klô-'nô-vēts\, Sebastian Fabian. *Lat. surname* Acer·nus \ə-'sər-nəs\. c.1545–1602. Polish poet. Author of works in Latin and Polish including *Roxolania* (1584, satire on Russia), *Victoria deorum* (1587, on the oppression of the poor), *Flis* (1595, on life of Vistula River raftsmen), and *Worek Judaszów* (1600, on corruption and exploitation of the time).

Kloos \'klōs\, Willem Johan Theodoor. 1859–1938. Dutch poet and critic. Central figure of 1880 Dutch literary revival; cofounder (1885) and mainstay of its periodical *De nieuwe gids;* championed aesthetic idea of beauty as having highest value in art and life. Best known for his early sonnets collected in *Verzen* (1894).

Klop·stock \'klȯp-shtȯk\, Friedrich Gottlieb. 1724–1803. German poet. Achieved sensational success with publication (1748) of first 3 cantos of his religious epic in unrhymed hexameters *Der Messias.* Private tutor at Langensalza (1748–50), where he fell in love with his cousin, the "Fanny" of his odes; lived in Copenhagen on royal pension (1751–70); m. (1754) Margarethe (Meta) Moller, the "Cidli" of his odes (d. 1758); in Hamburg (1770 ff.), where he published (1773) the last 5 of the 20-canto *Messias.* Other works included *Geistliche Lieder* (1757, 1769), *Oden* (1771); critical and theoretical writings, including the prose *Die deutsche Gelehrtenrepublik* (1774) on his own scheme of poetry; religious dramas as *Der Tod Adams* (1757) and *David* (1772); and *Hermanns Schlacht* (1769), *Hermann und die Fürsten* (1784), and *Hermanns Tod* (1787), a trilogy of historical prose dramas with bardic choruses.

Klotz *or* **Kloz** \'klȯts\. Family of Bavarian violinmakers in Mittenwald including: Mathias (1653–1743), active in Padua and (from 1683) in Mittenwald. His sons ¶Georg (1687–1737), ¶Sebastian (1696–c.1760), and ¶Johann Carl (1709–c.1770).

Kluck \'klu̇k\, Heinrich Rudolph Alexander von. 1846–1934. German general. Commanded 1st Army in attempt to take Paris (1914); defeated 13 miles from city by Anglo-French forces in First Battle of the Marne (Sept. 6–9, 1914); wounded (1915) and retired (1916). Wrote version of the battle in *Der Marsch auf Paris und die Marneschlacht* (1926).

Kluck·hohn \'klək-ˌhōn\, Clyde Kay Maben. 1905–1960. American anthropologist, b. Le Mars, Ia. Taught at Harvard (from 1935); noted for studies of the Navajo and of cultural value systems and patterns. Author of *Navaho Witchcraft* (1944), *Mirror for Man* (1949, with E.Z. Vogt and Leonard McCombe), etc.

Klu·ge \'klü-gə\, Hans Günther von. 1882–1944. German field marshal. Served in World War I (1914–18); occupied Polish Corridor (1939); served in France (1940); as commander on central Russian front (1941–43) was largely successful in containing Soviet offensives; as commander in chief in western Europe (July–Aug. 1944) was unable to stop Allied advance; committed suicide after being implicated in attempt (July 20, 1944) to assassinate Hitler.

Klug·hardt \'klük-härt\, August Friedrich Martin. 1847–1902. German composer. Works included operas as *Iwein* (1879) and *Gudrun* (1882), oratorios as *Zerstörung Jerusalems* (1899), symphonies, suites, overtures, chamber music, and songs.

Klyu·chev·sky \klyü-'chef-skəi\, Vasily Osipovich. 1841–1911. Russian historian. Professor at U. of Moscow (1879 ff.); known for his sociological approach to Russian history, as in his collected lectures *Kurs russkoy istori* (1911–31).

Knapp \'nap\, Seaman Asahel. 1833–1911. American agriculturist, b. Schroon Lake, N.Y. Professor (1879), president (1884–86), Iowa State Agricultural College; special agent of U.S. Dept. of Agriculture (from 1898). Originator (1904) of farm demonstration method in which an expert demonstrates, farm by farm, new agricultural discoveries and techniques; method became basis of USDA's Farmers Cooperative Demonstration Work program.

Kne·bel \'kne-bəl\, Karl Ludwig von. 1744–1834. German poet and translator. Associated (1775–81) with Goethe, Schiller, and their literary circle at Weimar. Author of sonnets and other poems collected in *Sammlung kleiner Gedichte* (1815) and *Distichen* (1827), and of translations into German of the *Elegiae* of Propertius (1798) and the *De rerum natura* of Lucretius (1821).

Knel·ler \'knel-ər, *Angl* 'nel-ər\, Sir Godfrey. Baronet. *Orig.* Gottfried Knil·ler \'knil-ər\. 1646 or 1649–1723. British painter, b. Germany. To England (1675); painted portraits of Duke of Monmouth, Charles II, and Louis XIV; principal painter to William III, of whom he did (1697) an equestrian portrait; retained favor under Anne and George I. Painted ten reigning monarchs in all, including Peter the Great, 42 portraits of members of the Kit Cat Club (1700–20), Hampton Court Beauties series, and portraits of British admirals and other British celebrities of his day.

Knick·er·bock·er \'nik-ər-ˌbäk-ər\, Harmen Jansen. 1650?–?1716. Dutch colonist in New Amsterdam (New York). Founder of Knickerbocker family in America; to New Amsterdam (1674) and settled on land near Albany (1682); moved to near Red Hook in Dutchess County (1704).

Knig·ge \'knig-ə\, Adolf Franz Friedrich von. Freiherr. 1752–1796. German writer. Active member of the Illuminati. Best known for *Über den Umgang mit Menschen* (1788), a practical guide to happiness and success; also author of didactic novels as *Die Reise nach Braunschweig* (1792), dramatic poems, etc.

Knight \'nīt\, Charles. 1791–1873. English publisher. Published *Penny Magazine* (1832–45), *Penny Cyclopaedia* (1833–44), *Pictorial History of England* (1837–44), *Pictorial Shakespeare* (1838–41), etc.

Knight, Gowin. 1713–1772. English scientist and librarian. Principal librarian of British Museum (1756–72). Developed improved method of magnetization and produced several compasses, including one used by Royal Navy for almost a century.

Knight, John Shively. 1894–1981. American newspaper publisher, b. Bluefield, W. Va. On staff (1920–33), proprietor (from 1933), Akron, Ohio, *Beacon Journal;* acquired Akron *Times-Press* (1938), Detroit *Free Press* (1940), Chicago *Daily News* (1944); later added Philadelphia *Inquirer,* New York *Daily News,* etc.; merged with Ridder Publications chain (1974) to form Knight-Ridder Newspapers, Inc., which grew to 34 dailies and 4 television stations (1981); as editorial chairman, wrote weekly column "Editor's Notebook" (Pulitzer prize, 1968).

Knight, Sarah, *nee* Kem·ble \'kem-bəl\. *Called* Mme. Knight. 1666–1727. American businesswoman and diarist, b. Boston. m. (before 1689) Richard Knight. Prosperous shopkeeper in New London, Conn. (c.1714 ff.). Known for *The Journal of Mme. Knight* (pub. 1825), a vivid and detailed account of her unchaperoned journey from Boston to New York in 1704 which contains important information on colonial life.

Knigh·ton \'nīt-ᵊn\, Henry. d. c.1396. English ecclesiastic and chronicler. An Austin canon at Abbey of St. Mary of the Meadows, Leicester. His chronicle (pub. 1652) consists of a compilation of earlier chronicles covering 1066–1337, an original history covering 1337–66, and an original chronicle covering 1377–95; important for its depiction of John Wycliffe and Lollardism and for favorable account of John of Gaunt.

Kno·bels·dorff \'knō-bəls-ˌdȯrf\, Georg Wenzeslaus von. 1699–1753. German architect and painter. Designed Berlin Opera House (1741–43), new wing of Charlottenburg Castle (1740–43), parts of Castle of Sans Souci at Potsdam (1745–47); helped plan gardens at Rheinsberg, Potsdam, and Sans Souci.

Knolles \'nōlz\, Richard. 1550?–1610. English historian. Master of secondary school at Sandwich (from c.1572); author of *Generall Historie of the Turkes* (1603).

Knollys \'nōlz\, Sir Francis. 1514?–1596. English courtier. M.P. (1542 ff.); privy councilor under Elizabeth (1558) and vice chamberlain of royal household; in charge of fugitive Mary, Queen of Scots (1568–69), and commissioner at her trial; treasurer of royal household (1572–96). His son ¶Sir William (1547–1632), Earl of Ban·bury \'ban-b(ə-)rē, 'bam-\, soldier and courtier; M.P. (1572 ff.); served in Low Countries under Leicester (1586) and against Spanish Armada (1588); privy councilor (1596); treasurer of royal household (1602); created earl (1626) by Charles I.

Knopf \kə-'nəpf, (kə-)'näpf\, Adolph. 1882–1966. American geologist, b. San Francisco. Professor at Yale (1920–51), Stanford U. (1951 ff.). Known for studies of economic and Precambrian geology and in petrology, esp. investigations of average chemical composition of Earth's crust.

Knorr \'knȯr\, Ludwig. 1859–1921. German chemist. Discovered antipyrine (1883); isolated two forms of ethyl acetoacetate (1911).

Knowles \'nōlz\, James Sheridan. 1784–1862. British playwright, b. Ireland. Cousin of Richard Brinsley Sheridan. Plays included *Caius Gracchus* (1815), *William Tell* (1825), *The Hunchback* (1832), and *The Love Chase* (1837); published also novels, poems, and miscellaneous works.

Knowl·ton \'nōlt-ᵊn\, Charles. 1800–1850. American physician, b. Templeton, Mass. Advocated birth-control methods in *The Fruits of Philosophy* (1832); prosecuted and imprisoned for three months at Cambridge, Mass. (1832); book made subject of a test case in England, eventually decided in favor of defendants (1877).

Knowlton, Frank Hall. 1860–1926. American paleobotanist, b. Brandon, Vt. Paleontologist (1900–07) and geologist (1907–26), U.S. Geological Survey. Made pioneering studies of prehistoric climates based on geologic evidence; discovered many species of fossilized plants. Founder and editor (1897–1904) of *The Plant World;* author of *Birds of the World* (1909), *A Catalogue of the Mesozoic and Cenozoic Plants of North America* (1919), *Plants of the Past* (1927).

Knox \'näks\, Edmund George Valpy. *Pseudonym* Evoe \'ē-(,)vē\. 1881–1971. English humorist. On staff (from 1921), editor of *Punch* (1932–49). Author of *The Brazen Lyre* (1911), *Fiction As She Is Wrote* (1923), *Quaint Specimens* (1925), *Folly Calling* (1932), etc.

Knox, Frank, *in full* William Franklin. 1874–1944. American newspaper publisher and politician, b. Boston. Publisher, *Chicago Daily News* (from 1931). Served in Spanish–American War and World War I. Republican nominee for vice president of the U.S. (1936); U.S. secretary of the navy (1940–44).

Knox, Henry. 1750–1806. American Revolutionary officer, b. Boston. Close friend and adviser of Washington; served through war and took part in all notable engagements; brought back (winter of 1775–76) 55 pieces of captured artillery from Ft. Ticonderoga, N.Y., to Boston, which formed basis of American artillery; brigadier general (Dec. 1776); major general (Nov. 1781); in command at West Point (1782); succeeded Washington as commander of the army (Dec. 1783–Jan. 1784). Founded Society of the Cincinnati (1783). U.S. secretary of war (1785–94).

Knox, John. 1513–1572. Scottish religious reformer. Ordained priest (1536); converted to Protestant cause by George Wishart (c.1545); became spokesman for Reformation in Scotland. Captured at St. Andrews and sent to French galleys (1548–49); to England, where he was appointed (1551) a royal chaplain. At Mary Tudor's accession (1553), fled to the Continent; at Geneva (1554, 1556–58), where he met Calvin; returned to Scotland (1559). Became foremost leader of the Scottish Reformation; set the austere moral tone of the Church of Scotland and shaped its democratic form of government. Published six tracts dealing with religious issues in Scotland, including *The First Blast of the Trumpet against the Monstrous Regiment of Women* (1558) and *Treatise on Predestination* (1560); issued prayer book *Book of Common Order* (1564). Shortly before death, received appointment as minister in Edinburgh. Author of *History of the Reformation in Scotland* (pub. 1586).

Knox, Philander Chase. 1853–1921. American politician, b. Brownsville, Pa. Practiced law, Pittsburgh (from 1875). U.S. attorney general (1901–04); won antitrust suit against Northern Securities Co. (1901–04); drew up legislation creating U.S. Department of Commerce and Labor (1903). U.S. senator (1904–09). U.S. secretary of state (1909–13); initiated "dollar diplomacy." U.S. senator (1917–21); prominent in opposition to League of Nations.

Knox, Ronald Arbuthnott. 1888–1957. English prelate and writer. Entered Roman Catholic church (1917); Roman Catholic chaplain, Oxford U. (1926–39). Published translation of the Bible (1944–48). Among his books were *Some Loose Stones* (1913), *A Spiritual Aeneid* (1918), *The Belief of Catholics* (1927), *Heaven and Charing Cross* (1935), *Let Dons Delight* (1939), *Captive Flames* (1940), *New Testament Commentaries* (1953–56), and detective novels as *Still Dead* (1934).

Knud·sen \'knüt-sən\, Gunnar. 1848–1928. Norwegian industrialist and politician. Minister president (1908–10, 1913–20); championed neutral policy during World War I.

Knud·sen \'knü-sən\, Martin. 1871–1949. Danish physicist and oceanographer. His study of seawater established the chlorinity–salinity–density relationship.

Knud·sen \'knü-sən, *Angl* (kə-)'nüd-sən\, William S., *orig.* Signius Wilhelm Paul. 1879–1948. American industrialist, b. Copenhagen, Denmark. To U.S. (1900, naturalized 1914). With Ford Motor Co. (1911–21); vice president (1922), president (1924), Chevrolet Motor Co.; vice president (1933–37), president (1937–40), General Motors Corp. Director of industrial production for National Defense Commission (1940); co-director, Office of Production Management (1941); director of production for War Department, with rank of lieutenant general (1942–45).

Knut. See CANUTE.

Knyp·hau·sen \'knip-,haù-zən\, Wilhelm von. Baron. 1716–1800. Prussian soldier. To America as commander of Hessian troops (1776); took part in battles of Ft. Washington and Brandywine, Pa., and Monmouth, N.J.; commanded at New York City in absence of Sir Henry Clinton (1779–80) and raided Hackensack. Returned to Germany (1782) and became military governor of Kassel.

Kō·a·mi \kō-äm-ē\. Family of Japanese lacquerware artists, including: Michinaga (1410–1478), personal attendant to shogun Ashikaga Yoshimasa; excelled in *taka-maki-e* and *togidashi* techniques of lacquer design; said to have begun practice of modelling lacquerware designs after famous paintings. His son ¶Michikiyo (1433–1500) created own designs for lacquered household furnishings of Emperor Tsuchimikado II. ¶Nagashige (1599–1651) made what is considered by some to be greatest piece of Japanese lacquerware in existence, a set of stands presented as wedding gift to daughter of shogun Tokugawa Iemitsu.

Ko·ba·ya·shi \kō-bä-yäsh-ē\ Issa. *Orig.* Kobayashi Nobuyuki. *Called also* Kobayashi Yatarō. *Pseudonym* Is·sa \ēs-sä\. 1763–1827. Japanese poet. Composed verse in unadorned language expressing through sentimental simplicity the concerns of common man. Collections included *Tabishūi* (1795), *Chichi no shūen nikki* (1803), *Oraga Haru* (1819).

Kobayashi Kiyochika. 1847–1915. Japanese print designer. Adopted Western techniques for his *kōsen-ga* ("pictures of sunbeams") landscapes of Tokyo; works included series *Tokyo and Its Suburbs* and *Cat on the Canvas;* ceased Western painting (c.1882) and produced educational prints and cartoons based on historical themes.

Kobayashi Kokei. *Orig.* Kobayashi Shigeru. 1883–1957. Japanese painter. Studied under Kajita Hanko; became prominent member of Restored Nippon Bijutsu-in. At first painted traditional subjects as *Tale of the Bamboo Cutter* (1914); later produced contemporary scenes and still lifes known for their serenity and classical poise as *The Amitabha Hall* (1914), *Hot Spring* (1918), and *Tresses* (1931).

Kobayashi Takiji. 1903–1933. Japanese writer. Greatest writer of the proletarian literary movement in pre-World War II Japan. Influenced by works of Shiga Naoya; established reputation with *Fuzai-jinushi* and *Kani-kōsen* (both 1929); participated in radical political activities; elected chief secretary of Japan League of Proletarian Writers; arrested and beaten to death by police.

Kōbō Daishi. See KŪKAI.

Ko·bo·ri \kō-bō-rē\ Enshū. *Orig.* Kobori Masakazu. 1579–1647. Japanese master of the tea ceremony. Known also for his poetry, landscape design, and flower arrangement.

Koch \'käch, 'käk\, Frederick Henry. 1877–1944. American educator and theater founder, b. Covington, Ky. Taught at U. of North Dakota (1905–18); professor of dramatic literature at U. of North Carolina (1918–44). Founded many theater groups, including Dakota Playmakers (1910), Carolina Playmakers (1918). Regarded as father of American folk drama for his promotion of rural community theater groups, directing of folk-play touring companies, and seminal part in Little Theater movement; edited 11 volumes of folk plays.

Koch \'kȯk\, Johannes. *Known by Lat. form* Johannes Coc·cei·us \kä-'kā-(y)əs, käk-'sā-\. 1603–1669. German theologian. Professor, Bremen (1630), Franeker (1636), Leiden (1650); principal exponent of covenant theology in Reformed church. Author of *Summa doctrinae de foedere et testamento Dei* (1648).

Koch \'kȯk\, Martin. 1882–1940. Swedish novelist. Among his works were *Ellen* (1911), *Arbetare* (1912), *Timmerdalen* (1913), *Guds vackra värld* (1916), *Mauritz* (1939).

Koch \'kȯk\, Robert, *in full* Heinrich Hermann Robert. 1843–1910. German physician and pioneer bacteriologist. Began bacteriological researches while practicing at Wollstein (1872–80); on mission to Egypt and India to study cholera (1883); professor at U. of Berlin and director of the Institute of Hygiene (1885); director of the Institute for Infectious Diseases, Berlin (1891). First to isolate and obtain a pure culture of the anthrax bacillus (1876), publishing a method of preventive inoculation against this disease (1883). Isolated tubercle bacillus (1882); identified the comma bacillus as the cause of cholera (1883); produced tuberculin, of value in diagnosing tuberculosis (1890). Studied rinderpest in South Africa and developed a means of vaccination against it (1896); also investigated bubonic plague in Bombay (1897) and malaria and sleeping sickness in Africa. Awarded 1905 Nobel prize for physiology or medicine.

Koch, Rudolf. 1876–1934. German calligrapher, type designer, and teacher. Type designer for Klingspor foundry, Offenbach (1906–34); taught at Kunstgewerbeschule, Offenbach (1908 ff.); founder (1918) of workshop Offenbach Penmen. A leader in 20th-century revival of interest in calligraphy;

designed typefaces Maximilan (1913), Neuland (1923), Kabel (1927); also made woodcuts, tapestries, rugs, and items for church use.

Ko·cha·now·ski \kō-kä-'nōf-skē\, Jan. 1530–1584. Polish poet. Author of the first Polish tragedy *Odprawa posłów greckich* (1578), cycle of elegies *Treny* (1580) on the death of his daughter, songs, Latin verse, etc.

Köch·el \'kœk-əl; *Angl* 'kə(r)-shəl, -kəl\, Ludwig Alois Ferdinand von. Ritter. 1800–1877. Austrian music bibliographer. Compiled *Chronologisch-thematisches Verzeichnis* (1862) in which he numbered all of Mozart's works to correspond to Mozart's life; Mozart's works are still identified by a prefatory "K." (for Köchel) or "K.V." (*Verzeichnis*) and the catalogue number.

Ko·cher \'kō-kər\, Emil Theodor. 1841–1917. Swiss surgeon. Professor, Bern (from 1872). Known esp. for work on the thyroid gland; first to excise it in treatment of goiter (1876); known also for work on dislocations of the shoulder, on hernia, and on osteomyelitis. Wrote textbook *Chirurgische Operationslehre* (1892). Awarded 1909 Nobel prize for physiology or medicine.

Ko·chow·ski \kō-'kōf-skyē\, Wespazjan. 1633–1700. Polish poet and historian. Soldier (1650–61); later, court historian to King John III Sobieski. Author of epic *Psalmodia polska* (1695) claiming Poland to be God's chosen nation.

Kock \kōk\, Charles-Paul de. 1793–1871. French novelist and playwright. Best known for his discreetly pornographic novels about Parisian life, including *L'Enfant de ma femme* (1812), *Georgette* (1820), *Gustave, ou le mauvais sujet* (1821), *La Femme, le mari et l'amant* (1829), *La Pucelle de Belleville* (1834), *La Fille aux trois jupons* (1861). Author also of a number of melodramas, light operas, vaudeville sketches, pantomimes, etc.

Ko·çu Bey \kō-'chü-'bā\. *Also spelled* Ko·çi Bey \kō-'chə-\. *In full* Kuricali Koçu Mustafa Bey. d. c.1650. Turkish politician, b. Albania. In service of several Ottoman sultans; adviser to sultans Murat IV and Ibrahim I. Wrote (1630) treatise *Risale-i Koçu Bey* analyzing causes of decline of Ottoman Empire and urging return to established principles of Ottoman government.

Kō·da \kō-dä\ Rohan. *Orig.* Kōda Shigeyuki. 1867–1947. Japanese writer. Author of novels employing heroic, idealized characters, *as Fūryū Botoke* (1889), *Gojū-no-tō* (1891), *Sora Utsu Nami* (1903–05, unfinished); also wrote poetry, plays, historical stories, literary criticism, essays.

Ko·dály \'kō-dī\, Zoltán. 1882–1967. Hungarian composer. Professor at Budapest Academy of Music (1907–41); made tours of Hungary collecting folk songs which he published (1906–21) with friend Béla Bartok; also wrote on Hungarian folk music. Created an individual style based on Hungarian folk music, contemporary French music, and Italian Renaissance religious music. Works included *Psalmus Hungaricus* (1923), comic opera *Háry János* (1926), the orchestral *Marosszék Dances* (1930) and *Dances of Galánta* (1933), a *Te Deum* (1936), *Concerto for Orchestra* (1941), *Missa Brevis* (1942), opera *Cinka Panna* (1948), *Symphony in C Major* (1961), and chamber music as two string quartets (1908, 1916–17), two cello sonatas (1909–10, 1915), and *Serenade* for two violins and violas (1919–20).

Ko·da·ma \kō-däm-ä\ Gentaro. 1852–1906. Japanese general. Chief of staff of Japanese army in Manchuria in Russo-Japanese War (1904–05); chiefly responsible for successful strategy of the war.

Koech·lin \kesh-lan, kek-\, Charles-Louis-Eugène. 1867–1950. French composer. Studied under and much influenced by Fauré; as teacher had strong impact on his own and younger generations of French composers; associate of Satie, Roussel, Milhaud, and others; wrote treatises on modal polyphony, harmony, and orchestration. Composed 2 symphonies, symphonic poems, esp. four on Kipling's *Jungle Book,* choral works as *La Fin de l'homme* (1895) and *L'Abbaye* (1895–1908), ballets, piano pieces, film music, chamber works, etc.

Koelreuter, Josef Gottlieb. See Kölreuter.

Koe·nig \kœ-nēg, kœ̄-\, Marie-Pierre-Joseph-François. 1898–1970. French soldier. Served in World War I; fought in Norway and France during early part of World War II; with de Gaulle's Free French forces (from June 1940); successfully defended Bir-Hakeim in Libya against Rommel (1942); head of French Forces of the Interior (June 1944). Commanded French army in Germany (1945–49); vice president of Supreme War Council (1950). Elected to National Assembly (1951, 1956); minister of defense (1954, 1955).

Koer·ber \'kœr-bər\, Ernest von. 1850–1919. Austrian politician. Prime minister and minister of interior (1900) and justice (1902). Tried to solve nationalist question and to carry through a German-Czech agreement in Bohemia; effected a compromise with Hungary (1902) which he later abandoned because of opposition; resigned (1904). Again Austrian prime minister (1916).

Koest·ler \'kes(t)-lər\, Arthur. 1905–1983. British writer, b. Budapest. Member of German Communist party (1931–38); reported (1936) on Spanish Civil War for British newspaper; imprisoned by Spanish Loyalists on spying charges; renounced Communist party at time of Moscow trials (1938); imprisoned by French at start of World War II; imprisonment inspired anticommunist works that examined Soviet mentality, including *The Gladiators* (1939) and *Darkness at Noon* (1940). To Britain (1941); wrote works on history of science and scientific community including *The Sleepwalkers* (1959); in later years turned toward study of mysticism and parapsychology.

Kōetsu. See Honami Kōetsu.

Koff·ka \'kôf-kä; *Angl* 'kôf-kə, 'käf-\, Kurt. 1886–1941. German psychologist. Taught at U. of Giessen (1911–24); served (1912) as subject with Wolfgang Köhler in experiments on perception conducted by Max Wertheimer; became a chief developer and spokesman of Gestalt psychology and applied it to child development, learning, memory, emotion, etc.; to U.S. (1924); professor at Smith College (1927–41). Author of *The Growth of the Mind* (1924), *Gestalt Psychology* (1929), *Principles of Gestalt Psychology* (1935).

Ko·foid \'kō-,fȯid\, Charles Atwood. 1865–1947. American zoologist, b. Granville, Ill. Taught at U. of California, Berkeley (1900–36; professor from 1910); played major role in establishment (1912) of what is now Scripps Institution of Oceanography at La Jolla; assistant director (1907–23). Known for studies and classification system of plankton; invented Kofoid horizontal net and Kofoid self-closing bucket, both for collection of plankton.

Ko·găl·ni·cea·nu \,kōg-əl-nē-'chä-nü\, Mihail. 1817–1891. Romanian politician and historian. First prime minister of united Romania (1863–65); carried out land and social reforms; minister of interior (1868–70, 1879–80), of foreign affairs (1877–78). Author of *Histoire de la Valachie et de la Moldavie* (1837); co-founded national literary review *Dacia literară* (1840); edited ancient Moldavian chronicles as *Letopisetele Moldoviei* (1845–52).

Koh \kō\ Hui-dong. 1886–1965. Korean painter and politician. Pioneered in application of Western techniques to traditional Korean painting; later painted in traditional style. Minister of House of Councilors (1960–61).

Koh·ler \'kō-lər\, Josef. 1849–1919. German jurist and writer. Author of works on jurisprudence and on German patent and copyright law; author also of poetry, as *Lyrische Gedichte und Balladen* (1892), the novel *Eine Faustnatur* (1907), essays on art history, etc.

Kohler, Kaufmann. 1843–1926. American rabbi and educator, b. Fürth, Bavaria. To U.S. (1869); rabbi of congregation in New York (1879–1903); an editor of and contributor to *Jewish Encyclopedia* (1901–06). President, Hebrew Union Coll. (1903–21). Leader of Reformed Judaism in America. Author of *Jewish Theology Systematically and Historically Considered* (1918) and *The Origins of the Synagogue and the Church* (1929).

Köh·ler \'kœ̄-lər\, Wolfgang. 1887–1967. German psychologist. A key figure in the development of Gestalt psychology; associate of Max Wertheimer and Kurt Koffka. Director of anthropoid research station at Canary Islands (1913–20); head of psychological institute and professor, U. of Berlin (1921–35); professor, Swarthmore (Pa.) College (1935–55); member of Institute for Advanced Study, Princeton (1955–56); professor, Dartmouth College (from 1958). Author of *Intelligenzprüfungen an Menschenaffen* (1917), *Die physischen Gestalten in Ruhe und im stationären Zustand* (1920), *Gestalt Psychology* (1929), *Dynamics in Psychology* (1940).

Kohl·ha·se \'kōl-,häz-ə\, Hans. d. 1540. German merchant and brigand. Had two horses confiscated by a Saxon nobleman (1532); after failure to obtain redress from courts, organized (1534) outlaw band and terrorized Saxony; captured (1540) by Joachim II of Brandenburg and broken on wheel in Berlin.

Kohl·rausch \'kōl-,raůsh\, Friedrich Wilhelm Georg. 1840–1910. German physicist. Professor at Darmstadt (1871), Würzburg (1875), Strasbourg (1888), Berlin (1895). Devised improvements in measuring methods in many branches of physics, esp. magnetism and electricity; investigated elasticity, electrolytes, the reflection of light, etc. Wrote *Leitfaden der praktischen Physik* (1870). His father ¶Rudolf Hermann Arndt Kohlrausch (1809–1858), physicist; known for his association with Wilhelm Weber in making the first measurements of an electric current using absolute units (1856).

Ko Hung \'gō-'hůŋ\. *Also called* Pao-p'u-tzu \'baů-'půd-zü\, *i.e.* He Who Holds to Simplicity. 283?–343. Chinese Taoist alchemist. Author of *Pao-p'u-tzu,* an attempt to combine Taoist alchemy with Confucian ethics.

Ko·hut \'kō-,hüt\, Alexander. 1842–1894. American rabbi, b. Felegyhaza, Hungary. Superintendent of Hungarian schools (1867); chief rabbi of Fünfkirchen, Hungary (1872–80); to U.S. (1885); with Sabato Morais founded (1886) Jewish Theological Seminary, New York, and taught there until death. Author of Talmudic lexicon *'Arukh ha-shalem* (1878–92).

Ko·i·so \kō-ē-sō\ Kuniaki. 1880–1950. Japanese general. Chief of staff of Kwantung army (1932); commander in chief in Korea (1935–38); prime minister (1944–45); sentenced as war criminal to life imprisonment (1948).

Koizumi Yakumo. See Lafcadio Hearn.

Ko·jong \kō-jōŋ\. *Orig.* Yi T'ae Wang \yē-ta-wäŋ\. d. 1907. Korean emperor. Ascended throne as a young boy; real power held by his father Taewŏn-gun (to 1882) and Kojong's queen Min (to 1895); proclaimed himself emperor and changed country's name to Taehan (1897); forced to sign treaty (1904–05) establishing Japanese suzerainty in Korea; abdicated in favor of son (1907).

Kok III \'käk,'kōk\, Adam. 1811–1875. African ruler. Head of Griqua nation of Orange Free State, South Africa (from 1837); led resettlement of his people in Griqualand East on east coast of South Africa (1861–63); aided British suppression of Hlubi tribe in Natal (1874); his country annexed by Cape Colony (1874).

Kō·ken \kō-ken\. *Later called* Shō·to·ku \shō-tō-kü\. 718–770. Japanese empress. Daughter of Shōmu; ruled as Kōken (749–758); her promotion of career of the monk Dōkyō (*q.v.*) led to deposition of Emperor Junnin and death of his chief minister Oshikatsu; ruled as Shōtoku (764–770) but actual power held by Dōkyō.

Kokh·ba \'kȯk-bä\, Bar. *Orig.* Sim·e·on bar Ko·zi·ba \'sim-ē-ən-bär-'kȯ-zē-ˌbä\. d. 135 A.D. Jewish leader in Palestine. Led revolt (131–135) against Roman domination, sparked by Hadrian's Hellenization campaign including building of temple to Jupiter Capitolinus on ruins of Temple of Jerusalem; given name Bar Kokhba by Rabbi Akiba ben Joseph; enjoyed initial success but gradually lost to Roman reinforcements under Gaius Julius Severus; killed in battle at Bethar.

Ko·kosch·ka \'kȯ-kȯsh-kä\, Oskar. 1886–1980. Austrian painter and dramatist. One of leading exponents of Expressionism. Contributed drawings to *Der Sturm* in Berlin; professor, Dresden Academy (1919–24); to London (1938); taught at International Summer Academy for Visual Arts, Salzburg (1953–63). His psychological portraits, lyric landscapes, panoramic cityscapes, and allegorical compositions included *Dent du Midi* (1909), *Double Portrait* (1912), *The Tempest* (1914), *Knight Errant* (1915), *The Power of Music* (1919), *London Bridge View of the Thames* (1926), *Tomaš G. Masaryk* (1936), *The Red Egg* (1941), *What We Are Fighting For* (1943), *Prometheus Saga* (1950), *View of Hamburg Harbor* (1951), *Thermopylae* (1954), *Herodotos* (1960–63). Author of poem *Die träumenden Knaben* (1908) and of the Expressionistic plays *Mörder, Hoffnung der Frauen* (1907; music by Hindemith, 1921), *Der brennende Dornbusch* (1911), *Hiob* (1917), and *Orpheus und Eurydike* (1923). Also designed tapestries and theatrical scenery and costumes and executed lithographs.

Kol·be \'kȯl-bə\, Hermann, *in full* Adolf Wilhelm Hermann. 1818–1884. German organic chemist. Professor at Marburg (1851–65) and Leipzig (1865–84); edited *Journal für praktische Chemie* (from 1865). Converted (1843–45) carbon disulfide to acetic acid, one of first syntheses of an organic compound from inorganic materials; expounded a theory of radicals; indicated the possibility of the existence of secondary and tertiary alcohols before their discovery; credited with first synthesis of salicylic acid; worked on the electrolysis of organic acids.

Kol·be \'kȯl-be\, Maximilian Maria. 1894–1941. Polish religious. Joined Franciscan Coventuals (1907); ordained priest (1918); founder (1927) and superior of religious center City of Mary Immaculate at Niepokalanów; arrested (1941) by Nazis for aiding Jewish refugees and the Polish underground; tortured and executed at Auschwitz; beatified (1971).

Kol·chak \(ˌ)kəl-'chäk\, Aleksandr Vasiliyevich. 1873–1920. Russian admiral and counterrevolutionary. Flag captain of Baltic fleet at outbreak of World War I; vice admiral in command of Black Sea fleet (1916–17). To Omsk as war minister in anti-Bolshevik government (Oct. 1918); led military coup (Nov. 1918) and became head of White army; at first successful but began to lose control when Omsk was captured by Bolsheviks (1919); retreated to Irkutsk; forced to resign; captured and shot.

Köl·csey \'kœl-chā\, Ferenc. 1790–1838. Hungarian poet, critic, and orator. Vigorous supporter of Ferenc Kazinczy's language reforms; member of Diet (1832–34); his critical essays laid foundation of systematic literary criticism and aesthetics in Hungary. Author of the Hungarian national hymn (1823) and of other lyric poetry.

Kold \'kōl\, Kristen Mikkelsen. 1816–1870. Danish educator. Established basic pattern for the folk high school by founding (1851) at Ryslinge first of several residential schools.

Kol·de·wey \'kȯl-də-ˌvī\, Robert. 1855–1925. German archaeologist. Conducted excavations in Asia Minor and Turkey (from 1882); directed excavation of the ruins of Babylon (1899–1917).

Kol·lár \'kȯl-lär\, Jan. 1793–1852. Slovak poet and clergyman. Pastor to Slovak Protestants in Pest (1819–49); advocate of nonpolitical Romantic Pan-Slavism. Author of an edition of Slovakian folk songs (1923–27), the sonnet cycle *Slávy dcera* (1824), a treatise advocating cultural unity among Slavonic peoples (1836), etc.

Koł·łą·taj \kȯl-'lōⁿ-tī\, Hugo. 1750–1812. Polish priest and politician. Rector of U. of Kraków (1782–86); his program of social and political reforms strongly influenced constitution of May 3, 1791; vice chancellor of Poland (1791–92); active in Kościuszko's rebellion (1794); imprisoned in Austria (1794–1802). Founded college of Krzemieniec at Volhynia (1805); imprisoned in Moscow (1807–08); patron of radical opposition in Duchy of Warsaw. Works included *Prawo polityczne narodu polskiego* (1790) and *Nil desperandum* (1808).

Kol·ler \'käl-ər, 'kȯl-\, Carl. 1857–1944. American ophthalmologist, b. Schüttenhofen, Bohemia (now Sušic, Czech.). Associate of Sigmund Freud at Vienna General Hospital; to U.S. (1888, naturalized 1902); practiced ophthalmic surgery in New York. His introduction of cocaine as a local anesthetic in eye operations (1884) inaugurated the use of local anesthesia in other types of surgery.

Köl·li·ker \'kœl-ə-kər\, Rudolf Albert von. 1817–1905. Swiss anatomist, histologist, and zoologist. Professor, Würzburg (from (1847); known esp. for researches in histology and embryology. With Carl von Siebold founded *Zeitschrift für wissenschaftlichen Zoologie* (1848); author of *Handbuch der Gewebelehre des Menschen* (1852) and *Entwicklungsgeschichte des Menschen und der höheren Tiere* (1861).

Kol·lon·tay \kəl-(ˌ)lən-'tī\, Aleksandra Mikhaylovna. 1872–1952. Soviet commissar and diplomat. Joined Bolsheviks (1915); first Soviet commissar of public welfare (1917); advocated radical changes in traditional social customs and institutions. Prominent in Workers' Opposition group within Bolshevik party (1920–21). Minister to Norway (1923–25, 1927–30), Mexico (1926–27), Sweden (1930–45); given (1943) rank of ambassador, first woman ambassador in the world.

Koll·witz \'kȯl-vits\, Käthe, *nee* Schmidt. 1867–1945. German painter, lithographer, and etcher. m. Karl Kollwitz (1891) and settled in Berlin. Her works, often representing life among the poor and the proletariat, included two series of etchings *Der Weberaufstand* (1894–98) and *Bauernkrieg* (1903–08), woodcuts, lithographs, illustrations for *Simplicissimus* (from 1910), and two sculptured figures for a German soldiers' cemetery in Flanders (erected 1932).

Ko·lo·ko·tró·nis \kȯ-lȯ-kȯ-'trȯn-yēs\, Theódoros. 1770–1843. Greek soldier. A leader in war for independence (1821 ff.); commander in chief of Peloponnesus (1823). Conspired against regency governing for King Otto I; imprisoned (1834); pardoned at Otto's accession to power (1835) and restored to rank of general.

Koloman. See KÁLMÁN.

Ko·lo·wrat-Lieb·stein·sky \'kȯ-lȯv-rät-'lēb-stän-skē\, Franz Anton von. Graf. 1778–1861. Bohemian politician. Governor of Bohemia (1809–26); promoted revival of Czech language and history. Ministerial chief of domestic affairs to Emperors Franz I and Ferdinand I in Vienna (1826–48); chief political rival of Metternich.

Köl·reu·ter *or* **Koel·reu·ter** \'kœl-ˌrȯit-ər\, Josef Gottlieb. 1733–1806. German botanist. Professor of natural history and curator of Botanical Gardens at Karlsruhe (1764–86). Pioneer in hybridization experiments with plants; recognized the importance of insects and the wind in pollinating flowers.

Kol·tsov \(ˌ)kəlʸt-'sȯf\, Aleksey Vasilyevich. 1808–1842. Russian poet. Known for lyrics of Russian peasant life; published *Stikhotvoreniya* (1835).

Ko·ma·rov \kə-(ˌ)mə-'rȯf\, Vladimir Mikhaylovich. 1927–1967. Soviet cosmonaut. In Soviet air force (from 1942); pilot of Voskhod 1 (Oct. 12–13, 1964), first craft to carry more than one person into space; pilot of Soyuz 1 (Apr. 23–24, 1967) and killed during landing, first man known to have died during a space mission.

Kō·mei \kō-mā\. 1821–1867. Emperor of Japan (1846–67). Under control of shoguns; after Commodore Perry's visits (1853, 1854) his influence gradually increased, opening way for his son Meiji's great reforms.

Ko·men·ský \kȯ-'men-skē\, Jan Ámos. *Lat.* Johann Amos Co·me·ni·us \kə-'mē-nē-əs\. 1592–1670. Czech theologian and educator. Influenced by German Protestant millenialists and Francis Bacon; fled Thirty Years' War to Poland (1621), settling with group of Bohemian Brethren at Leszno; developed new philosophy ("pansophy") of education and new methods; after great success of *Janua linguarum reserata* (1631, Gate of Languages Unlocked), innovative Czech–Latin textbook, invited to London (1641–42), Sweden (1642–48) to consult on educational matters; elected last bishop of Moravians (1648); fled Polish destruction of Leszno (1656) to Amsterdam. Author also of *Labyrint světa a Ráj srdce* (1618, Labyrinth of the World and the Paradise of the Heart), an allegory of consolation for dispossessed Moravians; numerous didactic and pedagogic works, esp. *Orbis sensualium pictus* (1658), first illustrated textbook, in use for two centuries, and *Didactica opera omnia* (1657).

Ko·mi·sar·jev·sky \ˌkäm-ə-'sär-yəf-skē\, Theodore. 1882–1954. British theatrical producer, b. Italy of Russian parents. Brother of Vera Komissarzhevskaya. Produced plays and operas in Russia (1906–19); to London (1919), naturalized British subject (1932); influential theatrical designer and producer in Great Britain, U.S., Paris, Italy, esp. of Russian and English classics; caused controversy with experimental designs, as aluminum scenery for *Macbeth* (1933).

Ko·mis·sar·zhev·ska·ya \kə-məs-(ˌ)sər-'zhef-skə-yə\, Vera Fyodorovna. 1864–1910. Russian actress and theatrical producer. Sister of Theodore Komisarjevsky. Joined (1896) Aleksandrinsky Theater and became one of its most famous actresses; produced (from 1905) modern plays in her own theater.

Ko·mu·ra \kō-mür-ä\ Jutarō. Marquis. 1855–1911. Japanese diplomat. Minister to U.S. (1898–1900) and to Russia (1900); foreign minister (1901–06 and 1908–11); negotiated Treaty of Portsmouth and second Anglo–Japanese alliance (both 1905); ambassador to Great Britain (1906–08). Created count (1907) and marquis (1911).

Ko·nar·ski \kō-'när-skē\, Stanisław. 1700–1773. Polish priest and writer. Entered Order of Piarist Fathers (1715); superior of Polish province (1741). Using John Locke's theories, instituted educational reforms as founding Collegium Nobilium in Warsaw (1741), stressing purity of the Polish language, emphasizing teaching of drama and the natural sciences. Wrote historical and political works, esp. collection of Polish laws *Volumina legum* (1732–68).

Kon·baung \'kōn-,baùŋ\. Name of last ruling dynasty (1752–1885) of Burma; founded by Alaungpaya (*q.v.*), who conquered the Mon nation and extended his suzerainty to the Shan States; succeeded by ten monarchs, including Hsinbyushin, Bodawpaya, Bagyidaw, Tharrawaddy Min, Pagan Min, Mindon Min, and Thibaw (*qq.v.*); dynasty ended when Burma was annexed by the British (1885) and Thibaw, the last ruler, was exiled to India.

Kon·dí·lis \kōn-'thē-lyēs\, Geórgios. 1879–1936. Greek general and politician. Served through Balkan Wars and World War I; general (1922); suppressed royalist revolt (Oct. 1923). Entered parliament (1923); minister of war, then (1924–25) of interior; engineered coup d'état and became prime minister (Aug. 1926); retired (Dec. 1926); changed support from liberal party to conservative Populist party; minister of war (1932–33, 1933–35); by coup d'état (Oct. 1935) aided in restoration of monarchy and return of George II to throne (Nov. 1935); acted as premier and temporary dictator.

Ko·nev \'kōn-yəf\, Ivan Stepanovich. 1897–1973. Soviet general. In World War II; marshal of Soviet Union (1944); commander in chief of Soviet army (1946–60); inspector, ministry of defense (1962–73).

Ko·niec·pol·ski \kōn-yet-'spōl-skē\, Stanisław. 1591–1646. Polish soldier. Appointed field commander of Polish forces (1619); defeated the Tatars at Martynow (1624) and made palatine of Sandomierz; transferred to Prussia (1626), where he won (1627) series of victories against the Swedes at Puck, Hamersztyn, and Tczew; withdrew from strategic strongholds in Prussia (1628) but defeated Gustav II Adolphus at Trzciana (1629). Commander in chief of Polish forces (1632); influential adviser of Władysław IV and played major role in directing foreign policy; repulsed Turko-Tatar army at Kamieniec (1633) and crushed the Tatars at Ochmatow (1644). Suppressed several Cossack rebellions in the Ukraine and founded (1633) there town and citadel of Brady.

Kö·nig \'kœ-nik\, Friedrich. 1774–1833. German printer. Inventor of the steam printing press. Built for London *Times* the first flatbed cylinder press (1806); cofounder (1817) of König & Bauer, manufacturers of steam printing presses.

Kö·nigs·mark \'kœ-nik-,smärk\. Swedish family of German origin, including notably: Hans Christoph (1600–1663), Graf; entered Swedish army (1630); commanded Swedish forces in Westphalia (1636 ff.), Swedish left wing at battle of Breitenfeld (1642), and Swedish forces in battle of Prague, the last battle of Thirty Years' War (1648); created field marshal in Swedish army. His grandson ¶Philipp Christoph (1665–1694), Graf; entered army of elector of Hanover; became lover of Sophia Dorothea, wife of the crown prince (later King George I of England); twice tried to help her escape from Hanover; was presumably murdered on discovery of the liaison. Philipp's sister ¶Maria Aurora (1662–1728), Gräfin; mistress of Elector Augustus II of Saxony and mother of Maurice of Saxony; a powerful figure at the Saxon court; later fell from favor and made coadjutor abbess and lady provost of Quedlinburg.

Ko·ninck \'kō-niŋk\ *or* **Ko·ning** \-niŋ\ *or* **Co·ningh** \-niŋ\ *or* **Con·ningh** \'kōn-iŋ\, Philips de. 1619–1688. Dutch painter. Associated with Rembrandt's artistic circle in Amsterdam. Painted portraits, biblical subjects, genre scenes, and esp. panoramic landscapes as *View over a Flat Landscape* (1664) and *Extensive Landscape with a Hawking Party.*

Ko·ni·shi \kō-nē-shē\ Yukinaga. d. 1600. Japanese general. Convert to Roman Catholicism. Spearheaded Toyotomi Hideyoshi's invasion of Korea (1592–98); at first successful in southern Korea but later stalemated by Chinese troops; returned to Japan (1598) to support Toyotomi Hideyori in civil war against Tokugawa Ieyasu; defeated at Battle of Sekigahara (1600) and executed.

Ko·noe \kō-nō-ye\ Fumimaro. Prince. 1891–1946. Japanese politician. Protégé of Saionji Kimmochi; entered House of Peers (1916); elected its president (1933). Prime minister (1937–39, 1940–41); tried unsuccessfully to restrict power of the military and to keep war with China from widening into a world conflict; concluded nonaggression pact with Soviet Union (1941); attempted to improve relations with U.S.; helped bring down Tōjō cabinet (1944); committed suicide when suspected of being war criminal.

Ko·nop·nic·ka \kō-nōp-'nēt-skä\, Marja, *nee* **Wa·si·low·ska** \vä-sē-'lōf-skä\. 1842–1910. Polish author. Her chief poem, *Pan Balcer w Brazylji* (1892–1909), was a popular epic on Polish emigration to the Americas; also known for poem cycle *Italia* (1901) and short stories as *Niemczaki* and *Nasza Szkapa.*

Konrad. See also CONRAD.

Kon·rad der Pfaf·fe \'kōn-rät-dərp-'fäf-ə\, *i.e.* the Priest. 12th century. Early Middle High German poet and priest. Author of the *Rolandslied* (1131?), free German version in verse of the Old French epic *Chanson de Roland,* and probably compiler of the *Kaiserchronik* (c.1150).

Konrad von Mar·burg \'mär-,bùrk\. c.1180–1233. German priest and papal inquisitor. Confessor (from 1225) to wife of landgrave of Thuringia, later St. Elizabeth of Hungary; made chief papal inquisitor in Germany by Gregory IX (1231); combated heretical movements; murdered near Marburg.

Konrad von Me·gen·berg \'mā-gən-,berk\. 1309?–1374. German writer. Author of *Planctus Ecclesiae in Germaniam* (1338), *Deutsche Sphära* (first German handbook of astronomy and physics), and *Das Buch der Natur* (1349–50).

Konrad von Würz·burg \'vuerts-,bùrk\. c.1225–1287. Middle High German poet. Author of epics *Partonopier und Meliur* and *Der Trojanerkrieg;* secular verse romances *Englehart, Daz Herzmaere,* and *Keiser Otto mit dem Barte;* religious legends *Silvester, Alexius,* and *Pantaleon;* the allegorical *Klage der Kunst; Die goldene Schmiede* (in praise of the Virgin); love lyrics, etc.

Konstantin. See CONSTANTINE.

Kook \'kük\, Abraham Isaac. 1865–1935. Palestinian rabbi, b. Latvia. Became (1904) rabbi of Jaffa, Palestine, and founded a yeshiva there; rabbi of Machzike Hadath congregation in London (1916–19); worked for support of Balfour Declaration. Rabbi of Ashkenazic communities in Jerusalem (1919–21); first chief rabbi of Palestine (1921–35) under British mandate. A mystic and a Talmudic scholar; his essays published as *Orot ha-qodesh.*

Koop·mans \'küp-mənz\, Tjalling Charles. 1910–1985. American economist, b. 's-Graveland, Netherlands. To U.S. (1940); worked for shipping firm, devising system of equations that minimized total cost of transporting goods from U.S. to specific British locations; joined Cowles Commission for Research in Economics, U. of Chicago (1944); moved with Commission to Yale U. (1955); professor of economics, Yale (1955–81). Shared 1975 Nobel prize for economics with Soviet Union's Leonid Kantorovich for contributions to theory of optimum allocation of resources.

Ko·per·nik \kō-'per-nēk\, Mikołaj. *Lat.* Nicolaus **Co·per·ni·cus** \kə-'pər-ni-kəs\. 1473–1543. Polish astronomer. Canon of cathedral of Frauenburg (1497); studied canon law, medicine in Italy; adviser and secretary to uncle, Lucas Waczenrode, bishop of Ermeland (1503–12). Made astronomical observations of orbits of sun, moon, planets (from 1497); gradually abandoned accepted Ptolemaic system of astronomy and worked out heliocentric system in which Earth rotates daily on axis and, with other planets, revolves around sun; circulated manuscript argument privately but was reluctant to publish theory; at urging of student Rhäticus published at last *De revolutionibus orbium coelestium* (1543) explaining new system, which in winning acceptance in scientific world constituted a revolutionary step.

Köpfel, Wolfgang Fabricius. See CAPITO.

Ko·pisch \kō-'pish\, August. 1799–1853. German painter and poet. Known for popular poetry based on legends and fairy tales, as *Gedichte* (1836) and *Allerlei Geister* (1848); translated parts of Dante's *Divine Comedy* (1837); given court position at Potsdam (1847), where he wrote *Die Schlösser und Gärten zu Potsdam* on royal commission (1854).

Kop·lik \'käp-lik\, Henry. 1858–1927. American pediatrician, b. New York City. Described Koplik's spots on mucous membrane of lips and cheeks, used in diagnosis of measles; established first milk depot in U.S. for distribution of milk to infants of the poor.

Kopp \'kōp\, Hermann Franz Moritz. 1817–1892. German chemist. Professor at Giessen (1843–63) and Heidelberg (1863–90). Investigated connection between physical properties and chemical composition of substances; set forth notion of specific volume. Wrote *Geschichte der Chemie* (1843–47).

Köp·pen \'kœp-ən\, Wladimir Peter. 1846–1940. German meteorologist and climatologist, b. Russia. Meteorologist at the German Naval Observatory, Hamburg (1874–1919). Produced a world map of temperature belts (1884); introduced (1900) Köppen climatic classification system based on monthly and annual averages of temperature and precipitation of the Earth's five climatic regions; co-editor of *Handbuch der Klimatologie* (1927–40) at Graz.

Kop·pers \'kōp-ərs\, Wilhelm. 1886–1961. German anthropologist. Ordained Roman Catholic priest (1911). Professor (1928–38, 1945–57) at U. of Vienna and director (1929–38, 1945–57) of its Institute for Ethnology. A chief proponent of *Kulturkreise* theory of origin of cultures; adopted (by 1931) a comparative historical methodology. Edited journal *Anthropos* (1923–39); wrote *Völker und Kulturen* (1924, with Wilhelm Schmidt), *Die Bihl in Zentralindien* (1948), *Der Urmensch und sein Weltbild* (1949).

Köp·ping \'kœp-iŋ\, Karl. 1848–1914. German engraver and glass designer. Known for his glassware designs in Art Nouveau style.

Kö·prü·lü \kœ-prue-'lue\. Illustrious Turkish family of viziers credited with arresting the Ottoman Empire's decline in the 17th century, including: Köprülü Mehmed Paşa (d. 1661), b. Albania; founder of the family; grand vizier (1656–61); despotic governor, restored central authority in government; defeated Venetian fleet in the Dardanelles (1657) and recovered Tenedos and Lemnos; suppressed revolts, esp. one of pashas (1659).

His son ¶Fazl Ahmed (1635–1676), governor general of Damascus (1660); grand vizier (1661–76); waged war with Austria (1663–64) for control of

Hungary and Transylvania; badly defeated at St. Gotthard (Aug. 1, 1664) but concluded at Vasvár treaty (Aug. 10, 1664) favorable to Ottomans. Conquered Crete (1669), thus ending war with Venice. Began war against Poles (1672); twice beaten by John Sobieski; secured peace by Treaty of Żórawno (1676). His brother ¶Fazıl Mustafa (1637–1691), grand vizier (1689–91); reorganized internal affairs and the army and navy; liberated (1690) Nish and Belgrade from Austrians; killed at battle of Slankamen. Mehmed Paşa's nephew ¶Amca-zâde Hüseyin (d. 1702), grand vizier (1697–1702); negotiated Treaty of Carlowitz (1699) by which Ottomans lost much territory.

Köprülüzade. See MEHMET FUAT KÖPRÜLÜ.

Ko·ra·ïs \kȯr-ä-ˈēs\, Adamantios. *Fr.* Co·raï *or* Co·ray \kȯ-rá-ē\. 1748–1833. Greek man of letters. Resident in Paris (from 1788). Devoted himself to inspiring national aspirations of the Greek people by reviving memory of their classical heritage; created a new Greek literary language by purifying foreign elements from Demotic vernacular and adding best elements from classical Greek; composed (1828–35) *Atakta,* first Modern Greek dictionary. Edited classical authors; translated Herodotus; issued *Library of Greek Literature* (17 vols., 1805–26) and *Parerga* (9 vols., 1809–27). Considered father of Modern Greek literature.

Kor·da \ˈkȯr-dä, *Angl* ˈkȯr-də\, Sir Alexander. 1893–1956. British motion-picture producer, b. Hungary. Produced in Hollywood and London such films as *The Private Life of Henry VIII* (1933), *The Scarlet Pimpernel* (1935), *The Shape of Things to Come* (1936), *The Thief of Bagdad* (1940), *To Be or Not to Be* (1942), *The Third Man* (1949), *Seven Days to Noon* (1950), *The Sound Barrier* (1952).

Kor·fan·ty \kȯr-ˈfán-tē\, Wojciech. 1873–1939. Polish politician. As member of secret nationalist society "Z," wrote and spoke against attempt to Germanize Poles of Upper Silesia; member of German Reichstag (1903–12, 1918) and Prussian Diet (1904–18). Headed struggle for independence of Upper Silesian Poles from Germany, including (May 1921) an armed uprising; his proposed Korfanty Line forced Allies to establish German–Polish border in location more favorable to Poland. Member of Polish Constituent Assembly (1919–22) and Parliament (1922–30); imprisoned (1930) for bitterly criticizing Piłsudski's dictatorial methods; elected to Senate (1930).

Kōrin. See OGATA.

Korn \ˈkȯrn\, Arthur. 1870–1945. German physicist. Pioneer in telephotography. Credited with first transmission of a photograph by telegraphy, from Munich to Nürnberg and return (1904).

Kor·ná·ros \kȯr-ˈnär-ȯs\, Vitzéntzos. 17th century. Cretan poet. Author in Greek of the romantic epic *Erotókritos* and the biblical drama *Thysia tou Avraam.*

Kör·ner \ˈkœr-nər\, Karl Theodor. 1791–1813. German poet, dramatist, and patriot. Joined Lützow Volunteer Corps at Breslau in war against Napoléon; killed in battle at Gadebusch. Author of librettos, plays as *Zriny* (1812) and *Hedwig* (1815), and the collection of patriotic lyrics *Leyer und Schwert* (1814) containing "Das Schwertlied," composed on the battlefield. His father ¶Christian Gottfried (1756–1831), jurist and literary critic, was friend of Schiller and correspondent of Goethe; prepared first collected edition of Schiller's works (1812–15).

Körner, Theodor. 1873–1957. Austrian soldier and politician. Served through World War I; inspector general of Austrian army (1918). Social Democratic member of Bundesrat (1925–34); military adviser to Schutzbund (early 1930s). Mayor of Vienna (1945–51); president of Austria (1951–57).

Körner, Wilhelm. 1839–1925. German organic chemist. Professor at Bonn (1867–70) and Milan (1870 ff.). Developed method of determining position of substituents on the benzene ring (1874); prepared 126 aromatic compounds, including pyridine (1869); synthesized asparagine (1887, with Angelo Menozzi).

Korn·gold \ˈkȯrn-ˌgȯlt\, Erich Wolfgang. 1897–1957. American composer and conductor, b. Brünn, Austria (now Brno, Czech.). Professor, Vienna State Academy of Music (1930); to U.S. (1934, naturalized 1943). His compositions included operas *Die tote Stadt* (1920), *Das Wunder der Heliane* (1927), and *Die Kathrin* (1939); orchestral works *Sinfonietta* (1912), *Tomorrow* (1942), *Violin Concerto* (1946), *Symphony in F Sharp* (1951–52); chamber music, songs, and scores for 19 films including *Anthony Adverse* (1936, Academy Award), *The Adventures of Robin Hood* (1938, Academy Award), *The Sea Wolf* (1941), *King's Row* (1942).

Kor·ni·lov \(ˌ)kər-ˈnyē-ləf\, Lavr Georgyevich. 1870–1918. Russian general. In World War I commanded division in Galicia (1914); assumed command (1916) of 20th army corps; in command of troops in Petrograd after Revolution (1917); commander in chief (Aug. 1917). Checked by Bolsheviks in attempt to make himself dictator; escaped to Caucasus; organized Cossack force; killed in action.

Ko·ro·len·ko \kə-(ˌ)rəl-ˈyān-kə\, Vladimir Galaktionovich. 1853–1921. Russian writer. Exiled to Siberia (1879–84) for advanced social ideas; settled in Nizhni Novgorod; editor of review *Russkaya Bogatstvo* (from 1895). Representative of older literary traditions; master of style. Author of stories including *Son Makara* (1883), *Slepoy Muzykant* (1886), *Les shumit* (1886), and of autobiographical *Istoriya moyego sovremennika* (1905–21).

Ko·rol·yov \kə-(ˌ)rəl-ˈyȯf\, Sergey Pavlovich. 1906–1966. Soviet aeronautical engineer. Studied engineering under A. N. Tupolev and V. A. Zhukovsky; with F. A. Tsander formed (1931) Moscow Group for Study of Reactive Motion and directed launching (1933) of Soviet Union's first liquid propellant rocket. Began (c.1945) designing rockets, guided missiles, and spacecraft; later placed in charge of systems engineering for Soviet spacecraft; directed Soviet Union's space program.

Ko·ro·šec \ˈkȯr-ȯ-shek\, Anton. 1872–1940. Slovene priest and politician. Took part in founding of Yugoslav nation (1918); held several ministries in cabinet; prime minister (1928); opposed dictatorship of Alexander I and imprisoned (1933–34) for insistence on Slovene autonomy.

Korsakov, Nikolay A. Rimsky-. See RIMSKY-KORSAKOV.

Kor·tum \ˈkȯr-tu̇m\, Karl Arnold. 1745–1824. German physician and satirist. Author of burlesque epic *Die Jobsiade* (1784).

Kor·win-Pio·trow·ska \ˈkȯr-vēn-pyȯ-ˈtrȯf-ská\, Maria. *Pseudonym* Gabriela Za·pol·ska \zá-ˈpȯl-ská\. 1860–1921. Polish writer. Known for Naturalistic novels *Káska Kariatyda* (1888), *Przedpiekle* (1889), *Sezonowa miłosc* (1905), *Kobieta bez skazy* (1913), etc., and bourgeois comedies including *Tamten* (1898), *Moralność pani Dulskiej* (1907), *Skiz* (1909), and *Panna Moliczewska* (1912).

Korzeniowski, Józef Teodor Konrad. See Joseph CONRAD.

Kor·zyb·ski \kȯ-ˈzhip-skē, *Angl* kȯr-ˈzip-skē\, Alfred Habdank Skarbek. 1879–1950. American semanticist, b. Warsaw, Poland. To U.S. (1916, naturalized 1940). President and director, Institute of General Semantics, Chicago (1938–46) and Lakeville, Conn. (from 1946). Originator of general semantics, a linguistic philosophy based on man's "time-binding capacity" to transmit ideas from generation to generation. Author of *Manhood of Humanity* (1921), *Science and Sanity: An Introduction to Nonaristotelian Systems and General Semantics* (1933).

Ko·sach-Kvit·ka \ˈkȯ-säk-ˈkvēt-kä\, Larisa Petrovna. *Pseudonym* Lesya Ukrain·ka \ü-ˈkrīn-kä\. 1871–1913. Ukrainian poet. Member of Ukrainian Modernist movement in poetry; her lyrics and dramatic poems published as *Na krylakh pisnya* (1893), *Nevilnychi pisni* (1895), and *Lisova pisnya* (1912).

Koś·ciusz·ko \kȯsh-ˈchüsh-kȯ, *Angl* ˌkäs-ē-ˈəs-ˌkō\, Tadeusz Andrzei Bonawentura. *Eng.* Thaddeus Kosciusko. 1746–1817. Polish patriot. Studied engineering and artillery in France. Went to America to offer services in American Revolutionary army (1776); appointed colonel of engineers in Continental army (Oct. 1776); in charge of construction of fortifications at West Point (1778–80); in charge of transportation during Greene's retreat (1781); engaged before Charleston, S.C. (1782); one of founders of Society of the Cincinnati (1783); brigadier general (1783). Returned to Poland (1784); major general in Polish army (1789); led rebellion against occupying forces (March 1794); captured and imprisoned by Russia (1794–96). In America again (1797–98). Resident of France (from 1798); continued efforts to gain freedom for Poland until his death in Switzerland.

Ko·se \kō-se\ Kanaoka. 802?–?897. Japanese painter. Held court rank and directorship of the Imperial garden. First major secular artist in Japan; reputed to have abandoned Chinese style and founded a Japanese school of painting; excelled in landscapes, portraits of officials, and animals; none of his documented works extant.

Kö·sem Sul·tan \kœ̄-ˈsem-su̇l-ˈtän\. c.1585–1651. Ottoman sultana. Exerted strong influence on Ottoman politics for half a century as wife of Sultan Ahmed I, mother of Murad IV and İbrahim I, and grandmother of Mehmed IV; attempted to kill Mehmed IV but was herself strangled.

Kosen. See SAKAI Toshihiko.

Ko·so·la \ˈkȯ-sȯ-lá\, Iisakki Vihtori. 1884–1936. Finnish politician. Founder (1929–30) of Lapua Movement, a Fascist nationalist organization opposed to Russian domination of Finland; movement declined after he was imprisoned (1932–35) for unsuccessful coup d'état (Feb. 1932).

Kos·sel \ˈkȯs-əl\, Albrecht, *in full* Karl Martin Leonhard Albrecht. 1853–1927. German biochemist. Professor at Heidelberg (1901–24). Known for investigations of the chemistry of protein, the cell, and the cell nucleus; discovered adenine (1885), thymine (1894), histidine (1896), agmatine, thymic acid, etc. Awarded the 1910 Nobel prize for physiology or medicine. His son ¶Walther Ludwig Julius Paschen Heinrich (1888–1956), professor of physics, Kiel (1921–32), Danzig (1932–45), Tübingen (from 1947); known for his theory of the physical nature of chemical valence and researches on the spectra of X-rays and gamma rays.

Kos·suth \'kō-shu̇t, *Angl* 'kä-ˌsüth, kä-'\, Lajos. 1802–1894. Hungarian patriot and statesman. Sent to National Diet (1832); developed a radical political and social philosophy; imprisoned on political charges (1837–40); editor of reform organ *Pesti Hirlap* (1840–44). Member of the Hungarian Diet (1847–49). Headed Hungarian insurrection (1848–49); persuaded Hungarian national assembly to declare independence of Hungary; appointed governor of Hungary with dictatorial powers (1848). As insurrection was crushed, resigned his powers (Aug. 1849) and fled into exile in Turkey (imprisoned there, 1849–51), U.S. (1851–52), and England. During Austro–Sardinian war (1859), organized a Hungarian legion in Italy; resided thereafter in Turin.

Koster. See COSTER.

Ko·sy·gin \(ˌ)kə-'sig-yin, *Angl* kə-'sē-gən\, Aleksey Nikolayevich. 1904–1980. Soviet politician. Joined Communist party (1927); mayor of Leningrad (1938); deputy chairman (1940–56, 1957–60), first deputy chairman (1960–64), Council of Ministers; minister of finance (1948), of light industry (1948–53); elected full member of Politburo (1948), removed (1953), reinstated (1960). Premier of Soviet Union (1964–80); exerted moderating influence on other Soviet leaders but overshadowed by party secretary Leonid Brezhnev.

Kosz·to·lán·yi \'kō-stō-ˌlän-yē\, Dezső. 1885–1936. Hungarian poet, novelist, and critic. Most outstanding Impressionist in Hungarian literature; advocated principle of art for art's sake; in later years campaigned for preservation of purity of Hungarian language. His works included verse *Négy fal között* (1907), *A szegény kisgyermek panaszai* (1910), and *A bús férfi panaszai* (1924); novels *A véres költö* (1921) and *Édes Anna* (1926); short stories, and translations.

Kot·lya·rev·sky \kōt-lyä-'ref-skē\, Ivan. 1769–1838. Ukrainian writer. Author of *Ereyida* (1798), a burlesque-travesty of Virgil's *Aeneid* which was first work written entirely in Ukrainian; also wrote musical comedies *Natalka Poltava* (1838) and *Moskal-charivnyk* (1841).

Kō·to·ku \kō-tō-ku̇\ Shūsui. 1871–1911. Japanese journalist and Socialist. Became newspaper writer (1893); one of first Socialists in Japan; organized (1901) Social Democratic party but it was immediately banned; founded newspaper *Heimin shimbun* (1901); paper closed by government after he opposed Russo–Japanese War (1904–05); began organizing workers for radical activities and denounced parliamentary system; executed on charge of attempting to assassinate the emperor.

Ko·tsyu·bin·sky \kōt-syü-'byēn-skē\, Mikhaylo. 1864–1913. Ukrainian novelist and short-story writer. Known for his impressionistic novel *Fata morgana* (1904–10).

Kot·ze·bue \'kōt-sə-ˌbü\, August Friedrich Ferdinand von. 1761–1819. German dramatist. In Russian civil service (1781–90), living in Paris and Mainz; dramatist and librettist to court theater, Vienna (1798–1800). Arrested on return to Russia (1800); won favor of Paul I; released (1801); became director of German theater in St. Petersburg. Returned to Germany (1801–06); won unpopularity through quarrels with Goethe and attacks on Romantic school; in Russia (1806–17); Russian consul general in Königsberg and political observer for Russia in Germany (1817); founded antiliberal journal *Literarisches Wochenblatt* in Mannheim (1818), continued in Weimar; stabbed to death for ridiculing Burschenschaft movement. Author of over 200 dramatic works, including *Adelheid von Wulfingen* (1788), *Menschenhass und Reue* (1789), *Die Indianer in England* (1790), *Spanier in Peru* (1796), *Der Wildfang* (1798), *Die deutschen Kleinstädter* (1803); also historical and biographical works and miscellaneous sketches and stories.

His son ¶Otto (1787–1846), naval officer and explorer; accompanied Krusenstern on voyage around world (1803–06); commanded *Rurik* in attempt (1815–18) to find passage across Arctic Ocean and explore Oceania; discovered some 400 islands in South Sea and Kotzebue Sound near Bering Strait (1816); visited California and Hawaii and discovered Romanzov Island of Marshall group (1817); commanded third round-the-world voyage (1823–26).

K'ou Ch'ien-chih \'kō-chē-'en-'ji(ə)r\. d. 448 A.D. Chinese Taoist. On basis of a vision (415), assumed Chang Ling's old title of *t'ien-shih* (celestial master) and set out to purge Taoism of its orgiastic practices and mercenary spirit and instill emphasis on hygienic rituals and good works; gained many followers; had title *t'ien-shih* conferred by Imperial decree (423), title later becoming designation of leader of Taoist church; persuaded Emperor T'ai Wu of Northern Wei to persecute Buddhists and adopt (444) Taoism as official state religion. After his death Buddhism returned as dominant religion in China.

Kou·moun·dhoú·ros \ˌkü-mün-'thü-rōs\, Aléxandros. 1814–1883. Greek politician. Elected to Chamber of Deputies (1851); minister of finance (1856–57, 1859); took part in overthrow of King Otto (1862); nine times prime minister of Greece at various periods (between 1865 and 1882); policies characterized by hostility toward Turkey.

Kous·se·vitz·ky \küs-(ˌ)yiv-'yēt-skəi, *Angl* ˌkü-sə-'vit-skē\, Serge. *Orig.* Sergey Aleksandrovich Kusevitsky. 1874–1951. American conductor, b. Vyshniy Volochëk, Russia. Director of Russian State Orchestra (1918–20); conductor in western Europe and England (1920–24); to U.S. (1924, naturalized 1941). Conductor of Boston Symphony Orchestra (1924–49); organized Berkshire Music Festivals (held each summer from 1934); organized Berkshire Music Center (1940). Champion of modern music; commissioned works by Ravel, Prokofiev, Gershwin, Stravinsky.

Kou·wen·ho·ven \'kō-vən-ˌhō-vən\, William Bennett. 1886–1975. American electrical engineer, b. New York City. Taught at Johns Hopkins (1914–75, professor from 1930). Developed several heart resuscitating mechanisms (as his defibrillator) and techniques; responsible for worldwide use of external heart massage.

Ko·va·lev·ska·ya \kə-(ˌ)vəl-'yäf-skə-yə\, Sofya Vasilyevna, *nee* Kor·vi·na Kru·kov·ska·ya \(ˌ)kər-'vye-nə-krü-'kōf-skə-yə\. *Known in West as* Sonya Ko·va·lev·sky \ˌkō-və-'lef-skē\. 1850–1891. Russian mathematician. m. (1868) Vladimir Kovalevsky, brother of Aleksandr O. Kovalevsky. Lecturer (1884–85), professor (1889–91), U. of Stockholm. Besides scientific papers, wrote autobiographical sketch *Recollections of Childhood* (1890) and novels including *The Sisters Rajavski* and *Vera Vorontzoff* (both 1895).

Ko·va·lev·sky \kə-(ˌ)vəl-'yäf-skəi\, Aleksandr Onufriyevich. 1840–1901. Russian embryologist. Brother-in-law of Sofya V. Kovalevskaya. Professor at St. Petersburg (1867, 1891–93), Kazan (1868–69), Kiev (1869–74), Odessa (1874–90). Founder of comparative embryology and experimental histology; established the existence of a common pattern in the development of all multicellular animals. Works included *Development of Amphioxus lanceolatus* (1885) and *Anatomy and Development of Phoronis* (1887).

Ko·va·řo·vic \'kō-vär-ˌzhō-vits\, Karel. 1862–1920. Czech conductor and composer. Conductor and head of opera, National Theater, Prague (1900–1920); composed operas including *Ženichové* (1884), *Psohlavci* (1898), and *Na starém bělidle* (1901), ballets, symphonic poem *Persephone* (1884), string quartets, sonatas for violin and piano, a piano concerto, songs and choruses.

Koxinga. See CHENG CH'ENG-KUNG.

Ko·že·luh \'kō-zhe-lük\ *or* **Ko·ze·luch** \-ze-\, Leopold, *orig.* Jan Antonín. 1747–1818. Bohemian composer. His ballets and pantomimes successfully produced in Prague (1771–78); fashionable piano teacher in Vienna (from 1778); succeeded Mozart as court composer in Vienna (1792–1818). Composed also operas, symphonies, some 50 piano concertos, keyboard sonatas, chamber music, cantatas, oratorios, masses, arrangements of Scottish songs, etc.

Kra·cho·lov \'krä-kə-ləv\, Peyo. *Pseudonym* Peyo Ya·vo·rov \'yä-və-rəv\. 1877–1914. Bulgarian poet and playwright. With rebel army in attempt to recover Macedonia from Turkish rule (1902–03); described experiences in *Haidushki Kopneniya* (1908); wrote for National Theater (1908–13). His verse at first realistic with social-political themes; later became first Bulgarian Symbolist poet. His works included verse collections *Stikhotvoreniya* (1901), *Bezsunitsi* (1907), and *Podir Senkite na Oblatsite* (1910), and plays *V Polite na Vitosha* (1911) and *Kogato Gram Udari* (1912).

Kraenz·lein \'kran(t)-ˌslīn\, Alvin C. 1876–1928. American athlete, b. Milwaukee. During 1900 Olympic Games in Paris, won 110-meter hurdles, 200-meter hurdles, 60-meter dash, and running broad jump, first to win four gold medals; later became an athletic coach and physical trainer.

Krae·pe·lin \ˌkrep-ə-'lēn\, Emil. 1856–1926. German psychiatrist. Professor at Dorpat (1885–91), Heidelberg (1891–1903), Munich (1903–22); director of Research Institute of Psychiatry, Munich (1922 ff.). Principal founder of modern psychiatric nosology; divided mental diseases into dementia praecox and manic-depressive groups; pioneered in psychopharmacology and in application of experimental psychological methods to clinical study. Wrote *Compendium der Psychiatrie* (1883).

Krafft-Ebing \'kräf-'tä-biŋ\, Richard von. Freiherr. 1840–1902. German neuropsychiatrist. Professor at Strasbourg (1872) and Vienna (1889). Made studies in sexual psychopathology, epilepsy, hemicrania; established relationship between syphilis and general paralysis; best known for his *Psychopathia Sexualis* (1886).

Kraft *or* **Krafft** \'kräft\, Adam. c.1455 or 1460–1508 or 1509. German sculptor. His works (all in Nürnberg) included a triptych of Christ's Passion and Resurrection in St. Sebaldus (1490–92), the elaborate late-Gothic tabernacle in the Church of St. Lawrence (1493–96), *The Seven Stations* (1505–08, reliefs of scenes from the life of Christ), and many reliefs for public and private buildings.

Král' \'kräl\, Janko. 1822–1876. Slovak poet. His participation in 1848 revolution gave him legendary status among his countrymen; his romantic ballads, lyrics, and epics helped popularize Slovak literary language codified by L'udevit Štúr.

Kraljević, Marko. See MARKO KRALJEVIĆ.

Kra·mář \'krä-märsh\, Karel. 1860–1937. Czech politician. Propounded Pan-Slavic and Neo-Slavic ideas; a leader in Young Czech movement; first prime minister of Czechoslovakia (1918–19).

Kra·mers \'krä-mərs\, Hendrik Anthony. 1894–1952. Dutch physicist. Professor at Utrecht (1926–34) and Leiden (1934–52). Predicted the existence of the Raman effect (1924); with Ralph de Laer Kronig, derived important equations relating the absorption to the dispersion of light (1927–29); demonstrated that the complex form of the mathematical functions in dispersion theory results from inability of a signal to be propagated faster than the speed of light (1927); also made researches in X-rays, ferromagnetism, and kinetic theory of gases.

Krapf \'kräpf\, Johann Ludwig. 1810–1881. German missionary, traveler, and philologist. Missionary in Abyssinia (1837–42); traveled with Erhardt and Rebmann through East Africa and discovered Mts. Kilimanjaro (1848) and Kenya (1849); joined English expedition to Abyssinia as interpreter (1867); introduced many Abyssinian manuscripts into Germany and England.

Krapp \'krap\, George Philip. 1872–1934. American educator, b. Cincinnati. Professor of English, Columbia (from 1910). Author of *The Elements of English Grammar* (1908), *Pronunciation of Standard English in America* (1919), *The English Language in America* (1925), etc.

Kra·sic·ki \krá-'sēts-kē\, Ignacy. 1735–1801. Polish poet and prelate. Bishop of Warmia (1767); chaplain to Stanisław II Poniatowski; archbishop of Gniezno (1795). Wrote fables and satires, esp. the mock-heroic *Myszeidos* (1775) and *Monachomachia,* a satire on cloistered life of monks (1778), and novels *Mikołaja Doświadczyńskiego przypadki* (1776) and *Pan Podstoli* (1778).

Kra·siń·ski \krá-'sēnʸ-skē\, Zygmunt. Count. 1812–1859. Polish poet and dramatist. With Mickiewicz and Słowacki, a member of Poland's triad of messianic poets. Known for tragedies *Nieboska komedja* (1835) and *Irydion* (1836) and poems *Przedświt* (1843) and *Psalmy przyszłości* (1845).

Kras·ner \'kraz-nər\, Lee. *Orig.* Lenore Krassner. 1908–1984. American artist, b. New York City. Studied (1936–40) with Hans Hofmann (*q.v.*); m. (1945) Jackson Pollock (*q.v.*). With her husband and other first-generation action painters of the New York school founded abstract expressionism; created energetic canvases marked by bold, outlined images.

Kra·szew·ski \krá-'shef-skē\, Józef Ignacy. 1812–1887. Polish novelist. Edited review *Ateneum* (1841–52) in Volhynia and daily *Gazeta Codzienna* (1859–62) in Warsaw. Author of 9 novels on peasant life, 7 historical novels of Poland under Saxon kings, and cycle of 29 novels (written 1876–86) covering Polish history in chronological order. Author also of plays, verse (including epic on history of Lithuania, *Anafielas,* 1840–43), criticism, and historical works.

Kraus \'kraůs\, Karl. 1874–1936. Austrian satirist, critic, and poet. Founder and editor of the polemical review *Die Fackel* (from 1899; sole contributor from 1911), attacking middle-class circles and the liberal press. Author of verse *Worte in Versen* (1916–30), dramas as *Die letzten Tage der Menschheit* (1918), aphorisms *Sprüche und Widersprüche* (1909) and *Nachts* (1919), essay collections *Sittlichkeit und Kriminalität* (1908), *Literatur und Lüge* (1929), and *Die Sprache* (1937), translations of Shakespeare, etc.

Krau·se \'kraů-zə\, Karl Christian Friedrich. 1781–1832. German philosopher. Advocated a union of mankind to work toward a goal of universal development; created the "all-in-God" philosophical system of panentheism, the doctrine that God includes the world as a part, though not the whole, of his being; his disciples in Spain influenced educational system. Works included *Entwurf des Systems der Philosophie* (1804), *System der Sittenlehre* (1810), *Das Urbild der Menschheit* (1811), *Abriss des Systems der Philosophie* (1825–28), *Vorlesungen über die Grundwahrheiten der Wissenschaft* (1829).

Krause, Wilhelm. 1833–1910. German anatomist. Credited with first description of nerve end organs in the skin.

Krav·chin·sky \kráv-'chēnʸ-skəi\, Sergey Mikhaylovich. *Pseudonym* S. Stepnyak *or* Step·niak \'styāp-nyák\. 1852–1895. Russian writer. Fled Russia (1878) and lived abroad because of terrorist activities. Author of *Underground Russia* (1882), *Russia Under the Tsars* (1885), *Andrey Kozhukhov* (1889; in Eng. as *The Career of a Nihilist*), *King Stork and King Log* (1895), etc.

Kray von Kra·jo·wa \'krī-fòn-'krä-yə-vä\, Paul. Baron. 1735–1804. Austrian general. Commanded in Netherlands against French, and defeated Pichegru at Catrou (1794) and Kléber near Wetzlar (1796); suffered reverses (1797), but won victories at Verona, Legnago, Magnano, and Mantua in Italian campaign (1799); succeeded Archduke Charles Louis as commander of army in Germany (1800); failed in German campaign and was removed from command.

Krebs \'krebs\, Sir Hans Adolf. 1900–1981. British biochemist, b. Germany. Privatdocent, Freiburg (1932); to England (1933); lecturer (1935–45), professor (1945–54), Sheffield U.; professor, Oxford (1954–67). Discovered the urea cycle (1932) and the citric acid cycle (1936, also called the Krebs cycle). Wrote *Energy Transformations in Living Matter* (1957, with Hans Kornberg). Awarded (with Fritz Lipmann) Nobel prize for physiology or medicine (1953).

Krebs \'kreps\, Johann Ludwig. 1713–1780. German organist and composer. Pupil of J.S. Bach; organist at Zwickau (1737), Zeitz (1744), Altenburg (1755). Composer of organ music, sonatas for flute and harpsichord, sacred vocal music, etc.

Kreh·biel \'krā-ˌbēl\, Henry Edward. 1854–1923. American music critic, b. Ann Arbor, Mich. With *New York Tribune* (from 1880). Championed Wagner and other Romantic composers, opposed modern school of composition. Revised and completed English edition of A.W. Thayer's *Life of Ludwig von Beethoven* (1921); author of *Studies in the Wagnerian Drama* (1891), *Afro-American Folk-Songs* (1914), etc.

Kreis·ler \'krī-slər\, Fritz. 1875–1962. American violinist and composer, b. Vienna. In Austrian army, World War I; to U.S. (naturalized 1943). Composer of many original violin pieces including *Caprice viennois* and *Schön Rosmarin,* a string quartet, and the operetta *Apple Blossoms* (1919).

Krell, Nikolaus. See CRELL.

Kre·mer \'krā-mər\, Gerhard. *Known by Lat. form* Gerardus Mer·ca·tor \(ˌ)mər-'kāt-ər\. 1512–1594. Flemish cartographer. In Louvain (1530–52); studied independently under mathematician Gemma Frisius and engraver Gaspar a Myrica; produced maps of Palestine (1537), of the world (1538), of Flanders (1540); produced terrestrial (1541) and celestial (1551) globes; imprisoned for 7 months on charge of heresy (1544). Opened cartographic workshop at Duisburg (1552); court cosmographer to Duke of Cleve (1564). Known esp. for his map of the world employing his Mercator projection (1569); began great *Atlas* by publishing collection of maps of Ptolemy (1578), following with maps of France, Germany, and the Netherlands (1585) and of Italy, Greece, and the Balkan states (1589); map of British Isles published (1595) after his death by his son.

Kress \'kres\, Samuel Henry. 1863–1955. American merchant, b. Cherryville, Pa. Founder (1896) of S.H. Kress & Co., operating a chain of five, ten, and twenty-five cent stores in U.S. Established (1929) foundation through which he donated most of his vast art collection to American museums.

Kretsch·mer \'krāch-mər, 'krech-\, Ernst. 1888–1964. German psychiatrist. Professor at Marburg (1926–46) and Tübingen (1946–59). Made researches into causes of schizophrenia, hysteria, compulsive criminality, mental illness in children, etc. In *Körperbau und Charakter* (1921) attempted to correlate body build and physical constitution with mentality and character; also wrote *Hysterie, Reflex und Instinkt* (1923), *Geniale Menschen* (1929), *Psychotherapeutische Studien* (1949), etc.

Kretschmer, Paul. 1866–1956. German linguist. Professor at Vienna (1899–1936). Adherent of Neo-grammarian school of linguistics; in *Einleitung in die Geschichte der griechischen Sprache* (1896) concluded that a non-Greek Mediterranean culture had preceded Greeks at Anatolia; also contributed to modern Greek dialectology and German linguistic geography; with Frans Skutsch founded linguistic journal *Glotta* (1907).

Kret·zer \'kret-sər\, Max. 1854–1941. German novelist. Disciple of Zola and founder of Naturalistic school in Germany. Author chiefly of realistic and social novels as *Die Betrogenen* (1882), *Die Verkommenen* (1883), *Meister Timpe* (1888), *Der Fassadenraphael* (1911), *Der alte Andreas* (1911).

Kreu·ger \'krūe-gər\, Ivar. 1880–1932. Swedish industrialist, financier, and swindler. Founded (1913) a match company; during World War I concentrated entire Swedish match industry under Swedish Match Company with himself as managing director; after the war, developed an international match monopoly; engaged in vast financing operations, including loans to various governments in return for industrial concessions. Financial stress beginning in 1929 forced collapse of his enterprises; committed suicide; subsequent investigation revealed vast irregularities in his finances.

Kreutz·berg \'kròits-ˌberk\, Harald. 1902–1968. German dancer. Joined (1922) Hanover Ballet and often toured with partner Yvonne Georgi; toured U.S. and Far East with Ruth Page (1932, 1934); thereafter primarily a soloist. A leading interpreter of modern dance; known esp. for solos combining dance with mime and pictorial costuming. Opened school in Bern, Switzerland (1955); retired from stage (1959) but continued as teacher and choreographer.

Kreut·zer \krœd-zer, krœ̄d-; *Ger* 'kròit-sər\, Rodolphe. 1766–1831. French violinist and composer. A founder of French school of violin playing and one of foremost improvisers and conductors of his day. Professor at Paris Conservatory (1795–1826); chamber musician to Napoléon and later to Louis XVIII; chief conductor (1817–24), music director (1824–26), Paris Opéra. Composer of 42 *Études ou caprices,* 19 violin concertos, about 40 operas including *Lodoïska* (1791), ballets, and much chamber music. Beethoven's *Kreutzer Sonata* was dedicated to him.

Kreutz·wald \'kròits-ˌvält\, Friedrich Reinhold. 1803–1882. Estonian physician, folklorist, and poet. Municipal health officer in Voru for over 40 years. Founded (1838) Estonian Learned Society to collect narrative folksongs for a national epic; combined collected material with original poetry to produce national epic of Estonia, *Kalevipoeg* (1857–61).

Krė·vė \'krā-vā\, Vincas. *Surname orig.* Krėvė-Mic·kie·vi·čius \-ˌmēts-kyav-'ē-chůs\. 1882–1954. Lithuanian philologist, poet, and dramatist. Professor of Slavonic languages and literature at Kaunas (1922–39) and Vilnius (1939–40); foreign minister and acting premier under Soviet occupation (1940–44); fled to Austria (1944); professor at U. of Pennsylvania (1947–53). One of greatest of Lithuanian authors. His works included historical dramas *Savunas* (1911), *Dainavos kunigaikstis* (1923), *Skirgaila* (1925), *Likimo keliais* (1926, 1929), *Karaliaus Mindaugo mirtis* (1935); village drama *Zentas* (1922); adaptation of Lithuanian legends *Dainavos salies senu zmoniu palavimai* (1912); short-story collections *Sutemose* (1921) and *Po siaudine pastoge* (1922–23); Oriental tales *Rytu pasakos* (1930); and unfinished biblical epic on Hebrew life in Herod's time *Dangaus ir zemes sunus* (1949).

Krie·ger \'krē-gər\, Adam. 1634–1666. German composer. Court organist in Dresden to Elector of Saxony (1658–66). Considered most varied and original master of the German Baroque song; his songs, some on his own texts, published in *Arien* (1657) and *Neue Arien* (1667).

Krieger, Johann Philipp. 1649–1725. German composer. Court organist at Bayreuth (c.1670); visited Italy (1673–75); court organist at Halle (1677–80); Kapellmeister at court of Weissenfels (1680–1725). Composed over 2,000 cantatas (only some 80 extant), fugues, keyboard suites, suites for wind instruments, about 200 secular songs, operas (only a few arias extant), etc.

Krim·pen \'krim-pən\, Jan van. 1892–1958. Dutch type designer. First successful design, lettering for a special commemorative stamp (1923); designed, for Enschedé firm, Lutetia (1927), Antigone Greek (1927), Romanée (1928), Romulus (1931), Cancelleresca Bastarda (1935), Spectrum (1943) typefaces for books.

Krish·na Men·on \'krish-nə-'men-ən\, Vengalil Krishnan. 1897–1974. Indian politician. Practiced law, London (from 1925); member of St. Pancras Borough Council (1934–47); secretary of India League (1927–47). Indian high commissioner in London (1947–52); returned to India (1952). President, India League (1947–74); Indian representative at United Nations (1952–60); member of Indian Parliament (1953–57, 1957–67, 1969–74); minister without portfolio (1956–57), of defense (1957–62); champion of anticolonialism and neutralism.

Krist·en·sen \'krē-sən-sən\, Knud. 1880–1962. Danish politician. Entered parliament (1920); became a leader of Venstre (Left) party; minister of interior (1940–42). Prime minister (1945–47); founded (1953) Independent party, advocating return of southern Schleswig to Denmark and repeal of most social welfare legislation.

Kri·ža·nić \'krē-zhä-nēty\, Juraj. 1618–1683. Croatian priest and scholar. Ordained Roman Catholic priest (1642); on mission to Moscow to promote unification of Roman and Russian Orthodox churches (1647); again to Moscow (1659) to promote personal dream of uniting all Slav peoples in a single political entity centered in Moscow; banished to Siberia (1661–76), where he wrote on political, economic, religious, linguistic, and philosophical topics; to Poland (1676). Sometimes called the "Father of Pan-Slavism."

Kroch·mal \'krōk-mäl\, Nachman Kohen. *Known as* Ra·nak \rä-'näk\. 1785–1840. Jewish scholar and philosopher, b. Austrian Poland (now Ukrainian S.S.R.). Merchant, later bookkeeper, at Nesterov, near Lvov; gathered disciples, esp. Solomon Rapoport. Known for *More nevukhe ha-zman* (pub. 1851), an analysis of Jewish history within framework of world history.

Kroe·ber \'krō-bər\, Alfred Louis. 1876–1960. American anthropologist, b. Hoboken, N.J. Taught at U. of California, Berkeley (1901–46; professor from 1919); known for work on languages, culture, religion, etc., of North American Indians. Author of *Anthropology* (1923), *Cultural and Natural Areas of Native North America* (1939), *Peruvian Archaeology in 1942* (1944), *Configurations of Culture Growth* (1945), *The Nature of Culture* (1952), *Style and Civilizations* (1957), *Yokuts Dialect Survey* (1963), etc.

Krogh \'krōg\, August, *in full* Schack August Steenberg. 1874–1949. Danish physiologist. Professor, Copenhagen (1916–45). Discovered the regulation of the motor mechanism of capillaries. Published *Mechanism of Gas Exchange in Lungs* (1910), *The Respiratory Exchange of Animals and Man* (1916), *The Anatomy and Physiology of Capillaries* (1922). Awarded the 1920 Nobel prize for physiology or medicine.

Krohg \'krōg\, Christian. 1852–1925. Norwegian painter. Pioneer in open-air painting in Norway; works included *Port the Helm, Leif Ericson Discovers America, Norwegian Pilot, The Seamstress.* His son and pupil ¶Per Lasson (1889–1965) was a major figure (from 1920) in the renaissance of mural painting in Norway; also studied under Henri Matisse (1907–09); taught in Oslo at State Art and Craft School (1935–46) and State Art Academy (1946 ff.). Works included frescoes for Maritime School and for Town Hall (both in Oslo) and a mural in the Security Council chamber of UN building, New York.

Kro·neck·er \'krō-ˌnek-ər\, Leopold. 1823–1891. German mathematician. Lecturer (1861–83), professor (1883 ff.), Berlin; known chiefly for work in elliptic numbers, the theory of algebraic equations, and the theory of algebraic numbers.

Kro·pot·kin \(ˌ)krə-'pōt-kyin\, Pyotr Alekseyevich. 1842–1921. Russian geographer, revolutionist, and philosopher. Made valuable contributions (1871–73) to geography by explorations in Siberia, Finland, and Manchuria. Joined (1872) extreme branch of International Workingmen's Association; became foremost leader and theorist of anarchist movement; imprisoned (1883–86) in Lyons for anarchistic activities and publications; lived in England (1886–1917) and in Russia (1917–21). Developed theory of "anarchist communism" based on replacement of private property and unequal incomes with free distribution of goods and services. Author of *Paroles d'un Révolté* (1885), *La Conquête du pain* (1892), *La Grande Révolution* (1893), *L'Anarchie, sa philosophie, son idéal* (1896), *Fields, Factories and Workshops* (1899), *Modern Science and Anarchism* (1903).

Krṣna De·va Rā·ya \'krish-nə-'dā-və-'rī-ə\. 16th century. Indian emperor. Ruler (1509–29) of the Vijayanagar empire in the Deccan; reigned during golden age of Telugu literature and patron of many poets; himself a poet, composed epic *Amuktamālyadā* (completed 1520).

Krucz·kow·ski \krüch-'kōf-skē\, Leon. 1900–1962. Polish writer. Author of novels *Kordian i cham* (1932), *Pawie pióra* (1935), and *Sidła* (1937), plays *Odwety* (1948), *Niemcy* (1949), *Pierwszy dzień wolności* (1960), and *Śmierć gubernatora* (1961), verse, and short stories.

Krü·de·ner \'krue-də-nər\, Barbara Juliane von, *nee* von Vie·ting·hoff \fōn-'fēt-iŋ-ˌhōf\. Freifrau. 1764–1824. Russian mystic. m. (1782; separated 1785) Freiherr Burchard von Krüdener; led carefree life in Germany, France, Russia, and Switzerland; intimate of Madame de Staël; published largely autobiographical novel *Valérie* (1804). Returned to Riga (1804); converted to teachings of Moravians, and influenced by chiliasts and Pietists and by association with Jung-Stilling in Germany (1808) and ideas of Swedenborg. Devoted herself to preaching and prophesying in Europe; brought Queen Louise of Prussia and Alexander I of Russia under her influence; played important part in furthering formation of Holy Alliance.

Krue·ger \'krü-gər\, Walter. 1881–1967. American army officer, b. Flatow, Germany. To U.S. (1889); joined U.S. army as private (1898); commissioned (1901); served in Spanish–American War, Philippine insurrection (1899–1903), Mexican border (1916), World War I; commander of 3d army (1941), 6th army (1943); occupied Hollandia, Dutch New Guinea (Apr. 1944); freed many islands on drive to the Philippines; on occupation duty in Japan (1945); retired as general (1946).

Kru·ger \'krue-(g)ər, *Angl* krü-gər\, Paul, *in full* Stephanus Johannes Paulus. 1825–1904. South African statesman. Migrated from Cape Colony to north of Orange River (the Great Trek, 1836–40); became a founder of Transvaal state, whose independence was acknowledged by Great Britain in Sand River Convention (1852). Elected commandant general of Transvaal forces (1864). Transvaal annexed by British (1877) and Kruger dismissed from service (1878) on account of opposition to British domination. A leader of Boer rebellion (1880) and associate of Piet Joubert and Marthinus Pretorius in negotiating peace (1881). President of Transvaal (1883–1900). Too old to take part in Boer War (1899–1902), went to Europe in vain attempt to get European powers to intervene. Died in Switzerland.

Kruif, Paul de. See DE KRUIF.

Krum \'krəm\. d. 814. Bulgarian khan (802–814). Gained power by victories over Avars; waged war (808–813) with Byzantine Empire; defeated and killed Emperor Nicephorus (811); besieged Constantinople (813–814); defeated by Leo the Armenian at Mesembria (813).

Krum·ba·cher \'krüm-ˌbäk-ər\, Karl. 1856–1909. German scholar. Taught at U. of Munich (from 1892). Largely developed the modern study of Byzantine culture. Founder (1892) and director (1892–1909) of *Byzantinische Zeitschrift;* author of *Geschichte der byzantinischen Literatur* (1891), *Das Problem der neugriechischen Schriftsprache* (1902), etc.

Krüm·mel \'kruem-əl\, Otto. 1854–1912. German oceanographer. Professor at Kiel (1883–1911) and Marburg (1911–12); his *Handbuch der Ozeanographie* (1897) established practice of recognizing only three oceans, the Atlantic, Pacific, and Indian.

Kru·pa \'krü-pə\, Gene. 1909–1973. American musician, b. Chicago. Jazz drummer with Eddie Condon, Red Nichols, Benny Goodman; led own band (1938–51) and toured as soloist; appeared in several films; recorded soundtrack for his movie biography *The Gene Krupa Story* (1959).

Krupp \'krüp, *Angl* 'krəp\, Friedrich. 1787–1826. German ironmaster. Founder (1811) of the Krupp Works at Essen. His son ¶Alfred (1812–1887) succeeded him; perfected process of making cast steel, begun by his father; began manufacture of ordnance (c.1847); his field guns a major reason for Prussia's victory in war with France (1870–71); supplied arms to at least 46 nations. His son ¶Friedrich Alfred (1854–1902) succeeded in management of the works; also manufactured machinery. At his death, control passed to his daughter ¶Bertha (1886–1957), whose husband (m. 1906) prefixed Krupp to his name and became ¶Gustav Krupp von Boh·len und Hal·bach \-fōn-'bō-lən-ünt-'häl-ˌbäk\ (1870–1950); Gustav assumed management of the works; after World War I, began secretly rearming Germany; supporter of Hitler and helped finance the Nazis in 1933 election. His son ¶Alfried (1907–1967) assumed control (c.1939); seized properties in countries conquered by Germany during World War II; ran his factories with inmates of concentration camps as slave laborers; imprisoned by Nürnberg tribunal and his property forfeited (1946); granted amnesty (1951); restored fortunes of Krupp works.

Krup·ska·ya \'krüp-skə-yə\, Nadezhda Konstantinovna. 1869–1939. Russian revolutionary. Active in aiding Lenin in revolutionary program in St. Petersburg (1891–98); m. (1898) Lenin; exiled to Siberia (1898). Joined Lenin in exile in Europe (1901); secretary of Bolshevik section of Social Democratic party (1900–17); returned to Russia (1917). Held (from 1917) several posts in education commissariat, including vice commissar (1929); member of Central Committee of Communist party (1927). Wrote memoirs *Vospominaniya o Lenin* (pub. in book form 1957).

Kru·sen·stern \'krüz-yin-shtyirn\, Adam Johann von. 1770–1846. Russian navigator. Commissioned by Czar Alexander I (1803) to explore north Pacific; made valuable geographical discoveries and was first Russian to circumnavigate the globe (1803–06).

Kru·sen·stjer·na \'krü-sən-ˌsher-nə\, Agnes von. 1894–1940. Swedish novelist. Known for autobiographical novel cycles *Tony* (3 vols., 1922–26), *Fröknarna von Pahlen* (7 vols., 1930–35), and *Fattigadel* (4 vols., 1935–38).

Krutch \'krüch\, Joseph Wood. 1893–1970. American critic and naturalist, b. Knoxville, Tenn. Drama critic, *The Nation* (1924–52); professor, Columbia (1937–1952). Author of *Comedy and Conscience After the Restoration* (1924), *Edgar Allan Poe* (1926), *The Modern Temper* (1929), *Samuel Johnson* (1944), *The Great Chain of Life* (1957), *Human Nature and the Human Condition* (1959), *More Lives Than One* (1962, autobiography), *The Most Wonderful Animals That Never Were* (1969), etc.

Kry·len·ko \kril-'yen-kə\, Nikolay Vasiliyevich. 1885–?1938. Russian revolutionary officer. Joined revolutionary movement (1904); commander of Bolshevist forces (1917–18); later private secretary to Lenin; people's commissar for justice (1922–38).

Kry·lov \kri-'lȯf\, Ivan Andreyevich. 1768–1844. Russian fabulist. Translated La Fontaine's fables; published 9 collections of his own fables (1809–43), extremely popular for their satirizing of bureaucrats and other social types; chief librarian in Imperial Public Library (1816–41).

Ksches·sin·ska·ya \kshchās-'yin^y-skə-yə\, Mathilde. 1872–1971. Russian dancer. Joined Maryinsky Theater, St. Petersburg (1890); made (1895) *prima ballerina assoluta* by Imperial Russian Ballet, only other holder of that title being Pierina Legnani; known for roles in *Cinderella, La Sylphide, Esmeralda, Nutcracker, Sleeping Beauty;* first Russian to accomplish 32 consecutive *fouettés en tournant;* settled in France (1920); opened dancing school in Paris (1929). Wrote autobiography *Souvenirs de la Kschessinska* (1960).

Kuang-hsü. See TSAI-T'IEN.

Kuang Tsung. See Chu Ch'ang-lo under CHU family.

Kuang Wu Ti. See Liu Hsiu under LIU family.

Kuan Han-ch'ing \'gwän-'hän-'chiŋ\. 1241?–?1320. Chinese playwright. Often considered greatest dramatist of Chinese classical theater; played important role in development of early Chinese drama; plays often dealt with everyday events and used female protagonists of low social standing; over 60 titles known but only 14 plays survive, including *Tou-o yüan, Tan tou huei,* and *Chiu feng chen.*

Kuan-hsiu \'gwän-shē-ü\. *Orig.* Chiang \jē-'äŋ\. 833–912. Chinese painter. Known esp. for his paintings of lohans; also a poet and Buddhist savant.

Ku·blai Khan \'kü-blə-'kän, -ˌblī-\. 1215–1294. Mongol khan and founder of Mongol dynasty in China. Son of Tolui and grandson of Genghis Khan, and brother of Mangu Khan and Hülegü. With his brothers undertook conquest of southern China (1251–59); advanced to borders of Tibet. Succeeded Mangu as khan (1260); completed subjugation of China by expelling Kin Tatars in the north and putting down various rebellions (1260–79); founded (1264–67) Ta-tu (now Peking) as his capital. Relinquished parts of Mongol empire to other descendants of Genghis Khan, but retained China; completed organization of China and founded Yüan dynasty (1280), succeeding the Southern Sung dynasty. In foreign wars, subdued Korea and Burma, but expeditions to Japan (1274, 1281) and Java (1293) failed. Visited by Marco Polo (*q.v.*) with father and uncle (1275–92). Ardent Buddhist, but tolerant of other faiths; patron of literature and arts.

Küch·lüq \kuek-'luek\ *or* **Kush·lek** \ku̇sh-'lek\. d. c.1218 A.D. Leader of Turkic Naimans. Defeated by Genghis Khan (1204) and fled to Karakitai; usurped throne of Karakitai Khan and again defeated by Genghis (1218); fled to Afghanistan, captured and killed.

Kud·ir·ka \ku̇d-'ir-kä\, Vincas. 1858–1899. Lithuanian physician, writer, and patriot. Founded (1889), edited, and contributed to literary-political journal *Varpas* at Tilsit; zealous protester against Russification attempts. Wrote satires, poems, and the Lithuanian national anthem; translated Byron, Schiller, Mickiewicz.

Kuei, Prince of. See Chu Yu-lang under CHU family.

Kü·gel·gen, von \fȯn-'kue-gəl-gən\. Family of German painters including: Gerhard (1772–1820), painted chiefly mythological and religious pictures, also portraits of Goethe, Schiller, Herder, and Wieland, etc. His twin brother ¶Karl (1772–1832) produced chiefly sketches of Crimean landscapes. Gerhard's son and pupil ¶Wilhelm (1802–1867) painted portraits of Goethe and Wieland.

Ku·gler \'kü-glər\, Franz. 1808–1858. German art historian. Teacher of Jacob Burckhardt; championed revival of Prussian art. Wrote *Handbuch der Geschichte der Malerei* (1837), *Handbuch der Kunstgeschichte* (1842), etc.

Kuhhorn, Martin. See Martin BUCER.

Kuh·lau \'kü-ˌlau̇\, Daniel Frederik Rudolph. 1786–1832. Danish composer, b. Germany. Works included operas as *Røverborgen* (1814) and *Lulu* (1824), music to Boye's *Shakespeare* (1826) and Johan Heiberg's Danish national play *Elverhøj* (1828), piano pieces, chamber music, songs, and male quartets.

Kuhl·mann \'kül-män\, Richard von. 1873–1948. German politician. Foreign minister (1917–18); represented Germany in peace negotiations with Russia at Brest-Litovsk and with Romania at Bucharest (1918). Publicly championed peace by agreement rather than decision by arms alone, and was forced to withdraw from office (1918).

Kuhn \'kün\, Adalbert, *in full* Franz Felix Adalbert. 1812–1881. German philologist and mythologist. Teacher (1841), director (1870), Kollnisches Gymnasium, Berlin. Founded a new school of comparative mythology based on comparative philology. Cofounder and editor (from 1851) of *Zeitschrift für vergleichende Sprachforschung,* and editor of a series of Brandenburg, North German, and Westphalian myths, customs, and legends (1843, 1848, 1859). Author of works on Indo-European language and history, as *Zur ältesten Geschichte der indogermanischen Volker* (1845), and essays on mythology as *Mythologischen Studien* (1886, 1912).

Kuhn, Richard. 1900–1967. Austrian chemist. Known for researches on vitamins and carotenoids; declined 1938 Nobel prize for chemistry in accordance with instruction of German government.

Kuhn, Walter Francis, *known as* Walt. 1877–1949. American painter, b. Brooklyn, N.Y. As a founder (1912) and secretary of Association of American Painters and Sculptors, was instrumental in staging New York Armory Show (1913) that introduced avant-garde painting to U.S. Known for his bold and unpolished paintings of clowns, show girls, and acrobats, as *The Blue Clown* (1931) and *Lavender Plumes* (1938); in later years painted still lifes and trees.

Kuh·nau \'kü-ˌnau̇\, Johann. *Surname orig.* Kuhn. 1660–1722. German composer, organist, and scholar. Organist (1684), cantor (1701 ff.) at St. Thomas's, Leipzig. Composed keyboard sonatas, as in *Neue Klavierübung* (1689–92) and *Musikalische Vorstellung einiger biblischen Historien in 6 Sonaten,* an example of early program music (1700); cantatas and other church music, etc. Also wrote satirical novel *Der musikalische Quacksalber* (1700) deriding Italian musical affectation.

Kū·kai \kü-kī\. *Posthumous name* Kō·bō Dai·shi \kō-bō-dī-shē\. 774–835. Japanese Buddhist priest. Studied in China (804–806); founded in Japan the popular Shingon school of Buddhism; established (816) in Kii province Mt. Kōya monastery. Author in Chinese of *Jūjū shinron* on Shingon. Contributed greatly to development of Japanese religious art; also noted as a sculptor, poet, and calligrapher.

Ku K'ai-chih \'gü-'kī-'ji(ə)r\. c.344–c.406. Chinese painter. One of the most famous of Chinese masters, esp. in figure painting; two handscrolls are extant, *Nymph of the Lo River* and *Admonitions of the Instructress to the Palace Ladies;* wrote essay *On Painting the Cloud Terrace Mountain;* known also as a wit and statesman.

Ku·le·shov \kül-yi-'shȯf\, Lev Vladimirovich. 1899–1970. Soviet film theorist and director. Known for use of montage and effective closeups, as in *The Project of Engineer Prite* (1917), *On the Red Front* (1920), *According to the Law* (1926); founded (1920) Kuleshov Workshop, Moscow, where he trained actors and directors; officially censured (1935) and produced no major films thereafter. Author of theoretical works *Art of the Cinema* (1929), *Practice of Film Direction* (1935), *Fundamentals of Film Direction* (1941).

Ku·lin \'kü-lin\. d. c.1204. Bosnian ruler. Ruled Bosnia (from c.1180) as *ban* or viceroy of the king of Hungary; converted from Roman Catholicism to Bogomil and led many of his subjects into that faith; forced by Pope Innocent II to recant (1203).

Kulmbach, Hans von. See Hans SÜSS.

Kül·pe \'kuel-pə\, Oswald. 1862–1915. German philosopher and experimental psychologist. Disciple of Wundt and exponent of the Würzburg school of psychology; professor at Würzburg (1894–1909), Bonn (1909–12), and Munich (1912–15); carried on researches in psychology of perception, judgment, and thought, seeking to find a critical realism. Wrote *Grundriss der Psychologie* (1893) and *Die Realisierung* (1912–23).

Ku·mā·ra Gup·ta I \ku̇-'mä-rə-'gu̇p-tə\. d. 455 A.D. Fourth king (c.415–455) of the Gupta dynasty of India. Son of Candra Gupta II. Ruler during India's golden age of literature.

\ə\ abut \ə\ kitten, *Fr.* table \ər\ further \a\ ash \ā\ ace \ä\ cot, cart \au̇\ out \ch\ chin \e\ bet \ē\ easy \g\ go \i\ hit \ī\ ice \j\ job \ŋ\ sing \ō\ go \ȯ\ law \ȯi\ boy \th\ both \t͟h\ the \ü\ loot \u̇\ foot \y\ yet \zh\ vision \á, b̲, g̃, k̲, ⁿ, œ, œ̄, ue, ue̅, ʸ\ *see* Guide to Pronunciation

Ku·mā·ra·jī·va \kü-ˈmä-rə-ˈjē-və\. 344–413. Indian Buddhist scholar and mystic. Famed for his encyclopedic knowledge of Indian and Vedantic learning; brought to China (c.383) by Chin emperor Fu Chien, where he introduced Indian culture.

Ku·mā·ri·la \kü-ˈmär-i-lə\. *Also called* Bhaṭ·ṭa \ˈbät-tə\ *or* Svā·min \ˈsvä-mēn\. fl. 730 A.D. Hindu philosopher, native of Bihar. Wrote a famous commentary on Mīmāmsā system of philosophy; a bitter opponent of Buddhism.

Ku·ma·za·wa \küm-äz-ä-wä\ Banzan. 1619–1691. Japanese political philosopher. Samurai in service of lord of Okayama (1634); adopted neo-Confucian philosophy of Wang Yang-min; chief minister of Okayama (1647–56); fostered agriculture; later kept in custody or under surveillance for works advocating reforms in government.

Ku·me \küm-ē\ Masao. 1891–1952. Japanese novelist and playwright. A founder (1916) of literary journal *Shinshichō;* disciple of novelist Natsume Sōseki. Known esp. for novel *Jūkensei-no-shūki* (1916).

Kum·mer \ˈküm-ər\, Ernst Eduard. 1810–1893. German mathematician. Professor at Breslau (1842–55) and Berlin (1855–83); contributed to development of differential geometry and the theory of numbers; originated the theory of ideal numbers.

Kun \ˈkün\, Béla. 1886–1937. Hungarian politician and revolutionary. Fought in Austrian army in World War I; captured by Russians (1916); became Bolshevist; returned to Hungary (1918); founded Hungarian Communist party (1918); edited *Red News* (1918–19); organized Communist revolution in Budapest (1919); succeeded Károlyi as premier (Mar. 21–Aug. 1, 1919); introduced radical changes in government; reconquered much territory from Czechs and Romanians; failed to control Slovakian peasants. In counterrevolution, was defeated with aid of Romanians (1919); fled to Vienna and later (1920) to Russia; as leader of Third International, attempted to foment revolutions in Austria and Germany during 1920s; liquidated in Stalinist purge.

Kuncevyč, Saint Josaphat. See JOSAPHAT KUNCEVYČ.

Kunck·el von Lö·wen·stjern \ˈkün̦-kəl-fón-ˈlœ-vən-ˌshtyern\, Johann. *Also spelled* Kun·kel. 1630–?1702. German chemist. Court chemist at Dresden; director of laboratory and glassworks at Brandenburg (1679–88); minister of mines in Stockholm for Charles XI (from 1688); created baron (1693). Discovered processes for making artificial ruby glass and preparing phosphorus; studied putrefaction, fermentation, and nature of salts.

Kundt \ˈkünt\, August Adolph Eduard Eberhard. 1839–1894. German physicist. Professor at Würzburg (1869), Strassburg (1872), Berlin (1888); discovered a method of determining the velocity of sound in gases; conducted researches on the conduction of heat and the friction of gases, and on the optical properties of metals.

Kundulun Khan. See NURHACHI.

Kung, Prince. See I-HSIN.

K'ung \ˈküŋ\, H. H. *Orig.* K'ung Hsiang-hsi \-shē-ˈäŋ-ˈshē\. 1881–1967. Chinese banker and politician. Active in revolutionary years (1911–17); friend and supporter of his wife's brother-in-law Sun Yat-sen; minister of industry in Nationalist government (1928–31); member of the Kuomintang executive committee (1926–28); minister of finance (1933–38); president (1938), vice president (1939–44). A man of great wealth; gave valuable aid to Chiang Kai-shek (who was married to another of his wife's sisters); resident in U.S. (from 1948). He married ¶Ai-ling Soong \ˈī-ˈliŋ-ˈsüŋ\, *Chin.* Sung Ai-ling \süŋ\ (1888–1973), eldest daughter of C. J. Soong (see SOONG family); joined revolutionary movement (1910); shrewd in business; of great influence over her husband, esp. in financial undertakings.

K'ung Ch'iu \ˈküŋ-chē-ˈü\. *Literary name* Chung-ni \ˈjüŋ-nē\. *Called* K'ung Fu-tzu \-füd-zü\, *i.e.* Master K'ung, *Latinized as* Con·fu·cius \kən-ˈfyü-shəs\. 551–479 B.C. Chinese philosopher. Dedicated life to achieving reform of government; failing to secure official post for himself, turned to teaching, gathering group of intelligent disciples whom he trained in literature, music, human relations, and above all ethics; taught that rulers exist to secure happiness of subjects, that family provides model for all human relations. Briefly held post in native state of Lu, but with no authority; enjoyed considerable success in placing his students in positions of power. Became in time the most revered person in Chinese history and, although he taught no system or religion, the eponym of a rich and complex philosophy and of a state cult of Confucianism. Wrote no surviving works, but many are traditionally attributed to him, and a great many more are traditionally called Confucian Classics.

Kung Hsien \ˈgüŋ-shē-ˈen\. c.1618–1689. Chinese painter. Most important artist of Eight Masters of Nanking; produced chiefly dense and somewhat forbidding landscapes.

Kung-sun Hung \ˈgüŋ-ˈsün-ˈhüŋ\. d. 121 B.C. Chinese scholar. According to tradition, a poor swineherd who did not begin to study the Confucian Classics until age of 40; became important adviser to Han emperor Wu (140); known esp. for ability to interpret omens, a quality he made a part of officially accepted Confucian doctrine; with Tung Chung-shu, established (124) first Imperial university, the predecessor of the Confucian civil service examination system.

Kung-sun Lung \-ˈlüŋ\. 320?–?250 B.C. Chinese philosopher. Representative of Dialectician school of philosophy; wrote *Kung-sun Lung-tzŭ,* whose 6 extant chapters (of 14) constitute sole surviving independent work of Chinese literature of logic.

Ku·ni·gun·de \ˌkü-nē-ˈgün-də\. Saint. c.980–1033 or 1039. German empress. Wife of Emperor Henry II of Germany; according to legend, when her reputation had been unjustly impugned she vindicated herself by walking barefoot over hot irons. After Henry II's death (1024), retired to a convent which she had founded, and devoted herself to pious works. Canonized (1200).

Ku·ni·ki·da \kün-ē-kē-dä\ Doppo. *Personal name orig.* Kamekichi, *later* Tetsuo. 1871–1908. Japanese short-story writer. Correspondent during Sino–Japanese War (1894–95); his dispatches published as *Aitei tsūshin.* Identified with Naturalist movement; his poetic but tragic stories dealing chiefly with downtrodden common people included *Gen oji* (1897), *Musashino* (1898), *Gyūniku to bareisho* (1901), *Haru-no-tori* (1904).

Ku·ni·yo·shi \ˌkü-ni-ˈyō-shē\, Yasuo. 1893–1953. American painter, b. Okayama, Japan. To U.S. (1906); taught at Art Students' League (from 1933) and New School for Social Research (from 1936; both in New York); first president of Artists Equity Association (1947). Influenced esp. by Jules Pascin; his mature style marked by sensuous physicality and use of pastel hues, later used brighter colors and ironic content; noted for paintings of women, carnival scenes, still lifes, landscapes, including *Child* (1923), *I'm Tired* (1938), *Upside Down Table and Mask* (1940), *Desert Woman* (1943), *Exit* (1950), and *Juggler* (1952).

Kunjae. See CH'OE Kyong.

Kunkel. See KUNCKEL.

Kuo Hsi \ˈgwō-ˈshē\. fl. 1060–1075. Chinese painter. Painted landscapes as *Early Spring of 1072* and handscroll *The Coming of Autumn;* author of treatise on painting *Lin-ch'uan kao-chih.*

Kuo Hsiang \-shē-ˈäŋ\. d. 312 A.D. Chinese philosopher. High government official; his *Chuang-tzu chu,* a Neo-Taoist commentary on the Chuang-tzu, is thought to have been started by the philosopher Hsiang Hsiu and is therefore sometimes called the Kuo-Hsiang commentary.

Kuo Mo-jo \-ˈmō-ˈjō\. *Orig.* Kuo K'ai-chen \-ˈkī-ˈjən\. 1892–1978. Chinese writer and politician. Studied medicine in Japan (1913–21), where he helped found (1921) art-for-art's-sake group Ch'ang-tsao; became Marxist (1924); a political commissar in Chiang Kai-shek's Northern Expedition (1926); purged from Kuomintang (1927); participated in Communist uprising in Nanking (1927); fled to Japan (1927–37); returned (1937) to take part in resistance to Japan; given important posts in government; held many important positions in People's Republic of China (from 1949). His works included verse *Nü-shên* (1921); collection of personal sketches *Kanlan* (1926); epistolary novel *Lo-yeh* (1928); short stories; plays as *Ch'ü Yüan* (1944) and *Hu fu* (1946); essays; 9 autobiographical works; historical treatises as *Chung-kuo ku tai she-hui yen-chiu* (1929) and *Liang Chou chin wen tz'u ta hsi t'u lu k'ao shih* (1935); and translations of Goethe, Schiller, Tolstoy, Turgenev, Upton Sinclair, and other Western authors.

Kuo Sung-tao \-ˈsüŋ-ˈdaü\. 1818–1891. Chinese diplomat. Minister to England (1877–78), first Chinese resident minister stationed abroad; recalled for advocating adoption of Western ideas and technology in China.

Kuo Tzu-i \ˈgwōd-ˈzü-ˈē\. 697–781. Chinese general. Suppressed (763) An Lu-shan Rebellion against the T'ang dynasty; helped establish Nestorian Christianity in China.

Kup·ka \ˈküp-kä\, František. *First name also given as* Frank *or* François. 1871–1957. Czech painter, satirist, and illustrator. Pioneer in abstract movement called Orphism; settled in Paris (1895). Works included *Disks of Newton* (1912) and *Fugue in Red and Blue* (1912).

Küp·per \ˈkæp-ər\, Christian Emil Marie. *Known as* Theo van Does·burg \vän-ˈdüs-bærḡ\. 1883–1931. Dutch painter. With Piet Mondrian, Jacobus Oud, and others founded the group de Stijl and art review *De Stijl* (1917); taught at Bauhaus (1921–23); published reviews *Mecano* (1923) and *Art concret* (1930).

Kuprili. See KÖPRÜLÜ.

Kup·rin \küp-ˈryēn, ˈküp-ryin\, Aleksandr Ivanovich. 1870–1938. Russian novelist and short-story writer. At times an army officer, journalist, hunter, actor, circus worker; emigré in Paris (1917–37). One of last exponents of Russian critical realism; best known for novels *Poyedinok* (1905) and *Yama* (1909–15).

Ku·ra·kin \kü-ˈrák-yin\, Boris Ivanovich. Prince. 1676–1727. Russian diplomat. Brother-in-law of Peter the Great; sometimes called "father of Russian diplomacy." Fought in Great Northern War against Sweden (1700–05). Represented Peter at Rome (1707), London, Hanover, and The Hague (1708–16); ambassador at Paris (1724 ff.); instrumental in preventing Great

Britain from siding with Sweden in war against Russia; his autobiography (1709) is an important historical document.

Ku·ra·tsu·ku·ri \kůr-ät-sůk-ůr-ē\ Tori. 7th century. Japanese sculptor. Executed several works in bronze, including 16-foot-high Buddha (*Jōrokubutsu*) at the Gangō-ji (606) and the Shaka Triad at the Golden Pavilion of Hōryū-ji (623, both in Nara).

Kurb·ski \'kürp-skəi\, Andrey Mikhaylovich. Prince. 1528–1583. Russian general. Member of Ivan IV's special advisory council (1547); distinguished himself in campaigns against Kazan (1549–53), Crimean Tatars (1556), Livonia (1557–64); defected (1564) to side of King Sigismund II of Poland, who commissioned him to fight against Ivan. Author of religious works, a history of Ivan's reign, and correspondence with Ivan, criticizing the czar.

Kur·cha·tov \kür-'chá-təf\, Igor Vasilyevich. 1903–1960. Soviet nuclear physicist. On staff (from 1927) of Physico-Technical Institute, Leningrad, and director (from c.1932) of its nuclear physics laboratory; directed development of first Soviet atomic bomb (1949), world's first thermonuclear bomb (1953), atomic electric power stations, cyclotrons, etc.; also directed research on fusion energy.

Kü·ren·ber·ger \'kue-rən-,ber-gər\. *Also called* the Knight of Kürn·berg \'kuern-,berk\. fl. c.1160. Austrian poet. Earliest known (by name) Minnesinger; member of knightly family; author of *Das Falkenlied* and of love songs, etc.; sometimes erroneously credited with authorship of original *Nibelungenlied.*

Ku·ro·da \kůr-ō-dä\ Kiyotaka, *orig.* Ryōsuke. 1840–1900. Japanese politician. In charge of colonizing and developing island of Hokkaido (1870–80); prime minister (1888–89); later held other cabinet positions.

Kuroda Nagamasa, *orig.* Kichibē. 1568–1623. Japanese general. In service of Toyotomi Hideyoshi and a leading general in his Korean campaign (1592–98); after Hideyoshi's death (1598), changed allegiance to Tokugawa Ieyasu and fought for him at Battle of Sekigahara (1600); given fief of Fukuoka as reward.

Ku·ro·pat·kin \kü-(,)rə-'pát-kyin\, Aleksey Nikolayevich. 1848–1921. Russian general. Distinguished himself in Russo-Turkish War (1877–78); lieutenant general and governor of Transcaspian territories (1890–98); minister of war (1898–1904). Given supreme command of Russian forces in Far East and fought in Manchuria (1904) but was opposed to war with Japan; defeated at Mukden (1905) and relieved of command. Wrote *The Russian Army and the Japanese War* (1909).

Kurz \'kůrts\, Hermann. 1813–1873. German novelist and translator. Author of historical novels *Schillers Heimatjahre* (1843) and *Der Sonnenwirt* (1854), satirically humorous tales of Swabian life *Erzählungen* (1858–63), and translations of Ariosto, Cervantes, Shakespeare, etc.

Ku·shān \ků-'shän\ *or* **Ku·ṣā·ṇa** \ků-'shän-ə\. Name of a nomadic clan of the Yüeh-chih Tatars in northern India and Afghanistan forming a dynasty of kings (c.78 A.D.–?220), esp. Kaniṣka (*q.v.*); acknowledged as one of four great powers of its time; instrumental in development of Mahāyāna Buddhism and the Gandhāra and Mathura schools of art. Dynasty disappeared as result of the rise of the Sassanians.

Kus·ser \'kůs-er\ *or* **Cous·ser** *Fr* kü-ser\, Johann Siegmund. 1660–1727. Hungarian composer. Lived in Paris (1674–82); orchestra conductor at Hamburg, where he presented his operas *Erindo* (1694), *Porus* (1694), *Pyramus und Thisbe* (1694), *Scipio Africanus* (1695), and *Jason* (1697); master of the chapel, Christ Church cathedral, Dublin (from 1710), and royal music master for Ireland (from 1717).

Ku·su·mi \kůs-ům-ē\ Morikage. 1610?–1700. Japanese painter. Representative of Kanō school but developed a more fluid and vivid style of painting; excelled in landscapes and paintings of farmers and common people; works included *Enjoying the Evening Cool Under a Gourd Trellis, Landscape Screen Depicting the Uji Bridge,* and *A Flock of Rooks.*

Ku·su·no·ki \kůs-ůn-ō-kē\ Masashige. 1294–1336. Japanese soldier. Supported Emperor Daigo II's attempt to restore Imperial supremacy over the shogunate (1331); brilliant military strategist; captured fortress of Chihiya near Nara and repulsed vastly superior shogunal army (1332); governor of Settsu, Kawachi, and Izumi provinces during brief Imperial restoration (1333–35); named commander in chief of Imperial forces against rebellion of Ashikaga Takauji (1335); defeated Takauji (Jan. 1336) but later lost to him (1336); committed suicide to avoid capture; his loyalty to the emperor made him a legendary figure in Japanese history.

Kutb-ud-Din Aibak. See QUṬB-UD-DĪN AYBAK.

Ku·tu·zov \kü-'tü-zəf\, Mikhail Illarionovich. *Surname also given as* Go·le·ni·shchev-Kutuzov \gəl-(,)yin-'yish-chəf-\. Prince. 1745–1813. Russian field marshal. Served in Poland (1764–69) and against Turks (1770–74, 1787–91); ambassador at Constantinople, governor of Finland, and governor of St. Petersburg (1801). Army commander in wars against Napoléon (1805–12); defeated at Austerlitz (1805); military governor of Kiev (1806–11); commander in chief against Turks (1811–12) and against French (1812); defeated at Borodino but won victory over Davout and Ney at Smolensk (Nov. 1812) during French retreat; pursued French into Poland and Prussia, where he died.

Küt·zing \'kuet-siŋ\, Friedrich Traugott. 1807–1893. German botanist. Taught at Nordhausen secondary school (1835–83). Known for studies of algae published in *Phycologia germanica* (1845), *Species algarum* (1849), *Tabulae phycologiae* (1845–71).

Kuu·si·nen \'kü-sin-en\, Otto Vilhelmovich. 1881–1964. Soviet politician, b. Finland. Joined Finnish Social Democratic party (1905); minister of education (1918); fled to Russia (1918–39), where he helped found (1918) Finnish Communist party and was secretary of the Communist International; head of puppet Finnish Socialist government (1939–40). President of Supreme Soviet of Karelo-Finnish Soviet Socialist Republic (1940–56); secretary and presidium member of Central Committee of Soviet Communist party (1946–53, 1957–64).

Ku·wat·li \kü-wät-'lē\, Shukri al-. 1891–1967. Syrian politician. Opposed French rule as member (from c.1930), leader (1940) of National Bloc; first president of independent Syrian republic (1943–49); signed treaty expelling French troops (1943); ousted by military coup (1949); again president (1955–59); took Syria into union with Egypt as United Arab Republic (1958); exile in Beirut (from 1959).

Ku Yen-wu \'gü-'yən-'wü\. 1613–1682. Chinese scholar. Founded Han school of learning that advocated abandonment of rigid Neo-Confucian thought and a return to original Confucian Classics and commentaries; compiled works on practical knowledge as *T'ien-hsia chün-kuo li-ping shu* and *Jih-chih lu.*

Kuy·per \'kœi-pər\, Abraham. *Called* Abraham the Mighty. 1837–1920. Dutch theologian and politician. Represented Anti-Revolutionary party in lower chamber (1874–77); founded (1880) Free University, Amsterdam, to train Calvinist ministers. Broke with national church and formed Free Reformed church (1886). Again member of lower house (1894); effected Conservative and Clerical alliance between Calvinist and Catholic parties; formed a Christian Conservative ministry (1901) and was minister of interior (until 1905); championed social reforms; sat in lower (1908–12) and upper (1912–20) chambers.

Kuyuk. See GÜYÜK.

Kuz·nets \'kəz-(,)nets\, Simon. 1901–1985. American economist, b. Kharkov, Ukraine. To U.S. (1922). Studied business cycles for National Bureau of Economics. Taught economics at U. of Pa. (1930–54), at Johns Hopkins U. (1954–60), and at Harvard U. (1960–71). Awarded 1971 Nobel prize for economics for originating concept of gross national product as measure of national income and economic growth. Author of *National Income and Its Composition, 1919 to 1938* (1941), etc.

Kva·ran \'kvá-rán\, Einar Hjörleifsson. 1859–1938. Icelandic writer. Newspaper journalist and editor in Canada (1885–95) and Reykjavík (1895–1906); converted to spiritualism and wrote and lectured much on it. Author of novels, short stories, plays, and poetry.

Kvitka, Larisa Petrovna Kosach-. See KOSACH-KVITKA.

Kyd \'kid\, Thomas. 1558–1594. English dramatist. Shared lodgings with Christopher Marlowe. Initiated the Elizabethan revenge play with *The Spanish Tragedie* (written c.1587; published undated, but probably 1592). Also translated Robert Garnier's *Cornélie* as *Cornelia* (1594); may have written an earlier version of *Hamlet.*

Kyn·as·ton \'kin-ə-stən\, Edward, *called* Ned. c.1640–1706. English actor. Probably last and best of boy actors playing female roles; last female role in Beaumont and Fletcher's *Maid's Tragedy* (1661); became (by 1665) a leading actor of male roles at Covent Garden Theatre, London; with Thomas Betterton's Lincoln's Inn Fields (1695–99).

Kyŏmja. See CHŎNG SŎN.

Kyriotes, John. See John GEOMETRES.

L

La Argentina. See Antonia MERCE.

La·ba·die \lȧ-bȧ-dē\, Jean de. 1610–1674. French religious reformer. Originally member of Jesuit order; became attracted to Pietism; converted to Calvinism (1650); zealously preached return to primitive Christianity and gained many followers in the Netherlands; because of his doctrines, excommunicated from Reformed church (1670); took his separatist group of Pietists to Germany. Last Labadist colony, at Wiewert, dissolved in 1732. Author of *La Réforme de l'église par le pastorat* (1667), etc.

La·ban \ˈlä-bän\, Rudolf. *Orig.* Rudolf Laban de Va·ral·jas \-de-ˈvär-äl-yäs\. 1879–1958. Hungarian choreographer, dance theorist, and teacher. Founded (1915) Choreographic Institute at Zürich, later establishing branches in Italy, France, and central Europe; worked in Germany (1919–37); as ballet director of Berlin State Opera (1930–34), noted for choreographing large "movement choirs." Joined (1938) former pupils Kurt Jooss and Sigurd Leeder at their school at Darlington Hall in Devon, England; made studies of industrial efficiency, devised corrective exercises for factory employees, and published *Effort* (1947); with Lisa Ullmann formed (1946) Art of Movement Studio at Manchester, later (1953) moved to Addlestone, Surrey. His theoretical systems of human motion, as choreutics and eukinetics, provided intellectual foundation for development of central European dance, esp. as developed further by his pupils Jooss, Leeder, and Mary Wigman; originated (1928) Labanotation, a system for recording human movement, used esp. for dance. Published *Die Welt des Tänzers* (1920), *Schrifttanz* (1928), *Modern Educational Dance* (1948), *The Mastery of Movement on the State* (1950), etc.

Lab·ar·nas I \ˈlab-ər-ˌnas\. *Also spelled* Lab·er·nash \-ˌnash\. d. c.1650 B.C. Hittite king (c.1680–c.1650 B.C.). Traditionally regarded as founder of Hittite Old Kingdom; his capital at Kussara in central Anatolia; extended his rule south to Mediterranean; conquered Tuwanuwa, Hupisna, Landa, Lusna, and other cities; may have also conquered Arzawa; succeeded by his son Hattusilis I (*q.v*).

Labarnas II. See HATTUSILIS I.

La·bat \lȧ-bȧ\, Jean-Baptiste. 1663–1738. French Dominican missionary. Served in French West Indies (1694–1705); author of *Nouveau voyage aux Îles de l'Amérique* (1722), etc.

La·bé \lȧ-bā\, Louise. *Known as* la Belle Cor·dière \lȧ-bel-kȯr-dyer\, *i.e.* the Beautiful Ropemaker. c.1524–1566. French poet. Her father and husband both ropemakers (hence nickname). Member of Lyons school of Humanist poets; author of many love lyrics, elegies, sonnets, etc.

Lab·eo \ˈlab-ē-ō\, Marcus Antistius. d. 10 or 11 A.D. Roman jurist. Regarded as founder of the Proculian school of law, named from his disciple Sempronius Proculus. His systematic exposition of Roman law was called *Libri posteriores* because it was published posthumously.

Labeo Notker. See NOTKER.

La·be·ri·us \lə-ˈbir-ē-əs\, Decimus. c.115–43 B.C. Roman knight and writer. Author of mimes (farces), verse satires, an epic on the Gallic War, etc.

Labernash I. See LABARNAS.

La·biche \lȧ-bēsh\, Eugène-Marin. 1815–1888. French playwright. Published novel *La Clef des champs* (1838); author of many farcical comedies including *Le Chapeau de paille d'Italie* (1851), *Le Misanthrope et l'Auvergnat* (1852), *Le Voyage de M. Perrichon* (1860), *La Poudre aux yeux* (1861).

Lab·i·e·nus \ˌlab-ē-ˈē-nəs\, Titus. d. 45 B.C. Roman politician. Tribune of the plebs (63 B.C.); legate of Caesar in Gaul (to 52); at outbreak of Civil War, joined Pompey; fled to Africa after battle of Pharsalus (48); killed in action at Munda in Spain. His son ¶Quintus (d. 39 B.C.) commanded a Roman army which invaded Syria and Asia Minor (40–39 B.C.).

La·blache \ˌlȧ-ˈblȧsh\, Luigi. 1794–1858. Italian singer. Most famous bass of his generation. Sang in Italy (1812–24), Vienna (1824–30), London (1830–52), Paris (1830–51); great success as Geronimo in Cimarosa's *Il matrimonio segreto,* Sir George Walton in Bellini's *I puritani,* and title role in Donizetti's *Marino Faliero;* Schubert, among others, wrote songs for him.

La Bo·é·tie \lȧ-bȯ-ā-sē\, Étienne de. 1530–1563. French writer. Judge at Bordeaux; intimate friend of Montaigne; author of sonnets, some Latin verses, translations, and treatises on politics and religion.

La·bo·ri \lȧ-bȯ-rē\, Fernand-Gustave-Gaston. 1860–1917. French lawyer. Defense counsel of Dreyfus (1894–99); secured acquittal of Mme Joseph Caillaux for murder (1914) of Gaston Calmette.

La·bou·chère \ˌlab-ü-ˈsha(ə)r, -ˈshe(ə)r\, Henry Du Pré. *Nicknamed* Lab·by \ˈlab-ē\. 1831–1912. English journalist and politician. In diplomatic service (1854–64); gained reputation as journalist on *The Daily News* during Franco–Prussian War, and with Edmund Yates on *The World;* founded (1877) and edited *Truth,* remarkable for exposures of sham and corruption; M.P. (1865–66, 1867–68, 1880–1906); advocate of Irish home rule; instrumental in exposing Richard Pigott; advocated abolition of House of Lords; opposed expansionist policies of Joseph Chamberlain.

La·bou·laye \lȧ-bü-lā\, Édouard-René Le·feb·vre de \lə-fevrᵊ-də\. 1811–1883. French journalist and politician. Founder of *Revue Historique de Droit* (1855); elected member of Chamber of Deputies (1871) and senator for life (1880). Administrator of Collège de France (from 1873). Author of *Questions constitutionnelles* (1872), *La Liberté religieuse* (1875), etc.

La Bour·don·nais \lȧ-bür-dȯ-ne\, Bertrand-François Ma·hé de \mȧ-ā-də-\. Comte. 1699–1753. French naval officer. Appointed governor of Mascarene Islands (1735); captured Madras from the English (1746); engaged in long dispute with Dupleix, French governor in India; imprisoned (1748–50) in the Bastille before being vindicated. His grandson ¶Louis-Charles Mahé de La Bourdonnais (1797–1840) was considered world's leading chess player after his defeat (1834) of Alexander Macdonnell.

La·bri·o·la \ˌlä-brē-ˈō-lä\, Antonio. 1843–1904. Italian philosopher. Professor, Rome (1874 ff.); adopted a radical Socialist philosophy (by 1885); first in Italy to lecture on Marxism (1889); undertook systematic study of Marxism. Works included *In memoria del Manifesto dei Communisti* (1895), *La concezione materialistica della storia* (1896), *Discorrendo di socialismo et di filosofia* (1897).

La·brouste \lȧ-brüst\, Henri, *in full* Pierre-François-Henri. 1801–1875. French architect. Known for use of iron frame construction in his designs of Bibliothèque Sainte-Geneviève (1843–50) and Bibliothèque Nationale (1862–68), both in Paris.

La·bru·nie \lȧ-brü̅e-nē\, Gérard. *Pseudonym* Gérard de Ner·val \ner-vȧl\. 1808–1855. French writer. One of first French Symbolists and Surrealists; traveled widely in Europe and the Levant; in later years insane; committed suicide. Author of travelogue *Voyage en Orient* (1851), short-story collections *La Main de gloire* (1832) and *Les Filles du feu* (1854; contains "Sylvie"), verse *Les Chimères* (1854), novel *Aurélia* (1855), and plays.

La Bru·yère \lȧ-brü̅e-yer\, Jean de. 1645–1696. French moralist. Tutor in history to Louis de Bourbon, grandson of the Great Condé (1684). Author of *Les Caractères de Théophraste traduits du grec, avec les caractères et les moeurs de ce siècle* (1688), which in later editions was largely expanded by additional "caractères" and commentaries.

La·caille \lȧ-kȧy, -käy\, Nicolas-Louis de. 1713–1762. French astronomer. Professor, Collège Mazarin (1739); astronomer, Collège de Lisieux (from 1746); led astronomical expedition to Cape of Good Hope (1750–54); made observations of approximately 10,000 southern stars; determined lunar and solar parallax (with Mars as intermediary); first to measure a South African arc of the meridian. Compiled *Coelum Australe Stelliferum* (1763).

La Cal·pre·nède \lȧ-kȧl-prə-ned\, Gautier de Costes de \kȯst-də-\. c.1610–1663. French novelist and playwright. Author of the tragedies *Le Comte d'Essex* (1638), *Édouard Roi d'Angleterre* (1639), etc., and the novels *Cassandre* (1642–45), *Cléopâtre* (1647–57), *Faramond* (1661–70), etc.

La·cé·pède \lȧ-sā-ped\, Bernard-Germain-Étienne De·la·ville de \də-lȧ-vēl-də-\. Comte. 1756–1825. French naturalist and politician. Member (1799), president (1801), of Senate; minister of state (1809); entered Chamber of Peers (1819). Author of *Essai sur l'électricité* (1781), *Physique générale et particulière*

(1782–84); contributed *Histoire naturelle des quadrupèdes ovipares et des serpents* (1789), *Histoire naturelle des poissons* (1798–1803), and *Histoire naturelle des cétacés* (1804) to Buffon's *Histoire naturelle.*

La·chaise \lá-shez\, Gaston. 1882–1935. American sculptor, b. Paris, France. To U.S. (1906, naturalized 1916). Known for sculptures of massively proportioned female nudes, including *Standing Woman* (1912–27), *Torso* (1928), *Floating Figure* (1935); executed portrait busts of John Marin, Marianne Moore, E.E. Cummings, etc.

La Cha·lo·tais \lá-shá-lò-te\, Louis-René de Ca·ra·deuc de \ká-rá-dœk-də\. 1701–1785. French magistrate. Advocate general (1730), attorney general (1752), to parlement of Brittany; published *Comptes rendus des Constitutions des jésuites* (1761–62), an attack on the Jesuits which was instrumental in causing order to be suppressed in France; wrote *L'Éducation nationale* (1763); imprisoned (1765–67) for leading Breton parlement's legal challenge (1763–65) to authority of Louis XV; his position restored on accession of Louis XVI (1774).

La Chaus·sée \lá-shō-sā\, Pierre-Claude Ni·velle de \nē-vel-də-\. 1692–1754. French playwright. Creator of the sentimental comedy (*comédie larmoyante*), as in *La Fausse Antipathie* (1733), *Le Préjugé à la mode* (1735), *Mélanide* (1741), *L'Homme de fortune* (1751), etc.

La·ches \'lä-,kēz\. c.475–418 B.C. Athenian general. Elected general (427); replaced (426) after unsuccessful mission to Sicily; prosecuted by Cleon, trial satirized by Aristophanes in *The Wasps.* In Peloponnesian War, commanded Athenian army at Mantinea (418), where he was killed in action.

Lachman Dās. See BANDĀ SINGH BAHĀDUR.

Lach·mann \'läk-,män\, Karl Konrad Friedrich Wilhelm. 1793–1851. German philologist. Professor at Friedrich Wilhelm U., Berlin (1825–51). A founder of modern textual criticism; delineated phonetic and metrical principles of Middle High German (1816–17). Edited Propertius (1816), Catullus (1829), Tibullus (1829), Lucretius (1850), and other classical authors; in *Betrachtungen über Homers Ilias* (1837–41), argued that the Iliad consists of 16 interpolated but independent poems.

Lach·ner \'läk-nər\. Family of German musicians, of Rain, Upper Bavaria: Franz Paul (1803–1890), intimate friend of Schubert; court Kapellmeister (1836–65) and general music director (1852) in Munich; composed operas including *Catarina Cornaro* (1841) and *Benvenuto Cellini* (1849), oratorios, 8 symphonies, orchestral suites in the tradition of Bach, church music, choruses, chamber music, and songs. His brother ¶Ignaz (1807–1895) composed operas, many songs, chamber music, masses, symphonies, etc. Another brother ¶Vincenz (1811–1893) composed overtures, chamber music, songs, etc.

Lackland, John. See JOHN, king of England.

La·clède \lá-kled, *Angl* lə-'klēd, -'kled\, Pierre. *Orig.* Pierre Laclède Li·guest \lē-ge\. 1724?–1778. French fur trader and pioneer. To America (1755); founder of St. Louis, Mo., establishing trading post on site of present city (1764). See René CHOUTEAU.

La·clos \lá-klō\, Pierre-Ambroise-François Cho·der·los de \shò-der-lō-də-\. 1741–1803. French soldier and writer. Commissioned in army (1761); lost commission upon publication of *Lettre à MM. de l'Académie Française sur l'éloge de M. le Maréchal de Vauban* (1786), criticizing army; returned to army (1792–1803); general (1800). Author of novels *Les Liaisons dangereuses* (1782) and *De l'éducation des femmes* (1785).

La·combe \lá-kōⁿb\, Louis Trouil·lon \trü-yōⁿ\. 1818–1884. French pianist and composer. Works included opera *Winkelried* (1892), the comic operas *La Madone* (1861) and *Le Tonnelier du Nuremberg* (1897), dramatic symphonies as *Sapho* (1878), chamber music, piano pieces, songs, a cappella choruses, etc.

La Con·da·mine \lá-kōⁿ-dá-mēn\, Charles-Marie de. 1701–1774. French naturalist and mathematician. On expedition to Peru to measure a meridional arc at the equator (1735–43); made first scientific exploration of the Amazon (1743); worked on establishment of a universal unit of length.

La·cor·daire \lá-kòr-der\, Jean-Baptiste-Henri. 1802–1861. French prelate. Ordained priest (1827); joined (1830) Félicité Lamennais's liberal Catholic group and helped found its organ *L'Avenir* which advocated separation of church and state; submitted after suppression of group by Pope Gregory XVI (1832); became famous for his sermons (known as Lenten Conferences) at Notre Dame (1836). Became convinced that restoration of religious orders was best way to strengthen French church; joined Dominicans (1838) and began restoring the order in France (1843); headed French Dominicans (1850–54); continued preaching liberty in church and state.

La·cre·telle \lá-krə-tel\, Pierre-Louis de. 1751–1824. French journalist and magistrate. Active in French Revolution; member of Commune of Paris and elected to Estates-General and Legislative Assembly; defended publicly constitution of 1791. Under the Empire, took little part in politics; under Restoration, became coeditor of *Minerve Française.* His brother ¶Jean-Charles-Dominique, *called* le Jeune \lə-zhœn\ (1766–1855) was a journalist and historian; on editorial staff of *Journal des Débats* (1790); imprisoned (1797–99) for monarchist sympathies; as royal censor, successfully opposed press censorship, causing loss of his office (1827). Pioneer in historical study of French Revolution. Published *Précis historique de la Révolution française* (1801–06), *Histoire de France pendant le XVIIIe siècle* (1808), *Histoire de France dupuis la restauration* (1829–35), etc.

La·croix \lák-rwä\, François-Antoine-Alfred. 1863–1948. French mineralogist. Professor, Muséum d'Histoire Naturelle, Paris (1893–1936); investigated volcanos of Mount Pelée after eruption of 1902 and Vesuvius after eruption of 1906. Author of *Minéralogie de la France et de ses colonies* (1893–1913), *La Montagne Pelée et ses eruptions* (1904), *Minéralogie de Madagascar* (1922–23), etc.

Lac·tan·ti·us \lak-'tan-sh(ē-)əs\, Lucius Caecilius Firmianus. c.240–320. Christian writer, b. North Africa. Teacher of rhetoric at Nicodemia; moved to the West (c.305); tutor at Trier to Constantine's son Crispus (from c.317). Author of *Divinae institutiones,* the first systematic Latin account of the Christian attitude toward life; called the "Christian Cicero" because of elegance of his style.

La·cy \'lā-sē\, Henry de. 3d Earl of Lin·coln \'liŋ-kən\. 1249?–1311. English soldier. Counselor of Edward I and Edward II. Accompanied Edward I to Gascony (1286–89); commanded army in France (1296–98); guardian of kingdom in Edward II's absence (1310).

Lacy, Hugh de. 5th Baron Lacy *and* 1st Lord of Meath \'mēth, 'mē<u>th</u>\. d. 1186. English soldier. Accompanied Henry II to Ireland (1171); governor of Ireland (1177–81, 1185–86); received submission of Roderic O'Connor, king of Connaught; secured good order; accused of ambition to be king of Ireland; murdered by a native.

Lacy, Peter. Count Lacy. 1678–1751. Irish soldier. Served with Irish Jacobite troops in France and Italy and on Rhine (1692–97); trained troops of Peter the Great (from 1697) and led them against Danes, Swedes, Turks (1705–21); commanded brigade at Poltava (1709); field marshal (1736). His son ¶Francis Maurice, *known also as* Franz Moritz (1725–1801), soldier in Austrian service in War of Austrian Succession and Seven Years' War; field marshal (1765); head of military advisory board (1766–73) with full confidence of Maria Theresa and Joseph II; with Laudon, joint Austrian commander in War of Bavarian Succession; suffered defeats in Turkish War (1788–90).

La·cy·des \lə-'sī-,dēz\ of Cy·re·ne \sī-'rē-(,)nē\. d. 206 or 205 B.C. Greek philosopher. Succeeded Arcesilaus as head of Greek academy (241 or 240–224 or 223); emphasized teaching of his predecessor.

Ladd \'lad\, George Trumbull. 1842–1921. American psychologist and philosopher, b. Painesville, Ohio. Influential in establishing experimental psychology in U.S.; professor, Yale (1881–1905). Author of *Elements of Physiological Psychology* (1887), *Psychology, Descriptive and Explanatory* (1894), *Philosophy of Religion* (1905), *The Secret of Personality* (1918), etc.

Ladd, William. 1778–1841. American pacifist, b. Exeter, N.H. Sea captain (to 1812), farmer (1812–19); devoted himself to cause of world peace (from 1819); founder (1828), American Peace Society. Author of *An Essay on a Congress of Nations* (1840), proposing a congress of nations and an international court, a plan later realized in the League of Nations and the World Court.

Ladd-Frank·lin \'lad-'fraŋ-klən\, Christine. 1847–1930. American psychologist and logician, b. Windsor, Conn. m. Fabian Franklin (1882). In logic, published original method for reducing all syllogisms to a single formula (1883); in psychology, advanced original theory accounting for development of man's color sense.

Ladislas. See also LÁSZLÓ (kings of Hungary), ULÁSZLÓ (kings of Hungary), and WŁADYSŁAW (kings of Poland).

Lad·is·las \'lä-dē-släs\. 1377–1414. King of Naples (1386–1414) and of Hungary (1390–1414). Son of Charles III of Durazzo, of the house of Anjou; at war with rival Louis II of Anjou (1391–99); led expedition into Dalmatia and crowned himself king (1404); planned conquests in central Italy (1400–14); twice seized Rome (1408–09, 1413); defeated at Roccasecca (1411).

Ladislav. King of Bohemia. See LÁSZLÓ V of Hungary.

Lae·li·us \'lē-lē-əs\, Gaius. d. after 160 B.C. Roman general and politician. Served with Scipio Africanus in Spain (210–206) and in Africa (204–202); commanded the cavalry in victory over Hannibal at Zama (202). Plebeian aedile (197); praetor of Sicily (196); consul (190); ambassador to Transalpine Gaul (170); met Polybius and supplied him with much information about Scipio Africanus (160). His son ¶Gaius, *surnamed* Sa·pi·ens \'sā-pē-ənz, 'sap-ē-\; friend of Panaetius and Scipio Aemilianus; named as one of the speakers in Cicero's *De senectute, De amicitia,* and *De republica;* tribune (151 B.C.); served against the Carthaginians in Africa (147) and Spain (145); consul (140); helped introduce Greek culture in Rome.

Laemm·le \ˈlem-lē\, Carl. 1867–1939. American motion-picture producer, b. Laupheim, Germany. To U.S. (1884); began producing films in New York (c.1908); an organizer (1912) and sole head (1920–36) of Universal Pictures Corp., Hollywood, Calif. Produced first full-length photoplay *Traffic in Souls* (1912), and first million-dollar picture *Foolish Wives* (1922).

Laën·nec \lā-nek\, René-Théophile-Hyacinthe. 1781–1826. French physician. Considered father of thoracic medicine; introduced practice of auscultation with the stethoscope, which he invented (c.1819). Published *De l'auscultation médiate* (1819); professor at Collège de France (1822); physician at Hôpital de la Charité, Paris (1823).

Laer \ˈlär\, Pieter van. *Called* Il Bam·boc·cio \ēl-bäm-ˈbōt-chō\. 1592 or 1595–1642. Dutch painter. To Rome (c.1625); originator of Bambocciati, a type of relatively small, often anecdotal, realistic painting of scenes from common or rustic life, as *The Quack* and *The Game of Ninepins.*

Laertius, Diogenes. See DIOGENES LAERTIUS.

La Farge \lə-ˈfärzh, -ˈfärj\, John. 1835–1910. American artist, b. New York City. Painted chiefly landscapes and flowers (1860–76). Commissioned for mural decoration of Trinity Church, Boston (1876–77), his success leading to other work of similar nature, including panels in St. Thomas's Church, New York City, *The Ascension* in the Church of the Ascension, New York City (1887), and lunettes in the Minnesota State Capitol at St. Paul. Developed opalescent glass; wrote *The American Art of Glass* (1893). His canvases included *Christ and Nicodemus, The Three Kings, The Muse of Painting.* Executed stained glass for Second Presbyterian Church, Chicago; Memorial Hall, Harvard U.; Columbia U. Chapel, New York City. Also wrote *Considerations on Painting* (1895), *An Artist's Letters from Japan* (1897), *The Higher Life in Art* (1908).

La Farge, Oliver Hazard Perry. 1901–1963. American author and anthropologist, b. New York City. Grandson of John La Farge; president, American Association of Indian Affairs (1933–42, 1948–63); wrote *Tribes and Temples* (with Frans Blom, 1927), *Laughing Boy* (1929, Pulitzer prize), *Sparks Fly Upward* (1931), *Long Pennant* (1933), *All the Young Men* (1935), *The Enemy Gods* (1937), *The Copper Pot* (1942), *The Door in the Wall* (1965), etc.

La·fargue \lá-fárg\, Paul. 1842–1911. French Socialist politician and writer. Son-in-law of Karl Marx; associated with Jules Guesde in organizing Marxian Socialist movement in France. Wrote *Le Communisme et l'évolution économique* (1892), etc.

La Fa·ri·na \lä-fä-ˈrē-nä\, Giuseppe. 1815–1863. Italian revolutionary and historian. Exiled from Sicily (1837–38) for participation in revolution; took part in Tuscan movement (1848); deputy and minister of public instruction and public works in Sicily (1848–49); again fled Sicily after Revolution of 1848. Associated with Cavour (from 1855) in National Italian Society, its president (1859); wrote (1858) *Credo politico* calling for Italian independence and unity; aided in deposition of Bourbons in Sicily (1860); deputy from Messina in Italian parliament (1861–63). Author of *Storia della rivoluzione italiana 1821–48* (1849), *Storia d'Italia, 1815–50* (1851–52), etc.

La·fa·yette *or* **La Fa·yette** \lá-fá-yet; *Angl* ˌläf-ē-ˈet, ˌlaf-\, Marie-Joseph-Paul-Yves-Roch-Gilbert du Mo·tier de \də-mō-tyā-də-\. 1757–1834. French statesman and officer. Entered French military service (1771); withdrew (1776) to enter American service in Revolutionary War (1777); commissioned major general in Continental army (1777); became intimate associate of George Washington. In France, advancing American cause (1778–80); served in Virginia (1780–81); instrumental in defeat of Cornwallis (July–Oct. 1781). Returned to France (1781); member of French National Assembly (1789); aided in organizing National Guard and elected (July 1789) its commander; sought transfer of power from the aristocracy to the bourgeoisie but supported a constitutional monarchy. In command of force that fired on the mob in the Champ de Mars (July 1791); resigned command of Guard (Oct. 1791). Appointed (Dec. 1791) commander of army at Metz in war with Austria. Opposed further advance of Jacobin party; declared a traitor by National Assembly; fled to Flanders and was imprisoned by Austrians (1792–97). Returned to France (1799); took no part in politics, being opposed to Napoleonic policies. Member, Chamber of Deputies (1815, 1818–24); leader of opposition (1825–30). Commander of the National Guard during revolution of 1830.

La Fa·yette \lá-fá-yet, *Angl* ˌläf-ē-ˈet, ˌlaf-\, Marie-Madeleine de, *nee* Pioche de La Vergne \pyȯsh-də-lá-vernʸ\. Comtesse. 1634–1693. French novelist. m. François Motier, comte de La Fayette (1655; d. 1683). Lived (1665–80) with La Rochefoucauld. Author of *La Princesse de Montpensier* (1662), *Zayde* (1670), *La Princesse de Clèves* (1678), and *La Comtesse de Tende* (1724).

La Fayette, Gilbert Mo·tier de \mȯt-yā-də\. c.1380–1462. French soldier. Served under Marshal Bouciquaut and later under John I, duc de Bourbon; created marshal of France (1420). Served with Joan of Arc at Orléans and Patay (1429). Friend and close adviser to King Charles VII; worked to reform army (1445–48); campaigned against English in Normandy (1449).

Laf·fite *or* **La·fitte** \lá-fēt, *Angl* lə-ˈfēt\, Jean. c.1780–c.1826. French pirate. In New Orleans, La. (c.1809); head of band of privateers and smugglers (1810); when British sought his aid in attack on New Orleans (1814) he revealed their plans to American authorities; in charge of American artillery in Battle of New Orleans (Dec. 1814–Jan. 1815), with many of his band serving under him. Returned to piracy after War of 1812, with headquarters at Galveston, Texas; captured and scuttled American merchant ship (1820); his headquarters raided and destroyed by American warship; continued piracy on Spanish main; disappeared about 1825.

Laf·fitte \lá-fēt\, Jacques. 1767–1844. French financier and politician. Regent (1809) and governor (1814–19) of the Bank of France; member of Chamber of Deputies (from 1816). Partisan of Louis-Philippe; premier and finance minister (1830–31); failed to reconcile parties with his policies.

Laffitte, Pierre. 1823–1903. French philosopher. Disciple of Auguste Comte, whom he succeeded (1857) as head of Comité Positiviste; professor at Collège de France (1892). Author of *Leçons de cosmographie* (1853), *Cours philosophique sur l'histoire générale de l'humanité* (1859), *Les Grands Types de l'humanité* (1874), *De la morale positive* (1880), etc.

La·fi·tau \lá-fē-tō\, Joseph-François. 1670–1740. French missionary. Entered Jesuit order; missionary among the Iroquois in Canada (1712–17). Wrote *Moeurs des sauvages américains comparés aux moeurs des premiers temps* (1724).

La Flesche \lə-ˈflesh\, Francis. 1857–1932. American ethnologist, b. near Bellevue, Neb. Brother of Susette La Flesche; ethnologist with Bureau of American Ethnology (1910–29); champion of rights of American Indians. Author of *The Middle Five* (1900, memoir of student life in a mission school), *The Omaha Tribe* (with Alice C. Fletcher, 1911), *A Dictionary of the Osage Language* (1932), *War Ceremony and Peace Ceremony of the Osage Indian* (1938).

La Flesche, Susette. *Indian name* Inshta Theumba, *i.e.* Bright Eyes. 1854–1903. American reformer, b. near Bellevue, Neb. Daughter of chief of Omaha Indians; sister of Francis La Flesche; made successful speaking tour of East (1879) on behalf of Ponca and Omaha tribes and against forced removal; helped obtain passage of Dawes Severalty Act (1887). Author of *Ploughed Under* (1881).

La Fol·lette \lə-ˈfäl-ət\, Robert Marion. 1855–1925. American politician, b. Primrose, Wis. Practiced law (from 1880), Madison, Wis. Member, U.S. House of Representatives (1885–91). Interested himself in reform of Wisconsin state politics; governor of Wisconsin (1900–06); known as leader among progressive Republicans; U.S. senator (from 1906); leader of progressives and radicals. Opposed U.S. entrance into World War I; critical of Wilson's policies; opposed League of Nations and admission of U.S. to World Court; sponsored resolution authorizing senatorial investigation into Teapot Dome. Candidate of League for Progressive Political Action, for U.S. presidency (1924); defeated. Founded (1909) *La Follette's Weekly Magazine* (later called *The Progressive);* an organizer of National Progressive Republican League (1911). His son ¶Robert Marion, Jr. (1895–1953), b. Madison, Wis.; U.S. senator from Wisconsin (1925–47).

La·fon·taine *or* **La Fon·taine** \lá-fōⁿ-ten\, Mlle. *Orig. name unknown.* 1655–1738. French dancer. First woman professional ballet dancer; made debut (1681) at Paris Opéra as première danseuse in Lully's *Le Triomphe de l'amour;* created many roles, including Lully's *Persée* (1682), *Amadis de Gaule* (1684), *Le Temple de la paix* (1685), and *Armide* (1686), and Desmaret's *Didon* (1693); admired for her grace and charm; later retired, apparently to a convent.

Lafontaine, Henri-Marie. 1854–1943. Belgian lawyer and politician. Elected (1895) to Senate and its vice chairman (1919–32). Authority on international law; helped bring about the Hague peace conferences of 1899 and 1907; president of International Peace Bureau (1907–43). Author of *Bibliographie de la paix et de l'arbitrage international* (1904), *The Great Solution* (1916), legal handbooks, etc. Awarded Nobel peace prize (1913).

La Fontaine, Jean de. 1621–1695. French poet. Inspector of forests and waterways (1651–71); member of Mme de La Sablière's Parisian household and salon (from 1673); known for his wit, charm, facile morals, and absent-mindedness. Author of *Fables* (1668–94), about 240 poems based largely on traditional fables; also wrote *Contes et nouvelles en vers* (1664–74), prose narrative *Les Amours de Psiché et de Cupidon* (1669), and with Champmeslé opera librettos and plays.

Lafontaine, Sir Louis Hippolyte. 1807–1864. Canadian politician, b. Boucherville (now in Que.). Elected to provincial assembly for Terrebonne (1830); leader of French Canadians; refused solicitor generalship but on death of Sydenham formed a first administration with Robert Baldwin (1842–43), and a second, acting as premier and attorney general for Lower Canada (1848–51); passed amnesty bill, which provoked riots in Montreal; chief justice of Lower Canada (1853–64); settled question of land tenure in Canada.

La Forge \lȧ-fȯrzh\, Louis de. d. before 1666. French philosopher. Annotated Descartes's *Traité de l'homme* and wrote *Traité de l'esprit de l'homme* (1666) as a continuation of that work.

La·forgue \lȧ-fȯrg\, Jules. 1860–1887. French poet. Reader to Empress Augusta in Berlin (1881–86). A Symbolist and master of lyrical irony; invented vers libre almost simultaneously with his friend Gustave Kahn. Works included verse *Les Complaintes* (1885), *L'Imitation de Notre-Dame la Lune* (1886), *Le Concile féerique* (1886), and *Les Derniers Vers* (1890); short-story collection *Moralités légendaries* (1887); art criticism *Mélanges posthumes* (1903).

La·fosse \lȧ-fōs\, Charles de. 1636–1716. French painter. Studied under Charles Le Brun. Known for decorative historical and allegorical murals painted in a light, brightly colored Baroque style; decorated Montagu House in London (1689–91) and the cupola of the church of Les Invalides in Paris (1705); also executed *Sacrifice of Iphigeneia, Sunrise,* and *The Finding of Moses.*

La Fres·naye \lȧ-fre-ne, -nā\, Roger de. 1885–1925. French painter. Developed (1910–13) interest in Cubism and became associated with Cubist group Section d'Or in Paris; in last years painted realistic works as *Portrait de Guynemer* (1921–23). His canvases included *Portrait de l'artiste* (1907), *Nature morte au coquetier* (1911), *La Partie de cartes* (1912), *Le 14-juillet* (1914).

La·ger·kvist \ˈläg-ər-kvist\, Pär Fabian. 1891–1974. Swedish novelist, playwright, and poet. Author of novels *Gäst hos verkligheten* (1925), *Dvärgen* (1944), *Barabbas* (1950), *Sibyllan* (1956), *Ahasverus död* (1960), *Pilgrim på havet* (1962); tales *Det eviga leendet* (1920) and long story *Bödeln* (1933; dramatized 1934); plays *Den osynlige* (1923), *Mannen utan själ* (1936), *Seger i mörker* (1939), *De vises sten* (1947), *Låt människan leva* (1949); verse *Ångest* (1916), *Hjärtats sånger* (1926), *Genius* (1937), *Sång och strid* (1940), *Hemmet och stjärnan* (1942); and philosophical prose works *Det besegrade livet* (1927), *Den knutna näven* (1934), *Den befriade människan* (1939). Awarded Nobel prize for literature (1951).

La·ger·löf \ˈläg-ər-ˌlœv\, Selma Ottiliana Lovisa. 1858–1940. Swedish novelist. Taught at Landskrona (1885–95); awarded Nobel prize for literature (1909); first woman member of Swedish Academy (1914). Author of novels *Gösta Berlings saga* (1891), *Antikrists mirakler* (1897), *Jerusalem* (1901–02), *Herr Arnes pennigar* (1904), *Liljecronas hem* (1911), and a trilogy comprised of *Löwensköldska ringen* (1925), *Charlotte Löwensköld* (1925), *Anna Svärd* (1928); collections of stories *Osynliga Länkar* (1894), *En herrgårdssägen* (1899), *Nils Holgerssons underbara resa genom Sverige* (1906–07), *Troll och människor* (1915–21); and autobiographical works *Mårbacka* (1922), *Ett Barns memoarer* (1930), *Dagbok för Selma Lagerlöf* (1932).

La Grange \lȧ-gräⁿzh\, Charles Var·let de \vȧr-le-də-\. 1639?–1692. French actor. Comedian in Molière's company; collaborated with Vinot in preparing first important edition of Molière's works (1682).

La·grange \lȧ-gräⁿzh\, Joseph-Louis. Comte. 1736–1813. French mathematician, b. Italy. Professor at Royal Artillery School, Turin (1755); communicated to Euler method of solving the isoperimetrical problem from which grew the calculus of variations (1755); a founder (1757) of society which became Turin Academy of Sciences; awarded prize by French Academy of Sciences for essay on libration of the moon (1764) and a theory of the satellites of Jupiter (1766). Succeeded Euler as director of the mathematics section of Berlin Academy of Sciences (1766–87); published works on celestial mechanics, differential and integral calculus, the numerical and algebraic solution of equations, and the theory of numbers. To Paris (1787) at invitation of Louis XVI; headed commission for reform of weights and measures (1793); professor, École Normale (1795) and École Polytechnique (1795–99); under Napoléon I, made senator and count. Publications included *Mécanique analytique* (1787), *Théorie des fonctions analytiques* (1797), and *Leçons sur le calcul des fonctions* (1806).

Lagrange, Marie-Joseph. 1855–1938. French biblical scholar. Joined Dominicans (1879); ordained priest (1883). In Jerusalem (1890–1910), where he founded École Pratique d'Études Bibliques (1890) and journal *Revue Biblique* (1892); began (1903) *Études bibliques,* a series of commentaries on the Bible to which he contributed several volumes; after World War I returned to École Pratique to teach. His works included *Le Judaïsme avant Jésus-Christ* (1931), *Histoire ancienne du canon du Nouveau Testament* (1933), and *Critique textuelle—La Critique rationelle* (1935).

La Guar·dia \lə-ˈg(w)ärd-ē-ə\, Fiorello Henry. *Called* the Little Flower. 1882–1947. American politician, b. New York City. Practiced law in New York (from 1910); member, U.S. House of Representatives (1917–21, 1923–33). Mayor of New York (1934–45); fought corruption, revised city charter, fostered civic improvements as slum clearance and low-cost housing. Chief, U.S. Office of Civilian Defense (1941–42); director general, U.N. Relief and Rehabilitation Administration (1946).

La Halle, Adam de. See ADAM DE LA HALLE.

La Harpe \lȧ-ȧrp\, Frédéric-César de. 1754–1838. Swiss politician. To St. Petersburg as tutor to future czar Alexander (1794); to France (1796); played important part in establishing the Helvetic Republic (1798), of which he became a director; secured deposition of Peter Ochs (June 1799) but was himself deposed (Jan. 1800). Fugitive in France (1800–14). Member of the Grand Council of the Canton of Vaud (1816–28).

La Harpe *or* **La·harpe** \lȧ-ȧrp\, Jean-François de. *Surname orig.* De·lharpe \də-lȧrp\ *or* De·la·harpe \də-lȧ-ȧrp\. 1739–1803. French playwright and literary critic. Wrote criticism for and was editor of *Mercure de France;* admitted (1786) to Académie Française and lectured at its Lycée; his lectures published as *Cours de littérature* (1799–1805). Author of unsuccessful tragedies as *Warwick* (1763), *Les Barmécides* (1778), and *Coriolan* (1784), and literary criticism as *Commentaire sur Racine* (1807).

La·haye \lȧ-e, -ā\, Louis-Marie de. Viscount de Cor·me·nin \kȯr-mā-naⁿ\. 1788–1868. French lawyer and political writer. Member of Chamber of Deputies (1828–46, 1848); opposed to Louis-Philippe; appointed councilor of state (after 1848). Author of *Droit administratif* (1821), *Les Entretiens de village* (1846), etc.

La Hire *or* **La Hyre** \lȧ-ēr\, Laurent de. 1606–1656. French painter. Commissioned by Richelieu to execute mythological paintings which decorated Palais-Royal (c.1640); a founder of French Royal Academy of Painting and Sculpture (1648). Painted *Pope Nicolas V at the Tomb of St. Francis* (1630), *St. Peter Healing the Sick* (1635), *The Conversion of St. Paul* (1637), etc. His son ¶Philippe (1640–1718), astronomer and mathematician, wrote on experimental astronomy, physics, natural history, and geometry.

La Hon·tan *or* **La·hon·tan** \lȧ-ōⁿ-täⁿ\, Louis-Armand de Lom d'Arce de \də-lōⁿ-dȧrs-də-\. Baron. 1666–1715. French officer and traveler. Served in Canada (1683–93); explored along the Wisconsin and Mississippi rivers (1688–89); deserted army (1693); traveled widely through Europe. Author of *Nouveaux voyages de M. le Baron de Lahontan dans l'Amérique septentrionale* (1703).

Lahor, Jean. See Henri CAZALIS.

Lahr \ˈlär\, Bert. *Orig.* Irving Lahr·heim \ˈlär-ˌhīm\. 1895–1967. American comedian, b. New York City. On vaudeville and burlesque stage (from 1910); scored success in Broadway musical *Hold Everything* (1928); continued success in musicals, dramas as *Burlesque* (1946) and as Estragon in *Waiting for Godot* (1956), radio, and television; appeared in many films, esp. as the Cowardly Lion in *The Wizard of Oz* (1939).

La Huerta, Adolfo de. See HUERTA.

Laid·law \ˈlād-ˌlȯ\, Sir Patrick Playfair. 1881–1940. English pathologist. On staff of Guy's Hospital, London (from 1913). Coauthor of important paper on distemper (1926); isolated (1933) influenza virus (type A).

Lai·do·ner \ˈlī-dȯ-ner\, Johan. 1884–?1952. Estonian soldier. Served in Russian army (1914–17); commanded Estonian army in war for independence (1918). Presiding officer, League of Nations commission investigating Mosul frontier dispute between Great Britain and Turkey (1925). Suppressed attempted coup by right-wing "Vap" movement (1934); supported regime of Konstantin Pats; deported to Soviet Union (1940) and believed to have died there.

Laing \ˈlaŋ, ˈlāŋ\, Alexander Gordon. 1793–1826. Scottish explorer. Sent by governor of Sierra Leone to Mandingo country to open up commerce and prepare for abolition of slave trade (1822); frequently defeated Ashantis (1823–24); sent to explore Niger Basin via Tripoli and Timbuktu (1825); first European to reach Timbuktu (Aug. 18, 1826); murdered there.

Laing, Malcolm. 1762–1818. Scottish historian. British M.P. (1807–12). Wrote in liberal tone last volume of Robert Henry's *History of England* (1793); published his own *History of Scotland* (1802).

Laird \ˈla(ə)rd, ˈle(ə)rd\, Macgregor. 1808–1861. Scottish merchant and explorer. Organized company for trade along lower Niger; on first expedition (1832–34), led by Richard Lander (*q.v.*), was first white man to ascend Benue River from confluence with Niger; promoted navigation company for running steamships between England and New York (1837), of which the *Sirius* was first to cross Atlantic from Europe entirely under steam; funded (1854) second expedition to the Niger, led by William Baikie (*q.v.*).

Laj·oie \ˈlash-ə-ˌwā\, Napoleon, *known as* Larry. 1875–1959. American baseball player, b. Woonsocket, R.I. Second baseman in National League, with Philadelphia (1896–1900), and in American League, with Philadelphia (1901, 1915–16) and Cleveland (1902–14). Had 3,242 hits and career batting average of .338. Elected to Baseball Hall of Fame (1937).

Lajos. See LOUIS, kings of Hungary.

Laj·pat Rai \ˈläj-pət-ˈrī\, Lala. 1865–1928. Indian writer and politician. Advocate of militant anti-British nationalism and a leader of the Hindu supremacy movement; presided over special session of Congress party that launched non-cooperation movement (1920); elected to legislative assembly (1923); introduced resolution for boycott of British Simon Commission on constitutional reform (1928). Author of *The United States of America: A Hindu's Impression* (1916), *Unhappy India* (1928), etc.

La·ka·nal \lá-ká-nál\, Joseph. *Name orig.* La·ca·nal \lá-ká-nál\, *changed to distinguish him from his Royalist brothers.* 1762–1845. French educator and politician. Member of National Convention (1792) and voted for execution of the king; member (1793), president (1794), Committee of Public Instruction; reformed educational system; member of Council of Five Hundred. Under Napoléon, occupied educational posts. In exile in U.S. (1816–33), and president of Louisiana State U. (1817–25).

Lake \'lāk\, Gerard. 1st Viscount Lake. 1744–1808. English general. Nephew of the elder George Colman. Served in Germany (1760–62), America (1781), Low Countries (1793–94); routed Irish rebels at Vinegar Hill (1798), received surrender of French at Cloone. Commander in chief in India (1800–05); made full general (1802); in Marāthā war in northwest India took Delhi and Agra, won battles of Laswari and Farrukhābād; pursued Holkar into Punjab and forced surrender (1805); created baron (1804), viscount (1807).

Lake, John. 1624–1689. English prelate. Bishop of Chichester (1685); one of the Seven Bishops (see William SANCROFT) who petitioned against James II's Declaration of Indulgence (1688), but were aquitted of a charge of seditious libel; refused to take oath of allegiance to William and Mary (1688).

Lake, Kirsopp. 1872–1946. English biblical scholar. Professor at Leiden (1904–14) and Harvard (1914–38). Identified textual family of biblical manuscripts known as Lake group. Author of *The Text of the New Testament* (1900), *The Historical Evidence for the Resurrection of Jesus Christ* (1905), *The Beginning of Christianity* (1920–33), etc.

Lake, Mother. See Leonora BARRY.

Lake, Simon. 1866–1945. American naval architect, b. Pleasantville, N.J. Inventor of even-keel type of submarine; built *Argonaut* (1897), first submarine to operate successfully in the open sea; his torpedo boat design adopted by U.S. navy during World War I; also invented submarine apparatus for recovering sunken vessels and their cargoes.

Lak·shmi Bai \'läk-shmē-'bī\. d. 1858. Indian queen. Rani of Jhānsi; in Indian Mutiny against British rule, aided Tantia Topi in capture of Gwalior (1857); killed fighting the British at Marar or Kotah.

La·lande \lá-lä^{n}d\, Joseph-Jérôme Le Fran·çais de \lə-frä^{n}-se-də-\. 1732–1807. French astronomer. Sent to Berlin by French Academy to determine moon's parallax (1751); professor at Collège de France, Paris (from 1762); director of Paris observatory (from 1768). Worked on planetary theory; improved planetary tables of Halley and others. Author of *Traité d'astronomie* (1764), *Histoire céleste française* (1801; containing catalog of nearly 50,000 stars), *Bibliographie astronomique* (1803), etc.

Lalande, Michel-Richard de. *Surname also spelled* De·la·lande \də-lá-lä^{n}d\. 1657–1726. French composer. Organist at four Paris churches; one of four superintendents of the Chapel Royal (1683); master of royal chamber music (1695); in sole control of Chapel Royal (by 1714). Leading composer of sacred music in France in his day; known esp. for his 42 motets for chorus and orchestra for Versailles chapel; also composed secular cantatas and pastorals, *Symphonies pour les soupers du roi* (1703), divertissements, and ballets as *Le Ballet de la jeunesse* (1686).

La·lique \lá-'lēk\, René. 1860–1945. French jeweler and glassmaker. Established jewelry firm at Paris (1885); produced in Art Nouveau style elegantly and fantastically designed jewelry, as brooches and combs, using relatively few precious stones. Began artistic experiments in rock crystal and architectural glass; acquired glass factory at Wingen-sur-Moder (1920); created personal style of molded glass for luxury articles which were height of fashion during 1920s; also produced lighting fixtures and other architectural glass items.

Lal·ly \lá-lē\, Thomas-Arthur de. Comte de Lally. Baron de Tol·len·dal \tò-lä^{n}-dál\. 1702–1766. French soldier. Served in Irish Brigade of French army under the maréchal de Saxe; took part in Charles Edward's invasion of British Isles (1745); commander in chief of French East Indies (1756); waged offensive war against the English (1758); defeated and forced to capitulate to Sir Eyre Coote (1761); beheaded on charge of treason and cowardice.

La·lo \lá-lō\, Édouard-Victor-Antoine. 1823–1892. French composer. Known for the clarity of his orchestration; his compositions included operas *Fiesque* (1867) and *Le Roi d'Ys* (1888), ballet *Namouna* (1882), violin concerto *Symphonie espagnole* (1875), cello concerto (1876), *Symphony in G Minor* (1887) and other orchestral works, church and chamber music, piano pieces, and songs.

La·lor \'lā-lər\, Peter. 1827–1889. Australian engineer and politician, b. Ireland. To Australia (1852); joined (1854) gold miners' Ballarat Reform League; led their uprising (Nov.–Dec. 1854) at Eureka Stockade in Ballarat, Victoria, which resulted in redress of grievances. Member of Victoria Legislative Assembly (1856–71, 1875–89), speaker (1880–89).

Lam·a·chus \'lam-ə-kəs\. d. 414 B.C. Athenian general. Distinguished himself as an associate of Alcibiades and Nicias in the Sicilian expedition (415 B.C.); killed in action fighting the Syracusans.

La·mar \lə-'mär\, Joseph Rucker. 1857–1916. American jurist, b. Elbert Co., Ga. Practiced law in Augusta (from 1880); member of state supreme court (1904–06). Associate justice, U.S. Supreme Court (from 1911).

Lamar, Mirabeau Buonaparte. 1798–1859. American politician, b. Louisville, Ga. In Texas (from 1836); served in Sam Houston's force at battle of San Jacinto. Vice president of Republic of Texas (1836) and president (1838–41); after 1844, advocated annexation to United States. His nephew ¶Lucius Quintus Cincinnatus Lamar (1825–1893), b. Putnam Co., Ga., was a lawyer; settled in Mississippi (1855); member of U.S. House of Representatives (1857–60); served in Confederate army in Civil War; appointed Confederate envoy to Russia (1862); again member of U.S. House of Representatives (1873–77); U.S. senator (1877–85); U.S. secretary of the interior (1885–88); associate justice, U.S. Supreme Court (1888–93).

La Marche \lá-mársh\, Olivier de. c.1425–1502. French chronicler and poet. In service of court of Burgundy (from 1439); wrote allegorical poems as *Le Chevalier délibéré;* remembered esp. for *L'État de la maison du duc Charles de Bourgogne* (1474) and for his *Mémoires* covering period 1435 to 1488 (complete c.1490).

La Marck \lá-márk\. French noble family descended from a son of Adolphe IV, comte d'Altena; family held duchy of Bouillon (1483–1591) which then passed to the house of La Tour d'Auvergne. Its members included: Robert I (d. 1489), duc de Bouil·lon \bwē-yō^{n}\. ¶Robert II (d. 1535), duc, accompanied Charles VIII in expedition against Naples (1495); fought at Novara (1513) and Pavia (1524). ¶Robert III (c.1491–1537), duc, fought in wars in Italy; marshal of France; defended Pérouse (1537); his *Mémoires* important source material for period 1490 to 1521. His son ¶Robert IV (1520?–1556), duc, marshal of France (1547).

La·marck \lá-márk\, Jean-Baptiste-Pierre-Antoine de Mo·net de \də-mò-ned-ə-\. Chevalier. 1744–1829. French naturalist. In French army (1761–68); studied medicine and then botany in Paris; published *Flore française* (1779), *Dictionnaire de botanique* (1783–95), and *Illustrations de genres* (1791–1800). Held several positions at Jardin du Roi (1788–93); professor of zoology, Jardin des Plantes (1793–1818). Forerunner of Darwin in evolutionary theory; proposed theory that changes in environment cause changes in animals and plants, resulting in adaptive modification or greater development, and that such acquired characters are transmitted to offspring; responsible for classification of animals into vertebrates and invertebrates; among invertebrates, first proposed the classes Infusoria, Annelida, Crustacea, Arachnida, and Tunicata. Author of *Système des animaux sans vertèbres* (1801), *Recherches sur l'organisation de corps vivans* (1802), *Philosophie zoologique* (1809), *Histoire naturelle des animaux sans vertèbres* (1815–22).

La Mar·mo·ra \lä-'mär-mō-rä\, Alfonso Fer·re·ro \fār-'re-rō\. Marchese. 1804–1878. Italian soldier and politician. Served in the war of independence (1848–49). As minister of war (1848–59, with a few interruptions), reorganized the Sardinian army; served in Crimean War (1855) and commanded the army in the war of 1859. Prime minister of Sardinia (1859–60, 1864–66); chief of staff (1866); concluded alliance with Prussia against Austria (1866); retired after being held responsible for defeat by Austrians at Custoza (June 1866).

La·marque \lá-márk\, Maximilien. Comte. 1770–1832. French general. Campaigned in Italy and captured Gaeta (1806); engaged under Napoléon at Wagram. Member of Chamber of Deputies (1828–32); outspoken in his opposition to the government. His funeral (June 5–6, 1832) was occasion seized by Republicans for an insurrection in Paris.

La·mar·tine \lá-már-tēn\, Alphonse-Marie-Louis de Prat \prá\ de. 1790–1869. French poet. Best known for his *Méditations poétiques* (1820), which was immensely popular and strongly influenced course of Romantic movement in French literature. Other poetic works were *Nouvelles méditations poétiques* (1823), *La Mort de Socrate* (1823), *Le Dernier Chant du pèlerinage d'Harold* (1825), *Harmonies poétiques et religieuses* (1830), and *Les Visions,* a projected Christian epic of which he only published *Jocelyn* (1836) and *La Chute d'un ange* (1838). Author also of prose works as *Histoire des Girondins* (1847), *Histoire de la Restauration* (1851–52), *Graziella* (1852). Known also as an orator; minister of foreign affairs in provisional government (1848).

Lamas, Carlos Saavedra. See SAAVEDRA LAMAS.

Lamb \'lam\, Lady Caroline, *nee* Pon·son·by \'pən(t)-sən-bē, 'pän(t)-\. 1785–1828. English novelist. m. (1805) William Lamb (*q.v.*); became notorious for her affair with Lord Byron (1812–13); author of novels *Glenarron* (1816, containing a caricature portrait of Byron), *Graham Hamilton* (1822), *Ada Reis* (1823). Mentally deranged after happening to meet Byron's funeral procession.

Lamb, Charles. 1775–1834. English essayist and critic. Clerk in India House (1792–1825); lived in straitened circumstances with parents and sister ¶Mary Ann (1764–1847), who in fit of insanity killed her invalid mother (1796); gave up projected marriage and devoted himself to guardianship of his sister.

Contributed four sonnets to his friend Coleridge's first volume (1796); wrote poem "The Old Familiar Faces," published with Charles Lloyd (1798); published prose romance *A Tale of Rosamund Gray* (1798). With sister Mary wrote *Tales from Shakespear,* Charles doing the tragedies and Mary the comedies (1807); wrote with her a child's *Ulysses* (1808), children's stories *Mrs. Leicester's School* (1809), and poetry for children. Contributed articles on Hogarth and Shakespeare to Leigh Hunt's *Reflector;* published his collected prose and verse (1818); on staff of *London Magazine,* to which he contributed (1820–25) the 25 *Essays of Elia* (reprinted; 1st series, 1823; 2d, 1833). Also known as a great letter writer.

Lamb, Sir Horace. 1849–1934. English mathematician and physicist. Professor at Adelaide U., Australia (1875–85) and Victoria U., Lancashire (1885–1920); made researches on wave propagation, electrical induction, theory of tides and waves, etc. Author of *Hydrodynamics* (1895), *Dynamical Theory of Sound* (1910), *Statics* (1912), *Dynamics* (1914), *Higher Mechanics* (1920), etc.

Lamb, William. 2d Viscount Mel·bourne \ˈmel-bərn, -ˌbȯ(ə)rn\. 1779–1848. English politician. m. (1805) daughter of 3d Earl of Bessborough (see Lady Caroline LAMB); Whig M.P. (1806); supported Catholic emancipation; Irish secretary (1827, 1828); succeeded to viscountcy (1829); home secretary under Grey (1830–34), employed in Ireland coercive measures. Prime minister (July–Nov. 1834 and 1835–41), eminently tactful political adviser of young Queen Victoria; opposed reduction of duties on imported grain; his firm stand averted war with France over Syria (1840).

Lam·balle \lä^{n}-bȧl\, Marie-Thérèse-Louise de, *nee* Sa·voie-Ca·ri·gnan \sȧv-wȧ-kȧ-rēn-yä^{n}\. Princesse. 1749–1792. French noblewoman. Intimate friend of Marie-Antoinette; m. Louis-Alexandre-Stanislas de Bourbon, prince de Lamballe (1766; d. 1767); imprisoned (1792), refused to subscribe to the oath against the monarchy and was torn to pieces by mob.

Lam·bart \ˈlam-ˌbärt\, Frederic Rudolph. 10th Earl of Cav·an \ˈkav-ən\. 1865–1946. British soldier. Entered army (1885); served in Boer War (1900–01); colonel on retired list (1912); corps commander in France in World War I; to Italy (1917), commander of all British troops in Italy (1918); repelled Austrian attack at Piave River (1918), launched successful offensive at Vittorio Veneto (Sept. 1918); chief of imperial general staff (1922–26); field marshal (1932).

Lam·beau \ˈlam-(ˌ)bō, lam-ˈbō\, Earl Louis, *known as* Curly \ˈkər-lē\. 1898–1965. American football coach, b. Green Bay, Wis. Cofounder (1919), head coach and general manager (1919–49), and halfback (1919–29) of Green Bay Packers; won 6 National Football League championships (1929–31, 1936, 1939, 1944); coach of Chicago Cardinals (1950–51) and Washington Redskins (1952–54); charter member of Professional Football Hall of Fame (1963).

Lam·ber·mont \lä^{n}-ber-mō^{n}\, August. Baron. 1819–1905. Belgian politician. Fought in Spain in Isabella II's army in First Carlist War (1834–39); in Belgian foreign affairs ministry (1842–1905); negotiated settlement of the Scheldt Question with the Netherlands (1863); created baron (1863); prominent at several international conferences (1874–90) on questions of war and Central African affairs.

Lam·bert \ˈlam-bərt\ of Spo·le·to \spə-ˈlāt-(ˌ)ō\. d. 898. Holy Roman emperor (892–898). Ruled with his father Guy of Spoleto (892–894) and alone (894–898); deposed when Pope Formosus crowned Arnulf of Carinthia emperor (896) but regained crown same year when Arnulf died; instigated Cadaver Synod (897) using Formosus's desecrated corpse; defeated Berengar, marquis of Friuli, near Marengo (898); may have been assassinated.

Lambert, Constant, *in full* Leonard Constant. 1905–1951. English composer. Instrumental in establishing ballet as art form in England. Commissioned by Diaghilev to compose ballet *Romeo and Juliet* (1926); conductor, Camargo Society (1930–31); director, Sadler's Wells Ballet (1931–47). Composed ballet *Horoscope* (1937), choral and orchestral works as *The Rio Grande* (1927, text by Sacheverell Sitwell) and *Summer's Last Will and Testament* (1936, setting of Thomas Nashe), song cycle *Eight Chinese Songs* (1926), piano pieces, etc. Published *Music Ho! a Study of Music in Decline* (1934), on 20th-century music.

Lambert, Daniel. 1770–1809. English fat man. So famous for his corpulence that his name became a synonym for immensity; at death stood 5′11″ and weighed 739 pounds.

Lam·bert \lä^{n}-ber, *Ger* ˈläm-ˌbert, *Angl* ˈlam-bərt\, François, *Ger.* Franz. *Known as* Lambert of A·vi·gnon \ȧ-vēn-yō^{n}\. 1486–1530. French theologian. Entered Franciscan monastery in his native Avignon (1501); converted to Protestantism (1522) and joined Luther at Wittenberg (1523); in service of Landgrave Philip of Hesse (from 1526); his *Reformatio ecclesiarum Hassiae* rejected by Synod of Homberg as too democratic (1526); first professor of theology at Marburg (1527).

Lam·bert \ˈläm-ˌbert\, Johann Heinrich. 1728–1777. German physicist, mathematician, astronomer, and philosopher. In Berlin under patronage of Frederick the Great (1764). Conducted researches on heat, light, and color; discovered method of measuring the intensity and absorption of light, the lambert (a unit of brightness) being named after him; constructed a color pyramid; measured the coefficient of expansion of air; formulated theorem on the motion of the planets; demonstrated the irrationality of π; responsible for concept of hyperbolic functions in trigonometry. Published *Photometria* (1760), *Neues Organon* (1764), *Die Theorie der Parallellinien* (1766), *Pyrometrie* (1779).

Lam·bert \ˈlam-bərt\, John. 1619–1683. English general. At outbreak of Civil War, joined Parliamentary army as captain; led cavalry at Marston Moor; major general (1647); commander of army in north (1647) and spokesman of the army; aided Cromwell in destroying Scottish army at Preston (1648); led van at Dunbar (1650); won victory of Inverkeithing; commanded troops on east bank of Severn at battle of Worcester (1651). Leader of council of officers that installed Cromwell as lord protector (1653); served on Council of State and was Cromwell's chief aide until ousted (1657) for vigorously protesting offer of crown to Cromwell. After deposition of Richard Cromwell (May 1659), became prominent in ensuing power struggle; regarded as leader of extreme republican party; virtual ruler of country until frustrated by Monck's advance to London; kept prisoner until his death.

Lambert, Louis. See Patrick S. GILMORE.

Lam·bert von Hers·feld \ˈläm-ˌbert-fȯn-ˈhers-ˌfelt\. 1025–1088. German historian. Joined Benedictine convent at Hersfeld (1058); moved to Abbey of Hasungen (1077). Author of *Annales,* a history of the world to 1077, containing a comprehensive treatment of contemporaneous events from the accession of of Henry IV; *Vita Lulli,* a biography of Archbishop Lullus of Mainz who founded the monastery at Hersfeld; and the epic *Carmen de Bello Saxonico.*

Lamb·ton \ˈlam(p)-tən\, John George. 1st Earl of Dur·ham \ˈdər-əm, ˈdə-rəm, ˈdu̇r-əm\. 1792–1840. English politician. Whig M.P. (1813–28); proposed scheme of parliamentary reform rejected as too advanced; created baron (1828); privy councilor and lord privy seal in administration of his father-in-law, Lord Grey (1830–33); one of four who drew up the first Reform Bill; created Viscount Lambton and Earl of Durham (1833); ambassador to St. Petersburg (1835–37). Governor general and lord high commissioner in Canada (1838); took statesmanlike action to placate rebellious Lower Canada but reviled in England for it; resigned (1838); attempted public justification by means of his *Report on the Affairs of British North America* (1839), outlining principles and schemes of British colonial policy adopted by his successors.

La·mé \lȧ-mā\, Gabriel. 1795–1870. French mathematician and engineer. Professor at École Polytechnique (1832–44) and U. of Paris (1851–62); engaged in building railroads from Paris to Saint-Germain and to Versailles; engineer in chief of mining (1836). Contributed to number theory, thermodynamics, algebra; introduced curvilinear coordinates into pure and applied mathematics.

La·men·nais \lȧm-ne\, Hughes-Félicité-Robert de. *Surname orig. spelled* La Men·nais \lȧm-en-e\. 1782–1854. French priest and philosopher. With his brother ¶Jean-Marie-Robert (1780–1860), produced a scheme of church reform (1808) and a defense of Ultramontanism (1814); ordained priest (1816); defended church tradition in *Essai sur l'indifférence en matière de religion* (1817–23). Changed position and began advocating alliance of Catholicism with political liberalism, esp. in *De la religion considérée dans ses rapports avec l'ordre politique et civil* (1825–26); with Henri Lacordaire, Charles de Montalembert, et al., founded (1830) journal *L'Avenir* to advocate democratic principles and separation of church and state; journal suppressed (1831) and its principles condemned by Pope Gregory XVI (1832); denounced the papacy and European monarchs in *Paroles d'un croyant* (1834) and severed all ties with the church. Served in constituent assembly after revolution of 1848.

La·me·rie \ˈlā-m(ə-)rē, ˈlam(-ə)-rē\, Paul de. 1688–1751. English silversmith, b. Netherlands. To England (by 1691); set up shop in London (1712); known for his Rococo cups, ewers, tankards, etc.

La·meth \lȧ-met\, Alexandre-Théodore-Victor. Comte. 1760–1829. French soldier and politician. Served under Rochambeau in American Revolution; elected to Estates-General (1789), soon joined Third Estate; with Antoine Barnave and Adrien Duport formed triumvirate which at first supported rights of common people but later (early 1791) advocated a constitutional monarchy and directed unsuccessful struggle of the Feuillants against the Jacobins. Served under Lafayette in war with Austria (1792); prisoner of war (1792–95); returned to France (1800); prefect (1802–15) and member of liberal parliamentary opposition to Louis XVIII and Charles X.

La Met·trie \lȧ-me-trē\, Julien Of·froy \ȯ-frā\ de. 1709–1751. French physician and philosopher. Forced to flee from France and then from Leiden because of materialistic teachings in his *Histoire naturelle de l'âme* (1745) and *L'Homme-machine* (1747); found asylum with Frederick the Great in Berlin. Held that psychical phenomena are due to organic changes in brain and

\ə\ abut \ᵊ\ kitten, *Fr.* **table \ər\ further \a\ ash \ā\ ace \ä\ cot, cart \au̇\ out \ch\ chin \e\ bet \ē\ easy \g\ go \i\ hit \ī\ ice \j\ job \ŋ\ sing \ō\ go \ȯ\ law \ȯi\ boy \th\ both \t͟h\ the \ü\ loot \u̇\ foot \y\ yet \zh\ vision \ȧ, b̲, g̲, k̲, ^{n}, œ, œ̄, ue, ue̅, ʸ\ *see* Guide to Pronunciation**

nervous system, that the only pleasures are those of the senses, that life should be spent in enjoyment of pleasures, that the soul ceases to exist with the death of the body. Also wrote *Discours sur le bonheur* (1748), *Les Animaux plus que machines* (1750), *Le Petit Homme à longue queue* (1751).

Lam·masch \'läm-äsh\, Heinrich. 1853–1920. Austrian jurist and politician. Professor of criminal and international law at Vienna (from 1889); four times member (from 1900) and president of International Court of Arbitration, The Hague. Opposed union with German Reich and later *Anschluss* movement; favored peace by agreement in World War I and a league of nations; last minister president of old Austria (Oct.–Nov. 1918).

La·moi·gnon \läm-wän-yōⁿ\. Prominent French family, including: Guillaume de Lamoignon (1617–1677), lawyer and first president of the parlement of Paris (1658); headed tribunal trying Nicolas Fouquet (1661) but withdrew in protest of trial's political nature; member (1667–72) of committee for reformation of French law; created marquis de Bâ·ville \də-bä-vēl\ (1670). His son ¶Nicolas de Lamoignon de Bâville (1648–1724), lawyer, intendant at Languedoc (1685–1718); much hated for his repressive measures against the Huguenots. His nephew ¶Guillaume de Lamoignon, seigneur de Blanc·mes·nil \blä-mā-nēl, -me-\ *and* de Males·herbes \mäl-zerb\ (1683–1772), chancellor of France (1750), father of Malesherbes (*q.v.*).

La·mont \'lä-mȯnt\, Johann von. 1805–1879. German astronomer, b. Scotland. On staff (1827–35), director (1835–79), Royal Observatory, Bogenhausen; professor, U. of Munich (1852–79). Provided orbital data on satellites of Saturn and Uranus; determined mass of Uranus; cataloged over 34,000 stars; discovered fluctuation of Earth's magnetic field (1850) and existence of Earth currents (1862). Chief publication *Handbuch des Erdmagnetismus* (1849).

La·mon·tagne-Beau·re·gard \lä-mōⁿ-tänʸ-bō-rə-gär\, Blanche. 1889–1958. Canadian poet, b. Les Escoumains, Que. First important woman poet in French Canada; author of collections of lyric poetry generally extolling her native Gaspé Peninsula, including *Visions gaspésiennes* (1913), *Par nos champs et nos rives* (1917), *Moisson nouvelle* (1926), *Ma Gaspésie* (1928).

La·mo·ri·cière \lä-mȯ-rēs-yer\, Christophe-Louis-Léon Ju·chault de \zhü-shō-də-\. 1806–1865. French general. Entered engineers (1829); to Algiers as captain in the Zouaves (1830); governor general of Algeria during incumbent's absence (1845); distinguished himself in campaign against Abdelkader (1847). Member of Legislative Assembly (1848–51); minister of war (1848); opposed Louis-Napoléon so vigorously that he was banished from France (1852). Entered military service of the papacy and was defeated at Castelfidardo (1860).

La Mothe \lä-mȯt\, Antoine Lau·met de \lō-me-də-\. Sieur de Ca·dil·lac \kä-dē-yäk\. 1658–1730. French soldier and colonialist. To Canada (1683); commandant at St. Ignace, Mackinac (1694–97); founded Fort-Pontchartrain du Détroit (1701; later city of Detroit); governor of Louisiana (1710–1716 or 1717).

La Mothe Le Va·yer \lä-mȯt-lə-vä-yā\, François de. 1588–1672. French philosopher. A leader among 17th-century French skeptics; tutor of King Louis XIV (1652–57); appointed historiographer of France and councilor of state. His works included *Considérations sur l'eloquence française* (1638), *De la vertu des païens* (1642), *De peu de certitude qu'il y a dans l'histoire* (1668).

La Motte \lä-mȯt\, Marc-Antoine-Nicolas de. Comte. 1754–1831. French adventurer. m. ¶Jeanne, *nee* de Saint-Ré·my de Va·lois \də-saⁿ-rā-mē-də-väl-wä\ (1756–1791); the comtesse became mistress of Prince Louis-René-Édouard de Rohan and pretended to be an intimate of Queen Marie-Antoinette. Rohan purchased (1785) a diamond necklace under the impression (given him by the comtesse) that he was authorized to do so by the queen; when the jewelers complained to the queen, Rohan was arrested, tried, and acquitted (1786); the comtesse was condemned to be whipped, branded, and imprisoned, but escaped from prison; the comte was believed to have fled with the necklace to London.

La Motte Fouqué de. See FOUQUÉ.

La Motte-Houdar. See Antoine HOUDAR DE LA MOTTE.

Lamp·man \'lamp-mən\, Archibald. 1861–1899. Canadian poet, b. Morpeth, Ont. Worked in post office department of Canadian civil service (1883–99). Member of Confederation group; known for his nature poems collected in *Among the Millet* (1888), *Lyrics of Earth* (1893), *Alcyone* (1899), *At the Long Sault* (1943).

Lam·precht \'läm-prekt\, Karl Gottfried. 1856–1915. German historian. Professor at Bonn (1885), Marburg (1890), Leipzig (1891); developed theory that science of history is social-psychological rather than exclusively political. Author of *Deutsches Wirtschaften im Mittelalter* (1885–86), *Deutsche Geschichte* (1891–1909), *Die kulturhistorische Methode* (1900), etc.

Lamprecht der Pfaf·fe \-derp-'fäf-ə\, *i.e.* the Priest. fl. 1120–1130. Frankish poet. Author of the Middle Frankish *Alexanderlied* (c.1130), an epic on the life of Alexander the Great.

La·my \lä-mē\, Bernard. 1640–1715. French ecclesiastic and scholar. Member of the Congregation of the Oratory; suffered ecclesiastical discipline for teaching Cartesian doctrines. Among his works were *Nouvelles réflexions sur l'art poétique* (1668), *Traité de la grandeur en général* (1680), *Harmonie évangélique* (1689).

Lamy, John Baptist, *orig.* Jean-Baptiste. 1814–1888. American prelate, b. Lempdes, France. Ordained Roman Catholic priest (1838); in U.S. (from 1839); missionary bishop in the Southwest (from 1850); bishop of Santa Fe (1853); built missions, schools, hospitals, a cathedral in Santa Fe; archbishop (1875–85); titular archbishop of Cyzicus (1885). Willa Cather's novel *Death Comes for the Archbishop* is based on his career in the Southwest.

Lan·cas·ter \'laŋ-kə-stər; 'lan-ˌkas-tər, 'laŋ-\, House of. English royal house derived from the fourth son of Edward III, John of Gaunt, created (1362) duke of Lancaster after marriage (1359) with daughter and heiress of Henry, 1st Duke of Lancaster; branch of Plantagenet family, rival (after 1399) of house of York. Symbol of house in War of the Roses was the red rose. Reigning Lancastrian kings were Henry IV, Henry V, Henry VI.

Lancaster, Earls and dukes of. See EDMUND, HENRY, JOHN of Gaunt, THOMAS.

Lancaster, Sir James. c.1554–1618. English navigator and pioneer of East Indian trade. Served under Drake against Armada (1588); sailed with earliest English oversea expedition to establish East Indian trade (1591–94); commanded first fleet of East India Company (1601–03), establishing at Bantam, Java, the first of company's trading posts in Southeast Asia; promoted search for Northwest Passage.

Lancaster, John of. See JOHN of Lancaster.

Lancaster, Joseph. 1778–1838. English educationist. Joined Society of Friends; taught free school of a thousand boys; organized corps of elder boys as monitors to oversee and instruct; the Lancasterian system of education adopted widely by nonconformists in competition with Andrew Bell's system supported by Church of England; emigrated to America (1818), where he lectured extensively and founded schools in Philadelphia, Baltimore, Boston, Washington, D.C.

Lan·ce·lot \läⁿs-lō\, Claude. 1615?–1695. French priest and educator. A Jansenist; taught at Petites Écoles, Les Granges (1645 or 1646–60), where he introduced a new method of teaching languages. Author of *Nouvelle méthode pour apprendre la langue latine* (1644), *Jardin des racines grecques* (1657), *Mémoires* (1738).

Lan·ches·ter \'lan-chəs-tər\, Frederick William. 1868–1946. English engineer. Built first automobile in Britain (1895); founded (1899) Lanchester Engine Co. and produced (1901) a car noted for graceful appearance and lack of vibration. Also pioneered in aeronautics; published *Aerodynamics* (1907) and *Aerodonetics* (1908) containing advanced aeronautical ideas which helped lay foundations of aircraft design.

Lan·cia·ni \län-'chän-ē\, Rodolfo Amadeo. 1847–1929. Italian archaeologist. Assisted in excavations at Ostia; director of Roman excavations (1875–95); professor at Rome (1882–1911); authority on topography of ancient Rome. Published *Ancient Rome in the Light of Modern Discoveries* (1888), *Forma Urbis Romae* (1893–1901), *Storia degli scavi di Roma* (1909–12), *Wanderings in the Roman Campagna* (1909).

Lan·ci·si \län-'chē-sē\, Giovanni Maria. 1654–1720. Italian physician, clinician, and botanist. Physician to popes Innocent XI, Innocent XII, Clement XI. Considered first modern hygienist; related prevalence of malaria in swamps to presence of mosquitoes and recommended drainage as preventive measure. Wrote *De subitaneis mortibus* on sudden deaths in Rome (1707), *De motu cordis et aneurysmatibus* on cardiac pathology (1728), treatises on influenza, malaria, rinderpest, etc.

Lan·cret \läⁿ-kre\, Nicolas. 1690–1743. French painter. Much admired as a decorator; known for his brilliant depiction of light comic subjects as balls, fairs, and village weddings.

Lan·dau \'län-daü\, Ezekiel. 1713–1793. Polish rabbi. Head of rabbinical court at Brody (1734–45); rabbi of Jampol, Podalia (1745–55), where he arbitrated dispute between Jacob Emden and Jonathan Eybeschütz; rabbi of Prague (1755–93). Implacable opponent of Ḥasidism and Haskala movements; known for his halakhic decisions, collected as *Nod'a be-Yehuda* (1776).

Lan·dau \(ˌ)lən-'daü\, Lev Davidovich. 1908–1968. Soviet physicist. Head of Theory Division of S.I. Vavilov Inst. of Physical Problems, Moscow (1937–68). Made significant contributions to atomic and nuclear physics, low-temperature physics, solid state, stellar, and plasma physics. Author of *Course of Theoretical Physics* (1948, with E.M. Lifshits). Awarded Nobel prize for physics (1962) for theories on condensed matter, esp. liquid helium.

Landau, Mark Aleksandrovich. *Pseudonym* M. A. Al·da·nov \(ˌ)əl-'dä-nəf\. 1886–1957. Russian writer. Following Russian Revolution emigrated to France (1919), thence to U.S. (1941); author of *Deux révolutions* (1921), tetralogy *Myslitel* (1923–25), *La Clef* (1930), *Évasion* (1932), anti-Soviet satire *Nachalo kontsa* (1939), *Istoki* (1947).

Lan·dells \'land-əlz\, Ebenezer. 1808–1860. English wood engraver. Conceived idea of *Punch*, projected magazine (first issue July 17, 1841); contributed to early numbers of *Illustrated London News*.

Lan·den \'lan-dən\, John. 1719–1790. English mathematician. Made researches on elliptic functions; produced Landen's theorem for expressing the arc of a hyperbola in terms of two elliptic arcs (1775). Published *Mathematical Memoirs* (1780–90).

Lan·der \'län-dər\, Harald. *Orig.* Alfred Bernhardt Stevns·borg \'stev-əns-bȯrḡ\. 1905–1971. Danish dancer and choreographer. Studied under Michel Fokine (1926–27); with Royal Danish Ballet as leading dancer (1929–45) and ballet master (1930–51); introduced own compositions as *Études* (1948) and esp. works by Fokine and Auguste Bournonville; developed company into a superb performing organization. Ballet master of Paris Opéra (1953–62); became French citizen (1956); opened studio in Paris (1964).

Lan·der \'lan-dər\, Richard Lemon. 1804–1834. English explorer. Made with Hugh Clapperton (*q.v.*) expedition to western Africa and published Clapperton's journal and records (1830). With his brother ¶John (1807–1839), traced (1830–31) the course of the Lower Niger River to its delta and published journal (1832) of the expedition. Richard led (1832–34) trading expedition up the Niger organized by Macgregor Laird (*q.v.*); killed by natives.

Lan·di·ni \län-'dē-nē\ *or* **Lan·di·no** \-nō\, Francesco. c.1325–1397. Florentine musician and composer. Blind from childhood; a leading representative of *ars nova* of 14th century. Famed during lifetime for his musical memory, skill in improvisation, virtuosity on the organetto. His extant works include 140 ballate, 10 madrigals, a French virelay, and a caccia.

Lan·dis \'lan-dəs\, Kenesaw Mountain. 1866–1944. American jurist, b. Millville, Ohio. Practiced law in Chicago (1891–1905). U.S. district judge, Northern District of Illinois (1905–22); presided at trial (1907) of Standard Oil of Indiana rebate cases, found defendants guilty, imposed fine of $29,240,000 (later reversed). First commissioner of professional baseball (1920–44); noted for uncompromising measures to preserve integrity of the game. Elected to Baseball Hall of Fame (1944).

Lan·do \'län-dō\. *Lat.* Lan·dus \'lan-dəs\. d. 914. Pope (913–914). His papal administration controlled by house of Theophylact.

Lan·don \'lan-dən\, Letitia Elizabeth. *Pseudonym* L.E.L. 1802–1838. English poet and novelist. m. (1838) George Maclean (*q.v.*). Published volumes of verse as *The Fate of Adelaide* (1821), *The Venetian Bracelet* (1829); four novels, including *Ethel Churchill* (1837); and a tragedy *Castruccio Castracani* (1837).

Lan·dor \'lan-,dȯ(ə)r, -dər\, Walter Savage. 1775–1864. English poet and prose writer. Gained friendship with Southey through poem *Gebir* (1798); went through fortune; fought as volunteer in Spain (1808); lived at Florence (from 1858), assisted by Robert Browning. Author of volumes of verse as *The Hellenics* (1847) and *Heroic Idylls* (1863); dramas including *Don Julian* (1812) and *Antony and Octavius* (1856); and esp. prose works as *Imaginary Conversations* (5 vols., 1824, 1828, 1829), *Pericles and Aspasia* (1836), and *The Pentameron* (1837).

Lan·dow·ska \lȧn-'dȯf-skȧ\, Wanda Louise. 1879–1959. Polish harpsichordist. Settled in Paris (1900); initiated 20th-century revival of the harpsichord and was principal exponent of 17th- and 18th-century harpsichord music, esp. of Bach and Couperin; published *Musique ancienne* (1909, with husband Henry Lew); founded (1925) École de Musique Ancienne near Paris; settled in U.S. (1941). Her theories of technique were basis of contemporary harpsichord playing; composer of songs, piano pieces, and orchestral works.

Lan·dru \läⁿ-drᵫ\, Henri-Désiré. 1869–1922. French murderer. Sometimes called the "modern Bluebeard"; defrauded at least 283 middle-aged women (from 1910); in sensational trial, convicted by circumstantial evidence of murdering 10 women and a boy, though no bodies were found; guillotined.

Land·seer \'lan(d)-,si(ə)r\, Sir Edwin Henry. 1802–1873. English painter. Extremely popular in his day for his animal paintings. His canvases included *Alpine Mastiffs Reanimating a Distressed Traveller* (1820), *The Cat's Paw* (1824), *High Life* (1829), *Low Life* (1829), *Jack in Office* (1833), *The Old Shepherd's Chief Mourner* (1837), *A Distinguished Member of the Humane Society* (1838), *Dignity and Impudence* (1839), *Rout of Comus* (1843), *Shoeing* (1844), *Stag at Bay* (1846), *A Random Shot* (1848), *Monarch of the Glen* (1851), *Titania and Bottom* (1851). Also painted Queen Victoria, Prince Albert, and members of the nobility. Completed lions at base of Nelson monument in Trafalgar Square (1866).

Land·stad \'län-städ\, Magnus Brostrup. 1802–1880. Norwegian pastor and poet. Published (1853) *Norske folkeviser,* the first collection of authentic Norwegian traditional ballads; compiled a national hymnal which included some 50 of his own hymns (1861).

Land·stei·ner \'länt-,shtī-nər, *Angl* 'lan(d)-,stī-nər\, Karl. 1868–1943. American immunologist and pathologist, b. Vienna, Austria. Professor at Vienna (1909–19); to U.S. (1922, naturalized 1929); professor at Rockefeller Institute for Medical Research, New York (1922–39). Discovered (1901) A, B, and O human blood types and developed ABO system of blood typing; discovered M and N blood groups (1927) and the Rhesus factor (1940); also studied poliomyelitis. Wrote classic *Die Spezifitaet der serologischen Reaktionen* (1936). Awarded 1930 Nobel prize for physiology or medicine.

Lan·dulph \'län-du̇lf\ of Car·ca·no \kär-'kän-ō\. d. 998. Italian prelate. Archbishop of Milan (979–998); his distribution of church lands to the lay aristocracy created a new privileged class (the *capitanei*) that played important part in 11th-century Milanese politics.

Lane \'lān\, Alfred Church. 1863–1948. American geologist, b. Boston. Professor at Tufts U. (1909–36); as chairman of committee on measurement of geologic time of National Research Council (1922–46), originated and directed research on Earth's age.

Lane, Sir Allen. *Orig.* Allen Lane Williams. 1902–1970. English publisher. Nephew of John Lane (1854–1925), whom he succeeded as managing editor of The Bodley Head, London (1925–35); founder (1935) and managing director (1935–69) of Penguin Books, Ltd., publisher of high-quality, low-priced paperbacks; published *The Penguin Shakespeare* (1937) and the Puffin Story Books (1941), latter of which revolutionized children's literature.

Lane, Edward William. 1801–1876. English Orientalist. Author of classic *Manners and Customs of the Modern Egyptians* (1836) and of first accurate version of *A Thousand and One Nights* (1838–40); compiled as life work Arabic thesaurus (5 parts, 1863–74; completed in 3 parts by grandnephew Stanley Lane-Poole, 1877–92).

Lane, Sir Hugh Percy. 1875–1915. Irish art dealer. Established a gallery of modern art in Dublin (c.1903); director of Irish National Gallery (1914–15). His death caused a controversy over the disposition of his collection of Impressionist paintings, which was finally divided between Dublin and London.

Lane, James Henry. 1814–1866. American soldier and politician, b. Kansas, probably Lawrenceburg. Lieutenant governor of Indiana (1849–53); moved to Kansas (1855); identified himself with the Free State movement; elected senator but not seated by U.S. Senate (1856). Headed an "army" of irregulars raiding Kansas proslavery districts (1856). U.S. senator (1861–66). Vigorously supported Lincoln; advocated emancipation and arming of Negroes.

Lane, John. 19th century. American blacksmith. Constructed (c.1833) a plow with moldboard and share formed of strips of steel, thus obtaining credit for inventing the first steel plow. Cf. John DEERE. His son ¶John (1824–1897), manufacturer of plows in Chicago, invented improvements in steel plows.

Lane, John. 1854–1925. English publisher. Cofounder with Elkin Mathews of Bodley Head Publishing Co. (1887); continued as sole proprietor after partnership dissolved (1894). Also founder of the *Yellow Book* (1894).

Lane, Jonathan Homer. 1819–1880. American physicist, b. Geneseo, N.Y. Examiner in U.S. Patent Office (1848–57); with U.S. Office of Weights and Measures (from 1869). Formulated Lane's law that gaseous bodies may from generation of heat by contraction grow hotter as they lose heat; in *On the Theoretical Temperature of the Sun* (1870), was first to investigate mathematically the sun as a gaseous body; invented a "visual telegraph," an electromagnetical governor, an air pump.

Lane, Joseph. 1801–1881. American soldier and politician, b. Buncombe Co., N.C. Fought in Mexican War; governor of Oregon Territory (1849–50); delegate from Oregon Territory to U.S. House of Representatives (1851–59); U.S. senator (1859–61). Candidate for vice president on Breckinridge ticket (1860), defeated.

Lane, Sir Ralph. 1530?–1603. English colonist. To Virginia (1585); in command of colony at Roanoke Island (1585); with colonists, returned to England (1586). Author of an account of the Virginia settlement published in Hakluyt's *Voyages* (1589).

Lane, Ralph Norman Angell. See Sir Norman ANGELL.

Lan·franc \'lan-,fraŋk\. 1005?–1089. Italian prelate. Became a Benedictine at Bec (1042), prior (1045); opened school in monastery, to which European scholars flocked; contended against Berenger in controversy over transubstantiation (1050) and again at council of Tours (1055). Opposed marriage of William the Conqueror with his cousin Matilda but later became reconciled and sought papal dispensation; because trusted counselor of William, who made him archbishop of Canterbury (1070–89); rebuilt cathedral, reformed and reorganized English church, raised standards of monasteries; created (c.1076) ecclesiastical courts separate from secular jurisdiction; warned William of conspiracy by earls of Norfolk and Hereford (1075); secured crown of William II against claims of Duke Robert of Normandy (1087).

Lan·fran·co \län-'fräŋ-kō\, Giovanni. 1582–1647. Italian painter. Pupil of Agustino and Annibale Carracci, influenced by Correggio; exponent of Baroque illusionism; bitter rival of Domenichino. Decorated dome of S. Andrea della Valle, Rome (1621–25), and dome of S. Gennaro chapel in Naples cathedral (1641–46).

Lang \'laŋ\, Andrew. 1844–1912. Scottish scholar and man of letters. Took lead in controversy with Max Müller over interpretation of mythology and folk tales;

proved folklore the foundation of literary mythology; published *Custom and Myth* (1884), *Myth, Ritual and Religion* (1897), *The Making of Religion* (1898). Author of verse, including *Ballads and Lyrics of Old France* (1872), *Helen of Troy* (1882), *Grass of Parnassus* (1888). Turned to history, writing *A History of Scotland From the Roman Occupation* (1900–07), *Historical Mysteries* (1904), *The Maid of France* (1908), etc. Published 12-volume collection of world fairy tales (1889–1910). Wrote novels *The Mark of Cain* (1886) and *The Disentanglers* (1902); fairy tales *The Gold of Fairnilee* (1888), *Prince Prigio* (1889), *Prince Ricardo of Pantouflia* (1893); literary studies *World of Homer* (1910) and *History of English Literature from "Beowulf" to Swinburne* (1912); and translations of Homer (*Odyssey,* with S. H. Butcher, 1879; *Iliad,* with E. Myers and Walter Leaf, 1882).

Lang \ˈläŋ\, Fritz. 1890–1976. American film director, b. Vienna, Austria. His films praised for their visual texture and intellectual rigor and sometimes criticized for frequent emphasis on terror and fatality. In Berlin directed *Der müde Tod* (1921), *Dr. Mabuse, der Spieler* (1922), *Die Nibelungen* (1924), *Metropolis* (1926), *M* (1931), *Das Testament des Dr. Mabuse* (1933). To U.S. (1934, naturalized 1939); in Hollywood directed *Fury* (1936), *You Only Live Once* (1937), *Western Union* (1941), *Scarlet Street* (1945), *Clash by Night* (1952), *Rancho Notorious* (1952), *Moonfleet* (1955), etc.

Lang \ˈlaŋ\, John Dunmore. 1799–1878. Australian ecclesiastic, b. Scotland. Entered Presbyterian ministry (1820); to Sydney (1823); founder of Australian Presbyterian church; bitter anti-Catholic; opposed influence of ex-convicts and arranged immigration of upper-working-class Protestants; instigated (1842) movement comparable to 1843 disruption of the Church of Scotland.

Lang, John Thomas, *called* Jack. 1876–1975. Australian politician. Entered New South Wales parliament (1913); rose to Labour party secretary and state treasurer (1920–22); premier of New South Wales (1925–27, 1930–32); his defiance of Prime Minister J.H. Scullin's economic policies led to Scullin's defeat (1931) and decline of Labour party's national power; expelled from Labour party (1943); in Parliament as independent (1943–49).

Lang, Matheson, *in full* Alexander Matheson. 1879–1948. British actor, b. Montreal. On London stage (from 1900); acted Benedick to Ellen Terry's Beatrice (1903); scored success in title roles of *Othello* (1907), *Romeo and Juliet* (1908), *Mr. Wu* (1913), *The Wandering Jew* (1920); produced and dramatized many works; toured for over 30 years throughout the English-speaking world. m. (1903) ¶Nellie Hutin Brit·ton \ˈbrit-ᵊn\ (1876–1965), who acted in many of his productions and with whom he inaugurated (1914) the Shakespeare seasons at Old Vic Theatre, London.

Lang \ˈläŋ\, Matthäus. 1468–1540. German ecclesiastic and politician. Of bourgeois origin; entered (c.1494) service of Emperor Maximilian I and rose to great power as the emperor's secretary and chief counselor; negotiated League of Cambrai against Venice (1508), alliance with Pope Julius II (1512), and settlement at Congress of Vienna (1512) that ultimately gave Bohemian and Hungarian thrones to the Habsburgs. Made bishop of Gurk (1505) and cardinal (1512) although not ordained priest until 1519. Prince-archbishop of Salzburg (1519–40); helped suppress Peasants' War (1524–25); took strong measures against spread of Reformation.

Lang \ˈlaŋ\, William Cosmo Gordon. 1st Baron Lang of Lam·beth \ˈlam-bəth\. 1864–1945. British prelate, b. Scotland. Bishop of Stepney (1901–08) and canon of St. Paul's; archbishop of York (1908–28); influential member of House of Lords. Archbishop of Canterbury (1928–42); active in social work in industrial centers; cleared of suspicion of having conspired to achieve abdication of Edward VIII (1936); created baron (1942).

Lang·dell \ˈlaŋ-dᵊl\, Christopher Columbus. 1826–1906. American lawyer and educator, b. New Boston, N.H. Practiced law, New York City (1854–70). Professor of law, Harvard Law School (1870–1900) and dean (1870–95); introduced (1870) the case method of teaching law, now generally used in the U.S. Author of *Selection of Cases on the Law of Contracts* (1871), *Selection of Cases on Sales of Personal Property* (1872), *Cases of Equity Pleading* (1875).

Lang·don \ˈlaŋ-dən\, Harry Philmore. 1884–1944. American actor, b. Council Bluffs, Ia. Known for his boyish, innocent comic roles in silent films *Tramp, Tramp, Tramp* (1926), *The Strong Man* (1926), *Long Pants* (1927), *The Chaser* (1928), *Heart Trouble* (1928), etc.

Langdon, John. 1741–1819. American Revolutionary leader, b. Portsmouth, N.H. Active in pre-Revolutionary agitation; member, Continental Congress (1775–76, 1783–84); naval agent for colonies (1776). Organized, financed, and served in John Stark's expedition against Burgoyne (1777). President of New Hampshire (1785–86, 1788–89); delegate to Constitutional Convention (1787); governor of New Hampshire (1805–09, 1810–12); U.S. senator (1789–1801); 1st pro tempore president of the U.S. Senate (1789).

Langdon, Samuel. 1723–1797. American clergyman, b. Boston. Congregational pastor at Portsmouth, N.H. (1747–74) and Hampton Falls, N.H. (1780–97); president of Harvard (1774–80).

Lan·ge \ˈlån-ge\, Antoni. 1861–1929. Polish poet and literary critic. A leader of Young Poland movement. Author of lyric and philosophical poems, historical dramas, and translations from Baudelaire and other French writers.

Lange \ˈläŋ-ə\, Carl Georg. 1834–1900. Danish physician and psychologist. Lecturer (1875–85), professor of pathological anatomy (1885–1900), Copenhagen; independently of William James, set forth (in *Om Sindsbevaegelser,* 1885) physiological theory of emotions, now known as James-Lange theory.

Lange \ˈläŋ-ə\, Christian Louis. 1869–1938. Norwegian pacifist. Secretary to Nobel Commission of Norwegian parliament (1900–09) and member of Nobel Prize committee; Norwegian representative at International Peace Conference, The Hague (1907); secretary general of International Parliamentary Union (1909–33); Norwegian delegate to League of Nations (1920–38); won Nobel peace prize (1921, with Karl Hjalmar Branting). Author of *The European Civil War* (1915), *History of Internationalism* (1919), *International Politics* (1924), *Imperialism and Peace* (1938), etc.

Lange \ˈlaŋ\, Dorothea. 1895–1965. American photographer, b. Hoboken, N.J. Known for her documentary photographs of indigent victims of the Depression, as "White Angel Breadline" (1932) and "Migrant Mother" (1936); published collection of photographs *An American Exodus* (1939); later photographed evacuations of Japanese-Americans to concentration camps (c.1942) and did photo-essays for *Life* magazine, including "Mormon Villages" and "The Irish Countryman."

Lange \ˈläŋ-ə\, Friedrich Albert. 1828–1875. German philosopher. Professor at Marburg (1872–75), where established tradition of Neo-Kantianism; introduced Darwinistic sociology and philosophy of history into Germany. Author of *Die Arbeiterfrage* (1865), *Die Grundlagen der mathematischen Psychologie* (1865), *Geschichte des Materialismus* (1866), *Neue Beiträge zur Geschichte des Materialismus* (1867), *Logische Studien* (1877), etc.

Lang·en \ˈläŋ-ən\, Eugen. 1833–1895. German engineer. Partner (from 1864) of N.A. Otto, with whom he designed an internal-combustion engine (1867) and a "silent engine" (pat. 1877), latter the first operating example of modern automobile engine; conceived idea of overhead suspension monorail.

Lang·en·ho·ven \ˈläŋ-ən-hü-fən\, Cornelius Jacob. 1878–1932. South African poet and politician. Senator in South African parliament; author in Afrikaans of poetry, plays, prose, and the national anthem "Die Stem van Suid-Afrika" (music by M.L. de Villiers).

Lang·er \ˈläŋ-ər\, František. 1888–1965. Czech dramatist. Physician in Czech army medical corps. Known for his dramas *Velbloud uchem jehly* (1923), *Periferie* (1925), *Jízdní Llídka* (1935); also wrote novels and short stories.

Lang·er \ˈläŋ-ər\, Johann Peter von. 1756–1824. German painter. Known for portraits and religious paintings; conducted school for tapestry painting (until 1801); director of Munich Acad. (1806). His son and pupil ¶Robert (1783–1846) was a painter; executed frescoes in churches in Munich.

Lang·er \ˈlaŋ-ər\, Susanne Knauth. 1895–1985. American philosopher, b. New York City. Taught philosophy at Harvard U. (1927–42) and at Connecticut Coll. (1954–62). Stressed importance of signs, symbols, and feelings in her study of language, art, and psychoanalysis. Author of *Philosophy in a New Key* (1942), *The Practice of Philosophy* (1930), *Feeling and Form* (1953), and *Mind: An Essay on Human Feeling* (1967, 1972, 1982).

Lang·er, William Leonard. 1896–1977. American historian, b. Boston. Taught at Harvard (1927–64; professor from 1936); consultant to federal agencies on intelligence matters. Author of *European Alliances and Alignments* (1931), *Diplomacy of Imperialism* (1935), *The Challenge to Isolation* (1952, with S.E. Gleason), *The Undeclared War* (1953, with Gleason); editor of *An Encyclopedia of World History* (1940).

Lang·er·hans \ˈläŋ-ər-ˌhäns\, Paul. 1847–1888. German pathologist. Discovered (1869) Langerhans's cell islands of the pancreas.

Lan·ge·ron \läⁿzh-rōⁿ\, Andrault de. Count. 1763–1831. French general in Russian service. General of division of Austerlitz (1805); distinguished himself at Leipzig (1813); stormed Montmartre and entered Paris with Allies (1814); governor general of New Russia (southern Russia, 1822 ff.).

Lan·ge·vin \läⁿzh-vaⁿ\, Paul. 1872–1946. French physicist. Taught at Collège de France (from 1902) and École Municipale de Physique et Chemie (from 1904); fled to Switzerland (1944). Known for work on secondary X-rays, the properties of ions in gases, the kinetic theory of gases, Brownian movement, the theory of magnetism, the theory of relativity.

Langey, Seigneur de. See Guillaume du BELLAY.

Lang·ford \ˈlaŋ-fərd\, Nathaniel Pitt. 1832–1911. American explorer and conservationist, b. Westmoreland, N.Y. To Montana (1862); helped organize vigilante committee at Bannack, later recounted in *Vigilante Days and Ways* (1890); appointed (1868) territorial governor but not confirmed by Senate. Helped organize and took part in expedition to Yellowstone Lake area (1870); instrumental in creation (1872) of Yellowstone National Park and its first superintendent and protector (to 1877).

Lang·ham \ˈlaŋ-əm\, Simon. 1310–1376. English prelate. Monk, prior, abbot of abbey of St. Peter at Westminster; treasurer of England (1360); bishop of

Ely (1361); chancellor of England (1363); archbishop of Canterbury (1366); cardinal (1368); forced to resign archbishopric (1368); died at Avignon.

Lang·hans \'läŋ-häns\, Carl Gotthard. 1732–1808. German architect. Director of royal buildings, Berlin (1788); designed the Hatzfeld Palace at Breslau (1766–74), the Brandenburg Gate (1788–91) and Bellevue Castle at Berlin, theaters at Charlottenburg, Potsdam, and Berlin, various Protestant churches in Silesia, etc.

Lang·horne \'laŋ-,hȯ(ə)rn\, John. 1735–1779. English poet. Rector of Blagdon, Somerset (1776–79). Best poem, *The Country Justice* (1774–77); known for translation, with his brother ¶William (1721–1772), of Plutarch's *Lives* (1770).

Lan·gie·wicz \län-'gye-vēch\, Marian Melchior. 1827–1887. Polish patriot. Leader of Polish insurgents in the district of Sandomierz (1863); dictator of Poland (March 10–21, 1863); defeated by Russians, fled to Austria, and was imprisoned (1863–65); later entered Turkish army under name Lan·gie Bey \län-'gye-'bā\. Wrote *Relacya o kampanii własney 1863 roku* (1905) and *Pisma wojskowe* (1920).

Lang·land \'laŋ-lənd\, William. c.1330–c.1400. English poet. Little known about his life; may have been native of Malvern Hills region and educated at Benedictine school at Great Malvern; may also have been a cleric in minor orders in London. Presumed author of the allegorical poem *The Vision of William concerning Piers the Plowman* (usually called *Piers Plowman*); the poem exists in three versions, the A text conjecturally dated 1370, the B text 1377–79, and the C text (which some scholars attribute to other author or authors) 1393–98.

Lan·glès \läⁿ-gles\, Louis-Mathieu. 1763–1824. French Orientalist. Instrumental in establishing École des Langues Orientales, in Paris, and its first administrator (1795).

Langley, Edmund of. 1st Duke of York. See EDMUND of Langley.

Lang·ley \'laŋ-lē\, Samuel Pierpont. 1834–1906. American astronomer and airplane pioneer, b. Roxbury, Mass. Professor of physics and astronomy, and director of Allegheny Observatory, Western U. of Pennsylvania, now U. of Pittsburgh (1867–87); invented bolometer for measuring distribution of heat in spectrum of sun (1878); measured solar radiation at various wavelengths and studied effect of solar activity on the weather. Secretary, Smithsonian Institution, Washington, D.C. (from 1887); there continued studies of solar radiation. Began study of possibilities of flight in heavier-than-air machines; built models of planes; his model no. 5 achieved a flight of 3000 ft. on Potomac River (May 1896), model no. 6 a flight of 4200 ft. (Nov. 1896), first flights of mechanically propelled heavier-than-air machines in the world. Full-sized machine, designed to carry an operator, failed in two trials (Oct. and Dec. 1903).

Lan·glois \läⁿ-glwå\, Charles-Victor. 1863–1929. French scholar. Authority on history of medieval France; professor, U. of Paris (1909); director, Archives Nationales (1913). Works included *Le Règne de Philippe III le Hardi* (1887), *Manuel de bibliographie historique* (1896–1904), *La Vie en France au moyen âge de la fin du XIIe siècle au milieu du XIVe siècle* (1924–27).

Langlois, Hippolyte. 1839–1912. French general. Noted for his classic treatise on artillery *L'Artillerie de campagne* (1891–92).

Langlois, Jean-Charles. 1789–1870. French soldier and painter. Best known for his paintings of military panoramas as *Bataille de la Moskova, Incendie de Moscou, Prise de Malakof.*

Lang·muir \'laŋ-,myu̇(ə)r\, Irving. 1881–1957. American chemist, b. Brooklyn, N.Y. Research chemist (1909–50), Research Laboratory, General Electric Co. Investigated electrical discharges in gases, atomic structure, thermionic emission and surfaces in vacuum, and chemical forces in solids, liquids, and surface films. Developed gas-filled tungsten electric lamp, a high-vacuum pump, high-vacuum electron tubes, an atomic-hydrogen welding torch. With Gilbert N. Lewis, originated the Lewis-Langmuir atomic theory; awarded the 1932 Nobel prize for chemistry for his work in surface chemistry.

Lang·ston \'laŋ-stən\, John Mercer. 1829–1897. American educator and diplomat, b. Louise Co., Va. Son of white planter Ralph Quarls and black slave Lucy Langston; professor of law and dean, Howard U. (1869–76); U.S. minister to Haiti and chargé d'affaires to Santo Domingo (1877–85). President, Virginia Normal and Collegiate Institute, Petersburg, Va. (from 1885). Member, U.S. House of Representatives (1890–91).

Lang·stroth \'laŋ-,strȯth\, Lorenzo Lorraine. 1810–1895. American apiarist, b. Philadelphia. Congregational pastor at Greenfield, Mass. (1844–48); interested himself in beekeeping; invented (1851) a movable-frame beehive which revolutionized the bee industry; developed methods of scientific management for large-scale honey production.

Lang·toft \'laŋ-,tȯft\, Peter. d. c.1307. English religious and chronicler. Canon of Augustinian priory at Bridlington; author of a chronicle in French verse dealing with history of England up to death of Edward I. The latter part of the chronicle was translated into English by Robert Mannyng (*q.v.*).

Lang·ton \'laŋ-tən\, Stephen. d. 1228. English prelate. Doctor in arts and theology, Paris (c.1181–1206); composed biblical commentaries and theological treatises. Made cardinal priest (1206); consecrated archbishop of Canterbury (1207) but kept out of see by King John (until 1213); at first sided with barons against John, and played important role in creation of the Magna Carta (1215); later withdrew and appeared as one of John's commissioners at Runnymede (June 1215); supported Henry III's party (1218–28) and responsible for reissue of Magna Carta (1225); promulgated (1222) set of constitutions still recognized as binding in English ecclesiastical courts.

Langton, Walter. d. 1321. English prelate and politician. A leading adviser of Edward I; greedy and unpopular as treasurer of the exchequer (1295–1307) and bishop of Lichfield (1296–1321); imprisoned (1307–12) and his holdings seized by Edward II; restored as treasurer (1312) in attempt by Edward to undermine power of lords ordainers, who forced Langton's dismissal from privy council (1315).

Lang·try \'laŋ(k)-trē\, Lillie. *Nee* Emilie Charlotte Le Bret·on \lə-'bret-ᵊn\. *Known as* the Jersey Lily. 1853–1929. British actress, b. Island of Jersey. m. 1st Edward Langtry (1874; d. 1897). First appeared professionally on stage in London (1881); most successful as Rosalind in *As You Like It;* toured provinces and U.S.; opened Imperial Theatre, London (1901); celebrated for her beauty.

Lan·guet \läⁿ-ge\, Hubert. 1518–1581. French diplomat and writer. Known for his *Vindiciae contra tyrannos* (1579), a treatise upholding daring theories on liberty of conscience and of thought, and rights of peoples against their rulers.

La·nier \lə-'ni(ə)r\, Nicholas. *Surname spelled with many variants, as* Laniere *and* Laneer. 1588–1666. English composer, singer, and painter. Court musician (from c.1613); painted scenery, composed music for, and sang in Ben Jonson's masque *Lovers Made Men* (1617), in which he was credited with introducing the Italian *stylo recitativo* into England; also composed music for Jonson's masques *The Vision of Delight* (1617), *The Gypsies Metamorphosed* (1621, with Robert Johnson), and *The Masque of Augurs* (1622, with Alfonso Ferrabosco); music master to Charles I and II.

Lanier, Sidney. 1842–1881. American poet, b. Macon, Ga. Served in Confederate army through Civil War; first flutist with Peabody Orchestra, Baltimore (1873); lecturer on English literature, Johns Hopkins U. (1879). Author of *Tiger-Lilies* (1867, novel), *Poems* (1877), *The Science of English Verse* (1880), *The English Novel* (1883). Among his best known poems were "The Symphony," "Corn," "The Song of the Chattahoochee," "The Marshes of Glynn," "Sunrise," "The Revenge of Hamish."

Lan·jui·nais \läⁿ-zhwʸē-ne\, Jean-Denis. Comte. 1753–1827. French politician. Member of Estates-General (1789) and National Assembly; Girondist member of the Convention (1792); member of the Council of the Ancients; elected senator (1800); opposed the Consulate (1802) and the establishment of the Empire (1804).

Lan·kes·ter \'laŋ-kəs-tər; 'lan-,kes-, 'laŋ-\, Sir Edwin Ray. 1847–1929. English zoologist. Professor at U. of London (1874–90), Oxford (1890–98), Royal Institution, London (1898–1900); director of British Museum of Natural History (1898–1907). Conducted important studies on protozoan parasites; contributed to comparative anatomy, embryology, parasitology, anthropology. Author of *Degeneration* (1880), *Science from an Easy Chair* (1908), *Great and Small Things* (1923), etc.

Lan·man \'lan-mən\, Charles Rockwell. 1850–1941. American Orientalist, b. Norwich, Conn. Professor of Sanskrit, Harvard (1880–1926). Author of *Sanskrit Reader* (1884); edited (from 1891) 31 volumes of "Harvard Oriental Series."

Lan·ner \'län-ər\, Joseph Franz Karl. 1801–1843. Austrian dance composer. Organized (1824) orchestra which achieved great popularity in Vienna; rival of the elder Johann Strauss, with whom he is credited with creating the modern Viennese waltz. Composed waltzes, galops, cotillions, quadrilles, polkas, and marches.

Lannes \lån\, Jean. Duc de Mon·te·bel·lo \də-mȯn-tā-bel-ō\. 1769–1809. French general. Son of a stable boy; joined national volunteers of Gers (1792); distinguished himself under Napoléon in the Italian campaign (1796) and the Egyptian expedition (1798–99). Took part in coup d'état which brought Napoléon to power (Nov. 9, 1799). Won victory of Montebello (1800); engaged at Marengo (1800), Austerlitz (1805), Jena (1806), Pułtusk (1806), Friedland (1807), and in Spanish campaign (1808–09). Created marshal of France (1804) and duc (1808); mortally wounded at Essling.

La Noue \lå-nü\, François de. *Nicknamed* Bras-de-Fer \brä-də-fer\, *i.e.* Arm of Iron. 1531–1591. French soldier. Became Protestant (1558) and took up Huguenot cause; lost an arm at Fontenay (1570) and had iron arm made. Commanded forces at La Rochelle (1572–73) and in Flanders (1578–80); captured and imprisoned (1580–85) by Spanish; mortally wounded at the siege of Lamballe. Published *Discours politiques et militaires* (1587) and *Observations sur Guicciardini* (1592).

Lan·re·zac \lä^{n}r-zák\, Charles-Louis-Marie. 1852–1925. French general. Commanded 5th army at outbreak of World War I; a capable tactician but driven back by German assaults; relieved of command (Sept. 1914).

Lans·bury \'lanz-bər-ē; -brē, *US also* -ˌber-ē\, George. 1859–1940. English politician. Joined Socialist party (1890); M.P. (1910–12, 1922 ff.). Leader of Labour party (1931–35); resigned because of extreme pacificism; visited (1937) Hitler and Mussolini in futile attempt to stop advance toward war.

Lans·dale \'lanz-ˌdāl\, Edward G. 1908–1987. American air force officer, b. Detroit. Joined U.S. army, rising to rank of major (1947); left army to join air force as captain, rising to rank of major general (1963). As U.S. adviser to Philippines, oversaw plan to counteract Communist insurgency; developed influential theory that Communist revolution could only be defeated by a program of social, economic, and political reforms as well as military operations; theory failed in Vietnam. Helped create the Special Forces (Green Berets).

Lansdowne, Marquis of. See William PETTY; Henry PETTY-FITZMAURICE.

Lan·sel \'län-sel\, Peider. 1863–1943. Romansh poet, b. Italy. Leader of revival of Raeto-Romance language and culture. Author of verse as *Il vegl chalamer* (1929), *La funtana chi staina* (1936), *Fanzögnas* (1939); short stories *Gruisaidas albas* (1931); critical study *Ils retoromans* (1935); and anthologies *La musa ladina* (1910) and *Musa rumantscha* (1950).

Lansfeld, Countess of. See Lola MONTEZ.

Lan·sing \'lan(t)-siŋ\, Robert. 1864–1928. American lawyer and public official, b. Watertown, N.Y. U.S. associate counsel, Bering Sea arbitration (1892); U.S. counsel, Alaskan Boundary Tribunal (1903), North Atlantic Fisheries Tribunal (1909–10); counselor, U.S. Department of State (1914–15). U.S. secretary of state (1915–20); arranged purchase (1917) of Danish West Indies (now Virgin Islands); negotiated Lansing-Ishii Agreement with Japan (1917); broke with Pres. Wilson by counseling importance of peace treaty over League of Nations.

Lan·ston \'lan-stən\, Tolbert. 1844–1913. American inventor, b. Troy, Ohio. Began (1883) working on typesetting machine; received (1887) patent for a "type forming and composing machine," and (1897) introduced commercially his perfected Monotype. Cf. Ottmar MERGENTHALER.

Lan·za \'länt-sä\, Giovanni. 1810–1882. Italian politician. Elected deputy to Piedmontese Chamber (1848); leader of center-left; held several ministries. Italian minister of interior (1864–65); prime minister of Italy (1869–73).

Lan·zi \'länt-sē\, Luigi. 1732–1810. Italian archaeologist and antiquary. Advanced theory of Greek influence on Etruscan civilization; his works included *Saggio di lingua etrusca* (1789), *Storia pittorica dell'Italia* (1792–96).

Lan·zo \'länt-sō\ *or* **Lan·zo·ne** \länt-'sō-nā\ of Milan. fl. 1042. Lombard noble. Led insurrection of common people that drove out noble classes from Milan (1041 or 1042); concluded peace treaty with nobles granting general amnesty (1043); subsequent fate unknown.

La·od·i·ce \lā-'äd-ə-sē\. 3d century B.C. Syrian queen. Wife of Antiochus II of Syria and mother of Seleucus II and Antiochus Hierax (*qq.v.*).

Lao She. See SHU SHE-YÜ.

Lao-tzu \'lau̇d-'zü\, *i.e.* Master Lao \'lau̇\. *Orig.* Li Erh \'lē-'ərk\. 6th century B.C. Chinese philosopher. Little of certainty known about his life, though unreliable information was provided by Ssu-ma Ch'ien (*q.v.*); many legends attached to him, as that he rebuked the young Confucius for his pride. Considered founder of Taoism; traditionally, author of *Tao-te Ching* ("Classic of the Way of Power"), now considered to be the work of many authors.

Lap·chick \'lap-(ˌ)chik\, Joseph Bohomiel, *called* Joe. 1900–1970. American basketball player and coach, b. Yonkers, N.Y. Played center for professional N.Y. Original Celtics (1923–27) and Cleveland Rosenblums (1927–30); coached St. John's U., Brooklyn (1936–47, 1956–65), won National Invitational Tournament four times; coached N.Y. Knickerbockers (1947–56).

La Pérouse, Comte de. See Jean-François de GALAUP.

La·place \lä-pläs\, Pierre-Simon de. Marquis. 1749–1827. French astronomer and mathematician. To Paris (1768); demonstrated his gift for mathematics to d'Alembert and through his influence obtained professorship in mathematics at École Militaire; minister of interior for 6 weeks (1799); entered Senate (1799), its vice president (1803). Announced (1773) discovery of the invariability of the planetary mean motions (a discovery of importance in establishing the stability of the solar system); with Lavoisier proved that respiration is a form of combustion (1780); devised theory of attraction between spheroids (1784–85); demonstrated that eccentricities and inclinations of planetary orbits to each other always remain small, constant, and self-correcting (1786); discovered dependence of the moon's acceleration on the secular changes in the eccentricity of the earth's orbit (1787); worked out laws of motion of the first three moons of Jupiter; set forth his nebular hypothesis in *Exposition du système du monde* (1796); discovered Laplace transform for solving partial differential equations; investigated tides, specific heats, capillary action, electricity, equilibrium of a rotating fluid mass; worked on theory of probability. Chief works: *Théorie du mouvement et de la figure elliptique des planètes* (1784), *Théorie des attractions des sphéroïdes et de la figure des planètes* (1785), *Traité de mécanique céleste* (1799–1825), *Théorie analytique des probabilités* (1812), *Essai philosophique sur les probabilités* (1814).

Lap·pa·rent \lä-pä-rä^n\, Albert-Auguste Co·chon de \kō-shō^n-də-\. 1839–1908. French geologist and mining engineer. Professor at Catholic Institute, Paris (from 1876); author of *Traité de géologie* (1882), *Leçons de géographie physique* (1896), etc.

Lap·worth \'lap-(ˌ)wərth\, Charles. 1842–1920. English geologist. Professor at Mason College, Birmingham (1881–1913). Published study of graptolite fossils of the Southern Uplands of Scotland (1873); established Ordovician System of geological strata (1879); made detailed study of the Durness-Eireboll region of the northwest Scottish Highlands (1882–83).

La Ra·mée \lä-rä-mā\, Pierre de. *Known by Lat. form* Petrus Ra·mus \'rā-məs\. 1515–1572. French philosopher and logician. Published (1543) *Aristotelicae animadversiones,* an attack on Aristotelian logic; in *Dialecticae partitiones* (1543) criticized university curriculum and argued for return to teaching of the seven liberal arts; works suppressed; forbidden to teach logic (1544–47); ban lifted by Henry II (1547); appointed professor at Collège de France (1551); embraced Calvinism (1561); persecuted thereafter by academic and ecclesiastic enemies; assassinated. His system of logic, known as Ramism, emphasized logic as method of disputation and had great influence in 16th and 17th centuries.

Lar·a·mie \'lar-ə-mē\, Jacques. d. 1821. American fur trapper, b. probably in Canada. Trapped (from c.1816) in Colorado and southeastern Wyoming; reached upper course of Laramie River. The Laramie Mountains, Fort Laramie, Laramie County, and Laramie, Wyo., were named after him.

Lar·baud \lär-bō\, Valéry-Nicolas. 1881–1957. French novelist and critic. Author of *Fermina Marquez* (1911), *A.O. Barnabooth, poésies et journal intime* (1913), *Enfantines* (1918), *Amants, heureux amants* (1923), *Jaune, bleu, blanc* (1927), *Aux couleurs de Rome* (1938), *Ce vice impuni, domaine française* (1941).

Lard·ner \'lärd-nər\, Nathaniel. 1684–1768. English biblical and patristic scholar. Founder of modern school of critical research in early Christian literature; chief work *Credibility of Gospel History* (1727).

Lardner, Ring, *in full* Ringgold Wilmer. 1885–1933. American short-story writer, b. Niles, Mich. Columnist for *Chicago Tribune* (1913–19) and Bell syndicate (1919–27). Author of humorous, satirical short stories collected in *You Know Me, Al* (1915), *Gullible's Travels* (1917), *Treat 'Em Rough* (1918), *The Big Town* (1921), *How to Write Short Stories* (1924), *The Love Nest* (1926), *Round Up* (1929), etc.; also wrote plays as *Elmer the Great* (1928, with George M. Cohan) and *June Moon* (1929, with George S. Kaufman).

La·re·do Brú \lä-'rā-thō-'brü\, Federico. 1875–1946. Cuban soldier and politician. Fought in war of independence (1898–99); led revolutionary movement against Pres. Zayas (1920–24); founder of Union Nationalist party; president of Cuba (1936–40).

La Ré·vel·lière-Lé·peaux \lär-väl-yer-lā-pō\, Louis-Marie de. 1753–1824. French politician. Member of Estates-General (1789), National Convention (1792), Council of Ancients (1795); president of the Directory (1795–99); proposed supplanting of Christianity with a deistic system.

La Rey, Jacobus Hercules De. See DE LA REY.

Lar·gil·lière *or* **Lar·gi·lierre** \lär-zhēl-yer\, Nicolas de. 1656–1746. French painter. Known for his portraits of important members of French and English courts, esp. Louis XIV and James II.

Lar·go Ca·bal·le·ro \'lär-gō-kä-bäl-'yā-rō\, Francisco. 1869–1946. Spanish labor leader and politician. Joined Socialist party (1894); imprisoned for political activities (1917–18); elected to parliament (1918); head of Unión General de Trabajadores (1925). Minister of labor in various governments (1931–33); his advocacy of an activist Socialist policy helped precipitate military coup (July 1936); prime minister (1936–37); undertook military reforms but unable to create a unified war effort among leftist parties; exile in France (1939); imprisoned by Nazis (1942–45).

La·ri·o·nov \lər-yi-'ō-nəf\, Mikhail Fyodorovich. 1881–1964. Russian painter and stage designer. Founder of Rayonism, an art movement synthesizing Cubism, Futurism, and Orphism and marked by its reduction of forms into rays of light; painted first Rayonist work *Glass* (1909) and published movement's manifesto (1913). To Paris (1914), where he produced abstract stage designs for Diaghilev's Ballets Russes, including *Le Soleil de nuit* (1915), *Contes russes* (1919), *Chout* (1922), *Le Renard* (1922). His wife ¶Natalya Sergeyevna Gon·cha·ro·va \gən-(ˌ)chə-'rō-və\ (1881–1962) was an original member of the Rayonist movement; to Paris with her husband (1914) and also executed stage designs for the Ballets Russes; designs included *Le Coq d'or* (1914), *Le Renard* (1922), *Les Noces* (1923), *Une Nuit sur le Mont Chauve* (1924), *Firebird* (1926), *Cendrillon* (1938).

La Rive \lä-rēv\, Auguste-Arthur de. 1801–1873. Swiss physicist. Professor (1823–46), secretary (1834–46), Académie de Genève; investigated specific heat of gases and temperature of the earth's crust; made discoveries in magnetism, electrodynamics, the voltaic cell, and the passage of electricity through gases; discovered a process for electrogilding. Author of *Traité d'électricité théorique et appliquée* (1854–58), etc.

La·ri·vey \lá-rē-ve\, Pierre de. *Orig. surname* Giun·ta \'jün-tä\. c.1540–1619. French playwright. Author of comedies adapted from Italian originals and written in prose, an innovation for the French stage at the time; regarded as one of creators of French comedy; his works included *Les Ésprits, Le Fidèle, Le Laquais, La Veuve, Les Jaloux* (all pub. 1579).

La Ri·vière \lá-rēv-yer\, Bureau de. d. 1400. French politician. Marmouset (trusted adviser) to King Charles V (1360–80); also provost of Paris and acted as premier chamberlain of France; designated custodian of the treasure (1374); a representative at peace talks with England (1376). Banished at beginning of Charles VI's reign; returned as real head of government (1388); imprisoned, his property confiscated by Charles's uncles (1392); pardoned (1394).

Lar·kin \'lär-kin\, Philip Arthur. 1922–1985. British poet. Librarian at several British universities. Considered by some the most gifted English poet of his time. Author of collected verse *The North Ship* (1945), *XX Poems* (1951), *The Less Deceived* (1955), *The Whitsun Weddings* (1964), *High Windows* (1974); edited *The Oxford Book of Twentieth Century Verse* (1973); published book of essays *Required Writing* (1983).

Lar·mi·nie \'lär-mə-nē\, William. 1849–1900. Irish poet. Associated with Irish literary revival; author of *Glanlua* (1889), *Fand and Moytura* (1892), *West Irish Folk Tales and Romances* (1893).

Lar·mor \'lär-mȯr\, Sir Joseph. 1857–1942. British mathematician, b. Ireland. Lecturer (1885–1903), professor (1903–32), Cambridge. Worked on mathematical problems in electrodynamics and thermodynamics; studied atomic structure. First to calculate rate of energy radiation from an accelerated electron and first to explain the splitting of spectrum lines by a magnetic field.

La Roche \lä-'rȯsh\, Sophie von, *nee* Gu·ter·mann \'gü-tər-ˌmän\. 1731–1807. German novelist. m. (1753) George M. F. von La Roche. Author of *Geschichte des Fräuleins von Sternheim* (1771), first German novel by a woman.

La Roche·fou·cauld \lá-rȯsh-fü-kō\, François de. Duc. 1613–1680. French moralist. Served in army in Italy (1629), Netherlands and Picardy (1635–36), Flanders (1639); intrigued against Richelieu (1635); joined the Fronde and was wounded at the siege of Paris; enjoyed the friendship of Mme de Longueville, Mme de Sévigné, and especially comtesse de La Fayette. His literary fame rests upon his *Réflexions ou sentences et maximes morales* (first pub. anonymously, 1665) and *Les Mémoires sur la régence d'Anne d'Autriche* (1662).

La Rochefoucauld-Lian·court \-lyäⁿ-kür\, François-Alexandre-Frédéric de. Duc. 1747–1827. French social reformer. Founded at Liancourt a school for the education of children of poor soldiers, later called École des Enfants de la Patrie. Member of the Estates-General (1789); émigré in England and U.S. (1792–99); during Empire served on state commissions on health, manufacturing, prisons; created a peer of France (1814).

La·ro·mi·guière \lá-rȯ-mēg-yer\, Pierre. 1756–1837. French philosopher. Censured by French parlement for holding that taxation was illegal; disciple of Condillac. Author of *Project d'éléments de métaphysique* (1793), *Les Paradoxes de Condillac* (1805), *Leçons de philosophie* (1815–18), etc.

La·rousse \lá-rüs, *Angl* lə-'rüs\, Pierre-Athanase. 1817–1875. French grammarian, lexicographer and encyclopedist. Founded publishing house and bookstore in Paris (1852); issued series of grammars, dictionaries, and other educational textbooks; founded journal for teachers *L'École Normale* (1859). Best known for his *Grand Dictionnaire universel du XIXᵉ siècle* (1866–76), in preparation of which he spent last years of his life.

Lar·ra y Sán·chez de Cas·tro \'lär-rä-ē-'sän-chāth-t͟hā-'käs-trō\, Mariano José de. *Pseudonym* Fí·ga·ro \'fē-gä-rō\. 1809–1837. Spanish journalist and satirist. Author of historical play *Macías* (1834) and novel *El doncel de Don Enrique el doliente* (1834); best known for bitter satires published over his pseudonym in various newspapers.

Lar·re·ta \lär-'rā-tä\, Enrique Rodríguez. 1875–1961. Argentinian novelist. Best known for historical novel *La gloria de Don Ramiro* (1908); also published novels *Zogoibi* (1926), *Gerardo o la torre de las damas* (1953), and *En la pampa* (1955), memoirs and essays *La naranja* (1948), plays, and poetry.

Lar·rey \lá-re\, Dominique-Jean. Baron. 1766–1842. French military surgeon. With Napoléon in Egypt and Russia; surgeon in chief, Hôpital du Gros-Caillou and Hôtel des Invalides. Credited with introducing field hospitals, ambulance service, and first-aid practices to the battlefield; first to note contagiousness of trachoma (1802); published first description of trench foot (1812).

Lar·sen \'lärs-ᵊn\, Esper Signius, Jr. 1879–1961. American petrologist, b. Astoria, Ore. Member of U.S. Geological Survey (1909–58); taught at Harvard (1923–49). Known for early investigations of radioactive dating and studies of igneous rocks. Wrote *The Microscopic Determination of the Nonopaque Minerals* (1934) and *Geology and Petrology of the San Juan Mountains, Colorado* (1935).

Lars Por·se·na \'lär-'spȯr-sə-nə\. 6th century B.C. King of Clusium. According to tradition, laid siege to Rome in attempt to restore Tarquinius Superbus as king of Rome and was forced to retreat by the heroism of Horatius Cocles and Mucius Scaevola (509 B.C.).

Lars·son \'lärs-sȯn\, Carl. 1853–1919. Swedish painter and etcher. Joined plein-airists at Paris; introduced Jugendstil into Sweden; later known for decorative genre scenes chiefly of his home and family life; also did mural paintings, portraits, witty drawings and caricatures, illustrations, etc. His home in Sundborn now a national museum.

Lar·tet \lár-te\, Édouard-Armand-Isidore-Hippolyte. 1801–1871. French archaeologist. One of founders of paleontology. Discovered fossils near Auch (1834); investigated anthropological remains in French caves; discovered evidence in cave of Aurignac that man existed contemporaneously with extinct mammals (1852); credited with discovering man's earliest art and with establishing a date for the upper Paleolithic period of the Stone Age. Published *Reliquiae Aquitanicae* (1865–75, with Henry Christy).

La Rue \lá-rue\, Pierre *or* Pierchon de. *Lat.* Petrus Pla·ten·sis \plə-'ten(t)-səs\. c.1460–1518. Flemish composer. In service of Philip the Handsome (1492–1506) and Margaret of Austria (from 1508); canon at Courtrai (1516). Representative of Flemish, or Netherlandish, style; composer of masses, motets, and other church music, French chansons, etc.

La Sale *or* **La Salle** \lá-sál\, Antoine de. c.1386–c.1460. French courtier and writer. In service of dukes of Anjou (1400–48) as soldier, administrator, tutor; governor of sons of Count Louis of Luxembourg (from 1448). Best known for his romance *Le Petit Jehan de Saintré* (1456); also wrote *La Salade* (1442), *Du Réconfort à Madame de Fresne* (1457), and *Lettre sur les tournois* (1459).

La Salle \lá-sál\, Jean-Baptiste de. Saint. 1651–1719. French religious and educator. Of noble family; ordained priest (1678); dedicated himself to education of the poor; with 12 companions founded (1684) Brothers of the Christian Schools (known as Christian Brothers), first purely teaching order of male non-clerics; founded schools, boarding schools, reformatories, training colleges for secular teachers. Canonized (1900) by Pope Leo XIII.

La Salle \lá-sál, *Angl* lə-'sal\, René-Robert Ca·ve·lier de \ká-vəl-yā-də-\. Sieur. 1643–1687. French explorer. Pioneer settler and trader near Montreal (1666); on expedition to Lake Ontario region (1669); later claimed to have discovered Ohio River at this time. Backed by Frontenac, obtained from Louis XIV grants (1673 and 1678) of lands and trading privileges in West. Descended Mississippi River to Gulf of Mexico (arrived Apr. 9, 1682), claiming whole valley for Louis XIV and naming the region Louisiana. Returned to France; named viceroy of North America; organized expedition for colonizing (1684); landed by error at what is now Matagorda Bay, Texas; on way to mouth of Mississippi, murdered by his men.

Lasca, Il. See Anton GRAZZINI.

Las·car·is \'las-kə-rəs\, Constantine. 1434–1501. Greek grammarian. Settled in Milan after fall of Constantinople (1453); taken under patronage of Duke Francesco Sforza; published elementary grammar *Erotemata,* first book printed in Greek (1476); taught Greek in Rome, Naples (1465–67), and Messina (1467–1501). His brother ¶John *or* Janus (c.1445–c.1535), Greek scholar and teacher; lived at Florence as librarian to Lorenzo de' Medici; after his patron's death, served French court in various diplomatic posts (from 1495); one of first teachers of Greek in France; collected many Greek manuscripts and produced editiones principes of the *Greek Anthology,* Callimachus, Musaeus, etc.

Lascaris, Theodore I and II. See THEODORE.

Las Ca·sas \läs-'käs-äs\, Bartolomé de. 1474–1566. Spanish missionary and historian. To Hispaniola as a planter (1502); ordained priest (1512 or 1513), first to be ordained in New World. Began (1514) to labor for Indians, preaching against slavery system; devoted life to this cause; to Spain (1515) to intercede with Ferdinand; unsuccessful in his model Indian colony at Cumaná, Venezuela (1520–22); became Dominican at Santo Domingo (1522); secured passage of laws to protect Indians (1542); bishop of Chiapas (1544–47); returned to Spain. Author of *Brevísima relación de la destrucción de las Indias* (1552) and *Historia de las Indias* (first printed 1875).

Las Cases \lás-käz\, Emmanuel-Augustin-Dieudonné-Joseph de. Comte. 1766–1842. French historian. Officer in royal navy; émigré in England (1790–1802); published *Atlas historique* (1802); given position on council of state (1809) and created count (1810) by Napoléon. Accompanied Napoléon to St. Helena and recorded his conversations (1815–16); the publication of his *Memorial de Sainte-Hélène* (1823) established the Napoleonic legend in Europe. Deputy for Saint-Denis (1831–34, 1835–39).

Lasco, Johannes à. See Jan ŁASKI.

La Ser·na y Hi·no·jo·sa \lä-'ser-nä-ē-ē-nō-'k̲ō-sä\, José de. 1770–1832. Spanish general. Major general, commanding Upper Peru (1816); viceroy (1821–24); captured by Sucre, with whole Spanish army, at battle of Ayacucho (Dec. 9, 1824).

Lash·ley \ˈlash-lē\, Karl Spencer. 1890–1958. American psychologist, b. Davis, W. Va. Professor at U. of Minnesota (1923–26), U. of Chicago (1929–35), Harvard (1935–55); director, Yerkes Laboratories for Primate Biology, Orange Park, Fla. (1942–55). Associated with John B. Watson on studies of animal behavior (1914–17); conducted pioneer quantitative investigations of relation between brain mass and learning ability; developed theory of equipotentiality of the cerebral cortex. Author of *Brain Mechanisms and Intelligence* (1929).

Las·ker \ˈlas-kər\, Albert Davis. 1880–1952. American advertising executive and philanthropist, b. Freiburg, Germany, of American parents. Joined (1898) Chicago advertising agency of Lord and Thomas; its sole owner (1912–42). Chairman, U.S. Shipping Board (1921–23). Established (1942) Albert and Mary Lasker Foundation for funding of medical research and public health projects.

Las·ker \ˈläs-kər\, Eduard. 1829–1884. German politician. Entered government service of Prussia (1856); member, Prussian Chamber of Deputies (1865–79), German Reichstag (1867–83); cofounder (1866) and a leader of National Liberal party; took part in consolidation of German empire and in many legislative and administrative enactments; withdrew from National Liberal party (1880) following differences with Bismarck over financial and economic policies, and joined secessionists (1881).

Lasker, Emanuel. 1868–1941. German chess master. Won world championship from Steinitz (1894) and held title until defeated by Capablanca at Havana (1921). Author of *Common Sense in Chess* (1896) and works on mathematics and philosophy.

Lasker-Schü·ler \-ˈshü-lər\, Else. 1869–1945. German writer. m. (1894) Jonathan Lasker; author of volumes of lyric verse, novels, and the play *Die Wupper* (1908).

Las·ki \ˈlas-kē\, Harold Joseph. 1893–1950. English political scientist. Professor at McGill U. (1914–16), Harvard (1916–20), London School of Economics (1926–50). Prominent member of Labour party, chairman (1945); embraced Marxism during 1930s in effort to explain Britain's "crisis in democracy." Author of *The Problem of Sovereignty* (1917), *Authority in the Modern State* (1919), *Communism* (1927), *Democracy in Crisis* (1933), *The State in Theory and Practice* (1935), *The Rise of European Liberalism* (1936), *Parliamentary Government in England* (1938), *The American Presidency* (1940), *Reflections on the Revolution of Our Time* (1943), *The American Democracy* (1948), etc.

Łas·ki \ˈläs-kē\, Jan. *Called* the Elder. *Lat.* Johannes à Las·co \ə-ˈlas-(ˌ)kō\. 1455–1531. Polish ecclesiastic and politician. Chancellor of Poland (1503–10); archbishop of Gniezno and thus primate of Poland (1510 ff.); undertook diplomatic missions to settle differences with Teutonic Knights; excommunicated (1530) by Pope Clement VII for supporting candidacy of John to Hungarian crown. Made extensive collections of Polish statutes, published as *Commune incliti Regni Poloniae privilegium* (1506) and *Statua provinciae Gnesnensis antiqua* (1525–28).

Łaski, Jan. *Called* the Younger. *Lat.* Johannes à Las·co \ə-ˈlas-(ˌ)kō\. 1499–1560. Polish religious reformer. Nephew of Jan Łaski the Elder; ordained priest (1521); friend and associate of Erasmus in Basel (1524–25). Became austere Calvinist; organized and preached throughout western Europe (from 1531); superintendent of London church of foreign Protestants (1550) and influential figure in Edward VI's court. To Poland (1556–60); aided in establishing and spreading principles of Reformation.

Las·ky \ˈlas-kē\, Jesse Louis. 1880–1958. American motion-picture producer, b. San Francisco. Organizer and head of Jesse L. Lasky Feature Play Co. (1914), which through merger later became Paramount–Famous Players–Lasky Corp. (1916–32); independent producer for Hollywood studies (to 1945); formed own company to make film biographies (1945). Produced over 1,000 pictures, including *Sergeant York* (1941), *The Adventures of Mark Twain* (1942), *Rhapsody in Blue* (1945), *The Great Caruso* (1951).

Las·salle \lä-ˈsäl\, Ferdinand. *Surname orig.* Las·sal \lä-ˈsäl\. 1825–1864. German Socialist. Disciple of Karl Marx (from 1848) and Socialist propagandist; took part in revolution of 1848–49 in Düsseldorf; settled in Berlin as political journalist (1859). Champion of the working classes (from c.1862); worked to change Germany from a bourgeois state based on private property to a democratic constitutional state; founded Der Allgemeine Deutsche Arbeiterverein (1863) to promote use of political power by workers; killed in a duel.

Las·sell \la-ˈsel, lə-ˈ\, William. 1799–1880. English astronomer. Became wealthy from his brewery business. Built observatory near Liverpool; catalogued many new nebulae. Discovered (Oct. 10, 1846) Triton, satellite of Neptune; Hyperion, satellite of Saturn (Sept. 19, 1848, simultaneously with George P. Bond); and (Oct. 24, 1851) Ariel and Umbriel, satellites of Uranus.

Las·sen \ˈläs-ən\, Eduard. 1830–1904. Belgian composer, b. Copenhagen. Succeeded Liszt as conductor of court theater in Weimar (1858–95). Composed operas *Frauenlob* (1860) and *Der Gefangene* (1865), two symphonies, songs, and music for Sophocles's *Oedipus*, Goethe's *Faust* and *Pandora*.

Las·se·ran Mas·sen·côme \lás-räⁿ-más-aⁿ-kòm\, Blaise de. Seigneur de Mon·luc \mōⁿ-lu̅e̅k\. c.1500–1577. French soldier. Fought in northern Italy (1521–22); with Francis I at Pavia (1525); aided in relief of Marseilles (1536) and distinguished himself at Ceresole (1544); governor of Moncalieri (1548–58); fought for Guise faction in Wars of Religion (1562 ff.); marshal of France (1574). Known for autobiographical *Commentaires* (1592).

Las·so \ˈläs-sō\, Orlando di. *Orig.* Orlande *or* Roland de Las·sus \ˈlä-su̅e̅s\. *Lat.* Orlandus Las·sus \ˈlas-əs\. 1532–1594. Flemish composer. Entered service of Ferrante Gonzaga (c.1544); in Italy (1544–54), esp. as maestro di capella of St. John Lateran at Rome (1553–54); called to Munich by Duke Albert V of Bavaria (1556); Kapellmeister (from 1563); ennobled by Maximilian II (1570); made knight of Golden Spur by the pope (1574). Regarded as leading composer (next to Palestrina) of 16th century; composed over 2000 works, including music for the seven penitential psalms, motets, masses, Magnificats, Italian madrigals and villanelle, French chansons, sacred and secular German songs, etc.

Lass·well \ˈlas-ˌwel, -wəl\, Harold Dwight. 1902–1978. American political scientist, b. Donnellson, Ill. Taught at U. of Chicago (1922–38); director of war communications research at Library of Congress (1939–45); professor, Yale Law School (1946–71). Revolutionized contemporary behaviorial political science by his pioneering studies of power relations and of personality and politics. Works included *Psycho-pathology and Politics* (1930), *World Politics and Personal Insecurity* (1935), *Politics: Who Gets What, When, How* (1936), *Politics Faces Economics* (1946), *Power and Personality* (1948), *Power and Society* (1950, with Abraham Kaplan), *The Policy Sciences* (1951, with D. Lerner), *The Future of Political Science* (1963), *The Signature of Power* (1979).

Last·man \ˈläst-män\, Pieter. 1583–1633. Dutch painter. Taught Rembrandt in Amsterdam (1624); works included mainly biblical and mythological subjects as *Odysseus and Nausicaa, Coriolanus and the Roman Woman, Baptism of the Chamberlain, Angel and the Prophet Balaam.*

La·sus \ˈlā-səs\ of Her·mi·o·ne \hər-ˈmī-ə-nē\. 6th century B.C. Greek poet. Rival of Simonides and teacher of Pindar; wrote hymns, dithyrambs, riddles; only 3 lines of a hymn extant.

Lász·ló \ˈläs-lō\. *Anglicized as* Lad·is·las \ˈlad-ə-ˌsläs\. Name of five kings of Hungary, first four of Árpád dynasty:

László I. Saint. 1040–1095. King (1077–95). Son of Béla I and brother of Géza I; conquered Croatia and Bosnia (1091); extended domain into Transylvania; supported Pope Gregory VII against Emperor Henry IV; established order and suppressed paganism; introduced a legal code; canonized (1192).

László II. 1131–1162. King (1161–62). Son of Béla II; supported by Byzantine Empire in his struggle with his nephew Stephen III.

László III. 1199–1205. King (1204–05). Son and successor of Emeric; reigned under regency of his uncle Andrew II.

László IV. *Called* the Cu·man \kü-ˈmän\. 1262–1290. King (1272–90). Son and successor of Stephen V; his mother a princess of the Cumans (a Turkic people that had settled in Hungary); allied with Rudolf I of Germany to defeat Otakar II of Bohemia in Battle of Dürnkrut (1278); adopted Cuman dress and customs; forced to wage war against Cumans, defeating them at Hódmezö (1282); involved in civil war against rival claimants to throne (1288–90); assassinated by a Cuman.

László V. *Bohemian* Lad·i·slav \lä-di-ˈsläf\. *Called* Post·hu·mus \ˈpäs-chə-məs, pä-ˈst(y)ü-, pōst-ˈhyü-\. 1440–1457. King of Hungary (1444–57) and of Bohemia (1453–57). Posthumous son of Emperor Albert II; under guardianship (1440–52) of the future Emperor Frederick III; guardianship later transferred to Ulrich, Count of Cilli; crowned king of Bohemia as Ladislav I (1453); under regency of George of Poděbrady in Bohemia and János Hunyadi in Hungary; caused murder of László Hunyadi (1457); fled to Prague, where he died.

László de Lom·bos \-de-ˈlòm-bòs\, Philip Alexius de, *Hung.* Fülöp Elek. 1869–1937. British painter, b. Budapest. To England (1907, naturalized 1914). Best known for his portraits of eminent men, as kings Edward VII and George V, Kaiser Wilhelm II, Theodore Roosevelt, Woodrow Wilson, Mussolini.

La Taille \lá-táy\, Jean de. c.1540–c.1607. French poet and dramatist. Author of tragedies *Saül le furieux* (1562) and *La Famine* (1573), comedies *Le Négromant* and *Les Corrivaux* (both 1573); poems *Le Courtisan retiré* and *Le Prince nécessaire;* and treatise on drama *De l'art de la tragédie* (1572), prescribing the Aristotelian unities of drama.

La·té·co·ère \lá-tā-kò-er\, Pierre. 1883–1943. French aircraft manufacturer. Founded (1917) aircraft-building firm; his Compagnie Latécoère began (Dec. 25, 1918) commercial air flights from Toulouse to Barcelona, later extended routes to Morocco (1919) and Dakar (1925); line renamed Compagnie Générale Aéropostale (1927), taken over by Air France after financial failure (1932).

La·teur \lá-tœ̄r\, Frank. *Pseudonym* Stijn Streu·vels \'strœ̄-vəls\. 1871–1969. Flemish writer. One of great masters of Flemish prose; nephew of Guido Gezelle; master baker at Avelgem (to 1905). Known for lyrical tales set in the villages of southwest Flanders; gained fame with short-story collection *Lenteleven* (1899); chief works included novels *Langs de wegen* (1902), *De vlaschaard* (1907), *De teleurgang van den Waterhoek* (1927), *Levensbloesem* (1937), and short-story collections *Zonnetij* (1900), *Dorpsgeheimen* (1904), *Het kerstekind* (1911), *Werkmenschen* (1926), and *Kerstwake* (1928).

La·tham \'lā-thəm, -t͟həm\, John. 1740–1837. English ornithologist. Author of *A General History of Birds* (11 vols., 1821–28), for which he designed, etched, and colored the illustrations himself.

La·throp \'lā-thrəp\, Julia Clifford. 1858–1932. American social-service worker, b. Rockford, Ill. Joined Hull-House, Chicago (1890); member, Ill. Board of Charities (1893–1901, 1905–09); helped found Chicago Institute of Social Science (1903–04); first chief, Children's Bureau, U.S. Department of Labor (1912–21).

Lathrop, Mary Alphonsa. *Known as* Mother Alphonsa. *Orig. name* Rose Hawthorne. 1851–1926. American religious, b. Lenox, Mass. Daughter of Nathaniel Hawthorne; m. (1871) George P. Lathrop. Author of stories, poems, *Story of Courage* on Visitation nuns (with her husband, 1894), *Memories of Hawthorne* on her father (1897). Founded sisterhood Servants of Relief for Incurable Cancer (1898), which became Dominican Congregation of St. Rose of Lima (1900); mother superior (1900–26); established Rosary Hill Home, Hawthorne, N.Y. (1901).

Lathyrus. See PTOLEMY IX.

Lat·i·mer \'lat-ə-mər\, Hugh. c.1485–1555. English religious reformer. Ordained priest (1515); gained reputation for his preaching at Cambridge; at first an orthodox Roman Catholic but later (c.1525) converted to Reformist doctrine; on question of lawfulness of Henry VIII's marriage to Catherine of Aragon, took king's side; on charge of heresy made complete submission (1532); after Henry VIII's repudiation of papal authority, cooperated with Cranmer and Thomas Cromwell in advising king (1534); bishop of Worcester (1535), resigned (1539) because he opposed Act of the Six Articles. By his preaching, established principles of Reformation in popular mind; for refusal to accept the Six Articles sent to Tower (1546); in Edward VI's reign resumed preaching but refused to resume his see; on Mary's accession committed to Tower; found guilty of heresy and burned at stake, with Nicholas Ridley.

La·ti·ni \lä-'tē-nē\, Brunetto. 1212?–?1294. Florentine writer and politician. Member of Guelf party; exile in France (1260–66); held public offices (from 1267), esp. chancellor of Florence (1273); friend and counselor of Dante. Chief work the prose encyclopedia *Li Livres dou trésor* written in Oïl dialect of northern France.

La Tour, Abbé de. See Isabelle de CHARRIÈRE.

La Tour \lá-tür\, Charles Tur·gis de Sainte-Étienne de \tü̅r-zhē-də-sa^{n}-tā-tyen-də-\. 1596–1666. French fur trader and colonial administrator. To Acadia (c.1600); built Fort La Tour at mouth of St. John River; made lieutenant governor of most of Acadia (1631); governor of Acadia (1653); kept post after English conquered territory (1654) and renamed it Nova Scotia.

La Tour, Georges de. 1593–1652. French painter. Known chiefly for candlelight subjects as *The Mocking of Job, The New-born, St. Joseph the Carpenter, The Lamentation over St. Sebastian;* also executed daylight compositions *The Hurdy-gurdy Player, The Sharper, The Fortune Teller.*

La Tour, Maurice Quen·tin de \kä^{n}-ta^{n}-də-\. 1704–1788. French painter. Portraitist to the king (1750–73); best known for pastel portraits as of Diderot, Voltaire, d'Alembert, Louis XV, Mme de Pompadour, and Jean-Jacques Rousseau.

La Tour d'·Au·vergne \-dō-vern^{y}\. Name of French noble family, originally from village of Latour in Auvergne, dating from 12th century; the senior branch held countships of Auvergne and Lauragais during 15th century; the junior branch held viscountcy of Turenne, duchy of Bouillon (from 1591), and principality of Sedan; Sedan ceded to France (1642) and family received (1651) duchies of Albret and Château-Thierry.

A leading member was ¶Henri de La Tour d'Auvergne (1611–1675), vicomte de Tu·renne \tü̅-ren\, soldier; served in Dutch War of Independence (1625–30); entered French army (1630); served with distinction in campaigns of Thirty Years' War against Imperial army in France and Italy (1635–40); secured reputation with capture of Turin (1640); made marshal of France (1643); given command of French army in Germany (1643); joined Swedes in conquering Bavaria (1645–48). Joined the Fronde (1649) but later reconciled to the court (1651); commanded royal armies against Condé (1652–58) and finally, in Battle of the Dunes (1658), completely defeated him; appointed marshal general (1660). Commanded armies of Louis XIV in invasion of Spanish Netherlands (1667); became a Roman Catholic (1668). Commanded French armies against the Empire (1672–75) in Holland, the Palatinate, and Alsace until killed in action at Sasbach.

La·treille \lá-trāy\, Pierre-André. 1762–1833. French entomologist. Father of modern entomology. Ordained priest (1786); head of entomology department (1799), professor (1829), Museum of Natural History, Paris. Established first detailed classification of crustaceans and insects. Published *Précis des caractères génériques des insectes disposés dans un ordre naturel* (1796) and *Histoire naturelle générale et particulière des crustacés et insectes* (1802–05).

La Tré·moille \lá-trā-müy\. Noble French family, including: Georges (c.1382–1446), member of king's council (1427) and grand chamberlain of France; exerted great influence over Charles VII; obstructed Joan of Arc's efforts against the English (1429–30); forced to retire from court by constable de Richemont (1433). His grandson ¶Louis (1460–1525), prince de Tal·mont \tál-mō^{n}\ *and* vicomte de Thou·ars \tü-är\, *called* Che·va·lier sans re·proche \shə-vál-yā-sä^{n}-rə-prȯsh\, defeated rebellious French princes at Saint-Aubin-du-Cormier (1488); commanded army of Italy and conquered the Milanese (1500); served gloriously in Italian campaigns until his death at Battle of Pavia. His grandson ¶François (1502–1541) succeeded to family estates; by marriage to granddaughter of Frederick of Aragon gained treatment as foreign prince at court.

François's sons founded three branches of the house: ¶Louis III (1522–1577) was made duc de Thouars and founded house of Thouars. ¶Georges established house of marquis of Rohan and comtes d'Olonne. ¶Claude (d. 1566) founded house of Noirmoutier.

La·trobe \lə-'trōb\, Benjamin Henry. 1764–1820. American architect and engineer, b. Fulneck, Yorkshire, England. To U.S. (1796). Introduced Greek Revival style to U.S. with design of Bank of Pennsylvania at Philadelphia (1798); designed and built Philadelphia city water supply system, first in America (1799). Surveyor of public buildings, Washington, D.C. (1803–17); designed south wing of the Capitol, made alterations in the White House, remodeled the Patent Office, and drew plans for the Marine Hospital. Designed and engaged in construction (1805–18) of Basilica of the Assumption of the Blessed Virgin Mary, Baltimore. In partnership with Robert Fulton to build steamboats (1813–15); lost his fortune on failure of scheme. Rebuilt Capitol (1815–17) after its destruction by British in 1814; died of yellow fever while directing work on New Orleans water supply system.

Lat·tre de Tas·si·gny \lá-trə-də-tá-sēn-yē\, Jean-Marie-Gabriel de. 1889–1952. French soldier. Entered army (1911); served in World War I and Morocco (1921–26); general (1939). Infantry division commander (1940); imprisoned by Germans (1942–43) but escaped to North Africa. Took command of French 1st army (1943); led it in Allied landing operations in southern France (Aug. 1944) and in drive across France, Germany, Austria. Commander of Western European Union ground forces (1948–50); successful as commander in French Indochina (1950–52).

Lau·be \'lau̇-bə\, Heinrich Rudolf Constanz. 1806–1884. German writer and theater director. Active in Young Germany movement and editor of its organ *Zeitung für die elegante Welt* (1833–34, 1843–44); director of Hofburgtheater, Vienna (1849–67), Leipzig Stadttheater (1869–70), and Vienna Stadttheater (1872–80). Author of works on the theater; travel sketches and stories as *Französische Lustschlösser* (1840); plays, including *Die Karlsschüler* on the young Schiller (1847) and the tragedy *Graf Essex* (1856); novels and stories, including trilogy *Das junge Europa* (1833–37).

Laud \'lȯd\, William. 1573–1645. English prelate. Ordained Anglican priest (1601); became zealous opponent of Puritanism; royal chaplain (from 1611); bishop of St. David's (1621–26). Intimate with Buckingham, gained free scope, from accession of Charles I, for his activities against Calvinists; supported Charles in conflict with Parliament; privy councilor (1626); bishop of London (1628); chancellor of Oxford U. (1630). Archbishop of Canterbury (1633); dedicated to absolutism in church and state; sought to root out Presbyterianism in Scotland and Calvinism in England; his attempt to impose Anglican liturgy in Scotland provoked riot in Edinburgh, which led to Bishops' Wars and the Long Parliament; accused of high treason; committed to Tower (1641); condemned and beheaded.

Lau·der \'lȯd-ər\, Sir Harry MacLennan. 1870–1950. Scottish music-hall comedian. To London (1900); gained great popularity for rendition of Scottish songs and ballads, many of his own composition, including "Just a Wee Deoch and Doris," "Roamin' in the Gloamin'," "Wee Hoose amang the Heather".

Lauder, William. d. 1771. Scottish Latin scholar and literary impostor. Sought to prove (1747), by means of forged, garbled, and interpolated quotations, *Paradise Lost* plagiarized from 17th-century Latin poets; exposed (1750) by John Douglas (*q.v.*).

Lauderdale, Earls and Duke of. See MAITLAND family.

Lau·don *or* **Lou·don** \'lau̇-dȯn, *Angl* 'lau̇d-ᵊn\, Gideon Ernst von. Freiherr. 1717–1790. Austrian field marshal. Joined Austrian army (1741); general in

Seven Years' War, distinguished himself at Prague and Kolín (1757) and at Hochkirch (1758); victorious at Kunersdorf (1759); defeated La Motte-Fouqué at Landeshut, stormed Glatz, but was defeated at Liegnitz (1760); captured Schweidnitz (1761). Commanded army in Bohemia as field marshal in War of Bavarian Succession (1778); commanded in Turkish war at capture of Belgrade (1789); commander in chief of Austrian armed forces (1790).

Lau·don·nière \lō-dòn-yer\, René Gou·laine de \gü-len-də-\. fl. 1562–1582. French colonist. Sent to establish colony in America (1562 and 1564); escaped to France when his settlement on St. Johns River, Florida, was devastated by Spaniards (1565); author of *L'Histoire notable de la Floride* (pub. 1586).

Laue \ˈlaů-ə\, Max Theodor Felix von. 1879–1960. German physicist. Professor, Berlin (1919–43); director, Max Planck Inst., Berlin (from 1951). Discovered (1912) the interference of X-rays in crystals and as a result was able to measure the wave lengths of X-rays and to study the structure of crystals; contributed to development of the theories of relativity, electromagnetism, and diffraction of light. Awarded 1914 Nobel prize for physics. Author of *Das Relativitätsprinzip* (1911), *Röntgenstrahleninterferenzen* (1941), etc.

Laugh·ton \ˈlòt-ən\, Charles. 1899–1962. American actor, b. Scarborough, Yorkshire, England. On stage and (from 1932) in motion pictures, chiefly in Hollywood, including *The Private Life of Henry VIII* (1933, Academy Award), *The Barretts of Wimpole Street* (1934), *Ruggles of Red Gap* (1935), *Mutiny on the Bounty* (1935), *Hunchback of Notre Dame* (1939), *Hobson's Choice* (1954), *Witness for the Prosecution* (1958). Naturalized U.S. citizen (1950).

Lau·mont \lō-mōn\, François-Pierre-Nicolas Gil·let \zhē-le\ de. 1747–1834. French mineralogist. Discovered the mineral laumontite, which is named for him.

Launay, Vicomte Charles de. See Delphine de GIRARDIN.

Lau·ra \lòr-ə\. 1308?–1348. French lady. Her praises were sung by Petrarch in his sonnets and canzoni; identified traditionally with Laure de Noves \də-nòv\, wife of Hugues de Sade, of Avignon.

Lau·ra·na \laů-ˈrä-nä\, Francesco da. c.1425–c.1502. Italian sculptor and medalist. Known esp. for his severely elegant portrait busts of women, including Beatrice of Aragon, Baptista Sforza, and Ippolita Maria Sforza; also executed series of medals for Duke René of Anjou, statues of the Madonna, and bas-reliefs in Italy and Sicily, and tombs and architectural sculpture in southern France.

Laurana, Luciano da. d. 1479. Italian architect. May have been related to Francesco da Laurana; named (1468) by Federigo, Duke of Urbino, chief architect of his ducal palace at Urbino; known esp. for executing palace's facade and courtyard; worked for Constanza Sforza on fortress in Pesaro (1476–79).

Lau·rel \ˈlaů-rel\, José Paciano. 1891–1959. Philippine politician. Elected to Senate (1925); associate justice of supreme court (1936). President of the Philippines (1943–45); defeated for presidency (1949); elected to Senate (1951).

Lau·rel \ˈlòr-əl, ˈlär-\, Stan, *in full* Arthur Stanley Jefferson (1890–1965), b. Ulverston, England, and his partner ¶Oliver Nowell Har·dy \ˈhärd-ē\ (1892–1957), b. Atlanta. American film comedians. Laurel came to U.S. (1910), joined Hal Roach studio as writer and director (1917); Hardy had acted in and directed comic films since 1913. During their partnership (from 1926), Laurel played the skinny, bumbling, innocent roles while Hardy took the fat, pompous, long-suffering parts; their 200 or so slapstick films included *Leave 'em Laughing* (1927), *Two Tars* (1928), *The Music Box* (1932), *Pack Up Your Troubles* (1932), *Babes in Toyland* (1934), *Way Out West* (1937), *A Chump at Oxford* (1940).

Laurence. See LAWRENCE.

Lau·ren·cin \lō-rän-san\, Marie. 1885–1956. French painter. Painted esp. delicate, idyllic pastels of young girls. Also known for her designs of decorations and costumes for the Comédie-Française and for the Ballets Russes of Diaghilev.

Lau·rens \ˈlòr-ən(t)s, ˈlär-\, Henry. 1724–1792. American Revolutionary statesman, b. Charleston, S.C. Export merchant in Charleston (1748?–64); planter (from 1764). Served in state assembly (1757–74, except for 1764–65); president, South Carolina Council of Safety (1775). Member, Continental Congress (1777–79), president (Nov. 1777–Dec. 1778). Captured by British (1780) on way to negotiate treaty with Dutch; exchanged for General Cornwallis (1782). On mission in France and England (1782–84). His son ¶John (1754–1782) was an officer on Washington's staff (from 1777); envoy extraordinary to France (1780); stormed British redoubt at Yorktown; negotiated terms of Cornwallis's surrender. Engaged in irregular warfare in South Carolina; killed in action.

Lau·rent \lò-rän, lō-\, Auguste, *orig.* Augustin. 1807–1853. French chemist. Professor at Bordeaux (1838–45); assayer at Paris mint (1848–53). Studied naphthalene and phenol and their derivatives; propounded the nucleus theory of organic radicals; with C.F. Gerhardt, worked on classification of organic compounds. Wrote *Méthode de chimie* (1854).

Laurent, François. 1810–1887. Belgian historian and legal scholar. Professor of civil law, Ghent (1836 ff.); championed liberalism and progressive ideas; worked on reforms of Belgian civil code and participated in philanthropic activities (after 1879). Author of *Études sur l'histoire de l'humanité* (18 vols., 1861–70), *Principes de droit civil* (33 vols., 1867–79), *Droit civil international* (1880–82), etc.

Laurentius. See also LAWRENCE.

Lau·ren·tius \lò-ˈren-sh(ē-)əs\. 5th–6th century. Antipope (498, 501–c.505). Elected in opposition to Pope Symmachus (498) but soon submitted; appointed bishop of Nocera in Campania, Italy; installed as pope by his followers after Symmachus fled Rome (501); civil chaos and factional wars ensued; eventually banished by Theodoric, king of the Goths.

Lau·ria \ˈlaůr-yä\ *or* **Lu·ria** \ˈlür-yä\ *or* **Lo·ria** \ˈlòr-yä\, Ruggiero di. 1250?–1305. Italian naval commander. Admiral of Aragonese fleet defeating French off Malta (1283), Angevin fleet in Bay of Naples (1284), French fleet off coast of Catalonia (1285); supported Frederick III's claim to Sicilian throne (1295); later changed allegiance to Angevin-Aragonese side and led its fleet to victory over Sicilians (1299, 1300).

Lau·ri·er \lòr-yā; *Angl* ˈlòr-ē-ˌā, ˈlär-\, Sir Wilfrid. 1841–1919. Canadian politician, b. Saint-Lin, Que. Member of Quebec legislature (1871–74) and of Dominion House of Commons (1874–1919); spoke in defense of Riel, for union between French and English in Canada, and against clerical intimidation in politics. Minister of inland revenue (1877–78). Leader of Liberal party (1887–1919). Prime minister of Canada (1896–1911); pursued policies of unrestricted reciprocity with U.S., protection of Canadian industry, construction of effective transportation system, development of western territories; defeated (1911) over reciprocity agreement with U.S.; thereafter leader of the opposition.

Lauriston, Marquis de. See Jacques LAW.

Laus·se·dat \lōs-då\, Aimé. 1819–1907. French army officer and geodesist. Served in army engineers (1840–79); professor at École Polytechnique (from 1856), Conservatoire des Arts et Métiers (from 1873); invented photogrammetry and the phototheodolite (1859); also invented several astronomical instruments.

Lau·ta·ro \laů-ˈtä-rō\. d. 1557. Chilean Indian chieftain. Led Araucanian Indians against Spaniards (1553–57); captured and executed Pedro de Valdivia (1553); killed in action at battle of Mataquito. His exploits are celebrated in *La Araucana* of the Spanish poet Ercilla y Zúñiga.

Lautreamont, le Comte de. See Isidore-Lucien DUCASSE.

Lau·trec \lō-trek\, Odet de Foix de \də-fwå-də-, -fwä-\. Vicomte. 1485–1528. French soldier. Marshal of France (1515); governor of Milan (1516–22); defeated by Spanish at Bicocca and forced to leave Italy (1522); returned and recaptured Milan (1527); died while besieging Naples.

Lauzun, Duc de. See Armand-Louis GONTAUT.

Lau·zun \lō-zœn\, Antonin-Nompar de Cau·mont de \də-kō-mōn-də-\. Duc. 1633–1723. French soldier. Colonel (1658), colonel general (1668) of foreign dragoons; sent to Bastille for insulting Louis XIV's mistress, Mme de Montespan (1669); captain of Louis's bodyguard (1669); imprisoned (1671–81) by Louis to prevent him from accepting the duchesse de Montpensier's offer of marriage; returned to Paris (1682), apparently married the duchesse in secret but estranged by 1684. Commanded French troops in Ireland in support of James II (1690); created duc (1692).

La·val \lå-vål\, André de Mont·fort de \də-mōn-fòr-də-\. 1411–1485 or 1486. French soldier. Served with Joan of Arc at siege of Orléans and at battle of Patay; marshal of France (1439); served faithfully in Charles VII's wars; raised siege of Beauvais (1472).

La·val \lä-ˈväl\, Carl Gustaf Patrik de. 1845–1913. Swedish engineer. With Klosters-Bruck Steel Works (from 1872); invented the centrifugal cream separator (1878). Pioneered in development of high-speed turbines (from 1882), esp. his Laval reaction turbine that spun at 42,000 rpm (pat. 1883); his inventions, as a divergent steam nozzle, the flexible shaft, and a special double-helical gear, formed foundation for most subsequent steam-turbine developments.

La·val \lå-vål\, François-Xavier de Mont·mo·ren·cy \mōn-mòr-än-sē\. 1623–1708. French prelate. Ordained priest (1647); vicar apostolic of New France with title of bishop of Petrea (1658); to Quebec (1659); first bishop of Quebec (1674–88). Laid foundation of Catholic church in Canada; founded (1663) Seminary of Quebec, later (1852) named Laval U. in his honor.

La·val \lå-vål, *Angl* lə-ˈvəl, -ˈväl\, Pierre. 1883–1945. French politician. Member of Chamber of Deputies (1914–19, 1924–27); mayor of Aubervilliers (1923–44); minister of public works (1925), of justice (1926), of labor (1930); senator (from 1927). Premier and minister of foreign affairs (1931–32); minister of labor (1932), of colonies (1934), of foreign affairs (1934–35); again premier and minister of foreign affairs (1935–36). Minister of state in Vichy government (July–Dec. 1940); as premier (from Apr. 1942) pursued policy of collaboration with Germany; executed for treason.

La Va•lette \lá-vá-let\, Jean Pa•ri•sot de \pá-rē-zō-də-\. 1494–1568. French soldier. Grand master (from 1557) of the Knights of Malta (Hospitalers); defended Malta brilliantly against Turkish assaults and siege (1565); built a new city and capital, named Valletta in his honor.

La Val•lière \lá-vál-yer\, Françoise-Louise de la Baume Le Blanc de \də-lá-bōm-lə-blä^n-də-\. Duchesse. 1644–1710. French noblewoman. Mistress of Louis XIV (1661–67), and mother by him of four children; superseded by marquise de Montespan but kept as official (although not actual) mistress (to 1674); retired to a convent (1674).

La•va•ter \'lä-vä-ter, lä-'vä-\, Johann Kaspar. 1741–1801. Swiss poet, mystic, and writer on philosophy and theology. Protestant pastor at Zürich (1786 ff.); founder of physiognomy. Author of *Aussichten in die Ewigkeit* (1768–78), *Geheimes Tagebuch von einem Beobachter seiner selbst* (1772–73), *Physiognomische Fragmente zur Beförderung der Menschenkenntnis und Menschenliebe* (1775–78); also lyric poems, dramas, epics, etc.

La•ve•ran \lá-vrä^n\, Charles-Louis-Alphonse. 1845–1922. French parasitologist. Military physician (1870–96); while in Algeria to study malarial fever (1878–83) discovered the blood parasite that causes it (1880); with Pasteur Institute, Paris (1896–1922). Awarded 1907 Nobel prize for physiology or medicine for his work on protozoal disease agents. Author of *Traité des fièvres palustres* (1884), *Traité d'hygiène militaire* (1896), etc.

La Vé•ren•drye \lá-vā-rä^n-drē\, Pierre Gaul•tier de Va•rennes de \gō-tyā-də-vá-ren-də-\. Sieur. 1685–1749. Canadian explorer, b. Trois-Rivières, now in Que. Joined French army (1697); took part in raid on Deerfield, Mass. (1704), and fought in War of Spanish Succession. Became fur trader at Lake Nipigon (1726); started western explorations in 1731; erected forts on Lake of the Woods (1732), Lake Winnipeg (1734), Assiniboine River (1738); pushed westward to upper Missouri (1738) and sent (1742) two of his sons to explore beyond the Missouri, thus becoming discoverers of Manitoba, the Dakotas, western Minnesota, perhaps part of Montana, and western Canada.

La•very \'läv-(ə-)rē, 'lav-\, Sir John. 1856–1941. British painter, b. Belfast. Known for portraits, interiors, and landscapes as *Polymnia, A Lady in Black, Spring, Game of Tennis.*

La•vi•ge•rie \lá-vēzh-rē\, Charles-Martial-Allemand. 1825–1892. French prelate. Ordained priest (1849); director of Oeuvre des Écoles d'Orient (1857); bishop of Nancy (1863), archbishop of Algiers (1867), cardinal (1882), primate of Africa and archbishop of Carthage (1884). Founded (1868) Society of Missionaries of Africa (White Fathers); opposed slave trade in Africa and founded (1888) Anti-Slavery Society.

La•visse \lá-vēs\, Ernest. 1842–1922. French historian. Professor at the Sorbonne (1888); director of École Normale (1909–19). Edited *Histoire de France depuis les origines jusqu'à la Révolution* (1908–11) and *Histoire de France contemporaine depuis la Révolution jusqu'à la paix de 1919* (1920–22).

La•voi•sier \láv-wáz-yā\, Antoine-Laurent. 1743–1794. French chemist. Founder of modern chemistry. Member of Ferme Générale (1768–91); director of state gunpowder works (1776); member of commission to establish uniform system of weights and measures (1790); arrested by order of the Convention and guillotined. Conducted quantitative experiments; disproved the phlogiston theory; explained combustion (1772) as the union of the burning substance with the part of the air that he later (1777) termed oxygen; with Pierre Laplace proved that respiration is a form of combustion (1780); propounded a theory of formation of chemical compounds; conducted experiments to determine composition of water and various organic compounds; with Berthollet, Guyton de Morveau, and Fourcroy, devised system of chemical nomenclature that served as basis of present system (pub. 1787); published chief work *Traité élémentaire de chimie* (1789).

La•von \'läv-ön\, Pinḥas. *Surname orig.* Lu•bia•ni•ker\ lü-'byän-i-kər\. 1904–1976. Israeli politician. Minister of defense (1954–55); accused of involvement in attempt to discredit Egypt by bombing U.S. and British installations in Cairo (Lavon Affair, 1954); later exonerated.

Lav•rov \(,)ləv-'röf\, Pyotr Lavrovich. 1823–1900. Russian revolutionist and scholar. Associated with revolutionary activities (1862); helped inspire the Narodnik (Populist) movement; in Geneva edited Socialist review *Forward* (1873–77).

Law \'lö\, Bonar, *in full* Andrew Bonar. 1858–1923. British politician, b. Kingston, N.B., Canada. To Scotland (1870); M.P. (from 1900); Conservative party leader (1911 ff.); secretary for the colonies (1915–16); leader of House of Commons (1916–21); chancellor of the exchequer (1916–18); lord privy seal (1919–21); prime minister of Great Britain (1922–23).

Law, Edward. 1st Baron El•len•bor•ough \'el-ən-,bər-ə, -,bə-rə, -brə\. 1750–1818. English judge. Leading counsel for Warren Hastings (1788–95); attorney general (1801); lord chief justice of England (1802–18).
His son ¶Edward (1790–1871), Earl of Ellenborough; M.P. (1813–18); entered House of Lords (1818); lord privy seal (1828); president of Board of Control for India (1828–30, 1834–35, 1841, 1858). Succeeded Lord Auckland as governor general of India (1841); entrusted war with the emirs of Sind to Sir Charles Napier, who neglected instructions and seized Sind for annexation (1842); invaded Gwalior and pacified the Marāthās at Maharajpur (1843); recalled by directors (1844). First lord of admiralty (1846). Author (1858) of home constitution of government of India carried into effect by his successor.

Law \lō\, Jacques-Alexandre-Bernard. Marquis de Lau•ris•ton \lò-rē-stō^n\. 1768–1828. French soldier. Grandnephew of John Law; aide-de-camp to Napoléon (1800); served in Austerlitz campaign, captured Ragusa (1807), and distinguished himself at Wagram (1809). Rallied to Bourbon cause at the Restoration; peer of France (1815); created marquis (1817); marshal of France (1823).

Law \'lö, *Fr* lō\ of Lauriston, John. 1671–1729. Scottish financier. Published banking reform plan *Money and Trade Considered* (1705); received permission to try plan in France; founded Banque Générale (1716), which issued paper currency and prospered; founded (1717) Compagnie d'Occident to finance his Mississippi Scheme for development of the lower Mississippi valley; director-general of finance (1720); fled on collapse of the scheme, due to overissue of stock (1720); died in Venice, poor and forgotten.

Law \'lö\, Sallie Chapman, *nee* Gordon. 1805–1894. American nurse, b. Wilkes Co., N.C. m. Dr. John S. Law (1825). Active in organization and management of Confederate hospitals during the Civil War.

Law, William. 1686–1761. English writer. Author of influential works on Christian ethics and mysticism, including *Practical Treatise Upon Christian Perfection* (1726), *Serious Call to a Devout and Holy Life* (1728), his best known work, which deeply influenced the Evangelical Revival, *The Spirit of Prayer* (1749), *The Spirit of Love* (1852), *The Way to Divine Knowledge* (1752).

Lawes \'löz\, Henry. 1596–1662. English composer. Gentleman of Chapel Royal (1626); a royal musician for lutes and voices (1631). Suggested to Milton composition of *Comus* and wrote music for it (performed 1634); composed music for the George Sandys version of *Psalms* (1638) and for *Choice Psalmes put into Musick* (with his brother William, 1648); published three books of airs (*Ayres and Dialogues for One, Two, and Three Voices,* 1653, 1655, 1658); best known for his continuo songs. His brother ¶William (1602–1645) composed music for some 25 dramatic productions, including Jonson's *Entertainment at Welbeck* (1633), Shirley's *The Triumph of Peace* (1634), Davenant's *The Triumph of the Prince d'Amour* (1635, with his brother Henry) and *Britannia Triumphans* (1638), Cartwright's *The Royal Slave* (1636, with Henry); also noted for his consort suites, fantasias, Psalms, anthems, keyboard music, etc.; killed fighting for Royalist cause.

Lawes, Sir John Bennet. 1814–1900. English agriculturist. Carried out agricultural experiments on estate at Rothamsted (from 1843, with J.H. Gilbert). Patented (1842) a mineral superphosphate for manure; established (1842) the first fertilizer factory, thus founding the artificial fertilizer industry.

Lawes, Lewis Edward. 1883–1947. American penologist, b. Elmira, N.Y. Warden of Sing Sing Prison, N.Y. (1920–41); author of works on prisons and penology, including *Twenty Thousand Years in Sing Sing* (1932).

Law•less \'lö-ləs\, Emily. 1845–1913. Irish writer. Among her books were *Hurrish* (novel, 1886), *Grania* (novel, 1892), *With the Wild Geese* (verse, 1902).

Law•rance \'lör-ən(t)s, 'lär-\, Charles Lanier. 1882–1950. American aeronautical engineer, b. Lenox, Mass. Designed (1921) the Lawrance J-1, the prototype of all modern radial air-cooled engines; chief engineer of Wright Aeronautical Co. (1923–29); developed the J-1 into the Wright "Whirlwind" series of engines that powered Lindbergh's *Spirit of St. Louis* and planes flown by Richard Byrd, Amelia Earhart, etc.; founded (1930) Lawrance Engineering & Research Corp. and served as its president (1930–44) and board chairman (to 1950).

Law•rence *or* **Lau•rence** \'lör-ən(t)s, 'lär-\. Saint. *Lat.* Lau•ren•tius \'lör-'ren-sh(e-)əs\. d. 258. Christian martyr. Deacon of Pope Sixtus II; according to tradition, burned alive on a gridiron.

Lawrence of Arabia. See Thomas E. LAWRENCE.

Lawrence *or* **Laurence** of Brin•di•si \'brin-də-(,)zē, 'brēn-\. Saint. *Orig.* Giulio Cesare de Ros•si \'rós-sē\ *or* Rus•so \'rüs-sō\. 1559–1619. Italian religious. Joined (1575) Capuchin Friars Minor, taking name Lawrence; ordained (1582); gifted linguist; a leading polemicist of the Counter-Reformation in Germany; established Capuchin houses at Madrid and Munich; canonized (1881); declared doctor of the church (1959).

Lawrence of Can•ter•bury \'kant-ə(r)-,ber-ē, -b(ə-)rē\. Saint. d. 619. Anglo-Saxon prelate. Accompanied St. Augustine of Canterbury on mission to Kent (597); succeeded Augustine as archbishop of Canterbury (604 or 605); attempted to convince Celtic Christians to adopt Roman customs; opposed by Edbald, whom he later converted.

Lawrence, Abbott. See under William LAWRENCE.

Lawrence, Sir Alfred Tristram. 1st Baron Tre·veth·in \tri-'veth-ən\. 1843–1936. English jurist. Lord chief justice of England (1921–22).

Lawrence, Amos *and* Amos Adams. See under William LAWRENCE.

Lawrence, David. 1888–1973. American journalist, b. Philadelphia. Published *United States Daily* (1926–33); founded *U.S. News* (1933), became *U.S. News & World Report* (1947). Author of widely syndicated political news column and *True Story of Woodrow Wilson* (1924), *Beyond the New Deal* (1934), *Nine Honest Men* (1936), *Diary of a Washington Correspondent* (1942), etc.

Lawrence, David Herbert. 1885–1930. English novelist. His novels, which analyzed the ills of modern industrial society and the role of sex in human conduct, included *The White Peacock* (1911), *The Trespasser* (1912), *Sons and Lovers* (1913), *The Rainbow* (1915), *Women in Love* (1920), *The Lost Girl* (1920), *Kangaroo* (1923), *The Plumed Serpent* (1926), *Lady Chatterley's Lover* (1928), *The Virgin and the Gipsy* (1930). Author also of plays as *The Widowing of Mrs. Holroyd* (1914), *David* (1926); verse as *Amores* (1916), *Birds, Beasts, and Flowers* (1923), *Pansies* (1929), *Nettles* (1930); short-story collections as *The Prussian Officer* (1914), *England, My England* (1922), *The Captain's Doll* (1923), *The Woman Who Rode Away* (1928), *Love Among the Haystacks* (1930); travel books *Twilight in Italy* (1916) and *Sea and Sardinia* (1921); literary criticism *Studies in Classic American Literature* (1923); and psychological works as *Fantasia of the Unconscious* (1922).

Lawrence, Ernest Orlando. 1901–1958. American physicist, b. Canton, S.D. Professor at U. of California, Berkeley (from 1930); founder and director (from 1936), Radiation Laboratory, Berkeley. Invented the cyclotron (1929); made researches into the structure of the atom, effected transmutation of certain elements, produced radioactive isotopes; applied radioactivity to the study of problems in biology and medicine. Awarded 1939 Nobel prize for physics and 1957 Fermi Award.

Lawrence, Sir George St. Patrick. 1804–1884. British soldier, b. Ceylon. Took part in Afghan War (1838–39); commanded forces in Rājputāna during Sepoy Mutiny; author of *Forty-three Years in India* (1874). His brother ¶Sir Henry Montgomery (1806–1857), soldier and Indian administrator, took part in first Afghan War (1838), Kābul expedition (1842), Sikh Wars (1846, 1848); president of board of administration of Punjab (1849–53); chief commissioner of Lucknow in charge of Oudh (1856); at outbreak of Sepoy Mutiny put in charge of troops in Oudh (1857); killed while holding Lucknow against mutineers.

Another brother ¶John Laird Mair (1811–1879), 1st Baron Lawrence, Indian administrator, became magistrate and land revenue officer, Delhi; commissioner and then lieutenant governor of Punjab (1853–57); curbed oppression by chiefs and devised land-tenure system; able to disarm mutineers in Punjab and to send loyal Sikh troops to relief of Delhi; viceroy of India (1863–69), developed sanitation, irrigation, railway extension, and opposed intriguing in Afghanistan; called "Savior of the Punjab" for his reforms.

Lawrence, Gertrude. *Orig.* Gertrud Alexandra Dagmar Lawrence Kla·sen \'klas-ᵊn\. 1898–1952. English actress. On stage (from 1910), chiefly in musical comedy and revue; first straight dramatic part in *Candlelight* (1929), later playing opposite Noel Coward in his *Private Lives* (1930) and *Tonight at Eight-Thirty* (1936–37) and leading roles in *Susan and God* (1935), *Skylark* (1939), *Lady in the Dark* (1940), *The King and I* (1951).

Lawrence, James. 1781–1813. American naval officer, b. Burlington, N.J. Entered navy as midshipman (1798); second in command to Stephen Decatur in raid to destroy the *Philadelphia* in Tripoli harbor (1804); in command of the *Hornet* (1812–13); raided British shipping; defeated British brig *Peacock* (Feb. 24, 1813). Transferred to the *Chesapeake;* was defeated and mortally wounded in engagement with British frigate *Shannon* (June 1, 1813), crying "Don't give up the ship" as he was carried below.

Lawrence, Stringer. 1697–1775. English soldier. Served at Gibraltar (1727), Flanders (c.1745), Culloden Moor (1746). Commanded all troops of East India Company (1748); with Clive as junior officer relieved Trichinopoly (1752, 1753–54); defended Madras during siege by French (1758–59); major general (1759); retired (1766). Credited as founder of the Indian army under British rule for his transformation of irregulars into an effective fighting force.

Lawrence, Sir Thomas. 1769–1830. English painter. Gained reputation for his portrait of Queen Charlotte (1789); limner to king (1791); painted Countess of Derby (1790), George III (1792). Principal painter to king in succession to Reynolds; went to Aix-la-Chapelle to paint sovereigns and diplomats (1818). Known for portraits of courtliness and social elegance, including those of Mrs. Siddons, Princess de Lieven, J.P. Kemble as Hamlet. Instrumental in securing the Elgin Marbles for the nation and in founding of National Gallery.

Lawrence, Thomas Edward. *Later (1927) changed surname to* Shaw. *Known as* Lawrence of Arabia. 1888–1935. British archaeologist, soldier, and writer, b. Wales. On expedition excavating Carchemish on the Euphrates River (1911–14). Served in World War I (1914–18), major (1917), lieutenant colonel (1918); attached to General Wingate's staff in the Hejaz expeditionary force (1917), to General Allenby's staff (1918); leader of the Arab revolt against the Turks (1917–18), which he described in *The Seven Pillars of Wisdom* (1926), and its abbreviated version *Revolt in the Desert* (1927). Adviser on Arab affairs at the Colonial Office (1921–22). Joined (Aug. 1922) Royal Air Force as an enlisted man under name John Hume Ross, discharged (Dec. 1922); joined (1923) Royal Tank Corps under name T.E. Shaw, transferred to RAF (1925), discharged (1935). Published prose translation of the *Odyssey* (1932); wrote memoir of RAF life *The Mint* (pub. 1955); killed in motorcycle accident.

Lawrence, William. 1783–1848. American merchant, b. Groton, Mass. An organizer of first incorporated company to manufacture woolen goods, with plant at Lowell, Mass. (c.1825); contributed to endowment of academy in Groton, named Lawrence Academy in his honor (1846). His brother ¶Amos (1786–1852), b. Groton, established (1807) in Boston a mercantile firm, headed it (to 1831), and made it into one of largest in U.S.; well known for his benefactions.

Another brother ¶Abbott (1792–1855), b. Groton, was in partnership with Amos (from 1814); founded and developed textile manufacturing city of Lawrence, Mass. (from 1845); promoted New England railways; member, U.S. House of Representatives (1835–37, 1839–40); U.S. minister to Great Britain (1849–52); contributed to Harvard College, where the Lawrence Scientific School was named in his honor. A son of Amos ¶Amos Adams (1814–1886), b. Boston, was commission merchant and textile manufacturer; contributed to various causes, establishing Lawrence Coll., Appleton, Wis., and a college at Lawrence, Kan., which became nucleus of U. of Kansas; identified himself with antislavery agitation, gave money to John Brown.

Lawrence Jus·tin·i·an \jə-'stin-ē-ən\. Saint. 1381–1456. Italian religious. Augustinian monk; general of his order (1424–31); bishop of Castello (1433); first patriarch of Venice (1451).

Laws \'lȯz\, Samuel Spahr. 1824–1921. American educator, b. Ohio Co., Va. (now W. Va.). President, Westminster College, Fulton, Mo. (1855–61); vice president, New York Gold Exchange (c.1865); invented the stock ticker. Professor of philosophy and president, U. of Missouri (1876–89); professor of natural science, Presbyterian Theol. Sem. (1893–98). Author of *Metaphysics* (1879), *Christianity: Its Nature* (1903), etc.

Law·son \'lȯ-sən\, Andrew Cowper. 1861–1952. American geologist, b. Anstruther, Scotland. Professor (1890–1928), U. of California, Berkeley. Headed commission investigating 1906 California earthquake. Worked in geology, petrography, economic geology, geomorphology, seismology, etc.

Lawson, Edward Levy- *and* Harry Lawson Webster. See Edward LEVY-LAWSON.

Lawson, Henry. *Orig. surname* Lar·sen \'lär-sən\. *Middle name sometimes given as* Hertzberg *or* Archibald. 1867–1922. Australian writer. Author of short stories and ballad-like verse noted for realistic portrayals of bush life; books included *In the Days When the World Was Wise* (1896), *While the Billy Boils* (1896), *On the Track and over the Sliprails* (1900), *Joe Wilson and His Mates* (1901), *Children of the Bush* (1902), *When I Was King* (1905), *Triangles of Life* (1913), etc.

Lawson, John. d. 1711. English colonist. Surveyor general of North Carolina (1708); helped settle North Carolina; a founder of New Bern, N.C. Author of *A New Voyage to Carolina* (1709).

Lawson, Thomas William. 1857–1925. American stock market speculator, b. Charlestown, Mass. Associated with J.E.O. Addicks in promotion of Amalgamated Copper Co. (1897). Author of *Frenzied Finance* (an account of stock market operations in Amalgamated Copper, 1902), *Friday, the Thirteenth* (1907), *The Remedy* (1912), etc.

Lawson, Victor Fremont *or* Freemont. 1850–1925. American journalist, b. Chicago. Bought from Melville E. Stone an interest in Chicago *Daily News* (1876), sole proprietor (1888–1925); took over Chicago *Evening Post* (1878); published Chicago *Record* (1881), later (1883) merged with *Times-Herald* to become Chicago *Record-Herald* (sold his interest, 1914). Director (1893–1925) and president (1894–1900), Associated Press. Pioneer in development of foreign news service.

Law·ton \'lȯt-ᵊn\, Henry Ware. 1843–1899. American soldier, b. Manhattan, Ohio. Volunteer in Union army through Civil War; entered regular army (1867); served in frontier Indian fighting; pursued and captured Geronimo (1886). Major general of volunteers, serving in Cuba in Spanish–American War (1898), and in Philippines suppressing rebellion (1899).

Lay \'lā\, Horatio Nelson. 1832–1898. English diplomat. Organized (1855) and headed (1855–64) Maritime Customs Bureau to collect tariffs for the Chinese government.

Lay·a·mon \'lī-ə-mən, 'lā-ə-\. fl. 1200. English poet. Priest of Areley Regis in Worcestershire. Using Wace's *Roman de Brut* as source, wrote (c.1200) the *Brut,* an unrhymed, alliterative romance-chronicle, earliest considerable English poem.

Lay·ard \'lā-ˌärd, -ərd\, Sir Austen Henry. 1817–1894. English archaeologist and diplomat. Excavated Assyrian city of Calah (1845–47); at Nineveh, discovered (1849–51) palace of Sennacherib, much artwork, and many cuneiform tablets from the state archives. Liberal M.P. (1852–57, 1860–69); minister at Madrid (1869–77) and Constantinople (1877–80). Author of *Nineveh and its Remains* (1848–49), *Discoveries in the Ruins of Nineveh and Babylon* (1853). See also Hormuzd RASSAM and Sir H. C. RAWLINSON.

La·za·rev \ˈlá-zər-yif\, Pyotr Petrovich. 1878–1942. Soviet physicist and biophysicist. Director of Biophysics Inst., Moscow (1920–31), and of Biophysical Laboratories of Soviet Academy of Sciences (1938–42). Investigated photochemistry and molecular physics; known for his physico-chemical theory of the movement of ions and the consequent theory of excitation in living matter.

La·zar Hre·bel·ja·no·vić \ˈlá-zár-hreb-el-ˈyá-nò-vētʸ\. 1329–1389. Prince of the Serbs (1371–89). Led allied army of Serbs, Bosnians, Albanians, etc., in defeat of Turks under Murad I at Pločnik (1386); totally defeated and slain at battle of Kosovo.

Laz·a·rus \ˈlaz-(ə-)rəs\, Emma. 1849–1887. American poet and essayist, b. New York City. Published *Admetus and Other Poems* (1871), *Alide: An Episode of Goethe's Life* (prose romance, 1874), *The Spagnoletto* (verse tragedy, 1876), *Songs of a Semite* (verse, 1882), *By the Waters of Babylon* (prose poems, 1887); best known for sonnet "The New Colossus" (1883) inscribed at base of Statue of Liberty. Championed oppressed Jews during persecution in Russia (1879–83); organized relief work.

Laz·a·rus \ˈlät-sä-rüs\, Moritz. 1824–1903. German philosopher. Professor at Bern (1860–66), Kriegsakademie, Berlin (1867–73), U. of Berlin (1873). Founder of comparative psychology (with H. Steinthal and W. Wundt); with Steinthal founded journal *Zeitschrift für Volkerpsychologie und Sprachwissenschaft* (1859); a leading defender of Judaism against anti-Semitic attacks. Author of *Das Leben der Seele* (1855–57), *Treu und Frei* (1887), *Die Ethik des Judenthums* (1898–1911), etc.

La·zear \lə-ˈzi(ə)r\, Jesse William. 1866–1900. American physician, b. Baltimore Co., Md. Entered U.S. army medical corps (1900). Member, with Walter Reed, James Carroll, and Aristides Agramonte, of the Yellow Fever Commission (1900); while in Cuba studying the disease, died from bite of infected mosquito.

La·zhech·ni·kov \(ˌ)lə-ˈzhāch-nyi-kəf\, Ivan Ivanovich. 1792–1869. Russian novelist and playwright. Among his many historical novels were *Posledniy Novik* (1831–33), *Ledyanov dom* (1835), *Basurman* (1838); his drama *Oprichniki* (1842) used as text of opera by Tchaikovsky.

Lea \ˈlē\, Homer. 1876–1912. American soldier, b. Denver. Aided in relief of Peking during Boxer rebellion; general in Chinese army (1909); adviser to Sun Yat-sen (1911–12). Author of novel *The Vermillion Pencil* (1908) and military analysis *The Valor of Ignorance* (1909) which predicted a U.S.–Japanese war much like that in World War II.

Leach \ˈlēch\, Bernard Howell. 1887–1979. British potter, b. Hong Kong. Trained in Oriental ceramic tradition; established (1920) Leach Pottery at St. Ives, Cornwall; greatly influenced contemporary ceramic design. Wrote *A Potter's Book* (1940), *A Potter's Portfolio* (1951), *The Kenzan Tradition* (1966), etc.

Lea·cock \ˈlē-ˌkäk\, Stephen Butler. 1869–1944. Canadian economist and humorist, b. Swanmore, Hampshire, England. Professor and head of economics department, McGill U., Montreal (1908–36). Author of *Elements of Political Science* (1906), *Humour: Its Theory and Technique* (1935), and many humorous publications, beginning with *Literary Lapses* (1910) and including *Nonsense Novels* (1911), *Sunshine Sketches of a Little Town* (1912), *Arcadian Adventures with the Idle Rich* (1914), *Moonbeams from the Larger Lunacy* (1915), *Frenzied Fiction* (1917), *My Discovery of England* (1922), *Afternoons in Utopia* (1932), *Laugh Parade* (1940), *My Remarkable Uncle* (1942).

Leadbelly. See Huddie LEDBETTER.

Lea·hy \ˈlā-(ˌ)hē\, William Daniel. 1875–1959. American naval officer, b. Hampton, Ia. Commissioned in navy (1897); served in Spanish–American War, Philippine insurrection, Boxer Rebellion, World War I. Rear admiral (1930); admiral (1936); chief of naval operations (1937–39); retired (1939). Governor of Puerto Rico (1939–40); ambassador to France (1940–42). Chief of staff to Pres. Roosevelt (1942–45), Pres. Truman (1945–49). Admiral of the fleet (1944).

Leake \ˈlēk\, William Martin. 1777–1860. English antiquarian and classical topographer. Army officer (1794–1815). Collected Greek coins and inscriptions; presented his collection of Greek marbles to British Museum (1839). Known for topographical researches recorded in *Athens* (1821), *Morea* (1830), *Northern Greece* (1835).

Lea·key \ˈlē-kē\, Louis Seymour Bazett. 1903–1972. British anthropologist, b. Kenya. Curator of Coryndon Museum, Nairobi (1945–61). His discovery of fossil hominids at Olduvai Gorge, Tanzania, proved that human evolution was centered in Africa, not Asia; propounded several controversial theories, as that *Homo habilis* was direct ancestor of modern man. Author of *Adam's Ancestors* (1934), *White African* (1937), *Olduvai Gorge* (1952), *Unveiling Man's Origins* (1969, with Vanne Goodall), etc.

Le·al \ˈlā-äl\, Antonio Duarte Go·mes \ˈgō-mish\. 1848–1921. Portuguese poet. Author of *Tributo de sangue* (1873), *Claridades do sul* (1875), *A fome de Camões* (1880), *O anticristo* (1886), *A mulher de lucto* (1902); also wrote political pamphlets supporting the Republican movement.

Le·an·der \lē-ˈan-dər\. Saint. d. c.1600. Spanish prelate. Older brother of saints Florentina, Fulgentius, and Isidore; friend of Gregory the Great; archbishop of Seville (c.1577); converted the Visigoths from Arianism; considered organizer of the church in Spain.

Lear \ˈli(ə)r\, Edward. 1812–1888. English painter and nonsense poet. Published *Illustrations of the Family of the Psittacidae* (1832); employed by 13th Earl of Derby to draw Knowsley menagerie (1832–36); composed his first *Book of Nonsense* (1846, enlarged 1861, 1863); set up studio as topographical landscape painter in Rome (1837); recounted travels through Mediterranean countries in 7 travel books with delicately penned sketches, including *Illustrated Excursions in Italy* (1846) and *Journal of a Landscape Painter in Greece and Albania* (1851); executed large oil paintings showing Pre-Raphaelite influence. Author also of *Nonsense Songs, Stories, Botany and Alphabets* (1871), *More Nonsense, Pictures, Rhymes, Botany, etc.* (1872), *Laughable Lyrics* (1877), *Queery Leary Nonsense* (1911).

Lear, Tobias. 1762–1816. American diplomat, b. Portsmouth, N.H. Private secretary (1785–92) and military secretary (1798–99) to George Washington. U.S. consul at Algiers (1803–12); negotiated treaty (1805) with pasha of Tripoli, agreeing to ransom American prisoners.

Lear, William Powell. 1902–1978. American electronic engineer and manufacturer, b. Hannibal, Mo. Founded (1934) Lear Avia Corp. to produce aircraft navigational equipment; formed and headed (1939–62) Lear, Inc., manufacturer of military and aircraft products; organized (1962) Lear Jet Corp. to produce his small jet aircraft for private use; his Lear Motors Corp. (1967) attempted to develop steam-powered automobiles and buses.

Learmont, Thomas. See THOMAS of Erceldoune.

Lease \ˈlēs\, Mary Elizabeth, *nee* Cly·ens \ˈklī-ənz, -ən(t)s\. 1853–1933. American reformer, b. Ridgway, Pa. m. Charles Lease (1873; div. 1902); vigorous and effective orator in Kansas for Populist movement (1890–96); political writer for *New York World* (1896); spoke in N.Y. for prohibition, woman suffrage, and other causes; lecturer for N.Y.C. Board of Education (1902–18). Wrote *The Problem of Civilization Solved* (1895).

Lea·ven·worth \ˈlev-ən-ˌwərth\, Henry. 1783–1834. American soldier, b. New Haven, Conn. Served in War of 1812; on frontier duty (from 1818); built (1827) post (now Fort Leavenworth) in Kansas; commander of Jefferson Barracks, near St. Louis (1829); commander of entire southwest frontier (1834). Leavenworth, Kans., was named in his honor.

Lea·vis \ˈlē-vəs\, Frank Raymond. 1895–1978. English literary critic. Founder and editor (1932–53) of literary quarterly *Scrutiny;* taught English literature at Cambridge (1936–62); controversial for maintaining that literature should be a criticism of life and that criticism should be based on an author's moral position. Author of *Mass Civilization and Minority Culture* (1930), *New Bearings in English Poetry* (1932), *Revaluation* (1936), *The Great Tradition* (1948), *The Common Pursuit* (1952), *D.H. Lawrence* (1955), *Anna Karenina and Other Essays* (1968), *Dickens the Novelist* (1970), etc.

Lea·vitt \ˈlē-vət\, Henrietta Swan. 1868–1921. American astronomer, b. Lancaster, Mass. On staff of Harvard Observatory (from 1895); chief of photographic photometry department. Discovered 4 novae and some 2,400 variable stars; discovered that periods of Cepheid variable stars are closely related to their true brightness (1912).

Le·bau·dy \lə-bō-dē\, Paul. 1858–1937. French industrialist. With his brother Pierre, built a number of semirigid dirigibles, among which were the first military dirigible (1902) and the first English dirigible, which made round trip across the English Channel (1910).

Lebbaeus, Saint. See JUDAS.

Le·be·dev \ˈlyā-byid-yif\, Pyotr Nikolayevich. 1866–1912. Russian physicist. Professor, Moscow U. (1900–11); proved existence of, and measured, minute pressure exercised on bodies by light; investigated the earth's magnetism. Published *Experimental Research on Light Pressure* (1901).

Lebedev, Sergey Vasilyevich. 1874–1934. Russian chemist. Professor at Military Medical Academy, St. Petersburg (1917–34); established (1925) Laboratory for Petroleum Refining at St. Petersburg U. Produced an elastic rubber by polymerizing butadiene; developed a method for industrial production of synthetic rubber (1927–30).

Le Bel, Jean. See JEAN LE BEL.

Le Bel \lə-bel\, Joseph-Achille. 1847–1930. French chemist. Investigated optical activity and fermentation; propounded theory of asymmetric carbon atom independently of van't Hoff (1874); sought to determine existence of optically active compounds of nitrogen (1891).

Le·besgue \lə-beg\, Henri-Léon. 1875–1941. French mathematician. Taught at the Sorbonne (1910–21); professor, Collège de France (1921). His Lebesgue integral (1901), a generalization of the Riemann integral, revolutionized the field of integration; also contributed to topology, Fourier series, and potential theory. Wrote *Leçons sur l'intégration et la recherche des fonctions primitives* (1904) and *Leçons sur les séries trigonométriques* (1906).

Le·blanc \lə-blä^n\, Maurice-Marie-Émile. 1864–1941. French novelist. Known for his detective fiction with Arsène Lupin as the central character.

Leblanc, Nicolas. 1742–1806. French chemist. Surgeon (1780–93) to the household of the duc d'Orléans (Philippe-Égalité); invented process for the manufacture of soda from common salt (1789).

Le Blon \lə-blō^n\, Jakob Christoph. 1670–1741. German painter and engraver. Noted for his miniatures; to London, where he set up process of printing engravings in color to imitate paintings (1720), described in *Il coloretto* (1730); inventor of modern system of chromolithography.

Le·blond \lə-blō^n\, Alexandre-Jean-Baptiste. 1679–1719. French landscape designer. Collaborated with André Le Nôtre in designs of parterres; designed the gardens, in manner of Versailles, of Peter the Great's Peterhof palace near St. Petersburg.

Leblond, Marius and Ary. See Georges ATHENAS.

Le·boeuf \lə-bœf\, Edmond. 1809–1888. French soldier. Distinguished himself in siege of Constantine (1837) and in Italian campaign (1859); aide-de-camp to Napoléon III. Minister of war (1869–70); marshal of France (1870). Took command of III army corps (1870); fought well at Mars-la-Tour against Prussians; captured at Metz and imprisoned in Germany (1870–71); lived in retirement in France thereafter.

Le Bon \lə-bō^n\, Gustave. 1841–1931. French sociologist. Known for his study of psychological characteristics of crowds and his elitist theory of social evolution. Author of *L'Homme et les sociétés* (1881), *Les Lois psychologiques de l'évolution des peuples* (1894), *La Psychologie des foules* (1895), *Psychologie du socialisme* (1898), *La Révolution française et la psychologie des révolutions* (1912), *L'Évolution actuelle du monde* (1927), etc.

Le·bon \lə-bō^n\, Philippe. 1767–1804. French chemist and civil engineer. His "thermolampe" (pat. 1799) was first to use gas for illumination; patented an engine using coal gas.

Le Bou·len·gé \lə-bü-lä^n-zhā\, Paul-Émile. 1832–1901. Belgian artillery officer. Known for his discoveries in science of ballistics, and for his invention of Le Boulengé chronograph.

Le Braz \lə-brä\, Anatole. 1859–1926. French writer. Professor, U. of Rennes (1901–24). Collected and edited legends and folklore of his native Brittany, as in *La Légende de la mort* (1893) and *Vieilles histoires du pays breton* (1897); also wrote works based on Breton life and traditions as verse *La Chanson de la Bretagne* (1892), stories *Contes du soleil et de la brume* (1905), and novels *Le Gardien du feu* (1890) and *Pâques d'Islande* (1912).

Le Bre·ton \lə-brə-tō^n\, Andre-François. 1708–1779. French publisher. Commissioned and published Diderot's *Encyclopédie* (1751–80).

Le·brun \lə-brœ^n\, Albert. 1871–1950. French politician. Mining engineer by profession. Deputy (1900–20); senator (1920–32); president of the Senate (1931–32). President of France (1932–40), 14th and last of the Third Republic; attempted to preserve unity but failed to provide effective leadership; resigned (July 1940) when the government headed by Pétain and Pierre Laval assumed power.

Le Brun *or* **Le·brun** \lə-brœ^n\, Charles. 1619–1690. French painter. Painted (1640) *Hercules and the Horses of Diomedes* in style of his teacher Simon Vouet; studied in Rome under Nicolas Poussin (1642–46); on return to Paris given large decorative and religious commissions, esp. for Hôtel de Lambert; commissioned by Louis XIV to paint at Fontainebleau series of subjects drawn from life of Alexander the Great, and later to decorate small gallery of Louvre; appointed first painter to the king; worked eighteen years on decoration of palace of Versailles; director of the Gobelins (1663); personally created or supervised production of most of the paintings, sculptures, and decorative objects commissioned by French government for three decades; also distinguished as portrait painter, as in *The Banker Jabach and His Family* (1647).

Lebrun, Charles-François. Duc de Plai·sance \ple-zä^{n}s\. 1739–1824. French politician. Translator of Tasso's *Gerusalemme liberata* and of Homer's *Iliad.* Inspector general of the crown lands (1768); member of the Estates-General, National Assembly, Council of Five Hundred. Third consul (1799–1804); treasurer of the Empire (1804–14); instituted Cours de Comptes (1804); created duc de Plaisance (1808); ruled wisely and moderately as governor general of Holland (1811–13); peer of France (1814).

Lebrun, Élisabeth Vigée-. See VIGÉE-LEBRUN.

Lebrun, Pigault-. See PIGAULT DE L'ÉPINEY.

Lebrun, Ponce-Denis-Écouchard. *Known as* Lebrun-Pin·dare \-pə^n-där\. 1729–1807. French poet. Known for his epigrams, elegies, and odes.

Lé·ca·ve·lé \lā-käv-ə-lā\, Roland. *Pen name* Roland Dor·ge·lès \dȯr-zhə-les\. 1886–1973. French writer. Author of *Les Croix de bois* (1919), *Le Réveil des morts* (1923), *Montmartre mon pays* (1928), *Ci c'était vrai?* (1934), *Carte d'identité* (1945), *Tout est à vendre* (1956), etc.

Le Cha·pe·lier \lə-shä-pəl-yā\, Isaac-René-Guy. 1754–1794. French politician. Member of Estates-General (1789); president of Constituent Assembly (1789); introduced (1791) loi Le Chapelier which prohibitied workers' and employers' unions; became moderate in doctrines (1791) and opposed Robespierre; guillotined.

Le Châ·te·lier \lə-shät-əl-yā\, Henry-Louis. 1850–1936. French chemist. Professor at École des Mines (1877–1919), Collège de France (1887–1908), and the Sorbonne (1907–25). Conducted researches on chemical equilibrium, the combustion of gaseous mixtures, on metals, alloys, etc.; enunciated (1884) Le Châtelier's law dealing with the equilibrium of a system when displaced by a stress; developed an optical pyrometer.

Lechoń, Jan. See Leszek SERAFINOWICZ.

Leck \'lek\, Barth Anthony van der. 1876–1958. Dutch artist. A founding member of de Stijl group (1917), withdrew (1918); known esp. for wall decorations, stained glass windows, and pottery.

Lecky \'lek-ē\, William Edward Hartpole. 1838–1903. Irish historian. Among his works were *History of Rationalism in Europe* (1865), *History of European Morals* (1869), *History of England in the Eighteenth Century* (1878–90), *Democracy and Liberty* (1896).

Le·clair \lə-kler\, Jean-Marie. *Called* the Elder. 1697–1764. French violin virtuoso and composer. Musician of royal chamber (1733); established the classical French violin school that supplanted the earlier Italian school. Composed opera *Scylla et Glaucus* (1746), violin sonatas, trios, and concertos, etc. His brothers ¶Jean-Marie, *called* the Younger (1703–1777), and ¶Pierre (1709–1784) were also violin virtuosos and composers of violin sonatas.

Le·clan·ché \lə-klä^n-shā\, Georges. 1839–1882. French engineer. Invented (1866) the Leclanché battery, the first dry cell.

Le·clerc \lə-kler\, Charles-Victor-Emmanuel. 1772–1802. French soldier. m. Maria Paulina Buonaparte, sister of Napoléon (1797); served under Napoléon in Egypt; sent by Napoléon (1801) to conquer Santo Domingo; defeated Toussaint L'Ouverture (1802) and sent him a prisoner to France; died of yellow fever.

Le Clerc *or* **Le·clerc** \lə-kler\, Jean. *Lat.* Johannes Cler·i·cus \'kler-ə-kəs\. 1657–1736. Swiss theologian and scholar. Professor at Remonstrant Seminary, Amsterdam (1684); champion of Arminianism. Broke with scholastic Calvinism and espoused advanced principles of exegesis and theological method. Wrote biblical commentaries; edited *Bibliothèque universelle et historique* (1686–93), *Bibliothèque choisie* (1703–13), *Bibliothèque ancienne et moderne* (1714–30).

Le Clerc du Tremblay, François. See TREMBLAY.

L'·Écluse \lā-klüz\, Charles de. *Lat.* Carolus Clu·si·us \'klü-zhē-əs\. 1526–1609. French botanist. Credited with introducing the potato into Europe; published *Rariorum plantarum historia* (1601) and other works on European and American plants.

Le·cocq \lə-kȯk\, Alexandre-Charles. 1832–1918. French composer. Known for his operettas in the style of Offenbach, including *Fleur de thé* (1868), *La Fille de Madame Angot* (1872), *Les Cent Vierges* (1872), *Giroflé-Girofla* (1874), *La Petit Mariée* (1875), *Le Petit Duc* (1878), *Le Jour et la nuit* (1881), and *Le Coeur et la main* (1882).

Le Conte \lə-'känt\, Joseph. 1823–1901. American geologist, b. Liberty Co., Ga. Professor, U. of California, Berkeley (1869–96); made studies of stream gradation and mountain folding. Wrote *Religion and Science* (1874), *Elements of Geology* (1878), *Sight* (1881), etc.

Le·conte de Lisle \lə-kō^{n}t-də-lēl\, Charles-Marie-René. *Orig. surname* Leconte. 1818–1894. French poet, b. Réunion. Settled in Paris (1846); Senate librarian (1873). Identified with modern Parnassian school; considered a poet of disillusionment and skepticism; found source of inspiration in the works of the ancients. Author of *Poèmes antiques* (1852), *Poèmes barbares* (1862), *Poèmes tragiques* (1884), *Contes en prose* (1911), etc.

Le·coq de Bois·bau·dran \lə-kȯk-də-bwä-bō-drä^n\, Paul-Émile, *called* François. 1838–1912. French chemist. Engaged in spectroscopic researches on the rare earths; discovered gallium (1875), samarium (1880), and dysprosium (1886).

Le Corbusier. See Charles-Édouard JEANNERET.

Le·cou·vreur \lə-kü-vrœr\, Adrienne. 1692–1730. French actress. Studied under Paul Legrand; made debut at Comédie-Française in Crébillon's *Électre* (1717); excelled in tragedy; known for her beauty and her natural acting style; mistress (from 1721) of Maurice, comte de Saxe; reputedly poisoned by her rival, the duchesse de Bouillon; subject of a play *Adrienne Lecouvreur* by Scribe and Legouvé.

Led·bet·ter \'led-,bet-ər\, Huddie. *Known as* Lead·bel·ly \'led-,bel-ē\. 1885–1949. American singer, b. Mooringsport, La. Of black and Cherokee descent;

one of greatest blues singers; discovered (1933) by John A. Lomax, whom he assisted in collection of Southern folk songs; his many recordings included "Good Morning Blues" (1940), his compositions included "Rock Island Line" (1942) and "Good Night, Irene" (1943).

Le·de·bour \'lā-də-ˌbür\, Georg. 1850–1947. German Socialist. Social Democrat member of Reichstag (1900–18); opposed war credits in World War I (1914); helped form Independent Social Democrats (1917); participated in revolution of 1918; took leading part in Communist revolt, Berlin (1919); joined Socialist Labor party (1931); emigrated to Switzerland (1933).

Le·de·rer \'lā-dər-ər\, Emil. 1882–1939. German economist and sociologist. Professor, Heidelberg (1920–23), Berlin (1931–33), New School for Social Research, N.Y.C. (1933–39). Author of *Grundzüge der Ökonomischen Theorie* (1922), *Konjunktur und Krisen* (1925), *The State of the Masses* (1940), etc.

Le·des·ma Bui·tra·go \lā-'thās-mä-bwē-'trä-gō\, Alonso de. 1562–1633. Spanish poet. His *Conceptos espirituales* (1600) and *Juegos de noche buena* (1611) established the school of literary mysticism known as *conceptismo*.

Le·dó·chow·ski \ˌled-ü-'kȯf-skē\, Mieczysław Halka. Count. 1822–1902. Polish prelate. Ordained Roman Catholic priest (1845); archbishop of Poznań and Gniezno (1866–86); imprisoned (1874–76) for his opposition to the May laws during the Kulturkampf. Consecrated cardinal (1875); prefect of propaganda, Rome (1892–1902). His nephew ¶Włodzimierz Ledóchowski (1866–1942) joined Jesuits (1889), ordained (1894); provincial of Galicia province (1902); superior general of Jesuit order (1915–42).

Le·doux \lə-dü\, Claude-Nicolas. 1736–1806. French architect. Architect to Louis XVI; designed, in Neoclassical style, Madame du Barry's pavilion at Louveciennes (1770–72) and house at Versailles (1772), Madeleine Guimaud's hôtel (1772), and theater at Besançon (1775–84); best known for his saltworks city at Arc-et-Senans (1775–79) and series of 46 highly original city gates for Paris, 4 of which survive. Wrote *L'Architecture considérée sous le rapport de l'art des moeurs et de la legislation* (1804); also left unexecuted projects for spherical, cylindrical, and pyramidal houses.

Le·dru-Rol·lin \lə-drue-rȯ-laⁿ\, Alexandre-Auguste. 1807–1874. French lawyer and politician. Member of Chamber of Deputies (from 1841) and identified with radical groups; associated with Lamartine and Louis Blanc in seeking reforms; a leader in the revolution (1848) and minister of the interior in the provisional government. Elected to Legislative Assembly (1849); led insurrection that resulted in his heading a provisional government for two hours (June 13, 1849); fled to England (1849–70). Continued issuing Republican manifestoes; advocated universal suffrage and was largely instrumental in causing its adoption in France; deputy (1874).

Led·widge \'led-ˌwij\, Francis. 1891–1917. Irish poet. Introduced by Lord Dunsany; served through Gallipoli campaign (1915); killed in Belgium. Author of *Songs of the Field* (1915), *Songs of Peace* (1916), *Last Songs* (1918).

Led·yard \'led-yərd\, John. 1751–1789. American explorer and adventurer, b. Groton, Conn. Shipped as common seaman (1774); as corporal of marines accompanied Cook on his last voyage (1776–79); wrote *A Journal of Captain Cook's Last Voyage to the Pacific* (1783). Failed in attempt to establish fur trade with China; expelled (1788) from Russia during attempt to walk across it; died in Cairo before he could leave in search of Niger River.

Lee \'lē\, Ann. *Known as* Mother Ann. 1736–1784. American religious and founder of Shaker society in U.S., b. Manchester, England. Joined Shaking Quakers, or Shakers (1758); became acknowledged leader of Shakers (1770); preached a gospel of celibacy and frugality and affirmed she embodied the female half of God's dual nature. To U.S. (1774); settled with followers at Watervliet, N.Y. (1776), forming first Shaker colony in U.S. Arrested for treason (1780) but soon released; made tour (1781–83) among Shaker colonies in New England.

Lee, Arthur. 1740–1792. American diplomat, b. Westmoreland Co., Va. Brother of Francis Lightfoot and Richard Henry Lee; published ten political "Monitor's Letters" in *Virginia Gazette* (1768); colonial agent for Massachusetts (1770–75). Appointed (1776) by Continental Congress one of three commissioners to negotiate treaty with France; treaty was negotiated and signed (1778) but his charges of disloyalty and embezzlement against associate Silas Dean led to recall of Dean (1777) and himself (1779). Member, Continental Congress (1781–85) and U.S. Treasury Board (1784–89). Opposed adoption of the Constitution.

Lee, Arthur Hamilton. 1st Viscount Lee of Fare·ham \'fa(ə)r-əm, 'fe(ə)r-\. 1868–1947. English politician. Conservative M.P. (1900–18); director general of food supplies (1917–18); created baron (1918), viscount (1922); minister of agriculture (1920–21); first lord of admiralty (1921–22). Gave estate of Chequers to nation as residence for prime minister.

Lee, Charles. 1731–1782. American soldier, b. Dernhall, England. To America (1773); at outbreak of Revolution, appointed second ranking major general of Continental army; slow in carrying out Washington's orders and severely criticized him. Captured by British (Dec. 1776); while prisoner, submitted secret plan to Gen. Howe for defeating Americans; exchanged (1778). In command of planned attack at Monmouth (June 1778); instead of attacking began a retreat, which was halted only by arrival of Washington; court-martialed, suspended from command. Continued to abuse Washington; dismissed from army (1780).

Lee, Charles. 1758–1815. American jurist, b. Prince William Co., Va. Brother of Henry Lee; friend and supporter of George Washington; attorney general of the U.S. (1795–1801).

Lee, Fitzhugh. 1835–1905. American army officer, b. Fairfax Co., Va. Grandson of Henry Lee; in U.S. army (1856–61); entered Confederate service (1861). Cavalry commander, served notably in Peninsular operations (1861–62), in Chancellorsville campaign (1863), and at Spotsylvania Court House (1864). Governor of Virginia (1886–90). Consul general, Havana (1896–98); major general of volunteers in Spanish–American War; military governor of Havana (1899). Author of *General Lee* (1894), a biography of his uncle Robert E. Lee.

Lee, Francis Lightfoot. 1734–1797. American politician, b. Westmoreland Co., Va. Brother of Arthur and Richard Henry Lee; member, Virginia House of Burgesses (1758–68, 1769–76); supported revolutionary measures. Delegate to Continental Congress (1775–79); a signer of the Declaration of Independence.

Lee, Gypsy Rose. *Orig.* Rose Louise Ho·vick \'hō-vik\. 1914–1970. American stripteaser, b. Seattle. On burlesque stage (from 1929), including *Ziegfeld Follies* (1936); known for grace and style of her act; also appeared in Broadway musical *Star and Garter* (1942), motion pictures, night clubs; published mystery novels *The G-String Murders* (1941) and *Mother Finds a Body* (1942) and autobiography *Gypsy* (1957).

Lee, Henry. *Known as* Light-Horse Harry Lee. 1756–1818. American soldier and politician, b. Prince William Co., Va. Brilliant cavalry commander in Revolutionary War, esp. known for capture of fort at Paulus Hook, N.J. (Aug. 19, 1779) and for operations covering Greene's retreat across North Carolina to Virginia (1781). Member, Virginia legislature (1785–88, 1789–91) and Continental Congress (1785–88). Governor of Virginia (1792–95); commanded troops that suppressed Whisky Rebellion in Pennsylvania (1794). Member, U.S. House of Representatives (1799–1801). In his eulogy of Washington (1799) occurred the famous words, "First in war, first in peace, and first in the hearts of his countrymen." Robert Edward Lee (*q.v.*) was his son, Fitzhugh Lee (*q.v.*) his grandson.

Lee, Ivy Ledbetter. 1877–1934. American public relations consultant, b. Cedartown, Ga. Consultant (from 1906) to various large interests, notably John D. Rockefeller, Bethlehem Steel Co., Pennsylvania Railroad; his advocacy of open and honest corporate policies almost single-handedly made public relations a respectable profession.

Lee, Jason. 1803–1845. American pioneer and missionary, b. near Stanstead, Que. Joined Methodist church (1826); missionary in Oregon country (from 1834); cooperated in drawing up petition for territorial government (1836–37); presided (1841) at preliminary meeting for territorial organization; influential in establishing provisional government (1843). A founder (1842) of Oregon Institute, later Willamette U.

Lee, Manfred Bennington. 1905–1971. American novelist, b. Brooklyn, N.Y. With ¶Frederic Dan·nay \'dan-ˌā\ (1905–1982, author under pseudonym Ellery Queen \'kwēn\ of over 40 detective novels including *The Roman Hat Mystery* (1929), *The Greek Coffin Mystery* (1932), *The Four of Hearts* (1938), *The Devil to Pay* (1938). Under pseudonym Barnaby Ross \'rȯs, 'räs\ wrote (also with Dannay) series of novels featuring detective Drury Lane. Lee and Dannay also published short-story collections, juvenile mysteries, mystery anthologies, and (from 1941) *Ellery Queen's Mystery Magazine.*

Lee, Mary Ann. 1823?–1899. American dancer, b. Philadelphia. One of first American ballet dancers; made debut (with Augusta Maywood) in Philadelphia in *The Maid of Cashmere* (1837); formed troupe with George Washington Smith and toured U.S. (1845–47), presenting authentic versions of *Giselle, La Fille du Danube,* etc.; retired (1847) but danced occasionally until 1854.

Lee, Nathaniel. 1653?–1692. English dramatist. Produced *Nero* (1674) and *Sophonisba* (1675); made reputation with blank-verse tragedy *The Rival Queens* (1677); continued series of plays from classical history with *Caesar Borgia* (1679), *Lucius Junius Brutus* (1680), *Theodisius* (1680), and *Constantine the Great* (1683); collaborated with Dryden in *Oedipus* (1679) and *The Duke of Guise* (1682).

Lee, Richard Henry. 1732–1794. American Revolutionary statesman, b. Westmoreland Co., Va. Brother of Arthur and Francis Lightfoot Lee; member, Virginia House of Burgesses (1758–75); prominent in defending colonial rights (from 1764); with Patrick Henry and Thomas Jefferson, initiated intercolonial committees of correspondence (1773). Virginia delegate to Continental Congress (1774–79); on June 7, 1776, moved resolution (adopted July 2) that "these united colonies are, and of right ought to be, free and independent states; that they are absolved from all allegiance to the British crown, and that all political connection between them and the State of Great Britain is, and ought to be, totally dissolved"; a signer of Declaration of Independence and of Articles of Confederation. Again member of Congress (1784–89); its president (1784–85); opposed new Constitution. Member, U.S. Senate (1789–92).

Lee, Robert Edward. 1807–1870. American soldier, b. Westmoreland Co., Va. Son of Henry Lee. On engineering duties, U.S. army (1829–46); served in Mexican War, notably at Vera Cruz, Churubusco, and Chapultepec (1847); superintendent, West Point (1852). Transferred from engineers to cavalry (1855); on frontier duty in Texas (1856–57, 1860–61); suppressed John Brown's raid at Harpers Ferry, Va. (1859). At outbreak of Civil War, resigned from U.S. army and accepted command of Virginia forces; military adviser to Jefferson Davis (1861–62). Assigned (June 1862) to command army of Northern Virginia; repulsed Federal forces near Richmond (June 25–July 1, 1862). Started campaign into Maryland; checked at Antietam (Sept. 17, 1862); turned back Federal move at Fredericksburg (Dec. 13, 1862) and again at Chancellorsville (May 14, 1863). Advanced into Pennsylvania, but was decisively defeated at Gettysburg (July 1–3, 1863). With inferior forces, conducted brilliant defensive operations against Grant (May 1864–April 1865); appointed general in chief of all Confederate armies (Feb. 6, 1865); surrendered to Grant at Appomattox Court House (April 9, 1865). President, Washington College (1865–70), now Washington and Lee University.

Lee, Samuel Phillips. 1812–1897. American naval officer, b. Fairfax Co., Va. Grandson of Richard Henry Lee; served in Union navy through Civil War; commanded *Oneida* in attack on New Orleans (1862) and at Vicksburg under Farragut; commanded North Atlantic blockading squadron (1862–64) and Mississippi squadron (1864–65); retired (1873).

Lee, Sir Sidney. 1859–1926. English editor and scholar. Assistant editor (1883–90), coeditor with Sir Leslie Stephen (1890–91), and editor in chief (1891–1917), *Dictionary of National Biography.* Prepared facsimile edition of First Folio of Shakespeare (1902); also wrote *Life of William Shakespeare* (1898), *Life of Queen Victoria* (1902), *Shakespeare and the Modern Stage* (1906), *Shakespeare and the Italian Renaissance* (1915).

Lee, Vernon. See Violet PAGET.

Lee, William. 1550?–1610. English inventor. Clergyman at Calverton; invented first knitting machine (1589); patent refused by Queen Elizabeth, so he set up frames at Rouen, France.

Leech \ˈlēch\, John. 1817–1864. English caricaturist. Published *Etchings and Sketchings by A. Pen, Esq.* (1835); made hit with caricature of Mulready's design for postal envelope (1840); illustrated *Portraits of Children of the Mobility* (1841), *Comic History of Rome* (1852), and works by Dickens and R.S. Surtees; on staff of *Punch* (1841–64).

Leeds, Duke of. See Thomas OSBORNE.

Lee·ser \ˈlē-sər\, Isaac. 1806–1868. American rabbi, b. Westphalia, Prussia. To U.S. (1824); a leader of Jewish traditionalism in U.S.; rabbi of congregations in Philadelphia (1829–50, 1857–68); founded (1843) and edited (1843–68) *The Occident and American Jewish Advocate;* established Maimonides Coll. (1868).

Leete \ˈlēt\, William. 1613?–1683. American pioneer, b. Huntingdonshire, England. Became Puritan and sailed to America (1639); a founder of Guilford, Conn.; town clerk (1639–62). Governor, New Haven Colony (1661–64) and Connecticut Colony (1676–83).

Leeuw \ˈläü\, Gerardus van der. 1890–1950. Dutch Reformed theologian. Professor at Groningen (1918–50); a leading representative of the phenomenological interpretation of religion; author of *Phänomenologie der Religion* (1933), *De primitieve Mensch en de religie* (1937), etc.

Leeu·wen·hoek \ˈlā-ven-hük\, Antoni van. 1632–1723. Dutch naturalist. Draper at Delft (from c.1652); usher to Delft aldermen (1660); surveyor to court of Holland (1669). Made microscopes through which he observed microorganisms (from 1674); first to give accurate description of red blood corpuscles (1674) and spermatozoa (1677); demonstrated the blood capillaries (1683); described striated muscle fibers, the crystalline lens of the eye, etc.; observed hydra, rotifers, bacteria, and yeast plants; disproved doctrine of spontaneous generation.

Le Fa·nu \ˈlef-ən-yü, lə-ˈfän-yü\, Sheridan, *in full* Joseph Sheridan. 1814–1873. Irish novelist. Editor and proprietor (1839–58), *Evening Mail,* Dublin. Author of novels and stories of the supernatural, including *The House by the Churchyard* (1863), *Uncle Silas* (1864), *In a Glass Darkly* (1872), *The Purcell Papers* (1880).

Le·feb·vre \lə-fevr^{ə}\, Charles-Édouard. 1843–1917. French composer. Works included comic opera *Le Trésor* (1883), operas *Zaïre* (1887) and *Djelma* (1894), choral works *Judith* (1877), *Melka* (1880), and *Éloâ* (1888), orchestral works, sonatas, psalms, etc.

Lefebvre, Pierre-François-Joseph. Duc de Dant·zig \dä^{n}t-sēg\. 1755–1820. French soldier. Entered French Guards (1773); general of brigade (1793) and of division (1794). Engaged at Fleurus (1794), the crossing of the Rhine (1795), Altenkirchen (1796), Neuwied (1797), Stockach (1799). Governor of Paris (1799); supported coup d'état of 18 Brumaire (Nov. 9, 1799); senator (1800); marshal of the Empire (1804). Fought at Jena (1806); besieged and captured Danzig (1807). Commander of the Imperial Guard (1812–14); engaged at Montmirail and Champaubert. At the Restoration, appointed peer of France; lost title after joining Napoléon during the Hundred Days.

Lefebvre-Des·nou·ettes \-dā-nwet\, Charles. Comte. 1773–1822. French soldier. General of brigade (1807) and of division; engaged in Spanish and Russian campaigns; distinguished himself at Bautzen (1813) and at Brienne, La Rothière, and Vauxchamps (1814); fought at Waterloo (1815).

Lefèvre, Pierre. See Peter FABER.

Le·fè·vre d'É·ta·ples \lə-fevr^{ə}-dā-täpl^{ə}\, Jacques. *Lat.* Jacobus Fa·ber Stap·u·len·sis \ˈfā-bər-ˌstap-yů-ˈlen-səs\. c.1455–1536. French theologian and reformer, b. Étaples. Leader of biblical humanism in pre-Reformation France. Taught philosophy in Paris (c.1490–1508); continued scholarly work at St.-Germain-des-Prés abbey under patronage of Guillaume Briçonnet (1508–20); vicar general at Meaux (1523); fled to Strasbourg following charges of Reformation sympathies (1525); recalled and appointed tutor in royal family and royal librarian at Blois (1526); under protection of Queen Margaret of Navarre in Nérac (from 1531). Produced translations of Aristotle and of the Bible into French (1530); wrote Latin commentaries on the Psalms (1509), Pauline Epistles (1512), the Gospels (1522), Catholic Epistles (1527); published works of Jan van Ruysbroeck, Nicholas of Caus, and other mystics.

Leffler, Anne Charlotte. See EDGREN.

Le Fort \lə-ˈfȯr\, Gertrud von. 1876–1971. German poet and novelist. Among her poetical works were *Hymnen an die Kirche* (1924), *Hymnen an Deutschland* (1932); among her novels, *Das Schweisstuch der Veronika* (1828–46), *Der Papst aus dem Ghetto* (1930), *Der Magdeburgische Hochzeit* (1938), etc.

Le·franc \lə-frä^{n}\, Jean-Jacques. Marquis de Pom·pi·gnan \pō^{n}-pēn-yä^{n}\. 1709–1784. French poet. His works included a translation of the Psalms of David (1751), tragedy *Didon* (1734), and verse *Ode sur la mort de Rousseau* (1742), *Poèmes sacrés* (1755), *Odes chrétiennes et philosophiques* (1771).

Le·fu·el \lə-fw^{y}el\, Hector-Martin. 1810–1881. French architect. Appointed architect of the château of Meudon, later of Fontainebleau; designed parts of restoration of the Louvre, succeeding Visconti (after 1853).

Le·garé \lə-ˈgrē\, Hugh Swinton. 1797–1843. American lawyer, b. Charleston, S.C. A founder and editor of literary journal *Southern Review* (1828–32); attorney general of the U.S. (1841–43).

Leg·ate \ˈleg-ət, -it, -(ˌ)āt\, Bartholomew. c.1575–1612. English religious. Preacher in a sect called the Seekers; found guilty of heresy; burned at the stake, last person in London so to die for religious opinions.

Le·gaz·pi \lā-ˈgäs-pē\, Miguel López de. c.1510–1572. Spanish explorer. To Mexico as government clerk (1545); established Spanish dominion over the Philippines (1565) and served as its governor (1565–72); founded Manila (1571).

Le·gen·dre \lə-zhä^{n}-dr^{ə}\, Adrien-Marie. 1752–1833. French mathematician. Member of commission to connect Paris and Greenwich geodetically; collaborated in preparing centesimal trigonometric tables; made important researches in the theory of elliptic functions, the theory of numbers, attractions of ellipsoids, and the method of least squares. Published *Éléments de géométrie* (1794), *Nouvelles méthodes pour la détermination des orbites des cometes* (1806), *Traité des fonctions elliptiques* (1825–37), and *Théorie des nombres* (1830).

Lé·ger \lā-zhā\, Fernan. 1881–1955. French painter. Influenced by Cézanne (1907), Cubism (1909), industrial technology (from 1919); developed a "machine art" characterized by monumental mechanistic forms in bold colors arranged in highly disciplined compositions. His canvases included *Soldiers Playing at Cards* (1917), *The City* (1919), *The Mechanic* (1920), *Le Grand Déjeuner* (1921), *Divers on a Yellow Background* (1941), *Les Loisirs* (1948–49), *Les Constructeurs* (1950), *The Great Parade* (1954); also executed murals for UN building, New York City (1952) and designed sets for ballets and films, stained glass windows, and mosaics.

Léger, Marie-René-Auguste-Alexis Saint-Léger. *Pseudonym* Saint-John Perse \pers\. 1887–1975. French poet and diplomat. Entered diplomatic service (1914); consul in Peking (1916–21); secretary to Aristide Briand (1921–32); secretary general of foreign ministry (1932–40); fled to U.S. (1940); consultant on French literature to Library of Congress; returned to France (1957). His poetry marked by precision and purity of language, liturgical meter, exotic vocabulary; works included *Éloges* (1911), *Anabase* (1924), *Exil* (1942), *Vents* (1946), *Amers* (1957), *Chronique* (1960), and *Oiseaux* (1962). Awarded Nobel prize for literature (1960).

Legge \ˈleg\. Name of an English family bearing titles of baron and earl of Dart·mouth \ˈdärt-məth\, including: William (1609?–1670), Royalist army leader; governor of Oxford (1645); helped Charles escape from Hampton Court (1647); imprisoned (1649–53). His son ¶George (1648–1691), 1st Baron Dartmouth, naval commander; served in Dutch war (1665–67) and in Flanders (1678); lieutenant governor of Portsmouth (1670–83); engaged in Tangier expedition (1683–84); commander in chief of fleet, but took oath of allegiance to William and Mary; died in Tower of London. His son ¶William (1672–1750), 1st Earl of Dartmouth; secretary of state for southern department (1710–13); lord keeper of privy seal (1713–14). His grandson ¶William (1731–1801), 2d earl; president of Board of Trade (1765–66); colonial secretary (1772–75); lord privy seal (1775–82); advocated (1776) use of force against American colonies; gave name to Dartmouth Coll. (1769).

Legge, James. 1815–1897. Scottish missionary and Sinologist. Missionary at Malacca and Hong Kong (1839–73); first professor of Chinese, Oxford (1876); published monumental edition of *Chinese Classics,* with translation, prolegomena, and notes (28 vols., 1861–86).

Le·gna·ni \län-ˈyän-ē\, Pierina. 1863–1923. Italian ballerina. In London first performed her celebrated 32 consecutive fouettés en tournant (1892); prima ballerina assoluta with Maryinsky Theater, St. Petersburg (1893–1901); created dual role of Odette-Odile in Petipa-Ivanov's *Swan Lake* (1895); also danced in *Coppélia, Blue Beard, Raymonda,* etc.

Le·gou·vé *or* **Le Gou·vé** \lə-gü-vā\, Gabriel-Marie-Jean-Baptiste. 1764–1812. French playwright. Author of *La Mort d'Abel* (1792), *Épicharis* (1793), *Etéocle et Polynice* (1799), *La Mort de Henri IV* (1806). His son ¶Gabriel-Jean-Baptiste-Ernest-Wilfrid (1807–1903) was also a writer; author of novel *Édith de Falsen* (1840) and plays *Louise de Lignerolles* (1848), *Adrienne Lecouvreur* (with Scribe, 1849), *Bataille de dames* (1851), *Un Jeune Homme qui ne fait rien* (1861).

Le·grain \lə-graⁿ\, Georges. 1865–1917. French Egyptologist. In charge of reconstruction of temple of Amon at Karnak (1895), where he discovered 800 statues of stone and 17,000 of bronze (1904).

Le·gren·zi \lā-ˈgrent-sē\, Giovanni. 1626–1690. Italian composer. Assistant chapelmaster (1681), chapelmaster (1685), St. Mark's, Venice. Composer of 19 operas, oratorios, psalms, masses, motets for 2 to 5 voices, many sonatas for 2 to 7 instruments, and books of chamber cantatas for 1 to 3 voices.

Le·gros \lə-ˈgrō\, Alphonse. 1837–1911. British painter and etcher, b. France. Encouraged by Whistler, settled in London (1863) and became naturalized (1881); Slade professor of fine art, University Coll., London (1876–92). Specialized in religious subjects and life of vagabonds in his paintings; produced some 600 graphics on fantastic and macabre themes; contributed to revival of draftsmanship in England. His canvases included *Angelus, Women at Prayer, Dead Christ, The Tinker.*

Le·guía y Sal·ce·do \lā-ˈgē-ä-ē-säl-ˈsā-t͟hō\, Augusto Bernardino. 1863–1932. Peruvian businessman and politician. Founded insurance company (1896); minister of finance (1903–08). President of Peru (1908–12); introduced fiscal and administrative reforms, improved health facilities, settled boundary disputes with Bolivia and Brazil; in London (1912–19). With aid of army seized power and expelled president José Pardo y Barreda (1919); president (1919–30); ruled dictatorially; overthrown by a military revolt (1930).

Le·hár \ˈle-hàr, *Angl* ˈlā-ˌhär\, Franz. 1870–1948. Hungarian composer. Bandmaster of various Austrian regiments (1890–1902); conductor of Theater an der Wien (1902). Composer of the opera *Kukuška* (1896), of the operettas *Der Rastelbinder* (1902), *Die lustige Witwe* (*The Merry Widow,* 1905), *Der Mann mit den drei Frauen* (1908), *Der Graf von Luxemburg* (1909), *Zigeunerliebe* (1910), *Endlich allein* (1914), *Cloclo* (1924), *Paganini* (1925), *Friederike* (1928), *Das Land des Lächelns* (1929), *Giuditta* (1934), etc., and of symphonic poems, sonatas, marches and dances for orchestra, etc.

Leh·man \ˈlē-mən\, Herbert Henry. 1878–1963. American banker and politician, b. New York City. Partner in Lehman Bros., bankers, New York (1908); lieutenant governor of New York (1928–32), governor (1932–42); director (1942–46) of Office of Foreign Relief and Rehabilitation; U.S. senator (1949–57); also known for philanthropic activities.

Leh·mann \ˈlā-män\, Ernst August. 1886–1937. German aeronautical engineer. Engaged in manufacture and piloting of Zeppelins (from 1913); accompanied Hugo Eckener on first Zeppelin trip to the U.S. in the *ZR3* (1924); commander of *Graf Zeppelin,* which made voyages to South America (1928–36), and of the *Hindenburg Zeppelin* (1936–37); died when the *Hindenburg* burned at Lakehurst, N.J.

Lehmann, Lilli. 1848–1929. German soprano. Interpreter esp. of Wagner and Mozart and of lieder; joined Berlin Opera (1870); studied under Wagner (1875) and sang at premières of *Ring* dramas, Bayreuth (1876); at Metropolitan Opera House, New York (1885–89, 1891–92); known for her dramatic presence, versatility, and power and flexibility of voice.

Lehmann, Lotte. 1888–1976. American soprano, b. Perleberg, Germany. One of most eminent lyric-dramatic sopranos of the day; sang in London (from 1913), Vienna (from 1914), U.S. (from 1930); to U.S. (1938) and naturalized. Known esp. for interpretations of Mozart, Beethoven's Leonore, Wagner, Richard Strauss, and songs of Robert Schumann.

Leh·mann \ˈli-män\, Orla, *in full* Peter Martin Orla. 1810–1870. Danish politician. Head of National Liberal movement in Copenhagen (1848) and member of "March Ministry"; leader of Schleswig movement; turned conservative and sat in the Folketing (1851–53), Landsting (1854–70), and Reichsrat (1856–66); minister of interior (1861–63).

Lehm·bruck \ˈlām-bru̇k\, Wilhelm. 1881–1919. German sculptor and etcher. A leading member of German Expressionist movement. His works featured nudes and elongated and exaggerated figures; sculptures included *The Bather* (1905), *Mankind* (1909), *Standing Woman* (1910), *Kneeling Woman* (1911), *Standing Youth* (1913), *The Fallen* (1915–16), *Seated Youth* (1918), and several portrait heads.

Le Hoan \ˈlā-ˈhwän\. d. 1005. Vietnamese king (980–1005). Founder of the Earlier Le dynasty; repulsed a Chinese invasion (981).

Leh·to·nen \ˈlek-tò-nen\, Joel. 1881–1934. Finnish poet and novelist. Best known for his novels *Putkinotko* (1919–20) and *Henkien taistelu* (1933).

Leibl \ˈlī-bəl\, Wilhelm. 1844–1900. German painter. Resident in Paris (1869–70), where he associated with Courbet and other realists, and in Munich (1870–73) as member of the Leibl circle; subsequently lived in Bavaria and the Lower Alps. His realistic works included portraits as *Frau Gedon* (1868–69) and genre scenes as *In the Kitchen, The Peasant Women of Dachau, The Village Politicians, Three Women in the Village Church.*

Leib·niz \ˈlīp-nits\, Gottfried Wilhelm. 1646–1716. German philosopher and mathematician. In service of archbishop elector of Mainz (1667–76); on diplomatic missions to Paris (1672–76) and London (1673), meeting many scholars; laid foundations (1675) of integral and differential calculus, published (1684) before Newton's, thus causing long-debated controversy; developed the dynamic theory of motion (1676). In service at Hanover of dukes of Braunschweig-Lüneburg as librarian and privy councilor (1676–1716); proposed basis for general topology (1679); wrote (1686, pub. 1819) *Systema theologicum,* an attempt to find common ground for Catholic and Protestant faiths; began (1687) history of Brunswick ducal house (pub. 1843–45); suggested founding of Acad. of Sciences (1700). Developed rationalistic system of metaphysics based on his theory of monads; also wrote on mathematics, natural science, philosophy, theology, history, law, politics, and other subjects; his principal work in theology *Essais de théodicée* (1710), in the main a discussion of problem of evil and a defense of optimism.

Leicester, Earls of. See (1) Robert de BEAUMONT; (2) Robert DUDLEY; (3) Simon de MONTFORT; (4) SIDNEY family.

Leicester of Holkham, Earl of. See Thomas William COKE.

Leich·hardt \ˈlīk-ärt\, Friedrich Wilhelm Ludwig. 1813–1848. German explorer. To New South Wales (1841) and began geological investigations; crossed Australian continent from Moreton Bay to Port Essington (1844–45) and described expedition in journal (1847); attempted expedition across continent from east to west but disappeared on Cogoon River without a trace.

Leich·ten·tritt \ˈlīk-tən-trit\, Hugo. 1874–1951. German composer and writer on music. Professor, Harvard (1933–41). Composer of dramatic music, orchestral works, chamber music, and songs. Author of *Chopin* (1905), *Geschichte der Motette* (1908), *Music, History, and Ideas* (1938), *Music of the Western Nations* (1956), etc.

Lei·dy \ˈlī-dē\, Joseph. 1823–1891. American zoologist, b. Philadelphia. Professor of anatomy (1853–91) and director of biology department (1884–91), Pennsylvania. Pioneer in researches in American vertebrate paleontology. Author of *On the Fossil Horse of America* (1847), *On the Extinct Mammalia of Dakota and Nebraska* (1869); also wrote on parasitology *Flora and Fauna within Living Animals* (1853), *Remarks on Parasites and Scorpions* (1886), and on protozoa *Fresh Water Rhizopods of North America* (1879); his *Elementary Treatise on Human Anatomy* (1861) a standard work.

Leif Er·iks·son *or* **Er·ics·son** \ˈlā-ˈver-ik-sən, *Angl* ˈlē-ˈfer-\. fl. 1000. Norwegian explorer. Son of Erik the Red. According to the *Groenlendinga saga,* learned of land to the west of Greenland from Bjarni Herjulfsson; sailed west (after 1000) and visited Helluland, Markland, and Vinland, which may be Labrador, Newfoundland, and Nova Scotia, although they are variously identified. In *Eiríks saga* he is sent by Olaf I Tryggvason to Christianize Greenlanders; sailing off course, landed in Vinland; returned to Greenland.

Leigh·ton \ˈlāt-ᵊn\, Frederick. Baron Leighton of Stret·ton \ˈstret-ᵊn\. 1830–1896. English painter. Won reputation with *Cimabue's Madonna Carried in Procession through the Streets of Florence* (1855); settled in London (1860). Excelled in draftsmanship, as in *Venus Disrobing for the Bath, Hercules*

Wrestling with Death, The Daphnephoria, Phryne, Captive Andromache, The Bath of Psyche, The Garden of the Hesperides.

Leighton, Robert. 1611–1684. Scottish prelate. Ordained Presbyterian minister (1641); signed Covenant (1643); principal of Edinburgh University (1653) and professor of divinity. Persuaded by Charles II to become bishop of Dunblane (1661); labored to preserve best of episcopacy and of Presbyterianism as basis for a union; because of persecution of Covenanters sought to resign (1665, 1669); continued his fruitless efforts as archbishop of Glasgow (1670–74).

Lein·ber·ger \'līn-ˌber-gər\, Hans. c.1480–1535. German sculptor. Active in Landshut (after 1510). His works marked a direct transition from Bavarian late Gothic to early Baroque.

Leino, Eino. See Armas LÖNNBOHM.

Leinster, Duke of. See James Fitzgerald (1722–1773), at FITZGERALD family.

Lei·poldt \'lā-pȯlt\, Christiaan Frederick Louis. 1880–1947. South African writer. Trained as doctor; journalist by profession. A leading poet of "Second Afrikaans Language Movement." Author esp. of metaphysical, personal poems he called "Slampamperliedjie"; verse included *Oom Gert Vertel en ander Gedigte* (1911), *Uit Drie Wêrelddele* (1923), *Skoonheidstroos* (1932), *Geseënde Skaduwees* (1949); also wrote plays as *Die Heks* (1923) and *Die Laaste Aand* (1930), travel books, detective stories, books on cookery.

Lei·se·witz \'lī-zə-ˌvits\, Johann Anton. 1752–1806. German dramatist. In Brunswick administrative service (from 1778). His *Julius von Tarent* (1776) was one of the best *Sturm und Drang* tragedies; author also of short dramatic sketches *Die Pfändung* and *Der Besuch um Mitternacht* (both 1775).

Leis·ler \'līs-lər\, Jacob. 1640–1691. American insurrectionary leader, b. Frankfurt am Main, Germany. To New Amsterdam (1660); successful merchant and trader in furs, tobacco, and wine. Led (1689) Leisler's Rebellion against British crown's agent Lt. Gov. Francis Nicholson; on flight of Nicholson, proclaimed William and Mary sovereign, assumed authority and administered the government with title of lieutenant governor (1689–91). Surrendered his powers to duly appointed governor, but was tried for treason and hanged.

Leith \'lēth\, Charles Kenneth. 1875–1956. American geologist, b. Trempealeau, Wis. Professor, Wisconsin (1903–45); writer on Precambrian, structural, and economic geology.

Leit·zel \'līt-səl\, Lillian. *Orig.* Leopoldina Alitza Pe·li·kan \ˌpā-lē-'kän\. 1892 or 1893–1931. American aerialist, b. Breslau, Germany. To U.S. with Barnum & Bailey Circus (1908); star with Ringling Brothers and Barnum & Bailey Circus (from 1919); famed for her "plange" in which she spun vertically 100 times while hanging by one arm from a high rope; m. (1928) Alfredo Codona (*q.v.*); plunged to her death during performance.

Lei·vick \'lā-vik\, Halper. 1888–1962. American poet and playwright, b. near Minsk, Russia. To U.S. (1913); author of Yiddish plays, including *Der Golem* (1921), and of volumes of poetry.

Le Jeune \lə-zhœ̄n\, Claude. c.1528–1600. French composer. Court musician to Duke François of Anjou and King Henry IV. A chief exponent of *musique mesurée,* setting Antoine de Baïf's poems in this style; also composed Psalm settings, sacred and secular chansons, madrigals, motets, a mass, and instrumental fantasias.

Le·jeune \lə-'jün\, John Archer. 1867–1942. American marine corps officer, b. Pointe Coupee Parish, La. Entered navy (1888); brigadier general (1916) and major general (1918). Served in Spanish–American War (1898), Philippine Islands (1908–09), at capture of Vera Cruz (1914), and in France as commander of 2d division (1918–19); commanding officer, U.S. Marine Corps (1920–29; retired); superintendent, V.M.I. (1929–37).

Le·jeune \lə-zhœ̄n\, Louis-François. Baron. 1775–1848. French general and painter. Served in Revolutionary and Napoleonic armies. Credited with introducing lithography into France; painted battle scenes, landscapes, and portraits.

Le Ju·mel de Bar·ne·ville \lə-zhü̅-mel-də-bȧr-nə-vēl\, Marie-Catherine. Comtesse d'Aul·noy \ȯ(l)n-wȧ\ *or* Au·noy \ōn-wȧ\. 1650 or 1651–1705. French writer. Author of fairy tales published as *Contes de fées* (1697), *Les Contes nouveaux* (1698) and pseudohistorical novels of court intrigue including *Hippolyte, conte de Douglas* (1690), *Memoirs de la cour d'Espagne* (1690), *Relation du voyage d'Espagne* (1691).

Le·kain \lə-kaⁿ\. *Orig.* Henri-Louis Cain \kaⁿ\. 1729–1778. French tragedian. Friend and disciple of Voltaire; made debut at Comédie-Française as Titus in Voltaire's *Brutus* (1754); although ugly and harsh-voiced, was extremely popular, esp. as Genghis Khan in *L'Orphelin de la Chine* and in title role of *Tancrède;* introduced more realistic costumes and scenery.

Le·keu \lə-kœ̄\, Guillaume-Jean-Joseph-Nicolas. 1870–1894. Belgian composer. Influenced by Beethoven and his teacher César Franck; composer of cantata *Andromède* (1891), orchestral *Fantaisie sur deux airs populaires angevins* (1892), two symphonic studies, a string quartet (finished by d'Indy), and other chamber music and orchestral works.

L.E.L. See Letitia Elizabeth LANDON.

Le·land \'lē-lənd\, Charles Godfrey. 1824–1903. American poet, b. Philadelphia. Author of humorous poems and sketches, including *Meister Karl's Sketch-Book* (1855); *Hans Breitmann's Barty* (1857), *The Breitmann Ballads* (1871), *The Gipsies* (1882), etc.

Leland, Henry Martyn. 1843–1932. American automobile manufacturer, b. Danville, Vt. Organized Leland & Faulconer Mfg. Co., Detroit (1890); merged it into Cadillac Motor Car Co. (founded by him, 1904); president of Cadillac (1909–17); founder (1917) of Lincoln Motor Co., later (1922) sold to Ford Motor Co.; known for maintaining rigorous standards in his automobiles.

Leland, John. 1506?–1552. English antiquary. King's antiquary (1533); toured England and Wales to search for records, manuscripts, relics of antiquity.

Leland, John. 1691–1766. English Presbyterian minister and Christian apologist. Replied to Matthew Tindal and to Thomas Morgan's *The Moral Philosopher;* attacked deists in *View of the Principal Deistical Writers* (1754–56).

Le·le·wel \le-'lev-el\, Joachim. 1786–1861. Polish historian, geographer, and politician. A leader of Polish revolution (1830–31); lived subsequently as exile in Paris and Brussels. His works in Polish included *History of Poland* (1829) and *The Rebirth of Poland* (1843); his works in French included *Numismatique du moyen âge* (1835), *La Pologne au moyen âge* (1846–51), *Géographie de moyen âge* (1852–57).

Le Loi \'lā-'lȯi\. *Reign title* Le Thai To \'lā-'tī-'tō\. d. 1443. Vietnamese emperor (1428–43). Leader (from 1418) of resistance movement against Chinese overlords; won independence of Vietnam from China (1428); became emperor and founded the Later Le dynasty (1428); promulgated land reforms.

Le·ly \'lā-lē, *Angl* 'lē-lē\, Sir Peter. *Orig.* Pieter Van der Faes \vän-dər-'fās\. 1618–1680. British painter, b. Westphalia. To England (1641); painted at first historical subjects and landscapes; known esp. for his portraits of the English aristocracy, including the royal family, *Windsor Beauties* series (1660s), and *Admirals* series (1666–67).

Le Ma·çon *or* **Le Mas·son** \lə-mȧ-sōⁿ\, Robert 1365?–1443. French politician. Chancellor of France (1418–22) and member of French council (to 1436) of Charles VII; supported Joan of Arc.

Le Maire \lə-mer\, Jacques. fl. 1720–40. French instrument maker. Invented the front-view reflecting telescope later developed by Herschel.

Le Maire \lə-'mer\, Jakob. 1585–1616. Dutch navigator. With Willem Schouten explored the South Seas (1615–16) and discovered Tonga, Staten Island (off Tierra del Fuego), Le Maire Straits, and New Hanover and New Ireland in the Bismarck Archipelago.

Le·maire de Belges \lə-'mer-də-belzh\, Jean. 1473–1525. Flemish poet and chronicler. Historiographer to Margaret of Austria and later to Louis XII. Last of poetic Rhetoriqueurs; attempted to reconcile Italian Renaissance with French tradition in *Concorde des deux langages* (1511); also known for humorous *Épitres de l'amant vert* (1505) and prose romance *Illustrations de Gaule et singularités de Troie* (1513).

Le Mais·tre \lə-metrᵊ\, Antoine. 1608–1658. French religious. Founded (1638) group of ascetics known as *solitaires* at Jansenist abbey of Port-Royal; wrote polemics defending Jansenism and devotional works. His brother ¶Isaac-Louis, *known as* Le Maistre de Sa·cy \-də-sȧ-sē\ (1613–1684) was spiritual director (1649–61) of Jansenist *solitaires* at Port-Royal; did much to popularize Jansenism, esp. with his *Nouveau Testament de Mons* (1667) and other translations from the Bible and the Church Fathers.

Le·maî·tre \lə-metrᵊ\, Georges-Henri. 1894–1966. Belgian astrophysicist. Professor, U. of Louvain (1927); formulated modern "big-bang" theory of origin of universe (1927); made researches on cosmic rays, three-body problem, theory of relativity. Works included *Discussion sur l'évolution de l'Univers* (1933) and *L'Hypothèse de l'atome primitif* (1946).

Lemaître, Jules, *in full* François-Élie-Jules. 1853–1914. French writer. Literary critic on staff of *Revue Bleue;* dramatic critic on *Journal des Débats* and *Revue des Deux Mondes;* his critiques appeared in book form, *Contemporains* (1885–99) and *Impressions du théâtre* (1888–98). Author also of plays as *Revoltée* (1889), *Les Rois* (1893), and *La Massière* (1904), and collections of stories *Serenus* (1886) and *En marge des vieux livres* (1905–07).

Le Masson, Robert. See LE MAÇON.

Le·may \lə-mā\, Léon-Pamphile. 1837–1918. French-Canadian poet and novelist, b. Lotbinière, Que. Among his volumes of verse were *Les Vengeances* (1875), *Fables canadiennes* (1881), *Les Gouttelettes* (1904); among his novels, *Le Pèlerin de Sainte Anne* (1877), *L'Affaire Sougraine* (1884).

Le·mer·cier \lə-mer-syā\, Jacques. 1585?–1654. French architect. Appointed architect of the king (1618); took charge of completion of the Louvre (1624); designed Palais Richelieu, later developed into the Palais Royal; designed the Sorbonne.

Lemercier, Népomucène, *in full* Louis-Jean-Népomucène. 1771–1840. French playwright and poet. Among his tragedies were *Agamemnon* (1794), *Ophis* (1798), *Charlemagne* (1816), *Frédégonde et Brunehaut* (1821), *Richard III et*

Jeanne Shore (1824); his comedy *Pinto* (1798) was first French historical comedy; also wrote epics and the satiric poem *La Panhypocrisiade* (1819–32).

Lé·me·ry \lām(-ə)-rē, lem-rē, *Angl* ˈlem-ər-ē\, Nicolas. 1645–1715. French chemist. Apothecary to the king (1674–81); noted teacher. Author of *Cours de chymie* (1675), *Pharmacopée universelle* (1697), *Traité des drogues simples* (1698), *Traité de l'antimoine* (1707), etc.

Lemnius, Simon. See MARGADANT.

Lem·on \ˈlem-ən\, Mark. 1809–1870. English journalist. Author of farces, melodramas, operas, novelettes, lyrics, songs, and novels; best known as one of the founders and first editors (later sole editor) of *Punch* (1841–70).

Le·mon·nier \ˈlə-mȯn-yā\, Camille, *in full* Antoine-Louis-Camille. 1844–1913. Belgian novelist. Author of Naturalistic novels as *Un Mâle* (1881), *L'Hystérique* (1885), *Happe-chair* (1886), *Le Petit Homme de Dieu* (1902), short stories, art criticism, etc.

Lemonnier, Pierre-Charles. 1715–1799. French astronomer. Assisted Maupertuis and Clairaut in measuring a degree of the meridian in Lapland (1736); professor, Collège Royal (1746); investigated disturbances of motion of Jupiter caused by Saturn; carried on lunar observations for 50 years; studied terrestrial magnetism and atmospheric electricity; determined positions of numerous stars; observed and recorded Uranus before its discovery as a planet.

Le·mot \lə-mō\, François-Frédéric. Baron. 1773–1827. French sculptor. Carved statues *Numa Pompilius, Cicéron, Brutus, Lycurgue, Léonidas aux Thermopyles;* also carved the huge bas-relief on the front of the Louvre.

Le Moyne \lə-mwän\, Charles. 1626–1685. French colonist. To Canada (1641) as soldier, trader, interpreter; ennobled by Louis XIV (1668) and presented with seigneury of Longueuil and other seigneuries which descended to his sons, including: ¶Charles (1656–1729), baron de Lon·gueuil \lōⁿ-gœy\, commandant general of Canada (1711); governor of Three Rivers (1720), of Montreal (1724).

¶Pierre (1661–1706), sieur d'·Iber·ville \dē-ber-vēl\, soldier and colonist; led raid on English forts on Hudson Bay (1686); continued expeditions against British settlements (1686–97). Commissioned to found French colony on Mississippi Delta; established (1699) colony at Mobile Bay; explored the Mississippi and discovered Lake Pontchartrain; moved colony to Biloxi, Miss., first permanent French settlement in Louisiana Territory; established (1700) unsuccessful colony near New Orleans; governor of Louisiana (1703).

¶Jean-Baptiste (1680–1747), sieur de Bien·ville \byaⁿ-vēl\, accompanied Pierre down Mississippi River; governor of Louisiana (1706–13, 1717–23, 1733–43); founded New Orleans (1718). ¶Antoine (1681–1747), sieur de Châ·teau·guay \shä-tō-gā\, in Louisiana with his brothers; governor of Guiana (1737–44); to Acadia and aided in defense of Louisbourg.

Le Moyne, François. 1688–1737. French painter. Best known work, decoration of the vault of the Salon d'Hercule at the Château de Versailles with 142 figures of superhuman proportions (1736).

Le·moyne \lə-mwän\, Jean-Baptiste. 1704–1778. French sculptor. Carved statues of Louis XV at Rennes and Bordeaux, tombs of Cardinal Fleury and Mignard at Saint-Roch, and many portrait busts, esp. of Voltaire, Montesquieu, Mme de Pompadour.

Le Nain \lə-naⁿ\, Antoine (c.1588–1648) and his brothers Louis (1593–1648) and Mathieu (1607–1677). French painters. Established common workshop in Paris (by 1630); often collaborated on paintings, making specific attribution difficult; best known for their realistic paintings of peasant life. Antoine esp. known for small paintings often on copper. Louis also painted religious scenes and *A Blacksmith in His Forge.* Mathieu became official painter of Paris (1633), was made chevalier, and excelled in large compositions and portraits.

Le·nard \ˈlā-närd\, Philipp Eduard Anton. 1862–1947. German physicist. Professor, Kiel (1898–1907) and Heidelberg (1907 ff.). Discovered (from 1898) many properties of cathode rays, esp. their creation by photoelectric effect (1899); also studied ultraviolet light, electrical conductivity of flames, and phosphorescence. Awarded 1905 Nobel prize for physics. Author of *Über Kathodenstrahlen* (1906), *Über Äther und Materie* (1910), *Quantitatives über Kathodenstrahlen aller Geschwindigkeiten* (1918), *Grosse Naturforscher* (1929), *Deutsche Physik* (1936–37), etc.

Le·nar·to·wicz \ˌlen-är-ˈtȯ-vēch\, Aleksander Teofil. 1822–1893. Polish poet. Published *Szopka* (1849), *Lirenka* (1851), *Gladiatorowie* (1857), *Rytmy narodowe* (1881), etc.

Lenau, Nikolaus. See Nikolaus NIEMBSCH VON STREHLENAU.

Len·bach \ˈlān-ˌbäk\, Franz von. 1836–1904. German painter. His works included copies of Rubens, Titian, and others for Schack's gallery in Munich, *The Arch of Titus, The Shepherd Boy,* and portraits of Emperor William I, Bismarck, Wagner, Liszt, Gladstone, and other famous men.

Len·clos \läⁿ-klō\, Anne de. *Known as* Ninon de Lenclos. 1620–1705. French courtesan. Her beauty and wit attracted many distinguished men of the day, including Richelieu, St.-Évremond, La Rochefoucauld, D'Estrées, Condé, and Sévigné; in later years, enjoyed the friendship of Mme de Maintenon, Mme de Lafayette, Queen Christina of Sweden, and her salon was attended by the most select society of the period. Defended herself in *La Coquette vengée* (1659).

L'·En·fant \läⁿ-fäⁿ\, Pierre Charles. 1754–1825. American architect and soldier, b. Paris, France. To America (1776) to serve in Continental army; captain of engineers (1778); served in southern army; major (1783), retired (1784). Remodeled building in New York City for temporary quarters of new federal government (1789). Invited by George Washington, laid out plans for the national capital on the Potomac (1791) and began construction; dismissed for his imperious attitude (Feb. 1792); excellence of plans recognized by Park Commission (1901) and development of city of Washington carried out in accordance with them.

Len·glen \läⁿ-glen, *Angl* ˈleŋ-(g)lən\, Suzanne. 1899–1938. French tennis player. In lawn tennis, won Wimbledon singles and doubles (1919–23, 1925) and mixed doubles (1920, 1922, 1925), French singles (1920–1923, 1925–26), doubles and mixed doubles (1925–26); won gold medals in singles and doubles in 1920 Olympics. In hard court, won world singles (1914, 1921–23), doubles (1914, 1921–22), mixed doubles (1921–23) titles.

Le·nin \ˈlyā-nyin\. *Orig.* Vladimir Ilich Ul·ya·nov \ül-ˈyä-nəf\. 1870–1924. Russian Communist leader. Born into middle-class family; became Marxist (1889); practiced law in Samara (1892). To St. Petersburg (1893), where he began Socialist propaganda work; arrested (1895), exiled (1897) to Siberia, where he married (1898) Nadezhda Krupskaya (*q.v.*) and completed his economic study *The Development of Capitalism in Russia* (1899). Lived mostly in Western Europe (1900–17); founded, edited, or controlled several revolutionary periodicals, esp. *Iskra* (1900–03), *Vperyod* (1905–06), *Zvezda* (1910–12), *Pravda* (1912–14), all intended for circulation in Russia. Collaborated with Plekhanov in working out program of organization and action for Marxian Socialists, accepted by Second Socialist Congress (1903), which, however, divided into Mensheviks and Bolsheviks; became leader of the Bolsheviks. Convened (1912) Bolshevik party conference at Prague which resulted in final split with Mensheviks; vigorously denounced World War I as imperialistic and urged Socialists in all countries to rise against their own governments; issued program (Nov. 1914) for creation of Third International; left for Petrograd upon hearing of overthrow of the czar (March 1917). In Russia (from April 1917), assumed leadership of revolutionary movement; declared that supreme power in Russia was vested in the soviets; overthrew Kerensky's provisional government (Nov. 7–8, 1917); became head of Soviet government as chairman of the Council of People's Commissars; dissolved constituent assembly (Jan. 7, 1918) and established the dictatorship of the proletariat. Accepted humiliating peace of Brest Litovsk with Germany (1918); defended Soviet government against counterrevolutionary armies (1918–21); founded Communist International (1919); introduced far-reaching socialistic reforms, later (1921) modified by New Economic Policy; died at Gorky of a stroke. Formulator of present official Communist ideology (Marxism-Leninism), esp. by writings as *What Is To Be Done?* (1902), *Two Tactics of Social-Democracy in the Democratic Revolution* (1905), *Imperialism, the Highest Stage of Capitalism* (1917), and *The State and Revolution* (1917).

Len·nep \ˈlen-ep\, Jacob van. 1802–1868. Dutch novelist and poet. Best known for historical novels *De pleegzoon* (1833), *De Roos van Dekama* (1836), *De lotgevallen van Ferdinand Huyck* (1840), etc.; also wrote *Nederlandsche legenden* (1828–31, verse), epic and burlesque poems, short stories, plays, histories, and translations.

Lenn·gren \ˈlen-grān\, Anna Maria, *nee* Malm·stedt \ˈmälm-stet\. 1754–1817. Swedish poet. m. Karl Lenngren (1780); known for pastoral idyls *Den glada fasten* (1796) and *Pojkarna* (1797), satires *Portraiterne* (1796) and *Grefvinnans besök* (1800).

Len·non \ˈlen-ən\, John Winston. 1940–1980. English singer and songwriter. Founder (1956), guitarist and singer with the Quarrymen, later (1958) known as the Beatles, most successful rock-and-roll group of the 1960s (disbanded 1970); composed, usually with fellow Beatle Paul McCartney, many of group's songs, as "I Want To Hold Your Hand," "She Loves You," "Yesterday," "Lucy In The Sky With Diamonds"; appeared in group's movies *A Hard Day's Night* (1964), *Help!* (1965).

Len·nox \ˈlen-əks\. Name of English family springing from union of Charles II and Louise-Renée de Kéroualle (*q.v.*), Duchess of Portsmouth, and including dukes of Rich·mond \ˈrich-mənd\ (peerage of England) and of Lennox (peerage of Scotland). Members included: Charles Lennox (1672–1723), 1st Duke of Richmond, Duke of Lennox (cr. 1675); changing politics and religion, became reconciled to King William; lord of bedchamber to George I (1714). His grandson ¶Charles (1735–1806), 3d duke; diplomat; minister at Paris (1765); secretary of state for southern department (1766–67), denounced ministerial policy toward American colonies; master general of ordnance with seat in cabinet (1782–95). His nephew ¶Charles (1764–1819), 4th duke; M.P. (1790); lord lieutenant of Ireland (1807–13); general (1814); governor general of British North America (1818).

¶Charles Gor·don-Lennox \'gȯrd-ᵊn-\ (1791–1860), 5th duke; eldest son of 4th duke; assistant military secretary to Wellington in Portugal (1810–14); postmaster general (1830–34); assumed on death (1836) of his uncle, last duke of Gordon in Gordon line (see under GORDON family), additional surname of Gordon. His son ¶Charles Henry Gordon-Lennox (1818–1903), 6th Duke of Richmond and 1st Duke of Gordon in Lennox line; Conservative political leader, aide to Wellington (1842–52), M.P. (1841), president of Board of Trade (1867–69), leader in House of Lords (1868–76); lord president of council (1874–80), secretary for Scotland (1885–86); promoted agricultural legislation.

Lennox, Earls and dukes of. See STEWART family.

Lennox, Countess of. See Margaret Douglas under DOUGLAS family.

Lennox, Charlotte, *nee* Ramsay. 1720–1804. British novelist and poet, b. New York City. Resident in England (from 1735); m. Alexander Lennox (1747); friend of Samuel Johnson and Samuel Richardson. Author of *Poems on Several Occasions* (1747), novel *The Female Quixote* (1752), *Shakespeare Illustrated* (1753), play *The Sister* (1769), and many translations from the French.

Le·no \'lē-(ˌ)nō\, Dan. *Orig.* George Gal·vin \'gal-vən\. 1860–1904. English entertainer. Extremely popular (by 1869) for his music-hall act consisting of clog dancing, singing, comic patter; star of Drury Lane's annual Christmas pantomime (1888–1904).

Le·noir \lən-wär\, Alexandre, *in full* Marie-Alexandre. 1761–1839. French antiquary. Collector of French monuments and works of art saved from convents and churches at the time of the Revolution; worked on restoration of tombs of French kings.

Lenoir, Étienne, *in full* Jean-Joseph-Étienne. 1822–1900. French inventor. Invented first practical internal combustion engine (c.1859); built first automobile with internal combustion engine (1862); also invented electric brake for trains (1855) and a boat using his engine (1886).

Le·nor·mand \lə-nȯr-mäⁿ\, Henri-René. 1882–1951. French playwright. Author of *Le Temps est un songe* (1919), *Le Simoun* (1920), *L'Homme et ses fantômes* (1924), *Une Vie secrète* (1929), etc.

Lenormand, Louis-Sébastien. 1757–1839. French chemist and aeronaut. Credited with first successful parachute descent, made from the tower of the Montpellier observatory, holding an umbrella five feet in diameter in each hand (1783).

Lenormand, Marie-Anne-Adélaïde. *Popularly known as* La Si·bylle du Faubourg Saint Ger·main \lä-sē-bēl-dü̅-fō-bür-saⁿ-zher-maⁿ\. 1772–1843. French fortune teller. Gained fame by prophesying marriage of Joséphine de Beauharnais and Napoléon Bonaparte; consulted by such personages as Mme de Staël, Talma, Alexander I of Russia, the duc de Berry.

Le·nor·mant \lə-nȯr-mäⁿ\, François. 1837–1883. French Assyriologist and numismatist. Professor of archaeology, Bibliothèque Nationale (1874); chief works, *La Monnaie dans l'antiquité* (1873–79), *Les Sciences occultes en Asia* (1874–75), and *Les Origines de l'histoire d'après la Bible et les traditions des peuples orientaux* (1880–82); recognized existence in cuneiform texts of a non-Semitic language now called Akkadian.

Le·nô·tre \lə-nō-trᵊ\, André. 1613–1700. French landscape architect. Director of royal gardens under Louis XIII (1637–43) and Louis XIV; designed, wholly or in part, many famous gardens, as at Versailles, Chantilly, Saint-Cloud, Saint-Germain-en-Laye, Fontainebleau, Kensington Gardens and St. James's Park (London), the Quirinal and the Vatican (Rome).

Len·ox \'len-əks\, James. 1800–1880. American bibliophile and philanthropist, b. New York City. Established and gave land and books to the Lenox Library (1870), later (1895) part of New York Public Library.

Len·thall \'len-ˌtȯl, 'len-təl\, William. 1591–1662. English parliamentarian. Member of Short Parliament (1640); speaker of Long Parliament (1640–53); refused to tell King Charles whether any of the Five Members was in the House of Commons (1642); speaker of Parliament of 1654; member of Parliament of 1656; speaker of restored Long Parliament (1659); cooperated with Monck in bringing about the Restoration.

Len·tu·lus \'len-t(y)ü-ləs\, Lucius Cornelius. *Surnamed* Crus \'krəs\. d. 48 B.C. Roman politician. Hostile to Caesar; consul (49); after battle of Pharsalus (48), fled to Egypt, where he was seized by Ptolemy and executed.

Lentulus, Publius Cornelius. *Surnamed* Su·ra \'s(y)ü-rə\. d. 63 B.C. Roman politician. Quaestor (81); praetor (75, 63); consul (71). Involved in Catiline's conspiracy; became leader of conspirators when Catiline fled Rome; executed.

Lentulus, Publius Cornelius. *Surnamed* Spin·ther \'spin-thər\. d. c.48 B.C. Roman politician. Curule aedile (63), aided Cicero in suppressing conspiracy of Catiline. Praetor (60); governor of Hispania Citerior (59); consul (57); governor of Cilicia (56–53). At outbreak of Civil War (49), joined Pompey; after battle of Pharsalus (48), fled to Rhodes; captured by Caesar and executed.

Len·ya \'lān-yä, *Angl* 'len-yə\, Lotte. *Orig.* Karoline Wilhelmine Bla·mau·er \blä-'mau̇-ər\. 1898–1981. Austrian singer and actress. m. (1926) Kurt Weill (*q.v.*); gained fame as Jenny in Berlin production (1928) and film version (1931) of Brecht's and Weill's *Die Dreigroschenoper;* also created roles of Anna in *Die sieben Todsünden* (1933), Miriam in *The Eternal Road* (1937), the Duchess in *The Firebrand of Florence* (1945; all by Weill). Resident in New York (from 1935); besides American stage roles, known for appearances in films *From Russia With Love* (1964), *Cabaret* (1966), etc.

Lenz \'lents\, Heinrich Friedrich Emil, *also called* Emil Khristianovich. 1804–1865. German physicist. Professor (1836–65), dean (1840–63), U. of St. Petersburg; studied electrical phenomena; enunciated Lenz's law on the direction of the induced current in electromagnetic induction (1833); credited with discovery of the dependence of electrical resistance on temperature (1842–43).

Lenz, Jakob Michael Reinhold. 1751–1792. German poet and dramatist. In Strasbourg (1771), joined Goethe's circle; followed Goethe to Weimar (1776), but forced to leave for eccentric manners; suffered mental breakdown and led wandering life. Author of lyric poems including *Die Liebe auf dem Lande,* realistic and social plays as *Der Hofmeister* (1774) and *Die Soldaten* (1776), the comedy *Die Freunde machen den Philosophen* (1776), the satire *Pandaemonium Germanicum* (pub. 1819), and critical works.

Lenz, Peter. *Religious name* Father De·si·de·ri·us \ˌdā-zē-'dā-rē-u̇s\. 1832–1928. German painter, architect, and sculptor. Benedictine monk at Beuron (1876); helped to found Beuron school of art (1894); sought to revive interest in religious art.

Leo \'lē-(ˌ)ō\. Name of thirteen popes:

Leo I. Saint. *Called* the Great. c.400–461. Pope (440–461). Influential as a deacon; sent on a mission to Gaul by Emperor Valentinian III (440). As pope, took great interest in affairs in all parts of the realm of the church; wrote *Tome* against Eutyches's doctrines (449); condemned Robber Synod of Ephesus (449); convened Council of Chalcedon (451); persuaded Attila to spare Rome (452) and kept Genseric (455) from destroying the city; exponent of primacy of papacy in church jurisdiction; held that papal power was passed on from St. Peter; sought to drive out all heresy; active in disciplinary reforms; wrote many sermons and letters of historic interest.

Leo II. Saint. d. 683. Pope (681–683). Confirmed canons of Council of Constantinople (680); healed schism between sees of Rome and Ravenna.

Leo III. Saint. d. 816. Pope (795–816). Crowned Charlemagne (800) emperor of the West, an act which established the temporal sovereignty of the pope over the Roman city and state and caused schism between Eastern and Western empires.

Leo IV. Saint. d. 855. Pope (847–855). Rebuilt Rome after its sacking by Saracens; crowned Louis II coemperor (850); censured Archbishop Hincmar of Reims; excommunicated Cardinal Anastasius (later antipope Anastasius Bibliothecarius).

Leo V. d. 903. Pope (July–Sept. 903). Deposed and murdered by antipope Christopher.

Leo VI. d. 928. Pope (May–Dec. 928). Pope John VIII's prime minister; elected by Marozia Crescentius; regulated jurisdiction of hierarchy of Dalmatia.

Leo VII. d. 939. Pope (936–939). Invited (936) St. Odo of Cluny to Rome to settle dispute between King Hugo and Duke Alberic II of Spoleto; promoted reform of German clergy.

Leo VIII. d. 965. Pope (963–965). First created pope (963) by Emperor Otto I but deposed (964) by synod favoring John XII; after death of John XII and election of Benedict V, again (964) placed by Otto in pontifical seat.

Leo IX. Saint. *Orig.* Bru·no \'brü-(ˌ)nō\ of Egis·heim \'ā-gəs-ˌhīm\. 1002–1054. Pope (1048–54), b. Alsace. Undertook church reforms while bishop of Toul (1027–49). Elected by influence of his cousin Emperor Henry III; enjoined celibacy of the clergy; called Hildebrand (later Pope Gregory VII), Frederick (later Pope Stephen IX), Humbert of Moyenmoutier, and others to Rome to help him revitalize the church; traveled through Italy, Germany, and France (1050); declared war against Normans in southern Italy (1053), captured and detained; created Schism of 1054 by excommunicating Michael I Cerularius, patriarch of Constantinople.

Leo X. *Orig.* Giovanni de' Medici. 1475–1521. Pope (1513–21). Second son of Lorenzo the Magnificent (see MEDICI); destined in childhood for the church; created cardinal deacon of Sta. Maria in Dominica (1488). As pope, an able administrator but used his influence to benefit his family; drove French from Italy, but later (1515) defeated by Francis I; made concordat (1516) with France; terminated 5th Lateran Council (1517) and prevented threatened schism; failed to realize importance of rise of Reformation (1519), although he issued (1521) bull excommunicating Luther; accelerated construction of St. Peter's Basilica and enlarged Vatican library; made Rome a center of European culture but depleted papal treasury by extravagant manner of living; a scholar and patron of art in all forms.

Leo XI. *Orig.* Alessandro Ottaviano de' Medici. 1535–1605. Pope (April 1605). Archbishop of Florence (1574); cardinal (1583); sent on mission to

France (1596) by Pope Clement VIII. As pope, assisted Emperor Rudolf II in Turkish War.

Leo XII. *Orig.* Annibale Francesco Clemente Melchiore Girolamo Nicola del·la Gen·ga \ˌdäl-lä-ˈjeŋ-gä\. 1760–1829. Pope (1823–29). Ordained (1783); nuncio to Lucerne (1793), Cologne (1794–1805), Paris (1814); cardinal (1816); bishop of Senigallia (1816–18); vicar general of Rome (1820). As pope attempted to reverse liberal policies of predecessor Pius VI; reinstated authoritarianism in Papal States; concluded concordats with Hanover (1824) and Holland (1827); condemned indifferentism and Freemasonry; revived jubilees; recognized reorganized Hispanic dioceses.

Leo XIII. *Orig.* Gioacchino Vincenzo Raffaele Luigi Pec·ci \ˈpet-chē\. 1810–1903. Pope (1878–1903). Ordained (1837); nuncio to Brussels (1843–46); bishop of Perugia (1846–78); cardinal (1853). His pontificate one of most notable in recent history of church; wrote important encyclicals on marriage, Freemasonry, study of the Bible, education, modern Socialism (*Rerum novarum,* 1891); continued assertion of predecessor as to papal authority; won advantage (1887) in struggle with Kulturkampf in Germany; opened Vatican archives (1883) to scholars; took conciliatory positions toward civil governments; constantly strove for promotion of peace.

Leo II. d. 1219. King of Armenia (1198–1219). Rallied Armenians after their dispersion by Seljuq Turks; consolidated Cilicia; cooperated with German emperors Frederick I Barbarossa and Henry VI; allied Lesser Armenia to the West.

Leo. Name of six rulers of the Eastern Roman Empire:

Leo I. c.400–474. Emperor (457–474). A Thracian, raised to power by Aspar (*q.v.*); installed Anthemius as Western emperor (467); made disastrous expedition against Vandals in Africa (468); caused murder of Aspar (471).

Leo II. d. 474. Infant grandson of Leo I; associated as ruler with his grandfather (473–474), but died a few months after him.

Leo III. *Called* the Isau·ri·an \ī-ˈsȯr-ē-ən\. c.680–741. Emperor (717–741), first of Isaurian dynasty. Helped Justinian II regain throne (705); commander of Anatolikon army; overthrew Theodosius III (717). Compelled Maslamah ibn ʿAbd al-Malik to give up siege of Constantinople (718), thus checking Arab expansion into southeastern Europe; defeated Arabs in great battle at Akroïnon in Phrygia (739); made many administrative reforms in army, finances, and various codes of law; issued (726) the *Ecloga,* a revised law code; in long strife with church over image worship; an Iconoclast, his actions caused insurrections in Greece and Italy (727), and confiscation of papal lands within the empire led to complete rupture with pope (730–732).

Leo IV. *Called* the Kha·zar \kä-ˈzär\. 749–780. Emperor (775–780). Son of Constantine V; continued energetic policy against Arabs and Bulgars and upheld a mild Iconoclasm; married Irene (later empress).

Leo V. *Called* the Armenian. d. 820. Emperor (813–820). A distinguished general under Nicephorus I and Michael I; proclaimed emperor (813) after deposing Michael. Conducted successful war against Bulgarians (814–817); carried out severe repressions of Paulicians and image worshipers; assassinated by followers of Michael the Amorian.

Leo VI. *Called* the Wise *and* the Philosopher. 866–912. Emperor (886–912). Coemperor (870–886) with his father Basil I; deposed Photius, patriarch of Constantinople (886); during his reign Bulgarians established independent church, Arab pirates captured Thessalonica (904), Arabs conquered Sicily (907); a scholar of some ability, wrote verse and *Orations* (chiefly on theological subjects), and issued *Basilica* (888?), a completion of the digest of the laws of Justinian; m. 1st Theophano (*q.v.*); 2d Zoe (Zautza); and 3d Zoe (Carbonopsina), whose son Constantine VII succeeded to the throne. See Zoe.

Leo \ˈlā-ō\, Heinrich. 1799–1878. German historian. Professor, Halle (1830–78); opponent of Ranke; conservative and extreme reactionary. Author of *Geschichte der italienischen Staaten* (1829–32), *Lehrbuch der Universalgeschichte* (1835–44), etc.

Leo \ˈlā-ō\, Leonardo (*or* Lionardo) Ortensio Salvatore de. 1694–1744. Italian composer. Member of Neapolitan school; composed over 60 operas, including serious operas *Demofoonte* (1735) and *L'olimpiade* (1737), comic operas *La 'mpeca scoperta* (1723) and *Amor vuol sofferenze* (1739), several oratorios, many sacred works, concertos, organ works, piano pieces, etc.

Leo Af·ri·ca·nus \ˈlē-ō-ˌaf-ri-ˈkā-nəs\, *i.e.* Leo the African. *Arab.* al-Ḥasan ibn Muḥammad al-Wazzān al-Zaiyātī *or* al-Fāsī. c.1485–c.1554. Arab traveler and geographer, b. Granada. Traveled through northern Africa and western Asia; captured by pirates and sent to Rome (1517); learned Latin and Italian and became a Christian; took name Giovanni Leone (John Leo); wrote *Descrittione dell' Africa* (1550), for long time only source of knowledge of geography of Sudan.

Le·och·a·res \lē-ˈäk-ə-ˌrēz\. 4th century B.C. Greek sculptor. Associated with his master Scopas in decorating the Mausoleum of Halicarnassus (c.350 B.C.); his gold and ivory statues of Philip of Macedon's family were installed in Philippium at Olympia (c.338).

Leo de Bagnolas. See Levi ben Gershom.

Leo Di·ac·o·nus \ˈlā-ō-dī-ˈak-ə-nəs\. 10th century. Byzantine historian. Wrote in ten books a chronicle of events between 959 and 976.

Leof·ric \ˈlā-ə-frik\. d. 1057. Earl of Mercia. Succeeded his father as one of three great earls of England (between 1024 and 1032); supported Edward the Confessor against Earl Godwin (1051); benefactor of the church, like his wife Godgifu, famed in legend as Lady Godiva (*q.v.*).

Leo Hebraeus. See Levi ben Gershom.

Leon of Modena. See Leone Modena.

León, Juan Ponce de. See Ponce de León.

Le·ón \lā-ˈōn\, Luis de. 1527–1591. Spanish poet and religious writer. Joined Augustinians (1544); held professorships at Salamanca (from 1561); imprisoned by Inquisition (1572–76); provincial of his order (1591). Master of classical style; best known for *De los nombres de Cristo* (1583), dialogue treatise on names given to Christ in Scripture; author also of translations with commentaries of Song of Solomon and Book of Job, theological treatises in Spanish and Latin, and lyrical poems as "La vida retirada" (1557) and "Noche serena" (1583).

Leon·ard \ˈlen-ərd\, Benny. *Orig.* Benjamin Lei·ner \ˈlī-nər\. 1896–1947. American boxer, b. New York City. Won world lightweight championship from Freddy Welsh in New York (May 28, 1917); defended title 7 times and held it until retirement (1925); lost only 5 of 209 career bouts.

Leonard, William Ellery. 1876–1944. American educator and poet, b. Plainfield, N.J. On English faculty, U. of Wisconsin (from 1906; professor from 1926). Author of *Sonnets and Poems* (1906), *The Lynching Bee* (1920), *Two Lives* (1925), *The Locomotive-God* (1927), *A Son of Earth* (collected verse, 1928), and a translation (1916) and study (1942) of Lucretius.

Le·o·nar·di \ˌlā-ō-ˈnär-dē\, John, *Ital.* Giovanni. Saint. 1541?–1609. Italian religious. Entered order of Apostolic Clerics of St. Jerome; ordained (c.1572); became active in charitable work and formed (1574) Clerks Regular of the Mother of God (papal approval 1595); formed (1579) Confraternity of Christian Doctrine; active in monastic reform, founding four other orders, and against Protestantism; helped found (1603) seminary for missionaries. Canonized (1938) by Pius XI.

Leonardo of Pisa. See Leonardo Fibonacci.

Le·o·nar·do da Vin·ci \ˌlā-ō-ˈnär-dō-dä-ˈvēn-chē, *Angl* ˌlē-ə-ˈnär-(ˌ)dō-də-ˈvin-chē\. 1452–1519. Italian painter, sculptor, architect, engineer, and scientist, b. Vinci. Illegitimate son of a Florentine notary; in Florence as apprentice to Andrea del Verrocchio (c.1467–77) and independent artist (1477–82); artist and technical adviser on architecture and engineering to Ludovico Sforza, Duke of Milan (1482–99); military engineer to Cesare Borgia (1502–03); worked in Florence (1503–06), Milan (1506–13), Rome (1513–16); painter and architect (from 1516) to King Francis I at Cloux, France, where he died. Famed for the astonishing breadth of his genius. Left many notebooks containing his researches into anatomy, architecture, hydraulics, hydrology, geology, meteorology, mechanics, machinery and gears, military weaponry and fortifications, human and avian flight, optics, mathematics, botany, etc. Designed palace and garden at Romorantin, France (1517–19), private residences, and many military constructions; worked (1482–94) on monumental bronze equestrian statue of Francesco Sforza at Milan (never cast, clay model produced 1493). Master of expression, use of light and shadow, and technical details in paintings; painted 2 *Annunciations* (c.1472–77), *Madonna and Child* (c.1474), *Portrait of a Young Lady* (c.1475–78), *St. Jerome* (c.1480), *Adoration of the Magi* (1481), 2 *Virgin of the Rocks* (1483, 1508), *Lady with an Ermine* (c.1490), *Last Supper* (1495–97, mural at monastery of Sta. Maria delle Grazie, Milan), *Virgin and Child with St. Anne* (1500), *Madonna with Yarn-winder* (1501), *Mona Lisa* (1503–06, portrait of Lisa del Giocondo), *Battle of Anghiari* (1503–06), and *St. John the Baptist* (c.1516); also left many pen and pencil drawings, including series *Visions of the End of the World.* His *Treatise on Painting* published in 1651 (complete ed. 1817).

Leonardo de Argensola, Bartolomé and Lupercio. See Argensola.

Le·on·ca·val·lo \lā-ˌōn-kä-ˈväl-lō\, Ruggero. 1858–1919. Italian composer. Composed, in verismo style, operas *Pagliacci* (1892), *Chatterton* (1896), *La bohème* (1897), *Zazà* (1900), *Der Roland* (1904), and their librettos.

Le·o·ne Mo·de·na \lā-ˈō-nā-mō-ˈdā-nä\. *Eng.* Leon of Modena. *Hebrew name* Judah Ar·yeh \ˈär-yə\. 1571–1648. Italian rabbi and writer. Precocious student, translated Pentateuch into Italian and 1st book of *Orlando furioso* into Hebrew; rabbi in Vienna (from 1594); addicted to gambling; author of verse, polemics, biblical exegesis, Hebrew–Italian dictionary, and esp. *Ari nohem,* scholarly and devastating attack on the *Sefer ha-zohar* of the Kabbala.

Le·on·hard \ˈlā-ȯn-ˌhärt\, Karl Cäsar von. 1779–1862. German mineralogist and geologist. Professor, Heidelberg (1818–62). Published *Charakteristik der Felsarten* (1823), *Die Basaltgebilde* (1832), etc.; founder (1807) and editor of journal *Taschenbuch für die gesammte Mineralogie;* leonhardite is named after him.

León Hebreo. See ABRABANEL.

Le·o·ni \lā-'ō-nē\, Franco. 1864–1949. Italian composer. Composed operas as *Rip Van Winkle* (1897), *L'oracolo* (1905), and *La terra del sogno* (1920), oratorios, and songs.

Leoni, Leone. 1509–1590. Italian medalist, goldsmith, and sculptor. Engraver in papal mint, Rome (1537–40), in mint at Milan (1542–45, 1550–90); in service of Charles V of Germany as sculptor and medalist. Works included bronze busts of Charles V and Philip II of Spain, marble statue of Charles V, tomb of Marquis of Marignano (in Milan cathedral), medals as of Michelangelo. His son ¶Pompeo (c.1533–1608) was also a sculptor; in service of Philip II of Spain; known for his expressive sculpture portraits.

Le·on·i·das \lē-'än-əd-əs\. d. 480 B.C. King of Sparta (490?–480 B.C.). Succeeded his half-brother Cleomenes I; famous for his defense of the pass of Thermopylae against a vast Persian army; slain with all his force at the pass.

Leonidas of Ta·ren·tum \tə-'ren-təm\. 3d century B.C. Greek poet. About 100 of his facile but influential epigrams survive in the *Greek Anthology.*

Lé·o·nin \lā-ō-naⁿ\ *or* **Le·o·ni·nus** \,lē-ə-'nī-nəs\. 12th century. French composer. Leading liturgical composer of his generation; associated with Notre Dame, or Parisian, school of composition. Credited with composing *Magnus liber* (c.1170), a collection of two-voiced organum settings in melismatic and discantus styles.

Le·on·na·tus \lē-ə-'nā-təs\. d. 322 B.C. Macedonian soldier. General under Alexander the Great; after Alexander's death (323 B.C.), received satrapy of Lesser Phrygia; killed in action near Lamia.

Le·o·nor \lyō-'nȯr\. *In full* Leonor Te·les de Me·ne·ses \-'tel-yish-thā-mə-'nā-zish\. d. 1405. Portuguese queen. Mistress, and later (1371) queen, of King Ferdinand I of Portugal; regent at his death (1383); driven out by John I; imprisoned in convent at Tordesillas (from 1386).

Le·on·ow·ens \'lē-ə-,nō-ənz\, Anna Harriette, *nee* Crawford. 1834–1914. Welsh teacher and writer. To Asia (1849); m. Thomas L. Leonowens (d. 1858); governess of children of King Mongkut (Rama IV) in Bangkok (1862–67). Wrote accounts of Siamese court life, *The English Governess at the Siamese Court* (1870) and *The Romance of the Harem* (1872).

Le·on·ti·us \lē-'än-shē-əs\. d. 705. Emperor of the Eastern Roman Empire (695–698). An army officer, led revolt against Justinian II, deposed and exiled him; overthrown by Tiberius III Apsimar (698); slain by Justinian.

Leontius of By·zan·ti·um \bə-'zan-sh(ē-)əm, -'zant-ē-əm\. d. 543. Byzantine monk and theologian. Took part (1531–36) at Constantinople in Christological controversy, assuming a moderate, orthodox position against the Nestorians and Monophysites; in *Libri tres contra Nestorianos et Eutychianos,* developed enhypostatic theory of Christ's nature that provided basis for settlement of Christological question by Council of Constantinople (553); unsuccessfully defended Origenism against orthodox position.

Le·o·par·di \,lā-ō-'pär-dē\, Alessandro. d. 1522? Venetian sculptor. Known particularly for his completion of Verrocchio's equestrian statue of Bartolommeo Colleoni in Venice; cast the statue in bronze and created its marble pedestal. Designed church of Sta. Giustina at Padua.

Leopardi, Giacomo. Conte. 1798–1837. Italian poet. Victim of physical deformities and chronic ailments from early childhood; distinguished as classical scholar and student of modern languages. Leading Italian lyric poet of pessimism. Among his works were *Canzoni* (1824), *Versi* (1826), philosophical prose *Operette morali* (1827), *I canti* (1831), long poem *La ginestra* (1836), poetic satire *I paralipomeni della batracomiomachia* (1842); best known lyrics, "A Silvia," "L'infinto," "Il passero solitario," etc.

Le·o·pold I \'lā-ō-,pȯlt, *Angl* 'lē-ə-,pōld\. Prince of An·halt-Des·sau \'än-hält-'des-,au̇\. *Called* der Alte Des·sau·er \der-'äl-tə-'des-,au̇-ər\, *i.e.* the Old Dessauer. 1676–1747. Prussian field marshal, b. Dessau. Commanded Prussian contingent through most of War of Spanish Succession; distinguished himself at Höchstädt (1703), Blenheim (1704), Cassano (1705), Turin (1706), Tournai and Malplaquet (both 1709). Defeated Charles XII of Sweden (1715) at Strakund and Rügen. A strict disciplinarian, molded (1715–40) Prussian army into a disciplined and efficient force that made possible Frederick II's later victories; introduced iron ramrod and modern bayonet into army. Retired after defeating Austrians at Kesselsdorf (1745).

Leopold. *Old High Ger.* Lu·it·pold \'lü-it-,pȯlt\. Name of several rulers of Austria: (1) Of the Babenberg family, four margraves (Leopold I to IV) and two dukes (Leopold V and VI), especially:

Leopold I. d. 994. Margrave (976–994). First Babenberg to hold Austrian rule; extended eastern frontier to Vienna Woods after war with Magyars.

Leopold III. Saint. 1075–1136. Margrave (1095–1136). Supported Emperor Henry V against papacy in investiture controversy; given Henry's daughter in marriage as reward; laid foundations of Austria's greatness; founded monasteries and (1133) Cistercian abbey at Heiligenkreuz; canonized (1485); declared national patron of Austria (1663).

Leopold VI. *Called* der Glor·rei·che \dər-'glōr-,rī-kə\, *i.e.* the Glorious. 1176–1230. Duke (1198–1230). Went on crusade (1212) in Spain against the Moors and (1217–19) to Palestine and Egypt; active supporter of Emperor Frederick II.

(2) Of the Habsburg family (from 1282), dukes and archdukes of Austria, especially:

Leopold I. 1293?–1326. Son of King Albert I of Habsburg and brother of Frederick, rival emperor of Louis IV of Bavaria; made duke of Austria and Styria; completely defeated by Swiss (1315) at Morgarten; after Frederick's capture at Mühldorf (1322) continued war against Louis.

Leopold V. 1586–1633. Archduke (1619–33). Son of Charles of Styria and brother of Emperor Ferdinand II; bishop of Passau (1605) and of Strassburg (1607); unsuccessful in administration of Jülich and Cleve (1609); received bishopric (1625) from the pope.

Le·o·pold \'lē-ə-,pōld\. Name of three kings of Belgium:

Leopold I. *Orig.* Georges Chrétien Frédéric. 1790–1865. First king of independent Belgium (1831–65). Fourth son of Francis Frederick, Duke of Saxe-Coburg-Saalfeld; uncle of Queen Victoria of England. Served in Russian army under Alexander I (1805–14); fought at Lützen, Bautzen, and Leipzig (1813); m. (1816) Princess Charlotte of England (d. 1817); lived in England (1817–30); refused throne of Greece (1830); chosen king of Belgium (1831) on its separation from Holland; m. (1832) Marie-Louise d'Orléans, daughter of Louis-Philippe. During his reign, treaty signed with Netherlands (1839); maintained neutral foreign policy and friendly relations with France until 1851 when they became difficult because of policies of Napoléon III.

Leopold II. *Orig.* Louis Philippe Marie Victor. 1835–1909. King (1865–1909). Son of Leopold I; m. (1853) Maria Henrietta of Austria. Enforced neutrality of Belgium during Franco–Prussian War (1870–71); organized African International Assoc. (1876); financed expedition of Stanley to the Congo (1879–84); granted sovereignty over Congo (1884–85); assumed title of sovereign of Congo Free State (1885); criticized (1903–05) for treatment of natives in Congo; Congo Free State annexed to Belgium (1908).

Leopold III. 1901–1983. King (1934–1951). Son of Albert I; m. (1926) Astrid of Sweden. Surrendered Belgian army to Germany (May 1940); regarded by some as a quisling; remained in Belgium during World War II under house arrest; liberated by U.S. forces near Salzburg, Austria; remained in Switzerland (1945–50) while brother Charles served as regent; abdicated (1951) in favor of his son Baudouin.

Leopold. 1835–1905. Prince of Hohenzollern-Sigmaringen. Brother of King Carol I of Romania. Candidate for throne of Spain (1870) after Revolution of 1868; at first refused, then accepted, then finally withdrew. This was immediate cause of Franco–Prussian War (1870–71), when Prussia refused to accede to France's demand that his candidacy should never be renewed.

Leopold. Name of two Holy Roman emperors:

Leopold I. 1640–1705. King of Hungary (1655–1705) and Bohemia (1656–1705), Holy Roman emperor (1658–1705). Second son of Emperor Ferdinand III; became Habsburg heir (1654). Waged war with the Turks (1661–64), ended by victory of Montecuccoli at St. Gotthard; second war (1682–97), in which Turks were assisted by Hungarian magnates; Turks defeated at Senta (1697) by Prince Eugene; signed Treaty of Karlowitz (1699) that ended Turk control of Hungary. Joined (1686) England and Holland in war against France; accepted unfavorable Treaty of Rijswijk (1697). Involved in War of the Spanish Succession (1701–14) through Habsburg claim to throne of Spain; his reign saw monarchial absolutism and administrative centralism gain ascendancy. Married 1st his niece Margaret Theresa, daughter of Philip IV of Spain; 2d Claudia Felicitas of Tirol; 3d Eleanora of Neuberg—their sons succeeding as Emperors Joseph I and Charles VI.

Leopold II. 1747–1792. Holy Roman emperor (1790–92). Third son of Francis I and Maria Theresa, and brother of Joseph II. Grand duke of Tuscany (1765–90) as Leopold I. Formed alliance with Prussia (1792) against revolutionary France; died just before war was declared.

Leopold. Name of two grand dukes of Tuscany:

Leopold I. See LEOPOLD II, Holy Roman emperor.

Leopold II. 1797–1870. Grand duke (1824–59). Son of Grand Duke Ferdinand III and father of Ferdinand IV; at first continued his father's liberal reforms, later adopted reactionary policy in response to radical agitation; granted (1848) new constitution (abolished 1852); refused to join in war on Austria; exiled a few months (1849) but restored by Austrian troops; driven out (1859) on refusing to make alliance with Sardinia; died in Bohemia.

Le·o·pold \'lē-ə-,pōld\, Aldo, *in full* Rand Aldo. 1886–1948. American forester, b. Burlington, Ia. With U.S. Forest Service (1909–28), chiefly in the Southwest; professor, U. of Wisconsin (1933–48). Fervent campaigner for preservation of wildlife and wilderness areas; director, Audubon Society (from 1935); a founder of Wilderness Society (1935). Author of *Game Management* (1933) and *A Sand County Almanac* (1949).

Le·o·pold \'lā-ō-ˌpōld\, Carl Gustaf af. 1756–1829. Swedish poet. A champion of French classicism in Sweden. Secretary, court poet, and dramatic collaborator of Gustav III (1788); author of narrative verse, didactic poems, panegyric odes, lyrics, tragedies, works on philosophy and aesthetics, etc.

Le·o·pold \'lā-ə-ˌpȯlt\, Jan Hendrik. 1865–1925. Dutch poet. Known for poems about spiritual loneliness, esp. epic *Cheops* (1915).

Le·o·tych·i·des \ˌlē-ō-'tik-ə-ˌdēz\ *or* **Le·o·tych·i·das** \-əd-əs\. c.545–c.469 B.C. King of Sparta (491–469 B.C.). Commanded Greek fleet and shared in the victory over the Persians at Mycale (479). Later convicted of accepting bribes from the enemy and banished.

Le·o·vi·gild \lē-'ō-və-ˌgild\. d. 589. King of the Visigoths in Spain (c.569–586). Did much to merge Visigoths and Romans in Spain into united people; steadfast Arian. His son ¶Her·men·e·gild \hər-'men-ə-ˌgild, 'hər-mə-nə-\ (d. 585) brought up in Arian faith; m. (579) In·gun·this \iŋ-'gən(t)-thəs, in-\, a Catholic princess, and was converted; revolted against his father but was defeated and executed; canonized.

Le·pe·le·tier de Saint-Far·geau \lə-pel-tyā-də-saⁿ-fár-zhō\, Louis-Michel. 1760–1793. French politician. Member of Estates-General (1789) and president of the National Assembly (1790); member of the National Convention (1792); assassinated.

Lep·i·dus \'lep-əd-əs\, Marcus Aemilius. d. 152 B.C. Roman general and politician. Consul (187 B.C.); pontifex maximus (180 ff.); censor (179); consul again (175). In war, distinguished himself against Antiochus III in Syria and against the Ligurians. Built the Via Aemilia from Ariminum (Rimini) to Placentia (Piacenza); settled colonies in Mutina (Modena) and Parma.

Lepidus, Marcus Aemilius. d. c.77 B.C. Roman politician. Praetor of Sicily (81 B.C.); consul (78). After Sulla's death, tried to abrogate the constitution which Sulla had passed. Incurred the enmity of the senate; left Rome, gathered an army, and returned to attack the city (77); defeated by Pompey and Catulus; fled to Sardinia and died soon thereafter. His son ¶Marcus Aemilius (d. 13 or 12 B.C.) joined Caesar's party at outbreak of Civil War (49); consul (46); at time of Caesar's assassination (44), commanded an army near Rome and sided with Mark Antony; with Antony and Octavian formed Second Triumvirate (43) to administer the Roman government; consul again (42); forced into a subordinate role, failed to incite a revolt against Octavian in Sicily (36).

L'·Epine \lā-pēn\, Ernest. 1826–1893. French dramatist. Collaborated with Alphonse Daudet in *La Dernière Idole* (1862), *Les Absents* (1863), etc.

Le Play \lə-ple, -plā\, Frédéric, *in full* Pierre-Guillaume-Frédéric. 1806–1882. French mining engineer and sociologist. Engineer in chief and professor (1840), inspector (1848), École des Mines; gave up engineering for sociology (c.1855). Divided family types into patriarch, stem, and individualist; propounded theory of cyclical changes in society based on rise or decline in family morale; his "monographic" method of collecting data influenced later statistical sampling; opposed idea of continuous evolutionary social progress. His works included *Les Ouvriers européens* (1855, rev. 1877–79), *La Réforme sociale en France* (1864), *L'Organisation du travail* (1870).

Lep·si·us \'lep-sē-ùs\, Karl Richard. 1810–1884. German Egyptologist. Headed expedition to Egypt (1842–45) and explored Nile valley into the Sudan; collected many archaeological artifacts and did much to establish Egyptian chronology. Professor, Berlin (1846); returned to Egypt and discovered the Canopus Decree (1866). Author of *Totenbuch der Ägypter* (1842), *Chronologie der Ägypter* (1849), *Denkmäler aus Ägypten und Äthiopien* (1849–59), *Königsbuch der alten Ägypter* (1858), etc.

Ler·do de Te·ja·da \'ler-t͟hō-t͟hā-tā-'kä-t͟hä\, Sebastián. 1827–1889. Mexican politician. Judge of Supreme Court (1855–57); held various cabinet positions (1857–67); strong supporter of Juárez through period of French invasion; chief justice of Supreme Court (1867–72); president of Mexico (1872–76); overthrown by Porfirio Díaz (Nov. 1876); exiled.

Lerma, Duque de. See Francisco SANDOVAL Y ROJAS.

Lermoliev, Ivan. See Giovanni MORELLI.

Ler·mon·tov \'lyär-mən-təf\, Mikhail Yuryevich. 1814–1841. Russian poet and novelist. Became a Guards officer (1834); at Pushkin's death (1837), addressed impassioned ode to czar which resulted in assignment to a line regiment in Caucasus (1837–38); again sent to Caucasus (1840); distinguished himself in battle at Valerik River; killed in a duel. Considered foremost Russian Romantic poet and second only to Pushkin among all Russian poets. His best known poems included *Pesnya pro tsarya Ivana Vasilyevicha* (1837), *Tambovskaya kaznacheysha* (1838), *Mtsyri* (1840), *Demon* (1841), "Listok" (1841), "Prorok" (1841); also wrote dramas as *Maskarad* (1842) and novel *Geroy nashego vremeni* (A Hero of Our Time, 1840).

Ler·ner \'lər-nər\, Alan Jay. 1918–1986. American dramatist and librettist, b. New York City. As librettist and lyricist collaborated with composer Frederick Loewe on some of American theater's most celebrated musicals, including *Brigadoon* (1947), *Paint Your Wagon* (1951), *My Fair Lady* (1956), and *Camelot* (1960); collaborated with Loewe on film *Gigi* (1958, Academy Award); wrote screenplays for films *Royal Wedding* (1951), and *An American in Paris* (1951, Academy Award); collaborated with composer Burton Lane on stage musical *On a Clear Day You Can See Forever* (1965).

Le·roux \lə-rü\, François-Pierre. 1832–1907. French physicist. Discovered phenomenon of "anomalous dispersion" in light; developed automatic timing for measuring velocity of sound in confined pipes.

Leroux, Gaston. 1868–1927. French novelist. Author of detective and mystery stories, including *Rouletabille* (1907), *Le Mystère de la chambre jaune* (1908), *Le Parfum de la dame en noir* (1909).

Leroux, Pierre. 1797–1871. French philosopher, journalist, and politician. Helped found *Le Globe* (1824); made it official organ of Saint-Simonian Socialists (1831); broke with Saint-Simonians (1832) but remained a Socialist; with George Sand founded *Revue Indépendante* (1841). Member of Constituent Assembly (1848) and Legislative Assembly (1849); opposed Louis-Napoléon's coup d'état; in exile (1851–59). Wrote *De l'humanité* (1840), *Sept discours sur la situation actuelle de la Société et de l'esprit humain* (1841), etc.

Leroux, Xavier-Henri-Napoléon. 1863–1919. French composer. Works included operas *Astarté* (1901), *La Reine Fiammette* (1903), *Le Chemineau* (1907), *Le Carillonneur* (1913), *La plus forte* (1924), dramatic overture *Harald,* a mass with orchestra, church music, piano pieces, motets, songs, etc.

Le Roy \lər-wä\, Édouard. 1870–1954. French philosopher and mathematician. Disciple of Henri Poincaré; a Pragmatist; professor, Collège de France (1921–41); his books included *Les Origines humaines et l'évolution de l'intelligence* (1928), *Le Problème de Dieu* (1929).

Ler·roux Gar·cía \ler-'rü-gär-'thē-ä\, Alejandro. 1864–1949. Spanish politician. Lawyer and journalist in Barcelona; member of parliament (1901–07, 1910–36); founded Radical party (1908) which soon became representative of moderate middle class liberalism. First foreign minister of second republic (1931); headed six governments (1933–35); his coalition with rightist groups and promulgation of conservative measures led to uprising of 1934, which he severely repressed, and to his ouster in 1936 elections; in self-exile (1936–47).

Le·sage \lā-sázh\, Alain-René. 1668–1747. French novelist and playwright. Author of the picaresque masterpiece *L'Histoire de Gil Blas de Santillane* (1715–35); among his lesser works were novel *Le Diable boiteux* (1707) and plays *Crispin, rival de son maître* (1707) and *Turcaret* (1709).

Lesbia. See Gaius Valerius CATULLUS.

Les·caze \les-'käz\, William. 1896–1969. American architect, b. Geneva, Switzerland. To U.S. (1920); practiced in New York with George Howe (1929–34) and in own firm (from 1934). Designed Philadelphia Savings Fund Society Building (with Howe, 1931–32), chancery building of Swiss embassy, Washington, D.C. (1959), Church Peace Center Building, N.Y.C. (1962).

Le·sche·tiz·ky \ˌlesh-ə-'tit-skē\, Theodor. *Orig.* Teodor Le·sze·tyc·ki \ˌlesh-e-'tit-skē\. 1830–1915. Polish pianist and teacher. Settled in St. Petersburg (1852) and Vienna (1878) as piano teacher; his pupils included Paderewski, Gabrilówitsch, Schnabel; one of greatest pianists and teachers of his time. Composer of opera *Die erste Falte* (1867) and of works for piano.

Les·cot \les-kō\, Élie. 1883–1974. Haitian politician. Minister to U.S. (1937–41); president of Haiti (1941–46).

Lescot, Pierre. c.1515–1578. French architect. Called the founder of the classic school in France; engaged on the Louvre (from 1546); his Hôtel Carnavalet (1545) survives in part.

Lesdiguières, Duc de. See François de BONNE.

Le·se \'lā-sā\, Benozzo di. *Known as* Benozzo Goz·zo·li \gȯt-'tsȯ-lē\. 1420–1497. Florentine painter. Collaborated with Ghiberti brothers on bronze door of Baptistery, Florence, with Fra Angelico on frescoes for chapel of Pope Nicholas V, Vatican, and on ceiling of Cappella di S. Brizio, Orvieto cathedral. Works included also altarpiece for Collegio Gerolominiano, Perugia (1456), frescoes for Palazzo Medici-Riccardi, Florence (1459–60), choir of S. Agostino, San Gimignano (1463–65), and Campo Santo, Pisa (1469–85).

Les·kien \les-'kēn\, August. 1840–1916. German philologist. Professor, Leipzig (1870–1916); a chief proponent of Neogrammarian school of linguistics. His works on Baltic and Slavic languages included a handbook (1871) and a grammar (1909) of Old Bulgarian, a Serbo-Croatian grammar (1914), and a Lithuanian grammar and reader (1919).

Le·skov \lyi-'skȯf\, Nikolay Semyonovich. *Pseudonym* Steb·nit·ski \styib-'nyit-skəi\. 1831–1895. Russian novelist. Author of novels *Nekuda* (1864), *Na nozhakh* (1870–71), *Soboryane* (1872, Cathedral Folk), and short stories *Ledi Makbet Mtgenskogo uezda* (1865), *Ocharovanny strannik* (1873), etc.

Les·lie \'lez-lē, 'les-lē\, Alexander. 1st Earl of Le·ven \'lē-vən\. c.1580–1661. Scottish soldier. Served in Swedish army (1605–38); defended Stralsund against Wallenstein (1628); took Brandenburg (1634); field marshal (1636). Returned to Scotland and took command (1638) of Scottish Covenanting army in war with England; occupied northeastern England (1640–41); made earl of Leven and Lord Bal·go·nie \bal-'gō-nē\ (1641). Led Scottish troops against Roman Catholic rebels in Ireland (1642–43). Commander of Scottish army fighting on Parliamentary side (1644–46); took part in battle of Marston Moor, stormed Newcastle; accepted surrender of Charles I at Newark (May 1646), turned him over to Parliament (Jan. 1647). After execution of Charles entered Royalist camp; commanded forces defending Scotland from Cromwell's army (1650–51); captured and held (1651–54); retired.

Leslie, David. 1st Baron New·ark \'n(y)ü-ərk, 'n(y)ů(-ə)rk\. 1601–1682. Scottish soldier. Served in army of Gustav Adolphus; returned (1643) to Scotland as major general under Alexander Leslie; brought Scottish horse to support of Cromwell at Marston Moor; besieged and took Carlisle; routed Montrose at Philiphaugh (1645). Second in command to Alexander Leslie of Scottish army levied on behalf of Charles II; fought stubborn defensive campaign against Cromwell until battle of Worcester (1651); created baron (1661).

Leslie, Frank. *Orig. (to 1857)* Henry Carter. 1821–1880. American publisher, b. Ipswich, England. To U.S. (1848); publisher (from 1855) of *Frank Leslie's Illustrated Newspaper;* published other periodicals for all ages and classes. His wife (m. 1874) ¶Miriam Florence, *nee* Fol·line \fä-'lēn \ (1836–1914), b. New Orleans, edited *Frank Leslie's Lady's Magazine* (1863) and other Leslie publications; at husband's death, took over management of his publishing business and made it a great success; changed name legally to Frank Leslie (1882).

Leslie *or* **Les·ley** \'lez-lē, 'les-lē\, John. 1527–1596. Scottish prelate and historian. Ordained Roman Catholic priest (1558); at Reformation championed Catholicism, disputed with Knox; one of commissioners sent to bring Mary, Queen of Scots, to Scotland (1561) and one of her staunchest partisans; her adviser in her ecclesiastical policy and ambassador at court of Elizabeth; bishop of Ross (1566); for his part in Ridolfi plot to depose Elizabeth in favor of Mary, imprisoned in Tower of London (1571), banished (1573); while representing Mary's interests in Paris and Rome, published his Latin history of Scotland *De origine, moribus, et rebus gestis Scotorum* (1578); suffragan and vicar general of diocese of Rouen (1579).

Leslie, Sir John. 1766–1832. Scottish mathematician and physicist. Professor, Edinburgh (from 1805). Gave first correct description of capillary action (1802); first to create artificial ice (1810). Published *An Experimental Inquiry into the Nature and Properties of Heat* (1804), *Philosophy of Arithmetic* (1817), etc.

Leś·mian \'lesh-myȧn\, Bolesław. *Surname orig.* Les·man \'les-mȧn\. 1878–1937. Polish poet. Spent most of life as lawyer in a provincial town. One of first to adapt Symbolism and Expressionism to Polish verse; his poetry distinguished by inventiveness of vocabulary, sensuous imagery, philosophic content. Published *Sąd rozstanjny* (1912), *Łąka* (1920), *Napój cienisty* (1936), *Dziejba leśna* (1938).

Leś·niew·ski \lesh-'nyef-skē\, Stanisław. 1886–1939. Polish mathematician and logician. Studied under Kazimierz Twardowski and Jan Lukasiewicz; professor (1919–39), U. of Warsaw, where he established (with Lukasiewicz) the Warsaw school of logic. Known for work on antinomies; developed an original and comprehensive system of logic consisting of three interrelated theories which he termed protothetic, ontology, and mereology.

Les·pi·nasse \les-pē-nȧs\, Julie-Jeanne-Éléonore de. 1732–1776. French hostess. Natural daughter of comtesse d'Albon; companion (1754–64) to Mme du Deffand; became hostess of one of most brilliant and emancipated Parisian salons (1764); remembered for her relations with d'Alembert, her liaisons with the marquis de Mora and the comte de Guibert, to the latter of whom were written the *Lettres de Mlle de Lespinasse,* first published in 1809 and valuable for accounts of contemporary life and customs.

Les·seps \lā-seps, le-, *Angl* lā-'seps, 'les-əps\, Ferdinand-Marie de. Vicomte. 1805–1894. French diplomat and promoter of the Suez Canal. In consular service at Lisbon (1825–28), Tunis (1828–32), Alexandria (1832–33), Cairo (1833–37), and European cities; minister at Madrid (1848–49). First thought of constructing canal across Suez in 1832; received concession for its construction from Sa'īd Pasha, viceroy of Egypt (1854); helped form company which carried out construction (1859–69). President of French company that worked on construction of Panama Canal (1881–88) but gave up project because of financial and political difficulties; sentenced to imprisonment by French government for misappropriation of funds, but decision reversed.

Les·sing \'les-iŋ\, Gotthold Ephraim. 1729–1781. German dramatist and critic. To Berlin (1748) as literary critic, translator, editor (1749–50) of own dramatic journal; associate of E. von Kleist and Gleim in Leipzig (1755–58); in Berlin (1758); contributed (1759–60) to Nicolai's journal *Briefe, die neueste Literatur betreffend* letters on Wieland and Klopstock, against Gottsched, and in praise of Shakespeare. Secretary to Gen. Tauentzien, Breslau (1760–65); drama critic to German National Theater, Hamburg (1767–68); librarian of ducal library, Wolfenbüttel (from 1770). His works included comedies *Der junge Gelehrte* (1748), *Der Freigeist* (1749), *Die Juden* (1749), and the classic German drama *Minna von Barnhelm* (1763, pub. 1767); the tragedies *Miss Sara Sampson,* 1st German tragedy of middle-class life (1755), and *Philotas* (1759) and *Emilia Galotti* (1772), both in prose; dramatic poem on toleration *Nathan der Weise* (1779); collection of epigrams and Anacreontic poems *Kleinigkeiten* (1751); *Fabeln* (1759); the analysis of the separate functions of poetry and the plastic arts *Laokoon* (1766); theatrical criticisms, esp. *Hamburgische Dramaturgie* (1767–68); archaeological treatise *Wie die Alten den Tod gebildet* (1769); religious treatise *Die Erziehung des Menschengeschlechts* (1780); extracts from papers of H.S. Reimarus *Fragmente eines Ungenannten* (1774–78), which involved him in a religious controversy with Johann M. Goeze (*q.v.*).

L'·Es·trange \lə-'strānj\, Sir Roger. 1616–1704. English journalist and pamphleteer. Wrote Royalist pamphlets from Holland (1648–51); attacked Milton in *No Blinde Guides* (1660). Surveyor of printing presses and licenser of the press (1663–88); issued *Public Intelligence* and *The News* (1663–66); attacked Whigs, Titus Oates, and dissenters in *The Observator* (1681–87); translator of Quevedo (*The Visions of Quevedo,* 1667), Seneca, Cicero (*Offices,* 1680), Aesop (*Fables,* 1692), and Josephus.

Le·sueur \lə-swʸœr\, Charles-Alexandre. 1778–1846. French naturalist. Explored coasts of Australia (1800–04); with naturalist François Péron, collected over 100,000 zoological specimens, including about 2500 new species; explored and collected specimens in U.S. (1816–17). Joined Robert Owen's community at New Harmony, Ind.; taught drawing there (1826–37). Author of monographs on reptiles, crustaceans, and esp. American fishes.

Le Sueur \lə-swʸœr\, Eustache. 1616–1655. French painter. One of founders (1648) and first professors of Académie Royale de Peinture; known for religious paintings, esp. *Life of St. Bruno* (series of 22 paintings, 1645–48) and *St. Paul Preaching at Ephesus* (1649).

Le Sueur *or* **Lesueur,** Jean-François. 1760–1837. French composer. Chapelmaster at several churches (1777–87), esp. Notre-Dame in Paris (1786–87); inspector (1795–1802), professor (1818–37), Paris Conservatoire; director of Tuileries Chapel (1804–30); teacher of Hector Berlioz, Ambroise Thomas, Gounod, etc. Composed eight operas, esp. *La Caverne* (1793), *Paul et Virginie* (1794), *Télémaque* (1796), and *Ossian ou les bardes* (1804), several oratorios, many masses, and other sacred vocal music.

Leszczyńska, Maria. See MARIE, queen of France.

Leszczyński, Stanisław. See STANISŁAW I.

Le Tel·lier \lə-tāl-yā, -tel-\, François-Michel. Marquis de Lou·vois \lüv-wä\. 1639–1691. French politician. Son of Michel Le Tellier; succeeded his father as minister of war (1677–91) and carried out his plans for reorganizing the army; after death of Colbert (1683) became Louis XIV's chief adviser; a competent but ruthless administrator; took important part in Louis's campaign against Huguenots and destruction (1688) of major cities of the Palatinate.

Le Tellier, Michel. 1603–1685. French politician. Minister of war (1643–67); loyal to Mazarin during the Fronde; reorganized and increased army. Chancellor of France (1677–85); an enemy of the Huguenots, signed revocation of Edict of Nantes (1685).

Le Thanh Tong \'lā-'tän-'tȯŋ\. *Known also as* Le Thanh Ton \-'tȯn\ *or* Thuan Hoang De \'twän-'hwäŋ-'dā\. d. 1497. Emperor of Vietnam (1460–97). Established a Chinese-style centralized administration; drew up civil and penal codes utilizing Confucian precepts; expanded his rule southward, defeating (1471) Champa.

Lethington, Lord. See MAITLAND family.

Let·tow-Vor·beck \'let-ō-'fōr-bek\, Paul von. 1870–1964. German soldier. Commanded colonial forces in German East Africa (1914–18); deputy to Reichstag (1929–30); unsuccessfully attempted to organize conservative opposition to Hitler.

Leu·ba \'ləb-ə\, James Henry. 1868–1946. American psychologist, b. Neuchâtel, Switzerland. To U.S. (1887); professor at Bryn Mawr College (1889–1933). Continued development of G. Stanley Hall's new experimental psychology. Author of *The Psychological Origin and the Nature of Religion* (1909), *The Psychology of Religious Mysticism* (1925), *God or Man?: A Study of the Value of God to Man* (1933).

Leuchtenberg, Duke of. See BEAUHARNAIS family.

Leu·cip·pus \lü-'sip-əs\. 5th century B.C. Greek philosopher. Originator of the atomistic theory and thus founder of the school of philosophy based thereon; teacher of Democritus; only fragments of works survive but believed to have written *The Great World System* and *On the Mind.*

Leuck·art \'lòi-ˌkärt\, Rudolf, *in full* Karl Georg Friedrich Rudolf. 1822–1898. German zoologist. Professor at Giessen (1850–69) and Leipzig (1869 ff.); pioneer in modern parasitology and animal ecology. Correctly described the structure of sponges and classified them as coelenterates; studied jellyfish; recognized parthenogenesis in numerous insects; first to study the life histories of many parasitic worms. Author of *Die menschlichen Parasiten* (1863–76), etc.

Leu·en·berg·er \'lȯi-ən-,ber-gər\, Nikolaus. c.1611–1653. Swiss rebel. Leader of peasant revolt at Bern (1653); secured some concessions but soon defeated at Herzogbuchsee (June 1653); arrested and executed.

Leut·ze \'lȯit-sə\, Emanuel Gottlieb. 1816–1868. American painter, b. Gmünd, Württemberg. To U.S. as a child. Studio in Germany (1841–59) and in New York and Washington, D.C. (from 1859). Known for historical paintings, esp. *Washington Crossing the Delaware* (1851), *Westward the Course of Empire Takes its Way* (1860, in the Capitol, Washington, D.C.), *Cromwell and Milton, The Landing of the Norsemen, The Settlement of Maryland.*

Le·vail·lant \lə-vȧ-yäⁿ\, François. 1753–1824. French traveler and ornithologist. Traveled in South Africa, studying the natives and collecting birds (1780–85). Author of *Voyages de Levaillant dans l'intérieur de l'Afrique* (1790–96) and *Histoire naturelle des oiseaux d'Afrique* (1796–1812).

Le·vant \lə-'vant, le-, lē-\, Oscar. 1906–1972. American pianist and composer, b. Pittsburgh. Known as jazz pianist and interpreter of Gershwin and as a wit; scored music for Broadway plays and Hollywood films. Composer of two string quartets, a piano concerto, a nocturne, and a number of songs. Author of *A Smattering of Ignorance* (1940) and *Memoirs of an Amnesiac* (1965).

Le·vas·sor \lə-vȧ-sȯr\, Emile. 1844?–1897. French automotive engineer. With René Panhard (*q.v.*) built first vehicle with an internal combustion engine mounted at front of chassis rather than under driver's seat (1891–92); killed in auto race.

Le Vau \lə-vō\, Louis. 1612–1670. French architect. Designed parts of the Louvre and of the Tuileries.

Leven, Earl of. See Alexander LESLIE.

Le·vene \lə-'vēn\, Phoebus Aaron Theodore. *Orig.* Fishel Aaronovich Le·vin \lə-'vēn\. 1869–1940. American chemist, b. Sagor, Russia. To U.S. (1892); member, Rockefeller Institute (1905–39). Known for pioneering work on nucleic acids; determined formation of nucleotides and how they combine in chains; isolated sugar D-ribose (1909), discovered 2-deoxyribose (1929); also did work on carbohydrates, lipoids, hexosamines, etc.

Le·ver \'lē-vər\, Charles James. 1806–1872. Irish novelist. Practiced medicine in Ireland and Brussels. Scored success with novels *The Confessions of Harry Lorrequer* (1837) and *Charles O'Malley* (1841); edited *Dublin University Magazine* (1842–45) and gathered round him Irish wits. Settled at Florence (1850); British consul at Spetsai (1857) and Trieste (1867). Author of lighthearted, rollicking novels, many on Irish life and characters, including *Jack Hinton* (1843), *Tom Burke of Ours* (1844), *Arthur O'Leary* (1844), *Roland Cashel* (1850), *The Daltons* (1852); historical romances *The O'Donoghue* (1845) and *The Knight of Gwynne* (1847); later, more analytical novels *The Fortunes of Glencore* (1857), *Luttrell of Arran* (1865), *Lord Kilgobbin* (1872).

Lever, William Hesketh. 1st Viscount Le·ver·hulme \'lē-vər-,hyüm\. 1851–1925. English soap manufacturer. With his brother James Darcy established soapworks (1884); made great success manufacturing "Sunlight" soap from vegetable oils instead of tallow; built (1888–89) model industrial village of Port Sunlight, site of Lever Brothers, Ltd.; instituted profit-sharing plan and other employee benefits. M.P. (1906–10); baron (1917), viscount (1922).

Lev·er·ett \'lev(-ə)-rət\, Frank. 1859–1943. American geologist, b. Denmark, Iowa. With U.S. Geological Survey (from 1886), geologist (1890–1929). Authority on glacial deposits in the upper Mississippi, Great Lakes regions, and Ohio Valley.

Leverett, John. 1616–1679. American colonial governor, b. Boston, England. To America (1633); Massachusetts colonial agent in England (c.1655–62); member, Massachusetts General Court (1663–65) and council (1665–70). Lieutenant governor (1671–73), governor (1673–79). His grandson ¶John Leverett (1662–1724) was president of Harvard (1707–24).

Leverhulme, 1st Viscount. See William H. LEVER.

Lev·er·more \'lev-ər-,mȯ(ə)r, -,mō(ə)r\, Charles Herbert. 1856–1927. American educator and peace advocate, b. Mansfield, Conn. Founded Adelphi College, Brooklyn, N.Y. (1896); its president (1896–1912). Devoted himself to propaganda for world peace (from 1912).

Le·ver·rier \lə-ver-yā\, Urbain-Jean-Joseph. 1811–1877. French astronomer. Produced improved tables of Mercury's orbit; investigated (1845) disturbance in the motion of Uranus, making calculations indicating the presence of an unknown planet which was discovered (1846) by J.G. Galle and named Neptune; carried out complete revision of planetary theories. Director of Paris Observatory (1854–70, 1873–77). Cf. John Couch ADAMS.

Le·ver·tin \'lā-vər-tēn\, Oscar Ivar. 1862–1906. Swedish poet, novelist, and critic. Began as Realist but became a leader of Romanticists (c.1890). Author of novels and stories *Konflikter* (1885), *Rococonoveller* (1899), *Magistrarna: Österås* (1900); verse *Legender och visor* (1891), *Nya dikter* (1894), *Kung Salomo och Morolf* (1905); works on literature and art as *Jacques Callot* (1911).

Leve·son-Gower \'lü-sən-'gȯ(ə)r\, Granville George. 2d Earl Gran·ville \'gran-vəl, -(,)vil\. 1815–1891. English politician. Nephew of George Granville Leveson-Gower; Whig M.P. (1836–46); undersecretary for foreign affairs; a free trader in House of Lords (from 1846); minister for foreign affairs (1851–52) under Lord John Russell; president of Privy Council (1852–54, 1859–66); leader of Liberals in House of Lords (from 1855); failed to form ministry (1859); colonial secretary (1868–70, 1886). Foreign secretary (1870–74, 1880–85) under Gladstone; a supple negotiator but lacking strength to cope with European statesmen, unable to take effective measures in troubles in Egypt and Sudan, against *Alabama* claims of U.S., or for maintenance of intermediate zone between Russia and Afghanistan; supported Gladstone's home rule policy; forced to yield to Bismarck over Angra Pequeña in southwest Africa (1883–84).

Leveson-Gower, George Granville. 1st Duke of Suth·er·land \'səth-ər-lənd\ and 2d Marquis of Staf·ford \'staf-ərd\. 1758–1833. English politician and philanthropist. Son of 1st marquis; M.P. (1778–84, 1787–98); ambassador in Paris (1790–92); m. (1785) Elizabeth, Countess of Sutherland; constructed roads and bridges in Sutherlandshire, Scotland; reduced rents and brought land under cultivation. Created duke (1833). See his son Francis (1800–1857) under EGERTON family.

Levi. See MATTHEW.

Le·vi \'lā-vē\, Carlo. 1902–1975. Italian physician, painter, and novelist. His novel *Cristo si è fermato a Eboli* (1945) began trend toward social realism in postwar Italian literature; other works included *Paura della libertà* (1947), *L'orologio* (1950), *Le parole sono pietre* (1955), *Il futuro ha un cuore antico* (1956), *La doppia notte dei tigli* (1959).

Lé·vi \lā-vē\, Sylvain. 1863–1935. French Orientalist. Professor at Collège de France (1894–1935). Author of *Le Théâtre indien* (1890), *La Doctrine du sacrifice dans les Brâhamanas* (1898), *Le Népal* (1905–08), *L'Inde et le monde* (1926); compiler of *Hôbôgirin, Dictionnaire du Bouddhisme d'après les sources chinoises et japonaises* (1928 ff.).

Le·vi ben Ger·shom \'lē-vī-ben-'gər-shəm, -'gər-səm\. *Also called* Ger·son·i·des \gər-'sän-ə-,dēz\, Leo de Ban·gno·las \bän-'yō-läs\, Leo He·brae·us \hē-'brā-əs\, *and* Ral·bag \'räl-,bäg\. 1288–1344. French Jewish mathematician and philosopher. Author of mathematic treatises *Sefer ha-mispar* (1321), *De sinibus, chordis et arcubus* (1342), *De numeris harmonicis* (1343); philosophical works *Milhamot Adonai* (Wars of God, 1317–29) and *Sefer ha-keshet ha-yashar* (1319); commentaries on the Bible and the Talmud. Invented Jacob's staff and used it to measure angular distance between celestial bodies.

Le·vi-Ci·vi·ta \le-vē-'chē-vē-tä\, Tullio. 1873–1941. Italian mathematician. Professor, Padua (1898), Rome (1918–38). Collaborated with Curbastro Ricci in founding absolute differential calculus (tensor analysis) with their *Méthodes de calcul differéntiel absolu et leurs applications* (1900); introduced concept of parallel displacement in general curved spaces (1917); also contributed to three-body problem, differential geometry, hydrodynamics, engineering. Also published *Lezioni di meccanica razionale* (1923–27), *Lezioni di calcolo differenziale assoluto* (1925), etc.

Lev·in·son \'lev-ən-sən\, Salmon Oliver. 1865–1941. American lawyer and peace advocate, b. Noblesville, Ind. Practiced law, Chicago (from 1891). Originator (1918) and publicist of "outlawry of war" movement; helped draft Kellogg-Briand Pact (1928); established (1929) William Edgar Borah Outlawry of War Foundation at U. of Idaho.

Lé·vis \lā-vē(s)\, François-Gaston de. Duc. 1720–1787. French soldier. Distinguished himself in the War of the Austrian Succession; served in Canada (1756), succeeded to command at Montcalm's death (1759); created marshal of France (1783) and duc de Lévis (1784).

Le·vi·ta \lə-'vē-tə\, Elijah. *Heb. in full* Eliyahu ben Asher Ha-Le·vi Ash·ke·na·zi \hä-'lē-,vī-'ash-kə-'nä-zē\. *Also called* Ba·ḥur \bə-'kür, 'bȯ-,kür\. 1469–1549. Jewish scholar, b. Bavaria. To Italy as young man; taught at Rome, Padua, Venice. Author of *Sefer ha-baḥur* (1518), *Pirqe Eliyahu* (1520), and other works on Hebrew grammar; Masoretic commentaries *Sefer ha-zakhronot* (unpublished) and *Massorot ha-massorot* (1538); lexical works, including *Sefer Meturgeman* (1541) and *Tishbi* (1542).

Levitsky, Ivan. See Ivan NECHUY.

Lev·nî \lev-'nī\, Ressam. d. 1732. Turkish painter. Chief court painter to Ottoman sultans Mustafa II and Ahmed III. Best known for his over 100 illustrations for *Surname-i Vehbi* (c.1720–25); also executed portraits of sultans and series of 50 plates of royal family.

Le·vy \'lē-vē\, Joseph Moses. 1812–1888. English newspaper proprietor. Chief proprietor of *Sunday Times* (1855–56). Acquired (1855) *Daily Telegraph and Courier* and, as the *Daily Telegraph,* turned it into first penny newspaper in London.

Le·vy \'lē-vē, 'lev-ē\, Uriah Phillips. 1792–1862. American naval officer, b. Philadelphia. Commissioned sailing master in navy (1812); captain (1844); flag officer of Mediterranean Squadron (1860); retired (1865). Purchased Jefferson's home, Monticello, and willed it to the nation, but successful contest of the will prevented fulfillment of the bequest.

Lé·vy-Bruhl \lā-vē-brüel\, Lucien. 1857–1939. French philosopher and sociologist. Professor at the Sorbonne (1899–1927); known for studies of mentality and religion of primitive peoples. Author of *La Morale et la science des moeurs* (1903), *Les Fonctions mentales dans les sociétés primitives* (1910), *La Mentalité primitive* (1922), *L'Âme primitive* (1927), *Le Surnaturel et la nature dans la mentalité primitive* (1931).

Le·vy-Law·son \'lē-vē-'lò-sən\, Edward. 1st Baron Burn·ham \'bər-nəm\. *Orig. surname* Levy. 1833–1916. English newspaper proprietor. Son of Joseph Moses Levy; adopted surname Lawson (1875). Editor (1855–1903), managing proprietor (1885–1903), *Daily Telegraph;* supported social reforms and empire; sponsored many charitable appeals; sponsored George Smith's Assyrian expedition (1873), Henry M. Stanley's African expedition (1874); created baron (1903). His son ¶Harry Lawson Webster, *surnamed* Lawson (1862–1933), was M.P. (1885–92, 1893–95); managing proprietor of *Daily Telegraph* (1903–28); again M.P. (1905–06, 1910–16); promoted Territorial Army; chairman of committee formulating teachers' pay scales (1920); chairman of International Labor Conferences, Geneva (1921, 1922, 1926). Succeeded to barony (1916), raised to viscount Burnham (1919).

Le·wald \'lā-,vält\, Fanny. 1811–1889. German novelist. Author of *Clementine* (1843), *Diogena* (1847), *Stella* (1883), *Die Familie Darner* (1887).

Le·wan·dow·ski \lā-vän-'dòf-skē\, Louis. 1821–1894. Polish cantor, chorus conductor, and composer. In Berlin directed music at Old Synagogue (1840–66) and New Synagogue (1866 ff.); taught at Jewish Free School and Jewish Teachers' Seminary. As composer of synagogue music, merged traditional Ashkenazi liturgical melodies with modern harmonies; composed solos for cantor, choral works, and Psalm settings for soloist, choir, and organ; also secular songs, overtures, and symphonies.

Le·wa·ni·ka \lə-wän-'ē-kə\. *Orig.* Ro·bo·si \rō-'bō-sē\ *or* Lu·bo·si \lü-\. c.1842–1916. Lozi king of Barotseland. Acceded to throne (1876) but deposed (1884); regained crown and ruled as Lewanika (1885–1916); accepted British protection; abolished slavery and slave trade.

Lew·es \'lü-əs\, George Henry. 1817–1878. English philosopher and critic. Contributed articles to reviews (1840–49), including many on drama later published as *The Spanish Drama* (1846) and *Actors and Acting* (1875); cofounder (1850) and literary editor of radical weekly *The Leader.* Met (1851) George Eliot (Mary Ann Evans, *q.v.*); separated from his wife (1854) and lived with Eliot for rest of his life. Published *Comte's Philosophy of the Sciences* (1853) and *Life of Goethe,* a biographical classic (1855); as popularizer of science, esp. physiology and psychology, published *Seaside Studies* (1858), *Physiology of Common Life* (1859–60), *Studies in Animal Life* (1862), and *The Problems of Life and Mind* (1874–79), claiming against Comte a place for introspection in psychology, and initiating study of mental phenomena in their relation to social and historical conditions. Edited *The Fortnightly Review* (1865–66).

Lew·in \'lü-ən\, Kurt. 1890–1947. American social psychologist, b. Mogilno, Prussia. Professor, Berlin (1922); to U.S. (1932); professor, U. of Iowa (1935–45); director, group dynamics research center at M.I.T. (1945–47). Author of *A Dynamic Theory of Psychology* (1935), *Principles of Topological Psychology* (1936), *Field Theory in Social Science* (1951), etc.

Lew·is \'lü-əs\, Alun. 1915–1944. Welsh poet. Author of works based on his army experiences, including short-story collection *The Last Inspection* (1942) and verse *Raiders' Dawn* (1942) and *Ha! Ha! Among the Trumpets* (1945); killed in action in Burma.

Lewis, Andrew. 1720–1781. American soldier, b. County Donegal, Ireland. To America (1732); major under Washington in expedition to Fort Duquesne (1754); commanded British contingent that defeated Indians at Point Pleasant (1774), resulting in peace with Indians during early years of Revolution and in the opening up of the way for George Rogers Clark campaign of 1778–79. Brigadier general in Continental army (1776–77).

Lewis, Cecil Day. See DAY-LEWIS.

Lewis, Clarence Irving. 1883–1964. American philosopher, b. Stoneham, Mass. Taught at Harvard (1920–53, professor from 1930). A conceptualistic Pragmatist within a Kantian framework; proposed system of logic based on strict implication. Author of *Symbolic Logic* (1932), *An Analysis of Knowledge and Valuation* (1947), *The Ground and Nature of the Right* (1955), etc.

Lewis, Clive Staples. 1898–1963. English scholar and writer. Fellow and tutor at Oxford (1925–54), professor of English, Cambridge (1954–63). Author of literary studies *Allegory of Love* (1936), *English Literature in the Sixteenth Century* (1954), *The Discarded Image* (1964); seven fantasy tales for children collectively titled *Chronicles of Narnia* (1950–56); autobiography *Surprised by Joy* (1955); novel *Till We Have Faces* (1956); and many works of Christian apologetics including *Pilgrim's Regress* (1933), *The Problem of Pain* (1940), *The Screwtape Letters* (1942, allegorical fiction), and, in science fiction-allegorical form, *Out of the Silent Planet* (1938), *Perelandra* (1943), *That Hideous Strength* (1945).

Lewis, Francis. 1713–1803. American merchant and patriot, b. Llandaff, Wales. To U.S. (1738); N.Y. delegate to Continental Congress (1774–79); signer of Declaration of Independence. His son ¶Morgan (1754–1844), b. New York, was chief of staff for General Gates at Ticonderoga and Saratoga; chief justice of New York Supreme Court (1801–04); governor of New York (1804–07); major general in War of 1812.

Lewis, Gilbert Newton. 1875–1946. American physical chemist, b. Weymouth, Mass. On faculty of M.I.T. (1905–12); professor (1912–46), dean of College of Chemistry (1912–40), U. of California, Berkeley. Did much work in valence theory; proposed (1916) that a chemical bond was a pair of electrons shared or held jointly by two atoms; also made studies on thermodynamics, isotopes, heavy water, fluorescence, color in organic substances, etc. Works included *Valence and the Structure of Atoms and Molecules* (1923) and *Thermodynamics and the Free Energy of Chemical Substances* (1923, with Merle Randall).

Lewis, Isaac Newton. 1858–1931. American army officer and inventor, b. New Salem, Pa. Commissioned in army artillery (1884); invented an artillery position finder (pat. 1891), Lewis machine gun (1911), artillery fire-control system, a gas-propelled torpedo, etc. Originated modern artillery corps organization, adopted by U.S. army in 1902; retired (1913); to Europe, where he manufactured his machine gun in Belgium and later England.

Lewis, John Llewellyn. 1880–1969. American labor leader, b. near Lucas, Iowa. Coal miner; legal representative (1905), vice president (1917), president (1920–60), United Mine Workers' Union. In disagreement with policies of American Federation of Labor (AFL), organized (1935) Committee for Industrial Organization, reorganized (1938) as Congress of Industrial Organizations (both known as CIO), around a nucleus of ten unions, and entered aggressively into competition with AFL; president of CIO (1935–40).

Lewis, Matthew Gregory. *Nicknamed* Monk \'məŋk\ Lewis. 1775–1818. English novelist and dramatist. Attaché at The Hague (1794), where, inspired by Ann Radcliffe's works, he wrote his famous Gothic romance *Ambrosio, or the Monk* (1796), in which the supernatural and horrible predominate; M.P. (1796–1802); produced musical drama *The Castle Spectre* at Drury Lane (1798); succeeded to large fortune and made tours of inquiry into treatment of slaves on West Indian estates, reported in his *Journal of a West Indian Proprietor* (pub. 1834). Author also of *Tales of Terror* (1799), *Tales of Wonder* (1801), and ballads.

Lewis, Meade Anderson. *Called* Lux \'ləks\. 1905–1964. American jazz pianist, b. Chicago. His "Honky Tonk Train Blues" (first issued 1929) was discovered in 1935 and chiefly instigated the boogie-woogie craze of late 1930s.

Lewis, Meriwether. 1774–1809. American explorer, b. Albemarle Co., Va. Private secretary to President Jefferson (1801–03). Named by Jefferson to lead expedition to explore the Louisiana Purchase; selected William Clark (*q.v.*) as coleader. Lewis and Clark expedition (1804–06) went up the Missouri River to its source, crossed the Great Divide, and descended Columbia River to the Pacific Ocean; brought back valuable information on natural features of country, its flora, fauna, Indian tribes, etc. Governor of Louisiana Territory (1807–09).

Lewis, Morgan. See under Francis LEWIS.

Lewis, Sinclair, *in full* Harry Sinclair. 1885–1951. American novelist, b. Sauk Centre, Minn. Journalist and editor (1907–16); m. (1928; div. 1942) Dorothy Thompson (*q.v.*). Author of *Our Mr. Wrenn* (1914), *The Trail of the Hawk* (1915), *The Job* (1917), *Main Street* (1920), *Babbitt* (1922), *Arrowsmith* (1925), *Mantrap* (1926), *Elmer Gantry* (1927), *The Man Who Knew Coolidge* (1928), *Dodsworth* (1929), *Ann Vickers* (1933), *Work of Art* (1933), *It Can't Happen Here* (1935), *Prodigal Parents* (1938), *Bethel Merriday* (1940), *Gideon Planish* (1943), *Cass Timberlane* (1945), *Kingsblood Royal* (1947), *World So Wide* (1951), etc. First American to be awarded the Nobel prize for literature (1930).

Lewis, Wyndham, *in full* Percy Wyndham. 1884–1957. English painter and writer. Founder of Vorticist movement, which sought to relate art to industrial process; founded and edited Vorticist review *Blast* (1914); served in World War I; notorious during 1930s for championing Fascism but later recanted; art critic for *The Listener* (1946–51). His paintings included *Surrender of Barcelona* (1937) and portraits of Dame Edith Sitwell (1935), T.S. Eliot (1938), Ezra Pound (1939). His books included novels *Tarr* (1918), *The Apes of God* (1930), *The Revenge for Love* (1937), *Self-Condemned* (1954), trilogy *The Human Age,* comprising *Childermass* (1928), *Monstre Gai* and *Malign Fiesta* (both 1955); short-story collections *The Wild Body* (1926) and *Rotting Hill* (1951); memoirs *Blasting and Bombardiering* (1937) and *Rude Assignment* (1950); critical works *The Art of Being Ruled* (1926), *Time and Western Man* (1927), *Men Without Art* (1934), *The Writer and the Absolute* (1952).

Ley \'lē, 'lā\, James. 1st Earl of Marl·bor·ough \'märl-,bər-ə, 'mòl-, -,bə-rə, -brə\. 1550–1629. English judge. Lord chief justice in Ireland (1604), in England

(1622–24); lord high treasurer (1624); succeeded Bacon as speaker of House of Lords (1621) and pronounced judgment of peers upon Bacon.

Ley \'lī\, Robert. 1890–1945. German Nazi leader. Entered Nazi party (1924); deputy (1928); leader of the Nazi organization in Munich (1931), in all Germany (1932); as head of Labor Front (from 1933) ruthlessly enforced obedience in labor ranks; committed suicide awaiting trial as war criminal.

Ley·bourn \'lē-ˌbərn\, William. 1626–?1700. English mathematician. Coauthor of *Urania Practica* (1648, first book on astronomy written in English); author of *The Compleat Surveyor* (1653), *Cursus Mathematicus* (1690), and *Panarithmologia* (1693, earliest English ready reckoner), etc.

Ley·den \'lād-ᵊn\, John. 1775–1811. Scottish poet and Orientalist. Contributed to Matthew Lewis's *Tales of Wonder* (1801); assisted Scott in gathering materials for his *Minstrelsy of the Scottish Border;* published poem *Scenes of Infancy* (1803). Collected linguistic and ethnographical information among Indochinese tribes of Malay Peninsula and East Indian islands, published in *Dissertation on the Languages and Literatures of the Indo-Chinese Nations* (1807).

Leyden, Lucas van. See LUCAS VAN LEYDEN.

Ley·dig \'lā-dik\, Franz. 1821–1908. German zoologist. Professor, Tübingen (1857–75) and Bonn (1875–87); discovered cell in interstitial tissue of the testes, gland in mesonephros of vertebrates, mucous cell in epidermis of fish (all named after him). Author of *Lehrbuch der Histologie des Menschen und der Tiere* (1857), *Zelle und Gewebe* (1885), etc.

Leygues \leg\, Georges, *in full* Jean-Claude-Georges. 1857–1933. French politician. Deputy (from 1885); minister of marine (1917–18), rendering important service in coordinating activities of Allied fleets. Premier of France (1920–21). Again minister of marine (1925–30, 1932–33).

Ley·poldt \'lī-ˌpōlt\, Frederick. 1835–1884. American publisher and bibliographer, b. Stuttgart, Germany. To U.S. (1854), naturalized. With Henry Holt established book firm Leypoldt & Holt (1866). Editor and publisher (from 1868) of *Literary Bulletin,* which became (1873) *The Publishers' Weekly,* and (from 1870) of annual catalogues of books published, which developed into *The Publishers' Trade List Annual.* A founder of the *Library Journal* (1876) and its publisher.

L'·Her·bier \ler-byā\, Marcel. 1888–1979. French film director. Pioneer in establishing film as art form; helped found Cinémathèque Française (1936) and Institut des Hautes Études Cinématographiques (1942). His films included *Eldorado* (1921), *L'Argent* (1928), *Le Mystère de la chambre jaune* (1930), *Le Parfum de la dame en noir* (1931), *La Comédie du bonheur* (1940), *La Nuit fantastique* (1942).

L'·Her·mite \ler-mēt\, François, *known as* Tristan. 1601–1655. French poet, playwright, and novelist. Author of verse *Plaintes d'Acante* (1633), *Les Amours de Tristan* (1638), *La Lyre* (1641); autobiographical novel *Le Page disgracié* (1643); comedy *La Parasite* (1653); and tragedies *Mariane* (1636), *La Mort de Sénèque* (1643), *La Mort de Crispe* (1645).

Lhé·vinne \lā-'vēn\, Josef. 1874–1944. Russian pianist. Known for Romantic style, masterly technique, careful musicianship. Debut at Moscow (1889); American debut, New York (1906); toured Europe and U.S. frequently; settled in U.S. (1919); taught privately and at Juilliard School of Music, N.Y.C. His wife (m. 1898) ¶Rosina, *nee* Bes·sie \'bes-ē\ (1880–1976) was an eminent pianist and teacher.

L'·Hos·pi·tal \lō-pē-tȧl, lō-\, Michel de. 1507–1573. French jurist and politician. Councilor to parlement of Paris (1537); Henry II's envoy to Council of Trent (1547); first president of Chambre des Comptes (1555). Chancellor of France (1560); secured passage of act granting toleration to the Huguenots (1562); policy of tolerance failed and religious wars followed, destroying his influence in government; dismissed from office (1568).

Lhote \lōt\, André. 1885–1962. French painter and writer. Initially a Fauvist, later associated with Cubism; contributor to *La Nouvelle Revue Française* (1917–40); established Académie Montparnasse, Paris (1922); published *Traité du paysage* (1939) and *Traité de la figure* (1950). His canvases included *Escale* (1913), *Femme à sa toilette* (1923), *Léda* (1930), *Le Grand Canal* (1934).

Li \'lē\. Name of family that supplied emperors of the T'ang dynasty (618–907) of China. Its more prominent rulers, usually known by their reign titles, included:

Li Yüan \-yue-'än\. *Reign title* Kao Tsu \'gau̇d-zü\, *i.e.* High Progenitor. 565–635. Founder and first emperor (618–626) of T'ang dynasty. Military governor under Sui dynasty; aided by son Li Shih-min and Turkish allies, rebelled and captured Sui capital of Ch'ang-an (617); proclaimed T'ang dynasty and assumed throne (618); reformed tax, monetary, and legal systems but retained Sui system of local government; abdicated in favor of Li Shih-min (626).

Li Shih-min \-'shi(ə)r-'min\. *Reign title* T'ai Tsung \'tīd-'zu̇ŋ\. 600–649. Second emperor (626–649). Instigated revolt in which his father Li Yüan overthrew Sui dynasty (617); expelled Turks (by 624); reconquered southern China and reunited the Chinese Empire; instituted thorough reforms in civil service examinations, army, finance, taxation, land tenure, provincial governments; promoted education and the arts; often considered the greatest Chinese emperor, and his reign a high point of Chinese culture and administration.

Li Chih \-'ji(ə)r\. *Reign title* Kao Tsung \'gau̇d-'zu̇ŋ\. 628–683. Third emperor (649–683). Son of Li Shih-min; constantly at war, esp. against Turks and Tibetans; conquered Korean peninsula and made Korea a vassal state (668); ended lavish expenditures on palace construction started by his father; a weak ruler, in later years dominated by his consort, the empress Wu (see WU CHAO).

Li Che \-'jə\. *Reign title* Chung Tsung \'ju̇ŋ-'dzu̇ŋ\. d. 731. Fourth emperor (683, 705–710). Son of Li Chih and Empress Wu; after reign of one month, forced to abdicate by his mother and replaced by his brother Li Tan (683); restored to throne (705); dominated by a palace faction centered around his wife, Empress Wei; forced to resign by palace coup (710).

Li Tan \-'dän\. *Reign title* Jui Tsung \'zhwēd-'zu̇ŋ\. 662–716. Fifth emperor (684–690, 710–712). Son of Li Chih and Empress Wu; brother of Li Che; placed on throne by Wu (684), later deposed by her (690); restored to throne by coup led by his son Li Lung-chi (710); abdicated.

Li Lung-chi \-'lu̇ŋ-'jē\. *Reign title* Hsüan Tsung \shue-'änd-'zu̇ŋ\. *Also known as* Ming Huang \'miŋ-'hwäŋ\, *i.e.* Brilliant Emperor. 685–762. Sixth emperor (712–756). Led coup to restore his father Li Tan to throne (710); ascended throne after father's abdication (712); carried out reforms of bureaucracy, finance, canal system, taxation, army; patron of arts and letters; established Hanlin Academy; yielded much power to chief minister Li Lin-fu (after 737); in later years dominated by his concubine Yang Kuei-fei (*q.v.*); attacked by forces of his general An Lu-shan (*q.v.*) and fled capital (756); abdicated (756). His reign saw greatest prosperity and power of T'ang dynasty.

Li Kua \-'gwä\. *Reign title* Te Tsung \'dəd-'zu̇ŋ\. 742–805. Ninth emperor (780–805). Determined to restore fortunes of the dynasty; reconstituted former administrative system; promulgated new tax system; failed to control provincial governors; in later years lost power to court eunuchs.

Li Ang \-'äŋ\. *Orig.* Li Han \-'hän\. *Reign title* Wen Tsung \'wənd-'zu̇ŋ\. 809–840. Fourteenth emperor (826–840). His attempts to free court from influence of palace eunuchs all failed, culminating in Sweet Dow Incident of 833 in which his chief ministers and other officials were murdered; afterwards power of eunuchs even greater.

Liadov, Anatoly Konstantinovich. See LYADOV.

Liang \lē-'äŋ\. Name of two Chinese dynasties: (1) Dynasty (502–557), sometimes called Earlier Liang, one of the Six Dynasties, founded by Hsiao Yen (*q.v.*) with its capital at Ku-tsang, succeeded by the Ch'en. (2) Later Liang (907–923), one of the Five Dynasties, founded by Chu Wen (*q.v.*).

Liang Ch'en-yü \-'chən-'yue\. 1510–1580. Chinese dramatist. His *Huan sha chi* initiated the K'un-shan school of dramatic singing that dominated Chinese theater until end of 18th century.

Liang Ch'i-ch'ao \-'chē-'chau̇\. 1873–1929. Chinese scholar and revolutionary leader. Disciple of K'ang Yu-wei; his and K'ang's writings used by emperor in Reform Movement of 1898; reforms suppressed by empress dowager; fled to Japan (1898); associated with Sun Yat-sen, working for reforms, and also with K'ang Yu-wei; returned (1912) to China and conducted a daily paper in Tientsin; held several government positions (1912–14); organized successful resistance to attempt of Yüan Shih-k'ai to establish himself as emperor (1915–16); spent later years teaching and writing books on history, education, literature, etc., placing Western ideas before the Chinese.

Liang K'ai \-'kī\. c.1140–c.1210. Chinese painter. Accorded highest honor (*tai-chao*) at Imperial painting academy; left to become a Ch'an Buddhist priest near Hangchow. His Ch'an paintings marked by vibrant intensity and masterly brush technique.

Li Ao \'lē-'au̇\. d. c.844. Chinese philosopher. High official in T'ang dynasty. Friend or disciple of Han Yu; integrated Buddhist ideas into Confucianism, laying foundations of Neo-Confucianism; helped make *Ta hsüeh, Chung Yung,* and *I Ching* part of Confucian Classics; helped raise reputation of Meng-tzu.

Liap·chev \'lyȧp-chef\, Andrei. 1866–1933. Bulgarian politician. Pioneer in cooperative movement; entered parliament (1908); minister of finance (1908–11, 1918), of war (1918). Prime minister (1926–31); pursued conciliatory foreign policy; avoided war with Yugoslavia.

Li·a·quat Ali Khan \lē-ä-'kwät-'äl-ē-'k̲än\. 1895–1951. Pakistani statesman. Barrister by profession; joined (1923) Muslim League, its general secretary (1936–47); member of United Province Legislative Council (1926–40); Mohammed Ali Jinnah's right-hand man in successful struggle to establish an independent Pakistan. First prime minister of Pakistan (1947–51); laid down domestic and foreign policies which guided country even after his death; assassinated by fanatics for his refusal to wage war on India.

Li·ba·ni·us \lə-'bā-nē-əs, lī-\. 314–393. Greek Sophist and rhetorician, b. Antioch, Syria. Established famous school at Antioch (354); his works included orations, letters, a life of Demosthenes.

Li·bau \'lē-bau̇\, Andreas. *Lat.* Li·ba·vi·us \lə-'bā-vē-əs\. c.1540–1616. German physician, alchemist, and chemist. Professor, Jena (1588–91); inspector of schools and town physician at Rothenburg (1592–1607); rector of Gymnasium Casimirianum, Coburg (from 1607). Pioneered in analytical approach to chemistry; attacked followers of Paracelsus; discovered methods for preparing ammonium sulfate, hydrochloric acid, tin tetrachloride, etc. His *Alchymia* (1606) considered first modern chemistry textbook.

Lib·by \'lib-ē\, Willard Frank. 1908–1980. American chemist, b. Grand Valley, Colo. Taught at U. of Calif., Berkeley (1933–41); member of Manhattan Project (1941–45); with Institute for Nuclear Studies, U. of Chicago (1945–59); professor, U.C.L.A. (1959–80). Awarded Nobel prize for chemistry (1960) for discovery (1947) of carbon-14 dating technique.

Li·be·ra·le da Ve·ro·na \ˌlē-bā-'rä-lā-däv-ā-'rō-nä\. *Also called* Liberale di Ja·co·po dal·la Bra·va \-ˌdē-jä-'kō-pō-ˌdäl-lä-'brä-vä\. c.1445–1526 or 1529. Veronese painter. Worked with Girolamo da Cremona illuminating choir books (1467–69); best known for his illuminated choir books of Siena cathedral (1470–74); also executed frescoes and religious paintings on wood.

Lib·e·ra·ce \ˌlib-ə-'rä-chē\, Wladziu Valentino. 1919–1987. American pianist, b. West Allis, Wis. Flamboyant showman known for a florid piano style and a repertoire mixing current popular songs, old parlor favorites, and up-tempo renditions of classics; appeared (from 1950s) on television and the popular concert circuit; famous for his custom-designed pianos, ubiquitous candelabra, extravagant costumes and jewels, and sentimental patter.

Li·be·ri \'le-bā-re\, Pietro. *Called* il Li·ber·ti·no \ēl-ˌlē-bār-'tē-nō\. 1614–1687. Venetian painter. Known chiefly for his *Battle of the Dardanelles.*

Li·be·ri·us \lī-'bir-ē-əs\. d. 366. Pope (352–366). Involved in controversy between Arians and Athanasius; exiled to Thrace (355) because of his support of Athanasius; replaced by antipope Felix II but reinstated (358).

Li Chin-chung. See WEI CHUNG-HSIEN.

Li Ch'ing-chao \'lē-'chiŋ-'jau̇\. 1081–after 1141. Chinese poet. Considered greatest female poet of China; wrote esp. *tz'u* poetry; only fragments survive of her six volumes of poetry and seven of essays.

Li·cin·i·us \lī-'sin-ē-əs\. *In full* Valerius Licinianus Licinius. d. 325 A.D. Roman emperor (308–324). Of Illyrian peasant stock; rose in army; made augustus in the East by Emperor Galerius (308); became sole emperor in the East (311); m. (313) Constantia, half-sister of Constantine the Great; with Constantine issued Edict of Milan (313) recognizing Christianity; defeated Maximinus (314) and in turn was beaten at Cibalae in Pannonia by Constantine (314); made peace but later resumed the war and was defeated at Adrianople (324) by Constantine; surrendered and was executed.

Lick \'lik\, James. 1796–1876. American financier and philanthropist, b. Fredericksburg, Pa. In California (from 1848); made fortune in real estate. Endowed Lick Observatory, Mount Hamilton, Calif.

Lid·dell \'lid-əl\, Henry George. 1811–1898. English classical scholar. Ordained in Anglican church (1838); headmaster of Westminster School (1846–55); dean of Christ Church, Oxford (1855–91). Joint author with Robert Scott of standard *Greek–English Lexicon* (1843), also wrote *History of Ancient Rome* (1855). It was for his daughter Alice that Lewis Carroll wrote *Alice in Wonderland.*

Lid·dell Hart \ˌlid-əl-'härt\, Sir Basil Henry. 1895–1970. English military historian and strategist. Served through World War I; wrote (1920) official *Infantry Training* manual for army, containing his "battle drill" system and "expanding torrent" method of attack; early advocate of air power and mechanized tank warfare; retired (1927). Military correspondent of *Daily Telegraph* (1925–35), *Times* (1935–39), *Daily Mail* (1941–45). Among his works were military biographies, *The Decisive Wars of History* (1929), *The Remaking of Modern Armies* (1927), *The Future of Infantry* (1933), *A History of The World War* (1934), *The Defence of Britain* (1939), *Dynamic Defence* (1940), *The Strategy of Indirect Approach* (1941), *Deterrent or Defence* (1960), *History of the Second World War* (1970).

Lid·don \'lid-ən\, Henry Parry. 1829–1890. English theologian. Ordained Anglican priest (1852); a leading spokesman of Oxford movement; Ireland professor of exegesis, Oxford (1870–82); canon of St. Paul's Cathedral (1870), chancellor (1886); defended Athanasian Creed. Published *The Divinity of Our Lord and Savior Jesus Christ* (1867), *Life of Edward Bouverie Pusey* (1893–97).

Lid·ner \'lēd-nər\, Bengt. 1757–1793. Swedish poet. Author of cantata text *Grefvinnan Spastaras Död* (1783), opera libretto *Medea* (1784), etc.

Lie \'lē\, Jonas Lauritz Idemil. 1833–1908. Norwegian novelist. Author of *Den fremsynte* (1870), *Tremasteren "Fremtiden"* (1872), *Lodsen og hans Hustru* (1874), *Livsslaven* (1883), *Familien paa Gilje* (1883), *Kommandørens Døtre* (1886); also *Trold* (1891–92, fairy tales), plays, and verse.

Lie, Sophus, *in full* Marius Sophus. 1842–1899. Norwegian mathematician. Professor at Kristiania (1872–86, 1898–99) and Leipzig (1886–98). Discovered contact transformations (1870); contributed to continuous transformation groups, differential geometry, differential equations. Published *Differentialgleichungen* (1891), *Vorlesungen über continuierliche Gruppen* (1893), *Theorie der Transformationsgruppen* (1893), *Geometrie der Berührungstransformationen* (1896).

Lie, Trygve Halvdan. 1896–1968. Norwegian statesman. Legal adviser to Norwegian Labor party (1922–40); minister of justice (1935–39), of shipping and supply (1939–41), of foreign affairs (1941–46). First secretary general, UN (1946–52); secured evacuation of Soviet troops from Iran (1946); undertook peace mission to capitals of major powers (1950); resigned due to Soviet resentment over his support of UN intervention in Korea.

Lie·ber \'lē-bər\, Francis. 1800–1872. American political scientist, b. Berlin, Germany. To U.S. (1827); planned and edited *Encyclopaedia Americana* (13 vols., 1829–33). Professor of history and political economy, South Carolina Coll. (1835–56), Columbia (1857–65), Columbia Law School (1865–72). Author of *Manual of Political Ethics* (1838–39), *Legal and Political Hermeneutics* (1839), *On Civil Liberty and Self-government* (1853), *A Code for the Government of Armies* (1863), which in a revised form was issued by U.S. War Department as *Instructions for the Government of Armies in the Field, General Orders No. 100.*

Lieber, Thomas. See LÜBER.

Lie·ber·kühn \'lē-bər-ˌkūēn\, Johann Nathanael. 1711–1756. German anatomist. A practicing physician; greatly contributed to microscopic technique; discovered (1745) the crypts of Lieberkühn (glands in the intestines).

Lie·ber·mann \'lē-bər-ˌmän\, Carl Theodore. 1842–1914. German chemist. Professor, Charlottenburg (from 1873). With Graebe, produced first synthetic alizarin (1868).

Liebermann, Max. 1847–1935. German painter and etcher. Studied under Steffeck (1866–68) and Millet (1873); founder (1899) and leader of Berliner Sezession. Known for objective paintings of the life and labor of the poor, including *The Flax Spinners, An Asylum for Old Men, Woman Plucking Geese, Country Tavern in Bavaria, Going to School in Edam.*

Lie·big \'lē-bik\, Justus von. Freiherr. 1803–1873. German chemist. Professor at Giessen (1824–52) and Munich (1852–73). Among his contributions to chemistry were the establishment at Giessen of the first practical chemical teaching laboratory, introduction of methods of analysis of carbon, hydrogen, and halogens in organic compounds, a method for manufacture of potassium cyanide, and work in collaboration with Wöhler on constitution of bitter oil of almonds and on uric acid. In biochemistry, investigated constitution of body fluids; considered founder of agricultural chemistry; held that transformation of inorganic into organic substance takes place exclusively in plants, and that plants receive carbon and nitrogen from carbon dioxide and ammonia in the atmosphere while they receive mineral elements from soil; experimented with artificial soil fertilizers.

Lieb·knecht \'lēp-ˌknekt\, Wilhelm. 1826–1900. German journalist and politician. Active in revolution of 1848; in exile (1849–62) in England, where he joined Marx's Communist League; in Leipzig (1865); formed friendship with August Bebel (*q.v.*); together they led German Socialism for rest of century; with him founded Social Democratic Labor party (1869). Member of Reichstag (1867–70, 1874 ff.). Editor, *Demokratisches Wochenblatt* (merged into *Volkstaat,* 1869) and (from 1890) *Vorwärts.* Helped draft Erfurt charter (1891) of German Social Democratic party.

His son ¶Karl (1871–1919) was also a Socialist leader; member, Reichstag (1912); violently opposed Germany's policy (1913–14) leading to World War I; organized antiwar demonstrations (1915, 1916); imprisoned (1916–18); on release (1918), took leadership with Rosa Luxemburg (*q.v.*) of Spartacus League which later became German Communist party; involved in the Spartacist insurrection (Jan. 1919); arrested and murdered (with Luxemburg).

Liebler, Thomas. See LÜBER.

Lieb·mann \'lēp-ˌmän\, Otto. 1840–1912. German philosopher. Professor, Strassburg (1872), Jena (1882); a leader of Neo-Kantianism, esp. with his book *Kant und die Epigonen* (1865).

Liech·ten·stein \'lik-tən-ˌshtīn\. Principality in central Europe and its ruling family; its chief members, holding the title Prince von und zu Liechtenstein, were: Joseph Wenzel (1696–1772), Austrian general; took prominent part in several wars of Austria, esp. that of the succession (1740–48); minister to France (1737–41); reigning prince (1748–72). His great-nephew ¶John I Joseph (1760–1836), Austrian field marshal; fought in Turkish war (1788–91) and in Napoleonic wars (1799–1814); covered retreat at Austerlitz (1805); ruled principality (1805–36). ¶John II (1840–1929), nephew of John I; prince (1858–1929), the longest known period of personal rule in European history. His brother ¶Francis I (1853–1938), prince (1929–38).

Lieh-tzu \lē-'ed-'zü\. *Orig.* Lieh Yü·k'ou \lē-'e-'yūē-'kō\. 4th century B.C. Chinese philosopher. One of three primary originators of Taoism; presumed author of the *Lieh-tzu;* regarded by some as imaginary.

Lietz·mann \'lēt-,smän\, Hans. 1875–1942. German church historian. Professor, Jena (1905–24) and Berlin (1924–42). Began and directed *Handbuch zum Neuen Testament* (1906–31); edited *Zeitschrift für neutestamentliche Wissenschaft* (1920 ff.); wrote *Geschichte der alten Kirche* (1932–44), etc.

Lie·vens *or* **Lie·vensz** *or* **Li·vens** \'lē-vəns\, Jan. 1607–1674. Dutch painter. Studio in Leiden (1621–31), England (1631–34), Antwerp (1635–44), Amsterdam (1644–74). Painter of biblical, mythological, genre, and allegorical scenes, landscapes, and portraits.

Li·far \li-fär\, Serge. 1905–1986. French dancer, choreographer, and ballet master, b. Kiev. Joined Sergey Diaghilev's Ballets Russes in France, becoming company's premier danseur (1925); joined (1929) Paris Opéra Ballet as premier danseur and ballet master; as ballet master (1930–58) staged ballets that were independent of opera; trained the ballet school to perform modern ballets; staged over 50 works, including *Promethée* (1929), *Les Mirages* (1947), *Phèdre* (1950), with themes drawn from mythology, legend, or the Bible. Wrote biographies of Auguste Vestris and Sergey Diaghilev and over 25 books on dance.

Lig·dan Khan \'lig-dän-'kän\. 1591–1634. Last Mongol great khan (1604–34). Attempted unsuccessfully to unify Mongol tribes and establish a monarchy strong enough to withstand Manchus.

Light \'līt\, Francis. c.1740–1794. English colonial administrator. Negotiated acquisition (1786) of Penang Island in Strait of Malacca for use as British naval base; served as its governor.

Light·foot \'līt-,fu̇t\, Joseph Barber. 1828–1889. English theologian. Professor, Cambridge (1861); canon of St. Paul's (1871); bishop of Durham (1879–89). Author of commentaries on Epistles, works on Apostolic Fathers defending authenticity of Epistles of Ignatius; influential member of committee for revision of New Testament (1870–80).

Ligne \lēnʸ\, Charles-Joseph de. Prince. 1735–1814. Belgian soldier. Distinguished himself in the Seven Years' War (1756–63); served in Austrian diplomatic service at various European courts; fought for Russia and Austria in Russo–Turkish War of 1787–92; created field marshal by Catherine II of Russia. Maintained correspondence with leading figures of his time, including Frederick the Great, Voltaire, Goethe. Selections from his writings form *Mélanges militaires, littéraires et sentimentaires* (34 vols., 1795–1811).

Li·go·rio \lē-'gōr-yō\, Pirro. c.1500–1583. Italian architect. Built and decorated Cardinal Ippolito's Villa d'Este of Tivoli (1550–69) and Casino of Pope Pius IV in Vatican Gardens (1558–62); published Roman antiquities.

Liguest, Pierre Laclède. See LACLÈDE.

Li·guo·ri \lē-'gwȯ-rē\, Alfonso Maria de'. Saint. 1696–1787. Italian prelate. Ordained priest (1726); bishop of Sant'Agata dei Goti (1762–75). Founder (1732) of Congregation of the Most Holy Redeemer, commonly known as Redemptorist Order. Author of works on moral theology as *Theologia moralis* (1748), and on ascetic, devotional, and dogmatic subjects. Canonized (1839); declared doctor of the church (1871).

Li Ho \'lē-'hō\. 791–817. Chinese poet. His verse characterized by vivid imagery, odd diction, striking juxtapositions, and unrelieved pessimism.

Liholiho. See KAMEHAMEHA II and IV.

Li Hou-chu. See LI YÜ.

Li Hsiu-ch'eng \'lē-shē-'ü-'chəŋ\. d. 1864. Chinese rebel. Leader (from 1859) of the Taiping Rebellion; unable to take Shanghai (1860–62); captured while defending Nanking and executed.

Li Hung-chang \'lē-'hu̇ŋ-'jäŋ\. 1823–1901. Chinese statesman. Associated with Gen. Gordon in suppression of Taiping rebellion (1861–64); governor of Kiangsu (1862); viceroy of Nanking (1865) and of Canton (1867); viceroy of Chihli (1870); promulgated Western ideas and modernizing projects; China's representative with foreign powers (1870–94); founded Chinese navy; negotiated peace with French (1884–85) over Tonkin difficulties; in supreme command of Chinese forces in Korea at time of outbreak of Chinese–Japanese War (1894); badly defeated; negotiated peace (1895); prime minister (1895–98); commissioner to restore peace after Boxer uprising (1900).

Lij Iya·su \'lē-ē-'yäs-ü\. 1896–1935. Emperor of Ethiopia (1913–17). Succeeded his grandfather Menelik II; deposed by Zauditu.

Li K'o-yung \'lē-'kō-'yu̇ŋ\. d. 908 A.D. Chinese general. Suppressed great peasant rebellion of Huang Cha'ao (884); on breakup of T'ang dynasty (907), established independent state of Chin in Shansi.

Li Kung-lin. See LI LUNG-MIEN.

Lil·burne \'lil-bərn\, John. 1614?–1657. English leader of the Levelers. Imprisoned (1638–40) for importing Puritan publications; fought in Parliamentary army; resigned as lieutenant colonel because of refusal to take the Covenant (1645). Became leading propagandist for Levelers; fierce critic of Parliament and Cromwell; repeatedly imprisoned; twice acquitted of treason (1649, 1655); joined Quakers.

Li·li·en·cron \'lē-lē-ən-,krōn\, Detlev von, *in full* Friedrich Adolf Axel Detlev von. Freiherr. 1844–1909. German writer. Served in Prussian army in Austro–Prussian War (1866) and Franco–Prussian War (1870–71); in German government service (to 1887). Among his volumes of verse were *Adjutantenritte* (1883), *Poggfred* (1896), *Nebel und Sonne* (1900), *Bunte Beute* (1903); among his novels, *Breide Hummelsbüttel* (1887), *Der Mäcen* (1889); among his dramas, *Der Trifels und Palermo* (1886), *Pokahuntas* (1905).

Li·li·en·thal \'lē-lē-ən-,täl\, Otto. 1848–1896. German aeronautical engineer. Studied flight of birds and built gliders in which he demonstrated advantages of curved surfaces over flat ones for wings; wrote pioneering books in aeronautics as *Der Vogelflug als Grundlage der Fliegekunst* (1889).

Li·li·u·o·ka·la·ni \li-,lē-ə-(,)wō-kə-'län-ē\. *Also known as* Lydia Paki Liliuokalani *and* Liliu Ka·ma·ka·e·ha \kə-,mä-kä-'ā-'hä\. 1838–1917. Queen of the Hawaiian Islands (1891–93). m. (1862) John O. Dominis (d. 1891). Succeeded her brother Kalakaua; attempted to restore authority of monarchy; fought annexation; deposed (1893). Composed song "Aloha Oe" (1898); wrote memoirs *Hawaii's Story by Hawaii's Queen* (1898).

Lil·le·bak·ken \'lil-ə-,bäk-kən\, Johan Petter. *Pseudonym* Johan Petter Falk·ber·get \'fälk-,ber-gət\. 1879–1967. Norwegian novelist. Known for realistic novels dealing with peasants, miners, and railway workers, including *Den fjerde nattevakt* (1923) and two sets of trilogies, *Christianus Sextus* (1927–35) and *Nattens brød* (1940–59).

Lil·lie \'lil-ē\, Frank Rattray. 1870–1947. American zoologist, b. Toronto, Ont. Professor, Chicago (1906–35). Director, Marine Biological Laboratory, Woods Hole, Mass. (1910–26); president (1925–42). Known for discoveries concerning fertilization of the ovum and role of hormones in sex determination.

Lil·lo \'lil-(,)ō\, George. 1693–1739. English dramatist. Author of *Silvia* (ballad opera, 1730), *The London Merchant* (domestic tragedy, 1731), *The Christian Hero* (1735), *Fatal Curiosity* (1736), *Marina* (1738). One of first to introduce middle-class characters on English stage.

Lil·ly \'lil-ē\, William. 1602–1681. English astrologer. Published almanac *Merlinus Anglicus Junior* (1644) and annual pamphlets of prophecy; author of *Christian Astrology* (1647); ridiculed as Sidrophel in Butler's *Hudibras.*

Li Lung-mien \'lē-'lu̇ŋ-mē-'en\ *or* **Li Kung-lin** \-'gu̇ŋ-'lin\. 1049–1106. Chinese painter. Official of Northern Sung court at K'ai-feng; painted landscapes and horses, and later chiefly Buddhist subjects; esp. skillful in contrasts of light and shade and in delicate lines.

Lily \'lil-ē\, William. 1468?–1522. English grammarian. Settled in London as private teacher of grammar, said to be first in city to teach Greek; first high master of St. Paul's school (1512–22); known for share in authorship of the old Eton Latin grammar *Brevissima Institutio,* a revision of Colet's *Aeditio.*

Li·man von San·ders \'lē-män-fȯn-'zän-dərs\, Otto. 1855–1929. German general. Entered German army (1874), rising to lieutenant general. Sent to reorganize Turkish army (1913); given command of 1st Turkish army at outbreak of World War I; commanded Turkish armies in Dardanelles (1915), Asia Minor and Syria (1918); defeated in Palestine (1918).

Lim·burg *or* **Lim·bourg** \'lim-,bu̇rk\, Pol and his brothers Hermann and Jehanequin. all b. after 1385–all d. by 1416. Belgian illuminators. In service of duc de Berry (c.1409–16); for him produced, in international Gothic style, brilliantly illuminated books of hours *Belles Heures* (or *Les Heures d'Ailly*) and *Très riches heures* (completed c.1485 by Jean Colombe).

Limerick, Earl of. See Thomas DONGAN.

Li·món \li-'mōn\, José Arcadio. 1908–1972. American dancer and choreographer, b. Culiacán, Sinaloa, Mexico. Founded (1947) José Limón American Dance Co.; on staff of Juilliard School of Music (1953); artistic director, American Dance Theater (1964). Works included *The Moor's Pavane* (1949), *La Malinche* (1949), *The Traitor* (1954), *Emperor Jones* (1956), etc.

Li·mo·sin \lē-mō-zaⁿ\ *or* **Li·mou·sin** \-mü-\, Léonard. c.1505–c.1577. French enameler. Painter and valet de chambre to Francis I (from 1530) and Henry II. Known for his enamelwork, monochromatic and richly colored, on portraits, plates, vessels, votive tablets, etc.; also an accomplished oil painter.

Lin·a·cre \'lin-i-kər\, Thomas. c.1460–1524. English Humanist and physician. One of first propagators of the New Learning in England. Lectured on medical subjects at Oxford; formed circle of scholars with John Colet and William Grocyn; had Erasmus and Sir Thomas More as students; appointed (1500) tutor to Prince Arthur; physician to Henry VIII (1509–20). Founder (1518) and first president of College of Physicians.

Li·na·res \lē-'nä-rās\, José María. 1810–1861. Bolivian politician. President of Bolivia (1857–61), assuming dictatorial powers; ousted by revolution.

Lincoln, Earl of. See Henry de LACY; John de la Pole (1464?–1487) under de la POLE family.

Lin·coln \'liŋ-kən\, Abraham. 1809–1865. Sixteenth president of the United States, b. near Hodgenville, Ky. Moved to Indiana (1816), to Macon County, Ill. (1830); had little formal schooling. Settled in New Salem, Ill., as storekeeper, rail splitter, postmaster, surveyor; studied law in leisure hours (1831–37); elected to Illinois legislature (1834–41). Moved to Springfield (1837); practiced law. Whig member, U.S. House of Representatives (1847–49). Rose to be prominent Illinois circuit-riding lawyer (from 1849); nominated for U.S. Senate (1858); during campaign, stumped Illinois in series of debates with his Democratic opponent, Stephen A. Douglas; took stand against slavery; though defeated for senatorship, campaign made him leading candidate for next Republican presidential nomination. Elected president (1860); after attack on Ft. Sumter, proclaimed blockade of southern ports (Apr. 1861). During Civil War, supported loyally his generals in the field, choosing successively to command the army of the Potomac McClellan, Burnside, Hooker, Meade, and Grant; issued Emancipation Proclamation (Jan. 1, 1863), declaring freedom of the slaves of all states in rebellion; made immortal Gettysburg address dedicating the national cemetery there (Nov. 19, 1863). Renominated and reelected (1864); five days after Lee's surrender at Appomattox Court House had ended Civil War, was shot (Apr. 14, 1865) in Ford's Theater, Washington, D.C., by John Wilkes Booth and died next day.

Lincoln, Benjamin. 1733–1810. American Revolutionary officer, b. Hingham, Mass. Major general in Continental army (1777) in command of militia in Vermont; in command of American army in southern department (Sept. 1778). Captured with his army in Charleston, S.C. (May 1779); exchanged; served in Yorktown campaign (1781); elected secretary of war by Congress (1781–83). Commanded force that suppressed Shays's Rebellion (1787).

Lincoln, Robert Todd. 1843–1926. American lawyer, b. Springfield, Ill. Son of Abraham Lincoln. Served on Grant's staff last few months of Civil War. U.S. secretary of war (1881–85); U.S. minister to Great Britain (1889–93); president, Pullman Co. (1897–1911).

Lind \ˈlind\, James. 1716–1794. Scottish physician. Called "father of naval hygiene in England." Naval surgeon (1739–48); physician at Haslar Naval Hospital, Gosport (1758–94). Experimented with remedies for scurvy; instrumental in admiralty decision to supply navy with lemon juice (1795).

Lind, Jenny, *orig.* Johanna Maria. *Known latterly as* Madame Jenny Lind-Gold·schmidt \-ˈgōlt-shmit, *Angl* -ˈgōl(d)-\. *Called* the Swedish Nightingale. 1820–1887. Swedish soprano singer. Unrivaled master of coloratura; made debut at Stockholm in *Der Freischütz* (1838); court singer (1840). Studied in Paris under García (1841); toured German cities; gained popularity in London (1847–48); retired from operatic stage (1849) and devoted herself to concert singing and oratorio. Engaged in America by P. T. Barnum (1850–52); m. (1852) Otto Goldschmidt; became naturalized British subject (1859); taught at Royal College of Music, London (1883–86).

Lind·bergh \ˈlin(d)-ˌbərg\, Charles Augustus. 1902–1974. American aviator, b. Detroit. Airmail pilot, St. Louis to Chicago (1926). Made first solo nonstop transatlantic flight, from Roosevelt Field, N.Y., to Le Bourget Air Field, Paris (May 20–21, 1927) in his monoplane *Spirit of St. Louis.* Became technical adviser to airlines; advocated U.S. neutrality in World War II, resigning (1941) commission in air corps reserve as result; consultant to Ford Motor Co. and United Aircraft Corp. during World War II; after war, consultant to Pan American Airways and U.S. Dept. of Defense; brigadier general in U.S. air force reserve (1954). Devised for French surgeon Alexis Carrel (*q.v.*) a sterilizable glass pump for circulating culture fluid through an excised organ; later active in conservation work. Author of *We* (1927), *Of Flight and Life* (1948); *The Spirit of St. Louis* (autobiography, 1953; Pulitzer prize).

Lind·blad \ˈlind-blăd\, Bertil. 1895–1965. Swedish astronomer. Director, Stockholm observatory (1927–65). Contributed to theory of galactic structure and motion and to methods of determining absolute magnitude of distant stars; explained star streaming (1926); devised a spectral classification system.

Lin·de \ˈlin-də\, Carl Paul Gottfried von. 1842–1934. German engineer. Professor, Technische Hochschule, Munich (1868–79); developed a methyl ether refrigerator (1874), an ammonia refrigerator (1876); discovered process of liquefying air in large quantities (1895); developed (1902) method of separating pure liquid oxygen from liquid air that resulted in widespread industrial conversion to processes utilizing oxygen.

Lin·de·gren \ˈlin-də-grən\, Erik Johan. 1910–1968. Swedish poet. His *Mannen utan väg* (1942) marked beginning of new Swedish poetry of 1940s; other verse included *Sviter* (1947) and *Vinteroffer* (1954); coeditor of anthology *40-talslyrik* (1947).

Lin·de·mann \ˈlin-də-ˌmän\, Ferdinand von, *in full* Carl Louis Ferdinand von. 1852–1939. German mathematician. Professor, Königsberg (1883) and Munich (1893–1923). Proved that the ratio π is a transcendental number (1882), and hence that it is impossible to "square the circle" by ruler-and-compass construction; originated a method of solving equations of any degree by means of transcendental functions (1892).

Linden, Pieter Cort van der. See CORT VAN DER LINDEN.

Lin·den·thal \ˈlin-dən-ˌthȯl\, Gustav. 1850–1935. American civil engineer, b. Brünn, Austria. To America (1874). Consulting engineer in bridge and railway construction, Pittsburgh (1877–90); commissioner of bridges, New York City (1902–03); consulting engineer for Pennsylvania R.R. tunnels under Hudson and East rivers, New York; consulting engineer and designer, Hell Gate steel-arch bridge over East River, New York (opened 1917).

Lin·det \laⁿ-de\, Jean-Baptiste-Robert. 1746–1825. French politician. Member of Legislative Assembly and National Convention; prepared report (1792) which was basis for act of accusation against Louis XVI; sided with Montagnards as member of Committee of Public Safety (1793–94); extremely efficient as director of Central Food Committee; minister of finance (1799).

Lind·gren \ˈlin(d)-grən\, Waldemar. 1860–1939. American geologist, b. Kalmar, Sweden. To U.S. (1883); with U.S. Geological Survey (1884–1912); professor, M.I.T. (1912–33). Stressed dominance of igneous processes in ore formation; introduced (1913) classification system of ore deposits; one of first to identify contact-metamorphic ore bodies in North America. Wrote *Mineral Deposits* (1913), a standard textbook in economic geology.

Lind·ley \ˈlin-(d)lē\, John. 1799–1865. English botanist and horticulturist. On staff, Horticultural Society of London (1822–62); professor, U. of London (1829–60). Campaigned for classification system of A.L. de Jussieu over that of Linnaeus. Published *A Synopsis of British Flora, Arranged According to the Natural Order* (1829), *An Introduction to the Natural System of Botany* (1830), *The Theory and Practice of Horticulture* (1840), *The Vegetable Kingdom* (1846).

Lindley, William. 1808–1900. English civil engineer. Engineer in chief, Hamburg–Bergedorf Railway (1838–60); chiefly responsible for rebuilding Hamburg after fire of 1842; consulting engineer in other cities (1865–79); constructed sewerage system for Frankfurt am Main that was widely imitated in Europe and America.

Lind·man \ˈlind-män\, Salomon Arvid Achates. 1862–1936. Swedish admiral and politician. Served in navy (1882–91); member of the Diet (1905); minister of the navy (1905) and prime minister of Sweden (1906–11); minister of foreign affairs (1917); again prime minister (1928–30).

Lin·do \ˈlin-dō\, Mark Prager. *Pseudonym* De Oude Heer Smits \də-ˌau̇-də-ˌhār-ˈsmits\, *i.e.* Old Mr. Smits. 1819–1879. Dutch writer, b. London. Settled in the Netherlands; translator of Scott, Fielding, Thackeray, Dickens, and others. Under pseudonym wrote humorous sketches, later collected and published (1877–79) as *Kompleete Werken van den Ouden Heer Smits.* His serious works included *The Rise and Development of the British People* (1868–74).

Lind·say \ˈlin-zē\. Name of Scottish family including the earls of Craw·ford \ˈkrȯ-fərd\ and earls of Bal·car·res \bəl-ˈkar-əs\. Among its members: David (1440?–1495), 5th Earl of Crawford, 1st Duke of Mont·rose \män-ˈtrōz, mən-\, lord high admiral (1476); lord chamberlain (1483); ambassador to England. ¶Patrick (d. 1589), 6th Baron Lindsay of the Byres \ˈbī(ə)rz\; supported plot for murder of Rizzio (1566); guardian of Mary, Queen of Scots (1567); aided in defeat of her adherents at Langside (1568); one of first of Scottish nobles to support cause of Reformers.
¶Colin (1654?–1722), 3d Earl of Balcarres; distinguished himself at Southwold Bay (1672); privy councilor (1680, 1705); joined Prince Charles Edward (1715). His grandson ¶Alexander (1752–1825), 6th earl; soldier; forced to surrender at Ticonderoga (1777); governor of Jamaica (1794–1801); general (1803); representative Scottish peer (1784–1825).

Lindsay *or* **Lynd·say** \ˈlin-zē\, Sir David. c.1490–c.1555. Scottish poet. Influential courtier and diplomat; on missions to European courts. Satirized vices of clergy and abuses in state; influential in turning common people toward the Reformation. Author of *The Dreme* (1528), *The Testament and Complaynt of Our Soverane Lordis Papyngo* (1530), *The Complaynt and Publict Confession of the Kingis Auld Hound* (c.1536), *Ane Satyre of the Thrie Estaitis* (1540).

Lindsay, David. 1856–1922. Australian explorer. Traversed Australia from north to south (1888); on journey across Victoria Desert, discovered auriferous area which led to discovery of goldfields of West Australia; explored Northern Territory (1916–20).

Lindsay, Howard. 1889–1968. American playwright, producer, and actor, b. Waterford, N.Y. Coauthor with Russel Crouse (*q.v.*) of musical comedies *Anything Goes* (1934), *Red, Hot, and Blue* (1936), *Hooray for What?* (1937), *Strip for Action* (1942), *State of the Union* (1946), *Call Me Madam* (1950), *Tall Story* (1959), *Sound of Music* (1959), *Mr. President* (1962), and a dramatization of Clarence Day's *Life with Father* (1939).

Lindsay, Norman Alfred William. 1879–1969. Australian cartoonist, illustrator, and novelist. Cartoonist on *Sydney Bulletin* (from 1901); produced erotic illustrations, principally in Art Nouveau manner, for many classics, including Theocritus, Boccaccio, Petronius, Casanova, Rabelais, and own novel *The Cautious Amorist.* Joint founder of Endeavour Press. Author of *A Curate in Bohemia* (1913), *The Magic Pudding* (1919), *Redheap* (1931), *Saturdee* (1933), *Pam in the Parlour* (1934), *Age of Consent* (1938), *The Cousin from Fiji* (1945), etc.

Lindsay, Vachel, *in full* Nicholas Vachel. 1879–1931. American poet, b. Springfield, Ill. Studied painting, Chicago (1900–03) and New York (1904–05). Tramped like a troubadour through the South (1906) and West (1912), exchanging his poems for bed and board. First volume of poems *General William Booth Enters into Heaven and Other Poems* (1913) was followed by the successful *The Congo and Other Poems* (1914). Lectured and chanted his own verses through the U.S. in attempt to revive poetry as oral art form among the common people. Later volumes *Adventures While Preaching the Gospel of Beauty* (1914), *Art of the Moving Picture* (1915; one of first serious evaluations of film), *The Golden Book of Springfield* (1920), *The Golden Whales of California* (1920), *Going-to-the Sun* (1923), *The Candle in the Cabin* (1926), etc.

Lind·sey \'lin-zē\, Benjamin Barr. 1869–1943. American jurist, b. Jackson, Tenn. Wrote statute establishing (1899) at Denver the first juvenile court in U.S.; its presiding judge (1900–27); introduced reforms, as that juvenile offenders should be treated rather than punished, that they should be protected as wards of the court. Judge, Superior Court of California (from 1934); helped establish at Los Angeles a conciliation court for divorce cases and served as its judge (1939–43). Author of *Problems of the Children* (1903), *The Revolt of Modern Youth* (with Wainwright Evans, 1925), *The Companionate Marriage* (with Evans, 1927), autobiography *The Dangerous Life* (with Rube Borough, 1931), etc.

Lin·gard \'liŋ-ˌgärd\, John. 1771–1851. English historian. Author of *The Antiquities of the Anglo-Saxon Church* (1806) and *History of England* (8 vols., 1819–30).

Ling·el·bach \'liŋ-əl-bäk\, Jan. 1622–1674. Dutch painter. Known esp. for genre scenes and landscapes.

Lin·guet \laⁿ-ge\, Simon-Nicolas-Henri. 1736–1794. French lawyer and journalist. Editor of *Annales Politiques* (1777–92); notorious for controversial writings as attacks on lawyers and the duc de Duras; confined in the Bastille (1780–82) and published *Mémoires sur la Bastille* (1783); fled to Brussels to escape the Revolution but returned too soon (1791); guillotined.

Li·niers \lē-'nyers, *Fr* lēn-yā\, Santiago Antonio María de. 1753–1810. Spanish naval officer, b. France. Seized Buenos Aires from British (1806); installed as viceroy; dismissed by Spanish Central Junta (1809); joined revolutionary movement attempting to reestablish royal authority (May 1810); captured and shot.

Link \'liŋk\, Edwin Albert. 1904–1981. American inventor and businessman, b. Huntingdon, Ind. With his brother George, invented (1929) the Link flight simulator for training pilots in the classroom; founder and president (1935–53), Link Aviation, Inc.; president, General Precision Corp. (1958–59). Also invented equipment for oceanographic use.

Link·la·ter \'liŋ-ˌklāt-ər, -klət-\, Eric Robert Russell. 1899–1974. Scottish novelist, dramatist, and historical writer. Author of *Poet's Pub* (1929), *Juan in America* (1931), *Ben Jonson and King James* (1931), *The Men of Ness* (1932), *Mary Queen of Scots* (1933), *Robert the Bruce* (1934), *Magnus Merriman* (1934), *Juan in China* (1937), *Private Angelo* (1946), *Position at Noon* (1958), *The Voyage of the Challenger* (1972), etc., and autobiographies *The Man on My Back* (1941), *A Year of Space* (1953), *Fanfare for a Tin Hat* (1970).

Lin·ley \'lin-lē\, Thomas. 1732–1795. English composer. With his son ¶Thomas (1756–1778), violinist and composer, composed or compiled music for his son-in-law R. B. Sheridan's comic opera *The Duenna* (1775); musical director at Drury Lane and composer of songs and operas (1776–81). For his daughter Elizabeth Ann, see Richard Brinsley SHERIDAN.

Linlithgow, Marquises of. See John Adrian Louis HOPE.

Linnaeus. See LINNÉ.

Linnankoski, Johannes. See Vihtori PELTONEN.

Lin·né \lin-'ā\, Carl von. *Lat.* Carolus Lin·nae·us \lə-'nē-əs, -'nā-\. 1707–1778. Swedish botanist. A father of modern systematic botany. Appointed lecturer in botany at Uppsala (1730); explored Lapland for Acad. of Sciences (1732), publishing scientific results in *Flora Lapponica* (1737); traveled through Dalecarlia, Sweden; took M.D. at Harderwijk, Holland (1735). Published *Systema Naturae* in which he presented his system of botanical nomenclature (1735); while still in Holland, wrote also *Fundamenta Botanica* (1736), *Bibliotheca Botanica* (1736), *Hortus Cliffortianus* (1737), *Critica Botanica* (1737), *Genera Plantarum* (1737), and *Classes Plantarum* (1738). Traveled to England and France; returned to Sweden and established himself as physician at Stockholm (1738); professor of medicine (1741) and botany (from 1742), Uppsala. Toured Öland and Gotland (1742), publishing results in *Olandska och gothländska resa* (1745), in which botanical specific names were first used. Other important publications included *Flora Suecica* and *Fauna Suecica* (1745), *Hortus Upsaliensis* (1748), *Philosophia Botanica* (1750), and *Species Plantarum,* which gave a full account of specific names and is considered foundation for modern system of botanical nomenclature (1753).

Lin·nell \'lin-əl\, John. 1792–1882. English painter. Painted portraits and landscapes; patron and friend of William Blake.

Lin Piao \'lin-bē-'au̇\. 1908–1971. Chinese soldier and politician. Joined Socialist Youth League (1925); served under Chiang Kai-shek (1926–27); joined (1928) Mao Tse-tung in south central China and soon established himself as one of ablest commanders in Red army; noted as a tactician; a leader of the Long March (1934–35). Commanded Communist forces against Japan and against Chiang in post-World War II civil war; captured all of Manchuria (by 1948), Peking (1949). Held high positions in government; elected to Politburo (1955) and Politburo's Standing Committee (1958); defense minister (1959); vice chairman of party (1969) and thus Mao's heir apparent; killed in a plane crash.

Lin·scho·ten \'lin-ˌskō-ten\, Jan Huyghen van. 1563–1611. Dutch traveler. In Goa, gathered information on Indonesia (1583–89); promoted Dutch attempts to find northeast passage to East Indies; took part in Barents's second voyage into Kara Sea (1594–95) and published journal (1601); also author of *Itinerario, voyage ofte schipvaert naer Oost ofte Portugaels Indien* (1596).

Lins do Rê·go \'lēⁿ(n)s-thü-'rā-gü\, José. 1901–1957. Brazilian novelist. Member of Brazilian "Northeast" school of Realists. Best known for "Sugar Cane" cycle of social novels comprised of *Menino de Engenho* (1932), *Doidinho* (1933), *Bangüê* (1934), *O moleque Ricardo* (1935), *Usina* (1936); also wrote *Pedra Bonita* (1938), *Fogo morto* (1943), *Os cangeceiros* (1953).

Lin Shu \'lin-'shü\. 1852–1924. Chinese translator. Ignorant of any foreign language and working through oral interpreters, produced over 170 translations of Western books; although criticized for their errors, his translations were important for introducing Western literature to China.

Linth, Hans Konrad von der Escher. See ESCHER VON DER LINTH.

Lin·ton \'lint-ən\, Ralph. 1893–1953. American anthropologist, b. Philadelphia. Professor, U. of Wisconsin (1928–37), Columbia (1937–46), Yale (1946–53). Contributed to development of cultural anthropology. Author of *The Material Culture of the Marquesas Islands* (1924), *The Tanala, a Hill Tribe of Madagascar* (1933), *The Study of Man* (1936), *The Cultural Background of Personality* (1945), *The Tree of Culture* (1955).

Linton, William James. 1812–1897. American wood engraver, reformer, and writer, b. London, England. Active in Chartist agitation (1841–42); wrote *To the Future* (1848), *The Plaint of Freedom* (1852), *Claribel and Other Poems* (1865). To U.S. (1866) and set up printing press at New Haven, Conn.; made engravings for *Frank Leslie's Illustrated News,* Whittier's *Snow-Bound,* Longfellow's *Building of the Ship,* Bryant's *Thanatopsis* and *The Flood of Years;* wrote *The Masters of Wood-Engraving* (1889). His wife (m. 1858) ¶Eliza, *nee* Lynn \'lin\ (1822–98) gained success as novelist with *Joshua Davidson* (1872), *Autobiography of Christopher Kirkland* (1885), and with *Girl of the Period* articles in *Saturday Review.*

Lin Tse-hsü \'lin-'dzə-shü\. 1785–1850. Chinese official. Entered government bureaucracy (1820); as governor general of Hunan and Hupeh, suppressed opium traffic (1837); sent by Emperor Min-ning to handle opium situation at Canton (1838); ordered (1839) destruction of $6,000,000 worth of opium owned by foreign merchants, which led to Opium War (1839–42); opposed to opening China to foreigners; proponent of revitalization of traditional Chinese thought and institutions, the "self-strengthening" movement; recalled by emperor (1841) because of difficulties due to his policies; banished to Kulja (1843); recalled (1845) and served as governor of different provinces (1846–50).

Li·nus \'lī-nəs\. Saint. d. 76 or 79. Pope (67–76 or 79). Generally considered as the successor to St. Peter.

Lin Yü-t'ang \'lin-'yœ̄-'täŋ\. *Commonly written* Lin Yutang. 1895–1976. Chinese author and philologist. Editor of several English-language journals; founded (1932) *Lun-yü pan-yüeh-kan,* first Western-style satirical magazine in China; inventor of Chinese indexing system and collaborator in official romanization plan. Lived chiefly in U.S. (from 1936). Author in Chinese and English of novels, critical and satirical essays, plays, short stories, works on philosophy and history, translations, etc.; works included *My Country and My People* (1936), *The Importance of Living* (1937), *Moment in Peking* (1939), *With Love and Irony* (1940), *A Leaf in the Storm* (1941), *Chinatown Family* (1948), *Lady Wu* (1956), etc.

Li·o·nel \'lī-ən-əl\ of Ant·werp \'ant-ˌwərp, 'an-ˌtwərp\. Duke of Clar·ence \'klar-ən(t)s\. 1338–1368. English prince. Third son of Edward III; m. (1341) Elizabeth, daughter of William de Burgh, Earl of Ulster; father's representative in England (1345, 1346); governor of Ireland (1361–66); created duke of Clarence (1362). Father of Philippa, who married (1368) Edmund Mortimer, 3d Earl of March.

Lionne \lyȯn\, Hugues de. 1611–1671. French diplomat. Adviser to Mazarin on foreign affairs (1643); assisted Mazarin in negotiating Treaty of Westphalia (1648); negotiated Treaty of the Pyrenees (1659). French ambassador at Rome

(1654), Madrid (1656), Frankfurt (1657), Turin (1658). Secretary of state for foreign affairs (1663–71); persuaded Louis XIV to claim most of Spanish Netherlands, which led to War of Devolution (1667–68) against Spanish; laid diplomatic groundwork for war (1672–78) against Dutch.

Lio·tard \lyȯ-tär\, Jean-Étienne. 1702–1789. Swiss painter. Produced notable pastel portraits of Pope Clement XII (1735), Empress Maria Theresa and her family (1743), Princess of Wales (1753), and others; also executed pastel drawings, genre scenes, enamels, copperplate engravings, glass paintings. Wrote *Traité des principes et des règles de la peinture* (1781).

Liou·ville \lyü-vēl\, Joseph. 1809–1882. French mathematician. Taught at École Polytechnique (1831–51), Collège de France (1837–43, 1851–79), Faculté des Sciences de Paris (1857–74). Founder and editor (1836–74) of *Journal de mathématiques pures et appliquées* (also known as *Journal de Liouville*). Worked in mathematical analysis; discovered transcendental numbers (1844) and developed theory of doubly periodic functions (1847); contributed to differential equations, boundry-value problems, differential geometry, and theory of numbers.

Lip·chitz \lēp-shēts, *Angl* ˈlip-(ˌ)shits\, Jacques. 1891–1973. French sculptor, b. Latvia of Polish-Jewish parents. To Paris (1909, naturalized 1925). One of first to produce Cubist sculpture; at first worked in solid blocks of material or low-relief still lifes, executing works as *Sailor with a Guitar* (1914); began (1925) working in more abstract forms called *sculptures transparentes,* including *Joie de vivre* (1927), *Harpist* (1928), *The Couple* (1928–29), *Chant des Voyelles* (1931), *Prometheus* (1936). Resident in U.S. (from 1941); reverted to more solid representations imbued with spiritual content, often on biblical or mythological themes; later works included *Prayer* (1943), *Dancing Girl with Braids* (1948), *Spirit of Enterprise* (1960), series of "semi-automatics" as *Only Inspiration* and *Gypsy Dancer* (1952–53), and series of bronzes called *À la limite du possible* including *The Artichokes* (1958) and *The Bone* (1959).

Lip·kin \ˈlip-kin\, Israel. *In full* Israel ben Ze'ev Wolf Lipkin. *Known as* Israel Sa·lan·ter \ˈsäl-än-tar\. 1810–1883. Lithuanian rabbi. Founder of the Musar movement of Jewish Orthodoxy which emphasized personal piety as a complement to Talmudic studies.

Lip·mann \ˈlip-mən\, Fritz Albert. 1899–1986. American biochemist, b. Königsberg, Germany. Professor at Harvard U. (1941–57) and at Rockefeller U. (1957–70). Shared 1953 Nobel prize for physiology or medicine for discovery of coenzyme A, a key substance in the human body's metabolism. Author of *Wanderings of a Biochemist* (1971).

Li Po \ˈlē-ˈbō\. *Literary name* Li T'ai-po \ˈlē-ˈtī-ˈbō\. 701–762. Chinese poet. Probably the greatest poet China has produced. Lived a dissipated life, part of the time at the court of the T'ang emperor and part wandering about in disgrace; one of a hard-drinking band known as "the Eight Immortals of the Wine Cup"; according to popular legend, drowned from a boat in an effort while tipsy to embrace the reflected moon. Famous for the exquisite imagery, richness of language, allusions, and cadence of his lyrics.

Lip·pe \ˈlip-ə\. A former German principality and its ruling family, which had its origin in the 12th century; founded (1123) by Bernhard I (1113–1144); became a county (1529); divided (1613) into two lines: Lippe-Det·mold \-ˈdet-ˌmȯlt\ and Lippe-Al·ver·dis·sen \-ˈäl-vər-ˌdē-sən\, which later (1643) became the Schaumburg-Lippe county (*q.v.*); became principality (1720).

Lip·pers·hey \ˈlip-ərs-ˌhī\, Hans. *Known also as* Hans *or* Jan Lip·pers·heim \ˈlip-ərs-ˌhīm\. c.1570–c.1619. Dutch spectacle maker. Credited with invention of the telescope (1608).

Lip·pi \ˈlēp-pē\, Filippo. *Known as* Fra Filippo Lippi. c.1406–1469. Florentine painter. Carmelite monk (1421 ff.); released from monastic vows by Pius II (c.1461). Influenced by Masaccio, later by Fra Angelico. His works included frescoes *Life of St. John the Baptist* and *Life of St. Stephen* (in Prato cathedral) and *Life of the Virgin* (in cathedral at Spoleto), and canvases as *Coronation of the Virgin, Madonna and Child Enthroned, Adoration of the Magi, Adoration of the Child with St. Hilary, Madonna and Child with Two Angels, Vision of St. Bernard, Annunciation, St. Lawrence.*

Lippi, Filippo, *known as* Filippino. c.1457–1504. Florentine painter. Son of Filippo Lippi; apprenticed to Botticelli (1469–73). Completed frescoes of Masaccio in the Brancacci chapel, as *SS. Peter and Paul Raising the Dead Youth;* other works included frescoes in church of Sta. Maria sopra Minerva at Rome, in the Strozzi Chapel at Florence, in Lorenzo de' Medici's villa at Poggio a Caiano; altarpiece in church of San Michele at Lucca; and canvases *Journey of Tobias, Vision of St. Bernard, Virgin Enthroned, Madonna with Saints, Crucifixion, Adoration of the Magi, The Virgin and Child, with St. Joseph and an Angel.*

Lippi, Lorenzo. *Anagrammatic pseudonym* Per·lo·ne Zi·po·li \pär-ˈlō-nāt-ˈsē-pō-lē\. 1606–1664. Florentine poet and painter. Known particularly for his comic epic *Il malmantile racquistato* (pub. 1676).

Lip·pin·cott \ˈlip-ən-kət, -ˌkät\, Joshua Ballinger. 1813–1886. American publisher, b. Juliustown, N.J. Began J. B. Lippincott & Co., Philadelphia (1836); notable publications, a *Pronouncing Gazetteer* (1855), a *Dictionary of Biography and Mythology* (1870). Founded *Lippincott's Magazine* (1868). His son ¶Joshua Bertram (1857–1940) was vice president of the J. B. Lippincott Co. (1886–1911), president (1911–26), chairman of the board (from 1926).

Lip·pisch \ˈlip-ish\, Alexander Martin. 1894–1976. American aeronautical engineer, b. Munich, Germany. His designs of tailless and delta-winged aircraft in 1920s and '30s important in development of jet and rocket airplanes; designed world's first successful rocket-propelled airplane (flown 1928); chief designer of Messerschmitt Me 163, first operational jet fighter (1944). To U.S. after war; established (1965) Lippisch Research Corp. at Cedar Rapids, Ia.

Lipp·mann \lēp-män\, Gabriel-Jonas. 1845–1921. French physicist. Professor at Sorbonne (from 1883). Invented capillary electrometer (1873); devised (1891) process of photography in natural colors in which light is reflected back on itself; for it was awarded 1908 Nobel prize for physics. Author of *Cours de thermodynamique* (1886) and *Cours d'acoustique et d'optique* (1888).

Lipp·mann \ˈlip-mən\, Walter. 1889–1974. American journalist and author, b. New York City. A founder (1914) and associate editor, *New Republic;* editorial writer (1921–29), editor (1929–31), New York *World;* columnist, New York *Herald Tribune* (1931–67; Pulitzer prize, 1958 and 1962). Assistant to secretary of war (1917); took part in Paris Peace Conference (1918–19). Author of *A Preface to Politics* (1913), *Drift and Mastery* (1914), *The Stakes of Diplomacy* (1915), *Public Opinion* (1922), *The Phantom Public* (1925), *A Preface to Morals* (1929), *The Method of Freedom* (1934), *The Good Society* (1937), *Essays in the Public Philosophy* (1955).

Lipps \ˈlips\, Theodor. 1851–1914. German philosopher. Professor at Bonn (1884–90), Breslau (1890–94), Munich (1894–1914). Developed theory of aesthetics based on concept of *Einfühlung* (empathy). Works included *Grundtatsachen des Seelenlebens* (1883), *Raumästhetik und geometrisch-optische Täuschungen* (1897), *Die ethischen Grundfragen* (1899), *Ästhetik* (1903–06).

Lips \ˈlips\, Joest. *Lat.* Justus Lip·si·us \ˈlip-sē-əs\. 1547–1606. Flemish Humanist and philosopher. Professor at Jena (1572), Leiden (1578), Louvain (1592). Opponent of Ciceronian prose style; instrumental in revival of Stoic philosophy, esp. with his *De constantia* (1584); caused controversy by presenting theory of toleration in *Politicorum libri sex* (1589). Published editions of Tacitus (1574), Valerius Maximus (1585), tragedies (1589) and philosophical works (1605) of Seneca.

Lips, Johann Heinrich. 1758–1817. Swiss painter and engraver. Best known for his engravings after the old masters; also engraved portraits of many of his contemporaries, including Goethe and Wieland.

Lipsius, Justus. See Joest LIPS.

Lip·si·us \ˈlip-sē-ůs\, Richard Adelbert. 1830–1892. German theologian. Professor, Vienna (1861), Kiel (1865), Jena (1871–92). Clarified origin and authorship of early Christian literature, esp. apocryphal Acts of the Apostles; integrated aspects of Kantian Idealism with systematic theology in *Philosophie und Religion* (1885). Cofounder of the Evangelical Union. Chief work *Lehrbuch der evangelisch-protestantischen Dogmatik* (1876).

Lip·sky \ˈlip-skē\, Louis. 1876–1963. American editor, b. Rochester, N.Y. Editor, *Maccabean Monthly,* official organ of Federation of American Zionists; editor, *The New Palestine.* A leader in the Zionist movement.

Lip·ton \ˈlip-tən\, Sir Thomas Johnstone. 1st Baronet. 1850–1931. British merchant and yachtsman, b. Glasgow of Irish parents. Worked in U.S. at various jobs (1865–75). Opened grocery store in Glasgow (1876) which expanded into a large chain of stores throughout Great Britain, dealing in tea, coffee, cocoa, and various groceries and meat products; acquired plantations in Ceylon, packing houses and factories in England and Chicago; incorporated (1898). Competed for the America's Cup with five yachts, each named *Shamrock* (1899, 1901, 1903, 1920, 1930).

Li Rois Adenes. See ADENET LE ROI.

Li·sa \ˈlē-sə, -(ˌ)sä\, Manuel. 1772–1820. American fur trader, b. New Orleans. Headquarters at St. Louis (from c.1790); explored upper Missouri River region, establishing trading posts in successive expeditions (from 1807), esp. Ft. Lisa near present Omaha, Neb. (1812); took part in famous exploration race against flotilla sent out by John J. Astor (1811).

Lis·boa \lēs-ˈbō-å\, Antônio Francisco. *Known as* Alei·ja·di·nho \ä-lā-zhá-ˈdēn-yü\, *i.e.* Little Cripple. 1738?–1814. Brazilian sculptor and architect. Designed, built, and decorated sanctuary of Bom Jesus de Matozinhos in Congonhas do Campo (1757–77), church of São Francisco in Ouro Preto (1766–94); noted for Rococo statuary.

Lisgar, Baron. See Sir John YOUNG.

Li Shang-yin \ˈlē-ˈshäŋ-ˈyin\. 813–858. Chinese poet. Had undistinguished career as government official. His poetry characterized by exotic imagery, abstruse allusions, political allegory, and personal satire involving both historical and contemporary events and figures.

Li Shao-chün \ˈlē-ˈshau̇-ˈjuen\. 2d century B.C. Chinese philosopher. In service of Emperor Wu Ti (from 133 B.C.). Responsible for much of the mystical content of Taoist thought; introduced hygienic exercises, worship of Tsao Chün the Furnace Prince, and claim that ultimate goal of the Taoist was to become a *hsien* (immortal sage).

Li Shih-chen \ˈlē-ˈshi(ə)r-ˈjən\. 1518–1593. Chinese pharmacologist. Compiled *Pen-ts'ao kang-mu* (completed 1578), a giant materia medica describing over 2000 drugs and some 8000 prescriptions.

Lisle, Viscounts. See (1) John DUDLEY; (2) SIDNEY family.

Lisle *or* **l'Isle, de.** See (1) DELISLE; (2) LECONTE DE LISLE; (3) ROUGET DE LISLE; (4) VILLIERS DE L'ISLE-ADAM.

Lisle \ˈlīl, ˈlēl\, Alice, *nee* Beck·en·shaw \ˈbek-ən-ˌshȯ\. 1614?–1685. English woman. m. (1630) John Lisle (1610?–1664), member of Cromwell's House of Lords and a regicide. Tried for sheltering two of Monmouth's supporters at her house overnight; beheaded at Winchester.

Lis·sa·jous \lē-sä-zhü\, Jules-Antoine. 1822–1880. French physicist. Known for researches in acoustics, esp. on vibratory movements, and in optics; investigated (1857–58) Lissajous figures (also called Bowditch curves) which had been studied earlier (1815) by Nathaniel Bowditch.

Lissandrino. See Alessandro MAGNASCO.

Lis·sitz·ky \lyi-ˈsyēt-skəi, *Angl* lə-ˈsits-kē\, Eliezer, *called* El. 1890–1941. Russian painter, typographer, and designer. Taught (1919–21) at revolutionary art school at Vitebsk, where he was influenced by Kasimir Malevich; produced (from 1919) series of abstract paintings collectively called *Proun.* In Germany (1921–28); helped edit Constructivist and other progressive art magazines and associated with members of de Stijl movement; designed on his *Proun* theory exhibition halls built in Berlin (1923), Dresden (1926), Hanover (1928); employing Constructivist methods of spatial photomontage, lettering, light, etc., devised innovations in typography, advertising, and exhibition design which had considerable influence in western Europe; published *Die Kunstismen* (1924, with Hans Arp). Returned to Moscow (1928), where he continued to produce innovative designs for exhibitions and architecture.

Li Ssu \ˈlē-ˈsü\. 280?–208 B.C. Chinese minister of state. Entered Ch'in government service (247); minister of Emperor Cheng (*q.v.*) and responsible for suggesting most of the emperor's radical political and cultural innovations after 221; instrumental in creating a unified writing system used in China until recent times; advised (213) the emperor to burn the classics in order to break off absolutely all connection with the past; killed as result of a court intrigue.

Li Ssu-hsün \ˈlē-ˈsü-ˈshüen\. 651–716. Chinese painter. Founder of Northern school of professional painters and chief exponent of a decoratively colored landscape style of the T'ang dynasty; no genuine works extant.

List \ˈlist\, Georg Friedrich. 1789–1846. American economist, b. Reutlingen, Germany. Founder and secretary of association of German industrialists that opposed tariff barriers between German states; imprisoned, charged with sedition (1824); to U.S. (1825, naturalized). Became a leader in advocacy of protective tariff; U.S. consul at Baden (1831–34), Leipzig (1834–37), Stuttgart (1843–45). Author of *Outlines of American Political Economy* (1827), *The National System of Political Economy* (1841), etc.

List, Siegmund Wilhelm Walther. 1880–1971. German soldier. Served in World War I; general (1930); commander of Austrian army (1938), of armies of occupation in Czechoslovakia (1939), of army which broke French defenses at Sedan (1940); field marshal; commander in Balkans (1941), on Moscow front (Dec. 1941), on Stalingrad front (Sept. 1942). Imprisoned for war crimes (1948–52).

Lis·ta y Ara·gón \ˈlēs-tä-ē-ä-rä-ˈgōn\, Alberto. 1775–1848. Spanish mathematician, poet, critic, and educator. Ordained priest (1803); founded and directed college of San Mateo (1820–23); editor, *Gaceta de Madrid* (1833 ff.). Works included *El império de la estupidez* (1798), *Poesías* (1822), *Lecciones de literatura española* (1836), *Ensayos literarios y críticos* (1844).

Lis·ter \ˈlis-tər\, Joseph. 1st Baron Lister of Lyme Re·gis \ˌlīm-ˈrē-jəs\. 1827–1912. English surgeon and medical scientist. Son of Joseph Jackson Lister; surgeon to Edinburgh Royal Infirmary (1856), to Glasgow Royal Infirmary (1861); professor at Glasgow (1859–69), Edinburgh (1869–77), King's College, London (1877–93). Founder of antiseptic surgery; made study of inflammation and suppuration following injuries and wounds and began experiments in asepsis (c.1861); influenced by Pasteur's discoveries; introduced carbolic acid as an antiseptic (1865); demonstrated conclusively that his method of antisepsis reduced danger to life from surgery (1877). Created baronet (1883), baron (1897).

Lister, Joseph Jackson. 1786–1869. English optician. Wine merchant by trade. Investigated principles of construction of the object glasses of microscopes and discovered fundamental principle (law of the aplanatic foci) of the modern instrument (1830); first to ascertain true form of red corpuscle of mammalian blood (1834).

Lister, Samuel Cunliffe. 1st Baron Mas·ham \ˈmas-əm, ˈmash-əm\. 1815–1906. English inventor. With his brother John, established (1838) at Manningham a worsted-milling business; invented a wool-combing machine (1845), a silk-combing machine utilizing silk waste (c.1865), a velvet loom for making piled fabrics (c.1878), and other clothmaking devices; created baron (1891); noted as art collector, philanthropist.

Lis·ton \ˈlis-tən\, Charles, *nicknamed* Sonny. 1917?–1970 or 1971. American boxer, b. St. Francis Co., Ark. Won world heavyweight championship by knocking out Floyd Patterson in Chicago (Sept. 25, 1962); lost title (Feb. 25, 1964) in Miami Beach, Fla., to Cassius Clay (later Muhammad Ali).

Liston, Robert. 1794–1847. Scottish surgeon. Renowned for surgical skill and for invention of the Liston splint used in cases of thigh dislocation.

Liszt \ˈlist\, Franz. 1811–1886. Hungarian piano virtuoso and composer. Studied in Vienna (1821–23) under Czerny and Salieri, and in Paris (1823) under Paer and Reicha; made sensational debut at Paris (1824); toured Europe as piano virtuoso, revolutionizing technique of piano playing; composed music at same time, inventing the symphonic poem and the method of transformation of themes; lived (1835–39) in partial retirement in Geneva with the comtesse d'Agoult, by whom he had three children (one of whom married Richard Wagner). Appointed (1843) director of court music at Weimar; settled there with Princess Carolyne Sayn-Wittgenstein (1848–61), and devoted himself to composition, writing, and work as conductor at court concerts. To Rome (1861); took four minor orders of Roman Catholic church (1865), thenceforth known as "Abbé Liszt"; passed remainder of his life between Rome and Weimar, with intervals of teaching in the Hungarian Conservatory of Music in Budapest. Among his compositions were *A Faust Symphony* (1857), *A Symphony to Dante's Divina Commedia* (1857), 13 symphonic poems including *Les preludes* (1854), *Hungaria* (1856), *Héroïde funèbre* (1857), *Hamlet* (1876); works for piano and orchestra as 2 *Concertos* (1855, 1857), *Fantasia on Hungarian Folk Tunes* (1853), *Totentanz* (1865); solo piano pieces *Apparitions* (1834), *Années de pèlerinage* (1835–77), *Études d'exécution transcendante* (1851), *Sonata in B Minor* (1852–53), *Legendes* (1863); sacred choral works including *Missa solemnis* (1856), *Hungarian Coronation Mass* (1857), oratorios *Christus* (1855–66) and *Die Legende von der heiligen Elisabeth* (1857–62), *Requiem* (1869), *Die heilige Cäcilia* (1875); secular choral works; 19 *Hungarian Rhapsodies* (1851–86); secular and sacred songs; and many transcriptions of his own and others' works.

Li Ta-chao \ˈlē-ˈdä-ˈjau̇\. 1888–1927. Chinese Communist leader. Chief librarian (1918), professor of history (1920), Peking U.; organized Marxist study groups, teaching and influencing many future Communist leaders, esp. Mao Tse-tung; cofounder (1921) of Chinese Communist party, its theoretician and party leader in north China; executed by Chang Tso-lin.

Li T'ai-po. See LI PO.

Li T'ang \ˈlē-ˈtäŋ\. c.1080–1130. Chinese painter. Earned highest ranking in art academy of Northern Sung empire; after fall of empire, went south and entered Southern Sung art academy. His style of painting a transition between Northern and Southern styles; painted chiefly landscapes; master of the ax stroke.

Lit·ke \ˈlyit-kə\, Fyodor Petrovich. Count. 1797–1882. Russian explorer and geographer. Joined navy (1812); on V. M. Golovnin's round-the-world voyage (1817–19); headed expedition (summers of 1821–24) that explored and mapped west coast of Novaya Zemlya and parts of Barents Sea; circumnavigated globe on scientific expedition (1826–29); a founder (1845) and president (1845–73 except 1850–57) of Russian Geographical Society.

Li Tsung. See Chao Yun under CHAO family.

Li Tsung-jen \ˈlēd-ˈzu̇ŋ-ˈzhən\. 1890–1969. Chinese general. Joined revolutionary forces (1925); member of Kuomintang (1928–29); dismissed from all posts (1929) for opposing Chiang Kai-shek; reinstated (1931); vice president of Nationalist China under Chiang Kai-shek (1948–49); self-exile in U.S. (1949–65); returned to Peking (1965).

Lit·tle \ˈlit-ᵊl\, Arthur Dehon. 1863–1935. American chemical engineer, b. Boston. Chemist and superintendent of first mill in U.S. making sulfite wood pulp (1884–85); organized (1886) in Boston a chemical consulting firm, later (1909) reorganized as Arthur D. Little, Inc., largest unendowed commercial industrial research laboratory in U.S. Invented processes of chrome tanning and of electrolytic manufacture of chlorates, artificial silk, gas, and petroleum.

Little, Charles Coffin. 1799–1869. American publisher, b. Kennebunk, Me. With James Brown as his chief associate (from 1837), established firm of Little, Brown & Co. (1847), publishers of legal and general works.

Little, Malcolm. See MALCOLM X.

Littleton, Mark. See John Pendleton KENNEDY.

Lit·tle·ton \ˈlit-ᵊl-tən\, Sir Thomas. *Surname also spelled* Lyttelton *or* Luttelton. 1422–1481. English jurist and legal author. Sergeant at law (1453); a justice of assize in northern circuit (1455); judge of common pleas (1466); knight of the Bath (1475). Gained fame through his treatise *Tenures* (in legal French), a complete view of English land law, one of earliest books printed in

London and the earliest treatise on English law ever printed (1481 or 1482). His text was a part of legal education for more than three centuries and was the basis of Sir Edward Coke's (*q.v.*) commentary *Institutes of the Lawes of England* (1628), known as *Coke upon Littleton.*

Lit·tle Tur·tle \ˌlit-ᵊl-ˈtərt-ᵊl\. c.1752–1812. American Indian leader, b. near Fort Wayne, Ind. Chief of Miami tribe; led raids on settlers in Northwest Territory; routed Gen. Josiah Harmar's militia (1790) and Gen. Arthur St. Clair's garrison (1791) before suffering defeats at Ft. Recovery and Fallen Timbers (both 1794); forced to sign Treaty of Greenville (1795), thereafter advocating peace.

Lit·tre \lētrᵊ\, Alexis. 1654–1725. French physician and anatomist. First described type of hernia and urethral mucous glands named after him.

Lit·tré \lē-trā\, Maximilien-Paul-Émile. 1801–1881. French lexicographer and philosopher. Ardent democrat, took part in insurrection against Charles X (1830); disciple of Comte (from c.1839) and publicist for his Positivist philosophy; recognized as head of the Positivist school after death of Comte (1857). Published *Paroles de philosophie positive* (1859) and *Auguste Comte et la philosophie positive* (1863). Chief work *Dictionnaire de la langue française* (1863–73).

Lit·vi·nov \lyi-ˈvyē-nəf, *Angl* lit-ˈvē-\, Maksim Maksimovich. *Orig.* Meir Wa·lach \ˈväl-äk\. 1876–1951. Russian Communist leader and diplomat. Joined Social Democratic party (1898); in Socialist schism (1903) joined Lenin and the Bolsheviks. After Russian Revolution (1917) represented Russian government in London; headed Russian delegations at disarmament commissions (1927–29), signing Kellogg Pact (1928); commissar for foreign affairs (1930–39). Soviet ambassador to U.S. (1941–43); deputy commissar for foreign affairs (1943–46).

Li Tzu-ch'eng \ˈlēd-ˈzü-ˈchəŋ\. 1605?–1645. Chinese rebel leader. During disturbances of last years of Ming dynasty, became bandit chieftain (1629–45); overran parts of Hupeh and Honan (1640); captured Kaifeng (1642) and conquered all of Shensi (1642–44); proclaimed himself emperor (1644) and seized Peking; defeated by Gen. Wu San-kuei; driven into Hupeh.

Liu \lē-ˈü\. Family name of the emperors of the Han dynasty (*q.v.*) of China. Its more prominent members, usually known by their reign titles, included:

Liu Pang \-ˈbäŋ\. *Posthumous title* Kao Tsu \ˈgau̇d-ˈzü\, *i.e.* High Progenitor. 256–195 B.C. Founder and first emperor (206–195). Born of peasant family; police officer under Ch'in dynasty; after death of Shih Huang Ti (210), became rebel leader under Hsiang Yü; received kingdom of Han in western China; defeated Hsiang Yü; founded Han dynasty; a pragmatic, effective ruler; revived rural economy and lightened tax burden of the peasants. One of his wives was Empress Lü (see LÜ).

Liu Heng \-ˈhəŋ\. *Reign title* Wen Ti \ˈwən-ˈdē\, *i.e.* Cultured Emperor. d. 157 B.C. Fourth emperor (179–157). Son of Liu Pang; reign marked by personal frugality, economy in government, and efforts to improve lot of common people; introduced *nien-hao* (designating year reign of emperors) and court scholars.

Liu Ch'i \-ˈchē\. *Reign title* Ching Ti \ˈjiŋ-ˈdē\. d. 140 B.C. Fifth emperor (156–140). Son of Liu Heng; helped his father crush Revolt of the Seven Kingdoms (154); limited power of feudal princes and consolidated power in the central government.

Liu Ch'e \-ˈchə\. *Reign title* Wu Ti \ˈwü-ˈdē\, *i.e.* Martial Emperor. 156–87 B.C. Sixth emperor (140–87). Son of Liu Ch'i; expanded Chinese empire (133–101), subjugating Hsiung-nu nomads of northern frontier, annexing parts of southern China and upper parts of Vietnam, reconquering northern and central Korea; reorganized government into closely supervised agencies; levied heavy taxes to finance military expeditions; made Confucianism the state religion.

Liu Ping-i \-ˈbiŋ-ˈē\. *Reign title* Hsüan Ti \shu̅e-ˈän-ˈdē\. d. 49 B.C. Eighth emperor (73–49). Not directly descended from Liu Ch'e; abated harshness and corruption of prior two reigns; his reign a period of great prosperity.

Liu Shih \-ˈshi(ə)r\. *Reign title* Yüan Ti \yu̅e-ˈän-ˈdē\. 75–33 B.C. Ninth emperor (48–33). Son of Liu Ping-i; vigorous supporter of Confucianism; failed to check power of his eunuch secretaries; ceded much power to his empress Wang Cheng-chün and other members of the Wang clan.

Power of the Liu family was interrupted after the reign of Emperor P'ing Ti (reigned 1 B.C.–6 A.D.) by the usurpation (9 A.D.) of the throne by Wang Mang (*q.v.*); power restored (25 A.D.) by Liu Hsiu as the Later, or Eastern, Han dynasty.

Liu Hsiu \-shē-ˈü\. *Reign title* Kuang Wu Ti \ˈgwäŋ-ˈwü-ˈdē\, *i.e.* Shining Martial Emperor. 4 B.C.–57 A.D. First emperor of the Later Han dynasty (25–57 A.D.). Raised army (22) against Wang Mang (*q.v.*) and with help from other Liu members defeated him (23), thus restoring Han dynasty; moved capital to Lo-yang in eastern China (hence name Eastern Han dynasty) and proclaimed himself emperor (25); consolidated his power and restored peace to empire; subdued domestic rebellions, including Red Eyebrows revolt; his reign saw rise in power of aristocratic families.

Liu Chuang \-jə-ˈwäŋ\. *Reign title* Ming Ti \ˈmiŋ-ˈdē\, *i.e.* Enlightened Emperor. 29–76 A.D. Emperor (58–76). Conquered Hsiung-nu tribes of northwest frontier; reestablished Chinese influence in Central Asia through generalship of Pan Ch'ao (see under PAN PIAO); Buddhism introduced.

Liu Ta \-ˈdä\. *Reign title* Chang Ti \ˈjäŋ-ˈdē\. 57–88 A.D. Emperor (76–88). Son of Liu Chuang; conquests of Pan Ch'ao continued; internally, pursued a peaceful policy; much power accumulated by court eunuch secretaries and landed families; his reign began weakening of Han rule.

Reign of Liu Ta followed by nine emperors, all of them losing power until the last, Hsien Ti (reigned 189–220), was overthrown by Ts'ao P'ei, founder of the Wei dynasty.

Liu An \lē-ˈü-ˈän\. Prince of Huai-nan. *Literary name* Huai-nan-tzu \ˈhwī-ˈnänd-ˈzü\. d. 122 B.C. Chinese ruler and scholar. Grandson of Liu Pang; student of Taoism; author of *Huai-nan-tzu,* a treatise that became a standard work of the Taoists; became deeply involved in occult studies, such as the search for an elixir of immortality; accused of conspiracy, committed suicide.

Liu Chi \-ˈjē\. 1311–1375. Chinese painter. Known esp. for bird and flower pieces.

Liu Chin \-ˈjin\. d. 1510. Chinese politician. With seven other eunuchs (known collectively as the Eight Tigers), gained control of government of the profligate Emperor Cheng-te; amassed fortune by corrupt practices; executed after his corruption was exposed.

Liud·ger \lē-ˈüt-ger\ *or* **Lud·ger** \ˈlüt-ger\. Saint. 744–809. Frisian prelate. Bishop of Münster (c.804–809); first to preach Christianity in Westphalia, later active in ecclesiastical organization of Saxony; founded monastery of Werden on Ruhr River.

Liu·dolf \lē-ˈü-ˌdȯlf\. 930–957. Duke of Swabia (950–957). Son of Emperor Otto I; joined with Conrad the Red of Lotharingia and Archbishop Frederick of Mainz in revolt against Otto (952); seized Regensburg and welcomed Magyar invaders into Germany (953); deserted by Conrad and Frederick (955) and reconciled to father.

Liudprand. See LIUTPRAND.

Liu E \lē-ˈü-ˈā\. *Called also* Liu O \-ˈō\. 1857–1909. Chinese novelist. Mathematician and water conservation expert by profession; banished to Ili (1908). Author of autobiographical novel *Lao Ts'an yu chi,* an attack upon government administration system.

Liu K'un-i \-ˈkü-ˈnē\. 1830–1902. Chinese politician. Entered Hunan army as officer (1855); governor of Liang-Kiang (1879–81, 1890–1902); an efficient administrator who rooted out corruption and supplied his troops with Western guns and ships; influential due to his position and as adviser to Imperial government on Western matters; kept South China free of Boxers and refused (1900) government orders to kill foreigners; with Chang Chih-tung, submitted (1902) to throne memoranda that led to Westernizing reforms.

Liu Pang. See under LIU family.

Liu Pei \-ˈbā\. 162–223. Chinese emperor (221–223). Claimed descent from Liu royal family but grew up in poverty; became soldier, distinguishing himself during Yellow Turban Rebellion; became a leading Han general. After fall of Han dynasty (220), seized area in central China around Szechwan and founded the Shu, or Minor Han, dynasty.

Liu Shao-chi \-ˈshau̇-ˈchē\. 1898–1974. Chinese politician. Joined Chinese Communist party while studying (1921–22) in Moscow; returned to China (1922); involved in labor movement and rose rapidly in party hierarchy; secretary general of Communist party (1943–54); vice chairman (1949–59), chairman (1959–68), People's Republic of China; stripped of all positions (1968).

Liu-Sung. See SUNG, 1.

Li·ut·prand \ˈlē-u̇t-ˌpränt\ *or* **Lu·it·prand** \ˈlü-ət-\. d. 744 A.D. King of the Lombards (712–744). Seized Ravenna (728); attacked Rome (730); made alliance with Charles Martel, defeated dukes of Spoleto and Beneventum, and again besieged Rome (739); brought Lombardy to zenith of her power; promulgated *Edicta Liutprandi.*

Li·ut·prand *or* **Li·ud·prand** \ˈlē-u̇t-ˌpränt\ of Cre·mo·na \kri-ˈmō-nə\. c.922–c.972. Lombard prelate and historian. Confidential secretary and protégé of Berengar II (947); ambassador to Byzantine court (949–955); on return, broke with Berengar and fled (955) to German court of Otto II, who made him bishop of Cremona (961–972). Among his works were *Antapodosis* (containing events in Italian history 888–958), *De Rebus Gestis Ottonis Magni Imperatoris* (covering period 960–964).

Liu Tsung-yüan \lē-ˈüd-ˈzu̇ŋ-yu̅e-ˈän\. 773–819. Chinese essayist and poet. Government official; banished to minor provincial post in Hunan. With his friend Han Yü, a leader in movement to replace highly formal "parallel" prose style (*p'ien-wen*) with the more flexible and simple classical prose of ancient times; author of poems and essays chiefly on nature.

Liu Yüan \lē-ˈü-yu̅e-ˈän\. d. 310 A.D. Chinese invader. Leader of the Hsiung-nu; invaded China, took title king of Han (304), and conquered most of northern

Shansi province. His invasion started barbarian conquest (304–589) of China.

Livens. See LIEVENS.

Liv·er·more \'liv-ər-ˌmō(ə)r, -ˌmò(ə)r\, Mary Ashton, *nee* Rice. 1820–1905. American reformer, b. Boston. m. Rev. Daniel P. Livermore (1845). With husband, edited church periodical *New Covenant,* Chicago (1857–69). Active in woman suffrage movement; founded (1869) and edited (1869–72) *The Agitator* and the *Woman's Journal* into which it was merged. Also interested in temperance cause.

Liverpool, Earls of. See Charles JENKINSON.

Liv·ia Dru·sil·la \'liv-ē-ə-drü-'sil-ə\. *Called* Julia Augusta *after death (30) of Augustus.* 58 B.C.–29 A.D. Roman empress. Daughter of Marcus Livius Drusus Claudianus; wife of her cousin Tiberius Claudius Nero, and by him mother of Tiberius and Nero Claudius Drusus; divorced husband to marry (38) Octavian (Augustus), thus becoming the first Roman empress. Secured succession of her son Tiberius; in the early part of his reign she was very influential in public affairs; deified (42 A.D.) by her grandson Claudius I.

Liv·ing·ston \'liv-iŋ-stən\. Name of an American family prominent in colonial and postcolonial periods. The founder Robert Livingston (1654–1728), b. Ancrum, Roxburghshire, Scotland. To America (1673); settled at Albany, N.Y.; established estate of 160,000 acres; secretary of Indian affairs (from 1695); member, N.Y. provincial assembly (1709–11, 1716–25).

His grandson ¶Phillip (1716–1778), b. Albany, was a successful New York merchant; one of first to advocate founding of King's College, now Columbia; established a professorship of divinity at Yale; member of Continental Congress (1774–78); signer of Declaration of Independence. His brother ¶William (1723–1790), b. Albany; lawyer; helped William Smith prepare a digest of laws of New York (pub. 1752, 1762); moved to Elizabethtown, N.J. (1772); member of Continental Congress (1774–76); governor of New Jersey (1776–90); delegate to Constitutional Convention (1787); signer of the Constitution. William's son ¶Henry Brockholst (1757–1823), b. New York City, served in American Revolution; practiced law in New York (from 1783); associate justice, U.S. Supreme Court (1806–23).

¶Robert R. (1746–1813), b. New York City; lawyer and politician; great-grandson of Robert; member of Continental Congress (1775–77, 1779–81); one of committee of five who drew up Declaration of Independence; first U.S. secretary of foreign affairs (1781–83); chancellor of New York State (1777–1801); administered oath of office to Washington (Apr. 30, 1789); U.S. minister to France (1801–04); aided Robert Fulton in building his steamboat and obtained a monopoly (later broken) of steam navigation. His brother ¶Edward (1764–1836), b. Columbia Co., N.Y., lawyer in New York (from 1785); member, U.S. House of Representatives (1795–1801); U.S. district attorney for New York State and mayor of New York (1801–03); moved to New Orleans (1804), on Jackson's staff at battle of New Orleans (1815); drew up legal code for Louisiana; member, U.S. House of Representatives (1823–29), U.S. senator (1829–31) from Louisiana; U.S. secretary of state (1831–33); U.S. minister to France (1833–35).

Livingston, Milton Stanley. 1905–1986. American physicist, b. Brodhead, Wis. Professor at M.I.T. (1938–70); director of accelerator project at Brookhaven National Laboratory; associate director of Fermi National Accelerator Laboratory (1967–70). With E.O. Lawrence developed (late 1920s) cyclotron, first effective atom-smashing device.

Liv·ing·stone \'liv-iŋ-stən\, David. 1813–1873. Scottish missionary and explorer. Operative in cotton mill from age of ten; ordained missionary (1840). Embarked as missionary, reached Bechuanaland in Africa (July 1841); repulsed by Boers in missionary efforts; m. (1844) Mary Moffat (d. 1862), daughter of Robert Moffat (*q.v.*); organized exploration expeditions into interior; discovered Lake Ngami (1849), Zambezi River (1851); on great expedition northward from Cape Town through west Central Africa to Luanda and back to Quilimane (1853–56) collected vast amount of information and discovered Victoria Falls of the Zambezi (1855); welcomed back in Britain with enthusiasm; published his *Missionary Travels* (1857); severed connection with missionary society. Returned as consul of Quilimane (1858–64); commanded expeditions exploring Zambezi, Shire, and Rovuma rivers, discovered lakes Chilwa and Nyasa (1859); recalled (1863) and on second visit to England published *The Zambesi and its Tributaries* (1865) with intent to expose Portuguese slave traders and get missionary and commercial settlement established near head of the Rovuma. Led expedition to explore watershed of Central Africa and sources of Nile (1866); discovered lakes Mweru (1867) and Bangweulu (1868), explored country to Nyangwe on the Lualaba River, returned almost dying to Ujiji, where he was rescued (1871) by Henry M. Stanley (*q.v.*); sought source of Nile, pushing eastward to Unyanyembe, then south to village of Chitambo's (now in Zambia), where he died. *The Last Journals of David Livingstone* were published in 1874.

Liv·i·us An·dro·ni·cus \'liv-ē-əs-ˌan-drə-'nī-kəs, -an-'drän-ik-əs\, Lucius. c.284–c.204 B.C. Roman poet and playwright. A Greek slave until freed by a member of Livian family; taught Latin and Greek in Rome. Founder of Roman epic poetry and drama; translated and imitated Greek originals; his *Odyssia,* a translation of Homer's *Odyssey,* was first major poem in Latin.

Livy \'liv-ē\. *Latin* Titus Liv·i·us \'liv-ē-əs\. 59 B.C.–17 A.D. Roman historian. Under patronage of Emperor Augustus wrote *The Annals of the Roman People* (142 books), a history of Rome from its foundation to the death (9 B.C.) of Drusus. Books I to X and XXI to XLV are extant, together with fragments or epitomes of all but two of the other books.

Li Yü \'lē-'yœ̄\. *Also called* Li Hou-chou \-'hō-'jō\. 937–978. Last emperor of Chinese Southern T'ang dynasty. Succeeded his father Li Ching (961); under suzerainty of Sung emperor T'ai Tsu, who invaded (974) and deposed him (975); imprisoned (975–978). Author of lyric poems (called *tz'u*) expressing grief at loss of kingdom; also a painter, collector, calligrapher, musician.

Li Yüan. See under LI family.

Li Yüan-hao \-yœ-'än-'hau̇\. 11th century A.D. Tibetan ruler. Leader of Tangut tribes inhabiting present Kansu Province, China; ceased tribute payments to Sung dynasty (1038); founded the Hsia dynasty (usually called Hsi Hsia or Western Hsia) and proclaimed himself emperor; attempted to establish a Chinese system of government.

Li Yuan-hung \'lē-yü-'än-'hu̇ŋ\. 1864–1928. Chinese politician. Naval officer in Chinese–Japanese War (1894–95); transferred to army; at first opposed to revolution (1911) of Sun Yat-sen, but later joined it; vice president of Chinese Republic (1912–16); on Yüan Shih-k'ai's death became president (1916–17); restored parliament; again president (1922–23) but again forced out by militarists under Gen. Ts'ao K'un; worked for reunification of China by negotiation.

Lizardi, José Joaquín Fernández de. See FERNÁNDEZ DE LIZARDI.

Llewelyn. See LLYWELYN.

Llo·ren·te \lyō-'rān-tā\, Juan Antonio. 1756–1823. Spanish priest and historian. General secretary of the Inquisition (1789–1801); on commission by Joseph Bonaparte, published in Paris his *Histoire critique de l'Inquisition d'Espagne* (1817–18).

Lloyd \'lȯid\, Edward. fl. 1688–1713. English coffeehouse owner. His coffeehouse in Lombard St., London, was resort of insurers against sea risk, and provided name for *Lloyd's List,* devoted to shipping news (from 1726), and for the commercial corporation Lloyd's.

Lloyd, Harold Clayton. 1894–1971. American film actor and producer, b. Burchard, Neb. Joined (1915) Hal Roach Studio as actor, later also writer and producer; established (1924) own production company. Famous for comic character of shy, insignificant little man with spectacles and straw hat; appeared in *Just Nuts* (1915), *My Wife* (1919), *Safety Last* (1923), *Girl Shy* (1924), *The Freshman* (1925), *The Kid Brother* (1927), *Speedy* (1928), *Mad Wednesday* (1947), etc.

Lloyd, Henry Demarest. 1847–1903. American journalist, b. New York City. On staff of Chicago *Tribune* (1872–85). Wrote for *Atlantic Monthly* magazine sensational "Story of a Great Monopoly" (1881), an exposé of the methods of the Standard Oil Company and the railroads; first of the muckrakers. Devoted himself to reform (from 1885); published *Wealth Against Commonwealth* (1894), *A Country Without Strikes* (1900), etc.

Lloyd, Marie. *Orig.* Matilda Alice Victoria Wood. 1870–1922. English music-hall comedienne. Known chiefly for character impersonations, esp. of Cockneys, low comedy roles, and as a popularizer of comic songs.

Lloyd, William. 1627–1717. English prelate. Bishop of St. Asaph (1680); one of the Seven Bishops (see William SANCROFT) who petitioned against James II's Declaration of Indulgence (1688) but were acquitted of charge of seditious libel; bishop of Lichfield and Coventry (1692), of Worcester (1700).

Lloyd George \ˌlȯid-'jȯ(ə)rj\, David. 1st Earl of Dwy·for \'dü-ē-ˌvȯ(ə)r\. 1863–1945. British politician, b. Manchester, of Welsh parents. Solicitor (1884); Liberal M.P. (from 1890), won recognition by brilliance in debate; president of Board of Trade (1905–08); as chancellor of the exchequer (1908–15), devised "People's Budget" (1909) raising taxes on upper incomes and large estates and designed (1911) Britain's first comprehensive health and unemployment insurance. Minister of munitions (1915–16); secretary of state for war (1916). Replaced Asquith as prime minister (1916–22) and, as virtual dictator, directed Britain's policies to victory in World War I and in settlement of terms of peace; arranged conference (1921) with Irish leaders and instituted negotiations which resulted in founding of Irish Free State. Author of *War Memoirs* (1933–36) and *The Truth about the Peace Treaty* (1938).

Llull \'lyülʸ\, Ramon. *Eng.* Raymond Lul·ly \'lul-ē\. c.1235–1316. Catalan mystic, philosopher, poet, and missionary. Reared at court of Majorca, writing lyrical troubadour poetry; experienced mystical visions (c.1263), abandoned courtly life and devoted himself to philosophy and missionary work; traveled throughout Asia Minor and North Africa attempting to convert Muslims;

according to legend, stoned to death at Bougie. As philosopher, influenced by Neoplatonic Augustinianism and opposed Averroism; in chief work *Ars magna* set out his theosophical attempt to encompass all knowledge in a Neoplatonic schema and to resolve all religious differences and establish a tranquil world. As mystic, reflected Neoplatonism of Victorine school and wrote *Llibre d'amic e amat.* Other works (in Catalan) included allegorical novels *Blanquerna* (c.1284) and *Felix* (c.1288), treatise on chivalry *Llibre de l'Orde de cavalleria,* animal fables *Llibre de las bèsties,* encyclopedia of medieval thought *Llibre de contemplació en Déu,* religious poetry; also many philosophical and theological works in Latin.

Llwyd \'(h)lüid\, Morgan. 1619–1659. Welsh writer. Puritan preacher, chaplain in Parliamentary army during Civil War. Best known for *Llyfr y Tri Aderyn* (1653), an allegorical treatise on religious liberty and theory of government; also wrote *Llythyr ir Cymryu Cariadus* (1653) and poetry.

Ly·wel·yn \(h)lə-'wel-in\. Name of two princes of Gwynedd in northern Wales:

Llywelyn ap Ior·werth \'yȯr-werth\. *Called* the Great. d. 1240. Returned from exile and drove his uncle Dafydd from throne (1194); brought most of northern Wales under his control (by 1202); m. (1205) Joan (d. 1237), illegitimate daughter of King John; invaded and deprived of most of Gwynedd by John (1211); won back (1212) most of losses with alliance with barons opposed to John; prince of all Wales not ruled by Normans (1216); secured in his rights by clauses in Magna Carta; forced to withdraw (1223) to north behind boundary between Cardigan, Dyfed, and Builth, Powys, but his rule still accepted by most Welsh princes in south; in last years turned government over to his son Dafydd ap Llywelyn.

Llywelyn ap Gruff·udd \'grif-ith\. d. 1282. Grandson of Llywelyn ap Iorwerth; on death of uncle Dafydd ap Llywelyn (1246), divided Gwynedd with his brother Owain; seized Owain's lands (1255); proclaimed himself prince of Wales and received homage of other Welsh princes (1258); allied himself (1262) with Simon de Montfort and in Barons' War made himself master of south and north Wales; recognized as overlord of Wales by Treaty of Shrewsbury (1265); refused to do homage to Edward I; invaded by Edward and subjugated (1277); rebelled (1282), killed in skirmish near Builth.

Lo·ba·chev·sky \lə-(,)bə-'chäf-skəi, *Angl* ,lō-bə-'chef-skē, ,läb-ə-, -'chev-\, Nikolay Ivanovich. 1792–1856. Russian mathematician. Founder, with János Bolyai, of non-Euclidean geometry. At U. of Kazan as professor (from 1814), university librarian (1825–35), rector (1827–46). Announced (1826) and published (1829) his non-Euclidean geometry; discovered method for approximation of the roots of algebraic equations (1834). Works included "O nachalakh geometrii" (1829–30), *Voobrazhaemaya geometriya* (1835), *Geometrische Untersuchungen zur Theorie der Parallellinien* (1840), *Pangéométrie* (1855–56).

Lo·ba·nov-Ro·stov·sky \(,)lə-'bá-nəf-(,)rə-'stȯf-skəi, *Angl* -skē\, Aleksey Borisovich. Prince. 1824–1896. Russian diplomat. Entered diplomatic service (1844); ambassador at Constantinople (1878–79), London (1879–82), Vienna (1882–94), Berlin (1894–95). Foreign minister of Russia (1895–96); sought friendly relations with France, Germany, Austria-Hungary; forced Japan to withdraw claim to Liaotung Peninsula; brought northern Manchuria into Russian sphere of influence.

Lobato, José Bento Monteiro. See MONTEIRO LOBATO.

Lo·ben·gu·la \,lō-beŋ-'gyü-lə, lō-'beŋ-gyə-lə\. c.1836–1894. King of the Matabele (Ndebele). Son of Mzilikazi; ascended throne (1870); granted farming (1886) and mineral (1888) concessions to British South African Company, but attacked the British as they established themselves (1893); in decisive battle (Oct. 23, 1893), the Matabele were slaughtered and Lobengula forced to yield his capital Bulawayo and flee.

Lob·ko·witz \'lȯp-kō-vits\, Wenzel Eusebius von. Fürst. 1609–1677. Bohemian politician. Fought in Thirty Years' War; helped consolidate Habsburg rule in Bohemia as president of the Landtag (1643–49); vice president (1644), president (1652), Hofkriegsrat. Chief minister (1669–74) of Emperor Leopold I's Aulic Council (Reichshofrat); suppressed rebellion in Hungary (1670–71) and continued repressive measures there; dismissed for his pro-French policy.

Lobo, Francisco Rodrigues. See RODRIGUES LOBO.

Lo·bo \'lō-bü\, Jerónimo. 1595–1678. Portuguese missionary. Entered Society of Jesus (1609); ordained (1621); missionary (from 1622) in India and Ethiopia. His manuscript account of his travels was translated into French as *Voyage historique d'Abissinie* (1728).

Lo·ca·tel·li \,lō-kä-'tel-lē\, Pietro Antonio. 1695–1764. Italian violinist and composer. Leading violin virtuoso of his day, known esp. for his use of double stops and special tunings for special effects. Composed concerti grossi, sonatas, and caprices.

Loch \'läk, 'läk\, Henry Brougham. 1st Baron Loch of Dry·law \'drī-,lȯ\. 1827–1900. British colonial administrator. Soldier, serving in India (1844–53), Crimean War (1853–56), 2d and 3d China wars (1857–58, 1860). Governor of Isle of Man (1863–82), of Victoria (1884–89), of Cape Colony and high commissioner of South Africa (1889–95); assisted in the annexation of Mashonaland and Matabeleland.

Lochiel. See CAMERON of Lochiel.

Loch·ner \'lōk-nər\, Stefan. c.1400–1451. German painter. Leading master of the Cologne school. His masterpiece was a three-paneled altarpiece in the cathedral at Cologne; also painted *St. Jerome in His Cell, Madonna with the Violet, Presentation in the Temple, Madonna in the Rose Bower,* and altarpiece for church of St. Laurenz, Cologne.

Locke \'läk\, Alain LeRoy. 1886–1954. American educator and critic, b. Philadelphia. First black Rhodes scholar (1907–11). Professor of philosophy, Howard U. (1917–53). Leader and chief interpreter of the Harlem Renaissance; encouraged and promoted many black writers, painters, musicians; developed a "cultural pluralism" philosophy. Author of *The New Negro* (1925), *Four Negro Poets* (1927), *The Negro in America* (1933), *Frederick Douglass* (1935), *The Negro and His Music* (1936), *Negro Art: Past and Present* (1936), *The Negro in Art* (1941), etc.

Locke, David Ross. *Pseudonym* Petroleum Vesuvius Nas·by \'naz-bē\. 1833–1888. American journalist, b. Vestal, N.Y. Editor, *The Jeffersonian,* Findlay, Ohio, to which he contributed (Mar. 21, 1861) the first of the Petroleum V. Nasby letters. Editor, Toledo (Ohio) *Blade* (1865–71); the Nasby letters, political satires marked by humor, caricatures, and aggressiveness, continued in Toledo *Blade* through 1887. Highly popular lecturer on lyceum circuit.

Locke, John. 1632–1704. English philosopher. Secretary to diplomatic mission to Brandenburg (1665); went to live in house of Anthony Ashley Cooper (later Earl of Shaftesbury) as physician and confidential adviser (from 1667) and tutor; secretary of Council of Trade and Plantations (1672–73). In France (1675–79); suspected of complicity in Shaftesbury plots (1684), fled to Holland; returned to become commissioner of appeal (1689–1704) and adviser to government on coinage. Spent some 20 years developing his empirical theory of epistemology, published in *An Essay Concerning Human Understanding* (1690); outlined his liberal constitutionalist ideas on government in *Two Treatises on Government* (1690). Author also of three *Letters on Toleration* (1689, 1690, 1692), *Some Thoughts Concerning Education* (1693), *The Reasonableness of Christianity* (1695). Known as the father of English empiricism.

Locke, Matthew. 1621 or 1622–1677. English composer. One of the earliest English writers of music for stage; joint composer with Christopher Gibbons of music for Shirley's masque *Cupid and Death* (1653); wrote part of music for Davenant's *Siege of Rhodes* (1656) and *Macbeth* (1663), Shadwell's *Psyche* (1673) and *The Tempest* (1674), and other contemporary plays. Also composed instrumental music, sacred and secular songs, anthems, motets, etc.; published (1673) *Melothesia,* containing keyboard music and earliest extant English rules for figured bass.

Locke, Richard Adams. 1800–1871. American journalist, b. East Brent, Somerset, England. To U.S. (1832); on staff of New York *Sun* (1835–36), in which he perpetrated famous "Moon Hoax," purporting to reveal Sir John Herschel's discovery of men and animals on the moon (Aug. 1835).

Lock·hart \'läk-ərt, 'läk-,(h)ärt\, John Gibson. 1794–1854. Scottish editor, novelist, and biographer. Called to Scottish bar (1816); one of chief contributors to *Blackwood's Magazine* (1817); sketched Edinburgh society in *Peter's Letters to his Kinsfolk* (1819); m. (1820) Sir Walter Scott's daughter Charlotte Sophia; editor of *The Quarterly Review* (1825–53). Author of novels *Valerius* (1821), *Adam Blair* (1822), *Reginald Dalton* (1823), and *Matthew Wald* (1824); verse translations *Ancient Spanish Ballads* (1823); biography of Burns (1828) and his magnum opus *Life of Sir Walter Scott* (7 vols., 1837–38), rated among the great biographies in English.

Lock·wood \'läk-,wu̇d\, Belva Ann, *nee* Bennett. 1830–1917. American lawyer, b. Royalton, N.Y. m. 2d (1868) Ezekiel Lockwood. Adm. to bar (1873); practiced, Washington, D.C.; first woman admitted to practice before the U.S. Supreme Court (1879). Leader in women's rights movement. Nominated by National Equal Rights party for president of the United States (1884, 1888); U.S. delegate to peace congresses in Europe (1906, 1908, 1911).

Lock·yer \'läk-yər\, Sir Joseph Norman. 1836–1920. English astronomer. Government official in War Office (1857–75), Science and Art Dept. (1875–90); director, Solar Physics Observatory, and professor of astronomical physics, Royal Coll. of Science (1890–1913). Studied sunspots and solar eclipses; discovered (1868, in Sun's atmosphere) and named helium; discovered and named Sun's chromosphere (1868). Founded (1869) and edited (1869–1919) scientific journal *Nature.* Author of *The Chemistry of the Sun* (1887), *The Sun's Place in Nature* (1897), *Inorganic Evolution* (1900), etc.

Ló·czy \'lōt-sē\, Lajos. 1849–1920. Hungarian geologist. Geologist in Béla Széchenyi's expedition to India and China (1877–80); published results in *Wissenschaftliche Ergebnisse der Reise in Ostasien* (1899). Professor at Budapest (1889); director, Hungarian Geological Inst. (1908). Known esp. for work on mountains of the Tibetan plateau and on steppe formations of the Gobi and the northern Yellow River territory.

Lo·der \ˈlō-dər\, Bernard Cornelius Johannes. 1849–1935. Dutch jurist. Judge, High Court of Justice, the Netherlands (1908–21); first president, Permanent Court of International Justice, The Hague (1922–25).

Lodge \ˈläj\, Henry Cabot. 1850–1924. American politician and author, b. Boston. Great-grandson of George Cabot. Member, U.S. House of Representatives (1887–93), U.S. Senate (1893–1924); led opposition to the Peace Treaty and the Covenant of the League of Nations (1919). Author of *The Story of the Revolution* (1898), *The Senate and the League of Nations* (1925), and biographies of Hamilton, Webster, and Washington.

Lodge, Henry Cabot. 1902–1985. American politician and diplomat, b. Nahant, Mass. Grandson of Henry Cabot Lodge (1850–1924). U.S. senator from Massachusetts (1937–44; 1947–53); U.S. ambassador to U.N. (1953–60); Republican candidate for U.S. vice president (1960); U.S. ambassador to South Vietnam (1963–64; 1965–67); ambassador to West Germany (1968–69); chief negotiator at Vietnam peace talks in Paris; special envoy to Vatican (1970–77). Author of *The Storm Has Many Eyes* (1973), etc.

Lodge, Sir Oliver Joseph. 1851–1940. English physicist. Professor, University Coll., Liverpool (1881–1900); principal, U. of Birmingham (1900–19). Investigated lightning, electromagnetic waves, wireless telegraphy; perfected the coherer used in wireless telegraphy; conducted experiment to determine whether moving matter exerts a drag on the ether, obtaining a negative result; first to suggest (1894) the Sun might be a source of radio waves (confirmed 1942); pursued psychical researches (after 1910); attempted to reconcile science and religion. Writings included *Modern Views of Electricity* (1889), *Life and Matter* (1905), *Man and the Universe* (1908), *The Ether of Space* (1909), *Raymond, or Life and Death* (1916), *Making of Man* (1924), *Atoms and Rays* (1924), *Evolution and Creation* (1927), *Beyond Physics* (1930), *Advancing Science* (1931), *Past Years* (autobiography, 1931), etc.

Lodge, Thomas. 1558–1625. English writer. Abandoned law for literature. One of founders of English drama; author of plays *The Wounds of Civile War* and, with Robert Greene, *A Looking Glasse for London and England* (both 1594). Author of lyric poems, including *Scillaes Metamorphosis* (1589), *Phillis* (sonnets, 1593), *A Fig for Momus* (eclogues with satiric cast, 1595); of romances *Rosalynde, Euphues Golden Legacie* (1590, supplying plot of Shakespeare's *As You Like It), Robert, Second Duke of Normandy* (1591), *Euphues Shadow* (1592), *William Longbeard* (1593), *A Margarite of America* (1596); of pamphlets *Catharos* (1591), *The Divel Conjured* (1596), etc.

Lo·dī \ˈlōd-ē\. Name of dynasty of Afghan kings of Delhi (1451–1526); founded by Bahlūl Lodī (reigned 1451–89), who conquered kingdoms of Mālwa and Jaurpur and extended his empire to the borders of Bengal; succeeded by his son Sikander Lodī and grandson Ibrāhīm Lodī (*qq.v.*).

Loeb \ˈlœb, *Angl* ˈlōb\, Jacques. 1859–1924. American biophysiologist, b. Mayen, Germany. Worked at Naples biological station (1889–91); to U.S. (1891); professor, Chicago (1892–1902), California (1902–10); member, Rockefeller Institute for Medical Research (1910–24). Published (1888) his tropism theory of animal behavior; did pioneer work on artificial parthenogenesis and in analysis of the process of egg fertilization; also made researches on physiology of the brain, regeneration of tissue, duration of life, theory of colloidal behavior of proteins; defended mechanism. Author of *The Dynamics of Living Matter* (1906), *The Mechanistic Conception of Life* (1912), *The Organism as a Whole* (1916), *Regeneration* (1924), etc.

Loeb \ˈlōb\, James Morris. 1867–1933. American banker, classicist, and philanthropist, b. New York City. Member of banking firm Kuhn, Loeb & Co. (1888–1901). Founded and endowed in New York City the Institute of Musical Art (1905), incorporated into Juilliard Musical Foundation (1923). Projected and subsidized (1910) publication of Loeb Classical Library, some 360 volumes from Greek and Latin authors; collected antique art objects, most bequeathed to museums; endowed centers of classical studies.

Loef·fler \ˈlef-lər\, Charles Martin Tornov. 1861–1935. American composer, b. Mulhouse, France. To U.S. (1881); violinist with Boston Symphony Orchestra (1882–1903). Composer of orchestral works *Night in the Ukraine* (1891), *Fantasia Concerto* (1894, with cello), *La Mort de Tintagiles* (1900), *La Villanelle du Diable* (1901), *A Pagan Poem* (1906), *Memories of My Childhood* (1925), *Evocation* (1931, with female chorus); *Canticum Fratris Solis* (1925, voice and chamber orchestra); chamber music, esp. *Music for Four Stringed Instruments* (1917); piano pieces and songs.

Loe·ning \ˈlō-niŋ\, Grover Cleveland. 1888–1976. American aircraft manufacturer, b. Bremen, Germany, of American parents. President, Loening Aeronautical Engineering Corp., New York (1917–28), and Grover Loening Aircraft Co. (1928–38). Invented strut-braced monoplane and an amphibian airplane; took out numerous airplane patents.

Loer·ke \ˈlœr-kə\, Oskar. 1884–1941. German poet. Author of *Wanderschaft* (1911), *Atem der Erde* (1930), *Der Silberdistelwald* (1934), etc.

Loes·ser \ˈles-ər\, Frank Henry. 1910–1969. American composer and lyricist, b. New York City. To Hollywood (1936) and composed film scores and songs, his songs including "Two Sleepy People" (1938), "On a Slow Boat to China" (1948), "Baby, It's Cold Outside" (1948, Academy Award); turned to composing Broadway musicals, writing *Where's Charley?* (1948, including "Once in Love with Amy"), *Guys and Dolls* (1950, "A Bushel and a Peck", "Luck Be a Lady"), *Most Happy Fella* (1956, "Standin' on the Corner," "Joey, Joey"), *How to Succeed in Business Without Really Trying* (1961, "I Believe in You"). Also remembered for song "Praise the Lord and Pass the Ammunition" (1942) and music for film *Hans Christian Andersen* (1953).

Loew \ˈlō\, Marcus. 1870–1927. American theater owner and motion-picture producer, b. New York City. Owned chain of nickelodeons (by 1905), later movie theaters. Formed Loew's, Inc., which purchased Metro Pictures (1920) and Goldwyn Pictures (1924), and became Metro-Goldwyn-Mayer.

Loe·we \ˈlœ̄-və\, Johann Carl Gottfried. 1796–1869. German composer. Municipal music director in Stettin (1821–66). Regarded as creator of German ballad as a distinct art form; works included ballads, 5 operas, oratorios, cantatas, piano sonatas, and chamber music.

Loe·wi \ˈlœ̄-vē, *Angl* ˈlō-ē\, Otto. 1873–1961. American pharmacologist, b. Frankfurt am Main, Germany. Professor, Graz (1909–38) and College of Medicine, New York U. (1940–61). Investigated chemical transmission of nerve impulses, for which he shared with Sir Henry Dale 1936 Nobel prize for physiology or medicine; also studied diabetes and the action of digitalis and adrenaline; devised Loewi's test for detection of pancreatic disease.

Loe·wy \ˈlō-ē\, Raymond Fernand. 1893–1986. American industrial designer, b. Paris. To U.S. (1919). Founded own design firm (1927); headed Raymond Loewy Associates (1930–61); chairman of Raymond Loewy International (1961–75); consultant to governments and many private companies; had major effect on the man-made environment by designing everything from automobiles, ships, airplanes, buildings, and appliances to everyday products as toothbrushes and pens; produced streamlined products of economy and grace. Author of *Never Leave Well Enough Alone* (1951).

Löff·ler \ˈlœf-lər\, Friedrich August Johannes. 1852–1915. German bacteriologist. On staff of Imperial Health Dept., Berlin (1879–84), where he worked with Robert Koch; professor, Greifswald (1888–1913); director, Inst. for Infectious Diseases, Berlin (1913–15). Discovered bacillus of glanders (1882) and that of swine erysipelas (1885); isolated and made culture of Klebs-Löffler bacillus, the organism causing diphtheria (1884), after it had been first described by Klebs (*q.v.*); developed successful protective serum against foot-and-mouth disease.

Loft·huus \ˈlu̇ft-hüs\, Christian Jensen. 1750–1797. Norwegian peasant leader. Petitioned (1786) Danish court to redress peasants' grievances; upon refusal, returned to Norway and gathered popular support; arrested (1787) and died in prison in Christiania. Considered a martyr of Norwegian agrarian reform.

Lof·ting \ˈlȯf-tiŋ\, Hugh. 1886–1947. English writer. Resident chiefly in U.S. (from 1912). Author and illustrator of "Dr. Dolittle" series of children's books, including *The Story of Dr. Dolittle* (1920), *The Voyages of Dr. Dolittle* (1922), *Doctor Dolittle's Caravan* (1926), *Doctor Dolittle's Return* (1933); also wrote *The Story of Mrs. Tubbs* (1923), *Porridge Poetry* (1924), *Gub Gub's Book* (1932), *Tommy, Tilly, and Mrs. Tubbs* (1934), etc.

Lo·gan \ˈlō-gən\, George. 1753–1821. American physician and politician, b. near Germantown, Pa. Undertook on own initiative and at own expense to visit France in effort to improve relations between France and U.S. (1798–99); efforts disapproved by U.S. government; Congress passed Logan Act (1799) forbidding a private citizen to undertake diplomatic negotiations without official authority. U.S. senator from Pennsylvania (1801–07).

Logan, James. 1674–1751. American public official and jurist, b. Lurgan, Ireland, of Scottish parentage. To America (1699) as secretary to William Penn; member of the provincial council (1703–47); mayor of Philadelphia (1722); acting executive of the province (1736–38). Chief justice, Pennsylvania supreme court (1731–39). Interested in botany; the family Loganiaceae and the genus *Logania* were so named by Linnaeus in his honor.

Logan, James. *Indian name* Tah-gah-jute. c.1725–1780. American Indian leader, b. Shamokin (now Sunbury), Pa. A leader, but not chief, among the Mingo bands on the Ohio and Scioto rivers; friendly with the whites until his family was massacred (1774); thereafter allied with the British.

Logan, James Harvey. 1841–1928. American lawyer and horticulturist, b. near Rockville, Ind. Judge, Superior Court, Santa Cruz Co., Calif. (1880–92). Produced in his garden a new variety of berry, the loganberry (1881).

Logan, James Richardson. d. 1869. British naturalist. Settled on island of Penang in Strait of Malacca (1830s); founded (1847) and edited *Journal of the Indian Archipelago and Eastern Asia;* contributed to it articles on natural science, languages, and cultures of Indonesian Archipelago; published some of these articles as *The Language and Ethnology of the Indian Archipelago*

(1857). Active in public affairs in Penang; editor of *Penang Gazette* (from 1853).

Logan, John. 1748–1788. Scottish clergyman and poet. Edited volume of poems by friend Michael Bruce (1770), but apparently withheld several (including "Ode to the Cuckoo") and published them in his own volume of poems (1781); best lyric, "The Braes of Yarrow."

Logan, John Alexander. 1826–1886. American soldier and politician, b. near what is now Murphysboro, Ill. Member, U.S. House of Representatives (1859–62). Raised Illinois regiment and served in Civil War; brigadier general and major general (1862). Helped found Grand Army of the Republic (1865); founder of Memorial Day (1868). Member, U.S. House of Representatives (1867–71), U.S. Senate (1871–77, 1879–86); candidate for vice president of the U.S. on Blaine ticket (1884).

Logan, Sir William Edmond. 1798–1875. Canadian geologist, b. Montreal. As manager (1831–38) of copper smelting company at Swansea, Wales, made map of coal basin, refuting drift theory of origin of coal by showing character of beds of stigmaria clay underneath coal seams of South Wales; head of Geological Survey of Canada (1842–70).

Lo·gau \ˈlō-gau̇\, Friedrich von. Freiherr. *Pseudonym* Salomon von Go·law \ˈgō-läf\. 1604–1655. German epigrammatist. Satirized contemporary society in *Erstes Hundert Teutscher Reimsprüche* (1638), *Deutscher Sinn-Gedichte Drey Tausend* (1654).

Lo·hen·stein \ˈlō-ən-ˌshtīn\, Daniel Casper von. 1635–1683. German writer. Author of tragedies as *Ibrahim Bassa* (1650), *Cleopatra* (1661), and *Agrippina* (1665), a book of lyrics, and novel *Grossmüthiger Feldherr Arminius* (1689).

Loi·sy \lwȧ-zē\, Alfred-Firmin. 1857–1940. French linguist, biblical scholar, and philosopher of religion. Ordained Roman Catholic priest (1879); excommunicated (1908) as a Modernist because of his books *L'Évangile et l'Église* (1902) and *Autour d'un petit livre* (1930); professor of history of religions, Collège de France (1909–26).

Lo Kuan-chung \ˈlō-ˈgwän-ˈju̇ŋ\. c.1330–1400. Chinese novelist. Best known for his historical novel *San Kuo chih yen-i* (Romance of the Three Kingdoms); controversy exists as to whether he was coauthor (with Shih Nai-an) or reviser (with Shih as author) of *Shui-hu chuan* (Story of the Water Margin; translated by Pearl Buck as *All Men Are Brothers*), a semihistorical picaresque novel in the colloquial style.

Lo·max \ˈlō-ˌmaks\, John Avery. 1867–1948. American folklorist, b. Goodman, Miss. Spent most of life collecting American folk songs and ballads, recording over 10,000 of them for Library of Congress. Edited *Cowboy Songs and Other Frontier Ballads* (1910), *Plantation Songs of the Negro* (1916), *Songs of the Cattle Trail and Cow Camp* (1919), *American Ballads and Folk Songs* (1934, with his son Alan), *Negro Folk Songs as Sung by Lead Belly* (1936, with Alan); wrote autobiography *Adventures of a Ballad Hunter* (1947).

Lomb \ˈläm\, Henry. 1828–1908. American optician, b. Burghaun, Germany. To U.S. (1849); cofounder (1853, with J.J. Bausch) of Bausch & Lomb Optical Co., Rochester, N.Y.

Lombard, Peter. See PETER LOMBARD.

Lom·bar·di \ləm-ˈbärd-ē\, Vincent Thomas, *called* Vince. 1913–1970. American football coach, b. Brooklyn, N.Y. One of "Seven Blocks of Granite" while a guard on Fordham U. football team (grad. 1937); as head coach of the Green Bay Packers (1959–67), won 5 National Football League championships (1961–62, 1965–67) and Super Bowls I and II (1967, 1968); head coach, Washington Redskins (1969).

Lom·bar·do \ləm-ˈbärd-(ˌ)ō\, Guy Albert. 1902–1977. American bandleader, b. London, Ont. To U.S. (1924, naturalized 1937). Formed dance band (1920) which, under name Royal Canadians (from 1927), became extremely popular as purveyor of "the sweetest music this side of heaven"; his broadcasts on New Year's Eve from New York became a national tradition; appeared in films and was a noted international speedboat racer.

Lom·bar·do \lōm-ˈbär-dō\, Pietro. c.1435–1515. Italian sculptor and architect. At Padua executed Roselli monument in church of S. Antonio (1464–67) and designed Casa Olzignan (1467); lived in Venice (from c.1467); also executed Dante's tomb at Ravenna (1482), tombs of Malipiero, Marcello, and Mocenigo at Venice, and tomb (begun 1485) of Zanetti in Treviso cathedral; architect and chief sculptor for church of Sta. Maria dei Miracoli, Venice (1481–89); master mason of Palazzo Ducale, Venice (1498–1515). His son ¶Antonio (c.1458–?1516), sculptor, collaborated with his father and brother; works included marble statues *Peter Martyr* and *Thomas Aquinas* in Venice. Another son ¶Tullio (c.1455–1532), also sculptor, among whose works were the choir chapel in Treviso cathedral, Vendramini tomb in Venice, and four marble angels in Venice.

Lom·bro·so \lom-ˈbrō-sō\, Cesare. 1836–1909. Italian physician and criminologist. Professor of psychiatry at Pavia (1862–76); professor of forensic medicine (1876), psychiatry (1896), criminal anthropology (1906), Turin. Held that a criminal represents a distinct anthropological type with definite physical and mental stigmata and that a criminal is the product of heredity, atavism, and degeneracy. Chief work *L'uomo delinquente* (1876).

Lo·mé·nie de Bri·enne \lō-mā-nēd-brē-en\, Étienne-Charles de. 1727–1794. French ecclesiastic and politician. Ordained (1752); bishop of Condom (1760); archbishop of Toulouse (1763); controller general of finance (1787–88), unable to stop worsening financial crisis. Archbishop of Sens (1788–91); cardinal (1788); one of few prelates who took oath to Civil Constitution of the Clergy of 1790; bishop of Yonne (1791–93); died in prison.

Lo·mo·no·sov \lə-(ˌ)mə-ˈnȯ-səf\, Mikhail Vasilyevich. 1711–1765. Russian scientist and man of letters. Studied in Germany (1736–41), esp. under Christian von Wolff and Johann Henckel; adjunct in physics (1742–45), professor of chemistry (from 1745), St. Petersburg Academy of Sciences; established (1748) first scientific chemical laboratory in Russia and introduced (1752) a course of instruction in physical chemistry; set up a colored-glass works (1753) and produced the first colored-glass mosaics in Russia. Drew up plans for Moscow State U. (opened 1755) and appointed a councilor (1757). While imprisoned (1743–44), wrote *276 Notes on Corpuscular Philosophy and Physics* containing dominant ideas of his scientific work; developed an atomistic theory of matter based on a materialistic monadology; evolved a corpuscular, mechanical theory of heat based on Boyle; did work on the law of the conservation of matter and energy, crystallization of liquids, electricity, meteorology, metallurgy, origin of icebergs; invented (1759) several astronomical and navigational instruments. Wrote poetry, much of it on scientific subjects; worked on unfinished heroic epic on Peter the Great; his tragedy *Tamira and Sellim* produced in St. Petersburg (1750). A leader in reformation of Russian language and versification, esp. with *Russian Grammar* (1755–57).

Lon·don \ˈlȯn-dȯn, *Angl* ˈlən-dən\, Fritz Wolfgang. 1900–1954. German physicist. Professor of chemical physics, Duke U. (1939–54). With Walter Heitler, devised (1927) first quantum mechanical treatment of the hydrogen molecule, their wave equations forming basis for valence-bond approach to molecular quantum mechanics; also made researches on superconductivity and superfluids.

Lon·don \ˈlən-dən\, John Griffith, *called* Jack. 1876–1916. American novelist and short-story writer, b. San Francisco. Lived life of sailor, waterfront loafer, and hobo (1891–94); became Socialist; joined Klondike gold rush (1897–98). Acceptance of stories by the *Overland Monthly* (Dec. 1898), *Atlantic Monthly* (July 1899) and of a book of collected stories *The Son of the Wolf* (1900) encouraged him in his writing. Wrote 50 books, including *A Daughter of the Snows* (1902), *The Call of the Wild* (1903), *The People of the Abyss* (1903), *The Sea Wolf* (1904), *White Fang* (1906), *The Road* (1907), *The Iron Heel* (1907), *Martin Eden* (1909), *Burning Daylight* (1910), *The Cruise of the Snark* (1911), *John Barleycorn* (1913), *The Abysmal Brute* (1913), *The Valley of the Moon* (1913), *The Strength of the Strong* (1914).

London, Meyer. 1871–1926. American Socialist and labor leader, b. Suwalki, Poland. To U.S. (1891); a founder of the Socialist party of America (1899–1901). Member, U.S. House of Representatives (1915–19, 1921–23).

Londonderry, Marquis of. See Robert STEWART.

Long \ˈlȯŋ\, Crawford Williamson. 1815–1878. American surgeon, b. Danielsville, Ga. Practiced in Jefferson, Ga. (from 1842); first to use ether as an anesthetic (8 operations between 1842 and 1846); published account of his experience (Dec. 1849). Previous to this publication, W.T.G. Morton (*q.v.*) made a public demonstration of the use of ether (1846) and claimed priority in the discovery.

Long, Earl. See under Huey P. LONG.

Long, Gabrielle Margaret Vere, *nee* Campbell. *Pseudonyms* Marjorie Bow·en \ˈbō-ən\, George Runnell Pree·dy \ˈprēd-ē\, *and* Joseph Shear·ing \ˈshi(ə)r-iŋ\. 1888–1952. English novelist. m. 2d (1917) Arthur L. Long. Wrote over 100 novels, plays, biographies, and historical studies; known esp. for novels *The Viper of Milan* (1917), *General Crack* (1928), *My Tattered Loving* (1937), *The Abode of Love* (1944), trilogy on the Renaissance *The Golden Root* (1934), *The Triumphant Beast* (1934), *Trumpets at Rome* (1937).

Long, Huey Pierce. *Nicknamed* the Kingfish. 1893–1935. American politician, b. near Winnfield, La. Governor of Louisiana (1928–31); implemented a successful program of public works and welfare legislation. U.S. senator (1932–35); assassinated. Noted for demagoguery, his radical Share-the-Wealth national program (with slogan "Every man a king"), and his dictatorial control over Louisiana through his political machine. His brother ¶Earl Kemp (1895–1960) was governor of Louisiana (1939–40, 1948–52, 1956–60).

Long, James. c.1793–1822. American adventurer, b. probably North Carolina. Led expedition to Texas (1819); formed republic with himself as president; declared independence (June 23, 1819). Captured and taken to Mexico City (1822); shot and killed by a sentry.

Long, John Luther. 1861–1927. American writer, b. Hanover, Pa. His short story, "Madame Butterfly" (in *Century Magazine,* Jan. 1898), was adapted for the stage by David Belasco, and used as a basis for the libretto of Puccini's opera.

Long, Stephen Harriman. 1784–1864. American army officer and explorer, b. Hopkinton, N.H. In U.S. army (1814–63) as topographical engineer; commanded exploring expeditions to upper Mississippi (1817), Rocky Mountain region (1820); discovered Longs Peak, Colorado. Explored northern U.S. boundary (1823).

Long·a·cre \'lȯŋ-ˌā-kər\, James Barton. 1794–1869. American engraver, b. Delaware Co., Pa. Known for his work in *The National Portrait Gallery of Distinguished Americans* (4 vols., 1834–39); chief engraver, U.S. Mint (1844–69).

Long·champ \lōⁿ-shäⁿ\, William. d. 1197. English prelate. Of Norman origin; in service of Richard I of England, who on accession (1189) made him chancellor of England and bishop of Ely; joint chief justiciar of England during Richard's participation in Third Crusade (1190–91); papal legate (1190). Forced by general uprising against his arrogance to withdraw to Normandy; went on diplomatic missions to Germany and France (1194–95).

Lon·er·gan \'län-ər-gən\, Bernard Joseph Francis. 1904–1984. Canadian theologian and philosopher, b. Buckingham, Que. Entered Society of Jesus (1922); taught at Jesuit seminaries and colleges. A leading Roman Catholic theologian and proponent of transcendental Thomism; applied philosophic method of Thomas Aquinas to contemporary issues; endeavored to modernize church thinking; sought unity of scientific, artistic, and common-sense cognition through emphasis on preconceptual intellect. Author of *Insight: A Study of Human Understanding* (1957), *Grace and Freedom* (1971), *Method in Theology* (1972), etc.

Longespée, William. See WILLIAM LONGSESPÉE.

Long·fel·low \'lȯŋ-ˌfel-(ˌ)ō\, Henry Wadsworth. 1807–1882. American poet, b. Portland, Me. Professor of modern languages, Bowdoin (1829–35), Harvard (1835–54); devoted himself wholly to his writing from 1854. Among his poetical works: *Voices of the Night* (including "The Psalm of Life," 1839), *Ballads and Other Poems* (including "The Wreck of the Hesperus," "The Skeleton in Armor," "The Village Blacksmith," 1841), *Evangeline* (1847), *The Seaside and the Fireside* (1850), *The Golden Legend* (1851), *The Song of Hiawatha* (1855), *The Courtship of Miles Standish* (1858), *Tales of a Wayside Inn* (including "Paul Revere's Ride," 1863); *The Divine Comedy of Dante Alighieri* (3 vols., 1865–67).

Lon·ghe·na \lōŋ-'ge-nä\, Baldassare. 1598–1682. Venetian architect. Known esp. for the domical church, Santa Maria della Salute, Venice (1631–87); other designs included Chioggia cathedral, Church of Sta. Maria degli Scalzi at Venice, Palazzo Pesaro and Palazzo Rezzonico (both Venice), staircase in monastery of S. Giorgio Maggiore.

Longhi. See also LUNGHI.

Lon·ghi \'lȯŋ-gē\, Pietro. *Orig. surname* Fal·ca \'fäl-kä\. 1702–1785. Venetian painter. Known for paintings of contemporary life, as *The Dancing Master* and *Exhibition of a Rhinoceros at Venice* (1751); also painted landscapes and portraits. His son ¶Alessandro (1733–1813), painter and engraver; known for his portraits and etchings; his biography of Venetian artists, *Compendio delle vite de' pittori veneziani istorici* (1762), is important source book.

Longimanus. See ARTAXERXES I.

Lon·gi·nus \län-'jī-nəs\. 1st century A.D. Greek critic. Name generally assigned to the author of *On the Sublime,* a seminal work of literary criticism and style.

Longinus, Johannes. See Jan DLUGOSZ.

Long·man \'lȯŋ-mən\. Name of an English family of book publishers founded by Thomas Longman (1699–1755); shared in publishing Boyle's *Works,* Ainsworth's *Latin Dictionary,* Ephraim Chambers's *Cyclopaedia,* and Johnson's *Dictionary;* took into partnership (1754) his nephew ¶Thomas Longman (1730–1797), who brought out a new edition of Chambers's *Cyclopaedia.* His son ¶Thomas Norton (1771–1842) published works of Wordsworth, Coleridge, Moore, Southey, and Scott; gained for firm sole proprietorship of *Edinburgh Review* (1826). His sons ¶Thomas (1804–1879) and ¶William (1813–1877) first published Macaulay's *Lays of Ancient Rome* (1842) and his *History of England* (1848); William was author of the *History of the Life and Times of Edward III* (1869). ¶Thomas Norton (1849–1930), son of Thomas (1804–1879), continued control of the firm (to 1919).

Longo. See LUNGHI.

Longomontanus. See Christian SEVERIN.

Long·street \'lȯŋ-ˌstrēt\, Augustus Baldwin. 1790–1870. American clergyman, author, and educator, b. Augusta, Ga. Contributed (from 1827) to Milledgeville (Ga.) *Southern Recorder* series of humorous sketches of Georgia life, *Georgia Scenes,* published in book form (1835 and 1840). Methodist minister (1838); ardent secessionist. President, Emory College (1839–48), U. of Mississippi (1849–56), U. of South Carolina (1857–65).

Longstreet, James. 1821–1904. American army officer, b. Edgefield District, S.C. Entered army (1842); served in Mexican War; resigned to enter Confederate service (1861). Commissioned brigadier general, then major general (1861); lieutenant general (1862). Commanded corps at second battle of Bull Run (1862), right wing of Lee's army at Antietam (Sept. 1862), corps at Gettysburg (July 1863), where his delay in carrying out Lee's orders to attack has been held responsible for the Confederate defeat, left wing of the Confederate army at Chickamauga; surrendered with Lee at Appomattox (Apr. 9, 1865). U.S. minister to Turkey (1880–81); U.S. marshal (1881–84); U.S. railroad commissioner (1898–1904). Author of military autobiography *From Manassas to Appomattox* (1896).

Longsword, William. See WILLIAM LONGESPÉE.

Longueuil, de. See Charles LE MOYNE.

Longue·ville \lōⁿg-vēl\, Anne-Geneviève de, *nee* de Bour·bon-Con·dé \də-bür-bōⁿ-kōⁿ-dā\. Duchesse. 1619–1679. French noblewoman. Sister of the Great Condé; m. duc de Longueville (1642; d. 1663); famed for her beauty and for her liaisons, esp. with La Rochefoucauld (1646).

Lon·gus \'läŋ-gəs\. 2d or 3d century A.D. Greek writer. Author of *Daphnis and Chloe,* the first pastoral romance.

Longus, Tiberius Sempronius. See SEMPRONIUS LONGUS.

Long·well \'lȯŋ-wəl, -ˌwel\, Chester Ray. 1887–1975. American geologist, b. Spalding, Mo. Taught at Yale (1920–56, professor from 1929); on staff, U.S. Geological Survey (1920–45, 1948–75); research associate, Stanford U. (1955–75). Known for studies of western U.S.; coauthor, *Physical Geology* (1932) and *Introduction to Physical Geology* (1955).

Long·worth \'lȯŋ-wərth\, Nicholas. 1869–1931. American politician, b. Cincinnati. Practiced law, Cincinnati (1894); member of U.S. House of Representatives (1903–13, 1915–31); m. Alice, daughter of President Theodore Roosevelt (1906); speaker of the House of Representatives (1925–31).

Lo·nit·zer \'lō-nit-sər\, Adam. *Lat.* Lo·ni·cer·us \lə-'nī-sə-rəs\. 1528–1586. German botanist. The genus *Lonicera* was named after him.

Lönn·bohm \'lœn-bȯm\, Armas Eino Leopold. *Pseudonym* Eino Lei·no \'lā-nō\. 1878–1926. Finnish poet. Known for his somber, lyrical verse as *Maaliskuum lauluja* (1896), *Helkavirsiä* (1903–16), *Simo Hurtta* (1904–19), *Talviyö* (1905), *Halla* (1908); also wrote novels, plays, animal fables, and essays.

Lon Nol \'län-'nōl\. 1913–1985. Cambodian army officer and politician. Joined (1952) Cambodian army and fought against the insurgent Viet Minh; became army chief of staff (1955), commander in chief (1960). Twice served as premier (1966–67, 1969); engineered coup (March 1970) overthrowing Prince Norodom Sihanouk; served as premier (to 1972) and then as president of Khmer Republic (1972–75). Failed to expel North Vietnamese and Viet Cong troops from Cambodia (now Democratic Kampuchea); fought civil war with Khmer Rouge; stayed until Phnom Penh fell (April 1975).

Lönn·rot \'lœn-rȯt\, Elias. 1802–1884. Finnish folklorist and philologist. District medical officer at Kajaani (1833–53); professor at Helsinki (1853–62). One of the founders of modern Finnish literature. Chief work, the collection and editing of Finnish epic songs, which he organized and systematized into a great national epic *Kalevala* (pub. 1835, enlarged 1849).

Lons·dale \'länz-ˌdāl\, Frederick. *Orig.* Lionel Frederick Leonard. 1881–1954. British playwright. Author of musical comedies and comedies of manners, including *The King of Cadonia* (1908), *The Best People* (1909), *The Balkan Princess* (1910), *The Maid of the Mountains* (1917), *Aren't We All?* (1923), *The Last of Mrs. Cheney* (1925), *On Approval* (1927), *Canaries Sometimes Sing* (1929), *Once is Enough* (1938); also wrote scripts for films.

Lonsdale, Dame Kathleen, *nee* Yard·ley \'yär-dlē\. 1903–1971. Irish crystallographer. m. (1927) Thomas Lonsdale; research assistant to Sir William H. Bragg (1922–27, 1937–42); professor, University Coll., London (1949 ff.). First woman elected to Royal Society (1945); created dame (1956). Developed various X-ray techniques for study of crystal structure; definitely established the hexagonal molecular arrangement of benzene compounds (1929) and accurately measured distance between carbon atoms in diamonds.

Lonsdale, William. 1794–1871. English geologist. Assistant secretary and curator, Geological Society of London (1829–42). Authority on corals; studied fossil remains from Great Britain, North America, Russia; made suggestion (1837) which formed basis of Devonian System of Adam Sedgwick and Sir Roderick I. Murchison.

Loos \'lōs\, Adolph. 1870–1933. Austrian architect, b. Moravia. Practiced chiefly in Vienna; his designs, esp. private residences, exerted strong influence on other European Modernist architects. Works included Villa Karma (Clarens, Switz., 1904–06), Steiner House (Vienna, 1910), Goldman and Salatsch Building (Vienna, 1910), Scheu House (Hietzing, Austria, 1912), Tristan Tzara's house (Paris, 1926).

Loos \'lüs\, Anita. 1893–1981. American writer, b. Sisson (now Mount Shasta), Calif. Author of many film scripts, including *Red-Headed Woman* (1932), *The Girl from Missouri* (1934), *San Francisco* (1936), *I Married an Angel* (1942); also wrote novels, esp. *Gentlemen Prefer Blondes* (1925) and *But Gentlemen Marry Brunettes* (1928).

Looy \'lō-ē\, Jacobus van. 1855–1930. Dutch painter and novelist. Leading painter of the Amsterdam school; among his novels were *De dood van mijn poes* (1889) and the trilogy *Jaapje* (1917), *Jaap* (1923), and *Jakob* (1930).

Lope de Vega. See VEGA.

Lo·pes \'lō-pish\, Fernão. c.1380–c.1460. Portuguese historian. Keeper of state archives (1418); court chronicler (1419–54). Commissioned (1434) by the king to chronicle the history of the kings of Portugal; produced three chronicles.

Ló·pez \'lō-pās\, Carlos Antonio. 1790–1862. Paraguayan dictator. Nephew of José de Francia; one of two consuls ruling the country (1841–44); president (dictator) of Paraguay (1844–62); extremely corrupt, ended Paraguay's isolation and sought to modernize its economy and society; interfered in Argentinian civil war of 1845–46. His son ¶Francisco Solano (1827–1870) succeeded as president (1862–70) with dictatorial powers; ambition to dominate South America led to difficulties with Brazil and Argentina (1864–65); declared war against them and Uruguay and invaded Argentina; at first successful but in 5-year war (1865–70) Paraguay devastated; killed by Brazilian troops.

López, José Hilario. c.1800–1869. Colombian general and politician. President of New Granada (1849–53).

López, Luis Carlos. 1883–1950. Colombian poet. Author of lyrical poems depicting life in his native city of Cartegena; works included *De mi villorio* (1908), *Posturas difíciles* (1909), *Por el atajo* (1928).

López Con·tre·ras \-kōn-'trā-räs\, Eleázar. 1883–1973. Venezuelan soldier and politician. Provisional president of Venezuela (1935) on death of Gómez; elected president (1936–41).

Ló·pez de Aya·la \'lō-pāth-thā-ä-'yä-lä\, Pedro. 1332–1407. Spanish politician, soldier, historian, and writer. Captain of Castilian fleet (1359); ambassador to France (1379–80, 1395–96); chancellor of Castile (1398–1407). Author of the historical work *Crónicas de los reyes de Castilla don Pedro, don Enrique II, don Juan I, don Enrique III* (pub. 1779–80), satiric poem *Rimado de palacio* (c.1400), and translations of Titus Livius, Boccaccio, etc.

López de Ayala y Her·re·ra \-ē-er-'rer-ä\, Adelardo. 1828–1879. Spanish dramatist and politician. Elected deputy (1857); prominent in revolution (1868); minister of colonies (1868, 1871, 1872, 1875); president of chamber of deputies (1878–79). Author of historical plays as *Un hombre de estado* (1851), *Los dos Guzmanes* (1851), *Rioja* (1854); musical plays as *El conde de Castralla* (1856); realistic and moralizing plays as *El tejado de vidrio* (1856), *El tanto por ciento* (1861), *El nuevo don Juan* (1863), *Consuelo* (1878).

López de Cár·de·nas \-thā-'kär-thā-näs\, García. fl. 1540. Spanish explorer. On Coronado's expedition (1540–42); first European to sight Grand Canyon.

López de Legazpi, Miguel. See LEGAZPI.

López de Mendoza, Íñigo. See MENDOZA.

López de Se·gu·ra \-thā-sā-'gü-rä\, Ruy. 16th century. Spanish bishop and writer on chess. Wrote (1561) *Libro de la invención liberal y arte de juego del axedrez*, first manual of chess instruction; developed, but did not invent, the Ruy López opening in chess.

López Do·mín·guez \-thō-'mēŋ-gāth\, José. 1829–1911. Spanish general and politician. Under the republic, captain general of Burgos (1873); captured Cartagena; minister of war (1892–95); president of senate (1905); premier of Spain (1906).

Ló·pez Ma·te·os \'lō-pā-smä-'tā-ōs\, Adolfo. 1910–1969. Mexican politician. Senator (1946–52); minister of labor (1952–57). President of Mexico (1958–64); increased industrialization and literacy, extended agrarian reform.

López Pu·ma·re·jo \-pü-mä-'rā-kō\, Alfonso. 1886–1959. Colombian politician. President of Colombia (1934–38, 1942–45); introduced social reforms.

López y Fuen·tes \-ē-'fwān-tās\, Gregorio. 1895–1966. Mexican novelist. Published poetry *La siringa de cristal* (1913) and *Claros de selva* (1922); turned to writing novels based on Mexican Revolution and Indian themes, including *El vagabundo* (1922), *El alma del poblacho* (1924), *Campomento* (1931), *Tierra* (1932), *Mi General!* (1934), *El indio* (1935), *Huasteca* (1939), etc.

Lo·rain \lə-'rān\, John. 1753–1823. American horticulturist, b. England. To America as a child; managed a farm in Maryland; moved to Germantown, Pa. (1795); experimented with cross-breeding of corn, first (1812) to create a hybrid by combining two types of corn. Described his experiments in *Nature and Reason Harmonized in the Practice of Husbandry* (1825).

Lorca, Federico García. See GARCÍA LORCA.

Lo·re·dan \'lō-rā-ˌdän\, Pietro. d. 1439. Venetian admiral. Captain of Venetian fleets that defeated Turks off Gallipoli (1416), Genovese fleet off Rapallo (1431); general (1436), generalissimo (1438) in war against the marchese of Mantua; reestablished Venetian dominance along Po River; murdered, perhaps as result of power struggle with doge Francesco Foscari.

Lo·rentz \'lō-rents\, Hendrik Antoon. 1853–1928. Dutch physicist. Professor of mathematical physics, Leiden (1878–1912); director, Teyler Inst., Haarlem (1912 ff.). Made important contributions to the electromagnetic theory of light; developed an electron theory of matter; with Pieter Zeeman (*q.v.*) discovered the Zeeman effect; shared with Zeeman the 1902 Nobel prize for physics; did work on phenomena of moving bodies, including the Lorentz transformations, that led to promulgation of the theory of relativity. See George FITZGERALD.

Lo·ren·za·na y Bu·trón \lō-rān-'thä-nä-ē-bü-'trōn\, Francisco Antonio. 1722–1804. Spanish prelate. Archbishop of Mexico (1766–72); archbishop of Toledo and primate of Spain (1772–1800); cardinal (1789). Chief work *Historia de Nueva España* (1770).

Lo·ren·zet·ti \ˌlō-ränt-'sāt-tē\, Ambrogio. c.1290–1348. Italian painter. One of greatest painters of Sienese school; known particularly for his series of frescoes *Good and Bad Government* in Palazzo Pubblico at Siena (1337–39); also executed four scenes from legend of St. Nicolas of Bari as part of altarpiece (c.1332), panels of *Presentation of Christ in the Temple* (1342), and *Annunciation* (1344). His brother and teacher ¶Pietro (c.1280–c.1348), also a leading representative of Sienese school; probably a pupil of Duccio; painted polyptych in Arezzo cathedral (1320), frescoes at Assisi (c.1338–40), triptych *Birth of the Virgin* (1342), etc.

Lo·ren·zi·ni \ˌlō-rant-'sē-nē\, Carlo. 1826–1890. *Pseudonym* Carlo Col·lo·di \kōl-'lō-dē\. Italian writer. Chief work a series of adventure tales finally brought out in book form as *Le avventure di Pinocchio* (1882).

Lorenzo the Magnificent. See MEDICI family.

Lo·ren·zo \lō-'rent-sō\, Fiorenzo di. c.1445–c.1525. Umbrian painter. Master of Perugino and Pinturicchio.

Lorenzo, Piero di. See PIERO DI LORENZO.

Lorenzo Mo·na·co \-'mō-nä-kō\. *Orig.* Piero di Gio·van·ni \dē-jō-'vän-nē\. c.1370–c.1425. Italian painter. Joined Camaldolese order (1391); lived mostly at monastery of Sta. Maria degli Angeli, Florence. His work, in the International Gothic style, combined graceful flow of line and decorative feeling of Sienese school with the Florentine traditions of Giotto's followers. Painted polyptych *Madonna and Child* (1406–10), *Coronation of the Virgin* for the altar of his monastery (1413), three predella pieces representing *Nativity, Life of a Hermit,* and stormy seascape (c.1415), *Adoration of the Magi* (c.1422), frescoes of *Life of the Virgin* and *Annunciation* altarpiece (both 1420–24); also a miniaturist.

Lorges, Comte de. See Guy-Aldonce II de Durfort de Duras, at DURFORT family.

Loria, Ruggiero di. See LAURIA.

Lor·i·mer \'lär-ə-mər\, George Horace. 1867–1937. American editor, b. Louisville, Ky. Editor in chief of *The Saturday Evening Post* (1899–1936); president (1932–34), chairman (from 1934), Curtis Publishing Co. Author of *Letters From a Self-made Merchant to His Son* (1902), etc.

Lorimer, James. 1818–1890. Scottish legal philosopher. Admitted to Scottish bar (1845); professor of public law, Edinburgh (1865 ff.). Held that natural law is founded on divine authority and is revealed in conscience and in history; concerned esp. with the application of natural law to international relations. Works included *The Institutes of Law* (1872), *The Institutes of the Law of Nations* (1883–84), *Studies National and International* (1890).

Lo·ris \'lōr-əs\, Heinrich. *Known by Lat. name* Henricus Gla·re·anus \ˌglar-ē-'ā-nəs\. 1488–1563. Swiss Humanist. Crowned poet laureate at Cologne by Emperor Maximilian I (1512); under influence of Erasmus, embraced the Reformation but soon rejected it; taught at Freiburg im Breisgau (1529 ff.). Published treatises on Greek and Roman writers, mathematics, descriptive geography, and music; known esp. for *Dodecachordon* (1547) on music theory, which proposed a system of 12 independent modes, later accepted widely.

Lo·ris-Me·li·kov \'lōr-yis-'myāl-yi-kəf\, Mikhail Tariyelovich. Count. 1825–1888. Russian general and politician. Entered army (1843); commanded regiment in Crimean War (1854–56); major general (1856); lieutenant general (1863); governor of Terek region (1863–75). Commanded army invading Turkey from Armenia (1877–78); captured Ardahan and Kars, won major victory at Aladja Dagh, laid siege to Erzurum. Chairman of Imperial Administrative Commission (1880), charged with combating Nihilism; minister of interior (1880–81).

l'Orme, de. See DELORME.

Lorrain, Claude. See Claude GELLÉE.

Lorrain, Jean. See Paul DUVAL.

Lor·raine \lō-ren; *Angl* lə-'rān, lō-\. Name of ducal family of France, ruling in Lorraine continuously from 1048 to its union with Habsburgs (1740; see HABSBURG-LORRAINE). Branch houses of Vaudémont and Aumale originated in 15th century with nephew of Charles II the Bold; Charles's daughter Isabelle married René I of Anjou, who became (1434) duke of Lorraine (see RENÉ I). René's line extended through eight generations to Emperor Francis I (*q.v.*). Branch of House of Guise (see below) originated when Claude I, son of René II, was made count, then duke (1528) of Guise; this male line became extinct (1765) with Emperor Francis I; duchy had been granted (1737) by Francis to Stanisław I Leszczyński, and on his death (1766) title passed to France.

For the more important dukes of Lorraine, see CHARLES. Other members of the house included: ¶Gérard (1024–1070), created first duc de Lorraine by

Henry III (1048); founder of the family. ¶Philippe-Émmanuel de Lorraine. Duc de Mer·coeur \mer-kœr\. 1558–1602. Cousin of Duke Charles III; succeeded to duchy (1577); governor of Brittany (1582); rebelled when Henry III assassinated members of house of Guise (1588); leader of resistance in Brittany to Henry IV (from 1589); set up a parlement at Nantes; won victory at Craon (1592); submitted after Henry converted to Catholicism (1593); served with Emperor Rudolf II's army against Turks in Hungary.

House of Guise \gēz\. Members included:

¶Claude I. 1496–1550. Son of René II, duc de Lorraine; as comte de Guise, fought under Francis I in Italy (1515) and the Champagne (1523); defeated imperial army at Neufchâteau (1523); member of council of regency during Francis I's captivity (1525–27); raised to duc de Guise (1528); claimed precedence over other nobility; helped conquer Luxembourg and served under Charles, duc d'Orléans, in Flanders (1542). His daughter Mary married (2d) James V of Scotland and was mother of Mary, Queen of Scots.

¶Jean de Lorraine. 1498–1550. Third son of René II; bishop coadjutor of Bar (1501); cardinal (1518); noted for lavish entertainments and gifts, by which he built pro-Guise party at French court; patron of Erasmus, Cellini, etc.

¶François de Lorraine. *Known as* le Ba·la·fré \lə-bà-lä-frā\, *i.e.* the Scarred. 1519–1563. 2d duc de Guise. Son of Claude I; as comte d'Au·male \dō-mál\ fought at Montmédy (1542), at sieges of Landrecies (1543) and Boulogne (1545); raised to duc d'Aumale (1547); m. (1549) Anne d'Este, daughter of Duke Ercole II of Ferrara. Especially efficient in defense of Metz (1552) against Charles V; made prince de Join·ville \zhwaⁿ-vēl\ (1552). Commanded French expedition against Spanish in Italy (1557); took Calais from English (1558). Grand master of royal household (1559); rival of Bourbons for influence; defeated conspiracy of Louis, prince de Condé (1560). After death of Francis II (1560), forced to retire by Catherine de Médicis. Opposed Huguenots; led Catholic forces in first of wars of religion (1562–63); while besieging Orléans, assassinated by Jean de Poltrot, seigneur de Méré.

¶Charles de Lorraine. 1524–1574. Brother of François; archbishop of Reims (1538); created (1547) cardinal of Guise and (1550) of Lorraine; powerful in political intrigues; with brother François virtual head of government (1559–60); persecuted Huguenots but attempted a compromise with them in order to win papal concessions to Gallican church.

¶Henri I de Lorraine. *Also known as* le Balafré. 1550–1588. 3d duc de Guise. Son of François; fought against Huguenots (1567–69); forced Coligny to raise siege of Poitiers (1569). Helped plan Massacre of St. Bartholomew and personally supervised murder of Coligny (1572); prime mover in establishing Holy League (1576) against Bourbons; revived League (1584) to exclude Henry of Navarre from succession; involved in Wars of the Three Henrys; defiance of King Henry III's order to keep away from Paris followed by Day of Barricades (May 12, 1588), resulting in Henry III's capitulation to demands of League; on Henry's order, assassinated by Royal Guard. His younger brother ¶Louis II (1555–1588), archbishop of Reims; cardinal (1578); assassinated at Blois the day after Henri's death (1588).

¶Charles de Lorraine. Duc de Ma·yenne \də-mà-yen\. 1554–1611. Brother of Henri I; fought in Huguenot Wars under his brother; after Henri's assassination, took command of Holy League forces. Proclaimed cardinal of Bourbon king in opposition to Henry of Navarre (1589) but defeated at Arques (1589) and Ivry (1590) by Henry IV. Submitted to Henry IV (1595) and remained loyal until his death. His son ¶Charles (1571–1640) was the 4th duc de Guise. Charles's son ¶Henri II (1614–1664) was archbishop of Reims before succeeding as 5th duc; twice attempted to gain crown of Naples. His nephew ¶Louis-Joseph (1650–1671) succeeded as 6th duc, and Louis-Joseph's son ¶François-Joseph (1670–1675) was 7th duc and last of male line.

Lorraine, Henri de. Comte de Har·court \dár-kür\. *Nicknamed* Ca·det la Perle \kà-del-à-perl\. 1601–1666. French soldier. Fought in wars against Spain in Catalonia, Flanders, Italy, France; served in Louis XIII's campaigns against the Huguenots, capturing Turin (1640); made master of horse by Louis (1643). A royalist leader in wars of the Fronde; established royal authority in Normandy; lifted siege of Cognac and assured obedience of Guyenne (1651); turned against the king, seizing several towns in Alsace; eventually reconciled with the court and made governor of Anjou.

Lorraine-Habsburg. See Habsburg-Lorraine.

Lor·re \'lór-ē, 'lär-\, Peter. *Orig.* László Loe·wen·stein \'lœ̄-vən-ˌshtīn\. 1904–1964. American actor, b. Rózsahegy, Hungary (now Ružomberok, Czechoslovakia). Known for his portrayals of sinister, soft-spoken villains. Scored success in German film *M* (1931); to Hollywood (1934) and appeared in films *Mad Love* (1935), *Crime and Punishment* (1935), *The Maltese Falcon* (1941), *Casablanca* (1942), *The Beast with Five Fingers* (1946), *Beat the Devil* (1954); also starred as Japanese detective Mr. Moto (1937–38).

Lorris, Guillaume de. See Guillaume de Lorris.

Lort·zing \'lórt-siŋ\, Gustav Albert. 1801–1851. German composer. Known esp. for his light operas *Zar und Zimmermann* (1837), *Der Wildschütz* (1842), *Undine* (1845), *Der Waffenschmied* (1846), *Rolands Knappen* (1849).

Lo·sey \'lō-zē\, Joseph. 1909–1984. American film director, b. La Crosse, Wis. Directed films dealing with human weaknesses, moral depravity, and ambiguous personal relationships. Blacklisted (1951) in Hollywood as a leftist, he moved to England to pursue career. Films included *The Boy With Green Hair* (1948), *The Prowler* (1950), *The Damned* (1961), *The Servant* (1963), *King and Country* (1964), *Accident* (1967), *The Go-Between* (1970), *Don Giovanni* (1979), and *Steaming* (1984).

Lot \lót\, Ferdinand. 1886–1952. French historian. Professor at the Sorbonne (1909–36); authority on the later Roman Empire and medieval Europe. Author of *Études sur le règne de Hugues Capet et la fin du Xᵉ siècle* (1904), *Les Invasions barbares et le peuplement de l'Europe* (1937), *L'Art militaire et les armées du Moyen Age* (1946), etc.

Loṭf 'Alī Khān Zand \'lót-fä-'lē-'kän-zänd\. 1769–1794. Persian ruler, last of Zand dynasty. Grandson of Karīm Khān Zand; succeeded his father Ja'far Khān (1789); involved constantly in civil war against Āghā Moḥammad Khān Qājār; scored several victories against Qājār forces but defeated at Kermān (1794) and executed soon afterwards.

Lo·thair \lə-'t(h)er, lō-\. *Fr.* Lo·thaire \lò-ter\. 941–986. King of France (954–986). Son of Louis IV. Next to the last of the Carolingians; dominated by Hugh the Great (to 956), then (to 965) by Otto I's brother Archbishop Bruno of Cologne; in attempt to recover Lorraine, fought with Otto II (978–980); quarreled with Hugh Capet (980–985); succeeded by son Louis V.

Lothair. *Ger.* Lo·thar \'lō-tär, *also* lo-'tär\. Name of two Holy Roman emperors:

Lothair I. 795–855. Emperor (840–855). Son of Louis I; given control of Italy (817); crowned co-emperor (823); with his brothers Pepin and Louis the German, briefly deposed his father (830, 833). On death of Louis I (840), attempted to seize all authority; defeated by brothers at Fontenoy (841); by Treaty of Verdun (843) granted title of emperor and sovereignty over northern Italy and Lorraine; divided his kingdom among his three sons (855); abdicated.

Lothair II (*or* **III**). 1075–1137. King of Germany and Holy Roman emperor (1125–37; crowned 1133). Son of Gebhard, Count of Supplinburg; took part in uprising of Emperor Henry IV (1088); for supporting Henry V, appointed duke of Saxony (1106); rebelled against Henry V (1112–15); waged war with the Hohenstaufens (1128–35); invaded Italy (1132–33, 1136–37).

Lothair II. d. 950 A.D. King of Italy. Ruled jointly with his father, Hugh, Count of Arles (931–947), alone (947–950); in conflict with Berengar II (945–950) finally overcome; his widow, Adelaide, married Emperor Otto I.

Lothair. *Sometimes called* Lothair II. *Ger.* Lothar. 835–869. King of Lotharingia (855–869). On death (855) of his father Emperor Lothair I, received Lotharingia (modern Lorraine); his attempts (from 857) to divorce his wife Theutberga and marry his mistress Waldrada resulted in much strife.

Lothian, Earls and marquises of. See Kerr family.

Lo·throp \'lō-thrəp\, Harriett Mulford, *nee* Stone. 1844–1924. American writer, b. New Haven, Conn. m. (1881) Daniel Lothrop. Author of juvenile books, esp. the Pepper family series as *Five Little Peppers and How They Grew* (1881), *Five Little Peppers Grown Up* (1892), etc.

Loti, Pierre. See Louis-Marie-Julien Viaud.

Lo·tich·i·us Se·cun·dus \lō-'tē-k̲ē-ùs-zā-'kùn-dùs\, Petrus. 1528–1560. German Humanist. Professor of medicine, Heidelberg (1557 ff.). Author of songs, elegies, and eclogues written in Latin.

Lot·ti \'lòt-tē\, Antonio. 1667–1740. Italian composer. Composed some 20 operas as *Il vincitor generoso* (1708), *Porsenna* (1712), *Giove in Argo* (1717).

Lot·to \'lòt-tō\, Lorenzo. c.1480–1556. Venetian painter. Known esp. for his mystical paintings of religious subjects, including *Madonna and St. Peter Martyr* (1503), *Entombment* (1512), *Susanna and the Elders* (1517), *St. Nicholas of Bari in Glory* (1529), *Crucifixion* (1531), *Madonna of the Rosary* (1539), *Madonna Enthroned with Four Saints* (c.1540), *St. Antonio Giving Alms* (1542), *Presentation in the Temple* (unfinished); also painted many perceptive portraits and altarpieces in churches at Bergamo and Venice.

Lot·ze \'lòt-sə\, Rudolf Hermann. 1817–1881. German philosopher. Professor, Leipzig (1842–44), Göttingen (1844–81), Berlin (1881); opposed the theory of a "vital force"; aided in founding science of physiological psychology; founder of Theistic Idealism. Chief work *Mikrokosmos* (1856–58).

Lou·bet \lü-be\, Émile-François. 1838–1929. French politician. Mayor of Montélimar (1870–99). Member, Chamber of Deputies (1876–84); senator (1885–87); minister of public works (1887–88); prime minister (1892); reelected to Senate (1894); its president (1896–99). Seventh president of Republic of France (1899–1906); administration marked by Dreyfus crises (1899, 1904), signing of Entente Cordiale with Great Britain (1904), and separation of church and state (1905); retired from public life (1906).

Loudon, Gideon Ernst von. See Laudon.

Lou·don \'laud-ᵊn\, John Claudius. 1783–1843. Scottish horticultural writer. Edited *Gardener's Magazine* (1826–43); established and edited *Architectural Magazine* (1834); compiler of several encyclopedic works.

Loughborough, Baron. See Alexander WEDDERBURN.

Louis, Saint. See LOUIS IX of France.

Lou·is \lwē, *Angl* 'lü-ē, 'lü-əs\. Name of three dukes of Anjou, claimants to throne of Naples:

Louis I. 1339–1384. Duke of Anjou and count of Provence (1339–84) and titular king of Sicily and Jerusalem (1382–84). Son of King John II of France; fought at Poitiers (1356); made lieutenant general of Languedoc and Guyenne (1364) by his brother Charles V; fought many years against the English; regent of France (1380–82) for his nephew Charles VI; crowned king by antipope Clement VII (1382); led invasion of southern Italy against rival claimant Charles III of Durazzo but died before fighting a decisive battle.

Louis II. 1377–1417. Duke of Anjou and count of Maine and Provence (1384–1417) and titular king of Naples, Sicily, and Jerusalem. Son of Louis I; crowned king of Naples by antipope Clement VII (1389); occupied Naples (1390–99), driven out by Ladislas; recognized antipope Alexander V, who crowned him king again (1409); conducted unsuccessful campaign against Naples (1409–10); defeated Ladislas at Roccaseca (1411) but lost papal support and returned to France.

Louis III. 1403–1434. Duke of Anjou and Touraine, count of Maine and Provence, titular king of Naples, Sicily, and Jerusalem (1417–34). Son of Louis II; crowned king of Naples by Pope Martin V (1419); waged struggle (from 1420) against rival claimant Alfonso V of Aragon, sometimes supported, sometimes opposed, by Queen Joan II of Naples; died before completely defeating Alfonso.

Louis I. *Ger.* Lud·wig \'lüt-vik̲\. 1174–1231. Duke of Bavaria (1183–1231). Succeeded his father Otto I; extended his territory; founded cities of Landshut, Landau, Iser, Straubing; supported Frederick II for throne of Holy Roman Empire; on Fifth Crusade in Egypt (1221); regent of Germany for Frederick (1225–28); rebelled (1228) against Frederick's son Henry; murdered, perhaps on Frederick's orders.

Louis. *Ger.* Ludwig. Name of three kings of Bavaria, of the Wittelsbach family:

Louis I. 1786–1868. King (1825–48). Son of King Maximilian I; a liberal and German nationalist before accession to throne; defended liberal Bavarian constitution of 1818 against Metternich. Turned conservative upon accession; enthusiastic patron of the arts; transformed Munich into the artistic center of Germany, erected many fine buildings; caused scandal by his affair with Lola Montez (*q.v.*); at outbreak of revolution of 1848 abdicated in favor of his son Maximilian II.

Louis II. 1845–1886. King (1864–86). Son of Maximilian II; supported Austria in Seven Weeks' War (1866); joined Prussia in war against France (1870–71); brought Bavaria into German Empire (1871); eccentric, participated less and less in state affairs; patron of art and music, esp. of Richard Wagner; lavish in expenditures for new public buildings, creating great public debt; declared insane, committed suicide by drowning three days later.

Louis III. *In full* Ludwig Leopold Joseph Maria Aloys Alfred. 1845–1921. King (1913–18). Son of Prince Regent Luitpold; m. (1868) Archduchess Maria Theresa of Austria-Este; regent (1912–13) and successor of his cousin Otto I; improved agriculture and transportation; patron of the arts; in exile after revolution of 1918; last reigning king of house of Wittelsbach.

Louis. 1773–1803. King of Etruria (1801–03). Son of Ferdinand, Duke of Parma; m. (1795) María Luisa, daughter of Charles IV of Spain; father of Charles, Duke of Parma and King of Etruria.

Louis. Name of three Flemish counts:

Louis of Flanders. Count of Ne·vers \nə-ver\. 1271?–1322. Fought with Philip IV of France for possession of county; defeated and imprisoned (1312) but escaped.

Louis I de Nevers. Count of Flanders. 1304?–1346. Son of Louis of Flanders; became count of Nevers (1322) but extravagance led to revolt; later (1328) a more serious revolt, led by Jacob van Artevelde, broke out in Flanders; forced to flee (1337) to Paris; killed at Crécy (1346).

Louis II de Male \də-mȧl\. Count of Flanders. 1330–1383. Son of Louis I de Nevers; wounded at Crécy; his rule a long struggle with communes, led by Ghent; caused three districts, previously seized by Philip the Fair, to be restored (1369) to Flanders; extravagances and harsh taxation led to revolt, partly suppressed by defeat of Artevelde at Roosebeke (1382). His daughter Margaret married (1369) Philip the Bold of Burgundy; on his death, Flanders passed to Burgundy.

Louis. Name of eighteen kings of France:

CAROLINGIAN (*q.v.*):

Louis I. 778–840. King (814–840). See LOUIS I, Holy Roman emperor.

Louis II. *Called* le Bègue \lə-beg\, *i.e.* the Stammerer. 846–879. King (877–879). Son of Charles II the Bald; made king of Aquitaine (867); attempted to redistribute offices of state but frustrated by Frankish magnates.

Louis III. 863–882. King (879–882), jointly with his brother Carloman; son of Louis II; ruled in Francia and Neustria; defeated the Normans at Saucourt, Pontheiu (881).

Louis IV. *Called* d'Ou·tre·mer \dü-trə-mer\, *i.e.* from beyond the sea. 921–954. King (936–954). Son of Charles III the Simple; carried to England on death of his father (929); spent most of reign struggling against Hugh the Great (see HUGH CAPET); invaded Lorraine (938); with support from Emperor Otto I, recovered Reims (946) and Laon (949) from Hugh.

Louis V. *Called* le Fai·né·ant \fā-nā-äⁿ\, *i.e.* the Sluggard. 967–987. King (986–987), last of Carolingians in France. Son of Lothair; led frivolous life; unsuccessfully sought Hugh Capet's aid against Otto III of Germany; succeeded by Hugh Capet.

CAPETIAN (*q.v.*):

Louis VI. *Called* le Gros \lə-grō\, *i.e.* the Fat. 1081–1137. King (1108–37). Son of Philip I; by continuous warfare for 24 years subdued robber barons around Paris; engaged in war against Emperor Henry V and Henry I of England (1116–20). Encouraged communal movement among his vassals; granted privileges to towns and aided the church.

Louis VII. *Called* le Jeune \lə-zhœn\, *i.e.* the Young. c.1120–1180. King (1137–80). Son of Louis VI; m. (1137) Eleanor of Aquitaine. Conquered Champagne (1142–44); joined Second Crusade (1147–49). Divorced Eleanor (1152), who married (1152) Henry of Anjou, later Henry II of England; gave up Aquitaine (1154). Long struggle (1157–80) with Henry II; not much actual fighting, but many parts of France held by English king.

Louis VIII. *Called* le Lion \lə-lyōⁿ\ *or* Coeur de Lion \kœr-də-lyōⁿ, *Angl* 'lē-ən\. 1187–1226. King (1223–26). Son of Philip Augustus; m. (1200) Blanche of Castile. A warrior prince, active in several campaigns (1213–15). Offered English crown by barons in opposition to John; led French expedition to England (1216–17); defeated; returned to France after death of John. Aided in war against Albigenses (1215–19); directed massacre at Marmande. As king, tried to destroy power of Plantagenets and to conquer the south of France; overpowered Avignon and received submission of the Albigenses of Languedoc (1226).

Louis IX. *Known as* Saint Louis. 1214–1270. King (1226–70). Son of Louis VIII; his mother, Blanche of Castile, regent during minority (1226–34); m. (1234) Margaret of Provence. Long and comparatively peaceful reign save for brief rising of nobles (1242–43). Led Seventh Crusade (1248–54); his mother again regent until her death (1252); defeated and captured (1250) at al-Manṣūrah, Egypt; remained in Syria (1250–54), strengthening its defenses. Signed Treaty of Corbeil (1258); gave up claims of France to Roussillon and Barcelona. By Treaty of Paris with England (1259), Normandy, Anjou, Touraine, Maine, and Poitou became French, while Henry III was recognized as duke of Aquitaine. Led another crusade to Tunisia (1270); took Carthage; died of the plague at Tunis. Canonized (1297).

Louis X. *Called* le Hu·tin \ǖe-taⁿ\, *i.e.* the Stubborn. 1289–1316. King of Navarre (1305–16) and of France (1314–16). Son of Philip IV; his reign marked by baronial unrest; granted charters to nobility.

VALOIS (*q.v.*):

Louis XI. 1423–1483. King (1461–83). Son of Charles VII; m. (1436) Margaret, daughter of James I of Scotland. Made unsuccessful attempts against his father's throne (1440, 1456); fled to Flanders (1456). As king, destroyed power of great feudatories; struggled esp. with Charles the Bold, Duke of Burgundy, who led a conspiracy of nobles (League of Public Weal, 1464–65); nobles detached by diplomacy and bribery, Charles defeated in war (1467–77); after Charles's death (1477), war continued with his daughter Mary of Burgundy. By Treaty of Arras (1482) Burgundian territories lapsed to king of France; also Anjou, Maine, Provence, and other regions united with the crown (1480–81), foundation of absolute monarchy of France.

Louis XII. 1462–1515. King (1498–1515). Son of Charles, duc d'Orléans; m. 1st Jeanne (1476), daughter of Louis XI; 2d Anne de Bretagne (1499), widow of Charles VIII; 3d Mary Tudor (1514), sister of Henry VIII of England. Duc d'Orléans (1465–98); imprisoned (1488–91) for revolt against Charles VIII; took part in French invasion of northern Italy (1494–95). A popular ruler; inaugurated widespread reforms in finance and justice. Led army into northern Italy, overthrew Ludovico Sforza (1499); with Ferdinand of Aragon conquered Naples (1500–01), but quarreled; French driven out (1503). Joined in League of Cambrai (1508) against Venice, won battle of Agnadello (1509), in which Venice was overwhelmed. Through jealousy of allies and England, Holy League formed (1511) against France, French driven out of Lombardy; defeated by Henry VIII in Battle of the Spurs (1513); peace concluded (1514).

BOURBON (*q.v.*):

Louis XIII. 1601–1643. King (1610–43). Son of Henry IV and Marie de Médicis; m. Anne of Austria (1615). His mother regent during his minority (1610–17); after murder (1617) of her favorite, Concino Concini (*q.v.*), suppressed her rebellion (1620) and thereafter maintained an uneasy truce with her. Personally timid and poor in health, for most of reign completely under influence of Richelieu; for uprising of Huguenots (1622–28) in south of France, foreign policy toward Habsburgs, and participation of France in Thirty Years' War (1618–48), see Armand-Jean du PLESSIS. Other events: his brother Gaston d'Orléans (see under ORLÉANS) attempted (1632) overthrow of Richelieu by expedition from Spain; conspiracy of Cinq-Mars unsuccessful (1641–42). His eldest son succeeded him as Louis XIV; his second son, Philippe I, duc d'Orléans, was founder of house of Orléans (*q.v.*).

Louis XIV. *Called* le Grand \lə-grä^{n}\, *i.e.* the Great, *and* le Roi So·leil \lə-rwä-sò-ley, -rwȧ-\, *i.e.* the Sun King. 1638–1715. King (1643–1715). Son of Louis XIII and Anne of Austria. Regency held by his mother, but power actually with Cardinal Mazarin (1643–61); Peace of Westphalia concluding Thirty Years' War (1648); civil wars of the Fronde (1648–53); war with Spain terminated by Peace of the Pyrenees (1659); France received Roussillon and part of Spanish Netherlands. Married Marie-Thérèse of Spain (1660). On death of Mazarin (1661), assumed control; aided by able ministers, especially Colbert (finance) and François Le Tellier (war). Engaged in long struggle with Spain and the Empire over Franche-Comté, parts of Netherlands, and Luxembourg; first stage, the Queen's War (1667–68), terminated by the Treaty of Aix-la-Chapelle; second, the Dutch War (1672–78), generally successful, esp. with the armies of Turenne up to his death (1675), and closed by the Treaty of Nijmegen; third (1683–97) marked by French invasion of Spanish Netherlands, devastation of the Palatinate, formation of first Grand Alliance against France under leadership of William III of England (1689), and French naval defeat off La Hogue (1692), and concluded by Treaty of Rijswijk, by which France lost certain territories; and fourth, the War of the Spanish Succession (1701–14); marked by struggle with second Grand Alliance and by several severe defeats of the French by the Duke of Marlborough and Prince Eugene in the battles of Blenheim, Oudenarde, Malplaquet, and concluded by treaties of Utrecht (1713) and Rastatt (1714), by which, although Philip of Anjou, his grandson, retained Spanish throne, French territories were given up, French prestige diminished, and the country burdened with debt. During reign, Huguenots gradually deprived of rights; Edict of Nantes revoked (1685) and thousands fled from France; power of church generally brought under control. Much under the influence of his mistresses Louise de La Vallière, Mme de Montespan, and Mme de Maintenon, whom he married after death of Marie-Thérèse (1683). Inordinately ambitious, his monarchical authority greatly increased and despotically used; condition of poor classes made worse. His idea of government summed up in words attributed to him: "L'état c'est moi" (I am the state). His reign longest in European history: France at its zenith, his court the most magnificent in Europe, French letters and arts in their golden age.

Louis XV. *Called* le Bien-Ai·mé \lə-byä^{n}-ne-mā\, *i.e.* the Well-Beloved. 1710–1774. King (1715–74). Son of Louis, duc de Bourgogne, and great-grandson of Louis XIV. During minority (1715–23), under regency of Philippe II, duc d'Orléans; actual administration by Dubois. Duc de Bourbon prime minister (1723–26); m. (1725) Maria Leszczyńska (see MARIE). Bourbon replaced by Fleury as minister (1726–43), whose policy for recovery partly successful while France kept out of war, but who involved France in War of Polish Succession (1733–35; closed by Treaty of Vienna, 1735, which added Lorraine to France), and brought France into Austrian Succession War (1740–48) as ally of Frederick of Prussia, and was blamed for results of Peace of Aix-la-Chapelle which brought no gains to France. After Fleury's death (1743), managed affairs personally but disordered finances were never relieved, administration generally became worse, and discontent and hatred of king by the masses grew steadily more bitter. Had several mistresses, especially Mme de Pompadour, whose influence (1745–64) was long continued and most harmful. Engaged in Seven Years' War (1756–63) which by Treaty of Versailles brought disaster in loss of Canada and India. Jesuits suppressed (1764). Parlement of Paris abolished (1771). In later years influenced by Mme du Barry, duc de Choiseul, and duc d'Aiguillon.

Louis XVI. 1754–1793. King (1774–92). Third son of Dauphin Louis (only son of Louis XV); m. (1770) Marie-Antoinette (*q.v.*). At time of accession, France much disturbed by misery and discontent. At first aided by able ministers as Turgot, Malesherbes, Vergennes, etc.; objectionable taxes remitted, evil laws abolished, and conditions somewhat improved, but soon overruled by extravagant queen and court. Necker made finance minister (1776); America aided in War of Independence (1778–81). Necker (dismissed 1781) was succeeded by Calonne (1783), whose unpopular borrowing methods caused opposition to new taxes and criticism of extravagance of court; Necker recalled (1788). Estates-General met (May 1789). Next four years (1789–92) coincident with French revolution. Wavering policy caused king loss of confidence of both Royalists and Revolutionists; with family, brought forcibly by Parisian mob (Oct. 1789) from Versailles to live in Tuileries; sought to escape from France (June 1791) but arrested at Varennes and brought back. Took oath as constitutional king (Sept. 1791); deposed by National Convention and Republic declared (Sept. 21, 1792); tried for treason (Dec. 1792); found guilty and condemned to death; guillotined.

Louis XVII. *Full name* Louis-Charles. 1785–1795. Titular king (1793–95). Second son of Louis XVI and Marie-Antoinette; became dauphin (1789); imprisoned in the Temple with royal family (1792). Many accounts (partly legendary) of ill treatment by guardians, Antoine Simon and J.J.C. Laurent; died in prison; later, many claimants as real Louis XVII arose.

Louis XVIII. *Full name* Louis-Xavier-Stanislas. 1755–1824. Titular king (1795–1814), king (1814–15, 1815–24). Grandson of Louis XV and brother of Louis XVI and Charles X; m. (1771) Louise Marie Joséphine of Savoy; took active part in politics, opposing revival of parlements (1774) and participating in 1787 Assembly of Notables; remained in Paris after outbreak of Revolution (1789–91); fled to Belgium (1791), later Germany; proclaimed himself regent after death of Louis XVI (1793); took title of Louis XVIII after death of Louis XVII (1795). During Napoleonic regime (1796–1814) led life of constant wandering, living in Germany, Russia, Poland, and England, always engaged in royalist conspiracies; on Napoléon's downfall and restoration of Bourbons (Mar.–Apr. 1814), issued Declaration of Saint-Ouen, promising a constitution to France; entered Paris (May 2); fled to Ghent during Hundred Days (1815); again entered Paris (July 8, 1815); influenced by Élie Decazes, minister of police (1816–20); general policy prudent and sensible; during last years government controlled by Villèle and ultraroyalists.

Louis. Name of three dauphins of France:

Louis. *Called* le Grand Dau·phin \lə-grä^{n}-dō-fa^{n}\ *and* Mon·sei·gneur \mō^{n}-sen-yœr\. 1661–1711. Son of Louis XIV of France and Marie-Thérèse; m. (1679) Marie Christine of Bavaria; given command of armies in Rhine campaign (1688) and in Flanders (1693); aided Villars in War of Spanish Succession (1709–10). Had three children: Louis, duc de Bourgogne; Philip V of Spain; Charles, duc de Berry.

Louis. Duc de Bour·gogne \də-bür-gōn^{y}\. 1682–1712. Son of Louis le Grand. Dauphin and father of Louis XV; educated by Fénelon, who composed for him *Télémaque* and *Fables;* became under his training a prince of exemplary character; m. (1697) Marie-Adélaïde of Savoy; dauphin (1711–12); after death of his father (1711) took part in councils of king.

Louis. 1729–1765. Son of Louis XV and Maria Leszczyńska; at battle of Fontenoy (1745); m. as second wife (1747) Marie-Josèphe of Saxony; pious, opposed to new ideas, friendly to Jesuits; had three sons, all of whom became kings of France: Louis XVI, Louis XVIII, and Charles X.

Louis. *Ger.* Lud·wig \'lüt-vik̲\. Name of three kings of Germany (East Franks):

Louis I. See LOUIS I, Holy Roman emperor.

Louis II. *Called* der Deut·sche \dər-'dòi-chə\, *i.e.* the German. c.804–876. King (843–876). Son of Louis I; given rule of Bavaria (825); took part in revolts against his father (830–833). On death of his father (840), joined with his half-brother Charles the Bald against his brother Lothair and defeated him at Fontenoy (841). By Treaty of Verdun (843) became king of all Germany east of the Rhine; commonly regarded as the founder of the German kingdom. Fought successful war against Moravia (846–847), unsuccessful war with Charles (855–858); divided kingdom (865) among sons Carloman, Charles the Fat, Louis the Younger; by Treaty of Mersen (870) divided Lotharingia with Charles.

Louis III. *Called* das Kind \däs-'kint\, *i.e.* the Child. 893–911. King (899–911). Son of Arnulf; his government administered by Archbishop Hatto of Mainz; country overrun by the Hungarians (900–910); last of the Carolingians in Germany.

Louis. *Ger.* Ludwig. *Called* der Jüng·ere \dər-'yu̵ŋ-ə-rə\, *i.e.* the Younger. c.830–882. German king. Son of Louis II the German; on father's orders invaded Aquitaine (854); on death of father (876), became ruler of Franconia, Thuringia, and Saxony; defeated his uncle Charles the Bald at Andernach (876), acquiring eastern Lotharingia; by Treaties of Verdun (879) and Ribémont (880) received western Lotharingia.

Louis. *Ger.* Ludwig. Name of four Holy Roman emperors:

Louis I. *Called* der From·me \dər-'fròm-ə\ *or* le Pieux \lə-pyœ̄\, *i.e.* the Pious. 778–840. King of France and of Germany (814–840) and emperor of the West (814–840; crowned 816). Third son of Charlemagne; ruled Aquitaine (781–814); crowned co-emperor (813). Divided the empire (817) among his sons Lothair, Pepin, and Louis the German, to take effect after his death; m. (819) as 2d wife Judith of Bavaria; son (born 823) became Charles the Bald. Reign marked by quarrels with sons and various changes in plans for succession; twice deposed by sons (830, 833) but each time restored; civil war (838–840) left the empire in disarray.

Louis II. c.822–875. Emperor (855–875). Son of Lothair I; crowned king of Lombards (844), receiving Italy on death of father; crowned joint emperor (850). Acquired territories in Lotharingia and Provence; waged campaign

(866–871) that checked Arab invasion of Italy; otherwise a weak ruler; the empire declined rapidly.

Louis III. *Called* der Blin·de \dər-'blin-də\, *i.e.* the Blind. c.880–928. King of Provence (887–928) and Holy Roman emperor (901–905). Son of King Boso of Provence and grandson of Emperor Louis II; conquered northern Italy (900–901); crowned emperor by Pope Benedict IV (901); ousted from Italy by Berengar (903); returned to Italy (904); took Lombardy but was captured (905) at Vernona by Berengar, who blinded him and sent him back to Provence.

Louis IV. *Called* der Bay·er \dər-'bī-ər\, *i.e.* the Bavarian. 1283?–1347. King of Germany and Holy Roman emperor (1314–47; crowned 1328). Duke of Bavaria (1294–1347) of the Wittelsbach line. Opposed at election of king by Frederick, Duke of Austria; waged war with Frederick (1314–22) and made him prisoner at battle of Mühldorf (1322); in conflict with papacy; invaded Italy (1327–30), seized Rome, and set up antipope Nicholas V; at Diet of Rense (1338) electoral princes declared that emperor did not need papal confirmation.

Louis. *Hung.* La·jos \'lä-yōsh\. Name of two kings of Hungary:

Louis I. *Called* the Great. 1326–1382. King of Hungary (1342–82) and of Poland (1370–82). Son of Charles I; entered into long struggle with Venice (3 wars: 1342–46, 1357–58, 1378–81) for control of Adriatic coast; finally successful (treaty 1381); maintained friendly relations with Holy Roman emperor; appointed successor to Polish crown by Casimir III (1370), but union of two countries not a success.

Louis II. 1506–1526. King of Hungary (1516–26). Son of Ulászló II; led a dissolute life, kept from affairs of state; lost Belgrade to Turks (1521); killed at battle of Mohács.

Louis. *Port.* Lu·ís \lü-'ēsh\. 1838–1889. King of Portugal (1861–89). Son of Ferdinand II and Maria II da Gloria. Duke of Saxony and duke of Oporto during brother Peter V's reign (1853–61); m. (1862) Maria Pia of Savoy. As king, attempted various reforms; freed slaves in Portuguese colonies (1868); reign progressive but disturbed by political strife and many ministerial changes.

Louis. Comte de Sois·sons \swä-sōⁿ\. *Known as* Mon·sieur le Comte \məs-yœ̄-lə-kōⁿt\. 1604–1641. French nobleman. Grandson of Louis I, Prince of Condé; persistent enemy of Cardinal Richelieu's regime; with other malcontents invaded France with a Habsburg army (1641); won battle at La Marfée but was mysteriously shot dead at his moment of victory.

Louis of Nas·sau \'nä-sō\. Count of Nassau-Dietz \-'dēts\. 1538–1574. Dutch soldier. Brother of William I the Silent; a leader in revolt against Spanish rule; led invasion of northern Netherlands (Apr. 1568), won at Heiligerlee (May) but, with William, routed at Jemgum (July); retreated to France. Launched second invasion (1572); captured Mons (May) but lost it (Sept.); killed at battle of Mook.

Louis of Ta·ran·to \tä-'rän-tō\. 1320–1362. King consort of Naples and count of Provence (1347–62). Also prince of Taranto and Achaia; believed to have taken major role in murder (1345) of Andrew, husband of Queen Joan I of Naples; m. (1347) Joan; fled to Avignon on invasion (1348) of Andrew's brother Louis I of Hungary; returned to Naples (1352); usurped royal power from Joan; regained most of Sicily from the Aragonese (1356–57); suppressed baronial revolt in Naples.

Lou·is \'lü-əs\, Joe. *Orig.* Joseph Louis Bar·row \'bar-(,)ō\. *Nicknamed* the Brown Bomber. 1914–1981. American boxer, b. Lexington, Ala. Won first professional fight by knockout in first round (Chicago; July 4, 1934). Won world's heavyweight championship by defeating James J. Braddock (June 22, 1937); defended title 25 times, winning all bouts, 21 by knockouts; retired undefeated (1949); made unsuccessful comebacks against Ezzard Charles (Sept. 27, 1950) and Rocky Marciano (Oct. 26, 1951).

Louis, Morris. *Orig.* Morris Bernstein. 1912–1962. American painter, b. Baltimore. With W.P.A. easel-painting project in New York (1937–40); early work Cubist; associated (from 1952) with New York school of Abstract Expressionism. His canvases characterized by use of brilliantly colored stripes or waves in a vertical pattern or flowing across the lower corners of otherwise blank fields; executed several series of paintings as *Veils* (1954, 1958), *Aleph* (1960–61), *Unfurled* (1961), *Pillar* (1961–62).

Louis \lwē\, Pierre. *Pseudonym* Pierre Louÿs \lwēs, lü-ēs\. 1870–1925. French poet and novelist. Founded *La Conque* (1891) and other short-lived literary reviews; sought in his verse to combine pagan sensuality with stylistic perfection. Author of *Astarté* (verse, 1891), *Les Chansons de Bilitis* (prose poems, 1894), *Aphrodite* (novel, 1896), *La Femme et le pantin* (novel, 1898), *Sanguines* (stories, 1903), etc.

Louis Amadeus. See LUIGI AMADEO.

Louis Bonaparte. See BONAPARTE.

Louis de Bourbon. See CONDÉ.

Lou·ise \lwēz, lü-ēz\ of Sa·voy \sə-'vȯi\. Duchesse d'An·gou·lême \däⁿ-gü-lem\. 1476–1531. French regent. Daughter of Philip II the Landless, Duke of Savoy; m. (1490) Charles de Valois-Orléans, comte d'Angoulême; mother of Francis I of France and of Margaret of Navarre. Regent while Francis was on Italian expeditions (1515, 1525–26); able to detach Henry VIII of England from alliance with Emperor Charles V; with Margaret of Austria signed (1529) Treaty of Cambrai (Ladies' Peace).

Louise Maximilienne Caroline. Countess of Al·ba·ny \'ȯl-bə-nē\. 1752–1824. British noblewoman. Daughter of Gustav Adolf, prince of Stolberg-Gedern; m. (1772) Charles Edward Stuart, the Young Pretender; left him (1780) for liaison with Vittorio Alfieri, Italian poet; lived and maintained salon in Florence; received at court by George III of England; after Alfieri's death (1803) lived with painter François Fabre.

Louis-Napoléon. See NAPOLÉON III.

Lou·is-Phi·lippe \lwē-fē-lēp, *Angl* 'lü-ē-fi-'lēp\. *Called* le Roi-Ci·toy·en \lər-wä-sēt-wä-yaⁿ\, *i.e.* the Citizen King. 1773–1850. King of the French (1830–48). Eldest son of Louis-Philippe-Joseph (Philippe-Égalité), duc d'Orléans; only sovereign of the Bourbon-Orléans line (see ORLÉANS). Duc de Valois (1773–85); duc de Chartres (1785–93); like his father, joined with revolutionists (1789); member of Jacobin Club (1790); lieutenant general in Revolutionary army, fought at Valmy and Jemappes (1792); deserted with Dumouriez to Austrians (1793); on death of father (1793) became duc d'Orléans. During Napoleonic regime (1796–1814) lived in Switzerland, Philadelphia (1797–1800), England, Sicily; m. (1809) Maria Amelia, daughter of Ferdinand IV of Naples. Lived in France (1817–30), administering estates and great wealth. On July revolution (1830) against Charles X, proclaimed "citizen king" by Thiers and elected by deputies (Aug. 7); at first democratic and bourgeois, but fundamentally Bourbon; power weakened by gradual attempts to restore monarchy and inability to win allegiance of the industrial classes; cooperated with British in forcing the Dutch to recognize Belgian independence; deserted by Liberals; overthrown by revolution (Feb. 1848); abdicated; escaped with wife to England.

Had eight children:

Ferdinand-Philippe; see ORLÉANS.

¶Marie-Louise (1812–1850), wife of Leopold I of Belgium.

¶Marie (1813–1839), wife of Prince Frederick of Württemberg; an artist, best known for her statue of Joan of Arc.

¶Louis-Charles-Philippe-Raphaël, duc de Ne·mours \nə-mür\ (1814–1896), colonel of cavalry (1826); at siege of Antwerp (1832), on expeditions to Algeria (1836, 1837, 1841); in England (1848–70), involved in attempts to restore Bourbon monarchy; returned to France (1871) and restored to rank of divisional general.

¶Clémentine (1817–1907), wife of Prince Augustus of Saxe-Coburg; mother of King Ferdinand I of Bulgaria.

¶François-Ferdinand-Philippe-Louis-Marie (1818–1900), prince de Join·ville \zhwaⁿ-vē\; in French navy (1831–48), rear admiral (1844); prominent in modernization of navy; to England (1848); on staff of Gen. McClellan in U.S. Civil War (1861–62). In France (from 1871); deputy in National Assembly (1871–75). Author of *Essais sur la marine française* (1852), *Études sur la marine* (1859), etc.

¶Henri-Eugène-Philippe-Louis, duc d'Au·male \dō-mál\ (1822–1897), governor general of Algeria (1847–48); general of division (1873); author of political and historical works.

¶Antoine-Marie-Philippe-Louis, duc de Mont·pen·sier \mōⁿ-päⁿs-yā\ (1824–1890), fought in African campaigns (1842–45); m. Luisa, sister of Queen Isabella II of Spain; in Spanish army (1857–59); offered himself as candidate for Spanish throne (1870) but failed.

Louis William I. *Ger.* Ludwig Wilhelm. *Called* Tür·ken·lou·is \,tuer-kən-'lü-ē\. 1655–1707. Margrave of Baden. Fought against French (c.1673–78), against the Turks with great distinction (1683–91); captured Heidelberg (1693); served under Marlborough in War of Spanish Succession; marshal (1704).

Lou·ka·ris \lü-'kär-ēs\, Kyrillos. *Eng.* Cyril Lu·ca·ris \lü-'kär-əs\. 1572–1638. Greek Orthodox prelate. Patriarch of Alexandria (1602); patriarch of Constantinople (1620–38), 5 times forced to resign but reinstated; often denounced for advocating church reforms on Calvinistic lines; presented (c.1625) to James I of England the Codex Alexandrinus, valuable 5th-century manuscript of Greek Bible; executed by strangling on charge of inciting the Cossacks to attack the Turks.

Louth, Robert. See LOWTH.

Lou·ther·bourg \lü-ter-bür\, Philip James de, *orig.* Philippe-Jacques de. 1740–1812. British painter, printmaker, and theatrical designer, b. Germany. Worked in Paris (from c.1755) under Charles Van Leo, the Tischbeins, Francesco Casanova; settled in England (1771) on Garrick's invitation to superintend scene painting at Drury Lane; naturalized British subject. As theatrical designer (to 1785), known for elaborate Romantic settings and his introduction of the act drop. As painter, known for landscapes and battle scenes, including *Lord Howe's Victory off Ushant, Destruction of the Armada, View of a Landscape in Cumberland.* Invented a polygraphic system for reproducing paintings in color and (1781) the Eidophusikon, a moving panorama combining moving pictures with dramatic lighting effects and music.

Louverture, Toussaint. See TOUSSAINT LOUVERTURE.

Lou·vet de Cou·vray \lü-ved-ə-küv-rā\, Jean-Baptiste. 1760–1797. French politician and novelist. Member of National Convention (1792); joined Girondists and attacked Robespierre (Oct. 1792); fled Paris to escape the guillotine; returned (1795) and became member of the Council of Five Hundred. Author of *Les Amours du chevalier de Faublas* (1786–91).

Louvois, Marquis de. See François LE TELLIER.

Louw \ˈlō\, Nicolaas Petrus van Wyk \fän-ˈvīk\. 1906–1970. South African poet, dramatist, and literary theorist. Considered greatest figure in Afrikaans literature; leader and theoretician of the Dertigers, group of poets during 1930s responsible for revival of Afrikaans poetry. Author of verse *Alleenspraak* (1935), *Die Halwe Kring* (1937), *Die Dieper Reg* (1938), *Raka* (1941), *Gestaltes en Diere* (1942), *Tristia* (1962); plays *Dias* (1952), *Germanicus* (1956), *Die Held* (1962), *Koning Eenoog* (1963); prose works *Lojale Verset* (1939), *Berigte te Velde* (1939), *Maskers van die Erns* (1956), *Swaarte en Ligpunte* (1958).

Louÿs, Pierre. See Pierre LOUIS.

Love \ˈləv\, Hough. 1863–1940. English geophysicist. Professor, Oxford (1899–1940). Discovered a major type of earthquake wave later named for him. Wrote *Treatise on the Mathematical Theory of Elasticity* (1892–93), *Some Problems of Geodynamics* (1911), etc.

Love·craft \ˈləv-ˌkraft\, Howard Phillips. 1890–1937. American writer, b. Providence, R.I. Known for his fantastic or macabre short novels and stories, esp. his "Cthulhu Mythos" tales; published most stories in *Weird Tales* magazine (from 1923). Works included *The Case of Charles Dexter Ward* (1928), *At the Mountains of Madness* (1931), *The Shadow over Innsmouth* (1936), *Beyond the Wall of Sleep* (1943).

Love·joy \ˈləv-ˌjȯi\, Arthur Oncken. 1873–1963. American philosopher, b. Berlin, Germany. Professor, Johns Hopkins U. (1910–38). His method for studying philosophy based on unit ideas common to Western philosophers. Author of *The Revolt Against Dualism* (1930), *Primitivism and Related Ideas in Antiquity* (with George Boas, 1935), *The Great Chain of Being* (1936), *Essays in the History of Ideas* (1948).

Lovejoy, Elijah Parish. 1802–1837. American abolitionist, b. Albion, Me. Presbyterian minister (1833); editor (from 1833) of *St. Louis Observer,* strongly supporting temperance and abolitionist causes; moved press (1836) to Alton, Ill., and continued abolitionist propaganda, press being destroyed several times; shot and killed by a mob in attempt to save his property; hence known as "the Martyr Abolitionist."

Love·lace \ˈləv-ˌlās\, Richard. 1618–1657. English poet. Took part in expeditions to Scotland (1639–40); imprisoned in Gatehouse at Westminster for presenting Kentish petition in king's favor (1642), wrote "To Althea, from Prison"; went abroad, fighting for French against Spanish at Dunkerque (1646); returned and was imprisoned (1648); published *Lucasta: Epodes, Odes, Sonnets, Songs, etc.* (1649). His graceful lyrics and dashing military career made him prototype of the perfect Cavalier.

Lov·ell \ˈləv-əl\, Francis. Viscount. 1454–?1487. English rebel. Chamberlain to Richard III (1483–85); fought at Bosworth Field (Aug. 1485); led unsuccessful revolt in Yorkshire against Henry VII (1486); to Ireland (1487) and took part in expedition to England of Lambert Simnel, the impostor "King Edward VI"; fled after defeat at East Stoke, Nottinghamshire (June 1487) and never heard of again.

Love·lock \ˈləv-lək, -ˌläk\, John Edward, *called* Jack. 1910–1949. New Zealand athlete. Set world record of 4 min. 7.6 sec. for the mile run (1933); won 1,500-meter race at 1936 Olympics in record time of 3 min. 47.8 sec.

Lov·er \ˈləv-ər\, Samuel. 1797–1868. Irish novelist and songwriter. Wrote Irish songs, including "Rory O'More," "The Angel's Whisper," "The Low-backed Car," "Molly Bawn," "Four-leaved Shamrock"; associated with Dickens in founding *Bentley's Miscellany.* Author of popular novels, including *Rory O'More* (1837) and *Handy Andy* (1842).

Lov·ett \ˈləv-ət\, Robert Morss. 1870–1956. American educator and reformer, b. Boston. Taught at U. of Chicago (1893–1936, professor from 1909); active in Hull-House settlement, American Civil Liberties Union, etc.; president (1921–38), League for Industrial Democracy; secretary of U.S. Virgin Islands (1939–44), dismissed by Dies committee of U.S. Congress. Author of textbooks as *History of English Literature* (with William Vaughn Moody, 1902); critical works as *Edith Wharton* (1925), *Preface to Fiction* (1930); novels *Richard Gresham* (1904), *Winged Victory* (1907); plays as *Cowards* (1914).

Lovett, William. 1800–1877. English Chartist leader. Cabinetmaker in London (after 1821); follower of Robert Owen; a founder (1836) of London Workingmen's Association and main author of its People's Charter of 1838; his influence became limited by his moderate policies; while imprisoned (1839) wrote (with John Collins) *Chartism: A New Organization of the People.* Founded (1841) National Association for Promoting the Political and Social Improvement of the People and thereafter devoted himself to it.

Low \ˈlō\, Sir David Alexander Cecil. 1891–1963. British cartoonist and caricaturist, b. New Zealand. On staff of *The Bulletin,* Sydney, Australia (1911), and, in London, of the *Star* (1919), *Evening Standard* (1927), *Daily Herald* (1950), *The Guardian* (1953). Famous for his political cartoons; created character Colonel Blimp. Cartoons collected in *Caricatures* (1915), *Lloyd George and Co.* (1922), *Low and I* (1923), *Low Again* (1938), *A Cartoon History of Our Times* (1939), *Europe at War* (1940), *A Cartoon History of the War* (1941), *The Years of Wrath* (1949), etc.

Low, Sir Hugh. 1824–1905. English colonial administrator. Civil servant in Labuan (1848–77); British resident of Perak (1877–89); his administrative methods became models for subsequent British colonial operations in Malay Peninsula.

Low, Juliette Magill Kinzie, *nee* Gordon. 1860–1927. American founder of Girl Scouts, b. Savannah, Ga. m. (1886) William M. Low; organized first troop of Girl Guides at Savannah, Ga. (Mar. 9, 1912; name changed to Girl Scouts, 1913, and headquarters moved to New York City).

Low, Seth. 1850–1916. American merchant, politician, and educator, b. Brooklyn, N.Y. With his father's mercantile house (1870–87). Mayor of Brooklyn (1882–86). President, Columbia U. (1890–1901), transforming it into a major university. Mayor of New York City (1901–03); replaced patronage with civil service and expanded public utilities and transportation.

Low·den \ˈlau̇d-ᵊn\, Frank Orren. 1861–1943. American politician, b. Sunrise City, Minn. Son-in-law of George M. Pullman; practiced law in Chicago (1887–1906). Member, U.S. House of Representatives (1906–11); governor of Illinois (1917–21); sponsored legislation aiding farmers and agriculture.

Lowe \ˈlō\, Sir Hudson. 1769–1844. British soldier, b. Ireland. Continuously active through Napoleonic wars; attached to Prussian army of Blücher, served with distinction. Governor of St. Helena, held strict vigilance against intrigues of Napoléon (1815–21), for which he was criticized by Barry O'Meara, physician to Napoléon; military commander in Ceylon (1825–30).

Lowe, Robert. Viscount Sher·brooke \ˈshər-ˌbru̇k\. 1811–1892. English politician. Practiced law, Sydney, Australia (1842); member of legislative council, New South Wales (1843–50). Liberal M.P. (1852–80); vice president of education board (1859–64); an Adullamite, helped to defeat Whig Reform Bill (1866). Gladstone's chancellor of exchequer (1868–73); home secretary (1873–74); created viscount (1880).

Lowe, Thaddeus Sobieski Coulincourt. 1832–1913. American aeronaut and inventor, b. Jefferson Mills (later Riverton), N.H. Interested in ballooning (from 1856); chief of aeronautic section, U.S. army (1861–65), during which time he made first airborne use of telegraph and camera. Reputed first to manufacture artificial ice in U.S. (1866). Invented and built apparatus for production of water gas (1873–75); constructed (1897) New Lowe Coke Oven system for producing high-grade coke.

Low·ell \ˈlō-əl\, Abbott Lawrence. 1856–1943. American political scientist and educator, b. Boston. Brother of Amy and Percival Lowell; practiced law, Boston (1880–97). Professor of government, Harvard (1900–09). President of Harvard (1909–33). Author of *Governments and Parties in Continental Europe* (1896), *The Government of England* (1908), *Conflicts of Principle* (1932), *At War with Academic Tradition in America* (1934), etc.

Lowell, Amy. 1874–1925. American poet and critic, b. Brookline, Mass. Sister of A.L. and Percival Lowell. A leading member (from c.1913) of Imagist school; wrote much in vers libre and in polyphonic prose. A brilliant and popular conversationalist and lecturer; noted for leading unconventional life. Her volumes of verse included *A Dome of Many-Coloured Glass* (1912), *Sword Blades and Poppy Seed* (1914), *Men, Women, and Ghosts* (1916), *Can Grande's Castle* (1918), *Pictures of the Floating World* (1919), *A Critical Fable* (1922), *What's O'Clock* (1925), *East Wind* (1926), *Ballads for Sale* (1927). Her critical works included *Six French Poets* (1915), *Tendencies in Modern American Poetry* (1917), and the biography *John Keats* (1925).

Lowell, Francis Cabot. 1775–1817. American industrialist, b. Newburyport, Mass. In mercantile business, Boston (1793–1810). With aid of Paul Moody, built at Waltham, Mass. (1812–14), first complete cotton spinning and weaving mill in U.S. Lowell, Mass., is named in his honor.

Lowell, James Russell. 1819–1891. American poet, essayist, and diplomat, b. Cambridge, Mass. Nephew of F. C. Lowell. Began career with *A Year's Life* (1841), followed by *Poems* (1844), *Biglow Papers* (collected 1848; second series 1867), *A Fable for Critics* (1848), and *The Vision of Sir Launfal* (1848). Succeeded to Longfellow's chair at Harvard (1855–86). Editor, *Atlantic Monthly* (1857–61); associate of Charles Eliot Norton in editing *North American Review* (1864–72). U.S. minister to Spain (1877–80), Great Britain (1880–85). His works also included poetry as *Commemoration Ode* (1865), *Under the Willows* (1869), *Three Memorial Poems* (1877), *Heartsease and*

Rue (1888); prose as *Conversations on Some of the Old Poets* (1845), *Fireside Travels* (1864), *Among my Books* (1870; second series 1876), *My Study Windows* (1871), *Democracy and Other Addresses* (1887), and *Political Essays* (1888).

Lowell, Percival. 1855–1916. American astronomer, b. Boston. Brother of A. L. and Amy Lowell; in business and traveling, chiefly in Japan (1877–93); author of *Chŏson* (1885), *Soul of the Far East* (1888), *Noto* (1891), and *Occult Japan* (1895). Built astronomical observatory near Flagstaff, Ariz. (1893–94); best known for his studies of Mars and for mathematical work predicting the discovery of Pluto (discovered by C. W. Tombaugh, 1930). Among his astronomical works were *Mars* (1895), *The Solar System* (1903), *Mars and Its Canals* (1906), *Mars as the Abode of Life* (1908), *The Evolution of Worlds* (1909), and *The Genesis of the Planets* (1916).

Lowell, Robert Traill Spence, Jr. 1917–1977. American poet, b. Boston. Great-grandnephew of James Russell Lowell and distant cousin of A. L., Amy, and Percival Lowell; imprisoned for refusing to serve in World War II (1944); taught at Harvard. Author of volumes of verse *Land of Unlikeness* (1944), *Lord Weary's Castle* (1946, Pulitzer prize), *The Mills of the Kavanaughs* (1951), *Life Studies* (1959), *Imitations* (1961), *For the Union Dead* (1964), *Near the Ocean* (1967), *Notebook 1967–68* (1969), *Day by Day* (1977); also trilogy of plays *The Old Glory* (1965) and translations.

Low·er \ˈlō-ər\, Richard. 1631–1691. English physician and physiologist. Made first direct transfusion of blood from one animal to the veins of another (in dogs, 1665); studied cardiopulmonary system; published *Tractatus de corde* (1669).

Lowes \ˈlōz\, John Livingston. 1867–1945. American scholar, b. Decatur, Ind. Professor of English, Harvard (1918–39). Author of *Convention and Revolt in Poetry* (1919), *The Road to Xanadu* (1927), *The Art of Geoffrey Chaucer* (1931), *Essays in Appreciation* (1936), etc.

Low·ie \ˈlō-ē\, Robert Harry, *orig.* Robert Heinrich. 1883–1957. American anthropologist, b. Vienna, Austria. To U.S. (1893); with American Museum of Natural History, N.Y.C. (1908–21); professor, U. of Calif., Berkeley (1921–50). Known for ethnological studies of the North American Plains Indians and of South American and German cultures. Works included *Primitive Society* (1920), *Primitive Religion* (1924), *The Crow Indians* (1935), *The History of Ethnological Theory* (1937), *The German People* (1945), *Social Organization* (1948).

Low·in \ˈlō-ən\, John. 1576–1653. English actor. Joined King's company (1603); played with Shakespeare, Burbage, John Heming, Condell; acted in chief plays of Shakespeare, Jonson, Beaumont and Fletcher, and Massinger.

Lowndes, Mrs. Belloc. See Marie Adelaide BELLOC.

Lowndes \ˈlaun(d)z\, William Thomas. 1798–1843. English bookseller and bibliographer. Spent fourteen years compiling *The Bibliographer's Manual of English Literature* (1834), first systematic work of its kind in England; left unfinished *The British Librarian* (1839–42).

Low·ry \ˈlau̇-rē\, Malcolm, *in full* Clarence Malcolm. 1909–1957. English novelist. Author of novels *Ultramarine* (1933), *Under the Volcano* (1947), *Dark as the Grave Wherein My Friend Is Laid* (unfinished, 1968), short-story collection *Hear Us O Lord from Heaven Thy Dwelling Place* (1961), and *Selected Poems* (1962).

Lowth *or* **Louth** \ˈlau̇th\, Robert. 1710–1787. English prelate and scholar. Professor of poetry at Oxford (1741–50); published his lectures *De Sacra Poesi Hebraeorum* (1753), pointing out parallelism as characteristic of Hebrew poetry, the beginning of modern literary study of sacred poetry as poetry. Bishop of Oxford (1766–77), of London (1777); dean of Chapel Royal (1777). Author of *Life of William of Wykeham* (1758), *A Short Introduction to English Grammar* (1762), and *Sermons and Other Remains* (1834).

Loyd \ˈlȯid\, Samuel. 1841–1911. American puzzlemaker, b. Philadelphia. Famous in his day for composing chess problems; invented board game Parcheesi and such puzzles as the Fifteen Puzzle (c.1878, also called Boss Puzzle, Jeu de Taquin, or Diablotin); assisted on some of his puzzles by and collaborated on a widely syndicated puzzle column with his son ¶Samuel (d. 1934), who continued producing chess problems after his father's death.

Loyola, Ignatius of. See IGNATIUS of Loyola.

Loy·son \lwȧ-zōⁿ\, Charles. *Known as* Père Hya·cinthe \yȧ-saⁿt\. 1827–1912. French religious. Ordained in Roman Catholic church (1851); excommunicated for heterodoxy (1869). Married (1872); although excommunicated, continued to profess faith; pastor of a liberal Catholic church in Geneva (1873–74); founded Gallican Catholic church in Paris (1879). Author of *De la réforme catholique* (1872–73), *Mon Testament, ma protestation* (1893), etc.

Lü \ˈlue̅\. d. 180 B.C. Empress of China. First woman ruler of China; wife of Liu Pang (see under LIU family); became real power behind throne with accession (195 B.C.) of their son Hui Ti; consolidated power by ignoring members of ruling Liu family and appointing her relatives to important posts; after death of Hui Ti (188), appointed another infant to succeed him, then replaced him with yet another. After her death, her family lost power to Liu family upon accession of Liu Heng, a son of Liu Pang by another wife.

Lub·bock \ˈləb-ək\, Sir John William. 1803–1865. English astronomer and mathematician. Banker by profession; gave uniform method for calculation of cometary and planetary orbits (1829); supplementing Laplace, demonstrated stability of solar system; claimed to have reduced tabular errors of moon below those of observation.

His son ¶Sir John (1834–1913), 1st Baron Ave·bury \ˈāv-b(ə-)rē, ˈā-bər-ē\, became partner in father's banking house (1856); Liberal M.P. (1870–1900); instrumental in carrying several banking reforms and measures dealing with shop hours regulation, public libraries, and ancient monuments. Vice chancellor for London U. (1872–80); president, London Chamber of Commerce (1890–92); created baron (1900). Known best as writer of popular science books, esp. in archaeology and entomology, including *Pre-historic Times,* long used as textbook on archaeology (1865), *The Origin of Civilization and the Primitive Condition of Man* (1870), *Origin and Metamorphoses of Insects* (1874), *British Wild-flowers* (1875), *Ants, Bees, and Wasps* (1882), *On the Senses, Instincts, and Intelligence of Animals* (1888). His nephew ¶Percy Lubbock (1879–1965), literary critic; author of *The Craft of Fiction* (1921) and of autobiographical books *Earlham* (1922), *Shades of Eton* (1929).

Lu·bec·ki \lüb-ˈyet-skəi, *Pol* -skē\, Ksawery Drucki. 1779–1846. Russian official. Officer in Russian army; member of provisional government of Duchy of Warsaw (1813–15); negotiated settlement of Polish foreign debt (1817–21). As minister of the treasury of Russian-controlled Congress Kingdom of Poland (1821–30), restored financial stability of government, created Land Credit Society (1825) and Bank of Poland (1828), developed state mines and foundries; returned to St. Petersburg (1830); member of State Council (1832).

Lü·ber \ˈlue̅-bər\ *or* **Lie·ber** \ˈlē-bər\ *or* **Lie·bler** \-blər\, Thomas. *Known as* Thomas Eras·tus \i-ˈras-təs, *Ger* ā-ˈräs-tu̇s\. 1524–1583. Swiss theologian and physician. Professor of medicine, Heidelberg (1557–80), Basel (1580–83). Privy councilor to Elector Frederick III (1559–64). Took part in theological conferences at Heidelberg (1560) and Maulbronn (1564), upheld Zwinglian doctrine of the Eucharist and denied right of excommunication as a divine ordinance in controversy with Olevianus, George Withers, and others; excommunicated on charge of Socinianism (1570–75). Author of a collection of theses on excommunication *Explicatio gravissimae quaestionis* (1568; pub. 1589). The doctrine known as Erastianism, which upholds state supremacy in ecclesiastical affairs, goes by his name, but was not held by him.

Lu·bin \ˈlü-bin\, David. 1849–1919. American agriculturist, b. Kłodowa, Poland. To U.S. (1855); successful in drygoods business, Sacramento, Calif. (1874–84), in fruitgrowing (1884); interested himself in national agricultural problems; organized fruitgrowers; advocated tariff protection for farmers; founded (1905) at Rome the International Institute of Agriculture, a world clearinghouse for data on crops, prices, and trade to protect the common interests of farmers of all nations.

Lu·bitsch \ˈlü-bich\, Ernst. 1892–1947. American motion-picture director, b. Berlin, Germany. Achieved success in Germany as director of historical costume films *Madame Dubarry* (1919, in U.S. called *Passion*), *Anna Boleyn* (1920, in U.S. *Deception*), *Das Weib des Pharao* (1921); to U.S. (1922, naturalized 1933) to direct Mary Pickford in *Rosita* (1923). Established reputation for his sophisticated comedies of manners notable for their graceful wit, understatement, sexual innuendo, and inventive camera work; films included *The Marriage Circle* (1924), *Forbidden Paradise* (1924), *Kiss Me Again* (1925), *Lady Windermere's Fan* (1925), *So This Is Paris* (1926), *The Love Parade* (1929), *Trouble In Paradise* (1932), *The Merry Widow* (1934), *Ninotchka* (1939), *The Shop Around the Corner* (1940), *That Uncertain Feeling* (1941), *To Be or Not to Be* (1942), *Heaven Can Wait* (1943), *That Lady in Ermine* (1948).

Lüb·ke \ˈlu̅ep-kə\, Heinrich. 1894–1972. German politician. Politically inactive during Nazi era; Christian Democratic member of North Rhine-Westphalia Landtag (1946–52), of federal Bundestag (1949–50, 1953–59); minister of food, agriculture, and forestry (1953–59); president of German Federal Republic (1959–69); popular for his dignified demeanor and discretion.

Lübke, Wilhelm Meyer-. See MEYER-LÜBKE.

Luca da Cortona. See Luca SIGNORELLI.

Luca d'Olanda. See LUCAS VAN LEYDEN.

Lucan, Earl of. See George Charles BINGHAM.

Lucan, Titular earl of. See Patrick SARSFIELD.

Lu·can \ˈlü-kən\. *Full Latin name* Marcus Annaeus Lu·ca·nus \lu̇-ˈkā-nəs\. 39–65 A.D. Roman poet, b. Corduba (modern Córdoba), Spain. Grandson of the elder Seneca, nephew of the younger; for a time enjoyed Nero's favor, losing it as his literary reputation grew, until the jealous Nero forbade his public recitals; joined conspiracy of Piso (*q.v.*) against Nero, was betrayed, committed suicide. His sole extant work is epic *Pharsalia* about the civil war between Caesar and Pompey.

Lucaris, Cyril. See LOUKARIS.

Lu·cas \'lü-kəs\, Frank Laurence. 1894–1967. English man of letters. Author of critical works *Seneca and Elizabethan Tragedy* (1922), *Tragedy in Relation to Aristotle's Poetics* (1927), *The Decline and Fall of the Romantic Ideal* (1936), *The Art of Living* (1959), etc.; also edited John Webster (1927) and wrote novels, poems, and plays.

Lu·cas van Ley·den \'lü̅-käs-vän-'lī-dən\. *Known also as* Lucas Hu·gensz \'hü̅-gəns\ *or* Ja·cobsz \'yä-kȯps\. *Ital. name* Luca d'·Olan·da \dō-'län-dä\. 1494–1533. Dutch painter and engraver. Trained by his father Huygh Jacobszoon and by Cornelis Engelbrechtsz; met (1521) Albrecht Dürer in Antwerp and was influenced by him; said to have developed technique of etching on copper, instead of iron, plates; among first to use aerial perspective in prints as *The Poet Virgil Suspended in a Basket* (1521). Among his engravings were *Muhammad and the Monk Sergius* (1508), *Susanna and the Elders* (1508), *The Circular Passion* series (1510), *The Milkmaid* (1510), *Ecce Homo* (1510), *Dance of the Magdalene* (1519), *Passion* series (1521), portrait of Emperor Maximilian (1521); his paintings included *Self-Portrait* (c.1508), *The Chess Players* (c.1508), *Last Judgment* (1526), *Moses Striking the Rock* (1527), *Blind Man of Jericho Healed by Christ* (1531).

Luce \'lüs\, Henry Robinson. 1898–1967. American editor and publisher, b. Tengchow (now P'eng-lai), China, of American parentage. Founder (1923, with Briton Hadden), editor, and publisher of weekly magazine *Time;* also of monthly *Fortune* (1930), weekly picture magazine *Life* (1936), weekly *Sports Illustrated* (1954); as editor in chief of Time, Inc. (1929–64), also produced television programs, operated radio and television stations, sponsored "March of Time" radio (1931) and newsreel (1935) series.

Luce, Stephen Bleecker. 1827–1917. American naval officer, b. Albany, N.Y. In navy (1841–89), rising to rear admiral (1886); author of textbook *Seamanship* (1863). Advocated and obtained (1884) establishment of Naval War College for postgraduate training of naval officers; its first president (1884–89).

Lucera, Duke of. See Matthias GALLAS.

Lu·chaire \lü̅-sher\, Achille, *in full* Denis-Jean-Achille. 1846–1908. French historian. Professor at Bordeaux (1879) and the Sorbonne (1899). Works included *Histoire des institutions monarchiques de la France sous les premiers Capétiens* (1883), *Étude sur les actes de Louis VII* (1885), *Louis VI le Gros* (1890), *Innocent III* (1904–08), *La Société française au temps de Philippe-Auguste* (1909).

Luchana, Count. See Baldomero ESPARTERO.

Luchetto, Il. See Luca CAMBIASO.

Lu Chi \'lü-'jē\. 261–303. Chinese poet and literary critic. First important writer of kingdom of Wu; to Chin capital of Lo-yang (290) where he became president of national university and occupied high government posts; executed for involvement in plot to overthrow the emperor. Excelled in writing *fu,* a mixture of poetry and prose, as his *Wen fu* on the art of letters; also wrote lyrical poetry and *Pien-wang lun,* a history of Wu.

Lu Chiu-yüan \'lü-jē-'ü-yü̅-'än\. *Also known as* Lu Hsiang-shan \-shē-'äŋ-'shän\. 1139–1193. Chinese philosopher. Teacher at the imperial academy; held several government posts. Contemporary and chief rival of Chu Hsi; with Chu, formed Idealist, Neo-Confucian school of Lu Wang, as opposed to Rationalist school of Ch'eng Chu; held that there is a single unifying principle in the world and that this principle is found within each person's mind.

Lu·cian \'lü-shən\. c.120–after 180 A.D. Greek satirist and rhetorician, b. Syria. Regarded as most brilliant writer of the revived Greek literature under the Roman Empire. Toured Greece, Italy, Gaul as public lecturer; settled in Athens, studied philosophy; attracted patronage of Emperor Verus; made (c.170) archistator (a kind of chief court usher) in Alexandria, Egypt; spent last years in Athens as public speaker. Among his works were *Dialogues of the Gods, Dialogues of the Dead, Banquet of Philosophers, Demonax, Auction of Philosophers, Prometheus, The False Prophet, The Eunuch, How to Write History.*

Lucian of An·ti·och \'ant-ē-,äk\. Saint. c.240?–312. Christian theologian and martyr, b. Syria. Founder of Antioch school which practiced a literal-historical method of biblical exegesis; analyzed the Greek text of the Old and New Testaments, producing a recension (known as the Lucianic Byzantine or Syrian text) which became the common one; held Adoptionist views; martyred at Nicomedia in Bithynia.

Lu·cia·ni \lü-'chän-ē\, Sebastiano. *Known as* Sebastiano del Piom·bo \'pyȯm-bō\. c.1485–1547. Italian painter. Pupil of Giorgione in Venice; to Rome (1511) to decorate Villa Farnesina; worked with Michelangelo, from whose designs he executed *Pietà* (c.1517) and *Flagellation* (1516–24); rival of Raphael; devised technique for painting with oils on stone and on plaster walls; keeper of papal seals (whence his nickname, 1531–47); known esp. for portraits.

Lucidor, Lasse. See Lars JOHANSSON.

Lucien Bonaparte. See BONAPARTE.

Lu·ci·fer \'lü-si-fər\. *Known also as* Lucifer Ca·lar·i·ta·nus \kə-,lar-ə-'tā-nəs\. d. c.371. Sardinian prelate. Bishop of Cagliari; known for his vehement opposition to Arianism; defended Athanasius at council of Milan; exiled by Emperor Constantius II (355); formed schismatic sect called Luciferians (363) to combat return of Arian bishops to former rank in orthodox church.

Lu·cil·i·us \lü-'sil-ē-əs\, Gaius. c.180–c.102 B.C. Roman poet. Prominent member of Scipio Aemilianus's literary circle in Rome; regarded as originator of the form of satirical composition later perfected by Horace, Persius, and Juvenal. Only fragments of his works are extant.

Lu·ci·us \'lü-sh(ē-)əs\. Name of three popes:

Lucius I. Saint. d. 254. Pope (253–254). Condemned the Novatian Schism; his martyrdom under Valerian unproven. Patron saint of Copenhagen.

Lucius II. *Orig.* Gherardo Cac·cia·ne·mi·ci \,kät-chä-'nä-mē-chē\. d. 1145. Pope (1144–45). Cardinal (1124); papal chancellor to Innocent II; opposed Giordano Pierleoni's attempt to establish an independent Roman republic; killed leading assault against the rebels.

Lucius III. *Orig.* Ubaldo Al·lu·cin·go·li \,äl-lü-'chēŋ-gō-lē\. 1097?–1185. Pope (1181–85). Cistercian monk; cardinal (1141); bishop of Ostia (1159); trusted counselor of Pope Alexander III. As pope, forced to leave Rome after establishment of city-republic free from papal interference; convened Synod of Verona (1184) that instigated attacks on the Cathari and established prosecution procedures against heretics later used in the Inquisition.

Lu·cre·tia \lü-'krē-sh(e-)ə\. *Eng.* Lu·crece \lü-'krēs, 'lü-(,)krēs\. d. c.509 B.C. Roman matron. According to tradition, the beautiful and virtuous wife of Lucius Tarquinius Collatinus; raped by Tarquinius Sextus; killed herself; the event caused Lucius Junius Brutus to lead revolt that drove the Tarquins from Rome, marking foundation of Roman Republic; legend told in Shakespeare's *Rape of Lucrece.*

Lu·cre·ti·us \lü-'krē-sh(ē-)əs\. *In full* Titus Lucretius Car·us \'kar-əs, kā-rəs\. c.100 to 90–c.55 to 53 B.C. Roman poet. A disciple of Epicurus; committed suicide, according to tradition, in a fit of madness caused by a love philter given to him by his wife. His great work was *De rerum natura,* a didactic and philosophical poem treating of physics, psychology, and ethics according to the Epicurean doctrine.

Lu·cul·lus \lü-'kəl-əs\, Lucius Licinius. c.117–58 or 56 B.C. Roman general. Quaestor in the East under Sulla (87); proquaestor (86–80); curule aedile (79); consul (74). Campaigned in Asia Minor and defeated Mithradates (74–71) and Tigranes (69). In Rome (from 66), lived in great luxury and established reputation by the splendor of his banquets and the magnificence of his surroundings; enjoyed the company of the leading poets, artists, and philosophers of his time.

Lu·cy \'lü-sē\. Saint. d. 304. Christian martyr. Suffered martyrdom at Syracuse, Sicily, probably under Diocletian's persecutions; her feast day, December 13, was shortest day of the year before Gregorian calendar reform.

Lucy, Richard de. d. 1179. English jurist. Supported King Stephen in civil war (1139); chief justiciar of England (with Robert de Beaumont, c.1155–68; alone 1168–79); as one of Henry II's chief councilors, helped formulate much important legislation, including property law and judicial procedure reforms; involved in Henry's struggle against Thomas Becket and twice excommunicated by Becket (1166, 1169); regent of England while Henry fought rebellions (1173–74); founded (1178) Lesnes Abbey in penance for his part in Becket's murder; resigned office shortly before death and entered Lesnes.

Lucy, Sir Thomas. 1532–1600. English squire. M.P. (1571, 1584); justice of peace in Warwickshire; according to story told by Nicholas Rowe (1710), prosecuted Shakespeare for stealing deer from Charlecote Park (1585); reputedly caricatured by Shakespeare as Justice Shallow.

Lud *or* **Ludd** \'ləd\, Ned. fl. 1779. English laborer. Perhaps mythical; reputedly a half-witted Leicestershire workman who, about 1779, broke up stocking frames; riots that occurred (1811–16) when workmen broke up labor-saving machinery were called "Luddite riots," and men who took part in them were known as "Luddites."

Lu·den·dorff \'lü-dən-,dȯrf\, Erich Friedrich Wilhelm. 1865–1937. German general and politician. At outbreak of World War I (1914), was appointed chief of staff of 8th army; quartermaster general (1916–18); worked with Hindenburg; responsible with him for defeat of Russia, and alone the cause of collapse of Serbians and Romanians and defeat of Italy at Caporetto (1917); his plan of campaign (1918) on the Western Front almost successful in crushing Allies; after German defeat, fled to Sweden. Returned to live at Munich (1919); took part in reactionary conspiracies, as the Kapp Putsch (1920) and the Hitler Beer Hall Putsch (1923); National Socialist member of Reichstag (1924–28); in last years led crusades against Jews, Catholics, Masons, and Protestants, supported Hitler and then deserted him; later became a pacifist. Author of several works on World War I.

Lud·ford \'lәd-fәrd\, Nicholas. c.1485–c.1557. English composer. Works included a set of seven daily Lady masses, four complete and three incomplete masses, and a Magnificat.

Lud·low \'lәd-(,)lō\, Edmund. c.1617–1692. English Parliamentary leader. Fought in Parliamentary army; M.P. (1646); one of chief promoters of Pride's Purge (1648); one of king's judges, signed death warrant. Member of Council of State (1649, 1650). Practically completed subjugation of Ireland (1651–52); arrested on refusal to acknowledge Cromwell as Protector, but allowed to retire to Essex; on recall of Long Parliament (1659) member of committee of safety and of council of state and commander in chief in Ireland; impeached by restored Parliament, escaped to Vevey, Switzerland, where he wrote *Memoirs* (1698–99).

Ludlow, John Malcolm Forbes. 1821–1911. English social reformer. One of founders of Christian Socialist movement; founder and editor of *Christian Socialist* (1850).

Ludlow, Roger. 1590–?1664. English colonist. To America (1630) as an assistant of Massachusetts Bay Company; deputy governor of Massachusetts (1634). Moved to Windsor, Conn., and presided (1636) over first court held in Connecticut. Collected and codified Connecticut laws in *The Code of 1650,* known as *Ludlow's Code.* First settler, Fairfield, Conn. (1639); magistrate of Connecticut colony (1639–54). Returned to England (1654).

Lud·mil·la \lüt-'mil-ä\ *or* **Lud·mi·la** \-'mē-lä\. Saint. c.860–921. Patron saint of Bohemia. Grandmother of St. Wenceslas; married Borivoj, first Czech prince to adopt Christianity; pioneered in establishing Christianity in Bohemia; strangled, purportedly on orders of her daughter-in-law, regent Drahomíra, who favored paganism.

Lud·wick \'lüt-vik\, Christopher. 1720–1801. American Revolutionary leader, b. Giessen, Germany. Baker in India and common sailor; opened bakery shop in Philadelphia (1754); prospered and financially supported the Revolution; volunteered for mission (1776) in which, disguised as a deserter, he induced hundreds of German mercenaries on Staten Island to join the American cause; superintendent of bakers and director of baking for Continental army (1777), became known as the "Baker General."

Ludwig. See also LOUIS.

Lud·wig \'lüt-vik, 'lüd-\, Carl Friedrich Wilhelm. 1816–1895. German physiologist. One of the founders of physicochemical school of physiology in Germany. Professor at Marburg (1846–49), Zürich (1849–55), Vienna (1855–65), Leipzig (1865–95). Developed the kymograph (1847) and a mercurial blood pump (1859) to study blood pressure and the circulation of blood; demonstrated the influence of nerves on the distribution of blood and on the secretion of glands; first to keep animal organs alive in vitro (1856); discovered depressor and accelerator nerves of the heart; located a blood vessel regulatory mechanism in the medulla oblongata; with Henry Bowditch formulated (1871) the "all-or-none" law of cardiac muscle action; postulated (1844) that the epithelium of the kidney tubules serves as a passive filter in urine production.

Ludwig, Emil. *Orig. surname* Cohn \'kōn\. 1881–1948. German writer. Name legally changed to Ludwig (1883). His works included novels *Manfred und Helene* (1911), *Diana* (1918), plays, poems, essays, and esp. biographies *Goethe* (1920), *Napoleon* (1925), *Wilhelm II* (1925), *Der Menschensohn* (1928), *Lincoln* (1929), *Cleopatra* (1937), *Roosevelt* (1938), *Beethoven* (1943), etc.

Ludwig, Otto. 1813–1865. German writer. A pioneer Realist; coined term *Poetischer Realismus.* Author of an opera *Die Köhlerin* (1838), the tragedies *Der Erbförster* (1850) and *Die Makkabäer* (1854), the novellas *Die Heiteretei* (1851), *Zwischen Himmel und Erde* (1856), and the critical work *Shakespeare-Studien* (1891).

Lue·ger \'lue-gәr\, Karl. 1844–1910. Austrian politician. Elected to Vienna municipal council (1875), to Austrian Reichsrat (1885); cofounder (1889) and leader of Christian Social party; as mayor of Vienna (1897–1910), transformed it into an efficient, modern metropolis; instrumental in introduction of universal suffrage in Austria (1907).

Lufft \'lu̇ft\, Hans. 1495–1584. German painter. Known as "the Bible Printer" because at Wittenberg he printed the first complete edition of Luther's Bible.

Lu·gal·zag·gisi \,lü-gәl-'zag-ә-sē\. *Also spelled* Lugal-Zaggisi *or* Lugalzaggesi. 24th century B.C. Mesopotamian king (c.2375–2350 B.C.). Ensi (sacred king) of southern Mesopotamian city of Umma; conquered cities of Lagash and Kish; united all of Sumer, subduing cities of Ur and Uruk; extended empire to Mediterranean coast; defeated by Sargon.

Lu·gard \lü-'gärd\, Frederick John Dealtry. 1st Baron Lugard. 1858–1945. British soldier and colonial administrator, b. India. Served in Afghan War (1879–80), Sudan campaign (1885), Burma campaign (1886–87); commanded West African frontier force, with rank of brigadier general (1897–99). High commissioner and commander in chief of Northern Nigeria (1900–06); governor of Hong Kong (1907–12); unified Nigeria (1912–14) and was its governor general (1914–19). Wrote *Dual Mandate in British Tropical Africa* (1922); created baron (1928).

Lu·geon \lü-zhōn\, Maurice. 1870–1953. Swiss geologist, b. France. Professor at Lausanne (1898 ff.); pioneer in development of modern Alpine geology; provided first comprehensive interpretation of the Alps as a whole (1901); consultant on dam sites. Wrote *Barrages et géologie* (1933).

Lu·gné-Poe \lue̅n-yä-pō\, Aurélian-Marie. 1869–1940. French actor and theatrical manager. As manager (1892–1929) of the Théâtre de l'Oeuvre, Paris, introduced works of many contemporary playwrights, including Ibsen, Hauptmann, Strindberg, Maeterlinck, Paul Claudel.

Lu·go·nes \lü-'gō-nās\, Leopoldo. 1874–1938. Argentinian poet and critic. Published volumes of Modernist verse *Las montañas del oro* (1897), *Los crepúsculos del jardín* (1905), *Lunario sentimental* (1909); edited *Revue Sudaméricaine* in Paris (1911–14). Rejected Modernism for a treatment of national themes in a realistic style; wrote *La guerra gaucha* (prose sketches, 1905), *El libro de los paisajes* (poems, 1917), *Cuentos fatales* (short stories, 1924), *El ángel de la sombra* (novel, 1926). Promoted Argentinian culture at home and abroad; also produced histories of Argentina, critical studies of classical Greek literature and culture, translations of Homer. Regarded as outstanding figure of his age in cultural life of Argentina.

Lu·go·si \lә-'gō-sē\, Bela. 1884–1956. American actor, b. Lugos, Hungary (now Lugoj, Romania). Played leading roles at Royal Hungarian National Theater, Budapest (by 1913); to U.S. (1921). Scored success as the vampire in stage version of *Dracula* (1927, New York); gained international fame by recreating role for film *Dracula* (1931). Continued to portray monsters or sinister characters in films *Murders in the Rue Morgue* (1932), *The Black Cat* (1934), *Mark of the Vampire* (1935), *The Wolf Man* (1941), *The Ape Man* (1943).

Lu·han \'lü-,hän\, Mabel, *nee* Gan·son \'gan-sәn\. *Known as* Mabel Dodge Luhan. 1879–1962. American writer, b. Buffalo, N.Y. m. 2d Edwin Dodge (1903), 4th Antonio Luhan (1923). Hosted many famous figures at her home at Taos, N.M., as John Reed, Amy Lowell, and D.H. Lawrence, the latter of whom she wrote about in *Lorenzo in Taos* (1932); also wrote an autobiographical series under title *Intimate Memories* (1933–37).

Lu Hsiang-shan. See LU CHIU-YÜAN.

Lu Hsün. See CHOU SHU-JEN.

Lu·i·gi Ame·deo \lü-'ē-jē-,äm-ä-'de-ō\. Duca d'Abruz·zi \dä-'brüt-tsē\ *and* Prince of Sa·voy-Aos·ta \sä-'vȯi-ä-'ȯs-tä\. 1873–1933. Italian explorer and naval officer. Son of King Amedeus of Spain. First to scale Mt. St. Elias in Alaska (1897); made Arctic expedition (1899) to record 86° 34′ N; first to scale Ruwenzori peaks in Africa (1906); reached 20,000 feet on K2 (1909); commanded Italian fleet (1914–17); later explored and colonized in Somaliland.

Luineach, Turlough. See O'NEILL family.

Lu·i·ni \lü-'ē-nē\, Bernardino. d. 1532. Italian painter. Member of Lombard school; excelled in religious and mythological frescoes; among his works *Beheading of John the Baptist, Jesus among the Doctors, Herodias, Birth of Christ.*

Luís. See LOUIS.

Lu·ís Pe·rei·ra de Sou·sa \lü-'ēsh-pā-'rā-rä-dä-'sü-sä\, Washington. 1869–1957. Brazilian politician. Mayor of São Paulo (1914–19); governor of state of São Paulo (1920–24); senator in National Congress (1924–26). President of Brazil (1926–30); tried with little success to improve finances and prevent collapse of coffee market; deposed in coup; exile in Europe (1930–46).

Luitpold. See also LEOPOLD.

Lu·it·pold \'lü-әt-,pōlt\. 1821–1912. Prince regent of Bavaria (1886–1912). Son of Louis I and uncle of Louis II and Otto; officer in Bavarian army (1866–86); chosen (1886) regent of Bavaria for Otto during his entire reign because of Otto's insanity; introduced liberal reforms; patron of the arts, made Munich a center of culture; succeeded by his son Louis III.

Luitprand. See LIUTPRAND.

Lu·kács \'lu̇k-äch\, György. 1885–1971. Hungarian philosopher and literary critic. Became Marxist (1918); commissar for culture and education (1919); member of Hungarian underground movement in Vienna (1919–29); in Moscow (1930–44); returned to Hungary (1945) as member of parliament and professor (1945–58) at U. of Budapest; minister of culture in Nagy's cabinet (1956). Formulated a Marxist system of aesthetics that opposed political control of artists and defended humanism; produced over 30 books and hundreds of essays, including *Theorie des Romans* (1920), *Geschichte und Klassenbewusstsein* (1923), *Der junge Hegel* (1948), *Die Zerstörung der Vernunft* (1954), *Die Eigenart des Ästhetischen* (1963), *Probleme des Realismus* (1964–65).

Lu·kas \'lü-kәs\, Paul. *Orig. surname* Lukács. 1895–1971. American actor, b. Budapest, Hungary. To U.S. (1927); successful on the legitimate stage and in motion pictures, including *Watch on the Rhine* (1943).

Łu·ka·sie·wicz \,lü-kä-'shā-vēch\, Jan. 1878–1956. Polish logician. Minister of education (1919); professor at Warsaw (1920–39), where he was a founder of the Warsaw school of logic; professor at Royal Irish Academy, Dublin (1946–56). Made detailed study of Aristotle's syllogistic in *O Zasadzie*

Sprzeczności u Arystotelesa (1910); reevaluated ancient and medieval logic by employing modern formal techniques of logic; developed a three-valued propositional calculus (1917) and made researches on many-valued logics; devised a notation system for syllogistic propositions.

Luke \'lük\. Saint. 1st century A.D. One of the twelve Christian apostles. A physician; companion of St. Paul, whom he accompanied to Greece and Macedonia (c.51), Jerusalem (c.58), and on Paul's prison voyage to Rome (c.66); traditionally regarded as author of the third Gospel and the Acts of the Apostles in the New Testament.

Lu·kin \'lü-kən\, Lionel. 1742–1834. English coach-builder and inventor. Patented (1785) an "unsubmergible" boat fitted with airtight and watertight projections of cork or hollow chambers, the prototype of the modern lifeboat; also invented a raft for rescuing persons under ice, an adjustable hospital bed, a rain gauge.

Luks \'ləks\, George Benjamin. 1867–1933. American painter, b. Williamsport, Pa. Staff artist on Philadelphia *Press* and Philadelphia *Bulletin;* originator of comic strip "Hogan's Alley" (featuring the Yellow Kid; cf. R. F. OUTCAULT) in New York *World.* Member (from 1908) in New York of the Eight (later called Ashcan School), group of painters depicting urban life in realistic manner. Among his canvases were *The Spielers* (1905), *The Wrestlers* (1905), *Little Madonna, Women and Black Cat, Ducks, Morris Canal, The Breaker Boys, Tango Artist.*

Luli \'ləl-ē, 'lül-ē\. *Gr.* Elu·lai·os \ˌel-yə-'lī-əs\. fl. 705 B.C. Phoenician king of cities of Tyre and Sidon. After death of Sargon II (705), joined Shabaka of Egypt and Hezekiah of Judah in a rebellion against Assyrian rule; defeated by Sennacherib and fled to Cyprus (c.702).

Lul·ly \lᵫ-lē\, Jean-Baptiste. *Orig.* Giovanni Battista Lul·li \'lül-lē\. 1632–1687. French composer, b. Italy. Called founder of national French opera. Brought to France by Roger de Lorraine, Duke of Guise (1646); member of corps of 24 violins attached to service of Louis XIV, whose favor he won; court composer (1653); superintendent of court music (1661); wrote masques and ballets in which he and Louis XIV himself took part; collaborated (1663–71) with Molière in comédies-ballets as *Le Mariage forcé* (1664), *La Princesse d'Élide* (1664), *Le Bourgeois Gentilhomme* (1670); head of Académie Royale de Musique, now the Grand Opéra (1672–87); became naturalized French citizen and one of king's secretaries (1681). Developed French form of the overture; introduced lively ballets, varied rhythms, simplicity and directness of expression in his operas. Composed operas, with Quinault as librettist, including *Alceste* (1674), *Thésée* (1675), *Atys* (1676), *Isis* (1677), *Proserpine* (1680), *Persée* (1682), *Amadis* (1684), and *Armide* (1686); also several pastorali, many ballets and masques, church music including the famous *Miserere* (1664) and 17 motets, dances for various instruments, suites for trumpets and strings, and *Suites de Symphonies et Trios.*

Lully, Raymond. See Ramon LLULL.

Lu·mière \lᵫ-myer\, Auguste-Marie-Louis-Nicolas (1862–1954) and his brother Louis-Jean (1864–1948). French chemists, industrialists, and motion-picture pioneers. Founded in Lyons a factory for producing photographic plates, paper, and chemicals; they invented the Lumière process of color photography and the Cinématographe, an early motion-picture camera (1895); produced films, esp. *La Sortie des usines Lumière,* considered the first movie (1895); also produced the first newsreels and the first documentaries.

Lum·mer \'lům-ər\, Otto Richard. 1860–1925. German physicist. Associate of Helmholtz (1884–1904); professor, Berlin (from 1904). Known for investigations in optics and thermal radiation; rediscovered (1884) interference in a plane-parallel glass plate, which developed (1901) into the Lummer-Gehrcke interference spectroscope; did work with Ernst Pringsheim on blackbody radiation, the results (1900) of which led Max Planck to develop the quantum theory.

Lum·mis \'ləm-əs\, Charles Fletcher. 1859–1928. American author and editor, b. Lynn, Mass. Settled in Los Angeles (1885); interested himself in preserving Spanish missions and other historical relics in California. Author of *A New Mexico David* (1891), *A Tramp Across the Continent* (1892), *The Land of Poco Tiempo* (1893), *The Spanish Pioneers* (1893), *The Awakening of a Nation: Mexico of Today* (1898), *A Bronco Pegasus* (1928), and volumes of Pueblo folk tales and old California Spanish songs.

Lu·mum·ba \lə-'məm-bə, -'mům-\, Patrice Hemery. 1925–1961. Zaire politician. Member of Batetela tribe and a Catholic; in postal service, became active in nationalist movement (1955); founded (1958) Mouvement National Congolais, the first nationwide Congolese political party. First prime minister of Zaire (June–Sept. 1960); aroused strong opposition by his attempt to end attempt of Katanga province to secede; dismissed; arrested by forces of Joseph Kasavubu and turned over to Katanga regime, where he was murdered.

Lu·na \'lü-nä\, Álvaro de. c.1390–1453. Spanish politician. Minister of John II of Castile; appointed constable of Castile (1422); consolidated monarchial power in Castile; created duke of Trujillo, count of Gormaz, of San Esteban, and of Ledesma, and lord of many cities and castles; lost power in last years and was executed.

Luna, Pedro de. See antipope BENEDICT XIII.

Lu·na·char·sky \lü-(ˌ)nə-'chär-skəi\, Anatoly Vasilyevich. 1875–1933. Russian Communist leader and writer. Joined Social Democratic party (1898); arrested (1899), escaped to Paris; joined Bolsheviks under Lenin (1903); at outbreak of Russian Revolution (1917), joined Lenin and Trotsky in Russia and aided in Bolshevik coup d'état (Nov. 1917). Commissar for education (1917–29); introduced widespread reforms in public education and did much to preserve works of art and historical buildings during civil war; ambassador to Spain (1933). Author of *Religion and Socialism* (1911), *Culture and the Working Class* (1919), etc.

Lu·na·li·lo \lü-nä-'lē-lō\, William C. 1832–1874. King of Hawaiian Islands (1873–74). Elected king to succeed Kamehameha V, last of the direct Kamehameha line; had liberal ideas, worked for improvements in constitution; favored reciprocity treaty with U.S.

Lu·na y Arel·la·no \'lü-nä-ē-ä-räl-'yä-nō\, Tristán de. 1510–1573. Spanish explorer. Served under Coronado in New Mexico expedition; named governor and captain general of Florida; led unsuccessful attempt to conquer Florida (1559–61); died in poverty in Mexico City.

Lun·de·berg \'lün-də-ˌberʸ\, Christian. 1842–1911. Swedish industrialist and politician. Member of Riksdag (1885–1911; speaker 1908–11); chairman of council of state (1896–1900, 1902–04). Prime minister (1905); negotiated end of Swedish-Norwegian union (1905).

Lun·dy \'lən-dē\, Benjamin. 1789–1839. American abolitionist, b. Hardwick, N.J. Organized Union Humane Society in St. Clairsville, Ohio (1815), one of the first antislavery societies; founded and edited antislavery newspapers *Genius of Universal Emancipation* (at various places, 1831–35) and *The National Enquirer* (at Philadelphia, 1836–38; later called the *Pennsylvania Freeman*); traveled, wrote, and spoke in various states against slavery; reestablished the *Genius* in Illinois (1839).

Lüneburg, Dukes of. See HANOVER.

Lung-ch'ing. See Chu Tsai-kou under CHU family.

Lun·ghi \'lüŋ-gē\ *or* **Lon·ghi** \'lȯŋ-gē\ *or* **Lon·go** \'lȯŋ-gō\. Family of Italian architects active chiefly in Rome, including: Martino, *called* the Elder (d. 1591), commissioned by Pope Sixtus V to build church of S. Girolamo degli Schiavoni (1588–90) and continued work on the Chiesa Nuova in S. Maria in Vallicella. His son ¶Onorio (1569–1619) began work on S. Carlo al Corso (1612). His son ¶Martino, *called* the Younger (1602–1657), continued work on S. Carlo after his father's death; other works included initial construction of church of S. Antonio de'Portoghesi (1638–56), a staircase in Ammanati's Palazzo Caetani (c.1640; now Ruspoli), and the facade of SS. Vincenzo ed Anastasio in Piazzi di Trevi (1646–50).

Lung-wu. See Chu Yü-chien under CHU family.

Lunn \'lən\, Sir Arnold Henry Moore. 1888–1974. British skier, b. India. Editor of *British Ski Year Book* (from 1919); introduced (1922) slalom gates, creating the modern Alpine slalom race; induced the Fédération Internationale de Ski to recognize competition in downhill as well as slalom skiing (1930). Author of works on skiing, esp. *The Story of Ski-ing* (1952), and on religion, as *Difficulties* (with Ronald Knox, 1932).

Lunt \'lənt\, Alfred. 1893–1977. American actor, b. Milwaukee. Stage debut in Boston (1913); scored huge success in *Clarence* (1919–21); m. (1922) Lynn Fontanne and with her starred in stage productions including *Sweet Nell of Old Drury* (1923), *The Guardsman* (1924), *Pygmalion* (1926), *Design for Living* (1933), *Idiot's Delight* (1936), *Amphitryon 38* (1938–39), *O Mistress Mine* (1945), *Quadrille* (1952–55), *The Visit* (1958–60).

Lu·pe·scu \lü-'pe-skü\, Magda. *Orig. surname* Wolff. *Called from 1947* Princess Elena. 1896?–1977. Romanian adventuress. m. an army officer; met Prince Carol (1921?); divorced her husband; left Romania (1925) to live with Carol in Paris; returned to Romania (1930) soon after Carol seized throne; during Carol's reign (1930–40) exerted great influence over political events; forced to flee with Carol to Spain (1940); m. (1947) Carol and lived mainly in Portugal.

Lu·pi·no \lů-'pē-nō\. *Orig. spelled* Lup·pi·no. Name of English family of actors tracing its ancestry to an Italian actor (fl. 1612) who billed himself as Signor Luppino. His descendant ¶George William Luppino (1632–1693), singer, reciter, and puppet master, emigrated to England. Other members included ¶Thomas Frederick Lupino (1749–1845), scenic artist and dancer, first to use present family spelling. ¶George (1853–1932), famous clown. His son ¶Barry (1884–1962) excelled in pantomime and musical comedy; appeared in films and often toured the U.S. His brother ¶Stanley (1894–1942) remembered for performances in revues and musical comedies; produced stage and screen plays;

wrote plays, novels, and reminiscences *From the Stocks to the Stars* (1934). His nephew ¶Henry George (1892–1959) took stage name Lupino Lane; known for Cockney comic roles; starred and toured in variety, musical comedy, pantomime; scored huge success as Bill Snibson in *Me and My Girl* (1937) in which he created a ballroom dance called the "Lambeth walk."

Lup·ton \'ləp-tən\, Thomas Goff. 1791–1873. English mezzotint engraver. One of first to employ steel in his art. Did best work in seascapes and landscapes, esp. in reproductions of J. M. W. Turner's work.

Lü Pu-wei \'lü̅e-'bü-'wā\. d. 235 B.C. Chinese politician. Originally a merchant; made minister of kingdom of Ch'in (250); an efficient administrator, responsible for many of Ch'in's conquests of its neighboring states; supervised compilation of *Lü-shih Ch'un Ch'iu* (c.240), a compendium of folklore and pseudoscientific and Taoist writings; reputed to be natural father of Emperor Cheng (*q.v.*); banished (237) on charge of plotting against the throne.

Lur·çat \lü̅er-sä\, Jean. 1892–1966. French painter and tapestry designer. Leading figure in 20th-century revival of French tapestry-making. Produced his first tapestries (1917); with Toussaint Dubreuil, Marcel Gromaire, and François Tabard, established at Aubusson a tapestry center (1939). Designed over 1,000 tapestries, including *Four Seasons* (1940), *Apocalypse Tapestry* (1948), *The Song of the World* (1957–64); also did theatrical set and costume designs, ceramics, book illustrations, lithographs, books on tapestry.

Lu·ria \'lür-yä\, Isaac ben Solomon. *Called* ha-Ari \hä-'är-ē\, *i.e.* the Lion. 1534–1572. Palestinian Hebrew mystic and Kabbalist. Spent youth in Egypt; studied the Zohar, central work of Kabbala; to Safed, Galilee (1570), to study under Moses ben Jacob Cordovero. Founded own school of Kabbala known as Lurianic Kabbala; wrote few works, composed three well known hymns. His disciple Ḥayyim Vital collected notes of his lectures and produced numerous works expounding his doctrines, notably *'Eẓ Ḥayyim* (1772).

Luria, Ruggiero di. See LAURIA.

Lur·ton \'lərt-ᵊn\, Horace Harmon. 1844–1914. American jurist, b. Newport, Ky. Served in Confederate army in Civil War. Practiced law, Clarksville, Tenn. (1867–86); justice on Tennessee Supreme Court (1886–93). Associate justice, U.S. Supreme Court (1910–14).

Luscinus, Gaius Fabricius. See FABRICIUS LUSCINUS.

Lu·si·gnan \lü̅e-zēn-yäⁿ\. Name of French noble family of Poitou, descended from Hugues VIII of Lusignan, which ruled Cyprus from 1192 to 1475 and also provided kings of Jerusalem. Hugues VIII's eldest son and successor ¶Hughes IX, comte de La Marche \là-màrsh\ (d. 1219) had his fiancée, Isabella of Angoulême, taken for wife by his feudal lord, King John of England (1200); formed alliance with Philip II Augustus of France that precipitated the Barons' War in England against John. His son ¶Hughes X, comte de La Marche (d. 1249), m. (1220) Isabella, then widow of John of England; waged war (1219–24) on Henry III of England (Isabella's son); rebelled against Louis IX (1241–42) and lost his principal strongholds, but later pardoned. For kings of Cyprus and Jerusalem, see AMALRIC II and GUY DE LUSIGNAN (both sons of Hugues VIII) and HUGH.

Lus·sy \lü̅e-sē\, Melchior. 1529–1606. Swiss soldier and religious promoter. Represented Catholic cantons at Council of Trent and at courts of popes Paul IV, Pius IV, Gregory XIII and XIV; served in papal (1557) and Venetian (1560) armies; played major role in implementing reforms of Trent in Catholic Switzerland; ruled as virtual dictator in his native Unterwalden.

Lu·te·ro \lü-'ter-ō\ *or* **Lu·te·ri** \-ē\, Giovanni. *Known as* Dos·so Dos·si \'dȯs-sō-'dȯs-sē\. 1479?–1542. Italian painter of Ferrarese school. In service of dukes of Ferrara. Works included frescoes (with his brother Battista) in Castello del Buon Conciglio, Trent, and Villa Imperiale, Pesaro; religious paintings; and esp. romantic and mythological landscapes; strongly influenced by Giorgione and Titian. His brother ¶Battista Lutero, *known also as* Battista Dossi (d. 1548), collaborated with him on chief artistic commissions.

Luṭ·fi as-Say·yid \lüt-'fē-əs-'sī-yəd\, Aḥmad. 1872–1954. Egyptian lawyer and journalist. Worked for legal department of government; founder (1907) and editor of newspaper *al-Jarīdah,* representing moderate wing of Egyptian nationalism; at end of World War I, served on delegation that negotiated end of British occupation of Egypt; a leading spokesman for modernization and introduction of Western technology and reforms.

Lu·ther \'lüt-ər, *Angl* 'lü-thər\, Hans. 1879–1962. German politician. Minister of food and agriculture (1922–23), of finance (1923–25); helped bring inflation under control; negotiated the Dawes loan for Germany (1924). Chancellor of Germany (1925–26); secured Germany's adhesion to Locarno Pact. Ambassador to U.S. (1933–37).

Luther, Martin. 1483–1546. German religious reformer. Founder of the Reformation and of Protestantism. Became an Augustinian friar (1506); ordained priest (1507); lectured in Wittenberg on dialectics, physics, and the Scriptures (1508). On mission to Rome (1510–11), where he was unfavorably impressed by conditions. Professor of biblical exegesis, Wittenberg (1512–46). Began to preach the doctrine of salvation by faith rather than by works; attacked the church's sale of indulgences; nailed to the church door at Wittenberg (Oct. 31, 1517) his 95 theses questioning the value of the indulgences and condemning the means used in selling them. Publicly defended his position in appearances before a chapter of his own Augustinian order (May 1518) and before Cardinal Legate Cajetan (Oct. 1518); appealed from the pope to a general council of the church. Publicly debated the issue in Leipzig with Johann Eck (July 1519) and went further than the mere indulgence issue by denying the supremacy of the pope and by asserting that the church council in condemning Jan Hus had been wrong. Publicized his arguments by pamphlets *An den christlichen Adel deutscher Nation, De captivitate Babylonica ecclesiae praeludium,* and *Von der Freiheit eines Christenmenschen* (all 1520). Excommunicated by Pope Leo X (1521); publicly burned the bull; appeared (Apr. 17–18, 1521) before Diet of Worms, which passed the Edict of Worms putting Luther under the ban of the empire. Luther's friend Frederick of Saxony concealed him for safety in a castle at Wartburg (1521–22); there he wrote scriptural and reformatory pamphlets, prepared an edition of sermons on the Epistles and Gospels at mass, and translated the New Testament from Greek into German. Returned to Wittenberg (1522) and devoted himself to organization of the church he had inaugurated; opposed the Peasants' War; denied freedom of the will in *De servo arbitrio* (1525), a response to an attack by Erasmus; m. (1525) Katharina von Bora, a former nun. Translated the Old Testament and wrote many commentaries, catechisms, sermons, hymns, etc.

Lu·ther \'lü-thər\, Seth. 1790?–?1850. American reformer, b. probably in Providence, R.I. Worked as carpenter and in cotton mills; vigorous campaigner for labor reforms and abolition of monopolies, capital punishment, debtors' prisons, militia system. Published *Address to the Working-men of New England* (1832), *Address on the Origin and Progress of Avarice* (1834), etc.

Lu·thu·li \lü-'t(h)ü-lē\ *or* **Lu·tu·li** \-'tü-\, Albert John Mvumbi. 1898–1967. South African reformer. Elected chief of Zulu community at Groutville (1936); joined (1945) African National Congress, its president (1952–60); leader of nonviolent struggle against the government's discriminatory racial policies; awarded Nobel peace prize (1960). Wrote *Let My People Go* (1962).

Lütke, Fyodor Petrovich. See LITKE.

Luttelton, Sir Thomas. See LITTLETON.

Lut·trell \'lə-trəl\, Henry. c.1765–1851. English poet. Noted conversationalist; known for his witty light verse satirizing London society as in *Letters to Julia, in Rhyme* (1822) and *Crockford House* (1827).

Lutuli, Albert John Mvumbi. See LUTHULI.

Lut·yens \'ləch-ənz, 'lət-yənz\, Sir Edwin Landseer. 1869–1944. English architect. Made reputation with design of a house at Munstead Wood, Godalming, Surrey (1896), and a series of romantic country houses; collaborated with Gertrude Jekyll on many garden designs; best known for his planning of New Delhi and his design of Viceroy's House there (1912); appointed (1917) to Imperial War Graves Commission, producing designs for the Cenotaph at London and the Great War Stone (both 1919) and military cemeteries in France; also designed British Embassy in Washington (1926–29) and began (1929) project for Roman Catholic cathedral at Liverpool left incomplete at his death.

Lüt·zow \'lʊet-sō\, Adolf von. Freiherr. 1782–1834. German general. Entered Prussian army (1795); present at defeat by French at Auerstädt (1806); at outbreak of Wars of Liberation (1813), organized and commanded a mounted free corps (Lützowsche Freikorps, known as the Schwarze Schar) that operated behind French lines; fought many partisan actions but generally ineffective; captured while leading cavalry regiment at Waterloo (1815); remained in Prussian army after release.

Luvini, Bernardino. See LUINI.

Luxembourg, Duc de. See MONTMORENCY-BOUTEVILLE.

Lux·em·burg \'lük-səm-ˌbůrk\, Rosa. 1870–1919. German Socialist agitator, b. Poland. Involved in underground activities in Poland; in Zürich (1889–98), where she became member of international Socialist movement and helped found the Polish Social Democratic party, nucleus of the Polish Communist party. To Berlin (1898); defended orthodox Marxism in *Sozialreform oder Revolution?* (1889); propounded her theory of revolutionary mass action in *Massenstreik, Partei und Gewerkschaften* (1906); associated with Karl Liebknecht (*q.v.*) as leader of the Spartacus League; involved with him in the Spartacist insurrection; arrested and killed while being taken to prison.

Luy·ken \'lœi-kən\, Jan. 1649–1712. Dutch poet and lithographer. Published volume of erotic verse *De duyste lier* (1671); embraced pietist Christianity; later wrote mystical religious poetry as *Jesus en de ziel* (1678).

Luynes, Duc de. See Charles d'ALBERT.

Lu Yu \'lü-'yü\. 1125–1210. Chinese poet. Most prolific and most important poet of the Southern Sung dynasty; wrote esp. on patriotic and nature themes; some 9,200 of his 20,000 poems are extant.

Lu·zán Cla·ra·munt de Suel·ves y Gur·rea \lü-'thän-klä-rä-'münt-dā-'swel-b̲ās-ē-gür-'rā-ä\, Ignacio. 1702–1754. Spanish writer. Chief work *Poética*

(1737), a critical work advocating observance of strict classic rules in Spanish literary composition.

Luz·zat·to \lüd-'dzät-tō\, Moshe Ḥayyim. 1707–1747. Italian Kabbalist and poet. One of founders of modern Hebrew poetry. Wrote hymns, study of Hebrew prosody *Leshon Limudim* (1724), allegorical drama *Migdal 'oz* (1727); took up Kabbalistic studies and wrote much on the subject; expelled by Italian rabbis, settled in Amsterdam (1736); there wrote ethical work *Messilath yesharim* (1740), morality play *La-yesharim tehillah* (1743), etc.; died in Palestine.

Luzzatto, Samuel David. *Known from his initials as* She·dal \'shā-,däl\. 1800–1865. Italian scholar. Professor, Collegio Rabbinico, Padua (1829). Master of Hebrew style, also wrote in Italian; presented an emotional, antiphilosophical concept of Judaism. Author of Hebrew poetry and scholarly works on biblical exegesis, Hebrew philology, and the history of Hebrew literature.

Lvov \'lʸvȯf, *Angl* l(y)ə-'vȯf\, Aleksey Fyodorovich. 1798–1870. Russian composer. Conductor of Imperial Court Choir (1837–55); commissioned by czar (1833) to compose music for Russian national anthem (words by Vasily Zhukovsky). Composer of operas, including *Undina* (1846), church music, songs, and many violin pieces.

Lvov, Georgy Yevgenyevich. Prince. 1861–1925. Russian politician. Member of 1st Duma (1905); joined right wing of Constitutional Democratic party; chairman of All-Russian Union of Zemstvos (1914) and a leader of Zemgor (1915), relief organizations. After outbreak of Russian Revolution and abdication of czar, became premier in provisional government (Mar. 1917); unable to satisfy radical demands of general population; resigned and succeeded by Aleksandr Kerensky (July 1917); settled in Paris (1918).

Lya·dov \'lyä-dəf\, Anatoly Konstantinovich. 1855–1914. Russian composer. Studied under Rimsky-Korsakov; taught at St. Petersburg Conservatory (from 1878); collected folksongs for Imperial Geographical Society (1897), publishing several volumes. Composed orchestral works as *Baba-Yaga* (1905), *Volshebnoya ozero* (Enchanted Lake, 1909), and *Kikimora* (1910), choral works, songs, and many piano pieces.

Lyall, Edna. See Ada Ellen BAYLY.

Lyau·tey \lyō-tā, -te\, Louis-Hubert-Gonzalve. 1854–1934. French soldier and colonial administrator. Early interested in social reform; influenced by Joseph Gallieni's ideas on conquest as a means of civilization. Conquered Madagascar as commander of all southern French forces (1900–02); in Morocco as commandant of Ain Sefra (1904–06), of Oran (1906–10); resident general of Morocco (1912–25, except for 1916–17 when he was French minister of war); pacified Morocco and firmly established French hegemony, fostered economic development, and promoted Casablanca as a port. Marshal of France (1921).

Ly Bon \'lē-'bȯn\. *Known also as* Ly Ban \-'bän\, Ly Bi \-'bē\, *and* Li Bi \'lē-'bē\. *Reign name* Li Nam-Viet De Bon \'lē-'näm-'vyet-'dā-'bȯn\. d. 549. Vietnamese ruler. Led successful revolt against Chinese rule, capturing capital at Long Bien (542); proclaimed himself emperor (544), founding the Earlier Ly dynasty, the first such dynasty in Vietnam; controlled most of northern and central Vietnam, his authority recognized southward to Cham border; defeated by Chinese at Chu Dien (547); fled to Laos but executed there.

Ly·con \'lī-kän\. 3d century B.C. Greek philosopher. Head of Peripatetic school (270–226 B.C.).

Ly·co·phron \'lī-kə-frän\ of Chal·cis \'kal-səs\. 3d century B.C. Greek poet and scholar. Worked in library at Alexandria (from c.285 B.C.); one of the Pleiad of Alexandria. Wrote a treatise on comedy and humerous tragedies, of which only a few fragments survive. His only extant poem is *Alexandra,* in which Cassandra prophesies the fall of Troy and the later adventures of the Greek and Trojan heroes.

Ly·cur·gus \lī-'kər-gəs\. According to tradition, a Spartan lawgiver of the 9th century B.C., who by decree imposed upon Sparta its characteristic institutions designed to produce tough and able warriors.

Lycurgus. c.390–324 B.C. Athenian orator and financier. Favored anti-Macedonian policy of Demosthenes; renowned for his wise administration of Athenian finances after the battle of Chaeronea (338–326); carried out extensive public works program and remodelled the fleet.

Ly·dek·ker \lə-'dek-ər\, Richard. 1849–1915. English naturalist and geologist. With Geological Survey of India (1874–82); catalogued fossil mammals, amphibians, reptiles, and birds for the British Museum. Author of *A Manual of Palaeontology* (with H. A. Nicholson, 1889); with W. H. Flower wrote *An Introduction to the Study of Mammals* (1891) and *The Royal Natural History* (1893–96).

Lyd·gate \'lid-,gāt, -gət\, John. c.1370–c.1450. English poet. Benedictine monk; prior of Hatfield Broad Oak in Essex (1421–32); court poet at courts of Henry IV, V, and VI. Wrote *Troy Book* containing reverent tributes to his "master" and friend Chaucer (written 1412–20, printed 1513), *The Falle of Princis* (written 1430–38, printed 1494), *The Siege of Thebes* (written c.1420, printed c.1500), *London Lickpenny,* describing contemporary London manners, and two allegorical poems, *Complaint of the Black Knight* and *Temple of Glass,* also devotional, hagiological, philosophical, scientific, historical, and satirical poems.

Ly·ell \'lī-əl\, Sir Charles. 1797–1875. British geologist, b. Scotland. Made geological expeditions to various regions of Europe; opposed catastrophic theory advanced to account for great geologic changes; published *Principles of Geology* (1830–33) to refute this theory; leading proponent of James Hutton's theory of uniformitarianism. Regarded as father of modern geology. Also wrote *Elements of Geology* (1838), *Travels in North America, with Geological Observations* (1845), *The Antiquity of Man* (1863).

Lyly \'lil-ē\, John. 1554?–1606. English writer. M.P. (1589–1601); supported the bishops in Martin Marprelate controversy. Known chiefly for his didactic romance in two parts *Euphues, the Anatomy of Wit* (1579) and *Euphues and his England* (1580), aiming at reform of education and manners, and its affected style (called Euphuism), marked by antithesis, alliteration, similes, and a pervading effort after elegance; ridiculed by Shakespeare and others but admired and imitated by large number of contemporaries, including Lodge and Greene. Author of several dramas beginning with *The Woman in the Moone* (produced 1583?), most on classical and mythological subjects, as *Alexander and Campaspe* (1584), *Sapho and Phao* (1584), *Endimion* (1591), *Midas* (1592), *Gallathea* (1592), *Mother Bombie* (1594).

Lynch \'linch\, Benito. 1880 or 1885–1951. Argentinian novelist. Author of novels on rural life, including *Los caranchos de la Florida* (1916), *Raquela* (1918), *El inglés de los güesos* (1924), *El romance de un gaucho* (1930); also novelette *El antojo de la patrona* (1925) and several collections of short stories.

Lynch, Charles. 1736–1796. American planter and justice of the peace, b. near Lynchburg, Va. Commanded Virginia volunteer regiment with General Greene at Guilford Court House; in Virginia senate (1784–89). During disorganized conditions accompanying American Revolution, presided over extralegal court to punish lawlessness, in which convictions were frequent and followed by summary punishment, usually flogging; hence the term *lynch law.*

Lynch, John Roy. 1847–1939. American lawyer, politician, and army officer, b. near Vidalia, La. Former slave; represented Mississippi in U.S. House of Representatives (1873–77, 1882–83); first black to preside over a national convention of Republican party (1884); in U.S. army (1901–11); practiced law in Chicago (from 1911). Author of *The Facts of Reconstruction* (1913).

Lynch, Thomas. 1749–1779. American planter and patriot, b. near Georgetown, S.C. Member of 2d Continental Congress (1776–77); a signer of the Declaration of Independence; lost at sea.

Lynd \'lind\, Robert Staughton. 1892–1970. American sociologist, b. New Albany, Ind. Professor, Columbia (1931–60). With collaboration of his wife (m. 1921) ¶Helen, *nee* Mer·rell \'mer-əl\ (1896–1982), b. La Grange, Ill., made sociological study of a Middle Western city (Muncie, Ind.) and published *Middletown: A Study in Contemporary American Culture* (1929) and *Middletown in Transition* (1937). He was sole author of *Knowledge for What?* (1939). She wrote *England in the 1880's* (1945), *On Shame and the Search for Identity* (1958), *Toward Discovery* (1965), and taught at Sarah Lawrence College (1929–64).

Lynd, Sarah, *nee* Dry·hurst \'drī-,hərst\. 1888–1952. English poet. m. (1909) Robert Lynd. Author of lyrical verse published in *The Thrush and the Jay* (1917), *The Goldfinches* (1920), *Collected Poems* (1944); also of novel *The Chorus* (1916), short stories *The Mulberry Bush* (1925), and *Autobiography* (1950).

Lyndhurst, Baron. See John Singleton COPLEY.

Lyndsay, Sir David. See LINDSAY.

Lynedoch, Baron. See Thomas GRAHAM (1748–1843).

Ly·nen \'lᵫ-nən\, Feodor Felix Konrad. 1911–1979. German biochemist. At U. of Munich (1942–79); awarded Nobel prize for physiology or medicine (1964, with Konrad Bloch) for his work on the metabolism of cholesterol and fatty acids.

Lyon \lyōⁿ\, Corneille de. c.1500–?1574. French painter, b. Holland. Became attached to French royal court in Lyons (1524); royal painter to Henry II and Charles IX. Known for series of portraits of the royal court.

Ly·on \'lī-ən\, Mary Mason. 1797–1849. American educator, b. near Buckland, Mass. Pioneer in providing advanced education for women. Taught at Ashfield, Mass., Londonderry, N.H., and Ipswich, Mass. (1821–34). Opened Mount Holyoke Seminary, South Hadley, Mass. (1837), which later became Mount Holyoke College; remained president (1837–49).

Lyon, Nathaniel. 1818–1861. American army officer, b. Ashford, Conn. Served through Mexican War and on western frontier duty. Brigadier general in command of Union forces at St. Louis, Mo. (May 1861); captured Jefferson City (June 15, 1861) and Boonville (June 17).

Lyo·net \ˈlyō-neˈ\, Pierre. 1706–1789. Dutch entomologist. Cipher clerk for the government. Illustrated Fréderick Lesser's *Théologie des insectes* (1742) and Abraham Trembley's treatise on the hydra (1744); known esp. for his skillful dissections and brilliant illustrations in his *Traité anatomique de la Chenille, qui ronge le bois de Saule* (1760).

Ly·ons \ˈlī-ənz\, Joseph Aloysius. 1879–1939. Australian politician. Premier of Tasmania and treasurer (1923–28); member of Federal House of Representatives (from 1929) and leader of United Australia party in legislature (from 1931). Prime minister and treasurer of Australia (1931–39).

Lyot \ˈlyō\, Bernard-Ferdinand. 1897–1952. French astronomer. On staff (from 1920), chief astronomer (1943), Meudon observatory. Inventor of the solar coronagraph (1930) and other instruments used to study the Sun's corona.

Ly·san·der \lī-ˈsan-dər\. d. 395 B.C. Spartan naval and military commander. Commanded fleet which defeated the Athenians off Notium (406 B.C.); replaced (406) by Callicratidas but chosen commander again and victorious at Aegospotami (405); captured Athens (404) and thus brought the Peloponnesian War to a triumphal end. Ambitious to establish himself as supreme in Sparta; instigated establishment of the Thirty Tyrants in Athens; aided Agesilaus II attain Spartan throne (399) but soon suffered decline in political power. Commanded army against the Boeotians (395); killed while attacking Haliartus.

Ly·sen·ko \li-ˈseŋ-kə\, Trofim Denisovich. 1898–1976. Soviet biologist and agronomist. As director of Institute of Genetics of Academy of Sciences of the U.S.S.R. (1940–65), virtually dictated the agricultural policies of the Soviet Union; developed a doctrine of genetics (Lysenkoism) based on theories of Lamarck and I.V. Michurin which denied the existence of genes and plant hormones and held that all parts of an organism took part in heredity; his doctrine eventually discredited, but not before greatly harming Soviet genetic research, agricultural practices, and scientific education. Presented his doctrine in *Heredity and Its Variability* (1946) and *The Science of Biology Today* (1948).

Lys·i·as \ˈlis-ē-əs\. c.445–after 380 B.C. Athenian orator. Settled in Athens (412 B.C.); fled from city when it fell under control of the Thirty Tyrants (404); when democracy was restored, returned to impeach Eratosthenes, one of the tyrants, in a speech (403) which is still extant. Of most of his orations, only fragments are extant.

Lysias. d. 162 B.C. Syrian general. Regent under kings Antiochus Epiphanes and Antiochus Eupator; appointed viceroy (165 B.C.); attempted to quell Jewish insurrection under Maccabees; his great army defeated (165?) by Judas Maccabaeus; seized Syrian throne on death of Antiochus Epiphanes; defeated Judas and besieged Jerusalem; compelled to make peace by insurrection in Antioch.

Ly·sim·a·chus \lī-ˈsim-ə-kəs\. c.355–281 B.C. Macedonian general. Served under Alexander the Great. At Alexander's death (323 B.C.), received Thrace; assumed title of king (306). Shared in victory at Ipsus (301) and gained large section of Asia Minor; gained Macedonia (287–286). Defeated by Seleucus Nicator (281). His 3d wife was Arsinoë II (*q.v.*).

Ly·sip·pus \lī-ˈsip-əs\. 4th century B.C. Greek sculptor. Head of school at Argos and Sicyon. Credited with developing new system of bodily proportions, making the head smaller, the legs longer, and adjusting details to these changes. Said to have executed over 1,500 bronze works, none extant although some survive in copies, esp. *Apoxymenos;* other works attributed to him include two versions of *Agias, Troilus, Coridas,* colossal bronze statue of Zeus at Tarentum, colossal bronze seated Heracles at Tarentum, and the chariot of the sun at Rhodes; made a number of portrait busts of Alexander the Great.

Ly·sis \ˈlī-səs\ of Ta·ren·tum \tə-ˈrent-əm\. 4th century B.C. Greek philosopher. Member of Pythagorean school in southern Italy; settled in Thebes (c.390); teacher of Epaminondas.

Lyt·tel·ton \ˈlit-ᵊl-tən\, George. 1st Baron Lyttelton of Frank·ley \ˈfraŋ-klē\. 1709–1773. English politician and man of letters. Direct descendant of Sir Thomas Littelton; first cousin to Earl Temple and to George Grenville and brother-in-law of William Pitt. M.P. (1735–56); a lord of the treasury (1744–54); chancellor of exchequer (1755–56); opposed repeal of Stamp Act (1766). Patron of poet Thomson and other literary men. Author of *Dialogues of the Dead* (1760), *The History of the Life of Henry the Second* (1767–71); in poetry remembered chiefly for the *Monody* (1747) on death of his wife and as having place in Johnson's *Lives of the Poets.* His brother ¶William Henry (1724–1808), 1st baron of second creation; M.P. (1748); as governor of South Carolina (1755–62), detained as hostages Cherokee chiefs sent to conference, precipitating renewal of Indian war and frontier ravages; governor of Jamaica (1762–66); ambassador to Portugal (1766–71).

Lyttleton, Sir Thomas. See LITTLETON.

Lyt·ton \ˈlit-ᵊn\, Edward George Earle Lytton Bul·wer- \ˌbu̇l-wər-\. 1st Baron Lytton of Kneb·worth \ˈneb-wərth\. 1803–1873. English novelist and politician. Brother of Sir Henry Bulwer. Began literary career with novels *Falkland* (1827) and *Pelham* (1828); editor, *New Monthly Magazine* (1831–32). M.P. (1831–41). Produced plays *The Lady of Lyons* (1838), *Richelieu* (1839), and *Money* (1840). Returned to politics; M.P. (1852–66); colonial secretary (1858–59); created baron (1866). Author of poems including *The New Timon* (1846), of short stories introducing the occult, of historical and romantic novels including *Devereaux* (1829), *Paul Clifford* (1830), *Eugene Aram* (1832), *The Last Days of Pompeii* (1834), *Rienzi* (1835; on which Wagner's opera *Rienzi* is based), *The Last of the Barons* (1843), *Harold* (1848), *The Caxtons* (1849), and of a prophetical romance *The Coming Race* (1871).

His son ¶Edward Robert Bulwer-Lytton (1831–1891), 1st Earl of Lytton, politician and poet (pseudonym Owen Meredith), had a career in diplomatic service; as viceroy of India (1875–80) effected internal reforms but failed to avert Second Afghan War (1878); ambassador at Paris (1887–91). Author of several volumes of verse, including autobiographical lyrics *Clytemnestra* (1855) and *The Wanderer* (1858), long romances *Lucile* (1860) and *Glenaveril* (1885), and the fantastic epic *King Poppy* (1892).

M

Ma·'ar·rī, al- \ul-mä-är-'rē\. *More completely* Abū al-'Alā' Aḥmad ibn 'Abd Allāh al-Ma'arrī. 973–1057. Arab poet. Won reputation with *Saqṭ az-zand;* led ascetic life; attracted followers and students by originality of thought and pessimistic moralism. Wrote *Luzūm mā lam valzam* or *Luzūmiyāt,* in which he noted the unnecessary complexity of traditional rhyme schemes; *Risālat al-ghufrān,* a Muslim *Divine Comedy; al-Fuṣūl wa al-ghāyāt,* collection of rhymed homilies.

Maartens, Maarten. See POORTEN-SCHWARTZ.

Maas, Nicolas. See Nicolaes MAES.

Ma·bil·lon \má-bē-yō^{n}\, Jean. 1632–1707. French scholar. Became Benedictine monk (1654); ordained (1660); lived at abbey of Saint-Germain-des-Prés, Paris (from 1664). Discovered many manuscripts throughout Europe; wrote *De re diplomatica* (1681), establishing science of diplomatics; considered founder of Latin paleography. Coeditor of *Acta sanctorum ordinis sancti Benedicti* (9 vols., 1668–1702); began edition of *Annales ordinis sancti Benedicti* (1703–07); other works included *Vetera analecta* (1675–85), *De liturgia gallicana* (1685), *Museum Italicum* (1687–89), *Traité des études monastiques* (1691–92).

Ma·bi·ni \mä-'bē-nē\, Apolinario. 1864–1903. Philippine revolutionary. Joined (1896) Emilio Aguinaldo's nationalist force, soon becoming his right-hand man; drew up (1898) constitution for short-lived Philippine republic of 1898–99; with Aguinaldo continued struggle against U.S. attempt to annex the Philippines; captured by American troops (1899) and banished to Guam.

Ma·bly \má-blē\, Gabriel Bon·not de \bó-nó-də-\. *Called* Abbé de Mably. 1709–1785. French philosopher and historian. Brother of Étienne Bonnot de Condillac (see CONDILLAC); secretary to Cardinal Pierre Guérin de Tencin and involved in diplomatic activities. Author of *Parallèles des Romains et des Français* (1740), *Droit public de l'Europe* (1748), *Observations sur l'histoire de France* (1765), etc.

Mabuse, Jan. See Jan GOSSAERT.

Mc·Ad·am \mə-'kad-əm\, John Loudon. 1756–1836. British engineer, b. Scotland. Made fortune in New York City in his uncle's countinghouse (1770–83). Surveyor general of roads, Bristol, England (1815); general surveyor of roads (1827); introduced improved roads built of crushed stone, known as "macadamized" roads.

Mc·A·doo \'mak-ə-,dü\, William Gibbs. 1863–1941. American railroad executive and public official, b. near Marietta, Ga. Practiced law, Chattanooga, Tenn. (1885–92), New York (from 1892). President, Hudson & Manhattan R.R. Co., which completed (1904) first tunnel under Hudson River. U.S. secretary of the treasury (1913–18); U.S. director general of railways (1917–19). Married Eleanor, daughter of President Wilson (1914). Prominent candidate for Democratic nomination for president (1920 and 1924). U.S. senator from California (1933–38).

Mc·Al·lis·ter \mək-'al-əs-tər\, Samuel Ward, *known as* Ward. 1827–1895. American lawyer and social leader, b. Savannah, Ga. Practiced, San Francisco (1850–52). Resident, New York City and Newport, R.I. (from 1852). Became arbiter of New York's social world; originated the Patriarchs, a group of heads of old New York families; responsible for phrase "the Four Hundred," referring to the number of people who belonged in New York Society. Author of *Society as I Have Found It* (1890).

MacAlpin, Kenneth I. See KENNETH.

Mc·Al·pine \mək-'al-pən, -pīn\, William Jarvis. 1812–1890. American civil engineer, b. New York City. Chief engineer or consulting engineer for various bridges, including Eads Bridge at St. Louis and George Washington Bridge in New York; built Riverside Drive, New York City.

Macarius. See also MAKARY.

Ma·car·i·us \mə-'kar-ē-əs\. *Called* the Egyptian *or* the Great. c.300–c.390. Egyptian ascetic. Lived for 60 years as ascetic hermit in desert of Scete; ordained priest (c.340); acquired fame as prophet, healer, ascetic, spiritual instructor; considered one of the Desert Fathers. Briefly banished (c.374) for his strong opposition to Arianism; reputed author of *To the Friends of God,* letter addressed to young monks. A written tradition of mystical theology survives under his name.

Macarius Mag·nes \-'mag-,nēz, -nəs\. 5th century. Eastern Orthodox cleric and polemicist. Usually identified with the bishop of Magnesia (modern Manisa, Turkey). Author of *Apokritikos ē monogenēs pro Hellēnas* (5 books, c.400), commonly called *Apocriticus,* an apology for Christianity preserving contemporary pagan attacks on Christian revelation.

Mac·Ar·thur \mə-'kär-thər\, Arthur. 1845–1912. American army officer, b. Chicopee Falls, Mass. Served through Civil War. Major general of volunteers in Spanish–American War, on duty in Havana (1898–99); defeated Philippine insurgent forces of Emilio Aguinaldo (1899); military governor of the Philippines (1900–01). Lieutenant general and assistant chief of staff (1906); retired (1909).

His son ¶Douglas (1880–1964), b. Little Rock, Ark.; commissioned, U.S. army (1903); commanded 42d (Rainbow) division in France during World War I (1918–19); brigadier general (1920); superintendent, U.S.M.A. (1919–22); major general (1925). In command of Philippine Department (1928–30); general and chief of staff, U.S. army (1930–35); director of organization of national defense for the Philippine government (1935–37). Recalled to active service (July 1941) as lieutenant general and commander of U.S. forces in the Far East; allied supreme commander in S.W. Pacific (1942) and of occupational forces in Japan (1945–51); general of the army (1944); accepted surrender of Japan aboard battleship *Missouri* (Sept. 2, 1945). Supreme commander of UN forces, Korea (1950–51); dismissed (Apr. 1951) by Pres. Truman for continued public statements advocating invasion of China; retired to private life.

MacArthur, Charles Gordon. 1895–1956. American playwright, b. Scranton, Pa. Newspaper reporter in Chicago and New York (1914–23); turned to writing plays (from 1924) and to writing and producing motion pictures and plays (from 1929); partner in Hecht-MacArthur, Inc. Collaborated with E. Sheldon in play *Lulu Belle* (1926), with Sidney Howard in *Salvation* (1927), and with Ben Hecht in *The Front Page* (1928), *Twentieth Century* (1932), *Ladies and Gentlemen* (1939), and *Swan Song* (1946).

Mac·ar·thur \mə-'kär-thər\, John. 1767–1834. Australian agriculturalist, b. England. To Australia (1789); banished to England for inspiring the Rum Rebellion (1808) against Gov. William Bligh; returned (1816) to promote Australian wool industry and acquired fortune in wool trade; spokesman for Exclusionists in Legislative Council of New South Wales (1825–32).

Ma·cart·ney \mə-'kärt-nē\, George. 1st Earl Macartney. 1737–1806. British diplomat, b. Ireland. British envoy at St. Petersburg (1764–67); chief secretary for Ireland (1769–72); governor of the Caribbean Islands (1775–79). Governor of Fort St. George (Madras, 1780–86). First British diplomatic representative to Peking (1792–94); governor of Cape of Good Hope (1796–98).

Ma·cau·lay \mə-'kó-lē\, Catharine, *nee* Saw·bridge \'só-,brij\. 1731–1791. English historian. m. 1st George Macaulay (1760; d. 1766). Author of *The History of England from the Accession of James I to that of the Brunswick Line* (8 vols., 1763–83).

Macaulay, Dame Rose, *in full* Emilie Rose. 1881–1958. English novelist. Author of novels *Potterism* (1920), *Dangerous Ages* (1921), *Told by an Idiot* (1923), *Orphan Island* (1924), *Crewe Train* (1926), *Keeping up Appearances* (1928), *They Were Defeated* (1932), *Going Abroad* (1934), *The World My Wilderness* (1950), *The Towers of Trebizond* (1956); literary criticism *Some Religious Elements in English Literature* (1931); travel books *They Went to Portugal* (1946), *Fabled Shore* (1949); and verse.

Macaulay, Thomas Babington. 1st Baron Macaulay. 1800–1859. English writer and politician. Called to bar (1826); M.P. (1830–34, 1839–47, 1852–56); raised to peerage (1857). Member, Supreme Council of India (1834–38); secretary of war (1839–41); paymaster of the forces (1846–47). Contributor to *Edinburgh Review* (from 1825). Author of *History of England,* covering reigns of James II and William III (5 vols., 1849–61). Author also of *Lays of Ancient Rome* (1842) and numerous essays (including one on Milton in *Edinburgh Review,* 1825), biographical sketches, speeches, etc.

Mc·Au·ley \mə-ˈkȯ-lē\, Catherine Elizabeth. 1787–1841. Irish religious. Founder of the House of our Blessed Lady of Mercy, Dublin (1827), which became (1831) the Order of the Sisters of Mercy; superior of the order (1831–41).

McAuley, James Phillip. 1917–1976. Australian poet. Founder (1955) and editor of literary journal *Quadrant;* professor of English at U. of Tasmania (from 1961). Noted for his classical approach, great technical skill, academic point of view. Author of volumes of poetry *Under Aldebaran* (1946), *A Vision of Ceremony* (1956), *Captain Quiros* (1964), *Surprises of the Sun* (1969), *Collected Poems* (1971); critical works *The End of Modernity* (1959) and *Christopher Brennan* (1973).

Mc·Au·liffe \mə-ˈkȯ-ləf\, Anthony Clement. 1898–1975. American army officer, b. Washington, D.C. Entered army (1919); brigadier general (1942); in command of the 101st Airborne division during successful defense of Bastogne (Dec. 1944), checking the German counterattack in the Ardennes and making famous reply "Nuts!" to surrender ultimatum of surrounding German force. Commanded 103d division into Alsace and Berlin (1945). General (1955); commander of U.S. army in Europe (1955–56).

Mac·beth \mək-ˈbeth\. d. 1057. King of Scotland (1040–57). Probably grandson of King Kenneth II; succeeded (c.1031) as moarmaer (chief) of Moray province. Killed his cousin Duncan in battle near Elgin and seized kingdom (1040); defeated rebel army near Dunkeld, Perth (1045); defeated and slain by Malcolm III.

Mc·Bride \mək-ˈbrīd\, Sir Richard. 1870–1917. Canadian politician, b. New Westminster, B.C. Member of British Columbian legislature (1898–1915); premier of British Columbia (1903–15); agent general for British Columbia in London (1915–17).

Mac·ca·bees \ˈmak-ə-(ˌ)bēz\. Family of Jewish patriots of 2d and 1st centuries B.C., more correctly called the Hasmonaeans (*q.v.*). Members of the family were:

¶Mat·ta·thi·as \ˌmat-ə-ˈthī-əs\. d. 166? B.C. Founder of family; priest of Modein, village near Lydda; defied decree of Antiochus IV Epiphanes of Syria to Hellenize the Jews; rose in revolt (167) and fled with five sons.

¶Ju·das \ˈjü-dəs\ *or* Ju·dah \-də\. d. 160 B.C. His third son; became leader (166–160 B.C.); received surname Mac·ca·bae·us *or* Mac·ca·be·us \ˌmak-ə-ˈbē-əs\ (perhaps meaning "the Hammerer"), later applied to all members of Hasmonaean family; able military leader; defeated several Syrian armies; purified the Temple of Jerusalem and restored Jewish worship (165 or 164 B.C.; now commemorated by the Jewish Feast of Dedication, or Hanukkah); secured recognition of Jewish religious liberty and worked for political independence; won victory over Syrian forces of Nicanor (160), but fell in battle of Elasa just before concluding alliance with Romans. Two other sons ¶John Gad·di \ˈgad-ē\ and ¶El·e·a·zar Ava·ran \ˌel-ē-ˈā-zə-rə-ˈvär-ən\ were killed (before 160) in the revolt.

¶Jon·a·than \ˈjän-ə-thən\. *Called* Ap·phus \ˈap-fəs\. d. 143 or 142 B.C. Youngest son of Mattathias; succeeded his brother Judas as leader (160–143 or 142 B.C.); successful as military leader; profited by intrigues at Syrian court; gradually changed Judea into independent principality under a Hasmonaean high priest (from 157); became high priest (152); supported Alexander Balas against Demetrius I (152–150); after Alexander's death (145) supported Antiochus VI; trapped at Bethshean and killed by Tryphon, Syrian usurper.

¶Si·mon \ˈsī-mən\. *Called* Thas·si \ˈthäs-ē\. d. 135 or 134 B.C. Second son of Mattathias; succeeded Jonathan as leader; won independence (142) of Jewish nation (Judea), establishing the Hasmonaean dynasty; drove all Syrians from citadel in Jerusalem; chosen civil governor and high priest (141); sent embassy to Rome; began coinage of money; treacherously murdered by his son-in-law. Later members (*qq.v.*) of the Hasmonaean family included Alexander Jannaeus, Antigonus I and II, Aristobulus I and II, John Hyrcanus I and II, Mariamne, Salome Alexandra.

Mc·Car·thy \mə-ˈkär-thē, *also* -ˈkärt-ē\, Joseph Raymond. 1908–1957. American politician, b. Grand Chute, Wis. State circuit judge (1940–42). U.S. senator from Wisconsin (1947–57); accused many individuals of subversive activities and roused considerable public support for investigations and persecutions carried on by his Senate subcommittee; his campaign of slander gave rise to term McCarthyism; influence declined rapidly after televised confrontation with U.S. army officials (1954); censured by Senate (1954).

McCarthy, Joseph Vincent. *Nicknamed* Marse Joe \ˌmärs-ˈjō\. 1887–1978. American baseball manager, b. Philadelphia. Manager of the New York Yankees (1931–46), leading them to 8 American League pennants and 7 World Series titles. Elected to Baseball Hall of Fame (1957).

M'·Car·thy \mə-ˈkär-thē, *also* -ˈkärt-ē\, Justin. 1830–1912. Irish writer and politician. On staff of *Northern Daily Times* (1853–59), *Morning Star* (1860–68), and *Daily News* (1870 ff.). M.P. and advocate of home rule for Ireland (1879–1900); chairman of the Irish Parliamentary party, the Anti-Parnellites (1890–96). Author of a number of novels as *Dear Lady Disdain* (1875) and *Miss Misanthrope* (1878), biographies, *History of Our Own Times* (1879–97), and *Reminiscences* (1899).

Mc·Cau·ley \mə-ˈkȯ-lē\, Mary, *nee* Lud·wig \ˈləd-ˌwig\. *Known as* Molly Pitch·er \ˈpich-ər\. 1754–1832. American Revolutionary heroine, b. Trenton, N.J. m. 1st John Casper Hays (1769; d. 1789); 2d George McCauley (1792). At battle of Monmouth (June 28, 1778), carried water to the weary and wounded soldiers (hence the sobriquet "Molly Pitcher"), and when her husband was overcome by the heat, manned his cannon through rest of battle.

Mc·Cay \mə-ˈkā\, Winsor. d. 1934. American cartoonist and pioneer of cartoon films. Began (1906) newspaper comic strip "Little Nemo in Slumberland," marked by use of color and highly imaginative illustration style; made animated film *Little Nemo* (1911), followed it (1914) with *Gertie the Trained Dinosaur;* produced *The Sinking of the Lusitania,* the first feature-length animated film (1918).

Macchiavelli, Niccolò. See MACHIAVELLI.

Mc·Clel·lan \mə-ˈklel-ən\, George Brinton. 1826–1885. American army officer, b. Philadelphia. Entered army (1846); served through Mexican War; on engineering duty (till 1855); invented (1855) the McClellan saddle used in U.S. army. At outbreak of Civil War, commissioned major general, U.S. army (May 1861), commanding department of the Ohio; influential in keeping Kentucky in the Union. Commanded army of the Potomac (July 1861), general in chief (Nov. 1861); reorganized army into an efficient force but was criticized for refusal to attack Confederate units in Virginia. Directed the Peninsula campaign (Mar.–Aug. 1862); won at Antietam (Sept. 17, 1862) but was removed from command by Lincoln for failure to continue pressure on Lee's army. Democratic candidate for president (1864); defeated by Lincoln. Governor of New Jersey (1878–81).

Macclesfield, Earls of. See Charles GERARD; Sir Thomas PARKER.

Mc·Clin·tic \mə-ˈklin-tik\, Guthrie. 1893–1961. American theatrical producer and director, b. Seattle. Produced and directed esp. plays starring his wife (m. 1921) Katherine Cornell (*q.v.*).

Mc·Clin·tock \mə-ˈklin-tək\, Sir Francis Leopold. 1819–1907. British naval officer and explorer, b. Ireland. Vice admiral (1877) and admiral (1884). Served in Arctic expeditions in search of Sir John Franklin (1848, 1850, 1852); commanded expedition in search of Franklin (1857–59) and published story (1859) of fate of the Franklin expedition.

Mc·Clos·key \mə-ˈkläs-kē\, John. 1810–1885. American prelate, b. Brooklyn, N.Y. Ordained Roman Catholic priest (1834); organized (1841) and became first president (1841–42) of St. John's College (later Fordham U.). Archbishop of New York (1864). Created first American cardinal (1875).

Mc·Clung \mə-ˈkləŋ\, Clarence Erwin. 1870–1946. American zoologist, b. Clayton, Pa. Taught at U. of Kansas (1898–1912); professor at U. of Pennsylvania (1912–40). Published hypothesis that an extra chromosome (labelled X) was the determiner of sex (1899–1902). Author of *Microscopical Technique* (1929).

Mc·Clure \mə-ˈklu̇(ə)r\, Sir Robert John Le Mesurier. 1807–1873. British naval officer, b. Ireland. Commanded an expedition in search for Sir John Franklin (1850–54) and in course of the search discovered the Northwest Passage.

McClure, Samuel Sidney. 1857–1949. American editor and publisher, b. Frocess, County Antrim, Ireland. To U.S. (1866). Established McClure Syndicate, first newspaper syndicate in U.S. (1884), purchasing manuscripts from authors and selling them to newspapers for simultaneous publication. Founder (1893) and editor, *McClure's Magazine.*

Mc·Con·nell \mə-ˈkän-ᵊl\, Francis John. 1871–1953. American clergyman, b. Trinway, Ohio. Entered Methodist ministry (1894); president of DePauw U. (1909–12). Elected bishop (1912); supported reforms in the steel industry. Author of *The Diviner Immanence* (1906), *The Christlike God* (1927), *Christianity and Coercion* (1933), *Evangelicals, Revolutionists, and Idealists* (1942), etc.

Mc·Cook \mə-ˈku̇k\, Alexander McDowell. 1831–1903. American army officer, b. Columbiana Co., Ohio. Commissioned in U.S. army (1852); served through Civil War; distinguished himself at Bull Run, Shiloh, Stones River, Chickamauga; major general (1862). On frontier duty after Civil War; brigadier general, U.S. army (1890); major general (1894).

McCook, Edward Moody. 1833–1909. American army officer and politician, b. Steubenville, Ohio. Cousin of Alexander M. McCook; cavalry commander in Civil War; brigadier general (1864). U.S. minister to Hawaii (1866–69); governor of territory of Colorado (1869–75). His brother ¶Anson George (1835–1917) was also an army officer and served with Ohio volunteers through

Civil War; brevetted brigadier general (1865); member of U.S. House of Representatives (1877–83).

Mc·Cor·mack \mə-'kȯr-mək, -mik\, John Francis. 1884–1945. American tenor, b. Athlone, Ireland. Naturalized American citizen (1919). Operatic debut as Turiddu in *Cavalleria rusticana,* London (1907); joined Manhattan Opera Company (1909) and later Chicago, Boston, Metropolitan, and Monte Carlo opera companies. Among his roles were Rodolpho in *La Bohème,* Faust, Pinkerton in *Madame Butterfly,* Don Ottavio in *Don Giovanni.* Well known as concert singer, esp. of Irish songs.

Mc·Cor·mick \mə-'kȯr-mik\, Anne Elizabeth, *nee* O'Hare \ō-'ha(ə)r,-'he(ə)r\. 1880–1954. American journalist, b. Wakefield, Yorkshire, England. To U.S. as a child; m. (1910) Francis J. McCormick. Foreign correspondent of *New York Times* (from 1922); first woman to receive (1937) Pulitzer prize for journalism. Author of *The Hammer and the Scythe* (1928), *The World at Home* (1956), *Vatican Journal* (1957).

McCormick, Cyrus Hall. 1809–1884. American inventor and industrialist, b. Rockbridge Co., Va. Invented a successful reaping machine (1831; patented 1834); opened factory in Chicago and began its manufacture on a large scale (1847); formed McCormick Harvesting Machine Co. with himself as president (1879–84). Succeeded as president (1884–1902) by his son ¶Cyrus Hall (1859–1936), who became first president (1902–19) and board chairman (1919–35) of International Harvester Co.

McCormick, Robert Rutherford. 1880–1955. American newspaper editor and publisher, b. Chicago. Grandson of Joseph Medill and grandnephew of the elder Cyrus Hall McCormick; president, Sanitary District of Chicago (1905–10). President of Chicago Tribune Co. (from 1911); editor and publisher of *Chicago Tribune* (with his cousin Joseph Medill Patterson, 1914–25; alone thereafter); also founded *New York Daily News* (1919, with Patterson) and *Washington* (D.C.) *Times-Herald* (1949); known for espousing his conservative views in his newspapers.

McCormick, Samuel Black. 1858–1928. American Presbyterian clergyman and educator, b. Westmoreland Co., Pa. President, Western U. of Pennsylvania (1904–20), which he transferred to Pittsburgh, renamed U. of Pittsburgh, and organized into a modern institution of learning.

Mc·Coy \mə-'kȯi\, Sir Frederick. 1817–1899. Australian geologist and paleontologist, b. Ireland. Professor at Queen's College, Belfast (1849–54), and U. of Melbourne (1854–99). Made paleontological studies of Ireland and Victoria; established National Museum of Victoria (1863). Author of *A Synopsis of the Silurian Fossils of Ireland* (with Richard Griffith, 1846), *Prodromus of the Palaeontology of Victoria* (1874–82), *Prodromus of the Zoology of Victoria* (1885–90), etc.

McCoy, Horace. 1897–1955. American novelist and screenwriter, b. Nashville, Tenn. Author esp. of novels of the hard-boiled school, including *They Shoot Horses, Don't They?* (1935), *Kiss Tomorrow Goodbye* (1948), *Scalpel* (1952).

McCoy, Joseph Geating. 1837–1915. American cattleman, b. Sangamon Co., Ill. Established (1866) a cattle-shipping business at Abilene, Kans., making it the center of the cattle industry; later founded other cattle markets. Wrote *Historic Sketches of the Cattle Trade of the West and Southwest* (1874).

McCoy, Kid. See Norman SELBY.

Mc·Crae \mə-'krā\, Hugh Raymond. 1876–1958. Australian poet. Author of sophisticated, highly polished lyrics about fauns, picaresque types from medieval tradition, everyday subjects; works included *Satyrs and Sunlight* (1909; rev. 1928), *Colombine* (1920), *Idyllia* (1922), *The Mimshi Maiden* (1938), *Poems* (1939), *Forests of Pan* (1944), *Voice of the Forest* (1945).

McCrae, John. 1872–1918. Canadian physician and poet, b. Guelph, Ontario. Surgeon to first brigade of Canadian artillery in World War I; killed in action. As poet, remembered chiefly for lyric "In Flanders Fields" (1915).

Mc·Cul·lers \mə-'kəl-ərz\, Carson, *in full* Lula Carson, *nee* Smith. 1917–1967. American novelist, b. Columbus, Ga. m. Reeves McCullers (1937); among her novels were *The Heart is a Lonely Hunter* (1940), *Reflections in a Golden Eye* (1941), *The Member of the Wedding* (1946), *The Ballad of the Sad Café* (1951), *Clock Without Hands* (1961).

Mc·Cul·loch \mə-'kəl-ək, -ək\, Hugh. 1808–1895. American lawyer and financier, b. Kennebunk, Me. Practiced law, Fort Wayne, Ind. (1833); bank official, Fort Wayne (1835–63). U.S. comptroller of the currency (1863–65); U.S. secretary of the treasury (1865–69, 1884–85).

McCulloch, Sir James. 1819–1893. Australian politician, b. Scotland. To Melbourne (1853); member of Legislative Assembly (1856–77); premier of Victoria (1863–68, 1868–69, 1870–71, 1875–77); retired to England (1877).

McCulloch, John Ramsay. 1789–1864. Scottish economist. Edited *The Scotsman* (1818–20); taught at University College, London (1828–32); comptroller of the stationery office (1838–64). Author of *Discourse on the Rise, Progress, Peculiar Objects and Importance of Political Economy* (1824); compiled *Dictionary...of Commerce and Commercial Navigation* (1832), *Statistical Account of the British Empire* (1837), *The Literature of Political Economy* (1845); did much to publicize economic views of David Ricardo.

Mc·Cutch·eon \mə-'kəch-ən\, George Barr. 1866–1928. American novelist, b. near Lafayette, Ind. City editor, Lafayette *Daily Courier* (1893–1901). Author of *Graustark* (1901), *Brewster's Millions* (1902), *Beverly of Graustark* (1904), *Mary Midthorne* (1911), *A Fool and his Money* (1913), *The Prince of Graustark* (1914), *The Merivales* (1929), etc. His brother ¶John Tinney (1870–1949), b. South Raub, Ind., cartoonist on staff of *Chicago Record* (1889–1901), *Chicago Record-Herald* (1901–03), *Chicago Tribune* (1903–45). Known for cartoons on political and Midwestern rural life subjects; awarded Pulitzer prize for a topical cartoon dealing with bank failure (1932).

MacDiarmid, Hugh. See Christopher M. GRIEVE.

Mac·Don·agh \mək-'dən-ə, -'dän-\, Thomas. 1878–1916. Irish poet. Involved in Easter Rebellion in Ireland (1916) and executed. Author of *John-John, Of a Poet-Patriot,* and *Wishes for my Son.* His son ¶Donagh (1912–1968) was a district judge (1946–68), popular radio and stage performer, and authority on traditional Irish ballads. Author of comedies as *Happy as Larry* (1946) and *God's Gentry* (1951) and of verse as *Veterans* (1941), *The Hungry Grass* (1947), *A Warning for Conquerors* (1968).

Mac·Don·ald \mək-'dän-əld\, Alexander. *Gael.* Alasdair mac Mhaigh·stir Alas·dair \mək-'vas-tər-,al-ə-'star\. 1700?–?1770. Scottish poet and patriot. Took part in Jacobite rising of 1745. Published a Gaelic vocabulary (1741) and *Aish-eiridh na Sean Chánoin Albannaich,* first Scottish Gaelic book of secular poetry (1751).

Macdonald, Dwight. 1906–1982. American writer, b. New York City. Staff writer, *The New Yorker* (1951–71); film critic, *Esquire* (1960–66); writer and editor, *Partisan Review* (1937–43); editor, *Politics* (1944–49). Wrote on sociopolitical and cultural issues from point of view of sardonic iconoclast and gadfly; avowed opponent of middle-class culture; variously embraced Trotskyism, anarchism, and pacifism; in collected essays *Against the American Grain* (1963) divided American culture into "mass-cult" and "mid-cult."

Macdonald, Flora. 1722–1790. Scottish Jacobite heroine. Aided Prince Charles Edward in his escape after the battle of Culloden Moor (1746); m. Allan Macdonald (1750); resident in North Carolina (1774–79); returned to Scotland.

Macdonald, George. 1824–1905. Scottish novelist and poet. Author of volumes of verse; books for children, including *At the Back of the North Wind* (1871), *The Princess and the Goblin* (1872), *The Princess and Curdie* (1873); a number of "Unspoken Sermons" (1866–89); novels, including *Phantastes* (1858), *Alec Forbes* (1865), *Robert Falconer* (1868), *Lilith* (1895).

Macdonald, Sir Hector Archibald. 1853–1903. British soldier, b. Scotland. Enlisted as private (1870), rising to major general (1900); served with distinction in Egypt, in Sudan campaign (1888–91), in expedition to Dongola (1896), at Omdurman (1898); served in the Punjab (1899–1900) and in South Africa (1900–01), where he captured Koodoesberg (Feb. 1900) and opened way to relief of Kimberley, and engaged in actions leading (Feb.–May 1900) to surrender of Boer generals Cronjé and Prinsloo.

Mac·do·nald \mák-dó-náld\, Jacques-Étienne-Joseph-Alexandre. Duc de Tarente \tá-räⁿt\. 1765–1840. French soldier, of Scottish descent. Served in French Revolutionary and Napoleonic armies; general of brigade (1795) and of division (1796). Governor of Rome (1799); won Napoléon's praise for his winter crossing (1800) of the Splügen Pass into Lombardy, which contributed to Treaty of Lunéville. Distinguished himself at Wagram (1809) and was created marshal of France and duc de Tarente. Served in Austria (1809–10), Catalonia (1810–11), and in the campaign for the defense of France (1813–14); negotiated with allies for abdication of Napoléon (1814).

Mac·Don·ald \mək-'dän-əld\, James Ramsay. 1866–1937. British politician, b. Scotland. Joined Labour party (1894), its secretary (1900–12), treasurer (1912–24). M.P. (1906–18) and leader of Labour party (1911–14). Pacifist by conviction, opposed England's participation in World War I; lost leadership of Labour party (1914) and seat in House of Commons (1918), but regained both (1922). Prime minister and secretary for foreign affairs (Jan. 1924), organizing first Labour ministry in history of Britain; defeated in elections (Oct. 1924). Again prime minister, head of the second Labour ministry (1929–31); remained prime minister as head of coalition cabinet (1931–35); lord president of the council in cabinet of Stanley Baldwin (1935–37). Author of *Socialism and Government* (1909), *The Social Unrest* (1913), etc.

Macdonald, Sir James Ronald Leslie. 1862–1927. British soldier and engineer, b. Scotland. In British army (1883–1913), major general (1908). As chief engineer for Uganda railroad, made geographical survey of British East Africa (1891); commanded exploring expedition (1897–99) that mapped territory between Lake Victoria and Fashoda.

Macdonald, Sir John Alexander. 1815–1891. Canadian politician, b. Glasgow, Scotland. Settled in Kingston, Canada (1820). Member of Legislative

Assembly (1844–54, 1856–91); premier of Province of Canada (1857). Leader of federation movement and influential in securing passage of British North America Act (1867). First prime minister of Dominion of Canada (1867–73); again prime minister (1878–91); supported trade protectionism, aided in completion of Pacific railway. Regarded as organizer of Dominion of Canada.

Macdonald, John Sandfield. 1812–1872. Canadian politician, b. St. Raphael, Upper Canada (now Ont.). Member of Legislative Assembly (1841–67); solicitor general (1849–51); attorney general (1858). Prime minister of Canada (1862–64). First premier, Province of Ontario (1867–71).

MacDonald, Lucy Maud, *nee* Montgomery. 1874–1942. Canadian novelist, b. Clifton, Prince Edward Island. m. Rev. Ewan MacDonald (1911). Among her books were *Anne of Green Gables* (1909), *Anne of Avonlea* (1909), *Anne of the Island* (1915), *Emily's Quest* (1928), *Anne of Ingleside* (1939).

MacDonald, Ramsay. See James Ramsay MACDONALD.

Macdonald, Ross. *Pseudonym of* Kenneth Mil·lar \ˈmil-ər\. 1915–1983. American writer, b. Los Gatos, Calif. Credited with elevating the hard-boiled detective novel to level of literature; used seedy backdrop of southern California to convey "hopeless pessimism." Under the name John Macdonald, introduced private eye Lew Archer in *The Moving Target* (1949); as John Ross Macdonald then as Ross MacDonald, penned such Archer mysteries as *The Drowning Pool* (1950), *The Barbarous Coast* (1956), *The Galton Case* (1959), *The Far Side of the Dollar* (1965), *The Underground Man* (1971), etc.

Mac·don·ald-Wright \mək-ˈdän-əl-ˈdrīt\, Stanton. 1890–1973. American painter, b. Charlottesville, Va. One of first American abstract painters; founder of Synchromism art movement (1912, with Morgan Russell); later also painted in more nonobjective style; directed W.P.A. projects (1935–42); taught at U.C.L.A. (1942–52). Works included *Synchromy* (1912), *Abstraction on Spectrum* (1914), *Synchromy in Green and Orange* (1916), *Embarkation* (1962).

Mac·Don·nell \mək-ˈdän-ᵊl\, Randal. 1st Marquis of An·trim \ˈan-trəm\. 1609–1683. Irish intriguer. Grandson of Sorley Boy MacDonnell; m. (1635) Katherine, widow of George Villiers, 1st Duke of Buckingham; planned abortive attack on Argyll in Bishops' War (1639); arrested several times for royalist schemes; created marquis (1644). Disappointed at not being made lord lieutenant for Ireland, offered services to Cromwell (1649); at sieges of Ross and Carlow (1650); imprisoned (1660–63) after Restoration, then pardoned.

Mac·Don·nell \mək-ˈdän-ᵊl, *Scot* ˌmak-də-ˈnel\, Sorley Boy, *Gael.* Somhairle Buidhe. c.1510–1590. Irish chieftain, of Scottish descent. Treated with Queen Elizabeth for security of settlement of Hebridean Scots on Antrim coast (1560); defeated and held captive by rival Shane O'Neill (1564–67); defeated by Walter Devereux, Earl of Essex (1575); escaped to Scotland (1585); submitted to English government on receipt of all country between Bann and Bush rivers (1586).

Mac·don·ough \mək-ˈdän-ə, -ˈdən-\, Thomas. 1783–1825. American naval officer, b. The Trap (now Macdonough), Del. Entered navy (1800); served in war with Tripoli, accompanying Stephen Decatur's raid to burn the *Philadelphia* (1804); commanded American fleet on Lake Champlain (1812–14); defeated and captured British squadron in battle of Plattsburg (Sept. 11, 1814).

Mc·Dou·gall \mək-ˈdü-gəl\, Alexander. 1732–1786. American Revolutionary general, b. island of Islay, Scotland. To America (1738); commanded British privateers (1756–63). Pamphleteer against British government in New York (1769); imprisoned (1770–71). Served in Revolution; brigadier general (1776); major general (1777); took command of West Point after Arnold's treason. Member, Continental Congress (1781–82, 1784–85).

McDougall, William. 1822–1905. Canadian politician, b. near York (now Toronto). A father of the Canadian Confederation. Became a leader of the Clear Grit (radical wing of Reform party), founding (1850) its organ *North American;* sold paper (1857) to George Brown and became his political associate. Member of Legislative Assembly (1858–72, 1878–82); attended conferences leading to British North America Act; minister of public works (1867–69); appointed (1869) lieutenant governor of Rupert's Land and the Northwest Territories but dismissed when the Red River settlers resisted his attempt to assume post; resumed legal practice (1873).

McDougall, William. 1871–1938. American psychologist, b. Chadderton, Lancashire, England. Professor, Harvard (1920–27), Duke (1927–38). Developed a "hormic" theory of human psychology opposed to current mechanistic and behavioristic theories. Author of *Physiological Psychology* (1905), *Introduction to Social Psychology* (1908), *Body and Mind* (1911), *The Group Mind* (1920), *Outline of Psychology* (1923), *Outline of Abnormal Psychology* (1926), *Energies of Men* (1932), *Psycho-Analysis and Social Psychology* (1936), etc.

Mac·Dow·ell \mək-ˈdau̇(-ə)l\, Edward Alexander. 1860–1908. American composer, b. New York City. Under patronage of Liszt, produced his *First Modern Suite* at Zürich (1882); professor of music, Columbia (1896–1904). Composer of symphonic poems *Hamlet and Ophelia* (1885), *Lancelot and Elaine* (1888), *Lamia* (1889), *The Saracens* (1891); piano sonatas *Tragica* (1893), *Eroica* (1895), *Norse* (1900), *Keltic* (1901); orchestral *Indian Suite* (1892); two concertos for piano and orchestra (1884, 1890); songs; and esp. piano pieces as *Woodland Sketches* (1896), *Sea Pieces* (1898), *New England Idylls* (1902), *Fireside Tales* (1902).

Mc·Dow·ell \mək-ˈdau̇(-ə)l\, Ephraim. 1771–1830. American surgeon, b. Rockbridge Co., Va. Practiced in Danville, Ky. Pioneer in abdominal surgery; performed (1809) first recorded ovarian surgery in United States.

McDowell, Irvin. 1818–1885. American army officer, b. Columbus, Ohio. Entered army (1838); served through Mexican War. Promoted brigadier general (1861) and put in command of department of Northeastern Virginia; lost battle of Bull Run (July 21, 1861); superseded by McClellan. Major general and corps commander in second battle of Bull Run (Aug. 29–30, 1862); relieved of command for his conduct in that battle but exonerated; no further field command in Civil War. Major general, U.S. army (from 1872).

Mc·Duf·fie \mək-ˈdəf-ē\, George. 1790?–1851. American politician, b. near Augusta, Ga. Member from South Carolina, U.S. House of Representatives (1821–34); governor of South Carolina (1834–36); member, U.S. Senate (1842–46). Noted orator; prominent in support of nullification.

Mace \ˈmās\, James, *called* Jem. 1831–1910. English boxer. Considered model of scientific boxing in England; won English heavyweight title (1861), lost it to Tom King (1862), but again recognized as champion when King refused to fight him; defeated Tom Allen (1870) for world championship.

Ma·ce·do \mə-ˈsā-t͟hü\, José Agostinho de. 1761–1831. Portuguese writer. Entered Augustinian order (1778) but later expelled. Court chaplain (1802); censor of books (1824–29); court chronicler (1830). Among his verse, *Os burros* (1812–14), *A meditação* (1813), *Newton* (1813), *O oriente* (1814); among his critical works, *Motim literário* (1811), *As pateadas* (1812).

Macedonicus. See Lucius Aemilius PAULUS.

Mac·e·do·ni·us \mas-ə-ˈdō-nē-əs\. d. c.362 A.D. Greek Orthodox prelate and theologian. Held Semi-Arian views; elected bishop of Constantinople by Arian bishops (c.339); deposed (346–351) but reinstated; repressed orthodox Nicene elements; expelled by Council of Constantinople (360) and exiled. His adherents formed a Christian sect called Macedonians.

Ma·ček \ˈmä-chek\, Vladimir. 1879–1964. Croatian nationalist. Joined (1905) Croatian Peasant party; became its leader on death of Radić (1928); negotiated agreement with government assuring autonomy of Croatia (Aug. 1939); deputy prime minister of Yugoslavia (1939–41); fled Communist takeover (1945), eventually settling in U.S. Wrote *In the Struggle for Freedom* (1957).

Ma·ceo y Gra·ja·les \mä-ˈsā-ō-ē-grä-ˈkäl-äs\, Antonio (1845–1896) and his brother José (1846–1896). Cuban patriots. Fought together in the Ten Years' War (1868–78); joined the rebellion together (1895) and defeated the Spaniards at Jobito and at Sao del Indio (1895).

Mc·Ew·en \mə-ˈkyü-ən\, Sir John Blackwood. 1868–1948. British composer, b. Scotland. Composer of symphonies, esp. *Solway* (1911), orchestral suites, chamber and instrumental music, songs, etc.

Mac·ew·en \mə-ˈkyü-ən\, Sir William. 1848–1924. Scottish surgeon. Known as a pioneer in field of bone surgery.

Mac·fad·den \mək-ˈfad-ᵊn\, Bernarr. *Orig.* Bernard Adolphus McFadden. 1868–1955. American physical culturist and publisher, b. near Mill Spring, Mo. Founded (1898) *Physical Culture* magazine and introduced a method of healing he called "Physcultopathy." Publisher of pulp magazines (from 1919) as *True Story, True Romances, True Detective, Photoplay, Movie Mirror.* Founded (1947) Cosmotorianism, "the happiness religion."

Mac·far·quhar \mək-ˈfär-kər\, Colin. 1745?–?1793. Scottish printer. Shop in Edinburgh; founder, with Andrew Bell, of *Encyclopaedia Britannica* (1768); edited early volumes of 3d edition.

Mac·far·ren \mək-ˈfar-ən\, Sir George Alexander. 1813–1887. English composer. His works included nine symphonies, operas *The Devil's Opera* (1838), *Don Quixote* (1846), *Robin Hood* (1860), oratorios *St. John the Baptist* (1873), *The Resurrection* (1876), *Joseph* (1877), chamber music and songs.

Mc·Gee \mə-ˈgē\, Thomas D'Arcy. 1825–1868. Canadian politician and writer, b. County Louth, Ireland. On staff of *Freeman's Journal* in London, and the *Nation.* A leader in the Young Ireland party (1846); fled to U.S. (1848) and founded *New York Nation* and *American Celt.* To Canada (1857); member of Parliament (from 1858); minister of agriculture (1864–68). Supported federation; member of the first Dominion Parliament (1867–68). Assassinated at Ottawa, probably because of his statements against the Fenian invasion. Among his books were *A History of the Irish Settlers in North America* (1851), *A Popular History of Ireland* (1862–69), *Poems* (1869).

McGee, William John. 1853–1912. American geologist and anthropologist, b. near Farley, Iowa. With U.S. Geological Survey (1883–93), Bureau of American Ethnology (1893–1903), Inland Waterways Commission (1907–12). Noted for studies of Pleistocene geology of upper Mississippi valley, stratigraphy of Atlantic coast plain, role of sheetfloods in pediment formation. Wrote *The Geology of the Head of Chesapeake Bay* (1888), *The Seri Indians* (1898), *Outlines of Hydrology* (1908).

Mc·Gill \mə-'gil\, James. 1744–1813. Canadian businessman and philanthropist, b. Glasgow, Scotland. Made fortune in fur trading, with headquarters (from c.1774) in Montreal; member of Legislative Assembly of Lower Canada (1792–96, 1800–04); bequeathed £10,000 and land for founding of McGill University (chartered 1821).

McGillicuddy, Cornelius. See Connie MACK.

Mc·Gil·li·vray \mə-'gil-ə-vrā, -vrē\, Alexander. 1759?–1793. American Creek Indian chief, b. Alabama. Son of Scottish father and French-Creek mother. Loyalist during American Revolution, associated with British trading firm as its agent with the Creeks. Sought to organize confederation of southern Indians to force back the whites (1783 ff.); incited attacks on American settlements (1785–87); played off Spanish against Americans in trying to advance Creek interests. Negotiated treaty with U.S. in New York (1790); repudiated it (1792) when he obtained better terms from the Spanish.

Mc·Giv·ney \mə-'giv-nē\, Michael Joseph. 1852–1890. American clergyman, b. Waterbury, Conn. Ordained Roman Catholic priest (1877); founded at New Haven, Conn., the Knights of Columbus (1882).

Mc·Graw \mə-'grȯ\, John Joseph. *Nicknamed* Little Napoleon. 1873–1934. American baseball player and manager, b. Truxton, N.Y. Third baseman, Baltimore Orioles (1891–99). Manager, New York Giants (1902–32), managing them to 10 National League pennants and World Series titles in 1905, 1921, 1922; won 2,840 games, second only to Connie Mack. Elected to Baseball Hall of Fame (1937).

Mac·Greg·or \mə-'greg-ər\, John. *Pseudonym* Rob Roy \'räb-'rȯi\. 1825–1892. Scottish traveler and writer. Designed (1865) a short, light, flat-decked canoe (called a Rob Roy) for river cruising, and made long cruises in it (from 1865). Author of *A Thousand Miles in the Rob Roy Canoe* (1866), etc.

MacGregor, Robert. *Later (1693) took surname* Camp·bell \'kam-(b)əl\. *Known as* Rob Roy \'räb-'rȯi\. 1671–1734. Scottish freebooter. Engaged in rustling cattle and exacting tribute for protection against thieves; arrested and sentenced to be transported, but pardoned (1727). Hero of Sir Walter Scott's novel *Rob Roy* (1818).

Mc·Guf·fey \mə-'gəf-ē\, William Holmes. 1800–1873. American educator, b. near Claysville, Pa. President, Cincinnati College (1836–39) and Ohio U. (1839–43); professor, U. of Virginia (1845–73). Best known for his series of *Eclectic Readers* (first and second readers, 1836; third and fourth readers, 1837). More than 120,000,000 copies of McGuffey's *Readers* in original and revised editions have been sold.

Mach \'mäk\, Ernst. 1838–1916. Austrian physicist and philosopher. Professor of physics at Prague (1867–95), of philosophy at Vienna (1895–1901). Investigated in his researches in physics the physiology and psychology of the senses, esp. in relation to the theory of knowledge; one of the founders of *Empiriokritizismus,* a realistic philosophy based on the analysis of sensations; established basic principles of modern scientific positivism; studied flight of projectiles, his name given to ratio of the speed of an object to the local speed of sound. Author of *Beiträge zur Analyse der Empfindungen* (1886), *Erkenntnis und Irrtum* (1905), *Kultur und Mechanik* (1915), etc.

Má·cha \'mä-kä\, Karel Hynek. 1810–1836. Czech poet and novelist. Representative of Czech Romanticism and one of greatest Czech poets. Best known for his lyrics and his epic *Máj* (1836).

Ma·cha·do \mə-'shä-thü\, Bernardino Luís. 1851–1944. Portuguese politician, b. Rio de Janeiro. Entered parliament (1882); supported republicanism; minister of foreign affairs (1910–11); premier (1914); president of Portugal (1915–17); banished by insurgents (1917); premier of a coalition ministry (1921); again president (1925–26); deposed by military revolt; exiled (1927–40).

Machado de As·sis \-thē-ä-'sēs\, Joaquim Maria. 1839–1908. Brazilian novelist. Rose from printer's apprentice to newspaper editor and high office in civil service. Master of Brazilian prose; his works marked by urbanity, wit, pessimism, and discursive and ambiguous narration. His works included novels *A mão e a luva* (1874), *Helena* (1876), *Memórias póstumas de Brás Cubas* (1881), *Quincas Borba* (1891), *Dom Casmurro* (1899), *Esaú e Jacó* (1904), *Memorial de Aires* (1908); story collections *Histórias sem data* (1884), *Páginas recolhidas* (1899), *Relíquias de casa velha* (1906); and poems and plays.

Ma·cha·do y Mo·ra·les \mä-'chä-thō-ē-mō-'rä-läs\, Gerardo. 1871–1939. Cuban politician. Took part in revolution against Spain (1895–98); Liberal party leader (1920). President of Cuba (1925–33); instituted massive program of public works, later assumed dictatorial powers; deposed by popular revolt (1933); fled to U.S.

Machado y Ru·iz \-ē-rü-'eth\, Antonio. 1875–1939. Spanish poet. Representative of Generation of 1898. Best known for austere, pessimistic, meditative poems in *Campos de Castilla* (1912) and *Nuevas canciones* (1924). His brother ¶Manuel (1874–1947) wrote verse inspired by Andalusian themes as *Cante hondo* (1912) and *Sevilla* (1919); also collaborated with his brother in plays as *La Lola se va a los puertos* (1930) and *La duquesa de Benamejí* (1932).

Ma·char \'mä-kär\, Josef Svatopluk. 1864–1942. Czech poet. Bank official in Vienna (1891–1918); inspector general of Czech army (1919–24). Author of lyric trilogy *Confiteor* (1887–92), sarcastic sonnets (1891–93), political poems as *Tristium Vindobona* (1893), novel in verse *Magdaléna* (1893), verse cycle *Svědomím věků* (1901).

Machaut *or* **Machault,** Guillaume de. See GUILLAUME DE MACHAUT.

Ma·chen \'mā-chən\, John Gresham. 1881–1937. American theologian, b. Baltimore. Ordained Presbyterian minister (1914); became a leader of the fundamentalists in the Presbyterian church; was refused a professorship at Princeton Theol. Sem. (1926) because of his opposition to liberal revision of Westminster Confession of Faith; withdrew (1929) to found, head, and teach at Westminster Theol. Sem., Philadelphia. Suspended from ministry (1935); seceded and, with followers, founded (1936) the Presbyterian Church of America (later named Orthodox Presbyterian church). Known as New Testament and Greek scholar; author of *Christianity and Liberalism* (1923), *The Virgin Birth of Christ* (1930), etc.

Mc·Hen·ry \mək-'hen-rē\, James. 1753–1816. American Revolutionary patriot and public official, b. Ballymena, County Antrim, Ireland. To America (1771); on medical staff in Continental army (1775–78). Private secretary to General Washington (1778–80), to Lafayette (1780–81). Member, Continental Congress (1783–86); Maryland delegate to Constitutional Convention (1787). U.S. secretary of war (1796–1800). Fort McHenry in Baltimore was named after him.

Ma·chia·vel·li \ˌmäk-yä-'vel-lē, *Angl* ˌmak-ē-ə-'vel-ē\, Niccolò. 1469–1527. Italian political philosopher. Entered service of chancery of Florence (1494); secretary (1498–1512) to Florentine executive council (*i Dieci*); carried out several diplomatic missions in the Italian states, France, and Germany. Deprived of office by the Medici when they regained power (1512), and imprisoned for a time; retired to his estate near San Casciano and devoted himself to study and writing; official historiographer of Florence (1520). Most famous work *Il principe* (1513), containing his theory of government and a number of maxims of practical statecraft; also wrote *Discorsi sopra la prima deca di Tito Livio* (1517), *La mandragola* (comedy, 1518), *Dell'arte della guerra* (1520), *Vita di Castruccio Castracani* (1520), *Istorie fiorentine* (1525).

Ma·chin \'mā-chən\, John. 1680–1751. English mathematician. Professor of astronomy, Cambridge (1713–51); secretary of Royal Society (1718–47). Made studies to determine area of a circle; first to compute pi (π) to 100 decimal places.

Ma·cià \mä-sē-'ä\, Francesc. 1859–1933. Spanish Catalan politician. Elected to parliament (1905); founded nationalist party Estat Català (1922) and worked for Catalan independence; attempted (1926) to raise rebellion in northern Spain; imprisoned and expelled. After amnesty (1931), returned to Barcelona; organized Republican Left of Catalonia and after collapse of the monarchy (Apr. 1931) proclaimed Catalonia a republic; chosen provisional president; negotiated compromise with Madrid government (1932) whereby Catalonia was recognized as an autonomous region.

Mac·In·nes \mə-'kin-əs\, Colin. 1914–1976. English novelist. Author of *June in Her Day* (1952), *City of Spades* (1957), *Absolute Beginners* (1959), *Mr. Love and Justice* (1960), *England, Half English* (essays, 1961), *All Day Saturday* (1966), *Loving Them Both* (1974).

MacInnes, Thomas Robert Edward, *called* Tom. 1867–1951. Canadian writer, b. Dresden, Ont. Author of prose works *Lonesome Bar* (1909), *Chinook Days* (1927), *The Teaching of the Old Boy* (translation of and commentary on Lao-tzu, 1927), and of verse *Complete Poems* (1923) and *In the Old of My Age* (1947).

Mc·In·tire \'mak-ən-tī(ə)r\, Samuel. 1757–1811. American architect and wood carver, b. Salem, Mass. Designed many of the colonial houses, churches, and public buildings of old Salem; also produced furniture, interior woodwork, busts, medallions.

Mac·in·tosh \'mak-ən-ˌtäsh\, Charles. 1766–1843. Scottish chemist and inventor. Best known as inventor of waterproof fabric (patented 1823) known as *mackintosh.*

Macintosh, Douglas Clyde. 1877–1948. American theologian, b. Breadalbane, Ont. Ordained in Baptist ministry (1907); professor, Yale (1916–42). Author of *The Problem of Knowledge* (1915), *Theology as an Empirical Science* (1919), *Social Religion* (1939), etc.

Mc·In·tosh \'mak-ən-ˌtäsh\, Lachlan. 1725–1806. American Revolutionary soldier, b. Raits, Scotland. To U.S. (1736). Brigadier general (Sept. 1776); killed Button Gwinnett in duel (1777); wintered with Washington at Valley Forge (1777–78); failed to carry out plans against Detroit (1778); captured by British at Charleston, S.C. (1780); brevetted major general (1783).

Mc·In·tyre \'mak-ən-ˌtī(ə)r\, James Francis Aloysius. 1886–1979. American prelate, b. New York City. Ordained priest (1921); archbishop of Los Angeles (1948–70); cardinal (1953).

McIntyre, Oscar Odd. 1884–1938. American journalist, b. Plattsburg, Mo. Started journalistic career at Gallipolis, Ohio; conducted syndicated column "New York Day by Day," appearing in over 500 newspapers (from 1912). Author of *White Light Nights* (1924), *The Big Town* (1935), etc.

Macip, Vicente Juan. See MASIP.

Ma·čiu·lis \mä-'chu̇l-is\, Jonas. *Pseudonym* Mai·ro·nis \mī-'rȯn-is\. 1862–1932. Lithuanian poet. Regarded as bard of the Lithuanian national renaissance. Ordained Roman Catholic priest (1888); taught at St. Petersburg theological academy (1894–1909). Best known for patriotic lyrics often set to music; works included lyric collection *Pavasario balsai* (1895), epic poems *Jaunoji Lietuva* (1907), *Raseiniu Magdė* (1909), and *Mūsu Vargai* (1920), and dramatic trilogy in verse *Kęstučio Mirtis* (1921), *Vytautas pas Kryžiuočius* (1924), and *Vytautas Karalius* (1930).

Mac·Iver \mə-'kē-vər, -'kī-\, Robert Morrison. 1882–1970. American sociologist, b. Stornoway, Outer Hebrides, Scotland. Professor at Toronto (1915–27), Barnard Coll. (1927–29), Columbia U. (1929–50); president (1963–65) and chancellor (1965–66), New School for Social Research, New York. Author of *The Modern State* (1926), *Leviathan and the People* (1939), *The Web of Government* (1947), *The Prevention and Control of Delinquency* (1966), etc.

Mack \'mak\, Connie. *Orig.* Cornelius Alexander Mc·Gil·li·cud·dy \mə-'gil-ə-ˌkəd-ē\. 1862–1956. American baseball player and manager, b. East Brookfield, Mass. Catcher with Washington (1886–89), Buffalo (1890), Pittsburgh (1891–96); manager, Philadelphia Athletics (1901–50); won 9 American League pennants and 5 World Series (1910–11, 1913, 1929–30); won 3,776 games and lost 4,025, both all-time records. Elected to Baseball Hall of Fame (1937).

Mackay, Clarence Hungerford. See under John W. MACKAY.

Mc·Kay \mə-'kā\, Claude. 1890–1948. American writer, b. near Clarendon Hills, Jamaica, West Indies. One of first and most militant writers of the Harlem Renaissance. Published *Songs of Jamaica* (1911) and *Constab Ballads* (1912), both in Jamaican dialect; to U.S. (1912, naturalized 1940); on staff of *Liberator* magazine (1919–22). Author of verse *Spring in New Hampshire* (1920) and *Harlem Shadows* (1922); novels *Home to Harlem* (1927), *Banjo* (1929), *Banana Bottom* (1933); short-story collection *Gingertown* (1932); autobiography *A Long Way from Home* (1937); study *Harlem: Negro Metropolis* (1940), etc.

McKay, David Oman. 1873–1970. American religious leader, b. Huntsville, Utah. Ninth president (1951–70) of the Church of Jesus Christ of Latter-day Saints.

McKay, Donald. 1810–1880. American shipbuilder, b. Shelburne Co., N.S. To U.S. (1827). Known for designing and building, in his East Boston yards, the finest and fastest packet and clipper ships of the period (1845–69), including *Flying Cloud, Sovereign of the Seas, Lightning, Great Republic* (burned before launch), *Glory of the Seas* (in service to 1923); also built iron ships for U.S. navy, as the *Nausett.*

Mack·ay \'mak-ē\, John William. 1831–1902. American businessman, b. Dublin, Ireland. To U.S. (1840), to California (1851); worked as miner; struck rich ore in Comstock Lode (1873) and accumulated fortune. With James Gordon Bennett, founded Commercial Cable Co. (1883) and laid two submarine cables to Europe (1884) to break Gould monopoly. Organized Postal Telegraph Cable Co. (1886) to lay land lines and break the Western Union monopoly. His son ¶Clarence Hungerford (1874–1938), b. San Francisco, succeeded him in his interests; supervised completion of first transpacific cable (1904); laid cables to southern Europe (1905), Cuba (1907), etc.; first to combine radio, cables, and telegraphs under one management (1928).

Mac·kay \mə-'kī\, Mary. *Pseudonym* Marie Co·rel·li \kə-'rel-ē\. 1855–1924. English novelist. Author of popular melodramatic novels as *Romance of Two Worlds* (1886), *Barabbas* (1893), *Sorrows of Satan* (1895), *Murder of Delicia* (1896), *The Master Christian* (1900), *God's Good Man* (1904), *Holy Orders* (1908), etc.

Mac·Kaye \mə-'kī\, James Morrison Steele, *known as* Steele. 1842–1894. American actor, dramatist, and producer, b. Buffalo, N.Y. Manager of Madison Square Theater, New York (1879), designed by him, first of modern "intimate" theaters; patented over 100 theatrical inventions, including overhead lighting, moving double stage, folding theater seats. Built Lyceum Theater; established there first dramatic school in America. Author of some 30 plays, including *Hazel Kirke* (1880), *Paul Kauvar* (1887), *Money Mad* (1889).

His son ¶Percy (1875–1956), b. New York City; poet and dramatist; author of *The Canterbury Pilgrims* (1903), *Fenris the Wolf* (1905), *Sappho and Phaon* (1907), *The Scarecrow* (1908), *The Playhouse and the Play* (essays, (1909), *St. Louis* (masque, 1914), *Caliban* (masque, 1916), *Rip Van Winkle* (folk opera, 1920), *The Sphinx* (1929), *The Mystery of Hamlet* (1945), etc. Another son ¶Benton (1879–1975), b. Stamford, Conn.; forester and regional planner; with U.S. Forest Service (1905–18); proposed establishment of Appalachian Trail (1921); worked on regional planning aspects of Tennessee Valley Authority (from 1934); on staff of Rural Electrification Administration (1942–45). Author of *The New Exploration* (1928) and *From Geography to Geotechnics* (1968).

Macke \'mäk-ə\, August. 1887–1914. German painter. Member of Der Blaue Reiter group of Expressionists. Works included *The Promenade* (1913), *Great Zoological Garden* series, *Landscape with Cows and Camel* (1914).

Mc·Kean \mə-'kēn\, Thomas. 1734–1817. American politician and jurist, b. New London, Pa. Member (1774–83), president (1781), Continental Congress; signer of Declaration of Independence; chief justice of Pennsylvania (1777–99); governor (1799–1808).

Mack·en \'mak-ən\, Walter. 1915–1967. Irish writer. Actor-manager-director of Gaelic Theatre, Galway; also connected with Abbey Theatre, Dublin. As novelist, known for *Rain on the Wind* (1950) and historical trilogy *Seek the Fair Land* (1959), *The Silent People* (1962), *The Scorching Wind* (1964); as dramatist, wrote *Mungo's Mansion* (1946, also called *Galway Handicap*) and *Home is the Hero* (1953).

Mc·Ken·na \mə-'ken-ə\, Joseph. 1843–1926. American jurist, b. Philadelphia. Practiced law in California (from 1865). Member, U.S. House of Representatives (1885–92). U.S. circuit judge (1892–97). U.S. attorney general (1897–98). Associate justice, U.S. Supreme Court (1898–1925).

McKenna, Reginald. 1863–1943. English politician. M.P. (1895–1918); financial secretary of the treasury (1905); president of board of education (1907–08); first lord of the admiralty (1908–11); initiated (1909) construction of 18 *Dreadnought*-class battleships; home secretary (1911–15); chancellor of exchequer (1915–16); chairman, Midland Bank, Ltd. (1919–43).

Mc·Ken·ney \mə-'ken-ē\, Ruth. 1911–1972. American writer, b. Mishawaka, Ind. Author of books of humorous sketches including *My Sister Eileen* (1938), *The McKenneys Carry On* (1940), *Loud Red Patrick* (1947), *All About Eileen* (1952).

Mack·en·sen \'mäk-ən-zən\, August von. 1849–1945. German soldier. Entered army (1869); general field marshal (1915). Commanded forces invading Poland (1914–15) and Romania (1916); achieved great German breakthrough in Gorlice-Tarnów (June 1915); defeated Russians at Brest-Litovsk and at Pinsk; retired (1920); made state councilor (1933).

Mac·ken·zie \mə-'ken-zē\, Sir Alexander. 1764–1820. Scottish explorer. Entered service of Northwest Fur Co. (1779); established Ft. Chipewyan on Lake Athabasca (1788). Explored in the northwest and discovered the Mackenzie River (1789); made overland journey from Ft. Chipewyan to the Pacific coast (1793), first European to cover this ground. Wrote an account of his explorations (1801).

Mackenzie, Alexander. 1822–1892. Canadian politician, b. Logierait, Perthshire, Scotland. To Canada (1842); editor of newspaper *Lambton Shield* (1852–54); associated with George Brown, supported confederation; member, Dominion House of Commons (1867–92); first Liberal prime minister of the Dominion of Canada (1873–78).

Mackenzie, Sir Alexander Campbell. 1847–1935. British composer, b. Edinburgh. Concert violinist and teacher; principal of Royal Acad. of Music (1888–1924); conductor of London Philharmonic Society (1892–99). His compositions included cantatas *The Bride* (1881), *Jason* (1882), and *The Story of Sayid* (1882); choral work *The Cotter's Saturday Night* (1888); oratorio *The Rose of Sharon* (1884); operas *Colomba* (1883) and *The Troubadour* (1886); orchestral works *La Belle Dame Sans Merci* (1883), *Scottish Concerto* for piano (1897), and the *Scottish Rhapsodies* comprising *Rhapsodie Ecossaise* (1880), *Burns* (1881) and *Tam o' Shanter* (1911); the *Pibroch* suite for violin (1889); piano pieces, songs, etc.

Mackenzie, Alexander Slidell. *Orig.* Alexander Sli·dell \'slīd-ᵊl\. 1803–1848. American naval officer, b. New York City. Brother of John Slidell; name Mackenzie added in 1838. In quashing a planned mutiny (1842), hanged three men from the yardarm of his brig *Somers;* court of inquiry and court-martial wholly exonerated him. Author of *A Year in Spain* (1829), *Popular Essays on Naval Subjects* (1833), *Spain Revisited* (1836), and biographies of John Paul Jones, Perry, and Decatur.

Mackenzie, Charles Frederick. 1825–1862. Scottish clergyman. Ordained Anglican priest (1851); first bishop of Central Africa (1861–62).

Mackenzie, Sir Compton, *in full* Edward Montague Compton. 1883–1972. English writer. Literary critic, London *Daily Mail* (1931–35); rector, Glasgow U. (1931–34); founder and editor, *Gramophone* magazine (1923–62). Author of *Poems* (1907); plays, including *The Gentleman in Grey* (1906), *Columbine* (1920), *The Lost Cause* (1931); novels, including *The Passionate Elopement* (1911), *Carnival* (1912), *Poor Relations* (1919), *Rich Relatives* (1921), *The Parson's Progress* (1923), *Vestal Fire* (1927), *Extraordinary Women* (1928), *The Four Winds of Love* (1937–45), *The Monarch of the Glen* (1941),

Whisky Galore (1947); and a ten-volume memoir *My Life and Times* (1963–71).

Mackenzie of Rose·haugh \ˈrōz-hȯ, rō-ˈzȯk̲\, Sir George. 1636–1691. Scottish lawyer. As king's advocate (1677), became instrument of Charles II in his policy of persecution of Covenanters, thereby gaining nickname "Bloody Mackenzie." On failure of hopes of his party (1689), retired to Oxford to do literary work; founder (1682) of Advocates' Library, Edinburgh. Author of graceful moral essays and legal, political, and antiquarian works.

Mackenzie, George Henry. 1837–1891. American chess player, b. North Kessock, Scotland. To U.S. (1863); recognized as American chess champion (1880), world champion (1887).

Mackenzie, Henry. 1745–1831. Scottish novelist. Attorney for the crown in management of exchequer business; comptroller of taxes (1804–31). Author of novels *The Man of Feeling,* series of sketches about a weak sentimental hero which gained instant success (anonymously, 1771), *The Man of the World,* tale of a villain and seducer (1773), *Julia de Roubigné,* novel in manner of Richardson (1777).

Mackenzie, John. 1835–1899. Scottish missionary. To South Africa (1858); did missionary work in Bechuanaland and was constant champion of rights of African tribes; advocated making Bechuanaland a British protectorate (from 1867); deputy commissioner of Bechuanaland (1884–85).

Mc·Ken·zie \mə-ˈken-zē\, Sir John. 1838–1901. New Zealand politician, b. Scotland. To New Zealand (1860); Liberal member of Parliament (1881–1900); as minister of lands and immigration (1891–1900) sponsored legislation that provided land and credit to small farmers and helped break up large estates.

Mac·ken·zie \mə-ˈken-zē\, Sir Morell. 1837–1892. English laryngologist. Helped found Hospital for Diseases of the Throat, London (1863); involved in controversy when he incorrectly diagnosed Emperor Frederick III's throat disease as noncarcinogenic (1887). Author of *Diseases of the Throat* (1880–84).

Mackenzie, Ranald Slidell. 1840–1889. American army oficer, b. New York City. Son of Alexander S. Mackenzie; entered Union army (1862); distinguished himself at Second Bull Run, Fredericksburg, Gettysburg; major general (1865) and cavalry corps commander. On frontier duty after Civil War; one of most effective Indian-fighters, defeating Red Cloud and Red Leaf in Nebraska and Dull Knife in Bighorn Mountains (1876); retired as brigadier general (1884).

Mackenzie, Sir William. 1849–1923. Canadian financier and railroad builder, b. Kirkfield, Ont. Built sections of the Canadian National and Canadian Pacific railways; with Sir Donald Mann (from 1886) organized and built Canadian Northern R.R., later merged into the Canadian National Railway system.

Mackenzie, William Lyon. 1795–1861. Canadian insurgent leader, b. Springfield, Scotland. To Canada (1820); published in Toronto the *Colonial Advocate* (1824–34), in which he assailed the government; member of Parliament (1828–36), six times expelled; led 800 insurrectionists in Toronto uprising with intention of setting up provisional government (Dec. 1837); on failure, fled to U.S., organized supporters in Buffalo, N.Y., and fortified Navy Island in Niagara River; caused international incident of the *Caroline,* American steamer fitted out to support the insurrectionists, which was destroyed by Canadians in Niagara River; agitation succeeded in drawing attention of home government to colonial abuses. Again in Parliament (1851–58), supported radical positions.

Mc·Ker·row \mə-ˈker-ō\, Ronald Brunlees. 1872–1940. English scholar and publisher. Managing director (from 1917), Sidgwick & Jackson, Ltd., publishers; editor of various English classics, including *Works of T. Nashe* (1904–10), and of a new edition of Shakespeare, for which he wrote *Prolegomena for the Oxford Shakespeare* (1939); noted for his work in bibliography; founder (1925) and first editor of *Review of English Studies.*

Mc·Kim \mə-ˈkim\, Charles Follen. 1847–1909. American architect, b. Isabella Furnace, Pa. Partner in McKim, Mead, and White (1879–1908). A leader in American Neoclassical revival. Among the works in which he took a chief part were: Boston Public Library (1887); Rhode Island state capitol (1892); Columbia U. Library (1893), University Club (1899), Morgan Library (1903), Pennsylvania Railway Station (1904–10), all in New York; restoration of the White House, Washington, D. C. (1902–03).

Mac·kin·der \mə-ˈkin-dər\, Sir Halford John. 1861–1947. English geographer. Director, Oxford School of Geography (1899–1904); director of London School of Economics (1903–08) and reader in economic geography there (1908–25). M.P. (1910–22). In paper "The Geographical Pivot of History" (1904) described his theory of Eurasia as the natural seat of geopolitical power with the "maritime lands" (i.e., other continents) as subordinate; expanded theory in *Democratic Ideals and Reality* (1919). Chairman of Imperial Shipping Committee (1920–45), of Imperial Economic Committee (1926–31). Also wrote *Britain and the British Seas* (1902).

Mc·Kin·ley \mə-ˈkin-lē\, John. 1780–1852. American jurist, b. Culpeper Co., Va. U.S. senator from Alabama (1826–31); member, U.S. House of Representatives (1833–35). Associate justice, U.S. Supreme Court (1837–52).

McKinley, William. 1843–1901. Twenty-fifth president of the United States, b. Niles, Ohio. Served through Civil War. Practiced law, Canton, Ohio (from 1867). Republican member, U.S. House of Representatives (1877–83, 1885–91); as chairman (1889–91) of Committee on Ways and Means, had major part in framing and passing the protective McKinley Tariff of 1890. With organization directed by Marcus Alonzo Hanna, elected governor of Ohio (1892–96) and president of the U.S. (1896 and 1900). Championed tariff protectionism and opposed free silver; after Spanish–American War (1898), acquired Cuba, Puerto Rico, Guam, the Philippines; annexed Hawaii (1898), Wake Island and Samoa (1899). Assassinated by Leon Czolgosz, an anarchist, at Buffalo.

Mack·in·tosh \ˈmak-ən-ˌtäsh\, Charles Rennie. 1868–1928. Scottish architect. A leader of Art Nouveau movement; designed Glasgow School of Art buildings (1894–1909), four Tea-Rooms in Glasgow celebrated for their interior decorations (1898–1904), Windyhill, Kilmacolm (1899–1901), Hill House, Helensburgh (1902), Scotland Street School (1904–06); noted also for designs for furniture, tapestries, etc.; exercised considerable influence on European decorative design. After withdrawal from architectural work (1913) devoted himself to painting, esp. in water colors.

Mackintosh, Elizabeth. *Pseudonyms* Gordon Dav·i·ot \ˈdav-ē-ət\ *and* Josephine Tey \ˈtā\. 1897–1952. Scottish writer. As Daviot, author of three novels and several plays, including *Richard of Bordeaux* (1933). As Tey, author of detective novels, including *Miss Pym Disposes* (1947), *The Franchise Affair* (1949), *The Daughter of Time* (1951), and *The Singing Sands* (1952).

Mack·lin \ˈmak-lən\, Charles. *Surname orig.* Mc·Laugh·lin \mə-ˈkläk̲-lən\. 1697?–1797. Irish actor and playwright. Celebrated for acting of Shylock; author of farce *Love à la Mode* (1759) and comedy *The Man of the World* (1781), creating burlesque character Sir Pertinax Macsycophant.

Mack·mur·do \mək-ˈmər-(ˌ)dō\, Arthur Heygate. 1851–1942. English architect and designer. Friend and disciple of John Ruskin and William Morris; pioneer in Arts and Crafts movement. Designed Savoy Hotel and about 12 private houses, London; founded (1882) Century Guild of artists to produce furniture and decorative accessories; designed textiles, tapestries, wallpaper, metalwork characterized by swirling plant forms; founder of art magazine *The Hobby Horse* (1884).

Mack von Lei·be·rich \ˈmäk-fȯn-ˈlī-bə-rik̲\, Karl. Freiherr. 1752–1828. Austrian general. Commanded army against the French (1798) and occupied Rome, but was forced to withdraw because of revolt in Naples. Commanded Austrian army in southern Germany (1805); forced to capitulate with 20,000 men at Ulm (1805).

Mc·Lach·lan \mə-ˈkläk̲-lən, -ˈkläk-\, Alexander. 1818–1896. Canadian poet, b. Johnstone, Scotland. To Canada (1840); farmer in Ontario. Author of poetry in Scots dialect dealing with homesickness of Scottish immigrants; books of verse included *The Spirit of Love* (1846), *Lyrics* (1858), *The Emigrant* (1861), *Poems and Songs* (1874).

Mc·Lar·en \mə-ˈklar-ən\, Bruce Leslie. 1937–1970. New Zealand racing driver and designer. Drove for Cooper racing team (1959–65); youngest driver to win a Formula I Grand Prix (U.S., 1959); won Canadian-American Challenge Cup road race series (1967, 1969) and 1968 Belgian Grand Prix; also noted as designer of racing cars; killed while testing a car.

Mac·lar·en \mə-ˈklar-ən\, Charles. 1782–1866. Scottish journalist. Cofounder (1817) and editor (1820–45) of Edinburgh *Scotsman,* first independent Scottish Liberal paper; editor of 6th edition of *Encyclopaedia Britannica* (1820–23); also did editing on 4th, 5th, and 7th editions of the *Britannica.*

Maclaren, Ian. See John WATSON.

Mac·lau·rin \mə-ˈklȯr-ən\, Colin. 1698–1746. Scottish mathematician. Professor at Marischal College, Aberdeen (1717) and at Edinburgh (1725). Author of *Geometrica Organica, sive Descriptio Linearum Curvarum Universalis* (1720) dealing with general properties of conics and of higher plane curves, *Treatise of Fluxions* (1742) containing his essay on tides, statement of the conception of level surfaces, and theory of maxima and minima, *A Treatise of Algebra* (1748), *An Account of Sir Isaac Newton's Philosophical Discoveries* (1748).

Mac·lay \mə-ˈklā\, William. 1734–1804. American lawyer, b. Chester Co., Pa. U.S. senator (1789–91). His journal (pub. 1880) of Senate debates during his term is the only continuous report of the proceedings.

Mac·lean \mə-ˈklān\, George. 1801–1847. British soldier and colonial administrator, b. Scotland. Officer in Royal African Colonial Corps, served in Sierra Leone and the Gold Coast (1826–28). Council president of Cape Coast, West

Africa (1830–44); made peace with Ashanti kingdom; established informal protectorate over coastal Fanti states; m. (1838) Letitia Landon (*q.v.*).

Mc·Lean \mə-'klān\, John. 1785–1861. American politician and jurist, b. Morris Co., N.J. Member, U.S. House of Representatives (1813–16). U.S. postmaster general (1823–29). Associate justice, U.S. Supreme Court (1829–61); dissented in Dred Scott decision (1857). Unsuccessful candidate for Republican nomination for the presidency (1856, 1860).

Mc·Lean \mə'-klēn\, William Lippard. 1852–1931. American newspaper proprietor, b. Mount Pleasant, Pa. Publisher of Philadelphia *Evening Bulletin* (1895–1931); director of Associated Press (1896–1924). His son ¶Robert (1891–1980), b. Philadelphia, succeeded him as publisher of *Evening Bulletin* (1931–59; chairman, 1959–80); president (1938–58), Associated Press.

Mac·Leish \mə-'klēsh\, Archibald. 1892–1982. American poet, b. Glencoe, Ill. Practiced law, Boston (1920–23); expatriate in France (1923–28); influenced by Pound and Eliot, published verse *The Happy Marriage* (1924), *The Pot of Earth* (1925), *Streets in the Moon* (1926), *The Hamlet of A. MacLeish* (1928). Began writing public verse concerned with social issues, esp. the threat to democracy from fascism, including *Conquistador* (1932, Pulitzer prize), *Frescoes for Mr. Rockefeller's City* (1933), *Public Speech* (1936), *America Was Promises* (1939), and verse plays *The Fall of the City* (1937) and *Air Raid* (1938). Librarian of Congress (1939–44); assistant secretary of state (1944–45); chairman of U.S. delegation to London Conference to draw up UNESCO charter (1945); professor, Harvard (1949–62); lecturer, Amherst Coll. (1963–67). Later works included verse *Act Five* (1948), *Collected Poems* (1952, Pulitzer prize), *Songs for Eve* (1954), *The Wild Old Wicked Man* (1968); verse plays *J.B.* (1958, Pulitzer prize), *Herakles* (1967), *Scratch* (1971), etc; prose *A Time to Speak* (1941), *Poetry and Experience* (1961), etc.

Mc·Len·nan \mə-'klen-ən\, John Ferguson. 1827–1881. Scottish sociologist. Author of papers on totemism, of *Primitive Marriage* (1865) setting up exogamy as primitive form of marriage and stimulating research in this field, and of *The Patriarchal Theory* (1885).

Macleod, Fiona. See William SHARP.

Mac·leod \mə-'klaůd\, Henry Dunning. 1821–1902. Scottish economist. Author of *The Theory and Practice of Banking* (1856), *Elements of Political Economy,* in which he first applied term "Gresham's law" (1858), and *The Theory of Credit* (1889–91).

Macleod, John James Rickard. 1876–1935. Scottish physiologist. Professor, Western Reserve U. (1903–18), U. of Toronto (1918–28), U. of Aberdeen (from 1928). For share in discovery (1921) of insulin, awarded jointly with F.G. Banting the 1923 Nobel prize for physiology or medicine. Author of *Practical Physiology* (1903), *Diabetes, Its Physiological Pathology* (1913), *Fundamentals in Physiology* (1916), *Physiology and Biochemistry in Modern Medicine* (1918), etc.

Macleod, Mary. *Sc. Gael.* Màiri Nighe·an Al·as·dair Ru·aidh \ˌnē-ən-'al-ə-stər-'rü-ə\, *i.e.* Mary, daughter of Alasdair the Red. c.1615–c.1706. Scottish poet. Known for her Scottish Gaelic eulogies and laments of distinguished members of the Macleod family.

Macleod, Norman. 1812–1872. Scottish clergyman and author. A founder of Evangelical Alliance (1847); minister of Barony Church, Glasgow (1851–72). Edited *Good Words* (1860–72); author of *The Earnest Student* (1854), *The Gold Thread* (1861), *Simple Truth Spoken to Working People* (1867), *Reminiscences of a Highland Parish* (1867).

Mac Li·am·móir \mə-'klē-ə-ˌmòr\, Micheál. 1899–1978. Irish actor, scenic designer, and theatrical producer. Founder (1928, with Hilton Edwards) and director (from 1928) of Gate Theatre, Dublin; produced, designed, and acted in over 300 plays there; known esp. for Shakespearean roles. Also founder (1928, with Edwards) and director (1928–31) of Galway Gaelic Theatre; his Gaelic drama *Diarmuid agus Gráinne* produced there (1928). Played Iago in film *Othello* (1955); developed and appeared in one-man stage shows as *The Importance of Being Oscar* (1960), *I Must Be Talking to My Friends* (1963), *Talking About Yeats* (1970).

Mac·lise \mə-'klēs\, Daniel. 1806–1870. Irish painter and illustrator. Made reputation with *All-Hallow Eve* (1833); designed book illustrations for Tennyson and some of Dickens's Christmas books.

Mc·Lough·lin \mə-'klȯf-lən\, John. 1784–1857. Canadian fur trader, b. Rivière du Loup, Que. Entered service of North West Company (c.1806), a partner (1814); chief factor for Hudson's Bay Company in charge of Columbia River district (1821–46); established (1825) headquarters at Ft. Vancouver (now Vancouver, Wash.) and controlled fur trading in Northwest region; often criticized by his superiors for providing assistance to American settlers. Founded (1842) Oregon City; often called "the father of Oregon."

Mc·Lu·han \mə-'klü-ən\, Marshall, *in full* Herbert Marshall. 1911–1980. Canadian communications theorist, b. Edmonton, Alberta. Professor of English (from 1946), U. of Toronto, and director (from 1963) of its Centre for Culture and Technology. Expert on mass communications; wrote *The Mechanical Bride* (1951), *Understanding Media* 1964), *The Medium is the Massage* (with Quentin Fiore, 1967), *From Cliché to Archetype* (with Wilfred Watson, 1970).

Mac·lure \mə-'klůr\, William. 1763–1840. American geologist, b. Ayr, Scotland. Visited U.S. (1782, 1796); became naturalized citizen of U.S. (before 1803). Member, U.S. commission to settle spoliation claims between U.S. and France (1803–07). Made geological chart of U.S. (1809; revised and enlarged 1817). Considered father of American geology.

Mac·Ma·hon \måk-må-ōⁿ\, Marie-Edme-Patrice-Maurice de. Comte de Mac-Mahon *and* duc de Ma·gen·ta \må-zhaⁿ-tå\. 1808–1893. French soldier and politician. In the Crimea, led the assault on Malakoff (1855); led successful campaign against the Kabyles in Algeria (1857–58); in war with Austria (1859) turned defeat into victory at Magenta and helped French win at Solferino; made marshal and duc de Magenta (1859). Governor general of Algeria (1864–70). In Franco–Prussian War (1870); defeated at Weissenburg, Wörth, and Sedan. Aided Thiers in suppressing Paris Commune (1871). Elected president of France (1873–79); lost confrontation with parliament over dismissal of ministry (1877), making the presidency largely an honorific office.

Mac·Ma·hon \mək-'mä(-ə)n\, Percy Alexander. 1854–1929. English mathematician, b. Malta. Professor of physics, Ordnance Coll. (1890–97); deputy warden of standards (1904–20). Specialist in algebraic forms; author of *Combinatorial Analysis* (1915–16).

Mc·Man·us \mək-'man-əs\, George. 1884–1954. American cartoonist, b. St. Louis. On staff of New York *American* (1912). Creator of the comic strip "Bringing up Father" (1913).

Mc·Mas·ter \mək-'mas-tər\, John Bach. 1852–1932. American historian, b. Brooklyn, N.Y. Taught engineering, Princeton (1877–83), history, Pennsylvania (1883–1920). Wrote *The History of the People of the United States* (9 vols., 1883–1927), *Benjamin Franklin as a Man of Letters* (1887), *The United States in the World War* (1918–20).

Mac·mil·lan \mək-'mil-ən\, Daniel. 1813–1857. Scottish bookseller and publisher. Bookseller at Glasgow (1831–33), Cambridge (1833–37), London (1837–43); opened shop with his brother Alexander in Cambridge (1843); added publishing (1844), assuming firm name Macmillan & Co.; won first successes with Kingsley's *Westward Ho!* (1855) and *Tom Brown's School Days* (1857). Succeeded (1857) by his brother ¶Alexander (1815–1896), who transferred business to London (1863) and opened branch in New York (1867); published *Macmillan's Magazine* (1859–1907), *Nature* (from 1869), and works of Tennyson, Lewis Carroll, Kipling, Yeats, among others. Daniel's son ¶Sir Frederick Orridge (1851–1936) became partner (1876), chairman (1893); president of Publishers Association (1900–02, 1911–13).

Mac·Mil·lan \mək-'mil-ən\, Donald Baxter. 1874–1970. American explorer, b. Provincetown, Mass. With Peary on north polar expedition (1908–09); led expeditions to Arctic lands (1913–37). Author of *Four Years in the White North* (1918), *Kahda* (1929), *How Peary Reached the Pole* (1932).

Macmillan, Harold, *in full* Maurice Harold, 1st Earl of Stock·ton \'stäk-tən\. Viscount Macmillan of Oven·den \'əv-ən-dən\. 1894–1986. British statesman. Heir to Macmillan publishing house. Member of House of Commons (1924–29, 1931–64). Appointed as parliamentary secretary to Minister of Supply (May 1940); during World War II British minister at Allied Headquarters in Africa. Appointed minister of defense (October 1954), foreign secretary (April 1955), chancellor of the exchequer (December 1955); succeeded (January 1957) Sir Anthony Eden as prime minister in wake of Suez crisis; as Conservative prime minister worked to improve Anglo-U.S. relations; helped Britain to adapt to end of colonialism and diminished role in world affairs; tried to be go-between for U.S. and U.S.S.R.; resigned (October 1963). Published several volumes of memoirs.

Macmillan, John. 1670–1753. Scottish minister. Founder (1743) of the Reformed Presbyterian church, composed mostly of Cameronians.

Mac·Mon·nies \mək-'män-ēz\, Frederick William. 1863–1937. American sculptor, b. Brooklyn, N.Y. Among his works were *Nathan Hale* in City Hall Park, New York; *Faun with Heron, Sir Henry Vane* in Boston Public Library; *Bacchante with Infant Faun, Venus and Adonis, Cupid,* equestrian statues of Gen. Slocum, Theodore Roosevelt, Gen. George B. McClellan.

Mac·nagh·ten \mək-'nȯt-ᵊn\, Sir William Hay. 1793–1841. British diplomat. Secretary to Lord William Bentinck (1830–33); adviser to Lord Auckland, governor general of India (1837); envoy and minister to Afghan court at Kābul (1838); tried unsuccessfully to replace Afghan ruler Dōst Moḥammad Khān with rival Shāh Shojā' (1841); killed by Afghans for suspected treachery.

MacMurrough, Dermot. See DERMOT MACMURROUGH.

Mc·Nair \mək-'na(ə)r, -'ne(ə)r\, Lesley James. 1883–1944. American army officer, b. Verndale, Minn. Entered army (1904); served with Pershing in Mexico (1916) and in World War I. Major general (1939), lieutenant general (1941). As chief of General Headquarters, U.S. army (1940; title changed to commander of Army Ground Forces, 1942), directed training and organization of ground combat troops; introduced simulation of battle conditions in training and standardized military doctrine and organization throughout army; killed in Normandy.

Mc·Nar·ney \mək-'när-nē\, Joseph Taggart. 1893–1972. American army officer, b. Emporium, Pa. Entered army (1915); deputy chief of staff, U.S. army (1942); general (1945). Commander of U.S. forces in the Mediterranean (1944–45), Europe (1945–47); retired (1952).

Mc·Naugh·ton \mək-'nôt-ᵊn\, Andrew George Latta. 1887–1966. Canadian army officer, b. Moosomin, Sask. Entered army (1910); artillery officer in World War I; chief of general staff (1929–35); commander of Canadian army in Great Britain (1942–44); retired with rank of general; minister of national defense (1944–45); chairman, Canadian section of International Joint Commission (1950–62). Co-inventor of cathode ray direction finder (1926).

Mac·Neice \mək-'nēs\, Louis, *in full* Frederick Louis. 1907–1963. Irish poet and playwright. Known for low-keyed, socially committed topical verse; wrote and produced radio plays for British Broadcasting Corp. (1941–61), esp. *The Dark Tower* (1947, with music by Benjamin Britten). His books of verse included *Blind Fireworks* (1929), *Poems* (1935), *The Earth Compels* (1938), *Autumn Journal* (1939), *Plant and Phantom* (1941), *Ten Burnt Offerings* (1952), *Solstices* (1961), *The Burning Perch* (1963); translated Aeschylus's *Agamemnon* (1936); wrote prose works *Letters from Ireland* (1937, with W.H. Auden), *Modern Poetry* (1938), *The Poetry of W.B. Yeats* (1941), *Varieties of Parable* (1965), *The Strings Are False* (1965, autobiography).

Mc·Neile \mək-'nē(ə)l\, Herman Cyril. *Pseudonym* Sap·per \'sap-ər\. 1888–1937. English army officer and novelist. In British army (1907–19). Author of *Bull-Dog Drummond* (1920), *Jim Maitland* (1923), *The Final Count* (1926), *Tiny Carteret* (1930), etc.

Mc·Neill \mək-'nē(ə)l\, James. 1869–1938. Irish politician. Member of committee to draft constitution for Irish Free State (1922); high commissioner for Irish Free State (1923–28) and governor general (1928–32).

Mac·Neill \mək-'nē(ə)l\, John Gordon Swift. 1849–1926. Irish politician and historian. Professor at King's Inn, Dublin (1882–88), and National U. of Ireland (from 1909). M.P. (1887–1918). Author of *Studies in the Constitution of the Irish Free State* (1925), memoirs *What I Have Seen and Heard* (1925), etc.

Ma·comb \mə-'kōm\, Alexander. 1782–1841. American army officer, b. Detroit. Entered army (1801); brigadier general (1814). In War of 1812, defended Plattsburg against British (Sept. 1814); commanding general, U.S. army (1828–41).

Ma·con \'mā-kən\, Nathaniel. 1758–1837. American politician, b. Edgecombe (now Warren) Co., N.C. Served in American Revolution. Member, U.S. House of Representatives (1791–1815; speaker 1801–07), U.S. Senate (1815–28); defended states' rights and opposed most legislation of the day.

Mc·Par·lan \mək-'pär-lən\, James. 1844–1919. American detective, b. Northern Ireland. To U.S. (1863); joined Pinkerton Detective Agency (early 1870s); gained fame for his instrumental part in breaking up the Molly Maguires (1873–77) and in suppressing strike of Western Federation of Miners (1905); hero of Conan Doyle's *The Valley of Fear* (1915).

Mac·Phail \mək-'fā(ə)l\, Agnes Campbell. 1890–1954. Canadian politician, b. Proton, Ont. A leader of Co-operative Commonwealth Federation of Canada; member of Canadian House of Commons (1921–40), first woman elected to Canadian legislature. Represented Canada in Assembly of League of Nations.

Mc·Pher·son \mək-'fərs-ᵊn\, Aimee Semple. *Nee* Aimee Elizabeth Kennedy. 1890–1944. American religious, b. near Ingersoll, Ont. m. 1st Robert J. Semple (1908; d. 1910), 2d Harold S. McPherson (1912; div. 1921). Missionary in China (1908–09); itinerant preacher (1916–18); settled in Los Angeles (1918). Conducted Pentecostal revivals throughout America and preached on radio, gaining fame and thousands of followers by her flamboyant preaching and fundamentalist, adventist theology; founded (1927) International Church of the Foursquare Gospel. Often involved in controversy, as with her sensational 5-week disappearance (1926) and many lawsuits. Wrote *This Is That* (1919), *In the Service of the King* (1927), *Give Me My Own God* (1936).

Mac·pher·son \mək-'fərs-ᵊn\, Sir David Lewis. 1818–1896. Canadian politician, b. Castle Leathers, Scotland. To Montreal (1835); amassed fortune in shipping; obtained contract to build a railway from Toronto to Sarnia (1853). Member of Legislative Council of Canada (1864–67) and of Canadian Senate (from 1867); minister of the interior (1883–85).

Macpherson, James. 1736–1796. Scottish poet. Collected Gaelic manuscripts and poems; published *Fragments of Ancient Poetry collected in the Highlands of Scotland* (1760); published *Fingal* (1762) and *Temora* (1763), alleged translations from Gaelic of 3d-century poet Ossian, admired (by Goethe among others) for romantic rhythm and occasional passages of striking beauty; asserted by Dr. Johnson to have woven romance himself from fragments of poems and stories (1775); never produced his originals or rebutted charge of forgery. M.P. (1780–96). Author also of *The History of Great Britain from the Restoration to the Accession of the House of Hanover* (1775).

Mc·Pher·son, \mək-'fərs-ᵊn\, James Birdseye. 1828–1864. American army officer, b. near Clyde, Ohio. Commissioned in Corps of Engineers (1853). Chief engineer on Grant's staff (1862); major general (Oct. 1862), serving through Vicksburg campaign (1862–63). Commanded army of the Tennessee (1864) cooperating with Sherman in Georgia; killed by skirmishers near Atlanta.

Mac·quar·ie \mə-'kwar-ē\, Lachlan. 1761–1824. British soldier and colonial administrator, b. Scotland. Entered British army (1777); brigadier general (1811), major general (1813). As governor of New South Wales (1809–21) fostered public works program, established a currency (1813), expanded opportunities for Emancipists.

Mc·Rae \mə-'krā\, Milton Alexander. 1858–1930. American newspaper publisher, b. Detroit. In partnership (from 1889) with Edward W. Scripps (*q.v.*), developed (1897) the Scripps-McRae Press Association which became (1907) the United Press. Author of *Forty Years in Newspaperdom* (1924).

Mac·rea·dy \mə-'krēd-ē\, William Charles. 1793–1873. English tragedian. Made London debut at Covent Garden (1816); gained leading place by his Richard III (1819); transferred to Drury Lane (1823); played successfully in America (1826) and in Paris (1828); during his management of Covent Garden (1837–39) produced Shakespeare, Browning's *Strafford,* and Bulwer-Lytton's *Lady of Lyons* and *Richelieu,* himself playing principal characters; manager of Drury Lane (1841–43); in America was confronted by mob and riot resulting from bitter jealousy of actor Edwin Forrest (1849); took farewell of stage at Drury Lane (1851). Numbered among chief roles Macbeth, Cassius, King Lear, Henry IV, Iago, and title roles in Sheridan Knowles's *Virginius* and *William Tell.*

Mc·Reyn·olds \mək-'ren-əl(d)z\, James Clark. 1862–1946. American jurist, b. Elkton, Ky. Practiced law, Nashville, Tenn. (from 1884). U.S. attorney general (1913–14). Associate justice, U.S. Supreme Court (1914–41).

Ma·cri·nus \mə-'krī-nəs\. *In full* Marcus Opellius Macrinus. c.164–218. Roman emperor (217–218), b. Caesarea (now Cherchell, Algeria). Rose rapidly in equestrian career; prefect of praetorians under Caracalla; plotted and brought about murder of Caracalla (217); succeeded him as emperor; fought inconclusive battle with Parthians, agreeing to unfavorable peace which cost him support of his Syrian troops; defeated near Antioch and succeeded by Elagabalus.

Ma·cro·bi·us \mə-'krō-bē-əs\, Ambrosius Theodosius. fl. c.400 A.D. Latin grammarian. Little known about his life; may have been a praetorian prefect in Sicily (399), proconsul in Africa (410), grand chamberlain (422). Extant works, *Commentarius ex Cicerone in somnium Scipionis* and *Conviviorum saturnaliorum libri septem* (usually called the *Saturnalia*).

M'·Tag·gart \mək-'tag-ərt\, John M'Taggart Ellis. 1866–1925. English philosopher. Lecturer, Cambridge (1897–1923); espoused a Hegelian philosophy of atheistic spiritual pluralism. Author of *Some Dogmas of Religion* (1906), *Commentary on Hegel's Logic* (1910), and *The Nature of Existence* (1921, 1927).

Mc·Tam·ma·ny \mək-'tam-ə-nē\, John. 1845–1915. American inventor, b. Kelvin Row, Scotland. To U.S. (1862); served in Civil War. Invented the mechanical player piano (c.1866; patented 1881); gave public exhibition of it in St. Louis (1876); also invented a voting machine employing a perforated roll (patented 1892).

Ma·cy \'mā-sē\, Anne Sullivan. *Nee* Joanna Sullivan. 1866–1936. American educator, b. Feeding Hills, Mass. Teacher (from 1887) and constant companion of Helen Keller. Her husband (m. 1905; sep. 1913) ¶John Albert Macy (1877–1932), b. Detroit; author and critic; edited Helen Keller's *Story of My Life* (1903); wrote *The Spirit of American Literature* (1913), *Socialism in America* (1916), *About Women* (1930), etc.

Ma·dách \'mä-dách\, Imre. 1823–1864. Hungarian poet and dramatist. Author notably of a dramatic poem dealing with the life and fall of the human race, *Az ember tragediája* (*The Tragedy of Man,* 1861); also wrote dramas *A civilizátor* (1859) and *Mózes* (1860).

Mad·an \'mad-ᵊn, 'mād-ᵊn\, Martin. 1726–1790. English barrister and clergyman. Methodist chaplain of Lock Hospital, London (1750–80); stirred storm of protest with his *Thelyphthora* ("ruination of women"), advocating polygamy as remedy for evils of prostitution (1780).

Ma·da·ria·ga y Ro·jo \mä-t͟här-'yä-gä-ē-'rō-k͟ō\, Salvador de. 1886–1978. Spanish writer and diplomat. Ambassador in Washington (1931); delegate to League of Nations (1931–36); ambassador to France (1932–34); self-exile in England (1936–76). Among his works were *Shelley and Calderón* (1920), *The Genius of Spain* (1923), *La fuente serena* (verse, 1927), *Englishmen, Frenchmen, Spaniards* (1927), *Anarchy or Hierarchy* (1937), *Hernán Cortés*

(1941), *Spain* (1942), *The Heart of Jade* (novel, 1944), *The Rise and Fall of the Spanish Empire* (1947), *Morning Without Noon* (memoirs, 1973).

Ma·de·lin \mȧd-laⁿ\, Louis, *in full* Émile-Louis-Marie. 1871–1956. French historian. Author of *La Rome de Napoléon* (1904), *La Révolution* (1911), *Danton* (1914), *Histoire du Consulat et de l'Empire* (1937–54), etc.

Ma·der·na \mä-'der-nä\, Bruno. 1920–1973. Italian composer. Known as composer of avant-garde and electronic music; with Luciano Berio founded (1954) at Milan the Studio di Fonologia Musicale, a major laboratory for electronic music. His works included opera *Satyricon* (1973); orchestral works as *Quadrivium* (1969), three oboe concertos (1962, 1967, 1973), concertos for piano (1959) and for violin (1969); chamber music, esp. *Serenata* (1954); vocal works; and electronic music as *Notturno* for tape (1956) and *Syntaxis* for four electronic timbres (1957). Known also as conductor and teacher, esp. in association with Internationale Ferienkurse für Neue Musik, Darmstadt.

Maderna *or* **Ma·der·no** \-nō\ *or* **Ma·der·ni** \-nē\, Carlo. 1556–1629. Italian architect. Exponent of Roman Baroque style; nephew and pupil of Domenico Fontana; protégé of Clement VIII and Paul V. Succeeded Fontana as architect of St. Peter's (1603–29); designed nave and façade, altered Michelangelo's Greek cross plan to that of present Latin cross. Among his other works were Palazzo Mattei di Giove, church of Santa Maria della Vittoria, continuation of Palazzo Quirinale and Palazzo Barberini.

Ma·de·ro \mä-'thā-rō\, Francisco Indalécio. 1873–1913. Mexican revolutionist and politician. A liberal and idealist; published *La sucesión presidencial de 1910* (1908) calling for restoration of constitution of 1857; opposed reelection of Díaz to presidency (1910), but failed of election; demanded effective suffrage and no reelection, and plotted against Díaz; fled to U.S. (Nov. 1910). Led military campaign ending in capture of Ciudad Juárez, where capital was established (May 11, 1911); forced resignation of Díaz and became president (1911–13); his administration ineffectual; after revolts and street fighting in Mexico City (Feb. 1913), overthrown by Huerta; arrested, shot while allegedly attempting escape.

Ma·de·to·ja \'mȧ-de-ˌtō-yȧ\, Leevi Antti. 1887–1947. Finnish composer. Professor, Helsinki Academy (1916–39); music critic, *Helsingin Sanomat* (1916–32). Composer of operas *Pohjalaisia* (1923) and *Juha* (1934), three symphonies, choral works, songs, cantatas, chamber music, and a Finnish national anthem.

Mā·dha·vā·cār·ya \'mäd-ə-vä-'kär-yə\. 1296?–?1386. Hindu scholar and royal counselor. Elder brother of Sāyana; lived at court in Vijayanagar as minister to the king; wrote on rhetorical, philosophical, and religious subjects.

Mā·dhav Rāo \'mäd-əv-'rau̇\. Name of two peshwas of the Marāthās: Mādhav Rāo I (1754–1772); fourth peshwa (1761–72); son and successor of Bālājī Rāo; nominal head of the first great Marāthā houses; defeated Hyder Ali of Mysore (1770–71). ¶Mādhav Rāo II (1774–1795); sixth peshwa (1774–95); during entire life, power held by Marāthā minister, Nāna Fadnavis; First Marāthā War (1775–82) against British occurred in his reign.

Madh·va \'mäd-və\. *Also called* Ānan·da·tīr·tha \'ä-nən-də-'tir-tə\ *and* Pūr·ṇa-praj·ña \ˌpu̇r-nə-'präj-nyə\. c.1199–c.1278. Indian philosopher. A Hindu; exponent of Dvaita; many miracles similar to those of Christ are attributed to him, as walking on water and multiplying loaves of bread. Wrote 37 works in Sanskrit, mostly commentaries on Hindu sacred texts and treatises on his own theological and philosophical system. His followers are called Mādhvas.

Mad·i·son \'mad-ə-sən\, Dolley, *nee* Payne. *Often spelled* Dolly. 1768–1849. American socialite, b. Guilford Co., N.C. m. 1st John Todd, Jr. (1790; d. 1793), 2d James Madison (1794). Famous Washington hostess while her husband was secretary of state (1801–09) and president (1809–17).

Madison, James. 1751–1836. Fourth president of the United States, b. Port Conway, Va. Member, Virginia legislature (1776–80, 1784–86), Continental Congress (1780–83); his proposals at and management of the Constitutional Convention (1787) earned him title "father of the U.S. Constitution." Cooperated with Hamilton and Jay in writing a series of papers (pub. 1787–88 under title of *The Federalist*) explaining the new Constitution and advocating its adoption. Member, U.S. House of Representatives (1789–97); sponsored the Bill of Rights; leader of Democratic-Republican party in opposition to Hamilton's financial measures. Drafted the Virginia Resolutions (1798) inspired by resentment at the Federalist alien and sedition laws. U.S. secretary of state (1801–09). President of the U.S. (1809–17); commander in chief during War of 1812; approved charter of Second Bank of the United States and nation's first system of protective tariffs. Rector, U. of Virginia (1826–36).

Mäd·ler \'med-lər\, Johann Heinrich von. 1794–1874. German astronomer. With Wilhelm Beer published first map of Mars (1830) and an authoritative map of the Moon (1836); popularizer of astronomy with his *Populäre Astronomie* (1841) and *Geschichte der Himmelskunde* (1873).

Ma·dog ab Owain Gwyn·edd \'mȧd-ȯg-ȧb-'ō-ˌwīn-'gwin-eth\. fl. 1170. Welsh prince. May not have existed; according to Richard Hakluyt's *Voyages* (1582) and David Powel's *Historia of Cambria* (1584), sailed away in ten ships and discovered America (c.1170); subject of Southey's poem *Madoc*.

Madonella. See Mary ASTELL.

Mad·ox \'mad-əks\, Thomas. 1666–1727. English legal antiquary and historian. Clerk in office of the exchequer and later in augmentation office; royal historiographer (1714). Author of *Formulare Anglicanum*, a landmark in diplomatic history of post-Conquest charters (1702), *History and Antiquities of the Exchequer of the Kings of England* (1711), *Firma Burga* on English municipal history (1722), and *Baroni Anglica* on tenures (1736).

Mad·vig \'mȧth-vēg\, Johan Nicolai. 1804–1882. Danish scholar and politician. Professor, Copenhagen (1829–80); worked esp. for improvement of classical schools. Entered parliament (1848), its president (1856–63); minister of education (1848–52). Published *Die Verfassung und Verwaltung des römischen Staates* (1881–82) and works on Latin grammar and Greek syntax.

Mae·ba·ra \mī-bär-ä\ Issei. *Called* Hi·ko·ta·rō \hē-kō-tär-ō\ *or* Ha·chi·jū·rō \hä-chē-ju̇r-ō\. 1834–1876. Japanese soldier and politician. Studied under Yoshida Shōin; active in antishogunate movement (by 1860); took part in overthrow of Tokugawa shogunate (1868); cabinet councilor (1868); minister of war (1869); helped suppress Saga rebellion of Etō Shimpei (1874); became dissatisfied with government policies, led (1876) unsuccessful rebellion of samurai in Chōshu; captured and executed.

Mae·ce·nas \mi-'sē-nəs\, Gaius. c.70–8 B.C. Roman statesman and patron of literature. Close friend of Horace and Virgil, and of Octavian (later Emperor Augustus). Entrusted by Octavian with administration of Rome while Octavian fought with Pompey the Younger (38–36); influential adviser during Augustus's reign. Presented Horace with the Sabine farm which Horace celebrated in his verse; requested Virgil to write his *Georgics*. Only fragments of his own writings are extant.

Mael·zel *or* **Mäl·zel** \'melt-səl\, Johann Nepomuk. 1772–1838. German musician and inventor. Settled in Vienna as music teacher (1792); won fame for mechanical inventions including a kind of orchestrion called the panharmonicon (1805), an automatic trumpeter (1808), and ear trumpets used by Beethoven among others; named court mechanician (1808). Commissioned (1813) Beethoven's *Wellington's Victory* for his panharmonicon; perfected (1815) Dietrich Winkel's metronome and manufactured it in Paris; settled in U.S. (1826).

Maer·lant \'mȧr-länt\, Jacob van. c.1225–c.1291. Flemish poet. Founder of the didactic school in the Netherlands. Details of his life in dispute; probably sexton at Maerlant (1255–?65); clerk to court at Damme (from c.1266). Author of rhymed versions of Latin and French originals, including *Alexanders Geesten, Historie van den Grale Merlyn* (c.1260), *Torec* (c.1262), *Historie van Troyen* (c.1264), *Der Naturen Bloeme* (1266–69), *Rijmbijbel* (1271), and *Spieghel Historiael* (begun 1282; chiefly after Vincent de Beauvais's *Speculum Historiale);* also wrote poems scourging social and clerical abuses, as *Wapene Martijn, Van den Lande van Oversee, Disputacie van Onser Vrouwen ende vanden Heilighen Cruce.*

Maes \'mȧs\, Nicolaes. *Also called* Nicolas Maas \'mȧs\. 1634–1693. Dutch painter. Studied under Rembrandt; known esp. for genre pictures and portraits. His works included *Girl at the Window, Reverie, Idle Servant, Woman Scraping Parsnips, The Card Players, The Listener, Old Woman at the Spinning Wheel, The Inquisitive Servant, Saying Grace, Hagar's Farewell.*

Maesa, Julia. See JULIA MAESA.

Mae·ter·linck *Flem* 'mȧ-tər-liŋk, *Fr* me-ter-laⁿk, *Angl* 'māt-ər-ˌliŋk, *also* 'met-, 'mat-\, Maurice-Polydore-Marie-Bernard. 1862–1949. Belgian poet, dramatist, and essayist. Settled in Paris (1896); gained reputation with Symbolist verse *Serres chaudes* (1899); established himself as leading writer of Symbolist drama with *La Princesse Maleine* (1899), *Pelléas et Mélisande* (1892), *Monna Vanna* (1902), *L'Oiseau bleu* (1908), *Le Bourgmestre de Stilmonde* (1918), etc.; author also of works on philosophy and nature as *Le Trésor des humbles* (1896), *La Sagesse et la destinée* (1898), *La Vie des abeilles* (1901), *L'Intelligence des fleurs* (1907), *La Vie des termites* (1926), *La Vie des fourmis* (1930). Awarded Nobel prize for literature (1911).

Maet·suy·ker \'mȧt-ˌsœi-kər\, Joan. 1606–1678. Dutch colonial administrator. Hired by Dutch East India Company as legal expert; sent to Batavia (1636), served on Council of Justice and wrote (1642) Statutes of Batavia; governor of Ceylon (1648–51). As governor general of Dutch East Indies (1653–78), drove out Spanish and Portuguese, acquired Macassar and most of Sumatra, established Dutch power in Java.

Maet·zu y Whit·ney \'mīt-sü-ē-'hwit-nē\, Ramiro de. 1875–1936. Spanish writer. Member of Generation of '98; supported dictatorship of Primo de Rivera; shot by Republicans in Civil War. Known for his work defending Spanish traditionalism *La defensa de la Hispanidad* (1934).

Maffei, Marchese di. See Francesco SCIPIONE.

Ma·ga·lhães \mə-gəl-'yīⁿsh\, Fernão de. *Known in Span. as* Fernando de Ma·gal·la·nes \mä-gä(l)-'yän-äs\ *and in Eng. as* Ferdinand Ma·gel·lan \mə-'jel-ən\. c.1480–1521. Portuguese navigator. Served in Portuguese expeditions to India and Malacca (1505–12) and to Azamor (1513–14). Offered services to Spain (1517); acquired approval of Charles V for voyage to Spice Islands

(Moluccas) by western route. Left Spain (Sept. 20, 1519) with five vessels; sighted South America near Pernambuco (Nov. 29); explored La Plata estuary; wintered at Port St. Julian (Mar.-Aug. 1520); crushed mutiny; sailed through strait now known as Strait of Magellan (Oct.–Nov. 1520); reached Guam (Mar. 6, 1521); discovered Philippines (Mar. 16), arriving Cebú (Apr. 7); made alliance with treacherous native sovereign; killed on expedition on his behalf to island of Mactan. One vessel commanded by Juan de Elcano (*q.v.*) completed circumnavigation of globe (1522).

Magdalene, Mary. See MARY MAGDALENE.

Ma·gen·die \mȧ-zha^{n}-dē\, François. 1783–1855. French physiologist. Professor, Collège de France (from 1831); pioneer in experimental physiology in France; demonstrated the functions of the spinal nerves; investigated the mechanisms of blood flow, deglutition, and vomiting; credited with introduction of strychnine, morphine, brucine, codeine, quinine, and compounds of iodine and bromine into medical practice. Wrote *Précis élémentaire de physiologie* (1816–17); founded (1821) *Journal de Physiologie Expérimentale,* first periodical devoted to experimental physiology.

Mag·gi·ni \mäd-ˈjē-nē\, Giovanni Paolo. c.1580–c.1632. Italian violinmaker. Pupil and associate of Gasparo da Salò; worked in Brescia.

Ma·ginn \mə-ˈgin\, William. 1793–1842. Irish writer. Contributed to *Noctes Ambrosianae* in *Blackwood's Magazine* (1822–35); with Hugh Fraser founded *Fraser's Magazine* (1830), contributing *Gallery of Literary Characters* and *Homeric Ballads* (from 1838); his best story, *Bob Burke's Duel with Ensign Brady* (1834).

Ma·gi·not \mȧ-zhē-nō, *Angl* ˌmazh-ə-ˈnō, ˌmaj-\, André-Louis-René. 1877–1932. French politician. Member of Chamber of Deputies (from 1910); served in World War I. Minister of colonies (1917, 1928–29), of pensions (1921–24), of war (1922–24, 1929–32). Vigorous advocate of military preparedness; principal creator of the Maginot line which was named in his honor.

Ma·gnan \mȧn-yä^{n}\, Bernard-Pierre. 1791–1865. French soldier. Served at Waterloo (1815), in Spain (1823) and Algeria (1830); general of brigade (1839) and of division (1845); suppressed uprising in Lyons (1849); took active part in ensuring success of coup d'état (Dec. 2, 1851); created marshal of France; senator (1852); commander of army of Paris (1859).

Ma·gna·ni \män-ˈyän-ē\, Anna. 1908–1973. Italian actress. Known for her earthy and sensual portrayals in films *La cieca di Sorrento* (1934), *Roma città aperta* (1945), *L'onorevole Angelina* (1947), *Il miracolo* (1948), *Bellissima* (1951), *The Rose Tattoo* (1955, Academy Award), *The Fugitive Kind* (1960), *The Secret of Santa Vittoria* (1968), etc.

Ma·gna·sco \män-ˈyäs-kō\, Alessandro. *Called* Lis·san·dri·no \ˌlēs-sän-ˈdrē-nō\. 1667–1749. Italian painter. Worked in Milan; known esp. for religious, landscape, and genre paintings as *The Baptism of Christ* and *The Synagogue.*

Mag·nen·ti·us \mag-ˈnen-sh(ē-)əs\, Flavius Popilius. d. 353 A.D. Roman emperor of the West (350–353). Of German pagan birth; in command of troops on the Rhine; plotted against and caused death of Constans (350); defeated by Constantius II at Mursa (351); fled to Gaul; committed suicide.

Mag·nes \ˈmag-nəs\, Judah Leon. 1877–1948. American religious leader and educator, b. San Francisco. Rabbi, Temple Emanu-El, New York (1906–10), B'nai Jeshurun, New York (1911–12). Leader, Society for Advancement of Judaism (1912–20). Chief founder (1925), chancellor (1925–35), and president (1935 ff.), Hebrew U., Jerusalem.

Ma·gnol \mȧn-yȯl\, Pierre. 1638–1715. French physician and botanist. Originated classification of plants by families; works included *Prodromus historiae generalis plantarum* (1689) and *Novus caracter plantarum* (1720). The genus *Magnolia* was named after him.

Magnus. King of Denmark. See MAGNUS I of Norway.

Mag·nus \ˈmäŋ-nu̇s, *Angl* ˈmag-nəs\. Name of seven kings of Norway:

Magnus I Olafs·son \ˈō-läfs-ˌsȯn\. *Called* the Good. 1024–1047. King of Norway (1035–47) and of Denmark (1042–47). Illegitimate son of Olaf II Haraldsson; defeated the Wends in battle at Lyrskog (1043); repulsed attempts of future Sweyn II to assume Danish throne; shared throne with his uncle Harold III Hardraade (1045); died during campaign against Denmark.

Magnus II Ha·ralds·son \ˈhä-räld-sȯn\. d. 1069. King (1066–69). Son of Harold III Hardraade; divided kingdom with brother Olaf III, taking north and west portion.

Magnus III. *Called* Bar·fot \ˈbär-fōt\, *i.e.* Barefoot. c.1073–1103. King (1093–1103). Son of Olaf III; at first ruled only southern third (1093–95); after death (1095) of Haakon Magnusson, ruled all Norway; harried Orkneys and Hebrides (1098–99); waged war with Sweden (1099–1101); led another expedition south; landed on Orkneys and Isle of Man; killed on coast of Ireland.

Magnus IV. *Called* the Blind. c.1115–1139. King (1130–35). Son of Sigurd I and grandson of Magnus III; succeeded to throne jointly with Harold IV Gille (1130); engaged in civil war with Harold (1134–35); defeated, had his eyes put out, and imprisoned; later, killed in naval battle with sons of Harold.

Magnus V Er·lings·son \ˈer-liŋ-ˌsȯn\. 1156–1184. King (1162–84). Son of Erling the Crooked; under regency (1162–64) of his father who remained real power behind throne until his death (1179); crowned (1163) by Roman Catholic church; fought long civil war with Sverrir Sigurdsson; finally defeated (1179) and fled to Denmark; slain in naval battle in attempt to recover kingdom.

Magnus VI. *Called* La·ga·bø·ter \ˈlä-gä-ˌbœt-ər\, *i.e.* Lawmender. 1238–1280. King (1263–80). Succeeded his father Haakon IV; made peace with Alexander III of Scotland, ceding Hebrides and Isle of Man; introduced (1274) national legal code that remained in use for over 400 years; instituted municipal code (1277); concluded Concordat of Tønsberg (1277).

Magnus VII Eriksson. See MAGNUS II, king of Sweden.

Mag·nus \ˈmäŋ-ˌnüs, *Angl* ˈmag-nəs\. Name of two kings of Sweden:

Magnus I. *Called* La·du·lås \ˈlä-dü-lōs\, *i.e.* Barn lock. 1240–1290. King (1275–90). Second son of Birger Jarl; deposed his brother Valdemar; opposed nobles and protected peasantry by wise legislation; increased trade relations with Europe.

Magnus II Eriks·son \ˈā-rik-sȯn\. 1316–1374. King of Norway as Magnus VII (1319–55) and of Sweden as Magnus II (1319–63). Son of Duke Erik and of Ingeborg, daughter of Haakon V of Norway; ruled under a regent (1319–32); lived almost all the time in Sweden; tried to control nobility and the church; named his son Haakon VI successor in Norway (1343); deposed (1356–59) by his son Erik XII; lost southern districts of Sweden to Valdemar IV of Denmark (1360); deposed by Royal Council of Swedes (1363); succeeded by Duke Albert of Mecklenburg; retired to Norway.

Mag·nus \ˈmag-nu̇s\, Heinrich Gustav. 1802–1870. German chemist and physicist. Professor, Berlin (1834–70); discovered periodic acid (1833), ethionic and isethionic acids (1833–39), polymerization of hydrocarbons on heating (1853); discovered (1853) Magnus effect, the generation of a sidewise force on a spinning cylinder or sphere in a fluid; also studied gases in the blood, theory of heat, expansion of gases, electrolysis, optics, magnetism, etc.

Mag·nus \ˈmäŋ-ˌnüs, *Angl* ˈmag-nəs\, Olaus. *Orig.* Olaf Mans·son \ˈmäns-sȯn\. 1490–1557. Swedish ecclesiastic and historian. Roman Catholic priest; left Sweden (1523); resident in Danzig and (from 1541) in Rome; director of St. Brigitta's monastery, Rome (from 1549); archbishop of Uppsala (1544–57). Published *Carta Marina* (1539), first detailed map of Scandinavia, and *Historia de gentibus septentrionalibus* (1555), long accepted as authoritative on Scandinavian history. His brother ¶Johannes (1488–1544), also ecclesiastic and historian; sent to Sweden by Pope Adrian VI as papal legate (1523); administrator of Uppsala archdiocese (1524); exiled for refusal to support Gustav I Vasa; archbishop of Uppsala (1533–44) but lived with his brother in Danzig and Rome. Author of *Historia de omnibus gothorum sueonumque regibus* (1554), primary source for history of several Scandinavian kings.

Mag·nús·son \ˈmäŋ-üs-sȯn\, Árni. 1663–1730. Icelandic antiquary and philologist. Professor, Copenhagen (from 1701); on royal mission to Iceland to value estates and report on economic conditions (1702–12). Established most important collection of early Icelandic manuscripts, which he donated (1720) to U. of Copenhagen.

Magnússon, Jón. c.1610–1696. Icelandic clergyman and writer. Parson at Eyri (1655); stricken by an illness, he accused two parishioners of practicing witchcraft on him, both burned at the stake (1656); wrote *Píslarsaga* (pub. 1914) describing his sufferings.

Ma·go \ˈmā-(ˌ)gō\ *or* **Ma·gon** \-(ˌ)gōn\. d. c.203 B.C. Carthaginian general. Youngest son of Hamilcar Barca; accompanied his brother Hannibal to Italy (218 B.C.); held key commands in great victories of early part of Second Punic War; supported Hasdrubal in Spain (215); defeated by Scipio Africanus at Ilipa (207); finally defeated in Cisalpine Gaul (203); died of wounds on return voyage to Carthage.

Ma·goon \mə-ˈgün\, Charles Edward. 1861–1920. American lawyer and administrator, b. Steele Co., Minn. Practiced in Nebraska. Governor of Canal Zone (1905–06); provisional governor of Cuba (1906–09).

Ma·gritte \mȧ-grēt\, René-François-Ghislain. 1898–1967. Belgian painter. One of foremost Surrealist painters; his works characterized by spatial manipulation, metamorphic themes, use of iconographic images as men in bowlers, birds, lions, horsemen, leaves. His canvases included *Threatening Weather* (1928), *The Wind and the Song* (1929), *Human Condition* (1934), *The Rape* (1934), *Time Transfixed* (1939), *The Companions of Fear* (1942), *The Rights of Man* (1945), *Pandora's Box* (1951), *Golconda* (1953), *The Listening Chamber* (1953), *Ready-made Bouquet* (1957), *The Castle of the Pyrenees* (1959), *The Tomb of the Wrestlers* (1960).

Mag·say·say \mäg-ˈsī-ˌsī, -ˌsī-ˈsī\, Ramón. 1907–1957. Philippine politician. Liberal congressman (1946–50); as secretary of defense (1950–53) crushed the Communist Hukbalahap (Huk) rebellion; president of the Philippines (1953–57).

Ma·han \mə-ˈhan\, Alfred Thayer. 1840–1914. American naval officer and historian, b. West Point, N.Y. In U.S. navy (1859–96); served in Civil War; president, Naval War College, Newport, R.I. (1886–89, 1892–93). Published *The Influence of Sea Power Upon History, 1660–1783* (1890) and *The Influence of Sea Power upon the French Revolution and Empire, 1793–1812* (1892), both of which profoundly influenced U.S. and worldwide naval buildups prior to World War I. U.S. delegate to first Hague Peace Conference (1899). Other works included *The Interest of America in Sea Power* (1897), *Sea Power in Its Relations to the War of 1812* (1905), *Naval Strategy* (1911), and biographies of Farragut and Nelson.

Mahāvīra. See VARDHAMĀNA.

Mahdi, al-. See MUḤAMMAD AḤMAD.

Ma·hen·dra \mə-ˈhān-drə\. *Pāli* Ma·hin·da \mə-ˈhēn-də\. c.270–c.204 B.C. Indian missionary. Generally held to be son of Aśoka; to Ceylon as Buddhist missionary (c.251); converted King Tissa and many of the common people.

Mahendra. 1920–1972. King of Nepal (1955–72). Promulgated constitution (1959) but next year suspended part of it and assumed power; banned political parties; introduced (1962) a new constitution, later (1967) amended it.

Mahendravarman. See CHITRASENA.

Ma·hil·lon \má-ē-yōⁿ\, Victor-Charles. 1841–1924. Belgian music scholar. Entered his father's instrument manufacturing firm (1865); founded and edited journal *L'Écho musical* (1869–86); as curator of Brussels Conservatory (from 1879) formed large collection of ancient and modern instruments and made copies of many of them. Published *Les Éléments d'acoustique musicale et instrumentale* (1874) and other works on acoustics and wind instruments.

Mā·hir Pa·sha \ˈmä-hir-ˈpäsh-ä\, ʿAlī. 1882–1960. Egyptian politician. Judge in native courts (1907); director of royal law school (1923); instrumental in framing of new constitution (1923). Entered parliament (1924); minister of education (1925–26), of finance (1928–29), of justice (1930–32); named chief of royal cabinet (1935, 1937). Prime minister (1936, 1939–40); maintained friendly relations with Italy at onset of World War II; again prime minister (Jan.–Mar. and July–Sept. 1952).

Mah·ler \ˈmä-lər\, Gustav. 1860–1911. Austrian composer, b. Bohemia. Director, Imperial Opera, Vienna (1897–1907); conducted in U.S. (1907–10). Among his compositions were ten symphonies (the last unfinished), cantata *Das klagende Lied* (1880), six songs with orchestra *Das Lied von der Erde* (1908), and song cycles *Lieder und Gesänge aus der Jugendzeit* (1880–88), *Lieder eines fahrenden Gesellen* (1883–85; texts by Mahler), *Des Knaben Wunderhorn* (1888–96), *Kindertotenlieder* (1901–04; texts by Friedrich Rückert), *Fünf Lieder nach Rückert* (1901–04; texts by Rückert).

Mah·mud \mä-ˈmüd\. Name of two sultans of Ottoman empire:

Mahmud I. 1696–1754. Sultan (1730–54). Restored order after Patrona Halil uprising in Istanbul (1730); suppressed Janissary rebellion (1731); waged intermittent and inconclusive war with Persia (1731–46); forced Austria to cede Belgrade (1739); patron of the arts.

Mahmud II. 1785–1839. Sultan (1808–39). Succeeded his brother Mustafa IV; waged unsuccessful war against Russia (1809–12); attempted to suppress Greeks in their struggle for freedom (1821–29) and was forced by Greek allies, France, England, and Russia, to sign Treaty of Adrianople securing Greek independence (1829); eliminated the Janissary corps (1826); introduced Western reforms in army, government, education, dress; started war with Egypt (1839).

Maḥ·mūd \ˈmäk̲-müd\ of Ghaz·na \ˈgäz-nä\. 971–1030. Muslim sultan (997–1030) of Ghazna (now Ghaznī; see GHAZNAVID). Son of Sebüktigin; extended small Afghan kingdom from the Tigris to the Ganges and northward to the Oxus; invaded India seventeen times (1001–26); overwhelmed Hindu ruler of Lahore; sacked Somnath (1024) in Gujarat; carried away much booty; annexed the Punjab; transformed Ghazna into a cultural center; patron of the arts; subject of many legends.

Mahmud Abdülbâkî. See BÂKÎ.

Mah·mud Mu·zaf·far Shah \ˈmäk̲-müd-mü-ˈzaf-ar-ˈshä\. 1823–1864. Last sultan (1834–57) of Riau and Lingga. Under father's regency (1834–41); attempted to restore authoritarianism; made claim to throne of Pahang; deposed by the Dutch, who established control in the region.

Mah·mud Ne·dim Pa·şa \mä-ˈmüd-nā-ˈdim-pə-ˈshä\. c.1818–1883. Turkish politician. Held ministries of commerce and of justice; as grand vizier (1871–72, 1875–76), supported reactionary policies, allowed Sultan Abdülaziz to become an absolute monarch; opposed Britain and France and curried friendship of Russia; minister of interior (1879–83).

Mah·mud Shah \ˈmäk̲-müd-ˈshä\. d. 1528. Founder of Johore. Sultan of Malacca (1488–1511); ineffective ruler; fled following capture of Malacca by Portuguese (1511). Founded kingdom of Johore with capital on island of Bintang (or Bintan); continued to receive tribute from surrounding states; led several unsuccessful attacks against Malacca; fled to Sumatra after his capital was razed by the Portuguese (1526).

Mahon, Ducs de. See CRILLON family.

Mahon, Viscount. See STANHOPE family.

Ma·hon \ˈmän, mə-ˈhün, mə-ˈhōn\, Charles James Patrick. 1800–1891. Irish adventurer and politician. M.P. (1847–52); served in Russian, Turkish, and Austrian armies; fought on government side in Uruguayan civil war; commanded Chilean fleet against Spain; colonel in Brazilian army; fought in Union army in American Civil War; M.P. (1879–91).

Ma·hone \mə-ˈhōn\, William. 1826–1895. American soldier, b. Southampton Co., Va. With Confederate army of Northern Virginia (from 1862); served at Malvern Hill, Second Manassas, the Wilderness; major general (1864). Leader of Readjuster party in Virginia (1879); U.S. senator (1881–87).

Mah·o·ny \ˈmä-ō-nē, ˈmä-nē\, Francis Sylvester. *Pseudonym* Father Prout \ˈpraůt\. 1804–1866. Irish humorist. Master of rhetoric at a Jesuit college; expelled from the Jesuit order (1830), abandoned priesthood for literary pursuits. Contributed to *Fraser's Magazine* and *Bentley's Miscellany* poems and translations from Horace and French writers.

Mai \ˈmä-ē\, Angelo. 1782–1854. Italian prelate and antiquary. Jesuit (from 1799); ordained (1808); Vatican librarian (1819–25); cardinal (1838). Known chiefly for his discovery and publication of old manuscripts and palimpsests, as Cicero's *De re republica,* Plautus's *Vidularia,* Fronto's letters, Eusebius of Caesarea's *Chronicon,* and Dionysius's *Roman Antiquities.*

Maiano, Benedetto da. See BENEDETTO DA MAIANO.

Maid of Norway. See MARGARET, Queen of Scotland.

Mai·grot \meg-rō\, Émile. *Pseudonym* Émile Hen·riot \äⁿr-yō\. 1889–1961. French writer. Author of verse *La Flamme et les cendres* (1909), novel *Aricie Brun* (1924), autobiographical works *Au bord du temps* (1958), *On n'est pas perdu sur la terre* (1960), travel books, essays, etc.

Mai·láth \ˈmȯi-lät\, János. Count. 1786–1855. Hungarian historian and poet. Known as interpreter of Magyar culture to the Germans; his works, in German, included verse (1824), *Magyarische Sagen, Märchen und Erzählungen* (1825), and histories of the Magyars (1828–31) and of the Austrian empire (1834–50).

Mail·lart \má-yár\, Louis, *known as* Aimé. 1817–1871. French composer. Among his works were the operas *La Croix de Marie* (1852), *Les Dragons de Villars* (1856), *Lara* (1864).

Maillart, Robert. 1872–1940. Swiss civil engineer. Known for his radical use of reinforced concrete which revolutionized masonry arch bridge design. His many bridges in the Swiss Alps included bridge over the Inn at Zuoz (1901) and the Schwandbach Bridge at Schwarzenburg; constructed factories and warehouses for Swiss companies in Russia (1912–19).

Mail·lol \má-yȯl\, Aristide. 1861–1944. French sculptor. Painter and tapestry designer before turning (c.1900) to sculpture; executed woodcut illustrations for fine editions of Latin poets (1920s and '30s). Known for large, graceful, emotionally restrained statues executed in tradition of classical Greece and Rome; works included *The Mediterranean* (c.1901), *Night* (1902), *Action in Chains* (1906), *Cyclist* (1907–08), *Flora* (1911), *The River* (c.1939–43).

Mail·ly-Nesle \má-yē-nel\, Marie-Anne de. Duchesse de Châ·teau·roux \shá-tō-rü\. 1717–1744. French courtier. Fifth daughter of marquis de Nesle; m. marquis de La Tournelle (1734; d. 1740); became official mistress of Louis XV (1742), succeeding two older sisters; created duchess (1743); a leader of court faction favoring involvement in War of Austrian Succession.

Maim·bourg \maⁿ-bür\, Louis. 1610–1686. French ecclesiastical historian. Entered Jesuit order (1626); dismissed from order because of his *Traité historique de l'établissement et des prérogatives de l'église de Rome* (1685), which defended Gallicanism; wrote also *Histoire du luthéranisme* (1680), *Histoire du calvinisme* (1682), etc.

Mai·mon \ˈmī-mȯn\, Salomon. *Orig.* Salomon ben Josh·ua \ben-ˈjäsh-ə-wə\. 1753–1800. German philosopher, b. Polish Lithuania of Jewish descent. Wrote unorthodox commentary on *More nevukhim* of Maimonides, from whom he took his surname; lived (from 1790) at Nieder-Siegersdorf at estate of Count Friedrich von Kalckreuth. Known as Skeptical critic of Kant, esp. in *Versuch über die Transcendentalphilosophie* (1790); his works included *Philosophisches Wörterbuch* (1791), *Über die Progressen der Philosophie* (1792), *Kritische Untersuchungen über den menschlichen Geist* (1797).

Maimonides. See MOSES BEN MAIMON.

Maine, Duc du. See Louis-August under Bourbon kings of France at BOURBON.

Maine \ˈmān\, Sir Henry James Sumner. 1822–1888. English jurist. Pioneered in study of comparative law, esp. primitive law and anthropological jurisprudence; professor of civil law, Cambridge (1847–54); published lectures as *Ancient Law* (1861), which made his reputation. Legal member of council in India (1863–69), shaped plans for codification of Indian law; member of secretary of state's council for India (1871–88); first professor of comparative jurisprudence at Oxford (1869–78); master of Trinity (1877–88), professor of international law (1887–88), Cambridge. Author of works on philosophy of law, history, and politics, including *Early History of Institutions* (1875), *Early Law and Custom* (1883).

Maine de Biran. See BIRAN.

Maintenon, Madame de. See Françoise d'AUBIGNÉ.

Mair, John. See MAJOR.

Mair, Simon. See MAYR.

Mai·ret \me-re\, Jean. 1604–1686. French dramatist. Forerunner and rival of Corneille. Author of pastorals *Chryséide et Arimand* (1625), *Sylvie* (1626), *La Silvanire* (1630); comedy *Les Galanteries du duc d'Ossonne* (1632); tragedies *Virginie* (1633), *Sophonisbe* (1634), *Le Marc-Antoine, ou La Cléopâtre* (1635), *Le Grand et dernier Solyman* (1637); tragicomedy *L'Illustre corsaire* (1637).

Maironis. See Jonas MAČIULIS.

Mai·son \me-zōⁿ\, Nicolas-Joseph. 1771–1840. French soldier. In Revolutionary army (1792) and under Napoléon; general of division (1812); remained loyal to Louis XVIII during the Hundred Days; created marquis (1817); commanded expedition (1828) to Peloponnesus and was created marshal of France; minister of foreign affairs (1830); ambassador at Vienna (1831) and St. Petersburg (1833); minister of war (1835–36).

Mai·son·neuve \mez-ōⁿ-nœv\, Paul de Cho·me·dey de \də-shȯm-dā-də-\. Sieur. 1612–1676. French colonial administrator. Founder (1642) and first governor (1642–65) of Montreal.

Mais·tre \mestrᵊ\, Casimir-Léon. 1867–1957. French soldier and explorer. Second in command of exploring expedition to Madagascar (1889–90); led expedition to Central Africa (1891–93), exploring along the Congo, Ubangi, Benue, and Niger rivers.

Maistre, Joseph-Marie de. Comte. 1753–1821. French polemical writer and diplomat. Entered Savoy senate (1788); emigrated to Switzerland during French Revolution (1792); ambassador of Victor Emmanuel I at St. Petersburg (1802–16); returned to Turin as chief magistrate and minister of state of Sardinia. Proponent of traditionalism. Among his works were *Considérations sur la France* (1796), *Essai sur le principe générateur des constitutions politiques* (1814), *Du pape* (1819), *Les Soirées de Saint Pétersbourg* (1821), and *Examen de la philosophie de Bacon* (1836).

Mait·land \'māt-lənd\. Name of a Scottish family possessing the ancestral keep of Thirle·stane \'thər(-ə)l-ˌstān\, the lands of Leth·ing·ton \'leth-iŋ-tən\, and the earldom and dukedom of Lau·der·dale \'lȯd-ər-ˌdāl\, which descended from an Anglo-Norman family that settled in Berwick during the late 12th century. The family included:

Sir Richard, Lord Lethington (1496–1586), lawyer, poet, and collector of Scottish verse; lost his sight (1561) but remained active as judge until 1584; an ordinary lord of session and privy councilor (1561); keeper of great seal (1562–67); author of poems of social and political satire and a history of family of Seton.

His eldest son ¶William Maitland of Lethington (c.1528–1573); secretary of state to queen regent of Scotland (1558), but joined lords of the congregation against her (1559); secretary of state (1561–66), entrusted with foreign policy of Mary, Queen of Scots, whom he supported against Knox; conciliatory toward England, worked for union between two crowns; shared in murder of Darnley; driven by enmity with Bothwell to side of insurgents against Mary at Langside, but after her flight (1568) worked to restore her to power; with Kirkcaldy held Edinburgh castle against the regent Morton (till 1573); died in prison.

Sir Richard's second son ¶Sir John (1545–1595), 1st Baron Maitland of Thirlestane; lord privy seal of Scotland (1567); supported cause of Mary, Queen of Scots, against Presbyterians; privy councilor (1583); became principal adviser to James VI (by 1586); chancellor of Scotland (1587–95); made alliance with England and a compromise with Scottish Presbyterians; sponsored "Golden Act" (1592) which sanctioned the Presbyterian hierarchy of church courts. His son ¶John (d. 1645), 2d baron, was created 1st earl of Lauderdale (1624).

The 1st earl's son ¶John (1616–1682), 2nd Earl and first Duke of Lauderdale; began career as zealous adherent of Presbyterian cause; commissioner for Solemn League and Covenant (1643–46) sent to Westminster Assembly; sent to confer with Charles I at Carisbrooke and gained from him the Engagement (1647); shifted to Royalist side (1647); joined Prince Charles in Holland and accompanied him to battle of Worcester, where he was captured (1651); imprisoned (1651–60). As secretary of state for Scottish affairs (1660–80), became virtual ruler of Scotland; made his object the bringing to the crown of absolute power of church and state in Scotland; persecuted Covenanters; goaded peasants of west country into rebellion (1666); drilled Episcopal church into submission; held seat in the Cabal ministry; aroused hatred of both countries by his ruthlessness, arrogance, and debauched life. His brother ¶Charles (d. 1691), 3d Earl of Lauderdale, assisted him in management of Scottish affairs (1674–80) and succeeded him as earl (1682).

Maitland, Edward. 1824–1897. English mystic. Published autobiographical *The Pilgrim and the Shrine* (1867); collaborated with Anna Kingsford (*q.v.*) in *Keys of the Creeds* (1875) and *The Perfect Way* (1882); with her, founded Hermetic Society (1884).

Maitland, Frederic William. 1850–1906. English legal historian. Reader (1884), professor of English law (1888), Cambridge; a founder (1887) of Selden Society for study of history of English law and edited several volumes for it. With Sir Frederick Pollock wrote *History of English Law Before the Time of Edward I* (1895), standard authority on the subject; author also of *Domesday Book and Beyond* (1897), *Roman Canon Law in the Church of England* (1898), *English Law and the Renaissance* (1901), etc.

Maizières, Philippe de. See MÉZIÈRES.

Majano, Benedetto da. See BENEDETTO DA MAIANO.

Majd ad-Dīn. See under IBN AL-ATHĪR.

Ma·jor \'mā-jər\, Charles. *Pseudonym* Sir Edwin Cas·ko·den \kas-'kōd-ᵊn\. 1856–1913. American novelist, b. Indianapolis. Practiced law, Shelbyville, Ind. (from 1877). Author of *When Knighthood Was in Flower* (1898), *Dorothy Vernon of Haddon Hall* (1902), *A Gentle Knight of Old Brandenburg* (1909), *The Little King* (1910), *The Touchstone of Fortune* (1912), etc.

Ma·jor \'mä-yōr\, Georg. 1502–1574. German Lutheran theologian. Court preacher (1537–45), dean of theological faculty (1558–74), Wittenberg. Expounded doctrine (Majorism) that good works are necessary to salvation as evidence of vital faith.

Ma·jor \'mā-jər\ *or* **Ma·ir** \'mā-ər, 'ma(ə)r, 'me(ə)r\, John. 1469–1550. Scottish Scholastic. Professor at Glasgow (1518), St. Andrews (1522); taught Patrick Hamilton, George Buchanan, John Knox; provost of St. Salvator's Coll., St. Andrews (1533–50). Maintained doctrinal position of Rome and the Scotist position that civil authority was derived from popular will; approved Gallicanism and reform of ecclesiastical abuses; one of last eminent Scholastic teachers.

Ma·jor·elle \må-yȯ-rel\, Louis. 1859–1926. French cabinetmaker. Trained as painter; took over management of his father's cabinetmaking shop in Nancy (1879); designed and produced (from 1890) elegant furniture in Art Nouveau style, reaching epitome of his style in a graceful writing desk (1899–1902).

Ma·jo·ri·an \mə-'jōr-ē-ən\. *Lat.* Julius Valerius Ma·jo·ri·a·nus \mə-ˌjōr-ē-'ā-nəs\. d. 461 A.D. Roman emperor in the West (457–461). Made emperor by Ricimer; won battle (458) over Vandals on coast of Campania; lost fleet off Spain (460); promulgated a number of laws for the reform of the empire; forced to abdicate and executed five days later on Ricimer's orders.

Ma·jum·dar \mə-'jəm-dər\, Dhirenda Nath. 1903–1960. Indian anthropologist. Founder (1947) and editor of journal *Eastern Anthropologist;* made studies of tribes of India, esp. the Khāsi. Author of *Fortunes of a Primitive Tribe* (1944), *The Affairs of a Tribe* (1950), *Race Realities in Cultural Gujarat* (1950), *Caste and Communication in an Indian Village* (1958), *Himalayan Polyandry* (1962).

Ma·ka·ren·ko \(ˌ)mə-'kår-yin-kə\, Anton Semyonovich. 1888–1939. Soviet social worker and educator. Organized Gorky Colony for indigent children (1920s); director (from 1931) of Dzerzhinsky Commune, a penal institution for young offenders. His books included an account of his work at Gorky Colony *Putevka v zhizn* (1933–35), a guide to child raising *Kniga dlya roditeley* (1937), and several works on education.

Ma·kar·ios III \mä-'kär-yȯs, *Angl* mə-'kär-ē-ˌōs, -'kar-\. *Orig.* Mikhail Khristodolou Mous·kos \'mō-skȯs\. 1913–1977. Cypriot prelate and politician. Ordained priest (1946); bishop of Kition (1948); archbishop and primate of Orthodox church of Cyprus (from 1950). A leader in movement seeking *énosis* (union) with Greece; dropped demands for *énosis* and accepted compromise that led to Cyprian independence (1959). First president of Republic of Cyprus (1959–77); worked for peace between Greek and Turkish communities in Cyprus.

Ma·ka·rov \(ˌ)mə-'kå-rəf\, Stepan Osipovich. 1849–1904. Russian admiral. Distinguished himself in Russo–Turkish War (1877–78); vice admiral and commander of Baltic fleet (1897); commanded Russian naval forces in Far East (1904); lost on flagship *Petropavlovsk* when it was blown up by a mine.

Ma·kart \'mä-kärt\, Hans. 1840–1884. Austrian painter. Known for his exuberant historical paintings full of pageantry, including *Caterina Cornaro* (1873), *Triumph of Ariadne* (1873), *Entry of Charles V into Antwerp* (1878).

Ma·ka·ry \(ˌ)mə-'kår-i\. *Lat.* Ma·car·i·us \mə-'kar-ē-əs, -'kär-\. c.1482–1564. Russian prelate. Archbishop of Novgorod (1526); metropolitan of Moscow and primate of Russian Orthodox church (1542–64). Worked to combine powers of church and state under an autocratic czar; implemented ideology of a Pan-Russian Christendom that would establish Moscow as successor to Rome and Constantinople in religious primacy; codified Orthodox law and liturgy; directed synods of 1547 and 1549 that canonized over 40 Russian saints and centralized local devotions; established first printing press in Russia; composed the first *Minei-Cetii* (mementos of Russian saints for daily meditation and devotion) and *Stepennaya Kniga* (history of Russian ruling families); urged Ivan IV to invade Eastern territories.

Ma·kem·ie \mə-'kem-ē, -'kā-mē\, Francis. c.1658–1707 or 1708. American clergyman, b. County Donegal, Ireland. Ordained Presbyterian minister

(1682); to America (1683). Founded first Presbyterian church in America (1683, at Snow Hill, Md.); evangelist (1683–98); settled in eastern Virginia (1699); organized first American presbytery (1706). Regarded as founder of Presbyterianism in America.

Ma·ła·chow·ski \mȧ-lȧ-ˈk̲ôf-skē\, Stanisław. 1736–1809. Polish politician. Named marshal (speaker) of the Sejm (1788); presided over historic Four Years' Sejm (1788–92); prime force behind liberal constitution of 1791; president of senate of Duchy of Warsaw (1807–09).

Mal·a·chy \ˈmal-ə-kē\. Saint. *Ir. Gael.* Máel Máedoc Úa Mor·gair \ˌü-ə-ˈmȯr-ˌgȯir\. 1094?–1148. Irish prelate and reformer. Ordained (1119); as vicar in Armagh (1120–c.22), persuaded church to accept Gregory VII's reforms; restored abbey of Bangor while bishop of Down (1123?–24); bishop of Connor (1124–c.27); abbot of Iveragh (1127–32). Archbishop of Armagh (1132–36); again bishop of Down (1136); journeyed to Rome (1139); died at Clairvaux in arms of St. Bernard, his future biographer. Promoted reform of Irish dioceses; founded (1142) Mellifont, first Cistercian abbey in Ireland; introduced Roman liturgy and a regular hierarchy into the Irish church. Canonized (1199).

Malakoff, Duc de. See Aimable PÉLISSIER.

Ma·la·las \mə-ˈlā-ləs\, John. c.491–c.578. Byzantine historian. Author of a chronicle of world history notable esp. because written in vulgar language for instruction of monks and common people.

Mal·a·mud \ˈmal-ə(ˌ)məd\, Bernard. 1914–1986. American writer, b. New York City. Taught at Oregon State U. (1949–61), Bennington Coll. (1961–86). In novels and short stories combined realism and symbolism to portray commonplace lives. Novels included *The Natural* (1952), *The Assistant* (1957), *The Fixer* (1966, Pulitzer Prize and National Book Award), *The Tenants* (1971). Short story collections included *The Magic Barrel* (1958, National Book Award), *Idiots First* (1963), and *Rembrandt's Hat* (1973).

Ma·lan \mə-ˈlan, -ˈlän\, Daniel François. 1874–1959. South African politician. Dutch Reformed minister (1905); involved in Afrikaans language movement; entered Parliament (1918). As minister of interior (1924–33), secured recognition of Afrikaans as an official language replacing Dutch and instituted laws establishing South African nationality and flag. Founded (1934) Purified Nationalist party which became official opposition; with J.B.M. Herzog, formed reunited Nationalist party (1939). Prime minister (1948–54), forming the first exclusively Afrikaner government; instituted policy of apartheid; paved way for establishment of republic.

Malan, François Stephanus. 1871–1941. South African politician. A leader of political party Afrikaner Bond; supported British offer of reconciliation after Boer War; minister of education (1910–21); acting prime minister (1918–19); supporter of Afrikaner political rights.

Malaparte, Curzio. See Kurt SUCKERT.

Ma·la·te·sta \ˌmä-lä-ˈtes-tä\. Italian family of Rimini, prominent from the 13th to the 16th century, and including: Malatesta da Ve·ruc·chio \dä-vā-ˈrük-kyō\ (d. 1312), expelled Ghibellines (1295) and became lord of the city; placed in Hell (*Inferno*) by Dante. His son ¶Gianciotto (d. 1304), husband and murderer of Francesca (see under POLENTA family), whose love for Gianciotto's brother Paolo was told by Dante. ¶Carlo (1364?–1429) governed Milan for a time; supported Pope Gregory XII; man of letters and patron of the arts. His nephew ¶Sigismondo Pandolfo (1417–1468), patron of art and letters and accomplished soldier; made war against the pope and was excommunicated (1460); defeated (1462) by forces of Pius II and lost much territory. His grandson ¶Pandolfo (1475–1534), last of the line to hold Rimini.

Malbodius, Jan. See Jan GOSSAERT.

Mal·bone \ˈmȯl-ˌbōn\, Edward Greene. 1777–1807. American painter, b. Newport, R.I. Considered greatest American miniaturist; his portraits of New England personalities admired for their delicate drawing and rich coloring.

Mal·colm \ˈmal-kəm\. Name of four kings of Scotland:

Malcolm I Mac·Don·ald \mək-ˈdän-əld\. d. 954. King (943–954). Given Cumbria by West Saxon king Edmund I (945); lost Northumbria (954).

Malcolm II Mac·ken·neth \mə-ˈken-əth\. c.953–1034. King (1005–34). Grandson of Malcolm I; annexed Lothian and Cumbria north of the Solway to Scotland; pledged allegiance to Canute (1031).

Malcolm III Mac·Dun·can \mək-ˈdəŋ-kən\. *Surnamed* Can·more \ˈkan-ˌmō(ə)r, -ˌmȯ(ə)r\. c.1031–1093. King (1058–93). Son of Duncan I; with help of Siward defeated (1054) and killed Macbeth (1057); m. (1070) Margaret of Scotland (*q.v.*); did homage to William the Conqueror (1072); carried on war with England; with Margaret, started transition from Celtic culture and Columban religious rites to feudal system and Roman ritual; killed while raiding Northumberland.

Malcolm IV. 1142–1165. King (1153–65). Succeeded his grandfather David I; surrendered Northumberland and Cumberland to Henry II of England.

Malcolm X \-ˈeks\. *Muslim name* el-Hajj Ma·lik el-Sha·bazz \el-ˈhaj-mə-ˈlēk-el-shə-ˈbaz\. *Orig.* Malcolm Little. 1925–1965. American religious leader, b. Omaha, Neb. While imprisoned for robbery (1946–52) converted to Black Muslim faith and changed his name; rose in Black Muslim organization, becoming (1963) its first "national minister"; brilliant orator, preached black separatism and nationalism and pride in race and racial achievements. Broke with Black Muslims and formed own religious group called Muslim Mosque, Inc. (1964); founded Organization of Afro-American Unity (1964); converted to orthodox Islām, softened his separatist views, and worked for social reforms; assassinated in Harlem. Author of *The Autobiography of Malcolm X* (1965).

Mal·czew·ski \mäl-ˈchef-skē\, Antoni. 1793–1826. Polish poet. Chief work, narrative poem *Marja* (1825).

Male·branche \mȧl-brä^{n}sh\, Nicolas de. 1638–1715. French philosopher. Entered Congregation of the Oratory (1660); ordained (1664); engaged in philosophical controversies, esp. with Arnauld and Bossuet. Principal disciple of Descartes; attempted to synthesize Cartesianism with Neoplatonism and thought of St. Augustine; his philosophical system embodied the doctrine that the mind cannot have knowledge of anything external to itself except through its relation to God. Chief work *De la recherche de la verité* (1674–78); also wrote *Traité de la nature et de la grâce* (1680), *Méditations chrétiennes* (1683), *Traité de morale* (1684), *Entretiens sur la métaphysique et la religion* (1688).

Males·herbes \mȧl-zerb\, Chrétien-Guillaume de La·moi·gnon de \də-lȧm-wȧn-yō^{n}-də-\. 1721–1794. French politician. Son of Guillaume de Lamoignon; made counsellor to Parlement of Paris (1744); president of Cour des Aides (1750); director of the press (1750–63); instrumental in securing publication of the *Encyclopédie;* banished (1771–74); secretary of state for royal household (1775–76); as minister of state supported Turgot's reforms (1787–88). Took no part in early stages of Revolution; helped conduct defense of Louis XVI (1792); arrested (1793) and tried for treason, executed.

Ma·let \mȧ-le\, Claude-François de. 1754–1812. French general. Entered army (1771); in Revolutionary and Napoleonic armies; attempted coup d'état against Napoléon that almost succeeded (Oct. 22–23, 1812); court-martialled and shot.

Ma·le·vich \(ˌ)məl-ˈyāv-yich\, Kazimir Severinovich. 1878–1935. Russian painter. Founded Suprematist school of abstract art (1913); his paintings included *Black Square on White* (1913), *White on White* (1918). Published his theory of art in *Die gegenstandslose Welt* (1926).

Mal·fat·ti \mäl-ˈfät-tē\, Gian Francesco. 1731–1807. Italian mathematician. Known for proposing (1802) and solving Malfatti's problem which is to inscribe in a given triangle three circles each tangent to the other two and to two sides of the triangle.

Malhār Rāo Holkar. See HOLKAR.

Mal·her·be \mə-ˈler-bə\, Daniel François. 1881–1969. South African writer. Professor of literature, Bloemfontein (1918–42); helped establish Afrikaans as cultural language of South Africa. Author of poetry, drama, and esp. novels as *Vergeet nil* (1913), *Saul* (trilogy, 1933–37), *Die Meulenaar* (1936).

Mal·herbe \mȧ-lerb\, François de. 1555–1628. French poet. Court poet to Henry IV and Louis XIII; composed odes, sonnets, and other lyrics stressing form, restraint, and purity of diction; prepared way for French classicism.

Mā·lik ibn An·as \ˈmäl-ik-ˌib-ə-nan-ˈas\. *In full* Abū ʿAbd Allāh Mālik ibn Anas ibn al-Ḥārith al-Aṣbaḥī. c.715–795. Muslim theologian. Passed most of life in Medina; noted as Islāmic jurist and founder of Mālikī school; flogged for declaring loyalty to caliph not a religious obligation. Author of *Muwaṭṭa'*, first compendium of Islāmic law.

Ma·lik-Shāh \ma-ˌlik-ˈshä\. 1055–1092. Sultan of Seljuq Turks (1073–92). Son of Alp-Arslan; affairs ably administered by his vizier, Niẓām al-Mulk; ruled an extensive empire, Seljuqs reaching zenith of power; conquered Mesopotamia and Azerbaijan, acquired Syria and Palestine, established a measure of control over Mecca, Medina, Yemen, and Persian Gulf territories; during his reign, fraternity of Assassins founded (see ḤASAN-E ṢABBĀḤ); calendar reformed (1079) at his suggestion by group of astronomers including Omar Khayyám.

Ma·lin·ov·sky \məl-yin-ˈôf-skəi\, Rodion Yakovlevich. 1898–1967. Soviet marshal. General during World War II; commanded on Stalingrad (1942) and southwestern (1943) fronts; made marshal (1944); head of all Soviet land forces (1956); minister of defense (1957–67).

Ma·li·now·ski \ˌmal-ə-ˈnȯf-skē, ˌmäl-, -ˈnȯv-\, Bronisław Kasper. 1884–1942. British anthropologist, b. Poland. Founder of social anthropology. Did field research in New Guinea (1914), Trobriand Islands (1915–18), Africa (1930s); reader in social anthropology (1924–27), professor (1927), U. of London. To U.S. (1938); at Yale (from 1939). Author of *Argonauts of the Western Pacific* (1922), *Myth in Primitive Psychology* (1926), *Crime and Custom in Savage Society* (1926), *Sex and Repression in Savage Society* (1927), *The Sexual Life of Savages in N.W. Melanesia* (1929), *A Scientific Theory of Culture* (1944), etc.

Malintzin. See MARINA.

Ma·li·pie·ro \ˌmä-lēp-ˈye-rō\, Gian Francesco. 1882–1973. Italian composer. Professor (1932) and director (1939–52), Venice Conservatory; edited Monteverdi's works (1926–42) and directed edition of Vivaldi's instrumental works (1947–72). His works influenced by pre-Romantic music and characterized by contrapuntal style and tonality based on diatonic material. His compositions included operas *L'orfeide* (1918–22), *San Francesco d'Assisi*

(1922), *Torneo notturno* (1929), *La favola del figlio cambiato* (1934), *I capricci di Callot* (1942), *Venere prigioniera* (1955); orchestral works as 11 sinfonias, 6 piano and 2 violin concertos, *Impressioni dal vero* (1910–22), *Pause del silenzio* (1917), *Fantasie di ogni giorno* (1953), *Notturno di canti e balli* (1957); choral works as *La Passione* (1935); chamber and instrumental music.

Mal·lar·mé \má-lȧr-mā\, Stéphane. 1842–1898. French poet. Taught English in provincial schools (1863–71) and in Paris (1871–94); a leader of the Symbolist movement. Author of *L'Après-midi d'un faune* (1876), *Poésies* (1887), *Vers et prose* (1893), *Un Coup de dés jamais n'abolira le hasard* (1897), etc.; translator of poems of Edgar Allan Poe (1888).

Mal·let \'mal-ət\, David. *Orig. surname* Mal·loch \'mal-ək, -ək\. 1705?–1765. Scottish poet. Gained reputation with ballad *William and Margaret* (1723); wrote, with James Thomson, *The Masque of Alfred* (1740, music by Thomas Arne), containing patriotic song "Rule Britannia"; also wrote poems, including *The Excursion* (1728) and *The Hermit* (1747).

Mal·lon \'mal-ən\, Mary. *Known as* Typhoid Mary. 1870?–1938. American typhoid carrier. Herself immune to typhoid, spread the disease while working as a cook in New York City area (from c.1904); institutionalized on North Brother Island, N.Y.C. (from 1914).

Mal·lo·ry \'mal-(ə-)rē\, Stephen Russell. 1813?–1873. American politician, b. Trinidad. To U.S. as a child. U.S. senator from Florida (1851–61); secretary of the navy, Confederate States of America (1861–65).

Mal·lo·wan \'mal-,ō-ən\, Sir Max Edgar Lucien. 1904–1978. English archaeologist. m. (1930) Agatha Christie. Directed excavations at Chaldean-Babylonian city of Ur (1925–30, with Leonard Woolley), Nineveh (1931–32, with R.C. Thompson), Tell Brak (1937–38), Nimrud (1949–58); professor, U. of London (1947–62); editor of Near Eastern and Western Asiatic series of Penguin Books (1948–65).

Malmesbury, Earl of. See James HARRIS.

Malmesbury, William of. See WILLIAM of Malmesbury.

Malm·ström \'mȧlm-strœm\, Bernhard Elis. 1816–1865. Swedish poet and critic. Known for his romance *Hvi suckar det så tungt uti skogen?* (1839) and elegy *Angelika* (1840).

Ma·lone \mə-'lōn\, Dumas. 1892–1986. American biographer, b. Coldwater, Miss. Taught at Yale U., Columbia U., and U. of Virginia. Regarded as foremost authority on Thomas Jefferson; author of comprehensive six-volume biography *Jefferson and His Time* (1948–81). Edited *Dictionary of American Biography* and *Political Science Quarterly* (1953–58).

Malone, Edmond. 1741–1812. Irish scholar. Settled in London (1777); member of Samuel Johnson's club; aided Boswell in revising *The Life of Samuel Johnson;* published (1778) "An Attempt to Ascertain the Order in Which the Plays of Shakespeare Were Written," his conclusions for most part still accepted; published own edition of Shakespeare (11 vols., 1790) and left to James Boswell the younger materials for a new octavo edition (Third Variorum Edition, 21 vols., 1821). Among first to detect Rowley forgeries of Chatterton and Ireland forgeries of Shakespeare mss.; edited works of Dryden (1800). The Malone Society (founded 1907) was named for him.

Malone, Kemp. 1889–1971. American philologist, b. Minter, Miss. Taught at Johns Hopkins (1924–56); cofounder of *American Speech;* etymologist for *American College Dictionary* (1947) and *Random House Dictionary* (1966). Author of *Literary History of England* (with others, 1948), *Chapters on Chaucer* (1951), *Studies in Heroic Legend* (1959).

Mal·o·ry \'mal-(ə-)rē\, Sir Thomas. fl. 1470. English writer. Author of English prose epic *Morte Darthur* (finished between March 1469 and March 1470; printed by Caxton, 1485), eight Arthurian romances chiefly translated from French sources in direct, idiomatic, elevated style. Identified by George Lyman Kittredge with Sir Thomas Malory (d. 1471), knight of Newbold Revell in Warwickshire, who was a retainer of Richard Beauchamp, Earl of Warwick, and who, as a result of quarrels with a neighboring priory, was imprisoned.

Ma·lou·et \mȧl-we\, Pierre-Victor. Baron. 1740–1814. French politician. Governor of French Guiana (1776–78); member of Constituent Assembly; defended royalist cause, fled from France (1792). Returned to France (1803) and was appointed commissary general of marine at Antwerp; councilor of state (1810); minister of marine (1814).

Mal·pi·ghi \mäl-'pē-gē\, Marcello. 1628–1694. Italian anatomist. Professor at Pisa (1656–59) and Messina (1662–66); personal physician to Pope Innocent XII (1691). Because of early use of microscope in biological studies, called founder of microscopic anatomy; studied structure of secreting glands; discovered capillary circulation in the lung of the frog (1661), the deeper portion of the epidermis known as the Malpighian layer, loops of capillaries (or Malpighian tufts) in the kidney, and masses of adenoid tissue (or Malpighian corpuscles) in the spleen; described taste buds, structure of human lung, development of the chick, structure of the brain and spinal cord, and the metamorphosis of the silkworm.

Mal·raux \mȧl-rō\, André-Georges. 1901–1976. French novelist. Involved in revolutionary movements while on archaeological expeditions in Indochina (1922–29); colonel in Republican air force during Spanish Civil War; with French Resistance during World War II; became supporter of Charles de Gaulle (1945); minister of cultural affairs (1958–69). Author of novels *Les Conquérants* (1928), *La Voie royale* (1930), *La Condition humaine* (1933), *Le Temps du mépris* (1935), *L'Espoir* (1937), *Les Noyers de l'Altenburg* (1943); art criticism *Psychologie de l'art* (1947–49), *Les Voix du silence* (1951), *Le Musée imaginaire de la sculpture mondiale* (1952–54); *Antimémoires* (memoirs, 1967) and *Les Chênes qu'on abat* (on his last conversation with de Gaulle, 1971).

Mal·te-Brun \mȧl-tə-brœⁿ\, Conrad. *Orig.* Malte Conrad Bruun \'brün\. 1775–1826. French geographer, b. Denmark. Banished from Denmark because of sympathy with French Revolution (1800); settled in Paris; founder of *Annales des voyages* (1808); author of *Précis de la géographie universelle* (1810–29).

Mal·thus \'mal-thəs\, Thomas Robert. 1766–1834. English economist. Curate at Albury, Surrey (1798); professor at East India Company's college at Haileybury (1805–34). Aroused controversy by his argument in *An Essay on the Principle of Population* (1798) that population when unchecked tends to increase in a geometric ratio while means of subsistence tend to increase only in an arithmetic ratio and that preventive checks on increase of population are necessary as an alternative to the exclusive operation of positive checks, such as overcrowding, disease, war, poverty, and vice; in second edition (1803), documented his argument, relinquished question of mathematical ratios, recognized influence of moral restraint as a preventive check, remained pessimistic of possibilities of future progress of mankind. Author also of *Principles of Political Economy* (1820).

Ma·lus \mȧl-üs\, Étienne-Louis. 1775–1812. French engineer and physicist. Military engineer (from 1796); with Napoléon's expedition to Egypt and Syria (1798–1801). Made researches in optics; discovered polarization of light by reflection (1808); won prize from the Institute with memoir on the theory of double refraction of light in crystalline substances (1810).

Mal·vy \mȧl-vē\, Louis-Jean. 1875–1949. French politician. Radical Socialist member of Chamber of Deputies (1906 ff.); minister of commerce (1913–14), of the interior (1914); forced to resign after Clemenceau's attacks upon his position against defeatists (1917). Accused of treason; acquitted by the Senate assembled as a high court but banished for five years for laxity in performance of his duties as minister of the interior (1918). Again member of Chamber of Deputies (1924–40) and minister of the interior (1926).

Mälzel, Johann Nepomuk. See MAELZEL.

Mamaea, Julia. See under JULIA MAESA.

Ma·me·li \mä-'me-lē\, Goffredo. 1827–1849. Italian poet and patriot. Volunteer under Garibaldi in Lombardy (1848); killed during defense of Rome against French army. Author of Italian national anthem "Fratelli d'Italia" (1847, music by Michele Novaro).

Ma·mer·ti·nus \,mā-mər-'tī-nəs, ,mam-ər-\, Claudius. 4th century A.D. Roman politician. Consul (362 A.D.); later governor of Italy, Africa, and Illyria; career ended by embezzlement charge (368). Author of panegyric on Emperor Julian delivered at Constantinople when Mamertinus was elevated to consulship.

Mam·lūk \'mam-,lük\. *Also spelled* Mam·e·luke \'mam-ə-,lük\. Name of dynasty of Central Asian slave origin which ruled in Egypt and Syria (1250–1517); dynasty reached peak of power during the Turkish or Baḥrī period (1250–1382), esp. under sultans Baybars I (*q.v.*) and al-Malik an-Nāṣir (see NĀṢIR); corruption and decline in power set in during Circassion or Burjī period (1382–1517) until the dynasty was subjugated by the Ottoman empire.

Ma'·mūn, al- \al-ma-'mün\. *More completely* Abū al-'Abbās 'Abd Allāh al-Ma'mūn. 786–833. Seventh 'Abbāsid caliph (813–833). Son of Harūn ar-Rashīd; gained throne by defeating his half-brother al-Amīn; captured Baghdad (813); attempted to reconcile Sunnites and Shi'ites; renowned patron of philosophy and astronomy; reign disturbed because of his imposition of Mu'tazilite doctrine on his subjects.

Ma·nas·seh \mə-'nas-ə\. *Gr.* Ma·nas·ses \-,ēz\. d. 639? B.C. King of Judah (692?–?639 B.C.). Son of Hezekiah; encouraged alien cults of Assyria; for some time captive in Babylon. The *Prayer of Manasses* (Old Testament Apocrypha) attributed to Manasseh when in prison.

Manasseh ben Is·ra·el \-ben-'iz-rā-əl, -'iz-rē-əl\. 1604–1657. Dutch Jewish theologian and cabalist. Rabbi at Amsterdam (from 1622); set up first Hebrew printing press in Holland (1626); in England (1655–57) petitioning Cromwell for abolition of legislation excluding Jews from England. Author of *El conciliador* (in Spanish, a harmony of the Pentateuch; 1632), *De la fragilidad humana* (1642), *Esperança de Israel* (1650), *Vindiciae judaeorum* (1656).

Ma·nas·ses \mə-'nas-ˌēz\, Constantine. d. 1187. Byzantine prelate and historian. Metropolitan of Naupactus; author of a world chronicle (to 1081) in political verse.

Mance \'mans\, Sir Henry Christopher. 1840–1926. English electrical engineer. With Persian Gulf Telegraph Dept. of government of India (1863–85). Invented the heliograph and a method of locating faults in submarine cables.

Mance \mä^{n}s\, Jeanne. 1606–1673. French philanthropist. Resident in Canada (from 1641); founded (1644) Hôtel Dieu, Montreal.

Manchester, Earls and dukes of. See MONTAGU.

Manchu. Chinese dynasty. See CH'ING.

Man·ci·ni \män-'chē-nē\, Olympe. Comtesse de Sois·sons \swȧ-sō^{n}\. 1639–1708. French noblewoman, of Italian descent. Niece of Cardinal Mazarin, wife (from 1657) of Eugène-Maurice de Savoie-Carignan, mother of Prince Eugene, mistress of Louis XIV; fled France after being charged with complicity in murder and black-magic scandal (Affair of the Poisons).

Mancini, Pasquale Stanislao. 1817–1888. Italian politician. Deputy in parliament of Naples (1848–49); fled to Turin (1849) after revolutionary activities; professor of international law, U. of Turin (1849 ff.). Member of Italian parliament (from 1861); minister of justice (1876–78), of foreign affairs (1881–85); concluded Triple Alliance (1882); accomplished occupation of Eritrea (1884–85).

Man·ci·ni-Ma·za·ri·ni \mä^{n}-sē-nē-mȧ-zȧ-rē-nē\, Louis-Jules. Duc de Ni·vernais \nē-ver-ne\. 1716–1798. French soldier and diplomat. Fought in Italy (1733) and Bohemia (1740); ambassador at Rome (1748–52), Berlin (1756), and London (1762–63); negotiated Treaty of Paris (Feb. 1763); minister of state in Necker's cabinet (1787).

Man·co Ca·pac \'mäŋ-(ˌ)kō-'kä-ˌpäk\. *Inca* Man·qo Qha·paq. fl. c.1200 A.D. Traditional founder of Inca dynasty in Peru. Supposed to have consolidated Indians (Quechuas) of highlands of Peru.

Manco In·ca Yu·pan·qui \-'iŋ-kə-yü-'päŋ-kē\. *Inca* Man·qo 'In·ka Yu·pan·ki. d. 1545. Inca ruler. Brother of Huáscar; recognized by Pizarro after death of Atahualpa and Huáscar (1533) and crowned at Cuzco. Raised army and attacked Spaniards (1536); defeated (1537) and fled to mountains.

Man·del \mä^{n}-del\, Georges. *Orig.* Louis-Georges Roth·schild \rȯt-shēld\. 1885–1944. French politician. *Chef de cabinet* to Clemenceau (1917–20); deputy in National Assembly (1919–24, 1928–40); minister of colonies (1938–40), of interior in Reynaud cabinet (Mar.–July 1940); arrested (1941) and executed by Vichy government.

Man·del·stam \mən-dyil-'shtȧm\, Osip Yemilyevich. 1891–1938. Russian poet. Best known for his classically restrained, terse, resonant verse collected as *Kamen* (1913) and *Tristiya* (1922); also produced novellas and translations.

Man·der \'män-dər\, Karel van. 1548–1606. Dutch painter and writer. Best known work *Het Schilderboeck* (1604), a collection of biographical studies of painters of various epochs.

Man·de·ville \'man-də-ˌvil\, Bernard. 1670–1733. British philosopher and satirist, b. Holland. Settled in London in medical practice. Known as author of *The Fable of the Bees, or, Private Vices, Public Benefits* (1714; first published as *The Grumbling Hive,* 1705), a political satire in octosyllabic verse maintaining that every virtue is at bottom some form of selfishness; other works included *Free Thoughts on Religion, the Church and Natural Happiness* (1720), *A Letter to Dion* (1732), *An Enquiry into the Origin of Honour, and the Usefulness of Christianity in War* (1734).

Mandeville, Geoffrey de. 1st Earl of Es·sex \'es-iks\ (cr. 1141). d. 1144. English baron. Constable of the Tower (c.1130); gained vast lands and great power by betraying first King Stephen, then Matilda; raised rebellion; turned bandit in Fens, where he was fatally wounded. His son ¶William (d. 1189), 3d earl, went to England (1166) from court of Philip of Flanders, with whom he went on crusade (1177–78); attended Henry II faithfully through rebellion and French wars; chief justiciar under Richard I (1189).

Mandeville, Sir John. 14th century. Name assumed by unknown author of *The Voyage and Travels of Sir John Mandeville, Knight,* a book of travels written in French (c.1356) describing journeys in the East, including India and the Holy Land, combining geography with romance; the author borrowed travel accounts largely from works of others and may not have traveled at all; the identification with a physician of Liége, Jean de Bourgogne, is very uncertain.

Ma·nes \'mā-(ˌ)nēz\ *or* **Ma·ni** \'mä-nē\ *or* **Man·i·chae·us** \ˌman-ə-'kē-əs\. 216–276 or 277. Persian religious leader. Founder of Manichaeism. Preached (from 240) a system compounded of Zoroastrian dualism and Christian soteriology; active at court of Persian king Shāpūr I and on long journeys in Turkestan, India, and China; claimed to have received divine revelations and that he was the final prophet of God in the world. The Magians bitterly opposed his preaching and finally caused his condemnation and death. His works have been lost.

Ma·net \mȧ-ne\, Édouard. 1832–1883. French painter. Studied under Couture (1850–56); his style a mixture of realism and impressionistic technique; his depictions of nudes and casual city life often scandalized Paris; encouraged Monet and other Impressionists and was an important forerunner of Impressionism. His canvases included *Spanish Singer* (1860), *La Musique aux Tuileries* (1862), *Olympia* (1863), *Le Déjeuner sur l'herbe* (1863), *The Races at Longchamp, Paris* (1864), *The Fifer* (1866), *The Execution of the Emperor Maximilian of Mexico* (1867), *The Balcony* (1869), *The Studio in the Batignolles* (1870), *Boating* (1874), *The Plum* (1877), *Chez le Père Lathuille* (1879), *The Artist's Garden in Versailles* (1881), *A Bar at the Folies-Bergère* (1882).

Man·e·tho \'man-ə-ˌthō\ *or* **Man·e·thon** \-ˌthän\ *or* **Man·e·thos** \-ˌthäs\. 3d century B.C. Egyptian priest and historian. Author of a history of Egypt written in Greek, of which only fragments are extant.

Man·fa·lū·ṭī \ˌmän-fä-lü-'tē\, Muṣṭafā Luṭfī al-. 1876–1924. Egyptian writer. Pioneer of modern Arabic prose; his smooth and classical style exerted great influence on later Arabic writers. Best known for his collected essays *Nazarat* (1902–10) and *Mukhtarat* (1912), and short stories *'Abarat* (1946).

Man·fred \'man-ˌfred, -frəd\. c.1232–1266. King of Naples and Sicily (1258–66). Natural son of Emperor Frederick II; prince of Tarentum (1250–57); regent for Conradin in southern Italy (1254); crowned at Palermo (1258); excommunicated by Pope Alexander IV (1258); defeated papal forces and seized Tuscany; his dominions bestowed as papal fief on Charles of Anjou by Pope Urban IV; defeated and killed at Benevento.

Man·gan \'maŋ-gən\, James Clarence. 1803–1849. Irish poet. Author of *German Anthology* (1845); known esp. for "Dark Rosaleen," "O'Hussey's Ode to the Maguire," "Twenty Golden Years Ago," and the tragic autobiographical ballad "The Nameless One."

Man·gin \mä^{n}-zha^{n}\, Charles-Marie-Emmanuel. 1866–1925. French soldier. General of division (1914); commanded defense of Verdun (1916) and offensive along Chemin des Dames (1917); commanded 10th army in its counterattack at Villers-Cotterets (July 1918) which halted German advance. Member of Conseil Supérieur de la Guerre (from 1921).

Man·grai \'män-ˌgrī\. fl. 1287–1311. Thai ruler. Founder (1296) and ruler (1296–1311) of independent kingdom of Lan Na (in northwest region of present Thailand) and its capital Chiengmai.

Man·gu Khan \'maŋ-gü-'kän\. 1208–1259. Mongol khan (1251–59). Eldest son of Tolui and grandson of Genghis Khan; as a general of his uncle Ögödei conquered the Kipchaks (1237); sent his brother Hülegü (*q.v.*) to Persia to quell disturbances; with other brother Kublai conquered (1252–59) nearly all of China; died of dysentery on return from campaign; succeeded by Kublai.

Man·gun·ku·su·mo \ˌmäŋ-ˌgu̇n-kü-'sü-mō\, Tjipto. 1884–1942. Indonesian nationalist. A founder (1912) of socialist Indische Partij; worked for Indonesian independence from Dutch rule; became member of parliamentary body Volksraad (1918); helped found Partai Nasional Indonesia (1927); exiled for revolutionary activities (1927–38).

Manhae. See HAN Yong-un.

Mani *or* **Manichaeus.** See MANES.

Ma·nil·i·us \mə-'nil-ē-əs\, Gaius. 1st century B.C. Roman politician. Tribune of the people (67 B.C.); sponsor of Manilian law to recall Roman commanders in Asia and extend power of Pompey over all the East. Cicero supported the law in his oration *Pro lege Manilia.*

Manilius, Marcus. 1st century A.D. Roman poet. Nothing known of his life; author of poem on astrology called *Astronomica,* of which five books are extant.

Ma·nin \mä-'nēn\, Daniele. 1804–1857. Italian patriot and politician. Imprisoned for opposition to Austrian rule (1847–48); led patriotic movement in Venice (1848) as president of restored Republic of St. Mark; led defense of Venice against Austrian siege (Apr.–Aug. 1849); lived in exile (Paris, 1849–57).

Man·ing \'man-iŋ\, Frederick Edward. 1811–1883. New Zealand jurist, b. Ireland. To New Zealand (1824); settled among Maoris (1833), was adopted into a native tribe, and married a native. Judge of native land courts (1865–81). Author of *The History of the War in the North Against the Chief Heke* (1862) and *Old New Zealand* (1863).

Manini. See Francisco MARÍN.

Ma·niu \män-'yü\, Iuliu. 1873–1953. Romanian politician. Member of Hungarian parliament (1906–10); president (1918) of Transylvania Directing Council which proclaimed union with Romania. Member of Romanian parliament (1919–38); a founder (1926) and leader of the National Peasant party. Prime minister of Romania (1928–30, 1932–33); a leader of August 1944 coup which brought Romania into Allied camp; imprisoned on charge of espionage and treason (from 1947).

Man·ley \'man-lē\, Mary de la Rivière, *nee* Manley. 1663–1724. English writer. Decoyed into bigamous marriage with her cousin John Manley (c.1688; d. 1714); achieved literary triumph with *Secret Memoirs and Manners of Several Persons of Quality of both Sexes, from the New Atalantis* (1709), a scandalous chronicle involving Whig notables; arrested for libel but discharged (1710); succeeded Swift as editor of *Examiner* (1711); author of plays, including *Lucius* (1717), of *Memoirs of Europe* (1710), autobiography *The Adventures of Rivella* (1714), and *The Power of Love, in Seven Novels* (1720).

Man·ly \'man-lē\, John Matthews. 1865–1940. American philologist, b. Sumter Co., Ala. Professor of English, U. of Chicago (1898–1933). Author of *Some New Light on Chaucer* (1926), *Chaucer and the Rhetoricians* (1926); collaborator in many textbooks in English; editor of *Specimens of Pre-Shakespearean Drama* (1897) and *The Canterbury Tales* (1940). His brother ¶Charles Matthews (1876–1927), mechanical engineer, was associated with Samuel P. Langley in experiments with airplanes; designed light 5-cylinder radial gasoline engine for airplane use, regarded as first modern aircraft engine; took out about fifty patents on power generation and transmission systems.

Mann \'man\, Sir Donald D. 1853–1934. Canadian railroad builder, b. Acton, Ont. Partner of William Mackenzie (*q.v.*) in contracting firm (1886); had important part (from 1895) in building and organizing Canadian Northern R.R.

Mann \'män, *Angl* 'man\, Heinrich. 1871–1950. German writer. Brother of novelist Thomas Mann; exile in France (1933–40); interned (1940) but escaped to U.S. Author of novels *Im Schlaraffenland* (1900), *Professor Unrat* (1905; filmed as *Der blaue Engel,* 1928), *Die kleine Stadt* (1909), *Das Kaiserreich* trilogy (*Die Armen,* 1917; *Der Untertan,* 1918; *Der Kopf,* 1925), *Henri Quatre* (1935–38); collections of political essays *Macht und Mensch* (1919) and *Geist und Tat* (1931); plays.

Mann \'man\, Sir Horace. 1701–1786. English diplomat. British envoy at Florence, Italy (1740–86); friend and correspondent of Horace Walpole in thousands of letters avowedly written, on both sides, for publication.

Mann, Horace. 1796–1859. American educator, b. Franklin, Mass. Considered father of American public education. Practiced law (1823–37); member of Mass. legislature (1827–37). First secretary, Massachusetts Board of Education (1837–48); revolutionized public school organization and teaching; instrumental in establishing first normal school in U.S. (1839). Member, U.S. House of Representatives (1848–53). President, Antioch College (1852–59).

Mann, James Robert. 1856–1922. American politician, b. near Bloomington, Ill. Member, U.S. House of Representatives (1897–1922). His name is associated with important laws, including the Mann-Elkins Act (1910) for railroad rate regulation, the Mann Act (or White-slave-traffic Act, 1910), etc.

Mann, Thomas, *called* Tom. 1856–1941. English labor leader. Joined Amalgamated Society of Engineers (1881) and Socialist party (1885); president of Dockers' Union (1889–93) and leader, with John Burns, of great London dock strike of 1889; secretary of Independent Labour party (1894–97). Union organizer in Australia (1901–10); helped Ben Tillett found National Transport Workers' Federation (1910); a founding member (1920) of British Communist party.

Mann \'män, *Angl* 'man\, Thomas. 1875–1955. German novelist. Brother of Heinrich Mann; recipient of Nobel prize for literature (1929); refugee from Germany (1933); to U.S. (1938, naturalized 1944). Author of novels *Buddenbrooks* (1900), *Königliche Hoheit* (1909), *Der Zauberberg* (1924; *The Magic Mountain*), tetralogy *Joseph und seine Brüder* (*Die Geschichten Jaakobs,* 1933; *Der junge Joseph,* 1934; *Joseph in Ägypten,* 1936; *Joseph der Ernährer,* 1943), *Lotte in Weimar* (1939), *Doktor Faustus* (1947), *Die Bekenntnisse des Hochstaplers Felix Krull* (1954); novellas *Tonio Kröger* (1903), *Tristan* (1903), *Der Tod in Venedig* (1912), *Unordnung und frühes Leid* (1926), *Mario und der Zauberer* (1930), *Der Erwählte* (1951), *Die Betrogene* (1953); literary, philosophical, and political essays *Betrachtungen eines Unpolitischen* (1918), *Goethe und Tolstoi* (1921), *Die Forderung des Tages* (1930), *Leiden und Grösse der Meister* (1935), *Das Problem der Freiheit* (1939), *Ansprache im Goethejahr* (1949).

Man·ner·heim \'mán-nər-ˌhām\, Carl Gustaf Emil von. Baron. 1867–1951. Finnish soldier and politician. In Russian army (1889–1917), distinguished himself in Russo-Japanese War (1904–05) and rose to rank of lieutenant general. To Finland, where he took command of White Guard (1918) and suppressed Finnish Bolsheviks. Regent of Finland (1918–19). Chairman of council of defense (1931–39); field marshal (1933); planned and supervised construction of Mannerheim line of defense against Russia (1939–40; again from 1941); marshal of Finland (1942). President of Finland (1944–46).

Man·ner·ing \'man-ər-iŋ\, Mary. *Orig.* Florence Friend \'frend\. 1876–1953. American actress, b. London, England. Stage debut in Manchester and London (1892); to U.S. (1896) and appeared under Daniel Frohman's management; m. (1897; div. 1910) James K. Hackett; starred in *Janice Meredith, The Truants, A Man's World,* and *The Garden of Allah.*

Man·ners \'man-ərz\. Name of English family possessing earldom and dukedom of Rut·land \'rət-lənd\ and marquisate of Gran·by \'gran-bē\, including among its members: John (1721–1770), Marquis of Granby; soldier; M.P. (1741); colonel and, later, commander of Leicester "blues" (1745–59); commander in chief of British contingent in Germany during Seven Years' War (from 1759); led British cavalry to victory over French at Warburg (1760); repulsed French attacks on Vellinghausen (1761); commander in chief of the forces (1766); subject of Junius's invectives. His son ¶Charles (1754–1787), 4th duke (1779); M.P. (1774); protested against government policy of taxing American colonies (1775); lord privy seal in Pitt's ministry; lord lieutenant of Ireland (1784), advocated legislative union of Ireland with England.

His grandson ¶John James Robert (1818–1906), 7th duke (1888); a Conservative leader in Parliament (1841–88); a leader of Young England party (1843–47); held offices in Conservative ministries (between 1852 and 1892); postmaster general (1874–80, 1885–86); advocate of factory reform, general system of allotments, Irish disestablishment; made Baron Roos of Bel·voir \'rōs-əv-'bē-vər\ (1896). Author of *England's Trust and other Poems* (1841), *English Ballads and other Poems* (1850), and notes on Irish and Scottish tours (1848–49).

For Manners-Sutton branch, see Charles MANNERS-SUTTON.

Manners, John Hartley. 1870–1928. American playwright, b. London, England. Actor in London (1899–1902); to U.S. (1902). Author of *Peg o' My Heart* (1912), *Happiness* (1914), *The National Anthem* (1922).

Manners-Sut·ton \-'sət-ᵊn\, Charles. 1st Viscount Can·ter·bury \'kant-ə(r)-ˌber-ē, -b(ə-)rē\. 1780–1845. English politician. Tory M.P. (1806–35; speaker from 1817); created viscount (1835). His father ¶Charles (1755–1828), bishop of Norwich (1792–1805), archbishop of Canterbury (1805–28), and his uncle ¶Thomas (1756–1842), 1st Baron Manners, solicitor general (1802), lord chancellor of Ireland (1807–27), were cousins of Charles Manners, 4th Duke of Rutland (see MANNERS family). His son ¶John Henry Thomas (1814–1877), 3d Viscount Canterbury, was lieutenant governor of New Brunswick (1854–61), governor of Trinidad (1864–66), of Victoria, Australia (1866–73).

Man·nes \'man-əs\, David. 1866–1959. American musician and educator, b. New York City. Violinist; conductor of New York Symphony (1898–1912); founded (1912) Music School Settlement for Colored Children; with wife founded (1916) David Mannes School, later Mannes Coll. of Music; conducted Metropolitan Museum concerts (1918–47). His wife (m. 1898) ¶Clara, *nee* Damrosch (1869–1948), b. Breslau, Prussia (now Wrocław, Poland); daughter of Leopold Damrosch; to U.S. (1871); pianist, performed frequently with husband (1901–17); accompanied Kneisel Quartet, Pablo Casals, etc.; helped found David Mannes School (1916), codirector (1916–48).

Mann·hardt \'män-ˌhärt\, Wilhelm. 1831–1880. German ethnologist. Made studies of folklore and culture of ancient Germanic and Baltic peoples. Author of *Die Korndämonen* (1868) and *Wald- und Feld-kulte* (1875).

Mann·heim \'män-ˌhīm\, Karl. 1893–1947. German sociologist. Taught at Heidelberg (1926–30), Frankfurt am Main (1930–33), U. of London (1933–47). Known for his "sociology of knowledge," study of science as a social organization, work on problems of leadership and consensus. Wrote *Ideologie und Utopie* (1929) and *Freedom, Power, and Democratic Planning* (1950).

Man·ni·nen \'mán-ni-nen\, Otto. 1872–1950. Finnish poet and translator. Published *Säkeitä* (1905–10), *Virrantyven* (1925), *Matkamies* (1938), *Runoja* (1950), and translations of works of Homer, Sophocles, Goethe, Ibsen, Molière, and others.

Man·ning \'man-iŋ\, Henry Edward. 1808–1892. English prelate. Ordained in Church of England (1832); archdeacon of Chichester (1840–51). Became Roman Catholic (1851); founder and superior (1857–65) of the Oblates of St. Charles, London; archbishop of Westminster (1865); cardinal (1875). Vigorous builder of Catholic schools and institutions; Ultramontanist; intervened to end 1889 London dock strike. Author of *The Unity of the Church* (1842), *The Grounds of Faith* (1852), *The Eternal Priesthood* (1883), etc.

Manning, James. 1738–1791. American clergyman and educator, b. Piscataway, N.J. Ordained Baptist minister (1763); a founder and first president, Brown U. (1765–91). Chief founder of Warren Association (1767); member of Congress of the Confederation (1786).

Man·nix \'man-iks\, Daniel. 1864–1963. Australian prelate, b. Ireland. Ordained Roman Catholic priest (1890); professor (1891), president (1903–12), St. Patrick's College, Maynooth. Titular archbishop of Pharsalus (1912); to Australia as coadjutor archbishop (1913); archbishop of Melbourne (1917–63). Caused controversy by opposing conscription during World War I and advocating Irish independence; promoted Catholic Action and the Catholic social movement; founded 181 schools and 108 parishes.

Mann·li·cher \'män-lik-ər\, Ferdinand von. Ritter. 1848–1904. Austrian firearms designer. Joined Austrian Arms Co., Styr (1866); known for inventions in small arms, esp. Model 1885 Austrian service rifle (1884) and the cartridge clip (1885).

Man·nuc·ci \män-'nüt-chē\ *or* **Ma·nu·zio** \mä-'nüts-yō\, Aldo, *in full* Teobaldo. *Lat.* Aldus Ma·nu·tius \mə-'n(y)ü-sh(ē-)əs\. 1449–1515. Italian scholar, editor, and printer. Founder of the Aldine Press. Settled in Venice (1490); gathered group of compositors and Greek scholars; produced first printed editions of many Greek and Latin classics; his first dated book, Constantine Lascaris's *Erotemata* (March 1495); first to use italic type (in

Virgil edition of 1501); founded Aldine Academy of Hellenic scholars (by 1502); known esp. for his editions of Aristotle (5 vols., 1495–98), Aristophanes (1498), Francesco Colonna's *Hypnerotomachia Poliphili* (1499), Juvenal (1501), and (in 1502) Catullus, Lucan, Sophocles, Herodotus, Dante's *Divina commedia.* His son ¶Paolo, *Lat.* Paulus (1512–1574), succeeded to management of Aldine Press (1533); produced esp. Latin classics, notably works of Cicero; directed press for Accademia Veneta (1558–61); to Rome (1561) to establish Vatican press. His son ¶Aldo, *Lat.* Aldus, *called* the Younger (1547–1597), took over management of Aldine Press (1561); published his *Epitome orthographiae* (1575) and commentary on Horace's *Ars poetica* (1576); to Bologna (1585), published there his life of Cosimo de' Medici (1586); appointed director of Vatican press (1590).

Man·ny \'man-ē\, Sir Walter de. Baron de Manny. d. 1372. English military commander, b. Hainaut. To England in retinue of Philippa of Hainaut (1327); distinguished himself in service of Edward III against Scots, Flemings, and French; M.P. (intermittently from 1347); accompanied John of Gaunt in invasion of France (1369). Founder of house of Carthusian monks, Charterhouse, in London (1371).

Man·nyng \'man-iŋ\, Robert. *Also known as* Robert de Brun·ne \də-brün-nə\. fl. 1288–1338. English chronicler and poet. Gilbertine canon at Sempringham, Lincolnshire (c.1302–17). Author of *Handlyng Synne* (1300–c.07), a verse translation with his own additions of a French text *Manuel des Pechiez* (written c.1250–70), including metrical homilies and stories on Commandments, Seven Deadly Sins, and Sacraments, and depicting social life of time; author also of chronicle *The Story of Inglande,* translation in verse of Wace's *Brut* and French chronicle of Peter Langtoft.

Manoel do Nascimento, Francisco. See NASCIMENTO.

Ma·no·har \'mən-ə-hər\. fl. 1580–1620. Indian painter. Son of Basāvan; a leading miniaturist of the Mughal school of painting in India; known for his manuscript illustrations, portraits, animal studies.

Manolete. See Manuel RODRÍGUEZ SÁNCHEZ.

Man·ri·que \män-'rē-kä\, Gómez. c.1415–1490. Spanish soldier, dramatist, and poet. Prominent in rebellious outbreaks during reigns of John II and Henry IV; author of lyrics and political satires, and most notably of dramatic compositions which were precursors of later dramatic forms. His nephew ¶Jorge Manrique (1440?–1479) was author of lyrics, satires, and acrostics, and most notably of *Coplas por la muerte de su padre* (1492), an elegy in 40 stanzas on the death of his father.

Man·sa Mū·sā \'män-sä-mü-'sä\. d. 1332? A.D. Emperor of Mali. Grandson or grandnephew of Sundiata; ascended throne (1307); accompanied by a fabulously opulent retinue, made pilgrimage to Mecca by way of Cairo (1324); conquered Songhai kingdom; expanded trade; patron of arts, education, architecture; an efficient administrator, left his kingdom strong and prosperous.

Man·sart \mä^{n}-sȧr, *Angl* 'man-särt\, François, *in full* Nicolas-François. 1598–1666. French architect. Apprenticed to Salomon de Brosse; instrumental in establishment of classicism in French Baroque architecture; his designs notable for their subtlety, elegance, harmony; did not invent but popularized the mansard roof. His works included the churches of Sainte-Marie de Chaillot and Visitation de Sainte-Marie, the Hôtel de la Vrillière and Hôtel de Nevers in Paris, and several châteaux, esp. Balleroy and Maisons-Laffitte. His grandnephew ¶Jules Har·douin-Mansart \ȧr-dwa^{n}-\, *orig. (to 1668)* Hardouin (1646–1708), was building superintendent and architect of Louis XIV (from 1675); enlarged Château de Saint-Germain; built Château de Clagny (1676–1680); completed the Palace of Versailles begun by Le Vau. His other works included the dome of the Hôtel des Invalides, the Place Vendôme, the Place des Victoires at Paris, and several châteaux as Château de Dampierre, de Luneville, de Sagonne.

Mans·bridge \'mans-brij\, Albert. 1876–1952. English educator. Pioneer of adult education; founded Workers' Educational Association in England (1903) and Australia (1913) and served as its secretary (1903–15); president of World Association for Adult Education.

Man·sel \'man-səl\, Henry Longueville. 1820–1871. English philosopher and clergyman. Professor, Oxford (1866); dean of St. Paul's (1868). Maintained duality of consciousness as testifying to existence of self and external world; followed Sir William Hamilton in holding limitation of knowledge to the finite and conditioned. Author of article on metaphysics in 8th edition of *Encyclopaedia Britannica* (1857), *The Limits of Religious Thought* (1858), *The Philosophy of the Conditioned* (1866), *The Gnostic Heresies of the First and Second Centuries* (1875).

Mans·feld \'mäns-felt\, Peter Ernst von. Fürst. 1517–1604. German soldier. Served under Emperor Charles V and under Philip II of Spain; governor of Luxembourg and of Netherlands. His natural son ¶Graf Peter Ernst (1580–1626), German general, saw military service in Austria and Netherlands (1603–09); in Thirty Years' War, fought on Protestant side, leading attack against Austria (1625); defeated by Wallenstein at Dessau (1626).

Mansfield, Earl of. See William MURRAY.

Mans·field \'man(t)s-ˌfēld, 'manz-\, Joseph King Fenno. 1803–1862. American army officer, b. New Haven, Conn. Commissioned in engineers (1822); served through Mexican War; inspector general of the army with rank of colonel (1853–61); brigadier general (1861); charged with defense of Washington, D.C.; major general of volunteers (1862). Took command of XII Corps (Sept. 1862); killed at Antietam.

Mansfield, Katherine. *Orig.* Kathleen Beau·champ \'bē-chəm\. 1888–1923. British writer, b. New Zealand. m. 2d (1918) John Middleton Murry (*q.v.*). Author of short stories collected in *In a German Pension* (1911), *Prelude* (1918), *Je ne parle pas français* (1919), *Bliss* (1920), *The Garden Party* (1922), *The Doves' Nest* (1923), and *Something Childish* (1924). Her *Poems* (1923), *Journal* (1927), and *Letters* (1928) were collected and published after her death.

Mansfield, Richard. 1854–1907. American actor, b. Berlin, Germany, of Anglo-Dutch parentage. To U.S. (1872); on English stage (1877–82); on American stage (from 1882). Played leading roles in *Dr. Jekyll and Mr. Hyde* (1887), *Richard III* (1889), *Beau Brummell* (1890), *Merchant of Venice* (1893), *Cyrano de Bergerac* (1898); staged first American productions of *Arms and the Man* (1895), *The Devil's Disciple* (1897), *Peer Gynt* (1906).

Man·ship \'man-ˌship, -shəp\, Paul. 1885–1966. American sculptor, b. St. Paul, Minn. His works included marble portraits *Pauline Francis—Three Weeks Old* (1914) and *John D. Rockefeller* (1918), statue *Dancer and Gazelles* (1916), Prometheus Fountain at Rockefeller Plaza, N.Y.C. (1934), and Paul J. Rainey Memorial Gateway at Bronx Zoo, N.Y.C. (1934).

Man·so de Ve·las·co \'män-sō-t͟hā-b͟ā-'läs-kō\, José Antonio. Conde de Su·pe·run·da \sü-pā-'rün-dä\. 1688–1767. Spanish colonial administrator. Governor of Chile (1737–44); viceroy of Peru (1745–61).

Man·son \'man(t)-sən\, Sir Patrick. 1844–1922. Scottish parasitologist. To Amoy, China, as head of Baptist Missionary Hospital and engaged in private practice (1871); settled in Hong Kong (1883); instituted school of medicine which developed into university and medical school of Hong Kong. To London (1890); instrumental in foundation (1899) of London School of Tropical Medicine and taught there (to 1914). First to enunciate (1877–78) hypothesis that the mosquito was the host of the malarial parasite at one stage of its existence, and thus an active agent in spreading malaria. Called father of tropical medicine.

Man·stein \'män-shtīn\, Fritz Erich von. *Orig. surname* von Le·win·ski \fȯn-lā-'vin-skē\. 1887–1973. German army officer. Entered army (1905); planned assault against France in World War II (plan adopted Feb. 1940); captured Sevastopol (1942); field marshal (1942); commanded in Soviet Union (1942–44); imprisoned for war crimes (1945–53).

Man·ṣūr \man-'sür\. *Called* Us·tād Manṣūr \u̇s-'täd-\, *i.e.* Master Manṣūr. 17th century. Mughal painter. Court painter to Emperor Jahāngīr; known for his paintings of animals, birds, flowers.

Man·ṣūr, al- \ˌal-ˌman-'su̇(ə)r\. *Sometimes Anglicized as* Al·man·zor \al-'man-zər, -ˌzȯ(ə)r\ *or* Al·man·sor \-sər, -ˌsȯ(ə)r\. Arabic surname meaning "victorious," assumed by many Muslim princes.

Manṣūr, al-. *More completely* Abū Ja'far al-Manṣūr. *Also known as* al-Manṣūr al-'Abbāsī. between 709 and 714–775. Second 'Abbāsid caliph (754–775). Succeeded his brother as-Saffāḥ; crushed last remnants of Umayyad resistance; began construction of Baghdad (762), to which he transferred seat of government; patron of learning; firmly established new dynasty; encouraged translation of Greek and Latin classics into Arabic.

Manṣūr, Abū 'Āmir al-. *More completely* Muḥammad ibn Abū 'Āmir al-Manṣūr. c.938–1002. Muslim regent of Córdoba, Spain. Rose from humble professional letter writer to minister of finance under Caliph Ḥakam II; seized power as vizier under Hishām II (978), thereafter was virtual ruler of the caliphate; replaced Slavs in army with Berber and Christian mercenaries; victorious in campaigns against Christian kingdoms in north; as a result of triumphs assumed (981) honorific title al-Manṣūr bi-Allāh; adopted title al-Malik al-Karīm (994). Checked separatist movements in religion; extended and sustained power of Umayyad caliphate just before its decline; patronized learning and literature.

Manṣūr, Abū Yūsuf Ya'qūb al-. *More completely* Abū Yūsuf Ya'qūb ibn 'Abd al-Mu'min al-Manṣūr. c.1160–1199. Third ruler of Mu'minid dynasty (1184–99). Pacified rebellious Algerian tribes (1184–88); decisively defeated Alfonso VIII of Castile at Battle of Alarcos (1195); advanced to Madrid (1196); brought Mu'minid dynasty to height of power; built many public works.

Man·te·gaz·za \ˌmän-tā-'gät-tsä\, Paolo. 1831–1910. Italian physiologist and anthropologist. Professor at Pavia (1860–70) and at Florence (from 1870), where he founded Museum of Anthropology and Ethnology and journal *Archivo par l'antropologia e la etnografia.* His publications included works on the physiology of pleasure, pain, and love, spontaneous generation, physiognomy, and political treatises and fiction.

Man·te·gna \män-'ten-yä\, Andrea. 1431–1506. Italian painter and engraver. Chief master of Paduan school; adopted son and pupil of Francesco

Squarcione. To Mantua (1459) as protégé of Lodovico Gonzaga; called to Rome (1488–90) by Innocent VIII to decorate Belvedere Chapel. Among his paintings were frescoes in Eremitari Church, Padua (1448–55), *The Agony in the Garden* (c.1450), *St. Luke Polyptych* (1454), *St. George* (c.1455–60), *Madonna Enthroned with Saints* (1456–59), *St. Sebastian* (c.1459), *Adoration of the Shepherds* (c.1460), *Death of the Virgin* (c.1465), *The Dead Christ* (c.1466), frescoes in Camera degli Sposi, Palazzo Ducale, Mantua (1473–74), *Madonna of the Caves* (c.1484), *Triumph of Caesar* (begun c.1486), *Madonna della Vittoria* (1495), *Parnassus* (1497), *Wisdom Overcoming the Vices* (1502); his engravings included *Battle of the Sea Gods* (c.1490), *Bacchanal* (c.1490), *The Entombment* (1490s), *The Risen Christ Between St. Andrew and Longinus* (1490s).

Man·tell \man-ˈtel\, Gideon Algernon. 1790–1852. English geologist and paleontologist. Studied paleontology of the Mesozoic Era, esp. in Sussex; demonstrated freshwater origin of the Wealden strata of the Cretaceous Period; discovered four of the five genera of dinosaurs known in his time. Author of *The Fossils of the South Downs* (1822), *The Wonders of Geology* (1838), *Medals of Creation* (1844), etc.

Man·teuf·fel \ˈman-ˌtȯi-fəl\, Edwin Hans Karl von. Freiherr. 1809–1885. Prussian soldier. Entered cavalry (1827); chief of Prussian military cabinet (1857); lieutenant general (1861); served in Danish War (1864) and Austro–Prussian War (1866); in Franco–Prussian War (1870–71), won Battle of Amiens (Nov. 27, 1870), occupied Rouen (Dec. 1870), and quickly overcame resistance in southern France; created field marshal and commander of Prussian army of occupation in France (1871–73); governor of Alsace-Lorraine (from 1879).

Man·u·el \ˈman-yu̇-əl\. Name of two emperors of the Eastern Roman Empire:

Manuel I Com·ne·nus \käm-ˈnē-nəs\. c.1122–1180. Emperor (1143–80). Son of John II; distinguished as a soldier; m. as first wife (1146) Irene (*q.v.*); took Corfu from Roger II of Sicily (1149); defeated at Brindisi (1156), ending Byzantine influence in Italy; regained lost territory in Cilicia (1158); forced Prince Renaud of Antioch and King Baldwin III of Jerusalem to recognize his suzerainty (1159); annexed Dalmatia, Croatia, and Bosnia (1167); launched several campaigns against Seljuq Turks, suffering disastrous defeat at Myriocephalon (1176); his unsuccessful attempt to restore the Roman Empire left Byzantium financially weak.

Manuel II Pa·lae·ol·o·gus \ˌpā-lē-ˈäl-ə-gəs\. 1350–1425. Emperor (1391–1425). Son of John V; crowned co-emperor (1373); helped his father regain Constantinople and the throne from his older brother Andronicus IV (1379); made journey (1399–1403) to Western countries to seek aid in establishing union of churches and in defending Constantinople, which was besieged by Turks; made peace treaty (1403) with Mehmed I, resulting in recovery of Thessalonica and peaceful relations until 1421; attacked by Murad II (1422); retired to a monastery after signing a humiliating peace treaty (1423).

Ma·nuel \mən-ˈwel, mȧn-\. Name of two kings of Portugal:

Manuel I. *Called* the Fortunate. 1469–1521. King (1495–1521). Created Duke of Beja and recognized as heir (1491) by cousin John II; m. 1st Isabella, daughter of Ferdinand and Isabella of Spain (1496; d. 1498); 2d her sister Maria (1498); 3d Eleanor of Austria, sister of Emperor Charles V (1518). His reign was golden age of Portuguese discovery and colonization; dispatched Cabral, da Gama, Lavrador, Côrte-Real on voyages; appointed Albuquerque governor in India (1508); amassed great wealth; promulgated new code of laws (1512); centralized public administration.

Manuel II. 1889–1932. King (1908–10). Second son of Carlos I; Duke of Beja; his reign a period of confusion and succession of ineffectual governments; overthrown by naval revolt (1910); lived in exile in England during rest of life.

Ma·nu·el \mȧn-wʸel\, Eugène. 1823–1901. French writer. Author of *Pages intimes* (verse, 1865), *Les Ouvriers* (social drama, 1870), *Poèmes populaires* (1872), *L'Absent* (comedy, 1873), *En Voyage* (verse, 1888), etc.

Ma·nuel \män-ˈwel\, Juan. *Known as* Don Juan Manuel. 1282–1348. Spanish prince, general, and writer. Nephew of Alfonso X; coregent for Alfonso XI during his minority (1320–25); deeply involved in political intrigues of the day; general in chief of the Spanish army fighting the Moors. Chief literary work *El libro del conde Lucanor* (1323–25), a collection of 51 prose tales in the Oriental manner, each with a little moral in verse at the end; other extant works include *Libro de los estados* and *Libro del caballero y del escudero*.

Ma·nu·el \ˈmän-ü-el\, Niklaus. *Sometimes erroneously called* Deutsch \ˈdȯich\. 1484–1530. Swiss painter, wood engraver, politician, and writer. Studied in Venice under Titian. Works included 45 frescoes of *Dance of Death* at Bern Dominican monastery (1516–19), *Pyramus and Thisbe, Enthauptung Johannes des Täufers*. Ardent supporter of Reformation; author of satirical comedies and polemical verse, including *Vom Papst und seiner Priesterschaft* (1522), *Der Ablasskrämer* (1525), *Barbali* (1526), *Krankheit und Testament der Messe* (1528).

Manutius, Aldus. See Aldo MANNUCCI.

Manuza. See MAVURA.

Manuzio, Aldo. See MANNUCCI.

Man·zo·ni \mänd-ˈzō-nē\, Alessandro Francesco Tommaso Antonio. 1785–1873. Italian novelist and poet. Leader of Italian Romantic school. To Paris (1805–07); influenced by Voltairism; later abandoned skepticism in favor of ardent religious orthodoxy; participated in Milanese revolt (1848); appointed senator of the kingdom (1860). Known especially for his novel *I promessi sposi* (1825–27), an historical study of 17th-century Italy and a model of modern Italian prose. Among his other works were *Inni sacri* (1815), *Osservazioni sulla morale cattolica* (1819), the tragedies *Il conte di Carmagnola* (1820) and *Adelchi* (1822), an ode on Napoléon's death "Il Cinque Maggio" (1822), and *Storia della colonna infame* (1842).

Mao Chʻang \ˈmau̇-ˈchäŋ\. fl. 145 B.C. Chinese scholar. Known for his revision of and commentary on the great Confucian Classic *Shih Ching;* his text, often called *Mao shih,* is still considered the authoritative version of the *Shih Ching*.

Mao Tse-tung \ˈmau̇d-ˈzə-ˈdu̇ŋ\. *Pin-yin* Mao Ze-dong. 1893–1976. Chinese soldier and statesman. Served in his native Hunan in revolutionary army (1911–12); at Peking U. (1919), where he participated in May Fourth Movement of students; embraced Marxism and helped found (1921) Chinese Communist party; began working with the Kuomintang (1923), chiefly as organizer of peasant unions in Hunan; expelled from Kuomintang by Chiang Kai-shek (1927). Chairman (1931–34) of Chinese Soviet Republic in Kiangsi Province; defeated by Chiang's forces (1934); led army of 200,000 on famed Long March from Kiangsi to northwestern mountains of Shensi Province (1934–35); wrote *Strategic Problems of China's Revolutionary War* (1936) and *On New Democracy* (1938), establishing himself as leading theoretician of the Chinese Communist party; adapted Marxism to Chinese conditions by placing the peasantry rather than the urban proletariat in the revolutionary vanguard; instituted Rectification Campaign (1942–44) to implement his theories; defeated the Nationalists at Nanking (Apr. 1949). Became chairman of Communist party and of the People's Republic of China (1949); launched (1957) the Great Leap Forward, an unsuccessful attempt to decentralize the economy, chiefly by establishing a nationwide system of people's communes; retired (1959) as chairman of the republic but remained as party chairman; instituted the Cultural Revolution (1966–69) in attempt to reinvigorate revolutionary principles in the party and nation; spent final years in virtual seclusion and declining health.

Mao Tun. See SHEN YEN-PING.

Map \ˈmap\, Walter. *Surname Latinized* Ma·pes \ˈmā-pēz\. c.1140–c.1209. English ecclesiastic, author, and wit. Clerk of royal household and itinerant justice; sent on missions abroad; canon of St. Paul's Cathedral, Lincoln; archdeacon of Oxford (from 1197). Author of *De nugis curialium* (i.e. Courtiers' Triflings, c.1182–1192), a miscellany of court gossip, daily events, theological arguments, etc. Credited (probably incorrectly) with lost Latin prose romance of *Lancelot du Lac* and prose romances *Mort Artus* and *Queste del Saint Graal*.

Ma·pu \ˈmäp-ü\, Abraham. 1808–1867. Lithuanian Jewish novelist. Taught religion and German; influential advocate of Haskalah (Enlightenment) movement. Author of first Hebrew novel *Ahavat Ziyyon* (1853), an idyllic historical romance set in ancient Israel; other novels included *ʻAyiṭ tzavuaʻ* (1858–69), *Ashmat Shomron* (1865), *Ḥoze ḥezyonot* (1869).

Maq·di·sī, al- \al-ˈmak-də-sē\. *Also called* al-Mu·qad·da·sī \al-mə-ˌkäd-də-ˈsē\. *More completely* Muḥammad ibn Aḥmad al-Maqdisī. c.946–c.1000. Arab geographer, b. Jerusalem. Traveled widely in Muslim countries (except India and Spain) gathering material for his geographical compendium *Kitāb aḥsan al-taqāsīm fī maʻrifat al-aqālīm* (completed 985).

Ma·quet \mȧ-ke\, Auguste. 1813–1888. French writer. Best known as collaborator with Alexandre Dumas père in many novels and plays, doing research to establish historical facts used by Dumas in his plots.

Mar, Earls of. See (1) earls of Douglas under DOUGLAS family; (2) John ERSKINE; (3) James Stewart (1531?–1570), Earl of Moray, under STEWART family.

Ma·rais \mȧ-re, -rā\, Marin. 1656–1728. French composer. Studied under Lully and was associated with production of his operas; in royal orchestra (1676–1725). Most celebrated virtuoso and teacher of viola da gamba in his day. Composer of operas *Alcide* (1693), *Ariane et Bacchus* (1696), *Alcione* (1706), and *Sémélé* (1709), and of several books of viol music.

Ma·ral·di \mä-ˈräl-dē\, Giacomo Filippo. 1665–1729. Italian astronomer. Nephew of J. D. Cassini; lived in Paris (from 1687). Discovered that the dark division observed by Cassini was the line of demarcation between two of Saturn's rings; recognized the variability of one of the stars in the constellation Hydra (1704); author of a star catalogue.

Maran. See KARO.

Ma·ran \má-rän\, René. 1887–1960. French novelist, b. Martinique. Awarded Goncourt prize (1921) for *Batouala.*

Ma·rat \má-rà\, Jean-Paul. 1743–1793. French politician and physician, b. Switzerland. Practiced medicine in London (1770s) and Paris (from 1777); took active part in prerevolutionary agitation; published (from Sept. 1789) radical paper *L'Ami du Peuple* inciting the people to violence. Member of National Convention (1792) and identified with radical Jacobins; attacked by Girondists, arrested, and tried, but acquitted (Apr. 1793). Joined Danton and Robespierre in overthrowing power of the Girondists. Assassinated by Charlotte Corday (*q.v.*) while in his bath.

Ma·rat·ti \mä-'rät-tē\ *or* **Ma·rat·ta** \-tä\, Carlo. 1625–1713. Italian painter. With G.B. Gaulli, leading painter of the Roman school; commissioned by Clement XI to restore Raphael's frescoes in Vatican (1702–03); chief master of Roman late Baroque style. Among his works were *Nativity* (1650), *Mystery of the Trinity Revealed to St. Augustine* (c.1655), *The Appearance of the Virgin to St. Philip Neri* (c.1675), *The Virgin with SS. Charles and Ignatius* (c.1685), frescoes for many Roman palaces, and portraits as of Clement IX.

Mar·beck \'mär-,bek\ *or* **Mer·becke** \'mär-\, John. d. c.1585. English composer and writer. Organist at St. George's Chapel, Windsor (from c.1531); early adherent of Calvinism; arrested and condemned to burn at stake (1544), but pardoned through Bishop Gardiner of Winchester. Published earliest concordance of whole English Bible (1550) and *The Boke of Common Praier Noted,* a setting of plainchant for the Anglican liturgy (1550).

Marbois, Marquis de Barbé-. See BARBÉ-MARBOIS.

Mar·bot \már-bō\, Jean-Baptiste-Antoine-Marcelin de. Baron. 1782–1854. French soldier. Entered army (1799); aide-de-camp of Augereau at Austerlitz, Jena, Eylau, of Lannes at Saragossa, of Masséna at Wagram; general at Waterloo (1815); exiled (1815–19); published *Remarques critiques* (1820) in reply to Gen. Joseph Rogniat's treatise on war; reentered army (1830) as general; wrote *Mémoires* (pub. 1891).

Marc \'märk\, Franz. 1880–1916. German painter. Joined Expressionist group Neue Künstlervereinigung (1909); with Wassily Kandinsky, founded Expressionist group Der Blaue Reiter (1911–14) and edited its organ; influenced by Delauney and Cubism, changed style from naturalistic to almost purely abstract; killed in action near Verdun. Known esp. for the intense nature mysticism of his animal paintings; works included *Cat Under a Tree* (1910), *Blue Horses* (1911), *Tiger* (1912), *Deer in the Wood, No. 1* (1913), *Stables* (1913–14), *Tyrol* (1913–14), *Fighting Forms* (1914).

Mar·ca \már-kà\, Pierre de. 1594–1662. French prelate. Ordained Roman Catholic priest (1642); governor of Catalonia (1644–51); bishop of Conserans (1648); archbishop of Toulouse (1652) and minister of state; archbishop of Paris (1662). Author of *Histoire de Béarn* (1640), *De concordantia sacerdotii et imperii* (1641), etc.

Mar·ca·bru \már-kà-brü\ *or* **Mar·ca·brun** \-brœ^{n}, -brü^{n}\. fl. c.1130–48. Gascon troubadour. One of earliest troubadours known; an innovator and reformer responsible for severity of classical troubadour style; 45 of his poems are extant.

Marcantonio. See Marcantonio RAIMONDI.

Mar·ceau \már-sō\, François-Séverin. *Orig.* Marceau-Des·gra·viers \-dā-gràv-yā\. 1769–1796. French soldier. Took part in assault on the Bastille (1789); participated in defense of Verdun (1792); made head of army of the West (1793); distinguished himself at Fleurus (1794) and along the Rhine (1795–96).

Mar·cel \már-sel\, Étienne. c.1316–1358. French bourgeois leader. Provost of the merchants of Paris (from 1354); leader in the Estates-General (1356); induced Dauphin Charles (later King Charles V) to issue an edict of reform; King John II, then a prisoner of the English, forbade execution of the edict, whereupon Marcel turned from the dauphin to support the claims of Charles the Bad, king of Navarre. Led the Paris mob into the palace of the dauphin (Feb. 22, 1358) and in the presence of the dauphin murdered the marshals of Champagne and Normandy; murdered by Jean Maillart, an agent of the dauphin, when on the point of opening the gates of Paris to the troops of the king of Navarre.

Marcel, Gabriel-Honoré. 1889–1973. French philosopher and dramatist. Taught philosophy intermittently; worked as publisher's reader, editor, writer, critic. Raised as an agnostic; converted to Roman Catholicism (1929). A Phenomenologist and a leading exponent of Christian Existentialism. His philosophical works included *Journal métaphysique* (1927), *Être et avoir* (1935), *Homo Viator* (1945), *Le Mystère de l'être* (1951), *Les Hommes contre l'humain* (1951), *Le Déclin de la sagesse* (1954), *L'Homme problématique* (1955), *La Dignité humaine et ses assises existentielles* (1964); his plays included *Le Coeur des autres* (1921), *Un Homme de Dieu* (1925), *La Chapelle ardente* (1925), *Le Chemin de crête* (1936), *Le Dard* (1936), *Rome n'est plus dans Rome* (1951), *Croissez et multipliez* (1955), *La Dimension Florestan* (1958).

Mar·cel·li·nus \mar-sə-'lī-nəs\. Saint. d. 304. Pope (296–304). Pontiff during the persecutions under Diocletian.

Mar·cel·lo \mär-'chel-lō\, Benedetto. 1686–1739. Italian composer and public official. Member of Venetian Grand Council (1707) and Council of Forty (1711); governor of Pola (1730–37); papal chamberlain of Brescia (1738–39). Chief work *Estro poetico-armonico,* settings in cantata style of G.A. Giustiniani's Italian paraphrases of the first 50 Psalms (1724–26); also composed some 400 cantatas, 10 masses, 15 motets, concertos, sonatas. Author of *Il teatro alla moda,* a pamphlet satirizing contemporary opera (c.1720). His brother ¶Alessandro (1684–1750) composed cantatas, violin sonatas, and concertos, esp. the *Oboe Concerto in D Minor* long attributed to his brother.

Mar·cel·lus \mär-'sel-əs\. Name of two popes:

Marcellus I. Saint. d. 309. Pope (308–309). His pontificate during persecutions under Diocletian; his imposition of penances on apostates of the persecutions led to rioting; banished (309) from Rome by Emperor Maxentius; died shortly afterward.

Marcellus II. *Orig.* Marcello Cer·vi·ni \cher-'vē-nē\. 1501–1555. Pope (April–May 1555). Protégé of Cardinal Alessandro Farnese; cardinal (1539); papal legate under Paul III; president (with Reginald Pole and the future Pope Julius III) of Council of Trent (1545–47); a leader in church reform.

Marcellus. Name of Roman plebeian family, including: Marcus Claudius Marcellus (268?–208 B.C.), general; consul five times (between 222 and 208); defeated Insubres (222), slaying their king, Viridomarus, with his own hand; defeated Hannibal at Nola (216); commanded army in Sicily (214–211), captured Syracuse (212) and subjugated whole island; fought Hannibal (210–208); ambushed and killed on reconnoitering expedition near Venusia. ¶Marcus Claudius Marcellus (d. 45 B.C.), orator and politician; consul (51 B.C.); a leader of Optimate party and opponent of Caesar; withdrew to Mytilene after Pompey's defeat at Pharsala (48); pardoned by Caesar after request by the Senate (46), Caesar being thanked in speech (*Pro Marcello*) by Cicero; murdered on way to Rome by one of his retinue.

¶Marcus Claudius Marcellus (42–23 B.C.), son of Augustus's sister Octavia; adopted by Augustus (25) and named as his successor; served under Augustus in Spain (25); his untimely death was referred to by Virgil in the *Aeneid* (Book VI).

Marcellus, Nonius. See NONIUS MARCELLUS.

March, Earls of (in English peerage). See MORTIMER family.

March, Earls of (in Scottish peerage). See Alexander Stewart under STEWART family; William Douglas (1724–1810) under DOUGLAS family.

March \'márk\, Ausiàs. 1397–1459. Catalan poet. Spent most of life in royal service. Known for poems describing the conflict between his sensuality and passionate idealism; his verse influenced by Petrarch and marked by personal expression, metaphysical subtlety, spare and original imagery; his poetic subjects also included death, religion, and morals.

March \'märch\, Francis Andrew. 1825–1911. American philologist, b. Millbury, Mass. A principal founder of modern comparative Anglo-Saxon linguistics. Professor, Lafayette Coll. (1857–1906); director of American staff of *Oxford English Dictionary* (1879–82); consulting editor of *Standard Dictionary* (1893–95). Author of *Method of Philological Study of the English Language* (1865), *A Comparative Grammar of the Anglo-Saxon Language* (1870), *Introduction to Anglo-Saxon: An Anglo-Saxon Reader* (1870), *The Spelling Reform* (1881). His son ¶Francis Andrew (1863–1928), b. Easton, Pa., was a lexicographer; taught at Lafayette (1882–1928, professor from 1891); in charge of etymological work for the *Standard Dictionary* (1893–95); coeditor with his father of *A Thesaurus Dictionary of the English Language* (1902). Another son ¶Peyton Conway (1864–1955), b. Easton, Pa., army officer; entered army (1888); served in World War I as artillery commander in France (1917); as general and chief of staff (1918–21) merged the various branches of the regular and volunteer armies and directed the mobilization program; retired (1921).

March, Fredric. *Orig.* Frederick McIntyre Bick·el \'bik-əl\. 1897–1975. American actor, b. Racine, Wis. On stage in *The Skin of Our Teeth* (1942), *A Bell for Adano* (1944), *Long Day's Journey Into Night* (1955), etc.; in motion pictures including *Dr. Jekyll and Mr. Hyde* (1932, Academy Award), *Death Takes a Holiday* (1934), *The Barretts of Wimpole Street* (1935), *A Star Is Born* (1937), *The Best Years of Our Lives* (1946, Academy Award), *Inherit the Wind* (1960), etc.

March, William. See William E.M. CAMPBELL.

Mar·chand \már-shä^{n}\, Jean-Baptiste. 1863–1934. French soldier and explorer. Enlisted in army (1883); commissioned sublieutenant (1887); sent to Africa (1889); fought in Senegal; traced Niger River to its source, explored region from Ivory Coast to Tengrela; commanded cross-continent expedition which reached and occupied Fashoda (July 1898), causing serious crisis in Anglo-French relations, and later (Dec. 1898–May 1899) marched through Ethiopia to Djibouti. Served during Boxer Rebellion in China. In World War I, general of brigade and of division; commanded 10th colonial division in Champagne offensive (1915), on the Somme (1916) and Chemin des Dames (1917), in battle of Verdun (1917), and on the Marne (1918). Retired (1919).

Marchand, Jean-Hippolyte. 1883–1941. French painter. Deserted conventional styles and exhibited at Salon des Indépendants (1908); painted *Portrait de femme à sa toilette,* landscapes, still lifes, etc.

Mar·che·si \mär-ˈkä-zē\, Salvatore. Cavaliere de Ca·stro·ne \dā-käs-ˈtrō-nā\. Marchese del·la Ra·ja·ta \ˌdāl-lä-rä-ˈyä-tä\. 1822–1908. Italian baritone, singing teacher, and composer. Expelled from Italy (1848); sang in U.S. and various cities of Europe and finally settled in Paris. Composed a number of songs and made Italian translations of French and German operas. His wife (m. 1852) ¶Mathilde, *nee* Grau·mann \ˈgrau̇-ˌmän\ (1826–1913), b. Germany; concert singer and singing teacher; studied under Manuel García; made debut (1849) as singer and often toured with her husband; taught at Vienna Conservatory (1854–61, 1868–78), Cologne, London; established École Marchesi in Paris (1881); author of *L'Art du chant* (1886) and *Marchesi and Music* (1897). Their daughter ¶Blanche (1863–1940) was also a concert and opera singer; wrote *A Singer's Pilgrimage* (1923).

Mar·chet·ti \mär-ˈkāt-tē\, Filippo. 1831–1902. Italian composer. His works included operas as *Gentile da Varano* (1856), *Ruy Blas* (1869), and *Don Giovanni d'Austria* (1880), songs, and sacred vocal music.

Marchmont, Earl of. See Sir Patrick HUME.

Mar·cian \ˈmär-shən\. c.392–457. Emperor of the Eastern Roman Empire (450–457). A Thracian of humble birth; on death of Theodosius II chosen consort by Pulcheria; refused tribute to Attila (450); successfully defended empire in Syria and Egypt (452) and on Armenian frontier (456); an able administrator, left empire in good financial condition. Council of Chalcedon (451) held in his reign.

Mar·ci·ano \ˌmär-s(h)ē-ˈan-(ˌ)ō, -ˈän-\, Rocky. *Orig.* Rocco Francis Mar·che·gia·no \ˌmär-shäg-ˈyän-(ˌ)ō\. 1923–1969. American boxer, b. Brockton, Mass. Had first professional fight (Mar. 1947); won world heavyweight championship by knocking out Jersey Joe Walcott in 13th round at Philadelphia (Sept. 23, 1952); successfully defended title six times; retired (Apr. 1956) with career record of 49 victories (43 by knockouts) and no defeats.

Mar·ci·on \ˈmär-s(h)ē-ən\. d. c.160 A.D. Christian Gnostic. Left his native Sinope for Rome (c.140); at first a disciple of Cerdo, later developed own religious system; excommunicated (144) as a quasi-Gnostic heretic. Founded sect (Marcionites) with churches in northern Africa, Gaul, Asia Minor, and Egypt; held that the God of Moses was imperfect and therefore distinct from the God of Jesus; compiled own New Testament, the *Instrumentum.*

Marcius, Ancus. See ANCUS MARCIUS.

Mar·co·ni \mär-ˈkō-nē\, Guglielmo. 1874–1937. Italian physicist and inventor. Carried out successful experiments with wireless telegraphy near Bologna (1895); to England (1896); made successful demonstrations (1896–97), finally sending signals 12 miles. To La Spezia at invitation of Italian government, where wireless station was erected (1897); Marconi's Wireless Telegraph Co., Ltd., formed in London (1897); established communication across English Channel between England and France (1898); formed American Marconi Co. (1900); filed (1900) British patent No. 7777 for wireless improvements that enabled several stations to operate on different wavelengths without interference. Succeeded in receiving and sending signals across the Atlantic between Poldhu, Cornwall, and St. John's, Newfoundland (1901); patented magnetic detector (1902) and horizontal directional aerial (1905); introduced timed-spark system for generating continuous waves (1912); in later years worked on development of shortwave wireless communication. Shared (with Karl F. Braun) the 1909 Nobel prize for physics.

Marco Polo. See POLO.

Mar·cous·sis \mär-kü-sē\, Louis. *Orig.* Ludwig Casimir Ladislas Mar·kus \ˈmär-küs\. 1883–1941. Polish painter. To Paris under Lefebvre (1903); associated with Picasso; one of the early Cubists. Works included *Still Life with Draughtsboard* (1912) and *Rain No. 1* (1927).

Mar·cus \ˈmär-ku̇s\, Siegfried. 1831–1898. German inventor. Established engineering laboratory at Vienna (1860); built and drove a one-cylinder automobile (1864); built (1874) a second automobile with an advanced electrical system, probably oldest gasoline-powered automobile extant; later built two more automobiles, neither extant; also invented a telegraphic relay system (c.1850), an electric lamp (1877), various other electrical devices, and a carburetor.

Mar·cus Au·re·li·us \ˈmär-kəs-ȯ-ˈrēl-yəs, -ˈrē-lē-əs\. *Surnamed* An·to·ni·nus \ˌan-tə-ˈnī-nəs\. *Orig.* Marcus An·ni·us Ve·rus \ˈan-ē-əs-ˈvir-əs\. 121–180. Roman emperor (161–180). Son of Annius Verus and nephew of Emperor Antoninus Pius, by whom he was adopted (138) and created caesar (139); m. (145) Annia Galeria Faustina, daughter of emperor. Consul (140, 145, 161); held other public offices (140–161). As emperor made Lucius Verus his colleague (161); his generals subdued Parthians (162–166) and revolting tribes in Pannonia (167–168); won victories (168–175) over Marcomanni and Quadi, restoring the Danubian frontier; visited Egypt and Athens; returned to Italy (176); again fought barbarians in the north (177–180); died at Vindobona (Vienna). One of the most eminent of Stoic philosophers; a man of gentle character and wide learning, yet an opponent of Christianity, supporting persecutions. Author of *Meditations* (written in Greek), a collection of precepts of practical morality.

Marcus Aurelius Antoninus. See ANTONINUS.

Mar·cu·se \mär-ˈkü-zə\, Herbert. 1898–1979. American political philosopher, b. Berlin, Germany. A founder of Frankfurt Institute of Social Research (1920s); to U.S. (1934, naturalized 1940); lectured at Columbia (1951–52) and Harvard (1952–54); professor at Brandeis U. (1954–65) and U. of California, San Diego (1965–70). Known for his studies of the repressive nature of contemporary society and advocacy of revolutionary changes to reform it. Author of *Reason and Revolution* (1941), *Eros and Civilization* (1955), *Soviet Marxism* (1958), *One-Dimensional Man* (1964), *Negations* (1968).

Mar·cy \ˈmär-sē\, William Learned. 1786–1857. American politician, b. Sturbridge, Mass. Member of dominant New York political group known as the "Albany Regency." Comptroller, New York State (1823–29); associate justice, New York Supreme Court (1829–31); U.S. senator (1831–32). Coined phrase "spoils system" (1832). Governor of New York (1833–39); U.S. secretary of war (1845–49); U.S. secretary of state (1853–57).

Mar·der·steig \ˈmär-dər-ˌshtīg\, Giovanni, *orig.* Hans. 1892–1977. Italian printer, b. Germany. Founded (1922) Officina Bodini at Montagnola, Italy; acquired international reputation for the exceptional quality of his books, as his 50-volume edition of Gabriele D'Annunzio's works (1927–32); later moved firm to Verona; also founder and head (from 1947) of printing house Stamperia Valdonèga, Verona; designer of typefaces Fontana, Dante, Griffo, and Zeno.

Mar·do·ni·us \mär-ˈdō-nē-əs\. d. 479 B.C. Persian general. Son-in-law of Darius I; made satrap of Ionia (492); led unsuccessful expedition (492) against Eretria and Athens. After accession of Xerxes, commanded army at time (480) of Persian defeat at Salamis; defeated and killed at Plataea.

Ma·ré·chal \ma-rā-shal\, Pierre-Sylvain. 1750–1803. French writer. Known for his antireligious writings as *Livre échappé au Déluge* (1784, parody of the Bible) and *Dictionnaire des athées anciens et modernes* (1800); his *Almanach des honnêtes gens* (1788) contained proposal for a new calendar which became basis for the French Republican calendar of 1793.

Ma·rées \mä-ˈrā\, Hans von. 1837–1887. German painter. Lived in Italy (from 1864); chief work, frescoes in library of zoological museum at Naples.

Ma·ren·co \mä-ˈreŋ-kō\, Carlo. 1800–1846. Italian dramatist. Influenced by the Romantic movement; wrote historical tragedies as *Buondelmonte* (1827), *Corso Donati* (1830), *Ezzelino III* (1832), and *Pia de' Tolomei* (1837). His son ¶Leopoldo (1831–1899) also wrote historical tragedies; best known for his comedy *Il falconiere di Pietra Ardena* (1870).

Ma·ren·zi·o \mä-ˈrents-yō\, Luca. 1553 or 1554–1599. Italian composer. In Rome in service of cardinals Luigi d'Este (1578–86) and Cinzio Aldobrandini (from c.1593). Developed individual technique noted for homophonic style and daring chromatic harmonies; composed madrigals, villanelles and airs, motets, and Magnificats.

Ma·ret \ma-re\, Hugues-Bernard. Duc de Bas·sa·no \də-bä-ˈsä-nō\. 1763–1839. French diplomat. Journalist during early stages of Revolution; ambassador to England (1792, 1797) and Naples (1793). Confidential adviser to Napoléon, who appointed him secretary of state; created duke (1809), minister of foreign affairs (1811–13); minister of state during Hundred Days; exiled after Waterloo (1815–20). Created peer of France (1831); prime minister (Nov. 1834).

Marets, Nicolas Des. See DESMARETS.

Mar·ett \ˈmar-ət\, Robert Ranulph. 1866–1943. English anthropologist. Reader in social anthropology at Oxford (1910–36); rector, Exeter Coll., Oxford (1928 ff.); works included *The Threshold of Religion* (1909), *Anthropology* (1912), *Psychology and Folklore* (1920), *Heart and Hands in Human Evolution* (1935), etc.

Ma·rey \ma-re\, Étienne-Jules. 1830–1904. French physiologist. Professor, Collège de France (from 1868). Known for work on the physiology of the heart and circulation, animal heat, human and animal locomotion, the flight of birds and insects, and the application of cinematography to physiological studies; invented the sphygmograph (1863).

Mar·ga·dant \ˈmär-gə-ˌdänt\, Simon. *Lat. pseudonym* Simon Lem·ni·us \ˈlem-nē-əs\ *from mother's name* Lemm \ˈlem\. c.1511–1550. German poet. Studied under Melanchthon at Wittenberg (1534–38); his two books of *Epigrams* (1538) antagonized Luther, who had him expelled (1538); further attacked Luther in third book of *Epigrams* (1538) and bitter dramatic satire *Monachopornomachia* (1540). Other works, all in Latin, included *Amores* (love poems, 1542), *Raeteis* (epic of Swiss war of 1499, pub. 1874), and first translation of the *Odyssey* (1549).

Mar·gai \'mär-ˌgī\, Sir Milton Augustus Striery. 1895–1964. Sierra Leone politician. Government medical officer (1928–50); founder (1951) and leader of Sierra Leone People's party; minister of health, agriculture, and forestry (1953); chief minister and minister of internal affairs (1954–61); premier (1958–61). First prime minister of independent Sierra Leone (1961–64); followed conservative, pro-British policies.

Mar·ga·ret \'mär-g(ə-)rət\. *Dan.* Mar·gre·te \mär-'grē-tə\. 1353–1412. Queen of Denmark, Norway, and Sweden. Daughter of King Valdemar IV of Denmark; m. (1363) Haakon VI, king of Norway. Regent of Denmark for her son Olaf (1376–87) and, on death of Haakon (1380), became regent of Norway, also for Olaf; on Olaf's death (1387), seized control of both kingdoms; elected as joint sovereign by Denmark (1387) and by Norway (1388); had Eric of Pomerania, her grandnephew, proclaimed her successor (1389); offered throne of Sweden by disaffected citizens; defeated and took prisoner (1389) Swedish king Albert of Mecklenburg; after complete conquest of Sweden (1389–97), effected Union of Kalmar, a dynastic union that nominally lasted until 1523; kept effective control, although Eric was crowned king (1397) of the three nations; no monarchy in Europe equal in extent at the time.

Margaret. 1282?–1318. Queen of Edward I of England. Daughter of Philip III of France; m. (1299) Edward as his second wife; never crowned queen.

Margaret. 1240–1275. Queen of Alexander III of Scotland. Eldest daughter of Henry III of England; m. Alexander (1251); looked upon with suspicion as representing English influence, confined in Edinburgh castle by guardians of king and queen until released through intervention by her father.

Margaret. *Known as* the Maid of Norway. 1283–1290. Queen of Scotland (1286–90). Daughter of King Erik II of Norway and granddaughter of Alexander III of Scotland and Margaret; affianced to Prince Edward, son of Edward I of England (1287); died in Orkneys en route to England.

Margaret of An·gou·lême \äⁿ-gü-lem\. *Fr.* Mar·gue·rite \mȧr-gə-rēt\ d'Angoulême. *Also known as* Margaret of Na·varre \nȧ-vȧr\. 1492–1549. Queen of Henry II of Navarre. Daughter of Charles de Valois-Orléans, comte d'Angoulême, and Louise of Savoy; sister of Francis I; m. 1st (1509) Charles, duc d'Alençon (d. 1525), 2d (1527) Henry II of Navarre. Active in politics and a supporter of Protestantism, but inclined to mysticism; a friend of literature and protector of Humanist Reformers; her courts at Nérac and Pau most brilliant intellectually in Europe at that time. Author of *Heptaméron,* collection of 72 tales modeled on the *Decameron* (1558), and of dramatic and religious poems published as *Le Miroir de l'âme pêcheresse* (1531), *Les Marguerites de la Marguerite des princesses* (1547), *Les Dernières poésies* (pub. 1895).

Margaret of An·jou \äⁿ-zhü, *Angl* 'an-jü\. *Fr.* Marguerite d'Anjou. 1430–1482. Queen of Henry VI of England. Daughter of René I of Anjou; m. Henry VI (1445) to confirm truce with France in Hundred Years' War; became a key member of Lancastrian party; during Henry VI's insanity, strove against Richard, Duke of York's protectorate; failed to crush Richard, who again became protector after first battle of St. Albans (1455), the inauguration of Wars of the Roses; finally ousted Richard from power (1456). After victory at Wakefield (1460), defeated Richard Neville, Earl of Warwick, at St. Albans (1461) and brutally executed her enemies; defeated at Towton (1461); retired to Scotland with Henry; invaded Northumberland with help from Louis XI, but failed (1462); given refuge in Flanders and Lorraine; her forces defeated at Hexham (1464); arranged with Warwick a temporarily successful invasion of England (1470–71) and placed Henry VI on throne; defeated at Barnet (1471), Henry VI becoming a prisoner; defeated and captured at Tewkesbury (1471), where her son Edward was killed; imprisoned (1471–76); ransomed by Louis XI (1476) on surrender of all rights of succession to French territory.

Margaret of An·ti·och \'ant-ē-ˌäk\. Saint. 3d or 4th century A.D. Christian martyr. One of most venerated saints of the Middle Ages; according to her legend, refused marriage offer of prefect Olybrius, suffered extravagant trials and tortures, and was beheaded at Antioch. Her story may have been based on that of St. Pelagia of Antioch and is essentially the same as St. Marina of the Eastern church.

Margaret of Austria. See also MARGARET of Parma.

Margaret of Austria. 1480–1530. Duchess of Savoy and regent of the Netherlands (1507–15, 1519–30). Daughter of Emperor Maximilian I and Mary of Burgundy; m. 1st (1497) Infante Juan of Spain, who died a few months later; 2d (1501) Philibert II (1480–1504), Duke of Savoy. Appointed (1507) by her father regent of the Netherlands and guardian of her nephew Charles (later Emperor Charles V); pursued pro-English foreign policy; reappointed as regent by Charles (1519); extended Habsburg dominion to Friesland (1515–24); annexed bishop of Utrecht's lands (1528); negotiated Treaty of Cambrai (1529) with Louise of Savoy for France.

Margaret of Burgundy. *Fr.* Marguerite de Bour·gogne \-də-bür-gȯnʸ\. 1290–1315. Queen of Navarre. Daughter of Robert II, Duke of Burgundy; m. Louis le Hutin (1305), king of Navarre (see LOUIS X of France). Convicted of adultery, imprisoned, and smothered to death by order of king.

Margaret of Ca·rin·thia \kə-'rin-thē-ə\. *Ger.* Mar·ga·re·te von Kärn·ten \ˌmär-gä-'rā-tə-fȯn-'kern-tən\. *Called* Maul·tasch \'mau̇l-ˌtäsh\. 1318–1369. Duchess of Carinthia and Countess of Tirol. Daughter of Henry, Duke of Carinthia; m. John Henry, Prince of Bohemia (1330); discarded this husband (1341) and m. Louis, son of the emperor (1342); inherited Carinthia and Tirol (1335) but forced to cede Carinthia to House of Habsburg; Tirolese rebellion supporting her was crushed and she was forced (1363) to cede Tirol to Habsburgs.

Margaret of Flan·\'flan-dərz\. *Fr.* Marguerite de Flan·dre \-də-fläⁿdrᵊ\. *Also known as* Margaret of Constantinople. 1202–1280. Countess of Flanders and Hainaut (1244–80). Daughter of Emperor Baldwin I; m. 1st Bouchard d'Avesnes and 2d (1223) William of Dampierre. Inherited Flanders and Hainaut; struggle ensued between children of two marriages; settled by Louis IX of France, who gave Hainaut to sons of Bouchard d'Avesnes and Flanders to sons of William of Dampierre (1246).

Margaret of Flanders. *Fr.* Marguerite de Flandre. 1350–1405. Countess of Flanders and Duchess of Burgundy. Daughter of Louis II de Male; m. 1st Philippe de Rouvre (1357), 2d Philip the Bold (1369); mother of Duke John; inherited (1384) Flanders, Artois, etc.

Margaret of France. See MARGARET of Valois.

Margaret of Navarre. See MARGARET of Angoulême.

Margaret of Par·ma \'pär-mə\. *Ital.* Mar·ghe·ri·ta di Par·ma \ˌmär-gä-'rē-tä-dē-'pär-mä\. *Also known as* Margaret of Austria. 1522–1586. Regent of the Netherlands. Natural daughter of Emperor Charles V; m. Alessandro, duca di Firenze (1536; d. 1537), 2d Ottavio Farnese, duca di Parma (1538). Governor general of Netherlands (1559–67); dismissed (1564) her chief adviser Antoine Perrenot de Granville, who had antagonized Dutch nobles; acceded to some demands of the Gueux, but suppressed (1567) Calvinist revolt; replaced by Duke of Alba. Head of civil administration of Netherlands under her son Alessandro Farnese (1580–83).

Margaret of Provence. *Fr.* Marguerite de Pro·vence \-də-prȯ-väⁿs\. 1221–1295. Queen of Louis IX of France. Daughter of Raymond Berengar IV, Count of Provence; m. Louis (1234); under strict supervision of mother-in-law Blanche of Castile; accompanied Louis on Seventh Crusade (1248–54); attempted, without success, to involve herself in politics.

Margaret of Savoy. *Ital.* Mar·ghe·ri·ta di Sa·vo·ia \ˌmär-gä-'rē-tä-dē-sä-'vȯ-yä\. 1851–1925. Queen of Humbert I of Italy. Daughter of Duke of Genoa; m. Crown Prince Humbert (1868) and became queen when he succeeded to throne (1878). Queen dowager (from 1900).

Margaret of Scotland. Saint. 1046–1093. Queen of Malcolm III of Scotland. Daughter of Anglo-Saxon prince Edward Atheling; reared at court of Hungary; m. (1070) Malcolm; persuaded Malcolm to initiate series of ecclesiastical reforms that transformed the religious and cultural life of Scotland; founded Holy Trinity Abbey at Dunfermline, restored many churches, devoted herself to care of the sick and poor. Canonized (1249). Considered patroness of Scotland.

Margaret of Va·lois \vȧl-wȧ\ *or* of France. *Fr.* Marguerite de Valois *or* de France. *Known as* Reine Mar·got \ren-mȧr-gō\. Queen consort of Navarre. 1553–1615. Daughter of Henry II of France and Catherine de Médicis; noted for her beauty and learning, notorious for her loose living; m. (1572) Henry of Navarre (later Henry IV of France); involved in political and religious conspiracies of the day; her marriage dissolved by pope (1599). Wrote *Mémoires* (pub. 1628) and *Lettres.*

Mar·ga·ret The·re·sa \'mär-g(ə)-rət-tə-'rā-sə, -'rä-zə\ of Spain. 1651–1673. Empress of Germany (1666–73). Daughter of Philip IV of Spain; first wife (m. 1666) of her uncle Emperor Leopold I; their daughter Maria Antonia married Maximilian II Emanuel of Bavaria.

Margaret Tu·dor \'t(y)üd-ər\. 1489–1541. Queen of James IV of Scotland. Daughter of Henry VII of England; m. (1503) James IV (d. 1513); supported English party against French; regent (1513) and guardian of her son James V; made peace with England; m. (1514) Archibald Douglas, 6th Earl of Angus; forced to give up regency to John Stewart, Duke of Albany (1515), and flee to England. Returned to Scotland, joined French party, allied herself with Albany, repeatedly shifted from one side to the other; on divorce (1527) from Angus, m. (1528) Henry Stewart, 1st Baron Methven; became chief adviser to James on fall of Angus (1528); fell out of royal favor (1534) after James discovered she had betrayed state secrets to her brother Henry VIII. Great-grandmother of James I of England.

Mar·ge·rie \mȧr-zhə-rē\, Emmanuel-Marie-Pierre-Martin Jac·quin de \zhȧ-kaⁿ-də-\. 1862–1953. French geologist. Known esp. for contributions to geomorphology; stated (independently of William M. Davis) that time was a major factor in development of landforms. Translated Eduard Suess's *Das Artlitz der Erde* as *La Face de la terre* (1897–1918); wrote *Les Formes du*

Terrain (with Gaston de La Nöe, 1888), *Le Jura* (1922–36), *Critique et géologie* (1943–48), *Études américaines* (1952), etc.

Marg·graf \'märk-ˌgräf\, Andreas Sigismund. 1709–1782. German chemist. Director, chemical laboratory of German Academy of Sciences of Berlin (1754–60); introduced the microscope as an aid in chemical work; distinguished between oxides of aluminum and calcium; discovered sugar in the sugar beet (1747), thus founding beet-sugar industry.

Mar·ghi·lo·man \ˌmär-gē-lō-'män\, Alexandru. 1854–1925. Romanian politician. Elected deputy (1884); minister of interior (1900–01), of finance (1912–14); leader of Conservative party (from 1914); during World War I, advocated Romanian neutrality; prime minister of Romania (1918); signed peace treaty with Central Powers (May 7, 1918; never ratified).

Mar·go·li·outh \mär-'gō-lē-əth, 'mär-gəl-yüth\, David Samuel. 1858–1940. English scholar. Professor of Arabic, Oxford (1889–1937); specialized in study of Arabic commentaries on Aristotle and history of Islām. Edited and translated Arabic works as the chronicle of Miskawayh published as *Eclipse of the 'Abbasid Caliphate* (with H. F. Amedroz, 1920–21); author of *Mohammed and the Rise of Islam* (1905), *The Early Development of Mohammedanism* (1914), *The Relations between Arabs and Israelites Prior to the Rise of Islam* (1924), etc.

Mar·go·lis \mär-'gō-ləs\, Max Leopold. 1866–1932. American philologist, b. Merech, Vilna, Russia. To U.S. (1889); professor of biblical philology, Dropsie Coll. (1909–32). Editor in chief of a Jewish translation of the Scriptures into English (1917). Author of *The Hebrew Scriptures in the Making* (1922), *A History of the Jewish People* (1927, with Alexander Marx), etc.

Marguerite. See MARGARET.

Mar·gue·ritte \már-gə-rēt\, Paul. 1860–1918. French novelist. Broke with Naturalists when he signed *Manifeste des cinq* (1887) against Zola; author of *Tous quatre* (1885), *Jours d'épreuve* (1889), *La Force des choses* (1890), *Ma Grande* (1892), *La Tourmente* (1893), *La Flamme* (1909), *L'Embusqué* (1916). Collaborator with his brother ¶Victor (1866–1942) in *Pariétaire* (1896), *Poum* (1897), *Le Désastre* (1898), *Femmes nouvelles* (1899), *Les Braves Gens* (1901), *La Commune* (1904), *Le Prisme* (1905). Victor published independently *La Prostituée* (1907), *La Garçonne* (1922), *Appel aux consciences* (1925).

Mar·gue·tel de Saint-De·nis \már-gə-tel-də-saⁿd-nē\, Charles de. Seigneur de Saint-Év·re·mond \saⁿ-tev-rə-mōⁿ\. c.1614–1703. French writer. Fought on royalist side in wars of the Fronde and was promoted by Cardinal Mazarin; on discovery of his facetious letter deriding Mazarin's Treaty of the Pyrenees, fled to London (1661) and was welcomed by Charles II; thereafter lived in England (1661–65, 1670 ff.) and Holland (1665–70). Author of poems; comedies in verse as *Les Académiciens* (1643) and in prose as *Sir Politick Would-Be* (c.1664); prose satires *Retraite de M. le duc de Longueville* (1649) and *Conversation du maréchal d'Hoquincourt avec le Père Canaye* (c.1663); literary criticism as *De la tragédie ancienne et moderne* (1672); discourses and letters.

Mar·gu·ni·os \mär-'gü-nē-ȯs\, Maximus. d. 1602. Greek Humanist and prelate, b. Crete. Became Orthodox monk (1579); made bishop of Kíthira but forced by Venetian authorities to live in Venice; headmaster of Greek College and leader of Greek community in Venice. Leading 16th-century Orthodox theologian; attempted unsuccessfully to achieve a compromise in *Filioque* controversy. Collected valuable library of classical Greek and Latin works; collaborated with Sir Henry Savile in 1613 standard edition of St. John Chrysostom's works; wrote *Brevis tractatus de consiliis atque praeceptis evangelicis* (1602) and a tract on the divine permission of evil.

Maria. See also MARIE and MARY.

Ma·ria \mə-'rē-ə\. Name of two reigning queens of Portugal:

Maria I. *In full* Maria Fran·cis·ca \fråⁿ-sēsh-kə\. 1734–1816. Queen (1777–1816). Eldest daughter of King Joseph I; m. (1760) her uncle Pedro (see PETER III of Portugal); crowned with him as joint sovereign (1777); both feeble and weak-minded; control of affairs seized by her mother, Marianna Victoria, who had Pombal banished from court; became demented after husband's death (1786); government taken over by her second son, John (1792), who was declared regent (1799–1816; see JOHN VI); died at Rio de Janeiro.

Maria II. *Usually known as* Maria da Gló·ria \thə-'glȯr-yə\. 1819–1853. Queen (1826–53). Daughter of Dom Pedro I, emperor of Brazil, and granddaughter of John VI of Portugal; became queen after her father had renounced his rights (1826); fled to England and Brazil because of civil war (1828–33) that resulted when her uncle Miguel (*q.v.*), regent, usurped the throne; with her father's help, forced Miguel to yield (1834); m. (1835) Duke Auguste of Leuchtenberg (d. 1835), and 2d (1836) Duke Ferdinand of Saxe-Coburg-Gotha. During her reign government dominated by duque de Saldanha, new constitution granted (1838–42), insurrections (1846, 1851). Succeeded by son Peter V.

Ma·ria Ade·la·ide \mä-'rē-ä-ä-ˌdel-ä-'ēd-ə\. 1894–1924. Grand duchess of Luxembourg (1912–19). Succeeded her father William IV; under German occupation (1914–18); abdicated (1919) in favor of her sister Charlotte and entered a convent in Italy.

Ma·ria An·na \mä-'rē-ä-'än-ä\ of Bavaria-Neu·burg \-'noi-ˌbu̇rk\. 1667–1740. Queen of Charles II of Spain. m. Charles (1689; d. 1700); heroine of Victor Hugo's *Ruy Blas.*

Ma·ria Ca·ro·li·na \mä-'rē-ä-ˌkä-rō-'lē-nä\. 1752–1814. Queen of Naples. Daughter of Francis I and Maria Theresa; m. (1768) Ferdinand IV of Naples (see FERDINAND I of the Two Sicilies); entered council of state (1777) and thereafter held real power in Naples; caused downfall of Tanucci; made her favorite Sir John Acton prime minister and under his influence adopted a pro-British, anti-French policy; joined Austro-British coalition against France; in exile during Parthenopean Republic (Dec. 1798–June 1799); again waged war on France (1805) and again forced to flee by French army (1806); exiled to Austria (1811).

Ma·ría Cris·ti·na \mä-'rē-ä-kres-'tē-nä\. Name of two queens consort of Spain:

María Cristina de Bor·bón \-t͟hā-bȯr-'bōn\. 1806–1878. Daughter of Francis I, king of the Two Sicilies; queen of Spain (1829–33) as fourth wife (m. 1829) of Ferdinand VII (*q.v.*); at his death (1833) became regent for her daughter Isabella; her regency marked by First Carlist War and government instability; antagonized many supporters by morganatic marriage to Fernando Muñoz (1833); forced to accept liberal 1812 constitution (1836); on signing law depriving communes of right to elect councils, forced to resign regency (1840); retired to France; after fall of Espartero (1843) returned to Madrid; because of intrigues, very unpopular; driven from Spain by revolution (1854).

María Cristina. 1858–1929. Daughter of Archduke Charles Ferdinand of Austria; m. Alfonso XII (1879); queen regent from his death (Nov. 1885) until their son Alfonso XIII was declared of age (1902); showed ability and tact; did not oppose real rulers—the army, church, and party leaders; her reign a period of peace and some progress, except for Spanish–American War (1898); American possessions lost; resigned at end of regency (1902) and devoted rest of life to social and charitable work.

Ma·ria E·le·o·no·ra \mä-'rē-ä-ā-lā-ō-'nō-rä\ of Brandenburg. 1599–1655. Queen of Sweden. Daughter of Elector John Sigismund of Brandenburg; m. Gustav Adolphus of Sweden (1620).

Ma·ria Fyo·do·rov·na \(ˌ)mər-'yē-yə-'fyȯ-dər(-ə)v-nə\. *Orig.* Marie Sophia Frederika Dagmar. 1847–1928. Empress of Russia. Daughter of King Christian IX of Denmark; m. (1866) Grand Duke Aleksandr Aleksandrovich, later (1881–94) czar of Russia as Alexander III. Widely known throughout Russia for her philanthropies.

Maria Leszczyńska. See MARIE.

Ma·ría Lu·i·sa \mä-'rē-ä-lü-'ē-sä\. 1782–1824. Queen of Etruria. Daughter of Charles IV of Spain; m. (1795) Louis de Bourbon, who was granted kingdom of Etruria (Tuscany) by Napoléon (1801); on his death (1803) became regent for her son Charles Louis (1803–07); lost kingdom (1807); granted Lucca by Congress of Vienna (1814).

María Luisa. Name of two queens consort of Spain:

María Luisa Te·re·sa \tā-'rā-sä\. 1751–1819. Daughter of Philip, Duke of Parma; m. Charles IV (1765); queen of Spain (1788–1808); had influence over weak-minded king and controlled affairs; made Godoy minister and with him ruined Spain's finances, finally (1808) bringing about intervention of Napoléon; spent last part of life in France and Italy.

María Luisa Ga·bri·e·la \gä-brē-'ā-lä\. 1688–1714. Daughter of Victor Amadeus II, Duke of Savoy; m. Philip V (1701); queen of Spain (1701–14), greatly aiding Philip in his administration of affairs; acted as regent during absence of Philip in Naples (1701–03) during War of Spanish Succession; mother of Louis I and Ferdinand VI of Spain.

Mar·i·am·ne \'mər-ē-'am-nē\. Name of two wives of Herod the Great: (1) Mariamne the Has·mo·nae·an \ˌhaz-mə-'nē-ən\ (c.57–29 B.C.), granddaughter of Hyrcanus II; m. Herod (37 B.C.); mother of Alexander and Aristobulus and grandmother of Herod of Chalcis and Herod Agrippa I; ordered executed by Herod in fit of jealousy; subject of various works of literature. (2) Mariamne (d. c.20 B.C.), daughter (or sister) of high priest Simon; mother of Herod Philip.

Ma·ria·na \mär-'yä-nä\, Juan de. 1536–1624. Spanish historian. Entered Jesuit order (1554); ordained (1561); taught in Jesuit schools in Rome (1561), Sicily (1565), and Paris (1569); lived in Toledo (from 1574). Chief work *Historia general de España* (1601), published originally in Latin (1592–1605) and translated into Spanish by himself.

Ma·ria·na de Aus·tria \mär-'yä-nä-t͟hā-'au̇s-trē-ä\. 1634–1696. Queen of Philip IV of Spain. Daughter of Emperor Ferdinand III; m. (1649) Philip; regent (1665–75) during minority of their son Charles II; made J.E. Nithard inquisitor general and minister (1665–69); recognized independence of Portugal (1668); at war with France (1673–75).

Mar·i·a·nus Sco·tus \ˌmar-ē-ˈā-nə-ˈskōt-əs\. *Ir. Gael. orig.* Moel-Brig·te \ˈmōil-ˈbrē-də\. 1028–1082 or 1083. Irish chronicler. Became Benedictine monk (1052); banished from Ireland (1052); entered Irish monastery at Cologne, Germany (1056); ordained (1059); lived as recluse at Fulda (1059–69) and Mainz (from 1069). Author of *Chronicon,* world history down to 1082 valuable for information on Irish monastic movement in 10th- and 11th-century Germany.

Ma·ría Pía \mä-ˈrē-ä-ˈpē-ä, *Port* mə-ˈrē-ə-ˈpē-ə\. 1847–1911. Queen of Portugal (1862–89). Daughter of Victor Emmanuel II of Italy; m. (1862) King Louis; unpopular because of her extravagances and absolutist ideas; dowager queen during reign of Charles I (1889–1908).

Ma·ria Stel·la \mä-ˈrē-ä-ˈstel-lä\. 1773–1843. Italian adventuress. Reared as daughter of Lorenzo Chiappini, constable of Modigliana; Chiappini left letter after his death (1821) stating that Maria Stella was actually the daughter of a nobleman who had exchanged her for Chiappini's son; Maria Stella then claimed that Louis-Philippe, duc d'Orléans and later king of France, was the exchanged son; her claim rejected by ecclesiastical court of Faenza (1824).

María Teresa de Austria. See MARIE-THÉRÈSE.

Ma·ria The·re·sa \mə-ˈrē-ə-tə-ˈrā-sə, -ˈrā-zə\. *Ger.* Ma·ri·a The·re·sia \mä-ˈrē-ä-tā-ˈrā-zē-ä\. 1717–1780. Archduchess of Austria and queen of Hungary and Bohemia. Daughter of Emperor Charles VI; m. (1736) Francis Stephen, Duke of Lorraine (later Francis I, Holy Roman emperor). By virtue of the Pragmatic Sanction, succeeded to the Habsburg dominions (1740); opposed by France, Prussia, Spain, etc., in War of Austrian Succession (1740–48); obtained imperial crown for her husband Francis (1745); lost Silesia to Frederick II of Prussia and Austrian lands in Italy to Naples (1748). By financial reforms and aids to commerce and agriculture, strengthened Austria's resources; reorganized army; made alliance with France which brought on Seven Years' War (1756–63), Austria humiliated. After death of Francis (1765) associated her son Joseph II, Holy Roman emperor, with her as ruler of hereditary states (1765–80). Joined Russia and Prussia in partition of Poland (1772). Mother of Emperor Leopold II and Marie-Antoinette.

Marie. See also MARIA and MARY.

Ma·rie \må-rē\. *Pol.* Maria Lesz·czyń·ska \lesh-ˈchin^{y}-skå\. 1703–1768. Queen of Louis XV of France. Daughter of King Stanisław I Leszczyński of Poland; m. Louis XV (1725); had no direct influence on French politics, but her Polish dynastic connections brought France into War of Polish Succession (1733–38).

Ma·rie \mə-ˈrē; *Brit also* ˈmär-ē, ˈmar-ē, ˈmer-ē\. *In full* Marie Alexandra Victoria. 1875–1938. Queen of Ferdinand I of Romania (1914–27). Daughter of Alfred, Duke of Edinburgh; m. (1893) Ferdinand, who became (1914) king of Romania; influential in determining government policies; on surrender of Romania to Germany (1917–18) showed great courage and heroism in working for the Red Cross and her people; crowned with Ferdinand (1922) as rulers of Greater Romania; retired from public life after death (1927) of Ferdinand. Author of *My Country* (1916), *Ilderim* (1925), and *The Mask* (1935), fiction; *The Story of My Life* (1934–35); and Romanian fairy tales.

Marie I. King of the Sedang tribe of Vietnam. See DAVID DE MAYRENA.

Ma·rie \må-rē\, Pierre. 1853–1940. French neurologist. Studied under Jean Charcot; professor, U. of Paris (1907–25); made fundamental contribution to endocrinology by his description of acromegaly (1886); first to describe Charcot-Marie muscular atrophy (1886), pulmonary osteoarthropathy (1890), cerebellar ataxia (1893), cleidocranial dysostosis (1897), rhizomelic spondylosis (1898).

Ma·rie-Amé·li de Bour·bon \må-rē-å-mā-lē-də-bür-bō^{n}\. *Ital.* Maria Amelia. 1782–1866. Queen of Louis-Philippe of France. Daughter of Ferdinand IV, king of Naples; m. Louis-Philippe (1809); took no interest in politics; exiled (1848), lived at Claremont, England (1848–66).

Ma·rie-An·toi·nette \må-rē-ä^{n}-twå-net, *Angl* mə-ˈrē-ˌan-t(w)ə-ˈnet; *Brit also* ˈmär-ē-, ˈmar-ē-\. *In full* Josèphe-Jeanne-Marie-Antoinette. 1755–1793. Queen of Louis XVI of France. Daughter of Emperor Francis I and Maria Theresa; m. Louis (1770) while he was dauphin. Disliked because of her love of luxury and extravagance, attempts to advance her favorites and Austrian interests, alleged extramarital affairs. Affair of Diamond Necklace (1785–86) increased feeling against her (see Louis-René-Édouard de Rohan under ROHAN family and comte de LA MOTTE). Strongly opposed summoning of Estates-General (1789); forced to live in Tuileries (1789); influenced Louis to resist attempts of National Assembly to abolish feudalism and restrict royal prerogative, thus becoming main target of agitation; worked to save the crown by negotiating with comte de Mirabeau and later with Antoine Barnave and asking for intervention of her brother Emperor Leopold II. Consigned to Temple as prisoner with king and children (1793); tried by Revolutionary Tribunal, found guilty of treason, and guillotined. Her courage and frankness at trial and her tragic fate the subject of much literature.

Marie-Caroline-Ferdinande-Louise. Duchess de Berry. See Charles-Ferdinand de BOURBON.

Marie de Bourgogne. See MARY of Burgundy.

Ma·rie de France \må-rē-də-frä^{n}s\. 12th century. French poet. Resident most of her life in England; sometimes identified with Marie, abbess of Shaftesbury and half-sister of Henry II of England. Earliest known French female poet; creator of the *lai Breton;* author of *Lais* (12 narrative poems, c.1170), *Ysopet* (75 Aesopic fables, 1180), and *L'Espurgatoire Seint Patriz* (c.1190).

Marie de Mé·di·cis \-də-mā-dē-sēs\. *Ital.* Ma·ria de' Me·di·ci \mä-ˈrē-ä-dā-ˈmed-ē-chē\. 1573–1642. Queen of Henry IV of France. Daughter of Francesco de' Medici, Grand Duke of Tuscany; m. as 2d wife Henry IV (1600). After murder of Henry (1610), made regent for her son Louis XIII (1610–17); confided in her favorite, Concino Concini, marquis d'Ancre; pursued pro-Spanish policy, squandered state revenues, bought loyalty of rebellious nobles; exiled to Blois by king on assumption of rule (1617). Restored to place in king's council (1622); after unsuccessful attempt to persuade Louis to dismiss Richelieu (Day of the Dupes, Nov. 10, 1630) was banished from France (1631); until her death, vainly plotted against Richelieu.

Ma·rie-Lou·ise \mə-ˈrē-lə-ˈwēz; *Brit also* ˈmär-ē-, ˈmar-ē-; *Fr* må-rē-lwēz\. *Ger.* Ma·ria Lu·i·sa \mä-ˈrē-ä-lü-ˈē-zä\. 1791–1847. Austrian princess. Daughter of Emperor Francis II; 2d wife (1810) of Napoléon I; mother of Napoléon II; on Napoléon's abdication, went with son to Vienna (1814–16). Made duchess of Parma, Piacenza, and Guastalla (1816–31); her rule mild but wholly without political sagacity. Contracted morganatic marriages with Adam Adalbert, Graf von Neipperg (1821; d. 1829), and with Charles-René, comte de Bombelles (1834).

Ma·rie-Thé·rèse \må-rē-tā-rez\. *Sp.* María Teresa de Au·stria \-thā-ˈaù-strē-ä\. 1638–1683. Queen of Louis XIV of France. Daughter of Philip IV of Spain; by Treaty of the Pyrenees (1659) renounced any claim to Spanish succession; m. (1660) Louis XIV; neglected by king for his mistresses.

Ma·ri·ette \mår-yet\, Auguste-Ferdinand-François. 1821–1881. French archaeologist. Joined Egyptian department of the Louvre (1849); in Egypt (1850–54), excavating the Avenue of the Sphinxes and the Sarapeum at Ṣaqqārah; settled in Egypt (1858) as conservator of monuments for Egyptian government; controlled archaeological excavations in Egypt. Among his discoveries were temple of Seti I, pyramid fields of Ṣaqqārah, great temples of Dandarah and Edfu, burial grounds of Maydūm, Abydos, and Thebes. Published *Abydos* (1869), *Aperçu de l'histoire d'Égypte* (1874), *Les Mastabas de l'Ancien Empire* (1889), etc.; suggested plot for Verdi's *Aïda.*

Ma·ri·gnac \må-rēn-yåk\, Jean-Charles-Galissard de. 1817–1894. Swiss chemist. Professor at Geneva (1841–78); known for determinations of atomic weights and researches in crystallography and on rare-earth elements; discoverer of ytterbium (1878) and codiscover of gadolinium (1880, with Lecoq de Boisbaudran).

Ma·ri·gnol·li \ˌmär-ēn-ˈyōl-lē\, Giovanni dei. fl. 1290–1357. Italian traveler. Franciscan friar; one of four legates sent on mission to court of Emperor Togon Temür of China by Pope Benedict XII (1338), reaching Peking (1342), where he remained three or four years; at Columbum (Quilon) in Malabar, founded a Catholic church (1348); visited Ceylon, Persia, Mesopotamia, Syria, Jerusalem; returned to Avignon (1353); later, chaplain to Emperor Charles IV; left fragmentary journal of travels.

Ma·ri·gny \må-rēn-yē\, Enguerrand de. 1260–1315. French politician. Favorite of Philip the Fair; grand chamberlain and chief minister of the king (1304 ff.); unpopular with nobility and the bourgeoisie; associated with policy of heavy taxation and debasement of the coinage; after death of Philip (1314), accused by Charles of Valois of mismanagement of royal finances and of sorcery, and hanged.

Ma·ril·lac \må-rē-yåk\. Name of a French family of Auvergne, including: Charles de Marillac (1501?–1560), ecclesiastic and diplomat; ambassador to Constantinople (to 1538) and to London (to 1543); archbishop of Vienna (1557) and an opponent of the Guises. His nephew ¶Michel (1563–1632), councilor of state, guardian of the seals (1626). His brother ¶Louis (1573–1632), soldier, marshal of France (1629); involved in intrigues against Richelieu; executed. His daughter ¶Saint Louise (1591–1660) was cofounder (1633, with St. Vincent de Paul) and superior of Daughters of Charity; canonized (1934).

Ma·rín \mä-ˈrēn\, Francisco de Paula. *Nicknamed* Ma·ni·ni \mä-ˈnē-nē\. 1774–1837. Spanish horticulturalist. To Hawaiian Islands (c.1791–94); given land in Honolulu by King Kamehameha I for horticultural experiments; introduced many plant species and scientific methods of agriculture to islands; amassed great fortune; interpreter to the king and later assumed many government duties.

Ma·rin \mə-ˈrin\, John Cheri. 1870–1953. American painter, b. Rutherford, N.J. In Europe (1905–10); influenced by Whistler, Cézanne, Cubism, German Expressionism; exhibited annually at Alfred Stieglitz's 291 Gallery in New York (1909–17). Known esp. for his expressionistic watercolor seascapes and views of Manhattan; his later oil paintings influenced by his earlier watercolor style. Works included *Brooklyn Bridge* (c.1912), *Lower Manhattan* (1920), *The*

Singer Building (1921), *Maine Islands* (1922), *Off York Island, Maine* (1922), *Tunk Mountains, Maine* (1945), *Sea Piece* (1951).

Ma·ri·na \mä-'rē-nä\. *Orig.* Ma·lin·tzin \mä-'lint-sən\. *Also called* Doña Marina *or* Ma·lin·che \mä-'lēn-chā\. c.1501–1550. Aztec princess. Given as slave to and became mistress of Hernán Cortés; acted as Maya and Nahua interpreter and otherwise aided Cortés in Spanish conquest of Mexico; m. Juan de Jaramillo, soldier, and with him went to Spain.

Ma·ri·na·tos \,mä-rē-'nä-tòs\, Spyridon Nikolaou. 1901–1974. Greek archaeologist. Professor, U. of Athens (1939 ff.); director of antiquities and monuments of Greece (1956); inspector general of archaeological services of Greece (1967). Discovered site of Battle of Thermopylae, burial ground of Battle of Marathon, and ancient port city on island of Thera. Author of *Cretan Civilisation* (1927), *Crete and Mycenae* (1959), etc.

Ma·ri·net·ti \,mär-ē-'nät-tē\, Emilio Filippo Tommaso. 1876–1944. Italian writer. Founded Futurist movement with publication (Feb. 20, 1909) of "Manifeste de Futurisme" in *Le Figaro* of Paris; war correspondent, Libya and the Balkans (1911–14); officer in World War I (1914–18); joined Fascist party (1919). Among his works were *La Conquête des étoiles* (1902), *Le Roi bombance* (1905), *Mafarka le Futuriste* (1910), *Le Futurisme* (1911), *Anti-neutralità* (1912), *Guerra sola igiene del mundo* (1915), *Otto anime in una bomba* (1919), *Tamburo di fuoco* (1922), *Futurismo e Fascismo* (1924).

Ma·ri·ni \mä-'rē-nē\ *or* **Ma·ri·no** \-nō\, Giambattista. 1569–1625. Italian poet. Protégé of Cardinal Pietro Aldobrandini in Rome, Ravenna (1605), and Turin (1608); won favor of Charles Emmanuel I (Turin). To Paris (1615); protégé of Marie de Médicis (Paris, 1615–23). Notable as leading exponent of concettism in Italian 17th-century literature; chief work *Adone,* a long narrative poem on love story of Venus and Adonis (1623); also published *Le rime* (1602), *La lira* (1608–14), *La murtoleide* (1619), *La sampogna* (1620), etc.

Marini, Marino. 1901–1980. Italian sculptor. Professor at Brera Academy, Milan (1940–70). Known esp. for expressionistic horse-and-rider series (from 1935); also executed nudes, portraits of Stravinsky, Chagall, Henry Miller, etc.

Ma·rin·ko·vić \má-'rēn-kà-vet^y, *Angl* -,vich\, Vojislav. 1876–1935. Yugoslav statesman. Member of Serbian legislature (1906 ff.); minister of national economy (1914–17); leader of Progressists (1915 ff.); aided in drafting Corfu Declaration (1917). Active in organization of the Democratic Union party (1919). Minister of trade (1919), interior (1921–22), foreign affairs (1924, 1927–32); premier of Yugoslavia (April–July 1932).

Ma·ri·nus \mə-'rī-nəs\. Name of two popes:

Marinus I. *Also mistakenly known as* Martin II. d. 884. Pope (882–884). Papal emissary to Fourth Council of Constantinople (869–870); later, bishop of Caere (now Cerveteri). As pope, attempted to settle Photian schism; absolved and restored Formosus (later pope).

Marinus II. *Also mistakenly known as* Martin III. d. 946. Pope (942–946). His pontificate dominated by Alberic II, Marquis of Spoleto; worked for church reform, esp. in discipline and monasticism.

Marinus of Tyre \'tī(ə)r\. 2d century A.D. Greek geographer. Regarded as founder of mathematical geography; predecessor of Ptolemy.

Mar·i·on \'mer-ē-ən, 'mar-ē-\, Francis. *Called* the Swamp Fox. 1732?–1795. American Revolutionary commander, b. Winyah, S.C. Fought Cherokee Indians (1759, 1761); member of South Carolina Provincial Congress (1775); commissioned captain (1775) and served through Revolutionary War; commanded militia troops in South Carolina, harassing British forces by raids and escaping into the swamps and forests when hard pressed; made daring rescue of Americans surrounded by British at Parkers Ferry, S.C. (Aug. 1781); brigadier general (1781); took part in battle of Eutaw Springs (Sept. 1781). Member of S.C. senate (1782–90).

Ma·ri·otte \màr-yòt\, Edme. c.1620–1684. French physicist. Roman Catholic priest; Founding member (1666) of Academy of Sciences, Paris. Published (1676) *Discours de la nature de l'air* in which he coined word barometer and independently stated Boyle's law (known in France as Mariotte's law); introduced experimental physics into France; also made studies in physiology of plants, hydrodynamics, fall of bodies, nature of color, freezing of water, etc.

Ma·ris \'mà-rəs\. Name of three brothers, Dutch painters, closely associated in their work: Jacob (1837–1899), best known as a landscape painter, esp. of Dutch scenes; painted *Landscape near Dordrecht, Seaweed Carts,* and *Grey Tower, Old Amsterdam.* ¶Matthijs (1839–1917); to London (1885) to design stained-glass windows; paintings included *Souvenir of Amsterdam, Bride of the Church, The Four Mills, Girl Feeding Chickens.* ¶Willem (1844–1910); resided chiefly in London; excelled in pastoral scenes as *Cows at a Watercourse.*

Mar·is \'mar-əs\, Roger Eugene. 1934–1985. American baseball player, b. Hibbing, Minn. Member of Cleveland Indians (1957–58), Kansas City Athletics (1958–60), New York Yankees (1960–66), St. Louis Cardinals (1967–68). Surpassed Babe Ruth's 1927 record for home runs in a season by hitting 61 homers for the 1961 season of 161 games.

Ma·ri·tain \mà-rē-taⁿ\, Jacques. 1882–1973. French philosopher. Brought up Protestant; became Roman Catholic (1906); professor at Institut Catholique, Paris (1914–39), Columbia (1941–44), Princeton (1948–60); ambassador to Holy See (1945–48). Known as interpreter of thought of St. Thomas Aquinas and for own system of philosophy based on Aristotelianism and Thomism. His books included *Art et scolastique* (1920), *Distinguer pour unir, ou les degrés du savoir* (1932), *Frontières de la poésie* (1935), *Humanisme intégral* (1936), *La Philosophie morale* (1960).

Ma·ritz \mə-'rēts\, Salomon Gerhardus. *Known also as* Gerrit Maritz. 1876–1940. South African general and rebel. Fought against British in Boer War; commander of South African troops stationed near German colony of South-West Africa (1914); at onset of World War I, defected to German side and precipitated a general rebellion of Boer troops throughout South Africa; rebellion quelled (1915), fled to Europe (1915–23); established an anti-Semitic, pro-Fascist movement in South Africa (1930s).

Mar·i·us \'mer-ē-əs, 'mar-\, Gaius. c.157–86 B.C. Roman general and politician. Tribune of plebs (119); praetor (115); consul (107, 104–100, 86). Fought against Jugurtha (107–106) and against the Cimbri and Teutones (104–101), winning decisive victories over Teutones at Aix (102) and over Cimbri near Vercellae (101). Rivalry with Sulla led to civil war (88); at first driven from Rome, but returned and, with aid of Cinna, captured city and revenged himself by proscribing leaders of aristocratic party. His adopted son ¶Gaius (109–82 B.C.), consul (82), failed in resistance against Sulla; committed suicide.

Marius, Marcus Aurelius. 3d century A.D. Roman emperor. On murder of Postumus (268 A.D.), set himself up in Gaul as rival emperor to Gallienus; uncertain whether his reign lasted two to three days or several months.

Marius, Simon. See Simon MAYR.

Marius Victorinus, Gaius. See VICTORINUS.

Ma·ri·vaux \má-rē-vō\, Pierre Car·let de Cham·blain de \kár-le-də-shäⁿ-blaⁿ-də-\. 1688–1763. French playwright and novelist. After studying law, turned to the theater; published periodical *Le Spectateur français* (1722–23). His plays, chiefly satirical and love comedies, included *L'Amour et la vérité* (1720), *Annibal* (tragedy, 1720), *La Surprise de l'amour* (1722), *La Double Inconstance* (1723), *Arlequin poli par l'amour* (1723), *Le Prince travesti* (1724), *L'Île des esclaves* (1725), *L'Île de la raison* (1727), *La Colonie* (1729), *Le Jeu de l'amour et du hasard* (1730), *L'École des mères* (1732), *L'Heureux stratagème* (1733), *La Mère confidente* (1735), *Le Legs* (1736), *Les Fausses Confidences* (1737), *L'Épreuve* (1740); his novels, *La Vie de Marianne* (1731–41) and *Le Paysan parvenu* (1735–36).

Mark \'märk\. Saint. *In full* John Mark. *Called* the Evangelist. 1st century A.D. One of the 12 Christian Apostles. Fellow worker with Paul and Barnabas; traditionally regarded as author of the second Gospel.

Mark. Saint. d. 336. Pope (Jan.–Oct. 336). Conferred on bishops of Ostia right to consecrate new popes; may have founded church of San Marco, Rome.

Mark the Hermit. *Lat.* Marcus Er·e·mi·ta \,er-ə-'mīt-ə\. d. after 430 A.D. Christian theological writer. May have been disciple of St. John Chrysostom; abbot of a monastery in Ancyra; later an anchorite in Syria and Palestine. Author of theological polemics *Contra Nestorianos* refuting Nestorianism and *De baptismo* against the Messalians, and of treatise *De lege spirituali* on asceticism.

Mark Antony *or* **Anthony.** See Marcus ANTONIUS.

Mark·ham \'mär-kəm\, Sir Clements Robert. 1830–1916. English geographer and historical writer. Served in navy (1844–52); member, Board of Control (1854), East India Co., and in charge of geographical work (1867–77); introduced the cinchona from Peru into India; secretary (1863–88), president (1893–1905), Royal Geographical Society; appointed Robert F. Scott to lead British South Pole expedition. Wrote *Travels in Peru and India* (1862), *Arctic and Antarctic Exploration* (1895), *Lands of Silence* (1921), etc.

Markham, Edwin, *orig.* Charles Edward Anson. 1852–1940. American poet, b. Oregon City, Ore. Teacher, school principal, and school superintendent in California; moved to New York (1899) and engaged in lecturing and writing. Achieved sensational success with poem of social protest "The Man with the Hoe" (1899). His books of verse included *The Man with the Hoe and Other Poems* (1899), *Lincoln and Other Poems* (1901), *The Shoes of Happiness* (1915), *California the Wonderful* (1915), *Gates of Paradise* (1920), etc.

Markham, Gervase *or* Jervis. 1568?–1637. English writer. Soldier in Low Countries and Ireland; translator, compiler, and original writer on forestry, agriculture, veterinary art. Author of *A Discource of Horsemanshippe* (1593), *The Most Honorable Tragedie of Sir Richard Grinvile, Knight* (1595, poem on the last fight of the *Revenge*), *The English Arcadia* (1607, poem in continuation of Sidney's *Arcadia*), *Country Contentments* (1611), and other poems and plays.

Mar·ko Kra·lje·vić \'mar-kò-'kràl-ye-,vēt^y, *Angl* -,vich\, *i.e.* Mark, son of the king. c.1335–1395. King of Serbia (1371–95). Son of King Vukašin; completed a monastery near Sušica; renowned for strength and drinking ability and as implacable foe of the Turks; killed in battle of Rovine against Turks. Hero of Serbian, Romanian, and Bulgarian folk literature.

Mar·kov \'mär-kəf\, Andrey Andreyevich. 1856–1922. Russian mathematician. Taught at St. Petersburg (1880–1905). Made studies in number theory, continued fractions, limits of integrals, approximation theory, convergence of series; contributed to probability theory, esp. with his introduction of Markov chains that helped launch modern theory of stochastic processes.

Mar·ko·vić \'mär-kō-vētʸ\, Svetozar. 1846–1875. Serbian political writer. Member of Socialist International; largely responsible for introducing Socialism into Serbia; edited several Socialist newspapers, including *Radnik* (1871), first such periodical in Serbia.

Mar·kov·ni·kov \(,)mər-'kòv-nyi-kəf\, Vladimir Vasilyevich. 1838–1904. Russian chemist. Professor at Kazan (1868–71), Odessa (1871–73), Moscow (1873–98). Known for studies of petroleum hydrocarbons and chemistry of alicyclic compounds; developed (1869) Markovnikov rule concerning addition reactions in unsymmetrical alkenes.

Marks \'märks\, Johnny. 1909–1985. American composer, b. Mount Vernon, N.Y. Best known for classic Christmas song "Rudolph the Red-Nosed Reindeer," which sold more than 150 million records and 8 million sheet-music copies. Also wrote "I Heard the Bells on Christmas Day," etc.

Marlborough, Dukes of. See John CHURCHILL; SPENCER family.

Marlborough, Earl of. See James LEY.

Mar·lowe \'mär-,lō\, Christopher. 1564–1593. English dramatist. Apparently engaged in espionage service for the government while at Cambridge (1580–87) and perhaps afterwards; attached himself early as dramatist to the Admiral's Men, which produced most of his plays; killed in a tavern brawl under mysterious circumstances. In *Tamburlaine the Great* (2 parts; acted 1587, pub. 1590), first dramatist to discover vigor and variety of blank verse; other plays (in conjectured order of composition; publishing dates given) were *Dido, Queen of Carthage* (1594, completed by Thomas Nashe), *The Tragicall History of Dr. Faustus* (1604), *The Troublesome Raigne and Lamentable Death of Edward the Second* (1594), *The Massacre at Paris* (1600), and *The Famous Tragedy of the Rich Jew of Malta* (1633). Translated Ovid's *Amores* and Lucan's *Pharsalia;* paraphrased part of Musaeus's *Hero and Leander* in heroic couplets (1598); author of short poems, including "The Passionate Shepherd to His Love."

Marlowe, Julia. *Orig.* Sarah Frances Frost \'frȯst\. 1866–1950. American actress, b. Cumberlandshire, England. To U.S. (1870); m. 2d (1911) Edward Hugh Sothern (*q.v.*). Stage debut (New York, 1887); directed and had first financially successful role as Henry VIII's sister in *When Knighthood Was in Flower* (1900); teamed (1904) with Sothern and together they were leading team of Shakespearean actors of the day; among roles were Viola in *Twelfth Night* and Julia in J.S. Knowles's *The Hunchback;* retired (1916) but made occasional appearances thereafter.

Mar·ma·duke \'mär-mə-,d(y)ük\, John Sappington. 1833–1887. American soldier and politician, b. Arrow Rock, Mo. Entered army (1857); resigned commission and joined Confederate army (1861); fought at Boonville and Shiloh; brigadier general (1863), major general (1864); commanded cavalry in Sterling Price's raid in Missouri (1864); fought at Little Blue and captured at Marais des Cygnes River. Governor of Missouri (1884–87); sponsored legislation providing for regulation of railroads.

Mar·mi·on \'mar-mē-ən\, Shackerley *or* Shakerley. 1603–1639. English dramatist. Imitated Ben Jonson. Author of allegorical poem *Cupid and Psyche* (1637) and comedies as *Holland's Leaguer* (1632), *A Fine Companion* (1633).

Már·mol \'mär-mōl\, José. 1818–1871. Argentine writer. Imprisoned (1839) for his opposition to dictator Rosas and eventually forced to flee to Montevideo and Rio de Janeiro; returned (1852) to Argentina as national hero; senator; director of National Library (1858–71). Author of plays *El poeta* and *El cruzado* (both 1842), verse collections *Cantos del Peregrino* (1846), *A Rosas: El 25 de mayo de 1850* (1850), *Armonías* (1851–54), and historical romance *Amalia* (1851), often considered first Argentine novel.

Mar·mont \mär-mōⁿ\, Auguste-Frédéric-Louis Viesse de \vyes-də-\. Duc de Ra·guse \də-rä-güez\. 1774–1852. French soldier. Entered artillery (1792); general (1798); served in Napoleonic campaigns, notably at Marengo (1800), Ulm (1805), Ragusa (1806), Wagram (1809), Salamanca (1812), and in Germany (1813–14); created duc (1808) and marshal of France (1809); surrendered Paris and deserted to Allied side (Mar. 1814), precipitating Napoléon's abdication. Honored by Louis XVIII at Restoration; created peer of France (1814) and commissioned major general; tried unsuccessfully to suppress Revolution of 1830. Retired thereafter to Vienna.

Mar·mon·tel \mär-mōⁿ-tel\, Jean-François. 1723–1799. French writer. Author of tragedies *Denys le Tyran* (1748), *Aristomène* (1749), *Cléopâtre* (1750), *Les Héraclides* (1752), and *Funérailles de Sésostris* (1753); contributed to the *Encyclopédie;* edited *Mercure de France* (1758–60); royal historiographer (1771); wrote also *Contes moraux* (1761), philosophical romances *Bélisaire* (1767) and *Les Incas* (1777), *Éléments de littérature* (1787), *Mémoires d'un père* (1804), and librettos for several light operas.

Mar·nix van Sint Al·de·gon·de \'mär-niks-vän-sint-,äl-də-'gōn-də\, Philips van. 1540–1598. Dutch theologian and writer. Dispatched on a number of missions by William of Orange and finally taken prisoner by the Spaniards. Published satire *De biencorf der H. Roomsche Kercke* (1569); translated the Psalms of David (1580); may have written national anthem "Wilhelmus van Nassauwe."

Maro, Publius Vergilius. See VIRGIL.

Ma·rob·o·dus \mə-'räb-əd-əs\. d. 37 A.D. King of the Marcomanni. Spent youth in Italy and received Roman education; emigrated with his people to Bohemia (c.9 B.C.); founded a kingdom and organized first confederation of Germanic tribes against the Romans; secured treaty with Emperor Tiberius (6 A.D.); defeated by Cherusi leader Arminius (17); deposed (19).

Ma·rot \mä-rō\, Clément. 1496?–1544. French poet. Valet de chambre to Francis I (1526–42); accused of heresy, fled to Geneva under protection of Calvin (1542) and later to Italy. One of first French poets to use Petrarchan sonnet form; originated the *blason* (1536) and introduced the elegy, eclogue, epigram, epithalamium, and *strambotto* into France. Among his works were *Le Temple de Cupido* (allegorical poem, 1515), *L'Enfer* (1532), *L'Adolescence Clementine* (1532), various *épîtres, rondeaux, épigrammes, ballades,* etc.; also, translations of the Psalms (1541–43) and of selections from Virgil, Ovid, and Petrarch. His father ¶Jean, *surname orig.* des Ma·res *or* des Ma·rets \dā-mä-rā\ (c.1463–1526), was also a poet; secretary to Anne of Brittany (1506); valet de chambre to Francis I (1514–26); wrote *La Vraydisante advocate des dames* (1506), and verse descriptions of Louis XII's expeditions to Genoa (1507) and Venice (1509).

Marot, Jean. c.1619–1679. French architect. Designed private houses as Hôtels de Monceau, de Mortemart, and de Pussort, and ornamentation for chimneys, ceilings, etc.; best known for *Le Petit Marot* and *Le Grand Marot,* series of architectural engravings essential for study of 17th-century French architecture. His son ¶Daniel (1661–1752), also an architect; fled France (1685) because of his Protestantism and entered service of William of Orange; accompanied William to London (1694); returned to Holland (c.1698) and continued working for royal family. Designed apartments and gardens at Het Loo palace (c.1692), Armistice, or Truce, Hall at The Hague (c.1697), private houses, royal library; contributed designs for gardens, decoration, and ornamentation of Hampton Court, London; also executed series of engravings providing excellent record of fashions of the times.

Ma·ro·zia \mä-'rȯts-yä, *Angl* mə-'rō-zh(ē-)ə\. d. before 945. Italian noblewoman. Daughter of Theodora and Theophylact; wife (1st) of Alberic, (2d) of Guido of Tuscany, and (3d) of Hugh, king of Italy; exercised great influence at the papal court and succeeded in elevating her son to the papal throne as John XI; imprisoned by her son Alberic II (932).

Mar·pa \'mär-'pä\. 1012–1096. Tibetan Buddhist mystic. Founder of the Bka'-brgyud-pa sect.

Mar·purg \'mär-,pu̇rk\, Friedrich Wilhelm. 1718–1795. German composer and writer on music. Director of Prussian state lottery (1766–95). Wrote much on music, esp. *Abhandlung von der Fuge* (1753–54) and *Legende einiger Musikheiligen* (1786); edited and largely wrote periodicals *Der critische Musicus an der Spree* (1749–50), *Historische-kritische Beyträge* (1754–62, 1778), and *Kritische Briefe über die Tonkunst* (1760–64). Composed *6 Sonaten für das Cembalo* (1756), *Fughe e Capricci* for keyboard (1777), and songs.

Mar·quand \mär-'kwänd\, John Phillips. 1893–1960. American novelist, b. Wilmington, Del. Author of *The Unspeakable Gentleman* (1922), *The Black Cargo* (1925), *Haven's End* (1933), several detective novels around the character Mr. Moto, *The Late George Apley* (1937, Pulitzer prize), *Wickford Point* (1939), *H. M. Pulham, Esquire* (1941), *So Little Time* (1943), *Repent in Haste* (1945), *B.F.'s Daughter* (1946), *Point of No Return* (1949), *Melville Goodwin, U.S.A.* (1951), *Sincerely, Willis Wayde* (1955), *Women and Thomas Harrow* (1958).

Mar·quet \mär-ke\, Albert, *in full* Pierre-Albert. 1875–1947. French painter. Pupil of Gustave Moreau; best known for cityscapes of Paris, Le Havre, Rouen, Rotterdam, etc.

Mar·quette \mär-ket, *Angl* mär-'ket\, Jacques. *Known as* Père Marquette. 1637–1675. French missionary and explorer. Entered Jesuit novitiate (1654); ordained (1666). To New France (1666); on mission among Ottawa Indians (1668); founded mission of St. Ignace on north shore of Straits of Mackinac (1671). Accompanied Jolliet on voyage down Wisconsin and Mississippi rivers, to the mouth of the Arkansas River, and back to Lake Michigan via the Illinois River (1673); on mission (1674–75) to Illinois Indians, reaching sites of present Chicago and Utica. Journal of voyage with Jolliet was first published in 1681.

Mar·quis \'mar-kwəs\, Don, *in full* Donald Robert Perry. 1878–1937. American journalist and humorist, b. Walnut, Ill. Associated with Joel Chandler Harris in editing *The Uncle Remus Magazine* (1907–09). On staff,

New York *Sun* (1912–22), conducted column "The Sun Dial," in which he introduced mehitabel the cat, archy the cockroach, the Old Soak, etc. On staff, New York *Tribune* (1922–25). Much of the material in his column was collected and printed in book form as *The Old Soak* (1921), *archy and mehitabel* (1927), *Off the Arm* (1930), *archy does his part* (1935), etc. Also wrote *Danny's Own Story* (1912), *Dreams and Dust* (1915), *Hermione* (1916), *Sonnets to a Red-Haired Lady* (1922), *The Dark Hours* (1924), *Out of the Sea* (1927).

Marr \'mär\, Nikolay Yakovlevich. 1865–1934. Russian linguist and archaeologist. Contributed to Caucasian archaeology and language studies; his eccentric theories, such as that language is a phenomenon of social class rather than nationality and that all languages developed from an original word-stock of four elements, dominated Soviet linguistics from about 1920 to 1950.

Mar·ra·di \mär-'rä-dē\, Giovanni. 1852–1922. Italian poet. Among his works were *Canzoni moderne* (1879), *Fantasie marine* (1880), *Ballate moderne* (1894), *Rapsodia garibaldiana* (1899), and prose criticisms.

Mar·ri·ott \'mər-ē-ət\, Sir John Arthur Ransome. 1859–1945. English historian. M.P. (1917–29). Author of *Makers of Modern Italy* (1889), *England since Waterloo* (1913), *The Eastern Question* (1917), *England under the Tudors* (1922), *The Mechanism of the Modern State* (1927), *Evolution of Modern Europe, 1453–1923* (1932), *The Evolution of the British Empire and Commonwealth* (1939), etc.

Mar·ro·quín \mär-rō-'kēn\, José Manuel. 1827–1908. Colombian politician and philologist. President of Colombia (1900–04); lost Panama by revolution (1903). Author of books on Castilian grammar and spelling.

Mar·ry·at \'mar-ē-ət\, Frederick. 1792–1848. English naval commander and novelist. Entered navy (1806); in Burmese War commanded successful expedition up Bassein River (1825); retired as captain (1830). Author of novels on sea life largely based on his own experiences, including *Frank Mildmay* (1829), *The King's Own* (1830), *Peter Simple* (1834), *Jacob Faithful* (1834), *Mr. Midshipman Easy* (1836); also of *Japhet in Search of a Father* (1836), *Snarleyyow, or the Dog Fiend* (1837), and *Poor Jack* (1840); in his last days, of books for children, including *Masterman Ready* (1841), *The Settlers in Canada* (1844), *The Children of the New Forest* (1847).

Mars \märs\, Mlle. *Orig.* Anne-Françoise-Hippolyte Bou·tet \bü-te\. 1779–1847. French actress. Daughter of Monvel (*q.v.*); renowned as comedienne; member of Théâtre Français company, and a favorite with Napoléon I; excelled in interpretations of plays of Molière and Marivaux; retired from stage (1841).

Marsch·ner \'märsh-nər\, Heinrich August. 1795–1861. German composer. Director, Dresden court opera (1824–27), Leipzig Stadttheater (1827–31), Hanover Hoftheater (from 1831). Among his compositions were operas *Der Vampyr* (1828), *Der Templer und die Jüdin* (1829), *Hans Heiling* (1833), *Das Schloss am Ätna* (1836), and *Kaiser Adolph von Nassau* (1845), chamber music, piano pieces, choruses, and songs.

Marsh \'märsh\, Sir Edward Howard. 1872–1953. English man of letters. In civil service (1896–1937), esp. as private secretary to Winston Churchill (1905–29); art collector and patron of artists as Stanley Spencer and Duncan Grant. Edited *Georgian Poetry* (5 vols., 1912–22) and *Collected Poems of Rupert Brooke* (1918); translated La Fontaine's *Fables* (1931) and Horace's *Odes* (1941); author of *A Number of People* (1939).

Marsh, George Perkins. 1801–1882. American lawyer, diplomat, and philologist, b. Woodstock, Vt. Member of U.S. House of Representatives (1843–49); U.S. minister to Turkey (1849–53), to Italy (1861–82). Scholar of Northern European languages and Middle Eastern and Mediterranean geography and agricultural practices; contributed to *Oxford English Dictionary;* author of *The Origin and History of the English Language* (1862) and *Man and Nature* (1864).

Marsh, John. 1752–1828. English composer. Apprenticed to solicitor (1768); gave up law and devoted himself to music after inheriting estate near Canterbury (1781); directed subscription concerts at Canterbury (1781–86) and Chichester (from 1787). Composed symphonies, overtures, chamber and keyboard music, anthems, hymns, glees. Wrote *Hints to Young Composers of Instrumental Music* (1807), *A Short Introduction to the Theory of Harmonics* (1809), etc.

Marsh, Dame Ngaio, *in full* Edith Ngaio. 1889–1982. New Zealand novelist. Produced plays in New Zealand (1938–64). Author of mystery novels centering around Inspector Roderick Alleyn of Scotland Yard, including *A Man Lay Dead* (1934), *Overture to Death* (1939), *Final Curtain* (1947), *Death of a Fool* (1956), *Dead Water* (1963), *Tied Up in Tinsel* (1972), *Grave Mistake* (1978).

Marsh, Othniel Charles. 1831–1899. American paleontologist, b. Lockport, N.Y. Nephew of George Peabody; professor, Yale (1866–99). Led expeditions to the West in search for fossils (from 1870); discovered over 1000 fossil vertebrates, including toothed birds; made large fossil collection which he donated to Yale. Author of "Fossil Horses in America" (1874), *Introduction and Succession of Vertebrate Life in America* (1877), and monographs including *Odontornithes* (1880) and "The Dinosaurs of North America" (1896).

Marsh, Reginald. 1898–1954. American painter, b. Paris, France, of American parents. Illustrator for New York journals; taught at Art Students' League, New York (from 1934) and Moore Institute, Philadelphia (from 1949). Known esp. for his paintings of New York City scenes, including *The Bowery* (1930), *Why Not Use the L?* (1930), *Tattoo and Haircut* (1932), *Twenty-Cent Movie* (1936); executed frescoes in Washington, D.C., post office (1935) and New York Custom House (1937).

Marsh, Sylvester. 1803–1884. American inventor, b. Campton, N.H. Built inclined railway up Mount Washington, N.H. (1866–69), inventing special designs of engines for ascending grades, a cog rail (patented 1867), and an atmospheric brake (patented 1870).

Mar·shal \'mär-shəl\. Name of an English family of hereditary marshals including among its members earls of Pembroke:

William Marshal (c.1146–1219), 1st Earl of Pem·broke \'pem-ˌbrůk, *US also* -ˌbrōk\ and Strig·ul \'strig-əl\ through marriage (1189) with daughter of Richard de Clare, 2d Earl of Pembroke and Strigul (see CLARE family); performed exploits as crusader in Holy Land (c.1185–87); helped drive regent William Longchamp into exile (1191); declared for King John (1199); supported royal side in Barons' War; one of John's executors and regent of kingdom (1216); led young King Henry III's army against Prince Louis and rebels at battle of Lincoln (1217) and effected settlement by Treaty of Lambeth (1217). His son ¶William (d. 1231), 2d earl; one of 25 executors of Magna Carta (1215); fought alongside his father at Lincoln (1217); as justiciar in Ireland, forced submission of Hugh de Lacy (1224); m. Henry III's sister Eleanor (1224); fought with Henry III in Brittany and conducted raids in Normandy and Anjou. His cousin ¶John Marshal (1170?–1235), 1st Baron Marshal of Hing·ham \'hiŋ-əm\; nephew of 1st earl; received grants of land for service in Flanders with his uncle and in Ireland, where he was marshal (1207); supported King John against barons; fought against French at Lincoln (1217); justice and diplomatic agent (after 1225).

Mar·shall \'mär-shəl\, Alfred. 1842–1924. English economist. A founder of school of neoclassical economists; first principal of University College, Bristol (1877–81); professor, Cambridge (1885–1908). Author of *Principles of Economics* (1890), *Industry and Trade* (1919), and *Money, Credit and Commerce* (1923).

Marshall, Christopher. 1709–1797. American patriot and diarist, b. prob. in Dublin, Ireland. To America (1727); pharmacist in Philadelphia (to 1774); member of Council of Safety (1777). Best known for his *Remembrancer,* a diary he kept during the Revolution (first pub. at length, 1877).

Marshall, Frank James. 1877–1944. American chess master, b. New York City. Won chess championship of U.S. from J. W. Showalter (1909) and held it continuously until his resignation (1936).

Marshall, George Catlett. 1880–1959. American army officer and statesman, b. Uniontown, Pa. Commissioned in army (1902); served in World War I (1917–19); aide-de-camp to Gen. Pershing (1919–24); served in China (1924–27). Chief of staff, U.S. army (1939–45; retired); general of the army (1944). Sent by Pres. Truman to attempt to mediate in civil war in China (1945–47). U.S. secretary of state (1947–49); originated (1947) European Recovery Program (Marshall Plan); U.S. secretary of defense (1950–51). Awarded Nobel peace prize (1953).

Marshall, James Wilson. 1810–1885. American carpenter and gold miner, b. Hunterdon Co., N.J. To California (1845). His discovery of gold (Jan. 24, 1848) during excavation for a sawmill that he was building in partnership with John A. Sutter (*q.v.*) started famous gold rush of 1849.

Marshall, John. 1755–1835. American jurist, b. near Germantown (now Midland), Va. Son of Thomas Marshall; served in Continental army through American Revolution; at Brandywine, Germantown, Monmouth, Valley Forge. Admitted to bar (1780); practiced, Richmond, Va. (from 1783). Member of Virginia executive council (1782–95), of House of Burgesses (1782–88). Became recognized Federalist leader in Virginia; one of three American commissioners to France (1797–98) to obtain redress for French hostile actions. Member, U.S. House of Representatives (1799–1800). U.S. secretary of state (1800–01). Chief justice of U.S. Supreme Court (1801–35). Principal founder of American system of constitutional law, including doctrine of judicial review; participated in over 1000 decisions, as *Marbury* v. *Madison* (1803), *McCulloch* v. *Maryland* (1819), *Dartmouth College* v. *Woodward* (1819), *Cohens* v. *Virginia* (1821), *Gibbons* v. *Ogden* (1824).

Marshall, Sir John Hubert. 1876–1958. English archaeologist. Director general of Indian Archaeological Survey (1902–31); directed large-scale excavations at Taxila (from 1913) and (from 1921) in Indus Valley, at latter unearthing prehistoric Harappan civilization centered about cities of Harappā (discovered 1921) and Mohenjo-daro (1922). Author of *Mohenjo-Daro and the Indus Civilization* (1931), *The Monuments of Sanchi* (with A. Foucher, 1939), and *Taxila* (1951).

Marshall, Louis. 1856–1929. American lawyer and civic leader, b. Syracuse, N.Y. Practiced law in Syracuse (1877–93) and New York (1894–1929); specialized in defending constitutional rights of members of minorities; mediator in effecting settlement in New York cloakmakers' strike (1910); arbitrator in clothingworkers' strike (1919). A founder of Jewish Welfare Board; a founder (1906) and president (from 1912) of American Jewish Committee. Championed minority protective clauses in Versailles peace treaties (1919); active in Zionist cause (from 1917).

Marshall, Stephen. c.1594–1655. English clergyman. Presbyterian vicar at Finchingfield, Essex (c.1629–51); town preacher at Ipswich (from 1651). Powerful preacher and popular Puritan leader; one of five clergymen who wrote (1641) as Smectymnuus (*q.v.*); swayed House of Commons by sermons on episcopal and liturgical reform; member of Westminster Assembly (1643); participated in preparation of Shorter Catechism (1647).

Marshall, Thomas. 1730–1802. American Revolutionary leader, b. Westmoreland Co., Va. Member, Virginia House of Burgesses (1761–67, 1769–73, 1775). Served in Continental army through American Revolution; at battle of Trenton and battle of Brandywine. Surveyor in Kentucky (1783); surveyor of revenue for the District of Ohio (to 1797). Father of John Marshall.

Marshall, Thomas Riley. 1854–1925. Twenty-eighth vice president of the United States, b. North Manchester, Ind. Practiced law, Columbia City, Ind. (1875–1908); governor of Indiana (1909–13). Vice president of the United States (1913–21), advocated neutrality prior to World War I, supported League of Nations, opposed woman suffrage and prohibition. Made remark "What this country needs is a really good five-cent cigar"; wrote *Recollections of Thomas R. Marshall: A Hoosier Salad* (1925).

Mar·si·li \mär-'sē-lē\ *or* **Mar·si·gli** \mär-'sēl-yē\, Luigi Ferdinando. 1658–1730. Italian naturalist, geographer, and soldier. Founded Accademia della Scienze dell'Istituto di Bologna (1712); published first treatise on oceanography, *Histoire physique de la mer* (1724).

Mar·sil·i·us \mär-'sil-ē-əs\ of Pad·ua \'paj-ə-wə\. *Ital.* Mar·si·lio da Pa·do·va \mär-'sēl-yō-dä-'pä-dō-vä\. c.1280–c.1343. Italian scholar. Professor of philosophy, Paris (1311 ff.); rector, U. of Paris (1313 ff.); participated in Ghibelline struggles in northern Italy. Wrote *Defensor Pacis* (1324, pub. 1522), a juridical treatise against temporal power of pope; forced to flee Paris (1326); excommunicated by Pope John XXII (1327); protégé of Louis IV of Bavaria; aided in patron's conquest of Rome (1328); remained for rest of life at Louis's court in Munich.

Mars·man \'mär-smən\, Hendrik. 1899–1940. Dutch poet, novelist, and critic. Under influence of German Expressionists published *Verzen* (1923); as editor of periodical *De Vrije bladen,* became foremost critic of the younger generation (1925); author also of verse collections *Paradise Regained* (1927), *Porta Negra* (1934), *Tempel en kruis* (1940), and novels *De dood van Angèle Degroux* (1933) and *Heden ik, morgen gij* (with S. Vestdijk, 1936).

Mar·ston \'mär-stən\, John. 1576–1634. English dramatist. Published erotic poem *The Metamorphosis of Pigmalion's Image* (1598) and *The Scourge of Villanie,* eleven coarse and vigorous satires (1598); attacked Ben Jonson in plays *Histriomastix* (1599) and *Jack Drum's Entertainment* (1600); pilloried by Johnson as Crispinus in *Poetaster* (1601); published (1602) *The History of Antonio and Mellida* and its tragic sequel *Antonio's Revenge;* became shareholder (1604) in Children of the Chapel and for them wrote his remaining plays; took orders (1609); incumbent of Christ Church, Hampshire (1616–31). Author also of bombastic and rather coarse tragedies *The Wonder of Women, or The Tragedy of Sophonisba* (1606) and *The Insatiate Countess* (with William Barksteed, 1613), and of gay and entertaining comedies *The Malcontent* (with additions by Webster, 1604), *Eastward Hoe* (with Jonson and Chapman, 1605, and including reflections on Scots for which the authors were confined in prison), *The Dutch Courtezan* (1605), *Parisitaster, or the Fawne* (1606), *What You Will* (1607).

Marston, John Westland. 1819–1890. English dramatist. Solicitor's clerk; belonged to mystical society and edited mystical periodical *Psyche;* author of dozen metrical dramas with well constructed plots and fine diction, including *The Patrician's Daughter* (1841), *Strathmore* (1849), *Mare de Méranie* (1850), *A Life's Ransom* (1857), *A Hard Struggle* (1858), *Life for Life* (1869), and a comedy *The Favourite of Fortune* (1866). His son ¶Philip Bourke (1850–1887), poet, lost his sight at early age; author of collections of poems *Song-tide* (1871), *All in All* (1875), *Wind Voices* (1883), *Garden Secrets* (1887), *A Last Harvest* (1891).

Mar·sus \'mär-səs\, Domitius. c.54–c.4 B.C. Roman poet. Author of epigrams, an epic poem, and a treatise *De urbanitate.*

Mar·sy·as Paint·er \mär-'sē-ə-'spānt-ər\. fl. c.350–325 B.C. Greek painter. Name given to painter, representative of Kerch style, of pelike *Peleus Taming Thetis* and vase *Nuptial Lebes.*

Martel, Charles. See CHARLES MARTEL.

Martel \màr-tel\, Édouard-Alfred. 1859–1938. French speleologist. Tribunal of commerce in Paris (1886–99); professor of subterranean geography, Sorbonne (1899); on staff of Department of Geological Maps of France (1901). Considered founder of speleology; explored caves of Cévennes (1883–87) and also of Ireland, Austria, Majorca, Greece, etc.

Martel de Janville, Comtesse de. See Sibylle de RIQUETI DE MIRABEAU.

Mar·tel·li \mär-'tel-lē\ *or* **Mar·tel·lo** \-lō\, Pier Jacopo. 1665–1727. Italian poet and dramatist. Attempted to create an Italian counterpart to classical French tragedy; invented verse of two seven-syllable hemistichs (now called *verso Martelliano*) as substitute for French alexandrines; author of *Il femia sentenziato,* a dramatic satire on Scipione Maffei (1724), epic, satiric, and religious verse, literary treatises as *Del verso tragico* (1709), and several tragedies in imitation of the French.

Mar·tens \'mär-təns\, Adolphe Adhémar Louis Michel. *Pseudonym* Michel de Ghel·de·ro·de \'gel-də-,rō-də\. 1898–1962. Belgian playwright. Pioneer in concept of total theater. His avant-garde, neo-Gothic, fantastic plays included *Images de la vie de Saint François d'Assise* (1927), *Barabbas* (1929), *Fastes d'enfer* (1929), *Pantagleize* (1930), *Magie rouge* (1934), *Mademoiselle Jaïre* (1934), *Hop, Signor!* (1935).

Mar·tens \'màr-tyins\, Fyodor Fyodorovich. *Called in Fr.* Frédéric de Mar·tens \də-màr-taⁿ\ *and in Ger.* Friedrich von Mar·tens \fòn-'mär-təns\. 1845–1909. Russian jurist and diplomat. On staff of Russian ministry of foreign affairs (1868–72); professor, Imperial School of Law and Imperial Alexander Lyceum (1872–1905); diplomatic representative of Russia in various international arbitration proceedings. Authority on international law; author of *International Law of Civilized Nations* (1882); editor of *Recueil des traités et conventions conclus par la Russie avec les puissances étrangères* (15 vols., 1874–1909).

Mar·tens \'mär-təns\, Georg Friedrich von. 1756–1821. German jurist and diplomat. Professor of law, Göttingen (1783). Published *Recueil des traités* (7 vols., 1791–1801; 4 supplements, 1802–08), *Nouveau recueil général des traités* (16 vols., 1817 ff.).

Mar·tí y Pé·rez \mär-tē-ē-'pä-rās\, José Julián. 1853–1895. Cuban patriot and writer. Involved in 1868 revolutionary uprising; deported to Spain (1871); continued political activities for Cuban independence while in France, Mexico, Guatemala; returned to Cuba (1878) but again exiled (1879), residing thereafter chiefly in New York; founded Cuban Revolutionary party (1892); inspired Cuban revolt (1895) and, with a few companions, landed in Cuba to command rebel troops; killed by Spanish in skirmish. Contributed regular column to *La Nación* of Buenos Aires; author of sensitive, deceptively simple poems on freedom collected as *Versos sencillos* (1891) and *Versos libres* (1913); also wrote essays *Nuestra América* (1881), *Emerson* (1882), *Whitman* (1887), *Bolívar* (1893).

Mar·tial \'mär-shəl\. *Full Latin name* Marcus Valerius Mar·ti·a·lis \,mär-shə-'ā-ləs\. c.40–c.103. Roman poet, b. Spain. Resident in Rome (from 64); friend of Juvenal; enjoyed patronage of emperors Titus and Domitian; commemorated opening of the Colosseum with *Liber spectaculorum* (80; 33 poems still extant); published (84 or 85) *Xenia* and *Apophoreta,* collections of mottoes for gifts; published (86–98) eleven books of epigrams in elegaic couplets depicting, with acute observation but often with obscenity, many aspects of contemporary Roman life; retired to Spain (98); published twelfth and last book of epigrams (102).

Martianus Capella. See CAPELLA.

Martignac, Vicomte de. See Jean-Baptiste-Sylvère GAY.

Martin. See also MARTYN.

Mar·tin \màr-taⁿ, *Angl* 'märt-ᵊn\. Saint. *Also known as* Saint Martin of Tours \tür\. c.316–397. French prelate. Born a pagan; converted to Christianity at age ten; served in Roman army; on discharge (356?) settled at Poitiers under guidance of St. Hilary; preached against Arianism in Pannonia and Illyricum; embraced monastic life at Milan and at island of Gallinaria. Rejoined Hilary at Poitiers (360); founded (c.361) community of hermits at Ligugé, first monastery in Gaul. Bishop of Tours (371); founder of the monastery of Marmoutier; opposed Priscillianism but protested execution of Priscillian, resulting in rupture with Spanish bishops. Patron saint of France; regarded as patron of publicans and innkeepers.

Mar·tin \'märt-ᵊn\. Name of three popes (Martin IV assumed that number because of erroneous reading of popes Marinus as Martin II and III):

Martin I. Saint. d. 655. Pope (649–655). Condemned Monotheletism at Lateran Synod (649); deposed (653) by Emperor Constans II; exiled to the Crimea.

Martin II and **III.** See MARINUS I and II.

Martin IV. *Orig.* Simon de Brie \də-brē\ *or* Bri·on \brē-ōⁿ\. 1210?–1285. Pope (1281–85), b. France. Of noble birth; member of council of Louis IX of

France; chancellor and keeper of great seal (1260); cardinal (1261). Excommunicated (1281) Michael Palaeologus, emperor of the East, thus weakening union of Eastern and Western churches; labored to save Sicily for France after Sicilian Vespers (1282).

Martin V. *Orig.* Oddo Co·lon·na \kō-lōn-nä\. 1368–1431. Pope (1417–31). Elected at the Council of Constance after the deposition of Benedict XIII, Gregory XII, and John XXIII; condemned conciliar theory; restored papal power in Papal States, esp. by overcoming Braccio da Montone (1424); worked to restore papal authority in England and France and to organize crusades against the Hussites; made special concordats with several countries; brought peace to the papacy and the end of the Western Schism.

Martin I. 1374–1409. King of Sicily (1392–1409). Son of Martin the Humanist of Aragon; prince of Aragon; m. 1st Queen Maria of Sicily (1391; d. 1402), 2d Blanche of Navarre (1403); suppressed popular revolt supported by the pope; reformed administration.

Mar·tin \mȧr-ta^{n}\. Name of four brothers, French artisans: Guillaume (d. 1749), ¶Julien (d. 1752), ¶Robert (1706–1765), and ¶Étienne-Simon (d. 1770); remembered for perfecting the composition and application of vernis Martin (patented by Guillaume and Robert, 1730); among their commissions were coaches and rooms at Versailles.

Martin, Albert-Alexandre. *Known as* Albert l'Ou·vri·er \lü-vrē-ā\, *i.e.* the Worker. 1815–1895. French politician. Mechanic and member of many secret political and labor societies; leader of Society of the Seasons (1846); elected to provisional government in Revolution of 1848; elected to National Assembly (1848); played leading role in May–June uprising; imprisoned (1848–59). First industrial worker elected to office in France.

Martin, Bon-Louis-Henri. 1810–1883. French historian. Member of National Assembly (1871) and senator (1876). Published *Histoire de France,* containing selections from important chroniclers and historians (15 vols., 1833–36) and its sequel *Histoire de France depuis 1789 jusqu'à nos jours* (6 vols., 1878–83).

Mar·tin \'märt-ᵊn\, Edward Sandford. 1856–1939. American editor and writer, b. near Auburn, N.Y. A founder of *Harvard Lampoon* (1876); founder and first editor of *Life* magazine (1883) and editorial writer for it (1887–1933). On editorial staff, *Harper's Weekly* (1893–1913), and writer of the "Easy Chair" in *Harper's Magazine* (1920–35). Author of *A Little Brother of the Rich* (verse, 1890), *Reflections of a Beginning Husband* (1913), *What's Ahead, and Meanwhile* (1927), etc.

Martin, Glenn Luther. 1886–1955. American airplane manufacturer, b. Macksburg, Iowa. Established one of first airplane factories in U.S. (Santa Ana, Cal., 1909); built aircraft for U.S. army (from 1914); formed (1917) Glenn L. Martin Co., Cleveland, Ohio; located at Baltimore (1929). Chief business, manufacture of bombers (esp. the B-10 and the B-26 Marauder of World War II) and transoceanic flying boats; designer and builder (from 1935) of clipper airplanes used in transpacific service. Retired (1953).

Martin, Gregory. c.1540–1582. English biblical translator. Helped convert his friend Edmund Campion to Catholicism; tutor to Philip Howard (1569–70); entered William Allen's Roman Catholic college at Douai, France (1570); ordained (1573); taught at Allen's college (1573–76); sent to help organize new English college at Rome (1577); moved (1578) with Douai Coll. to Reims, where he spent rest of life translating Bible into English from the Latin Vulgate; his translation published (New Testament, 1582; Old Testament, 1609–10) as Douay Bible.

Martin, Hipsch *or* Hübsch. See Martin SCHONGAUER.

Martin, Homer Dodge. 1836–1897. American painter, b. Albany, N.Y. At first painted in manner of Hudson River school; after stay in France (1882–86), adopted aspects of Impressionism; his landscapes characterized by spacious design, brilliant color, underlying gravity or gentle melancholy. His canvases included *Ontario Sand Dunes, The Sun Worshippers, Westchester Hills, Adirondack Scenery, Normandy Farm, Evening on the Seine, Harp of the Winds.*

Martin, John. 1789–1854. English painter. Known chiefly for *Belshazzar's Feast* (1821), *The Fall of Nineveh* (1828), *The Deluge* (1826), and *The Eve of the Deluge* (1840), showing wild imaginative power.

Martin, Joseph William, Jr. 1884–1968. American politician, b. North Attleboro, Mass. Publisher of North Attleboro *Evening Chronicle* (from 1908). Member of U.S. House of Representatives (1925–67), speaker (1947–49, 1953–55).

Martin, Luther. 1748?–1826. American lawyer and public official, b. near New Brunswick, N.J. Practiced in Maryland (from c.1772); first attorney general of Maryland (1778–1805). Member, Continental Congress (1785) and Federal Constitutional Convention (1787); opposed plan of strong central government and adoption of Constitution. Defended Samuel Chase in impeachment trial before U.S. Senate (1804) and Aaron Burr in treason trial in Richmond, Va. (1807). Chief judge, court of oyer and terminer, Baltimore (1813–16); again attorney general of Maryland (1818–22); losing prosecutor in *McCulloch* v. *Maryland* case (1819).

Mar·tin \mȧr-ta^{n}\, Pierre-Émile. 1824–1915. French engineer. Director of the steel mills of Sireuil; employing ideas of Sir William Siemens, invented the Siemens-Martin process of making steel from pig iron.

Mar·tin \'märt-ᵊn\, Violet Florence. *Pseudonym* Martin Ross. 1862–1915. Irish novelist. Collaborated with her cousin Edith Somerville (*q.v.*) on vivid tales of Irish life, including *An Irish Cousin* (1889), *Naboth's Vineyard* (1891), *The Real Charlotte* (1894), *The Silver Fox* (1897), and a series of sporting stories beginning with *Some Experiences of an Irish R. M.* (1899).

Mar·tín Dí·az \mär-'tēn-'thē-äth\, Juan. *Called* el Em·pe·ci·na·do \el-em-pā-thē-'nä-thō\, *i.e.* the Stubborn. 1775–1825. Spanish patriot. Led guerrilla bands against French in Peninsular War (1808–14); Constitutionalist in Revolution of 1820; continued activities against absolutists, captured (1823) and publicly displayed in an iron cage; executed.

Mar·tin du Gard \mȧr-ta^{n}-dü̅-gȧr\, Roger. 1881–1958. French writer. Author of novels, including *Devenir!* (1903), *Jean Barois* (1913), *Le Testament du père Leleu* (1913), *Les Thibault* (in 8 parts, 1922–40), *La Gonfle* (1928); also *Un Taciturne* (drama, 1931), *Confidence africaine* (1931), *Vieille France* (1933), *Notes sur André Gide* (1951); awarded 1937 Nobel prize for literature.

Mar·ti·neau \'märt-ᵊn-,ō\, Harriet. 1802–1876. English writer. Delicate and deaf from childhood; gained success and became authority on economics upon publication of *Illustrations of Political Economy* (1832–34), *Poor Laws and Paupers* (1833), and *Illustrations of Taxation* (1834). Visited America (1834–36), where she gave offense by abolitionist views and by *Society in America* (1837); visited Middle East (1846); in *Eastern Life, Present and Past* (1848) expounded philosophic atheism; issued condensed translation of Comte's *Philosophie positive* (1853). Author also of novels *Deerbrook* (1839) and *The Hour and the Man* (1840), of popular tales for children, of *History of England during the Thirty Years' Peace, 1816–46* (1849) and *Autobiographical Memoir* (1877).

Her brother ¶James (1805–1900), Unitarian theologian; preacher in Liverpool (1832–57); professor of mental and moral philosophy, Manchester New Coll. (1840–69), and principal (1869–85); author of influential philosophical works, including *Rationale of Religious Inquiry* (1836), *Ideal Substitutes for God* (1879), *Types of Ethical Theory* (1885), *A Study of Religion* (1888), *The Seat of Authority in Religion* (1890).

Mar·ti·net \mȧr-tē-ne, *Angl* ,märt-ᵊn-'et\, Jean. 17th century. French army officer. Lieutenant colonel and inspector general in army of Louis XIV; devised a new system of military drill given his name.

Mar·ti·nez \mär-'tē-(,)nās, -(,)nez\, Maria Antonita, *nee* Mon·toya \män-'tȯi-ə\. 1887–1980. American potter, b. San Ildefonso Pueblo, N.M. m. (1913) Julian Martinez; known for her lustrous black-on-black ware; instrumental in revitalization of ancient Indian art of pottery making.

Mar·tí·nez \mär-'tē-näs\, Tomás. 1812–1873. Nicaraguan general and politician. Fought against William Walker (1856–57); president of Nicaragua (1857–67); defeated in war with Honduras and El Salvador.

Mar·tí·nez de Cam·pos \mär-'tē-nāth-thā-'käm-pōs\, Arsenio. 1834–1900. Spanish soldier and politician. Served in Morocco (1859), Mexico (1861), and Cuba (1869–72). Aided in restoring monarchical government in Spain (1874–75), seated Alfonso XII on the throne and defeated the Carlists (1876). Suppressed Cuban insurrection (1878). Premier of Spain (1879); minister of war (1881–84); president of the Senate (1886, 1891, 1899). Again commanded in Cuba (1895–96).

Martínez de Ira·la \-ē-'rä-lä\, Domingo. 1509?–1556. Spanish conquistador. With Pedro de Mendoza to New World (1536); took part in founding of Buenos Aires; explored region of La Plata and Paraná rivers; governor of Spanish colonies (1538–40, 1544–48); founded Asuncíon (1537) and moved colonial administration there from Buenos Aires.

Martínez de la Ro·sa \-'rō-sä\, Francisco de Paula. *Full surname* Martínez de la Rosa Ber·de·jo Gó·mez y Ar·royo \-ber-'thā-kō-'gō-mā-thē-ä-'rȯi-ō\. 1787–1862. Spanish politician and writer. Liberal; elected to Cortes of Cádiz (1812); imprisoned (1814–20) for opposing absolutism of Ferdinand VII. Premier of Spain (1820–23, 1834). Political exile in Paris (1823–31); ambassador to Paris (1844–47), to Vatican (1848–51). Author of plays including tragedy *Edipo* (1829) and historical drama *La conjuración de Venecia* (1834; first successful Spanish Romantic play), poetry, historical works, and the historical novel *Doña Isabel de Solís* (1837).

Martínez de To·le·do \-tō-'lā-thō\, Alfonso. 1398?–?1468. Spanish prelate and writer. Archpriest of Talavera; chaplain to John II of Castile. Author of a satirical work on worldly love and the foibles of women, *Reprobación del amor mundano* (1438, better known as *Corbacho*).

Mar·tí·nez Pas·qua·lis \mər-ˈtē-nēsh-pəsh-ˈkwäl-ēsh\. 1727–1779. Portuguese mystic. Founder (1754) of a society of mystics later led by Louis-Claude de Saint-Martin (*q.v.*).

Mar·tí·nez Ru·iz \mär-ˈtē-näth-rü-ˈēth\, José. *Pen name* Azo·rín \ä-thō-ˈrēn\. 1873–1967. Spanish writer. Member of Generation of '98; foremost literary critic of his day. Author of novels as *La voluntad* (1902), *Antonio Azorín* (1903), *La confesiones de un pequeño filósofo* (1904), *Don Juan* (1922), and *El caballero inactual* (1929), dramas, short stories, literary studies as *La ruta de Don Quijote* (1905), *Clásicos y modernos* (1913), *Al márgen de los clásicos* (1915), and *España clara* (1966), and essays on Spanish life as *El alma castellana* (1900), *Los pueblos* (1905), *Castilla* (1912), and *Una hora de España 1560–1590* (1924). Edited *Revista de Occidente* (1923–36).

Martínez Sier·ra \-ˈsyer-rä\, Gregorio. 1881–1947. Spanish playwright and novelist. Edited several Modernist periodicals in Madrid; operated publishing house Renacimiento, which introduced many foreign playwrights into Spain; introduced the art theater into Spain while director (1917–28) of Eslava Theater, Madrid. Author of verse collections *Flores de escarcha* (1900) and *La casa de la primavera* (1907), plays *Teatro de ensueño* (1905), *Canción de cuna* (1911), *Primavera en otoño* (1911), *Madame Pepita* (1913), *El reino de Dios* (1916), and *Don Juan de España* (1921), novels *Tú eres la paz* (1906) and *El amor catedrático* (1907), prose *Un teatro de arte en España* (1926), and the libretto for Manuel de Falla's *El amor brujo* (1915).

Mar·tí·nez Zu·vi·ría \mär-ˈtē-näs-sü-vē-ˈrē-ä\, Gustavo. *Pseudonym* Hugo Wast \ˈväst\. 1883–1962. Argentine novelist. Lawyer by profession; member, House of Deputies (1916–20); director, National Library, Buenos Aires (1931–54); minister of justice and public education (1943–44). Among his novels were *Flor de durazno* (1911), *La casa de los cuervos* (1916), *Valle negro* (1918), *Ciudad turbulenta, ciudad alegre* (1919), *La corbata celeste* (1920), *Desierto de piedra* (1925), *El jinete de fuego* (1926), *Tierra de jaguares* (1927), *Lo que Dios ha unido* (1945).

Martin-Harvey, Sir John. See Sir John Martin HARVEY.

Mar·ti·ni \mär-ˈtē-nē\, Ferdinando. 1841–1928. Italian writer. Minister of education (1892–93); colonial minister (1914–16). Author of comedies, including *L'uomo propone e la donna dispone* (1862), *Chi sa il gioco non l'insegni* (1871), *Il peggio passo è quello dell'uscio* (1873), *La vipera* (1894), and *Peccato e penitenza* (stories, 1913).

Martini, Giovanni Battista. *Known as* Padre Martini. 1706–1784. Italian composer and music scholar. Became Franciscan monk (1721); maestro di cappella at San Francesco in Bologna (from 1725); ordained priest (1729). Renowned as teacher, his pupils included J.C. Bach, Mozart, Gluck, Sarti, Jomelli, Grétry; authority on music history and theory, writing *Storia della musica* (1757–81), *Saggio di contrappunto* (1774–75), etc. Prolific composer of secular and sacred music; wrote in homophonic and contrapuntal styles; his works included oratorios, *Litaniae* (1734), some 32 masses, 24 sinfonias, 12 concertos for various instruments, 96 keyboard sonatas including 12 *Sonate d'intavolatura* (1742) and 6 *Sonate d'intavolatura per l'organo ed il cembalo* (1747), and some 1,000 canons.

Mar·ti·ni \mår-tē-nē, *Ger* mär-ˈtē-nē\, Jean-Paul-Egide. *Orig.* Johann Paul Ägidius Mar·tin \ˈmär-tən\. *Also known as* Mar·ti·ni il Te·de·sco \mär-ˈtē-nē-ēl-tā-ˈdā-skō\. 1741–1816. French composer, b. Germany. Settled at Nancy (1760) and later (1764) in Paris, where he became music director successively for prince de Condé and comte d'Artois. Composer of operas as *L'Amoureux de quinze ans* (1771), *Henry IV* (1774), and *Le Droit du seigneur* (1783), military pieces, and choral music; his best known composition was the song "Plaisir d'Amour".

Mar·ti·ni \mär-ˈtē-nē\, Simone. c.1284–1344. Italian painter. One of leading representatives of Sienese school; probably a pupil of Duccio di Buoninsegna; employed at papal court of Benedict XII at Avignon (1339–44). Among his works were *Maestà* fresco in Palazzo Pubblico, Siena (1315), altarpiece *St. Louis of Toulouse Crowning His Brother, King Robert of Anjou* (c.1317), *Madonna* polyptych in Sta. Caterina, Pisa (1319), frescoes illustrating life of St. Martin in Lower Church of S. Francesco, Assisi (c.1325–26), fresco equestrian portrait of Guidoriccio da Fogliano in Palazzo Pubblico, Siena (1328), and altarpiece *Annunciation* (1333, in collaboration with his brother-in-law Lippo Memmi).

Mar·tin·son \ˈmär-tēn-ˌsȯn\, Harry Edmund. 1904–1978. Swedish novelist and poet. Spent early adulthood as merchant seaman, laborer, vagrant; m. (1929; div. 1940) Moa Martinson (*q.v.*). His books included verse *Spökskepp* (1929), *Nomad* (1931), *Natur* (1934), *Passad* (1945), *Cikada* (1953), *Aniara* (1956, epic poem on space travel); novels *Nässlorna blomma* (1935), *Vägen ut* (1936), *Vägen till Klockrike* (1948); travel sketches *Resor utan mål* (1932), *Kap Farväl* (1933). Awarded 1974 Nobel prize for literature (with Eyvind Johnson).

Martinson, Moa. *Nee* Helga Maria Swartz \ˈsvärts\. 1890–1964. Swedish novelist. m. 2d (1929; div. 1940) Harry E. Martinson. Known for her trilogy about the *statare* (agricultural laborer) comprised of *Mor gifter sig* (1936), *Kyrkbröllop* (1938), *Kungens rosor* (1939).

Mar·ti·nů \mär-ˈtē-nü\, Bohuslav Jan. 1890–1959. Czech composer. Pupil of Joseph Suk; to Paris (1923), where he studied under Albert Roussel; fled German invasion to U.S. (1941); professor at American Academy, Rome (1957). His compositions included operas *Voják a tanečnice* (1928), *Tři přání* (1929), *Mirandolina* (1954), *Ariadne* (1958); ballets *Istar* (1922), *Vzpoura* (1925), *Kuchyňská revue* (1927); orchestral works including *Polička* (1925), *La Bagarre* (1928), *Concerto grosso* (1937), *Double Concerto* (1938), *Memorial to Lidice* (1943), 6 symphonies, and concertos for piano (5), violin (2), oboe, flute; choral works, with and without orchestra; piano pieces; and much chamber music including 6 string quartets and 3 piano trios.

Mar·ti·nus \mär-ˈtē-nüs\ *or* **Martinus Go·sia** \-ˈgō-sē-ä\. c.1100–c.1166. Italian jurist. One of the Four Doctors of Bologna law school; a successor of Irnerius, although probably not his pupil; advocated a more liberal interpretation of the law than his contemporary Bulgarus; friend and adviser of Emperor Frederick I; wrote a commentary on the *Corpus juris.*

Mar·ti·nuz·zi \ˌmär-tē-ˈnüt-tsē\, György. *Orig.* Juraj Utie·še·no·vić \ˌüt-je-ˈshe-nȯv-ētʸ, *Angl* -vich\. *Known as* Fráter György. 1482–1551. Hungarian statesman. Son of Croatian father and a Venetian mother surnamed Martinuzzi; became Paulist friar (1510); chief adviser (from c.1529) to King John I Zápolya of Hungary. Bishop of Nagyvárad (1534); concluded Treaty of Nagyvárad (1538) with Ferdinand of Austria (later Emperor Ferdinand I); after death of Zápolya (1540), served as guardian and regent for Zápolya's son John Sigismund. Attacked by alliance headed by Isabella, the queen mother (1550); defeated the alliance and concluded treaty whereby Isabella renounced rights to Transylvania in favor of Ferdinand I (1551); secured unity of Hungary, but was forced to pay tribute to Turkey because Ferdinand was too weak to defend Hungary. Made cardinal and archbishop of Esztergom (1551); suspected of disloyalty and assassinated by order of Ferdinand.

Martov, L. See Yuly TSEDERBAUM.

Mar·tyn \ˈmärt-ᵊn\, Edward. 1859–1923. Irish playwright. Associated with Lady Gregory, W. B. Yeats, and George Moore in founding Irish Literary Theatre (1899); founded Irish Theatre at Dublin (1914) for presentation of plays in Irish language. Author of plays *The Heather Field* (1899), *Maeve* (1899), *The Tale of a Town* (1902), *The Dream Physician* (1914), etc.

Martyn, Henry. 1781–1812. English missionary. Chaplain under East India Co. (1805); translated New Testament and Prayer Book into Hindustani, New Testament and Psalms into Persian, and Gospels into Judaeo-Persian.

Martyn, John. 1699–1768. English botanist. Professor, Cambridge (1732–62), and at same time practicing physician. Author of *Historia plantarum rariorum* (1728–37); translator of Virgil's *Georgics* (1741) and *Bucolics* (1749), with agricultural and botanical notes. His son ¶Thomas (1735–1825) was professor of botany, Cambridge (1762–1825), and introduced Linnaean system; published translation and continuation of Rousseau's *Letters on the Elements of Botany* (1785), long a standard work.

Martyr, Peter. See PETER MARTYR; Pietro Martire d'ANGHIERA; Pietro Martire VERMIGLI.

Ma·ru·lić \mȧ-ˈrü-lētʸ\, Marko. 1450–1524. Croatian poet and philosopher. Classical scholar at his native Split; his vernacular verse marked beginnings of Croatian literature. Author of epic poems on biblical subjects, esp. *Istorija svete udovice Judit u versih hrvacki složena* (1521), and of didactic moral works in Latin.

Marvel, Ik. See Donald Grant MITCHELL.

Mar·vell \ˈmär-vəl\, Andrew. 1621–1678. English poet and politician. Traveled on the Continent (c.1642–46); tutor to daughter of Lord Fairfax (c.1651–52), to William Dutton, Cromwell's ward (1653–57); Milton's colleague in Latin secretaryship (1657); M.P. (1660–78), with republican leanings, but favorite of Charles II. As political writer, vigorously opposed government after Restoration in verse satires as *Last Instructions to a Painter* (1667) and prose satires as *The Rehearsal Transpros'd* (1672–73), *Mr. Smirke* (1676), and *Growth of Popery and Arbitrary Government in England* (1677). One of greatest of the Metaphysical poets; wrote on nature, garden, country life, moral and political themes. His poems included "An Horatian Ode upon Cromwell's Return from Ireland (1650)," "The First Anniversary" (1655), "On the Death of O.C.," "The Definition of Love," "Eyes and Tears," "Flecknoe," "The Emigrants in the Bermudas," "The Nymph Complaining for the Death of her Fawn," "Thoughts in a Garden," "To his Coy Mistress."

Mar·wān \mar-ˈwän\. Name of two Umayyad caliphs of Baghdad:

Marwān I. *In full* Marwān ibn al-Ḥakam. d. 685. Caliph (683–685). Founder of Marwānid branch and father of ʿAbd al-Malik.

Marwān II. d. 750. Last of Umayyad caliphs (744–750). Overthrown by ʿAbbāsids.

Marx \ˈmärks\. Name of five brothers, all b. New York City, forming comedy team extremely popular on the American stage, screen, and radio: Julius Henry, *known as* Groucho (1890–1977), ¶Leonard, *known as* Chico (1891–1961), ¶Arthur, *orig.* Adolph, *known as* Harpo (1893–1964), ¶Milton, *known as* Gummo (1894–1977), and ¶Herbert, *known as* Zeppo (1901–1979). On vaudeville stage (except Zeppo; from c.1904); Gummo left act and entered garment business (c.1918), replaced by Zeppo. As "The Four Marx Brothers," gained huge success with Broadway comedies *I'll Say She Is* (1924), *The Cocoanuts* (1925; film 1929), *Animal Crackers* (1928; film 1930); also appeared in motion pictures *Monkey Business* (1931), *Horsefeathers* (1932), *Duck Soup* (1933); Zeppo left team to become a highly successful theatrical agent and airplane parts manufacturer. Remaining three brothers starred in films *A Night at the Opera* (1935), *A Day at the Races* (1937), *Room Service* (1938), *Go West* (1940), *The Big Store* (1941), *A Night in Casablanca* (1946), *Love Happy* (1949). Groucho, the leering, mustachioed, bushy-browed, cigar-smoking member, was master of the wisecrack and non sequitur; Harpo, the mute, curly-headed cherubic kleptomaniac, played the harp and communicated by pantomime or by horn; Chico, con man and monologist, spoke in an ersatz Italian accent; Zeppo was the straight man. Groucho appeared alone in films as *Copacabana* (1947), *It's Only Money* (1951), *A Girl in Every Port* (1952), *Skidoo* (1968); emceed quiz show "You Bet Your Life" on radio (1947–50) and television (1950–61). Author of *Beds* (1930), *Many Happy Returns* (1942), *Groucho and Me* (1959), *Memoirs of a Mangy Lover* (1963).

Marx, Adolf Bernhard. 1795–1866. German composer and music scholar. Composer of an opera, oratorio *Moses* (1841), choral works, symphony, piano sonata, and songs; cofounder (1850) with Julius Stern and Theodor Kullak of Berlin (later Stern) Conservatory.

Marx, Karl Heinrich. 1818–1883. German political philosopher. Editor of *Rheinische Zeitung* at Cologne (1842), which was suppressed by the government (1843). Exile in Paris (1843–45) and Brussels (1845–48); returned to Cologne at outbreak of revolutionary activity and founded *Neue rheinische Zeitung* (1848); with his friend and lifelong collaborator Friedrich Engels (*q.v.*), published (1848) *Manifest der kommunistichen Partei* (*The Communist Manifesto*); expelled from Prussia (1849). Settled in London; devoted himself to development of his theory of Socialism which, based on Hegel's dialectical method and Ludwig Feuerbach's materialism, become known as historical materialism or Marxism; worked for social reforms and the spread of Socialism; European correspondent for *New York Tribune* (1851–62); instrumental in founding of International Workingmen's Association (later called First International) at London (1864); struggled with Mikhail Bakunin for control of the International, finally defeating him at its congress at The Hague (1872). His great work *Das Kapital* (1867, 1885, 1894), an analysis of the economics of capitalism, was carried to completion by Engels; also wrote *Die heilige Familie* (with Engels, 1845), *Misère de la philosophie* (1847), *Die Klassenkämpfe in Frankreich 1848 bis 1850* (1850), *Der Achtzehnte Brumaire des Louis Napoleon* (1852), *Zur Kritik der politischen Ökonomie* (1859).

Marx, Wilhelm. 1863–1946. German politician. Member of Prussian Landtag (1899–1918) and the Reichstag (1910–32); founder (1911) and first president of Catholic Schools Organization; chairman of Roman Catholic Center party (1921–28); chancellor of Germany (1923–24, 1926–28).

Mary \ˈme(ə)r-ē, ˈma(ə)r-ē, ˈmā-rē\. 1st century B.C. –1st century A.D. Mother of Jesus. Lived in Nazareth; m. Joseph; other biblical references too sparse to construct a coherent biography. Object of veneration in the Christian church since apostolic times; favorite subject in art, music, literature.

Mary. Name of two queens of England:

Mary I *or* **Mary Tudor.** *Often called* Bloody Mary. 1516–1558. Queen of England and Ireland (1553–58), of house of Tudor. Daughter of Henry VIII and Catherine of Aragon; succeeded to throne on death of her half-brother Edward VI and after deposition of Lady Jane Grey; m. Philip II of Spain (1554); repealed laws establishing Protestantism in England and reestablished Roman Catholicism (1555); persecuted Protestants, total number martyred about 300; accepted Cardinal Pole as chief adviser; lost Calais (1558), last English foothold on the Continent.

Mary II. 1662–1694. Queen of England, Scotland, and Ireland (1689–94), of house of Stuart. Eldest child of James II and Anne Hyde; reared a Protestant; m. (1677) her cousin William, Prince of Orange; with husband, invited by English nobles to assume English crown in order to prevent James II from establishing Roman Catholicism in country; landed in England (1688); crowned joint sovereign with William (1689).

Mary. *Also known as* Mary of An·jou \äⁿ-zhü, *Angl* ˈan-ˌjü\. 1370–1395. Queen of Hungary (1382–85). Daughter of Louis the Great; became queen on death of father; m. Sigismund of Luxembourg; deposed (1385) by Charles III of Naples; imprisoned (1386) but freed by Sigismund (1387); queen with Sigismund (1387–95).

Mary *or* **Mary Stu·art** \ˈst(y)ü-ərt, ˈst(y)ů(-ə)rt\. *Known as* Mary, Queen of Scots. 1542–1587. Queen of Scotland (1542–87). Daughter of James V of Scotland and Mary of Guise; next heir (through her grandmother, Margaret Tudor) to English throne after Henry VIII's children. Became queen when six days old on death of James V; brought up with royal children of France in Roman Catholic faith; m. (1558) Francis II of France (d. 1560). Returned to Scotland (1561); distrusted for her religion and regarded as frivolous because of her culture; victim of intrigues among nobles for disposal of her hand; m. (1565) her cousin Henry Stewart, Lord Darnley (see under STEWART family) and gave him title of king; quelled consequent insurrection by her half-brother James, Earl of Moray. Set out to make herself absolute monarch and to impose Roman Catholicism, with David Rizzio as her secretary and chief minister; refused Darnley's demand that crown be secured to him for life and to his heirs, whereupon he formed compact with other nobles, who murdered Rizzio (1566); bore son (1566), later James I of England; abducted (Apr. 1567) by James Hepburn, Earl of Bothwell, probably at her own instigation; m. Bothwell (May 1567). Having provoked Scottish nobles to rebellion by this marriage, and deserted by her army at Carberry Hill (June 1567), was forced to dismiss Bothwell, deliver herself up to confederate lords, and sign an abdication in favor of her son; escaped from imprisonment at Loch Leven, gathered army of six thousand, but was defeated by Moray at Langside (1568). Fled to England; held prisoner there rest of her life by Elizabeth; imperiled by a number of unsuccessful Catholic risings in her behalf; consented to divorce from Bothwell; charged with being an accomplice in Babington's plot (1586); tried and condemned to death; beheaded at Fotheringhay.

Mary of Bur·gun·dy \ˈbər-gən-dē\. *Fr.* Ma·rie de Bour·gogne \må-rē-də-bür-gònʸ\. 1457–1482. Duchess of Burgundy (1477–82). Daughter and heiress of Charles the Bold; her duchy seized by Louis XI, who sought her in marriage for the dauphin, Charles; declined; m. (1477) Maximilian of Austria, later Holy Roman emperor (1493); signed (1477) the Great Privilege, the Magna Carta of the Netherlands. Mother of Philip I of Spain and of Margaret of Austria.

Mary of France. *Nee* Mary Tu·dor \ˈt(y)üd-ər\. 1496–1533. Queen of Louis XII of France. Daughter of Henry VII and Elizabeth; betrothed (1508–14) to Charles, prince of Castile (later Emperor Charles V); m. (1514) Louis XII (d. 1515); secretly m. (1515) Charles Brandon, 1st Duke of Suffolk, with whom she went to Field of Cloth of Gold (1520). Her daughter Frances was mother of Lady Jane Grey.

Mary of Guise \gwʸēz, gēz, *Angl* gēz, gwēz\. *Also known as* Mary of Lor·raine \lò-ren, *Angl* lə-ˈrān, lò-\. 1515–1560. Queen of Scotland. Daughter of Claude, Duke of Guise; m. (1534) Louis d'Orléans (d. 1537) and 2d (1538) James V of Scotland; mother of Mary, Queen of Scots; regent of Scotland (1554–59); attempted suppression of Protestantism in Scotland.

Mary of Hungary. 1505–1558. Queen of Hungary (1522–26) and regent of the Netherlands (1531–52). Daughter of Philip I of Spain and sister of Emperor Charles V; m. (1522) Louis II of Hungary. Ably administered affairs of Netherlands for twenty years under direction of Charles.

Mary of Mo·de·na \ˈmò-dā-nä\. *Nee* Marie Beatrice d'·Es·te \ˈdes-tā\. 1658–1718. Queen of James II of England. Daughter of Alfonso IV, Duke of Modena; 2d wife of James II (m. 1673); after invasion of England by William and Mary (1688), joined James in his refuge in France.

Mary of Teck \ˈtek\. *In full* Mary Augusta Louise Olga Pauline Claudine Agnes. 1867–1953. Queen of George V of Great Britain. Daughter of Francis, Duke of Teck; m. (1893) George, Duke of York (George V from 1910); mother of Edward VIII and George VI; popular with British people.

Mary of the Incarnation. *Orig.* Barbe-Jeanne Aca·rie \å-kå-rē\, *nee* Av·ril·lot \åv-rē-yō\. 1566–1618. French religious. m. (1582) Pierre Acarie, comte de Villemore; introduced Discalced Carmelite order into France (1604); worked for reform of Benedictine convents and for expansion of Ursulines; after husband's death (1613), entered Carmelite convent at Amiens; took vows with name of Mary of the Incarnation (1615).

Mary Mag·da·lene \-ˈmag-də-lən, -ˌlēn; -ˌmag-də-ˈlē-nē\. Saint. *Also known as* Mary of Mag·da·la \ˈmag-də-lə\. 1st century A.D. Galilean woman. Native of Magdala, village near Tiberias; cleansed of evil spirits by Jesus; accompanied and aided Jesus in Galilee; present at Jesus's crucifixion and burial; according to John 20:14–17, was first to see the resurrected Christ. Distinct from, but sometimes erroneously identified with, Mary of Bethany and the repentant woman of Luke 7:36–50.

Mary Stuart. See MARY, Queen of Scots.

Mary Tudor. See (1) MARY I of England; (2) MARY of France.

Masaccio. See TOMMASO DI GIOVANNI DI SIMONE GUIDI.

Ma·sa·mu·ne \mä-sä-mün-e\ Hakuchō, *orig.* Tadao. 1879–1962. Japanese novelist and critic. Baptized into Christian faith (1897); drama critic for newspaper *Yomiuri shimbun* (1903–10); devoted himself to writing (from 1910). Among his novels, most marked by pessimism, were *Jinai* (1907), *Doko-e* (1908), *Doro ningyō* (1911), *Ushibeya-no-nioi* (1916), *Shisha seisha* (1916), *Umare zarishi naraba* (1924), *Kotoshi-no-aki* (1959); also wrote plays as *Jinsei-no-kōfuku* (1924) and *Ichimanen* (1928), and criticism as *Bundan jimbutsu hyōron* (1932), *Shisō mushisō* (1938), and *Bundanteki Jishōden* (1938).

Masaniello. See Tomasso ANIELLO.

Ma·sa·o·ka \mä-sä-ō-kä\ Shiki, *orig.* Tsunenori. 1867–1902. Japanese poet. On editorial staff of newspaper *Nihon* (1892); war correspondent in Sino–Japanese War (1895); contracted tuberculosis (1895) and was ill rest of life. Responsible for revitalization of *haiku* and *tanka* poetic forms; considered best *haiku* poet of modern times; verse included *Botan kuroku* (1899) and *Shiki kushū* (1909).

Ma·sa·ryk \'mä-sä-rik\, Tomáš Garrigue. 1850–1937. Czechoslovak statesman and philosopher. m. (1878) an American, Charlotte Garrigue (d. 1923); professor, Prague (1882); founded monthly reviews *Athenaeum* (1883) and *Naše Doba* (1893). Member of Austrian Reichsrat (1891–93, 1907–14); vigorous critic of Austrian policy. At outbreak of World War I escaped from Austria (1914); organized (1917) Czechoslovak Legion, which gained recognition (1918) as the de facto government of the future state of Czechoslovakia. First president of Czechoslovakia (1918–35). Among his philosophical and political writings were *Der Selbstmord als soziale Massenerscheinung der modernen Zivilisation* (1881), *Zakladove konkretni logiky* (1885), *Česka Otazka* (1895), *Otazka socialni* (1898), *Zaklady marxismu filosoficke a sociologicke* (1898), *Jan Hus* (1899), *Rusko a Evropa* (1913), *The New Europe* (1918), *Světova Revoluce za valky a ve valce* (1925). His son ¶Jan Garrigue (1886–1948); in diplomatic service (from 1919); minister to Britain (1925–38); lectured in U.S. (1939–40); foreign minister (1940–48) and vice premier (1941–45) of Czechoslovak provisional government in London.

Ma·sca·gni \mäs-'kän-yē\, Pietro. 1863–1945. Italian composer. Musical director of La Scala, Milan (1929). Composer of the famous one-act opera *Cavalleria rusticana* (1890) which started vogue for "verismo" operas, and of less successful operatic works including *L'amico Fritz* (1891), *Silvano* (1895), *Iris* (1898), *Le maschere* (1901), *Isabeau* (1911), *Il piccolo Marat* (1921), *Nerone* (1935); also symphonic works, chamber and church music, songs.

Mas·cart \mås-kår\, Eleuthère-Elie-Nicolas. 1837–1908. French physicist. Professor, Collège de France (from 1872); known for work in spectroscopy, optics, on electrical units, atmospheric electricity, and terrestrial magnetism.

Ma·sche·ro·ni \,mäs-kā-'rō-nē\, Lorenzo. 1750–1800. Italian mathematician. Ordained priest (1767); professor, Pavia (1786); his works included *Geometria del compasso* (1797), a collection of geometrical constructions in which the compass is used exclusively.

Mas·deu \mäs-'thā-ü\, Juan Francisco de. 1744–1817. Spanish historian. Entered Jesuit order (1759); author of *Historia crítica de España y de la cultura española* (20 vols., 1783–1805).

Mase·field \'mās-,fēld\, John Edward. 1878–1967. English poet, playwright, and fiction writer. Ran away to sea (1891); worked in menial jobs while traveling around America; settled in London and devoted himself to writing (1897). Poet laureate (from 1930); member of Order of Merit (1935). Among his works were *Salt Water Ballads* (1902), *A Mainsail Haul* (stories of the sea, 1905), *Captain Margaret* (romance, 1908); dramas *The Tragedy of Nan* (1909) and *The Tragedy of Pompey the Great* (1910); verse narratives *The Everlasting Mercy* (1911), *The Widow in the Bye Street* (1912), and *Dauber* (1913); *The Story of a Roundhouse and Other Poems* (1912), *Philip the King* (drama, 1914), *Gallipoli* (prose sketches, 1916), *Reynard the Fox* (narrative poems, 1919); novels of adventure as *Sard Harker* (1924), *Odtaa* (1926), *Dead Ned* (1938), and *Live and Kicking Ned* (1939); children's books as *The Midnight Folk* (1927) and *The Box of Delights* (1935); *Basilissa* (fictional biography of Empress Theodora, 1940); autobiographies *So Long to Learn* (1952) and *Grace Before Ploughing* (1966); *In Glad Thanksgiving* (poems, 1967).

Masham, Baron. See Samuel Cunliffe LISTER.

Mas·ham \'mas-əm\, Lady Abigail, *nee* Hill. d. 1734. English courtier. Through influence of guardian Duchess of Marlborough entered household of Queen Anne (c.1704); m. (1707) Samuel Masham, later (1712) Baron Masham; held strong Tory views and gradually turned queen against Marlborough; interceded for Robert Harley, Earl of Oxford, and secured dismissal of ministry (1710); given charge of privy purse; deserted Oxford and secured his dismissal (1714) in favor of Bolingbroke; lived in retirement after Anne's death (1714).

Mas·i·nis·sa *or* **Mas·si·nis·sa** \'mas-ə-'nis-ə\. c.240–148 B.C. King of Numidia. Son of chieftain of Massyli tribe; fought as a Carthaginian ally (212–206) and as a Roman ally (from 206); under Roman protection, gained mastery over all of Numidia (201). See SOPHONISBA.

Ma·sip \mä-'sēp\, Juan Vicente. *Known as* Juan de Jua·nes \thā-kwän-ās\. d. 1579. Spanish painter. His religious paintings included a cycle from the legend of St. Stephen, *Holy Family* for Valencia cathedral, *Last Supper,* several versions of *Virgin with Child.* His father ¶Vicente (c.1480–c.1545) was also a painter; best known for his altarpiece for Segorbe cathedral (1530) and *Baptism of Christ* in Valencia cathedral (1535).

Mas·ke·lyne \'mas-kə-,lin, -kəl-ən\, John Nevil. 1839–1917. English magician. Trained as watchmaker; became famous by exposing Davenport Brothers as fraudulent spiritualists (1865); on tour, featuring his box trick, juggling, and automata (with George A. Cooke, 1896–1904); took David Devant as partner (1904); with Devant published *Our Magic* (1911).

Maskelyne, Nevil. 1732–1811. English astronomer. Ordained minister (1755); deputed to observe transit of Venus at St. Helena (1761); experimented en route on determination of longitude by method of lunars, which method he introduced in his *British Mariner's Guide* (1763); astronomer royal (1765); invented prismatic micrometer; supervised publication of annual *Nautical Almanac* (1766–1811); suggested and carried out Mt. Schiehallion experiment for determining earth's density from deviations of the plumb line (1774).

Masoch, Leopold von Sacher-. See SACHER-MASOCH.

Masolino. See Tommaso di CRISTOFORO FINI.

Ma·son \'mās-ᵊn\, Charles. 1728–1786. English astronomer. Assistant at Greenwich Observatory (1756–60); with Jeremiah Dixon, employed by proprietors of Maryland and Pennsylvania to survey boundary line between these states (1763–68), the line afterwards known as the Mason and Dixon Line; with Dixon, measured arc of the meridian in America; engaged in astronomical projects in England (from 1769).

Mason, Daniel Gregory. See Lowell MASON.

Mason, George. 1725–1792. American planter and Revolutionary statesman, b. Fairfax Co., Va. Member (1752–73) of Ohio Company for development of western lands; elected to House of Burgesses (1759); active in opposition to the Stamp Act and the Townshend duties; drew up nonimportation resolutions (Fairfax Resolves) eventually adopted by Continental Congress; member of Virginia Constitutional Convention (1776) and prepared the Declaration of Rights and most of the constitution for Virginia; member of Virginia House of Delegates (1776–88); outlined (1780) plan, later adopted, by which Virginia ceded her western land claims to the United States; member of federal Constitutional Convention (1787) but did not sign Constitution and opposed Virginia's ratification; his criticism of the Constitution largely responsible for adoption of the Bill of Rights; chosen first U.S. senator from Virginia but refused to serve.

His grandson ¶James Murray Mason (1798–1871), b. Fairfax Co., Va.; practiced law in Winchester, Va. (from 1820); member, U.S. House of Representatives (1837–39) and U.S. Senate (1847–61); drafted Fugitive Slave Law (1850); member of Confederate Congress (1861); commissioner of the Confederacy to Great Britain and France (1861–65); seized (with John Slidell, *q.v.*) on board British mail steamer *Trent* (Nov. 1861); released (Jan. 1862) and proceeded to London; lived in Virginia (1868–71).

Mason, Henry. See Lowell MASON.

Mason, James Murray. See George MASON.

Mason, James. 1909–1984. British actor. Known esp. for playing flawed characters; memorable for his rich voice and urbane manner. His films included *The Seventh Veil* (1945), *Odd Man Out* (1947), *The Desert Fox* (1951), *Five Fingers* (1952), *A Star Is Born* (1954), *Lolita* (1962), *Georgy Girl* (1966), and *The Verdict* (1982).

Mason, Sir John. 1503–1566. English diplomat. Sent on missions to the Continent by Henry VIII, Edward VI, Mary, and Elizabeth; chancellor of Oxford (1552–56, 1559–64); under Elizabeth, directed foreign policy.

Mason, John. 1588–1635. English colonist. Governor of Newfoundland (1615). Joined Gorges and others in organizing Laconia Company (1629) to found settlement on Piscataqua River, thus becoming a founder of New Hampshire.

Mason, John Mitchell. 1770–1829. American clergyman and educator, b. New York City. Ordained Presbyterian minister (1793); pastor of two churches in New York; famed for his preaching. Raised standards of Protestant theological education in U.S.; founded (1804) seminary in New York; provost, Columbia College (1811–16); president, Dickinson College (1821–24).

Mason, Lowell. 1792–1872. American musician, b. Medfield, Mass. Published *Boston Handel and Haydn Society's Collection of Church Music* (1822); organizer of Boston Academy of Music (1833). Devised system of musical instruction for children based on Pestalozzian methods and published *Manual of Instruction* (1834); established first public school music program in U.S. (Boston, 1838); teacher of music in Boston schools (1838–41). Compiler of several collections of music, esp. church music, and author of tunes for many hymns, including "Nearer, My God, to Thee," "From Greenland's Icy Mountains," "My Faith Looks Up to Thee." His son ¶William (1829–1908) b. Boston, was a concert pianist, teaching and giving piano recitals in New York (from 1855); author of books on piano method and technique, of *Memoirs of a Musical Life* (1901), valuable source on Liszt's circle at Weimar; composer of piano pieces. Another son ¶Henry (1831–1890), b. Brookline, Mass.; piano manufacturer, founded, with Emmons Hamlin, the Mason and Hamlin Organ Co., Boston (1854), extended into piano manufacturing (from 1882) and reorganized as Mason and Hamlin Organ and Piano Co. His son ¶Daniel Gregory (1873–1953), b. Brookline; composer; taught at Columbia (1905–42; professor from 1929); his music conservative in form and influenced by German Romantics; composer of three symphonies, *Chanticleer Overture* (1926), chamber music, songs, and piano pieces; author of *From Grieg to Brahms* (1902), *Beethoven and his Forerunners* (1904), *Contemporary Composers* (1918), *From Song to Symphony* (1924), etc.

Mason, Max. 1877–1961. American mathematician, b. Madison, Wis. Professor, U. of Wisconsin (1908–25); president, U. of Chicago (1925–28); president (1929–36), Rockefeller Foundation, N.Y. Inventor of devices for submarine detection; made researches in differential equations, calculus of variations, electromagnetic theory; wrote *The New Haven Mathematical Colloquium* (1910).

Mason, Otis Tufton. 1838–1908. American ethnologist, b. Eastport, Me. Curator of ethnology in National Museum (1884–1902); head curator of anthropology (1902–08). Author of *Woman's Share in Primitive Culture* (1894), etc.

Mason, William. 1724–1797. English poet. Wrote *Musaeus* (lament for Pope in imitation of *Lycidas,* 1747), plays *Elfrida* (1752) and *Caractacus* (1759), *Heroic Epistle* to Sir William Chambers, satirizing fashions in gardening (1773), *The English Garden* in blank verse (1772–81). As Gray's executor, wrote *Life and Letters of Gray* (1774).

Mason, William. 1829–1908. See Lowell MASON.

Mas·pe·ro \más-pā-rō\, Gaston-Camille-Charles. 1846–1916. French Egyptologist. Director general of excavations and antiquities for Egyptian government (1881–86, 1889–1914); discovered 40 royal mummies near Dayr al-Baḥrī (1881). His works included *Les Contes populaires de l'Égypte ancienne* (1882), *L'Archéologie égyptienne* (1887), *Les Momies royales de Deir-el-Bahari* (1889), *Histoire ancienne des peuples de l'Orient classique* (1895–97), *Causeries d'Égypte* (1907).

Mas·sa·soit \ˌmas-ə-ˈsȯit\. d. 1661. American Indian chief, b. near present Bristol, R.I. Grand sachem of Wampanoag Indians, living in Massachusetts between Cape Cod and Narragansett Bay. Negotiated peace (1621) with the Pilgrims, and remained friendly with the whites all his life. His son was King Philip (*q.v.*).

Mas·sé \má-sā\, Félix-Marie, *called* Victor. 1822–1884. French composer. Chorus master at Paris Opéra (1860–76). His compositions included the cantata *Le Renégat de Tanger* (1844) and operas as *Galathée* (1852), *Les Noces de Jeannette* (1853), *Les Saisons* (1856), *Fior d'Aliza* (1866), *Paul et Virginie* (1876), and *Une Nuit de Cléopâtre* (1885).

Mas·sé·na \má-sā-ná\, André. Duc de Ri·vo·li \rē-vó-lē\ *and* Prince d'·Ess·ling \des-liŋ\. 1758–1817. French general. Entered army (1775); general of division (1793); played important part in French victory at Loano (1795); triumphed under Napoléon in Italy (1796–97), esp. in battle of Rivoli (1797). Commanded French army in Switzerland and won battle at Zürich (1799). Defended Genoa (1800); marshal of France (1804). Commanded army in Italy (1805); defeated Austrians at Caldiero (Oct. 30, 1805); reconquered Calabria from British (1806); created duc (1808). Distinguished himself in battles of Aspern-Essling and Wagram (1809); created prince (1810). Commander in chief of French army in Spain (1810–11); defeated by Arthur Wellesley, Duke of Wellington, at Bussaco, Portugal (Sept. 27, 1810) and at Fuentes de Oñoro, Spain (May 5, 1811); relieved of command. Supported restoration of Louis XVIII.

Mas·se·net \más-ne, *Angl* ˌmas-ᵊn-ˈā, ma-ˈsnā\, Jules-Émile-Frédéric. 1842–1912. French composer. Professor, Paris Conservatory (1878–1912); wrote autobiography *Mes Souvenirs* (1912). His compositions included operas as *La Grand' Tante* (1867), *Don César de Bazan* (1872), *Le Roi de Lahore* (1877), *Hérodiade* (1881), *Manon* (1884), *Le Cid* (1885), *Esclarmonde* (1889), *Werther* (1892), *La Navarraise* (1894), *Thaïs* (1894), *Sapho* (1897), *Le Jongleur de Notre-Dame* (1902), *Ariane* (1906), and *Don Quichotte* (1910), incidental music to Leconte de Lisle's *Les Érinnyes* containing the "Elégie" (1873), oratorios as *Marie-Magdeleine* (1873) and *Ève* (1875), cantatas, biblical dramas, a requiem mass, a piano concerto, overtures, notably to Racine's *Phèdre* (1873), seven orchestral suites including *Scènes hongroises* (1871) and *Scènes alsaciennes* (1881), ballets, chamber music, songs, etc.

Mas·sey \ˈmas-ē\, Charles Vincent. 1887–1967. Canadian diplomat, b. Toronto. Associate secretary of cabinet war committee (1918); minister without portfolio (1925); Canadian minister to U.S. (1926–30); high commissioner for Canada in U.K. (1935–46); chancellor of U. of Toronto (1947–53); governor general of Canada (1952–59).

Massey, Gerald. 1828–1907. English poet. Joined Chartists and Christian Socialist movement. Author of *Voices of Freedom and Lyrics of Love* (1850), *The Ballad of Babe Christabel* (1854), *War Waits* (1855), *Havelock's March* (1860), *A Tale of Eternity* (1869), etc.; in closing years, sought source of psychic and spiritualistic phenomena in ancient Egyptian civilization and produced *A Book of the Beginnings* (1881), *The Natural Genesis* (1883), and *Ancient Egypt: the Light of the World* (1907).

Massey, William Ferguson. 1856–1925. New Zealand politician, b. Ireland. To New Zealand (1870) and settled as farmer near Auckland. Member of House of Representatives (1894–1925); opposition whip (1895–1903); leader of Conservative opposition (1903–12); prime minister of New Zealand (1912–25); lifelong spokesman of agrarian interests, opponent of militant industrial unionism; signed Treaty of Versailles (1919) on behalf of New Zealand.

Mas·sil·lon \má-sē-yōⁿ\, Jean-Baptiste. 1663–1742. French prelate. Bishop of Clermont (1717); pronounced funeral orations for prince de Conti, the grand dauphin, and Louis XIV.

Mas·sine \(ˌ)mə-ˈsēn\, Léonide. *Orig.* Leonid Fedorovich Mias·sin \(ˌ)myə-ˈsēn\. 1896–1979. Russian dancer and choreographer. One of most important figures in ballet history. With Diaghilev's Ballets Russes (1914–21, 1924–29); made Paris debut by creating title role in Fokine's *La Légende de Joseph* (1914); choreographed his first ballet *Le Soleil de nuit* (1915), followed by *Les Femmes de bonne humeur* (1917), *La Boutique fantasque* (1919), *Le Tricorne* (1919), etc.; collaborated with Jean Cocteau, Picasso, and Satie on *Parade* (1917), bringing the avant-garde into ballet. Solo dancer and ballet master of Roxy Theater, N.Y. (1927–30). Principal dancer and choreographer of Ballet Russe de Monte Carlo (1932–38); created (1933) the symphonic ballet with *Les Présages,* using Tchaikovsky's *Fifth Symphony;* other symphonic ballets *Choreártium* (1933, music of Brahms), *Symphonie fantastique* (1936, Berlioz), *Seventh Symphony* (1938, Beethoven), etc. Founder and head of new Ballet Russe de Monte Carlo (1938–42); directed National Ballet Theater, N.Y. (1942–45); toured with own Ballet Russe Highlights (1945–46); worked primarily in Europe (from 1947). Extended Fokine's choreographic reforms in narration and characterization; often used folk dance and demi-caractère dance in his ballets; as dancer, known for character roles (esp. as Petrouchka) and commanding stage presence. His other ballets, about 100 in all, included *Le Beau Danube* (1924), *Jeux d'enfants* (1932), *Union Pacific* (1934), *Gaîté Parisienne* (1938), *Rouge et noir* (1939), *Labyrinth* (1941), *Aleko* (1942), *Mademoiselle Angot* (1943), *Clock Symphony* (1948), *Harold in Italy* (1951), *Mario and the Magician* (1954), *Don Juan* (1959); also choreographed and danced in films as *The Red Shoes* (1948), *Tales of Hoffmann* (1951), and *Carosello Napoletano* (1954).

Mas·sin·ger \ˈmas-ᵊn-jər\, Philip. 1583–1640. English dramatist. Collaborated with Nathaniel Field, Cyril Tourneur, Dekker, and Fletcher (1613–25) for the King's Men; succeeded Fletcher as chief dramatist for King's Men (1625–40). With Dekker wrote *The Virgin Martyr* (1620?) and with Field *The Fatal Dowry* (1632); introduced thinly veiled reflections on current politics into his plays; denounced Buckingham in *The Bondman* (1623); rhetorical and picturesque in expression, fluent and flexible in verse, had few rivals in art of plot construction. Sole author of fifteen plays, chiefly romantic dramas, including (in probable order of composition; date of 1st printing given): *The Duke of Milan* (1623), *The Unnatural Combat* (1639), *The Renegado* (1630), *The Parliament of Love* (1805), *The Roman Actor* (1629), *The Maid of Honour* (1632), *The Picture* (1630), *The Great Duke of Florence* (1635), *The Emperor of the East* (1631), *The City Madam* (1658), *The Guardian* (1655), *The Bashful Lover* (1655), and comedy *A New Way to Pay Old Debts* (1632) featuring Sir Giles Overreach. For his eleven plays written in collaboration with Fletcher, see John FLETCHER.

Mas·sing·ham \ˈmas-iŋ-əm\, Henry William. 1860–1924. English journalist. Editor, London *Daily Chronicle* (1895–99) and the *Nation* (1907–23), which he molded into an influential liberal organ. His son ¶Harold John (1888–1952), journalist; author of literary criticism, writings on bird and animal life, studies of the English countryside, folklore, mythology, etc., including *St. Francis of Assisi* (1913), *Dogs, Birds and Others* (1919), *Pre-Roman Britain* (1927), *The Heritage of Man* (1929), *Genius of England* (1937), *Wisdom of the Fields* (1945), *Faith of a Fieldsman* (1951).

Massinissa. See MASINISSA.

Mas·sio \ˈmäs-syō\, Niccolo di Giovanni di. *Known as* Gen·ti·le da Fa·bri·a·no \jen-ˈtē-lā-dä-ˌfäb-rē-ˈän-ō\. c.1370–1427. Italian painter, b. Fabriano. First great representative of Umbrian school; worked in International Gothic style. Commissioned to decorate Doges' Palace in Venice with historical frescoes (1409; completed by Pisanello); in Brescia worked for Pandolfo III Malatesta (1414–19); executed his masterpiece *Adoration of the Magi* for Sta. Trinità, Florence (1423); painted several aristocratic Madonnas, Quaratesi Polyptych (1425); began cycle of frescoes for St. John Lateran, Rome (1427; completed by Pisanello).

Mas·son \mä-sōⁿ, má-\, Antoine. 1636–1700. French engraver. Best known for portraits as *Comte d'Harcourt, Olivier d'Ormesson, Marie de Lorraine, Duchesse de Guise;* his *Pèlerins d'Emmaüs,* after Titian, is also well known and is often called in English *The Tablecloth* because of the delicacy with which texture of the table linen is rendered.

Mas·son \ˈmas-ᵊn\, David. 1822–1907. Scottish scholar. Edited *Macmillan's Magazine* (1859–68); professor, Edinburgh (1865–95); historiographer royal for Scotland (1896). Edited works of Goldsmith (1869), Milton (1874), and De Quincey (1889–90). Author of *Essays, Biographical and Critical* (1856),

British Novelists (1859), *Drummond of Hawthornden* (1873), *Chatterton* (1873), *De Quincey* (1878), and his magnum opus *Life of Milton* (1859–80).

Mas·son \mä-sōⁿ, má-\, Frédéric. 1847–1923. French historian. Friend and secretary to Prince Napoléon; entrusted with family papers of Napoléon for classification; from these papers drew material for a number of books on Napoléon I, including *Napoléon inconnu* (1895), *Napoléon et sa famille* (1897–1919), *Napoléon et son fils* (1904), *Napoléon à Sainte-Hélène, 1815–1821* (1912).

Mas·sue \má-sue\, Henri de. Marquis de Ru·vi·gny \də-rue-vēn-yē\. 1605–1689. French soldier. Zealous Protestant, deputy general of Huguenots at French court (1653); friend of Turenne; naturalized in England (1680), to which he emigrated (1686) after revocation of Edict of Nantes. His son ¶Henri (1648–1720), 2d Marquis de Ruvigny and 1st Earl of Gal·way \'gȯl-,wā\, soldier, was aide-de-camp to Turenne (1672–75); retired to England (1688); commanded cavalry regiment of French refugees in service of William III (1691); commander in chief in Ireland (1692); created viscount (1692), earl (1697); one of lords justices of Ireland (1697–1701); commander of English forces in Portugal in War of Spanish Succession, entering Madrid (1706); defeated at Almansa (1707); lord justice in Ireland (1715–16).

Mas·sys \'mäs-īs\ *or* **Mat·sys** \'mät-sīs\ *or* **Mes·sys** \'mes-īs\ *or* **Met·sys** \'met-sīs\, Quentin. c.1466–1530. Flemish painter. A leading representative of the early Flemish school of Antwerp. Painted biblical and genre pictures, portraits, and decorations, including *The Money Changer and His Wife, The Old Man and the Courtesan, Christus Salvator Mundi, Virgin and Child, The Crucifixion* (in collaboration with Joachim Patinir), portraits of Erasmus. His son ¶Jan (1509–1575), religious and genre painter; master in Antwerp guild (1531); banished for heretical opinions (1543–58); painted at first in imitation of his father and then after the Roman masters; works included *Lot and His Daughters* (1563), *Virgin Kissing the Child,* and *Judith with the Head of Holofernes.* Another son ¶Cornelis (1513–79) became master painter (1531); painted landscapes in his father's styles; also executed engravings.

Mas·ters \'mas-tərz\, Edgar Lee. 1869–1950. American writer, b. Garnett, Kans. Successful lawyer in Chicago. Author of verse *A Book of Verses* (1898), *Spoon River Anthology* (1915), *The Great Valley* (1916), *Starved Rock* (1919), *Domesday Book* (1920), *The New Spoon River* (1924), *Fate of the Jury* (1929), *Invisible Landscapes* (1935), *The New World* (1937); novels *Mitch Miller* (1920), *Children of the Market Place* (1922), *The Nuptial Flight* (1923), *The Tide of Time* (1937); autobiography *Across Spoon River* (1936); and biographies *Lincoln—the Man* (1931), *Vachel Lindsay* (1935), *Whitman* (1937), *Mark Twain* (1938).

Mas·ter·son \'mas-tər-sən\, William Barclay, *known as* Bat \'bat\. 1853–1921. American peace officer, b. Iroquois Co., Ill. To Kansas (1870); became known as Indian fighter, scout, gambler; sheriff of Ford Co., Kans. (1877); U.S. marshal (1878); associated with Wyatt Earp in Tombstone, Ariz. (1880); gained national reputation as defender of order on the frontier. Sportswriter on New York *Morning Telegraph* (1902–21).

Mas·'ū·dī, al- \al-,mas-ü-'dē\. *In full* Abū al-Ḥasan 'Alī al-Mas'ūdī. d. 957. Arab historian and traveler. Traveled widely to Africa, Ceylon, Armenia, etc.; renowned as scholar; wrote lost 30-volume "History of Time" *Akhbār az-zamān;* also *Kitāb al-awsaṭ;* achieved fame as historian with abridged *Murūj adh-dhahab wa ma'ādin al-jawāhir,* combining history, science, local customs, geography, etc.

Ma·ta Ha·ri \'mä-tə-'hä-rē\. *Orig.* Margaretha Geertruida MacLeod, *nee* Zel·le \'zel-ə\. 1876–1917. Dutch dancer, courtesan, and spy. m. (1895) Campbell MacLeod, captain in Dutch colonial army; with him lived in Java and Sumatra (1897–1902); assumed name Mata Hari (perhaps from Malayan word for sun) and became successful dancer in Paris (from 1905); had numerous lovers, many military officers; although the truth remains unclear, apparently acted as a spy for Germany (from c.1916); arrested by the French for espionage (Feb. 1917); executed by firing squad.

Ma·ta·mo·ros \mä-tä-'mō-rōs\, Mariano. 1770–1814. Mexican priest and patriot. Served with insurgents under command of Morelos (1811–14); captured in battle at Purvarán (Jan. 5, 1814) and executed at Valladolid. Matamoros, Mex., is named in his honor.

Math·er \'math-ər, 'math-\. Name of family of American Congregational clergymen, prominent in 17th-century New England for their zealous Puritanism, scholarship, and intellect, and involvement in controversial causes: Richard Mather (1596–1669), b. Lowton, Lancashire, England; ordained in Anglican church (1618); suspended from ministry for his Puritanism (1633); reinstated but again suspended (1634). To America (1635); pastorate at Dorchester (1636–69). Leader of Congregationalism in Massachusetts; author of *The Bay Psalm Book* (with John Eliot, 1640) and of *A Platform of Church Discipline* (1649) which, under title of the *Cambridge Platform,* was basic document of New England Congregationalism; chief proponent of Half-Way Covenant of 1662.
His son ¶Increase (1639–1723), b. Dorchester, Mass.; preached in England (1658–61); pastor, Second Church, Boston (1664–1723). President of Harvard (1685–1701). In England represented Massachusetts colonial interests and secured new charter and new governor (1688–92). His *Cases of Conscience Concerning Evil Spirits* (1693) credited with ending executions for witchcraft; continued until his death a leader in his church and a spokesman for Congregationalism. Author of many religious treatises, political pamphlets, sermons, and *A Brief History of the Warr with the Indians* (1676).
His son ¶Cotton (1663–1728), b. Boston; ordained (1685); assisted his father at Second Church, Boston (1685–1723); succeeded to pastorate (1723–28). Active in opposition to royal governor Andros (1689) and in support of Andros's successors. Countenanced Salem witchcraft trials and executions (1692–93) but later supported view they were unfair; interested in science, incurring popular disapproval for his support of smallpox inoculation; his *Curiosa Americana* (1712–24) won him membership in Royal Society of London. Active in charitable work and promotion of education. Published over 400 works on religious, historical, scientific, and moral subjects, including *Wonders of the Invisible World* (1693), his masterpiece *Magnalia Christi Americana* (ecclesiastical history of New England, 1702), *Bonifacius* or *Essays to Do Good* (1710), *Christian Philosopher* (1721), *Manuductio ad Ministerium* (1726), *Ratio Disciplinae* (1726).

Mather, Stephen Tyng. 1867–1930. American conservationist, b. San Francisco. Descendant of Richard Mather; a founder (1903) of Thorkildsen-Mather Borax Co.; president of Sterling Borax Co. (from c.1920). Organizer and first director, National Park Service (1917–29); established coordinated system of national parks and principles for their preservation and use.

Math·e·son \'math-ə-sən\, Samuel Pritchard. 1852–1942. Canadian prelate, b. Kildonan, Man. Ordained Anglican priest (1876); chancellor, U. of Manitoba (1900–34); archbishop of Rupert's Land (1905–31); primate of all Canada (1909–31).

Math·ew \math-(,)yü, *also* 'math-(,)ü\, Theobald. 1790–1856. Irish temperance missionary. Entered Capuchin order (1808); ordained Roman Catholic priest (1813); provincial of Capuchins (1822–51); joined total-abstinence movement (1838) and carried on crusades in Irish, English, and Scottish cities and (1849–51) in America.

Mathews. See also MATTHEWS.

Math·ews \math-(,)yüz\, Charles. 1776–1835. English comedian. Played in chief London houses (from 1803); created some 400 new roles; best known as Sir Fretful Plagiary in R.B. Sheridan's *Critic;* introduced (1808) one-man shows known as "At Homes," including songs, recitations, ventriloquial imitations; joint manager with Frederick Henry Yates of Adelphi (from 1828). His son ¶Charles James (1803–1878), actor and playwright, practiced architecture several years; made London debut as George Rattleton in own play *The Humpbacked Lover* (1835); excelled as light comedian; author of many slight plays, largely adaptations; m. (1838) Lucia Elizabeth Vestris (*q.v.*); with her managed Covent Garden (1839–42), Lyceum (1847–54), and other theaters; produced and starred with her in Boucicault's *London Assurance* (1841); toured U.S., Paris, Australia, India.

Mathews, Shailer. 1863–1941. American theologian, b. Portland, Me. Professor (1894–1908) and dean (1908–33), divinity school of U. of Chicago; a leader of Social Gospel movement. Author of *The Social Teaching of Jesus* (1897), *The Messianic Hope in the New Testament* (1905), *The Spiritual Interpretation of History* (1916), *The Faith of Modernism* (1924), *Creative Christianity* (1935), etc.

Math·ew·son \'math-(y)əs-ən\, Christopher, *known as* Christy. *Also known as* Matty *and* Big Six. 1880–1925. American baseball player, b. Factoryville, Pa. Pitcher for National League team, New York Giants (1900–16); pitched 3 shutouts against Philadelphia Athletics in 1905 World Series; won 35 or 37 games in 1908 season; had career totals of 367, 372, or 373 victories and 186 or 188 losses. Manager, Cincinnati Reds (1916–18); president, Boston Braves (1923–25). One of the first elected to Baseball Hall of Fame (1936).

Ma·thi·as \mə-'thī-əs\, Thomas James. 1754?–1835. English satirist and scholar. Caused sensation with satirical poem *The Pursuits of Literature* (1794); edited Gray (1814); passed latter part of life at Naples; wrote Italian verse, edited works of Italian authors.

Ma·thieu \mát-yœ\, Albert-Xavier-Émile. 1874–1932. French historian. Author of *La Révolution et l'Église* (1911), *Études robespierristes* (1917–18), *La Révolution française* (1922–24), *Autour de Robespierre* (1925), *Girondins et Montagnards* (1930), etc.

Mathieu, Émile-Louis-Victor. 1844–1932. Belgian composer. Director, Louvain Music School (1881–98) and Royal Conservatory, Ghent (1898–1924). Composed operas, including *Georges Dandin* (1876), *La Bernoise* (1880), and *L'Enfance de Roland* (1895), ballet *Les Fumeurs de Kiff* (1876), choruses, cantatas, symphonic poems, concertos for piano and for violin, songs, etc.

Ma·til·da \mə-'til-də\. Saint. 895–968. Queen of Henry I of Germany. Daughter of Saxon Count Dietrich; m. Henry the Fowler (909), who became king of Germany (919). Noted for philanthropies; founded many convents.

Matilda. Name of three queens consort of England:

Matilda of Flanders. d. 1083. Wife (m. c.1053) of William I the Conqueror; crowned (1068) on her arrival in England after serving ably as regent in Normandy during William's absences.

Matilda *or* **Maud** \'mȯd\. 1080–1118. Daughter of Malcolm III of Scotland; first wife (m. 1100) of Henry I of England.

Matilda. 1103?–1152. Daughter of Eustace III, Count of Boulogne; wife (m. before 1125) of Stephen of England.

Matilda *or* **Maud** \'mȯd\. 1102–1167. English princess. Daughter of Henry I of England and Matilda; m. Holy Roman emperor Henry V at Mainz (1114); returned to England after his death (1125); recognized by barons as Henry I's successor; m. (1128) Geoffrey Plantagenet of Anjou. On assumption by Stephen of English throne, invaded England with her half-brother Robert, Earl of Gloucester (1139); captured Stephen (1141); established herself as "Lady of England and Normandy"; after six months, driven from London by citizenry as result of her greed; returned to Normandy (1148); from there exercised considerable influence on her son King Henry II of England.

Matilda of Tuscany. *Called* la Gran Con·tes·sa \lä-'grän-kōn-'tes-sä\, *i.e.* the Great Countess. 1046–1115. Countess of Tuscany (1055–1115). Daughter of Boniface of Canossa; inheritor of power over large part of northern Italy; strong supporter of Pope Gregory VII against Emperor Henry IV; it was at her castle at Canossa that Gregory received Henry's barefoot penance (Jan. 1077); waged war intermittently against Henry (1080–1106).

Ma·tisse \mȧ-tēs\, Henri-Émile-Benoît. 1869–1954. French painter and sculptor. Studied under Gustave Moreau (1892–99); influenced by Post-Impressionism; revolted against Pointillism and became (1905) a leader among the Fauvists; resident chiefly at Nice (from c.1914); designed sets and costumes for Diaghilev's production of ballet *Le Chant du Rossignol* (1920); illustrated edition of Mallarmé's *Poésies* with 29 etchings (1932); supervised installation at Barnes Foundation, Merion, Pa., of his large mural *Dance II* (1933). Continued illustrating books as Montherlant's *Pasiphaé* (1944), Baudelaire's *Fleurs du mal* (1947), Ronsard's *Florilège des Amours* (1948), Charles d'Orléans's *Poèmes* (1950). In last years worked extensively with gouache and colored paper cutouts; published *Jazz* (1947), reflections on art and life; designed Chapelle du Rosaire, Vence, France (1948–51). His canvases included *La Desserte* (1897), *Joie de vivre* (1905–06), *Open Window* (1905), *Woman with the Hat* (1905), *Le Luxe* (1907), *La Desserte Rouge* (1908), *Red Studio* (1911), *Piano Lesson* (1916), *Odalisque with Magnolias* (1924), *Pink Nude* (1935), *Lady in Blue* (1937), *Large Interior in Red* (1948), *Sorrow of the King* (1952), *Souvenir of Oceania* (1953); his sculptures included *Jaguar Devouring a Hare* (1899), *Madeleine I* (1901), *The Back* (four versions, 1909–30), *Seated Nude* (1925).

Ma·tos Fra·go·so \'mä-tōs-frä-'gō-sō\, Juan de. 1608–1688. Spanish dramatist, b. Portugal. Author esp. of comedies, including *El redentor cautivo, La dicha por el desprecio, El yerro del entendido.*

Ma·tos Guer·ra \'mȧ-tüsh-'ger-rȧ, -rə\, Gregório de. 1633–1696. Brazilian poet. Lawyer by profession; in Lisbon, Portugal (1652–81), holding posts of magistrate of criminal and of orphans' courts; returned to Bahia, Brazil (1681), and practiced law; wrote bitter, sarcastic verse satirizing political and social life of Portugal and Brazil; produced no great single work but considered first native Brazilian poetic voice.

Mat·shi·ki·za \,mäch-ē-'kē-zə\, Todd T. 1921–1968. South African writer and musician. Contributed monthly column to magazine *Drum* (from 1951); jazz critic and pianist; wrote vocal compositions for solo, quartet, and chorus; wrote score for musical *King Kong* (1959); radio announcer and producer in Zambia (1965–68). Also author of autobiographical sketches *Chocolates for My Wife* (1961) and short stories.

Ma·tsu·dai·ra \mät-süd-ī-rä\ Sadanobu. *Surname orig.* Ta·ya·su \tī-ä-sü\. 1758–1829. Japanese politician. Related to Tokugawa family. Chief minister under shogun Tokugawa Ienari (1787–1801); instituted Kansei reforms (1787–93), a series of conservative fiscal measures intended to reinvigorate Japan which were ultimately unsuccessful.

Matsudaira Tsuneo. 1877–1949. Japanese diplomat. Vice minister for foreign affairs (1923); ambassador to U.S. (1925–28) and Great Britain (1928–36); minister to Imperial household (1936–45); attempted to moderate Japan's anti-Western foreign policy; first chairman of Diet under new constitution (1947).

Matsudaira Yoshinaga. *Also known as* Matsudaira Keiei. 1829–1890. Japanese noble and politician. Related to Tokugawa family; inherited Fukui fief in central Japan (1838); adviser to government during confrontation crisis with Matthew C. Perry; advised government to open relations with rest of world and embark on policy of foreign conquest. Acting prime minister (1862); strong supporter of Imperial authority and national solidarity; later served in high positions in Meiji government.

Ma·tsu·ka·ta \mät-sü-kät-ä\ Masayoshi. Prince. 1835–1924. Japanese politician. Minister of finance (1881–91, 1898–1900); instituted financial reforms that stabilized currency and revitalized government finances; premier of Japan (1891–92, 1896–98); keeper of privy seal (1917–22). Created prince (1922).

Ma·tsu·na·ga \mät-sün-ä-gä\ Teitoku, *orig.* Katsuguma. 1571–1654. Japanese poet. Founder of the Teimon school of *haiku* poetry.

Ma·tsuo \mät-sü-ō\ Munefusa. *Pseudonym* Matsuo Bashō. *Known as* Ba·shō \bä-shō\. 1644–1694. Japanese poet. Abandoned life of samurai for poetry (1666); revitalized poetic form of *haiku* with spirit of Zen Buddhism and style of evocative contrasts of natural phenomena; excelled also at *renga* form of linked verses. Author of travel description *Oku-no-hosomichi* (1694).

Ma·tsu·o·ka \mät-sü-ō-kä\ Yōsuke. 1880–1946. Japanese politician. Member of Diet (1930–34); represented Japan in Geneva at League of Nations (1932) in pleading for recognition of Japanese policy in Manchuria; lost his case, led Japanese delegation out of League (1933). President, South Manchurian railway (1935–39). Minister of foreign affairs (1940–41); allied Japan with Axis powers and concluded nonaggression pact with Russia. Died while on trial as war criminal.

Ma·tsu·ya·ma \mät-sü-yä-mä\ Motonori. 1884–1958. Japanese geophysicist. Taught at Kyōto U. (1911–49), president (1949); known for studies of remanent magnetization in Japanese and Korean volcanic extrusions and of reversals of geomagnetic poles; authority on physical methods of locating ore bodies. Wrote *Physics of Lithospheres and the Interior of the Earth.*

Mat·syen·dra·nā·tha \məts-,yen-drə-'nät-ə\. *Known also as* Mī·na·nāth \'mē-nə-'nät\. 10th century? Indian religious. First human guru of the Nātha cult; subject of many legends and considered semi-divine by his Buddhist and Hindu followers; master of Gorakhnāth.

Matsys, Quentin. See Quentin MASSYS.

Mattathias. See ANTIGONUS II of Judea; MACCABEES.

Mat·teo Se·ra·fi·ni da Ba·scio \mät-'tā-ō-,sä-rä-'fē-nē-dä-'bäsh-ō\ *or* **di Bas·si** \-dē-'bäs-sē\. c.1495–1552. Italian monk, b. Bascio. Joined Observant Franciscans (c.1511); ordained priest (c.1520); founder of Friars Minor Capuchin, commonly called Capuchins (c.1525; order approved by Pope Clement VII, 1528); first vicar general of the order (1529); on apostolic missionary work (from c.1530); accompanied (1546–47) papal troops assisting Emperor Charles V against Schmalkaldic League.

Mat·te·ot·ti \,mät-tā-'ȯt-tē\, Giacomo. 1885–1924. Italian politician. Member of Chamber of Deputies (from 1919); secretary general of Socialist party (1924); denounced Fascist party (May 30, 1924); 12 days later murdered by six Fascists, causing a worldwide scandal and shaking Mussolini's regime.

Mat·te·uc·ci \,mät-tā-'üt-chē\, Pellegrino. 1850–1881. Italian explorer. Physician by profession; traveled up the Blue Nile (1877); first European to traverse Africa north of the Equator from Egypt to Gulf of Guinea (1880–81).

Mat·thay \'mat-(,)ā\, Tobias Augustus. 1858–1945. English composer, pianist, and teacher. Taught at Royal Academy of Music (1876–1925) and at own piano school (founded 1900); composed an overture, a piano quartet, and much piano music. Expounded his theories of piano technique and teaching in *The Act of Touch* (1903), *The First Principles of Pianoforte Playing* (1905), *Relaxation Studies* (1908), *Musical Interpretation* (1913), *On Method in Teaching* (1921), etc.

Mat·thes \'mät-əs, 'mat-\, François Emile. 1874–1948. American geologist, b. Amsterdam, Netherlands. To U.S. (1891); with U.S. Geological Survey (1896–1947); known esp. for his maps of western areas including Bighorn Mountains, Glacier National Park, Grand Canyon, Yosemite Valley, Mt. Rainier; later concentrated on geomorphology and study of glaciers. Author of classic *Geologic History of the Yosemite Valley* (1930).

Mat·the·son \'mät-ə-,zȯn\, Johann. 1681–1764. German composer and writer on music. Studied under Praetorius; tenor opera singer in Hamburg (1697–1705); befriended Handel (1703); Kapellmeister (1715–28) and canon at Hamburg cathedral; contributed to development of church cantata. Author of *Der vollkommene Kapellmeister* (1739), biographical dictionary of composers *Grundlage einer Ehrenpforte* (1740), and translations of English works. Composer of operas, oratorios and cantatas, suites for clavier, flute sonatas, a Passion, a mass, etc.

Mat·thew \'math-(,)yü, *also* 'math-(,)ü\. Saint. 1st century A.D. One of 12 Christian Apostles. A collector of customs at Capernaum; at the summons of Jesus became an apostle; commonly identified with Le·vi \'lē-,vī\, the son of Alphaeus; traditionally regarded as author of the First Gospel.

Matthew, Thomas. See John ROGERS (c.1500–1555).

Matthew, William Diller. 1871–1930. American paleontologist, b. Saint John, N.B. To U.S. (1889); with American Museum of Natural History, N.Y.C. (1895–1927); professor, U. of California, Berkeley (1927–30). Argued in "Climate and Evolution" (1915) that a majority of mammalian orders and families originated in Northern Hemisphere and subsequently spread southward.

Matthews. See also MATHEWS.

Mat·thews \'math-(,)yüz\, Brander, *in full* James Brander. 1852–1929. American educator and author, b. New Orleans. Professor of literature (1892–1900) and of dramatic literature (1900–24), Columbia; a founder of the Authors' (1882) and Players (1889) clubs. Author of plays as *Margery's Lovers* (1884) and *A Gold Mine* (1887, with G. H. Jessop), novels as *A Confident To-morrow* (1899) and *Vistas of New York* (1912), essays, and books on the drama, including *French Dramatists of the 19th Century* (1881), *The Development of the Drama* (1903), *Molière* (1910), *Shakspere as a Playwright* (1913), *Playwrights on Playmaking* (1923).

Matthews, Stanley. 1824–1889. American jurist, b. Cincinnati. Practiced law, Cincinnati (from 1844); U.S. senator (1877–79); associate justice, U.S. Supreme Court (1881–89).

Mat·thi·as \mə-'thī-əs\. Saint. 1st century A.D. Christian apostle. Chosen by lot to fill the place of Judas Iscariot; may have been missionary in Judea and foreign lands; according to legends, martyred by crucifixion or by being hacked to pieces.

Mat·thi·as \mə-'thī-əs, *Ger* mä-'tē-äs\. 1557–1619. Holy Roman emperor (1612–19). Younger son of Maximilian II; governor general of Spanish Netherlands (1577–81); appointed governor of Austria (1593) by his brother Emperor Rudolf; supported Counter-Reformation and suppressed several peasant rebellions. After formidable insurrection of Hungarian Protestants (1606), declared head of the Habsburg house; forced from Rudolf by treaty (1608) cession of Austria, Hungary, and Moravia, and (1611) crown of Bohemia. Chosen emperor (1612); left most affairs of state in hands of chief adviser Melchior Klesl; attempted to establish peace between Protestant states and Catholic League but failed. Crowned king of Bohemia (1617) and of Hungary (1618); Bohemians revolted (1617); uprising in Prague (1618) was beginning of Thirty Years' War.

Mat·thi·as Cor·vi·nus \mə-'thī-əs-kȯr-'vī-nəs\. *Hung.* Mátyás Hun·ya·di \hu̇n-'yäd-i\. 1443–1490. King of Hungary (1458–90). Second son of János Hunyadi; his claim to throne challenged throughout his reign by his uncle Emperor Frederick III; fought successfully against Turks (c.1462–68); waged long war against Bohemia (1468–78); proclaimed king of Bohemia (1469); by Treaty of Olomouc (1478) obtained cession of Moravia, Silesia, and Lusatia; in war with Frederick III, seized Vienna (1485); built up most powerful kingdom of Central Europe; improved internal conditions and strengthened army; held annual diets; patron of science and literature; established one of finest libraries (Bibliotheca Corvina) in Europe. Chose as heir to throne of Hungary his natural son ¶Johannes Corvinus, *Hung.* János Hunyadi (1473–1504), but Ulászló II was elected instead; Johannes became *ban* of Croatia and Dalmatia.

Mat·thies·sen \'math-əs-ən\, Francis Otto. 1902–1950. American scholar, b. Pasadena, Calif. Taught English at Harvard (1929–50, professor from 1942). Author of *Translation: An Elizabethan Art* (1931), *The Achievement of T.S. Eliot* (1935), *American Renaissance* (1941), *Henry James* (1944), *The James Family* (1947), etc.

Mat·this·son \'mat-i-sȯn\, Friedrich von. 1761–1831. German poet. In service (1794 ff.) of Princess Louise of Anhalt-Dessau; chief librarian in service of king of Württemberg at Stuttgart (1812). His verse praised for its melancholy sweetness and pastoral descriptive passages; author of *Gedichte* (1787), poem "Adelaide" (set to music by Beethoven), and *Erinnerungen* (1810–15).

Mat·ti·o·li \mät-tē-'ō-lē\, Ercole Antonio. Conte. 1640–1703. Italian diplomat. Settled at Mantua and served as secretary of state under Charles III and Charles IV. Regarded by many as the famous secret prisoner known as "the Man in the Iron Mask," incarcerated in the Bastille (1698–1703) for revealing secret negotiations for sale of the Mantuan fortress of Casale to France.

Mat·to de Tur·ner \'mät-tō-thā-'tər-nər\, Clorinda. 1854–1909. Peruvian novelist. Best known for *Aves sin nido* (1889), novel about exploitation of Peruvian Indians; also wrote novels *Índole* (1890) and *Herencia* (1895), plays, and poetry.

Ma Tuan-lin \mäd-'wän-'lin\. 13th century. Chinese historian. Author of *Wen hsien t'ung k'ao*, a huge encyclopedia of general knowledge.

Mā·tu·rī·dī, al- \al-,mä-tu̇r-ē-'dē\, Abū Manṣūr Muḥammad. *More fully* Abū Manṣūr Muḥammad ibn Maḥmūd al-Ḥanafī al-Mutakallim al-Māturīdī as-Samarqandī. d. 944. Muslim theologian. Defended traditional orthodoxy against Hellenist rationalism of Mu'tazilite sect; became accepted leader of Māturīdīyah school.

Mat·u·rin \'mat-chu̇-rən\, Charles Robert. 1780–1824. Irish novelist and dramatist. Protestant curate of St. Peter's, Dublin (1804–24). Author of Gothic romances *The Fatal Revenge* (1807), *The Wild Irish Boy* (1808), *The Milesian Chief* (1812), *Women* (1818), *Melmoth the Wanderer* (1820), and *The Albigenses* (1824), and of tragedies *Bertram* (1816), *Manuel* (1817), and *Fredolfo* (1819).

Mat·ve·yev \(,)mət-'vyā-yif\, Artamon Sergeyevich. 1625–1682. Russian politician. Friend and influential adviser of Czar Alexis. Rose through bureaucratic ranks to head Moscow household troops (1654); head of department of Ukrainian affairs (1669), pressed for annexation of Ukrainian lands from Poland; head of department of foreign affairs (1671); negotiated with Poland treaty of cooperation against Turks (1672); did much to introduce Western culture to Russia; on death of Alexis (1676), stripped of rank and possessions and exiled to Siberia for promoting succession of future Peter I.

Mátyás Hunyadi. See MATTHIAS CORVINUS.

Mat·zel·ig·er \mət-'sel-ə-gər\, Jan Ernst. 1852–1889. American inventor, b. Paramaribo, Dutch Guiana (now Surinam). Son of Dutch colonial engineer and a black Guianese mother; to U.S. (c.1872), settled in Lynn, Mass.; worked in shoe factory; invented (c.1880, patented 1883) shoe-lasting machine that soon supplanted hand-lasting method; received other patents for shoe-manufacturing machinery.

Mauch \'mau̇k\, Karl Gottlieb. 1837–1875. German explorer. To South Africa (1865); discovered goldfields in Hartley Hills (1867) and ruins of ancient city of Zimbabwe (1871), both in modern Zimbabwe.

Mauch·ly \'mäk-lē\, John William. 1907–1980. American physicist and engineer, b. Cincinnati. Co-inventor (with John P. Eckert) of Electrical Numerical Integrator and Computer (ENIAC), first electronic computer (1946), and later models Binac and Univac I. With Eckert formed (1948) corporation to build computers; sold interests (1950) to Remington Rand (later Sperry Rand Corp.), remaining with Rand as director of special projects.

Mauclerc. See PETER of Dreux.

Maud. See MATILDA.

Maude \'mȯd\, Sir Frederick Stanley. 1864–1917. British soldier, b. Gibraltar. Entered army (1884); fought in South African War (1899–1902); commander of 13th Division at Dardanelles (1915); took division to Mesopotamia and there assumed command of army (1916); drove Turks out of al-Kūt, Iraq, and captured Baghdad (1917); died of cholera.

Mauds·lay \'mȯdz-lē\, Henry. 1771–1831. English engineer. Worked for Joseph Bramah (1789–98); set up own engineering business in London (1798); took out patents for printing calico (1805–08); invented the metal lathe; perfected a measuring machine accurate to a millionth of an inch; designed other precision tools; designed and built stationary and marine engines. Considered father of the machine-tool industry. His son ¶Thomas Henry (1792–1864) built up father's firm, which constructed engines for ships of British navy for quarter century. Another son ¶Joseph (1801–1861) patented marine engines, built engines for first screw steamer for admiralty, patented feathering screw propeller and direct-acting annular-cylinder screw engine.

Maugham \'mȯm\, Somerset, *in full* William Somerset. 1874–1965. English novelist and playwright. Author of novels, including *Liza of Lambeth* (1897), *Mrs. Craddock* (1902), *Of Human Bondage* (1915), *The Moon and Sixpence* (1919), *Ashenden* (1928), *Cakes and Ale* (1930), *First Person Singular* (1931), *The Hour Before Dawn* (1942), *The Razor's Edge* (1944); short stories, including *Rain* (1932); plays, including *A Man of Honour* (1903), *Lady Frederick* (1907), *The Circle* (1921), *Our Betters* (1923), *The Constant Wife* (1927), *The Sacred Flame* (1929), *Sheppey* (1933); and autobiographies *The Summing Up* (1938), *Strictly Personal* (1941), *A Writer's Notebook* (1949).

Mau·guin \mō-gaⁿ\, Charles-Victor. 1878–1958. French mineralogist and crystallographer. Taught at the Sorbonne, Paris (1919–48, professor from 1933). Made first study of structure of mica group minerals by X-ray diffraction analysis; devised system of symbols for designation of symmetry properties of crystals, adopted (1935) as international standard.

Mau·nou·ry \mō-nü-rē\, Michel-Joseph. 1847–1923. French soldier. Entered army (1867); in World War I commanded 6th army and checked von Kluck's drive on Paris (Aug.–Sept. 1914); military governor of Paris (1915).

Mau·pas·sant \mō-pä-säⁿ\, Guy de, *in full* Henri-René-Albert-Guy de. 1850–1893. French writer. Civil service clerk (1872–80); protégé of Flaubert. First gained attention with short story "Boule de Suif" (1880), followed by collections of short stories establishing him as supreme in this field, *La Maison Tellier* (1881), *Mademoiselle Fifi* (1882), *Contes de la bécasse* (1883), *Les Sœurs Rondoli* (1884), *Contes et nouvelles* (1885), *Le Horla* (1887), *Le Rosier de Madame Husson* (1888), *La Main gauche* (1889), *L'Inutile beauté* (1890). Among his novels were *Une Vie* (1883), *Bel-Ami* (1885), *Mont-Oriol* (1887), *Pierre et Jean* (1888), *Fort comme la mort* (1889), *Notre cœur* (1890).

Mau·peou \mō-pü\, René-Nicolas-Charles-Augustin de. 1714–1792. French politician. President of Parlement of Paris (1763); chancellor of France (1768–74); joined with duc d'Aiguillon and Joseph-Marie Terray in forming triumvirate to administer government; overthrew Parlement of Paris and replaced it with smaller and more limited courts (1771–74); forced into retirement at accession of Louis XVI (1774).

Mau·per·tuis \mō-per-twʸē\, Pierre-Louis Mo·reau de \mȯ-rō-də-\. 1698–1759. French mathematician and astronomer. Head of expedition sent by Louis XV into Lapland to measure a degree of longitude (1736–37); supported

Newtonian theory of Earth's shape; originated principle of least action (1744); involved in numerous quarrels, esp. with Voltaire, who satirized him.

Mau·ra y Mon·ta·ner \'maù-rä-ē-mòn-tä-'när\, Antonio. 1853–1925. Spanish politician. Member of the Cortes (1881 ff.); minister of colonies (1892–94), of interior (1902); prime minister of Spain (1903–04, 1907–09, 1918, 1919, 1921–22); instituted series of democratic reforms to prevent revolution and foster a constitutional monarchy; his attempt to promote Spanish political influence and commerce in Morocco provoked Rif War and a general strike (July 1909) in Barcelona.

Mau·rel \mò-rel\, Victor. 1848–1923. French baritone. Sang in Paris Opéra (1879–94); chosen by Verdi to create role of Iago in his *Otello* (1887) and role of Falstaff (1893) at La Scala, Milan; with Metropolitan Opera Co. (1894–96); returned to Opéra Comique (1896–1904), where he created role of Mathias in Erlanger's *Le Juif polonais* (1901); settled in New York City as voice teacher (1909).

Mau·re·pas \mòr-pä, mō-rə-\, Jean-Frédéric Phé·ly·peaux de \fā-lē-pō-də-\. Comte. 1701–1781. French politician. Secretary of state of king's household (1718–49) and of marine (1723–49); reorganized navy; his dismissal caused by Mme de Pompadour; in exile (1749–74). Prime minister at accession of Louis XVI (1774); restored powers of Parlement of Paris (1774); alarmed at Turgot's reforms, helped bring about his downfall (1776) and later, dismissal of Necker (1781).

Mau·riac \mòr-yàk\, François. 1885–1970. French novelist. Published verse *Les Mains jointes* (1909); wrote polemical works against totalitarianism and Fascism (1930s) and worked with Resistance during World War II; awarded Nobel prize for literature (1952). Best known for somber, austere psychological novels set in the provinces and exploring religious struggle of a sinner, including *L'Enfant chargé de chaînes* (1913), *La Robe prétexte* (1914), *Le Baiser au lépreux* (1922), *Le Désert de l'amour* (1925), *Thérèse Desqueyroux* (1927), *Le Noeud de vipères* (1932), *Le Mystère Frontenac* (1933), *Les Anges noirs* (1936), *Les Chemins de la mer* (1939), *La Pharisienne* (1941), *Galigaï* (1952), *L'Agneau* (1954), *Un Adolescent d'autrefois* (1969). Author also of plays as *Asmodée* (1939), *Les Mal Aimés* (1945), *Le Feu sur la terre* (1951), and *Le Pain vivant* (1955); essays as *Souffrances et bonheur du chrétien* (1929), *Le Romancier et ses personnages* (1933), and *Le Rencontre avec Barrès* (1945); and *Journal* (1934–51) and *Mémoires* (1959–67).

Mau·rice \'mòr-əs, 'mär-; mō-'rēs\. Saint. *Lat.* Mau·ri·tius \mò-'rish(-ē)-əs\. d. c.286. Christian martyr. Commander of Theban Legion, a group of Egyptian Christians serving in Roman army; ordered by Maximian (later Roman emperor) to help quash revolt of Christian peasants in Gaul; refused order; executed at Agaunum (now Saint-Maurice-en-Valais, Switzerland) with his entire Legion, including SS. Vitalis, Candidus, and Exuperius. The cult of St. Maurice and the Theban Legion still exists in Switzerland and northern Italy.

Maurice. *Lat. in full* Mau·ri·cius Fla·vi·us Ti·be·ri·us \mò-'rish(-ē)-əs-'flā-vē-ə-stī-'bir-ē-əs\. c.539–602. Emperor of the Eastern Roman Empire (582–602). Commander of Imperial forces in East (578); made emperor by Tiberius II; m. (582) Tiberius's daughter Constantina. Successfully concluded Persian war (591); through his general Priscius, defeated Avars several times (598–601); instituted exarchates at Ravenna and Carthage; overthrown and killed by Phocas.

Maurice. *Commonly known as* Maurice of Nas·sau \'nas-ò, *Ger* 'näs-,aù\. 1567–1625. Stadholder of the Dutch Republic (1584–1625). Son of William the Silent. Prince of Orange (1618) and Count of Nassau. Elected stadholder by northern provinces (1584–91); in command of armed forces; a great military leader; seized Zutphen, Deventer, and Nijmegen (1591), Gertruydenberg (1593), and province of Groningen (1594); defeated Spaniards at Turnhout (1597) and Nieuport (1600); lost Ostend (1604); agreed to truce with Spain (1609) but renewed struggle (1621); worked with Johan van Oldenbarnevelt from 1587 to 1609 but thereafter his enemy; caused his death (1619).

Maurice. *Ger.* Mo·ritz \'mō-rits\. 1521–1553. Duke of Saxony (1541–53) and elector in the Albertine line (1547–53). Son of Henry the Pious; supported Reformation and aided Charles V in various wars (1542–44) and esp. against Elector John Frederick (1546–47). In opposition to Charles, granted favorable terms to Magdeburg (1550), concluded treaty with Henry II of France (1552), and refused to recognize Augsburg Interim (1548); finally forced Charles to leave Germany and to conclude the Treaty of Passau (1552); rule ended by struggle with Albert II Alcibiades; mortally wounded at Sievershausen.

Maurice. *Ger.* Mo·ritz \'mōr-its\. *Full given name* Hermann Moritz. Comte de Saxe \sàks\. *Known as* Maurice of Saxony. 1696–1750. French general. Natural son of Frederick Augustus I of Saxony (later Augustus II of Poland). Served under Prince Eugene of Savoy against the French in Flanders (1709–10). Commanded a German regiment in French service (1719) and made innovations in military training, esp. in musketry. Served in French army against his half-brother Augustus III of Poland in War of Polish Succession (1733–38). In War of Austrian Succession captured Prague (1741) and conquered the Austrian Netherlands with victories at Fontenoy (1745), Brussels, Antwerp, Mons, and Raucoux (1746); invaded Holland (1747), defeating Duke of Cumberland at Lauffeld and capturing fortress of Bergen-op-Zoom. Created marshal (1744) and marshal general (1747) of France. Author of *Mes Rêveries* (pub. 1756–57), a military treatise.

Maurice, Frederick Denison, *in full* John Frederick Denison. 1805–1872. English theologian. Ordained Anglican priest (1834); wrote novel *Eustace Conway* (1834); professor of English history and literature, King's Coll., London (1840), and of theology (1846–53), but deprived (1853) for denial of eternity of hell in *Theological Essays*. Organizer and first principal, Working Men's Coll. (1854); professor of moral philosophy, Cambridge (1866–72). Active supporter of all attempts at cooperation among working men; with Thomas Hughes and Charles Kingsley founded Christian Socialism movement (1848). Author of *The Kingdom of Christ* (1838), *The Religions of the World and their Relations to Christianity* (1847), *Moral and Metaphysical Philosophy* (1850–62), *What Is Revelation?* (1859), *The Claims of the Bible and of Science* (1863), and *Social Morality* (1869). His son ¶Sir John Frederick (1841–1912), soldier; in army (1862–1903), serving in South Africa, Egypt, the Sudan; major general (1895); author of essay that influenced army reform at beginning of twentieth century, and of books on military history.

Maurice, Furnley. See Frank L.T. WILMOT.

Maurois, André. See Émile-Salomon-Wilhelm HERZOG.

Mau·ro·pus \mò-'rō-pəs\, John. 11th century. Byzantine scholar and ecclesiastic. Private tutor at Constantinople; at Constantine IX's court; later a monk and archbishop of Euchaita. Author of sermons, poems in classical meter, letters, a saint's life, and canons.

Maur·ras \mò-räs, mō-; mò-ràs\, Charles. 1868–1952. French writer and political theorist. Founder with Jean Moréas of *école romane,* group of poets opposed to Symbolists (1891); became monarchist after Dreyfus affair; a founder of (1899) and regular contributor to review *L'Action Française,* which became (1908) daily paper and royalist party organ with himself and Léon Daudet as editors; imprisoned (1945–52) for supporting Pétain government. Espoused theory of "integral nationalism," which advocated supremacy of the state, primacy of French interests in international relations, and return to political and religious forms of former French greatness. Among his works were *Le Chemin de paradis* (1895), *Enquête sur la monarchie* (1900), *Anthinéa* (1901), *Les Amants de Venise* (1902), *L'Avenir de l'intelligence* (1905), *L'Allée des philosophes* (1924), *La Musique intérieure* (verse, 1925), *Barbarie et poésie* (1925), *Au signe de Flore* (1931), *La Balance intérieure* (verse, 1952).

Maurus, Terentianus. See TERENTIANUS MAURUS.

Mau·ry \mò-rē, mō-\, Jean-Siffrein. 1746–1817. French prelate. Ordained priest (1770); member of Estates-General (1789) and Constituent Assembly (1789–91); emigrated from France (1791). Created cardinal (1794); returned to France under Napoléon; archbishop of Paris (1810–14); fled to Rome at Restoration. Among his writings, best known was *Essai sur L'éloquence de la chaire* (1777).

Maury, Louis-Ferdinand-Alfred. 1817–1892. French scholar and archaeologist. General director of the national archives (1868–1888). Works included *Essai sur les légendes pieuses du Moyen Âge* (1843) and *Croyances et légendes de l'Antiquité* (1863).

Mau·ry \'mòr-ē, 'mär-\, Matthew Fontaine. 1806–1873. American naval officer and oceanographer, b. near Fredericksburg, Va. Entered navy (1825); circumnavigated the globe (1826–30). Superintendent, Depot of Charts and Instruments and of the Naval Observatory (1842–61); conducted researches on ocean winds and currents; made wind and current charts of Atlantic, Pacific, and Indian oceans; published (1855) *The Physical Geography of the Sea*, first textbook of modern oceanography; prepared chart of Atlantic seabed to show practicability of submarine cable. Resigned from U.S. navy to enter Confederate service (1861); agent of Confederacy in England (1862–65). Professor of meteorology, V.M.I. (1868–73). Author of *First Lessons in Geography* (1868), *The World We Live In* (1868), etc.

Maur·ya \'mä-ùr-yə\. A dynasty (c.321–c.185 B.C.) of Hindu kings of India, founded by Candragupta (*q.v.*). Its greatest ruler was Aśoka (*q.v.*), whose kingdom comprised nearly all of India.

Mau·ser \'maù-zər\, Peter Paul (1838–1914) and his brother Wilhelm (1834–1882). German inventors. To Liége (1867), where they perfected breech-loading gun which became "Mauser model 1871" after its adoption by Prussian government in 1871; purchased arsenal at Oberndorf am Neckar to manufacture their guns; invented a pistol, a revolver, and repeating rifle. Peter invented the Mauser magazine rifle (1897).

Mau·so·lus \mò-'sō-ləs\. d. 353 or 352 B.C. Persian satrap of Caria (377 or 376–353 or 352 B.C.). Moved capital from Mylasa to Halicarnassus; joined (362) revolt of satraps against Artaxerxes II but abandoned it before its defeat; his rule virtually autonomous; annexed part of Lycia and several Ionian Greek cities. Chiefly known because of magnificent monument Mausoleum erected in his memory at Halicarnassus by his sister and widow, Artemisia (*q.v.*).

Mauss \mōs\, Marcel. 1872–1950. French sociologist and anthropologist. Assisted his uncle Émile Durkheim on number of works, esp. *Le Suicide* (1897); professor of primitive religion, École Pratique des Hautes Études, Paris (1902); a founder of Institut d'Ethnologie at U. of Paris (1925); taught at Collège de France (1931–39). Made original study of forms of exchange and contract of peoples of Melanesia, Polynesia, and northwestern North America; also studied magic, mourning rites, concept of the self. Author of *Essai sur le don* (1925), *Sociologie et anthropologie* (1950), etc.

Mauth·ner \'maůt-nər\, Fritz. 1849–1923. German writer. Theater critic for *Berliner Tageblatt* (1876–1905); exponent of philosophical Skepticism. Author of collection of parodies on contemporary poets, of satirical novels, historical novels, and philosophical works, esp. *Wörterbuch der Philosophie* (1910) and *Der Atheismus und seine Geschichte im Abendlande* (1921–23).

Mau·ve \'maů-və\, Anton. 1838–1888. Dutch painter. Influenced by Corot and Barbizon school; settled (1885) at Laren, where he became leader of Dutch Barbizon school of painting. Known for landscapes and scenes of rural life, both in oils and water colors; works included *Cows in Meadow* and *Dune Landscape*.

Mauvissière, Sieur de la. See Michel de CASTELNAU.

Mav·er·ick \mav-(ə-)rik\, Samuel Augustus. 1803–1870. American cattleman and politician, b. South Carolina. In Texas (from 1835); engaged in revolutionary agitation and fighting which led to Texan independence; member of convention which established Republic of Texas (1836); mayor of San Antonio (1839); member of Texas congress (1845) and of first legislature of State of Texas. Owned large cattle ranch. The term maverick (for an unbranded animal) arose from his practice of not branding his calves.

Ma·vor \'mā-vər\, Osborne Henry. *Pseudonym* James Bri·die \'brī-dē\. 1888–1951. Scottish physician and playwright. Credited with reviving Scottish theater with witty comedies including *Sunlight Sonata* (1928), *The Anatomist* (1931), *Jonah and the Whale* (1932), *A Sleeping Clergyman* (1933), *Marriage Is No Joke* (1934), *Colonel Wotherspoon* (1934), *King of Nowhere* (1938), *One Way of Living* (1939), *Mr. Bolfry* (1943), *Dr. Angelus* (1947), *The Queen's Comedy* (1950).

Ma·vro·kor·dá·tos \,mäv-rò-kòr-'thät-òs\, Aléxandros. Prince. 1791–1865. Greek politician and patriot. Devoted himself to cause of Greek independence; president of first national assembly (1821–22) and instrumental in drafting of constitution; elected first president of Hellenic Republic (1822); distinguished himself in defense of Missolonghi (1822–23); governor general of Missolonghi (1823–25); prime minister of Greece (1833–34, 1841, 1843–44, 1854–55).

Ma·vu·ra \mə-'vůr-ə\ *or* **Ma·nu·za** \mə-'nü-zə\. 17th century. Ruler of Mwene Mutapa empire. With aid of Portuguese, deposed his uncle Kapranzine as emperor (1629); converted to Christianity and took name Felipe; swore vassalage to Portugal; during his reign Portugal established missionary and trading stations in Central Africa for first time.

Mā·war·dī, al- \,al-mä-'war-dē\. *More completely* Abū al-Hasan 'Alī ibn Muḥammad al-Māwardī. d. 1058. Arab jurist. In service of caliph at Baghdad; author of *Ordinances of Government,* an exposition of prerogatives of the caliph sanctioned by religious law.

Mawlānā. See JALĀL AD-DĪN AR-RŪMĪ.

Maw·son \'mò-sᵊn\, Sir Douglas. 1882–1958. Australian explorer and geologist, b. England. To Australia as a child; on scientific staff of Sir Ernest Shackleton's Antarctic expedition (1907); leader of Australasian Antarctic expedition (1911–14) and British, Australian, and New Zealand Antarctic expedition (1929–31); professor, U. of Adelaide (1920–52).

Max \mäks\, Adolphe. 1869–1939. Belgian politician. Burgomaster of Brussels (1909–39); stubbornly opposed German abuses of power and requisitions on the people of the occupied city (1914) until the Germans removed him to an internment camp in Germany. Returned (1918); elected to the Chamber of Representatives (1919) and appointed minister of state.

Max·en·ti·us \mak-'sen-sh(ē-)əs\, Marcus Aurelius Valerius. d. 312. Roman emperor (306–312). Son of Maximian; passed over in appointment of new caesars on abdication (305) of his father and Diocletian; led uprising in Rome (306) and was proclaimed caesar by praetorians; overthrew Severus and drove Galerius out of Italy; quarreled with his father and banished him (308); engaged in war (312) with Constantine; defeated and killed at Battle of Milvian Bridge.

Max·im \'mak-səm\, Sir Hiram Stevens. 1840–1916. British inventor, b. Sangerville, Me. In engineering works, Fitchburg, Mass. (c.1865); chief engineer, United States Electric Lighting Co., first company of its kind in America (1878). To England (1881, naturalized 1900); organized Maxim Gun Co. (1884), merged with Nordenfeldt Co. (1888), absorbed into Vickers' Sons and Maxim (1896); knighted (1901). Invented the Maxim recoil-operated machine gun (1884), an electric pressure regulator, a mousetrap, an automatic steam-powered water pump, vacuum pumps, engine governors, gas motors, etc. His brother ¶Hudson, *orig.* Isaac (1853–1927), b. Orneville, Me.; inventor and explosives expert; American representative of his brother's company (1888–91); organized Maxim Powder Co. in New Jersey (1893); sold out his plant and smokeless powder patents to E. I. Du Pont de Nemours & Co. (1897); consultant for this company (1897–1927); invented high explosive maximite, smokeless powder stabillite, torpedo propellant motorite, a process for making calcium carbide, etc.

Sir Hiram's son ¶Hiram Percy (1896–1936), b. Brooklyn, N.Y.; invented Maxim silencer for firearms; adapted principle to mufflers, safety valves, air compressors, blowers; designed Columbia electric automobile.

Max·im·i·an \mak-'sim-ē-ən\. *Lat.* Marcus Aurelius Valerius Max·im·i·a·nus \mak-,sim-ē-'ā-nəs\. d. 310. Roman emperor (286–305, 306–308), b. of humble origin in Pannonia. Made caesar by Diocletian (285) and augustus (286); ruled in Italy and Africa (293–305); abdicated simultaneously (305) with Diocletian; recalled to aid his son Maxentius (306) who proclaimed himself emperor at Rome; again emperor (306–308); expelled by Maxentius (308); fled to Gaul and lived at court of his son-in-law Constantine; killed or committed suicide after unsuccessfully raising revolt against Constantine.

Max·i·mil·ian \mäk-sē-'mē-lē-än, *Angl* ,mak-sə-'mil-yən\. *In full* Ferdinand Maximilian Joseph. 1832–1867. Archduke of Austria and (1864–67) emperor of Mexico. Brother of Francis Joseph, emperor of Austria. Trained for naval service; in command of Austrian navy (1854). Married (1857) Princess Carlota (*q.v.*), daughter of Leopold I of Belgium. Viceroy of Lombardo-Venetian kingdom (1857–59). After French had partially conquered Mexico, an assembly of Mexican notables in exile met under French auspices and offered throne to Maximilian (1863); accepted throne (1864); reached Mexico City (June 1864); with aid of French troops, drove Juárez over northern frontier; attempted liberal reforms; U.S. government refused to recognize empire and demanded (1866) that French withdraw their army; Napoléon III ordered troops withdrawn, breaking his pledge of military support for Maximilian. Besieged by Juárez at Querétaro and captured (May 15, 1867); condemned by court-martial and shot at Querétaro.

Maximilian. Name of two kings of Bavaria:

Maximilian I. *In full* Maximilian I Joseph. 1756–1825. King (1806–25), of house of Wittelsbach. Served in French regiment in Alsace (1777–89); duke of Zweibrücken (1795). Elector of Bavaria as Maximilian IV Joseph (1799–1806); forced to enter war against France (1799) but signed separate peace (1801); sided with France against allied powers (1805); gained territory by Treaty of Pressburg (Dec. 1805) and by its terms assumed title of king (1806). Remained loyal to Napoléon until just before battle of Leipzig (1813); negotiated alliance with Austria (1813). Aided by chief minister Graf von Montgelas, made Bavaria into a consolidated, well administered state; granted liberal constitution (1818).

Maximilian II. *In full* Maximilian II Joseph. 1811–1864. King (1848–64). Son of King Louis I of Bavaria; unsuccessfully attempted alliance of small German states as counterweight to Austria and Prussia (1848–49); introduced some liberal reforms; patronized scholars, esp. Leopold von Ranke, and made Munich a center of culture; aggressively supported claim of Frederick of Augustenburg to duchies of Schleswig and Holstein.

Maximilian. Name of three electors of Bavaria:

Maximilian I. 1573–1651. Duke of Bavaria (1597–1651); elector (1623–51). Restored Bavaria to solvency and sound government; revised law code and made army efficient. Active opponent of Protestant cause; established Catholic League (1609) and served as its head. In Thirty Years' War (1618–48) allied himself with Emperors Ferdinand II and III; his army under Graf von Tilly defeated that of Elector Frederick V at White Mountain (1620); effected Wallenstein's dismissal (1630); driven from Munich by Swedish army (1632); fought against Swedes and French (1637–38); made separate peace (Truce of Ulm, 1647).

Maximilian II Emanuel. 1662–1726. Elector (1679–1726). Son of Elector Ferdinand Maria; m. (1685) Maria Antonia, daughter of Emperor Leopold I and Margaret Theresa. Fought for Austria against Turks (1683–88), making his reputation with capture (1688) of Belgrade. Habsburg ally during War of the Grand Alliance (1689–97); governor of Spanish Netherlands (1692–99). Aided France in War of the Spanish Succession (1701–14), but after defeat of Höchstädt (1704), forced to take refuge in Netherlands; restored (1714).

Maximilian III Joseph. 1727–1777. Elector (1745–77). Son of Emperor Charles VII; forced to renounce candidacy for imperial election; sided with Maria Theresa in Seven Years' War (1756–63).

Maximilian. Name of two Holy Roman emperors:

Maximilian I. 1459–1519. King of Germany (1486–1519) and Holy Roman emperor (1493–1519). Son of Frederick III; m. Mary of Burgundy (1477). Successfully defended his Burgundian lands from French attacks (1477–93); by Treaty of Pressburg (1491) secured Bohemian and Hungarian successions for the Habsburgs. Inaugurated many administrative reforms (1495–1512).

Became involved in war with France (1494) for sovereignty of Milan and Naples; defeated in war with Swiss Confederacy (1499), which meant practical independence of the latter. Joined League of Cambrai (1508) against Venice and (1513) the Holy League against France; as ally of Henry VIII of England, helped win battle of the Spurs (1513) against France. After victory of Francis I of France at Melegnano (1515), forced to cede Milan to the French. Author of several autobiographical works and a work on hunting.

Maximilian II. 1527–1576. King of Bohemia (1562–76) and Hungary (1563–76) and Holy Roman emperor (1564–76). Son of Ferdinand I; concluded disadvantageous truce (1568) with Turks. Held tolerant attitude toward Protestants of Germany.

Maximilian. Prinz zu Wied \'vēt\. 1782–1867. German traveler and naturalist. From travels wrote *Reise nach Brasilien* (1820–21), *Beiträge zur Naturgeschichte von Brasilien* (1825–33), *Reise durch Nordamerika* (1838–41).

Maximilian. *Known as* Prince of Ba·den \'bäd-ən\. *Full Ger. name* Maximilian Alexander Friedrich Wilhelm. 1867–1929. German politician. Heir presumptive to grand ducal throne of Baden; president of Baden diet (1907–18); during World War I, did much to improve conditions of British prisoners in Germany and of German prisoners in Russia. Appointed chancellor of German empire (Oct. 3, 1918); democratized the constitution; initiated negotiations for armistice and insisted that Emperor William II abdicate; resigned (Nov. 1918).

Maximilian Franz \'fränts\. 1756–1801. Archbishop-elector of Cologne (1784–1801). Youngest son of Empress Maria Theresa; raised Bonn academy to university status (1786).

Max·i·mi·nus \,mak-sə-'mē-nəs\. *Also known as* Max·i·min \'mak-sə-mən\. Name of two Roman emperors:

Maximinus. *In full* Gaius Julius Verus Maximinus. *Surnamed* Thrax \'thraks\, *i.e.* the Thracian. 173–238. Emperor (235–238). A Thracian of unusual size and strength; made emperor by soldiers on the Rhine after murder of Alexander Severus; spent much of reign fighting tribes along Danube and the Rhine; suppressed revolt of landowners in Africa under Gordian (238); deposed by Roman Senate; unsuccessfully besieged Aquileia (238); slain by his own soldiers.

Maximinus. *In full* Gaius Galerius Valerius Maximinus. *Orig. surname* Daia \'dī-ə\. d. 313. Roman emperor (308–313), b. Illyria. Nephew of Galerius; made caesar (305) and given government of Syria and Egypt; made augustus (308); persecuted Christians; on death of Galerius (311) occupied Asia Minor; invaded Licinius's dominions in Thrace (313) but totally defeated by him at Tzurulum.

Max·i·mus \'mak-sə-məs\. Saint. *Called* the Confessor. c.580–662. Byzantine theologian. Secretary to Emperor Heraclius; entered monastery at Scutari (613 or 614); to Carthage (628), where he was vigorous opponent of Monothelite doctrine; banished to Thrace (655); recalled to Constantinople (662) and commanded to accept Monothelite heresy; on refusal, tortured and banished to Lazica. Developed a Christocentric theology based on classical philosophy and teachings of Pseudo-Dionysius the Areopagite. Author of some 90 works on theology and mysticism, esp. *400 Capita de caritate* on asceticism and charity, *Mystagogia* on mystical meaning of the liturgy, commentaries on Gregory of Nazianzus and Pseudo-Dionysius.

Maximus. Name of four Roman emperors:

Maximus. *In full* Magnus Clemens Maximus. d. 388. Emperor (383–388), b. Spain. Led insurrection in Britain (383); defeated Gratian in Gaul (383); recognized as augustus in Gaul, Spain, and Britain by Theodosius and Valentinian II; invaded Italy (387), driving out Valentinian; defeated and killed at Aquileia by Theodosius.

Maximus. *In full* Marcus Clodius Pupienus Maximus. See PUPIENUS MAXIMUS.

Maximus. *Surnamed* Ty·ran·nus \tə-'ran-əs, tī-\. d. 422. Emperor (409–411). Proclaimed in Spain (409) by rebel Gerontius; defeated and deposed by Constantine the usurper (411); killed in a second insurrection (418–422).

Maximus. *In full* Petronius Maximus. 396–455. Emperor (455). Prefect of Rome (420); twice consul; with eunuch Heraclius engineered assassination of Aetius (454); forced Valentinian's widow Eudoxia to marry him the day after Valentinian's murder; emperor from March 17 to May 31, 455; slain by Roman mob.

Maximus. *Also* Mak·sim \(,)məks-'yēm\. *Called* the Greek *or* the Ha·ghi·o·rite \ha-'gē-ə-,rīt\. 1480–1556. Greek monk and Humanist scholar. Studied at Paris, Venice, Florence; entered Orthodox monastery of Vatopedi on Mt. Athos (1504). To Moscow (c.1515) as librarian and translator to Grand Prince Vasily III; built up Russian church libraries; translated the Scriptures and philosophical-theological literature into Russian; became leader of liberal Nonpossessors (or Transvolgans) in Russian church controversy, opposed by Joseph of Volokolamsk; arrested (1525) and imprisoned (to 1551) by Joseph's followers. Author of anti-Latin church treatise *Eulogy for the Holy Apostles Peter and Paul,* commentaries on the Psalms and on New Testament Acts of the Apostles, etc.

Maximus of Eph·e·sus \'ef-ə-səs\. d. 370 A.D. Greek philosopher. A Neo-Platonist; had reputation as theurgic magician, said to have animated a statue of Hecate; gained great influence over the future Roman emperor Julian, joining his court at Constantinople (361); imprisoned by Valens (364); executed on charge of conspiring against Valens's life.

Maximus, Valerius. See VALERIUS MAXIMUS.

Maximus Pla·nu·des \plā-'n(y)üd-,ēz\. 1260–c.1310. Greek Orthodox monk and scholar. In Constantinople established a laic monastery and a school famed for its humanities curriculum; unsuccessful in diplomatic mission to Venice for Andronicus II Palaeologus (1295–96). Author of *De processione Spiritus Sancti* (c.1281) and *Tractatus de Spiritu Sancto adversus Latinos* (1282); his Greek translations of classical Latin literary and philosophical works spread such knowledge through Byzantine world.

Max·ton \'mak-stən\, James. 1885–1946. British politician, b. Scotland. Teacher (1906–16); organizer in Scotland for Independent Labour party (1919–22) and chairman of this party (1926–31, 1934–39); M.P. (from 1922). Author of *Lenin* (1932) and *If I were Dictator* (1935).

Max·well \'mak-,swel, -swəl\. Name of Scottish family holding titles of earl of Mor·ton \'mȯrt-ᵊn\, earl of Niths·dale \'niths-,dāl\, Lord Maxwell, Lord Her·ries \'her-əs\, and including among its members:

William Maxwell (1676–1744), 5th Earl of Nithsdale; joined English Jacobites (1715); taken prisoner at Preston (1715); joined Chevalier James Edward at Rome after escaping (1716) by aid of his wife ¶Winifred (m. 1699; d. 1749), Countess of Nithsdale, daughter of William Herbert, 1st Marquis of Powis (see HERBERT family), who wrote an account of her husband's escape.

¶Sir John Maxwell of Ter·reg·les \tə-'reg-əlz\ (1512?–1583), 4th Baron Herries; partisan of Mary, Queen of Scots; warden of west marches (1552–53, 1561, 1579); joined Mary with strong force at Dunbar (1566); called to peerage as Baron Herries in right of his wife (1566); commanded Mary's horse at Langside (1568); assisted in depriving Morton of regency (1578).

Maxwell, Elsa. 1883–1963. American columnist, songwriter, and professional party-giver, b. Keokuk, Ia. Organized parties for royalty and high society in Europe and U.S. (from c.1907); appeared in several films, including *Elsa Maxwell's Hotel for Women* (1939) and *The Lady and the Lug* (1940); hosted radio program "Elsa Maxwell's Party Line" (1942 ff.) and wrote syndicated gossip column.

Maxwell, Gavin. 1914–1969. Scottish writer and conservationist. Best known for autobiographical novels *Ring of Bright Water* (1960) and *The Rocks Remain* (1963); also wrote *Harpoon at a Venture* (1952), *God Protect Me from My Friends* (1956), *A Reed Shaken by the Wind* (1957), *The Pains of Death* (1959), *Raven Seek Thy Brother* (1968), etc.

Maxwell, James Clerk. 1831–1879. Scottish physicist. Professor, Marischal Coll., Aberdeen (1856–60) and King's Coll., London (1860–65); first professor of experimental physics, Cambridge (from 1871), where he supervised building of Cavendish laboratory. Investigated color perception and color blindness, kinetic theory of gases, nature of Saturn's rings, geometrical optics, viscoelasticity; worked on theory of electromagnetism, publishing his *Treatise on Electricity and Magnetism* (1873); demonstrated that light is an electromagnetic wave; developed fundamental equations describing electrical and magnetic forces and fields. Other books were *Theory of Heat* (1870), *Matter and Motion* (1877), and *Elementary Treatise on Electricity* (1881).

May \'mī\, Karl Friedrich. 1842–1912. German novelist. Author of travel and adventure stories for juveniles, dealing with desert Arabs or American Indians, including *Durch die Wüste* (1892), *Winnetou* (1893), *Der Schatz im Silbersee* (1894), *Im Lande des Mahdi* (1896), *Ardistan und Dschinnistan* (1909).

May \'mā\, Philip William, *called* Phil. 1864–1903. English caricaturist. Made reputation with *Phil May's Winter Annual* (1892–1903), depiction of low life in *Daily Graphic* and other papers, *Sketch Book* (1895), and *Guttersnipes: Fifty Original Sketches* (1896); on staff of *Punch* (from 1896); East London types his specialty, such as habitués of the racecourse, the prize ring, the stage.

May, Thomas. 1595–1650. English poet and parliamentary historian. Published comedy *The Heir* (1622) and tragedies *Antigone* (1631), *Julia Agrippina* (1639), *Cleopatra* (1639); translator of Virgil's *Georgics* and of Lucan; produced at command of Charles I verse histories of King Henry II (1633) and Edward III (1635); secretary to Long Parliament and its historian in *The History of the Parliament of England Which Began Nov. the Third, 1640* (1647).

May, Sir Thomas Erskine. 1st Baron Farn·bor·ough \'färn-,bər-ə, -,bə-rə, -b(ə-)rə\. 1815–1886. English jurist. Clerk of House of Commons (1871–86). Author of *Treatise on the Law, Privilege, Proceedings and Usage of Parliament* (1844), *Rules, Orders, and Forms of Procedure of the House of Commons*

(1854), *The Constitutional History of England since the Accession of George III* (1861–63), *Democracy in Europe* (1877), etc.

Ma·ya·kov·ski \mə-yi-'kôf-skəi, *Angl* -skē\, Vladimir Vladimirovich. 1893–1930. Russian poet. Member of Bolshevik party (from 1908); vigorous spokesman for Communist party, esp. after the Revolution. Leader of Futurist movement in Russia; sought to "depoetize" poetry by use of technical innovations, crude language, grotesquely hyperbolic images, declamatory manner. Best known poems were "Oblako v shtanakh" (1915), "Fleyta-pozvonochnik" (1916), "Oda revolutsi" (1918), "Levy marsh" (1919), *150,000,000* (1920), "Lyublyu" (1922), "Pro eto" (1923); also book of travel sketches *Moye otkrytiye America* (1926) and plays *Misteriya-buff* (1921), *Klop* (1929), *Banya* (1930).

May·bach \'mī-,bäk\, Wilhelm. 1846–1929. German automobile builder. In partnership with Gottlieb Daimler at Cannstatt (1883), where they produced one of first gasoline motors; with Daimler formed Daimler-Motoren-Gesellschaft (1890); its technical director (from 1895). Constructed first Mercedes automobile (1900–01); credited with invention of spray-nozzle carburetor, honeycomb radiator, and change-speed gear. With his son Carl organized at Friedrichshafen company to build aircraft engines (1909); Maybach automobiles were produced from 1922 to 1939.

May·beck \'mā-,bek\, Bernard Ralph. 1862–1957. American architect, b. New York City. Settled in San Francisco (1889); in private practice there; on faculty, U. of Calif., Berkeley (1894–1903, professor from 1898). Eclectic designer, employed Gothic, Roman, Tudor, Baroque styles and reinforced concrete and wood materials; designed Hearst Hall (1899), Town and Gown Club (1899), Men's Faculty Club (1900), all at U. of Calif.; also designed First Church of Christ, Scientist (Berkeley, 1910), Palace of Fine Arts (San Francisco, 1915), residential town of Clyde, Calif. (1917), Principia College campus, Elsah, Ill. (from 1938).

Mayebre Sheshi. See SALITIS.

Mayenne, Duc de. See Charles de Lorraine under LORRAINE family.

Mayer. See also MAYR.

May·er \'mī-ər\, Johann Tobias. 1723–1762. German mathematician, physicist, and astronomer. With Homann Cartographic Bureau, Nürnberg (1746–50); professor, Göttingen (1751 ff.). Introduced improvements in map making; discovered libration of moon (1747–48); known esp. for lunar tables.

Mayer, Julius Robert von. 1814–1878. German physician and physicist. His work on nature of heat helped lay foundation for discovery of first law of thermodynamics; calculated mechanical equivalent of heat (1842).

May·er \'mā-ər, 'ma(ə)r, 'me(ə)r\, Louis Burt. 1885–1957. American motion-picture producer, b. Minsk, Russia. To Canada (1888); opened nickelodeon at Haverhill, Mass. (1907); owned largest chain of movie theaters in New England (by 1918); naturalized U.S. citizen (1912). Founded (1918) in Los Angeles, Calif., Metro Pictures Corp. and Louis B. Mayer Pictures Corp.; merged (1924) with Goldwyn Co. to become Metro-Goldwyn-Mayer Corp. Vice president in charge of production, M-G-M (1924–48); developed star system, discovered Clark Gable, Greta Garbo, Joan Crawford, Rudolph Valentino, etc.; produced films *Ben Hur* (1926), *Grand Hotel* (1932), *Dinner at Eight* (1933), *The Good Earth* (1937), etc.

May·er \'mī-ər\, Maria Gertrude, *nee* Goep·pert \'gœp-ərt\. 1906–1972. American physicist, b. Kattowitz, Germany (now Katowice, Poland). m. (1930) Joseph Mayer; to U.S. (1930, naturalized 1933); taught at Johns Hopkins (1931–39), Columbia (1939–46), U. of Chicago (1946–60); professor, U. of Calif., San Diego (1960–72). Author of *Statistical Mechanics* (with her husband, 1940) and *Elementary Theory of Nuclear Shell Structure* (with Johannes H.D. Jensen, 1955). Awarded Nobel prize in physics (1963) with Jenson and E.P. Wigner for studies on nuclear shell structure.

May·hew \'mā-,hyü\, Henry. 1812–1887. English journalist. With Gilbert à Beckett started comic weekly *Figaro in London* (1831–39); a founder of *Punch* (1841), its coeditor (1841–43); made hit with one-act farce *The Wandering Minstrel* (1834); published his chief work *London Labour and the London Poor* (1851–62). With his brother ¶Augustus Septimus (1826–1875) wrote clever works of fiction, including *The Greatest Plague of Life* (1847) and *The Good Genius that Turned Everything to Gold* (1847).

Mayhew, Thomas. 1593–1682. American colonist, b. Tisbury, England. To Medford, Mass. (c.1632); bought (1641) Martha's Vineyard, Nantucket, and the Elizabeth Islands; moved to Martha's Vineyard (1646) and acted as magistrate there. Commissioned governor of Martha's Vineyard (1671–82). His great-great-grandson ¶Jonathan (1720–1766), b. Chilmark, Martha's Vineyard; Congregational pastor, West Church, Boston (1747–66); known for his liberalism in religious doctrine and his defense of liberal theories of government.

May·nard \me-nár\, François. 1582–1646. French poet. Chief disciple of Malherbe and associated with him in attempts to reform French language and literary forms; held office in presidial court of Aurillac (1611–28). Author of sonnets, odes, and epigrams, published in *Les Oeuvres de Maynard* (1646).

Mayne \'mān\, Jasper. 1604–1672. English dramatist and clergyman. Author of *The City Match* (comedy, 1639) and *The Amorous War* (tragicomedy, 1648). After Restoration, appointed canon of Christ Church, Oxford, archdeacon of Chichester, and chaplain in ordinary to the king.

Mayo, Earl of. See Richard S. BOURKE.

Mayo \'mā-(,)ō\, George Elton. 1880–1949. American psychologist, b. Adelaide, Australia. Professor, U. of Queensland (1919–22); to U.S. (1922); taught at U. of Pennsylvania (1923–26) and Harvard Graduate School of Business Administration (1926–47, professor from 1929). Pioneer in industrial sociology; emphasized dependence of productivity on small-group unity. Author of *The Human Problems of an Industrial Civilization* (1933) and *The Social Problems of an Industrial Civilization* (1945).

Mayo, William Worrall. 1819–1911. American physician, b. near Manchester, England. To U.S. (1845); provost surgeon for southern Minnesota, headquarters at Rochester, Minn. (from 1863). With his sons (see below), helped Sisters of St. Francis found (1889) St. Mary's Hospital, Rochester, with the Mayos as its sole staff.

His son ¶William James (1861–1939), b. Le Sueur, Minn.; surgeon in Rochester (from 1883); with his brother Charles developed a cooperative group clinic at St. Mary's Hospital which evolved into the Mayo Clinic; cofounder (1915, with Charles) of the Mayo Foundation for Medical Education and Research in affiliation with the U. of Minn.; known esp. for operations of the abdomen, pelvis, and kidney.

Another son ¶Charles Horace (1865–1939), b. Rochester, Minn.; also a surgeon in Rochester (from 1888); surgeon, Mayo Clinic (to 1930); cofounder of the Mayo Foundation (see above); professor of surgery at U. of Minn. (1915–36); originated modern procedures in goiter surgery and in neurosurgery. Charles Horace's son ¶Charles William (1898–1968), b. Rochester; surgeon at Mayo Clinic (1931–63); member of clinic's board of governors; professor of surgery (from 1933) at Mayo Foundation.

May·ow \'mā-(,)ō\, John. 1641–1679. English physiologist and chemist. Known for work on atmospheric composition, respiration, chemistry of combustion, and muscular action; his investigation (1674) of part played by *spiritus nitroaerus* in combustion is sometimes considered as discovery of oxygen.

Mayr *or* **May·er** \'mī(-ə)r\, Johann Simon, *Ital.* Giovanni Simone. 1763–1845. German composer. To Italy (1787); one of foremost opera composers in Italy of his day; maestro di capella in Bergamo (1802–45) and director (1805–45) of cathedral choir school where Donizetti was his pupil; said to have been first to introduce crescendo of the orchestra, much used by Rossini. Composed about 70 operas, including *Un pazzo ne fa cento* (1796), *Che originali* (1798), *Ginerra di Scozia* (1801), *I cherusci* (1808), *La rosa bianca e la rosa rossa* (1813), *Meden in Corinto* (1813); also oratorios, cantatas, and other church music.

Mayr, Simon. *Also spelled* Mair *or* Mayer. *Known by Lat. form* Simon Mar·ius \'mär-yùs\. 1573–1624. German astronomer. Assistant to Tycho Brahe (1601); claimed to have discovered (c.1610) largest moons of Jupiter and named them Io, Europa, Ganymede, and Callisto (discovery generally credited to Galileo); made first telescopic observation of Andromeda spiral nebula (1611).

Ma Yü·an \'mä-'yü-'än\. 14 B.C.–49 A.D. Chinese general. Began military career in service of minister Wang Mang; later entered service of Emperor Kuang Wu Ti and helped him establish the Later Han dynasty; appointed governor of South China (35 A.D.); reinstituted Chinese rule southward to Vietnam; sent (45) to northern frontier, where he helped subdue Hsiung-nu tribes; worshipped as god after his death.

Ma Yüan. c.1160–1225. Chinese painter. Court painter to Sung emperors; received the Golden Belt, the highest Chinese honor. His works, together with those of his contemporary Hsia Kuei, formed basis of Ma-Hsia school of painting; painted figures and flowers, but best known for his landscapes; master of one-cornered painting. His works included *Early Spring, Two Sages and an Attendant Beneath a Plum Tree, Watching the Deer by a Pine-shaded Stream, On a Mountain Path in Spring, The Four Sages of Shang-shan.*

May·wood \'mā-,wùd\, Augusta. *Surname orig.* Williams. 1825–1876. American dancer, b. New York City. Acquired stepfather's name (1828); made debut in Auber's *Le Dieu et la Bayadère* (Philadelphia, 1837); Paris debut in *Le Diable boîteax* (1839); danced with Paris Opéra (1839–40), San Carlo Opera, Lisbon (1843–45), Kärntnertor Theater, Vienna (1845–47); prima ballerina at La Scala, Milan (1849–58); opened ballet school in Vienna and taught there (to 1873). First American ballerina to achieve international acclaim; best known roles were in *Giselle, La Gypsy, Le Diable amoureux, Faust, La Dame aux Camélias, Rita Gauthier.*

Ma·za·rin \må-zå-raⁿ, *Angl* ,maz-ə-'raⁿ\, Jules. *Orig.* Giulio Ma·za·ri·ni \mäd-zä-'rē-nē\. 1602–1661. French cardinal and statesman, b. Italy. Captain of infantry under Calonna (1624); executed several diplomatic missions for papacy (1627–34), esp. settlement of War of Mantuan Succession (1630); took minor orders (1632) but never ordained priest; nuncio to France (1634–36). Entered service of Richelieu and became naturalized Frenchman (1639). Made cardinal (1641); succeeded Richelieu as prime minister (1642); retained by queen regent, Anne of Austria, after Louis XIII's death (1643–61). Foreign policy, based on that of Richelieu, generally successful during final period of Thirty Years' War (1643–48). War of the Fronde (1648–53) for a while upset his domestic policy; twice exiled (1651–52 and 1652–53). Destroyed remaining power of feudal nobles. By alliances and treaties (esp. Treaty of the Pyrenees, 1659) greatly strengthened France as a power in Europe; laid foundation for Louis XIV's later successes. Amassed a great private fortune; pensioned literary leaders and founded (1642) great library, Bibliothèque Mazarine.

Ma·zas \má-säs\, Jacques-Féréol. 1782–1849. French violin virtuoso and composer. Works included violin studies, concertos, and the one-act comic opera *Le Kiosque* (1842).

Maz·dak \ˈmaz-ˌdak\. 5th century A.D. Persian religious leader. Originally a Magian priest; founded Mazdakism, a dualistic sectarian religion derived from Manichaeism; preached community of property (including women), simplicity of life, and abstinence from meat.

Ma·ze·pa \(ˌ)mə-ˈz(y)ā-pə, mə-ˈzep-ə\, Ivan Stepanovich. c.1644–1709. Cossack hetman. Brought up in Polish court; returned to Ukraine, entering service of hetman Pyotr Doroshenko (1663); transferred allegiance to Ivan Samoilovich (1674); became hetman of the Ukraine (1687); fought against Crimean Tartars (1689). Gained favor of Peter I the Great but later became alienated from him; sought to gain independence of the Ukraine, intriguing (1700) with Poles and Swedes; fled to Turkey with Charles XII of Sweden after his defeat at Poltava (1709).

Ma·zo \ˈmä-thō\, Juan Bautista Martínez del. c.1612–1667. Spanish painter. Pupil and son-in-law of Velázquez; chief court painter of Philip IV (from 1661); painted figures, portraits, and landscapes, esp. *Vista de Zaragoza* (1647).

Ma·žu·ra·nić \má-ˈzhü-rá-nēt^{y}, *Angl* -nich\, Ivan. 1814–1890. Croatian poet and politician. Chancellor of Croatia and Slavonia (1861); governor (*ban*) of Croatia (1873–80). Chief poetical work, epic *Smrt Smail-Age Čengića* (1846).

Maz·ze·i \mät-ˈtse-ē\, Philip. 1730–1816. Italian physician and merchant. Wine merchant in London (1755–73); in Virginia, trying to introduce viticulture (1773–78). Colonial American agent in Europe (1779–83), sending information to Jefferson. Recipient of a letter from Jefferson (1796) in which Jefferson bitterly attacked Federalist leaders, publication of which caused a political scandal in U.S.

Maz·zi·ni \mat-ˈtsē-ne, mad-ˈdzē-nē\, Giuseppe. 1805–1872. Italian patriot. Practiced law in Genoa (1827–30); associated himself with the democratic movement in Italy; joined the Carbonari (1830); imprisoned for six months and then exiled (1831) to France. Made his home in Marseilles; wrote a letter to Charles Albert of Sardinia which caused a decree of perpetual banishment to be announced against him. Organized (1831) secret revolutionary society, Giovine Italia (Young Italy), whose purpose was the unification of Italy under a republican form of government. Settled in London (1837) and continued his revolutionary activities; on outbreak of revolution in Italy (1848) returned to become a member of the triumvirate, with Aurelio Saffi and Armellini, in the Republic of Rome (1849), but went into exile when papal control of the city was reestablished. Instigated rebel manifestations in Mantua (1852), Milan (1853), Genoa (1857); involved in revolutionary movement at Palermo and was captured (1870), but soon released; remained until his death an uncompromising republican.

Maz·zo·la \mät-ˈtsȯ-lä\ *or* **Maz·zuo·li** \-ˈtswȯ-lē\, Girolamo Francesco Maria. *Known as* Par·mi·gia·ni·no \ˌpär-mē-jä-ˈnē-nō\ *or* Par·mi·gia·no \-ˈjä-nō\. 1503–1540. Italian painter, b. Parma. Influenced by Correggio, esp. in *Mystic Marriage of St. Catherine* (c.1521) and frescoes in S. Giovanni Evangelista, Parma (1522–23); worked chiefly at Parma, also at Rome (1524–27) and Bologna (1527–31); reacted against High Renaissance classicism and initiated Mannerism. Known esp. for portraits as *Self-Portrait* (1524), *Gian Galeazzo Sanvitale* (1524), *Antea* (c.1535–37), and also *Vision of St. Jerome* (1527) and *Madonna dal Collo Lungo* (1534).

Maz·zo·li \mat-ˈtsō-lē\, Ludovico. *Called* Maz·zo·li·no \ˌmät-tsō-ˈlē-nō\. c.1478–1528. Italian painter. Member of Ferrara school; known for *Nativity, Adoration of the Magi, Resurrection of Lazarus, Massacre of the Innocents, The Miraculous Draught of Fishes, Christ Among the Doctors.*

Maz·zo·ni \mät-ˈtsō-nē\, Guido. *Called* Il Mo·da·ni·no \ēl-ˌmō-dä-ˈnē-nō\. c.1450–1518. Italian sculptor. Employed at Naples (to 1495); accompanied Charles VIII to France (1495–1516); worked chiefly in terra cotta. Designed tomb of Charles VIII, bronze bust of King Ferdinand, and a group *Adoration.*

Mazzuoli, Girolamo Francesco Maria. See MAZZOLA.

M'ba-Der·li·non \$^{ə}$m-ˈbä-der-lē-ˈnō^{n}, *Angl* em-ˈbä-\. 1902–1967. Gabonese politician. Elected to Territorial Assembly (1952); mayor of Libreville (1956); prime minister (1958–61); first president of independent Gabon (1961–67); pursued strong pro-French policy; became increasingly authoritarian; ousted by army coup (Feb. 1964) but quickly restored by French troops.

Mbi·re \$^{ə}$m-ˈbir-e, *Angl* em-ˈbi(ə)r-(ˌ)ā\ *or* **Nem·bi·re** \nem-ˈbi(ə)r-(ˌ)ā\. 14th century. Founder of the Mwene Motapa empire. Brought his Karanga people from vicinity of Lake Tanganyika and established his empire at Zambezi River (c.1325).

Mboya \$^{ə}$m-ˈbȯi-ə, *Angl* em-\, Thomas Joseph, *called* Tom. 1930–1969. Kenyan politician and nationalist leader. Member of Luo tribe; early involved in nationalistic activities; general secretary of Kenya Federation of Labour (1953–63); elected to Legislative Council (1957) and led successful movement there for increase in black representation. A founding member of Kenya African National Union party (1960); minister of justice (1963), of economic affairs (1964–69); assassinated.

Mc-. Names beginning with this prefix are alphabetized as if spelled MAC-.

Mead \ˈmēd\, George Herbert. 1863–1931. American philosopher and social psychologist, b. South Hadley, Mass. Professor, U. of Chicago (1894–1931). As psychologist, a behavioralist emphasizing role of spoken language in the development of the self; as philosopher, contributed to development of American pragmatism with his philosophy of "objective realism." His mss. and lecture notes posthumously edited and published as *The Philosophy of the Present* (1932), *Mind, Self, and Society* (1934), *Movements of Thought in the Nineteenth Century* (1936), and *The Philosophy of the Act* (1938).

Mead, Larkin Goldsmith. 1835–1910. American sculptor, b. Chesterfield, N.H. Works included *Ethan Allen* in capitol at Montpelier, Vt., *Lincoln Monument* in Springfield, Ill, *The Father of Waters* in Minneapolis.

Mead, Margaret. 1901–1978. American anthropologist, b. Philadelphia. Assistant curator of ethnology, American Museum of Natural History (1926–42); associate curator (1942–64), curator (1964–69). Adjunct professor, Columbia (from 1954). On field trips to Samoa (1925–26, 1928–29), New Guinea (1931–33), Bali and New Guinea (1936–39); known also as popular and controversial lecturer on contemporary social issues. Author of *Coming of Age in Samoa* (1928), *Growing Up in New Guinea* (1930), *Sex and Temperament in Three Primitive Societies* (1935), *Balinese Character* (with Gregory Bateson, 1941), *And Keep Your Powder Dry* (1942), *Male and Female* (1949), *Childhood in Contemporary Cultures* (with Martha Wolfenstein, 1955), *New Lives for Old* (1956), *Anthropology* (1964), *Continuities in Cultural Evolution* (1964), *Culture and Commitment* (1970), *Blackberry Winter* (autobiography, 1972).

Mead, Richard. 1673–1754. English physician. Recognized as foremost physician of his day; author of *Mechanical Account of Poisons* (1702) and works on plague, smallpox, measles, scurvy.

Meade \ˈmēd\, George Gordon. 1815–1872. American army officer, b. Cádiz, Spain, of American parents. Artillery officer (1835–36); after work as civilian engineer (1836–42), reentered army (1842). Brigadier general of volunteers (1861), major general (1862); at second Bull Run, Antietam, and Chancellorsville. Placed in command of army of the Potomac (1863–65); repulsed Confederate army under Lee at Gettysburg (July 1–4, 1863), but was criticized for lack of aggressiveness in following up repulse to obtain decisive victory. Commanded several military departments after the war.

Mea·gher \ˈmä(-ə)r; ˈmä-hər, -gər\, Thomas Francis. 1823–1867. American politician and soldier, b. Waterford, Ireland. Member, Young Ireland party (from 1845); a founder of the Irish Confederation (1847). Banished to Tasmania (1849) for advocating insurrection; escaped to U.S. (1852); became naturalized citizen and leader of Irish-Americans in New York City. Union officer through Civil War; engaged at first Bull Run, Peninsular Campaign, second Bull Run, Antietam, Fredericksburg, Chancellorsville; brigadier general (1864). Territorial secretary of Montana (1865) and acting governor (1865–66).

Means \ˈmēnz\, Gaston Bullock. 1879–1938. American detective and swindler, b. Blackwelder's Spring, N.C. Cotton salesman (to 1914); spy for Germany during early part of World War I; with William J. Burns Detective Agency (1914–21); bilked Chicago widow Maude King of her fortune and in sensational trial was acquitted (1917) of her murder; while imprisoned for extortion and forgery, wrote *The Strange Death of President Harding* (with May Thacker, 1930). Attempted to swindle socialite Evalyn W. McLean by claiming he could recover Charles Lindbergh's kidnapped son (1932); convicted of grand larceny and spent rest of life in prison.

Mea·ny \ˈmē-nē\, George. 1894–1980. American labor leader, b. New York City. President, N.Y. State Federation of Labor (1934–39), American Federation of Labor (1952–55), American Federation of Labor–Congress of Industrial Organizations (1955–79).

Meath, Earl of. See Reginald BRABAZON.

Meath, Lord of. See Hugh de LACY.

Meccherino. See Domenico BECCAFUMI.

Me·chain \me-sha^{n}\, Pierre-Françoise-André. 1744–1804. French astronomer and hydrographer. With Jean Delambre measured the meridian arc from

Dunkirk to Barcelona (1792–98) to establish a basis for a metric system; also discovered comets and observed eclipses.

Mechnikov. See Élie METCHNIKOFF.

Meck·el \'mek-əl\, Johann Friedrich. 1781–1833. German anatomist. Professor at Halle (1808–33); discovered Meckel's diverticulum of the small intestine and Meckel's cartilage. Published *Handbuch der pathologischen Anatomie* (1812–16) and *System der vergleichenden Anatomie* (1821–31).

Meck·len·burg \'mek-lən-ˌbùrk, 'mā-klən-\. A former German duchy and its ruling family, founded by the Slavic Obodrite ruler Niklot (d. 1160); ruler made prince of the empire (1170); made a duchy (1348); Duke Albert III (*q.v.*) made king of Sweden (1363); possessions divided (1701) into duchies of Mecklenburg-Schwerin and Mecklenburg-Strelitz; both made grand duchies (1815).

Me·di·ci \'med-ē-chē, *Angl* 'med-ə-(ˌ)chē\. Name of an Italian family powerful in Florence and Tuscany, esp. from 14th to 16th century; name recorded in Florence as early as 1201. Real founder of family was Giovanni di Bic·ci de' Medici \dē-bēt-chē-dā-\ (1360–1429), Florentine merchant; amassed very large fortune by skill in trade; strong supporter of smaller guilds and common people; virtual ruler of Florence (1421–29). From his two sons, Cosimo (1389–1464) and Lorenzo (1395–1440), derived the two great branches of the Medici family:

ELDER BRANCH:

¶Cosimo (1389–1464), *known as* the Elder. Florentine banker; patron of the arts and ruler of the republic; after death given title Pater Patriae, i.e. father of his country; acquired great wealth from his father and ruled through controlling appointments to chief offices; rival of the Albizzi; expelled from Florence (1433) but returned (1434); for 30 years patron of literature and fine arts. His son ¶Piero (1414–1469), *known as* the Gouty, was ruler of Florence (1464–69); his grandson Giulio (1478–1534) became pope as Clement VII (*q.v.*).

¶Lorenzo (1449–1492), *known as* il Ma·gni·fi·co \ˌēl-män-'yē-fē-kō\, *i.e.* the Magnificent; eldest son of Piero. Florentine statesman, ruler, and patron of arts and letters; conjointly with his brother Giuliano succeeded (1469) to great wealth and power of Medici family; engaged in struggle with Pazzi family and Pope Sixtus IV; after assassination of Giuliano (1478) became sole ruler (1478–92); with help of King Ferdinand of Aragon, made peace with pope (1480). Immoral and tyrannical ruler, but contributed greatly to make Florence prosperous; a polished prose writer and original poet; participated actively in intellectual achievements of Florence; esp. influential in causing the Tuscan dialect to become national speech of Italy.

His sons: ¶Piero (1471–1503) ruled two years only, driven from Florence (1494) by Savonarola and his followers. Giovanni (1475–1521), pope as Leo X (*q.v.*). ¶Giuliano (1479–1516), duc de Ne·mours \nə-'mür\, whose natural son ¶Ippolito (1511?–1535) became a cardinal.

¶Lorenzo (1492–1519), son of Piero; created (1516) duke of Ur·bi·no \ür-'bē-nō\ by his uncle Pope Leo X; for his daughter Caterina, see CATHERINE DE MÉDICIS. ¶Alessandro (1510–1537), passed off as Lorenzo's son but probably illegitimate son of Pope Clement VII; last of the direct male line of elder branch of family; first duke of Florence (1531–37); under imperial patent of Charles V; murdered for his tyrannical rule by a kinsman Lorenzino (see below).

YOUNGER BRANCH:

¶Lorenzo (1395–1440), *known as* the Elder, second son of Giovanni di Bicci; confined himself to family's banking interests. His grandsons: ¶Lorenzo, *known as* the Younger (1463–1507), enemy of Savonarola, and ¶Giovanni (1467–1498), who married Caterina Sforza.

¶Giovanni (1498–1526), *known as* Giovanni del·le Ban·de Ne·re \ˌdāl-lā-'bän-dā-'nā-rā\, *i.e.* John of the Black Bands; son of Giovanni and Caterina; Italian general, killed at battle of Mantua. ¶Lorenzo, *known as* Lorenzino (1514–1548), grandson of Lorenzo the Younger; murdered his kinsman Alessandro (1537; see above); author of comedy *Aridosia* (1536).

¶Cosimo I (1519–1574), *known as* the Great, son of Giovanni delle Bande Nere; granted title of duke of Florence (1537–74) on extinction of elder branch; capable ruler, but despotic and cruel; conquered Siena (1555); given title of grand duke of Tuscany by the pope (1569), but title generally dated from its bestowal under imperial grant (1576) on his son Francesco; patron of the arts; erected many buildings; established the Florentine Academy.

His son ¶Francesco (1541–1587), tool of Emperor Maximilian II and of Philip II of Spain; also a capable but despotic ruler; founded Accademia della Crusca; m. 1st Joanna, sister of Maximilian II, 2d Bianca Cappello, his long-time mistress; father, by Joanna, of Maria (see MARIE DE MÉDICIS), wife of Henry IV of France. For another son Ferdinand I, Grand Duke of Tuscany, see at FERDINAND.

¶Cosimo II (1590–1621), son of Ferdinand I; grand duke (1609–20); gave up all practice of banking and commerce; protected Galileo Galilei; m. Maria Magdalena of Austria, sister of Emperor Ferdinand II, by whom he had seven children, including Ferdinand II, grand duke; see at FERDINAND.

¶Cosimo III (1642–1723), son of Ferdinand II; grand duke (1670–1723); weak ruler, under whom Tuscany's power further declined; m. Marguerite-Louise d'Orléans (d. 1721), daughter of Gaston, duc d'Orléans. Their children included ¶Gian Gastone (1671–1737), last grand duke of Tuscany (1723–37), weak and disolute ruler, who was driven out of Tuscany at its annexation by Austria (1737), and ¶Anna Maria Ludovica (1667–1743), known as "the last of the Medici."

Médicis, Catherine de and Marie de. See CATHERINE DE MÉDICIS and MARIE DE MÉDICIS.

Me·dill \mə-'dil\, Joseph. 1823–1899. American journalist, b. near St. John, N.B. To U.S. (1832); adm. to bar (1846) in Ohio. Founded Cleveland *Leader* (1852); a founder (1854) of the Republican party. Bought interest in Chicago *Tribune* (1855); vigorously supported Lincoln in campaign for presidency and during his administration; gained control of the *Tribune* (1874) and continued as publisher and editor until his death. Mayor of Chicago (1871–74); reorganized municipal government and helped establish Chicago Public Library. Grandfather of Robert Sanderson McCormick, Joseph Medill Patterson, and Eleanor Medill Patterson (*qq.v.*).

Me·di·na \mā-'t͟hē-nä\, Bartolomé de. 1527 or 1528–1580. Spanish theologian. Entered Dominican order; taught at Alcalá and later (1576–80) at Salamanca; zealous exponent of Thomism; formulated the casuistical theory of probabilism.

Medina, Bartolomé de. d. c.1580. Spanish metallurgist. To Mexico (1554); while mining at Pachuca, invented (1557) the patio process for extracting silver from ore.

Medina, José Toribio. 1852–1930. Chilean bibliographer and historian. Published some 300 books on South American subjects, including *Historia de la literatura colonial de Chile* (1878), *Colección de documentos inéditos para la historia de Chile* (30 vols., 1888–1902), *Biblioteca hispanoamericana* (1898–1917), *La Araucana* (1910–18).

Medina An·ga·ri·ta \-ˌäŋ-gä-'rē-tä\, Isaías. 1897–1953. Venezuelan soldier and politician. Minister of war and the navy (1936–41); general (1940); president of Venezuela (1941–45).

Medina-Sidonia, Duke of. See Alonso PÉREZ DE GUZMÁN.

Medt·ner \'met-nər\, Nikolay Karlovich. *Also spelled* Metner. 1880–1951. Russian pianist and composer. Settled in Paris (1925); composed chamber music, about 100 songs, and much piano music.

Med·wall \'med-ˌwȯl\, Henry. fl. 1490. English dramatist. Chaplain to John Morton, archbishop of Canterbury. Author of morality play *Nature* (c.1495) and of earliest secular play in English *Fulgens and Lucres,* from medieval Latin original, with comic underplot (c.1497).

Med·win \'med-wən\, Thomas. 1788–1869. English biographer. Cousin and schoolfellow of Shelley; associated with Shelley and Byron in Italy (1821) and from notes of their conversations wrote *Memoir of Shelley* (1833), later expanded into *The Life of Shelley* (1847).

Mee \'mē\, Arthur. 1875–1943. English journalist, editor, and writer. Editor of *The Children's Encyclopedia* (1908–33), *Harmsworth Self-Educator* (1906), *Harmsworth History of the World* (1907), *Harmsworth Popular Science* (1912), etc. Author of *Joseph Chamberlain* (1900), *The Rainbow Books* (1939), etc.

Mee·ker \'mē-kər\, Nathan Cook. 1817–1879. American journalist and reformer, b. Euclid, Ohio. Early associated with Fourierists and Campbellites in Ohio; agricultural editor of Horace Greeley's *New York Tribune* (c.1865); with support from Greeley, founded (1869) Union Colony, a utopian farm cooperative at Greeley, Colo.; lived there and published *Greeley Tribune* (1870–78); became Indian agent (1878); slain by Ute Indians after failing in attempt to convert them from hunters to farmers.

Meer \'mār\, Jan van der. *Usually called* Jan van der Meer *or* Jan Ver·meer van Haar·lem \vər-'mār-vän-'här-ləm\. Name of two Dutch painters, father (1628–1691) and son (1656–1705), b. Haarlem. The former painted the downs and flatlands of Holland in brown-green tones; his son and pupil painted chiefly landscapes with animals.

Meersch \'märz\, Jean-André Van Der. 1734–1792. Belgian soldier. Served in armies of France (1757) and Austria; retired (1779). During revolt against Austrian rule, took command (Aug. 1789) of army raised by J.-F. Vonck; won several battles against Austrians; concluded armistice (Dec. 1789). Arrested (Apr. 1790) by followers of Henri van der Noot; fled to France on restoration of Austrian rule (Dec. 1790) but later was amnestied and returned.

Meer van Delft, Jan van der. See Jan VERMEER.

Me·gab·y·zus \mə-'gab-ə-zəs\. 5th century B.C. Persian general. Son of Zopyrus and brother-in-law of King Xerxes I; sent (482) to quell uprising in Babylon, razed the city; accompanied Xerxes to Greece; one of conspirators in assassination of Xerxes (465). Satrap of Syria under Artaxerxes I; suppressed Egyptian revolt led by Inaros; twice quarrelled with Artaxerxes but each time reconciled.

Meg·a·cles \'meg-ə-klēz\. 6th century B.C. Athenian political leader. Member of great family of the Alcmaeonidae; head of Paralioi regional political grouping; twice helped oust Peisistratus (c.560, c.556); grandfather of Pericles.

Me·gas·the·nes \mə-'gas-thə-nēz\. c.350–c.290 B.C. Greek historian. Sent (302 B.C.) by Seleucus I as ambassador to court of Indian king Candragupta Maurya. Wrote *Indika,* a description of Indian customs, flora, and fauna; only fragments of his work are extant.

Megerle, Johann Ulrich. See ABRAHAM A SANCTA CLARA.

Me·her Ba·ba \'mā-hər-'bäb-ä\, *i.e.* Compassionate Father. *Orig.* Merwan Sheheriarji Ira·ni \ē-'rän-ē\. 1894–1969. Indian religious leader. Achieved (c.1920) a realization of his own nature as *avatāra,* or divine incarnation, latest in a series of such enlightened leaders pointing toward unity with the divine; proclaimed no dogma or organization but attracted many followers in India and abroad; established himself at Meherābad, near Ahmadnagar; traveled widely; observed strict silence (from 1922).

Meh·med \me-'met\. Name of six sultans of the Ottoman Empire:

Mehmed I. *Called* Çelebi Sultan Mehmed. d. 1421. Sultan (1402–21). Son of Bayezid I; in division of Ottoman lands following Timur's defeat of Bayezid at Ankara (1402), received Amasya; defeated brother İsa and seized Bursa (1404–05); sent brother Mûsa against brother Süleyman in Rumelia (1410) and then, aided by Emperor Manuel II Palaeologus, defeated Mûsa at Camurlu (1413); proclaimed himself sultan of Anatolia and Rumelia (1413); gained territory in Albania (1417), raided Hungary.

Mehmed II. *Called* Fa·tih \fä-'tēk\, *i.e.* the Conqueror. 1432–1481. Sultan (1444–46, 1451–81). Son of Murad II; placed on throne on father's abdication (1444); faced crusade of Europeans, defeat by father at Varna (1444), intrigue of viziers, revolt of Janissaries; displaced by father (1446) but succeeded him (1451); after careful diplomatic and military preparations, laid siege to Constantinople (April 1453); personally commanded breaching of the walls with cannon of unprecedented size and capture of the city (May 29, 1453); as first act, converted Hagia Sophia into mosque; renamed city Istanbul; repopulated city, encouraged Italian and Greek scholars to settle; restored Greek Orthodox partriarchate (1454), established a Jewish grand rabbi; collected large library, fostered flowering of Islāmic theology and science. Extended empire by expeditions in Hungary, Walachia, Moldavia, Anatolia, Rhodes, Crimea; defeated Turkmen at Bashkent (1473); raided Otranto, Italy (1480), and died while preparing Italian invasion. Considered true founder of Ottoman Empire.

Mehmed III. 1566–1603. Sultan (1595–1603). Succeeded Murad III; continued arduous war with Austria, capturing Erlau, Hachova, Kanizsa; suppressed revolts in Anatolia; faced war with Iran (1603).

Mehmed IV. *Surnamed* Av·ci \äv-'jē\, *i.e.* Hunter. 1642–1693. Sultan (1648–87). Succeeded father İbrahīm; power at first held by competing factions led by mother, grandmother, Janissaries; administration reformed by emergence of Köprülü (*q.v.*) viziers; conducted campaigns against Austria, Poland; deposed following failure of siege of Vienna (1683) and several defeats.

Mehmed V. *Orig.* Mehmed Re·şad \-rā-'shäd\. 1844–1918. Sultan (1909–18). Succeeded brother Abdülhamid II; ruled largely under influence of liberal-nationalist Committee of Union and Progress; during his reign nearly all Ottoman territory in Europe was lost.

Mehmed VI. *Orig.* Mehmed Va·hi·ded·din \-vä-hē-ded-'dēn\. 1861–1926. Sultan (1918–22). Succeeded brother Mehmed V; accepted Allied occupation of Constantinople; dissolved parliament, banned nationalist movement, attempted to assert personal rule; allowed elections (1919) but forced by Allies to dissolve new parliament; signed Treaty of Sèvres (1920); forced to flee Turkey (1922) by nationalists under Mustafa Kemal.

Mehmed Ağa *or* **Aghā** \-ä-'gä\. 16th–17th century. Ottoman architect. Studied under Sinan; royal architect (1606); built (1609–16) Sultan Ahmed Cami, or Blue Mosque, Istanbul.

Mehmed Es'ad \-äs-'äd\. *Pen names* Gâ·lib De·de \gä-'lēb-dā-'dā\ *and* Şeyh Gâlib \'shāk-gä-'lēb\. 1757–1799. Turkish poet. One of last great classical poets of Ottoman literature; member of Ottoman imperial council; head of the Galata monastery in Istanbul. Known for allegorical romance *Hüsn ü Aşk* (Beauty and Love) and poems on mystical religious themes.

Mehmed Si·yah-Ka·lam \-sē-'yäk-kä-'läm\. 15th century. Turkish artist. Known for vigorous paintings of animals and men, esp. in military occupations; noted for realism, use of perspective, adaptation of Chinese traditions.

Mehmed Talât Paşa. See TALÂT PAŞA.

Meh·met Fu·at Kö·prü·lü \me-'met-fü-'ät-kœ-prü-lü\. *Also known as* Kö·prü·lü·za·de \kœ-prü-lü-zä-'dā\. 1890–1966. Turkish scholar and politician. Descendant of Köprülü viziers; professor, Istanbul (from 1913); member of parliament (from 1936); foreign minister of Turkey (1950–54). Author of authoritative and influential studies of Turkish history and literature including *Türk edebiyatında ilk Mutasavviflar* (1919), *Türk edebiyatı tarihi* (1926), *Erzurumlu emrah* (1930), *Les Origines de l'empire Ottoman* (1935), *Türk saz saileri antolojisi* (1940).

Meh·ring \'mā-riŋ\, Franz. 1846–1919. German Socialist historian and journalist. Edited *Berliner Volkszeitung* (1883–88); joined Social Democrats (1890) and edited its *Leipziger Volkszeitung;* joined Liebknecht and Luxemburg in opposition at outbreak (1914) of World War I and became member of early Spartacist group (1916). Author of *Geschichte der deutschen Sozialdemokratie* (1897–98), *Karl Marx* (1918).

Meh·ta \'mā-tä\, Sir Pherozeshah Merwanji. 1845–1915. Indian lawyer and politician. First Parsi to be called to the English bar (1868); successful practitioner in Bombay; justice of the peace (1869); largely responsible for creation of Bombay municipal government (1872) and member of the new Bombay Corporation (1873–1915; chairman 1884–85, 1905); member of Bombay legislature (1886–1915); member of governor's council (1893); helped found Central Bank of India (1911).

Mé·hul \mā-üel\, Étienne-Nicolas. 1763–1817. French composer. Composed over 40 operas, including *Euphrosine et Coradin* (1790), *Mélidore et Phrosine* (1794), *Le Jeune Henry* (1797), *Adrien* and *Ariodant* (1799), *L'Irato* (1801), *Les Deux Aveugles de Tolède* (1806), *Joseph* (1807), and *La Journée aux aventures* (1816); also wrote ballets, cantatas, symphonies, piano sonatas, and many songs, including patriotic hymns as *Hymne à la Raison* (1793), *Chant du départ* (1794), *Hymne du IX thermidor* (1795).

Mei·di·as Paint·er \'mād-ē-ə-'spänt-ər\. 5th–4th century B.C. Name assigned to Greek vase painter known for florid style and depictions of "flying drapery."

Mei·er·o·vics \,mā-er-'ō-vits\, Zigfrids Anna. 1887–1925. Latvian politician. First foreign minister of independent Latvia (1918) and held office almost continuously until death; prime minister (1921–23, 1923–24).

Meiggs \'megz\, Henry. 1811–1877. American businessman, b. Catskill, N.Y. Made fortune in lumber business in California (1849 ff.); became political and cultural leader in San Francisco; fled debts to Chile (1854); recouped fortune as builder of railroads in Chile and Peru, including the Valparaiso–Santiago route, the Callao, Lima & Oroya Railroad with its Mount Meiggs tunnel at 15,658 feet altitude; lost fortune in bankruptcy of Peruvian government.

Meigh·en \'mē-ən\, Arthur. 1874–1960. Canadian politician, b. near Anderson, Ont. Member, Canadian House of Commons (1908–21, 1922–26); solicitor general of Canada (1913), secretary of state (1917), minister of the interior (1917); member of imperial war cabinet (1918); prime minister of Canada (1920–21, 1926); minister without portfolio (1932–35) and government leader in the Senate.

Meigs \'megz\, Josiah. 1757–1822. American lawyer and educator, b. Middletown, Conn. Practiced law in New Haven, Conn. (1783–89), St. George, Bermuda (1789–94); a founder of *New Haven Gazette* (1784–88); professor, Yale (1794–1800); professor (1801–11), president (1801–10), U. of Georgia. Surveyor general of the U.S. (1812–14); commissioner of U.S. General Land Office (1814). President of Columbian Institute, Washington, D.C. (1819–22); a founder of Columbian Coll. (now George Washington U., 1821).

Meiji. See MUTSUHITO.

Mei·kle \'mē-kəl\, Andrew. 1719–1811. Scottish millwright and inventor. Patented machine for dressing grain (1768); invented drum threshing machine (1784; patented 1788).

Mei·kle·john \'mik-əl-jän, 'mī-kəl-\, Alexander. 1872–1964. American educator, b. Rochdale, England. To U.S. (1880). Professor, Brown U. (1897–1912); president, Amherst (1912–24); professor (1926–38), director of experimental college (1927–32), U. of Wisconsin; instructor in School for Social Studies, San Francisco (1933–36). Author of *The Liberal College* (1920), *The Experimental College* (1932), *Education Between Two Worlds* (1942), *Free Speech* (1948).

Mei Lan-fang \'mā-'län-'fäŋ\. 1894–1961. Chinese actor. A performer of female roles; considered perhaps greatest singer-actor-dancer in history of Chinese theater; credited with revitalization of Chinese theater in 20th century, esp. with reinstating dance as a principal dramatic element.

Meil·hac \me-yák\, Henri. 1831–1897. French playwright. Author of vaudevilles and comedies as *Le Petit-fils de Mascarille* (1861), *La Vertu de Célimène* (1861); collaborated with a number of other playwrights, including Delavigne, Gille, Massenet, and esp. with Ludovic Halévy, as in comedies *Froufrou* (1869), *La Boule* (1874), and operatic libretti for Offenbach's *La Belle Hélène* (1864), *Barbe-Bleu* (1866), *La Vie Parisienne* (1866), *La Grande-Duchesse de Gérolstein* (1867), *La Périchole* (1868), *Le Petit Duc* (1878), and for Bizet's *Carmen* (1875).

Meil·let \me-ye\, Antoine. 1866–1936. French linguist. Professor, École des Hautes Études (1891–1906), Collège de France (1906–36); known for comprehensive comparative studies of Indo-European language family. Author of *Esquisse d'une grammaire comparée de l'arménien classique* (1903), *Introduction à l'étude comparative des langues indo-européennes* (1903), *Les dialectes indo-européennes* (1908), *Aperçu d'une histoire de la langue grecque*

(1913), *Grammaire du vieux perse* (1915), *Esquisse d'une histoire de la langue latine* (1928), etc.

Mei·necke \'mī-nə-kə\, Friedrich. 1862–1954. German historian. Professor, Strassburg (1901–06), Freiburg (1906–14), Berlin (1914–28); editor of *Historische Zeitschrift* (1893–1935); first president, Free U. of Berlin (1948–54); noted esp. for studies of power and morality as embodied in nations. Author of *Das Zeitalter der deutsche Erhebung* (1906), *Weltbürgertum und Nationalstaat* (1908), *Die Idee der Staatsraison* (1924), *Die Entstehung des Historismus* (1936), *Die deutsche Katastrophe* (1946).

Mein·gre \maⁿgrᵊ\, Jean I le. *Called* Bou·ci·caut \bü-sē-kō\. d. 1367. French soldier. Served under John II and Charles V; marshal of France. His son ¶Jean II (c.1366–1421), *also called* Boucicaut, was made marshal of France by Charles VI (1391); taken prisoner at Nicopolis during Hungarian campaign (1396); with troops and fleet defended Byzantine Empire against Turkish fleet at Gallipoli (1399) and prevented capture of Galata; sent to strengthen French administration in Genoa (1401–09), which involved a brief war with Venice; taken prisoner at Agincourt (1415); died in England. Noted as a tournament knight and upholder of chivalric code; founded order of Dame blanche à l'écu vert.

Mei·nong \'mī-nȯŋ\, Alexius. Ritter von Hand·schuchs·heim \fȯn-'hänt-shu̇ks-ˌhīm\. 1853–1920. Austrian philosopher and psychologist. Professor, Graz (from 1882), where he established (1894) first psychological institute in Austria; established a general theory of value and a theory of objects on psychological grounds. Works included *Über Gegenstände* (1899), *Über Annahmen* (1902), *Über Möglichkeit und Wahrscheinlichkeit* (1915), *Über emotionale Präsentation* (1917).

Me·ïr \mā-'ir\. *Orig. perhaps* Mi·a·sa \mē-'äs-ə\ *or* Moi·se \'mȯi-shə\. 2d century A.D. Palestinian rabbi, b. Asia Minor. Student of Rabbi Akiba; became renowned *tanna,* or master of oral law, and continued Akiba's work of compiling and codifying the Halakhot; helped reestablish Sanhedrin after Hadrianic persecutions; known as great dialectician and fabulist.

Me·ir \mā-'ir\ of Roth·en·burg \'rōt-ən-ˌbu̇rk\. *Known also as* Meir ben Ba·ruch \-ˌben-bär-'ük\. c.1215–1293. German rabbi. Opened Talmudic school at Rothenburg; renowned as authority on rabbinic law, esp. as glossator of Rashi's Talmudic commentary; considered supreme judge of appeal for German Jewry; captured while fleeing Emperor Rudolph I's persecution and imprisoned in Alsace (1286–93).

Meir, Golda. *Nee* Goldie Ma·bo·vitch \'mäb(-əv)-ˌyich\. *Known (1917–56) as* Goldie Mey·er·son \'mī-ər-sən\. 1898–1978. Israeli politician, b. Kiev, Russia. To U.S. (1906); teacher in Milwaukee; m. (1917) Morris Meyerson; emigrated to Palestine (1921); executive secretary (1928–32), U.S. representative (1932–34), Women's Labor Council; member of executive committee of Histadrut (from 1934); chairman, Workers' Sick Fund (1936 ff.); head of political department, Jewish Agency (1946–48). Israeli minister to Moscow (1948); member of Knesset (1949–74); minister of labor (1949–56); foreign minister (1956–66), adopting (1956) Hebraized name Meir; secretary general of Mapai party (1966), helped form Labor party (1967); prime minister (1969–74).

Mei·re·les \mā-'rā-lish\, Cecília. 1901–1964. Brazilian poet. Influenced by Symbolists, wrote highly individual poetry of great lyricism. Works included *Espectros* (1919), *Nunca mais* (1923), *Baladas para el-Rei* (1925), *Viagem* (1939), *Vaga música* (1942), *Mar absoluto* (1945), *Retrato natural* (1949), *Romanceiro da Inconfidência* (1953).

Meissen, Heinrich von. See HEINRICH VON MEISSEN.

Meis·sner \'mīs-nər\, Georg. 1829–1905. German physiologist and anatomist. Professor, Basel (1855–57), Freiburg (1857–59), Göttingen (1860–1901); known for work relating to the skin, organs of sight, and respiration. Meissner's corpuscles, small tactile end organs in the skin, are named after him.

Meis·so·nier \mes-ȯn-yā\, Jean-Louis-Ernest. 1815–1891. French painter. Studied under Cogniet; best known for small genre pictures painted with great delicacy and often representing military subjects. Among his famous canvases were *Hallebardier, La Partie d'échecs, Le Grand Fumeur, Le Liseur, Solferino, La Rixe,* and a Napoleonic cycle comprising *Campagne de France, Castiglione, Les Cuirassiers, Iéna, 1807.*

Meis·son·nier \mes-ȯn-yā\, Juste-Aurèle. 1693 or 1695–1750. French goldsmith and decorator, b. Italy. Regarded as a master of Rococo; appointed goldsmith and furniture designer to King Louis XV (1726).

Meit·ner \'mīt-nər\, Lise. 1878–1968. Austrian physicist. Member of Kaiser-Wilhelm Inst., Berlin (1912–38); professor, U. of Berlin (1926–38); fled to Stockholm (1938); known for her work on disintegration products of radium, thorium, and actinium and on behavior of beta rays; with Otto Hahn discovered (1918) protactinium and accomplished (1938) with Hahn and Fritz Strassmann the fission of uranium. Fermi Award (1966) with Hahn and Strassmann.

Me·khi·tar *or* **Me·chi·tar** \ˌmek-ə-'tär\. *Orig.* Peter Ma·noug \mä-'nōg\. 1676–1749. Armenian religious. Ordained Roman Catholic priest (1696); founded (1701) at Constantinople the Order of St. Anthony, which became (1711) a Benedictine order known as Mekhitarists; order designed to introduce western culture among Armenian people; abbot of monastery which he founded (1702) in the Morea (then ruled by Venice) and transferred (1715) to San Lazzaro, near Venice, and widely known for its work in printing Armenian classics and an Armenian translation of the Bible.

Me·la \'mē-lə\, Pomponius. 1st century A.D. Latin geographer. His *De situ orbis* (c.43 A.D.) is earliest known description of ancient world written in Latin.

Me·lanch·thon \mā-'läŋk-tȯn, *Angl* mə-'laŋ(k)-t(h)ən\, Philipp. *Orig. surname* Schwartz·erd \'shvärt-sərd\. 1497–1560. German scholar and religious reformer. Influenced by Rudolf Agricola, William of Ockham; first professor of Greek (1518), Wittenberg, where he met and joined with Luther; at Luther's urging published *Loci communes rerum theologicarum* (1521), first great Protestant treatise on dogmatic theology. Noted for vast learning, skill in dialectics and exegesis, and a moderation that tempered Luther's vehemence. Wrote *Unterricht der Visitatoren* (1527), guidelines for governance of churches and schools that were enacted (1528) in Saxony, creating first public school system of modern times; trained teachers, wrote textbooks, helped found universities of Königsberg, Jena, Marburg. Drafted the Augsburg Confession (1530) and Apology of the Confession of Augsburg (1531), both of which became authoritative statements of Lutheran faith. Forced to flee Wittenberg (1548) but invited by Maurice of Saxony to return and reorganize university. Rejected Augsburg Interim (1548). Sought consistently to reconcile Protestantism with Roman Catholicism and thus attain Christian unity.

Me·las \'mā-läs\, Michael Friedrich Benedikt von. Freiherr. 1729–1806. Austrian general. Commanded Austrian army in Italy; with Suvorov at Cassano d'Adda, the Trebbia River, and Novi (1799), and alone at victory over French at Genola; defeated by Napoléon in battle of Marengo (June 14, 1800); commanding general in Bohemia (1801–03).

Mel·ba \'mel-bə\, Dame Nellie. *Orig.* Helen Porter Mitchell. 1861–1931. Australian soprano. Operatic debut as Gilda in *Rigoletto* at Brussels (1887), adopting name of Melba from Melbourne, Australia; London debut at Covent Garden as Lucia in *Lucia di Lammermoor* (1888); first appeared at Metropolitan Opera, New York City, as Lucia (1893); regular performer at Covent Garden and Metropolitan (to 1926). Outstanding coloratura of her day. Created dame of the British Empire (1918).

Melbourne, Viscount. See William LAMB.

Mel·chers \'mel-chərz\, Gari, *in full* Julius Gari. 1860–1932. American painter, b. Detroit. Excelled in genre pictures of Dutch peasant life, religious paintings, portraits, and mural decorations. His mural *Peace and War* is in the Library of Congress, Washington, D.C.

Mel·chers \'mel-kərs\, Paulus. 1813–1895. German prelate. Bishop of Osnabrück (1857); archbishop of Cologne (1866). Imprisoned six months during Kulturkampf (1874) and declared removed from office by tribunal for church affairs (1876); fled to Holland (1875–85), whence he administered his diocese. Resigned as archbishop (1885) and was created cardinal at Rome; joined Jesuits (1892).

Melchett, Baron. Sir Alfred Moritz Mond. See under Ludwig MOND.

Melchiades. See MILTIADES.

Mel·chior \'mel-kyȯr\, Johann Peter. 1742–1825. German porcelain modeller. Master modeller at Höchst porcelain factory (1767–79), at Frankenthal (1779–93), Nymphenburg (1797–1822); noted chiefly for earlier work, transitional between Rococo and Neoclassical, including religious groups, pastoral and mythological figures, figures of children; later produced Neoclassical portrait reliefs.

Mel·chi·or \'mel-kē-ˌȯ(ə)r\, Lauritz Lebrecht Hommel. 1890–1973. American singer, b. Copenhagen, Denmark. Debut at Danish Royal Opera in *Pagliacci* (1913), at Covent Garden (1924), at Metropolitan Opera, New York City (1926); regular in Wagnerian tenor roles at Covent Garden (1926–39), Bayreuth (1924–31), Metropolitan (1929–50); naturalized U.S. citizen (1947). Considered the outstanding *heldentenor* of the day.

Melcombe, Baron. See George BUBB DODINGTON.

Mel·do·la \'mel-də-lə\, Raphael. 1849–1915. English chemist. Known for researches on triphenyl methane dyes; produced first oxazine dyestuff, Meldola's blue (1879).

Mel·dol·la \mel-'dōl-lä\, Andrea. *Known as* Lo Schia·vo·ne \ˌlō-skyä-'vō-nā\. 1522–1563. Italian painter. Collaborated with Tintoretto in decorating the Palazzo Zen in Venice (c.1540); works included *Adoration of the Magi, Bacchus and Nymphs, St. John the Baptist.*

Mel·e·a·ger \mel-ē-'ā-gər\. 1st century B.C. Greek epigrammatist. Compiled earliest known anthology, *Stephanos* (The Garland), containing epigrams of many authors and including 130 epigrams of his own composition.

Me·lén·dez Val·dés \mā-'lān-dāth-ˌbäl-'dās\, Juan. 1754–1817. Spanish poet and politician. Professor, Salamanca (1778–89); member of judiciary (from 1789); supported and held office under Napoleonic regime (1808–13); fled to France (1813). Author of classical pastoral verse, often foreshadowing Spanish

Romanticism in its sentimentality; philosophical odes; romantic ballads as "Doña Elvira."

Me·le·ti·os Pe·gas \mē-ˈlē-tē-ȯs-ˈpeg-äs\. *Also spelled* Me·le·ti·us \mə-ˈlē-shē-əs\. 1549–1601. Greek prelate. Monk and scholar at Candia, Crete; patriarch of Alexandria (1590–1601); a leader of opposition to Union of Brest-Litovsk (1596) joining Ukrainian and Belorussian Orthodox churches with Roman Catholic church.

Me·le·ti·us \mə-ˈlē-shē-əs\. Saint. d. 381 A.D. Greek prelate. Bishop of Sebaste (358), of Antioch (360); orthodox in doctrine, he was subject to attack from the Arians; banished (360) by Emperor Constans II; appointment of an Arian bishop caused schism in Antioch that persisted to 401; finally established in Antioch under Emperor Theodosius (379); died while presiding over Council of Constantinople.

Meletius. 4th century. Greek prelate. Bishop of Lycopolis; engaged in dispute with Peter, bishop of Alexandria, over penances imposed on Christians who lapsed during persecutions of Diocletian; deposed by Peter (c.306); exiled to Palestine in new persecutions (308–311); formed (328) schismatic sect, Meletians, holding to ascetic, monastic regimen.

Mel·ga·re·jo \mel-gä-ˈre-kō\, Mariano. 1818–1871. Bolivian general and politician. President of Bolivia (1865–71), deposing José María de Achá; gave up much of Bolivia's claim to nitrate regions of Atacama Desert; left Bolivia financially ruined.

Me·li \ˈme-lē\, Giovanni. 1740–1815. Sicilian physician and poet. Wrote chiefly in dialect; author of *La fata galanti* (1761–62), *La buccolica* (1767–87), mock epic *Don Chisciotti e Sanciu Panza* (1785–87), *Favuli murali* (1810–14), canzonets, odes, pastorals, and collections of Sicilian proverbs.

Mé·liès \māl-yes\, Georges. 1861–1938. French film director. Trained as magician; manager of Théâtre Robert-Houdin; built (1897) motion picture studio; first to film fictional narratives, using scripts, actors, sets, etc.; experimented in camera tricks as slow and stop motion, dissolves, superimposition, double exposure; made over 400 films (1899–1913), as *Cleopâtre* (1899), *Le Christ marchant sur les eaux* (1899), *Le Voyage dans la lune* (1902), *Le Voyage à travers l'impossible* (1904), *Hamlet* (1908), *Les Hallucinations du baron de Munchhausen* (1911).

Melikov, Count Loris-. See LORIS-MELIKOV.

Mé·line \mā-lēn\, Félix-Jules. 1838–1925. French politician. Deputy (1872–1903); minister of agriculture (1883–85); opponent of Boulanger; premier of France (1896–98); elected to senate (1903); minister of agriculture (1915–16).

Me·liq-Ha·ko·bi·an \ˈmel-ēk-hä-ˈkȯb-ē-ən\, Hakob. *Pseudonym* Raf·fi \ˈräf-fē\. 1835–1888. Armenian novelist. Worked as schoolmaster, salesman, trader; journalist with Russian-Armenian paper *Mshak* (1872–84); ardent nationalist. His chief novels were *Jalaleddin* (1878), *Khent* (1880), *Davith-Bek* (1881–87), and *Samuel* (1888).

Me·lis·sus \mə-ˈlis-əs\. 5th century B.C. Greek philosopher. Disciple of Parmenides, last important representative of Eleatic school; commanded fleet of Samos in victory over Athens (441 or 440 B.C.). Only fragments of his works are extant.

Mel·i·to \ˈmel-ə-(ˌ)tō\. 2d century. Greek prelate. Bishop of Sardis; a chief theologian and apologist of post-apostolic age; extant works include an important treatise on Easter.

Mel·li·tus \ˈmel-ət-əs\. Saint. d. 624. English prelate. Leader of band of missionaries sent by Pope St. Gregory I to join St. Augustine in Britain (601); consecrated by Augustine first bishop of London (between 601 and 604); archbishop of Canterbury (619).

Mel·lon \ˈmel-ən\, Andrew William. 1855–1937. American financier, b. Pittsburgh. Entered father's banking house (1874); acquired large interests in coal, coke, and iron enterprises, aluminum manufacture, and banking; president, Mellon National Bank of Pittsburgh (from 1902). U.S. secretary of the treasury (1921–32); U.S. ambassador to Great Britain (1932–33). Endowed National Gallery of Art, Washington, D.C.

Me·lo \ˈmā-lü, *Sp* -lō\, Francisco Manuel de. 1608–1666. Portuguese soldier, historian, and poet. Served in Spanish army (to 1640), and then under the house of Bragança (after 1640); imprisoned (1644–55) and then banished to Brazil (1655–58); lived thereafter in Lisbon. Wrote principally in Spanish; chief work *Historia de la guerra de Cataluña* (1645); collected poems first published under title *Las tres musas de Melodino* (1649); also published verse *Obras métricas* (1665), treatise on marriage *Carta de guia de casados* (1650), collected letters *Cartas familiares* (1664).

Me·loz·zo da For·lì \mā-ˈlȯt-tsō-dä-fȯr-ˈlē\. 1438–1494. Italian painter of Umbrian school. Known for skill in perspective, esp. in foreshortening; influenced by Piero della Francesca; assisted in decorating library of ducal palace, Urbino; to Rome (c.1475); executed frescoes in library of Sixtus IV, Vatican (1477 ff.), fresco *The Ascension,* SS. Apostoli (c.1480); designed mosaics for Sta. Croce in Gerusalemme, cupola frescoes for Cappella del Tesoro at Loreto, decoration of Cappella Feo in S. Biagio at Forlì.

Me·lus \ˈmā-ləs, ˈmē-\ *or* **Me·lo** \-(ˌ)lō\ of Ba·ri \ˈbär-ē,ˈbar-\. d. 1020. Lombard noble. Led uprising (1009) against Byzantine governor of Bari; defeated and forced to flee; enlisted aid of Norman knights and led invasion of Byzantine Italy (1018); defeated at Canne by Emperor Basil II's Varangian Guard; died while attempting to enlist aid of Emperor Henry II, who created him duke of Apulia.

Melville, Viscounts. See DUNDAS of Arniston.

Mel·ville *or* **Mel·vill** \ˈmel-ˌvil\, Andrew. 1545–1622. Scottish religious reformer. Principal of Glasgow U. (1574–80), of St. Mary's Coll., St. Andrews (1580–1606); reorganized Scottish universities; promoted study of Aristotle and taste for Greek. Had principal part in drawing up *The Second Book of Discipline* (1578, sanctioned 1581), shaping Presbyterian church; preached boldly before General Assembly against absolute spiritual authority of king and hierarchy (1582); escaped to England until after Arran's fall (1585). Headed deputation to remonstrate with James VI (1596) against encroachments of government; summoned before English privy council to suggest solution to problem of Scottish church, delivered two long speeches on behalf of freedom of assemblies; composed a satirical Latin poem on king's religious practice, for which he was sent to Tower for four years; released through Henri de la Tour d'Auvergne, duc de Bouillon, and made professor of theology in U. of Sedan (1611). His nephew ¶James Melville *or* Melvill (1556–1614), religious reformer; professor, St. Andrews (1580); devoted himself (from 1586) to church controversy and antagonism toward episcopal schemes of king; attended his uncle to London (1606); detained (1607–13). Remembered for his *Diary,* giving portrait of Knox.

Melville, George John Whyte-. See WHYTE-MELVILLE.

Melville, George Wallace. 1841–1912. American naval officer and explorer, b. New York City. Entered navy (1861); chief engineer of the *Jeanette,* George W. De Long's ship in Arctic exploration (1879); after wreck of ship, led a detachment to safety through Siberia. Headed relief expedition which discovered bodies of De Long and his companions and rescued ship's records. Chief engineer on the *Thetis* of Greely relief expedition (1884). Chief, bureau of steam engineering, U.S. navy (1887–1903); rear admiral (1899); retired (1903). Author of *In the Lena Delta* (1884).

Melville, Herman. 1819–1891. American writer, b. New York City. Went to sea as cabin boy (1839); sailed on whaler *Acushnet* (1841–42); deserted his ship at the Marquesas Islands and found temporary refuge among cannibal natives; escaped on Australian whaler *Lucy Ann* but left her at Papeete; shipped as seaman on frigate *United States* (1843–44). Devoted himself to writing stories based on his experiences: *Typee* (1846), *Omoo* (1847), *Mardi* (1849), *Redburn* (1849), *White-Jacket* (1850), *Moby Dick* (1851), *Pierre: or the Ambiguities* (1852), *Israel Potter* (1855), *The Piazza Tales,* including "The Encantadas," "Bartleby," "Benito Cereno" (1856), *The Confidence-Man* (1857); published verse *Battle-Pieces* (1866), *Clarel* (1876), *John Marr* (1888), *Timoleon* (1891). U.S. customs inspector on New York docks (1866–85). Left unpublished at his death novel *Billy Budd, Foretopman* (pub. 1924).

Melville of Hall·hill \ˈhȯl-ˌhil\, Sir James. 1535–1617. Scottish soldier and diplomat. Offered allegiance to Mary, Queen of Scots (1561); ambassador to Queen Elizabeth, sought to win her approval of Darnley marriage; loyal to Mary Stuart up to her commitment to Loch Leven Castle. Sent on diplomatic missions during James VI's minority; privy councilor under Queen Anne. Presented historical data in autobiography *Memoirs* (pub. 1683).

Melville, Jean-Pierre. See Jean-Pierre GRUMBACH.

Melzi, José de Palafox y. See PALAFOX Y MELZI.

Mem·ling \ˈmem-liŋ\ *or* **Mem·linc** \-liŋk\, Hans. c.1430 or 1435–1494. Flemish painter. Studied in Cologne and under Rogier van der Weyden in Brussels; lived in Bruges (from 1465). Works included portraits and religious paintings as the triptych of *The Marriage of St. Catherine, Adoration of the Magi, Virgin and Child with Saints and Donors, Bathsheba, Passion Triptych, St. Christopher* altarpiece, *Last Judgment* altarpiece, *Thomas Portinari and Wife, Man with an Arrow,* etc.

Me·na \ˈmā-nä\, Juan de. 1411–1456. Spanish poet. Secretary to King John II of Castile. Chief work *El laberinto de fortuna* (1444), popularly called *Las trescientas,* written in 12-syllable lines of *arte mayor.*

Mena, Pedro de. *Full surname* Mena y Me·dra·no \-ē-māth-ˈrä-nō\. 1628–1688. Spanish sculptor. Known for works in polychromed wood; carved in high relief figures of 40 saints for the choir stalls in Málaga cathedral, *St. Francis* for Toledo cathedral, *Dolorosa* for Cuenca cathedral, *Virgin of Bethlehem* for Santo Domingo, Málaga.

Men·aech·mus \mə-ˈnēk-məs\. 4th century B.C. Greek mathematician. Credited with discovering and describing the conic sections.

Mé·nage \mā-nȧzh\, Gilles. 1613–1692. French scholar. A lawyer and later cleric; sponsored (from 1656) weekly *mercuriales,* Wednesday literary meetings. Author of *Origines de la langue française* (1650), *Origines de la langue italienne* (1669), *Observations sur la langue française* (1672), *Menagiana* (1693–1715), etc.

Men·a·hem \'men-ə-k̲əm, mā-'näk̲-əm\. 8th century B.C. King of Israel (c.746–c.736 B.C.). Reign noted for cruelty; forced to pay tribute to Assyria.

Menahem ben Sa·ruq \-,ben-'sär-ək\. c.910–c.970. Spanish poet and lexicographer. Secretary to Ḥisdai ibn Shaprut; compiled *Maḥberet,* a Bible lexicon, the first dictionary in Hebrew, which provoked controversy that helped spark a golden age of Hebrew philology.

Me·nan·der \mə-'nan-dər\. 342–292 B.C. Athenian dramatist. Student of Theophrastus and friend of Epicurus. Author of more than 100 comedies noted for literary style, ingenuity of plot, and wit, and considered the zenith of Greek New Comedy. Works included *Dyscolus* and, extant in fragments, *Orgē, Perikeiromenē, Samia, Epitrepontes;* his plays were adapted by Plautus and Terence.

Menander. *Pāli* Mi·lin·da \mə-'lin-də\ *or* Mi·ne·dra \mə-'nā-drə\ *or* Me·na·dra \mə-'nä-drə\. fl. 160–135 B.C. A Greek king in India. One of a powerful Greco-Bactrian dynasty set up at Kabul; invaded India, conquered and apparently held for some time the valley of the Indus, the Punjab, Gujarat, etc.; probably converted to Buddhism; subject of Buddhist classic *Milinda-pañha.*

Menander Pro·tec·tor \-prə-'tek-tər\. 6th century A.D. Byzantine historian. At instance of Emperor Maurice, wrote a history of period 558–582, continuing that of Agathias; work extant in fragments.

Me·nard \'mā-nərd, -,närd; mə-'närd\, John Willis. 1838–1893. American politician, b. Kaskaskia, Ill. Clerk in U.S. Department of Interior (1861–65); active in Republican party in New Orleans; elected to fill unexpired term in House of Representatives, first Negro so elected (1868); denied seat in challenge; active in Florida Republican politics (from 1871).

Mé·nard \mā-nȧr\, Louis-Nicolas. 1822–1901. French scholar, poet, and artist. Active in insurrection of 1848 and imprisoned for his *Prologue d'une révolution* (1849); a gifted painter in Barbizon manner; influenced Parnassians with mythological studies in Greek. Author of *Prométhée délivré* (1843), *Poèmes* (1855), *De la morale avant les philosophes* (1860), *La Legende de Saint-Hilarion* (1875), *Rêveries d'un païen mystique* (1876), etc.

Me·nard \mā-nȧr, *Angl* mə-'närd\, Michel Branamour. 1805–1856. American fur trader, b. Laprairie, Que. Nephew of Pierre Menard; trader with Shawnee and Delaware tribes (from 1823); moved westward and located claim (1834) to about six square miles of land on Galveston Island, Texas, and organized company (1838) to settle it, thus founding the city of Galveston. Menard County, Texas, was named after him.

Menard, Pierre. 1766–1844. American fur trader and pioneer, b. St. Antoine, Que. To Vincennes, Ind. (c.1787) and then to Kaskaskia, Ill. (1789); an organizer of St. Louis Missouri Fur Co. (1809); president, Ill. legislative council (1812–18); first lieutenant governor of State of Illinois (1818).

Menasseh ben Israel. See MANASSEH BEN ISRAEL.

Mencius. See MENG-TZU.

Mencke \'meŋ-kə\ *or* **Menck·en** \'meŋ-kən\. Family of German scholars including: Otto Mencke (1644–1707), professor of moral philosophy, Leipzig, and cofounder (1682) and editor of *Acta Eruditorum,* first literary and scientific periodical in Germany. His son ¶Johann Burkhard (1674–1732), writer and historian, succeeded his father as editor of *Acta Eruditorum* and founded *Neue Zeitungen von gelehrten Sachen* (1715); editor of *Scriptores rerum Germanicarum, praecipue Saxonicarum* (1728–30); author of poems under pseudonym Philander von der Lin·de \,fōn-dər-'lin-də\.

Menck·en \'meŋ-kən, 'men-\, Henry Louis. 1880–1956. American journalist and writer, b. Baltimore. On staff of Baltimore *Morning Herald* (1899–1905), Baltimore *Evening Herald* (1905–06). On staff of Baltimore *Sun* (1906–10), *Evening Sun* (1910–16, 1918–36), and on both *Sun* and *Evening Sun* (from 1936). Literary critic, *Smart Set* (1908–24), and coeditor (1914–24). Founder, with George Jean Nathan (*q.v.*), coeditor, and editor, *American Mercury* (1924–33). Contributing editor, *The Nation* (1921–32). Author of *Ventures into Verse* (1903), *George Bernard Shaw—His Plays* (1905), *In Defense of Women* (1917), *The American Language* (1918; supplements 1945, 1948), *Prejudices* (in 6 series, 1919–27), *Notes on Democracy* (1926), *Treatise on the Gods* (1930), *Treatise on Right and Wrong* (1934), *A New Dictionary of Quotations* (1942), the autobiographical *Happy Days* (1940), *Newspaper Days* (1941), and *Heathen Days* (1943), etc.

Men·da·ña de Nei·ra \mān-'dän-yä-t̲h̲ā-'nā-rä\, Álvaro de. 1541–1595. Spanish mariner and explorer. Discovered and explored Solomon Islands (c.1567) and Marquesas Islands (c.1595).

Mendel, David. See Johann August Wilhelm NEANDER.

Men·del \'men-dəl\, Gregor Johann. 1822–1884. Austrian botanist. Entered order of Augustinians at Brünn (1843); ordained (1847); taught in technical high school (1854–68); abbot (1868). Known for breeding experiments with peas in monastery garden (from 1856); discovered Mendel's laws of segregation and of independent assortment, based on his inference that heritable characteristics are paired units and that their appearance in hybridized offspring obeys statistical laws; his work was published by natural history society of Brünn (1866) but not widely recognized until brought into prominence by De Vries and others (1900).

Men·del \'men-dᵊl\, Lafayette Benedict. 1872–1935. American physiological chemist, b. Delhi, N.Y. Professor, Yale (1897–1935). Known for researches with Thomas Osborne on digestion and nutrition, protein metabolism, growth; simultaneously with Elmer McCollum discovered vitamin A (1913); contributed to discovery (1915) of B-complex vitamins.

Mendele Mokher Sefarim. See Shalom ABRAMOVICH.

Men·de·le·yev \myin-dyil-'yā-yəf; *Angl* ,men-də-'lā-əf\, Dmitry Ivanovich. 1834–1907. Russian chemist. Professor, St. Petersburg (1867–90); director, bureau of weights and measures (from 1893). Known for devising periodic table classification of chemical elements by atomic weight, on basis of which system he was able to predict properties of yet-undiscovered elements. Author of *The Principles of Chemistry* (1868–70).

Men·dels·sohn \'men-dəls-zōn, *Angl* 'men-dᵊl-sən\, Arnold Ludwig. 1855–1933. German composer. Cousin of Felix Mendelssohn. Professor at conservatories of Cologne (1885–90), Darmstadt (1891–1912), Frankfurt (1912–33). Known for choral and orchestral works, including *Abendkantate* (1881), *Frühlingsfeier* (1891), and *Psalm 137* (1913); also of three operas, including *Elsi, die seltsame Magd* (1896); incidental music to Goethe's *Paria* (1906) and *Pandora* (1908); symphonies, chamber music, and songs.

Mendelssohn, Dorothea. See Dorothea SCHLEGEL.

Mendelssohn, Erich. 1887–1953. American architect, b. Allenstein, East Prussia (now Olsztyn, Poland). Achieved fame with Expressionist masterpiece Einstein Tower, Potsdam (1919–21); built hat factory at Luckenwalde (1920–23), Schocken stores at Stuttgart (1927) and Chemnitz (1928); fled Germany (1933) to Belgium and then Great Britain; designed De La Warr Pavilion, Bexhill (with S. Chermayeff, 1933), hospitals in Haifa (1937) and Jerusalem (1938); to U.S. (1941); designed Maimonides Hospital, San Francisco (1946), synagogues and community centers in St. Louis, St. Paul, Cleveland, etc.

Mendelssohn, Felix. *In full* Jakob Ludwig Felix Mendelssohn-Bar·thol·dy \-bär-'tōl-dē, *Angl also* -'thōl-\. 1809–1847. German composer. Grandson of Moses Mendelssohn; with family, added name Bartholdy on inheritance from a maternal uncle; converted in childhood to Christianity. Made first public appearance as pianist (1818) and presented original compositions at musical gatherings in father's house. Formed close friendships with Weber and Goethe (1821) and Moscheles. Gave initial impetus to Bach revival by successfully conducting Bach's *St. Matthew Passion* in Berlin (1829), first time since death of the composer. Appeared successfully as pianist and conductor in London (1829); toured (until 1832) in England and on the Continent; again to London in 1833 and repeatedly thereafter. Musical director in Düsseldorf (1833); director of Gewandhaus concerts in Leipzig (from 1835), which became musical center of Europe; cofounder (1843) and director of Leipzig Conservatory. Collapsed from overwork and from nervous prostration following death of his sister Fanny. Composed five symphonies, including *C Minor* (1824), *Reformation* (1829–30), *Italian* (1833), *Scottish* (1842), and symphony cantata *Lobgesang* (1840); overtures, including *A Midsummer Night's Dream* (1826), *The Hebrides* or *Fingal's Cave* (1830–32), *Meeresstille und glückliche Fahrt* (1828–32), *Die schöne Melusine* (1833); concertos, including a violin concerto (1844) and two piano concertos (1831, 1837); comic opera *Die Hochzeit des Camacho* (1825), operetta *Die Heimkehr aus der Fremde* (1829); much chamber music, esp. string quartets and quintets, piano trios; piano works, including eight books of *Lieder ohne Worter* (1830–45), three sonatas, five books of *Variations,* seven preludes and fugues; organ works; vocal music, including oratorios *St. Paul* (1836) and *Elijah* (1846), and songs, Psalms, motets, and other choral works, etc.

Mendelssohn, Moses. *Orig.* Moses Des·sau \'des-,au̇\. 1729–1786. German Jewish philosopher. Formed close friendship with Lessing (1754), which inspired latter's *Nathan der Weise,* and was befriended by Nicolai, Lavater, and others. Author of *Philosophische Gespräche* (1755), the satire *Pope ein Metaphysiker* (1755), the essay *Abhandlung über die Evidenz in den metaphysischen Wissenschaften* (1763; Berlin Acad. prize), *Phädon* (in support of immortality of the soul, 1767), translations into German of the Psalms and the Pentateuch (1783), which helped advance assimilation of the Jews, *Jerusalem oder über religiöse Macht und Judentum* (plea for religious tolerance, 1783), *Morgenstunden oder über das Dasein Gottes* (1785), etc.

Men·den·hall \'men-dən-,hȯl\, Thomas Corwin. 1841–1924. American physicist, b. near Hanoverton, Ohio. Professor, Ohio State U. (1873–78, 1881–84); president, Rose Polytechnic Institute, Terre Haute, Ind. (1886–89), Worcester Tech. (1894–1901); superintendent, U.S. Coast and Geodetic Survey (1889–

94). Known for his researches in gravity, seismology, electricity, and atmospheric electricity.

Men·dès \maⁿ-des\, Catulle, *in full* Abraham-Catulle. 1841–1909. French man of letters. To Paris and founded (1859) *Revue Fantaisiste;* actively associated with Parnassian school of poetry, the origins of which he described in *Légende du Parnasse contemporain* (1884). Dramatic critic of *Le Journal* (from 1893). Wrote verse as *Philoméla* (1864), *Hespérus* (1869), *Poésies* (1876), *Poésies nouvelles* (1893); plays as *La Femme de Tabarin* (1887), *La Reine Fiammette* (1898), *Medée* (1898), *Glatigny* (1906); romances as *Le Roi vierge* (1881), *Monstres parisiens* (1882), *Zo'har* (1886); critical work *Rapport sur le mouvement poétique français de 1867–1900* (1902); biography of Richard Wagner (1886).

Mendès-France \-fräⁿs\, Pierre. 1907–1982. French politician. Lawyer by training; Radical-Socialist deputy (1932–40, 1946–58, 1967–68). Imprisoned (1940) by Vichy government but escaped (1941) and joined Free French Air Force; commissioner for finance in French Provisional government (1943–44); minister of national economy (1944–45). Prime minister and minister of foreign affairs (1954–55); ended French involvement in Indochina (1954); made concessions leading to Tunisian autonomy; instrumental in defeat of European Defense Community, accepting instead a British plan for German rearmament; attempted to strengthen executive power. Deputy premier without portfolio in Mollet's government (1956). Author of several books on political and economic topics.

Men·die·ta \mān-'dyā-tä\, Carlos. 1873–1960. Cuban politician. Active in revolution against Spain (1896–98); deputy (1901–23); opposed administrations of Menocal and Machado; arrested (1931) and went into exile in New York; after Machado's fall (1933), led opposition to radical government of Grau San Martín. Provisional president of Cuba (1934–35).

Men·do·za \mān-'dō-thä, -sä\, Antonio de. c.1490–1552. Spanish colonial governor. First viceroy of New Spain (Mexico; 1535–49) and viceroy of Peru (1551–52). Brought first printing press to New World (1535); did much to alleviate exploitation of Indians; built schools, churches; fostered agriculture; sent out expedition under Coronado which explored much of what is now New Mexico and Colorado.

Men·do·za \men-'dō-zə\, Daniel. 1764–1836. English boxer. Acknowledged English heavyweight champion on retirement of Benjamin Brain (1791); lost title to "Gentleman" John Jackson (1795); first great fighter to combine scientific boxing with rapid, rather than hard, punching; operated successful boxing school, London.

Mendoza, Diego Hurtado de. See HURTADO DE MENDOZA.

Men·do·za \mān-'dō-thä\, Íñigo López de. Marqués de San·til·la·na \sän-tē(l)-'yä-nä\. 1398–1458. Spanish poet. Led expeditions against the Muslims in Spain; supported John II of Castile after ouster of Álvaro de Luna; patron of the arts. Commissioned translations of Homer, Plato, Virgil, and Seneca into Spanish; first to compose sonnets in Spanish (in imitation of Petrarch); first to write formal literary criticism, in *Proemio e carta al condestable de Portugal* (1449); collected proverbs. His poetry, much of it influenced by Italian models, included allegories as *Infierno de los enamorados* and the panegyric *Comedieta de Ponza* (1436), didactic poems as *Diálogo de Bías contra Fortuna* (1448), and lyrics as his 10 *serranillas* (pastoral songs).

Mendoza, Juan de Palafox y. See PALAFOX Y MENDOZA.

Mendoza, Juan Gonzales de. c.1540–1617. Spanish prelate. To Mexico as soldier, and there entered Augustinian order. On mission from Philip II to China (1580–83); bishop of Lipari Islands (1593), of Chiapas (1607), and of Popayán (1608). Published (1586) an account of China.

Mendoza, Pedro de. 1487–1537. Spanish soldier and explorer. Appointed by Charles V military governor of lands between Plata River and Strait of Magellan. Equipped expedition largely at own expense (1535); sailed up Plata River and founded first colony of Buenos Aires (1536).

Mendoza, Pedro González de. 1428–1495. Spanish prelate, statesman, and soldier. Son of Íñigo López de Mendoza, marqués de Santillana. Bishop of Calahorra (1454), of Sigüenza (1468); created cardinal (1473); a supporter of Henry IV, who made him chancellor of Castile (1473); archbishop of Seville (1474); aided Isabella I in securing throne of Castile (1474); archbishop of Toledo and primate of Spain (1482).

Mendoza de la Cer·da \-thä-lä-'ker-thä\, Ana. Princesa de Ebo·li \ā-'bō-lē\. 1540–1592. Spanish courtier. m. (1559) Ruy Gómez de Silva, later prince of Eboli. Became mistress of Philip II and also of his secretary, Antonio Pérez; involved in court intrigues; banished from court (1579). A character in Schiller's *Don Carlos.*

Men·e·de·mus \,men-ə-'dē-məs\. c.339–c.265 B.C. Greek philosopher, of Eretria. Reputed student under Phaedo, whose Elian school he transferred to Eretria, where it became known as Eretrian school. His doctrines are said to have resembled those of Megarian school.

Men·e·la·us \,men-ᵊl-'ā-əs\. 1st century A.D. Greek mathematician, of Alexandria. Author of *Sphaerica* on geometry of the sphere, including his original definition of and theorems concerning spherical triangles; stated Menelaus's theorem, a fundamental theorem of spherical trigonometry.

Me·ne·lik II \'mā-nə-lik, *Angl* 'men-ᵊl-(,)ik\. *Orig.* Sah·le Ma·ri·am \'säl-em-'är-yäm\. 1844–1913. Emperor of Ethiopia (1889–1913). Son of Haile Malakof, king of Shewa; held captive by Tewodros II of Ethiopia (1855–65); assumed throne of Shewa (1865); expanded realm southward; succeeded Yohannes IV as emperor. Signed Treaty of Wachile (1889) with Italy, interpreted by Italy as placing empire under Italian domination; abrogated treaty (1893); defeated Italians at Aduwa (Mar. 1, 1896); established independence of Ethiopia. Negotiated boundary settlements with British Sudan (1902) and Italian Somaliland (1908). Unable to continue rule because of apoplectic attacks, succeeded by a regency (1910).

Me·nén·dez de Avi·lés \mā-'nān-dāth-thā-ä-bē-'lās\, Pedro. 1519–1574. Spanish mariner. Captain general of the Indies fleet (1554); made three trips to America (between 1555 and 1563); imprisoned (1563–65) but regained royal favor. *Adelantado* of Florida (1565), charged with exploration, colonization, and defense of the province; built fort at St. Augustine and defeated and massacred French Protestant colony of Ft. Caroline on St. Johns River (1565); firmly established Spanish power in Florida.

Menéndez Pi·dal \-pē-'thäl\, Ramón. 1869–1968. Spanish philologist. Professor of Romanic philology, Madrid (1899–1939); founder and editor (from 1914) of *Revista de filología española.* Author of *Manual de gramática histórica española* (1904), *Cantar de Mio Cid* (1908–12), *Los orígines de español* (1926), *La España del Cid* (1929), *Romancero hispánico* (1953), etc.

Menéndez y Pe·la·yo \-ē-pā-'lä-yō\, Marcelino. 1856–1912. Spanish critic and historian. Professor, Madrid (1878–98); director, Biblioteca Nacional (1898–1912). Author of *La ciencia española* (1876–88), *Historia de los heterodoxes españoles* (1880–82), *Historia de las ideas estéticas en España* (1883–91), *Estudios de crítica literaria* (1883–1908), etc.

Me·nes \'mē-,nēz\. *Sometimes* Me·na \'mē-nə\. fl. 3100 B.C. First king of unified Egypt. Credited with uniting north and south kingdoms under one scepter and founding city on site of Memphis; traditional founder of 1st dynasty; reigned 62 years.

Meng·el·berg \'meŋ-əl-,berk\, Willem, *in full* Josef Willem. 1871–1951. Dutch orchestra conductor, pianist, and composer. A leading interpreter of Beethoven, Richard Strauss, and Gustav Mahler; conductor of Amsterdam Concertgebouw Orchestra (1895–1945) and of London Symphony Orchestra and Royal Philharmonic Society (1911–14); conductor of National Symphony Orchestra of New York and its successor the New York Philharmonic Orchestra (1921–30), latterly as co-conductor with Toscanini.

Meng·er \'meŋ-ər\, Carl von. 1840–1921. Austrian economist. A leading theorist of Austrian school of economics; professor, Vienna (1879–1903). Contributed to marginal utility theory and subjective theory of value. Author of *Grundsätze der Volkswirtschaftslehre* (1871).

Men·gli Gi·ray *or* **Men·gli Gi·rai** \'meŋ-glē-gē-'rī\. c.1440–1515. Tatar ruler. Khan of the Crimean Tatars (from c.1468); vassal of Ottoman sultan (from c.1475); allied with Ivan III of Muscovy against Lithuania and Tatar khan Ahmed; later joined Lithuania against Muscovy.

Mengs \'meŋ(k)s\, Anton Raphael. 1728–1779. German painter. To Dresden (1744) as court painter to Elector Augustus III; worked in Rome (1755–61); in Madrid as first painter to Charles III (1761–69, 1773–77) and in Rome (1769–72, from 1777). Considered greatest living painter in his day; chief exponent of Neoclassicism; works included fresco *Parnassus* in Villa Albani, Rome (1761), decoration of Camera dei Papiri in Vatican (1769–72), frescoes in royal palace in Madrid.

Meng T'ien \'məŋ-tē-'ən\. d. 209 B.C. Chinese general. Commander in chief of Emperor Shih Huang Ti; appointed by the emperor to superintend the building of the Great Wall (214–209 B.C.); reputed to have been the inventor of the pen or writing brush.

Meng-tzu \'məŋ-dzü\. *Orig.* Meng K'o \'məŋ-'kō\. *Known in West by Latinized form* Men·ci·us \'men-shē-əs\. c.371–c.289 B.C. Chinese philosopher. Pupil of Tzu Ssu, grandson of Confucius; lived during turbulent period of the Warring States; traveled among various states but found no patron among contemporary princes. Taught ethical system similar to that of Confucius, based on *jen,* or magnanimity, and on belief in man's innate goodness; counseled princes to rule lightly, with regard to needs and wishes of the people. Records of his doings and sayings compiled by disciples in book *Meng-tzu.* Revered second only to Confucius as cofounder of Confucianism.

Me·nip·pus \mə-'nip-əs\. 3d century B.C. Greek Cynic philosopher and satirist. Originally a slave; bitterly satirized, in verse varied with prose, foibles of men, esp. of fellow philosophers; style influenced Varro, Seneca, Lucian.

Men·ken \'meŋ-kən\, Adah Isaacs. *Nee* Adah Bertha The·o·dore \'thē-ə-,dȯr\. 1835?–1868. American actress, b. New Orleans. m. A. I. Menken (1856) and then, under impression that she was divorced, John C. Heenan (1859), pugilist; became central figure in divorce scandal. Stage debut (1857), New York (1859); enjoyed huge success in sensational productions of *Mazeppa* (first produced in Albany, N.Y., 1861) in New York, Baltimore, San Francisco, London (1864), etc.; successful in Paris in *Les Pirates de la Savane* (1866). Wrote poems later collected and published (1868) under title *Infelicia*.

Men·ku·re \men-'kü-rā\ *or* **Men·kau·re** \-'kau̇-\. *Gr.* Myk·e·ri·nos \,mik-ə-'rī-nəs\. *Lat.* Myc·e·ri·nus \,mis-ə-'rī-nəs\. 26th century B.C. King of Egypt. Fifth (or sixth) king of 4th dynasty; son of Khafre; builder of third pyramid of Giza, smallest but most perfect of the pyramids.

Men·no Si·mons \'men-ō-'sim-ōns\. 1469–1561. Dutch religious reformer. Ordained Roman Catholic priest (1524); priest in his native Witmarsum (1531–36); came under influence of Lutheran and Anabaptist thought and withdrew from church (1536); was rebaptized and ordained elder at Groningen (1537); active as organizer and leader of peaceful Anabaptist groups in East Friesland, Holland, and Germany. Mennonite church took its name from him.

Menocal, Mario García. See GARCÍA MENOCAL.

Me·nod·o·tus \mə-'näd-ət-əs\. fl. c.120 A.D. Greek physician and philosopher, of Nicomedia. Practiced medicine as an art while espousing Skeptical philosophy; attacked Asclepiades for atomism, etc.

Menon, V.K. Krishna. See KRISHNA MENON.

Me·nou \mə-'nü\, 'Abd Allāh, *orig.* Jacques-François de. Baron. 1750–1810. French soldier. General (1792); commanded French army in Egypt after death of Kléber (1800); adopted Islām and changed name (1800); defeated by English at Alexandria (Mar. 21, 1801) and capitulated. Tribune (1802); governor general in Tuscany (1808), Venice (1809).

Men·shi·kov \'myänʸ-shi-kəf\, Aleksandr Danilovich. Prince. c.1670–1729. Russian soldier. Attracted notice of Peter the Great and rose rapidly from obscurity; governor of St. Petersburg (1703); general (1704); commanded cavalry in Lithuania (1705); created prince for winning battle of Kalisz (1706); made field marshal for Poltava (1709). At death of Peter the Great (1725), was instrumental in having empress dowager proclaimed empress under title of Catherine I; established and controlled a secret supreme council; contrived betrothal of daughter to future Peter II; at Catherine's death (1727), became regent for Peter II but soon exiled to Siberia by Peter II (1727).

Menshikov, Aleksandr Sergeyevich. Prince. 1787–1869. Russian soldier. Great-grandson of A.D. Menshikov. Served against Napoléon (1812–15) and the Turks (1828–29); major general (1816). Governor general of Finland (1830); minister of marine (1836). Commanded Russian naval and military forces in the Crimea (1854–55); defeated by British and French at Alma (Sept. 20, 1854), Inkerman (Nov. 5); failed to relieve Sevastopol.

Men·te·lin \'men-tə-lin\, Johann. c.1410–1478. German printer. Probably associated with Gutenberg at Mainz after latter's quarrel with Fust; citizen of Strassburg (from 1447), where he was first to establish a press; printed the 49-line Bible (1460–61) and a German Bible (1466).

Men·tu·ho·tep \'men-tü-'hō-,tep\. Name of four kings of Egypt of the 11th dynasty, especially:

Mentuhotep II. *Also known as* Neb·ha·pet·re \'neb-hä-'pā-trə\. *Orig.* San·khib·ta·wy \'sän-kib-'tä-wē\. 21st century B.C. King (2060–10 B.C.). At accession ruled Upper Egypt from Thebes; undertook (c.2047) campaign against Heracleopolis, capital of Middle and Lower Egypt; conquered Heracleopolis (c.2040) and reunited Egypt; his reign marked beginning of Middle Kingdom period.

Mentuhotep III. *Also known as* Sankh·ka·re Mentuhotep \säŋk-'kär-ə-\. 21st–20th century B.C. Successor of Mentuhotep II; reopened desert trade route through Wadi Hammamat to Red Sea and resumed sea trade with Punt.

Men·zel \'ment-səl\, Adolph Friedrich Erdmann von. 1815–1905. German painter, illustrator, and lithographer. Produced six pen-and-ink-drawings for lithographs illustrating Goethe's *Künstlers Erdenwallen,* over 400 designs for woodcuts illustrating Kugler's *Geschichte Friedrichs der Grosse* (from 1839), 200 sketches for woodcuts for an edition of the works of Frederick the Great on commission of Frederick William IV (1844–49), etc.; as a painter, known for patriotic historical works and for small genre scenes.

Menzel, Wolfgang. 1798–1873. German critic and historian. Helped found Burschenschaft at Jena (1818); exile in Switzerland (1820–24); resident mostly in Stuttgart (from 1825), where he edited *Literaturblatt* (1825–48) and a paper of the same name published by himself (1852–69). Member of Württemberg parliament (1831, 1848); actively opposed Young Germany and was bitterly attacked by Börne, Heine, and others. Author of witty poems *Streckverse* (1823) and of *Geschichte der Deutschen* (1824–25), *Die deutsche Literatur* (1828), *Die deutsche Dichtung* (1858–59), *Allgemeine Weltgeschichte* (1862–70), the novel *Furore* (1851), romances, fairy tales, etc.

Men·zies \'men-(,)zēz\, Sir Robert Gordon. 1894–1978. Australian politician. Member of Victoria legislature (1929–34), federal Parliament (1934–66); attorney general of Australia (1934–39); treasurer (1939–40); prime minister (1939–41, 1949–66); organized Liberal party (1944); led Australia into ANZUS pact (1951) and SEATO (1954).

Merbecke, John. See John MARBECK.

Mer·ca·dan·te \,mär-kä-'dän-tā\, Saverio, *in full* Giuseppe Saverio Raffaele. 1795–1870. Italian composer. Director of royal conservatory in Naples (1840–62); totally blind (from 1862). Composed 60 operas, including *L'apoteosi d'Ercole* (1820), *Elisa e Claudio* (1821), *Caritea* (1826), *Gabriella di Vergy* (1828), *Zaïra* (1831), *I normanni a Parigi* (1832), *Il giuramento* (1837), *Il reggente* (1843), *Orazi e Curiazi* (1846); also wrote some 17 masses, many Psalms, motets, and other church music, cantatas, orchestral pieces, fantasias, funeral symphonies, songs, etc.

Mer·cal·li \mär-'käl-lē\, Giuseppe. 1850–1914. Italian geologist. Revised scale for measuring intensity of earthquake shocks (1902); studied glacial action in northern Italy and volcanoes at Etna and Vesuvius.

Mer·ca·ti \mär-'kä-tē\, Michele. 1541–1593. Italian physician and naturalist. Director of Vatican botanical garden (from 1561); physician to Pope Clement VIII; established natural history museum in Vatican and wrote a description of it in *Metallotheca Vaticana* (1574). Also wrote *Istruzione sopra la peste* (1576), *Degli obelischi di Roma* (1589).

Mercator, Gerardus. See Gerhard KREMER.

Mercator, Nicolaus. See Nikolaus KAUFFMANN.

Mer·cé \mer-'sā\, Antonia. *Stage name* La Ar·gen·ti·na \lä-är-gän-'tē-nä\. 1888?–1936. Argentine dancer. *Première danseuse,* Madrid Opera (1899–1902); studied native dances of Spain; originated Neoclassical style of Spanish dance, established it as theatrical art; toured Europe, America, the Orient.

Mer·cer \'mər-sər\, Cecil William. *Pen name* Dornford Yates \'yāts\. 1885–1960. English novelist. Works included *The Brother of Daphne* (1914), *Courts of Idleness* (1920), *Berry and Co.* (1921), *Jonah and Co.* (1922).

Mercer, John. 1791–1866. English calico printer and chemist. Discovered dyes suitable for printing calico orange, yellow, and bronze; discovered process for treating cotton named *mercerization* after him (1850).

Mercer, John H., *called* Johnny. 1909–1976. American songwriter, b. Savannah, Ga. Author of lyrics for hundreds of popular songs including "Jeepers Creepers," You Must Have Been a Beautiful Baby," "Too Marvelous for Words," "Blues in the Night," "Accentuate the Positive," "Laura," "Skylark," "Lazy Bones," "Goody Goody," "Satin Doll," "Old Black Magic"; won Academy Awards for "On the Atchison, Topeka, and Santa Fe" (with Harry Warren, 1946), "In the Cool, Cool, Cool of the Evening" (with Hoagy Carmichael, 1951), "Moon River" (with Henry Mancini, 1961), "Days of Wine and Roses" (with Mancini, 1962).

Mercer, Mabel. 1900–1984. American singer, b. Burton-on-Trent, Staffordshire, England. Cabaret singer famed for her unique singing style mixing cadenced speech with vocalizing as a way of emphasizing the lyrics; inspired such singers as Leontyne Price, Billie Holiday, and Frank Sinatra; sang at Paris cabarets between the world wars; to U.S. (1938).

Mer·cié \mers-yā\, Antonin, *in full* Marius-Jean-Antonin. 1845–1916. French sculptor. Works included *Le Génie des arts,* tomb of Louis-Philippe, monuments to William Tell at Lausanne, Joan of Arc at Domrémy.

Mer·cier \mers-yā\, Désiré-Joseph. 1851–1926. Belgian prelate and philosopher. Professor of Thomist philosophy, Louvain (1882–1906), where he was founder of Institut Supérieur de Philosophie and founder and editor of *Revue Néo-scolastique* (1894–1906). Archbishop of Malines and primate of Belgium (1906); cardinal (1907). Spiritual leader and spokesman of Belgians during German occupation of Belgium in World War I.

Mercier, Honoré. 1840–1894. Canadian politician, b. St. Athanase, Que. Edited Conservative newspaper *Courrier de St. Hyacinthe* (1862); opposed confederation; helped form Parti National (1871); member of federal House of Commons (1872–74). Member of Quebec assembly (1879–91); solicitor general (1879); leader of Liberal party of Quebec (1883–91); premier and attorney general of Quebec (1887–91); pursued nationalist policy; known esp. as champion of French-Canadian interests; dismissed on charges of financial mismanagement.

Mercier, Louis-Sébastien. 1740–1814. French man of letters. Champion of Rousseau; outlined a didactic theater of *drames bourgeois* in *Traité du théâtre* (1773). Author of plays as *Jenneval* (1767), *Le Deserteur* (1770), *Le Faux Ami* (1772), *La Brouette du vinaigrier* (1775), *La Destruction de la ligue* (1782); also wrote prophetic *L'An 2440* (1770) and critical *Tableau de Paris* (1781–89).

Merck \'merk\, Johann Heinrich. 1741–1791. German writer and critic. In government service in Hesse-Darmstadt. Helped found (1772) *Frankfurter Gelehrte Anzeigen;* highly influential as critic, helped further *Sturm und Drang* movement; friend of Goethe, whose *Götz von Berlichingen* he published at his own expense.

Mercoeur, Duc de. See Philippe-Émmanuel under LORRAINE family.

Mer·cy \mer-'sē\, Franz von. Freiherr. c.1590–1645. Bavarian field marshal. Served in Austrian army (c.1606–37); distinguished himself in defense of

Rheinfelden (1634); in Bavarian service (from 1638); defeated French at Tuttlingen (1643), Freiburg (1644), Mergentheim (1645); mortally wounded in action at Nördlingen (1645). His grandson ¶Graf Claudius Florimund von Mercy (1666–1734) was an Austrian field marshal; served in Hungary, Italy; in War of Spanish Succession distinguished himself at Cremona (1702), on the Rhine (1702–03), in Bavaria (1704); aided Eugene of Savoy against Ottomans at Peterwardein (1716), Belgrade (1717); killed in action near Parma. The nephew and adopted son of Claudius ¶Graf Anton Mercy d'Ar·gen·teau \där-zhäⁿ-tō\ (1691–1767) was also an Austrian field marshal. A grand-nephew of Claudius ¶Graf Florimund Mercy d'Argenteau (1727–1794) was in the Austrian diplomatic service (1751–94); ambassador in Paris (1766–90), London (1794); adviser of Marie-Antoinette.

Mère Agnès, Mère Angélique. See under ARNAULD family.

Mer·e·dith \'mer-əd-əth\, George. 1828–1909. English novelist and poet. Articled to London solicitor (1845) but turned to journalism; m. (1847; d. 1861) Mary Ellen, daughter of Thomas Love Peacock. Contributed to *Household Words, Chambers's Edinburgh Journal, Fraser's Magazine;* published *Poems* (1851), novels *The Shaving of Shagpat* (1855), *Farina* (1857), *Ordeal of Richard Feverel* (1859), *Evan Harrington* (1860), *Emilia in England* (1864, later called *Sandra Belloni*). Met Swinburne and Pre-Raphaelite group; lodged with Rossetti and Swinburne in Cheyne Walk, Chelsea (1861–62); published *Modern Love, and Poems of the English Roadside* (1862), considered his best poetical work. Reader to Chapman & Hall (1860–94). Subsequent novels included *Rhoda Fleming* (1865), *Vittoria* (1867), *Adventures of Harry Richmond* (1871), *Beauchamp's Career* (1875), *The Egoist* (1879), *The Tragic Comedians* (1880), *Diana of the Crossways* (1885), *One of Our Conquerors* (1891), *Lord Ormont* (1894), *The Amazing Marriage* (1895). Published characteristic poems of natural realism, including volumes *Poems and Lyrics of the Joy of Earth* (1883), *Ballads and Poems of Tragic Life* (1887), *A Reading of Earth* (1888), *Poems. The Empty Purse* (1892), *A Reading of Life* (1901), *Last Poems* (1909). Criticized for obscurity and affectation, accentuated in later novels; acclaimed for stimulative thought on politics, sociology, and ethics, penetrating character analysis, lively humor, and resilient optimism.

Meredith, Owen. See E. R. Bulwer-LYTTON.

Me·ren·re \mer-'en-(,)rā\. *Also called* Merenre An·tyem·saf \an-'tyem-,saf\. 23d? century B.C. King of Egypt of the 6th dynasty. Son of Pepi I, with whom he was probably co-regent for 9 years; ruled 4 years alone; extended Egyptian boundaries southward and placed all Upper Egypt under a single official. Succeeded by half-brother Pepi II.

Meres \'mi(ə)rz\, Francis. 1565–1647. English clergyman. Schoolmaster at Wing (1602); author of *Palladis Tamia: Wits Treasury* (1598), reviewing 125 English authors each in comparison with a Latin, Greek, or Italian author, listing Shakespeare's plays, and narrating Marlowe's death.

Me·rezh·kov·sky \myir-yish-'kôf-skəi, *Angl* ,mer-əsh-'käf-skē\, Dmitry Sergeyevich. 1865–1941. Russian writer. In critical essays became a chief spokesman for Modernism in Russian literature; edited magazine *Novy put* (1903–04); published critical works *Tolstoy: Dostoyevsky* (1901–02), *Gogol i chort* (1906), novels *Khristos i Antikhrist* (trilogy 1896–1905), *Aleksandr I* (1911–12), *14 Dekabrya* (1918), play *Pavel I* (1908). Opposed Bolshevik revolution and fled Russia (1919), settling in Paris. Later works included biographies of Napoléon (1929), Michelangelo (1930), Jesus (1933), Leonardo da Vinci (1938); novel *Rozhdenie bogov* (1924–25). His wife ¶Zinaida Nikolayevna Me·rezh·kov·ska·ya \myir-yish-'kôf-skə-yə\, *pseudonym* Hip·pi·us *or* Gip·pi·us \'gyēp-pē-üs\ (1869–1945), poet, novelist, and critic; author of Symbolist verse, plays, novels, stories, and biting critical essays as in *Literaturny dnevnik* (1908), *Zhivye litsa* (1925); with husband wrote *Le Tsar et la révolution* (1907).

Mer·gen·tha·ler \'mər-gən-,thäl-ər, 'mer-gən-,täl-\, Ottmar. 1854–1899. American inventor, b. Hachtel, Germany. To U.S. (1872, naturalized 1878). After many experiments, invented first Linotype typesetting machine (patented 1884); produced improved machine (1885) with automatic justification; later patented further improvements.

Me·ri·an \'mā-rē-än\, Matthäus. 1593–1650. Swiss engraver and bookseller. Took over business of his father-in-law, Jean Théodore de Bry (1623), in Frankfurt. Produced copperplate engravings for J.L. Gottfried's *Historische Chronica,* the Bible, Abelin's *Theatrum Europaeum* (begun 1635), *Basler Totentanz* (1644), and, esp., began series of *Topographia* with text by the Austrian topographer Martin Zeiller, showing perspective views of various European cities, towns, castles, etc. (16 vols., 1642–88); completed (1624) de Bry's *Collectiones Peregrinationum in Indiam.* His son and successor ¶Matthäus (1621–1687) was a portrait and religious painter and engraver. Another son ¶Kaspar (1627–1686), etcher and engraver, produced portraits, landscapes, views of cities, and festive scenes. Matthäus the elder's daughter ¶Anna Maria Sibylla (1647–1717), painter, engraver, and naturalist, m. (1668) the painter J. A. Graff; traveled in Surinam and made study of native insect and plant life (1699–1701); painted flowers, fruits, and insects; author of works on natural science, often with original copperplate illustrations.

Me·ri·ci \mā-'rē-chē\, Angela. Saint. 1470 or 1474–1540. Italian religious. Entered Third Order Franciscans; experienced vision (1506) foretelling her founding an order; renowned in Brescia for charitable work, humility; gathered group of followers (1531) and formed Company of St. Ursula (1535), first teaching order for young girls; elected superior (1537). Canonized (1807).

Me·ri·kan·to \'mer-i-,kän-tō\, Oskar, *in full* Frans Oskar. 1868–1924. Finnish organist and composer. Works included operas, concerto for violin, clarinet, horn, and string quartet, works for organ, piano, and violin, choruses, and many Finnish songs. His son ¶Aarre (1893–1958) taught at Sibelius Academy, Helsinki (1936–58); composed symphonies, concertos for piano and for violin, suites including *Kyllikin ryöstö* (1935), vocal and chamber works, and esp. opera *Juha* (1922).

Mé·ri·mée \mā-rē-mā\, Prosper. 1803–1870. French man of letters. Appointed inspector general of historical remains in France (1833); elected senator (1853). Author of works exhibiting classical style in expressing Romantic themes, including: plays as *Le Théâtre de Clara Gazul* (collection, 1825), *La Jacquerie* (1828), *L'Occasion* (1830), *Le Carosse du Saint-Sacrement* (1830); tales and nouvelles as *Mosaïque* (1833), *Columba* (1840), *Carmen* (1846), *Lokis* (1869), *La Chambre bleu* (1872); novels as *La Chronique du temps de Charles IX* (1829), *Arsène Guillot* (1844), *L'Abbé Aubain* (1846); historical studies as *Études sur l'histoire romaine* (1844), *Histoire du Don Pèdre Ier, Roi de Castille* (1848); also series of *Notes de voyages* (1835–40), *Lettres à une inconnue* (1874).

Me·ring \'mā-riŋ\, Joseph von. Freiherr. 1849–1908. German physician, physiologist, and pharmacologist. Professor at Strassburg (1886–90), Halle (1890–1908); with Oskar Minkowski discovered (1889) that removal of pancreas caused diabetes in dogs; with Emil Fischer developed (1902–05) the barbiturates barbital, veronal, proponal.

Me·ri·si \mā-'rē-zē\, Michelangelo. *Known as* Ca·ra·vag·gio \,kär-ä-'väd-jō\. 1573–1610. Italian painter, b. Caravaggio. Worked in Rome (c.1595–1606); achieved fame with series of paintings on life of St. Matthew for Contarelli Chapel (1597–1602); caused astonishment and often criticism with intensely naturalistic depictions; works imbued with light, often of supernatural quality, and with tense drama; fled Rome after killing a man in a brawl (1606), to Naples, Malta, Sicily. Works included *Lute Player, Basket of Fruit, Crucifixion of St. Peter, Deposition of Christ, Madonna dei Palafrenieri, Death of the Virgin, St. Jerome, Supper at Emmaus, Madonna of the Rosary, Seven Works of Mercy, Beheading of St. John, Burial of St. Lucy, Resurrection of Lazarus.*

Mer·kys \'mar-kēs\, Antanas. 1887–1955. Lithuanian politician. In Lithuanian army (1919 ff.); member of right-wing Nationalist League, several times minister of defense; governor of Klaipeda (Memel, 1927–32); last prime minister of Lithuania (1939–40); deported by occupying Soviet forces (1940).

Mer·leau-Pon·ty \mer-lō-pōⁿ-tē\, Maurice. 1908–1961. French philosopher. Professor, Lyons (1945–49), Sorbonne (1949–52), Collège de France (1952–61); a chief exponent of philosophy of Phenomenology. Author of *La Structure du comportement* (1942), *Phénoménologie de la perception* (1945), *Sens et non sens* (1948), *Signes* (1961), etc., and Marxist essays *Humanisme et terreur* (1947), *Les Aventures de la dialectique* (1955).

Merle d'·Au·bi·gné \merl-dō-bēn-yā\, Jean-Henri. 1794–1872. Swiss Protestant theologian. Pastor in Hamburg (1818); court preacher, Brussels (1823); professor of church history in Geneva (1832). Wrote *Histoire de la Réformation du XVIe siècle* (1835–53) and *Histoire de la Réformation en Europe au temps de Calvin* (1863–78).

Mer·lin \mer-laⁿ\, Antoine-Christophe. *Called* Merlin de Thi·on·ville \-də-tyōⁿ-vēl\. 1762–1833. French politician. Member of Legislative Assembly (1791–92); a radical, member of Club Cordeliers; as member of National Convention (1792–95) drafted convention demanding execution of king; fought Vendée uprising (1793); conspired in downfall of Robespierre (1794); member of Council of Five Hundred (1795–98); director general of posts (1798–99).

Merlin, Philippe-Antoine. Comte. *Called* Merlin de Dou·ai \-də-dwā\. 1754–1838. French jurist and politician. Member of Estates-General (1789) and president of criminal court of the North (1791). Member of National Convention (1792), of the Committee of Public Safety (1794–95); under the Directory, minister of justice (1795–99) and a director (1797–99); *procureur général* at the Court of Cassation (1801–14); councilor of state (1808); created comte by Napoléon (1810). Expelled from France at the Restoration (1815), returning fifteen years later.

Merlo, Aimé. See Georges ATHENAS.

Mer·man \'mər-mən\, Ethel. *Orig. surname* Zimmerman. 1908?–1984. American singer and actress, b. New York City. Debuted on Broadway in *Girl Crazy* (1930); starred in Broadway musicals *Anything Goes* (1934), *Red, Hot and Blue* (1936), *Panama Hattie* (1940), *Annie Get Your Gun* (1946), *Call Me Madam* (1950), *Gypsy* (1959), *Hello, Dolly!* (1970), etc.; film appearances included *Anything Goes* (1938), *Call Me Madam* (1953), *There's No Business Like Show Business* (1954); reigned as "queen of Broadway" for three decades; known for her clarion voice, flawless diction, brassy gusto, and belting delivery.

Mer·mil·lod \mer-mē-yō\, Gaspard. 1824–1892. Swiss prelate. Established (1857) first Roman Catholic parish in Geneva since time of Calvin; named titular bishop (1864), cantonal administrator (1871), sparking Swiss *Kulturkampf;* expelled on being named vicar apostolic (1873); returned to Switzerland on being named bishop of Lausanne and Geneva by Pope Leo XIII (1883); cardinal in Rome (from 1890).

Mer·ne·ptah \'mer-,nep-,tä\. 13th century B.C. King of Egypt (1236–23 B.C.) of the 19th dynasty. Son of Ramses II. In a great battle (1232) defeated coalition of Libyans and Sea Peoples.

Me·ro·dach-bal·a·dan II \mi-'rō-,dak-'bal-ə-,dan, 'mer-ə-\. *Assyrian* Mar·duk-apal-id·di·na \'mär-,dük-ə-'pal-ə-'dē-nə\. d. c.694 B.C. King of Babylonia (721–710). As ruler of a part of Chaldea, submitted to Tiglath-pileser III (729–728); at a moment of Assyrian weakness, claimed Babylonian throne; made alliance with Elamites (721) against Sargon II of Assyria; defeated and driven out by Sargon (710); after Sargon's death (705), renewed alliance against Assyria; sent embassy to Hezekiah of Judah; again briefly seized Babylon before being defeated by Sargon's son Sennacherib (703); fled to Elam.

Mer·o·vech *or* **Mer·o·wech** \'mer-ə-,vech\. *Fr.* Mé·ro·vée \mā-rȯ-vā\. *Also spelled* Merowig, Merwich, Meroveus. fl. c.450 A.D. Frankish ruler. King of Salian Franks, from whom Merovingian dynasty took its name; father of Childeric I.

Mer·o·vin·gi·an \,mer-ə-'vin-jē-ən\. Name of the first Frankish dynasty, taking its name from Merovech (*q.v.*), son of Chlodion, kings of Salian Franks; dynasty firmly established by Clovis I and lasted through reign of Childeric III (to 751). See CLOVIS, CHARIBERT, CHILDERIC, CHILDEBERT, CHILPERIC, CHLODOMER, CHLOTAR, DAGOBERT, GUNTRAM, SIGEBERT, THEUDEBALD, THEUDEBERT, THEUDERIC.

Mer·ri·am \'mer-ē-əm, 'mir-\, Clinton Hart. 1855–1942. American naturalist, b. New York City. In medical practice (1879–85); chief, U.S. Biological Survey (1885–1910). Author of *The Birds of Connecticut* (1877), *Life Zones and Crop Zones of the United States* (1898), *Indian Population of California* (1905), *Review of the Grizzly and Big Brown Bears of America* (1917), *The Buffalo in Northern California* (1926), etc.

Merriam, Florence Augusta. See Florence A. BAILEY.

Merriam, George (1803–1880) and his brother Charles (1806–1887). American publishers, b. respectively Worcester and West Brookfield, Mass. Joined family printing business; formed Merriam, Little & Co. (1831), reorganized as G. & C. Merriam Co. (1832) in Springfield, Mass. Purchased (1843) copyright of Noah Webster's *American Dictionary of the English Language;* published first version (1847) of Merriam-Webster dictionary series.

Merriam, John Campbell. 1869–1945. American paleontologist, b. Hopkinton, Iowa. Taught at U. of Cal. (1894–1920); president, Carnegie Institution (1920–38). Author of *Triassic Ichthysauria* (1908), *The Occurrence of Human Remains in California Caves* (1909), *Relation of Paleontology to the History of Man* (1910), *The Emergence of Man* (1919), *The Living Past* (1930), *Spiritual Values and Constructive Life* (1933), *Science and Belief* (1939), etc.

Mer·rick \'mer-ik\, Leonard. *Orig. surname* Miller. 1864–1939. English writer. Author of novels, including *Cynthia* (1897), *The Actor-Manager* (1898), *The Worldlings* (1900), *Conrad in Quest of his Youth* (1903), *The Man Who Understood Women* (stories, 1908), *A Chair on the Boulevard* (1921), etc.

Mer·rill \'mer-əl\, Frank Dow. 1903–1955. American army officer, b. Hopkinton, Mass. Entered army (1929); intelligence officer on staffs of Gen. Douglas MacArthur (1941–42), Gen. Joseph Stilwell (1942–43); brigadier general (1943); organized (1943) volunteer regiment known as "Merrill's Marauders," trained for jungle warfare; fought behind Japanese lines in Burma; captured Myitkyina airfield (May 1944) and city (Aug. 1944); chief of staff, Tenth army (1944–45), Sixth army (1946–47); retired as major general (1948).

Merrill, George Perkins. 1854–1929. American geologist, b. Auburn, Me. On staff, U.S. National Museum (1881–1929), curator (from 1887), head curator of geology section (from 1897); developed geological and paleontological collection in museum; known esp. for his studies of meteorites, of building stone, and of rock weathering. Author of *Stones for Building and Decoration* (1891), *Treatise on Rocks, Rock Weathering, and Soils* (1897).

Merrill, Stuart Fitzrandolph. 1863–1915. American poet, b. Hempstead, Long Island, N.Y. Resident in Paris (from (1889). His chief works, all written in French, were *Les Gammes* (1887), *Les Fastes* (1891), *Petits poèmes d'automne* (1895), *Les Quatre Saisons* (1900), *Une voix dans la foule* (1909).

Merriman, Henry Seton. See Hugh Stowell SCOTT.

Mer·ri·man \'mer-i-mən\, John Xavier. 1841–1926. South African politician, b. England. To South Africa as a child. Diamond dealer in Kimberley, wine merchant in Cape Town; member of assembly of Cape Colony (1869–1910); held cabinet posts (1875–78, 1881–84, 1890–93, 1898–1900); prime minister (1908–10); broke with long-time friend Cecil Rhodes after Jameson Raid (1895) and opposed British imperialism; leader of South African party (1903–10); member of Parliament of Union of South Africa (1910–24).

Mer·ritt \'mer-ət\, Anna, *nee* Lea \'lē\. 1844–1930. American artist, b. Philadelphia. m. Henry Merritt (1877); resident chiefly in London (from 1871). Her paintings included *Camilla, Eve Overcome by Remorse, Eve Repentant, Love Locked Out, Piping Shepherd, James Russell Lowell.*

Merritt, Wesley. 1834–1910. American army officer, b. New York City. Entered army (1860); served through Civil War, rising to major general of volunteers (1865); on frontier duty (1866–79); superintendent, U.S.M.A., West Point (1882–87); major general (1895). Commanded first Philippine expedition (1898); occupied Manila (Aug. 1898).

Mer·ry \'mer-ē\, Robert. 1755–1798. English poet. Settled in Florence (c.1784) and there was made member of Accademia della Crusca. Under pseudonym Del·la Crus·ca \,del-ə-'krəs-kə\ wrote affected verse in England; carried on sentimental correspondence in verse with Mrs. Hannah Cowley (1787); inspired a school of dilettantish versifiers, the Della Cruscans, who were savagely satirized in William Gifford's *Baviad* (1794).

Mer·ry del Val \'mer-rē-thel-'bäl\, Rafael. 1865–1930. Spanish prelate, b. London. Ordained priest (1888); served as papal diplomat; titular archbishop of Nicaea (1900). Papal secretary of state (1903–14) under Pope Pius X; cardinal (1903); secretary of the Holy Office (1914–30).

Mer·senne \mer-sen\, Marin. 1588–1648. French mathematician. Fellow pupil of Descartes; entered mendicant order of Minims (1611); taught at Nevers (1614–20), Paris (from 1620); defended Descartes and Galileo against clerical critics; made researches in mathematics, physics, and astronomy; discovered Mersenne numbers (1644), major contribution to study of prime numbers.

Mer·ton \'mərt-ᵊn\, Thomas. *Also known as* Father M. Louis. 1915–1968. American religious and writer, b. Prades, France, of New Zealand and American parents. To U.S. (1916); entered Trappist order (1941); ordained priest (1949). Author of *Thirty Poems* (1944), *Figures for an Apocalypse* (verse, 1948), *The Seven Storey Mountain* (1948), *Seeds of Contemplation* (1949), *Ascent to Truth* (1951), *No Man Is an Island* (1955), *Thoughts in Solitude* (1958), *The New Man* (1962), *Life and Holiness* (1963), *Faith and Violence* (1968), etc.

Merton, Walter de. d. 1277. English prelate. Chancellor of England (1261–63, 1272–74) and justiciar (1271); bishop of Rochester (1274). Founded (1264) Merton Coll., Oxford.

Me·ru·lo \'mer-ü-lō\, Claudio. *Orig. surname* Mer·lot·ti \mär-'lȯt-tē\. 1533–1604. Italian organist and composer. Organist at St. Mark's, Venice (1557–84); court organist at Parma (1586–91). Composed ricercari, canzoni, and toccatas for organ; also, many madrigals, motets, and masses for five to twelve voices.

Mé·ry·on \mār-yōⁿ\, Charles. 1821–1868. French etcher and engraver. Best known for etchings of Parisian scenes, *Eaux-fortes sur Paris* (1850–54).

Mes·dag \'mes-däk\, Hendrik Willem. 1831–1915. Dutch painter. Known chiefly for seascapes. Presented to The Hague (1903) the Mesdag Museum together with his collection of French and Dutch paintings, bronzes, porcelains, and other objets d'art.

Me·sha \'mē-shə\. fl. c.850 B.C. King of Moab. Paid tribute to Ahab, but after Ahab's death, ceased payments; resisted attack by Jehoram and Jehoshaphat; sacrificed his first-born son to avert defeat. The Moabite stone (discovered 1868) on which this event is recorded is oldest known Semitic monument.

Mes·mer \'mes-mər, *Angl* 'mez-\, Franz *or* Friedrich Anton. 1734–1815. German physician. Practiced in Vienna; explored ideas on magnetic and gravitational influences on health; developed a theory of "animal magnetism" and experimented in magnetic therapeutics; denounced in Vienna, moved to Paris (1778), where he devoted himself to curing diseases; his séances investigated (1784) by government commission of physicians and scientists; denounced as impostor; later moved to London. Although he did not employ hypnotism, the term mesmerism was attached to that technique.

Me·so·ne·ro Ro·ma·nos \mā-sō-'nā-rō-rō-'mä-nōs\, Ramón de. 1803–1882. Spanish writer. Founder and editor (1836–42) of *Semanario Pintoresco Español.* Exponent of *costumbrismo,* portrayal of local customs; collections of essays included *Escenas matritenses* (1836–42), *Tipos y caracteres* (1843–62), *El antiguo Madrid* (1861), *Memorias de un setentón* (1880).

Mes·rob *or* **Mes·rop** \mes-'rōp\. *Also called* Mash·tots \mash-'tōts\. Saint. c.350–439 or 440 A.D. Armenian religious. Became monk (c.395); founded several monasteries; later served as chancellor to King Vramshapuh. Established (c.406) definitive alphabet for Armenian, used to translate from Greek the "Merobian" Bible (c.410), to which he contributed; credited with translating biblical commentaries, patristic works, liturgical works, hymns, etc.; also contributed to creation of Georgian alphabet.

Mes·sa·ger \mes-à-zhā\, André-Charles-Prosper. 1853–1929. French composer and conductor. Director of Opéra-Comique, Paris (1898–1903); artistic director of Covent Garden Theatre, London (1901–07); co-director of Paris Opéra (1907–14); conductor of conservatory concerts (1908–19); again director of Opéra-Comique (1919–20). Composed comic operas and operettas, including *La Béarnaise* (1885), *La Basoche* (1890), *Madame Chrysanthème* (1893), *Les p'tites Michu* (1897), *Véronique* (1898), *Béatrice* (1914), and *Monsieur Beaucaire* (1919), many ballets, piano pieces, songs, etc.

Messager, Charles. *Pseudonym* Charles Vil·drac \vēl-dràk\. 1882–1971. French writer. A founder of group L'Abbaye (1906, with Georges Duhamel). Author of verse *Poèmes* (1905), *Le Livre d'amour* (1910), *Découvertes* (1912), *Chants du désespéré* (1920), *Poèmes de l'Abbaye* (1925); plays *Le Paquebot 'Tenacity'* (1920), *Le Pèlerin* (1922), *Madame Béliard* (1925), *La Brouille* (1930), *Le Jardinier de Samos* (1932), *Trois mois de prison* (1934), *L'Air du temps* (1938), *Dommages de guerre* (1961); essays *Notes sur la technique poétique* (1910), *Récits* (1926), *D'après l'écho* (1949); children's books, etc.

Mes·sa·la *or* **Mes·sal·la Cor·vi·nus** \mə-'sä-lə-,kȯr-'vī-nəs, -'sal-ə-\, Marcus Valerius. c.64 B.C.–8 A.D. Roman general and patron of letters. Held a command in republican army at battle of Philippi (42 B.C.); commanded center of Octavian's fleet in battle of Actium (31); consul (31); as proconsul of Aquitania, subjugated that province. Patron of Albius Tibullus, Sulpicia, Ovid.

Mes·sa·li Hajd \me-'säl-ē-'hīd\, Ahmed. 1898–1974. Algerian nationalist. Founded (1937) nationalist party that became (1946) Mouvement pour le Triomphe des Libertés Démocratiques (MTLD).

Mes·sa·li·na *or* **Mes·sal·li·na** \,mes-ə-'lī-nə\, Valeria. c.22–48 A.D. Roman empress. Daughter of Marcus Valerius Messala Barbatus; 3d wife of Emperor Claudius. Noted for licentiousness; caused death of number of persons who attempted to thwart her desires. Executed by order of the emperor after she had, during his temporary absence from Rome, married her favorite, Silius. See NARCISSUS.

Mes·ser·schmitt \'mes-ər-shmit\, Willy. 1898–1978. German aircraft designer and manufacturer. Designed his first plane (1916) and founded manufacturing firm under own name (1923); designed all-metal M 18 (1926), the Me 109 fighter (1935), the Me 262, first jet flown in combat (1944), etc.

Mes·sier \mes-yā, mās-\, Charles. 1730–1817. French astronomer. Draftsman, clerk, and observer to J.-N. Delisle (1751–60); thereafter worked alone; credited with discovery of 15 comets; compiled and published (from 1770) catalogue of nebulae, many of whose designations are still used.

Mes·si·ko·mer \'mes-i-,kō-mər\, Jakob. c.1828–? Swiss farmer and archaeologist. Excavated lake dwelling sites on Lake Pfäffikon (from 1858), recovering great number of artifacts.

Messina, Antonello da. See ANTONELLO.

Messys, Quentin. See Quentin MASSYS.

Meš·tro·vić \'mesh-trō-,vēt^y, *Angl* 'mes(h)-trə-,vich\, Ivan. 1883–1962. American sculptor, b. Vrpolje, Slavonian Austria (now Yugoslavia). Begun exhibiting with Vienna Sezession (1902); exhibited at London, Paris, Rome, Venice; to U.S. (1947, naturalized 1954); professor at Syracuse U. (1947–55), Notre Dame (1955–62). Works included memorial chapel to unknown soldier (Belgrade), monument to Brătianu (Bucharest), *The Archangel Gabriel, Job, Despair, Jacob's Well,* portraits and busts of Lady Cunard, Sir Thomas Beecham, President Masaryk, Pius XI, Herbert Hoover, etc.

Metacomet. See PHILIP.

Metagenes. See CHERSIPHRON.

Me·ta·sta·sio \,mā-tä-'stäz-yō\, Pietro. *Orig.* Pietro Antonio Domenico Bonaventura Tra·pas·si \trä-'päs-sē\. 1698–1782. Italian poet and dramatist. Protégé of Gravina, a jurist. To Naples (1719); gained patronage of singer Marianna Bulgarelli; called to Vienna (1730) as court poet to Charles VI, Holy Roman emperor. Known particularly for melodramas, in development of which he succeeded Apostolo Zeno; his 26 melodramas (set to music by various composers) included *Didone abbandonata, Catone in Utica, Ezio, Semiramide, Alessandro nell'Indie, Artaserse, Demetrio, Olimpiade, Demofoonte, La clemenza di Tito, Achille in Sciro, Attilio Regolo;* also wrote canzonette, including *La libertà* (1733) and *La partenza* (1746), oratorios, poems for cantatas, critical works, etc.

Me·ta·xas \,met-äk-'säs, *Angl* me-,tak-'säs\, Ioannis. 1871–1941. Greek general and politician. Served in Turkish war (1897), Balkan War (1912–13); chief of staff (1913–17), general (1916); opposed Greek participation in World War I and Asia Minor campaign (1921–22); a leader of monarchists, held cabinet posts (1928, 1932–33, 1935–36); on restoration of monarchy (1936), named premier (1936); with royal authority instituted dictatorship (1936–41); led Greece into Western alliance (1940).

Met·calfe \'met-,kaf, -,käf, -kəf\, Charles Theophilus. Baron Metcalfe. 1785–1846. English colonial administrator, b. Calcutta. Entered service of East India Co. (1801); envoy to Lahore (1808); as envoy to Sikh states signed (1809) boundary treaty with Ranjit Singh; member of governing council (1827); as acting governor general (1835), instituted freedom of press and English as official language; lieutenant governor of North West Provinces and Oudh (1836–38); governor of Jamaica (1839–42); governor general of Canada (1843–45).

Metch·ni·koff *Fr* mech-nē-kȯf\, Élie. *Russ.* Ilya Ilich Mech·ni·kov \'myäch-nyik-əf\. 1845–1916. Russian zoologist and bacteriologist. Professor of zoology and comparative anatomy, Odessa (1870–82); resigned to devote himself to research; while conducting research on starfish in Messina, Italy (1882–86), observed and named phenomenon of phagocytosis; to Paris, where Pasteur gave him a laboratory (1888); succeeded Pasteur as director of Pasteur Inst. in Paris (1895–1916). Investigated intracellular digestion; formulated theory of phagocytosis as first line of immunologic defense; made microscopic studies of diseases of the blood. Shared (with Paul Ehrlich) 1908 Nobel prize for physiology or medicine. Author of *Leçons sur la pathologie comparée de l'inflammation* (1892), *L'Immunité dans les maladies infectieuses* (1901), *Études sur la nature humaine* (1903).

Me·tel·lus \mə-'tel-əs\. Name of prominent Roman family of Caecilian gens, including among members: Lucius Caecilius Metellus (d. 221 B.C.); consul (251, 247); as general defeated Carthaginians at Panormus (250 B.C.) by panicking Hasdrubal's elephants. ¶Quintus Caecilius Metellus, *surnamed* Mac·e·don·i·cus \,mas-ə-'dän-i-kəs\ (d. 115 B.C.), praetor (148); distinguished for victories in Macedonia and Greece (148–146 B.C.); consul (143), censor (131); opponent of Gracchi. ¶Quintus Caecilius Metellus, *surnamed* Nu·mid·i·cus \n(y)ü-'mid-ə-kəs\ (d. c.91 B.C.), nephew of Metellus Macedonicus; consul (109 B.C.) and proconsul (108); defeated Jugurtha in Numidia (109–108); censor (102); went into exile (100) as opponent of Saturninus. ¶Quintus Caecilius Metellus, *surnamed* Pi·us \'pī-əs\ (d. c.63 B.C.), son of Metellus Numidicus; praetor (89); served Sulla; defeated Q. Pompaedius Silo in Social War (88); defeated Norbanus (82); consul (80); commanded in Spain against Sertorius (80–71). ¶Quintus Caecilius Metellus Ce·ler \'sē-lər\ (d. 59 B.C.), legate in Asia under Pompey (66); praetor (63 B.C.); opponent of Catiline and hostile to his conspiracy; consul (60). His brother ¶Quintus Caecilius Metellus Ne·pos \'nē-,päs\ (d. c.55 B.C.) sided with Pompey in civil wars; tribune (62 B.C.), consul (57). ¶Quintus Caecilius Metellus Pius Scip·io \'sip-ē-,ō\ (d. 46 B.C.), adopted son of Metellus Pius; consul with son-in-law Pompey (52 B.C.); commanded armies for Pompey in Syria and Egypt; commanded center of Pompey's army at Pharsalus (48); defeated by Caesar at Thapsus (46); captured, committed suicide. ¶Quintus Caecilius Metellus, *surnamed* Cre·ti·cus \'krē-tə-kəs\ (d. c.56 B.C.), consul (69 B.C.); subjugated Crete (68–67) after refusing to heed Pompey's order to suspend offensive.

Met·ford \'met-fərd\, William Ellis. 1824–1899. English inventor. Invented explosive rifle bullet, adopted by government (1863) but outlawed by St. Petersburg convention (1869); produced breech-loading rifle (1871); his type of bore combined by an American, James P. Lee, with bolt action and detachable magazine in the Lee-Metford rifle, selected for British use (1888).

Met·ge \'met-yā\, Bernat *or* Bernardo. 1350–1413. Catalan poet. At various times in service of kings Peter IV, John I, Martin. Author of *Libro de fortuna y prudencia* (1381) and esp. *Lo somni* (1398), verse philosophical reflection on death, immortality, etc.

Methodius, Saint. See under Saint CYRIL (c.827–869 A.D.).

Meth·u·en \'meth-yə-wən\, Paul Sanford. 3d Baron. 1845–1932. British soldier. Served in Ashanti War (1874), Egyptian War (1882); lieutenant general (1898). In Boer War commanded 1st division of the 1st army corps; defeated by Cronjé at Magersfontein (Dec. 11, 1899) and later (1902) taken prisoner by De La Rey. General (1904); field marshal (1911). Commander in chief in South Africa (1908–12); governor of Natal (1910); governor of Malta (1915–19).

Methuen, Sir Algernon Methuen Marshall. *Orig. surname* Sted·man \'sted-mən\. 1856–1924. English publisher. Opened small publishing office in London under name Methuen & Co. (1889); made initial publishing success by issuing Kipling's *Barrack-Room Ballads* (1892); became publisher for Belloc, Chesterton, Conrad, Anthony Hope, W.W. Jacobs, Lankester, Sir Oliver Lodge, Maeterlinck, Masefield, Gilbert Parker, Stevenson, Oscar Wilde, and many others. Compiled *An Anthology of English Verse* (1921) and *Shakespeare to Hardy* (1922).

Me·to·chi·tes \,met-ə-'kīt-,ēz\, George. c.1240–c.1328. Byzantine theologian. Emissary of Emperor Michael VIII to Pope Gregory X to seek union of Greek and Latin churches; assisted Patriarch John XI Beccus in drawing up decree of union at Council of Lyons (1274); wrote numerous polemics and apologies on union; imprisoned and banished by anti-union Emperor Andronicus II Palaeologus (1282). Works included *Historia dogmatica.*

Metochites, Theodore. c.1260–1332. Byzantine politician and diplomat. Son of George Metochites. In service of Emperor Andronicus II Palaeologus;

negotiated marriage of emperor's daughter to Serbian czar Milutin (1298); later m. Irene Palaeologus and was made imperial chancellor (1321); deprived and exiled by Andronicus III (1328); retired (1331) to Chora monastery, whose restoration and decoration in outstanding mosaics he directed. Author of essays on philosophical, literary, historical subjects, many collected in *Hypomnēmatismoi kai sēmeiōseis gnōmikai;* also of commentaries on Plato, scientific treatises.

Me·ton \'mē-,tän\. fl. 432 B.C. Greek astronomer of Athens. Discovered 19-year Metonic cycle of solar years and synodic months.

Mé·traux \mā-trō\, Alfred. 1902–1963. Swiss anthropologist. Professor, Tucumán (1928–34); with Bishop Museum, Honolulu (1935–41), Bureau of American Ethnology (1941–45), UNESCO (1946–62); made expeditions to Easter Island (1934–35), the Amazon (1947–48), Haiti (1949–50). Author of *La Civilisation matérielle des tribus Tupi-Guarani* (1928), *L'Île de Pâques* (1935), *Myths and Tales of the Matako-Indians* (1939), *Ethnology of Easter Island* (1940), *Myths of the Toba and Pilagá Indians* (1946), *Le Vaudou haïtien* (1958), etc.

Met·ro·cles \'me-trə-,klēz\. 4th century B.C. Greek philosopher. Pupil of Theophrastus and Crates of Thebes; an exponent of Cynic philosophy; first philosopher known to have compiled collection of instructive anecdotes and sayings.

Met·ro·do·rus \,me-trə-'dōr-əs, -'dòr-\. 4th century B.C. Greek philosopher of Chios. A leading representative of atomistic school.

Metrodorus. 5th century B.C. Greek philosopher of Lampsacus. Pupil of Anaxagoras; produced an allegorical interpretation of Homer's *Iliad* and of the Olympian pantheon.

Metrodorus. *Called* the Younger. c.330–278 or 277 B.C. Greek philosopher of Lampsacus. Chief pupil of Epicurus; author of numerous polemics against other schools. Works included *Eurylochus* and *Metrodorus.*

Met·ro·pha·nes Kri·top·ou·los \me-'träf-ə-,nēz-kri-'täp-ə-ləs\. 1589–1639. Greek prelate. Monk of Mt. Athos; sent by Patriarch Cyril Lucaris of Constantinople to tour Anglican and Protestant universities of Europe (1617–30); bishop in Egypt (1631); patriarch of Alexandria (1636). Author of a Greek confession (1624–25) that attempted to achieve acceptance by all churches.

Me·tsu *or* **Me·tzu** *or* **Me·tsue** \met-'sœ\, Gabriel. 1629–1667. Dutch painter. Known for genre works as *The Duet, The Sportsman, Music Lovers, Old Poultry Seller, The Music Lesson, Visit to the Nursery,* and *Artist and his Wife.*

Metsys, Quentin. See Quentin MASSYS.

Met·ter·nich \'met-ər-(,)nik\, Klemens Wenzel Nepomuk Lothar von. Fürst. *Family name* Metternich-Win·ne·burg \-'vin-ə-,bůrk\. 1773–1859. Austrian statesman and diplomatist. Brought up in courts of Rhine electorates where his father (Prince Georg Karl, 1746–1818) was Austrian ambassador. Westphalian representative at Congress of Rastadt (1797–99); Austrian envoy to Saxony (1801–03) and ambassador at Berlin (1803–05) and Paris (1806–09); after war declared between France and Austria (1809), returned to Vienna. Austrian minister of foreign affairs (1809–48); influential in securing Marie Louise as 2d wife of Napoléon (1810), thereby relieving French pressure on Austria. By skillful diplomacy and deceit, kept Austria out of war between France and Russia (1812–13) but finally joined alliance with Russia against France (1813); created hereditary prince of Austrian Empire (1813). At Congress of Vienna (1814–15), at height of his power. Largely responsible for policy of balance of European power to ensure stability of European governments, but failed to achieve a system of federated states based on historical regions; acquiesced in the suppression of liberal ideas or revolutionary movements. Weakened somewhat by revolutions of 1830 but did not resign until forced by Vienna mob (1848); lived in retirement in England and Belgium (1848–51) and in Vienna (1851–59). His son ¶Fürst Richard (1829–1895), Austrian diplomat, was ambassador in Paris (1859–70); m. (1856) Pauline, Countess Sándor (1836–1921), with whom he played important role in the political and social life at the court of Napoléon III.

Mettrie, Julien Offroy de la. See LA METTRIE.

Metz \'mets\, Christian. 1794–1867. American religious leader, b. Neuwied, Prussia. Leader of sect known as Community of True Inspiration (from 1817); established communistic colony on site near Buffalo, N.Y. (1842–54); colony emigrated to Iowa frontier site, christened Amana (1855); community incorporated (1859) as Amana Society, with Metz as its head until his death.

Met·zin·ger \met-saⁿ-zhā\, Jean. 1883–1956. French painter. An early follower of Picasso and Braque in Cubism. Author of *Du Cubisme* (1910, with A. Gleizes).

Metzu, Gabriel. See Gabriel METSU.

Meu·len \'mœ-lən\, Adam Frans van der. 1632–1690. Flemish painter. Court painter to Louis XIV of France (c.1666), whom he accompanied on campaigns; painted chiefly battles and sieges engaged in by Louis XIV, and landscapes.

Meun, Jean de. See Jean CHOPINEL.

Meu·nier \mœn-yā\, Constantin. 1831–1905. Belgian sculptor and painter. Known esp. for monumental figures of miners and factory workers, as *Le Marteleur* (1890), *Débardeur du port* (1890), *La Glèbe* (1892), *Le Puddleur* (1893).

Meu·rice \mœ-rēs\, François-Paul. 1820–1905. French dramatist. Editor of Victor Hugo's *L'Événement* (1848); helped found Hugo journal *Le Rappel* (1869); a literary executor of Victor Hugo, whose works he edited (46 vols., 1880–85). Works included *Falstaff* (1842, with T. Gautier and A. Vacquerie), metrical translation of *Hamlet* (1847, with A. Dumas), dramas *Benvenuto Cellini* (1852), *Schamyl* (1854), *Struensée* (1898), dramatic version of *Les Misérables* (1878), romances *La Famille Aubry* (1857) and *Le Songe d'amour* (1889), etc.

Meus·nier de la Place \mœn-yā-də-là-plàs\, Jean-Baptiste-Marie-Charles. 1754–1793. French general and mathematician. Engineer in army (from 1775); derived Meusnier's theorem on curvature at a point on a surface (1776); published (1783) theory of dynamics and equilibrium in aerostation; designed (1784) dirigible balloon; joined Jacobins (1790); field marshal (1792); killed in defense of fortress of Kassel, Mainz.

Mew \'myü\, Charlotte Mary. 1869–1928. English poet. Frequent contributor to *Temple Bar, The Nation, The New Statesman, The Englishwoman,* and *The Chap-book.* Published two volumes of verse, *The Farmer's Bride* (1916) and *The Rambling Sailor* (1929).

Mey·er \'mī(-ə)r\, Adolf. 1866–1950. American psychiatrist, b. Niederweningen, Switzerland. To U.S. (1892). Psychiatrist at Kankakee, Ill. (1893–95), Worcester, Mass. (1895–1902); teacher at Clark U. (1895–1902); director of pathology, Pathological Inst., New York City (1902–10); professor, Cornell (1904–09); professor, Johns Hopkins U. (1910–41) and director, Henry Phipps Psychiatric Clinic (1914–41); leading exponent of psychobiology, emphasizing behavioral disorders and social pathology against neuropathology as basis of psychiatric problems.

Meyer, Annie Florance, *nee* Na·than \'nā-thən\. 1867–1951. American educator and writer, b. New York City. Cousin of Benjamin Cardozo and Emma Lazarus; m. Alfred Meyer (1887). Known as founder of Barnard College, Columbia U. (opened 1889). Author of *Woman's Work in America* (1891), *The Dominant Sex* (play, 1911), *The District Attorney* (play, 1920), *The Advertising of Kate* (play, 1921), *Black Souls* (play, 1932), *Barnard Beginnings* (1935), etc.

Meyer, Conrad Ferdinand. 1825–1898. Swiss writer. Author of verse including *Zwanzig Balladen* (1864), *Romanzen und Bilder* (1870), lyrical epic *Huttens letzte Tage* (1871), narrative *Engelberg* (1873), and collected *Gedichte* (1882), in which he approached Symbolism; several *novellen* including *Das Amulett* (1873), *Jürg Jenatsch* (1876), *Der Heilige* (1880), *Plautus im Nonnenkloster* (1881), *Gustav Adolfs Page* (1882), *Das Leiden eines Knaben* (1883), *Die Hochzeit des Mönchs* (1884), *Angela Borgia* (1891).

Meyer, Eduard. 1855–1930. German historian. Professor, Leipzig (1884–85), Breslau (1885–89), Halle (1889–1902), Berlin (1902–23). Author of *Geschichte des Altertums* (1884–1902), *Ägyptische Chronologie* (1904), *Cäsars Monarchie* (1918), *Ursprung und Anfänge des Christentums* (1921–23), etc. His brother ¶Kuno (1858–1919) was professor of Celtic, Liverpool (1895–1911) and Berlin (from 1911); cofounder and director, Summer School of Irish Learning, Dublin (1903) and founder (1904) of its journal *Ériu;* contributed to promotion of Celtic scholarship; edited many middle Irish texts with translations, as *The Vision of MacConglinne* (1892), *Voyage of Bran* (1895–97), *Cáin Adamnáin* (1905), *Fianaigecht* (1910).

Meyer, Joseph. 1796–1856. German publisher, industrialist, and publicist. Founded at Gotha publishing house Bibliographisches Institut (1826), which he removed to Hildburghausen (1828); compiled and published *Der grosse Konversationslexicon* (1840–52) and other reference works. His son ¶Hermann Julius (1826–1909) was at first active in his father's enterprises; to U.S. as political fugitive (1849), founded book business in N.Y.; returned to Germany (1854) and took over at Hildburghausen his father's Bibliographisches Institut (1855), which he reorganized and removed to Leipzig (1874); retired (1885). Hermann's son ¶Hans (1858–1929) entered the Bibliographisches Institut (1884), of which he was director (1885–1914); traveled in Africa; climbed Kilimanjaro (1889) and reached top of Kibo and found crater; member of German colonial council (1901); studied volcanoes and glaciation of Ecuadorian cordilleras (1903); traveled in German East Africa (1911); professor of colonial geography, Leipzig (1915–28). Hans's brother ¶Hermann (1871–1932), traveler and explorer, accompanied anthropologist Karl Ranke to central Brazil and headwaters region of the Xingú (1895–97) and discovered the Atelchú, tributary of the Ronuro; visited German colonies in Rio Grande do Sul (1898–1900) and, with Koch-Grünberg and others, navigated upper course of the Ronuro as far as mouth of the Xingú (1899); founded and financed colonies for Germans in Rio Grande do Sul; co-owner (1903–32) and chief director (after 1915) of Bibliographisches Institut in Leipzig.

Meyer, Julius Lothar. 1830–1895. German chemist. Professor, Eberswalde (1866–68), Karlsruhe (1868–76), Tübingen (1876–95); studied physiology of blood; known for attempts, independent of Mendeleyev, to construct periodic table of elements (from 1864). Author of *Die modernen Theorien der Chemie* (1864).

Meyer, Kuno. See under Eduard MEYER.

Me·yer \mā-yer\, Paul, *in full* Marie-Paul-Hyacinthe. 1840–1917. French philologist and literary historian. Secretary (1872–76) and director (1882), École des Chartes; professor, Collège de France (1876–1906); authority on Provençal and Romance literatures; cofounder (1872) of review *Romania.* Edited many old French texts and published *Les Derniers Troubadours de la Provence* (1872), *La Chanson de la croisade contre les albigeois* (1875–79), *Recueil d'anciens textes bas-latins, provençaux, et français* (1874–77), etc.

Mey·er \'mī(-ə)r\, Viktor. 1848–1897. German chemist. Professor, Zürich (1872–85), Göttingen (1885–89), Heidelberg (1889–97); studied aromatic nitro compounds; devised method of measuring vapor densities of inorganic substances at high temperatures (1871); discovered thiophene (1883); named and pioneered field of stereochemistry; discovered (1878) oximes.

Mey·er·beer \'mī(-ə)r-ˌbār, *Angl* -ˌbi(ə)r\, Giacomo. *Orig.* Jakob Liebmann Meyer Beer \'bār\. 1791–1864. German composer. Brother of Michael and Wilhelm Beer. To Italy (1816), where he composed Italian operas in Rossini's style; frequent visitor to Paris (from 1825), and soon composed in French style; general music director, Berlin Opera (1842). His operas included *Il crociato in Egitto* (1824), *Robert le Diable* (1831), *Les Huguenots* (1836), *Ein Feldlager in Schlesien* (1844), *Le Prophète* (1849), *Le Pardon de Ploërmel* or *Dinorah* (1859), *L'Africaine* (first performed 1865); composed also cantatas, overtures, orchestral marches, ceremonial music, etc.

Mey·er·heim \'mī(-ə)r-ˌhīm\, Eduard, *in full* Friedrich Eduard. 1808–1879. German painter. Known for genre scenes from German peasant and middle-class life in oils and water colors. His son and pupil ¶Paul (1842–1915) painted chiefly animal pictures, genre scenes, landscapes, and portraits.

Mey·er·hof \'mī(-ə)r-ˌhōf\, Otto. 1884–1951. German biochemist. Professor at Kiel (1918–24); member of Kaiser Wilhelm Inst. for Biology, Berlin-Dahlem (1924–29); director of department of physiology, Kaiser Wilhelm Inst. for Medical Research, Heidelberg (1929–38); fled Germany (1938); at Inst. of Physico-Chemical Biology, Paris (1938–40); professor, U. of Penn. (1940–51). Investigated conversion of energy and process of spasm in muscle; shared (with A.V. Hill) 1922 Nobel prize for physiology or medicine.

Mey·er·hold \'mī(-ə)r-ˌhōlt\, Vsevolod Yemilyevich. 1874–1940. Russian actor and theatrical producer. On staff of Moscow Art Theater (1898–1902); pioneered in nonrepresentational theater, producing Symbolist plays for Vera Komissarzhevskaya (1906–08), utilizing "biomechanics," constructivist sets, and other experimental devices and techniques; staged works for Mariinsky and Aleksandrinsky theaters, Leningrad, and for own theater (from 1924); arrested and imprisoned (1938).

Mey·er-Lüb·ke \'mī(-ə)r-'lue̅p-kə\, Wilhelm. 1861–1936. German linguist, b. Switzerland. Professor, Jena (1887–90), Vienna (1890–1915), Bonn (1915–36); known for developmental studies of Latin dialects and Romance languages. Author of *Grammatik der romanischen Sprachen* (1890–1902), *Italienische Grammatik* (1890), *Einführung in das Studium der romanischen Sprachwissenschaft* (1901), *Historische Grammatik der französischen Sprache* (1908–21), *Romanisches etymologisches Wörterbuch* (1911), *Das Katalanische* (1925), etc.

Me·yer·son \mā-yer-sōⁿ\, Émile. 1859–1933. French philosopher, b. Poland. Settled in France (1882). Author of *Identité et Réalité* (1907), *La Déduction relativiste* (1925), *Du cheminement de la pensée* (1931), etc.

Meyn·ell \'men-ᵊl\, Wilfrid. 1852–1948. English journalist and writer. Editor of works of Francis Thompson (1913); author of books of verse and biographies of Disraeli (1903) and Johnson (1913). His wife (m. 1877) ¶Alice Christiana Gertrude, *nee* Thompson (1847–1922), poet and essayist, published her first poems in *Preludes* (1875), praised by Ruskin, Rossetti, and Browning; aided her husband in editing the Catholic periodical *Weekly Register* (1881–98) and *Merry England* (1883–95), through which the Meynells discovered and aided Francis Thompson, the poet; gained literary fame with prose essays collected in *The Rhythm of Life* (1893), *The Colour of Life* (1896), etc.; published anthologies and a life of Ruskin (1900), also poems in *A Father of Women* (1917) and essays in *Hearts of Controversy* (1917). Their son ¶Sir Francis Meredith Wilfrid (1891–1975), book designer and writer on typographical subjects; founder of Nonesuch Press (1923); author of *Typography* (1923), *Seventeen Poems* (1945), *Poems and Pieces* (1961), etc.

Mey·rink \'mī-riŋk\, Gustav. 1868–1932. German writer, b. Vienna. Banker in Prague (1889–1902); in Vienna on staffs of *Lieben Augustin* and *Simplicissimus;* left Protestant church for Mahayana Buddhism (1927). Author of often grotesque and mystic works, including collections *Der heisse Soldat* (1903), *Das Wachsfigurenkabinett* (1907), *Des deutschen Spiessers Wunderhorn* (1913), *Fledermäuse* (1916); novels *Der Golem* (1915), *Das grüne Gesicht* (1916), *Walpurgisnacht* (1917), and *Der Engel vom westlichen Fenster* (1927).

Mé·zières *or* **Mai·zières** \māz-yer\, Philippe de. c.1327–1405. French crusader. Served under Humbert II, dauphin de Vienne, against Turks (1345–47); founded Order of the Passion of Jesus Christ to fight the infidels (1347); an associate of Peter I of Cyprus, whose chancellor he became (1359); with Peter led new crusade, sacked Alexandria (1365); councilor of Charles V (1373) and tutor of the dauphin; devoted himself to thoughts and plans for crusades to restore Holy Land to Christian power. Author of *Vita Sancti Petri Thomasii,* the *Nova religio passionis,* and an allegory *Le Songe du vieil pèlerin.*

Mi·all \'mī-əl\, Edward. 1809–1881. English clergyman and journalist. Lifelong advocate of disestablishment of Church of England; founded and edited weekly *Nonconformist* (1841); sought to amalgamate with Chartists (1842); led in founding of British Anti-State Church Assoc. (1844). M.P. (1852–57, 1869–74).

Mi·an·to·no·mo \mī-ˌan-tə-'nō-mō\. 1565?–1643. American Indian leader. Sachem of the Narragansetts; friendly with English settlers; deeded Rhode Island to William Coddington and his associates (1638); captured and executed by Uncas, a sachem of the Mahicans.

Mi·aou·lis \mē-'au̇l-yəs\, Andreas Vokos. 1769–1835. Greek naval commander. In war for Greek independence, commanded Greek fleet (1822–27) and successfully engaged Turkish squadrons (1822, 1826, 1827); involved in uprising of 1831; destroyed his fleet to keep it from Russians; one of delegation sent (1832) to offer Greek crown to Prince Otto of Bavaria.

Mi·cah *or* **Mi·chah** \'mī-kə\ *or* **Mi·che·as** \mī-'kē-əs\. 8th century B.C. Hebrew prophet. Prophesied impending judgment on Israel and esp. Judah, with proffer of Messianic hope, recorded in the Old Testament book of Micah.

Mi·chael I \'mī-kəl\. d. 1257. Czar of the Bulgarian empire (1246–57) of Asen dynasty. Son of Ivan Asen II; succeeded brother Kaliman I; in his reign loss of Bulgarian territory and power to Greeks continued.

Michael. Name of nine emperors of Eastern Roman Empire:

Michael I. *Orig.* Michael Ran·ga·be \räŋ-'gä-bā, rän-\. d. 843. Emperor (811–813). Son-in-law of Nicephorus I; proclaimed emperor in coup d'état against Nicephorus's son Stauracius; suppressed iconoclast rebellions; recognized Charlemagne as Holy Roman emperor in return for possession of Adriatic cities including Venice; undertook campaign to recapture territory from Bulgarians (813); defeated by Krum at Versinikia; deposed by Leo the Armenian (Leo V); retired to monastery.

Michael II. d. 829. Emperor (820–829). Soldier, companion of Leo the Armenian; imprisoned by Leo (820); freed by partisans and proclaimed emperor (820); reign marked by revolt of Thomas the Slavonian and by Arab conquests of Crete and parts of Sicily. Founder of Amorian or Phrygian dynasty.

Michael III. *Called* the Amorian, the Phrygian, the Drunkard. 838–867. Emperor (842–867). Son of Theophilus; under regency of mother Theodora and minister Theoctistus (842–856); use of icons restored (843); campaigns against Slavs and Arabs undertaken (843), leading to recovery of Crete and capture of Damietta; seized power with aid of uncle Bardas, who became chief figure in government; deposed Patriarch Ignatius and installed Photius (858); led campaign to the Euphrates (859). Under influence of Basil the Macedonian turned against Bardas and allowed him to be murdered (865); made Basil co-emperor (866); assassinated at instance of Basil. Last of Amorian or Phrygian dynasty.

Michael IV. *Called* the Paph·la·go·ni·an \ˌpaf-lə-'gō-nē-ən\. d. 1041. Emperor (1034–41). Introduced to court by brother, John the Orphanotrophus; became favorite of Empress Zoe, who married him on death of Emperor Romanus III (1034); established peace with Egypt and the Fāṭimid caliphate (c.1037); reign marked by Byzantine conquests of Messina (1037), Syracuse (1040); late in reign fell ill, retired to monastery.

Michael V Cal·a·pha·tes \-ˌkal-ə-'fāt-ˌēz\. *Called also* the Caulker. d. after 1042. Emperor (1041–42). Nephew of Michael IV; adopted by Empress Zoe; succeeded Michael IV; exiled Zoe to convent but forced by popular revolt to recall her; deposed, blinded, sent to monastery.

Michael VI Strat·i·ot·i·cus \-ˌstrat-ē-'ät-i-kəs\. 11th century. Emperor (1056–57). An elderly court official when named successor by Empress Theodora; antagonized military leaders, who proclaimed Isaac Comnenus; abdicated after his supporters were defeated by Isaac.

Michael VII Du·cas \-'d(y)ü-kəs\. *Called* Par·a·pin·a·ces \ˌpar-ə-pə-'nā-ˌsēz\. 1059–1078. Emperor (1067–78). Son of Constantine X Ducas; under regency of mother, who married (1068) Romanus Diogenes, who became co-emperor as Romanus IV; sole emperor on defeat of Romanus by Seljuq Turks (1071); at height of rioting and civil war between rival commanders, abdicated and entered monastery.

Michael VIII Pa·lae·ol·o·gus \-ˌpā-lē-ˈäl-ə-gəs\. 1224?–1282. Emperor (1259–82). Son of Andronicus Palaeologus and descended from Alexius III; assumed regency for John IV (1258) and was crowned co-emperor (1259); liberated Constantinople from Latins (1261); sole emperor (from 1261); maneuvered diplomatically to prevent any attempt on Constantinople by Charles of Anjou, a campaign culminating in submission of Greek church to Roman church at Council of Lyons (1274); ruthlessly suppressed opposition to union; defeated one of Charles's armies at Berat, Albania (1281); excommunicated by Pope Martin V, a tool of Charles; helped provoke uprising of the Sicilian Vespers (March 1282), which ended Charles's plans. Founder of Palaeologus dynasty.

Michael IX Palaeologus. c.1277–1320. Emperor (1295–1320). Son of Andronicus II; made co-emperor (1295); led mercenary troops against Turks; engaged (1303) Roger de Flor and his Catalan Company to fight Turks; arranged murder of Roger (1305); predeceased his father.

Michael. *In full* Michael Korybut Wiś·nio·wiec·ki \ˌvish-nyȯv-ˈyāt-skē\. 1640–1673. King of Poland (1669–73). Son-in-law of Emperor Leopold I; opposed by anti-Habsburg faction of John Sobieski; in revolt of Cossacks lost Podolia and much of Ukraine to Turks (1672–73).

Michael. *Russ.* Mikhail Fyodorovich Ro·ma·nov \(ˌ)rə-ˈmän-əf\. 1596–1645. Czar of Russia (1613–45), first of the Romanov house. Son of Patriarch Philaret. Elected (1613) to bring unity at time when Russia was being invaded from west and torn by internal anarchy; made peace with Sweden (1617) and Poland (1618), and reorganized government of Russia; had father as co-ruler (1619–33); called in experts from other lands to improve army and country's industrial methods; advanced Russian power in Siberian regions.

Michael. *Serb.* Mihailo III Ob·re·no·vić \ȯ-bren-ˈō-vētʸ\. 1823–1868. Prince of Serbia. Second son of Miloš I Obrenović; succeeded his brother Milan (1839) and was driven from throne (1842); again on throne, succeeding his father (1860–68); with help of Great Powers, succeeded in freeing Balkans from Turkish rule; assassinated (1868).

Michael I and **II.** Princes of Transylvania. See APAFI.

Michael. *Called* the Brave. *Rom.* Mihai Vi·tea·zul \vē-tyä-ˈzül\. 1558–1601. Prince of Walachia (1593–1601). In alliance with Moldavia and with Sigismund Báthory of Transylvania, conducted war against Turks (1594–98), defeating them at Călugăreni (Aug. 1595) and Giurgiu (Oct. 1595); swore fealty to Emperor Rudolf II (1598); defeated Andreas Báthory at Şelimbăr (Oct. 1599) and proclaimed himself prince of Transylvania; conquered Moldavia (1600) and briefly united much of future Romania; deprived of Transylvania by Rudolf and lost Moldavia to Polish (1600); executed by imperial general Giorgio Basta.

Michael Ce·ru·la·ri·us \-ˌser-yə-ˈlar-ē-əs\. c.1000–1059. Greek prelate. Civil servant in Constantinople; entered monastery (1040); named patriarch of Constantinople (1043) by Constantine IX Monomachus; rejected primacy of Rome and, on being excommunicated by papal legate Cardinal Humbert of France (1054), became popular symbol of independence of Byzantine church; persuaded Constantine to support schism; deposed and exiled (1058) by Emperor Isaac I Comnenus.

Michael Constantine Psel·lus \-ˈ(p)sel-əs\. 1018–c.1078. Byzantine philosopher, theologian, and politician. Imperial secretary to Michael V (1041–42); secretary of state to Constantine IX (1042–54); professor of philosophy at Constantinople (1045–54); prime minister under Theodoro (1055–56) and Michael VII Ducas (1071–78). Known for his encyclopedic knowledge; vigorous advocate of study of Greek classics, esp. Plato; wrote voluminously in many fields, but known esp. for his correspondence and for *Chronographia,* a history covering 976–1078.

Mi·cha·e·lis \ˌmik-ä-ˈā-ləs\, Georg. 1857–1936. German politician. In Prussian civil service (1879–85, 1892 ff.); undersecretary of finance (1909–15); in food ministry (1915–17); chosen by Hindenburg and Ludendorff to succeed Bethmann-Hollweg as imperial chancellor and Prussian minister president (July 1917), but was replaced by Hertling (Nov. 1917) following loss of support in Reichstag over peace terms; president of Pomerania (1918–19).

Michaelis, Johann David. 1717–1791. German theologian and Orientalist. Pioneer in use of historico-critical study in biblical interpretation; professor, Göttingen (1746–91). Author of an introduction to the New Testament (1750) and of *Mosäisches Recht* (1770), a Hebrew grammar (1778), etc.

Mi·cha·e·lis \mē-kä-ˈil-ēs\, Karin Marie, *nee* Bech-Brøn·dum \ˈbek-brœn-dəm\. 1872–1950. Danish writer. m. 1st Sophus Michaelis (1895; div.), 2d C. E. Stangeland (1912). Author of stories and novels including *Højt Spil* (1898), *Barnet* (1902), *Trold* (1904), *Tommelise* (1906), *Den farlige Alder* (1910), *Elsie Lindtner* (1912), *Grev Sylvains Hoevn* (1913), *Lille unge Kone* (1921), *Mette Trap og hendes Unger* (1922), *Traeet paa Godt og Ondt* (1924–30), *Mor* (1935), *Den grønne Ø* (1937).

Mi·cha·e·lis \ˌmik-ä-ˈā-ləs, *Angl* mi-ˈkā-ləs\, Leonor. 1875–1949. American chemist, b. Berlin, Germany. Assistant to Paul Ehrlich (1898–99); with Berlin Municipal hospital (1899–1902, 1906–22); professor, U. of Berlin (1908–22), Nagoya Medical School, Japan (1922–26), Johns Hopkins U. (1926–29), Rockefeller Inst. (1929–40); known esp. for Michaelis-Menten hypothesis on enzyme-catalyzed reactions (1913).

Mi·cha·e·lis \mē-kä-ˈil-ēs\, Sophus August Berthel. 1865–1932. Danish writer. Author of lyric poetry, including *Digte* (1889), *Solblomster* (1893), *Sirener* (1898), *Livets Fest* (1900), *Palmerne* (1904), *Blaaregn* (1913), *Romersk Foraar* (1921); novels, including *Synd* (1891), *Dødedansen* (1900), *Den evige Søvn* (1912), *Hellener og Barbar* (1914), *Himmelskibet* (1921).

Mi·chaud \mē-shō\, Joseph-François. 1767–1839. French journalist and historian. Editor of *La Quotidienne,* ultraroyalist journal (1815); author of *Histoire des Croisades* (1811–22); with his brother ¶Louis-Gabriel (1773–1858), compiled *Biographie universelle* (1811–28); Louis became director of the royal press (1823) and published several biographies, as of Louis-Philippe (1849) and Talleyrand (1853).

Mi·chaux \mē-shō\, André. 1746–1802. French botanist and traveler. In Tigris and Euphrates valleys (1782–85), in U.S. (1785–96), and in Madagascar (1800–02). From his collections and field notes were prepared *Histoire des chênes de l'Amérique Septentrionale* (1801) and *Flora boreali-americana* (1803). His son ¶François-André (1770–1855) accompanied him to U.S. and managed his botanical garden; traveled extensively beyond the Alleghenies and along the Atlantic coast; published *Histoire des arbres forestiers de l'Amérique septentrionale* (1810–13).

Micheas. See MICAH.

Miche \mēsh\, Jean-Claude. d. 1873. French missionary. Catholic missionary to Cochinchina (from 1836); imprisoned by Emperor Minh Mang (1836–43); gained confidence of King Norodom of Cambodia and induced him to accept French protectorate status (1864); chief apostolic vicar of Cambodia (from 1864).

Mi·chel \ˈmī-kəl, ˈmich-əl\ of North·gate \ˈnȯ(ə)rth-ˌgāt, -gət\. *Known as* Dan (*i.e.* Master) Michel. fl. 1340. English translator and monk. Translator into Kentish dialect of French treatise *La somme des vices et des vertues* by Laurentius Gallus (1279), known as *Ayenbite of Inwyt* (or *Remorse of Conscience*) and valued philologically as dated example of southern dialect.

Mi·chel \mē-shel\, Claude. *Pseudonym* Clo·dion \klȯd-yōⁿ\. 1738–1814. French sculptor. Known for small sculptures, usually in terra-cotta, of classical subjects as fauns, satyrs, nymphs, bacchantes, portrayed in quintessential Rococo manner.

Michel, Louise, *in full* Clémence-Louise. 1830–1905. French anarchist. Teacher in Paris; took part in the Commune of Paris (1871) and was deported to New Caledonia (1873); returned after amnesty (1880) and at once engaged in anarchist lecturing and plotting; sentenced to six years' imprisonment (1883) and refused to accept a pardon (1885); in London (1886–96), and returned to Paris, always continuing to spread anarchist propaganda. Among her books were *Le Livre du jour de l'an* (1872), *Les Microbes humains* (1886), *Mémoires* (1886), *La Commune* (1898).

Mi·chel·an·ge·lo \ˌmē-kä-ˈlän-jä-lō, *Angl* ˌmī-kə-ˈlan-jə-ˌlō, ˌmik-ə-ˈlan-, ˌmē-kə-ˈlän-\. *Full Ital. name* Michelangelo di Lodovico Buo·nar·ro·ti Si·mo·ni \ˌbwȯ-när-ˈrȯ-tē-sē-ˈmō-nē\. 1475–1564. Italian sculptor, painter, architect, and poet, b. Caprese. Apprenticed to painter Ghirlandajo (1488); studied esp. ancient paintings and sculptures in Medici collection; lived in palace of Lorenzo de' Medici (1490–92). Fled shortly before downfall of the Medici to Bologna (1494–95); at Rome (1496–1501); at Florence (1501–05) studied Leonardo's art. Summoned by Pope Julius II to Rome; decorated ceilings of Sistine Chapel (1508–12); worked on Julius memorial (1513–16). Sent (1516) by Pope Leo X to Florence to work on new façade for San Lorenzo (to 1520; not completed) and to procure marbles from quarries of Carrara and Seravezza. Active chiefly in Florence (to 1534); one of nine citizens in charge of defense of city (1529). Again at Rome (from 1534); in service of popes Clement VII, Paul III, Paul IV; succeeded Sangallo as architect of St. Peter's, Rome (1547). Friend of painter Sebastiano del Piombo (1516–34), of Roman nobleman Tommaso Cavalieri (from 1532), and of Vittoria Colonna (1538–47); for the last two, wrote religious and love sonnets and made allegorical chalk drawings. Among his sculptures were the bas-relief *Battle of the Centaurs* and *Madonna of the Steps* (Case Buonarroti, Florence); statuettes *Kneeling Angel, St. Proculus,* and *St. Petronius* (all at Bologna); *Bacchus; Pietà* (St. Peter's, Rome); colossal figure of young David carved out of single marble block and incomplete statue of Matthew (both in Florence Acad.); a Madonna for Church of Notre Dame, Bruges; bronze statue of Pope Julius II (Bologna; destroyed 1511); the "tragedy of his life," the Julius tomb for Pope Julius II with the famous statue of Moses (now in San Pietro in Vincoli, Rome); and the figure *Victory* (Florence Acad.); the athletic nude *Christ Bearing the Cross* for Santa Maria sopra Minerva, Rome; tombs of several Medici in San Lorenzo, Florence; *Youth Crouching; Cupid Kneeling; Pietà* or *Deposition from the Cross* (Florence cathedral; later restored) and the Rondanini *Pietà* (Rondanini Palace, Rome), both intended for his own tomb. Among his paintings were the circular painting *Holy Family,* also called *Doni-Madonna;* cartoon *Battle of Cascina,* executed in rivalry with Leonardo da Vinci and intended for a gigantic fresco of Florentine history for council room of Palazzo Vecchio in Florence; ceiling decorations in Sistine Chapel for Julius II; colossal fresco for Clement VII and Paul III, *The Last Judgment* on altar wall of Sistine Chapel; for Paul III, frescoes *Conversion of Paul* and *Crucifixion of Peter* (both in Pauline Chapel of Vatican). Among his pen and chalk drawings and sketches were *Phaeton, Tityus, Ganymede,* and the series *Crucifixion, Entombment,* and *Resurrection.* His architectural works included façade for Medici sepulchral chapel, Florence; for Clement VII, plans for Laurentian Library in Florence (built 1530–34); plans for completion of St. Peter's, Rome, begun by Sangallo, and alterations in Bramante's original Greek cross plan; plans for Farnese Palace (1546 ff.) and general plans for new Capitoline Place (begun 1546), Rome, with equestrian statue of Marcus Aurelius in center; plans for Porta Pia (building begun 1564), for transformation of Baths of Diocletian into Church of Santa Maria degli Angeli, both at Rome, and for new fortifications of Rome. His poetry included many lyric poems, mostly sonnets and madrigals, love poems, and religious and philosophical poems. Frequently considered the creator of the Renaissance.

Mi·che·let \mēsh-le\, Jules. 1798–1874. French historian. Head of historical section in National Archives (1831–52); professor, Collège de France (1838–51). First and greatest of the nationalist and romantic historians of France. His works included *Tableau chronologique de l'histoire moderne* (1825), *Introduction à l'histoire universelle* (1831), *Histoire romaine* (1831), *Histoire de France* (17 vols., 1833–67), *Origines du droit français* (1837), and *Histoire de la Révolution française* (1847–53). His wife ¶Adèle-Athénaïs, *nee* Mia·la·ret \myȧ-lȧ-re\ (1826–1899), writer, collaborated with her husband in *L'Oiseau* (1856), *L'Insecte* (1858), and *La Mer* (1861); also wrote *Les Mémoires d'un enfant* (1866) and *La Nature* (1872).

Mi·che·lin \mēsh-laⁿ\, André (1853–1931) and his brother Édouard (1859–1940). French industrialists and philanthropists. Partners in Michelin & Cie (founded by father Jules, 1831); formed (1888) firm to manufacture rubber tires for use on bicycles; first to apply pneumatic tires to automobiles (1895); instituted scheme of making family allowances among employees based on the size of the family. André created (1900) the *Guide Michelin.*

Mich·ell \'mich-əl\, John. 1724–1793. English geologist and astronomer. Professor, Cambridge (1762–64); rector of Thornhill (from 1767); credited with invention of torsion balance (1784) and founding of seismology; described method of magnetization.

Mi·che·loz·zo \mē-kā-'lȯt-tsō\ *or* **Mi·che·loz·zi** \-tsē\. *In full* Michelozzo di Bar·to·lom·me·o \dē-ˌbär-tō-lōm-'me-ō\. 1396–1472. Florentine architect, sculptor, and goldsmith. After Brunelleschi, principal Florentine architect of early Renaissance. Aided Ghiberti on doors of baptistery; associate of Donatello (1425–35); protégé of Cosimo de' Medici; succeeded Brunelleschi as superintendent of cathedral of Florence (1446). Sculptural works included *St. John the Baptist* and an undetermined part of the works of Donatello and Luca della Robbia. Architectural works included the Riccardi Palace for Cosimo de' Medici, Medici chapel in Church of Santa Croce, and Convent of San Marco (all in Florence), San Giorgio Maggiore Library (Venice), Palazzo Rettorale (Ragusa, Dalmatia), Holy Cross tabernacle in Church of San Miniato (Florence), and reconstruction of Medici Bank (Milan) and of Palazzo Vecchio (Florence).

Mi·chels \'mik-əls\, Robert. 1876–1936. German economist and sociologist. Professor at Paris, Turin, Basel, Perugia; known for enunciation of "iron law of oligarchy." Author of *Storia del marxismo in Italia* (1909), *Zur Soziologie des Parteiwesens in der modernen Demokratie* (1911), *Probleme der Sozialphilosophie* (1914), *Italien von Heute* (1930), etc.

Mi·chel·sen \'mik-kəl-sən\, Christian, *in full* Peter Christian Hersleb Kjerschow. 1857–1925. Norwegian politician. Practiced law (1879–85); member of Storting (from 1891); minister of finance (1903–05); formed new cabinet following Hagerup's resignation (1905) and received support of Storting in bringing about dissolution of union with Sweden; played a leading part in election of Prince Charles of Denmark as King Haakon VII; first premier of independent Norway (1905–07).

Mi·chel·son \'mī-kəl-sən\, Albert Abraham. 1852–1931. American physicist, b. Strelno, Prussia (now Strzelno, Poland). To U.S. (1854); professor, Case School of Applied Science (1883–89), Clark U. (1889–92); professor and head of the department of physics, U. of Chicago (1892–1931). Determined with a high degree of accuracy the speed at which light travels; invented (1881) an interferometer for measuring distances by means of the length of light waves; measured a meter in terms of the wave length of cadmium light for the Paris Bureau International des Poids et Mesures. Performed experiment (1887, with E. W. Morley) which showed that there is no absolute motion of the earth relative to an ether; this demonstration served as a starting point in the development of the theory of relativity. Received 1907 Nobel prize in physics.

Mi·chiel \mē-'kyel\, Vitale II. d. 1172. Venetian leader. Doge of Venice; maintained general neutrality between Guelfs and Ghibellines; resisted attempt of Byzantine Emperor Manuel I Comnenus to exact subsidy for war with Norman Sicily (1166); forced by popular sentiment to go to war following Byzantine seizure of Venetian shipping (1171); naval expedition proved disastrous, and returning ships spread plague to city; assassinated by a mob. Episode led to revision of constitution of Venetian Republic limiting power of doge.

Michinaga. See under FUJIWARA family.

Mi·chu·rin \myi-'chür-yin\, Ivan Vladimirovich. 1855–1935. Russian horticulturist. Operated orchard that became a state institution (1918); gained political support for his theories of crossbreeding; postulated complete heritability of acquired characteristics, a theory that, as "Michurinism," became state doctrine and was furthered by Lysenko.

Mi·cip·sa \mə-'sip-sə\. d. 118 B.C. King of Numidia (148–118 B.C.). Eldest son of Masinissa; pursued policy of friendship with Rome.

Mic·kie·wicz \mēts-'kye-vēch\, Adam Bernard. 1798–1855. Polish poet. Taught in Kovno (1819–23); arrested in Vilna as a revolutionary (1824) and sent to St. Petersburg; to Odessa (1825) as teacher in lyceum; in service of governor general at Moscow (1825–28); allowed to travel abroad (1829); settled in Paris (1832); first professor of Slavic literatures, Collège de France, Paris (1840–44). Attempted to organize military unit in Italian revolution (1848); edited radical newspaper *La Tribune des peuples* (1849). Regarded as greatest of Polish poets; wrote *Poezye I* (1822), *Poezye II* (1823), *Dziady* (1823–32), *Sonety Krymskie* (1826), *Konrad Wallenrod* (1828), epic *Pan Tadeusz* (1834); prose *Księgi narodu i pielgrzymstwa polskiego* (1833).

Mick·le \'mik-əl\, William Julius. 1735–1788. Scottish poet. Published *The Concubine* (or *Syr Martyn*) in manner of Spenser (1765); won success with his translation of *The Lusiad* from the Portuguese of Camões (1775); author of ballad *Cumnor Hall* (1784), which suggested to Sir Walter Scott the writing of *Kenilworth.*

Mi·con *or* **Mi·kon** \'mī-ˌkän\. 5th century B.C. Athenian painter and sculptor. Associate of Polygnotus (*q.v.*) in decoration of the Stoa Poikile, executing *Battle of Theseus and the Amazons;* also worked on decoration of the Theseum, or Temple of Theseus, and Temple of the Dioscuri, in Athens.

Middlesex, Earl of. See (1) Lionel CRANFIELD; (2) Charles Sackville, under SACKVILLE family.

Mid·dle·ton \'mid-ᵊl-tən\, Arthur. 1681–1737. American colonial leader, b. Charleston, S.C. In South Carolina House of Commons, led movement overthrowing proprietary control (1719). Acting governor during absence of crown representative (1725–31); administration marked by conflict with House of Commons. His son ¶Henry (1717–1784) was a member of Continental Congress (1774–76) and its president (Oct. 1774–May 1775). Henry's son ¶Arthur (1742–1787) was a member of Continental Congress (1776–78 and 1781–83) and signer of Declaration of Independence. A son of Arthur ¶Henry (1770–1846) was governor of South Carolina (1810–12); member of U.S. Congress (1815–19); U.S. minister to Russia (1820–30).

Middleton, Conyers. 1683–1750. English clergyman and controversialist. Librarian, Cambridge U. (1719); attacked Roman Catholic ritual in *Letter from Rome* (1729); assailed on ground of latitudinarianism in his remonstrance with Daniel Waterland on historical accuracy of the Bible; criticized for latitudinarian treatise on miracles (1748); increased reputation with *Life of Cicero* (1741), largely borrowed from William Bellenden.

Middleton, John. 1st Earl of Middleton. 1619–1674. Scottish soldier. Served in France; second in command of Parliamentary army at Philiphaugh (1645); suppressed Royalist uprising (1647); distinguished himself at Preston (1648); led highland force dispersed by Monck (1654); created earl (1656); commander in chief, governor of Edinburgh Castle, lord high commissioner to Scottish parliament (1660); deprived as result of accusations by Earl of Lauderdale (1663).

Middleton, Thomas. 1570?–1627. English dramatist. One of Philip Henslowe's established playwrights (1602); collaborated with Munday, Drayton, Webster, etc.; collaborated on part I of Dekker's *The Honest Whore* (1604); produced satirical comedies of contemporary London manners; later, with Rowley, turned to romantic comedy; devised pageant for installation of lord mayor (1613, and repeatedly afterwards); wrote entertainment for opening of New River by Hugh Myddelton (1613); city chronologer, London (1620), his ms. history extant in 18th century; for satirizing policy of court on matter of Spanish marriage in political drama *A Game at Chesse* (1624), censured along with actors. Author of *Michaelmas Terme* (1607), *The Phoenix* (1607), *A Tricke to Catch the Old One* (1608), *The Famelie of Love* (1608), *A Mad World, my Masters* (1608), *The Roaring Girl* or *Moll Cut-Purse* (1611, with

Dekker), *A Faire Quarrell* (1617, with Rowley), *A Chast Mayd in Cheapeside* (pub. 1630), *More Dissemblers besides Women* (pub. 1657), *No Wit, No Help like a Woman's* (pub. 1657), *Women Beware Women* (pub. 1657), *The Spanish Gipsie* (tragicomedy, pub. 1653), *The Changeling* (performed 1621; pub. 1653; with Rowley), and *Any Thing for a Quiet Life* (pub. 1662; with Rowley).

Middleton, Thomas Fanshaw. 1769–1822. English missionary. Ordained Anglican priest (1792); archdeacon of Huntingdon (1812); first bishop of Calcutta (1814); founded Bishop's Coll., Calcutta (1820). Author of *Doctrine of the Greek Article* (1808) and other scholarly works.

Midg·ley \'mij-lē\, Thomas, Jr. 1889–1944. American chemist, b. Beaver Falls, Pa. On staff of C.F. Kettering's Dayton Engineering Laboratories (1916–23); discovered (1921) antiknock property of tetraethyl lead in gasoline; vice president, Ethyl Corp. (from 1923); discovered (1930) Freon refrigerant; vice president, Kinetic Chemicals, Inc. (from 1930); also did research on hydrocarbon cracking, synthetic rubber.

Mid·hat Pa·şa \mid-'hät-pə-'shä\. 1822–1883. Ottoman politician. Civil administrator; restored order in Rumelia (1854), Bulgaria (1857); vizier of Niš (1861); governor of Baghdad (1869); instituted numerous reforms; named grand vizier to replace anti-reform Mahmud Nedim (1872); soon removed to posts of justice minister, then president of Council of State; took part in deposing of Sultan Abdülaziz (1876) and of Murad V (1876); made grand vizier by Abdülhamid II (1876); encouraged promulgation of first Ottoman constitution (1876); banished (1877); recalled, made governor of Izmir (1878–81); convicted (1881) of complicity in death of Abdülaziz and banished.

Mieczysław. See MIESZKO.

Miel·zi·ner \mel-'zē-nər\, Jo. 1901–1976. American theatrical designer, b. Paris, France. Designer of Broadway sets for dramas, musicals, ballets, etc. (from 1924), producing over 360 designs including those for *Winterset, Pal Joey, Glass Menagerie, Annie Get Your Gun, Streetcar Named Desire, Death of a Salesman, South Pacific, Guys and Dolls, The King and I;* also designed for motion pictures, winning Academy Award for art direction of *Picnic* (1955).

Mie·re·velt *or* **Mie·re·veld** \'mē-rə-ˌvelt\, Michiel Janszoon van. 1567–1641. Dutch painter. Worked chiefly in Delft and The Hague; court painter to house of Orange. Painted portraits of William of Orange and other princes of Orange-Nassau and hundreds of other notables; with assistants produced upwards of 2000 portraits.

Mie·ris \'mē-ris\. Family of Dutch painters of Leiden including: Frans van Mieris, *called* the Elder (1635–1681); studied with Gerrit Dou, Abraham van den Tempel; known for highly polished small genre pictures and portraits. His sons and pupils ¶Jan (1660–1690), painter of portraits and genre pictures, and ¶Willem (1662–1741), painter of portraits and genre and mythological pictures. Willem's son ¶Frans (1689–1763), genre and portrait painter, etcher, and historian.

Mie·ro·sław·ski \ˌmye-rō-'slàf-skē\, Ludwik. 1814–1878. Polish revolutionist. Took part in Polish insurrection (1830–31); imprisoned (1846–48) for revolutionary plotting; led Polish uprisings in Poznań (1848), Baden (1849); briefly styled "dictator" in Polish uprising of 1863. Author of a history of revolution in Poland.

Mie·scher \'mē-shər\, Johann Friedrich. 1844–1895. Swiss physiologist. Professor, Basel (1871–95); founded first physiological institute in Switzerland, the Vesalianum (1885). Discovered (1869) and isolated (1874) nucleic acid.

Mies van der Rohe \ˌmēs-ˌvän-də-'rō(-ə), ˌmēz-\, Ludwig. 1886–1969. American architect, b. Aachen, Germany. Learned stonecutting and masonry from father, furniture design from Bruno Paul (1905–07); in architectural office of Peter Behrens (1908–11); opened own office, Berlin (1913); designed multiple-dwelling unit for Weissenhof exhibit (1927), German pavilion for Barcelona Exposition (1929), Tugendhat House, Brno, Czechoslovakia (1930); developed line of tubular-steel furniture, notably the Barcelona chair (1929). Director of Bauhaus (1930–33); to U.S. (1937); director of School of Architecture, Illinois Inst. of Technology (1938–58). Known esp. for developing neoclassical designs featuring exposed supports, glass-curtain walls, simple forms; leading exponent of International Style; works included Farnsworth house, Plano, Ill. (1946–50); apartment houses (1949–50), Federal Center (1964), Chicago; Seagram Building (1956–58, with Philip Johnson), New York City; Public Library (1967), Washington, D.C.; Gallery of the Twentieth Century (1968), New National Gallery (1968), Berlin.

Miesz·ko \'myesh-kō\. *Later spelling* Mie·czy·sław \'myech-i-slàf\. Name of three rulers of Poland:

Mieszko I. c.930–992. Prince or duke of Poland (c.963–992) of Piast dynasty. Accepted Christianity (966); expanded Polish dominion into Galicia, annexed Pomerania; organized Polish state.

Mieszko II. *Also called* Lam·bert \'làm-bert\. 990–1034. King of Poland (1025–34). Son of Bolesław I; lost territory to coalition of Germany and Kievan Russia.

Mieszko III. *Called* Sta·ry \'stär-i\, *i.e.* the Old. c.1126–1202. Prince of Great Poland (1138–1202), prince of Kraków (1173–77, 1198–1202). Son of Bolesław III, from whom he inherited Poznań principality; claimed Kraków on death of older brother.

Mi Fei \'mē-'fā\. *Orig.* Mi Fu \-'fü\. *Also called* Yüan-chang \yü-'än-'jäŋ\, Hai-yüeh Wai-shih \'hī-yü-'e-'wī-'shi(ə)r\, *and* Hsiang-yang Man-shih \shē-'äŋ-'yäŋ-'män-'shi(ə)r\. 1051–1107. Chinese scholar, poet, and artist. Reared at imperial court; through life held various offices; known for personal eccentricity, occasionally caustic criticisms, and uprightness. An innovative painter of landscapes, introducing techniques of "Mi dots" and "splashed ink"; historian, critic, and practitioner of calligraphy. Writings included verse *Shan-lin chi* (lost), critical works *Pao-chang tai-fang lu* on calligraphy, *Hua shih* on painting, and posthumous collections.

Miff·lin \'mif-lən\, George Harrison. 1845–1921. American publisher, b. Boston. On staff of publishing house Hurd & Houghton (1867); admitted to firm (1872) and continued as partner in successor firms; president, Houghton Mifflin Co. (1908–21).

Mifflin, Thomas. 1744–1800. American Revolutionary officer, b. Philadelphia. Member, Continental Congress (1774–76, 1782–84), president (1783). Aide-de-camp to Washington (1775); quartermaster general, Continental army (1775–77); major general (1777); member of Board of War (1777–78). Involved in Conway cabal to replace Washington with Gates (1777–78), but upon failure of plan repudiated his connection with it. Member, Constitutional Convention (1787); governor of Pennsylvania (1790–99).

Mi·gnard \mēn-yàr\, Pierre. *Called* le Ro·main \lə-rō-maⁿ\. 1610 or 1612–1695. French painter. In Italy (1630–52); court painter (from 1657); rival of Charles Le Brun; head of Academie Royale (1690–95). Best known as painter of portraits, as of Louis XIV, Mme de Maintenon, Mme de Montespan, Mme de La Vallière, Mme de La Fayette, Mme de Sévigné, Bossuet, Turenne, Colbert, Molière. His brother ¶Nicolas, *called* Mi·gnard d'Avi·gnon \-dà-vēn-yōⁿ\ (1606–1668), also a painter, was commissioned by king to decorate certain chambers in the Tuileries; painted also portraits of many members of the court.

Migne \mēnʸ\, Jacques-Paul. 1800–1875. French cleric and editor. Settled in Paris (1833) and founded and edited *L'Univers Religieux;* established (1836) publishing house for religious books; among important publications of this house were the 28 volumes of *Scripturae sacrae cursus completus,* 100 volumes of *Collection ... des orateurs sacrés,* 383 volumes of *Patrologiae cursus completus,* and 171 volumes of *Encyclopédie théologique.*

Mi·gnet \mēn-ye\, François-Auguste-Marie. 1796–1884. French historian. Friend and associate of Thiers; with Thiers and Carrel founded and edited *Le National,* an anti-Bourbon journal (1830); director of archives in ministry of foreign affairs (1830–48). Among his histories were *Histoire de la révolution française* (1824), *Antonio Perez et Philippe II* (1845), *Histoire de Marie Stuart* (1851), *Histoire de la rivalité de François I et Charles-Quint* (1875).

Mi·gnon \mēn-yōⁿ\, Abraham. 1640–1679. Dutch painter. Worked in Baroque manner; known for pictures of flowers, fruit, animals, birds, and insects.

Mi·guel \mē-'gel\. *In full* Miguel Maria Evaristo de Bra·gan·ça \thə-brə-'gàⁿ-sə\. *Usually known as* Dom Miguel. 1802–1866. Pretender to Portuguese throne. Third son of John VI of Portugal; brought up in Brazil; returned to Portugal (1821); plotted against father (1821–26); on accession (1826) of niece, Maria da Gloria, betrothed to her and made regent (1827) by Maria's father, Dom Pedro of Brazil; usurped throne and brought on civil war (1828–33); overthrown by Dom Pedro and followers (1834) and forced by England and France to give up all claims to throne; lived in Italy and Germany in exile.

Mihai. See MICHAEL.

Mi·haj·lo·vić \mē-'hī-lō-vētʸ\, Dragoljub. *Called* Dra·ža \'drà-zhà\. 1893–1946. Serbian soldier. Distinguished for bravery during World War I. Following German conquest of Yugoslavia (1941), organized Chetniks, royalist underground army to carry on guerilla warfare against German and Italian armies; minister of war in Yugoslavian government in exile, and head of Free Yugoslavian army (1942); rival of Communist partisans led by Tito; abandoned in favor of Tito by Allies and King Peter (1944); captured and executed by partisans.

Mi·ha·la·che \ˌmē-hä-'läk-ē\, Ion. 1882–?1953. Romanian politician. Founded (1918) Peasant party and elected to parliament (1919); minister of agriculture (1919–20); vice president of fusion National Peasant party (1926); minister of agriculture (1928–30), of interior (1930–33); opposed dictatorship of King Carol II and in World War II was active in underground opposition to government of Gen. Antonescu; arrested and imprisoned by Communist regime (1947).

Mi·ka·el Se·hul \mik-ä-'el-se-'hül\. c.1692–1784. Ethiopian ruler. Nobleman; aided King Iyoas in subduing rebellion of Islāmic Galla tribes; occupied capital, proclaimed himself regent, deposed and executed Iyoas (1769), ending 27-century reign of Solomonic kings of Ethiopia; installed successively as puppet kings John II, Teklq Haimanot II, Tekle Giorgis; defeated in battle with Galla rebels (1784), retired from regency.

Mikhail. See MICHAEL.

Mi·khay·lov·sky \myi-k̲ī-'lôf-skəi\, Nikolay Konstantinovich. 1842–1904. Russian sociologist. On staff of journal *Otechestvennye zapiski* (1868–84); editor, *Russkoye bogatstvo* (1892–1904); romanticized peasant life and culture; recognized as leader of *narodnik* (populist) movement and countenanced terrorist tactics of extreme *Narodnaya volya* (People's Will) wing.

Mi·ki \mē-kē\ Kiyoski. 1897–1945. Japanese philosopher. Professor, Hosei U., Tokyo (1927–42); founded Marxist journal *Shinkō kagaku no hata-no-moto-ni* (1928); developed synthesis of Marxism and liberal democracy; expelled from Communist organization (1930); arrested as Communist (1930, 1945).

Mik·kel·sen \'mēk-əl-sən\, Ejnar. 1880–1971. Danish explorer. On expeditions to east coast of Greenland (with Amdrup, 1900), Franz Josef Land (1901–02), etc.; commanded expeditions to northeastern Greenland (1909–12), Scoresby Sound (1924), west Greenland (1925), and east Greenland (1932). Author of *Conquering the Arctic Ice* (1909), *Lost in the Arctic* (1913), *Frozen Justice* (1920).

Mi·klas \'mik-,läs\, Wilhelm. 1872–1956. Austrian politician. Leader in Christian Socialist party (1907–38) and member of Austrian parliament (1907–28); president of the Nationalrat (1923–28); president of Austrian republic (1928–38); resigned (Mar. 1938), Austria being proclaimed a part of the German Reich.

Mi·klo·šić \'mē-klō-,shetʸ, *Ger* -,shich\, Franz Xaver von. 1813–1891. Slavic philologist. Professor, Vienna (1849–85); regarded as founder of modern Slavic philology. Author of *Vergleichende Grammatik der slawische Sprachen* (1852–75), etc.

Mi·ko·łaj·czyk \mē-kòl-'ī-chik\, Stanisław. 1901–1966. Polish politician. Member of Sejm (1930–35); vice chairman of Peasant party (1931–39); to London (1939); prime minister of Polish government in exile (1943–44); returned to Poland (1945); second deputy premier and minister of agriculture and land reform in provisional government (1945–47); attempted to secure democratic government but his Peasant party terrorized by Stalinists; fled to England and U.S. (1947).

Mi·ko·yan \myi-(,)kə-'yän\, Anastas Ivanovich. 1895–1978. Soviet politician. Bolshevik leader in Baku (1917–19); member of Central Committee (from 1923), of Politburo (from 1935; later known as Presidium); commissar for trade (1926–31), supplies (1931–34), food industry (1934–38), foreign trade (1938–49); deputy premier (1946–64); supporter of Khrushchev; chairman of Presidium (1964–65).

Mik·száth \'mik-sát\, Kálmán. 1847–1910. Hungarian novelist. Political journalist; member of national assembly (from 1887). Author of often Romantic novels, anecdotal or historical in plot, later also exhibiting trend to satire and realism; works included *A két koldusdiák* (1885), *A beszélő köntös* (1889), *Beszterce ostroma* (1894), *Szent Péter esernyője* (1895), *A gavallérok* (1897), *Különös házasság* (1900), *A vén gazember* (1906), *A noszty fiu esete Tóth Marival* (1908), *A fekete város* (1910).

Mi·ku·licz-Ra·dec·ki \mē-'kü-lyich-rá-'det-skē\, Johann von. 1850–1905. Polish surgeon. Professor, Kraków (1882–87), Königsberg (1887–90), Breslau (1890–1905); introduced innovations in abdominal surgery, notably suturing perforated gastric ulcer (1885), restoring part of esophagus (1886), removing malignant section of colon (1903); introduced improved esophagoscope and gastroscope (1881); championed antiseptic technique; described Mikulicz's disease.

Mi·lan \'mē-län\. *In full* Milan Obre·no·vić \ób-re-'nò-vētʸ\. 1854–1901. Prince (1868–82) and king (1882–89) of Serbia. Succeeded cousin Michael as prince (1868); assumed rule from regency (1872); forced by popular pan-Slavist sentiment to declare war on Turkey (1876); defeated, but owing to Russia's victory over Turks and with Austrian support secured Serbian independence (1878); took title of king (1882); engaged in unsuccessful war against Bulgaria (1885); abdicated (1889) in favor of son Alexander; in Paris (1892–97); returned to Belgrade and became commander in chief of Serbian army (1897); again withdrew from Serbia after Alexander's marriage (1900).

Mi·lán \mē-'län\, Luis. c.1500–after 1561. Spanish musician and composer. Noted player on the vihuela; courtier to Germaine de Foix at Valencia. Author of *El maestro* (1536), containing many pieces for vihuela and songs with vihuela accompaniment; also wrote *El cortesano* (1561), manual of courtly behavior.

Mi·la·nés y Fuen·tes \mē-lä-'nä-sē-'fwän-täs\, José Jacinto. 1814–1863. Cuban poet. Best known for his lyrics as in *El aguinaldo habanero* (1837), *El conde Alarcos* (1838).

Milbanke, Anne Isabella. See under George Gordon BYRON.

Milch \'milk̲\, Erhard. 1892–1972. German airman. Army pilot in World War I; civilian aviator (1920); associated with Lufthansa (1926–33); protégé of Goering; secretary of state in air ministry (1933–44); inspector general of Luftwaffe (1941–44); imprisoned for war crimes (1947–54).

Miles \'mī(ə)lz\, Nelson Appleton. 1839–1925. American army officer, b. near Westminster, Mass. Served through Civil War; major general of volunteers (1865); custodian of Jefferson Davis at Fortress Monroe (1865–66). Colonel, U.S. army (1866); engaged in frontier Indian fighting (1869–80); brigadier general (1880) and major general (1890); led successful campaigns against Apache, Sioux, Nez Percé tribes; captured Geronimo (1886); senior commander, U.S. army (1895); occupied Puerto Rico (1898); lieutenant general, U.S. army (1901); retired (1903).

Mi·les·cu \mē-'les-kü\, Nicolae. 1626–1708. Romanian traveler and scholar. Mutilated (1668) after failure of intrigue to gain princely throne of Moldavia, left Romania forever; to Moscow (1671); ambassador of czar to Peking (1675–78). Produced Romanian translation of Greek Bible; left manuscript description of China journey (pub. 1882).

Milford Haven, Marquis of. See Louis Alexander MOUNTBATTEN.

Mi·lhaud \mē-yō\, Darius. 1892–1974. French composer. Secretary to Paul Claudel in Brazil (1916–18); to Paris (1918) and became member of "Les Six"; in U.S. (1940–47); professor at Mills Coll. (1940–71), Paris Conservatoire (from 1947). A pioneer of polytonality; works included operas *La Brebis égarée* (1923), *Les Malheurs d'Orphée* (1925), *Le pauvre matelot* (1927), *Christoph Colomb* (1930), *Médée* (1939), *David* (1954), *Saint Louis* (1972); ballets *L'Homme et son désir* (1918), *Le Boeuf sur le toit* (1919), *La Création du monde* (1923), *Salade* (1924), *Le Train bleu* (1924), *Moïse* (1940), *Les Cloches* (1945), *La Rose des vents* (1957); much dramatic music, esp. for Claudel's translations of Aeschylus; 13 symphonies; concertos for piano, oboe, violin, etc.; choral works, songs; chamber music including 18 string quartets; keyboard works; works for children.

Mi·líč \'mil-ēch\, Jan. *Known as* Milíč of Kro·mě·říž \króm-'yer-zhēsh\. c.1305–1374. Bohemian theologian and prelate. Ordained (c.1350); court archivist to Emperor Charles IV (1358); began preaching reform (c.1363) in Czech and German, calling for vernacular Bible; in Rome (1367), expounding his criticism of ecclesiastical abuses; imprisoned by Inquisition; released by Pope Urban V (1367), returned to Prague and continued preaching. Regarded as a predecessor of Jan Hus and the Reformation.

Milinda. See MENANDER.

Mill \'mil\, Hugh Robert. 1861–1950. Scottish geographer and meteorologist. Librarian, Royal Geographical Society (1892–1900); director, British Rainfall Organization (1901–19). Editor of *British Rainfall* and *Symons's Meteorological Magazine* (1901–19). Author of *Realm of Nature* (1892), *The English Lakes* (1895), *The Siege of the South Pole* (1905), *The Life of Sir Ernest Shackelton* (1923), etc.

Mill, James. 1773–1836. Scottish philosopher, historian, and economist. To London (1802) with Sir John Stuart, M.P.; became editor of *St. James's Chronicle* (1805), and wrote for *Edinburgh Review* (1808–13) and other reviews; devoted 11 years to his highly critical *History of India* (1817); appointed official in East India Co. (1819), rose to examiner and head of office (1830). Met Jeremy Bentham (1808), adopted his principles, became his companion and chief promulgator of Bentham's utilitarian philosophy in England; contributed utilitarian articles to *Encyclopaedia Britannica* (1816–23) and to *Westminster Review,* Benthamite organ (from 1824). As head of association for setting up "chrestomathic" school for higher education, took leading part in founding London U. (1825). Known as founder of philosophic radicalism, author of *Elements of Political Economy,* developing Ricardo's labor theory of value (1821), *Analysis of the Mind,* his magnum opus, providing in associationism a psychological basis for utilitarianism (1829), and *Fragment on Mackintosh,* supporting doctrine that morality is based on utility (1835).

Mill, John Stuart. 1806–1873. English philosopher and economist. Son of James Mill, who subjected him to a systematic education from age of three with a view to his succession as chief exponent of utilitarian philosophy; at ten read Plato and Demosthenes with ease; on visit to France (1820), gained interest in French literature, politics, and social conditions; became junior clerk in India House (1823), in charge of relations with native states (1836–56), chief of office (1856), retired on dissolution of East India Co. (1858). Formed Utilitarian Society for reading and discussion at Bentham's house (1823–26); member of Speculative Society (1826–29); chief contributor to *Westminster Review* and recognized as champion of utilitarian school before age of twenty; edited Bentham's *Rationale of Judicial Evidence* (1825), but after period of mental crisis and self-analysis (1826–27), departed from utilitarianism of Bentham by recognizing differences in quality as well as quantity of pleasure and by further humanizing and widening the inherited philosophy by infusing an element of idealism. Edited (1835–40) *London* (from 1836 *London and Westminster*) *Review;* contributed to *Edinburgh Review.* Created profound impression with his *System of Logic* (1843), treating methods of inductive logic; followed Ricardo's abstract theory in *Principles of Political Economy* (1848) but applied economic doctrines to social conditions. Best known treatises included *On Liberty* (1859), *Thoughts on Parliamentary Reform* (1859), *Representative Government* (1861), *Utilitarianism* (1863), and *Examination of Sir William Hamilton's Philosophy* (1865). M.P. (1865–68), voted with advanced Radical party and advocated women's suffrage. Returned to literary pursuits with *The Subjection of Women* (1869), *The Irish Land Question* (1870), and *Autobiography* (1873); lived last years at Avignon.

Mil·lais \'mil-,ā, mil-'ā\, Sir John Everett. 1829–1896. English painter. Exhibited at Royal Acad. *Pizarro Seizing the Inca of Peru* (1846). Originated, with Holman Hunt and D. G. Rossetti, Pre-Raphaelite Brotherhood (1848); developed Pre-Raphaelite principles and own reputation with banquet scene from Keats's *Isabella* (1849), *Christ in the House of His Parents* (1850), which drew upon him a storm of abuse because of its unconventionality, *The Return of the Dove to the Ark* and *Mariana of the Moated Grange* (1851), *The Huguenot* and *Ophelia* (1852), *The Proscribed Royalist* and *The Order of Release* (1853). Works of transitional period included *The Blind Girl, Autumn Leaves,* and *Peace Concluded* (1856), *Sir Isumbras at the Ford* and *The Escape of a Heretic* (1857), *Apple Blossoms* and *The Vale of Rest* (1859), *The Black Brunswicker* (1860). Illustrated Trollope's works (1860–69) and Tennyson's poems; exhibited *The Eve of St. Agnes* (1863), *Jephthah* (1867), *Rosalind and Celia* (1868). Developed greater individuality and breadth and brilliant coloring of his mature phase (from 1870), as in *The Boyhood of Raleigh* (1870), *Chill October* (1870). Turned to portraits, landscapes, and figures; painted portraits of Gladstone, Lord Beaconsfield, Wilkie Collins, Carlyle, John Bright, Irving, Tennyson.

Millar, Kenneth. See Ross MACDONALD. .

Mil·lar·det \mē-yȧr-de\, Alexis, *in full* Pierre-Marie-Alexis. 1838–1902. French botanist. Professor, Strasbourg (1869–72), Nancy (1872–76), Bordeaux (1876–99); originated plan of hybridization of French and American grapevines to combat Phylloxera infestation; developed (1885) Bordeaux mixture, first successful fungicide.

Mil·lay \mil-'ā\, Edna St. Vincent. 1892–1950. American poet, b. Rockland, Me. Author of volumes of verse as *Renascence and Other Poems* (1917), *A Few Figs from Thistles* (1920), *Second April* (1921), *The Harp Weaver and Other Poems* (1923, Pulitzer prize), *The Buck in the Snow* (1928), *Wine from these Grapes* (1934), *Conversation at Midnight* (1937), *Huntsman, What Quarry?* (1939), *There Are No Islands, Any More* (1940), *Mine the Harvest* (1954); plays *Aria da Capo* (1919), *The Lamp and the Bell* (1921), *Two Slatterns and a King* (1921); libretto for *The King's Henchman,* opera composed by Deems Taylor (produced 1927).

Mil·ler \'mil-ər\, Alice, *nee* Duer \'d(y)ů(ə)r\. 1874–1942. American novelist, b. New York City. m. Henry W. Miller (1899). Author of *The Modern Obstacle* (1903), *The Blue Arch* (1910), *Are Women People?* (satirical verse, 1915), *Come Out of the Kitchen* (1916), *The Charm School* (1919), *The Beauty and the Bolshevist* (1920), *Priceless Pearl* (1924), *Reluctant Duchess* (1925), *Forsaking All Others* (1930), *Gowns by Roberta* (1931), *Death Sentence* (1934), *The White Cliffs* (narrative poem, 1940), etc.

Miller, Cincinnatus Hiner *or* Heine. *Pen name* Joaquin Miller. 1837–1913. American poet, b. Liberty, Ind. Led adventurous life in California mining camps, among Digger Indians, with horse thieves (1856–59); adm. to bar, Portland, Ore. (1861); edited newspaper in Eugene, Ore. (1863), which was suppressed because of his Confederate sympathies. Published two volumes of poetry, *Specimens* (1868) and *Joaquin et al* (1869); visited England (1871) and published *Pacific Poems* and *Songs of the Sierras* (1871); attracted attention in literary circles both by his verse and by his western attire and manners; subsequently published *Songs of the Sunlands* (1873), *Life Among the Modocs* (1873), *The Ship in the Desert* (1875), *The Baroness of New York* (1877), *Songs of Italy* (1878), *Shadows of Shasta* (1881), etc.

Miller, David Hunter. 1875–1961. American lawyer, b. New York City. Legal adviser to American commission at Paris Peace Conference (1919); collaborated in drawing up final draft of Covenant of the League of Nations; with U.S. Dept. of State (1929–44). Author of *My Diary at the Conference of Paris, with Documents* (21 vols., 1924–26), *The Drafting of Covenant* (1928), *Treaties and Other International Acts of the United States* (1931–48).

Miller, Ferdinand von. 1813–1887. German bronze founder. Director of Royal Foundry, Munich (from 1844); among works cast there was the bronze door of the Capitol at Washington. His son and pupil ¶Ferdinand (1842–1929), cast statues of Humboldt, Shakespeare, and Columbus for St. Louis, figures for a fountain at Cincinnati, statues of a soldier for Soldiers' Monument, Charleston, S.C., and of William I at Metz (1892), etc. Another son ¶Oskar (1855–1934), electrical engineer; organized first German electrical exposition, Munich (1882); cofounder (with Rathenau) and director of German Edison Co., from which developed Allgemeine Elektrizitäts-Gesellschaft (A.E.G.), or General Electric Co., and Berlin Electrical Works (1883–90); president and technical director of International Electrical Engineering Exhibition at Frankfurt; contributed to development of high-tension electric power transmission.

Miller, Glenn. 1904–1944. American bandleader, b. Clarinda, Iowa. Trombonist with dance bands including those of Ben Pollack (1926), Dorsey brothers (1934), Ray Noble (1935); organized orchestra (1938) that became one of most popular "Big Bands" playing swing dance music; hits, all with characteristic arrangements, included "In the Mood," "Moonlight Serenade," "Sunrise Serenade," "Tuxedo Junction," "Chattanooga Choo-Choo." Leader of U.S. Army Air Force band in Europe (1944); disappeared in flight from England to Paris.

Miller, Harriet, *nee* Mann \'man\. *Pen name* Olive Thorne Miller. 1831–1918. American ornithologist, b. Auburn, N.Y. m. Watts T. Miller (1854; d. 1904). Writer esp. of children's books on birds, as *Little Folks in Feathers and Fur, and Others in Neither* (1875), *Bird-Ways* (1885), *The Bird Our Brother* (1908), *The Children's Book of Birds* (1915), etc.

Miller, Henry John. 1860–1926. American actor and director, b. London, England. To Canada as a boy; leading man at Charles Frohman's Empire Theatre, New York City (1890–96); great success in *The Only Way* (1899); producer-director of Princess Theatre (1906–18), scoring success with W.V. Moody's *The Great Divide* (1906), *Servant in the House* (1908), *Faith Healer* (1910); manager of Henry Miller Theatre (1918–26).

Miller, Henry Valentine. 1891–1980. American author, b. New York City. Author of autobiographical novels notable for sexual candor and concern for self-realization, including *Tropic of Cancer* (1934), *Tropic of Capricorn* (1939), both long banned in U.S., *The Colossus of Maroussi* (1941), *Air-Conditioned Nightmare* (1945), *Rosy Crucifixion* trilogy comprising *Sexus* (1949), *Plexus* (1953), *Nexus* (1959); also essays *The Cosmological Eye* (1939), *Wisdom of the Heart* (1941), *Big Sur and the Oranges of Hieronymus Bosch* (1956).

Miller, Hugh. 1802–1856. Scottish geologist and man of letters. Accountant in bank at Cromarty; contributed to Mackay Wilson's *Tales of the Borders;* wrote *Scenes and Legends in the North of Scotland* (1835); editor of *The Witness,* organ of nonintrusionists (1840–56), in which he began geological articles collected as *The Old Red Sandstone* (1841). Presented anti-evolutionary interpretation of fossil record. Pioneer in popularizing of geology by means of chief works *Footprints of the Creator* (1847), *The Testimony of the Rocks* (1857), *Sketch Book of Popular Geology* (1859); wrote *First Impressions of England and its People* (1846) and *My Schools and Schoolmasters* (1854).

Miller, Joaquin. See Cincinnatus MILLER.

Miller, Johann Martin. 1750–1814. German novelist and poet. Clergyman and schoolmaster in Ulm. Works included *Siegwart, eine Klostergeschichte* (1776), imitation of Goethe's *Werther,* and volume of lyric poems *Gedichte* (1783), containing "Was frag ich viel nach Geld und Gut."

Miller, John Preston. 1923–1961. American geologist, b. Smithville, Mo. With U.S. Atomic Energy Commission, Los Alamos, N.M. (1943–46); professor, Penn. State U. (1950–54), Harvard (1954–61); known for studies of stream channels, chemistry of weathering, sediment transport.

Miller, Joseph *or* Josias, *commonly* Joe. 1684–1738. English comedian. Member of Drury Lane company (from 1709); a favorite as Trinculo in *The Tempest,* First Gravedigger in *Hamlet,* Marplot in *The Busybody.* His name unwarrantably used after his death in title *Joe Miller's Jest-book, or The Wit's Vade Mecum* (by John Mottley; pub. 1739), collection of coarse jests, only three of which are told of Miller.

Miller, Leonard. See Leonard MERRICK.

Miller, Max. 1901–1967. American writer, b. Traverse City, Mich. Author of *I Cover the Waterfront* (1932), *The Man on the Barge* (1935), *Fog and Men on Bering Sea* (1936), *Mexico Around Me* (1937), *Reno* (1941), *Land Where Time Stands Still* (1943), *It's Tomorrow Out Here* (1945), *No Matter What Happens* (1949), *Cruise of the Cow* (1952), *Holladay Street* (1962), etc.

Miller, Olive Thorne. See Harriet MILLER.

Miller, Oskar von. See under Ferdinand von MILLER.

Miller, Patrick. 1731–1815. Scottish inventor. Conducted experiments with steamboat (1788–89); credited by some with invention of steamboat.

Miller, Perry Gilbert Eddy. 1905–1963. American scholar, b. Chicago. At Harvard U. (1931–63); wrote *The New England Mind* (1939), *Roger Williams* (1953), *Consciousness in Concord* (1958), etc.

Miller, Samuel Freeman. 1816–1890. American jurist, b. Richmond, Ky. Practiced law, Keokuk, Iowa (1850–62); associate justice, U.S. Supreme Court (1862–90); first construed 14th Amendment in Slaughterhouse Cases (1873).

Miller, William. 1782–1849. American religious leader, b. Pittsfield, Mass. In study of biblical prophetic books, believed he discovered that Christ was to return to earth about 1843; lectured and preached on the Second Coming of Christ (from 1831); published *Evidence from Scripture and History of the Second Coming of Christ, about the Year 1843* (1836). His followers, known as Millerites, or Adventists, prepared for Christ's coming, both in 1843 and 1844; following the "Great Disappointment" Millerites organized Advent Christian church (1860), Seventh-Day Adventists (1863), etc.

Miller, William. 1810–1872. Scottish poet. Made reputation by contributions of songs in *Whistle Binkie* (1832–53); author of "Wee Willie Winkie" and other nursery lyrics.

Mil·le·rand \mē-rä^{n}\, Alexandre. 1859–1943. French politician. Proprietor and editor of Socialist journals (1883–98); elected as Radical Socialist to Chamber of Deputies (1885–1920); minister of commerce (1899–1902), of public works (1909–10), of war (1912–13, 1914–15); commissioner general of Alsace (1919–20); prime minister (1920); elected president of France (1920–24); forced to resign by parties of the left; senator (1925–40).

Mil·les \'mel-əs\, Carl, *in full* Vilhelm Carl Emil. *Orig. surname* An·ders·son \'än-dər-sȯn\. 1875–1955. American sculptor, b. Uppsala, Sweden. Professor at Stockholm Art Acad. (1920–31), Cranbrook Acad., Mich. (1931 ff.); naturalized U.S. citizen (1945). Works included colossal Sten Sture monument near Uppsala (1925), statue of Gustav Vasa, *Playing Bears* groups in granite for Berzelius Park, Stockholm, *Europa* fountain in Halmstad (1926), *Poseidon* fountain in front of Göteborg museum, *Orpheus* fountain in Stockholm (1936), *Meeting of the Waters* fountain, St. Louis (1940).

Mil·let \mē-ye, -le, *Angl* mē-'yā, mi-'lā\, Jean-François. *Often called* Fran·cisque \frä^{n}-sēsk\. c.1642–1679. French painter, b. Antwerp. Settled in Paris (1660); painted Italian and Arcadian landscapes in imitation of Poussin.

Millet, Jean-François. 1814–1875. French painter. Lived alternately in Normandy and Paris (1840 ff.) and painted religious, classical, and esp. peasant subjects; settled in Barbizon (1849), joined Fontainebleau group of landscape artists; intimate friend of Rousseau. Works included *The Winnower, The Sower, The Water Carrier, The Binders, The Shepherdess, The Gleaners, The Angelus, Spring, Harvesters Resting, Shepherdess Seated, Planting Potatoes, Breaking the Flax, Man with the Hoe, Woman Feeding Chickens, Death and the Woodcutter.* His brother ¶Jean-Baptiste (1831–1906), sculptor and painter, produced watercolors and landscapes of Fontainebleau and environs of Paris and sculptures at Notre Dame de Paris and Madeleine de Vézelay.

Mil·li·kan \'mil-i-kən\, Robert Andrews. 1868–1953. American physicist, b. Morrison, Ill. Taught at U. of Chicago (1896–1921; professor from 1910); director, Norman Bridge Laboratory of Physics, Calif. Inst. Tech. (from 1921). First to isolate the electron and measure its charge (1911); investigated cosmic rays, absorption of X-rays, Brownian movement in gases; verified Einstein's photoelectric equation; obtained precise value for Planck's constant. Received 1923 Nobel prize for physics. Author of textbooks and *The Electron* (1917), *Evolution in Science and Religion* (1927), *Science and the New Civilization* (1930), *Time, Matter, and Value* (1932), *Protons, Photons, Neutrons and Cosmic Rays* (1935), etc.

Mil·lin \'mil-ən\, Sarah Gertrude, *nee* Lieb·son \'lēb-sən\. 1889–1968. South African writer, b. Lithuania. To South Africa as infant; m. (1912; d. 1952) Philip Millin. Author of *Rhodes, a Life* (1933), *General Smuts* (1936), and novels including *The Dark River* (1920), *God's Stepchildren* (1924), *Mary Glenn* (1925), *The Coming of the Lord* (1928), *What Hath a Man?* (1938), etc.

Mil·lis \'mil-əs\, Harry Alvin. 1873–1948. American economist, b. Paoli, Ind. Professor (1916) and head of economics department, U. of Chicago (1928–38); noted for studies of taxation, industrial relations; member of first National Labor Relations Board (1934–35), its chairman (1940–45).

Mil·löck·er \'mil-œk-ər\, Karl. 1842–1899. Austrian composer. Conductor at Theater an der Wien, Vienna (1869–83). Composed popular operettas as *Das verwunschene Schloss* (1878), *Apajune der Wassermann* (1880), *Der Bettelstudent* (1882), *Der Feldprediger* (1884), *Der arme Jonathan* (1890), *Der Probekuss* (1894).

Mills \'milz\, Bertram Wagstaff. 1873–1938. English circus proprietor. Produced (1920–37) annual Christmas circus show at Olympia, London; formed (1929) touring tent circus.

Mills, Charles Wright. 1916–1962. American sociologist, b. Waco, Tex. Professor, Columbia U. (1946–62). Author of *The New Man of Power* (1948), *White Collar* (1951), *The Power Elite* (1956), *Causes of World War Three* (1958), *Sociological Imagination* (1959), *Images of Man* (1960), *The Marxists* (1962).

Mills, Clark. 1815–1883. American sculptor and bronze founder, b. Onondaga Co., N.Y. Executed bronze equestrian statue of Andrew Jackson, the first large bronze statue cast in U.S., dedicated (1853) in Lafayette Square, Washington, D.C.; cast (1863) Thomas Crawford's *Liberty* for Capitol dome; executed portrait busts of Calhoun and Washington.

Mills, Robert. 1781–1855. American architect and engineer, b. Charleston, S.C. Studied under James Hoban, Thomas Jefferson, Benjamin Latrobe; considered first professional architect in U.S.; architect of public buildings, Washington (1836–51); designed the Treasury building, General Post Office, Patent Office building, Washington Monument.

Mills, Sir William. 1856–1932. English inventor. Pioneer in researches on alloys; invented (1915) Mills hand grenade.

Mills, William Corless. 1860–1928. American archaeologist, b. Pyrmont, Ohio. Curator and librarian of Ohio State Archaeological and Historical Society (1898–1928); curator of Ohio State U. Museum (1899–1928); known for excavations of Indian burial grounds in Ohio, esp. the Adena Mound (1901). Author of *Certain Mounds and Village Sites in Ohio* (1907–22), *Archaeological Atlas of Ohio* (1914).

Mil·man \'mil-mən\, Henry Hart. 1791–1868. English clergyman and historian. Professor of poetry, Oxford (1821–31); dean of St. Paul's (1849). Edited (1838) Gibbon's *Decline and Fall of the Roman Empire;* known chiefly for historical works, including *History of the Jews* (1829), *History of Christianity* (1840), and *History of Latin Christianity* (1854–55).

Milne \'mil(n)\, Alan Alexander. 1882–1956. English poet and playwright. Author of plays, including *Make-Believe* (1918), *Mr. Pim Passes By* (1919), *The Romantic Age* (1920), *The Truth about Blayds* (1921), *The Dover Road* (1922), *Ariadne* (1925), *Michael and Mary* (1930), *Toad of Toad Hall* (1930), *Miss Elizabeth Bennet* (1936), *Gentleman Unknown* (1938); of detective novel *The Red House Mystery* (1922); and esp. of the series of juveniles (verse and prose) *When We Were Very Young* (1924), *Winnie-the-Pooh* (1926), *Now We Are Six* (1927), and *The House at Pooh Corner* (1928).

Milne, Edward Arthur. 1896–1950. English astronomer. Professor of mathematics, Manchester (1924–28), Oxford (from 1928); known for studies of stellar composition and dynamics and for development of theory of kinematic relativity. Author of *Thermodynamics of the Stars* (1930), *The White Dwarf Stars* (1932), *Relativity, Gravitation, and World-Structure* (1935), *Kinematic Relativity* (1948).

Milne, John. 1850–1913. English mining engineer and seismologist. Engineer in Labrador, Newfoundland; professor of geology, Imperial Coll. of Engineering, Tokyo (1875–94); invented (1880) seismograph; returned to England (1894); instrumental in establishing seismological stations throughout world. Author of *Earthquakes* (1883), *Seismology* (1898).

Milne-Ed·wards \mēl-nā-dwȧrs, *Angl* miln-'ed-wərds\, Henri. 1800–1885. French zoologist. Professor, École Centrale des Arts et Manufactures (1832), Muséum d'Histoire Naturelle (1841 ff.), Sorbonne (1843 ff.); studied physiological division of labor in the economy of organisms; worked esp. on mollusks, crustaceans, and anthozoans. Author of *Histoire naturelle des crustacés* (1834–40), *Leçons sur la physiologie et l'anatomie comparée de l'homme et des animaux* (1857–81), *Introduction à la zoologie générale* (1858), etc.

Mil·ner \'mil-nər\, Alfred. 1st Viscount Milner. 1854–1925. British colonial administrator, b. Hesse-Darmstadt. On staff of *Pall Mall Gazette* (1881–85); private secretary to the chancellor of the exchequer (1886–89); undersecretary for finance in Egypt (1890–92); governor of Cape of Good Hope (1897–1901), notable for intransigent attitude toward Boers; demanded, after conference with Kruger at Bloemfontein (1899), enfranchisement of British settlers; administrator (1901–02) and governor (1902–05) of the Transvaal and Orange River colonies; also, high commissioner for South Africa (1897–1905). Created baron (1901) and viscount (1902). Member of War Cabinet (1916–18); secretary for war (1918–19); colonial secretary (1919–21); recommended Egyptian independence (1921).

Milner, John. 1752–1826. English clergyman and controversialist. Ordained (1777); established at Winchester refugee Benedictine nuns from Belgium; obtained substitution of oath not contrary to Roman Catholic doctrine in Pitt's Catholic relief bill (1791); titular bishop of Castabala (1803); opposed crown's claim of veto power over appointment of Roman Catholic bishops. Author of *Antiquities of Winchester* (1798–1801), *The End of Religious Controversy* (1818).

Milner-Gibson, Thomas. See GIBSON.

Milnes \'mil(n)z\, Richard Monckton. 1st Baron Hough·ton \'hau̇t-ən\. 1809–1885. English man of letters. At Cambridge, a leader in the Union and member of Apostles Club, with Tennyson, Hallam, and Thackeray. M.P. (1837–63); interested in copyright legislation; advocated penny banks; left Peel's party on account of corn-law controversy; made peer (1863); championed Oxford Movement, oppressed nationalities, and slaves. Remembered as a patron of young writers: secured laureateship for Tennyson; helped to make Emerson known to Britons; one of first to recognize Swinburne's gifts and Keats as of first rank. Author of volumes of graceful verse and *Life of Keats* (1848).

Mi·lo \'mī-(,)lō\ *or* **Mi·lon** \'mī-,län\. 6th century B.C. Greek athlete of Crotona. Renowned for his strength; victor in wrestling six times at Olympic games and six times at Pythian games.

Milo, Titus Annius Papianus. 95–48 B.C. Roman politician. Tribune of the people (57); praetor (55); his bitter rivalry with Publius Clodius culminated in murder of Clodius by Milo's followers; tried for murder, found guilty, and condemned to exile; killed in action near Thurii, southern Italy.

Mi·lo·ra·do·vich \myi-(,)lə-'rä-də-vyich\, Mikhail Andreyevich. 1771–1825. Russian general. Distinguished himself under Suvorov in Italy and Switzerland (1799); general of division at Austerlitz (1805); captured Bucharest (1806), defeated Turks on Danube (1807); engaged at Borodino (1812) and Lützen (1813); governor of St. Petersburg (1818–25); killed while attempting to crush Decembrist uprising.

Mi·loš \'mē-lōsh\. *In full* Miloš I Ob·re·no·vić \-ō-bren-'ō-vēt^y\. *Orig.* Miloš Te·o·do·ro·vić \-tā-ōd-ór-'ō-vēt^y\. 1780–1860. Prince of Serbia (1815–39, 1858–60). A peasant; joined rebels under Karageorge (1804); turned against Karageorge (1813), cooperated with Turks; led Serbian war of liberation (1815) and won Turkish recognition as prince; proclaimed hereditary prince (1817); secured full Serbian autonomy (1830); abdicated (1839); succeeded (1839) by son Milan (who died same year), then by another son, Michael; deposed Alexander Karageorgevič (1858); regarded as creator of modern Serbia.

Mi·lo·slav·ska·ya \myil-(,)ə-'sláf-skə-yə\, Mariya Ilinichna. d. between 1666 and 1671. Russian czarina. First wife of Czar Alexis; at her death her relatives formed a political faction that dominated reign of her son Fyodor and regency of daughter Sophia.

Mi·lo·va·no·vić \,mē-lō-'vä-nō-vēt^y, *Angl* -vich\, Milovan. 1863–1912. Serbian jurist and politician. Professor, Belgrade; drafted liberal constitution (1888); minister of justice (1896); minister of foreign affairs (1908–11); premier of Serbia (1911–12); initiated negotiations for formation of a Balkan league.

Mil·ti·a·des \mil-'tī-ə-,dēz\. Saint. *Also* Mel·chi·a·des \mel-'kī-ə-,dēz\. d. 314. Pope (310 or 311–314). Persecution of Christians ended during his pontificate, following Constantine the Great's defeat of Maxentius (312); condemned Donatists (313).

Miltiades. *Called* the Elder. 6th century B.C. Athenian politician. Opponent of tyrant Peisistratus; founded Athenian colony in the Thracian Chersonese.

Miltiades. *Called* the Younger. c.554–?489 B.C. Athenian general. Nephew of Miltiades the Elder; archon (524–523); inherited Chersonese dominion of uncle; established there as tyrant (c.516); became vassal of Darius I and served in his Scythian expedition (513); supported Ionian revolt against Darius (499) and at that time seized Lemnos and Imbros; fled to Athens (494); impeached for earlier tyranny, acquitted (493). One of 10 generals of Athenian land forces (from 493); argued for and commanded successful attack on Persian invasion force at Marathon (490); led unsuccessful naval expedition to reassert control of Aegean (489); died of wound.

Mil·tiz *or* **Mil·titz** \'mil-tits\, Karl von. 1490–1529. German ecclesiastic. Papal chamberlain and notary (1515); presented golden rose to Prince Frederick the Wise of Saxony (1518); conferred with Luther in Saxony on matter of indulgences (1519–20).

Mil·ton \'milt-ᵊn\, John. 1608–1674. English poet. Noted as Latin poet and orator while at Christ's Coll., Cambridge; wrote first English poem on death of sister's first child, "On the Death of a fair Infant" (1626); wrote at university ode "On the Morning of Christ's Nativity" (1629), sonnet to Shakespeare (1630), the companion poems "L'Allegro" and "Il Penseroso" (1631). Having given up idea of entering the church, devoted himself to study of classics at father's home (1632–38), where he wrote "Arcades" (1633), *Comus* (a masque, 1634; pub. 1637), and the elegy "Lycidas" (1637; pub. 1638); traveled in France and Italy (1638–39). Settled in London as tutor to his nephews Edward and John Phillips; published series of pamphlets against episcopacy, including *Of Reformation Touching Church Discipline in England* (1641), *The Reason of Church-government Urg'd against Prelaty* (1642), and his replies to Bishop Hall, and in defense of Smectymnuus (*q.v.*). Married (1642) Mary Powell, daughter of Oxfordshire Cavalier, a girl of seventeen, who returned to her father's house after a month, became reconciled (1645), died (1652). Published pamphlets relating to divorce, including *The Doctrine and Discipline of Divorce* (1643) and *Tetrachordon: The Four Chief Places of Scripture Which Treat of Marriage* (1645), which provoked enmity of Presbyterians and threat of prosecution by parliamentary committee; replied to this threat in his most famous prose work, *Areopagitica* (1644), on liberty of the press; published *Tractate of Education* (1644) and defended execution of Charles in *The Tenure of Kings and Magistrates* (1649); Latin (or foreign) secretary to Council of State (1649); officially replied to Dr. Gauden's *Eikon Basilike* in *Eikonoklastes* (1649) and to Salmasius in *Pro Populo Anglicano Defensio* (1650). Having become blind (1652), was assisted in official duties by Andrew Marvell until Restoration; published 2d *Defensio* (1654); in this period composed sonnets on massacre of Vaudois in Piedmont, on his blindness, to Fairfax, to Cromwell, also Greek and Latin poems. At Restoration, lost greater part of fortune but, through intercession of Marvell and perhaps Davenant, was included in amnesty; bitterly disappointed in republican principles. Completed, by dictation to an amanuensis, long-contemplated blank verse epic on the fall of man, *Paradise Lost* (completed by 1665, pub. 1667 in 10 books; enlarged to 12 books, 1674), of which 1300 copies were sold in 18 months. Published (1671) *Paradise Regained,* written at suggestion of Thomas Ellwood, and the lyrical drama *Samson Agonistes,* lamenting his own old age and his nation's apostasy.

Mi·lyu·kov \myil-yü-'kóf\, Pavel Nikolayevich. 1859–1943. Russian politician and historian. Taught at Moscow U. (to 1895); a leader of liberal sentiment; a founder (1905) of Kadet or Constitutional Democratic party; aided in drafting Vyborg Manifesto (1906); member of 3d and 4th Dumas (1907–17) and a leader of opposition groups; minister of foreign affairs in Prince Lvov's provisional government (1917); fled after Bolshevik revolution; settled in Paris after the peace (1919). Works included *Ocherk: po istorii russkoy kultury* (1896–1903).

Mi·lyu·tin \myil-'yü-tyin\, Dmitry Alekseyevich. Count. 1816–1912. Russian general. As minister of war (1861–81), put into effect program for army reform and reorganization; created field marshal (1888). Author of *Istoriya voyny Rossi s Frantsiyey* (1852–53). His brother ¶Nikolay Alekseyevich (1818–1872) assisted Alexander II in introducing important administrative reforms and in effecting emancipation of the serfs; secretary of state for Poland (1866–68).

Mim·ner·mus \mim-'nər-məs\. fl. c.630 B.C. Greek elegiac poet of Colophon. Only fragments of his works are extant.

Mina, Francisco Espoz y. See ESPOZ Y MINA.

Mi·na·mo·to \mē-nä-mō-tō\. *Also known, esp. contemporaneously, by Chinese name* Gen·ji \gen-jē\. A Japanese military feudal family, whose shoguns were in power 1192–1219. The family originated with younger princes of an emperor of 9th century A.D. Prominent members included: Minamoto Yorinobu (968–1048); hired (1028) by Fujiwara family to quell rebellion in Eastern Japan; his success (1031) added greatly to family's power and influence. ¶Yoriyoshi (988–1075) helped quell Ainu rebellions and for government fought Earlier Nine Years' War (1051–62), suppressing rebellion of Abe clan in northern Japan; established Minamoto power in Honshu. His son ¶Yoshiie (1039–1106) fought in Earlier Nine Years' War, earning nickname Ha·chi-man-Ta·rō \häch-ē-män-tär-ō\, *i.e.* firstborn of the God of War; defeated rival Kiyowara family in series of battles (1083–87) and established absolute rule of Minamotos in north; unrivalled as military leader, noted for ferocity; revered by later generations of the family.

¶Minamoto Tameyoshi (1096–1156) became head of Seiwa branch of family in Kantō region; supported Sutoku in attempted coup d'état against Emperor Shirakawa II (1156); in ensuing Hōgen War, defeated by son Yoshitomo; executed. His son ¶Yoshitomo (1123–1160) supported Kiyomori, leader of Taira clan, in war on insurper Sutoku; defeated father but refused order to kill him, whereupon another Minamoto officer did so; attempted to overthrow Kiyomori in Heiji War (1159); defeated, escaped, killed by disloyal retainer. Yoshitomo's son ¶Yoritomo (1147–1199) was banished after father's defeat and held in confinement (1159–79); formed political alliance with Hōjō Tokimasa and married his daughter (1180); joined and quickly became principal in rebellion against rule of Taira Kiyomori (1180), rallying much of Minamoto clan and many disgruntled Taira and establishing himself at Kamakura; at invitation of emperor, crushed revolt of cousin Minamoto Yoshinaka (1183) and thereby secured position in Kyōto; established military and civil government independent of Taira; aided by brother Yoshitsune, defeated Taira (1184–85); expelled and later eliminated Yoshitsune; built system of provincial administrators independent of local and imperial government and created thereby a parallel feudal system; on death of Emperor Shirakawa II (1192) proclaimed himself supreme commander, thus establishing shogunate, or *Bakufu.*

His brother ¶Yoshitsune (1159–1189) was reared in monastery after being spared execution by Taira Kiyomori; joined brother (1174) and became invaluable military leader in revolt against Kiyomori; defeated revolt of cousin Yoshinaka (1183), occupied Kyōto; defeated Taira forces (1184–85); became favorite of emperor and incurred brother's enmity; attempted to rebel but defeated and forced to flee; wandered incognito for some years, hunted by Yoritomo's agents; betrayed by a friend, committed suicide.

Minchō. See KICHIZAN Minchō.

Min·dau·gas \min-'daú-gäs\. *Also called* Min·do·ve \min-dó-va\ *or* Men·dovg \men-'dóvg\. d. 1263. Lithuanian ruler. Established authority over other nobles and chiefs (1236) and created Lithuanian state; accepted baptism from Livonian Knights (1250 or 1251); received royal crown from Pope Innocent IV (1253); expanded domain eastward into Russian lands, helping thereby to check Mongol expansion westward; murdered by Samogitian rivals.

Min·don Min \'mēn-dón-'mēn\. 1814–1878. King of Burma (1853–78). Succeeded brother Pagan Min; negotiated end of Second Anglo–Burmese War; forced to cede Pegu; ceded commercial privileges in Upper Burma (1867). Instituted reforms in tax assessment, government salaries, etc.; fixed weights and measures; first Burmese king to issue coinage. Built new capitol at Mandalay (1857) and fostered golden age of Burmese art and religion.

Mind·szen·ty \mēⁿ(n)d-'shen-tē\, József. *Orig.* József Pehm \'pām\. 1892–1975. Hungarian prelate. Ordained (1915); a leader of opposition to totalitarian government; bishop of Veszprém (1944); primate of Hungary and archbishop of Esztergom (1945); cardinal (1946); for refusing to permit secularization of Catholic schools by Communist regime, arrested (1948), convicted (1949) of treason, and given life sentence; freed during uprising of 1956; given asylum in U.S. embassy, Budapest (1956–71); consented to leave Hungary (1971), settling in Vienna; retired as primate and archbishop (1974).

Mi·ner \'mī-nər\, John Thomas, *called* Jack. 1865–1944. Canadian naturalist, b. Dover Centre, Ohio. To Ontario (1878); established (1904) bird sanctuary on his farm in Kingsville and conducted studies of migratory birds; his friends founded (1931) Jack Miner Migratory Bird Foundation to carry on his work. Author of *Jack Miner and the Birds* (1934), etc.

Ming \'miŋ\. A Chinese dynasty (1368–1644), founded by Chu Yüan-chang, successor to the Yüan dynasty, that extended Chinese rule into Korea, Mongolia, Turkistan, Vietnam, and Burma; noted for its civil service system, high level of culture and art, esp. bronze vases and porcelain, and a stable but autocratic government; dynasty weakened by factionalism among civil officials, growing power of palace eunuchs, and a succession of weak and inattentive rulers; dynasty overthrown by Manchu tribesmen who established the Ch'ing dynasty. For its emperors, see the CHU family.

Min·ghet·ti \mēŋ-'gät-tē\, Marco. 1818–1886. Italian politician and scholar. Member of government of Roman Republic (1847); served in Piedmontese army under Charles Albert; under Cavour served as minister of exterior (1860–61), interior (1861–62), finance (1862–63), agriculture and commerce (1869); premier (1863–64, 1873–76); ambassador to London (1868) and Vienna (1870–73). Among his works were *Dell'economia pubblica* (1859), *Stato e chiesa* (1878), a biography of Raphael (1885).

Ming Huang. See Li Lung-chi under LI family.

Ming Ti. See Liu Chuang under LIU family.

Min·gus \'miŋ-gəs\, Charles. 1922–1979. American musician, b. Nogales, Ariz. Played in bands of Louis Armstrong (1941–43), Kid Ory (1943–46), Lionel Hampton (1946–48); later associated with Charlie Parker, Art Tatum, Stan Getz, Bud Powell, etc.; known as virtuoso bassist and, from mid-1950's, as jazz composer of remarkable breadth in experimental, expressionistic vein. Author of autobiography *Beneath the Underdog* (1971).

Minh Mang \'min-'mäŋ\. *Orig.* Ngu·yen Phuoc Chi Dam \'nī-en-'pwȯk-'kē-'däm\. 1792–1841. Vietnamese ruler. Son of Emperor Gia Long; succeeded as emperor of Annam (1820); persecuted Christian missionaries (from 1825) and, following Saigon revolt (1833), Christians generally; discouraged Western trade; largely prepared ground for French invasion (1858).

Mi·nié \mēn-yā, *Angl* 'min-ē-,ā\, Claude-Étienne. 1804–1879. French army officer. Invented (1849) conical-pointed cylindrical bullet (the Minié ball) for use in muzzle-loading rifles.

Minikh. See MÜNNICH.

Min·kow·ski \miŋ-'kȯf-skē\, Hermann. 1864–1909. German mathematician, b. Russia. Professor, Königsberg (1894), Zürich (1896), Göttingen (1902). Made studies in field of theory of numbers; credited with laying mathematical foundation for theory of relativity. Author of *Geometrie der Zahlen* (1896), *Diophantische Approximationen* (1907), *Raum und Zeit* (1907) and *Zwei Abhandlungen über die Grundgleichungen der Elektrodynamik* (1909).

Minkowski, Oskar. 1858–1931. German physiologist, b. Lithuania. Brother of Hermann Minkowski. Professor, Strassburg (1891–1904), Cologne (1904), Greifswald (1905–09), Breslau (1909–26); studied diabetes; discovered cause and treatment of diabetic acidosis (1884); with Joseph von Mering showed (1889) that pancreas produces anti-diabetic substance.

Min·naert \'min-ärt\, Marcel Gilles Jozef. 1893–1970. Belgian astronomer and physicist. Director (1937–63), Sonnenborgh Observatory, Utrecht; studied solar spectrophotometry. With assistants prepared standard *Photometric Atlas of the Solar Spectrum* (1940). Also author of *De Natuurkunde van het vrije veld* (1937–42), *De sterrekunde en de mensheid* (1946), etc.

Min·nel·li \mə-'nel-ē\, Vincente. 1913–1986. American film director, b. Chicago. Noted for his direction of classic Hollywood musicals including *Cabin in the Sky* (1943), *Meet Me in St. Louis* (1944), *The Pirate* (1948), *An American in Paris* (1951), *The Band Wagon* (1953), and *Gigi* (1958, Academy Award); also directed nonmusical films as *The Clock* (1945), *Father of the Bride* (1950), *The Bad and the Beautiful* (1952), and *Lust for Life* (1956); m. (1945) singer-actress Judy Garland; directed their daughter Liza Minnelli in *A Matter of Time* (1976).

Minnewit, Peter. See Peter MINUIT.

Min-ning \'min-'niŋ\. *Reign title* Tao-kuang \'daů-'gwäŋ\. *Temple name* Hsüan Tsung \shue-'änd-'zůŋ\. *Posthumous name* Ch'eng Huang-ti \'chəŋ-'hwäŋ-dē\. 1782–1850. Chinese emperor (1821–50), sixth of the Ch'ing dynasty. Son of Yung-yen; unsuccessful in attempts to prevent dynastic decline; attempted to stop opium trade by Western merchants, resulting in first Opium War with Great Britain (1839–42); ceded Hong Kong to Great Britain (1842).

Mi·no·be \mē-nō-be\ Tatsukichi. 1873–1948. Japanese jurist. Professor of law, Tokyo U. (c.1900–32); developed theory that emperor is highest organ of the state rather than divine embodiment of state and is thus subject to law; held that sovereignty resides ultimately in the people; his views attacked by nationalists and his books banned; member of House of Peers (1932–35).

Mi·no da Fie·so·le \'mē-nō-dä-fyā-'zō-lā\. 1430–1484. Italian sculptor. Probably pupil of Desiderio da Settignano; worked in Rome (1454, 1463, 1473–80), often with Andrea Bregno. Carved many monuments, altars, reliefs, and tabernacles; worked with Giovanni Dalmata on tomb of Pope Paul II in St. Peter's; known esp. for portrait busts.

Mi·no·mu·ra \mē-nō-mủr-ä\ Rizaemon. 1821–1877. Japanese businessman. Joined Mitsui brokerage firm, rising to leadership of it; built Mitsui into largest banking firm in Japan; branched into other businesses as well, creating the largest of the *zaibatsu*, or industrial combines.

Mi·not \'mī-nət\, George Richards. 1885–1950. American physician, b. Boston. Associated with Massachusetts General Hospital (1912–13, 1915–23), Huntington and Peter Bent Brigham hospitals (1923–28); professor of medicine, Harvard (1928–48); developed raw-liver diet for treatment of pernicious anemia (1926); later helped develop liver extract. Awarded, jointly with William P. Murphy and George H. Whipple, Nobel prize for physiology or medicine (1934) for researches on liver treatment of the anemias.

Minot, Laurence. 1300?–?1352. English poet. Author of 11 spirited war songs celebrating battle of Halidon Hill (1333), capture of Berwick, battle of Crécy, siege of Calais, and other triumphs of Edward III (first pub. 1795).

Min·sheu \'min-shü\, John. fl. 1617. English lexicographer. Teacher of languages in London; published *Guide into Tongues,* a lexicon with equivalents in eleven languages (1617), first English book published by subscription.

Minto, Baronets, barons, and earls of. See ELLIOT family.

Min·ton \'mint-^{ə}n\, Sherman. 1890–1965. American jurist, b. Georgetown, Ind. Member, U.S. Senate (1935–41); judge of U.S. circuit court of appeals (1941–49); associate justice, U.S. Supreme Court (1949–56).

Minton, Thomas. 1765–1836. English pottery manufacturer. Established business (1789) at Stoke on Trent; maker of majolica, bone china, and reproductions of works of della Robbia and Palissy; reputedly developed willow pattern for tableware. His son ¶Herbert (1793–1858), his partner (1817–36), sole proprietor thereafter, produced under direction of Léon Arnoux porcelain rivaling that of Sèvres.

Mi·nu·ci·us Fe·lix \mə-'n(y)ü-sh(ē-)əs-'fē-liks\, Marcus. d. c.250 A.D. Latin writer, b. Africa? Lawyer in Rome; converted to Christianity and wrote dialogue *Octavius* (earliest known work of Latin Christian literature), purporting to be a colloquy between a Christian and a pagan in which the Christian refutes all charges brought by people against the new religion.

Min·u·it \'min-yə-wət\ *or* **Min·ne·wit** \'min-ə-,wit\, Peter. 1580–1638. Dutch colonial official. Director general of Dutch colony of New Netherland (1626–31); purchased Manhattan Island from the Indians for trinkets valued at sixty guilders ($24); established forts for colonial defense; recalled (1631). Sent by West India Company to establish Swedish colony on Delaware Bay; bought (1638) land, built Ft. Christina (now Wilmington, Del.), named country New Sweden and served as its governor. Lost at sea.

Mio·man·dre \myō-mä^{n}dr^{ə}\, Francis de. 1880–1959. French writer. Author of *Écrit sur de l'eau* (1908, Goncourt prize), *L'Aventure de Thérèse Beauchamp* (1914), *Voyage d'un sédentaire* (1918), *L'Ombre et l'amour* (1925), *Baroque* (1930), *L'Âne de Buridan* (1949), *Rencontres dans la nuit* (1954), etc.

Mi·quel \'mē-kel\, Johannes von. 1828–1901. German politician. Converted to socialism by writings of Karl Marx; a founder of German Nationalverein (1859); leader of right wing of National Liberal party in Prussian parliament (1867–82); member of Reichstag (1867–77, 1887–90), Prussian upper house (from 1882); minister of finance (1890–97); reformed Prussian system of taxation; tried to help poor; vice president of ministry (1897–1901).

Mī·rā Bāī \'mē-rä-'bä-ē\. 1450?–?1547. Indian Hindu mystic and poet. Rājput princess; frequently persecuted for devotion to cult of Kṛṣṇa; undertook pilgrimages; author of lyrical songs of devotion marked by use of everyday language and images.

Mirabeau, Comte de. See Honoré-Gabriel RIQUETI.

Mirabeau, Marquis de. See Victor RIQUETI.

Mirabeau, Vicomte de. See André Riqueti under Honoré-Gabriel RIQUETI.

Mi·ra de Ames·cua \'mē-rä-t͟hā-ä-'mäs-kwä\, Antonio. 1574?–1644. Spanish ecclesiastic and playwright. Chaplain to Cardinal Prince Ferdinand of Austria (from 1619). Among his dramas were *El esclavo del demonio, El galan valiente y discreto,* and *El palacio confuso.*

Miraflores, Marqués de. See Manuel PANDO FERNÁNDEZ DE PINEDA.

Mīr 'Alī \'mē-rä-'lē\ of Ta·briz \tə-'brēz\. c.1360–1420. Islāmic calligrapher. Developed cursive *nasta'līq* script, regarded as most elegant of Persian scripts.

Mi·ram·bo \mi-'räm-bō\. d. 1884. Nyamwezi leader. A warlord of Nyamwezi tribe, united clans and built powerful kingdom in present Tanzania; dominated trade routes of central Africa and checked Arab expansion.

Mi·ra·món \mē-rä-'mōn\, Miguel. 1832–1867. Mexican soldier. Head of reactionary political faction (1859) and commander of forces fighting against Juárez (1859–60); temporary president succeeding Zuloaga (1860); defeated (Dec. 1860), fled into exile. Conferred with Napoléon III on Mexico; named grand marshal of Mexican empire (1863) by Maximilian; supported Maximilian (1866–67); captured and shot with him.

Miranda, Bartolomé de. See Bartolomé de CARRANZA.

Mi·ran·da \mē-'rän-dä\, Francisco de. 1750–1816. Venezuelan revolutionist. Served in Spanish army (1773–83); served in Cuba; fled to U.S. (1783); secured limited aid from William Pitt in London for revolutionary activities; general of division in French revolutionary armies (1792–93). Led abortive invasion of Venezuela (1806); met Bolívar in London (1810); commanded rebel army in Venezuela (1810); generalissimo and dictator of Venezuela (Apr. 1812); fought vainly against royalists and finally forced to sign treaty (July 1812) yielding country to them; arrested, sent to Spain; died in prison.

Miranda, Sá de. See SÁ DE MIRANDA.

Mirandola. See PICO DELLA MIRANDOLA.

Mir·beau \mēr-bō\, Octave-Henri-Marie. 1850–1917. French journalist and writer. Dramatic critic on *L'Ordre*; a founder of satirical paper *Grimaces* (1882); known as a radical, attacking vigorously all forms of social organization. Among his satirical novels were *Le Calvaire* (1886), *La Famille Cannettes* (1888), *L'Abbé Jules* (1888), *Sébastien Roch* (1890), *Le Jardin des supplices* (1898), *Le Journal d'une femme de chambre* (1900), and *Dingo* (1912); among his plays, *Les Mauvais Bergers* (1897), *L'Épidémie* (1898).

Mir·bel \mēr-bel\, Charles-François Bris·seau de \brē-sō-də-\. 1776–1854. French botanist. At Musée d'Histoire Naturelle (1798–1803); director of gardens at Malmaison (from 1803); a founder of plant cytology and physiology. Author of *Traité d'anatomie et de physiologie végétale* (1802).

Mir·cea \'mēr-chä\. *Surnamed* Cio·ba·nul \chò-'bän-ül\, *i.e.* the Shepherd. d. 1418. Prince of Walachia (1386–1418). Struggled to maintain independence of Walachia in spite of designs of Hungary, Poland, and Turkey; forced to acknowledge sovereignty of Turkey (1412).

Mīr Dā·mād \'mēr-dä-'mäd\. *More completely* Muḥammad Bāqir ibn ad-Dāmād. d. 1631 or 1632. Iranian philosopher and teacher. Contributed to debate over eternality of creation the notion of "eternal origination"; given title Mu'allim-Thalith (Third Teacher, after Aristotle and al-Fārābī). Author of *Taqwīm al-īmān* and other treatises and of poetry.

Miriam. See Zenon PRZESMYCKI.

Mīr Ja·'far \'mēr-'jäf-ər\. *In full* Mīr Muḥammad Ja'far Khān. 1691?–1765. Indian general and ruler. Helped brother-in-law 'Alī Vardī Khān seize Bengal (1740); plotted overthrow of Sirāj-ud-Dawlah (1756); made secret alliance with Clive and the British; made ruler of Bengal (1757–60); granted large concessions to British; deposed by British (1760); reinstated (1763–65).

Mīr·khwānd \mērk-'vänd\ *or* **Mir·khond** \mēr-'ḵönd\. *More completely* Muḥammad ibn Kavand-Shāh ibn Maḥmud. 1433–1498. Persian historian. Author of *Rowzat oṣ-ṣafā'* (Garden of Purity), containing brief biographies of Persian notables from legendary times to his own day.

Mi·ró \mē-'rō\, Gabriel. *Full surname* Miró Fer·rer \-fer-'er\. *Occasional pseudonym* Si·güen·za \sē-'gwān-thä\. 1879–1930. Spanish novelist. Author of finely wrought, stylistically brilliant novels including *Hilván de escenas* (1903), *Del vivir* (1904), *Las cerezas del cementerio* (1910), *El abuelo del rey* (1912), *Figuras de la Pasión del Señor* (1916), *El libro de Sigüenza* (1917), *Nuestro padre San Daniel* (1921), *El obispo leproso* (1926).

Miró, Joan. 1893–1983. Spanish painter. To Paris (1919); met Pablo Picasso; early works show influence of Cubism; associated with the Surrealists (from 1924); returned to Barcelona (1932–36); eventually divided time between Paris and Barcelona. A seminal contributor to modern art; perhaps the greatest of the Surrealists; influenced abstract expressionists as Pollock, Rothko, and Motherwell; known for his use of bright colors and hallucinatory figures to create a poetic vision of the subconscious. Besides canvases, created sculptures, stage designs, mosaics, tapestries, and murals for public buildings.

Mīr Qā·sim \'mēr-'käs-ēm\. d. 1777. Indian ruler. Son-in-law of Mīr Ja'far; placed on throne of Bengal (1760); resisted British control and instigated massacre at Patna (1763); deposed by British (1763); defeated at Baksar (1764).

Mīr Say·yid 'Alī \'mēr-'sī-yēd-al-'ē\. 16th century. Persian painter. To India (c.1545) at invitation of Emperor Humāyūn; with 'Abd-uṣ-Ṣamad helped found Mughal school of painting; superintended production of some 1400 illustrations for *Dāstān-e Amīr Ḥamzeh;* himself noted as a miniaturist.

Mīr·zā 'Alī \mēr-'zä-ä-'lē\. 16th century. Persian artist. Employed at Ṣafavid court in Isfahan; noted as miniaturist, illustrator and illuminator, and esp. as designer of arabesque ornament.

Mir·za Ghul·am Ah·mad \mēr-'zä-gül-'äm-'äk-mäd\. c.1839–1908. Indian Muslim leader. Proclaimed himself the *mahdī* and, for Hindus, the incarnation of Kṛṣṇa; aimed to unite all religions in Islām; founded militant sect of Aḥmadiyah.

Mīr·zā Ta·qī Khān \mēr-'zä-tä-'kē-'ḵän\. *Also called* Amīr Ka·bīr \ä-'mēr-kä-'bēr\, *i.e.* Great Minister. c.1798–1852. Iranian politician. Rose through civil administration to prime minister (1848–51) under Shāh Nāṣer od-Dīn; instituted reforms in public finance, administration; fostered trade, education, adoption of Western technology, etc.; dismissed, exiled, murdered as result of plot of disaffected nobles.

Mi·ses \'mē-zes\, Ludwig von. Edler. 1881–1973. American economist, b. Lemberg, Austria (now Lvov, Ukrainian S.S.R.). Professor, Vienna (1913–38); to U.S. (1940); professor, N.Y.U. (1945–69). Author of *Theorie des Geldes und der Umlaufsmittel* (1912), *Liberalismus* (1927), *Grundprobleme der Nationalökonomie* (1933), *Bureaucracy* (1944), *Planned Chaos* (1947), *Human Action* (1949), *The Anti-Capitalistic Mentality* (1956), etc.

Mises, Richard von. Edler. 1883–1953. American mathematician, b. Lemberg, Austria (now Lvov, Ukrainian S.S.R.). Brother of Ludwig von Mises. Professor, Strassburg (1909–18), Dresden (1919), Berlin (1920–33), Istanbul (1933–39), Harvard U. (from 1939). Worked on aerodynamics, statistics, probability.

Mishima Yukio. See KIMITAKE Hiraoka.

Mis·tin·guett \mē-staⁿ-get\. *Orig.* Jeanne-Marie Bour·geois \bürzh-wä, -wä\. 1875–1956. French entertainer. Attained international popularity as music hall entertainer noted for vivacity; appeared in *L'Âne de Buridan* (1909), *Tais-toi mon coeur* (1910), *La Vie parisienne* (1911), etc.; regular at Moulin Rouge, the Casino, Folies-Bergère; identified esp. with songs "Mon Homme," "J'en ai marre," "En douce," "La Java."

Mis·tral \mē-sträl\, Frédéric. 1830–1914. Provençal poet. Helped found Félibrige organization of modern Provençal poets (1854) and became active leader in Provençal renaissance and its establishment as literary language; shared Nobel prize for literature with José Echegaray y Eizaguirre (1904). Works included Provençal–French dictionary *Lou Tresor dóu Félibrige* (1878–85), pastoral poems *Mirèio* (1859), *Calendau* (1867), collection of lyrics and narrative poems *Lis Isclo d'or* (1875), historical epic *Nerto* (1884), dramatic poem *La Rèino Jano* (1890), epic *Lou Pouèmo Jóu Rose* (1897), and collection *Lis Oulivado* (1912).

Mistral, Gabriela. See Lucila GODOY ALCAYAGA.

Mitch·el \'mich-əl\, John. 1815–1875. Irish nationalist. Practiced law (from 1840); joined Young Ireland movement (1845); founded and edited *United Irishman* (1847) to advocate repeal of the Act of Union and armed resistance to England; tried, convicted, and transported (1848); escaped from Van Diemen's Land to America (1853); returned to Ireland (1874); elected to English Parliament from Tipperary (1875) but declared ineligible. Author of *Jail Journal* (1854). His grandson ¶John Purroy Mitchel (1879–1918), b. Fordham, N.Y., was a lawyer; mayor of New York (1914–18).

Mitchel, Ormsby MacKnight. 1809–1862. American astronomer, b. Morganfield, Ky. Professor, Cincinnati Coll. (1836–59); did much to popularize astronomy; director, Dudley Observatory, Albany, N.Y. (1859–61); general in Civil War; led raid that captured Huntsville, Ala. (Apr. 1862). Author of *Planetary and Stellar Worlds* (1848), *Popular Astronomy* (1860).

Mitch·ell \'mich-əl\, Donald Grant. *Pseudonym* Ik Mar·vel \'mär-vəl\. 1822–1908. American author, b. Norwich, Conn. Author of *Reveries of a Bachelor* (1850), *Dream Life* (1851), *Doctor Johns* (1866), *English Lands, Letters and Kings* (1889–97), *American Lands and Letters* (1897–99), etc.

Mitchell, John. d. 1768. American physician, botanist, and cartographer, b. Great Britain? Appeared in Virginia about 1725; notable success in treating yellow-fever victims; returned to England (c.1746); best known for his large-scale *Map of the British and French Dominions in North America* (1755), a map used in various boundary negotiations in later history.

Mitchell, John. 1870–1919. American labor leader, b. Braidwood, Ill. Coal miner (from 1882); member, Knights of Labor (1885–90), United Mine Workers of America (from 1890); president, United Mine Workers (1898–1908); organized and directed successful anthracite coal miners' strike (1902). Chairman, New York State Industrial Commission (1915–19). Author of *Organized Labor* (1903), *The Wage Earner and His Problems* (1913).

Mitchell, John Ames. 1845–1918. American artist, editor, and novelist, b. New York City. Founded and edited *Life* magazine (1883–1918).

Mitchell, John Thomas Whitehead. 1828–1895. English reformer. Secretary of Rochdale Society (1857 ff.); founder (1863), chairman (from 1874), Cooperative Wholesale Society; developed theoretical and practical aspects of consumer cooperative movement.

Mitchell, Margaret Munnerlyn. 1900–1949. American writer, b. Atlanta, Ga. Author of the novel *Gone With the Wind* (1936, Pulitzer prize).

Mitchell, Margaret Julia, *known as* Maggie. 1832–1918. American actress, b. New York City. Excelled in comedy roles, esp. as Fanchon in *Fanchon the Cricket* (1861), a play adapted for her from George Sand's "La Petite Fadette."

Mitchell, Maria. 1818–1889. American astronomer, b. Nantucket I., Mass. Librarian of Nantucket Atheneum (1836–60); working alone, established orbit of a newly discovered comet (1847), for which she became first woman elected to American Academy of Arts and Sciences (1847); on staff of *American Ephemeris and Nautical Almanac* (1849–68); professor, Vassar Coll. (1865–88).

Mitchell, Sir Peter Chalmers. 1864–1945. British zoologist, b. Scotland. Secretary of Zoological Society of London (1903–35). Author of *Outlines of Biology* (1894), *The Nature of Man* (1904), *Materialism and Vitalism in Biology* (1930), *My House in Málaga* (1938).

Mitchell, Reginald Joseph. 1895–1937. English aircraft designer. Engineer and designer for Supermarine Aviation Works (1916–37), chief engineer (from 1919); known for design of series of flying boats and high-speed seaplanes and esp. of the Spitfire fighter (1936).

Mitchell, Silas Weir. 1829–1914. American physician and author, b. Philadelphia. Practiced, Philadelphia; surgeon in Union army in Civil War; specialized in study and treatment of neurological disorders. Author of *Gunshot Wounds* (1864), *Wear and Tear* (1871), *Injuries of Nerves and Their Consequences* (1872), *Fat and Blood* (1887), etc.; also wrote poetry as *The Hill of Stones* (1882), *A Psalm of Deaths* (1890), *The Mother and Other Poems* (1893), *The Comfort of the Hills* (1909); fiction as *In War Time* (1885), *Roland Blake* (1886), *Hugh Wynne, Free Quaker* (1898), *The Adventures of François* (1899), *The Autobiography of a Quack* (1900), *Constance Trescott* (1905), *The Red City* (1907), *John Sherwood, Inn Master* (1911), *Westways* (1913).

Mitchell, Sir Thomas Livingstone. 1792–1855. Scottish explorer. Deputy surveyor general, New South Wales (1828); known for four expeditions into interior of Australia (1831–45); seeking overland route to Gulf of Carpentaria, found sources of Barcoo River (1845–47).

Mitchell, Wesley Clair. 1874–1948. American economist, b. Rushville, Ill. Professor, U. of California (1909–12), Columbia (1914–19, 1922–44), New School for Social Research (1919–21). Helped organize (1920) National Bureau of Economic Research; director of research (1920–45); served on many government boards. Author of *A History of the Greenbacks* (1903), *Gold Prices and Wages Under the Greenback Standard* (1908), *Business Cycles, the Problem and its Setting* (1927), *The Backward Art of Spending Money* (1937), etc.

Mitchell, William. 1879–1936. American army officer, b. Nice, France, of American parents. Entered army as private (1898); promoted through grades to brigadier general (1920); served in Spanish–American War, Philippines, on Mexican border; in World War I commander of the air forces, A.E.F. (1917–18). Outspoken advocate of air power; demonstrated ability of aerial bombing to sink battleships (1921–23); court-martialed because of his criticism of War and Navy departments for mismanagement of aviation service (1925); convicted; resigned (1926). Author of *Our Air Force* (1921), *Winged Defense* (1925), *Skyways* (1930).

Mit·ford \ˈmit-fərd\, John. 1781–1859. English clergyman. Editor of *Gentleman's Magazine* (1834–50); author of *Miscellaneous Poems* (1858); did chief critical work and research for *Works of Thomas Gray* (1814) and eleven memoirs for "Aldine" edition of English poets (1835–43).

Mitford, Mary Russell. 1787–1855. English novelist and dramatist. Daughter of spendthrift physician; at age of ten, drew £20,000 in a lottery; published *Miscellaneous Poems* (1810), narrative poem *Christina* (1811), and other volumes; reduced to poverty by father's improvidence, wrote for magazines and stage; contributed to *Lady's Magazine* sketches of country life that ultimately became *Our Village* (5 vols., 1824–32), her best known work. Author also of *Belford Regis* (novel, 1835), *Country Stories* (1837), *Recollections of a Literary Life* (1852), *Atherton* (novel, 1854), and four tragedies, *Julian* (1823), *The Foscari* (1826), *Rienzi* (1828), and *Charles I* (1834).

Mitford, Nancy. 1904–1973. English writer. Known esp. for witty novels of upper-class life as *Pursuit of Love* (1945), *Love In a Cold Climate* (1949), *The Blessing* (1951), *Don't Tell Alfred* (1960); also wrote biographies *Madame de Pompadour* (1954), *Voltaire in Love* (1957), *The Sun King* (1966), *Frederick the Great* (1970); edited *Noblesse Oblige* (1956), which popularized "U" and "non-U" usages.

Mitford, William. 1744–1827. English historian. On advice of Gibbon, undertook *History of Greece* (1784–1810), which enjoyed long popularity and held highest place among scholars until superseded by histories of Grote and Thirlwall. M.P. (1785–1818).

Mith·ra·da·tes \ˌmith-rə-ˈdāt-ˌēz\. *Also spelled* Mith·ri·da·tes. Name of five kings of Parthia, of Arsacid dynasty, especially:

Mithradates I. *Called also* Ar·sa·ces VI \ˈär-sə-ˌsēz\. d. 138 B.C. King (171–138 B.C.). Brother of Phraates I. Assumed title Phil·hel·lene \ˈfil-ˌhel-ˌēn, fil-ˈhel-\, *i.e.* Greek-loving. Real founder of Parthian Empire; conquered Babylonia and Media, defeating the Seleucids; held Demetrius II Nicator captive.

Mithradates II. *Called* the Great. d. 88 B.C. King (123–88 B.C.). Succeeded father Artabanus II; defeated Scythians; established trade with China along Silk Route; made treaty with Rome (92 B.C.); conquered Mesopotamia (90) and Artavasdes of Armenia.

Mithradates III. d. 54 B.C. King (56–55 B.C.). Usurped throne from brother Orodes; killed after short reign.

Mithradates. Name of six kings of Pontus, especially:

Mithradates II. d. 266 or 265 B.C. Conquered Cappadocian and Paphlagonian territory on Halys River to form nucleus of Pontus.

Mithradates III. d. c.185 B.C. King (c.255–c.185). Succeeded father Ariobarzanes; m. Laodice, sister of Seleucus II Callinicus, and received Greater Phrygia as dowry; fought with Antiochus Hierax against Seleucus at Ancyra (c.240); attempted to conquer Sinope (from 220).

Mithradates IV Phi·lop·a·tor Phil·a·del·phus \fil-ˈäp-ə-ˌtȯ(ə)r-ˌfil-ə-ˈdel-fəs\. d. c.150 B.C. King (c.170–c.150). Son of Mithradates III; possibly regent for son of elder brother Pharnaces.

Mithradates V Eu·er·ge·tes \yə-ˈwər-jə-ˌtēz\. d. 121 or 120 B.C. King (c.150–c.120). Son of Pharnaces; ally of Rome, assisting in 3d Punic War; seized Phrygia; assassinated.

Mithradates VI Eu·pa·tor \ˈyü-pə-ˌtȯ(ə)r\. *Called* the Great. d. 63 B.C. King (120–63 B.C.). Son of Mithradates V; overthrew regency of mother (115); gradually became master of Cappadocia, Paphlagonia, Bithynia, and all southern and eastern coast regions of Black Sea; conflict with Nicomedes of Bithynia aroused opposition of Romans. Waged three wars against Rome: First Mithradatic War (88–85 B.C.); successful at first until his general in Greece was defeated by Sulla at Chaeronea and at Orchomenus (86); forced to sign peace by Sulla and pay heavy damages. Second Mithradatic War (83–82 B.C.); defeated Roman army that invaded Pontus. Third Mithradatic war (76–64 B.C.); occupied Bithynia, which had been bequeathed to Rome; driven out of Pontus (72–71) by L. Licinius Lucullus to court of son-in-law Tigranes of Armenia; reconquered Pontus (68–67), but defeated by Pompey (66); fled to the Crimea (65); committed suicide. Had great military ability; one of most formidable opponents Rome ever had.

Mi·tre \ˈmē-trā\, Bartolomé. 1821–1906. Argentine soldier, politician, and writer. As fugitive from Rosas regime, lived as journalist in Bolivia, Chile, and Peru (1837–52); returned at head of Uruguayan forces at battle of Monte Caseros (1852); a leader of secessionist government of Buenos Aires (1853–61); defeated Urquiza at Pavon (1861); president of Argentina (1862–68); in alliance with Brazil and Uruguay, conducted successful war against Paraguay (1864); senator (from 1868); defeated for presidency, unsuccessfully rebelled (1874). Author of *Historia de Belgrano y de la independencia Argentina* (1858–59) and *Historia de San Martín y de la emancipación Sud-Americana* (1887–88).

Mi·tro·pou·los \mē-ˈtrȯ-pü-lȯs\, Dimitri. 1896–1960. American orchestra conductor and composer, b. Athens, Greece. Principal conductor (1929), professor (1930), Odeion Conservatory, Athens; conductor of Minneapolis Symphony (1937–49); naturalized (1946); conductor of New York Philharmonic (1949–58), Metropolitan Opera (1954–60); unorthodox in style; noted esp. for introducing modern works as by Schoenberg, Berg, Krenek. Compositions included opera *Soeur Béatrice* (1919), symphonic works *La mise au tombeau de Christ* (1916) and *Fête crétoise* (1928), song cycle *Hedonica* (1927), etc.

Mitsch·er \ˈmich-ər\, Marc Andrew. 1887–1947. American naval officer, b. Hillsboro, Wis. Entered navy (1910); pilot (1916); captain (1938), rear admiral (1941); commanded carrier *Hornet* (1941–42), engaged at Battle of Midway (June 1942); commanded all air forces in battles for Solomon Islands (1943); commander of fast carrier Task Force 38 (or 58) attached to Third (or Fifth) fleet, central Pacific (1944–45); engaged in battles of Philippine Sea, Leyte Gulf, at Iwo Jima and Okinawa; admiral (1946).

Mitsch·er·lich \ˈmich-ər-(ˌ)lik\, Eilhardt. 1794–1863. German chemist. Professor, Berlin (from 1822); discovered (1818) phenomenon of isomorphism and developed theory; discovered monoclinic sulfur (1823), selenic acid (1827); synthesized nitrobenzene (1832); obtained and named benzene (1834).

Mit·tag-Lef·fler \ˈmit-ˌtäk-ˈlef-lər\, Magnus Gösta. 1846–1927. Swedish mathematician. Professor, Helsinki (1877–81), Stockholm (1881–1927); founded and edited (1882–1927) journal *Acta Mathematica;* contributed to general theory of functions, derived Mittag-Leffler theorem.

Mi·vart \ˈmī-ˌvärt, -vərt; ˈmiv-ərt\, St. George Jackson. 1827–1900. English biologist. Taught anatomy at St. Mary's Hosp. Medical School, London (1862–84); professor, Roman Catholic University Coll., Kensington (1874–84), Louvain (1890–93); an evolutionist, insisting upon action of divine power in development of man's mind; critic of Darwin and Huxley as regards natural selection theory; sought to reconcile science and religion; excommunicated for liberalism and repudiation of ecclesiastical authority (1900). Author of *The Genesis of Species* (1871), *Nature and Thought* (1882), *Origin of Human Reason* (1889), etc.

Mix \'miks\, Thomas Edwin, *called* Tom. 1880–1940. American actor, b. Mix Run, Pa. Cowboy; appeared in Wild West shows; entered silent films (1910); made into highly popular star of some 100 silent Westerns (to 1928); toured with own Wild West show and circus; unsuccessful in talking pictures.

Mi·ya·ga·wa \mē-yä-gä-wä\ Chōshun. *Also known as* Chō·za·e·mon \chō-zä-em-ōn\ *and as* Ki·hei·ji \kē-hā-jē\. 1682–1752. Japanese painter. Influenced by Hishikawa Moronobu; became a leading exponent of *Ukiyo-e* manner, noted esp. as brilliant colorist; founder of Miyagawa school.

Mi·ya·mo·to \mē-yä-mō-tō\ Musashi, *orig.* Masana. *Pseudonym* Ni·ten \nē-ten\. 1584–1645. Japanese soldier and artist. Noted swordsman, invented *nitō-ryū* or fencing with two swords; exponent of *sumi-e* ink painting technique, noted esp. for paintings of birds, rendered with great economy in ink monochrome.

Mi·ya·za·ki \mē-yä-zä-kē\ Yūzen *or* Yūzensai. 1654–1736. Japanese painter. Invented *yūzen-zome* process for imparting rich colors to silk with rice-paste dyes; his name also attached to elaborate designs, *yūzen-moyō,* he created.

Mi Yu-jen \'mē-'yü-'zhən\. *Also called* Yüan-hui \yü̅e-'än-'hwē\. 1086–1165. Chinese painter. Known for ink landscapes in Mi style developed by his father Mi Fei (*q.v.*).

Miz·ner \'mīz-nər\, Addison. 1872–1933. American architect, b. Benicia, Cal. Designed series of ornate pseudo-Spanish hotels and homes in Florida, including Everglades Club, Boca Raton Club, homes for Harold Vanderbilt, Rodman Wanamaker, A.J.D. Biddle, etc.; made and lost fortune in Florida land bubble (1925–26). His brother ¶Wilson (1876–1933) was noted wit and bon vivant in New York City; managed Hotel Rand (1906 ff.); associated with Addison in land speculation; later a screenwriter in Hollywood.

Mi·zo·gu·chi \mē-zō-gu̇ch-ē\ Kenji. 1898–1956. Japanese motion-picture director. Noted for films dealing with conflict of modern and traditional values, social problems, nature of reality, including *Gaitō no suketchi* (1925), *Kami-Nengyo haru no sasayaki* (1926), *Tōkyo koshinkyoko* (1929), *Zangiku monogatari* (1939), *Joyu sumako-no-koi* (1947), *Yoru-no-on-natachi* (1948), *Ugetsu monogatari* (1953), *Akasen chitai* (1956).

Mi·zu·no \mē-zün-ō\ Tadakuni. 1794–1851. Japanese politician. Tutor to Tokugawa Ieyoshi (1828); adviser to shogun (1834); as adviser to shogun Ieyoshi (1837–43) virtually controlled government; attempted to restore martial values; discouraged trade, introduced extreme sumptuary laws, ordered peasants from cities back to countryside; unpopularity of these Tempō reforms led to his dismissal (1843).

Mnemon. See ARTAXERXES II.

Mnes·i·cles \'nes-i-ˌklēz\. *Also spelled* Mnes·i·kles. 5th century B.C. Greek architect. Designer (c.437 B.C.) of Propylaea of the Acropolis, Athens; believed by some scholars to have designed also the Erectheum.

Mo·bā·rez od-Dīn Mo·ḥam·mad \mȯ-'bär-ez-ůd-'dēn-mu̇-ḳäm-mäd\. d. 1358? Iranian ruler. Made governor of Fārs and Yazd by Il-Khanid ruler Abū Sa'īd (1314); by marriage gained (1340) Kermān; conquered most of southern Iran (by 1356), establishing dynasty known as Moẓaffarid after his father; deposed by sons (1358). Dynasty extinguished by Timur (1393).

Mo·berg \'mü-berʸ\, Vilhelm, *in full* Carl Artur Vilhelm. 1898–1973. Swedish novelist. Author of novels of Swedish peasant life and its hardships, including *Raskens* (1927), *De knutna händerna* (1930), *Mans kvinna* (1933); the Knut Toring trilogy *Sänkt sedebetyg* (1935), *Sömnlös* (1937), *Giv oss jorden* (1939); *Rid i Natt!* (1941), *Soldat med brutet gevär* (1944); tetralogy on emigration to America *Utvandrarna* (*The Emigrants,* 1949), *Invandrarna* (*Unto a Good Land,* 1952), *Nybyggarna* (1956), *Sista brevet till Sverige* (1959).

Mö·bi·us \'mœ-bē-ůs\, August Ferdinand. 1790–1868. German mathematician and astronomer. Professor, Leipzig (from 1815); director of observatory (from 1848); wrote astronomical texts including *Die Elemente der Mechanik des Himmels* (1843); chief mathematical publication *Der barycentrische Calcul* (1827), in which he introduced homogenous coordinates and projective transformations into analytical geometry; developed idea of Möbius net; discovered (1858) one-sided figure the Möbius strip.

Möbius, Karl August. 1825–1908. German zoologist. Professor, Kiel (1868–87); director of natural history museum, Berlin (1887–1905); a pioneer in ecological research, introduced concept of "life community" or ecosystem.

Mo·cat·ta \mō-'kat-ə\, Frederic David. 1828–1905. British philanthropist and scholar. Director of family firm of bullion brokers (1857–74); contributed to improved workers' housing, hospitals, education in London; subsidized publication of *Zur Geschichte und Literatur* by Leopold Zunz (1845) and of English translation of H. Graetz's *History of the Jews* (1891–92). Author of *The Jews of Spain and Portugal and the Inquisition* (1877) and other historical works.

Moch·nac·ki \mȯḵ-'nät-skē\, Maurycy. 1804–1834. Polish writer. As critic championed literary Romanticism in Poland; took part in revolt of 1830; exiled to France. Author of critical *O literaturze polskiej wieku XIX* (1830), and eyewitness account of revolt *Powstanie narodu polskiego w latach 1830–1831* (1834).

Moc·kel \mȯ-kel\, Albert Henri Louis. 1866–1945. Belgian poet and critic. Founder and editor (1886–93) of journal *La Wallonie,* organ of Belgian Symbolists. Author of verse *Chantefable un peu naïve* (1891), *Clarté* (1901), *La Flamme immortelle* (1924).

Moc·que·reau \mȯ-krō\, André. 1849–1930. French religious and music scholar. Entered Benedictine order (1877); prior at Solesmes (1902–08); founder and editor of *Paléographie musicale* (13 vols., 1889–1928), which published photographic reproductions of medieval manuscripts with researches on history of liturgical chants of Roman Catholic church.

Moctezuma. See MONTEZUMA.

Mo·der·sohn-Beck·er \'mōd-ər-zōn-'bek-ər\, Paula, *nee* Becker. *Also called* Becker-Modersohn. 1876–1907. German painter. m. (1898?) landscapist Otto Modersohn; in Paris (from 1900); noted esp. for still lifes, self-portraits, pictures of mothers and children, executed in naturalistic style in broad areas of color showing influence of Gauguin and Cézanne.

Mo·di·glia·ni \ˌmō-dēl-'yä-nē\, Amedeo. 1884–1920. Italian painter and sculptor. Settled in Paris (1906); known esp. for portraits and nudes, executed in characteristic planar, asymmetric, elongated manner in broad expanses of color; executed some 25 directly carved stone sculptures and many drawings.

Mo·djes·ka \mȯ-'jes-kə\, *orig.* Mo·drze·jew·ska \mȯ-je-'yef-skä\, Helena. *Nee* Jadwiga Opid \'ō-pēt\. 1840–1909. American actress, b. Kraków, Poland. Took name (perhaps by marriage) Modrzejewski (1861) for stage; appeared at Comédie-Française (1866); leading actress at Imperial Theatre, Warsaw (1866–76); to U.S. (1876) and settled in California; on American stage (from 1877); excelled in serious dramatic roles, including Lady Macbeth, Juliet, Ophelia, Imogen, Ibsen's Nora, Dumas's Camille.

Mo·djes·ki \mȯ-'jes-kē\, Ralph. *Orig. surname* Mo·drze·jew·ski \mȯ-je-'yef-skē\. 1861–1940. American engineer, b. Kraków, Poland. Son of Helena Modjeska; to U.S. (1876). Consulting bridge engineer in Chicago (from 1892); chief engineer of McKinley Bridge (St. Louis), Broadway Bridge (Portland, Ore.), Benjamin Franklin Bridge (Philadelphia), Huey P. Long Bridge (New Orleans), etc. Member, board of engineers, Quebec Bridge (reconstruction) and Oakland Bay Bridge (San Francisco).

Mo·drzew·ski \mȯ-'jef-skē\, Andrzej. *Full surname* Frycz-Modrzewski \'frich-\. c.1503–1572. Polish writer. Author of various pamphlets urging legal and religious reforms, esp. *Commentariorum de republica emendanda libri quinque* (1551–54) outlining utopian ideas.

Moe \'mō\, Jørgen Engebretsen. 1813–1882. Norwegian poet, folklorist, and theologian. With Peter Asbjørnsen edited collections of Norwegian folk tales *Nor* (1837), *Norske folkeeventyr* (1841); wrote Romantic verse *Digte* (1850), children's classic *I brønden og i kjaernet* (1851). Bishop of Christiansand (1875–81). His son ¶Moltke (1859–1913), folklorist and scholar, collaborated with Asbjørnsen and continued collections of tales and folksongs.

Moel·ler van den Bruck \'mœl-ər-vän-dən-'bru̇k, -fän-\, Arthur. 1876–1925. German critic. Editor, in German, of Poe's works (1901–04) and coeditor of first German edition of Dostoyevsky's works (1906–15; with Merezhkovsky); author of cultural history *Die Deutschen* (1904–10), *Das Recht der jungen Völker* (1919), and *Das dritte Reich* (1923), title of which became slogan of the Nazis.

Moe·ran \'mȯr-ən\, Ernest John. 1894–1950. English composer. Influenced by Delius and by folksongs of Ireland and East Anglia; orchestral works included rhapsodies (1922, 1924, 1943), *Whythorne's Shadow* (1931), *Lonely Waters* (1932), *Symphony* (1937); chamber and instrumental works *3 Piano Pieces* (1919), a string trio (1931), violin sonatas, etc.; set many songs of Shakespeare, A.E. Housman, Herrick, James Joyce.

Mof·fat \'mäf-ət\, David Halliday. 1839–1911. American financier, b. Washingtonville, N.Y. Engaged in banking, mining, real estate, and other investments in Denver (from 1860); interested esp. in making Denver a railroad center; planned Moffat Tunnel (completed 1920) through Continental Divide.

Moffat, Robert. 1795–1883. Scottish missionary. Sent to Namaqualand (1817); moved mission station to Kuruman in Bechuanaland (1825); completed translation of New Testament into Tswana (1839); established mission among Matabeles; translated Old Testament into Tswana (1857), also *Pilgrim's Progress* and hymns.

Mof·fatt \'mäf-ət\, James. 1870–1944. American theologian, b. Glasgow, Scotland. Ordained in Free Church of Scotland (1896); professor, Oxford (1911–15), United Free Church Coll., Glasgow (1915–27); to U.S. (1927); professor of church history at Union Theol. Sem., New York (from 1927). Author of *Historical New Testament* (1901), *Introduction to the Literature of* *the New Testament* (1911), etc.; translator of the New Testament (1913), Old Testament (1924–26).

Mof·fett \ˈmäf-ət\, William Adger. 1869–1933. American naval officer, b. Charleston, S.C. Entered navy (1890); served under Dewey in battle of Manila Bay (1898); at Veracruz (1914); chief, bureau of aeronautics, with rank of rear admiral (1921–33); largely created navy's air wing; secured adoption of dirigibles; died in crash of dirigible *Akron.*

Mo·fo·lo \mō-ˈfō-lō\, Thomas Mokopu. 1877–1948. Bantu novelist, b. Lesotho. Author in Sesotho language of novels *Moeti oa Bochabela* (1906), *Pitseng* (1910), *Chaka* (1925); first important 20th-century African novelist.

Mo·gi·la \(ˌ)mə-ˈgyē-lə\, Peter. 1596–1646. Russian prelate, b. Moldavia. Entered monastery in Kiev (1625), archimandrite (1627); metropolitan of Kiev (1633); composed (1640) *Orthodox Confession of Faith,* which was accepted by patriarchs of Constantinople, Jerusalem, Alexandria, and Antioch (1642–43), and by synod of Jerusalem (1672).

Mogul. See MUGHAL.

Mohammad. See also MAHMUD, MEHMED, MOHAMMED, MUḤAMMAD.

Mo·ḥam·mad ʿAlī Shāh \mō-ˈk̲äm-mäd-ä-ˈlē-ˈshä\. 1872–1925. Shah of Iran (1907–09). Son of Moẓaffar od-Dīn; attempted to suppress constitution of 1906; deposed.

Mo·ḥam·ma·dī \mō-k̲äm-mäd-ˈē\. *Also called* Ostād Moḥammadī \ō-ˈstäd-\. 16th century. Persian painter. Resident of Isfahan; known for original style in depictions of open-air scenes of everyday life.

Moḥammad Khodābanah. See ÖLJEITÜ.

Mo·ḥam·mad Reza Pa·hla·vi \mō-ˈk̲äm-mäd-ˈrä-zä-pä-ˈhläv-ē\. 1919–1980. Shah of Iran (1941–79). Son of Reza Shah Pahlavi; placed on throne at instance of Great Britain and Soviet Union; forced to flee country by supporters of Mohammad Mosaddeq (1953); resumed rule after overthrow of Mosaddeq (1954); promoted development through oil revenues; built large army and a secret police force (Savak); after a period of growing popular opposition led mainly by Islāmic fundamentalists, left Iran (1979); lived in exile in Morocco, Mexico, Panama, Egypt.

Moḥammad Shams od-Dīn Ḥāfez. See ḤĀFEZ.

Mo·ham·med I As·kia \mu̇-ˈham-med-as-ˈkē-ə\. d. 1538. Ruler of Songhai (1493–1528). At battle of Anfao (April 1493) defeated son of Sonni ʿAlī and gained throne of Songhai Empire; established civil rule and administration in Songhai; established Islām as state religion and made celebrated pilgrimage to Mecca (1495–97); subdued many neighboring tribes and states; made Songhai into major civilizing influence. Deposed by son Musa (1528) and exiled to island (1528–37); recalled to capital Gao by son Askia Ismaïl (1537). His tomb remains one of the most venerated mosques in West Africa.

Mohammed Shah, Sultan Sir. See AGA KHAN III.

Mohl \ˈmōl\, Hugo von. 1805–1872. German botanist. Professor, Tübingen (1835–72); named colloidal substance of plant cells protoplasm (1846); studied cell nucleus; first to propose that new cells are formed by division; elucidated role of osmosis; investigated stomata of leaves.

Möh·ler \ˈmœ̄-lər\, Johann Adam. 1796–1838. German theologian. Ordained priest (1819); professor, Tübingen (1826–35), Munich (1835–38); advocate of uniting Catholic and Protestant churches. Author of *Die Einheit in der Kirche* (1825), *Symbolik* (1832), *Neue Untersuchung der Lehrgegensätze zwischen Katholiken und Protestanten* (1834).

Mohn \ˈmōn\, Henrik. 1835–1916. Norwegian meteorologist. Director, Norwegian Meteorological Inst. (1866–1935); professor, Christiania (Oslo, 1866–1913); investigated dynamics of the atmosphere, storms, meteorology of the North Atlantic, and climate of Norway.

Mo·holy-Nagy \ˈmō-hōi-ˈnädʸ\, László, *Eng.* Ladislaus. 1895–1946. Hungarian painter, designer, and photographer. Member of Constructivist school; head of metal shop, Bauhaus school, Germany (1923–29); developed "photogram" medium; fled Germany (1935); in London designed sets for film *Shape of Things to Come;* to U.S. (1937); director of New Bauhaus, or American School of Design, Chicago, with Walter Gropius (1937–39), reorganized as Institute of Design (1939; now part of Ill. Inst. of Tech.). Worked in painting, drawing, photography, stage sets, sculpture, film cartoons, and other arts.

Mo·ho·ro·vi·čić \mō-ˌhȯr-ō-ˈvē-chēch\, Andrija. 1857–1936. Croatian geophysicist. Taught at Technical School, Zagreb (1891–1921); director of Zagreb meteorological observatory (1892–1921); known for investigation of Croatian earthquake of 1909; from analysis of seismic waves, discovered Mohorovičić discontinuity, boundary between Earth's crust and mantle.

Mohr \ˈmōr\, Carl Friedrich. 1806–1879. German pharmacist. Professor, Bonn (1867–79); one of first to suggest law of conservation of energy (1837); known esp. for contributions to analytical techniques in chemistry as titration, for which he invented the pinchcock; also devised Mohr's balance.

Mohr, Joseph. 1792–1848. Austrian clergyman and poet. Author of Christmas song "Stille Nacht, heilige Nacht" (1818; set to music by Franz Gruber).

Mohs \ˈmōs\, Friedrich. 1773–1839. German mineralogist. Professor, Graz (1812–17), Freiburg (1818–26), Vienna (1828–35); introduced (1812) Mohs scale of hardness still commonly used.

Moi·naux \mwä-nō\, Georges. *Pseudonym* Georges Cour·te·line \ku̇r-tə-lēn\. 1858–1929. French humorist. Author of vigorously satirical stories and novels as *Les Gaîtés de Pescadron* (1886), *Le Train de 8 heures 47* (1888), *Lidoire* (1891), *Messieurs les ronds-de-cuir* (1893); also wrote comedies as *Boubouroche* (1893), *Un Client sérieux* (1897), *Le Gendarme est sans pitié* (1899), *L'Article 330* (1900), *La Paix chez soi* (1903).

Moir \ˈmȯi(ə)r\, David Macbeth. *Pseudonym* Δ \ˈdel-tə\. 1798–1851. Scottish physician. Wrote essays and poems for *Blackwood's,* novel *The Life of Mansie Wauch* (1828), and *Outlines of Ancient History of Medicine* (1831).

Moira, Earl of. See Francis RAWDON-HASTINGS.

Mois·san \mwä-säⁿ\, Henri, *in full* Ferdinand-Frédéric-Henri. 1852–1907. French chemist. Professor, École de Pharmacie, Paris (1886–1900), Sorbonne (1900). First to isolate fluorine (1886); developed electric arc furnace (1892); discovered silicon carbide and believed he had produced (1893) minute artificial diamonds; awarded 1906 Nobel prize for chemistry.

Mo·is·si \ˈmō-ə-sē\, Alexander. 1880–1935. Italian actor, b. Trieste, Austria (now Italy). Won fame chiefly in Max Reinhardt productions in Berlin; played many roles, including Hamlet, Romeo, Othello, Mark Antony, Shakespeare's fools, Faust, Orestes, Cyrano de Bergerac, Everyman.

Moj·mír I \mȯi-ˈmēr\. 9th century. Prince of Moravia (830–846). Emerged at end of period of domination by Avars to rule Moravia; founded a state that expanded to encompass Bohemia and parts of Poland, Slovakia, Hungary.

Mokṣadeva. See HSÜAN-TSANG.

Mo·ku·an \mō-ku̇-än\ *or* **Mokuan Rei·en** \-rā-en\. d. 1343? Japanese painter. Zen Buddhist priest; studied painting while on pilgrimage in China; influenced by work of Mu-ch'i Fu-ch'ang; one of first Japanese artists to adopt Chinese monochrome ink style.

Mo·la \ˈmō-lä\, Emilio. *Full surname* Mola Vi·dal \-b̲ē-ˈdäl\. 1887–1937. Spanish soldier. Served in Morocco (1909–26); joined insurrection led by General Franco; under Franco, held command of northern army in Spain during first year of civil war; killed in airplane accident.

Mo·la \ˈmō-lä\, Pier Francesco. 1612–1666. Italian painter. Notable for mythological and religious paintings, esp. for their landscape backgrounds.

Mo·lay \mō-le\, Jacques de. 1243–1314. French knight. Entered Order of Knights Templars (1265); elected grand master (c.1298); arrested on order of Philip IV of France, confessed to certain charges, later retracted on plea of torture (1307); appealed to Pope Clement V (1309, 1310); condemned by papal commission (1314) after Clement had suppressed order (1312); again retracted confession and burned at stake by Philip.

Mol·cho \ˈmȯl-kō\, Solomon. *Orig.* Diogo Pi·res \ˈpē-rish\. c.1500–1532. Portuguese Jewish martyr. Of *marrano* family (forced converts to Christianity); under influence of David Reubeni (*q.v.*), experienced mystic vision of coming of the Messiah; openly proclaimed Judaism, traveled and preached in Turkey, Palestine, Italy; sought aid of Emperor Charles V in arming *marranos* to crusade against Turks in Palestine; given over to Inquisition in Mantua; on refusing to return to Christianity, burned at stake.

Mo·lé \mō-lā\, Louis-Mathieu. Comte. 1781–1855. French politician. For pro-monarchial *Essais de morale et de politique* (1806) made member of Council of State by Napoléon I; minister of justice (1813); created peer of France during Restoration; minister of marine (1817–18) and member of privy council; minister for foreign affairs (1830); premier of France (1826–39); failed in attempt to form a second ministry (1848); one of deputies who opposed the coup d'état (Dec. 2, 1851).

Molé, Mathieu. Seigneur de Cham·plâ·treux \shäⁿ-plä-trœ̄\. 1584–1656. French jurist and politician. *Procureur général* (1614); upheld authority of Parlement of Paris against royal usurpation (1631) and was for a time suspended from office as a result; first president of Parlement (1641–53) and keeper of the seals (1651–56).

Mo·le·naer *or* **Mo·le·naar** \ˈmō-le-när\, Jan Miense. c.1610–1668. Dutch painter. Known esp. for genre scenes and portraits.

Mo·len·graaff \ˈmō-lən-ˌgräf\, Gustaaf Adolf Frederik. 1866–1942. Dutch geologist. Known for studies of geology of Indonesia. Author of *Verkennings-Tochten in Zentral Borneo* (1900).

Mo·le·schott \ˈmō-le-sk̲ȯt\, Jacob. 1822–1893. Dutch physiologist. Professor, Zürich (1856), Turin (1861), Rome (1879). Did research on blood, diet, respiration, innervation of the heart, etc. Advocate of scientific materialism, expressed in his controversial *Kreislauf des Lebens* (1852).

Moles·worth \ˈmōlz-wərth\, Mary Louisa, *nee* Stew·art \ˈst(y)ü-ərt, ˈst(y)u̇(-ə)rt\. *Pseudonym* Ennis Graham. 1839–1921. Scottish writer, b.

Rotterdam. m. Major R. Molesworth (1861). Best known as writer of children's books as *Carrots: Just a Little Boy* (1876), *The Cuckoo Clock* (1877).

Molesworth, Sir William. 8th Baronet Molesworth. 1810–1855. English politician. M.P. (1832–41, 1845–55); founded *London Review* (1835); acquired *Westminster Review* (1836) and was associated with John Stuart Mill in editing it; ardent champion of measures for colonial self-government; denounced penal transportation; colonial secretary (1855).

Mo·ley \ˈmō-lē\, Raymond Charles. 1886–1975. American journalist, educator, and political figure, b. Berea, Ohio. Professor of government (1923–28), of public law (1928–54), Columbia U.; assistant secretary of state (1933) and member of the "brains trust" group of advisers to President F.D. Roosevelt. Editor of magazine *Today* (1933–37); contributing editor to *Newsweek* (1937–68); author of *Lessons in American Citizenship* (1917), *Parties, Politics, and People* (1921), *Tribunes of the People* (1932), etc.

Mo·lière \mȯl-yer\. *Orig.* Jean-Baptiste Po·que·lin \pȯ-klaⁿ\. 1622–1673. French actor and playwright. Formed own company and performed in Paris and in the provinces (from 1643); gained patronage of the duc d'Orléans (1658) and that of Louis XIV (1765), the troupe becoming known as King's Comedians. As playwright, made first outstanding success with *Les Précieuses ridicules* (1659), followed by a series of comedies which established his reputation as supreme in this field. Among his most notable comedies were *Sganarelle* (1660), *École des maris* (1661), *Les Fâcheux* (1661), *École des femmes* (1662), *Le Mariage forcé* (1664), *Dom Juan* (1665), *Le Misanthrope* (1666), *Le Médecin malgré lui* (1666), *Tartuffe* (1667), *Amphitryon* (1668), *L'Avare* (1668), *Le Bourgeois gentilhomme* (1670), *Les Fourberies de Scapin* (1671), *Les Femmes savantes* (1672), *Le Malade imaginaire* (1673). Regarded as the greatest of French comedic writers and by many as the greatest of all French writers.

Mo·li·na \mō-ˈlē-nä\, Luis de. 1535–1600. Spanish theologian. Entered Jesuit order (1553); taught at Coimbra (1563–67), Évora (1568–83); propounded doctrine of Molinism, that divine grace is open to all, but that its efficacy depends upon the will that accepts it; caused theological controversy. Works included *Concordia liberi arbitrii cum gratiae donis* (1588–89), *Commentaria in primam partem divi Thomae* (1592), *De jure et justitia* (1593–1609).

Molina, Tirso de. See Gabriel TÉLLEZ.

Mo·li·net \mȯ-lē-ne\ *or* **Mou·li·net** \mü-\, Jean. 1435–1507. French poet and chronicler. Succeeded Georges Chastellain as historiographer of Charles the Bold; retained post under Mary of Burgundy and Philip the Handsome; continued Chastellain's *Chronique* for years 1474 to 1504; a leader among the "Rhétoriqueurs," Burgundian school of poetry.

Mo·li·nos \mō-ˈlē-nōs\, Miguel de. 1628–1696. Spanish priest and mystic. Ordained (1652); to Rome (1663); published (1675) *Guida spirituale,* outlining an extreme form of Quietism; imprisoned for heresy (1685) and his book condemned by the Inquisition (1687).

Mo·lique \mō-ˈlēk\, Wilhelm Bernhard. 1802–1869. German violinist and composer. Music director and conductor, Stuttgart (1826–49); in London (1849–66) as successful teacher and concert violinist. Compositions included six violin concertos, a violin concertino, a violoncello concerto, eight string quartets and other chamber music, and the oratorio *Abraham* (1860).

Mo·li·tor \mȯ-lē-tȯr\, Gabriel-Jean-Joseph. Comte. 1770–1849. French soldier. Entered Napoleonic army (1791); general (1799); occupied Dalmatia (1806); governor of Swiss Pomerania (1807); governor general of Holland (1811–13); created count (1808), marshal of France and a peer (1823).

Mol·ler \ˈmȯl-ər\, Georg. 1784–1852. German architect. Court architect to grand duke of Hesse-Darmstadt (from 1810); his works included the Opera House (1819), Ludwigskirche (1822–26), new chancellery (1826), and other public buildings in Darmstadt, and the ducal palace at Wiesbaden.

Møl·ler \ˈmœl-ər\, Poul Martin. 1794–1838. Danish writer. Professor, Christiania (Oslo, 1828–31), Copenhagen (from 1831). Author of *Strøtanker* (Aphorisms), etc.; a founder of poetic Realism in Denmark; best known for unfinished novel of student life *En dansk students eventyr* (pub. posthumously).

Mol·let \mȯl-e\, Guy. 1905–1975. French politician. Joined Socialist party (1921); served in army and Resistance in World War II; deputy (from 1945); secretary general of Socialist party (from 1946); minister of state (1946–47, 1950–51); with Mendès-France organized Republican Front (1950); premier of France (1956–57); joined England in occupation of Suez Canal (1956); failed to solve Algerian crisis; again minister of state (1958–59).

Möll·hau·sen \ˈmœl-ˌhaü-zən\, Heinrich Balduin. 1825–1905. German traveler and author. On scientific expeditions in western U.S. (1851–52, 1853–54, 1857–58); befriended by Alexander von Humboldt; appointed custodian of royal libraries, Potsdam (1854). Author of 45 novels and 80 *novellen,* mainly of adventure based on experiences in the western U.S.

Mol·lien \mȯl-yaⁿ\, François-Nicolas. Comte. 1758–1850. French politician. Tax official (from 1775); under Napoléon, administrator (1799), director general (1801) of sinking fund; councilor of state (1804) and finance minister (1806–14); count of the Empire (1808); again finance minister during Hundred Days; created peer of France (1819).

Mollien, Gaspard-Théodore. 1796–1872. French explorer and diplomat. Explored Senegal, Guinea, Portuguese Guinea (1817–19); failed to locate source of the Niger; first European to make contact with peoples of interior West Africa; consul to Haiti (1828), consul general to Cuba (1831). Author of *Voyage dans l'intérieure de l'Afrique* (1820).

Mollison, Amy Johnson. See JOHNSON.

Mol·lis·on \ˈmäl-əs-ᵊn\, James Allan. 1905–1959. British aviator, b. Scotland. m. (1932; div. 1938) Amy Johnson (*q.v.*). Established numerous records for airplane flights, including that from Australia to England (8 days, 19 hours; 1931), England to Cape Town via west coast (4 days, 17 hours; 1932), England to India (with wife; 22 hours, 1934); made first solo westward flight across North Atlantic (1932), first flight from England to South America (1933), first flight from England to U.S. (with wife; 1933).

Mol·nár \ˈmȯl-när\, Ferenc. 1878–1952. Hungarian playwright and novelist. War correspondent on German–Austrian front (1914–18); to U.S. (1940). Author of short stories and novels as *Az éhes város* (1900), *Éva* (1903), *A Pálutcai fiúk* (1907), *Rabok* (1907), *Andor* (1918), *A zenélo angyal* (1933), *A zőld huszár* (1937); plays as *Az ördög* (1907), *Liliom* (1909), *A vörös malom* (1923), *A hattyú* (1926), *Olympia* (1928), *Harmonia* (1932), *Arthur* (1943).

Mo·lo·tov \ˈmäl-ə-ˌtȯf, ˈmȯl-, ˈmōl-, -ˌtȯv\, Vyacheslav Mikhaylovich. *Orig. surname* Skryabin. 1890–1986. Soviet political leader, b. Nolinsk, Russia. Organizer of Bolshevik party (from 1906). Secretary of Central Committee (from 1921); staunch supporter of Stalin as Lenin's successor; granted full membership in Politburo (1926); assumed control of Moscow party committee and purged it of anti-Stalinists; served as Soviet Union's prime minister (1930–41); also served (from May 1939) as commissar of foreign affairs, negotiating German-Soviet Nonaggression Pact (August 1939). After German invasion of Soviet Union (June 1941) served on special war cabinet; arranged alliances with Great Britain and U.S.; served as Soviet spokesman at Allies' conferences at Teheran (1943), Yalta (1945), and Potsdam (1945), as well as San Francisco conference creating the U.N. Resigned as foreign minister (1949) but resumed post from Stalin's death (March 1953) until dismissal by Khrushchev (June 1956); lost all high offices following failure to depose Khrushchev (June 1957); appointed ambassador to Mongolia. Expelled from Communist party (1962); reinstated (1984). During World War II ordered production of bottles of inflammable liquid now known as "Molotov cocktails."

Molt·ke \ˈmȯlt-kə\, Adam Gottlob. Graf. 1710–1792. Danish politician, b. Germany. Made page to future king Christian VI (1722), chamberlain to future Frederick V (1730); court marshal (1743–46); privy councilor (1747); created count (1750); most influential of Frederick's advisers; dismissed by Christian VII (1766). His grandson ¶Graf Adam Wilhelm (1785–1864) entered government service (1809); minister of finance (1831); president of exchequer (1845); first prime minister of Danish parliamentary government (1848–52); introduced constitution (1849); member of Landsting (1849–60).

Moltke, Helmuth Karl Bernhard von. Graf. 1800–1891. Prussian soldier. In youth entered Danish service; transferred to Prussian army (1821); on general staff (1833); traveled widely; as chief of Prussian general staff (1858–88), reorganized Prussian army (1858–63); devised strategic and tactical command methods for modern mass armies engaged on broad fronts; directed strategy in war against Denmark (1864), against Austria (1866), and against France (1870–71); created field marshal (1871).

Moltke, Helmuth Johannes Ludwig von. 1848–1916. German soldier. Nephew of Helmuth von Moltke. Adjutant to uncle (1882); quartermaster general (1903); chief of general staff (from 1906) and director of German strategy at outbreak of World War I (1914); lost the first battle of the Marne (Sept. 1914); relieved of his command (Nov. 1914).

Mol·za \ˈmȯlt-sä\, Francesco Maria. 1489–1544. Italian Humanist and poet. Known esp. for his *Ninfa Tiberina* in *ottave rime* (1538).

Mom·bert \ˈmȯm-ˌbert\, Alfred. 1872–1942. German poet. Member of "Kosmiker" group and a forerunner of the Expressionists. Works included *Tag und Nacht* (1894), *Der Glühende* (1896), *Der Denker* (1901), *Die Blüte des Chaos* (1905), *Der Held der Erde* (1919), *Sfaire der Alte* (1936–42).

Momm·sen \ˈmȯm-zən\, Theodor, *in full* Christian Matthias Theodor. 1817–1903. German classical scholar and historian. Professor of law, Leipzig (1848); dismissed (1850) for participation in liberal movement; professor of Roman law, Zürich (1852) and Breslau (1854), and of ancient history, Berlin (1858); member of Progressive party (1863–67) and National Liberal party (1873–79) in Prussian Landtag and strong opponent of Bismarck; member of Liberal Union (1881 ff.) and German Liberal party (1884 ff.) in Reichstag; awarded Nobel prize for literature (1902). Editor in chief (from 1854) of *Corpus inscriptionum Latinarum* (1863 ff.) for Berlin Acad., and editor of *Auctores antiquissimi* section of *Monumenta Germaniae historica,* to which he also contributed editions of Cassiodorus (1861), Solinus (1864), etc.; author of *Römische Geschichte* (1854–56, supplementary vol. 1886), *Die Geschichte* *des römischen Münzwesens* (1860), *Römisches Staatsrecht* (1871–88), *Römisches Strafrecht* (1899), editions of Edict of Diocletian (1851), Justinian's *Digest* (1866), *Codex Theodosianus* (1905, with P. Meyer), and other works chiefly on epigraphy, archaeology, and Roman law.

Mo·na·gas \mō-'nä-gäs\, José Tadeo. 1784–1868. Venezuelan general and politician. Fought under Bolívar in War of Independence (1812–21); military leader of Venezuelans when union with Gran Colombia dissolved (1830); broke with Páez (1847); president of Venezuela (1847–50, 1855–58); actually a dictator; revised constitution (1857); overthrown by a revolution (1858) and banished. Returned to power (1868) as leader of Blue faction, but died soon after. His brother ¶José Gregorio (1795–1858) was president of Venezuela (1851–55; placed in office by brother); signed law abolishing slavery (1854).

Mona Lisa. See Lisa del GIOCONDO.

Mo·nash \'män-,ash\, Sir John. 1865–1931. Australian engineer and soldier. Brigade commander at Gallipoli (1915) and in defense of Suez Canal; commanded 3d Australian division in France (1916–18); lieutenant general (1918) commanding Australian army corps in France during final months of the war; retired (1930) with rank of general.

Monboddo, Lord. See James BURNETT.

Mon·cey \mōⁿ-sā\, Bon-Adrien-Jeannot de. Duc de Co·ne·glia·no \,kō-nāl-'yän-ō\. 1754–1842. French soldier. Commander of army which defeated Spaniards and forced peace (1795); created marshal of the Empire (1804) and duc (1808); commanded national guard in Paris (1814) and defended city against allied forces; created peer of France by Louis XVIII; commanded corps in French expedition in Spain (1823).

Monck *or* **Monk** \'məŋk\, George. 1st Duke of Al·be·marle \'al-bə-,märl\. 1608–1670. English soldier. Served with Dutch against Spanish (1629–38); commanded regiment against Irish rebels (1642–43). In Royalist army until capture at Nantwich (1644); imprisoned in Tower (1644–46); after imprisonment, took negative oath of covenant; as major general in Ulster and at Dunbar (1650), commended himself to Cromwell; entrusted by Cromwell with subjugation of Scotland (1652); won two sea fights over Tromp (1653) which ended First Dutch War. Governor of Scotland (1654); at Coldstream, Berwick, organized regiment known as Coldstream Guards (1659–60); promised support to Parliament, crossed border, and marched to London (1660); general in chief of land forces and joint commander of navy; forced dissolution of John Lambert's army and restored Rump Parliament; entered into direct communication with Charles II; caused election of new parliament, which restored monarchy (May 1, 1660); welcomed Charles II at Dover. Created Baron Monck, Earl of Tor·ring·ton \'tór-iŋ-tən, 'tär-\, and Duke of Albermarle; privy councilor, chamberlain, lord lieutenant of Devon and Middlesex; soon withdrew from political affairs. Maintained order and supervised preventive measures through plague in London (1665); in Second Dutch War took to sea with Rupert; defeated by de Ruyter off Dunkirk (1666); month later won complete victory over de Ruyter off North Foreland.

Moncrieff. See also SCOTT-MONCRIEFF.

Moncrieff, Alexander. 1695–1761. See under Ebenezer ERSKINE.

Mon·crieff \mən-'krēf\, Sir Alexander. 1829–1906. British army engineer. Originated (about 1868) Moncrieff system of disappearing gun mountings for heavy batteries.

Mond \'mänd\, Ludwig. 1839–1909. British chemist and industrialist, b. Germany. To England (1862, naturalized 1867). Partner in firm at Widnes, where his patented method for recovering sulfur lost in Leblanc alkali process was used; with J. T. Brunner, started alkali works (1873) which became firm of Brunner, Mond, and Co., manufacturers of alkali by ammonia-soda process; developed Mond gas, a producer gas; devised a gas battery; discovered nickel carbonyl and a method of extracting nickel from its ores; formed Mond Nickel Co. with mines in Canada; founded Davy-Faraday Research Laboratory at Royal Institution (1896). His son ¶Sir Alfred Moritz (1868–1930), 1st Baron Mel·chett \'mel-chət\, industrialist, financier, and politician; chairman of Mond Nickel Co.; Liberal M.P. (1906–28); first commissioner of works (1916–21); minister of health (1921–22); Zionist; instituted Mond-Turner conferences to discuss problems between employers and Trades Union Congress (1927).

Mon·di·no dei Liuc·ci \mōn-'dē-nō-dāl-yüt-chē\. *Also called* Rai·mon·di·no dei Liuz·zi \,rī-mōn-'dē-nō-dāl-yüt-tsē\ *and* Mun·di·nus \(,)mən-'dī-nəs\. c.1270–c.1326. Italian anatomist. Author of textbook *Anothomia* (1316), which remained authoritative until appearance of Vesalius's anatomical work.

Mondory. See MONTDORY.

Mon·dri·an \'mòn-drē-än\, Piet. *Orig.* Pieter Cornelis Mon·dri·aan \'mōn-drē-än\. 1872–1944. Dutch artist. From a traditional Dutch landscape style, evolved through Divisionism, Luminism, Cubism (from his move to Paris, 1912); with Theo van Doesburg, Bart van der Leck, Vilmos Huszar formed the de Stijl group (1917); developed "neoplastic" aesthetic involving reduction of paintings to elements of straight lines, primary colors, noncolors; fled Paris to London (1938), New York City (1940).

Mo·net \mó-ne\, Claude. 1840–1926. French painter. Introduced by Eugène Boudin to novel practice of painting in open air; developed technique of rendering light and color as actually perceived, perfecting style (c.1872) known as Impressionism; settled at Giverny (1883), where he cultivated a celebrated garden and built water-lily pond that inspired his huge last paintings. Among his many notable canvases were *Un Déjeuner sur l'herbe, La Robe vert, Déjeuner dans un intérieur, Impression, soleil levant, La Gare Saint-Lazare, La Seine à Lavacourt, Les Meules,* a series of landscapes along the Seine, a series on Rouen cathedral.

Mo·ne·ta \mō-'ne-tä\, Ernesto Teodoro. 1833–1918. Italian journalist and pacifist. Staff officer under Garibaldi; in Italian army (1861–67). Director of Milan newspaper *Il Secolo* (1867–96); became interested in cause of international peace, founding Società Internazionale per la Pace: Unione Lombarda (c.1887) and other peace societies; president, International Peace Congress at Milan (1906); shared Nobel peace prize (1907) with Louis Renault.

Monge \mōⁿzh\, Gaspard. Comte de Pé·luse \pā-lūez\. 1746–1818. French mathematician and physicist. Taught at École Militaire de Mézières (1768–83); developed in that period techniques of descriptive geometry; professor of hydraulics, the Louvre (1780 ff.); naval examiner (1783–89); on committee that established metric system (1791); minister of marine and colonies (1792–93); helped found (1795) École Polytechnique and for it wrote texts *Géométrie descriptive* and *Feuilles d'analyse appliquée à la géométrie* (both 1799); accompanied Napoléon to Egypt (1798–1801) and helped found (1798) Institut d'Egypt; deprived of all offices (1814).

Mongkut. See RAMA IV.

Mo·nier \mòn-yā\, Joseph. 1823–1906. French gardener and inventor. Patented (1867) idea of using iron rods in concrete for strengthening; considered principal inventor of reinforced concrete.

Mon·i·er-Wil·liams \,mən-ē-ər-'wil-yəmz, ,män-\, Sir Monier. *Orig. surname* Williams. 1819–1899. English Sanskrit scholar, b. Bombay. Professor, Haileybury (1844–59), Oxford (1860–87); conceived and established Indian Inst. (begun 1875, completed 1896). Author of Sanskrit grammars and dictionaries, and works on Indian poetry, philosophy, religious and sacred books.

Mo·ñi·no y Re·don·do \mōn-'yē-nō-ē-rā-'thón-dō\, José. Conde de Flo·ri·da·blan·ca \flō-rē-thä-'bläŋ-kä\. 1728–1808. Spanish politician. Prime minister of Spain (1776–92); instituted reform program of Charles III; dismissed for hostility towards France. President of Central Junta of Spanish government during uprising against Napoleonic invasion (1808).

Mo·niusz·ko \mòn-'yüsh-kō\, Stanisław. 1819–1872. Polish composer. Composed operas including *Halka* (1848, rev. 1857), *Flis* (1858), *Hrabina* (1859), *Verbum nobile* (1860), *Straszny dwór* (1864); operettas; sacred music as *Litanie Ostrobramskie* (1843), 7 masses; secular cantatas as *Milda* (1848), *Nijola* (1852), *Widma* (1858?); 360 songs including those in *Śpiewnik domowy* (1843–59).

Moniz, António Egas. See EGAS MONIZ.

Monk. See also MONCK.

Monk \'məŋk\, Maria. 1816–1849. Canadian impostor, b. St. John's, Que. In two books, *Awful Disclosures by Maria Monk* (1836) and *Further Disclosures* (1837), claimed to reveal revolting practices in Hôtel Dieu convent at Montreal from which she said she had escaped; books sold several hundred thousand copies and helped fan anti-Catholic bigotry.

Monk, Thelonious Sphere. 1920–1982. American musician, b. Rocky Mount, N.C. Pianist in bands of Lucky Millander (1942), Coleman Hawkins (1944); led own small groups thereafter; with Dizzy Gillespie, Charlie Parker, etc., one of principal creators of "bop" style; as composer and arranger, noted for harmonic and rhythmic sophistication and humor; songs included "Epistrophy," "Straight No Chaser," "Blue Monk," "Round Midnight."

Monk·house \'məŋk-,haùs\, Allan Noble. 1858–1936. English dramatist and novelist. Plays included *Mary Broome* (1912), *The Conquering Hero* (1923), *Grand Cham's Diamond* (1925), *O Death, Where Is Thy Sting?* (1927), *Cecilia* (1932); novels *A Deliverance* (1898), *My Daughter Helen* (1922), *Marmaduke* (1924).

Monluc, Seigneur de. See Blaise de LASSERAN MASSENCÔME.

Monmouth, Duke of. See James SCOTT.

Monmouth, Earl of. See Robert Carey, under Henry CAREY (1524?–1596).

Monmouth, Geoffrey of. See GEOFFREY of Monmouth.

Mon·net \mó-ne, -nā\, Jean-Omer-Marie-Gabriel. 1888–1979. French economist and diplomat. Engaged in family brandy distilling firm; member of Inter-Allied Maritime Commission (1915–17); deputy secretary general, League of Nations (1919–23); chairman of Franco-British Economic Coordination Committee (1939–40); proposed plan for Franco-British union (1940);

minister of commerce in provisional French government (1944); secured establishment of National Planning Council and was its head (1945–47); commissioner general for implementation of "Monnet Plan" for economic reconstruction (1947); with Robert Schuman proposed European common market for coal and steel (1950); president (1952–55) of High Authority of European Coal and Steel Community; founder and president (1955–75), Action Committee for the United States of Europe.

Mon·nier \mòn-yā\, Henri-Bonaventure. 1805–1877. French caricaturist and playwright. Creator of famous characters Mme Gibou and Joseph Prudhomme; author and illustrator of *Scènes populaires* (1830), *Nouvelles scènes populaires* (1835–39), *Scènes de la ville et de la campagne* (1841), *Les Bourgeois de Paris* (1854), *Les Mémoires de M. Joseph Prudhomme* (1857); also wrote vaudevilles and comedies.

Mon·noy·er \mòn-wä-yā\, Baptiste, *in full* Jean-Baptiste. 1634–1699. French painter. Known esp. for his pictures of flowers; assisted in decoration of Versailles, Trianon, Marly, Saint-Cloud, Mendon, and in England Montagu House, Kensington and Hampton Court palaces.

Mo·nod \mò-nō\, Adolphe-Louis-Frédéric-Théodore. 1802–1856. French clergyman, b. Denmark. Reformed minister in Naples, Lyons; founded (1833) Free Evangelical church; professor, Montauban (1836–47); minister at Oratoire, Paris (1847–56). Author of *Sermons* (1844), *Saint Paul* (1851), etc. His brother ¶Frédéric-Joël-Jean-Gérard (1794–1863), Reformed minister in Paris (from 1820), founded (1849) a Free Evangelical church, Paris.

Monod, Gabriel-Jean-Jacques. 1844–1912. French historian. Founder and director of *Revue historique* (1875); lectured at École des Hautes Études, École Normale Supérieure; professor, Collège de France (1905). Author of *Allemands et Français* (1872), *Études critiques sur les sources de l'histoire mérovingienne* (1872–85), etc.

Monod, Jacques-Lucien. 1910–1976. French biochemist. Member (1945–76), director (1971–76), Pasteur Institute, Paris; professor, U. of Paris (from 1959), Collège de France (from 1967); proposed mechanism by which some genes might regulate other genes through medium of "messenger" RNA synthesis; proposed mechanism of protein synthesis in ribosomes also involving messenger RNA molecules; awarded Nobel prize for physiology or medicine (1965, with François Jacob and André Lwoff). Author of *Le Hasard et la nécessité* (1970).

Mon·rad \'mòn-räth\, Ditlev Gothard. 1811–1887. Danish clergyman and politician. Lutheran minister; a leader of National Liberal party; head of government of 1848; bishop of Lolland-Falster (1848–54); member of Riksdag (1849–65); minister of culture and interior (1859–63); prime minister (1863–64), dismissed following war with Prussia; lived in New Zealand (1865); returned to Denmark (1869); again bishop of Lolland-Falster (1871); member of opposition party in Riksdag (1882–86).

Mon·rad \'mòn-räd\, Marcus Jakob. 1816–1897. Norwegian philosopher. Professor, Christiania (Oslo; from 1851); sought to unite Hegelian point of view with Christian doctrine. Author of *Tankeretninger i den nyere tid* (1874), etc.

Monro. See also MUNRO.

Mon·ro \mən-'rō\, Alexander. *Called* Monro pri·mus \-'prī-məs\. 1697–1767. Scottish anatomist. First professor of anatomy, Edinburgh (1720); helped make Edinburgh a major center for medical training; demonstrated cause of jaundice. His youngest son ¶Alexander Monro, *called* Monro se·cun·dus \-sə-'kən-dəs\, of Craiglockhart (1733–1817), anatomist, succeeded to his father's chair (1759–1808); first to perform paracentesis and to use stomach pump; described (1783) communication between lateral ventricles of the brain, called after him *foramen of Monro;* described bursea mucosae (1788); author of works on the nervous system, physiology of fishes, the brain, eye and ear. His son ¶Alexander Monro, *called* Monro ter·ti·us \-'tər-shē-əs\ (1773–1859), joint professor with his father (1800) and alone (1817–46); lectured mainly from grandfather's notes; wrote on hernia, the stomach, the brain.

Mon·roe \mən-'rō\, Harriet. 1860–1936. American poet and editor, b. Chicago. Founded (1912) and edited (1912–36) *Poetry: a Magazine of Verse.* Author of *Valeria and Other Poems* (1891), *The Columbian Ode* for opening of World's Columbian Exposition, Chicago (1892), *The Passing Show—Modern Plays in Verse* (1903), *You and I* (1914), *The Difference and Other Poems* (1924), *A Poet's Life* (1938).

Monroe, James. 1758–1831. Fifth president of the United States, b. Westmoreland Co., Va. Served in American Revolution; member, Continental Congress (1783–86); practiced law, Fredericksburg, Va.; U.S. senator (1790–94); U.S. minister to France (1794–96); governor of Virginia (1799–1802); one of negotiators of the Louisiana Purchase (1803); U.S. minister to England (1803–07); again governor of Virginia (1811); U.S. secretary of state (1811–17), of war (1814–15). President of the U.S. (1817–25); period known as "era of good feeling" because of lack of vigorous factional quarrels; Florida acquired (1819); Missouri Compromise legislation enacted (1820); Monroe Doctrine promulgated (1823).

Monroe, Marilyn. *Orig.* Norma Jean Mor·ten·son \'mòrt-ᵊn-sən\, *later used surname* Baker. 1926–1962. American actress, b. Los Angeles. Appeared in films including *All About Eve* (1950), *Monkey Business* (1952), *Niagara* (1953), *Gentlemen Prefer Blondes* (1953), *River of No Return* (1954), *Seven-Year Itch* (1955), *Bus Stop* (1956), *Prince and the Show Girl* (1957), *Some Like It Hot* (1959), *The Misfits* (1961); world famous as "sex symbol" and later as a tragic figure.

Monsieur le Comte. See LOUIS, comte de Soissons.

Mon·si·gny \mōⁿ-sēn-yē\, Pierre-Alexandre. 1729–1817. French composer. Regarded with Grétry and Philidor as a creator of French comic opera. Composed operas *Les Aveux indiscrets* (1759), *On ne s'avise jamais de tout* (1761), *Le Roy et le fermier* (1762), *Le Déserteur* (1769), *Félix, ou l'enfant trouvé* (1777), etc., with librettos mostly by Sedaine (from 1761).

Mon·son \'mən(t)s-ᵊn\, Sir William. 1569–1643. English naval commander. Distinguished himself in Cádiz expedition (1596); vice admiral of squadron sent to intercept Spanish treasure fleet (1602); admiral of narrow seas (1604–16); arrested Lady Arabella Stuart (1611); deprived of command on suspicion of complicity in Overbury murder; vice admiral (1635) in Dutch campaign. Author of valuable *Naval Tracts* (printed in full 1704).

Mons·tre·let \mōⁿ-strə-le\, Enguerrand de. c.1390–1453. French chronicler. In service of John of Luxembourg and present at Compiègne when Joan of Arc was captured by Burgundians. Author of *Chronique* (covering period 1400–44), a continuation of Froissart.

Mon·ta·gna \mōn-'tän-yä\, Bartolommeo. c.1450–1523. Italian painter. Founder of school of Vicenza. Among works were altarpiece for S. Michele, Vicenza, frescoes illustrating life of St. Blasius in SS. Nazaro e Celso, Verona, *Madonna and Child,* and *Madonna with Saints.*

Mon·ta·gna·na \ˌmōn-tän-'yä-nä\, Domenico. c.1687–1750. Italian instrument maker. Opened shop in Venice (c.1711); noted for violins and esp. cellos.

Montagu. See also MONTAGUE.

Mon·ta·gu \'mänt-ə-ˌgyü, 'mənt-\. English family of earls and dukes of Man·ches·ter \'man-ˌches-tər, -chə-stər\, including:

Henry (c.1563–1642), 1st Earl of Manchester; brother of Edward, 1st Baron Montagu of Boughton; sergeant-at-law and king's sergeant (1611); opened case against Earl and Countess of Somerset (1616); as chief justice of King's Bench, condemned Sir Walter Raleigh (1618); lord high treasurer (1620); created Viscount Man·de·ville \'man-də-ˌvil, -vəl\ (1620), earl (1626); lord privy seal (1628).

¶Edward (1602–1671), 2d earl, son of 1st earl; M.P. (1623); created Baron Montagu of Kim·bol·ton \kim-'bōlt-ᵊn\ (1626); a leader of Puritans in House of Lords; one of 12 peers who petitioned king to summon Long Parliament (1640); impeached by king for high treason (1642), acquitted; major general of eastern counties (1643); nominally in command at Marston Moor (1644); charged by Cromwell with incompetency and neglect, resigned (1645); opposed trial of Charles II and formation of Commonwealth (1649); supported Restoration; privy councilor and lord chamberlain (1660).

¶Charles (c.1660–1722), 1st Duke of Manchester, grandson of 2d earl; supported William III in Ireland (1690); ambassador to Venice (1697), Paris (1699), Venice (1707); created duke (1719).

Montagu. English family of barons and dukes of Montagu, including:

Sir Edward Montagu (d. 1557), judge; chief justice of King's Bench (1539); transferred to Court of Common Pleas (1545); member of council of regency under Henry VIII's will. His grandson ¶Edward (1562–1644), 1st Baron Montagu of Bough·ton \'bòt-ᵊn, 'baůt-\; brother of Henry Montagu (*q.v.*), 1st Earl of Manchester; imprisoned as a Royalist; died in Tower of London. Edward's son ¶Edward (1616–1684), 2d baron, conducted Charles I to Holmby House and aided him in escape (1647).

¶Ralph Montagu (1638–1709), 1st Duke of Montagu, son of 2d baron; took part in negotiations with Louis XIV (1669) and in arranging neutrality of England in war between France and Holland (1676); privy councilor (1672); lost favor (1678) by conducting affairs with Duchess of Cleveland and her daughter the Countess of Sussex simultaneously; precipitated impeachment of Earl of Danby (1678); created earl by William III (1689), duke by Anne (1705).

Montagu *or* **Mon·ta·cute** \'mänt-ə-ˌkyüt, 'mənt-\. Name of English family holding the earldom of Salis·bury \'sòlz-ˌber-ē, -b(ə-)rē\ (1337–1428), including:

William (1301–1344), 3d Baron Montagu; partisan of Edward II; carried off Earl of March from Nottingham Castle (1330); created earl of Salisbury (1337); marshal of England (1338); wrested Isle of Man from Scottish (c.1340).

¶William (1328–1397), 2d earl, son of 1st earl; fought at Crécy and Poitiers (1346); one of the original knights of the Order of the Garter; attended Richard II in meeting with Wat Tyler's rebels at Smithfield (1381).

¶John (1350?–1400), 3d earl, nephew of 2d earl; notorious as a Lollard; conspired against Henry IV, beheaded.

¶Thomas (1388–1428), 4th earl, son of 3d earl; restored to title (1409) and dignities (1421); fought at Agincourt (1415) and Harfleur (1416); lieutenant general of Normandy (1419); until 1428, chief English commander in France; completed conquest of Champagne and Maine; killed in siege of Orléans.

Montagu *or* **Moun·ta·gu** \'mänt-ə-,gyü, 'mənt-\. English family of earls of Sand·wich \'san-(,)(d)wich\, including:

Edward Montagu (1625–1672), 1st Earl of Sandwich; nephew of Henry Montagu, 1st Earl of Manchester, and of Edward Montagu, 1st Baron Montagu of Boughton (*qq.v.*). Joined Parliamentary army (1643); raised regiment with which he fought at Marston Moor (1644), Naseby (1645), Bristol (1645). M.P. (1645–48); member of Cromwell's council of state (1653); general at sea (1656), colleague of Robert Blake; at odds with General Monck, as revealed in diary of his secretary, Samuel Pepys; sent with fleet to arrange peace with Sweden and Denmark (1659). Assisted in restoration of Charles II; general at sea (1660), carried fleet to side of Charles and conducted Charles to England from Holland. In command of squadron in battle with Dutch off Lowestoft (1665); ambassador to Madrid (1666–69), concluded treaty with Spain (1667); in renewal of Dutch war, took conspicuous part in action in Southwold Bay, where he was blown up with his flagship *Royal James.*

¶John Montagu (1718–1792), 4th earl; succeeded his grandfather, 3d earl (1729); took seat in House of Lords (1739); a lord commissioner of the admiralty (1744–49); plenipotentiary to congress at Breda (1746); first lord of admiralty (1749–51, 1763, 1771–82); a principal secretary of state (1763–65); notorious for part he took in prosecution of Wilkes, for association with Mad Monks of Medmenham Abbey (see Francis DASHWOOD), and for bribery and corruption in management of the admiralty, whence his nickname Jemmy Twitch·er \'twich-ər\. Sandwich (now Hawaiian) Islands named after him by Captain Cook. Traditionally held to be inventor (1762) of the sandwich for eating at the gaming table.

Montagu, Charles. 1st Earl of Hal·i·fax \'hal-ə-,faks\. 1661–1715. English wit, politician, and patron of literature. Grandson of Sir Henry Montagu, 1st Earl of Manchester. M.P. (1689–99); as lord of treasury (1692), originated English national debt by inducing Parliament to raise a million pounds by life annuities; carried through a bill proposed earlier by William Paterson to raise loan, the subscribers to which were to form a corporation, thus originating the Bank of England (1694); chancellor of exchequer and privy councilor (1694); member of Whig Junto; reformed the currency (1695) with help of Somers, Locke, and Newton; first introduced exchequer bills; carried through scheme for forming consolidated fund to meet interest on government loans (1696); first lord of treasury and prime minister (1697); obliged to resign on account of unpopularity (1699); created Baron Halifax (1700); impeached (1701) for obtaining grants from William III in trust for himself and for promoting second Partition Treaty, and (1703) for neglect of duties as auditor, but not prosecuted. On George I's accession, created earl of Halifax (1714) and 1st lord of treasury. Collaborated with Matthew Prior in *The City Mouse and the Country Mouse* (1687), a parody on Dryden's *Hind and the Panther.* Friend and patron of Addison, Steele, and Congreve.

His nephew ¶George Montagu (d. 1739) succeeded him as Baron Halifax; created earl of Halifax (1715). Succeeded by his son ¶George Montagu Dunk \'dəŋk\ (1716–1771), 2d earl; took name of Dunk on marriage (1741) with heiress of large fortune of Sir Thomas Dunk; as president of Board of Trade (1748–61), aided founding of colony of Nova Scotia, the chief town of which was named Halifax after him (1749), and zealously extended American commerce; lord lieutenant of Ireland (1761–63); first lord of admiralty (1762); secretary of state (1762); joined triumvirate with Grenville and Egremont; dismissed (1765); lord privy seal in administration of his nephew Lord North (1770).

Montagu, Edwin Samuel. 1879–1924. English politician. Son of Samuel Montagu. M.P. (1906–22); secretary to H.H. Asquith (1906–16); parliamentary undersecretary to India office (1910–14); financial secretary to the treasury (1914–15); privy councilor, chancellor of duchy of Lancaster (1915); minister of munitions (1916); secretary of state for India (1917–22); helped prepare Montagu-Chelmsford Report on Indian government (1918); helped draft and carry Government of India Act (1919) which first granted ministerial responsibilities to native Indians.

Montagu, Elizabeth, *nee* Robinson. 1720–1800. English author, wit and beauty. m. (1742) Edward Montagu (d. 1775), grandson of 1st Earl of Sandwich and cousin of Edward Wortley Montagu. Made her salon in Mayfair center of literary and social life; held assemblies for literary discussion, to which epithet *bluestocking* was first applied; among guests were Lord Lyttelton, Burke, Garrick, Sir Joshua Reynolds, Hannah More, Fanny Burney. Contributed three dialogues to Lord Lyttelton's *Dialogues of the Dead* (1760); author of essay *Writings and Genius of Shakespear* (1769), defending him against strictures of Voltaire.

Montagu, Lady Mary Wort·ley \'wərt-lē\. 1689–1762. English poet and letter writer. Daughter of Evelyn Pierrepont, 1st Duke of Kingston; precocious child, taught herself Latin; m. (1712) Edward Wortley Montagu (d. 1761), grandson of 1st Earl of Sandwich; accompanied husband on embassy to Constantinople (1716–18), on which she wrote sparkling *Letters from the East* (unauthorized publication, 1763); on return, introduced into England inoculation for smallpox, which she had observed in Turkey. Settled in Twickenham as leader of society and fashion, and renewed friendship with Pope and Swift; quarreled with Pope (1722); bitterly attacked by Pope and Swift; left husband and country to live in Italy (1739–61), whence she wrote letters to her daughter, Countess of Bute. Author also of *Town Eclogues* (1716), play *Simplicity* (c.1735).

Montagu *or* **Moun·ta·gue** \'mänt-ə-,gyü, 'mənt-\, Richard. 1577–1641. English prelate and controversialist. Archdeacon of Hereford and chaplain to James I (1617); defended himself against charges of Arminianism and popery in *Appello Caesarem* (1625); through influence with Laud, became bishop of Chichester (1628), of Norwich (1638). Also wrote *Immediate Addresse unto God Alone* (1624), *Acts and Monuments of the Church Before Christ Incarnate* (1642).

Montagu, Samuel. *Orig.* Montagu Sam·uel \'sam-yə(-wə)l\. Baron Swayth·ling \'swāth-liŋ\. 1832–1911. English financier and philanthropist. Founded with brother and brother-in-law foreign-exchange and banking firm (1853); profited in arbitrage; instrumental in making London clearinghouse of international money market. Liberal M.P. (1885–1900); member of gold and silver commission (1887–90), supported bimetallism. Zealous supporter of Jewish religious, social, and charitable work. Created baron (1907).

Montague. See also MONTAGU.

Mon·ta·gue \'mänt-ə-,gyü, 'mənt-\, Charles Edward. 1867–1928. British journalist and man of letters. Member of staff of *Manchester Guardian* (1890–1914, 1919–25); chief editorial writer and dramatic critic on *Guardian.* Author of the novels *A Hind Let Loose* (1910), *Rough Justice* (1926), *Right off the Map* (1927); stories *Fiery Particles* (1923), *Action* (1928); essays *Disenchantment* (1922), *The Right Place* (1924); etc.

Mon·taigne \mōⁿ-tenʸ, *Angl* män-'tān\, Michel Ey·quem de \ek-em-də-\. 1533–1592. French essayist. Thoroughly educated in Humanist learning; counsellor of Parlement of Bordeaux (1557–70); retired to his estate, Château de Montaigne, and wrote *Essais* (1572–80); mayor of Bordeaux (1581–85); wrote third book of *Essais* (1588). Fame rests on these *Essais,* reflecting spirit of scepticism and inspired by his studies in the classics, esp. Plutarch, and by his consideration of lives and ideals of leading figures in his own time; in form, style, and thought, the *Essais* exercised important influence on French and English literature.

Montalbán, Juan Pérez de. See PÉREZ DE MONTALBÁN.

Mon·ta·le \mōn-'tä-lā\, Eugenio. 1896–1981. Italian poet. A founder of journal *Primo tempo* (1922); director of Gabinetto Vieusseux library, Florence (1929–38); poetry critic, *La Fiera letteraria* (1938–48); literary and then music editor, *Corriere della sera* (from 1948). Author of verse early classed as Hermeticist but later notable for directness of expression. Wrote *Ossia di seppia* (1925), *La casa dei doganieri* (1932), *Le occasioni* (1939), *Finisterre* (1943), *La bufèra e altro* (1956), *Satura* (1962), *Accordi e pastelli* (1963), *Il colpevole* (1966), *Xenia* (1972); published translations from Shakespeare, Eliot, G.M. Hopkins, etc., in *Quaderno di traduzione* (1948). Elected senator for life (1967); awarded Nobel prize for literature (1975).

Mon·ta·lem·bert \mōⁿ-tá-läⁿ-ber\, Charles-Forbes-René de. Comte. 1810–1870. French journalist and politician. Founder with Lamennais of journal *L'Avenir* (1830); wrote for *L'Univers* (from 1833); entered House of Peers (1835); champion of liberalism in the state and in the Roman Catholic church; member of Constituent Assembly (1848) and Corps Législatif; opposed Napoléon III's policies from date of the coup d'état (1851). Among notable works were *Des intérêts catholiques au XIXᵉ siècle* (1852), *De l'avenir politique de l'Angleterre* (1856), *Les Moines d'Occident* (1863–77).

Montalembert, Marc-René de. Marquis. 1714–1800. French military engineer. Entered army (1732); served in War of Polish Succession, War of Austrian Succession, Seven Years' War; developed ideas for simplified polygonal fortifications to replace complex plans of Vauban; ideas long resisted by engineering establishment but finally published in *La Fortification perpendiculaire* (1776–78); émigré for a time after Revolution, later consultant to Lazare Carnot.

Montalvo, Garci Rodríguez de. See RODRÍGUEZ DE MONTALVO.

Mon·tal·vo \mòn-'täl-bō\, Juan. 1832–1889. Ecuadoran writer. Spent much of life in exile for opposition to Ecuadoran regime. Author of essays on liberalism and ethics as *Catilinarias* (1880–82), *Siete tratados* (1882), *El espectador* (1886–88), and of *Capítulos que se le olvidaron a Cervantes* (1895), a pastiche of *Don Quixote.*

Montalvo, Luis Gálvez de. See GÁLVEZ DE MONTALVO.

Mon·ta·nel·li \ˌmōn-tä-ˈnel-lē\, Giuseppe. 1813–1862. Italian politician. Founded nationalist newspaper *L'Italia* (1847); formed Tuscan ministry; with Mazzini and Guerrazzi, a triumvir of Florentine republic after uprising of 1849; at Paris (1849–59). On return to Italy unsuccessfully advocated formation of central Italian kingdom; member, Italian parliament (1861–62).

Mon·ta·ñés \mōn-tän-ˈyās\, Juan Martínez. 1568–1649. Spanish sculptor. Worked in Seville (from 1587); leading Spanish sculptor of his day and a principal creator of Spanish Baroque style. Known for gilded and polychromed wood altars and altar figures in Seville cathedral, church of Santiponce, San Miguel in Jérez de la Frontera.

Mon·ta·nus \män-ˈtā-nəs\. 2d century. Christian schismatic of Phrygia. Claimed to be incarnation of the Paraclete and proclaimed a further revelation; prophesied the Millenium; gathered followers (known as Montanists, Phrygians, or Cataphrygians) and established ascetic rule. Most distinguished convert to Montanism was Tertullian (*q.v.*). Sect suppressed during the reign of Justinian (527–565), but remnants survived to 9th century.

Montauban, Charles Cousin-. See COUSIN-MONTAUBAN.

Montausier, Duc de. See Charles de SAINT-MAURE.

Montbazon, Duc de. See ROHAN family.

Mont·calm-Go·zon \mōⁿ-kålm-gò-zōⁿ\, Louis-Joseph de. Marquis de Montcalm de Saint-Vé·ran \-də-saⁿ-vā-räⁿ\. 1712–1759. French soldier. Entered army (1724); distinguished himself at Prague (1742), Piacenza (1746); field marshal (1756) and commander of French troops in North America; fought heroically to save Canada from the British; captured Oswego (1756), Ft. William Henry (1757); repulsed Abercrombie at Ticonderoga (July 8, 1758); defeated and mortally wounded in the battle of Quebec (Sept. 13, 1759).

Mont·chres·tien \mōⁿ-krā-tyaⁿ\, Antoine de. c.1575–1621. French playwright and economist. An adventurer; exile in England and Holland (1605–11); established steel foundry; killed while taking part in Huguenot uprising. Credited with introduction of the term *political economy* into French by publication of his book *Traicté de l'économie politique* (1615); author of a number of tragedies, including *Sophonisbe* (1596), *L'Ecossaise* (1601), *Les Lacènes* (1601).

Montcorbier, François de. See François VILLON.

Mont·do·ry *or* **Mon·do·ry** \mōⁿ-dò-rē\. *Orig.* Guillaume des Gil·berts \dā-zhēl-ber\. 1594–1651. French actor. Joined company of Valleran le Conte (1612); member of company of Prince of Orange (1622–29); with Charles Le Noir established (1629) playhouse in Paris and enjoyed immediate success with Corneille's *Mélite;* opened (1634) Théâtre Marais; continued to present works of Corneille; considered first great French actor.

Monte \mōⁿt\, Philippe de. 1521–1603. Flemish composer. Court Kapellmeister, Vienna (1568–1603). Composed 38 masses, 319 motets, and some 1200 secular madrigals in 42 books.

Monteagle, Baron. See William PARKER.

Montebello, Duc de. See Jean LANNES.

Mon·té·clair \mōⁿ-tā-kler\, Michel Pi·gno·let de \pēn-yò-led-ə\ *or* Pi·no·let de \pē-nò-led-ə-\. 1667–1737. French composer. Double bass player at Paris Opéra (from 1699). Leading French composer of dramatic and instrumental music in period between Lully and Rameau. Works included opera *Jephté* (1732), opera ballet *Les Festes de l'été* (1716), cantatas as *Adieu de Tircis à Climène* (1695, perhaps first French cantata), airs, sacred music; also noted as a teacher and writer of pedagogic works as *Nouvelle méthode pour apprendre la musique* (1709).

Montecorvino, Giovanni da. See GIOVANNI DA MONTECORVINO.

Mon·te·cuc·co·li \ˌmōn-tā-ˈkük-kō-lē\ *or* **Mon·te·cuc·cu·li** \-kü-lē\, Raimundo. Prince. 1609–1680. Italian soldier. Entered Austrian army (1625); distinguished himself at Breitenfeld (1631), Lützen (1632); prisoner in Sweden (1639–42); fought for Modena in War of Castro (1642–44). As field marshal, drove Swedes from Germany, Denmark, Pomerania (1658–60); defeated Turks (1664) in battle of St. Gotthard (Szentgotthard); imperial generalissimo (1664), president of Hofkriegsrat (1668); commanded imperial army in war of empire and Holland against France (1672–75), opposing Turenne. For his services, made prince of the empire (1679) and given duchy of Melfi by the king of Naples (1679).

Mon·te·fel·tro \ˌmōn-tā-ˈfāl-trō\ *or* **Mon·te·fel·tre** \-trā\. Distinguished Italian family of Renaissance period holding power in Urbino (from 1234) and prominent in Ghibelline cause, including: Antonio (d. 1403), added Gubbio and Cantiano to family domain. His son ¶Guidantonio (d. 1443) married a niece of Pope Martin V, who extended family lands in direction of Tuscany, beginning long rivalry with Malatesta family. His illegitimate son ¶Federigo (1422–1482) was one of greatest condottieri of the day; led papal armies against Sigismondo Malatesta (1463); created duke of Ur·bi·no \ür-ˈbē-nō\ by Pope Sixtus IV (1474). His son ¶Guidobaldo (1472–1508) was expelled from Urbino by Cesare Borgia (1502), but regained power there (1503); last of Montefeltro line.

Mon·te·fi·o·re \ˌmänt-ē-fē-ˈōr-ē, -ˈòr-\, Claude Joseph Gold·smid- \ˈgōl(d)-(ˌ)smid-\. 1858–1938. British Jewish leader. Grandson of Sir Isaac Lyon Goldsmid (*q.v.*); assumed surname Goldsmid by letters patent; a founder and joint editor (1888–1908) of *Jewish Quarterly Review;* Hibbert lecturer, Oxford (1892); active in educational and philanthropic work; president of Anglo-Jewish Association (1896–1921); founded (1902) Jewish Religious Union; president of University College, Southampton (1915–34), World Union for Progressive Judaism (1926–38). Author of *Liberal Judaism* (1903), *The Synoptic Gospels* (1909), *Judaism and St. Paul* (1914), *Rabbinic Anthology* (with H. Loewe, 1938), etc.

Montefiore, Sir Moses Haim. 1784–1885. British Jewish philanthropist, b. Leghorn, Italy, of Anglo-Italian family. Brother-in-law of Benjamin Gompertz. Amassed fortune in London Stock Exchange; retired (1824); devoted himself to alleviating hardships of his coreligionists; journeyed seven times to Palestine (1827–75) in behalf of his people; founded girls' school and hospital at Jerusalem (1855); obtained from sultan of Morocco edict giving equality to Jews (1864); interceded with Prince Carol of Romania in behalf of Moldavian Jews (1867). Made baronet (1846).

Mon·tei·ro Lo·ba·to \mōⁿ(n)-ˈtā-rü-lō-ˈbä-tü\, José Bento. 1883–1948. Brazilian writer. Lawyer and coffee planter in São Paulo interior, whence he contributed sketches and articles collected in *Urupés* (1918), featuring backland character Jeca Tatú; founded *Revista do Brasil;* a forerunner of Modernism in Brazil. Author also of *Ideias de Jeca Tatú* (1919), *Cidades mortas* (1919), *Negrinha* (1920).

Mon·te·jo \mōn-ˈtā-kō\, Francisco de. c.1479–1553. Spanish conquistador. To New World (1514); took part in conquest of Cuba; a founder of Veracruz (1519); named adelantado and captain general of Yucatán (1526); began (1527) conquest of Yucatán, completed (1535–45) by his son ¶Francisco (1508–1574), who founded (1542) capital city of Mérida.

Mon·te·li·us \mòn-ˈtā-lē-əs\, Oscar, *in full* Gustav Oscar Augustin. 1843–1921. Swedish archaeologist. On staff (from 1863), professor (from 1888), director (1907–13), Museum of National Antiquities, Stockholm; known for work on prehistoric chronology, esp. of Bronze Age. Author of *Om tidsbestämming inom Bronsåldern* (1888), *Civilization of Sweden in Heathen Times* (1888), etc.

Mon·te·ma·yor \mōn-tā-mä-ˈyòr\ *or* **Mon·te·mor** \mōn-tā-ˈmòr\, Jorge de. 1520?–?1561. Spanish romancer and poet, b. Portugal. To Spain (1543) to join entourage of the principe (later Philip II); traveled in Italy and Flanders. Author of the unfinished pastoral romance *Diana* (1559), written in prose with passages of verse included and widely popular in Europe; an English translation by Bartholomew Young (1598) was used by Shakespeare in *Two Gentlemen of Verona.*

Mon·te·mez·zi \ˌmōn-tā-ˈmed-dzē\, Italo. 1875–1952. Italian composer. Composed operas including *Giovanni Gallurese* (1905), *L'amore dei tre re* (1913), *La notte de Zoraima* (1931); orchestral works as *Paolo e Virginia* (1929), *Italia mia!* (1944).

Mon·té·pin \mōⁿ-tā-paⁿ\, Xavier de. 1823–1902. French novelist and playwright. Author of popular novels, including *Les Chevaliers du Lansquenet* (1847), *Les Viveurs de province* (1860), *La Sorcière blonde* (1876), *La Porteuse de pain* (1884), *Chanteuse des rues* (1902); his plays included *La Policière* (1890), *Le Médecin des folles* (1891), *La Joyeuse d'orgue* (1897), *La Marchande de fleurs* (1901), and dramatizations of many of his novels.

Monterrey, Conde de. See Gasper de ACEVEDO Y ZÚÑIGA.

Mon·tes \ˈmòn-tās\, Ismael. 1861–1933. Bolivian politician. Took part in revolution of 1898; president of Bolivia (1904–09, 1913–17); minister to England (1911) and France (1917); lived in exile in France (from 1920); returned to become head of Liberal party (1928).

Montespan, Marquise de. See Françoise ROCHECHOUART DE MORTEMART.

Montesquieu, Baron de La Brède et de. See Charles-Louis de SECONDAT.

Mon·tes·so·ri \mōn-tās-ˈsò-rē, *Angl* ˌmänt-ə-ˈsōr-ē, -ˈsòr-\, Maria. 1870–1952. Italian physician and educator. First woman in Italy to receive medical degree (1894); became interested in education as assistant physician at university psychiatric clinic, and studied psychiatry and pedagogy; founder and principal (1899–1901) of Orthophrenic School for feeble-minded and defective children; successfully put into practice educational ideas of Édouard Seguin, and determined to apply similar principles and methods to education of normal children; lecturer on pedagogy (1900–07), professor of anthropology (1904–08), U. of Rome. Opened first Montessori school for children (Casa dei Bambini) in slum districts of Rome (1907); her method emphasized development of child's initiative and sense and muscle training by means of specially prepared teaching materials and games, and stressed freedom of child. Director of Montessori Institute, Barcelona (1917), and of training courses in London (1919); government inspector of schools in Italy (1922–34); founder of Montessori Training Center, Laren, the Netherlands (1938). Author of *Il metodo della pedagogia scientifica* (1909), *Antropologia pedagogica* (1910), *Il* *segreto dell'infanzia* (1938), *Formazione dell'uomo* (1949), *La mente del bambino* (1952), etc.

Mon·tet \mō^{n}-te\, Pierre. 1885–1966. French Egyptologist. Professor, Strasbourg (1919–48), Collège de France (1948–56); director of excavations at Byblos in Syria, where oldest alphabetical inscriptions discovered up to that time were found (1921–24); engaged in study of ruins of Tanis in Lower Egypt (1929–51). Author of *Byblos et l'Égypte* (1928), *La Nécropole royale de Tanis* (1947–51), etc.

Mon·teux \mō^{n}-tœ̄\, Pierre. 1875–1964. American conductor, b. Paris, France. Conductor of Diaghilev's Ballets Russes (1911–14), leading premieres of Stravinsky's *Petrouchka* (1911) and *Sacre du Printemps* (1914), etc. In French army (1914–16); to U.S. (1916); conductor at the Metropolitan Opera House (1917–19); conductor, Boston Symphony (1919–24), Paris Symphony (1929–38), San Francisco Symphony (1936–52); naturalized (1942); conductor of London Symphony (1961–64); noted as interpreter of 20th century music.

Mon·te·ver·di \ˌmōn-tā-ˈvār-dē\ *or* **Mon·te·ver·de** \-dā\, Claudio. 1567–1643. Italian composer. In service of Duke of Mantua (c.1590–1612), maestro di capella (from 1601); maestro di capella, St. Mark's, Venice (from 1613); became priest (1633). Leading figure in musical revolution of 16th century; highly influential in establishing new genres of opera and oratorio. Composer of 9 books of madrigals, esp. 5-part madrigals; canzonets; operas as *Orfeo* (1607), *L'Arianna* (1608, lost except for the "Lamento"); *L'incoronazione di Poppea* (1642); also ballets, masses, Psalms, motets, and other sacred music.

Mon·tez \ˈmän-ˌtez\, Lola. *Orig.* Marie Dolores Eliza Rosanna Gilbert. 1818–1861. American dancer and adventuress, b. Limerick, Ireland. Three times married; London debut as Lola Montez (1843); successful in Europe; mistress of Louis I of Bavaria (1847–48), who made her Baroness Ro·sen·thal \ˈrō-zən-ˌtäl\ and Countess Lans·feld \ˈläns-ˌfelt\; controlled Bavarian government (1847–48); opposed Jesuits; ousted by revolution (1848). On stage in U.S. (1851) and Australia (1855–56); settled in New York. Author of *Anecdotes of Love* (1858), *Arts of Beauty* (1858), etc.

Mon·te·zu·ma \mȯn-tā-ˈsü-mä *Angl* ˌmänt-ə-ˈzü-mə\ *or* **Moc·te·zu·ma** \ˈmȯk-tā-ˈsü-mä\. *Nahuatl* Mo·te·cuh·zo·ma \ˌmȯ-tā-kwä-ˈsō-mä\. Name of two Aztec rulers:

Montezuma I. d. 1469. Emperor of Mexico (1440–69). Domain said to have extended from Atlantic to Pacific; enlarged and beautified Mexico City.

Montezuma II. 1466–1520. Emperor (1502–20). Succeeded uncle Ahuitzotl; waged wars with Tlascalans; tried to persuade Cortés not to come to Mexico City (1519); seized by Cortés in Tenochtitlán and held as hostage; after uprising of Aztecs against Spaniards, wounded as he addressed them; died a few days later.

Mont·fau·con \mō^{n}-fō-kō^{n}\, Bernard de. 1655–1741. French scholar. Entered Benedictine Congregation of Saint-Maur (1676); called to Paris (1687) to prepare edition in Latin of works of Greek church fathers; his *Palaeographia graeca* (1708) won him recognition as founder of science of paleography. Also published editions of Athanasius (1698), John Chrysostom (1718–38); wrote *L'Antiquité expliquée et représentée en figures* (15 vols., 1719).

Montferrat, Count of. See BONIFACE.

Mont·fort \mō^{n}-fȯr\, Louis-Marie Gri·gnion de \grēn-yō^{n}-də-\. Saint. 1673–1716. French cleric. Ordained priest (1700); preacher in Nantes, Poitiers; apostolic missionary for France (1706). Founded Daughters of Wisdom (1700) and Company of Mary, known as Montfort Fathers (1705). Canonized (1947).

Montfort, Simon de. *Also known as* Simon IV de Montfort l'Amau·ry \-lȧ-mō-rē\. 1165?–1218. French soldier. Grandson, through mother, of Robert de Beaumont, Earl of Leicester; m. (1190; d. 1221) Alice de Montmorency. Took part in Fourth Crusade (1202–04); at call of Pope Innocent III led crusade against Albigenses, or Cathari (1209–18); conquered Béziers, Carcassonne, won battle of Muret (1213); awarded lands of Raymond, Count of Toulouse (1215); killed while besieging Toulouse.

Mont·fort \ˈmänt-fərt, *Fr* mō^{n}-fȯr\, Simon de. Earl of Leices·ter \ˈles-tər\. c.1208–1265. English soldier, b. Normandy. Son of Simon de Montfort (1165?–1218); inherited claim to earldom of Leicester; to England (1229) and formally gained earldom (1236); m. (1238) Eleanor, sister of Henry III; became reconciled with Henry III, after quarrel provoked by other nobles, and after accompanying Richard, Earl of Cornwall, on crusade (1240), by covering Henry's escape from disastrous Poitevin campaign (1242); king's deputy in disaffected province of Gascony (1248); put down with severity excesses of seigneurs; acquitted on charges of oppression but yielded to demand of jealous Henry III for his resignation (1252). In parliament led opposition in resisting king's demand for subsidy (1254); in Mad Parliament at Oxford headed opposition, with Earl of Gloucester, and was one of fifteen signers of Provisions of Oxford (1258); on Henry's revocation of assent to provisions withdrew to France in despair (1261). On invitation of barons who accused king of falseness to his oath, led rebellion against all violators of the provisions, in the Barons' War (1263–65); injudiciously accepted arbitration of Louis IX of France, who declared the provisions invalid (1264); renewed rebellion, triumphed over royal forces and captured king at battle of Lewes (1264); virtually governor of kingdom, summoned (Jan. 1265) parliament of churchmen, barons, four knights from each shire, and two citizens from each borough, the beginning of the modern Parliament. Made alliance with Welsh that aroused resentment of Welsh Marchers, who united with Prince Edward against him; defeated and killed at Evesham (Aug. 4, 1265). Long popularly revered as a martyr and saint, known as "Simon the Righteous."

Mont·ge·las \mō^{n}zh-lȧ\, Maximilian Joseph von. Graf. *Original family name* de Gar·ne·rin \gȧr-nə-ra^{n}\. 1759–1838. Savoyard statesman. Entered service of Duke Charles II Augustus of Zweibrücken; under successor Elector Maximilian Joseph, served as Bavarian prime minister (1799–1817); also minister of finance (1803–17), of the interior (1807–17); introduced first German written constitution (1808); failed to win complete independence for Bavaria but considered founder of the state.

Mont·gol·fier \mō^{n}-gȯl-fyā, *Angl* mänt-ˈgäl-fē-ər\, Joseph-Michel (1740–1810) and his brother Jacques-Étienne (1745–1799). French inventors. Built first practical balloon, inflated with heated air, which made ascent of ten minutes at Annonay on June 5, 1783; built balloon in which first manned ascent was made, over Paris (Nov. 21, 1783).

Mont·gom·er·ie \(ˌ)mən(t)-ˈgəm-(ə-)rē, män(t)-, -ˈgäm-\, Alexander. c.1545–1611. Scottish poet. One of the last of the *makaris,* poets writing in Lowland Scots; pensioned by James VI (1583); later disgraced for involvement in pro-Catholic Ladyland plot (1597). Best known for allegorical "The Cherrie and the Slaye" (printed 1597); also wrote "The Flytting Betwixt Montgomerie and Polwart," sonnets, lyrics, songs.

Montgomery. (1) Earls of (cr. 1605). See HERBERT family. (2) Countess of. See Anne Clifford, under CLIFFORD family.

Mont·gom·ery \(ˌ)mən(t)-ˈgəm-(ə-)rē, män(t)-, -ˈgäm-\, Sir Bernard Law. 1st Viscount Montgomery of Ala·mein \ˌal-ə-ˈmān\. 1887–1976. British soldier. Commissioned in army (1908); distinguished himself in World War I; commanded a division in France (1939–40); as commander of 8th army in Egypt (1942) began offensive at el-Alamein (Nov. 1942) which drove Rommel's forces from Egypt, Libya, and Tripolitania and forced him to abandon Mareth Line in southern Tunisia (May 1943); led 8th army in Sicily and Italy (1943–44). Following Allied invasion of France, made field marshal (1944) and commander of British-Canadian 21st army group in northern France (1944); commander, British-occupied zone in Germany (1945–46); created viscount (1946); chief of imperial general staff (1946–48); deputy commander of NATO forces (1951–58).

Mont·go·me·ry \mō^{n}-gȯm-rē\, Gabriel de. Comte. c.1530–1574. French soldier. By accident, mortally wounded King Henry II in a joust (1559); became Protestant; served under prince de Condé; captured and executed at Paris.

Mont·gom·ery \(ˌ)mən(t)-ˈgəm-(ə-)rē, män(t)-, -ˈgäm-\, James. 1771–1854. British poet, b. Scotland. Editor and proprietor (1794–1825) of paper in Sheffield, the *Sheffield Iris.* Author of descriptive poems *The Wanderer of Switzerland* (1806), *Greenland* (1819), *The Pelican Island* (1828), and of hymns and verse renderings of the Psalms.

Montgomery, Lucy Maud. See Lucy Maud MACDONALD.

Montgomery, Richard. 1736–1775. American Revolutionary officer, b. Swords, County Dublin, Ireland. In British service (1756–72), serving much in America; emigrated to America (1773). At outbreak of Revolution, appointed brigadier general in Continental army (1775); commander of expedition against Montreal; captured Montreal (Nov. 1775); major general; killed leading assault on Quebec (Dec. 31, 1775).

Montgomery, Robert. 1807–1855. English poet. Ordained (1835); held various preferments. Touched popular religious sentiment in *Omnipresence of the Deity* (1828) and *Satan* (1830). Immortalized by Macaulay's attempt to demolish his reputation in *Edinburgh Review.*

Mon·ther·lant \mō^{n}-ter-lä^{n}\, Henry-Marie-Joseph Mil·lon de \mē-yō^{n}-də-\. 1896–1972. French writer. Author of novels, essays, and plays mainly of trenchant social criticism aimed esp. at democratic and "feminine" values. Novels included *Le Songe* (1922), *Les Olympiques* (1924), *Les Bestiaires* (1926), *La Petite Infante de Castille* (1929), *Les Célibataires* (1934); tetralogy *Les Jeunes Filles* (1936), *Pitié pour les femmes* (1936), *Le Démon du bien* (1937), *Les Lépreuses* (1939); *Les Auligny* (1956), *Le Chaos et la nuit* (1963), *Les Garçons* (1969). Essays included *La Relève du matin* (1920), *Mors et vita* (1932), *Service inutile* (1935), *L'Équinoxe de septembre* (1938), *Le Solstice de juin* (1941), *Carnets* (1947), *Le Fichier parisien* (1951), *Va jouer avec cette poussière* (1966), *Le Treizième César* (1970). Plays included *L'Exile* (1929), *La Reine morte* (1942), *Malatesta* (1946), *Le Maître de Santiago* (1947), *La Ville dont le prince est un enfant* (1951), *Port-Royal* (1954), *Don Juan* (1958), *La Guerre civile* (1965).

Mon·tho·lon \mō^{n}-tȯ-lō^{n}\, Charles-Tristan de. Comte. 1783–1853. French soldier. Entered army (1798); general of brigade (1811); aide-de-camp to Napoléon at Waterloo (1815); accompanied Napoléon to St. Helena and was named an executor of his will. Editor of *Mémoires pour servir à l'histoire de France sous Napoléon* (with General Gourgaud, 1822–23). Aided Louis-Napoléon in attempt to seize throne (1840); imprisoned (1840–47); member of Constituent Assembly (1849). Author of *Récits de la captivité de Napoléon à Ste. Hélène* (1847).

Mon·ti \'mōn-tē\, Vincenzo. 1754–1828. Italian poet. Secretary to Cardinal Braschi (1781–97); professor of eloquence, U. of Pavia (1802 ff.); historiographer of the kingdom of Italy under Napoléon (1806–14). Author of Neoclassical verse celebrating his many enthusiasms, including "Il pelegrino apostolico" (1782), "Al signor di Montgolfier" (1783), "La Bassvilliana" (1793), "Il fanatismo" and "La superstizione" (1797), "Prometeo" (1797), "La mascheroniana" (1800); published three tragedies, love poetry, and an outstanding blank verse *Iliade* (1810).

Mon·ti·cel·li \mōn-tē-sā-lē, -se-\, Adolphe-Joseph-Thomas. 1824–1886. French painter. Known esp. for scenes of courtly revels executed in characteristic impasto manner; painted also landscapes, portraits, circus scenes, floral studies.

Mont·mo·ren·cy \mō^{n}-mȯ-rä^{n}-sē, *Angl* ˌmänt-mə-'ren(t)-sē\. Name of distinguished French family originating in Montmorency in northern France, seigneury of which was granted (996) to Bouchard I; prominent members included: Baron Mathieu II (c.1174–1230); distinguished himself in wars under Louis VIII and entrusted by him with guardianship of his children; constable of France (1218). ¶Baron Charles (1325–1381); marshal (1343) and chamberlain (1346) of France, and captain general of the Flemish borders; helped negotiate peace of Brétigny (1360). ¶Baron Jean II (1402–1477); chamberlain of France; at his death family divided into three branches (see also Filips van MONTMORENCY; MONTMORENCY-BOUTEVILLE). From the senior line came ducs de Montmorency:

¶Anne (1493–1567), 1st duc de Montmorency, was reared with future King Francis I; marshal of France (1522); captured with Francis at Pavia (1525); governor of Languedoc and grand master of France (1526); led French against Charles V in Provence (1536); constable of France (1537); created duke by Henry II (1551); Catholic leader against Protestants (1551–67); defeated at St.-Quentin (1557); commanded at Dreux (1562), mortally wounded at St.-Denis. His son ¶François (1530–1579), duc, m. (1559) Diane de Valois, illegitimate daughter of Henry II; marshal (1559). Succeeded as duke by his brother ¶Henri I (1534–1614); governor of Languedoc (from 1563); marshal (1567), constable of France (1593). His son ¶Henri II (1595–1632) succeeded as duke, governor of Languedoc; marshal of France (1630); joined Gaston d'Orléans in revolt against Richelieu; captured and beheaded.

Montmorency, Filips van. Graaf van Hoorne *or* Hoorn \'hōrn\. 1524?–1568. Dutch nobleman. Courtier to Emperor Charles V; led imperial troops against League of Schmalkalden (1546–47); commander of Flemish guard of Philip II of Spain (1550); stadholder of Gelder and Zutphen (1555–67); admiral of Spanish fleet (1559); member of council of state of the Netherlands (1561–65); with William I the Silent and the Graaf van Egmond, secured recall of Cardinal Archduke Antoine de Granvelle (1564); withdrew from council in protest of continuing persecution of Protestants and helped form League of Nobles (1565); refused to join William I in armed opposition to Spanish authorities and retired to estate (1566); lured to Brussels by Duke of Alba (1567); with Egmond, seized, convicted of treason and heresy, executed.

Montmorency-Boute·ville \-büt-vēl\, Francois-Henri de. Duc de Lux·em·bourg \lūk-sä^{n}-bür\. 1628–1695. French soldier. Posthumous son of François de Montmorency-Bouteville, executed by Richelieu; reared with Louis II de Bourbon, the prince de Condé; fought with Condé at Lens (1648) and in Fronde uprising (1650–53); in Spanish army (1653–59); pardoned and returned to France (1659); by marriage acquired title of duc de Luxembourg (1661); lieutenant general (1668); commanded army occupying Cologne (1672); occupied Utrecht (1672–73), executing masterful retreat from William of Orange's forces; marshal of France (1675); commander of army of the Rhine (1676–78); surrendered Philippsburg to Charles V of Lorraine (1677); defeated William of Orange at Saint-Denis (1678). Imprisoned (1680) for alleged complicity in Affair of the Poisons; exiled but recalled (1681) as captain of king's guards; commander in chief (1689); crushed army of Prince George Frederick of Waldeck at Fleurus (July 1, 1690); defeated armies of William (now William III) at Mons (1691), Namur and Steenkerke (1692), Neerwinden (1693).

Montpensier. See ORLÉANS.

Montreuil, Gerbert de. See GERBERT.

Montrose, Earl and Marquis of. See James GRAHAM.

Monts, Sieur de. See Pierre du GUA.

Montt \'mȯnt\, Manuel. 1809–1880. Chilean politician. Member of Congress (1840–51); minister of interior and of justice under Pres. Bulnes; founded (1843) U. of Chile; president of Chile (1851–61) ruling as authoritarian conservative; administration marked by progress in education, construction of railways and telegraphs, tax reform, etc.; president of supreme court (1861–80). His son ¶Jorge (1846–1922) was naval officer; commanded naval forces in revolt against Pres. Balmaceda (1891); provisional president (1891), elected president of Chile (1891–96). Another son ¶Pedro (1849–1910) was member (1876–91), president (1885–91), Chamber of Deputies; took part in revolt against Balmaceda (1891); senator (1900); president of Chile (1906–10).

Mon·tu·cla \mō^{n}-tue-klȧ\, Jean-Étienne. 1725–1799. French mathematician. Published treatise on history of the quadrature of the circle (1754) and classic *Histoire des mathématiques* (1758, rev. 1799–1802).

Mon·tú·far y Ri·ve·ra Mae·stre \mōn-'tü-fä-rē-rē-'vā-rä-'mī-strā\, Lorenzo. 1823–1898. Guatemalan politician and historian. Frequently exiled for opposition to dictatorship of Rafael Carrera; lawyer, magistrate, and publisher in Costa Rica; as foreign minister of Costa Rica, helped organize Central American defense against William Walker (*q.v.*); ran unsuccessfully for president of Guatemala (1891). Author of *Reseña historica de Centro America* (1878–88).

Mon·tyon \mō^{n}-tyō^{n}\, Jean-Baptiste-Antoine Au·get de \ō-zhed-ə-\. Baron. 1733–1820. French lawyer, economist, and philanthropist. Councilor of state (1775); chancellor to Monsieur, brother of the king (1780); émigré (1789–1814). Instituted by bequest two prizes awarded annually by French Academy, one for a literary work of high moral character and the other for a poor citizen who has performed a notably virtuous deed.

Mon·vel \mō^{n}-vel\. *Orig.* Jacques-Marie Bou·tet \bü-te\. 1745–1812. French actor and playwright. Excelled as comedian; author of several comic operas and comedies, including *L'Amant bourru* (1777), *Les Amours de Bayard* (1786).

Monzaemon, Chikamatsu. See CHIKAMATSU.

Mon·zie \mō^{n}-zē\, Anatole de. 1876–1947. French politician and scholar. Deputy (1909–19, 1929–40); senator (1920–29); minister of finance (1925), of education (1925), of justice (1925), of public works (1925–26, 1938–40); founder and president, *Encyclopédie française*.

Moo·die \'müd-ē\, Susannah, *nee* Strick·land \'strik-lənd\. 1803–1885. Canadian writer, b. Bungay, Suffolk, England. Sister of Agnes Strickland, Catherine Traill; m. (1831) Lt. J.W.D. Moodie; to Canada (1832); related lessons of life in Upper Canadian wilderness in *Roughing It in the Bush* (1852); also wrote *Life in the Clearings* (1853) and several novels.

Moo·dy \'müd-ē\, Dwight Lyman. 1837–1899. American evangelist, b. Northfield, Mass. Shoe salesman, Boston and Chicago (to 1860); gave up business to devote himself to evangelism; organized North Market Sabbath School (1858) in Chicago; met Ira D. Sankey (1870); with him made two tours in Great Britain (1873–75 and 1881–83); campaigned in many cities in U.S. Founded Northfield Seminary for girls (1879), Mount Hermon School for boys (1881), Chicago (now Moody) Bible Institute (1889). With Sankey published *Sacred Songs and Solos* (1873), *Gospel Hymns* (1875).

Moody, John. 1868–1958. American financial analyst, b. Jersey City, N.J. On staff of Spencer Trask & Co., bankers (1890–1900); founded (1900) *Moody's Manual of Industrial and Miscellaneous Securities;* founded (1905) and edited *Moody's Magazine;* founded (1909) annual *Moody's Analyses of Investments;* merged his operation (1919) with that of late Henry V. Poor; firm became (1941) Standard and Poor. Author of *The Truth about Trusts* (1904), *How to Analyze Railroad Reports* (1911), *The Railroad Builders* (1919), *Masters of Capital* (1921), etc.

Moody, William Henry. 1853–1917. American jurist, b. Newbury, Mass. Special prosecutor in trial of Lizzie Borden (1893); member, U.S. House of Representatives (1895–1902); U.S. secretary of the navy (1902–04); U.S. attorney general (1904–06); associate justice, U.S. Supreme Court (1906–10).

Moody, William Vaughn. 1869–1910. American poet and playwright, b. Spencer, Ind. Teacher of English, U. of Chicago (1895–1907). Author of *Poems* (1901); two dramas in verse, *The Masque of Judgment* (1900) and *The Fire-Bringer* (1904); and two important plays, *The Great Divide* (1906) and *The Faith Healer* (1909). With Robert Morss Lovett wrote a *History of English Literature* (1902) and *A First View of English Literature* (1905).

Moon \'mün\, William. 1818–1894. English inventor. Blind (from 1840); devised (1845) a system of embossed type (Moon's type) for the blind, easier to learn than Braille but requiring more space; issued Bible in his system, which he extended to Irish and Chinese.

Moo·ney \'mü-nē\, James. 1861–1921. American ethnologist, b. Richmond, Ind. On staff, Bureau of American Ethnology (1885–1921), esp. as investigator of Indians of the South and West. Author of *The Siouan Tribes of the East* (1894), *The Ghost Dance Religion* (1897), *Myths of the Cherokee* (1900), *The Cheyenne Indians* (1907), etc.

Mooney, Thomas Joseph. 1882–1942. American labor leader, b. Chicago. Joined Socialist party; active in labor organization in San Francisco. With ¶Warren K. Bil·lings \'bil-iŋz\ (1893–1972), convicted of responsibility for bomb explosion that killed nine persons and wounded about 40 others in San

Francisco during Preparedness Parade (July 22, 1916). Mooney condemned to death and Billings to life imprisonment; Mooney's sentence commuted by governor (1918) to life imprisonment. Both Mooney and Billings protested their innocence; case subject to several investigations. Mooney pardoned and released (1939); Billings released (1939), pardoned (1961).

Moore \'mō(ə)r, 'mȯ(ə)r, 'mu̇(ə)r\, Alfred. 1755–1810. American jurist, b. New Hanover Co., N.C. Nephew of James Moore; served in uncle's regiment in Revolution (1775–81); planter and politician in N.C.; judge of state superior court (1798–99); associate justice, U.S. Supreme Court (1799–1804).

Moore, Benjamin. 1748–1816. American clergyman, b. Newtown, Long Island, N.Y. Ordained Episcopal priest (1774); loyal to Great Britain through the Revolution; rector of Trinity Church (1800) and bishop of New York (from 1801); professor at Columbia (1784–86) and president (1801–11). His son ¶Clement Clarke (1779–1863), b. N.Y.C.; professor, General Theological Seminary (1823–50); best known for authorship of the ballad "A Visit from St. Nicholas," known also as "'Twas the Night Before Christmas" (pub. anonymously in Troy, N.Y., *Sentinel,* Dec. 23, 1823).

Moore, Clement Clarke. See under Benjamin MOORE.

Moore, Daniel McFarlan. 1869–1936. American electrical engineer, b. Northumberland, Pa. Took out over 100 U.S. patents in the fields of radio, X-ray, and lighting; patented (1917) neon gas-discharge lamp.

Moore, Douglas Stuart. 1893–1969. American composer, b. Cutchogue, N.Y. Composed operas *The Devil and Daniel Webster* (1939), *Giants in the Earth* (1950), *Ballad of Baby Doe* (1956), *Wings of the Dove* (1961), *Carry Nation* (1966); also songs, chamber music, etc.

Moore, George Augustus. 1852–1933. Irish novelist. Studied art in Paris, joining group including Manet, Degas, Renoir, Monet; deserted brush for poetry under influence of Gautier, Baudelaire, Mallarmé, Verlaine, and produced *Flowers of Passion* (1878) and *Pagan Poems* (1882). Wrote novels *A Modern Lover* (1883) and *A Mummer's Wife* (1885), showing influence of Flaubert and Zola; succeeded with realistic novels including *Esther Waters* (1894), *Evelyn Innes* (1898), *Sister Teresa* (1901). Wrote autobiographical *Confessions of a Young Man* (1888); championed Impressionist painters in *Impressions and Opinions* (1891), *Modern Painting* (1893). Returned to Ireland (1901) and joined Edward Martyn and W. B. Yeats with Irish literary revival. Published stories *The Untilled Field* (1903) and novel *The Lake* (1905). Resumed autobiography in masterly trilogy *Hail and Farewell,* comprising *Ave* (1911), *Salve* (1912), *Vale* (1914). Returned to London (1911); produced *Brook Kerith* (the story of Jesus, 1916), *Story-Teller's Holiday* (1918), *Héloïse and Abélard* (1921), *Daphnis and Chloe* (1924), *Ulick and Soracha,* an Irish story of Middle Ages (1926).

Moore, George Edward. 1873–1958. English philosopher. Fellow of Trinity Coll. (1898–1904), lecturer (1911–25), professor (1925–39), Cambridge; editor of journal *Mind* (1921–47). Developed system of Ideal Utilitarianism, a chief modern theory of ethics; author of *Principia Ethica* (1903), *Philosophical Studies* (1922), *Some Main Problems of Philosophy* (1958), etc.

Moore, George Foot. 1851–1931. American Orientalist, b. West Chester, Pa. Ordained Presbyterian minister (1878); professor, Andover Theol. Sem. (1883–1902), Harvard (1902–28). Author of *Literature of the Old Testament* (1913), *History of Religions* (1913–19), *Metempsychosis* (1914), *Judaism in the First Centuries of the Christian Era* (1927–30).

Moore, Henry Ludwell. 1869–1958. American economist, b. Charles Co., Md. Professor, Columbia (1902–29); a pioneer in mathematical and statistical economics; considered a founder of econometrics. Author of *Laws of Wages* (1911), *Economic Cycles* (1914), *Synthetic Economics* (1929), etc.

Moore, Henry Spencer. 1898–1986. British sculptor, b. Castleford, Yorkshire, England. Created abstract sculptures esp. in bronze and stone, often on a monumental scale; best known for his undulating reclining nudes; major commissions included sculptures for UNESCO headquarters, Paris (1957–58); Lincoln Center, New York (1963–65); and National Gallery of Art, Washington, D.C. (1978). Smoothly fused elements of abstract art with those of primitive art; also known for his watercolors and drawings, esp. those depicting the underground shelters during the London blitz. Considered by many the greatest sculptor of his time.

Moore, James. 1737–1777. American soldier, b. New Hanover Co., N.C. Served in French and Indian War (1755–63); a leader of colonial cause in N.C.; colonel of N.C. regiment of Continental army (1775); won major victory at Moore's Creek Bridge (Feb. 27, 1776); brigadier general (1776).

Moore, James Hobart. See at William Henry MOORE.

Moore, Sir John. 1761–1809. British general, b. Glasgow. Served in America (1779–83); assisted in reduction of French garrisons in Corsica (1794); served in West Indies, Ireland, and Holland; distinguished himself before Alexandria and Cairo (1801); served in Sicily (1802), Sweden (1808). Acquired reputation as great trainer of men and as tactician; named commander in chief in Portugal (1808); ordered to expel French from Peninsula; approached Madrid only to find that Napoléon had occupied Madrid and cut off his retreat to Portugal; forced to retreat through mountainous country to La Coruña in winter; attacked by Soult at beginning of embarkation, defeated French, but fell mortally wounded (Jan. 16, 1809).

Moore, John Bassett. 1860–1947. American jurist and publicist, b. Smyrna, Del. With U.S. Department of State (1885–91); professor of international law and diplomacy, Columbia (1891–1924); member, Hague Tribunal (1912–28); judge, Permanent Court of International Justice (1921–28). Author of *History and Digest of International Arbitrations* (1898), *A Digest of International Law* (1906), *International Adjudications* (1936).

Moore, Julia A. 1847–1920. American poet. Known as the "Sweet Singer of Michigan"; published *The Sentimental Song-Book* (1878).

Moore, Marianne Craig. 1887–1972. American poet, b. Kirkwood, Mo. Edited *The Dial* (1925–1929). Author of *Poems* (1921), *Observations* (1924), *Selected Poems* (1935), *The Pangolin* (1936), *What Are Years* (1941), *Nevertheless* (1944), *Collected Poems* (1951, Pulitzer prize), *Like a Bulwark* (1956), *O To Be a Dragon* (1959), *The Arctic Ox* (1964), *Tell Me, Tell Me* (1966); also wrote essays *Predilections* (1955), translated *Fables of La Fontaine* (1954).

Moore, Roger. See Rory O'MORE.

Moore, Stanford. 1913–1982. American biochemist, b. Chicago. On staff of Rockefeller Inst. for Medical Research (now Rockefeller U.; 1939–82); known for studies of enzymes; with William H. Stein, first to fully demonstrate structure of a human enzyme (pancreatic nuclease, 1959); corecipient with Stein and C.B. Anfinsen of 1972 Nobel prize for chemistry.

Moore, Thomas. *Pseudonyms* Thomas Little *and* Thomas Brown the younger. 1779–1852. Irish poet. Published translation of *Odes of Anacreon* (1800), *Poetical Works of late Thomas Little* (1801), and *Odes and Epistles* (1806); gained reputation as national lyrist of Ireland by his *Irish Melodies,* with music by Sir John Stevenson (irregularly pub. 1807–34), and *National Airs* (1818–27). Found vent for his wit in pungent satirical verses collected (1813) in *The Twopenny Post-bag.* Contracted with Longmans for metrical romance on Eastern subject and produced *Lalla Rookh* (1817), which earned him European reputation. Traveled in Italy with Lord John Russell; visited Byron, whose memoirs he received in trust and later destroyed; wrote in Paris *The Loves of the Angels,* an Oriental poem (1823); after *The Epicurean,* an imaginative work (1827), confined himself to prose, including lives of Sheridan (1825), Byron (1830), Lord Edward Fitzgerald (1831), and *History of Ireland* (1827); edited Byron's works. Author also of satirical *The Fudge Family in Paris* (1818), *Fables for the Holy Alliance* (1823), *The Fudges in England* (1835).

Moore, William Henry (1848–1923), b. Utica, N.Y., and his brother James Hobart (1852–1916), b. Berkshire, N.Y. American promoters and stock market operators. Active (1890–1904) in reorganizing or merging corporations; reorganized and promoted Diamond Match Co., the failure of which closed Chicago Stock Exchange for 3 months (1896); promoted formation (1898) of National Biscuit Co.; acquired or organized several steel firms, selling them (1901) to J.P. Morgan's U.S. Steel; acquired and systematically overcapitalized railroad empire; forced into receivership (1914).

Moore-Brabazon, John. See BRABAZON.

Mor, Anthonis. See Sir Anthony MORE.

Mo·raes \mü-'rīsh\, Francisco de. *Full surname* Moraes Ca·bral \kȧ-'bräl\. c.1500–1572. Portuguese romancer. Courtier to John III; author of famous romance of chivalry *Palmeirim de Inglaterra.*

Mo·rais Bar·ros \mü-'rīs-'bȧr-rüs\, Prudente José de. 1841–1902. Brazilian politician. A founder of Republican party (1870); president of senate (1891–94); first civil president of Brazil (1894–98).

Mo·ra·is \mō-'rā-əs\, Sabato. 1823–1897. American clergyman, b. Leghorn, Italy. To U.S. (1851); rabbi of congregation in Philadelphia (1851–97); founder and president, Jewish Theological Seminary, N.Y. (1886–97).

Mo·ra·les \mō-'rä-läs\, Cristóbal de. 1500?–1553. Spanish composer. Maestro de capilla, Ávila cathedral (1526–29); member of papal choir (1535–45); maestro de capilla, Toledo cathedral (1545–47), Málaga (1551–53). Composed 23 masses, 16 Magnificats (2 in each mode), some 90 motets, etc.; first major Spanish composer.

Morales, Luis de. *Called* El Di·vi·no \el-dē-b̲ē-nō\. c.1509–1586. Spanish painter. Called (1563) by Philip II to assist in decorating the Escorial. Greatest of Spanish Mannerist painters; his works include *Ecce Homo, Sagrada familia, Virgen con el Niño, Piedad, Presentación en el templo,* and series of 20 panels on life of Christ for church of Arroyo del Puerco (1563–68).

Mo·rand \mō-rä^n\, Paul. 1888–1976. French diplomat and writer. Attaché in London, Rome, Madrid (1912–19); in foreign office (1919–25); minister to London (1940), Bucharest (1943); ambassador at Bern (1944); dismissed (1945) for Vichy collaboration. Author of stories and novels of postwar cosmopolitan Europe as *Ouvert la nuit* (1922), *Fermé la nuit* (1923), *Lewis et Irène* (1924), *L'Europe galante* (1925), *Magie noire* (1928), *France la douce* (1934), *L'Homme pressé* (1941), *Hécate et ses chiens* (1954).

Mo·ran·di \mō-ˈrän-dē\, Giorgio. 1890–1964. Italian painter. Early associated with Futurists, later with De Chirico and Surrealists; developed highly individual style thereafter; known esp. for landscapes and still lifes exhibiting great formalism of design, executed in subtly muted colors, imbued with sense of repose and contemplation. Instructor at Bologna Academy of Fine Arts (1930–56).

Mo·ra·tín \mō-rä-ˈtēn\, Nicolás Fernández de. 1737–1780. Spanish playwright and poet. Introduced principles of French literary classicism in Spanish play construction. Among his poetical works were *La Diana* (1765), epic *Las naves de Cortés destruidas* (1785); theatrical works included comedy *La petimetra* (1762), tragedies *Lucrecia* (1763), *Hormesinda* (1770), *Guzmán el Bueno* (1777). His son ¶Leandro Fernández de (1760–1828) was also a playwright and poet; among his comedies were *El viejo y la niña* (1790), *La comedia nueva o El cafe* (1792), *El barón* (1803), *La mojigata* (1804), and *El sí de las niñas* (1806); wrote also a history of the Spanish stage.

Moray, Earls of. See (1) Sir Thomas RANDOLPH; (2) STEWART family.

Mo·ra·zán \mō-rä-ˈsän\, Francisco. 1792–1842. Central American politician, b. Honduras. After Honduras gained independence (1821), aided in organizing new government; led army in victories over reactionaries in El Salvador (1828) and Guatemala (1829); elected president of Central American Confederation (1830–40); failed to keep country united, fled to Peru; organized army and invaded Costa Rica with intention of restoring Confederation (1842); captured and shot.

Mor·car \ˈmȯr-kär\ *or* **Mor·ke·re** \ˈmȯr-ˌke-re\. fl. 1066. Earl of the Northumbrians. Aided Northumbrians to expel Tostig (1065) and was chosen earl; defeated by Norsemen at Fulford Gate; left Harold to fight alone at Hastings; submitted to William the Conquerer, but later (1068) rebelled; joined insurgents in Isle of Ely.

Mor·daunt \ˈmȯr-dənt, -ˌdȯnt\, Charles. 3d Earl of Pe·ter·bor·ough \ˈpēt-ər-ˌbər-ə, -ˌbə-rə, -b(ə-)rə\. 1658–1735. English military and naval commander and diplomat. Accompanied expeditions to Barbary Coast (between 1674 and 1680); intrigued against James II in Holland; on William III's accession, became privy councilor, first lord of treasury, and Earl of Mon·mouth \ˈmän-məth\ (1689); imprisoned (1697) on suspicion of complicity in Sir John Fenwick's plot; sent to command in Spain in War of Spanish Succession (1705), captured Barcelona, made triumphal entry into Valencia (1706), returned to assume command of fleet and raised siege of Barcelona; recalled (1707); joined Tories; sent on special embassies to southern Europe; commander in chief of naval forces under George I; shortly before death acknowledged as countess Anastasia Robinson (d. 1755), famous operatic singer whom he had married secretly (1722?); patron of letters; friend of Swift, Pope, Arbuthnot, Gay.

More \ˈmō(ə)r, ˈmȯ(ə)r\, Sir Anthony. *Known as* Antonio Mo·ro \ˈmȯ-rō\. *Orig.* Anthonis Mor \ˈmȯr\. 1512 or 1525–1575. Dutch painter. Invited to Madrid by Emperor Charles V; sent to England, where he painted his masterpiece, portrait of Queen Mary for her bridegroom, Philip of Spain (1553), also portraits of Sir Thomas Gresham and Sir Henry Lee.

More, Hannah. 1745–1833. English religious writer. Daughter of village schoolmaster; wrote verse early and came before the public with the pastoral drama *The Search after Happiness* (1762) and *The Inflexible Captive* (1774); frequent visitor to London, where she was welcomed by circle of Johnson, Reynolds, and Garrick; taken up by Elizabeth Montagu. Had two dramas produced, *Percy* (1777) and *Fatal Falsehood* (1779); after Garrick's death forsook stage and on publication of *Sacred Dramas* (1782) and *Thoughts on Importance of the Manners of the Great to General Society* (1788) devoted herself to social and religious amelioration; set up Sunday schools in Cheddar neighborhood (1789); shared evangelical views of William Wilberforce and Zachary Macaulay; wrote *An Estimate of the Religion of the Fashionable World* (1791), *Strictures on the Modern System of Female Education* (1799), and, to counteract teachings of Tom Paine and the French Revolution, a tract *Village Politics* (1792), the beginning of the series known as "Cheap Repository Tracts," including the *Shepard of Salisbury Plain*. Author of many other ethical books and tracts including *Hints Towards Forming the Character of a Young Princess* (1805), *Coelebs in Search of a Wife* (nominally a novel, 1809), *Practical Piety* (1811), *Moral Sketches* (1819).

More, Henry. 1614–1687. English philosopher and poet. Became a leading member of Cambridge Platonists; argued against Descartes and Hobbes; composed books in verse and prose under spiritual stimulus of one of his pupils, Anne, Viscountess Conway. Author of *Psychozoia Platonica* (verse, 1642), *Philosophicall Poems* (1647), *Antidote Against Atheism* (1652), *Conjectura Cabbalistica* (1653), *Immortality of the Soul* (1659), *Explanation of the Grand Mystery of Godliness* (1660), *Enchiridion Ethicum* (1667), *Divine Dialogues* (1668), *Enchiridion Metaphysicum* (1671).

More, Paul Elmer. 1864–1937. American critic, b. St. Louis, Mo. Taught Sanskrit, Harvard (1894–95), Bryn Mawr (1895–97). Literary editor, *The Independent* (1901–03), New York *Evening Post* (1903–09); editor, *The Nation* (1909–14); lecturer at Princeton U. (1914–34). Associated with Irving Babbitt as champion of humanism. Author of critical essays published in *Shelburne Essays* (11 vols., 1904–21), and of *Life of Benjamin Franklin* (1900), *Nietzsche* (1912), *Platonism* (1917), *The Religion of Plato* (1921), *Hellenistic Philosophies* (1923), *The Greek Tradition* (1924–31), *New Shelburne Essays* (1928–36), *The Sceptical Approach to Religion* (1934), etc.

More, Sir Thomas. Saint. 1478–1535. English statesman and author. Page in household of Archbishop Morton (1491), who sent him to Oxford; friend of Erasmus, Colet, and Lyly and pupil of Linacre and Grocyn; called to bar, where he was eminently successful; subjected himself to discipline of Carthusian monk (1499–1503); M.P. (1504); successfully opposed Henry VII's demand for aid in money on marriage of Princess Margaret; M.P. and undersheriff of London (1510). While envoy to Flanders sketched description in Latin of imaginary island of Utopia which he completed and published (1516). Impressed king by arguments in a celebrated Star Chamber case; master of requests (1514); privy councilor (1518); at Field of Cloth of Gold met Guillaume Budé (1520); accompanied Wolsey to Calais and Bruges (1521); recommended by Wolsey, elected speaker of House of Commons (1523); chancellor of duchy of Lancaster (1525). Appeared as champion of king against Luther's measures of reform (1523); directed his first English controversial book, *Dialogue Concerning Herecies and Matters of Religion,* against Tyndale's writings (1529). On fall of Wolsey succeeded against his will as lord chancellor of England, the first layman commoner to hold the office (1529); dispatched cases with unprecedented rapidity. Quarreled with Henry VIII over relaxation of heresy laws, refused to take oath renouncing jurisdiction of any but the sovereign over the church; resigned (1532). Charged with high treason, along with Elizabeth Barton, the "holy maid of Kent"; steadfastly refused (1534) along with John Fisher, bishop of Rochester, to take oath impugning pope's authority; sent to Tower; during imprisonment prepared a *Dialogue of Comfort against Tribulacyon;* convicted of treason for refusal to affirm Act of Supremacy; sentence to be hanged commuted by king to decapitation; his head fixed upon London Bridge. Beatified by Leo XIII (1886), canonized (1935). As writer, best known for his *Utopia,* describing communal ownership of land, educations of men and women alike, and religious toleration; author also of *Lyfe of Iohan Picus Erle of Myrandula* (1510), *Apologye of Syr Thomas More Knyght* (1533).

Moréas, Jean. See Yánnis PAPADIAMANTÓPOULOS.

Mo·reau \mȯ-ˈrō\, Gustave. 1826–1898. French painter. Professor, École des Beaux-Arts (1892). Known for Symbolist canvases, in later years exhibiting fascination for exotic eroticism and violence, including *Oedipe et le Sphinx* (1864), *Orphée* (1865), *Diomède dévoré par ses chevaux* (1865), *L'Apparition* (1876), *Hésiode et la Muse* (c.1891), *Jupiter et Sémélé* (1896). Left home and works to form Musée Gustave Moreau, Paris.

Moreau, Louis-Gabriel. *Called* l'Aî·né \len-ā\, *i.e.* the Elder. French painter. Known for landscapes as *Vue du coteau de Bellevue, Vue des environs de Vincennes, Paysage vallonné.* His brother ¶Jean-Michel, *called* le Jeune \lə-zhœ̄n\, *i.e.* the Younger (1741–1814), was an engraver and illustrator; painted elegant court scenes; best known for illustrations of Molière, Voltaire, and Rousseau.

Moreau, Victor, *in full* Jean-Victor-Marie. 1763–1813. French soldier. Volunteer (1791); general of division (1794); commander of army of the North (1795); commanded armies of the Rhine and Moselle (1796) and drove Austrians back to the Danube; relieved of command (1797) for concealing evidence of conspiracy of his friend Pichegru; commanded army in Italy (1799) and was defeated at Cassano d'Adda; commanded army of the Rhine (1800) and won battle of Hohenlinden (Dec. 3, 1800); headed Republican and Royalist conspiracy against Napoléon and was exiled (1804) after being convicted of complicity in the Cadoudal and Pichegru plots; lived near Trenton, N.J. (1805–13); entered Russian service and was mortally wounded at battle of Dresden (Aug. 27, 1813).

Mo·reell \mōr-ˈē(ə)l, mȯr-\, Ben. 1892–1978. American naval officer, b. Salt Lake City. Entered navy as engineer (1917); rear admiral, chief of Bureau of Yards and Docks and of Civil Engineer Corps (1937–45); organized Construction Battalions (known as Seabees) for duty in World War II (1941–45); vice admiral (1944); chief of Material Division (1945–46); directed coal mines federalized by Truman administration (1946); admiral (1946); retired (1946). President (1947–52), chairman (1947–58), Jones & Laughlin Steel Co.

Mo·reel·se \mō-ˈrāl-sə\, Paulus. 1571–1638. Dutch painter. Known for Mannerist portraits and for architectural decoration in Utrecht.

More·house \ˈmō(ə)r-ˌhau̇s, ˈmȯ(ə)r-\, Daniel Walter. 1876–1941. American astronomer, b. Mankato, Minn. Professor (from 1900), president and dean (1923–30), Drake U. Discovered comet named after him (1908).

Mo·rel \mȯ-rel\. Family of French printers and scholars, including: Fédéric (1523–1583), royal printer (1571–83); known for his excellent editions of ancient classics. His son ¶Fédéric (1558–1630) was royal printer (1581) and a noted scholar; professor of eloquence, Collège de France (1586). Two sons of Fédéric the younger ¶Fédéric III (c.1573–1624), royal printer (1602–24), and ¶Claude (1574–1626), royal printer (1625–26). Claude's two sons ¶Charles (c.1612–after 1640), royal printer (1635–39) and secretary to the king (1639), printed works of Gregory of Nazianzus, Cyril of Jerusalem, John Chrysostom; and ¶Gilles (c.1616–1675), who took over the press from Charles (1639), printed *Magna bibliotheca patrum* (1643), transferred the business to his partner Simon Piget and became counselor to the Grand Council (1650–75).

Morella, Conde de. See Ramón CABRERA.

Mor·el·let \mȯr-le\, André. 1727–1819. French economist and man of letters. A wit and pamphleteer, a leader of *philosophe* circle; contributor to Diderot's *Encyclopédie.*

Mo·rel·li \mō-'rel-lē\, Domenico. 1826–1901. Italian painter. Professor, Naples Academy (from 1869); a leader of the Realist movement in Italy; known especially for his historical and genre paintings and later for his biblical scenes.

Morelli, Giovanni. *Pseudonym* Ivan Ler·mol·iev \lyir-'mȯl-yəf\. 1816–1891. Italian art critic. Member, Italian parliament (1861–70); senator (1873 ff.); secured art conservation law now bearing his name; developed successful principles of art criticism based chiefly on observation that rendition of details is conventional and uniform for each master and hence an accurate means of identification. Author of *Die Werke italienischen Meister in den Galerien von München, Dresden und Berlin* (1880), *Kunstkritische Studien über italienischer Malerei* (1890–93).

Mo·rel·ly \mȯ-rel-ē\. 18th century. French philosopher. Nothing known of his life. Promulgated a view of communist utopia in *Essai sur l'esprit humain* (1743), *Essais sur le coeur humain* or *Principes naturels de l'éducation* (1745), *Physique de la beauté* (1748), *Naufrage des îles flottantes* (1753), *Le Code de la nature* (1755).

Mo·re·los y Pa·vón \mō-'rā-lōs-ē-pä-'b̲ōn\, José María. 1765–1815. Mexican priest and revolutionist. Joined insurrection led by Hidalgo (1811) and succeeded Hidalgo as leader of rebels; called Congress of Chilpancingo and issued a declaration of independence from Spain (Nov. 6, 1813); finally defeated by royalists, captured, and shot.

Moreno, Alfredo Baquerizo. See BAQUERIZO MORENO.

Mo·re·no \mō-'rā-nō\, Mariano. 1778–1811. Argentinian political leader. Lawyer, held various posts in colonial administration; published *Representación de los hacendados* (1809) against oppressive trade restrictions; secretary for political and military affairs to provisional junta of Buenos Aires (1810); soon became leader of junta; promoted revolution, founded national library, edited junta newspaper; advocated complete independence; forced out of junta by conservative members (1810); died en route to diplomatic post in England.

Mo·re·ri \mȯ-rā-rē\, Louis. 1643–1680. French Roman Catholic priest and scholar. Compiler of *Grand Dictionnaire historique ou Mélange curieux de l'histoire sacrée et profane* (1674).

Mo·re·to y Ca·ba·ña \mō-'rā-tō-ē-kä-'b̲än-yä\, Agustín. 1618–1669. Spanish playwright. Friend of Calderón; among his highly popular plays were *El valiente justiciero, El lindo don Diego, El desdén con el desdén,* and *Rico hombre de Alcalá.*

Moretto. See Alessandro BONVICINO.

Mor·ga·gni \mōr-'gän-yē\, Giovanni Battista. 1682–1771. Italian physician. Practiced in Bologna (1701–07), Forlì (1709–11); professor, Padua (1711–71); considered the founder of pathological anatomy. Published *Adversaria anatomica* (1706–19), *De sedibus et causis morborum per anatomen indagatis* (1761).

Morgan, Augustus de. See DE MORGAN.

Mor·gan \'mȯr-gən\, Charles Langbridge. 1894–1958. English novelist and dramatic critic. Dramatic critic for London *Times* (1926–39). Author of *The Gunroom* (1919), *My Name Is Legion* (1925), *Portrait in a Mirror* (1929), *The Fountain* (1932, Hawthornden prize), *Sparkenbroke* (1936), *The Flashing Stream* (play, 1938), *The Voyage* (1940), *The Empty Room* (1941), *The Judge's Story* (1947), *The River Line* (1949; play 1952), *The Burning Glass* (play, 1953), *Challenge to Venus* (1957).

Morgan, Conwy Lloyd. 1852–1936. English zoologist and psychologist. Professor (1884–1919), principal (1887–1909), first vice chancellor, U. of Bristol; sometimes called founder of comparative psychology. Author of *Animal Life and Intelligence* (1890), *Introduction to Comparative Psychology* (1895), *Habit and Instinct* (1896), *Animal Behaviour* (1900), *The Interpretation of Nature* (1905), *Instinct and Experience* (1912), *Emergent Evolution* (1923), *Life, Mind, and Spirit* (1926), *Mind at the Cross-ways* (1929), *The Animal Mind* (1930), *The Emergence of Novelty* (1933).

Morgan, Daniel. 1736–1802. American Revolutionary soldier, b. Hunterdon Co., N.J. Served in militia in Pontiac's War (1763–64); entered Continental army (1775); served under Arnold in assault on Quebec (Dec. 31, 1775), under Gates in opposing Burgoyne (1777); as brigadier general, commanded troops in western North Carolina and defeated British at Cowpens (Jan. 17, 1781); commanded Virginia militia in suppressing Whisky Insurrection (1794) in western Pennsylvania. Member, U.S. House of Representatives (1797–99).

Morgan, Sir Henry. 1635–1688. British buccaneer, b. Wales. Early life obscure; probably member of British expedition that seized Jamaica (1655); with buccaneers in Caribbean in Second Anglo-Dutch War (1665–67); chosen commander of buccaneers (1668); commissioned by governor of Jamaica, captured Puerto Principe (now Camagüey) in Cuba and Portobelo, Panama; took large sum from governor of Panama, ravaged coast of Cuba, sacked Maracaibo and Gibraltar (1669), recaptured Santa Catalina (1670), and took Panama City (1671); after treaty between Spain and England, called to England to answer for conduct (1672); gained favor of king; appointed lieutenant governor of Jamaica and commander in chief (1674).

Morgan, John. 1735–1789. American physician, b. Philadelphia. Founded U. of Pennsylvania Med. Coll. (1765), first in American colonies; professor there (1765–75); director general of hospitals and physician in chief of American army (1775–77); removed by Congress (1777); exonerated of neglect or wrongdoing by Washington and by Congress; practiced, Philadelphia (from 1777).

Morgan, John Hunt. 1825–1864. American soldier, b. Huntsville, Ala. Served in Mexican War; entered Confederate service (1861); famed for cavalry raids (1862–63) in Tennessee and Kentucky; brigadier general (1862); raided outskirts of Cincinnati (July 1863); killed in action near Greenville, Tenn.

Morgan, John Pierpont. 1837–1913. American banker and financier, b. Hartford, Conn. Son of Junius S. Morgan; apprentice with representatives of his father's firm in London and New York (1857–60); New York agent for this firm (1860–64); member, Dabney, Morgan & Co. (1864–71) and Drexel, Morgan & Co. (1871–93). Formed J. P. Morgan & Co. (1895) closely linked with Drexel & Co. of Philadelphia, with Morgan, Harjes & Co. of Paris and J. S. Morgan & Co. of London. Best known for his government financing, for his breaking of Jay Cooke's government bond monopoly (1873), for his reorganization of important American railroads, and for his industrial consolidations, esp. formation of United States Steel Corporation (1901). Enjoyed great prestige as symbol of financial stability; renowned as collector of art and rare books; president, Metropolitan Museum of Art, New York City. Benefactor of the Cathedral of St. John the Divine, Metropolitan Museum of Art, New York Public Library, New York hospitals, and many other institutions.

His son ¶John Pierpont, Jr. (1867–1943), b. Irvington, N.Y., succeeded to his father's position as head of J. P. Morgan & Co. (1913); agent of Allied governments in floating large loans in U.S. during World War I; floated $1.7 billion in loans for postwar reconstruction. The elder Morgan's daughter ¶Anne Tracy (1873–1952) was a noted philanthropist; with Mrs. August Belmont founded (1909) Working Girls Vacation Society (from 1922, America Women's Assoc.; president, 1928–43); founded (1917) American Friends for Devastated France and collected over $5 million for French relief; first American woman made commander of Legion of Honor (1932); organized (1939) American Friends of France.

Morgan, Junius Spencer. 1813–1890. American banker and financier, b. West Springfield, Mass. Merchant in New York, Hartford, and Boston (to 1854); partner in George Peabody & Co. (1854), international bankers of London, England; on retirement of Peabody (1864), reorganized firm as J. S. Morgan & Co.; president (1864–90).

Morgan, Lewis Henry. 1818–1881. American ethnologist, b. near Aurora, N.Y. Practiced law (1844–62); in N.Y. legislature (1861–69). Interested himself in study of the American Indian culture, esp. the Seneca, by whom he was adopted (1846); studied kinship systems, property, etc., and evolved comprehensive theory of cultural evolution. Author of *League of the Ho-dé-no-sau-nee, or Iroquois* (1851), *Systems of Consanguinity and Affinity* (1871), *Ancient Society* (1877), *Houses and House-Life of the American Aborigines* (1881), etc.

Morgan, Lady Sydney, *nee* Ow·en·son \'ō-ən-sən\. 1776–1859. Irish woman of letters. Wrote volume of sentimental poetry (1801); attracted attention with a novel, *St. Clair* (1804); made reputation with *The Wild Irish Girl* (1806), extolling Ireland; m. (1812) Sir Thomas Charles Morgan; continued to produce verse, travel books, and novels, including *O'Donnel* (1814), *Florence M'Carthy* (1816), *France* (1817), etc.

Morgan, Thomas Hunt. 1866–1945. American geneticist, b. Lexington, Ky. Professor, Columbia (1904–28); director, Kerckhoff Laboratories of Biological Sciences, Calif. Inst. Tech. (from 1928); carried on studies (from 1909) of heredity in *Drosophila* fruit fly; awarded Nobel prize for physiology or medicine (1933) for discoveries relating to laws and mechanism of heredity, esp. the existence of genes for specific traits located at specific sites on chromosomes. Author of *Regeneration* (1901), *Evolution and Adaptation* (1903), *Experimental Zoology* (1907), *Heredity and Sex* (1913), *Mechanism of Mendelian Heredity* (1915), *The Physical Bases of Heredity* (1919), *Evolution and Genetics* (1925), *The Theory of the Gene* (1926), *Scientific Basis of Evolution* (1932), *Embryology and Genetics* (1933), etc.

Morgan, William. c.1545–1604. Welsh prelate. Ordained Anglican priest (1568); bishop of Llandaff (1595), of St. Asaph (1601). Produced translation of the Bible into Welsh (1588) that helped fix Welsh literary language.

Morgan, William. 1774?–?1826. American Freemason, b. prob. in Culpeper Co., Va. Jailed in Canandaigua, N.Y., and then kidnapped (Sept. 1826) after it became known that he was writing a book to expose the secrets of Freemasonry. Charges were made that he was murdered to prevent the publication of the book; charges strongly denied by Freemasons. His disappearance became a political issue, leading to formation of Anti-Masonic party (1827). The book, *Illustrations of Masonry,* appeared late in 1826.

Morgan, William de. See DE MORGAN.

Morganfield, McKinley. See Muddy WATERS. .

Mor·gen·stern \'mȯr-gən-ˌshtern\, Christian. 1871–1914. German poet. Author of lyrical verse as *Ich und die Welt* (1898), *Einkehr* (1910), *Ich und Du* (1911), and *Epigramme und Sprüche* (1920); of grotesque and nonsense verse *Galgenlieder* (1905, 1908), *Palmström* (1910), *Palma Kunkel* (1916), *Der Gingganz* (1919), *Die Schallmühle* (1928); and of translations of Ibsen, Strindberg, Hamsun.

Morgenstern, Lina, *nee* Bau·er \'bau̇-ər\. 1830–1909. German writer and reformer. m. Dr. Theodor Morgenstern (1854); worked esp. in field of women's and children's education and protection of young girls. Author of *Der häusliche Beruf* (1875), *Universalkochbuch* (1881), *Frauenarbeit in Deutschland* (1893), and of books for children.

Morgenstern, Oskar. 1902–1977. American economist, b. Görlitz, Germany. Professor, Vienna (1935–38), Princeton (1938–70), New York U. (1970–77). Author of *Wirtschaftsprognose* (1928), *Theory of Games and Economic Behavior* (with John von Neumann, 1944), *On the Accuracy of Economic Observations* (1950), *Prolegomena to a Theory of Organization* (1951), *Economic Activity Analysis* (1954), *The Question of National Defence* (1959), *Predictability of Stock Market Prices* (with C. J. Granger, 1970).

Mor·gen·thau \'mȯr-gən-ˌthȯ\, Henry. 1856–1946. American diplomat, b. Mannheim, Germany. To U.S. (1865); practiced law, New York City (1879–99); in real estate business (1899–1913). U.S. ambassador to Turkey (1913–16), taking over at outbreak of World War I diplomatic interests of various allied countries; U.S. ambassador to Mexico (1920); U.S. technical expert, London monetary and economic conference (1933). Author of *Ambassador Morgenthau's Story* (1918), *All in a Lifetime* (1922), *I Was Sent to Athens* (1929), etc. His son ¶Henry, Jr. (1891–1967), b. New York City; publisher of *American Agriculturist* (1922–33); governor, Farm Credit Administration (1933); U.S. secretary of the treasury (1934–45).

Mor·hof \'mōr-hōf\, Daniel George. 1639–1691. German literary historian. Professor, Rostock (1660), Kiel (1665). Author of *Unterricht von der Teutschen Sprache und Poesie* (1682), first historical treatment by a German of German grammar and European literature, and *Polyhistor litterarius* in Latin (1688–92), first history of universal literature by a German writer, etc.

Mo·ri \mō-rē\ Arinori. 1847–1899. Japanese government official. One of first Japanese educated in West; became enthusiastic promoter of westernization; help form (1873) westernizing Meirokusha society; as first minister of education (1885) developed new centralized education system.

Mori Rintarō. *Pseudonym* Mori Ōgai. 1862–1922. Japanese novelist. A samurai; studied in Germany; army surgeon (to 1916). Author of *Maihime* (1889), *Asobi* (1910), *Fushinchū* (1910), *Gan* (1911–13), *Abe Ichizoku* (1913), *Sanshō dayū* (1915), *Takasebune* (1916); also wrote stories, plays as *Kamen* (1909), *Ikutagawa* (1910).

Mo·rice \mȯ-rēs\, Charles. 1861–1919. French writer. Author of *La Littérature de tout à l'heure,* supposed to contain a theory of symbolism (1899); biographies *Paul Verlaine* (1887), *Rodin* (1899), *Tristan Corbière* (1912), etc.; *Quincaille: poèmes en prose* (1919), *Le Rideau de pourpre* (1921).

Mó·ricz \'mō-rits\, Zsigmond. 1879–1942. Hungarian novelist. Known esp. for starkly realistic novels of peasant life as *Sárarany* (1910), *Légy jó mindhalálig* (1920), *Kivilágos kivirradtig* (1924), *Pillangó* (1925), *Rokonok* (1930), *A boldog ember* (1930); also wrote historical novels as *Eroély trilógia* (1922–35) and *Rózsa Sándor* (1940–42), stories, and plays.

Mor·i·er \'mȯr-ē-ˌā\, James Justinian. c.1780–1849. British diplomat and novelist. Served at court of Persia as secretary of legation and envoy (1809–15); described journeys in Turkey, Armenia, Asia Minor; known for his *Adventures of Hajji Baba of Ispahan* (1824) and *The Adventures of Hajji Baba of Ispahan in England* (1828), satire on Western civilization.

Mö·ri·ke \'mœ-rē-kə\, Eduard Friedrich. 1804–1875. German poet and novelist. His works included collection of lyrics *Gedichte* (1838), verse *Idylle am Bodensee* (1846), the romantic novel *Maler Nolten* (1832), folk tale *Das Stuttgarter Hutzelmännlein* (1853), the novelle *Mozart auf der Reise nach Prag* (1856).

Mo·rin \mȯ-raⁿ\, Jean. *Lat.* Joannes Mo·ri·nus \mə-'rī-nəs\. 1591–1659. French theologian and Orientalist. Joined the Oratory (1618) and became head of a college at Angers; summoned to Rome (1640) to discuss union of Greek and Roman churches, but soon recalled by Richelieu; writer on church history and esp. on textual criticism. Produced first edition of Samaritan Pentateuch and Targum for Polyglot Bible (1645); wrote *Histoire de la deliverance de l'église chrétienne* (1630), *Exercitationes biblicae* (1633), etc.

Morin, Paul d'·Equil·ly \dā-kē-lē\. 1889–1963. Canadian poet, b. Montreal. Taught at colleges in U.S., Canada, and at Istanbul. Author of verse collections *Le Paon d'émail* (1911), *Poèmes de cendre et d'or* (1922), *Oeuvres poétiques* (1961).

Morison. See also MORRISON.

Mor·i·son \'mȯr-ə-sən, 'mär-\, James. 1816–1893. Scottish clergyman. Excluded (1841) by United Secession church for preaching universal atonement; with three other ministers deposed for anti-Calvinistic views, founded (1843) the Evangelical Union, whose members are sometimes called Morisonians.

Morison, Robert. 1620–1683. Scottish botanist. Fled as Royalist to France (1644); gardener to Gaston, duc d'Orléans (1649); senior physician and botanist to Charles II and superintendent of royal gardens (1660); first professor of botany, Oxford (1669). Revived study of systematic botany in *Praeludia botanica* (1669), *Historia plantarum* (1680–99). The genus *Morisonia* was named for him.

Morison, Samuel Eliot. 1887–1976. American historian, b. Boston. On staff, Harvard (from 1915, professor from 1925); Harmsworth professor of American history, Oxford U. (1922–25). Author of *Life of Harrison Gray Otis* (1913), *Oxford History of the United States* (1927), *Builders of the Bay Colony* (1930), *Tercentennial History of Harvard University* (1930–36), *Growth of the American Republic* (with Henry Steele Commager, 1930), *Admiral of the Ocean Sea* (1942, Pulitzer prize), *History of U.S. Naval Operations in World War II* (1947–62), *John Paul Jones* (1959, Pulitzer prize), *Two-Ocean War* (1963), *Oxford History of the American People* (1965), *European Discovery of America* (1971–74), etc.

Morison, Stanley. 1889–1967. English typographer. Typographic adviser to Monotype Corp. (1923 ff.), Cambridge U. Press (1923–59); editor of journal *The Fleuron* (1926–30); on staff of London *Times* (1929–60), including term (1945–47) as editor of *Times Literary Supplement.* Known esp. for design of Times New Roman typeface (1932). Author of *Four Centuries of Printing* (1924), *First Principles of Typography* (1936), etc.

Mo·ri·sot \mȯ-rē-zō\, Berthe. 1841–1895. French painter. Granddaughter of J.-H. Fragonard; studied with Corot, Manet; painted in Impressionist manner, with emphasis on design; exhibited at the Salon and with Impressionist group; works noted also for delicate coloring in landscapes, figure studies, portraits, etc.

Moritz. See also MAURICE.

Mo·ritz \'mō-rits\. *Known as* der Ge·lehr·te \dər-gə-'lār-tə\, *i.e.* the Scholar. 1572–1632. Landgrave of Hesse-Kassel (1592–1627). Founded (1599) Collegium Adelphicum Mauritianum at Kassel for sons of nobility; planned union of all Protestant sects; attacked by Catholic army during Thirty Years' War; abdicated (1627).

Moritz, Karl Philipp. 1757–1793. German writer. Professor of archaeology at Academy of Art, Berlin (1789). Author of aesthetic writings, of contributions on psychology, of the mainly autobiographical novels *Anton Reiser* (1785–90) and *Andreas Hartknopf* (1786), and of travel books.

Morkere. See MORCAR.

Mor·lac·chi \mōr-'läk-kē\, Francesco Giuseppe Baldassare. 1784–1841. Italian composer. Kapellmeister (1811–41) in Dresden, where he was a rival of Karl von Weber; composed some 25 operas, including *Il poeta in campagna* (1807), *Il Corradino* (1808), *Le Danaidi* (1810), *Il nuovo barbiere di Siviglia* (1816), *La simplicetta di Pirna* (1817), *Il Colombo* (1828), *Il rinnegato* (1832); also several oratorios, masses with orchestra, and other church music.

Mor·land \'mȯr-lənd\, George. 1763–1804. English painter and engraver. Exhibited at age of ten at Royal Academy; gained reputation as copyist of Flemish and Dutch masters; his first original engraving, *The Angler's Repast* (1780). Produced some 4000 pictures, specializing in *galanteries,* inn yards, pastoral scenes, animals, esp. pigs. Known esp. for the *Laetitia* series of moralities after Hogarth (1786) and for his masterpiece *The Interior of a Stable* (1791).

Mor·ley \'mȯr-lē\, Christopher Darlington. 1890–1957. American writer, b. Haverford, Pa. On editorial staff, Doubleday, Page & Co. (1913–17), *Ladies' Home Journal* (1917–18), Philadelphia *Evening Public Ledger* (1918–20), New York *Evening Post* (1920–24); contributing editor, *Saturday Review of Literature* (1924–41). Among his books were *Parnassus on Wheels* (1917), *The Haunted Book Shop* (1919), *Kathleen* (1920), *Tales from a Rolltop Desk*

(1921), *Thunder on the Left* (1925), *Off the Deep End* (1928), *Human Being* (1932), *Mandarin in Manhattan* (1933), *The Trojan Horse* (1937), *Kitty Foyle* (1939), *Thorofare* (1942). Editor of 11th edition of *Bartlett's Quotations* (1937).

Morley, Edward Williams. 1838–1923. American chemist and physicist, b. Newark, N.J. Professor, Western Reserve (1869–1906). Conducted researches in the variations of atmospheric oxygen content, thermal expansion of gases, vapor tension of mercury, densities of oxygen and hydrogen; best known for collaboration with A. A. Michelson (*q.v.*) on ether-drift experiment (1887).

Morley, Henry. 1822–1894. English man of letters. Assisted Charles Dickens in editing *Household Words* and *All the Year Round* (1850–65); edited the *Examiner* (1859–65); professor, University Coll., London (1865–89) and Queen's Coll., London (1878); edited classics in Morley's Universal Library (63 vols., 1883–88), Cassell's National Library (214 vols., 1886–90), and Carisbrooke Library (14 vols., 1889–91). Wrote monographs on *Palissy the Potter* (1852), *Jerome Cardan* (1854), *Cornelius Agrippa* (1856), *Clément Marot* (1870), and a monumental history of English literature down to death of Shakespeare, *English Writers* (11 vols., 1864–95).

Morley, John. Viscount Morley. 1838–1923. English politician and writer. Journalist in London (1860 ff.); editor of *Fortnightly Review* (1867–82) and *Pall Mall Gazette* (1880–83); M.P. (1883–95, 1896–1908); raised to peerage (1908). Supporter of Gladstone; chief secretary for Ireland (1886, 1892–95); secretary for India (1905–10). Among his works were *Edmund Burke* (1867), *Voltaire* (1872), *Rousseau* (1876), *Diderot and the Encyclopaedists* (1878), *Richard Cobden* (1881), *Ralph Waldo Emerson* (1884), *Studies in Literature* (1891), *Oliver Cromwell* (1900), *Life of Gladstone* (1903), *Critical Miscellanies* (1908), and *Recollections* (1917).

Morley, Thomas. 1557 or 1558–1602. English composer. Organist and master of choristers, Norwich cathedral (1583–87); organist, St. Paul's, London (1591); gentleman of the Chapel Royal (1592–1602); succeeded William Byrd as holder of patent of monopoly on music publishing (1598 ff.). Responsible for the great popularity and flowering of Italian madrigal in England; published books of own madrigals (1594, 1598) and edited *Triumphes of Oriana* (by various composers, 1603); published collections of canzonets, airs, balletti.

Mor·nay \mȯr-ne\, Philippe de. Seigneur du Ples·sis-Mar·ly \plā-sē-mȧr-lē\. *Known as* Duplessis-Mornay. 1549–1623. French Huguenot leader. Escaped Massacre of St. Bartholomew (1572); as Protestant publicist wrote *Discours au roi Charles* (1572), *Remonstrances aux estats pour la paix* (1576), *Vindiciae contra tyrannos* (1579), and other pamphlets; became trusted adviser to Henry of Navarre (1576); after Prince Condé's death (1588), his power and influence gained him nickname of "Huguenot Pope"; governor of Saumur (1589–1621); disappointed by Henri IV's abjuration of Protestantism (1593), withdrew from the court and devoted himself to writing.

Mör·ner af Mor·lan·da \ˈmœr-nə-räv-ˈmȯr-län-də\, Carl Otto. Baron. 1781–1868. Swedish soldier and diplomat. Suggested name of and conducted negotiations (1810) with Jean Bernadotte to fill vacant Swedish throne.

Mornington, Earl of. See Richard WELLESLEY.

Mor·ny \mȯr-nē\, Charles-Auguste-Louis-Joseph de. Duc. 1811–1865. French noble and politician. Half-brother of Napoléon III; deputy (1842–48, 1849); chief agent in successful coup d'état (Dec. 2, 1851); minister of interior (1851–52); president of Corps Législatif (1854–65); created duc (1862).

Mo·ro \ˈmōr-ō\, Aldo. 1916–1978. Italian politician. Professor, Bari (1940–46); deputy (1946–78); minister of justice (1955–57), of public instruction (1957–59); general secretary of Christian Democrat party (1959–63); prime minister (1963–68); foreign minister (1970–72); prime minister (1974–76); kidnapped and murdered by terrorists.

Moro, Antonio. See Sir Anthony MORE.

Mo·ro·ne \mō-ˈrō-nā\, Giovanni. 1509–1580. Italian prelate and diplomat. Bishop of Modena (1529); papal ambassador to Germany (1536); cardinal (1542); governor of Bologna (1544); bishop of Novarra (1553–60); imprisoned (1557–59) by Pope Paul IV; named by Pius IV president of Council of Trent (1563), successfully settling dispute over nature of authority of bishops; bishop of Ostia (from 1570).

Mo·ro·ni \mō-ˈrō-nē\ *or* **Mo·ro·ne** \-nā\, Giovanni Battista. c.1525–1578. Italian painter. Member of the Brescian school; notable for working almost exclusively as portraitist.

Mo·ro·si·ni \mō-rō-ˈsē-nē\. Name of patrician family of Venice, including notably: Domenico (d. 1156), doge of Venice (1148–56); extended Venetian power to Istria, Dalmatia, the Adriatic. ¶Marino (d. 1253), doge of Venice (1249–53). ¶Michele (d. 1382), doge of Venice (1382). ¶Antonio (c.1366–c.1434) compiled a valuable chronicle of his times. ¶Andrea (1558–1618), historian of Venice and its eastern possessions for period 1521–1615. ¶Francesco (1618–1694), soldier; commander of fleet (1657); distinguished himself several times against Turks; forced to yield Candia to Turks (1667–69); again named commander (1684), won several victories over Turks, reconquering Peloponnesus and Athens; doge of Venice (1688).

Morpeth, Viscount. See earls of Carlisle, under HOWARD family.

Mor·phy \ˈmȯr-fē\, Paul Charles. 1837–1884. American chess player, b. New Orleans. Matches in U.S., England, and France, esp. against Adolf Anderssen, established him as world's chess master (1857–59); on staff of *Chess Monthly* and New York *Ledger* (1859–60); in later life, mentally deranged.

Mor·rell \ˈmȯr-əl, ˈmär-\, Lady Ottoline Violet Anne, *nee* Cav·en·dish-Ben·tinck \ˈkav-ən-dish-ˈben-(ˌ)tiŋk\. 1873–1938. English hostess. m. (1902) Philip E. Morrell. In London (1902–13, 1924–38) and at Garsington Manor, Oxfordshire (1913–24), hostess and patron of notable circle of artists and intellectuals, including Bertrand Russell, D. H. Lawrence, Aldous Huxley, Augustus John, Virginia Woolf, T. S. Eliot, Siegfried Sassoon, W. B. Yeats, etc.

Mor·rill \ˈmȯr-əl\, Justin Smith. 1810–1898. American politician, b. Strafford, Vt. Member, U.S. House of Representatives (1855–67); author of Morrill Tariff Act (1861), first of protective tariff acts, and Morrill Land-Grant College Act (1862), giving lands to states and territories which would provide colleges for teaching agriculture and the mechanic arts; U.S. senator (1867–98).

Mor·ris \ˈmȯr-əs, ˈmär-\, Alexander. 1826–1889. Canadian politician, b. Perth, Upper Canada (Ont.). Conservative member of legislature of United Province of Canada (1861–72); champion of confederation; minister of inland revenue (1869–72); chief justice, Manitoba Court of Queen's Bench (1872); lieutenant governor of Manitoba and Northwest Territories (1872–77); in Ontario legislature (1878–86).

Morris, Clara. *Orig.* Clara Morrison. between 1846 and 1848–1925. American actress, b. Toronto, Ont. To U.S. as a child; stage debut in Cincinnati (1869); in New York City with Augustin Daly's company (1870–73); toured extensively (to 1890s); noted esp. for roles in *Man and Wife, Camille, Miss Multon, Jane Eyre, The New Magdalen;* achieved recognition as great emotional actress. Wrote *Life on the Stage* (1901), *A Pasteboard Crown* (1902), *The Life of a Star* (1906), etc.

Morris, Edward Patrick. 1st Baron Morris. 1858–1935. Canadian jurist and politician, b. St. John's, Nfd. Member of Newfoundland assembly (1885–1918); acting attorney general (1890–95); leader of Independent Liberals (1898–1908), People's party (1908–19); attorney general and minister of justice (1902–07); premier of Newfoundland (1909–18); member of imperial war cabinet (1916–18); created baron (1918). Edited *Newfoundland Law Reports, 1800–1900,* commonly referred to as *Morris' Reports.*

Morris, George Pope. 1802–1864. American journalist and poet, b. Philadelphia. Founded (1823) and edited (1824–42) *New York Mirror and Ladies' Literary Gazette;* with N. P. Willis edited the daily *Evening Mirror* (1844 ff.) and the weekly *Home Journal* (1846–64). His poems included "Woodman, Spare that Tree," "Near the Lake," "My Mother's Bible," "We Were Boys Together," "A Long Time Ago."

Morris, Gouverneur. 1752–1816. American politician and diplomat, b. Morrisania, N.Y. Practiced law, New York City; associated with colonial cause from outbreak of Revolution; member of New York provincial congress (1775–77); member of Continental Congress (1777–79); assistant superintendent of finance (1781–85), in which post he prepared report that proposed system of decimal coinage using terms dollar and cent; member of Constitutional Convention (1787). U.S. commissioner to England (1790–91); U.S. minister to France (1792–94). U.S. senator (1800–03). Chairman, Erie Canal Commission (1810–13). His half-brother ¶Lewis Morris (1726–1798) was member of Continental Congress (1775–77) and a signer of the Declaration of Independence. A nephew ¶Lewis Richard (1760–1825) engaged in business at Springfield, Vt.; Vermont secretary of foreign affairs (1781–83); member of U.S. House of Representatives (1797–1803); by withholding his vote on the 36th ballot in the Jefferson–Burr contest for the presidency, turned the election to Jefferson.

Morris, Lewis. See under Gouverneur MORRIS.

Morris, Lewis Richard. See under Gouverneur MORRIS.

Morris, Michael. 3d Baron Morris. *Known as* Lord Morris and Kil·lan·in \kil-ˈan-ən\. 1826–1901. Irish jurist. M.P. (1865–67); solicitor general and attorney general for Ireland (1866); puisne judge of common pleas (1867–87, chief judge from 1876); lord chief justice of Ireland (1887–1900); created baronet (1885), life peer (1889), baron (1900).

Morris, Robert. 1734–1806. American financier and politician, b. Liverpool, England. To America (1747); in commission shipping business, Philadelphia (from c.1748). Favored colonial cause at outbreak of Revolution; member, Continental Congress (1775–78) and signer of the Declaration of Independence; performed important service to American cause by arranging for financing the purchases of supplies for Washington's armies (1776–78); superintendent of finance under the Articles of Confederation (1781–84);

founded and organized the Bank of North America (1782); delegate, Constitutional Convention (1787); U.S. senator from Pennsylvania (1789–95); financially ruined by speculation in western lands.

Morris, Thomas, *called* Old Tom. 1821–1908. Scottish golfer. Professional and greenskeeper at St. Andrews (from 1863); won British championship (later British Open; 1861, 1862, 1864, 1867). His son ¶Thomas, *called* Young Tom (c.1851–1875), won the Open 4 consecutive times (1868, 1869, 1870, 1872; no contest in 1871).

Morris, William. 1834–1896. English poet and artist. Close friend of Burne-Jones from Oxford days; worked at architecture and painting (1856–62); one of originators of *Oxford and Cambridge Magazine,* through which he became friend of D. G. Rossetti; published his first poetry, *The Defence of Guenevere* (1858); m. (1859) Jane Burden, a model; with Philip Webb designed and built home, the Red House, at Upton, Kent; with Rossetti, Burne-Jones, and others, helped to found decorating firm which effected reform of Victorian taste in color and design; designed esp. furniture, fabrics, wallpapers. Translated into English verse the *Aeneid* (1875), the *Odyssey* (1887); after travel in Iceland produced *Three Northern Love Stories* (1875) and the epic *Sigurd the Volsung* (1877). Founded, with Philip Webb, Society for the Protection of Ancient Buildings (1877). Joined Democratic Federation (1883); led group of seceders (1884) in organizing the Socialist League, and edited its organ *The Commonweal;* relinquished membership and editorship when anarchist faction became dominant; described a Socialist commonwealth in England in *News from Nowhere* (1891) and *A Dream of John Ball* (1888). Started the Kelmscott Press (1890) at Hammersmith, for which he designed special type and ornamental letters and borders for use in publishing medieval French romances, Shelley, Keats, Rossetti, Herrick, his own works, and finally his magnificent *Kelmscott Chaucer* (1896). Author of other volumes of verse, *The Life and Death of Jason* (1867), *The Earthly Paradise* (1868–70), *Love is Enough* (1872), and *Poems by the Way* (1891), and of prose romances including *The House of the Wolfings* (1889), *The Roots of the Mountains* (1890), *The Story of the Glittering Plain* (1891), *The Wood Beyond the World* (1895), *The Well at the World's End* (1896), *The Water of the Wondrous Isles* (1897), *Story of the Sundering Flood* (1898).

Morris, William. 1873–1932. American theatrical agent, b. Schwarzenau, Germany. Employed by theatrical booking firm of Klaw and Erlanger; later led opposition of independent agents to monopoly over vaudeville theaters held by Keith-Albee United Booking Office; after lengthy struggle, aided by *Variety* newspaper, broke monopoly; organized William Morris Agency.

Morris, William Richard. 1st Viscount Nuf·field \ˈnəf-ˌēld\. 1877–1963. English automobile manufacturer. Entered bicycle business (1893); developed Morris-Oxford automobile (1912) and Morris-Cowley (1914); incorporated Morris Motors, Ltd. (1919); introduced MG sports car (1923), Morris Minor (1931); acquired other firms; merged with Austin Motor Co. to form British Motor Corp. (1952). Created baron (1934), viscount (1938). Noted philanthropist; endowed Oxford medical school (1936), Nuffield Coll. (1937), Nuffield Foundation (1943), etc.

Mor·ris-Jones \ˈmȯr-əs-ˈjōnz, ˈmär-\, Sir John. *Orig. surname* Jones. 1864–1929. Welsh poet and scholar. Professor, U. Coll. of North Wales (1895–1929); one of the leaders in the revival of Welsh literature; adjudicated national eisteddfodau (1896–1929). Author of *A Welsh Grammar* (1913), *Cerdd Dafod* (a study of Welsh metric art, 1925), *Orgraff yr Iaith Gymraeg* (on orthography, 1928); also published Welsh poems and translations, esp. from Omar Khayyam and Heine, as *Caniadau* (1907).

Morrison. See also MORISON.

Mor·ri·son \ˈmȯr-ə-sən, ˈmär-\, Arthur. 1863–1945. English journalist, novelist, and playwright. On staff of *National Observer;* author of *Tales of Mean Streets* (1894), *A Child of the Jago* (1896), *To London Town* (1899), *The Hole in the Wall* (1902), *The Green Eye of Goona* (1904), and a series of detective stories centered about the character Martin Hewitt; coauthor of plays including *That Brute Simmons* (1904).

Morrison, Herbert Stanley. Baron Morrison of Lam·beth \ˈlam-bəth\. 1888–1965. English politician. Active in Independent Labour party (1906) and London Labour party (1915); M.P. (1923–24, 1929–31, 1935 ff.); chairman, National Labour party (1928–29); minister of transport (1929–31); alderman and leader, London County Council (from 1934); minister of supply (1940); home secretary and minister of home security (1940–45); member of war cabinet (1942–45); lord president of the council and leader of House of Commons (1945–51); foreign secretary (1951); created baron (1959).

Morrison, Richard James. *Pseudonym* Zad·ki·el \ˈzad-kē-əl\. 1795–1874. English astrologer. Served in British navy (1806–29); issued *Herald of Astrology* (1831), continued annually as *Zadkiel's Almanac.*

Morrison, Robert. 1782–1834. Scottish missionary. Ordained in Presbyterian church (1807); became first Protestant missionary to China on being sent by London Missionary Society to Canton (1807); translator to East India Company (1809–34); translated into Chinese New Testament (1813) and, with some help, Old Testament (1821); completed his *Chinese Grammar* (1815), *Chinese Dictionary* (1823); established Anglo-Chinese College at Malacca (1818).

Morrison, William Shepherd. Viscount Dun·ros·sil \dən-ˈräs-əl\. 1893–1961. British politician, b. Scotland. M.P. (1929–59); minister of agriculture and fisheries (1936–39), of food (1939–40); postmaster general (1940–42); minister of planning (1943–45); speaker, House of Commons (1951–59); created viscount (1959); governor general of Australia (1959–61).

Mor·row \ˈmär-(ˌ)ō, ˈmȯr-\, Dwight Whitney. 1873–1931. American lawyer, banker, and diplomat, b. Huntington, W.Va. Partner in N.Y. law firm (1905–14), J. P. Morgan & Co. (1914–27); organized Kennecott Copper Co.; U.S. ambassador to Mexico (1927–30); U.S. delegate to London Naval Conference (1930); U.S. senator from New Jersey (1930–31).

Morse \ˈmȯ(ə)rs\, Charles Wyman. 1856–1933. American promoter, b. Bath, Me. In New York (from 1897); organized merger of ice companies into American Ice Co. (1899); merged several coastwise shipping companies; gained control of chain of banks in New York; indicted, tried, and convicted (1908) of making false entries in books of the Bank of North America and misapplying its funds; in prison (1910–12). Reentered New York financial field (1913) with consolidation of shipping interests; at U.S. entrance into World War I, contracted with U.S. Shipping Board to build vessels for government use; indicted (1922) for conspiracy to defraud the government, tried, and acquitted; later civil suit resulted in judgment of $11.5 million against him; placed under guardianship as an incompetent (1926).

Morse, Edward Sylvester. 1838–1925. American zoologist, b. Portland, Me. Professor, Bowdoin (1871–74), Imperial U., Tokyo (1877–80); director, Peabody Museum, Salem, Mass. (from 1880); curator of Japanese ceramics, Boston Museum of Fine Arts (from 1892). A founder of Japanese archaeology. Author of *First Book of Zoology* (1875), *Japanese Homes and Their Surroundings* (1886), *Glimpses of China and Chinese Homes* (1902).

Morse, Jedidiah. 1761–1826. American clergyman, b. Woodstock, Conn. Congregational pastor, Charlestown, Mass. (1789–1819); active in maintaining orthodoxy and forcing Unitarian believers out of Congregational church. Published (1784) *Geography Made Easy,* the first geography appearing in U.S.; also *The American Geography* (1789), *Elements of Geography* (1795), *American Gazetteer* (1796), *A Compendious History of New England* (with Elijah Parish, 1804), *Annals of the American Revolution* (1824).

Morse, Samuel Finley Breese. 1791–1872. American artist and inventor, b. Charlestown, Mass. Son of Jedidiah Morse; portrait painter in Boston, Charleston, S.C., and New York (1815–c.1837); a founder and first president (1826–45, 1861) of National Academy of Design; professor, N.Y.U. (from 1832). Interested himself in possibilities of magnetic telegraph (from 1832); conducted experiments with technical aid of Leonard D. Gale (1800–1883) and financial aid of Alfred Vail; invented Morse code for use in telegraph instrument; filed a caveat at patent office (1837) and endeavored in vain to get European patents; made public exhibitions of his apparatus (from 1837). U.S. congress (1843) voted him $30,000 for experimental line between Washington and Baltimore; line built by Ezra Cornell, and Morse sent (May 24, 1844) the first message, "What hath God wrought!" Involved in much litigation over rights to his invention, but courts upheld him and he enjoyed prosperity in his later years.

Mor·ta·ra \mōr-ˈtä-rä\, Edgar. 1851–1940. Italian religious. Born to a Jewish family; taken (1858) from his father's house in Bologna by papal guards on ground that, while gravely ill, he had been secretly baptized by a Roman Catholic maid servant; held despite parents' repeated attempts at recovery, widespread public indignation in Europe, and appeals to pope; discovered during occupation of Rome (1870), but decided to remain Roman Catholic; became monk of Canons Regular of the Lateran; ordained (1873).

Mor·tier \mȯr-tyā\, Édouard-Adolphe-Casimir-Joseph. Duc de Tré·vise \də-trā-vēz\. 1768–1835. French soldier. Entered volunteers (1791); general (1799); occupied Hanover (1803); created marshal of France (1804); distinguished himself esp. at Friedland (1807), in Spain (1808–11); commanded Young Guard in Russian campaign (1812); defended Paris (1814); rejoined Napoléon in Hundred Days (1815); peerage suspended (1815–19); ambassador to Russia (1830–31); premier and minister of war (1834–35); mortally wounded at side of Louis-Philippe by Fieschi's bomb.

Mor·til·let \mȯr-tē-ye\, Gabriel de, *in full* Louis-Laurent-Marie-Gabriel de. 1821–1898. French archaeologist. On staff of Musée des Antiquités Nationales, Saint-Germain-en-Laye (1867–85); deputy (1885–89); professor, École d'Anthropologie, Paris (1876–98). Created system of epochs of cultural history as Chellean, Acheulean, Mousterian, Solutrean, etc. Author of *Géologie et minéralogie de la Savoie* (1858), *La Préhistorique* (1882), etc.

Mor·ti·mer \ˈmȯrt-ə-mər\. Name of Anglo-Norman family of Welsh marches holding earldoms of March \ˈmärch\ and Ul·ster \ˈəl-stər\, including among members: Roger de Mortimer (fl. 1054–1074), the founder; son of Hugh, bishop of Coutances (c.990); named from his castle, Mortemer-en-Brai. His son ¶Ralph (d. 1104?); to England with William I; settled on Welsh marches; enriched by award of forfeited lands of Earl of Hertford, including Wigmore, henceforth the family seat (1074), which were entered in Domesday Book.

¶Roger (1231?–1282), 6th Baron of Wig·more \'wig-ˌmō(ə)r, -ˌmȯ(ə)r\; further added to estates by marriage (1247) with Maude de Breuse (Matilda de Braose); sided with barons against Henry III (1258); became royalist (1261), fought against Llewelyn ap Gruffydd; after battle of Lewes, exiled to Ireland but prepared resistance and aided Prince Edward to escape from de Montfort (1265); commanded rear guard at Evesham (1265); became a guardian of realm (1272).

His grandson ¶Roger de Mortimer (1287–1330), 8th Baron of Wigmore and 1st Earl of March; acquired Irish estates by marriage with Joan de Geneville; defeated kinsfolk, the Lacys, in Ireland; lieutenant (1316) and justiciar (1319) of Ireland; helped uncle in fight to maintain independent position of house of Mortimer in Wales against threat of the Despensers (1320), Edward II's favorites; forced to surrender to king at Shrewsbury (1322); escaped after imprisonment to France (1323), where Isabella, queen of England, became his paramour and joined him in invasion of England (1326) and execution of the Despensers; acquired lands of Despensers and of Arundel; compelled Edward II to abdicate (1327) in favor of his son Edward III; with Isabella, ruled the realm, procured murder of Edward II; responsible for failure of Scots expedition (1327); justiciar of Wales (1327); created earl (1328); by his arrogance, excited jealousy of Henry, Earl of Lancaster, who persuaded young Edward III to assert his independence and seize and imprison his mother's paramour; condemned without trial by his peers; hanged, drawn, and quartered at Tyburn.

¶Edmund de Mortimer (1351–1381), 3d earl; great-grandson of 1st earl; m. (1368) Philippa, daughter of Lionel of Antwerp, Duke of Clarence, 3d son of Edward III, thereby becoming representative of one of chief Anglo-Norman lordships in Ireland and, on death of his wife's father, next in succession to English crown after the Black Prince and his son; lieutenant of Ireland (1379); handed on to house of York claim to throne, which was contested in Wars of the Roses; his elder daughter, Elizabeth, married Henry Percy (Hotspur).

¶Roger de Mortimer (1374–1398), 4th Earl of March and Ulster; son of 3d earl; proclaimed heir presumptive to English throne (1385); m. niece of King Richard II (1388); lieutenant of Ireland (1397); killed in battle of Kells in Ireland; his grandson Richard, Duke of York (offspring of his daughter Anne and Richard, Earl of Cambridge, grandson of Edward III), was father of King Edward IV, who acquired Mortimer estates.

¶Edmund de Mortimer (1391–1425), 5th Earl of March and 3d Earl of Ulster; son of 4th Earl of March; recognized as heir presumptive by Richard II (1398); during Lancastrian revolution, held in custody with his brother by Henry IV (1399–1413); restored to estates (1413) by Henry V, whom he accompanied through wars in France (1415–21); member of council of regency; lieutenant of Ireland (1423), died of plague while negotiating with native septs, leaving earldom to become merged with crown on accession of his nephew's son to throne as Edward IV.

Morton, Earls of. See (1) DOUGLAS family; (2) MAXWELL family.

Mor·ton \'mȯrt-ᵊn\, Ferdinand Joseph La Menthe, *called* Jelly Roll. 1885–1941. American musician, b. Gulfport, La. Professional pianist in New Orleans (from 1902), traveling widely; made first recordings (1923); with group Red Hot Peppers made series of recordings (1926–30) that are among earliest examples of disciplined jazz ensemble work; later noted also as raconteur of marked braggadocio, claiming among other accomplishments the invention of jazz. Compositions included "Jelly Roll Blues," "Wolverine Blues," "Dead Man Blues," "Black Bottom Stomp," "Harmony Blues," "King Porter Stomp."

Morton, John. c.1420–1500. English prelate and statesman. Present with Lancastrians at battle of Towton (1461); attainted by Yorkists; lived with exiled court of Margaret of Anjou (c.1463–70); aided formation of coalition between Richard Neville, Earl of Warwick, and George, Duke of Clarence; landed with Warwick at Dartmouth (1470) but after battle of Tewkesbury (1471), submitted to Edward IV. Master of rolls (1473); a negotiator of Treaty of Picquigny (1475); bishop of Ely (1479); one of executors of Edward IV's will (1483); escaped imprisonment by Richard III and aided Earl of Richmond (later Henry VII), whose adviser he became. Archbishop of Canterbury (1486–1500); lord chancellor (1487); cardinal (1493); chancellor of Oxford (1495).

Morton, John. 1724?–1777. American patriot, b. Ridley, Pa. Delegate to Stamp Act Congress (1765); member, Continental Congress (1774–77) and signer of the Declaration of Independence.

Morton, John Cameron Andrieu Bingham. 1893–1979. British journalist. Joined *Daily Express* (1922); took over from Wyndham Lewis the humorous column "By The Way," which he wrote as "Beachcomber" (1924–75).

Morton, John Maddison. See under Thomas MORTON (1764–1838).

Morton, Joy. 1855–1934. American merchant, b. Detroit, Mich. Son of Julius S. Morton; entered salt business in Chicago (1880); gained control of and reorganized firm as Joy Morton & Co. (1885), which became Morton Salt Co. (1910); experimented in scientific husbandry at farm estate in Lisle, Ill., where he also established (1921) Morton Arboretum.

Morton, Julius Sterling. 1832–1902. American agriculturist, b. Adams, N.Y. Secretary of Nebraska Territory (1858–61); U.S. secretary of agriculture (1893–97); originator of Arbor Day (1872). His son ¶Paul (1857–1911) was U.S. secretary of the navy (1904–05); chairman of board and later president, Equitable Life Assurance Association (1905–11).

Morton, Levi Parsons. 1824–1920. American banker and politician, b. Shoreham, Vt. Established banking firm in New York (1863); member, U.S. House of Representatives (1879–81); U.S. minister to France (1881–85); vice president of the U.S. (1889–93); governor of N.Y. (1895–97).

Morton, Oliver Hazard Perry Throck. 1823–1877. American politician, b. Salisbury, Ind. A founder of Indiana Republican party (1856); lieutenant governor of Indiana (1860), succeeding to governorship (1861) and being elected governor (1864); known for his able and vigorous war policies in support of Union cause; U.S. senator (1867–77).

Morton, Sarah Wentworth, *nee* Ap·thorp \'ap-ˌthȯ(ə)rp\. *Pseudonym* Phi-len·ia \fi-'lēn-yə, fī-, -'lē-nē-ə\. 1759–1846. American poet, b. Boston. m. Perez Morton (1781); contributed lyric and narrative verse to the periodicals of the time; long believed to have written novel *The Power of Sympathy* (1789; see William H. BROWN).

Morton, Thomas. 1590?–?1647. American colonist, b. England. To America (1624), settled in Quincy, Mass.; built house at Merry Mount, where his licentious life, anti-Puritan polemics, and successful Indian trade brought him in bad repute with the Pilgrim fathers; arrested and sent to England (1628, again 1630); arrested and imprisoned at Boston (1644–45). Author of *New English Canaan* (1637), a partly satirical description of New England.

Morton, Thomas. 1764–1838. English playwright. Produced comedies in which John Emery, Charles and John Kemble, and Macready played, including *A Cure for Heartache* (1797), *Speed the Plough* (with its invisible Mrs. Grundy, 1798), *The Blind Girl* (1801), *The School of Reform* (1805), *Town and Country* (1807), *A Roland for an Oliver* (1819), *School for Grown Children* (1827). His son ¶John Maddison (1811–1891), playwright, showed facility in adapting French pieces; scored a hit with farce *Box and Cox* (1847); author of a hundred other farces.

Morton, Thomas. 1781–1832. Scottish shipbuilder. Inventor of the patent slip (patented 1819) for docking vessels, a submerged carriage on an inclined railway, used as a substitute for a dry dock.

Morton, William Thomas Green. 1819–1868. American dentist, b. Charlton, Mass. Practiced in Boston (from 1842); associated one year (1842–43) with Horace Wells (*q.v.*); from Charles T. Jackson, a professor of chemistry, learned of experiments with sulfuric ether as an anesthetizing agent; tested ether on animals and on himself, and finally (Sept. 30, 1846) on a patient; a fortnight later (Oct. 16, 1846) at Mass. General Hospital, Dr. John C. Warren removed tumor from the neck of a patient anesthetized by Morton's process. Morton and Jackson received patent for use of "letheon" (1846); Morton's claims and attempts to profit largely by the discovery brought conflicting claims from Jackson, Horace Wells, and Crawford W. Long; last years embittered by controversy, litigation, and poverty.

Mor·us *or* **Mor·ys** \'mȯr-is\, Huw. *Pseudonym* Eos Ceir·iog \'ā-ȯs-'kär-yȯg\, *i.e.* Nightingale of Ceiriog. 1622–1709. Welsh poet. Brought new level of craftsmanship and dignity to popular free meters supplanting bardic verse.

Morveau, Guyton de. See GUYTON DE MORVEAU.

Mo·sad·deq \'mōs-ad-ˌdek\, Mohammad. *Surname also spelled* Mossadegh, Masaddiq. 1880–1967. Iranian politician. Governor general of Fars (1914); minister of justice (1920), finance (1921), foreign affairs (1923); member of Majles (1923–27); opposed Reza Shah; in private life (1927–44); again elected to Majles (1944–53); sponsored bill nationalizing Anglo-Iranian Oil Co. (1951); premier of Iran (1951–53); the attempt of Shah Mohammad Reza Pahlavi to dismiss him (Aug. 1953) led to mob violence and the shah's forced flight from Iran; regime overthrown a short time later by opponents aided by U.S., and shah returned; imprisoned (1953–56) and under house arrest (1956–67).

Mo·san·der \mō-'sän-dər\, Carl Gustaf. 1797–1858. Swedish chemist. In charge of laboratory (1826), professor (1832–58), Caroline Medical Inst., Stockholm; credited with discovery of the elements lanthanum (1839), erbium and terbium (1843); discovered (1843) didymium, later (1885) shown to be mixture of neodymium and praseodymium.

Mos·by \'mōz-bē\, John Singleton. 1833–1916. American soldier, b. Edgemont, Va. Enlisted in Confederate army (1861); scout on Gen. J. E. B. Stuart's staff in the Peninsula Campaign, at Manassas, and at Antietam (1862); commanded (1863–65) independent cavalry unit, Mosby's Rangers, raiding federal pickets and supplies; captured Gen. E. H. Stoughton and his staff behind Federal lines at Fairfax Court House (Mar. 9, 1863); harassed Sheridan in Shenandoah valley (1864); colonel (1864). After war, resumed practice of law; U.S. consul, Hong Kong (1878–85); assistant attorney, U.S. Department of Justice (1904–10). Author of *Mosby's War Reminiscences* (1887), *Stuart's Cavalry in the Gettysburg Campaign* (1908). Credited by some with coining phrase "the Solid South" (1878).

Mo·sca \'mō-skä\, Gaetano. 1858–1941. Italian political scientist. Professor, Palermo (1885–88), Rome (1888–96), Turin (1896–1908); deputy (1908–19); senator (1919 ff.). Among his works were *Sulla teorica dei governi e sul governo parlamentare* (1884), *Elementi di scienza politica* (1896), *Diritto costituzionale* (1908).

Mo·sche·les \'mō-shə-ləs\, Ignaz *or* Isack. 1794–1870. German pianist, composer, and teacher, b. Prague. To Vienna (1808); achieved high reputation as virtuoso pianist; prepared piano reduction of Beethoven's *Fidelio* (1814); settled as composer and teacher in London (1825); taught at Leipzig Conservatory (from 1846). Composed piano concertos, sonatas, three *Allegri di bravura,* chamber music, variations, and studies for pianoforte. Known as a gifted improvisator and as inventor of the "singing tone," later developed by the Liszt school.

Mo·sche·rosch \'mō-shə-ˌrōsh\, Johann Michael. *Pen name* Philander von Sit·te·wald \fōn-'zit-ə-vält\. 1601–1669. German satirist. Author of the satirical "book of visions" *Wunderliche und wahrhafftige Gesichte Philanders von Sittewald* (1640–43) and other satires on the customs and manners of his day, and *Insomnis cura parentum* (1643), a work of Lutheran piety.

Mos·cho·pou·los \mōs-'kōp-ů-ˌlōs\, Manuel. 13th–14th century. Byzantine grammarian. Author of *Erotemata grammatika* (pub. 1493), a lexicon *Sylloge onomaton Attikon,* recensions of Sophocles.

Mos·chus \'mäs-kəs\. fl. c.150 B.C. Greek pastoral poet. His extant works include fragments of a *Bucolica;* short epic *Europa* is attributed to him, as by some is *Lament for Bion.*

Moschus, John. c.550–619. Byzantine religious. Entered monastery of St. Theodosius near Jerusalem (c.565); later moved to Rome. Author of *Neos paradeisos* (Lat. title *Pratum spirituale*), known as "The Spiritual Meadow," a long-popular collection of descriptions of monastic and ascetic practices and spiritual experiences.

Mościc·ki \mōsh-'chēts-kē\, Ignacy. 1867–1946. Polish chemist and politician. Taught at Freiburg (1897–1912), the technical high school in Lwów (1912–26); long a partisan of Piłsudski; president of Poland (1926–39); in exile and Swiss citizen (from 1939).

Mose·ley \'mōz-lē\, Henry Gwyn Jeffreys. 1887–1915. English physicist. Worked under Rutherford at U. of Manchester (1910–14); studied X-ray spectra; discovered Moseley's law of characteristic X-ray spectra of elements (1913); established significance of atomic number; predicted unknown element hafnium.

Mo·sen \'mō-zən\, Julius. 1803–1867. German poet, novelist, and playwright. Dramaturgist of court theater, Oldenburg (1844–48). Author of the epics *Lied vom Ritter Wahn* (1831) and *Ahasver* (1838); verse collection *Gedichte* (1836); tales *Georg Venlot* (1831), *Bilder im Moose* (1846); novel *Der Kongress von Verona* (1842); tragedies *Herzog Bernhard* (1855), *Der Sohn des Fürsten* (1858).

Mo·ser \'mō-zər\, Gustav von. 1825–1903. German writer. Author of some 70 comedies and farces, including *Ultimo* (1874), *Der Hypochonder* (1877), *Der Bibliothekar* (1878), *Der Registrator* (1879, with L'Arronge), *Krieg im Frieden* (1881, with Franz von Schönthan).

Moser, Johann Jakob. 1701–1785. German jurist and publicist. Professor, Tübingen (1720–24, 1729–34); district counsellor, Württemberg (1751–59); first legal scholar to bring out a complete presentation of German constitutional law. Author of *Teutsches Staatsrecht* (50 vols., 1737–54), *Deutsches Staatsarchiv* (13 vols., 1751–57), etc.

Mö·ser \'mœ-zər\, Justus. 1720–1794. German historian, jurist, and publicist. In service of prince-bishop of Osnabrück (from 1747); opposed French Revolution, influenced Goethe and Herder on questions of history and economics. Author of *Osnabrücke Geschichte* (1768), *Patriotischen Phantasien* (1774–76), etc.

Mo·ses \'mō-zəz, -zəs\. *Hebrew* Mo·she \'mō-shə\. 14th–13th century B.C. Hebrew prophet and lawgiver. According to biblical book of Exodus, led Israelites from Egypt through the wilderness to Canaan; received Covenant; established religious community of Israel and organized its cult and judicial traditions. Traditionally held to be author of the Pentateuch.

Moses of Kho·ren \kōr-'en\. *Armenian* Mov·ses Kho·re·na·tzi \'mō-səs-kōr-en-'ät-sē\. 5th? century A.D. Armenian writer. Generally considered father of Armenian literature; author of a *History of Armenia,* only work to treat pre-Christian Armenia.

Moses of Nar·bonne \när-'bän, -'bən\ *or* **Moses Nar·bo·ni** \när-'bō-nē\. *Also* Moses ben Josh·ua \'jäsh(-ə)-wə\. d. 1362. French-Jewish physician and philosopher. Author of commentaries on Maimonides, Averroës, Ibn Ṭufayl, al-Ghazālī.

Moses, Anna Mary, *nee* Robertson. *Known as* Grandma Moses. 1860–1961. American painter, b. Greenwich, N.Y. m. Thomas Moses (1887; d. 1927); farmed in Staunton, Va., and Eagle Bridge, N.Y.; took up painting in her 70s; gained fame for her primitive paintings, mainly on board, documenting rural scenes and life of 19th–20th century America; works included *Sugaring Off, Catching the Thanksgiving Turkey, Old Oaken Bucket, Black Horses, Old Checkered House.*

Moses, Robert. 1888–1981. American public official, b. New Haven, Conn. Adviser to N.Y. Gov. A.E. Smith (1918–29); chairman, State Council of Parks (1924–62), Metropolitan Conference on Parks (1926–30); secretary of state of N.Y. (1927–28); New York City park commissioner (1934–60); held numerous other posts in public authorities. Planned and built large number of public works, including Jones Beach (1930) and dozens of state and city parks; hundreds of playgrounds; 416 miles of parkways, including Northern and Southern State parkways, Henry Hudson, Palisades; urban expressways as the Bruckner, Long Island, Major Deegan, Whitestone; bridges as Bronx-Whitestone, Henry Hudson, Throgs Neck, Triborough, Verrazano-Narrows; Queens Midtown Tunnel; Co-op City and other housing projects; Shea Stadium, Lincoln Center, United Nations complex, etc. President, N.Y. World's Fair (1964–65).

Moses ben Mai·mon \-ˌben-mī-'mōn\. *Arab. name* Abū 'Imran Mūsā ibn Maymūn ibn 'Ubayd Allāh. *Known by Gr. form* Mai·mon·i·des \mī-'män-ə-ˌdēz\ *and by acronym* RaM·BaM \räm-'bäm\. 1135–1204. Jewish philosopher, b. Spain. Foremost intellectual figure of medieval Judaism. Emigrated (c.1159) from his native Córdoba, finally settling (1166) at Fostat, Egypt, near Cairo; became physician to Saladin, sultan of Egypt, and head of Jewish community. His philosophical system attempted to reconcile rabbinic Judaism with Aristotelianism as modified by Arabic interpretation; believed in freedom of the will; condemned asceticism. Except for Hebrew commentary on the Mishna (*Mishne Torah,* 1168), wrote main works in Arabic; chief work on religious philosophy *Dalālat al-ḥā'irīn* (1190, *The Guide of the Perplexed;* Hebrew title *More nevukhim*); also wrote rabbinical letters on contemporary problems and treatises on logic, mathematics, medicine, law, and theology.

Moses ben Naḥ·man \-ben-'näk-mən\. *Called* Naḥ·ma·ni·des \näk-'män-ə-ˌdēz\ *and* Naḥmanides Ram·ban \räm-'bän\. c.1195–1270. Spanish Talmudist. Author of biblical and Talmudic commentaries influenced by Kabbalistic doctrines; exiled (1263).

Moses ben Samuel ibn Tibbon. See IBN TIBBON.

Mo·ses de Le·ón \'mō-sās-thā-lā-'ōn\. *More completely* Moses ben Shem Tov de León \-bān-shem-'tōb-\. 1250–1305. Spanish Kabbalist. Presumed author of *Sefer ha-zohar,* which he ascribed to 2d-century rabbi Simeon ben Yoḥai; work became one of most important to Kabbalistic mysticism.

Moses ibn Ezra. See IBN EZRA.

Mo·ses·sohn \'mō-zəz-ˌzōn\, Nehemiah. 1853–1926. American clergyman, b. Crimea, Russia. To U.S. (1887); rabbi in Philadelphia, Dallas, Tex., and Portland, Ore. (to 1902). Founded and edited, with his sons as publishers, *The Jewish Tribune,* in Portland, Ore. (1902–18) and New York City (1918–26). His son ¶David Nehemiah (1883–1930) was a lawyer and editor; planned and effected reorganization of garment industry in New York, and became executive director (1918–23), chairman (1923–30), of Associated Dress Industries of America; edited *The Jewish Tribune* (1926–30). Another son ¶Moses Dayyan (1884–1940), law partner of his brother David in Portland, Ore. (to 1918), and New York City (from 1918), succeeded his brother as executive chairman of Associated Dress Industries of America (1930–33); published *The Jewish Tribune* (1903–31).

Mosharref od-Dīn. See SA'DĪ.

Mos·heim \'mōs-ˌhīm\, Johann Lorenz von. 1694–1755. German theologian. Helped found U. of Göttingen, where he became professor and chancellor (1747); pioneer in modern preaching and founder of modern pragmatic ecclesiastical historical writing in Germany.

Moshesh. See MSHWESHWE.

Mosleḥ od-Dīn Sa'dī. See SA'DĪ.

Mos·ley \'mōz-lē\, Sir Oswald Ernald. 6th baronet. 1896–1980. British politician. M.P. (1918–24, 1926–31); deserted Labour party (1931); founded (1932) British Union of Fascists, known as Blackshirts; interned (1940–43); founded (1948) Union Movement.

Mos·que·ra \mōs-'kā-rä\, Tomás Cipriano de. 1798–1878. Colombian soldier and politician. Joined army of Simon Bolívar (1815); brigadier general (1828); deputy (1834 ff.); president of New Granada (1845–49); headed liberals' revolt (1859–61); captured Bogotá and assumed power (1861); called assembly which created United States of Colombia (1863); elected president (1863–67); assumed dictatorial powers, but was deposed (1867) and banished for two years; president of Cauca state (1871–73); senator (1874).

Mossadegh. See MOSADDEQ.

Mos·taert \ˈmȯs-tärt\, Jan. c.1475–1555 or 1556. Dutch painter. Known esp. for *Deposition* triptych, *Adoration of the Kings, Tree of Jesse.*

Mosz·kow·ski \mȯsh-ˈkȯf-skē\, Moritz. 1854–1925. German pianist and composer. To Paris (1879); composed the opera *Boabdil* (1892), the ballet *Laurin* (1896), the symphonic poem *Jeanne d'Arc,* overtures, concert suites, *Spanische Tänze* for piano (1876), etc.

Mo·ten \ˈmōt-ᵊn\, Benjamin, *called* Bennie. 1894–1935. American musician, b. Kansas City, Mo. Pianist; led jazz bands in and around Kansas City (from 1922); principal developer of "Southwestern" style of orchestral jazz; influenced esp. his second pianist, Count Basie.

Mo Ti. See MO-TZU.

Mot·ley \ˈmät-lē\, John Lothrop. 1814–1877. American historian, b. Dorchester, Mass. Secretary, U.S. legation at St. Petersburg (1841). Published *The Rise of the Dutch Republic* (1856), *The History of the United Netherlands* (1860–67), *The Life and Death of John of Barneveld* (1874). U.S. minister to Austria (1861–67), to Great Britain (1869–70).

Mo·to·da \mō-tō-dä\ Eifu. 1818–1891. Japanese educator. Confucian scholar; joined imperial household as tutor (1870); tutor and later councilor to Emperor Meiji; principal author of highly conservative Imperial Rescript on Education (1890).

Mo·ton \ˈmōt-ᵊn\, Robert Russa. 1867–1940. American educator, b. Amelia Co., Va. Head of military department, Hampton Institute (1890–1915); succeeded Booker T. Washington as principal of Tuskegee Normal and Industrial Institute (1915–35); Spingarn medal (1932). Author of *Racial Good Will* (1916), autobiography *Finding a Way Out* (1920), *What the Negro Thinks* (1929).

Motonobu. See KANO.

Mo·to·o·ri \mō-tō-ō-rē\ Norinaga. 1730–1801. Japanese scholar and poet. Authority on customs, poetry, and religion of ancient Japan and a major contributor to Shintō theology; chief work, his 49-volume *Kojiki-den* (commentary on the *Kojiki,* completed 1798).

Mott \ˈmät\, Frank Luther. 1886–1964. American journalist, b. What Cheer, Iowa. Taught at U. of Iowa (1921–42); dean, School of Journalism, U. of Mo. (1942–51). Author of *Six Prophets out of the Middle West* (1917), *Rewards of Reading* (1926), *A History of American Magazines* (1930–57; Pulitzer prize, 1939), *The News in America* (1952), etc.

Mott, John Raleigh. 1865–1955. American religious leader, b. Livingston Manor, N.Y. Student secretary, International Committee, YMCA (1888–1915); general secretary (1915–31); president, World Alliance of YMCA's (1926–37). Founder and general secretary, World's Student Christian Federation (1895–1920), and chairman (1920–28); chairman, International Missionary Council (1921–42); shared with Emily G. Balch (*q.v.*) 1946 Nobel prize for peace.

Mott, Lucretia, *nee* Cof·fin \ˈkȯ-fən\. 1793–1880. American reformer, b. Nantucket, Mass. m. James Mott (1811; d. 1868); taught school; traveled as Quaker lecturer; minister (1821); a founder (1833) and president, Philadelphia Female Anti-Slavery Society; with Elizabeth Cady Stanton called women's-rights convention at Seneca Falls, N.Y. (1848); active in Underground Railroad (from 1850); a founder and first president (1866), American Equal Rights Association; a founder of Free Religious Association (1867).

Mot·ta \ˈmȯt-tä\, Giuseppe. 1871–1940. Swiss politician. Member of Nationalrat (1899–1911), of Bundesrat (from 1911); president of the Swiss Confederation (1915, 1920, 1927, 1932, 1937); opened first session of the Assembly of the League of Nations (1920) and was president of the Assembly (1924).

Motte Guyon, Jeanne-Marie de la. See GUYON.

Mot·teux \mä-ˈtə(r), ˈmä-ˌ\, Peter Anthony, *orig.* Pierre-Antoine. 1660–1718. British playwright and translator, b. France. Settled in London after revocation of Edict of Nantes (1685); edited *The Gentleman's Journal* (1692–94); edited Thomas Urquhart's translation of first three books of Rabelais, translated books IV and V (1693–1708); published free translation of *Don Quixote* (1700–03).

Mot·te·ville \mȯt-vēl\, Françoise Ber·taut de \ber-tō-də-\. c.1621–1689. French courtier. Member of court of Anne of Austria; m. Nicolas Langlois, seigneur de Motteville (1639; d. 1641); remained as *femme de chambre* of queen until queen's death (1666). Author of *Mémoires pour servir à l'histoire d'Anne d'Autriche* (first printed 1723).

Mottl \ˈmȯt-ᵊl\, Felix Josef. 1856–1911. Austrian composer and conductor. Protégé of Wagner; conductor of court opera, Karlsruhe (1881–1903), Munich Opera (1903–11); appeared regularly at Bayreuth (from 1886), in London (1894 ff.), and at Metropolitan Opera House (1903–04); edited works of Berlioz, Bach, Wagner, and other classics, and composed operas, the festival play *Eberstein* (1881), a string quartet (1898), songs, etc.

Mot·tram \ˈmät-rəm\, Ralph Hale. 1883–1971. English writer. Known esp. for novel *The Spanish Farm* (1924, Hawthornden prize) and its sequels *Sixty-four, Ninety-four* (1925) and *The Crime at Vanderlynden* (1926).

Mo-tzu \ˈmōd-ˈzü\, *i.e.* Master Mo. *Orig.* Mo Ti \ˈmō-ˈdē\. *Lat.* Mi·cius \ˈmish(-ē)-əs\. 470?–?391 B.C. Chinese philosopher. By tradition, originally a Confucian; evolved philosophy emphasizing simplicity, universal love, revival of religious sensibility; revered for having exemplified his own philosophy. Chief written work the *Mo-tzu.* Moism for a time rivaled Confucianism as leading Chinese school of thought.

Mou·che·ron \müsh-rōⁿ\, Frederik de. 1633–1686. Dutch painter. Painted chiefly Italian rivers and mountain landscapes. His son and pupil ¶Isaac (1667–1744) painted landscapes in his father's style and etched views of gardens and landscapes.

Mou·hot \mü-ō\, Henri, *in full* Alexandre-Henri. 1826–1861. French naturalist and explorer. Traveled in Europe, Russia; for British Royal Geographical Society and Zoological Society of London, traveled to Indochina (1858); explored Mekong River and tributaries; discovered (1858) ruins of Angkor. Author of *Voyage dans les royaumes de Siam, de Cambodge, de Laos et autres parties centrales de l'Indo-Chine* (1863).

Mou·lay Abd al-Ha·fid \mō-ˈlī-əb-dul-ˈhä-fēd\. c.1875–1937. Sultan of Morocco (1908–12). Revolted and deposed brother Abd-al-Aziz IV (1908); forced to recognize French protectorate over Morocco (1912), abdicated.

Mou·lin \mü-laⁿ\, Jean. 1899–1943. French patriot. Civil servant; youngest subprefect (1930) and prefect (1937); removed from prefecture of Eure-et-Loire (1940) by German occupation; joined Resistance; to England; returned as Gen. de Gaulle's delegate general to unoccupied France; helped organize maquis; first chairman of National Council of the Resistance (May 1943); legendary under nom de guerre Max; captured, tortured to death.

Mou·lins \mü-laⁿ\, Master of. fl. c.1480–c.1500. Name given otherwise unknown French painter, the outstanding artist of French late Gothic; works attributed to him include *Moulins Triptych* (c.1498) in Moulins cathedral, *Nativity with Cardinal Rolin, Portrait of a Praying Child, Female Donor with St. Magdalen.*

Moul·ton \ˈmōlt-ᵊn\, Forest Ray. 1872–1952. American astronomer, b. Le Roy, Mich. Taught at U. of Chicago (1898–1926, professor 1912); associate editor, *Transactions of American Mathematical Society* (1907–12). With Thomas C. Chamberlin, propounded (1904) the planetesimal hypothesis of the origin of the solar system. Author of *Celestial Mechanics* (1902), *Descriptive Astronomy* (1912), *Periodic Orbits* (1920), *Consider the Heavens* (1935), etc. His brother ¶Harold Glenn (1883–1965), economist; teacher at U. of Chicago (1909–22); director, Institute of Economics, Washington, D.C. (1922–29); president of Brookings Institution, Washington, D.C., from its founding (1927–52). Author of *Principles of Money and Banking* (1916), *Financial Organization of Society* (1921), *The American Transportation Problem* (1933), *Income and Economic Progress* (1935), etc.

Moul·trie \ˈmül-trē, ˈmōl-\, William. 1730–1805. American Revolutionary general, b. Charleston, S.C. Repulsed British attack on Sullivan's Island, now Fort Moultrie, in Charleston harbor (June 28, 1776); brigadier general in Continental army (1776); defended Charleston (1779); held prisoner by British (1780–82); major general (1782); governor of South Carolina (1785–87, 1792–94).

Mou·nier \mün-yā\, Emmanuel. 1905–1950. French philosopher and writer. Founded (1932) and edited journal *Esprit;* developed philosophy of personalism. Author of *La Pensée de Charles Péguy* (1931), *Révolution personnaliste et communautaire* (1935), *Manifeste au service du personalisme* (1936), *De la propriété capitaliste à la propriété humaine* (1936), *L'Affrontement chrétien* (1944), *Introduction aux existentialismes* (1947), etc.

Mount \ˈmau̇nt\, William Sidney. 1807–1868. American painter, b. Setauket, Long Island, N.Y. Painted portraits of Daniel Webster, Robert Schenck, Benjamin F. Thompson; known esp. for idyllic genre scenes as *Rustic Dance, Eel Spearing at Setauket, Raffling for the Goose, Bargaining for a Horse.*

Mountagu *or* **Mountague.** See MONTAGU.

Moun·tain \ˈmau̇nt-ᵊn\, Jacob. 1749–1825. Canadian prelate, b. Norfolk, England. First Anglican bishop of Quebec (1793). His son ¶George Jehoshaphat (1789–1863), b. Norwich, England, was ordained priest in Canada (1814); bishop of Montreal (1836); bishop of Quebec (1837).

Mount·bat·ten \mau̇nt-ˈbat-ᵊn\, Louis. 1st Earl Mountbatten of Burma. *Known until 1917 as* Prince Louis Francis Albert Victor Nicholas of Bat·ten·berg \ˈbat-ᵊn-ˌbərg\. 1900–1979. British naval commander and statesman. Son of Louis Alexander Mountbatten and great-grandson of Queen Victoria. Entered navy (1913); promoted through the grades to captain (1932), vice admiral (1942); commanded carrier *Illustrious* (1941); chief of Combined Operations (Commandos, 1942–43); supreme allied commander, Southeast Asia theater (1943–46); directed recapture of Burma; viceroy of India overseeing rapid transfer of power to native government and partition of Pakistan (1947); governor general of India (1947–48); created viscount (1946), earl (1947); commander of Mediterranean fleet (1952–54); first sea lord

(1955–59); admiral of the fleet (1956); chairman, UK Defense Staff and Chiefs of Staff Committee (1959–65).

Mountbatten, Louis Alexander. 1st Marquis of Mil·ford Ha·ven \'mil-fərd-,hā-vən\. *Known to 1917 as* Prince Louis of Battenberg. 1854–1921. British admiral, b. Austria. Son of Prince Alexander of Hesse; naturalized British subject (1868); entered navy (1868); rear admiral (1904); vice admiral (1908); commanded Atlantic fleet (1908–10); second sea lord (1911), first sea lord (1912–14); brought navy to peak of readiness; forced to resign by public outcry against his German background (1914); assumed surname Mountbatten, renounced German titles, created marquis (1917); admiral (1919).

Mountjoy, Baron. See Charles BLOUNT.

Mou·ret \mü-re\, Jean-Joseph. 1682–1738. French composer. Orchestra director at Paris Opéra (1714–18); composer-director at New Italian Theater (1717–37); artistic director of Concert Spirituel (1728–34). Composed stage works *Les Fêtes ou Le Triomphe de Thalie* (1714), *Le Mariage de Ragonde* (1714), *Ariane* (1717), *Les Amours des dieux* (1727); motets, cantatas, cantatilles, airs, etc.

Mou·ron \mü-rōⁿ\, Adolphe-Jean-Marie. *Pseudonym* Cas·san·dre \kå-säⁿdrᵊ\. 1901–1968. French artist and designer, b. Ukraine. Established reputation with posters as "Étoile du Nord" and "Dubo Dubon Dubonnet"; founded advertising agency Alliance Graphique (1926); designed typefaces Bifur (1929), Acier Noir (1935), Piegnot (1937); later a scenic designer and painter.

Moussorgsky. See MUSSORGSKY.

Mou·ton \mü-tōⁿ\, Jean. c.1459–1522. French composer. Chorister (1477–83), maître de chapelle (1483–?), Nesle; at cathedrals of Amiens (1500–01), Grenoble (1501–02); member of Royal Chapel (from c.1502). Composed over 100 motets, 15 masses, over 20 extant chansons; noted for use of canon and counterpoint techniques.

Mow·att \'mau̇-ət\, Anna Cora, *nee* Ogden. 1819–1870. American writer and actress, b. Bordeaux, France, of American parents. m. James Mowatt (1834, d. 1851). Wrote plays, novels, cookbooks, books on etiquette, etc.; best known play *Fashion; or Life in New York* (produced 1845); also wrote *Armand, the Child of the People* (1847). On stage (1845–54), often playing opposite E. L. Davenport.

Mow·bray \'mō-(,)brā, -brē\. Name of an Anglo-Norman baronial house derived from Montbray, Normandy, which was founded at the Conquest by Geoffrey de Montbray (d. 1093), bishop of Coutances; a principal adviser of William I in England (from 1066). His nephew and heir ¶Robert de Mowbray (d. 1125?), became earl of North·um·ber·land \nȯr-'thəm-bər-lənd\ (c.1080), rebelled against William II Rufus (1088); killed Malcolm of Scotland at Alnwick (1093); imprisoned for rebellion in favor of Count Stephen of Aumâle (1095).

Robert's wife Mathilde was allowed by the pope to marry Nigel d'Aubigny, another nephew of Bishop Geoffrey of Coutances; Nigel founded the second house of Mowbray, and his son ¶Roger de Mowbray (d. 1188), 2d Baron Mowbray, having changed his name, went on crusades (1147, 1164); joined Scots in rebellion (1174); founded Newburgh priory, benefactor of other houses; went on third crusade (1186). Roger's grandson ¶William (d. 1224), 4th baron, was a leader of rising against King John and one of 25 executors of Magna Carta (1215); captured fighting against Henry III at Lincoln (1217). William's great-grandson ¶John (1286–1322) became involved in dispute with Despensers (1320) over the lordship of Gower in South Wales, received through his wife; harried Glamorgan, with other lords marchers; pardoned on temporary fall of Despensers (1321), but on king's taking up arms was captured, with Thomas, Earl of Lancaster, at Boroughbridge and executed. John's grandson ¶John (1328?–1368) acquired by marriage earldom of Not·ting·ham \'nät-iŋ-əm, *US also* -,ham\ and marshalship of England.

The latter John's second son ¶Thomas (1366?–1399), 12th Baron Mowbray and 1st Duke of Nor·folk \'nȯr-fək\, was summoned to Parliament as Earl of Nottingham (1383); created marshal of England for life (1385); joined his brother-in-law Arundel and the Duke of Gloucester in routing royal favorite Robert de Vere, Earl of Oxford (1388); one of five appellants in proscribing king's friends in the Wonderful Parliament (1388); detached from other appellants by Richard II, who appointed him warden of Scottish marches (1389), captain of Calais (1391), and emissary to arrange Richard's marriage with Isabella, daughter of Charles VI of France (1396); helped arrest his former fellow appellants, Gloucester, Arundel, and Warwick, perhaps responsible for murder of Gloucester in prison; received as reward Arundel's lands and was created duke of Norfolk (1397); sought to protect himself by allying with Duke of Hereford (later Henry IV), who betrayed him to king; banished, died at Venice; his downfall recounted in act I of Shakespeare's *Richard II*.

Thomas's son ¶Thomas (1386–1405), earl marshal and 3d Earl of Nottingham, in resentment at exclusion from his father's dukedom and marshalship joined Archbishop Scrope in denouncing Henry IV as usurper and in treasonable movement to join Northumberland (1405); seized with Scrope at Shipton's Moor and beheaded. His brother ¶John (1389–1432), 2d Duke of Norfolk, became earl marshal and 4th Earl of Nottingham; prominent in French wars (1417–30); one of protector's council (1422); restored to dukedom (1425). His grandson ¶John (1444–1476), 4th duke, last of the line; created earl of War·renne and Sur·rey \'wär-ən-ən(d)-'sə-rē, -'sər-ē\ (1451); figured in Paston letters; exchanged Gower and Chepstow estates with William Herbert, 1st Earl of Pembroke, for manors in Norfolk and Suffolk. On death (1481) of his daughter Anne, dukedom of Norfolk passed to the Howard family (*q.v.*), descendants of Margaret, daughter of 1st Duke of Norfolk; the earldom of Nottingham was revived for Charles Howard (1596) of the eldest of cadet branches of the ducal house.

Mowbray, George Mordey. 1814–1891. American industrialist, b. Brighton, England. To U.S. (1854); produced first refined oil in Titusville (Pa.) field (c.1859); manufactured nitroglycerin for blasting purposes (from (1866); received many patents for improvements in explosives. His nephew and adopted son ¶Henry Siddons Mowbray, *orig.* Henry Sid·dons \'sid-ənz\ (1858–1928), b. Alexandria, Egypt, was an artist; studio in New York (1886); excelled in mural painting as in the J. P. Morgan Library, New York; U.S. courtroom, Federal Building, Cleveland; University Club Library, New York City.

Mo·winck·el \'mō-,viŋ-kəl\, Johan Ludwig. 1870–1943. Norwegian politician and shipowner. A founder of Norwegian-American line (1911); Liberal member (1906–09, 1912–18, 1921–40), president (1915–18, 1927), and vice president (1928), Storting; minister of commerce (1921–22), for foreign affairs (1923); prime minister and minister for foreign affairs (1924–26, 1928–31, 1933–35); member (1925) and president (1928–30, 1933–34) of delegation to Assembly of League of Nations; to England (1940), later to U.S. as representative of government-in-exile.

Mowinckel, Sigmund Olaf Plytt. 1884–1965. Norwegian scholar. Professor, Oslo (1922–65); a leading student of Old Testament literature, esp. Psalms. Author of *Psalmenstudien* (1921–24), *Prophecy and Tradition* (1946), *Offersang og sangoffer* (1951), *Han som kommer* (1951), *Religion og kultus* (1952), *Tetrateuch—Pentateuch—Hexateuch* (1964), etc.

Moyano, Sebastián. See Sebastián de BELALCÁZAR.

Moyne, Baron. See under GUINNESS family.

Moy·ni·han \'mȯin-yən, 'mȯi-nē-ən, *US usu* 'mȯi-nə-,han\, Berkeley George Andrew. 1st Baron Moynihan. 1865–1936. English surgeon, b. Malta. Practiced in Leeds (from 1890); on staff of Leeds General Infirmary (1890–1926); professor, U. of Leeds (1909–26); considered outstanding British surgeon of the day, greatly influential on surgical practice; president, Royal Coll. of Surgeons (1926–32); created baron (1929). Author of *Abdominal Operations* (1905), *Duodenal Ulcer* (1910), etc.

Mo·ẓaf·far ʽAlī \mō-'zäf-fär-ä-'lē\. 16th century. Persian artist. Pupil of Behzād; noted for portraits, miniatures, architectural decorations; helped illustrate manuscript of works of Neẓāmī for Shah Ṭahmāsp I.

Moẓaffarid dynasty. See MOBĀREZ.

Moẓaffar od-Dīn Shāh \-əd-'dēn-shä\. 1852–1907. Shāh of Iran (1896–1907). Son of Naṣer od-Dīn Shāh; made governor of Azerbaijan (1861); passed years as crown prince in pursuit of pleasure; unpopular and incompetent ruler; secured large loans from Russia, leading to political concessions; court corruption added to popular unrest, which forced him to convene a Majles (national assembly) and to grant a constitution (1906).

Mo·zart \'mōt-,särt\. Name of a family of Austrian musicians of German origin, including: Leopold, *in full* Johann Georg Leopold (1719–1787), violinist, composer, and teacher, b. Bavaria; court composer (1757) and assistant conductor (1762), and teacher at the cathedral choir school (1777) in Salzburg; works included a celebrated early violin method *Versuch einer gründlichen Violinschule* (1756), piano pieces, much church music, oratorios, operas, symphonies, trio sonatas, pieces for violin and for organ, etc. His daughter ¶Maria Anna Walburga Ignatia, *nicknamed* Nan·nerl \'nän-ərl\ (1751–1829), pianist and teacher; toured leading capitals of Europe (1762–66) as child prodigy with father and brother (see below); taught at Salzburg until marriage (1784) to Baron von Berchthold zu Sonnenberg, and after his death (1801). Leopold's son ¶Wolfgang Amadeus, *christened* Joannes Chrysostomus Wolfgangus Theophilus (1756–1791), showed unusual musical ability as child, esp. on harpsichord and as composer; toured as child prodigy with his father and sister (from 1762); composed his first published violin sonatas and improvisations in Paris; published two symphonies and six violin sonatas in London after style of J. C. Bach and Abel; returned to Salzburg (1766) and studied counterpoint under father's direction; again in Vienna (1767–69), where he received imperial commission to compose and conduct an opera; given honorary appointment as concertmaster to archbishop of Salzburg (1769); to Italy with his father (1769); in Milan saw his opera *Mitridate, rè di Ponto* produced at La Scala (1770); strongly influenced by Haydn in Vienna (1773); broke with archbishop (1781); settled in Vienna as teacher and composer; m. (1782) Constanze Weber (1763–1842), soprano; lived in poverty in spite of position as royal chamber composer to Emperor Joseph II of Austria (1787);

traveled (1789) to Berlin, visiting Dresden and Leipzig on the way; at work on his *Requiem* at the time of his death in Vienna; his grave is unknown. He composed over 600 works in virtually every form, creating a body of work unexcelled in beauty, diversity, and profundity. Among his works were: operas as *La finta semplice* (1767), *Idomeneo, rè di Creta* (1781), *Die Entführung aus dem Serail* (1782), *Le nozze di Figaro* (1786, *The Marriage of Figaro*), *Don Giovanni* (1787), *Così fan tutte* (1790), *Die Zauberflöte* (1791, *The Magic Flute*), *La clemenza di Tito* (1791); operettas, ballet music, dramatic cantatas, 57 arias, duets, tercets, and quartets with orchestral accompaniment; church music, including oratorios and cantatas, 18 orchestral masses (1768–83), the unfinished *Requiem* (1791), over 40 litanies, vespers, offertoriums, kyries, hymns, and other smaller works; major orchestral works as 41 symphonies, 21 piano concerti, 5 violin concerti, concerti for bassoon, for flute, for horn, for clarinet, 2 sinfonie concertanti, 23 divertimenti, 13 serenades as *Eine kleine Nachtmusik* (1787); piano music including 20 sonatas, 14 minuets, fantasies, fugues, rondos; chamber music including 6 string quintets, 25 quartets, 35 violin sonatas, piano quartets and trios, flute quartets.

Mozelekatse. See MZILIKAZI.

Mpa·di \ᵊm-'päd-ē\, Simon-Pierre. c.1900–? Congolese religious leader. Active in white missions and Salvation Army; broke with them (1936) and joined Gounzist movement of Simon Kimbangu; developed movement into militant, separatist African church; created (1939) subsidiary Mission des Noirs; fled to French Congo and deported back (1943, 1944); disappeared. His movement gradually dwindled, but gave impetus to Congolese nationalism.

Mpe·ze·ni \ᵊm-pā-'zä-nē\. c.1830–1900. South African ruler. Son of Zwangendaba, king of Ngoni; at father's death (1848), led group of his people into present Zambia; forced (from 1889) to defend diplomatically his territory against colonial ambitions of Great Britain, Germany, Portugal; succeeded until 1897, when he was forced to accede to rash attack on British Nyasaland; forced to surrender (1898) to heavy British counterattack.

Mqha·yi \ᵊm-'kī-(-ē), -'kä-yē\, Samuel Edward Krune. 1875–1945. South African writer. Schoolteacher, newspaper editor, translator; did much to standardize Xhosa grammar and orthography; became dominant figure in Xhosa literature known as Imbongi Yesizwe Jikelele (Xhosa poet laureate). Works included biblical translation *U-Samson* (1910), *Ityala lama Wele* (1914), verse *Imihobe nemi-Bongo* (1927), memoir *U-Don Jadu* (1927), autobiography *U-Mqhayi wase- Ntab' ozuko* (1939).

Mshwe·shwe \ᵊm-'shwäsh-wä\. *Also called* Mo·shoe·shoe \məsh-'wäsh-wä\ *or* Mo·shesh \mə-'shesh\. c.1786–1870. Sotho chief. Son of a chieftain of the Sotho (Basuto or Basotho); became renowned military leader; united small groups to form Sotho nation with capital at Thaba Bosiu (c.1830); dealt with European missionaries; for a time played off British against Boers; allied himself with British (1843); defeated British in war following their annexation of his territory (1848); later involved in conflict with Orange Free State and sought British aid; obtained British annexation (1868) but saw Basutoland given to Cape Colony by treaty (1869). Basutoland held by Britain (1884–1966), then became independent as Lesotho.

Msi·ri \ᵊm-'sir-ē\. *Also called* Nge·leng·wa \ŋā-'lāŋ-wä\ *or* Mwen·da \'mwen-dä\. d. 1891. Central African ruler. A leader of Nyamwezi, a group of whom he led into Katanga (c.1856); gained control of large kingdom from previous Lunda rulers (by 1870); prospered on copper trade and on slaves and ivory; killed in rebellion encouraged by traders from Belgian Congo.

Mswa·ti \ᵊm-'swä-tē\ *or* **Mswa·zi** \ᵊm-'swä-zē\. c.1820–1868. South African ruler. Son of Sobhuza I of Swaziland; succeeded as king (1840); gained control of Bantu tribes, extended influence north into Rhodesia and Mozambique; organized Ngwane people (later called Swazi after him) into powerful warrior nation; ceded land in Transvaal to Boers (1845) and encouraged cooperation with them.

Mu·'ā·wi·yah \mu̇-'ä-wē-ya\. Name of two Umayyad caliphs:

Mu'āwiyah I. *More completely* Mu'āwiyah ibn Abī Sufyān. c.602–680. First Umayyad caliph (661–680). Early opposed Muḥammad and submitted only after conquest of Mecca; scribe to Muḥammad; conquered Syria; made governor of Damascus by caliph 'Umar (640); broke with caliph 'Alī and met him in battle of Ṣiffīn (657); organized opposition to 'Alī's caliphate and gained control of Egypt; chosen caliph on assassination of 'Alī (661); made capital at Damascus; organized Arab tribal army and sent numerous expeditions against Byzantines; conquered territory to the east and in North Africa; began centralization of caliphal government.

Mu'āwiyah II. d. 684. Caliph (683–684). Son and successor of Yazīd I.

Mu·bā·rak \mu̇-'bär-ak\, 'Alī Pasha. c.1823–1893. Egyptian administrator. Entered ministry of war (1850); with Public Works Commission (1863–67); assistant director of education (1867–83); minister of public works (1883–88), of education (1888–91); effective in modernizing and unifying educational system; founded (1870) Dār al-'ulūm teacher training college. Compiled *Khiṭaṭ at-tawfīqiyah al-jadīdah* (1886), an encyclopedia of Egyptian culture and history.

Mu·bar·rad, al- \u̇l-mu̇-'bar-rad\. *Orig.* Abū al-'Abbās Muḥammad ibn Yazīd. 826–898. Arab grammarian and scholar. Compiled *al-Kāmil,* anthology of poetry and proverbs, with grammatical commentary.

Mu·cha \'mu̇k̲-ä\, Alphonse, *orig.* Alfons Maria. 1860–1939. Czech painter and illustrator. In Paris (from 1888); designed posters, costumes, etc. for Sarah Bernhardt (1894–1900); became a leading designer and painter of Art Nouveau style; returned to Czechoslovakia (1922).

Mu-ch'i Fa-ch'ang \'mü-'chē-'fä-'chäŋ\. 13th century. Chinese painter. Known for landscapes, still lifes, flower studies, and esp. for works on Ch'an (Zen) Buddhist themes; his works highly influential in Japan.

Muck \'mu̇k\, Carl. 1859–1940. German conductor. Conductor of Royal Opera (1892–1912) and general music director (1908) in Berlin; guest conductor of opera and concerts in London, Vienna, Paris, and other cities; conductor of Boston Symphony (1912–18), of Philharmonic concerts in Hamburg (1922–33); known esp. as an interpreter of Wagner, Bruckner.

Muel·ler \'mᵫl-ər; *Angl* 'mu̇l-, 'məl-, 'mil-\, Erwin Wilhelm. 1911–1977. American physicist, b. Berlin, Germany. Professor, Kaiser-Wilhelm Institut (1947–52), Penn State U. (1952–76); invented (1956) field ion microscope, with which he produced first images of single atoms.

Muel·ler \'mᵫl-ər\, Otto. 1874–1930. German painter. Joined (1910) Die Brücke group; taught at Breslau Academy (1919–30); a leader among Expressionist painters, noted for nudes, figures of gypsy women, etc., executed as elongated figures in characteristically muted colors.

Muench \'minch\, Aloisius Joseph. 1889–1962. American prelate, b. Milwaukee. Ordained (1913); bishop of Fargo, N.D. (1935–59); papal nuncio to Germany (1951–59); cardinal (1959).

Mue·sa·re·te \ˌmyü-sə-'ret-ē\. *Nicknamed* Phry·ne \'frī-nē\, *i.e.* Toad. 4th century B.C. Athenian courtesan. Noted for her beauty; reputedly the model for Apelles's painting *Aphrodite Anadyomene* and for the statue of the Cnidian Aphrodite by Praxiteles, her lover.

Muf·fat \'mu̇f-ät\, Georg. 1653–1704. German composer, b. Savoy. Organist in Molsheim, later to archbishop of Salzburg (1678–90); Kapellmeister to bishop of Passau (1690–1704). Works included *Armonico tributo,* a set of trio sonatas (1682), *Apparatus musico-organisticus,* 12 toccatas and other pieces for organ (1690), two sets of orchestral suites titled *Florilegium* (1695, 1698), *Ausserlesene Instrumental-Music,* 12 concerti grossi (1701). His son ¶Gottlieb (1690–1770) was imperial court organist in Vienna (from 1717); published *72 Versetl sammt 12 Toccaten* for organ (1726), *Componimenti musicali* (c.1739) from which Handel borrowed heavily.

Müg·ge \'mᵫg-ə\, Theodor. 1806–1861. German novelist. Author of *Toussaint* (1840), *Der Voigt von Silt* (1851), *Afraja* (1854), etc.

Mug·gle·ton \'məg-əl-tən\, Lodowicke. 1609–1698. English Puritan. Tailor by trade; presented himself and his cousin John Reeve (1608–1658) as messengers of a new dispensation (1651); made converts, called Muggletonians, a sect lasting into 18th century; denied Trinity; held that devil became incarnate in Eve; imprisoned (1653), fined (1677) for blasphemy; quarreled with Quakers; prepared autobiography and doctrinal letters.

Mu·ghal \'mü-gəl\. *Also spelled* Mo·gul \'mō-\. Muslim dynasty ruling large parts of India (1526–1857), founded by Ẓahīr-ud-Dīn Muḥammad (*q.v.*); noted for administrative efficiency, religious toleration, patronage of arts. Other rulers included Humāyūn, Akbar, Jahāngīr, Shāh Jahān, 'Ālamgīr, Bahādur Shāh, Muḥammad Shāh, Aḥmad Shāh (*qq.v.*); domain reduced to Delhi region, held under suzerainty of Marāthās (1785–1803), British (1803–57).

Mu·ḥam·mad \mü-'ḵam-mad; *Angl* mō-'ham-əd, mü-, -'häm-\. *In full* Abū al-Qāsim Muḥammad ibn 'Abd Allāh ibn 'Abd al-Muṭṭalib ibn Hāshim. c.570–632. Founder of Islām, b. Mecca. Orphaned at six and reared by grandfather and later by uncle, who trained him as a merchant; m. wealthy widow Khadījah (c.595; d. 619), who bore him several children including Fāṭimah; experienced (c.610) vision in which he received prophetic call; received thereafter periodic revelations he held to be of God, some 650 of which were written down to become the Qur'ān, the sacred scripture of Islām; gathered followers and began (c.613) to preach publicly a message of Allāh's power and goodness, the duty of worship and generosity, and a doctrine of last judgment; this new religion became known as Islām, i.e. submission (to Allāh), and its adherents Muslims, i.e. those submitting. Opposition to Islām, economic, political, and personal, led to withdrawal of clan protection and Muḥammad's leaving Mecca (619); took up residence with followers in Medina (622), an event called *hijrah* and marking beginning of Islāmic Era calendar; established as mediator among Arab clans of Medina; sent or led several raids on Meccan caravans; heavily engaged Meccan forces at Badr (624), Uḥud (625); repelled siege (627); expelled or executed Jewish and Arab opponents in Medina; made treaty with Mecca (629) and peacefully received city's submission (630); defeated coalition of nomadic tribes at Ḥunayn (630); led large army to Syrian border (630); held sway over all of Arabia; died at Mecca. Of his later wives, 'Ā'ishah was the daughter of his friend and successor Abū Bakr; Ḥafsah was the daughter of 'Umar (successor of Abū Bakr as caliph); Umm Ḥabībah was the daughter of Abū Sufyān, his chief opponent in Mecca until 629. His daughter Fāṭimah married 'Alī (fourth caliph), his daughter Umm Kulthūm married 'Uthmān (third caliph).

Muḥammad. Name of 11 sultans of Granada of the Naṣrid dynasty, including:

Muḥammad I al-Ghā·lib \ūl-'gä-lēb\. 1231–1273. Sultan (1238–73). Founder of the Naṣrid dynasty (*q.v.*); grandson of Naṣr; vassal of Ferdinand III and later Alfonso X of Castile; began construction of the Alhambra.

Muḥammad XI. *More completely* Abū 'Abd Allāh Muḥammad. *Known in Spanish as* Bo·ab·dil \bō-äb-'dēl\. d. 1527. Last sultan (1482–92) of dynasty. Prompted by his mother, rebelled against father Abū al-Ḥasan 'Alī (*called* Muley Hacén *or* Alboacen), seized Alhambra, and was proclaimed sultan (1482); reign marked by continual civil wars with relatives; captured on expedition against Castile (1483) and forced to cede territory; continued to lose territory until reduced to town of Granada; lost Granada to siege by forces of Isabella and Ferdinand (1492), ending Muslim rule in Spain; granted small district in southern Spain; in exile in Morocco (from 1493).

Muḥammad V. *Orig.* Si·di Mu·ḥam·mad ben Yū·suf \'sē-dē-mü-'kam-mad-ben-'yü-sủf\. 1909–1961. Sultan (1927–57) and king (1957–61) of Morocco. Son of Sultan Moulay Yūsuf; chosen over elder brothers to succeed by French authorities; gradually emerged as leader of nationalist sentiment; deported by French to Corsica and then Madagascar (1953); allowed to return (1955); negotiated full independence of Morocco (1956); took title king (1957); relinquished power to son Hassan II (1960).

Mu·ham·mad \mō-'ham-əd, -'häm-, *also* mü-\, Elijah. *Orig.* Elijah Poole \'pül\. 1897–1975. American religious leader, b. near Sandersville, Ga. Became assistant to Wallace Fard (1931) and established (1934) Mosque No. 2 of the Nation of Islam in Chicago; succeeded Fard as leader of movement (1934) with title "Messenger of Allah"; imprisoned (1941–47) for opposing military conscription; directed growth of Black Muslim movement and of many related business activities.

Muḥammad, Mīrzā. See SIRĀJ-UD-DAWLAH.

Muhammad, Wallace. See Wallace D. FARD.

Muḥammad 'Abduh. See 'ABDUH.

Mu·ḥam·mad Aḥ·mad \mü-'kam-mad-'ak-mad\. *In full* Muḥammad Aḥmad ibn as-Sayyid 'Abd Allāh. *Known as* al-Mahdī \ül-mak-'dē\. 1844–1885. Sudanese religious and nationalist leader. Born to a family claiming descent from the prophet Muḥammad; became member of ascetic Sammani order (1861); gathered body of disciples, to whom he announced (1881) that he was the expected Mahdī, divinely appointed to purify Islām and destroy unbelievers; led followers to stronghold in Nuba Mountains; destroyed Egyptian forces sent to arrest him; defeated army under Gen. William Hicks at Kashgil (Nov. 1883); undertook siege of Khartoum (Oct. 1884) and took city, massacring inhabitants (Jan. 1885). Died probably of typhus.

Muḥammad 'Alī Pa·sha \-ä-'lē-'päsh-ä\. 1769–1849. Egyptian ruler. Perhaps of Albanian descent; member of contingent of Macedonian Albanians in Ottoman force sent to oppose Napoléon's Egyptian invasion (1798); gained power and secured (1805) appointment as *wālī* (viceroy) of Egypt with rank of pasha; ruthlessly eliminated Mamlūk beys, expropriated large estates, laid groundwork for modern administrative state; greatly extended agriculture and irrigation; adopted European methods in education, military organization, etc. Sent son Ibrāhīm Pasha to suppress Wahhābī movement (1816–18); dispatched expeditions into Sudan (1820–21), Syria (1831); defeated imperial Ottoman forces at Nezib (June 24, 1839), provoking intervention of European powers (1840); forced to give up Syria but gained hereditary rule of Egypt and Sudan (1841); retired in favor of Ibrāhīm (1848).

Muḥammad al-Mah·dī al-Ḥuj·jah \-ül-mä-'dē-ül-kūj-'ä\. *Also called* Muḥammad al-Muntazar. d. 878? Islāmic religious. Twelfth and last *imām* of the Ithnā 'Asharīyah, the main body of Shī'ah Muslims; disappeared; expected by Shī'ites to reappear as the *mahdī*.

Muhammad Bello. See under USMAN DAN FODIO.

Muḥammad Ghūrī. See MU'IZZ-UD-DĪN MUḤAMMAD.

Muḥammad ibn al-Ḥa·ni·fī·yah \-,ib-ən-ül-,kan-i-'fē-yä\. 637–710. Islāmic leader. Son of 'Alī, the fourth caliph, but not by Fāṭimah; attracted unsought support of various groups as successor to caliphate; eventually pledged allegiance to 'Abd al-Malik.

Muḥammad ibn Fa·lāh \fa-'lä\. c.1400–1461. Muslim theologian. Reputed descendant of seventh *imām;* early excommunicated by Shī'ites for extreme views; sought disciples among disaffected Arab tribesmen (from 1436), claiming to be representative of 'Alī; forged coalition of tribesmen that became core of Musha'sha' sect; captured and established himself in Hoveyzeh, Iran. Author of sect's code *Kalām al-mahdī.*

Muḥammad ibn Tugh·luq \-,təg-'lək\. c.1290–1351. Indian ruler. Son of Ghiyās-ud-Dīn Tughluq, sultan of Delhi; led successful expedition against Hindus of Warangal in the Deccan (1321–22); succeeded to throne (1325); ruthlessly suppressed numerous rebellions, but lost territory and influence steadily through reign; moved capital to Deogin (1327), promoting spread of Urdu in the Deccan but further weakening Delhi; instituted reforms, esp. in agriculture, but their effects vitiated by droughts; killed during an expedition against rebels.

Muḥammad Qāsim Hindūshāh. See FIRISHTAH.

Muḥammad Shāh \-'shä\. *In full* Nāṣir-ud-Dīn Muḥammad Shāh. *Orig.* Rawshan Akhtar. 1702–1748. Mughal emperor of India (1719–48). Grandson of Bahādur Shāh I; placed on throne by Sayyids, who retained power; gained power with death of the Sayyids (1720); a weak, pleasure-loving ruler; allowed provinces to escape central authority; lost territory to Marāthās under Bājī Rāo and esp. to Nāder Shāh, who looted Delhi (1739).

Muḥammad Shay·bā·nī \-shī-bä-'nē\. *Also called* Shaybānī Khān Uz·bek \-'kän-'üz-bek\. 1451–1510. Uzbek ruler. Conquered and established himself in Bukhara, where his line ruled to 1599; captured Samarkand and Fergana from Bābur (1501).

Muhammed bin Hamid. See TIPPU TIB.

Mu·ḥā·si·bī, al- \ül-mü-,kä-sē-'bē\. *In full* Abū 'Abd Allāh al-Ḥārith ibn Asad al-Muḥāsibī al-'Anazī. c.781–857. Muslim Ṣūfī mystic and theologian. Emphasized rationalism and severe self-examination as accompaniments of ascetic and mystic life; major written work *Ar-rī 'āyah li-ḥūqūq Allāh;* teachings banned in anti-Mu'tazilite reaction to inquisition of 833–851.

Müh·len·berg \'mūē-lən-,berk, *Angl* 'myü-lən-,bərg\, Henry Melchior. 1711–1787. American clergyman, b. Einbeck, Hanover, Germany. Ordained in Lutheran church (1739); to U.S. (1742) to serve as pastor to congregations in Pennsylvania; did constructive pioneer work in organizing Lutheran churches in Pennsylvania, New Jersey, Maryland, New York; organized (1748) Evangelican Lutheran Ministerium of Pennsylvania, first American synod; known as virtual founder of Lutheranism in America. Three of his sons, ¶John Peter Gabriel Muhlenberg (1746–1807), ¶Frederick Augustus Conrad Muhlenberg (1750–1801), and ¶Gotthilf Henry Ernest Mühlenberg (1753–1815), all b. Trappe, Pa., became Lutheran clergymen. John was ordained (1772); served in American Revolution; brigadier general (1777); supported Anthony Wayne in assault on Stony Point; second in command under von Steuben (1780); stormed British redoubts at Yorktown (1781); brevetted major general (1783); vice president of Pennsylvania (1785–88); member, U.S. House of Representatives (1789–91, 1793–95, 1799–1801) and U.S. Senate (1801). Frederick Augustus, ordained (1770), was a member of Continental Congress (1779–80); member of U.S. House of Representatives (1789–97) and first speaker. Gotthilf Henry, ordained (1770), served as pastor of Holy Trinity Church, Lancaster, Pa. (1780–1815); first president of Franklin College (1787); interested himself in botanical studies. Gotthilf Henry's son ¶Henry Augustus Philip (1782–1844), also a Lutheran clergyman (from 1804); member of U.S. House of Representatives (1829–38); first U.S. minister to Austria (1838–40). Gotthilf Henry's grandson ¶Frederick Augustus (1818–1901), also a Lutheran clergyman (from 1855); taught at Franklin Coll. (1840–50), Pennsylvania Coll. (1850–67); first president, Muhlenberg Coll. (1867–76); professor, U. of Pennsylvania (1876–88); president, Thiel Coll. (1891–93). A grandson of Frederick Augustus Conrad ¶William Augustus (1796–1877) was a Protestant Episcopal clergyman (from 1820); rector in New York City (1846–58); founder of first American order of deaconesses (1852; see Anne AYRES) and of St. Luke's Hospital, New York, with which he was associated from 1858; author of a number of hymns.

Muḥyī' ad-Dīn. See ABŪ KĀLĪJĀR.

Muḥyī' ad-Dīn 'Arabī. See IBN AL-'ARABĪ.

Muir \'myủ(ə)r\, Edwin. 1887–1959. Scottish poet and critic. Worked as editor and, with his wife, as translator, esp. of Kafka; contributed to various periodicals criticism collected as *Latitudes* (1924), *Transition* (1926), etc.; also wrote *Structure of the Novel* (1928), *Scott and Scotland* (1936), *The Present Age* (1939), *The Estate of Poetry* (1962). Wrote novels as *The Marionette* (1927); meditative, visionary verse in *Chorus of the Newly Dead* (1926), *Journeys and Places* (1937), *The Voyage* (1946), *The Labyrinth* (1949), *Collected Poems* (1960).

Muir, John. 1838–1914. American naturalist, b. Dunbar, Scotland. To U.S. (1849); toured Wisconsin, Illinois, and Indiana studying botanical specimens; tramped from Indianapolis to Gulf of Mexico, keeping a diary of his observations and thoughts (1867–68); to California (1868); centered his studies in Yosemite Valley (1868–74), then in Nevada, Utah, and Alaska; settled on fruit farm near Martinez, Calif. (1881–91). With Robert U. Johnson, campaigned (from c.1880) for establishment of Yosemite National Park, finally provided for by Congress (1890); conducted propaganda to save forest reserves (from 1897); on camping trip with President Theodore Roosevelt (1903), gained his support, and had influence in Roosevelt's acts setting aside

148,000,000 acres of additional forest reserves. Among his books were *The Mountains of California* (1894), *Our National Parks* (1901), *Stickeen* (1909), *My First Summer in the Sierra* (1911), *The Yosemite* (1912), *Travels in Alaska* (1915), etc.

Muir, William. 1819–1905. British colonialist and scholar. In Bengal civil service (1837–76); foreign secretary to Indian government (1865); lieutenant governor of North-West provinces (1868–74); member of Council of India in London (1876–85); principal of Edinburgh U. (1885–1905); helped found and endow Muir Coll. and U. of Allahabad. Author of long-standard *Life of Mahomet* (1858–61), *The Corân* (1878), *The Caliphate* (1891), etc. His brother ¶John (1810–1882) also served in Bengal (1829–53); founded chair of Sanskrit at Edinburgh (1862).

Mu'·izz, al- \u̇l-ˈmü-iz\. d. 975. Islāmic caliph of the Fāṭimid dynasty (953–975). Ruled area comprising present Tunisia, Sicily, Algeria, Morocco; sent expedition westward to conquer Fez (958–959).

Mu·ʻizz ad-Daw·lah \ˈmü-iz-əd-ˈdau̇-lä\. *Orig.* Aḥmad ebn Bū·yeh \ˈbü-ye\. 10th century. Persian ruler. A leader of Daylamī people; in decline of caliphal power, entered Baghdad (945), assumed title of amīr, and established Būyid dynasty; effectively reduced ʻAbbāsid caliphs to puppets.

Muʻizz-ud-Dīn Mu·ḥam·mad \-u̇d-ˈdēn-mü-ˈk̲am-mad\ of Ghūr \ˈg̲ür\. *More completely* Muʻizz-ud-Dīn Muḥammad ibn Sām. *Also known as* Muḥammad Ghūrī \g̲ü-ˈrē\ *and* Shihāb-ud-Dīn Muḥammad Ghūrī. d. 1206. Indian ruler. Supported brother Ghiyas-ud-Dīn in conquest of Ghūr (c.1162) and in conflict with Khwārezm; conquered much of Hindustan, annexed Lahore (1186); defeated Rājput kings (1192); established Muslim rule over northern Indian plain.

Mu·kam·mas \mü-ˈkam-mas\, David al-. *In full* David Abū Sulaymān ibn Marwān ar-Raqqī al-Mukammas. *Also called* David ha-Bav·li \hä-ˈbäv-lē\. fl. 900. Syrian Jewish philosopher. Early converted to Christianity but later attacked Christianity and Islām; perhaps resumed Judaism; first Jewish philosopher to cite Aristotle; adapted Greek and Arab ideas. Chief work *ʻIshrūn maqālāt.*

Muk·ta·fī, al- \u̇l-mu̇k-taf-ˈē\. d. 908. Islāmic caliph of the ʻAbbāsid dynasty (902–908). Defeated Qarmaṭians in Syria (904); recovered Egypt from Ṭūlūnids (905); lost Tunisia to Fāṭimids.

Mul·ca·hy \məl-ˈkā-hē\, Richard James. 1886–1971. Irish politician. Lieutenant in Easter Rebellion (1916); Sinn Féin M.P. (1918–22); member of Dáil Éireann (1921–37, 1938–43, 1944–61); Irish Free State minister of defense (1922–24); commander in chief of Free State army, succeeding Michael Collins (1922–23); minister for local government (1927–32), for education (1948–51, 1954–57); president of Fine Gael party (1944–60).

Mul·cas·ter \ˈməl-ˌkas-tər\, Richard. 1530?–1611. English schoolmaster. First headmaster of Merchant-Taylors' school, London (1561–86); high master of St. Paul's school, London (1596–1608). Author of *Positions* (on the training of children, 1581) and *Elementaire* (on the writing of English, 1582).

Mul·ford \ˈməl-fərd\, Clarence Edward. 1883–1956. American writer, b. Streator, Ill. Author of Western novels, including *Bar 20* (1907), *The Orphan* (1908), *Hopalong Cassidy* (1910), *Man From Bar 20* (1918), *Hopalong Cassidy Returns* (1924), *Hopalong Cassidy Takes Cards* (1937), etc.

Mulgrave, Barons and earls of. See (1) PHIPPS family; (2) John SHEFFIELD.

Mul·lā Sad·rā \mu̇l-ˈlä-sa-ˈdrä\. *Also called* Ṣadr ad-Dīn ash-Shī·rā·zi \ˌsad-ru̇d-ˈdē-nu̇sh-shē-ˈrä-zē\. c.1571–1640. Iranian philosopher. Evolved a partly mystical cosmology, involving eternality of nature; criticized as heretical, but played major role in Iranian cultural renascence. Chief work *Asfār.*

Mül·len·hoff \ˈmue̅l-ən-ˌhȯf\, Karl. 1818–1884. German philologist. Professor, Kiel (1846–58), Berlin (from 1864); succeeded J. Grimm at Prussian Acad. of Sciences (1864). Author of works chiefly on Germanic philology and antiquities; editor of *Denkmäler deutscher Poesie und Prosa aus dem 8.–12. Jahrhundert* (1864, with W. Scherer), *Deutsche Heldenbuch* (1866–73, with others), including his own edition of *Laurin* (1871), *Deutsche Altertumskunde* (1870 ff.). His glossary to Klaus Groth's *Quickborn* (1853) was the first grammatical and lexicographical treatment of Plattdeutsch.

Mül·ler \ˈmue̅l-ər\, Adam Heinrich. Ritter von Ni·ters·dorf \fȯn-ˈnē-tərs-ˌdȯrf\. 1779–1829. German economist. Representative of Romantic school of German political economy; friend of Friedrich von Gentz and disciple of Edmund Burke; cofounder, with Heinrich von Kleist, of journal *Phöbus* (1808). As Austrian consul general for Saxony in Leipzig (1816–27), opposed Prussian customs policy; active in Vienna (1827) as journalist and political correspondent of state chancellery. Author of *Die Lehre von Gegensätzen* (1804), *Elemente der Staatskunst* (1810), *Versuche einer neuen Theorie des Geldes* (1816), etc.

Müller, Eduard. 1848–1919. Swiss politician. Member of Nationalrat (1884–95), Bundesrat (1895–1919); president of Swiss Confederation (1899, 1907, 1913); contributed to unification of Swiss civil and penal law and to procedure in military courts.

Müller, Ferdinand Jakob Heinrich von. Freiherr. 1825–1896. German naturalist. To Australia (1847); government botanist for Victoria (1853); director of Melbourne botanical garden (1857); instrumental in introducing Australian blue-gum tree (*Eucalyptus globulus*) into California, Africa, Europe, and South America. Author of *Fragmenta Phytographiae Australiae* (1858–82), *Flora Australiensis* (1863–78, with George Benson), *Select Plants Readily Eligible for Industrial Culture* (1876).

Müller, Frederik Paludan-. See PALUDAN-MÜLLER.

Müller, Friedrich. *Called* Ma·ler \ˈmäl-ər\ Müller, *i.e.* Painter Müller. 1749–1825. German poet, painter, and engraver. Court painter at Mannheim (1777); to Italy (1778); turned to literature, deeply influenced by *Sturm und Drang* movement. Author of idylls *Der Satyr Mopsus* (1775), *Bacchidon und Milon* (1775), *Die Schafschur* (1775), *Das Nusskernen* (1811); dramatic works *Situation aus Fausts Leben* (1776), *Fausts Leben dramatisiert* (1778), *Niobe* (1778), *Golo und Genoveva* (1808), trilogy *Adonis, Die klagende Venus,* and *Venus Urania* (1825).

Müller, Fritz Johann Friedrich Theodor. 1821–1897. German zoologist. To Brazil (1852); traveling naturalist for National Museum of Rio de Janeiro (1876–91); became a major champion of Darwinism, esp. in *Für Darwin* (1864); studied development of crustaceans, mimicry, olfactory apparatus of butterflies, etc.

Müller, Georg Elias. 1850–1934. German psychologist. Professor, Göttingen (1881–1934); known esp. for work relating to psychophysical method, memory, and color perception. Author of *Grundlegung der Psychophysik* (1878), *Zur Analyse der Unterschiedsempfindlichkeit* (1899, with L. J. Martin), *Gesichtspunkte und Tatsachen der psychophysischen Methodik* (1903), *Zur Analyse der Gedächtnistätigkeit und des Vorstellungsverlaufnis* (1911–17), etc.

Müller, Hermann. 1876–1931. German politician. Editor of Social Democratic paper *Görlitzer Zeitung* (1899–1906); member of the executive committee of the Social Democratic party (1906 ff.); member of the Reichstag (1916–18, 1920–31) and of the National Assembly at Weimar (1919); succeeded Graf von Brockdorff-Rantzau as minister of foreign affairs (1919–20) and signed the Treaty of Versailles (1919); chancellor of Germany (Mar.–June 1920); again chancellor at head of a coalition cabinet (1928–30).

Mul·ler \ˈməl-ər\, Hermann Joseph. 1890–1967. American geneticist, b. New York City. Professor, U. of Texas (1921–32), U. of Edinburgh (1938–40), Amherst Coll. (1940–45), Indiana U. (1945–67); on staff, U.S.S.R. Inst. of Genetics (1933–37); awarded 1946 Nobel prize for physiology or medicine for work on artificial transmutation of the gene by X-rays (first produced in *Drosophila* fruit fly, 1927).

Mül·ler \ˈmue̅l-ər\, Johann. *Known as* Re·gi·o·mon·ta·nus \rā-gē-ō-mȯn-ˈtä-nu̇s, *Angl* ˌrē-jē-ō-män-ˈtā-nəs\, *Latin for Königsberg, his birthplace.* 1436–1476. German mathematician and astronomer. Assisted Georg Purbach in work on Ptolemy's astronomy (completed 1463); established (1471) at Nürnberg, with the help of the wealthy patrician Bernhard Walther, an observatory, a mechanical workshop, and a printing plant; observed the comet afterwards known as Halley's comet (1472); published, with Walther, *Ephemerides ab Anno 1475–1506* (1473), used by Columbus and other navigators; advanced the study of algebra and trigonometry in Germany; called (1472, 1476) to Rome by Pope Sixtus IV to assist in reforming the calendar.

Müller, Johannes Peter. 1801–1858. German physiologist and comparative anatomist. Professor, Bonn (1826–33), Berlin (from 1833); introduced concept of specific energy of nerves; gave explanation of color sensations produced by pressure on retina; investigated blood, lymph, chyle, and mechanism of voice; discovered fetal pronephric ducts (Müllerian ducts, 1825) and lymph-hearts in the frog (1832); explained nature of hermaphroditism; studied embryology and metamorphoses of echinoderms. Chief publication *Handbuch der Physiologie des Menschen* (1833–40).

Müller, Johannes von. 1752–1809. Swiss historian. In service of archbishop of Mainz (1786–92), imperial chancery, Vienna (1793–98); custodian of imperial library (1800–04); historiographer at Berlin in Prussian service (1804); introduced to Napoléon (1806), under whom he became secretary of state in new kingdom of Westphalia (1807) and director-general of public education (1807–09). Author of *Reisen der Päpste* (1782), *Geschichten Schweizerischer Eidgenossenschaft* (1786–1808), *Darstellung des Fürstenbundes* (1787), *24 Bücher Allgemeiner Geschichten* (1809), etc.

Müller, Karl Otfried. 1797–1840. German philologist and archaeologist. Professor, Göttingen (1819–40). Author of *Geschichten hellenischer Stämme und Städte* (1820, 1824), *Prolegomena zu einer wissenschaftlichen Mythologie* (1825), *Handbuch der Archäologie der Kunst* (1830), and treatises on ancient Dorians (1824) and Etruscans (1828).

Mül·ler \'mɶl-ər, *Angl* 'myül-ər, 'mil-, 'məl-\, Max, *in full* Friedrich Max. 1823–1900. British Orientalist, b. Germany. Son of Wilhelm Müller; to England (1848); professor, Oxford (1850–75). Published edition of the *Rigveda* (1849–74), the 51-volume *Sacred Books of the East* (1879–1910); wrote *History of Ancient Sanskrit Literature* (1859–60), *Lectures on the Science of Language* (1861–64), *Contributions to the Science of Mythology* (1897), etc.

Mül·ler \'mɶl-ər\, Paul Hermann. 1899–1965. Swiss chemist. Research chemist for firm J. R. Geigy AG., Basel (1925–65); discovered insecticidal properties of DDT (1939); awarded Nobel prize in physiology or medicine (1948).

Mül·ler \'mɶ̄l-ər\, Sophus Otto. 1846–1934. Danish paleontologist. Director of prehistoric, ethnological, and antique collections (1892–1921) in new National Museum; specialized in study of Bronze and Iron ages and Oriental influence on prehistoric Europe. Author of *Ordning af danmarks oldsager* (1888–95), *Vor oldtid* (1897), *Oldtidens kunst i danmark* (1918–33).

Mül·ler \'mɶl-ər\, Wenzel. 1767–1835. German composer. Kapellmeister, Leopoldstädter-Theater, Vienna (1786–1807, 1813–30), German Opera, Prague (1807–13). Composed many popular operas and Singspiels, including *Das Sonnenfest der Braminen* (1790), *Der Fagottist* (1791), *Das Neusonntagskind* (1793), *Die Schwestern von Prag* (1794), *Die Teufelsmühle am Wienerberg* (1799), *Tankredi* (1817), *Aline* (1822).

Müller, Wilhelm. 1794–1827. German poet. Took part in Prussian uprising against Napoléon; teacher (1819) and ducal librarian in Dessau. Author of lyric poems in *77 Gedichte aus den hinterlassenen Papieren eines reisenden Waldhornisten* (1821–24), which included cycles "Die schöne Müllerin" and "Winterreise" (both set to music by Schubert, 1824); *Lieder der Griechen* (1821–24); *Neugriechische Volkslieder* (1825); *Lyrische Reisen* (1827); stories, works on philology, translations, etc.

Mül·ler \'myül-ər, 'mil-, 'məl-\, William John. 1812–1845. English painter. Known for landscapes of Gloucestershire, Wales, Europe.

Mül·ler \'mɶl-ər\, Wolfgang. *Called* Müller von Kö·nigs·win·ter \-fön-ˌkɶ̄-niks-'vin-tər\. 1816–1873. German writer. Practiced medicine in Düsseldorf (1842–48); settled in Cologne (1853) and Wiesbaden (1869). Author of songs, ballads, tales, etc. of the Rhine country.

Müller-Gut·ten·brunn \-'gu̇t-ən-ˌbru̇n\, Adam. *Pseudonym* Ig·no·tus \ig-'nōt-u̇s, *Angl* -əs\. 1852–1923. Austrian writer and theater director. Critic and literary editor, *Deutsche Zeitung,* Vienna (1873–88); director of Raimund Theater (1892–96) and Kaiser Jubiläum Theater (1898–1903); author of dramas, novels, historical, literary, and theatrical treatises, etc.

Müller-Ly·er \-'lē-ər\, Franz. 1857–1916. German sociologist and psychiatrist. Described (1889) the Müller-Lyer optical illusion. Author of *Phasen der Kultur* (1908), *Die Entwicklungsstufen der Menschheit* (1910–24), *Die Familie* (1912), *Phasen der Liebe* (1913), *Soziologie der Leiden* (1914), etc.

Mul·li·ken \'məl-ə-kən\, Robert Sanderson. 1896–1986. American chemist and physicist, b. Newburyport, Mass. Taught at N.Y.U. (1926–28), U. of Chicago (1928–86). Developed (from 1928) a molecular orbital theory explaining chemical bond that holds atoms together in a molecule; considered molecule as a distinct entity defined by orbit of outermost electrons not around nuclei of individual atoms but around whole molecule; developed (1952) a quantum-mechanical theory of the behavior of electron orbitals as different atoms merge to form molecules.

Müll·ner \'mɶl-nər\, Adolf. 1774–1829. German playwright. Founded private theater for which he wrote "fate tragedies" as *Der 29 Februar* (1812), *Die Schuld* (1813); also wrote *Yngurd* (1817), *Die Albaneserin* (1820), etc.

Mulock, Dinah Maria. See CRAIK.

Mul·ready \məl-'red-ē, 'məl-ˌred-ē\, William. 1786–1863. Irish painter. Achieved popularity in London with genre scenes of cottage life; known also for book illustrations; designed Rowland Hill's first postal envelope (1840).

Multatuli. See Eduard DOUWES DEKKER.

Mum·mi·us \'məm-ē-əs\, Lucius. *Surnamed* A·cha·i·cus \ə-'kā-i-kəs\. 2d century B.C. Roman general and politician. As praetor (153 B.C.) defeated Lusitanians in Spain; consul (146); commanded Roman army in Achaean war; captured Corinth, thus completing (146) Roman conquest of Greece.

Mumtāz Maḥal. See under SHĀH JAHĀN.

Mun \mɶⁿ\, Albert de, *in full* Adrien-Albert-Marie de. Comte. 1841–1914. French politician. Founder of Circles of Catholic Workmen (1871); member of Chamber of Deputies (1876–78, 1881–93, 1894–1914); opponent (1905) of bill for separation of church and state. Among his books were *La Loi des suspects* (1900), *Contre la séparation* (1905), *Ma vocation sociale* (1908), and *L'Heure décisive* (1913).

Mun \'mən\, Thomas. 1571–1641. English writer. Early definer of theory of balance of trade; director of East India Co. (1615); defended East India Co. against charge of bullionists, that such foreign trade as did not yield direct balance of bullion (specie) was harmful, in his *Discourse of Trade, from England unto the East Indies* (1621).

Mun·a·ka·ta \mu̇n-ä-kä-tä\ Shikō. 1903–1975. Japanese artist. Known for woodblock prints, often on Buddhist themes, marked by bold and vivid execution.

Munch \mɶ̄nsh\ *or* **Münch** \'mɶnk\, Charles. 1891–1968. French conductor. Professor of violin, Strasbourg (1919–26); professor and orchestra leader, Leipzig (1926–33); a founder and conductor (1935–38), Paris Philharmonic; conductor of Boston Symphony (1949–62) and director of Berkshire Music Center, Tanglewood (1951–62); a founder and conductor (1967–68), L'Orchestre de Paris; known esp. for interpretations of Brahms, Debussy, Ravel.

Munch \'mu̇ŋk\, Edvard. 1863–1944. Norwegian painter and printmaker. A forerunner of Expressionism in numerous boldly subjective paintings expressing emotional distress in macabre scenes as *The Sick Child* (1886), *The Cry* (1893), *The Vampire* (1893–94), *Ashes* (1894), *In Hell, Self-Portrait* (1895); later painted many landscapes; a leading figure in printmaking revival.

Munch, Peter Andreas. 1810–1863. Norwegian historian and philologist. Professor in Christiania; leader of Norwegian historical school; demonstrated that Old Norse language was of specifically Norwegian origin; maintained that Icelandic literature was really Old Norse. Author of *Det norske Folks Historie* (1852–63), etc.

Munch, Peter Rochegune. 1870–1948. Danish historian and politician. Radical member of parliament (1909–40); minister of interior (1909–10), of defense (1913–20); foreign minister (1929–40); attempted to maintain Danish neutrality and to secure German recognition of 1920 border; forced by popular sentiment to resign after German occupation (1940). Author of *Købstadsstyrelsen i Danmark* (1900), *Dansk politik under krig og besaettelse* (1946–47).

Münch-Bel·ling·hau·sen \'mɶnk-'bel-iŋ-ˌhau̇-zən\, Eligius von. Freiherr. *Pseudonym* Friedrich Halm \'hälm\. 1806–1871. German playwright. Director of Vienna Royal Theater (1867–70). Author of *Griseldis* (1835), *Der Sohn der Wildnis* (1843), *Der Fechter der Ravenna* (1857), etc.

Münch·hau·sen \'mɶnk-ˌhau̇-zən\, Börries von. Freiherr. 1874–1945. German poet. A reviver of ballad writing; author of *Gedichte* (1897), *Balladen* (1901), *Ritterliche Liederbuch* (1903), *Meister-Balladen* (1923), *Idyllen und Lieder* (1928), etc.

Münchhausen, Karl Friedrich Hieronymus von. Freiherr. *Eng. corruption* Baron Mun·chau·sen \'mən-ˌchau̇z-ᵊn, 'mu̇n-, -ˌchȯz-\. 1720–1797. German soldier. Served with distinction in Russian campaign against Turks; noted raconteur, famed for stories of his adventures and exploits; a collection *Vademecum für lustige Leute* (1781–83) was attributed to him; his name is now proverbially associated with absurdly exaggerated stories. Baron Munchausen tales subsequently elaborated and published in London (1785) by Rudolph Erich Raspe (*q.v.*).

Mun·day \'mən-dē\, Anthony. 1560?–1633. English poet, playwright, and compiler. To Rome (1578), a journalist, if not a spy, reporting activities and designs of English Roman Catholics in France and Italy in *The English Romayne Lyfe* (1582); actor in Earl of Oxford's company (1579–84). Author of many pamphlets; wrote plays, the few extant including *Fedele and Fortunio* (c.1584, from Italian), *John a Kent and John a Cumber* (1589), *Sir Thomas More* (with emendations believed to be by Shakespeare); translator of *Palladino of England* (1588), *Amadis de Gaule* (1589–95), and other French romances; wrote most of London city pageants (1592–1623); rival of Ben Jonson and Middleton.

Mun·de·lein \'mən-də-ˌlīn\, George William. 1872–1939. American prelate, b. New York City. Ordained (1895); archbishop of Chicago (from 1915); cardinal (1924).

Mundt \'mu̇nt\, Theodor. 1808–1861. German novelist and critic. A leader of the Young Germany school. Among his novels were *Madonna* (1835), *Carmela* (1844), *Mendoza* (1846–47), *Die Matadore* (1850), *Graf Mirabeau* (1858); also wrote works on history, cultural history, travel, and aesthetics.

Mun·dy \'mən-dē\, John. between 1550 and 1554–1630. English composer. Son of William Mundy. Organist of St. George's Chapel, Windsor (from c.1586); composed sacred and secular songs, anthems, etc., including those published in *Songs and Psalms* (1594), and keyboard pieces, including 4 in the Fitzwilliam Virginal Book.

Mundy, William. *Surname also spelled* Moondaye, Munday, Mondy, Monday, Mondie, *etc.* c.1529–?1591. English composer. Head chorister of Westminster Abbey (1543–47); vicar-choral of St. Paul's and gentleman of the Chapel Royal (from 1564). Composed liturgical services, anthems, some 22 polyphonic motets, etc.; several works signed "Mundy" cannot be certainly attributed to him or to his son John (*q.v.*).

Mü·nec·cim·ba·şi \mɶ̄-näj-jēm-'bäsh-ə\, Ahmed Dede. 1631–1702. Turkish historian. Court astrologer to Sultan Mehmed IV (1665–87); exiled. Author in Arabic of a valuable universal history *Jāmi' ad-duwal,* published in a Turkish translation as *Sahaif-ül-Ahbar.*

Mungo, Saint. See KENTIGERN.

Mu·ni \'myü-nē\, Paul. *Orig.* Muni Wei·sen·freund \'wīz-ᵊn-ˌfrend\. 1895–1967. American actor, b. Lemberg, Austria. To U.S. (1902, naturalized 1923);

member of company in Yiddish Art Theatre, New York (1918–25); entered motion pictures (1929); noted for roles in *Scarface* (1932), *I am a Fugitive from a Chain Gang* (1932), *Story of Louis Pasteur* (1936, Academy Award), *The Good Earth* (1937), *Life of Émile Zola* (1937), *Juárez* (1939), *Song to Remember* (1945), *Last Angry Man* (1959).

Munk \'muŋk\, Kaj Harald Leininger. 1898–1944. Danish playwright and patriot. Roman Catholic priest; revived heroic and religious drama with plays as *En idealist* (1928), *Cant* (1931), *Henrik VIII* (1931), *Ordet* (1932) *De Udvalgte* (1933), *Han sidder ved Smeltediglen* (1938), *Egelykke* (1940); active in resistance to German occupation; killed by Gestapo.

Mün·nich \'mœn-ik\, Burkhard Christoph von. Graf. 1683–1767. German soldier and politician. Entered service of Czar Peter I (1721); commander in chief of Russian army (1728); field marshal and president of war council (1732). Captured Danzig (Gdańsk) in War of Polish Succession (1734) and won distinction in Crimean campaigns (1736–39). Overthrew regent Biron (1740) and became chief minister in regency of Anna Leopoldovna (1740–41); given sentence of death (1741) following accession to throne of Elizabeth; sentence commuted to exile in Siberia; recalled by Peter III (1762); director general of Baltic ports under Catherine II.

Mun·nings \'mən-iŋz\, Sir Alfred James. 1878–1959. English painter. Known esp. for sporting scenes, pictures of horses, portraits; president of Royal Academy (1944–49).

Mu·ñoz Ma·rín \'mün-yōs-mä-'rēn\, Luis. 1898–1980. Puerto Rican politician. Son of Luis Muñoz Rivera; reared in New York City and Washington, D.C.; returned to Puerto Rico (1926); editor of *La Democracia* (1926–28, 1932); member of Puerto Rico senate (1932–36, 1940–48); founded Popular Democratic party (1938); with Gov. Rexford Tugwell developed Operation Bootstrap for economic development; first elected governor of Puerto Rico (1948–64); secured commonwealth status (1952); again in senate (from 1964).

Muñoz Ri·ve·ra \-rē-'ver-ä\, Luis. 1859–1916. Puerto Rican publisher and politician. Founded newspaper *La Democracia* (1889), in which he campaigned for Puerto Rican independence; instrumental in obtaining Spanish charter for home rule (1897); secretary of state, minister of justice, and later president of autonomist cabinet (1898–99); to U.S. (1899); published magazine in New York City; resident commissioner for Puerto Rico in Washington, D.C. (1910–16).

Munro. See also MONRO.

Mun·ro \mən-'rō\, George. 1825–1896. American publisher, b. West River, N.S. To New York City (1856); formed (c.1863) Munro's Ten Cent Novels to produce pulp fiction, including highly successful "Old Sleuth" series; produced "Seaside Library" of ten-cent reprints from Scott, Dickens, the Brontës, etc.; published weekly *Fireside Companion* (1866–1907).

Munro, Hector Hugh. *Pseudonym* Sa·ki \'säk-ē\. 1870–1916. Scottish writer, b. Burma. Wrote political satires for *Westminster Gazette;* published his only serious book, *The Rise of the Russian Empire* (1900); correspondent for *Morning Post* in Balkans, Russia, and Paris (1902–08). Began series of witty, satirical, sometimes fantastic short stories with *Reginald* (1904) and *Reginald in Russia* (1910), about an irrepressible young man of the world, followed by *The Chronicles of Clovis* (1911), *Beasts and Super-Beasts* (1914), *The Square Egg* (1924); author of novels *The Unbearable Bassington* (1912) and *When William Came* (1913). Killed in France in World War I.

Munro, Neil. 1864–1930. Scottish novelist and journalist. Art, dramatic, and literary critic, Glasgow *Evening News;* editor in chief (1918). Began as novelist with *The Lost Pibroch* (1896) and *John Splendid* (1898); others included *Gilian the Dreamer* (1899), *Doom Castle* (1901), *Children of Tempest* (1903), *Erchie* (1904), *The Vital Spark* (1906), *Daft Days* (1907); also wrote verse, essays.

Munro *or* **Mon·ro** \mən-'rō\, Robert. d. 1680? Scottish soldier. Served in Scottish rebellion against Charles I; sent on expedition against Catholic rebels in Ireland (1642); commanded (1644) Parliamentary forces in Ulster; captured Belfast (1644); defeated by O'Neill at Benburb (1646); on making of terms between Parliament and Ormonde, refused to surrender Carrickfergus and Belfast, and was imprisoned and superseded by Monck (1648).

Mun·sell \mən(t)-'sel\, Albert Henry. 1858–1918. American portrait painter, b. Boston, Mass. Inventor of instruments for color measurement and a system of classifying colors described in *Atlas of the Munsell Color System* (1915) that has remained a standard used by artists, chemists, etc.

Mun·sey \'mən(t)-sē, 'mən-zē\, Frank Andrew. 1854–1925. American publisher, b. Mercer, Me. To New York and started publishing magazines with *Golden Argosy* (1882) for children; added *Argosy* (pulp fiction, 1896), *All-Story* (which first serialized E. R. Burroughs's *Tarzan,* 1912), *Munsey's Weekly* (1889; from 1891 *Munsey's Magazine*); expanded into newspaper field, acquiring New York *Star* (1891), *Press* (1912), *Sun* and *Evening Sun* (1916), *Herald* and *Evening Telegram* (1920), *Globe* (1924).

Mun·son \'mən(t)-sən\, Walter David. 1843–1908. American shipping magnate, b. Cheshire, Conn. With one schooner, began freight service between New York and Havana (1873), the beginning of the Munson Steamship Line (incorporated 1899), which became largest firm in U.S. coastal and Caribbean shipping; expanded interests to include lines to Mexican, Central American, Haitian, Jamaican, Colombian, and Canadian ports.

Mün·ster \'mœn-stər\, Sebastian. 1489–1552. German scholar. Professor of theology and Hebrew at Heidelberg (1524–27), of Hebrew at Basel (from 1529); edited Hebrew Bible (1534–35), Ptolemy's *Geographia* (1540); known esp. for *Cosmographia* (1544), first detailed description of the world in German.

Mün·ster·berg \'mụn(t)-stər-,bərg, 'myün(t)-, 'mən(t)-\, Hugo. 1863–1916. American psychologist, b. Danzig. Taught at Freiburg (1887–92); to U.S. at invitation of William James, taught at Harvard (1892–95, 1897–1916); superintended construction of laboratory at Harvard especially equipped for experimental psychology; known as pioneer in field of applied psychology. Among his books were *Die Willenshandlung* (1888), *Beiträge zur experimentellen Psychologie* (1889–92), *Psychology and Life* (1899), *Psychology and the Teacher* (1909), *Psychology and Industrial Efficiency* (1913), *Psychology and Social Sanity* (1914), etc.

Mun·ta·ner \,mün-tä-'nər\, Ramón. 1265–1336. Catalonian soldier, minstrel, and chronicler. Wrote *Crónica catalana,* valuable as source for history of his period.

Mun·the \'mən-,te\, Axel Martin Fredrik. 1857–1949. Swedish physician and writer. Practiced Paris and Rome; author of *Letters from a Mourning City* (1887), *Memories and Vagaries* (1898), *Red Cross and Iron Cross* (1916), a highly popular memoir *The Story of San Michele* (1929).

Mun·the \'mụn-tə\, Gerhard Peter Frants Wilhelm. 1849–1929. Norwegian painter and illustrator. Works included landscapes, fantastic designs influenced by Norwegian fairy tales and sagas and reproduced in figured tapestries, decorative water colors, woodcuts illustrating Snorri Sturluson's *Heimskringla* (1893–1900), decorations for residences and public buildings, etc.

Mün·zer *or* **Mün·tzer** \'mœnt-sər\, Thomas. *Lat.* Mo·ne·tar·i·us \,mō-nə-'tar-ē-əs\. 1468 or 1489/90–1525. German religious reformer. Teacher and clergyman; came under influence of Luther (1518); evolved position based on conviction of supremacy of inner light over Scripture; linked theology to political view of common people as instrument of divine will; preached in and expelled from Zwickau, Nordhausen, Allstedt, Mühlhausen, etc.; allied himself with Peasants' Revolt (1524–25); defeated at Frankenhausen (1525), captured and beheaded. Long subject of controversy, legend, and competing ideological interpretation.

Mun·zing·er \'mœnt-siŋ-ər\, Werner. 1832–1875. Swiss explorer. Traveled among Bogos (1854–61); member of German expeditions to eastern Sudan (1861) and north and northwest Ethiopia (1864); British consul at Mesewa (1865) and served as guide to British forces in Abyssinian War (1868); named governor by khedive of Egypt (1870); pasha and governor general of eastern Sudan (1872).

Muqaddasī, al-. See MAQDISĪ.

Muqanna', al-. See HASHIM IBN HAKIM.

Muq·ta·fī, al- \ụl-,mụk-tä-'fē\. 1096–1160. Islāmic caliph of 'Abbāsid dynasty (1136–60). On accession, began campaign to wrest political power from Seljuqs; gained control of numerous provinces in Iraq; recognized Seljuq sultan in return for concession of autonomy in Iraq (1156); later besieged in Baghdad.

Mu·rad \mü-'räd\. Name of five sultans of the Ottoman Empire:

Murad I. 1326?–1389. Sultan (1360–89). Son of Orhan; conquered Adrianople (1362), which he renamed Edirne and made his capital, Philippopolis (1363), Gallipoli (1367); defeated Serbian coalition at Cirnomen and Bulgarians at Samakow (1371); reduced Byzantine Emperor John V Palaeologus to vassalage; captured Sofia (1385), Niš (1386); consolidated hold on Anatolia; killed in battle with Serbians and Bosnians at Kosovo.

Murad II. 1404–1451. Sultan (1421–51). Son of Mehmed I; forced to deal with several rival claimants to throne; reasserted Ottoman power over Turkmen principalities and Byzantines; captured Salonika after five-year campaign (1425–30); lost Niš and Sofia (1443) to coalition of Hungarians, Poles, Germans, Albanians, Serbians; abdicated (1444) in favor of son Mehmed II; led army in defeat of European forces at Varna (1444); resumed throne (1446); defeated Hungarians at Kosovo (1448).

Murad III. 1546–1595. Sultan (1574–95). Son of Selim II; captured Fez from Portuguese (1578); in war (1578–90) with Iran captured Azerbaijan, Tiflis, Nehāvand, Hamadan; began long war (1593–1606) with Austria. Reign saw weakening of administrative offices, Janissaries, economy.

Murad IV. *In full* Murad Oglu Ahmed. 1612–1640. Sultan (1623–40). Son of Ahmed I; succeeded brother Osman II; reasserted power of sultanate, suppressed lawlessness and power of Janissaries and other military groups;

rooted out corruption; suppressed tobacco and wine shops, coffeehouses; restored state finances; reconquered Baghdad (1638).

Murad V. 1840–1904. Sultan (1876). Succeeded uncle Abdülaziz at behest of Midhat Paşa; soon suffered mental collapse; deposed after three months in favor of brother Abdülhamid II.

Mu·ralt \mūē-rält\, Béat-Louis de. 1665–1749. Swiss writer. Served in French army; traveled in England (1694–95). Wrote *Lettres sur les Anglais et les Français* (1725), which helped introduce English thought to Europe, influencing esp. Rousseau and Voltaire; *Lettres sur les voyages* (1725); and works on pietism and mysticism.

Mu·ra·sa·ki \mür-ä-säk-ē\ Shikibu. 978?–?1026. Japanese courtier and writer. Real name and much of life unknown; served at court of Empress Akiko (from 1005). Author of *Genji monogatari* (*Tale of Genji*), generally considered to be first full novel in the world and the greatest classic of Japanese literature.

Mu·rat \mūē-ra\, Joachim. 1767–1815. French cavalry commander. Served in Italy (1796–97) and Egypt (1798–99), rising to rank of general of division; aided Napoléon Bonaparte in coup d'état (1799); m. (1800) Napoléon's sister Maria Annunciata. Helped win battle of Marengo (1800); appointed governor of Paris; created marshal of France (1804) and prince and high admiral (1805). Commanded cavalry at Austerlitz (1805), Jena (1806), Eylau and Friedland (1807). Became king of Naples under title Joachim I Napoléon (1808); introduced Code Napoléon and other reforms, encouraged Italian nationalism. Took part in Russian campaign and distinguished himself at Borodino (1812). Joined Napoléon's cause on emperor's return from Elba; defeated by Austrian army at Tolentino (May 2–3, 1815); captured and executed. His son ¶Prince Napoléon-Lucien-Charles (1803–1878) emigrated to U.S. (1825), but made continued efforts to recover for himself father's throne in Naples; settled in France (1848); ambassador to Turin (1849–50); senator (1852); created prince (1853).

Mu·ra·to·ri \ˌmü-rä-ˈtō-rē\, Lodovico Antonio. 1672–1750. Italian antiquary and historian. Ordained priest (1694); employed in Ambrosian library, Milan, where he published *Anecdota* (1697–98); librarian to Duke Rinaldo I of Modena (from 1700). Compiled *Rerum Italicarum Scriptores* (28 vols., 1723–51), documents on medieval Italian history; *Antiquitates Italicae Medii Aevi* (1738–42), containing the 2d-century Muratorian Canon; *Annali d'Italia* (12 vols., 1744–49).

Mu·ra·vyov \mü-(ˌ)rəf-ˈyóf\, Mikhail Nikolayevich. Count. 1796–1866. Russian soldier. Governor general of Wilno (1863–65); became known as "hangman of Wilno" for brutal suppression of Polish uprising (1863); made count (1865). His grandson ¶Mikhail Nikolayevich (1845–1900) entered foreign ministry (1864); minister to Denmark (1893); minister of foreign affairs (1896–1900); recommended Russian seizure of Port Arthur and Dalny on Liaotung Peninsula, Manchuria (1897), which led to Russo-Japanese War (1904–05); issued call for disarmament conference at The Hague (1899).

Muravyov-Apos·tol \-(ˌ)ə-ˈpós-təl\, Sergey Ivanovich. 1796–1826. Russian soldier. Member of noble family; played leading role in planning Decembrist uprising (1825); executed.

Mur·chi·son \ˈmər-chis-ᵊn, -kis-\, Sir Roderick Impey. 1792–1871. British geologist, b. Scotland. Secretary (1827–31), president (1831–33, 1841–43), Geological Society. Investigated lower fossiliferous strata of England and Wales; established (1835) Silurian system; with Adam Sedgwick, established (1839) Devonian system; collaborated with Édouard P. de Verneuil and Keyserling in geological survey of Russia (1841); proposed (1841) Permian system; studied geology of Scottish Highlands; director general of Geological Survey and director of Royal School of Mines (1855). Founded (1871) chair of geology and mineralogy at Edinburgh. Author of *The Silurian System* (1839, rev. 1854), *Geology of Russia* (1845). Murchison Falls, Uganda, and Murchison River, Western Australia, named for him.

Mur·doch \ˈmər-ˌdäk\, James Edward. 1811–1893. American actor, b. Philadelphia. Made amateur debut in *Lovers' Vows* (1829); although a semi-invalid (from 1832) became outstanding actor and perhaps finest light comedian of the day; made notable appearances opposite Fanny Kemble (1833), in San Francisco (1853) and London (1856); last appearance in Cincinnati (1883).

Mur·dock \ˈmər-dək, -ˌdäk\, William. 1754–1839. British engineer and inventor, b. Scotland. Entered firm of Boulton and Watt (1777); superintendent of fitting Watt's engines in Cornwall; developed method of distilling coal gas and illuminated his home with it (1792); lighted exterior of factory at Soho with coal gas (1802); invented improvements in steam engine; made working model of locomotive steam engine (1784); worked on a steam carriage or road locomotive; invented D slide valve (1799) and apparatus for utilizing compressed air; credited with invention of sun-and-planet motion patented by Watt.

Mure \ˈmyür\, Sir William. 1594–1657. Scottish poet. Member of Scottish Parliament (1643); wounded at Marston Moor (1644). Author of *The True Crucifixe for True Catholickes* (1629), a paraphrase of the Psalms (1639), and *The Cry of Blood and of a Broken Covenant* (1650).

Murel, John A. See MURRELL.

Mu·re·na \myü-ˈrē-nə\, Lucius Licinius. 1st century B.C. Roman general. Commanded army against Mithradates (83–82 B.C.). His son ¶Lucius Licinius, consul (62 B.C.), was accused of bribery by a defeated rival for office; defended by Cicero and acquitted.

Mur·et \mūē-re\, Marc-Antoine. *Lat.* Mu·re·tus \myü-ˈrēt-əs\. 1526–1585. French poet and Humanist. Teacher of the classics in Bordeaux, Paris, Toulouse; fled charge of heresy to Italy (1554); taught at Rome; ordained priest (1576); editor of many Latin classics and author of important commentaries.

Mur·free \ˈmər-ˌfrē\, Mary Noailles. *Pseudonym* Charles Egbert Crad·dock \ˈkrad-ək\. 1850–1922. American novelist, b. near Murfreesboro, Tenn. Established reputation as short-story writer by her stories in the *Atlantic Monthly* (from 1878), afterwards published in book *In the Tennessee Mountains* (1884). Other works included novels *Where the Battle was Fought* (1884), *Down the Ravine* (1885), *The Despot of Broomsedge Cove* (1889), *His Vanished Star* (1894), *The Juggler* (1897), *A Spectre of Power* (1903), *The Frontiersman* (1904), *The Storm Centre* (1905), *The Windfall* (1907), *The Ordeal* (1912).

Mur·ger \mūēr-zher\, Henri, *in full* Louis-Henri. 1822–1861. French writer. Best known for sketches of Bohemian life in Paris, as in *Scènes de la vie de bohème* (1847–49; source of operas by Leoncavallo and Puccini), *Le Pays latin* (1851), *Scènes de la vie de jeunesse* (1851).

Mu·rie·ta \mür-ˈyā-tä\ *or* **Mur·riet·ta** \mür-ˈryā-tä\, Joaquín. d. 1853? Mexican outlaw. Of unknown origin; identity uncertain as name was used by more than one man on occasion; led band of outlaws in California, becoming notorious esp. for attacks on miners, settlers, etc. Generally assumed killed in gunfight between Mexican band and a special posse deputized by the legislature.

Mu·ril·lo \mü-ˈrē(l)-yō, *Angl* myü-ˈril-(ˌ)ō, m(y)ü-ˈrē-(ˌ)ō\, Bartolomé Esteban. 1617–1682. Spanish painter. Succeeded Pacheco as head of Seville school (1654); a founder and first president of Seville Acad. (1660 ff.); influenced by Velázquez, Flemish and Venetian schools; known esp. as colorist, particularly as a master of color contrast. Painted chiefly religious works, often softening Baroque manner with homely or genre details of great sentimental appeal; works included *Ecstasy of St. Diego of Alcalá; Founding of Santa Maria Maggiore* (Santa María Blanca, Seville), *Immaculate Conception; St. Leandro, St. Isidoro, Vision of St. Anthony,* and *La Purísima* (Seville cathedral); *St. John of God Attending the Sick* and *Miracle of the Loaves and Fishes* (Church of St. George, Seville); *Adoration of the Shepherds, St. Elizabeth of Hungary, Birth of the Virgin, St. John on Patmos, The Two Trinities.*

Mu·ril·lo \mü-ˈrē-yō\, Gerardo. *Also called* Dr. Atl \ˈät-ᵊl\. 1875–1964. Mexican painter and writer. A pioneer of *méxicanismo* movement for artistic nationalism; known esp. for landscapes and depiction of Indian culture; invented Atl colors.

Muris, Johannes de. See JEHAN DES MURS.

Murnau, F. W. See Friedrich W. PLUMPE.

Mur·ner \ˈmür-nər\, Thomas. 1475–c.1537. German religious and satirist. Franciscan priest, opponent of Reformation; author of humorous satires *Narrenbeschweerung* (1512), *Der schelme zunfft* (1512), and *Geuchmatt* (1519), the biting anti-Lutheran attack *Von dem grossen Lutherischen Narren* (1522), translation of the *Aeneid* (1515), textbook on logic, metrics, and law, etc.

Mu·ro \mür-ō\ Kyūsō. 1658–1734. Japanese scholar. Held office under shogun Tokugawa Yoshimune; propagated Confucian thought of Chu Hsi, emphasizing duty, righteous behavior, loyalty to the ruler, by which he meant the shogun rather than the emperor.

Mur·phy \ˈmər-fē\, Arthur. 1727–1805. Irish actor and playwright. Acted roles of Richard III, Othello, Biron, and Osmyn. Author of many farces and satires, as *The Apprentice* (1756), *The Upholsterer* (1757), *Know Your Own Mind* (1777); wrote biographies of Fielding and Garrick, an essay on the genius of Samuel Johnson (1792), and translations of Sallust and Tacitus (1793).

Murphy, Audie. 1924–1971. American soldier, b. near Kingston, Tex. Enlisted in army (1942); served in 7th army in Tunisia, Sicily, Italy, France, Germany (1942–45), rising to lieutenant; most decorated American soldier of World War II, winning Distinguished Service Cross, Legion of Merit, two Silver Stars, Bronze Star, Croix de Guerre, and, for actions in Colmar Pocket (Jan. 1945), Medal of Honor. Appeared in films as *Beyond Glory* (1948), *To Hell and Back* (1955).

Murphy, Charles Francis. 1858–1924. American political leader, b. New York City. Head of Tammany Hall (1902–24).

Murphy, Frank, *in full* William Francis. 1890–1949. American politician and jurist, b. Harbor Beach, Mich. Mayor of Detroit (1930–33), resigning to become governor general of Philippine Islands; U.S. high commissioner to Philippine Islands (1935–36); governor of Michigan (1936–38); attorney general of the U.S. (1939–40); associate justice, U.S. Supreme Court (1940–49).

Murphy, Isaac. 1856–1896. American jockey, b. Fayette Co., Ky. Won 628 races of 1412 entered in career (1873–96), including 4 of first 5 American derbies (1884, 1885, 1886, 1888); first jockey to ride 3 Kentucky Derby winners (1884, 1890, 1891).

Murphy, John Benjamin. 1857–1916. American surgeon, b. Appleton, Wis. Professor, Northwestern U. (1901–05, 1908–16), Rush Medical Coll. (1905–08); specialist in abdominal surgery; invented (1892) Murphy's button for rapid and accurate intestinal anastomosis; promoted early appendectomy; first to induce immobilization and collapse of lung for pulmonary tuberculosis (1898).

Murphy, John Francis. 1853–1921. American painter, b. Oswego, N.Y. Known for landscapes as *October, Indian Summer, The Old Barn.*

Murphy, Michael Charles. 1861–1913. American athletic trainer, b. Westborough, Mass. Trainer of track and football athletes at Yale (1887–89, 1892–96, 1900–05) and at U. of Pennsylvania (1896–1900, 1905–13); coach of American Olympic teams of 1908 and 1912.

Murphy, Robert Daniel. 1894–1978. American diplomat, b. Milwaukee. Entered Foreign Service (1917); vice consul, Zürich (1921), Munich (1921–25); consul, Paris (1930–36); chargé d'affaires to Vichy government (1940); liaison with French in North Africa, laying groundwork for cooperation in Allied invasion (1942); helped negotiate Italian armistice (1943); political adviser for Germany (1944–49), helping to organize Berlin Airlift (1948); ambassador to Belgium (1949–52), Japan (1952–53); helped negotiate Korean armistice (1953); assistant secretary (1953), deputy undersecretary (1953), undersecretary of state (1959); continued to serve on governmental boards.

Mur·ray \ˈmər-ē, ˈmə-rē\. Scottish noble family that held (from 1595) titles of earls, marquises, and dukes of Atholl (or Athole), derived from the related Stewart family (*q.v.*) and including:
John Murray (d. 1642), 1st Earl of Ath·oll \ˈath-əl\ of Murray line; grandson of 5th and last earl in Stewart line; led men on king's side in Civil War; imprisoned (1640) by Marquis of Argyll. His son ¶John (1631–1703), 2d earl and 1st marquis; Royalist leader; supported rising in favor of Charles II, under command of 9th Earl of Glencairn (1653); held high offices after Restoration, including justice-generalship of Scotland (1661–75); created marquis of Atholl (1676); deprived on joining in remonstrance to king against Lauderdale's severities inflicted on Covenanters (1678); lord lieutenant of Argyll (1684); captured Earl of Argyll (1685); wavered at revolution; implicated in Jacobite plots and intrigues; pardoned; acted as negotiator in pacification of Highlands. His son ¶John (1660–1724), 2d marquis and 1st duke (created 1703); supported William and Glorious Revolution (1688) in spite of urging of his brother, Lord Charles Murray, Earl of Dunmore, to support King James; kept clear of Jacobite plot against Queen Anne despite intrigues of Simon Lord Lovat and his tool, Duke of Queensberry; secured Queensberry's downfall (1703); privy councilor, lord privy seal (1703); opposed union (1705–07); took no part in invasion of 1708; deprived on accession of George I; remained faithful to government despite sons' participation in Jacobite rebellion (1715); captured (1717) Rob Roy Macgregor. His son ¶James (1690–1764), 2d duke; lord privy seal (1733–63); keeper of the great seal and lord justice general (1763). James's brother George was a Jacobite general (see Lord George MURRAY) and father of ¶John (1729–1774), 3d duke; M.P. (1761–64); sold the sovereignty of Isle of Man to the treasury (1765). His son ¶John (1755–1830), 4th duke, was created Earl Strange in peerage of Great Britain (1786). Later holders of the dukedom adopted the surname Stewart-Murray.

Murray, Earl of. See earls of Moray: (1) Sir Thomas RANDOLPH; (2) STEWART family.

Murray, Charles. 1864–1941. Scottish poet and engineer. Secretary for public works (1910), director of defense (1917), South Africa. Author of *Hamewith* (1900), *A Sough o' War* (1917), and *In Country Places* (1920).

Murray, Lord George. 1694–1760. Scottish Jacobite commander. Son of 1st Duke of Atholl; fought in rebellion of 1715 under Earl of Mar and in highland expedition of 1719; pardoned; joined Prince Charles Edward and won victory at Prestonpans (Sept. 21, 1745); during retreat from Derby, kept Cumberland's dragoons in check; defeated General Hawley at Falkirk (Jan. 17, 1746); commmanded (1746) right wing at Culloden Moor; died in exile.

Murray, Gilbert, *in full* George Gilbert Aimé. 1866–1957. British classical scholar, b. Sydney, Australia. Professor of Greek, Glasgow (1889–99); regius professor of Greek, Oxford (1908–36). Sat on foreign office committee that participated in drafting covenant of League of Nations; member of South African delegation to Assembly of League of Nations (1921–23), of British delegation (1924); interested in protection of minorities by League; chairman (1923–38) of League of Nations Union; president (1945–57) of United Nations Association. Author of *Ancient Greek Literature* (1897), plays *Carlyon Sahib* (1899) and *Andromache* (1900), and works on Greek drama, including *Rise of Greek Epic* (1907), *Four Stages of Greek Religion* (1912), *Euripides and his Age* (1913), *The Classical Tradition in Poetry* (1927), *Aristophanes* (1933), *Aeschylus, Creator of Tragedy* (1940), *Greek Studies* (1946), *Hellenism and the Modern World* (1954). Known chiefly for his critical editions of Euripides (1901–10) and Aeschylus (1937) and verse translations of Euripides, acted successfully in England and America. Also wrote *Faith, War, and Policy* (1918), *The Ordeal of this Generation* (1929), *Liberality and Civilization* (1938).

Murray, James. 1721–1794. British soldier, b. Scotland. Son of 4th Baron Elibank. Entered army (1740); commander of brigade at Louisbourg (1758); one of Wolfe's three brigadiers in expedition against Quebec (1759); commander of left wing in battle for Quebec (1759); military governor of city (1759); military governor (1760–63), civil governor (1763–66) of province of Quebec; urged conciliatory policy toward French-Canadians. Governor of Minorca (1774); obliged to surrender to besieging French and Spaniards under De Crillon (1782); general (1783).

Murray, Sir James Augustus Henry. 1837–1915. British lexicographer, b. Scotland. As author of article on English language in *Encyclopaedia Britannica* and *The Dialect of the Southern Counties of Scotland* (1873), gained reputation as philologist; president of Philological Society (1878–80, 1882–84). Engaged (from 1879) in the planning and editing of Philological Society's *New English Dictionary,* now called *Oxford English Dictionary* (based on materials accumulated since 1857 and completed, except supplements, 1928); moved to Oxford (1885); editorially responsible for half the dictionary.

Murray, Sir John. Baronet. *Called* Murray of Brough·ton \ˈbrȯt-ᵊn\. 1715–1777. Scottish Jacobite. In Rome became secretary to Prince Charles Edward; an efficient aide until a nervous collapse (March 1746), after which his disability threw rebel commissariat into confusion; turned king's evidence against Jacobite rivals; pardoned (1748).

Murray, John. 4th Earl of Dun·more \(ˌ)dən-ˈmō(ə)r\. 1732–1809. British administrator, b. Scotland. Succeeded to title (1756); representative peer of Scotland (1761–69); governor of New York (1770–71), Virginia (1771–76); dissolved Virginia House of Burgesses (1773, 1774); raised militia and undertook Lord Dunmore's War against Shawnee Indians of Ohio country (1774). Precipitated colonial uprising by seizing powder store (April 1775); moved government to man-of-war offshore, declared martial law (June); defeated by colonists at Great Bridge (Jan. 1, 1776); bombarded Norfolk; returned to England (July 1776). Again representative peer (1776–87); governor of Bahamas (1787–96).

Murray, John. 1741–1815. American clergyman, b. Alton, England. Converted to Universalism by preaching and teaching of James Relly (c.1759); to America (1770). Began itinerant preaching of universal salvation; chaplain in American Revolution; first settled pastorate in newly organized Independent Church of Christ, Gloucester, Mass. (1779–93); pastor of Universalist society in Boston (1793–1809). Regarded as father of American Universalism. His wife ¶Judith, *nee* Sar·gent \ˈsär-jənt\ (1751–1820), was known for her essays, poems, and plays collected and published (1798) as *The Gleaner.*

Murray, John. *Orig. surname* Mac·Mur·ray \mək-ˈmər-ē, -ˈmə-rē\. 1745–1793. British publisher, b. Scotland. Retired lieutenant of marines; bought bookselling business of William Sandby in Fleet Street (1768); started monthly *English Review;* published Mitford's *Greece,* Langhorne's *Plutarch's Lives,* and first part of Isaac D'Israeli's *Curiosities of Literature.* His son ¶John (1778–1843), called by Byron "the Anak of publishers," as London agent for A. Constable shared in publication of *Marmion* (1807); launched *Quarterly Review* (1809) in competition with *Edinburgh Review;* published works of Byron, his close friend, of Jane Austen, Crabbe, Lyell, Borrow, Moore, Campbell, Irving. His son ¶John (1808–1892) projected the series of Murray "Handbooks for Travelers" or "Murray's Red Guides" (begun 1836); published works of Hallam, Gladstone, Lyell, Dean Stanley, Darwin, Livingstone, and Campbell's *Lives of the Chancellors,* Smith's dictionaries, and many books of travel.

Murray, Sir John. 1841–1914. British zoologist and oceanographer, b. Ontario, Canada. Naturalist to *Challenger* expedition (1872–76), studying esp. sea bottom sediments; after death of C.W. Thomson, editor of reports of expedition's scientific results (1882–95); carried out bathymetrical survey of freshwater lochs of Scotland (1897); explored North Atlantic (1910).

Murray, John Courtney. 1904–1967. American religious and theologian, b. New York City. Entered Jesuit order (1920); ordained (1933); professor, Woodstock Coll. (1937–57); editor of *Theological Studies* (from 1941); advocate of dialogue among churches and social groups; principal author of Declaration on Religious Liberty adopted by Second Vatican Council (1962–65). Wrote *We Hold These Truths* (1960), *The Problem of God* (1964), etc.

Murray, Lindley. 1745–1826. American grammarian, b. Sevatra Creek, Pa. Prospered as lawyer and merchant in New York City; to England to regain health (1784); devoted himself to gardening and production of schoolbooks, including *Grammar of the English Language* (1795) with corresponding

Exercises and *Key* (1797), *English Reader* (1799), and *An English Spelling Book* (1804), all widely circulated in England and U.S.; author of religious tracts as *Power of Religion on the Mind* (1787).

Murray, Margaret, *nee* **Pol·son** \ˈpōl-sən\. 1844–1927. Canadian patriot, b. Paisley, Scotland. m. John Clark Murray (1865); founder of Imperial Order of the Daughters of the Empire (1900).

Murray, Philip. 1886–1952. American labor leader, b. Blantyre, Lanarkshire, Scotland. To U.S. (1902); coal miner in Pennsylvania; vice president, United Mine Workers of America (1920–42); head of Steel Workers' Organizing Committee (1936–42); vice president (1938–40), president (1940–52, succeeding John L. Lewis) of Congress of Industrial Organizations; president (1942–52), United Steel Workers of America.

Murray *or* **Mor·ay** \ˈmər-ē, ˈmə-rē\, Sir Robert. 1600?–1673. Scottish statesman. Secret envoy to negotiate treaty between Scotland and France; formed plan for escape of Charles I from Newcastle which Charles failed to take advantage of (1646); joined Charles II in Paris (1654). After Restoration, lord of exchequer for Scotland and deputy secretary (1663); one of triumvirate, with Lauderdale and king, that ruled Scotland (to 1670); a founder of Royal Society (1662).

Murray, William. 1st Earl of **Mans·field** \ˈman(t)s-ˌfēld, ˈmanz-\. 1705–1793. British jurist, b. Scotland. Son of 5th Viscount Stormont; M. P. (1742–56); solicitor general (1742), attorney general (1754); privy councilor (1756); lord chief justice (1756–88); created baron (1756); found technical flaw allowing substitution for fine and imprisonment for Wilkes's outlawry (1768); on unpopular side in cases of seditious libel, bitterly attacked by Junius; created earl (1776); during Gordon riots (1780) his house was burned, but nonetheless conducted scrupulously fair trial in which Lord George Gordon was acquitted. Reduced commercial law and doctrine of quasi-contract to coherent body of rules; developed new law to replace land-centered law in covering commerce; called by Macaulay "father of modern toryism."

Mur·rell *or* **Mur·rel** *or* **Mu·rel** \mə-ˈrel\, John A. 1804?–?1850. American desperado, b. Tenn. Organized criminal bands in several states and established cooperation in disposing of stolen goods (1826–34); captured (1834) and sentenced to ten years' imprisonment for stealing Negro slaves; testimony introduced during his trial indicated he was planning a Negro uprising in the southwest.

Mur·row \ˈmər-(ˌ)ō, ˈmə-(ˌ)rā\, Edward Roscoe, *orig.* Egbert Roscoe. 1908–1965. American journalist, b. Greensboro, N.C. With CBS (1935–61); director of CBS European bureau (1937–46); made notable broadcasts from London during Blitz (1941); vice president, director of public affairs (1946–47); produced and narrated "Hear It Now" series on radio (1950–51), "See It Now" on televison (1951–58); producer and host of "Person to Person" (1953–60), "Small World" (1958–60); head of U.S. Information Agency (1961–64).

Mur·ry \ˈmər-ē, ˈmə-re\, John Middleton. 1889–1956. English critic. Editor, the *Athenaeum* (1919–21) and *Adelphi* (1923–48); m. (1918) Katherine Mansfield. Author of *Dostoevsky* (1916), *Still Life* (1917), *The Evolution of an Intellectual* (1920), *The Things We Are* (1922), *Pencillings* (1923), *To the Unknown God* (1924), *Keats and Shakespeare* (1925), *Things to Come* (1928), *God* (1929), *Son of Woman* (1931), *The Necessity of Communism* (1932), *Katherine Mansfield* (with R. E. Mantz, 1933), *Between Two Worlds* (autobiographical, 1935), *Shakespeare* (1936), *The Necessity of Pacifism* (1937), *The Mystery of Keats* (1949), *Jonathan Swift* (1954), *Unprofessional Essays* (1956), *Love, Freedom and Society* (1957), etc.

Mur·sil·is \mu̇r-ˈsil-əs\ *or* **Mur·shil·ish** \-ˈshil-əsh\. Name of two Hittite kings:

Mursilis I. 17th–16th century B.C. King (c.1620–c.1590 B.C.). Succeeded grandfather Hattusilis I; continued campaign in Syria, destroying Halap (Aleppo) and Mari; attacked Babylon and ended Amorite dynasty; killed in palace coup.

Mursilis II. 14th century B.C. King (c.1334–c.1306 B.C.). Son of Suppiluliumas; succeeded brother Arnuwandas III; conducted numerous campaigns against Arzawa, Kaska, Azzi-Hayasa; set down annals of his and his father's campaigns and exploits.

Mur·ta·ḍā \ˌmu̇r-tä-ˈdä\, Muḥammad al-. d. c.1790. Yemenite scholar. Exponent of thought of al-Ghazālī; contributed to reform in orthodox Islām that paralleled Wahhābī revival.

Mus \mᵫ\, Paul. 1902–1969. French scholar. Secretary and librarian, Research Institute of French School of the Far East, Hanoi (1927–40); helped rally anti-Japanese resistance in Vietnam in World War II; as political adviser to Gen. Leclerc, negotiated with Ho Chi Minh (1945); director, School for Overseas Administration (1945–50); professor, Collège de France (1945–50), Yale U. (1950 ff.). Author of *Barabudur* (1935), *La Lumière sur les Six Voies* (1939), *Vietnam: sociologie d'une guerre* (1952), etc.

Mus, Publius Decius. See DECIUS MUS.

Mūsā, Mansa. See MANSA MŪSĀ.

Mu·sae·us \myu̇-ˈzē-əs\. *Surnamed* Gram·mat·i·cus \grə-ˈmat-i-kəs\. 5th? century A.D. Greek poet. Author of love epic *Hero and Leander* (340 verses extant).

Mū·sa ibn Nu·ṣayr \ˈmü-sä-ˌib-ən-nu̇-ˈsīr\. c.640–714. Arab ruler. Appointed by Calīph al-Walīd I governor of Ifrīqīyah (Tunisia, 708); extended Muslim rule to Tangier and overcame Berbers; sent general Ṭāriq ibn Ziyād at head of Berber army to Spain, beginning Muslim conquest of Iberia; led army to Spain (712), taking Mérida, Toledo, Saragossa; recalled by caliph.

Mu·sä·us \mü-ˈze-u̇s\, Johann Karl August. 1735–1787. German writer. Author of satirical novels, including a parody on Richardson's *Grandison* called *Grandison der Zweite* (1760–62); also wrote *Physiognomische Reisen,* satire on Lavater's theories (1778–79) and ironical and fanciful tales *Volksmärchen der Deutschen* (1782–86), etc.

Mu·say·li·mah \mu̇-ˌsī-lē-ˈmä\. d. 633 A.D. Arab leader. Chief opponent of Abū Bakr, first caliph; killed in battle.

Mush·et \ˈməsh-ət\, Robert Forester. 1811–1891. English metallurgist. Invented process of adding spiegeleisen during Bessemer process (1856) and a manganese-tungsten process (1868) for making self-hardening steel for engineer's tools.

Mu·sil \ˈmü-zil\, Robert von. Edler. 1880–1942. German writer. Served in World War I, in Austrian war office (1920–22); lived in Berlin, Vienna, Geneva. Known esp. for monumental unfinished novel *Der Mann ohne Eigenschaften* (1930–43), ironic analysis of the ills of the age; also wrote *Die Verwirrungen des Zöglings Törless* (1906), *Vereinigungen* (1911), *Die Frauen* (1924), plays, essays, etc.

Mus·lim ibn al-Ḥaj·jāj \mu̇s-ˈlē-ˌmib-ə-nal-ka̱j-ˈjäj\. *In full* Abū al-Ḥusayn Muslim ibn al-Ḥajjāj al-Qushayrī. c.817–875. Islāmic scholar. A chief authority on Ḥadīth, accounts of sayings and deeds of Prophet Muḥammad; traveled widely to collect some 300,000 traditions, compiled in *Ṣaḥīḥ,* which became accepted as one of six canonical collections.

Musorgsky. See MUSSORGSKY.

Mus·sa·to \müs-ˌsä-tō\, Albertino. 1261–1329. Italian statesman and poet. Member of ruling council of Padua; ambassador to Pope Boniface VIII (1302); member of embassy to Emperor Henry VIII (1311); crowned poet of Padua (1314); exiled (1325). Author of Latin poems, Latin tragedy *Ecerinis,* and historical works *Historia Augusta* and *De gestis italicorum post Henricum VII Caesarem.*

Mus·schen·broek \ˈmᵫs-ən-ˌbrük\, Pieter van. 1692–1761. Dutch mathematician and physicist. Member of notable Leiden family of instrument makers; practiced medicine; professor at Duisburg (1719–23), Utrecht (1723–40), Leiden (1740–61); discovered (1746) principle of Leyden jar (called also Kleistian jar) at about same time as E. G. von Kleist and others.

Mus·sert \ˈmᵫs-ərt\, Anton Adriaan. 1894–1946. Dutch engineer and political leader. Leader of National Socialist party in Netherlands (from 1931); named by German commissar leader of the Netherlands people (1942); executed for treason.

Mus·set \mᵫ-se\, Alfred de, *in full* Louis-Charles-Alfred de. 1810–1857. French writer. Achieved recognition with precocious poetry, Romantic but leavened by ironic and even flippant wit, as *Contes d'Espagne et d'Italie* (1830) and *Un Spectacle dans un fauteuil* (1832); conducted fitful affair with George Sand (1833–39); wrote verse and prose plays including *La Nuit vénitienne* (1830), *André del Sarto* (1833), *Fantasio* (1833), *Les Caprices de Marianne* (1833), *On ne Badine pas avec l'amour* (1834), *Lorenzaccio* (1834), *Il ne faut jurer de rien* (1836), *Un Caprice* (1837). Verse included *Rolla* (1833), four lyrical *Nuits* (1835–37), *Souvenir* (1841); wrote autobiographical novel *La Confession d'un enfant du siècle* (1836), stories as *Pierre et Camille* (1844), *Mimi Pinson* (1845), *La Mouche* (1853). Elected to French Academy (1852).

Mus·so·li·ni \ˌmüs-sō-ˈlē-nē, *Angl* ˌmü-sə-ˈlē-nē, ˌmu̇s-ə-\, Benito Amilcare Andrea. 1883–1945. Italian dictator. Expelled from Switzerland because of Socialist party activities (1904); engaged in journalism in Italy and continued political agitation; imprisoned at various times; left-wing leader of Socialist party (1912) and editor of *Avanti* (1912–14), official organ of Socialist party in Italy; expelled from party for supporting World War I, founded (1914) own paper *Il Popolo d'Italia;* after Italy entered war, volunteered and served (1915–17) as private until wounded; returned to editorship of *Popolo d'Italia.* Organized first Fasci di Combattimento at Milan (1919); conducted campaign of violence against Socialists, Communists, Republicans, etc.; elected to parliament (1921); organized (Nov. 1921) Partito Nazionale Fascista, of which he became known as *il duce* (leader). Directed Fascists in march on Rome (1922); when Facta cabinet resigned, he was summoned by king to form ministry (1922); took over a number of ministries himself; changed electoral law to assure Fascist control of government; openly instituted dictatorship (1925); suppressed all opposition parties and newspapers. Signed treaty (1929) with papacy, ending 59-year-old dispute; denounced (1930) provisions of Versailles Treaty, causing strained relations with France; conquered Ethiopia (1935–36) and annexed it to Italy; withdrew from League of Nations (1937) because it approved sanctions against Italy; aided Franco in Spanish civil war (1936–39); conquered and annexed Albania (1939); signed military alliance with Germany (1939); declared war on Britain and France (June 1940); suffered defeat in attack on Greece (1940); lost African colonies (1941); after severe reverses, deposed by Fascist Grand Council (July 1943); arrested by king but rescued in daring German parachute raid; established puppet regime in northern Italy; captured and shot by partisans.

Mus·sorg·sky \'mü-sərg-skəi, *Angl* mu̇-'sȯrg-skē, -'zȯrg-\, Modest Petrovich. 1839–1881. Russian composer. Officer in aristocratic Preobrazhensky Guards (1856–59); civil servant (from 1863); experienced great difficulties with money and his health; associated at times with Balakirev, Rimsky-Korsakov. One of the most original and influential composers of the day. Works included operas *Zhenitba* (one act only, 1868), *Boris Godunov* (1874), *Khovanshchina* (completed by Rimsky-Korsakov, 1886), *Sorochinskaya yarmarka* (unfinished, 1874–80); orchestral works *Ivanova noch na Lysoy gore* (*St. John's Night on the Bare Mountain,* 1867), *Vzyatiye Karsa* (1880); piano works including *Intermezzo in modo classico* (1861), *Shveja* (1871), suite *Kartinki s vystavki* (*Pictures at an Exhibition,* 1874; later orchestrated by Ravel); over 60 songs including cycles *Detskaya* (*The Nursery,* 1868–72), *Bez Solntsa* (*Sunless,* 1874), *Pesni i plyaski smerti* (*Songs and Dances of Death,* 1875–77).

Mus·ta·fa \mü-stä-'fä\. Name of four sultans of the Ottoman empire:

Mustafa I. 1591–1639. Sultan (1617–18, 1622–23). Succeeded brother Osman II; a weak ruler; dethroned (1618) but restored (1622) by Janissaries; again deposed in favor of Murad IV.

Mustafa II. *In full* Mustafa oglu Mehmed IV. 1664–1703. Sultan (1695–1703). Son of Mehmed IV; continued war against Holy League, recovering Chios and other areas; lost Azov to Russia (1696), defeated by Austrians at Senta (1697); forced in Treaty of Carlowitz (1699) to give up much of Balkan holdings; faced with domestic revolts; deposed by military mutiny.

Mustafa III. 1717–1774. Sultan (1757–74). Succeeded Osman III; attempted with mixed success to reform administration of empire, esp. in fiscal matters; instituted military reforms aided by Baron François de Tott; avoided European alliances; declared war on Russia (1768) and suffered loss of Ottoman fleet at Çeşme (1770).

Mustafa IV. 1779–1808. Sultan (1807–08). In league with Janissaries and religious conservatives, overthrew cousin Selim III (1807); ended Selim's reforms; killed Selim to prevent his restoration; deposed and later murdered on orders of brother and successor Mahmud II.

Muṣṭafā an-Naḥḥās Pasha. See NAḤḤĀS PASHA.

Mustafa Kemal. See Kemal ATATÜRK.

Mustafa Reşid Paşa. See REŞID PAŞA.

Mus·tan·ṣir, al- \al-mu̇s-'tän-sir\. 1029–1094. Egyptian caliph of Fāṭimid dynasty (1036–94). Reign beset by wars of military factions; offered military command to Armenian general Badr al-Jamali, who defeated all factions and restored peace but secured for himself actual rule of Egypt; lost control of other portions of North Africa; lost Syria to Seljuq Turks.

Mus·ta'·ṣim, al- \al-ˌmu̇s-'tä-sim\. 1221–1258. Caliph of Baghdad of the 'Abbāsid dynasty (1242–58). Last of 'Abbāsid line; killed at Baghdad by Hülegü.

Mus·tel \mœs-tel\, Victor. 1815–1890. French manufacturer and inventor of musical instruments. Established harmonium factory in Paris (1853) and patented a "double expression" (1854) and made other improvements in the harmonium; invented the typophone, métaphone, etc.

Mu·su·rus \myu̇-'sü-rəs\, Marcus. *Gr.* Markos Mou·sou·ros \mü-sü-rȯs\. 1470?–1517. Greek scholar. Associated with Aldus Manutius (from 1493) and others in promoting Greek studies; supervised publication of many of the Aldine classics.

Mu'·ta·ḍid, al- \al-mu̇-'tad-id\. d. 902. Caliph of Baghdad of 'Abbāsid dynasty. Son of al-Muwaffaq; forced uncle al-Mu'tamid to disinherit son in his favor; instituted reforms in caliphal government; died following defeat by Qarmaṭians.

Mu'·ta·mid, al- \al-mu̇-'täm-id\. *More completely* Muḥammad II al-Mu'tamid. 1027–1095. Muslim ruler of Seville (1069–90). Conquered and annexed Córdoba (1071); gained control of Murcia; threatened by Alfonso VI of León and Castile, reluctantly invited Yūsuf ibn Tāshufīn, Almoravid sultan, to send aid (1085); afforded respite by Yūsuf's victory over Christian forces (1086); again invited Yūsuf, who deposed him and sent him a prisoner to Morocco (1090); last 'Abbādid ruler of Seville.

Mu·ta·nab·bī, al- \al-ˌmü-tä-'näb-bē\. *In full* Abū aṭ-Ṭayyib Aḥmad ibn Ḥusayn al-Mutanabbī. 915–965. Islāmic poet. Early life notable for adventures; in Iraq and later in Egypt became renowned for panegyrics exhibiting great artistry; considered by some the greatest poet in Arabic in Islāmic times.

Mu'·ta·sim, al- \al-mu̇-'tas-im\. 794–842. Caliph of Baghdad (833–842), of 'Abbāsid dynasty. Son of Hārūn ar-Rashīd; first caliph to employ Turkish mercenaries; crushed Persian rebels led by Bābak (837); defeated Byzantine Emperor Theophilus and destroyed fortresses of Ancyra and Amorium (838).

Mu·ta·wak·kil, al- \al-mu̇-tä-'wäk-kil\. 822–861. Caliph of Baghdad of the 'Abbāsid dynasty. Instituted persecution of non-Islāmics and of unorthodox Islāmics; razed shrine of Shī'i martyr al-Ḥusayn ibn 'Alī; continued indecisive wars with Byzantines; murdered by Turkish mercenaries at instigation of oldest son.

Mü·te·fer·ri·ka \mœ̄-ˌtä-fär-rē-'kä\, Ibrahim. 18th century. Ottoman printer, b. Hungary. Convert to Islām; at Istanbul printed first Turkish-language books (from 1727).

Mu·te·sa \mü-'tā-sä\. Name of two rulers of Buganda:

Mutesa I. *In full* Mutesa Walugembe Mukaabya. c.1838–1884. Established a bureaucratic autocracy; strengthened military power, which was used to raid and extort tribute from neighboring states; accepted and played off influences of Arabs, Europeans.

Mutesa II. *Also known as* Sir Edward Frederick Mutesa. 1924–1969. *Kabaka* (king, 1939–53, 1955–66). Unpopular owing to dependence on British; demanded separation of Buganda from Uganda and eventual independence, for which he was deposed and deported (1953); restored by Bugandan supporters (1955); came into conflict with Milton Obote, prime minister of Uganda, and was forced to flee (1966); died in Great Britain.

Muth \'müt\, Konrad. *Lat.* Conradus Mu·ti·a·nus Ru·fus \ˌmu̇t-sē-'än-u̇s-rü-fu̇s, *Angl*, ˌm(y)ü-shē-'ā-nəs-'rü-fəs\. *Also called* Mu·tian \ˌmüt-sē-'än, *Angl* 'm(y)ü-shən\. 1471–1526. German Humanist. Fellow pupil with Erasmus; canonicus in Gotha (from 1503); became center of Mutianischen Kreis (circle), which opposed Scholasticism and favored Humanism and which was probably responsible for *Epistolae obscurorum virorum;* championed Reuchlin in Reuchlinian controversy.

Mu·tis \'mü-tēs\, José Celestino Bruno. 1732–1808. Spanish naturalist. One of first disciples of Linnaeus in Spain; physician to household of Ferdinand VI (1757–60); to New Granada (Colombia) as physician to Spanish viceroy (1760); given formal appointment as botanist (1782); created botanical garden at Mariquita, collected thousands of specimens; assembled major botanical library; compiled *Flora de Bogotá o de Nueva Granada* (unpublished).

Mu·tsu·hi·to \mu̇t-su̇-hē-tō\. *Reign name* Mei·ji \mā-jē\. 1852–1912. Emperor of Japan (1867–1912), 122d in direct lineage. Son of Kōmei; named crown prince (1860); crowned at Osaka (1868); transferred capital to Tokyo (1869). His accession provided occasion for ending shogunate, the "Meiji Restoration" consisting of return of power to the emperor; his reign saw feudal system abolished and fiefs of great clans surrendered (1871); samurai regulated (1871); Western ideas, arts, laws, customs, schools, business methods, etc., introduced; Gregorian calendar adopted (1873); Satsuma rebellion (1877) put down; new constitution promulgated (1889); Chinese–Japanese War (1894–95), Anglo–Japanese alliance (1902), and Russo–Japanese War (1904–05). Succeeded by his son Yoshihito.

Mu Tsung. See (1) Chu Tsai-kou under CHU family; (2) TSAI-CH'UN.

Mu·waf·faq, al- \al-mu̇-'wäf-fäk\. d. 891. Islāmic soldier. Brother of and regent for caliph al-Mu'tamid; restored order in Iraq, defeated Ṣaffārid uprising (876).

Mu·wa·tal·lis \ˌmü-(w)ə-'tal-əs\ *or* **Mu·wa·tal·lish** \-əsh\. 14th–13th century B.C. King of Hittite New Kingdom (c.1306–c.1282 B.C.). Son and successor of Mursilis II; fought celebrated battle against Ramses II of Egypt at Kadesh (1299); moved capital to Dattassa, leaving brother Hattusilis as viceroy in the north.

Muy·bridge \'mī-ˌbrij\, Eadweard. *Orig.* Edward James Mug·ger·idge \'məg(-ə)-rij\. 1830–1904. American motion-picture pioneer, b. Kingston on Thames, England. To U.S. as a boy; in photographic survey work for U.S. Coast and Geodetic Survey; gained attention with large composite photographs of Yosemite Valley (1868); requested (1872) by Leland Stanford to prove by photography that a running horse at one period of his stride has all four feet off the ground, devoted himself to photographic studies of motion; invented the zoopraxiscope, by which he reproduced moving pictures on a screen; continued experiments (1884–87) under auspices of U. of Pennsylvania.

Mu·ẓaf·far 'Alī \mu̇-'zäf-fär-ä-'lē\. fl. c.1540–c.1576. Persian artist. Known esp. as portraitist; contributed to illustration of manuscript of works of Neẓāmī for Ṭahmāsp I; executed wall paintings for royal palace and Cihil Sutūn, Isfahan.

Mu·zaf·far Shah \mu̇-'zäf-fär-'shä\. 15th century. Sultan of Malacca (1445–?1459). Ended traditional tribute to Siam and defeated Siamese punitive expeditions (1445, 1456); made Malacca a thriving commercial power; gained control of Selangor and parts of Sumatra coast.

Mu·žá·ko·vá \mü-zhä-ˈkò-vä\, Johanna, *nee* Rot·to·vá \ròt-ˈtò-vä\. *Pseudonym* Karolina Svět·lá \ˈsvet-lä\. 1830–1899. Czech novelist. Best known for novels describing Prague society and the north Bohemian countryside, as *Vesnický román* (1867), *Kříž u potoka* (1868), and *Kanturčice* (1869).

Muz·zey \ˈmәz-ē\, David Saville. 1870–1965. American historian, b. Lexington, Mass. Professor, Barnard Coll. (1912–23), Columbia (1923–40). Author of *An American History* (1911), *History of the American People* (1927), etc.

Mwan·ga \ˈmwäŋ-(g)ä\. 1866–1901. Ruler of Buganda (1884–97). Son of Mutesa I, whom he succeeded as *kabaka* (king); instituted massacre of Ganda Christians (1885–86); driven from capital by rebellious Muslim faction (1888–90); forced to accept British protectorate (1893); power circumscribed by Christian oligarchy; rebelled against British (1897) but won little support among people; fled to exile.

Mwenda. See MSIRI.

Myconius, Oswald. See Oswald GEISHÜSLER.

Myd·del·ton *or* **Myd·dle·ton** \ˈmid-ᵊl-tәn\, Sir Hugh. 1560–1631. Welsh goldsmith, banker, and clothmaker. M. P. (1603–28); on authority of Parliament, took over project of supplying London with water from springs in Hertfordshire by means of canal 38 miles long discharging into a reservoir called New River Head (completed 1613).

My·er \ˈmī-әr\, Albert James. 1829–1880. American army officer, b. Newburgh, N.Y. Army surgeon (1854); proposed (1858) wigwag signalling system; assigned task of organizing and commanding a signal corps for U.S. army (1860); commanded Signal Corps (1863, 1866–80); proposed, founded, and supervised U.S. Weather Bureau (1870–80). Fort Myer, Va., is named in his honor.

My·ers \ˈmī-әrz\, Frederic William Henry. 1843–1901. English poet and essayist. Classical lecturer, Cambridge (1865–72); school inspector under education department (1872–1900); took lead among founders of Society for Psychical Research (1882); helped to revise society's proceedings, which were published as *Phantasms of the Living* (1886). Author of poems, including *Saint Paul* (1867), *Renewal of Youth* (1882); also *Essays, Classical and Modern* (1883), *Science and a Future Life* (1893), *Human Personality and its Survival of Bodily Death* (1903).

Myers, Leopold Hamilton. 1881–1944. English novelist. Author of philosophical novels expressing spiritual turmoil and despair, including *The Orissers* (1922), *The Clio* (1925), and Indian tetralogy *The Near and the Far* (1929), *Prince Jali* (1931), *The Root and the Flower* (1935), *Pool of Vishnu* (1940).

Mykerinos. See MENKURE.

Myles na gCopaleen. See Brian O'NOLAN.

My·li·us-Erich·sen \ˈmūē-lē-u̇s-ˈi-rēk-sәn\, Ludvig. 1872–1907. Danish explorer. Led Danish literary expedition (1902–04) to explore unknown shores of Melville Bay, Greenland, and study language, customs, and traditions of Eskimos; led *Danmark* expedition (1906–07) to chart coastline of northeast Greenland; perished there. Author of *Grønland* (with H. Moltke, 1906).

Myr·dal \ˈmuer-ˌdäl, *Angl* ˈmәr-, ˈmiәr-\, Alva, *nee* Rei·mer \ˈrī-mәr\. 1902–1986. Swedish sociologist, government official, and peace activist. m. (1924) economist Gunnar Myrdal. With husband helped to implement (1930s) national program of state responsibility for welfare of children regardless of parents' means. Served as principal director of U.N. Dept. of Social Affairs (1949–50), director of UNESCO Dept. of Social Sciences (from 1951); Swedish ambassador to India, Burma, and Ceylon (1955–61); Sweden's chief multinational disarmament negotiator (1961–73); outspoken critic of the arms race; with Alfonso García Robles of Mexico awarded 1982 Nobel prize for peace; received numerous other international peace awards. Publications included *The Game of Disarmament: How the United States and Russia Run the Arms Race* (1976).

My·ron \ˈmī-rәn\. fl. c.480–440 B.C. Greek sculptor. Considered in his time one of greatest of Attic sculptors; works certainly identified are the Athena and Marsyas group and *Discobolus* (*Discus Thrower*), both extant in copies of bronze originals; attributed works include *Anadumenus,* a standing Herakles, head of Perseus, *Hecate;* lost works include *Ladas* and the bronze cow for Athenian marketplace.

Mys·li·ve·çek \mis-li-ˈvech-ek\, Josef. *Also spelled* Misliveçek, Mysliweczek. 1737–1781. Czech composer. Achieved great success in Italy, esp. Naples, with operas including *Medea* (1767), *Il Bellerofonte* (1767), *Il Demofoonte* (1769), *Montezuma* (1771), *Romolo ed Ersilia* (1773), *Ezio* (1775); also wrote oratorios as *Adamo ed Eva* (1771), *La liberazione d'Israele* (1775), *Abramo ed Isacco* (1777), orchestral and chamber works.

Mzi·li·ka·zi \ᵊm-ˌzē-lē-ˈkä-zē\. *Also spelled* Umsiligasi, Mozelekatse. c.1790–1868. South African ruler. Chief of Kumalo tribe of Bantu people; a lieutenant of Shaka; revolted and led tribe northward (1823); traveled into Mozambique, Transvaal, Botswana, Zambia (1837), and settled finally in present Rhodesia (c.1840); growing body of followers formed Ndebele (Matabele) nation; repelled Boer attacks and concluded peace with Transvaal (1852).

N

Nā·bi·ghah, an- \ən-,nä-bē-'gä\. *In full* an-Nābighah adh-Dhubyānī. *Orig.* Zi·yād ibn Mu·'ā·wi·yah \zē-'yäd-,ib-ən-mü-'ä-wē-yä\. fl. c.600. Arab poet. Poet at courts of Nu'mān and Ghassān; one of seven pre-Islāmic poets whose works were collected in *Mu'allaqāt.*

Na·bis \'nā-bəs\. d. 192 B.C. Tyrant of Sparta (207–192 B.C.). Attacked by Achaeans and defeated at Scotitas (201); attacked by Romans under Flamininus (195) and forced to surrender control of Argos; murdered; last ruler of independent Sparta.

Na·bo·kov \nə-'bó-kəf, 'nab-ə-kóf\, Vladimir Vladimirovich. 1899–1977. American writer, b. St. Petersburg, Russia. Lived in England (1919–22), Germany and France (1922–40); to U.S. (1940, naturalized 1945); professor, Wellesley Coll. (1941–48), Cornell U. (1948–58). In Berlin and Paris published verse, stories, dramas, etc., under pseudonym V. Si·rin \'syir-yin\; later wrote chiefly novels; works included *Mashenka* (*Mary,* 1926), *Korol-dama-valet* (1928), *Zashchita luzhina* (*The Defense,* 1930), *Podvig* (*Glory,* 1932), *Camera obscura* (1933), *Otchayaniye* (*Despair,* 1934), *Priglasheniye na kazn* (1935), *Dar* (*The Gift,* 1935), *Soglyadatay* (collection, 1938), *The Real Life of Sebastian Knight* (1941), *Bend Sinister* (1947), *Lolita* (1955), *Pnin* (1957), *Pale Fire* (1962), *Ada* (1969), *Transparent Things* (1972); also wrote memoirs as *Speak, Memory* (1967), and critical works; translated works of Gogol, Pushkin, Lermontov. Also a noted lepidopterist.

Nab·o·nas·sar \,nab-ə-'nas-ər\. *Assyrian* Nabu-nasir. d. 734 B.C. King of Babylon (747–734 B.C.). A vassal of Tiglath-pileser III of Assyria; his reign supposed to have begun a new Babylonian astronomical era, later adopted by the Greeks.

Nab·o·ni·dus \,nab-ə-'nī-dəs\. *Assyrian* Nabu-na'id. d. 539? B.C. Last king of Babylonia (556–539 B.C.). Showed only partial devotion to gods Marduk and Nebo and thus incurred enmity of priesthood; made son Belshazzar co-regent with him. Joined Croesus, king of Lydia, against rising power of Cyrus the Great, but was conquered (540–539) and Babylon taken by Cyrus's general Gobryas.

Nab·o·po·las·sar \,nab-ə-pə-'las-ər\. *Assyrian* Nabu-apal-usur. d. 605 B.C. King of Babylonia (reigned 625–605 B.C.). Founder of Chaldean dynasty; as viceroy of Chaldea, declared Chaldea's independence and began long struggle to throw off control of Assyria; with allies, captured and destroyed Nineveh (612); founded new Babylonian empire with Chaldea the dominant power.

Na·bu·co de Arau·jo \nä-bü-kō-t͟hā-á-'raù-zhō\, Joaquim Aurelio Baretto. 1849–1910. Brazilian politician and diplomat. Deputy (1878–89); founder of Brazilian Anti-Slavery Society; retired after success of abolition movement (1888). Ambassador to U.S. (1905–10). Author of *Camões e os Lusíadas* (1872), *O abolicionismo* (1883), *Pensées détachées et souvenirs* (1906).

Na·bu·ri·man·ni \'näb-ü-rə-'män-ē\. *Also called* Naburianos, Naburiannuos, Naburiannu, Naburimannu. fl. c.491 B.C. Babylonian astronomer. Earliest Babylonian astronomer known by name; devised so-called System A of ephemerides of sun, moon, planets; calculated synodic month.

Nach·ti·gal \'näk-tē-,gäl\, Gustav. 1834–1885. German explorer. Received commission to deliver gifts from Prussian king to sultan of Bornu; traveled to Fezzan and, as the first European, to Tibesti (1869), Kuka (1870), Kanem and Borku (1871), Baguirmi (1872), Wadai (1873), Darfur (1874), and returned over Egypt to Germany (1875). German consul in Tunis (1882–84); visited western Africa as imperial commissioner (1884) and annexed Togo, Cameroon. Author of *Sahara und Sudan* (1879–81).

Na·dab \'nā-,dab\. d. 900 B.C. King of Israel (901–900 B.C.). Son and successor of Jeroboam I.

Nadar. See Gaspard-Félix TOURNACHON.

Na·del \'näd-əl, *Angl* 'nād-ᵊl\, Siegfried Frederick. 1903–1956. Austrian anthropologist. Reader, U. of Durham, England (1948–50); professor, U. of Canberra, Australia (1950–56); known for studies of Nupe and other Nigerian peoples and for theoretical works. Author of *Black Byzantium* (1942), *The Nuba* (1947), *Foundations of Social Anthropology* (1951), *Nupe Religion* (1954), *Theory of Social Structure* (1958).

Na·del·man \'näd-ᵊl-mən\, Elie. 1882–1946. American sculptor, b. Warsaw, Poland. Worked in Paris (1903–14); to U.S. (1914, naturalized 1927); noted esp. for mannered, often humorous figures and mannikins in characteristic curvilinear style; also executed architectural decoration, Impressionistic portrait heads.

Nā·der Khān \'näd-er-'k̲än\. *Orig.* Muḥammad Nāder Khān. 1880–1933. King of Afghanistan (1929–33). Minister at Paris (1924–26); organized revolt that overthrew usurper Ḥabībollāh (1929); elected king; assassinated.

Nā·der Shāh \'ná-dər-'shá\. *Also known as* Ṭahm·āsp Qo·lī Khān \tá-'másp-kó-'lē-k̲án\. *Orig.* Nāder Qolī Beg \-'beg\. 1688–1747. King of Persia (1736–47). A Turk; became leader of large band of bandits, whom he led in support of Ṭahmāsp II against Afghan usurper (1726–31); granted government of several provinces; deposed Ṭahmāsp (1732) and made Ṭahmāsp's infant son, 'Abbās III, shāh (1732–36); assumed throne; to win support of Afghans, made Sunnī form of Islām the state religion; renewed war with Turks successfully; to revenge murder of embassy, ravaged Northwest Provinces, took and sacked Delhi (1739); carried off Koh-i-noor diamond and the Peacock Throne; subjugated Bokhara and Khwarezm; assassinated.

Nae·vi·us \'nē-vē-əs\, Gnaeus. c.270–c.199, 202, or 204 B.C. Roman poet and playwright. Author of some 30 comedies, notably *Tarentilla,* a few tragedies; created the Roman historical drama as in *Romulus* and *Clastidium;* wrote epic of the First Punic War, *Bellum Poenicum.*

Na·gai \nä-gī\ Sōkichi. *Pseudonym* Nagai Kafū. 1879–1959. Japanese novelist. Traveled and studied in U.S. and France; professor, Keiō U., Tokyo (1910–16). Author of lyrical, occasionally Naturalistic, novels of Tokyo life, including *Sumidagawa* (1909), *Ude kurabe* (1917), *Ajisai* (1931), *Tsuyu no atosaki* (1931), *Bokutō kidan* (1937).

Na·ga·no \nä-gä-nō\ Osami. 1880–1947. Japanese admiral. Naval attaché in Washington, D.C. (1920–23); representative at naval conferences and League of Nations; minister of the navy (1936–37); commander in chief, Japanese fleet (1937); chief of naval staff (1941); planned and executed Pearl Harbor attack (Dec. 7, 1941); fleet marshal (1943); died on trial as war criminal.

Nā·gār·ju·na \nä-'gär-jə-nə\. fl. c.150–250 A.D. Indian religious. By tradition, a Hindu Brahmin; converted to Buddhism; attracted followers to his critical examinations of Hindu and Buddhist doctrines; considered founder of Mādhyamika or Mādhyamaka school of Buddhism. Works attributed to him include *Mūlamadhyamakakārikā* and *Vigrahavyāvartanī* in Sanskrit, *Ta-chih-tu-lun, Shī-chu-p'i-p'o-sha-lun,* and *Shih-erh-men-lun* in Chinese, *Rigs pa drug ca paḥi tshig leḥur byas pa shes bya ba, Ston pa ñid bdun cu paḥi tsig leḥur byas pa shes bya ba,* and *Shib mo rnam par ḥtag pa shes bya baḥi mdo* in Tibetan. Subject of many later legends, perhaps owing to confusion with sorcerers, alchemists, and others of same name.

na gCopaleen, Myles. See Brian O'NOLAN.

Nä·ge·li \'neg-ə-lē\, Hans Franz. c.1497–1579. Swiss politician and military leader. Captain of Bernese military forces; took part in numerous campaigns, notably against adventurer-baron Giangiacomo Medici (1531), in liberation of Vaud (1536); chief magistrate of Bern (1540–68).

Nägeli, Karl Wilhelm von. 1817–1891. Swiss botanist. Professor, Freiburg (1852), Zürich (1855), Munich (from 1858); studied cell division and osmosis; discovered (1844) antheridia and spermatozoids of ferns; originated concept of meristem and the micellar theory to account for the structure of organized bodies.

Na·gle \'nā-gəl\, Nano Honoria. c.1718–1784. Irish religious. Opened schools for poor children; founded (1775) Society of Charitable Instruction, which subsequently grew into the Order of the Presentation of the Blessed Virgin Mary, devoted to visitation of the sick and education of poor children.

Nagy \'nädʸ\, Imre. 1896–1958. Hungarian politician. Joined Russian Red army in World War I; lived in Moscow (1929–44); held various posts in Hungarian government (1944–48); ardent supporter of peasants' interests; premier of Hungary (1953–55); recalled as premier during revolt of 1956; appealed to Western powers for aid against Soviet occupation; tried and executed.

Nagybánya, Miklós Horthy de. See HORTHY DE NAGYBÁNYA.

Naharro, Bartolomé de Torres. See TORRES NAHARRO.

Naḥ·ḥās Pa·sha \nä-'kās-'päsh-ä\, Muṣṭafā an-. 1876–1965. Egyptian politician. Member (from 1919), chairman (1927–52) of nationalist Wafd party; prime minister (1928, 1929–30, 1936–37, 1942–44, 1950–52); clashed frequently with British and with King Fu'ād I and King Farouk I over proposals to limit power of colonial commissioners and the monarchy; negotiated Anglo-Egyptian alliance (1936), which he attempted to abrogate (1950).

Na·hi·ena·ena \nä-,hē-ā-nä-'ā-nä\. 1815–1836. Hawaiian princess. Daughter of Kamehameha I; educated in mission schools; acceded to demand of chiefs that she marry her half-brother Kamehameha III (1834); alienated missionaries and the large body of Christian converts among her people; received back into church shortly before her death.

Nahl \'näl\, Johann August. 1710–1781. German sculptor and decorator. Worked on Rohan château, Strasbourg; for Frederick II decorated castles and palaces, esp. Charlottenburg in Potsdam; to Kassel (1755), director of the Academy there (from 1777).

Na·hum \'nā-(h)əm\. 7th century B.C. Hebrew prophet. One of the minor prophets; flourished before the fall of Nineveh (612 B.C.), his prediction of which is recorded in the Old Testament book of Nahum.

Nai·du \'nīd-(,)ü\, Sarojini, *nee* Chat·to·padh·yay \,chät-tō-'pəd-,yī\. 1879–1949. Indian poet and reformer. m. (1898) Dr. M. G. Naidu; organized flood-relief work in Hyderābād (1908), lectured widely in India and (1928–29) in U.S.; first Indian woman president (1925) of the Indian National Congress; several times imprisoned for nationalist agitation; governor of United Provinces (now Uttar Pradesh, 1947–49). Known as the "nightingale of India" for her verse, published in *The Golden Threshold* (1905), *The Bird of Time* (1912), and *The Broken Wing* (1915–16).

Nai·ma \nī-'mä\, Mustafa. 1655–1716. Turkish historian. Held various official posts in Constantinople; made official chronicler by grand vizier (1709). Author of chronicle *Tarih* (pub. 1730) of period 1591–1659.

Nair, Sir Chettur Sankaran. See SANKARAN NAIR.

Nairne \'ne(ə)rn\, Carolina, *nee* Ol·i·phant \'äl-ə-fənt\. Baroness Nairne. 1766–1845. Scottish songwriter. Daughter of a Jacobite leader. Her poems published as *Lays from Strathearn* (1846); excelled in humorous ballads, Jacobite anthems, and songs of pathos, including "Land o' the Leal," "Charlie is My Darling," "The Laird o' Cockpen," "The Hundred Pipers," "Will Ye No' Come Back Again?"

Nai·smith \'nā-,smith, 'nāz-məth\, James A. 1861–1939. American physical educator, b. Almonte, Ont. On staff of McGill U. (1887–90), of Y.M.C.A. College, Springfield, Mass. (1890–95), of Y.M.C.A., Denver, Colo. (1895–98), and of U. of Kansas (1898–1937); originated the game of basketball (1891).

Na·kae \nä-kī\ Tōju, *orig.* Gen. *Pseudonym* Mok·ken \mōk-ken\. 1608–1648. Japanese scholar. A Neo-Confucian, originally an adherent of Rationalist school of Chu Hsi; introduced into Japan Idealist thought of Wang Yang-ming.

Nakae Tokusuke. *Pseudonym* Nakae Chōmin. 1847–1901. Japanese writer. Studied in France; ran a French language school; founded daily newspaper *Tōyō jiyū shimbun* (1881) in which he expounded Western democratic ideas; elected to Diet (1890); translated and popularized works of J.-J. Rousseau.

Nakatomi Kamatari. See FUJIWARA family.

Na·ki·an \'näk-ē-ən\, Reuben. 1897–1986. American sculptor, b. College Point, N.Y. Used heroic subject matter to create quasi-abstract art; early sculpture included realistic portraits of Pres. Franklin D. Roosevelt and his cabinet; under influence of Arshile Gorky, turned to abstract expressionism; reinterpreted themes from classical mythology; best-know works include bust of artist Marcel Duchamp and nine-foot-high bronze *Hiroshima.*

Nał·kow·ska \nál-'kóf-ská\, Zofia. 1884–1954. Polish novelist and playwright. Among her Symbolist and psychological novels were *Kobiety* (1906), *Książe* (1907), *Narcyza* (1910), *Romans Teresy Hennert* (1924), *Choucas* (1927), *Niedobra miłość* (1928), *Granica* (1935), *Węzły życia* (1948); plays *Dom kobiet* (1930), *Dzień jego powrotu* (1931); also *Medaliony* (1946).

Namatianus. See Claudius RUTILIUS NAMATIANUS.

Nām·dev \'näm-dəv\. 1270?–?1350. Indian poet and religious. Converted by vision from life of thief and murderer to one of devotion; became leading exponent of Vārakarī (Pilgrim) school of Hinduism; author of devotional lyrics and hymns in Marathi that inspired a long-lived tradition; some of his verses included in Sikh scripture *Ādi Granth.*

Na·mier \'nā-(,)mi(ə)r\, Sir Lewis Bernstein. *Orig. surname* Bern·stein \'bərn-,stīn\. 1888–1960. British historian, b. Poland. To England (1906, naturalized 1913); adopted surname Namier (1913); in Foreign Office (1915–20); engaged in commerce, journalism, etc., to support research; professor, Manchester (1931–53). Author of *Structure of Politics at the Accession of George III* (1929), *England in the Age of the American Revolution* (1930), *1848: The Revolution of the Intellectuals* (1946), *Diplomatic Prelude* (1948), *Europe in Decay* (1950), etc. His 2d wife (m. 1947) ¶Julia Michaelovna, *nee* Ka·za·rin \(,)kə-'zär-yin\ (1893–1977), published under pseudonym Iulia de Beau·sobre \də-bō-söbrᵊ\ *The Woman Who Could Not Die* (1938) on her imprisonment in the Soviet Union, *Flame in the Snow* (1945) on St. Seraphim of Sarov, etc.

Nā·nak \'nän-ək\. *Called* Gu·rū \'gu̇-rü\, *i.e.* Teacher. 1469–?1539. Indian religious leader. In early years a Hindu in beliefs; visited Hindu and Muslim religious centers; settled in Punjabi village of Kartārpur; evolved devotional, contemplative religion of salvation known as Sikhism; wrote devotional hymns later included in scriptural *Ādi Granth;* chose disciple Angad to succeed him as Gurū.

Na·na Sa·hib \'nä-nä-'sä-hib\. *Orig.* Dhon·du Pant \'dən-du̇-'pənt\. c.1820–c.1859. Indian leader. A Marāthā; adopted (1827) by Bāji Rao II, last peshwa of Poona, but not allowed to inherit his pension; when mutiny broke out (1857) assumed leadership of sepoys in Cawnpore; promised English troops safety if they would capitulate, but treacherously murdered the men and later directed that the women and children be killed and cast in a well; often defeated by British and finally (1859) driven into Nepal; probably perished in Nepal hills.

Nan·da Ba·yin \'nän-dä-'bī-(y)in\. 16th century. King of Burma (1581–99). Son and successor of Bayinnaung; beset by rebellions of various relatives, of Siam, of the Mon people; besieged in capital Pegu by Siamese (1595); captured and deposed by brother with Mon aid, ending father's empire.

Nan·da·ku·mar \,nən-də-'kəm-ər\. *Also known as* Nun·co·mar \,nən-'kəm-ər\. d. 1775. Bengali Brahmin official. Governor of Hugli (1756); replaced Warren Hastings as collector of Burdwan (1764); accused Hastings of peculation as governor general but was indicted and executed for forgery.

Na·ni·ni \nä-'nē-nē\ *or* **Na·ni·no** \-nō\, Giovanni Maria. 1543 or 1544–1607. Italian composer. Associated with Palestrina; maestro di cappella, Santa Maria Maggiore, Rome (1567?–75), San Luigi dei Francesi (1575–77); member of papal choir (from 1577); with brother ¶Giovanni Bernardino (c.1560–1623) taught singing and composition; composed motets, madrigals, canons, etc.

Nan·ni di Ban·co \'nän-nē-dē-'bäŋ-kō\. 1380? or 1385?–1421. Florentine sculptor. Exemplified transition from Gothic to Renaissance styles; works included *Isaiah,* life-size marble statue for Florence cathedral (c.1408), *Quattro Coronati* for Or San Michele (c.1411–13), *Assumption* for Porta della Mandorla (begun c.1414; probably finished by Lucca della Robbia).

Nan·sen \'nän-sən\, Fridtjof. 1861–1930. Norwegian explorer, zoologist, and statesman. Curator, Museum of Natural History, Bergen (1882); headed first expedition to cross ice fields of Greenland (1888); headed expedition (1893) aiming to reach across North Pole by drifting; made fast his exploring vessel *Fram* to an ice floe, New Siberian Islands; drifted to about 84° N; left the *Fram* and, accompanied by F. H. Johansen (1895), pushed across to 86° 14′ N, then the highest latitude reached by man. Professor, Royal Frederick U. (from 1897); director, International Commission for Study of the Sea (1901); took active part in separation of Norway and Sweden (1905); first Norwegian minister to Great Britain (1906–08); made further oceanographic expeditions, chiefly in North Atlantic Ocean (1910–14). Led Norwegian delegation to first League of Nations assembly (1920); for League, directed repatriation of World War I prisoners; directed famine relief in Russia sponsored by Red Cross (1921–23) and relief work of League of Nations for Russian, Armenian, and Greek refugees; awarded Nobel peace prize (1922). Author of *Auf Schneeschuhen durch Grönland* (1891), *Eskimoliv* (1891), *Norwegian North Polar Expedition* (1893–96), *In Nacht und Eis* (1897), *Northern Waters* (1906), *Russland und der Friede* (1923), *Betrogenes Volk* (1928), etc.

Nan·teuil \näⁿ-tœy\, Robert. 1623 or 1630–1678. French engraver. Advanced engraving technique by his own precise style; appointed engraver and illustrator to the king (1657); mainly responsible for edict (1660) giving engravers the privileges of artists; executed portraits of Louis XIV, Mazarin, etc.

Nao·ro·ji \nau̇-'rō-jē\, Dadabhai. 1825–1917. Indian politician. Prime minister to Prince of Baroda (1874–76); president, Indian National Congress (1886, 1893, 1906); Liberal M.P. (1892–95), first Indian M.P.

Na·pier \'nā-pē-ər, -,pi(ə)r; nə-'pi(ə)r\, Sir Charles. 1786–1860. Scottish naval commander. Midshipman in British navy (1800); served in Napoleonic War, War of 1812; to Azores (1831) to assist supporters of Princess María of Portugal; made commander of Portuguese loyalist fleet (1833); destroyed fleet of pretender Dom Miguel off Cape St. Vincent (July 1833); created conde Napier de São Vicente in Portuguese peerage (1833); defended Lisbon (1834). Rejoined British navy (1839); took part in Syrian expedition (1840–41); commanded Turkish forces in capture of Beirut and Acre (1840); M.P. (1841); rear admiral (1846); commander of Channel fleet (1847–49); vice admiral (1853); commander of Baltic fleet (1854–55) at beginning of Crimean War; disappointed extravagant public expectations of him by declining to attack Russian naval base at Kronshtadt, removed; M.P. (1855–60); admiral (1858).

Napier, Sir Charles James. 1782–1853. British army officer. Served in Portugal (1810), against U.S. (1813); as military resident of Cephalonia (1822–33) met Byron and declined offer to become commander of Greek army; general in command in northern England during Chartist riots (1839–41); undertook (1842) the conquest of Sind; completed it by victory of Hyderābād (1843); governor of Sind (1843–47); subdued hill tribes (1844–45); given command in war against Sikhs but arrived after victory of Gujarat (1849); left India (1851). His brother ¶Sir George Thomas (1784–1855) entered army (1800); major general (1837); governor of Cape of Good Hope (1837–43); general (1854). A third brother ¶Sir William Francis Patrick (1785–1860) entered army (1800); served in Portugal (1809–11); retired (1819); lieutenant governor of Guernsey (1842–47); lieutenant general (1851). Author of *History of the War in the Peninsula* (1828–40) and *History of Conquest of Scinde* (1844–46), a defense of his brother Sir Charles James's decision to annex the Sind.

Napier *or* **Ne·per** \ˈnā-pər\, John. Laird of Mer·chis·ton \ˈmər-kə-stən\. 1550–1617. Scottish mathematician. A staunch Protestant; addressed to King James VI his *Plaine Discovery of the Whole Revelation of St. John* (1594). Invented logarithms, which he described in his *Mirifici Logarithmorum Canonis Descriptio* (1614), explaining in his *Mirifici Logarithmorum Canonis Constructio* (pub. 1619) their method of construction; pioneer in use of present system of decimal notation; invented "Napier's bones," mechanical devices for computing, described in his *Rabdologiae* (1617).

Napier, MacVey. 1776–1847. Scottish lawyer and editor. Signet librarian, Edinburgh (1805–37); professor, U. of Edinburgh (from 1824); edited Supplement (1815–24) to 4th, 5th, 6th editions of *Encyclopaedia Britannica;* edited 7th edition (1830–42); edited *Edinburgh Review* (from 1829).

Napier, Robert. 1791–1876. Scottish marine engineer. Built engines for first four steamers of Cunard Company (1840); built the *Persia* for Cunard Company (1854) and one of the earliest ironclad warships, H.M.S. *Black Prince* (1860).

Napier, Robert Cornelis. 1st Baron Napier of Mag·da·la \ˈmag-də-lə\. 1810–1890. British army officer, b. Ceylon. Engineer, chiefly of public works (1826–45); showed special engineering skill in first (1845) and second (1848) Sikh wars; built roads, canals, and defenses; in the Sepoy Mutiny (1857), instrumental in relieving and in recapturing Lucknow; by cutting road through jungle, effected capture of rebel leader Tantia Topi (1859); commanded 2d division in Chinese expedition (1860); on Indian governor general's council (1861–65); acting viceroy and governor general (1863); commander of Bombay army (1865–70); lieutenant general (1867); commanded punitive expedition against Ethiopia (1868) and took stronghold of Magdala; created baron (1868); commander in chief in India (1870–76); general (1874); governor of Gibraltar (1876–82); field marshal (1883).

Na·po·lé·on I \nȧ-pȯ-lā-ō^{n}, *Angl* nə-ˈpōl-yən, -ˈpō-lē-ən\. *Full name* Napoléon Bo·na·parte \bȯ-nȧ-pȧrt, *Angl* ˈbō-nə-ˌpärt\. *Ital.* Na·po·le·o·ne Buo·na·par·te \ˌnä-pō-lā-ˈō-nāb-wȯ-nä-ˈpär-tā\ *used by Napoléon until 1796. Called* le Pe·tit Ca·po·ral \ləp-tē-kȧ-pȯ-rȧl\, *i.e.* the Little Corporal. 1769–1821. Emperor of the French, b. Corsica. For family see BONAPARTE. At military schools of Brienne le Château (1779–84) and Paris (1784–85); second lieutenant in La Fère regiment of artillery (1785–91); in French revolutionary forces in Paris (1792), in Corsica (1792), at Marseilles, and in command of artillery that decided the conflict at siege of Toulon (1793); made general of brigade; as a Jacobin, held in prison after downfall of Robespierre (1794); took part in defense of Tuileries, driving Parisian mob from the streets with a "whiff of grapeshot" from his artillery (13 Vendémiaire, i.e. Oct. 5, 1795); commander of the army of the Interior (1795).

Italian and Egyptian Campaigns, First Consulate: m. Joséphine de Beauharnais (1796); sent by Directory to conduct Italian campaign (1796); won brilliant victory at Lodi; occupied Milan, defeated Austrians at Arcole (1796), and captured Mantua (1797); conquered northern Italy for France and forced Austrians beyond Alps; established Cisalpine and Ligurian republics; negotiated Treaty of Campo Formio (Oct. 17, 1797), contrary to orders of Directory. Returned to France; proposed conquest of Egypt as first step toward India; occupied Malta, landed at Alexandria, occupied Nile delta (July 1798); his fleet destroyed by Nelson in battle of the Nile (Aug. 1–2, 1798); invaded Syria and halted by British at Acre (1799); returned to Egypt, won victory at Aboukir (July 25, 1799), and suddenly returned to France on learning of formation of Second Coalition of powers (1799). Aided by Sieyès and Lucien Bonaparte, carried out coup d'état of 18 Brumaire (Nov. 9, 1799); overthrew Directory, dispersed Council of Five Hundred. With Sieyès and Roger Ducos as second and third consuls, formed provisional government; promulgated Constitution of Year VIII (1799). Raised new army, crossed Alps by Great St. Bernard pass, defeated Austrians at Marengo (June 14, 1800); signed Treaty of Lunéville (1801), and Treaty of Amiens with England (1802), favorable to France. Reorganized government on grand scale; negotiated Concordat of 1801 with Pius VII; reconstructed educational system; established Legion of Honor (1802); effected codification of laws of France as *Code Napoléon* (1804–10). Acclaimed consul for life (1802). Secured cession of Louisiana from Spain (1800) but failed to conquer Haiti (1802–03); abandoned dream of empire overseas by selling Louisiana to United States (1803). Third Coalition formed (1804), led by Pitt in England. Conspiracies against him hastened decision to make France a hereditary empire; crowned himself emperor at Paris (Dec. 2, 1804); assumed title of king of Italy (1805).

Empire: Planned invasion of England from Boulogne (1805), but finally recognized it as impossible; turned to campaign in Bavaria and Austria; won at Austerlitz (Dec. 2, 1805) over Austria and Russia; forced Treaty of Pressburg on Austria, ending Third Coalition; dissolved Holy Roman Empire (Aug. 6, 1806); virtual master of the Continent, but lost supremacy of the seas to England in defeat of Villeneuve by Nelson at Trafalgar (Oct. 21, 1805). Made his brother Joseph king of Naples (1806) and brother Louis king of Holland. Faced Fourth Coalition formed (1806–07) by Prussia, Russia, England, and Sweden; defeated Prussians at Jena and Auerstedt (Oct. 14, 1806); entered Warsaw; victorious in Polish campaign (1807) at Eylau and Friedland; met Alexander I of Russia on raft at Tilsit; forced Treaty of Tilsit (1807) that humbled Russia and ended Fourth Coalition. Issued decrees of Berlin (1806) and Milan (1807) establishing "continental system," closing Europe to British commerce; to enforce blockade, sent army under Junot into Portugal; later sent another army into Spain under Murat; invited Ferdinand of Spain to conference at Bayonne and imprisoned him (1808–14); proclaimed Joseph Bonaparte king of Spain (June 1808); Peninsular War (1808–14) begun. Fifth Coalition (Austria and England) formed (1809); led army into Austria, entered Vienna; fought indecisive battles of Aspern and Essling (May 1809); decisively defeated Austrians at Wagram (July 6); signed Treaty of Vienna (Schönbrunn). Erected kingdom of Westphalia for Jérôme Bonaparte; enlarged France by many annexations (Tuscany, Papal States, Holland, etc.); made Murat king of Naples (1808). Divorced Joséphine (1809) and m. Archduchess Maria Luisa of Austria (1810).

To enforce Treaty of Tilsit, led army of 400,000 across Russian frontier; won Borodino against Kutuzov; entered Moscow (Sept. 14); retreated with terrible losses (Oct.–Nov. 1812); lost prestige, found strong nationalist uprisings in Europe; defeated Allies at Bautzen (1813). Faced strong Sixth Coalition of powers; won last great victory at Dresden (Aug. 26–27, 1813); attacked by Allies and defeated in "Battle of the Nations" at Leipzig (Oct. 16–19); retreated to France; defeated Blücher and Schwarzenberg in brief brilliant defensive campaign (Jan.–Feb. 1814) but was later overwhelmed by numbers of Allies; Paris taken by Allies (Mar.); his generals (Ney, Soult, Suchet, Eugène de Beauharnais) defeated; deserted by Murat; abdicated at Fontainebleau (April 6); sent to Elba; Louis XVIII placed on throne by Allies.

The Hundred Days: Left Elba; landed at Cannes (Mar. 1, 1815); entered Paris (Mar. 20; beginning of Hundred Days); raised new armies; defeated Blücher at Ligny (June 16) while Ney fought Wellington at Quatre Bras on same day; defeated at Waterloo (June 18); fled to Paris; abdicated second time (June 22); Allies entered Paris (July 7); surrendered to British (July 15) on board the *Bellerophon;* landed on St. Helena (Oct. 16, 1815); under British governor, Sir Hudson Lowe (1816–21); remains removed (1840) by direction of Louis-Phillipe to Hôtel des Invalides, Paris.

Napoléon II. *Full name* François-Charles-Joseph Bonaparte. *Called* l'·Ai·glon \leg-lō^{n}\, *i.e.* the Eaglet. 1811–1832. Titular king of Rome, b. Paris. Son of Napoléon I; named as successor on abdication of his father (Apr. 1814), but Allies refused to accept him; lived at court of Vienna (1814–32); created duc de Reich·stadt \də-ˈrik-ˌshtät\ (1818); under control of Metternich.

Napoléon III. *Known as* Louis-Napoléon. *Full name* Charles-Louis-Napoléon Bonaparte. 1808–1873. Emperor of the French. Son of Louis Bonaparte, king of Holland, and nephew of Napoléon I; lived in exile with his mother in Germany and Switzerland (1815–30); took part in uprisings in Romagna (1830–31); forced to flee to France. On death of Napoléon II (1832), assumed headship of Bonaparte family; attempted to foment military coup d'état in Strasbourg (1836); discovered, sent to America, but soon returned (1837); attempted another coup (Boulogne, 1840); arrested, condemned to life imprisonment at fortress of Ham (1840), but escaped (1846) to England. Welcomed Revolution of 1848 in Paris; elected to National Assembly (1848) and later president of the Republic (Dec. 1848); opposed by royalists in call for revision of constitution to allow his reelection (1851); by coup d'état (Dec. 2, 1851), made himself dictator; elected president for 10 years (Dec. 21). Proclaimed himself emperor as Napoléon III (Dec. 2, 1852); at first (1852–56) successful in policy of concentration of power in emperor and of subordination of elected assemblies; m. (1853) Eugénie de Montijo, a Spanish countess. Caused France to join in Crimean War (1854–56); joined Sardinia against Austria (1859–60), aiding Italy in attaining unity; Savoy and Nice annexed

(1860); installed Archduke Maximilian of Austria as emperor of Mexico (1864), but his notion of a "Latin empire" was frustrated by Juárez, the Mexican people, and the threatening attitude of the U.S. Attacked by opposition parties; successful in a managed plebiscite that approved a constitutional monarchy (1870). Several imprudent acts and foolish boasts (1866–70) gave opportunity to Bismarck to involve France in the disastrous Franco–Prussian War (1870–71); joined army, captured at Sedan (Sept. 2, 1870); held as prisoner near Kassel, Germany, until end of war; deposed by National Assembly at Bordeaux (Mar. 1, 1871); retired with wife and son to Chislehurst, England.

Napper-Tandy, James. See TANDY.

Ná·prav·ník \'nä-práv-nyēk\, Eduard Francevič. 1839–1916. Czech pianist, conductor, and composer. Chief conductor (from 1869) of Imperial Russian Opera at St. Petersburg; also conducted Russian Musical Society (1869–81); composer of operas, including *Harold* (1886), *Dubrovsky* (1895), and chamber and orchestral works.

Na·rai \'när-,ī\ *or* **Na·ra·ya·na** \nä-'rī-ə-nə\. d. 1688. King of Siam (1657–88). Attempted unsuccessfully to curtail Dutch power; forced by blockade to grant further concessions (1664); encouraged French missionaries and cultivated French alliance; forced to accept French garrison in Bangkok (1687).

Na·ra·meikh·la \när-ä-'mīk-lä\. *Also called* Meng Soam·wun \'meŋ-'swäm-wu̇n\. d. 1434. King of Arakan (1404–34). Son of King Rajathu; driven from Arakan by Burmese–Mon conflict (1404); became vassal of Aḥmad Shāh of Gaur; regained Arakan (1430); built new capital Mrohaung and established Mrohaung dynasty, which lasted to 18th century.

Na·ram-Sin \nä-'räm-'sin\. c.2254–c.2218 B.C. King of Akkad. Fourth king of the Akkadian dynasty founded by Sargon; events of his reign uncertain, but records indicate that he made wide conquests, invading Arabia and Syria.

Narasimhavarman. See PALLAVA.

Na·ra·yan \nə-'rī-ən\, Jaya Prakash. *Also written* Jai Prakash Narain. 1902–1979. Indian politician. Imprisoned for civil disobedience (1932–33); led in founding Congress Socialist party (1933); imprisoned (1939, 1943–46) for opposition to World War II; founded Indian Socialist party (1952); abandoned politics (1954) to work in Bhoodan Yajna agrarian reform movement; resumed political activity as opponent of Indira Gandhi (1974); imprisoned (1975); formed coalition Janata party to oppose Gandhi in elections (1977).

Narboni, Moses. See MOSES of Narbonne.

Nar·cis·sus \när-'sis-əs\. d. 54 A.D. Roman freedman. Secretary to Emperor Claudius; with Empress Messalina, established ascendancy over Claudius; assisted Messalina in procuring death of a number of persons; after Messalina's marriage to Silius, betrayed her to Claudius and secured order for her execution; subsequently fell from favor; imprisoned, committed sucide after Nero's accession.

Nar·di \'när-dē\, Jacopo. 1476–after 1563. Florentine politician and historian. Held various municipal posts after expulsion of Medici (1494); supporter of Savonarola; exiled on fall of republic (1531), lived thereafter in Venice. Author of valuable *Istorie della citta' di Firenze* (1582); also wrote verse comedies.

Nar·di·ni \när-'dē-nē\, Pietro. 1722–1793. Italian violinist. Soloist at court of Stuttgart (1753–67); director of music at Tuscan court (1770–93); renowned for beauty of his playing; composer of concertos, sonatas, string quartets, etc.

Nares \'ne(ə)rz, 'na(ə)rz\, Sir George Strong. 1831–1915. British naval officer, b. Scotland. Entered navy (1845); captain of *Challenger* (1872–74) in southern seas expedition; commanded *Alert* and *Discovery* in Arctic expedition (1875–76); commanded *Alert* in survey of Magellan Straits (1878); rear admiral (1887), vice admiral (1892).

Na·res·uan \,när-e-'swän\. *Orig.* Phra Na·ret \'prä-när-'et\. *Known as* the Black Prince. c.1555–1605. King of Siam (1590–1605). Son of King Maha Dhammaraja, a vassal of Bayinnaung of Burma; governor of Phitsanulok province (1571); renounced allegiance to Burma (1584) and defeated Burmese armies sent to restore power; as king assumed offensive; established rule over Cambodia and seized Burmese territory; laid foundation for later Siamese power and prosperity. Regarded as national liberator.

Narottama. See NORODOM.

Nar·ses \'när-,sēz\ *or* **Nar·seh** \'når-,se\. d. c.302 A.D. King of Persia (293–302) of Sāsānian dynasty. Son of Shāpūr I; seized throne from his grandnephew Bahrām III; made war on Rome; defeated Galerius but, badly beaten in Armenia (296), concluded a peace with Romans that lasted 40 years.

Narses. c.480–574. Byzantine general. A eunuch; rose to command of Justinian I's imperial bodyguard; aided Belisarius in putting down Nika riot (532); sent to Italy (538) to support and spy on Belisarius; commanded forces against barbarians in Balkans and Italy (551–553); conquered Totila, leader of the Ostrogoths, and finally the last Gothic army in Italy; by subduing Alemanni and Franks (553–555), brought Italy again under Justinian's rule; prefect of Italy (554–567); dismissed by Justin II.

Na·ru·sze·wicz \,nå-rü-'shev-ēch\, Adam Stanisław. 1733–1796. Polish prelate, historian, and poet. Entered Jesuit order (1748); bishop of Smolensk (1788), of Lutsk (Łuck, 1790); court poet and historiographer to Stanisław II; chief work *Historja narodu polskiego* (History of the Polish Nation, 1780–86). Also wrote verse idylls and satires.

Na·ru·to·wicz \,nå-rü-'tȯ-vēch\, Gabriel. 1865–1922. Polish engineer and politician. Minister of public works (1920–22); foreign minister (1922); elected president of Poland to succeed Piłsudski; assassinated by a madman a few days after he assumed office.

Nar·vá·ez \när-'b̲ä-āth, -ās\, Pánfilo de. c.1480–1528. Spanish soldier. To America (c.1498); aided in conquest of Cuba (1511); sent to Mexico to arrest Cortés and bring him back (1520); surprised near Veracruz by Cortés, captured, and kept prisoner for two years (1520–22); returned to Spain; secured permission to conquer and govern territory of Florida; sailed from Spain (1527); reached Florida (1528) after great hardships and losses; constructed small boats at Apalachee Bay and set out for Mexico; lost at sea in Gulf of Mexico.

Nar·vá·ez \när-'b̲ä-āth\, Ramón María. Duque de Va·len·cia \b̲ä-'lān-thyä\. 1800–1868. Spanish general and politician. As supporter of Isabella II fought in Catalonia against Carlists (1834–36); opposed Espartero in Cortes (from 1838); succeeded him in the council (1843); created duke (1844); prime minister (1844–46); promulgated constitution of 1845; again prime minister (1847–51); reactionary in his policy, lost support, and quarreled with former Queen Maria Christina; in power (1856–57, 1864–65, and 1866–68), his chief rival being O'Donnell; died shortly before deposition of Isabella II.

Na·rysh·ki·na \(,)nə-'rish-kyin-ə\, Natalya Kirillovna. 1651–1694. Consort of Czar Alexis of Russia. Daughter of nobleman, educated in Western manner; m. as 2d wife Czar Alexis (1671); following birth of son Peter, her family and adherents formed court faction; on death of Alexis (1676) Naryshkin party promoted succession of Peter; lost influence to Miloslavsky faction supporting elder son Fyodor; on death of Fyodor (1682) became regent for Peter, who won succession through aid of Patriarch Ioakim; forced to recognize Ivan V as co-ruler and Sophia as regent; rallied supporters and forced Sophia to yield throne to Peter alone (1689); largely in control of government (1689–94).

Nasby, Petroleum V. See David Ross LOCKE.

Nas·ci·men·to \nåsh-sē-'mãⁿ(n)-tü\, Francisco Manoel do. *Pseudonym* Filinto Eli·sio \ā-'lē-zyü\. 1734–1819. Portuguese poet. Ordained priest (1754); ordered arrested by Inquisition on charge of heterodoxy, fled to France (1778); settled in Paris; his poetry, highly varied in theme and style and developing from early Neoclassicism to full Romanticism, was subsequently collected in 22 vols. (1836–40).

Nāṣer. See also NĀṢIR.

Nā·ṣer-e Khos·row \'nás-er-e-'k̲ȯs-rō\. *In full* Abū Mo'īn Nāṣer-e Khosrow al-Marvāzī al-Qubādiyānī. 1004–c.1072 or 1077. Persian poet and theologian. Traveled (1045) to Mecca, Palestine, and Egypt, where he became a missionary for Ismā'īlī form of Islām; after return home, forced to flee to Badakhshān for heresy. Author of prose travel description *Safarname,* philosophical verse *Rawshana'ināme* and *Jāmi' al-ḥikmatayn.*

Nā·ṣer od-Dīn \'nás-er-u̇d-'dēn\. 1831–1896. Shāh of Iran (1848–96). Son of Moḥammad Shāh; instituted numerous reforms through chief minister Mīrzā Taqī Khān; later became more conservative; seized Herāt (1856) but forced by British to return it; granted various concessions to Europeans, causing growing nationalist sentiment; assassinated.

Nash \'nash\, Francis. 1742?–1777. American Revolutionary officer, b. Prince Edward Co., Va. Served in North Carolina militia against Regulators (1771); lieutenant colonel (1775), colonel (1776) of 1st N.C. regiment; brigadier general, Continental army (1777); mortally wounded at battle of Germantown (Oct. 4, 1777). Nash Co., N.C., and Nashville, Tenn., named for him.

Nash, John. 1752–1835. English architect. Known for street improvements in London; under patronage of Prince of Wales (later George IV), laid out Regent's Park and its terraces (1811); designed Regent Street (1813–20); redesigned Buckingham House, which became known (1825) as Buckingham Palace; redesigned St. James's Park (1827–29).

Nash, Ogden, *in full* Frederic Ogden. 1902–1971. American writer, b. Rye, N.Y. Author esp. of humorous and prosodically unorthodox verse, as in *Hard Lines* (1931), *The Primrose Path* (1935), *I'm a Stranger Here Myself* (1938), *Good Intentions* (1942), *Musical Zoo* (1947), *Versus* (1949), *You Can't Get There From Here* (1957), *Everyone But Thee and Me* (1962); wrote libretto for musical *One Touch of Venus* (1943, with S.J. Perelman).

Nash, Paul. 1889–1946. English painter, printmaker, photographer. Official war artist (1917, 1940); known chiefly for landscapes, influenced by Cubism and Surrealism but intensely personal in style; in last years did notable series of flower studies. Works included *The Menin Road, Wall Against the Sea, Oxenbridge Pond, Totes Meer.* Also did book illustrations, wood engravings.

Nash, Richard. 1674–1762. English gamester and social arbiter. Known as "Beau Nash" and "King of Bath"; master of ceremonies at Bath (from 1705); made Bath highly fashionable watering-place; virtually abolished dueling; invented new games of chance to evade gaming laws (until stricter legislation of 1745).

Nash *or* **Nashe** \'nash\, Thomas. 1567–?1601. English pamphleteer and dramatist. Became professional writer in London (1588); produced *Anatomie* *of absurditie* (1589); joined in Martin Marprelate controversy (1589–90) on side of the episcopacy, under pseudonym Pas·quil \'pas-kwəl\; waged bitter controversy with Gabriel Harvey, defending both Robert Greene, author of *Menaphon,* and himself, with *Pierce Penilesse, his supplication to the divell* (1592), *Strange newes* (1592), *Christes teares* (1593), *Have with you to Saffron Walden* (1596), until controversy was suppressed by archbishop of Canterbury (1599). Pioneered English picaresque novel in *The unfortunate traveller, or the life of Jack Wilton* (1594); wrote satirical masque *Summers last Will* (1592); finished Marlowe's tragedy *Dido* (1596); imprisoned because of satire of the state in comedy *The Isle of Dogs;* last work a burlesque panegyric of red herring of Yarmouth, *Lenten stuffe* (1599).

Nash, Sir Walter. 1882–1968. New Zealand politician, b. England. To N.Z. (1909); Labourite member of N.Z. Parliament (1929–68); minister of finance (1935), of marketing (1936–40), of social security (1940–41); minister to U.S. (1942–44); member of Pacific War Council (1942–44); leader of Labour party (from 1950); prime minister of New Zealand (1957–60).

Na·si \'nás-ē\, Joseph, *baptized* João Miguez. 1520–1579. Portuguese Jewish financier and statesman. Gained competence in employ of Mendes banking house in Antwerp; settled in Istanbul (1554) and declared himself a Jew; gained high favor with Sultan Süleyman; made duke of Naxos by Sultan Selim II (1566); prompted Ottoman attack on Cyprus (1571).

Nasier, Alcofribas. See François RABELAIS.

Nā·ṣir, an- \ən-'nä-sər\. d. 1225. Caliph of Baghdad (1180–1225). Longest reign of all caliphs; reign noted for lavish display and ambitious building.

Nā·ṣir \'nä-sər\, al-Malik an-. 1284–1340. Mamlūk sultan of Egypt (1293–1340) of Bahri dynasty. His reign one of longest in Muslim annals; his army defeated (1299) by Mongols, who for a time occupied northern Syria; subdued Druzes and Maronites of Lebanon (1300–02).

Nāṣir ad-Daw·lah \-ùd-'daù-lä\. d. 969. Muslim prince. Son of governor of Mosul; succeeded (929) to leadership of Ḥamdānid family; expanded family authority in Syria and Iraq; failed in attempts (934, 938) to gain Azerbaijan; rivaled the caliph in power; pursued ruinous tax policies, amassing vast wealth at expense of subjects and family; deposed, imprisoned, killed by other Ḥamdānid princes.

Nas·myth \'nā-ˌsmith, 'nāz-məth\, Alexander. 1758–1840. Scottish painter. Intimate of Robert Burns and painted his portrait; became "father of Scottish landscape art"; invented bowstring bridge (1794).

Nasmyth, James. 1808–1890. Scottish engineer. Son of Alexander Nasmyth; began manufacture of machine tools at Manchester (1834), developed Bridgewater Foundry; invented steam hammer (1839), constructed and patented it (1842); devised a planing machine, a nut-shaping machine, a steam pile driver, a hydraulic punching machine; also studied astronomy.

Naṣ·rid \'näs-rēd\. Name of last Muslim dynasty in Spain, ruling in Granada (1238–1492); founded by Muḥammad I al-Ghālib (*q.v.*) and named for his grandfather Naṣr.

Nas·sau \'näs-ˌaù, *Angl* 'nas-ˌò\. Princely family of Europe, deriving its name from a county on the east bank of the Rhine, north of Mainz; founded by Walram I (d. 1198); divided (1255) into two branches.

I. The elder line (German), founded by Walram II; occupied south part of region continuously till its absorption by Prussia (1866); Adolf of Nassau (*q.v.*), son of Walram II, was king of Germany (1292–98); later, line divided into several branches but by 1816 all extinct except Nassau-Weil·burg \-vīl-bùrk\; erected into a duchy (1806); when Duke Adolf (1817–1905, *q.v.*) sided with Austria (1866), Prussia seized duchy; grand duchy of Luxembourg passed to duke of Nassau (1890).

II. The cadet line (Dutch), founded by Otto I (d. about 1292); occupied north part of region; division of territory among Otto's three sons gave rise to several branches: (1) Engelbert (or Engelbrecht) I, of Nassau-Dil·len·burg \-'dil-ən-ˌbùrk\ branch, acquired by marriage (1404) lands in the Low Countries; a descendant, Henry III, inherited both German and Dutch possessions; Henry's son René (*q.v.*) also inherited the principality of Orange; at René's death without issue, all lands went to his cousin William I, Count of Nassau (*q.v.*), who founded first line of Or·ange-Nassau \ō-'rän-zhə-; *Angl* 'òr-inj-, 'är-, -ənj-\. Stadholders of the Netherlands who, as princes of Orange-Nassau, succeeded William I were: Maurice, Frederick Henry, William II, and William III (*qq.v.*). (2) The four sons of John VI, Count of Nassau, a brother of William I, who ruled Nassau-Dillenburg (to 1606), founded new branches, two of these being extinct by 1739; the eldest son was John Maurice (*q.v.*), Graaf van Nassau-Sie·gen \-'zē-gən\, this branch being extinct by 1743; the third son, Ernest Casimir, founded (1606) line of Nassau-Dietz \-dets\; a descendant, John William Friso (*q.v.*), inherited possessions of Orange in the Netherlands; his son William IV reunited (1743) all lands of house of Orange and became hereditary stadholder (1747); title lost by William V (1795) when driven out by Napoléon; his son William VI lost Nassau (1806) by refusing to adhere to Confederation of the Rhine, but became king of the Netherlands (1815) as William I; family continued as house of Orange (sometimes still called Orange-Nassau) on throne of the Netherlands (from 1815); see WILLIAM I, II, and III; WILHELMINA.

Nas·ser \'näs-ər, *Angl also* 'nas-\, Gamal Abdel. 1918–1970. Egyptian soldier and politician. Founded secret nationalist society of army officers and led it in overthrowing King Farouk (1952); head of ruling revolutionary council (1952–56); prime minister (1954–56); promulgated constitution (1956); president of Egypt (1956–58); nationalized Suez Canal (1956); formed United Arab Republic (1958; included Syria 1958–61) and was its president (1958–70); built Aswan High Dam on Nile (completed 1968); defeated in war with Israel (1967).

Nast \'nast\, Condé Montrose. 1873–1942. American publisher, b. New York City. Joined *Collier's Weekly* (1898); bought *Vogue* (1909), *Vanity Fair* (1914), *House and Garden* (1915), etc.; began British (1916) and French (1920) editions of *Vogue;* formed Condé Nast Publications (1922); introduced *Glamour* (1939).

Nast, Thomas. 1840–1902. American cartoonist, b. Landau, Germany. To U.S. (1846); illustrator on staff of *Frank Leslie's Illustrated Newspaper* (1855–59); staff artist of *Harper's Weekly* (1862–86); at height of career, attacked (1869–72) Tweed Ring in New York; his cartoons largely responsible for overthrow of the ring; credited with devising elephant and donkey symbols of Republican and Democratic parties, with creating American image of Santa Claus, etc.; U.S. consul, Guayaquil, Ecuador (1902).

Natalis, Alexander. See Alexandre NOËL.

Na·than \'nā-thən\, George Jean. 1882–1958. American editor and critic, b. Fort Wayne, Ind. Drama critic for *Outing* and *Bohemian* magazines (1906–14); with H.L. Mencken, coeditor of *Smart Set* (1914–23); with Mencken founded and edited (1924–30) *The American Mercury;* contributing editor (1925–30); a founder and editor, with Dreiser, O'Neill, Sherwood Anderson, etc., of *The American Spectator* (1932). Author of *The Eternal Mystery* (1913), *Another Book on the Theatre* (1916), *The Theatre, the Drama, the Girls* (1921), *The Critic and the Drama* (1922), *The New American Credo* (1927), *Passing Judgments* (1934), *The Morning After the First Night* (1938), *Encyclopedia of the Theatre* (1940), *The Entertainment of a Nation* (1942), *Theatre Book of the Year* (annually 1943–51), etc.

Nat·horst \'nát-hòrst\, Alfred Gabriel. 1850–1921. Swedish geologist, paleobotanist, and explorer. Director of a division of the Riks-Museum of Natural History, Stockholm (1885–1917); explored in Greenland (1883); led expedition to Bear Island, Spitsbergen, and King Charles Island (1898); visited (1899) Jan Mayen, eastern Greenland, and Franz Josef Fjord, and discovered King Oscar Fjord.

Na·tion \'nā-shən\, Carry Amelia, *nee* Moore. 1846–1911. American temperance agitator, b. Garrard Co., Ky. m. 2d David Nation (1877; div. 1901). Resident in Kansas (from 1889), a prohibition state; maintained that, since the saloon was illegal in Kansas, any citizen could destroy liquor, furniture, and fixtures in a place selling intoxicants; armed with a hatchet, went on wrecking expeditions through Kansas cities and towns (1899–1909), including one "hatchetation" of Kansas State senate saloon (1901); often arrested, imprisoned, fined, and clubbed or shot at.

Na·torp \'nä-ˌtòrp\, Paul Gerhard. 1854–1924. German philosopher. Professor, Marburg (from 1885); a leader of Marburg neo-Kantian school. Author of *Sozialpädagogik* (1899), *Philosophie und Pädagogik* (1909), *Die logischen Grundlagen der exakten Wissenschaft* (1910), *Sozialidealismus* (1920), etc.

Na·tsu·me \nät-sùm-e\ Kinosuke. *Pseudonym* Natsume Sōseki. 1867–1916. Japanese novelist. Lecturer in English at Tokyo U. (1903–07); author of novels of manners and of the isolation of modern man, including *Wagahai-wa Neko-de aru* (1905–06), *Botchan* (1906), *Kusamakura* (1906), *Mon* (1910), *Kōjin* (1912–13), *Kokoro* (1914).

Nat·ta \'nät-tä\, Giulio. 1903–1979. Italian chemist. Professor, Milan Polytechnic Inst. (1938–74); awarded Nobel prize in chemistry (1963) with K. Ziegler for studies on the chemistry and technology of high polymers, esp. polypropylenes.

Nat·tier \nát-yā\, Jean-Marc. 1685–1766. French painter. Summoned by Peter the Great to paint portraits of him and Empress Catherine (1715); also for Peter executed *Battle of Poltava;* achieved great success with classical portraits of members of family and court of Louis XV.

Nau, John-Antoine. See Eugène TORQUET.

Nau·dé \nō-dā\, Gabriel. 1600–1653. French physician, librarian, and historian. Honorary physician to Louis XIII (1633); librarian to Cardinal Mazarin (from 1642) and collector of the 40,000-volume Bibliothèque Mazarine. Author of influential *Avis pour dresser une bibliothèque* (1627).

Nau·mann \'naù-män\, Friedrich, *in full* Joseph Friedrich. 1860–1919. German clergyman, publicist, and politician. Early a follower of Stoecker's

Christian Social movement; a contributor to *Die Hilfe;* founder (with Hellmuth von Gerlach and others, 1896) and first president, National Social Union; member of the Reichstag (1907–12, 1913–18); cofounder and a leader (1918) of the German Democratic party. Founded and edited *Die Zeit* (1896–97, 1901–03). Wrote *Mitteleuropa* (1915), etc.

Naumann, Johann Gottlieb. 1741–1801. German composer. Kapellmeister in Dresden (1776–77); appointed to reform Hofkapelle of Gustav II in Stockholm, for whom he wrote opera *Gustaf Wasa* (1786); returned to Dresden as Oberkapellmeister (1786). Other operas included *La clemenza di Tito* (1769), *Solimano* (1773), *Orpheus og Eurydike* (1786, for Copenhagen Royal Opera), *La dama soldato* (1791); also wrote much sacred music.

Naumann, Karl Friedrich. 1797–1873. German mineralogist and geologist. Son of Johann G. Naumann; professor, Freiburg (1826–42), Leipzig (1842–72); identified monoclinic series of crystals in *Grundriss der Krystallographie* (1825); also wrote *Lehrbuch der reinen und angewandten Krystallographie* (1830), *Elemente der Mineralogie* (1846), *Lehrbuch der Geognosie* (1850–54).

Naun·dorff *or* **Naun·dorf** \'naůn-ˌdôrf\, Karl Wilhelm. 1787–1845. French clockmaker. In Germany (1812–28); assumed title duc de Normandie (1824) and claimed to be the Dauphin Louis-Charles (son of Louis XVI and Marie-Antoinette), whom he greatly resembled in appearance; went to Paris (1833) to push claims; expelled from France (1836). See LOUIS XVII.

Na·va·'i \nä-vä-'ē\, Mir Ali Shir. 1441–1501. Turkish poet and scholar. Held offices at caliphal court of Herāt; disciple of dervish master Jāmī; wrote early works in Persian but later turned to native Chagatai Turkish, becoming outstanding exponent of Chagatai literature. Works included a version of Islāmic romance *Farhād and shīrīn,* prose *Muhakamat al-lugatayn, Majālis an-nafāis, Mizan al-awzan.*

Na·var·re·te \nä-b̲är-'re-tā\, Domingo Fernández. 1610–1686. Spanish missionary. Entered Dominican order (1635); to Philippines (1648); worked in Fukien and Chekiang provinces, China (1658–69); archbishop of Santo Domingo (1677 ff.).

Navarrete, Juan Fernández de. *Called* el Mu·do \el-'mü-t̲h̲ō\, *i.e.* the Mute. c.1526–1579. Spanish painter. Influenced by Titian; painted in Mannerist style; court painter to Philip II (from 1568); employed (from 1576) on decoration of the Escorial, completing eight altarpieces before his death.

Na·var·ro \nä-'b̲är-rō\, Pedro. 1460?–1528. Spanish soldier. Known for his developments in use of mines in warfare, esp. against castles of Naples (1503); in service of Gonzalo de Córdoba against Naples (1500–07); with Cardinal Cisneros in conquest of Oran (1509); commanded in conquest of Tripoli (1510).

Navero, Emiliano González. See GONZÁLEZ NAVERO.

Na·vez \ˌnä-'vez\, François Joseph. 1787–1869. Belgian painter. Influenced esp. by David, of whom he painted a notable portrait; inaugurated 19th-century renaissance in Belgian painting.

Na·vier \nȧv-yā\, Claude-Louis-Marie-Henri. 1785–1836. French civil engineer. Entered Corps des Ponts et Chaussées (1806); edited works of his granduncle Emiland Gauthey (from 1807); also edited works of Bernard Bélidor; pioneer in application of mathematical analysis to engineering; published equations for equilibrium and vibration of elastic solid (1821); published systematic treatment of strength of materials and structural analysis (1826); derived Navier-Stokes equation on momentum of fluids.

Na·ville \nȧ-vēl\, Édouard-Henri. 1844–1926. Swiss Egyptologist. Conducted excavations in Egypt (1883–1913); discovered tomb of Hatshepsut; professor, Geneva (from 1891); president, International Red Cross (1916–19). Author of *Das ägyptische Todtenbuch* (1886), *Bubastis* (1889), *La Religion des anciens Égyptiens* (1906), *Archaeology of the Old Testament* (1913), *The Law of Moses* (1920), etc.

Nawānagar, Maharaja of. See RANJITSINHJI VIBHAJI.

Nay·ler \'nā-lər\, James. c.1617–1660. English religious leader. Served in Parliamentary army (1642–50); joined Quakers; convinced that he was incarnation of Christ, rode into Bristol in imitation of Christ; convicted of blasphemy (1656) and sentenced to pillory, whipping, branding, and imprisonment.

Na·zi·mo·va \(ˌ)näz-'yē-mə-və, *Angl* nə-'zim-ə-və\, Alla. *Orig.* Alla Le·ven·ton \'lyāv-yin-tən\. 1878–1945. American actress, b. the Crimea, Russia. Studied under Stanislavsky in Moscow; debut in St. Petersburg (1904); to New York with Paul Orlenev company (1905); best known for interpretation of Ibsen roles; outstanding also in O'Neill's *Mourning Becomes Electra* (1931); appeared in motion pictures.

Naẓ·ẓām, an- \an-naz-'zäm\, Ibrāhīm. *In full* Abū Isḥāq Ibrāhīm ibn Sayyār ibn Hanī' an-Naẓẓām. c.775–c.845. Muslim theologian. Championed traditional orthodoxy against Hellenism of Mu'tazilites; dealt with problem of free will.

Nea·gle \'nē-gəl\, John. 1796–1865. American painter, b. Boston. Studio in Philadelphia; son-in-law of Thomas Sully; known as portraitist; works included *Gilbert Stuart, Washington, Pat Lyon at the Forge.*

Neal, Neale. See also NEILL.

Neal \'nē(ə)l\, Daniel. 1678–1743. English clergyman and historian. Author of *History of the Puritans* (1732–38).

Neal, John. 1793–1876. American writer, b. Portland, Me. His works included novels as *Keep Cool* (1817), *Logan* (1822), *Seventy-Six* (1823), *The Down-Easters* (1833), *True Womanhood* (1859), etc.; influential as a critic, esp. during English sojourn (1823–27); first to praise Poe in print.

Neale \'nē(ə)l\, Edward Vansittart. 1810–1892. English reformer. Pioneer in Christian Socialist and cooperative movements (from 1851); founded first cooperative store in London; founder (1851), general secretary (1875–91), Central Co-operative Board; instrumental in passing the Consolidation Act of 1862.

Neale, John Mason. 1818–1866. English hymnologist. Ordained (1842); founded Anglican nursing sisterhood of St. Margaret's (1854); translated ancient and medieval hymns, and Bernard of Cluny's *De contemptu mundi* including the hymns "For thee, O dear, dear country," "Jerusalem the golden," "O happy band of pilgrims." Author of *An Introduction to the History of the Holy Eastern Church* (1850).

Ne·an·der \nā-'än-dər\, Johann August Wilhelm. *Orig.* David Men·del \'men-dəl\. 1789–1850. German historian and theologian, of Jewish parentage. Pupil of Schleiermacher; embraced Christianity (1806); professor of church history, Berlin (from 1813). Author of *Allgemeine Geschichte der christliche Religion und Kirche* (1825–52).

Ne·ar·chus \nē-'är-kəs\. d. 312? B.C. Macedonian soldier. Satrap of Lycia and Pamphylia (333 B.C.); for Alexander the Great, commanded fleet in its journey from mouth of the Indus to head of Persian Gulf (325–324); after death of Alexander (323), joined Antigonus and regained Lycia and Pamphylia.

Neb·u·chad·rez·zar \ˌneb-(y)ə-kə-'drez-ər\. *Also spelled* Neb·u·chad·nez·zar \-'nez-ər\. *Bab.* Nabu-kudurri-usur. *Gr.* Nab·u·cho·don·o·sor \nab-(y)ə-kō-'dän-ə-ˌsȯr\ *or* Nab·u·go·don·o·sor \-gō-\. Name of two kings of Babylon:

Nebuchadrezzar I. 12th century B.C. King (c.1124–1103 B.C.) of 2d Isin dynasty. Conquered Elam, ruled most of Mesopotamia.

Nebuchadrezzar II. c.630–562 B.C. Chaldean king of Babylon (605–562 B.C.). Son of Nabopolassar; sent by father on expedition against Necho II of Egypt (610); defeated Necho at Carchemish (605); conquered Palestine, capturing Jerusalem (597); carried Jewish king Jehoiachin and many Jews as prisoners to Babylon; appointed Zedekiah king as his vassal; after Zedekiah's rebellion (588), besieged Jerusalem (587–586), destroyed it, and for second time carried Jews in exile to Babylon; took Tyre (573) after siege of 13 years; conducted campaign against Egypt (568); restored Babylon and other cities; rebuilt walls, palaces, temples, etc. Succeeded by his son AWIL-MARDUK.

Ne·ca·ti \nā-jä-'tə\ *or* **Ne·ja·ti** \-zhä-\, Īsa. d. 1509. Turkish poet. Probably born a slave; to Istanbul (c.1480), in service of Ottoman princes; wrote graceful and refined verse that earned him reputation as first great lyric poet in Ottoman literature.

Ne·cha·yev \nyi-'chȧ-yəf\, Sergey Gennadiyevich. 1847–1882. Russian revolutionary. An agitator from student days; founded (1869) professional revolutionary group; notorious for ruthless murder of a fellow member (1869); fled to Switzerland, arrested and returned (1872), died in prison. Model for Pyotr Verkhovensky in Dostoyevsky's *The Possessed.*

Ne·cho \'nē-ˌkō\. *Sometimes known as* Necho I. fl. c.672–664 B.C. Egyptian ruler. Installed as governor of Sais by Esarhaddon of Assyria (671 B.C.); deposed by Taharqa but restored by Ashurbanipal (667); survived further conquests by Kushites and Assyrians; ancestor of 26th dynasty of Egypt, founded by his son Psamtik I.

Necho II. d. 595 B.C. King of Egypt (610–595 B.C.) of 26th dynasty. Son of Psamtik I; in aid of Assyrians, completely defeated (608 B.C.) Jews under Josiah at Megiddo in Palestine; lost Asiatic possessions when defeated (605) by Nebuchadrezzar at Carchemish; maintained fleet at Nile delta and on Red Sea; attempted to dig canal from Bubastis to Red Sea; said by Herodotus to have sent an expedition (c.600) under Phoenician leaders that circumnavigated Africa.

Ne·chuv \'nyā-chüf\, Ivan. *Pseudonym* Ivan Le·vits·ky \lyiv-'yit-skəi\. 1838–1918. Ukrainian novelist. Author of realistic novels *Prichepa* (1869), *Khmari* (1871), *Burlachka* (1876), *Kaydasheva simya* (1878).

Neck·am \'nek-əm\ *or* **Nech·am** \'nek-əm\, Alexander. *Punningly nicknamed* Ne·quam \'nē-ˌkwam\, *Latin* wicked. 1157–1217. English scholar. Abbot of Cirencester (1213). Author of *De naturis rerum* and of *De utensilibus,* in which he recorded for first time outside of China use of a magnetic needle by mariners.

Neck·er \nā-ker, ne-; *Angl* nā-'ke(ə)r, 'nek-ər\, Jacques. 1732–1804. French financier and statesman, b. Geneva. Apprentice in Paris banking house (1750–62); set up banking business (1762) and gained fortune during Seven Years' War (1756–63); resident minister of Geneva in Paris (from 1768); retired from banking (1772). Named director of royal treasury (1776), director general of finance (1777); introduced mild reforms; incurred opposition in financing American Revolution and forced to resign (1781). Recalled as director general of finance (1788); virtually premier of France; presented program of liberal reform to Estates-General (1789) but failed to press it effectively; his second dismissal was an immediate cause of storming of Bastille (July 12–14, 1789); held third ministry under Talleyrand and Mirabeau (1789–90); retired to his estate near Geneva. Best known work *Administration des finances* (1784). His wife (m. 1764) ¶Suzanne, *nee* Cur·chod \kœr-shō\ (1739–1794), daughter of a pastor near Lausanne, had been engaged to Edward Gibbon; a talented author, and hostess to political, financial, and literary leaders of the time. Their daughter was Madame de Staël.

Nec·ta·ne·bo \nek-'tan-ə-,bō, -tə-'neb-(,)ō\. Name of two kings of Egypt of the 30th dynasty:

Nectanebo I. *Also called* Nekht·nebf *or* Nekht·neb·ef \nekt-'neb-əf\. d. 363 B.C. King (380–363 B.C.). Orig. a general; usurped throne of Nepherites II and founded 30th dynasty (380); repelled Persians at Mendes (373) when Pharnabazus hesitated in his attack.

Nectanebo II. *Also called* Nekht·har·heb \nekt-'här-,(h)eb\ *or* Nekht·ha·reh·be \-'här-,eb-ə\. d. after 343 B.C. King (360–343 B.C.). Nephew of Tachos, whom he deposed (360) with aid of Agesilaus II of Sparta; repelled Persians under Artaxerxes III (350) but forced to flee to Memphis and thence to Nubia from successful Persian invasion (343). Last ruler of 30th dynasty.

Ned·bal \'ned-bäl\, Oskar. 1874–1930. Czech violist, conductor, and composer. Played with Czech Quartet (1891–1906); conductor of Czech Philharmonic (1896–1906), Tonkünstlerorchester, Vienna (1906–18), etc. Composed orchestral, chamber, piano music, ballets, and popular operettas as *Die keusche Barbora* (1911), *Karl* (1913), *Die Winzerbraut* (1916).

Ne·der·burgh \'nā-dər-,bœrḡ\, Sebastian Cornelius. 1762–1811. Dutch politician. Lawyer for Dutch East Indies Co. (1787); governor general in Batavia (1791 ff.); author of charter under which East Indian colonies came under direct control of Dutch government (1801).

Ne·dim \nā-'dēm\, Ahmed. 1681–1730. Turkish poet. Friend and protégé of Ibrahim Paşa; author of vivid and charming odes, lyrics, and songs reflecting peace and elegance of the Tulip Age of Sultan Ahmed III's reign.

Need·ham \'nēd-əm\, John Turberville. 1713–1781. English naturalist. Ordained Roman Catholic priest (1738); staunch advocate of spontaneous generation and of vitalism.

Nee·fe \'nā-fə\, Christian Gottlob. 1748–1798. German musician and composer. Music director and organist (1779–96) at Bonn, where he taught Beethoven.

Neer \'nār\, Aart *or* Aert *or* Aernout van der. 1603 or 1604–1677. Dutch painter. Active in Amsterdam (from c.1640); known for nocturnal landscapes esp. of canal and river scenes. His son and pupil ¶Eglon Hendrick (1634?–1703), court painter to the elector palatine at Düsseldorf (from 1690), painted group and genre scenes, landscapes with biblical or mythological figures, and small portraits.

Nees von Esen·beck \'nās-fón-'ā-zən-,bek\, Christian Gottfried Daniel. 1776–1858. German botanist and naturalist. Physician; professor of botany, Bonn (1818–30), Breslau (1830–52); president of Leopoldina (Imperial German Academy of Natural Science, 1818–58). Author of books on fungi, mosses, natural philosophy, etc.

Nef \'nef\, John Ulric. 1862–1915. American chemist, b. Herisau, Switzerland. To U.S. (1868); professor, Purdue (1887–89), Clark (1889–92), Chicago (1892–1915); pioneer investigator of bivalent carbon, fulminates, and mechanism of organic reactions.

Ne·fer·ti·ti \,nef-ər-'tēt-ē\ *or* **Nof·re·te·te** \,näf-rə-'tēt-ē\. 14th century B.C. Egyptian queen. Wife of Akhenaton; probably of Asiatic (Mitanni) birth; noted for beauty and influence on her husband's religious ideas.

Neff·tzer \neft-ser\, Auguste. 1820–1876. French journalist. Founder and editor (1861–71) of *Le Temps.*

Nef'i. See ÖMER.

Neghelli, Marchese di. See Rodolfo GRAZIANI.

Ne·gri \'nā-grē\, Ada. 1870–1945. Italian poet. Works included *Fatalità* (1892), *Maternità* (1904), *Dal profondo* (1910), *Il libro di Mara* (1919), *I canti dell'isola* (1924), *Sorelle* (1929), *Il dono* (1936), *Fons amoris* (1945); prose works included *Le solitarie* (1917), *Le strade* (1926).

Ne·grín \nāḡ-'rēn\, Juan. 1894–1956. Spanish politician. Professor of pharmacology, Madrid (1923–31); Democratic Socialist member of Cortes (1931–39); minister of finance (1936–37); last prime minister of Republican government (1937–39); prime minister of Republican government in exile (1939–45).

Ne·gruz·zi \ne-'grüt-sē\, Costache. 1808–1868. Romanian writer. Author of *Alexandru Lăpușneanul* (1840), first Romanian historical novel; translator of works of Victor Hugo, Pushkin, and others.

Ne·he·mi·ah \,nē-(h)ə-'mī-ə\ *or* **Ne·he·mi·as** \-əs\. 5th century B.C. Jewish leader. Appointed by Artaxerxes I governor of Judea (445) and authorized to rebuild Jerusalem.

Neh·ru \'ne(ə)r-(,)ü, 'nā-(,)rü\, Motilal, *called* Pandit Motilal. 1861–1931. Indian political leader. Practiced law in Allāhābād (from 1883); member of United Provinces legislative council; active in Indian National Congress; became associated with Gandhi in non-cooperation movement (1919); founded its paper, the *Independent;* president of Indian National Congress (1920); with C. R. Das organized Swaraj party (1923); member of Indian Legislative Assembly 1923–24, 1926); framed Nehru report, formulating plan for dominion status for India (1928); advocated campaign of civil disobedience (1930); imprisoned (1930). His son ¶Jawaharlal (1889–1964) was educated in England (1905–12); with father, radicalized by Amritsar massacre (1919); joined Gandhi's movement, becoming his chief political heir; imprisoned several times for a total of nearly 10 years (1921–45); secretary (1923–25, 1927–29), president (1929 ff.), Indian National Congress; first prime minister of independent India (1947–64); a chief architect of politics of nonalignment. Author of an autobiography (1936), *The Unity of India* (1941), *Nehru on Gandhi* (1948), etc.

Neid·hart von Reu·en·thal \'nīt-härt-fón-'rói-ən-täl\. c.1180–c.1250. Bavarian knight and Middle High German poet. c.1180–c.1250. Introduced poetic genre of *höfische Dorfpoesie,* courtly verse on village life and esp. on village maidens, set as summer or winter dancing songs; inspired a later strain of poems ridiculing the rude life and manners of the peasantry, for which he was nicknamed Neidhart Fuchs \'füks\, *i.e.* Neidhart the Fox.

Nei·hardt \'nī-,härt\, John Gneisenau. 1881–1973. American poet, b. Sharpsburg, Ill. Professor, U. of Nebraska (1923), U. of Mo. (1948–66); literary editor, St. Louis *Post-Dispatch* (1926–38); named poet laureate of Nebraska (1921). His works included *The Divine Enchantment* (1900), *The Lonesome Trail* (1907), *Man-Song* (1909), *The River and I* (1910), *The Song of Three Friends* (1919), *Song of the Indian Wars* (1925), *Black Elk Speaks* (1932), *The Song of the Messiah* (1935), *Song of Jed Smith* (1941), *When the Tree Flowered* (1951), *Eagle Voice* (1953), etc.

Neill. See also NEAL, NEALE.

Neill \'nē(ə)l\, James George Smith. 1810–1857. British army officer, b. Scotland. Joined army of East India Co. (1827); organized and reformed Turkish contingent in Crimean War (1854–56); at outbreak of Sepoy Mutiny ruthlessly crushed mutineers at Benares (1857); led famous march from Cawnpore to join in assault upon Lucknow, where he led the assault and was killed in action.

Neil·son \'nē(ə)l-sən\, James Beaumont. 1792–1865. Scottish inventor. With Glasgow Gasworks (1817–47); introduced and patented (1828) use of the hot blast in the manufacturing of iron, greatly increasing productivity; also made improvements in the manufacturing of gas.

Neilson, Julia Emilie. 1868–1957. English actress. First appeared in *Pygmalion and Galatea* (1888); toured U.S. and Canada; as Rosalind in *As You Like It,* played longest run on record in a London theater (1896–98); theater manager with her husband.

Neilson, William Allan. 1869–1946. American scholar, b. Doune, Scotland. Teacher in Upper Canada Coll., Toronto (1891–95); instructor, Bryn Mawr (1898–1900), Harvard (1900–04), Columbia (1904–06); professor of English, Harvard (1906–17); president, Smith Coll. (1917–39). Author of *Essentials of Poetry* (1912), *The Facts About Shakespeare* (with A. H. Thorndike, 1913), *Robert Burns* (1917), *A History of English Literature* (1920); editor of the Cambridge edition of Shakespeare's works (1906, 1942); editor in chief, *Webster's New International Dictionary, Second Edition* (1934).

Neira, Álvaro Mendaña de. See MENDAÑA DE NEIRA.

Neis·ser \'nī-sər\, Albert Ludwig Sigesmund. 1855–1916. German physician. Professor, Breslau (from 1882); specialist in dermatology and venereal diseases; discovered (1879) gonococcus; demonstrated (1879) the existence of the bacillus of leprosy.

Neithardt von Gneisenau, Count. See August GNEISENAU.

Ne·kra·sov \nyi-'krá-səf\, Nikolay Alekseyevich. 1821–1877. Russian poet. Worked as journalist and critic; bought and published (1846–66) *Sovremennik;* editor and publisher of *Otechestvennye zapiski* (1868–77). Known for poems on life and suffering of the peasantry as "Moroz krasny-nos" (Red-Nosed Frost, 1863); published collections as *Mechty i zvuki* (1840) and unfinished long narrative *Komu na Rusi zhit khorosho?* (Who Can Be Happy and Free in Russia?, 1879).

Nell \'nel\, William Cooper. 1816–1874. American author, b. Boston. A leading advocate of removal of discriminations against Negro children in Massachusetts public schools; clerk in Boston post office (1861–74), first Negro to be given a federal position. Author of *Services of Colored Americans in the Wars of 1776 and 1812* (1851), *The Colored Patriots of the American Revolution* (1855).

Nel·li·gan \nel-ē-gäⁿ\, Émile. 1879–1941. Canadian poet, b. Montreal. Became a leading figure in Montreal literary school with poems published (1896–99) in various periodicals; confined to asylum (from 1899). Well known poems included "Le Vaisseau d'or" and "La Romance du vin"; verse collected as *Émile Nelligan et son oeuvre* (1903).

Nel·son \'nel-sən\, Horatio. Viscount Nelson. 1758–1805. British naval officer. Entered navy (1770); lieutenant (1777); saw first active service in West Indies (1780); commanded H.M.S. *Boreas* in West Indies (1784); served under Hood in taking of Bastia and of Calvi (where sight of his right eye was destroyed), completing the reduction of Corsica (1794); served later under Jervis; met (1793) Emma Hamilton, wife of British ambassador at court of Naples; appointed commodore (1796); returned from mission at Elba in time to join Jervis in victory off Cape St. Vincent over French and Spanish fleets (Feb. 1797); rear admiral (1797). Failed in desperate attempt to take Santa Cruz de Tenerife (July 1797); shot through right elbow, suffered badly performed amputation; returned to fleet (1798) in *Vanguard;* pursued French fleet in eastern Mediterranean; discovered them in Abu Qir (Aboukir) Bay, and allowed only two frigates to escape (battle of the Nile; Aug. 1, 1798); created baron. Blockaded Malta and Naples, held by French and Neapolitan Jacobins; annulled Cardinal Ruffo's proposed terms to rebels, received absolute surrender; restored Neapolitan royal family to power; created duke of Bron·te \'brōn-tā\ by Ferdinand I of Naples; returned overland to England with Sir William and Lady Hamilton (1800); separated from his wife (1801). Vice admiral (1801); although second-in-command to Sir Hyde Parker, attacked Copenhagen (1801); created viscount (1801); shared houses with Hamiltons in London and at Merton in Surrey. Appointed on reopening of war to Mediterranean command (1803); blockaded French in Toulon for two years; on their escape pursued to West Indies and back to Cádiz; in battle of Trafalgar (Oct. 21, 1805) formed fleet in two columns; with his ship *Victory,* restrained enemy's van; in breaking through enemy's center ran afoul of the French ship *Redoutable* from whose mizzentop he was struck by a sharpshooter's musket ball that broke his spine; died as victory was completed with annihilation of enemy fleet.

Nelson, Samuel. 1792–1873. American jurist, b. Hebron, N.Y. Associate justice (1831–37), chief justice (1837–45), N.Y. supreme court; associate justice U.S. Supreme Court (1845–72).

Nelson, Thomas. 1738–1789. American Revolutionary politician, b. Yorktown, Va. Member of Continental Congress (1775–77, 1779); signer of the Declaration of Independence; governor of Virginia (1781).

Nelson, Thomas. 1780–1861. Scottish publisher. Founder of firm of Thomas Nelson & Sons. His son ¶William (1816–1887) entered the business (1835); improved Edinburgh, restoring Old Scottish Parliament House and other buildings. Another son ¶Thomas (1822–1892) established a London branch of the firm (1844), invented a rotary press (1850).

Nelson, William Rockhill. 1841–1915. American journalist, b. Fort Wayne, Ind. Founder and editor (1880–1915), Kansas City *Evening Star;* bought *Times* (1894); effective promoter of urban planning, beautification; chief benefactor of Nelson Gallery of Art (opened 1933).

Ne·ma·nja \'nem-än-yä\. Name of a family of Serbian princes that governed from late 12th to late 14th century; founded by Stefan Nemanja (ruled c.1167–96); dynasty reached its height during the reign of STEPHEN DUŠAN.

Ne·me·si·a·nus \nə-,mē-zhē-'ā-nəs, -shē-\, Marcus Aurelius Olympius. fl. c.280 A.D. Roman poet, b. Carthage. Extant works include four Virgilian eclogues, incomplete *Cynegetica* on hunting; fragments of *De aucupio* on bird catching are attributed to him.

Ne·me·si·us \nə-'mē-zhē-əs, -shē-əs\ of Em·e·sa \'em-ə-sə\. 4th century. Christian philosopher. Bishop of Emesa (Homs), Syria; author of influential treatise *Periphyseōs anthrōpou* (On the Nature of Man), a Christian psychology synthesizing Platonic, Aristotelian, Galenic elements.

Ne·mir·ov·ich-Dan·chen·ko \nyim-'yir(-əv)-,yich-dän-chäŋ-kə\, Vladimir Ivanovich. 1858–1943. Russian playwright and theatrical producer. Influential as playwright, director, and teacher in evolving modern stage practices as long rehearsal times, new acting styles; with Stanislavsky founded (1897) Moscow Art and Popular Theater; also founded an opera workshop (1919), Moscow Art Musical Studio, etc.

Ne·mours \nə-mür\. Name of a French lordship, created a county by Charles V in latter part of 14th century; granted as peerage-duchy to Charles III of Navarre (1404); after long dispute, confirmed to Jacques d'Armagnac, a grandson of Bernard VII, comte d'Armagnac (*q.v.*); his line failing, duchy was granted (1507) to Gaston de Foix (d. 1512), then to Giuliano de' Medici (d. 1516). Second ducal house of Nemours held by a branch of the house of Savoy (1528–1659, *q.v.*). Duchy was given by Louis XIV to his brother Philippe, duc d'Orléans (1672), with whose descendants it remained.

Nemours, Louis-Charles d'Orléans, duc de. See under LOUIS-PHILIPPE.

Nen·ni \'nen-nē\, Pietro Sandro. 1891–1980. Italian politician. Jailed for opposing Italo–Turkish War (1911–12); joined Italian Socialist party (1921), edited its organ *Avanti!* (1923–26); attacked Fascists; served with Garibaldi Brigade in Spanish Civil War; imprisoned in Germany (1940–43), Italy (1943); vice premier in Parri government (1945); member of Constitutional Assembly (1946); vice premier and foreign minister (1946); leader of left-wing Socialists (from 1947); repudiated alliance with Communists (1956) and led Socialists back into coalition government (1963); vice premier (1963–68); foreign minister (1968–69); senator (1971), president of Senate (1979).

Nen·ni·us \'nen-ē-əs\. fl. c.800 A.D. Welsh compiler. Traditionally credited with miscellaneous history *Historia Britonum,* containing perhaps earliest known reference to Arthur.

Neper, John. See John NAPIER.

Nepomuk, Saint John of. See JOHN of Nepomuk.

Ne·pos \'nē-,päs, 'nep-,äs\, Cornelius. c.100–c.25 B.C. Roman historian. Friend of Cicero and Catullus; only extant work is a fragment of a Roman biographical compendium *De viris illustribus;* also wrote a *Chronica,* an *Exempla,* and perhaps a geography.

Nepos, Julius. d. 480. Roman emperor in the West (474–480). Sent by Leo I as magistrate over Italy; deposed Glycerius and proclaimed himself emperor; forced to flee by rebellion of Orestes, one of his generals (475), who placed his son Romulus Augustulus on the throne; continued to be recognized as emperor in Gaul and the East; killed in Dalmatia.

Nep·veu *or* **Ne·veu** \nə-vœ\, Pierre. *Known as* Trin·queau \traⁿ-kō\. d. 1542. French architect. Designer of several of the finest châteaux in the Loire valley, notably Amboise, Chenonceaux, and Chambord.

Ne·ri \'nā-rē\, Philip. Saint. *Ital.* Filippo Neri. 1515–1595. Italian clergyman and mystic. In Rome followed course of studies and lay devotion (1533–51); organized (1548) lay Confraternitá di SS. Trinità; ordained (1551); at San Giovanni founded (1564) the society Fathers of the Oratory; granted by Pope Gregory XIII a church at Vallicella, where he founded (1575) Institute of the Oratory; first provost (from 1577). From musical services held in the oratory, many by Palestrina, came name *oratorio* for one form of musical composition.

Néricault, Philippe. See DESTOUCHES.

Neri Tanfucio. See Renato FUCINI.

Nernst \'nernst\, Walther Hermann. 1864–1941. German physicist and chemist. Professor, Göttingen (1891–1904), Berlin (1905 ff.); director (1924–33), Inst. for Experimental Physics; a founder of modern physical chemistry; did research on the theories of ions, chemical equilibrium, and solutions, and on the generation of current in the galvanic cell; enunciated (1906) third law of thermodynamics concerning the energy change in a reaction; awarded 1920 Nobel prize for chemistry. Author of influential textbook *Theoretische Chemie* (1893), etc.

Ne·ro \'nē-(,)rō, 'ni(ə)r-(,)ō\. *In full* Nero Claudius Caesar Drusus Ger·man·i·cus \jər-'man-i-kəs\. *Originally* Lucius Domitius Ahe·no·bar·bus \ə-,hē-nə-'bär-bəs, ə-,hen-ə-\. 37–68 A.D. Roman emperor (54–68). Son of Domitius Ahenobarbus, Roman consul, and Agrippina, daughter of Germanicus Caesar; educated by Seneca and Burrus; adopted by his stepfather Emperor Claudius (50); m. 1st Octavia, daughter of Claudius (53). Proclaimed emperor by praetorian guard at behest of Agrippina; caused death of Britannicus (55) and procured assassination of his mother (59); first few years of reign in general marked by wise conduct of public affairs, with Seneca and Burrus as advisers; private life profligate and dissipated; murdered Octavia and her sister Antonia; m. Poppaea Sabina (62) and later caused her death; accused of kindling fire (64) that destroyed a great part of Rome; instituted persecutions of Christians; discovered plot against him (65) and brought about deaths of many Romans, including Seneca; visited Greece (67–68); competed for prizes at festivals; emptied the public treasury by extravagances; declared a public enemy by the Senate; committed suicide.

Nero, Gaius Claudius. 3d century B.C. Roman general and politician. Consul (207 B.C.); with his colleague in the consulship, Marcus Livius Salinator, defeated Hasdrubal in decisive battle of Metaurus (207).

Ne·ru·da \'ner-üd-á\, Jan. 1834–1891. Czech poet, novelist, and journalist. Critic for newspaper *Národní listy.* Works included lyrical verse and ballads *Hřbitovni kvítí* (1858), *Knihy veršů* (1868), *Pisně kosmické* (1878), *Balady a romance* (1883), *Prosté motivy* (1883), *Zpěvy páteční* (1896); stories *Povídky malostranské* (1878); novel *Trhani* (1888).

Ne·ru·da \nā-'rü-thä\, Pablo. *Orig.* Neftalí Ricardo Re·yes Ba·soal·to \'rā-yäs-bä-'swäl-tō\. 1904–1973. Chilean poet and diplomat. Honorary consul in Rangoon, Colombo, Batavia, Singapore (1927–33); consul in Buenos Aires (1933–34), Barcelona and Madrid (1934–36); ambassador to Mexico (1940–42), to France (1971–72); senator (1945–48); in exile (1948–52). Author of *Crepusculario* (1923), *Veinte poemas de amor y una canción desesperada* (1924), *El habitante y su esperanza* (1925), *Tentativa del hombre infinito* (1926), *Anillos* (1926), *Residencia en la tierra* (1933, 1935, 1947), *Canto general* (1950), *Las uvas y el viento* (1954), *Odas elementales* (1954, 1956, 1957), *Estravagario* (1958), *Cantos ceremoniales* (1961), *La barcarola* (1967), *Las piedras del cielo* (1970), etc. Awarded Nobel prize for literature (1971).

Ner·va \'nər-və\, Marcus Coc·ce·ius \käk-'sē-(y)əs\. c.30–98. Roman emperor (96–98). Held offices of trust under Vespasian and Titus (71–81); consul (71, 90); banished by Domitian to Tarentum (93); as emperor, unable to repress excesses of praetorian guard; adopted Trajan as successor (97).

Nerval, Gérard de. See Gérard LABRUNIE.

Ner·vi \'ner-vē\, Pier Luigi. 1891–1979. Italian architect. Known for designs utilizing reinforced concrete cast in place or from prefabricated forms, achieving unprecedented versatility and beauty in this material; partner in Nervi and Bartoli (from 1932); professor, U. of Rome (from 1947). Designs included those for a Naples cinema (1926–27), Berta stadium in Florence (1930–32), series of hangars for Italian air force (1935–41), complex for Turin Exhibition (1949–50), UNESCO headquarters, Paris (1950, with Marcel Breuer and others), Gatti wool factory, Rome (1953), Pirelli building, Milan (1955, with others), sport palaces for 1960 Rome Olympics (1957–60), George Washington Bridge Terminal, N.Y.C. (1961–62), Australia Square, Sydney (1962–69), Place Victoria, Montreal (1962–65), San Francisco cathedral (1970), Vatican auditorium (1971).

Ner·vo \'nār-b̲ō\, Amado. *Orig.* Juan Crisóstomo Ruiz de Nervo. 1870–1919. Mexican poet and diplomat. Served in Mexican legation in Madrid (1905–18); minister to Argentina and Uruguay (1918–19). Author of Modernist verse imbued with moral and religious feeling as *Perlas negras* (1898), *Lira heroica* (1902), *Los jardines interiores* (1905), *En voz baja* (1909), *Serenidad* (1914), *Elevación* (1917), *Plenitud* (1918), etc.; wrote novel *El bachiller* (1894); a founder (1898) of review *Revista moderna.*

Nes·be·neb·ded \ˌnes-bə-'neb-dəd, -'ben-əb-\. *Also known as* Smen·des \'smen-(ˌ)dēz\. 11th century B.C. King of Egypt (c.1085 B.C.). Probably acquired claim to throne through wife Tentamon; founded 21st dynasty with capital at Tanis; acknowledged as pharaoh by priests of Amon who ruled Upper Egypt from Thebes.

Nes·bit \'nez-bət\, Edith. 1858–1924. English novelist, poet, and writer of juvenile books. Attained success with stories of the "Bastable Children" as *The Wouldbegoods* (1901), *Five Children and It* (1902), and *New Treasure Seekers* (1904); best known novel *The Red House* (1903), her last *The Lark* (1922).

Ne·si·mi \nā-sē-'mē\, Seyid İmadeddin. d. c.1418. Turkish mystic and poet. Disciple of Faḍl Allāh, founder of heretical Islāmic sect of Ḥurūfīs; Ḥurūfī missionary; executed for heresy. Author of *dīvāns* (verse collections) in Persian and Turkish and some Arabic poems; Turkish verse included many *ghazals* and *rubāʿīs* on Ṣūfī and Ḥurūfī topics.

Nesiotes. See CRITIUS.

Neş·ri \nesh-'rē\. *In full* Hüseyin ibn Eyne Beg. d. c.1520. Turkish historian. Author of *Cihannüma,* a universal history drawn critically from earlier histories, from court records, and in part from eyewitness knowledge.

Nes·sel·ro·de \nyis-syilʸ-'rȯd-yi\, Karl Robert von. Graf. 1780–1862. Russian politician, b. Portugal, of German descent. Entered Russian navy (1797); as junior diplomat served in Prussia, Netherlands, France; attended Congress of Vienna (1814–15); minister of foreign affairs (1822–56); chancellor (1845–62); counseled aid to Austria in crushing Hungarian uprising (1848); his policies toward Ottoman Empire and France helped precipitate Crimean War (1853–56); concluded Treaty of Paris (1856).

Nes·tlé \nes-lā, *Angl* 'nes-lē\, Henri. *Orig. surname* Nest·le \'nest-lə\. 1814–1890. Swiss businessman, b. Germany. Established chocolate manufactory (1867) at Vevey, Switzerland; sold his interest in the business (1875).

Nes·tor \'nes-tō(ə)r, -tȯ(ə)r, -tər\. c.1056–1113. Russian monk and chronicler. In monastery at Kiev (from c.1074); traditionally held to have compiled *Povesti vremennykh let,* first Russian chronicle of a national character.

Nes·to·ri·us \ne-'stōr-ē-əs, -'stȯr-\. d. c.451 A.D. Persian prelate. Patriarch of Constantinople (428–431); preached the doctrine (Nestorianism) that in Jesus Christ a divine person and a human person were joined in perfect harmony of action but not in the unity of a single individual; deposed for heresy by the Council of Ephesus (431) and banished (c.436) to the Libyan desert. Nestorianism spread widely in Persia, India, Mongolia, and China.

Nes·troy \'nes-ˌtrȯi\, Johann Nepomuk Eduard Ambrosius. 1801–1862. Austrian dramatist. Opera singer, comic actor; in Vienna (from 1831); a brillant comedian, esp. in his own works; manager of Carl-Theater, Vienna (1854–60). Plays included *Der böse Geist Lumpazivagabundus* (1833), *Die beiden Nachtwandler* (1836), *Der Talisman* (1840), *Das Mädl aus der Vorstadt* (1841), *Einen Jux will er sich machen* (1842), *Der Zerrissene* (1844), *Der Schützling* (1847), *Höllenangst* (1849), etc.

Ne·to \'nā-tü\, António Agostinho. 1922–1979. Angolan leader. Gained recognition through protest poetry and became a leader of Angolan nationalist sentiment; frequently imprisoned by Portuguese authorities; physician (from 1959); imprisoned (1960–62), escaped to Morocco; president of Movimento Popular de Libertação de Angola (MPLA; from 1962); proclaimed People's Republic of Angola (1975), president (1975–79).

Net·scher \'nech-ər\, Caspar. c.1635–1684. German painter. Settled at The Hague (1662); became known for genre works in manner of Terborch; later a fashionable portraitist. His sons ¶Theodor (1661–1732) and ¶Constantijn (1668–1723) were also portrait and genre painters.

Neu·ber \'nȯi-bər\, Friederike Caroline, *nee* Weis·sen·born \'vīs-ən-ˌbȯrn\. 1697–1760. German actress and theatrical manager. m. Johann Neuber (1718; d. 1759) and with him was member of various theatrical troupes; formed own company (1727); patronized by Frederick Augustus I of Saxony (1727–33); with J. C. Gottsched, considered a creator of modern German theater, introducing careful learning of roles and rehearsal; to Russia for Empress Anna (1740–41); later broke with Gottsched; retired (1747) but formed new company (1748) that failed to prosper.

Neu·berg \'nȯi-ˌberk\, Carl. 1877–1956. German biochemist. Professor, Berlin (1916–38); director of Kaiser-Wilhelm Institute for Biochemistry (1920–38); professor, Jerusalem (1939–41), New York U. (1941–50), Brooklyn Polytechnic (from 1951). Founded (1906) *Biochemische Zeitschrift;* discovered (1911) carboxylase in yeast, made other contributions to understanding of fermentation.

Neu·bur·ger \'nȯi-ˌbu̇r-gər\, Max. 1868–1955. Austrian physician. Professor, Vienna (1917–39); founder and director (1917–39) of first institute for the history of medicine. His works included *Handbuch der Geschichte der Medizin* (with J. L. Pagel, 1902–05) and *Geschichte der Medizin* (1906–11).

Neufchâteau, François de. See Nicholas-Louis FRANÇOIS.

Neu·hof *or* **Neu·hoff** \'nȯi-ˌhōf\, Theodor von. Baron. 1694–1756. German adventurer. Soldier and diplomat in French, Bavarian, Swedish, Spanish service; indefatigable intriguer; conspired with Corsican exiles and was crowned Theodore I, king of Corsica (1736); driven out by the Genoese (1736) and defeated in attempts to return to Corsica (1738, 1743).

Neu·komm \'nȯi-ˌkȯm\, Sigismund von. Ritter. 1778–1858. Austrian composer, pianist, and scholar. Pupil (1797 ff.) of Joseph Haydn in Vienna; Kapellmeister, German Theater in St. Petersburg (1804–08); to Paris (1809); became friend of Grétry, Cherubini; made chevalier of the Legion of Honor (1815) for his requiem in honor of Louis XVI. Kapellmeister to Dom Pedro in Rio de Janeiro (1816–21); patronized esp. by Talleyrand; traveled widely. Composed theatrical, church, vocal, instrumental music.

Neu·mann \'nȯi-ˌmän\, Alfred. 1895–1952. German writer. Known for historical novels as *Der Teufel* (1926), *Rebellen* (1927), *Der Held* (1930), *Der Narrenspiegel* (1933), *Die Goldquelle* (1938), *Der Pakt* (1949); also wrote tales, dramas, essays, and translated many works from French.

Neumann, Balthasar, *in full* Johann Balthasar. 1687–1753. German architect. A master of the German Baroque school, noted also as an engineer and an organizer; designed archbishop's residence at Würzburg with its staircase (1719–44), summer castle at Werneck (1733–45), church of Vierzehnheiligen, Lichtenfels (1743–72), episcopal palaces at Bruchsal (1731) and Werneck (1733), the abbey church at Neresheim (1749–92), etc.

Neumann, Franz Ernst. 1798–1895. German physicist and mineralogist. Professor, Königsberg (from 1829); formulated law of molecular heat (1831); formulated law of electromagnetic induction (1845, 1847) from results of experiments of Faraday and Henry; worked on reflection, refraction, and double refraction of light, and on conduction of heat. His son ¶Carl Gottfried (1832–1925) was also a mathematician; professor, Halle (1863), Basel (1863), Tübingen (1865), Leipzig (1868); developed the potential theory; founder of logarithmic potentials.

Neu·mann \'nȯi-ˌmän, *Angl* 'n(y)ü-mən\, John Nepomucene. Saint. 1811–1860. American prelate, b. Prachatice, Bohemia. To U.S. (1836); ordained priest (1836); entered Redemptorist order (1842); bishop of Philadelphia (1852); built many churches, asylums, schools; organized first U.S. diocesan school system, including some 100 parochial schools; founded U.S. branches of several orders of teaching nuns. Canonized by Pope Paul VI (1977).

Neu·mann \'nȯi-ˌmän\, John von. 1903–1957. American mathematician, b. Budapest, Hungary. Professor, Hamburg (1929–30), Princeton (1931–33), Inst. for Advanced Study (1933–57); contributed to theory of numbers and theory of games, cybernetics (term coined by him); received Fermi award (1956) for work on theory, design, and construction of computers. Author of *Theory of Games and Economic Behavior* (with O. Morgenstern, 1944), *Theory of Self-reproducing Automata* (1966), etc.

Neumann, Stanislav Kostka. 1875–1947. Czech poet and editor. Active in revolt against cultural and literary tradition as editor of reviews *Moderní revue* and *Nový kult;* later member of Communist party. Verse included *Nemesis, bonorum custos* (1895), *České zpěvy* (1910), *Kniha lesů, vod a strání* (1914), *Nové zpěvy* (1918), *Rudé zpěvy* (1923), *Láska* (1933).

Neumann, Therese. 1898–1962. German stigmatic. Exhibited stigmata and bleeding, experienced visions and ecstasies, esp. during Lent of each year (from

1926; diminished after 1950); her case inconclusively investigated by church authorities, explained by some in terms of her earlier history of hysteria.

Neu·mark \'nöi-ˌmärk\, Georg. 1621–1681. German writer. Librarian in Weimar (from 1652); author of poetic works as *Filamon* (1640), *Davidischen Regentenspiegel* (1655), *Poetisch-historischer Lustgarten* (1666), etc.; best known poem "Wer nur den lieben Gott lässt walten."

Neu·rath \'nöi-rät\, Konstantin von. Freiherr. 1873–1956. German diplomat. Entered diplomatic service (1908); minister to Denmark (1919); ambassador to Italy (1922), Britain (1930–32); minister of foreign affairs (1932–38); "protector" for Bohemia and Moravia (1939–41); imprisoned (1946–54) for war crimes.

Neurath, Otto. 1882–1945. German philosopher and sociologist. Developed neo-Positivist foundation for behaviorist sociology and economics; director of International Union of Pedagogy. Author of *Vollsozialisierung* (1920), *Empirische Soziologie* (1931), *Foundations of the Social Sciences* (1944).

Neu·reu·ther \'nöi-ˌröi-tər\, Eugen Napoleon. 1806–1882. German painter, etcher, and illustrator. Assisted Cornelius in decoration of the Glyptothek, Munich; art director, Nymphenburg porcelain manufactory (1848–56). His works included illustrations for German legends, ballads, and romances, notably those of Goethe (1829–40), woodcut designs for Herder's *Cid* (1838), oil paintings, etc.

Neu·tra \'nöi-trä, *Angl* 'n(y)ü-trə\, Richard Josef. 1892–1970. American architect, b. Vienna, Austria. Collaborated on Berliner Tageblatt building, then tallest in Berlin (1921); with Erich Mendelsohn designed prize-winning city planning project for Haifa, Palestine (1923; now in Israel); to U.S. (1923, naturalized 1929); achieved renown with Lovell House, Los Angeles (1927–29); became a leading exponent of International Style; other works included Corona School, Los Angeles (1935), Channel Heights development in San Pedro, Cal. (1942–44), Kauffmann Desert House, Palm Springs, Cal. (1946–47), Tremaine House, Santa Barbara, Cal. (1947–48), churches, university buildings, civic and cultural buildings, etc. Author of *Mystery and Realities of the Site* (1951), *Survival through Design* (1954), *Life and Human Habitat* (1956), *Therapy by Design* (1965).

Neu·ville \nœ-vēl\, Alphonse-Marie de. 1836–1885. French painter. Known for battle scenes.

Ne·vā'ī \nā-vä-'ē\, 'Alī Shīr. 1441–1501. Turkish poet and scholar. Patronized by kings of Khorāsān and Herāt; author of four *divans* (collections of verse) and treatises on Turkish poetry and poets, Turkish and Persian languages, etc. Considered outstanding representative of Chagatai Turkish literature.

Nev·ers \'nev-ərz\, Ernest Alonzo. 1903–1976. American athlete, b. Willow River, Minn. All-American fullback at Stanford U. (1924, 1925); pitcher for St. Louis Browns (1926–28); professional football player for Chicago Cardinals (1929–31); set National Football League single-game scoring record of 40 points (6 touchdowns, 4 conversions against Chicago Bears, 1929).

Neveu, Pierre. See NEPVEU.

Nev·ille *or* **Nev·ill** \'nev-əl\. Family name of an English noble house of many branches, most notably that of Durham, which was descended from Dolfin, receiver of a grant of territory in Durham (1131), and which had Raby as its seat and, after union with Bulmer family, with Brancepeth as second seat. Ralph de Neville (1291?–1367), 2d Baron Neville, participated in victory of Neville's Cross (1346) and capture of David Bruce; governor of Berwick (1355). His son ¶John (d. 1388), 3d baron, fought in French wars of Edward III (1345, 1349, 1360); admiral of fleet (1370); a powerful supporter of John of Gaunt (from 1370); as lieutenant of king in Aquitaine (1378) recovered towns, castles, and forts; warden of Scottish border (after 1381); built Raby Castle, erected Neville screen in Durham cathedral.

His son ¶Ralph (c.1364–1425), 4th baron, was created Earl of West·mor·land \'wes(t)-mər-lənd, *US also* wes(t)-'mō(ə)r- *or* -'mȯ(ə)r-\ (1397); m. (as 2d wife) a daughter of John of Gaunt; took part against Richard II (1399) and made marshal of England by Henry IV; warden of west marches after battle of Shrewsbury and death of Hotspur (1403); put down a rebellion by Northumberland, Mowbray, and Archbishop Scrope (1405); one of regents for Henry V's son. ¶Charles Neville (1542 or 1543–1601), 6th Earl of Westmorland, joined Northumberland in abortive attempt to release Mary, Queen of Scots (1569); was attainted (1571) and lost estates.

¶Richard Neville (1400–1460), Earl of Salis·bury \'sȯlz-ˌber-ē, -b(ə)-rē\; son of 1st Earl of Westmorland; m. (1425) Alice, daughter of Thomas de Montagu, Earl of Salisbury, whose title and holdings he inherited (1429); warden of both marches (1434); chancellor during protectorate of Richard Plantagenet, 3d Duke of York (1454–55); fled to France with York on their defeat at Ludford; returned (1460) with his son the Earl of Warwick (see below); became chamberlain; captured after battle of Wakefield and murdered.

His son ¶Richard Neville (1428–1471), Earl of Salisbury and, through marriage to daughter of Richard Beauchamp, Earl of War·wick \'wär-ik, *US also* 'wȯr-ik, 'wȯr-(ˌ)wik\ (from 1450); *known as* the Kingmaker; with father, aided Yorkists in War of the Roses to win battle of St. Albans (1455); was rewarded with captaincy of Calais (1455); aided the Yorkists to victory at Northampton (1460) and took Henry VI captive; opposed Duke of York's claim to throne till the latter's death in Lancastrian success at Wakefield (1460); defeated by Queen Margaret at 2d battle of St. Albans (1461); joined Edward, Duke of York's son, in march on London and victory at Towton (1461) and proclaimed him Edward IV, becoming himself virtual ruler of England during first three years of Edward's reign; displaced during mission to France by Woodville (1467), plotted revenge; married his daughter to George, Duke of Clarence (1469); instigated revolt of Yorkshire rebel known as Robin of Redesdale (1469), forced Edward IV to flee to Flanders; joined Lancastrians and aided Queen Margaret in invasion of England (1470–71); in meantime placed Henry VI on throne (1470); defeated and slain by Edward IV's forces at Barnet (1471). His daughter ¶Anne (d. 1485) m. (1472) Richard, Duke of Gloucester (later Richard III), whereby her share of Neville estates was absorbed by the crown.

Warwick's brother ¶John Neville (d. 1471), Marquis of Mon·ta·gu \'mänt-ə-ˌgyü, 'mənt-\ *and* Earl of Nor·thum·ber·land \nȯr-'thəm-bər-lənd\; took part in Yorkist battles (1453, 1457); imprisoned after 2d battle of St. Albans but liberated by Edward IV after battle of Towton (1461); defeated Lancastrians at Hexham (1464); joined Lançastrians upon restoration (1469) to Percy of earldom of Northumberland, which had been promised to him; killed at Barnet (1471), fighting on Lancastrian side.

Another brother ¶George Neville (1433?–1476) was bishop of Exeter (1458), chancellor of England (1460–67), archbishop of York (1464), chancellor to Henry VI (1470–71); surrendered himself and Henry VI to Edward IV after battle of Barnet (1471); imprisoned in France (till 1475).

Nev·in \'nev-ən\, Ethelbert Woodbridge. 1862–1901. American composer, b. Edgeworth, Pa. Debut as pianist, Pittsburgh (1886); composed songs and short piano pieces published in *Sketch Book* (1888), *Water Scenes* (1891, including "Narcissus"), *In Arcady* (1892), *May in Tuscany* (1896), *A Day in Venice* (1898); songs included "Rosary" (1898), "Mighty lak' a Rose" (1900). His brother ¶Arthur Finley (1871–1943) studied Blackfoot Indians and composed Indian operas *Poia* (1910) and *Daughter of the Forest* (1918), and piano and orchestral works.

Nevin, John Williamson. 1803–1886. American theologian, b. Upper Strasburg, Pa. Professor of biblical literature, Western Theol. Seminary (1830–40), German Reformed Seminary at Mercersburg, Pa. (1840–53); president, Franklin and Marshall Coll. (1866–76). His teachings with regard to sacraments, mystical union, liturgy, etc., became basis of Mercersburg theology; founded *Mercersburg Review* (1849, with Philip Schaff). Author of *The Anxious Bench* (1844), *The Mystical Presence* (1846), etc.

Nev·ins \'nev-ənz\, Allan. 1890–1971. American historian, b. Camp Point, Ill. On editorial staff, New York *Evening Post* (1913–23), *The Nation* (1913–18), New York *World* (1925–31); professor of American history, Columbia (1928–58), where he organized an oral history project. Author of biographies of Frémont (1928), John D. Rockefeller (1940), Henry Ford (with F.E. Hill, 1954–63), and *Grover Cleveland—A Study in Courage* (1932, Pulitzer prize), *Hamilton Fish—The Inner History of the Grant Administration* (1936, Pulitzer prize); also wrote Civil War history *Ordeal of the Union* (1947–71).

Nevsky, Alexander. See ALEXANDER NEVSKY.

New·all \'n(y)ü-əl\, Cyril Louis Norton. Baron Newall. 1886–1963. British general. Entered army (1905); joined Royal Flying Corps (1914); deputy chief of the air staff (1926–31), chief (1937–40); marshal of Royal Air Force (1940); governor general of New Zealand (1941–46); created baron (1946).

Newark, Baron. See David LESLIE.

New·bery \'n(y)ü-bər-ē\, John. 1713–1767. English publisher. Set up bookshop and publishing house in London (1744); started newspapers and had among contributors Goldsmith and Dr. Johnson; one of the first to publish children's books, including *Giles Gingerbread, Goody Two Shoes, Tommy Trip;* published *Mother Goose's Nursery Rhymes* (c.1760). Commemorated by the Newbery Medal, annually awarded since 1922 for most distinguished contribution to literature for children in U.S.

New·bolt \'n(y)ü-ˌbōlt\, Sir Henry John. 1862–1938. English poet and man of letters. Practiced law (1887–99); editor of *Monthly Review* (1900–04). Author of novels as *Taken from the Enemy* (1892), *The Old Country* (1906), *New June* (1909); gained renown as poet with *Admirals All,* containing "Drake's Drum" (1897), followed by *The Island Race* (1898), *The Sailing of the Long-Ships* (1902), *Songs of the Sea* (1904), etc. Wrote *Naval History of the Great War* (1920) and two vols. of *Naval Operations,* official history of the British navy.

Newburgh, William of. See WILLIAM of Newburgh.

Newcastle, Duke of. See (1) William Cavendish (1592–1676) under CAVENDISH family; (2) Thomas PELHAM-HOLLES.

New·comb \'n(y)ü-kəm\, Simon. 1835–1909. American astronomer and mathematician, b. Wallace, N.S. Taught country school in Maryland (1853–57); with aid of Joseph Henry, became computer, *Nautical Almanac* office (1857–77); superintendent, *American Ephemeris and Nautical Almanac* (1877–97); professor of mathematics, U.S. navy (1861–97), stationed at the Naval Observatory; professor of mathematics and astronomy, Johns Hopkins U. (1884–94, 1898–1900); secured international adoption of system of astronomical constants (1896); founder and first president (1899–1905), American Astronomical Society; rear admiral, retired (1906). Author of *Popular Astronomy* (1878), *The Stars* (1901), *Astronomy for Everybody* (1902), *Reminiscences of an Astronomer* (1903), etc.

Newcomen, Matthew. 1610?–1669. See SMECTYMNUUS.

New·co·men \'n(y)ü-kə-mən, n(y)ü-'kəm-ən\, Thomas. 1663–1729. English blacksmith and inventor. In association with John Calley (or Cawley), invented (1705) an engine in which steam admitted to a cylinder was condensed by a jet of cold water and the piston driven by atmospheric pressure; entered partnership with Thomas Savery, whose primitive steam engine for pumping water from mines (patented 1698) he improved and built into a practical working engine in common use in collieries (from 1712).

New·di·gate \'n(y)ü-də-gət, -ˌgāt\, Sir Roger. 1719–1806. English antiquary. M.P. (1741–47, 1750–80); collected ancient marbles, vases, casts of statues; founded at Oxford the Newdigate prize for English verse (1805).

New·ell \'n(y)ü-əl\, Frederick Haynes. 1862–1932. American civil engineer, b. Bradford, Pa. Hydraulic engineer, U.S. Geological Survey (1888–1902); chief engineer (1902–07), director (1907–14), U.S. Reclamation Service; head, civil engineering department, U. of Illinois (1915–20); author of works on water supply and irrigation engineering.

Newell, Peter Sheaf Hersey. 1862–1924. American cartoonist and illustrator, b. near Bushnell, Ill. Contributed comics and illustrations to *Harper's Weekly* and *Harper's Bazaar;* illustrated John K. Bangs's *A House-Boat on the Styx* (1896), *The Pursuit of the House-Boat* (1897), Lewis Carroll's *Alice in Wonderland* (1901); creator of illustrated books for children as *Topsys and Turvys* (1893), *Jungle Jangle* (1909), etc.

New·lands \'n(y)ü-lən(d)z\, Francis Griffith. 1848–1917. American politician, b. Natchez, Miss. Member from Nevada, U.S. House of Representatives (1893–1903), U.S. Senate (1903–17); responsible for creation of U.S. Reclamation Service (1902), for Newlands Act (1913) providing for mediation and conciliation in labor disputes, and for creation of Federal Trade Commission (1914).

Newlands, John Alexander Reina. 1837–1898. English chemist. Noted patterns in atomic weights of chemical elements of similar properties and published (1864) a table of elements illustrating his "law of octaves"; contributed to development of true periodic table by Mendeleyev.

New·man \'n(y)ü-mən\, Barnett. 1905–1970. American painter, b. New York City. Associated with Abstract Expressionist movement; with Rothko, Motherwell, Baziotes, founded (1948) Subject of the Artist school. Known for canvases of simplified forms, large color fields.

Newman, Ernest. *Orig.* William Roberts. 1868–1959. English music critic. Music critic for Manchester *Guardian* (1905–06), *Birmingham Daily Post* (1906–18), *Observer* (1919–20), *Sunday Times* (1920–58); author of studies of Gluck (1895), Elgar (1906), Hugo Wolf (1907), Richard Strauss (1908), Beethoven (1927), Liszt (1934), monumental *Life of Richard Wagner* (1933–47), *Opera Nights* (1943), *Testament of Music* (1962), etc.

Newman, Francis William. 1805–1897. English scholar. Brother of John Henry Newman; in college lost sympathy with Anglicanism and became nonconformist; unsectarian missionary to Baghdad (1830–33); tutor, Bristol Coll. (1834–40); professor, Manchester New Coll. (1840–46), U. Coll., London (1846–69); took part in religious controversy on the rationalistic side, opposed to his brother. Author of *History of the Hebrew Monarchy* (1847), *The Soul* (1849), *Phases of Faith* (1850), and numerous scholarly, educational, social, and political works.

Newman, John Henry. 1801–1890. English prelate and theologian. Fellow (1822) and tutor (1826–32) of Oriel Coll., Oxford, where he was associated with Edward Pusey and John Keble, and later R. H. Froude; vicar of St. Mary's, Oxford (1828–43); published volume of verse *Lyra Apostolica* (1834). Acknowledged leader of the Tractarian, or Oxford, movement; published *The Arians of the Fourth Century* (1833) and contributed 24 tracts to and edited series of *Tracts for the Times* (from 1833), especially *Tract XC* (1841), opposing religious liberalism, urging Anglican reaffirmation of the doctrine of apostolical succession, maintaining that the Thirty-nine Articles were opposed only to abuses, not to Roman Catholic doctrine; after three years of seclusion wrote *Essay on Development of Christian Doctrine* (1845) and became a Roman Catholic (1845); ordained priest in Rome (1847); established in Birmingham the Congregation of the Oratory (1847). Rector of Dublin Catholic U. (1851–58); replied to Charles Kingsley's charge of Roman Catholic indifference to truthfulness in *Apologia pro Vita Sua* (1864), an exposition of his spiritual history, recognized as a literary masterpiece. Elected honorary fellow of Trinity Coll. (1877). On the side of the Inopportunists, opposed pronouncement of pope's infallibility as likely to alienate Anglicans; created, by Pope Leo XIII, cardinal of St. George in Velabro (1879). Author of several volumes of sermons and lectures including *Parochial and Plain Sermons* (1834–42), *Lectures on the Present Position of Catholics in England* (1851), *Idea of a University* (1873); *The Dream of Gerontius* (dramatic monologue in verse, 1866), *Verses on Various Occasions* (1874); *The Grammar of Assent* (1870); religious novels *Loss and Gain* (1848) and *Callista* (1856).

Newnes \'n(y)ünz\, Sir George. 1851–1910. English publisher. Founded *Tit-Bits* (1881), *Strand Magazine* (1891). Gladstonian Liberal M.P. (1885–95), started *Westminster Gazette* as Liberal organ (1893); founded *Country Life* (1897), *Wide World Magazine* (1898), etc. Baronet (1895).

New·ton \'n(y)üt-ᵊn\, Alfred. 1829–1907. English zoologist. First professor of zoology and comparative anatomy, Cambridge (from 1866); edited journals *Ibis* (1865–70), *Zoological Record* (1870–72); author of *Dictionary of Birds* (1893–96), etc.

Newton, Sir Charles Thomas. 1816–1894. English archaeologist. Joined staff of British Museum (1840); superintended excavations at Bodrum, discovered site of ancient Halicarnassus, and recovered chief remains of the Mausoleum (1855–56); first keeper of Greek and Roman antiquities, British Museum (1861–85); professor, U. Coll., London (1880–88).

Newton, Hubert Anson. 1830–1896. American astronomer, b. Sherburne, N.Y. Professor of mathematics, Yale (1853–96); a pioneer in study of meteoroids, meteors, comets, etc.; helped determine orbit of Leonid swarm (1864).

Newton, Sir Isaac. 1642–1727. English physicist and mathematician. Developed binomial theorem (1665); invented method of fluxions, early form of differential calculus, and a form of integral calculus (1665–66); conceived idea of universal gravitation after seeing apple fall in his garden (1665), according to Voltaire, who is reputed to have had the story from Newton's stepniece; deduced from Kepler's third law that the force between the earth and the moon must be inversely proportional to the square of the distance between them, and showed that Kepler's three laws could each be derived from single law of gravitation; discovered composite nature of white light and ability of prism to separate colors owing to their different refrangibilities; studied chromatic aberration and to eliminate it invented a form of reflecting telescope (1668); developed an emission, or corpuscular, theory of light, later modifying it to include some wave phenomena. Professor, Cambridge (1669–1701); M.P. (1689–90, 1701); warden (1695–99), master (1699–1727) of the mint; president of Royal Society (1703–27). Published works included *De Motu* (1684), *Philosophiae Naturalis Principia Mathematica,* the seminal work for modern science (published by Edmund Halley, 1687), *Opticks* (1704).

Newton, John. 1725–1807. English clergyman. Impressed on board a man-of-war (c.1743), made midshipman, deserted; spent ten years in African slave trade; tide surveyor at Liverpool (1755–60); ordained (1760) and made curate of Olney; intimate friend of Cowper and joint producer of the *Olney Hymns* (1779), including his "Glorious things of thee are spoken" and "One there is above all others." Author of *Cardiphonia* (1781).

Nexø \'nik-sœ̄\, Martin Andersen. 1869–1954. Danish writer. Author of novels championing the working class, including the cycles *Pelle erobreren* (4 vols., 1906–10) and *Ditte mennskebarn* (3 vols., 1917–21), and *En moder* (1900), *Dryss* (1902), *Midt i en Jaerntid* (1929), *Morten hin Røde* (1945); also wrote volumes of short stories as *Skygger* (1898), *Af dybets lovsang* (1908), *Barndommens kyst* (1911), *Lykken* (1913), *Under himlen blaa* (1915), *Undervejs* (1919); memoirs *Et lille Krae* (1932), *Under aaben himmel* (1935), *For lud og koldt vand* (1937), *Vejs ende* (1939); travel books and essays as *Soldage* (1903), *Mod dagningen* (1923), *Haenderne vaek* (1934), *Lenin* (1947).

Ney \'nī\, Elisabet, *in full* Franzisca Bernadina Wilhelmina Elisabeth. 1833–1907. American sculptor, b. Münster, Westphalia. Court sculptor to Louis II of Bavaria (1867–70); to U.S. (1870); settled in Texas. Among her works: busts of Schopenhauer, Garibaldi, Bismarck, Stephen F. Austin, Samuel Houston; the Albert Sidney Johnston Memorial at Austin, Tex.; and the heroic figure *Prometheus Bound.*

Ney \nē, nā\, Michel. Duc d'·El·ching·en \del-k̲iŋ-ən\. Prince de La Mos·ko·va \də-lȧ-mȯs-kō-vȧ\. 1769–1815. French soldier. Entered army (1788); general of brigade (1796); distinguished himself under Bernadotte in capture of Mannheim (1797); organized army of the Rhine (1799); again prominent at Hohenlinden (1800); created marshal of France (1804); won victory of Elchingen (Oct. 14, 1805) for which he was created duc (1808); engaged at Jena (1806), Königsberg, Eylau, and Friedland (1807), in Spain (1808–11); commanded center at Borodino (1812) and was created prince; commanded rear guard in retreat from Russia and distinguished himself at Smolensk and Kovno (1812); engaged at Lützen, Bautzen, and Leipzig (1813), and the campaign for the defense of France (1814); created peer by Louis XVIII at the Restoration, but rallied to Napoléon during the Hundred Days; commanded the Old Guard at Waterloo (June 18, 1815); tried and condemned for treason by the Chamber of Peers; shot.

Nez·ā·mi \ˌnez-ä-ˈmē\. *More completely* Elyās Yūsof Neẓāmī Ganjavī. c.1141–1203 or 1217. Persian poet. Considered greatest romantic Persian poet; lived as an ascetic. Known for *Khamseh* (The Quintuplet), a pentalogy of romantic epic poems in rhymed couplets consisting of *The Treasure-house of Mysteries, Khosrow and Shīrīn, Leyla and Majnun, The Seven Beauties* (his masterpiece), and *The Book of Alexander the Great.*

Nga·ta \ˈŋä-tä, *Angl* en-ˈgät-ə\, Sir Apirana Turupa. 1874–1950. Maori leader. First Maori to graduate from a New Zealand university (1897); active in Young Maori party; in Parliament (1905–44); minister of native affairs (1928–34), inaugurated (1931) Maori land development plan; fostered educational and cultural development; a founder and chairman (1928–34) of Maori Board of Ethnological Research. Compiled *Nga Moteatea* (1929), anthology of Maori tribal songs and chants.

Ngo Dinh Diem \ˈŋō-ˈdin-de-ˈem, *Angl* en-ˈgō-\. 1901–1963. Vietnamese politician. Member of a royal family; served in government of Emperor Bao Dai; in exile (1945–54); president of Republic of Vietnam (1954–63), holding dictatorial powers; with heavy U.S. aid, conducted long struggle with Communist regime of North Vietnam; persecuted opponents, esp. Buddhists; assassinated in military coup d'état.

Ngo Quy·en \-kī-ˈen\. 896 or 897–944. Vietnamese leader. Prefect of a northern province under Chinese rule; defeated Chinese and proclaimed independent kingdom of Nam Viet (939); established capital at Co Loa. His dynasty lasted only to 954, but Nam Viet retained independence to 19th century.

Ngo Van Chieu \-ˈvän-jē-ˈü\. *Also called* Le Van Trung \ˈlā-ˈvän-ˈtru̇ŋ\. 1878–1926. Vietnamese religious leader. Founded Cao Dai sect with theology compounded of elements of Confucianism, Buddhism, Taoism, Roman Catholicism; first pope of the sect.

Ng Poon Chew \ˈwü-ˈpän-ˈjəu̇\. 1866–1931. American clergyman and editor, b. South China. To U.S. (1881); in Presbyterian ministry (1892–99); founder and editor of *Chinese Western Daily* (*Chung Sai Yat Po*), first Chinese daily newspaper published in U.S. (1900–31).

Nguy·en \ŋī-ˈen, *Angl* en-gī-ˈen, nī-\. Name of a family prominent in Vietnamese affairs from 16th century; after long struggle with rival Trinh family, accepted de facto partition (1673) and ruled southernmost part of Vietnam; gained control of Champa and Mekong delta (see Hien Vuong); family survived Tay Son rebellion (1771) and provided rulers of the Nguyen dynasty of unified Vietnam (1802–1945). See Gia Long, Khai Dinh, Minh Mang, Tu Duc.

Nguyen Du \-ˈdü\. *In full* Nguyen-Du Thanh-Hien. *Pen name* To Nhu \ˈtōn-ˈhü\. 1765–1820. Vietnamese poet. In service of Le dynasty until its fall (1787); joined court of Gia Long (1802); undertook diplomatic missions to China. Author of verse in Chinese and in Vietnamese, notably the epic *Kim Van Kieu,* adapted from a Chinese novel and considered a chief ornament of Vietnamese literature.

Nguyen Hue \-ˈhwā\ (c.1752–1792) and his brothers Nguyen Lu \-ˈlü\ (c.1752–1792) and Nguyen Nhac \-ˈnäk\ (c.1752–1793). *Known collectively, from their home village, as* the Tay Son \-ˈtī-ˈsȯn\ brothers. Vietnamese revolutionaries and rulers. Leaders (from 1771) of national insurrection known as Tay Son Rebellion; conquered central and southern parts of Vietnam (by 1778); overthrew Trinh ruling house of northern Vietnam (1787), achieving reunification of country. Each brother ruled (1788–93) a part of Vietnam, with Hue taking northern part; Chinese invading force defeated by Hue (1788–89); brothers defeated by Nguyen Anh (Gia Long).

Nguyen Tri Phuong \-ˈtrē-ˈpwȯŋ\. 1806–1873. Vietnamese general. Repelled Siamese invasion and succeeded Truong Minh Giang as commander in chief (1841); viceroy of lower Cochinchina (1841); became father-in-law and close adviser of Emperor Tu Duc; kept Vietnam closed to Western influences and contacts; defeated French naval attack at Da Nang (1859); defeated in subsequent battles and captured at Hanoi (1873).

Nguyen Truong To \-tru̇-ˈȯŋ-ˈtō\. 1828–1871. Vietnamese politician. Convert to Roman Catholicism; traveled in Europe; ardent proponent of Westernization, but lost influence with Emperor Tu Duc to court mandarins who counseled closing Vietnam to the West.

Nguyen Van Thinh \ˈvän-ˈtin\. d. 1946. Vietnamese politician. Installed as figurehead president of French-controlled Republic of Cochinchina (1946); committed suicide.

Niall. King of Ireland. See O'Neill family.

Nib·lo \ˈnib-(ˌ)lō\, William. 1789–1878. American hotel and theater proprietor, b. Ireland. To U.S. in youth; opened (1829) Niblo's Garden, long one of most fashionable theaters in New York City.

Ni·can·der \nə-ˈkan-dər, nī-\. 2d century B.C. Greek poet, physician, and grammarian. Member of the Pleiad of Alexandria; extant poems are *Theriaca* and *Alexipharmaca* on venomous animals and antidotes for poisons.

Ni·can·der \nē-ˈkän-dər\, Karl August. 1799–1839. Swedish poet. Author of verse, mainly Romantic, including *Sånger av August* (1819), *Runor av Norna Gest* (1824), *Dikter* (1825), *Hesperider* (1835); also wrote plays as *Runasvärdet* (1820).

Nic·co·li·ni \ˌnēk-kō-ˈlē-nē\, Giovanni Battista. 1782–1861. Italian playwright. Among his plays were *Polyxena* (1811), *Nabucco* (1816), *Antonio Foscarini* (1827), *Lodovico Sforza* (1834), *Arnaldo da Brescia* (1838), and *Filippo Strozzi* (1847).

Nic·co·lò dell'·Ar·ca \ˈnēk-kō-ˌlō-del-ˈär-kä\. *Also known as* Niccolò da Ba·ri \-dä-ˈbär-ē\. fl. c.1460–94. Bolognese sculptor. Combined Gothic and early Renaissance elements in works as canopy and figures for tomb of St. Dominic, group of lamenting figures in S. Maria della Vita, Madonna and saints group for Palazzo Comunale, all in Bologna.

Niccolò de' Nic·co·li \-dä-nē-ˈkōl-lē\. c.1364–1437. Florentine Humanist. Contributed to growth of interest in antiquity through large personal collection of ancient art objects and library of classical works; noted also as a calligrapher.

Ni·ce·fo·ro \ne-ˈchā-fō-rō\, Alfredo. 1876–1960. Italian sociologist. Professor at Lausanne, Brussels, Paris, Messina, Naples, and (from 1931) Rome; developed theory of unconscious antisocial "deep ego" and socialized "superior ego" (1902); pioneered in statistical studies of social phenomena, esp. crime. Author of *L'Italia barbara contemporanea* (1898), *Antropologia delle classi povere* (1908), *La misura della vita* (1919), *Criminologia* (1942–53), *L'io profondo e le sue maschere* (1949).

Ni·ceph·o·rus I \nī-ˈsef-(ə-)rəs\. *Gr.* Ni·keph·o·ros \nē-ˈkef-ō-rōs\. Saint. c.758–829. Greek prelate. Served in imperial secretariat; representative of Emperor Constantine VI at Council of Nicaea (787); took charge of welfare activities for Empress Irene; patriarch of Constantinople (806–815); deposed by iconoclastic opponents, sought monastic retreat. Author of theological works, chiefly anti-iconoclastic, and of historical works *Breviarium Nicephori* on Byzantine history 602–769 and *Chronological Tables.*

Nicephorus. Name of three rulers of Eastern Roman Empire:

Nicephorus I. d. 811. Emperor (802–811). Official in government of Empress Irene; proclaimed emperor on her deposition; crushed revolts of rivals (803, 808); refused to pay tribute to Hārūn ar-Rashīd, caliph of Baghdad, and was defeated by Islāmic troops at Crasus (805); lost Heraclea, Tyana, etc., to Hārūn (806) and agreed to pay. Reached preliminary agreement (810) with Charlemagne on return of Venice, Istria, Dalmatian coast to Byzantine control; campaigned against Bulgars (807–809); killed in massacre of Byzantine army by Krum during invasion of Bulgaria.

Nicephorus II Pho·cas \-ˈfō-kəs, -ˌkäs\. 912–969. Emperor (963–969). Son of Bardas Phocas, a general; succeeded father as commander of Byzantine forces in the East (954–955); instilled new discipline and organization; for Romanus II commanded expedition that captured Crete (961); captured much of Cilicia and Syria (962); as result of intrigue by his lieutenant John Tzimisces, proclaimed by army to succeed Romanus instead of minor heirs Basil and Constantine; m. Romanus's widow Theophano; continued wars against Arabs for a time, but, beset by continuing intrigue, gradually withdrew into retirement; assassinated in plot involving Theophano and John Tzimisces. Considered the greatest of Byzantine military emperors and a principal architect of the empire.

Nicephorus III Bo·tan·ei·a·tes \-bə-ˌtan-ē-ˈāt-ˌēz\. 11th century. Emperor (1078–81). Military commander in Anatolia; proclaimed emperor during revolt against Michael VII Ducas; entered Constantinople, defeated rival Nicephorus Bryennius, and secured throne; opposed by numerous other rivals; owing to constant civil strife, lost much of Anatolia to Seljuq Turks; abdicated and entered a monastery.

Nicephorus Bryennius. See Bryennius.

Nicephorus Cal·lis·tus Xan·thop·ou·los \-kə-ˈlis-təs-zan-ˈthäp-ə-ləs\. c.1256–c.1335. Byzantine historian. Cleric attached to Hagia Sophia, Constantinople; taught rhetoric and theology; in late years a monk. Author of a monumental *Ecclesiasticae historiae,* narrating history of the church down to 912 and written in stylized florid prose of early Byzantine Humanism; also wrote treatises on hymnody and liturgy, commentaries on patristic writings, verse catalogues of Byzantine emperors and patriarchs, etc.

Nicephorus Gregoras. See Gregoras.

Ni·ce·tas \nī-ˈsēt-əs\ of Re·me·si·ana \rə-ˌmā-zē-ˈan-ə\. 4th–5th century. Greek prelate, theologian, and poet. Bishop of Remesiana (c.366); active missionary among Serbian Slavs; known chiefly through writings of Paulinus, bishop of Nola. Author of a major doctrinal work "Six Books of Instructions for Baptismal Candidates"; apparently introduced term "communion of saints"; reputedly also author of numerous liturgical hymns, possibly including the "Te Deum Laudamus."

Nicetas Ste·tha·tos \-steth-'ät-(,)ōs\. c.1000–c.1080. Byzantine mystic and theologian. Monk in the Studius monastery, Constantinople; follower of Symeon the New Theologian, of whom he wrote a biography; also wrote treatises on Hesychasm and ascetical mysticism; theologian-polemist to Patriarch Michael Cerularius in dispute with Cardinal Humbert that led to definitive Latin–Orthodox schism of 1054.

Ni·chi·ren \nē-chē-ren\. *Orig.* Zen-ni·chi \zen-nē-chē\. *Priestly name* Zen-shō·bō Ren·chō \zen-shō-bō-ren-chō\. 1222–1282. Japanese Buddhist leader. Entered monastery (1233); undertook rigorous study to recover genuine teaching of historic Buddha from welter of sects and cults; proclaimed the *Lotus Sūtra* as true doctrine (1253) and was forced to flee; became militant critic of sects and suffered persecution; published tract *Risshō ankoku-ron* (1260) ascribing ills of the nation to false religion; exiled by government (1261–63); resumed attacks, arrested and condemned to death (1271); instead, exiled to island of Sado (1271–74); there wrote systematic treatise *Kaimokushō* (1272); retired with disciples to Minobu-san. His intractable arguments helped reshape Buddhism in Japan to Japanese ways of thought and action.

Nich·o·las \'nik-(ə-)ləs\. *Also known as* Nicholas of My·ra \'mī-rə\. Saint. 4th century. Christian prelate. Bishop of Myra, in Lycia, Asia Minor; nothing certain known of his life; subject of many legends of his miracles, often in behalf of children; his remains transferred in 11th century from Myra to Bari, Italy. Patron saint of Greece and Russia; also considered patron saint of mariners, thieves, virgins, and children; gradually became identified with custom of giving gifts at Christmas.

Nicholas. Name of five popes and one antipope:

Nicholas I. Saint. *Sometimes called* Nicholas the Great. c.819 to 822–867. Pope (858–867). Supported Ignatius, patriarch of Constantinople, and excommunicated Photius (863); in turn excommunicated by Photius (867), precipitating Photian Schism; conducted long struggle with Lothair, king of Lorraine, forbidding his divorce; upheld right of bishops to appeal to Rome against their archbishops; recognized the False, or pseudo-Isidorian, Decretals (865); one of major contributors to establishment of Roman see as supreme in the church and primacy of spiritual over temporal authority.

Nicholas II. *Orig.* Gerard of Burgundy. 980?–1061. Pope (1059–61). Bishop of Florence; elected to succeed Stephen X in opposition to antipope Benedict X; a reformer; issued bull (1059) establishing procedure for papal elections by cardinals, which precipitated break with emperor and German bishops.

Nicholas III. *Orig.* Giovanni Gaetano Or·si·ni \ōr-'sē-nē\. c.1225–1280. Pope (1277–80). Cardinal (1244), protector of Franciscans (1261); as pope sought to balance influence of Angevins and Habsburgs and to extend church's holdings in Sicily, Italy.

Nicholas IV. *Orig.* Girolamo Ma·sci \'mäsh-shē\. 1227–1292. Pope (1288–92). A Franciscan; minister general (1274–79); cardinal bishop of Palestrina (1281); first Franciscan pope; sought to maintain balance of Angevin and Habsburg power; failed to revive crusade; sent missionaries to Mongols, Balkans, Near East.

Nicholas V. *Orig.* Tommaso Pa·ren·tu·cel·li \,pä-rān-tü-'chel-lē\ *or* Tommaso da Sar·za·na \dä-särd-'zä-nä\. 1397–1455. Pope (1447–55). Bishop of Bologna (1444), cardinal (1446); by patience and conciliation obtained resignation of antipope Felix V (1449); instituted Peace of Lodi (1455); fostered church reforms; great patron of arts; had Vatican rebuilt and walled, St. Peter's restored; restored senatorial palace on Capitoline Hill; patron of Humanists, founded Vatican library.

Nicholas V. *Orig.* Pietro Rai·nal·duc·ci \,rī-näl-'düt-chē\. d. 1333. Antipope (1328–30) in Rome under imperial sponsorship in opposition to John XXII at Avignon.

Nicholas. Name of several patriarchs of Constantinople, including:

Nicholas I. *Called* the Mystic. 852–925. Patriarch (901–907, 912–925). Entered Byzantine civil service; became monk (886) under patronage of Patriarch Photius; secretary counsellor to Emperor Leo VI; made patriarch (901); deposed (907) for opposing Leo's fourth marriage; recalled (912) and named regent for Constantine VII; by harsh retaliation against Euthymius, patriarch during his exile, began bitter factional rivalry within church (912–917); issued decree (920) settling question of fourth marriages for Greek Orthodox members.

Nicholas III. 11th–12th century. Patriarch (1084–1111). Monk of Prodromos monastery in Constantinople before appointment as patriarch; mediated disputes between clergy and Emperor Alexius I Comnenus; a noted theologian and supporter of orthodoxy; condemned Bogomil sect and its leader Basil the Physician; renewed contacts with Western church but refused to compromise Orthodox doctrine; composed prayer and response texts for several Byzantine liturgical services.

Nicholas I. 1841–1921. Prince (1860–1910) and king (1910–18) of Montenegro. Succeeded uncle Danilo I as prince; led army against Turks (1862, 1876); obtained great increase in territory and recognition of Montenegran sovereignty from Congress of Berlin (1878); introduced Western ideas and methods; attempted by diplomacy to create a South Slav state. In later years became more despotic; forced to grant constitution (1905); declared himself king (1910); took part in Balkan War against Turkey (1912–13); in World War I supported Serbia against Austria-Hungary and was defeated; concluded peace and went into exile (1916); deposed by national assembly (1918).

Nicholas. Name of two czars of Russia:

Nicholas I. *Russ.* Nikolay Pavlovich. 1796–1855. Czar (1825–55). 3d son of Paul I; by training and temperament a soldier; m. (1817) Princess Charlotte (changed to Alexandra) of Prussia; succeeded his brother Alexander I, the moment being marred by the abortive Decembrist uprising; came to represent autocracy, post-Napoleonic reaction, militarism, bureaucracy; quelled uprising in Poland (1830–31); aided Austria in quelling uprising in Hungary (1849). His designs upon Constantinople provoked war with Turkey (1853) into which other European powers were drawn (Crimean War, 1854–56).

Nicholas II. *Russ.* Nikolay Aleksandrovich. 1868–1918. Czar (1894–1917). Eldest son of Alexander III; made peace proposals (1898) which led to International Peace Conference at The Hague (1899) and to the founding of the Hague Tribunal; directed construction of the Trans-Siberian railroad; waged unsuccessful war with Japan (1904–05); forced to grant constitution of 1905 but quickly dissolved first two dumas and made only token efforts to still popular discontent by liberal reforms under prime minister Stolypin; joined Allies in World War I (1914). Dissatisfaction with both his foreign and his domestic policies culminated in Russian Revolution (1917); abdicated (Mar. 1917); executed at Yekaterinburg with his whole family by the Bolsheviks (July 1918).

Nicholas. *Russ.* Nikolay Nikolayevich. 1831–1891. Russian grand duke. 3d son of Czar Nicholas I; commanded Russian army of the Danube in Russo–Turkish War (1877–78). His son ¶Grand Duke Nicholas, *Russ.* Nikolay Nikolayevich (1856–1929) was commander in chief, St. Petersburg military district (1905–14); in World War I, commander in chief against Germany and Austria-Hungary (1914–1915); viceroy and commander in chief in the Caucasus (1915–17); after Revolution lived in the Crimea (1917–19) and in France (from 1919); chosen leader of Russian monarchists in exile in France (1926).

Nicholas of Au·tre·court \ō-trə-kür\. c.1300–after 1350. French philosopher and theologian. Follower of William of Ockham, whose Nominalist doctrine he developed to logical extreme, denying universals, causality, rational proofs of God's existence, etc.; maintained that faith may assent to propositions reason rejects; tried for heresy by Pope Benedict XII at Avignon (1340); condemned, forced to resign professorship at Sorbonne (1347), works burned; dean of cathedral of Metz (1350).

Nicholas of Clé·manges \klā-mäⁿzh\. *Orig.* Nicolas Poille·vilain \pwȧy-vlaⁿ\. c.1363–1437. French theologian. Known as a liberal Humanist; rector, U. of Paris (1393); secretary to Benedict XIII at Avignon (1397–1408); retired to Carthusian monastery (1408–32); professor, College of Navarre (from 1432); supported Gallicanism, subordination of popes to councils. Author of *De fructu rerum adversarum* and *De fructu eremi* on church schism, *De studio theologico, De lapsu et reparatione justitiae* on church reform, biblical commentaries, etc.

Nicholas of Cu·sa \'k(y)ü-sə\. *Ger.* Ni·ko·la·us von Cu·sa \,nē-kō-'laús-fòn-kü-zȧ, -'lä-ús-\. *Lat.* Nic·o·la·us Cu·sa·nus \,nik-ə-'lā-əs-k(y)ü-'sā-nəs\. 1401–1464. German prelate and philosopher. Ordained (c.1440); created cardinal (1448), bishop of Bressanone (1450). Author of *De concordantia catholica* (1433, on supremacy of church councils, written for the Council of Basel), *De docta ignorantia* on learning (1440), and philosophical and mathematical treatises. Anticipated Copernicus by his belief in the earth's rotation and revolution around the sun; conducted botanical experiments; collected manuscripts and discovered lost comedies of Plautus.

Nicholas of Da·mas·cus \də-'mas-kəs\. *Lat.* Nic·o·la·us Dam·a·sce·nus \,nik-ə-lā-əs-,dam-ə-'sē-nəs\. 1st century B.C. Greek historian. Friend of Augustus and Herod the Great. Only fragments of his universal history have been preserved.

Nicholas of Flüe \'flūē-ə\. *Ger.* Nikolaus von der Flüe. *Orig.* Nikolaus Lö·wen·brug·ger \'lœ-vən-,brůg-ər\. *Often called* Bru·der Klaus \'brü-dər-klaús\. 1417–1487. Swiss religious. Abandoned family (1467) and lived as hermit in Ranft ravine near Basel; saved Swiss Confederation by plea for union at Diet of Stans (1481). Canonized (1872).

Nicholas of Her·e·ford \'her-ə-fərd, *US also* 'hər-fərd\. d. after 1417. English theologian. Disciple of John Wycliffe; denounced hierarchy, clerical laxity, supported English preaching and liturgy; assisted Wycliffe in translation of Bible into English; condemned with Wycliffe and Lollards (1382), excommunicated; appealed to Pope Urban VI but sentenced to confinement.

Abjured Lollardism (1391) and made inquisitor of suspected heretics; chancellor of Hereford cathedral (1391), St Paul's (1395).

Nicholas of Ly·ra \'lī-rə\. *Lat.* Nic·o·la·us Ly·ra·nus \ˌnik-ə-'lā-ə-slī-'rā-nəs, -slə-\. c.1270–1349. French scholar. Entered Franciscan order (c.1300); professor, Sorbonne (1309); Franciscan provincial for France (1319–49); founded College of Burgundy, Paris (1325). Author of 50-vol. *Postillae perpetuae in universam S. Scripturam,* earliest printed biblical commentary and long a standard manual of exegesis.

Nicholas of Ver·dun \ver-dœⁿ, *Angl* (ˌ)vər-'dən\. fl. c.1150–1210. Flemish goldsmith and enamellist. Outstanding exponent of his crafts in his day, important in transition from late Romanesque to early Gothic style. Works included altarpiece for abbey church of Klosterneuberg, Austria (1181); Dreikönigsschrein in Cologne cathedral (c.1200); reliquary of SS. Piatus and Nicasius in Tournai cathedral (1205).

Nicholas Oresme. See ORESME.

Nich·ols \'nik-əlz\, Anne. 1891–1966. American playwright, b. Dales Mill, Ga. Author of *Abie's Irish Rose,* which ran continuously in New York from 1922 to 1927 (2327 performances), the longest run on record up to that time (revived 1937, 1954; film versions 1928, 1946); also wrote *The Gilded Cage* (1920), *Love Dreams* (1921), and *Just Married* (with Adelaide Matthews, 1921).

Nichols, Edward Leamington. 1854–1937. American physicist, b. Leamington, England, of American parents. Professor, U. of Kansas (1883–87), Cornell (1887–1919); founder and editor, *Physical Review* (1893–1912). Author of *Elements of Physics* (1896–97), and collaborator in studies of luminescence and fluorescence.

Nichols, Ernest Fox. 1869–1924. American physicist, b. Leavenworth, Kans. Professor, Dartmouth (1898–1903), Columbia (1903–09), Yale (1916–20); president, Dartmouth (1909–16), M.I.T. (1920); director of research, National Electric Light Assoc., Cleveland (1920–24); esp. known for his experiments in measuring planetary heat, determining light pressure, etc., by means of an extremely sensitive radiometer devised by him.

Nichols, John. 1745–1826. English printer and author. Apprentice (1757), partner (1766), successor (1777) of William Bowyer, the "learned printer"; edited *Gentleman's Magazine* (1778–1826); published *Bibliotheca Topographica Britannica* (1780–90); edited works of Swift and Hogarth; published *Anecdotes* (1812–15) and *Illustrations* (1817–31) on 18th-century literary history, *History and Antiquities of the County of Leicester* (1795–1815); issued Samuel Johnson's *Lives of the English Poets.* His son ¶John Bowyer (1779–1863) became proprietor of *Gentleman's Magazine* (1833); added two volumes to his father's *Illustrations* (1848, 1856); published county histories; wrote antiquarian and topographic works. His son ¶John Gough (1806–1873), editor of *Gentleman's Magazine* (1851–56), printed many volumes for the Camden Society, of which he was a founder (1838); edited *The Topographer and Genealogist* (1846–58) and *The Herald and Genealogist* (1863–73); wrote antiquarian works.

Nich·ol·son \'nik-əl-sən\, Ben. 1894–1981. English painter. Early influenced by Vorticism, Cubism; known esp. for abstract or semi-abstract still lifes and landscapes, sometimes rendered in relief, in which the plane of the picture is emphasized by various formal means.

Nicholson, John. 1821–1857. British soldier and administrator, b. Ireland. Entered Bengal army (1839); deputy commissioner (1851–56) in Punjab; became among natives object of hero worship under title of Nik·kul Seyn \'nik-əl-'sān\; in Sepoy Mutiny (1857) led first column in assault on Delhi; fell mortally wounded in successful storming of Kashmir Gate.

Nicholson, Joseph Shield. 1850–1927. English economist. Professor, Edinburgh (1880–1925); authority on currency and banking. Author of *Principles of Political Economy* (1893–1901), *Bankers' Money* (1902), *Inflation* (1919), *Revival of Marxism* (1920), etc.

Nicholson, Reynold Alleyne. 1868–1945. English Orientalist. Lecturer in Persian (1902–26), professor (1926–33), Cambridge; noted esp. as student of Islāmic literature and mysticism. Author of *Literary History of the Arabs* (1907), *Mathnawi of Jalalu'ddin Rumi* (1925–40); admired for English versions of Persian and Arabic poetry.

Nicholson, Seth Barnes. 1891–1963. American astronomer, b. Springfield, Ill. On staff of Mt. Wilson Observatory (1915–57); discovered four satellites of Jupiter: IX (1914), X and XI (1938), XII (1951); also studied sunspots.

Nicholson, William. 1753–1815. English scientist. With East India Co. (1769–76); conducted a mathematics school, London; waterworks engineer for Portsmouth and Gosport; invented a hydrometer and a machine for printing on linen (1790); discovered electrolytic decomposition of water (1800); founded and published (1797–1813) *Journal of Natural Philosophy, Chemistry and the Arts.* Author of *Introduction to Natural Philosophy* (1781), *First Principles of Chemistry* (1790), etc.; compiled *Dictionary of Practical and Theoretical Chemistry* (1808).

Nicholson, William. 1816–1865. Australian politician, b. England. To Melbourne (1841); mayor (1850); member of the council (1852–56, 1859–64) and premier of Victoria (1859); credited with introducing the ballot (1855).

Nicholson, Sir William Newzam Prior. 1872–1949. English painter and engraver. Designed striking commercial posters with his brother-in-law, James Pryde, under name of Beggarstaff Brothers, which led to a series of original and witty books; published series of woodcuts including *The Square Book of Animals* (1896), *An Almanac of Twelve Sports* (with Rudyard Kipling, 1898), *Twelve Portraits,* etc. Painter of portraits, figure subjects, still life and landscape studies.

Ni·ci·as \'nis(h)-ē-əs\. d. 413 B.C. Athenian general and politician. Political opponent of Cleon and Alcibiades; negotiated short-lived Peace of Nicias with Sparta (421 B.C.); with Alcibiades and Lamachus, placed in command of Sicilian expedition (415), although he had opposed project; undertook siege of Syracuse; captured by Syracusans and executed.

Nicias of Ath·ens \'ath-ənz\. 4th century B.C. Greek painter. Contemporary of Praxiteles, some of whose statues he painted; none of his works extant.

Nic·o·de·mus \ˌnik-ə-'dē-məs\. Saint. *Called* the Ha·gio·rite \'haj(-ē)-ə-ˌrīt, 'hā-jē(-ə)-\. 1748–1809. Greek religious. Monk of Mt. Athos; edited works of Macarius of Corinth, helping to revive interest in Hesychasm; author of *Pedalion* (*Rudder of the Ship of Knowledge*) on Greek church law, Greek version of Ignatius of Loyola's *Spiritual Exercises, Philocalia* and *Enchiridion* on monasticism; proclaimed saint (1955).

Nic·ol \'nik-əl\, William. 1744?–1797. Scottish schoolmaster. Host to Robert Burns (1787, 1789), who immortalized him in "Willie Brewed a Peck o'Maut."

Nicol, William. 1768–1851. Scottish physicist. Invented the Nicol prism (1828) for producing and analyzing polarized light.

Ni·co·lai \ˌnē-kō-'lä-ē\, Christoph Friedrich. 1733–1811. German writer, critic, and bookseller. Champion of German enlightenment (*Aufklärung*); defended Milton against Gottsched; literary associate of Lessing and Moses Mendelssohn, with the latter of whom he founded (1757) Berlin critical journal *Bibliothek der schönen Wissenschaften und Freien Kunste;* with both collaborated in the literary review *Briefe, die Neueste Literatur betreffend* (1759–65); edited *Allgemeine deutsche Bibliothek* (1765–92) and wrote satirical novels, notably *Die Freuden des jungen Werthers* (1775), attacks on Goethe, Schiller, Kant, Fichte, and his other literary critics, several biographies, etc.

Nicolai, Otto, *in full* Carl Otto Ehrenfried. 1810–1849. German composer and conductor. Kapellmeister (1837–38), conductor (1841–47), Hoftheater, Vienna; director of cathedral choir and Kapellmeister of royal opera, Berlin (1848). Composed operas, notably *Die lustigen Weiber von Windsor* (1849); sacred music, esp. *Te Deum* (c.1831), a mass, Psalm settings; choral, vocal, orchestral works.

Ni·co·lai·er \ˌnē-kō-'lī-ər\, Arthur. 1862–1942. German physician. Professor, Göttingen (1894), Berlin (1901); discovered bacillus of tetanus (1894).

Nicolas. See also NICHOLAS.

Nic·o·las \'nik-(ə-)ləs\, Sir Nicholas Harris. 1799–1848. English antiquary. Author of *Synopsis of the Peerage of England* (1825), *History of the Orders of Knighthood of the British Empire* (1841–42), etc.

Nicolaus. See NICHOLAS.

Nic·o·lay \'nik-ə-lā\, John George. 1832–1901. American biographer, b. Essingen, Bavaria. To U.S. (1838); private secretary to Abraham Lincoln (1860–65); U.S. consul at Paris (1865–69); marshal of U.S. Supreme Court (1872–87). Collaborator with John Hay in a biography of Abraham Lincoln (1890) and in an edition of *Complete Works of Abraham Lincoln* (1894).

Ni·cole \nē-kōl\, Pierre. 1625–1695. French theologian. Teacher at Port-Royal and writer and editor of polemical Jansenist tracts; wrote *La Logique ou l'art de penser,* better known as *La Logique de Port-Royal* (1662, with A. Arnauld); also wrote tracts against Protestantism; author of *Essais de morale* (1671). Involved in important theological controversies of his time, as against Fénelon and Mme Guyon, against Quietism, against the Jesuits, etc.

Ni·co·let \nē-kō-le\, Jean. 1598–1642. French explorer. Brought to New France by Champlain (1618); lived among Indians on upper Ottawa River; made expedition to Lake Michigan and Wisconsin region (1634), first European to reach that region.

Nic·oll \'nik-əl\, Sir William Robertson. *Pseudonym* Claudius Clear \'kli(ə)r\. 1851–1923. Scottish man of letters. Free Church minister (1874); founded (1891) literary journal *Bookman;* edited *The Expositor's Greek Testament* (1897) and works of Charlotte Brontë (1902).

Ni·colle \nē-kōl\, Charles-Jean-Henri. 1866–1936. French bacteriologist. Director, Pasteur Institute, Tunis (1902–32); professor, Collège de France (1932); discovered (1909) that typhus fever is transmitted by the body louse; awarded 1928 Nobel prize for physiology or medicine.

Nic·olls \'nik-əlz\, Richard. 1624–1672. British colonialist. Commanded troop of horse in Royalist army (1643); in exile with the Stuarts; first governor of New York, taken over from the Dutch (1664–68); issued "the Duke's Laws" (1665).

Nicolson. See also NICHOLSON.

Nic·ol·son \'nik-əl-sən\, Sir Harold George. 1886–1968. British diplomat and man of letters. Son of 1st Baron Carnock; entered foreign office (1909); m. (1913) Victoria Mary Sackville-West (*q.v.*); served on British delegation to Paris Conference (1919); M.P. (1935–45). Author of biographies of Paul Verlaine (1921), Tennyson (1923), Byron (1924), Swinburne (1926), Lord Curzon (1934), Dwight Morrow (1935), King George V (1952), Sainte-Beuve (1957); of novels as *Sweet Waters* (1921), *Public Faces* (1932); of essays as *Some People* (1927), *Diplomacy* (1939), *The English Sense of Humour* (1947), *Good Behaviour* (1955), *Age of Reason* (1960); his valuable *Diaries and Letters* edited and published by his son (1966–68).

Ni·com·a·chus \nə-'käm-ə-kəs, nī-\. 4th century B.C. Greek painter. Overshadowed by more celebrated contemporaries but highly praised by Vitruvius.

Nicomachus of Ger·a·sa \'jer-ə-sə\. fl. c.100 A.D. Greek philosopher and mathematician. Author of *Arithmētikē eisagōgē*, first work to treat arithmetic independent of geometry; also wrote neo-Pythagorean treatises *Encheiridion harmonikēs* and *Theologumena arithmetikēs*.

Nic·o·me·des \,nik-ə-'mē-,dēz\. Name of three kings of Bithynia: Nicomedes I (reigned 278–250 B.C.); founder (264) of Nicomedia, capital of Bithynia. ¶Nicomedes II, *surnamed* Epiph·a·nes \ə-'pif-ə-nēz\ (reigned 149–91 B.C.), hero of Corneille's *Nicomède*. ¶Nicomedes III, *surnamed* Phi·lo·pa·ter \'fī-lō-,pat-ər\ (reigned 91–74 B.C.), opponent of Mithradates and loyal friend of the Romans; reduced Bithynia to the status of a Roman province.

Nicomedes. fl. c.250 B.C. Greek mathematician. Reputed discoverer of the conchoid curve, by which he was able to trisect an angle and double a cube.

Ni·cot \nē-kō\, Jean. c.1530–1600. French diplomat and scholar. Ambassador in Portugal (1559–61); introduced use of tobacco from Portugal into France. The terms *nicotine* and *Nicotiana* derive from his name.

Nie·buhr \'nē-,bür\, Barthold Georg. 1776–1831. German historian. Son of Carsten Niebuhr; secretary to director of Danish national bank (1804–06), to Baron von Stein in Prussian service (1806–10); state historiographer (1810–16); Prussian ambassador to Vatican (1816–23). Chief work the enormously influential *Römische Geschichte* (1811–32), which virtually created scientific historical scholarship and began new era of historiography.

Niebuhr, Carsten. 1733–1815. German traveler and explorer. Invited to join Danish expedition (1761–67) to explore Arabia, Palestine, Syria, Persia, and Asia Minor; only surviror; published *Beschreibung von Arabien* (1772), *Reisebeschreibung nach Arabien und andern umliegenden Ländern* (1774).

Nie·buhr \'nē-,bu̇(ə)r, -bər\, Reinhold. 1892–1971. American clergyman and theologian, b. Wright City, Mo. Ordained in Evangelical Synod (1915); pastor in Detroit (1915–28); professor, Union Theol. Sem. (1928–60); known for doctrine of Christian Realism, criticisms of "social gospel" liberalism. Author of *Does Civilization Need Religion?* (1927), *Moral Man and Immoral Society* (1932), *Beyond Tragedy* (1937), *The Nature and Destiny of Man* (1941–43), *Faith and History* (1949), *Irony of American History* (1952), *The Self and the Dramas of History* (1955), *Structure of Nations and Empires* (1959), *Man's Nature and his Communities* (1965), etc. His brother ¶Helmut Richard (1894–1962), clergyman; professor, Yale Divinity School (1931–62); author of *The Kingdom of God in America* (1937), *The Meaning of Revelation* (1941), *Christ and Culture* (1951), *Radical Monotheism* (1960), etc.

Nie·der·mey·er \'nē-dər-,mī-ər\, Abraham Louis. 1802–1861. Swiss composer. Composed operas *Stradella* (1837), *María Estuardo* (1844), *La Fronda* (1853); sacred music; music for poems as by Victor Hugo, Deschamps, Lamartine.

Nie·haus \'nē-,hau̇s\, Charles Henry. 1855–1935. American sculptor, b. Cincinnati, O. His sculptures included portrait busts in rotunda of the Capitol, Washington, D.C., statue of William McKinley for his tomb in Canton, Ohio, and the John Paul Jones monument in Washington, D.C.

Nieheim, Dietrich von. See DIETRICH VON NIEHEIM.

Niel \nyel\, Adolphe. 1802–1869. French soldier. Distinguished himself in the Crimean War, esp. at the siege of Sevastopol (1855), and became aide-de-camp to Emperor Napoléon III; engaged at Magenta and Solferino (1859); marshal of France (1859); minister of war (1867–69).

Niels \'nils\. 1063–1134. King of Denmark (1104–34). Son of Sweyn II; reign marked by struggles with the church over extent of royal power.

Niel·sen \'nē(ə)l-sən\, Arthur Charles. 1897–1980. American businessman, b. Chicago. Founded (1923) A.C. Nielsen Co. to conduct consumer surveys, marketing research, radio ratings, and (from 1950) television surveys.

Niel·sen \'nil-sən, *Angl* 'nē(ə)l-sən\, Carl August. 1865–1931. Danish composer. Conductor of the music society and codirector of the conservatory, Copenhagen (1915–27). Composed 6 symphonies, the operas *Saul og David* (1903) and *Maskerade* (1907), orchestral fantasy *Pan og Syrinx* (1926), concertos for violin (1911), flute (1926), and clarinet (1928), violin sonatas, string quartets, piano pieces, songs, etc.

Nielsen, Morten. 1922–1944. Danish poet. Killed during Danish resistance to German occupation; his poetry collected in *Krigere uden Vaaben* (1943) and *Efterladte Digte* (1945).

Niem, Dietrich von. See DIETRICH VON NIEHEIM.

Niembsch von Streh·le·nau \'nēmpsh-fōn-'shtrā-lə-,nau̇\, Nikolaus Franz. *Pseudonym* Nikolaus Le·nau \'lā-,nau̇\. 1802–1850. Austrian poet, b. Hungary. In U.S. (1832–33); wrote in tradition of German Romantic pessimism; became insane (1844). Known for his lyric verse (first published as *Gedichte*, 1832) and dramatic-narrative poems *Faust* (1836), *Savonarola* (1837), *Die Albigenser* (1842), and *Don Juan* (1844).

Niem·ce·wicz \nyemt-'sev-ēch\, Julian Ursyn. 1758–1841. Polish patriot and man of letters. Aide and adviser of Kościuszko; in U.S. (1796–1807); returned to Poland (1807); involved in revolution (1830–31), was forced into exile; died in Paris. Among his works were *Powrót posła* (1790, political comedy), *Śpiewy historyczne* (1816, song poems), *Lebje i Siora* (1821, novel), *Jan z Tęczyna* (1825, first Polish historical novel).

Nie·möl·ler \'nē-,mə(r)l-ər, -,mœl-\, Martin, *in full* Friedrich Gustav Emil Martin. 1892–1984. German Protestant theologian. Joined German navy (1910); won Iron Cross for exploits as submarine commander; ordained minister of Evangelical Chuch (1924); appointed pastor of Berlin congregation (1931); outspoken opponent of Hitler and Nazism; interned in Dachau and Sachsenhausen concentration camps (1937–45); after World War II became passionate advocate of international disarmament and rebuilder of protestant church in Germany; president of World Council of Churches (1961–68).

Nien·huys \'nēn-,hœis\, Jacobus. 1836–1927. Dutch businessman and planter. To Sumatra (1863) where he established the tobacco industry.

Niepce \nyeps\, Joseph-Nicéphore. 1765–1833. French physicist. With his brother Claude, invented an internal combustion engine which powered a boat (1807); produced permanent "heliotypes" by means of glass plates coated with bitumen (1822); credited with making world's first photograph (1826); associated with Daguerre (from 1829) in experiments with photography. His nephew ¶Claude-Félix-Abel Niepce de Saint-Vic·tor \-də-saⁿ-vēk-tȯr\ (1805–1870), physicist, devoted himself to furthering development of photography as invented by Joseph Niepce and Daguerre, and was first to use albumen, one of first to try fixing images on glass, and one of first to produce steel engravings by photographic means.

Nie·rem·berg \'nē-rem-berḡ\, Juan Eusebio. 1595–1658. Spanish Jesuit naturalist and author. Works included *Historia natural* (1635), *De la diferencia entre lo temporal y lo eterno* (1640), *Corona virtuosa y virtud coronada* (1643). The genus *Nierembergia* is named after him.

Nie·to Ca·bal·le·ro \'nyā-tō-kä-b̲ä-(l)-yä-rō\, Luis Eduardo. 1887–1957. Colombian politician and author. Helped overthrow Rafael Reyes (1909); ambassador to Switzerland and Mexico; author of *Ideas liberales* (1922), *Libros Colombianos* (1928), *Críticas* (1936), *Hombres del pasado* (1944), etc.

Nietz·sche \'nē-chə, *Angl also* -chē\, Friedrich Wilhelm. 1844–1900. German philosopher and poet. Professor of classical philology, Basel (1869–79), where he was at first the friend and follower and later (from c.1878) a strong opponent of Wagner in art and philosophy; opponent of Schopenhauer's philosophy; suffered mental breakdown (1889); spent last years in care of his mother at Naumburg and his sister Elisabeth Förster-Nietzsche (*q.v.*) at Weimar. Known for denouncing religion, for espousing doctrine of perfectibility of man through forcible self-assertion, and for glorification of the superman or overman (*Übermensch*). His works, chiefly on philology, music, Greek antiquity, and esp. philosophy, included *Die Geburt der Tragödie aus dem Geiste der Musik* (1872), *Unzeitgemässe Betrachtungen* (1873–76), *Menschliches-Allzumenschliches* (1878–80), *Morgenröte* (1881), *Die fröhliche Wissenschaft* (1882), *Also sprach Zarathustra* (1883–92), *Jenseits von Gut und Böse* (1886), *Zur Genealogie der Moral* (1887), *Der Fall Wagner* (1888), *Götzendämmerung* (1889), *Der Antichrist* (1895), the autobiography *Ecce Homo* (1908).

Nieu·port \nyœ̄-pȯr\, Édouard. 1875–1911. French aviator and airplane builder. Pioneer in the development of the airplane; constructed biplanes of a type much used in World War I.

Nieuw·land \'nyü-lənd\, Julius Arthur. 1878–1936. American chemist and botanist, b. Hansbeke, Belgium. Ordained Roman Catholic priest (1903); taught at Notre Dame (from 1904); known for synthesis of organic compounds, esp. synthetic rubber, from acetylene.

Nie·vo \'nyā-vō\, Ippolito. 1831–1861. Italian novelist and poet. Author of *Lucciole* (1858, poems); known esp. for his historical novel *Confessioni di un ottuagenario* (1867).

Ni·fo \'nē-fō\, Agostino. *Lat.* Augustinus Ni·phus \'nī-fəs\ *or* Niphus Sues·sa·nus \swes-'ā-nəs\. 1473?–?1538. Italian philosopher. Taught at U. of Padua (1496 ff.), Pisa; abandoned early Averroism of his *De intellectu et demonibus* (1492) for Christian and Thomist version of Aristotelianism; for Pope Leo X wrote *Tractatus de immortalitate animae contra Pomponatium* (1518) refuting

Pietro Pomponazzi; author also of *De Pulchro et Amore* (1531), commentaries, and *De regnandi peritia* plagiarized from Machiavelli.

Ni·gel \'nī-jəl, *earlier* 'nē-(,)jel\. d. 1169. English prelate and statesman. Bishop of Ely (1133); in charge of exchequer of Henry I (from 1130); offered resistance to King Stephen (1139) but was reconciled and restored (1142); summoned by Henry II to reorganize exchequer, the work of his life; chief justiciar (1165); probable compiler of the *Black Book of the Exchequer.*

Nigel. *Lat.* Ni·gel·lus \ni-'gel-əs\. *Surnamed* Wir·ek·er \'wir-(,)ek-ər, -ik-\. fl. 1190. English monk and satirist. Author of *Speculum stultorum* in Latin elegiac verse, ridiculing vices of both clergy and society, and of *Contra curiales et officiales clericos* in prose. Quoted by Chaucer in *Nonnes Preestes Tale.*

Ni·ger \'nī-jər\, Pescennius. *In full* Gaius Pescennius Niger Jus·tus \'jəs-təs\. d. 194 A.D. Roman general and rival emperor. Promoted to senator (c.180); consul (c.189); governor of Syria (c.190). Proclaimed emperor by his legions on death of Pertinax (192) and accepted as such by the Asiatic provinces; slain by Septimius Severus after loss of Battle of Issus.

Nig·gli \'nig-lē\, Paul. 1888–1953. Swiss mineralogist. Professor at Leipzig (1915), Tübingen (1918), Zürich (1920). Originated application of X-ray techniques to mathematical crystallography for crystal-structure analysis. Author of *Lehrbuch der Mineralogie und Kristallchemie* (1920).

Night·in·gale \'nīt-ᵊn-,gāl, -iŋ-\, Florence. *Known as* the Lady with the Lamp. 1820–1910. English nurse, hospital reformer, and philanthropist, b. Florence, Italy. Trained as nurse; superintendent of hospital for invalid women, London (1853); took 38 nurses to Üsküdar (1854) early in Crimean War and organized barrack hospital; introduced sanitation, lessened cases of typhus, cholera, and dysentery; by means of £50,000 testimonial fund, founded institution for training of nurses (1860), first such in world; first woman to receive Order of Merit (1907).

Ni·gra \'nē-grä\, Constantino. Conte. 1828–1907. Italian diplomat. Secretary to Cavour at Congress of Paris (1856); minister (later ambassador) to France (1861–76); ambassador, St. Petersburg (1876–82), London (1882–85), Vienna (1885–1904); senator (1890); Italian representative at first International Peace Conference (1899).

Nij·hoff \'nī-,hȯf\, Martinus. 1894–1953. Dutch poet. Author of verse *De wandelaar* (1916), *Vormen* (1924), *Nieuwe gedichten* (1934), *Het uur U* (1942); plays *Pierrot aan de lantaan* (1918), *Het heilige* (1950); essays *Gedachten op dinsdag* (1931).

Ni·jin·ska \nyi-'zhēn-skə\, Bronisława Fominitshna. 1891–1972. Russian dancer, choreographer, and teacher, of Polish descent. With Mariinsky Theater, St. Petersburg (1908), and Ballets Russes, Paris (from 1909), with brother Vaslav Nijinsky; choreographed (from 1921) many works, esp. of Stravinsky, Poulenc, Ravel, Milhaud; ballet mistress of several companies, esp. Colon Theater, Buenos Aires (from 1926) and Grand Ballet de Monte Carlo (from 1947); opened school in Los Angeles (1938).

Ni·jin·sky \nyi-'zhēn-skəi, *Angl* nə-'zhin-skē, -'jin-\, Vaslav Fomich. 1890–1950. Russian dancer and choreographer, of Polish descent. Debut in Mariinsky Theater, St. Petersburg (1907); first appeared in Paris (1909) with Diaghilev's Ballets Russes. Among ballets in which he appeared were *Les Sylphides, Pétrouchka, L'Après-midi d'un faune, Schéhérazade, Le Spectre de la rose, Le Sacre du printemps.* Rejected conventional forms of classical ballet in search of a free form of expression; noted for powerful and graceful technique. Became insane (1919) and was confined in several asylums.

Nij·len \'nī-lən\, Jan van. 1884–1965. Flemish poet. His works, such as *Het aangezicht der aarde* (1923), *De vogel Phoenix* (1928), *Het oude kind* (1938), *Te laat voor deze wereld* (1957), etc., reflected the disillusionment of modern life.

Nikias. See NICIAS.

Ni·kisch \'ni-kish\, Arthur. 1855–1922. Hungarian musician and conductor. Conductor, Leipzig Opera (1879–89), Boston Symphony Orchestra (1889–93), Gewandhaus Orchestra of Leipzig (1895–1922), Berlin Philharmonic Orchestra, with which he toured Europe (from 1897); toured U.S. with London Symphony Orchestra (1912); composed a symphony, a string quartet, a cantata, etc.

Nikita. See ROMANOV.

Ni·ki·tin \nyik-'yē-tyin\, Afansay. fl. 1466–72. Russian author and traveler. Earliest known Russian visitor to India; author of *Khozhdeniye za tri morya.*

Nikitin, Ivan Savvich. 1824–1861. Russian poet. Best known for patriotic poem *Russia* (1853) and realistic narrative poem of peasant life *Kulak* (1857).

Nikolai *or* **Nikolay.** See NICHOLAS.

Nikolas *or* **Nikolaus.** See NICHOLAS.

Ni·kon \'nyē-kən\. *Orig.* Nikita Mi·nin \'myin-yin\. 1605–1681. Russian prelate. Metropolitan of Novgorod (1648); patriarch of Moscow (1652–58); convened synod at Moscow (1654) to institute reforms in church ceremonial and in the text of church books; reforms were unpopular and caused schism in the church, and the founding of the Raskolnik sect; exiled to Byelozero (1666).

Niles \'nī(ə)lz\, Hezekiah. 1777–1839. American editor, b. Jefferis's Ford, Pa. Editor, Baltimore *Evening Post* (1805–11); founder and editor, *Niles' Weekly Register* (1811–36); author of *Principles and Acts of the Revolution in America* (1822).

Nil·son \'nil-sȯn\, Lars Fredrik. 1840–1899. Swedish physicist. Professor, Uppsala (1878), Stockholm (1883); discoverer (1879) of the metallic element scandium.

Ni·lus \'nī-ləs\ of An·cy·ra \an-'sī-rə\. Saint. *Also called* Nilus the Ascetic. d. c.430 A.D. Greek Byzantine abbot and author. Supported mentor St. John Chrysostom in refuting Arianism; became monk and later abbot of monastery near Ancyra; author of *De monastica exercitatione, De voluntaria paupertate,* and many letters.

Nilus of Ros·sa·no \rȯs-'sä-nō\. Saint. *Also known as* Nilus the Younger. c.905–1005. Italian abbot. Founded several communities of monks in Calabria, as well as abbey of Grottaferrata (1004); defended papal crown (esp. Gregory V) against antipopes; author of some letters and liturgical poems.

Nim·bār·ka \nim-'bär-kə\. *Also called* Nim·bā·dit·ya \nim-'bäd-ēt-yə\ *or* Ni·ya·mā·nan·da \,nē-(y)ə-mə-'nän-də\. fl. 12th or 13th century? Indian Brahmin, philosopher, and astronomer. Adherent of *dvaitadvaita;* founder of Nimanda sect (called Nimbārkas or Nimāvats) which flourished in the 13th and 14th centuries in eastern India and practiced *bhakti* yoga. Sometimes identified with Bhāskara, a 9th- or 10th-century philosopher and commentator on the *Brahma-sūtra.*

Nim·itz \'nim-əts\, Chester William. 1885–1966. American naval officer, b. Fredericksburg, Tex. Commander of 1st battleship division (1938–39); chief of bureau of navigation (1939–41); commander in chief of U.S. Pacific fleet (1941–45); admiral (1941); fleet admiral (1944); chief of naval operations (1945–47).

Nim·zo·witsch \nimt-'sō-vich\, Aron. 1886–1935. Russian chess master. Developed "hypermodern" school of play, as expounded in his *Mein System* and *Die Blockade* (both 1925).

Nin \'nin\, Anaïs. 1903–1977. American author, b. Paris. Daughter of Joaquín Nin y Castellano. Lived mainly in New York City (from 1914) and Paris (esp. in 1930s and 1940s). Influenced by Surrealism and psychoanalysis; her works included a collection of short stories *Under a Glass Bell* (1944); criticism *D.H. Lawrence: An Unprofessional Study* (1932), *The Future of the Novel* (1968); novels *House of Incest* (1936), *Winter of Artifice* (1939), *Ladder to Fire* (1946), *Children of the Albatross* (1947), *Four-Chambered Heart* (1950), *Spy in the House of Love* (1954), *Solar Barque* (1955), *Seduction of the Minotaur* (1961), *Collages* (1964); and her lifelong *Diary* (begun 1914; pub. 1966–80).

Ning Tsung. See Chao K'uo under CHAO family.

Nin·i·an \'nin-ē-ən, 'nin-yən\. Saint. *Also called* Ninias, Ninus, Ninnidh, Rigna, Ringan, Trignan, *and* Dinan. c.360–c.432. Scottish apostle of Christianity. Son of a British chieftain; made pilgrimage to Rome; after fifteen years' study consecrated bishop; founded church at Whithorn (397); evangelized the southern Picts.

Ni·ño \'nēn-yō\, Pedro Alonso. *Called* el Ne·gro \el-'nā-grō\. 1468?–?1505. Spanish navigator. Accompanied Columbus on first and third voyages; associated with Cristóbal Guerra in first successful commercial voyage to America (1499–1500).

Ni·no·mi·ya \nē-nō-mē-(y)ä\ Sontoku, *orig.* Kinjarō. *Called* Hōtoku Sensei *late in life.* 1787–1856. Japanese agrarian reformer. Developed agricultural system, called Hōtoku-kyō, that greatly improved peasant farming and saved hundreds of villages from ruin, esp. during 1836 famine.

Ninon de Lenclos. See Anne de LENCLOS.

Ninsei. See NONOMURA Ninsei.

Nin·to·ku \nin-tō-kü\. *Orig.* Osa·sa·gi-no-Mi·ko·to \ō-sä-sä-gē-nō-mē-kō-tō\. 290–399. 16th emperor of Japan (313–399). Noted for concern with welfare of subjects and promotion of agriculture by building of canals, dikes, etc. Father of emperors Richū, Hanshō, and Ingyō. Interred at Sakai in largest Imperial mausoleum in Japan.

Nin y Cas·tel·la·no \'nēn-ē-käs-tā(l)-'yän-ō\, Joaquín. 1879–1949. Spanish pianist, composer, and writer, b. Cuba. Compositions included *Suite de valses lyriques, Danza Ibérica, En el jardín de Lindaraja, Suite espagnole,* and *Chants d'Espagne.*

Ni·o·bid Paint·er \nī-,ō-bid-'pānt-ər\. fl. c.475–450 B.C. Greek vase painter. Known and named for a painted calyx krater depicting death of the children of Niobe; paintings thought to reflect lost murals of Polygnotus.

Niphus, Augustinus. See Agostino NIFO.

Nip·kow \'nip-kō\, Paul Gottlieb. 1860–1940. German engineer. Developed railroad signalling systems; invented scanning disk (1884) which made possible a mechanical television system.

Ni·sard \nē-zár\, Désiré, *in full* Jean-Marie-Napoléon-Désiré. 1806–1888. French journalist and literary critic. On staff of *Journal des Débats* and *Le National;* professor at the Sorbonne; director of École Normale Supérieure

(1857–67). Author of *Études sur les poètes latins de la décadence* (1834), *Histoire de la littérature française* (1844–61), etc.

Nis·bett \'niz-bət\ *or* **Nes·bitt** \'nez-bət\, Louisa Cranstoun. 1812–1858. English comedy actress. First London appearance in Andrew Cherry's *Soldier's Daughter* (1829); won triumph in Sheridan Knowles's *Love Chase* (1837); the original Lady Gay Spanker in *London Assurance* (1841).

Ni·shi \nē-shē\ Amane. Baron. 1829–1897. Japanese scholar and politician. Studied at Leiden (1862–65); professor at Kaieisho College in Tokyo; president, Tokyo Academy (1890); member of Senate (1882) and House of Peers (1890). As cofounder of Meirokusha Society helped introduce Western philosophy, esp. British Empiricism, to Japan; created modern philosophical terminology in Japanese permitting comparison of Oriental and Western thought.

Ni·shi·da \nē-shē-dä\ Kitarō. 1870–1945. Japanese philosopher. Early education in Chinese Confucian Classics; professor at Gakushūin U. in Tokyo (1909) and Kyōto U. (1910–28). His attempts to assimilate Western thought into Oriental spiritual tradition expounded in *Zen-no-kenkyū* (1911), *Jikaku-ni okeru chokkan to hansei* (1917), and *Hataraku-mono kara miru-mono e* (1927).

Ni·shi·ka·wa \nē-shē-kä-wä\ Sukenobu, *orig.* Yūsuke. *Also known as* Ji·to·kus·ai \jē-tō-ku̇s-ī\ *and* Bun·so·do \bu̇n-sō-dō\. 1671–1751. Japanese painter. Studied with masters of Kano and Taso schools; later influenced by *Ukiyo-e* painters, esp. Hishikawa Moronobu; established own school of *Ukiyo-e* in Kyōto. His wood-block prints, esp. of kimono designs, best seen in illustrated book *Hyakunin jorō shinasadame.*

Niten. See MIYAMOTO.

Nit·hard \'nēt-,härt\. 790?–844. Frankish historian. Natural son of St. Angilbert and of Bertha, daughter of Charlemagne. Sided with Charles the Bald in quarrels between sons of Louis the Pious; fought at Fontenoy (841); wrote history of the times, *Historiarum libri IV* (c.843); lay abbot of Saint-Riquier (843).

Nithsdale, Earls and countess of. See MAXWELL family.

Ni Tsan \'nēd-'zän\. 1301–1374. Chinese painter. Born wealthy, led life of cultivated retirement; became a wandering Taoist recluse in later life. One of Four Great Masters of Yüan dynasty; known for spare, monochromatic ink landscapes.

Nit·ta \nēt-tä\ Yoshisada. 1301–1338. Japanese warrior. Key supporter of Daigo II in destruction of Kamakura shogunate (1332); lost power struggle to Ashikaga Takauji who deposed Daigo (1336); helped Daigo regain power briefly (1338) but soon died in battle. His death resulted in the end of the Imperial restoration and led to establishment of Ashikaga shogunate.

Nit·ti \'nēt-tē\, Francesco Saverio. 1868–1953. Italian economist and politician. Member of parliament (1904–20, 1921–24); minister of commerce and agriculture (1911–14); minister of finance (1917–19); prime minister (1919–20); senator (1948). Wrote *Il capitale straniero in Italia* (1915), *Europa senza pace* (1921), *The Decadence of Europe* (1922), *Bolshevism, Fascism, and Democracy* (1927), *L'Inquiétude du monde* (1934).

Nit·tis \'nēt-tēs\, Giuseppe de. 1846–1884. Italian painter. To Paris (1868); associated with Gérôme and Meissonier; known for scenes of Parisian life.

Nitzsch \'nēch\, Karl Immanuel. 1787–1868. German Protestant theologian. Professor at Bonn (1822–47), Berlin (1847–54); rector of university and provost of St. Nikolai (1854). A founder of the meditation theology; champion of the Evangelical Union. Author of *System der christlichen Lehre* (1829), *Praktische Theologie* (1847–67), and *Akademische Vorträge über die christliche Glaubenslehre* (1858).

Ni·velle \nē-vel\, Robert-Georges. 1856–1924. French soldier. General of brigade (1914) and of division (1915); replaced Pétain in command of the 2d army (1916); succeeded Joffre as commander in chief of the French armies of the North and Northeast (Dec. 1916); relieved of command when his offensive (Apr. 1917) failed; exonerated by committee of inquiry from blame for the failure.

Nivelle de La Chaussée. See LA CHAUSSÉE.

Niv·en \'niv-ən\, Frederick John. 1878–1944. Scottish author, b. Valparaiso, Chile. Educated in Scotland; settled in Canada after World War I. Wrote over 30 novels, many of them historical romances set in Scotland and Canada; known esp. for collection of autobiographical essays *Coloured Spectacles* (1938) and for trilogy on settlement of western Canada comprising *The Flying Years* (1935), *Mine Inheritance* (1940), *The Transplanted* (1944).

Nivernais, Duc de. See Louis-Jules MANCINI-MAZARINI.

Niyamānanda. See NIMBĀRKA.

Ni·za \'nē-sä\, Marcos de. *Called* Fray Marcos. c.1495–1558. Savoyard Franciscan missionary and explorer. Served in Peru (1531–35), Guatemala (1535–36), and Mexico (1537–58), where he was provincial of his order (1540–43). Discovered Arizona and New Mexico and claimed to have sighted the "Seven Cities of Cibola" while leading expedition commissioned by Antonio de Mendoza (1539); guided Coronado's expedition which proved "Seven Cities" to be ordinary Indian pueblos (1540).

Ni·ẓām al-Mulk \nē-'zä-mül-'mülk\, *i.e.* Regulator of the Kingdom. *Personal name* Abū 'Alī Ḥasan ibn 'Alī. 1018 or 1019–1092. Persian politician. Vizier of Persia under sultans Alp-Arslan (1063–72) and Malik-Shah (1072–92); wrote *Seyasāk-nā'meh* (The Book of Government) containing political and religious views.

Nizami. See NEẒĀMĪ.

Niz·zo·li \'nēt-tsō-(,)lē\, Mario. *Lat.* Marius Ni·zo·li·us \ni-'zō-lē-əs\. 1498–1576. Italian Humanist. Author of *Observationes in M. Tullium Ciceronem* (1536) and *Antibarbus philosophicus* (1553), an argument against Scholasticism.

Nkru·mah \en-'krü-mə, (^{ə}ŋ-)'krü-\, Kwame. 1909–1972. Ghanaian politician. Leader in liberation of Gold Coast from British rule; founded Accra *Evening News* (1948); formed Convention People's party (1949); elected to parliament (1951); prime minister (1952–60); first president of Ghana republic (1960–66); overthrown by military coup (1966) and granted asylum in Guinea, where he became co-head of state. Author of *Towards Colonial Freedom* (1946), *Consciencism* (1946), *Neo-Colonialism, The Last Stage of Imperialism* (1965), *Handbook of Revolutionary Warfare* (1968), and *Class Struggle in Africa* (1970).

No·ah \'nō-ə\, Mordecai Manuel. 1785–1851. American journalist, b. Philadelphia. As consul to Tunis and special agent to Algiers (1813–15), secured release of American prisoners held by Algerian pirates; founder and editor, New York *Enquirer* (1826), New York *Evening Star* (1834), New York *Union, Noah's Times and Weekly Messenger;* surveyor of port of New York (1829–33).

No·ailles \nȯ-ȧy\. Distinguished French family, including: Antoine de Noailles (1504–1562), admiral of France, ambassador to England (1553–56). His brother ¶François (1519–1585), bishop of Dax (from 1555); ambassador to England (1556–57), Venice (1557–69), Ottoman Empire (1572). ¶Duc Anne-Jules (1650–1708), marshal of France (from 1693). Anne-Jules's brother ¶Louis-Antoine (1651–1729), archbishop of Paris (1695), cardinal (1700). Anne-Jules's son ¶duc Adrien-Maurice (1678–1766), marshal of France (from 1734). His son ¶duc Louis (1713–1793), marshal of France (from 1766). His brother ¶Philippe (1715–1794), duc de Mou·chy \mü-shē\, marshal of France. His son ¶vicomte Louis-Marie (1756–1804) served under his brother-in-law Lafayette in America; member of the Estates-General (1789); initiated measures there whereby the nobles stripped themselves of their rights and privileges (1789); emigrated to America (1792); fought under Rochambeau against the British in Santo Domingo (1802–04). ¶Duc Paul (1802–1885), peer of France (from 1827); ambassador to Russia (1871); author of *Histoire de Mme de Maintenon* (1848–58).

Noailles, Anna-Élisabeth Ma·thieu de \mȧ-tyœ̄-də-\. Comtesse. Princesse Bran·co·van \brȧn-kō-vä^{n}, brä-\. 1876–1933. French author. Member of Bibescu family; m. grandson of duc Jules de Noailles. Her literary salon was frequented by most writers of her time, including Proust, Collette, Valery, Cocteau. Author of books of lyrical poetry *Le Coeur innombrable* (1901), *Les Éblouissements* (1907), *L'Honneur de souffrir* (1927); novels *La Nouvelle Espérance* (1903), *Le Visage émerveillé* (1904), *La Domination* (1905); and memoirs *Le Livre de ma vie* (1932).

Nō·a·mi \nō-äm-ē\. *Orig.* Na·kao \nä-kä-ō\ Sanenori. *Also called* Shin·nō \shēn-nō\. 1397–1494. Japanese poet, painter, and art critic. Curator of the Ashikaga art collection; compiled (1476) catalog *Kundaikan sayū chōki,* important for appraisal of Chinese artists. His paintings, in the *suiboku* (monochromatic ink) style of Mu-ch'i Fa-ch'ang, included *The Pines of Miho* and *The White-robed Kannon.* He was succeeded as curator by his son ¶Ge·ia·mi \gā-äm-ē\ (d. 1485), *orig.* Nakao Shingei, a *suiboku* painter influenced by Shūbun and best known for *The Waterfall* (1480); and grandson ¶Sō·a·mi \sō-äm-ē\ (1472–1525), *orig.* Nakao Shinsō, a *suiboku* painter, master of the tea and incense ceremonies, reviser of Nōami's catalog (1511), and designer of the Ryōan-ji and Daisei-in gardens, two of the most celebrated Zen temple gardens in Japan. Together these three artists are known as the San Ami (Three Amis).

No·bel \nō-'bel, *attributively often* 'nō-,bel\, Alfred Bernhard. 1833–1896. Swedish manufacturer, inventor, and philanthropist. Invented dynamite (1866), ballistite, one of the first smokeless powders (1887), artificial gutta-percha, and over 100 other patented items; acquired wealth through the manufacture of dynamite and other explosives in various parts of the world and through his interests in the Baku oil fields in Russia; bequeathed fund of $9,200,000 for establishment of Nobel prizes, first awarded in 1901.

No·bi·le \'nō-bē-(,)lā\, Umberto. 1885–1978. Italian aeronautical engineer and explorer. Designed airships *Norge* and *Italia;* flew across North Pole in *Norge* with Amundsen and Ellsworth (1926); commanded polar expedition in dirigible *Italia* (1928); rescued after wreck of *Italia* (1928), for which he was later adjudged responsible; resigned commission as general (1929); to U.S.S.R. (1932), U.S. (1936); reinstated in Italian air service (1945); deputy in Italian assembly (1946). Wrote account of his Arctic adventures *Gli italiani al Polo Nord* (1959).

No·ble \'nō-bəl\, Sir Andrew. 1st Baronet. 1831–1915. Scottish physicist and artillerist. His experiments in ballistics led to changes in composition of gunpowder and in design of guns; invented the chronoscope for measuring shot velocity in gun barrels (c.1862); with ordnance firm Sir W.G. Armstrong, Whitworth, and Co. (from 1863), chairman (1900). Created baronet (1902).

No·bre \'nō-brā\, António. 1867–1900. Portuguese poet. His lyrical and subjective poems in *Só* (1892), *Despedidas* (1902), and *Primeiros versos* (1921), were influenced by French Symbolism absorbed while in Paris (1890–95).

Nó·bre·ga \nü-'breg-ə, -ä\, Manuel de. 1517–1570. Portuguese Jesuit missionary. Founder (1549) and first provincial (1553–59) of Jesuit mission in Brazil; planned foundation of São Paulo (1554); instrumental in expulsion of French Protestants from southern Brazil (1555–63); founder (1567) and first rector of Colégio de Rio de Janeiro.

Nobunaga. See ODA Nobunaga.

No·card \nȯ-kär\, Edmond-Isidore-Étienne. 1850–1903. French veterinarian and biologist. Credited with discovering the bacteria of bovine farcy, of ulcerative lymphangitis of the horse, etc., and with identifying bacillus of avian tuberculosis with that of mammalian tuberculosis; demonstrated transmission of tuberculosis to man through the milk and meat of infected cattle.

Nock \'näk\, Albert Jay. 1870–1945. American author, b. Brooklyn, N.Y. Essayist (from 1910) for many magazines, esp. his column "The State of the Nation" in *American Mercury* (1930s); editor, *Freeman* (1920–24); books included *Jefferson* (1926), *The Theory of Education in the United States* (1932), *Our Enemy, the State* (1935), *Henry George: An Essay* (1939), and *Memoirs of a Superfluous Man* (1943, autobiography).

No·dier \nȯd-yā\, Charles, *in full* Jean-Charles-Emmanuel. 1780–1844. French man of letters. Exerted great influence on French Romantics such as Hugo, Musset, and Sainte-Beuve after appointment as director of Bibliothèque de l'Arsenal (1824); author of tales *Jean Sbogar* (1818), *Les Vampires* (1820), *Smarra* (1821), *La Fée aux miettes* (1832), *Le Chien de Brisquet* (1844), etc.

Noel. See NOWELL.

No·ël \nȯ-el\, Alexandre. *Lat.* Alexander Na·ta·lis \nā-'tal-əs\. 1639–1724. French theologian. Entered Dominican order (1654); regent of studies at Saint-Jacques, Paris. His *Selecta historiae ecclesiasticae capita* (1676–86) was condemned (1684) by Pope Innocent XI for its expression of Gallicanism; wrote revised version as *Historia ecclesiastica veteris et novi testamenti* (1699). Signed *Cas de conscience* (1701) favoring Jansenists; submitted to its condemnation by Pope Clement XI. Appealed against Clement's bull *Unigenitus* (1713); again submitted.

No·el-Ba·ker \ˌnō-əl-'bā-kər\, Philip John. Baron. *Surname orig.* Baker. 1889–1982. English statesman. Competed in 1912 and 1920 Olympic Games, captained 1924 British Olympic team; added wife's surname to his own (c.1926). Lifelong campaigner for international peace and disarmament; member of British delegation to 1919 Paris Peace Conference; with League of Nations secretariat (to 1922); assisted Fridtjof Nansen in famine relief in Russia and resettlement of wartime refugees; member of British delegation to League (1929–30); principal assistant to Arthur Henderson at International Disarmament Conference, Geneva (1932–33). Labour M.P. (1929–31, 1936–70); secretary of state for air (1946–47), for Commonwealth relations (1947–50); minister of fuel and power (1950–51). Helped draft UN charter; member of British delegation to UN (1946–47); president of International Council on Sport and Physical Recreation, UNESCO (from 1960). Awarded 1959 Nobel prize for peace. Created life peer (1977). Author of *The Private Manufacture of Armaments* (1936), *The Arms Race: A Programme for World Disarmament* (1958), etc.

Noe·ther \'nœ-tər\, Emmy, *in full* Amalie Emmy. 1882–1935. German mathematician. Professor at Göttingen (1919–33); to U.S. (1933) after Nazi dismissals of Jewish academics. Developed a general theory of ideals for all cases (1920–26); her work (from 1927) on noncommutative algebras made her known as the most creative abstract algebraist of modern times.

Nofretete. See NEFERTITI.

No·ga·ret \nȯ-gȧ-re\, Guillaume de. 1260 or 1270–1313. French jurist and politician. Chief adviser to Philip IV in his struggle with the papacy and the Templars; excommunicated (1304) by Pope Benedict XI for part in unsuccessful coup against Boniface VIII at Agagni, Italy (1303).

Nogaret de La Va·lette \-də-lȧ-vȧ-let\, Jean-Louis de. Duc d'É·per·non \dā-per-nōⁿ\. 1554–1642. French politician. Favorite of Henry III, who created him duke and peer of France (1582); with Anne de Joyeuse virtual prime minister; colonel general of infantry (1587); effectively defended crown in civil wars; at first refused to serve Henry IV after murder of Henry III (1589) but later reconciled; governor of Limousin (1596); active in conspiracies against Henry IV; may have helped arrange assassination of Henry IV (1610); arranged for Marie de Médicis to be regent for Louis XIII; exiled by Louis XIII (1617); engineered escape of Marie de Médicis from Blois (1619); governor of Guienne (1622–38); exiled by Richelieu (1641).

No·gu·chi \nō-gu̇ch-ē, *Angl* nō-'gü-chē\, Hideyo, *orig.* Seisaku. 1876–1928. American bacteriologist, b. Inawashiro, Japan. To U.S. (1900) and entered laboratory of pathology at U. of Pennsylvania; published *The Action of Snake Venom upon Cold-blooded Animals* (1904); at Rockefeller Institute (from 1904); discovered *Treponema pallidum* (the causative agent of syphilis) in brains of persons afflicted with paresis; devised Noguchi test for diagnosis of syphilis; succeeded in producing culture medium for development of spirochetes, thus forwarding study of these organisms.

Noir \nwär\, Victor. *Orig.* Yves Sal·mon \säl-mōⁿ\. 1848–1870. French journalist. His slaying (Jan. 10) by Prince Pierre-Napoleón Bonaparte and funeral (Jan. 12) provoked republican demonstrations against the Second Empire.

Nolasco, Peter. See PETER NOLASCO.

Nol·de \'nȯl-də\, Emil. *Orig. surname* Hansen. 1867–1956. German painter and printmaker. Influenced by Impressionists while in Paris (1900) and later by primitive art while in New Guinea (1913–14); member of Expressionist group Die Brücke (1906–07). Known for violent religious pictures, such as *Dance Around the Golden Calf* (1910) and *The Life of Christ* (1911–12), landscapes, watercolors, and graphic works.

Nöl·de·ke \'nœl-də-kə\, Theodor. 1836–1930. German Orientalist. Professor, Kiel (1868), Strassburg (1872–1906). Author of *Geschichte des Qorâns* (1859), *Das Leben Mohammeds* (1863), *Geschichte der Perser und Araber zur Zeit der Sassaniden* (1879), and works on Semitic languages.

No·lhac \nȯ-läk\, Pierre de, *in full* Anet-Marie-Pierre Gi·rauld de \zhē-rō-də\. 1859–1936. French writer. Curator of museum at Versailles (1892–1920); director of museum Jacquemart-André, Paris (1920). Among his books were *Le Dernier Amour de Ronsard* (1882), *Érasme en Italie* (1888), *La Reine Marie-Antoinette* (1889), *Pétrarque et l'humanisme* (1892), *Louis XV et Mme de Pompadour* (1904), *Versailles sous Louis XIV* (1911), *Ronsard et l'humanisme* (1921).

Nol·le·kens \'nȯl-ə-kənz\, Joseph. 1737–1823. English sculptor. Executed portrait busts of Sterne, Garrick, George III, Pitt, Canning, Lord Castlereagh, Benjamin West, etc., and numerous mythological statues.

Nol·let \nȯ-le\, Jean-Antoine. 1700–1770. French physicist. Ordained deacon (c.1728); taught first experimental physics classes in Paris (1735); first professor of physics at Collège de Navarre, Paris (1753). Invented electroscope (1747); discovered osmosis (1748); improved Leyden jar (1750).

No·mi·noë \nō-mē-'nō-e\ *or* **No·men·oë** \nō-mēn-'ō-e\. d. 851. Breton king. Named count (819) and duke (826) of Vannes by Louis the Pious to pacify Brittany; supported (840) and later (844–845) defeated Charles the Bald, thus becoming independent ruler of Brittany; replaced French bishops with Bretons after their refusal to crown him and established (849) own archbishopric at Dol which never received papal sanction; conquered Anjou, Nantes, and Rennes to augment his power (849–51).

No·nell y Mon·tu·ri·ol \nō-'nel-ē-mōn-tü-rē-'ōl\, Isidro. 1873–1911. Spanish painter. Began as Impressionist landscape painter but turned (1890) to realistic portraits of gypsies and poor people; leader of Barcelonian group of young artists, "Els Quatre Gats" (c.1898), which included Picasso; adopted more abstract style after study of Daumier and Toulouse-Lautrec; had successful show in Barcelona (1910). Considered a pioneer of Spanish modern painting.

Nonius, Petrus. See Pedro NUNES.

No·ni·us Mar·cel·lus \'nō-nē-əs-ˌmär-'sel-əs\. 4th century A.D. African Latin grammarian and lexicographer. Author of *De compendiosa doctrina,* a lexicon important for preserving extracts from earlier writers, esp. the satires of Lucilius and Marcus Terentius Varro.

Non·nus \'nän-əs\. 5th century A.D. Greek epic poet. Author of the *Dionysiaca,* an epic of 48 books in hexameters recounting Dionysus's journey to India; converted to Christianity in later life and wrote a paraphrase in hexameters of St. John's Gospel.

No·no·mu·ra \nō-nō-mu̇r-ä\ Ninsei. *Known as* Nin·sei \nin-sā\ *or* Sei·bei \sā-bā\ *or* Sei·su·ke \sā-su̇k-e\. c.1574–1660 or 1666. Japanese potter. His pottery, known as *Ninsei-yaki* or *Omuro-yaki,* consisted mainly of delicate, finely glazed tea ceremony wares; regarded with Aoki Mokubei and Ogata Kenzan as greatest Japanese potters.

Noon \'nün\, Sir Firoz Khan. 1893–1970. Pakistani politician. High commissioner for India in United Kingdom (1936–41); prime minister of Pakistan (1957–58). Author of *Canada and India* (1939), *Wisdom from Fools* (1940), *Scented Dust* (1941), *From Memory* (1962).

Noo·nan \'nü-nən\, Fred J. 1893–1937. American aviator, b. Chicago. Navigator on trail-blazing flight of Pan American Clipper from San Francisco to Honolulu (1935) and on fatal flight of Amelia Earhart (July 1937).

Noot \'nōt\, Henri van der. 1731–1827. Belgian politician. Organized Brabant revolution against liberal reforms of Joseph II (1787); joined Jean-François Vonck and Jean-André van der Meersch to defeat Austrian forces at Turnhout (Oct. 1789); as leader of oligarchic "statist" party exiled progressive rival Vonck and arrested Meersch; failure to unify country led to Austrian reconquest of Belgium (1790) and Noot's exile (1790–92).

Noot, Jan Baptista van der. Jonker. c.1540–c.1595. Dutch poet. Political exile in London, Germany, France (1567–78); author of *Het theatre oft toon-neel* (1568), a prose defense of Calvinism prefaced by sonnets and epigrams translated by Spenser for English version (1569); *Het bosken* (1570 or 1571), a collection of poetry influenced by Petrarch and Ronsard; and esp. the allegorical dream epic *Cort Begryp der XII Boeken Olympiados* (1579). Considered first true Renaissance poet in Holland.

Nor·bert \'nór-bərt\. Saint. c.1080–1134. German ecclesiastic. At request of Pope Calixtus II, founded at Prémontré, France, religious order of Premonstratensians (also called Norbertines or White Canons), devoted to pastoral work, education, and preaching (1121); archbishop of Magdeburg (1126); defended Pope Innocent II against antipope Anacletus II (1130). Canonized (1582).

Nor·dau \'nór-,daù\, Max Simon. *Orig. surname* Süd·feld \'sūed-,felt\. 1849–1923. German physician and author, b. Hungary. Practiced medicine in Budapest (1878–80) and Paris; became Zionist leader in Europe (from 1895) and supported Herzl in approving acceptance of East Africa as a Jewish settlement. Author of critical and satirical works on moral and social questions including *Die konventionellen Lügen der Kulturmenschheit* (1883), *Paradoxe* (1886), and *Entartung* (1892–93); novels and stories including *Gefühlskomödie* (1891), *Die Drohnenschlacht* (1897), and *Morganatisch* (1904); and essays, plays, travel books, fairy tales, etc.

Nor·den \'nór-dən\, Carl Lukas. 1880–1965. Dutch inventor, b. Java. To U.S. (1904); as private consulting engineer to U.S. navy (from 1915) developed flight instruments, a radio-controlled target airplane, a drone flying bomb, and the catapults and arresting gears for aircraft carriers; began design of Norden bombsight (1921), which he perfected with Frederick I. Entwistle (1931).

Nor·den·flycht \'nür-dən-,flʉekt\, Hedvig Charlotta. 1718–1763. Swedish poet. Champion of feminist movement and (with Dalin) of French taste in Swedish literature; founder of the first Swedish literary salon, center (from 1753) of the literary "Order of Thought Builders," to which Creutz and Gyllenborg belonged. Author of *Den sorjande Turturdufwan* (collection of lyrics inspired by the death of her husband; 1743), *Qwinligt tankespel* (1744–50), and other lyric love poems.

Nor·den·skiöld \'nür-dən-,shœld\, Nils Adolf Erik. Baron. 1832–1901. Swedish geologist and explorer. Went on several expeditions to Spitsbergen (first in 1858); led expedition that reached highest northern latitude (81° 42′) then attained in the eastern hemisphere (1868); accomplished Northeast Passage in the *Vega* (1878–80); visited Greenland, studying the icecap (1870, 1883). His son ¶Baron Nils Erland Herbert (1877–1932), ethnologist, professor at Göteborg (1924–32); traveled in various South American countries (from 1899) and wrote on the cultural development of South American Indians, esp. *Comparative Ethnographical Studies* (1918–38). His cousin ¶Nils Otto Gustaf Nor·den·skjöld \-,shœld\ (1869–1928), geologist and explorer, traveled in Tierra del Fuego (1895–97), Alaska (1898), Greenland (1900, 1909), the Andes (1904–05, 1920–21); led expedition to the Antarctic (1901); rescued by the Argentine government after his ship, the *Antarctica,* was crushed by ice (1903).

Nord·hoff \'nórd-,häf, -,hóf\, Charles. 1830–1901. American writer, b. Erwitte, Westphalia, Prussia. To U.S. (1835); in U.S. navy (1844–47) and merchant marine and fishing vessels (1847–53). Author of *Man-of-War Life* (1855), *The Merchant Vessel* (1855), *Whaling and Fishing* (1856), *Stories of the Island World* (1857), *Politics for Young Americans* (1875), etc.

Nordhoff, Charles Bernard. 1887–1947. American writer, b. London, England, of American parents. Author of *The Fledgling* (1919), *The Pearl Lagoon* (1924), *Picaro* (1924), *The Derelict* (1928). Collaborator in a number of books with James N. Hall (*q.v.*), including *Mutiny on the Bounty* (1932), *Hurricane* (1935), *Botany Bay* (1941). Edited, under title of *In Yankee Windjammers* (1940), journals of his grandfather Charles Nordhoff (*q.v.*).

Nor·di·ca \'nór-dik-ə\, Lillian. *Orig.* Lillian Norton. 1857–1914. American soprano, b. Farmington, Me. After debuts with Milan Opera (1879) and as prima donna with Paris Opéra (1882), became first American singer to be acclaimed in Europe; devoted herself esp. to Wagnerian roles (from 1894), chiefly with Metropolitan Opera House, New York (1896–1907), Oscar Hammerstein's Manhattan Opera Co. (1907–08); on concert tours (after 1908).

Nor·draak \'nór-drók\, Rikard. 1842–1866. Norwegian composer. Studied and collected Norwegian folk songs; met Grieg (1864) and inspired him to develop a Norwegian national school for music; composed the music for the national anthem "Ja, vi elsker dette landet" (1864), written by his cousin Bjørnstjerne Bjørnson, incidental music to Bjørnson's *Mary Stuart* and *Sigurd Slembe,* piano pieces, etc.

Nord·ström \'nürd-strœ̄m\, Ludvig Anselm. 1882–1942. Swedish writer. Published short stories "Fiskare" (1907) and "Borgare" (1909), using realism and local color; his anti-individualistic *Petter Svensks historia* (1923–27), influenced by H.G. Wells, preached a socialist philosophy called "totalism"; his essays *Bonde-Nöden* (1933) and *Lort-Sverige* (1938) inspired reforms to clean up the Swedish countryside.

Nor·folk \'nór-fək, *US also* -,fók\, Earls and dukes of. Titles in English peerage. Title of earl of Norfolk held first by Ralph de Guader (fl. 1070); conferred by Stephen (1136) upon Hugh Bigod and held by members of the Bigod family (*q.v.*) until it became extinct (1306) with death of Roger Bigod, 5th earl; granted (1312) by Edward II to his half-brother Thomas of Brotherton (1300–1338), from whom it descended to the latter's daughter Margaret (cr. duchess of Norfolk, 1397), then to dukes of Norfolk, becoming extinct with death of Anne, daughter of 4th duke and wife of young Richard, Duke of York, who was murdered in the Tower. Ducal title created (1397) for Margaret, Countess of Norfolk, and her grandson Thomas Mowbray (1366?–1399), held by members of Mowbray family (*q.v.*) until death (1476) of John, 4th duke; recreated (1483) for Richard (1472–1483), the younger of the princes doomed by Richard III in the Tower, and held (from 1483) by members of Howard family (*q.v.*); still the premier dukedom of England, ranking next after princes of the blood.

Normanby, Viscount and marquises of. See PHIPPS family.

Nor·mand \'nór-mənd\, Mabel Ethelreid. 1893?–1930. American actress, b. R.I. or Mass. Acted for Mack Sennett (1909–17, 1921–23), playing lead in series of *Mabel* films, esp. *Mabel's Strange Predicament* (1914), *Tillie's Punctured Romance* (1914), *Mickey* (1918), *The Extra Girl* (1923), etc.; with Goldwyn Co. (1917–20), making *The Venus Model* (1918), *Sis Hopkins* (1919), etc.; reputed to have originated custard pie throwing scene (c.1913) in a Sennett film; career ruined by association with murder scandals (1922, 1924).

Nor·man·dy \'nór-mən-dē\, Dukes of. Rulers of duchy of northern France set up in 912 with Rollo as first duke. See esp. WILLIAM I the Conqueror (duke 1035–87) who conquered England (king 1066–87). See also other rulers of Normandy under RICHARD, ROBERT, WILLIAM.

No·ro·dom \'nór-ə-dəm\. *Also called* Na·rot·ta·ma \,när-ə-'täm-ə\. 1834–1904. King of Cambodia (1860–1904). Signed treaty at gun point relinquishing control of Cambodia's foreign relations and trading concessions to France, becoming her deputy in effect and ending the possibility of Cambodian independence (Apr. 1864); initiated land reforms and abolished slavery.

Nor·ris \'nór-əs, 'när-\, Frank, *in full* Benjamin Franklin. 1870–1902. American novelist, b. Chicago. War correspondent in South Africa for San Francisco *Chronicle* (1895–96) and in Cuba for *McClure's Magazine* (1898–99); assistant editor, San Francisco *Wave* (1896–97); on staff of Doubleday, Page & Co. (from 1899). A pioneer of American Naturalism; wrote *Blix* (1899), *McTeague* (1899), *A Man's Woman* (1900), *The Third Circle* (1909, short stories), *Vandover and the Brute* (1914), and *The Octopus* (1901) and *The Pit* (1903), the first parts of his projected "epic of the wheat" trilogy of which the unwritten *Wolf* was to be the third. His brother ¶Charles Gilman (1881–1945), magazine editor and author of *Brass* (1921), *Bread* (1923), *Seed* (1930), *Hands* (1935), *Bricks Without Straw* (1938), etc.

Norris, George William. 1861–1944. American politician, b. Sandusky, O. Member, U.S. House of Representatives (1903–13); U.S. senator from Nebraska (1913–43). Led contest for overthrow of arbitrary rule of Speaker Joseph G. Cannon in the House (1910); opposed U.S. entry into World War I; led long struggle for federal power control in Tennessee Valley and secured passage of act creating Tennessee Valley Authority (1933), the first TVA-built dam being called Norris Dam in his honor (1936). Author of 20th Amendment to the Constitution (ratified 1933); coauthor of Norris-LaGuardia Act (1932) restricting use of injunctions in labor disputes.

Norris, Sir John. 1547?–1597. English military commander. Won fame under Essex in guerrilla war against Irish (1573–75); in service in Netherlands (1577–85); ambassador to Dutch States (1588); commanded with Sir Francis Drake fleet that ravaged coasts of Spain and Portugal (1589); returned to Ireland (1597) to aid in reducing Tyrone; failed to pacify Connaught.

Norris, John. 1657–1711. English philosopher and clergyman. Elected fellow of Oxford U. (1680); vicar of Newton St. Loe (1689–92), Bemerton (1692–1711). Exponent of Cambridge Platonism in writings such as *An Idea of Happiness* (1683); sole English advocate of Malebranche's theory of divine illumination, esp. in *Two Treatises Concerning the Divine Light* (1692) and *An Essay Towards the Theory of the Ideal or Intelligible World* (1701–04); also author of political tract *A Murnival of Knaves* (1683) and other theological, philosophical, and literary works.

Norris, Kathleen, *nee* Thompson. 1880–1966. American novelist, b. San Francisco. m. Charles G. Norris (1909; *q.v.*); wrote (from 1910) short stories for magazines; author of many novels, including *Saturday's Child* (1914), *Sisters* (1919), *The Sea Gull* (1927), *Lost Sunrise* (1939), and *Through a Glass Darkly* (1955).

Nor·rish \'nór-ish, 'när-\, Ronald George Wreyford. 1897–1978. English chemist. At U. of Cambridge (1930–65), where he developed flash photolysis and flash spectroscopy to study rapid reactions of free atoms and radicals, for which he was awarded Nobel prize for chemistry (1967) with Manfred Eigen and George Porter.

North \'nó(ə)rth\. Name of an English family, some of whose members bore the title of Baron North, including: Sir Thomas (1535–?1603), 2d son of 1st Baron North (cr. 1554); served in army in Ireland (1582, 1596–97), Holland (1585–87); translator of *The Diall of Princes* (1557; from a French version of Guevara's *Reloj de príncipes*) with mannerisms and antitheses foreshadowing euphuism, of *The Morall Philosophie of Doni* (1570), Eastern fables from the Italian, and of Plutarch's *Lives* from the French of Amyot (1579, with added *Lives* 1595, 1603), the chief source from which Shakespeare drew his knowledge of ancient history. ¶Roger (1585?–?1652), great-grandson of 1st baron; accompanied Raleigh to Guiana (1617), forced to return by disaffection; made successful voyage to the Amazon (1620–21) and established settlement in Guiana (1627). ¶Francis (1637–1685), 1st Baron Guil·ford \'gil-fərd\; son of 4th Baron North; solicitor general (1671), attorney general (1673), chief justice of common pleas (1675–82), lord chancellor (1682); participated in coronation of James II (1685). ¶Sir Dudley (1641–1691), economist, brother of Francis North; agent at Smyrna and at Constantinople (1662–80), amassing a fortune; commissioner for customs and for treasury; anticipated Adam Smith in *Discourses Upon Trade* (1691); advocated free trade. ¶Roger (1653–1734), lawyer, brother of Francis and Sir Dudley North; solicitor general to Duke of York (1684); attorney general to James II's queen (1686); quit politics (1688) and turned to writing. Author of *Memoires of Musick* (1728); eulogistic biographies of three of his brothers, *Lives of the Norths* (1742–44); and an *Examen* (1740) or criticism of White Kennett's *Compleat History of England.* ¶Frederick (1732–1792), 2d Earl of Guilford; son of 7th Baron North; known as Lord North (by courtesy until 1790); entered House of Commons at 22; a lord of the treasury (1759–65); chancellor of the exchequer (1767); as prime minister (1770–82), made himself pliant agent of George III, who dominated the ministry and, against protests of Fox and Burke, pursued ruinous policy leading to revolt and loss of American colonies; opposed Wilkes, supported American stamp tax and Townshend's tea duty; resigned (1782) upon hearing of Cornwallis's surrender; united with Fox to overthrow Shelburne ministry (1783). ¶Brownlow (1741–1820), clergyman, half-brother of Frederick North; dean of Canterbury (1770); bishop of Coventry and Lichfield (1771), of Worcester (1774), of Winchester (1781).

North, Christopher. See John WILSON (1785–1854).

North, Frank Joshua. 1840–1885. American soldier and frontiersman, b. Ludlowville, N.Y. To Nebraska Territory (1865), where he learned language and customs of Pawnee tribe; led Pawnee units against attacks of other tribes, mainly Cheyenne, on U.S. forts and Union Pacific Railroad workers (1864–77); with Buffalo Bill Cody's Wild West Show (1877–84); considered best revolver shot on plains, having beaten "Wild Bill" Hickok and others in competition (1873).

North, Simeon. 1765–1852. American firearms manufacturer, b. Berlin, Conn. Supplied pistols (from 1799) and rifles (from 1823) to U.S. government; devised 10-round repeating rifle (1825); developed use of interchangeable parts in manufacturing at about same time as Eli Whitney (c.1798).

North·amp·ton \nórth-'(h)am(p)-tən\, Earls of. Title held by a number of English families: first by a Norman noble Simon de Sen·lis \də-sän-lēs, *Angl* -'sen-ləs\, builder of Northampton Castle, and his son ¶Simon (d. 1153), who fought for Stephen at Lincoln (1141); by ¶William de Bohun (d. 1360), captain general in Brittany, who fought at Cressy; by Henry Howard (cr. 1604; see earl of Northampton under HOWARD family); by members of Compton family, including William Compton (d. 1630), 1st earl, and his son Spencer Compton (*q.v.*), 2d earl.

Northbrook, Baron and 1st earl of. See BARING family.

Northcliffe, Viscount. See Alfred Charles William HARMSWORTH.

North·cote \'nó(ə)rth-kət, -,kōt\, James. 1746–1831. English painter. Pupil of and assistant to Sir Joshua Reynolds (1771–75); best known for portraits and *The Emperor of Russia Rescuing a Boy from Drowning* (1820); also wrote lives of Reynolds (1813) and Titian (1830).

Northcote, Sir Stafford Henry. 1st Earl of Iddes·leigh \'idz-lē, 'ij-\. 1818–1887. English politician and financier. M.P. (1855–85), in the confidence of Disraeli; secretary for India (1867); chairman of Hudson's Bay Company (1869–74); chancellor of exchequer (1874–80); leader of House of Commons (1876), of the opposition (1880–85); foreign secretary (1886). His son ¶Henry Stafford (1846–1911), 1st baron; colonial administrator; M.P. (1880–99); as governor of Bombay (1899–1903) dealt with plague and famine and obtained passage of land revenue reform measures; as governor general of Australia (1903–08) contributed to imperial unity and encouraged immigration.

Nor·throp \'nór-thrəp\, John Knudsen. 1895–1981. American engineer and industrialist, b. Newark, N.J. Helped found Lockheed Aircraft Co. (1927); founded Avion Corp. (1928), Northrop Corp. (1932), Northrop Aircraft (1939). Designed Vega monoplane, A-17, P-61 Black Widow, F-89 Scorpion jet, C-125 Raider, B-49 bomber, Flying Wing, etc.

Northumberland, Earls and dukes of. See John and Robert DUDLEY; PERCY and NEVILLE families.

Nor·ton \'nórt-ᵊn\, Caroline Elizabeth Sarah, *nee* Sheridan. 1808–1877. English author. Granddaughter of Richard Brinsley Sheridan; m. 1st (1827) Hon. George Chapple Norton (d. 1875). Led by marital troubles to issue eloquent defenses instrumental in passage of Infant Custody (1839) and Marriage and Divorce (1857) acts; George Meredith's model for Diana in *Diana of the Crossways* (1885). Wrote poetry *The Dream, and Other Poems* (1840), *Aunt Carry's Ballads* (1847); novels *Stuart of Dunleath* (1851), *Lost and Saved* (1863), *Old Sir Douglas* (1867); and many popular songs.

Norton, Charles Eliot. 1827–1908. American author and educator, b. Cambridge, Mass. Editor, with James Russell Lowell, of *North American Review* (1864–68); with E.L. Godkin and others, founded *The Nation* (1865); professor, Harvard (1873–97), beginning first course in the fine arts as associated with social, cultural, and literary development of a people. Friend of Carlyle, Emerson, Ruskin, Longfellow, and other literary figures. Author of *Historical Studies of Church-Building in the Middle Ages* (1880); translator into English prose of Dante's *Divine Comedy* (1891–92); editor of *Poems of John Donne* (1895), *Poems of Mrs. Anne Bradstreet* (1897), Thomas Carlyle's *Correspondence,* etc.

Norton, John. 1606–1663. American Puritan clergyman, b. Hertfordshire, England. To America (1635) and settled at Ipswich; pastor in Ipswich (1638–56) and Boston (1656–63); active in persecution of Quakers in Massachusetts colony; author of a Latin treatise *Responsio ad totam quaestionum syllogen* (1645; printed in London 1648), on New England church government, first Latin book composed in the colonies.

Norton, Thomas. 1532–1584. English lawyer and poet. Amanuensis to Protector Somerset; eloquent debater in Parliament (from 1558) for anti-Catholic measures; as censor, conducted examinations of Catholics under torture. Translated Calvin's *Institutes* (1561); contributed to Tottel's *Miscellany;* collaborated with Thomas Sackville in blank-verse *Tragedy of Gorboduc,* the earliest English tragedy (1561), probably writing first three acts.

Nor·way \'nó(ə)r-,wā\, Nevil Shute. *Pseudonym* Nevil Shute \'shüt\. 1899–1960. English novelist. Trained as aeronautical engineer; noted for combining technical detail with fictional narrative; novels included *Marazan* (1926), *So Disdained* (1928), *What Happened to the Corbetts* (1939), *Landfall* (1940), *No Highway* (1948), *A Town Like Alice* (1950), *Round the Bend* (1951), *On the Beach* (1957); autobiography *Slide Rule* (1954).

Norwich, Earl of. See George GORING.

Norwich, Edward of. 2d Duke of York. See EDWARD.

Nor·wid \'nór-vēd\, Cyprian Kamil. 1821–1883. Polish writer. Lived in Paris (1849–52, 1855–83) and U.S. (1852–54); unknown in his time; his revival (from 1901 by Zenon Przesmycki) greatly influenced modern Polish writers, esp. anti-Romantic lyric poems which introduced free verse and everyday vocabulary into Polish poetry. Writings included verse *Poezye* (1863), *Vademecum* (1866), *Rzecz o wolnosci słowa* (1869), *Assunta* (1908); plays *Krakus* (1863), *Wanda* (1863), *Kleopatra* (1904); a treatise on aesthetics *Promethidon* (1863); and short stories.

Nos·ke \'nós-kə\, Gustav. 1868–1946. German politician. On staff of various Social Democratic periodicals (from 1897); member of Reichstag (from 1906); to Kiel during November revolution of 1918, where he reestablished order; member, ruling Council of National Deputies (1918); commanded troops which brutally suppressed Berlin Spartacist revolts (1919); became first Reichsminister of defense (1919) but resigned following the Kapp Putsch (1920); president, Hanover province (1920–33); took part in the unsuccessful coup against Hitler (July 1944). Author of *Kolonialpolitik und Sozialdemokratie* (1914) and *Von Kiel bis Kapp* (1920).

Nos·kow·ski \nós-'kóf-skē\, Zygmunt. 1846–1909. Polish composer. Invented a system of musical notation for use of the blind; conductor of Warsaw Philharmonic Orchestra (1881–1902). Composed operas *Livia Quintilla* (1900), *Wyrok* (1907), *The Quarrel about the Boundary Wall* (1909); a ballet, two cantatas, three symphonies, a symphonic poem, etc.

Nos·tre·dame \nó-trə-dám\, Michel de. *Lat.* Nos·tra·da·mus \,näs-trə-'dā-məs, ,nō-strə-'däm-əs\. 1503–1566. French physician and astrologer. Published book of rhymed prophecies under title *Centuries* (1555); prophesied correctly the manner of the death of Henry II of France; gained favor of Catherine de Médicis; became physician to Charles IX.

Noth \'nōt\, Martin. 1902–1968. German biblical scholar. Professor of theology at Bonn (1945–65); author of *Das System zwölf Stämme Israels* (1930), *Die Welt des Altes Testament* (1940), and *Überlieferungsgeschichte des Pentateuch* (1948).

No·thomb \nò-tōⁿ\, Jean-Baptiste. 1805–1881. Belgian politician. Premier of Belgium (1843–45); ambassador at Berlin (1845–81).

Not·ker \'nòt-ker, -kər\. *Called* Bal·bu·lus \'bal-byə-ləs\, *i.e.* the Stammerer. 840?–912. Swiss monk. Author of *Brevarium regum Francorum* (c.881), *Gesta Caroli* (c.884), four hymns to St. Stephen, and esp. *Liber hymnorum* (c.884), important in the development of the sequence. Beatified (1512).

Notker. *Called* Lab·eo \'lab-ē-,ō\, *i.e.* the thick-lipped. c.950–1022. Swiss-German Benedictine scholar. His translations of Latin classics into German influential in fixing the form of the German language.

Notredame, Michel de. See NOSTREDAME.

Nottingham, Earl of. English title held by MOWBRAY family (1383–1476), HOWARD family (1596–1681), FINCH family (1681–1729), united (since 1729) with earldom of Winchilsea.

Noue. See LA NOUE.

No·va \'nō-vä\, Juan de, *Port.* João da. d. 1509. Spanish navigator. While in service of Portugal discovered islands of Ascension and St. Helena and established first commercial concessions in East Indies (1501).

No·vák \'nò-väk\, Vítězslav Augustín Rudolf. 1870–1949. Czech composer. Pupil of Dvořák; professor at Prague Conservatory (1909–20), Czech State Conservatory (from 1920); one of principal proponents of Czech nationalism in music. Composed operas *Zvíkovský rarášek* (1915), *Karlštejn* (1916), *Lucerna* (1923), *Dědův odkaz* (1926); orchestral works, esp. *V Tatrách* (1902), *Slovácká svita* (1903), *De Profundis* (1941); two ballets; choral works, esp. *Bouře* (1910), *Podzimní symfonie* (1934), *Májová symfonie* (1943); chamber music and songs.

No·va·ko·vić \nò-'väk-ò-vētʸ\, Stojan. 1842–1915. Serbian writer and politician. Premier (1895, 1909); minister to Turkey (1886–92), to St. Petersburg (1900–05); writer on Serbian literature, history, and grammar.

Novalis. See Friedrich von HARDENBERG.

No·va·tian \nə-'vā-shən\. *Latin* No·va·ti·a·nus \nə-,vā-shē-'ā-nəs\. c.200–c.258. Roman Christian sectarian. Became leader of Roman clergy (c.250); on election of Cornelius as pope, became champion of rigorism and had himself proclaimed bishop of Rome (251), thus becoming the second antipope and founding the Novatian sect which spread throughout Roman Empire and lasted until 7th century; excommunicated (251); fled Rome during persecutions of Christians (251–53) and suffered martyrdom under Valerian.

No·vel·lo \nə-'vel-ō\, Ivor. *Orig.* David Ivor Davies. 1893–1951. English actor, composer, and playwright. Son of Clara Novello Davies. Composer of over sixty songs, including "Keep the Home Fires Burning" (1915); actor-manager (1924) with *The Rat,* written in collaboration with Constance Collier, and with his own plays *The Truth Game* (1928) and *Symphony in Two Flats* (1929); to Hollywood for writing and acting (1931); actor-manager with his musicals *Glamorous Night* (1935), *Careless Rapture* (1936), *Crest of the Wave* (1937), *Perchance to Dream* (1945), *King's Rhapsody* (1949).

Novello, Vincent. 1781–1861. English organist and composer. Arranged collection of sacred music (1811), which marked founding of publishing house of Novello & Co.; introduced to England unknown compositions of Haydn, Mozart, and Palestrina; original member and frequent conductor of Philharmonic Society. His son ¶Joseph Alfred (1810–1896), bass singer and music publisher, inaugurated, with success, many popular concert enterprises, introduced Mendelssohn's works to English public, and devised a system of printing cheap editions of standard musical works. His daughter ¶Clara Anastasia (1818–1908), Countess Gi·gliuc·ci \jēl-'yüt-chē\, oratorio and operatic singer, at age of 14 took soprano part in Beethoven's *Missa Solemnis;* praised by Mendelssohn and Schumann; m. Count Gigliucci (1843).

Novello Davies, Clara. See Clara Novello DAVIES.

No·verre \nò-ver\, Jean-Georges. 1727–1810. French dancer and choreographer. Ballet master and leading dancer for several European theaters including London's Drury Lane (1755–57) and King's (1780–94), Stuttgart (1760–67), Vienna (1767–74), Grand Opéra, Paris (1776–80); choreographed many ballets, esp. *Les Fêtes chinoises, Medée et Jason, Psyche et l'Amour, Les Petits Riens;* wrote *Lettres sur la danse et sur les ballets* (1760) which brought about major reforms in ballet, esp. in stage costume and the introduction of dramatic action.

No·vi·kov \'nòv-yi-kəv\, Nikolay Ivanovich. 1744–1818. Russian journalist and philanthropist. Satirized foreign influence in Russia, the institution of serfdom, etc., in his magazines *The Drone* (1769–70), *The Painter* (1772–73), *The Purse* (1774); leased Moscow *Gazette,* with its printing plant (1779–89), and tried to inculcate a love for good literature by publishing many low-priced editions of classics; imprisoned by Catherine II (1792–96).

Novius. See under Lucius POMPONIUS.

No·vo·sil·tsev \nə-(,)vəs-'yilts-yəf\, Nikolay Nikolayevich. Count. 1736–1836. Russian politician. Confidant of Czar Alexander I, who made him member of the Secret Committee (1801–03) for planning of reforms; imperial commissar of Russian Poland (1815–31).

No·vot·ný \'nòv-òt-nē\, Antonín. 1904–1975. Czech politician. Joined Communist party (1921) and elected to its Central Committee (1946), Politburo (1951); first secretary (1953). Leader in Stalinist takeover of Czech government (1948). Assumed presidency on death of Zápotocký (1957) and reelected (1964). Forced to resign presidency and party membership during Dubček's nationalistic reforms (1968), but reinstated to party (1971) after latter's downfall.

No·vy \'nō-vē\, Frederick George. 1864–1957. American bacteriologist, b. Chicago. Taught at U. of Michigan (1887–1935, professor from 1902). Developed Novy jar for cultivation of anaerobic bacteria; gave (with Victor Vaughan) first college course in bacteriology in U.S. (1889); discovered *Clostridum novyi* (1894) and *Spirocheta novyi* (1906); known esp. for work on trypanosomes and spirochetes. Model (with Jacques Loeb) for Max Gottlieb in Sinclair Lewis's *Arrowsmith.*

Now·ell *or* **Now·el** *or* **No·el** \'nō-əl\, Alexander. c.1507–1602. English clergyman. Dean of St. Paul's, London (1560–1602); inclined to Calvinism; author of the *Large Catechism,* the *Middle Catechism* (both printed 1570), and the *Small Catechism* (1549, supplemented 1604), which last is practically that of the *Book of Common Prayer.*

No·wo·wiej·ski \nò-vòv-'yā-skē\, Feliks. 1877–1946. Polish composer. Composed oratorios *Return of the Prodigal Son* (1901), *Quo Vadis* (1903), *The Finding of the Holy Cross* (1905), operas *Emigranci* (1917), *Legenda Bałtyku* (1924), *Ondraszek,* ballets, symphonies, masses, choral works, songs, and the Polish national hymn "Rota."

Noyes \'nòiz\, Alfred. 1880–1958. English poet. Professor of English, Princeton (1914–23); published first volume of poems *The Loom of Years* (1902); gained popularity with *The Flower of Old Japan* (1903); turned to poetry of the sea in *Forty Singing Seamen* (1907) and *Drake* (1908); treated Elizabethan poets in *Tales of Mermaid Tavern* (1912). Author also of poetic plays, including *Sherwood, or Robin Hood and the Three Kings* (1912), *Rada: A Belgian Christmas Eve* (1915); short stories, including *Walking Shadows* (1917); novels, including *The Winepress* (1913), *The Sun Cure* (1929); and an epic trilogy *The Torch Bearers* (1922, 1925, 1930).

Noyes, Arthur Amos. 1866–1936. American chemist, b. Newburyport, Mass. Professor at M.I.T. (1890–1919), esp. with the Laboratory of Physical Chemistry (1903–17) which he founded; at Cal. Inst. of Technology (from 1919). Author of *A Detailed Course of Qualitative Chemical Analysis* (1895) and *General Principles of Physical Science* (1902), which revolutionized the teaching of analytical and physical chemistry, and of *A System of Qualitative Analysis for the Rare Elements* (1927, with W.C. Bray). Also known for work on electrolyte solutions.

Noyes, Clara Dutton. 1869–1936. American nurse, b. Port Deposit, Md. Involved in nurses training in Mass. and N.Y. (1897–1916); director, department of nursing service, American Red Cross (1919–36); awarded Florence Nightingale medal by International Committee of the Red Cross (1923) and French medal of honor (1929).

Noyes, John Humphrey. 1811–1886. American social reformer, b. Brattleboro, Vt. Studied for ministry; announced (1834) that he had attained sinlessness, or perfection; expounded gospel of perfectionism and formed society of Bible communists (1836), attempting to return to the communism of the early Christian church; his views on marriage and his belief in free love caused his arrest (1846). Fled to central New York State, followed by the Bible communists, and established (1848) Oneida Community. Under his leadership, community flourished, abandoned free love, or complex marriage (1879); community was capitalized at $600,000 when incorporated (1881) and became known esp. for manufacture of traps and silverware. Fled to Canada to escape prosecution for adultery. His views were set forth in *The Berean* (1847), *Bible Communism* (1848), *Male Continence* (1848), *Scientific Propagation* (1873), *Home Talks* (1875).

Noyes, La Verne. 1849–1919. American manufacturer and inventor, b. Genoa, N.Y. Invented wire dictionary holder and opened factory in Chicago to manufacture it (1879); obtained patents on improved agricultural machinery; improved steel windmill and organized and headed Aërmotor Company, Chicago, to manufacture his windmills (1889).

Nu·bar Pa·sha \nü-'bär-'pá-shä\. *Also called* Nubar Pasha Nu·bar·i·an \nü-'bär-ē-ən\. 1825–1899. Egyptian politician. Premier of Egypt (1878–79, 1884–88, 1894–95); negotiated several treaties with Europe, including a system of mixed courts administrating a body of law compiled by an international commission (effected 1875).

Nuffield, 1st Viscount. See William Richard MORRIS.

Nu·gent \'nü-jənt\, Sir George. 1757–1849. English military officer. Served in American Revolution (1777–83), in Flanders under Duke of York (1793); lieutenant governor of Jamaica (1801–06); commander in chief in India (1811–13); field marshal (1846).

Nugent, John Charles. 1878–1947. American actor and playwright, b. Niles, Ohio. Acted in vaudeville and esp. in plays *Kempy* (1922), *The Dumb-Bell* (1923), *The Rising Sun* (1924), *Poor Nut* (1925), which he co-wrote with his son ¶Elliott (1899–1980), b. Dover, Ohio, actor and playwright; director of Broadway plays as *Without Love* (1942) and *The Voice of the Turtle* (1943–45); co-wrote *The Male Animal* (1940) with James Thurber.

Nugent, Laval. Count Nugent von West·meath \-fŏn-'west-mēth\. 1777–1862. Irish soldier. General chief of staff of Austrian army (1809); conquered Croatia, Istria, and the Po region (1813); commanded forces in Italy (1815), besieged Rome, and conquered Murat at Ceprano and San Germano; became a prince of the Holy Roman Empire (1816); supported Radetzky against the Piedmontese (1848); field marshal (1849); took part in Italian campaign of 1859.

Nuitter. See Charles TRUINET.

Nu·ma Pom·pil·i·us \'n(y)ü-mə-päm-'pil-ē-əs\. 8th–7th century B.C. Second legendary king (715–673 B.C.) of early Rome. Sabine; often credited with formulation of the religious calendar and with the founding of nearly all the earliest religious institutions, esp. the Vestal Virgins, cults of Mars, Jupiter, Romulus, and the office of *pontifex maximus.*

Nu·me·ni·us \n(y)ů-'mē-nē-əs\. 2d century A.D. Greek philosopher. Chiefly responsible for the transition from Platonist Idealism to a Neoplatonic synthesis of Hellenistic, Persian, and Jewish intellectual systems; only fragments of his works are extant.

Nu·mer·i·an \n(y)ů-'mer-ē-ən\. *In full* Marcus Aurelius Numerius Nu·mer·i·a·nus \n(y)ů-ˌmer-ē-'ā-nəs\. d. 284. Roman emperor (283–284) jointly with his brother Carinus. Younger son of Emperor Carus; accompanied his father on expedition against Persians (283); after death of Carus, died in camp on returning from the East; succeeded by Diocletian.

Nuncomar. See NANDAKUMAR.

Nu·nes \'nü-nēsh\, Pedro. *Lat.* Petrus No·ni·us \'nō-nē-əs\. 1492–1577. Portuguese mathematician. Appointed royal cosmographer (1529) and adviser for reformation of weights and measures (1572–75); discovered loxodromic curves (1533) before Mercator; invented device (the nonius) for graduating instruments, later improved into the vernier. Wrote on physics, geography, cosmology, and navigation, esp. *De arte atque ratione navigandi* (1546).

Nú·ñez \'nün-yās\, Rafael. 1825–1894. Colombian politician. President of Colombia (1880–82, 1884–86, 1887–88); supported new constitution of 1886 and instigated series of reforms which centralized the government and restored the power of the Catholic church.

Núñez Cabeza de Vaca, Álvar. See CABEZA DE VACA.

Nú·ñez de Ar·ce \'nün-yāth-thā-'är-thā\, Gaspar. 1834–1903. Spanish poet, playwright, and politician. Foreign correspondent for *La Iberia* in African campaign (1859–60); deputy to Cortes (1865 ff.); civil governor of Barcelona (1868); minister of colonial affairs (1882). Author of lyrics *Gritos del combate* (1875), *Idilio* (1879), *Elegía* (1879), *Última lamentación de Lord Byron* (1879), *Vértigo* (1879), *La visión de Fray Martín* (1880), and *La pesca* (1884), and tragedy *El haz de leña* (1872).

Núñez de Bal·boa \-bäl-'bō-ə, *Angl* bal-'bō-ə\, Vasco. 1475–1519. Spanish explorer. Explored coast of Colombia with Rodrigo de Bastidas (1500); settled in Hispaniola but fled creditors to join expedition which founded first stable settlement on continent at Darien (1510); governor of settlement (1511). Discovered Pacific Ocean (Sept. 25, 1513) and, as "El Mar del Sur," i.e. South Sea, took formal possession of it for Spain; made other journeys of exploration (1513–17). Served (1514–19) under Pedro Arias Dávila, new governor of Panama, with whom he had unfriendly relations and disputes; accused (probably falsely) of sedition; condemned and beheaded.

Núñez Ve·la \-'bā-lä\, Blasco. d. 1546. Spanish colonialist. Named by Charles V first viceroy of Peru (1543); attempted to control abuses of native population; killed by colonists led by Gonzalo Pizarro.

Nu·nó \nü-'nō\, Jaime. 1824–1908. Catalan conductor and composer. Director, National Conservatory of Music, Mexico City (1854–55); in U.S. (from 1855). Composer of music of Mexican national anthem (text by Francisco González Bocanegra; officially adopted 1854).

Nur·ed·din \ˌnü-red-'dēn\. *In full* Nūr ad-Dīn Abū al-Qāsim Maḥmūd ibn 'Imād ad-Dīn Zangī. *Also called* al-Malik al-'Ādil, *i.e.* the Just Ruler. 1118–1174. Sultan of Syria and Egypt. Succeeded his father Zangī in control of northern Syria (1146) and changed capital from Mosul to Aleppo; defeated the Christian armies of the Second Crusade, before Damascus; extended his dominion over all Syria and Egypt.

Nur·ha·chi \'nůr-'häch-ē\. *Formal title* Kun·du·lun Khan \'kün-'dü-'lün-'kän\. *Reign title* T'ien-Ming \tē-'en-'miŋ\. *Full Juchen title* Ge·ren Gu·run Be Uji·re Geng·gi·yen \'ger-'en-'gü-'rün-'bā-'ü-'jē-'rā-'geŋ-gē-'(y)en\. *Temple name* T'ai-tsu \'tīd-'zü\. *Posthumous name* Wu Huang-ti \'wü-hü-'äŋ-'dē\, *later altered to* Kao Huang-ti \'kaů-\. 1559–1626. Manchurian chieftain. Leader of Chien-chou Juchen tribe (from 1586); conquered (1599–1618) and united other Juchen tribes into a Manchu state which became the Manchu, or Ch'ing, dynasty of China (1644–1911). Directed creation, by Erdeni, of a Manchu system of writing (1599); moved capital to Mukden (1625); took Fu-shun (1618) in attempt to conquer China, but slain at Ningyuan; succeeded by his sons Abahai and Dorgon (*qq.v.*).

Nu·ri as-Sa·id \ˌnůr-ē-ås-så-'ēd\. 1888–1958. Iraqi politician. Began lifelong support of Hashemite dynasty by joining army of Amīr Fayṣal I (1916); served as prime minister on 14 occasions (from 1930) and also held other cabinet posts; negotiated treaty with Great Britain which granted independence to Iraq (1930); instrumental in formation of Arab League (1945) and in creation of Baghdad Pact (1955).

Nūr Jahān *or* **Nūr Mahāl.** See under JAHĀNGĪR.

Nur·mi \'nůr-mē\, Paavo Johannes. 1897–1973. Finnish long-distance runner. Won 7 gold medals in Olympics (1920, 1924, 1928); held world record for mile, 4 min. 10.4 sec. (1923–31).

Nut·tall \'nət-(ˌ)ȯl\, George Henry Falkiner. 1862–1937. British biologist, b. San Francisco. Brother of Zelia Nuttall. Professor, Cambridge U. (from 1906); founder and chief editor, *Journal of Hygiene* (1901) and *Journal of Parasitology* (1908); discoverer (1892) of *Bacillus aerogenes;* author of *The Bacteriology of Diphtheria* (with others, 1908) and papers in bacteriology, parasitology, and physiology.

Nuttall, Thomas. 1786–1859. American botanist and ornithologist, b. Settle, Yorkshire, England. To U.S. (1808); discovered many North American plants; wrote *The Genera of North American Plants* (1818); curator, Botanical Garden, Harvard (1822–32); turned attention to ornithology and published *A Manual of the Ornithology of the United States and Canada* (1832).

Nuttall, Zelia Maria Magdalena. 1857–1933. American archaeologist, b. San Francisco. Sister of George H.F. Nuttall. Authority on ancient and colonial history of Mexico; author of *The Fundamental Principles of Old and New World Civilizations* (1901), *The Book of the Life of the Ancient Mexicans* (1903), etc.; editor of *Codex Nuttall* (1902).

Nut·ting \'nət-iŋ\, Wallace. 1861–1941. American clergyman, painter, and antiquarian, b. Marlboro, Mass. In Congregational ministry (1888–1905); author of *Old New England Pictures* (1913), *The Clock Book* (1924), *Furniture Treasury* (1928, 1933), and a series of illustrated descriptive books on the beauties of several states (as *Maine Beautiful, Vermont Beautiful,* etc.).

Nu·vo·la·ri \ˌnü-vō-'lär-ē\, Tazio Giorgio. 1892–1953. Italian racing driver. Drove mainly for the Italian Alfa Romeo and German Auto Union teams; won Mille Miglia (1930), Le Mans (1933), Ulster Tourist Trophy (1933), U.S. Vanderbilt Cup (1936), numerous European Grands Prix; champion of Italy (1932, 1935–36); retired (1947); often considered greatest driver in auto racing history.

Nuyssen, Janssens van. See Abraham JANSSENS.

Nye \'nī\, Edgar Wilson, *known as* Bill. 1850–1896. American humorist, b. Shirley, Me. Wandered westward to Laramie City, Wyoming Territory (1876); founded and edited *Laramie Boomerang* (1881–84), in which appeared first the humorous pieces later collected in his books; on staff, New York *World* (1887–91); popular as lecturer, with James Whitcomb Riley (1887–90). Author of *Bill Nye and Boomerang* (1881), *Forty Liars and Other Lies* (1882), *Baled Hay* (1884), *Bill Nye's History of the United States* (1894), *Bill Nye's History of England* (1896).

Nyem, Dietrich von. See DIETRICH VON NIEHEIM.

Ny·gaards·vold \'nūē-gōrs-vōl\, Johan. 1879–1952. Norwegian politician. Laborite member of the Storting (from 1916); Labor party leader (1932); president of the Storting (1934); prime minister and minister of public works (1935–40); following German invasion of Norway, prime minister of the Norwegian government in exile (1940–45).

O

Oake·ley \'ōk-lē\, Frederick. 1802–1880. English ecclesiastic. Joined the Tractarian movement; introduced ritualism into Margaret Chapel, London (1839–45); followed Newman into Roman Catholic communion (1845); canon of Westminster diocese (1852–80); translator of Latin hymn "Adeste Fideles" ("O Come All Ye Faithful"; 1841).

Oak·ley \'ōk-lē\, Annie. *Orig.* Phoebe Anne Oakley Moses. 1860–1926. American markswoman, b. Darke Co., O. Toured vaudeville circuits and circuses with husband Frank E. Butler (m. 1876), also a noted marksman; starred in Buffalo Bill's Wild West Show (1885–1902).

Oast·ler \'ōst-lər\, Richard. 1789–1861. English reformer. Led agitation against employment of children in factories and for ten-hour working day resulting in passage of Ten Hours Act of 1847; imprisoned (1840–44) for a debt, which was paid by subscription; published *Fleet Papers* (1841–43) from prison.

Oates \'ōts\, Lawrence Edward Grace. 1880–1912. English explorer. Member of Antarctic expedition led by Captain R.F. Scott (1910); member of party that reached South Pole (Jan. 1912); on return trip, when his illness threatened to delay whole party, he deliberately walked to his death in blizzard in unavailing attempt to facilitate companions' return.

Oates, Titus. 1649–1705. English impostor and fabricator of the Popish Plot. Son of an Anabaptist preacher; employed by Israel Tonge, English divine obsessed with notion of popish plots; feigned conversion to Catholicism; expelled from two Jesuit seminaries (1677, 1678). "Uncovered" (1678) plot forged by him and Tonge, whereby Roman Catholics were supposed pledged to massacre Protestants, burn London, assassinate the king; swore to its truth before a magistrate, Sir Edmund Berry Godfrey; gained credence of populace on murder of Godfrey (1678), with result that about 35 persons were judicially murdered; implicated Queen Catherine and her physician, on whose acquittal he lost prestige; convicted and fined for calling Duke of York a traitor, and imprisoned; found guilty (1685) of perjury and sentenced to be pilloried and flogged and imprisoned for life. Pardoned (1689) on accession of William of Orange and allowed a pension.

O·ba·di·ah \,ō-bə-'dī-ə\. One of the minor Hebrew prophets, of uncertain date, whose judgment on Edom for siding with Israel's enemy the Old Testament book of Obadiah records.

Obadiah Ya·reh ben Abra·ham \-'yär-e-,ben-'ä-brə-,ham\ of Ber·ti·no·ro \,ber-tē-'nōr-ō\. c.1450– before 1516. Italian rabbi. Author of commentary on the Mishnah that has been part of printed text of most editions since 1549.

Oban·do \ō-'b̲än-dō\, José Maria. 1795–1861. Colombian politician. Fought (from 1822) with independence forces; led revolt which overthrew (1831) dictator Rafael Urdaneta; named vice president (1831–32); in exile after unsuccessful revolt against Conservative government of José Marquez (1838–40); elected president (1853) and overthrown (1854), but effected adoption of the liberal constitution of 1853.

Oberge, Eilhart von. See Eilhart von Oberge.

Ober·holt·zer \'ō-bər-,hōlt-sər\, John H. 1809–1895. American Mennonite religious leader. Ordained as bishop (1847) and founded (1860) General Conference of the Mennonite Church of North America.

Ober·lin *Fr* ȯ-ber-la^{n}, *Ger* 'ō-bər-,lēn, *Angl* 'ō-bər-lən\, Johann Friedrich. 1740–1826. Alsatian pastor and philanthropist. Lutheran pastor at Walderbach (from 1767); famed for success in improving agriculture (esp. by crop rotation), industry, education (esp. in forerunner of kindergarten), and morals in his pastorate in the Steintal. Oberlin, Ohio, and its college are named for him.

Ober·to I \ō-'ber-ō\. d. 975. Italian feudal lord. Created marquis of eastern Liguria for service under Berengar II (951); switched allegiance (960) to Otto I, who created him count palatine (962). The Este, Malaspina, Pallavicina, and Massa Parodi families of Italy are believed to have descended from his sons.

Obertus, Jakob. See Obrecht.

Obizzo of Ferrara. See Este family.

Obra·do·vić \ȯ-'brȧ-dȯ-vēt^{y}\, Dositej. 1742–1811. Serbian writer. His *Život i priključenija* (Life and Adventures, 1793) was first book published in the Serbian popular language; translated *Aesop's Fables* (1788); recognized as founder of modern Serbian literature.

Obrecht \'ō-brek̲t\ *or* **Ho·brecht** \'hō-brek̲t\, Jacob. *Lat.* Ober·tus \ō-'bərt-əs\ *or* Ho·ber·tus \hō-'bərt-əs\. c.1450–1505. Dutch conductor, composer, and contrapuntist. A master of the Franco-Flemish or Netherlandish school; composed masses, motets, a *Passion,* chansons.

Obre·gón \ō-b̲rā-'gȯn\, Álvaro. 1880–1928. Mexican soldier and politician. Planter in Sonora (1910–12); entered service of Madero against revolutionists (1912); suppressed Pascual Orozco (1912) and supported Carranza against Victoriano Huerta (1913–14); also aided Carranza against Villa and Emiliano Zapata (1915); defeated Villa at Celaya and León (1915). Overthrew Carranza and was elected president of Mexico (1920–24); put down revolt of Adolfo de la Huerta (1923–24); reelected president (1928) but soon assassinated by José de León Toral.

Obre·no·vić \ȯ-'bren-ȯ-vēt^{y}\. Name of a Serbian dynasty founded (1815) by Prince Miloš. For its ruling members, Miloš (prince 1815–39, 1858–60), Michael (prince 1839–42, 1860–68), Milan (prince 1868–82, king 1882–89), and Alexander (king 1889–1903), see these names. Rule of dynasty interrupted (1842–58) by Prince Alexander of the rival Karađorđević (*q.v.*) dynasty.

O'·Bri·en \ō-'brī-ən\. Name of Irish family of northern Munster descended from Turlough O'Brien (1009–1086) and his line of Irish chieftains, kings of Tho·mond \'tü-mənd, 'thō-\, including:

¶Conor O'Brien (d. 1539), last independent prince of Thomond; sided with Fitzgeralds in their feud with the Butlers. His brother ¶Murrough (d. 1551), 1st Earl of Thomond and Baron In·chi·quin \'in-chə-,kwin\, gave up his kingship to Henry VIII on creation as earl and baron (1543). Conor's grandson ¶Conor (1534?–1581), 3d earl; intrigued with Fitzgerald against English, was defeated, and formally surrendered (1571). The younger Conor's son ¶Donough (d. 1624), Baron of Ibrick·an \ē-'brik-ən\ and 4th Earl of Thomond, *known as* the Great Earl; assisted English in suppressing Tyrone's Rebellion (1595); obtained transfer of Clare to jurisdiction of Munster (1602); president of Munster (1605); governor of Clare (1619). With death of ¶Henry, 8th earl (d. 1741), earldom of Thomond became extinct.

¶Murrough O'Brien (1614–1674), 1st Earl of Inchiquin and 6th Baron Inchiquin; attended Strafford into Leinster at outbreak of Irish rebellion (1641); governor of Munster (1642); compelled to submit to Parliament (1644) and became president of Munster; gathered force in southern Ireland, fortified southern ports against Parliament, and was joined by Ormonde; driven westward by Cromwell, fled to France (1650); created earl of Inchiquin (1654); served with French in Catalonia (1654); captured by Algerines (1660); high steward of Queen Henrietta Maria's household. ¶Murrough (1724?–1808), 5th earl, was created marquis of Thomond. His brother ¶James (1769–1855), 3d Marquis of Thomond and 7th Earl of Inchiquin; admiral in British navy (1847); at his death, marquisate became extinct.

O'Brien, Edward Joseph Harrington. 1890–1941. American author, editor, and anthologist, b. Boston. Author of *White Fountains* (verse, 1917), *The Bloody Fool* (play, 1917), *Son of the Morning* (1932), etc. Originator and editor of *The Best Short Stories* (1915–40) and of *The Best British Short Stories* (1921–40).

O'Brien, Fitz-James. c.1828–1862. American writer, b. County Limerick, Ireland. To New York City (1852); wrote stories for periodicals and plays for James W. Wallack, esp. *A Gentleman from Ireland* (1854); died in Civil War. His short stories, esp. "The Diamond Lens," "What Was It?" and "The Wondersmith" (all 1859), are considered forerunners of modern science fiction.

O'Brien, Flann. See Brian O'Nolan.

O'Brien, James, *later* James Bronterre. 1805–1864. Irish journalist and Chartist. Moved to London (1829) where he became a leader of the Chartist working class movement; editor, *Poor Man's Guardian* (1831–35); imprisoned for seditious speaking (1840–41); joint founder of socialist National Reform League (1850).

O'Brien, William. 1852–1928. Irish journalist and Nationalist leader. Appointed by Parnell editor of *United Ireland* (1881); arrested when paper was suppressed (1881); in jail, drew up the "No Rent" manifesto; M.P. (1883–95); started the "No Reduction, No Rent" slogan (1887); imprisoned under Coercion Act of 1887; initiated new agrarian movement, the United Irish League (1898); participated in conference (1902) that led to Land Purchase Act (1903), abolishing Irish landlordism; founded "All for Ireland" party (1910) with motto "Conference, Conciliation, Consent"; in general election (1918), caused his party to retire, thereby securing Sinn Féin victory and extinction of Irish party.

O'Brien, William Smith. 1803–1864. Irish political insurgent. M.P. (1828–48); joined with Daniel O'Connell in movement for repeal of legislative union between Great Britain and Ireland (1843); broke with O'Connell and joined Thomas Francis Meagher in advocating violent revolution (1848); led abortive insurrection in County Tipperary, Ireland (July 29, 1848); death sentence commuted to exile in Tasmania; released (1854) and granted full pardon (1856).

O'·Bry·an \ō-'brī-ən\, William. 1778–1868. English clergyman. Founded (1815) the Bible Christian church, a Wesleyan Methodist sect which eventually became part of the United Methodist church in 1907; left group over administrative differences and became itinerant evangelist in U.S. (1831).

Obst·fel·der \'ōpst-ˌfel-dər\, Sigbjørn. 1866–1900. Norwegian writer. Traveled widely during youth; model for Rilke's hero in *Aufzeichnungen des Malte Laurids Brigge.* Author of verse *Digte* (1893); plays *De røde draaber* (1897), *Om vaaren* (1898), *Esther* (1899); and prose works.

Ocam·po \ō-'käm-pō\, Florián de. 1490 or 1495–c.1558. Spanish chronicler. Canon of Zamora, and historiographer (from 1539) to Charles V; wrote *Crónica general de España* (1543, 1553).

O'·Car·o·lan \ō-'kar-ə-lən\ *or* **Car·o·lan** \'kar-ə-lən\, Turlough. *Gaelic name* Toirdhealbhach Ó Cear·bhal·láin \ō-'kyar-ə-ləin\. 1670–1738. Irish bard. Became blind from smallpox (1688); itinerant among houses of gentry, repaying hospitality with songs to harp accompaniment; wrote and composed about two hundred songs in Irish; ten were adapted by Thomas Moore.

O'·Ca·sey \ō-'kā-sē\, Sean. *Orig.* John Casey. 1880–1964. Irish playwright. Wrote working-class plays for Abbey Theatre in Dublin, including *Shadow of a Gunman* (1923), *Juno and the Paycock* (1924), *The Plough and the Stars* (1926); broke with the Abbey (esp. W.B. Yeats) after its rejection of Expressionistic anti-war play *The Silver Tassie* (1928); in England (from 1926). Other plays included *Within the Gates* (1933), *Purple Dust* (1940), *The Star Turns Red* (1940), *The Bishop's Bonfire* (1955), *The Drums of Father Ned* (1958), *Behind the Green Curtains* (1961). His 6-volume autobiography (1939–56) was published in U.S. as *Mirror in My House* (1956).

Occam, William of. See OCKHAM.

Occleve, Thomas. See HOCCLEVE.

Ochi·no \ō-'kə-nō\, Bernardino. 1487–1564. Italian theologian and reformer. Franciscan (1504–34), then Capuchin; elected vicar general of Capuchins (1538–42); confessor of Pope Paul III; influenced toward Protestantism by Juan de Valdés and converted (1536); fled to Geneva (1542); at odds with Calvin; to Augsburg (1545–47), London (1547–53), Zürich (1555), Basel, Nürnberg, etc. Antitrinitarian; upheld polygamy. His works included *Tragoedie or Dialoge of the Unjuste Usurped Primacie of the Bishop of Rome* (1549), reputed to have influenced Milton's *Paradise Lost.*

Ochoa \ō-'chō-ä\, Eugenio de. 1815–1872. Spanish writer and scholar. Edited, with F. Baudry, *Colección de los mejores autores españoles* (1838–72); published a historical novel *El auto de fe* (1837), a collection of poems *Ecos del alma* (1841), and translations, as of Virgil's complete works, Victor Hugo's *Hernani, Notre Dame de Paris,* etc.

Ochozias. See AHAZIAH.

Ochs \'äks\, Adolph Simon. 1858–1935. American newspaper publisher, b. Cincinnati. Proprietor and publisher, Chattanooga *Times* (1878–1935); publisher, *New York Times* (1896–1935); proprietor, Philadelphia *Times* (1902–12) and Philadelphia *Public Ledger* (1902–12); director, Associated Press (1900–35); his innovations included the rotogravure printing of pictures and the book review supplement. By gift of $500,000 made possible publication of *Dictionary of American Biography.*

Ochs \'ōks\, Peter. 1752–1821. Swiss politician, b. Nantes, France. To Basel (1769). Instrumental in the establishment of the Helvetian Republic (Apr. 12, 1798), esp. in writing most of its constitution; first president of Helvetian Senate and later president of Helvetian Directory; deposed by party of La Harpe (1799); retired to Basel.

Ochs, Siegfried. 1858–1929. German choral conductor and composer. Founder, Philharmonischer Chor (1882); wrote comic opera *Im Namen des Gesetzes* (1888), operettas, vocal canons, and song cycles.

Och·sen·bein \'ōk-sən-ˌbīn\, Johann Ulrich. 1811–1890. Swiss soldier and politician. Led abortive coup against government of Luzern (1845), which precipitated formation of the Sonderbund; president of Bernese government and the Confederation Diet (1847); headed the constitutional reform committee (1848); president of the Nationalrat (1848); in Franco-Prussian War on French side (1870).

Ochus. See ARTAXERXES III; DARIUS II.

Ockeghem. See OKEGHEM.

Ockenfuss, Lorenz. See OKEN.

Ockenheim, Johannes. See OKEGHEM.

Ock·ham *or* **Oc·cam** \'äk-əm\, William of. *Known as* Doc·tor In·vin·cib·i·lis \'däk-tər-ˌin-vin-'sib-ə-ləs\ *and* Ven·er·ab·i·lis In·cep·tor \'ven-ər-'ab-ə-ləs-in-'sep-tòr\. c.1285–?1349. English Scholastic philosopher. Joined Franciscans; pupil, later rival, of Duns Scotus. To Avignon, France (1324). In Franciscan controversy defended evangelical poverty against Pope John XXII, esp. in *Opus nonaginta dierum* (c.1330); excommunicated and fled (1328) to Italy and later (1330) to Munich, where he spent rest of life. With Michael of Cesena, general of the Franciscan order, joined side of Emperor Louis of Bavaria in contesting temporal power of the pope; laid foundations in *Dialogus* (1343) of modern theory of independence of civil rule. Practically closed the Scholastic controversy over universals with his Nominalistic doctrine that the real is always individual, not universal, that universals have no real existence but are only abstract terms, and the corollary that "entities must not be unnecessarily multiplied" (called Ockham's Razor), thus preparing the way for Francis Bacon's philosophy.

O'·Cle·ry \ō-'kli(ə)r-ē\, Michael, *orig.* Tadhg. 1575–1643. Irish chronicler. Took name Michael on becoming Franciscan friar; with other scholars composed *Réim Rioghroidhe* (1630; a genealogy of Irish kings and saints), *Leabhar Gabhála* (1631; an account of the settlements of Ireland), and *Annála Rioghachta Éireann* (1636; a digest of old Irish annals).

O'·Con·nell \ō-'kän-əl\, Daniel. *Known as* the Liberator. 1775–1847. Irish nationalist leader. United Irish Roman Catholics under leadership of their priests into a league for urging Irish claims; originated the Catholic Association (1823) and perfected its constitutional method of agitation for repeal of civil disabilities by mass meetings. Elected M.P. (1828); took seat only after Wellington and Peel, forced by public opinion, carried through Catholic emancipation (1829); fought Coercion Act (1833); led agitation for abolition of tithes and of established church in Ireland; opposed poor law and movement against rent. Lord mayor of Dublin (1841); revived earlier demand for repeal of union of Great Britain and Ireland; recreated the Catholic Association and held mass meetings (1842–43); arrested for seditious conspiracy (1843) but released (1844) on writ of error by House of Lords. Found his power broken by dissension, opposition by revolutionaries of Young Ireland (1845), distress from potato famine, and ill health; died at Genoa on way to Rome.

O'Connell, William Henry. 1859–1944. American prelate, b. Lowell, Mass. Rector, American Coll., Rome (1895); bishop of Portland, Me. (1901); archbishop of Constance and coadjutor with succession of Boston (1906); bishop of Boston (1907); cardinal (1911).

O'·Con·nor \ō-'kän-ər\, *Ir. Gael.* Ui Con·cho·bhair \ō-'kòn-kə-vəir\. Name of an ancient Irish clan that shared with the O'Rourkes the sovereignty of Connaught into the eleventh century, including the following kings: ¶Cathal O'Connor (d. 1010), king of Connaught (from 980); bridged the Shannon (1000); retired to a monastery (1003). His grandson ¶Aedh (d. 1067); fought continually with rival O'Rourkes; killed near Oranmore. His great-grandson ¶Roderic, *Ir. Gael.* Ruaidhri (d. 1118), king from 1076; won victory at Cunghill (1087); was treacherously blinded (1092). Roderic's son ¶Turlough, *Ir. Gael.* Toirdhealbhach (1088–1156); assumed kingship of Ireland (1120); deposed (1135); regained kingship (1141–49). His son ¶Roderic *or* Rory (1116?–1198), king of Connaught (from 1156); regained high kingship of Ireland (1166); forced by Anglo-Norman invasion to submit to Henry II (1175) and pay tribute as vassal of England; last of high kings of Ireland. ¶Cathal (1150?–1224) succeeded as king (1201); resisted English expeditions (1220, 1224) under Walter de Lacy, elder son of Hugh de Lacy, 5th Baron Lacy.

O'Connor, Feargus Edward. c.1796–1855. Irish Chartist leader. M.P. (1832), unseated as radical through Daniel O'Connell's influence (1835); joined Chartists in England and became undisputed leader by 1841; advocated physical violence in his paper the *Northern Star;* presented the Chartist petition in Parliament, where it was defeated (1848).

O'Connor, Flannery, *in full* Mary Flannery. 1925–1964. American writer, b. Savannah, Ga. Author of novels *Wise Blood* (1952), *The Violent Bear It Away* (1960); collections of short stories *A Good Man Is Hard To Find* (1955), *Everything That Rises Must Converge* (1965); and essays *Mystery and Manners* (1969).

O'Connor, Frank. See Michael O'DONOVAN.

O'Connor, Thomas Power. *Popularly known as* Tay Pay \'tā-'pā\. 1848–1929. Irish journalist and nationalist leader. While freelance journalist wrote a scathing *Life of Lord Beaconsfield* (1876); in Parliament (from 1880) a supporter of Parnell; founded radical newspapers (1887, 1893), a literary paper *T. P.'s Weekly* (1902), and other weeklies; privy councilor (1924). Author of *The Parnell Movement* (1886) and *Memoirs of an Old Parliamentarian* (1929). Called "Father of the House of Commons" because of unbroken period of service.

O'Connor, William Douglas. 1832–1889. American journalist, b. Boston. Close friend and benefactor of Walt Whitman (from 1862); author of *Harrington* (1860), *The Good Gray Poet* (1866), *Three Tales* (1892).

O'·Con·or \ō-'kän-ər\, Charles. 1804–1884. American lawyer, b. New York City. As special deputy attorney general, State of New York, prosecuted William M. Tweed and his associates (1871–75), causing dissolution of Tweed Ring. Nominated by Straight-Out Democrats for president of the United States (1872).

Oc·ta·vi·a \äk-'tā-vē-ə\. *Called* Octavia Minor. 69–11 B.C. Roman matron. Sister of Octavian (Emperor Augustus) and 2d wife (40 B.C.) of Mark Antony, who divorced her (32) after he had become infatuated with Cleopatra.

Octavia. 42?–62 A.D. Roman empress. Daughter of Emperor Claudius and Messalina, and wife (53) of Nero; executed by order of Nero.

Octavian *or* **Octavianus.** See Emperor AUGUSTUS.

Oc·ta·vi·us \äk-'tā-vē-əs\. Family of Roman soldiers and politicians, including: Gnaeus Octavius (d. 162 B.C.), general and politician; distinguished himself in campaign against Persians (172–168); consul (165 B.C.); assassinated in Syria. ¶Marcus (2nd century B.C.), tribune (133) who opposed agrarian reform measures of Tiberius Gracchus, for which he was deposed. ¶Gnaeus (d. 87 B.C.), consul (87 B.C.); adherent of Sulla and opponent of his colleague in the consulship, Lucius Cornelius Cinna; murdered by followers of Cinna. ¶Gaius (d. 58 B.C.), general and politician, praetor (61), proconsul of Macedonia (60); m. Atia, niece of Julius Caesar; father of the Emperor Augustus. ¶Marcus (1st century B.C.), general; belonged to Senate party during Civil War; defeated Dolabella at sea; joined Pompey and fought at Thapsus (46 B.C.) and Actium (31).

Octavius, Gaius. See Emperor AUGUSTUS.

O'·Cur·ry \ō-'kər-ē\, Eugene. 1796–1862. Irish antiquary and Gaelic scholar. Transcribed many Irish manuscripts of the Royal Irish Academy, Trinity College, and British Museum; his lectures were published as *The Manuscript Materials of Ancient Irish History* (1861) and *On the Manners and Customs of the Ancient Irish People* (1873).

Oda \ōd-ä\ Nobunaga. *Earlier names* Kip·pō·shi \kip-pō-shē\ *and* Sa·burō \sä-bu̇r-ō\. 1534–1582. Japanese general. Succeeded to father's fief (1549); allied with Hideyoshi (1558) and Ieyasu (1562); began drive to destroy power of the daimyos and unify country by subjugating Owari Province and defeating Imagawa Yoshimoto (1560); supported (1567) and later deposed (1573) Ashikaga Yoshiaki, ending Ashikaga shogunate; destroyed political power of Buddhism by defeating Buddhist priests at Osaka (1580) after 10 years' war; conquered central Japan (1582). At his death controlled half the provinces of Japan, thus paving the way for its unification.

Od·ae·na·thus *or* **Od·e·na·thus** \ˌäd-i-'nā-thəs\, Septimus. *Aramaic* Odainath. d. 267 or 268 A.D. Prince of Palmyra. Ally of Rome; defeated Persians and restored large part of the East to Roman Empire; acknowledged by Rome as independent ruler; assassinated; succeeded by his wife Zenobia (*q.v.*).

Odell \ō-'del\, Jonathan. 1737–1818. American Loyalist, b. Newark, N.J. Served as surgeon in British army; became Anglican priest (1767). During Revolutionary War wrote satirical anti-American verses and served as chaplain to a Pennsylvania Loyalist regiment; go-between in correspondence of Benedict Arnold and the British (from 1779). Writings were collected in *The Loyal Verses of Joseph Stansbury and Doctor Jonathan Odell* (1860).

Ode·ri·gi \ˌō-dā-'rē-jē\ *or* **Ode·ri·si** \-zē\ **da Gub·bio** \-dä-'güb-byō\. 1240–1299. Italian miniaturist and manuscript illuminator. Noted by Dante in his *Divina commedia.*

Odets \ō-'dets\, Clifford. 1906–1963. American playwright, b. Philadelphia. On stage in minor roles (1923–30); a founder of Group Theatre, New York City, for which he wrote plays of social protest, esp. *Waiting for Lefty* (1935), *Awake and Sing!* (1935), *Golden Boy* (1937); to Hollywood (1936) for directing and writing, esp. screenplays of *The General Died at Dawn* (1936), *Sweet Smell of Success* (1961), *Wild in the Country* (1961); also author of *Till the Day I Die* (1935), *Paradise Lost* (1935), *The Silent Partner* (1938), *Rocket to the Moon* (1938), *Night Music* (1940), *Clash by Night* (1941), *The Big Knife* (1949), *The Country Girl* (1950), and *The Flowering Peach* (1954).

Odo. Count of Paris. See EUDES.

Odo \'ō-(ˌ)dō\ *or* **Eudes** \œd\ of Bayeux. 1036?–1097. Anglo-Norman prelate. Half-brother of William the Conqueror; bishop of Bayeux (1049); fought at Hastings (1066); was granted Dover Castle and earldom of Kent; as regent during William's absence, ruled tyrannically; left England after rebelling against his nephew William II Rufus (1088); died on way to join First Crusade.

Odo of Cluny. Saint. c.879–942. French abbot. Elected abbot of Cluny (927); granted privilege of exemption and authorized to reform monasteries of Gaul and Italy by Pope John XI (931); credited (perhaps falsely) with developing method of designating musical pitches by letters; author of moral works, esp. two hagiographies and religious poem *Occupatio,* anthems, and hymms.

Odo·a·cer \ˌō-dō-'ā-sər\. *Also* Odo·va·car *or* Odo·va·kar \ˌō-dō-'vā-kər\. c.433–493. First barbarian king of Italy (476–493). Joined Roman army (c.470); as German tribal leader (a king of the Heruli) in the army, led insurrection (476) and was proclaimed king; caused death of Roman general Orestes and abdication of his son the puppet emperor Romulus Augustulus, whose title and office were abolished, thus terminating the Western Roman Empire. Conquered Dalmatia (482); became opponent of Emperor Zeno (from 484). Shut up in Ravenna (489–493) and several times defeated by Theodoric, king of the Ostrogoths; treacherously slain by the latter.

O'·Don·nell \ō-'dän-əl\. Name of an ancient Irish family, lords of Tyr·con·nel \tər-'kän-əl\, *Ir. Gael.* Tir Conaill (approximately modern Donegal), rivals of the O'Neills in Ulster, and including: Manus O'Donnell (d. 1564), deputy governor of Tyrconnel during father's pilgrimage to Rome (1510–11); chief (1537); united with Con O'Neill to overthrow English rule in Ireland but was defeated (1539); harassed (from 1547) by his eldest son ¶Calvagh (d. 1566), who, with aid obtained from Scotland, imprisoned him and usurped authority (1558) and was later surprised, captured, and tortured by Shane O'Neill (1561), being restored by arrival of supporting forces sent in response to appeal to Queen Elizabeth (1566). ¶Hugh Roe O'Donnell (1572–1602), nephew of Calvagh; held as hostage by English lord deputy; escaped (1591) and received chieftainship from his father, Hugh MacManus (1592); secretly worked against the English and appealed to Philip II of Spain for assistance; invaded Connaught (1595, 1597); helped Tyrone to defeat English at Yellow Ford (1598); lost fortresses of Lifford and Donegal by treachery of Niall Garv (1600); failed in attack on English besiegers of newly landed Spanish forces; laid complaint before Philip III of Spain but died in Spain of poison. ¶Sir Niall Garv O'Donnell (1569–1626), grandson of Calvagh; in resentment at election of his cousin Hugh Roe, made terms with English government, was promised grant of Tyrconnel, but quarreled with deputy over lordship of Inishowen (1601); his claims of chieftainship (1602) passed over in favor of Rory O'Donnell by English government; charged with complicity in seizure of Culmore Castle and sacking of Derry (1608); died in Tower of London. ¶Rory O'Donnell (1575–1608), 1st Earl of Tyrconnel, younger brother of Hugh Roe, assumed chieftainship on brother's flight to Spain (1602); gave allegiance to English lord deputy, but fled with Hugh O'Neill when his designs for tribal independence and seizure of Dublin were known (1607); reached Rome, where his grievances, emphasizing religious disabilities, were heard; died of Roman fever.

O'·Don·nell \ō-'t͟hō-nel\, Leopoldo. Conde de Lu·ce·na \t͟hā-lü-'thā-nä; -'sā-\. Duque de Te·tuán \tā-'twän\. 1809–1867. Spanish marshal and politician of Irish descent. Fought for Isabella II against Carlists (1833–39); general in army of Queen Maria Christina and accompanied her into exile (1840); fought against Espartero (1843); governor of Cuba (1843–48); minister of war under Espartero (1854–56); led successful revolution against him (1856); prime minister of Spain (1856, 1858); led successful expedition into Morocco (1859); again prime minister (1863, 1865–66).

O'·Do·no·jú \ō-t͟ho-nō-'k̲ü\, Juan. 1762–1821. Spanish soldier. Captain general and acting viceroy (1821) of New Spain (Mexico); on arrival at Vera Cruz, found the country conquered by Iturbide, with whom he signed a treaty at Córdoba (Aug. 24, 1821) surrendering Mexico; served as one of the five regents governing Mexico until regular constitutional government could be inaugurated.

O'·Don·o·van \ō-'dän-ə-vən, -'dən-\, John. 1809–1861. Irish archaeologist. Edited Michael O'Clery's *Annála Ríoghachta Èireann* (1851); with Eugene O'Curry compiled ancient laws of Ireland; author of works on Irish history and antiquities and *Grammar of the Irish Language* (1847).

O'Donovan, Michael. *Pseudonym* Frank O'Connor. 1903–1966. Irish writer. Member of Irish Republican army (1921–22); imprisoned during civil war; gained instant fame with publication of short stories *Guests of the Nation* (1931); director of Abbey Theatre, Dublin (1936–39); broadcaster for Ministry of Information, London, in World War II; published stories in *The New Yorker* (1945–61); visiting professor at Northwestern, Harvard, Chicago (1952–60). Known mainly for collections of short stories, including *The Wild Bird's Nest* (1932), *Bones of Contention* (1936), *Crab Apple Jelly* (1944), and *The Common Chord* (1947). Also author of autobiographies *An Only Child*

(1961), *My Father's Son* (1969); plays *In The Train* (1937), *Time's Pocket* (1939), *The Statue's Daughter* (1940), etc.; translations of Gaelic literature, esp. Brian Merriman's *The Midnight Court* (1945), included in *Kings, Lords, and Commons* (1959); and criticism *The Lonely Voice* (1963), *The Backward Look* (1967), etc.

O'Donovan, William Rudolf. 1844–1920. American sculptor, b. Preston Co., Va. Executed busts of Winslow Homer, Gen. Joseph Wheeler, Walt Whitman, etc.; his statue of Washington stands at the top of Battle Monument, Trenton, N.J.

Odo·ric \'ōd-ə-rik\ of Por·de·no·ne \ˌpȯrd-ᵊn-'ō-nē\. *Ital.* Odo·ri·co \ˌō-dō-'rē-kō\. c.1265–1331. Italian Franciscan missionary. His journal of travels (c.1314–30) in Turkey, Persia, India, Java, China, and other Asian parts enjoyed wide popularity in Europe and was plagiarized by the author of *The Travels of Sir John Mandeville;* beatified (1755).

O'·Dowd \ō-'dau̇d\, Bernard Patrick. 1866–1953. Australian poet. Worked as teacher, librarian, parliamentary draftsman. Espoused belief that poets should be socially involved; author of verse *Downward?* (1903), *The Silent Land* (1905), *Dominion of the Boundary* (1907), and prose pamphlet "Poetry Militant" (1909); also author of *The Bush* (1912; long poem about Australia) and *Alma Venus! and Other Verses* (1921; social satire in verse).

O'·Duf·fy \ō-'dəf-ē\, Eoin. 1892–1944. Irish soldier. Member of Irish Republican army (1917), chief of staff (1921–22); in charge of forces of Irish Free State (1924–25); director of Blue Shirt organization; helped found United Ireland party (1933); organized and led Irish brigade fighting on side of General Franco in Spain (1936–37); brigadier general in Spanish army.

Odum \'ōd-əm\, Howard Washington. 1884–1954. American sociologist, b. Bethlehem, Ga. While professor at U. of North Carolina (1920–54) pioneered Southern sociological education by founding departments of sociology and public welfare (both 1922), the Institute for Research in Social Science (1924), and scholarly journal *Social Forces* (1922); wrote extensively on folk sociology (esp. of the American Negro) and social problems of the South, including *The Negro and His Songs* (1925, with Guy B. Johnson), *Southern Regions of the U.S.* (1936), *American Regionalism* (1938, with Harry E. Moore), and *Understanding Society* (1947); also wrote a fictional trilogy with a black hero, *Rainbow Round My Shoulder* (1928), *Wings On My Feet* (1929), and *Cold Blue Moon* (1931).

O'·Dwy·er \ō-'dwī-ər\, Joseph. 1841–1898. American physician, b. Cleveland. Pioneer in successful use of intubation to prevent asphyxia in diphtheria (1885), and in use of diphtheria serum.

O'Dwyer, William. 1890–1964. American politician, b. Bohola, Ireland. To U.S. (1910); as Brooklyn district attorney prosecuted Murder, Inc.; mayor, New York City (1946–50); ambassador to Mexico (1950–52).

Oe·ben \'œ̄-ben\, Jean-François. c.1715–1763. French cabinetmaker, b. Germany. Entered workshop of André-Charles Boulle (1751); patronage of Mme. de Pompadour assured his appointment as royal cabinetmaker (1754). Known for outstanding marquetry and ingenious mechanical devices; his masterpiece was the *bureau du roi,* begun in 1760 and finished after his death by his associate Jean-Henri Riesener.

Oecolampadius. See Johannes HUSZGEN.

Oeconomus. See Sebastian HOFMEISTER.

Oeh·len·schlä·ger \'œ̄-lən-shleg-ər\, Adam Gottlob. 1779–1850. Danish poet and dramatist. A pioneer of the Romantic movement in Denmark, having been converted by Henrick Steffens; engaged in literary feuds notably with Baggesen (1813–19) and J. L. Heiberg (1827–30); crowned as "king of the Scandinavian singers" by Tegnér at Lund (1829), and publicly acclaimed as national poet (1849). Author of *Guldhornene* (symbolic poem, 1802), *Sanct-Hansaften-spil* (lyric drama, 1803), *Aladdin* (verse fantasy, 1805); the historical tragedies *Hakon Jarl* (1807), *Baldur hin Gode* (1808), *Palnatoke* (1809), and *Axel og Valborg* (1810); *Correggio* (drama, in German, 1809), *Nordens Guder* (an Eddaic epic cycle, 1819), *Helge* (a cycle of verse romances, 1814), reminiscences, etc.

Oen·gus *or* **Aen·gus** \'aŋ-gəs\ *or* **Oengus Mac Oen·go·ba·na** \-mək-'aŋ-gə-ˌbän-ə\. *Also called* Oengus the Culdee. Saint. 8th–9th century. Irish monk. Member of Irish monastic reform movement Céli Dé (in English, Culdees) and pupil of Máelrúain of Tallaght; founded own church, Dísert-Oengusa, in County Leix. Author of the *Félire* (c.800), a religious verse calendar of the early Irish church.

Oe·nop·i·des \i-'näp-ə-ˌdēz\ *or* **Oi·nop·i·des** \'ȯi-\ of Chi·os \'kī-ˌäs\. 5th century B.C. Greek astronomer and mathematician. Had knowledge of the obliquity of the ecliptic; fixed length of solar year at 365 days and somewhat less than nine hours; credited with discovering 12th and 23rd propositions of the first book of Euclid and the quadrature of the meniscus.

Oersted. See ØRSTED.

Oer·tel \'ür-təl\ *or* **Or·tell** \'är-təl\, Abraham. *Lat.* Or·te·li·us \ȯr-'tē-lē-əs, -'tēl-yəs\. 1527–1598. Flemish cartographer. Appointed (1575) geographer to Philip II of Spain; his atlas *Theatrum orbis terrarum* (1570) long remained basis for geographic works.

Oer·tel \'œr-təl\, Hanns. 1868–1952. German linguist. Professor at Yale (1896–1915), Basel (1915–21), Marburg (1921–25), Munich (from 1925); wrote principally on the Hindu Vedas and *Syntax of Cases in the Narrative and Descriptive Prose of the Brahmanas* on Sanskrit (1926).

Oertel, Max Joseph. 1835–1897. German physician. Known for his method of treating heart and circulatory diseases, obesity, etc., by regulation of diet, restriction of fluid intake, and exercise.

Oe·ser *or* **Öser** \'œ̄-zər\, Adam Friedrich. 1717–1799. German painter, sculptor, and etcher. Champion of reform in art on antique lines; in Leipzig (from 1759), director of the art academy (1764), where he taught Winckelmann and Goethe. His works included frescoes, allegorical murals, decorative ceilings, and etchings.

Oe·ting·er \'œ̄-tiŋ-ər\, Friedrich Christoph. 1702–1782. German theologian and theosophist. Leader of Pietists and disciple of Böhme and Swedenborg; author of *Inquisitio in sensum communem et rationem* (1753), *Theologia ex idea vitae deducta* (1765), etc.

Of·fa \'ȯ-fə\. d. 796. King of Mercians in Anglo-Saxon England (757–796). Wrested Bensington from Cynewulf of Wessex (779); took territory beyond Severn from Welsh; built Offa's Dyke from mouth of Wye to mouth of Dee, against Welsh; formed bishopric of Lichfield with sanction of Pope Hadrian I (788); caused beheading (794) of Aethelberht, king of East Anglia; traded and corresponded with Charlemagne as an equal.

Offa of An·gel \'äŋ-(g)əl\. 4th century A.D. Ruler of Angel. According to Old English poem *Widsith,* saved his father, King Wermund, from Saxon domination by defeating a Saxon prince in single combat; probably same Offa mentioned in *Beowulf;* the Anglo-Saxon Mercian dynasty claimed descent from him.

Offaly, Barons of. See FITZGERALD family.

Of·fen·bach \'ȯ-fən-ˌbäk, *Fr* ȯ-fen-bȧk\, Jacques, *orig.* Jacob. 1819–1880. French musician and composer, b. Cologne. To Paris (1833); orchestra conductor at Théâtre Française (1850); opened his own theater, Bouffes-Parisiens (1855) and played (until 1866) one-act operettas of his own composition, as *Les deux aveugles* (1855), *Les Violoneux* (1855), *Le Mariage aux lanternes* (1857), *Orphée aux enfers* (1859). Contributed successful operettas and opéra bouffe to other theaters in Paris, as *La Belle Hélène* (1864), *La Vie parisienne* (1866), *La Grande-Duchesse de Gérolstein* (1867), *La Périchole* (1868), *Les Brigands* (1869). Managed the Théâtre de la Gaîté in Paris (1873–76) and toured the U.S. (1876). His only grand opera *Contes d'Hoffmann* (*Tales of Hoffman*), finished by Ernest Guiraud, was not produced until after his death.

Ogadai. See ÖGÖDEI.

Oga·ta \ō-gä-tä\ Kenzan. *Signed works* Kenzan, Shisui, Shinshō, Shōkosai, Shuseidō, Tōin. 1663–1743. Japanese potter and painter. Studied pottery with Nonomura Ninsei; opened his first kiln at Narutaki (1699), later moved to Nijō (1712) and Edo (1731). Produced *raku* ware, ceramics, and porcelains; known esp. for *iro-e* (color painting) ornamentation, often from designs supplied by his brother Ogata Kōrin. Also known for paintings, some bearing his poems.

Ogata Kōrin. *Orig. prename* Ichinojo. 1658–1716. Japanese painter. Influenced by Kōetsu, Sōtatsu, and Kanō and Tosa schools; given honorific rank of Hokkyō (1701); one of two great masters of the Sōtatsu-Kōrin school of decorative painting; known for screen paintings, lacquerwork, textile designs, and pictorial decorations supplied for ceramics of his brother Ogata Kenzan.

Og·burn \'äg-(ˌ)bərn\, William Fielding. 1886–1959. American sociologist, b. Tallahassee, Fla. Authority on social changes due to technological advances; known esp. for application of statistical methods to problems of social sciences and for idea of "cultural lag" to describe cultural readjustments. Professor at Columbia (1919–27) and U. of Chicago (1927–51); writings included *Social Change* (1922) and *Sociology* (1940, with Meyer F. Nimkoff).

Og·den \'ȯg-dən, 'äg-\, Aaron. 1756–1839. American lawyer, b. Elizabethtown, N.J. U.S. senator (1801–03); governor of New Jersey (1812). His operation of steamboat line between Elizabethtown and New York brought litigation with Thomas Gibbons, conducting a rival line under monopoly rights originally granted by the New York legislature to Livingston and Fulton. The Gibbons-Ogden case was carried to U.S. Supreme Court, where Chief Justice Marshall's decision (1824) established the principle of freedom of interstate commerce.

Ogden, Charles Kay. 1889–1957. British psychologist and linguist. Founded intellectual journal *The Cambridge Magazine* (1912); inventor of Basic English, simplified system of learning English through a selected vocabulary of 850 words (took final form in 1928); coauthor of *Foundations of Aesthetics* (with I.A. Richards and James Wood, 1921) and *The Meaning of Meaning* (with I. A. Richards, 1923); author of *The Basic Vocabulary* (1930), *Debabelization* (1931), *The System of Basic English* (1934).

Ogden, Peter Skene. 1794–1854. Canadian fur trader, b. Quebec. Fur trader with North West Company and (after merger) Hudson's Bay Company; during trading expeditions explored much of the American West, discovering the Humboldt River in Nevada (1828) and making first reconnaissance of eastern face of Sierra Nevada (1829); rescued survivors of Marcus Whitman's expedition from Cayuse Indians (1847); author of *Traits of American-Indian Life and Character* (1853). Ogden, Utah, and the Ogden River are named for him.

Ogden, Rollo. 1856–1937. American journalist, b. Sand Lake, N.Y. Editor, New York *Evening Post* (1903–20), New York *Times* (1922–37).

Ogden, William Butler. 1805–1877. American railroad executive, b. Walton, N.Y. To Chicago (1835); first mayor of city of Chicago (1837–41); interested in railroad development out of Chicago; first president, Union Pacific Railroad (1862).

Ogé \ō-'zhā\, Jacques Vincent. 1750–1791. Haitian insurgent. Organized (1790) in U.S. a secret expedition to emancipate Haitian slaves; after a few successful battles was captured and executed. Regarded as a martyr by the natives of Haiti, who rose in rebellion to avenge his death and nearly exterminated the whites on the island.

Og·gio·no \ōd-'jō-nō\ *or* **Og·gio·ne** \-nā\ *or* **Ug·gio·ne** \üd-'jō-nā\, Marco da. 1475?–?1530. Italian painter. Pupil and imitator of Leonardo da Vinci; known chiefly for his copies of Leonardo's *Last Supper*.

Ogil·by \'ō-gəl-bē\, John. 1600–1676. British translator and printer, b. near Edinburgh. A pioneer in the making of road atlases with *Britannia...a Geographical and Historical Description of the Principal Roads thereof* (1675); published translations in verse of Virgil, Homer, Aesop's *Fables;* satirized by Dryden in *MacFlecknoe* and by Pope in the *Dunciad*.

Ogil·vie \'ō-gəl-vē\, John. 1797–1867. Scottish lexicographer. Compiler of *The Imperial Dictionary, English, Technological, and Scientific* (1850), including encyclopedic features.

Ogiń·ski \ō-'gēnʸ-skē\, Michal Kleofas. 1765–1833. Polish politician and composer. Commanded his own regiment of cuirassiers in the Kosciusko rebellion (1794); refugee (1794–1802); served as mediator for his people with Czar Alexander after the Treaty of Tilsit (1807); became Russian senator (1810); withdrew to Italy (1815); composed polonaises, mazurkas, waltzes, songs, and an opera *Zélis et Valcour* (1799).

Ogles·by \'ō-gəlz-bē\, Richard James. 1824–1899. American politician, b. Oldham Co., Ky. Served in Mexican War and in Union army in Civil War; major general (1863); governor of Illinois (1865–69, 1873); U.S. senator (1873–79); again governor (1885–89), first man to be elected three times governor of Illinois.

Ogle·thorpe \'ō-gəl-,thȯrp\, James Edward. 1696–1785. English soldier and philanthropist. M.P. (1722–54); interested himself in prison reform; planned project for colonizing unemployed men freed from debtor's prison on lands in America; received charter (1732) for a colony of Georgia. Accompanied first band of emigrants to America (1733) and administered affairs of colony until return to England (1734); founded Savannah. Again in Georgia (1735–36, 1738–43); fought against Spaniards; repulsed Spanish attack on Georgia (1742). In England (from 1743); general (1765). Surrendered Georgia charter to British government (1752).

Ögö·dei \'ō-gō-'dā\. *Also spelled* Ogadai, Ogdai, Ogotai, Ugedei. 1185–1241. Mongol Khan (1229–41). Third son of Genghis Khan; attempted organization of empire set up by Genghis; built a palace at Karakorum; put down revolts in Korea, China, and Turkistan; aided by wise counsels of Yeh-lü Ch'u-ts'ai, who advised preservation of conquered cultures; sent great army under Batu Khan and Subotai into Russia (1237–41), plundered Moscow, destroyed Kiev, and overran Poland and Hungary, reaching the Adriatic Sea; an intended invasion of western Europe was called off after his death during a drinking bout. His death followed by a confused period of 10 years, which included short reigns of his widow ¶Töregene (1241–46), son ¶Güyük (1246–48), and grandson ¶Kaidu (1248); his family displaced (1251) by Mangu Khan and Kublai Khan.

O'·Gor·man \ō-'gȯr-män\, Juan. 1905–1982. Mexican architect and muralist. Built private houses in International Style in Mexico City (1928–mid-1930s); later active as easel and mural painter. Planned and built (1950–52) library of National University of Mexico, Mexico City, employing as exterior decoration imaginative mosaics depicting history of Mexico; created mosaics *Homage to Cuauhtemoc* at Hotel de la Mision, Taxco (1957), and *Fraternity of Indo-American Peoples* at Parque San Cristobal, Santiago, Chile (1963–64); also known for murals at library of Patzcuaro, Michoacan (1941–42), and for his own house outside Mexico City (1953–56).

O'·Gra·dy \ō-'grā-dē\, Standish James. 1846–1928. Irish man of letters. Called "father of the Irish literary revival"; influenced young Irish writers (including Yeats) with historical works as *History of Ireland: The Heroic Period* (1878), *History of Ireland: Cuculain and His Contemporaries* (1880), *Finn and His Companions* (1892); also wrote historical novels, esp. *The Bog of Stars* (1893) and *The Flight of the Eagle* (1897).

Og·yū \ōg-yü\ Sorai. 1666–1728. Japanese Confucian scholar. Advocated pragmatic application of Confucianism to promote social and political reforms by means of uniform, rational laws; also noted for appreciative commentary on shogun Tokugawa Ieyasu.

O'·Ha·gan \ō-'hā-gən\, Thomas. 1st Baron O'Hagan. 1812–1885. Irish jurist. Lord chancellor of Ireland (1868–74, 1880–81), first Roman Catholic in the office since time of James II.

O'·Hara \ō-'har-ə\, Geoffrey. 1882–1967. American composer and songwriter, b. Chatham, Ont. To U.S. (1904, naturalized 1919). Among his works were the operettas *Peggy and the Pirate* (1927), *Riding Down the Sky* (1928), *Harmony Hall* (1933); the songs "There Is No Death," "K-K-K-Katy," "Wreck of the Julie Plante," "Leetle Bateese," "If Christ Came Back."

O'Hara, John Henry. 1905–1970. American writer, b. Pottsville, Pa. Wrote criticism and features for newspapers and magazines; author of novels as *Appointment in Samarra* (1934), *Butterfield 8* (1935), *A Rage to Live* (1949), *Ten North Frederick* (1955), *From the Terrace* (1958), *Sermons and Soda Water* (1960), *The Lockwood Concern* (1965); short stories as *The Doctor's Son* (1935), *Files on Parade* (1939), *Pal Joey* (1940; adapted as musical comedy, 1940), *The Hat on the Bed* (1963), *Waiting for Winter* (1966); plays and screenplays; and a newspaper column collected in *My Turn* (1966).

O'Hara, Mary. See Mary Alsop.

O'Hara, Theodore. 1820–1867. American soldier and poet, b. Danville, Ky. Served in Mexican War and in Confederate army through Civil War; known esp. for one poem, "The Bivouac of the Dead," a dirge commemorating the reburial at Frankfort, Ky. (1847), of Kentuckians killed in the battle of Buena Vista.

O'·Hig·gins *Eng* ō-'hig-ənz, *Span* ō-'ē-gēns\, Ambrosio. Marqués de Osor·no \t͟hā-ō-'sȯr-nō\. *Orig. name* Ambrose Hig·gins \'hig-ənz\. 1720?–1801. Irish soldier and administrator. Captain of cavalry in Chilean service; defeated Araucanian Indians and founded fort of San Carlos (1770); built road from Santiago to Valparaíso; captain general of Chile (1789–96); rebuilt Osorno (1792) and was created marquis; as viceroy of Peru (1796–1801), improved defenses and lines of communications.

O'Higgins, Bernardo. 1778–1842. Chilean soldier and statesman. Natural son of Ambrosio O'Higgins; known as "Liberator of Chile". Military leader of Chilean patriots (from 1810); made commander of army (1813); with Carrera was defeated at Rancagua (1814) but after joining with San Martín, decisively defeated the Spanish at Chacabuco (Feb. 12, 1817); liberal dictator of Chile (1817–23); deposed by revolution, retired to Peru.

O'·Higgins \ō-'hig-ənz\, Harvey Jerrold. 1876–1929. American journalist and novelist, b. London, Ont. Author of *The Smoke-Eaters* (1905), *A Grand Army Man* (1908), *The Beast* (nonfiction, with Ben B. Lindsey, 1910), *Julie Crane* (1924), *Clara Barron* (1926).

O'Higgins, Kevin Christopher. 1892–1927. Irish politician. Joined the Sinn Féin movement (1916) and was interned; minister of the interior and vice president of the executive council in the provisional government of Ireland (1922); minister for home affairs and justice (1923) and for external affairs (1927); helped draft Irish Free State constitution and secured its passage; established the Civic Guard and restored order in Ireland; assassinated.

Ohi·ra \ō-hē-rä\ Masayoshi. 1910–1980. Japanese politician. Joined finance ministry (1936); member, House of Representatives (from 1952); chief cabinet secretary (1960–62); minister for foreign affairs (1962–64, 1972–74), of international trade and industry (1968–70), of finance (1974–76); prime minister (1978–80).

Oh·lin \'ō-lin\, Bertil Gotthard. 1899–1979. Swedish economist and politician. Member of parliament (1938–70); minister of trade (1944–45); leader of Liberal party (1944–67); awarded (with James E. Meade) Nobel prize for economics (1977).

Ohm \'ōm\, Georg Simon. 1789–1854. German physicist. Professor, Polytechnische Schule of Nürnberg (1833–49), Munich (1849–54); discovered the relationship between the strength of an unvarying electrical current, the electromotive force, and the resistance of a circuit, now known as Ohm's law, and summarized it in *Die galvanische Kette, mathematisch bearbeitet* (1827). The ohm, the practical unit of electrical resistance, was named in his honor.

Oinopides. See Oenopides.

Ois·trakh \'ȯi-strək, *Angl* -,sträk, -strək\, David Fyodorovich. 1908–1974. Russian violinist. Debut in Moscow (1933); taught (from 1934) at Moscow Conservatory; toured in Europe (from 1951), U.S. (from 1955); acclaimed for exceptional technique and tone.

Oje·da \ō-'kā-thä\, Alonso de. 1465–1515. Spanish explorer. To America with Columbus (1493); active in conquest of Hispaniola (1493–95); with Juan de la Cosa and Amerigo Vespucci explored northern coast of South America (1499–1500); as governor of Nueva Andalucía (Darien) unsuccessfully attempted settlement near Cartagena (1508–09); colonized Darien.

Ojet·ti \ō-'yāt-tē\, Ugo. 1871–1946. Italian writer and art critic. Editor in chief, *Corriere della Sera* (1926–27); works included criticisms, a collection of essays *Cose Viste* (1923–39), novels, esp. *L'amore e suo figlio* (1913) and *Mio figlio ferravierre* (1922), short stories, and plays.

Ōjin \ō-jēn\. 200?–?310. 15th emperor (from 270) of Japan. During his reign immigrant Chinese and Koreans introduced Confucianism and helped develop Japanese culture; deified as Hachiman, god of war.

Oka \ō-kä\ Asajirō. 1866–1944. Japanese biologist. Known for introduction of Darwin's theory of evolution into Japan, esp. with *Lectures on Evolutional Theory* (1904); expert on freshwater jellyfish, frogs, and other marine life.

Oka·da \ō-kä-dä\ Beisanjin. *Also known as* Hi·ko·bē \hē-kō-be\. 1744–1820. Japanese painter. Influenced by Uragami Gyokudō; known for landscapes in Chinese *bunjin-ga,* or literati style.

Okada Tamechika. *Name at birth* Shinzō; *later called* Rei·zei \rā-zā\ Saburō. 1823–1864. Japanese painter. A leader in revival of *Yamato-e* style (paintings stressing Japanese themes and techniques instead of Chinese); also proficient in calligraphy and Buddhist painting; a member of the Imperial court; slain after being falsely accused of pro-shogunate sentiments.

Oka·ku·ra \ō-kä-kü-rä\ Kakuzō. *Pseudonym* Ten·shin \ten-shēn\. 1862–1913. Japanese art critic. Under influence of Ernest Fenollosa worked for re-appreciation of Japanese art; director (1888–98) of Tokyo Fine Arts School, which he helped found (1887); also helped found Japan Academy of Fine Arts. Author of *The Ideals of the East* (1903), *The Awakening of Japan* (1904), etc.

Ōka·wa \ō-kä-wä\ Shūmei. 1886–1957. Japanese politician. One of foremost proponents of nationalism; founded the political group Yūzonsha (1919, with Kita Ikki) and *Nippon* (1924), magazine advocating military government and takeover of Manchuria; led two unsuccessful military coups (1931); imprisoned (1932–37) for involvement in assassination of Premier Inukai Tsuyoshi; famous for helping shape and broadcasting government domestic propaganda (1939–45); arrested (1945) as war criminal but charges dropped on grounds of insanity.

Okazaki Genshichi. See KAIGETSUDŌ.

Okba. See 'UQBAH IBN NĀFI'.

O'·Keeffe \ō-'kēf\, Georgia. 1887–1986. American painter, b. near Sun Prairie, Wis. Became acquainted with Alfred Stieglitz and his circle in New York City (from 1907); m. Stieglitz (1924); developed own romantic style featuring abstract studies of color and light; began (1924) painting abstract floral forms suggestive of human anatomical parts; after visiting (1929) New Mexico, began lifelong series of paintings of desert terrain and bleached animal skulls. Regarded as a leading American artist of the 20th century.

O'Keeffe, John. 1747–1833. Irish playwright. Gained reputation as author of *Tony Lumpkin in Town* (produced 1778); author of farces, comedies, esp. *Wild Oats* (1791), comic operas, esp. *The Agreeable Surprise* (1781), *The Castle of Andalusia* (1782), *The Poor Soldier* (1783), and of the song "I am a Friar of Orders Grey" in his opera *Merry Sherwood.*

Oke·ghem \'ō-kə-gem\ *or* **Ock·e·ghem** \'äk-ə-\, Jean d' *or* Jan van. *Also known by numerous other variants, including* Johannes Ock·en·heim \'ōk-ən-hīm\. c.1410–1495. Flemish composer and contrapuntist. A master of the Franco-Flemish or Netherlandish school; at court of Charles VII in Paris (from 1453) and head of the chapel (1454); served under Louis XI as treasurer of St. Martin's abbey, Tours (1459); again in Paris (from 1461); royal Kapellmeister (from 1465). His compositions included masses (*Missa cuiusve toni, Missa prolationum*), motets, canons, and chansons.

O'·Kel·ly \ō-'kel-ē\, Seán Thomas. *Ir. Gael.* O Ceal·laigh \ō-'kyel-ē\. 1883–1966. Irish politician. One of founders of Sinn Féin; speaker of first Dáil Éireann (1919–21); Irish envoy to U.S. (1924–26); vice president of executive council and minister for local government and public health (1932–39), minister of finance (1939–45); president (1945–59), Republic of Ireland.

O'Kelly, Seumas. 1881–1918. Irish writer. Editor of several papers, including the Sinn Féin *Nationality* (1918); author of plays *The Shuiler's Child* (1910), *The Bribe* (1914), *The Parnellite* (1917), etc.; short stories, esp. *The Weaver's Grave* (1919); and a novel *The Lady of Deerpark* (1917).

Oken \'ō-kən\, Lorenz. *Orig. surname* Ock·en·fuss \'ō-kən-,füs\. 1779–1851. German naturalist and philosopher. Sought to unify the natural sciences; in his speculations, foreshadowed theories of the cellular structure of organisms and of the protoplasmic basis of life.

Okhlop·kov \(,)ək-'lóp-kəf\, Nikolay Pavlovich. 1900–1967. Russian theater manager and producer. While director (1931–37) of Moscow's Realistic Theater was one of first to use a round stage; producer at Vakhtangov (1938–43) and Mayakovsky (1943–66) theaters.

Okig·bo \ō-'kig-(,)bō\, Christopher. 1932–1967. Nigerian poet. Worked as civil servant, librarian, editor; killed while fighting in Biafran army. His poetry influenced by classical training, native Ibo mythology and landscape, and belief he was reincarnation of his grandfather, a priest of river goddess Idoto; poems included *Heavensgate* (1962), *Limits* and *Distances* (1964), *Silences* and *Path of Thunder* (1965).

Oku \ō-kü\ Yasukata. Count. 1846–1930. Japanese soldier. Served in war with China (1894–95); general (1903); took important part in Russo-Japanese War (1904–05); considered one of Japan's great military strategists; chief of staff (1906–12); count (1907); field marshal (1911).

Ōku·bo \ō-kü-bō\ Toshimichi. 1831–1878. Japanese politician and reformer. Member of Satsuma clan; one of five leaders in restoration of emperor to power (1867–68); cabinet officer (1870–78); aided government in putting down Satsuma rebellion of Saigō Takamori (1877); murdered by followers of Saigō.

Ōku·ma \ō-kü-mä\ Shigenobu. Marquis. 1838–1922. Japanese politician. One of younger leaders in Restoration period (1867–68); as minister of finance (1869–81) organized fiscal system on sound basis; established (1882) the Rikken Kaishintō (Progressive party); prime minister (1898 and 1914–16); founder (1882) and president of Waseda U. at Tokyo.

Oku·mu·ra \ō-küm-ür-ä\ Masanobu. *Also known as* Gen·pa·chi \gen-pä-chē\. 1686–1764. Japanese painter and wood-block printer. Taught himself painting and print design; publisher (from 1724) of illustrated books; one of first to adopt Western perspective, esp. in his large-scale *uki-e* ("looming picture") prints of interiors of stores, theaters, homes; said to have originated format of wide, vertical prints called *habahiro hashira-e.*

Ōku·ra \ō-kür-ä\ Kihachirō. 1837–1928. Japanese businessman. Founder (c.1872) of the Ōkura-Gumi Company, one of largest *zaibatsu* (industrial-financial combines); one of first in foreign trade, it later branched into mining and engineering enterprises.

Ōkyo \ō-kyō\. *Full name* Ma·ru·ya·ma \mä-rü-yä-mä-\ Ōkyo. *Also called* Maruyama Masataka. 1733–1795. Japanese painter. Influenced by Chinese masters; founded Maruyama school that incorporated Occidental principles of realism with traditional Japanese style.

Olaf. See also OLOF.

Olaf \'ō-läf, *Angl* 'ō-,läf, -ləf\. Name of two kings of Denmark:

Olaf I. d. 1095. King (1086–95). Son of Sweyn II; nicknamed "Hunger" because of famines during reign.

Olaf II. 1370–1387. Son of Haakon VI Magnusson of Norway and Margaret of Denmark; king of Denmark (1376–87) and of Norway, as Olaf V or sometimes IV (1380–87), his mother ruling as regent of both countries. See MARGARET.

Olaf \'ō-läf, *Angl also* 'ō-ləf\ *or* **Olav** \'ō-läv\. Name of five kings of Norway:

Olaf I Trygg·va·son \'trüg-və-sōn\. c.964–1000. King (995–1000). Born while parents were in exile; brought up at court of Vladimir I, Grand Prince of Russia; m. Gyda, a princess of Dublin, and lived in England and Ireland several years (c.990–993); converted to Christianity in Scilly Islands; led Viking expedition, ravaging coasts of France, England, and Ireland (994); sailed to Norway and was accepted as king (995); began to convert country to Christianity; quarreled with King Sweyn of Denmark; in an expedition to Wendish country, waylaid off Svöld, near Rügen, by combined Swedish and Danish fleets; on total defeat of Norwegians, leaped overboard and disappeared. A great warrior and popular sovereign; subject of many legends.

Olaf II Ha·ralds·son \'här-räl-sōn\. *Called also* Saint Olaf. 995?–1030. King (1016–28). Son of Harald Grenske and a descendant of Harald I. Took part in Viking expeditions; accepted Christianity (1013); endeavored to complete conversion of Norway; with Bishop Grimkell devised religious code of 1024, from which time the church of Norway may be dated; made enemies of petty kings of Norway who sought help of Canute the Great of Denmark; fled to Russia (1028); tried to reconquer Norway but was defeated and killed at Stiklestad; national hero and patron saint of Norway; canonized (1164).

Olaf III Haraldsson. *Also called* Olaf Kyr·re *Norw* 'kür-rə, *Old Norse* 'kür-rə\, *i.e.* the Quiet. d. 1093. King (1066–93). Son of Harald III Haardraade; after death of father at Stamford Bridge (1066), brought back fleet to Norway; divided kingdom with brother Magnus II Haraldsson; reigned jointly with him (1066–69) and alone (1069–93); entire reign marked by peace and progress and growth of Christianity.

Olaf IV Mag·nus·son *Norw* 'mäŋ-nü-sōn, *Old Norse* 'mäg-nü-sōn\. 1100?–1115. Son of Magnus III; king (1103–15) jointly with his two brothers, Eystein and Sigurd; sometimes not counted as a king.

Olaf V. See OLAF II, king of Denmark.

Olaf Guth·frith·son \'ō-ləf-'güth-frith-sən\. d. 941. Danish king of Northumbria and Dublin. Kinsman of Olaf Sihtricson; leader of Ostmen; king of Dublin (934), of Deira (southern Northumbria, 940).

Olaf Siht·ric·son \'ō-ləf-'sit-rik-sən\ *or* **An·laf Siht·ric·son** \'än-läf-\ *or* **Olafr Sig·tryggs·son** \'ō-läv-ər-'sēg-trüg-sōn\. *Known in sagas as* Olaf the Red. d. 981. Danish king of Northumbria and Dublin. Leader of Ostmen; one of princes defeated by Aethelstan at Brunanburh (937); driven from

Northumbria by Edmund (944); his dominion in Ireland destroyed by defeat of Danes at Tara (980).

Ólafs·son \'ō-läf-sȯn\, Eggert. 1726–1768. Icelandic poet and antiquarian. One of leaders in preservation of Iceland's language and culture; *Reise igiennem Island* (1772) recorded his scientific and cultural survey of Iceland in 1752–57.

Olaus Magnus. See MAGNUS.

Ola·ya Her·re·ra \ō-'lä-yä-er-'re-rä\, Enrique. 1880–1937. Colombian politician. President of Colombia (1930–34); administration notable for financial measures to combat economic depression.

Ol·bers \'ōl-bers\, Heinrich Wilhelm Matthäus. 1758–1840. German physician and astronomer. Devised method of determining the orbit of a comet (1779); discovered 5 comets (the one of 1815 with a period of 72 years being named after him), rediscovered the asteroid Ceres, and discovered the asteroids Pallas (1802) and Vesta (1807); advanced Olbers's hypothesis accounting for origin of asteroids by explosion of a primordial planet.

Ol·brich \'ōl-,brik\, Joseph Maria. 1867–1908. German architect. Champion of modernism in architecture and handicraft; cofounder (1897) of Wiener Sezession, the Austrian manifestation of Art Nouveau movement. Author of *Ideen* (1899), *Architektur* (1901–14), *Der Frauenrosenhof* (1907), etc.

Ol·cott \'ōl-kət\, Chauncey, *orig.* Chancellor John. 1860–1932. American singer and actor, b. Buffalo, N.Y. Successful as star in Irish musical dramas (from 1891), some of which he wrote himself; introduced song "Mother Machree" in U.S.; wrote and sang "My Wild Irish Rose."

Olcott, Henry Steel. 1832–1907. American theosophist, b. Orange, N.J. Studied occult science under Madame Blavatsky (1874); cofounder (with Madame Blavatsky, 1875) and first president of the Theosophical Society. With Madame Blavatsky traveled and made converts in India and Ceylon (1879–84); after challenge (1885) to Madame Blavatsky's claims, devoted himself to developing Theosophical Society on legitimate basis. Lectured widely in India, Ceylon, Japan; opened free schools in India for pariahs; cooperated with Annie Besant in work of British Theosophical Society.

Old·berg \'ōld-bərg\, Arne. 1874–1962. American composer, b. Youngstown, O. Composed chamber music, symphonies, a symphonic poem *The Sea* (1934), overtures, esp. *Paolo and Francesca* (1908), rhapsodies, concertos, and piano pieces.

Old·cas·tle \'ōl(d)-,kas-əl\, Sir John. 1377?–1417. English Lollard leader. Titled Baron Cob·ham \'käb-əm\ after his marriage to Joan, Lady Cobham (1409). Won friendship of Henry, Prince of Wales (later Henry V), during Welsh campaigns; a leader of force sent to France by Henry (1411). Arrested by Henry's orders and convicted of heresy (1413); escaped; headed a Lollard conspiracy and other plots; captured, hanged as heretic and traitor, and burned while hanging. Portrayed as boon companion of the prince in *The Famous Victories of Henry V*, adapted by Shakespeare in *Henry IV*, in which Falstaff was originally named Oldcastle. Also central figure in anonymous play *The First Part of the True and Honorable Historie, of the Life of Sir John Old-castle* (1600). Cf. Sir John FASTOLF.

Ol·den·bar·ne·velt \,äl-dən-'bär-nə-,velt\, Johan van. 1547–1619. Dutch statesman. A founding father of Dutch independence. Participated (from 1568) in revolt of Netherlands against Spain; helped William I negotiate Union of Utrecht (1578–79); as Grand Pensionary (1586) mobilized Dutch resources for Maurice of Nassau; negotiated Triple Alliance with England and France against Spain (1596); negotiated Twelve Years' Truce with Spain (1609). Sided (1617) with Remonstrants (Arminians) in religious strife against Maurice and the Gomarists (Calvinists); arrested (1618), condemned for religious subversion, and beheaded.

Ol·den·burg \ȯl-dən-,bu̇rk\. A German family of nobility which became prominent in the 15th century. It is divided into several lines:

(1) Counts of Oldenburg (region in northwestern Germany), extinct (1667).

(2) Dynasties of Denmark: (a) Rulers of Denmark (1448–1863) and Norway (1450–1814), and at times of Sweden; began with Christian I, Count of Oldenburg (ruled 1448–81), who descended through his mother from Eric V Klipping, and who was offered crown of Denmark (1448) on death of Christopher III (of Bavaria); succeeded by John (*or* Hans) (1481–1513) and thereafter by 14 sovereigns alternately named Christian (II–VIII) and Frederick (I–VII), becoming extinct with Frederick VII (1863). (b) Glücks·burg \'glu̇ks-,bu̇rk\ line, the present reigning house of Denmark (Christian IX, Frederick VIII, and Christian X). See 4(b) below.

(3) Got·torp \'gȯ-,tȯrp\ or Hol·stein-Got·torp \'hōl-,shtīn-\ line (named from a castle in Schleswig), a branch of the Danish line; founded (1586) by Duke Adolf, a younger son of King Frederick I of Denmark; line ruled (as counts, 1568–1773) in a part of Schleswig-Holstein under Danish kings; their county became a duchy (1777); held by Napoléon (1806–13); became a grand duchy (1815) but title not adopted until later (1829); last rulers: Nicholas Frederick Peter (1827–1900) and Frederick Augustus (1852–1931; ruled 1900–18; abdicated). Two other royal lines have branched from this: (a) *Russian:* Holstein-Gottorp-Romanov, founded by Peter III (czar, 1762), son of Anna (daughter of Empress Catherine I) and Charles Frederick of Holstein-Gottorp. See ROMANOV. (b) *Swedish:* Holstein-Gottorp line (see VASA), founded by Adolf Frederick of Holstein (ruled 1751–71), uncle of Peter III and brother of Charles Frederick.

(4) Holstein-Sön·der·borg \-'sœn-ər-bȯrg\ line, originating (1582) with Duke John (Hans) (1545–1622), third son of Christian III of Denmark; divided into two lines: (a) Sönderborg-Au·gu·sten·burg \-au̇-'gu̇s-tən-,bu̇rk\ beginning (1770); recent head, Prince Christian (1831–1917); (b) Schleswig-Holstein-Sönderborg-Glücksburg, beginning (1825), of which one branch is 2(b) above, another (through George I) the royal line of Greece.

Old·field \'ōld-,fēld\, Anne. 1683–1730. English actress. Made reputation as Lady Betty Modish in Cibber's *Careless Husband* (1704); excelled as Lady Townley in the *Provoked Husband;* created many parts in genteel comedy; in tragedy created role of Jane Shore (1714); excelled as Cleopatra and as Calista in Rowe's *Fair Penitent;* created role of Sophonisba (1730).

Oldfield, Berna Eli, *known as* Barney. 1878–1946. American auto racer, b. Wauseon, Ohio. Chief driver (from 1902) of Henry Ford's racing car, the *999;* winner of many races and first to achieve mile-a-minute performance (June 15, 1903, at Indianapolis); retired (1918); later involved in tire manufacturing and auto safety engineering.

Old·ham \'ōl-dəm\, John. c.1600–1636. English colonist. To America (1623), landing at Plymouth; his report of explorations of Connecticut River (1633) induced Massachusetts colonists to found first English settlements in Connecticut; his murder by Pequot Indians was one of causes of Pequot War.

Oldham, John. 1653–1683. English poet. A pioneer in the imitation of classical satire in English, esp. with *Satires Upon the Jesuits* (1681); also wrote Pindaric odes.

Oldham, Richard Dixon. 1858–1936. British geologist and seismologist. Member, Geological Survey of India (1879–1903); famous for report on Assam earthquake of June 12, 1897, wherein he identified primary, secondary, and tertiary waves; first to establish existence of Earth's core from seismic data (1906).

Old·mix·on \'ōld-,mik-sən\, John. 1673–1742. English historian. Author of poems and plays, esp. *The Governor of Cyprus* (1703); published partisan histories of England, Scotland, Ireland, and America; attacked Clarendon in his *Critical History of England* (1724–26); provoked Pope's retaliation in the *Dunciad.*

Olds \'ōldz\, Ransom Eli. 1864–1950. American automobile inventor and manufacturer, b. Geneva, O. Founded Olds Motor Works (1899) which made the Oldsmobile (from 1901), the first commercially successful American car; founder and president, Reo Motor Car Co. (1904–24), chairman (1924–36).

Oldstyle, Jonathan. See Washington IRVING.

Ol·dys \'ōl-dəs, 'ōldz\, William. 1696–1761. English antiquary. Collaborated with Samuel Johnson in compilation of the *Catalogue of the Harley Library* (1743–45) and on *Harleian Miscellany* (1744–46); Norroy king-of-arms (1755–61); wrote *Life of Raleigh* (1736).

Oleg \'ō-(,)leg\. d. c.912. Viking warrior and prince of Kiev. Founder of Kievan Rus state. Succeeded kinsman Rurik as Novgorod ruler (c.879); conquered Smolensk and Kiev (882), making latter his capital; united local Slav and Finnish tribes under his rule; defeated Constantinople (907), extracting a large indemnity; negotiated treaty with Constantinople (911) which was basis of permanent trade activity between it and Kievan Rus.

Olenin, Boris. See Viktor CHERNOV.

Ole·sha \(,)əl-'yesh-ə\, Yury Karlovich. *Pseudonym* Zu·bi·lo \zü-'byē-lə\. 1899–1960. Soviet writer. Wrote articles for railwaymen's paper *Gudok* in early 1920s; achieved fame with novel *Zavist* (1927); imprisoned in late 1930s for criticism of Socialist Realist literature; also author of *Tri Tolstyaka* (1928), play *Spisok blagodeyaniy* (1931), short story collections, humorous verse, screenplays.

Oleś·nicki \ȯ-lesh-'nē-kə\, Zbigniew. 1389–1455. Polish politician and prelate. Became leading member of Privy Council after saving life of King Władysław II at Battle of Grunwald (1410); bishop of Kraków (1423); negotiated nobles' recognition of king's son as heir in exchange for limitation of power, thus beginning Polish elective monarchy (1430); as regent of Poland (1434–47) opposed Hussite religious movement and defeated Hussite nobles (1439); appointed first Polish cardinal (1439); on death of Władysław III (1444) ruled country until coronation of Casimir IV (1447).

Ole·vi·a·nus \ō-lā-vē-'än-u̇s\, Caspar. 1536–1587. German theologian. A founder of the German Reformed church; with Zacharius Ursinus compiled the Heidelberg Catechism (1562).

Ol·ga \'ōlʸ-gə, *Angl* 'ōl-gə, 'äl-, 'ōl-\. Saint. c.890–969. First Russian saint of the Orthodox church. Wife of Prince Igor I of Kiev; ruled Kiev (945–964) after Igor's death as regent for her minor son; baptized at Constantinople (c.957).

Olga Con·stan·ti·nov·na \-kən-(,)stən-'tyē-nəv-nə\. 1851–1926. Queen of Greece. Daughter of Grand Duke Constantine of Russia; m. (1867) George I of Greece; mother of Constantine I of Greece.

Olgierd. See ALGIRDAS.

Olid \ō-'lēth\, Cristóbal de. 1488–1524. Spanish soldier. With Cortés in conquest of Mexico (1519–21); attempted to conquer Honduras for own gain but slain by Cortés's followers.

Olier \ōl-yā\, Jean-Jacques. 1608–1657. French priest. Founder (1641) of Sulpician order for training men for the priesthood and (1642) of the Seminary of Saint Sulpice in Paris.

Oliphant, Carolina. See Carolina NAIRNE.

Oli·phant \'äl-ə-fənt\, Laurence. 1829–1888. English writer, b. Cape Town, South Africa. Published *A Journey to Khatmandu* (1852), *The Narrative of the Earl of Elgin's Mission to China and Japan* (1859), and the satirical novel *Piccadilly* (1870). Fell under influence of Thomas Lake Harris, spiritualist prophet in U.S. (1867–81). With his wife wrote *Sympneumata* (1884), advocating a purified sex life; wrote mystical novels *Altiora Peto* (1883) and *Massollam* (1885); also *Episodes in a Life of Adventure* (1887). Proposed plan to establish a Jewish state in Palestine (1878) that was rejected by Ottoman sultan.

Oliphant, Margaret Oliphant, *nee* Wilson. 1828–1897. Scottish writer. m. (1852) Francis W. Oliphant. Author of *Mrs. Margaret Maitland* (1849), *Merkland* (1851), *Adam Graeme* (1852), a series of four novels entitled *Chronicles of Carlingford* (1863–66), *The Primrose Path* (1878), *A Beleaguered City* (1880), *A Little Pilgrim in the Unseen* (1882), *Kirsteen* (1890), *A Widow's Tale* (1898). Author also of *The Makers of Venice* (1887), *Literary History of England 1790–1825* (1882), and *Annals of a Publishing House* (1897).

Olivares, Conde de. See GUZMÁN Y PIMENTAL.

Ol·i·ver \'äl-ə-vər\, Andrew. 1706–1774. American political leader, b. Boston. Member of Massachusetts Provincial Council (1746–65); secretary of the province (1756–71); appointed stamp officer after passage of the Stamp Act (1765), he was unpopular, hanged in effigy, his house damaged by mob violence; lieutenant governor of Massachusetts (1771–72); again suffered unpopularity when Benjamin Franklin secured and published (1773) certain private letters of his describing unrest in the colonies and suggesting remedies.

Oliver *or* **Oliv·i·er** \ō-'liv-ē-ər, -'liv-ē-ā\, Isaac. 1556?–1617. English painter of French extraction. Known for miniatures, including portraits and religious and classical scenes. His eldest son ¶Peter (1594–1648) was employed by Charles I to make copies in miniature of paintings in his collection.

Oliver, James. 1823–1908. American industrialist, b. Scotland. To U.S. (1835); invented process for manufacturing hard-faced plows (patents 1868, 1869); president of Oliver Chilled Plow Works in South Bend, Ind., until his death.

Oliver, Joseph. *Called* King Oliver. 1885–1938. American jazz musician, b. Abend, La. Played cornet with various bands in New Orleans (1907–17); to Chicago (1917), where he organized own band (1920), reorganized as King Oliver's Creole Jazz Band (1922–24), with Louis Armstrong on second horn; after move to New York City (1928) his fortunes declined and he died in obscurity. Composed many songs, including "Doctor Jazz," "West End Blues," "Dixieland Blues," "Dippermouth," "High Society."

Oliver, Paul Ambrose. 1830–1912. American soldier and inventor, b. at sea. Credited with inventing dynamite and black powder explosives, contemporaneously with and independently of Nobel and Schultze.

Oli·vé·tan \ō-lē-vā-täⁿ\, Pierre-Robert. *Lat.* Oliv·e·ta·nus \ō-,liv-ə-'tā-nəs\. c.1506–1538. French Protestant scholar. Published (1535) translation of the Bible with a preface by his kinsman John Calvin.

Olivia, Conde de. See Rodrigo CALDERÓN.

Olivier, Isaac and Peter. See OLIVER.

Oli·vier \ō-lēv-yā\, Juste Daniel. 1807–1876. Swiss writer. Author of books on Swiss history and patriotic poems, hymns, and short stories.

Öl·jei·tü \,œl-jā-'tœ\. *Muslim name* Moḥammad Kho·dā·ba·nah \kō-,dä-ban-'ä\. 1280–1316. 8th Il-Khan ruler of Iran (1304–16). Great-grandson of Hülegü; baptized Christian and named Nicholas by mother; converted to Islam in youth; conquered province of Gilan (1307); made Shī'ism state religion (1309–10); active patron of arts; built capital at Soltānīyeh.

Ol·li·vier \ō-lēv-yā\, Émile. 1825–1913. French politician. Elected to legislative assembly (1857); one of "The Five" republican delegates; as Napoléon III's minister of justice (Jan.–Aug. 1870), drew up constitution, instituted liberal reforms; maneuvered by Bismarck into declaring war on Prussia; forced to resign after French defeats revealed folly of the ministry in plunging country into war. Wrote histories, esp. *L'Empire libéral* (1894–1902), a novel, ecclesiastical works, etc.

Ol·me·do \ōl-'mā-thō\, José Joaquín. 1782–1847. Ecuadorian politician and poet. Delegate of Guayaquil to Cortes de Cádiz (1811); declined election as first vice president of Ecuador (1830). Best known for his lyrics, as in *La victoria de Junín: Canto a Bolívar* (1825).

Olm·sted \'ōm-,sted, 'äm-, -stəd\, Frederick Law. 1822–1903. American landscape architect, b. Hartford, Conn. Received appointment as superintendent of Central Park, then under construction in New York City (1857); in association with Calvert Vaux, designed new plans for the park; also planned Prospect Park in Brooklyn, South Park in Chicago, Belle Isle Park in Detroit, Stanford U. grounds, the grounds of the Capitol at Washington, the Boston park system, and many others. Instrumental in securing the Yosemite as a national reservation. His reports to *New York Times* on South (1852–55) published as *The Cotton Kingdom* (1861).

Ol·ney \'äl-nē, 'ō(l)-\, Richard. 1835–1917. American statesman, b. Oxford, Mass. U.S. attorney general (1893–95); U.S. secretary of state (1895–97); while directing U.S. policy in settlement of Venezuela boundary dispute with Great Britain (1895) formulated Olney Corollary to Monroe Doctrine, which maintained U.S. right to intervene in international disputes in Western Hemisphere.

Olof \'ü-lōv, -lōf\. *Called* Olof Sköt·ko·nung \'skœt-,kō-nüŋ\, *i.e.* Olof the Tax King. d. 1022. King of Sweden. Joined with Sweyn I of Denmark in successful war against Norway (1000); made peace with Olaf II Haraldsson, to whom he married daughter Astri; attempted to impose Christianity but impeded by pagan chieftains.

Oló·za·ga \ō-'lō-thä-gä\, Salustiano. 1805–1873. Spanish politician. Involved in conspiracy to assassinate King Ferdinand VII (1831); took refuge in Paris; returned to Spain after Ferdinand's death and became supporter of Queen Maria Christina; ambassador in Paris (1840, 1855–65, 1868 ff.).

Ol·son \'ōl-sən\, Charles John. 1910–1970. American poet, b. Worcester, Mass. Instructor (from 1948) and rector (1951–56), Black Mountain College; leader (with Robert Creeley) of Black Mountain school of poetry; his avant-garde theories of poetry contained in *Projective Verse* (1959), from which title Projectivistic poetry derives; major poems published in *The Maximum Poems* and *The Distances* (both 1960).

Olyb·ri·us \ō-'lib-rē-əs\, Anicius. d. 472. Roman emperor (April–November 472). Native of Rome but fled to Constantinople (after 455); m. (c.464) Placidia, daughter of Valentinian III; sent to Italy by Emperor Leo; made emperor of the West by Ricimer (472).

Olym·pi·as \ō-'lim-pē-əs, ə-\. c.375–316 B.C. Macedonian queen. Daughter of Neoptolemus, king of Epirus; m. (359 B.C.) Philip II of Macedon; mother of Alexander the Great. Retired to Epirus when Philip married (337) Cleopatra; gained much influence during Alexander's reign (337–323); said to have caused death of Cleopatra and her daughter; again withdrew to Epirus (c.331); joined Polyperchon in alliance against Cassander; besieged in Pydna by Cassander, captured and killed.

Olym·pio \ō-'lim-pē-ō\, Sylvanus. 1902–1963. Togolese politician. As prime minister (1958–60) led Togo to independence and was elected first president (1961–63) of the new republic; assassinated in army coup.

Olym·pi·o·do·rus \ō-,lim-pē-ə-'dōr-əs, -'dȯr-\. 5th century A.D. Greek historian, b. Egypt. Long resident at court of Theodosius; author of a history of the Western Roman Empire from 407 to 425, an abstract of which (by Photius) is extant.

Olympiodorus of Alexandria. *Called* the Elder. 5th century A.D. Greek Peripatetic philosopher. Remembered chiefly as a teacher of Proclus.

Olympiodorus of Alexandria. *Called* the Younger. 6th century A.D. Greek Neoplatonic philosopher. Maintained Platonic tradition in Alexandria after suppression of Athenian school (529) by Justinian; wrote commentaries on Plato and Aristotle.

O'·Ma·ho·ny \ō-mə-'hō-nē\, John. 1816–1877. American political leader, b. County Cork, Ireland. To New York City (1852); suggested (1856) and aided in organizing the Irish Republican Brotherhood under James Stephens (1858); headed American branch known as Fenian Brotherhood, popularly Fenians (1858–66); resigned after dissension following fiasco of Fenian attack on Canada (1866); again Fenian leader (1872–77).

Oma·lius d'Hal·loy \ō-mȧl-yü̅s-dȧ-lȯi\, Jean-Baptiste-Julien d'. 1783–1875. Belgian geologist. Authority on geology of the Netherlands and Belgium; did work on metamorphism and ethnography; known esp. for his systematic subdivisions of geologic formations in Earth's crust (proposed 1830).

Oman \ō-'mən\, Sir Charles William Chadwick. 1860–1946. British historian, b. India. Author of histories of Greece (1888), of Europe from 476 to 918 (1893), of the art of war in Middle Ages (1898) and in 16th century (1937), of Peninsular War (1902–30), of England before the Norman Conquest (1910), and of *Warwick the Kingmaker* (1891), *Wellington's Army* (1912), *Napoleonic Studies* (1929), *On the Writing of History* (1939), etc.

Oman, John Wood. 1860–1939. Scottish Presbyterian theologian. Professor (from 1907) and principal (1922–35), Westminster College, Cambridge;

author of *Vision and Authority* (1902), *The Problem of Faith and Freedom* (1906), *The Church and Divine Order* (1911), *Grace and Personality* (1917), *The Natural and the Supernatural* (1931).

Omar. See 'UMAR.

Omar Khay·yám \ˌō-ˌmär-ˌkī-ˈ(y)äm, ˌō-mər-, -kī-, -ˈ(y)am\. *Arab.* Gheyās od-Dīn Abū ol-Fatḥ 'Omar ebn Ebrahīm ol-Khayyāmī. 1048?–?1131. Persian poet, mathematician, astronomer, and philosopher. Member of group of eight scholars appointed by Sultan Malik-Shāh to reform the Muslim calendar (1079); their reform inaugurated the Jalalaean era. Published a series of astronomical tables known as *Zīj Malik-shāhī* and a treatise on algebra. Best known as a poet for his *Robā'īyāt* ("quatrains"), a collection of quatrains in which the 1st, 2d, and 4th lines rhyme, known to English readers esp. through the translation by Edward FitzGerald (*q.v.*).

Omayyad. See UMAYYAD.

Ömer \œ-ˈmer\. *Pseudonym* Nef'i \nef-ˈē\. *Known also as* Nef'i of Erzurum. d. 1635 or 1636. Ottoman poet. Court panegyrist to Sultan Murad IV; known also as a powerful satirist; attacked many high figures in vituperative, often obscene verse; executed on order of one such victim, the deputy prime minister. Considered one of greatest of classic Ottoman poets and esp. a master of the *qaṣīdah* (ode) form.

Omer Pa·sha \ˈō-mər-pä-ˈshä\. *Also* Omar \ˈō-mər, -mär\ Pasha. *Orig.* Michael Lat·tas \lä-ˈtäs\. 1806–1871. Turkish general, b. Croatia. Fled to Bosnia (1828) and became Muslim; governor of Lebanon (1842); suppressed several revolts; defeated Russians at Oltenița (1853); commanded army in Crimea (1855); governor of Baghdad (1857–59); put down insurrections in Montenegro (1862) and in Crete (1867); created marshal (1864).

Omodeo. See Giovanni Antonio AMADEO.

O'·More \ō-ˈmō(ə)r, -ˈmȯ(ə)r\, Rory. *Ir. Gael.* Ruaidh·ri og ua Mor·dha \ˈrȯi-rē-ō-ə-ˈmȯr-ə\. Name of three Irish rebel chieftains of Laoighis (formerly Leix): Rory (fl. 1554), captain of Leix. His son ¶Rory (*or* Rury) Oge (d. 1578) fought against forces of both Elizabeth and Earl of Ormonde (1572); participated in Kildare plots (1574); pardoned; rebelled again on hope of help from Spain; defeated by Sir Henry Sidney; finally caught and killed by the Fitzpatricks. ¶Rory (fl. 1620–1652), *called often* Roger Moore; organized a conspiracy to recover lands of Irish families; failed to seize Dublin Castle (1641), but led Ulster rebellion; won victory at Julianstown (1641); commanded forces in Kings and Queens counties (1643), in Connaught and Leinster; after failure of uprising of 1650, was driven away to island of Bofin (1652).

Omp·te·da \ˈȯmp-tā-ˌdä\, Georg von. Freiherr. *Pseudonym* Georg Ege·storff \ˈā-gəsh-ˌtȯrf\. 1863–1931. German writer. Author of novels *Sylvester von Geyer* (1897), *Eysen* (1899), *Cäcilie von Sarryn* (1902), etc.; also of stories, poems, dramas, translations of de Maupassant, etc.

Om·ri *or* **Om·rai** \ˈäm-ˌrī, ˈȯm-\. *Hebrew* 'Amri. d. 875? B.C. King of Israel (876–869 B.C.). Proclaimed king by army; gained control of Israel by overcoming Tibni, claimant to throne, and made Samaria his capital; made Moab subject to him; succeeded by his son Ahab.

Ōmura \ō-mu̇r-ä\ Masujirō. 1824–1869. Japanese military scholar and soldier. Gained fame as military strategist during battles between his Choshū clan and shogunate (1864–65); as minister of military affairs (1869) planned elimination of samurai as warrior class and conscription system for new Imperial Army, of which he is considered father; assassinated by samurai opposed to reforms.

Oña \ˈōn-yä\, Pedro de. 1570?–?1643. Chilean poet. Author of *Primera parte de Arauca domado* (1596), verse epic in rhymed couplets based on Ercilla's *La Araucana;* of *El Ignacio de Cantabrice* (1639), religious poem on St. Ignatius Loyola, and *Temblor de Lima en 1609.*

Onas·sis \ō-ˈnä-sēs, *Angl* ō-ˈnas-əs\, Aristotle Socrates. 1900?–1975. Greek businessman, b. Turkey. To Argentina (1923); made first million by 1930 as tobacco importer; entered (1932) shipping business with purchase of 6 freighters, which he parlayed into 90-ship fleet; his half-billion dollar fortune included Olympic Airlines (1956), real estate, oil tankers, etc.; m. (1968) Jacqueline Kennedy, widow of Pres. John F. Kennedy.

Ona·tas \ō-ˈnāt-əs\. 5th century B.C. Greek sculptor. Famous for statues of athletes; works highly praised by Pausanias. The Aeginetan marbles, or sculptures, may be in part his work or represent his style.

Oña·te \ōn-ˈyä-tā\, Juan de. 1550?–1630. Spanish explorer, b. New Spain (now Mexico). Appointed first governor of New Mexico (1595), into which he led expedition to explore and conquer territory (1598); sent exploring parties into Kansas (1601) and to Gulf of California (1605); resigned (1607); convicted (1614) of cruelty, immorality, and false reporting while governor.

Oncken, August. See under Wilhelm ONCKEN.

Onck·en \ˈȯŋ-kən\, Hermann. 1869–1946. German historian. Professor at Heidelberg (1907–23), Munich (1923–28), Berlin (1928–35). Author of political biographies of Ferdinand Lassalle (1904) and Rudolf von Bennigsen (1910), and of *Deutschlands Weltkrieg und die Deutschamerikaner* (1914), *Das deutsche Reich und die Vorgeschichte des Weltkrieges* (1933), etc.

Oncken, Wilhelm. 1838–1905. German historian. Professor at Giessen (1870–1905). Author of *Athen und Hellas* (1865–66), *Österreich und Preussen im Befreiungskrieg* (1876–79), etc. His brother ¶August (1844–1911), economist, wrote *Adam Smith und Immanuel Kant* (1877), *Geschichte der Nationalökonomie* (1902), etc.

O'Neale, Margaret, *known as* Peggy. See Margaret EATON.

O'·Neill \ō-ˈnē(ə)l\. An Irish family descended, through his son Owen (*Ir. Gael.* Eoghan), from Niall \ˈnē(ə)l\ (d. 405), king of Ireland, who fought against rulers in Ireland, Britain, and Gaul. Of the O'Neills, who were chief rivals in Ulster of the O'Donnells, the following were important leaders: ¶Con O'Neill (1484?–?1559), *called* Ba·cach \ˈbäk-ək\, *i.e.* the Lame, 1st Earl of Ty·rone \ti-ˈrōn\; thrice invaded the Pale, English-controlled district (1520, 1539, 1541); made submission at Greenwich after three invasions of Tyrone (1542) and was created earl of Tyrone by Henry VIII; privy councilor of Ireland (1543). His son ¶Shane (1530?–1567), 2d earl; captured Calvagh O'Donnell and harassed English army until Elizabeth recognized him chieftain of Tyrone and granted his terms (1563); attacked Scottish settlements in Antrim, took chiefs of MacDonnells prisoner (1565); invaded the Pale (1566), but was defeated by O'Donnells (aided by English under Sidney) at Letterkenny (1567); took refuge with MacDonnells, by whom he was slain for the reward. ¶Sir Turlough Luineach (1530?–1595), Earl of Clan·con·nell \klan-ˈkän-ᵊl\; cousin of Shane; resisted Earl of Essex through alliances with O'Donnells, MacDonnells, and MacQuillans; created earl of Clanconnell (1578), but continued to intrigue against English; resigned (1593) in favor of his cousin Hugh (see next). ¶Hugh (1540?–1616), 3d Baron of Dun·gan·non \dən-ˈgan-ən, dəŋ-\ and 2d Earl of Tyrone; on inauguration, united with Hugh Roe O'Donnell in petitions to Spain for help in behalf of religious and political liberty for Irish; destroyed English force at Yellow Ford on Blackwater (1598); received supplies and supporting troops from Spain (1601); failed in attack on Mountjoy (1601–02); made submission and was confirmed in title and estates by James I (1603); fell under suspicion and, with Rory O'Donnell, Earl of Tyrconnel, fled to Spanish Netherlands (1607), thence to Rome, where he died. ¶Sir Phelim *or* Felim, *Ir. Gael.* Fei·dli·midh ru·adh \ˈfā-li-mē-ˈrü-ə\ (1604?–1653); participated with Randal MacDonnell, Earl of Antrim, and nobles of the Pale in insurrection (1641), seized Charlemont Castle (1641); as commander in chief of Northern Irish forces, responsible for failure to capture Drogheda after siege (1641–42); yielded command to Owen Roe O'Neill; went into hiding after surrender of Charlemont (1650); betrayed, captured, executed as a traitor. ¶Owen Roe (1590?–1649), nephew of Hugh; served thirty years in Spanish army; became general of Ulsterman (1642); defeated Scottish army under Munro (1646); was cooperating with Ormonde and Catholic confederates at arrival of Cromwell in Ireland (1649). ¶Daniel (1612?–1664), nephew of Owen; became a Protestant at court of Charles I; impeached for participation in army plots; escaped from Tower and served with Prince Rupert at Marston Moor, battles of Newbury (1643, 1644), and Naseby (1645); negotiated between Ormonde and Owen Roe O'Neill in Ireland (1649); commanded Ulster army temporarily; joined Charles II at The Hague, accompanied him to Scotland (1650), and carried on active intrigue for him until Restoration; postmaster general (1663).

O'Neill, Eugene Gladstone. 1888–1953. American playwright, b. New York City. In early life (1907–13) a seaman, derelict, reporter for New London *Times;* awarded Pulitzer prize for *Beyond the Horizon* (1920), *Anna Christie* (1922), *Strange Interlude* (1928), *Long Day's Journey into Night* (1957), and Nobel prize for literature (1936). Other plays included *Bound East for Cardiff* (1916), *The Moon of the Caribbees* (1919), *Emperor Jones* (1921), *The Hairy Ape* (1922), *Desire Under the Elms* (1924), *The Great God Brown* (1925), *Marco Millions* (1927), *Mourning Becomes Electra* (trilogy, 1931), *Ah, Wilderness!* (1932), *The Iceman Cometh* (1946), *A Moon for the Misbegotten* (written 1943, pub. 1952), *More Stately Mansions* (written 1935–41, pub. 1964).

O'Neill, John. 1834–1878. American Fenian leader, b. County Monaghan, Ireland. To U.S. (1848); led Fenian raid into Canada from Buffalo (1866); raided Canada again (1870) and was arrested and put in jail; made final attempt against Canada (1871) but again failed.

O'Neill, Norman Houstoun. 1875–1934. English composer. Music director, Haymarket Theatre (1908–19, 1920 ff.); composed music for Maeterlinck's *Blue Bird* (1909), Barrie's *Mary Rose* (1920), and other plays, as well as ballets, orchestral works, chamber music, and songs.

O'Neill, Rose Cecil. 1874–1944. American illustrator and author, b. Wilkes-Barre, Pa. m. (1902) Harry Leon Wilson. Illustrator for *Puck, Harper's, Good Housekeeping, Ladies Home Journal;* originator (1909) and designer of kewpies; author of *The Loves of Edwy* (1904), *The Lady in the White Veil*

(1909), *Garda* (1929), *The Goblin Woman* (1930), and several "Kewpie" books.

Onesander. See ONOSANDER.

Ones·i·mus \ō-ˈnes-ə-məs\. 1st century A.D. Phrygian slave. Escaped from his master Philemon; converted to Christianity by St. Paul, who wrote Epistle to Philemon on his behalf; said to have suffered martyrdom.

Ongaro, Francesco dall'. See DALL'ONGARO.

Ong Boun \ˈòŋ-ˈbün\. *Also spelled* Ong Bun; *also known as* King Si·ri·bun·ya-sarn \ˌsē-ri-ˈbün-yə-(ˌ)sərn\ *or* Si·ri·bun·ya·san \-(ˌ)sən\ *or by royal title* Phra Maha Bunya-Saya-Sethathirath. c.1730–1781. King of Laotian principality of Vien Chang (now Vientiane). On assuming throne (1760) made unwise alliance with Burma and quarrelled with powerful advisers Phra Vor and Phra Ta; crushed (1778) rebellions of these advisers, on which pretext Siamese King Phra Taksin invaded and sacked Vien Chang (1779), enthralling it to Siam; fled country but allowed to return.

Oni·as \ō-ˈnī-əs\. Name of several Jewish high priests of time of the Second Temple in 3d and 2d centuries B.C., esp. Onias III, high priest (185–173 B.C.), foiled attempt of Seleucus IV to confiscate temple treasury. His son ¶Onias IV built a temple at Leontopolis after being driven from Jerusalem by Alcimus.

On·ions \ˈən-yənz\, Charles Talbut. 1873–1965. English philologist and lexicographer. Member of editorial staff of *Oxford English Dictionary* (from 1895); editor of *Shorter Oxford English Dictionary* (1933, 1936); editor of *Medium Aevum* (1932–56); revising editor of Sweet's *Anglo-Saxon Reader.*

Onions, Oliver, *in full* George Oliver. 1873–1961. English novelist. Author of *The Compleat Bachelor* (1901), *The Odd-Job Man* (1903), *Little Devil Doubt* (1909), *Whom God Has Sundered* (1926), *The Story of Ragged Robyn* (1945), *Poor Man's Tapestry* (1946), *Bells Rung Backward* (1953), etc.

Onkel Adam. See Carl Anton WETTERBERGH.

On·ke·los \ˈäŋ-kə-läs\. *Often called* the Proselyte. 1st century A.D. Palestinian Jewish scholar. Reputed author of the Aramaic paraphrase of the Pentateuch known as the Targum of Onkelos.

Onn bin Ja'·afar \ōn-bēn-jä-fär\, Dato. 1895–1962. Malayan politician. A leader in Merdeka (independence) movement; founded (1946) United Malays National Organization, first political party to represent purely Malay interests; appointed (1948) member for home affairs for Federation of Malaya.

Onnes, Heike Kamerlingh. See KAMERLINGH ONNES.

O'·No·lan \ō-ˈnō-lən\, Brian. *Ir. Gael.* Ó'Nual·láin \ō-ˈnō-lən\. *Pseudonyms* Flann O'Brien *and* Myles na gCo·pal·een \ˈmī(ə)lz-nä-ˈgō-pə-ˌlēn\. 1911–1966. Irish writer. As Myles na gCopaleen wrote a column, "Cruiskeen Lawn," for the Dublin *Irish Times* for 26 years; as Flann O'Brien wrote novels *At Swim-Two-Birds* (1939), *An Béal Bocht* (1941; translated in English as *The Poor Mouth*), *The Dalkey Archive* (1964; adapted as a play, *When the Saints Go Cycling In*), and *The Third Policeman* (1967).

On·o·mac·ri·tus \ˌän-ō-ˈmak-rət-əs\. 530?–?480 B.C. Athenian prophet and mystic poet. Said to have influenced development of Orphic mysteries; banished when he made his own additions to an oracle of Musaeus.

Ono \ō-nō\ Tōfū. 894–964. Japanese calligrapher. With Fujiwara Yukinari and Fujiwara Sukemasa (collectively known as the *sanseki,* "three best writing brushes") perfected writing style *jōdai-yō* ("ancient style").

Ono-no \ō-nō-nō\ Imoko. 7th century A.D. Japanese courtier. First envoy of Sui dynasty to China (607); founder of the Ikenobō, the oldest school of floral art.

On·o·san·der \ˌän-ō-ˈsan-dər\. 1st century A.D. Greek writer. Author of commentaries on Plato's *Republic* and a treatise on military art.

On·sa·ger \ˈön-ˌsäg-ər\, Lars. 1903–1976. American chemist, b. Oslo, Norway. To U.S. (1928, naturalized 1945); taught at Yale (1934–72, professor from 1945); devised gaseous diffusion method for manufacture of uranium 235; awarded Nobel prize for chemistry (1968) for discovery of reciprocal relations (which bear his name) fundamental to the thermodynamics of irreversible chemical processes, often called the fourth law of thermodynamics.

Ons·low \ˈänz-(ˌ)lō\, Georges, *in full* André-Georges-Louis. 1784–1853. French composer. Composed operas *L'Alcalde de la Vega* (1824), *Le Colporteur* (1827), *Le Duc de Guise* (1837), 4 symphonies, and chamber music.

Ō·ka \ō-ō-kä\ Tadasuke. 1675–1751. Japanese jurist. Most famous judge of Tokugawa period (1603–1867); appointed magistrate of Yamada (1712), of Edo (1717), of Shrines and Temples (1736); gained reputation as fairest and ablest judge, for which shogun Yoshimune granted him a small hereditary fief.

Oost \ˈōst\, Jakob van. 1600?–1671. Flemish painter. Influenced by Rubens; painted portraits and religious pictures, esp. *Resurrection, Ecclesiastic Dictating an Epistle, Philosopher Meditating.* His son ¶Jakob van Oost (1639–1713), *called* the Younger, also known for religious paintings and portraits, as *Holy Family, Martyrdom of St. Barbara.*

Opel \ˈō-pəl\, Fritz von. 1899–1971. German automotive industrialist. Director (from 1929), Adam Opel AG., maker of automobiles, bicycles, etc.; with Max Valier and Friedrich Sander experimented with rocket propulsion for automobiles and aircraft; piloted second rocket airplane to fly (1929).

Ophüls, Max. See Maximilian OPPENHEIMER.

Opie \ˈō-pē\, Amelia, *née* Al·der·son \ˈöl-dər-sən\. 1769–1853. English writer. m. (1798) John Opie (*q.v.*). Wrote *Father and Daughter* (1801) and volume of poems (1802); friend of Byron, Scott, Wordsworth, Wollstonecraft, and others; other works included 4 volumes of verse and novels *Adeline Mowbray* (1804), *Valentine's Eve* (1816), and *Madeline* (1822).

Opie, John. 1761–1807. *Known as* the Cornish Wonder. English painter and illustrator. Taken (1780) to London by John Wolcot ("Peter Pindar"); did portraits of authors, including Johnson, Burke, Southey, William and Mary Godwin, and court ladies; illustrated Boydell's *Shakespeare;* also did historical paintings, as *Assassination of James I of Scotland* (1786), *The Murder of Rizzio* (1787); wrote *Lectures in Painting* (1809).

Opie, Peter Mason. 1918–1982. British folklorist, b. Cairo. Foremost authority on childhood lore, pursuits, and customs. With wife Iona, who did the field research, edited *Oxford Dictionary of Nursery Rhymes* (1951), *The Oxford Nursery Rhyme Book* (1955), and *The Classic Fairy Tales* (1974) and wrote *The Lore and Language of Schoolchildren* (1959) and *Children's Games in Street and Playground* (1969), etc.

Opim·i·us \ō-ˈpim-ē-əs\, Lucius. 2d century B.C. Roman politician. Consul (121 B.C.); opposed reforms of Gaius Gracchus and led the mob of Optimates that killed Gracchus and 3000 of his followers; exiled (109) for accepting bribes from Jugurtha.

Opitz \ˈō-pits\, Martin. *Sometimes called* Opitz von Bo·ber·feld \-fón-ˈbō-bər-ˌfelt\. 1597–1639. German poet, critic, and metrical reformer. Founder of the so-called first Silesian school of poets; secretary and historiographer to King Władysław IV of Poland (from c.1635). Author of *Aristarchus,* which championed purity of German language, verse, style, etc. (in Latin 1617), *Buch von der deutschen Poeterey* (on versification and style, 1624), the didactic poems *Zlatna* (1623) and *Vesuvius* (1633), the prose idyl *Hercinia* (1630), *Daphne,* a German version of Rinuccini's Italian text, which became the oldest German opera (1627; music by Heinrich Schütz), hymns, translations, etc.

Op·pel \ˈò-pəl\, Albert. 1831–1865. German geologist and paleontologist. Professor at Munich (1861–65); in studying Swabian Jura discovered paleontologic and lithologic zones need not be identical or mutually dependent; developed use of ammonite fossils in dating Jurassic rocks.

Op·pen·heim \ˈäp-ən-ˌhīm\, Edward Phillips. 1866–1946. English writer. Published first novel, *Expiation* (1886); author of over 150 novels, short stories, and plays of espionage and intrigue, esp. *The Long Arm of Mannister* (1910), *The Moving Finger* (1911), *The Great Impersonation* (1920).

Op·pen·heim \ˈäp-ən-ˌhim, *Ger* ˈòp-\, Lassa Francis Lawrence. 1858–1919. English jurist, b. Germany. Naturalized in England (1900); Whewell professor of international law, Cambridge (1908–19); known for positivist approach to international law as propounded in *International Law: A Treatise* (1905–06).

Op·pen·hei·mer \ˈäp-ən-ˌhī-mər\, Sir Ernest. 1880–1957. South African industrialist, b. Germany. To South Africa (1902) as diamond broker; formed companies for mining of gold (1917), diamonds (1919, 1930), copper (1929); gained control of De Beers diamond mines (1929); member, South African parliament (1924–38).

Op·pen·hei·mer \ˈò-pən-ˌhī-mər\, Franz. 1864–1943. German economist and sociologist. Champion of liberal socialism in *Grossgrundeigentum und die soziale Frage* (1898) and other works.

Oppenheimer, Maximilian. *Known as* Max Ophüls \ˈō-fæls\. 1902–1957. German film director. In Germany and France as actor, director, and producer for stage (1921–30), and as writer and producer for radio (1925–41). Directed films in Germany, *Liebeli* (1932); Italy, *La signora di tutti* (1934); France, *La Tendre Ennemie* (1936), *Sarajevo* (1940), *La Ronde* (1950), *Le Plaisir* (1952); and U.S., *The Exile* (1947), *Letter from an Unknown Woman* (1948), *Caught* (1949), *The Reckless Moment* (1949).

Oppenheimer, Robert, *in full* Julius Robert. 1904–1967. American physicist, b. New York City. At U. of Cal. and Cal. Inst. Tech. (1929–47); director, Inst. for Advanced Study, Princeton, N.J. (1947–66). Director (1942–45), Manhattan Project, Los Alamos, N.M., which developed atomic bomb; received Enrico Fermi award (1963).

Op·per \ˈäp-ər\, Frederick Burr. 1857–1937. American illustrator and cartoonist, b. Madison, O. At various times on staffs of *Frank Leslie's Magazine, Puck,* and New York *Journal;* illustrated books by Bill Nye, Mark Twain, Finley Peter Dunne, etc. Creator of comic-strip characters Happy Hooligan, Alphonse and Gaston, etc.

Op·pert *Fr* ò-per, *Ger* ˈò-pərt\, Jules. 1825–1905. French Orientalist, b. Hamburg. To France (1847), naturalized (1854). Wrote *Éléments de la grammaire assyrienne* (1860), *Babylone et les Babyloniens* (1869), *Études sumériennes* (1881), etc.

Op·pi·an \ˈäp-ē-ən\. Name of two poets once considered the same: Oppian (fl. c.180 A.D.), b. Corycus or Anazarbus in Cicilia; author of poem on fishing, *Halieutica.* ¶Oppian (fl. c.211 A.D.), b. Apamea, Syria; author of poem on hunting, *Cynegetica.*

Op·pi·us \'äp-ē-əs\, Gaius. 1st century B.C. Roman writer. Close friend of Julius Caesar, who, during his absences from Rome, entrusted to him the management of his private affairs.

Op·pol·zer \'ō-pōlt-sər\, Theodor von. 1841–1886. Austrian astronomer. Professor, Vienna (from 1875). Author of *Canon der Finsternisse* (1887), giving a table of lunar and solar eclipses from 1207 B.C. to 2163 A.D.

Optic, Oliver. See William Taylor ADAMS.

Op·zoo·mer \'ōp-sō-mər\, Cornelis Willem. 1821–1892. Dutch philosopher and jurist. Professor, Utrecht (from 1846); leader of the empirical-positivistic school of philosophy and champion of modern theology; wrote on jurisprudence and philosophy, as *De weg der wetenschap* (1851) and *Wetenschap en wijsbegeerte* (1857).

Oquen·do \ō-'kān-dō\, Antonio de. 1557–1640. Spanish navigator. Admiral (1623); commanded armada defeated by Dutch force under Maarten Tromp at Battle of Downs (1639).

Or·age \'ór-ij\, Alfred Richard, *orig.* Alfred James. 1873–1934. English editor and social thinker. Joint (1907), later sole (from 1909) editor, *The New Age,* in which he expounded guild socialist views; became supporter (after World War I) of Social Credit theories of Clifford H. Douglas and established (1930) *The New English Weekly* as movement's organ; also lectured (1923–30) on behalf of Russian mystic George Gurdjieff. Wrote *Nietzsche in Outline and Aphorism* (1907), *Friedrich Nietzsche: The Dionysian Spirit of the Age* (1911), *Readers and Writers* (1922), *Social Credit and the Fear of Leisure* (1935).

Or·ange \'ór-inj, 'är-, -ənj\. Princely family of Europe, deriving its name from a principality (from c.11th century) forming an enclave in the ancient province of Venaissin, near the Rhone north of Avignon. Its rulers were: 9 princes of the house of Baux (1174–1393); 5 princes of the Burgundian house of Chalon (1393–1530), the last of whom, Philibert (*q.v.*), for services to Emperor Charles V, was granted (1522) extensive possessions in the Low Countries; and René (*q.v.*), who succeeded Philibert (1530) and on whose death (1544) all possessions passed to William I, Count of Nassau (later stadholder as William the Silent). Principality of Orange seized by Louis XIV (1660) and incorporated in France; by Treaty of Utrecht (1713) title of prince of Orange granted only to John William Friso, his son William IV, and successors; now name of reigning house of the Netherlands (see NASSAU, II). One sovereign of England, William III, was a prince of Orange; see WILLIAM III of the Netherlands.

Orange-Nassau. See NASSAU, II.

Or·bi·gny \ór-bēn-yē\, Alcide-Charles-Victor Des·sa·lines \dā-sá-lēn\ d'. 1802–1857. French naturalist. On scientific mission to South America (1826–34), findings of which he summarized in *Voyage dans l'Amérique méridionale* (1834–47); drew first comprehensive map of that continent (1842). Result of his mission was founding of science of stratigraphical paleontology; author also of *Paléontologie française* (begun in 1840 and continued by others after his death).

Or·bil·i·us Pu·pil·lus \ór-'bil-ē-əs-p(y)ü-'pil-əs\. 1st century B.C. Roman schoolmaster. Teacher of Horace, who described him as fond of flogging and by his reference made him typical of such a teacher.

Orcagna. See Andrea di CIONE.

Or·chard \'ór-chərd\, William Edwin. 1877–1955. English clergyman. Ordained Presbyterian minister (1904); advocated rapprochement between Anglican and Roman Catholic churches; converted to Roman Catholicism (1932) and was ordained (1935). Works included *The Temple* (1913) and sequel *Sancta Sanctorum* (1955).

Or·chard·son \'ór-chərd-sən\, Sir William Quiller. 1832–1910. Scottish painter. To London (1862); took subjects from history and literature; won wide acclaim with *Napoleon on Board the Bellerophon* (1880) and *Her Mother's Voice* (1888); also won success as portrait painter.

Or·czy \'órt-sē\, Emmuska Magdalena Rosalia Marie Josepha Barbara. Baroness. 1865–1947. British novelist and playwright, b. Hungary. Wrote series of detective stories *The Old Man in the Corner* (1900); won reputation with *The Scarlet Pimpernel* (1902, dramatized 1905), first of a series of adventure stories with background of French Revolution including *The Elusive Pimpernel* (1908) and *The Way of the Scarlet Pimpernel* (1933). Author also of *A Son of the People* (1906), *Beau Brocade* (1908), *Lady Molly of Scotland Yard* (1910), *Castles in the Air* (1921), *Nicolette* (1923), *Unravelled Knots* (1925), *The Divine Folly* (1937).

Or·de·laf·fi \ór-dā-'läf-fē\. A noble Italian family that ruled town of Forlì and surrounding areas of Romagna. Members included: Scarpetta Ordelaffi, who became (1307) head of Forlì with title of *capitano del popolo.* ¶Francesco (d. 1374) waged war (1356–59) against Guelf (papal) faction and lost most of the Ordelaffi lands, which were recovered (1376) by his son Sinibaldo. ¶Pino III (d. 1480) seized the throne by murdering his brother Cecco III, as well as his mother and first two wives; murdered by third wife, Lucrezia Pico. Pope Sixtus IV reclaimed Forlì and awarded it to his nephew, after which the Ordelaffi ceased to rule.

Or·de·ri·cus Vi·ta·lis \,ór-də-'rī-kəs-vī-'tā-ləs\ *or* **Or·de·ric Vi·tal** *Fr* ór-də-rēk-vē-tál, *Angl* 'ór-də-rik-\. 1075–?1142. Anglo-Norman chronicler. Son of French priest and Englishwoman. Spent life as monk in Norman abbey of St. Évroult; completed (1141) his *Historia ecclesiastica,* valuable for Norman, French, and English history of 1082–1141.

Or·dó·ñez \ór-'thōn-yāth\, Bartolomé. c.1490–1520. Spanish sculptor. An originator of the Spanish school of Renaissance sculpture; probably studied with Andrea Sansovino in Florence; collaborated with Diego de Siloé on *Caraccioli Altarpiece* (1514–15) and tomb of Andrea Boniface (c.1518), both in Naples; commissioned (1517) by Barcelona cathedral to make wooden and marble reliefs for choir area. His work influenced sculptors of 16th century Naples and (through collaborator Jehan Mone) Flanders.

Ordóñez de Montalvo, Garci. See RODRÍGUEZ DE MONTALVO.

Or·do·ño \ór-'thōn-yō\. Name of three kings of Asturias and León:

Ordoño I. d. 866. King of Asturias (850–866). Son of Ramiro I; won territory from the caliphate of Córdoba.

Ordoño II. d. 924. King of Galicia, including León (914–924). Son of Alfonso III; given Galicia by his father.

Ordoño III. d. 956. King (951–956). Son of Ramiro II; at war with his father-in-law, Fernán González, Count of Castile.

Or·dyn-Na·shcho·kin \'ór-dyin-(,)nəsh-'chók-yin\, Afanasy Lavrentyevich. d. 1680 or 1681. Russian diplomat and politician. Successfully defended Lithuanian and Livonian borders in war with Poland (1654); virtual ruler of occupied Livonian territory; arranged armistice with Sweden (1658); governor of Pskov (1665); called upon by Czar Alexis to negotiate Treaty of Andrusovo with Poland (1667); minister of foreign affairs (1667–71); advocated adoption of western Europe as model for Russian development; advocated expansion into Baltic region; entered monastery (1672). As chief advisor to Alexis, often regarded as Russia's first prime minister.

Or·dzho·ni·kid·ze \ər-jən-yik-'yēd-zə\, Grigory Konstantinovich. 1886–1937. Russian politician. Joined Communist party (1903); exiled to Siberia; released under general amnesty at outbreak of Revolution (1917). As chairman of party's Caucasian bureau brought Georgia into Soviet Union (1922); friend and associate of Stalin; member of Politburo of Central Executive Committee (1926); one of organizers of first Five-Year Plan (1928–32); commissar for heavy industries (1932–37).

O'·Reil·ly \ō-'rī-lē\, Alexander. 1725–1794. Irish soldier in Spanish army. Headed Spanish army which punished rebels in Louisiana (1768–69) and drew up regulations for government of the country; intrigued against Floridablanca and was banished to Galicia (1786).

O'Reilly, John Boyle. 1844–1890. American poet and editor, b. County Louth, Ireland. Joined Fenians and enlisted (1863) in British army unit with intention of inciting a revolt; discovered (1866), tried, sentenced to death, but sentence commuted to 23 years' penal servitude; deported to Australia (1867). Escaped to U.S. (1869); on editorial staff of Boston *Pilot* (from 1870); proprietor and editor (1876–90); became naturalized American citizen. Author of *Songs from Southern Seas* (1873), *Songs, Legends and Ballads* (1878), *The Statues in the Block* (1881), *In Bohemia* (1886), *Moondyne* (1889), etc.

O'Rell, Max. See Paul BLOUET.

Orel·la·na \ō-rā(l)-'yän-ä\, Francisco de. c.1490–c.1546. Spanish soldier and explorer. With Francisco Pizarro in conquest of Peru (1535); lieutenant in Gonzalo Pizarro's expedition to the Napo (1540–41); continued journey down the Napo to the valley of the Amazon and explored the course of the Amazon from the Andes to the Atlantic Ocean (1541–42).

Orel·la·na \ō-rā-'yän-ä\, José María. 1872–1926. Guatemalan general and politician. Chosen provisional president (1921–22) on deposition of Carlos Herrera; elected president (1922–26).

Oresme \ó-rem\, Nicole d'. c.1325–1382. French prelate. Bishop of Lisieux (1377); his translations of Aristotle served to popularize science and to fix the form of the French language; advised Charles V on tax and coinage reforms; important in development of mathematics (esp. analytical geometry) and kinematics (by proving Merton theorem geometrically); his theory of earthly motion propounded in *Livre du ciel et du monde;* his *Livre du divinacions* written against astrology; often called greatest medieval economist for his *De moneta,* written against debasement of the coinage.

Ores·tes \ór-'es-(,)tēz, ō-'res-\. d. 476 A.D. Roman soldier. Served for some years under Attila; deposed (475) Julian Nepos while commander of his army; placed son Romulus Augustulus on throne and ruled as regent (475–476); killed by Odoacer.

Or·fi·la \ȯr-fē-lȧ\, Matthieu-Joseph-Bonaventure. 1787–1853. French chemist of Spanish descent. Reputed founder of toxicology; founder of Musée Orfila, museum of comparative anatomy; known esp. for *Traité des poisons...ou toxicologie générale* (1813–15).

Orff \'ȯrf\, Carl. 1895–1982. German composer. Musical director of various theaters (1915–19); influential teacher of music; with Dorothee Günther founded (1924) Güntherschule, Munich, to teach children by his own method, which was subsequently widely adopted. As composer known chiefly for lavish theatrical works combining elements of Greek theater, Baroque opera, peasant life, Christian mystery, as *Carmina burana* (1937), *Der Mond* (1939), *Catulli carmina* (1943), *Die Kluge* (1943), *Trionfo di Afrodite* (1953), *Oedipus der Tyrann* (1959), *Prometheus* (1966), *De temporum fine comoedia* (1973).

Orford, Earls of. See (1) RUSSELL family; (2) Horace and Sir Robert WALPOLE.

Or·get·o·rix \ȯr-'jet-ə-riks\. 1st century B.C. Helvetic chieftain. Formed conspiracy (61 B.C.) to gain Roman throne and persuaded his countrymen to migrate; died suddenly before being brought to trial.

Or·han \ȯr-'hän\. *Also spelled* Or·khan \ȯr-'kän\. *Known as* Orhan Ga·zi \-gä-'zē\. c.1288–c.1360. 2d ruler of Ottoman Empire. Succeeded father Osman I (1326); conquered western part of Asia Minor (1326–45); supported John VI Cantacuzenus (1346) and married his daughter Theodora; crossed into Europe and settled in Thrace (1354); reorganized army and built mosques and theological colleges in newly conquered towns.

Orhan Ve·li Ka·nik \-'vel-ē-'kän-ik\. 1914–1950. Turkish poet. Editor, literary review *Yaprak* (1950); his volume of verse *Garip* (1941) revolutionized Turkish poetry by introducing free verse, vernacular idiom, and folklore; other works included *Vazegecemediğim* (1945), *Destan Gibi* (1946), *Yenisi* (1947), and *Karşi* (1949).

Ori·a·ni \ōr-'yän-ē\, Alfredo. 1852–1909. Italian writer. Author of novels *Memorie inutili* (1876), *Quartetto* (1883), *La disfatta* (1896), *Olocausto* (1902), etc.; also wrote criticism, essays, plays, and a volume of poems. His works were greatly admired during Fascist era for nationalistic bent.

Oriani, Barnaba. 1752–1832. Italian priest and astronomer. Showed by calculating its orbit that Uranus is a planet, not a comet as at first supposed.

Or·i·ba·si·us \ˌär-ə-'bā-zh(ē-)əs, ˌȯr-\. c.325–c.400 A.D. Greek physician of Pergamum. Personal physician of Emperor Julian; compiled a medical encyclopedia; reputed discoverer of the salivary glands.

Ori·be \ō-'rē-bā\, Manuel Ceferino. 1792–1857. Uruguayan general and political leader. Entered patriot army of Rio de la Plata as a boy; later was one of the "thirty-three immortals" who liberated Uruguay (1825–28); minister of war under Rivera (1833–35); president of Uruguay (1835–38); deposed by Rivera and fled to Buenos Aires; allied with Rosas, began long civil war (1842–51), marked esp. by siege of Montevideo; leader of the Blancos; finally defeated by combined Colorados, Brazilians, and Argentine revolutionists under Urquiza.

Or·i·gen \'är-ə-jən, 'ȯr-\. *Lat.* O·rig·e·nes \ȯ-'rij-ə-ˌnēz, ə-\, *surnamed* Ad·a·man·ti·us \ˌad-ə-'man-sh(ē-)əs\. 185?–?254 A.D. Christian writer and teacher. One of the Greek Fathers of the church; head of the catechetical school in Alexandria (c.211–232); later founded a school in Caesarea. His many works included textual studies on Old Testament (*Hexapla* and *Tetrapla*), *On Prayer* (c.233), *Exhortation to Martyrdom* (c.235), *Commentaries* and *Homilies,* and a defense of Christianity against attacks by the philosopher Celsus (*Contra Celsum,* c.248).

Orinda. See Katharine PHILIPS.

Oriol, Pierre. See PETRUS AUREOLI.

O'·Rior·dan \ō-'ri(ə)r-dᵊn, -'rī(ə)r-\, Conal Holmes O'Connell. *Pseudonym* Norreys Con·nell \'kän-ᵊl\. 1874–1948. Irish dramatist and novelist. Won reputation with *The Fool and his Heart* (1896); succeeded J.M. Synge as director of Abbey Theater (1909). Author of *The Pity of War* (1905), *The Age of Miracles* (1925), *Soldier's Wife* (1935), *Judith Quinn* (1939); plays, including *Shakespeare's End* (1912), *Captain Falstaff* (1936).

Orizzonte. See Jan Frans, under Pieter van BLOEMEN.

Ør·ja·sae·ter \'œr-jə-ˌsī-tər\, Tore. 1886–1968. Norwegian poet. His verse, esp. poetic trilogy *Gudbrand langleite* (1913–27), carried on tradition of the ballad and of folk and nature lyrics; other verse included *Manns Kvaede* (1915), *Elvesong* (1932), *Ettersommar* (1953), *Klårhaust* (1963); also wrote plays, as *Anne på Torp* (1930), *Christophorus* (1948), and prose.

Orkan, Władysław. See Franciszek SMRECZYŃSKI.

Orkhan. See ORHAN.

Orkney, Earls of. See Lord George HAMILTON (1666–1737); STEWART and SINCLAIR families.

Or·lan·do \ōr-'län-dō\, Vittorio Emanuele. 1860–1952. Italian politician. Served in cabinet positions (from 1903); prime minister (1917–19); led Italian delegation at Paris Peace Conference (1919–20); president, Chamber of Deputies (1919), resigned in protest against Fascist electoral fraud (1925); president, Constituent Assembly (1946–47).

Or·lé·ans \ȯr-lā-äⁿ\. Name of cadet branch of Valois and Bourbon houses of France; there have been four distinct houses:

I. Philippe (1336–1375); 5th son of Philip VI, Valois king of France, and Jeanne de Bourgogne; made duc d'Orléans by Philip VI (1344); having no heirs, title lapsed.

II. Chief members: ¶Louis I (1372–1407); 2d son of King Charles V and brother of Charles VI; comte de Valois; made duc d'Orléans (1392); m. (1386) Valentina Visconti of Milan; sat on brother's council; when Charles VI went mad, engaged in a long power struggle with his uncle Philip the Bold of Burgundy and Philip's son John, the latter of whom caused his assassination, thus bringing about civil war between Burgundians and Armagnacs (supporters of Orléans). Had nine children (one illegitimate), including: ¶Charles (1394–1465), the eldest son, who succeeded (1407) his father as duc d'Orléans; fought against Burgundians; joint commander at Agincourt (1415); defeated and taken prisoner to England until 1440; returned to France; m. (1441) Mary of Cleves as 3d wife; retired to Blois where he received literary figures, as Villon, Chastellain, Meschinot; one of greatest of courtly poets; wrote many love poems in French and English; father of Louis XII of France. ¶John (1399–1467), comte d'An·gou·lême \däⁿ-gü-lem\; grandfather of Francis I and Margaret of Navarre. ¶Jean (1403–1468), comte de Du·nois \də-dü̅en-wȧ\; known as "the Bastard of Orléans" for his illegitimate birth; soldier and diplomat; trusted adviser and grand chamberlain of his cousin, the dauphin Charles (from 1420); defeated English at Montargis (1427); defended Orléans (1428–29) until siege lifted by Joan of Arc; captured Chartres and Lagny (1432); made triumphant entry into Paris (1436); drove English northward, reconquering Normandy (1449–50) and Guyenne (1451); made count of Dunois (1439) and of Longueville (1443); joined (1465) League of Public Weal against Louis XI but later made peace with him. ¶Charles (1522–1545), duc d'Orléans; 3d son of Francis I, grandson of Louis XII, and great-grandson of John, comte d'Angoulême; in command of armies in Low Countries (1542–44).

III. Chief members: ¶Gaston (1608–1660), 3d son of Henry IV and Marie de Médicis and brother of Louis XIII; made duc d'Orléans (1626); m. (1626) Marie de Bourbon, duchesse de Montpensier; spent most of his life conspiring against Richelieu and Mazarin; after death of Louis XIII, led armies against Spain; joined Condé against court in the Fronde (1648–52). His daughter ¶Anne-Marie-Louise (1627–1693), duchesse de Mont·pen·sier \də-mōⁿ-päⁿ-syā\; opposed by Mazarin; aided Condé in revolt of the Fronde (1651–52); commanded troops which occupied Orléans (1652); banished from court (1652–57, 1662–64); had love affair with the comte de Lauzun, who as a result was imprisoned in the Bastille (1670–80); later (1681 or 1682) married him; wrote *Mémoires* (pub. 1729).

IV. Bourbon-Orléans (see also BOURBON). Chief members: ¶Philippe I (1640–1701), son of Louis XIII and brother of Louis XIV; succeeded his uncle Gaston (see branch III) as duc d'Orléans (1660); thus became founder of present house of Orléans; m. (1661) Henrietta Anne (*q.v.*), sister of Charles II of England, and 2nd (1671) Elizabeth Charlotte, daughter of the Elector Palatine; distinguished himself in War of Devolution (1667–68); defeated William of Orange at Cassel (1677) during Dutch War. His son ¶Philippe II (1674–1723) became duc d'Orléans (1701); distinguished himself in battles (1692–97) against England and Grand Alliance; in command in Italy (1706) and Spain (1707–08); regent of France (1715–23) during minority of Louis XV; unsuccessfully attempted to destroy authority of secretaries of state and restore it to the high nobility (1715–18); in alliance with England to force Philip V of Spain to renounce French claims and recognize him as heir to Louis XV (1719); during last years led a very profligate life. His son ¶Louis (1703–52), made duc d'Orléans (1723); governor of Dauphiné (1719–42); student of literature and sciences; retired (1742) from public life. His son ¶Louis-Philippe (1725–85), made duc d'Orléans (1752); served in Austrian wars and Seven Years' War (1742–57). His son ¶Louis-Philippe-Joseph (1747–1793), *known as* Philippe Éga·li·té \-ā-gȧ-lē-tā\, made duc de Montpensier (1747), duc de Chartres \də-shȧrtrᵊ\ (1752), duc d'Orléans (1785); liberal in views; temporarily banished from court for challenging the king's authority (1787) before the parlement of Paris; aided French Revolutionists (1789); on mission to England (1790) but returned to work against the monarchy (1791–92); renounced title and accepted name of Philippe Égalité from the Paris Commune on fall of monarchy (1792); accused of being accomplice of Dumouriez, arrested, and guillotined. His son Louis-Philippe (*q.v.*) became king of France (1830–48). Louis-Phillipe's eldest son ¶Ferdinand-Philippe-Louis-Charles-Henri (1810–42), soldier, made duc d'Orléans (1830); helped suppress revolution in Lyons (1831); served in Algeria (1835–40). His son ¶Louis-Philippe-Albert (1838–1894), comte de Paris, was pretender to crown of France; lived in England and traveled (1848–61); served as captain of volunteers on staff of Gen. McClellan in U.S. Civil War (1861–62); returned to France (1871) and relinquished claim of his family to throne (1873); on death of comte de Chambord (1883) became head of Legitimists; exiled

(1886); author of *Histoire de la guerre civile en Amérique* (1874–89). His brother ¶Robert-Philippe-Louis-Eugène-Ferdinand (1840–1910), duc de Chartres, lived in Germany and England (1848–58); with brother on McClellan's staff (1861–62); in French army (1870–71) under a pseudonym; later in active service as officer (until 1883); expelled from army by law forbidding service of princes of former reigning families. ¶Prince Louis-Philippe-Marie-Ferdinand-Gaston (1842–1922), comte d'Eu \dœ̄\, eldest son of Louis-Charles-Philippe-Raphaël, son of Louis-Philippe (*q.v.* under Louis-Philippe); m. (1864) Isabel of Brazil; entered Brazilian army; commander in chief (1869–70) of allied forces in war with Paraguay; unpopular because of extreme clerical views; forced to leave Brazil on downfall of empire (1889). ¶Louis-Philippe-Robert (1869–1926), son of Louis-Philippe-Albert, b. Twickenham, England; banished from France by law of 1886, made home in England; offered his services to France (1890) but was arrested and imprisoned; traveled in Asia (1890–95); became duc d'Orléans (1894) and pretender to throne of France; in vain offered services to France and other Entente countries at outbreak of World War I (1914); a scientist of distinction; led expeditions to Arctic regions (1905, 1907, 1919) and to British East Africa (1922–23). See under LOUIS-PHILIPPE for his other children.

Or·ley \'ór-lē\, Bernaert van, *also* Barend *or* Bernard. 1492?–1542. Flemish painter. Painted religious subjects as *Virgin and Child with Angels,* altarpieces, portraits; designed tapestries as *Hunts of Maximilian* and *Victory of Pavia.*

Or·lik \'ór-lik\, Emil. 1870–1932. German painter, etcher, and lithographer, b. Prague. His works included stage scenery for Reinhardt's productions, portrait etchings of Gustav Mahler, Haeckel, Richard Strauss, Bach, Beethoven, and others, genre pictures of Bohemian village life, portfolios of etchings, etc.

Or·lov \(,)ər-'lóf\. Russian noble family, including: Count Grigory Grigoryevich (1734–1783), general and statesman; leader in plot (1762) to dethrone and assassinate Peter III and place Catherine on throne; paramour of Czarina Catherine II; advocate of improvement in condition of the serfs. His brother ¶Aleksey Grigoryevich (1737–1808); also involved in the plot against Peter III; said to have carried Peter away and strangled him; commanded fleet which defeated Turks at Çeşme (1770); commanded a militia district in war against Napoléon (1806–07). Another brother, ¶Fyodor Grigoryevich (1741–1790); also involved in plot against Peter III; distinguished himself as naval commander in first Turkish war (1770); retired (1775). ¶Prince Aleksey Fyodorovich (1786–1861), natural son of Fyodor; engaged in wars against Napoléon (1805–07, 1812–14) and in Turkish war (1828–29); helped suppress Decembrist uprising (1825); ambassador to Turkey (1833); negotiated Treaty of Hünkâr İskelesi (1833); Russian diplomat at conference which negotiated Peace of Paris (1856); adviser to Nicholas I and Alexander II. ¶Prince Nikolay Alekseyevich (1827–1885), son of Prince Aleksey; represented Russia in Belgium (1860–70), France (1870–82), and Germany (1882–85).

Orm \'órm\ *or* **Or·min** \'ór-mən\. fl. c.1200. English Augustinian monk. Author of the *Ormulum,* metrical paraphrases (c.10,000 lines) of gospels for the year, followed by metrical homilies in English vernacular, written in an invented orthography based on phonetic principles.

Or·man·dy \'ór-mən-dē\, Eugene. *Orig.* Jeno Blau \'blau̇\. 1899–1985. American conductor, b. Budapest. To U.S. (1921) for aborted violin recital tour. Debuted (1924) as conductor at Capitol movie theater, New York City; substituted for Arturo Toscanini with Philadelphia Orchestra (1931); conducted Minneapolis Symphony (1931–36); coconductor with Leopold Stokowski of Philadelphia Orchestra (1936–38), sole conductor (1938–80); 44-yr. music directorship was longest in U.S. history; developed lush velvety quality that epitomized "Philadelphia sound."

Orme, Philibert de l'. See Philibert DELORME.

Ormea, Marchese d'. See FERRERO DI ROASIO.

Ormizd. See HORMIZD.

Ormonde, Earls, marquises, and dukes of. See BUTLER family.

Or·na·no *Fr* ór-ná-nō, *Ital* ōr-'nän-ō\, Alphonse d'. 1548–1610. French soldier of Corsican birth. In Charles IX's service, loyal to royalist cause in struggle against Catholic League; was one of first to recognize Henry IV; created marshal of France (1595). His son ¶Jean-Baptiste (1581–1626) was also a soldier in French service; followed Henry IV in the war in Savoy (1600–01); kept Guienne and Languedoc loyal to Louis XIII (1610); tutor in administration of Gaston d'Orléans (1619) and created marshal of France.

Ornano, Philippe-Antoine d'. Comte. 1784–1863. French soldier, b. Corsica. General in the French army; distinguished himself at Austerlitz (1805) and Jena and Lübeck (1806); engaged at Borodino; rallied to Napoléon during the Hundred Days and was exiled at the second restoration (1815); returned to France (1818) and French service (1828); member of the Corps Législatif (1848) and supporter of cause of Louis-Napoléon; marshal of France (1861).

Oro·des II \ó-'rō-(,)dēz\. *Parthian* Wrwd, *Pahlavi* Wyrwd *or* Wyrwy. d. c.36 B.C. King of Parthia. Helped his brother Mithradates III murder their father Phraates III; murdered and succeeded Mithradates (c.57); murdered by his son Phraates IV.

Orontius Fineus. See Oronce FINE.

Oro·si·us \ó-'rō-zh(ē-)əs, ə-\, Paulus. 5th century A.D. Spanish priest. With St. Augustine at Hippo (c.414); sent (415) by Augustine to Palestine to oppose Pelagianism; wrote *Liber apologeticus contra Pelagianos;* to Hippo (416) where Augustine asked him to write *Historiarum adversus paganos libri VII,* an account of universal history, translated into Old English by Alfred the Great.

Oroz·co \ō-'rōs-kō, *Angl* ō-'rós-(,)kō\, José Clemente. 1883–1949. Mexican painter. Most important 20th-century muralist to work in fresco. Satirical artist for revolutionary paper *La Vanguardia* (1914–17); exiled to U.S. (1917–20) for *House of Tears* paintings; with Rivera, Siqueiros, and others initiated Mexican muralist movement, esp. with murals *Cortés and Malinche* and *The Trench,* on Escuela Nacional Preparatoria in Mexico City (1923–27); exiled (1927–34) to U.S.; gained international fame with murals *Prometheus* at Pomona College and *Quetzalcoatl* at Dartmouth College; later murals at Guadalajara (1937–39, 1949) and *National Allegory* at Escuela Normal, Mexico City (1947–48); also known for paintings *Zapatistas* (1931) and *Metaphysical Landscape* (1948).

Or·pen \'ór-pən\, Sir William Newenham Montague. 1878–1931. British painter, b. Ireland. Appointed an official artist by British government during World War I; his paintings included portraits of Wilson, Foch, Viscount Bryce, and others.

Orr \'ó(ə)r, 'ō(ə)r\, James Lawrence. 1822–1873. American politician, b. Craytonville, S.C. Member (1848–59) and speaker (1857–59), House of Representatives; popular in North for anti-secessionist views; after failure to obtain Democratic presidential nomination (1860), advocated South Carolina's secession; senator (1861) in Confederacy; governor, South Carolina (1865–68); federal circuit court judge (1868–72); minister to Russia (1872–73).

Or·ren·te \ór-'rān-tā\, Pedro. 1588–1645. Spanish painter. Called "the Spanish Bassano." Known esp. for his religious paintings as *Martirio de san Sebastian* (1616) and *Imposición de la casulla a san Ildefonso* (1617).

Orrery, Earls of. See BOYLE family.

Or·ry \ó-rē\, Jean. 1652–1719. French economist. As representative in Spain (1700–06, 1713–15) of Louis XIV, centralized the financial administration and reorganized government on French model of ministers of state; as *veedor general* was real power in Spain.

Or·say \ór-sā\, Alfred-Guillaume-Gabriel d'. Comte. 1801–1852. French society leader in Paris and London. Wit, painter, sculptor, conversationalist, and arbiter of fashion; friend of Lady Blessington.

Or·si \'ór-sē\, Paolo. 1859–1935. Italian archaeologist. Museum director (1888 ff.), Syracuse, Sicily; responsible for excavation and research of sites in Sicily and southern Italy; expert in Siculan period.

Or·si·ni \ōr-'sē-nē\. Roman princely family, including: Giacinto Bobo-Orsini, elected Pope Celestine III (*q.v.*). ¶Matteo Rosso (d. 1246) as senator saved Rome from capture by Frederick II (1241). Family became head of Guelf faction opposed to Ghibelline leaders, the Colonna family. Other members included Giovanni Gaetano, who became Pope Nicholas III and Pierfrancesco, who became Pope Benedict XIII (*qq.v.*). ¶Flavio, Duca di Brac·cia·no \brät-'chän-ō\ (d. 1695), and his wife ¶Anne Marie de la Tré·mouillé \də-lá-trā-müy\ (1635–1722), a supporter of French policy at the papal court and a confidential adviser of King Philip V of Spain.

Orsini, Felice. 1819–1858. Italian revolutionary. Member of Young Italy; active in revolution of 1848–49; attempted (Jan. 14, 1858) assassination of Napoléon III; executed with an accomplice, Joseph Pieri, at Paris.

Orsini, Giulio. See Domenico GNOLI.

Ør·sted \'œr-stəd\, Hans Christian. 1777–1851. Danish physicist. Discovered (1820) that a magnetic needle aligns itself perpendicularly to a current-carrying wire, thus founding science of electromagnetism; discovered (1820) piperidine; prepared (1825) metallic aluminum; founded (1824) Society for the Promotion of Natural Science.

Or·szágh \'ór-säg\, Pavol. *Pseudonym* Hviez·do·slav \'hvyez-dó-sláf\. 1849–1921. Slovak poet. Author of epics *Hájnikova žena* (1886) and *Ežo Vlkolinský* (1890) and lyrical poetry as *Krvavé sonety* (1919).

Ortala, Count of. See Lennart TORSTENSON.

Or·te·ga y Gas·set \ór-'tā-gä-ē-gä-'set\, José. 1883–1955. Spanish philosopher and writer. Professor at Madrid (1910 ff.); founded periodicals *España* (1915), *El Sol* (1917), *Revista de Occidente* (1923); in voluntary exile (1936–45); founded Instituto de Humanidades in Madrid (1948). Among his works were *Adán en el paraíso* (1910), *Meditaciones del Quijote* (1914), *España invertebrada* (1922), *El tema de nuestro tiempo* (1923), *Espíritu de la letra* (1927), and *La rebelión de las masas* (1929).

Or·teig \'ór-,teg\, Raymond. 1870–1939. American restaurateur, b. Louvie-Juzon, France. To U.S. (1882); proprietor of the Lafayette and Brevoort hotels,

New York. Offered (1919) prize of $25,000 for first nonstop New York to Paris flight; prize won by Charles Lindbergh (1927).

Ortelius. See Abraham OERTEL.

Or·ti·gão \ȯr-tē-'gaüⁿ\, José Duarte Ramalho. 1836–1915. Portuguese essayist and journalist. Member, Academia Real das Ciências (1868–1910); founded (with Eça de Queiros) satirical review *As Farpas* (1871); works included a novel *Histórias cor de rosa* (1870) and travel books *John Bull* (1870) and *A Holanda* (1885).

Or·tiz \ȯr-'tēs\, Roberto M. 1886–1942. Argentine politician. Minister of finance (1935–37); president of Argentina (1938–40).

Ortiz Ru·bio \-'rü-byō\, Pascual. 1877–1963. Mexican politician. Minister to Germany (1923); ambassador to Brazil (1926); president of Mexico (1930–32), elected to succeed provisional president Emilio Portes Gil and to fill out the unexpired term of Álvaro Obregón; resigned (1932).

Or·ton \'ȯrt-ᵊn\, Arthur. *Alias* Thomas Cas·tro \'kas-trō\. *Known as* the Tich·borne Claimant \'tich-,bȯ(ə)rn, -bərn\. 1834–1898. English butcher and imposter. Emigrant to Australia (1852); returned to England (1866) on invitation of widow of Sir James Francis Doughty Tichborne, 10th baronet; impersonated her eldest son, Robert Charles Tichborne, who had been lost at sea, and convinced Lady Tichborne and many others; brought action (1871–72) for ejectment against the 12th baronet; on collapse of his suit after trial of 102 days, was committed for perjury after trial of 188 days; confessed his imposture (1895).

Orton, Edward, Jr. 1863–1932. American potter and industrial chemist, b. Chester, N.Y. Established (1894) first department for instruction in technology of clay, glass, and cement industries, at Ohio State U., and was its director (1894–1916).

Orton, Joe, *in full* John Kingsley. 1933–1967. English playwright. Known for "black comedies" *The Ruffian on the Stair* (1964), *Entertaining Mr. Sloane* (1964), *Loot* (1965), and *What the Butler Saw* (1969).

Or·vie·to \ōr-'vye-tō\, Angiolo. 1869–1967. Italian poet. His volumes of poetry included *Il velo di Maia* (1898), *Le sette leggende* (1912), *Le primavere della cornamusa* (1925), *Il vento di Sion* (1928).

Orwell, George. See Eric Arthur BLAIR.

Ory \'ȯr-ē\, Edward, *called* Kid. 1886–1973. American trombonist and composer, b. Laplace, La. Perhaps first to codify role of trombone in three-part contrapuntal jazz improvisation; bandleader (from 1911), playing with Mutt Carey, King Oliver, Louis Armstrong, and others; acted in movies *Crossfire* (1947), *New Orleans* (1947), and *The Benny Goodman Story* (1956); composed "Muskrat Ramble" (1926) and other jazz tunes.

'Oryān. See BĀBĀ ṬĀHER.

Orzesz·ko·wa \,ȯ-zhesh-'kȯ-vȧ\, Eliza, *nee* Paw·łow·ska \pȧv-'lȯf-skȧ\. 1841–1910. Polish writer. Ran bookshop and publishing house in Grodno (1879–82); wrote works of positive realism, advocating education for women, better treatment for Jews and peasants, and other social ideals; known esp. for novels *Meir Ezofowicz* (1878), *Dziurdziowie* (1885), *Cham* (1888), *Nad Niemnem* (1888), and *Bene nati* (1892).

Os·born \'äz-bərn, -,bȯ(ə)rn\, Fairfield, *in full* Henry Fairfield. 1887–1969. American conservationist, b. Princeton, N.J. Son of Henry Fairfield Osborn; trustee (from 1922) and president (1940–68), New York Zoological Society; founder (1947), Conservation Foundation. Author of conservationist articles, *Our Plundered Planet* (1948), and *The Limits of Our Earth* (1953).

Osborn, Henry Fairfield. 1857–1935. American paleontologist, b. Fairfield, Conn. Professor, Columbia (1891–1935); curator of vertebrate paleontology (1891–1910), president (1908–35), American Museum of Natural History; associated with U.S. Geological Survey (1900–35). Introduced instructional approach to museum display. Author of *The Age of Mammals* (1910), *Men of the Old Stone Age* (1915), *Origin and Evolution of Life* (1917), *Evolution and Religion in Education* (1926), etc.

Osborn, Sherard. 1822–1875. English naval officer and explorer, b. Madras, India. Commanded vessels on two expeditions (1850–51, 1852–54) in search of Sir John Franklin; took leading part in Chinese war of 1857–59; helped to lay cable between Great Britain and Australia.

Os·borne \'äz-bərn, -,bȯ(ə)rn, -,bō(ə)rn\, Dorothy. 1627–1695. English letter-writer. Letters written to Sir William Temple (m. 1655) during their courtship (1652–54) valued for their easy, conversational style and depiction of life in Commonwealth period.

Osborne, George Alexander. 1806–1893. Irish pianist and composer. Intimate with Berlioz and Chopin; composed chamber music, duets for violin and piano, two operas, and a popular piano solo *La Pluie de perles.*

Osborne, Thomas. 1st Earl of Dan·by \'dan-bē\. Marquis of Car·mar·then \kär-'mär-t͟hən, kə(r)-\. Duke of Leeds \'lēdz\. 1632–1712. English politician. M.P. (1665); treasurer of navy (1671); lord high treasurer (1673) and earl of Danby (1674); tried in House of Commons to maintain national credit and neutralize predominance of France; pressed for enforcement of laws against Roman Catholics and dissenters; contrived marriage of Mary, daughter of Duke of York, to William of Orange (1677); made peace with Holland. Engaged in corrupt politics; betrayed by Ralph Montagu as Charles II's negotiator with Louis XIV for increased bribes, and was impeached (1678) for treasonable negotiations with foreign powers and concealment of Popish Plot; although pardoned by Charles, was imprisoned in Tower of London (till 1684). Reconciled with Whigs, signed invitation to William of Orange; rewarded with marquisate; lord president of council (1689–99) and virtually prime minister; created duke (1694); accused of Jacobite intrigues; again impeached (1695) for accepting bribe from East India Company in connection with grant of a charter, but escaped condemnation when charge was not pressed; deprived of all offices (1699).

Osborne, Thomas. d. 1767. English bookseller. Proposed, with Charles Rivington, having their friend Samuel Richardson write a series of letters, the inception of *Pamela* (1740); was satirized by Pope in the *Dunciad* and beaten for impertinence by Dr. Johnson.

Osborne, Thomas Burr. 1859–1929. American biochemist, b. New Haven, Conn. On staff of Conn. Agricultural Experiment Station and professor at Yale (from 1886); developed Osborne beaker method for mechanical analysis of soil; known esp. for investigations of vegetable proteins, and discovery of vitamin A in cod-liver oil (1913, shortly after similar discovery by E. V. McCollum).

Osborne, Thomas Mott. 1859–1926. American penologist, b. Auburn, N.Y. Chairman, New York State Commission for Prison Reform (1913); served secretly a week in Auburn prison to know conditions at firsthand; warden, Sing Sing prison (1914–16); commanding officer, Portsmouth Naval Prison (1917–20); organized Mutual Welfare League, whereby prisoners had a measure of self-government and responsibility. Author of *Within Prison Walls* (1914), etc.

Os·bourne \'öz-bərn, -,bȯ(ə)rn, -,bō(ə)rn\, Lloyd. 1868–1947. American writer, b. San Francisco. Stepson of Robert Louis Stevenson and his collaborator in *The Wrong Box* (1889), *The Wrecker* (1892), and *The Ebb Tide* (1894). Author of *Memories of Vailima* (with his sister Isobel Strong, 1902), *Wild Justice* (1906), *An Intimate Portrait of R.L.S.* (1925), etc.

Os·car \'ȯs-kər\. *Swed.* Oskar. Name of two kings of Sweden and Norway:

Oscar I. *Orig.* Joseph-François. 1799–1859. King (1844–59). Son of King Charles XIV John; became duke of Sö·der·man·land \'sœ-dər-mȧn-,lȧnd\ (1810); sympathized with Liberals; on accession, introduced reforms as freedom of the press and penal reform; improved Sweden's economic position; on account of ill health, relinquished rule to Charles XV, his eldest son (1857–59); m. (1823) Joséphine Beauharnais (Leuchtenberg), granddaughter of Empress Joséphine.

Oscar II. 1829–1907. King of Sweden (1872–1907) and of Norway (1872–1905). Son of Oscar I and brother of Charles XV; m. (1857) Princess Sophia Wilhelmina, youngest daughter of Duke William of Nassau. Found problem of preserving union between Sweden and Norway increasingly difficult; supported (after 1866) Germany in hopes of strengthening Sweden against Russia; gave up throne of Norway (1905) to Haakon VII; served as mediator in several international disputes; wrote a play, poems, a number of historical works, and translations from the German.

Oscar of the Waldorf. See Oscar TSCHIRKY.

Os·ce·o·la \,äs-ē-'ō-lə, ,ō-sē-\. c.1804–1838. American Indian leader, b. Georgia. Leader of Seminoles in Florida during Second Seminole War (1835–37); seized when he appeared for a conference (Oct. 1837) and died in prison at Fort Moultrie, near Charleston, S.C.

Osee. See HOSEA.

Osei Tu·tu \ō-'sā-'tü-,tü\. d. 1712. Ashanti ruler. As chief of Kumasi (in present Ghana) united (c.1680–90) surrounding kingdoms into Ashanti nation and became Asantehene, i.e. king of Ashanti; led successful campaign against traditional enemy, the Denkyera (c.1698–1701); during reign tripled area of Ashanti by means of wars.

Öser. See OESER.

Os·good \'äz-,gu̇d\, Frances Sargent, *nee* Locke \'läk\. 1811–1850. American poet, b. Boston. m. Samuel Stillman Osgood, a portrait painter (1835); closely associated with Edgar Allan Poe (1845–47); author of *A Wreath of Wild Flowers from New England* (1838), *The Cries of New York* (1846), etc.

Osgood, Samuel. 1748–1813. American Revolutionary officer and politician, b. Andover, Mass. Served at Lexington and Concord; aide to Gen. Artemas Ward; member of Continental Congress (1781–84); first commissioner, U.S. Treasury (1785–89); postmaster general (1789–91); naval officer, port of New York (1803–13).

O'Shaugh·nes·sy \ō-'shȯ-nə-sē\, Arthur William Edgar. 1844–1881. English poet. Associated with Rossetti, Swinburne, and the Pre-Raphaelites; author of *The Epic of Women* (1870), *Lays of France* (1872), *Music and Moonlight* (1874).

O'Shaughnessy, Michael Maurice. 1864–1934. American hydraulic engineer, b. Limerick, Ireland. To U.S. (1885); city engineer of San Francisco (1912–32); builder of Hetch-Hetchy Water and Power Supply for San Francisco and a number of dams, aqueducts, tunnels, etc. O'Shaughnessy Dam in California named in his honor.

O'·Shea \ō-'shā\, William Henry. 1840–1905. Irish home rule advocate. M.P. (1880–86); tried to bring about compromise between Parnell and Liberal leaders (1882–84); his divorce (1890) from wife Katherine Page on charge of adultery with Parnell led to latter's downfall.

Osi·an·der \ō-zē-'än-dər\, Andreas. *Orig. surname* Ho·se·mann \'hō-zə-ˌmän\. 1498–1552. German Lutheran theologian. First Evangelical preacher in Nürnberg (1522–48), where he helped introduce the Reformation; opposed the Augsburg Interim (1548); preacher and professor of theology, Königsberg (from 1549); engaged in theological disputes (carried on after his death, until 1567, by his followers, the Osiandrists) with Martin Chemnitz and Melanchthon; published astronomical work of Copernicus, a *Harmoniae* of the Gospels (1537), etc., and wrote theological treatises.

Os·ler \'ōs-lər\, Sir William. 1849–1919. Canadian physician, b. Bond Head, Ont. Professor, McGill Medical School (1875–84) and physician to Montreal General Hospital (1878–84); professor, U. of Pennsylvania (1884–88); physician in chief, Johns Hopkins Hospital, Baltimore (1889–1905) and professor of medicine, Johns Hopkins U.; regius professor of medicine, Oxford U. (1905–19); created a baronet (1911). His teaching and personality strongly influenced medical progress, esp. clinical teaching and warmer relation between physicians and patients. Author of *Aequanimitas* (1889), *Principles and Practice of Medicine* (1892), *The Master Word in Medicine* (1903), *Science and Immortality* (1904), and *The Student Life* (1905).

Os·man \äs-'män\. *Arab.* 'Uth·mān \üth-'män\. Name of three rulers of the Ottoman empire:

Osman I. *Also called* Osman Ga·zi \-gä-'zē\. 1258–c.1326. Founder of Ottoman empire. Succeeded father Ertugrul as leader of Seljuq Turks; waged long and stubborn war against Byzantines, gradually gaining control of much Anatolian territory; conquered Bursa shortly before his death. Father of Orhan.

Osman II. *Also called* Genç Osman \'gench-\. *In full* Osman Og·lu Ah·med I \-äg-'lü-ä-'med\. 1603–1622. Ottoman sultan (1618–22). Defeated in military campaign against Poland (1620); assassinated by Janissaries during his attempt to break their power.

Osman III. 1699–1757. Ottoman sultan (1754–57). Son of Mustafa II, brother and successor of Mahmud I. Attempted to curb powers of grand viziers; regulated dress of women and Christians.

Osman Ali \-ä-'lē\. *Also called* Us·mān 'Alī Khān \us-'män-ä-'lē-k͟hän\. 1886–1967. Ruler (1911–48) and president (1948–56) of Hyderābād. Strengthened financial position of state, including issue of own currency; argued for full independence of Hyderābād after British departure (1947) from India, but surrendered (1948) to Indian authority.

Os·man Dig·na \us-'män-'dig-nə, üth-\. c.1840–1926. Sudanese soldier. Follower (from 1883) of the Mahdī; led Mahdist activities of Beja tribe in eastern Sudan (1883–91), capturing Tokar (1884); captured and imprisoned (1900–08).

Os·man Nu·ri Pa·şa \äs-'män-nu-'rē-pä-'shä\. 1832–1900. Turkish general. Served in Crimean War (1853–56), Lebanon (1860), Crete (1866–69), and in suppression of insurrection in Yemen (1871); general of army corps (1876); marshal (1876). In Russo–Turkish War (1877–78), became national hero by his defense of Pleven against Russian attacks; forced to surrender (Dec. 9, 1877). Commander in chief of the Imperial Guard (1878); minister of war (1878–85), and grand marshal of the palace.

Osman Pasha. See RIPPERDA.

Os·me·ña \ōs-'män-yä\, Sergio. 1878–1961. Philippine politician. Founder (1907) and leader (1907–22) of Nationalist party. Speaker of first Philippine assembly (1907–16), of House of Representatives (1916–22); senator (1922 ff.); vice president of Commonwealth of Philippines (1935–44) and secretary of public instruction (1936–44); president (1944–46).

Os·mund \'äz-mənd\. Saint. d. 1099. Norman prelate. Nephew and chaplain of William the Conqueror; chancellor of England (c.1072–78); bishop of Salisbury (1078–99); helped compile the Domesday Book; noted chiefly for formation of the Sarum use.

Osor·kon \ō-'sor-kän\. Name of four kings of Egypt:

Osorkon I. 10th century B.C. King (c.924–895 B.C.). Son and successor of Sheshonk I, founder of 22d dynasty.

Osorkon II. 9th century B.C. King (c.874–853 B.C.). Faced Libyan threat in western delta; witnessed beginning of disintegration of dynasty.

Osorkon III *and* **IV.** 8th century B.C. Kings of declining 22d dynasty.

Ossian. See James MACPHERSON.

Os·sian·nils·son \'ü-shän-'nils-son\, Karl Gustav. *Orig. surname* Ossian-Nilsson. 1875–1970. Swedish lyric poet and novelist. Chiefly known for early poetry, as *Masker* (1900), *Hedningar* (1901), *Flygskeppet* (1910), and autobiographical novel *Barbarskogen* (1908).

Os·si·etz·ky \ˌo-sē-'et-skē\, Carl von. 1889–1938. German pacifist and writer. Served in German army through World War I; on staff of *Berliner Volks-Zeitung* and later (1928) editor of *Weltbühne;* wrote vigorously in defense of pacifism. Imprisoned on charge of revealing military secrets (1931–32) and on charge of being an enemy of the state (1933–36); while in prison, awarded Nobel prize for peace (1935); the Hitler government considered the award a "challenge and an insult" and prohibited Germans thenceforth from accepting such awards.

Ossius of Córdoba. See HOSIUS.

Ossoli, Marchioness. See Margaret FULLER.

Ossory, Earls of. See BUTLER family.

Os·ta·de \ós-'tä-də\, Adriaen van. 1610–1685. Dutch painter and etcher. Pupil of Frans Hals; influenced by Brouwer and Rembrandt; known esp. for genre pictures of peasant life, as *Carousing Peasants in an Interior* (c.1638) and *The Itinerant Fiddler* (1672); also did religious subjects, portraits, and landscapes. His brother and pupil ¶Isack (1621–1649) was also a genre painter and etcher, esp. of Dutch village and tavern scenes, interiors, and winter scenes.

Ostād Moḥammadī. See MOḤAMMADĪ.

Os·tai·jen \'ós-tī-(y)ən\, Paul van. 1896–1928. Flemish poet and critic. Published *Music-Hall* (1916), poems about modern city life; second book of verse, *Het Sienjaal* (1918), inspired the Humanitarian Expressionist movement in Flanders; poems in rhythmic typography, *Bezette Stad* (1921), expressed nihilism and Dadaism acquired as political exile in Berlin (1918–21); developed poetic system called "organic expressionism," embodied in *Gedichten* (1928); translated Kafka (1925). Also wrote criticism *Krities proza* (1929–31) and creative prose, as *Vogelvrij* (1927), *De bende van de stronk* (1932), and *Diergaarde voor kinderen van nu* (1932).

Öst·berg \'œst-bərʸ\, Ragnar. 1866–1945. Swedish architect. Designer of the Stockholm Town Hall (1911–23), the Stockholm Marinmuseum, a restoration of the old Uppsala castle, etc.

Os·ten·so \'äs-tən-ˌsō\, Martha. 1900–1963. American novelist, b. Bergen, Norway. To U.S. as a child; author of *A Far Land* (poetry, 1924), *Wild Geese* (1925), *The Mad Carews* (1927), *Waters Under the Earth* (1930), *Prologue to Love* (1931), *White Reef* (1934), *The Stone Field* (1937), *The Sunset Tree* (1949), etc.

Os·ter·man \əs-tyir-'män\, Andrey Ivanovich. Count. *Orig.* Heinrich Johann Friedrich Os·ter·man \'ōs-tər-ˌmän\. 1687–1747. Russian statesman, b. Westphalia. To Russia (1704); member of Foreign Office (from 1708); played major role in peace conferences with Sweden (1718, 1721); served Catherine I and Peter II as vice chancellor, postmaster general, member of Supreme Privy Council, and president of special commission for commerce; created count and "first cabinet minister" by Anna Ivanovna (1731) and guided foreign policy during her reign (1730–40); with Burkhard Münnich overthrew (1740) regent Ernst Biron; disgraced and exiled to Siberia after coup of Elizabeth Petrovna (1741).

Ost·hoff \'ōst-ˌhóf\, Hermann. 1847–1909. German philologist. Specialist in phonetics and morphology; a leader of the "New Grammarians" (Junggrammatiker); professor, Heidelberg (from 1877); wrote *Forschungen im Gebiete der indogermanischen nominalen Stammbildung* (1875–76), etc.

Ostro·gor·sky \əs-(ˌ)trə-'gór-skəi, *Angl* ˌäs-trə-'gór-skē\, Moisey Yakovlevich. 1854–1919. Russian political scientist. Best known for treatise on English and American political parties, *Democracy and the Organization of Political Parties* (1902).

Ostrog·sky \(ˌ)əs-'trog-skəi, *Angl* äs-'träg-skē\, Konstantin Vasily. Prince. 1526–1608. Voivode (governor) of Kiev (1559–1608). At his home in Ostrog, founded an academy with a printing press on which the Ostrog Bible, first complete Bible printed in Slavonic, was printed (1581).

Ostrov·sky \(ˌ)əs-'tróf-skəi\, Aleksandr Nikolayevich. 1823–1886. Russian playwright. Considered greatest dramatist of Russian realistic period. *Kartiny semeynogo schastya* (1847) was first of over 50 plays, mainly comedies about merchant class; dismissed from civil service for *Svoi lyudi sochtemsya* (1850); *Snegurochka* (1873) adapted as opera by Rimsky-Korsakov (1880–81); supervised production of own plays at Maly Theater, Moscow; artistic director of Moscow imperial theaters (1885–86).

Ostrovsky, Nikolay Alekseyevich. 1904–1936. Soviet author. In spite of paralysis and blindness, wrote an optimistic autobiographical novel *Kak zakalyalas' stal'* (1932–34).

Ost·wald \'ōst-ˌvält\, Friedrich Wilhelm. 1853–1932. German physical chemist. With Arrhenius and van't Hoff established physical chemistry as separate discipline of science; professor at Leipzig (1887–1906); discovered Ostwald's law of dilution of an electrolyte (1888); conducted research on the electrical conductivity of organic acids, relationship between electrolytic dissociation and strength of chemical reaction; developed a quantitative color theory; invented a process for the preparation of nitric acid by oxidizing ammonia, important in the production of explosives in Germany during World War I; awarded 1909 Nobel prize for chemistry. Wrote *Lehrbuch der allgemeinen Chemie* (1885–87) and founder (with van't Hoff) of *Zeitschrift für physikalische Chemie* (1887). His son ¶Carl Wilhelm Wolfgang (1883–1943) was a founder of colloid chemsitry; professor, Leipzig (1923–43); author of *Grundriss der Kolloidchemie* (1909), etc.

O'Sullivan, Seumas. See James S. STARKEY.

O'·Sul·li·van \ō-'səl-ə-vən\, Timothy H. c.1840–1882. American photographer, b. New York City. Apprentice to Mathew Brady (c.1855) and Alexander Gardner (from 1856); with them (and independently) photographed many battles in Civil War; with surveys of 40th parallel of U.S. (1867–69), Panama (1870), and southwestern U.S. (1871, 1873, 1874); chief photographer, Treasury Dept. (1880).

Osuna, Duke of. See Pedro TELLEZ-GIRON.

Os·wald \'äz-wəld, -ˌwȯld\. Saint. c.605–641. King of Northumbria (633–641). Converted to Christianity during exile in Iona (from 616); aided brothers to drive out Anglian invaders, defeated and killed Cadwallae (633) and succeeded older brother on throne; introduced Christianity with aid of St. Aidan; killed in battle against pagan king Penda of Mercia.

Oswald of York. Saint. c.925–992. Anglo-Saxon prelate. Benedictine monk at Fleury, France; bishop of Worcester (961–992) and archbishop of York (972–992), administering both sees; cooperated with Saints Dunstan and Aethelwold in restoring ecclesiastical discipline in England; founded monasteries.

Os·wald \'äz-ˌwȯld, -wəld\, Lee Harvey. 1939–1963. American presumed assassin, b. New Orleans. In Soviet Union (1959–62); presumably assassinated John F. Kennedy in Dallas (Nov. 22, 1963); while under arrest, shot to death (Nov. 24) by Jack Ruby.

Os·wald \'äz-wəld, -ˌwȯld\, Richard. 1705–1784. British diplomat, b. Scotland. As Shelburne's agent, conducted negotiations with Franklin at Paris concluding American Revolution (1782); chief negotiator of treaty with U.S.

Os·wald von Wol·ken·stein \'ȯs-ˌvält-fȯn-'vȯl-kən-ˌshtīn\. 1377?–1445. German lyric poet and adventurer. Soldier for much of life; one of the last of the Minnesingers.

Os·wiu \'ōs-wē-ü\ *or* **Os·wy** \'äs-wē, 'äz-\. d. 670. Anglo-Saxon king. King of Bernicia on death of brother Oswald (641); defeated and killed (655) King Penda of Mercia; king of Northumbria (655–670); gained supremacy over all Mercia, the South Angles, East Angles, East Saxons, as well as many Britons and Scots; presided at Synod of Whitby (664).

Ota·kar \'ō-tä-ˌkär\. *Also spelled* Ot·to·kar \'ō-tō-\. *More fully* Přem·ysl Otakar \'przhem-ēs-əl-\. Name of two kings of Bohemia:

Otakar I. c.1155–1230. King (1198–1230). Confirmed (1192) duke of Bohemia by Henry VI; deposed (1193) but restored (1197); created king of Bohemia by Philip of Swabia; weakened by long struggle with clergy (1214–21).

Otakar II. 1230–1278. Son and successor of Wenceslas I; king of Bohemia and Moravia (1253–78) and duke of Austria (1253–74); led crusades to East Prussia (1254) and Lithuania (1266–67); extended (1260–69) his domain from Silesia to the Adriatic; divested (1274, 1276) of all territories save Bohemia and Moravia by Rudolf I; rebelled, slain at Battle of Dürnkrut.

Ote·scu \ō-'tes-kü\, Ion Nonna. 1888–1940. Romanian composer. His compositions included operas *L'Ilderim* (1919) and *De la Matei cetire* (1928); ballets *Ileana Cosînzeana* (1918) and *Rubinul miraculos* (1919); symphonic poems and other orchestral pieces.

Ot·frid *or* **Ot·fried** \'ōt-ˌfrēt\. 9th century. German monk and religious poet. Author of *Evangelienbuch* (completed c.870), an Old High German poetical version of the life of Jesus based on the Gospels, the oldest German poem using the end rhyme.

Othman. See 'UTHMĀN IBN 'AFFĀN.

Otho. See also OTTO.

Otho \'ō-thō\, Marcus Salvius. 32–69. Roman emperor (Jan.–Apr. 69). Governor of Lusitania under Nero (58–68); at first supported, later overthrew Galba by a conspiracy (68–69); proclaimed emperor by soldiers; defeated in battle by generals of Vitellius; committed suicide.

Otis \'ōt-əs\, Bass. 1784–1861. American painter, b. Bridgewater, Conn. Did portraits of James Madison (1817), Thomas Jefferson (1818), etc.; said to have made first lithograph in U.S. (1818).

Otis, Elisha Graves. 1811–1861. American inventor, b. Halifax, Vt. Devised automatic safety appliance for elevators (1852–53); patented a steam elevator (1861), the foundation of the Otis elevator business.

Otis, Elwell Stephen. 1838–1909. American army officer, b. Frederick, Md. Served through Civil War and against Indians on northwestern plains (1867–80); commander of Department of the Pacific and military governor of the Philippines (1898–1900); suppressed Philippine insurrection (1899–1900).

Otis, Harrison Gray. 1765–1848. American politician, b. Boston. Nephew of James Otis; practiced law, Boston (from 1786); member, U.S. House of Representatives (1797–1801); a leader of the Hartford Convention (1814–15); U.S. senator (1817–22); mayor of Boston (1829–32).

Otis, Harrison Gray. 1837–1917. American army officer and journalist, b. Marietta, O. Served through Civil War and in the Philippines in Spanish–American War; to California (1876); edited Santa Barbara *Press* (1876–79); editor (from 1882) and owner (from 1886), Los Angeles *Times*.

Otis, James. 1725–1783. American Revolutionary statesman, b. West Barnstable, Mass. Practiced law in Boston (from 1750). Was king's advocate general (1760) when royal customs collectors applied for writs of assistance to search for evidence of violation of Sugar Act of 1733; resigned his office and appeared as counsel for Boston merchants to oppose issuance of writs; made brilliant speech basing opposition on principles of natural law, superior to acts of Parliament (1761). In Massachusetts legislature (from 1761); among leaders of those upholding colonial cause; published *The Rights of the British Colonies Asserted and Proved* (1764). With Samuel Adams and Joseph Hawley, led majority in Massachusetts legislature (1766–69) in opposition to various revenue acts.

Ot·let \'ōt-lət\, Paul. 1868–1944. Belgian lawyer. With Henri-Marie Lafontaine devised (1899) the Universal Decimal Classification of subject groups for library collections.

Otrante, Duc d'. See Joseph FOUCHÉ.

Ott \'ät\, Mel, *in full* Melvin Thomas. 1909–1958. American baseball player, b. Gretna, La. First to hit 500 home runs in National League; player (1926–47) and manager (1942–48) for New York Giants; had batting average of .304 and 511 home runs for career; elected (1951) to Baseball Hall of Fame.

Ot·ter·bein \'ät-ər-ˌbīn\, Philip William. 1726–1813. American clergyman, b. Dillenburg, Germany. To U.S. (1752); in German Reformed pastorates in Pennsylvania and Maryland (1752–1813); with Martin Boehm and six lay evangelists formed (1789) the United Brethren in Christ.

Ot·to \'ȯt-(ˌ)ō, *Angl* 'ät-\. 1865–1906. Archduke of Austria. Son of Archduke Charles Louis, nephew of Emperor Francis Joseph, and father of Charles I; m. (1886) Princess Maria Josepha of Saxony; cavalry general in Austrian army.

Otto. 1848–1916. King of Bavaria (1886–1913). Son of Maximilian II Joseph. Became insane (1873); succeeded his brother Louis II as king (1886) under regency of his uncle Prince Luitpold (1886–1912) and of his cousin Louis (1912–13); deposed (1913) and succeeded by cousin as King Louis III.

Otto. Name of three dukes of Bavaria:

Otto von Nord·heim \fȯn-'nȯrt-ˌhīm\. d. 1083. Named duke (1061) by Agnes of Poitou acting as regent for King Henry IV; took part in kidnap of Henry (1062); led expedition against Hungarians (1063); deprived of duchy (1070); took command of Saxon uprising against Henry IV (1073); restored to duchy of Bavaria (1074); supported Rudolf against Henry for throne (1077–83).

Otto I von Wit·tels·bach \fȯn-'vit-əls-ˌbäk\. c.1120–1183. Duke (1180–83). Accompanied Emperor Frederick I to Italy; made count palatine (1156); founder of Wittelsbach dynasty in Bavaria. His nephew ¶Otto (d. 1209), count palatine, was murderer of King Philip of Swabia (1208).

Otto II. *Called* der Er·lauch·te \der-er-'laủk-tə\, *i.e.* the Illustrious. 1206–1253. Duke (1231–53). Grandson of Otto I, son of Louis I.

Otto. Name of five margraves of Brandenburg of 12th to 14th centuries, especially Otto III (d. 1267), who ruled jointly with his brother John I (1220–67) and made important acquisitions to the territory; and ¶Otto, *called* der Faule \der-'faủ-lə\, *i.e.* the Lazy (d. 1379); margrave (1350–73); son of King Louis of Bavaria.

Otto. *Called* das Kind \däs-'kint\, *i.e.* the Child. 1204–1252. First Duke of Brunswick-Lüneburg (see BRUNSWICK). Grandson of Henry the Lion; inherited Brunswick (1218) and Lüneburg (1227); held captive after defeat by Waldemar of Denmark; joined his lands in a single duchy (1235); made prince of the empire by Emperor Frederick II (1235).

Otto. Name of two counts of Gelderland and Zutphen: Otto I (1164–1207) succeeded father as count (1182); on crusade to Jerusalem (1188–91); attempted to conquer Brabant, Limburg, and bishopric of Liège (1195–1202); captured (1202) by Henry I of Brabant and ransomed. ¶Otto II (c.1220–1271), *called* the Lame; grandson of Otto I, son and successor (1229) of Gerhard III; awarded (1247) Nijmegen for support of claim of cousin Count William II to throne of Germany.

Otto I *or* **Otho.** *In full* Otto Friedrich Ludwig. 1815–1867. King of Greece (1832–62). Second son of Louis I of Bavaria. Chosen king of the Hellenes by London conference (1832); ruled under regency of three Bavarian advisers (1832–35); unpopular throughout his reign because of his religion, his taxation, his use of German officials, and interference of his wife, Princess Amalie of Oldenburg; forced by insurrection to grant a constitution (1843); deposed by a revolutionary government (1862).

Otto. Name of four Holy Roman emperors:

Otto I. 912–973. *Called* the Great. King of Germany and Holy Roman emperor (936–973; crowned 962). Son of Henry I the Fowler. Spent early years of reign in subduing revolts of nobles; m. (930; d. 946) Edith, daughter of Edward the Elder; aided Adelaide, Queen of Lombardy, against Berengar II (951); m. Adelaide (951); defeated Magyars in great battle on the Lechfeld (955); defeated Berengar II (961); marched into Rome and Byzantium (966–972). Coronation (962) revived the empire of Charlemagne. Deposed Pope John XII (963). His son Otto crowned as joint emperor (967) by Pope John XIII.

Otto II. 955–983. Holy Roman emperor (973–983). Son of Otto I. Subdued revolt of cousin Henry II of Bavaria (978); drove French out of Lorraine but was unsuccessful in siege of Paris (978); claimed provinces in southern Italy but was disastrously defeated by Saracens and Greeks (982); m. at Rome (972) ¶The·o·pha·no \tā-'ō-fän-(,)ō, *Angl* thē-'äf-ə-(,)nō\ (955?–991), daughter of Byzantine emperor Romanus II, who had great influence at his court, introducing much of the refinement of Constantinople, and who, after his death, ruled (983–991) for her son Otto III as coregent with the boy's grandmother Adelaide.

Otto III. 980–1002. Holy Roman emperor (983–1002). Son of Otto II. During minority under coregency of mother Theophano (983–991) and grandmother Adelaide (991–994); installed cousin Bruno of Carinthia as Pope Gregory V (996); lived in Rome (998–1002) and sought to make it the capital of a new Roman empire; established Sylvester II as pope (999).

Otto IV of Brunswick. 1174?–1218. Holy Roman emperor (1198–1215; crowned 1209). Son of Henry the Lion, Duke of Bavaria and Saxony. Put forward (1198) by Guelfs as rival to Philip, Duke of Swabia, as king and emperor; fought civil war against Philip (1198–1208); crowned emperor after Philip's death; excommunicated (1210) by Pope Innocent III; conquered southern Italy (1210). With John of England, defeated at Bouvines (1214) by Philip II Augustus of France supported by Innocent III; forced to retire (1215) to estates in Brunswick.

Otto of Bam·berg \'bam-,berk, *Angl* 'bam-(,)bərg\. Saint. *Called* Father of the Monks. 1060?–1139. German religious. Bishop of Bamberg and apostle of the Pomeranians. Appointed bishop (1102) by Emperor Henry IV; consecrated at Rome (1106); devoted himself to work of his bishopric, founding more than 20 monasteries; made journeys to Pomerania (1124–25, 1128), converting many; canonized (1189).

Otto of Frei·sing \'frī-ziŋ\. c.1111–1158. German bishop and historian. Grandson of Emperor Henry IV and half-brother of Conrad III; abbot of Cistercian monastery of Morimond in Burgundy (1137); made bishop of Freising (1137) in Bavaria; took part in Conrad's disastrous crusade (1147–49). Wrote (1143–46) *Historia de duabus civitatibus,* a philosophical interpretation of world history, following in part Augustine and Orosius; began chronicle of reign of Frederick I, *Gesta Friderici imperatoris.*

Otto of Nordheim. See OTTO, Duke of Bavaria.

Otto, Bodo. 1711–1787. American physician, b. Hanover, Germany. To America (1755); surgeon in Continental army (1776–82). His grandson ¶ John Conrad Otto (1774–1844) was also a physician; known for original description of hemophilia (1803); succeeded Benjamin Rush as physician to Pennsylvania Hospital (1813–34).

Otto, Nikolaus August. 1832–1891. German engineer. Built his first gas engine (1861); inventor of an early form of internal-combustion engine (with Langen, 1867); built first four-stroke cycle engine (1862).

Otto, Rudolf. 1869–1937. German theologian and philosopher. Professor at Göttingen (1897–1914), Breslau (1914–17), Marburg (1917–29); member, Prussian parliament (1913–18) and Constituent Chamber (1918). His works on man's experience with the holy included *Naturalistische und religiöse Weltansicht* (1904), *Das Heilige* (1917), *West-Östliche Mystik* (1926), *Die Gnadenreligion Indiens und das Christentum* (1930), and *Reich Gottes und Menschensohn* (1934).

Ottokar. See OTAKAR.

Ot·way \'ät-,wā\, Thomas. 1652–1685. English dramatist and poet. First play *Alcibiades* (1675); scored success with *Don Carlos* (1676); adapted plays by Racine and Molière. His first blank verse tragedy, *The Orphan,* was produced in 1680; his masterpiece, *Venice Preserved,* in which he caricatured Shaftesbury as Antonio and in which Elizabeth Barry played Belvidera, in 1682; also wrote comedies *Friendship in Fashion* (1678), *The Souldier's Fortune* (1680), *The Atheist* (1684), and an autobiographical poem *The Poet's Complaint of His Muse* (1680).

Ouaphris. See APRIES.

Oud \'aůt\, Jacobus Johannes Pieter. 1890–1963. Dutch architect. A leader (with Theo van Doesburg) of the de Stijl group and champion of modernism in architecture; city architect, Rotterdam (1918–33); wrote *Höllandische Architektur* (1926).

Ou·di·né \ü-dē-nā\, Eugène-André. 1810–1887. French sculptor and engraver of medals. Among his sculptures were *La Vierge et l'Enfant Jésus* at the church of Saint Gervais in Paris, *Hébé* in the palace of the Tuileries; among his medallions *Prince Napoléon, Le Duc d'Orléans, Berthollet, Deux Décembre 1851.*

Ou·di·not \ü-dē-nō\, Nicolas-Charles. Duc de Reg·gio \də-'rād-jō\. 1767–1847. French soldier. General of division (1799); in command of elite grenadiers, distinguished himself at Austerlitz (1805), Friedland (1807), Wagram (1809); created marshal of France and duc de Reggio (1809); engaged in the Russian campaign (1812), at Bautzen (1813), and in the defense of France (1813–14); remained loyal to the monarchy during the Hundred Days; appointed to command the National Guard and created a peer of France. His son ¶Nicolas-Charles-Victor (1791–1863), duc de Reggio, served in the Napoleonic armies, esp. in the defense of France (1813–14); commanded expedition against Rome and captured the city (1849).

Ou·dry \ü-drē\, Jean-Baptiste. 1686–1755. French Rococo painter, tapestry designer, and illustrator. Known esp. for animal paintings; headed (1734–36) Beauvais tapestry works; inspector general and designer, Gobelins factory (from 1736); illustrated books.

Ough·tred \'ö-,tred, -trəd\, William. 1574–1660. English mathematician. Invented (c.1632) earliest form of slide rule; invented trigonometric abbreviations and introduced signs of multiplication and proportion in his *Clavis Mathematicae* (1631).

Ouida. See Marie Louise de la RAMÉE.

Oui·met \'wē-,met\, Francis. 1893–1967. American golfer, b. Brookline, Mass. Winner, U.S. Open (1913), after a sensational playoff with Harry Vardon and Ted Ray, and U.S. Amateur championship (1914, 1931); on Walker Cup teams as player (1922–36) and captain (1936–49); did much to popularize golf in U.S.

Oun Kham \'ün-'käm\. 1811 or 1816–1895. Laotian ruler of Luang Prabang (1872–87, 1889–94). During exile (1887–89) in Bangkok assisted by Frenchman Auguste Parie, for which reason he turned over his region to France (1893) as a protectorate.

Ours·ler \'aů(r)z-lər\, Fulton, *in full* Charles Fulton. 1893–1952. American journalist and writer, b. Baltimore. Editor of various magazines published by Barnarr Macfadden (1922–42). Author of novels as *The Great Jasper* (1930), *Joshua Todd* (1935), *The Greatest Story Ever Told* (1949); detective stories under pseudonym Anthony Abbot; plays as *The Spider* (1927), *All the King's Men* (1929); and motion-picture scenarios.

Out·cault \'aůt-,költ\, Richard Felton. 1863–1928. American cartoonist, b. Lancaster, O. Cartoonist for New York City newspapers *World* (1885–96), where he originated the "Yellow Kid" (1896); *Journal* (1896–97); and *Herald* (1897 ff.), where he created "Buster Brown" (1902).

Ou·tram \'ü-trəm\, Sir James. 1803–1863. British army commander in India. Known as "the Bayard of India." Joined Bombay native infantry (1819); defended his residency at Hyderābād against 8000 Sikhs (1843); conducted brilliant war against Persia and made lieutenant general (1857); in Sepoy Mutiny, a volunteer under his old lieutenant Havelock in first relief of Lucknow; commanded Lucknow garrison through siege until relieved by Sir Colin Campbell; held the city through evacuation until third relief (1857); created baronet (1858); chief commander of Oudh (1858).

Out·re·meuse \ü-trə-mœ̄z\, Jean d'. 1338–1399. French writer. Lawyer at episcopal court of Liège; author of romanticized histories *La Geste de Liège* and *Ly Myreur des Histors.*

Ou·vard \üv-rär\, Gabriel-Julien. 1770–1846. French speculator and financier. Advanced large sums to finance Napoléon's campaigns; later (1807) incurred enmity of Napoléon and was imprisoned (1809–13); during the Hundred Days was appointed supply officer to Napoléon's army; convicted of illegal transactions on the Paris Bourse, was again imprisoned (1823–28).

Ouwe, Hartman von. See HARTMANN VON AUE.

Ou-yang Hsiu \'ō-'yäŋ-shē-'ü\. *Courtesy name* Yung-shu \'yůŋ-'shü\, *literary name* Tsui-weng \dzü-'ē-'wəŋ\, *canonized* Wen-chung \'wən-'chůŋ\. 1007–1072. Chinese poet, historian, and statesman. Served (1030–71) as judge and counsellor in various provinces; often demoted for criticism of bureaucratic policies but always reinstated; sought to reform political life through Confucian principles. Reintroduced unadorned "ancient style" in literature, esp. as head (1057–60) of civil service examinations; chronicler to Emperor Sung Jen Tsung; in later life opposed reforms of Wang An-shih. His writings included "New History of the Five Dynasties" and "New History of the T'ang Dynasty."

Ovan·do \ō-'vän-dō\, Nicolás de. c.1451–c.1511. Spanish colonial administrator. Succeeded Francisco de Bobadilla as governor of Spanish possessions in America (1502–09); established *encomienda* system of Indian forced labor; founded (1502) Spanish community in Santo Domingo.

Ovens \'ō-vəns\, Jürgen. 1623–1678. Danish painter. Pupil of Rembrandt; known esp. for group portraits, nocturnal scenes, and historical and allegorical subjects.

Over·beck \'ō-vər-ˌbek\, Johann Friedrich. 1789–1869. German religious painter. With Franz Pforr founded (1809) the Lucas Brotherhood, or Nazarenes, to renew the arts through Christian faith; in 1810 the Brotherhood (joined by Cornelius, Carolsfeld, Veit, Schadow, et al.) moved to Rome; became Roman Catholic (1813); his works, which influenced the Pre-Raphaelites, included frescoes as *Rose Miracle of St. Francis* (1829), paintings as *Italia and Germania* (1811–28), and portraits as *Vittoria Caldoni* (1821). His nephew ¶Johannes Adolf (1826–1895), archaeologist, wrote *Pompei* (1856), *Geschichte der griechischen Plastik* (1857–58), etc.

Over·bury \'ō-vər-ˌber-ē, -b(ə-)rē\, Sir Thomas. 1581–1613. English poet. Protégé (from 1606) of Robert Carr, Viscount Rochester (later Earl of Somerset); confidant to intrigue between Rochester and the profligate Frances Howard, Countess of Essex; opposed marriage of Rochester and Lady Essex, esp. in didactic poem *A Wife* (written 1611, pub. 1614); imprisoned in Tower (1613) on charge of disrespect to king, and slowly poisoned with blue vitriol by Lady Essex's agents. Known for the prose *Characters,* sketches modeled upon Theophrastus and important in development of the English essay.

Øver·land \'œ̄-vər-län\, Arnulf. 1889–1968. Norwegian poet, novelist, and playwright. Wrote poetry for social change as *Brød og vin* (1919) and *Berget det blå* (1937), and against Fascism as *Den røde front* (1937); in concentration camp (1941–45) for poetry (collected in 1945 as *Vi overlever alt*) against Nazi occupation of Norway. Also known for *Hustavler* (1929, verse) and *Gud plantet en have* (1931, short stories).

Over·ton \'ō-vərt-ᵊn, -vər-tən\, Richard. fl. 1642–63. English pamphleteer. A leader of Leveller movement; often imprisoned for religious pamphlets as *New Lambeth Fayre* (1642), *Man's Mortalitie* (1644), *A Remonstrance of Many Thousand Citizens* (1646), etc.

Over·weg \'ō-vər-ˌvāk\, Adolf. 1822–1852. German geologist and traveler. On British expedition to Central Africa (1849–52); mapped Lake Chad.

Ov·id \'äv-əd\. *Full Latin name* Publius Ovid·i·us Na·so \ō-'vid-ē-əs-'nā-sō\. 43 B.C.–17 A.D. Roman poet. Educated for the law, but devoted himself to literature; wrote love poems *Amores* (c.20 B.C.), *Epistulae heroidum, Ars amatoria* (c.1 B.C.), and *Remedia amoris,* also the etiological poem *Fasti;* banished by Augustus (8 A.D.), perhaps for passages in *Ars amatoria,* from Rome to Tomi (Constanta), near Black Sea, where he remained until death and where he wrote *Tristia, Epistulae ex Ponto,* and *Ibis.* Chief work, *Metamorphoses* (1–8 A.D.), a narrative poem recounting legends involving miraculous transformations of form from the creation to time of Julius Caesar.

Oviedo, Gonzalo Fernández de. See FERNÁNDEZ DE OVIEDO.

Oving·ton \'ō-viŋ-tən\, Earle L. 1879–1936. American aeronautical engineer. First U.S. Air Mail pilot (1911); invented various electrical appliances, including Ovington high-frequency apparatus.

Ovon·ram·wen \ˌō-vən-'räm-wən\. *Also called* Ove·ra·mi \ō-və-'räm-ē\. d. 1914. West African ruler. Last independent king of Benin (now part of Nigeria); attempted to repulse European encroachment, but murder of British official led to British takeover (1897); died in exile.

Owain Cy·feil·iog \'ō-ˌwīn-kə-'vāl-ˌyòg\. c.1130–1197. Welsh warrior-prince and poet. Prince of Powys (1149–95); joined Owain Gwynedd in repelling Henry II (1165); obtained outside help to expel Rhys ap Gruffydd, prince of South Wales, from Powys (1167–71); founded Cistercian house of Strata Marcella, where he died a monk. Author of *Hirlas Owain,* a poem in praise of members of his warband.

Owain Gwy·nedd \-'gwin-eth\. d. 1170. King of Gwynedd (North Wales). Succeeded father Gruffydd ab Cynan (1137); submitted to Henry II after invasion (1157); helped repel Henry II's invasion of South Wales (1165).

Ow·en \'ō-en, *Angl* 'ō-ən\, Daniel. 1836–1895. Welsh writer. Considered the national novelist of Wales; early career as tailor and Methodist preacher. Wrote novels *Y Dreflan* (1881), *Hunangofiant Rhys Lewis* (1885), *Profedigaethau Enoc Huws* (1891), *Gwen Tomos* (1894); also *Offrymau Neilltuaeth* (1879), *Y Siswrn* (1888), and *Straeon y Pentan* (1895).

Owen, Goronwy. 1723–1769. Welsh clergyman and poet. Held curacies in England; grammar school master, Williamsburg, Va. (1757–60); rector, St. Andrew's, Brunswick County, Va. (1760–69). Revived classical Welsh poetic forms, as the *cywydd* and *awdl;* best known poems "The Day of Judgment," "The Gem of the Precious Stone," "The Lineage and Attributes of the Muse," and "*Cywydd* in Answer to Huw the Red Poet."

Owen, Sir Hugh. 1804–1881. Welsh promoter of education. Helped establish teacher-training colleges; founded Aberystwyth University College (opened 1872); reformed and revived the eisteddfod.

Owen, John. *Lat.* Au·do·e·nus \ò-dō-'ē-nəs\ *or* Ove·nus \ō-'vē-nəs\. 1560?–1622. Welsh epigrammatist. Master of Latin idiom and pointed epigrams.

Ow·en \'ō-ən\, John. 1616–1683. English clergyman and theologian. Advocate of Congregationalism; vice chancellor of Oxford (1652–57); aide and chaplain to Cromwell (1653–58); dean of Christ Church Cathedral (1651–60). Author of *Eschol* (1648) and other religious works.

Owen, Sir Richard. 1804–1892. English anatomist and paleontologist. Superintendent of natural history department of British Museum (1856–84); early opponent of Darwin's thesis of evolution; follower of Cuvier. Among his many works on comparative anatomy were *Memoir on the Pearly Nautilus* (1832) and *On the Anatomy of Vertebrates* (1866–68).

Owen, Robert. 1771–1858. Welsh Socialist and philanthropist. Bought New Lanark mills at Manchester from David Dale (1799); with William Allen, Quaker philanthropist, and Jeremy Bentham as partners (1814), initiated program of amelioration in conditions of operatives; stopped employment of children; established sickness and old-age insurance, opened educational and recreational facilities. Contended in *A New View of Society* (1813) that man's character is wholly determined by environment; instrumental in drafting Factory Act of 1819, emasculated in House of Commons. Founded several communities of "Owenites" on the cooperative principle in Great Britain and the United States, including one at New Harmony, Indiana (1825–28), all unsuccessful. Withdrew from New Lanark after disagreements with partners (1829). Spent fortune on social schemes; devoted himself to preaching his educational, moral, secularist, and other ideas; at age of 82 took up spiritualism. Author of *Revolution in Mind and Practice* (1849) and autobiography (1857–58). A son ¶Robert Dale (1801–1877) accompanied his father to U.S. (1825) and to New Harmony, Ind.; taught school and edited New Harmony *Gazette;* to New York (1829) and edited *Free Enquirer;* again in New Harmony (1832); member of U.S. House of Representatives (1843–47); U.S. minister to Italy (1855–58); advocate of emancipation of slaves; author of *The Policy of Emancipation* (1863), *The Wrong Slavery* (1864), *Beyond the Breakers* (novel, 1870), *Threading My Way* (autobiography, 1874).

Owen, Robert Latham. 1856–1947. American politician, b. Lynchburg, Va. U.S. senator from Oklahoma (1907–25); aided in drafting Federal Reserve Act, known as the Glass-Owen Currency Act (1913), and Farm Loan Act (1916); advocated initiative, referendum, recall, and cloture in U.S. Senate.

Owen, Ruth. See Ruth ROHDE.

Owen, Wilfred. 1893–1918. English poet. Served in France (1916–17); company commander on Western front (1918); killed in action. His poems against war edited by Siegfried Sassoon (23 titles in 1920 ed.).

Ow·ens \'ō-ənz\, Jesse, *orig.* James Cleveland. 1913–1980. American athlete, b. Danville, Ala. Set three track and field world records and tied one on May 25, 1935; won four gold medals in Olympic Games (1936).

Owens, Michael Joseph. 1859–1923. American inventor and manufacturer, b. Mason Co., Va. (now W. Va.). Invented automatic bottle-blowing machine (patented 1895 and 1904); organized Owens Bottle Machine Co. (1903); vice president (1915–23); also organized Libbey-Owens Sheet Glass Co. (1916).

Owenson, Sydney. See Sydney MORGAN.

Ow·ings \'ō-iŋz\, Nathaniel Alexander. 1903–1984. American architect, b. Indianapolis. Founded (1936) with Louis Skidmore architectural firm of Skidmore and Owings (from 1939 Skidmore, Owings & Merrill); during World War II built secret town of Atom City, Oak Ridge, Tenn., for U.S. atomic energy project; designed New York City's Lever House, influential glass skyscraper; also designed New York City's Chase Manhattan Bank and Chicago's John Hancock Center and Sears Tower, etc. Author of *The American Aesthetic* (1969) and *The Spaces in Between* (1973).

Owon. See CHANG SUNG-OB.

Ox·en·ford \'äk-sən-fərd, -ˌfō(ə)rd, -ˌfò(ə)rd\, John. 1812–1877. English critic, playwright, and translator. Drama critic, London *Times* (1850 ff.); author of over 70 plays, esp. *My Fellow Clerk* (1835) and *The Hemlock Draught* (1848).

Oxenham, John. See also William DUNKERLEY.

Ox·en·ham \'äk-sən-əm, 'äks-nəm\, John. d. 1575. English mariner. With Drake in Central America (1572); headed a second expedition to the New World; was defeated by the Spaniards, captured, and hanged at Lima, Peru.

Ox·en·stier·na \'u̇k-sen-ˌsher-nä\, Axel Gustafsson. Count. 1583–1654. Swedish statesman. Appointed chancellor by Gustav Adolphus (1612); arranged peace treaties with Denmark at Knäred (1613) and with Russia at Stolbova (1617); took part in campaigns against Poland (1621); governor general of Prussia (1626); negotiated a truce with Poland (1629) by which Sweden retained Livonia; held supreme control in Rhine region in Thirty Years' War (from 1631); director of Swedish foreign policy in Germany (after 1632); director of the Evangelical League, Heilbronn (1633); negotiated treaty of Wismar with France (1636); guardian of Queen Christina (1636) and virtual director of Swedish policy after her ascension (1644); negotiated peace of Brömsebro with Denmark (1645); ennobled (1645).

Oxenstierna, Bengt Bengtsson. Baron. 1591–1643. Swedish statesman and traveler. Traveled in Palestine (1613) and in Asia Minor, Persia, Egypt, etc. (1616); in diplomatic service of Gustav Adolphus of Sweden (1620); governor general of Livonia and Ingria (1634). His nephew ¶Count Bengt Gabrielsson

Oxenstierna (1623–1702) was a statesman and diplomat in the service of Charles X and Charles XI; as governor of Poland led the defense of Thorn (1657); governor general of Livonia (1662–66); negotiated alliance with the Netherlands and Holy Roman Empire (1681); chancellor president and director of Swedish foreign policy (1680–97); member of regency council of Charles XII (1697).

Oxenstierna, Johan Gabriel. Count. 1750–1818. Swedish poet. Court poet to Gustav III and Charles XIII; author of poem cycles, the comic poem *Disa,* lyrics, epigrams, epistles, a translation of Milton's *Paradise Lost,* etc.

Oxford, Earls of. See Robert HARLEY; VERE family.

Oxford and Asquith, Earl of. See ASQUITH.

Ox·ley \ˈäk-slē\, John Joseph William Molesworth. 1783–1828. English naval officer. Surveyor general of New South Wales, Australia (from 1812); led expeditions (1817, 1818) to interior of that colony and (1823–24) to mouth of Brisbane River.

Ox·nam \ˈäk-ˌsnam, -snəm\, Garfield Bromley. 1891–1963. American clergyman, educator, and author, b. Sonora, Cal. Ordained (1916) Methodist minister; president, De Pauw U. (1928–36); bishop (1936); president, World Council of Churches (1948–54). Known for support of liberal causes, esp. of rights of labor and minorities. His many writings included *Facing the Future Unafraid* (1944) and *The Church and Contemporary Change* (1950).

Oya·ma \ō-yä-mä\ Iwao. Prince. 1842–1916. Japanese soldier. General (1891), field marshal (1898); in Chinese–Japanese War (1894–95), commanded second army and captured Port Arthur and Weihaiwei; in Russo–Japanese War (1904–05), commanded the Manchurian army and defeated the Russians under Kuropatkin in the battles of Liaoyang, the Shaho, and Mukden; created count (1884), marquis (1895), prince (1907).

Ōyōmei. See WANG YANG-MING.

Oza·ki \ō-zä-kē\ Kōyō. *Orig.* Ozaki Tokutarō. 1867–1903. Japanese novelist. Helped found (1885) literary magazine *Kenyūsha;* his romantic realism style influenced by study of Saikaku Ihara; helped introduce colloquial language in literature; among his works were *The Perfumed Pillow* (1890), *Tears and Regrets* (1896), *The Heart* (1903), and his masterpiece *The Gold Demon* (1897–1902).

Ozaki Yukio. 1858–1954. Japanese politician. Called the father of parliamentary politics of Japan. Elected (from 1890) 24 consecutive times to House of Representatives; a follower of Ōkuma Shigenobu, esp. as his minister of education (1898) and of justice (1914–16); mayor of Tokyo (1904); a leading advocate of universal manhood suffrage (est. 1925).

Oza·nam \ō-zȧ-nȧm\, Antoine-Frédéric. 1813–1853. French historian. A leader in the Catholic movement; a founder of the Society of Saint Vincent de Paul (1833); cofounder (1848) of *Ère nouvelle.* Author of *Essai sur la philosophie de Dante* (1839), *Études germaniques* (1847–49), etc.

Öz Beg \ˈœz-ˈbeg\. *Also spelled* Uz·bek \ˈüz-ˌbek, ˈəz-\. d. 1341. Mongol khan (1313–41) of the Golden Horde, or Kipchak empire, of southern Russia. Although Muslim, encouraged Christianity in his realm; his name survives in Uzbeks of Soviet Union.

Ozen·fant \ō-zäⁿ-fäⁿ\, Amédée. 1886–1966. French painter. With Le Corbusier founded Purism school of art and published its manifesto *L'Ésprit nouveau* (1920–25); also collaborated with him in writing *Après le cubisme* (1918) and *La Peinture moderne* (1925); in U.S. (1938–55).

Ozias. See UZZIAH.

Ozo·lua \ō-ˈzō-lə-wə\. *Called* the Conqueror. d. 1504. King (1481–1504) of Benin. Son of Ewuare the Great; extended boundaries of Benin (in present Nigeria) from Niger River in east to Lagos in west; encouraged trade with the Portuguese.

Ozu \ō-zü\ Yasujirō. 1903–1963. Japanese film director. Originator of the *shomin-geki,* films about lower-middle-class families such as *Umarete wa mita kevedo* (1932), *Toda-ke-no-kyodai* (1941), *Nagaya shinshi roku* (1947), *Banshun* (1949), *Bakushu* (1951), and *Tokyo monogatari* (1953).

P

Paaltjens, Piet. See François HAVERSCHMIDT.

Paap \'päp\, Willem Anthony. 1856–1923. Dutch novelist and playwright. Known esp. for satirical novels *Jeanne Collette* (1896) and *Vincent Haman* (1898).

Paa·sche \'päsh-ə\, Hermann. 1851–1925. German economist. Developed Paasche index for measuring current price or quantity levels relative to those of a selected base period.

Paa·si·ki·vi \'päs-ik-iv-ē\, Juho Kusti. 1870–1956. Finnish politician. Member of parliament (1907–13); minister of finance (1908–09); prime minister (1918, 1944–46); president (1946–56). Advocate of friendly relations with U.S.S.R.; negotiated (1940) end to Russo–Finnish War.

Pabst \'päpst\, George Wilhelm. 1885–1967. German film director. Preeminent director of German "new realism" films as *Die freudlose Gasse* (1925), *Geheimnisse einer Seele* (1926), *Die Liebe der Jeanne Ney* (1927), *Abwege* (1928), *Tagebuch einer Verlorenen* (1929), *Die Dreigroschenoper* (1931), and *Kameradschaft* (1931); later films included *Komödianten* (1941), *Paracelsus* (1943), *Der Letzte Akt* (1954).

Pa·ca \'pā-kə, 'pak-ə\, William. 1740–1799. American Revolutionary leader, b. near Abingdon, Md. Practiced law (from 1764); member of Continental Congress (1774–79) and signer of Declaration of Independence; governor of Maryland (1782–85); U.S. district judge for Maryland (1789–99).

Pa·ca·tus Dre·pa·ni·us \pə-'kāt-əs-drə-'pā-nē-əs\, Latinius *or* Latinus. fl. 390 A.D. Gallo-Roman orator and poet. Friend of Ausonius and Symmachus; delivered (389) a panegyric (still extant) to Theodosius I at Rome after latter's defeat of usurper Maximus.

Pac·ca \'päk-kä\, Bartolommeo. 1756–1844. Italian prelate and diplomat. Cardinal (1801); secretary of state, Papal States (1806 ff.); imprisoned by Napoléon for anti-French policies (1809–13); induced Pius VII to break concordat of Fontainebleau (1813); banished by Napoléon (1814); recalled after fall of the Empire; camerlengo, nuncio to Vienna (1816); governor of Rome (1817); bishop of Ostia and Velletri (1830 ff.). Author of memoirs important as historical source material.

Pac·ca·na·ri \,päk-kä-'nä-rē\, Niccolò. 1773–? Italian monk. Founded order of Regular Clerks of the Faith of Jesus (approved 1798 and absorbed by Society of Jesus, 1814), known generally as Paccanarists.

Pac·card \pák-kár\, Michel-Gabriel. 1757–1827. French physician. With Jacques Balmat made first ascent of Mont Blanc (1786).

Pac·chio·ni \päk-'kyō-nē\, Antonio. 1665–1726. Italian anatomist. Investigated the structure of dura mater, including the Pacchionian bodies named after him.

Pace \'pās\, Richard. 1482?–1536. English diplomat. Dean of St. Paul's (1519); sent by Wolsey to induce Swiss to attack forces of Francis I (1515), to influence imperial electors in favor of Henry VIII as successor to Emperor Maximilian (1519), and to further Wolsey's papal ambition (1521, 1523). His dispatches are historically important.

Pacelli, Eugenio. See Pope PIUS XII.

Pa·cha·cu·ti \,pä-chä-'kü-tē\ *or* **Pa·cha·cu·tec In·ca Yu·pan·qui** \,pä-chä-'kü-,tek-'iŋ-kə-yü-'päŋ-kē\. d. 1471. Inca emperor (1438–71). Extended his empire to southern Peru and northwest to Quito, Ecuador; said to have devised plans for his capital Cuzco; succeeded by his son Topa Inca Yupanqui.

Pa·che·co \pä-'chā-kō\, Francisco. 1564–1654. Spanish painter. Directed academy in Seville; pupils included Alonso Cano and Velázquez, who was also his son-in-law; known for portraits and religious works. Author of *Arte de la pintura* (1649).

Pacheco, Juan Manuel Fernández. Marqués de Vil·le·na \ve(l)-'yā-nä\. 1650–1725. Spanish scholar. A founder and first director (1713–25) of the Spanish Academy; guided preparation of its first dictionary, *Dictionario de autoridades* (1726–39).

Pacheco, María. See Juan López de PADILLA.

Pa·che·co Pe·rei·ra \pá-'shā-kō-pe-'rā-rə\, Duarte. 15th–16th century. Portuguese explorer. Called "Aquilles Lusitano" (i.e. the Portuguese Achilles) by Camões. Explored southwestern coast of Africa (1488); with Pedro Álvares Cabral to Brazil (1500); military governor in Portuguese East Africa (1520–22); wrote account of Portuguese explorations *Princípio do Esmeraldo "de Situ Orbis."*

Pa·chel·bel \päk-'el-,bel\, Johann. 1653–1706. German organist and composer. Held posts as organist in Vienna (1673–77), Eisenach (1677–78), Erfurt (1678–90), Württemberg court at Stuttgart (1690–92), Gotha (1692–95), St. Sebalduskirche at Nürnberg (1695–1706); an early model for J.S. Bach; composed contrapuntal organ fugues, suites, chaconnes, chorale-preludes, etc.; his *Hexachordum Apollinis* (1699), 6 sets of variations, considered best work.

Pach·er \'päk-ər\, Michael. c.1435–1498. German painter and woodcarver. One of first to introduce principles of Renaissance painting into Germany; known esp. for his altarpieces; also did *Betrothal of the Virgin* and *Flagellation* (both c.1484).

Pach·mann \'päk-mən\, Vladimir von. *Known also as* Vladimir de Pachman. 1848–1933. Russian pianist. Debut in Odessa (1869); toured in Europe and U.S.; known for performances of Chopin.

Pa·cho·mi·us \pə-'kō-mē-əs\. Saint. c.290–346. Christian monk. Founded (c.318 A.D.) on bank of Nile first cenobitic monastery, whose book of observances is earliest extant.

Pachymeres, George. See GEORGE PACHYMERES.

Pa·cif·i·co \pə-'sē-fē-kü, *Angl* pə-'sif-ə-(,)kō\, David. 1784–1854. Portuguese Jewish merchant. A British subject owing to birth in Gibraltar; Portuguese consul general in Greece (1837–42); made claim against Greek government for burning of his house by a mob (1847); almost precipitated a war when French and Russians protested British attempt to compel settlement of his claim (1850).

Pa·ci·ni \pä-'chē-nē\, Filippo. 1812–1883. Italian anatomist. Professor, Florence (from 1849). Rediscovered (1835) nerve terminations (described earlier by Abraham Vater) that came to be called Pacinian corpuscles after him; discovered (1854) bacillus of cholera.

Pacini, Giovanni. 1796–1867. Italian composer. Composed oratorios, masses, cantatas, chamber music, a *Dante* symphony, and esp. operas as *Saffo* (1840), *Medea* (1843), *La Regina di Cirpo* (1846), and *Niccolò de' Lapi* (1855). His brother ¶Emilio (1810–1898) wrote the libretto of Verdi's *Il trovatore.*

Pa·ci·not·ti \,pä-chē-'nòt-tē\, Antonio. 1841–1912. Italian physicist. Invented dynamo with ring winding (1860), same type of winding independently discovered and used in dynamo by Z. T. Gramme (1869).

Pa·cio·li \pä-'chō-lē\, Luca. *Called also* Luca di Bor·go \-dē-'bōr-gō\. 1445?–?1514. Italian mathematician and Franciscan friar. Author of *Summa de arithmetica, geometria, proportioni et proportionalita* (1494), which contained the first printed description of bookkeeping by double entry, and *De Divina proportione* with plates engraved by his friend Leonardo da Vinci (1509).

Pa·ci·us \'pá-sē-ùs\, Fredrik. 1809–1891. Finnish violinist and composer. Composed first Finnish opera *Kung Karlsjakt* (1852) and Finnish national anthem "Maamme"; also opera *Lorelei* (1887), a violin concerto, choruses, patriotic songs, etc.

Pack \'päk\, Otto von. 1480?–1537. German politician. In service of George, Duke of Saxony; author of several fraudulent schemes, esp. his report (1528) of a Catholic alliance against German Protestant rulers which led to attacks on Würzburg and Bamberg and nearly caused a general war.

Pack·ard \'pak-ərd\, Alpheus Spring. 1839–1905. American entomologist, b. Brunswick, Me. A founder and editor in chief of *American Naturalist* (1867–87); professor, Brown U. (1878–1905). Author of *The Cave Fauna of North America* (1888), *The Labrador Coast* (1891), *Textbook of Entomology* (1898), *Monograph of the Bombycine Moths* (1895–1914), etc.

Packard, Frank Lucius. 1877–1942. Canadian writer, b. Montreal. Author of novels as *Greater Love Hath No Man* (1913), *The Miracle Man* (1914), *The Beloved Traitor* (1916), *The Night Operator* (1919), and detective fiction, including the Jimmie Dale series.

Packard, James Ward. 1863–1928. American engineer and inventor, b. Warren, Ohio. With brother ¶William Doud (1861–1923), founded Packard Electric Co. (1890); designed and built first Packard automobile (1899); president, Packard Motor Car Co. (to 1915).

Pa·co·rus \pə-'kōr-əs, -'kȯr-\. *Parthian* Pkwr. *Sometimes called* Pacorus I. d. 38 B.C. Parthian warrior-prince. Army leader for his father, King Orodes II; invaded Syria (51–50); assisted Pompey's forces at Apamea (45); defeated and slain in Syria by Publius Ventidius for support of Quintus Labienus.

Pacorus II. *Parthian* Pkwr II. 1st–2nd century A.D. King (78–c.116) of Parthia. Reign filled with rebellions and counterkings; sold (110) client kingdom of Osroëne to Abgar VII.

Pa·cu·vi·us \pə-'k(y)ü-vē-əs\, Marcus. 220–c.130 B.C. Roman playwright, poet, and painter. Nephew of Ennius; noted esp. for tragedies. Only fragments of his works are extant.

Pa·de·loup \päd-lü\, Antoine-Michel. 1685–1758. French bookbinder. Most famous member of a Parisian bookbinding family; known for his mosaics and dentelle borders.

Pa·de·rew·ski \päd-e-'ref-skē, *Angl* ,pad-ə-, -'rev-\, Ignacy Jan. 1860–1941. Polish pianist, composer, and statesman. Studied under Leschetizky; professional debut in Vienna (1887); established himself as interpreter of Schumann, Chopin, Liszt, and Beethoven. Composed an opera *Manru* (1901), a symphony in B minor, concertos, and many orchestral and piano pieces, including well known *Minuet in G.* During World War I devoted himself to the Polish cause; aided in organizing a "general committee of assistance for the victims of the war in Poland" (1914); toured U.S. raising funds by concerts for Polish relief. After war, went to Warsaw and formed coalition ministry, in which he was prime minister and minister of foreign affairs, and which held office for ten months (Jan.–Nov. 1919).

Pa·dil·la \pä-'thē(l)-yä\, Juan. 1500?–1542. Spanish Franciscan missionary. To New Spain (1528); accompanied Cortés into southern Mexico (1533) and Coronado into New Mexico (1540–41); established first missions in the Southwest; murdered by Indians.

Padilla, Juan de. 1490?–1521. Spanish revolutionist. Led uprising of the *Comuneros* against the government of Charles V (1520–21); defeated, captured, and executed at Villalar. His wife ¶María Pa·che·co \pä-'chā-kō\ (d. 1531) led rebellion after husband's death and defended Toledo (1521–22); took refuge in Portugal after fall of Toledo.

Pad·ma·sam·bha·va \'pəd-mə-səm-'bəv-ə\, *i.e.* born of the lotus. *Also called* Guru Rimpoche. 8th century A.D. Indian Buddhist scholar and monk. Introduced Tantric Buddhism to Tibet and established first Buddhist monastery there (749).

Padovanino, Il. See Alessandro VAROTARI.

Pae·o·ni·us \pē-'ō-nē-əs\. fl. 450–400 B.C. Greek sculptor. Chiefly known for his Nike (Victory), carved for Messenians and Naupactians and placed at Olympia as a trophy, discovered in 1875.

Pa·er \'pä-er\, Ferdinando. 1771–1839. Italian composer. Kapellmeister at Dresden (1802–07), at Paris (from 1807) to Napoléon; director, Théâtre Italien in Paris (1812–27). A principal composer of Italian opera buffa; among his 43 operas were *Camilla* (1799), *Sargino* (1803), *Leonora* (1804), *Agnese* (1809), *Le Maître de chapelle* (1821); also composed religious and chamber music and secular cantatas.

Paes \'pīsh\, Sidônio Bernardino Cardosa da Silva. 1872–1918. Portuguese politician. Active in republican movement; minister to Germany (1913–16); president of Portugal (1917–18); assassinated.

Paesiello. See PAISIELLO.

Paetus, Thrasea. See THRASEA PAETUS.

Pá·ez \'pä-ās\, José Antonio. 1790–1873. Venezuelan soldier and political leader. In War of Independence (1810–22), won victories over Spanish that were chiefly responsible for bringing Venezuela into new republic of Great Colombia; led revolt against Bolívar (1829) and became first president of new republic of Venezuela (1830); president and dictator (1831–46); led revolt, as leader of conservatives, against President Monagas (1847); captured and imprisoned (1847–50); in exile (1850–58); minister to U.S. (1860). Again proclaimed dictator (1861), but forced to resign (1863) and go into exile.

Páez Xa·ra·mil·lo \-kär-ä-'mē(l)-yō\, Pedro. 1564–1622. Spanish Jesuit missionary. Captured and enslaved by Turkish pirates (1589–96); known as second apostle of Ethiopia for his many conversions (from 1603) in that country; first European to visit Lake Tana, source of Blue Nile.

Pa·ga·ni·ni \,päg-ä-'nē-nē, *Angl* ,pag-ə-, ,päg-ə-\, Niccolò. 1782–1840. Italian composer and violinist. Toured Europe with great success (1798–1801, 1805 ff.); revolutionized violin technique with wide use of harmonics and pizzicato effects and new methods of fingering. Among his compositions were 6 violin concertos, 24 caprices, 12 sonatas for violin and guitar, and sets of variations for violin.

Pa·gan Min \pä-'gän-'min\. d. 1880. King of Burma (1846–53). Deposed (1846) his father, Tharrawaddy; defeated in Second Anglo-Burmese War (1852–53), losing Rangoon and Lower Burma to British; deposed (1853) by his brother Mindon Min.

Page \'pāj\, Sir Earle Christmas Grafton. 1880–1961. Australian politician. M.P. (1919–61); held cabinet positions for 30 years; leader of Country party (1920–39); formed coalition (1923–29) with S.M. Bruce to lead government, their ministry noted for economic development; established the Australian Agricultural Council (1934); first chancellor (from 1955) of U. of New England.

Page, Frederick Handley. 1885–1962. English airplane manufacturer. Founded (1909) first British aircraft manufacturing firm, Handley Page, Ltd.; designed (1915) first twin-engine bomber, Handley Page 0/400.

Page, Thomas Jefferson. 1808–1899. American naval officer, b. Matthews Co., Va. Commanded *Water-Witch* in exploration of Plata River (1853–55); fired on by Paraguayan fort (1855); agitated for and second in command under W.B. Shubrick of punitive expedition (1858–59). In Confederate navy (1861–65); commanded *Stonewall.*

Page, Thomas Nelson. 1853–1922. American novelist and diplomat, b. Hanover Co., Va. U.S. ambassador to Italy (1913–19). Among his books were *In Ole Virginia* (1887), *Two Little Confederates* (1888), *The Old South* (1892), *Social Life in Old Virginia* (1897), *The Old Gentleman of the Black Stock* (1897), *Red Rock* (1898), *The Old Dominion* (1908), *Robert E. Lee, Man and Soldier* (1911).

Page, Walter Hines. 1855–1918. American journalist and diplomat, b. Cary, N.C. On staff of the *Forum* (1887–95), *Atlantic Monthly* (1895–98), of which he was editor (1898–99); partner in Doubleday, Page & Co., publishers (from 1900); founded and edited *The World's Work* (1900–13). As ambassador to Great Britain (1913–18) urged U.S. intervention in World War I. Author of *The Rebuilding of Old Commonwealths* (1902), *A Publisher's Confession* (1905), and *The Southerner* (1909), a novel published under the pseudonym Nicholas Worth \'wərth\.

Page, William. 1811–1885. American portrait painter, b. Albany, N.Y. Trained by Samuel F. B. Morse; while in Rome (1849–60) painted portraits of the Brownings; known esp. for *Self-Portrait* (1860) and *Portrait of Mrs. William Page* (1860–61).

Pag·et \'paj-ət\, Sir Henry William. 1st Marquis of An·gle·sey \'aŋ-gəl-sē\. 1768–1854. English military commander. Served in Flanders (1794), Holland (1799), Peninsula (1808); commanded cavalry and lost leg at Waterloo; M.P. (1790–1810); lord lieutenant of Ireland (1828–29, 1830–33); favored Catholic emancipation; opposed by O'Connell; field marshal (1846). His son ¶Lord George Augustus Frederick (1818–1880) served brilliantly in Crimean War; commanded third line in famous cavalry charge at Balaklava; general (1877); author of *Crimean Journals* (1875). The marquis's nephew ¶Sir Augustus Berkeley Paget (1823–1896) was a diplomat; held posts throughout Europe; envoy extraordinary (1867–76), ambassador (1876–83), to King Victor Emmanuel; ambassador at Vienna (1884–93).

Paget, Sir James. 1814–1899. English surgeon and pathologist. At St. Bartholomew's hospital, London, discovered (1834) *Trichinella spiralis,* the cause of trichinosis; professor of anatomy at Royal Coll. of Surgeons (1847–52); published *Lectures on Surgical Pathology* (1853); specialized in pathology of tumors and diseases of bones and joints; first to advocate enucleation of tumors; described (1877) *osteitis deformans,* later called Paget's disease; vice chancellor of U. of London (1883–95). Successor to John Hunter in surgery and, with Rudolf Virchow, one of founders of modern science of pathology.

Paget, Violet. *Pseudonym* Vernon Lee \'lē\. 1856–1935. English essayist and art critic. Lived in Italy (from 1871); author of essays, philosophic dialogues, stories, novels, including *Studies of the Eighteenth Century in Italy* (1880), *Limbo* (essays, 1897), *Ariadne in Mantua* (a play, 1903), *Satan the Waster* (1920), *Music and its Lovers* (1932).

Paget, William. 1st Baron Paget of Beau·de·sert \,bō-də-'za(ə)r\. 1505–1563. English statesman. Sent on diplomatic missions by Henry VIII; privy councilor and secretary of state (1543) and one of Henry's chief advisers; committed to Tower, with Somerset, on charge of conspiring against Warwick's life (1551); degraded from Order of Garter (1552) ostensibly because of discovery of low birth; restored to privy council by Queen Mary (1553); lord privy seal (1556–58).

Paglia, Antonio della. See PALEARIO.

Pag·ni·nus \päg-'nē-nəs\ *or* **Pa·gni·ni** \pän-'yē-nē\ *or* **Pa·gni·no** \-nō\, Santes. 1470–1536. Italian scholar. Entered Dominican order (1487); a disciple of Savonarola; published (1528) a Latin translation of the Bible, the first to divide chapters into numbered verses, which influenced later 16th-century scriptural translators.

Pa·gnol \pȧn-yȯl\, Marcel. 1895–1974. French playwright and film director. Best known for his film trilogy of the Marseille waterfront: *Marius* (1931), *Fanny* (1932), and *César* (1936).

Pahlavi. See Reza Shah Pahlavi; Mohammad Reza Pahlavi.

Paige \'pāj\, Leroy Robert, *Called* Satch·el \'sach-əl\. 1906–1982. American baseball player, b. Mobile, Ala. Pitcher in Negro leagues (1924–47), barnstorming throughout U.S., the Caribbean, and Central America; gained legendary status for pitching feats, reportedly winning 104 of 105 games in 1934 and pitching 55 career no-hitters. Pitcher for Cleveland Indians (1948–49), St. Louis Browns (1951–53), and Kansas City Athletics (1965), winning 28 games and losing 31; elected to Baseball Hall of Fame (1971).

Pail·le·ron \pȧy-rō^{n}\, Édouard. 1834–1899. French playwright and poet. Among his best plays were *Le Monde où l'on s'amuse* (1868), *L'Âge ingrat* (1878), *L'Étincelle* (1879), and *Le Monde où l'on s'ennuie* (1881).

Paine \'pān\, Albert Bigelow. 1861–1937. American author and editor, b. New Bedford, Mass. Friend and literary executor of Mark Twain; author of *The Mystery of Evelin Delorme* (1894), *The Autobiography of a Monkey* (1897), *The Commuters* (1904), *Mark Twain, a Biography* (1912), etc.

Paine, John Knowles. 1839–1906. American organist, music teacher, and composer, b. Portland, Me. Teacher of music, Harvard (1862–1906, professor from 1875); first professor of music in an American university; composer of oratorios, symphonies, cantatas, songs, chamber music, organ pieces.

Paine, Robert Treat. 1731–1814. American jurist, b. Boston. Member of Continental Congress (1774–78) and signer of Declaration of Independence; first attorney general of Massachusetts (1777–90); judge, Massachusetts supreme court (1790–1804); a founder (1780) of the American Academy of Arts and Sciences. His son ¶Robert Treat (1773–1811) was a poet; founded and edited *Federal Orrery* (1794–96), in which his satirical attacks on personages of the day brought social ostracism and physical attacks; best known poems were *The Invention of Letters* (1795), *The Ruling Passion* (1797), *Adams and Liberty* (1798).

Paine, Thomas. 1737–1809. American political philosopher and author, b. Thetford, England. After various occupations went bankrupt (1774) and emigrated to America; published *Common Sense* (1776), a 47-page pamphlet urging immediate declaration of independence, which had wide circulation and great influence; served in Continental army (1776); during Revolutionary War published 16 numbers of *Crisis,* a periodical upholding the colonial cause (1776–83); secretary to Congress's committee on foreign affairs (1777–79); clerk of Pennsylvania assembly (1779–81). To England (1787); wrote *The Rights of Man* (1791–92), defending revolutionary France and appealing to the English to overthrow their monarchy and organize a republic; tried, convicted of treason, and outlawed from England (1792); member of French Convention (1792–93); arrested and imprisoned in Paris as an Englishman (1793–1794); released on request of American minister, James Monroe, who said Paine was an American citizen; remained in Paris, writing and studying (to 1802); published *The Age of Reason* (Part I, 1794; Part II, 1796), a philosophical discussion of his deist belief. Returned to America (1802); lived last years in ostracism and poverty.

Pain·le·vé \pa^{n}l-vā\, Paul. 1863–1933. French mathematician and politician. Member of Chamber of Deputies (from 1910); minister of public instruction (1915–16), of war (1917), and premier of France (1917); president of Chamber of Deputies (1924) and unsuccessful candidate for presidency of France; again premier (1925); minister of war (1925–29) and of air (1930–32). Also known as a patron of French aviation.

Pain·ter \'pānt-ər\, William. 1540?–1594. English translator. Published *The Palace of Pleasure* (1566), a collection of tales translated from Boccaccio, Bandello, Cynthius, and other Italian and classical authors, freely used by Elizabethan dramatists.

Pais \'pīs\, Ettore. 1856–1939. Italian historian. Disciple of Theodor Mommsen; professor at Palermo, Pisa, Naples, and (1906–31) Rome; author of *Storia di Roma,* a multi-volume history of the ancient Roman republic (1898–1931).

Pa·i·siel·lo \ˌpä-ē-zē-'yel-lō\ *or* **Pa·e·siel·lo** \ˌpä-äz-\, Giovanni. 1740–1816. Italian composer. Called to St. Petersburg by Catherine the Great (1776–84); Kapellmeister to Ferdinand IV in Vienna (1784); called to Paris (1802) by Napoléon to organize chapel music; returned to Naples (1804) under patronage of Joseph Bonaparte and Murat. Among operas were *Il Barbiere di Siviglia* (1782), *Il Re Teodoro* (1784), *Le Gare generose* (1786), *La Molinara* (1788), and *Nina* (1789); also composed oratorios, masses, cantatas, symphonies, piano concertos, chamber music, etc.

Paisley, Baron. See Claud Hamilton, under Hamilton family.

Paix·hans \pek-sä^{n}\, Henri-Joseph. 1783–1854. French artillery officer. General of division (1848); inventor of the Paixhans gun, one of earliest guns throwing explosive shells.

Pa·jol \pȧ-zhȯl\, Claude-Pierre. Comte. 1772–1844. French general. Won distinction in battles of Austerlitz, Jena, and Wagram, and in Russian campaign; general of division (1812) and engaged at Lützen, Dresden, and Leipzig; rallied to Napoléon during the Hundred Days; engaged at Waterloo; took active part in Revolution of 1830; appointed peer of France and governor of Paris by Louis-Philippe.

Pa·jou \pȧ-zhü\, Augustin. 1730–1809. French sculptor. Under commission from Louis XVI, carved decorations for façades of Palais Royal and Palais Bourbon and decorated the opera house at Versailles; executed portrait busts of Descartes, Turenne, Pascal, Bossuet, Buffon, and other notables. His *Psyché* stands in the Louvre.

Pak·en·ham \'pak-ən-əm\, Sir Edward Michael. 1778–1815. British soldier, b. Ireland. Served with Wellington in the Peninsular War; distinguished himself at Salamanca (1812); defeated by Andrew Jackson and killed in attack upon New Orleans (1815).

Pal \'pal\, Bipin Chandra. 1858–1932. Indian journalist. An early leader of the Indian nationalist movement; in newspaper articles and speaking tours (1912–20) popularized concepts of *swadeshi* (exclusive use of Indian-made goods) and *swarāj* (Indian self-rule).

Pa·la·cio Val·dés \pä-'läth-yō-väl-'dās\, Armando. 1853–1938. Spanish novelist. Edited *La Revista Europea* (1875–78); known esp. for psychological and naturalistic novels as *El Señorito Octavio* (1881), *Marta y María* (1883), *José* (1885), *Riverita* (1886), *Maximina* (1887), *La hermana San Sulpicio* (1889), *La fe* (1892), *La aldea perdida* (1903), *Tristán o el pesimismo* (1906), *Los papeles del Doctor Angélico* (1911), and *La novela de un novelista* (1921).

Pa·lac·ký \'pȧ-lats-kē\, František. 1798–1876. Czech historian and politician. The founder of modern Czech historiography; chairman of Slavic congress at Prague (1848); deputy in first Austrian Reichstag; sought creation of an autonomous Czech nation to include Bohemia, Moravia, and Silesia; member of Austrian Herrenhaus (from 1861); chief works, *Geschichte von Böhmen* (1836–67) and *Dějiny národu českého* (1848–76).

Pa·lae·ol·o·gus \ˌpā-lē-'äl-ə-gəs, ˌpal-ē-\. *Plural* Pa·lae·ol·o·gi \-ˌjī\. Name of a (Greek) Byzantine family which furnished the last eight emperors of the Eastern Roman Empire (1259–1453): Michael VIII, Andronicus II and III, John V, VII, and VIII, Manuel II, and Constantine XI (*qq.v.*). Branch families of the Palaeologi ruled in the Italian marquisate of Montferrat (1305–1533) and in the Morea (1383–1460).

Pa·la·fox y Men·do·za \ˌpäl-ä-'fȯks-y-mān-'dō-thä\, Juan de. 1600–1659. Spanish prelate. To Mexico (1610); appointed bishop of Puebla de los Ángeles, Mexico (1639); viceroy (1642); pursued charitable policy toward Indians; laid Jesuits under interdict (1647); transferred to bishopric of Osma, Castile (1653). Author of historical, judicial, and theological works.

Palafox y Mel·zi \-ē-'mel-thē\, José Re·bol·le·do de \rā-b̲ō(l)-'yā-t̲h̲ō-t̲h̲ā\. Duque de Sar·a·gos·sa \ˌsar-ə-'gäs-ə\. 1775–1847. Spanish soldier. Known particularly for his defense of Saragossa in Peninsular War (1808–09); captain general of Aragon (1841 ff.); ardent defender of absolutism under Ferdinand VII; created duke of Saragossa and grandee of Spain (1836).

Pal·a·mas \'pal-ə-məs, päl-ä-'mäs\, Gregory. Saint. 1296–1359. Greek Orthodox monk and theologian. Entered monastery at Mt. Athos (1316); ordained priest (1326); chief defender (from 1332) of Hesychasm, esp. against Barlaam the Calabrian; archbishop of Thessalonica (1347); proclaimed saint and titled "Father and Doctor of the Orthodox Church" (1368).

Pa·la·mas \päl-ä-'mäs\, Kostis. 1859–1943. Greek poet. Supporter of demotic movement of late 19th-century; author of *Asalefti zoï* (1904), *Dodekalogos tou gyftou* (1907), *Parakaira* (1919), *Vradini fotia* (1946), play *Trisevgeni* (1903), etc.

Pa·lan·der \pȧ-'lȧn-dər\, Louis. 1842–1920. Swedish naval officer and explorer. Knighted and took name Palander af Ve·ga \-äv-'vā-ˌgȧ\ because he commanded ship *Vega* on Nordenskiöld's expedition (1878–80) to discover Northeast Passage; admiral (1910).

Pa·la·prat \pȧ-lȧ-prȧ\, Jean. 1650–1721. French playwright. Coauthor of comedies with David-Augustin de Brueys (*q.v.*).

Pa·le·a·rio \ˌpä-lā-'är-yō\, Aonio. *Also known as* Antonio del·la Pa·glia \ˌdāl-lä-'päl-yä\. *Lat.* Aonius Pal·e·ar·i·us \ˌpal-ē-'ar-ē-əs, ˌpā-lē-, -'er-\. 1503?–1570. Italian Humanist. Author of works branded as heretical; objected chiefly to doctrine of purgatory; after two previous trials for heresy, seized by Inquisition; imprisoned for three years and burned at stake. His works included didactic poem *De immortalitate animorum* (1536) and tracts.

Pa·lé·o·logue \pȧ-lā-ȯ-lȯg\, Maurice. 1859–1944. French diplomat. Minister to Bulgaria (1907–12); ambassador to Russia (1914–17); director general of French foreign office (1921–25). Author of *La Russie des Tsars pendant la Grande Guerre* (1921) and *Un Grand Réaliste* (biography of Cavour, 1926).

Pa·lés Ma·tos \pä-'lāz-'mä-tōs\, Luis. 1898–1959. Puerto Rican lyric poet, b. Guayama. After publishing Modernist poems in *Azaleas* (1915), turned to African and Afro-American themes and language for *Tuntún de pasa y grifería* (1937) and *Poesía, 1915–56* (1957).

Pa·le·stri·na \ˌpä-lā-'strē-nä, *Angl* ˌpal-ə-'strē-nə\, Giovanni Pierluigi da. c.1525–1594. Italian composer, b. Palestrina. Protégé of Pope Julius III; maestro di cappella, Cappella Giulia, Rome (1551), St. John Lateran (1555–60), and

Santa Maria Maggiore (1561 ff.); composer to papal chapel (1565); master of music, Cappella Giulia (1571 ff.). Composed exclusively in medieval church modes; works marked apex of attainment in field of older music; compositions included masses as *Missa Papae Marcelli,* lamentations as *Lamentations of Jeremiah,* hymns as *Stabat Mater,* motets, litanies, Magnificats, and madrigals.

Pa·ley \'pā-lē\, William. 1743–1805. English theologian and utilitarian philosopher. Archdeacon of Carlisle (1782); subdean of Lincoln (1795); published lectures *The Principles of Moral and Political Philosophy* (1785), which became textbook at Cambridge; his most original essay, *Horae Paulinae* (1790), showed improbability of hypothesis that New Testament is a "cunningly devised fable"; author also of *View of the Evidences of Christianity* in refutation of the deists (1794), and *Natural Theology* (1802).

Pal·frey \'pòl-frē\, John Gorham. 1796–1881. American Unitarian clergyman and historian, b. Boston. Proprietor and editor, *North American Review* (1835–43); member, U.S. House of Representatives (1847–49); author of *History of New England* (1858–75).

Pal·grave \'pal-,grāv, 'pòl-\, Sir Francis. 1788–1861. English historian. Son of Meyer Cohen, a stockbroker in London; changed name by royal permission (1823); deputy keeper of public records (1838–61); author of *History of Normandy and England* (1851–64). His son ¶Francis Turner (1824–1897), poet and critic; friend of Tennyson, Browning, Arnold, and William Gladstone; official of education department (1855–84); professor of poetry, Oxford (1885–95); published volumes of poetry, including *Visions of England* (1880–81) and *Amenophis* (1892), critical essays, including *Landscape in Poetry* (1897); edited well known anthologies *Golden Treasury of the Best Songs and Lyrical Poems in the English Language* (1861, 1897) and *Treasury of Sacred Song* (1889). Another son ¶William Gifford (1826–1888), traveler and diplomat, became a Jesuit missionary in Syria and Arabia, often traveling in disguise as a Syrian doctor; held many posts through the Orient; minister to Uruguay (1884); author of travel narratives. Another son ¶Sir Robert Harry Inglis (1827–1919), banker and economist, edited *The Economist* (1877–83) and *Dictionary of Political Economy* (1894–99); author of books on banking and taxation.

Palikao, Comte de. See COUSIN-MONTAUBAN.

Pa·li·sa \päl-'ē-zä\, Johann. 1848–1925. Austrian astronomer. At Pola observatory (1872–80), Vienna observatory (1880–1919); discovered 121 minor planets, 83 visually; prepared several star catalogs (1899, 1902, 1908).

Pa·lis·sot de Mon·te·noy \pá-lē-sōd(-ə)-mōⁿ-tən-wá\, Charles. 1730–1814. French writer. Attacked the Encyclopedists, notably Rousseau and Diderot, in his comedies *Le Cercle* (1755) and *Les Philosophes* (1760) and his poem *La Dunciade ou la Guerre des sots* (1764).

Pa·lis·sy \pá-lē-sē\, Bernard. 1510–1589. French potter. Persecuted as a Protestant; known for his lead-glazed rustic ware, decorated with plants, animals, and mythological scenes; published lectures on natural history as *Discours admirables* (1580); *De l'art de la terre* (1580) contained a description of his investigations in ceramics.

Pa·litzsch \'päl-ich\, Johann Georg. 1723–1788. German amateur astronomer. First discovered Halley's comet (1758) and the periodic variability of the star Algol (1782).

Pa·liz·zi \pä-'lēt-sē\, Filippo. 1818–1899. Italian painter. Cofounder (with Domenico Morelli) of Neapolitan Naturalist school; known esp. for paintings of animals.

Pal·la·dio \pä-'läd-yō\, Andrea. *Orig.* Andrea di Pietro della Gon·do·la \'gōn-dō-lä\. 1508–1580. Italian architect. Adapted principles of Roman architecture, esp. use of temple front as a portico; revolted against ornamentation; responsible for popularity of Palladian motif of the bay with a round-headed opening flanked by two square-headed openings. Works included, in Venice, San Giorgio Maggiore and Il Redentore churches, and palaces on Grand Canal. Published *Le antichità di Roma* (1554) and *I quattro libri dell' architettura* (1570).

Pal·la·di·us \pə-'lā-dē-əs\. c.363–before 431. Greek prelate and writer. Bishop (400) of Helenopolis and (417) of Aspuna; defended (from 400) mentor St. John Chrysostom, esp. with *Dialogus de vita Sancti Joannis Chrysostomi* (406–408); his *Historia Lausiaca* (419–420), dedicated to Lausus, chamberlain of Theodosius II, is most valuable single source for origins of Christian asceticism.

Palladius, Rutilius Taurus Aemilianus. 4th–5th century A.D. Roman writer. Author of a calendar of Roman agriculture, *De re rustica,* widely read in the Middle Ages.

Pal·las \'päl-,äs\, Peter Simon. 1741–1811. German naturalist. Professor, St. Petersburg (from 1768); collected fossils on scientific expedition (1768–74) in Russia and Siberia; published findings in *Reise durch verschiedene Provinzen des russichen Reichs* (1771–76); advanced (1777) a theory of mountain formation based on temporal sequence of rocks from the center to flanks of a range; important contributor to botany, zoology, geography, palaeography, ethnography and philology.

Pal·la·va \'pəl-lə-və\. A warrior dynasty of Hindu kings, of uncertain origin, ruling (300?–888 A.D.) in the Tamil country of southern India; used both Prākrit and Sanskrit languages; capital at Kanchi (modern Conjeeveram), near Madras; overcame Cholas and Cheras; height of their power (550–750); disputed control of Deccan with Chalukyas for more than two centuries; made great contributions to art and architecture; two greatest rulers were Chitrasena (*q.v.*) and Narasimhavarman I Mahāmalla (reigned c.630–668); defeated (740) and declined; completely overthrown by Chalukyas and Cholas (end of 9th century); especially important for their voyages to and settlements in Malay lands.

Pal·la·vi·ci·no \,päl-lä-vē-'chē-nō\, Pietro Sforza. 1607–1667. Italian prelate and writer. Joined Society of Jesus (1637); cardinal (1659); known esp. for *Istoria del concilio di Trento* (1656–57), written to refute the history by Fra Paolo Sarpi which had been placed on the Index.

Pal·len \'pal-ən\, Condé Benoist. 1858–1929. American editor, b. St. Louis. A projector and (1904–13) managing editor, *Catholic Encyclopedia;* author of *The Philosophy of Literature* (1897), *Death of Sir Launcelot and Other Poems* (1902), *Ghost House* (1928), etc.

Pal·li·ser \'pal-ə-sər\, John. 1807–1887. Canadian geographer and explorer, b. Ireland. Explored (from 1847) western British America; made topographical determination of boundary between U.S. and Canada from Lake Superior to Pacific Coast. His brother ¶Sir William (1830–1882), British cavalry officer, invented method of converting smooth bores into rifled guns (1862); invented chilled cast-iron shot (1863).

Palm \'pälm\, Johann Philipp. 1768–1806. German bookdealer. Published (1806) pamphlet *Deutschland in seiner tiefen Erniedrigung* (by an unknown author) attacking Napoléon and conduct of French army in Germany; arrested by order of Napoléon, tried by military court, and shot.

Pal·ma \'päl-mä\, Jacopo. *Orig.* Jacopo Ne·gre·ti \nā-'grā-tē\. *Called* Palma Vec·chio \'vāk-kyō\ *or* Il Vecchio \ēl-\, *i.e.* the Elder. c.1480–1528. Italian painter of Venetian school. Specialized in contemplative religious pictures called *sacra conversazione;* among his works were the *Sta. Barbara Altarpiece* in Venice and *Three Sisters;* many of his paintings were finished by his pupils after his death. His grandnephew ¶Jacopo (1544–1628), *called* Palma Gio·va·ne \-'jō-vä-nā\ *or* Il Giovane \ēl-\, *i.e.* the Younger, was also a Venetian painter; among his works were *Resurrection of Lazarus, The Brazen Serpent,* and 27 engravings.

Palma, Ricardo. 1833–1919. Peruvian writer. Director, National Library (1884–1910); known esp. for multi-volumed *Tradiciones peruanas* (1872–1910), prose sketches blending colonial Peruvian fact and fiction; also wrote *Anales de la inquisición de Lima* (1863) and several volumes of poems.

Palma, Tomás Estrada. See ESTRADA PALMA.

Palmela, Duque de. See SOUSA HOLSTEIN.

Pal·mer \'päm-ər, 'päl-mər\, Alexander Mitchell. 1872–1936. American politician, b. Moosehead, Pa. Member, U.S. House of Representatives (1909–15); alien property custodian (1917–19); as attorney general of the U.S. (1919–21) led government attack on radicals during "Red Scare" period.

Palmer, Alice Elvira, *nee* Free·man \'frē-mən\. 1855–1902. American educator, b. Colesville, N.Y. m. (1887) George Herbert Palmer. Professor of history, Wellesley Coll. (1879–82); president, Wellesley (1882–88); dean of women, U. of Chicago (1892–95).

Palmer, Austin Norman. 1859–1927. American penman and educator. Originated Palmer method of handwriting taught widely in American schools.

Palmer, Charles Skeele. 1858–1939. American chemist, b. Danville, Ill. Invented basic process for cracking oils to obtain gasoline (1900).

Palmer, Daniel David. 1845–1913. American founder of chiropractic, b. near Toronto. Practiced magnetic healing, Burlington (1883–95) and Davenport, Iowa (1895); developed system of adjusting the joints and esp. the spine by manual manipulation for the cure of disease; opened (1898) Palmer School of Chiropractic in Davenport. Author of *Textbook of the Science, Art and Philosophy of Chiropractic* (1910), *The Chiropractor* (1914).

Palmer, Edward Henry. 1840–1882. English Orientalist. Professor of Arabic, Cambridge (1871–81); during Egyptian rebellion (1882) sent by Gladstone on goodwill mission among Arabs; interpreter in chief to force in Egypt; ambushed and murdered by Arab robbers. Author of *Oriental Mysticism* (1867), *The Desert of the Exodus* (1871), *The Song of the Reed and Other Pieces* (1877), etc.

Palmer, Erastus Dow. 1817–1904. American sculptor, b. Pompey, N.Y. Among his works were *Indian Girl* and *White Captive* and portrait busts of Washington Irving, Erastus Corning, Henry Burden, etc.

Palmer, George Herbert. 1842–1933. American scholar and educator, b. Boston. m. (1887) Alice E. Freeman. Teacher at Harvard of Greek (1870–72), philosophy (from 1872); professor (1883–1913). Author of *The Odyssey of Homer* (translation, 1884), *The Antigone of Sophocles* (1899), *The Field of Ethics* (1901), *The Nature of Goodness* (1903), *The Life of Alice Freeman Palmer* (1908), *The Problem of Freedom* (1911), *Autobiography of a Philosopher* (1930), etc.

Palmer, Horatio Richmond. 1834–1907. American composer and music director, b. Sherburne, N.Y. Dean of School of Music at Chautauqua, N.Y. (1877–91); composer of church music, esp. hymns; author of words and music for "Yield not to temptation," "Galilee, blue Galilee," and music for "Just for Today," etc.

Palmer, James Shedden. 1810–1867. American naval officer, b. New Jersey. During Civil War, in command of *Iroquois* under Farragut in passing Vicksburg batteries (June 1862) and of Farragut's flagship *Hartford* in passing Port Hudson (Mar. 1863); rear admiral (1866).

Palmer, John McCauley. 1817–1900. American politician, b. Scott Co., Ky. Served through Civil War; major general (1862); governor of Illinois (1869–73); U.S. senator (1891–97); presidential candidate of Gold Democrats (1896).

Palmer, Potter. 1826–1902. American merchant, b. Albany Co., N.Y. Operated (1852–67) Chicago drygoods store (forerunner of Marshall Field & Co.) employing "Palmer system" of merchandising; built up State Street and other parts of Chicago (1870 ff.); built Palmer House hotel.

Palmer, Roger. Earl of Cas·tle·maine \ˌkás-əl-ˈmān, *US usu* ˌkas-\. 1634–1705. English Royalist and Roman Catholic pamphleteer. m. (1659) Barbara Villiers; accused of complicity in Popish Plot; member of James II's secret council; exempted from Act of Indemnity, escaped to Continent.

Palmer, Roundell. 1st Earl of Sel·borne \ˈsel-ˌbȯrn, -bərn\. 1812–1895. English jurist. M.P. (1847–52, 1853–57, 1861–72); solicitor general (1861); attorney general (1863–65); opposed Gladstone's Irish church policy; lord chancellor (1872–74, 1880–85); author of the Supreme Court of Judicature Act of 1873, which established a single hierarchy of courts; edited a hymnal, *The Book of Praise* (1863). Created earl (1882). His son ¶William Waldegrave (1859–1942), 2d earl, Viscount Wol·mer \ˈwu̇l-mər\; M.P. (1885–95); undersecretary for colonies (1895–1900); as 1st lord of admiralty (1900–05) helped modernize navy; as high commissioner for South Africa and governor of Transvaal and Orange River colonies (1905–10), facilitated reconstruction requisite for setting up responsible government in those colonies; uncompromising opponent of Parliament Bill; minister of agriculture (1915–16), resigned because of Asquith's policy of compromise with Irish.

Palmer, Samuel. 1805–1881. English landscape painter and etcher. Influenced by William Blake, as in *Repose of the Holy Family* (1824–25) and series of sepia drawings (1825) in Ashmolean Museum, Oxford; known for his illustrations of *L'Allegro* and *Il Penseroso.*

Palmer, Timothy. 1751–1821. American bridge builder, b. Newburyport, Mass. A pioneer builder of covered timber truss bridges, esp. with his Permanent Bridge (c.1806) over Schuylkill River, Philadelphia.

Palmer, Vance, *in full* Edward Vance. 1885–1959. Australian writer. Helped organize (1922–26) the Pioneer Players theatrical company in Melbourne; author of novels as *The Passage* (1930) and the political trilogy *Golconda* (1948), *Seedtime* (1957), and *The Big Fellow* (1959); short-story collections *Separate Lives* (1931), *Sea and Spinifex* (1934), *Let the Birds Fly* (1955), *The Rainbow Bird* (1956); ballad-like poetry as *The Forerunners* (1915); political plays; essays, etc.

Palmerston, Lord. See Henry John TEMPLE.

Palm·gren \ˈpälm-ˌgrān\, Selim. 1878–1951. Finnish pianist and composer. Conductor, Åbo Music Society (1909–12); professor, Eastman School of Music, Rochester, N.Y. (1923–26), Sibelius Academy, Helsinki (1939–51). Composed operas *Daniel Hjort* (1910) and *Peter Schlemihl,* symphonic poem *Floden,* 5 piano concertos, and many piano pieces, esp. *Finnische Lyrik.*

Pal·mie·ri \päl-ˈmyer-ē\, Luigi. 1807–1896. Italian physicist. Inventor of the mercury tube seismograph (1855), a rain gauge, an electrometer, etc.

Pa·lo·mi·no de Cas·tro y Ve·las·co \päl-ō-ˈmē-nō-thā-ˈkäs-trō-ē-bā-ˈläs-kō\, Antonio. 1655–1726. Spanish painter. Court painter at Madrid (1688 ff.). Paintings included frescoes in churches of San Juan del Mercado and Nuestra Señora de los Desamparados at Valencia. Known esp. for *El museo pictórico y escala óptica* (1715–24), containing a history and theory of Spanish painting and a biographical dictionary of Spanish artists.

Pa·lóu \pä-ˈlō-ü\, Francisco. 1722–1789. Spanish missionary. Entered Franciscan order (1739); ordained (1747). Accompanied Junípero Serra to Mexico (1749); with Serra, headed Franciscan group that replaced Jesuits in Lower California (1767); went northward (1773); set boundary stone between Lower and Upper California, used (1848) to fix boundary between U.S. and Mexico; explored San Francisco peninsula and founded (1776) mission still standing in heart of San Francisco. Author of a chronicle of the Franciscans in California *Noticias de la Nueva California* (1774) and *Relación histórica de la vida y apostólicas tareas del venerable padre Fray Junípero Serra* (1787).

Pals·grave \ˈpalz-ˌgrāv, ˈpȯlz-\, John. 1480?–1554. English grammarian. Author of one of earliest French grammars for English use, *Lesclarcissement de la langue Francoyse* (1530).

Pal·tock \ˈpȯl-tək\, Robert. 1697–1767. English attorney. Author of the utopian romance *The Life and Adventures of Peter Wilkins, a Cornish Man* (1751).

Pa·lu·dan-Mül·ler \ˈpá-lu̇-dán-ˈmu̅e̅-lər\, Frederik. 1809–1876. Danish poet. Achieved fame with Byronic epic *Danserinden* (1833); became a moralist and critic of Romanticism; other works included *Amor og Psyche* (1834), *Venus* (1841), and esp. the satirical epic *Adam Homo* (1841–48).

Pam·pa \ˈpäm-pä\. *Also called* Ādipampa, Nadoja, Jha, Oja, Ojha, Ovaja, Upadhayaya. fl. 940. Indian poet. Called *ādikavi* (first poet) in the Kanarese language; author of the epics *Ādipurāna,* in which the Jaina faith is expounded, and the *Pampa-Bhārata* (c.950), in which his patron Arikēsarī was likened to the hero of the *Mahābhārata.*

Pamphili, Eusebius. See EUSEBIUS of Caesarea.

Pam·phi·lus \ˈpam-fə-ləs\. fl. c.390–350 B.C. Greek painter. Succeeded Eupompus as head of Sicyonian school; teacher of Apelles and Melanthus; said to have been first to base the teaching of art on scientific principles.

Pamphilus. 1st century A.D. Greek grammarian and lexicographer. Prepared in collaboration with Zo·pyr·i·on \zō-ˈpir-ē-ən\ a Greek lexicon (95 books, all now lost), an epitome of which, by Diogenianus, is extant.

Pamphilus of Caes·a·rea \ˌsē-zə-ˈrē-ə; ˌses-ə-, ˌsez-\. d. 310. Christian writer and teacher. Reopened a school founded by Origen at Caesarea; imprisoned (307–309) during persecution under Emperor Maximinus and martyred. Collaborated with Eusebius of Caesarea (*q.v.*) in edition of the Septuagint from text in Origen's *Hexapla;* wrote an apology for Origen (5 books, now lost).

Pa·nae·ti·us \pə-ˈnē-sh(ē-)əs\. c.180–109 B.C. Rhodian Greek Stoic philosopher. Studied under Diogenes; taught in Athens and Rome; friend of Laelius and the younger Scipio; succeeded Antipater of Tarsus as head of the Stoa in Athens (129).

Pan Chao and **Pan Ch'ao.** See under PAN PIAO.

Panc·koucke \päⁿ-ku̇k\. Family of French booksellers and writers, including: André-Joseph (1700–1753), who founded the business in his native city, Lille. His son ¶Charles-Joseph (1736–1798), who established the business in Paris, bought and directed the *Mercure de France* (with his brother-in-law J.B.A. Suard), founded (1789) *Moniteur.*

Pan·cras \ˈpaŋ-krəs\. Saint. *Lat.* Pan·cra·tius \pan-ˈkrā-sh(ē-)əs, paŋ-\. c.290–304. Christian martyr. Suffered martyrdom at Rome in reign of Diocletian; later regarded as patron saint of children.

Pan·der \ˈpän-dər\, Christian Heinrich. 1794–1865. German anatomist. Regarded as a founder of science of embryology; discovered (1817) the trilaminar structure of the chick blastoderm; a coworker of Karl Ernst von Baer.

Pan·do \ˈpän-dō\, José Manuel. 1848–1917. Bolivian soldier and political leader. Head of revolt (1898); president of Bolivia (1899–1904); settled boundary disputes with Brazil and Chile.

Pan·do Fer·nán·dez de Pi·ne·da \ˈpän-dō-fer-ˈnän-dāth-thā-pē-ˈnā-thä\, Manuel. Marqués de Mi·ra·flo·res \mē-rä-ˈflō-rās\. 1792–1872. Spanish statesman. Ambassador in London (1834) and Paris (1838–40); premier of Spain (1846, 1863–64); author of works on contemporary Spanish history.

Pan·dulph *or* **Pan·dulf** \ˈpan-(ˌ)dəlf\ *or* **Pan·dol·pho** \pan-ˈdȯl-fō\. d. 1226. Roman papal envoy to England. Excommunicated King John (1211); received King John's submission (1213), supported him during baronial rebellion, and helped avert invasion from France; elected bishop of Norwich (1216); exercised practically royal authority in England during minority of Henry III (1219–21).

Pandulph III. c.987–1049. Prince of Capua. Dethroned and imprisoned (1022) by Henry II for aiding Byzantine invasion of south Italy; recaptured Capua (1026); fled (1036) to Constantinople from invasion of Conrad II; returned (1041) and restored (1045) to Capuan throne by Henry III; died during war with Gaimar of Salerno.

Pandulph Ironhead. d. 981. Prince of Capua and Benevento. Co-ruler with his father Landulph II (944–961) and with his brother Landulph III (from 961); faithful supporter (from 963) of Otto I, who gave him duchy of Spoleto (967); annexed Salerno (977), thus uniting Lombard states.

Pan·du·ran·ga \ˌpən-du̇-ˈrəŋ-gə\, Ramchandra. *Known as* Tan·tia To·pi \ˈtan-tē-ə-ˈtō-pē\ *or* Tat·ya To·pe \ˈtät-yə-ˈtō-pā\. c.1819–1859. Indian rebel. A leader of Indian Mutiny of 1857–58; a Marāthā Brahmin in service of Bājī Rāo and Nana Sahib; present at Nana Sahib's massacre of British colony at Cawnpore (1857); led Gwalior contingent that defeated Gen. C. A. Windham's forces at Cawnpore (Nov. 1857) but was routed by Sir Colin Campbell a few days later; joined forces with rani of Jhansi (1858); defeated at siege of Jhansi by Sir Hugh Rose (1858); fled to jungles of Rajputana; captured and hanged.

Pāṇ·dya \ˈpän-dyə\. An early Hindu (Tamil) dynasty ruling (from c.4th century B.C.) in extreme south of India (modern Madura); became Śaivas and were celebrated in the earliest Tamil poetry; carried on trade with Romans at beginning of Christian Era; the "Five Pāṇḍyas" flourished 12th to 14th centuries and ruled from Nellore to plains of extreme south; succeeded by Cōlas and Cēras but retained control of small kingdom until overthrown by Muslims (1304 A.D.), thus boasting continuous succession for more than 2000 years.

Pa·neth \'pän-ət\, Friedrich Adolf. 1887–1958. Austrian chemist. Professor at Berlin (1922), Königsberg (1929), Durham (1939); director of Max-Planck-Institut, Mainz (1953–58). With George de Hevesy introduced radioactive tracer techniques (1912–13); prepared bismuth, lead, and polonium hydrides with radioactive isotopes (1918–22); proved existence of methyl and ethyl free radicals (1922–35); determined the composition of the stratosphere as a function of altitude up to 45 miles; developed methods for dating rocks and meteorites by helium content.

Pan·ga·los \'päŋ-gä-ˌlȯs\, Theodoros. 1878–1952. Greek soldier and politician. Commander in chief of army in Thrace (1923); seized power as dictator (1925–26); proclaimed president of Republic of Greece (1926); overthrown (1926) and imprisoned (1926–28).

Pan·hard \pän-är\, René. 1841–1908. French automotive engineer. With Levassor built first vehicle with an internal combustion engine mounted at front of the chassis, rather than under the driver's seat (1891–92); founder and director of firm of Panhard and Levassor, an early automobile manufactory.

Pa·nik·kar \'pän-(y)ək-ˌkär\, Kavalam Madhava. 1895–1963. Indian statesman and author. Ambassador to China (1948–52), Egypt (1952–53), France (1956–59); wrote *Asia and Western Dominance* (1953), *In Two Chinas* (1955), plays, and novels.

Pa·nin \'pän-yin\. Russian noble family, including: Count Nikita Ivanovich (1718–1783), ambassador to Denmark (1747) and Sweden (1748–60); as minister of foreign affairs under Catherine II (1763–81) urged alliance with Poland and developed concept of "Northern Accord." His brother ¶Count Pyotr Ivanovich (1721–1789), general, distinguished himself in Seven Years' War. Pyotr's son ¶Count Nikita Petrovich (1770–1837), minister to the Netherlands and later to Prussia, vice chancellor and foreign minister at beginning of Paul I's reign; banished (1804). The second Nikita's son ¶Count Viktor Nikitich (1801–1874), minister of justice (1841–62).

Pā·ni·ni \'pän-(y)ə-(ˌ)nē\. fl. c.400 B.C. Indian grammarian. Author of *Aṣṭādhyāyī,* the oldest Sanskrit grammar, and perhaps the oldest extant grammar in the world; systematized all preceding works; marked the line between Vedic and classical Sanskrit.

Pa·niz·zi \pä-'nēt-tsē\, Sir Anthony. *Orig.* Antonio Genesio Maria Panizzi. 1797–1879. British librarian, b. Italy. Implicated in conspiracy against Modenese government and escaped to England (1823). Assistant (1831) and chief (1856–66) librarian, British Museum, which he greatly improved, as by planning general catalogue and designing Reading Room. Edited Boiardo's *Orlando innamorato,* Ariosto's *Orlando furioso.*

Pankhi. See PIANKHI.

Pank·hurst \'paŋk-ˌhərst\, Emmeline, *nee* Goulden \'gül-dən\. 1858–1928. English suffragist. m. (1879) Richard Marsden Pankhurst (d. 1898), barrister, a radical and a woman-suffrage advocate, author of first woman-suffrage bill in Great Britain (late 1860s) and of the Married Women's Property acts (1870, 1882). Mrs. Pankhurst founded (1889) the Women's Franchise League, which secured (1894) for married women the right to vote for local offices; founder (1903) and director (from 1906), Women's Social and Political Union, which used (from 1912) extreme militancy to further its goals; lived to see full and equal suffrage given to men and women; wrote autobiography *My Own Story* (1914). She was supported by daughters ¶Christabel Harriette (1880–1958) and ¶Estelle Sylvia (1882–1960), who published biography of her mother (1935).

Pan Ku. See under PAN PIAO.

Pan·nartz \'pän-ˌärts\, Arnold. d. c.1476. German printer. With Konrad Sweynheym introduced printing into Italy.

Pan·ne·ton \pȧn-tōⁿ\, Philippe. *Pseudonym* Rin·guet \raⁿ-ge\. 1895–1960. Canadian novelist, b. Trois Rivières, Que. Practiced medicine in Montreal; ambassador to Portugal (1956–60). Author of novels of rural life *Trente arpents* (1938), *Fausse monnaie* (1947), *Le Poids du jour* (1948); also of a short-story collection, *L'Héritage et autres contes* (1946).

Pan·ni·ni \pän-'nē-nē\ *or* **Pa·ni·ni** \pä-'nē-nē\, Giovanni Paolo. 1691–1765. Italian painter. Settled in Rome (1711); executed frescoes at Villa Patrizi (1718–25) and Palazzo del Senato (c.1725). Noted esp. for paintings of Roman topography, as *View of the Roman Forum* (1735) and *Piazza del Quirinale* (1743).

Pann·witz \'pän-vits\, Rudolf. 1881–1969. German philosopher. Cofounder (1904) with Otto zur Linde of periodical *Charon;* author of *Kultur, Kraft und Kunst* (1906), *Deutschland und Europa* (1918), *Kosmos atheos* (1926), *Logos, Eidos, Bios* (1931), *Der Friede* (1950), etc.

Pa·nof·sky \pän-'ȯf-skē, *Angl* pə-'nȯf-, pa-\, Erwin. 1892–1968. American art historian, b. Hanover, Germany. Professor at Hamburg (1926–33) and Institute for Advanced Study, Princeton, N.J. (1935–68); among his many books on medieval and Renaissance art were *Studies in Iconology* (1939), *Albrecht Dürer* (1943), *Gothic Architecture and Scholasticism* (1951), *Early Netherlandish Painting* (1953), and *Meaning in the Visual Arts* (1955).

Pan Piao \'bän-bē-'au̇\. 3–54 A.D. Chinese official of the Han dynasty. Began the *Han shu,* or *History of the Former Han Dynasty,* as a supplement to the *Shih-chi* of Ssu-ma Ch'ien. His son ¶Pan Ku \'bän-'gü\ (31–92) wrote the majority of the work, which became a model for later dynastic histories; later joined Tou Hsien in his campaigns in northern China; imprisoned on downfall of Tou and died there. Pan Ku's sister ¶Pan Chao \'bän-'jau̇\ (c.45–c.115) put finishing touches on the *Han shu;* was a lady-in-waiting to the empress; wrote poems and essays, as *Lessons for Women* (106), a work on feminine morality. In 101 she successfully petitioned the Emperor for the return of her brother ¶Pan Ch'ao \'bän-'chau̇\ (31–101), twin to Pan Ku, one of greatest Chinese generals; pacified (73–76) the Hsiung-nu tribes; protector general (from 91) of western Chinese regions; his conquests extended across the Pamirs to the Caspian Sea.

Pan·tae·nus \pan-'tē-nəs\. d. c.190 A.D. Greek Christian philosopher. Head of Catechetical School in Alexandria (c.180–190); master of Clement of Alexandria.

Pan·ta·le·on \pan-'tā-lē-ən\. Saint. d. 303. Roman physician. Personal physician to Emperor Galerius; martyred because of his Christian faith; patron saint of physicians.

Pan·ta·le·o·ne di Mau·ro \ˌpän-tä-lā-'ō-nē-dē-'mau̇-rō\. c.1030–c.1071. Italian merchant and statesman. Native of Amalfi. Attempted unsuccessfully (from 1062) to unite Henry IV, Constantine X Ducas, and antipope Honorius II against the Normans and Pope Alexander II.

Pan·ta·le·o·ni \ˌpän-tä-lā-'ō-nē\, Maffeo. 1857–1924. Italian economist. Professor at Rome (from 1901); finance minister of Fiume under D'Annunzio; senator (1923); supported Fascist movement; author of *Principi di economia pura* (1889).

Pan·to·ja de la Cruz \pän-'tō-kä-t͟hā-lä-'krüth\, Juan. 1553–1608. Spanish painter. Court painter to Philip II and Philip III. Among his works were *Nacimiento de la Virgen* (1603), *Resurrección* (1605), and portraits, as of Philip II, Archduke Albert, and Infanta Ana.

Pan·y·as·sis \ˌpan-ē-'as-əs\. 5th century B.C. Greek epic poet. Chief works, *Heracleia* and *Ionica;* only fragments extant.

Pan·zi·ni \pänt-'sē-nē\, Alfredo. 1863–1939. Italian writer. Author of novels *Io cerco moglie* (1920), *Il mondo e rotondo* (1921), *Il bacio di Lesbia* (1937); also two biographies of Cavour, children's books, etc.

Pa·o·li \'pä-ō-(ˌ)lē\, Pasquale. 1725–1807. Corsican patriot. Son of Giacinto Paoli, leader in revolt of 1734. Commanded Corsican forces in expulsion of Genoese (1755); as ruler (1755–64) suppressed vendetta system, built up navy, instituted schools; continued struggle for independence after cession of Corsica by Genoa to France; defeated (1769), took refuge in England, where he was welcomed as friend by Dr. Johnson and pensioned. Recalled to Corsica (1790) as military governor; led revolt against France (1793); with British help expelled the French and turned island over to England; disappointed in hope of being viceroy, retired to England (1795).

Paolo, Fra. See Paolo SARPI.

Paolo Veronese. See CALIARI.

Pao-p'u-tzu. See KO HUNG.

Pa·pa·dia·ma·dis \ˌpä-pät͟h-'yä-mä-(ˌ)t͟hēs\, Alexandros. 1851–1911. Greek writer. Author of short stories and a novella, *I Fomissa,* on rural themes.

Pa·pa·di·a·man·tó·pou·los \ˌpȧ-pȧ-t͟hē-ȧ-mȧn-'dȯp-ü-ˌlȯs\, Yánnis. *Pseudonym* Jean Mo·ré·as \mȯ-rā-ȧs\. 1856–1910. Greek poet. To Paris (1879); after publishing *Syrtes* (1884) in Parnassian mode became a leader of Symbolists; formulated Symbolist principles in journal articles (1885–86); founded periodical *Le Symboliste* (1886); published Symbolist verse *Les Cantilènes* (1886), *Le Pèlerin passionné* (1891); abandoned Symbolism and founded *école romane* (1891) dedicated to Greek and Latin classic traditions; published *Énone au clair visage* (1893), *Eriphyle* (1894), *Sylves* (1896), *Stances* (1899–1905); also wrote play *Iphigénie* (1904).

Pa·pa·gos \'pä-pä-ˌgȯs\, Alexandros. 1883–1955. Greek soldier and politician. As commander in chief (from 1940) checked Italian invasion but was defeated (1941) and held (1943–45) by Germans; successfully directed postwar operations in Greece against Communist guerrillas; field marshal (1949). Formed (1951) the Greek Rally, which became strongest political force in Greece; premier (1952–55).

Pa·pan·dre·ou \ˌpä-pän-ˈdrā-ü\, Georgios. 1888–1968. Greek politician. Head of government-in-exile (Oct.–Dec. 1944); vice premier (1950–51); premier (1963, 1964–65).

Pa·pen \ˈpäp-ən\, Franz von. 1879–1969. German diplomat, soldier, and politician. Military attaché in Mexico (1913–15) and Washington (1915); recalled by request of U.S. because of espionage charges (1915); deputy in Reichstag (1921–32); chancellor of Germany (June–Dec. 1932); premier of Prussia (to Apr. 1933); vice chancellor of Germany under Hitler (1933–34); ambassador to Austria (1934–38) and Turkey (1939–44); acquitted (1946) of major war crimes.

Paph·nu·tius \paf-ˈn(y)ü-sh(ē-)əs\. Saint. 4th century A.D. Greek prelate. Bishop of Thebes, in Upper Egypt; renowned for sanctity of his life; participated in Council of Nicaea (325) and Synod of Tyre (335).

Pa·pi·as \ˈpā-pē-əs\. 2d century A.D. Greek Christian prelate and writer. Bishop of Hierapolis in Phrygia; his chief work, *Explanation of the Sayings of the Lord,* extant in fragments, provides information on primitive Christianity and the origins of the Gospels.

Pa·pin \pá-pa^{n}\, Denis. 1647–?1712. French physicist. Pupil and assistant of Huygens; lived (after 1675) mostly in England; assistant of Boyle in physical experiments; experimented with hydraulics and pneumatic transmission of power; made improvements in air pump; invented the condensing pump; invented (1679) a "steam digester" (a pressure cooker), with which he showed that boiling point is raised or lowered as the pressure exceeds or falls below atmospheric pressure; invented the safety valve; credited with being the first (1690) to apply steam to raise a piston; constructed (1709) boat equipped with paddle wheels driven by a waterwheel.

Pa·pi·neau \pá-pē-nō\, Louis Joseph. 1786–1871. Canadian politician, b. Montreal. Elected (1808) to legislative assembly of Lower Canada; speaker (1815–37); member of Executive Council (1820–23); successful in mission of protest to England against projected union of Upper and Lower Canada (1823); led French-Canadian demand for financial reform and an elective provincial council; led legislative assembly of Lower Canada in denial of supplies to governor, and arranged for cooperation of William Lyon Mackenzie and Reform party of Upper Canada (1835); attended meeting of delegates at St. Charles that decided upon rebellion (1837); charged with high treason, fled to U.S.; declared a rebel; returned by benefit of general amnesty (1847); member of lower house of Canadian Parliament (1848–54).

Pa·pi·ni \pä-ˈpē-nē\, Giovanni. 1881–1956. Italian philosopher and writer. Founded and managed literary periodicals *Leonardo* (1903–07) and *Lacerba* (1913–15), latter to promote Futurism; at first, caustic opponent of Christianity and iconoclast; later converted (1920) to Roman Catholic orthodoxy. Works included *Il crepuscolo dei filosofi* (1906), his autobiography *Un uomo finito* (1912), *Maschilità* (1915), *L'esperienza futurista* (1919), *Storia di Cristo* (1921), *Pane e vino* (1926), *Gog* (1929), *Dante vivo* (1933), *Storia della letteratura italiana* (1937), *Lettere agli uomini di papa Celestino VI* (1946), and *Il diavolo* (1953).

Pa·pin·i·an \pə-ˈpin-ē-ən\. *Full Latin name* Aemilius Pa·pin·i·a·nus \pə-ˌpin-ē-ˈā-nəs\. c.140–212 A.D. Roman jurist. Friend of Emperor Septimius Severus, who appointed him praetorian prefect (203); executed by Emperor Caracalla. Chief works, *Quaestiones* and *Responsa.* Regarded as one of the greatest of Roman jurists.

Pa·pir·i·us \pə-ˈpir-ē-əs\, Lucius. *Surnamed* Cur·sor \ˈkər-sər, -sȯ(ə)r\. 4th century B.C. Roman general and politician. Consul (325, 319, 318, 314, 312 B.C.); dictator (323, 308); campaigned successfully against Samnites (309); his name became a byword for great strictness and severity. His son ¶Lucius Papirius Cursor (3d century B.C.) was consul (293, 272) and a general in Third Samnite War.

Pap·pen·heim \ˈpäp-ən-ˌhīm\, Gottfried Heinrich zu. Graf. 1594–1632. German imperial general. In Thirty Years' War became famed as cavalry commander; fought in Bohemian War (1620), against Ernst von Mansfeld (1621–22), and with Spaniards at Lombardy and with the Grisons (1623–26); suppressed peasant revolt in Upper Austria (1626); took part in storming of Magdeburg (1631) and battle of Breitenfeld (1631); mortally wounded at battle of Lützen.

Pap·pus \ˈpap-əs\ of Alexandria. fl. c.320 A.D. Greek geometer. Regarded as last of great Greek mathematicians. Chief work, *Synagoge,* or *Collection,* extant in incomplete form, contains systematic account of important ancient Greek mathematical works. Centrobaric method of reckoning area and volume of revolutes is also called theorem of Pappus.

Paracelsus. See BOMBAST.

Pa·ra·di·si \pä-rä-ˈdē-sē\ *or* **Pa·ra·dies** \pä-ˈräd-ēs\, Pietro Domenico. 1707–1791. Italian composer and music teacher. In London (from 1747) as teacher of harpsichord and singing; composed operas *Il decreto del fato* (1740) and *Fetonte* (1747), symphonies, organ concertos, and esp. 12 sonatas for harpsichord (1746).

Paradol. See PRÉVOST-PARADOL.

Pa·rāk·ra·ma·bā·hu I \pä-ˌräk-rä-mä-ˈbä-hü\. c.1123–1186. Sinhalese king of Ceylon (1153–86). United Ceylon under one rule; reformed the Buddhist establishment by expelling lax monks and building new temples; sent successful expeditions to India and Burma.

Pa·ra·ma·nu·chit \ˌpä-rä-ˈmän-ü-ˌchēt\ *or* **Pa·ra·ma·nu·ji·ta Ji·no·ra·sa** \ˌpä-rä-ˌmän-ü-ˈjē-tä-ˌjin-ō-ˈräs-ä\. 1791–1852. Siamese prelate and writer. Abbot of Watpha Jetubon; later created prince-patriarch of the Siamese Buddhist church; author of works in prose as the *Pathomasombodhi,* and in verse as the *Taleng Phai,* an epic about Naresuan's liberation of Siam.

Paramesvara. See also JAYAVARMAN II.

Pa·ra·mes·va·ra \ˌpä-ˌräm-es-ˈvär-ä\. *After conversion to Islām* Me·gat Is·kan·dar Shah \ˈmā-ˌgät-ēs-ˈkän-där-ˈshä\. d. 1424. Founder and ruler of Malacca (1403–24). Established relations with Thai kingdom of Ayutthaya and (in 1405) with Ming China.

Parapinaces. See MICHAEL VII DUCAS.

Pa·rás·khos \pä-ˈräs-k̲ōs\, Akhillés. 1838–1895. Greek poet. Central figure of Greek Romantic school of poetry in its second period (c.1850–80); influenced by Musset, Hugo, and Byron; his lyric poems published in 1881 and 1904.

Par·do \ˈpär-t̲h̲ō\, Manuel. 1834–1878. Peruvian politician. First civilian president of Peru (1872–76); attempted to restore financial stability; made treaty with Bolivia (1873) which led to War of the Pacific; president of the Senate (1876–78); assassinated. His son ¶José (1864–1947) was president of Peru (1904–08, 1915–19); deposed by Leguía.

Pardo Ba·zán \-b̲ä-ˈthän\, Emilia de. Condesa. 1852–1921. Spanish novelist and critic. Championed Naturalism with essay *La cuestión palpitante* (1883); founded review *Nuevo teatro crítico* (1891–93); professor, U. of Madrid (1916 ff.). Her works included realistic novels as *Un viaje de novios* (1881), *Los pazos de Ulloa* (1886), *La madre naturaleza* (1887), *Insolación* (1889), *La prueba* (1890), *Adán y Eva* (1894), *La quimera* (1905), *La sirena negra* (1908), *Dulce dueño* (1911); critical works *La literatura francesa moderna* (1910–14); and short stories *Cuentos sacroprofanos* (1899), *Un destripador de antaño* (1900).

Pa·ré \pá-rā\, Ambroise. 1510–1590. French surgeon. Often called father of modern surgery; served as army surgeon and physician to Henry II, Francis II, Charles IX, Henry III; introduced use of ligature of arteries instead of cauterization in treatment of wounds. Author of works on anatomy, surgery, treatment of wounds, plague, generation, obstetrics, and monsters.

Paredes, Diego García de. See Diego GARCÍA DE PAREDES.

Pa·re·des y Ar·ril·la·ga \pä-ˈrā-t̲h̲ēs-ē-är-rē-ˈyäg̲-ä\, Mariano. 1797–1849. Mexican general. Leader of extreme conservative group; supported Santa Anna (1841), but later revolted against him and (1845) led attack against Herrera; president of Mexico (Jan.–July 1846); his actions largely responsible for war with U.S.; went into exile (1847).

Pa·re·ja \pä-ˈre-kä\, Juan de. *Called* el Es·cla·vo \el-äs-ˈkläb̲-ō\, *i.e.* the Slave. c.1605–c.1670. Spanish painter, b. Seville, of slave parents of West Indian descent. Pupil and assistant to Velázquez, who painted his portrait (c.1650); painter of religious pictures as *La vocación de san Mateo* (1661) which contains a self-portrait.

Pa·re·to \pä-ˈre-tō\, Vilfredo. 1848–1923. Italian economist and sociologist. Professor, Lausanne (from 1893); developed methods of mathematical analysis in study of economic and sociological problems; argued for the superiority of the elite in *Trattato di sociologia generale* (1916); the ideology of Italian Fascism was largely based on his theories; other works included *Cours d'économie politique* (1896–97), *Les Systèmes socialistes* (1902), *Manuale d'economia politica* (1906), *Compendio di soziologia generale* (1920).

Par·faict \pár-fe\, François. 1698–1753. French historian. Collaborated with his brother ¶Claude (1705–1777) in publishing *Histoire générale du Théâtre-Français* (1734–49), *Dictionnaire des théâtres de Paris* (1749–56), etc.

Pa·ri·ni \pä-ˈrē-nē\, Giuseppe. 1729–1799. Italian poet. Editor, *Gazzetta di Milano* (1768–69); professor at Palatine and Brera schools (1769–99). His writings included *Alcune poesie di Ripano Eupilino* (1752), *Odi* (1757–91), *Dialogo sopra la nobilità* (1757, prose satire), *Ascanio in Alba* (1771, a play for which Mozart composed an operatic score), *Dei principi generali e particolari delle belle lettere* (1801), and *Il giorna,* a satiric poem on the Milanese aristocracy in four parts: *Mattino* (1763), *Mezzogiorno* (1765), *Vespro* (1801), and *Notte* (1801).

Paris, Comte de. See Louis-Philippe-Albert under ORLÉANS IV.

Pa·ris \pá-rēs\, Alexis-Paulin. 1800–1881. French scholar. Professor of medieval French literature, Collège de France (1853–72); editor and publisher of several chansons de geste. His son ¶Gaston, *in full* Bruno-Paulin-Gaston (1839–1903), romance philologist and medievalist, was professor at Collège de France, succeeding his father (1872), and director of the school (1895); helped found *Revue critique* (1866) and *Romania* (1872); author of *Histoire poétique de Charlemagne* (1865), *Chansons du XVe siècle* (1875), *La Poésie du moyen âge* (1885), *François Villon* (1901), etc.

Par·is \ˈpar-əs\, Matthew. d. 1259. English historian. Entered monastery of St. Albans (1217); succeeded (1236) Roger of Wendover as chronicler; carried on

(1235–59) and expanded scope of the *Chronica majora,* adding foreign events; reorganized and reformed an abbey in Norway on commission from Innocent IV (1248–49); wrote an abridgment of longer chronicles called *Historia anglorum,* extending from 1067 to 1253; author also of lives of monks and a book of *Additamenta.*

Par·ish-Al·vars \'par-əsh-'al-ˌvärz\, Elias. 1808–1849. English harpist. Composer of two harp concertos, fantasias, romances; compiler of Greek, Bulgarian, and Turkish melodies.

Parisot de La Valette, Jean. See LA VALETTE.

Park \'pärk\ Chung Hee. *Original family name* Pak \'päk\. 1917–1979. South Korean soldier and politician. Served in armies of Japan (1940–45) and South Korea (1946–63); general (1961); leader of military junta which overthrew government of John M. Chang (1961); acting president (1962–63); as president (1963–79) guided economic growth of South Korea; assassinated.

Park, Maud, *nee* Wood. 1871–1955. American reformer, b. Boston. m. (1897) Charles E. Park. Founded (from 1900) several woman suffragist organizations, as College Equal Suffrage League, Women's Joint Congressional Committee; first president, National League of Women Voters (1920–24).

Park, Mungo. 1771–1806. Scottish explorer. Surgeon in mercantile marine (1792); ascended Gambia River, crossed Senegal, followed course of Niger (1795–96); captured by Arab chief and escaped after four months' imprisonment; after nineteen months in interior, reached England (1799) and wrote *Travels in the Interior of Africa* (1799); on second expedition to the Niger (1805), reached Bussa, where he drowned during attack by natives.

Park, Robert Ezra. 1864–1944. American sociologist, b. Luzerne Co., Pa. Newspaper reporter (1887–98); professor at Harvard (1904–05), U. of Chicago (1914–33), Fisk (1936–43); secretary to Booker T. Washington; a noted authority on the American Negro and on human ecology. Author of *Introduction to the Science of Sociology* (1921, with Ernest W. Burgess), *The Immigrant Press and Its Control* (1922), *Race and Culture* (1950), *Human Communities* (1952), etc.

Par·ker \'pär-kər\, Alton Brooks. 1852–1926. American jurist, b. Cortland, N.Y. Judge, New York court of appeals (1889–96), appellate division of supreme court (1896–97); chief justice, court of appeals (1898–1904); Democratic candidate for the presidency (1904).

Parker, Charlie, *in full* Charles Christopher, Jr. *Also known as* Bird *or* Yardbird. 1920–1955. American jazz musician, b. Kansas City, Kan. Played professionally (from 1937) with many musicians, esp. Dizzy Gillespie and Thelonius Monk, and with own quintet (from 1947); often called greatest alto saxophonist and jazz improviser; a leading exponent of bebop; exerted great influence on later saxophonists.

Parker, Dorothy, *nee* Roths·child \'rȯth(s)-ˌchīld, 'rȯs-\. 1893–1967. American writer, b. West End, N.J. m. Edwin P. Parker (1917; div. 1928). On staff of *Vogue* (1916) and *Vanity Fair* (1917–20); book reviewer for *New Yorker* (1927–33); member (in 1920s) of "Algonquin Round Table" with Benchley, Thurber, and others; known for acerbic wit. Author of verse collected in *Enough Rope* (1926), *Sunset Gun* (1928), *Death and Taxes* (1931), and of short stories as in *Laments for the Living* (1930), *After Such Pleasures* (1933), *Here Lies* (1939); also collaborated on screen writing, as *A Star is Born,* and on three plays.

Parker, Eric. See Frederick Moore SEARLE.

Parker, Francis Wayland. 1837–1902. American educator, b. Bedford, N.H. Public school superintendent, Quincy, Mass. (1875–80), Boston (1880–83); principal, Cook Co. Normal School, Chicago (1883–99); leading advocate of progressive education. Founder of Chicago Inst. (1899; became U. of Chicago School of Education, 1901).

Parker, Sir Gilbert, *in full* Horatio Gilbert. 1862–1932. Canadian novelist, b. Camden East, Ont. Associate editor, *Sydney Herald,* Australia (1885–89); settled in London; Conservative M.P. (1900–18), champion of imperialism; in charge of British propaganda in America (1914–17). Known for portrayal of Canadian life and characters; works included plays *Vendetta* (1889), *No Defence* (1889); a volume of poems *A Lover's Diary* (1894); short stories, including *Pierre and his People* (1892), *Northern Lights* (1909), *Wild Youth* (1919); novels, including *Mrs. Falchion* (1893), *When Valmond Came to Pontiac* (1895), *Seats of the Mighty* (1896), *Right of Way* (1901), *The Weavers* (1907).

Parker, Horatio William. 1863–1919. American composer, b. Auburndale, Mass. Professor of music, Yale (1894–1919), and dean of Yale Music School (1904–19); composer of oratorios as *Hora Novissima* (1893), operas *Mona* (1911), *Fairyland* (1915), odes as *Hymnos Andron* (1901), a morality *The Dream of Mary* (1918), choral works *A Star Song, The Legend of St. Christopher,* organ and piano pieces, chamber music, and orchestral works; author of *Music and Public Entertainment* (1911).

Parker, Sir Hyde. 1739–1807. English admiral. Commander in chief at Jamaica (1796–1800); commanded fleet sent to Baltic against coalition of Russia, Sweden, and Denmark; showed irresolution, whereupon Nelson engaged, contrary to orders, in battle of Copenhagen (1801).

Parker, John. 1729–1775. American Revolutionary patriot, b. Lexington, Mass. Fought in French and Indian War; commanded the force of Minutemen in the battle of Lexington (April 19, 1775).

Parker, Martin. c.1600–1652. English ballad writer. Author of many popular ballads, esp. the Royalist "When the king enjoys his own again" (1643).

Parker, Matthew. 1504–1575. English prelate. Chaplain to Anne Boleyn (1535) and Henry VIII (1537); dean of Lincoln (1552); deprived of preferments during reign of Mary; appointed second Anglican archbishop of Canterbury by Elizabeth (consecrated 1559). Joining party later called Anglicans, sought to establish ecclesiastical forms midway between Romanism and Puritanism; revised Edwardian articles of convocation (1562), reducing the 42 articles to 39 and shaping them into final form (adopted 1571); proposed, supervised (1563–68), and published a revised translation, the *Bishops' Bible* (1572); drew up ecclesiastical enactments, called *Advertisements* (1565), in controversy over regulation of the service; prepared earliest editions of Gildas, Asser, Aelfric, Matthew Paris, and other chroniclers; author of a Latin treatise *De antiquitate britannicae ecclesiae* (1572), said to be first privately printed English book.

Parker, Sir Peter. 1721–1811. British naval officer. Commanded squadron in unsuccessful attack on Fort Moultrie, Charleston (1776); aided Howe in capture of New York; reduced Rhode Island; admiral of fleet (1799); remembered as patron of Nelson.

Parker, Quanah. See QUANAH.

Parker, Theodore. 1810–1860. American clergyman, b. Lexington, Mass. Pastor of West Roxbury (Mass.) Unitarian Church (1837–45); resigned due to opposition to his liberal sermons (as "The Transient and Permanent in Christianity," 1841) and lectures (published 1842 as *A Discourse of Matters Pertaining to Religion*); minister (from 1845) of 28th Congregational Society of Boston; associate of Emerson, Channing, and other Transcendentalists; engaged in social causes as abolition, prison reform, temperance, women's education, etc.; on secret committee that aided John Brown.

Parker, Sir Thomas. 1st Earl of Mac·cles·field \'mak-əlz-ˌfēld\. 1666?–1732. English judge. Lord chief justice (1710); favorite of George I on account of vehemence against Jacobites; lord chancellor (1718); impeached and found guilty of defalcation (1725).

Parker, William. 4th Baron Mont·ea·gle \'mänt-ˌē-gəl\ *and* 11th Baron Mor·ley \'mȯr-lē\. 1575–1622. English nobleman. Imprisoned briefly for supporting rebellion of Earl of Essex (1601); member of House of Lords (from 1605). Reported to Robert Cecil letter warning of Gunpowder Plot, probably written by his brother-in-law Francis Tresham (1605). Subscriber to, and member of council of, Virginia Company (1609).

Parker, Sir William. 1781–1866. English naval commander. As vice admiral, captured Amoy, Ningpo, and other ports, bringing Opium War to end (1842); commander in chief in Mediterranean (1845–52); retired (1852); admiral of fleet (1863).

Parkes \'pärks\, Alexander. 1813–1890. English chemist and inventor. Discovered cold vulcanization process (1846), the Parkes process of using zinc for desilverizing lead (1850); invented a form of celluloid (1855).

Parkes, Sir Harry Smith. 1828–1885. English diplomat. Employed in negotiating first European treaty with Siam (1855); precipitated with his vigorous protest capture of Canton (1856) and became virtual governor of city (1858–61); consul at Shanghai; minister to Japan (1865–83), where he forwarded cause of the reformers of Liberal party; minister to China (1883–85), concluded treaty opening Korea to British trade.

Parkes, Sir Henry. 1815–1896. Australian politician, b. England. Emigrated to Sydney (1839); led agitation against transportation of convicts (1849); edited (1850–57) liberal newspaper the *Empire,* demanding responsible government; colonial secretary (1866–68); premier of New South Wales (1872–75, 1878–82, 1887–89); instituted free-trade policy; reformed civil service; established compulsory free education; excluded Chinese immigrants; advocated Australian Commonwealth; author of verse and works on Australian political history.

Park·hurst \'pärk-ˌhərst\, Charles Henry. 1842–1933. American clergyman, b. Framingham, Mass. Pastor, Madison Square Presbyterian Church, New York City (1880–1918); president, Society for Prevention of Crime (1891); attacked political corruption and organized vice in sermon (1892) that aroused New York, caused the Lexow Investigation (1894), Tammany's defeat, and the election of the reform administration of Mayor William L. Strong.

Par·kin·son \'pär-kən-sən\, James. 1755–1824. English surgeon and paleontologist. Writer of first article (1812) on appendicitis and first to recognize perforation as cause of death; described Parkinson's disease (1817). Author of *Organic Remains of a Former World* (1804–11) and medical works.

Parkinson-Fortescue, Chichester Samuel. See FORTESCUE.

Park·man \'pärk-mən\, Francis. 1823–1893. American historian, b. Boston. Made trip over the old Oregon Trail westward out of St. Louis (1846) and wrote an account of it, *The California and Oregon Trail* (1849). In spite of severe nervous trouble, devoted himself to historical study and writing, publishing *History of the Conspiracy of Pontiac* (1851), *Pioneers of France in the New World* (1865), *The Jesuits in North America* (1867), *The Discovery of the Great West* (1869), *The Old Régime in Canada* (1874), *Count Frontenac and New France under Louis XIV* (1877), *Montcalm and Wolfe* (1884), *A Half-Century of Conflict* (1892).

Par·léř \'pär-lerzh\, Petr. *Orig.* Peter Par·ler \'pär-lər\. 1330–1399. German mason. Architect on the St. Vitus Cathedral, Prague (from 1353); first to build net vaults on the Continent; first to use an even number of sides for the polygon of a choir (at Kuttenberg, Czech., 1360).

Parley, Peter. See Samuel Griswold GOODRICH.

Par·ma \'pär-mä, *Angl* -mə\, Dukes of. Rulers of the duchy of Parma and Piacenza, northern Italy, esp. the Farnese (*q.v.*) family (1545–1731); Spanish Bourbons (1731–96; twice temporarily interrupted by Austrian rule); French empress Marie-Louise (1814–47); Spanish Bourbons again (1847–60). Duchy became part of Italy (1860). See CHARLES, dukes of Parma.

Par·men·i·des \pär-'men-ə-ˌdēz\. b. c.515 B.C. Greek philosopher of Elea. Founder of Eleatic School; author of a didactic poem *Nature*, which contained essential elements of his doctrines; only fragments of his work are extant. One of Plato's dialogues was named after him.

Par·me·nio \pär-'mē-nē-ō, -'mēn-yō\. c.400–330 B.C. Macedonian general. Served under Philip and Alexander the Great. Defeated the Illyrians (356); became Alexander's second in command in conquest of Persia; engaged in battles of Granicus, Issus, and Gaugamela; assassinated by order of Alexander because of conspiracy charges against his son Philotas (*q.v.*).

Par·men·tier \pär-mäⁿ-tyā, *Angl* ˌpär-mən-'tyā\, André, *also called* Andrew. 1780–1830. American horticulturist, b. Enghien, Belgium. To U.S. (1824); importer of plants for his commercial nursery and botanical garden in New York City; contributor to horticultural journals.

Parmigianino *or* **Parmigiano.** See Girolamo MAZZOLA.

Parmoor, Baron. See Charles Alfred CRIPPS.

Par·nell \pär-'nel, 'pärn-ᵊl\, Charles Stewart. 1846–1891. Irish nationalist leader. M.P. (1875–91); initiated calculated policy of obstruction in House of Commons in order to obtain concessions; elected president, Home Rule Confederation (1878); united nationalists, including Fenians of Ireland and America and Land League (organized 1879), in a fight for home rule; imprisoned (1881–82) on charge of obstructing operation of new land act; from prison directed tenants to pay no rent in retaliation for outlawing of Land League; released from prison upon Kilmainham treaty by which he agreed to work to reduce violence (1882); frustrated in legislative policy by Phoenix Park murders of Lord Cavendish and Thomas Burke by Irish Invincibles (1882); denounced the murders, which were followed by dynamiting outrages in England; brought about defeat of Gladstone government (1885) in protest against fresh coercive legislation; reached apex of career on return of Gladstone to power with definite commitment to adoption of Irish home-rule measure (1886); urged tenants' relief bill (1886); denied in House of Commons authenticity of letter printed in *The Times* purporting to express his extenuation of Phoenix Park murders; was vindicated (1890) by special commission of judges of high court after letter was proved a forgery of Richard Pigott (*q.v.*). Ruined (1890) by proof of his adultery with wife of Capt. William O'Shea, a former follower, in divorce suit; lost support of English liberals; abandoned by majority of parliamentary colleagues; led a minority in bitter losing fight.

Parnell, Thomas. 1679–1718. Irish poet. Contributor of allegorical papers to the *Spectator* and *Guardian* (1712–13); member of Scriblerus Club; wrote *Essay on Homer* prefixed to Pope's translations; known for his poems "The Hermit," "The Fairy Tale," "An Elegy to an Old Beauty," and "Night Piece on Death."

Pa·ro·di \pá-rô-dē\, Dominique-Alexandre. 1842–1901. French poet and playwright, b. Greece. Became naturalized French citizen (1881). Author of *Passions et idées* (1865), *Vaincus et vainqueurs* (1898), etc., and the plays *Ulm le parricide* (1872), *Rome vaincue* (1876), *La Reine Juana* (1893), *Le Pape* (1899), etc. His son ¶Dominique (1870–1955) known as a philosopher; author of *Traditionalisme et démocratie* (1909), *Du positivisme à l'idéalisme* (1930), etc.

Parr \'pär\, Catherine. 1512–1548. Sixth wife of Henry VIII of England. Married 1st Edward Borough; 2d John Neville, Lord Latimer; 3d (1543) Henry VIII. Tried to lessen religious persecution; acted kindly toward Prince Edward and Princesses Elizabeth and Mary; after Henry's death married (1547) Sir Thomas Seymour, Baron Seymour of Sudeley.

Parr, Thomas. *Known as* Old Parr. 1483?–1635. English centenarian. Celebrated by John Taylor, the "water poet"; said to have gone into service (1500) and to have done penance for incontinence at age of 105; exhibited at court by Earl of Arundel (1635).

Par·ran \'par-ən\, Thomas, Jr. 1892–1968. American physician, b. St. Leonard, Md. On staff of U.S. Public Health Service (1917–30); commissioner, New York State Dept. of Health (1930–36); U.S. surgeon general (1936–48); leader in efforts to control and eradicate venereal diseases; a founder of World Health Organization (1940).

Par·ratt \'par-ət\, Sir Walter. 1841–1924. English organist and composer. Taught organ at Royal College of Music, London (1883–1923); professor at Oxford (1908–18); composed incidental music and choral and organ works; helped restore original style to Bach's works.

Par·rha·si·us \pə-'rā-zh(ē-)əs, -sh(ē-)əs\. 5th century B.C. Greek painter. Worked in Athens; recognized as one of greatest painters of antiquity; noted for his mythological paintings, as of Theseus and of Demos, the personified people of Athens.

Par·ri \'pär-rē\, Ferruccio. 1890–1981. Italian politician. Leading anti-Fascist during Mussolini regime; in exile in France founded resistance group Giustizia e Libertà; leader of partisan brigade against Germans in northern Italy (1943–45); founder of Action party (1945); prime minister of first postwar government (June–Dec. 1945); a founder of Republican party (1946).

Par·ring·ton \'par-iŋ-tən\, Vernon Louis. 1871–1929. American educator, b. Aurora, Ill. Professor of English, U. of Washington (1908–29); author of *Main Currents in American Thought* (1927–30), known for its political liberalism and economic determinism; also wrote *The Connecticut Wits* (1926) and *Sinclair Lewis* (1927).

Par·ris \'par-əs\, Samuel. 1653–1720. American Congregational clergyman, b. London, England. To America (before 1674); pastor in Salem (1689–96). From him and his family originated the accusations of witchcraft that started the famous Salem witchcraft delusions (1692–94) and were responsible for the trials of many persons and the execution of twenty.

Par·rish \'par-ish\, Anne. 1760–1800. American philanthropist, b. Philadelphia. Founded in Philadelphia a House of Industry for employment of needy women (1795; incorporated 1815), the first charitable organization for women in America.

Parrish, Anne. 1888–1957. American novelist, b. Colorado Springs, Colo. Author of *The Perennial Bachelor* (1925), *Tomorrow Morning* (1926), *All Kneeling* (1928), *Floating Island* (1930), etc.

Parrish, Maxfield Frederick. 1870–1966. American painter and illustrator, b. Philadelphia. Best known as an illustrator for advertisements, magazines, and such books as *Mother Goose in Prose*, *Knickerbocker's History of New York*, and Kenneth Grahame's *Dream Days* and *The Golden Age*.

Par·rott \'par-ət\, Robert Parker. 1804–1877. American army officer and inventor, b. Lee, N.H. Resigned from army (1836) and entered foundry business (1836–77); invented a method of strengthening cast-iron guns by shrinking wrought-iron hoops on the breech (patented 1861), and an expanding projectile for rifled cannon (patented 1861). Parrott guns were used by Union forces through the Civil War.

Par·ry \'par-ē\, Sir Charles Hubert Hastings. 1848–1918. English composer and musical historian. Professor (1883) and director (1894–1918), Royal College of Music, London; professor, Oxford (1899–1908). Composer of an opera *Guinevere* (1885–86), five symphonies, a piano concerto (1878–79), *Symphonic Variations* (1897), and other orchestral works, but better known for choral compositions, including *Scenes from Prometheus Unbound* (1880), *Blest Pair of Sirens* (1887), *Ode to St. Cecilia's Day* (1889), *Invocation to Music* (1895), *Jerusalem* (1916); oratorios, including *Judith* (1888), *Job* (1892), *King Saul* (1894); incidental music to *The Birds* (1883) and *The Frogs* (1892) of Aristophanes; also chamber music, hymns, songs, piano and organ pieces, etc. Author of *The Evolution of the Art of Music* (1896), *Johann Sebastian Bach* (1909), and *Style in Musical Art* (1911).

Parry, Joseph. 1841–1903. Welsh composer. Composer of operas *Blodwen* (1878), *Virginia* (1882), *Sylvia* (1889), *Arianwen* (1890), *King Arthur* (1897), and oratorios, cantatas, overtures, a string quartet, hymn tunes, and anthems.

Parry, Sir William Edward. 1790–1855. English explorer. In search of Northwest Passage (1819–20, 1821–23, 1824–25); attempted to reach North Pole by sledge boats from Spitzbergen (1827) and reached latitude 82° 45′, which was not reached again until 1876; rear admiral (1852).

Par·se·val \'pär-zā-ˌväl\, August von. 1861–1942. German aeronautical engineer. Designed medium-sized nonrigid airship, known as a *Parseval*, having single large gasbag from which a car was suspended (1901–03).

Parsons, Sir Charles Algernon. See under William PARSONS.

Par·sons \'pärs-ᵊnz\, Elizabeth. 1749–1807. English imposter. Known as "the Cock Lane Ghost"; made certain scratchings supposed to be signals from ghost answering questions (1762); exposed by Dr. Johnson in *Gentleman's Magazine*.

Parsons, Elsie Worthington, *nee* Clews \'klüz\. 1875–1941. American anthropologist, b. New York City. m. (1900) Herbert Parsons. Wrote feminist sociological studies *The Family* (1906), *Religious Chastity* (1913, under pseudonym John Main), *The Old Fashioned Woman* (1913, as John Main), *Fear and Conventionality* (1914), *Social Freedom* (1915), *Social Rule* (1916); under influence of Franz Boas and P. E. Goddard took up study of Indian tribes; published studies *Social Organization of the Tewa of New Mexico* (1929), *Hopi and Zuñi Ceremonialism* (1933), *Mitla: Town of the Souls* (1936), *Pueblo Indian Religion* (1939); also wrote on West Indian and American Negro folklore.

Parsons, Louella, *nee* Oet·tin·ger \'et-iŋ-ər, 'et-ᵊn-jər\. 1893–1972. American newspaper columnist, b. Freeport, Ill. m. (1910) John Parsons. Wrote first movie column in U.S. (for the *Chicago Record-Herald,* 1914–18); wrote a movie gossip column for Hearst publications (1922–65), syndicated in over 400 newspapers; archrival of Hedda Hopper (*q.v.*); author of memoirs *The Gay Illiterate* (1944) and *Tell It to Louella* (1961).

Parsons *or* **Per·sons** \'pärs-ᵊnz\, Robert. 1546–1610. English Jesuit missionary and plotter. Joined Jesuits (1575); as missionary to England (1580), with Edmund Campion carried on political intrigue toward subjection of England to papal authority; escaped to Continent (1581); urged invasion of England by Philip II of Spain to restore Catholic church; founded seminaries for English Catholics in France and Spain; rector of English Coll., Rome (1597); wrote *Christian Directorie* (1585).

Parsons, Talcott. 1902–1979. American sociologist, b. Colorado Springs, Colo. On faculty of Harvard (1927–73); his general theoretical system for the analysis of society was developed in *Structure of Social Action* (1937), *Social System* (1952), *Structure and Process in Modern Societies* (1960), *Sociological Theory and Modern Society* (1968), *Politics and Social Structure* (1969), etc.

Parsons, Theophilus. 1750–1813. American jurist, b. Byfield, Mass. Wrote *The Essex Report* (1778), used by John Adams in writing the Massachusetts constitution of 1780; as chief justice (1806–13) of Massachusetts supreme court was instrumental in establishment of the English common-law tradition in the U.S. His son ¶Theophilus (1797–1882) practiced law in Boston (1827 ff.); professor at Harvard Law School (1848–69); author of many legal treatises, including *Law of Contracts* (1853–55), *Elements of Mercantile Law* (1856), and *Treatise on Maritime Law* (1859).

Parsons, William. 3d Earl of Rosse \'räs\. 1800–1867. Irish astronomer. M.P. (1821–34); Irish peer in House of Lords (from 1841). Studied methods of improving construction of speculum of reflecting telescope (from 1827); discovered way to obviate cracking of surface on cooling; built "Leviathan," giant telescope incorporating speculum 6 feet in diameter and 54 feet in focal length at Parsonstown (Birr), Ireland (1845); resolved certain spiral nebulae into groups of stars; studied and named Crab Nebula; discovered binary and triple stars. His eldest son ¶Laurence (1840–1908), 4th earl, astrophysicist, studied radiations of heat from moon (from 1868). Another son ¶Sir Charles Algernon (1854–1931) became proprietor of engineering works at Newcastle upon Tyne; invented Parsons compound steam turbine (introduced c.1884), added a condenser (1891), adapted it to maritime use (1897); invented nonskid automobile chains, a geared turbine (1910).

Parsons, William Barclay. 1859–1932. American civil engineer, b. New York City. Designed and built first units of New York's subway railway system (1899–1904); built East River Tunnel, New York City; chief engineer, Cape Cod Canal (1905–14); chairman, Chicago Transit Commission (1916). Author of *An American Engineer in China* (1900), *The American Engineers in France* (1920), *Robert Fulton and the Submarine* (1922), etc.

Pārś·va·nā·tha \,pärs-vä-'nä-tä\, *i.e.* Lord Serpent *in Sanskrit. Also called* Parś·va \'pärs-vä\. c.8th century B.C. Indian Jainist saint. The 23d Tīrthankara (*i.e.* saint) of the present age, according to Jaina beliefs; introduced four of the vows of Jainism, the fifth introduced by his successor Mahāvīra.

Partch \'pärch\, Harry. 1901–1974. American composer, b. Oakland, Cal. Composed avant-garde microtonal works based on his own 43-interval octave and devised esoteric instruments to play them; among his compositions were *Oedipus* (1951), *Plectra and Percussion Dances* (1952), *The Bewitched* (1955), and *And on the Seventh Day Petals Fell on Petaluma* (1963–64); summarized his theories in *The Genesis of a Music* (1949).

Par·te·cia·co \pär-tä-'chä-kō\, Agnello. *Also* Angelo Par·te·ci·pa·zio \,pär-tä-si-'päz-yō\. d. 827. Doge of Venice. Founded a dynasty that produced seven doges (810–942); moved seat of government from Malamocco to present site; built many bridges and began (814) Doges' Palace; obtained important commercial privileges from Leo V and Michael II. Succeeded by his sons Giustiniano and Giovanni I.

Par·the·ni·us \pär-'thē-nē-əs\ of Ni·caea \nī-'sē-ə\. 1st century B.C. Greek grammarian and poet. Captured by Romans in war against Mithradates (72 B.C.) and taken to Rome; became Virgil's teacher in Greek. Only extant work is *Love's Woes,* a collection of 36 love stories.

Par·ton \'pärt-ᵊn\, James. 1822–1891. American writer, b. Canterbury, England. To U.S. (1827); wrote esp. biographies, including *Horace Greeley* (1855), *Aaron Burr* (1857), *Andrew Jackson* (1859–60), *Benjamin Franklin* (1864), *John Jacob Astor* (1865), *Thomas Jefferson* (1874). His wife (m. 1856) ¶Sara Payson, *nee* Wil·lis \'wil-əs\ (1811–1872), b. Portland, Me., sister of N. P. Willis, was also an author, best known under her pseudonym Fanny Fern \'fərn\; on staff of *New York Ledger* (1856–72); author of novel *Ruth Hall* (1855) and several books for children.

Par·tridge \'pär-trij\, Alden. 1785–1854. American educator, b. Norwich, Vt. Taught at West Point (1806–17); founded a military academy at Norwich, Vt. (1819), beginning of the present Norwich U., and other similar academies in Virginia, Pennsylvania, Delaware, New Hampshire; regarded as founder of elementary and secondary grade military academies.

Partridge, Sir Bernard. 1861–1945. English caricaturist and illustrator. Worked at decorative painting and church ornament (1880–84); at illustration for press and book illustration (from 1884); joined staff of *Punch* (1891) and became chief cartoonist.

Partridge, Eric Honeywood. 1894–1979. British linguist and lexicographer, b. New Zealand. Among his books were *A Dictionary of Slang and Unconventional English* (1937), *A Dictionary of Clichés* (1940), *Usage and Abusage* (1942), *Shakespeare's Bawdy* (1947), *Dictionary of the Underworld* (1950), *Origins* (1958), and *Dictionary of Catch Phrases* (1977).

Partridge, John. 1644–1715. English astrologer and almanac maker. Shoemaker by trade; issued an almanac *Merlinus Liberatus* (from 1680) with patently equivocal predictions, which was parodied by Jonathan Swift under name of Isaac Bickerstaff (1708) in almanac predicting Partridge's death, and in pamphlet and epitaph recording his death; tried in vain to convince public that he was still alive.

Partridge, William Ordway. 1861–1930. American sculptor, b. Paris, France, of American parentage. Among his works were portrait busts of Chief Justice Fuller, Robert Peary, Whittier, and statues of Grant, Nathan Hale, Horace Greeley. Author of *Art for America* (1894), *Technique of Sculpture* (1895), etc.

Parvīz. See KHOSROW II.

Pa·rys·a·tis \pə-'ris-ə-təs\. d. 395? B.C. Persian queen. Daughter of Artaxerxes I, wife of Darius II Ochus, and mother of Artaxerxes II Mnemon and Cyrus the Younger; aided Cyrus in unsuccessful usurpation of the throne; gained revenge on his slayers.

Pas·cal \pås-kål, *Angl* pas-'kal, päs-'käl\, Blaise. 1623–1662. French scientist and philosopher. Mathematical prodigy as a child; completed original treatise on conic sections at age of sixteen; studied infinitesimal calculus; solved problem of general quadrature of the cycloid; contributed to development of differential calculus; originated, with Fermat, mathematical theory of probability. Invented a mechanical calculator (1642–45), the syringe, and the hydraulic press; wrote (1651–54) treatises on the equilibrium of liquid solutions, on the weight and density of air, and on the arithmetic triangle. Significant literary work began with his entrance into Jansenist community at Port-Royal (1655) and resulted from his exegesis and defense of Jansenism against Jesuitic attacks in which he established the principle of intuitionism; works included *Lettres écrites par Louis de Montalte á un provincial de ses amis,* popularly known as *Provinciales* (1656–57), and *Pensées,* published (1670) from manuscript notes left by him.

Pa·sca·rel·la \,päs-kä-'rel-lä\, Cesare. 1858–1940. Italian poet. Chief representative of Roman dialect poetry after Giuseppe Belli; books of verse included *Il morto di campagna* (1882), *Villa Gloria* (1886), and *La scoperta dell'America* (1893).

Pasch \'päsh\, Moritz. 1843–1930. German mathematician. Professor, Giessen (1873–1911); author of *Vorlesungen über neuere Geometrie,* containing system of axioms for descriptive geometry (1882), and works on differential and integral calculus, analysis, and variables and functions. Pasch's axiom is named after him.

Pas·chal *or* **Pas·cal** \pas-'kal, päs-'käl\. *Lat.* Pas·cha·lis \pas-'kā-ləs\. Name of two popes and two antipopes:

Paschal I. Saint. d. 824. Pope (817–824). Secured from Frankish Emperor Louis I the Pious independence of Roman see; sovereignty over papal territories, and freedom of papal elections; suspected of involvement in anti-Frankish plot and forced by Louis to take oath of purgation; built many churches.

Paschal II. *Orig.* Rai·ne·ri·us \rī-'nir-ē-əs\. d. 1118. Pope (1099–1118). Conducted long struggle with emperors Henry IV and Henry V over investitures seized by Henry V (1111) and released on promise to restore right of lay investiture; under pressure from Curia, revoked privilege (1112).

Paschal. d. 692. Antipope (687). Elected by a portion of Roman populace, along with rival Theodore, in opposition to Sergius I; refused to submit, imprisoned in monastery.

Paschal III. *Orig.* Guido of Cre·ma \'krem-ä\. d. 1168. Antipope (1164–68). Established by Emperor Frederick I Barbarossa to succeed antipope Victor IV in opposition to Pope Alexander III; at imperial command canonized Charlemagne (1165); enthroned on Frederick's capture of Rome (1167).

Pas·cha·sius Rad·ber·tus \pas-'kā-zh(ē-)əs-rad-'bert-əs\. Saint. c.785–c.860. French Benedictine abbot and theologian. Abbot of Corbie, near Amiens (c.843–c.851); attended synods of Paris (847) and Quercy (849). Wrote first monograph on the Eucharist, *De corpore et sanguine Christi* (831, revised 844), in which he argued for transubstantiation; opposed by Ratramnus in *De corpore et sanguine Domini* (c.850); also wrote biblical commentaries and other religious works.

Pas·cin \pás-kaⁿ\, Jules. *Orig.* Julius Pin·cas \'piŋ-kəs\. 1885–1930. French painter, b. Bulgaria of Italian, Spanish-Jewish parentage. Worked for satirical journals *Lustige Blätter* and *Simplicissimus* in Austria and Germany; to Paris (1905); became U.S. citizen during World War I; noted esp. for large-scale paintings of biblical and mythological scenes and bitterly ironic yet tender studies of women.

Pa·sco·li \'päs-kō-(,)lē\, Giovanni. 1855–1912. Italian lyric poet. Succeeded Carducci as professor at Bologna (1905); among his volumes of verse were *Myricae* (1891–97), *Canti di Castelvecchio* (1903), *Poemi conviviali* (1904), *Primi poemetti* (1904), *Nuovi poemetti* (1909), and *Poemi del Risorgimento* (1913); also translations from Greek and Latin poets and critical studies of Dante.

Pas·de·loup \päd-lü\, Jules-Étienne. 1819–1887. French conductor. Founded (1851) Société des Jeunes Artistes du Conservatoire, a symphony orchestra which gave public concerts for some years; conducted popular concerts (1861–84) at Cirque d'Hiver which introduced many works by contemporary composers, as Saint-Saëns, Massenet, Bizet, etc.

Pa·sek \'pä-sek\, Jan Chryzostom. 1636–1701. Polish soldier. Follower of King John II of Poland; his *Pamiętniki,* or memoirs (covering period 1656–88) furnish curious and lively picture of the times.

Pa·šić \'pä-shētʸ, *Angl* 'päsh-(,)ich\, Nicola. 1845–1926. Serbian and Yugoslav statesman. Helped found Radical party (1881); member of legislature (1878 ff.); condemned to death on charge of plotting against King Milan, but escaped into Austria; remained in exile (1883–89); premier of Serbia (1891–92); ambassador to Russia (1893–94); banished from Serbia (1899) for conspiracy against king; returned to Serbia (1903) and supported Karageorgević house in its accession to throne; minister of foreign affairs (1904); premier of Serbia and of its successor state, Yugoslavia (1906–26, with few interruptions); guided Serbian policy through World War I (1914–18) and creation and organization of Yugoslavia; gained reputation as "Old Fox of the Balkans."

Pasiphilus. See Hermann von dem BUSCHE.

Pa·sit·e·les \pə-'sit-ᵊl-,ēz\. 1st century B.C. Greek sculptor. Native of Magna Graecia, Italy; said to have originated the pointing machine and copying of statues by means of plaster casts; wrote a 5-volume book on works of art of the world.

Pa·ske·vich \(,)pəs-'kyāv-yich\, Ivan Fyodorovich. Count of Eri·van \ir-yi-'vänʸ\, Prince of Warsaw. 1782–1856. Russian soldier. Field marshal (from 1829); suppressed Polish rebellion (1830–31), captured Warsaw, and was appointed viceroy of Poland (1832–56); commanded Russian army sent to aid Austria in suppressing rebellion in Hungary (1849) and received Hungarian surrender at Világos. Commanded army of the Danube (1854); defeated at Silistra (1854).

Pas·ley \'pāz-lē\, Sir Charles William. 1780–1861. British army officer and engineer, b. Scotland. Introduced (1811) course of instruction for noncommissioned officers in military engineering, which was established at Chatham with him as director (1812–41); general (1860); author of treatises on military engineering.

Pa·so·li·ni \päs-ō-'lē-nē\, Pier Paolo. 1922–1975. Italian writer and film director. Editor, *Officina* (1955–58); his writings (some in Friulan) included verse as *Poesie a Casarsa* (1942), *La meglio gioventù* (1954), *La ceneri di Gramsci* (1957), *Poesia in forma di rosa* (1964); novels as *Ragazzi di vita* (1955), *Una vita violenta* (1959), *Donne di Roma* (1960); and essays as *Passione e ideologia* (1960), *Empirismo eretico* (1972). His socialistic films included *Accattone* (1961), *Mama Roma* (1962), *The Gospel According to St. Matthew* (1964), *Oedipus Rex* (1967), *The Decameron* (1971), and *The Canterbury Tales* (1971).

Pasqualis, Martínez. See MARTÍNEZ PASQUALIS.

Pas·quier \päk-yā, päs-kyā\, Étienne. 1529–1615. French jurist. Practiced law in Paris (from 1549); advocate general at Paris Chambre des Comptes (1585); spent much of his life fighting the Jesuits; author of *Recherches de la France* (1560 ff.), *Interprétation des "Institutes" de Justinien* (pub. 1847), *Catéchisme des Jésuites* (1602), etc.

Pasquier, Étienne-Denis de. Duc. 1767–1862. French politician. Descendant of Étienne Pasquier; named by Napoléon councilor of state and prefect of police (1810); minister of state (1815) and president of Chamber of Representatives (1816) at the Restoration; peer of France (1821) and president of Chamber of Peers under Louis-Philippe; chancellor of France (1837); created duke (1844).

Pas·sa·glia \päs-'säl-yä\, Carlo. 1812–1887. Italian theologian. Joined Society of Jesus (1827); professor of canon law (1844) and dogmatic theology (1845 ff.), Collegium Romanum; broke with Jesuits (1859) and attacked temporal power of pope; professor at Turin (1861); member of Turin parliament (1863–64). Author of *Commentarium theologicorum* (1850–51), *De ecclesia Christi* (1853–56), *Il pontifice ed il principe* (1860), etc.

Pas·sar·ge \pä-'sär-gə\, Siegfried. 1866–1958. German geographer. Professor at Breslau (1905–08) and Hamburg (1908–35); wrote on climate and physical morphology of southern Africa in *Die Kalahari* (1904), *Südafrika* (1908), *Physiologische Morphologie* (1912), *Vergleichende Landschaftskunde* (1921–30), etc.

Pas·sa·vant \,päs-ä-'väⁿ\, Johann David. 1787–1861. German painter and art scholar. Best known as author of *Rafael von Urbino und sein Vater Giovanni Santi* (1839–58) and *Le Peintre-graveur* (1860–64).

Pas·se·rat \päs-(ə-)rȧ, pás-\, Jean. 1534–1602. French Humanist and poet. Succeeded Ramus at Collège de France (1572); a main contributor to *Satire Ménippée* (1594), a manifesto which supported Henry of Navarre; wrote love poetry and scholarly commentaries on Latin poets.

Passfield, Baron. See Sidney James WEBB.

Passos, John Dos. See DOS PASSOS.

Pas·sy \pá-sē\, Frédéric. 1822–1912. French economist and politician. Member, Chamber of Deputies (1881–89); interested himself in promoting of international peace; founded (1867) Ligue Internationale de la Paix; aided Sir W. R. Cremer in founding Interparliamentary Union (1889); shared with Jean-Henri Dunant first Nobel peace prize (1901). His son ¶Paul-Édouard (1859–1940), phonetician, was assistant director of École des Hautes Études, Paris; founder of International Phonetic Association, chief originator of its phonetic alphabet, and editor of *Le Maître Phonétique* (1889–1940). Wrote *Les Sons du français* (1887), *Dictionnaire phonétique de la langue française* (with H. Michaelis, 1897), and *International French–English and English–French Dictionary* (with G. Hempl, 1904).

Pa·sta \'päs-tä\, Giuditta, *nee* Ne·gri \'nā-grē\. 1798–1865. Italian operatic soprano. Created many roles expressly written for her by Bellini (*La Sonnambula* and *Norma*), Donizetti (*Anna Bolena*), and Pacini (*Niobe*).

Pa·ster·nak \pəs-tyir-'nák, *Angl* 'pas-tər-,nak, 'päs-, -,nák\, Boris Leonidovich. 1890–1960. Russian poet and author. Influenced by Symbolists and later by Futurists; castigated by government for winning Nobel prize for literature (1958). Author of lyrical poetry as *Temy i variatsii* (1923), *Poverkh Baryerov* (1931), *Vtoroye rozhdenie* (1932); prose works *Detstro Luvers* (1918), *Okhrannaya Gramota* (1931), and *Doctor Zhivago* (1957); also translations of Shakespeare, etc.

Pas·teur \päs-tœr, *Angl* pas-'tər, -'t(y)ů(ə)r\, Louis. 1822–1895. French chemist and microbiologist. Professor of physics at Dijon (1848) and Strasbourg (1849); dean and professor of chemistry, Lille (1854–57); director, École Normale Supérieure (1857–67); professor of geology, physics, and chemistry, École des Beaux-Arts (1863–68); director of Institut Pasteur, Paris (1888–95). Did pioneer work in modern stereochemistry in proving that racemic acid is a mixture of two optically different forms of tartaric acid; investigated problems encountered in fermentation of wine and beer; demonstrated that lactic, alcoholic, and other fermentations are caused by minute organisms; proved that these organisms do not arise by spontaneous generation; discovered the bacilli causing two distinct diseases of silkworms and found method of preventing spread of the diseases (1868), thus saving silk industry in France; discovered bacteria to be cause of anthrax; developed (1881) method of inoculating with attenuated cultures of germs of anthrax and chicken cholera to protect animals against severe attacks of these diseases; developed curative and preventive treatment for hydrophobia in man and for rabies in dogs (1885).

Pas·ton \'pas-tən\. Name of a well-to-do English family of Norfolk, whose private correspondence from 1422 to 1509, collected and published (first two vols. 1787) along with state papers and other documents, provide historical material upon interfamily violence, domestic conditions, and lawsuits prevalent in reigns of Henry VI, Edward IV, and Richard III. Members of the family included: ¶Sir William (1378–1444), *known as* the Good Judge, and his son ¶John (1421–1466), letter writer and friend of Sir John Fastolf. ¶Sir Robert (1631–1683), 1st Earl of Yar·mouth \'yär-məth\, who entertained his friend Charles II at Oxnead (1676). His son ¶Sir William (1652–1732), 2d earl, last representative of the family, married a natural daughter of Charles II, sold some of the family correspondence to an antiquary, Peter Le Neve.

Pas·tor \'pas-tər\, Antonio, *known as* Tony. 1837–1908. American actor and theater manager, b. New York City. On stage from childhood; opened own theater in New York City (1865) and made vaudeville a respectable and popular family entertainment; acquired Fourteenth Street Theater, thereafter known as Tony Pastor's (1881).

Pas·tor \'päs-tōr\, Ludwig von. Baron von Cam·pers·fel·den \'käm-pərs-,fel-dən\. 1854–1928. German historian. Professor at Innsbrück (1881–1901); author of *Geschichte der Päpste seit dem Ausgang des Mittelalters* (1886–1933).

Pas·to·rius \päs-'tōr-ē-əs, pas-\, Francis Daniel. 1651–?1720. American lawyer and colonizer, b. Sommerhausen, Germany. Practiced law in Germany; as agent for Quaker group founded (1683) Germantown, Pa., and became its first mayor, chief citizen, and schoolmaster.

Pa·tañ·ja·li \pə-'tən-jə-lē\. *Also called* Go·nar·di·ya \,gȯn-är-'dē-(y)ä\ *and* Go·ni·kā·pu·tra \,gȯn-ē-kä-'pü-trä\. 2d century B.C. Indian scholar and grammarian. Wrote *Mahābhāsya,* the "Great Commentary" on Pāṇini's grammar and Kātyāyana's emendations to it; also generally identified by Hindu scholars with the founder of the Yoga system and author of at least part of the *Yoga sūtras.*

Patch \'pach\, Alexander McCarrell. 1889–1945. American soldier, b. Arizona Terr. As major general, organized (1942) Americal Division; took part in landing on Guadalcanal (1942); lieutenant general (1944); commanded Seventh army in landing in southern France (1944) and advance into Germany.

Patch, Sam. 1807?–1829. American daredevil, b. Rhode Island. Famous for dives (from 1827) from cliffs, bridges, and ship masts, sometimes with his pet bear; killed while diving into Genesee River at Rochester, N.Y.

Patch·en \'pach-ən\, Kenneth. 1911–1972. American poet, b. Niles, O. His experimental poems published in *Before the Brave* (1936), *First Will and Testament* (1939), *Hurrah for Anything* (1957), *Because It Is* (1960), *Collected Poems* (1969), *Out of the World of Patchen* (1970), etc. Author of novels *Journal of Albion Moonlight* (1941), *Memoirs of a Shy Pornographer* (1945), and *Sleepers Awake* (1946).

Pa·tel \pə-'täl\, Viththalbhai Jahverbhai. 1873?–1933. Indian nationalist leader. Practiced law in Bombay; represented Indian National Congress at London Conference (1919) on Government of India Act; joined Gandhi's non-cooperation movement (1920); a leader of Swarajist party; opposed to British rule; died in exile in Switzerland. His younger brother ¶Sardar Vallabhbhai Jahverbhai Nadiād (1875–1950) studied law in India and England; practiced law at Ahmadābād and was its municipal president (1924–28); entered politics (1916) as supporter of Gandhi; successfully led tax revolt of Bārdoli landowners (1928); a leader in the Indian National Congress; deputy prime minister and minister of home affairs, of information, and of states (1947–50).

Patenier. See PATINIR.

Pa·te·nô·tre \pát-nōtrᵊ\, Jules. 1845–1925. French diplomat. Minister to Sweden (1880–83), China (1883–86), Tangiers (1888–91), U.S. (minister 1891–93, ambassador 1893–97); ambassador to Spain (1897–1902). Author of *Souvenirs d'un diplomate* (1913).

Pa·ter \pá-ter\, Jean-Baptiste-Joseph. 1695–1736. French painter. Painted genre pictures in manner of his teacher Watteau, as *La Fête champêtre, La Balançoire, Conversation galante.*

Pa·ter \'pāt-ər\, Walter Horatio. 1839–1894. English essayist and critic. Fellow (from 1864) of Brasenose Coll., Oxford, which was his principal home. Made his life work the interpretation to his age of the Humanism of the Renaissance in art and literature; published collection of reviews of da Vinci, Botticelli, Pico della Mirandola, and Michelangelo as *Studies in the History of the Renaissance* (1873); associated with Pre-Raphaelites; published essays upon aesthetic poetry, style, Shakespeare, Lamb, Sir Thomas Browne in *Appreciations* (1889); published (1885) his masterpiece *Marius the Epicurean,* a philosophical romance of the time of Marcus Aurelius.

Paterculus, Velleius. See VELLEIUS PATERCULUS.

Pat·er·son \'pat-ər-sən\, Sir Alexander Henry. 1884–1947. English penologist. As prison commissioner (1922–47), reformed Borstal system for juvenile offenders, emphasizing rehabilitation aspects.

Paterson, Andrew Barton. *Nicknamed* Ban·jo \'ban-(,)jō\. 1864–1941. Australian journalist and poet. Editor and journalist for Sydney newspapers (from 1900); his books of verse included *The Man from Snowy River* (1895), *Rio Grande's Last Race* (1902), *Saltbush Bill, J.P., and Other Verses* (1917, in which "Waltzing Matilda" first appeared), *The Animals Noah Forgot* (1933, children's poems); also wrote short stories.

Paterson, Robert. 1715–1801. Scottish stonecutter. Deserted his family and devoted 40 years to repairing and erecting headstones on Covenanters' graves; the original of Scott's character "Old Mortality."

Paterson, William. 1658–1719. British financier, b. Scotland. Acquired fortune in trade; made first overtures to government for establishment of Bank of England (1691), adopted by Parliament (1694); organized bank (1694) but a year later resigned from directorate on issue of narrow scope of bank's operations; persuaded Scottish Parliament to create company for settlement of Darién on Isthmus of Panama; accompanied expedition (1698) and returned with survivors a broken man (1699); took prominent part in promoting Scottish union with England and framing articles of the treaty (1701–07); advocated (from 1701) financial measures forming basis of Walpole's sinking fund and the scheme for conversion of national debt (1716).

Paterson, William. 1745–1806. American jurist, b. County Antrim, Ireland. To America (1747); practiced law (from 1769); attorney general of New Jersey (1776–83); member of Constitutional Convention (1787); a leader in introducing the New Jersey Plan which, though rejected, was effectual in forcing a compromise on methods of representation in U.S. Senate and House of Representatives; U.S. senator (1789–90); governor of New Jersey (1790–93); associate justice, U.S. Supreme Court (1793–1806); published *Laws of the State of New Jersey* (1800).

Pa·thé \pá-tā, *Angl* pa-'thā, pä-\, Charles. 1863–1957. French motion-picture executive. With brother ¶Emile (1860–1937) founded (1896) Pathé Fréres, which produced and distributed films worldwide; originated (1909; in U.S. 1910) the newsreel *Pathé Gazette* with symbol of crowing rooster; produced screen series *The Perils of Pauline* (1914); retired (1929).

Pa·ti·nir \pá-tə-'nir\ *or* **Pa·ti·nier** *or* **Pa·te·nier** \-'nēr\, Joachim de. c.1485–1524. Dutch painter. Known for his religious landscape paintings, as *Crossing the Styx, Flight into Egypt, St. Christopher, The Temptation of St. Anthony, The Underworld,* and *The Baptism of Christ.*

Pa·ti·ño \pä-'tēn-yō\, José. 1666–1736. Spanish politician. In service of Philip V (from 1707); minister of navy and of colonies (1726–36), with additional control over financial and foreign affairs; successfully reorganized navy.

Patiño, Simón Ituri. 1862–1947. Bolivian industrialist and diplomat. Owned tin mines in Bolivia; minister plenipotentiary to Spain (1920–26), France (1926–41); reputed to have financed Bolivian war against Paraguay (1932–35).

Pa·tis·sier \pá-tēs-yā\, Charles-Joseph. Marquis de Bus·sy-Cas·tel·nau \bu̅e-sē-ká-stel-nō\. 1720–1785. French diplomat. Agent of French East India Co.; to East Indies (1741); representative at court of Ṣalābat Jang, niẓām of Hyderabad, whose chief adviser he became (1751–58).

Pat·kul \'pät-ku̇l\, Johann Reinhold von. 1660–1707. Livonian nobleman and adventurer. Entered service of Augustus II, elector of Saxony and king of Poland, and proposed alliance against Sweden (1698 ff.). After peace was finally negotiated at Altranstädt (1706), Patkul was delivered to Charles XII of Sweden and broken alive on the wheel as a traitor.

Pat·man \'pat-mən\, Wright, *in full* John William Wright. 1893–1976. American politician, b. near Hughes Springs, Tex. Democratic member, U.S. House of Representatives (1929–76); sponsored legislation for veterans' benefits (1936), fair trade practices (1936), and creation of the Small Business Administration (1953).

Pat·more \'pat-,mō(ə)r, -,mȯ(ə)r\, Coventry Kersey Dighton. 1823–1896. English poet. Assistant librarian, British Museum (1846–65); contributed to Pre-Raphaelite organ *The Germ;* published poems *Tamerton Church Tower* (1853); issued his masterpiece, a poetic celebration of married love, *The Angel in the House,* comprising *The Betrothal* (1854), *The Espousals* (1856), *Faithful For Ever* (1860), *The Victories of Love* (1863). Became a Roman Catholic (1864). Published *English Metrical Law* (1857), *The Unknown Eros,* odes on exalted themes (1877), *Amelia,* an idyll (1878), *Principle in Art* (1889), *Religio Poetae* (1893), *Rod, Root, and Flower,* meditations chiefly upon religious subjects (1895).

Pat·rick \'pa-trik\. Saint. *British name* Suc·cat \'su̇k-ət\. *Lat.* Pa·tri·ci·us \pə-'trish-(ē-)əs\. 5th century A.D. Apostle and patron saint of Ireland, b. Britain. Son of Calpurnius, a decurion of Celto-Roman family of high rank. Captured at age of sixteen by Irish marauders, sold as a slave in Antrim, escaped after six years into Gaul; returned to parents in Britain. Heeded call which came to him in a dream to preach to Irish; spent about fourteen years at Auxerre, France, in preparation. Entrusted by Pope Celestine I with conversion of Irish race and consecrated bishop (432). Although opposed by Druids, secured protection of local kings. Founded churches and planted the faith through west and north of Ireland; introduced Latin as language of church; founded church and monastery at Armagh; left writings in rude Latin, the *Confessio,* an account of his career, and a letter to Coroticus, a British king of Strathclyde who had killed some neophytes in a raid.

Patrick, Mary Mills. 1850–1940. American educator, b. Canterbury, N.H. Specialized in study of Near Eastern languages; president, Istanbul Woman's Coll. (1890–1924). Author of *Sappho and the Island of Lesbos* (1912), *Under Five Sultans* (1929), *A Bosporus Adventure* (1934), etc.

Päts \'pats\, Konstantin. 1874–1956. Estonian politician. Head of provisional government (1918); head of the government of Estonia (1921–22, 1923,

1932–33); dictator (1934–38); elected president (1938–40); deported to Russia on occupation by Soviets (1940).

Patsayev, Viktor Ivanovich. See under Georgy DOBROVOLSKY.

Pat·ten \'pat-ᵊn\, Gilbert. *Pseudonym* Burt L. Stan·dish \'stan-dish\. 1866–1945. American writer, b. Corinna, Me. Wrote over 200 adventure stories for boys, centering around the fictional hero Frank Merriwell.

Pat·ter·son \'pat-ər-sən\, John Henry. 1844–1922. American manufacturer, b. near Dayton, O. Owner (from 1884) of National Cash Register Co. in Dayton; known for merchandising innovations, as idea of exclusive sales territory.

Patterson, Joseph Medill. 1879–1946. American journalist, b. Chicago. Grandson of Joseph Medill. On staff of *Chicago Tribune* (1901–05); commissioner of public works, Chicago (1905–06); correspondent in World War I; coeditor of *Chicago Tribune* with his cousin Robert McCormick (1914–25); with McCormick founded (1919) New York *Daily News* and became its sole editor and publisher (from 1925). His sister ¶Eleanor Medill (1884–1948), also a newspaper editor; inherited an interest in *Chicago Tribune;* a member of its board of directors; owner and publisher of Washington (D.C.) *Herald* and Washington *Times* (from 1939), combining them into *Times-Herald;* author, under pen name Eleanor M. Gi·zyc·ka \gi-'zits-kä\, of *Glass Houses* (1926), *Fall Flight* (1928).

Pat·ti \'pät-tē\, Adelina, *orig.* Adela Juana Maria. 1843–1919. American operatic soprano, b. Madrid, Spain, of Italian parentage. Debut in New York (1859); with Covent Garden, London (1861–85); sang roles in operas of Bellini, Rossini, Gounod, etc.; considered one of greatest coloratura singers of 19th century.

Pat·tie \'pat-ē\, James Ohio. 1804–?1850. American frontiersman, b. Bracken Co., Ky. On several exploratory and trapping expeditions to southwestern U.S. (from 1824); his *Personal Narrative* (1830), an account of his travels, became famous despite being denounced as mostly false by his travelling companions.

Pat·ti·son \'pat-ə-sən\, Mark. 1813–1884. English scholar. Associate of John Newman until latter's conversion to Catholicism; investigated Continental systems of education (1859–60); rector of Lincoln College (1861); wrote *Life of Isaac Casaubon* (1875), *Life of John Milton* (1879), and *Memoirs* (1885). His sister ¶Dorothy Wyndlow (1832–1878), *known as* Sister Dora, philanthropist, joined sisterhood of the Good Samaritan (1864); became a surgical nurse; resigned from sisterhood to become head of municipal hospital at Walsall.

Pat·ton \'pat-ᵊn\, George Smith. *Known as* Old Blood and Guts. 1885–1945. American army officer, b. San Gabriel, Calif. Aide-de-camp to Gen. Pershing in Mexico (1916–17) and in Europe (1917); first man detailed to tank corps, U.S. army (1917); in command of 2d armored division (1940); in command, under Gen. Eisenhower, of U.S. forces in Morocco (1942); commanded II army corps in Tunisia (1943); commanded U.S. Seventh army in Sicily (1943); as commander of Third army swept across France and Germany (1944–45); one of finest practitioners of mobile tank warfare; general (1945). Wrote memoirs *War As I Knew It* (1947).

Paul \'pȯl\. Saint. *Roman name* Pau·lus \'pȯl-əs\. *Jewish name* Saul \'sȯl\. d. between 62 and 68 A.D. Born a Jew at Tarsus in Cilicia (now in Turkey); trained as rabbi and tentmaker; zealous opponent of Christianity until his conversion through a vision on road to Damascus. Became apostle to the Gentiles; with Barnabas and Titus to Jerusalem to plan missions with Christian leaders James, Peter, and John. Went on three missionary journeys throughout Asia Minor and Greece; founded many churches, to which he sent epistles (the "Pauline epistles" of New Testament). Arrested at Jerusalem and imprisoned at Caesarea for two years; appealed (as a Roman citizen) to emperor and transferred to Rome (60); after further imprisonment, said to have been martyred under Nero.

Paul. Name of six popes:

Paul I. Saint. d. 767. Pope (757–67). Member of Curia of his brother, Pope Stephen II, whom he succeeded; secured support of Pepin III against Lombard king Desiderius and Byzantine emperor Constantine V Copronymos; protested Constantine's revival of Iconoclasm and transported relics of many saints from catacombs to Roman churches.

Paul II. *Orig.* Pietro Bar·bo \'bär-bō\. 1417–1471. Pope (1464–71). Persuaded Louis XI to abolish Pragmatic Sanction of Bourges (1461); opposed Hussite church of Bohemia, excommunicating George of Podebrady (1466) and crowning Matthias Corvinus king of Bohemia (1469); supported crusade against Turks. Built Palazzo Venezia (begun 1455); encouraged founding of printing houses at Rome (1465); persecuted the Fraticelli (1466); although a patron of scholars, dissolved Roman Academy and arrested its members (1468).

Paul III. *Orig.* Alessandro Farnese. 1468–1549. Pope (1534–49). Protégé of Pope Alexander VI; encouraged reforms which began Counter-Reformation; commissioned Michelangelo to construct St. Peter's Basilica and paint *The Last Judgment* and ceiling of Sistine Chapel; excommunicated Henry VIII of England (1538); approved decree (1540) establishing order of Jesuits; aided Emperor Charles V in his wars against the Protestants of Germany; introduced Inquisition into Italy (1542); convened Council of Trent (1545).

Paul IV. *Orig.* Gian Pietro Ca·ra·fa \kä-'räf-ä\. 1476–1559. Pope (1555–59). Founded (with Cajetan of Thiene) order of Theatines (1524); as pope, continued reforms of Paul III; allied with France (1555) in pursuit of his anti-Spanish policy; made peace with Spain (1557) after march on Rome by Duke of Alba; deprived Cardinal Reginald Pole of his authority (1557); opposed Elizabeth's rule in England; unpopular because of his zeal for the Inquisition.

Paul V. *Orig.* Camillo Borghese. 1552–1621. Pope (1605–21). Forbade English Catholics to take oath of allegiance to James I (1606); engaged in struggle with Venice (1606–07); encouraged missions, esp. to Latin America; refused to support Catholic side in Thirty Years' War (from 1618); founded privy Vatican archives; authorized new version of *Rituale Romanum* (pub. 1614).

Paul VI. *Orig.* Giovanni Battista Mon·ti·ni \mōn-'tē-nē\. 1897–1978. Pope (1963–78). Ordained priest (1920); with Vatican secretariat of state (1924–54); archbishop of Milan (1954); cardinal (1958). As pope issued encyclicals for clerical celibacy (1967) and against artificial birth control (1968); visited many countries; worked for social justice and church reunion.

Paul I. 1901–1964. King of Greece (1947–64). Son of Constantine I. Refused crown on death of brother Alexander (1920); in exile (1923–35) during Hellenic Republic; succeeded his brother George II as king.

Paul I. *Russ.* Pavel Petrovich. 1754–1801. Emperor of Russia (1796–1801). Son of Peter III and Catherine the Great; succeeded Catherine (1796); reversed many of Catherine's policies; provoked hostility of the nobility and the army; inaugurated some reforms in treatment of serfs; joined Second Coalition against France (1798) and his army under Survorov aided in expelling French from northern Italy (1799); later, participated in organization of northern maritime league of Russia, Sweden, and Denmark against Great Britain (1800–01); assassinated.

Paul of Ae·gi·na \i-'jī-nə\. *Lat.* Pau·lus Ae·gi·ne·ta \'pȯ-ləs-ˌē-jə-'nēt-ə\. c.625–c.690 A.D. Greek surgeon. His *Epitomae medicae libri septem* contained nearly everything known of medicine in his time and greatly influenced Arab physicians.

Paul of Sa·mos·a·ta \sə-'mäs-ət-ə\. 3d century A.D. Christian ecclesiastic. Bishop of Antioch (260 A.D.); deposed from his see (268); denied a distinction of persons in God; taught that Christ was a mere man, raised above other men by the indwelling Logos (the impersonal power of God). His followers, regarded as heretics, were called Paulianists. Fragments of his writings are extant.

Paul of Thebes \'thēbz\. Saint. *Called also* Saint Paul the Hermit. c.230–c.343 A.D. Christian hermit. Said to have lived 113 years; lived as hermit in desert in Upper Egypt; teacher of Saint Anthony; called by Saint Jerome the founder of monasticism.

Paul of the Cross. Saint. *Orig. name* Paolo Francesco Da·nei \'dän-ā-(ˌ)ē\. 1694–1775. Italian priest. Ordained (1727); founder of Passionist order (approved 1741); established 12 monasteries in Italy; canonized (1867).

Paul the Deacon. *Lat.* Pau·lus Di·a·co·nis \'pȯ-ləs-ˌdī-ə-'kō-nəs\. c.720–c.799. Lombard historian and poet. Served as councilor to King Desiderius; member of Charlemagne's palace school; inmate (from 786) of Benedictine abbey of Monte Cassino. Author of *Historia Langobardum* (a history of the Lombards from 568 to 744) and *Historia Romana* (a continuation of Eutropius's Roman history).

Paul the Hermit, Saint. See PAUL of Thebes.

Paul, Alice. 1885–1977. American social reformer, b. Moorestown, N.J. A founder (1913) of the Congressional Union for Woman Suffrage, which became the National Woman's party; campaigned throughout her life for equal rights for women, esp. for the 19th Amendment; chairman (1942), National Woman's party.

Paul, Elliot Harold. 1891–1958. American writer, b. Malden, Mass. An expatriate in Paris after World War I; founder (with Eugene Jolas) of literary journal *transition* (1927); author of novels as *The Life and Death of a Spanish Town* (1937) and *The Last Time I Saw Paris* (1942), mystery stories, and screenplays as *Rhapsody in Blue* (1946).

Paul, Herbert Woodfield. 1853–1935. English biographer and historian. Author of *Men and Letters* (1901), *History of Modern England* (1904–06), and biographies of Gladstone, Matthew Arnold, Lord Acton.

Paul \'paůl\, Hermann. 1846–1921. German philologist. Professor, Freiburg (1874) and Munich (1893). Among his works were *Prinzipien der Sprachgeschichte* (1880), *Mittelhochdeutsche Grammatik* (1881), and *Deutsche Grammatik* (1916–20).

Paul, Jean. See Johann RICHTER.

Paul, John. See Pope JOHN PAUL I; John Paul JONES.

Paul \'pȯl\, Kegan, *in full* Charles Kegan. 1828–1902. English publisher and author. Published biography of William Godwin (1876); took over publishing business of H.S. King (1877); published *Last Journals of General Gordon,* works of Tennyson, Hardy, Meredith, Stevenson; was joined (1881) by Alfred Trench and (1889) by Messrs. Trübner & Co. and George Redway, to form

Kegan Paul, Trench, Trübner & Co., Ltd., later incorporated as Geo. Routledge & Sons, Ltd. Wrote *Biographical Sketches* (1883), *Maria Drummond* (1891).

Paul, Robert W. 1869–1943. British engineer. Exhibited (1896) a theatrograph (later called an animatograph), an early form of the motion-picture projector, following Edison's kinetoscope (1893).

Paul, Saint Vincent de. See VINCENT DE PAUL.

Paul-Bon·cour \pȯl-bōⁿ-kür\, Joseph. 1873–1972. French lawyer and politician. Deputy (1909–31); minister of labor (1911); joined Socialist party (1919); resigned from Socialist party, formed Union Socialiste Républicaine, and was elected to senate (1931); minister of war (1932); premier of France (1932–33); foreign minister (1932–34, 1936, 1938); senator (1946–48). Known for his support of League of Nations; member of League council (1933–36). In World War II member of resistance to German occupation. Member, later head, of French delegation to UN conference at San Francisco (1945). Author of *Le Fédéralisme économique* (1900), *Art et démocratie* (1912), and *Entre deux guerres* (1946).

Paul·ding \'pȯl-diŋ\, Hiram. 1797–1878. American naval officer, b. Westchester Co., N.Y. Acting lieutenant of the *Ticonderoga* at the battle of Lake Champlain (1814); served against Barbary pirates; cruised in the South Seas (1825) in pursuit of mutineers; visited China (1844–47); suppressed Walker's filibustering expedition against Nicaragua (1857).

Paulding, James Kirke. 1778–1860. American writer, b. Putnam Co., N.Y. Associated with Washington Irving in publication of humorous periodical *Salmagundi* (1807–08); published *Diverting History of John Bull and Brother Jonathan* (1812) and *The United States and England* (1815), a defense against English criticisms; prominent in literary war with English writers, publishing *A Sketch of Old England* (1822) and a burlesque *John Bull in America* (1825); urged use of native American material in literature, as in his poem "The Backwoodsman" (1818), novels *Koningsmarke* (1823), *Westward Ho!* (1832), *The Old Continental* (1846), and a play *The Lion of the West* (1831). U.S. secretary of the navy (1838–41).

Pau·let *or* **Paw·let** *or* **Pou·lett** *or* **Pow·lett** \'pȯl-ət\. An English family named from the parish of Pawlett, Somerset, different branches of which have held the baronies of St. John of Basing (from 1539), of Poulett of Hinton St. George (from 1627), and of Pawlet of Basing (1717–54); the earldoms of Wiltshire (from 1550) and of Poulet (from 1706); the marquisate of Winchester (from 1551); and the dukedom of Bolton (1689–1754). Its members included: Sir Amias Paulet (1536?–1588), lieutenant governor of Jersey, commissioner at trial of Mary, Queen of Scots, and famous as her Puritan guardian who refused to take suggestion to murder her privately. ¶Sir William Paulet (1485?–1572), 1st Marquis of Win·ches·ter \'win-,ches-tər, -chə-stər\; honored by Henry VIII; lord president of council and one of council of regency; lord treasurer (1547); joined lords at Baynard Castle who proclaimed Queen Mary in place of Lady Jane Grey; gained favor of Queen Elizabeth and was treasurer (1550–72). His grandson ¶Sir William (1535?–1598), 3d Marquis of Winchester; one of commissioners at trial of Mary, Queen of Scots, and lord steward of her funeral. ¶John Paulet (1598–1675), 5th Marquis of Winchester; grandson of the 3d marquis; known as "the great Loyalist" after fortifying and garrisoning Basing House, in Hampshire, against Cromwell's forces (1643–45); suffered long imprisonment and loss of property. ¶Charles (1625?–1699), 1st Duke of Bol·ton \'bōlt-ᵊn\ and 6th Marquis of Winchester; son of 5th marquis; deserted Stuart cause, supported Whigs and William of Orange on his landing; said to have precipitated Marlborough's disgrace by disclosures to king. ¶Charles (1661–1722), 2d Duke of Bolton and 7th Marquis of Winchester; son of the 1st duke; privy councilor (1690); lord chamberlain (1715); lord lieutenant of Ireland (1717–22). ¶Sir Charles Paulet *or* Powlett (1685–1754), 3d Duke of Bolton and 8th Marquis of Winchester; son of 2d duke; deprived of offices because of opposition to Sir Robert Walpole; married Lavinia Fenton, actress (1751).

Pau·li \'pau̇-lē\, Wolfgang. 1900–1958. American physicist, b. Vienna, Austria. Professor, Zürich (1928–40); with Inst. for Advanced Study, Princeton, (1940–45, 1949–50, 1954). Naturalized U.S. citizen (1946). Postulated existence of neutrinos (1931); won 1945 Nobel prize for physics for his discovery (1925) of the Pauli exclusion principle.

Pau·li·nus \pȯ-'lī-nəs\. Saint. *Known as* Saint Paulinus of Nola. *Full Latin name* Meropius Pontius Anicius Paulinus. 353–431. Christian prelate, b. Bordeaux. A Roman senator, consul, and (c.379) governor of Campania; ordained priest (395); bishop of Nola (c.409). Author of 35 poems, esp. one on the feast day of St. Felix, and about 50 letters addressed to Augustine, Jerome, Sulpicius Severus, and others.

Paulinus. Saint. 584?–644. Roman missionary to England. Joined Augustine in Kent (601); consecrated bishop (625); converted Edwin, king of Northumbria, who made him bishop of York (received archbishop's pallium 634); on death of Edwin (632), fled to Kent and became bishop of Rochester.

Paul Kar·a·geor·ge·vić \-,ká-rá-'jȯr-jə-vētʸ\. Prince. 1893–1976. Regent of Yugoslavia. Cousin of King Alexander I; m. (1923) Princess Olga of Greece. Appointed first regent for his nephew Peter II on death of Alexander (1934); forced to align Greece with Axis powers; deposed with other members of regency (1941); fled Greece; lived thereafter in Paris.

Paulmy, Marquis de. See VOYER family.

Paul·sen \'pau̇l-zən\, Friedrich. 1846–1908. German philosopher and educator. Professor at Berlin (1878–1908); elaborated theory of Panpsychism. Wrote on philosophy, as *System der Ethick* (1889), *Immanuel Kant* (1889), and *Einleitung in die Philosophie* (1892), and on education, as *Geschichte des gelehrten Unterrichts auf den deutschen Schulen und Universitäten* (1885).

Pau·lus \'pau̇-lu̇s\, Friedrich. 1890–1957. German field marshal. Commander (1942–43) of 6th army, which was captured by Russians at Stalingrad (Feb. 1943), thus ending Germany's offensive role in Russia.

Pau·lus \'pȯl-əs\, Julius. 2d–3d century A.D. Roman jurist. Appointed praetorian prefect by Emperor Alexander Severus. Author of commentaries on civil law and praetorian (or equity) law. Ranked with Papinian and Ulpian among the greatest of Roman jurists.

Paulus *or* **Paul·lus** \'pȯl-əs\, Lucius Ae·mil·i·us \i-'mil-ē-əs, -'mil-yəs\. d. 216 B.C. Roman soldier. Consul (219 and 216 B.C.); colleague of Varro in battle of Cannae (216), where he was killed. His son ¶Lucius Aemilius Paulus (229?–160 B.C.), *surnamed* Mac·e·don·i·cus \,mas-ə-'dän-ə-kəs\, Roman general; praetor in Spain (191–189); consul (182, 168); defeated Perseus in battle of Pydna (168), ending Third Macedonian War; given triumph in Rome (167); censor (164).

Paulus Aegineta. See PAUL of Aegina.

Paulus Diaconus. See PAUL the Deacon.

Paulus Jovius. See Paolo GIOVIO.

Pau·ly \'pau̇-lē\, August. 1796–1845. German classical philologist. Editor of Pauly's *Real-Encyclopädie der classischen Altertumswissenschaft* (1837 ff.). A new edition was edited (1893 ff.) by Georg Wissowa (*q.v.*).

Paunce·fote \'pän(t)s-,fu̇t, -fət\, Julian. 1st Baron Pauncefote. 1828–1902. English diplomat. Negotiated successfully disputes over Canadian seal fishing in Bering Sea (1892) and over boundary between Venezuela and British Guiana (1895–99); signed Hay-Pauncefote Treaty providing equal passage for all nations through Panama Canal (1901).

Pau·sa·ni·as \pȯ-'sā-nē-əs\. d. c.470 or 465 B.C. Spartan general. Son of King Cleombrotus; regent for Pleistarchus (479 B.C.); commanded allied Greek army in decisive victory at Plataea (479); admiral of Greek fleet (478); subjugated most of Cyprus and captured Byzantium from the Persians; became tyrannical and overbearing, alienating his Greek allies; entered into treasonable correspondence with Persian king; recalled to Sparta, where he plotted a revolt against the government; on discovery of his plot, fled to sanctuary on the Spartan Acropolis, where he was starved to death.

Pausanias. fl. 143–176 A.D. Greek traveler and geographer. Author of *Periegesis of Greece,* a valuable source of information on topography, local history, religious customs, architecture, and sculpture in Greece.

Pau·si·as \'pȯ-sē-əs\. 4th century B.C. Greek painter. Studied under Pamphilus; renowned as a decorative artist, esp. in encaustic.

Pau·stov·sky \pō-'stȯf-skəi\, Konstantin Georgiyevich. 1892–1968. Soviet writer. Author of novels and short stories in the Romantic tradition; esp. noted for his 6-volume *Rasskaz zhizni* (Story of a Life, 1946–62), novel *Rozhdenie morya* (1952), and novellas *Kara-Bugaz* (1932) and *Kolhkida* (1934).

Pa·ve·lić \'pa-ve-,lētʸ\, Ante. 1889–1959. Croatian politician. President of the senate of Yugoslavia (1932); organized (1929) terrorist group Ustashe, which assassinated King Alexander in Marseilles (1934); appointed by Hitler head of the small Croat state set up under German-Italian protection after the Axis conquest of the Balkans (1941); fled to Argentina after defeat of Germany (1945).

Pa·ve·se \pä-'vā-zā\, Cesare. 1908–1950. Italian writer. Translated many American writers of 1920s and 1930s and wrote essays on them in *La letteratura americana e altri saggi* (1951); founded publishing house Einaudi; imprisoned (1935) for anti-Fascist activities, as editing review *La Cultura;* with Resistance partisans in World War II. Author of works on alienation and disillusionment in modern life, including novels *Il compagno* (1947), *La luna e i falò* (1950), collections of stories *La bella estate* (1949), *Notte di festa* (1953), *Racconti* (1960), poetry *Lavorare stanca* (1936), *Verrà la morte e avrà i tuoi occhi* (1951), essays *Dialoghi con Leucò* (1947), and autobiographical *Il mestiere de viviere, diario 1935–1950* (1952).

Pa·vía y La·cy \pä-'b̲ē-ä-ē-'lä-thē, -sē\, Manuel. 1814–1896. Spanish general. Fought for Isabella II in First Carlist War (1833–39); helped Narvaez overthrow Espartero (1843); minister of war (1847); as captain general of the

Philippines crushed revolt of José Cuesta (1853); his defeat by Serrano y Domínguez at Alcolea (Sept. 28, 1868) insured deposition of Isabella.

Pavía y Ro·drí·guez de Al·bur·quer·que \-ē-rōth-'rē-gāth-thā-äl-bür-'ker-kā\, Manuel. 1827–1895. Spanish general. On staff of General Prim y Prats (1865) and engaged with him in deposition of Isabella II (1868); used his troops to gain control of political situation in Madrid (1874) and turned over power to Serrano y Domínguez to organize a coalition government; appointed senator for life (1880); captain general of Catalonia (1880–81) and New Castile (1885–86).

Pa·vie \pá-vē\, Auguste-Jean-Marie. 1847–1925. French diplomat and explorer. To Cochinchina (1869); as vice consul in Luang Prabang (1886–91) and consul general in Bangkok (1891–93) secured French control of kingdoms of Laos; explored upper Mekong Valley and defined border of Laos; wrote *Mission Pavie* (1898–1919) and *À la conquête des coeurs* (1921).

Pa·vlov \'páv-ləf, *Angl* 'päv-,lôf, 'pav-, -,lôv\, Ivan Petrovich. 1849–1936. Russian physiologist. Professor (from 1890) and director (1895–1925), department of physiology, Institute of Experimental Medicine, and professor in the Military Medical Acad. (1890–1925), St. Petersburg. Made researches on the physiology of the heart, digestion, and the brain and higher nervous system; conducted famous experiment demonstrating conditioned reflex in a dog; awarded 1904 Nobel prize for physiology or medicine.

Pa·vlo·va \'páv-ləv-ə, *Angl* 'pav-lə-və, pav-'lō-\, Anna Pavlovna. 1882–1931. Russian ballerina. Studied at Imperial Ballet School, St. Petersburg; toured Europe and U.S. (from 1907). Famed for dance creations, among best known of which were *Le Cygne,* composed especially for her by Michel Fokine, *Papillons,* and her only choreographic piece, *Autumn Leaves* (1918). Settled in Paris; m. (1914) Victor d'André (d. 1944); founded school for teaching interpretative dancing.

Pawlet. See PAULET.

Pax·ton \'paks-tən\, Sir Joseph. 1801–1865. English architect and horticulturist. Designed conservatory in gardens at Chatsworth (1836–40), which served as a model for his design of the Crystal Palace, built of glass and iron for the London Exhibition of 1851 and re-erected into a palace at Sydenham (1853–54).

Pa·yen \pá-yaⁿ\, Anselme. 1795–1871. French industrial chemist. His discovery of production of borax from boric acid broke Dutch monopoly on borax; discovered use of charcoal to filter out coloring impurities in beet sugar (1822); discovered diastase (1833), cellulose (1838), pectin, and dextrin. Professor at École Centrale des Arts et Manufactures (1829 ff.) and at Conservatoire des Arts et Métiers (1839 ff.).

Pay·er \'pī-ər\, Julius von. 1842–1915. Austrian explorer and painter. With Weyprecht led the Austro-Hungarian North Polar expedition which resulted in discovery of Franz Josef Land (1872–74); upon return to Europe, devoted himself to painting pictures relating to his polar experiences.

Payn \'pān\, James. 1830–1898. English novelist. Editor of *Chambers's Journal* (1859–74) and of *Cornhill Magazine* (1883–96); author of novels as *Lost Sir Massingberd* (1864), *Carlyon's Year* (1868), *The Talk of the Town* (1885), *Another's Burden* (1897).

Payne \'pān\, John. 1842–1916. English poet and translator. Author of *A Masque of Shadows* (1871), *Lautrec* (narrative poem, 1878), and *New Poems* (1880); translator of Villon's poems (1878), *Arabian Nights* (1882–84).

Payne, John Howard. 1791–1852. American actor and playwright, b. New York City. Succeeded in his play *Brutus, or the Fall of Tarquin* (1818); in Europe as actor and theater manager (1813–32); immortalized by a single song, "Home, Sweet Home," in his opera *Clari, or, the Maid of Milan* (1823). Collaborated with Washington Irving in plays, esp. *Charles the Second* (1824) and *Richelieu* (1826). U.S. consul at Tunis (1842–45, 1851–52). Author, translator, and adapter of more than sixty plays.

Payne, Peter. c.1380–1455. English Hussite theologian and diplomat. Follower of John Wycliffe; fled to Bohemia (1415) where he became a leading figure of the Hussite church; wrote theological tracts.

Payne Smith \'pān-'smith\, Robert. 1819–1895. English theologian and Orientalist. Published first part of his Syriac dictionary, the *Thesaurus Syriacus* (1868), which occupied him the rest of his life; regius professor of divinity, Oxford (1865–70); dean of Canterbury (1870–95); member of Old Testament revision committee (1870–85).

Payson, Howard. See Edward STRATEMEYER.

Páz·mány \'páz-mänʸ\, Péter. 1570–1637. Hungarian prelate and writer. Cardinal (1629); leader of Counter-Reformation in Hungary; wrote over 40 books on religion, esp. *Hodoegus* (1613).

Paz Sol·dán \'päs-sōl-'dän\, Mariano Felipe. 1821–1886. Peruvian politician and historian. Minister of foreign affairs (1858–63) and of justice (1868–72); wrote *Atlas geográfico del Perú* (1861), *Historia del Perú independiente* (1866), etc.

Pea·body \'pē-,bäd-ē, -bəd-ē\, Elizabeth Palmer. 1804–1894. American educator, b. Billerica, Mass. Mistress of private schools (1820–23, 1825–34); secretary to William Ellery Channing (1825–34); assistant to Bronson Alcott in Temple School, Boston (1834–36). Opened bookshop in Boston (1839) which became center for Transcendentalist activities, including publication of the *Dial* (1842–43); interested herself in educational theory and methods; published elementary textbooks in grammar and history. Studied Froebel and (1860) opened first American kindergarten, Boston; published the magazine *Kindergarten Messenger* (1873–75). Lectured at Alcott's Concord School of Philosophy (1879–84). Wrote a life of William Ellery Channing, an account of Bronson Alcott's school methods, *Records of a School* (1835).

Peabody, Endicott. 1857–1944. American educator, b. Salem, Mass. A founder (1884) and the first headmaster (1884–1940) of Groton School, Groton, Mass.

Peabody, George. 1795–1869. American merchant and philanthropist, b. South Danvers, now Peabody, Mass. Partner in Riggs and Peabody, wholesale drygoods house, Baltimore (1815–37); settled in London, England (1837), as banker and broker; admitted Junius Spencer Morgan to partnership (1854). Used his credit to support American credit abroad in years following panic of 1837; fitted out Elisha Kane's ship to search for John Franklin in the Arctic (1853). Founded and endowed Peabody Institute, Baltimore; Peabody Institute, Peabody, Mass.; Peabody Museum, Yale; Peabody Museum, Harvard; Peabody Education Fund to advance education in the South, etc.

Peabody, Josephine Preston. 1874–1922. American poet and playwright, b. Brooklyn, N.Y. Author of *The Wayfarers* (1898), *Fortune and Men's Eyes* (1900), *The Singing Leaves* (1903), *Pan, a Choric Idyl* (1904), *The Book of the Little Past* (1908), *The Piper* (1909), *The Singing Man* (1911), *The Wings* (1912), *The Wolf of Gubbio* (1913), *Harvest Moon* (1916), *Portrait of Mrs. W.* (1922).

Peach \'pēch\, Charles William. 1800–1886. English naturalist and geologist. Found fossils off coasts of Norfolk and Cornwall; found first fossils in Cambrian limestone of Scotland (1854); discovered many species of sponges, coelenterates, and mollusks.

Pea·cham \'pē-chəm\, Henry. 1576?–?1643. English author, painter, engraver, composer, mathematician. First book, *Graphice* (1606), treatise on pen and water-color drawings, reissued under title *The Gentleman's Exercise;* made reputation with his epigrams; his magnum opus *The Compleat Gentleman* (1622), from the last edition of which (1661) Dr. Johnson drew the heraldic definitions in his dictionary.

Pea·cock \'pē-,käk\, George. 1791–1858. English mathematician. With Herschel, Babbage, and Woodhouse, translated Lacroix's *Differential and Integral Calculus* (1816) and furthered introduction of Continental mathematical notation into Cambridge; published his *Algebra* (1830); dean of Ely (1839–58); member of commission on weights and measures, advocated system of decimal coinage.

Peacock, Thomas Love. 1785–1866. English novelist and poet. Close friend of Shelley (from 1812), and Shelley's executor; clerk and examiner to East India Company (1819–56). His satirical novels, of scanty plot but full of odd characters and interspersed with lyrics, included *Headlong Hall* (1816), *Melincourt* (1817), *Nightmare Abbey* (1818), *Crotchet Castle* (1831), and *Gryll Grange* (1860); his more Romantic novels included *Maid Marian* (1822), *The Misfortunes of Elphin* (1829). *Rhododaphne* (1818), his best long poetical composition, shows Shelley's influence; his essay *The Four Ages of Poetry* (1820) provoked Shelley's *Defence of Poetry.*

Peake \'pēk\, Mervyn Laurence. 1911–1968. English writer and illustrator, b. China. His writings included novels *Mr. Pye* (1953) and the Gothic fantasy trilogy *Titus Groan* (1946), *Gormenghast* (1950), *Titus Alone* (1959), books of verse *Shapes and Sounds* (1941), *The Glassblowers* (1950), a play *The Wit to Woo* (1957), and children's books; illustrated his own works.

Peale \'pē(ə)l\. Name of a family of American artists, including: Charles Willson Peale (1741–1827), portrait painter; an officer in American Revolution, at battles of Trenton and Princeton; an engraver in Philadelphia (c.1781–90); opened Peale Museum (1786); painted over 1000 portraits, including Washington, Franklin, Jefferson, and John Adams. His brother ¶James (1749–1831), miniaturist with studio in Philadelphia; painted miniatures of Martha and George Washington (1782) and one of George Washington (1788). Charles's three children: ¶Raphaelle (1774–1825), best known for his miniatures and still-life paintings. ¶Rembrandt (1778–1860), best known for his portraits and historical scenes; painted portrait of Washington from life (1795), Jefferson (1804), Napoléon Bonaparte (1810); opened a museum and portrait gallery in Baltimore; author of *Notes on Italy* (1831), *Portfolio of an Artist* (1839). ¶Titian Ramsay (1799–1885), painter and naturalist with Stephen Long's expedition to the Upper Missouri (1819–20); agent in Florida for Charles Lucien Bonaparte to collect specimens and make drawings for Bonaparte's *American Ornithology* (1825–33); on staff of Wilkes's exploring expedition to the South Seas (1838–42); examiner, U.S. Patent Office (1849–72). James Peale's two children: ¶Anna Claypoole (1791–1878), miniaturist, did portraits of Andrew Jackson, James Monroe, Henry Clay; and

¶Sarah Miriam (1800–1885), painted portraits of Lafayette, Commodore Bainbridge, Caleb Cushing, Senator Benton.

Pé·an \pā-ä^{n}\, Jules-Émile. 1830–1898. French surgeon. A founder of modern gynecological surgery; invented several surgical instruments and wrote medical books.

Pe·a·no \pā-'än-ō\, Giuseppe. 1858–1932. Italian mathematician and linguist. Professor, Turin (1890–98); a founder of symbolic logic, expounded in *Formulaire de mathematiques* (1894–1908); also wrote works on the general theory of functions in calculus (1884, 1893) and on mathematical logic (*Calcolo geometrico,* 1888). Devised an artificial language known as *Latino sine flexione,* or *Interlingua,* whose vocabulary consists of words common to Latin, French, German, and English (1903).

Pearl \'pərl\, Raymond. 1879–1940. American biologist, b. Farmington, N.H. Professor, Johns Hopkins medical school (from 1923), School of Hygiene and Public Health (from 1930). A founder of biometry; founded *Quarterly Review of Biology* (1926) and *Human Biology* (1929). Author of *The Biology of Death* (1922), *Introduction to Medical Biometry and Statistics* (1923), *The Biology of Population Growth* (1925), *The Ancestry of the Long-lived* (with his daughter Ruth DeWitt Pearl, 1934), *The Natural History of Population* (1939), etc.

Pearse \'pi(ə)rs\, Patrick Henry. 1879–1916. Irish educationist, author, and nationalist leader. Director of Gaelic League and editor of its newspaper *An Claidheamh Soluis* (1903–09); promoted use of Irish language, in which he wrote poems and stories; founded St. Enda's College in Dublin (1908). As a leader of the Irish Republican Brotherhood planned and commanded its forces in Easter Rising (Apr. 24, 1916); surrendered and was executed.

Pear·son \'pi(ə)rs-ᵊn\, Sir Cyril Arthur. 1866–1921. English publisher. Published magazines as *Pearson's Weekly* and *Home Notes* and newspapers as *Daily Express* (from 1900); also known for philanthropic work, esp. for blind persons.

Pearson, Drew, *in full* Andrew Russell. 1897–1969. American newspaper columnist, b. Evanston, Ill. With *Baltimore Sun* (1929); fired for writing (with Robert Allen) exposé *The Washington Merry-Go-Round* (1931); wrote (from 1932) muckraking column of same name with Allen (until 1942) and Jack Anderson (from 1959); exposed many government scandals.

Pearson, Hesketh. 1887–1964. English biographer. Author of numerous biographies, including *Doctor Darwin* (1930), *Gilbert and Sullivan* (1935), *G.B.S.* (1942), *Life of Oscar Wilde* (1946), and *Johnson and Boswell* (1958).

Pearson, John. 1613–1686. English prelate and theologian. Royalist chaplain until collapse of royal cause; defended Anglican church against Catholic and Puritan attacks and promoted London Polyglot Bible. At Restoration was showered with honors; defended authenticity of the letters of Ignatius; bishop of Chester (1673). Author of *Exposition of the Creed* (1659).

Pearson, Karl. 1857–1936. English mathematician. Professor at U. of London (1884–1933). Associate of Francis Galton and Walter Weldon; applied statistics to biological problems, esp. evolution and heredity. Editor, *Biometrika* (1901–36), *Annals of Eugenics* (1925–36); author of *The Ethic of Free Thought* (1888), *The Grammar of Science* (1892), *The Chances of Death, and other Studies in Evolution* (1897), *The Life, Letters, and Labours of Francis Galton* (1914); also literary works *The New Werther* (1880) and *The Trinity* (1882).

Pearson, Lester Bowles. 1897–1972. Canadian politician, b. Toronto. Taught at U. of Toronto (1924–28); entered diplomatic service (1928); ambassador to U.S. (1945–46); M.P. (1948–68); secretary of state for external affairs (1948–57); president, U.N. General Assembly (1952–53); prime minister (1963–68). Awarded Nobel peace prize (1957) for efforts to solve Suez crisis of 1956.

Pearson, Weetman Dickinson. 1st Viscount Cow·dray \'kaù-(ˌ)drā, -drē\. 1856–1927. English contractor. Partner in family firm (1875); to Mexico (1889); gained profitable contracts, acquired oil properties, and helped develop the Mexican petroleum industry. His firm built Blackwall Tunnel under Thames River, London (1894), four railroad tunnels under the East River, New York, dam on Blue Nile (1926). M.P. (1895–1910); created baron (1910), viscount (1917).

Pea·ry \'pi(ə)r-ē\, Robert Edwin. 1856–1920. American explorer, b. Cresson, Pa. Civil engineer, U.S. navy (from 1881); retired with rank of rear admiral (1911). Started Arctic exploration with voyages to Greenland (1886, 1891–92); on third voyage failed to reach North Pole (1893–95); his fourth voyage (1898–1902) reached 84° 17′ N., furthest north in the American Arctic. Granted three years' leave (1903); sailed in the *Roosevelt* (1905–06) in attempt to reach the North Pole; reached 87° 6′ N., only 174 miles from the Pole, before he had to turn back. Final and successful expedition (1908–09); reached the North Pole (Apr. 6, 1909). On announcing success of expedition, learned that Dr. Frederick A. Cook, had claimed five days earlier that he had reached the Pole a year before Peary. Scientific investigation later discredited Cook and recognized Peary's attainment. Author of *Northward over the Great Ice* (1898), *Nearest the Pole* (1907), *The North Pole* (1910), *Secrets of Polar Travel* (1917). His wife (m. 1888) ¶Josephine, *nee* Die·bitsch \'dē-bich\ (1863–1955), accompanied him on his 1891 and 1893 expeditions; wrote *My Arctic Journal* (1894), *The Snow Baby* (1901).

Pease \'pēz\, Edward Reynolds. 1857–1955. English Socialist. Left business career to help found Fabian Society (1884) and was its secretary (1890–1913); helped form (1900) Labour Representation Committee that became (1906) Labour party; wrote *History of the Fabian Society* (1916).

Pease, Francis Galdheim. 1881–1938. American astronomer, b. Cambridge, Mass. Optician and observer, Yerkes Observatory (1901–04); instrument designer (1904–07, 1908–13), astronomer (from 1911), Mt. Wilson Observatory. Known for direct photographs and spectrograms of nebulae, star clusters, the moon, and planets, measurement of stellar diameters with the interferometer, and measurement of ether drift and of the velocity of light; designed 100-inch telescope and other instruments; developed method for grinding mirror of the 200-inch telescope of Mt. Palomar.

Peat·tie \'pēt-ē\, Donald Culross. 1898–1964. American naturalist, b. Chicago. Author of *Almanac for Moderns* (1935), *Singing in the Wilderness* (1935), *The Road of a Naturalist* (1941), *American Heartwood* (1949), *The Rainbow Book of Nature* (1957), etc.

Peau·cel·lier \pō-sel-yā\, Charles-Nicolas. French military engineer. Invented (1873) a linkage, known by his name, capable of describing a circular arc of any radius, including a straight line.

Pech·stein \'pek-ˌshtīn\, Max. 1881–1955. German painter and printmaker. Member of German Expressionist group Die Brücke (1906–10) and of Neue Sezession group (from 1910) in Berlin; known for nudes and landscapes, as *Horse Market at Moritzburg* (1910), *Indian and Woman* (1910), *Nude under the Tent* (1911); after trip to South Pacific (1914) painted in more primitive style. Also a designer of stained glass and mosaics.

Peck \'pek\, Annie Smith. 1850–1935. American mountain climber, b. Providence, R.I. Public lecturer (from 1890) on archaeology, mountain climbing, and South America. Ascended the Matterhorn (1895), Popocatepetl and Orizaba (1897); made first ascent of Mt. Huascarán, Peru, 21,812 ft., highest point in America ever reached by an American (1908). Author of *A Search for the Apex of America* (1911), *The South American Tour* (1914), *Flying over South America* (1932), etc.

Peck, George Wilbur. 1840–1916. American journalist, humorist, and politician, b. Henderson, N.Y. In Milwaukee published the *Sun* (1878–90), in which appeared Peck's Bad Boy stories; mayor of Milwaukee (1890); governor of Wisconsin (1891–95). Author of *Peck's Bad Boy and His Pa* (1883), *Peck's Bad Boy with the Cowboys* (1907), etc.

Peckham, John. See JOHN PECKHAM.

Peck·ham \'pek-əm\, Rufus Wheeler. 1838–1909. American jurist, b. Albany, N.Y. Practiced law in Albany (1859 ff.); justice, New York State supreme court (1883–86) and court of appeals (1886–95); associate justice, U.S. Supreme Court (1896–1909).

Pe·cock \'pē-ˌkäk\, Reginald. 1395?–?1460. British theologian, b. Wales. Bishop of St. Asaph (1444), of Chichester (1450); privy councilor (1454). Issued (1455?) his chief work, *Repressor of Over-Much Weeting* [blaming] *of the Clergie,* directed against Lollard teachings, and of importance as a model of 15th-century English; wrote *Book of Faith,* also in the vernacular. In the *Provoker* denied authenticity of Apostles' Creed; in general, exalted authority of reason and denied Scriptures to be only standard of right and wrong; found guilty of heresy (1457); died in confinement.

Pec·quet \pe-ke\, Jean. 1622–1674. French physician and anatomist. Credited with discovery of course of lacteal vessels, of the cistern chyli (or reservoir of Pecquet), and of the termination of the thoracic duct at the opening into the left subclavian vein.

Pe·der·sen \'pith-ər-sən\, Christiern. 1480?–1554. Danish theologian and historian. Accompanied Christian II in exile; joined Reformation and made first translation of New Testament into Danish (1529). Returned to Denmark (1532) and collaborated in translating Bible into Danish (published 1550 as Christian III's Bible). By his work, furnished Denmark with beginnings of a national and theological literature in language of the people.

Pedersen, Holger. 1867–1953. Danish philologist and Celtic scholar. Author of *Vergleichende Grammatik der keltischen Sprachen* (1909–13), *Concise Comparative Celtic Grammar* (1937, with H. Lewis), and many books on European and Asian languages.

Pedersen, Johannes Peder Ejler. 1883–1951. Danish scholar and philologist. Professor of Semitic philology at Copenhagen (1922–50); his chief work *Israel: Its Life and Culture* (1920–34), valuable for his conception of the importance of the cult in ancient Israel.

Pe·der·sen \'pā-dər-sən\, Knut. *Pseudonym* Knut Ham·sun \'häm-su̇n\. 1859–1952. Norwegian writer. Worked at many jobs, as grade-school teacher, laborer; in U.S. (1882–84, 1886–88) as streetcar conductor in Chicago and farmhand in North Dakota. Author of Neo-Romantic novels generally stressing individualism, as *Sult* (1890), *Mysterier* (1892), *Pan* (1894), *Victoria* (1898), *Markens grøde* (1917), *Konerne ved Vandposten* (1920), *Landstrykere* (1927), *August* (1930), and *Men livet lever* (1933). Reputation damaged as result of support of Quisling regime, but later restored. Awarded Nobel prize for literature (1920).

Pedo. See ALBINOVANUS PEDO.

Pedrarias *or* **Pedrarias Dávila.** See Pedro ARIAS DÁVILA.

Pe·drell \pā-'t͟hrel\, Felipe. 1841–1922. Spanish composer and musicologist. Leader of nationalist music movement in Spain; his manifesto *Por nuestra música* (1891) advocated a Spanish opera based on native folksongs; founder and editor of several publications as *Salterio sacro-hispano* (1882) and *Música religiosa* (1896); edited *Hispanae schola musica sacra* (1894–98) and *Cancionero musical popular español* (1919–20); wrote critical and historical works on music. Professor at Madrid Conservatory (1895–1903); teacher of Albéniz, Anglés, Falla, Gerhard, and Granados. Composed symphonic poems, choral music, chamber music, choral works, songs, and esp. operas *El último abencerraje* (1869), *Quasimodo* (1875), *Cleopatra* (1881), *Los Pirineos* (1902), and *La Celestina* (1904). His nephew ¶Carlos (1878–1941), b. Uruguay; inspector of music in Buenos Aires schools (from 1906); settled in Paris (1921); composed operas as *Ardid de amor* (1917) and *La guitare* (1924), two ballets, symphonic and choral works, chamber music, and songs.

Pedro. See PETER for kings of Portugal and Spain.

Pe·dro \'pā-t͟hrü\. *Called* Dom Pedro. Name of two emperors of Brazil:

Pedro I, Dom. *Also* Dom Pedro IV of Portugal. *Full name* Antonio Pedro de Al·cân·ta·ra Bour·bon \-t͟hē-äl-'kän-tə-rə-bür-'bōn\. 1798–1834. Emperor (1822–31). Second son of John VI of Portugal; fled to Brazil (1807) to escape French; made regent of Brazil by King John (1821); took sides with Brazilians against Portuguese reactionary policy; declared independence of Brazil (Sept. 7, 1822); crowned emperor (Oct. 1822); at first popular, his influence weakened by despotic regime; promulgated new constitution (1824); abdicated (1831) and went to Europe; proclaimed king of Portugal (1826); resigned in favor of his daughter Donna Maria da Glória (see MARIA II of Portugal); waged successful war against the usurper, his brother Dom Miguel (1832–34); m. 1st Archduchess Maria Leopoldina of Austria (1818); 2d Princess Amélie of Leuchtenberg (1829).

Pedro II, Dom. *Full name* Pedro de Al·cân·ta·ra \-t͟hē-äl-'kän-tə-rə\. 1825–1891. Emperor (1831–89). Son of Dom Pedro I; became emperor on abdication of his father; in early years of reign, many revolutionary disturbances; aided Urquiza (1851–52) against Rosas in Argentina and joined Argentina and Uruguay in war (1864–70) against Paraguay; opened Amazon to commerce (1867) and worked for abolition of slavery (1871–88); absent several times in Europe, during which periods his daughter Isabella acted as regent. Forced to abdicate on proclamation of republic (Nov. 1889). Sent to Europe; died in Paris. A man of wide culture; visited U.S. (1876; first monarch to visit North America), where he met and encouraged Alexander Graham Bell and was first to use the telephone; his rule marked by great progress of Brazil.

Pedro. Duque de Coim·bra \kōin(m)-brə\. 1392–1449. Portuguese nobleman. 3d son of King John I and brother of King Edward; traveled in Asia and Africa; regent during minority of Afonso V (1438–48); accused of intending deposition and forced from office; encouraged voyages of younger brother Henry the Navigator; translated Latin classics; rebelled against Afonso's government and was killed in battle at Alfarrobeira. His son ¶Pedro (1429–66), constable of Portugal; in exile in Castile (1449–56) after downfall of father; proclaimed (1464) king by Catalonian rebels and aided their rebellion; author of prose and verse in Spanish as *Menosprecio del mundo* and *Satira de felice e infelice vida.*

Peel \'pē(ə)l\, Sir Robert. 1788–1850. English politician. Tory M.P. (1809–50); undersecretary for war and colonies (1810–12); chief secretary for Ireland (1812–18); combated successfully advocates of Roman Catholic emancipation; instituted Irish constabulary, nicknamed after him *peelers.* Began to build financial reputation upon carrying resolutions embodying recommendations of Huskisson, Ricardo, and other economists for resumption of cash payments (1819). As home secretary (1822–27), defeated upon question of Roman Catholic emancipation, carried bills embodying reform of criminal law. Joined cabinet of Duke of Wellington as home secretary and leader of House of Commons (1828–30); instituted (1829) first disciplined police force in London (*bobbies* nicknamed after him); forced by circumstances to propose Roman Catholic emancipation. First lord of treasury, chancellor of exchequer, and prime minister (1834–35); set about building up the Conservative party with policy of maintaining intact constitution of church and state. As first lord of treasury and prime minister (1841–46), with majority in both houses, imposed income tax and abated import duties on food and raw materials, with result that national debt and taxes were reduced; reorganized Bank of England; initiated reforms in Ireland; removed penal laws against Roman Catholics and municipal disabilities of Jews; carried measure repealing the corn laws (1846); defeated on Irish coercion bill by protectionists led by Lord Bentinck and Benjamin Disraeli and Whigs (1846). Supported Whigs in free-trade principles, emancipation of Jews; made last speech on Greek question in opposition to Palmerston's policy of interference (1850); mortally injured by fall from his horse.

His son ¶Arthur Wellesley (1829–1912), 1st Viscount Peel, M.P. (1865–95), was speaker of House of Commons (1884–95) in a stormy period and first invoked closure in combating Irish obstruction; created viscount (1895). His son ¶William Robert Wellesley (1867–1937), 2d Viscount and 1st Earl Peel, was M.P. (1900–06, 1909–12); minister of transport (1921–22); secretary for India (1922–24, 1928–29); first commissioner of works (1924–28); made earl (1929); lord privy seal (1931); member of Indian joint committee (1933), Palestine royal commission (1936–37).

Peele \'pē(ə)l\, George. 1556–1596. English dramatist and poet. Author of *The Arraignment of Paris* (a pastoral comedy presented to Queen Elizabeth by the chapel children c.1581, printed 1584); a chronicle play *Edward I* (1593); *The Battle of Alcazar* (acted 1588–89, printed 1594); *The Old Wives' Tale* (1595), characterized by a play within a play, and thought to have suggested subject of Milton's *Comus; The Love of King David and Fair Bethsabe* (1599); also of *Polyhymnia* (1590) and *The Honour of the Garter* (1593), and other occasional poems, and pageants, esp. *Device of the Pageant Borne Before Woolstone Dixi* (1585), earliest extant complete lord mayor's show.

Peg·ler \'peg-lər\, Westbrook, *in full* James Westbrook. 1894–1969. American journalist, b. Minneapolis. On staff of United Press as war correspondent (1916–18) and sports commentator (1919–25); with Chicago *Tribune* (1925–33); columnist for New York *World-Telegram* (1933–44) and King Features Syndicate (1944–62); known for caustic attacks on public figures.

Pe·go·lot·ti \pā-gō-'lȯt-tē\, Francesco Balducci. fl. 1315–1340. Florentine merchant. Commercial agent for Bardi family of Florence; his *Pratica della mercatura* (compiled 1335–43) valuable for information on trading routes, customs, and currencies.

Pé·goud \pā-gü\, Adolphe. 1889–1915. French aviator. Known for acrobatic flying feats; credited with first "looping the loop" in an aircraft; killed in aerial combat.

Pé·guy \pā-gē\, Charles-Pierre. 1873–1914. French writer. Vigorous defender of Dreyfus; a Socialist; pupil of Henri Bergson; founded (1900) the journal *Cahiers de la Quinzaine,* in which his chief works appeared. Author of studies on Joan of Arc, Victor Hugo, and Henri Bergson, and of religious meditations, esp. *Ève* (1913). Killed at first battle of the Marne.

Peirce \'pərs, 'pi(ə)rs\, Benjamin. 1809–1880. American mathematician and astronomer, b. Salem, Mass. Professor, Harvard (1833–80); consulting astronomer for *American Ephemeris and Nautical Almanac* (1849–67); superintendent, U.S. Coast Survey (1867–74). Renowned for accurate computation of the general perturbations of Uranus and Neptune, for his researches on the rings of Saturn, and for his papers in a new mathematical field *Linear Associative Algebra* (1870). Author of many mathematical textbooks and *A System of Analytic Mechanics* (1855).

Peirce, Benjamin Osgood. 1854–1914. American mathematician and physicist. Distant cousin of Charles Sanders Peirce; taught at Harvard (1881–1914), professor (from 1888); conducted researches in electricity, magnetism, and hydrodynamics; wrote *Short Table of Integrals* (1889).

Peirce, Charles Sanders. 1839–1914. American physicist, mathematician, and logician, b. Cambridge, Mass. Son of Benjamin Peirce. On staff of U.S. Coast Survey (1861–91); prepared numerous technical papers on logic (1867–85), laying foundations of the logic of relations, the instrument for logical analysis of mathematics, and contributing to the theory of probability and the logic of scientific methodology; lectured on logic, Johns Hopkins U. (1879–84). Founder of pragmatism, first outlined in paper contributed to *Popular Science Monthly* (1878) and developed later by William James, and of pragmaticism, which Peirce differentiated from James's philosophy; a founder of semiotics; now regarded as most original thinker and greatest logician of his time.

Pei·resc \pe-resk\, Nicolas-Claude Fab·ri de \fȧb-rē-də-\. 1580–1637. French antiquarian and patron of learning. Traveled to Italy (1599–1602) and met Galileo; senator at parliament of Aix (1605); corresponded with Rubens; discovered Orion Nebula (1610) and observed motions of the planets; encouraged Grotius; emphasized numismatics for historical research.

Peirse \'pi(ə)rs, 'pi(ə)rz\, Sir Richard Edmund Charles. 1892–1970. British air chief marshal. Commander in Palestine and Transjordan (1933–36); head of Bomber Command (1940–42); commander in India (1942–43); allied air chief in southeast Asia (1943–45).

Peisander. See PISANDER.

Pei·sis·tra·tus *or* **Pi·sis·tra·tus** \pī-'sis-trət-əs, pə-\. d. 527 B.C. Athenian tyrant. Distinguished himself in war with Megara (570–565); seized power

(561, 556–555) but driven out; gained definitive control with victory at Pallene (546) and ruled until death. Effected religious reforms, esp. the promotion of cult of Athena; built shrines and temples; improved water supply and the agora; reign noted for expansion of industry and commerce, internal tranquility, and neutrality in external relations.

Pei·xo·to \pā-'shō-tü\, Floriano. 1842–1895. Brazilian general. A leader in establishment of Brazilian independence (1889); vice president (1891); president (1891–94); put down naval revolt of Admiral Mello (1893–94).

Pek·ka·nen \'pek-kän-en\, Toivo. 1902–1957. Finnish writer. Known for realistic portrayals of the urban poor, as novels *Tehtaan varjossa* (1932) and *Isänmaan ranta* (1937); also wrote short stories, poems, plays, and memoirs *Lapsuuteni* (1953).

Pé·la·dan \pā-lá-däⁿ\, Joseph, *called* Joséphin. 1859–1918. French writer. Established reputation as mystic and master of the occult; founded order of "Rose-Croix" (1892–98); claimed descent from Babylonian kings, assuming title Sar, and called attention to himself by his eccentricities. Published series of strange novels under general title *La Décadence latine* (1885–1907); also wrote plays and art criticism.

Pe·la·gia \pə-'lā-j(ē-)ə\ of Antioch. Saint. d. c.311. Christian martyr. A 15-year-old virgin who, during persecutions of Diocletian, threw herself from a housetop to save her chastity.

Pe·la·gi·us \pə-'lā-j(ē-)əs\. Name of two popes:

Pelagius I. d. 561. Pope (556–561). As deacon, accompanied Agapetus to Constantinople (535–536) to dissuade Justinian I from reconquering Italy; became counselor to Justinian; during Vigilius's absence persuaded Totila to spare lives of citizens after his conquest of Rome (546); excommunicated (554) and imprisoned (554–555) for opposing Vigilius on "Three Chapters" controversy; elected pope on Justinian's insistence; as pope, rebuilt much of Rome, attempted to prevent schisms, and increased political power of the papacy.

Pelagius II. d. 590. Pope (579–590). Appealed for Frankish aid to stem Lombard invasions (580); unsuccessful in attempts to settle schism over "Three Chapters" controversy; quarreled with Byzantine emperor Maurice over granting of title "ecumenical patriarch" to St. John IV the Faster.

Pelagius. c.354–after 418. British monk and theologian. Led theological disputation in Rome, refuting the Augustinian doctrines of predestination and total depravity, asserting freedom of the will, and emphasizing primacy of human effort in spiritual salvation. Joined by Coelestius, a bold preacher, crossed to Africa (after sack of Rome by Goths, 410), and met Augustine; proceeded to Palestine. Accused of heresy (415); acquitted by synod of Jerusalem; called upon by Innocent I to abjure his teachings; his excommunication (417) by Innocent upheld by Zosimus; banished from Rome (418). His tenets (Pelagianism) persisted in modified form as semi-Pelagianism. Author of *Expositiones XIII Epistularum Pauli* (c.405), *De libero arbitrio* (416), *Libellus fidei* (417).

Pe·la·vi·ci·no \pā-lä-vē-'sē-nō\ *or* **Pal·la·vi·ci·no** \päl-lä-\, Oberto. 1197–1269. Italian politician. Served Frederick II as imperial vicar in northern Italy (1239–50); a leader of the Ghibelline party; made captain general by Della Torre rulers of Milan (1260); driven from Milan by Charles of Anjou's Guelf army (1264–65).

Pe·la·yo \pā-'lä-yō\. d. 737. First Christian king (718–737) in Asturias after the conquest of Spain by the Arabs. A Gothic chieftain in the mountains, defeated Moslems at Covadonga (718), marking the beginning of the Christian recovery; deeds partly legendary.

Pè·le·rin de Ma·ri·court \pel-(ə-)raⁿ-də-má-rē-kür\, Pierre Le. *Lat.* Petrus Peregrinus de Maricourt. 13th century. French crusader and scholar. His *Epistola ad Sigerum de Foucaucourt militem de magnete* (1269) was first detailed description of the compass as an instrument of navigation; considered by Roger Bacon the greatest experimental scientist of his time.

Pe·le·tier \pel-(ə-)tyā\ *or* **Peletier du Mans** \-dü̅e-mäⁿ\, Jacques. 1517–1582. French poet and mathematician. Member of French poetical reform group La Pléiade; insisted in *Art poétique française* (1555) that poets must imitate the classics; his chief verse collection, *L'Amour des Amours* (1555), contained lyrical sonnets and scientific poems.

Pel·ham \'pel-əm\. Name of an English family of Hertfordshire dignified by the barony of Pelham, earldoms of Clare \'kla(ə)r, 'kle(ə)r\, Chich·es·ter \'chich-əs-tər\, and Yar·bor·ough \'yär-ˌbər-ō, -bər-ə, -b(ə-)rə\, and the dukedom of New·cas·tle \'n(y)ü-ˌkas-əl, *locally* nyü-'kas-əl\, including: Sir William Pelham (d. 1587), soldier; served on the Continent; strengthened defenses of kingdom; lord justice of Ireland (1579–80), joined with Ormonde in crushing Munster; became marshal of Leicester's forces in Netherlands, wounded at Doesburg (1586); from Sir William were descended the earls of Yarborough; from his half-brother were descended the dukes of Newcastle. ¶Henry Pelham (1696–1754), politician; a lord of treasury (1721) on recommendation of Walpole; secretary for war (1724); paymaster of the forces (1730); by union of parties, prime minister and chancellor of exchequer (1743–54); in Parliament reigned supreme with his brother, Sir Thomas Pelham-Holles; introduced financial reforms; dismissed (1744) John Carteret for attempts to involve England more deeply in War of Austrian Succession. ¶Thomas Pelham (1756–1826), 2d Earl of Chichester; surveyor general of ordnance (1782); Irish secretary (1795–98); home secretary (1801–03); joint postmaster general (1807–23), postmaster general (1823–26). His brother ¶George (1766–1827), bishop successively of Bristol (1803), Exeter (1807), and Lincoln (1820). ¶Henry Francis (1846–1907), scholar and historian, grandson of 2d Earl of Chichester; professor of ancient history at Oxford (1889); curator of Bodleian (1892), president of Trinity Coll. (1897); author of *Outlines of Roman History* (1893).

Pel·ham-Hol·les \'pel-əm-'häl-əs\, Thomas, 1st Duke of Newcastle. 1693–1768. English politician. Brother of Henry Pelham; added name of Holles when he succeeded to estates of his maternal uncle John Holles (1711). Supported Whigs and Walpole, who chose him secretary of state (1724–54); succeeded his brother Henry as prime minister (1754–56); returned as prime minister (1757–62), with William Pitt as leader in House of Commons and director of foreign affairs; credited with holding Whig party together despite George III's opposition.

Pé·lis·sier \pā-lēs-yā\, Aimable-Jean-Jacques. Duc de Ma·la·koff \də-má-lá-kôf\. 1794–1864. French soldier. General of brigade (1846); governor general of Oran (1848–51). Supported coup d'état of Napoléon III (1851); commanded 1st army corps in Crimean War (1854–55) and succeeded Marshal Canrobert in supreme command; stormed the Malakoff and captured Sevastopol (Sept. 8, 1855); created marshal of France, duc de Malakoff (1858), and senator. French ambassador at London (1858–59); governor general of Algeria (1860–64).

Pell \'pel\, John. 1611–1685. English mathematician. Professor, Amsterdam (1643–46), Breda (1646–52); diplomat for Cromwell in Switzerland (1654–58). Introduced the sign "÷" into England. Gave solutions to the Diophantine equation $x^2 - Dy^2 = 1$ (known as the Pellian equation where D is a positive integer that is not a perfect square).

Pel·le·gri·ni \pel-lā-'grē-nē\, Carlo. *Pseudonym* Ape \'āp\. 1839–1889. Italian caricaturist. To England (1864); drew (from 1869) humorous portraits of prominent Englishmen (as of Thomas Carlyle in 1870) for *Vanity Fair*.

Pel·le·tier \pel-tyā\, Pierre-Joseph. 1788–1842. French chemist. Professor (1815) and director (from 1832), École de Pharmacie, Paris. With J.B. Caventou isolated chlorophyll (1817) and discovered strychnine, brucine, quinine, cinchonine, and other alkaloids (1817–21).

Pel·lew \pəl-'yü\, Edward. 1st Viscount Ex·mouth \'ek-sməth\. 1757–1833. English naval officer. Took part in Burgoyne's expedition in American Revolution (1777); captured first frigate taken in war with France (1793); quelled mutiny on *Impétueux* (1799); rear admiral (1804). M.P. (1802–04). Commander of East India station (1804–09); destroyed Dutch fleet off Java (1807); vice admiral (1808); commander in North Sea (1810), Mediterranean (1811); raised to peerage and promoted to admiral (1814); commanded Anglo-Dutch fleet that destroyed Algerine fleet and silenced shore batteries of Algiers (1816); created viscount (1816).

Pel·li·ca·nus \ˌpel-i-'kän-ůs, *Angl* ˌpel-i-'kā-nəs\, Konrad. *Orig. surname* Kürsch·ner \'kœrsh-nər\. 1478–1556. Swiss scholar. Originally a Franciscan monk, joined Reformation (c.1526) and became professor of theology and librarian in Zürich. First Christian to publish a Hebrew grammar (1504); wrote *Commentaria Bibliorum* (1532–37) and autobiography *Chronicon* (1544).

Pel·li·co \'pel-i-(ˌ)kō\, Silvio. 1789–1854. Italian writer and patriot. A founder and editor (1818–19) of liberal patriotic journal *Il Conciliatore;* sentenced as a Carbonarist to 15 years at hard labor (1822); released (1830); lived at Turin (from 1834) as librarian to the marchesa di Barolo, reformer of Turin prisons. Known esp. for memoirs of his imprisonment *Le mie prigioni* (1832); author also of tragedies as *Francesca da Rimini* (1815; translated by Byron), *Laodamia, Ester d'Engaddi,* and *Tommaso Moro* (1833), a translation of Byron's *Manfred*, mystic and religious poetry, and *Cantiche*.

Pel·liot \pēl-yō\, Paul. 1878–1945. French traveler and Orientalist. Explored central Asia (1906–09), returning with collection of Chinese, Tibetan, Sanskrit, and Uigur manuscripts of dates earlier than 11th century; professor, Collège de France (from 1911).

Pel·lou·tier \pel-ü-tyā\, Fernand. 1867–1901. French labor leader. Disillusioned by the French Marxist party (1892) and became an advocate of anarcho-syndicalist labor unionism; secretary, Fédération des Bourses du Travail (1895 ff.); founded (1900) Office Nationale de la Statistique et de la Placement; author of *Histoire des bourses du travail* (1902).

Pel·loux \pāl-'lü\, Luigi Girolamo. 1839–1924. Italian soldier and politician. Served in Africa (1885–89); elected deputy (1880); senator (1896); minister of war (1891–93, 1896–97); premier (1898–1900); resigned over failure to pass a repressive bill; given command of army corps at Turin (1900–02).

Pe·lop·i·das \pə-'läp-əd-əs\. d. 364 B.C. Theban general. Saved by his friend Epaminondas at battle of Mantineia (385); helped liberate Thebes from Spartans (379); elected chief magistrate; leader of the Sacred Band, an elite infantry that distinguished itself against Spartans at Tegyra (375) and Leuctra (371); defeated the tyrant Alexander at Cynoscephalae (364) but was killed in combat.

Pe·louze \pə-lüz\, Théophile-Jules. 1807–1867. French chemist. Assistant to Gay-Lussac in Paris; professor, École Polytechnique (1831–46) and Collège de France (1831–50); collaborated with Liebig in Germany in work on organic chemistry. Discovered nitrocellulose (1838), oxidation of borneol to obtain camphor (1840), synthesis of butyrin (1843), and glycerophosphoric acid (1845).

Pel·tier \pel-tyā\, Jean-Charles-Athanase. 1785–1845. French physicist and meteorologist. Discovered the Peltier effect, the production or absorption of heat at the junction of two metals on the passage of an electric current (1834); introduced concept of electrostatic induction (1840).

Pel·ton \'pelt-ᵊn\, Lester Allen. 1829–1918. American engineer, b. Vermilion, O. Inventor of the Pelton water turbine, a rotor driven by the impulse of a jet of water upon curved buckets fixed to its periphery (patented 1889).

Pel·to·nen \'pel-tȯ-nen\, Vihtori. *Pseudonym* Johannes Lin·nan·kos·ki \'lin-nän-ˌkȯ-skē\. 1869–1913. Finnish author. His works, which helped form Finnish national consciousness in the early 20th century, included the novels *Laulu tulipunaisesta kukasta* (1905), *Pakolaiset* (1908), and plays *Ikuinen taistelu* (1903), *Simson ja Delila* (1911).

Pem·ber·ton \'pem-bərt-ᵊn\, Sir Francis. 1625–1697. English judge. Lord chief justice (1681); chief justice of common pleas (1683); removed from bench probably for lack of zeal in trial of Lord William Russell (1683); defended successfully (1688) the Seven Bishops (see William SANCROFT), precipitating the revolution which placed William of Orange upon British throne.

Pemberton, John Clifford. 1814–1881. American army officer, b. Philadelphia. In Florida Indian wars, Mexican War, and western frontier duty (1837–61). Resigned from U.S. army to enter Confederate service (1861); lieutenant general (1862); in charge of defense of Vicksburg, besieged by Grant; surrendered (July 4, 1863).

Pemberton, Sir Max. 1863–1950. English novelist. Editor of *Cassell's Magazine* (1896–1906). Author of many romances, including *The Iron Pirate* (1893), *The Hundred Days* (1905), *The Mad King Dies* (1928), and of plays, including *The Finishing School* and revues.

Pembroke, Countess of. See (1) Anne Clifford, under CLIFFORD family; (2) Mary Herbert, under HERBERT family.

Pembroke, Earl of. Title first conferred (1138) by King Stephen of England upon Gilbert de Clare and held, by several different creations, by members of de Clare family (see CLARE), Marshal family (*q.v.*), de Valence family (see William de VALENCE), Hastings family (*q.v.*), by Humphrey, Duke of Gloucester (see HUMPHREY), William de la Pole (see de la POLE family), Jasper Tudor (*q.v.*), and thenceforth by members of Herbert family.

Pe·na \'pā-nȧ\, Afonso Augusto Moreira. 1847–1909. Brazilian politician. Member of commission that drafted Brazilian Civil Code (1888); supported new republic (1889); senator (1894); vice president (1902–06) and president (1906–09) of Brazil; created Bank of Conversion.

Pe·ña·ran·da Cas·til·lo \pān-yä-'rän-dä-käs-'tē(l)-yō\, Enrique. 1892–1969. Bolivian soldier and politician. Commander in chief of army (1933, 1935–38); minister of defense (1939); elected president (1940); deposed by coup (1943).

Pe·ña y Pe·ña \'pān-yä-ē-'pān-yä\, Manuel de la. 1789–1850. Mexican jurist. Judge of supreme court (from 1824) and later its president; cabinet officer (1837, 1845); senator (1843–47); provisional president of Mexico (Sept.–Nov. 1847, Jan.–June 1848). During latter term, Treaty of Guadalupe Hidalgo signed (Feb. 2), ending war with U.S.

Penck \'peŋk\, Albrecht. 1858–1945. German geographer. Professor at Vienna (1885–1906), Berlin (1906–26) and director of the Institute of Geography. His researches in the Bavarian Alps were the foundation of Pleistocene stratigraphy; also studied climates, regional ecology, and political geography; promoted a map of the world on a scale of one to 1,000,000 (1891). Author of *Morphologie der Erdoberfläche* (1894) and *Die Alpen im Eiszeitalter* (1901–09, with Eduard Brückner). His son ¶Walther (1888–1923) was a geologist for the Dirección General de Minas, Buenos Aires (1912–14); professor at Constantinople (1915–18) and Leipzig (1918 ff.); expounded theories of tectonic movements, contrary to prevailing ideas, in *Die morphologische Analyse* (1924).

Pencz \'pents\, Georg. 1500?–1550. German painter and engraver. One of group known as "the Little Masters." Painter of portraits and religious and mythological subjects.

Pen·da \'pen-də\. d. 655. King of Mercia. Defeated West Saxons (the Hwicce) at Cirencester (628); became king (632 or 633) on defeating and killing Edwin of Northumbria; champion of paganism against Christianity; defeated and slew (642) Oswald of Northumbria; drove King Cenwalh out of Wessex (645); routed East Angles and slew their king, Anna (654); on invasion of Northumbria, was defeated and slain by Oswiu.

Pen·der \'pen-dər\, Harold. 1879–1959. American electrical engineer, b. Tarboro, N.C. Proved existence of magnetic field around a moving electrically charged body (1903); author of *Principles of Electrical Engineering* (1911), *Direct Current Machinery* (1921), etc.

Pen·dle·ton \'pen-dᵊl-tən\, Edmund. 1721–1803. American jurist, b. Caroline Co., Va. Leader in pre-Revolutionary activities; member, Committee of Correspondence (1773); member of Continental Congress (1774, 1775); president, Committee of Safety (1775); governor of Virginia (1774–76); presiding judge, Virginia supreme court of appeals (1779–1803). A great-grandnephew ¶George Hunt Pendleton (1825–1889), b. Cincinnati; member of U.S. House of Representatives (1857–65) and U.S. Senate (1879–85); as chairman of Senate committee on civil service, secured passage of bill (1883) providing for Civil Service Commission and for competitive examinations; U.S. minister to Germany (1885–89).

Pendleton, Ellen Fitz. 1864–1936. American educator, b. Westerly, R.I. Professor of mathematics (1901–10), president (1911–36), Wellesley College; responsible for the construction of many buildings.

Pen·field \'pen-ˌfē(ə)ld\, Wilder Graves. 1891–1976. Canadian neurologist, b. Spokane, Wash. Founder and director (1934–60), Montreal Neurological Institute; devised a surgical method for treating epilepsy.

Pen·gel·ly \peŋ-'gel-ē\, William. 1812–1894. English educator and geologist. His excavations in Devonshire (1858–59, 1865–83) proved that early man coexisted with now-extinct animals, such as the mammoth.

Pen·hal·low \pen-'hal-ō\, Samuel. 1665–1726. American merchant and historian, b. Cornwall, England. To America (1686) and settled (1687) at Portsmouth, N.H.; treasurer of the province (1699–1726); chief justice, superior court (1717). Author of *The History of the Wars of New-England with the Eastern Indians...1703–1713 and 1722–1725* (1726), a valuable historical source book.

Pé·ni·caud \pā-nē-kō\. A 16th-century family of French enamellers of Limoges noted for monochromatically painted enamel works intended to look like sculpture (grisaille enamel), including: Nardon (d. 1542 or 1543), worked in the French Gothic style. His brother or son ¶Jean (fl. 1510–40) introduced motifs of the Italian Renaissance; used transparent enamel colors on copper. ¶Pierre (1515–1590), an enamellist and also a painter of religious and mythological subjects.

Pen·kov·sky \pyin-'kȯf-skəi\, Oleg Vladimirovich. 1919–1963. Soviet intelligence officer and spy. Colonel in the Soviet army intelligence directorate (GRU); passed more than 5000 photographed documents to British and U.S. intelligence forces; arrested and executed; his journal, *The Penkovsky Papers,* published in 1965.

Penn \'pen\, John. 1741?–1788. American Revolutionary leader, b. Caroline Co., Va. Practiced law in Virginia (1762–74) and North Carolina (from 1774); member, Continental Congress (1775–80), and a signer of Declaration of Independence (1776).

Penn, Sir William. 1621–1670. English Parliamentary naval commander. Engaged in pursuit of Prince Rupert (1651–52); as vice admiral under Robert Blake took part in victory off Portland (1653); commanded fleet sent against Spanish possessions in America; took Jamaica (1655); corresponded secretly with Royalists; at Restoration became Pepys's superior officer; captain of the fleet (with the Duke of York) in Second Dutch War (1665–67), won victory over Dutch near Lowestoft (1665).

Penn, William. 1644–1718. English religious reformer and colonialist. Son of Adm. Sir William Penn. Studied law; in charge of family estates in Ireland (1666). Joined Society of Friends; preached and wrote 42 books and pamphlets, esp. *No Cross No Crown* (1669); imprisoned for nonconformity (1667, 1669, 1670). Engaged in English political campaigns, championing religious tolerance, frequent elections, and uncontrolled parliaments (1675–80). As a trustee to manage West Jersey colony in America, had important part in framing its charter (1677) with its famous Concessions and Agreements. Inherited from his father a large financial claim against Charles II; petitioned the king for a grant of land in the New World as payment of the debt; received grant of Pennsylvania (1681); visited the colony in person (1682) and took to the colonists his Frame of Government. In Pennsylvania, amended Frame of Government to meet popular demands; made peace treaties with the Indians; superintended laying out of Philadelphia. In England (1684–99) through accession of James II (1685) and revolution of 1688; ordered foundation of a public grammar school in Philadelphia (1689), which still exists as the William Penn Charter School; presented (1697) to London Board of Trade a plan for union of American colonies. Again in Pennsylvania (1699–1701); renewed peace treaties with Indians; granted a liberal charter (1701) to the colony. Suffered a stroke (1712); his affairs managed by his wife, Hannah, until his death. He bequeathed his proprietary interests in Pennsylvania to his widow as executrix for their four sons, John, Thomas, Richard (1706–1771), and Dennis (d. before 1727). His son ¶Thomas (1702–1775) managed the proprietorship in person in the colony (1732–41), and thereafter resided in England. Richard's son ¶John (1729–1795) was lieutenant governor of Pennsylvania (1763–71, 1773–76) and was a Loyalist during American Revolution. A second son of Richard ¶Richard (1735–1811) served as lieutenant governor of Pennsylvania during John's absence (1771–73); to England (1775).

Pen·nant \'pen-ənt\, Thomas. 1726–1798. British naturalist, b. Wales. Author of *British Zoology* (1766), *History of Quadrupeds* (1781). Chiefly remembered for *Tours in Scotland* (1771–90), *Tours in Wales* (1778); praised as traveler by Dr. Johnson.

Pen·nell \'pen-ᵊl, pə-'nel\, Joseph. 1857–1926. American etcher, b. Philadelphia. First drawings in *Scribner's Monthly* (1881) won him commission to illustrate articles by George W. Cable, published in *The Creoles of Louisiana* (1884); sent to Italy to illustrate articles by William Dean Howells on Tuscan cities. He and his wife (m. 1884) ¶Elizabeth, *nee* Rob·ins \'räb-ənz\ (1855–1936), published *A Canterbury Pilgrimage* (1885), with text by Mrs. Pennell and etchings by Pennell; continued this series in *Italian Pilgrimage* (1886), *Our Journey to the Hebrides* (1889), *To Gipsyland* (1893), *Over the Alps on a Bicycle* (1898), etc., reflecting their trips in various parts of Europe; they also co-wrote a life of his friend James Whistler (1908). Settled in London (1884); etchings appeared in *Century, Harper's,* and leading English periodicals (from 1885). Interested himself in lithography (from 1895) and produced notable work in this medium. Returned to U.S. (1917) and made vivid drawings depicting industrial war activities.

Pen·ne·thorne \'pen-i-,tho(ə)rn\, John. 1808–1888. English architect. First discovered curved lines in Parthenon and upset belief that Greek architecture was absolutely rectilinear.

Pen·ney \'pen-ē\, James Cash. 1875–1971. American businessman, b. Hamilton, Mo. President (1913–17) and board chairman (1917–46), J.C. Penney Co.; began with one-third interest in drygoods store in Kemmerer, Wyo. (1902); instituted profit-sharing with employees (1907); involved in philanthropic work. Published *50 Years with the Golden Rule* (1950) and *View from the Ninth Decade* (1960).

Pen·ni \'pān-nē\, Gianfrancesco. *Called* Il Fat·to·re \ēl-fät-'tō-rā\. 1488?–?1528. Italian painter. Pupil of Raphael; aided master in many of his frescoes; after Raphael's death, continued, with Giulio Romano, his uncompleted works, as *The Baptism of Constantine by Pope Sylvester* (in the Vatican) and the *Cupid and Psyche* frescoes in the Villa Farnesina, Rome.

Pen·ni·man \'pen-i-mən\, James Hosmer. 1860–1931. American educator and historian, b. Alexandria, Va. Collector of Washingtoniana and authority on 18th-century American history. Author of books on education and *George Washington as Commander-in-Chief* (1917), *George Washington as Man of Letters* (1918), *George Washington at Mount Vernon* (1921), etc.

Pen·ning·ton \'pen-iŋ-tən\, William. 1796–1862. American politician, b. Newark, N.J. Practiced law (1817 ff.); Whig governor of New Jersey (1837–43); member and speaker of the U.S. House of Representatives (1858–61).

Pen·rose \'pen-,rōz, pen-'rōz\, Boies. 1860–1921. American politician, b. Philadelphia. U.S. senator from Pennsylvania (1897–1921); identified with high protective tariff legislation; opposed prohibition, woman suffrage, and measures regarded popularly as progressive. Republican boss of Pennsylvania after Matthew Quay's death (1904).

Penrose, Francis Cranmer. 1817–1903. English architect, archaeologist, and astronomer. Detected alteration in pitch of pediment of Pantheon at Rome; practiced exact mensuration of Greek classical buildings, supported theories of John Pennethorne (*q.v.*), and expounded entasis. Published *Principles of Athenian Architecture* (1851).

Penrose, Richard Alexander Fullerton, Jr. 1863–1931. American geologist, b. Philadelphia. Brother of Boies Penrose. On faculty of U. of Chicago (1892–1917); with National Research Council (1917–23); known for explorations for manganese and iron ore deposits. Author of *Geology of the Gulf Tertiary of Texas* (1889), *Last Stand of the Old Siberia* (1922), etc.

Pen·ry \'pen-rē\, John. 1559–1593. Welsh Puritan pamphleteer. With his Puritan colleagues John Udall, Job Throckmorton, and the printer Robert Waldegrave, published *Martin Marprelate* tracts (1588) satirizing the bishops and defending the Presbyterian system of discipline; hanged on charge of inciting rebellion.

Pe·pe \'pā-(,)pā\, Guglielmo. 1783–1855. Neapolitan soldier. As a Carbonarist, led Liberal revolution (1820); defeated by Austrians at Rieti (1821); banished under penalty of death; assumed command over Neapolitan troops sent to Lombardy against Austrians (1848); after recall of Neapolitan troops, participated as volunteer in defense of Venice (1849). Author of *Relations des événements politiques et militaires à Naples, 1820–21* (1822) and memoirs (1846). His brother ¶Florestano (1778–1851) served in army of Murat in Spain (1809), in Russia (1812), and in Italy (1814, 1815); lieutenant general (1815); commanded Bourbon troops sent to quell Sicilian uprising (1820); retired to private life (1821) as an opponent of the reaction.

Pe·pi \'pā-pē\. Name of two kings of ancient Egypt of 6th dynasty:

Pepi I *or* **Phi·os** \'fī-(,)äs\ *or* **Mer·i·re** \'mer-ē-,rā\. 24th century B.C. Son of Teti, founder of the 6th dynasty; third and greatest king of the dynasty; sent several punitive expeditions against Bedouins of Sinai and into Palestine; left many monuments throughout Egypt, esp. pyramid MeneferPepi at Ṣaqqārah, which gave name to Memphis, later Egyptian capital.

Pepi II Nef·er·ka·re \,nef-ər-'kär-ā\ *or* **Phi·ops** \'fī-(,)äps\. 23d century B.C. Son of Pepi I; reigned 94 years (c. 2294–2200 B.C.), longest reign known in history, generally uneventful, a period of decline with king much of time controlled by influential nobles. His pyramid at Ṣaqqārah (opened 1881) contained religious texts.

Pé·pin \pā-paⁿ, *Angl* 'pep-ən\. Name of two kings of Aquitaine:

Pépin I. 803?–838. King (817–838). Son of Louis the Pious, who bestowed the kingdom upon him; united with his brother Charles (later Charles the Bald) in wars against his father.

Pépin II. c.823–c.865. King (845–852). Son of Pépin I; defeated in war with Charles the Bald and deposed, relegated to monastery; escaped, became wanderer, once joining a Viking attack on Toulouse (864); captured and died in prison.

Pépin. *Ger.* Pip·pin \pi-'pēn\. Name of three Frankish mayors of the palace, ancestors of the Carolingian kings:

Pépin I. *Called* the Elder *or* Pépin of Lan·den \'län-dən\. d. 640. Mayor of the palace (628–639) for the Merovingian king Dagobert I; with Arnulf, bishop of Metz, controlled the policy of the state.

Pépin II. *Called* the Younger *or* Pépin of Her·stal \er-stål\. d. 714. Grandson of Pépin the Elder; became ruler of Austrasia (c.679); mayor of the palace and ruler over all Franks (687–714).

Pépin III. *Called* le Bref \lə-bref\, *i.e.* the Short. 714?–768. King of the Franks (751–768). Son of Charles Martel (who was illegitimate son of Pépin II); mayor of the palace (741–751); m. Bertha, daughter of Caribert, Count of Laon; deposed Childeric III (751), last of the Merovingian kings; founded the Carolingian dynasty (*q.v.*); aided Pope Stephen II against the Lombards (754–756); conquered them and bestowed upon the pope the sovereignty of the exarchate of Ravenna (Donation of Pépin); anointed by Stephen (754); fought against the Saxons but left completion of their subjugation to his son Charlemagne.

Pépin. d. 810. King of Italy (781–810). 2d son of Charlemagne; campaigned against Duke Tassilo III of Bavaria (787), against Avars (796), and in Venice (809–810).

Pe·po·li \'pep-ō-(,)lē\. Distinguished Italian noble family of Bologna, including: Romeo de' Pepoli (d. 1321), leader of Guelf (papal) party; ruled Bologna but fled with family during an insurrection; died in exile. His son ¶Taddeo (d. 1347) returned to Bologna (1327); proclaimed lord of the city (1337); recognized as papal vicar by Pope Benedict XII. A descendant ¶Gioacchino Napoleone (1825–1881); statesman; grandson of Murat; participated in defense of Bologna against Austrians (1848); headed provisional government of Bologna (1859); deputy to Italian parliament; minister of agriculture (1862); ambassador to St. Petersburg (1863–64) and Vienna (1868–70); senator (1868 ff.).

Pep·per·rell \'pep-ər-əl\, Sir William. 1696–1759. American merchant and general, b. Kittery, Me. Member of governor's council (1727–59); chief justice of Massachusetts (1730); commanded American force cooperating with British in capture of French fortress of Louisbourg on Cape Breton (1745); promoted to colonel (1745) and created baronet (1746), first native American so honored; raised regiment to serve in French and Indian War; lieutenant general (1759).

Pe·pusch \'pā-(,)pu̇sh\, John Christopher, *Ger.* Johann Christoph. 1667–1752. British musician and composer, b. Berlin. To London (1700); director (from c.1713), Lincoln's Inn Theatre; composed masques, cantatas, and chamber music; arranged tunes and composed overture for Gay's *Beggar's Opera* and *Polly* and other ballad operas.

Pepys \'pēps\, Samuel. 1633–1703. English diarist. Clerk of the king's ships and clerk of the privy seal (1660); surveyor general of victualing office (1665) through naval war with Holland, sticking at his post through plague of 1666; secretary of the admiralty (1673); imprisoned during fanatical period of the Popish Plot, chiefly because of being trusted servant of the Duke of York (1679–80); visited Tangier and arranged for its evacuation (1683–84); reappointed secretary of admiralty (1684–89); increased strength and efficiency of royal navy; friend of Newton, Wren, Evelyn, and Dryden. Left to

Magdalene College collection of books, manuscripts, prints, including 2000 ballads. Author of *Memoirs of the Royal Navy* (1690) and of a unique diary (Jan. 1, 1660–May 31, 1669), written in Thomas Shelton's system of shorthand, complicated with foreign words and invented ciphers, and offering an honest presentation of conduct of naval administration, ways of court and everyday life, as well as a candid self-portrait.

Pe·ral·ta \pā-'räl-tä\, Pedro de. 1585?–1666. Spanish colonial official. To Mexico (1608); named governor of New Mexico (1609); founded Santa Fe (1610); imprisoned (1612–13) during quarrel with church officials; in Caracas, Venezuela (1637–52).

Per·ce·val \'pər-sə-vəl\, Sir John. 1st Earl of Eg·mont \'eg-,mänt, -mənt\. 1683–1748. British political leader, b. Ireland. British M.P. (1727–34); aided James Oglethorpe in founding Georgia colony. His son ¶Sir John (1711–1770), 2d earl, 1st Baron Lov·el and Hol·land \'ləv-əl-ən(d)-'häl-ənd\, was M.P. (1741–61 with interruptions); first lord of admiralty (1763–66). ¶Spencer Perceval (1762–1812), son of 2d earl; in Parliament supported Pitt's policy of war with France (from 1796); solicitor general (1801); attorney general (1802–06); opponent of Catholic emancipation; chancellor of exchequer under Duke of Portland (1807), whom he succeeded as prime minister (1809); insisted on continuance of war; made bank notes legal tender (1811); assassinated by a bankrupt broker, John Bellingham.

Per·cier \per-syā\, Charles. 1764–1838. French architect. Collaborator with Pierre Fontaine in remodeling Malmaison and in designing the Opéra (1794) and the Louvre and Tuileries (1802).

Per·ci·val \'pər-sə-vəl\, John. *Known as* Mad Jack *or* Roaring Jack. 1779–1862. American naval officer, b. West Barnstable, Mass. Renowned for exploits in War of 1812 and in later commands against West Indian pirates, in the South Seas, on a cruise around the world (1844–46). Hero in H. A. Wise's *Tales for the Marines* (1855).

Per·cy \'pər-sē\. Name of a North of England noble family, originally Norman, whose founder William de Percy (1030?–1096), 1st Baron Percy, accompanied William the Conqueror to England; the family's honors included dukedom and earldom of North·um·ber·land \nȯr-'thəm-bər-lənd\ and earldom and barony of Percy, and its chief members were:

¶Richard de Percy (1170?–1244), 5th baron; one of the 25 barons entrusted with execution of Magna Carta. ¶Henry de Percy (1272?–1315), 1st Baron Percy of Aln·wick \'an-ik\ (from 1309 principal seat of family); aided Edward I in subjugation of Scotland. His son ¶Henry (1299?–1352), 2d baron; took prisoner David II of Scotland at victory of Neville's Cross (1346).

¶Sir Henry Percy (1342–1408), 1st Earl of Northumberland (created 1377); grandson of the 2d Baron Percy of Alnwick; earl marshal of England (1377); at first supported Richard II in his despotism (1397); joined Henry of Lancaster (1399); was given Isle of Man in fief; revolted with his son (1403), submitted (1404), and was restored to offices and lands; conspired with Owen Glendower and Edmund, son of 3d Earl of March, to place the latter on the throne (1405); slain on Bramham Moor while invading England. His brother ¶Sir Thomas (1344?–1403), Earl of Worces·ter \'wu̇s-tər\; served on mission to Flanders with Geoffrey Chaucer (1377); served on French and Spanish expeditions; deserting Richard II for Henry IV (1399), joined his brother's rebellion; captured at Shrewsbury and beheaded.

¶Sir Henry Percy (1364–1403), *called* Hot·spur \'hät-,spər\; eldest son of 1st Earl of Northumberland; associated with his father as warden of the marches (1384) and in placing Henry IV on throne (1399); led English force in battle of Otterburn (1388); with George Dunbar, Earl of March, defeated Scots at Homildon Hill (1402), taking Douglas prisoner; forbidden by Henry IV to ransom his brother-in-law Sir Edmund de Mortimer, revolted (1403) with his father and Owen Glendower; slain at battle of Shrewsbury (1403); introduced as a fiery-tempered soldier in Shakespeare's *Henry IV, Part I.* ¶Sir Henry (1394–1455), 2d Earl of Northumberland; son of Hotspur; liberated by Henry V and restored to titles and estates, from which time the family was loyal to house of Lancaster; furnished wardens of eastern and western marches. ¶Sir Henry (1446–1489), 4th earl; grandson of 2d earl; temporarily deprived of titles and estates by Edward IV in favor of John Neville, Lord Montagu; restored (1469); murdered by populace on attempting to enforce a subsidy by order of Henry VII. ¶Sir Thomas Percy (1528–1572), 7th earl; great-grandson of 4th earl; favored by Mary as a Roman Catholic and restored (1557) to earldom, which had been forfeited after the Pilgrimage of Grace insurrection (1537); beheaded after failure of revolt (1569) against Elizabeth in behalf of Mary, Queen of Scots. His brother ¶Sir Henry (1532?–1585), 8th earl, was shot in prison under charge of participating in the Throckmorton conspiracy with Mary, Queen of Scots. ¶Thomas Percy (1560–1605), great-grandson of 4th earl; upon nonfulfillment of James I's assurances of toleration for Roman Catholics, took active part in Gunpowder Plot and was mortally wounded in flight. ¶Sir Henry (1564–1632), 9th earl; son of 8th earl; father of Lucy Hay (*q.v.*); called the "Wizard Earl" because of his scientific experiments; was imprisoned 15 years on condemnation for implication in the Gunpowder Plot. His brother ¶George (1580–1632) was deputy governor of Virginia Colony (1609–10, 1611). ¶Sir Algernon (1602–1668), 10th earl; son of 9th earl; lord high admiral (1638); endeavored to negotiate reconciliation with Charles I and opposed, in House of Lords, Charles's trial; with death of his son, the 11th earl, the family became extinct in direct line (1670).

¶Sir Hugh Percy, *orig.* Sir Hugh Smith·son \'smith-sən\ (1715–1786), 1st Duke of Northumberland (3d creation); married (1740) granddaughter of 6th Duke of Somerset and his wife, Lady Elizabeth Percy (1667–1722), heiress of 11th Earl of Northumberland; assumed surname and arms of Percy; succeeded to earldom (1750) and was made duke (1766); lord lieutenant of Ireland (1763–65). His son ¶Sir Hugh (1742–1817), 2d duke, fought in American Revolution (1774–77). ¶Sir Algernon (1792–1865), 4th duke, 1st Baron Prud·hoe \'prüd-,(h)ō, 'prəd-\; 2d son of 2d duke; first lord of admiralty (1852–53); admiral (1862); sponsored publication (1863) of Edward William Lane's Arabic thesaurus.

Percy, Florence. See Elizabeth ALLEN.

Percy, John. 1817–1889. English metallurgist. Discovered process of extracting silver from its ores and improved process of making Bessemer steel; his chief work was *A Treatise on Metallurgy* (1864–80).

Percy, Thomas. 1729–1811. English antiquary and poet. Bishop of Dromore (1782–1811); edited *Reliques of Ancient English Poetry* (1765), usually called *Percy's Reliques,* which awakened interest in English and Scottish traditional songs and influenced the Romantic poets; published a translation from French, *Northern Antiquities* (1770); author of *The Hermit of Warkworth* (1771) and other ballads. His nephew ¶Thomas (1768–1808) edited the *Reliques* and defended genuineness against Ritson's criticism.

Per·dic·cas \pər-'dik-əs\. Name of three kings of Macedonia: Perdiccas I (fl. 700 B.C.), founder of Macedonian dynasty, an Argive who emigrated to Macedonia. ¶Perdiccas II (d. about 413 B.C.), king during Peloponnesian War. ¶Perdiccas III (d. 359 B.C.), brother of Philip.

Perdiccas. c.365–321 B.C. Macedonian general under Alexander the Great. On death of Alexander (323 B.C.), appointed regent for Roxana (*q.v.*) and her infant son Alexander IV; exercised wide authority in Asia as "supreme general"; when Antipater, Antigonus, Craterus, and Ptolemy formed league against him (322), invaded Egypt; killed in mutiny of his soldiers.

Pe·re·da \pā-'rā-t͟hä\, Antonio. c.1608–1678. Spanish painter. Executed paintings for Philip IV; known for religious pictures as *Anunciación* (1637), *San Jerónimo* (1643), and *Aparición de la Virgen* (1665).

Pereda, José María de. 1833–1906. Spanish novelist. Noted for his realistic novels set mainly in Montaña, as *El buey suelto* (1877), *Don Gonzalo González de la Gonzalera* (1879), *De tal palo tal astilla* (1880), *Pedro Sánchez* (1883), *Sotileza* (1884), *La Montálvez* (1888), *La Puchera* (1889), *Nubes de estío* (1891), and *Peñas arriba* (1893).

Peregrina, La. See GÓMEZ DE AVELLANEDA.

Peregrinus de Maricourt, Petrus. See PÈLERIN DE MARICOURT.

Per·e·gri·nus Pro·teus \,per-ə-'grīn-əs-'prōt-,yüs, -ē-əs\. 100–165 A.D. Greek Cynic philosopher. In Egypt as pupil of Agathobulus; a wandering preacher in Rome and Greece. Realizing his popularity was passing, immolated himself on a funeral pyre at Olympic games (165). Subject of a novel by Wieland.

Pe·rei·ra \pə-'rā-ē-rə\, Nuno Álvares. 1360–1431. Portuguese soldier. As constable of Portugal (1385) engaged in the battle of Aljubarrota and aided in conquest of Ceuta (1415); retired to a Carmelite monastery (1423). Beatified by Pope Benedict XV (1918).

Pereira Gomes, Wenceslau Braz. See BRAZ PEREIRA GOMES.

Per·el·man \'per-əl-mən (*his own pron.*), 'pər(-ə)l-mən\, Sidney Joseph. 1904–1979. American humorist, b. Brooklyn, N.Y. Published humorous pieces in *New Yorker* (from 1931) and *Holiday* (in 1950s) magazines; wrote film scripts, esp. *Monkey Business* (1931) and *Horsefeathers* (1932) for Marx Brothers and *Around the World In Eighty Days* (1956, Academy Award); author of plays as *One Touch of Venus* (1943, with Ogden Nash) and *The Beauty Part* (1962), and many books, including *Strictly from Hunger* (1937), *Crazy Like a Fox* (1944), *Acres and Pains* (1946), *Westward Ha!* (1948), *The Swiss Family Perelman* (1950), *The Road to Miltown* (1957), *The Rising Gorge* (1961), and *Baby, It's Cold Inside* (1970).

Pe·res·ve·tov \pyir-yis-'vyā-tôf\, Ivan Semyonovich. 16th century. Russian author and politician. Councilor to Ivan IV; advocated a strong, centralized autocracy supported by the lower nobility.

Per·etz \'per-ets\, Isaac Leib. 1852–1915. Polish Jewish writer. Called "Father of modern Yiddish literature." Author of social works in Yiddish, including Ḥasidic tales as the *Silent Soul* series, plays as *The Golden Chain* (1907), poems, and satires. Engaged in social work in the Warsaw Jewish community; influenced Jewish writers in Yiddish, esp. Sholem Asch.

Pe·rey \per-e\, Marguerite. 1909–1975. French physicist. Worked with Marie Curie while at Radium Inst., Paris (1929–39); with National Center for Scientific Research (1940–49); professor at Strasbourg (from 1949). Discovered element francium (1939); first woman member of French Academy of Science (1962).

Pe·rey·ra \pä-ˈre-ē-rä\, Carlos. 1871–1942. Mexican historian. Diplomat for governments of Díaz and Huerta; author of histories on Hispanic-American topics, esp. *Historia de la América española* (1920–24).

Pé·rez \ˈpä-räth\, Antonio. 1539–1611. Spanish statesman. Secretary of state to Philip II (1568); for Philip II, procured assassination of Juan de Escovedo, agent of John of Austria (1578); lost Philip's favor through relationship with Princesa de Éboli, mistress of the king (1579); escaped to Aragon (1590), receiving protection of Aragonese courts. Prosecuted by Inquisition on instigation of Philip (1591); liberated by Aragonese people, whose constitutional privileges were abolished by Philip II in consequence; fled to London and Paris; his *Relaciones* published in 1598.

Pé·rez \ˈpä-räs\, José Joaquín. 1800–1889. Chilean politician. Senator (1852–61); president of Chile (1861–71).

Pérez, Santiago. 1830–1900. Colombian politician. Minister of foreign affairs (1864–66); ambassador to U.S. (1868–73); president of Colombia (1874–76).

Pé·rez de Aya·la \ˈpä-räth-thā-ä-ˈyä-lä\, Ramón. 1880–1962. Spanish novelist, poet, critic, and diplomat. Correspondent in World War I for Buenos Aires periodical *La Prensa;* ambassador to London (1931–36). Author of lyrics as *La Paz del sendero* (1904), *El sendero innumerable* (1916), and *El sendero andante* (1921), and novels as *Tinieblas en las cumbres* (1907), *AMDG* (1910), *La pata de la raposa* (1912), *Troteras y Danzaderas* (1913), *Prometeo* (1916), *Belarmino y Apolonia* (1921), and *Tigre Juan* and sequel *El curandero de su honra* (1926).

Pérez de Guz·mán \-güth-ˈmän\, Alonso. *Called* el Bue·no \el-ˈbwā-nō\. 1256–1309. Spanish soldier. In service of Sultan of Morocco, later of Alfonso X (1282–84) and Sancho IV (from 1284); defended Tarifa (1294) against Moors led by rebel Infante Don Juan; captured Gibraltar from Moors (1308); progenitor of noble Castilian family of Medina-Sidonia. A descendant ¶Alonso Pérez de Guzmán, duque de Medina-Sidonia (c.1550–1619), placed by Philip II in command (1588) of "Invincible Armada" despite his lack of training or ability; completely defeated by English; named (1595) captain general of the ocean; responsible for loss of Cádiz (1596) to the English, also for defeat of Spanish squadron off Gibraltar (1606).

Pérez de Guzmán, Fernán. c.1378–c.1460. Spanish poet and historian. Nephew of Pedro López de Ayala and uncle of Iñigo López de Mendoza. After imprisonment (1432) in civil wars of John II, devoted himself to letters. Author of liturgical and love poetry, *Mar de historias,* which contained the first Spanish examination of the theories of historiography, and *Generaciones y semblanzas,* character sketches of the important men of his time.

Pérez de Hi·ta \-thā-ˈē-tä\, Ginés. 1544?–?1619. Spanish writer and soldier. Participated in war against Moriscos in the Alpujarras (1568–71). Author of historical novel *Historia de los bandos de los zegríes y abencerrajes,* better known as *Las guerras civiles de Granada* (Part I, 1595; Part II, 1619), important as antecedent of similar works in various literatures.

Pérez de Mon·tal·bán \-mòn-täl-ˈbän\, Juan. Spanish writer. Ordained priest (1625); follower of Lope Vega. Author of *Sucesos y prodigios de amor* (1624, collection of novellas), *Para todos* (1632, miscellany), and over 50 plays as *El segundo Séneca de España, El mariscal de Virón,* and *Los amantes de Teruel.*

Pérez Gal·dós \-gäl-ˈdōs\, Benito. 1843–1920. Spanish novelist and playwright. His fiction included a series of historical romances (1873–1912) under the title *Episodios nacionales* (46 volumes in all), and many novels reflecting contemporary life and its problems as *Doña Perfecta* (1876), *Fortunata y Jacinta* (1886–87), *Miau* (1888), *Angel Guerra* (1890–91), *Nazarín* (1895), *Misericordia* (1897); plays included *La Loca de la casa* (1893), *La de san Quintín* (1894), *Electra* (1900), *Mariucha* (1903); considered greatest Spanish novelist since Cervantes.

Per·fall \ˈper-ˌfäl\, Karl von. Freiherr. 1824–1907. German theater manager and composer. Director of court music (from 1864) and of court theater (1867–93) in Munich; composed operas as *Raimondin* (1881) and *Junker Heinz* (1886) and choral works; author of *Die Entwicklung des modernen Theaters* (1899).

Per·go·le·si \ˌpār-gō-ˈlā-sē\, Giovanni Battista. 1710–1736. Italian composer. Composer of operas, including *Lo frate innammorato* (1732), *Adriano in Siria* (1734), and *Il prigionier superbo* (1733), latter of which contained a comic intermezzo, *La serva pardona,* which precipitated the *guerre des bouffons* between advocates of French and Italian opera when performed in Paris in 1752. Composed also church music, esp. *Mass in F* and *Stabat Mater,* and chamber music.

Pe·ri \ˈpe-rē\, Jacopo. 1561–1633. Italian composer. Music director at court of the Medici in Florence. In effort to reconstruct musical forms used by Greeks in representation of their tragedies, developed new recitative style adapted to stage use and with libretto of poet Rinuccini wrote *Dafne* (1594), now regarded as the first opera; also composed opera *Euridice* (1600).

Per·i·an·der \ˌper-ē-ˈan-dər\. d. 586 B.C. Greek statesman. Son of Cypselus; tyrant of Corinth (c.627–586); promoted Corinthian commerce; conquered Epidaurus; annexed Corcyra (Corfu); patron of men of letters. One of the Seven Wise Men of Greece.

Pe·rib·sen \pə-ˈrib-sən, -ˌsen\. 27th century B.C. Egyptian king (reigned c.2675 B.C.) of the 2d dynasty. Promoted cult of god Seth over Horus; his ascendancy said to have been accompanied by persecution of worshipers of Horus.

Per·i·cles \ˈper-ə-ˌklēz\. c.495–429 B.C. Athenian statesman. Son of Xanthippus; leader of democratic party. Secured ostracism of his political opponents, Cimon and Thucydides, and gained complete ascendancy over city (from c.460 B.C.). While preparing Athens for inevitable conflict with Sparta, strove also to make city the center of art and literature and most beautiful city architecturally in world; responsible for building Parthenon, Propylaea, Odeon, and other noted buildings; gathered about himself group of noted people, including Anaxagoras and Phidias. His conduct of Peloponnesian War (begun 431) was vigorous and successful; stricken by plague (430) and died the next year.

Pe·ri·co·li \pā-ˈrē-kō-(ˌ)lē\, Niccolò. *Known as* Il Tri·bo·lo \ēl-ˈtrē-bō-(ˌ)lō\. 1500–1550. Italian sculptor and architect. Pupil of Jacopo Sansovino; architect to Grand Duke Cosimo I of Tuscany; later superintendent of bridges, rivers, and streets of Florence; works included marble statues *Sibyls* and *Assumption of the Virgin* (Bologna), and tomb of Adrian VI (with Michelangelo, at Pisa).

Pé·rier \pār-yā\, Casimir-Pierre. 1777–1832. French statesman. With brother ¶Antoine-Scipion (1776–1821), engaged in banking business in Paris (1801–17). Chosen deputy from Paris (1817); a leading member of opposition to Charles X (1824–30); after revolution of July 1830, became prime minister to Louis-Philippe (1831–32); restored civic order in France; forced Portugal to compensate French merchants (1831); sent army to defend Belgium against the Dutch (1831); ordered occupation of Ancona to check Austrian predominance in Papal States (1832). His son ¶Auguste-Casimir Périer (1811–1878), politician and minister in Thiers administration (1871–72); adopted (1873) the surname Casimir-Périer; father of Jean-Paul-Pierre Casimir-Périer (*q.v.*).

Pé·ri·gnon \pā-rēn-yōⁿ\, Dominique-Catherine de. Marquis. 1754–1818. French general. Campaigned against Spain (1793–96) and Italy (1799–1801); as ambassador to Madrid negotiated Spanish alliance (1796); senator (1801); marshal of France (1804); governor general of Parma (1806); supported Louis XVIII after Napoléon's abdication; commanding officer at Toulouse (1816) and Paris (1816); created marquis (1817).

Pérignon, Pierre. *Known as* Dom Pérignon. 1638–1715. French Benedictine monk. Put in charge of the vineyards at his monastery; reputed discoverer of method for making sparkling wines (champagne, etc.).

Perino del Vaga. See Pietro BONACCORSI.

Per·kin \ˈpər-kən\, Sir William Henry. 1838–1907. English chemist. Produced mauve, the first synthetic dye (1856); with father and brother, established works near Harrow for manufacture of mauve, thus founding aniline dye industry (1857). Developed process for producing alizarin; first to synthesize an amino acid (glycine, 1858, with B.F. Duppa), tartaric acid (1860, with Duppa), coumarin (1868); discovered the Perkin reaction for making aromatic unsaturated acids, such as cinnamic acid (1867); studied relation between chemical constitution and rotation of polarized light in a magnetic field.

Per·kins \ˈpər-kənz\, Frances. 1882–1965. American public official, b. Boston. Member of N.Y. Industrial Commission (1919–21, 1929–33), of N.Y. Industrial Board (1923–33; chairman 1926–29); as U.S. secretary of labor (1933–45) supervised New Deal labor legislation, esp. the Fair Labor Standards Act; member, Civil Service Commission (1946–52).

Perkins, George Walbridge. 1862–1920. American financier, b. Chicago. Instituted agency system while with N.Y. Life Insurance Co. (1876–1901); partner in J. P. Morgan & Co. (1901–10). Joined Progressive party in support of Theodore Roosevelt (1912); wrote and spoke on current political and industrial problems.

Perkins, Jacob. 1766–1849. American inventor, b. Newburyport, Mass. Invented machine to cut and head nails and tacks in one operation (c.1790), a steel check plate for printing bank notes (c.1808), the horizontal steam engine (1827); obtained (1834) one of first patents for a refrigerating machine. Established factory in England for printing bank notes; received contract (1840) for printing first penny postage stamps.

Perkins, Justin. 1805–1869. American missionary. Missionary to Nestorian Christians in northwestern Persia (1833). Established mission in Urmia (now Rezā'īyeh, 1835); opened schools, established printing press, reduced modern Syriac to writing, and issued books for the people. Author of *Missionary Life in Persia* (1861), etc.

Perkins, Maxwell Evarts. 1884–1947. American editor, b. New York City. Editor (from 1910), later vice president of publishing house Charles Scribner's Sons; encouraged and edited many American authors as Fitzgerald, Hemingway, and esp. Thomas Wolfe; appeared as "Foxhall Edwards" in Wolfe's *You*

Can't Go Home Again; his correspondence published as *Editor to Author* (1950).

Perkins, Thomas Handasyd. 1764–1854. American merchant, b. Boston. Amassed fortune in trading ventures, esp. in Chinese goods; benefactor of Massachusetts General Hospital and Boston Athenaeum; deeded his home to New England Asylum for the Blind (1833), later renamed the Perkins Institute and Massachusetts School for the Blind.

Perkins, William. 1558–1602. English Puritan theologian. Fellow of Christ's College, Cambridge (1584–94); noted for powerful sermons; author of many tracts as *Armilla Aurea* (1590) and *Reformed Catholike* (1597).

Per·ley \'pər-lē\, Sir George Halsey. 1857–1938. Canadian businessman and politician, b. Lebanon, N.H. Naturalized Canadian citizen; in family lumber business in Ottawa; member, Canadian House of Commons (1904, 1908, 1911, 1925–38); minister without portfolio (1912–16, 1930–35) and acting premier (1912–13, 1933); secretary of state (1926).

Per·mo·ser \per-'mō-zər\, Balthasar. 1651–1732. German sculptor. Court sculptor at Dresden (1689); exponent of German Baroque style; executed sculptures of mythological figures; also *Apotheose des Prinzen Eugen* (1718).

Pé·ro·chon \pā-rȯ-shō^{n}\, Ernest. 1885–1942. French writer. Author of novels *Nêne* (1920), *La Parcelle 32* (1922), *Barberine des Genêts* (1933), *Le Chanteur de villanelles* (1943), etc.

Pe·rón \pā-'rȯn\, Juan Domingo. 1895–1974. Argentine politician. Entered army (1913); participated in military coup (1943); minister of war and vice president (1945); president (1946–55); deposed in military coup and exiled in Madrid (1955–73); again president (1973–74). His presidency effected economic reforms as nationalization of railroads, benefits to laborers, and large-scale public works, but also marked by graft and suppression of civil liberties; extended Argentina's influence throughout Latin America. He was aided by his 2d wife (m. 1945) ¶María Eva Duarte, *nee* Ibar·gu·ren \ē-bär-'gü-ren\ (1919–1952), *called* Evi·ta \ā-'bē-tä\; de facto minister of health and labor; organized female workers; secured woman suffrage; instituted welfare programs; revered by lower classes.

Pe·ro·si \pā-'rȯ-zē\, Lorenzo. 1872–1956. Italian secular priest and composer. Music director, St. Mark's, Venice (1894) and Sistine Chapel, the Vatican (1897–1915). Among his compositions were oratorios *La passione di Cristo* (1897), *La transfigurazione* (1898), and *L'entrata di Cristo in Gerusalemme* (1900), choral works as *Mosè* and *Stabat Mater,* masses, motets, orchestral suites, quartets, etc.

Pé·ro·tin \pā-rȯ-ta^{n}\. *Lat.* Pe·ro·ti·nus \ˌper-ə-'tī-nəs\. d. 1238? French composer. A master (with Léonin) of the Notre-Dame school; maître de chapelle at church later built as Notre-Dame cathedral. Said to have introduced the composition of polyphony in four parts into western music; composed *Sederunt* and *Viderunt* organa.

Pérouse, Comte de La. See Jean-François de GALAUP.

Per·rault \pe-rō\. Name of four French brothers, prominent in the 17th century: Pierre (1611?–1680), receiver general of finances for Paris; his *De l'origine des fontaines* (1674) proved that rainfall was sufficient to sustain the flow of rivers. ¶Nicolas (1611?–?1661), dismissed from faculty of the Sorbonne for Jansenist views; author of *La morale des jésuites extraite fidèlement de leurs livres* (1667). ¶Claude (1613–1688), physician and architect; a founder of Académie des Sciences (1666); with other Académie members performed dissections and physiological experiments on animals and fish, results published as *Mémoires pour servir a l'histoire naturelle des animaux* (1671, 1676); designed Louvre colonnade (1667), Paris Observatory (1667), and two chapels. ¶Charles (1628–1703); in charge of royal buildings; member (from 1671), Académie Française; championed moderns (against Boileau-Despréaux) in *querelle des anciens et des modernes,* esp. with poem *Le Siècle de Louis le Grand* (1687); best known for *Contes de ma mere l'oye* (1697), retellings of folk fairy tales for children which included "Little Red Riding Hood," "Sleeping Beauty," "Puss in Boots," etc.

Per·rers \'per-ərz\ *or* **de Wind·sor** \də-'win-zər\, Alice. d. 1400. Mistress of Edward III of England. As lady of honor of Queen Philippa (from 1366), acquired influence over king; her banishment by Good Parliament (1376) for influencing judge's decisions revoked (1379).

Per·ret \pe-re\, Auguste. 1874–1954. French architect. Designed many reinforced concrete buildings, as church of Notre-Dame at Le Raincy (1922–23) and École Normale de Musique, Paris (1929); chief architect for reconstruction of Le Havre after World War II.

Per·rier \per-yā\, Édmond, *in full* Jean-Octave-Édmond. 1844–1921. French zoologist. Professor (1876) and director (from 1900), Muséum d'Histoire Naturelle; a principal French defender of theory of evolution, as in *Les Colonies animales et la formation des organismes* (1881), *Philosophie zoologique avant Darwin* (1884), *Le Transformisme* (1888).

Per·rin \pe-ra^{n}\, Ami. d. 1561. Swiss politician. Diplomat for Geneva (1544–55); champion of Guillaume Farel; leader of anti-Calvinist Libertine movement; fled to Bern after abortive Libertine rebellion against Geneva government (1555).

Perrin, Claude. *Called* Vic·tor \vēk-tȯr\ *or* Victor-Perrin. Duc de Bel·lune \bel-ūen\. 1764–1841. French general. Distinguished himself at Marengo (1800); commander in Batavia (1800–04); ambassador to Denmark (1805); created marshal of France for service at Friedland (1807); created duke (1808); fought in Spain (1809–10), Russia (1812), Germany (1813). Remained loyal to Bourbons during Hundred Days (1815); minister of war (1821–23).

Perrin, Jean-Baptiste. 1870–1942. French physicist and chemist. Professor, École Normale Supérieure of Paris (1910–40); established that cathode rays are electrons; investigated Brownian movement of minute particles suspended in liquids, thereby confirming the atomic nature of matter; awarded 1926 Nobel prize for physics for work on the discontinuous structure of matter and for discovery of equilibrium of sedimentation. Publications included *Traité de chimie physique* (1903), *Les Atomes* (1913), and *Les Éléments de la physique* (1930).

Perrin, Pierre. 1620–1675. French poet. Wrote librettos for Robert Cambert's *La Pastorale* (1659), *Pomone* (1671), and *Ariane* (1672), the first musical comedies in French.

Per·rine \pə-'rīn\, Charles Dillon. 1867–1951. American astronomer, b. Steubenville, O. Astronomer (1893–1909), Lick Observatory; director, Córdoba Astronomical Observatory, Argentina (1909–36). Discovered thirteen comets, motion in nebulosity about the new star in Perseus (1901), and the sixth and seventh satellites of Jupiter (1904, 1905); investigated solar eclipses.

Per·ron \'per-ˌōn, pə-'rōn\, Charles Edgar du. 1899–1940. Dutch writer and critic, b. Java. With Menno ter Braak founded literary journal *Forum* (1932–35). His writings included novels *Een voorbereiding* (1927), *Het land van herkomst* (1935), *Schandaal in Holland* (1939); poetry *Parlando* (1941); essays *De smalle mens* (1934); a biography of Multatuli, *De man van Lebak* (1937); and a translation of Malraux's *Condition humaine,* which had been dedicated to him.

Per·ro·ne \pār-'rō-nā\, Giovanni. 1794–1876. Italian Jesuit theologian. Active in condemnation of Hermesian heresy and in formulation of doctrines of papal infallibility and of Immaculate Conception. Known particularly for *Praelectiones theologicae* (1835–42).

Per·ro·net \pe-rȯ-nā\, Jean-Rodolphe. 1708–1794. French civil engineer. Director, École des Ponts et Chaussées (1747–94); inspector general (1750) and head (1763), Corps des Ponts et Chaussées. Known for his stone-arch bridges, esp. the Pont de Neuilly (1774) and the Pont de la Concorde in Paris (1791).

Per·rot \pe-rō\, Georges. 1832–1914. French archaeologist. On archaeological expedition to Asia Minor (1861) which resulted in his reconstruction of text of *Monumentum ancyranum.* Coauthor of *Histoire de l'art dans l'Antiquité* (1881), etc.

Per·rot \'per-ət\, Sir John. c.1527–1592. English governor in Ireland. Reputed son of Henry VIII by Mary Berkley. President of Munster (1570–73); forced submission of the Irish rebel James Fitzmaurice Fitzgerald (1573); lord deputy of Ireland (1584–88); established an English colony in Munster; recalled on trumped-up charges of treasonable negotiations with Spain; died in prison.

Per·rot \pe-rō\, Jules-Joseph. 1810–1894. French dancer and choreographer. One of foremost dancers of his time; exponent of expressive ballet. With Paris Opéra (1830–35); toured Europe (1835–40); in London (1842–48); ballet master, Imperial Theatre, St. Petersburg (1848–59). Choreographer of many Romantic ballets as *Giselle* (1841), *Ondine* (1843), *Esmeralda* (1844), *Pas de quatre* (1845), *Faust* (1848).

Perrot, Nicolas. 1644–1717. French explorer and fur trader in North America. Traded with North American tribes and secured their loyalty to France (from 1680s); built forts; claimed upper Mississippi River region for France (1689).

Per·ry \'per-ē\, Antoinette, *in full* Mary Antoinette. 1888–1946. American actress and director, b. Denver. On stage (from 1905) in *Music Master* (1906, 1908), *Mr. Pitt* (1924), *Masque of Venice* (1926), *Electra* (1927), etc.; director (from 1928) of plays as *Strictly Dishonorable* (1929–30), *Red Harvest* (1937), *Harvey* (1944). Founder (1941), American Theatre Wing; their Tony Award named after her.

Perry, Bliss. 1860–1954. American educator and critic, b. Williamstown, Mass. Professor, Williams (1886–93), Princeton (1893–1900), Harvard (1907–30); editor, *Atlantic Monthly* (1899–1909); general editor, series of Cambridge editions of the poets (1905–09). Author of *The Powers at Play* (1899), *Walt Whitman* (1906), *Whittier* (1907), *The American Mind* (1912), *Carlyle* (1915), *The American Spirit in Literature* (1918), *A Study of Poetry* (1920), *The Praise of Folly* (1923), *Pools and Ripples* (1927), *And Gladly Teach* (1935), etc.

Perry, Matthew Calbraith. 1794–1858. American naval officer, b. Newport, R.I. Brother of Oliver Hazard Perry; pioneer advocate of naval steamships; with rank of captain, commanded the *Fulton,* one of the first naval steamships (1837). Served (1843) on African coast in suppression of the slave trade; in command of squadron that captured (1846) Frontera, Tabasco, Laguna, Túxpam, and cooperated (1847) with Scott in siege of Veracruz during Mexican War. Sent (1852) in command of squadron to Japan to negotiate a treaty which would open up that country to commerce; delivered his message and papers to representatives of the emperor (July 1853) and sailed to China to give Japanese time to consider proposals; returned and obtained treaty (signed Mar. 1854) granting U.S. trading rights at ports of Hakodate and Shimoda; from this treaty dates the contact of Japan with western powers.

Perry, Oliver Hazard. 1785–1819. American naval officer, b. South Kingston, R.I. Brother of Matthew Calbraith Perry. Served in West Indies and the Mediterranean (1799–1807). In War of 1812, ordered to Erie, Pa. (1813), to build, equip, and man a fleet to contest control of Lake Erie with the British; fought battle of Lake Erie (Sept. 10, 1813); the *Lawrence,* his flagship, was so badly damaged that he left it during the battle and was rowed to the *Niagara* where he continued the fight and forced the surrender of the British fleet. After the battle, he sent the famous dispatch to General Harrison: "We have met the enemy and they are ours." For his victory he received the thanks of Congress and a gold medal. Commander of the *Java* in the Mediterranean (1816–17). On mission to Venezuela with small fleet (1819); contracted yellow fever on the Orinoco River and died.

Perry, Ralph Barton. 1876–1957. American philosopher and educator, b. Poultney, Vt. Professor, Harvard (1913–46); noted for his personalist revision of Pragmatism. Author of *The New Realism* (1912), *The Present Conflict of Ideals* (1918), *General Theory of Value* (1926), *The Thought and Character of William James* (1935, Pulitzer prize biography), *Puritanism and Democracy* (1944), *The Humanity of Man* (1956).

Perry, Roland Hinton. 1870–1941. American painter and sculptor, b. New York City. Specialized in portrait painting (from 1917). Among his sculptures were *Fountain of Neptune* in the Library of Congress; statue of Dr. Benjamin Rush in Washington, D.C.; statue of Gen. George S. Greene at Gettysburg, Pa.

Perry, William James. 1868–1949. English anthropologist. Believed that Egypt of 4000 B.C. was original and sole source of culture, which was then diffused throughout the world. Author of *The Origin of Magic and Religion* (1923), *The Growth of Civilisation* (1924), *Gods and Men* (1927), *The Primordial Ocean* (1935).

Perse, St.-John. See Marie LÉGER.

Per·seus \'pər-ˌsüs, -sē-əs\. c.212–c.165 B.C. Last king of Macedonia (179–168 B.C.). Commanded troops against Rome (199) and Aetolia (189); contrived execution of his brother Demetrius; succeeded his father, Philip V (179); attempt to dominate Greece precipitated Third Macedonian War (171–168); defeated at Pydna (168), dethroned and taken captive to Rome (167).

Per·shing \'pər-shiŋ, -zhiŋ\, John Joseph. *Nicknamed* Black Jack. 1860–1948. American army commander, b. Laclede, Mo. On frontier duty (1886–98); served in Cuba (1898) and the Philippines (1899–1903). U.S. military attaché, Tokyo (1905–06), and with Kuroki's army in Manchuria (1905); brigadier general (1906); in command of Department of Mindanao; suppressed Moro uprising (1913); commanded expeditionary force sent into Mexico in pursuit of Pancho Villa (1916). Major general (1916); commander in chief, American Expeditionary Forces (1917–19); general (1917); his Meuse-Argonne offensive destroyed German resistance (1918); chief of staff, U.S. army (1921–24); retired from active service. Author of *My Experiences in the World War* (1931, Pulitzer prize).

Persigny, Duc de. See Jean-Gilbert-Victor FIALIN.

Per·sius \'pər-sh(ē-)əs, -sē-əs\. *In full* Aulus Persius Flac·cus \'flak-əs\. 34–62 A.D. Roman satirist. Friend of Stoic philosopher Cornutus and poet Lucan. Author of six satires of a high moral tone, composed in hexameters.

Perth, Earls and dukes of. See DRUMMOND family.

Per·thes \'per-(ˌ)tes\, Johann Georg Justus. 1749–1816. German publisher. Founded (1785) a publishing house in Gotha; published esp. geographical works and the *Almanach de Gotha.* His nephew ¶Friedrich Christoph (1772–1843) founded a firm in Hamburg (1796) and the national museum there (1810); moved to Gotha (1822), where he specialized in publication of historical and theological works.

Per·ti·nax \'pərt-ᵊn-ˌaks\, Publius Helvius. 126–193 A.D. Roman emperor (Jan.–March 193). Commanded army units in Syria, Britain, Germany; held consulship twice; chosen emperor against his will to succeed Commodus; killed in a mutiny of the praetorian guard.

Pertz \'perts\, Georg Heinrich. 1795–1876. German historian. Archivist in Hanover (from 1816); chief librarian in Berlin (from 1842); editor of *Monumenta Germaniae historica* (1823–73).

Perugino. See Pietro VANNUCCI.

Pe·ruz·zi \pā-'rüt-tsē\. Family of Italian financiers prominent in the 13th and 14th centuries, including: Filippo di Amadeo de' Peruzzi (late 13th century), leader (1260) of Guelf (papal) League against Ghibelline leader Farinata degli Uberti; elected prior of Florence (1284). ¶Bonifazio di Tommaso (d. 1341) financed Scottish and French wars of Edward III of England (1330s). The failure of Edward and kings of Naples and France to repay their loans bankrupted the family (1343) and contributed to the European economic depression of mid-14th century.

Peruzzi, Baldassare Tommaso. 1481–1536. Italian architect and painter. Leading artist of High Renaissance; one of earliest to attempt illusionist architectural painting (*quadratura*); to Rome (1504); appointed architect of St. Peter's by Leo X (1520); to Siena after sack of Rome (1527); returned to Rome (1532). Among his paintings were frescoes in Church of Sant'Onofrio, on the ceiling of the Stanza d'Eliodoro in the Vatican, and in Church of Santa Maria della Pace (all in Rome); his architectural works included designs for Villa Farnesina and Ossoli Palace at Rome, fortifications of Siena, and (his chief work) Palazzo Massimi alle Colonne at Rome.

Pescara, Marqués de. See Fernando de ÁVALOS.

Pescennius Niger. See NIGER.

Pesellino, Il. See FRANCESCO DI STEFANO.

Pesh·kov \'pyāsh-kəf\, Aleksey Maksimovich. *Pen name* Maksim Gor·ky \'gȯrʸ-kəi, *Angl* 'gȯ(ə)r-kē\. 1868–1936. Russian writer. Reared in poverty with little education; held various menial jobs from age eight, began writing stories for provincial newspapers (1892), adopting pseudonym "Gorky," i.e. bitter; achieved fame with tale "Chelkash" (1895); other stories of underside of Russian society included "Byvshye lyudi" (1897), "Malva" (1897), "Dvadtsat shest i odna" (1899). Became supporter of Lenin and Bolshevik party, to which he contributed much of his income; in political exile (1906–13), lived on Capri; opposed Revolution (1917) and for a time criticized Lenin's dictatorship in journal *Novaya zhizn* (1917–18); joined government (1919) and helped protect and support other artists. Lived in Italy (1921–28); returned to Soviet Union (1929); first president of Soviet Writers' Union (1934); helped develop official aesthetic of Socialist Realism. Author of novels including *Foma Gordeyev* (1899), *Troye* (1900), *Mat* (1906), *Zhizn nenuzhnago cheloveka* (1907–08), *Ispoved* (1908), *Gorodok Okurov* (1909), *Khozyain* (1913), *Delo Artamonovykh* (1925), *Zhizn Klima Samgina* (1927–36); plays *Meshchane* (1901), *Na dne* (*The Lower Depths,* 1902), *Dachniki* (1905), *Vragi* (1906), *Vassa Zheleznova* (1910), *Zykovy* (1913), etc.; autobiographical works *Detstvo* (1913–14), *V lyudyakh* (1915–16), *Moi universitety* (1923). Native city of Nizhny Novgorod renamed (1932) Gorky in his honor.

Pesne \pen\, Antoine. 1683–1757. French painter. Studied in Paris and Italy, esp. with Andrea Celesti in Venice; court painter (from 1707) to Frederick I and II of Prussia; noted for Rococo coloristic style. Executed mythological and allegorical ceiling paintings and murals for palaces of Berlin, Charlottenburg, Potsdam, Rheinsberg, Sanssouci; also known for portraits and paintings of French and Italian actresses and dancers of Berlin Opera.

Pes·san·ha \pes-'ǟⁿn-yȧ\, Camilo. 1867–1926. Portuguese lyric poet. High school teacher in Macao (1893 ff.); learned Chinese language and culture; translated elegies (*Oito elegias chinesas*) and wrote *Introdução a um estudo sobre a civilização chinesa.* His Symbolist poems collected in *Clépsidra* (1920); a chief precursor of Modernist poetry.

Pes·soa \pā-'sō-ȧ\, Epitacio da Sil·va \thā-'sil-və\. 1865–1942. Brazilian political leader and jurist. Minister of justice (1898); president of Brazil (1919–23); member of Permanent Court of International Justice at The Hague (1924–30).

Pes·soa \'pes-wȧ, 'pes-ü-ȧ\, Fernando António Nogueira. 1888–1935. Portuguese poet. Greatest literary figure in Portuguese Modernism. Raised in South Africa and educated in English (1896–1905); earned living translating letters for business firms (1908–35); editor of review *Athena* (1924–25). Frequent contributor to avant-garde reviews, esp. Modernist organ *Orpheu* (1915); published poems in English *Antinous* (1918), *35 Sonnets* (1918), *Inscriptions* (1920); wrote literary and political manifestos *Ultimatum* (1917), *Aviso por causa da moral* (1923), *Interregno* (1928); a collection of poems *Mensagem* (1934) prophesied a resurgence of Portugal's greatness. Besides using own name, published poetry under other names (which he called heteronyms) that contained their own distinct poetic personalities: Alberto Caeiro (a materialistic rationalist), Ricardo Reis (a Stoic), and Álvaro de Campos (a Whitmanesque poet).

Pes·ta·loz·zi \ˌpes-tä-'lȯt-sē\, Johann Heinrich. 1746–1827. Swiss educational reformer. Established (1774) school for poor children on his estate at Neuhof and endeavored to put in practice educational theories of Jean-Jacques Rousseau; although school failed (1780), derived from his experience a knowledge of certain principles for effective education; explained doctrines in didactic novel *Lienhard und Gertrud, ein Buch für das Volk* (1781–87). Principal of a school at Burgdorf (1799–1804); moved to Münchenbuchsee (1804) and Yverdon (1805–25). His emphasis upon concrete approach in education, with objects used to develop powers of observation and reasoning, influenced strongly methods of instruction in elementary schools throughout Europe and America. His theories also expounded in *Abendstunde eines Einsiedlers* (1780) and *Wie Gertrud ihre Kinder lehrt* (1801).

Pes·tel \'pyäst-yil\, Pavel Ivanovich. 1793–1826. Russian soldier and revolutionary. A leader of Decembrist revolutionary movement; head of secret Southern Society; planned to overthrow Russian autocracy and found a centralized republic; arrested before Decembrist uprising (1825) and executed.

Pé·tain \pā-taⁿ\, Philippe. 1856–1951. French soldier. General of division (1914); commanded corps that broke German front in battle of Artois (1915); successful defense of Verdun (1916) made him national hero; commander in chief of the French armies, under Marshal Foch (1918); marshal of France (1918); vice president, Higher Council of War (1920–30); commanded French troops in Morocco (1925–26); minister of war (1934); ambassador to Spain (1939). Premier of Fascist-dominated Vichy government in unoccupied France (1940–44); fled to Switzerland after Allied invasion; returned for trial; convicted (1945) of collaboration with enemy; death sentence commuted by de Gaulle to life imprisonment.

Pe·tau \pə-tō\, Denis. *Lat.* Pe·ta·vi·us \pə-'tā-vē-əs\. 1583–1652. French theologian and scholar. Entered Jesuit order (1605); taught at Collège de Clermont in Paris (1621–44). A leading proponent of positive theology, esp. in his *Dogmata theologia* (1644–50).

Peter. See also PEDRO.

Pe·ter \'pēt-ər\. Saint. *Lat.* Pe·trus \'pē-trəs\. *Originally called* Sim·e·on \'sim-ē-ən\ *or* Si·mon \'sī-mən\. *Later* Simon Peter. *Sometimes* Ce·phas \'sē-fəs\. d. c.64 A.D. One of twelve Christian Apostles. During Jesus's ministry lived in Capernaum as a fisherman in partnership with James, John, and brother Andrew. After the Crucifixion, became the leader of the Christian community and made Jerusalem headquarters for preaching and proselyting in Palestine (c.33–44 A.D.); imprisoned by Herod Agrippa I, but escaped; established see of Antioch. By well founded tradition, went to Rome and died a martyr during persecutions of Nero. Probably wrote two Epistles included in the New Testament canon.

Peter. *Span.* Pe·dro \'pā-thrō\. Name of four kings of Aragon:

Peter I. 1068–1104. King of Aragon and Navarre (1094–1104). Son of Sancho V Ramírez; fought with father against Moors and continued struggle during reign; renewed alliance with El Cid (1094); conquered Huesca (1096) and Barbastro (1100).

Peter II. 1174–1213. King (1196–1213). Had himself crowned by Pope Innocent III and declared his kingdom a feudatory of Holy See (1204); fought against Moors, esp. at victory of Las Navas de Tolosa (1212); killed in battle.

Peter III. *Called* the Great. 1239–1285. King (1276–85). Son of James I; known for great stature and physical strength; conquered Sicily and became its king (1282); repelled French invasion (1285); forced by nobles and towns to lessen rights of the crown.

Peter IV. *Called* el Ce·re·mo·nio·so \el-thā-rā-mōn-'yō-sō\, *i.e.* the Ceremonious. 1319–1387. King (1336–87). Reincorporated Balearic Islands and Roussillon (1343–44); crushed rebellion of Aragon nobles (1348); supported claims of Henry of Trastámara to Castilian throne (1356–66); thereafter remained neutral in Hundred Years' War.

Peter. *Span.* Pedro. *Called* el Cru·el \el-krü-'el\, *i.e.* the Cruel. 1334–1369. King of Castile and León (1350–69). Son of Alfonso XI; right to throne challenged by half-brother Henry of Trastámara; deposed (1366) by the French but restored (1367) by the English led by Edward the Black Prince; defeated and slain by Henry at Monteil; depicted as harsh and unprincipled by Castilian historians favorable to house of Trastámara.

Peter I. 1329–1369. French king of Cyprus (1359–69). Led last serious crusade to regain Palestine from Muslims; captured Antalya (1361) and Alexandria (1365); murdered by one of his knights.

Peter. *In full* Peter Or·se·o·lo \ȯr-'zä-ə-(,)lō\. 1011–after 1050. King of Hungary (1038–46), second of the Árpád dynasty. Son of sister of St. Stephen and the doge of Venice; declared successor by Stephen; driven out (1041) by Samuel Aba, brother-in-law of Stephen, but restored (1044) with aid of Emperor Henry III.

Peter I of Montenegro. *Montenegrin* Pe·tro·vić Nje·goš \pe-'trȯ-vētʸ-'nyeg-ȯsh\. c.1747–1830. Prince-bishop of Montenegro. Succeeded his great-uncle in power (1782); allied himself with Russia and Austria against Turkey; defeated Turkish invasion (1796–99) and won full independence of Montenegro from Sultan Selim III (1799); added territories, esp. Brda; later (1813) allied with Russia against France, and forced French out of Kotor; involved in further wars with Turkey (1819, 1821). Published a code of civil and administrative law for his country. His nephew ¶Peter II (1812–1851) succeeded him (1830) as prince-bishop, defended country against Turks, maintained civil order, opened schools, built roads, and made himself known as a poet by writing an epic, a five-act historical play, and a number of lyrics.

Peter. *Port.* Pe·dro \'pā-thrü\. Name of five kings of Portugal, Peter I being of house of Burgundy (*q.v.*), the others of house of Bragança (*q.v.*):

Peter I. *Called* el Ju·sti·cie·ro \ēl-yü-stēs-'yer-ü\, *i.e.* the Severe. 1320–1367. King (1357–67). Son of Afonso IV; m. (1336) Constança (d. 1345), daughter of infante Juan Manuel; his mistress Inês de Castro (*q.v.*) was murdered on orders of Afonso (1355); as king, took revenge on Inês's assassins, dispensed strict justice in person, maintained neutrality with other kingdoms.

Peter II. 1648–1706. King (1683–1706). Dethroned (1667) his feebleminded brother Afonso VI and became regent until Afonso's death (1683); m. (1668) Marie-Françoise of Savoy-Nemours and (1687) Maria Sophia of Neuburg; concluded peace with Spain (1668); improved Portugal's financial condition; consolidated royal power; negotiated commercial treaty with England (1703); on Anglo-Austrian side in War of Spanish Succession.

Peter III. 1717–1786. King (1777–86). 2d son of John V and brother of King Joseph Emanuel; m. (1760) his niece Maria (see MARIA I); joint ruler with her.

Peter IV. See PEDRO I of Brazil.

Peter V. 1837–1861. King (1853–61). Son of Maria II (*q.v.*) and Ferdinand II; under regency of father (1853–55); m. (1858) Stephanie of Hohenzollern; promoted higher education.

Peter. Name of three rulers of Russia:

Peter I. *Russ.* Pyotr Alekseyevich. *Known as* Peter the Great. 1672–1725. Czar (1682–1725). Son of Alexis; reigned jointly with half-brother Ivan (1682–89) and alone thereafter. Married (1689) Eudoxia (*q.v.*), sent her to a monastery, and later (1712) married Catherine (*q.v.*). Captured Azov and founded Taganrog (1696). Traveled in Germany, Netherlands, England, and Austria (1697–98); returned to Russia and suppressed rebellion of the Strelitzi (1698). Engaged in long northern war (1700–21) with Sweden to establish ports on Baltic Sea; defeated by Charles XII of Sweden at Narva (1700) and in turn decisively defeated him at Poltava (1709); concluded peace (1721) with Sweden at Nystad and acquired Livonia, Estonia, Ingermanland (Ingria), and part of Karelia. Invaded Persia (1722–23), which ceded him southern and western shores of the Caspian. Founded new capital, St. Petersburg (1703); reorganized the government and military system; built up industry and naval fleet; increased power of the monarchy at expense of nobles and Orthodox church; renowned for introducing western European civilization into Russia and raising Russia to recognized place among great European powers.

Peter II. *Russ.* Pyotr Alekseyevich. 1715–1730. Czar (1727–30). Grandson of Peter the Great; succeeded Catherine I (1727; crowned 1728); fell under influence of Dolgoruky family and was betrothed to one of its members; died on day set for the wedding.

Peter III. *Russ.* Pyotr Fyodorovich. *Originally* Karl Peter Ulrich, Duke of Holstein-Gottorp. 1728–1762. Czar (1762). Grandson of Peter the Great; succeeded his aunt Elizabeth Petrovna; mentally weak; withdrew from Seven Years' War; formed alliance with Prussia; attempted to force Lutheran practices on Orthodox church; deposed by group of nobles (see ORLOV) with connivance of his wife (1762); abdicated and assassinated; succeeded by his wife, Catherine II (*q.v.*).

Peter I. 1844–1921. King of Serbia (1903–21). Son of Prince Alexander of Karageorgevič line. Trained in French military schools; fought in French army in Franco-Prussian War (1870–71); commanded a corps in rebellion of Bosnia and Hercegovina against Turkey (1875); lived most of time in exile until, after assassination of Alexander Obrenovič V, proclaimed king by the army and elected unanimously by parliament; a liberal and advocate of constitutional government; allied with Russia and France; named heir Prince Alexander as regent (1914); proclaimed king of Serbs, Croats, and Slovenes (1918–21).

Peter II of Yugoslavia. *Originally* Pe·tar Pe·tro·vič \'pe-tär-'pe-trȯ-,vētʸ\. 1923–1970. King (1934–45). Son of King Alexander and grandson of King Peter I of the Karageorgevič line. Succeeded to the throne on death of Alexander (1934); government under a regency headed by his uncle Prince Paul (1934–41); assumed sovereignty (Mar. 1941); after German invasion (Apr. 1941), set up government in London; reign ended when Yugoslavia became republic (1945); afterwards worked in public relations in N.Y.

Peter of Al·cán·ta·ra \äl-'kän-tä-rä\. Saint. *Originally* Pedro Ga·ra·vi·to \gä-rä-'bē-tō\. 1499–1562. Spanish ecclesiastic. Of noble birth; ordained (1524); provincial of province of Saint Gabriel (1538); founded new branch of Franciscan order (known as Alcantarines) which stressed an austere life; wrote *Tratado de la oración y meditación;* canonized (1669) by Pope Clement IX.

Peter of Amiens. See PETER the Hermit.

Peter of Blois \blwä\. *Lat.* Petrus Ble·sen·sis \blə-'sen-səs\. c.1135–c.1212. French writer. Tutor to William II of Sicily (1167–70); diplomat of Henry II of England; chancellor to archbishop of Canterbury (c.1175); sent on missions to Rome; secretary to Queen Eleanor (1191–95); his *Epistolae* an important historical source.

Peter of Bruys \brūē-ē\. *Lat.* Petrus Bru·sius \'brü-sh(ē-)əs\. d. 1126 or 1132/33. French religious reformer. Itinerant priest in Dauphiné and Languedoc;

advocated abolition of infant baptism, prayers for the dead, the mass and other ceremonies, church buildings, and hymns; followers known as Petrobrusians; burned as a heretic.

Peter of Cas·tel·nau \kȧs-tel-nō\. *Fr.* Pierre de Castelnau. d. 1208. French martyr. Archdeacon (1199); joined Cistercian order (1202); appointed (1207) by Innocent III apostolic legate and inquisitor against Raymond VI of Toulouse and the Albigenses; his assassination by Raymond led to the Albigensian Crusade.

Peter of Cour·te·nay \kür-tə-nā\. *Fr.* Pierre de Courtenay. d. 1219? Latin emperor of Constantinople (1216–17). Grandson of Louis VI of France; m. Yolande, sister of Emperor Baldwin I. Accompanied Philip Augustus on Third Crusade (1189–91); fought at Bouvines (1214). Chosen emperor (1216) but made prisoner on his journey east by Theodore Ducas, despot of Epirus, and died in captivity. Yolande ruled as regent (1217–19).

Peter of Dreux \drœ\. *Called* Mau·clerc \mō-kler\. 1190–1250. French duke of Brittany (1213–1237). Married Alix, heiress to Brittany; as duke introduced usages of Capetian chancery and annexed new fiefs; renounced Brittany and became count of Braine on majority of son John I (1237); on crusades (1239–40, 1248–50) as penance for quarrels with episcopate.

Peter of Montboissier. See PETER the Venerable.

Peter of Sa·voy \sə-'vȯi\. Earl of Rich·mond \'rich-mənd\ between 1203 and 1213–1268. Savoyard diplomat in English service. Son of Thomas I, Count of Savoy. Resigned ecclesiastical preferments, married, received in England by Henry III with earldom and estates (1240); associated with Simon de Montfort and barons (from 1252); sent by Henry III on diplomatic missions to pope and Louis IX of France; assumed title of count of Savoy (1263).

Peter of Verona. See PETER MARTYR.

Peter the Hermit. *Known also as* Peter of Amiens \ȧm-yaⁿ\. c.1050–1115. French ascetic and crusader. One of the preachers of the First Crusade (1095); led one section of the crusade to Constantinople (1096), where he joined section led by Walter the Penniless and crossed over to Asia Minor. His followers were destroyed by the Turks; returned to Constantinople, joined the army of the princes (1097), and accompanied them through Asia Minor to Jerusalem. After the conquest of Jerusalem (1099) by the crusaders under Godfrey of Bouillon, Peter founded and became prior (1100) of monastery of Neufmoutier, at Huy, Belgium.

Peter the Venerable. *Known also as* Peter of Mont·bois·sier \mōⁿ-bwȧs-yā\. c.1092–1156. French monk. Abbot of Cluny (from 1122); reputed instrumental in placing Innocent II on the papal throne and in gaining general church recognition of him instead of the antipope Anacletus; papal ambassador to Aquitaine, Italy, England; befriended Peter Abelard and reconciled him to St. Bernard and Innocent II; wrote poems, hymns, and letters.

Peter, Hugh. *Surname often* Pe·ters \'pēt-ərz\. 1598–1660. English clergyman. To America (1635); succeeded Roger Williams as preacher, Salem, Mass. (1636); active in establishment of colony at Saybrook, Conn., and in the building of Harvard College. Appointed (1641) to represent Massachusetts Bay Colony in England. Served as chaplain with Parliamentary forces (1642–49), and as a preacher before the Council during the Protectorate; reprimanded for attempts to mediate Dutch War (1652–54). At Restoration, arrested, tried as an accomplice in the execution of Charles I, condemned, and executed at Charing Cross.

Peterborough, Earl and countess of. See Charles MORDAUNT.

Peter Chry·sol·o·gus \-kris-'äl-ə-gəs\. Saint. c.400–450. Doctor of the Church. Archbishop of Ravenna (433); friend of Pope Leo I; famed for his orthodoxy; refused to defend Eutyches (449) when latter condemned for founding Eutychianism; many of his sermons survive.

Peter Cla·ver \-'kläv-ər\. Saint. *Span.* Pe·dro Cla·ver \'pā-thrō-klä-'ver\. 1581–1654. Spanish Jesuit missionary. To Cartagena, Colombia (1610); administered food, medicine, and religious instruction to newly-arrived African slaves despite official opposition; known as "Apostle of the Negroes." Canonized (1888).

Peter des Roches \-dā-'rȯsh\. d. 1238. English prelate, b. Poitou, France. Knight and clerk under Richard I; bishop of Winchester (from 1205); stood by King John through struggle with barons; chief justiciar (1214–15). Led a royal division at battle of Lincoln (1217); on crusade of Emperor Frederick II (1228–29); negotiated truce between Henry III and French (1231); patron of son or nephew Peter des Rivaux; lost power (1234) due to baronial opposition; assisted Gregory IX to defeat Romans (1235) at Viterbo. His son or nephew ¶Peter des Ri·vaux \dā-rē-'vō\ (c.1190–1262), b. Poitou, France; tutor (1216) and clerk (1218–23) to Henry III of England; exiled (1227–30); as treasurer of royal household (1232–34) in effect ran government; lost power (1234) in baronial revolt; baron of the exchequer (1253); keeper of the wardrobe (1257–58).

Pe·ter·kin \'pēt-ər-ˌkin\, Julia, *nee* Mood \'müd\. 1880–1961. American novelist, b. Laurens Co., S.C. Author of *Green Thursday* (1924), *Black April* (1927), *Scarlet Sister Mary* (1928, Pulitzer prize; subsequently dramatized), *Bright Skin* (1932), *Roll, Jordan, Roll* (1933), *Plantation Christmas* (1934).

Peter Lom·bard \'läm-ˌbärd, -bərd\. *Lat.* Petrus Lom·bar·dus \ləm-'bärd-əs, läm-\. c.1095–1160. Italian theologian. Taught in school of Notre Dame, Paris (1136–50); bishop of Paris (1159). Chief work, *Sententiarum libri IV* (1148–51), a collection of teachings of Church Fathers and opinions of medieval masters, was the official textbook in medieval theological schools and an important influence in crystallizing the doctrine concerning the sacraments of the Church. Also wrote letters, sermons, and commentaries on Holy Scripture.

Pe·ter·mann \'pā-tər-ˌmän\, August. 1822–1878. German geographer and cartographer. Promoted geographical expeditions to Africa and to polar regions; founder (1855) and editor of geographic journal *Petermanns Geographische Mitteilungen.* Chief works included an atlas of physical geography and maps of inner Africa and the Transvaal.

Peter Martyr. See also Pietro Martire d'ANGHIERA; Pietro Martire VERMIGLI.

Peter Mar·tyr \-'märt-ər\. Saint. *Known also as* Peter of Ve·ro·na \və-'rō-nə, *Ital* vā-'rō-nä\. c.1205–1252. Italian preacher and inquisitor. Entered Dominican order (c.1221); preached in Lombardy; as general inquisitor (1232, 1251), preached against Catharists; helped Seven Founders of Servites at Florence (1244–45); killed near Como by members of Catharist sect. Canonized (1253); patron saint of Spanish Inquisition.

Peter No·las·co \nō-'läs-kō\. Saint. *Fr.* Pierre No·lasque \nȯ-lȧsk\. c.1182–c.1256. French philanthropist. In Barcelona (from 1208) helped ransom Christian captives in hands of the Moors; founded (between 1218 and 1234), with aid of James I of Aragon and Raymond of Peñafort, religious Order of Our Lady of Mercy for the Redemption of Captives; members of the order became known as Mercedarians.

Pe·ters \'pā-tərs\, Carl. 1856–1918. German explorer. Founded German Colonization Society (1884) which established German protectorate of Tanganyika; made treaties with native chiefs in East Africa (1884); returned to Europe and formed German East Africa Co. (1885). Imperial high commissioner to district of Kilimanjaro (1891); dismissed for misuse of official power (1897). Formed company in London for exploitation of Rhodesia and Portuguese East Africa (1898); discovered deserted gold mines and traces of ancient cities along the Zambezi (1899).

Pe·ters \'pēt-ərz\, Curtis Arnoux. *Pseudonym* Peter Ar·no \'är-(ˌ)nō\. 1904–1968. American cartoonist, b. New York City. Known for satirical cartoons, esp. of New York café society, for *New Yorker* magazine (from 1925); wrote musical revues as *Here Comes the Bride* (1931); cartoons collected in *Hullabaloo* (1930), *Man in the Shower* (1944), *Sizzling Platter* (1949), etc.

Peters, Hugh. See Hugh PETER.

Peters, Samuel Andrew. 1735–1826. American Anglican clergyman, b. Hebron, Conn. Loyalist in American Revolution; fled to England (1774) and lived (until 1804) on government pension; returned to America (1805) to press land claims along Mississippi River; claims disallowed by Congress (1826). Author of *A General History of Connecticut* (1781), containing the famous blue laws said to have been enacted in early days of New Haven Colony.

Pe·ter·son \'pēt-ər-sən\, Henry. 1818–1891. American editor, b. Philadelphia. Edited *Saturday Evening Post* (1846–74); author of poetry and novels.

Peth·e·rick \'peth-ə-ˌrik\, John. 1813–1882. English trader and explorer. Explored western tributaries of Nile River; made zoological and ethnological discoveries in the Sudan and Central Africa; first European to encounter tribes of northeastern Congo; published account of his travels *Egypt, the Soudan and Central Africa* (1861).

Peth·ick-Law·rence \'peth-ik-'lȯr-ən(t)s, -'lär-\, Frederick William. 1st Baron. *Surname orig.* Lawrence. 1871–1961. English politician. Married (1901) Emmeline Pethick and added her surname to his; with wife became a leader of woman suffrage movement in 1910s and 1920s. M.P. (1923 ff.); secretary of state for India and Burma (1945–47); unsuccessful in attempts to reconcile Nehru and Jinnah. Created baron (1945).

Pet·i·gru \'pet-ə-ˌgrü\, James Louis. 1789–1863. American lawyer and politician, b. Abbeville District, S.C. State attorney general (1822–30); member, South Carolina House of Representatives (1830–33) and head of Union party opposed to nullification; opposed secession (1860) but remained loyal to Southern cause after decision was made.

Pé·tion \pā-tyōⁿ\, Alexandre Sabès. 1770–1818. Haitian general and politician. A mulatto, well educated; fought in rebellion under Toussaint L'Ouverture and Rigaud (1791–97); in France (1800–02); served under Dessalines (1802–06); with Christophe assassinated Dessalines (1806); became president of independent republic in southern Haiti (1807); at war with Christophe (1811–18); his rule comparatively moderate and progressive.

Pé·tion de Ville·neuve \pā-tyōⁿ-də-vēl-nœv\, Jérôme. 1756–1794. French revolutionist. Deputy to Estates-General (1789); member of Jacobin Club and ally of Robespierre; mayor of Paris (1791–92); first president of National Convention (1792); joined Girondins and was expelled from Convention by Jacobins (1793); escaped arrest and committed suicide.

Pe·ti·pa \pā-tē-pá\, Marius. 1819–1910. French dancer and choreographer. Pupil of his father Jean-Antoine (1796–1855); toured U.S. and Europe as dancer and pantomimist (1831–47). Associated (until 1903) with Mariinsky Theatre, St. Petersburg, as dancer (1847), stage manager (1858), choreographer (1862), and choreographer-in-chief (1869). Choreographed over 60 ballets, including *La Fille du pharaon* (1862), *Don Quixote* (1869), *The Talisman* (1889), *Raymonda* (1898), Glazunov's *Seasons* (1900), and Tschaikovsky's *Sleeping Beauty* (1890), *Nutcracker* (1892), *Swan Lake* (1895). Considered father of classical ballet.

Pe·tit \pə-tē\, Alexis-Thérèse. 1791–1820. French physicist. With P.-L. Dulong, developed methods for determining thermal expansion and specific heat of solid bodies; also with Dulong, enunciated law of Dulong and Petit, that elements in the solid state have nearly the same gram-atomic heat (1819).

Pe·ti·tot \pə-tē-tō\, Jean. 1607–1691. Swiss painter. First great miniature portraitist in enamel. Pupil of Jean and Henri Toutin in France (1633–37); attached to court of Charles I of England; after Charles I's execution, moved to France, patronized by Louis XIV; executed many portraits of the king and his court; a Protestant, fled to Geneva after revocation of Edict of Nantes (1685).

Pet·lyu·ra \pyet-'lyü-rá\, Symon. 1879–1926. Ukrainian political and military leader. Published Socialist newspapers in Kiev (1905–09) and Moscow (1912–14); led unsuccessful fight for Ukrainian independence from Soviet regime (1918–20); defeated, fled to Poland and later to Paris; assassinated in Paris.

Pe·to \'pēt-ō\, John Frederick. 1854–1907. American painter, b. Philadelphia. Friend and follower of William Harnett; studio in Philadelphia (1875–89) and Island Heights, N.J. (1889–1907). Known for realistic paintings of everyday subjects, as books, guns, and letter racks.

Pe·tő·fi \'pet-œ-fē\, Sándor. *Orig.* Alexander Pe·tro·vics \'pe-trò-vich\. 1823–1849. Hungarian poet. Early lyrics (*Versek,* 1844) were sponsored by the poet Vörösmarty, and his later work firmly established his place among the finest of Hungary's lyric poets; with Mór Jókai edited (1847–49) magazine *Életképek;* active in Hungarian revolution (1848–49) and by his patriotic songs gained recognition as Hungary's national poet; his "Talpra magyar" became anthem of 1848 revolution; believed killed in battle of Segesvár. Works included epic *János vitéz* (1845).

Pe·trarch \'pē-,trärk, 'pe-\. *Ital.* Francesco Pe·trar·ca \pā-'trär-kə\, *orig.* Pe·trac·co \pā-'träk-kō\. 1304–1374. Italian poet. Studied law at Montpellier (1316–20) and Bologna (1320–26); devoted himself thereafter to study of classics. Assumed minor ecclesiastical orders (1326); lived at Avignon, where (1327) he met Laura (*q.v.*), who inspired his *Rime.* Visited Flanders, Brabant, the Rhineland, and France (1333), where he discovered copies of two lost speeches of Cicero; visited Rome (1337); retired to Vaucluse; crowned poet laureate (Rome, 1341); entrusted with diplomatic mission by Clement VI (1343); settled in Milan (1353); on diplomatic missions for Duke of Visconti (1356, 1360). Friend of Boccaccio; protégé of Colonna and Visconti families. Known particularly for *Canzoniere* or *Rime,* a collection of his Italian lyrics, chiefly sonnets and odes written to Laura; other works included in Italian, allegory *I trionfi,* and, in Latin, epic poem *Africa, Epistolae metricae, Bucolica,* the treatises *De contemptu mundi, De vita solitaria, De remediis utriusque fortunae, De vera sapientia, De otio religiosorum,* and *De viris illustribus,* letters, orations, etc.

Pe·tre \'pēt-ər\, Sir Edward. 1631–1699. English religious. Entered Society of Jesus (1652); imprisoned for suspected complicity in Popish Plot (1679–80); confessor of James II; often accused of promoting policies leading to Revolution of 1688.

Pe·tri \'pā-trē\, Olaus. 1493–1552. Swedish clergyman. Chancellor (1531); opposed autocratic policies of Gustav Vasa; exerted great influence on Swedish Reformation by writing sermons, a hymnbook, a Lutheran church manual, and theological tracts; wrote one of earliest prose histories of Sweden; collaborated with his brother ¶Laurentius (1499–1573), first Lutheran archbishop of Uppsala (1531), in translation of the New Testament into Swedish.

Pe·trie \'pē-trē\, Sir Flinders, *in full* William Matthew Flinders. 1853–1942. English Egyptologist. Grandson of Capt. Matthew Flinders; studied ancient British remains at Stonehenge (1875–80); wrote *Inductive Metrology* (1875); investigated pyramids at Giza and other Egyptian antiquities (1880–1914); excavated Tanis, discovered Naukratis (1885) and Daphnae (1886); uncovered funeral portraits and collections of papyri in Fayyūm; excavated ancient Hawara, Kahun, Lachish; discovered temple at Medum (1891). Developed principle of sequence dating by potsherds (1890). Professor of Egyptology, University Coll., London (1892–1933); founded British School of Archaeology in Egypt (1894); discovered remains of a prehistoric race at Nagada (1895); uncovered stele of Merneptah at Thebes (1896), containing earliest known Egyptian reference to Israel; investigated tombs of 1st dynasty at Abydos (1899) and site of palaces of Memphis, Tarkhan; excavated in Palestine (1927–38). Also wrote *Methods and Aims in Archaeology* (1904) and *The Formation of the Alphabet* (1912).

Petronila. See RAMÓN BERENGUER IV.

Pe·tro·ni·us \pə-'trō-nē-əs\. *Full name probably* Titus Petronius Niger. *Surnamed* Ar·bi·ter \'är-bət-ər\. Roman writer. d. 66 A.D. Governor of Bithynia; consul (62 or 63); director of entertainment at Nero's court; accused by Nero's guard, Tigellinus, of plotting to kill Nero; committed suicide. Called by Tacitus Arbiter Ele·gan·ti·ae \,el-ə-'gan-chē-,ē\ or Ele·gan·ti·a·rum \-,gan-chē-'ā-rəm\, *i.e.* judge of elegance. Generally regarded as author of *Satyricon,* satirical picaresque romance in prose interspersed with verse, extant only in fragments.

Petrov, Yevgeny. See Yevgeny KATAYEV.

Pe·trov·sky-Sit·ni·an·ov·ich \pyi-'tròv-skəs-yit-'yän(-əv)-,yich\, Samuil Yemelyanovich. *Pseudonym* Simeon Po·lot·sky \(,)pə-'lòt-skəi\. 1629–1680. Byelorussian monk and writer. Tutor of Czar Alexis's children; westernizing influence at court; author of panegyrics, two biblical dramas, and a rhymed Psalter (1680).

Pe·truc·ci \pā-'trüt-chē\, Ottaviano dei. 1466–1539. Italian music publisher. Operated music publishing monopolies in Venice (1498–1511, 1536–39) and Fossombrone (1513–23); his *Harmonice Musices Odhecaton A* (1501) was first polyphonic music printed from movable type; publisher of Josquin des Prez, Okeghem, Compère, etc.

Petrucci, Pandolfo. c.1452–1512. Sienese despot. Returned (1487) from exile to become *signore* (lord) of Siena; stopped sale of public offices, improved monetary system, patronized arts and sciences; fled after implication in plot against Cesare Borgia (1503); returned (1507) again as despot; formed alliance with Spanish and Pope Julius II against French.

Pe·trun·ke·vitch \pyi-trün-'kyāv-,yich, *Angl* ,pe-trəŋ-'kā-(,)vich\, Alexander. 1875–1964. American zoologist, b. Pliski, Russia. Instructor (1910), professor (1917–44) at Yale. One of foremost authorities on spiders and other arachnids; author of *Index Catalogue of North, Central and South American Spiders* (1911), *Inquiry Into the Natural Classification of Spiders* (1933), *Treatise on Invertebrate Paleontology* (1955), etc.

Pe·trus Au·re·ol·us \'pē-trəs-ȯr-ē-'ō-ləs\ *or* **Au·re·o·li** \-'ō-lē\. *Fr.* Pierre Au·ri·ol \ȯr-yȯl\, Or·i·ol \ȯr-yȯl\, *or* D'Or·i·ol \dȯr-\. c.1280–1322. French Franciscan monk and scholastic philosopher. Lector at Bologna (1312), Toulouse (1314–15), Paris (1316–18); archbishop of Aix; attacked realist doctrines of Duns Scotus; regarded as precursor of William of Ockham in revival of nominalism; author of religious treatises.

Petrus de Vinea. See PIETRO DELLA VIGNA.

Pétrus Ky. See TRUONG VINH KY.

Petrus Lombardus. See PETER LOMBARD.

Petrus Venerabilis. See PETER the Venerable.

Pet·taz·zo·ni \,pet-täd-'dzō-nē\, Raffaele. Italian religious historian. 1883–1959. Professor at Bologna (1914–23) and Rome (1923–53); co-founder and president (1950–59), International Association for the History of Religions. His original phenomenologico-historical comparative method for study of religions exemplified in *La confessione dei peccati* (1929–35) and *L'omniscienza di Dio* (1955).

Pet·ten·ko·fer \'pet-ən-,kō-fər\, Max Josef von. 1818–1901. German hygienist. Founder of experimental hygiene; professor at Munich (from 1847) and director of Institute of Hygiene (from 1879); made researches on ventilation of dwellings, on gaseous metabolism in man, and on the function of clothing; as result of his observations on cholera, developed theory emphasizing importance of ground water and contamination of soil in origin of epidemics; planned effective drainage and sewerage systems for Munich; in chemistry, originated method for detecting bile acids; also for quantitative determination of carbon dioxide.

Pet·ter·sen \'pet-tər-sən\, Sverre. 1898–1974. Norwegian meteorologist. Specialist in dynamic and synoptic meteorologies; with Norwegian Meteorological Service (1924–39); professor at MIT (1939–42) and U. of Chicago (1952–63). Author of *Weather Analysis and Forecasting* (1940), *Introduction to Meteorology* (1941).

Pet·tie \'pet-ē\, George. 1548–1589. English writer. Author of *A Petite Pallace of Pettie his Pleasure* (1576), including twelve modernized classical tales, titled by publisher in imitation of Painter's *Palace of Pleasure* (1566).

Pet·ti·grew \'pet-ə-,grü\, James Johnston. 1828–1863. American Confederate general, b. Tyrrell Co., N.C. Served under Johnston through Peninsular campaign; in command of defenses of Petersburg (1862); in command of an advance on left of Pickett in charge at Gettysburg (July 3, 1863).

Pet·ty \'pet-ē\, Sir William. 1623–1687. English economist. Professor of anatomy at Oxford and of music at Gresham College, London (1651);

physician to army in Ireland (1652); completed (1654) "Down Survey" of Irish lands forfeited in 1641; served as commissioner of distribution of land grants to soldiers; secretary to Henry Cromwell (lord deputy of Ireland, 1657); made surveyor general of Ireland by Charles II; set up ironworks, opened mines, quarries, and fisheries. A founder of the Royal Society; designed a twin-hulled ship (1662). One of authors of first book on vital statistics (1662); one of first to point out errors in mercantilist position that abundance of precious metals sets standard of prosperity; showed unsoundness of prohibition upon exportation of money; his *Treatises of Taxes and Contributions* (1662, 1667, 1685) stated doctrine that price depends upon labor necessary for production; his *Verbum sapienti* (1691) contained first estimate of national incomes and first discussion of the velocity of money.

Petty, William. 1st Marquis of Lans·downe \ˈlanz-ˌdau̇n\ *and* 2d Earl of Shel·burne \ˈshel-(ˌ)bərn\. 1737–1805. British politician. Son of Thomas Fitzmaurice, 1st Earl of Kerry, and grandson of Sir William Petty; assumed (1751) name Petty. President of Board of Trade (1763); opposed Stamp Act (1764); as secretary of state under Pitt, thwarted in effort toward conciliation of American colonies (1766–68); opposed government, chiefly on American policy (1768–82); home secretary (1782); prime minister (1782–83); helped negotiate Treaty of Paris (1783).

Petty-Fitz·mau·rice \-fits-ˈmȯr-əs, -ˈmär-\, Henry Charles Keith. 5th Marquis of Lansdowne. 1845–1927. British politician. Great-grandson of William Petty (1737–1805). Held minor posts in Gladstone administrations (1868–83); as governor general of Canada (1883–88) effected settlement of Riel Rebellion (1885); as viceroy of India (1888–94) stabilized the rupee by closing Indian mints to free coinage, abolished presidential army system, reorganized police and legislative councils, and extended railway and irrigation works. As secretary for war (1895–1900) was blamed for early mistakes of Boer War; as foreign secretary (1900–05) accomplished alliance with Japan (1902) and Anglo-French Entente (1904), handled affairs of Venezuela blockade (1903) and Alaskan boundary with U.S. (1903). Minister without portfolio (1915–16) in Asquith's government; repudiated by the government and by his party for "Lansdowne Letter" to *Daily Telegraph* (Nov. 1917) outlining possible peace terms.

Pét·urs·son \ˈpyet-œr-sȯn\, Hallgrímur. 1614–1674. Icelandic Lutheran pastor and poet. Greatest religious poet of Iceland; worked as laborer and fisherman; pastor at Saurbaer (1651–69). Author of hymns on Passion of Christ, *Passiusálmar* (1666), which remain most cherished devotional songs in his country.

Peu·er·bach \ˈpȯi-ər-ˌbäk\ *or* **Peur·bach** \ˈpoir-ˌbäk\ *or* **Pur·bach** \ˈpür-\, Georg von. 1423–1461. Austrian astronomer and mathematician. Lectured in Germany, France, Italy (1448–53); court astrologer to Frederick III (1457 ff.); teacher and associate of Regiomontanus; observed comets and lunar eclipses; credited with early Occidental use of sines in trigonometry; compiled a table of sines; wrote *Theoricae novae planetarum* (1454) and first six books of *Epitoma magesti Ptolemaei* (1496).

Peu·ting·er \ˈpȯi-tiŋ-ər\, Conrad. 1465–1547. German Humanist and antiquary. Syndic of Augsburg (1493); known esp. as owner of a parchment map (called *Peutingerian table* after him) showing military roads of ancient Roman empire, which was bequeathed to him by Conrad Pickel (*q.v.*), who discovered it in a Benedictine monastery of Tegernsee, Upper Bavaria.

Pev·sner \ˈpef-snər\, Antoine. 1886–1962. French sculptor and painter, b. Orël, Russia. Naturalized Frenchman (1930). With brother Naum Gabo, a pioneer of Constructivist style, employing metal, glass, and wire and eschewing mass for space intervals and sense of movement; among his works were *Portrait of Marcel Duchamp* (1926), *Construction for an Airport* (two works of 1934 and 1935), *Developable Surface* (1936).

Pey·er \ˈpī-ər\, Johann Konrad. 1653–1712. Swiss physician and anatomist. Professor in Schaffhausen; first to describe lymphatic nodules in walls of small intestine, now known as Peyer's patches (1682).

Pey·ré \pe-rā\, Joseph. 1892–1968. French novelist. His adventure novels included *L'Escadron blanc* (1931), *Sang et lumières* (1935), *Les Lanciers de Jerez* (1961).

Pey·ro·net *or* **Pey·ron·net** \pe-rȯ-ne\, Charles-Ignace de. Comte. 1778–1854. French politician. Ultraconservative in sympathies, became minister of justice (1821–28) and of interior (1830); countersigned Ordinances of July 25, which were immediate cause of outbreak of the July revolution (1830). Convicted of treason and sentenced to life imprisonment and loss of civil rights; in prison (1830–34), pardoned (1834).

Pez·za \ˈpet-tsä\, Michele. *Known as* Fra Dia·vo·lo \frä-ˈdyä-vō-(ˌ)lō\. 1771–1806. Italian brigand chief. Leader of band of robbers; employed by Cardinal Ruffo against Parthenopean Republic (1799) and by English against French at Naples (1806); captured and hanged by French. Celebrated as popular guerrilla leader in folk legends, novels of Dumas *père*, and Auber's opera *Fra Diavolo* (1830).

Pfaff \ˈpfäf\, Johann Friedrich. 1765–1825. German mathematician. Professor at Helstedt (1788–1810) and Halle (1810 ff.). Proposed first general method of integrating partial differential equations of the first order (1814–15); also studied theory of series; term *Pfaffian problem* named for him.

Pfef·fer \ˈpfef-ər\, Wilhelm Friedrich Philipp. 1845–1920. German botanist. Taught at Leipzig (1877–1920); developed method for measuring osmotic pressure in plant cells (1877); measured size of giant molecules; author of *Pflanzenphysiologie* (1881).

Pfef·fer·korn \ˈpfef-ər-ˌkȯrn\, Johannes. 1469–1524. German controversialist. A converted Jew; attempted to purge Germany of Jewish literature; opposed by Reuchlin and other Humanists; instigated preparation and publication by Humanists of great satirical work *Epistolae obscurorum virorum*.

Pfi·ster \ˈpfis-tər\, Albrecht. d. c.1466. German printer. One of earliest printers in Germany; supposed printer of the "Bible of 36 lines," sometimes called *Pfister's Bible*.

Pfitz·ner \ˈpfits-nər\, Hans Erich. 1869–1949. German composer. Director of Conservatory of Music, municipal concerts, and (from 1909) the opera, Strasbourg (1908–18); teacher at Acad. of Art, Berlin (1919–29) and Munich (1930–33). Among his operas were *Der arme Heinrich* (1895), *Die Rose vom Liebesgarten* (1901), *Palestrina* (1917), and *Das Herz* (1931); among his choral works, *Kolumbus* (1905), *Das dunkle Reich* (1930); also wrote chamber music, concertos, songs.

Pflei·de·rer \ˈpflī-də-rər\, Otto. 1839–1908. German Protestant theologian. Professor at Jena (1871–75) and Berlin (1875 ff.). Chief work, *Die Religion, ihr Wesen und ihr Geschichte* (1868), attempt at classification of religions.

Pflü·ger \ˈpflᵫ-gər\, Eduard Friedrich Wilhelm. 1829–1910. German physiologist. Succeeded Helmholz at Bonn (1859); known for work on sensory function of the spinal cord, on intestinal nerves, on the embryonal development of the ovary, on gas exchange in the blood and in the cells, on electrical stimulation of motor nerves, and on digestive and metabolic processes; founder and editor (1868–1910), *Archiv für die gesammte Physiologie*.

Pford·ten \ˈpfȯr-tən\, Ludwig von der. Freiherr. 1811–1880. Bavarian jurist and statesman. Professor, Würzburg (1834), Leipzig (1847), März (1848–49); minister of foreign affairs for Saxony (1848), for Bavaria (1849); premier of Bavaria (1849–59, 1864–66).

Pforr \ˈpfȯr\, Franz. 1788–1812. German painter. A leader of the Nazarenes; painted religious subjects as *Der Graf von Habsburg und der Priester* (1810).

Pfyf·fer \ˈpfœf-ər\, Ludwig. 1524–1594. Swiss soldier and politician. Long in service of France as soldier; as chief magistrate (1570–94) made Luzern center of Catholic Counter-Reformation activities; formed Golden League (1586) of seven Catholic cantons; supported Philip II of Spain and Henri, duc de Guise, against Henry of Navarre.

Phae·do \ˈfē-(ˌ)dō\ *or* **Phae·don** \-(ˌ)dän\. b. c.417 B.C. Greek philosopher of Elis. Captured in war with Sparta (400–399) and sold as slave to an Athenian; freed; disciple of Socrates; founder of Elian school of philosophy; only his dialogues *Zopyrus* and *Simon* survive. Appears as principal speaker in Plato's dialogue *Phaedo*, which treats of immortality of the soul and purports to record Socrates's last conversation.

Phae·drus \ˈfē-drəs\. 5th century B.C. Greek philosopher. Contemporary of Socrates and Plato; one of Plato's dialogues (attacking prevailing conception of rhetoric) bears his name.

Phaedrus. c.15 B.C.–c.50 A.D. Roman fabulist. A freedman of Augustus, originally a Macedonian slave; author of *Fabulae Aesopiae*, chiefly versifications of fables of the Aesop cycle.

Phaenias *or* **Phainias**. See PHANIAS.

Phaer \ˈfā(ə)r, ˈfe(ə)r\ *or* **Phay·er** \ˈfā(-ə)r, ˈfa(ə)r, ˈfe(ə)r\, Thomas. 1510?–1560. English lawyer, physician, and translator. Translated nine books of Virgil's *Aeneid* into English verse (1558, 1562); first Englishmen to attempt translation of whole epic.

'Phags-pa \ˈfäg-spä\. 1235–1280. Tibetan scholar-monk. Advisor to Kublai Khan; as Sa-skya lama, head of Buddhist theocracy in Tibet under Mongol rule; invented an alphabet for Mongol language.

Phal \fäl\, Louis. *Known as* Battling Si·ki \ˈsē-kē\. 1897–1925. Senegalese boxer. Defeated (Sept. 24, 1922) Georges Carpentier for world light-heavyweight title; held it until defeated by Mike McTigue (Mar. 17, 1923); first African-born black to win a world professional boxing championship.

Phal·a·ris \ˈfal-ə-rəs\. d. c.554 B.C. Greek tyrant of Agrigento in Sicily (570–554 B.C.). According to tradition, he was notoriously cruel, burning human sacrifices inside a brazen bull; finally overthrown and executed by being burned in the same brazen bull.

Phan Boi Chau \ˈpän-ˈbȯi-ˈchau̇\. *Orig. name* Phan Van San \ˈpän-ˈvän-ˈsän\, *also known as* Phan Giai San \-ˈgyī-ˈsän, -gē-ˈī-\, Phan Sao Nam \-ˈsä-ō-ˈnäm\,

Phan Thi Han \-'tē-'hän\, *or* Hai Thu \'hī-tü\. 1867–1940. Vietnamese nationalist. Formed (1904) resistance group Duy Tan Hoi to overthrow French rule and install Cuong De on throne; organized (1912) another nationalist group, Viet Nam Quang Phuc Hoi; imprisoned (1912–17) for assassination attempt on Albert Saurraut. Author of two autobiographies, volumes of poetry, a historical novel, and *Viet Nam vong quoc su* (1906), Vietnam's first revolutionary history book.

Phan Chau Trinh \'pän-'chau-'trin(-yə)\. 1872–1926. Vietnamese nationalist. Prominent (from 1885) in nationalist movement against French rule; advocated an autonomous, democratic republic, urged replacement of mandarinal civil service system with vocational schools and commercial firms; imprisoned (1908–11) for anti-colonial agitations.

Phan Dinh Phung \'pän-'din(-yə)-'fuŋ\. 1847–c.1896. Vietnamese nationalist. Mandarin at court of emperor Tu Duc (to 1883); banished for opposition to accession of Ham Nghi to throne (1884); died during unsuccessful rebellion against French presence in Vietnam (1894–96).

Phan·i·as \'fan-ē-əs\ *or* **Phae·ni·as** \'fē-nē-\ *or* **Phai·ni·as** \'fī-\. fl. c.300 B.C. Greek philosopher of Eresus. Pupil of Aristotle and friend of Theophrastus; author of works on logic, botany, poetry, and esp. on history, as *Prytaneis of Eresus* and *Tyrants of Sicily;* only fragments of his works extant.

Phan Khoi \'pän-'kói\. 1888?–1958. Vietnamese scholar. Early follower of Phan Chau Trinh (*q.v.*); became most illustrious intellectual of North Vietnam; editor of literary reviews *Nhan Van* and *Giai Pham Mua Xuan;* imprisoned for criticizing corruption of the government and anti-intellectualism of the army.

Phan Thanh Gian \'pän-'tän(-yə)-'gyäŋ\ *or* **Phan Thang Giang** \-'täŋ-'gyäŋ\. c.1803–1867. Vietnamese diplomat. High official in court of Emperor Minh Mang; negotiated treaty (1862) with France aimed at halting French takeover of Vietnam; negotiated second treaty (1863) agreeing to French protectorate status; committed suicide after French repudiation of treaty.

Phao Sri·ya·nond \'paù-,rē-yä-'nónd\. 1910–1960. Thai politician. A leader of coup that restored Pibul Songgram to power (1947); his directorship of the national police notorious for corruption and attempt at genocide of Thai Chinese; ousted (1957) from power by rival Sarit Thanarat.

Phar·na·ba·zus \,fär-nə-'bā-zəs\. 5th–4th century B.C. Persian commander. Negotiated alliance with Sparta against Athens (413 B.C.); later aided Athenians under Conon in defeating Spartan fleet at Cnidus (394); engaged in expeditions against Egypt (385 and 373), but failed.

Phar·na·ces \'fär-nə-,sēz\. Name of two kings of Pontus:

Pharnaces I. 2d century B.C. King (c.183–170 B.C.).

Pharnaces II. 1st century B.C. King (63–47 B.C.). Son of Mithradates the Great; sided with Pompey in the Roman Civil War and was defeated by Caesar in battle near Zela (47), after which Caesar sent to the senate at Rome his famous laconic message announcing victory, "Veni, vidi, vici."

Phat Song. See HUYNH PHU SO.

Phaul·kon \'faùl-(,)kän\, Constantine. 1647–1688. Greek politician in Siam. In southeast Asia (from 1660); chief minister of government of King Narai of Siam (1678–88); encouraged Catholic missions and presence of France, Netherlands, and Portugal in Siam; executed by General Bedraja.

Phayre \'fa(ə)r, 'fe(ə)r\, Arthur Purves. 1812–1885. English colonial administrator. Served with army in India and Burma (1828–46); commissioner of Burmese provinces of Arakan (1849) and Pegu (1852), and of entire country (1862–67); concluded a commercial treaty and attempted to introduce European education; author of *History of Burma* (1883).

Pheidias. See PHIDIAS.

Phei·dip·pi·des *or* **Phi·dip·pi·des** \fī-'dip-ə-,dēz\ *or* **Phi·lip·pi·des** \fī-'lip-ə-,dēz\. 5th century B.C. Athenian long-distance runner. Dispatched to Sparta to ask for aid just before battle of Marathon. Often confused with unknown Greek runner who reputedly carried news of Greek victory at Marathon (490 B.C.) from field of battle to Athens, the feat after which the modern marathon race is named.

Phei·don \'fī-(,)dän\. 7th century B.C. Greek king of Argos. Made Argos an important power in the Peloponnese; captured Olympia (c.670); instituted a system of standard measures.

Phelps, Elizabeth Stuart. See Elizabeth S. WARD.

Phelps \'felps\, John Wolcott. 1813–1885. American soldier, b. Guilford Centre, Vt. Cooperated with Farragut in clearing lower Mississippi River (1862); organized, in New Orleans, first Negro troops for service in federal armies (1862); resigned (Aug. 1862) when federal government disavowed his act and ordered troops disbanded and used as common laborers. American Party nominee for president of U.S. (1880).

Phelps, William Lyon. 1865–1943. American educator and critic, b. New Haven, Conn. On Yale faculty (1892–1933), professor (1901–33). Author of *Essays on Modern Novelists* (1910), *Essays on Russian Novelists* (1911), *The Advance of the English Novel* (1916), *The Advance of English Poetry* (1918), *The Twentieth Century Theatre* (1918), *As I Like It* (1923), *What I Like in Poetry* (1934), *What I Like in Prose* (1934), *Autobiography with Letters* (1939).

Phe·rec·ra·tes \fə-'rek-rət-,ēz\. fl. c.430–410 B.C. Greek playwright. Author of Attic comedies on topical matters, as *Agrioi, Korianno, Chiron;* inventor of a meter called Pherecratic or Pherecratean, after him.

Pher·e·cy·des \,fer-ə-'sī-,dēz\ of Le·ros \'li(ə)r-,äs\. 5th century B.C. Greek chronicler. Contemporary of Herodotus and Thucydides; his chronicle in 10 books of early Attic myths extant only in fragments.

Pherecydes of Sy·ros \'sī-,räs\. fl. c.550 B.C. Greek philosopher. Sometimes counted among Seven Wise Men of Greece; reputed originator of doctrine of metempsychosis; reputed teacher of Pythagoras; author of *Heptamychos,* extant in fragments, describing origin of the world.

Phid·i·as \'fid-ē-əs\. fl. c.490–430 B.C. Greek sculptor. Regarded as greatest of ancient Greek sculptors. Studied under Ageladas; commissioned, during ascendancy of Pericles at Athens, to execute greatest of city's monuments and charged with general supervision of all public works under construction; charged, by political enemies of Pericles, with sacrilege because he represented himself and Pericles on shield of goddess Athena; said to have been imprisoned on this charge. Among his notable works were sculptures on the Parthenon and the Propylaea, statue of Olympian Zeus at Elis, statue *Athene Parthenos,* and statue of an Amazon at Ephesus.

Phidippides. See PHEIDIPPIDES.

Philadelphus. See (1) ANTIOCHUS XI of Syria; (2) ATTALUS II; (3) PTOLEMY II.

Philalethes. See JOHN, King of Saxony.

Philander von Sittewald. See MOSCHEROSCH.

Phi·la·ret \fyi-(,)lər-'yet\. *Orig.* Fyodor Nikitich Ro·ma·nov \(,)rə-'mà-nəf\. c.1553–1633. Patriarch of Moscow. Cousin of Czar Theodore I and father of Czar Michael. Forced by Czar Boris Godunov to take monastic vows under the name of Philaret (c.1601); metropolitan of Rostov (1605); patriarch of Moscow (1619); reformed church administration, established divinity colleges in each diocese, minimized Roman Catholic influence, and sponsored legislation to reform tax structure and reorganize the army.

Philaret. *Orig.* Vasily Mikhaylovich Droz·dov \(,)drəs-'dóf\. 1782–1867. Metropolitan of Moscow (1821–67). Archbishop of Tver (1819); served as final authority in theological and legal questions; directed translation of Slavonic Bible and basic liturgical prayers into modern Russian; author of standard catechism adopted (1829) by Holy Synod of Church of Russia.

Phi·lastre \fē-làstrᵊ\, Paul-Louis-Félix. 1837–1902. French colonial administrator. Inspector of native affairs in Saigon under Marie-Jules Dupré (1873–76); stopped invasion of Hanoi led by Dupuis and Garnier (1873); chargé d'affaires at Hué (1877–79).

Phil·by \'fil-bē\, Harry St. John Bridger. 1885–1960. British explorer in Arabia. Became a Muslim and adviser to King Ibn Sa'ūd of Saudi Arabia; author of *The Heart of Arabia* (1922), *Sheba's Daughters* (1939), etc.

Philelphus. See Francesco FILELFO.

Phi·le·mon \fə-'lē-mən, fī-\. c.368–c.264 B.C. Greek playwright. Author of Athenian New Comedies; rival of Menander, defeating him several times in contests; of 97 comedies, some 60 titles survive in Greek fragments and Latin adaptations.

Philemon. 1st century A.D. Christian of Colassae. Master of runaway slave Onesimus converted by St. Paul; recipient of Paul's Epistle to Philemon.

Philenia. See Sarah W. A. MORTON.

Phi·les \'fī-,lēz\, Manuel. c.1275–1345. Byzantine poet of Ephesus. Court poet under emperors Michael VIII Palaeologus and Andronicus I and II; author of poems on church festivals, works of art, and animals.

Phil·e·tae·rus \,fil-ə-'tē-rəs\. c.343–263 B.C. Paphlagonian ruler. Made guardian of Pergamum by Lysimachus of Thrace (302); transferred allegiance to Seleucus I (282); won independence of Pergamum and reigned there (282–263); founder of the Attalid dynasty (282–133 B.C.), named after his nephew Attalus, who defeated the Gauls (c.230 B.C.).

Phi·le·tas \fə-'lēt-əs, fī-\ of Cos \'kós, 'käs\. c.330–c.270 B.C. Greek poet. Tutor in Alexandria to son of Ptolemy I of Egypt and to Theocritus and Zenodotus; regarded as founder of Hellenistic school of poetry; author of numerous elegies, esp. *Demeter,* and a dictionary of rare words.

Phi·li·bert \fē-lē-ber\. Name of two dukes of Savoy:

Philibert I. *Called* le Chas·seur \lə-shà-sœr\, *i.e.* the Hunter. 1465–1482. Duke (1472–82). Son of Amadeus IX; reigned under regency of mother Yolande of France.

Philibert II. *Called* le Beau \lə-bō\, *i.e.* the Handsome. 1480–1504. Duke (1497–1504). Son of Philip II the Landless.

Philibert of Orange-Châ·lon \ó-räⁿzh-shà-lōⁿ\. 1502–1530. Prince of Orange. Last prince of Burgundian house of Châlon. Entered service of Emperor Charles V to regain lands of Orange seized by Francis I of France; successful at siege of Fuenterrabia (1523); granted duchy of Brabant, made stadholder of

Holland, Zeeland, and Utrecht by Charles V, who also forced Francis to return Orange (1526); viceroy of Naples (1520); killed at siege of Florence.

Philibert, Emmanuel. See EMMANUEL PHILIBERT.

Philidor. See DANICAN.

Phil·ip \'fil-əp\. Saint. 1st century B.C.–1st century A.D. One of the 12 Christian apostles, b. Galilee. Known only through accounts in the New Testament; given apostolate of Scythia; according to one tradition, died by crucifixion.

Philip. Saint. *Called* the Evangelist *and* the Deacon. 1st century A.D. Christian religious, b. Caesarea? One of seven deacons of the Jersualem church; evangelized in Samaria; in Greek tradition, bishop of Tralles.

Philip. (1) Son of Herod the Great and Mariamne; see HEROD PHILIP. (2) Son of Herod the Great and Cleopatra; see PHILIP the Tetrarch.

Philip. 8th century. Italian antipope (768). Monk in monastery of St. Vito; set up as pope (July 768) by Lombard King Desiderius on deposition of antipope Constantine II; ejected on election of Stephen III (Aug. 768); retired to his monastery.

Philip. *Fr.* Philippe. Name of three dukes of Burgundy:

Philip I de Rou·vres \rüvrᵊ\. 1346–1361. Duke (1349–61). Succeeded grandfather Eudes IV; under regency of mother Jeanne de Boulogne and her second husband, John II; m. (1357) Marguerite of Flanders; died without issue, whereupon Burgundy, Artois, Auvergne were divided among different heirs.

Philip II. *Called* le Har·di \lə-är-dē\, *i.e.* the Bold. 1342–1404. Duke (1363–1404). Fourth son of John the Good, king of France (1350–64); present at Poitiers (1356), where he earned his nickname for bravery in trying to save his father. Granted duchy of Burgundy (1363) after the Capetian line of dukes became extinct (1361). m. (1369) Margaret, daughter of Louis II de Male, Count of Flanders. On death of King Charles V of France (1380), appointed one of four guardians of Charles VI. Put down Flemish revolt (1382); inherited Flanders, Artois, Rethel, Nevers, Franche-Comté, and some lands in Champagne (1384). Appointed, with his brother Jean de France, duc de Berry, as regent to govern France when Charles VI became insane (1392); formed alliance with England (1396); supported Pope Boniface IX.

Philip III. *Called* le Bon \lə-bōⁿ\, *i.e.* the Good. 1396–1467. Duke of Burgundy (1419–67). Son of Duke John the Fearless; made alliance with Henry V of England (Treaty of Troyes, 1420), in which Henry was recognized as heir to throne of France. Gradually withdrew from this alliance (1429–35) and made peace with Charles VII of France (1435); increased holdings by additions of Namur (1420), Hainaut (1427), duchies of Brabant (1430) and Luxembourg (1443), and counties of Holland and Zeeland (1433). Retired to his court during latter part of life; a patron of arts. Founded Order of Golden Fleece (1429) in honor of marriage with Isabella of Portugal. Burgundy most wealthy and prosperous of all Europe at this time.

Philip. *Fr.* Philippe. Name of six kings of France, five Capetians, the sixth of the house of Valois:

Philip I. 1052–1108. King (1059–1108). Son of Henry I. Reigned (1059–66) under regency of his mother, Anne of Russia, and Baldwin V of Flanders. Kingdom at low ebb of strength because of powerful feudatories, especially Normandy, but royal domain increased by policy of devious alliances (esp. with Fulk IV of Réchin and Duke Robert II of Normandy), sale of his neutrality in quarrels among powerful vassals, and practice of simony. Excommunicated (1095) for disowning first wife, Bertha of Holland, and for marriage with Bertrada, wife of Fulk IV.

Philip II *or* **Philip Au·gus·tus** \ó-'gəs-təs, ə-\. 1165–1223. King (1179–1223). Son of Louis VII; engaged in various wars (1181–85), increasing kingdom; persecuted Jews (1182); waged war with England (1187–89). Set out on Third Crusade (1190) with Richard I of England, but they quarreled in Sicily and in Syria; on return to France (1191), conspired with Richard's brother John to seize English lands in France. War lasted six years (1194–99). Attacked John and deprived him of Normandy, Maine, and other English provinces in France, which were annexed to the kingdom (1202–04). War with Flanders (1213–14) resulted in alliance against France of Otto IV of Brunswick, John of England, and counts of Flanders and in defeat of Allies at Bouvines (1214). Consolidated new possessions (1214–23). One of the greatest of Capetian kings; built many churches and institutions, encouraged trade, and gave first charter to University of Paris (1200). Made France a power in Europe. Married three times: 1st (1180) Isabella of Hainaut, who brought him as dowry the province of Artois, 2d (1193) Ingeborg, whom he repudiated, and 3d (1196) Agnes (d. 1201), daughter of Bertold IV, Duke of Meran, from whom he was obliged to separate (1201).

Philip III. *Called* le Har·di \lə-är-dē\, *i.e.* the Bold. 1245–1285. King (1270–85). Son of Louis IX; a weak sovereign, pious but uneducated; influenced by favorites, by his wife, Marie of Brabant, by his mother, Margaret of Provence, and by Charles of Anjou; engaged in unsuccessful war for crown of Aragon (1283–85).

Philip IV. *Called* le Bel \lə-bel\, *i.e.* the Fair. 1268–1314. King (1285–1314). Son of Philip III; held long controversy with papacy, especially with Pope Boniface VIII (1294–1303). Forbidden to tax clergy by papal bull *Clericis laicos* (1296). Royal authority challenged by bulls *Ausculta fili* (1301) and *Unam sanctam* (1302). First Estates-General summoned for support (1302). His creature, Clement V, pope (1305–14), resided at Avignon; eventually established his authority over ecclesiastical matters. Reign one of most momentous of medieval history, marked by new developments of French monarchy and restriction of feudal usages. Instituted large-scale consultation of royal subjects in assemblies; reformed coinage (1306). Increased expenditures brought about confiscations, seizure of Guienne (1294; later restored), wars with England (1294–98) and with Guy de Dampierre, Count of Flanders (1297–1305), in which French were badly defeated at Courtrai (1302), expulsion of Jews (1306), and cruel suppression of Order of Templars in France (1307–13). m. (1284) Jeanne de Navarre, daughter of Henry, King of Navarre, whereby that kingdom annexed to France. Their three sons became kings of France and Navarre.

Philip V. *Called* le Long \lə-lōⁿ\, *i.e.* the Tall. 1294–1322. King (1316–22). Son of Philip IV; received Poitiers as appanage. Appointed regent on death of Louis X (1316); became king on death of infant John I. Assembly confirmed succession (1317) by adopting Salic law. Ended war with Flanders (1320). Fined Jews heavily; effected some administrative reforms but opposed by Estates-General in others. Tried especially to unify coinage, weights and measures.

Philip VI. 1293–1350. First king (1328–50) of the house of Valois. Son of Charles de Valois; before accession held several countships (Valois, Maine, Anjou, etc.); m. 1st (1313) Jeanne de Bourgogne (d. 1348) and 2d (1349) Blanche of Navarre. Appointed regent at death of Charles IV. Won battle of Cassel and reinstated count of Flanders (1328). Disputes over several matters with Edward III of England led to beginning of Hundred Years' War (1337), in which French navy defeated at Sluis (1340); Normandy invaded by Edward and French defeated at Crécy (1346); Calais taken by English (1347); Dauphiné added to France (1349).

Philip. *Ger.* Philipp. *Called* der Gross·mü·ti·ge \dər-gró-'smüe-tig-ə\, *i.e.* the Magnanimous. 1504–1567. Landgrave of Hesse (1509–67). Son of William II; declared of age (1518); m. (1523) Christina of Saxony. Won to cause of Reformation (1524) and one of its leaders in Germany; with John, Elector of Saxony, formed (1526) Protestant League of Gotha and Torgau in support of Martin Luther; founded first Protestant university at Marburg (1527); arranged disputation between Luther and Zwingli at Marburg (1529); signed Augsburg Confession and, with other Protestant leaders, formed (1530–31) League of Schmalkalden against Charles V; m. (1540) Margaret of Saale as second wife although first wife was still living; this bigamy, although consented to by Luther and Melanchthon, caused great scandal. Made peace with Charles (1541) but later badly defeated by him in Schmalkaldic War (1546–47); taken prisoner at Mühlberg and held in confinement (1547–52); liberated by Maurice. Divided Hesse among four sons.

Philip. *Known also as* Philip of Swa·bia \'swā-bē-ə\. *Ger.* Philipp. 1178–1208. Holy Roman emperor and king of Germany (1198–1208). Youngest son of Frederick I; educated for the church but resigned his see (1192); made Duke of Tuscany (1195) and of Swabia (1196); chosen king and emperor (1198), but never crowned as emperor. Entire reign a struggle with Otto, leader of the Guelfs. Murdered at Bamberg by Otto of Wittelsbach.

Philip. Name of five kings of Macedon:

Philip I. 8th century B.C. King (c.700 B.C.).

Philip II. 382–336 B.C. King (359–336 B.C.). Son of Amyntas II; m. (359) Olympias; proved himself military genius; carried out aggressive campaigns in Greece, calling forth from Demosthenes the famous orations of warning known as the *Philippics;* defeated Illyrians (358); defeated at Thessaly (353) but recaptured it (352); captured Olynthus (348); annexed much of Thrace (342–340); crushed combined Athenian and Theban army Chaeronea (338) and completed conquest of all Greece by overrunning the Peloponnesus; organized League of Corinth and was chosen (337) commander of the Greek forces against Persia; assassinated (336) by Pausanias, a Macedonian youth; succeeded by his son Alexander the Great.

Philip III Ar·rhi·dae·us \,ar-ə-'dē-əs\. 4th century B.C. King (323–317). Natural son of Philip II; proclaimed by army after Alexander's death; murdered at instance of Olympias, Alexander's mother.

Philip IV. 3d century B.C. King only for a few months (c.297 B.C.). Son of Cassander.

Philip V. 238–179 B.C. King (221–179 B.C.). Son of Demetrius II; warred against Rome (215–205, 200–197); was decisively defeated at Cynoscephalae (197) and forced to renounce hegemony in Greece (196). Reorganized finances, reopened mines, and issued central and local currencies (189–179); campaigned in the Balkans (184–181).

Philip. 1720–1765. Duke of Parma (1748–65). Second son of Philip V of Spain and of Elizabeth Farnese; m. (1738) Louise-Elisabeth of France, daughter of Louis XV; aided by French, conquered Parma, Piacenza, Milan (1745); recognized as duke (1748); his daughter María Luisa became queen of Spain (1788–1808).

Philip. Kings of Portugal. See PHILIP II, III, IV of Spain.

Philip. *Lat.* Marcus Julius Phi·lip·pus \fi-'lip-əs\. *Called* the Arabian. d. 249. Roman emperor (244–249). Became praetorian prefect after death of Misitheus; caused death of young emperor, Gordianus III (244); after being proclaimed emperor made disgraceful peace with Persians; founded Philippopolis; celebrated 1000th anniversary of founding of Rome by great exhibition of secular games (248); killed in struggle with Decius.

Philip. *Fr.* Philippe. Name of a count and a duke of Savoy:

Philip I. 1207–1285. Count (1268–85). Son of Thomas I; bishop of Valence; archbishop of Lyon (1246); succeeded brother Peter as count.

Philip II. 1438?–1497. Duke (1496–97). Son of Louis I.

Philip. *Sp.* Felipe. Name of five kings of Spain, four of the house of Habsburg, the last a Bourbon:

Philip I. *Called* el Her·mo·so \el-er-'mō-sō\, *i.e.* the Handsome. 1478–1506. King of Castile (1506). Son of Habsburg Emperor Maximilian I and Mary of Burgundy. Archduke of Austria; as Duke of Burgundy inherited vast domains of Burgundy on death of his mother (1482); m. (1496) Joan, daughter of Ferdinand II (V of Aragon) and Isabella, who succeeded to throne of Castile at Isabella's death (1504); joint ruler with Joan (1504–06), although her father, Ferdinand, was actual ruler because of their absence in Flanders; returned with wife to Spain (June 1506); died three months later, perhaps poisoned; Joan became insane. Founded Habsburg dynasty in Spain; their sons later became emperors Charles V and Ferdinand I of the Holy Roman Empire.

Philip II. 1527–1598. King (1556–98). Only son of Emperor Charles V and Isabella of Portugal. Educated by clergy; married four times: Maria of Portugal (1543), Mary I of England (1554), Elizabeth of Valois, daughter of Henry II of France (1560), and Anna, daughter of Emperor Maximilian II (1570); given government of Milan (1540), of Naples and Sicily (1554), of Netherlands (1555), and of Spain (1556); inherited also vast possessions in New World; ruled from Netherlands (1556–59); from there waged successful war against France, won battle of St. Quentin (1557). Ruled from Madrid (1559–98); put down revolt of Moriscos and expelled them (1569–70); sent expedition under his half-brother, Don John of Austria, who, with the Genoese, defeated the Turks at Lepanto (1571); determined to crush all opposition to Roman Catholicism; developed Inquisition and at great cost failed to put down revolt in Netherlands (1568–1609); supported Guises against Henry of Navarre (1562–98); conquered Portugal (1580–81); lost naval supremacy in defeat of Armada (1588) in war with England (1587–89); Treaty of Vervins (1598) ended war with France; encouraged art and built Escorial (1563–84). By first wife (Maria) left son Don Carlos, and by fourth wife his successor, Philip III.

Philip III. 1578–1621. King (1598–1621); ruled Portugal as Philip II. Son of Philip II; inherited Spanish possessions and problems of a declining power, but took no interest in government; left all direction of affairs to his favorite, Duke of Lerma (1598–1618) and later to Duke of Uceda, Lerma's son; spent time in court festivities; had reputation for extreme piety; final expulsion of Moriscos decreed (1609), an event of economic disaster to Spain; independence of Northern Provinces (Netherlands) recognized (1609).

Philip IV. 1605–1665. King (1621–65); ruled Portugal (to 1640) as Philip III. Eldest son of Philip III; left administration to Olivares (1623–43) and Luis de Haro (1643–61); during his reign Spain's industry and commerce continued to decline and country impoverished by disastrous foreign wars, especially with France, Germany, and Holland; independence regained by Portugal (1640); rebellion of Masaniello in Naples put down (1647) by Don John of Austria; Holland lost by Treaty of Westphalia (1648); Catalonia revolted (1640) and declared allegiance to Louis XIII of France; Roussillon lost permanently; Treaty of the Pyrenees (1659) a victory for France. A poet and patron of the arts, esp. of Velázquez.

Philip V. 1683–1746. King (1700–24, 1724–46). Grandson of Louis XIV and son of Dauphin Louis. Duke of Anjou (to 1700); educated by Fénelon; named heir to throne by Charles II; accession was beginning of War of Spanish Succession (1701–14); m. (1701) María Luisa of Savoy and (1714) Isabella Farnese of Parma, both of whom strongly influenced him. Spain invaded by Archduke of Austria; lost Gibraltar to England (1704). Recognized as king by Treaty of Utrecht (1713), but Italian possessions and Netherlands given up to Austria. French ideas in control at the court and French institutions introduced; intrigued against House of Orléans; abdicated (Jan. 1724) in favor of his son Louis but, when Louis died (Aug.), again took the throne (1724–46); joined in War of Austrian Succession against Maria Theresa (1741). Founder of Bourbon dynasty in Spain.

Philip. *Indian name* Metacomet. 1639?–1676. American Indian chief. Son of Massasoit; sachem of the Wampanoags (from 1662). Encroachments by English settlers on Indian lands and execution (1675) of three of his warriors caused him to make war, King Philip's War (1675–76), upon the New England colonists; killed by raiding party; his defeat ended Indian resistance to further white settlement in New England.

Philip the Tetrarch. *Lat.* Philippus. 20 B.C.–34 A.D. Tetrarch of Batanaea, Trachonitis, etc. (4 B.C.–34 A.D.). Son of Herod the Great and Cleopatra of Jerusalem; educated in Rome with half-brothers Archelaus and Antipas; appointed tetrarch by Augustus; m. Salome, daughter of Herod Philip and Herodias; just ruler, built towns, promoted Hellenization. Sometimes confused with Herod Philip.

Philip, John. 1775–1851. Scottish missionary. Championed rights of South African native races, securing enactment of British ordinance granting them equal rights (1828); reviled by white settlers; aroused British sentiment with lecture tour (1826) and *Researches in South Africa* (1828).

Philip Augustus. See PHILIP II of France.

Philip Neri, Saint. See NERI.

Phi·li·pon \fē-lē-pōⁿ\, Charles. 1800–1862. French journalist and caricaturist. Publisher of political-satirical periodicals *La Caricature* (1830–34, 1838 ff.), *Le Charivari* (1832 ff.), *Le Journal Amusant* (1849 ff.); popularized lithographic caricatures in these papers; remembered esp. for a drawing of the head of Louis-Philippe turning into a pear.

Phi·lip·pa of Hai·naut \fi-'lip-ə-əv-en-'ō\. c.1314–1369. Queen of Edward III of England. Daughter of William the Good, Count of Holland and Hainaut; m. (1327) to her second cousin, Edward III. Brought Flemish weavers to England; encouraged coal mining; said to have harangued English troops before battle of Neville's Cross (1346); patron of Froissart, her secretary (1361–1366); Queen's College, Oxford, named after her.

Philippa of Lan·cas·ter \'laŋ-kə-stər\. 1359–1415. Queen of John I of Portugal. Daughter of John of Gaunt; mother of Edward I of Portugal, Don Pedro the traveler and regent, Prince Henry the navigator, and Ferdinand the saint.

Philippe. See also PHILIP.

Phi·lippe \fē-lēp\, Charles-Louis. 1874–1909. French novelist. Shop inspector for Parisian municipal service. Author of Naturalist novels of humble folk of Paris or Bourbonnais, as *La Mère et l'enfant* (1900), *Bubu de Montparnasse* (1901), *Le Père perdrix* (1902), *Charles Blanchard* (1913, unfinished).

Philippe Égalité. See ORLÉANS, IV.

Phi·lip·pi \fi-'lip-ē\ *or* **Phi·lip·son** \'fē-lip-sən\, Johannes. *Known as* Johannes Slei·dan \'zlī-,dän\ *or* Slei·da·nus \zlī-'dän-əs\. 1506–1555. German historian. Protestant annalist of the Reformation; patronized by Philip the Magnanimous; author of *De Statu Religionis et Reipublica Carolo Quinto Caesare Commentarii* (1555).

Phi·lip·pi·cus \fi-'lip-ə-kəs\. *Surnamed* Bar·da·nes \bär-'dā-,nēz\. *Orig.* Vardan \'vär-dän\. Emperor of the Eastern Roman Empire (711–713). Sent by Justinian II to suppress revolt in Cherson; sided with rebels and proclaimed emperor; sailed to Constantinople and killed Justinian; defeated by Arabs; overthrown by conspiracy of Anastasius.

Philippides. See PHEIDIPPIDES.

Phil·ips \'fil-əps\, Ambrose. *Nickname* Nam·by-Pam·by \'nam-bē-'pam-bē\. 1674–1749. English poet. Friend of Steele and Addison; involved in long quarrel with Alexander Pope after praise by the *Guardian* of his *Pastorals* (1709) over Pope's. Author of *The Distrest Mother,* an adaptation of Racine's *Andromaque* (1712), and other plays.

Philips, John. 1676–1709. English poet. Author of *The Splendid Shilling* (1701), mock-heroic poem in Miltonic verse; composed *Blenheim* (1705) on commission of Harley and St. John to offset Addison's *Campaign;* imitated Virgil's *Georgics* in *Cyder* (1708), didactic poem.

Philips, Katherine, *nee* Fowler. *Pseudonym* Orin·da \ə-'rin-də\. 1631–1664. English poet. Called "Matchless Orinda"; instituted a Society of Friendship, a literary salon for discussion of poetry and religion, described in *Letters of Orinda to Poliarchus.* Her translation of Corneille's *La Mort de Pompée* was acted in Dublin (1662); published *Poems* (1667).

Phi·lips \'fē-ləps\, Obbe. c.1500–1568. Dutch religious leader. Founded (1534) a peaceful, independent Anabaptist sect, the Obbenites, later led (1537) by Menno Simons.

Phil·ips \'fil-əps\, Peter. 1561–1628. English composer. Organist for English College in Rome (1582–85) and for royal chapel of Archduke Albert of Austria (1597–1628). Composed polyphonic madrigals, motets, and keyboard music; his masses are not extant.

Phi·lis·tus \fi-'lis-təs\. c.430–356 B.C. Greek historian. Helped Dionysius I seize power in Syracuse (405) and became his right-hand man and commander of the citadel; exiled (386–366); recalled by Dionysius the younger and entrusted with command of fleet operating against Dion and Syracusan rebels; defeated and killed. Author of history of Sicily.

Philitas. See PHILETAS.

Phil·lip \ˈfil-əp\, Arthur. 1738–1814. English naval commander and founder of New South Wales. Commanded fleet carrying convicts to Sydney Cove, Australia, landing Jan. 26, 1788 (subsequently celebrated as Foundation Day); established and administered penal colony (1788–92); admiral (1814).

Phillipps, James Orchard Halliwell-. See HALLIWELL-PHILLIPS.

Phil·lips \ˈfil-əps\, Bert Greer. 1868–1952. American painter, b. Hudson, N.Y. Best known for paintings of Indian subjects and for murals. Studio at Taos, N. Mex.; known as founder of the Taos art colony.

Phillips, David Graham. 1867–1911. American novelist, b. Madison, Ind. Wrote novels designed to expose current evils in society, business, and government, as *The Cost* (1904), *The Husband's Story* (1910), *The Conflict* (1911), *Susan Lenox: Her Fall and Rise* (1917).

Phillips, Edward. 1630–?1696. English writer. Son of Milton's only sister, Ann; educated by Milton; tutor (1663–72) to son of John Evelyn and to Philip Herbert (later Earl of Pembroke); hack writer in London. Compiler of *The New World of Words* (a philological dictionary, 1658), and of *Theatrum Poetarum* (a catalogue of poets of all countries, 1675); published (1694) valuable short biography of Milton. His brother ¶John (1631–1706) was an assistant to Milton; later known for satirical attacks on the Puritans, *A Satyr Against Hypocrites* (1655), and the clergy, *Speculum Crape-Gownorum* (1682).

Phillips, George. 1593–1644. American clergyman, b. South Rainham, England. To America (1630); pastor at Watertown (1630–44). Credited by some with being first minister of Massachusetts Bay Colony to introduce the Congregational form of church polity. Among his descendants were Samuel, John, and Wendell Phillips (*qq.v.*).

Phillips, Horatio Frederick. 1845–1912. English aviation inventor. Patented (1884 ff.) first designs for thick wing sections with curved upper and lower sections, now used on all airplanes.

Phillips, John. 1719–1795. American merchant and philanthropist, b. Andover, Mass. Settled in Exeter, Mass.; contributed liberally to establishment and development of Phillips Academy, Andover; was founder and benefactor of Phillips Exeter Academy, Exeter (incorporated 1781, opened 1783). His nephew ¶Samuel Phillips (1752–1802) was an industrialist and political leader; manufactured powder for Continental army (from 1775); founder and benefactor of Phillips Academy, Andover (opened 1778), first of the great endowed academies in America.

Phillips, John. 1800–1874. English geologist. Nephew of geologist William Smith, with whom he made geological studies of various parts of England. Works included *Geological Map of the British Isles* (1842).

Phillips, Philip. *Known as* the Singing Pilgrim. 1834–1895. American gospel singer and music editor, b. Cassadaga, N.Y. Head of Philip Phillips & Co., Cincinnati, a music publishing house (1863–67); author or compiler of many collections of sacred songs, as *New Hymn and Tune Book* (1867), *American Sacred Songster* (1868), *The Gospel Singer* (1874).

Phillips, Stephen. 1868–1915. English poet and playwright. Member of Frank R. Benson's theatrical company (1885–92); published *Eremus* (1894), a long philosophical poem in blank verse; won fame with *Poems* (1897); wrote successful plays *Paolo and Francesca* (1900), *Herod* (1901), *Ulysses* (1902), *Nero* (1906).

Phillips, Wendell. 1811–1884. American reformer, b. Boston. Prominent abolitionist (from 1837), associated with William Lloyd Garrison; president of Anti-Slavery Society (1865–70). In later years, advocated prohibition, penal reforms, woman suffrage, regulation of corporations, and organization of the laboring class.

Phillips, William. 1731?–1781. British soldier. Major general (1777); commander of artillery under Burgoyne at Saratoga (Oct. 7, 1777); taken prisoner and exchanged (1781) for Continental general Benjamin Lincoln; later served in Rhode Island and Virginia.

Phillips, William. 1775–1828. English mineralogist and geologist. Wrote textbooks and (with W. D. Conybeare) *Outlines of the Geology of England and Wales* (1822), which defined the Carboniferous System.

Phill·potts \ˈfil-ˌpäts\, Eden. *Early pseudonym* Harrington Hext \ˈhekst\. 1862–1960. English novelist and playwright, b. India. Studied for the stage; clerk in London (1880–90). In his early novels *Lying Prophets* (1896) and *Children of the Mist* (1898), described Devonshire with charm and romantic coloring. Author also of realistic, often tragic, novels of Devonshire, including *Sons of the Morning* (1900), *Widecombe Fair* (1913), *Children of Men* (1923), *The Jury* (1927); wrote also historical novels, including *Evander* (1919), *The Treasures of Typhon* (1924); mystery stories and fairy stories, short stories, and poems, including *The Iscariot* (1912), *Pixies' Plot* (1922), *Sonnets from Nature* (1935), *The Enchanted Wood* (1948), and plays, including *The Farmer's Wife* (1917), *Yellow Sands* (1926, with daughter Mary Adelaide), *Buy a Broom* (1929), *A Cup of Happiness* (1933).

Phillpotts, Henry. 1778–1869. English prelate. Bishop of Exeter (1830–69); a leading spokesman for High Church conservatism; engaged in polemic in opposition to Catholic emancipation (1825); opposed Reform Bill in House of Lords.

Phi·lo \ˈfī-(ˌ)lō\, Quintus Publilius. 4th century B.C. Roman politician. Consul (339 B.C.) and sponsor of three Publilian laws enlarging power of plebeians.

Philo Byb·li·us \-ˈbib-lē-əs\ *or* **Philo** of Byblus *or* **He·ren·ni·us Byblius** \hə-ˈren-ē-əs\. 1st–2d century A.D. Greek scholar and teacher, of Byblus. Compiled information on religions along coast of Palestine; only fragments of his works are extant.

Phi·loch·o·rus \fə-ˈläk-ə-rəs\. d. c.260 B.C. Athenian politician and historian. Opposed policies of Demetrius Poliorcetes and his son Antigonus Gonatas; executed by Antigonus Gonatas. Author of a history of Athens, extant only in fragments.

Phil·o·de·mus \ˌfil-ə-ˈdē-məs\. c.110–c.35 B.C. Greek poet and Epicurean philosopher. Pupil of Zeno of Sidon; taught in Rome; friend of Calpurnius Piso. Thirty-four of his love epigrams are in the Palatine Anthology; thirty-six treatises attributed to him were discovered in the ruins of Herculaneum; developed the theory that the arts should be judged on aesthetic, not moral, grounds.

Phi·lo Ju·dae·us \ˈfī-lō-jü-ˈdē-əs\ *or* **Philo** of Alexandria. c.13 B.C.–between 45 and 50 A.D. Jewish philosopher of Alexandria. Known as "the Jewish Plato"; headed embassy of five Jews to Rome (c.40 A.D.) to plead with Caligula not to demand divine honors from Jews. As philosopher, sought to reconcile revealed religion of Pentateuch with philosophical reason as influenced by Plato, Aristotle, Neo-Pythagoreans, Cynics, and Stoics; often regarded as forerunner of Christian theology, esp. in his view of Logos as intermediary between God and man.

Phil·o·la·us \ˌfil-ə-ˈlā-əs\. 5th century B.C. Greek Pythagorean philosopher. Said to have anticipated Copernicus with theory that the center of the universe is occupied by a great fire (not the sun) around which the Earth revolved; only fragments of his works extant.

Philometor. See ATTALUS III of Pergamum; DEMETRIUS III of Syria; PTOLEMY VI.

Philopator. See SELEUCUS IV; PTOLEMY IV.

Philopator Philometor Caesar. See PTOLEMY XV.

Phil·o·poe·men \ˌfil-ə-ˈpē-mən\. 253?–182 B.C. Greek general of Achaean League. Known as "last of the Greeks"; distinguished himself at battle of Sellasia (222 or 221); appointed general (208), he improved armor and discipline of league's army; victorious over Spartans at Mantinea (207) and defeated Nabis, tyrant of Sparta (192); captured in skirmish before Messina and executed.

Philoponus, John. See JOHN PHILOPONUS.

Phil·o·stor·gi·us \fil-ə-ˈstȯr-gē-əs\. c.368–c.433 A.D. Byzantine historian. Follower of Eunomius; his church history in 12 books, covering period 300 to 425, was an apology for extreme Arianism and is extant in a summary by Photius.

Phi·los·tra·tus \fə-ˈläs-trət-əs\. Name of at least three members of a family of Greek writers; their identities and works are often confused among each other: Flavius Philostratus (c.170–c.245 A.D.), *called* the Athenian; member (c.202) of circle of Julia Domna; author of *Gymnasticus, Lives of the Sophists,* and a biography of Apollonius of Tyana. His son-in-law ¶Philostratus (b. c.190 A.D.), *called* the Lemnian; author of a letter to Aspasius of Ravenna and of first series of *Imagines,* descriptions of real or imaginary paintings on mythological themes at Naples. His grandson ¶Philostratus (3d century), *called* the Younger, wrote a second series of *Imagines.*

Phi·lo·tas \fə-ˈlōt-əs, fī-\. d. 330 B.C. Macedonian general. Son of Parmenio; served under Alexander the Great; on campaign in the East, was charged with conspiracy, tried by army, convicted, and executed.

Phi·lo·the·us Coc·ci·nus \fə-ˈläth-ē-ə-skäk-ˈsē-nəs\. c.1300–1379. Byzantine prelate and theologian. Bishop of Heraclea (1347); patriarch of Constantinople (1353–54, 1364–76); canonized Gregory Palamas (1368); principal opponent of Greek Orthodox movement for union with Roman church. His writings constituted the chief defense of Palamas and his doctrine of Hesychasm, as the *Hagioritic Tome* (c.1339), a biography of Palamas, and diatribes against Palamite opponents Gregorios Akindynos and Nicephorus Gregoras. Also wrote liturgical verse, hymns, and exegetical works.

Phi·lox·e·nus \fə-ˈläk-sə-nəs\. *Syriac* Akh·sĕn·ā·yā \äk-ˈsen-ˌī-(y)ə\. c.440–c.523 A.D. Syrian Christian leader of Eastern Church. Vigorous defender of Monophysite doctrine; bishop of Mabbug-Hierapolis (485); attempted to replace Orthodox bishops with Monophysites; banished from his see by Justin I (519). Produced (with Polycarp) Philoxenian version of the New Testament in Syriac (c.508), used during 6th century by Monophysites; wrote thirteen homilies on Christian life.

Phintias. See DAMON AND PHINTIAS.

Phiops. See Pepi II.

Phios. See Pepi I.

Phipps \'fips\. Name of an English family bearing titles of earl of Mul•grave \'məl-,grāv\, viscount and marquis of Nor•man•by \'nȯr-mən-bē\, descendants of Sir Constantine (1656–1723), defender of Henry Sacheverell (1710), and lord chancellor of Ireland (1710–14), including: ¶Sir Henry (1755–1831), 3d Baron Mulgrave, 1st Viscount Normanby, 1st Earl of Mulgrave; military commander; great-grandson of Sir Constantine; Pitt's chief military adviser; general (1809); chancellor of duchy of Lancaster (1804); foreign secretary (1805–06); first lord of admiralty (1807–10); master of the ordnance (1810–18) and cabinet member (1810–20); patron of art. His brother ¶Constantine John (1744–1792), 2d Baron Mulgrave; naval captain; commanded a polar expedition (1773); distinguished himself off Ushant (1778). ¶Sir Constantine Henry (1797–1863), 1st Marquis of Normanby and 2d Earl of Mulgrave; eldest son of 1st earl; governor of Jamaica (1832–34); lord lieutenant of Ireland (1835–39); colonial secretary (1839); home secretary (1839–41); ambassador at Paris (1846–52); minister at Florence (1854–58); conflicted with Palmerston and Gladstone on French and Italian policy. ¶Sir George Augustus Constantine (1819–1890), 2d Marquis of Normanby; son of 1st marquis; became liberal whip in House of Commons; lieutenant governor of Nova Scotia (1858–63); governor of Queensland (1871–74), of New Zealand (1875–79), of Victoria (1879–84).

Phips *or* **Phipps** \'fips\, Sir William. 1651–1695. American colonial governor, b. Maine. Ship's carpenter by trade; cousin of Sir Constantine Phipps (see Phipps family). Financed by Charles II and the Duke of Albemarle in search for sunken treasure; recovered treasure from a vessel sunk off Haiti (1686); knighted (1687). Associated with Increase Mather in seeking return to charter government in Massachusetts Colony (from 1687). Commanded Massachusetts troops in capture of Port Royal (1690) and in unsuccessful attack on Quebec. As royal governor of Massachusetts (1692–94) advocated free trade; came into conflict with various religious groups, and appointed a special court for trying the Salem witchcraft cases.

Phiz. See Hablot Knight Browne.

Pho•cas \'fō-kəs\. d. 610. Emperor of the Eastern Roman Empire (602–610). A Thracian centurion of army fighting Avars on the Danube; raised to emperor (602) by mutinous soldiers; had Emperor Maurice slain; notorious for cruelty; persecuted Monophysites and Jews; defeated by Persians under King Khosrow II, who penetrated even to Bosporus; overthrown by plot against him by Heraclius, exarch of Africa, and his son Heraclius, who became emperor (610); tortured and beheaded.

Phocas, Nicephorus II. See Nicephorus.

Pho•ci•on \'fō-shē-,än\. c.402–318 B.C. Athenian general and statesman. Pupil of Plato and friend of Xenocrates. First distinguished himself in naval battle of Naxos (376); saved Athenian force in Euboea by his victory at Tamynae (348); opposed anti-Macedonian policy in Athenian assembly; negotiated favorable terms for Athens after her defeat at Chaeronea by Philip II of Macedon (338). After Alexander's death (323), became virtual dictator in Athens under Antipater's domination; ruled with great moderation; on restoration of democracy (318), condemned to death by democratic party in Athens on false charge of treason; executed.

Pho•cyl•i•des \fə-'sil-ə-,dēz\. fl. c.540 B.C. Greek poet. Only a few fragments of his hexametric gnomic maxims are extant.

Phoebus. See Foix family.

Phoenix, John. See George Horatio Derby.

Phor•mi•on \'fȯr-mē-,än\. d. c.428 B.C. Athenian admiral. Active during Peloponnesian War; laid siege to Potidaea (432–431); sent (432) to block entrance to Gulf of Corinth where he routed 47 Peloponnesian ships and destroyed Cnemus's fleet (429).

Pho•ti•sa•rath \pȯ-tē-'sä-rät\ *or* **Pho•thi•sa•ra** \-'sä-rä\ *or* **P'o•t'i•sa•rat** \pȯ-tē-'sä-rät\. 1501–1547. Ruler of Laotian kingdom of Lan Chang (1520–47). Left monastic order to head government; built monasteries, temples, and became chief promulgator of Buddhism in Laos; his claim to principality of Chiengmai resulted in a long war.

Pho•ti•us \'fō-shē-əs\. c.820–891. Patriarch of Constantinople. Made patriarch by Emperor Michael III (858–867), replacing Ignatius; offended Pope Nicholas I by refusal to restore former Roman dioceses; excommunicated by Nicholas (863); issued encyclical (867) against pope and the doctrines (especially the filioque doctrine) of Western church, thereby precipitating Photian Schism between the East and West. Formally deposed by Council of Constantinople (869), Ignatius having been reinstated as patriarch after Michael's death (867). Again made patriarch (877); called council (879) that passed upon all theological issues between East and West; again excommunicated (882); abdicated (886). Wrote *Amphilochia,* treating doctrinal and exegetical questions and many other topics, and *Myriobiblion* or *Bibliotheca,* a summary of 280 works of classical authors now mostly lost; also *Mystagogia Spiritus Sancti,* homilies, letters, etc.

Phra•a•tes \frā-'āt-ēz\. *Parthian* Prdty. *New Persian* Farhād. Name of five kings of Parthia of Arsacid dynasty:

Phraates I. 2d century B.C. King (c.176–171). Attacked Media; conquered Mardi tribe; passed over sons to designate brother Mithradates as successor.

Phraates II. d. 128 B.C. King (c.138–128). Son of Mithradates I; after several losses finally defeated Antiochus VII Sidetes in Media (129), ending Seleucid power east of Euphrates; killed in battle with Tochari tribesmen.

Phraates III. d. c.57 B.C. King (70–58 or 57). Son of Sanatruces; formed alliance with Roman general Pompey (66) and invaded Armenia; suffered occupation of Parthian border states by Pompey (64–62). Murdered by sons Orodes II and Mithradates III.

Phraates IV. d. 2 B.C. King (37–2). Son of Orodes II, whom he murdered to gain throne; defeated Roman invasion under Mark Antony (36); reoccupied Media; driven out by Rome-supported Tiridates of Armenia (c.30), but returned to power with Scythian aid; concluded peace with Rome (20); poisoned by Musa, concubine given him by Augustus.

Phraates V. d. c.4 A.D. King (2 B.C.–c.4 A.D.). Son of Phraates IV; placed on throne by mother Musa after her murder of his father; married her (2 A.D.) and ruled jointly; by treaty (1 A.D.) recognized Roman control of Armenia.

Phrantzes, George. See George Sphrantes.

Phra•or•tes \frā-'ȯrt-ēz\. *Greek form of Iranian* Fravartish. *Name applied by Herodotus to* Khshathrita. d. 653 B.C. King of Media (675–653 B.C.). Subjugated Persians and other Asian peoples, forming an anti-Assyrian coalition of Medes and Cimmerians; defeated and killed in war on Assyrians.

Phyrne. See Muesarete.

Phryn•i•chus \'frin-ə-kəs\. fl. c.500 B.C. Athenian playwright. Author of tragedies, including *Capture of Miletus* and *Phoenissae;* credited with first use of female characters.

Phrynichus. fl. c.420 B.C. Athenian playwright. Writer of comedies, including *Solitary* and *Muses;* accused by Aristophanes, in his *Frogs,* of using vulgar tricks for their comic effect and of plagiarism and poor versification.

Phrynichus. 5th century B.C. Athenian general. Fought in Peloponnesian War; took leading part in establishing the Four Hundred in Athens (411); according to Thucydides, assassinated.

Phrynicus. *Surnamed* Ara•bi•us \ə-'rā-bē-əs\. 2d century A.D. Greek grammarian of Bithynia. Wrote *Sophistike Paraskeue* and *Ekloge,* criticizing contemporary deviations from Old Attic; only fragments of his work extant.

Phyfe \'fīf\, Duncan. *Surname orig.* Fife. 1768–1854. American cabinetmaker, b. Scotland. To America (c.1783); apprenticed to cabinetmaker near Albany (1784); had joiner's shop in New York (from c.1792); one of first to use factory method successfully to manufacture furniture; retired from business (1847). Renowned for excellence and artistic beauty of his Neoclassical furniture, esp. mahogany chairs, couches, and tables.

Phy•lar•chus \fi-'lär-kəs, fī-\. 3d century B.C. Greek historian, b. Egypt, but long resident in Athens. Chief work, history of Greece of period 272–220 B.C., only fragments of which are extant.

Physcon. See Ptolemy VIII.

Phys•ick \'fiz-ik\, Philip Syng. 1768–1837. American surgeon, b. Philadelphia. One of the first to use animal ligatures in surgery and leave them in the tissues to be absorbed; esp. successful in operating for stone in the bladder; devised a number of new surgical instruments of great service, as the needle forceps and the guillotine tonsillotome.

Piaf \pyȧf, *Angl* 'pē-,äf\, Edith. *Orig.* Edith Giovanna Gas•sion \gȧs-yōⁿ\. *Nicknamed* La Môme \lȧ-mōm\, *i.e.* the Kid. 1915–1963. French chanteuse. Sang in Paris streets; discovered (c.1930) by cabaret owner Louis Leplée, who changed her name to Piaf (slang for "sparrow"); gained international fame with *chansons* of tragic love affairs, as "Les trois cloches," "La Vie en rose," "L'Hymne a l'amour," etc.

Pia•get \pyȧ-zhe\, Jean. 1896–1980. Swiss psychologist. Professor at Geneva (1929–54); director, International Center for Epistemology, Geneva (1955–80). Known for investigations of thought processes, esp. in children; his books included *The Language and Thought of the Child* (1926), *Judgement and Reasoning in the Child* (1928), *The Origin of Intelligence in Children* (1954), and *The Early Growth of Logic in the Child* (1964).

Piag•gia \'pyäd-jä\, Carlo. 1827–1882. Italian explorer. In Sudan collecting animal specimens (1856, 1860–61); made first study of Zande tribes of Sudan and Zaire (1863–65); explored Upper Nile (1875) and discovered Lake Kyoga (1876); died during exploration of Blue Nile.

Pian del Carpini, Giovanni da. See Carpini.

Pian•khi \'pyaŋ-kē\ *or* **Pan•khi** \'paŋ-\. 8th century B.C. King of Kush (c.751–716). Invaded Egypt from the south and conquered nearly all Nile Valley; captured Memphis and most of delta cities; in control during nominal rule of 23d dynasty; erected granite stele, which still exists, covered with inscriptions describing his campaign in Egypt; brother of Shabako.

Piast \'pyäst\. Name of first Polish dynasty; so called from its legendary founder of 9th century, a peasant named Piast. Its first historical personage was Mieszko (c.963–992); it ended with Casimir III (1370), although branches ruled in Mazovia (to 1526) and in Silesia (to 1675). See entries under BOLESŁAW, CASIMIR, LOUIS, MIESZKO, and WŁADYSŁAW.

Pia·ti·gor·sky \pyət-yi-'gȯr-skəi, *Angl* ˌpyät-ə-'gȯr-skē\, Gregor. 1903–1976. American cellist, b. Ekaterinoslav, Russia. First cellist of Bolshoi orchestra (1919–21); fled Russia (1921); with Warsaw (1921–23) and Berlin (1924–28) orchestras. Gave virtuoso concerts throughout world (1929 ff.); American debut (1929); appeared frequently with Horowitz, Milstein, Rubinstein, Heifetz, etc.; cofounder (1961) of Heifetz-Piatigorsky Concerts in Los Angeles; known as master of 19th-century Romantic tradition.

Pi·att \'pī-ət\, Donn. 1819–1891. American journalist, b. Cincinnati. Founder and coeditor of the Washington, D.C., *Capital* (1871–80), a weekly paper in which he tried to expose the weaknesses and corruption of politicians. Indicted (Feb. 1877) on charge of inciting insurrection, but case was dropped after Hayes's inauguration.

Piatt, John James. 1835–1917. American journalist and poet, b. Milton, Ind. Author of *Poems of Two Friends* (with William Dean Howells, 1860), *Poems in Sunshine and Firelight* (1866), *Landmarks* (1872), *Idyls and Lyrics of the Ohio Valley* (1881), *Little New-World Idyls* (1893), *Odes in Ohio* (1897), etc. His wife ¶Sarah Morgan, *nee* Bryan (1836–1919), b. Lexington, Ky., was also a poet; author of *Child's World Ballads* (1887), *An Irish Wild-Flower* (1891), *An Enchanted Castle* (1893), etc.

Piaz·zet·ta \pyät-'tsāt-tä\, Giovanni Battista. 1682–1754. Italian painter. Pupil of Molinari and Crespi; worked in Venice; influenced Tiepolo; director, Venetian Academy (1750). His paintings, which evolved from a Baroque to a Rococo style, were of soldiers, peasants, and religious and classical subjects and included *Ecstasy of St. Francis* (c.1732), *Assumption* (c.1735), *Fortune Teller* (1740), *The Pastoral* and *Idyll by the Seashore* (both c.1740).

Piaz·zi \'pyät-tsē\, Giuseppi. 1746–1826. Italian Theatine monk and astronomer. Professor, Palermo (from 1780), where he was founder and director of the observatory; director of government observatory in Naples (from 1817). Discovered and named Ceres, first known asteroid (1801); published catalogues of fixed stars, the second (1813) listing 7646 stars.

Pi·bul Song·gram \'pē-'bu̇l-'sȯŋ-'gräm\, Luang. 1897–1964. Thai soldier and politician. Participated in coup that abolished monarchy (1932); as prime minister of a military government (1938–44), declared war on U.S. and Great Britain (1942) and followed pro-Japanese policies. Again prime minister (1948–57); allied with West, supported SEATO, repressed civil liberties; overthrown (1957) and fled to Tokyo.

Pi·ca·bia \pē-kȧb-yȧ\, Francis. 1879–1953. French painter. Originally an Impressionist; in forefront of Cubist, Orphist, and Dadaist movements; exhibited in New York Armory Show (1913); collaborated with Tristan Tzara in Zürich on magazine *Dada* (1918); published Parisian review *Cannibale* (1920); contributed to avant-garde journals, as *291;* rejected abstractionism for paintings based on human figure (1927). His canvases included *Udnie* (1913), *Catch as Catch Can* (1913), *Universal Prostitution* (1916–19), and *Transparencies* (1920s and 30s).

Picander. See C. F. HENRICI.

Pic·ard \pē-kȧr\, Charles-Émile. 1856–1941. French mathematician. Professor at the Sorbonne (1898 ff.); secretary, Académie des Sciences (1917–41). Proved Picard theorem (1879); worked on theory of functions and on algebraic surfaces; developed method of successive approximations for proving existence of integrals of differential equations; studied harmonic vibrations. Works included *Traité d'analyse* (1893), *Théorie des fonctions algébriques de deux variables indépendantes* (with Simart, 1897–1906).

Picard, Edmond. 1836–1924. Belgian jurist and author. Founder of review *L'art moderne;* exponent of Socialism, Symbolism, Impressionism. Works included *Scènes de la vie judiciare* (1893), *Ainsi naît, vit, meurt l'Amour* (1904).

Picard, Jean. 1620–1682. French astronomer. First to apply telescope to measurement of angles; known esp. for accurate measurement of a degree of a meridian, from which he computed size of the Earth (1668–70); credited with first use of telescopic sights and of pendulum clocks in astronomical observations; made first recorded observation of barometric light (1675); determined latitude and longitude of Tycho Brahe's observatory Uraniborg.

Picard, Louis-Benoît. 1769–1828. French playwright. Manager of Théâtre Louvois, the Odéon and the Opéra at various times. Author of many comedies, including *Les Visitandines* (comic opera, 1792), *Médiocre et Rampant* (verse comedy, 1797), *La Petite Ville* (prose comedy, 1801), etc.

Picard, Louis-Joseph-Ernest. 1821–1877. French lawyer and politician. Member of the Corps Législatif (1858) and opponent of imperial policies. After fall of the empire, became member of government of national defense (1870) as minister of finance (1870) and of interior (1871); senator for life (1875).

Pi·cas·so \pē-'käs-ō, *Angl* pi-'käs-(ˌ)ō, -'kas-\, Pablo. *In full* Pablo Ru·iz y Picasso \rü-'ēth-ē-\. 1881–1973. Spanish painter and sculptor. Studied in Barcelona and Madrid; settled in France (1904 ff.); produced decors for Diaghilev's Ballets Russes (1917–24); friend of many European artists and writers, as Braque, Matisse, Cocteau, Sartre, Camus; with Braque created Cubism. His artistic style evolved throughout his life, generally categorized as: Early Years (1900–01), use of strong colors; subjects generally of bourgeois life as cabarets, dance halls, etc.; *Le Moulin de la Galette* (1900). Blue Period (1901–04), use of blue color; despairing moods; subjects prostitutes, drunkards, etc.; *La Vie* (1903), *Old Guitarist* (1903). Rose Period (1904–06), warmer colors; subjects family groups, dancers, harlequins; *Woman with a Fan* (1905), *La Toilette* (1906), *Gertrude Stein* (1906). Cubist Period (1906–25), influenced by Cézanne, Greco-Iberian art, and African sculpture; *Les Demoiselles d'Avignon* (1906–07), *Seated Nude* (1909–10), *Aficionado* (1912). Classical Period (1915–25), *Two Seated Women* (1920), *Three Musicians* (1921). Later Years (1925 ff.), briefly influenced by Surrealists; use of personal symbols, as minotaurs; use of various themes as violence, eroticism, politics, the artist and his powers, etc.; revived interest in sculpture; paintings included *Three Dancers* (1925), *Seated Bather* (1930), *Guernica* (1937), *Woman Dressing Her Hair* (1940), *War and Peace* (1952); sculpture, *Guitar* (1926), *Bull's Head* (1943), *Goat* (1950), *Steel Sculpture* (1967, Chicago Civic Center). His technique, styles, and output (over 20,000 works) won him general recognition as the greatest and most influential artist of the 20th century.

Pic·card \pē-kȧr\, Auguste. 1884–1962. Swiss physicist. Investigated radioactivity and atmospheric electricity; with his assistant Kipfer, made balloon ascent of 51,775 feet into the stratosphere in airtight gondola of own invention, Augsburg, Germany (1931); made other balloon ascents up to 61,221 feet (1932–37); made observations of cosmic rays and other scientific phenomena; invented a bathyscape (1948) which dove to new record of 10,168 feet (1953). His twin brother ¶Jean-Félix (1884–1963), chemist and aeronautical engineer; to U.S. (1916, naturalized 1931); professor of aeronautical engineering (from 1936), Minnesota; with his wife, made stratosphere ascent in balloon from Dearborn, Michigan, reaching altitude of 57,564 feet (1934).

Pic·ci·ni·no \pēt-chē-'nē-nō\, Niccolò. 1386–1444. Italian soldier of fortune. Became condottiere (1424); entered service of the Visconti of Milan (1425); fought against Venice and Florence; helped drive Pope Eugene IV from Rome (1434); escaped capture by old comrade Francesco Sforza of Venice (1438); defeated by Florentines at Anghiari while invading Tuscany (1440); died soon after final defeat by Sforza.

Pic·cin·ni \pēt-'chēn-nē\, Niccolò. 1728–1800. Italian opera composer. Made debut with opera buffa *Le donne dispettose* in Naples (1754); composed over 130 serious and comic operas; called to Paris by Marie-Antoinette (1776) and became nonparticipating rival of Gluck in public feud between his followers (Piccinists) and admirers of Gluck (Gluckists). Returned to Naples at outbreak of French Revolution (1789) and lived on pension from king; returned to Paris (1798) and obtained inspectorship of music at National Conservatory. Among his works were Italian operas as *La buona figliuola* (1760), *L'olimpiade* (1761), and *I viaggiatori* (1774), and French operas as *Roland* (1778), *Atys* (1780), *Didon* (1783); also several oratorios, psalms, and other church music.

Pic·co·lo·mi·ni \ˌpēk-kō-'lō-mē-(ˌ)nē\. Illustrious Italian family of Siena, including: Enea Silvio, who became Pope Pius II (*q.v.*). His nephew Francesco Todeschini was Pope Pius III (*q.v.*). ¶Alessandro (1508–1578), prelate and writer, coadjutor to archbishop of Siena (1574), author of *La Raffaella* (1540), *Cento sonetti* (1549), and two comedies, *Alessandro* (1545) and *Amor costante* (1549), translations of works by Ovid and Virgil, commentaries on Aristotle, and *De le stelle fisse* (1540), first book of printed star charts. ¶Francesco (1520–1604), philosopher, author of *Universa philosophia de moribus* (1583), *Libri de scientiae natura* (1596), *Comes politicus* (1601). ¶Octavio (1600–1656), duca d'·Amal·fi \-dä-'mäl-fē\, soldier; a general in the Thirty Years' War in the imperialist service, passing (1643) to the Spanish service; recalled to imperial service and promoted field marshal (1648); operated against the Swedes in Bavaria and Bohemia, represented Austria at the Congress of Nürnberg (1649); created prince of the Holy Roman Empire (1649).

Pi·che·gru \pēsh-grüe\, Jean-Charles. 1761–1804. French general. Commanded armies of the Rhine and the Moselle (1793–94) and army of the North (1794); conquered the Netherlands and suppressed an insurrection in Paris (1795); president of Council of Five Hundred; plotted overthrow of government (1797); arrested and deported, but escaped and returned to France. Involved in Cadoudal plot against Napoléon (1804); committed suicide, or was murdered, in prison.

Pich·ler \'pik-lər\, Karoline, *nee* von Grei·ner \fōn-'grī-nər\. 1769–1843. Austrian novelist. Among her novels were *Agathokles* (1808), *Die Belagerung Wiens 1683* (1824), *Die Schweden in Prag* (1827), and *Die Wiedereroberung von Ofen* (1829).

Pi·chon \pē-shōⁿ\, Stéphen-Jean-Marie. 1857–1933. French journalist, politician, and diplomat. Deputy (1885–93); held various diplomatic posts (1893–

1906); senator (1906–24); minister of foreign affairs (1906–11, 1917–20); friend and consistent supporter of Clemenceau.

Pick·el \'pik-əl\, Conrad. *Known by Lat.* Con·rad·us Cel·tis \kȯn-'rät-əs-'kel-tis\ *or* Cel·tes \-'kel-tes\. 1459–1508. German Humanist and poet (in Latin). Studied under Agricola at Heidelberg; crowned first German poet laureate (1487); professor at Ingolstadt (1491–97) and Vienna (1497 ff.); promoted and systematized study of German antiquities and of classics, esp. Greek; discovered Peutinger Table and Latin plays of Hrosvitha. His musical masques *Ludus Dianae* (1501) and *Rhapsodia* (1505) were forerunners of Baroque opera. Author of *Ars versificandi* (1486), histories (esp. of Nürnberg), editions of classical authors, and lyrical poetry, as *Amores* (1502) and *Odae* (1513).

Pick·ens \'pik-ənz\, Andrew. 1739–1817. American Revolutionary commander, b. near Paxtang, Pa. Settled in South Carolina (1763). In the Revolution, served with distinction at Cowpens (1781); promoted brigadier general, captured Augusta, Ga. (1781); wounded at Eutaw Springs. Member of U.S. House of Representatives (1793–95).

Pick·er·ing \'pik-ər-iŋ\, Timothy. 1745–1829. American politician, b. Salem, Mass. Adjutant general of Continental army (1777–78); quartermaster general (1780–85); U.S. postmaster general (1791–95); U.S. secretary of war (1795); U.S. secretary of state (1795–1800). U.S. senator (1803–11); member, U.S. House of Representatives (1813–17). His son ¶John (1777–1846) was a lawyer and philologist; compiler of a lexicon of the Greek language (1826) and the first dictionary of Americanisms. A grandson of Timothy and nephew of John, ¶Charles Pickering (1805–1878), was a naturalist; chief zoologist in U.S. exploring expedition under Lieut. Charles Wilkes (1838–42); author of *Races of Men and Their Geographical Distribution* (1848), *The Chronological History of Plants* (1879), etc. A great-grandson of Timothy and nephew of Charles, ¶Edward Charles Pickering (1846–1919), was an astronomer; director, Harvard observatory (1876–1919); renowned for his work in stellar photometry and stellar spectroscopy, invented the meridian photometer; established *Harvard Photometry* (1884), the first great photometric catalogue; established observation station at Arequipa, Peru (1891), to study southern stars. Edward's brother ¶William Henry (1858–1938) was also an astronomer; led expeditions to observe solar eclipses; discovered Phoebe, 9th satellite of Saturn (1899); predicted existence of 9th planet (1919); cooperated with Edward in establishing observation station at Arequipa, Peru (1891); erected observatory and telescope at Flagstaff, Ariz. (1894), for Percival Lowell.

Pick·ett \'pik-ət\, George Edward. 1825–1875. American army officer, b. Richmond, Va. Resigned from U.S. army to enter Confederate service (1861); major general (1862). Held Confederate center at Fredericksburg; his command (4300 men) made famous charge at Gettysburg (July 3, 1863) across half a mile of broken ground against Union positions on Cemetery Ridge, only to be repulsed with loss of three-fourths of his division, often considered turning point of Civil War.

Pickett, Joseph. 1848–1918. American painter, b. New Hope, Pa. After career as carpenter, shipbuilder, carny, and shopkeeper, began painting at 65; executed naive paintings of town and landscape around New Hope, as *Manchester Valley* (1914–18); works not discovered until 1930s.

Pick·ford \'pik-fərd\, Mary. *Orig. name* Gladys Mary Smith. 1893–1979. American actress, b. Toronto. Known as "America's Sweetheart" for ingénue roles in such films as *Tess of the Storm Country* (1914), *Rebecca of Sunnybrook Farm* (1917), *Poor Little Rich Girl* (1917), *Pollyanna* (1920), and *Coquette* (1929, Academy Award). Married 2d Douglas Fairbanks (1920; div. 1935), 3d Charles (Buddy) Rogers (1937). With Fairbanks, Charlie Chaplin, and D.W. Griffith formed United Artists Corp. (1919).

Pi·co del·la Mi·ran·do·la \'pē-kō-,dāl-lä-mē-'rän-dō-(,)lä\, Giovanni. Conte. 1463–1494. Italian Humanist. A leading scholar of Italian Renaissance; settled at Florence (1484) as protégé of Lorenzo de' Medici and Marsilio Ficino; studied Hebrew, Arabic, and the Kabbala; posted publicly (Rome, 1486) a list of 900 theses dealing with logic, ethics, theology, mathematics, Kabbalistic lore, physics, etc., which he proposed to defend publicly against any opponent; accused by Innocent VIII of heresy (1487; cleared in 1492 by Alexander VI); reconverted to orthodoxy by Savonarola. Emphasized human dignity based on free will, as in *De hominis dignitate oratio* (1486); early death prevented construction of projected complete philosophical system; other works included *Heptaplus* (1489), *Disputationes contra astrologiam* (1496), and *De ente et uno* (1496).

Pi·cón \pē-'kōn\, Jacinto Octavio. 1852–1923. Spanish novelist and art critic. His novels, on themes of anti-clericalism and defence of natural love, included *La hijastra del amor* (1884), *La honrada* (1890), *Dulce y sabrosa* (1891), *Juanita Tenorio* (1910), and *Sacramento* (1914).

Pi·cot \pē-kō\, Auguste-Henri-Marie. Marquis de Dam·pierre \dä^{n}-pyer\. 1756–1793. French soldier. Commanded a division at Valmy and Jemappes (1792) and Neerwinden (1793); succeeded to command of the army of Belgium after the desertion of Dumouriez; killed in action.

Pic·quart \pē-kär\, Georges. 1854–1914. French general. Played important part in defense of Dreyfus, for which he was retired from army (1898) and imprisoned; upon Dreyfus's vindication, Picquart was restored to active service with commission of general of division (1906); minister of war (1906–09).

Pic·tet \pēk-te\, Raoul-Pierre. 1846–1929. Swiss physicist. Known for work on production of low temperatures and for liquefaction of oxygen, nitrogen, and carbon dioxide about the same time as it was accomplished by Cailletet (1877); professor, Geneva (1879–86); studied properties of substances at low temperatures.

Pictet de Roche·mont \-də-rȯsh-mō^{n}\, Charles. 1755–1824. Swiss politician and writer. With provisional government of Genevan Republic (1813); helped secure Geneva's membership in Swiss Confederation at Congress of Vienna (1814); as the Confederation's representative at the Paris Peace Conference prepared declaration of Switzerland's permanent neutrality ratified by European powers (Nov. 20, 1815); secured rectification of Swiss–Sardinian border (1816); wrote on politics and agronomy.

Pic·ton \'pik-tən\, Sir Thomas. 1758–1815. British army officer. Distinguished himself in capture of St. Lucia (1796); governor of Trinidad; tried in court of King's Bench on charge of cruelty in permitting torture, allowed under Spanish law; found guilty (1806) but vindicated in second trial (1808); served as one of Wellington's principal subordinates in Portugal (from 1810); took prominent part in battle of Fuentes d'Oñoro (1811) and conducted siege of Badajoz (1812); held command in battles of Pyrenees; killed at Waterloo.

Pictor, Quintus Fabius. See under FABIUS family.

Pidal, Ramón Menéndez. See MENÉNDEZ PIDAL.

Pid·ding·ton \'pid-iŋ-tən\, Henry. 1797–1858. English meteorologist and ship captain. Collected logs and information from ship captains on storms of the Indian seas; wrote *Sailor's Horn-book for the Laws of Storms in all parts of the World* (1848), in which he coined term "cyclone" for these storms.

Pierce. See also PEARCE, PEARSE, PEIRCE.

Pierce \'pi(ə)rs\, Franklin. 1804–1869. Fourteenth president of the United States, b. Hillsboro, N.H. Democratic member of state legislature (1829–33), of U.S. House of Representatives (1833–37), of U.S. Senate (1837–42); served in Mexican War (1846–48); brigadier general (1847); president of the United States (1853–57). His administration marked by unsuccessful attempt to buy Cuba, reorganization of diplomatic and consular corps, creation of U.S. Court of Claims, Gadsden Purchase (1853), opening of Northwest for settlement, and passage of Kansas-Nebraska Act of 1854.

Pierce, George Washington. 1872–1956. American physicist, b. Webberville, Texas. On faculty at Harvard (1901–40); his work in electrical communications led to development of Pierce oscillator and underwater detection devices; with A.E. Kennelly discovered motional impedance (1912). Author of *Principles of Wireless Telegraphy* (1910) and *Electric Oscillators and Electric Waves* (1919).

Pierce, Gilbert Ashville. 1839–1901. American politician and author, b. East Otto, N.Y. Governor of Territory of Dakota (1884–86); first U.S. senator from North Dakota (1889–91). Author of the play *One Hundred Wives* (1880), the novels *Zachariah, the Congressman* (1876) and *A Dangerous Woman* (1883), and compiler of *The Dickens Dictionary* (1872).

Pier·ma·ri·ni \,pyer-mä-'rē-nē\, Giuseppe. 1734–1808. Italian architect. Official architect and inspector general of architecture at Milan (1770–94); among his works were the La Scala Theater, Porta Orientale, and façade of Belgioioso Palace (all at Milan).

Pier·né \pyer-nā\, Gabriel, *in full* Henri-Constant-Gabriel. 1863–1937. French conductor and composer. Among his operas were *La Coupe enchantée* (1895, rev. 1905) and *Vendée* (1897); among his ballets, *Le Docteur Blanc* (1893) and *Salomé* (1895); composer also of orchestral suites, piano concertos, chamber music, oratorios and other choral works, and songs.

Pie·ro del·la Fran·ce·sca \'pyer-ō-'dāl-lä-frän-'chā-skä\ *or* **de' Fran·ce·schi** \-dā-frän-'chā-skē\. c.1420–1492. Italian painter. First Humanist artist of the Quattrocento; master of perspective. Pupil of Domenico Veneziano (1439–42); worked for d'Estes in Ferrara (c.1448), for Sigismundo Malatesta in Rimini (1451), for Count Montefeltro in Urbino (late 1450s–c.1474); wrote treatises on painting as *De prospectiva pingendi,* on proportions as *De quinque corporibus regularibus,* on mathematics as *Del abaco.* Works included frescoes as *Sigismundo Malatesta Before St. Sigismund* (1451), *The Legend of the True Cross* (1452–66, narrative cycle in Arezzo), *Resurrection* (c.1463, Sansepolcro), and paintings as *Flagellation of Christ* (late 1450s), *Portraits of Federico da Montefeltro, Duke of Urbino and of his Wife, Battista Sforza* (1465), *The Nativity* (c.1480).

Piero di Giovanni. See LORENZO MONACO.

Piero di Lo·ren·zo \-,dē-lō-'rent-sō\. *Known as* Piero di Co·si·mo \'kō-zē-mō\. 1462–1521. Florentine painter. Pupil of Cosimo Rosselli; noted for mythological paintings in a distinctive bizarre, romantic style, as *Vulcan and Aeolus* (c.1486), *Battle of the Centaurs and the Lapiths* (1486), *Discovery of Wine* (c.1500), *Death of Procris* (c.1500), *Rescue of Andromeda* (1515); also for portraits, as of Simonetta Vespucci (c.1498).

Pié·ro·la \'pyā-rō-(,)lä\, Nicolás de. 1839–1913. Peruvian general and politician. Stirred up revolts against both Pardo (1874) and Prado (1877–78); took part in War of the Pacific (1879–83) and assumed presidency of Peru when Prado left country (1879–81); finally driven from office by defeats of Peruvian army; overthrew government (1894) when Cáceres was deposed. Again president (1895–99); administration marked by strengthening of army and advances in legislation.

Pierozzi, Antonio. See Saint ANTONINUS.

Pieterszoon, Nicolaes *or* Claes. See TULP.

Pieterz, Barent and Carel. See FABRITIUS.

Piet Paaltjens. See François HAVERSCHMIDT.

Pietro, Guido di. See GUIDO DI PIETRO.

Pie·tro da Cor·to·na \'pye-trō-dä-kōr-'tō-nä\. *Orig. name* Pietro Ber·ret·ti·ni \,bār-rā-'tē-nē\. 1596–1669. Italian painter and architect, b. Cortona. An outstanding exponent of Baroque. Known for frescoes in Pitti Palace, Florence (1637, 1640) and (in Rome) in churches of Sta. Maria in Vallicella and of Sta. Bibiana (1624–26), in Barberini Palace (1633–39) and Pamphili Palace (1651–54). As architect, designed church of SS. Luca e Martina (1635–50), façades of churches of Sta. Maria della Pace (1656–57) and Sta. Maria in Via Lata (1658–62, all in Rome). Also painted religious and mythological canvases; head of Academy of St. Luke, Rome (1634–38).

Pietro del·la Vi·gna \-,dāl-lä-'vēn-yä\. *Lat.* Pe·trus de Vin·ea \'pē-trəs-də-'vin-ē-ə\. 1190?–1249. Italian jurist and statesman. In service of Emperor Frederick II (1221 ff.); as judge of Magna Curia of Sicily (1225–34) was principal author of Constitution of Melfi (1231); chief minister (1230 ff.), undertaking many missions, esp. to the Vatican; chancellor of Sicily (1246–49); suddenly imprisoned on charges of seeking to poison the emperor, committed suicide; his extant letters and speeches are sources for history of the period.

Pi·ga·fet·ta \,pē-gä-'fāt-tä\, Antonio. 1491–?1534. Italian traveler. Accompanied Magellan on trip around world and completed journey in the *Victoria* (1519–22); wrote for Charles V an account of the voyage, *Primo viaggio intorno al globo terraqueo.*

Pi·galle \pē-gāl\, Jean-Baptiste. 1714–1785. French sculptor. Pupil of Le Lorrain and Lemoyne; patronized by Madame de Pompadour and Louis XV; known for realistic style. Among his works were *Mercure attachant ses talonnières* (1744), *Vénus* (1748), *L'Amour et l'Amitié,* the mausoleum of Marshal Maurice de Saxe in Strasbourg (1777).

Pi·gault de l'Épi·ney \pē-gō-də-lā-pē-nā\, Charles-Antoine-Guillaume. *Known as* Pigault-Le·brun \-lə-brœⁿ\. 1753–1835. French writer. Author of comedies *Les Rivaux d'eux-mêmes* (1773), *Charles et Caroline* (1790); novels *L'Enfant du carnaval* (1792), *Mon oncle Thomas* (1799), and *Monsieur Botte* (1802).

Pig·neau de Bé·haine \pē-nʸō-də-bā-īn\, Pierre-Joseph-Georges. 1741–1799. French missionary. Established Catholic seminary in Cochinchina (now Vietnam, 1767); driven out by Siamese invasion (1769), reestablished school at Pondicherry, India; made bishop (1770); compiled dictionary and wrote catechism in Vietnamese; again in Vietnam (1775–77); sheltered Prince Nguyen Anh from rebels (from 1777) and helped him gain throne as Emperor Gia Long.

Pig·ot \'pig-ət\, George. Baron Pigot. 1719–1777. British merchant and colonial administrator. With East India Co. (1736 ff.); governor of Madras (1755–63, 1775–77); defended Madras against French attack (1758–59); created baron (1766); attempted to suppress corruption and restore the raja of Tanjore, but was arrested by his council; died in prison.

Pig·ott \'pig-ət\, Richard. 1828?–1889. Irish journalist and forger. Dublin newspaper proprietor and violent nationalist (until 1879); sold (1886) to Loyal and Patriotic Union, an Irish anti-home-rule society, papers incriminating Parnell in Phoenix Park tragedy and forming basis of *Times* articles *Parnellism and Crime;* confessed that papers were forged by him; fled to Madrid, shot himself.

Pig·ou \'pig-(,)ü\, Arthur Cecil. 1877–1959. British economist. Succeeded (1908) Alfred Marshall as professor of political economy, Cambridge, and was instrumental in dissemination of his ideas; noted for studies of tariff policy, unemployment, public finance, and esp. welfare economics with *The Economics of Welfare* (1920).

Pike \'pīk\, Zebulon Montgomery. 1779–1813. American army officer and explorer, b. Lamberton, N.J. Led exploring party to headwaters of Mississippi River (1805–06) and of Arkansas and Red rivers (1806–07); discovered (1806) peak now named Pikes Peak in his honor; his report on Santa Fe stimulated expansion into Texas. Brigadier general (1813); commanded troops against York (now Toronto), Canada; killed in the assault (Apr. 27, 1813).

Pi·late \'pī-lət\, Pontius. d. after 36 A.D. Roman procurator of Judaea (26–c.36 A.D.) under Emperor Tiberius. Tried and condemned Jesus; incurred enmity of Jews for insulting their religious sensibilities; attacked Samaritans on Mt. Garizin; recalled to Rome (36 A.D.) for trial for cruelty and oppression.

Pi·lâ·tre de Ro·zier \pē-lätrᵊ-də-rō-zyā\, Jean-François. 1756–1785. French physicist and aeronaut. First human being to ascend in a balloon (Oct 15, 1873); associated with Montgolfier brothers; killed with companion in attempt to cross English Channel in an apparatus composed of two balloons, one filled with hydrogen and the other with warm air.

Pil·cher \'pil-chər\, Percy Sinclair. 1866–1899. English aeronautical engineer. Influenced by studies of Otto Lilienthal; pioneer (from 1895) in construction and flights of heavier-than-air craft, esp. gliders; died of injuries from glider crash.

Pil·king·ton \'pil-kiŋ-tən\, Francis. c.1562–1638. English composer. Cantor (1602), precentor (1623) at Chester cathedral; published sets of madrigals (1613, 1624) and of songs for voice and lute, *First Book of Ayres* (1604).

Pil·lers·dorf \'pil-ərs-,dȯrf\, Franz. Freiherr. 1786–1862. Austrian politician. As interior minister (1848) gave name to Pillersdorf Constitution; head of government for a few weeks (1848); his conciliatory policy was disapproved, and he was retired.

Pills·bury \'pilz-,ber-ē, -b(ə-)rē\, Charles Alfred. 1842–1899. American businessman, b. Warner, N.H. Bought (1869) a small flour mill in Minneapolis and developed it into largest flour producer in world (C.A. Pillsbury & Co.); sold mills to English syndicate (1889).

Pillsbury, Harry Nelson. 1872–1906. American chess expert, b. Somerville, Mass. U.S. champion (from 1898); excelled in blindfold exhibition games.

Pilnyak, Boris. See VOGAU.

Pi·lon \pē-lōⁿ\, Germain. 1535–1590. French sculptor. His style a link between Gothic and Baroque periods; among his works were statues of the king and the queen on monument of Henry II in the Church of St. Denis (1563–70), a bronze statue of Cardinal René de Birague (1583–85), and *Trois Grâces* in marble (c.1561; latter two in the Louvre). Regarded as one of leading sculptors of the Renaissance in France.

Pi·lo·ty \pē-'lō-tē\, Karl von. 1826–1886. German painter. Foremost representative of realistic school of painting in Germany; director, Munich Academy (1874 ff.). Among his canvases were *Seni at the Dead Body of Wallenstein* (1855), *Galileo in Prison* (1861), *Columbus Discovers America* (1866), *The Triumph of Germanicus* (1873), and *The Death of Alexander the Great in Babylon* (1886).

Pil·sud·ski \pēl-'süt-skē\, Józef Klemens. 1867–1935. Polish general and statesman. Sentenced to five years' penal servitude in Siberia on false charge of conspiring to assassinate Czar Alexander III (1887). On return to Poland (1892), became a leader of Polish Socialist party; founded radical journal *Robotnik* (1894); arrested (1900), but escaped to England. Returned to Poland (1902) and continued political agitation; organized secretly a private Polish army; at outbreak of World War I (1914), offered army of 10,000 under his command to Austria, and fought against Russians; resigned command (1916) because of German and Austrian interference in Polish affairs; worked actively for Polish independence; gained recognition by Central Powers (Nov. 5, 1916) of independence of Russian Poland, and accepted position as head of military commission there. Imprisoned by Germans (1917–18) when his troops refused to join Central Powers in war. After collapse of Central Powers, returned to Warsaw; elected (1918) chief of state, generalissimo of Polish army, and (1920) first marshal of Poland. Directed war against Lithuanians, Ukrainians, and Bolsheviks (1919–20); absolute dictator of Poland as provisional president until Polish constitution drafted and accepted by Polish parliament (1922). Again intervened in Polish political affairs by moving troops into Warsaw (May 1926), overturning the Wojciechowski government, and installing a new cabinet under Ignacy Mościcki, in which he himself accepted position as minister of war; in this position, he was virtual dictator of Poland; premier of Poland (1926–28, 1930) and continued to keep position as minister of war and commander in chief of army, thereby absolutely controlling Polish policies until his death.

Pinch·back \'pinch-,bak\, Pinckney Benton Stewart. 1837–1921. American politician, b. Macon, Ga. Son of a white planter and a Negro slave; raised volunteer Negro company for service with Union army in Civil War (1862–63); engaged in postwar Louisiana politics; lieutenant governor (1871); acting governor (1872–73). Elected to U.S. House of Representatives (1872), but not seated, and to U.S. Senate (1873), but again not seated.

Pinch·beck \'pinch-,bek\, Christopher. 1670?–1732. London watchmaker and toymaker. Invented copper and zinc alloy (pinchbeck) resembling gold.

Pin·chot \'pin-(,)shō\, Gifford. 1865–1946. American conservationist and politician, b. Simsbury, Conn. Studied forestry in Europe; became first professional American forester; chief of Forest Service, U.S. Department of

Agriculture (1898–1910). Professor of forestry, Yale (1903–36); founder, with his brother Amos, of Pinchot School of Forestry at Yale; commissioner of forestry, Pennsylvania (1920–22). Governor of Pennsylvania (1923–27, 1931–35); prominent in initiating measures to settle great coal strike of 1923. Author of *A Primer of Forestry* (1899), *The Fight for Conservation* (1909), *Breaking New Ground* (1947, autobiography), etc.

Pinck·ney \'piŋk-nē\, Charles. 1757–1824. American politician, b. Charleston, S.C. 2d cousin of Charles Cotesworth Pinckney. Served in American Revolution; member, Continental Congress (1784–87); submitted to Constitutional Convention of 1787 a plan for a constitution, known as the "Pinckney Draught," containing more than thirty provisions later incorporated in the finished Constitution. Governor of South Carolina (1789–92, 1796–98, 1806–08); U.S. senator (1798–1801); U.S. minister to Spain (1801–05) during period when Louisiana was relinquished to France and then sold to U.S.; member, U.S. House of Representatives (1819–21).

Pinckney, Charles Cotesworth. 1746–1825. American diplomat, b. Charleston, S.C. 2d cousin of Charles Pinckney; member, Council of Safety (1776) and one of committee to draft plan for temporary government of South Carolina; served in Revolution; aide to George Washington at Brandywine and Germantown; captured by British at fall of Charleston (1780), exchanged (1782); brigadier general (1783); member of Constitutional Convention (1787). Minister to France (1796) but not recognized by France. Returned to France (1797) with Elbridge Gerry and John Marshall; approached by emissary of French government with request for bribe before negotiations might be begun; his report on "XYZ Affair" aroused intense feeling both in U.S. and in France; commissioned major general when war with France was expected (1798–1800). Federalist candidate for vice president (1800) and for president (1804, 1808). His brother ¶Thomas (1750–1828), b. Charleston, also served in Revolution, escaped capture at Charleston and joined Continental army; on Gates's staff, wounded and captured at Camden; governor of South Carolina (1787–89); U.S. minister to Great Britain (1792–94) and special commissioner to Spain (1795–96), where he negotiated Treaty of San Lorenzo (1795) settling southern U.S.–Spanish boundary line and navigation rights on Mississippi River; Federalist candidate for vice president (1796); member of U.S. House of Representatives (1797–1801); major general in War of 1812.

Pin·dar \'pin-dər, -ˌdär\. c.522–c.438 B.C. Greek lyric poet, b. near Thebes. Little is known of his life. Among his extant works are 44 complete *Epinicia (Odes of Victory),* celebrating victories in great national games. Among fragments of other works are *Hymns* (to Persephone, to Fortune, etc.), *Paeans* (to Apollo and to Zeus), *Choral Dithyrambs* (to Dionysus), *Processional Songs, Choral Songs for Maidens, Choral Dance Songs, Encomia* or *Laudatory Odes, Scolia* or *Festive Songs,* and *Dirges.*

Pindar, Peter. See John WOLCOT.

Pin·de·mon·te \ˌpēn-dā-'mōn-tā\, Ippolito. 1753–1828. Italian poet. Author of melancholy, pre-Romantic books of verse, esp. *Poesie campestri* (1788); also wrote *Abaritte* (1790, political prose satire), *Prose campestri* (1794), *Sermoni* (1819), and two tragedies; also known for translation into blank verse of Homer's *Odyssey* (1809–22). His brother ¶Giovanni (1751–1812) was a lyric poet, dramatist, and politician; his successful tragedies included *I baccanali, Lucio Quinzio Cincinnato,* and *Ginevra di Scozia.*

Pine \'pīn\, Robert Edge. 1730–1788. English painter. Successful painter in England (to 1784); to U.S. (1784); exhibited a series of pictures illustrating scenes from Shakespearean drama. Other works included *Mrs. Reid in the Character of a Sultana,* portrait of George Washington in Independence Hall, Philadelphia, portrait of Martha Washington.

Pi·neau \pē-nō\, Nicolas. 1684–1754. French woodcarver and interior designer. Pupil of Mansart and Boffrand; in service of Peter the Great as architect and interior designer (1716–28); returned to Paris as important designer; launched vogue for Rococo rooms in private dwellings.

Pi·nel \pē-nel\, Philippe. 1745–1826. French physician. A founder of psychiatry. Chief physician of Bicêtre (1793–95) and director of Saltpêtrière (1795–1826), both Parisian asylums; pioneered humane treatment of the insane; considered insanity result of psychological and physiological causes, rather than demonic possession; distinguished various psychoses and described hallucinations, withdrawal, and other symptoms. His *Nosographie philosophique* (1798) and *Traité médico-philosophique sur l'aliénation mentale ou la manie* (1801) laid much of foundation for establishment of psychiatry as a field of medicine.

Pi·ne·ro \pi-'ni(ə)r-(ˌ)ō, -'ne(ə)r-\, Sir Arthur Wing. 1855–1934. English dramatist. Actor (1874–81). His first play acted on stage, *£200 A Year* (1877); won financial independence with *The Money Spinner* (1880), *Sweet Lavender* (1888), and a series of farces, esp. *The Magistrate* (1885), *The Schoolmistress* (1886), *Dandy Dick* (1887); attempted serious drama in *The Squire* (1881) and returned to it in *The Profligate* (1889); marked off a new era of modern drama with *The Second Mrs. Tanqueray* (1893), first of a series of problem plays, including *The Notorious Mrs. Ebbsmith* (1895), *The Benefit of the Doubt* (1895), *Iris* (1901), *The Thunderbolt* (1908), *Mid-Channel* (1909). Author also of plays reflecting contemporary manners and morals, including *The Gay Lord Quex* (1899); satirical comedies, including *The Princess and the Butterfly* (1897); later plays mostly in lighter vein, including *The Enchanted Cottage* (1922), *Child Man* (1930), *Dr. Harmer's Holidays* (1930), *A Cold June* (1932).

Pi·net·ti de Wil·dal·le \pē-'nāt-tē-dā-wēl-'däl-lā\, Giuseppe. *Known as* Pinetti. 1750–1800. Italian magician. Considered founder of classical school of conjuring magic; introduced (1780s) second-sight trick, automata, and escape tricks.

Pin·gré \paⁿ-grā\, Alexandre-Gui. 1711–1796. French astronomer. Made observations of lunar eclipses and transits of Venus across the sun; author of *Cométographie* (1783–84).

P'ing Ti. See under LIU family.

Pin·ker·ton \'piŋ-kərt-ᵊn, -kər-tən\, Allan. 1819–1884. American detective, b. Glasgow, Scotland. To U.S. (1842); settled in Illinois; established private detective agency, first in U.S., at Chicago (1850); gained national prominence by solving Adams Express robberies; guarded Lincoln on his trip to Washington for the inauguration (1861); during Civil War, organized and conducted secret service activities for General McClellan (1861–62). Prominent for work against labor unions and labor movements, esp. in breaking up "Molly Maguires." Author of *Strikers, Communists, Tramps, and Detectives* (1878), *The Spy of the Rebellion* (1883), *Thirty Years a Detective* (1884), etc.

Pink·ham \'piŋk-əm\, Lydia, *nee* Estes. 1819–1883. American patent-medicine manufacturer, b. Lynn, Mass. Concocted (c.1865) an herbal patent medicine (called Mrs. Lydia E. Pinkham's Vegetable Compound) supposed to cure feminine ailments; became most widely advertised product in U.S. and extremely profitable.

Pink·ney \'piŋk-nē\, William. 1764–1822. American politician, b. Annapolis, Md. In England as joint commissioner to adjust American claims against British government for maritime losses (1796–1804); U.S. minister to Great Britain (1807–11); U.S. attorney general (1811–14); member, U.S. House of Representatives (1815–16); U.S. minister to Russia (1816–18); U.S. senator from Maryland (1819–22); influential in securing the Missouri Compromise.

Pin·sker \'pyin-skyir\, Leo, *orig.* Judah Leib. 1821–1891. Russian Jewish physician and nationalist. Practiced medicine in Odessa. Early advocacy of Jewish assimilation into Russian society destroyed by 1881 pogrom; became vigorous proponent of an autonomous Jewish state with publication of pamphlet *Auto-Emanzipation* (1882); leader of Zionist group Ḥibbat Ẓiyyon, which established some colonies in Palestine.

Pin·ski \'pin-skē\, David. 1872–1959. American dramatist and novelist, b. Mogilev, Russia. To U.S. (1899); to Israel (1949); author of six volumes of plays and fourteen volumes of stories, all written in Yiddish. Also published in English *Temptations* (short stories, 1919), *Ten Plays* (1919), *The Final Balance* (play, 1928), *The Generations of Noah Edon* (novel, 1931), etc.

Pin·to \'pēn-tō\, Aníbal. 1825–1884. Chilean politician. Deputy (1852–58, 1864–70), senator (1870–79); minister of war and marine (1871); president of Chile (1876–81); began war with Peru and Bolivia (1879).

Pin·to \'pēⁿ(n)-tü\, Fernão Mendes. c.1510–1583. Portuguese adventurer and writer. Traveled, traded, and fought in Far East (from 1537), esp. in China; returned to Portugal (1558) and wrote account of his travels *Peregrinação* (1614).

Pinto, Serpa. See SERPA PINTO.

Pinturicchio. See BETTO DI BIAGO.

Pin·zón \pēn-'thōn\, Martín Alonso. c.1441–1493. Spanish navigator. Part owner of *Pinta* and *Niña;* with brothers helped Columbus prepare expedition; commanded the *Pinta* on first voyage (1492); after landfall at Guanahani separated from Columbus; on return voyage attempted to beat Columbus home with news. A younger brother ¶Vicente Yáñez (c.1460–c.1523?) commanded the *Niña* on first voyage; made later voyages (1497–1500), exploring coast of Brazil (1500) and sailing north as far as Costa Rica; made voyage with Juan Díaz de Solís (1508–09) along Atlantic coast of South America, perhaps as far south as La Plata. Another brother ¶Francisco Martín (1440?–?1493) was master of the *Pinta* under Martín Alonso.

Piombo, Sebastiano del. See Sebastiano LUCIANI.

Pioz·zi \'pyȯt-tsē\, Hester Lynch, *nee* Salus·bury \'sȯlz-ˌber-ē, -b(ə-)rē\. *Known mostly as* Mrs. Thrale \'thrā(ə)l\. 1741–1821. British writer and friend of Dr. Johnson, b. Wales. m. (1763) Henry Thrale, Southwark brewer; began (1765) a twenty-year intimacy with Dr. Johnson, who became more or less domesticated in home of the Thrales and accompanied them to Wales (1774) and to France (1775); saved her husband from threatened bankruptcy and disposed of business on his death (1781); m. (1784) Gabriel Piozzi, Italian musician, which resulted in estrangement from Dr. Johnson; traveled in Italy (till 1787), where she associated with the Della-Cruscans and contributed verses; retained her vivacity through last days at Bath. Second only to Boswell in fame among writers on Dr. Johnson, editing his letters (1788) and writing

Anecdotes of the late Samuel Johnson, LL.D., during the last Twenty Years of his Life (1786).

Pi·per \'pē-pər\, Carl. Count. 1647–1716. Swedish politician. Appointed (1697) to council of state of Charles XII; only high councilor to accompany Charles in field during Northern War; captured (1709) at Poltava and held prisoner by Russians until death.

Pip·pi de' Gia·nuz·zi \'pē-pē-dā-jä-'nüt-tsē\, Giulio. *Surname a contraction of* Pietro di Filippo de' Gianuzzi. *Known as* Giulio Ro·ma·no \rō-'män-ō\. c.1499–1546. Italian painter and architect. After Raphael, chief master of the Roman school; an initiator of the Mannerist style. Pupil and heir of Raphael, assisting him at Rome, esp. with frescoes in Stanza dell'Incendio (1517) and in Logge (1519, both in Vatican); with Penni, continued Raphael's uncompleted work; settled in Mantua (1524 ff.). His frescoes included *Madonna and Saints* (c.1523, Rome), *Stoning of St. Stephen* (1523, Genoa), *Apollo and the Muses* (Pitti Palace), *Story of Psyche* and *Fall of Titans* (1534, Palazzo del Tè), and scenes from Trojan War (Reggia dei Gonzaga, Mantua). As architect, designed and built Reggia dei Gonzaga, Palazzo del Tè (1525–34), and own house (1544–46), all in Mantua.

Pippin. See PÉPIN.

Pip·pin \'pip-ən\, Horace. 1888–1946. American painter, b. West Chester, Pa. Worked as ironworker, junk dealer, porter, and other jobs; right arm paralyzed (1918) during World War I; considered greatest Negro painter of his time. Known for primitivist depictions of Negro life as *Cabin in the Cotton,* of episodes in life of John Brown as *John Brown Going to His Hanging* (c.1942), and of antiwar themes as *End of the War: Going Home* (1931–34) and many versions of *Holy Mountain.*

Pi·ran·del·lo \,pē-rän-'del-lō\, Luigi. 1867–1936. Italian novelist and dramatist. Lecturer in literature, Rome (1897–1922); visited U.S. (1923, 1935); toured and directed own company, Teatro d'Arte (1925–28); awarded Nobel prize for literature (1934). A revolutionary innovator in literature, esp. with invention of "theater within the theater" and use of themes of psychology. Among his works were poems as *Mal giocondo* (1889), criticism *L'umorismo* (1908), short stories as *Amori senza amore* (1894), *Beffe della morte e della vita* (1902–03), *Quand'ero matto* (1902), *Bianche e nere* (1904), *La vita nuda* (1910), *La trappola* (1915), *Un cavallo nella luna* (1918), and *Il carnevale dei morti* (1919), novels as *L'esclusa* (1901), *Il fu Mattia Pascal* (1904), *I vecchi e i giovani* (1913), *Uno, nessuno e centomila* (1925–26), and plays as *Così è si vi pare* (1917), *Sei personaggi in cerca d'autore* (1921), *Tutto per bene* (1920), *L'innesto* (1921), *Enrico IV* (1922), *Vestire gli ignudi* (1923), *La vita che ti diedi* (1924), *La nuova colonia* (1928), *Come tu mi vuoi* (1930), *Non si sa come* (1935).

Pi·ra·ne·si \,pē-rä-'nā-sē\, Giambattista. 1720–1778. Italian architect, decorative painter, and engraver. Known for series of copperplate engravings such as *Carceri d'invenzione* (1745), *Le antichità romane* (1748), views of Greek ruins at Paestum (1777–78), and esp. *Vedute di Roma* (1748–78) which depicted classical and contemporary Roman sites. As architect rebuilt church of Sta. Maria Aventina in Rome (1764–65). His prints of classical architecture contributed to 18th-century Neoclassical movement.

Pire \pēr\, Dominique Georges. 1910–1969. Belgian cleric and humanitarian. Taught philosophy at Dominican monastery of La Sarte (1937–47); active in World War II resistance movement. Awarded Nobel peace prize (1958) for aid to postwar displaced persons through founding of organizations as Aide aux Personnes Déplacées (1949), Homes of Welcome in Belgium (1950–54), University of Peace, Huy (1960), and Island of Peace projects in East Pakistan (1962) and India (1967); also founded World Friendships and World Sponsorships.

Pi·rel·li \pē-'rel-lē\, Giovanni Battista. 1848–1932. Italian industrialist. Established in Milan first Italian rubber factory (1872); pioneer in manufacture of electric cable (1884) and automobile tires (1899). His sons ¶Piero (1881–1956) and ¶Alberto (1882–1971) expanded the factory into an international enterprise. Alberto served with Supreme Council of Versailles (1919), the International Labor Office (1920–22), League of Nations (1923–27), and as minister of state (1938).

Pi·renne \pē-ren\, Henri. 1862–1935. Belgian historian. Professor, Ghent (1886–1930); imprisoned (1916–18) by Germans for refusal to teach during their occupation of Belgium. Among his books were *Histoire de Belgique* (1900–32), *Les anciennes démocraties des Pays-Bas* (1910), *Les Villes du moyen âge* (1927), *La Fin du moyen âge* (1931), *Mahomet et Charlemagne* (1937).

Pirk·hei·mer \'pirk-,hī-mər\, Willibald. 1470–1530. German Humanist. At outbreak of Reformation, associated himself with Reuchlin and Dürer. Author of a history of the Swiss War, books on science and politics, and translations of Greek classics into Latin.

Pir·mez \pēr-mes, -mez\, Octave. 1832–1883. Belgian writer. Precursor of Belgian literary renaissance; author of lyrical, elegant, contemplative essays and letters, as *Pensées et maximes* (1862), *Heures de philosophie* (1873), *Esquisses psychologiques* (1884).

Pi·ron \pē-rōⁿ\, Alexis. 1689–1773. French poet and playwright. Author of many epigrams, the dramatic monologue in three acts *Arlequin-Deucalion* (1722), comic opera *Endriaque* (1723; music by Rameau), and several plays, esp. *Gustave Vasa* (1733, historical tragedy) and *La Métromanie* (1738, comedy).

Pir·rie \'pi(ə)r-ē\, William James. 1st Viscount. 1847–1924. British shipbuilder, b. Quebec of Irish parents. Partner (1874) and later chairman of board of Harland & Wolff, sole builders for White Star line; built ships such as *Britannic* and *Titanic;* controller general of merchant shipping (1918); mainly responsible for introducing idea of standardizing ships. Created baron (1906), viscount (1921).

Pirs·son \'pi(ə)r-sən\, Louis Valentine. 1860–1919. American geologist, b. Fordham, N.Y. Taught at Yale (1893–1919). Author of *Rocks and Rock Minerals* (1908), *Textbook of Geology* (1915), and *Quantitative Classification of Igneous Rocks* (with Cross, Iddings, and Washington, 1903), which introduced CIPW system of classification and new terminology.

Pi·san·der *or* **Pei·san·der** \pī-'san-dər\. 7th century B.C. Greek epic poet. Author of *Heracleia,* only a few lines of which are extant.

Pisander *or* **Peisander.** 5th century B.C. Athenian politician. A leader of oligarchical party in Peloponnesian War (431 B.C. ff.); a commander of Greek fleet (412); helped establish Council of the Four Hundred at Athens (411); fled to Sparta when oligarchy fell.

Pi·sa·nel·lo \,pē-sä-'nel-lō\ *or* **Pi·sa·no** \pē-'sän-ō\, Antonio. c.1395–1455. Veronese painter and medalist. Collaborated with Gentile da Fabriano on frescoes in Doges' Palace in Venice (c.1415–22) and in St. John Lateran in Rome (c.1428); surviving frescoes include *Annunciation* at Bergonzi tomb (c.1424, Verona) and *St. George and the Princess* in church of S. Anastasia, Verona (c.1433–38); paintings included *St. Eustace* and *Madonna with SS. Anthony and George,* and portraits. Also known for his medals and drawings (esp. of horses) in Codex Vallardi. His works reflected the transition in Italy from International Gothic to Early Renaissance style.

Pi·sa·ni \pē-'sän-ē\, Niccolò. 14th century. Venetian admiral. During 3d war between Venice and Genoa concluded an alliance with Byzantine Empire at Constantinople (1350); defeated Paganino Doria at mouth of Bosphorus (1352), routed Genoese fleet (1353), and was defeated and captured by Doria at Portolungo (1354). His son ¶Vettore (1324–1380) was also an admiral; fought with father against Genoa (1350–55); during 4th war against Genoa given command of Venetian fleet (1378); defeated Genoese fleet and sacked Cattaro and Sebenico (1378); captured at Pola (1379); released and later captured Genoese-held port of Chioggia.

Pi·sa·no \pē-'sän-ō\, Andrea. *Also called* Andrea da Pon·te·de·ra \-dä-,pōn-tā-'der-ä\. c.1270–?1348. Italian sculptor of Pisan school, b. Pontedera. Succeeded Giotto as chief artist for cathedral of Florence (1337); chief artist for cathedral of Orvieto (1347); known esp. for the bronze doors of the baptistery of the cathedral of Florence, consisting of twenty reliefs from life of St. John the Baptist and eight representing Christian virtues. His son ¶Nino (1315?–?1368) was a sculptor, goldsmith, and architect; leading representative of mature Gothic style; collaborated with his father.

Pisano, Giunta. See GIUNTA PISANO.

Pisano, Leonardo. See Leonardo FIBONACCI.

Pisano, Nicola. c.1220–1278 or 1284. Italian sculptor. Works marked apex of Romanesque style; first important precursor of Renaissance; operated workshop in Pisa; known esp. for his hexagonal marble pulpit of the baptistery at Pisa, particularly the bas-reliefs from the life of Christ, as *Nativity* and *Adoration of the Kings* (c.1255–60). Among his other works were an octagonal pulpit in Siena cathedral (1265–68), designs for *Arca di San Domenico* in Church of San Domenico, Bologna (1264–67), and sculptural decorations for fountain at Perugia (1278). His son ¶Giovanni (c.1250–after 1314) was a sculptor, painter, and architect; chief Italian sculptor of Middle Ages; founder of Italian Gothic sculpture; chief architect, cathedral of Pisa (1278 ff.) and cathedral of Siena (1284–99, 1314 ff.); assisted father in execution of pulpit in Siena cathedral and of fountain of Perugia; among his architectural works were the Campo Santo at Pisa and the façade of Siena cathedral; sculptural works included font of San Giovanni Fuorcivita, pulpit of Sant'Andrea Pistoia at Siena (c.1297–1301), a pulpit in cathedral of Pisa (1302–10), statues of Madonna, monument of Urban IV (Perugia).

Pi·sa·rev \'pyē-sər-yiv\, Dmitry Ivanovich. 1840–1868. Russian critic. Foremost representative of Russian nihilism; proponent of utilitarianism in judging the arts and enemy of Pushkin; imprisoned (1862–67) for defense of Aleksandr

Herzen. His politico-literary articles included *Realisti* (1864) and *Borba za zhizn* (1867–68).

Pis·ca·tor \'pis-kə-,tôr\, Erwin. 1893–1966. German theatrical producer and director. Famed for Expressionistic staging techniques, such as films and newsreels and other optical, acoustical, and mechanical devices. During Weimar Republic (1919–33) used theater for radical political instruction; head of Dramatic Workship of New York's New School for Social Research (1939–51); director, Volksbühne, West Berlin (1951 ff.).

Pi·sem·sky \'pyĕs-im-skəi\, Aleksey Feofilaktovich. 1820–1881. Russian writer. Twenty years in government service. As author, his realist style marked also by naturalism. Among his novels were *Tyufyak* (1850), *Tysyacha dush* (A Thousand Souls, 1858), *Vzbalamuchennoye more* (1863); wrote peasant tragedy *Gorkaya sudbina* (1859).

Pi Sheng \'bē-'shəng\. 11th century. Chinese alchemist and blacksmith. Reputed inventor of movable type for printing (c.1041–48).

Pisida *or* **Pisides.** See GEORGE PISIDES.

Pisistratus. See PEISISTRATUS.

Pi·so \'pī-sō\. Roman plebeian family, gens Calpurnius, including notably: Lucius Calpurnius Piso, *surnamed* Fru·gi \'frü-jī\ (2d century B.C.); tribune of the plebs (149 B.C.) and sponsor of first law against extortion; praetor (136), consul (133), censor (120); opposed reforms of the Gracchi; author of a history of Rome, extant only in a few fragments. ¶Lucius Calpurnius Piso Cae·so·ni·nus \,siz-ə-'nī-nəs\ (1st century B.C.); father-in-law of Julius Caesar; consul (58 B.C.); involved in plot with Clodius to get rid of Cicero; governor of Macedonia (57–55); at outbreak of civil war, offered to mediate between Caesar and Pompey; after assassination of Caesar, opposed Mark Antony, but later joined his party. ¶Gaius Calpurnius Piso (d. 65 A.D.); robbed of his wife (37 A.D.) by Caligula and banished from Rome; conspired to take Nero's life.

Pis·sar·ro \pē-sȧ-rō\, Camille. 1830–1903. French painter, b. St. Thomas, Danish West Indies. Influenced early by Courbet and Millet; in London with Monet to escape Franco–Prussian War (1870–71); identified with Impressionist school and, later (late 1880s), with pointillism. Executed over 1600 landscapes and town scenes and nearly 200 prints; among canvases were *Vue de Pontoise* (1868), *Les Toites rouges* (1877), *Place du Théâtre Français* (1898), and *Self-Portrait* (1903).

Pis·se·leu \pē-sā-lœ̄\, Anne de. Duchesse d'Étampes \dā-tāⁿp\. 1508–c.1580. French courtier. Became (c.1526) mistress of Francis I; championed cause of Charles, duc d'Orléans against that of the Dauphin (later Henry II); accused of betraying Dauphin's military plans to Emperor Charles V; on accession of Henry II (1547) dismissed from court.

Pistoia, Cino da. See SIGHIBULDI.

Pis·ton \'pis-tən\, Walter Hamor. 1894–1976. American composer, b. Rockland, Me. Pupil of Nadia Boulanger and Paul Dukas in Paris (1924–26); taught music at Harvard (1926–60; professor from 1944); author of *Principles of Harmonic Analysis* (1933), *Harmony* (1941), *Counterpoint* (1947), and *Orchestration* (1955). Composed in Neoclassical style with Romantic overtones; works included 8 symphonies, *The Incredible Flutist* (1938, ballet), *Three New England Sketches* (1959, orchestral suite), *Capriccio* for harp and string orchestra (1963), chamber music, and concertoes for viola, for violin (2), for clarinet, for 2 pianos, and for string quartet and orchestra.

Pi·struc·ci \pē-'strüt-chē\, Benedetto. 1784–1855. Italian gem engraver and medalist in England. To England (1816); executed the St. George and the dragon used on the reverse of British gold coins; chief engraver (from 1817); chief medalist (1828).

Pit·cairn \'pit-,ka(ə)rn, -,ke(ə)rn\, John. 1722–1775. British officer of the Royal Marines. In command of advance detachment engaged by Americans at Lexington and Concord (1775); mortally wounded at Bunker Hill (June 17, 1775). His son ¶Robert (1747?–?1770), midshipman on the *Swallow,* was first to sight (July 2, 1767) the island later to be called Pitcairn Island and to become the refuge of the mutineers of the *Bounty* (1789).

Pitcher, Molly. See Mary MCCAULEY.

Pi·thou \pē-tü\, Pierre. 1539–1596. French jurist and historian. At first a Calvinist, converted (1573) to Catholicism; procurer general for parlement (1593); renowned as a supporter of Gallicanism and as a Humanist; among his works were a number of legal treatises written in Latin, *Satire Ménippée* (1593, polemical tract against Holy League), and *Les Libertéz de l'Église gallicane* (1594), which was used as the basis for the Declaration of the Clergy of France (1682).

Pit·kin \'pit-kən\, Walter Boughton. 1878–1953. American writer, b. Ypsilanti, Mich. Professor of journalism, Columbia U. (1912–1943); author of *How to Write Stories* (1922), *The Psychology of Happiness* (1929), *Life Begins at Forty* (1932), *Making Good before Forty* (1939), *On My Own* (1944), etc.

Pit·man \'pit-mən\, Sir Isaac. 1813–1897. English educator and phonographer. Invented an original system of shorthand based upon phonographic or phonetic, rather than orthographic, principles and published it as *Stenographic Sound-Hand* (1837); established Phonetic Institute for shorthand instruction at Bath; advocated spelling reform; proposed a phonetic printing alphabet with new letters; author of *Phonography* (1840). His brother ¶Benjamin, *known in U.S. as* Benn (1822–1910), was sent by Isaac to U.S. to teach shorthand system (1852); founded Phonographic Institute, Cincinnati (1853); refusal to adopt certain minor changes by Isaac caused his system to differ somewhat; invented electrochemical process of relief engraving (1855); teacher at Cincinnati Art School (from 1873).

Pit·ney \'pit-nē\, Mahlon. 1858–1924. American jurist, b. Morristown, N.J. Practiced law, Dover, N.J. (1882–89), and Morristown (from 1889); member, U.S. House of Representatives (1895–99); chancellor of New Jersey (1908–12); associate justice, U.S. Supreme Court (1912–22).

Pi·to·ni \pē-'tō-nē\, Giuseppe Ottavio. 1657–1743. Italian composer of Roman school. Choirmaster at Collegio di S. Marco, Rome (1677–1743), and at various churches, esp. St. Peter's (1719–43); composer of masses, motets, litanies, hymns, Matthew and Luke Passions, etc.

Pi·tot \pē-tō\, Henri. 1695–1771. French hydraulic engineer. Supervised draining of swamps in Languedoc (1740); built aqueduct for Montpellier; invented (1735) Pitot tube, which measures flow velocity of fluids.

Pi·tra \pē-trȧ\, Jean-Baptiste-François. 1812–1889. French prelate. Bishop of Frascati (1879), of Porto (1884); discovered (1863) secret of Greek hymnography and published it in *Hymnographie de l'Église grecque* (1867); author of *Analecta Sacra* (1876–83), etc.

Pitt \'pit\, Thomas. *Known as* Diamond Pitt. 1653–1726. English merchant. Carried on East Indian trade (from 1674) as interloper until East India Company, unable to check him in courts, received him into service (1694); governor of Madras (1697–1709); M.P. (1689–93, 1709 ff.); obtained Regent (or Pitt) diamond (1701), sold it (1717) to French regent to be placed with state jewels of France.

Pitt, William. 1st Earl of Chat·ham \'chat-əm\. *Called* the Elder Pitt *and later* the Great Commoner. 1708–1778. English politician. Grandson of Thomas Pitt. Entered Parliament (1735) and gained power over Commons with his oratory; opposed Carteret's Hanoverian policy and system of subsidies to Continental powers (1742–44); paymaster general and privy councilor (1746); dismissed (1755) for opposition to foreign policy of Newcastle cabinet; called reluctantly (1756) by George II as secretary of state and leader of House of Commons, virtually prime minister; dismissed (1757), but immediately recalled and given full control in foreign and military affairs; by vigorous prosecution of war brought about defeats of French in India, Africa, Canada, and on the seas, thus securing Britain a vast empire; compelled to resign by refusal of majority of cabinet to declare war on Spain (1761). Pensioned; continued to oppose attempts to tax American colonists; formed new ministry (1766) with office only as privy seal on account of poor health as result of gout, which caused resignation (1768). Created earl (1766). Collapsed in House of Lords protesting disruption of empire by peace-at-any-price policy and Duke of Richmond's motion for withdrawal of forces from America.

His eldest son ¶Sir John Pitt (1756–1835), 2d Earl of Chatham; lord privy seal (1794–96); president of council (1796–1801); commander of Walcheren Expedition (1809) and charged with its failure; general (1812).

Pitt, William. *Called* the Younger Pitt. 1759–1806. English politician. Second son of 1st Earl of Chatham. Entered Parliament (1781); assailed Tory ministry of Lord North but declined office until becoming chancellor of exchequer under Shelburne (1782); declined to form cabinet on fall of Shelburne's ministry (1783); brought forward scheme for parliamentary reform, only to be defeated, as also upon bill for modifying East India Company's charter. On dismissal of Fox-North coalition ministry (Dec. 1783), took office as chancellor of exchequer, 1st lord of treasury, and prime minister, the only member of cabinet in House of Commons; despite hostile votes, refused to dissolve Parliament until public feeling was on his side; received huge majority in general election (1784). Undertook ordering of finances by funding and reducing national debt, abating customs duties, instituting sinking fund for paying national debt; established new constitution for East India Company (1784); lost third parliamentary reform bill (1785); first statesman to attempt adoption of teachings of Adam Smith; failed in attempt to effect commercial union of British Isles (1785); negotiated favorable commercial treaty with France (1786); failed to carry House of Commons in favor of Wilberforce's proposed abolition of slave trade (1792). Formed (1793) First Coalition with Russia, Sardinia, Spain, Naples, Prussia, Austria, Portugal, granting these allies subsidies in struggle against France; suspended Habeas Corpus act, forced to levy income taxes; formed Second Coalition against France (1798), including Portugal, Naples, Russia, the Ottoman empire, and Austria, facilitated by victory of Nile; compelled by George III to withdraw proposal of Catholic emancipation introduced for quieting Irish rebellion of 1798, temporarily allayed by union with Ireland (1800–01) secured through political corruption. Resigned (1801) during Treaty of Amiens negotiations; assisted ministry of Addington until its weakness and declaration of war on France (1803) required him to return to office (1804); formed Third Coalition with Russia, Austria, and Sweden (1805); increased property tax by 25 per cent (1805); raised loan of twenty million pounds; seriously affected in health by charge of misappropriation of public funds against his friend Melville, head of admiralty (1805); broken by news of capitulation at Ulm (Oct. 1805); dealt death blow by defeats of Austria and Russia at Austerlitz (Dec. 1805).

Pit·ta·cus \'pit-ə-kəs\. c.650–c.570 B.C. Greek ruler of Mytilene. One of Seven Wise Men of Greece; overthrew Melanchrus, tyrant of Lesbos (c.611); distinguished himself in war against Athens for Sigium, killing Athenian commander single-handedly; became tyrant of Mytilene (589–579); voluntarily resigned power (579).

Pittendreich, Lord. See Sir James BALFOUR.

Pit·ti \'pēt-tē\. Prominent 15th-century Florentine family, a rival of the Medicis, including notably: Buonaccorso (1354–c.1431), ambassador of Florence to Duke Rupert of Bavaria, newly elected king of Germany (1400–10); author of *Cronaca* on personal adventures and Florentine politics. ¶Luca (1394–1472), who began building (c.1440) the Pitti Palace in Florence.

Pitt-Riv·ers \'pit-'riv-ərs\, Augustus Henry. *Orig. surname* Lane-Fox \'lān-'fäks\. 1827–1900. English army officer and archaeologist. Served in Crimean War; on his estate in Wiltshire made excavations of prehistoric, Roman, and Saxon sites; adopted a sociological approach to excavated objects and emphasized value of common artifacts; author of *Excavations in Cranborne Chase* (1887–1903). Often called "father of British archaeology."

Pi·us \'pī-əs\. Name of twelve popes:

Pius I. Saint. d. 155. Pope (142–155). Opposed Gnosticism and Marcionism; excommunicated Marcion (144).

Pius II. *Orig.* Enea Silvio Pic·co·lo·mi·ni \,pēk-kō-'lō-mē-nē\. *Known in literature as* Aeneas Sil·vi·us *or* Syl·vi·us \'sil-vē-əs\. 1405–1464. Pope (1458–64). In service to Council of Basel (1431–37); engaged in various missions of the church to German states; resided at court of Emperor Frederick III of Germany (1442–47), where he was poet laureate; ordained priest (1446); bishop of Trieste (1447), of Siena (1449). As pope, took the name Pius as a reminiscence of Virgil's "pius Aeneas"; became a leader of the Humanists; issued bull (1460) against belief that councils were superior to popes; quarreled (1461) with Louis XI of France and with George of Poděbrad of Bohemia (1462–64) on questions of doctrine; sought to lead crusade against Turks but died of fever at Ancona. A patron of learning and prolific writer, his works including a novel *De duobus amantibus historia,* a play *Chrysis,* poems (in Latin), letters and dialogues, a valuable history of his times *Historia Frederici imperatoris,* and a work on geography that is said to have influenced Columbus.

Pius III. *Orig.* Francesco Todeschini Pic·co·lo·mi·ni \,pēk-kō-'lō-mē-nē\. c.1440–1503. Pope (Sept.–Oct. 1503). Made archbishop of Siena and cardinal deacon (1460) by his uncle Pope Pius II; as papal legate, sent to Diet of Regensburg (1471) and to restore ecclesiastical authority in Umbria; elected pope despite attempt by Cesare Borgia to control conclave.

Pius IV. *Orig.* Giovanni Angelo de' Me·di·ci \'med-ē-(,)chē, *Angl* 'med-ə-(,)chē\. 1499–1565. Pope (1559–65). Archbishop of Ragusa (1547); papal vice legate for Bologna (1547); cardinal priest (1549). As pope, adopted policy of conciliation toward Emperor Ferdinand I and Philip II of Spain; reconvened the suspended Council of Trent (1562); issued bull (1564) confirming its decisions (*Benedictus Deus*); instituted Index of Forbidden Books (1564); authorized revisions of the catechism, missal, and breviary; encouraged St. Teresa of Avila; reduced powers of the Inquisition; patron of Michelangelo; revived Roman University; built many buildings and public works.

Pius V. Saint. *Orig.* Antonio Ghis·lie·ri \gēz-'lyer-ē\. 1504–1572. Pope (1566–72). Commissary general of Roman Inquisition (1551); bishop of Nepi and Sutri (1556); grand inquisitor (1558). As pope, endeavored to enforce reforming decrees of Council of Trent; instituted moral and ecclesiastical reforms; strengthened powers of Inquisition; eliminated Protestantism in Italy; excommunicated Elizabeth of England and declared her a usurper (1570); aided Catholics in France against the Huguenots and helped Spain in Netherlands; with Spain and Venice, formed the Holy League (1570) against the Turks; revised the breviary (1568) and missal (1570).

Pius VI. *Orig.* Giovanni Angelo Bra·schi \'bräs-kē\. 1717–1799. Pope (1775–99). Released American clergy (after 1781) from jurisdiction of vicar apostolic in England; established see of Baltimore (1789); during his pontificate, church reached nadir in modern times, losing papal authority to anticurial policies of Emperor Joseph II and the king of Naples; deprived of parts of papal dominions by the French (1791, 1796, 1798); carried a prisoner to Valence, France (1798), where he died.

Pius VII. *Orig.* Barnaba Gregorio Chia·ra·mon·ti \,kyär-ä-'mōn-tē\. 1742–1823. Pope (1800–23). Ratified concordat with France (1801); visited Paris and crowned Napoléon (1804); gradually came to oppose Napoléon's aggressions (1805–09); lost several provinces to French (1809); held prisoner by Napoléon at Savona and Fontainebleau (1809–14); reentered Rome (1814); restored Jesuit order (1814); suppressed Carbonari and restored order (1815–23).

Pius VIII. *Orig.* Francesco Saverio Ca·sti·glio·ni \,käs-tēl-'yō-nē\. 1761–1830. Pope (1829–30). Bishop of Montalto (1800), of Cesena (1816), of Frascati (1821); imprisoned for refusal to take oath of allegiance to Napoléon (1808). As pope, supported new French regime under Louis-Philippe; approved decrees of Council of Baltimore, Md. (1829).

Pius IX. *Orig.* Giovanni Maria Ma·stai-Fer·ret·ti \mäs-'tä-ē-fār-'rāt-tē\. 1792–1878. Pope (1846–78). Archbishop of Spoleto (1827); bishop of Imola (1832); cardinal (1840). As pope, proclaimed political amnesty (1846) to meet critical conditions in Papal States; granted a constitution and embarked on policy of wide reforms; after insurrection at Rome (1848), forced to flee to Gaeta; restored by French (1850); henceforth became extremely reactionary; supported ultramontanism; proclaimed dogma of the Immaculate Conception (1854); in Italian War (1859–60), lost greater part of papal dominions; convened Vatican Council (1869–70), which promulgated the dogma of papal infallibility (*Pastor aeternus*); lost temporal power to Victor Emmanuel (1870); pontificate longest in history of the church.

Pius X. Saint. *Orig.* Giuseppe Melchiorre Sar·to \'sär-tō\. 1835–1914. Pope (1903–14). Bishop of Mantua (1884); cardinal (1893). As pope, greatly interested in social questions, esp. improving the condition of the poor; abolished traditional right of veto at papal elections (1903); inaugurated reforms in church music; began revision (1904) of ecclesiastical laws (Codex Juris Canonici); issued encyclical (*Pascendi*) against Modernism (1907); antagonistic to Christian democracy. Canonized (1954).

Pius XI. *Orig.* Ambrogio Damiano Achille Rat·ti \'rät-tē\. 1857–1939. Pope (1922–39). Taught at Milan (1882–88); director and prefect of Ambrosian Library, Milan (1888–1910); subprefect and prefect of the Vatican Library (1911–18); sent to Poland (1918); nuncio (1919–20); cardinal and archbishop of Milan (1921). As pope, signed (Feb. 11, 1929) Lateran Treaty with Mussolini by which Vatican City was established and arrangement made for recognition by Italian government of the Roman Catholic religion; wrote protests against Third Reich (1933–36); denounced Mussolini's anti-Semitism; issued encyclicals against Communism and Nazism (1937); supported overseas missions; consecrated first Chinese bishops (1926); advocated measures for world peace.

Pius XII. *Orig.* Eugenio Pa·cel·li \pä-'chel-lē\. 1876–1958. Pope (1939–58). Nuncio in Bavaria and Germany (1917–29); cardinal (1929); secretary of state to Holy See (1929–39). As pope, maintained neutrality in World War II; opposed Catholic collaboration with Communists; issued encyclical *Divino Afflante Spiritu* (1943) which accepted modern biblical scholarship; maintained traditional Catholic social doctrine.

Pix·é·ré·court \pēk-sā-rā-kür\, René-Charles Guil·bert de \gēl-ber-də-\. 1773–1844. French playwright. Known as the "father of melodrama"; author of more than 100 melodramas, as *Le Château des Appennins* (1797), *Victor* (1798), *Coelina* (1801), and *Le Chien de Montargis* (1816).

Pi y Mar·gall \'pē-ē-mär-'gäl\, Francisco. 1824–1901. Spanish politician. Follower of Proudhon; organized radical Spanish Republican Federal party; as head of government, attempted to establish a decentralist, or "cantonalist," political system (1873).

Pi·zar·ro \pē-'thär-rō, -'sär-, *Angl* pə-'zär-(,)ō\, Francisco. c.1475–1541. Spanish conqueror of Peru. Sailed to America (1509); made journey with Ojeda in Caribbean (1510); with Balboa on his discovery of the Pacific (1513); mayor of Panama (1519–23); joined Diego de Almagro (1523) in plan to explore west coast of South America; first expedition (1524–25) a failure; second (1526–27) after great hardships explored Gulf of Guayaquil. Returned to Spain (1528) and secured from Charles V authority to conquer and govern new territory; enlisted 180 men, including his three half-brothers; arrived in Panama (1530) and started for Peru (1531); overcame Atahualpa (1532), Inca chieftain, and executed him (1533) at Cajamarca for refusal to accept Christian faith; marched to Cuzco (1533), captured it, and secured immense amount of gold; founded new capital, Lima (1535). Waged civil war with Almagro (1537–38), who was defeated and killed; slain by followers of Almagro in revenge (1541). His half-brothers: ¶Gonzalo (1502?–1548); went with Francisco to Peru (1531); governor of Quito (1539–46); after Spanish government abridged their rights, led conquistadores in revolt (1546–48), winning battle of Anaquito (1546); defeated and executed by Gasca. ¶Hernando (1475?–1578); went with Francisco to Peru (1531); returned to Spain with royal fifth ransom of Atahualpa (1534); again in Peru; seized at Cuzco by Almagro (1537); released; commanded brother's army, defeated Almagro (1538), and executed him; imprisoned in Spain (1540–60). ¶Juan (1505–1536); went with Francisco to Peru (1530); governor of Cuzco (1535); killed in fighting at Cuzco.

Piz·zet·ti \pēt-'tsāt-tē\, Ildebrando. 1880–1968. Italian composer. Professor at Istituto Musicale, Florence (1909–25), at S. Cecilia Academy, Rome (1936–

51). His works included operas as *Debora e Jaele* (1922), *Fra Gherardo* (1928), *La Figlia di Jorio* (1954), *Assassinio nella cattedrale* (1958, after T.S. Eliot's *Murder in the Cathedral*); symphonic scores as *Concerto dell' estate* (1928), *Canti dalla stagione alta* (1930); choral works as *Requiem* (1922), *Cantico di gloria* (1948); also incidental and chamber music, piano pieces, concertos, and songs, esp. "I pastore" (1908).

Plaat·je \'plä-chə\, Solomon Tshekiso. 1877–1932. South African writer and politician. A leader of the black community in South Africa. Correspondent in South African War (1899–1902); editor of *Koranta ea Becoana* (1901–08) and of *Tsala ea Batho* (1912 ff.); member of delegations to Europe; lectured in Europe, U.S., and Canada on situation in South Africa. Besides articles on native problems and translations of Shakespeare into Tswana, also wrote *Native Life in South Africa* (1915), *Sechuana Proverbs and Their European Equivalents* (1916), *Sechuana Phonetic Reader* (1916, with Daniel Jones), and a novel, *Mhudi* (1930).

Place \'plās\, Francis. 1771–1854. English reformer. Journeyman leather-breeches maker; member of London Corresponding Society (1794–97); led successful campaign to repeal legislation forbidding trade unionism (1814–24); campaigned against national sinking fund (1816–23); framed placard "To Stop the Duke, go for Gold," producing run on banks, forcing Wellington from office, and assuring passage of Reform bill (1832). Author of pamphlets and articles on social and economic questions; drafted the National, or People's, Charter in the form of an act of Parliament (1838) setting forth the platform of the Chartists.

Pla·cide \plä-sēd\, Alexander. 1750–1812. French dancer and impresario. Gained fame and toured Europe as tightrope walker; performed ballet *The Bird Catcher* in New York (1792); established a dance and mime company in Charleston, S.C., where he produced such ballets as Noverre's *Caprices de Galathée* and Gardel's *Chercheuse d'esprit;* also producer in Savannah and Augusta, Ga. (1798 ff.).

Pla·cid·ia \plə-'sid-ē-ə\, Galla, *in full* Aelia Galla. c.390–450. Roman princess. Daughter of Theodosius I and sister of Flavius Honorius. Taken prisoner by Alaric (410); held hostage (410–414); m. (414) Ataulphus, successor of Alaric; upon Ataulphus's death, restored to Honorius (416); m. (417) Constantius III; mother of Valentinian III and regent for him during his minority (425–c.440).

Plácido. See Gabriel VALDÉS.

Plaisance, Duc de. See Charles-François LEBRUN.

Plan·ché \plan-'shā\, James Robinson. 1796–1880. English playwright and antiquary. His first play a burlesque, *Amoroso, King of Little Britain* (1818); gained reputation for knowledge of costume and heraldry; translated or adapted plays and wrote original plays, at his best bringing out pieces for Madame Vestris (1831–56); wrote libretto for Weber's opera *Oberon* (1826); author of *History of British Costumes* (1834).

Planck \'pläŋk\, Max Karl Ernst Ludwig. 1858–1947. German physicist. Professor, Munich (1880–85), Kiel (1885–89), Berlin (1889–1928). As result of work on radiation from black bodies, originated and developed quantum theory (from 1900); awarded 1918 Nobel prize for physics; known also for work relating to thermodynamics and mechanics and to electrical and optical problems associated with radiation of heat and with the quantum theory.

Plan·cus \'plaŋ-kəs\, Lucius Munatius. 1st century B.C. Roman soldier and politician. Served under Caesar in Gaul; after assassination of Caesar (44 B.C.), joined Mark Antony; consul with Lepidus (42); in civil war between Octavian and Antony, sided with Octavian; sponsored in Senate motion to confer on Octavian title of Augustus (27). One of Horace's odes is addressed to him.

Plan·quette \plä^{n}-ket\, Robert, *in full* Jean-Robert-Julien. 1848–1903. French composer. Best known for light operas, including *Les Cloches de Corneville* (1877; commonly known in English as *The Chimes of Normandy), Le Chevalier Gaston* (1879), *Rip Van Winkle* (1884), *Le Talisman* (1893), *Le Paradis de Mahomet* (1906).

Plan·tag·e·net \plan-'taj-(ə-)nət\. Surname, originally a nickname, historically associated with English royal house called house of An·jou \'an-jü, *Fr* ä^{n}-zhü\ or the An·ge·vin \'an-jə-vən\ royal house, founded by Geoffrey, Count of Anjou (d. 1151), and his wife Matilda, daughter of Henry I of England, and occupying English throne (1154–1399) in persons of Henry II (ruled 1154–89), Richard I (1189–99), John (1199–1216), Henry III (1216–72), Edward I (1272–1307), Edward II (1307–27), Edward III (1327–77), Richard II (1377–99) in the direct line of descent and thereafter through its descendants in two contending branches, the houses of Lancaster and of York (*qq.v.*), until the death of Richard III (1485). First official use of Plantagenet as surname was in 1460 when Richard, Duke of York (see RICHARD), claimed the throne in name of Richard Plantagenet.

Plantagenet, George. Duke of Clarence. See GEORGE.

Plantagenet, Richard. Duke of York. 1472–1483. Second son of Edward IV of England. Given up (1483) by queen mother, in sanctuary of Westminster, through persuasion of Cardinal Bourchier; placed in Tower of London with his brother Edward V, where both were murdered, purportedly at order of Richard III.

Plan·té \plä^{n}-tā\, Gaston. 1834–1889. French physicist. Professor, Association Polytechnique, Paris (1860 ff.); invented first practical storage battery (1860).

Plan·tin \plä^{n}-ta^{n}\, Christophe. c.1520–1589. French bookbinder, printer, and publisher. Settled in Antwerp (1549); published *Biblia polyglotta* (1569–72), which fixed original text of Old and New Testaments; in Leiden (1583–85) as typographer for the university. Books published by him became famous for typographical excellence and beauty.

Planudes, Maximus. See MAXIMUS PLANUDES.

Plas·kett \'plas-kət\, John Stanley. 1865–1941. Canadian astronomer, b. Woodstock, Ont. Director, Dominion Astrophysical Observatory, Victoria, B.C. (1917–35); authority on the motion of faint stars, rotation of the Milky Way, and matter in interstellar space; discovered double star now known as Plaskett's star (1922).

Pla·teau \plä-tō\, Joseph Antoine Ferdinand. 1801–1883. Belgian physicist. Professor, Ghent (1835–72); invented (1832) one of earliest stroboscopes; investigated physiological optics and molecular forces; Plateau's problem is named after him.

Pla·ten \'plä-tən\, August. Graf von Platen Hal·ler·mund \'häl-ər-ˌmu̇nt\. 1796–1835. German writer. Among his poetical works were *Ghaselen* (1821), *Sonette aus Venedig* (1825), and *Die Abbassiden* (epic, 1834); among plays, *Der gläserne Pantoffel* (1823), *Die verhängnisvolle Gabel* (1826), *Der Schatz der Rhampsinit* (1828) and *Die Liga von Cambrai* (1833).

Plath \'plath\, Sylvia. 1932–1963. American poet, b. Boston. m. (1956) English poet Ted Hughes; instructor of English, Smith College (1957–58); committed suicide. Her confessional poems, often on death and oblivion, were published in *The Colossus* (1960), *Ariel* (1965), *Crossing the Water* (1971), *Winter Trees;* her semi-autobiographical novel *The Bell Jar* (1963) published under pseudonym Victoria Lucas.

Platina. See Bartolomeo SACCHI.

Pla·to \'plāt-(ˌ)ō\. *Orig. name* Aris·to·cles \ə-'ris-tə-ˌklēz\. c.428–348 or 347 B.C. Greek philosopher. Surnamed Plato because of his broad forehead or wide range of knowledge. Disciple of Socrates and teacher of Aristotle, with them laid philosophical foundations of Western culture. Studied under and with Socrates until Socrates's execution (399 B.C.), then left Athens; stayed for a while in Megara; traveled in Egypt, Cyrene, Sicily, and Magna Graecia. Returned to Athens permanently (387) and there founded his school of philosophy known as the Academy. His extant works are in form of dialogues, in each of which his master, Socrates, is represented in a leading role; these dialogues include *Republic* (generally regarded as his greatest work; a search for justice in construction of an ideal state), *Laws* (on same theme; unfinished), *Symposium* (on ideal love), *Phaedrus* (attacking prevailing conception of rhetoric), *Timaeus* (embodying a theory of the universe and containing story of the lost Atlantis), *Apology* (purporting to give Socrates's speech in own defense at his trial), *Phaedo* (on immortality of the soul; purporting to be a record of Socrates's last conversation before death), also *Charmides, Cratylus, Critias, Crito, Euthydemus, Euthyphro, Gorgias, Ion, Laches, Lesser Hippias, Lysis, Menexenus, Meno, Parmenides, Philebus, Politicus, Protagoras, Sophist, Theaetetus.*

Plato. fl. 428–389 B.C. Athenian playwright. Carried on poetic contest with Aristophanes; reputed author of 28 comedies (only fragments extant).

Pla·ton \(ˌ)plə-'tōn\. *Orig. name* Peter Lev·shin \lyif-'shēn\. 1737–1812. Russian prelate. Became monk, adopting name of Platon; religious instructor to future Czar Paul I (1762); bishop of Tver (1770); archbishop of Moscow (1775); metropolitan of Moscow (1787).

Platt \'plat\, Orville Hitchcock. 1827–1905. American politician, b. Washington, Conn. U.S. senator (1879–1905). Sponsor of Platt Amendment (1901), requiring Cuba to enter into no foreign agreements contrary to interests of the U.S., and to grant to U.S. the right to intervene in Cuban affairs, if necessary to keep order.

Platt, Thomas Collier. 1833–1910. American politician, b. Owego, N.Y. Political associate of Roscoe Conkling (from 1870); member, U.S. House of Representatives (1873–77); U.S. senator (1881); resigned along with Conkling in disagreement with President Garfield over a civil service appointment; again U.S. senator (1897–1909); in move to remove Theodore Roosevelt from state politics, promoted his nomination for vice president (1900).

Plat·ter \'plät-ər\, Thomas. 1499–1582. Swiss writer. Taught Hebrew at Basel; partner of Basel printer Andrew Cratander. His autobiography (completed 1575) is a valuable historical source.

Plau·tus \'plȯt-əs\, Titus Maccius. c.254–184 B.C. Roman playwright, b. Umbria. Little is known of his life; settled in Rome as writer of comedies adapted from Greek originals; credited with freeing Roman drama from slavish imitation of Greek and with creating Roman literary idiom. Of 21 plays commonly accepted as genuine, following are extant (some in incomplete form): *Amphitruo, Asinaria, Aulularia, Bacchides, Captivi, Casina, Cistellaria,*

Curculio, Epidicus, Menaechmi, Mercator, Miles Gloriosus, Mostellaria, Persa, Poenulus, Pseudolus, Rudens, Stichus, Trinummus, Truculentus. Only parts of *Vidularia* extant.

Play·fair \'plā-ˌfa(ə)r, -ˌfe(ə)r\, John. 1748–1819. Scottish mathematician and geologist. Professor in Edinburgh (1785 ff.). Author of *Elements of Geometry* (1795), *Illustrations of the Huttonian Theory of the Earth* (1802), and *Outlines of Natural Philosophy* (1812–16); proponent of Huttonian theory of the earth; first to propose that a river cuts its own valley; first to attribute transport of erratics to glaciation.

Play·ford \'plā-fərd\, John. 1623–1686. English music publisher. Publisher in London (1648–84) of collections of music and dance steps, as *The English Dancing-Master* (1650) and *Select Musical Ayres and Dialogues* (1653); author of *Briefe Introduction to the Skill of Music* (1654; revised 1683 by Henry Purcell). His collections remain the principal source of knowledge of English country dances and songs. His son ¶Henry (1657–1709) continued the family business.

Pleh·ve \'plāv-yi\, Vyacheslav Konstantinovich. 1846–1904. Russian government administrator. Director of secret police, ministry of the interior (1881); secretary of state for Finland (1899); minister of the interior (1902); his administration noted for harsh suppression of liberal and ethnic nationality movements and for policies which led to Russo–Japanese War; assassinated.

Ple·kha·nov \plyi-'k̲ä-nəf\, Georgy Valentinovich. 1857–1918. Russian political philosopher. Chief exponent in Russia of philosophic Marxism. In exile, chiefly at Geneva (1880–1917); founded (1883) Liberation of Labor, first Russian Marxist revolutionary organization, which became (1898) Russian Social Democratic Workers' party; chief theoretician; influenced thought and philosophy of Lenin; after split (1903) of Social Democratic party, headed Menshevik wing against Lenin's Bolsheviks. During World War I advocated defense of Russia, contrary to Bolshevik policy of working for defeat of government; thereafter opposed Bolshevik revolution. Credited with exercising great influence on development of socialist thought and policy in Russia, esp. his theory that Russia would undergo a two-phase revolution.

Ples·sis \plā-sē, ples-ē\, Armand-Emmanuel du. Duc de Rich·e·lieu \rē-shəl-yœ̄\. 1766–1822. French soldier and politician. Grandson of Louis de Vignerot du Plessis. In Russian army (1790–91), fought Turks at Izmail. In French Revolution fought on royalist side. In Russia (1795–1814); governor of Odessa (1803); governor general of New Russia (1805); transformed Odessa into a modern city, constructing port facilities, encouraging agriculture and commerce, cleaning up corrupt administration. Prime minister of France (1815–18, 1820–21); represented France at Congress of Aix-la-Chapelle (1818); obtained withdrawal of Allied occupation army and inclusion of France into Quadruple Alliance.

Plessis, Armand-Jean du. Cardinal and duc de Richelieu. 1585–1642. French statesman and cardinal. Bishop of Luçon (1607); elected deputy of the clergy for Estates-General (1614). Became adviser to Marie de Médicis (c.1615); secretary of state (1616); cardinal (1622). Appointed (1624) chief of royal council and thereafter controlled Louis XIII; first minister (1628); actually directed domestic and foreign policies of France. In domestic policy his major goal was establishment of royal absolutism. Led siege and capture of La Rochelle (1628–29), thus suppressing political power of Huguenots. Suppressed plots of Gaston d'Orléans (1626), duc de Montmorency (1632), and Cinq Mars (1642). Foiled attempt of Marie de Médicis to dismiss him (Day of Dupes, Nov. 11, 1630). Influence of nobility reduced. Rebuilt the Sorbonne; established Académie Française (1634). In foreign affairs his major goal was to weaken Habsburgs. In Thirty Years' War intervened by subsidizing (1631) Gustav Adolphus of Sweden to fight the emperor. After Treaty of Prague (1635) led Catholic France to join with Sweden and German Protestants in war against Catholic Imperialist armies, made alliances with Oxenstierna and Bernhard of Saxe-Weimar, sent armies into Spain and Italy. Laid down principles upon which Peace of Westphalia was later (1648) made; with his guidance Bourbons had gained balance of power from Habsburgs.

Plessis-Marly, Seigneur du. See Philippe de MORNAY.

Plethon, George Gemistus. See George GEMISTUS PLETHON.

Plet·ten·berg \'plet-ən-ˌberk\, Wolter von. 1450?–1535. Prince of Livonia, Kurland, and Estonia. Defended his country against Russian invasion (1494); defended the Teutonic Knights against the Poles (1515), and received from the head of the order the title of grand master; designated by Emperor Charles V a prince of the empire (1527).

Pley·el \'plī-əl, *Fr* ple-yel\, Ignaz Joseph. 1757–1831. Austrian composer and piano manufacturer. Pupil and friend of Haydn; deputy (1783), head Kapellmeister (1789–91), Strasbourg cathedral; settled (1795) in Paris and founded (1807) a piano factory that still bears his name. Composed 29 symphonies, concertos, 6 grand sonatas for piano, and chamber music.

Pli·ek·šāns \'plē-ek-shäns\, Jānis. *Pseudonym* Ra·i·nis \'ra-ē-nis\. 1865–1929. Latvian writer. Proponent of social justice and national freedom; edited newspaper *Dienas Lapa* (1891–95); exiled by Russian government for political activities (1897–1903); took part in unsuccessful revolution of 1905; in Switzerland (1905–20); on return, elected to parliament; director of national theater (1921–25); minister of education (1926–28). His verse included *Tālas noskanas zilā vakarā* (1903), *Vētras sēja* (1905), *Gals un sākums* (1913); his plays, which used folklore motifs as symbols for his political ideals, included *Uguns un nakts* (Fire and Night, 1905), *Zelta zirgs* (1910), *Jāzeps un vina brāli* (Sons of Jacob, 1919).

Plim·soll \'plim(p)-səl, 'plim-ˌsȯl\, Samuel. 1824–1898. English reformer. Known as "the Sailors' Friend." Coal merchant in London (1853); M.P. (1868–80); with his book *Our Seamen* (1873), helped overcome obstruction of shipowners to Merchant Shipping Act (1876), giving powers of inspection to Board of Trade; gave his name to Plimsoll mark, the load line allowed by law.

Pliny \'plin-ē\. *Lat.* Gaius Plin·i·us Se·cun·dus \'plin-ē-əs-sə-'kən-dəs\. *Known as* the Elder. 23–79 A.D. Roman scholar. To Rome in youth; served as cavalry commander in Africa and Germany; procurator in Spain (c.70–72); studied and wrote in fields of history, rhetoric, natural science, military tactics; died while trying to observe closely an eruption of Vesuvius. Of his 7 works, only one is extant, *Historia naturalis* (37 books), an encyclopedia of natural science esp. as it touches human life. His nephew ¶Gaius Plinius Cae·cil·i·us \sə-'sil-ē-əs\ Secundus, *known as* the Younger (61 or 62–c.113 A.D.); praetor (93); consul (100); head of military and senatorial treasuries (94–100); head of drainage board of Rome (104–06); governor of Bithynia and Pontica (c.110); best known for his 9 books of letters (published 100–109) on literary, social, political, and domestic themes.

Plis·nier \plēs-nyā\, Charles. 1897–1952. Belgian writer. Author of novels *Mariages* (1936), *Faux passeports* (1937, Goncourt prize), *Meurtres* (1939–41), and *Mères* (1946–49); also of verse *Les Voix entendues* (1913), *Prière aux mains coupées* (1931).

Plo·mer \'plü-mər\, William Charles Franklyn. 1903–1973. South African writer. Farmer and trader in South Africa; settled in London (late 1920s); editor with publishing firm. Author of novels *Turbott Wolfe* (1925), *Sado* (1931), *The Case Is Altered* (1932), *The Invaders* (1934), *Museum Pieces* (1952), collections of short stories, esp. *I Speak of Africa* (1927), *Four Countries* (1949), verse *Collected Poems* (1960), *Taste and Remembrance* (1966), *Celebrations* (1972), and autobiographical works as *Double Lives* (1943), *At Home* (1958), *Autobiography* (1975). Also wrote librettos for Benjamin Britten's opera *Gloriana* (1953) and cantatas *Curlew River* (1964), *The Burning Fiery Furnace* (1966), *The Prodigal Son* (1968).

Plo·ti·nus \plō-'tī-nəs\. 205–270 A.D. Roman Neoplatonic philosopher, b. Egypt of Roman parentage. Studied at Alexandria under Ammonius Saccas (223–234); with expedition of Gordian III in Persia (242–243); lectured in Rome on philosophy (from 244); biographized by his friend Porphyry, who also edited his works under title *Enneads;* chief exponent of Neoplatonism.

Plück·er \'plu̅e-kər\, Julius. 1801–1868. German mathematician and physicist. Professor in Bonn (from 1829). Known in mathematics for work in analytical geometry, esp. the introduction of abridged notation and developments which led to discovery of principle of duality; in physics, studied behavior of crystals in a magnetic field and the properties of magnetic bodies; made investigations in spectroscopy. Author of *Analytisch-geometrische Entwicklungen* (1828–31), *Theorie der algebraischen Curven* (1839), *Neue Geometrie des Raumes* (1868–69), etc.

Plu·mer \'plü-mər\, Herbert Charles Onslow. 1st Viscount Plumer. 1857–1932. English military commander. Served in Matabele campaign (1896) and Boer War; in World War I, commanded of 2d army on western front (1915–17), held Ypres salient and won victory at Messines ridge (1917); commanded Italian expeditionary force (1917–18); general (1916), field marshal (1919); governor of Malta (1919–25); high commissioner for Palestine (1925–28).

Plum·pe \'plu̇m-pə\, Friedrich Wilhelm. *Pseudonym* F.W. Mur·nau \'mu̇r-ˌnau̇\. 1889–1931. German motion-picture director. Achieved wide influence through inventive camera techniques and Expressionistic style in films as *Satanas* (1919), *Der Januskopf* (1920), *Schloss Vogelöd* (1921), *Nosferatu* (1921), *Der brennender Acker* (1922), *Phantom* (1922), *Der letzte Mann* (1924), *Tartuffe* (1925), *Faust* (1926); in U.S. made *Sunrise* (1927), *Four Devils* (1928), *Our Daily Bread* (1929), *City Girl* (1930), *Tabu* (with Robert Flaherty, 1931).

Plun·ket \'pləŋ-kət\, Oliver. Saint. 1629–1681. Irish prelate. Archbishop of Armagh and primate of Ireland (1669); in hiding after passage of Test Act (1673); accused of share in Irish branch of Titus Oates plot (1678); convicted of treason by London jury on inadequate evidence; hanged, drawn, and quartered; canonized (1975).

Plunket, William Conyngham. 1st Baron Plunket. 1764–1854. Irish lawyer and judge. Led Whigs in Irish Parliament (1798–1800); fiercest of adversaries of

Pitt's project of union (1798); solicitor general (1803) and attorney general for Ireland (1805–07); prosecuted Emmet (1803); M.P. (1807, 1812–27); succeeded Grattan (1820) as foremost champion of emancipation and recognized as one of best orators in House of Commons; opposed agitation by O'Connell and Catholic Association (1825); as Irish attorney general (1822), attempted to put down Orange faction; chief justice of common pleas in Ireland (1827); created baron (1827); lord chancellor of Ireland (1830–41).

Plun·kett \'plən-kət\, Edward John Moreton Drax. 18th Baron of Dun·sa·ny \(,)dən-'sā-nē\. *Known as* Lord Dunsany. 1878–1957. Irish writer. Nephew of Sir Horace Plunkett. Served in South African War and World War I; noted traveler and big-game hunter. Published stories *Gods of Pegana* (1905), *Time and the Gods* (1913), *A Dreamer's Tales* (1916), etc., novels *The Chronicles of Rodriguez* (1922), *The Blessing of Pan* (1927), *Curse of the Wise Woman* (1933), etc., verse *Fifty Poems* (1929), *A Journey* (1943), plays *The Glittering Gate* (1909), *Gods of the Mountain* (1911), *A Night at the Inn* (1916), *If* (1921), autobiography *Patches of Sunlight* (1938).

Plunkett, Sir Horace Curzon. 1854–1932. Irish agricultural reformer and politician. Cattle rancher in Wyoming (1879–89); returned to Ireland and devoted himself to the agricultural cooperative movement; founded (1894) Irish Agricultural Organization Society. M.P. (1892–1900); commissioner of congested-districts board in Ireland (1891–1918); endowed trust in his name for development of agriculture (1919); presiding officer of Irish convention (1917–18), strove for understanding with British government; senator of Irish Free State (1922–23). Author of *Ireland in the New Century* (1904), *Home Rule and Conscription* (1918), etc.

Plu·tarch \'plü-,tärk\. c.46– after 119 A.D. Greek biographer. Studied in Athens under Ammonius; traveled widely; taught in Rome; in later life, returned to native Chaeronea. Author of *Moralia* (a collection of more than 60 essays on all manner of questions). Best known for his *Parallel Lives,* in which he presented character studies of distinguished Greeks and Romans in pairs, from the age of Theseus and Romulus down to his own time.

Plutarch of Athens. d. 431 or 432 A.D. Greek philosopher. Preceded Syrianus as head of Platonic school at Athens; a teacher of Proclus; said to have combined Aristotle's psychology with Platonic doctrine of recollection.

Plymley, Peter. See Sydney SMITH.

Po·be·do·nos·tsev \pəb-yi-(,)də-'nóst-sif\, Konstantin Petrovich. 1827–1907. Russian government administrator. Tutor to Alexander III and Nicholas II; member of council of empire (1872); placed in high state positions, esp. director general of the Most Holy Synod of Russian Orthodox church (1880). Believer in absolutism; consistent opponent of liberal reforms; upheld influence of Orthodox church on Russian policy.

Po·ca·hon·tas \,pō-kə-'hänt-əs\. *Indian name* Matoaka. c.1595–1617. American Indian princess, b. near Jamestown, Va. Daughter of Powhatan. Said by Captain John Smith in his *Generall Historie of Virginia* (1624) to have saved his life (1608) by holding his head in her arms to prevent Powhatan's warriors from clubbing him to death. Taken prisoner by the English (1612); converted to Christianity and baptized Rebecca; married (1614) John Rolfe, colonist, whom she accompanied to England (1616); received with royal honors and presented to the king and queen. Died of smallpox while preparing to return.

Poc·ci \'pót-chē\, Franz von. Graf. 1807–1876. German artist, musician, and poet. As artist, attained fame with humorous silhouettes and drawings for *Fliegende Blätter;* as musician, composed an opera *Der Alchemist* (1840), songs, and music for marionette shows; as playwright, wrote folk plays.

Po Chü-i \'bó-'jü̅e̅-'ē\. 772–846 A.D. Chinese poet. Government official in several capacities (808–833), esp. governor of provinces and mayor of Lo-yang (829–833); close friend of Yüan Chen. Author of ballads and poems written in a simple, direct style, protesting social and political evils, esp. *Song of Everlasting Remorse* (806) and *Lute Song* (816).

Po·cock \'pō-,käk\, Reginald Innes. 1863–1947. English zoologist. Superintendent of Zoological Garden, London (1904–23); one of first to use external features, as feet and ears, in classification of mammals.

Podebrady, George of. See GEORGE, king of Bohemia.

Pod·gor·ny \päd-'gór-nē\, Nikolay Viktorovich. 1903–1983. Soviet politician. Joined Communist party (1930); deputy commissar of Ukraine's food industry (1939–40; 1944–46); chairman of Ukrainian Communist party (1957–63); elected alternate member (1958) and full member (1960) of Presidium of Central Committee (Politburo); chairman of Presidium of Supreme Soviet (1965–77); removed from Politburo and demoted to deputy of Supreme Soviet (1977).

Poe \'pō\, Edgar Allan. 1809–1849. American poet and short-story writer, b. Boston. Creator of the American Gothic tale and detective fiction genre. Reared in family of John Allan (1780–1834), a merchant of Richmond, Va.; after quarrel with foster father, ran away from home (1827); in Boston published *Tamerlane and Other Poems* (1827). His resources exhausted, enlisted in U.S. army (1827–29). Published at Baltimore *Al Aaraaf, Tamerlane, and Minor Poems* (1829). Student at West Point (1830–31); dismissed for neglect of duty and disobedience of orders; published *Poems by Edgar A. Poe* (1831). With his story *A MS. Found in a Bottle* won a short-story competition (1833). Edited *Southern Literary Messenger,* Richmond, Va. (1835–37), and contributed poems, essays, short stories, and critical reviews; gained meager living by his writing, as *The Narrative of Arthur Gordon Pym* (1838). Associate editor, *Burton's Gentleman's Magazine,* Philadelphia (1839–40), to which he contributed some of his most famous stories (*The Fall of the House of Usher, Ligeia,* etc.). Published *Tales of the Grotesque and Arabesque* (1840). Literary editor, *Graham's Magazine* (1841–42). Again won short-story prize with *The Gold Bug* (1843), considered first detective story; developed genre in *The Murders in the Rue Morgue* and *The Mystery of Marie Rogêt.* In New York published "The Raven" (1845), which brought him fame; published later in book form *The Raven and Other Poems* (1845). Editor of the *Broadway Journal* (1845–46). Period of abject poverty and despondency followed, aggravated by alcoholism (1847–49); in intermittent periods of sanity wrote "For Annie," "Ulalume," "Annabel Lee," "The Bells," "El Dorado."

Poel \'pōl\, William. *Orig. surname* Pole \'pōl\. 1852–1934. English actor and theatrical manager. Revolutionized Shakespearean production by returning to Elizabethan staging. Revived *Hamlet* with text of First Quarto and without scenery (1881); founded Elizabethan Stage Society (1895); revived plays of Shakespeare, Marlowe, Ben Jonson, Beaumont and Fletcher; produced for first time Swinburne's *Locrine* (1900), *Fratricide Punished* (1924); dramatized Howells's *A Foregone Conclusion* (1884).

Poel·zig \'pœlt-sik\, Hans. 1869–1936. German architect. Taught at Breslau Kunstakademie (1900–16), Technische Hochschule, Berlin (1920–35). Known esp. for his Grosses Schauspielhaus (1919) in Berlin, one of finest German Expressionist designs.

Po·e·rio \pō-'er-yō\, Alessandro. 1802–1848. Italian poet and patriot. Volunteer under Pepe against Austrians (1821) and exiled after Austria regained control of Naples; mortally wounded serving under Pepe against the Austrians (1848). Author of lyrics, esp. of the patriotic poem *Il Risorgimento.* His brother ¶Carlo (1803–1867) was a lawyer and patriot; active in revolution of 1848; sentenced (1851) to 24 years in irons and served 9 years before being released and exiled; returned to Italy and was elected (1861) member of Turin parliament.

Pog·gen·dorff \'póg-ən-,dórf\, Johann Christian. 1796–1877. German physicist. Editor of *Annalen der Physik und Chemie* (1824–77); investigated problems in electricity and magnetism; published *Biographisch-literarische Handwörterbuch zur Geschichte der exakten Wissenschaften* (1863) and works on history of science, esp. physics; the Poggendorff visual illusion is named after him.

Pog·gio Brac·cio·li·ni \'pód-jō-,brät-chō-'lē-nē\, Gian Francesco. 1380–1459. Italian Humanist. Papal secretary (1404 ff.); chancellor of Florence (1453 ff.); invented the Humanist script; known chiefly for discoveries, in various monasteries in Germany, Switzerland, and France, of lost Latin classics, including ten orations of Cicero, Lucretius's *De rerum natura,* Quintilian's *Institutio oratoria,* Ammianus Marcellinus's history, Statius's *Silvae,* part of Valerius Flaccus's *Argonautica,* and Tacitus's *Dialogus* and *Germania.* His own writings in Latin included *Facetiae* (1438–52, collection of humorous tales), letters, and moral dialogues as *De avarita* (1428–29), *Contra hypocritas* (1447–48), and *De miseria humanae conditionis* (1455).

Pohl \'pōl\, Richard. 1826–1896. German writer. Friend of Liszt in Weimar (1854–64); author of studies on Wagner, Liszt, and Berlioz; translator of Berlioz's works.

Poin·ca·ré \pwaⁿ-kä-rā\, Jules-Henri. 1854–1912. French mathematician. Cousin of Raymond Poincaré. At U. of Paris (from 1881), professor of physical mechanics (1885), of mathematical physics and calculus of probabilities (1886), and, finally, of celestial mechanics. Reconstituted analytical mathematics; developed automorphic functions; introduced Fuchsian functions; applied analysis to rational mechanics, physics, and astronomy; published *Les Méthodes nouvelles de la mécanique céleste* (1892–99); worked on electromagnetic theory of light, electric oscillations, and diffraction of hertzian waves; contributed to theory of numbers, topology, and theory of orbits. Wrote *La Valeur de la science* (1905) and *Science et méthode* (1908), etc.

Poincaré, Raymond. 1860–1934. French politician. Elected deputy (1887–1902); a leader of the progressive Republicans, esp. as an economist; held several cabinet offices (1893–1903); senator (1903–12); prime minister and foreign minister (1912–13); vigorously supported entente with Great Britain and alliance with Russia. Elected president (1913–20); influenced legislation much more than previous presidents; strengthened French defenses; served through entire period of World War I, sustaining patriotism by his oratory and by fighting defeatism. After termination of presidency returned to Senate (1920); stood for strong nationalist policy; again prime minister (1922–24); disagreed with Great Britain on reparations; sent French army to occupy the Ruhr (1923); was defeated by Radicals and Socialists (1924). Again prime minister and minister of finance (1926–29) to meet financial crisis; his stabilization of the franc resulted in a period of prosperity. Member of French Academy (1909).

Poin·sett \ˈpȯin-ˌset, ˌpȯin-ˈ, ˈpoin-sət\, Joel Roberts. 1779–1851. American politician and diplomat, b. Charleston, S.C. Member, U.S. House of Representatives (1821–25); first U.S. minister to Mexico (1825–29); U.S. secretary of war (1837–41); reorganized military forces and successfully directed second Seminole War. The poinsettia, which he brought back from Mexico (1829), is named in his honor.

Poi·ré \pwä-rā\, Emmanuel. *Pseudonym* Ca·ran d'Ache \kȧ-räⁿ-dȧsh\. 1858–1909. French illustrator and caricaturist. Contributed to numerous periodicals; a pioneer of episodic strip cartoon; noted for humor and for forceful simplicity of drawing. Published collections of works as *Nos soldats du siècle* (1889), *Le Carnet de chèques* (1892), *Pages d'histoire* (1904), etc.

Poi·ret \pwȧ-re\, Paul. 1879–1944. French dress designer. Proprietor of dress shop in Paris (1903 ff.); known for introduction of hobble skirt and for simple, flowing Greek costumes.

Poise \pwȧz\, Ferdinand, *in full* Jean-Alexandre-Ferdinand. 1828–1892. French composer. Known esp. for comic operas, including *Les Charmeurs* (1855), *La Surprise de l'amour* (1877), *Joli Gilles* (1884), etc.

Poi·seuille \pwȧ-zœy\, Jean-Léonard-Marie. 1797–1869. French physician and physiologist. Known for investigations of circulation of the blood, for his work *Le Mouvement des liquides dans des tubes de petits diamètres* (1844), and for discovery (1843) of Poiseuille's law concerning velocity of flow of a liquid through a capillary tube.

Pois·son \pwȧ-sōⁿ\, Jeanne-Antoinette. Marquise de Pom·pa·dour \pōⁿ-pȧ-dür, *Angl* ˈpäm-pə-ˌdō(ə)r, -ˌdȯ(ə)r, -ˌdů(ə)r\. 1721–1764. Mistress of Louis XV of France. m. (1741) Charles-Guillaume d'Étoiles; legally separated (1745). Established at Versailles as mistress (1745) and made marquise; made duchess (1752). Exerted considerable influence on Louis XV, esp. in internal affairs; had brother appointed director of royal buildings; sponsored many buildings, as the École Militaire, Place de la Concorde (both in Paris), and Petit Trianon palace (Versailles); patronized authors and artisans, esp. Voltaire and the Encyclopedists; her years of power considered apogee of taste in France. Changed Richelieu's purpose of weakening house of Austria to one of alliance with Austria which brought on Seven Years' War.

Poisson, Siméon-Denis. 1781–1840. French mathematician. Professor at École Polytechnique (1802 ff.); known for application of mathematics to physics, esp. to electrostatics and magnetism; author of works on definite integrals, Fourier's series, calculus of variations, probability; studied stability of planetary orbits and gravitational attraction of spheroidal and ellipsoidal bodies. His *Traité de mécanique* (1811, 1833) was a standard work for years; also wrote *Recherches sur la probabilité des jugements* (1837).

Poitiers, Diane de. See DIANE DE POITIERS.

Poitiers, Guillaume de. See GUILLAUME DE POITIERS.

Poi·vre \pwȧvrᵊ\, Pierre. 1719–1786. French missionary and merchant. To Orient as missionary (1740); returned to France and formed French East India Co. (1747); began mercantile activities in Cochinchina (Vietnam) but was expelled for illegal activities (1749); to Timor, whence he smuggled fruit and spice plants to Mauritius and Réunion; governor of Mauritius (1765).

Po·kor·ny \pō-ˈkȯr-nē\, Julius. 1887–1970. German philologist and Celtic scholar. Professor at Berlin (1920–36), Zürich (1944–58); author of *Altirische Grammatik* (1925), *Zur Urgeschichte der Kelten und Illyrier* (1938), *Altkeltische Dichtungen* (1944), *Indogermanisches etymologisches Wörterbuch* (1948–69), etc.

Po·krov·sky \(ˌ)pə-ˈkrȯf-skəi\, Mikhail Nikolayevich. 1868–1932. Russian historian and politician. Joined Bolsheviks (1905); forced to live abroad (1908–17). After Bolshevik revolution (1917), became delegate of Moscow workmen's council and member of peace conference at Brest Litovsk; general director of government archives, Moscow (1921). Among his works were *An Outline History of Russian Culture* (1915–18), *Russian History* (1924) and *Sketches of the History of the Revolutionary Movement in Russia in the 19th and 20th Centuries* (1924).

Pol \ˈpȯl\, Wincenty. 1807–1872. Polish poet. Author of patriotic verse as *Pieśni Janusza* (1833), *Pieśn o ziemi naszej* (Songs of our Land, 1843); also *Mohort* (1855) and *Wit Stwosz* (1857).

Polano, Pietro Soave. See Paolo SARPI.

Po·lan·yi \ˈpō-län-yi\, Michael. 1891–1976. British chemist and philosopher, b. Budapest. Professor at Berlin (1925–33), U. of Manchester (1933–58). Made researches in thermodynamics, X-ray analysis, and reaction kinetics; later turned to social studies and philosophy. His works included *Atomic Reactions* (1932), *The Logic of Liberty* (1951), *The Study of Man* (1959), *Beyond Nihilism* (1960), and *Scientific Thought and Social Reality* (1974).

Polastron, Yolande-Martine-Gabrielle de. See POLIGNAC.

Pol·der·vaart \ˈpōl-dər-ˌfärt\, Arie. 1918–1964. American geologist, b. Bandung, Java. Taught at U. of Cape Town (1946–49), Columbia U. (1951 ff.). Noted for investigations of the petrogenesis of igneous and metamorphic rocks and Precambrian geology; specialized in application of petrologic techniques to problems of Earth history; edited *Crust of the Earth* (1955); wrote *Basalts* (1967).

Pol·ding \ˈpōl-diŋ\, John Bede. 1794–1877. English prelate. First Roman Catholic bishop in Australia as bishop of Sydney (1835); established new dioceses, churches, schools, and brought in priests; named archbishop and metropolitan of Australia (1842).

Pole \ˈpōl\. Name of English family descended from Geoffrey Pole, Buckinghamshire squire, whose son ¶Sir Richard (d. 1505) married (1491?) a princess of the royal house ¶Margaret Pole (1473–1541), Countess of Salis·bury \ˈsȯlz-ˌber-ē, -b(ə-)rē\, daughter of George Plantagenet (1449–78), Duke of Clarence. She was given family lands of earldom of Salisbury by Henry VIII as some amends for judicial murder of her brother Edward, Earl of Warwick; was discharged as governess to Princess Mary on refusal to give up Princess Mary's jewels after Henry VIII's marriage to Anne Boleyn; beheaded as consequence of Henry's antagonism toward her son Reginald.

¶Reginald Pole (1500–1558), Roman Catholic prelate. Friend of Sir Thomas More; sent by Henry VIII to Rome to study (1521–27); made dean of Exeter and initiated by Thomas Cromwell into statesmanship (1527); while traveling abroad, criticized Henry VIII in his book *Pro ecclesiasticae unitatis defensione* (1536), giving adverse opinion on question of Henry's divorce and warning of temporal punishment in event of nonsubmission to papal authority, thus provoking execution of his mother and brother Henry in England; created cardinal by Pope Paul III (1536) and sent as emissary to incite Francis I and Charles V to send expedition to depose Henry VIII (1537, 1539); governor of Patrimony of St. Peter and legate at Viterbo (from 1541) amid scholars interested in discussion of justification by faith; one of presiding legates at Council of Trent, which embodied in its decree Pole's views of original sin and his doctrines of justification by faith; just missed election as pope (1549). Papal legate to Queen Mary on her accession and, on reversal of attainder, returned to England (1554); cardinal priest (1555); absolved kingdom and those ordained under old rite or in schism, instituted reforms; archbishop of Canterbury (1556) on Cranmer's deprivation; attempted to restore ecclesiastical system disrupted by Henry VIII; deprived of legatine authority (1557) and charged with heresy (1558) by Pope Paul IV; died hours after Queen Mary.

Pole, de la \ˌdel-ə-ˈpōl\. Name of a rich English family descended from a Hull merchant, Sir William de la Pole *or* at·te Pool \ˌat-ə-ˈpōl\ (d. 1366), who held offices under Edward III in recognition of loans of money, and including earls and dukes of Suffolk:

¶Michael de la Pole (1330?–1389), 1st Earl of Suf·folk \ˈsəf-ək\. Eldest son of Sir William; took part in Black Prince's siege of Limoges (1370); became most trusted personal adviser of Richard II; chancellor of England (1383); impeached (1386) by organized opposition of Thomas of Woodstock (Duke of Gloucester) on a charge of misappropriation of funds and, after brief reinstatement by Richard II, compelled to flee the realm (1387). ¶William (1396–1450), 4th Earl and 1st Duke of Suffolk, and, by reversion of title, Earl of Pem·broke \ˈpem-ˌbrůk\ (1447). Grandson of 1st earl; served in French wars (1417–31), first under Henry V, later under Duke of Bedford, and in chief command (1428); taken prisoner by Joan of Arc at Jargeau (1429). Occupied himself with home politics (from 1431), joining faction of Cardinal Beaufort; became chief adviser to Henry VI (1443); negotiated successfully match between Henry VI and Margaret of Anjou and two-year truce (1444); promoted to dukedom (1448); banished Richard of York as lieutenant of Ireland, replacing him with Edmund Beaufort, Duke of Somerset, in French command; became unpopular after ceding to France as part of truce all of Anjou and Maine and after renewal of war, partly in consequence of treacherous attack on Fougères during truce; accused by House of Commons of maladministration and of selling the realm to France; banished by Henry VI; intercepted off Dover and beheaded at sea; his farewell letter to his son included in the Paston letters.

¶John (1442–1491), 2d Duke of Suffolk. Son of 1st duke; joined Yorkists and married Elizabeth, sister of Edward IV and Richard III; became steward of England at coronation of Edward IV (1461) and was trusted by Richard III and Henry VII despite fact that three of his sons were pretenders to throne on death of Richard III, as follows: ¶John (1464?–1487), Earl of Lin·coln \ˈliŋ-kən\; lord lieutenant of Ireland (1484); promoted Simnel's plot; killed at battle of Stoke. ¶Sir Edmund (1472?–1513), Earl of Suffolk; repaired to Emperor Maximilian in Tyrol on promise of help to throne (1501); was delivered to Henry VII by king of Castile and beheaded on accession of Henry VIII. ¶Richard (d. 1525); recognized as king of England by Louis XII (1512); fought for French in Spain and Netherlands; prepared for invasion of England with German mercenaries; killed at battle of Pavia.

\ə\ **abut** \ᵊ\ **kitten**, *Fr.* **table** \ər\ **further** \a\ **ash** \ā\ **ace** \ä\ **cot, cart** \aů\ **out** \ch\ **chin** \e\ **bet** \ē\ **easy** \g\ **go** \i\ **hit** \ī\ **ice** \j\ **job** \ŋ\ **sing** \ō\ **go** \ȯ\ **law** \ȯi\ **boy** \th\ **both** \t͟h\ **the** \ü\ **loot** \ů\ **foot** \y\ **yet** \zh\ **vision** \ȧ, ḇ, g̱, ḵ, ⁿ, œ, œ̄, ue, ue̅, ʸ\ *see* **Guide to Pronunciation**

Po·len·ta \pō-ˈlān-tä\. Italian noble family of Ravenna, including: Guido da Polenta (d. 1310), leader of Guelf faction; recaptured Ravenna from Ghibellines (1275); resisted papal attempts to control Romagna (1285 ff.); elected chief magistrate of Ravenna (1286–90, 1292–93). His daughter ¶Francesca (d. 1283 or 1284) was married (c.1275) to Gianciotto Malatesta (*q.v.*) to unite Polenta and Malatesta families; engaged in adulterous affair with brother-in-law Paolo; both lovers discovered and slain by her husband. Known in literature as Francesca da Rimini; her story immortalized in Dante's *Inferno,* in plays by Pellico, Paul Heyse, D'Annunzio, et al., in operas by Götz, Ambroise Thomas, Rachmaninoff, paintings by Ingres, Watts, et al., symphonic poem by Tchaikovsky, poem by Leigh Hunt, etc. Guido's grandson ¶Guido Novello da Polenta (d. 1330) was a scholar and poet; hosted Dante while latter was in exile (c.1318–21); captain of Bologna (1322); defeated (1323) by his cousin Otasio who had seized Bologna in his absence; died in exile.

Pol·ia·koff \pəl-(ˌ)yə-ˈkȯf\, Serge. 1906–1969. French painter and lithographer, b. Moscow. Settled in Paris (1923); for next 20 years made living as cabaret guitarist; as painter, influenced by Kandinsky and Robert Delaunay; one of foremost abstract colorists in 1950s.

Po·li·doú·ri \ˌpȯl-i-ˈdü-rē\ *or* **Pol·y·doú·re** \-ˈdü-rā\, Maria. 1905–1930. Greek poet. Published two volumes of poems notable for alternately bitter and resigned recognition of impending death.

Po·li·gnac \pȯ-lēn-yȧk\. An ancient French family of nobility, including: Melchior de Polignac (1661–1742); diplomat under Louis XIV and XV; ambassador to Poland (1695–97); retired, but recalled to favor at court (1702); plenipotentiary at Congress of Utrecht (1712–13); cardinal (1713), minister at Rome (1725–32), archbishop of Auch (1726); member of French Academy. His grandnephew ¶Armand-Jules-François, duc de Polignac (1745–1817); m. (1767) Yolande-Martine-Gabrielle de Po·las·tron \də-pȯ-lȧs-trōⁿ\ c.1749–1793), intimate friend of Marie-Antoinette. Through court favor they received huge pensions which aroused popular hatred; their extravagance a direct cause of the revolution; emigrated to the Ukraine (1789). Their son ¶Auguste-Jules-Armand-Marie, comte (*later* prince) de Polignac (1780–1847); ultraroyalist politician; implicated in conspiracy against Napoléon (1804), imprisoned for two years; became intimate (1814) with comte d'Artois; held several offices under Bourbon restoration and was ambassador to London (1823–29); minister of foreign affairs under Charles X (1829–30); promulgated the Ordinances of July 1830 that caused the revolution driving out Charles; arrested and imprisoned at Ham (1830–36).

Poliorcetes, Demetrius. See DEMETRIUS I of Macedonia.

Politian. See Angelo AMBROGINI.

Po·li·tis \pȯl-ˈyē-tēs\, Nikolaos Sokrates. 1872–1942. Greek jurist and diplomat. Associate of Venizelos and on staff of ministry of foreign affairs (1914–16); minister of foreign affairs (1916–20, 1922, 1936); delegate to Peace Conference at Paris (1919); Greek minister in Paris and Madrid (1924–36, 1938–40); president, Institute of International Law (1937–42); published works on jurisprudence, as *La Justice internationale* (1924) and *Les Nouvelles Tendences du droit international* (1927).

Polk \ˈpōk\, James Knox. 1795–1849. Eleventh president of the United States, b. Mecklenburg Co., N.C. Member from Tennessee, U.S. House of Representatives (1825–39), speaker (1835–39); governor of Tennessee (1839–41). As first "dark horse" candidate for president, campaigned on "54°40′ or fight" slogan. As president of the United States (1845–49), settled Oregon boundary with Great Britain (1846), secured passage of Walker Tariff Act (1846), and successfully conducted the Mexican War (1846–48), which resulted in annexation of California and most of Southwest.

Polk, Leonidas. 1806–1864. American clergyman and Confederate army commander, b. Raleigh, N.C. Cousin of James K. Polk. Resigned U.S. army commission (1827) and studied theology; appointed Protestant Episcopal missionary bishop of the Southwest (1838) and bishop of Louisiana (1841); a founder of U. of the South, Sewanee, Tenn. (1860); entered Confederate army as major general (1861); in command of Mississippi River defenses (1861–62); lieutenant general (1862); fought at Shiloh, Murfreesboro, Chickamauga; killed at Pine Mountain.

Pol·lai·uo·lo \ˌpōl-lī-ˈwȯ-lō\, Antonio. c.1431–1498. Florentine painter, goldsmith, sculptor, and engraver. Protégé of the Medici and the Florentine signory; as an engraver, associate of Finiguerra; headed large atelier from which issued works in niello, sculptures, paintings, goldsmith's work, etc.; leading bronze sculptor after Verrocchio; pioneer in study of anatomy by dissection for artistic purposes; called to Rome (1484) by Innocent VIII. Works included bronze reliquary of S. Giovanni, tombs of Sixtus IV and Innocent VIII, bronze groups *Hercules and Antaeus* and *Hercules Strangling Cacus,* terracotta bust *The Young Warrior,* engraving *Ten Fighting Nudes,* and paintings as *Martyrdom of St. Sebastian* and *Apollo and Daphne.* His brother ¶Piero (c.1443–1496) collaborated with Antonio in painting; his own paintings included *Coronation of the Virgin, Three Saints, Prudence,* and *Annunciation.*

Pollaiuolo *or* **Pol·lai·o·lo** \-lī-ˈȯ-lō\, Simone del. *Known as* Il Cro·na·ca \ˌēl-krō-ˈnäk-ä\, *i.e.* the Chronicler. 1457–1508. Florentine architect. Admirer and describer of ancient Roman works (hence his nickname); his style emphasized planes and linear design; his works included the courtyard and monumental cornice of Palazzo Strozzi and the church of S. Salvatore al Monte in Florence.

Pol·lard \ˈpäl-ərd\, Alfred William. 1859–1944. English bibliographer. Librarian, British Museum (1883–1924); professor of English bibliography, King's Coll., London (1919–32). Editor of the Globe *Chaucer* (1898) and *The Library* (1903–34); author of *Early Illustrated Books* (1893), *Shakespeare Folios and Quartos* (1909), *A Census of Shakespeare Quartos* (1916), *A Short Title Catalogue of Books Printed in England, Scotland, & Ireland 1475–1640* (1926, with G. R. Redgrave et al.), etc.

Pol·lio \ˈpäl-ē-ˌō\, Gaius Asin·i·us \ə-ˈsin-ē-əs\. 76 B.C.–4 A.D. Roman soldier, orator, and politician. Sided with Caesar in civil war; campaigned in Greece, Africa, and Spain with Caesar (49–45) and against Sextus Pompeius in Spain (44). Later joined fortunes with Mark Antony; governor of Cisalpine Gaul; helped negotiate peace of Brundisium (40), reconciling Antony and Octavian for a time. Consul (40); campaigned in Illyria (39); constructed first public library in Rome. Patron of literature; author of tragedies and a history of civil wars; only few fragments of his orations extant. Virgil addressed fourth eclogue to him.

Pollio, Marcus Vitruvius. See VITRUVIUS.

Pol·lock \ˈpäl-ək\, Sir Frederick. 1845–1937. English legal scholar. Professor of jurisprudence at Oxford (1883–1903); professor of common law, Inns of Court (1884–90); judge of admiralty court of Cinque Ports (from 1914); king's counsel (1920). Corresponded for over 60 years with Oliver Wendell Holmes. Founded and edited *Law Quarterly* (1885–1919); edited *Law Reports* (1895–1935); author of authoritative textbooks *Principles of Contract* (1876), *Digest of the Law of Partnership* (1877), and *The Law of Torts* (1887), and with F. W. Maitland of *History of English Law Before the Time of Edward I* (1895).

Pollock, Jackson, *in full* Paul Jackson. 1912–1956. American painter, b. Cody, Wyo. Pupil of Thomas Hart Benton in N.Y.C. (1930–33); worked for Federal Arts Project (1935–43); held first of many one-man shows in N.Y.C. (1943). A leading exponent of Abstract Expressionism and Action Painting; known for technique (1947 ff.) of dripping or pouring paint onto canvas; influenced by Jungian symbolism and Surrealism. Among his canvases were *Guardian of the Secret* (1943), *Mural* (1943), *Blue Unconscious* (1946), *Full Fathom Five* (1947), *Autumn Rhythm* (1950), *Echo* (1951), *Blue Poles* (1952), *Easter and the Totem* (1953), *White Light* (1954).

Pollock, Oliver. 1737?–1823. American merchant, b. Ireland. To U.S. (1760); became wealthy from trading business in Louisiana Territory. During Revolutionary War, incurred heavy debts by furnishing supplies to Continental commanders, esp. George Rogers Clark, and paying bills of Virginia; reimbursed after several years.

Pol·lux \ˈpäl-əks\, Julius. 2d century A.D. Sophist and lexicographer, of Naukratis, Egypt. Appointed professor of rhetoric at Athens by Emperor Commodus. Only extant work is *Onomasticon,* a Greek dictionary.

Polo, Gaspar Gil. See GIL POLO.

Po·lo \ˈpȯ-lō, *Angl* ˈpō-(ˌ)lō\, Marco. 1254–1324. Venetian traveler. Accompanied (1271 ff.) his father Niccolò and uncle Maffeo on a trip from Acre through Sivas, Mosul, Baghdad, Hormuz, Khurasan to the Oxus River (Amu Darya), up the Oxus to The Pamirs, and by way of Kashgar, Yarkand, and Khotan to Lop Nor, then across the Gobi desert to Kansu and Shang-tu, where they found Kublai Khan (1275). Entered the diplomatic service of Kublai Khan and was used on missions to various parts of the Mongol empire. Left China (1292) and returned by way of Sumatra, India, and Persia to Venice (1295). Captured by Genoese and imprisoned for a year at Genoa (1298), where he dictated to a fellow prisoner, Rusticiano or Rustichello, the story of his travels, published under the title of *Divisament dou monde* (later known as *Il milione*).

Polotsky, Simeon. See PETROVSKY-SITNIANOVICH.

Po·lus \ˈpō-ləs\. 4th century B.C. Greek actor. Most famous tragic actor of his day; reputedly Demosthenes's elocution teacher; in striving for realism and conviction in acting, said to have carried an urn filled with the ashes of his recently deceased son during role in Sophocles's *Electra.*

Pol·y·ae·nus \ˌpäl-ē-ˈē-nəs\. 2d century A.D. Greek scholar of Macedonia. Lived in Rome as rhetorician. Author of *Strategica,* or *Strategemata,* a compilation of military stratagems written in Greek and presented in anecdotal form.

Po·lyb·i·us \pə-ˈlib-ē-əs\. c.200–c.118 B.C. Greek historian. In service in Achaean League; taken as political prisoner to Rome (168) and remained in exile about seventeen years; became friend of Scipio Aemilianus and, through him, an associate of leading literary figures in Rome; accompanied Scipio to Spain (151) and Africa (147) and was present at destruction of Carthage (146); after defeat of Corinth by Rome (146), worked to secure a favorable settlement for his countrymen; occupied himself thereafter with writing *Histories,* a general history of Rome and nearby countries from 220 to 146 B.C. (40 books, of which only first 5 and a few fragments are extant).

Pol·y·carp \'päl-ē-ˌkärp\. Saint. 2d century A.D. Greek Christian martyr. One of the Apostolic Fathers; bishop of Smyrna; author of letter to the Philippians (extant); because of his righteousness and through his attacks on heresies, esp. Marcionism and Valentinian communities, became very influential in Smyrna and neighboring regions; burned at stake on demand of mob during a period of persecutions of Christians in Asia.

Pol·y·cli·tus *or* **Pol·y·clei·tus** \ˌpäl-i-'klīt-əs\ *or* **Pol·y·cle·tus** \-'klēt-əs\. 5th century B.C. Greek sculptor and architect of Sicyon. Credited with developing to highest perfection the abstract proportion which characterizes Greek sculpture; carved a figure *Doryphorus,* embodying athletic type in accepted correct proportions, which was called the "canon." Also carved *Diadumenus* and the chryselephantine *Hera* at Argos. A younger ¶Polyclitus (4th century B.C.) of the same family was a sculptor and architect; known esp. for the Tholos and the theater at Epidaurus.

Po·lyc·ra·tes \pə-'lik-rə-ˌtēz\. d. c.522 B.C. Tyrant of Samos (c.535–c.522 B.C.). Collected and armed a fleet of 100 ships and made himself master of the Aegean basin; became notorious for acts of piracy. Lured to mainland by Oroetes, Persian satrap of Lydia, and crucified (c.522 B.C.).

Pol·y·do·rus \ˌpäl-i-'dȯr-əs, -'dōr-\. 1st century B.C. Greek sculptor of Rhodes. Collaborated with Agesander and Athenodorus in carving the Laocoön group.

Polydoúre, Maria. See POLIDOÚRI.

Pol·y·euc·tos \päl-ē-'yük-tōs\. Saint. 3d century A.D. Christian martyr. A Roman military officer, became a Christian on example of a martyred friend; refused orders to worship Roman idols; destroyed several Roman temples; executed by sword in Armenia (probably 250); greatly venerated by Greek Orthodox adherents; patron saint of oaths.

Pol·yg·no·tus \ˌpäl-ig-'nōt-əs\. c.500–c.440 B.C. Greek painter. Received Athenian citizenship as reward for his paintings in the Poecile and Theseum; associated with Cimon in rebuilding Athens; also painted *Iliupersis* and *Nekyia* in hall of Cnidian, Delphi. Regarded as leading representative of Greek painting of his century.

Polyhistor, Alexander. See ALEXANDER POLYHISTOR.

Pol·y·per·chon \ˌpäl-i-'pər-ˌkän\ *or* **Pol·y·sper·chon** \-'spər-ˌkän\. c.380–c.303 B.C. Macedonian general. Served under Alexander the Great; succeeded Antipater as regent of Macedonia (319 B.C.); superseded by Cassander (317).

Po·ma·re \pō-'mär-ā\, Sir Maui Wiremu Pita Naera. 1876–1930. Maori physician and politician. M.P. (1911–30); as minister for Maori race (1912–28) helped form royal commissions that allowed the Taranaki Maori to buy back ancestral lands; minister of health (1923–26); as minister of Cook Islands (1916–28) improved educational and legal systems and fought monopoly trading interests.

Pombal, Marquês de. See CARVALHO E MELLO.

Pomeranus. See Johannes BUGENHAGEN.

Pom·fret \'pəm-frət, 'päm-\, John. 1667–1702. English poet. His poems included in Dr. Johnson's *Lives of the Poets* (1779); the most popular, *The Choice* (1700), achieved great popularity and was praised by Dr. Johnson.

Pompadour, Madame de. See Jeanne-Antoinette POISSON.

Pom·pe·ia \päm-'pē-ə\. 1st century B.C. Second wife of Julius Caesar. Married Caesar (67 B.C.), who repudiated her (61 B.C.) on suspicion of adultery on the grounds that "Caesar's wife must be above suspicion."

Pom·pe·ius \päm-'pē-əs\. *Eng.* Pom·pey \'päm-pē\. A Roman gens to which belonged several distinguished soldiers and politicians:

Gnaeus Pompeius Stra·bo \-'strā-bō\. d. 87 B.C. Politician. Father of Pompey the Great; quaestor in Sardinia (103 B.C.); praetor (94); propraetor in Sicily (93); consul (89); sponsored law conferring on inhabitants of Gallia Transpadana privileges accorded to Latin colonies.

¶Gnaeus Pompeius Mag·nus \-'mag-nəs\. *Eng.* Pompey the Great. 106–48 B.C. General and statesman. Ally of Sulla against Marius (83 ff.); aided in crushing Servile Insurrection (71); consul with Crassus (70); cleared sea of pirates (67); took command in the East (66), where he defeated Mithradates and annexed Syria and Palestine; enjoyed a triumph (61). Organized, with Julius Caesar and Crassus, First Triumvirate (61); consul (55). Became champion of Senate and conservative party; as sole consul (52) secured passage of reform laws; broke with Caesar (51); brought on civil war and was decisively defeated at Pharsalus (48); fled to Egypt for protection, but was murdered by order of Ptolemy. His son ¶Gnaeus Pompeius Magnus (75?–45 B.C.) commanded his father's fleet in Adriatic (48); after battle of Pharsalus (48), went to Africa and then to Spain; defeated at Munda by Caesar (45), captured and executed. A second son ¶Sextus Pompeius Magnus, *called* Pompey the Younger (75–35 B.C.) crossed into Spain after father's defeat at Thapsus (46); defeated by Caesar at Munda (45); proscribed by the triumvirate (43). Collected fleet and gained control of Sicily, whence he harassed shores of Italy. Defeated by Agrippa at Naulochus (36); fled to Asia Minor; captured and executed by Antony's troops.

Pompeius Trogus, Gnaeus. See TROGUS.

Pom·pi·dou \pōⁿ-pē-dü, *Angl* 'päm-pi-ˌdü\, Georges-Jean-Raymond. 1911–1974. French politician. Aide to Charles de Gaulle (1944–46); deputy director general of tourism (1946–49); as chief personal assistant to de Gaulle (1958–59) helped draft constitution of Fifth Republic and prepare economic plans; negotiated a cease-fire with Algerian nationalists (1961). Premier of France (1962–68); as president of France (1969–74) continued policies of de Gaulle.

Pompignan, Marquis de. See Jean-Jacques LEFRANC.

Pompilius, Numa. See NUMA POMPILIUS.

Pom·po·naz·zi \ˌpōm-pō-'nät-tsē\, Pietro. 1462–1525. Italian philosopher. Professor of philosophy at Padua (1488–96, 1499–1509), Ferrara (1496–99, 1510), Bologna (1511–25); a leading exponent of Aristotelianism; known chiefly for his anti-Thomistic *Tractatus de immortalitate animi* (1516), which provoked controversy involving Thomists, Averroists, and followers of Alexander of Aphrodisias; replied to attacks with *Apologia* (1518) and *Defensorium* (1519); also author of *De incantationibus* (1556) and *De fato* (1567).

Pom·po·ni·us \päm-'pō-nē-əs\, Lucius. *Surnamed* Bo·no·ni·en·sis \bə-ˌnō-nē-'en-səs\, *i.e.* of Bononia (Bologna). fl. c.90 B.C. Latin writer. With Novius first to give literary form and expression to *Fabulae atellanae,* rude popular farces of rural or urban life; only fragments of their works extant.

Pomponius Mela. See MELA.

Pomponne, Marquis de. See Simon ARNAULD.

Pomuk, Saint John of. See JOHN of Nepomuk.

Pon·ce \'pōn-sā\, Manuel María. 1886–1948. Mexican composer. Professor at Conservatorio Nacional, Mexico City (1909–45). His compositions included orchestral works as *Estampas nocturnas* (1923), *Chapultepec* (1929, rev. 1934), *Poema elegiaco* (1935), *Concierto del Sur* (1941), concertos for piano (1912), for violin (1943), chamber music, piano pieces, and songs, esp. "Estrellita" (1914).

Pon·ce de Le·ón \'pȯn-thā-t͟hā-lā-'ȯn, 'pȯn-sā-; *Angl* ˌpän(t)s-də-'lē-ən, ˌpän(t)-sə-ˌdā-lē-'ōn\, Juan. 1460–1521. Spanish explorer. Went to America with Columbus on second voyage (1493); to Puerto Rico (1508); made governor (1509); founded San Juan (1511); with three ships set out (1513) to search for Bimini, a fabulous island on which was said to be located the Fountain of Youth; discovered Florida at Easter time (Span. *Pascua Florida*) and coasted along east and west sides; visited Bahamas (1513); campaigned against Carib Indians and occupied Trinidad (1514). Made second expedition to Florida (1521); attempted settlement, but was driven off by natives and wounded; died on return to Cuba. Ponce, Puerto Rico, is named in his honor.

Pon·ce·let \pōⁿ-sle\, Jean-Victor. 1788–1867. French mathematician and engineer. Military engineer at Metz (1815–25); professor of mechanics, École de l'Application, Metz (1825–35); professor of applied mechanics, Paris (1838–48). A founder of modern projective geometry. Published *Traité des propriétés projectives des figures* (1822) and *Applications d'analyse et de géométrie* (1862–64); developed principle of duality; named and vindicated geometrical continuity; discovered the circular points at infinity.

Pon·cet \pōⁿ-se\, Charles-Jacques. d. 1706. French pharmacist. Practiced in Cairo (1687 ff.); in Gonder, Ethiopia, cured Emperor Iyasu I and son of leprosy (1699–1700); his account of journey, *A Voyage to Ethiopia in the Years 1698, 1699 and 1700,* is only European source of history of Ethiopia in that period.

Pon·chiel·li \pōŋ-'kyel-lē\, Amilcare. 1834–1886. Italian composer. Music director, Bergamo cathedral (1881–86); best known among his operas were *I promessi sposi* (1856; rev. 1872), *La gioconda* (1876) and *Il figliuol prodigo* (1880); also composed ballets *Le due gemelle* and *Clarina* (both 1873) and sacred music.

Pond \'pänd\, James Burton. 1838–1903. American lecture manager, b. Cuba, N.Y. Began managing lecturers (c.1873); copurchaser of Redpath Lyceum Bureau, Boston (1875–79); opened independent office, New York (1879). Among lecturers under his management were Henry Ward Beecher, Samuel Clemens, Charles Sumner, Sir Arthur Conan Doyle, Henry M. Stanley, Matthew Arnold, Ian Maclaren, Anthony Hope.

Pond, John. 1767–1836. English astronomer. Astronomer royal (1811–35); installed mercury horizon (1821) and otherwise improved and modernized equipment; published catalogue of 1112 stars, determined with superior accuracy (1833).

Po·nia·tow·ski \ˌpȯn-yä-'tȯf-skē\. Name of Polish princely family of Italian origin, including: Prince Stanisław Poniatowski (1676–1762), general and diplomat; joined Charles XII of Sweden in support of Stanisław Leszczyński in Great Northern War (1700–21); after war reconciled with Augustus II; grand treasurer of Lithuania (1722); commander in chief of Polish army (1728 ff.). His son Stanisław became king of Poland (see STANISŁAW II AUGUST). Another son ¶Andrzej (1735–1773) was a general in the Austrian army. ¶Prince Józef Antoni (1763–1813), son of Andrzej; commander in Napoléon's army; fought against Russia and aided Kościuszko (1792–94); joined French army (1800); active against Russians, esp. as minister of war in duchy of Warsaw (1807) and in campaign against Moscow; wounded at Smolensk (1812) and showed great valor at Leipzig; marshal of France (1813). ¶Prince Józef Michał (1816–1873), nephew of Józef Antoni, was a composer; naturalized Tuscan subject (1847); later resided in Paris; made senator by Napoléon III. Wrote many operas, as *Don Desiderio* (1840), *Ruy Blas* (1843), and *L'Aventurier* (1865), and several masses.

Pon Nya \pōn-'nyä\, U. fl. c.1850–66. Burmese writer. A courtier; author of plays, songs, and epistles with themes of court life; created a freer form of dramatic verse; his play *Water Seller* noted for realistic portrayal of the court.

Pons \pōⁿs\, Jean-Louis. 1761–1831. French astronomer. Director of Lucca (Italy) observatory (1819) and Florence observatory (1825); credited with discovery of 37 comets (1801–27).

Pons, Lily, *orig.* Alice-Joséphine. 1904–1976. American soprano, b. Draguignan, France. m. 2d Andre Kostelanetz (1938; div. 1958). Operatic debut as Lakmé at Mulhouse (1928); at Metropolitan Opera, N.Y.C., as Lucia (1931); reigning diva at the Met for 25 years. Chief roles, Lucia in *Lucia di Lammermoor,* Rosina in *The Barber of Seville,* Gilda in *Rigoletto.*

Pon·sard \pōⁿ-sȧr\, François. 1814–1867. French playwright. Vigorous opponent of Romanticism and leader of *école du bon sens;* author of a translation of Byron's *Manfred,* and the plays *Lucrèce* (1843), *Agnès de Méranie* (1846), *Charlotte Corday* (1850), *L'Honneur et l'argent* (1853), *Lion amoureux* (1866), etc.

Pon·son·by \'pən-sən-bē\. English family in Ireland, descended from Sir John (1608–1678), who as colonel of a regiment of cavalry accompanied Cromwell to Ireland (1649); received grants of land in Ireland; M.P. (1661). His great-grandson ¶John (1713–1789), Irish political leader; commissioner of revenue (1744–71); speaker of Irish House of Commons (1756–71); one of principal "undertakers," members of great families monopolizing government of Ireland; lost in contest for supremacy to adherents of Marquis of Townshend, viceroy of Ireland (1767–72). His son ¶George (1755–1817) became a Whig leader; chancellor of Irish exchequer (1782); urged claims of Irish Catholics; led opposition to union of parliaments; lord chancellor of Ireland (1806); official leader of opposition in British House of Commons (1808–17). ¶John William (1781–1847), 4th Earl of Bess·bor·ough \'bez-b(ə-)rə\ *and* Viscount Dun·can·non \(,)dən-'kan-ən, (,)dəŋ-\; grandson of John (1713–1789); a Whig leader in House of Commons (1805–34); member of House of Lords (from 1834); home secretary under Lord Melbourne (1834–35); lord lieutenant of Ireland (1846–47). ¶Sir Henry Frederick (1825–1895), nephew of 4th earl; served in Crimea (1855–56); major general (1868); private secretary to Queen Victoria (1870 ff.). ¶Vere Brabazon (1880–1956), 9th Earl of Bessborough and Viscount Duncannon; M.P. (1913–20); served in Gallipoli (1915) and on staff in France (1916–18); governor general of Canada (1931–35).

Ponsonby, William. 1546?–1604. English publisher. Proprietor of printing house in London (1577 ff.); among his publications were Robert Greene's *Mamillia* (1582), Sidney's *Arcadia* (1590), and 10 volumes of Spenser's works, including *The Faerie Queen* (1590, 1596).

Pon·son du Ter·rail \pōⁿ-sōⁿ-dü̅e-te-rȧy\, Pierre-Alexis. Vicomte. 1829–1871. French novelist. Author of adventure stories as *Les Coulisses du monde* (1853), *Les Exploits de Rocambole* (1859), and many sequels of the latter.

Pon·ta·no \pōn-'tän-ō\, Giovanni, *often called* Gioviano. *Lat.* Jovianus Pon·ta·nus \pän-'tā-nəs\. 1426–1503. Italian Humanist, poet, and statesman. Held offices under Aragonese dynasty in Naples (1447 ff.); state secretary to Ferdinand I of Naples (1486–95); head of Academia Pontaniana in Naples (1471 ff.). His writings, all in Latin, included a history *De bello Neapolitano,* philosophical treatises *De prudentia* and *De fortuna,* an astrological poem *Urania,* moral and literary dialogues, and lyrical poems, esp. *Lepidina* and the collection *De amore coniugali.*

Pon·te \'pōn-tā\, Antonio da. 1512–c.1595. Italian architect-engineer. Designed and built the Rialto Bridge (1587) and the Bridge of Sighs (1589), both in Venice.

Ponte, Jacopo da. See Jacopo BASSANO.

Ponte, Lorenzo da. See DA PONTE.

Pon·ti·ac \'pänt-ē-,ak\. c.1720–1769. American Ottawa Indian chief, b. in Ohio. Organized a general Indian attack, historically known as Pontiac's War, upon the British (1763), in which he led the Indians attacking Detroit; made peace (1766) and remained friendly with British.

Pon·tian \'pän-sh(ē-)ən\ *or* **Pon·ti·a·nus** \,pän-shē-'ā-nəs\. Saint. d. 235 A.D. Pope (230–235). Convened a synod that reaffirmed excommunication of Origen (231–232); banished (235) with antipope St. Hippolytus to Sardinia by Emperor Maximinus; abdicated in favor of St. Antherus.

Pontius Pilate. See PILATE.

Pon·ton \'pänt-ᵊn\, Mungo. 1802–1880. Scottish inventor. His discovery that sunlight renders potassium dichromate insoluble (1839) formed basis of development of photoengraving.

Pon·top·pi·dan \pȯn-'tȯp-ē-dän\, Erik. 1698–1764. Danish theologian. Bishop of Bergen (1747–55). Among his works were an exposition on Luther's catechism, *Truth unto Godliness,* and *A Natural History of Norway* (1752–53).

Pontoppidan, Henrik. 1857–1943. Danish novelist. Originally an engineer, began work in fiction (1881); shared with Karl Gjellerup the Nobel prize for literature (1917). Among his novels were *Skyer* (1890), *Det Forjaettede Land* (1891–95), *Den Gamle Adam* (1895), *Lykke-Per* (1898–1904), *De dødes rige* (1912–16), and *Mands Himmerig* (1927); also wrote short stories, plays, and 4 volumes of memoirs (1933–40).

Pon·tor·mo \pōn-'tōr-mō\, Jacopo da. *Also called* Jacopo Car·ruc·ci \kär-'rüt-chē\. 1494–1557. Italian painter of Florentine Mannerist school. Pupil of Leonardo da Vinci, Piero di Cosimo, and Andrea del Sarto. His works included *Visitation, Deposition, Adam and Eve Driven from Paradise, St. Sebastian, Venus and Cupid,* and portraits as of Andrea del Sarto and Cosimo de' Medici.

Pontus de Tyard. See TYARD.

Poole \'pül\, William Frederick. 1821–1894. American librarian, b. Salem, Mass. Began *Poole's Index to Periodical Literature* (1848; 3rd edition, 1882); librarian, Boston (1852–69), Cincinnati (1871–73), Chicago (1874–94); author of monographs on American colonial times.

Poor \'pu̇(ə)r, 'pō(ə)r\, Charles Lane. 1866–1951. American astronomer, b. Hackensack, N.J. Professor at Columbia U. (1903–44). Known for work on comets and polemical stand against theory of relativity. His works included *Gravitation versus Relativity* (1922), *The Relativity Deflection of Light* (1926), *What Einstein Really Did* (1930).

Poor, Henry Varnum. 1812–1905. American economist, b. Andover, Me. Editor of *American Railroad Journal* (1849–62); wrote *History of the Railroads and Canals of the United States* (1860). With his son ¶Henry William (1844–1915) began compilation and publication of railway statistics, the first "Poor's Manual," *Manual of the Railroads of the United States,* appearing in 1868; supplemented the manual with *Poor's Directory of Railway Officials* (1886–95), *Poor's Handbook of Investment Securities* (1890–92).

Poor Richard. See Benjamin FRANKLIN.

Poor·ten-Schwartz \'pōr-tən-'shvärts\, Joost Marius Willem van der. *Pseudonym* Maarten Maar·tens \'mär-təns\. 1858–1915. Dutch novelist. Wrote in English realistic and moral novels and stories, chiefly of Holland, including *The Sin of Joost Avelingh* (1889), *An Old Maid's Love* (1891), *God's Fool* (1892), *The Greater Glory* (1894), *The New Religion* (1907), *The Price of Lis Doris* (1909), etc.

Poot \'pōt\, Hubert Korneliszoon. 1689–1733. Dutch poet. Of peasant birth; self-taught; published *Mengeldichten* (1716, 1727) and became known as "the Dutch Hesiod."

Po·pé \pō-'pā, 'pō-(,)pā\. d. 1692. American Tewa Pueblo Indian leader. A medicine man; led an attack (Aug. 10, 1680) of Pueblo Indian tribes on Santa Fe, N.M., killing almost 500 and driving the Spanish out; erased Spanish-Christian influences and restored native customs and religion; became despotic; Spanish rule reestablished after his death.

Pope \'pōp\, Albert Augustus. 1843–1909. American manufacturer, b. Boston. After service in Civil War made fortune in Boston shoe supply business; founded (1877) in Hartford, Conn., a bicycle factory that produced thousands of vehicles; began (in 1890s) producing gasoline and electric automobiles in Hartford, Indianapolis, and Toledo, Ohio.

Pope, Alexander. 1688–1744. English poet. Developed physical deformity as result of severe illness at age 12; attracted Wycherley's attention with his verse (1704); came to public notice on publication of *Pastorals* in Tonson's *Miscellany* (1709); won Addison's praise for the *Essay on Criticism* (1711) and wide reputation with brilliant mock-heroic poem *The Rape of the Lock* (1712); gained friendship of Swift with *Windsor Forest* (1713); with Swift, Gay, Arbuthnot, formed Scriblerus Club (1713) and collaborated on the *Memoirs of Martinus Scriblerus* (1741); earned independence with his translations of the *Iliad* (1715–20) and *Odyssey* (1725–26). Jointly with Swift published *Miscellanies* (1727–32), parodies upon writers, which evoked storm of abusive and scurrilous retorts from those who thought themselves injured; answered these in famous lampoon *Dunciad* (1728, 1742). Under influence of his friend Lord Bolingbroke, attempted systematic survey of human nature, completing *Essay on Man* (1733), lines and couplets of which have become household quotations, and four *Moral Essays;* in his last works, *Imitations of Horace* (1733–38), satirized contemporary social and political scene and defended himself; by a stratagem, secured publication of his letters (1735) as though they were pirated; published a "corrected" edition of letters (1737); began a blank verse epic, *Brutus,* incomplete at his death.

Pope, John. 1822–1892. American army commander, b. Louisville, Ky. Brigadier general of Union volunteers (1861); commanded army of the Mississippi in operations to open up navigation (1862); major general of volunteers (1862);

cooperated with Grant, Buell, and Halleck in move against Corinth, Miss. (1862); commanded army of Virginia, and was defeated at Second Bull Run (1862); relieved of command and sent to department of the Northwest; major general, U.S. army (1882); retired (1886).

Pope, John Russell. 1874–1937. American architect, b. New York City. A leading exponent of academic eclecticism. Among buildings designed by him were Scottish Rite Temple in Washington, D.C.; Lincoln Memorial in Hodgenville, Ky.; American Battle Monument at Montfaucon, France; City Hall in Plattsburg, N.Y.; Terminal Station, Richmond, Va.; National Gallery of Art, Washington, D.C.

Pope, Sir Thomas. 1507?–1559. English court clerk. Privy councilor in Queen Mary's reign; retained Queen Elizabeth's favor; bought Oxford house of abbey of Durham and with this initial site and building founded and endowed Trinity Coll., Oxford (chartered 1556).

Pope, Sir William Jackson. 1870–1939. English chemist. Professor at Cambridge (1908–39); known for work in crystallography and in organic chemistry; prepared first optically active sulfur, tin, and selenium compounds; developed method for producing mustard gas in great quantities.

Pop·ham \ˈpäp-əm\, Sir John. 1531?–1607. English judge. Solicitor general (1579); speaker of House of Commons (1580); attorney general (1581); lord chief justice (1592); presided at trials of Sir Walter Raleigh and Guy Fawkes; advocate of transportation system for convicts.

Po·pov \(ˌ)pəp-ˈóf\, Aleksandr Stepanovich. 1859–1905. Russian physicist and electrical engineer. Working independently of Marconi, constructed sensitive filings coherer for receiving electromagnetic signals (1895); developed (1898) this device into a ship-to-shore radio for Russian navy; acclaimed in Soviet Union as the inventor of radio.

Pop·paea Sa·bi·na \pä-ˈpē-ə-sə-ˈbī-nə\. d. 65 A.D. Roman woman. Wife of Rufius Crispinus; became mistress of Otho, divorced her husband, and married Otho; became mistress of Nero, divorced Otho, and married Nero (62); usually blamed as chief instigator of Nero's crimes; died as result of a kick from Nero.

Pöp·pel·mann \ˈpœp-əl-ˌmän\, Matthäus Daniel. 1662–1736. German architect. Architect of Augustus the Strong (1705); regarded as one of greatest masters of Baroque style. Chief work, pavilion of the Zwinger (unfinished) in Dresden.

Poquelin, Jean-Baptiste. See MOLIÈRE.

Porbus. See POURBUS.

Por·cia \ˈpōr-sh(ē-)ə, ˈpór-\. d. 42 B.C. Roman woman. Daughter of Cato of Utica; wife of Bibulus, then of Brutus, assassin of Julius Caesar; committed suicide after battle of Philippi, reputedly by swallowing live coals. Introduced (under spelling Portia) by Shakespeare in *Julius Caesar.*

Porcupine, Peter. See William COBBETT.

Pordenone. See Giovanni de' SACCHIS.

Por·phy·ry \ˈpór-f(ə-)rē\. *Lat.* Por·phyr·i·us \pór-ˈfi(ə)r-ē-əs\. *Orig. name* Mal·chus \ˈmal-kəs\. c.234–c.305. Greek scholar and Neoplatonic philosopher, b. Palestine. Studied under Cassius Longinus and, in Rome (263–268?), under Plotinus; lectured on philosophy in Rome; vigorously defended paganism and opposed Christianity. Author of *Adversus Christianos* (15 books, only fragments of which are extant), of lives of Plotinus and Pythagoras, of commentaries on Aristotle and on Homer, and of *Chronicles* (from capture of Troy down to 270 A.D.); edited works of Plotinus as *Enneads* (301).

Por·po·ra \ˈpōr-pō-(ˌ)rä\, Nicola Antonio Giacinto. 1686–1768. Italian composer and teacher of singing. Teacher in Naples (1719), Venice (1725, 1744), Vienna and Dresden (1728), London (1733–36), Vienna (1745–47). His pupils included Antonio Uberti, Farinelli, Caffarelli, and Pietro Metastasio; taught composition to Haydn (1752). In London (1733–36) as chief composer to Opera of the Nobility, formed to compete with Handel. Composer of 53 operas, esp. *Berenice* (1718, with Scarlatti), *Ermenegilda* (1729), *Polifemo* (1735), *Ifigenia in Aulide* (1735), and *Il trionfo di Camilla* (1740, rev. 1760), 6 oratorios, 6 chamber symphonies, 12 violin sonatas, and much church music.

Por·ras \ˈpór-räs\, Belisario. 1856–1942. Panamanian politician. Minister to U.S. (1910); president of Panama (1912–16, 1920–24), acting president (1918–20).

Porrée, Gilbert de La. See GILBERT DE LA PORRÉE.

Por·res \ˈpór-räs\, Martín de. Saint. 1579–1639. Peruvian Dominican friar. Son of a Spanish grandee and a black woman; became a Dominican oblate (1601) and friar (1610); noted for his kindness, nursing of the sick, obedience, and caring for the poor; considered national patron of social justice; canonized (1962).

Porsena, Lars. See LARS PORSENA.

Por·son \ˈpórs-ən\, Richard. 1759–1808. English classical scholar. Became widely known by his *Letters to Archdeacon Travis* (1788–89), an acute piece of criticism in defense of Gibbon's position on the genuineness of John i:7; regius professor of Greek, Cambridge (1792). Edited four plays of Euripides; edited Aeschylus (1792); made distinct contributions to knowledge of iambic and trochaic verse; by minute collations of Greek texts made valuable emendations.

Porta, Baccio della. See Fra BARTOLOMMEO.

Por·ta \ˈpór-tä\, Carlo. 1775–1821. Italian poet. Leading Milanese dialect poet; known esp. for dialect satires against nobility, clergy, and classicists, as *Fraa Diodatt, Fraa Zenever, Le desgrazzi di Giovannin Bougee,* and *Ninetta del Verzee.*

Porta, Giacomo della. c.1537–1602. Italian architect. Pupil of Vignola; completed various works begun by Vignola, including the façades of the churches Santa Caterina de'Funari and Il Gesù; completed the cupola of St. Peter's (1588–90) according to Michelangelo's model and the Palazzo Farnese (begun by Michelangelo). Other works included Villa Aldobrandini (1598–1604, at Frascati) and several fountains in Rome.

Porta, Giambattista della. 1535?–1615. Italian natural philosopher. Founded Accademia dei Segreti (c.1578) and helped in reconstitution of Accademia dei Lincei (1610); made important physical observations, although much of his work was from point of view of magic and alchemy; first to recognize heating effect of light rays; made improvements in the camera obscura, although he did not invent it. His writings included *Magia naturalis* (1558), *Arte del ricordare* (1566), *Villae* (1583–92, agricultural encyclopedia), *De' spiritali* (1606, containing description of a steam engine), and *De distillatione* (1609).

Por·taas \ˈpór-tós\, Herman Theodor. *Pseudonym* Herman Wil·den·vey \ˈvil-dən-ˌvā\. 1886–1959. Norwegian poet. Author of light, melodic verse published as *Campanula* (1902), *Nyinger* (1907), *Ringsgang* (1910), *Kjaertegn* (1916), *Hemmeligheter* (1919), *Ildorkestret* (1923), *Der falder stjerner* (1926), *Høstens lyre* (1931), *En ung manns flukt* (1936), *Ved sangens kilder* (1947), *Ugler til Athen* (1953), *Soluret* (1956); also wrote short stories, plays, reminiscences.

Por·tal \ˈpōrt-əl, ˈpórt-\, Charles Frederick Algernon. 1st Viscount Portal of Hun·ger·ford \ˈhəŋ-gə-fərd\. 1893–1971. British air chief marshal. Entered Royal Flying Corps (1915); director of organization in air ministry (1937–38); chief of bomber command (1940); chief of air staff (1940–46); created viscount (1946); controller of atomic energy, Ministry of Supply (1946–51); chairman, British Aircraft Corp. (1960 ff.).

Por·ta·les \pór-ˈtäl-ās\, Diego José Victor. 1793–1837. Chilean politician. A leader in revolution of 1829; as chief minister (1830–37) of ruling Conservative party was virtual dictator of Chile; hated by populace for repressive measures; credited with establishment of political order and instituting economic progress; initiated war with Peru–Bolivian confederation (1836); after his assassination became a symbol of Chilean unity.

Por·ta·lis \pór-tȧ-lēs\, Jean-Étienne-Marie. 1746–1807. French jurist and politician. Member of Conseil des Anciens (1795); one of four members of commission that drafted the Code Napoléon (1800–04). His son ¶Comte Joseph-Marie (1778–1858) was a councilor of state and count of the Empire under Napoléon; a peer of France, guardian of the seals, and minister of foreign affairs under Louis XVIII; first president of Court of Cassation (1829–51); senator (1851).

Por·te·ous \ˈpór-tē-əs, -tyəs, ˈpōr-\, John. d. 1736. Scottish soldier. Captain of Edinburgh city guard who fired on crowd at execution of a smuggler, killing or wounding nearly 30 persons (1736); sentenced to death, reprieved by Queen Caroline, taken from prison and hanged by an armed group in disguise. Incident (frequently called the Porteous riots) developed in Scott's *Heart of Midlothian.*

Porter, Charlotte E. See under Helen A. CLARKE.

Por·ter \ˈpōrt-ər, ˈpórt-\, Cole Albert. 1891–1964. American composer and lyricist, b. Peru, Ind. While at Yale composed football songs "Bingo Eli Yale" and "Bulldog." Widely known for his urbane, witty lyrics and sinuous music composed for such musicals as *Fifty Million Frenchmen* (1929, included "You Do Something to Me"), *Wake Up and Dream* (1929, "What Is This Thing Called Love"), *Gay Divorce* (1932, "Night and Day"), *Anything Goes* (1934, title song, "I Get a Kick Out of You," "You're the Top," "All Through the Night"), *Jubilee* (1935, "Begin the Beguine," "Just One of Those Things"), *Leave It to Me* (1938, "My Heart Belongs to Daddy"), *Dubarry Was a Lady* (1939, "Do I Love You"), *Panama Hattie* (1940), *Kiss Me Kate* (1948, "Wunderbar"), *Can-Can* (1953, "I Love Paris, " "C'est Magnifique," "It's All Right with Me"), and *Silk Stockings* (1955); other songs, many written for films, included "Let's Do It" (1928), "I've Got You Under My Skin" (1936), "In the Still of the Night" (1937), "I Concentrate on You" (1940).

Porter, David. 1780–1843. American naval officer, b. Boston. Served in wars against France (1799) and Tripoli (1801–05); in War of 1812 commanded the *Essex,* which became first U.S. naval vessel in Pacific waters; captured Nuku Hiva Island (1813); was captured off Valparaiso, Chile (1814). Member of

Board of Naval Commissioners (1815–23); commander in chief, West India squadron suppressing piracy (1823–25); court-martialed and suspended from duty for retaliatory action against Spanish authorities in Puerto Rico (1825–26); resigned from U.S. navy (1826). Commander in chief of Mexican navy (1826–29). U.S. consul general to Algiers (1830); U.S. chargé d'affaires at Constantinople and later (1839) U.S. minister to Turkey; died at Constantinople; David Glasgow FARRAGUT was his adopted son. His son ¶David Dixon (1813–1891) was also a naval officer; served under his father in the West Indies and in the Mexican navy; in Civil War, commanded mortar fleet under Farragut at New Orleans and on the Mississippi (1862), aided in reduction of Vicksburg and forts at Grand Gulf (1863); promoted rear admiral (1863); commanded naval forces in attack on Fort Fisher (Dec. 1864–Jan. 1865); superintendent of U.S. Naval Academy (1865–69), improved curriculum; admiral (1870); chaired naval board of inspection (1877–91).

Porter, Edwin Stanton. 1870–1941. American director-photographer, b. Connellsville, Pa. Joined (1899) Thomas A. Edison as cameraman and motion-picture director; for Edison made *The Life of an American Fireman* (1903), first American documentary and first film to use dramatic editing; also for Edison made *The Great Train Robbery* (1903), which used first close-up and set pattern for Westerns. Headed own film company, Rex (1909–12); chief director, Famous Players Film Co. (1912–16).

Porter, Eleanor, *nee* Hodg·man \ˈhäj-mən\. 1868–1920. American writer, b. Littleton, N.H. m. John Lyman Porter (1892). Author of many short stories and the novels *Cross Currents* (1907), *The Story of Marco* (1911), *Pollyanna* (1913), *Pollyanna Grows Up* (1915), *Just David* (1916), *The Road to Understanding* (1917), *Dawn* (1919), *Mary-Marie* (1920), etc.

Porter, Endymion. 1587–1649. English courtier. Groom of the bedchamber to Charles I and one of his most trusted advisers; undertook several diplomatic missions to Spain; patron of literature, esp. Davenant.

Porter, Gene, *nee* Strat·ton \ˈstrat-ᵊn\. 1868–1924. American author, b. Wabash County, Ind. m. Charles D. Porter (1886). Author of sentimental novels and stories as *Freckles* (1904), *At the Foot of the Rainbow* (1908), *A Girl of the Limberlost* (1909), *The Harvester* (1911), *Laddie* (1913), *Michael O'Halloran* (1915), *A Daughter of the Land* (1918), *The White Flag* (1923), *The Keeper of the Bees* (1925), and a volume of poems *The Fire Bird* (1922).

Porter, George Richardson. 1792–1852. English statistician. Headed statistical department of Board of Trade (1834 ff.); author of *The Progress of the Nation* (1836–43), a valuable source of early 19th century information.

Porter, Henry. fl. 1596–1599. English dramatist. Associate of Henry Chettle and Ben Jonson; wrote *The Two Angry Women of Abington* (1599).

Porter, Jane. 1776–1850. English novelist. Gained popularity with romances, *Thaddeus of Warsaw* (1803) and *The Scottish Chiefs* (1810); later novels included *The Pastor's Fireside* (1815), *Sir Edward Seaward's Narrative* (1831), and *The Field of Forty Footsteps* (1828).

Porter, Katherine Anne, *in full* Katherine Anne Maria Veronica Callista Russell. 1890–1980. American writer, b. Indian Creek, Tex. Newspaper reporter in Denver (1918–19); lived in Mexico (early 1920s); writer-in-residence at several colleges. Author of novel *Ship of Fools* (1962), collection of essays *The Days Before* (1952), and collections of short stories *Flowering Judas* (1930), *Pale Horse, Pale Rider* (1939), *The Leaning Tower* (1944), and *Collected Short Stories* (1965, Pulitzer prize and National Book Award).

Porter, Noah. 1811–1892. American clergyman and educator, b. Farmington, Conn. President of Yale (1871–86). Editor in chief, *Webster's American Dictionary of the English Language,* popularly known as *Webster's Unabridged* (1864), and of *Webster's International Dictionary of the English Language* (1890). Author of *The Human Intellect* (1868), *The Sciences of Nature versus the Science of Man* (1871), etc. His sister ¶Sarah (1813–1900) was founder (1843) of Miss Porter's School for Girls at Farmington, Conn.

Porter, Quincy, *in full* William Quincy. 1897–1966. American composer, b. New Haven, Conn. Studied under David Stanley Smith, Horatio Parker, Vincent d'Indy, and Ernest Bloch; dean (1938–42) and director (1942–46), New England Conservatory, Boston; professor, Yale (1946–65). Composer of orchestral works, esp. *Suite in C Minor* (1926), *Symphony* (1927), *Poem and Dance* (1932), *Concerto for Two Pianos* (1954), and *New England Episodes* (1958), and of chamber music, esp. 9 string quartets.

Porter, Rodney Robert. 1917–1985. British biochemist. With National Institute for Medical Research (1949–60); professor of immunology, London (1960–67); professor of biochemistry, U. of Oxford (1967–85); developed (1958) system of using enzymes to split antibodies and determined (1960) the peptide chains in antibody molecules; propounded concept of a four-chain structure in antibodies and facilitated understanding of relation between different classes of antibody. With Gerald M. Edelman awarded 1972 Nobel prize for physiology or medicine.

Porter, Sarah. See under Noah PORTER.

Porter, William Sydney. *Pseudonym* O. Hen·ry \ˈō-ˈhen-rē\. 1862–1910. American short-story writer, b. Greensboro, N.C. Employed in drugstore (to 1882); settled in Austin, Texas, as clerk and bookkeeper (1885–87), draftsman in a land office (1887–91), and bank teller (1891–94). Failed in editorship of humorous weekly the *Rolling Stone* (1894–95); columnist on Houston *Daily Post* (1895–96). Imprisoned (1898) for 3 years for embezzlement when he was bank teller. To New York (1902) and devoted himself to short-story writing, achieving great success. His stories, characterized by trick endings, appeared in magazines and the *New York World,* and were collected in *Cabbages and Kings* (1904), *The Four Million* (1906), *Heart of the West* (1907), *The Trimmed Lamp* (1907), *The Gentle Grafter* (1908), *The Voice of the City* (1908), *Options* (1909), *Roads of Destiny* (1909), *Whirligigs* (1910), *Strictly Business* (1910), *Sixes and Sevens* (1911), *Rolling Stones* (1913), *Waifs and Strays* (1917), *Postscripts* (1923).

Por·than \pȯr-ˈtän\, Henrik Gabriel. 1739–1804. Finnish scholar. Professor of rhetoric at Åbo U. (1777 ff.); regarded as founder of study of Finnish language and literature.

Portia. See PORCIA.

Por·ti·na·ri \ˌpōr-tē-ˈnär-ē\, Beatrice. 1266–1290. Florentine noblewoman. Wife of Simone de' Bardi. Seen by Dante when he was 9, she became his ideal lady and inspired most of his poetry, esp. *La vita nuova,* which is a chronicle of their relationship, and *Divina commedia,* where she guides him through "Paradiso."

Por·ti·na·ri \pȯr-tē-ná-ˈrē\, Cándido. 1903–1962. Brazilian painter. Influenced by Mexican fresco painting and by Picasso; known for his canvases of peasants and laborers and for his wall paintings in Library of Congress, Washington, D.C. (1941–42), and in UN building, New York (1950–56).

Port·land \ˈpōrt-lənd, ˈpȯrt-\, Earls and dukes of. English earldom held (1633–88) by Weston family (see Richard WESTON), revived (1689) and bestowed by William III upon William Bentinck (*q.v.*); held by Bentinck family when merged (1716) with dukedom of Portland.

Portogallo, Marcantonio. See FONSECA PORTUGAL.

Por·to·lá \pȯr-tō-ˈlä\, Gaspar de. c.1723–c.1784. Spanish soldier in America. Appointed governor of the Californias (1767); made thousand-mile march from Velicatá in Lower California, exploring site of present-day Los Angeles and San Francisco Bay and founding San Diego and Monterey (1769); left region (1770); governor of Puebla (1776).

Por·to-Riche \pȯr-tō-rēsh\, Georges de. 1849–1930. French playwright. Author of psychological dramas about the eternal triangle of wife, husband, and lover, including *La Chance de Françoise* (1889), *Amoureuse* (1891), *Le Passé* (1897), *Le Vieil Homme* (1911), *Le Marchand d'estampes* (1917).

Portsmouth, Duchess of. See Louise-Renée de KÉROUALLE.

Portugal, Marcos Antônio da Fonseca. See FONSECA PORTUGAL.

Po·rus \ˈpōr-əs\. d. between 321 and 315 B.C. Indian king who ruled a country in the Indus valley (in modern northern Punjab). Opposed Alexander in his invasion of India; completely defeated (326 B.C.) in the battle of the Hydaspes by Alexander's small Macedonian force; his life spared and kingdom restored; became supporter of Alexander; assassinated by agents of Eudamus.

Po·sa·da \pō-ˈsäth-ä\, José Guadalupe. 1851–1913. Mexican printmaker. His woodcut and lead cut illustrations, many in expressionistic or surrealistic styles, appeared in broadsides depicting lurid crimes and political scandals; also illustrated popular book and song covers; exerted considerable influence on Mexican revolutionary artists, esp. Orozco.

Po·sey \ˈpō-zē\, Thomas. 1750–1818. American Revolutionary officer and politician, b. Fairfax Co., Va. Served through the Revolution; brigadier general in war against Indians in the Northwest (1793–94); U.S. senator from Louisiana (1812–13); governor of Indiana Territory (1813–16).

Pos·i·do·ni·us \ˌpäs-ə-ˈdō-nē-əs\ *or* **Pos·ei·do·ni·us** \ˌpäs-ˌī-\, *called* the Athlete. c.135–c.51 B.C. Greek Stoic philosopher, b. Syria. Pupil of Panaetius; traveled in Gaul, Spain, Italy, Liguria, Africa, and Sicily; settled and taught in Rhodes; teacher (78–77) and friend of Cicero; did more to spread stoicism in Roman world than anyone except Panaetius; wrote general history of period 146–88 B.C., treatise on natural philosophy, essay on the gods, etc. Reputed the most learned man of his time. None of his works is extant.

Post \ˈpōst\, Charles Williams. 1854–1914. American manufacturer, b. Springfield, Ill. Established (1891) a sanitarium, La Vita Inn, at Battle Creek, Mich.; experimented with various health and prepared food products; made fortune selling a coffee substitute Postum (1895) and a line of breakfast foods as Grape Nuts (1897), Post Toasties, Post's Bran Flakes, etc.; opponent of organized labor; founded (1905) town of Post, Texas.

Post \ˈpȯst\, Christian Frederick. 1710?–1785. Moravian missionary in America, b. Konitz, East Prussia. Cabinetmaker by trade; to America (1742); performed missionary work among Indians of New York and Pennsylvania (1740s and 50s); secured allegiance to British authorities of Indians in western Pennsylvania (1758), resulting in French retreat from Fort Duquesne; continued missionary work in Ohio and Nicaragua.

Post \ˈpōst\, Emil Leon. 1897–1954. American mathematician, b. Augustów, Poland. To U.S. (1904); professor at City College of New York (1935–54); gave

(1921) a decision procedure for classical propositional calculus which is considered the beginning of modern proof theory.

Post, Emily, *nee* Price \'prīs\. 1872–1960. American writer and columnist, b. Baltimore, Md. m. Edwin M. Post (1892; div. 1906). Contributor to newspapers and magazines, esp. of articles on manners and social etiquette; author of *Etiquette* (1st ed., 1922), and other books.

Post, Melville Davisson. 1871–1930. American lawyer and detective-story writer, b. Romines Mills, W. Va. Author of *The Strange Schemes of Randolph Mason* (1896), *The Man of Last Resort* (1897), *Uncle Abner: Master of Mysteries* (1918), *The Mystery at the Blue Villa* (1919), *The Man Hunters* (1926), *The Bradmoor Murder* (1929), etc.

Post \'pòst\, Pieter. 1608–1669. Dutch architect. Secretary to Constantijn Huygens; architect to Prince Frederick Henry (1645 ff.). His designs in The Hague included Mauritshuis (c.1633, with Jacob van Campen), Swanenburg House (1645), Huis ten Bosch (1645–47, with van Campen), and Nieuwkoop almshouses (1658); also designed the Maastricht town hall (1656 ff.) and the weighthouse in Leiden (1658).

Post \'pōst\, Wiley. 1899–1935. American aviator, b. Grand Saline, Tex. With Harold Gatty (*q.v.*) as navigator, flew around the world (June 23–July 1, 1931) and published a book about it, *Around the World in Eight Days* (1931); made first solo flight around world, proving value of automatic pilot and other instruments (1933); designed a pioneer version of the pressure suit; killed with Will Rogers in airplane crash.

Postl, Karl Anton. See Charles SEALSFIELD.

Pos·tu·mus \'päs-t(y)ə-məs\, Marcus Cassianius Latinius. d. 268 A.D. Roman general and emperor. General in Cologne; set himself up as emperor of Gaul (c.258–268), thus becoming a rival to Gallienus; created a senate and struck own coinage; supported and succeeded by Victorinus; killed in mutiny of legion at Mogontiacum.

Po·ta·gos \pò-'täg-òs\, Panayotis. 1839–1903. Greek physician and traveler. Visited Mesopotamia, Persia, Afghanistan, the Gobi Desert, and India (1867–76); ascended the Nile to southern Sudan, crossed into the Congo River Basin, and explored the Uele River system in northern Zaire (1876–77), penetrating deeper into east central Africa than any European of his time.

Po·tem·kin \(,)pə-'tyòm-kyin\, Grigory Aleksandrovich. 1739–1791. Russian statesman. Officer in Horse Guards (1755); conspirator in plot against Peter III (1762); distinguished himself against Turks (1768–74) and became chief favorite of Catherine II (1774); created field marshal (1784); constructed fleet in Black Sea; planned colonization of Ukrainian steppes; annexed Crimea; built arsenal of Kherson (1778) and harbor of Sevastopol (1784); commander in chief of Russian army against Turkey (1787–91); created prince of Tauris (1787).

Pot·gie·ter \'pòt-,kēt-ər\, Andries Hendrik. 1792–1852. Boer colonizer. Led farmers in exodus (1836) to Vet River; expelled the Matabele (1837) with heavy losses and occupied the country across Vaal River; migrated (1838) to Mooi River and (1845) towards Delagoa Bay; founded several settlements in Transvaal region; after British annexation of Natal received more independent Boers; joined (1852) in pact with Pretorius for cooperation in uniting the Transvaal.

Pot·gie·ter \'pòt-,gēt-ər\, Everhardus Johannes. 1808–1875. Dutch writer. By trade a commercial agent in Amsterdam. Cofounder of magazine *De muzen* (1834–36), later superseded by *De gids* (*The Guide*), which became leading literary monthly of the Netherlands; contributor to this periodical. Among his books in prose were *Het Noorden* (1836–40), *Jan, Jannetje en hun jongste* (1842), *Het Rijksmuseum* (1844), *Een novelle?* (1864), *Onder weg in den regen* (1864); his verse included *Liedekens van Bontekoe* (1840), *Ter Gedachtenis* (1863), *Florence* (1868), and *De nalatenschap van den landjonker* (1875).

Po·thier \pò-tyā\, Joseph, *called* Dom Joseph. 1835–1923. French monk and music scholar. Prior of Ligugé (1893); abbot of Saint-Wandrille (1898); helped found *Paléographie musicale* (1889); editor, *Revue du chant grégorien* (1892–1914); appointed by Pope Pius X chairman of commission for reconstitution of music for church masses. With Dom Paul Jausions (d. 1870) did pioneer work in restoration of Gregorian chants and published *Les Mélodies grégoriennes d'après la tradition* (1880) and *Liber gradualis* (1883).

Pothier, Robert-Joseph. 1699–1772. French jurist. Author of legal treatises which were incorporated almost verbatim in the French Code Civil.

Po·toc·ki \pò-'tòt-skē\. Distinguished Polish family, including: Count Ignacy (1750–1809), statesman; as leader of Patriots faction engineered national alliance with Prussia (1790), pressed for administrative reforms, and, with Hugo Kołłątaj (*q.v.*), wrote major provisions of constitution of May 3, 1791; fled to Dresden after Russian invasion (1792); supported Kościuszko in his rebellion (1794); foreign minister of insurrectionary government (1794); state prisoner in St. Petersburg (1794–96); died while on diplomatic mission to Napoléon. His brother ¶Stanisław Kostka (1757?–1821) collaborated with Ignacy and others in drafting constitution of May 3, 1791; became head of educational system in duchy of Warsaw (1807) and minister of public instruction in kingdom of Poland (1815). ¶Alfred (1817–1889); Austrian minister of agriculture (1867–68); premier (1870–71); supporter of imperial federalism; parliamentary boycott of Czechs and Poles forced his resignation; governor of Galicia (1875–83).

Potocki, Wacław. 1625–c.1697. Polish poet. A country squire; author of devotional verse, epigrams (written 1670–95, published in 1907 as *Ogród fraszek*), *Argenida* (1697, allegorical verse novel), and, most notably, an epic, *Wojna chocimska* (completed 1670, published 1850) on the victory over the Turks at Chocim.

Pott \'pòt\, August Friedrich. 1802–1887. German philologist. Professor, Halle (1833–87). Established modern etymological studies on basis of correspondence of sounds occurring in related words in Indo-European languages; chief works, *Etymologische Forschungen* (1833–36), *Die Zigeuner in Europa und Asien* (1844–45), etc.

Pott \'pät\, Percivall. 1714–1788. English surgeon. Introduced improvements making surgery more humane, took steps toward abolishing extensive use of escharotics and cautery; suffered (1756) a particular kind of fracture of ankle, still called Pott's fracture; gave (1779) clinical description of a spinal affliction known as Pott's disease.

Pot·ter \'pät-ər\, Alonzo. 1800–1865. American clergyman, b. Dutchess Co., N.Y. Consecrated Episcopal bishop of Pennsylvania (1845); established Episcopal hospital (1860) and a divinity school (1863) in Philadelphia. His son ¶Henry Codman (1835–1908) was also a Protestant Episcopal clergyman; pastorates, Troy, N.Y. (1859–66), Trinity Church, Boston (1866–68), Grace Church, New York (1868–83); assistant bishop (1883), bishop (1887) of New York; initiated work (1892) on Cathedral of St. John the Divine; protested vice and corruption in New York (1899), resulting in investigation by Committee of Fifteen and election of Seth Low as a mayor pledged to reform; established respectable places where poor could buy intoxicating liquors (1904), protected liberal churchmen in his diocese. Author of *The Scholar and the State* (1897), *The Modern Man and His Fellow Man* (1903), etc.

Potter, Beatrice. See under Sidney WEBB.

Potter, Beatrix, *in full* Helen Beatrix. 1866–1943. English writer and illustrator. Famous for children's books featuring animal characters and her watercolor illustrations; first book began (1893) as a letter to a sick child and was privately published (1900) as *The Tale of Peter Rabbit;* followed by *The Tailor of Gloucester* (1902), *The Tale of Squirrel Nutkin, The Tale of Benjamin Bunny, The Tale of Jemima Puddle-Duck,* etc.

Potter, Edward Clark. 1857–1923. American sculptor, b. New London, Conn. Collaborated with Daniel Chester French in sculptures for Chicago World's Fair (1893); also in statues of Grant in Philadelphia, Hooker in Boston, and Devens in Worcester, Mass. Best known for animal sculptures and equestrian statues, esp. the *Sleeping Faun* in Chicago Art Institute and *Lions* on either side of the entrance to New York Public Library.

Pot·ter \'pò-tər\, Paul *or* Paulus. 1625–1654. Dutch painter. Famous for paintings of animals in rural settings; best known canvases *Young Bull* (1647), *Early Morning* (1647), and *Orpheus Charming the Beasts* (1650).

Pot·tier \pò-tyā\, Eugène. 1816–1887. French songwriter and politician. Member of the Paris Commune (1871); his poems collected under title *Chants révolutionnaires* (1887); among his songs was the "Internationale" (1871, music by Adolphe Degeyter), adopted as the rallying song of Communism.

Pot·tin·ger \'pät-ᵊn-jər, -iŋ-\, Sir Henry. 1789–1856. British soldier and diplomat, b. Ireland. Served during Marāthā War; political agent in Sindh (1836–40); led forces in first Opium War (1839–42); negotiated Treaty of Nanking (1842), by which China ceded Hong Kong; first British governor of Hong Kong (1843); governor of Cape of Good Hope (1846–47); governor of Madras (1847–54).

Pou·chet \pü-she\, Félix-Archimède. 1800–1872. French naturalist. Professor at École de Médecine, Rouen (1838 ff.); his *Hétérogénie ou traité de la génération spontanée* (1859), in which he advocated doctrine of spontaneous generation, gave rise to controversy with Pasteur.

Pouil·let \pü-je\, Claude-Servais-Mathias. 1790–1868. French physicist. Professor of physics, the Sorbonne (1838–52); invented a pyrheliometer; studied electric currents and compressibility of gases; measured solar heat and atmospheric absorption (1837).

Pou·lenc \pü-laⁿk\, Francis-Jean-Marcel. 1899–1963. French composer. Influenced by Ravel and Satie; with Auric, Honegger, Milhaud, et al., grouped as "Les Six"; on piano accompanied baritone Pierre Bernac in a series of tours (1934 ff.); his songs among finest of 20th century. His orchestral, choral, and vocal compositions included *Rapsodie nègre* (1917), *Sonata for Piano Duet* (1918), *Trois mouvements perpétuels* (1918), *Les Biches* (1924, ballet), song cycles *Poèmes de Ronsard* (1924) and *Chansons galliardes* (1926), *Concert champêtre* (1928), *Concerto for 2 Pianos* (1932), *Mass in G Major* (1937), *Organ Concerto* (1938), *Figure humaine* (1945, cantata), *Les Mamelles de Tirésias* (1947), *Piano Concerto* (1950), *Stabat Mater* (1951), and *Oboe Sonata* (1962).

Poulett. See PAULET.

Poul·sen \'paủl-sən\, Valdemar. 1869–1942. Danish electrical engineer. Invented telegraphone, an instrument for recording and reproducing sound by magnetization of a steel wire, disk, or ribbon (1898); invented an arc generator for high-frequency continuous electrical oscillations, used in wireless telegraphy and telephony (1903).

Pound \'paủnd\, Sir Dudley, *in full* Alfred Dudley Pickman Rogers. 1877–1943. British admiral. Commanded *Colossus* in battle of Jutland (1916); rear admiral, commander in chief in the Mediterranean (1936–39); admiral of the fleet (1939); first sea lord and chief of naval staff (1939–43).

Pound, Ezra Loomis. 1885–1972. American poet, critic, and editor, b. Hailey, Idaho. Traveled in Spain, Italy, and France (1907–08); lived in London (1909–19), Paris (1920–24), Italy (1924–45, 1958–72). An editor with magazines *Poetry* and *The Little Review;* leader of Imagist movement of 1912–14, edited first Imagist anthology *Des Imagistes* (1914); a major influence on twentieth century U.S. and English literature, esp. Yeats, T.S. Eliot, Joyce, Frost, Hemingway, and D.H. Lawrence; became obsessed with monetary reform, as in *What Is Money For?* (1939). During World War II, broadcast for Italian Fascist regime; brought to U.S. (1945), charged with treason; held in mental hospital until 1958, then allowed to return to Italy. Major poetical works included *Cantos,* a cycle written over many decades, and *A lume spento* (1908), *Personae* (1909), *Exultations* (1909), *Ripostes* (1912), *Lustra* (1916), *Homage to Sextus Propertius* (1919), *Hugh Selwyn Mauberley* (1920). Literary executor of Ernest Fenollosa, with the aid of whose notes he produced *Cathay* (1915), *Certain Noble Plays of Japan* (1916), and *Noh, or Accomplishment* (1917). Major prose works included translations and criticism, esp. *The Spirit of Romance* (1910) and *Pavannes and Divisions* (1918).

Pound, Roscoe. 1870–1964. American educator, b. Lincoln, Nebr. Chief U.S. advocate of sociological jurisprudence. Taught law, U. of Nebraska (1890–1903); professor, Northwestern (1907–09), Chicago (1909–10), Harvard (1910–37); dean of Harvard Law School (1916–36). After World War II, reorganized the Nationalist Chinese judicial system. Author of *Readings on the History and System of the Common Law* (1904), *Readings on Roman Law* (1906), *Outlines of Lectures on Jurisprudence* (1914), *The Spirit of the Common Law* (1921), *Introduction to the Philosophy of Law* (1922), *Law and Morals* (1924), *Criminal Justice in America* (1930), *The Lawyer from Antiquity to Modern Times* (1953), etc. His sister ¶ Louise (1872–1958), also educator, teacher of English, U. of Nebraska (1897–1945); known as folklorist and authority on the English ballad; senior editor, *American Speech* (1925–33).

Pound·mak·er \'paủnd-,mā-kər\. 1826–1886. Canadian Cree chief, b. near Battleford, N.W.T. Led agitation of Indians of north Saskatchewan for redress of grievances (1881–85); took prominent part in Riel Rebellion of 1885; surrendered (1885) and died in prison.

Pounds \'paủndz\, John. 1766–1839. English shoemaker. Crippled by accident (1781); took up teaching of poor children; considered originator of the idea of ragged schools.

Pou·part \pü-pȧr\, François. 1661–1709. French physician and naturalist. Author of works on cantharis, leeches, and mussels, as well as on osteology. Poupart's ligament, of the abdomen, is named after him.

Pour·bus \'pür-bœs\ *or* **Por·bus** \'pȯr-\. Name of family of Dutch painters, including: Pieter (1510–1584), painter of religious pictures and portraits. His son ¶Frans (1545–1581), noted esp. as portrait painter. Frans's son ¶Frans (1569–1622), portrait painter with studio at court in Mantua (to 1600) and king's court in Paris.

Pour·ta·lès \pür-tȧ-les\, Guy de. 1884–1941. French writer, b. Switzerland. Author of *Marins d'eau douce* (1919), *Montclar* (1926), *Nietzsche en Italie* (1929), *La Pêche miraculeuse* (1937), and biographies of Liszt (1925), Chopin (1927), Wagner (1932), and Berlioz (1939).

Pourtalès, Louis François de. 1823–1880. American naturalist, b. Neuchâtel, Switzerland. To U.S. (1847) with J.L.R. Agassiz; on staff of U.S. Coast Survey (1848–73); keeper, Harvard Museum of Comparative Zoology (1873–80), associated with Alexander Agassiz; studied marine life dredged from great depths; author of *Deep-Sea Corals* (1871).

Poussin, Gaspard. See Gaspard DUGHET.

Pous·sin \pü-saⁿ\, Nicolas. 1594–1665. French painter. Most significant 17th-century French painter; a master of the Classical school; painted chiefly in Rome; noted for scriptural and mythological subjects; works included *The Assumption of the Virgin* (c.1626), *The Rape of the Sabine Women* (2 canvases, c.1635 and c.1637), *Holy Family on the Steps* (1648), *Landscape with Diogenes* (1648), *Self-Portrait* (1650), *The Arcadian Shepherds* (c.1655), and *Apollo and Daphne* (1664).

Pow·der·ly \'paủd-ər-lē\, Terence Vincent. 1849–1924. American labor leader, b. Carbondale, Pa. Machinist by trade; joined Knights of Labor (1874) and became general master workman (1883–93); instrumental in obtaining alien contract-labor law (1885) and in establishing labor bureaus and public arbitration systems in many states; pursued conciliatory policy in labor disputes and tried to reconcile differences between Knights and American Federation of Labor; mayor of Scranton, Pa. (1878–84); U.S. commissioner general of immigration (1897–1902); chief, Division of Information in Bureau of Immigration (1907–21). Author of *Thirty Years of Labor, 1859–1889* (1889).

Pow·der·mak·er \'paủd-ər-,mā-kər\, Hortense. 1900–1970. American cultural anthropologist, b. Philadelphia. Taught at Queen's Coll., New York (1938–68, professor from 1954). Known for studies of a rural Mississippi community, *After Freedom* (1939), of the Hollywood film industry, *The Dream Factory* (1950), and of cultural changes in South Africa, *Copper Town* (1962); her autobiography, *Stranger and Friend* (1966).

Pow·ell \'paủ(-ə)l\, Adam Clayton, Jr. 1908–1972. American clergyman and politician, b. New Haven, Conn. Member, U.S. House of Representatives (1945–67, 1969–71) from New York; authored over 50 pieces of social legislation; barred from House seat (1967) on accusation of misusing public funds but seated on reelection.

Powell, Robert Baden-. See BADEN-POWELL.

Pow·ell \'pō-əl, 'paủ(-ə)l\, Cecil Frank. 1903–1969. English physicist. Prof., U. of Bristol (1948–63); awarded Nobel prize in physics (1950) for work on photography of nuclear processes; proved existence of the pion (1947); discovered antipion and (1949) modes of decay of kaons.

Pow·ell \'paủ(-ə)l\, Dawn. 1897–1965. American novelist, b. Mt. Gilead, Ohio. Author of *She Walks in Beauty* (1928), *Dance Night* (1930), *The Story of a Country Boy* (1934), *Turn, Magic Wheel* (1936), *The Locusts Have No King* (1948), *A Cage for Lovers* (1957), *The Golden Spur* (1962), and the plays *Jig Saw* and *Big Night.*

Powell, Earl, *nicknamed* Bud. 1924–1966. American jazz musician, b. New York City. A pioneer of bebop jazz; one of greatest jazz soloists, helped establish the piano as an authentic solo voice in jazz; composer of songs as "Tempus Fugue It," "Hallucinations," "Bouncing with Bud."

Powell, John Wesley. 1834–1902. American geologist, b. Mount Morris, N.Y. Pioneer explorer of Green and Colorado rivers (1869–75); on staff of U.S. Geological Survey (1875–94); succeeded Clarence King as director (1881); inaugurated (1883) publication of bulletins and (1890) monographs, and series of folio atlases (from 1894) presenting geologic and topographic charts. First director, Bureau of Ethnology in Smithsonian Institution (1879–1902); published first classification of American Indian languages in *An Introduction to the Study of Indian Languages* (1877); founded *Contributions to North American Ethnology* (1877); also wrote *Exploration of the Colorado River of the West and Its Tributaries* (1875) and *Report on the Lands of the Arid Region of the United States* (1878).

Pow·ell \'pō-əl, 'paủ(-ə)l\, Martin. fl. 1710–1729. English puppet showman. Director of Punch's Theatre at Covent Garden, London (1710–13), a popular attraction for high society; established form of Punch and Judy drama.

Pow·ell \'paủ(-ə)l\, William Henry. 1823–1879. American painter, b. New York City. His *Discovery of the Mississippi River by De Soto* (1853) fills a panel in the rotunda of the Capitol, Washington, D.C.; his *Oliver Hazard Perry at the Battle of Lake Erie* (1863) is in the Ohio State capitol.

Pow·er \'paủ(-ə)r\, Leonel *or* Lionel *or* Lyonel. d. 1445. English composer. After Dunstable, the leading 15th-century English composer; associated with Christ Church Priory, Cambridge (1423 ff.); composer of masses and motets in chanson style.

Power, Marguerite. See Marguerite GARDINER.

Power, Tyrone, *in full* William Grattan Tyrone. 1797–1841. Irish comedian. Joined strolling players at age of 14; succeeded (1826) Charles Connor as leading Irish comedian at Drury Lane; went down in *President,* lost in storm en route from America. His grandson ¶Frederick Tyrone (1869–1931), American actor, b. London, England, was member of Augustin Daly's company (1890–98); chief success in poetic drama or in heroic roles; player in moving pictures in Hollywood (after 1927). The latter's son ¶Tyrone Edmond (1914–1958), motion-picture actor, b. Cincinnati; entered motion pictures (1932) in *Tom Brown of Culver;* player of leading parts (from 1936), appearing in *Lloyd's of London* (1936), *Suez* (1938), *The Rains Came* (1939), *Blood and Sand* (1941), *The Razor's Edge* (1946), *Captain from Castile* (1947), etc.

Pow·ers \'paủ(-ə)rz\, Hiram. 1805–1873. American sculptor, b. Woodstock, Vt. Artist for waxworks museum, Cincinnati (1829–1834); to Washington, D.C. (1834), and executed portrait busts of noted men, including Jackson, Calhoun, Webster, Marshall; established studio in Florence, Italy (1837). Among his important works, in Neoclassical style, were *Greek Slave* (1843), *Il Penseroso* (1856), *Eve Disconsolate* (1871), *The Last of the Tribe* (1872), statues of Franklin and Jefferson in the Capitol, Washington, D.C.

Poweski, Piotr Skarga. See Piotr SKARGA.

Pow·ha·tan \ˌpaú-ə-'tan, paú-'hat-ᵊn\. *Indian name* Wa-hun-sen-a-cawh *or* Wahunsonacock. 1550?–1618. American Indian chief. Father of Pocahontas (*q.v.*); head of a federation of Algonquian tribes known as Confederacy of Powhatan in eastern Virginia; after marriage of Pocahontas to John Rolfe (1614), maintained friendly relations with white settlers.

Powis, Earls, marquises, and dukes of. See HERBERT family.

Powlett. See PAULET.

Pow·nall \'paún-ᵊl\, Thomas. 1722–1805. English colonial administrator. To New York as secretary to the governor (1753); lieutenant governor of New Jersey (1755); governor of Massachusetts (1757–60); urged vigorous measures toward driving French from America; led expedition to Penobscot (1759) to block French; unable to win confidence of Shirley party in Massachusetts. Returned to England (1760); M.P. (1767–80); urged government to treat with colonies (1775). Author of *The Administration of the Colonies* (1764) proposing union of all British possessions in America.

Pow·ys \'pō-əs\. Family of English brothers: John Cowper (1872–1963), author of novels including *Wood and Stone* (1915), *Wolf Solent* (1929), *A Glastonbury Romance* (1932), *Owen Glendower* (1940); poetry *Wolfsbane Rhymes* (1916), *Mandragora* (1917), *Samphire* (1922); philosophical and critical works, including *The Meaning of Culture* (1929), *In Defense of Sensuality* (1930), *A Philosophy of Solitude* (1933), *The Pleasures of Literature* (1938), *The Art of Growing Old* (1943); also an autobiography (1934). ¶Theodore Francis (1875–1953), author of allegorical novels of good and evil, life and death, set in a rural village, as *Mark Only* (1924), *Mr. Tasker's Gods* (1925), *Mr. Weston's Good Wine* (1927), *Unclay* (1931); also of short-story collections as *The House with the Echo* (1928) and *The White Paternoster* (1930). ¶Llewelyn (1884–1939), manager of stock farm in British East Africa (1914–19); author of *Ebony and Ivory* (stories and impressions of African life, 1922), *Thirteen Worthies* (1923), *Black Laughter* (1924), *Skin for Skin* (1925), *The Verdict of Bridlegoose* (1926), *Cradle of God* (1929), *A Pagan's Pilgrimage* (1931), *Apples Be Ripe* (novel, 1930), *Life and Death* (novel, 1939).

Poy·nings \'pȯin-iŋz\, Sir Edward. 1459–1521. English soldier and diplomat. Took part in rebellion against Richard III; escaped and attached himself to Earl of Richmond (Henry VII); governor of Calais (1493). As deputy to Prince Henry (Henry VIII), governor of Ireland, summoned Drogheda Parliament (1494) that enacted Poynings's law providing that every act of Irish Parliament must be approved by English privy council to become valid; expelled Perkin Warbeck, the Pretender (1495). Warden of Cinque Ports (c.1500); executed military undertakings in France and performed diplomatic missions.

Poyn·ter \'pȯint-ər\, Sir Edward John. 1836–1919. English historical painter. Director of National Gallery (1894–1904). Executed decorative designs in fresco, mosaic, stained glass, pottery; known for classic oil paintings, including *Israel in Egypt* (1867), *Atalanta's Race* (1876), *Lesbia and Her Sparrow* (1907).

Poyn·ting \'pȯint-iŋ\, John Henry. 1852–1914. English physicist. Professor, Mason Coll., which later became U. of Birmingham (from 1880); investigated radiation and pressure of light; developed (1884–85) theorem on flow of electromagnetic energy, now known as Poynting's vector; determined the mean density (1891) and gravitational constant (1893) of the Earth; suggested (1903) theory now known as Poynting-Robertson effect. Author of *Text-Book of Physics* (with J.J. Thomson, 1899–1914) and *The Earth: Its Shape, Size, Weight, and Spin* (1913).

Poz·zo \'pōt-tsō\, Andrea dal. 1642–1709. Italian Jesuit, architect, and painter of the Milanese school. Master of illusionism in painting; known chiefly for his decoration of the ceiling of the Church of Sant'Ignazio, Rome (completed 1694).

Pozzo di Bor·go \-dē-'bȯr-gō\, Carlo Andrea. Count. 1764–1842. Corsican diplomat in Russian service. Opposed Napoléon in Corsican politics (from c.1792); fled Corsica to England; member of British embassy staff in Vienna (1798–1804); entered Russian diplomatic service (1804). Consistently opposed Napoléon; obtained Swedish support against French; entered Paris with allied armies (1814) and became commissary general to provisional government. As Russian ambassador to France (1814–35), championed French interests, including urging Alexander I to decrease burdens placed on France by anti-Napoleonic allies and to shorten term of foreign occupation; Russian ambassador to Great Britain (1835–39).

Pra·do \'prät͟h-ō\, Mariano Ignacio. 1826–1901. Peruvian general and politician. Fought under Castilla in revolution of 1854; disagreed with President Juan Antonio Pezet's policy of compromise toward Spain (1865) and overthrew him; president (dictator) of Peru (1865–68); declared war against Spain (1865). Forced to leave country (1868); returned and was elected president (1876–79); defeated in War of the Pacific (1879). Spent most of rest of life in Europe.

Prado, Pedro. 1886–1952. Chilean writer. Advocate of Modernism; author of novels *La reina de Rapa Nui* (1914), *Alsino* (1920), *Un juez rural* (1924), and of verse *Flores de Cardo* (1908), *La casa abandonada* (1912), *El llamado del mundo* (1913), *Los pájaros errantes* (1915), and *Androvar* (1925, verse drama).

Pra·don \prȧ-dō^{n}\, Jacques. 1644–1698. French dramatist. Author of tragedies *Pyrame et Thisbé* (1674) and *Phèdre et Hippolyte* (1677), the latter advanced by enemies of Racine as a worthy competitor with Racine's *Phèdre;* the rivalry produced the War of the Sonnets, waged in verse between friends of the two playwrights. Other plays by Pradon were *Tamerlan* (1676), *La Troade* (1679), *Régulus* (1688), and *Scipion l'Africain* (1697).

Pra·do Ugar·te·che \'prät͟h-ō-ü-gär-'tā-chā\, Manuel. 1889–1967. Peruvian politician. Son of Mariano I. Prado. President, Central Reserve Bank of Peru (1934–39); president of Peru (1939–45, 1956–62).

Pradt \prȧt\, Dominique-Georges-Frédéric de Riom de Prol·hiac de Fourt de \də-ryō^{n}-də-prōl-yȧk-də-fūr-də-\. 1759–1837. French prelate and diplomat. Member of Estates-General (1789); an émigré (1791–99); personal chaplain to Napoléon (1800) and a negotiator of Treaty of Bayonne dethroning the Bourbon king of Spain (1808). Archbishop of Malines (1808); failed in diplomatic mission in Poland (1812). Turned from Napoléon to favor Bourbon restoration; appointed by Louis XVIII grand chancellor of Legion of Honor.

Praeconinus. See STILO PRAECONINUS.

Praed \'prād\, Winthrop Mackworth. 1802–1839. English poet. M.P. (from 1830); known as author of bright, witty skits and satirical pieces as "Stanzas to the Speaker Asleep," "The Country Ball," and "Good Night to the Season"; preeminent in vers de société; emulator of Hood in "The Red Fisherman" and "Arminius."

Prae·to·ri·us \pre-'tō-rē-ˌu̇s\, Michael. *Adopted Latinized form of orig. name* Schult·heiss \'shu̇lt-(ˌ)hīs\. 1571?–1621. German composer and writer on music. Kapellmeister to Duke of Brunswick-Wolfenbüttel (from 1604). Best known for his settings of Protestant hymns. Among his compositions were *Musae sioniae* (9 parts, 1605–10), *Hymnodia sionia* (1611), *Terpsichore* (1612), *Polyhymnia* (1619), and *Puericinium* (1621); chief among his writings on music was *Syntagma musicum* (1614–20).

Pra·ga \'präg-ä\, Emilio. 1839–1875. Italian poet. Wrote poetry influenced by Hugo, Baudelaire, Musset, Heine, and the Italian Romantics, as *Tavolozza* (1862), *Penombre* (1864), *Fiabe e leggende* (1867), and *Trasparenze* (1877); author also of drama *Le madri galanti* (1863).

Prajadhipok. See RAMA VII.

Prand·tau·er \'prän-ˌtau̇-ər\, Jakob. 1660–1726. Austrian Baroque architect. Worked primarily for monastic orders; most famous designs were the abbey of Melk (1702–38) and the monastery of Sankt Florian at Linz (begun 1708).

Prandtl \'prän-tᵊl\, Ludwig. 1875–1953. German physicist. Considered the father of aerodynamics. Professor at Göttingen (1904–53); director, Kaiser Wilhelm (later Max Planck) Institute for Fluid Mechanics (1925 ff.). His discovery of the boundary layer (1904) and studies in wing theory (1918–19) were basis of modern aerodynamics. Early pioneer in streamlining dirigibles and advocating monoplanes; made researches in supersonic flow and turbulence and innovations in wind tunnel design; also made studies in theory of plasticity and on meteorology.

Pra·pan·ca \prä-'pän-kä\. 14th century. Indonesian poet. Author of *Nāgarakertāgama* (1365), a long laudatory poem describing life in the kingdom of Java under Hayam Wuruk.

Pra·sad \prə-'säd\, Rajendra. 1884–1963. Indian nationalist leader. Practiced law in Calcutta; founded *Bihār Law Weekly* (1916); member (1912 ff.) and president (1934, 1939, 1947) of Congress party; left legal practice (1920) to follow Gandhi's noncooperation movement; founder and editor, Hindi weekly *Desh;* lifelong advocate of Hindi as national language; presided (1946–49) over Indian Constitutional Assembly and helped shape the constitution; first president of Republic of India (1950–62).

Pra·su·ta·gus \pre-'s(y)üt-ə-gəs\. d. 60 A.D. King of the Iceni in Britain. Ruled as client under Roman suzerainty; succeeded by his queen Boudicca (*q.v.*).

Pra·tel·la \prä-'tel-lä\, Francesco Balilla. 1880–1955. Italian composer. Director, Istituto Musicale, Lugo (1910–29), and of Liceo Musicale G. Verdi, Ravenna (1927–45); representative of Futurism in music. Works included operas as *Lilia* (1903), *L'aviatore Dro* (1920), and *Fabiano* (1939), the orchestral poem *Romagna,* the orchestral dance *La guerra,* and piano and organ works.

Pra·ti \'prä-tē\, Giovanni. 1815–1884. Italian poet. Ardent partisan of house of Savoy in Italian unification movement; court poet to house of Savoy; senator (1876 ff.). Among his works were Romantic epic *Edmenegarda* (1841), *Canti lirici, Canti del popolo, Memorie e lacrime* (1844), *Psiche* (1875), and *Iside* (1878).

Prat·i·nas \'prat-ᵊn-əs\. 6th–5th century B.C. Athenian tragic poet. A rival of Aeschylus; said to have first introduced satyric drama in Greek theater as a kind of play distinct from tragedy.

Pratt \'prat\, Sir Charles. 1st Earl **Cam·den** \'kam-dən\. 1714–1794. English jurist and political leader. Attorney general (1757); chief justice of court of common pleas (1761); in case of John Wilkes (1763) decided on illegality of general warrants; in House of Lords, opposed taxation of American colonies and Stamp Act as unconstitutional; lord chancellor (1766–70); in opposition until death of Chatham; president of council (1782, 1784–94). His son ¶Sir John Jeffreys (1759–1840), 2d Earl and 1st Marquis of Camden; as lord lieutenant of Ireland (1795–98), blocked remedial legislation and carried out cabinet's policy, which resulted in rebellion of 1798; appealed for military intervention and turned over control to Cornwallis; secretary of war (1804–05); president of council (1805–06, 1807–12); created Marquis of Camden and Earl of Breck·nock \'brek-nək\ (1812); chancellor of Cambridge U. (1834–40).

Pratt, Charles. 1830–1891. American oil magnate, b. Watertown, Mass. With Henry H. Rogers founded Charles Pratt & Co. (1867) for refining crude oil; business acquired by John D. Rockefeller (1874); became executive in Standard Oil Company. Benefactor of Amherst College and U. of Rochester; founded Pratt Institute, Brooklyn (1887); established Pratt Institute Free Library, first free public library in Brooklyn or New York City.

Pratt, Edwin John. 1883–1964. Canadian poet and educator, b. Western Bay, Nfd. Leading Canadian poet of his time; professor of English literature, Victoria Coll., U. of Toronto (1919–53); editor, *Canadian Poetry Magazine.* Among his books were *Newfoundland Verse* (1923), *The Witches' Brew* (1925), *Titans* (1926), *The Iron Door* (1927), *The Roosevelt and the Antinoe* (1930), *The Titanic* (1935), *Brébeuf and His Brethren* (1940), *Dunkirk* (1941), *Still Life* (1943), *They Are Returning* (1945), *Behind the Log* (1947), and *Towards the Last Spike* (1952).

Pratt, Francis Ashbury. 1827–1902. American inventor, b. Woodstock, Vt. With Amos Whitney founded Pratt & Whitney Co., Hartford, Conn. (1865), for manufacture of machine tools; president (1865–98). Instrumental in bringing about adoption of standard system of gauges; invented metal-planing machine (1869), gear cutter (1884), milling machine (1885).

Pratt, John Henry. 1809–1871. British clergyman and geophysicist. Missionary in India (1838 ff.); archdeacon of Calcutta (1850–71). Discovered (1855) there is a constant value for gravity at sea level at any given latitude and calculated the average depth of density compensation to be 100 kilometers; postulated (1856) a theory of isostasy.

Pratt, Richard Henry. 1840–1924. American army officer and educator, b. Rushford, N.Y. In Union army through Civil War; on frontier duty (to 1875). With government aid and approval, organized first nonreservation Indian school at Carlisle, Pa. (1879), from which developed Carlisle Indian Industrial School; remained head of this school until retired (1904).

Pratt, Silas Gamaliel. 1846–1916. American composer, b. Addison, Vt. Director, Chicago Grand Opera festival (1884); founder and president (1906–16), Pratt Institute of Music and Art, Pittsburgh (1906). Composer of operas *Zenobia* (1882), *Lucille* (1887), and *Ollanta* (unperformed); symphony *Prodigal Son* (1875), *Lincoln* symphony (undated), *Centennial Overture* (1876), cantata *The Inca's Farewell* (1891), *Triumph of Columbus* (1892), and many songs and piano pieces.

Pratt, Thomas Willis. 1812–1875. American civil engineer, b. Boston. Invented the bridge and roof truss known as "Pratt truss" (patented 1844).

Pratt, Waldo Selden. 1857–1939. American musician and teacher, b. Philadelphia. Professor of music and hymnology (1882–1917) and of public worship (1917–25) at Hartford (Conn.) Theol. Sem. Musical editor for *Century Dictionary;* editor of American Supplement (1920) to Grove's *Dictionary of Music and Musicians* and *New Encyclopedia of Music and Musicians* (1924). Author of *History of Music* (1907), *Music of the Pilgrims* (1921), etc.

Prax·ag·o·ras \prak-'sag-ə-rəs\. 4th century B.C. Greek physician. Defender of doctrine of humoralism; supposed by some to have been first to point out distinction between arteries and veins; teacher of Herophilus.

Prax·it·e·les \prak-'sit-ᵊl-ˌēz\. fl. 370–330 B.C. Athenian sculptor. Regarded as greatest Attic sculptor of his century. Only known extant work is marble statue *Hermes Carrying the Infant Dionysius;* other statues surviving in Roman copies are *Aphrodite of Cnidus, Apollo Sauroctonus,* and a number of satyrs.

Pré·ault \prā-ō\, Antoine-Auguste. 1809–1879. French Romantic sculptor. Among his notable works were *Charlemagne* (1836), *Carthage* (1838), *Le Christ en croix* (1840), *Clémence Isaure* (1848), and *Ophélie* (1873).

Pre·ble \'preb-əl\, Edward. 1761–1807. American naval officer, b. Portland, Me. Commissioned captain (1799); commander (1803) of third squadron sent to Mediterranean in war with Tripoli; sent Lt. Stephen Decatur to burn *Philadelphia* (1804); created effective squadron tactics for operations against Tripoli.

Preece \'prēs\, Sir William Henry. 1834–1913. British electrical engineer. Engineer in Post Office telegraphic system (1870–99); did pioneer work in railway signaling and in wireless telegraphy; encouraged Marconi and obtained for him Post Office assistance; introduced first telephones into Great Britain.

Preedy, George Runnell. See Gabrielle Margaret LONG.

Pregl \'prā-gəl\, Fritz. 1869–1930. Austrian chemist. Professor in Graz (1913–30); developed method of quantitative microanalysis of organic compounds; developed a sensitive microbalance and micromethods for measuring atomic groups; awarded 1923 Nobel prize for chemistry.

Prem Chand. See RAI SRIVASTANA.

Přemysl Otakar. See OTAKAR.

Prence \'pren(t)s\ *or* **Prince** \'prin(t)s\, Thomas. 1600–1673. English colonist. A pilgrim on the *Mayflower;* governor of Plymouth colony, Massachusetts (1634–35, 1638, 1657–73); advocated free public schools.

Pren·der·gast \'pren-dər-ˌgast\, Maurice Brazil. 1859–1924. American painter, b. St. John's, Nfd. Excelled in watercolor genre pictures, as of street scenes in Boston and impressions of Venetian and Neapolitan life; his later work moved from Postimpressionism toward abstraction; a member of The Eight; exhibited in New York Armory Show (1913). Among his canvases were *Ponte della Paglia* (1899), *Umbrellas in the Rain* (1899), *Central Park* (1901), *Promenade* (1914–15), and *Four Girls in Meadow* (c.1919).

Pre·o·bra·jen·ska \pryi-ə-(ˌ)brə-'zhen-skə\, Olga. 1871–1962. Russian ballet dancer and teacher. Joined (1889) Mariinsky Theater, Leningrad, and became its prima ballerina (1900–14); danced in over 700 performances of ballet classics; toured extensively in Europe (1895 ff.). Taught in Leningrad (1917–21); settled in Paris and taught there (1924–60); her pupils among best European dancers.

Pre·ra·do·vić \pre-'rä-dȯ-vētʸ\, Petar. 1818–1872. Croatian poet. Officer in Austrian army, rising to rank of general (1866); wrote early verse in German, but later in Croat; regarded as one of the greatest of Croatian poets; lyric and epic works included *Prvenci* (1846), *Nove pjesme* (1851), and *Pjesnička djela* (1873).

Pres·cott \'pres-kət, *also* -ˌkät\, Samuel. 1751–?1777. American patriot, b. Concord, Mass. With Paul Revere when Revere was captured on his famous ride (Apr. 18, 1775), escaped and carried the warning to Concord; served at Ticonderoga (1776); captured by British (1777) and died at Halifax.

Prescott, William. 1726–1795. American Revolutionary soldier, b. Groton, Mass. Colonel of a regiment of Minutemen (1775); fortified Breed's Hill (night of June 16, 1775) and commanded redoubt there the next day in battle known as the battle of Bunker Hill.

Prescott, William Hickling. 1796–1859. American historian, b. Salem, Mass. Grandson of William Prescott. Devoted himself to study of Spanish history; established reputation with first book *History of the Reign of Ferdinand and Isabella the Catholic* (1838); also wrote *History of the Conquest of Mexico* (1843), *Biographical and Critical Miscellanies* (1845), and *History of the Conquest of Peru* (1847). Published three volumes of *History of the Reign of Philip the Second* (1855–58), but did not live to complete the work.

Pre·šer·en \prə-'sher-ən\, France. 1800–1849. Slovene poet. Considered finest Slovene poet of Romantic movement. Held posts in Ljublana and Kranj as civil servant and lawyer. Known for epic poem *Krst pri Savici* (1836) and lyrical love verse *Gazele* (1833), *Sonetni venec* (1834), and *Sonetni nesrece* (1834).

Pres·ley \'pres-lē, 'prez-\, Elvis Aaron. 1935–1977. American entertainer, b. Tupelo, Miss. Known as the "King of Rock and Roll" and "Elvis the Pelvis" for hip gyrations which accompanied his singing. Worked as truck driver in Memphis, Tenn.; first commercial recording "That's All Right, Mama" (1954), first major success "Heartbreak Hotel" (1956); singing style was blend of black rhythm and blues with white rockabilly; sold over 600 million copies of such recordings as "Hound Dog," "All Shook Up," "Don't Be Cruel," "Love Me Tender," "It's Now or Never," and "Are You Lonesome Tonight?"; starred in 33 motion pictures, *Love Me Tender* (1956) being first.

Pres·sen·sé \pres-äⁿ-sā\, Edmond De·haut de \də-ō-də-\. 1824–1891. French clergyman and politician. Founded (1854) Protestant journal *Revue chrétienne;* member of National Assembly (1871); senator for life (1883). Among his works were *L'Église et la Révolution française* (1864) and *Histoire des trois premiers siècles de l'Église chrétienne* (1858–77).

Pres·ter John \'pres-tər-'jän\, *i.e.* Priest (*or* Presbyter) John. A legendary Christian king and priest of the Middle Ages, sometimes also identified with John the Elder of the New Testament, whose kingdom was believed to be either in Asia or Africa. (1) *Of Asia:* A king and priest first described in chronicle (1145) of Otto, Bishop of Freising, as dwelling in the Orient far beyond Persia and Armenia, a Nestorian Christian who attempted to come to the aid of Jerusalem during the Crusades. His connection with India due to legends of earlier origin (c.1122) applied to this later Nestorian ruler. Believed to have sent to Byzantine Emperor Manuel I (c.1165) a letter, now held to be spurious, containing accounts of the many marvels of his kingdom. Asiatic legends died out and, because of vague geographical knowledge of the times, legends and name were transferred to Africa by Portuguese explorers. (2) *Of Africa:* A king of Ethiopia (Abyssinia) of the 14th century or 15th century. Monarchs of Ethiopia had long possessed a chapel and altar at the Church of the Sepulcher in Jerusalem; one of these monarchs became known as Prester

John and on the map of Fra Mauro, a Venetian monk (fl. 1459), his kingdom was located in Abyssinia.

Pres·ton \ˈpres-tən\, Margaret, *nee* **Jun·kin** \ˈjəŋ-kən\. 1820–1897. American writer, b. Milton, Pa. m. John T. L. Preston (1857). Author of *Silverwood* (novel, 1856) and volumes of poetry, including *Beechenbrook* (1865), *Old Songs and New* (1870), *Colonial Ballads* (1887), etc.

Preston, Thomas. 1537–1598. English dramatist. Author of *Cambises, King of Percia* (1569), a bombastic tragedy of murder and bloodshed generally taken to mark the beginning of historical drama.

Preston, Thomas. 1860–1900. Irish scientist. Studied heat, magnetism, and spectroscopy; noted for experiments with effects of magnetic fields on spectral lines.

Prest·wich \ˈprest-(,)wich\, Sir Joseph. 1812–1896. English geologist. London wine merchant; studied Thames basin; published work on water-bearing strata round London (1851) which became standard authority; professor of geology, Oxford (1874–88).

Pre·ti \ˈpre-tē\, Mattia. 1613–1699. *Known as* Il **Ca·va·lie·re Ca·la·bre·se** \ēl-ˌkäv-äl-ˈyer-ā-ˌkäl-ä-ˈbrā-sā\ *or* Il Calabrese. Italian painter. Works included frescoes in Church of Sant'Andrea della Valle (Rome), frescoes from the life of St. Catherine in Church of San Pietro a Maiella (Naples), *Belshazzar's Banquet, Clarinda Freeing Olindo and Sofronia,* and *Martyrdom of St. Bartholomew.*

Pre·to·ri·us \prə-ˈtü-rē-œs\, Andries Wilhelmus Jacobus. 1798–1853. South African Dutch colonizer and soldier. One of leaders (1838) of the great trek for Natal; beat off attack of 10,000 Zulus at Blood River with force of 500 (1838); persuaded Boer settlements in Transvaal to enter into federal union with Natal (1840); led Natal Boers in opposition to British and crossed to north of Vaal River (1847) to be free of British sovereignty; led anti-British war in attempt to consolidate independent Boer states; defeated at Boomplaats (1848); went to aid of malcontents of Orange River (1851); won from British acknowledgment of independence of Transvaal Boers (1852); reconciled to his rival, General A. H. Potgieter; new district and town of Pretoria named in his honor. His eldest son ¶Marthinus Wessels (1819–1901) succeeded him as commandant general (1853); led punitive expedition against Chief Makapan (1854); was elected first president of newly constituted South African Republic (1857, again 1864, 1869); president (1859–63) of Orange Free State; strove to reconcile Free State burghers to amalgamation with Transvaal; attempted annexation of Bechuanaland and Delagoa Bay (1868) but yielded to Portugal's claim upon Delagoa Bay; resigned when Volksraad refused to ratify arbitration award which deprived Boers of their claim to diamond fields of lower Vaal (1871); after first annexation of Orange Free State by Great Britain (1877), joined insurgent Boer leaders, winning recognition of independence of the republic (1881); member of the ruling triumvirate until election of Paul Kruger as president (1883); lived to see British reannexation of his country.

Pretyman, Sir George. See TOMLINE.

Preuss \ˈpròis\, Hugo. 1860–1925. German jurist and politician. Follower of the organic-state philosophy of Otto von Gierke; contributor to liberal organs as *Nation* and *Die Hilfe;* minister of interior in Scheidemann's cabinet (1919); member of Weimar National Assembly (1919–20) and chief author of republican constitution adopted by that assembly; chief work *Die Entwicklung des deutschen Städtewesens* (1906).

Pre·vert \prā-ver\, Jacques. 1900–1977. French poet and screenwriter. Known for humorous, iconoclastic "song poems" of social hope and sentimental love, as *Tentative de description d'un dîner de têtes à Paris-France* (1931); these poems collected in *Paroles* (1945) and many achieved wide popularity after being set to music by Josef Kosma; other volumes of verse included *Histoires* (1946), *Spectacle* (1951), and *Imaginaires* (1970). His film scripts, all written for director Marcel Carné, included *Drôle de drame* (1937), *Les Visiteurs du soir* (1942), and *Les Enfants du Paradis* (1945).

Pré·vost \prā-vō\, Eugène-Marcel. 1862–1941. French novelist. Civil engineer by profession (to 1890), then devoted himself to writing moralizing and feminist fiction. Among his many novels were *Le Scorpion* (1887), *Mademoiselle Jauffre* (1889), *Cousin Laura* (1890), *Les Demi-vierges* (1894), *L'Heureux Ménage* (1900), *La Princesse d'Erminge* (1905), *Mon cher Tommy* (1920), *La Retraite ardente* (1927), and *L'Homme vierge* (1930). For the stage he wrote *Les Demi-vierges* (1895), *La Plus faible* (1904), *Pierre et Thérèse* (1909).

Prévost, Françoise. c.1680–1741. French dancer. Foremost ballerina of her generation. Made debut (1699) in Lully's *Atys* at Paris Opéra and was its prima ballerina until 1730; known for precision, lightness, and grace, as well as mime and dramatic ability; succeeded by her pupils Marie Camargo and Marie Sallé.

Prev·ost \ˈprev-ˌō(st)\, Sir George. 1767–1816. British colonial administrator. Governor general of Upper and Lower Canada (1811–15); known for conciliatory policies toward French Canadians; made unsuccessful attack on Sackets Harbor, N.Y. (1813); repulsed at Plattsburg, N.Y., by Americans under Macomb (1814).

Pré·vost \prā-vō\, Pierre. 1751–1839. Swiss philosopher and physicist. Professor of philosophy and physics at Geneva (1793–1823); known for work relating to heat and magnetism; formulated theory of exchanges dealing with radiation from one body to another (1791).

Prévost d'Ex·iles \-dāg-zēl\, Antoine-François. *Known as* Abbé Prévost. 1697–1763. French novelist. Entered Benedictine order (1721); left the order (1728) for life of travel and adventure, supporting himself by his writings. Notable among his works were *Les Mémoires d'un homme de qualité* (1728), *Histoire du Chevalier des Grieux et de Manon Lescaut* (1731), *Histoire d'une Grecque moderne* (1740), and *Mémoires d'un honnête homme* (1745).

Prévost-Pa·ra·dol \-pà-rà-dòl\, Lucien-Anatole. 1829–1870. French journalist, politician, and diplomat. On staff of *Journal des Débats* (1856 ff.), and a founder of *Courrier du Dimanche* (1866); opponent of Napoléon III until more liberal governmental policies developed; ambassador to U.S. (1870).

Prey·er \ˈprī-ər\, Wilhelm Thierry. 1841–1897. German physiologist and psychologist, b. England. To Germany (1857); professor at Jena (1869–93). Made investigations in hemoglobin, curare, and gases in the blood; formulated lactic acid theory of sleep (1876); a founder of modern developmental psychology, esp. with *Die Seele des Kindes* (1882).

Pri·bi·će·vić \prē-ˈbēt-yev-ētʸ\, Svetozar. 1875–1936. Yugoslav politician. Minister of interior (1919–20, 1921), of education (1920–21, 1924–26). During troubled years following, allied himself with Croatians under Radić and Maček and demanded Croatian autonomy; temporarily interned (1929) and then withdrew to France. Author of *La Dictature du roi Alexandre* (1932).

Pri·by·lov \pri-bi-ˈlòf\, Gavril. 18th century. Russian sea captain. First visitor (1786) to group of islands in Bering Sea called Pribilof Islands in his honor.

Price \ˈprīs\, Richard. 1723–1791. Welsh moral philosopher. Dissenting minister in London; established reputation with his *Review of the Principal Questions in Morals* (1758), foreshadowing Kantian theories; admitted (1765) to Royal Society for work on probability; his *Observations on Reversionary Payments* (1771) laid foundation of scientific system for life insurance and old-age pensions, and, coupled with *An Appeal to the Public on the Subject of the National Debt* (1772), led William Pitt to establish sinking fund; attacked the justice and policy of American war in *Observations on Civil Liberty and War with America* (1776); his eulogy to French Revolution, *Discourse on The Love of Our Country* (1789), answered by Burke's *Reflections on the Revolution in France.*

Price, Sterling. 1809–1867. American politician and army commander, b. Prince Edward Co., Va. Governor of Missouri (1853–57); major general in Confederate army in Civil War, serving in Missouri, Arkansas, and Texas; defeated at Westport, Mo. (Oct. 23, 1864).

Price, Thomas. 1852–1909. Australian politican, b. North Wales. Stonecutter in Liverpool; to Australia (1883); worked on Parliament buildings in Adelaide; Labour member of House of Assembly (1893); parliamentary leader of Labour party (1901); as prime minister (1905–09), unified Adelaide public transportation system, created wage boards, liberalized voting franchise, and initiated transfer of Northern Territory to Commonwealth.

Price, Sir Uvedale. 1747–1829. English landscape designer. A leading advocate of the picturesque style in the laying out of grounds and gardens; his *Essay on the Picturesque* (1794) involved him in controversy with followers of Lancelot Brown.

Price-Mars \prē-smärs\, Jean. 1876–1970. Haitian physician, historian, and diplomat. Chargé d'affaires in Washington, D.C. (1908–11); inspector of public education (1912–15); minister to France (1915–16). Author of collection of essays on Haitian folklore *Ainsi parla l'oncle* (1928) and a history *La République du Haïti et la République dominicaine* (1953).

Prich·ard \ˈprich-ərd\, Harold Arthur. 1871–1947. English philosopher. Fellow (1895–1924) and professor (1928–37) at Oxford. A leading member of the Oxford intuitionist school of moral philosophy; chief works *Kant's Theory of Knowledge* (1909), *Duty and Interest* (1928), *Moral Obligation* (1949), and *Knowledge and Perception* (1950).

Prichard, James Cowles. 1786–1848. English physician and ethnologist. Physician in Bristol (1810 ff.); argued for a single human species in *Researches Into the Physical History of Man* (1813) and *Natural History of Man* (1843). Introduced concept of moral insanity as a distinct disease; traced early connection between Hindus and Egyptians (1819); his *Eastern Origin of the Celtic Nations* (1831) established Celtic as an Indo-European language.

Prichard, Rhys. 1579–1644. Welsh clergyman and poet. Vicar of Llandovery (1602 ff.); famous for sermons written in a folksong meter, later published as *Canwyll y Cymry* (1646; complete ed. 1672).

Pride \ˈprīd\, Thomas. d. 1658. English Parliamentarian commander. Commanded regiment at Naseby (1645); conducted expulsion of about 140

Presbyterian and Royalist members of Long Parliament (Pride's Purge, 1648); one of judges in trial of Charles I and a signer of death warrant; commanded brigade at Dunbar (1650) and Worcester (1651); opposed Cromwell's appointment as king.

Prid·vo·rov \pryid-'vô-rəf\, Yefim Alekseyevich. *Pseudonym* Dem·yan Bed·ny \dyim-'yän-'byed-nyē\, *i.e.* Demyan the Poor. 1885–1945. Russian poet. Early a contributor to Socialist press; after Revolution gained great popularity with satirical fables and verse, latter often in form of songs glorifying Revolution.

Priest·ley \'prēst-lē\, John Boynton. 1894–1984. English author. Began career as publisher's reader and free-lance journalist; achieved great success with second novel *The Good Companions* (1929); other novels included *Angel Pavement* (1930), *Margin Released* (1962), *Lost Empires* (1965), and *The Image Men* (1969); wrote plays as *Dangerous Corner* (1932), *I Have Been Here Before* (1937), and *An Inspector Calls* (1946); also published essays *The English Comic Character* (1925), *English Journey* (1934), and *The English* (1973) and autobiographical works. Depicted ordinary people in over 100 books and plays; came to epitomize the archetypal Englishman.

Priestley, Joseph. 1733–1804. English clergyman and chemist. Tutor in belles lettres in Nonconformist academy of Warrington; also lectured on anatomy and astronomy and introduced teaching of modern history and practical instruction in sciences (1761); minister in Leeds (1767–72); librarian to Lord Shelburne (1772–79); minister in Birmingham (1780–91), where his house and effects were burned because of his sympathy with French Revolution; emigrated to U.S., settling at Northumberland, Pa. (1794). Published *The History and Present State of Electricity* (1767), in which he explained the rings (Priestley rings) formed by an electrical discharge on a metallic surface and proposed an explanation of the oscillatory character of the discharge from a Leyden jar. Announced discovery of "dephlogisticated air," now called oxygen (1774); adhered to phlogistic theory of combustion; isolated and described properties of nitrous oxide, ammonia, sulfur dioxide, hydrogen sulfide, carbon monoxide, nitrogen, etc.; discovered decomposition of ammonia by electricity (1781). His theological treatises included *A General History of the Christian Church* (1790–1802) and *Notes on All the Books of Scripture* (1803–04). His *Essay on the First Principles of Government* (1768) suggested to Jeremy Bentham "the greatest happiness of the greatest number" as the criterion of moral goodness.

Pri·e·to \prē-'ā-tō\, Joaquín. 1786–1854. Chilean soldier and politician. Led revolt of Conservatives (1829–30); defeated (1830) Freire, Liberal leader; president of Chile (1831–41); with aid of Diego Portales, minister of war, administration was an era of peace and progress; constitution was adopted (1833); revolt of Freire suppressed (1836); warred with Peru (1839).

Pri·eur \prē-œr\, Pierre-Louis. *Called* Prieur de la Marne \-də-lä-märn\. 1756–1827. French lawyer and politician. Elected to National Assembly (1789); advocated radical democratic reforms; member of National Convention (1792), Committee of General Defense (1793), and Committee of Public Safety (1793); suppressed counter-Revolutionary insurrections in Brittany and the Vendée (1793–94); member of Napoléon's Hundred Days' government (1815); exiled by Louis XVIII (1816).

Prieur-Du·ver·nois \-dü̅-ver-nwä\, Claude-Antoine. *Called* Prieur de la Côte-d'Or \-də-lä-kōt-dôr\. 1763–1832. French military engineer and politician. Elected member of National Assembly (1791) and of National Convention; member of Committee of Public Safety (1793); in charge of procurement of armaments and nationalization of war industries; in Council of Five Hundred under the Directory; a founder of École Polytechnique; responsible for adoption of metric system and foundation of bureau of longitude.

Prim, Juan. See PRIM Y PRATS.

Pri·ma·tic·cio \ˌprē-mä-'tēt-chō\, Francesco. *Fr.* Le Pri·ma·tice \lə-prē-mä-tēs\. 1504–1570. Italian painter and architect. Aided Giulio Romano in decoration of Palazzo del Tè, Mantua (1526–32); called to Fontainebleau by Francis I (1532), where he succeeded (1540) Il Rosso as head artist; appointed abbé of St. Martin of Troyes (1544) and court architect by Catherine de' Médicis; decorated the Château de Fontainebleau; also designed Henry II's tomb (1563–70) and the Archives Nationales in Paris.

Pri·mo de Ri·ve·ra y Or·ba·ne·ja \'prē-mō-t͟hā-rē-'b̲ā-rä-ē-ôr-bä-'nek̲-ä\, Miguel. Marqués de Es·tel·la \-t͟hā-ā-'stāl-yä\. 1870–1930. Spanish general and politician. In Spanish–American War, served in Cuba and Philippines (1898); in Morocco (1909–13); military governor of Cádiz (1915–19), of Valencia (1919–22), of Barcelona (1922–23). After coup d'état became dictator (1923–30); dissolved parliament, suspended constitutional guarantees, and proclaimed martial law; successfully ended Moroccan War (1927); settled labor disputes and undertook public works but failed to implement agrarian reforms; forced to resign after loss of army support. His son ¶José Antonio Primo de Rivera, Marqués de Estella (1903–1936), founded (1933) the Spanish fascist party, the Falange Española; expounded his views in his periodicals *F.E.* (1934) and *Arriba* (1935); imprisoned and executed by the Popular Front (1936).

Prim·rose \'prim-ˌrōz\. Name of a Scottish family including the earls and viscounts of Rose·bery \'rōz-b(ə-)rē\:

Sir Archibald Primrose (1616–1679), Lord Car·ring·ton \'kar-iŋ-tən\, supported Royalist cause in civil war; lord clerk register (1660–76), a privy councilor (1661); justice general (1676–78). His son ¶Archibald (1661–1723), 1st Viscount and 1st Earl of Rosebery; Scottish representative peer (1707, 1708, 1710, 1713); a commissioner for union with England. ¶Archibald Philip (1847–1929), 5th earl; succeeded to earldom (1868); undersecretary for home department with special charge of Scottish affairs (1881–83); foreign secretary under Gladstone (1886, 1892–94), holding to policy of distrust of Russia, firmness with France during trouble in Egypt, consideration of common interests of Germany and Great Britain. Liberal prime minister after Gladstone (1894–95); sought curtailment of hereditary right to seat and other reforms in House of Lords, also Welsh and Scottish disestablishment. Leader of Liberal opposition (1895–96); opposed Irish home rule; during Boer War led imperialist school in split from insular school of Liberal party.

Prim y Prats \'prēn-ē-'präts\, Juan. 1814–1870. Spanish soldier and politician. Lieutenant colonel of Cristinos during Carlist war (1833–39); opposed dictatorship of Espartero; exiled (1839); defeated Espartero (1843); major general (1843); captain general of Puerto Rico (1847–48); deputy in Cortes (1850–56), supporting O'Donnell; led successful campaigns in Morocco (1859–60); made (1860) marqués de los Cas·til·le·jos \t͟hā-lōs-käs-tēl-'yek̲-ōs\; commanded joint English, French, and Spanish expedition to Mexico (1861–62); with Serrano y Domínguez started revolution that overthrew Isabella II and Narváez (1868); held four different ministries (1869–70); secured election of Amadeus of Savoy to Spanish throne (1870); murdered.

Prince \'prin(t)s\, Morton. 1854–1929. American neurologist and psychologist, b. Boston. Authority on abnormal psychology; formulated such concepts as the neurogram and the co-conscious; among first to use hypnosis for psychological treatment; founded and edited *Journal of Abnormal Psychology* (1906–29). Author of *The Nature of Mind and Human Automatism* (1885), *The Dissociation of a Personality* (1906), *The Unconscious* (1913), *Clinical and Experimental Studies in Personality* (1929).

Prince, Thomas. See PRENCE.

Prin·cip \'prēnt-sēp\, Gavrilo. 1894–1918. Serbian nationalist and assassin. Proponent of unification of South Slav peoples into a federal nation; assassinated Archduke Francis Ferdinand and his wife at Sarajevo (June 28, 1914), thus precipitating World War I after Austria-Hungary invaded Serbia.

Prin·gle \'priŋ-(g)əl\, Sir John. 1707–1782. British physician. Physician general to forces in Flanders (1744), in London (from 1748); physician to George III (1774). Known as founder of modern military medicine for reforms in army hospital and camp sanitation; recognized forms of dysentery as one disease; coined term influenza; wrote *Observations on the Diseases of the Army* (1752).

Pringle, Thomas. 1789–1834. Scottish poet. Started (1817) magazine that became parent of *Blackwood's Magazine*; through friendship of Sir Walter Scott, obtained grant of land in South Africa for brothers (1819) and became (1820) government librarian at Cape Town. Returned to London (1826) and worked in antislavery movement. Author of *South African Sketches* (1834), a volume of poems *Ephemerides* (1828), and an autobiography *Narrative of a Residence in South Africa* (1835). Called father of South African poetry.

Prings·heim \'priŋs-ˌhīm\, Ernst. 1859–1917. German physicist. Professor, Berlin (1896–1905), Breslau (1905–17); known for work with Otto Lummer on radiation of heat from black bodies; verified Stefan-Boltzman law (1900); results of this work led Max Planck to develop the quantum hypothesis.

Pringsheim, Nathanael. 1823–1894. German botanist. One of first to demonstrate sexual reproduction in algae (1855); with Julius von Sachs, first to describe plastids (1868); published paper on alternation of generations in mosses and thallophytes (1876); founder and editor of *Jahrbücher für wissenschaftliche Botanik* (1858–94).

Prin·sep \'prin-(ˌ)sep\, James. 1799–1840. English antiquary and colonial administrator in India. Architect by training; assay master at mints at Calcutta (1819, 1832–38) and at Benares (1820–30); at Calcutta introduced a uniform coinage and reformed system of weights and measures; as secretary of Asiatic Society of Bengal (1832–38) amassed large collection of Indian coins.

Prinsterer. See GROEN VAN PRINSTERER.

Printz \'prins\, Johan Björnsson. 1592–1663. Swedish administrator in America. Governor of New Sweden colony on the Delaware River (1643–53).

Pri·or \'prī(-ə)r\, Edward Schröder. 1852–1932. British architect. Professor of fine arts, Cambridge (1912–32); a leader of Arts and Crafts movement; among his Neo-Gothic designs, Harrow Music School (1891), Home Place, Holt, Norfolk (1903–05), St. Andrew's Church, Roker, County Durham (1906–07).

Prior, Matthew. 1664–1721. English poet and diplomat. Friend of Charles Montagu (afterwards Earl of Halifax), with whom he wrote (1687) *The City Mouse and the Country Mouse* in ridicule of Dryden's *Hind and the Panther;* secretary in negotiations at Rijswijk (1697); went over to Tories (1702), allying himself with Harley and St. John; employed through Queen Anne's reign in negotiations with France; took leading part in framing Treaty of Utrecht (1713), called "Matt's Peace"; on Queen Anne's death impeached by Sir Robert Walpole and imprisoned (1715–17). In prison composed long humorous poem *Alma, or the Progress of the Mind* (1718). Known for his occasional poems, for his neat epigrams, for elegance and easy grace of his familiar verse, as in *To a Child of Quality, The Female Phaeton.*

Pri·scian \'prish-(ē-)ən\. *Full Lat. name* Pri·sci·a·nus Cae·sar·i·en·sis \ˌprish-ē-'ā-nəs-si-ˌzar-ē-'en-səs, -si-ˌzer-\. fl. 500 A.D. Latin grammarian at Constantinople. Author of *Institutionis grammaticae,* an exposition of Latin grammar that became the standard textbook for the teaching of grammar in medieval European schools; also wrote a verse panegyric on Anastasius, treatises on Terence and on weights and measures, and minor grammatical works.

Pris·cil·lian \prə-'sil-yən, -'sil-ē-ən\. *Lat.* Pris·cil·li·a·nus \prə-ˌsil-ē-'ā-nəs\. c.340–385. Spanish religious reformer. As layman, founded religious sect, now called Priscillianists; ordained priest and consecrated bishop of Ávila (380); some of his tenets condemned as heretical by synod of Saragossa (380); exiled by Emperor Gratian; condemned to death for sorcery and executed along with other Priscillianist leaders.

Priscus, Helvidius. See HELVIDIUS.

Pritch·ard \'prich-ərd\, Charles. 1808–1893. English astronomer. Professor at Oxford (1870), where he established observatory; determined libration of the moon; used wedge photometer in stellar photometry, measuring brightness of numerous stars; used photography in determination of stellar parallax.

Pritchard, Hannah, *nee* Vaughan \'vȯn\. 1711–1768. English actress. Member of Garrick's company for twenty years; excelled in characters of intrigue, including Lady Betty Modish and Lady Townly; also in tragedy as the Queen in *Hamlet,* Cleopatra in *All for Love,* Zara in *The Mourning Bride,* and not surpassed as Lady Macbeth until Mrs. Siddons.

Prith·vi Na·ra·yan Shah \'prit-vē-nə-'rä-yän-'shä, -'shȯ\. 1730–1775. Nepalese ruler. Ruler (1742–75) of Gorkha; conquered Malla kingdoms and Kāthmāndu Valley of Nepal and consolidated them into modern state of Nepal (1769); established his capital at Kāthmāndu.

Pro, Miguel. See PRO JUÁREZ.

Pro·bus \'prō-bəs\, Marcus Aurelius. d. 282. Roman emperor (276–282). Distinguished soldier under emperors Valerian, Claudius, and Aurelian; made governor of the East by Tacitus; proclaimed emperor in opposition to Florian by soldiers; waged successful wars in Gaul and Illyricum and put down usurpers; killed in mutiny of his soldiers.

Probus, Marcus Valerius. 1st century A.D. Latin grammarian and critic. Prepared annotated editions of Roman classics, as of Virgil, Plautus, Terence, Horace, Lucretius, etc.; wrote a biography of Persius; only a commentary on Virgil's *Eclogues* and *Georgics* is extant.

Pro·cac·ci·ni \ˌprō-kät-'chē-nē\. Family of Italian painters, including: Ercole (1520?–1595), pupil of Annibale Carracci; opened a school of painting in Milan; best works in Bologna churches. His son ¶Camillo (1551–1629) painted religious subjects as *The Last Judgment* (Church of Saint Procolo, Reggio). Another son ¶Giulio Cesare (c.1570–1626), among whose works were *Transfiguration* (Milan) and *St. Francis of Assisi* (the Louvre). A third son ¶Carlo Antonio (c.1555–1605) was a religious painter. Carlo's son ¶Ercole, *called* the Younger (1596–1676) was known for still-life paintings; succeeded to direction of the Milan academy.

Prochorus Cydones. See under DEMETRIUS CYDONES.

Pro·clus \'prō-kləs, 'präk-ləs\. 410?–485. Greek Neoplatonic philosopher. Regarded as last of great teachers of Neoplatonism. Pupil of Olympiodorus the Elder, Plutarch, and Syrianus; succeeded latter as head of Plato's Academy at Athens (c.450). His philosophy derived from Iamblichus; vigorously defended paganism and opposed Christianity. Chief works commentaries on dialogues of Plato, a work on Platonic theology, a brief statement of principles of Neoplatonism, essays on *Providence and Fate, Doubts about Providence,* and *The Nature of Evil,* a compendium of part of Aristotle's works, and treatises in fields of mathematics and astronomy.

Procop *or* **Procopius** the Great. See PROKOP HOLÝ.

Pro·co·pi·us \prə-'kō-pē-əs\. 6th century. Byzantine historian. Adviser to Belisarius (527–531, 536–540); accompanied him on his Persian and Italian campaigns; with expeditions against Vandals (533–534) and in Africa (534–536). Chief works *Polemon,* narratives of Persian, Vandal, and Gothic wars of time of Justinian; *Peri ktismaton,* account of chief public works during reign of Justinian; *Anecdota,* attacking Justinian, Theodora, Belisarius and his wife Antonina, and a number of high government officials.

Proc·ter \'präk-tər\, Bryan Waller. *Pseudonym* Barry Corn·wall \'kȯrn-wəl, -ˌwȯl\. 1787–1874. English poet. Practiced as conveyancer and barrister in London; metropolitan commissioner in lunacy (1832–61). Author of poetry as *Dramatic Scenes* (1819), *A Sicilian Story* (1820), and *The Flood of Thessaly* (1823), many songs, the tragedy *Mirandola* (produced 1821), and a biography of Charles Lamb (1864). His daughter ¶Adelaide Anne (1825–1864), poet, contributed verses under pseudonym Mary Ber·wick \'ber-ik\ to Dickens's periodicals; author of *Legends and Lyrics* (1858), including "The Lost Chord" (set to music by Sir Arthur Sullivan), and of hymns.

Proc·tor \'präk-tər\, Richard Anthony. 1837–1888. English astronomer and writer. Founder of *Knowledge,* a popular scientific magazine (1881); drew maps of Mars, Venus, and the Galaxy. His publications included *Saturn and His System* (1865), *Half-hours with the Telescope* (1868), *Other Worlds than Ours* (1870), *Myths and Marvels of Astronomy* (1877), etc.

Prod·i·cus of Ce·os \'präd-ə-kəs-əv-'sē-ˌäs\. 5th century B.C. Greek Sophist. Taught in Athens, a contemporary of Socrates; only a few fragments of his works extant.

Prodromus, Theodore. See THEODORE PRODROMUS.

Profiat, Don. See Jacob ben Machir IBN TIBBON.

Pro Juá·rez \prō-'k̲wär-äs\, Miguel Agustín. *Known as* Miguel Pro. 1891–1927. Mexican Jesuit martyr. Entered Society of Jesus (1911); studied outside Mexico because of religious persecutions (1914–25); ordained (1925) and returned to Mexico (1926); ministered secretly despite government ban on all religious practices; captured and executed on false charge of bomb plot against Pres. Obregón.

Pro·kof·iev \(ˌ)prə-'kȯf-yif, *Angl* prə-'kȯf-ˌyef, -ˌyev, -yəf\, Sergey Sergeyevich. 1891–1953. Russian composer. Studied with Glière, Rimsky-Korsakov, et al.; made debut (1908) as pianist in St. Petersburg and gave concerts throughout his life; awarded Anton Rubenstein prize for *Piano Concerto No. 1* (1911); first important orchestral work, *Scythian Suite* (1914–15), caused a scandal at its premiere in Petrograd (1916); began (1914) a long association with Diaghilev, writing ballets *Skazka pro shuta* (Tale of the Buffoon, 1915), *Le Pas d'acier* (1925), and *Bludniy sïn* (Prodigal Son, 1928) for his company. Lived abroad (1918–32), mainly in U.S., Paris, and Germany; returned to Russia (1933); composed *Petya i volk* (Peter and the Wolf, 1936) for a children's theater in Moscow; composed music for Eisenstein's films *Alexander Nevsky* (1938) and *Ivan the Terrible* (1944, 1948); worked (1941–52) on epic opera *Voyna i mir* (War and Peace) based on Tolstoy. Last years clouded by illness, but still productive with such works as opera *Povest' o nastoyashchem cheloveke* (Story of a Real Man, 1947–48), ballet *Skaz o kammenom tsvetke* (Stone Flower, 1948–53), and symphonies Nos. 6 (1945–47) and 7 (1951–52). Other works included operas *Lyubov k tryom apelsinam* (Love for Three Oranges, 1919), *Obrucheniye v monastïre* (Betrothal in a Monastery, also called The Duenna, 1946); ballets *Romeo i Dzhuletta* (1938), *Zolushka* (Cinderella, 1945); symphonies Nos. 1 (*Classical,* 1916–17) and 5 (1944); orchestral works *Lieutenant Kijе* suite (1934), *Egyptian Nights* suite (1934), *Russian Overture* (1936); 5 concertos for piano (esp. No. 3, 1917–21), violin (2), cello (2); cantatas *Semero ikh* (They are Seven, 1917–18), *20th Anniversary of the October Revolution* (1937); chamber music; piano music, esp. 10 sonatas, *Sarcasms* (1912–14), *Mimoletnosti* (Visions fugitives, 1915–17); and about 60 songs, esp. "Gadkiy utenok" ("The Ugly Duckling," 1914).

Pro·kop Ho·lý \'prȯ-kȯp-'hȯ-lē\. *Also called* Prokop the Bald, Prokop the Shaven *or* Pro·co·pi·us \prə-'kō-pē-əs\ the Great. c.1380–1434. Bohemian Hussite leader. Originally member of conservative (Utraquist) wing of Hussite movement; defended Bohemia against Romanist crusaders (1426, 1427, 1431); invaded Silesia, Saxony, Thuringia, and Hungary; joined peasant-worker (Taborite) branch of Hussite forces (1434); killed by combined Utraquist–Romanist force at Lipany. Another Taborite commander, Prokop the Lesser, also slain in same battle.

Pro·ko·po·vich \prə-(ˌ)kə-'pȯv-ˌyich\, Feofan. 1681–1736. Russian prelate and statesman. Adviser on church and educational affairs to Peter the Great, who called him from Kiev to St. Petersburg (1716); bishop of Pskov (1718); archbishop of Novgorod (1724). Restructured Russian Orthodox church as political arm of the state by writing new church constitution (1720); replaced patriarchate with Holy Synod; formulated a conservative theology with a Lutheran orientation.

Prony, Baron de. See Gaspard RICHE.

Pro·per·tius \prō-'pər-sh(ē-)əs\, Sextus. c.50–c.15 B.C. Roman elegiac poet. Left native Umbria and settled in Rome (c.34). His poems chiefly amatory; his first book (pub. 29), dedicated to his mistress Cynthia (real name Hostia), gained him admission to literary circle centering about Maecenas, where he enjoyed friendship of Ovid and Virgil. Four books of his poems, containing altogether over 4000 lines, are extant.

Prophet. See under TECUMSEH.

Pros·per \'präs-pər\ of Aq·ui·taine \ˌak-wə-'tān\. Saint. *Also* Prosper Ti·ro \-'tī-ˌrō\. c.390–c.463. French Christian writer. Lived in Marseilles as a monk; in Rome as secretary to Pope Leo I (435 ff.). Author of polemical literature, including a poem *De ingratis,* against Semi-Pelagians, a series of defenses of Saint Augustine, and a treatise against the *Collatio* of John Cassian. Also wrote

Epitoma chronicorum, a chronicle valuable as source book, esp. for years 425–455 A.D., and compiled a collection of Augustinian propositions.

Prosser, Gabriel. See GABRIEL.

Pro·tag·o·ras \prō-'tag-ə-rəs\. c.485–410 B.C. Greek philosopher. Taught in Athens; known as first of the Sophists; friend of Pericles; appointed lawgiver for colony of Thurii in Italy; accused of impiety; his books were publicly burned and he was exiled (c.415). His philosophy was epitomized in famous saying "Man is the measure of all things: of those which are, that they are; of those which are not, that they are not." Credited with being first to systematize study of grammar, distinguishing parts of speech, tenses, and moods.

Pro·tić \'prō-tēty\, Stojan. 1857–1923. Yugoslav editor and politician. Editor of Serbian Radical party newspaper *Samouprava;* also editor of *Odjek* (1884) and *Delo* (1894). Member of Serbian parliament (1887–97, 1901 ff.); joined Pašić as leader of Radical party (1903); home secretary and minister of finance. First prime minister of Kingdom of Serbs, Croats, and Slovenes (1918–19, 1920); as minister in charge of constituent assembly (1920–21) argued for moderate decentralization and broke with Pašić on that issue.

Pro·tog·e·nes \prō-'täj-ə-nēz\. 4th century B.C. Greek painter. Studio in Rhodes; rival of Apelles; noted for the extreme care which he devoted to every detail of his paintings. Among his notable works were *Ialysus* in Rhodes, *Resting Satyr* (painted during siege of Rhodes by Demetrius Poliorcetes, 305–304 B.C.), and portraits of King Antigonus and Aristotle's mother.

Pro·to·po·pov \prə-(,)tə-'pō-pəf\, Aleksandr Dmitriyevich. 1866?–1918. Russian politician. Large landholder in Simbirsk province; member of 3d and 4th Dumas (1907, 1912); considered reactionary by his party colleagues and dismissed from Moderate Liberal party; as minister of interior (1916–17), urged dissolution of the Duma and repressive measures to prevent food riots; latter actions actually caused strikes and riots which resulted in overthrow of government (March 1917); arrested and executed.

Proud \'prau̇d\, Joseph. 1745–1826. English clergyman. One of organizers (1787–88) in London of New Jerusalem Church which held beliefs of Emanuel Swedenborg; composed over 300 hymns still used in Swedenborgian worship.

Prou·dhon \prü-dōn\, Pierre-Joseph. 1809–1865. French journalist and Socialist. Regarded as father of anarchism. Became a mutualist while working in Lyons (1843); took active part in Socialist movement in Paris (1848); founded and edited radical journals *Le Représentant du Peuple* (1848–49), *La Voix du Peuple* (1849–50), and *Le Peuple de 1850* (1850); in exile (1858–62) after publication of *De la justice dans la révolution et dans l'église* (1858); pardoned by Napoléon III. Student and critic of all existent forms of political organization, he wrote *Qu'est-ce que la propriété?* (1840), *Contradictions économiques* (1846), *La Philosophie de la misère* (1846), *Confessions d'un révolutionnaire* (1849), *L'Idée générale de la révolution au XIX*e *siècle* (1851), *La Guerre et la paix* (1861), *La Capacité des classes ouvrières* (1863), etc.

Proust \prüst\, Joseph-Louis. 1754–1826. French chemist. Director of royal laboratory, Madrid (1799); lost position with fall of Charles IV, his patron, and returned to France (1808). Established law of definite proportions known also as Proust's law; first to prepare sugar from grapes, proving its identity with that obtained from honey (1799); discovered leucine in cheese (1818).

Proust, Marcel. 1871–1922. French novelist. Retired (c.1905) from fashionable society due to asthma attacks, death of parents, and disillusionment with world; author of a series of novels under the general title *À la recherche du temps perdu,* comprising *Du côté de chez Swann* (1913), *À l'ombre des jeunes filles en fleurs* (1919, Goncourt prize), *Le Côté de Guermantes* (1921), *Sodome et Gomorrhe* (1921), *La Prisonnière* (1923), *Albertine disparue* (1925), *Le Temps retrouvé* (1927); also published *Les Plaisirs et les jours* (1896, short stories) and miscellaneous works. Introduced exhaustive psychological analysis as a recognized element in fiction.

Prout, Father. See Francis Sylvester MAHONY.

Prout \'prau̇t\, Ebenezer. 1835–1909. English musical theorist and composer. Author of *Harmony* (1889), *Counterpoint* (1890), *Fugue* (1891), *The Orchestra* (1897); composed 4 symphonies, 2 overtures, 2 organ concertos, cantatas, and chamber and church music.

Prout, Samuel. 1783–1852. English watercolorist. Known for series of paintings of English landscape and marine scenes and of Continental streets and market places; author of several handbooks for art students.

Prout, William. 1785–1850. English chemist and physician. Practiced in London; suggested that hydrogen is the fundamental unit from which all elements are built (1815–16); prepared pure urea (1818); discovered hydrochloric acid in gastric juices (1824); among first to classify food components into fats, carbohydrates, and proteins (1827); made significant determinations of the density of air (1822–23).

Prou·ty \'prau̇t-ē\, Olive, *nee* Hig·gins \'hig-ənz\. 1882–1974. American novelist, b. Worcester, Mass. Author of *Bobbie, General Manager* (1913), *Stella Dallas* (1922), *White Fawn* (1931), *Lisa Vale* (1938), etc.

Pro·voost \'prō-,vōst\, Samuel. 1742–1815. American clergyman, b. New York City. Loyal to American Revolution; organized Protestant Episcopal church after Revolution; minister in Trinity parish (from 1784); consecrated first bishop of New York (1787).

Pru·den·ti·us \prü-'den-sh(ē-)əs\, Aurelius Clemens. 348–after 405. Latin Christian poet, b. Spain. Held two provincial governorships; held official position under Emperor Theodosius; retired to write poems on Christian themes (c.392). Author of *Cathemerinon* (including twelve long hymns for devotional use), *Psychomachia* (depiction of the struggle between virtue and vice for the soul of a Christian, considered first purely allegorical poem in European literature), *Peristephanon* (hymns praising martyrs and martyrdom), *Hamartigenia* (on the origin of evil), and *Apotheosis* (defense of the doctrine of the divinity of Christ).

Prud·homme \prūē-dôm\, René-François-Armand. *Pseudonym* Sul·ly Prudhomme \sūēl-lē-\. 1839–1907. French poet. A leader of French Parnassian movement; known for short philosophical, didactic, and symbolic poems inspired by Positivism; awarded first Nobel prize for literature (1901). Verse collections included *Stances et poèmes* (1865), *Les Solitudes* (1869), *Les Destins* (1872), *La France* (1874), *Le Prisme* (1886), *La Bonheur* (1888), *Épaves* (1908).

Pru·d'hon \prūē-dōn\, Pierre-Paul. 1758–1823. French painter. Employed intermittently as portraitist and decorator at court of Napoléon; regarded as leading painter of the Empire period. Known for allegorical or mythological paintings, as *La Justice et la Vengeance divine poursuivant le crime* (1808) and *Venus et Adonis* (1812), and for portraits, as of Empress Joséphine (1805).

Prus, Bolesław. See Aleksander GLOWACKI.

Pru·si·as \'prü-sh(ē-)əs\. Name of two kings of Bithynia:

Prusias I. *Known as* the Lame. d. 192 B.C. King (237–192 B.C.). Warred with Attalus I of Pergamum, married the sister of Philip of Macedon, and aided Philip in fighting the Romans.

Prusias II. *Known as* the Horseman. d. 148 B.C. King (192–148 B.C.). Son of Prusias I; summoned Hannibal to his court and planned under Roman influence to assassinate him, but Hannibal discovered the plan and committed suicide (183); was forced by the Romans to return (154) conquests he had made of territory in Pergamum.

Prussia, House of. For rulers of Prussia, see houses of BRANDENBURG and HOHENZOLLERN.

Prutz \'prüts\, Robert Eduard. 1816–1872. German writer. Among his works were *Gedichte* (1841), the novels *Die Schwägerin* (1851), *Das Engelchen* (1851), *Oberndorf* (1862), the literary histories *Geschichte des deutschen Theaters* (1847), *Die deutsche Literatur der Gegenwart 1848–58* (1859), and plays.

Prynne \'prin\, William. 1600–1669. English Puritan pamphleteer. Wrote controversial pamphlets assailing Arminianism and ceremonialism (1627 ff.); attacked popular amusements and particularly stage plays in *Histrio-Mastix* (1633); sentenced to life imprisonment and loss of his ears in pillory for supposed aspersion upon Charles I and Queen Henrietta Maria. Assailed Wren and the bishops in pamphlets written in Tower of London; deprived of stumps of his ears and branded on cheeks SL (*Seditious Libeler,* but interpreted by Prynne *Stigmata Laudis,* i.e. of Archbishop Laud). Released from prison by Long Parliament (1640); attacked Laud with vindictiveness (1644); M.P. (1648); opposed Independents and execution of Charles I; expelled by Pride's Purge; readmitted to Parliament as a Royalist (1661); made keeper of the records by Charles II; published *Brevia parliamentaria rediviva* (1662), most valuable of his compilations of constitutional history.

Przes·myc·ki \pshes-'mit-skē\, Zenon. *Pseudonym* Mi·riam \'mēr-yäm\. 1861–1944. Polish man of letters. Editor of weekly magazine *The Life,* Warsaw (1887–88), and monthly *Chimera* (1901–08); through these periodicals, exercised strong influence on development of Polish literature, esp. the introduction of Symbolism. Author of verse, and translations from Leconte de Lisle, Verlaine, Maeterlinck, et al.

Przhe·val·sky \pər-zhi-'väl-skəi\, Nikolay Mikhaylovich. 1839–1888. Russian explorer. Traveled to west central China (1870–73); rediscovered (1876–77) Lake Lop Nor, formerly visited by Marco Polo; explored (1879–80) eastern Tibet and sources of Hwang Ho; on last trip (1883–85), crossed Gobi desert and located watershed between Hwang Ho and Yangtze. Among his discoveries were a wild camel and an early type of horse, now known as Przhevalski's horse.

Przy·by·szew·ski \pshib-i-'shef-skē\, Stanisław. 1868–1927. Polish writer. Among his novels were *Homo Sapiens* (1895–98) and *Krzyk* (1917); among his prose poems, *De Profundis* (1896) and *Androgyne* (1900); among his plays, *Das grosse Glück* (1900) and *Śnieg* (1903).

Przy·sucha \pshi-'sü-kȧ\, Jacob Isaac ben Asher. 1766–1814. Polish Jewish Hasidic leader. Sought to turn Polish-Jewish community away from reliance on miracle workers by urging more rationalistic approach to Ḥasidism and speculative study of the Torah.

Psal·ma·naz·ar \,sal-mə-'naz-ər\, George. c.1679–1763. French literary impostor in London. Real name unknown; posed as a pagan Formosan; imposed upon many in London, including bishop of London, for whom he translated the catechism into "Formosan"; confessed to his imposture after serious illness (1728); became a Hebraist and worked as hack writer; highly esteemed by Dr. Johnson.

Psam·tik \'sam-tik\. *Libyan* Psam·a·tik \'sam-ə-tik\. *Gr.* Psam·met·i·chos \sə-'met-ə-kəs\. Name of three kings of Egypt of 26th dynasty:

Psamtik I. 7th century B.C. King (664–610). Founder of dynasty; son of Necho I and father of Necho II; established as regent of Egypt under Assyrians by Ashurbanipal (663); renounced allegiance to Assyria, subdued other Assyrian princes in Delta, and restored independence of Egypt (658–51); made capital at Sais; introduced Greek and Carian mercenaries into armies and permitted Greeks to settle in the Delta; seized Thebes (654); strengthened frontiers; promoted commerce; reign marked by extraordinary renaissance in art.

Psamtik II. 6th century B.C. King (595–589). Son of Necho II and father of Apries. Invaded Kush; reign remarkable for inscriptions of Greek and other mercenaries on colossi of temple at Abu Simbel.

Psamtik III. 6th century B.C. King (526–525). Son of Ahmose II; defeated by Cambyses II at Pelusium, Egypt becoming Persian province; executed for conspiracy against Persians.

Psellus, Michael Constantine. See MICHAEL CONSTANTINE PSELLUS.

Pseudo-Areopagite *or* **Pseudo-Dionysius.** See DIONYSIUS the Areopagite.

Pseudo-Demetrius. See DMITRY.

Psi·cha·ri \psē-kȧ-rē\, Jean. *Orig.* Ioannis Psi·cha·ris \psē-'kär-ēs\. 1854–1929. French philologist of Greek descent. A leader of demotic movement to establish modern Greek as a legitimate literary language; author of *To taxidi mou* (1888) and other works in this language. His son ¶Ernest Psichari (1883–1914); French writer; soldier in Africa (1906–12), recorded experiences in novel *L'Appel des armes* (1913); his conversion (1913) from agnosticism to Roman Catholicism basis of autobiographical novel *Le Voyage de centurion* (1916).

Ptah·ho·tep \(pə-)tä(k)-'hō-tep\. fl. 2400 B.C. Sage and vizier of ancient Egypt. Author of *The Proverbs of Ptahhotep,* oldest monument of Egyptian literature extant, used in later reigns as school book.

Ptochoprodromus. See THEODORE PRODROMUS.

Ptol·e·my \'täl-ə-mē\. *Lat.* Ptol·e·mae·us \,täl-ə-'mē-əs\. Name of fifteen kings of Egypt, comprising the Ptolemaic or Macedonian dynasty (323–30 B.C.):

Ptolemy I. *Called* Ptolemy So·ter \-'sōt-ər\, *i.e.* Preserver. 367, 366 or 364–283 or 282 B.C. King (323–285 B.C.), founder of the dynasty. General of army of Alexander the Great and one of his successors (Diadochoi) in partition of his empire (323), receiving Egypt and Libya. Nominally satrap (323–306) but from the first actual ruler; defended his province in continuous wars with Alexander's generals; formed alliance with Antipater against Perdiccas, who was killed (321) by his own soldiers when he invaded Egypt; lost Syria to Antigonus (315), but won back southern Syria by victory over Demetrius at Gaza (312). Assumed title of king (305); supported Rhodians against Demetrius I (304), whence the title *Soter;* concluded alliance with Cassander, Seleucus, and Lysimachus against Antigonus, who was defeated and killed at Ipsus (301). Made Alexandria his capital and foremost city in world; founded its library and museum and made it a haven for scholars; extended boundaries of kingdom; wrote a life of Alexander the Great. Resigned (285) in favor of his son Ptolemy Philadelphus.

Ptolemy II. *Called* Ptolemy Phil·a·del·phus \-,fil-ə-'del-fəs\. 308–246 B.C. King (285–246 B.C.). Son of Ptolemy I and brother of Ptolemy Ceraunos (see below); m. 1st Arsinoe I, daughter of Lysimachus of Thrace, 2d (276) his own sister Arsinoe II. Except for wars with Antiochus I and II of Syria, enjoyed peaceful reign; encouraged commerce, gaining maritime supremacy in Mediterranean and developing trade in Red Sea; developed agriculture; built canal from Red Sea to Nile; established colony of Ptolemaïs Epitheras (near modern Suakin); encouraged literature (the Pleiad) and arts; made Alexandria center of Hellenistic culture; built lighthouse on Pharos.

Ptolemy III. *Called* Ptolemy Eu·er·ge·tes \-yü-'er-jət-ēz\, *i.e.* Benefactor. d. 221 B.C. King (246–221 B.C.). Son of Ptolemy II; m. Berenice II of Cyrene. To avenge death of his sister Berenice, fought war (246–245) with Seleucus II of Syria and invaded Seleucid dominions; captured and retained Orontes River region, Antioch, Ephesus, and Thrace; recalled (243) by revolt in Egypt; reign for next twenty years generally one of peace; replaced Macedonian calendar with Egyptian solar year; restored temple statues; controlled eastern Mediterranean but allowed army to decline. Liberal patron of arts; added many books to great library in Alexandria; began temple at Idfu and erected many buildings elsewhere; left Egypt at peak of its political power.

Ptolemy IV. *Called* Ptolemy Phi·lop·a·tor \-fi-'läp-ə-,tȯr\, *i.e.* loving his father. d. 205 B.C. King (221–205 B.C.). Son of Ptolemy III; m. his sister Arsinoe III. Weak ruler, under influence of court favorites, esp. Sosibius; persuaded by them to murder his mother, uncle, and brother; his army defeated by Antiochus III of Syria (218), but won decisive victory over Antiochus at Raphia (217); his reign troubled by Egyptian rebellions (c.210 ff.).

Ptolemy V. *Called* Ptolemy Epiph·a·nes \-i-'pif-ə-nēz\, *i.e.* Illustrious. 210?–180 B.C. King (203–180 B.C.). Son of Ptolemy IV. Kingdom attacked by Antiochus III; Coele Syria and Palestine seized, and Egypt threatened, but saved by intervention of Rome; betrothed (198; m. 193) to Cleopatra I, daughter of Antiochus; declared of age (197), celebrated in a decree inscribed (196) by the Egyptian priesthood on the Rosetta stone; joined Rome in war against Antiochus; reign also troubled with native revolts begun in father's reign.

Ptolemy VI. *Called* Ptolemy Phil·o·me·tor \-fil-ə-'mē-tȯr\, *i.e.* loving his mother. d. 145 B.C. King (180–145 B.C.). Son of Ptolemy V; m. his sister Cleopatra II. During his minority, country ruled by his mother; crowned king (173); defeated and made prisoner (170) by Antiochus IV; restored by Rome as joint ruler (170–164) with his brother Ptolemy VIII; quarreled and obliged to flee; restored by Rome (163), but Cyrenaica given to brother; supported Demetrius II of Syria against Alexander Balas (148–145); killed in battle.

Ptolemy VII. *Called* Ptolemy Ne·os Phi·lop·a·tor \-'nē-,äs-fi-'läp-ə-tȯr\, *i.e.* New Philopator. d. 144 B.C. King (145–144). Son of Ptolemy VI. Served as co-ruler with his mother; killed by his uncle, Ptolemy VIII.

Ptolemy VIII. *Called* Ptolemy Euergetes II. *Nicknamed* Phys·con \'fis-,kän\, *i.e.* fat paunch. d. 116 B.C. King (145–116 B.C.). Brother of Ptolemy VI; m. 1st his own sister Cleopatra II, widow of Ptolemy VI, 2d his niece Cleopatra III. Joint ruler with Ptolemy VI (170–164); sole ruler (163) after expelling his brother; king of Cyrenaica (163–144); represented as extremely vicious and dissolute; expelled from Egypt by revolution led by his wife (131–129), but returned. Instituted economic and civil reforms (118); encouraged Roman interference in Egypt. Friendly to culture; improved Alexandrian library; restored many temples.

Ptolemy IX. *Called* Ptolemy Soter II, *also* La·thy·rus \lə-'thī-rəs\, *i.e.* Chick-pea. d. 80 B.C. King (116–110, 109–107, 88–80 B.C.). Son of Ptolemy VIII; twice married, both times to his own sisters, Cleopatra IV and Cleopatra V Selene. Ruled jointly (116–107) with his mother, Cleopatra III; expelled by her, fled to Cyprus, where he reigned (107–88); on death of his brother Ptolemy X, recalled to rule in Egypt (88–80); suppressed a revolt in Upper Egypt; refused to aid Romans against Pontus.

Ptolemy X. *Called* Ptolemy Alexander I. d. 88 B.C. King (107–88 B.C.). Brother of Ptolemy IX. Governor of Cyprus (114–108); ruled with his mother after expulsion of Ptolemy IX; caused mother's death (101); driven from Egypt (88) after plundering tomb of Alexander the Great and killed in unsuccessful attack on Cyprus.

Ptolemy XI. *Called* Ptolemy Alexander II. c.115–80 B.C. King (80 B.C.). Son of Ptolemy X. Captured by Mithradates VI (88–84); fled to Rome (84); sent by Sulla to marry (80) Berenice, his stepmother; murdered her after 20 days' reign; killed by enraged populace; last of legitimate male line of Ptolemies.

Ptolemy XII. *In full* Ptolemy XII Theos Philopator Philadelphus Neos Dionysos. *Nicknamed* Au·le·tes \ȯ-'lēt-ēz\, *i.e.* flute player. c.112–51 B.C. King (80–51 B.C.). Natural son of Ptolemy IX. m. his own sister Cleopatra V Tryphaena. Vicious and debauched; friendly to Rome; bribed Julius Caesar in return for securing law acknowledging his kingship (59); divested of Cyprus by Rome (58); driven into exile (58–55) but restored by Rome; bequeathed kingdom to his eldest son Ptolemy XIII and daughter Cleopatra VII (*q.v.*).

Ptolemy XIII. *Called* Ptolemy Theos Philopator. 63–47 B.C. King (51–47 B.C.). m. his sister Cleopatra VII; ruled jointly with her (51–49); expelled her (49); allied himself with Pompey the Great; defeated by Caesar and drowned during flight.

Ptolemy XIV. *Called* Ptolemy Theos Philopator II. c.59–44 B.C. King (47–44 B.C.). Younger brother of Cleopatra VII; coregent with her; murdered by her to make room for her son Caesarion.

Ptolemy XV. *Called* Ptolemy Philopator Philometor Caesar, *or commonly* Cae·sar·i·on \si-'zar-ē-ən, -'zer-\. 47–30 B.C. Son of Cleopatra VII by Julius Caesar. Coregent with his mother (44–30 B.C.); after Actium, put to death by Octavian.

Ptolemy. *Lat.* Claudius Ptol·e·mae·us \,täl-ə-'mē-əs\. 2d century A.D. Astronomer, mathematician, and geographer of Alexandria. His *Megalē Syntaxis tēs Astronomias,* commonly known as *Almagest* from title of Arabic translation, described a system (Ptolemaic system) of astronomy and geography based on theory that the sun, planets, and stars revolve around the earth. His *Geography* contained an estimate of size of the earth, description of its surface, and list of places located by latitude and longitude. Also wrote *Analemma* and *Planisphaerium* on geometry, *Optica* on optical phenomena, and *Harmonica* on music.

Ptolemy of Mau·re·ta·nia \,mȯ-rə-'tā-nē-ə\. d. 40 A.D. King of Mauretania (23–40). Son of Juba II and grandson of Mark Antony and Cleopatra VII.

Ruled under suzerainty of Rome; helped Roman forces suppress a Berber revolt in Numidia and Mauretania (24); assassinated by order of Caligula; last descendant of Cleopatra VII and of Ptolemaic dynasty.

Ptolemy Ap·i·on \-'ap-ē-,än, 'āp-\. d. 96 B.C. King of Cyrenaica (c.116–96). Natural son of Ptolemy VII; ruled under protection of Rome; bequeathed Cyrenaica to Rome in his will.

Ptolemy Ce·rau·nus \-si-'rò-nəs\. d. 279 B.C. King of Macedonia (280–279). Eldest son of Ptolemy I Soter; repudiated for succession in Egypt by his father; attached to court of Lysimachus of Thrace (283); killed Seleucus I (280); defeated Antigonus; slain by Gauls.

Ptolemy Phil·a·del·phus \-,fil-ə-'del-fəs\. 36–after 30 B.C. Son of Mark Antony and Cleopatra VII. Proclaimed king of Syria and Asia Minor during father's triumph at Alexandria (34); captured (30) by Octavian and adopted by his sister Octavia, wife of Antony; nothing known of subsequent life.

Pub·lil·i·us \pə-'blil-ē-əs\, Volero. 5th century B.C. Roman tribune. Sponsor (471 B.C.) of legislation (Publilian laws) increasing the powers of the plebeians.

Publilius Philo, Q. See PHILO.

Publilius Sy·rus \'sī-rəs\, *i.e.* the Syrian. 1st century B.C. Latin writer. Freed after arriving in Rome as slave; defeated Decimus Laberius in mime contest (45); acted with great success in his mimes; known for versified aphorisms extracted from mimes by later scholars (c.1st century A.D.).

Puc·ci·ni \püt-'chē-nē, *Angl* pü-'chē-\, Giacomo Antonio Domenico Michele Secondo Maria. 1858–1924. Italian operatic composer. Studied at Milan conservatory; patronized by Giulio Ricordi. His operas, most with tragic love themes, were *Le villi* (1884), *Edgar* (1889), *Manon Lescaut* (1893), *La Bohème* (1896), *Tosca* (1900), *Madama Butterfly* (1904), *La fanciulla del west* (1910), *La rondine* (1917), and *Il trittico* (1918; trilogy composed of *Il tabarro, Suor Angelica,* and *Gianni Schicchi*), and the incomplete *Turandot,* completed by Franco Alfano (*q.v.*).

Pu·celle \pᵫ-sel\, Jean. 1300?–?1355. French miniature painter and illuminator. Master of an illuminator's workshop in Paris; excelled in drolleries and traditional iconography; noted for his illuminations of the Belleville Breviary and the Hours of Jeanne d'Evreux.

Pucelle d'Orléans, La. See JOAN of Arc.

Püch·ler-Mus·kau \'pᵫk-lər-'mùs-,kaù\, Hermann Ludwig Heinrich von. Fürst. 1785–1871. German soldier, traveler, and writer. Became famous for his travel books, as *Briefe eines Verstorbenen* (1830, 1832), *Tutti Frutti* (1834), *Jugendwanderungen* (1835), *Semilasso in Afrika* (1836), and *Die Rückkehr* (1846–48).

Pu·dov·kin \pü-'dòv-kyin\, Vsevolod Illarionovich. 1893–1953. Russian film director. Pupil of Lev Kuleshov (*q.v.*). His silent films included *Mechanics of the Brain* (1925–26), *Mother* (1926), *The End of St. Petersburg* (1927), *Storm Over Asia* (1928); sound films included *Deserter* (1933), *General Suvorov* (1941), *Admiral Nakhimov* (1946–47); author of *Film Technique* (1933) and *Film Acting* (1935).

Pudsey, Hugh de. See PUISET.

Pu·fen·dorf \'pü-fən-,dòrf\, Samuel von. Freiherr. 1632–1694. German jurist and historian. Professor of natural law at Heidelberg (1661–68) and at Lund, Sweden (1670–77); historiographer to Charles XI of Sweden (1677–88) and at Berlin to elector of Brandenburg (1688–94). Known for his theory of natural law that all men have a right to equality and freedom, expounded in *Elementorum jurisprudentiae universalis* (1660) and *De jure naturae et gentium* (1672); also wrote *De statu imperii germanici* (1667) and *De habitu religionis christianae ad vitam civilem* (1687).

Pu·ga·chov \pü-(,)gə-'chòf\, Yemelyan Ivanovich. 1726–1775. Russian Cossack soldier. Served in Russian army (c.1762–70); proclaimed (1773) himself Peter III and led a Cossack and peasant rebellion against Catherine II; after initial victories, he was decisively defeated and captured (1774), taken to Moscow in an iron cage, and executed.

Pu·get \pᵫ-zhe\, Pierre. 1620–1694. French architect and sculptor. Employed by Pietro da Cortona to work on ceiling decorations of Barberini Palace in Rome and Pitti Palace in Florence (1640–43); worked mainly in Toulon and Marseilles. Designed portico of Hôtel de Ville at Toulon (1656–57) and Halle au Poisson and Hospice de Charité in Marseilles. Other works included statues *Hercule Gaulois, Persée délivrant Andromède, Milon de Crotone,* and bas-relief *Alexandre et Diogène.*

Pu·gin \'p(y)ü-jən, *Fr* pᵫ-zhaⁿ\, Augustus-Charles. 1762–1832. French architectural draftsman and archaeologist in London. Known for his works on medieval architecture, esp. *Specimens of Gothic Architecture* (1821–23) and *Architectural Antiquities of Normandy* (1827). His son ¶Augustus Welby Northmore (1812–1852), English architect and designer, was employed (1836–43) by Sir Charles Barry upon detail drawings for houses of Parliament; had extensive practice in designing Roman Catholic churches, esp. St. Oswald's, Liverpool (1839), and St. Augustine's, Ramsgate, Kent; instrumental in reviving Gothic architecture in England in 19th century; author of *Contrasts* (1836), *True Principles* (1841), etc. Many of his designs of churches completed by his son ¶Edward Welby (1837–1875), who built cathedral at Cóbh, Ireland.

Pu·gna·ni \pün-'yän-ē\, Gaetano, *in full* Giulio Gaetano Gerolamo. 1731–1798. Italian violinist and composer. Composed operas as *Adone e Venere* (1784) and *Werther* (1796), chamber music, ballets, oratorios, orchestral overtures, and violin pieces.

P'u-i \'pü-'ē\. *Later known in West as* Henry P'u-i. *Reign titles* Hsuan-t'ung \shü-'än-'tùŋ\ *and* K'ang-te \'käŋ-'də\. 1906–1967. Tenth and last emperor (1908–12) of the Ch'ing dynasty of China. Son of Prince Ch'un; succeeded (1908) his uncle Tsai-t'ien as emperor under regency of his father and with reign title Hsuan-t'ung; abdicated (1912) on establishment of republic; permitted to continue living in palace at Peking; chose Henry as given name; restored as "nominal ruler" for a few days (1917) by a coup d'état. To Japanese concession at Tientsin (1924); installed as president (1932–34) and emperor (1934–45, with reign title K'ang-te) of Japanese puppet state of Manchoukuo; captured by Soviet army (1945); imprisoned by Chinese government as war criminal (1950–59); worked in mechanical repair shop of a botanical garden at Peking (from 1959). Wrote autobiography *From Emperor to Citizen* (pub. in English, 1964–65).

Pui·set \pwʸē-ze\ *or* **Pud·sey** \'pəd-zē\, Hugh de. 1125?–1195. English prelate, b. in France. Nephew of King Stephen; archdeacon to his uncle Henry of Blois, bishop of Winchester; through ecclesiastical politics in north of England, assisted by his mistress, Adelaide de la Percy, became bishop of Durham (1153); tried to join rebellion against Henry II (1174); on accession of Richard I, purchased earldom of Northumberland; worsted in struggle with Longchamps for the justiciarship; compelled to make submission to Geoffrey, archbishop of York (1192), and surrendered earldom (1194). Patron of learning; ordered survey of rents and customs recorded in the Durham Domesday Book, popularly known as the *Boldon Buke.*

Pui·seux \pwʸē-zœ\, Victor-Alexandre. 1820–1883. French mathematician and astronomer. Taught at Rennes (1841–44), Besançon (1844–49), École Normale Supérieure, Paris (1849–55, 1862–68); professor, Sorbonne (1857–82); introduced new methods in algebraic functions; worked on celestial mechanics. His son ¶Pierre-Henri (1855–1928), astronomer, head of Paris observatory (1893); professor, Sorbonne (1897 ff.); studied the secular acceleration of the moon's motion, and asteroids; made determination of the constant of aberration; collaborated on map of the moon; published work on kinematics.

Pu·la·ke·śin II \,pùl-ə-'kā-shin\. 7th century A.D. Indian ruler. Most important member of the Cālukya dynasty ruling in the Deccan; reigned (610–642); conquered many territories around his kingdom; defeated Harṣa in the north and Pallava king Mahendravarman I; defeated by Pallava king Narasimhavarman (642).

Pu·łas·ki \pül-'äs-kē\, Kazimierz. *Anglicized* Casimir Pu·las·ki \pə-'las-kē, pyü-\. 1747–1779. Polish nobleman. Involved in rebellion in Poland (1768–72); fled to Turkey (1772), France (1775). To America with letter of introduction from Franklin to Washington (1777); served as volunteer at Brandywine and Germantown; made general and commissioned by Congress to organize independent cavalry corps (1778); ordered (1779) to support Gen. Lincoln in South Carolina; defended Charleston (May 1779); mortally wounded at siege of Savannah.

Pulcher, Appius Claudius. See CLAUDIUS gens.

Pulcher, Publius Claudius. See CLAUDIUS gens.

Pul·che·ri·a \pəl-'kir-ē-ə\. Saint. *In full* Ae·lia Pulcheria Au·gus·ta \'ē-lē-ə-pəl-'kir-ē-ə-ò-'gəs-tə\. 399–453. Byzantine empress. Daughter of Emperor Arcadius; regent (414–416) for and joint ruler (416–450) with her brother Theodosius II; advised Theodosius to marry Eudocia (*q.v.*), who later became a rival for power and was exiled to Jerusalem (443). On death of Theodosius (450) married Marcian, who became her colleague on the throne. (See THEODOSIUS II and MARCIAN for events of reigns.) An enemy of Nestorianism and Monophysitism; a saint of the Eastern church.

Pul·ci \'pül-chē\, Luigi. 1432–1484. Italian poet. Protégé of Cosimo and Piero de' Medici; friend of Lorenzo il Magnifico; known particularly for his romantic chivalric epic *Il Morgante maggiore* (28 cantos, 1483).

Pul·gar \pül-'gär\, Hernando del. 1436?–?1499. Spanish historian. Author of *Crónica de los reyes católicos* (1481–90), a history of Castilian rulers, chief source of material concerning Ferdinand and Isabella.

Pul·itz·er \'pùl-ət-sər (*family's pron.*), 'pyü-lət-\, Joseph. 1847–1911. American journalist and newspaper publisher, b. Makó, Hungary. To U.S. (1864, naturalized 1867) and served in Union army; reporter on *Westliche Post,* German-language daily of St. Louis (1868); elected to Missouri legislature (1869); purchased St. Louis *Dispatch* (1878) and merged it with the *Post* to form the St. Louis *Post-Dispatch,* first of the Pulitzer journals. Moved to New York and bought New York *World* (1883). Member of U.S. House of Representatives from New York (1885–86); founded New York *Evening World* (1887). Founded and endowed by bequest in his will a school of journalism at Columbia U. (opened 1912); also established the Pulitzer prizes "for the encouragement of public service, public morals, American literature, and the advancement of education." His son ¶Ralph (1879–1939) was also a journalist; president of Press Publishing Co., publishers of New York *World* and New York *Evening World* (1911–30); accomplished sale of papers to Scripps-Howard chain (1931). Another son ¶Joseph (1885–1955) succeeded his father as president of Pulitzer Publishing Co., publisher of St. Louis *Post-Dispatch* (from 1912).

Pull·man \'pu̇l-mən\, George Mortimer. 1831–1897. American inventor, b. Brocton, N.Y. Cabinetmaker in Albion, N.Y. (1848–55); contractor in Chicago (1855–59); storekeeper in Colorado (1859–63). Again in Chicago, with his friend Ben Field designed Pullman railroad car with folding upper berth (patented 1864) and extensible seat cushions to make lower berth (patented 1865); organized Pullman Palace Car Co. (1867). Also devised dining cars (1868), chair cars (1875), and vestibule cars (1887). Built town of Pullman, near Chicago, for workers; his company focus of violent strike (1894).

Pulte·ney \'pəlt-nē, 'pōlt-\, William. 1st Earl of Bath. 1684–1764. English politician. Whig M.P. (1705–42); secretary at war (1714–17) under Walpole; alienated from Walpole on failure to receive cabinet position (1721); antagonist of Walpole in speeches and journalistic war; by fanning agitation against Spain (1739), contributed to downfall of Walpole government. Requested to form a government but refused (1742); created earl (1742); failed of appointment as first lord of the treasury on death of Wilmington (1743); failed to form cabinet excluding Pitt (1746); retired. Remembered for oratorical eloquence.

Pulu. See TIGLATH-PILESER III.

Pum·pel·ly \pəm-'pel-ē\, Raphael. 1837–1923. American geologist, b. Owego, N.Y. Made trip up Yangtze and overland through Siberia to St. Petersburg (1864–65); engaged in exploration of copper and iron resources in Michigan and Lake Superior region (1865–70); first professor of mining, Harvard (1866–73); made study of mineral resources of United States for the tenth U.S. census (1875–80); conducted expeditions under Carnegie Institution auspices in Central Asia (1903, 1904).

Pun·nett \'pən-ət\, Reginald Crundall. 1875–1967. English geneticist. Professor of biology (1910–12) and genetics (1912–40), Cambridge; using poultry and sweet peas, discovered (with William Bateson) genetic linkage, sex determination, sex linkage, and autosomal linkage; with Bateson founded (1910) and edited *Journal of Genetics.* Author of *Mendelism* (1905) and *Heredity in Poultry* (1923).

Pu·pi·e·nus Max·i·mus \ˌpyü-pē-'ē-nəs-'mak-sə-məs\, Marcus Clodius. d. 238. Roman emperor (238). Joint ruler with Balbinus, appointed by Senate; murdered by praetorians. See GORDIANUS III.

Pu·pin \'pü-pēn, *Angl* p(y)ü-'pēn\, Michael Idvorsky. 1858–1935. American physicist and inventor, b. Idvor, Hungary (now in Yugoslavia). To U.S. (1874); professor of electromechanics, Columbia (1901–31). His inventions included a system of multiplex telegraphy accomplished by electrical tuning (1894); the Pupin coil, which extended range of long-distance telephony; a means of overcoming static resistance to wireless telegraphy. Developed method for short-exposure X-ray photography by means of a fluorescent screen and discovered secondary X-ray radiations. Wrote *Electro-Magnetic Theory* (1895), *From Immigrant to Inventor* (1923, Pulitzer prize).

Purbach. See PEUERBACH.

Pur·cell \'pər-səl, (ˌ)pər-'sel\, Henry. c.1659–1695. English composer. Chorister of Chapel Royal, London (1669); appointed composer to Charles II's string orchestra (1677); succeeded Dr. John Blow as organist at Westminster Abbey (1679); organist to Chapel Royal (from 1682); composer in ordinary to king, composed ode or anthem for every public event. Wrote incidental music for 43 plays, beginning with Lee's *Theodosius* (1680); began composition of chamber music with a series of fantasias for viols (1680); produced opera *Dido and Aeneas* (1689), written to libretto by Nahum Tate; composed music to Betterton's opera *Diocletian* (1690), to Dryden's *King Arthur* (1691), and to *The Fairy Queen* (1692), an adaptation of Shakespeare's *Midsummer Night's Dream;* composed *Te Deum and Jubilate* for St. Cecilia's Day (1694); also composed 8 harpsichord suites (1696) and over 100 sacred and secular songs. His brother ¶Daniel (c.1660–1717), organist of Magdalen College, Oxford (1688–95), completed music begun by Henry for *Indian Queen* (1664) of Dryden and Sir Robert Howard; composed incidental music for 30 dramas in London (1695–1707).

Pur·chas \'pər-chəs\, Samuel. c.1577–1626. English compiler of travel books. Known esp. for *Purchas, his Pilgrimage* (1613), treating religions of all ages; *Purchas, his Pilgrim. Microcosmus or the Histories of Man* (1619); *Hakluytus Posthumus or Purchas his Pilgrimes* (1625), based in part upon manuscripts left by Hakluyt, and often the only source of information upon explorations.

Pur·due \pər-'d(y)ü\, John. 1802–1876. American merchant, b. Huntingdon Co., Pa. Merchant in Lafayette, Ind.; benefactor of a land grant college located at Lafayette (1869), thereafter named Purdue U.

Pur·ky·ně \'pu̇r-kin-ye\, Jan Evangelista. *Surname often spelled* Pur·kin·je \-yā\. 1787–1869. Bohemian physiologist. Professor in Breslau (1823–50) and Prague (1850–69). Known for observations and discoveries in physiology and microscopic anatomy, esp. relating to ophthalmology and embryology; credited with discovery of subjective visual figures and recurrent images, germinal vesicle in birds' eggs (1825), sudoriferous glands of the skin and their ducts (1833), ciliary movement in vertebrates, pear-shaped cells in middle layer of cerebellar cortex known as Purkinje's cells (1837), network of fibers made up of large muscle cells in cardiac muscles of children, etc., known as Purkinje's network, system, or tissue (1839), ganglionic bodies in the brain, the lumen of the axis cylinder in nerves. Recognized fingerprints as means of identification (1823); made improvements in microtechnic. Proposed word "protoplasm" for formative material of young animal embryos.

Pūrṇaprajña. See MADHVA.

Pur·nell \pər-'nel\, Benjamin. 1861–1927. American religious leader, b. Jasper Co., Ky. Organizer (1903) and head (known as "king") of a communistic religious colony called the House of David, established at Benton Harbor, Mich.

Pursh \'pərsh\, Frederick. *Orig.* Friedrich Traugott Pursch \'pu̇rsh\. 1774–1820. American botanist and horticulturist, b. Saxony. To U.S. (1799); curator of botanical gardens at Baltimore (1799–1802), near Philadelphia (1802–05), New York (1806–10); to England (c.1812). Author of *Flora Americae Septentrionalis* (1814), *Journal of a Botanical Excursion in the Northestern Parts of the States of Pennsylvania and New York* (pub. 1869).

Pur·vits \'pu̇r-vits\, Vilhelms Karlis. 1872–1945. Latvian landscape painter. Introduced Impressionism into northeastern Europe.

Pu·sey \'pyü-zē\, Edward Bouverie. 1800–1882. English theologian. Fellow of Oriel College, Oxford (1823), joining Keble and Newman; regius professor of Hebrew, Oxford, and canon of Christ Church (from 1828). Alarmed by prevalence of rationalism in Anglican church, made common cause with Keble and Newman on *Tracts for the Times* (1834); produced tracts on baptism (1835) and on the Holy Eucharist (1836); supported Newman's interpretation of the Thirty-nine Articles in Tract 90 and became henceforth leader of Oxford Movement; suspended as university preacher on charge of heresy (1843); influential in revival of confession in Church of England through sermons on *Absolution* (1846) and the *Presence of Christ in the Holy Eucharist* (1853) and books *The Doctrine of the Real Presence* (1855) and *The Real Presence* (1857); endeavored to bring about union of English and Roman churches (from 1865), as in *Eirenicon* (1865, 1869, 1870); opposed university reform.

Push·kin \'püsh-kyin, *Angl* 'pu̇sh-kən\, Aleksandr Sergeyevich. 1799–1837. Russian poet. On staff of ministry of foreign affairs (1817 ff.); his "Ode to Liberty" (1820) caused his exile to south Russia, but he continued to hold government office. Studied Byron's verse; visited Caucasus region; finally dismissed from public service because of liberalism of views. Involved in Decembrist uprising (1825), but escaped punishment; later restored to staff of ministry of foreign affairs (1832); mortally wounded in duel. Introduced Romanticism and the Byronic hero into Russian literature. Among his works were *Ruslan and Lyudmila* (1820), *Kavkazskiy plennik* (Captive of the Caucasus, 1822), *Boris Godunov* (completed 1825; pub. 1831), *Bakhchisaraiski Fontan* (1827), *Bratya razboiniki* (Robber Brothers, 1827), *Tsygane* (Gypsies, 1827), *Poltava* (1829), *Evgeni Onegin* (1833), *Pikovaya dama* (Queen of Spades, 1834), *Skupoi rytsar* (Covetous Knight, 1836), *Kapitanskaya dochka* (Captain's Daughter, 1836), *Medny Vsadnik* (Bronze Horseman, 1837), *Kamenny gost* (Stone Guest, 1839), *Dubrovsky* (1841), etc.

Push·ma·ta·ha \ˌpu̇sh-mə-'tä-ˌhä, pu̇sh-'mä-tə-ˌhä\. c.1765–1824. American Choctaw Indian chief, b. Noxubee Co., Miss. Signed (1805) Treaty of Mount Dexter, ceding much tribal land in Alabama and Mississippi for white settlement; opposed Tecumseh's confederation (1811); allied his tribe with U.S. government during Creek War (1813–14); made further land cessions (1816, 1820).

P'u Sung-ling \'pü-'süŋ-'liŋ\. 1640–1715. Chinese writer. Known for novel *Hsing shih yin yüan* ("Tale of a Conjugal Union to Arouse the World") and collection of supernatural tales *Liao-chai chih-i* ("Strange Stories from the Liao Studio").

Put·nam \'pət-nəm\, Anne. 1680?–1716. American woman of Salem, Mass. As a child of 12, figured prominently in witchcraft trials and by her testimony caused conviction of several persons.

Putnam, Frederic Ward. 1839–1915. American anthropologist, b. Salem, Mass. Curator, Peabody Museum of American Archaeology and Ethnology, Harvard (1875–1909); curator of anthropology, American Museum of Natural History, New York City (from 1894), and professor at Harvard (from 1887); organizer (1891–93) of anthropological section of World's Columbian Exposition of

1893, Chicago, which became basis of Chicago's Field Museum of Natural History; organized department and museum of anthropology, U. of California, Berkeley (1903).

Putnam, George Palmer. 1814–1872. American publisher, b. Brunswick, Me. Settled in London, England (1841), and opened store selling American books in English market (1841–48); returning to New York (1848), started a book-publishing business; established business as G. P. Putnam & Son (1866); founded and published *Putnam's Monthly Magazine* (1853–57, 1868–70). Conducted campaign for international copyright agreements (from 1837). Father of Mary Corinna Jacobi (*q.v.*). His son ¶George Haven (1844–1930), b. London, England, served in Union army through Civil War; became partner in G. P. Putnam & Son (1866) and president (1872–1930); continued international copyright struggle, organized American Publishers' Copyright League (1886), and was instrumental in securing copyright act of 1909. Author of *Books and Their Makers During the Middle Ages* (1896–97), *A Prisoner of War in Virginia 1864–65* (1912), and two volumes of *Memoirs.* Another son ¶Herbert (1861–1955) was librarian of Congress (1899–1939); transformed Library of Congress from a reference collection to a great national library; president, American Library Association (1898, 1904). A grandson of George Palmer, also named ¶George Palmer (1887–1950), was treasurer, G. P. Putnam's Sons (1919–30); chairman of editorial board, Paramount Productions (1932–35); m. (1931) as 2d wife Amelia Earhart (*q.v.*) and edited her book *Last Flight* (1938).

Putnam, Israel. 1718–1790. American Revolutionary commander, b. Danvers, Mass. Served through French and Indian War (1754–63) and in Pontiac's War (1764); active in pre-Revolutionary agitation; volunteered (April 1775) after news of Lexington. Appointed major general, Continental army; engaged at Bunker Hill; in chief command at New York just before Washington's arrival and during defeat in battle of Long Island (1776); commanded at Philadelphia (1776), in the highlands of the Hudson (1777), in Connecticut recruiting service (1778–79); incapacitated by stroke (1779).

Putnam, Rufus. 1738–1824. American Revolutionary officer and pioneer, b. Sutton, Mass. Cousin of Israel Putnam. Served in French and Indian War; in command of defensive works around Boston (1775), and around New York (1776); served under Gates against Burgoyne; reconstructed West Point redoubts (1779); brigadier general (1783). One of organizers of Ohio Company to colonize tract on north bank of Ohio River; led colony to Marietta (1788) and laid out the town, first organized settlement in Northwest Territory; judge, Northwest Territory (1790–96). Surveyor general of United States (1796–1803).

Putnam, Samuel. 1892–1950. American scholar, b. Rossville, Ill. Literary critic for Chicago *Evening Post* (1920–26); contributor to Communist periodicals *Daily Worker* and *New Masses* (1936–44); wrote extensively on Brazilian history and literature; known esp. for his translations of works in Romance languages, as *Don Quixote* (1948).

Put·nik \ˈpüt-nēk\, Radomir. 1847–1917. Serbian general. Chief of staff, Serbian army (1903–16), except when serving as war minister (1904–05, 1906–08, 1912); defeated Bulgarian forces at Bregalnica (1913); during World War I, defeated Austrians on the Jadar, the Drina, and at Rudnik Mountains (1914); continued in command during defense of Serbia (1915), but was retired when armies of Central Powers overran Serbia (1915–16).

Put·te \ˈpœt-ə\, Isaac Dignus Fransen van de. 1822–1902. Dutch politician. Sugar planter in Java (1849–60); Liberal leader in parliament (1862); minister of colonies (1863); prime minister (1866); opposed forced labor and communal ownership of land in Dutch East Indies.

Put·ten·ham \ˈpət-ᵊn-əm\, George. c.1529–1590. English courtier and critic. Probable author of the anonymous *Arte of English Poesie* (1589), first detailed survey of English poetry; the authorship is sometimes ascribed to his brother ¶Richard (c.1520–c.1601).

Pu·vis de Cha·vannes \pᵫ-vēd-shȧ-vȧn, -vēs-də-shȧ-\, Pierre-Cécile. 1824–1898. French painter. Best known for his murals for the museums of Amiens, Marseilles, and Lyons, the amphitheater of the Sorbonne (1887–89), the Hôtel de Ville (1893), and Boston (U.S.A.) public library (1894–98).

Pyat \pyȧ\, Félix, *in full* Aimé-Félix. 1810–1889. French playwright and politician. Radical journalist; member of Constituent Assembly (1848) and Legislative Assembly (1849); signed appeal to arms (1849) and was forced to flee France; returned to France (1870) and became a leader of Commune of Paris (1871); again had to flee France, not to return until the amnesty (1880); Revolutionary Socialist member of Chamber of Deputies (1888). Opponent of Romanticism in literature; wrote plays as *Les Deux Serruriers* (1841) and *Le Chiffonnier de Paris* (1847).

Pya·ta·kov \pyə-(ˌ)tə-ˈkȯf\, Grigory Leonidovich. 1890–1937. Soviet politician. Assistant commissar for heavy industries (1931–37); executed for treason after conviction for having conspired with Trotsky for overthrow of government.

Pye \ˈpī\, Henry James. 1745–1813. English poet. Justice of peace at Westminster; poet laureate (1790) through favor of Pitt; author of ludicrously tame patriotic verses and one ambitious epic *Alfred* (1801).

Pyle \ˈpī(ə)l\, Charles C. *Known as* "Cash and Carry" Pyle. 1882?–1939. American promoter. Manager of football player Red Grange and promoted his national tour (1925); established first professional tennis circuit (1926); other promotions included transcontinental walking race known as the "Bunion Derby" (1928).

Pyle, Ernest Taylor, *known as* Ernie. 1900–1945. American journalist, b. near Dana, Ind. Journalist (from 1928) and columnist (from 1935) for Scripps-Howard newspaper chain; during World War II, covered American campaigns in North Africa, Sicily, Italy, and France; famous for columns about ordinary soldiers; killed during Okinawa campaign. Many of his columns compiled in *Ernie Pyle in England* (1941), *Here Is Your War* (1943), *Brave Men* (1944), *Last Chapter* (1946).

Pyle, Howard. 1853–1911. American illustrator and author, b. Wilmington, Del. Studio in New York (1876–80) and Wilmington (from 1880). Wrote and illustrated in Art Nouveau style a number of books for children as *The Merry Adventures of Robin Hood* (1883), *Pepper and Salt* (1886), *Otto of the Silver Hand* (1888), *The Wonder Clock* (1888), *Twilight Land* (1895), *The Garden Behind the Moon* (1895), *Jack Ballister's Fortunes* (1895), *Stolen Treasure* (1907).

Pym \ˈpim\, John. 1584–1643. English politician. M.P. (1621–43); made his first important speech in Parliament (1621) against relinquishing disabilities of Roman Catholics; took stand in opposition to monopolies, papistry, absolutism; took leading part in impeachment of Buckingham (1626); second to Sir John Eliot in support of Petition of Right (1628). As acknowledged leader, opened Short Parliament (1640) with speech on national grievances and urged Parliament to withhold supplies pending removal of grievances; petitioned king to make terms with Scots, thus provoking king to dissolve Parliament. By petitioning, caused king to open Long Parliament (1640); rode with Hampden through England, urging voters to their duty; assumed leadership in attack upon government; moved impeachment of Strafford and of Laud; decided Strafford's fate by revealing to Parliament plot to bring army up to Westminster to overawe Parliament; voted for Root and Branch Bill (1641) providing abolition of bishops as instruments of arbitrary government; promoted the Grand Remonstrance (1641); thwarted king's attempt to get control of Tower by calling up trainbands to guard Parliament; at opening of Civil War, a member of committee of safety (1642); took up matter of impeachment of Queen Henrietta Maria to House of Lords; led Parliament in seizing power of taxation and instituting an unprecedented excise tax and in rejecting peace negotiations; urged Essex to relief of Gloucester; persuaded Parliament to accept Scottish alliance (1643).

Pyn·chon \ˈpin-chən\, William. 1590?–1662. English colonist in America. Sailed from England (1630) and settled at Dorchester in Massachusetts colony; treasurer, Massachusetts colony (1632–34); one of first settlers of Springfield, Mass. (1636). Returned to England (1652) after church authorities denounced him as a heretic because of views expressed in a tract *The Meritorious Price of Our Redemption* (1650).

Pyn·son \ˈpin(t)-sən\, Richard. d. 1530. Norman printer in London. Successor to William de Machlinia as printer of English law books (c.1490); printer to Henry VIII (1509 ff.); introduced roman type into England (1509).

Pyr·rho \ˈpir-(ˌ)ō\ *or* **Pyr·rhon** \-ˌän\. c.360–c.272 B.C. Greek philosopher. Generally considered the father of Skepticism. Pupil of Anaxarchus of Abdera; traveled in India and Persia with Alexander the Great; founded a Skeptic school in Elis (c.330).

Pyr·rhus \ˈpir-əs\. 319–272 B.C. King of Epirus. Succeeded to the throne (306); lost his throne (302) but was restored to it (297) with the aid of Ptolemy I Soter. Went to Italy (281) to aid Tarentum against the Romans; proved himself a military genius, defeating the Romans at Heraclea (280) and Asculum (279). His heavy losses in victory gave rise to the phrase "Pyrrhic victory." Defeated by the Romans at Beneventum (275); killed in battle at Argos, Greece. Author of memoirs and books on art of war.

Py·thag·o·ras \pə-ˈthag-ə-rəs, pī-\. c.580–c.500 B.C. Greek philosopher and mathematician, b. Samos (hence known as "the Samian Sage"). Said to have traveled widely in search of wisdom; settled (c.530) in Crotona, Greek colony in southern Italy. Around him, inspired by his teaching, developed an association or brotherhood, strongly religious in nature, devoted to reformation of political, moral, and social life; Pythagoreanism maintained its organization until middle of 4th century B.C. Generally credited with the theory of the functional significance of numbers in the objective world and in music; other doctrines ascribed to him, as metempsychosis, may have been formulated by his disciples. Pythagoras left no writings; all that is known of his doctrines comes from his disciples. Pythagoreans are known to have made considerable advances in mathematics and astronomy.

Pythagoras of Rhe·gi·um \ˈrē-jē-əm\. 5th century B.C. Greek sculptor. Noted for his statues of athletes, as the boxer Euthymus (472). None of his work survives.

Pyth·e·as \ˈpith-ē-əs\. fl. 300 B.C. Greek navigator and geographer. Explored coasts of western Spain, Gaul, and British Isles; explored a large part of Britain on foot; first Greek to formulate a correct theory of tides, their periodical fluctuation, and their relation with the moon.

Pythias. See DAMON AND PHINTIAS.

Pyth·i·us \ˈpith-ē-əs\ *or* **Pyth·i·os** \-ē-ˌós\ *or* **Pyth·e·os** \-ā-ˌós\. 4th century B.C. Greek architect. Built the temple of Athena Polias at Priene; with Satyrus, built the Mausoleum of Halicarnassus, one of Seven Wonders of the World.

Q. See Sir Arthur QUILLER-COUCH.

Qā·jār \kä-'jär\. Name of a dynasty ruling Iran (1779–1925), founded by Āghā Moḥammad Khān of Qājār tribe; succeeding rulers included Fatḥ 'Alī Shāh, Nāṣer od-Dīn Shāh, Moẓaffar od-Dīn Shāh, Moḥammad 'Alī Shāh, Aḥmad Shāh (*qq.v.*); dynasty overthrown by Reza Khan (Reza Shah Pahlavi).

Qa·lā·'ūn \,käl-ä-'ün\. *In full* al-Manṣūr Sayf ad-Dīn Qalā'ūn al-Alfī. d. 1290. Mamlūk sultan of Egypt (1280–90). Consolidated Mamlūk position in Middle East by driving crusaders from Tripoli and eliminating the Mongol threat to Egypt (1289).

Qaro. See KARO.

Qāssim. See KASSEM.

Qobād. See KAVADH.

Qua·dra·tus \kwä-'drāt-əs\. Saint. 2d century A.D. Christian apologist in Asia Minor. Thought to be disciple of Ignatius of Antioch and Polycarp of Smyrna; a fragment of his *Apology for Christianity,* addressed to Emperor Hadrian during persecutions of 124 or 129, is preserved in the *Ecclesiastical History* of Eusebius of Caesarea and is considered earliest apology for Christianity.

Qua·nah \'kwän-ə\. *Known in later life as* Quanah Par·ker \'pär-kər\. 1845?–1911. American Comanche leader, b. northern Texas. Son of Chief Peta Nocone and Cynthia Ann Parker, a white captive. Led Indian alliance in raids against white settlements in Texas (1867–75); after surrender (1875), settled in Oklahoma reservation and preached advantages of white civilization, as education and agriculture, to Indians; became rich as business manager for Comanche, Kiowa, and Apache tribes.

Quan·trill \'kwän-trəl\, William Clarke. 1837–1865. American Confederate guerrilla, b. Canal Dover, Ohio. Farmer, gambler, schoolteacher, desperado, in Kansas region (to 1861); chief of irregular guerrilla band operating in Kansas and Missouri (1861–62); mustered into Confederate service (1862); sacked Lawrence, Kansas, killing at least 150 inhabitants (Aug. 21, 1863); defeated federal cavalry unit (Oct. 1863) and brutally slaughtered those captured; mortally wounded in a Kentucky raid.

Quantz \'kvänts\, Johann Joachim. 1697–1773. German flutist and composer. Pupil of Zelenka and Fux in Vienna (1717); flutist, teacher (1728), and court composer (1741) to Frederick the Great in Berlin; composed about 500 pieces, including about 300 concertos, for the flute; wrote *Versuch einer Anweisung die Flöte traversière zu spielen* (1752); added second key and sliding end to flute.

Quare \'kwär, 'kwa(ə)r\, Daniel. 1648–1724. English clockmaker. Invented (1680) a repeating watch mechanism, the forerunner of the modern alarm watch; invented (1695) a portable barometer; appointed clockmaker to King George I.

Quar·itch \'kwär-əch\, Bernard. 1819–1899. English bookseller, b. Prussian Saxony. Developed largest antiquarian book trade in world in his time; published among catalogues of foreign and English books his valuable *General Catalogue of Old Books and Manuscripts* (1887–97).

Quarles \'kwȯr(ə)lz, 'kwär(ə)lz\, Francis. 1592–1644. English poet. Secretary to Archbishop Ussher in Ireland (1626–30); chronologer to city of London (1639). Took Royalist side; wrote pamphlets in defense of Charles I, esp. *The Loyall Convert* (1644). Published series of biblical paraphrases collected as *Divine Poems* (1630); first secular work a heroic romance *Argalus and Parthenia* (1629). His emblem books *Emblemes* (1635) and *Hieroglyphikes of the life of Man* (1638) were most popular books of verse in 17th century; a prose book of aphorisms *Enchiridion* (1640) was also popular.

Quarton, Enguerrand. See CHARONTON.

Qua·si·mo·do \,kwäz-ē-'mō-dō\, Salvatore. 1901–1968. Italian poet and critic. Draftsman with government (1926–38); professor of Italian literature, Milan Conservatorio di Musica (1941–64). A leading Hermetic poet, writing introverted and symbolistic books of verse as *Acque e terre* (1930), *Oboe sommerso* (1932), *Odore di eucalyptus* (1933), *Erato e Apollion* (1936), and *Ed è subito sera* (1942). After World War II, dealt with more general, social themes in a simpler, realistic style as *Giorno dopo giorno* (1947), *Il falso e vero verde* (1956), *La terra impareggiabile* (1958), and *Dare e avere* (1966). Also published *Il poeta e il politico* (1960, critical essays) and translations, esp. of classical works. Awarded Nobel prize for literature (1959).

Qua·tre·fages de Bré·au \kȧ-trə-fȧzh-də-brā-ō\, Jean-Louis-Armand de. 1810–1892. French naturalist and anthropologist. Established incorrect and controversial theory of *phlebentérisme;* opponent of Darwinian theory. Author of *Histoire de l'homme* (1867), *Charles Darwin et ses précurseurs français* (1870), etc.

Quay \'k(w)ā\, Matthew Stanley. 1833–1904. American politician, b. Dillsburg, Pa. Secretary of Pennsylvania (1872–78, 1879–82), treasurer (1885–87); political boss of the state (from 1885); U.S. senator (1887–99, 1901–04).

Queen, Ellery. See Manfred LEE.

Queensberry, Earls, marquises, and dukes of. See DOUGLAS family.

Queirós *or* **Quirós.** See FERNANDES DE QUEIRÓS.

Queirós, José Maria Eça de. See EÇA DE QUEIRÓS.

Quel·li·nus \kve-'lē-nœs\, Artus. 1609–1668. Flemish Baroque sculptor. Works included architectural decorations, notably reliefs and caryatids for the town hall, now the royal palace, in Amsterdam (1648–55).

Que·neau \kə-nō\, Raymond. 1903–1976. French writer. Reader, later director (1955 ff.), *Encyclopédie de la Pléiade.* Author of humorous but pessimistic novels as *Le Chiendent* (1933), *Zazie dans le métro* (1959), and *Les Fleurs bleues* (1965), and verse as *Chêne et chien* (1937), *Les Ziaux* (1943), *Petite cosmogonie portative* (1950), and *Si tu t'imagines* (1952).

Quen·stedt \'kven-,shtet\, Friedrich August. 1809–1889. German paleontologist, mineralogist, and geologist. Authority on the Jurassic formations in Swabia; professor at Tübingen (1837–89); chief work *Petrefaktenkunde Deutschlands* (1846–84).

Quen·tal \kāⁿ(n)-'täl\, Antero Tarquínio de. 1842–1891. Portuguese poet. Leader of the Generation of Coimbra of 1860s; became a Socialist and helped found (1872) a Portuguese branch of the International. Opponent of Romanticism; known esp. for sonnets; among his works, darkly pessimistic in tone, were *Odes modernas* (1865, 1875), *Primaveras românticas* (1872), *Os sonetos completos* (1886), and the essay *Bom-senso e Bom-gusto* (1865).

Queranus, Saint. See CIARAN.

Qué·rard \kā-rȧr\, Joseph-Marie. 1797–1865. French bibliographer. Compiler of *La France littéraire,* a bibliography of 18th- and 19th-century French authors (1827–42, and a supplement, 1854–64).

Quercetanus, Andreas. See André DUCHESNE.

Quercia, Jacopo della. See JACOPO DELLA QUERCIA.

Que·ri·do \'kvā-rē-,dō\, Israël. 1874–1932. Dutch writer. Author of realistic and socialistic novels and stories as *De Jordaan* (1914) and *Menschenwee* (1903); also wrote historical novels as *De oude wereld* (1919).

Quesada, Gonzalo Jiménez de. See JIMÉNEZ DE QUESADA.

Ques·nay \kā-nā, ke-\, François. 1694–1774. French physician and economist. Physician to King Louis XV at Versailles. In economics, a contributor to the *Encyclopédie,* where his articles formulated the basis of the theory of the physiocrats; author also of *Tableau économique* (1758), *Maximes* (1758), *Physiocratie* (1768).

Ques·nel \kā-nel, ke-\, Pasquier. 1634–1719. French theologian. Member of the Oratory (1657) and director of its Paris congregation; expelled (1684). His edition of Leo the Great's *Opera omnia* (1675), with his annotations, was put on the *Index Expurgatorius,* and Quesnel was attacked for Gallicanism. His refusal to condemn Jansenism led to further attacks on him, esp. by the Jesuits; fled to Brussels (1685) and published *Réflexions morales* (1692); identified as a Jansenist, he was imprisoned (1703), but escaped to Amsterdam; established a Jansenist church in the Netherlands.

Qué·te·let \kāt-(ə-)le, ket-\, Lambert Adolphe Jacques. 1796–1874. Belgian statistician and astronomer. Founder (1828) and director, Royal Observatory, Brussels; secretary, Belgian Royal Academy (1834–74); organized first International Statistical Congress (1853). Conducted statistical researches on the development of the physical and intellectual qualities of man, formulating a theory of the "average man" as a basic type in *Sur l'homme* (1835); also through statistics attempted to find the relative penchant for crime in specific age groups.

Que·ve·do y Vil·le·gas \kā-'vā-t͟hō-ē-vē(l)-'yā-gäs\, Francisco Gó·mez de \'gō-māth-t͟hā-\. 1580–1645. Spanish writer. Personal agent and counselor of Duke of Osuna (1613–20); imprisoned after fall of Osuna (1620–23); a secretary to Philip II (1632); imprisoned (1639–42) for his political attacks. Known chiefly as a prose satirist; master of Baroque style called *conceptismo;* works in prose included the picaresque novel *La vida del Buscón* (1626), moral discourses *Política de Dios* (1626–55), and fantasies of hell and death *Los sueños* (1627); also wrote religious, amorous, and burlesque verse, published as *El parnaso español* (1648–70).

Que·zon y Mo·li·na \'kā-sȯn-ē-mō-'lē-nä\, Manuel Luis. 1878–1944. Philippine statesman. Member of Philippine assembly (1907–09); Philippine commissioner in U.S. Congress (1909–16); president of Philippine Senate (1916–35). As president of Commonwealth of the Philippines (from 1935), reorganized military defenses, promoted settlement of Mindanao, and fought corruption in government; following Japanese conquest of the Philippine Islands, became head of the Philippine government in exile. Quezon City is named after him.

Qui·che·rat \kēsh-rà\, Jules-Étienne-Joseph. 1814–1882. French historian and archaeologist. Professor (1847) and director (1871–82), École des Chartes. Wrote on medieval France; edited texts of trial and rehabilitation of Joan of Arc (1841–49); one of the founders of archaeology in France.

Quick \'kwik\, Armand James. 1894–1978. American hematologist, b. Theresa, Wis. Professor of biochemistry, Marquette U. School of Medicine (1944–66). Authority on blood diseases; developed (1932) a prothrombin time test (Quick test) that assesses the clotting ability of blood; also devised a prothrombin consumption time test for diagnosing hemophilia. Author of *Hemorrhagic Diseases* (1957), *Bleeding Problems in Clinical Medicine* (1970), etc.

Quickswood, Baron. See Hugh Gascoyne-Cecil under CECIL family.

Quid·de \'kvid-ə\, Ludwig. 1858–1941. German historian and politician. A leader in the German peace movement (from 1892); founded and edited (1889–95) *Deutsche Zeitschrift für Geschichtswissenschaft;* imprisoned briefly (1896) on charge of lese majesty for writing *Caligula* (1894). President, German Peace Society (1914–29) and German Peace Cartel (1920–29); awarded, with Ferdinand Buisson, Nobel peace prize for 1927. Author of *Völkerbund und Demokratie* (1920), *Völkerbund und Friedensbewegung* (1920), *Die Schuldfrage* (1922), etc.

Qui·dor \'k(w)ē-ˌdȯr, kē-'\, John. 1801–1881. American painter, b. Tappan, N.Y. Began as painter of tavern signs, parade pennants, and fire engines. Known esp. for series of imaginative paintings suggested by his friend Washington Irving's *History of New York by Diedrich Knickerbocker* and "Rip Van Winkle"; also painted landscapes of Hudson River valley.

Quidort, Jean. See JEAN DE PARIS.

Quil·ler-Couch \'kwil-ər-ˌküch\, Sir Arthur Thomas. *Pen name* Q. 1863–1944. English man of letters. Journalist in London and assistant editor of *The Speaker* (1887–92); professor of English literature, Cambridge (from 1912). Published most of his poetical work in *Poems and Ballads* (1896); edited *Oxford Book of English Verse* (1900), *Oxford Book of Ballads* (1910), and *Oxford Book of English Prose* (1925). Author of many romances, short stories, and novels, esp. of Cornwall and the sea, including *Dead Man's Rock* (1887), *The Splendid Spur* (1889), *Noughts and Crosses* (1891), *The Delectable Duchy* (1893), *The Ship of Stars* (1899), *The Westcotes* (1902), *Fort Amity* (1904), *Lady Good-for-Nothing* (1910), *Corporal Sam and other Stories* (1910), *Foe-Farrell* (1918), *Q's Mystery Stories* (1937); author also of several volumes of criticism, including *Adventures in Criticism* (1896), *On the Art of Writing* (1916), *On the Art of Reading* (1920), *Charles Dickens and other Victorians* (1925), *The Poet as Citizen* (1934).

Quil·ter \'kwil-tər\, Roger. 1877–1953. English composer. Known for songs and settings of English lyrics, including *Song Cycle to Julia* (1905), *Seven Elizabethan Lyrics* (1908), and settings of Tennyson; composed also orchestral music as *Serenade* (1907), *Three English Dances* (1910), and *A Children's Overture* (1920), and the operetta *Julia* (1936).

Quim·by \'kwim-bē\, Phineas Parkhurst. 1802–1866. American mental healer, b. Lebanon, N.H. Clockmaker by trade; gave hypnotic exhibitions (1838–47); devoted himself to mental healing (from 1847). In later years, endeavored to work out religious philosophy and a science of health and happiness to account for results achieved by mental healing. Among his consultants was Mary Baker Eddy (in 1862 and 1864); from him Mrs. Eddy may have gained basic ideas of her system of Christian Science. Regarded as the father of the New Thought movement.

Quin \'kwin\, James. 1693–1766. Irish actor, b. London. Appeared first in Dublin (1712); played small parts at Drury Lane, London, before first success as Bajazet in Rowe's *Tamerlane* (1715); rival to Garrick in such parts as Richard III and Falstaff; retired (1751) to Bath.

Qui·nault \kē-nō\, Philippe. 1635–1688. French dramatist and librettist. Wrote many verse tragedies, tragicomedies, comedies, as *Les Rivales* (1653), *Amalasonte* (1657), *La Mère coquette* (1665); turned to writing librettos (1671), esp. for operas of Lully (*q.v.*); credited with creating the lyric tragedy.

Quincke \'kviŋ-kə\, Georg Hermann. 1834–1924. German physicist. Professor, Berlin (1865–72), Würzburg (1872–75), Heidelberg (1875–1908); investigated molecular forces of fluids, esp. capillary phenomena, also optical properties of metals and acoustics; constructed an apparatus for measuring the length of sound waves by means of interference.

Quin·cy \'kwin-zē, 'kwin(t)-sē\, Josiah. 1744–1775. American lawyer and political leader, b. Boston. Pamphleteer in pre-Revolutionary agitation; on mission to England to argue the cause of the colonies (1774–75); died at sea on his return trip. His son ¶Josiah (1772–1864) was a politician and educator; member of U.S. House of Representatives (1805–13); opposed the Embargo Act, admission of Louisiana, and War of 1812; member of Massachusetts State senate (1804–05, 1813–20); mayor of Boston (1823–29); president of Harvard (1829–45); author of *The History of Harvard University* (1840), *A Municipal History ... of Boston* (1852), etc.

Qui·net \kē-ne\, Edgar. 1803–1875. French writer and politician. Translated (1827) Herder's *Ideen zur Philosophie der Geschichte der Menschheit;* traveled widely in Greece, Italy, and Spain, and wrote of his observations; author of epic poems *Napoléon* (1836) and *Prométhée* (1838) and a prose drama *Ahasvérus* (1833). Involved in revolutionary activities (1848) and banished from France (1852); again in France (after 1870). Opponent of Catholicism; advocated banishment of religious instruction from public schools. Other books by him were *Le Génie des religions* (1842), *Les Révolutions d'Italie* (1848–52), *Les Esclaves* (verse, 1853), *La Révolution* (1865), *L'Esprit nouveau* (1874).

Qui·ñó·nez y Mo·li·na \kēn-'yō-nās-ē-mō-'lē-nä\, Alfonso. 1873–1950. Salvadoran politician. Provisional president of El Salvador (1914–15); vice president (1915–23); president (1923–27).

Quin·ta·na \kēn-'tän-ä\, Manuel. 1835–1906. Argentinian politician. Minister of interior (1892); president of Argentina (1904–06); suppressed a radical revolution (1905).

Quintana, Manuel José. 1772–1857. Spanish writer and politician. Active in Napoleonic Wars; imprisoned for liberal activities (1814–20); president of public instruction (1820–23); tutor to Queen Isabella (1833); senator (1835); crowned national poet (1855). Known particularly for his *Vidas de españoles célebres* (1807–33); also wrote patriotic odes and tragedies as *El Duque de Viseo* (1801) and *El Pelayo* (1805).

Quintero, Serafín and Joaquín. See ÁLVAREZ QUINTERO.

Quin·til·ian \kwin-'til-yən\. *Full Lat. name* Marcus Fabius Quin·til·i·a·nus \kwin-ˌtil-ē-'ā-nəs\. c.35–c.100 A.D. Roman rhetorician, b. Spain. Practiced law in Rome; in Spain (c.57–68); taught oratory in Rome (68–c.88); tutor to Domitian's grandnephews; raised to rank of consul. Author of *Institutio oratoria* containing, in addition to principles of rhetoric, a practical exposition of the whole education of a Roman and a description of methods used in the best Roman schools.

Quin·til·lus \kwin-'til-əs\. *Full Lat. name* Marcus Aurelius Claudius Quintillus. d. 270 A.D. Roman soldier. Brother of Emperor Claudius II. Proclaimed emperor by his troops at Aquileia on death of Claudius II (270); committed suicide or was killed when his soldiers deserted to rival Aurelian (*q.v.*).

Quintus, Gaius Valens Hostilianus Messius. See HOSTILIAN.

Quintus Aurelius Symmachus. See SYMMACHUS.

Quintus Caecelius Metellus. See METELLUS.

Quintus Caepio Brutus. See Marcus Junius BRUTUS.

Quintus Cassius Longinus. See CASSIUS LONGINUS.

Quintus Fabius Ambustus. See FABIUS.

Quintus Fabius Maximus. See FABIUS.

Quintus Fabius Pictor. See FABIUS.

Quintus Horatius Flaccus. See HORACE.

Quintus Roscius Gallus. See ROSCIUS.

Quin·tus Smyr·nae·us \'kwin-tə(s)-(ˌ)smər-'nē-əs\. fl. c.375 A.D. Greek epic poet. Author of a hexameter poem in 14 books, called *Ta met' Homeron* or *Posthomerica,* narrating events at Troy from Hector's funeral to the departure of the Achaeans.

Qui·ri·no \kē-'rē-nō\, Elpidio. 1890–1956. Philippine politician. Member of Philippine House of Representatives (1919–25); senator (1925–31); secretary of state and vice president under Roxas; succeeded to presidency on death of Roxas (1948); elected president (1948–1953); his administration marked by suppression of Communist Huk movement, economic gains, widespread graft and corruption, and failure to solve social problems, esp. in rural areas.

Qui·ro·ga \kē-'rō-gä\, Horacio. 1878–1937. Uruguayan short-story writer. Known for his tales of men and animals struggling to survive in the tropical jungle, esp. *Cuentos de amor, de locura y de muerte* (1917), *Cuentos de la selva* (1918), *El salvaje* (1920), *Anaconda* (1921), *El desierto* (1925), and *Los desterrados* (1926).

Quis·ling \'kvis-liŋ, 'kwiz-\, Vidkun Abraham Lauritz Jonsson. 1887–1945. Norwegian army officer and politician. Military attaché in Petrograd (1918–19) and Helsinki (1919–21); minister of defense (1931–33); resigned to found fascist political party (the National Union) with a platform calling for the suppression of Communism and unionism. Actively collaborated in German conquest of Norway (1940); proclaimed sole political head of Norway (1940), as head of State Council of thirteen Nazi-dominated commissioners; attempts to convert Norway to National Socialism aroused fervent opposition; after liberation of Norway (1945), found guilty of treason and shot.

Qus·ṭā ibn Lū·qā al-Ba·'la·bak·kī \'kus-tä-,ib-ən-'lü-kä-äl-,bäl-ä-'bäk-kē\. fl. 860–900. Arab scientist and translator. Helped transmit Greek science to the West, esp. with translations of Aristotle and the *Mechanica* of Hero of Alexandria; also wrote more than 30 original works on medicine, astronomy, arithmetic, logic, and natural science.

Qu·tay·bah ibn Mus·lim \,kü-,tī-'bä-,ib-ən-müs-'lēm\. d. 715. Arab general. As governor of Khorāsān in Iran (704–15), conquered large parts of Central Asia for the Umayyads.

Quṭb-ud-Dīn Ay·bak \,küt-büd-'dēn-ī-'bäk\. d. 1210. Muslim ruler in India. Sold as slave in childhood; bought by Mu'izz-ud-Dīn Muḥammad of Ghūr (*q.v.*) and became his general; conquered areas between Ganges and Yamuna rivers; campaigned against the Rājputs (1195–1203); succeeded Muḥammad of Ghūr as ruler (1206).

R

Raab \'räp\, Julius. 1891–1964. Austrian politician. Member of National Assembly (1927 ff.); member of Federal Economic Council (1934–38); minister of commerce and transportation (1938). As chancellor (1953–61), guided Austria's economic rehabilitation.

Raa·be \'räb-ə\, Wilhelm. *Pseudonym* Jakob Cor·vi·nus \kòr-'vē-nùs\. 1831–1910. German poet and novelist. Author of *Die Chronik der Sperlingsgasse* (an idyl, 1856), *Halb Mär, Halb Mehr* (tales, 1859), *Der Hungerpastor* (1864), *Abu Telfan* (1868), *Der Schüdderump* (1870), *Deutscher Mondschein* (tales, 1873), *Horacker* (1876), *Alte Nester* (1880), *Odfeld* (1889), *Stopfkuchen* (1891), etc.

Rab. See ABBA ARIKA.

Rabad. See Abraham IBN DAUD.

Ra·ba·nus Mau·rus \rä-'bän-ùs-'maù-rùs\. *Also* Hra·ba·nus \rä-'bän-ùs\ *or* Rha·ba·nus Mag·nen·ti·us \-mag-'nen-tē-əs, -'nen-shəs\. c.780–856. Frankish theologian, scholar, and teacher. Educated at Fulda and at Tours (802) under Alcuin, who surnamed him "Maurus." Head of school at Fulda (803), developed it into a leading center of learning; abbot of Fulda (822–842); archbishop of Mainz (from 847); helped spread Romance learning in Germany; opposed Gottschalk's theories of predestination. Author of poems and of many commentaries and theological and pedagogical writings, esp. *De arte grammatica, De institutione clericorum* (c.810), and *De rerum naturis* (842–847).

Ra·baud \rá-bō\, Henri-Benjamin. 1873–1949. French conductor and composer. Director, Paris Conservatory (1922–41). Composer of operas, esp. *Marouf* (1914) and *Antoine et Cléopâtre* (1917), oratorio *Job* (1900), 2 symphonies, chamber music, piano pieces, and songs.

Ra·baut \rá-bō\, Paul. 1718–1794. French Huguenot leader. Certified preacher (1738); on death of Antoine Court (1760), succeeded to leadership of Huguenots.

Rabban Bar Sauma. See BAR SAUMA.

Rabbit, William. See KATAY DON SASORITH.

Rab·bu·la \'rab-yə-lə\. c.350–c.435. Syrian bishop. Son of pagan father; converted to Christianity and became a monk (c.400); bishop of Edessa (411); issued reform directives for clergy and monks; suppressed Gnostic sects and pagan and Jewish influences; at first supported Antiochan school of Nestorianism, later supported their foe, Cyril of Alexandria.

Ra·bé·a·ri·ve·lo \rá-bā-á-rē-vā-lō\, Jean-Joseph. 1901–1937. Malagasy poet. Considered father of modern Malagasy literature. Author of poems in French with surrealistic settings and themes of death and alienation; among his 7 volumes were *La Coupe de cendres* (1924), *Presque-Songes* (1934), *Traduit de la nuit* (1935), and *Vieilles chansons du pays Imérina* (1939).

Ra·be·lais \rá-ble, *Angl* 'rab-ə-,lā, ,rab-ə-'lā\, François. c.1483–1553. French writer. Became a Franciscan novice; member of convent of Fontenay-le-Comte (c.1510–24); joined Benedictine monastery at Maillezais. Studied medicine at Montpellier (1530); practiced at Lyons (1532). Wandered widely in France and Italy; returned to take parish of Meudon (1550–52). Edited various medical treatises. Fame rests on novels, first published under pseudonym Al·co·fri·bas Na·sier \ál-kò-frē-bás-náz-yā\ (an anagram of *François Rabelais*), collectively known as *Gargantua and Pantagruel* and noted for their racy humor and satire on contemporary events and doctrines: *Pantagruel* (1532), *Gargantua* (1534), *Tiers Livre* (1546), *Quart Livre* (1552), and *Cinquième Livre* (1564).

Ra·be·ner \'räb-ə-nər\, Gottlieb Wilhelm. 1714–1771. German satirist. Contributed, chiefly to *Bremer Beiträge* (from 1741), prose satires on middle-class life.

Rā·bi·'ah al·'Ada·wī·yah \,rab-ē-'ä-al-,ad-a-'wē-(y)ä\. *Known as* Rābi'ah of Bas·ra \bəs-'rä\. 713?–801. Arab mystic and poetess. First formulated the Ṣūfī ideal of a love of God that was disinterested in hope for paradise or fear of hell, thus changing Islāmic asceticism into mysticism.

Rā·biḥ az-Zu·bayr \'rab-ik-az-'zü-,bīr\. *Full name* Rābiḥ az-Zubayr ibn Faḍl Allāh. d. 1900. Muslim military leader in central Africa. Entered military service of Sudanese prince az-Zubayr Pasha and rose to position of command; with 400 followers, fled to central Africa after defeat of his master by Egyptians; established his capital at Dikwa, east of Lake Chad, and built up a large suzerainty; defeated by French forces at Kusseri in west Africa.

Ra·bi·no·witz \,räb-ə-'nò-vits, rə-'bin-ə-,vits\, Sholem Yakov. *Pseudonym* Sha·lom \shä-'lōm\ *or* Sho·lem \'shō-ləm\ Alei·chem \ä-'lā-ḵem\. 1859–1916. Russian-Jewish humorist, b. Pereyaslav, Ukraine. Government rabbi in Lubin (1880); from 1883 devoted himself to writing; used inherited wealth to encourage Yiddish writers and to edit (1888–89) *Die Yiddishe Folksbibliotek;* left Russia (1905) and settled in Switzerland; lectured in Europe and U.S.; settled in New York (1914). Author of over 40 volumes of novels, stories, and plays in Yiddish; works translated into English included *Jewish Children, The Old Country, Tevye's Daughters, The Bewitched Tailor,* and *Adventures of Mottel, the Cantor's Son.*

Ra·bu·tin \rá-bue̅-taⁿ\, Roger de. Comte de Bus·sy \-də-bue̅-sē\. *Called* Bussy-Rabutin. 1618–1693. French soldier, libertine, and writer. Served briefly in rebel forces in Fronde uprising, then in government forces; purchased rank of lieutenant colonel general of light cavalry (1653); noted for raffish adventures and tales based on them; elected to Académie Française (1665). Imprisoned (1665–66) and thereafter exiled from court following unauthorized publication of his *Histoire amoureuse des Gaules,* scandalous tales of court ladies; from exile conducted large correspondence, in part with cousin the marquise de Sévigné.

Racan, Seigneur de. See BUEIL.

Ra·chel \rá-shel\, Mlle. *Orig.* Élisa Fé·lix \fā-lēks\. 1820–1858. French actress. Acted for Comédie-Française, Paris (1837 ff.); excelled in tragic roles as Camille, Roxane, Phèdre, Lucrèce, Cléopâtre.

Rach·ma·ni·noff \(,)rək-'män-yi-nəf, *Angl* rak-'man-ə-,nóf, räk-'män-, -,nòv\, Sergey Vasilyevich. 1873–1943. Russian composer, pianist, and conductor. Conductor at Bolshoi Theater (1904–06); appeared as pianist and conductor in principal European and American cities; resident in Dresden (1907–10) and U.S. (1917–43). His orchestral works included 3 symphonies (1895, 1907, 1936), 4 piano concertos, esp. Nos. 2 (1901) and 3 (1909), symphonic poem *The Island of Death* (1909), *Rhapsody on a Theme of Paganini* (1934), *Symphonic Dances* (1941); vocal works included operas *The Miser Knight* and *Francesca da Rimini* (both 1941), choral symphony *The Bells* (1913), *Vesper Mass* (1915), songs; also wrote chamber music and piano pieces, esp. *Prelude in C-Sharp Minor* (1892).

Ra·cine \rá-sēn, *Angl* ra-'sēn, rə-\, Jean. 1639–1699. French dramatist. At court (from 1663), member of group including La Fontaine, Boileau, and Molière; had his first two plays, *La Thébaïde* (1664) and *Alexandre* (1665), produced by Molière's company at the Palais Royal; dissatisfied with production, submitted plays thenceforth to rival company, the Hôtel de Bourgogne, which successfully played his masterpieces of tragedy, *Andromaque* (1667), *Britannicus* (1669), *Bérénice* (1670), *Bajazet* (1672), *Mithridate* (1673), *Iphigénie* (1674), *Phèdre* (1677), and his only comedy *Les Plaideurs* (1668). Retired from playwriting (1677) but later wrote for a girls' school two religious tragedies, *Esther* (1689) and *Athalie* (1691). His biography was written (1747) by his son ¶Louis (1692–1763), who also won distinction as a religious poet.

Rack·ham \'rak-əm\, Arthur. 1867–1939. English illustrator. Known for imaginative, stylized illustration esp. for children's books, as *Grimms' Fairy Tales* (1900), *Rip van Winkle* (1905), *Peter Pan* (1906), *Midsummer Night's Dream* (1908), *Wagner's Ring of the Nibelung* (1910–11), *Aesop's Fables* (1912), *Mother Goose* (1913), *Dickens' Christmas Carol* (1915), *Comus* (1921), *The Tempest* (1926), *Pied Piper of Hamelin* (1934), *Peer Gynt* (1936), etc.

Racz·kie·wicz \rách-'kyev-ēch\, Władysław. 1885–1947. Polish politician. In Russian army (1914–17), later organizing Polish forces on Eastern front; Polish minister of interior; president of senate (1930–35); president of Polish government in exile (1939–45).

Rad·a·gai·sus \ˌrad-ə-ˈgī-səs\ *or* **Rad·a·gais** \ˈrad-ə-ˌgīs\. d. 406. Germanic chieftain. Invaded Italy (405 A.D.) and besieged Florence, where he was defeated by Stilicho; surrounded at Fiesole and captured.

Radak. See David KIMHI.

Ra·da·ma \ˈräd-ə-ˌmä\. Name of two kings of Merina, Madagascar:

Radama I. d. 1828. King (1810–28). Formed alliance with British governor of Mauritius, Sir Robert Farquhar, with whose aid he annexed territory and held off French; helped end slave trade; welcomed British missionaries.

Radama II. King (1861–63). Son of Radama I and Ranavalona I; succeeded mother on throne; readmitted Europeans; overthrown by oligarchy.

Radbertus, Paschasius. See PASCHASIUS RADBERTUS.

Rad·bod \ˈräd-bȯt\ *or* **Rat·bod** \ˈrät-\. d. 719 A.D. King of Frisia. Lost western Frisian territories to Pepin II of Herstal (689); reconquered lost lands after Pepin's death (714).

Radbot, Count. See HABSBURG.

Rad·cliffe \ˈrad-ˌklif\, Ann, *nee* Ward \ˈwȯ(ə)rd\. 1764–1823. English novelist. m. (1787) William Radcliffe. Most original and distinguished writer of school of Gothic romance, characterized by vivid scenic description and by startling events and horrors seemingly supernatural but ultimately traced to natural causes. Author of *A Sicilian Romance* (1790), *The Romance of the Forest* (1791), *The Mysteries of Udolpho* (1794), and *The Italian* (1797).

Radcliffe *or* **Rad·clyffe** \ˈrad-ˌklif\, Sir James. 3d Earl of Der·went·wa·ter \ˈdər-wənt-ˌwȯt-ər, -ˌwät-\. 1689–1716. English Jacobite nobleman. Brought up as companion of Prince James Edward, Old Pretender, in France (till 1710); leader in Stuart rising (1715), taken prisoner at Preston, attainted, beheaded.

Radcliffe, John. 1650–1714. English physician. Attended William III, Queen Mary, and Princess Anne, despite his Jacobitism; M.P. (1713); bequeathed property to Radcliffe Library, Infirmary, and Observatory, Oxford.

Radcliffe *or* **Rad·clyffe** \ˈrad-ˌklif\ *or* **Rat·clyffe** \ˈrat-\, Sir Thomas. 3d Earl of Sus·sex \ˈsəs-iks\. 1526?–1583. English governor. Lord deputy of Ireland (1556–66); vigorously subjugated various parts of island and reintroduced spiritual supremacy of the crown and the English liturgy; failed to subdue O'Neill; defeated opponents of Conor O'Brien, ally of England; appointed lord lieutenant of northern England (1569); suppressed rebellion of earls of Northumberland and Westmorland (1569–70).

Radcliffe-Brown \-ˌbrau̇n\, Alfred Reginald. 1881–1955. British social anthropologist. Director of education for Tonga (1916); taught at Cape Town (1920–25), Sydney (1925–31), U. of Chicago (1931–37), and Oxford (1937–46). Known for formulating a methodology for the study of social structures; author of *The Andaman Islanders* (1922), *The Social Organisation of Australian Tribes* (1931), *Structure and Function in Primitive Society* (1952), and *Method in Social Anthropology* (1958).

Ra·de·gun·da \ˈräd-ə-ˌgu̇n-dä\. Saint. d. 587 A.D. Frankish queen and nun. Thuringian princess; captured (529) by Chlotar I, who had her educated and married her; noted for humility and tending of the sick and poor; became a nun (c.555) after death of her brother; with help of Chlotar, built a convent at Poitiers and lived a life of simplicity there.

Ra·dek \ˈräd-yik\, Karl Bernhardovich. *Orig. surname* So·bel·sohn \(ˌ)sə-ˈbel-syən\. 1885–?1939. Russian Communist politician. Joined Social Democratic party of Poland and Lithuania (1901); participated in Russian Revolution of 1905; imprisoned (1906); journalist on Social Democratic papers in Poland and Germany (1906–14); in Switzerland during early part of World War I. After Russian Revolution (1917), accompanied Lenin across Germany; after German Revolution (1918), went to Germany and aided in reorganizing German Communist party; imprisoned in Germany (1919). To Russia (1920), and rose to leadership in the Communist International, but lost his influence (c.1923); charged with being an adherent of Trotsky and dismissed from the party (1927; readmitted 1930); became a Stalinist apologist; member of editorial board of state newspaper *Izvestiya* (1931–36); tried in Moscow (1937) for treasonable activities and condemned to ten years' imprisonment.

Ră·des·cu \rə-ˈdes-kü\, Nicolae. 1874–1953. Romanian army officer and politician. Served in World War I; chief of staff of Romanian army (1944); named premier and also minister of interior (Dec. 1944); attempted to counter growing dominance of Communist partisans in government; after suppression of a mass political demonstration was dismissed from office under Soviet pressure (March 1945); fled to Cyprus and to New York (1947).

Ra·detz·ky \rä-ˈdet-skē\, Joseph. Graf. *In full* Johann Joseph Wenzel Anton Franz Karl Radetzky von Ra·detz \-fȯn-ˈrä-dets\. 1766–1858. Austrian soldier. Served against Napoléon at Hohenlinden, Aspern, Wagram; chief of staff for Prince Schwarzenberg (1813–14, 1815). Created field marshal (1836). Commanded Austrian army which defeated Sardinians at Custoza (1848) and Novara (1849) and captured Venice (1849). Governor general of Lombardy-Venetia (1850–57).

Ra·de·wyns \ˈrä-də-vəns\, Florentius. c.1350–1400. Dutch religious leader. Ordained priest and became vicar of Deventer; became disciple of Gerhard Groote (c.1380); helped Groote found Brethren of Common Life and assumed its leadership on Groote's death (1384); founded (1387) Congregation of Windesheim which also practised *devotio moderna*.

Ra·dha·krish·nan \räd-ə-ˈkrish-nən\, Sarvepalli. 1888–1975. Indian educator and politician. Professor of Eastern religions and ethics, Oxford (1936–52); vice chancellor, Benares Hindu U. (1939–48); chancellor, U. of Delhi (1953–62). Led Indian delegation to UNESCO (1946–52); ambassador to Soviet Union (1949–52); elected vice president of India (1952); president of India (1962–67). Among his many works were *Indian Philosophy* (1923–27), *The Philosophy of the Upanishads* (1924), *Eastern Religions and Western Thought* (1939), *East and West* (1955).

Ra·dić \ˈrä-dētʸ\, Stjepan. 1871–1928. Croatian politician. Organized (1904) and headed Croatian Peasant party; vigorous advocate of autonomy for Croatia; member of legislature in newly organized Yugoslavia and for a short time (1925–26) minister of education; assassinated in parliament.

Ra·di·guet \rȧ-dē-ge\, Raymond. 1903–1923. French poet and novelist. Protégé of Jean Cocteau; author of *Les Joues en feu* (verse, 1920), *Devoirs de vacances* (verse, 1921), *Les Pélicans* (play, 1921), *Le Diable au corps* (novel, 1923), *Le Bal du comte d'Orgel* (novel, 1924).

Ra·din \ˈrā-dən\, Paul. 1883–1959. American anthropologist, b. Łódź, Poland. To U.S. (1884); taught at Mills Coll., U. of California (1920, 1931–41), Fiske U. (1927–31), Black Mountain Coll. (1941–45), etc. Authority on culture of primitive societies, esp. North American Indian tribes; pioneered culture-personality studies and use of autobiographical documents. Among his works were *The Winnebago Tribe* (1915–16), *The Genetic Relationship of the North American Indian Languages* (1919), *Primitive Man as a Philosopher* (1927), *Method and Theory of Ethnology* (1933), *Primitive Religion* (1938), *Indians of South America* (1942), *The World of Primitive Man* (1953), *The Trickster* (1956), etc.

Ra·di·shchev \(ˌ)rəd-ˈyēsh-chif\, Aleksandr Nikolayevich. 1749–1802. Russian writer. Civil servant; best known for his *Voyage from St. Petersburg to Moscow* (1790), in which he criticized serfdom, autocracy, and censorship; exiled to Siberia.

Ra·dis·son \rȧ-dē-sōⁿ\, Pierre Es·prit \es-prē\. c.1636–c.1710. French fur trader and explorer. To Canada (1651); captured and adopted by Iroquois Indians (1652–1654). Made fur-trading trips to western country (1654–1660), reaching Wisconsin and upper Mississippi Valley. Entered English service (1663); made expedition to Hudson Bay Region; inspired organization of Hudson's Bay Company (chartered 1670) for fur trade in this region. Served with French fleet in Guinea and Tobago (1674); led French expedition against the English on Hudson Bay (1682). His accounts of his voyages were published as *Voyages of Peter Esprit Radisson* (1885).

Rad·lov \ˈräd-ləf\, Vasily Vasilyevich. *Ger.* Wilhelm Rad·loff \ˈrät-ˌlȯf\. 1837–1918. Russian philologist, b. Berlin. Teacher, Siberia (1859–70); inspector of Muslim schools in Kazan (1871–84); curator of Asiatic museum, St. Petersburg (1884 ff.); government adviser on Central Asian affairs. Published ethnographic studies of Turkic peoples of Central Asia in *Proben der Volkslitteratur der türkischen Stämme* (1866–1907); also wrote *Aus Sibirien* (1884) and a comparative dictionary of Turkic languages (1893–1911).

Ra·do·sla·vov \ˌrȧ-dȯ-ˈslȧ-vȯf\, Vasil. 1854–1929. Bulgarian politician. Premier of Bulgaria (1913–18); instrumental in causing Bulgaria to enter World War I on side of Central Powers; fled to Berlin (1918).

Ra·do·witz \ˈräd-ō-vits\, Joseph Maria von. 1797–1853. Prussian general and statesman. Friend and adviser of crown prince (later Frederick William IV). Leader of ultraconservatives in Frankfurt National Assembly (1848); lieutenant general (1849). At Erfurt Parliament (1850), championed a union of German states under Prussian leadership; foreign minister (1850); director of military education (1852).

Ră·du·le·scu \rə-dü-ˈles-kü\, Ioan Heliade. 1802–1872. Romanian writer. Founded and edited first Romanian periodical in Bucharest, the literary journal *Albina Românească* (1829–48). Involved in revolutionary activities (1848); lived abroad, but returned (1859). Author of plays, literary history and criticism, a national epic poem *Mihaida* (1846), and translations from works of Dante, Tasso, Molière, Lamartine, Byron, etc.

Ra·dzi·will \rȧ-ˈjē-vēl\. Lithuanian Polish family raised to rank of princes of the realm in 16th century, including notably: Mikołaj I (d. 1509), palatine of Wilno and chancellor of Lithuania. His son ¶Mikołaj II (1470–1522) succeeded him to both offices; named prince of Holy Roman Empire. Mikołaj II's nephew ¶Mikołaj (1515–60), *called* the Black, was marshal of Lithuania (1544 ff.); chancellor (1550) and palatine (1551) of Wilno; inherited the princeship; an ardent Calvinist, published a translation of the Bible into Polish. The musician and composer ¶Prince Anton Heinrich (1775–1833); patron of Beethoven and Chopin; composed a musical adaptation of Goethe's *Faust*.

Rae \'rā\, John. 1813–1893. Scottish explorer. Doctor to Hudson's Bay Co. (1835–45); joined expedition of Sir John Richardson in search of Sir John Franklin (1847); on several exploring expeditions, eventually surveying and mapping some 1400 miles of Canadian Arctic coast (1846–64); proved King William's Land to be an island and learned fate of Franklin (1853–54).

Rae·burn \'rā-(,)bərn\, Sir Henry. 1756–1823. Scottish painter. Called the Scottish Reynolds. Fashionable Edinburgh portrait painter (from 1787), including among his sitters Scott, Hume, Boswell, Christopher North, Lord Melville, Henry Mackenzie, and Dugald Stewart.

Rae·der \'red-ər\, Erich. 1876–1960. German admiral. Chief of staff under Admiral von Hipper during World War I; admiral (1928); commander in chief of navy (1928–43); advocated construction of submarines and fast cruisers; grand admiral (1939); supervised invasion of Denmark and Norway (1940); dismissed from command for strategic differences with Hitler (1943); imprisoned by Nürnberg tribunal (1946–53).

Raed·wald \'rad-,wȯld\ *or* **Red·wald** \'red-,wȯld\. d. 624 or 625 A.D. King of East Anglia. Gained independence from control of Aethelberht and became fourth bretwalda; defeated Aethelfrith (616) and set Edwin on throne of Northumberland; perhaps buried or commemorated in Sutton Hoo ship burial.

Raeg·nald \'räg-näld, 'räḡ-\. 10th century. King of York. A Norse leader from Dublin; proclaimed himself king at York (919); submitted to authority of Edward the Elder (920).

Rae·mae·kers \'rä-,mä-kərs\, Louis. 1869–1956. Dutch political cartoonist and artist. His works included landscapes, portraits, posters, and esp. anti-German cartoons which appeared chiefly in the Amsterdam *Telegraaf* during and after World War I and were published in *The Great War in 1916, The Great War in 1917, Devant l'histoire* (1918), *Cartoon History of the War* (1919); also a cartoonist during World War II.

Rafael, Raffael, Raffaello, Raffaelo. See RAPHAEL.

Raff \'räf\, Joseph Joachim. 1822–1882. German composer, b. Switzerland. Director, Hoch Conservatory, Frankfurt (from 1877). Composer of chamber music, works for piano, symphonies, operas, orchestral suites, overtures, concertos, string quartets, violin sonatas, songs, stage music, etc.

Raf·fa·ël·li \rä-fä-el-lē\, Jean-François. 1850–1924. French painter, of Italian descent. Identified with Impressionists; painter esp. of street scenes.

Raffaellino. See Raffaello dal COLLE.

Raffi. See MELIQ-HAKOBIAN.

Raf·fles \'raf-əlz\, Sir Thomas Stamford. 1781–1826. English colonial administrator. Sent to Penang as assistant secretary to first governor (1805); persuaded Lord Minto of necessity of taking Java from French and accompanied expedition; as lieutenant governor of Java (1811–16), introduced new system of land tenure and removed fetters imposed on trade; as lieutenant governor of Bengkulu in Sumatra (1818–23), by acquisition and founding of Singapore (1819), checked threatened control by Dutch of Eastern Archipelago.

Ra·fi·nesque \rä-fē-nesk\, Constantine Samuel. *Called himself* Rafinesque-Schmaltz \-shmälts\ *to 1814.* 1783–1840. American naturalist, b. Constantinople, of French parentage. In U.S. (1802–04); Palermo, Sicily (1804–14); again U.S. (1815–40); traveled throughout U.S. on collecting trips; described many new species of plants and fishes. Partly anticipated Darwin by belief that each variety of a species is a deviant which, through reproduction, may become a permanent species. Author of *Ichthyologia Ohioensis* (1820), *Medical Flora of the United States* (1828–30), etc.

Rafn \'räv-ᵊn, 'räf-\, Carl Christian. 1795–1864. Danish philologist. Published works on Norse sagas and antiquities as *Antiquitates Americanae* (1837) on discovery of America by Vikings in 10th century.

Ra·ghu·nā·tha Śi·ro·ma·ṇi \'rə-gu̇n-'ä-tä-'syir-ō-'män-ē\. c.1475–c.1550. Indian philosopher. Leading representative of New Nyāya school of formal logic; his analysis of relations revealed true nature of number; chief work in logic, *Tattva-cintāmani-dīdhiti,* a commentary on works of Gangeśa (*q.v.*).

Ra·ghu·nath Rāo \'rəg-u̇-'nät-'rä-u̇\. d. 1783. Marāthā leader. Brother of Bālājī Rāo. Seized Lahore and control of the Punjab (1758); defeated Mughal forces (1763); caused murder of Narayan Rāo (1773), the fifth peshwa; became involved in civil war (1773–74); asked aid of British at Bombay, promising cession of Salsette and Bassein (1774); signed Treaty of Surat (1775).

Raglan, 1st Baron. See SOMERSET family.

Raguse, Duc de. See MARMONT.

Rah·bek \'räb-ek\, Knud Lyne. 1760–1830. Danish poet, writer, and literary critic. Directed literary periodical *Minerva* (1785–1809) and edited (1791–1808, 1815–22) *Den Danske Tilskuer,* modeled after the English *Spectator;* his home was the leading literary salon of the day; published editions of Scandinavian poets, criticism, stories, dramas, lyric poetry, etc.

Rah·man \'räm-än\, Mujibur. *Called* Sheikh Mu·jib \'shäk-'mü-yēb\. 1920–1975. Bengali politician. Cofounder of Awami League (1949); proponent of independence for East Pakistan; his arrest (late 1960s) sparked riots which eroded Pakistani authority in East Pakistan; first prime minister of Bangladesh (1972); assumed presidency (Jan. 1974); assassinated in coup d'état.

Rah·ner \'rä-nər\, Karl. 1904–1984. German theologian. Joined Society of Jesus (1922); ordained a priest (1932); professor of dogmatic theology and philosophy of religion at colleges in Austria and West Germany (from 1936); propounded "theology of liberation," doctrine applying theology to social and political problems esp. in Third World; advocated pluralistic approach to theology and supported theologians with dissenting views; adviser at Vatican Council II. Works included *Geist in Welt* (1939) and *Grundkurs des Glaubens* (1976).

Rahv \'räv\, Philip. 1908–1973. American literary critic, b. Kupin, Ukraine. Cofounder (with William Phillips) of journal *Partisan Review* (1933); often wrote on the role of the intellectual and the artist in society; author of *Image and Idea* (1957), *Myth and the Powerhouse* (1965), and *Literature and the Sixth Sense* (1969).

Ra·i·bo·li·ni \,rä-ē-bō-'lē-nē\, Francesco di Marco di Giacomo. *Known as* Fran·cia \frän-'chē-ä\. 1450–1517 or 1518. Italian painter. The major Bolognese painter of late 15th century; influenced by Umbrian school; known for religious painting as *Assumption* (1504) and several Madonnas, and for portraits as *Portrait of Federico Gonzaga as a Boy* (1510).

Raiff·ei·sen \'rī-,fī-zən\, Friedrich Wilhelm. 1818–1888. German economist. Founder of German agricultural cooperative credit societies following agricultural crisis of 1846–47; retired to Neuwied (1865) and founded the system of agricultural cooperative banks (Raiffeisen banks).

Raikes \'räks\, Robert. 1736–1811. English publisher and founder of Sunday schools. Proprietor of the *Gloucester Journal* (1757–1802); advocated prison reforms; with the aid of a local curate, Thomas Stock (1749–1803), set up first Sunday school for children (1780).

Rai·mon·di \rī-'mōn-dē\, Marcantonio. *Often called* Marc·an·to·nio \,mär-kän-'tȯn-yō\. c.1480–c.1534. Italian engraver. Pupil of Francesco Raibolini; also influenced by works of Lucas van Leyden and Dürer; leading Italian line engraver of the Renaissance; first to reproduce designs of other artists, esp. Raphael and Michelangelo, rather than own; employed at Rome (1510–27). Among his works were *The Climbers* (after Michelangelo), and *Poetry, Massacre of the Innocents, Quos Ego, Judgment of Paris, Death of Dido* (all after Raphael).

Raimondi, Pietro. 1786–1853. Italian composer. Known esp. for compositions in counterpoint; composer of operas, ballets, and religious music, esp. the sacred trilogy *Giuseppe* (1852).

Raimondino dei Liuzzi. See MONDINO DEI LIUCCI.

Rai·mund \'rī-,mu̇nt\, Ferdinand. *Orig. surname* Rai·mann \-,män\. 1790–1836. Austrian actor and playwright. Appeared chiefly in local comedy roles at the Leopoldstädter Theater, Vienna (1817–30), where he was director (1828–30); committed suicide. Author of romantic dramas and comedies, esp. *Der Barometermacher auf der Zauberinsel* (1823), *Der Alpenkönig und der Menschenfeind* (1828), and *Der Verschwender* (1834).

Rai·mun·do \rī-'mün-dō\ *or* **Ray·mond** \re-mōⁿ\. *Known as* Don Raimundo. d. 1152. French prelate in Spain. Chancellor to Alfonso VII of León and Castile; archbishop of Toledo and primate of Spain (1124–52); patronized and encouraged Toledan school of translators, who translated into Latin many Arabic and Jewish texts.

Rai·nald \'rī-,nält\ of Das·sel \'däs-əl\. c.1118–1167. German prelate and politician. As imperial chancellor (1156–59) to Frederick I Barbarossa, played a leading part in formation and execution of imperial policy, esp. against Adrian IV; archbishop of Cologne (1159); championed antipopes Victor IV and Paschal III; excommunicated (1163); died while on Italian campaign.

Rai·nal·di \rī-'näl-dē\, Girolamo *or* Hieronimo. 1570–1655. Italian architect. Appointed chief architect in Rome (1602) and papal architect (1644); among churches he designed were S. Silvestro at Caprarola, S. Lucia at Bologna (1623), S. Agnese at Rome (1652); also designed Palazzo Pamphili in Rome (c.1650) and worked on Palazzo Ducale in Modena (1631–34). He often collaborated with his son ¶Carlo (1611–1691), a Baroque architect; designed churches of S. Maria, Campitelli (1663–67), S. Maria dei Miracoli, and S. Maria in Monte Santo (both Rome), and the façade of S. Andrea della Valle (1661–65).

Rain·bor·ow \'rān-,bər-ə, -,bə-rə, -b(ə-)rə\ *or* **Rains·bor·ough** \'ränz-\, Thomas. d. 1648. English soldier. Commanded a Parliamentary regiment and fought at Naseby and Bristol (1645); M.P. (1646); took part in army council debates concerning negotiations with Charles I (1647); supported Agreement of the People; killed in battle at Doncaster.

Rain·ey \'rā-nē\, Gertrude, *nee* Pridg·ett \'prij-ət\. *Known as* Ma Rainey \'mä-\. 1886–1939. American singer, b. Columbus, Ga. m. (1904) Will Rainey. First of great black blues singers; influenced Bessie Smith; among her records were "See See Rider," "Trust No Man, " "Slave to the Blues," and "Slow Driving Moan."

\ə\ abut \ᵊ\ kitten, *Fr.* **table \ər\ further \a\ ash \ā\ ace \ä\ cot, cart \au̇\ out \ch\ chin \e\ bet \ē\ easy \g\ go \i\ hit \ī\ ice \j\ job \ŋ\ sing \ō\ go \ȯ\ law \ȯi\ boy \th\ both \t͟h\ the \ü\ loot \u̇\ foot \y\ yet \zh\ vision \à, ḇ, ḡ, ḵ, ⁿ, œ, œ̄, ue, ue̅, ʸ** *see* **Guide to Pronunciation**

Rainey, Henry Thomas. 1860–1934. American politician, b. near Carrollton, Ill. Democratic member, U.S. House of Representatives (1902–21, 1923–34); speaker of the House (1933–34); secured passage of New Deal measures.

Rainey, Joseph Hayne. 1832–1887. American politician, b. Georgetown, S.C. Barber by trade; first Negro to serve in U.S. House of Representatives (1870–79); defender of civil rights; special agent for Treasury Dept. for South Carolina (1879–81).

Rainis. See Jānis PLIEKŠĀNS.

Rai·nulf \'ren-əlf\ of Aver·sa \ä-'ver-sä\. *Also called* Ran·ulph Dren·go \'ran-əlf-'dreŋ-gō\. d. 1045. Norman leader. Led Norman mercenary force that fought for Melus of Bari (1017–18) and Duke Sergius IV of Naples (1027 ff.); received town of Aversa for services; reinforced by Hauteville brothers (c.1035); supported Gaimar V.

Rain·wa·ter \'rān-ˌwȯt-ər, -ˌwät-\, James, *in full* Leo James. 1917–1986. American physicist, b. Council, Idaho. Member of the Manhattan Project that developed atomic bomb. Began (1949) formulating theory that not all atomic nuclei are spherical; his theory tested and confirmed by Danish physicists Aage Bohr and Ben Mottelson; with them he shared 1975 Nobel prize for physics. Conducted valuable research on X-rays.

Rai·ny \'rā-nē\, Robert. 1826–1906. Scottish religious leader. Principal (1874–1901), Free Church Coll.; as champion of liberal party carried union of the Free and United Presbyterian churches (1900); first moderator of United Free Church of Scotland.

Rais *or* **Rays** *or* **Retz,** \re\, Gilles de. 1404–1440. French soldier. Distinguished himself in wars against English; fought with Joan of Arc, including relief of Orléans (1429), and was member of her guard; created marshal of France (1429); patron of the arts; arrested, convicted, and hanged for satanism and the murder of over 140 children. His name was later connected with the story of Bluebeard.

Rai Sri·vas·ta·na \'rīs-rē-və-'stän-ə\, Dhanpat. *Pseudonym* Prem Chand \'prem-'chänd\. *Called* Mun·shi \'mən-shē\. 1880–1936. Indian writer. Considered finest writer of modern Hindi fiction. A teacher (to 1921), later joined Gandhi's Noncooperation movement. Began writing in Urdu, later turned to Hindi; among his realistic novels were *Sevasdan* (1918), *Premashram* (1922), *Rangabhoomi* (1924), *Ghaban* (1928), *Karmabhoomi* (1931), and *Godān* (1936); his more than 300 short stories were collected as *Mānasarovar.*

Rai·su·li \ra-'sü-lē\, Aḥmad ibn Muḥammad. 1875?–1925. Moroccan brigand. Kidnapped Walter Harris, London *Times* correspondent in Tangier, Ion Perdicaris, naturalized American citizen (1904), and Sir Harry Maclean (1907); his demands for ransom met by sultan of Morocco, in order to avoid disastrous war with other nations; subject of U.S. Secretary of State John Hay's message "Perdicaris alive or Raisuli dead."

Ra·ja·go·pa·la·cha·ri \'räj-ə-gō-'päl-ä-'chä-rē\, Chakravarti. 1879–1972. Indian nationalist leader. Closely associated with Gandhi (from 1918); served on Working Committee of Indian National Congress (1922–42); prime minister of Madras (1937–39, 1952–54); governor general of India (1948–50); founder of conservative *Swatantra* (Freedom) party (1959).

Ra·ja Ha·ji \'räj-ä-'häj-ē\. d. 1784. Buginese soldier and politician. Served in military campaigns in Sumatra; captured capital of Malay state of Kedah (1770); became under-king of Johore (1777); developed port of Riau; slain during attack on Malacca.

Rajanubhab, Damrong. See DAMRONG.

Rā·ja·rā·ja I \'räj-ə-ˌräj-ə\. d. 1014. Indian king (985–1014), of the Cōla dynasty. Attacked the Pāṇdyas; extended his power north to the Tungabhadra River; conquered Northern Ceylon, Malabar Coast, Maldive Islands. His son and successor ¶Rā·jen·dra \rä-'jän-drə\ (d. 1044); king (1014–44); annexed the Raichūr Doab and moved into Mānyakheṭa; launched (1021–22) campaign that conquered lands eastward to Bengal and then north to the Ganges River; defeated the Śrivijaya kingdom (1025), reestablishing his trading routes with South China. He and his father were greatest rulers of the Cōla dynasty.

Rā·ja·rā·ja I \'räj-ə-ˌräj-ə\. d. 1014. Indian king (985–1014), of the Cōla dynasty. Attacked the Pāṇdyas; extended his power north to the Tungabhadra River; conquered Northern Ceylon, Malabar Coast, Maldive Islands. His son and successor ¶Rā·jen·dra \rä-'jän-drə\ (d. 1044); king (1014–44); annexed the Raichūr Doab and moved into Mānyakheṭa; launched (1021–22) campaign that conquered lands eastward to Bengal and then north to the Ganges River; defeated the Śrivijaya kingdom (1025), reestablishing his trading routes with South China. He and his father were greatest rulers of the Cōla dynasty.

Rajasanagara. See HAYAM WURUK.

Rá·kó·czi \'rá-kōt-sē\. Noble Magyar family prominent in the history of Hungary and Transylvania, including: Zsigmond (1544–1608), important supporter of István Bocskay's uprising against Catholic encroachment in northern Hungary (1604); prince of Transylvania (1607–08). His son ¶György I (1593–1648), prince of Transylvania (1630–48); allied himself with Swedes in invading Austria (1644–45) and gained territory in western Hungary and religious freedom for Hungarian Protestants. His son ¶György II (1621–1660), prince of Transylvania (1648–60); joined Charles X Gustavus of Sweden in attack on Poland (1656); driven from Poland by Crimean Tatars (1657); killed at Gyalu by invading Turks. His son ¶Ferenc I (1645–1676) became a Roman Catholic (1662); joined father-in-law Péter Zrínyi of Croatia in unsuccessful revolt against Habsburg rule. His son ¶Ferenc II (1676–1735), prince of Transylvania (1704–11); headed a Hungarian uprising for independence from Habsburg empire (1703); after initial success, defeated by Austrians (1711).

Rá·ko·si \'rá-kō-shē\, Mátyás. 1892–1971. Hungarian politician. Commissar for production under Béla Kun (1919); imprisoned for Communist activities (1927–40); extradited to Moscow (1940); returned as secretary of Hungarian Communist party (1944–56); head of party (1949–53); prime minister (1952–53); confirmed Stalinist; removed from party office by Moscow for offense to Marshal Tito (1956); fled to Moscow during Hungarian revolution.

Ra·kov·ski \'rá-kȯf-skē\, Georgi Sava. 1821–1867. Bulgarian revolutionary leader and writer. Vigorous proponent of Bulgarian liberation from Ottoman Turkish rule. While employee of Turkish war ministry (1853–56) secretly organized armed revolt in Bulgaria; arrested but escaped death sentence; lived abroad thereafter and continued to call for Bulgarian independence.

Ra·kov·sky \(ˌ)rə-'kȯf-skəi\, Khristian Georgiyevich. 1873–after 1938. Russian politician and diplomat, b. Bulgaria, of Romanian descent. Grandson of Georgi Raskovski. Imprisoned in Romania for subversive activities (1916–17); released by Russians; became (1919) member of the Central Committee of the Soviet Communist party. President, Council of People's Commissars of the Ukraine (1919–23). Soviet chargé d'affaires in London (1924); Soviet ambassador to France (1926–27). In struggle between Trotsky and Stalin, opposed Stalin; expelled from the Communist party (1927); reinstated (1935); arrested and convicted of espionage and treason; probably died in a labor camp.

Ra·leigh *or* **Ra·legh** \'rȯl-ē, 'räl-, *also* 'ral-\, Sir Walter. *Spelled his name consistently* Ralegh (*from 1581*) *but never* Raleigh, *the prevailing modern form.* 1554–1618. English courtier, navigator, historian, and poet. Joined his half-brother Sir Humphrey Gilbert in piratical expedition against Spaniards (1578); active and cruel in suppression of Desmonds in Munster (1580). At court as protégé of Leicester, caught Queen Elizabeth's fancy. Granted patent to take unknown lands in America in queen's name; sent expedition which explored coast from Florida to North Carolina (1584) and named coast north of Florida "Virginia"; sent settlers (1585) who occupied Roanoke Island, North Carolina, but deserted colony (1586); made later unsuccessful attempts to colonize Virginia. Succeeded in introducing potatoes and tobacco into England and Ireland, where he became friend of poet Spenser; eclipsed as favorite by Essex and banished for four years from queen's presence because of intrigue and secret marriage with one of her maids. Fitted out expedition to seek fabulous wealth of Guiana, explored coasts of Trinidad and sailed up the Orinoco (1595); took brilliant part in expedition against Cádiz (1596) and attack on the Azores (1597). On death of Elizabeth (1603) was stripped of his offices and estates; on charge of conspiring against James I, sent to Tower of London, where he lived with wife and son (till 1616) and composed his *History of the World* (1614; carried down to 130 B.C.). Released in order to seek gold along the Orinoco; lost his fleet by storms, lost men by desertion and disease, stricken with fever, lost his son Walter, returned (1618). On demand of Spanish minister, angered by destruction of new Spanish town San Tomás, beheaded at Whitehall under the old sentence. Wrote poems, of which only fragments survive, including *Cynthia, the Lady of the Sea; Methought I saw the Grave where Laura lay; The Lie; The Pilgrimage;* works on the fight over the Azores (1591) and the discovery of Guiana (1596); and political essays.

Ra·leigh \'rȯl-ē\, Sir Walter Alexander. 1861–1922. English critic and essayist. Professor of literature, Liverpool (1889), Glasgow (1900), and Oxford (1904). Author of *The English Novel* (1894), *Style* (1897), *Milton* (1900), *Wordsworth* (1903), *Shakespeare* (1907), *Six Essays on Johnson* (1910), *Romance* (1917), and *War in the Air* (first volume of history of Royal Air Force, 1922).

Ralph \'ralf\ of Cog·ge·shall \'käg-ə-shəl\. d. c.1227. English chronicler. Monk, later abbot (1207–1218), of Cistercian abbey at Coggeshall, Essex; continued the abbey's *Chronicon Anglicanum* to cover period 1187–1224 in English history; also wrote short annals and continued (covering 1162–1178) chronicle of Ralph Niger.

Ralph, James. 1695?–1762. American writer, b. probably in New Jersey. Accompanied Benjamin Franklin to London (1724). Imitated James Thomson in blank-verse poems *The Tempest* and *Night* (1727); attacked Pope in *Sawney;* staged ballad-opera *The Fashionable Lady,* first play by an American on London stage (1730); in employ of George Bubb Dodington and Frederick Louis, Prince of Wales, as political writer and liaison officer; given pension by Pelham ministry to purchase his silence. Author of *The History of England* (1744, 1746) and *The Case of Authors by Profession* (1758).

Ra·ma \'räm-ä\. Name of eight kings of Siam (Thailand) of the Chakkri dynasty:

Rama I. *Orig.* Chao Phra·ya Chak·kri \ˌchau̇-ˌprī-(y)ə-'chäk-krē\. 1737–1809. King (1782–1809). Founder of the Chakkri dynasty; drove out Burmese invaders (1776); repelled another Burmese invasion (1785); extended his domain by annexing parts of Cambodia and Malay Peninsula (1795); made Bangkok capital; patron of literature; wrote first version of dance-drama *Inao;* restored Siam to a position of power and prestige.

Rama II. 1768–1824. King (1809–24). Reopened relations with England; author of final versions of dance-dramas *Rāma* and *Inao;* his reign a golden age for arts and letters.

Rama III. d. 1851. King (1824–51). Signed treaties of commerce with Britain (1826) and U.S. (1833); extended his influence into eastern Malay Peninsula, Laos, and much of Cambodia.

Rama IV. *Orig. title* Chao Fa Mong·kut \ˌchau̇-ˌfä-ˌmȯŋ-ˈküt\, *i.e.* high crown prince; *reign title* Phra Chom Klao \ˌprä-ˌkȯm-ˈklau̇\. 1804–1868. King (1851–68). Son of Rama II; a monk; began work of modernizing Siam; made new treaties with Britain (1855) and U.S. (1856) and similar treaties with nine other countries; relinquished Cambodia to French (1867).

Rama V. *Better known as* Chu·la·long·korn \ˈchü-ˈlä-ˈlȯŋ-ˈkȯn\. *Orig.* Somdeth Phra Paraminda Maha Chulalongkorn. 1853–1910. King (1868–1910; under regency 1868–73). Son of Rama IV; abolished feudal system and slavery; improved education, laws, and communications; introduced telegraph (1883); established standard coinage and postal and education departments; reorganized government on European models (1892); opened first railway (1893); forced to yield Malay states to British and Luang Prabang and Cambodian provinces to French; visited European capitals (1897–1907).

Rama VI. *Orig.* Chao Fa Ma·ha Va·ji·ra·vudh \ˌchau̇-ˌfä-mä-ˈhä-ˌvä-jē-rä-ˈvüd\. 1881–1925. King (1910–25). Son of Rama V. Continued progressive policy of father; made monogamy only legal form of marriage; adopted Gregorian calendar; established Thai Red Cross; founded Chulalongkorn University (1916), first in Siam; instituted reforms in taxation; started many irrigation projects; refused to grant a constitution; maintained primacy of monarchy. Declared war on Germany and Austria (1917); made treaty with Allies, abolishing their extraterritorial rights. Introduced Western forms into Thai literature; wrote plays and translated English and French dramatists.

Rama VII. *Orig.* Praj·adh·i·pok \ˌprī-(y)äd-ē-ˈpȯk\. 1893–1941. King (1925–35). Brother of Rama VI. Set up a council of state to aid in government; brought consular courts to an end; temporarily dethroned by coup d'état (1932) of People's party, which established constitutional government; agreed to the change but (1933) suspended the new constitution; again forced to submit to the supporters of constitutional government; left the country (1934); abdicated (1935), retiring to England.

Rama VIII. *Orig.* Anan·da Ma·hi·dol \ä-ˈnän-dä-ˌmä-hē-ˈdȯl\. 1925–1946. King (1935–46). Nephew of Rama VII; made first state visit to Thailand in 1938; assassinated.

Ra·ma·krish·na \ˈräm-ə-ˈkrish-nə\. *Also called* Gadadhar Chatterji *and* Gadadhar Chattopadhyaya. 1836–1886. Hindu religious. Spent much of adult life in service of a temple to the goddess Kālī on the banks of the Ganges near Calcutta; later became an ascetic in a forest; preached the essential unity of all religions; looked upon as a sainted wise man by Hindus. The Ramakrishna Mission (a Vedantic order) founded (1897) by his followers.

Ra·man \ˈräm-ən\, Sir Chandrasekhara Venkata. 1888–1970. Indian physicist. Professor, Calcutta U. (1917–33) and at Indian Institute of Science (1933–48); director, Raman Research Institute, Bangalore (1948 ff.). Awarded Nobel prize in physics (1930) for researches in diffusion of light, esp. discovery of the Raman effect (announced 1928); founded *Indian Journal of Physics* (1926) and Indian Academy of Science (1934).

Ra·ma·na Ma·ha·ri·shi \ˈrəm-ə-nə-ˌmə-hə-ˈrē-shē\. *Called* Sri \ˈshrē\. *Orig. name* Ven·ka·tar·man Aiyer \ˌvəŋ-kə-ˈtär-mən-ˈī-ˌ(y)er\. 1879–1950. Indian Hindu philosopher and yogi. Experienced *samādhi* (state of bliss) at 17 and became a guru at Mt. Aranachala; preached that death and evil were illusions which could be dissipated by practice of *vicara* (self-pondering inquiry).

Rā·mā·nand \ˈräm-ə-ˌnänd\ *or* **Rā·mā·nan·da** \ˌräm-ä-ˈnän-də\ *or* **Rā·ma·dat·ta** \ˌräm-ä-ˈdät-ə\. c.1400–c.1470. North Indian Brahmin. Wandered about India preaching in Hindi; settled in Benares; founded a devotional cult of god Rāma known as the Rāmānandī, which appealed to all castes; main disciple was Kabīr.

Rā·ma·nā·tha \ˈräm-ə-ˌnä-tə\. d. 1295. Ruler of Hoysala kingdom in southern India. Driven from his domain by the Pāṇḍyas (1279); made war against his brother Narasimha III, who ruled northern half of Hoysala kingdom, and occupied part of his territory.

Rā·mā·nu·ja \rä-ˈmän-u̇j-ə\. *Also* Rā·mā·nu·jā·cār·ya \rä-ˈmän-u̇j-ə-ˈkär-yə\. c.1017–1137. Indian religious teacher. Founder of the Vaiṣṇava sect, and commentator on the Upanishads. Lived at Srirangam; driven out by hostile king, fled to Mysore; converted ruler of Mysore and is said to have founded 700 monasteries; taught a monistic philosophy based on a belief in the incarnation of Viṣṇu.

Ra·ma·nu·jan \rä-ˈmän-u̇-jən\, Srinivasa Aaiyangar. 1887–1920. Indian mathematician. To England (1914), where he engaged in original research. Best known for studies on theory of numbers, theory of partitions, and theory of continued fractions.

Ra·ma·thi·bo·di I \ˌräm-ə-tē-ˈbȯ-dē\. 1312–1369. Thai warrior chief and ruler. Through conquests, set up a unified Thai kingdom extending to Malacca in south and Burma in west, with capital known as Ayutthaya (1347 ff.); composed text (1350–59) that became foundation of Siamese legal system to 19th century.

Ra·ma·tir·tha \ˌräm-ə-ˈtir-tə\. *Orig. name* Ti·rath Ra·ma \ˈtir-ät-ˈräm-ə\. 1873–1906. Indian Hindu religious. Professor of mathematics, Foreman Christian College, Lahore (1895–1901); left wife and children (1901) and became a guru; taught system he called "Practical Vedānta."

Ra·maz·zi·ni \ˌrä-mät-ˈtsē-nē\, Bernardino. 1633–1714. Italian physician. Professor of medicine at Modena (1682–1700), Padua (1700–14). Advocated use of cinchona bark in treatment of malaria; his *De morbis artificum diatriba* (1700, 1713) was first comprehensive study of occupational diseases.

RaMBaM. See MOSES BEN MAIMON.

Ram·bert \ˈram-bərt\, Dame Marie. *Orig.* Cyvia Ram·bam \ˈräm-bäm\, *later* Miriam Ram·berg \ˈram-ˌbərg\. 1888–1982. British ballet producer, director, and teacher, b. Warsaw, Poland. Studied with Émile Jacques-Dalcroze (1910); eurhythmics teacher and dancer with Diaghilev's Ballets Russe (1912–17), influencing Nijinsky's choreography for *L'Apres-midi d'un faune* and *Le Sacre du printemps;* studied with Enrico Cecchetti; m. (1918) Ashley Dukes; naturalized British citizen (1918). Opened dance school in London (1920); produced her student Frederick Ashton's ballet *A Tragedy of Fashion* (1926). Founder (1926) and director of Marie Rambert Dancers, later known as Dame Marie's Ballet Club (1930) and (from 1935) Ballet Rambert, the oldest English ballet company still performing; helped found Camargo Society (1930); published autobiography *Quicksilver* (1972). One of most influential figures in development of 20th-century British ballet; teacher and promoter of many leading British dancers, choreographers, and stage designers.

Ramboldini, Vittorino. See VITTORINO RAMBOLDINI.

Rambouillet, Marquise de. See ANGENNES.

Rām Dās \ˈräm-ˈdäs\. *Also called* Bhai Jetha \ˈbī-ˈje-tə\. 1534–1581. Sikh leader. Succeeded Amar Dās as fourth Sikh Gurū (1574–81); founded Amritsar, now center of Sikhism; urged Emperor Akbar to punish graft and endow charitable undertakings; succeeded as Gurū by his son Arjun (*q.v.*).

Ra·meau \rȧ-mō\, Jean-Philippe. 1683–1764. French composer. Considered greatest French musical dramatist. Church organist at Clermont-Ferrand (1702–05, 1715–22), Paris (1705–08), Dijon (1709–14), and Lyons (1714–15). Settled in Paris (1723); gained success with opera-ballet *Les Indes galantes* (1735); succeeded Lully as leading composer of French opera; participated in musical controversy known as "La Guerre des Bouffons," between his adherents and the "Encyclopédistes"; appointed composer of the King's chamber music (1745). Considered leading musical theorist of the day; wrote *Traité de l'harmonie* (1722), *Nouveau système de musique théorique* (1726), etc. Among his 35 operas and opera-ballets were *Hippolyte et Aricie* (1733), *Castor et Pollux* (1737), *Dardanus* (1739), *Platée* (1745). *Pygmalion* (1748), and *Zoroastre* (1749); also composed music for harpsichord, *Pièces de clavecin* (1706, 1724, 1731) and *Pièces de clavecin en concerts* (1741).

Ra·mée \rə-ˈmā\, Marie Louise de la. *Pseudonym* Oui·da \ˈwēd-ə\: *nursery pron. of Louise.* 1839–1908. English novelist. Published melodramatic romances of fashionable life, including *Held in Bondage* (1863), *Strathmore* (1865), *Chandos* (1866), *Under Two Flags* (1867), *Puck* (1870), *Moths* (1880), *Street Dust* (1901). To Florence (1874); depicted Italian peasant life, as in *A Village Commune* (1881); wrote also animal stories, esp. *A Dog of Flanders* (1872), and children's stories as *Bimbi* (1882).

Ramée, Pierre de La. See LA RAMÉE.

Ra·men·ghi \rä-ˈmeŋ-gē\, Bartolommeo. *Known as* Il Ba·gna·ca·val·lo \ˌēl-ˌbän-yä-kä-ˈväl-lō\. 1484–1542. Italian painter. Student or follower of Francia, Raphael, Dosso Dossi; executed *Dispute of St. Augustine, Madonna and Child, Circumcision, Crucifixion,* etc.

Rameses. See RAMSES.

Ra·mí·rez \rä-ˈmē-räs\, Pedro Pablo. 1884–1962. Argentine cavalry officer and politician. Minister of war (1942–43); resigned to join Arturo Rawson in coup that overthrew Castillo government (1943); president (1943–44).

Ra·mi·ro \rä-ˈmē-rō\. Name of two kings of Aragon:

Ramiro I. d. 1063. King (1035–63). Natural son of Sancho III of Navarre; became first king of Aragon on death of father; annexed from brother Gonzalo and conquered from Moors additional territory.

Ramiro II. *Called* el Mon·je \el-ˈmoŋ-kā\, *i.e.* the Monk. d. 1154. King (1134–37). Son of Sancho V Ramírez; monk and bishop-elect of Barbastro when he succeeded elder brother Alfonso I; with aid of Ramón Berenguer IV crushed revolt of Aragonese nobles (1135); abdicated.

Ramiro. Name of three kings of León:

Ramiro I. 791–850. King (842–850).

Ramiro II. d. 951. King (931–951). Won great victory at Simancas over caliph 'Abd ar-Raḥman III (939) and negotiated truce with him (944); failed to suppress Castilian separatist movement led by Fernán González.

Ramiro III. 961–985. King (966–984). Under regency of his aunt and mother; defeated by Abū al-Manṣūr at Rueda (981).

Ram·kham·haeng \ˌräm-ˌkäm-ˈhaŋ\. *Also called* Rama the Strong. fl. c.1279–c.1317. 3d king of Sukhothai. Maintained alliance with Kublai Khan (1282 ff.); expanded domain into parts of Cambodia, Burma, Luang Prabang, Malay Peninsula; adopted Mongol military and political institutions; patron of arts and Buddhism; credited with inventing Thai alphabet; his reign one of great cultural and intellectual development.

Ram·ler \ˈräm-lər\, Karl Wilhelm. 1725–1798. German poet. Master of poetic diction; wrote odes, the cantata *Der Tod Jesu* (1755; music by Graun), etc.

Ramón. See Ramón GÓMEZ DE LA SERNA.

Ra·mon \rá-mōⁿ\, Gaston-Léon. 1886–1963. French bacteriologist. With Pasteur Inst., Paris (1911–49); head of Bureau of Epizootic Diseases, Paris (1949–58); developed antitoxins for vaccination against diphtheria and tetanus, and a process achieving several immunities with a single vaccination.

Ra·món Be·ren·guer \rä-ˈmón-bā-reŋ-ˈger\. Name of four counts of Barcelona, esp. Ramón Berenguer III (1082–1131), *called* the Great; count of Barcelona (1096–1131) and of Provence (1112–31); undertook joint expedition with Pisans against Balearic Islands (1114–15); fought against Muslim Almoravids (1115 ff.). His son ¶Ramón Berenguer IV (c.1114–1162), count of Barcelona (1131–62); married ¶Pe·tro·ni·la \ˌpā-trō-ˈnē(l)-yä\ (1136–1174), queen of Aragon (1137–74) and daughter of Ramiro II the Monk, thus becoming prince of Aragon and uniting crowns of Aragon and Catalonia under house of Barcelona; signed treaty of alliance with Henry II of England (1154); gained territories by conquest; father of Alfonso II of Aragon and of Berengaria, queen of Castile.

Ra·món y Ca·jal \rä-ˈmón-ē-kä-ˈkäl\, Santiago. 1852–1934. Spanish histologist. Professor at Valencia (1884–87), Barcelona (1887–92), Madrid (1892–1922). With Camillo Golgi, awarded Nobel prize for physiology or medicine (1906). Known esp. for work on histology of brain and nerves; isolated the neuron; discovered (1889) laws governing structure and connection of nerve cells in gray matter of brain and spinal cord; discovered (1890) primary changes in neurons as functional units; developed (1913) gold stain for histological research on nervous system. Author of *Textura del sistema nervioso del hombre y de los vertebrados* (1894–1904) and *Estudios sobre la degeneración y regeneración del sistema nervioso* (1913–14).

Ra·mos \ˈräm-ós\, Graciliano. 1892–1953. Brazilian novelist. Proprietor of general store in Palmeira dos Índios; imprisoned for supposed complicity in left-wing revolt (1936); later a journalist and federal inspector of education in Rio de Janeiro. Author of *Infância* (1945, memoirs) and of psychological novels of the poor set mainly in northeast Brazil, as *Caetés* (1933), *São Bernardo* (1934), *Augústia* (1936), and *Vidas Sêcas* (1938).

Ram·pol·la \räm-ˈpōl-lä\, Mariano. Marchese del Tin·da·ro \däl-ˈtēn-där-ō\. 1843–1913. Italian prelate. Entered diplomatic service of Roman Curia (1869); nuncio in Madrid (1882–87); created cardinal (1887); papal secretary of state (1887–1903) under Leo XIII; championed temporal power of pope against restrictions of Italian government.

Ram·say \ˈram-zē\. Name of a Scottish family holding titles of earl and marquis of Dal·hou·sie \dal-ˈhau̇-zē\ in peerage of Scotland, including among its chief members: William Ramsay (d. 1674), 2d Baron Ramsay and 1st Earl of Dalhousie (cr. 1633); aided Argyll against Montrose and supported Charles II (1651).

¶James Andrew Broun (1812–1860), 10th Earl and 1st Marquis of Dalhousie; British colonial administrator; entered House of Lords (1837); succeeded Gladstone as president of Board of Trade (1845); youngest governor general of India ever appointed (1847–56), was successful in acquiring territory, developing Indian resources, reforming administration. After Second Sikh War, annexed the Punjab (1849); annexed province of Pegu, Lower Burma (1853); by application of doctrine of lapse, annexed Satara, Jaitpur, Sambalpur (1849), Jhansi, Nagpur (1853); established public works and engineering colleges; built railways (first link, 1855), roads, and bridges; installed imperial system of telegraph and post offices, of irrigation; opened Ganges Canal; improved civil service and opened it to Indians; took action against suttee, thuggee, dacoity, slave trade, crime of meriahs; annexed Oudh (1856) and returned to England, broken in health.

¶Fox. *Orig. surname* Maule \ˈmól\ (1801–1874), 2d Baron Pan·mure \pan-ˈmyu̇(ə)r\ and 11th Earl of Dalhousie; served in army (1820–32); M.P. (1835–37, 1838–52); undersecretary for home affairs (1835–41); secretary for war (1846–52, 1855–58); censured for management of Crimean War; added surname Ramsay (1861).

Ramsay, Allan. 1686–1758. Scottish poet. Wigmaker in Edinburgh; as original member of Easy Club, was inspired to write verses and became club laureate (1715). Turned bookseller; published additional canto to *Christ's Kirk on the Green* (1718), his collected poems (1721), and Scots songs to old melodies in *Tea-Table Miscellany* (1724–27); edited old Scots poems in *Ever Green* (1724–27); produced his dramatic pastoral *The Gentle Shepherd* (1725), a popular success; first to introduce circulating library in Scotland. His eldest son ¶Allan (1713–1784) painted portraits in Edinburgh, including Duke of Argyll; to London (c.1756); court painter to George III (1767), having as subjects king, queen, Lord Bute, Gibbon, Chesterfield, and Hume.

Ramsay, Sir John. Viscount Had·ding·ton \ˈhad-iŋ-tən\ *and* Earl of Hol·der·ness \ˌhōl-dər-ˈnes\. 1580?–1626. Scottish conspirator and court favorite. Assisted in rescuing James VI from Gowrie conspirators by killing Earl of Gowrie and his brother (1600); accompanied James VI to England.

Ramsay, Sir William. 1852–1916. British chemist. Professor at Bristol (1880–87) and London (1887–1913); investigated molecular complexity of pure liquids; discovered noble gases argon (1894, with Baron Rayleigh), neon, krypton, and xenon (1898, with Morris W. Travers), helium (1895), and radon (1910); advanced proof that emanation of radium produces helium during its atomic disintegration (1903). Awarded Nobel prize for chemistry (1904). Author of *The Gases of the Atmosphere* (1896), *Modern Chemistry* (1900), *Elements and Electrons* (1913), etc.

Rams·den \ˈramz-dən\, Jesse. 1735–1800. English astronomical instrument maker. Opened shop in London (1762); took out patents for improvements in the sextant, theodolite, barometer, micrometer; specialized in divided circles; devised the mural circle.

Ram·ses \ˈram-ˌsēz\ *or* **Ram·e·ses** \ˈram-ə-ˌsēz\. Name of eleven kings of 19th and 20th dynasties of ancient Egypt:

Ramses I. 14th century B.C. King (1320–1318 B.C.). Founder of 19th dynasty, beginning reign at advanced age; named his son Seti I as coregent; planned and began great hypostyle hall at Karnak.

Ramses II. 14th–13th century B.C. 3d king (1304–1237 B.C.) of 19th dynasty. Son of Seti I. In early years of reign, engaged in important campaign against Hittites; fought (c.1300) indecisive battle at Kadesh on the Orontes in Syria; after several more years of war with Hittites in Palestine and Syria, arranged treaty of permanent peace (1283); m. daughter of Hittite king; remainder of long reign peaceful. Built residence city called Per-Ramesse; completed Seti's temple at Abydos; added to temples at Karnak and Luxor; constructed at Thebes great mortuary temple of the Rameseum with its colossal statues of himself; built the rock-cut temple at Abu Simbel; built other temples and also town of Per-Atum. His reign marked last peak of Egyptian imperial power.

Ramses III. 12th century B.C. 2d king (1198–66 B.C.) of 20th dynasty. Son of Setnakht. Effectively checked invasions of Libyans (1193, 1189) and Sea Peoples (1191); most of reign thereafter peaceful and prosperous. Reorganized society into classes grouped by occupation; erected mortuary temple at Madinat Habu; added to temple at Karnak; encouraged trade and industry; exploited copper mines at Sinai and gold mines at Nubia. Last years of reign filled with internal disturbances and attempted assassination by a secondary wife.

Ramses IV. 12th century B.C. King (1166–60 B.C.). Son of Ramses III. Erected many buildings; opened new quarries; built funerary temple near his father's; added to Karnak temple complex; much of power arrogated by high priest Ramsesnakht.

Ramses V. 12th century B.C. King (1160–56 B.C.). Son of Ramses IV. Added to father's temple in western Thebes; reign marked by growing power of high priest.

Ramses VI. 12th century B.C. King (1156–48 B.C.). Probably grandson of Ramses III. Apparently deposed Ramses V; usurped monuments of Ramses IV and V; last Egyptian king to work copper mines in Sinai; did little building; power remained in high priest.

Ramses VII. 12th century B.C. King (1148–47 B.C.). Son of Ramses VI.

Ramses VIII. 12th century B.C. King (1147–40 B.C.). Reign documented only by two surviving papyri indicating inflation in grain prices.

Ramses IX. 12th century B.C. King (1140–21 B.C.). Power in government centered in high priest, Amenhotep; Theban region invaded by Libyans; reign plagued by civil problems.

Ramses X. 12th century B.C. King (1121–13 B.C.). Power continued in high priest, Amenhotep; civil problems of predecessor still present, including presence of Libyan marauders.

Ramses XI. 12th century B.C. Last king (1113–1085 B.C.) of 20th dynasty. Reign saw downfall of high priest Amenhotep and rise to power of successor Herihor (*q.v.*); tombs at Thebes plundered; at end of reign new dynasties founded in Upper and Lower Egypt.

Ram·sey \'ram-zē\, Frank Plumpton. 1903–1930. British mathematical logician. Fellow of King's College, Cambridge (1923 ff.); known for systematic attempt to base mathematical theory of probability on partial belief; proved existence of family of numbers now known as Ramsey's numbers.

Rām Singh \'räm-'sin(-hə)\. 1816–1885. Indian Sikh leader. Succeeded (1862) Balak Singh as head of Sikh sect Nāmdhārī; introduced austere reforms and practice of chanting hymns culminating in shrieks; sought resurgence of Sikh rule in the Punjab; advocated boycott of British goods and services; exiled to Burma after his private army made attacks on Muslim community (1872).

Ramus, Petrus. See Pierre de LA RAMÉE.

Ra·mu·sio \rä-'müz-yō\, Giovanni Battista. 1485–1557. Italian geographer. With Venetian public service; known chiefly for collection of accounts of explorations and travels, *Delle navigationi e viaggi* (1550–59).

Ra·muz \rá-mue\, Charles-Ferdinand. 1878–1947. Swiss novelist. Author of tragic novels set in the Rhôneland as *La Vie de Samuel Belet* (1913), *La grande peur dans la montagne* (1925), *Beauté sur la terre* (1927), *Derborence* (1934), and *Le Garçon savoyard* (1936); wrote text for Stravinsky's *Histoire du soldat* (1918).

Ra·na·de \'rän-ə-dā(n)\, Mahadev Govind. 1842–1901. Indian Brahman lawyer and reformer. Judge of High Court of Bombay; instructor of history, Elphinstone College, Bombay (1866 ff.); founder, Indian National Social Conference (1887); advocate of social and economic reforms; wrote *Rise of the Maratha Power* (1900).

Ranak. See Nachman KROCHMAL.

Rā·nā Sān·gā \'rän-ä-'säŋ-ä\. 16th century. King of Mewār. Leader of Indian Rājput clans resisting conquests of Mughal emperor Bābur; defeated by Bābur at Khandwa (1527).

Ra·na·va·lo·na \,rän-ä-və-'lō-nä\. Name of three queens of Merina, Madagascar, esp. Ranavalona I (d. 1861), wife of King Radama I; on his death ruled alone (1828–61); reversed his Europeanizing policy, expelled Christian missionaries; repelled Anglo-French invasion (1845); failed to conquer independent Malagasy kingdoms.

Ran·cé \rän-sā\, Armand-Jean Le Bou·thil·lier de \lə-bü-tē-yā-də-\. 1626–1700. French monk. Abbot of La Trappe monastery (1664–95); instituted reforms and strict discipline in his order; known as founder of the Trappists (since 1892 united with the Cistercians); wrote *Traité de la sainteté et des devoirs de la vie monastique* (1683); engaged in controversy with Jean Mabillon (*q.v.*).

Rand \'rand\, Ayn. 1905–1982. American writer, b. St. Petersburg (now Leningrad), Russia. To U.S. (1926, naturalized 1931). Espoused her philosophy of objectivism and "rational selfishness" in novels *We, the Living* (1936), *Anthem* (1938), *The Fountainhead* (1943), *Atlas Shrugged* (1957), and in nonfiction books *For the New Intellectual* (1961), *The Virtue of Selfishness* (1965), *Capitalism: The Unknown Ideal* (1966), *The New Left* (1971), etc.

Rand, Sally. *Orig.* Helen Gould Beck \'bek\. 1904–1979. American entertainer, b. Elkton, Mo. Acrobatic dancer in carnivals and film actress in Hollywood (before 1930s); gained notoriety at Chicago's World Fair (1933) with a fan dance; continued to perform for over 30 years.

Ran·dall \'ran-dᵊl\, James Ryder. 1839–1908. American journalist and song writer, b. Baltimore. Intensely southern in sympathy, wrote "Maryland, My Maryland" (1861) upon hearing of Baltimore mob resistance to the passage of Union troops through the city.

Randall, Samuel Jackson. 1828–1890. American politician, b. Philadelphia. Democratic member, U.S. House of Representatives (1863–90), and speaker of the house (1876–81). Codified rules of the House of Representatives and greatly strengthened speaker's power.

Randall-Mac·Iver \-mə-'kī-vər, -'kē-\, David. 1873–1945. British archaeologist and anthropologist. Excavated at Abydos, Egypt, under Flinders Petrie (1899–1901); conducted first systematic excavation of Southern Rhodesian Zimbabwe remains (1905) and argued they were built at time of European Middle Ages; curator of Egyptology, U. of Pennsylvania museum (1907–11); settled in Rome and concentrated on Italian archaeology (after World War I). Published *Medieval Rhodesia* (1906), *The Iron Age in Italy* (1927), *Italy Before the Romans* (1928), etc.

Ran·dolph \'ran-,dä(l)f, -,dò(l)f, -də(l)f\, Asa Philip. 1889–1979. American labor leader, b. Crescent City, Fla. Founded monthly *The Messenger* (1917) advocating greater militancy by Negroes in industrial and military positions; organized (1925) Brotherhood of Sleeping Car Porters, president (1925–68); secured inclusion of railway porters and maids in Federal Railway Labor Act (1934); exerted pressure on President Roosevelt, resulting in Executive Order 8802 prohibiting discrimination in defense industries and federal bureaus and creating Fair Employment Practices Committee (1941); vice president of AFL–CIO (1955 ff.); director of March on Washington for Jobs and Freedom (Aug. 28, 1963), largest civil rights demonstration in U.S. history.

Randolph, Edmund Jennings. 1753–1813. American politician, b. Williamsburg, Va. Great-grandson of William Randolph and nephew of Peyton Randolph. Aide-de-camp to Gen. Washington (1775–76); attorney general of Virginia (1776). Member, Continental Congress (1779–82); governor of Virginia (1786–88). Delegate to Constitutional Convention (1787) and proposer of famous Virginia Plan; refused to sign Constitution because of belief it was not adequately republican in its provisions, but advocated acceptance in Virginia ratification convention (1788). U.S. attorney general (1789–94); U.S. secretary of state (1794–95). Practiced law, Richmond, Va. (from 1795); was chief counsel for Aaron Burr when Burr was tried for treason (1807).

Randolph, Edward. 1632–1703. British agent in America. In Massachusetts colony (1676); appointed by king collector of customs in New England (1678); in constant trouble with colonial authorities. As a result of his reports, Massachusetts charter was declared forfeited (1684) and he was commissioned secretary and register of the Dominion of New England (1685). Arrested (1689) after rebellion had overthrown government of the Dominion, and sent to England; freed and appointed surveyor general of customs for North America (1691). Again in colonies (1692–97) and in conflict with colonial authorities; imprisoned in Bermuda (1699–1700); in England (1700) made bitter attack on both charter and proprietary colonies for violations of the laws of trade.

Randolph, John. d. 1346. See under Sir Thomas RANDOLPH.

Randolph, John. *Known as* John Randolph of Roanoke. 1773–1833. American politician, b. Prince George Co., Va. Great-grandson of William Randolph. Member, U.S. House of Representatives (1799–1813, 1815–17, 1819–25, 1827–29), and U.S. Senate (1825–27). Chairman, Ways and Means Committee, and administration leader (1801–05); vigorous proponent of states' rights; opposed Jefferson (after 1805); brilliant orator and master of biting invective; bitter opponent of War of 1812 and Missouri Compromise; marked eccentricities in speech and act (after 1818) indicated mental abnormality, which in last years passed into actual insanity. Fought harmless duel with Henry Clay (1826). U.S. minister to Russia (1830).

Randolph, Peyton. 1721?–1775. American lawyer and politician, b. Williamsburg?, Va. Grandson of William Randolph; king's attorney for Virginia (1748–66); member, Virginia House of Burgesses (1748–49, 1752–75); on Virginia Committee of Correspondence (1759–67), chairman (1773); first president, Continental Congress (1774, 1775).

Randolph, Sir Thomas. 1st Earl of Mor·ay *or* Mur·ray \'mər-ē, 'mə-rē\. d. 1332. Scottish statesman. Nephew through his mother of King Robert Bruce. Captured at Methven; saved his life by deserting Bruce (1306). Captured by Sir James Douglas (1308); made submission to Bruce; created earl of Moray (one of seven original earldoms of Scotland) and became Bruce's most trusted adviser. Captured Edinburgh Castle by escalade (1314); commanded a division at Bannockburn (1314); took part in Edward Bruce's expedition into Ireland (1315); with Sir James Douglas, raided northern English counties and secured truce with Edward II; concluded offensive and defensive alliance with France (1326); became regent on death of Bruce (1329). His son ¶John (d. 1346), 3d earl, defeated Edward de Baliol at Annan (1332); joint regent (c.1334); liberated rest of country by subduing Edward de Baliol's lieutenant in Scotland; captive of English (1335–41); killed at battle of Neville's Cross (1346).

Randolph, Thomas. 1605–1635. English poet and dramatist. Writer of English and Latin verse; friend of Ben Jonson; author of comic plays *Aristippus, or the Joviall Philosopher* (1630), *The Conceited Pedler* (1630), *The Jealous Lovers* (1632), *The Muses' Looking-Glasse* (pub. 1638), *Amyntas* (pastoral drama, pub. 1638), and *Hey for Honesty* (pub. 1651).

Randolph, William. 1651?–1711. American planter and administrator, b. Warwickshire, England. To America (c.1673) and settled in Virginia, on James River below Richmond. Became large landowner and slave-owner, and one of leading planters of Virginia. Attorney general for the crown in Virginia (1694–98); a founder of College of William and Mary.

Randulf de Blundeville. See RANULF.

Rang·ström \'räŋ-strœm\, Ture, *in full* Anders Johan Ture. 1884–1947. Swedish composer. Composed 4 symphonies, symphonic poems, the opera *Kronbruden* (1919), *Ballad* for piano and orchestra (1937), chamber music, piano pieces, songs, etc.

Ran·jit Singh \'rən-jit-'sin-hə\. *Called* the Lion of the Punjab. 1780–1839. Founder of the Sikh kingdom. Succeeded his father (1792) as head of Sikh confederacy; seized Lahore and proclaimed himself maharaja of the Punjab (1799); annexed Amritsar (1802); his ambition clashed with British claims but war was avoided; treaty as to boundaries signed (1809) with Charles Metcalfe, English agent; organized powerful army; added Kangra (1813), Multan (1818), Kashmir (1819), and Peshawar (1823); campaigned successfully against Afghans and Pathans, traditional enemies; consolidated most of Punjab into a Sikh kingdom; cooperated with British in invasion of Afghanistan (1838). His son and successor ¶Da·lip *or* Dhu·lip \də-'lēp\ Singh (1837–1893) was proclaimed maharaja (1843) under regency of his mother; deposed (1849) as result of two anti-British outbreaks and pensioned; lived in England.

Ran·jit·sinh·ji Vi·bha·ji \'rən-jit-'si^{n}(-hə)-jē-'vē-bə-jē\. Maharaja Jam Saheb of Na·wā·na·gar \,nə-vä^{n}-'nəg-ər\. 1872–1933. Rajput nobleman. Maharaja (1907–33). Won renown in England as a cricketer; played for Sussex in first-class county competition (1895–97, 1899–1904, 1908, 1912); champion batsman for All England (1896, 1900). As maharaja of Nawānagar (1907 ff.) was progressive ruler; modernized capital Jāmnagar; developed seaport Nawānagar; built roads, railways, and irrigation facilities; chancellor, Indian Chamber of Princes (1932).

Rank \'raŋk\, Joseph Arthur. 1st Baron Rank. 1888–1972. British industrialist and film magnate. Entered (1905) family flour milling business, Ranks Hovis McDougall, Ltd. (chairman, 1952–69); founder (1935), General Film Distributors, Ltd., that by 1950s controlled virtually all film production and distribution in Great Britain.

Rank \'räŋk\, Otto. 1884–1939. Austrian psychoanalyst. Protégé of Sigmund Freud; editor (1912–24) of psychoanalytic journals *Imago* and *Internationale Zeitschrift für Psychoanalyse;* in *Das Trauma der Geburt* (1924) advanced theory that anxiety neurosis results from trauma of birth; other works included *Der Künstler* (1907), *Der Mythus von der Geburt des Helden* (1909), and *Das Inzest-Motiv in Dichtung und Sage* (1912).

Ran·ke \'räŋ-kə\, Leopold von. 1795–1886. German historian. A founder of the modern school of history; champion of objective writing based on source material rather than on legend and tradition. Professor, Berlin (1825–71); historiographer of Prussia (1841). His works included *Geschichte der romanischen und germanischen Völker von 1494–1535* (1824), *Die römischen Päpste* (1834–36), *Deutsche Geschichte im Zeitalter der Reformation* (1839–47), *Neun Bücher preussischer Geschichte* (1847–48), *Französische Geschichte* (1852–61), *Englische Geschichte* (1859–68), *Geschichte Wallensteins* (1869), *Weltgeschichte* (1881–88; completed by his assistants).

Ran·kin \'raŋ-kən\, Jeannette. 1880–1973. American reformer, b. near Missoula, Mont. Social worker (from 1909); active in woman-suffrage work (from 1910); first woman member of U.S. House of Representatives (1917–19, 1941–43); only member of the House to vote against declaration of both World Wars (1917, 1941); protested U.S. involvement in Vietnam.

Ran·kine \'raŋ-kən\, William John Macquorn. 1820–1872. Scottish civil engineer and physicist. Professor of civil engineering in Glasgow (1855–72). Known for researches on metal fatigue of railway axles, on steam-engine theory, and on earth pressures and stability of retaining walls. Author of manuals *Applied Mechanics* (1858), *The Steam Engine* (1959), *Civil Engineering* (1862), etc. The Rankine cycle is named after him.

Ran·som \'ran(t)-səm\, John Crowe. 1888–1974. American critic and poet, b. Pulaski, Tenn. Teacher of English, Vanderbilt (1914–37); professor of poetry, Kenyon Coll. (1937–58). Member of poetical circle The Fugitives, and contributed to manifesto *I'll Take My Stand* (1930); founder and editor, *The Kenyon Review* (1939–59). Author of volumes of verse *Poems about God* (1919), *Chills and Fever* (1924), *Grace After Meat* (1924), *Two Gentlemen in Bonds* (1927), *Selected Poems* (1945). Critical works included *God Without Thunder* (1930), *The World's Body* (1938), *New Criticism* (1941), and *Poems and Essays* (1955).

Ran·some \'ran(t)-səm\, Arthur Mitchell. 1884–1967. English author. Known chiefly for children's adventure novels as *Old Peter's Russian Tales* (1916), *Racundra's First Cruise* (1923), *Swallows and Amazons* (1931), *Pigeon Post* (1936), *We Didn't Mean to Go to Sea* (1937), *Missee Lee* (1941), etc.

Rant·zau \'ränt-,sau̇\, Johan. 1492–1565. German soldier. Prefect of Gottorp; persuaded Frederick I to accept the crown of Denmark and led Frederick's armies into Copenhagen and Malmö (1523); in Count's War (1533–36), led forces of Christian III to victories at Öxneberg (1535) and in siege of Copenhagen (1535–36).

Ran·ulf \'ran-əlf\ *or* **Ran·dulph** \'ran-dəlf\ *or* **Ralph** \'ralf, 'rāf, 'rä(l)f\ **de Blunde·ville** \də-blœnd-'vēl\. 6th Earl of Chester. c.1172–1232. English feudal leader. Grandson of Ranulf de Gernons. Led armies in wars against Welsh (from 1210); sided with King John against barons; created earl of Lincoln (1217); on 5th Crusade, taking part in capture of Damietta, Egypt (1219).

Ranulf de Ger·nons \-də-zher-nō^{n}\. 4th Earl of Chester. c.1100–1153. Anglo-Norman military leader. Grandnephew of Hugh of Avranches. Initially supported Matilda's claim to English throne against King Stephen; fought for her at Battle of Lincoln (1141) and captured Stephen; transferred (1149) allegiance to Stephen in return for city and castle of Lincoln.

Ran·vier \rä^{n}-vyā\, Louis-Antoine. 1835–1922. French histologist. Director of histological laboratory (1875) and professor of general anatomy (1886), Collège de France; noted for description (1878) of constrictions in nerve fibers, now known as nodes of Ranvier; discovered nerve terminals now known as Ranvier's tactile disks.

Raoul. See RUDOLF (d. 936 A.D.).

Ra·oul de Hou·denc *or* **Hou·dan** \rȧ-ül-də-ü-dä^{n}\. fl. c.1200–1230. French poet. Itinerant minstrel; imitator or competitor of Chrétien de Troyes; author of Arthurian allegorical romance *Méraugis de Portlesguez,* courtly romance *Roman des ailes,* and satirical allegory *Songe d'eufer.*

Ra·oult \rȧ-ül\, François-Marie. 1830–1901. French physicist and chemist. Taught at Grenoble (1867–1901); known esp. for work on the freezing point and vapor pressure of solutions in relation to the concentration and molecular weight of the dissolved substance.

Ra·pa·cki \rȧ-'pȧ-kē\, Adam. 1909–1970. Polish economist and politician. In German prisoner-of-war camps (1939–45); joined Polish Communist party (1948); minister for higher education (1950–56); while minister of foreign affairs (1956–68) presented to United Nations (1957) plan establishing denuclearized zone in central Europe, never implemented.

Raph·a·el \'raf-ē-əl, 'rā-fē-, 'räf-ē-\. *Ital.* Raf·fa·el·lo \,räf-fä-'el-lō\. *Surnamed* San·zio \'sänt-syō\. *Also* Raf·fa·el *or* Raf·a·el *or* Raf·fa·e·lo \,räf-fä-'el-ō\. 1483–1520. Italian painter. A master of the Italian High Renaissance. Assistant to Perugino (c.1495–1504); to Florence (1504) and Rome (1508 ff.); in service to Pope Julius II; later, protégé of Leo X; appointed chief architect of St. Peter's (1514); conservator of excavations at Rome (1515). Works included *Vision of a Knight* (c.1501), *St. Michael* (c.1501), *Marriage of the Virgin* (1504), *Portrait of Agnolo Doni* (c.1505), *Madonna of the Goldfinch* (c.1505), *Madonna del Prato* (c.1505), *La Belle Jardinière* (1507), *Deposition of Christ* (1507), frescoes in the Vatican (1508–11), including *Disputa* and *School of Athens, Sistine Madonna* (1513), tapestry cartoons in Sistine Chapel (c.1516), *Portrait of Balthasar Castiglione* (1516), and *Transfiguration* (c.1520). As architect, designed Palazzo Pandolfi in Florence and Villa Madama in Rome, etc.

Ra·pi·sar·di \,räp-ē-'zär-dē\, Mario. 1844–1912. Italian poet. Among his works were *La palingenesi* (1868), *Lucifero* (1877), *Giobbe* (1884), *Poesie religiose* (1887), *Poemetti* (1885–1907), *Atlantide* (1892), and translations, as of Shelley's *Prometheus Unbound.*

Rapp \'räp, *Angl* 'rap\, George, *orig.* Johann Georg. 1757–1847. American religious leader, b. Württemberg, Germany. Linen weaver by trade. As head of group of separatists, emigrated to U.S. (1803) and settled town of Harmony, Butler Co., Pa. Moved to Indiana and settled new town called Harmony in Wabash Valley (1814–24). Moved again and settled town called Economy, in Beaver Co., Pa. (from 1825). Members of this religious communistic society called Harmonites, or sometimes Rappites. Colony successful under Rapp's guidance. Rule of celibacy finally led to its extinction (1906).

Rapp \rȧp\, Jean. 1772–1821. French general. Aide-de-camp to Desaix de Veygoux and later to Napoléon; distinguished himself at Leipzig and Wagram and in the Russian campaign, esp. in the defense of Danzig (1813–14); rallied to Napoléon during the Hundred Days; in exile (1815–17).

Rasch \'räsh\, Albertina. 1896–1967. American dancer and choreographer, b. Vienna. Ballerina for various American companies (1911 ff.); opened ballet school in N.Y. (1923); formed (1924) first of several troupes, called Albertina Rasch Girls, noted in 1920s and 1930s for appearances in films and Broadway musicals which she choreographed.

Rashba. See Solomon ADRET.

Rashbaz. See Simeón DURÁN.

Rashi. See SHLOMO YITZHAQI.

Ra·shīd ad-Dīn \ra-'shēd-ad-'dēn\. 1247–1318. Persian physician, politician, and historian. Physician to the Mongol sovereigns of Persia; vizier of the empire (1298 ff.); composed encyclopedic universal history *Jāmi 'at-tawārīkh.*

Ra·shīd Ri·ḍā \ra-'shē-drē-'dä\, Muḥammad. 1865–1935. Syrian Muslim theologian. Disciple of Muḥammad 'Abduh (*q.v.*) and leading exponent of his ideas; founder and publisher of newspaper *al-Manār* (1898–1935); advocated Muslim acceptance of modern practices, as scientific and technological advancements and taking of interest in banking.

Ra·šin \'rȧ-shin\, Alois. 1867–1923. Czech politician. Member of Young Czech party (1895 ff.) and close associate of its leader, Karel Kramář; member of Austrian Reichsrat (1911–15); a leader of Prague revolution (Oct. 28, 1918) that established independent republican government; minister of finance (1918); assassinated by Communist revolutionary.

Rask \'räsk\, Rasmus Kristian. 1787–1832. Danish philologist and Orientalist. A founder of modern science of comparative linguistics. Professor (1825) and librarian (1829), U. of Copenhagen. Showed in *Undersögelse om det gamle Nordiske eller Isklandske Sprogs Oprindelse* (1818) that Old Norse and other Celtic languages are Indo-European; set forth principle of consonantal sound shifting in Germanic languages, later formulated as a law by Jacob Grimm; same work first to establish relation of Old Norse to Gothic. Wrote grammars of Icelandic (1811), Anglo-Saxon (in Swedish, 1817), Spanish (1824), Frisian (1825), Danish (1830), Old Norse (1832), and other languages. Traveled throughout Middle East and Asia (1816–23), collecting manuscripts in Persian, Pāli, Sinhalese, etc.

Ras·mus·sen \'räs-,mu̇s-ᵊn, *Angl* 'ras-mə-sən\, Knud Johan Victor. 1879–1933. Danish explorer and ethnologist, b. Greenland of an Eskimo mother. Authority on the Greenland Eskimo; held theory that Eskimos spring from same stock as North American Indians. Took part in Danish literary Greenland expedition (1902–04) under Mylius-Erichsen; studied the Eskimo of North Greenland, and made first recorded sledge crossing across Melville Bay; made ethnological expeditions to North Greenland (1906–08, 1909, 1910–11) and established (1910) Cape York station at Thule; led several Thule expeditions (from 1912) to North and East Greenland and the American Arctic. Author of *The People of the Polar North* (1908), *Myths and Legends from Greenland* (1921–25), *In the Home of the Polar Eskimos* (1923), *Across Arctic America* (1927), etc.

Raspe, Henry. See HENRY RASPE.

Ras·pe \'räs-pə\, Rudolph Erich. 1737–1794. German scholar and adventurer. Author of *Baron Munchausen's Narrative of His Marvellous Travels and Campaigns in Russia* (1785). Librarian and curator of museum at Kassel (1767–75); charged with stealing and selling medals, fled to England (1775); masquerading as mining expert, swindled Sir John Sinclair by pretending to discover gold and silver on his estate (1791); original of Douster-swivel in Scott's *Antiquary.* Revealed as author of *Munchausen* only in 1824 by biographer of Bürger (editor of first German version, 1786). See MÜNCHHAUSEN.

Ras·pu·tin \rə-'spüt-yin, *Angl* ra-'sp(y)üt-ᵊn, -'spu̇t-\, Grigory Yefimovich. *Orig. surname* No·vykh \'no̊v-yik̲\; *given name* Rasputin, *i.e.* Debauchee, *in youth.* 1872–1916. Russian mystic and court favorite. Received little education; peasant farmer in his native village; left family (1904) and devoted himself to religion; gained reputation as a holy man among the peasantry. In St. Petersburg (1905 ff.), gained ascendancy over the czar and esp. czarina by ability to improve hemophiliac condition of their son; interfered in church politics as well as in secular politics; notorious for debauchery and ignorance. Assassinated by a group of Russian noblemen in a patriotic endeavor to rid Russia of his baneful influence.

Ras·sam \räs-'säm\, Hormuzd. 1826–1910. Turkish Assyriologist. Assisted Sir A. H. Layard in archaeological excavations near Nineveh (1845–47, 1849–51) and succeeded him (1852) as British agent in excavations; discovered (1853) palace of Ashurbanipal at Nimrud; excavated palace of Shalmaneser II; discovered (1880) Mesopotamian tablet at Sippar identifying site as temple of sun god; made other important investigations in Assyria and Babylonia (1876–82).

Ras Tafari. See HAILE SELASSIE.

Ras·tell \ras-'tel\, John. c.1475–1536. English printer and dramatist. Associated with beginnings of English drama with morality plays *The Nature of the Four Elements* (1519), *Gentleness and Nobility* (c.1527), and *Calisto and Melebea* (c.1527). His son ¶William (1508–1565) worked as a scribe in father's office, later (1529) set up his own press; after execution of Sir Thomas More, rescued from Tower of London More's manuscripts and letters; published More's works in English (1557) and Latin (1565); wrote a biography of More, only a fragment of which is extant. Called to bar (1539) and rose to justice of queen's bench (1558). Also known for publishing law books and the plays of John Heywood.

Ra·ta·na \rä-'tän-ə\, Tahupotiki Wiremu. 1870–1939. New Zealand Maori political and religious leader. Originally a farmer; turned to faith healing and founded (1925) the Ratana church that controlled the four Maori seats in Parliament.

Ratclyffe, Sir Thomas. See RADCLIFFE.

Rat·dolt \'rät-,do̊lt\, Erhard. 1447–1528. German printer and type cutter. Printed chiefly liturgical, mathematical, and astronomical works with ornamental borders and initial letters, including an edition of Euclid (1482) containing over 400 wood engravings and over 200 diagrams; originated the decorated title page and was among first to use several colors on one page.

Ra·teau \rá-tō\, Camille-Édmond-Auguste. 1863–1930. French engineer. Invented the pressure-stage impulse turbine (1901); also known for manufacture of turbines (as multicellular turbines) and study of the use of turbines in aviation.

Ra·the·nau \'rä-tə-,nau̇\, Emil. 1838–1915. German industrialist. Founder of the German Edison Company (1883), forerunner of the Allgemeine Elektrizitäts-Gesellschaft, or A. E. G. (1887), of which he was general director; with Werner von Siemens founded (1903) Telefunken Gesellschaft. His son ¶Walther (1867–1922) became director of electrochemical enterprises, Bitterfeld (1893), a director of A. E. G. (1899), and president of A. E. G. (1915); directed distribution of war raw materials in Prussian war ministry (1914–15); minister of reconstruction in Wirth's first cabinet (1921); represented Germany at Cannes Conference (1922) and secured diminution of reparation payment of 1922; as foreign minister in Wirth's second cabinet (1922), participated in conference at Genoa and signed Rapallo Treaty with Russia (1922); assassinated by reactionaries.

Rath·ke \'rät-kə\, Martin Heinrich. 1793–1860. German anatomist. Physician in Danzig (1818–29); professor, Dorpat (1829–34), Königsberg (1835–60). First to describe gill slits and gill arches in embryos of mammals and birds; first (1839) to describe embryonic structure now known as Rathke's pouch; also did pioneering work in marine zoology, as being first to describe lancet fish.

Ra·tia \'rá-tē-á\, Armi. 1912–1979. Finnish textile designer. Founder (1951) of Marimekko, an international fabric concern that introduced bold abstract prints used on bed sheets, furniture, wallpaper, etc.

Rat·ke \'rät-kə\ *or* **Ra·tich** \'rä-tik̲\ *or* **Ra·ti·chi·us** \rä-'tik̲-ē-ùs\, Wolfgang. 1571–1635. German educational reformer. In Holland (1603–11) devised new system of teaching languages, based on Baconian theory of induction; attempted to introduce system in Augsburg, Kassel, Hanau, Frankfurt, and Basel.

Ra·tram·nus \rə-'tram-nəs\. d. c.868. French theologian. Priest and teacher at Benedictine abbey of Corbie in Somme (from c.825); pupil of Paschasius Radbertus. In *De corpore et sanguini Domini* (c.850), opposed Paschasius by arguing for a symbolic interpretation of the Eucharist; in *De praedestinatione* (850) opposed Hincmar of Reims and defended St. Augustine's theory of predestination; also wrote *Contra Graecorum* defending Western church from attacks by Photius of Constaninople during "Filioque" controversy, and *De nativitate Christi* arguing in opposition to Paschasius that Christ's birth was natural.

Rat·taz·zi \rät-'tät-tsē\, Urbano. 1808–1873. Italian Piedmontese politician. Joined with Cavour (1851); president, Chamber of Deputies (1852–53); minister of justice (1853–54) and interior (1854–58, 1858–60); prime minister (Mar.–Dec. 1862; Apr.–Oct. 1867); his resignations from premiership caused by opposition to Garibaldi's marches on Rome.

Rat·ti·gan \'rat-ə-gən\, Sir Terence Mervyn. 1911–1977. English dramatist. Gained success with farces *French Without Tears* (1936) and *While the Sun Shines* (1946); other plays included *Separate Tables* (1945), *The Winslow Boy* (1946), *Ross* (1960), *A Bequest to the Nation* (1970), *Cause Célèbre* (1977); also wrote screenplays as *The Yellow Rolls Royce* (1965) and *Goodbye Mr. Chips* (1968).

Rat·zel \'rät-səl\, Friedrich. 1844–1904. German geographer and ethnographer. Professor, Munich (1875–86), Leipzig (1886–1904); on tour of North and Central America as correspondent for *Kölnische Zeitung* (1874–75). A founder of ethnography; originated concept of *Lebensraum,* which relates human groups to the spatial units where they develop; made important contributions to political geography. Author of *Städte und Kulturbilder aus Nordamerika* (1876), *Die Vereinigten Staaten von Nordamerika* (1878–80), *Völkerkunde* (1885–88), *Politische Geographie* (1897), *Die Erde und das Leben* (1901–02), etc.

Rat·zen·ho·fer \'rät-sən-,hō-fər\, Gustav. 1842–1904. Austrian general, philosopher, and sociologist. Lieutenant general and president of the military supreme court (1898–1901). A social Darwinist; conceived of society as universe of conflicting ethnic groups that could be guided into higher forms of association by sociology. Author of *Wesen und Zweck der Politik* (1893), *Die soziologische Erkenntnis* (1898), *Der Positive Monismus* (1899), *Positive Ethik* (1901), etc.

Rau \'rau̇\, Sir Benegal Narsing. 1887–1953. Indian jurist. Entered Indian civil service (1910); revised entire Indian statutory code (1935–37); judge of Bengal High Court (1939); prime minister of state of Jammu and Kashmir (1944–45); helped draft constitutions of Burma (1947) and India (1950); Indian representative to UN Security Council (1950–52); judge on Permanent Court of International Justice, The Hague (1952–53).

Raun·kaier \'rau̇n-ker\, Christen. 1860–1938. Danish botanist. Devised (c.1900) a terminology for plant life forms now known as Raunkaier's categories; collection of his papers published (in English trans., 1934) as *Life Forms of Plants and Statistical Plant Geography.*

Rau·pach \'rau̇-,päk̲\, Ernst Benjamin Salomon. 1784–1852. German dramatist. Author of the tragedy *Die Leibeigenen* (1826), the popular play *Der Müller und sein Kind* (1835), the cycle *Die Hohenstaufen* (16 parts), *Der Nibelungen-Hort* (1828), etc.

Rau·schen·busch \'rau̇-shən-,bu̇sh\, Walter. 1861–1918. American clergyman, b. Rochester, N.Y. Professor at Rochester Theological Seminary (1897–1918). Leader of Social Gospel movement, stressing social transformation and economic betterment as purpose of Christianity. Author of *Christianity and the Social Crisis* (1907), *Prayers of the Social Awakening* (1910), *Christianizing the Social Order* (1912), *The Social Principles of Jesus* (1916), etc.

Rau·scher \'rau̇-shər\, Joseph Othmar von. 1797–1875. Austrian prelate. Tutor to future emperor Francis Joseph (1844); archbishop (1853) and cardinal

(1855) of Vienna. Chief architect of Austro-papal concordat of 1855; at first opposed dogma of papal infallibility in Vatican Council (1870) and favored a liberal government.

Ra·vail·lac \rá-vá-yák\, François. 1578–1610. French assassin. Schoolmaster, later entered monastery of Feuillants and was expelled for eccentric behavior; assassinated King Henry IV of France (May 14, 1610).

Ra·vais·son-Mol·lien \rá-ve-sō^{n}-mȯl-ya^{n}\, Jean-Gaspard-Félix La·cher \lá-sher\. 1813–1900. French philosopher. Inspector general of higher education (1859–88). Author of *Essai sur la métaphysique d'Aristote* (1837, 1846), *De l'habitude* (1839), and *La Philosophie en France au XIXe siècle* (1868).

Ra·vel \rá-vel, *Angl* rə-'vel, ra-\, Maurice, *in full* Joseph-Maurice. 1875–1937. French composer. Pupil of Fauré; lived mainly as semi-recluse at country retreat, Montfort-L'Amaury. His compositions included: operas *L'Heure espanole* (1911), *L'Enfant et les sortilèges* (1925, libretto by Colette); ballets *Daphnis et Chloé* (1912), *Ma Mère l'Oye* (1915), *La Valse* (1920), *Boléro* (1928); orchestral works *Pavane pour une infante défunte* (1899), *Rapsodie espagnole* (1907), *Tzigane* (1924), 2 piano concertos (both 1931); chamber music *String Quartet* (1903), *Piano Trio* (1914), *Sonatas* for violin and cello (1922) and for violin and piano (1927); piano music *Sonatine* (1905), *Gaspard de la nuit* (1908), *Valses, nobles et sentimentales* (1911), *Le Tombeau de Couperin* (1917); vocal music *Shéhérazade* (1903), *Chansons madécasses* (1926), *Don Quichotte à Dulcinée* (1932); songs; an orchestration of Mussorgsky's *Pictures at an Exhibition* (1922).

Ra·vens·croft \'rā-vənz-ˌkrȯft\, George. 1618–1681. English glassmaker. Known for development (patented 1674) of flint glass, which used raw materials native to England and was more durable than Venetian glass.

Ravenscroft, Thomas. c.1583–c.1633. English composer. Music master, Christ's Hospital, London (1618–22); author of *Pammelia,* earliest collection of rounds and catches printed in England (1609), and supplementary collections *Deuteromelia* (1609, including "Three Blind Mice"), *Melismata* (1611), and *The Whole Booke of Psalmes* (1621).

Raw·don-Has·tings \'rȯd-^{ə}n-'hā-stiŋz\, Francis. 1st Marquis of Hastings *and in Irish peerage* 2d Earl of Moi·ra \'mȯi-rə\. 1754–1826. British soldier and colonial administrator. Served (1775–82) against Americans at Bunker Hill, Camden, and Hobkirk's Hill. Championed Prince of Wales on regency question (1789); added Hastings to surname (1790); general (1803); master general of the ordnance (1806–07). Governor general of Bengal and commander in chief in India (1813–22); waged successful wars against Gurkhas (1816) and Pindaris and Marāthās (1817–18), establishing British supremacy in central India; purchased island of Singapore (1819); resigned because of imputations arising from indulgence to a banking house. Governor of Malta (1824).

Raw·lings \'rȯ-liŋz\, Marjorie, *nee* Kin·nan \kə-'nan\. 1896–1953. American novelist, b. Washington, D.C. m. Charles A. Rawlings (1919; div. 1933). Author of *South Moon Under* (1933), *Golden Apples* (1935), *The Yearling* (1938, Pulitzer prize), *Cross Creek* (1942), *Cross Creek Cookery* (1942), *The Sojourner* (1953).

Raw·lin·son \'rȯ-lən-sən\, Sir Henry Creswicke. 1810–1895. English army officer and Orientalist. In East India Company's military service (1827 ff.), studied Persian and the Indian vernaculars; as political agent at Kandahar (1840–42) and Baghdad (1843), completed transcript of cuneiform inscription of Darius I the Great at Bīsitūn, which he deciphered and interpreted (1846); received grant from British Museum to continue Assyrian and Babylonian excavations begun by Layard; director of East India Co. (1856); M.P. (1858, 1865–68); British minister in Persia (1859–60); member of India Council (1858, 1868–95), favored forward policy in Afghanistan. His son ¶Henry Seymour (1864–1925), 1st Baron Rawlinson; soldier; served with Roberts in India (1887–90), in Sudan with Kitchener (1898), and through Boer War; in World War I commanded forces sent to aid Antwerp (1914) and 4th army in battle of the Somme (1916); defeated Germans near Amiens (1918); British representative on Supreme War Council (1918); commanded forces in northern Russia (1919); created baron (1919); commander in chief in India (1920).

Raw·son \'rau̇-sȯn\, Arturo. 1884–1952. Argentine cavalry officer. Succeeded Pedro Ramírez as commander of cavalry (1942); led military coup that overthrew Castillo government (1943); acting president for two days before turning over government to Ramírez.

Ray \'rā\, John. *Wrote his name* Wray *till 1670.* 1627–1705. English naturalist. Often called "father of English natural history." Taught at Cambridge (1649–62); lost his fellowship for refusal to take oath of Act of Uniformity. With a pupil, Francis Willughby (*q.v.*), toured England, Wales, Low Countries, Germany, Italy, and France, making collections on which to base complete systematic descriptions of animal and vegetable life (1662–66); published *Catalogus Plantarum Angliae* (1670); demonstrated nature of buds and made division of flowering plants into dicotyledons and monocotyledons in *Methodus Plantarum Nova* (1682); first introduced a feasible limitation of term *species;* made great contributions to taxonomy; published masterwork *Historia Generalis Plantarum* (1686–1704); later devoted himself to study of insects; wrote, besides botanical and zoological works, some theological works and a collection of proverbs (1670).

Ray \'rāy\, Man. *Orig. name* Emmanuel Rud·nit·sky \rəd-'nit-skē\. 1890–1976. American painter, photographer, and film maker, b. Philadelphia. Member of Dadaist and Surrealist movements in New York (until 1921) and Paris (1921–40, 1951 ff.); associate of Duchamp, Picabia, and André Breton (*qq.v.*). Produced art objects, called "ready mades," as *Le Cadeau* (1921) and *Object to be Destroyed* (1923), and paintings as *Admiration of the Orchestrelle for the Cinematograph* (1919) and *Observatory Time–The Lovers* (1932–34). Experimented with abstract photography, developing "cameraless" pictures he called "rayographs," many collected in *Les Champs délicieux* (1922); made portrait photographs of Parisian celebrities. Produced surrealistic films *Le Retour à la raison* (1923), *Anemic Cinema* (1924), *L'Étoile de mer* (1928–29).

Ray, Rammohan. 1772–1833. Indian religious and social reformer. Settled in Calcutta (1814); translated Vedānta writings and the *Upaniṣads* into Bengali, Hindi, and English (1815–19); wrote works in Bengali on the Vedānta philosophy; organized a protest against British censorship of Calcutta press (1823); founded Vedānta College, Calcutta (1826); advocated a modern Western curriculum for schools; active in abolishing suttee (1818–29); founded (1828) the Brahmo Samaj, a Hindu theistic society.

Ray·burn \'rā-bərn\, Samuel Taliaferro. 1882–1961. American politician, b. Roane Co., Tenn. Moved to Texas (1887); Democratic member, U.S. House of Representatives (1913–61), speaker (1940–46, 1949–53, 1955–61); responsible for passage of much of Roosevelt's New Deal program.

Ra·yet \rá-ye\, Georges-Antoine-Pons. 1839–1906. French astronomer. Discovered, in collaboration with C. J. E. Wolf, three small stars, the first of a class of peculiar stars called Wolf-Rayet stars (1867).

Rayleigh, Baron. See John William STRUTT.

Ray·mond \rā-mō^{n}\. Name of counts of Tou·louse \tü-lüz\, including: Raymond IV, *called* Raymond de Saint-Gilles \-də-sa^{n}-zhēl\ (1042–1105), succeeded his older brother (1093); commanded a large army in the First Crusade (1095); helped capture Antioch (1098) and Jerusalem (1099); blocked southern expansion of Bohemond (1100–05); considered founder of Latin countship of Tripoli. His great-grandson ¶Raymond VI (1156–1222) succeeded his father Raymond V (1196); m. (1196) Joan, Queen of Sicily; fought with the Albigenses against the Crusaders under Simon de Montfort, was decisively defeated in the battle of Muret (1213) and had his possessions handed over to Montfort by the Fourth Lateran Council (1215); resumed war against Montfort; gained back most of his territory. His son ¶Raymond VII (1197–1249) succeeded to countship (1222); fought the Albigenses until he negotiated a truce (1223); invaded by Louis VIII and lost most of his possessions in Treaty of Meaux (1229); allied himself with Henry III of England and rebelled against France, but defeated at Saintes (1242); last count of Toulouse.

Raymond III. c.1140–1187. French count of Tripoli. Great-great-grandson of Raymond de Saint-Gilles, Count of Toulouse. Succeeded to countship (1152); campaigned against Nureddin and imprisoned by him (1164–72); regent for Baldwin IV (1174–77) and Baldwin V (1184–85); supported Guy de Lusignan against invasion of Saladin; mortally wounded in Battle of the Horns of Ḥaṭṭin.

Ray·mond \'rā-mənd\ of Peñafort. Saint. *Span.* Rai·mun·do de Pe·ña·fort \ri-'mün-dō-thā-pān-yä-'fȯrt\. c.1185–1275. Spanish Dominican monk and theologian. Canon of Barcelona (1219); aided Peter Nolasco in founding order for ransom of Christian captives; wrote *Summa de casibus penitentiae* (c.1222–29); called to Rome to serve as papal chaplain to Gregory IX (1230); codified canon law; his *Decretales Gregorii* formed vol. V of *Corpus Juris Canonici;* bishop of Tarragona (1235); general of Dominican order (1238–40). Canonized (1601).

Raymond of Poi·tiers \pwá-tyā\. 1099–1149. French prince of Antioch. Married Constance of Antioch and became prince (1136); resisted attempts of Byzantine emperor John II to control Antioch (1137–43); slain in battle against Nureddin.

Raymond of Sabunde. *Span.* Rai·mun·do Sa·bun·de \ri-'mün-dō-sä-'bün-dā\. d. 1436. Spanish theologian. Chiefly remembered for *Theologia naturalis* (written 1434–36), translated into French by Montaigne.

Raymond, Alexander Gillespie. 1909–1956. American cartoonist, b. New Rochelle, N.Y. Joined King Features Syndicate (1930); created (with Dashiell Hammett) comic strip "Secret Agent X-9" (1930); created comic strips "Flash Gordon" (1934), "Jungle Jim" (1934), and "Rip Kirby" (1946).

Raymond, Antonin. 1888–1976. American architect, b. Kladno, Bohemia. To U.S. (1910, naturalized 1916); with Frank Lloyd Wright (1916–17); practiced in Japan (1921–37); pioneer of modern architecture in Orient.

Raymond, Don. See RAIMUNDO.

Raymond, Henry Jarvis. 1820–1869. American journalist and politician, b. Lima, N.Y. Worked for Horace Greeley's *New Yorker* (1840) and *Tribune*

(1841–48). With George Jones, founded *New York Times* (1851) and was its editor (1851–69). Lieutenant governor of New York (1855–57). Member of meeting that founded Republican party (1856) and drafted statement of its principles. Member, U.S. House of Representatives (1865–67). Author of *A Life of Daniel Webster* (1853), *A History of the Administration of President Lincoln* (1864), etc.

Raymond, Percy Edward. 1879–1952. American paleontologist and stratigrapher, b. New Canaan, Conn. Professor of paleontology and curator of Museum of Comparative Zoology, Harvard (1912–45); known for studies on trilobites, red beds, sedimentation, and for textbook on vertebrate paleontology, *Prehistoric Life* (1947).

Ray·nal \re-näl\, Guillaume-Thomas-François de. Abbé. 1713–1796. French historian and philosopher. Regarded as a leader among the French freethinkers; educated for priesthood. Wrote histories of Netherlands (1747) and of English Parliament (1748); edited literary periodical *Mercure de France* (1750–54). With Denis Diderot wrote *Histoire philosophique et politique des établissements et du commerce des Européens dans les deux Indes* (1770), which was publicly burned (1781) by order of the parliament because of its attacks on the clergy and on Europeans for their conduct and policies toward the natives in the Indies.

Raynal, Paul. 1885–1971. French playwright. Author of the comedy *Le Maître de son coeur* (1920), and the tragedies *Le Tombeau sous l'Arc de Triomphe* (1924), *Au soleil de l'instinct* (1932), *Napoléon unique* (1937), and *A souffert sous Ponce-Pilate* (1939).

Raynald of Châtillon. See REGINALD.

Ray·nou·ard \rān-wär\, François-Juste-Marie. 1761–1836. French scholar and playwright. Author of the plays *Caton d'Utique* (1794), *Templiers* (1805), *Les États de Blois* (1810); best known for his studies in Provençal language and literature, as his collection of troubadour poetry *Choix de poésies originales des troubadours* (1816–21), his *Lexique roman* (1839–44), etc.

Ray·nov *or* **Rai·nov** \'rī-nȯf\, Nikolay Ivanov. 1889–1954. Bulgarian poet, painter, and art historian. Professor at Academy of Fine Arts, Sofia (1928 ff.); author of Symbolist poetry and prose and a 12-volume history of world art.

Rays, Gilles de. See RAIS.

Rā·zī \'rä-zē\, Abū Bakr Muḥammad ibn Zakarīyā' ar-. *Known in West by Lat. form* Rha·zes \'rä-(,)zēz\. c.865–between 923 and 935. Persian physician and philosopher. Considered greatest physician of Islāmic world. Chief physician of hospitals in Rayy and Baghdad; believed in atomist theory of nature. Author of numerous treatises in medicine, esp. a survey of Greek, Syrian, and early Arabic medicine and a treatise on smallpox and measles, on philosophy, and on alchemy. Some of his works were translated into Latin and had great influence on medical science in Middle Ages.

Ra·zin \'rä-zyin\, Stepan Timofeyevich. *Known as* Stenka Razin. d. 1671. Russian Cossack rebel. Headed small band of raiders that attacked Russian and Persian settlements near Caspian Sea (1667–69); leader of a Cossack and peasant rebellion in Volga River region (1670–71); captured Volgograd, Astrakhan, and Saratov; defeated by czarist army, tortured, and executed. Immortalized in folk songs and legends.

Ra·zi·ya \ra-'zē-yə\ *or* **Ra·ziy·yat-ud-din** \ra'zē-ya-tu̇d-'dēn\. d. 1240. Queen of Delhi of the Slave dynasty (1236–40). The only woman ruler of Muslim India. Daughter of Iltutmish and appointed by him as his successor; according to Muslim sources, a wise and just ruler and benefactor to her realm, but her reign disturbed by revolts; slain by Hindu followers.

Read \'rēd\, Albert Cushing. 1887–1967. American naval officer, b. Lyme, N.Y. Commissioned in U.S. navy (1908); commander of NC-4 aircraft in first transatlantic flight, from Long Island to Lisbon, Portugal (May 1919); served in both World Wars; rear admiral (1941); retired (1946).

Read, George. 1733–1798. American lawyer and Revolutionary leader, b. Cecil Co., Md. Member, Continental Congress (1774–77) and signer of Declaration of Independence. Presiding officer, Delaware constitutional convention (1776). Judge, U.S. court of appeals in admiralty cases (1782–86). Delegate to Constitutional Convention (1787) and vigorous upholder of rights of the smaller states. Instrumental in causing Delaware to be first state to ratify the Constitution. U.S. senator from Delaware (1789–93). Chief justice of Delaware (1793–98).

Read, Sir Herbert. 1893–1968. English poet and art critic. Edited *Burlington Magazine* (1933–39); chief advocate and interpreter of British art movements (from 1930s); influenced "New Apocalypse" poetic circle of 1940s. Author of autobiographical *The Innocent Eye* (1933), *The Contrary Experiences* (1963); poetry *Naked Warriors* (1919), *Collected Poems* (1966); critical works *The Meaning of Art* (1931), *Art and Society* (1936), *The Philosophy of Modern Art* (1952), *The True Voice of Feeling* (1953), etc.

Read, Herbert Harold. 1889–1970. British geologist. Member of Royal Geological Survey (1914–31); professor at Liverpool (1931–39) and U. of London (1939–55). Known for researches on the origins of granite; author of *Geology* (1949), *The Granite Controversy* (1957), and *Beginning Geology* (1966).

Read, Opie Percival. 1852–1939. American writer, b. Nashville, Tenn. Founded and edited the humorous journal *Arkansas Traveler* (1883–91); author of books employing homespun humor and usually set in the mid-South, as *Len Gansett* (1888), *A Kentucky Colonel* (1890), *The Jucklins* (1895), *My Young Masters* (1896), *In the Alamo* (1900), *The Starbucks* (1902), *Old Lim Jucklin* (1905).

Reade \'rēd\, Charles. 1814–1884. English novelist and dramatist. Began career by writing plays, the most successful being *Masks and Faces* (1852), *Gold* (1853), *The Courier of Lyons* (1854), *Sera Nunquam* (1865), *Drink* (1879). Employed fiction to attack prison conditions in *It Is Never too Late to Mend* (1856); followed five lesser novels with his masterpiece, the historical novel about the father of Erasmus, *The Cloister and the Hearth* (1861). Drew attention to abuses in private asylums for insane in *Hard Cash* (1863), to the marriage problem in *Griffith Gaunt* (1866), to terrorism by trade unions in *Put Yourself in His Place* (1870); published autobiographical *A Terrible Temptation* (1871); pictured degrading features of village life in *A Woman Hater* (1877); left behind at death a completed novel, *A Perilous Secret*.

Reading, 1st Marquis of. See Rufus ISAACS.

Read·ing \'red-iŋ\, John. 1677–1764. English composer. Organist at Lincoln cathedral and (after 1707) in London; composer of tune "Adeste Fideles."

Ré·au·mur \rā-ō-mu̅e̅r\, René-Antoine Fer·chault de \fer-shō-də-\. 1683–1757. French naturalist and physicist. Constructed (1730) a thermometer (Réaumur thermometer) so graduated that 0° marks the freezing point and 80° the boiling point of water; invented (1740) an opaque white glass known as Réaumur porcelain, also a method of tinning steel; worked on the production of steel and improvements in the manufacture of iron; isolated gastric juice (1752) and investigated its role in digestive process; investigated the action of the electric ray, regeneration of lost parts in crustaceans, artificial incubation of eggs, auriferous rivers, turquoise mines, etc. Author of *Mémoires pour servir à l'histoire des Insectes* (1734–42).

Re·ber \rə-ber\, Napoléon-Henri. 1807–1880. French composer. Author of 4 symphonies, chamber music, a suite of orchestral pieces, comic operas *La Nuit de Noël* (1848), *Le Père Gaillard* (1852), *Les Dames capitaines* (1857), etc., the ballet *Le Diable amoureux* (1840), and songs.

Re·bi·kov \'ryā-byi-kəf\, Vladimir Ivanovich. 1866–1920. Russian composer. Composer of operas as *In the Thunderstorm* (1894) and *The Christmas Tree* (1903), orchestral suites, symphonic poems, piano pieces, and choral works.

Reb·mann \'rāp-,män\, Johannes. 1820–1876. German missionary, traveler, and explorer. Discovered Mt. Kilimanjaro with Krapf (1848) and investigated Swahili and other native languages.

Re·brea·nu \reb-'ryän-ü\, Liviu. 1885–1944. Romanian novelist. Author of novels mainly with themes of nationalism and social reform as *Ion* (1920), *Pădurea spânzuraților* (1921), *Răscoala* (1932).

Recaizade Mahmud Ekrem Bey. See EKREM BEY.

Ré·ca·mier \rā-käm-yā\, Jeanne-Françoise-Julie-Adélaïde, *nee* Ber·nard \ber-när\. 1777–1849. French society beauty and wit. m. (1792) Jacques Récamier. Her salon in Paris attracted the notables of the day during the Consulate and the Empire; after the Restoration, she retired to Abbaye-aux-Bois, where she maintained close friendship with Chateaubriand. Portrayed in novel *Corinne* by her friend Mme de Staël. The récamier daybed was so named in her honor.

Rech·berg und Ro·then·lö·wen \'rek-berk-ünt-'rō-tən-,lœ-vən\, Johann Bernhard von. Graf. 1806–1899. Austrian politician. Helped Metternich in Revolution of 1848; represented Austria at Frankfurt (1849); associate of Radetzky in government of Lombardy-Venetia (1853); Austrian representative and president, Federal Council (1855), where he opposed Bismarck; foreign minister (1859–64) and minister president (until 1860).

Reck·ling·hau·sen \'rek-liŋ-,hau̇-zən\, Friedrich Daniel von. 1833–1910. German pathologist. Professor at Würzburg (1866–72), Strasbourg (1872–1906). Known for descriptions of lymph channels (canals of Recklinghausen) in connective tissue (1862), of multiple neurofibromatosis (1882), and of osteitis fibrosa cystica (1891).

Re·clus \rə-klu̅e̅\, Jean-Jacques-Élisée. 1830–1905. French geographer. Author of many books of travel and description, including *La Terre* (1867–68), *Nouvelle Géographie universelle* (1876–95), *L'Afrique australe* (in collaboration, 1901).

Rec·orde \'rek-,ȯ(ə)rd\, Robert. c.1510–1558. English mathematician. Taught mathematics at Oxford and Cambridge; physician to Edward VI and Queen Mary. Introduced algebra into England; first to write mathematical and astronomical works in English; in *The Whetstone of Witte* (1557), first to use equals sign (=); also wrote *The Ground of Artes* (c.1542), *The Castle of*

Knowledge (1551; wrote favorably of Copernican theory), and *Pathewaie to Knowledge* (1551).

Rec·to \'rek-tō\, Claro Mayo. 1890–1960. Philippine politician. Senator (1949–57); led "Filipino-first" movement against U.S. influence in Philippines (1953 ff.); founded Nationalist Citizen's party (1957) which advocated neutrality in foreign affairs and economic independence from U.S.

Red Cloud \'red-ˌklau̇d\. *Indian name* Mahpiua Luta. 1822–1909. American Indian chief, b. Nebraska. Chief of the Bad Face band of the Oglalas and leader of Sioux and Cheyenne bands; resisted U.S. government's development of the Bozeman Trail in Wyoming and Montana (1865–67); slew 82 whites in Fetterman Massacre (Dec. 21, 1866); signed Treaty of Ft. Laramie (1868).

Red Ea·gle \(ˈ)red-'ē-gəl\. *Known also as* William Weath·er·ford \'weth-ər-fərd\. 1780?–1825. American Indian leader, b. Alabama. Of mainly European heritage; led Upper Creeks in Creek War (1813–14), including massacre of 500 whites at Fort Mims; defeated by Gen. Andrew Jackson at Horseshoe Bend (March 27, 1814).

Red·field \'red-ˌfēld\, Robert. 1897–1958. American cultural anthropologist, b. Chicago. On faculty of U. of Chicago (1927 ff.); research associate, Carnegie Institution, Washington, D.C. (1934–46). Did fieldwork in Mexico, Central America, China, and India; authority on cultural and social changes of a folk peasant community affected by urban influences. Author of *Tepoztlán* (1930), *Chan Kom* (1934, with Alfonso Villa Rojas), *The Folk Culture of the Yucatán* (1941), *Peasant Society and Culture* (1956), etc.

Red·grave \'red-ˌgrāv\, Sir Michael. 1908–1985. British actor. Began acting at Liverpool Playhouse (1926); debuted on London stage at Old Vic (1936); debuted on New York stage as Macbeth (1948); other stage roles included Uncle Vanya, Hamlet, Antony, King Lear; among his films were *The Lady Vanishes* (1938), *Dead of Night* (1945), *The Browning Version* (1951), and *Nicholas and Alexandra* (1971). Known for regal bearing, sonorous voice, expressive face, and air of tragic poignancy. Published autobiography *In My Mind's Eye* (1983).

Re·di \'red-ē\, Francesco. 1626–1697. Italian physician, naturalist, and poet. One of first to test scientifically the theory of spontaneous generation; showed that no maggots developed in meat protected so that flies could not lay their eggs on it (1668). Author of the dithyrambic *Bacco in Toscana* (1685), etc.

Re·ding \'rā-diŋ\, Aloys. 1765–1818. Swiss politician. Participated in defense against French invasion (1798); elected head of Helvetian Republic (1801–02); overthrown by coup; headed rival insurrectionary government (Aug.–Sept. 1802); later involved in cantonal politics of Schwyz.

Reding, Ital. d. 1447. Swiss politician. Chief magistrate of canton of Schwyz (1412–44); his quarrel with Rudolf Stussi of Zürich over the landed inheritance of Count Frederick VII of Toggenburg led to civil wars (1439–40, 1443–50); laid siege to Greifensee and massacred its survivors (May 1444).

Red Jack·et \'red-ˌjak-ət\. *Orig. name* Otetiani, *changed to* Sagoyewatha *on elevation to chief.* 1756?–1830. American Indian chief, b. Seneca Co., N.Y. A chief of the Senecas. Friendly with whites, but opposed cession of Indian lands to U.S. and efforts to train Indians in white man's civilization.

Red·lich \'rāt-ˌlik\, Joseph. 1869–1936. Austrian jurist and politician. Authority on English government; member, Austrian parliament (1907–18) and German Progressive party; minister of finance in last imperial cabinet of Lammasch (1918); professor of comparative law, Harvard (1926–31); again minister of finance (1931). Author of *Englische Lokalverwaltung* (1901), *Das österreichische Staats- und Reichsproblem* (1920–26), and *Schicksaljahre Österreichs, 1908–1919* (political diaries).

Red·mond \'red-mənd\, John Edward. 1856–1918. Irish politician. M.P. (1881, 1891–1918); prominent organizer of Home Rule propaganda; leader of Parnellite group on death of Parnell (1891). Adopted conciliatory attitude toward government and anti-Parnellites, and brought about amalgamation of the two Irish Nationalist parties (1900). Used balance of power in House of Commons to force through constitutional resolutions removing veto power of House of Lords (1909–11); procured Irish acceptance of Home Rule bill (1912); opposed attempted separation of Ulster. Supported Great Britain in World War I and promoted recruiting in Ireland but declined place in Asquith's coalition cabinet (1915); expressed detestation of Easter Rebellion (1916); attempted conciliatory role in Irish convention (1917–18) but lost control to de Valera and extreme nationalists.

Re·don \rə-dōⁿ\, Odilon. 1840–1916. French painter, lithographer, and engraver. A forerunner of Surrealists with fantastic Symbolist prints inspired by Poe and Goya; also known for postimpressionistic paintings of flowers.

Red·path \'red-ˌpath\, James. 1833–1891. American journalist, b. Berwick upon Tweed, Scotland. To U.S. (c.1850); on staff, New York *Tribune* (1852–82). Vigorous abolitionist; aided in transporting ex-slaves to Haiti and in securing U.S. recognition of independence of Haiti; war correspondent with Union armies in Civil War. Editor *North American Review* (1886–87). Author of *The Roving Editor, or Talks with Slaves in the Southern States* (1859), *The Public Life of Captain John Brown* (1860), etc.

Redwald. See RAEDWALD.

Reed \'rēd\, Sir Carol. 1906–1976. English film director. Theatrical actor (1924) and director (1927–32); film director (1935 ff.). Among films he directed were *The Stars Look Down* (1939), *Night Train to Munich* (1940), *The True Glory* (1945), *Odd Man Out* (1947), *The Fallen Idol* (1948), *The Third Man* (1949), *Outcast of the Islands* (1951), *Our Man In Havana* (1959), and *Oliver!* (1968, Academy Award).

Reed, Isaac. 1742–1807. English editor. Practiced as conveyancer; devoted himself to literature and archaeology; revised Dr. Johnson and George Steevens's edition of Shakespeare (1785); edited the "first variorum" Shakespeare from Steevens's notes (1803).

Reed, John. 1887–1920. American journalist and poet, b. Portland, Ore. On staff of radical magazine *The Masses* (1913). War correspondent (1914) for *Metropolitan* magazine with Pancho Villa in Mexico and (1914–16) with armies on eastern front in Europe in World War I. In Russia in time to observe revolution of October 1917. Organized and led Communist Labor party (1919) and edited its journal *The Voice of Labor.* Indicted for sedition, escaped to Russia; buried in the Kremlin, Moscow. Author of *Sangar* (1912, verse), *The Day in Bohemia* (1913, verse), *Insurgent Mexico* (1914), *The War in Eastern Europe* (with Boardman Robinson, 1916), *Tamburlaine and Other Poems* (1916), *Red Russia* (1919), *Ten Days that Shook the World* (1919).

Reed, Joseph. 1741–1785. American Revolutionary commander and politician, b. Trenton, N.J. President, second Provincial Congress, Philadelphia (1775). Military secretary to Gen. Washington (1775), and adjutant general of Continental army. Member, Continental Congress (1777, 1778). President, supreme executive council of Pennsylvania (1778–81).

Reed, Stanley Forman. 1884–1980. American jurist, b. Maysville, Ky. General counsel, Federal Farm Board (1929–32), Reconstruction Finance Corp. (1932–35); solicitor general of U.S. (1935–38); associate justice, U.S. Supreme Court (1938–57).

Reed, Thomas Brackett. 1839–1902. American politician, b. Portland, Me. Republican member, U.S. House of Representatives (1877–99) and speaker of the House (1889–91, 1895–99); responsible for adoption by the House of Reed's Rules (1890), increasing speaker's power to expedite legislation favored by majority party; criticized as "Czar Reed" for his iron control of the House.

Reed, Walter. 1851–1902. American army surgeon, b. Belroi, Va. Entered Army Medical Corps (1875); on frontier duty (1875–90); curator, Army Medical Museum, and professor of bacteriology and microscopy at Army Medical College (1893); promoted major (1893). Head of commission (including James Carroll, Jesse Lazear, Aristides Agramonte) sent to Cuba to investigate cause and mode of transmission of yellow fever (1900); proved that yellow fever is transmitted by the mosquito *Aëdes aegypti.* With this knowledge, it was possible to eradicate the disease by destroying the carriers. Walter Reed Hospital, Washington, D.C., was named in his honor.

Reese \'rēs\, Lizette Woodworth. 1856–1935. American poet, b. Baltimore Co., Md. Taught in Baltimore public schools (1873–1921). Author of volumes of lyric verse, including *A Handful of Lavender* (1891), *Wayside Lute* (1909), *Spicewood* (1920), *Wild Cherry* (1923), *White April* (1930), *Pastures* (1933).

Reeve \'rēv\, Clara. 1729–1807. English novelist. Author of *The Champion of Virtue, a Gothic Story* (1777), renamed *The Old English Baron,* avowedly in imitation of Sir Horace Walpole's *Castle of Otranto.*

Reeve, Tapping. 1744–1823. American lawyer and educator, b. Brookhaven, N.Y.. Practiced, Litchfield, Conn. (1772 ff.); opened Litchfield Law School (1784), first in U.S.; judge on Conn. Superior Court (1798–1814).

Reeves \'rēvz\, William Pember. 1857–1932. New Zealand journalist, politician, and economist. Editor, *Canterbury Times* (1885–89), *Lyttelton Times* (1889–91). M.P. (1887–96); minister of education, labor, and justice (1891–96); introduced progressive labor measures, including first legislation to provide for compulsory arbitration of labor disputes (1894). Agent general for New Zealand (1896–1905), and high commissioner (1905–08). Director, London School of Economics (1908–19). Author of *The Long White Cloud* (1898) and *State Experiments in Australia and New Zealand* (1902).

Re·ge·ner \'rā-gə-nər\, Erich Rudolph Alexander. 1881–1955. German physicist. Professor, Stuttgart (1920–37, 1946–55); determined (1909) unit electric charge; studied cosmic rays in deep water, oxygen in the stratosphere, etc.

Re·ger \'rā-gər\, Max, *in full* Johann Baptist Joseph Maximillian. 1873–1916. German composer. Professor of composition, Leipzig Conservatory (1907–16); director of court orchestra (1911–15) and general music director (1913), Meiningen. Noted esp. for contrapuntal organ works as *Ein feste Burg* (1898), *Sonata in F sharp minor* (1899), *Phantasia und Fuge über BACH* (1900); other compositions included orchestral works as *Konzert im alten Stil* (1912), *Tondichtungen nach Arnold Böcklin* (1913), *Variationen und Fuge über ein Thema von Mozart* (1914), and violin and piano concertos; chamber music, esp. violin sonatas and cello suites; piano pieces; choral works; sacred music.

Reggio, Ducs de. See Nicolas-Charles OUDINOT.

Reg·i·nald \'rej-ən-əld\ *or* **Ray·nald** \re-nàld\ of Châ·til·lon \shä-tē-yōⁿ\. d. 1187. French crusader. Left for Holy Land (1147); m. (1153) Constance of Antioch, becoming prince of Antioch (1153–63); invaded Cyprus; captive of Muslims (1160–76). m. (1177) Stephanie of Outre-Jourdain, becoming prince of Kerak and Montréal; plundered Muslim caravans during periods of truce, provoking war with Saladin; defeated by Saladin and beheaded.

Re·gi·no von Prüm \'rā-gē-ˌnō-fòn-'prᵫm\. *Also* Re·gi·non \'rā-gē-ˌnòn\. d. c.915. German monk and chronicler. Educated in the monastery of Prüm, of which he was abbot (892–899); abbot of St. Martin's, Trier (899–915). Author of a *Chronicon* (a history of the world from the dawn of the Christian era to 906).

Régio, José. See REIS PEREIRA.

Regiomontanus. See Johann MÜLLER.

Re·gnard \rən-yàr\, Jean-François. 1655–1709. French playwright. Traveled widely; romanticized his capture (1678–79) by Algerian pirates in novel *La Provençale;* treasurer of France (1683–1703). Author of light comedies modeled on Molière, as *La Sérénade* (1694), *Le Joueur* (1696), *Les Folies amoureuses* (1704), *Le Légataire universel* (1708).

Re·gnault \rən-yō\, Henri-Victor. 1810–1878. French chemist and physicist. Professor, École Polytechnique (1840), Collège de France (1841–54); director, Sèvres porcelain manufactory (1854–70). Made determinations of coefficients of expansion, specific heats, and vapor pressures of mixtures; showed approximating nature of Boyle's law; conducted researches on unsaturated hydrocarbons; introduced an air thermometer and a hygrometer.

Regnault de Saint-Jean d'An·gé·ly \-də-saⁿ-zhäⁿ-däⁿ-zhā-lē\, Michel-Louis-Étienne. Comte. 1761–1819. French politician. Elected to Estates-General (1789); aided Napoléon in coup d'état of 18 Brumaire (1799); minister of interior (1802–14); helped prepare commercial code of law (1807); vice president of Conseil d'État during Hundred Days (1815); persuaded Napoléon to abdicate (1815); in exile thereafter.

Ré·gnier \rā-nyā\, Claude-Ambroise. Duc de Mas·sa \də-mà-sà\. 1746–1814. French politician. Member of Estates-General (1789) and Council of Ancients (1796); appointed by Napoléon councilor of state, minister of justice (1802–13), president of the Corps Législatif (1813). Created duke (1809).

Régnier, Henri-François-Joseph de. 1864–1936. French poet, critic, and novelist. Regarded as one of the leaders of the Symbolists. Among his volumes of verse were *Lendemains* (1885), *Les Jeux rustiques et divins* (1897), *Les Médailles d'argile* (1900), *La Sandale ailée* (1906), and *Flamma tenax* (1922–28). Among his critical works were *Sujets et paysages* (1906), *Portraits et souvenirs* (1913), and *Nos rencontres* (1931); among his novels *La Double Maîtresse* (1900), *La Peur de l'amour* (1907), *La Pécheresse* (1912), *L'Escapade* (1926), and *Le Voyage d'amour* (1930).

Régnier, Mathurin. 1573–1613. French poet. Nephew of Philippe Desportes. Private secretary to Cardinal de Joyeuse in Rome (1593–1604); canon of Chartres cathedral (1609). Best known for his satires as *Macette, Le Goût décide de tout, La Folie est générale, Le Mauvais repas, Le Mauvais lieu.*

Reg·u·lus \'reg-yə-ləs\, Marcus Atilius. d. c.250 B.C. Roman hero. Consul (267 and 256). Defeated Carthaginian fleet, invaded Africa, and defeated Carthaginian army (256); defeated and captured by the Carthaginians (255). According to tradition, on his promise to return to Carthage, he was sent with an embassy to Rome (250) to negotiate peace or the exchange of prisoners; failed in his mission and, true to his promise, returned to Carthage, where he was tortured to death.

Re·han \'rē-ən\, Ada. *Orig. surname* Cre·han \'krē-ən\. 1857–1916. American actress, b. Limerick, Ireland. To U.S. (1865); made acting debut (1873). In Augustin Daly's company, New York (1879–99); excelled in comedy roles.

Re·ho·bo·am \ˌrē-(h)ə-'bō-əm\. 10th century B.C. King of Judah (c.934–917 B.C.). Son of King Solomon. During the early years of his reign the northern tribes revolted under Jeroboam and succeeded in dividing Israel into two kingdoms, Rehoboam becoming first king of southern kingdom, Judah; both kingdoms invaded by Sheshonk of Egypt (c.926).

Reich \'rīk\, Wilhelm. 1897–1957. Austrian psychoanalyst. Taught psychoanalytic seminars in Vienna (1922–39); to U.S. (1939), where he founded private psychoanalytic institute; known for theory of repressive action of society on personality and restoration of integrity through "orgone" energy. Author of *Die Funktion des Orgasmus* (1927), *Charakteranalyse* (1933), *Die Massenpsychologie des Faschismus* (1933), *Dialektische Materialismus und Psychologie* (1934), *Die sexuelle Revolution* (1936–45).

Rei·cha \'rī-kà\, Anton. 1770–1836. Czech composer and music theorist. In Vienna (1801–08); to Paris (1808). Friend of Beethoven and Haydn; teacher of Liszt and Gounod. Composed symphonies, chamber music, and comic operas *Cagliostro* (1810), *Natalie* (1816), and *Sapho* (1822).

Rei·chardt \'rī-ˌkärt\, Johann Friedrich. 1752–1814. German composer, conductor, and writer. Kapellmeister and court composer to Frederick the Great (1775); dismissed by Frederick William II for sympathy with French Revolution (1794). His compositions included the first German Liederspiel *Liebe und Treue* (1800), Singspiele, settings for many of Goethe's poems, operas, chamber music, piano concertos, symphonies, etc.

Rei·che·nau \'rī-kə-ˌnaù\, Walther von. 1884–1942. German field marshal. Commanded German army which captured Warsaw (1939) and the 6th army (1940); commanded army on southern sector of Russian front (1941).

Rei·chen·bach \'rī-kən-bäk\, Georg von. 1772–1826. German scientific instrument maker. Famous for the high quality of his astronomical instruments. Designed (1796) a dividing machine for marking precision instruments; built (1819) a telescope combining the transit and the mural circle; also invented a rifled cannon and a water-pressure pump; engaged in building hydraulic machinery (after 1820).

Reichenbach, Hans. 1891–1953. German philosopher and educator. Professor at Berlin (1926–33), Istanbul (1933–38), U.C.L.A. (1938–53). Founder of Berlin school of Logical Positivism; with Rudolf Carnap founded journal *Erkenntnis* (1930); contributed to logical interpretations of probability theories, theories of induction, and philosophical bases of science. Author of *Elements of Symbolic Logic* (1947), *The Rise of Scientific Philosophy* (1951), and *The Direction of Time* (1956).

Reichenbach, Karl Ludwig. 1788–1869. German natural philosopher and industrialist. Discovered creosote and paraffin in wood tar; later, conducted researches on what he designated as "od," an alleged force permeating all nature.

Reichstadt, Duc de. See NAPOLÉON II.

Reid \'rēd\, Forrest. 1875–1947. Irish novelist and critic. Author of an autobiography *Apostate* (1926) and of romantic and mystical novels about boyhood and adolescence as *The Bracknels* (1911), *The Spring Song* (1916), *Pirates of the Spring* (1919), *Uncle Stephen* (1931), *Brian Wesby* (1934), *The Retreat* (1936), and *Young Tom* (1944).

Reid, Sir George Houston. 1845–1918. Australian politician, b. Scotland. To Australia (1852). Premier of New South Wales (1894–99); member of first Commonwealth Parliament and leader of free traders (1901); prime minister of Commonwealth (1904–05); directed an economic recovery program and maintained free trade. Led opposition in Parliament (1905–08); high commissioner in London (1910–16); member of British Parliament (1916–18).

Reid, Harry Fielding. 1859–1944. American geologist, b. Baltimore. Professor, Johns Hopkins (1896–1930); authority on dynamic geology, seismology, and glaciology; developed (1911) elastic rebound theory of earthquake mechanics.

Reid, Ogden Mills. See under Whitelaw REID.

Reid, Samuel Chester. 1783–1861. American naval officer, b. Norwich, Conn. Commanded privateer in War of 1812, and in Faial harbor in the Azores repulsed three attacks from British warships; finally scuttled his ship to escape capture. Designed U.S. flag in its present form, and the first one, made by his wife Mary, was raised on the Capitol Apr. 12, 1818.

Reid, Thomas. 1710–1796. Scottish philosopher. Founder of the Scottish or common-sense school. Presbyterian pastor, New Machar (1737–51); professor, Aberdeen (1751–64). Made reply to Hume in *Inquiry into the Human Mind on the Principles of Common Sense* (1764); succeeded Adam Smith as professor of moral philosophy at Glasgow (1764–81). Published *Essays on the Intellectual Powers of Man* (1785), *Essays on the Active Powers of Man* (1788).

Reid, Mayne, *in full* Thomas Mayne. 1818–1883. Irish writer. To U.S. (1840); served in Mexican War. To England (1849) and devoted himself to writing. Among his many romances and adventure stories were *The Rifle Rangers* (1850), *The Scalp Hunters* (1851), *The War Trail* (1857), *Afloat in the Forest* (1865), *The Castaways* (1870), *Free Lances* (1881). His *The Quadroon* (1856) was basis of Boucicault's successful play *The Octoroon.*

Reid, Sir Thomas Wemyss. 1842–1905. English journalist and biographer. Edited *Leeds Mercury* (1870–87); manager of Cassell's publishing firm (1887–1905); biographer of Charlotte Brontë (1877), Gladstone (1899); author of novels *Gladys Fane* (1884) and *Mauleverer's Millions* (1886).

Reid, Whitelaw. 1837–1912. American journalist and diplomat, b. near Xenia, Ohio. On staff, *Cincinnati Gazette* (1861–68); made reputation as war correspondent with Union armies. On staff, *New York Tribune* (1868); succeeded Horace Greeley as managing editor (1869); editor (1872–1905), publisher (1872–1912). U.S. minister to France (1889–92); member, American commission to negotiate peace with Spain (1898); U.S. ambassador to Great Britain (1905–12). His son ¶Ogden Mills (1882–1947) became associated with *New York Tribune* (1908); editor and publisher (from 1913); purchased *New York Herald* and combined it with *Tribune* (1924).

Reid, Sir William. 1791–1858. British meteorologist, soldier, and colonial administrator. Served as engineer in Peninsular War (1810–14), in expeditions against New Orleans (1815) and against Algiers (1816). Governor of Bermuda

(1839–46), Windward Islands (1846–48), Malta (1851–58); major general (1856). Contributed to development of circular theory of hurricanes.

Rei·dy \'rā-dē\, Affonso Eduardo. 1909–1964. Brazilian architect. A pioneer of the modern architectural movement in Brazil. Designed mainly museums, schools, and blocks of office buildings; among his works in Rio de Janiero were the Marechal Hermes Theater (1950) and the Pedregulho Residential Neighborhood (1947–55).

Reil \'rīl\, Johann Christian. 1759–1813. German physician. Published works on the anatomy of the nervous system, fever, and mental diseases; founded *Archiv für die Physiologie* (1795); proposed psychological method for treatment of mental disorders (1803).

Reille \rāy\, Honoré-Charles-Michel-Joseph. 1775–1860. French soldier. Under Napoléon at Jena and Friedland (1806); aide-de-camp to Napoléon (1808); distinguished himself at Essling and Wagram (1809) and in Napoléon's service at Waterloo (1815). Created peer of France (1819) and marshal of France (1847); supported the coup d'état of Napoléon III (1851); senator (1852).

Rei·ma·rus \rī-'mär-ůs\, Hermann Samuel. 1694–1768. German theologian and naturalistic philosopher. Teacher in Hamburg (from 1727). Author of the rationalistic *Apologie oder Schutzschrift für die vernünftigen Verehrer Gottes,* a series of anonymous critical essays on the gospel history, fragments of which were published (1774 ff.) by Lessing in Brunswick as the "Wolfenbüttel fragments."

Rei·na Bar·rios \'rā-nä-'b̠är-ryōs\, José María. 1853–1898. Guatemalan politician. Nephew of Justo Rufino Barrios. President of Guatemala (1892–97); pursued liberal policies; assassinated.

Rei·necke \'rī-nə-kə\, Carl Heinrich Carsten. 1824–1910. German pianist, composer, conductor, and teacher. Conductor of Gewandhaus concerts (1860–95); teacher at Leipzig Conservatory (1860–1902). Composed about 250 pieces, including operas and operettas as *König Manfred* (1867), choral works, as the oratorio *Belsazar,* much chamber music, symphonies, orchestral overtures, concertos, children's songs, etc.

Rei·ner \'rī-nər\, Fritz. 1888–1963. American conductor, b. Budapest. To U.S. as conductor of Cincinnati Symphony (1922–31); musical director of Pittsburgh Symphony (1938–48), of the Metropolitan Opera (1948–53), and of Chicago Symphony (1953–62); orchestra leader and head of opera department, Curtis Inst. of Music, Philadelphia (1931–41).

Rein·hard \'rīn-,härt\, Hans. 1755–1835. Swiss politician. Member (1796–1801), president (1800–01), of government of Zürich; negotiated Act of Mediation (Feb. 19, 1803) with Napoléon; mayor of Zürich (1803–30); president of Swiss *landammann* (chief executive) of Switzerland (1807, 1813); president of Swiss Diet (1814–15, 1816, 1822, 1828); led Swiss delegation at Congress of Vienna (1814–15).

Rein·hardt \'rīn-,härt\, Ad, *in full* Adolf Frederick. 1913–1967. American painter, b. Buffalo, N.Y. Member of Abstract Expressionists in early 1940s; after World War II led reductionist movement that sought to remove self-expression, content, and meaning from art; known for monochrome paintings, last ones done in black; forerunner of Minimal Art; wrote "Twelve Rules for a New Academy" (1957) expounding reductionist philosophy.

Reinhardt, Django, *orig.* Jean-Baptiste. 1910–1953. French guitarist, b. Belgium of gypsy parentage. Considered sole European jazz musician of true originality. Became co-leader (with Stéphane Grappelly) of Quintet de Hot Club de France (1934); toured U.S. with Duke Ellington orchestra (1946); wrote guitar compositions as "Nuages" and "Manoir de mes rêves."

Reinhardt, Max. *Orig. surname* Gold·mann \'gōlt-,män\. 1873–1943. Austrian theatrical director and stage manager. Specialist in impressionistic mass effects. Director of the Deutsches Theater (1905–20, 1924–32) and the Kammerspiele (1906); known for productions of *Mirakel* (1911), *Oedipus Rex* (1910; initiated revival of Greek drama), *Rosenkavalier* (1911; premier), and Hofmannsthal's *Jedermann* (1920). Produced the Salzburg Festspiele (1920–34); toured United States (1923) and produced the pageant spectacle *The Miracle;* opened (1924) the Komödie in Berlin and the Theater in der Josefstadt in Vienna; active in Kurfürstendamm Theater, Berlin (1925–26) and Berlin Theater (1928–29); guest producer, New York (1927–28). In U.S. (1938 ff.); filmed *Midsummer Night's Dream* (1934–35).

Rein·hold \'rīn-,hōlt\, Erasmus. 1511–1553. German astronomer. After Copernicus, the leading mathematical astronomer of 16th century. Professor at Wittenberg (1536–52); known for *Tabulae prutenicae* (1551), astronomical tables computed by Copernican methods.

Rein·ken \'rīŋ-kən\, Johann Adam. 1623–1722. German organist and composer of Dutch ancestry. Compositions included *Partite diverse* for organ, *Hortus musicus* for 2 violins, viola, and bass (1687), variations for the clavier, arrangements for the organ, etc. Influenced J.S. Bach.

Rein·kens \'rīŋ-kəns\, Joseph Hubert. 1821–1896. German theologian and bishop. Professor (1853) and rector (1866), Breslau; became associated with Old Catholic movement (1870) and was suspended (1870) because of opposition to dogma of papal infallibility; excommunicated (1872). Chosen first Old Catholic bishop of Germany (1873); resident thereafter in Bonn. Author of works on ecclesiastical history, etc.

Rein·mar von Ha·ge·nau \'rīn-,mär-fōn-'häg-ə-,naů\. *Called also* Reinmar der Al·te \-dər-'äl-tə\, *i.e.* the Old. d. c.1205. Minnesinger and knight of Alsace. Active at court in Vienna, where Walther von der Vogelweide came under his influence; accompanied Leopold V on crusade (1190); his verses on unrequited love constituted the ultimate refinement of the *Minnesang.*

Reis \'rīs\, Johann Philipp. 1834–1874. German physicist. Designed several instruments for transmission of sound, forerunners of Bell's telephone; first described publicly an electrical telephone (1861).

Reis·ke \'rī-skə\, Johann Jakob. 1716–1774. German philologist. Authority on Greek literature; edited Plutarch (1774–79) and other Greek classical authors. His *Abulfedae Annales Moslemici* (1754) laid foundation for Arabic historical scholarship. Also established science of Arabic numismatics.

Reis·ner \'rī-snər\, George Andrew. 1867–1942. American archaeologist, b. Indianapolis. Curator, Egyptian dept., Boston Museum of Fine Arts (1910–42); professor, Harvard (1905–42). Directed many excavations in Egypt and Nubia (1899 ff.); discovered tomb of Queen Hetepheres at Giza. Wrote *Mycerinus* (1931), *A History of the Giza Necropolis* (1942), etc.

Reis Pe·rei·ra \'rās-pə-'rā-rə\, José Maria dos. *Pen name* José Ré·gio \'rezh-ē-ü\. 1901–1969. Portuguese writer. High school teacher by profession. Known for volumes of lyrical verse as *Poemas de Deus e do diabo* (1925), *As encruzilhadas de Deus* (1936), *Fado* (1941), *Filho do homen* (1961); also author of plays as *Benilde ou a virgem-mãe* (1947) and *A salvação do mundo* (1954), and of social novels as *O príncipe com orelhas de burro* (1942) and *A velha casa* (1945–66).

Reis·si·ger \'rī-sig-ər\, Karl Gottlieb. 1798–1859. German composer. Wrote operas as *Turandot* (1835) and *Adèle de Foix* (1841), masses and church music, oratorio *David* (1850), orchestral and chamber music, piano pieces, and many songs.

Reith \'rēth\, Sir John Charles Walsham. 1st Baron Reith of Stonehaven. 1889–1971. British government official. Engineer by profession. General manager (1922), director general (1927–38), British Broadcasting Company; inaugurated empire shortwave broadcasting service and first regular high-definition television service in world (1936). Chairman, Imperial Airways (1938–39); first chairman, British Overseas Airways Corp. (1939–40). Minister of information (1940), of transport (1940), of works and buildings, and first commissioner of works (1940–42). Chairman of Commonwealth Telecommunications Board (1946–50) and of Colonial Development Corp. (1950–59). Created baron (1940).

Rej \'rā\, Mikołaj. 1505–1569. Polish writer. One of first to use Polish as literary language. Author of plays *Żywot Józefa* (1545), *Kupiec* (1549); verse *Wizerunek* (1558), *Zwierzyniec* (1562); prose translations of Psalms (1546); prose works *Posilla* (1557), *Żywot człowieka poczciwego* (1558).

Rej·lan·der \'rā-län-der\, Oscar Gustav. Swedish photographer. Settled in England (1853); attempted to elevate photography to status of an art by making photographs in imitation of paintings; chief work *The Two Ways of Life* (1857).

Rejment. See REYMONT.

Re·lan·der \re-'län-der\, Lauri Kristian. 1883–1942. Finnish politician. President of Finland (1925–31).

Rel·ly \'rel-ē\, James. 1722?–1778. British religious leader. Coworker of George Whitefield, but broke away because of his belief in salvation for all men; preached Universalism in London till death; his convert John Murray was the founder of Universalist churches in America.

Re·mak \'rā-,mäk\, Robert. 1815–1865. German physician and physiologist. Discovered (1838) the nonmedullated nerve fibers with a neurilemma (hence called fibers of Remak); discovered (1842) the three germ layers of the early embryo and (1844) the nerve cells in the heart (Remak's ganglia); pioneered in electrotherapy.

Re·marque \rə-'märk\, Erich Maria. 1898–1970. German novelist. Served in World War I; lived in Switzerland (1929–39); to U.S. (1939), naturalized. Author of the war novel *Im Westen nichts Neues* (*All Quiet on the Western Front,* 1929), *Der Weg Zurück* (1931), *Flotsam* (1941), *Der funke Leben* (1952), *Zeit zu leben, Zeit zu sterben* (1954), *Die Nacht von Lissabon* (1962), etc.

Rem·brandt \'rem-,bränt, *Angl* -,brant\. *In full* Rembrandt Harmensz (*or* Harmenszoon) van Rijn *or* Ryn \-vän-'rīn\. 1606–1669. Dutch painter and etcher. Leading representative of the Dutch school of painting and master of light and shadow. Settled in Amsterdam (1631) as portrait painter and teacher; m. (1634) the wealthy Saskia van Uy·len·burgh \'ōi-ləm-,bœrk\ (d. 1642), mother of his son Titus (1641–1668). Suffered financial reverses, was declared bankrupt (1656). His many paintings, etchings, drawings, and prints included chiefly group and single portraits, also biblical and mythical representations, landscapes, still lifes, genre pictures. Among his portraits were many of himself and his wife, his son Titus, Hendrickje Stoffels, scores of self-portraits, studies of old women and of Jewish rabbis, the groups *The Anatomy Lesson of Dr. Tulp* (1632), *The Nightwatch* (1642), and *The Anatomical Lesson of Dr. Joan Deyman* (1656); among his religious and mythological subjects, *The Flight into Egypt* (1627), *Abduction of Ganymede* (1635), *Danaë* (1636), *Susanna and the Elders* (1647), *Aristotle Contemplating the Bust of Homer* (1653), *The Polish Rider* (c.1655), and *Simeon Holding the Christ Child in the Temple* (1669); among his landscapes, *Stormy Landscape* (c.1638), *Winter Landscape* (1646). His etchings included *The Angel Appearing to the Shepherds* (1634), *The Return of the Prodigal Son* (1636), *The 100 Guilder Print* (c.1639–49), *Jan Six* (1647), and *The Three Crosses* (1653); over 1600 drawings also survive.

Ré·mi *or* **Re·my** \rə-mē, rā-\. Saint. *Lat.* Re·mig·i·us \rə-ˈmij-ē-əs\. 437?–?533. Frankish prelate. Archbishop of Reims (459); baptized Clovis in the Christian faith, and became known as "the Apostle of the Franks."

Rem·ing·ton \ˈrem-iŋ-tən\, Eliphalet. 1793–1861. American firearms manufacturer, b. Suffield, Conn. Established factory for making rifles, at what is now Ilion, N.Y. (1828); purchased arms manufactory of Ames & Co., Springfield, Mass. (1845); contracted for government work. Marketed Remington pistol (from 1847). Expanded into manufacture of agricultural implements (from 1856). His son ¶Philo (1816–1889), b. Litchfield, N.Y., was associated with his father in gun-manufacturing business; president of company (1861–65); reorganized factory (1865), separating agricultural implement works from gun factory, and becoming president of E. Remington & Sons, gun manufacturers (1865–89). Expanded operations to include manufacture of Remington sewing machines (from 1870) and Remington typewriters (from 1873); forced by financial conditions to sell sewing machine business (1882), typewriter plant (1886), and agricultural implement factory (1887).

Remington, Frederic. 1861–1909. American painter, illustrator, and sculptor, b. Canton, N.Y. Traveled in western U.S. and worked as cowboy; artist and correspondent in Cuba in Spanish–American War (1898). Known as animal painter and illustrator of scenes from the American West. Works included bronze sculptures *Broncho Buster* and *Wounded Bunkie,* paintings *Cavalry Charge on the Southern Plains, A Dash for the Timber, The Last Stand, The Emigrants, Conjuring the Buffalo Back.* Author and illustrator of *Pony Tracks* (1895), *Crooked Trails* (1898), *The Way of an Indian* (1906), etc.

Re·mi·zov \ˈryā-myi-zəf\, Aleksey Mikhaylovich. 1877–1957. Russian novelist and short-story writer. Left Russia (1921), resided in Paris (1923 ff.). Author of Symbolist stories in colloquial Russian, often with grotesque or whimsical elements, chronicles, novels, etc., including *Sochineniya* (1910–12), *Ukrepa* (1916), *Trava-Murava* (1920), *Ognennaya Rossiya* (1921), *Olya* (1927), *Plyashushchiy demon* (1949), *Povest' o dvukh zveryakh Ikhnelat* (1950), etc.

Rem·sen \ˈrem(p)-sən, ˈrem-zən\, Ira. 1846–1927. American chemist and educator, b. New York City. First professor of chemistry, Johns Hopkins U. (1876–1913); president, Johns Hopkins U. (1901–13). Founded *American Chemical Journal* (1879) and edited it (1879–1913). Conducted investigations both in organic and in inorganic chemistry; discovered saccharin; discovered Remsen's law on prevention of oxidation in methyl and other groups.

Remy, Saint. See RÉMI.

Re·nan \rə-nä^{n}\, Joseph-Ernest. 1823–1892. French philosopher, philologist, and historian. A leader of the school of critical philosophy in France. Among his earlier books were *Averroès et l'Averroïsme* (1852), *Études d'histoire religieuse* (1857), and *De l'origine du langage* (1858). His most famous works were those in the series entitled *Histoire des origines du christianisme,* including *La Vie de Jésus* (1863), *Les Apôtres* (1866), *Les Évangiles et la seconde génération chrétienne* (1877), *L'Église chrétienne* (1879), *Marc Aurèle et la fin du monde antique* (1880). Among other works were *Histoire du peuple d'Israël* (1887–94), *Drames philosophiques* (1888), etc.

Re·nard \rə-nȧr\, Alphonse François. 1842–1903. Belgian geologist. Reported (with Sir John Murray, 1891) on the rock specimens and oceanic deposits collected by the *Challenger* expedition.

Renard, Charles. 1847–1905. French military engineer. With Arthur Krebs, built first true dirigible "La France," which made a circular journey of 7 or 8 kilometers at Chalais-Meudon (Aug. 9, 1884).

Renard, Jules. 1864–1910. French writer. One of founders of *Mercure de France* (1890); among his many novels were *L'Écornifleur* (1892), *Histoires naturelles* (1896), *Poil de Carotte* (1894), *Bucoliques* (1898), *Les Philippe* (1907), *Nos frères farouches* (1908), *Ragotte* (1908); among his plays *Le Plaisir de rompre* (1897), *Le Pain de ménage* (1899), *La Bigote* (1909).

Renart, Jean. See JEAN RENART.

Renatus, Flavius Vegetius. See VEGETIUS.

Re·nau·dot \rə-nō-dō\, Théophraste. 1586?–1653. French physician and journalist. Physician to the king; received appointment as commissary general of the poor and established (1630) an information and publicity agency on their behalf; began publishing news and thus established a regular journal called the *Gazette* (1631), first French newspaper. Opened first free medical clinic for the poor (1635); also first pawnshop (1637).

Re·nault \rə-nō\, Louis. 1843–1918. French jurist. Professor at Dijon and (from 1873) at Paris; professor of international law (from 1881). France's representative at international conferences, notably at The Hague (1907); awarded, with Ernesto T. Moneta, Nobel prize for peace (1907). Wrote legal treatises.

Renault, Louis. 1877–1944. French industrialist. Founder (1899) of Renault Frères, which became one of largest manufacturers of automobiles in Europe.

Renault \rə-ˈnō\, Mary. *Orig. surname* Chal·lans \ˈchal-ənz\ 1905–1983. South African author, b. London. Known esp. for historical novels set in ancient Greece. Works included *The Last of the Wine* (1956), *The King Must Die* (1958), *The Bull from the Sea* (1962), *Fire From Heaven* (1969), *The Persian Boy* (1972), and *Funeral Games* (1981).

Re·né I \rə-nā\. *Lat.* Re·na·tus \rə-ˈnāt-əs\. *Called* le Bon \lə-bō^{n}\, *i.e.* the Good. 1409–1480. Duke of Anjou (1434–80) and Lorraine (1434–53). Son of Louis II of Anjou. Duke of Bar (1430–56), Count of Provence and Piedmont (1431–80), and titular king of Naples (1435–42); m. Isabella of Lorraine (1420); claimed succession to duchy of Lorraine (1431) but defeated by Count of Vaudémont and held as prisoner (1431–32, 1435–38); confirmed as Duke of Lorraine by the emperor (1434). Inherited Naples from his brother Louis III (1435); joined Isabella there (1438) but was driven out by Alfonso of Aragon (1442). Retired to Provence (1442); patron of poets and artists; m. Jeanne de Laval (1454); accepted title of king of Aragon and Count of Barcelona from Catalan rebels (1466). Author of poems, romances, etc.; called the "last of the troubadours." His daughter Margaret married Henry VI of England.

René of Nas·sau \nȧ-sō\ *or* of Châ·lon \shä-lō^{n}\. 1518–1544. Prince of Orange. From uncle Philibert of Orange-Châlon inherited (1530) Orange; from father inherited (1538) countship of Nassau-Dillenburg; by emperor Charles V appointed stadholder of Holland, Zeeland, and Utrecht (1538) and of Gelderland (1543); died at siege of St. Dizier in France.

Re·née \rə-nā\ of France. 1510–1574. Daughter of Louis XII of France. m. Ercole II, Duke of Ferrara (1528), member of Este family. Her court at Ferrara a refuge for French Protestants and liberal thinkers; accepted Calvinism; imprisoned during Inquisition (1554), confessed and attended mass; returned to Protestantism when released from prison.

Ren·ger-Patzsch \ˈreŋ-ər-ˈpäch\, Albert. 1897–1966. German photographer. Known for objective photographs of landscapes, forests, industrial subjects, etc.; his books of photographs included *Die Welt ist schön* (1928).

Re·ni \ˈren-ē\, Guido. 1575–1642. Italian painter. Employed at Rome (c.1600–22); forced by intrigues of jealous rivals to return to Bologna (1622). Known for classical idealism of his religious and mythological subjects. His frescoes included stories of Virgin Mary in Palazzo del Quirinale (c.1610), *Phoebus and the Hours* (1613–14, Palazzo Rospigliosi), and *The Glory of St. Domenic* (1614, church of St. Domenic, Bologna); his canvases included 4 *Labors of Hercules* (c.1620) and *Madonna with Rosary* (c.1630).

Ren·nell \ˈren-^{ə}l\, James. 1742–1830. English geographer. Surveyor general of Bengal for East India Co. (1764–77); published his *Bengal Atlas* (1779). Provided illustrations and route map for Mungo Park's *Travels in the Interior Districts of Africa* (1797); also published *Memoir of a Map of Hindoostan* (1783) and *A Treatise on the Comparative Geography of Western Asia* (1831). Author of works on hydrography; a pioneer in oceanography, after whom Rennell's current was named.

Ren·nen·kampf \ryin-nin-ˈkämp\, Pavel Karlovich. 1854–1918. Russian general of cavalry. Served in Russo–Japanese War and in World War I; defeated Germans at Insterburg (Aug. 7, 1914), but was defeated by Hindenburg at Tannenberg (Aug. 26–30, 1914). Governor of St. Petersburg (1915); commander in chief on the northern front (1916). Shot by the Bolsheviks.

Ren·ner \ˈren-ər\, Karl. 1870–1950. Austrian politician. Deputy (from 1907); chancellor (1918–19, 1919–20); headed Austrian delegation at peace negotiations (1919); minister of foreign affairs (1920); member, national council (1920–34), president (1931–33); imprisoned following Social Democratic revolt (1934); president, 2d republic (from 1945). Author (sometimes under pseudonyms Sy·nop·ti·cus \zue-ˈnȯp-ti-ˌku̇s\ and Rudolf Spring·er \ˈshpriŋ-ər\) of works chiefly on economics, government, law, and socialism, as *Österreichs Erneuerung* (1916–17) and *An der Wende zweier Zeiten* (1946, memoirs).

Rennie \ˈren-ē\, John. 1761–1821. Scottish civil engineer. Drained Lincolnshire fens; constructed or improved harbors of Wick, Holyhead, Grimsby, and Hull; designed Waterloo, Southwark, and London bridges (the last completed by his sons); designed London dock and East India dock on Thames among others, and Plymouth breakwater. His sons ¶George (1791–1866) and ¶Sir John (1794–1874), civil engineers, carried on their father's business; George built the *Dwarf,* first screw vessel in British navy; John was knighted on completion of London Bridge (1831).

Ren·nyo \ren-yō\. 1415–1499. Japanese Buddhist leader. 8th patriarch of the Jōdo Shinshū movement (1457 ff.); built temples at Kyōto (1478), etc.

Re·no \'rē-(,)nō\, Jesse Lee. 1823–1862. American army officer, b. Wheeling, W.Va. Brigadier general of volunteers (1861); major general (1862); engaged at Manassas and Chantilly; killed in action at South Mountain. Reno, Nev., was named in his honor.

Re·noir \rən-wär\, Jean. 1894–1979. French film director. Son of Pierre-Auguste Renoir. Served in World War I; wrote script for first film *Une vie sans joie* (1924); fled Nazis and settled in Hollywood (1940); returned to work in Europe (1951). Among his 36 films were *La Fille de l'eau* (1924), *La Grande Illusion* (1937), *La Bête humaine* (1938), *La Règle de jeu* (1939), *Le Carrosse d'or* (1952), *French-Cancan* (1955), *Eléna et les hommes* (1956).

Renoir, Pierre-Auguste. 1841–1919. French painter. A leader among the Impressionists; closely associated with Monet; after trips to Algeria, Italy, and Provence (1881–82), broke with Impressionism for more formal technique. Best known for his figure paintings, landscapes, and flower pictures. Among his notable canvases were *Portrait de Bazille* (1867), *La Loge* (1874), *Portrait de Monet* (1875), *Le Moulin de la Galette* (1876), *Mme Charpentier et ses enfants* (1878), *Le Déjeuner des canotiers* (1881), *Les Parapluies* (c.1883), and *Les Baigneuses* (1884–87).

Re·nou·vier \rə-nüv-yā\, Charles-Bernard. 1815–1903. French idealistic philosopher. A leader in neocriticism; founded journals *Critique philosophique* and *Critique religieuse* (1878). Among his many books were *Manuel de philosophie moderne* (1842), *Manuel de philosophie ancienne* (1844), *Les Dilemmes de la métaphysique* (1900), *Le Personnalisme* (1902).

Ren·shaw \'ren-,shò\, William. 1861–1904. English tennis player. Won Wimbledon singles championship 7 times (1881–86). His twin brother ¶Ernest (1861–1899) was Wimbledon singles champion in 1888. Together they won the British doubles championship 7 times (1879 ff.).

Rens·se·laer \'ren-sə-,lär\, Kiliaen *or* Killian van. 1595–1644. Dutch merchant. Dealer in precious stones in Amsterdam; a founder and organizer of Dutch West India Company (chartered 1621); bought and colonized huge tract of land, called Rensselaerswyck, comprising present counties of Albany, Columbia, and Rensselaer in New York.

Ren·wick \'ren-ik, -(,)wik\, James. 1662–1688. Scottish Covenanter. Joined Cameronians (1681); proclaimed Lanark declaration (1682); ordained (1683); field preacher; outlawed for his *Apologetic Declaration* (1684) disavowing authority of Charles II; refused to join rising under Earl of Argyll (1685); captured and hanged, last of Covenanting martyrs.

Ren·wick \'ren-(,)wik\, James. 1818–1895. American architect, b. New York City. Known for Gothic Revival designs. Won competition for design of Grace Church, New York City (1843); also designed Saint Patrick's Cathedral (1853) and other churches. Other works, Smithsonian Institution, Washington, D.C. (1848), Corcoran Art Gallery, Washington, D.C. (1859), Vassar College (1865), and Booth Theater, New York City (1869).

Repgau *or* **Repgow** *or* **Repegouw,** Eike von. See EIKE VON REPGAU.

Re·pin \'ryā-pyin\, Ilya Yefimovich. 1844–1930. Russian painter. Professor at St. Petersburg Academy (1893–1907). Painted episodes from Russian history as *Religious Procession in Kursk Gubernia* (1880–83), *Ivan Grozny and His Son Ivan* (1885), and *The Reply of the Cossacks to Sultan Mahmoud IV* (1891).

Rep·nin \ryip-'nyēn\, Anikita Ivanovich. Prince. 1668–1726. Russian general. Participated in Peter the Great's two Azov campaigns (1695, 1696) and in Northern War against Sweden (1700–21); commanded Russian center in victory at Poltava (1709); governor general of Riga; created field marshal by Catherine I. His grandson ¶Prince Nikolay Vasilyevich Repnin (1734–1801) was a general (from 1762); resident in Poland (1763–68), which became a virtual Russian protectorate; engaged in the war with Turkey (1768); defeated Turks at Budapest (1771); participated in peace negotiations (1774). Appointed ambassador to Turkey (1775–76). Distinguished himself in second war with Turkey (1787–91); negotiated partition of Poland (1792); governor general of Estonia and Livonia (1794–96); field marshal (1796); on diplomatic missions to Austria and Prussia (1798).

Rep·plier \'rep-,li(ə)r\, Agnes. 1855–1950. American writer, b. Philadelphia. Author esp. of essays as in *Books and Men* (1888), *Points of View* (1891), *Essays in Miniature* (1892), *Essays in Idleness* (1893), *Varia* (1897), *Compromises* (1904), *Americans and Others* (1912), *Counter-Currents* (1916), *Points of Friction* (1920), *Under Dispute* (1924), *In Pursuit of Laughter* (1936), *Eight Decades* (1937), etc.

Rep·ton \'rep-tən\, Humphrey. 1752–1818. English landscape designer. Succeeded Lancelot Brown as leading English landscape designer (from 1788); known for thickly planted landscapes with gradual transitions between houses and gardens; designed Uppark in Sussex and Sheringham Hall in Norfolk. Author of books on landscape gardening as *Observations on the Theory and Practice of Landscape Gardening* (1803).

Re·que·séns y Zú·ñi·ga \rā-kā-'säns-ē-'thün-yē-gä\, Luis de. 1528–1576. Spanish soldier. Succeeded Duke of Alba as governor of the Low Countries, then (1573) in revolt; promised an amnesty and remission of taxes, but could not grant religious freedom to the Dutch people; failed in attempts to capture Leiden or conquer Holland.

Resende, García de. See GARCÍA DE RESENDE.

Re·şid Pa·şa *or* **Re·shid Pa·sha** \re-'shēd-pä-'shä\, Mustafa. 1800–1858. Turkish statesman. Grand vizier (1837–38); envoy to London, Berlin, Paris; minister of foreign affairs (1839); chief adviser to young sultan Abdülmecid I (from 1839); helped draft and promulgate reform edicts known as the Tanzimat. Turkish representative in Paris (1841–45). Again minister of foreign affairs (1845) and grand vizier (1846 ff., with several interruptions), serving through the early part of the Crimean War (1854–55).

Re·spi·ghi \rā-'spē-gē, *Angl* rə-'spē-gē, re-\, Ottorino. 1879–1936. Italian composer. Known for his orchestral colorism. Studied under Rimsky-Korsakov and Max Bruch; professor of composition at Sta. Cecilia Academy, Rome (from 1913). His works included operas *Re Enzo* (1905), *Semirama* (1910), *Belfagor* (1923), *Maria Egiziaca* (1932), *La fiamma* (1934), *Lucrezia* (1937), orchestral works *Fontane di Roma* (1917), *Antiche arie e danze* (1916, 1923, 1931), *Pini di Roma* (1924), *Rossiniana* (1925), *Vetrate di chiesa* (1927), *Trittico Botticelliano* (1927), *Gli uccelli* (1927), *Feste romane* (1929), *Concerto a cinque* (1932), the ballet *La Boutique fantasque* (1919), choral and chamber music, and songs.

Res·sel \'res-əl\, Josef Ludwig Franz. 1793–1857. Austrian inventor. Considered first to develop a practical screw propeller for ships (1829).

Res·tif \rā-tēf\, Nicolas-Edme. *Known as* Restif de La Bre·tonne \-də-lä-brə-tòn\. 1734–1806. French novelist. Author of realistic and erotic novels of contemporary low life, from which he drew morals and proposed reforms, as *Le Paysan perverti* (1776), *La Vie de mon père* (1779), *Les Contemporaines* (1780–85), *La Paysanne pervertie* (1784), and *Monsieur Nicolas* (1794–97).

Res·tre·po \rā-'strā-pō\, Carlos E. 1867–1937. Colombian politician. President of Colombia (1910–14); minister of interior (1930–34); ambassador to Vatican City (1934).

Restrepo, José Manuel. 1781–1863. Colombian historian. Friend of Bolívar and other leaders in struggle for independence; held several ministerial positions (1821–30); chief work *Historia de la revolución de la república de Colombia* (1827, 1858).

Re·thel \'rā-təl\, Alfred. 1816–1859. German historical painter. Works included drawings of episodes from the life of St. Boniface, portraits of emperors Maximilian I and II, Charles V, and others, *Daniel in the Lions' Den, Saints Peter and John Healing the Lame,* fresco designs for the Aachen Rathaus representing the life of Charlemagne (1847–51), series of 6 water colors depicting *Hannibal Crossing the Alps* (1842–44), drawings for woodcuts *Death the Destroyer* and *Death the Friend* (1847–51) and for woodcut illustrations to *The Dance of Death,* etc.

Ré·ti \'rā-tē\, Richard. 1889–1929. Hungarian chess master. A chief exponent of hypermodern school; wrote on chess problems; devised the Réti opening (N–KB3).

Ré·ti \'re-tē\, Rudolph. 1885–1957. Serbian music critic and composer. Settled in U.S. (1938); wrote *The Thematic Process in Music* (1951) and *Tonality, Atonality, Pantonality* (1958); composed ballet-opera *David and Goliath* (1935), piano concerto (1948), piano pieces, songs.

Re·tief \rə-'tēf\, Pieter, *called* Piet. 1780–1838. South African Boer leader. Farmer and building contractor; fought in frontier wars of Cape Colony (from 1814); elected governor and head commandant of the Great Trek (1837); slain by Zulu king Dingane.

Retz, Cardinal de. See Jean-François-Paul de GONDI.

Retz, Gilles de. See Gilles de RAIS.

Ret·zi·us \'ret-sē-əs\, Anders Adolf. 1796–1860. Swedish anatomist and anthropologist. A pioneer in craniometry. Professor of anatomy and physiology, Karolinska Institut, Stockholm (1824–60); invented the cranial index (1842); described convulsions of the cerebral cortex (gyri of Retzius). His son ¶Gustaf Magnus (1842–1919), anthropologist and anatomist; professor of histology (1877) and of anatomy (1889–1900) at Stockholm; known for researches on the nervous systems of men and animals and on cranial anthropology; wrote *Das Menschenhirn* (1896).

Reu·be·ni \rü-'bā-nē\, David. d. after 1532. Arabian Jewish adventurer. Claimed to be brother of an Arabian Jewish king; supported by Pope Clement VII and John III of Portugal in plan to lead a Jewish army against Turks in Palestine; followed by Solomon Molcho (*q.v.*), a messianic preacher; rebuffed by John III; with Molcho, attempted to gain support from Emperor Charles V; arrested and died in Spanish prison.

Reuch·lin \'ròik-,lēn, ròik-'lēn\, Johannes. *Grecized form* Cap·nio \'kap-nē-,ō\. 1455–1522. German Humanist. Promoter of Greek and Hebrew studies in Germany and champion of modern (Reuchlinian) pronunciation of Greek. In service of Duke Eberhard of Württemberg (1481); count of German Empire (1492); judge in Swabian League (1502–13); in controversy (1510–16) with Dominicans of Cologne and the obscurantists, on whom he wrote satire *Epistolae obscurorum virorum* (1515–17); taught Greek and Hebrew, Ingolstadt (1519) and Tübingen. Author of the first Hebrew grammar *De rudimentis hebraicis* (1506), an edition of the seven penitential Psalms (1512), *De accentibus et orthographia linguae hebraicae* (1518), Latin satirical comedies *Sergius* (1496) and *Henno* (1497), cabalistic works *De verbo mirifico* (1494) and *De arte cabbalistica* (1517), etc.

Reu·ter \ˈrȯit-ər\, Christian. 1665–?1712. German dramatist and novelist. Author of satirical comedies, the satirical novel *Schelmuffskys Reisebeschreibung* (1696), and festival plays for the court at Berlin (1703–10).

Reuter, Ernst. 1889–1953. German politician. Joined Social Democratic party (1912); mayor of Magdeburg (1931); member of Reichstag (1932–35); lived in England and Turkey (1935–46); became leader of Social Democrats (1946); mayor of West Berlin (1948–53); exhibited strong leadership during Soviet blockade of Berlin (1948–49); presided over Deutsche Städtetages (1951 ff.).

Reuter, Fritz. 1810–1874. German writer. Author of Plattdeutsch dialect tales and poems chiefly of village life, the epic *Kein Hüsung* (1858), *Hanne Nüte* (1859), and *Schurr-Murr* (1861), the collection of largely autobiographical stories *Olle Kamellen* containing *Ut de Franzosentid* (1859), *Ut mine Festungstid* (1862), and *Ut mine Stromtid* (1864).

Reuter, Paul Julius von. *Orig.* Israel Beer Jo·sa·phat \ˈyō-zä-ˌfät\. 1816–1899. German journalist. Adopted name Reuter (1844). Founded in Aachen (1849) a central telegraphic and pigeon-post bureau for collecting and transmitting news, forerunner of Reuter's News Agency with headquarters in London (from 1851); removed to England (1851) and became naturalized British subject; created baron (1871) by Duke of Saxe-Coburg-Gotha.

Reu·ther \ˈrü-thər, -t͟hər\, Walter Philip. 1907–1970. American labor leader, b. Wheeling, W. Va. Tool and die maker by trade; began union activities (1935); president, United Automobile Workers (1946–70), Congress of Industrial Organizations (1952–55); gained many benefits for his union; advocate of liberal social and political causes.

Rev·ell \ˈrev-el\, Viljo. 1910–1964. Finnish architect. A leading exponent of Functionalism. His designs included Teollisuuskeskus Hotel in Helsinki (1952, with Keijo Petäjä), apartment buildings in Tapiola (1959–60), apartment house in Helsinki-Munkkiniemi (1961–62), and city hall of Toronto, Canada (1965).

Révellière-Lépeaux, La. See La Révellière-Lépeaux.

Rev·els \ˈrev-əlz\, Hiram Rhoades. 1822–1901. American clergyman, educator, and politician, b. Fayetteville, N.C. Church pastor and school principal in Baltimore; chaplain to Union black regiment stationed in Mississippi (1864–65); settled in Natchez, Miss., after Civil War. First Negro elected to U.S. Senate (1870–71); president, Alcorn A.&M. Coll., Lorman, Miss. (1871–74, 1876–83).

Revelstoke, 1st Baron. See Baring family.

Re·vent·low \ˈrā-vənt-lō\, Christian Ditlev Frederick. Count. 1748–1827. Danish state official. In Danish state service (1773–1813); became head of agricultural department (1784); effected agrarian reforms, including abolition (1788) of serfdom.

Re·ver·dy \rə-ver-dē\, Pierre. 1889–1960. French poet. An instigator of Cubism and Surrealism; founded Cubist review *Nord-Sud* (1916); retired to Abbaye de Solesmes (1926). Author of hermetic-like volumes of verse, as *Étoiles peintes* (1921), *Les Épaves du ciel* (1924), *Le Gant de grin* (1927), *Flaques de verre* (1929), and *Le Livre de mon bord* (1948).

Re·vere \ri-ˈvi(ə)r\, Paul. 1735–1818. American patriot, b. Boston. Silversmith and engraver by trade. Took part in Boston Tea Party (1773). Appointed official courier for Massachusetts Provincial Assembly (1774). Rode from Boston to Lexington to warn countryside that the British were on the march (Apr. 18, 1775), a ride celebrated by Longfellow in *The Midnight Ride of Paul Revere.* Designed and printed first issue of Continental money; designed and engraved first official seal for the colonies, and the state seal for Massachusetts. Member, Committee of Correspondence (1776). In command at Castle William (1778–79); took part in unsuccessful Penobscot expedition (1779). Discovered process for rolling sheet copper and opened a rolling mill at Canton, Mass.

Revillagigedo, Conde de. See Güemes de Horcasitas.

Re·vi·us \ˈrā-vē-œs\, Jacobus. 1586–1658. Dutch writer. Reformed church minister; proponent of Calvinism; author of historical works, the play *Haman* (1630), and a collection of scriptural or moralistic poems *Over-IJsselsche sangen en dichten* (1630).

Rex·roth \ˈreks-ˌrȯth\, Kenneth. 1905–1982. American writer, b. South Bend, Ind. In youth a wanderer, casual laborer, political radical; associated with various leftist and avant-garde movements, esp. with the literary Beat generation. Translated much French, Spanish, Greek, Chinese, Japanese verse; San Francisco correspondent of *The Nation* (1953–68); columnist, *San Francisco Examiner* (1960–68); cofounder of San Francisco Poetry Center. Books included *In What Hour* (1940), *Art of Worldly Wisdom* (1949), *The Dragon and the Unicorn* (1952), *The Bird in the Bush* (1959), *Assays* (1962), *Natural Numbers* (1965), *An Autobiographical Novel* (1966), *Alternative Society* (1970), *The Elastic Retort* (1973), *New Poems* (1974), etc.

Rey, Jacobus Hercules De la. See De la Rey.

Re·yes \ˈrā-yäs\, Alfonso. 1889–1959. Mexican poet, critic, and diplomat. Considered foremost Mexican scholar and man of letters of 20th century. In diplomatic service (1913–39), esp. as ambassador to Argentina (1927, 1936–37), Brazil (1930–36, 1938–39). Authority on literature of ancient Greece and Spanish Golden Age. Wrote on aesthetics, as *Cuestiones estéticas* (1911), history, literary criticism; prose works included *El plano oblicuo* (1920), *Reloj de sol* (1926), *La experiencia literaria* (1942). Author of translations of English and French works and of volumes of poetry as *Visión de Anáhuac* (1917), *Ifigenia cruel* (1924), *Pausa* (1926), and *Otra voz* (1936).

Reyes Pri·e·to \-prē-ˈā-tō\, Rafael. 1850–1921. Colombian explorer, soldier, author, and political leader. With his brothers Enrique and Néstor explored the tributaries of the Amazon in southeast Colombia (1874–84); made commander in chief of Colombian army; Colombian representative in Washington (1903) in relation to loss of Panama. President of Colombia (1904–09); assumed dictatorial power; made many improvements, but lost popularity; resigned (1909) when his treaty with U.S. recognizing independence of Panama was not approved. Wrote *A través de la América del Sur* (1902) and *Las dos Américas* (1914).

Rey·les \ˈrā-läs\, Carlos. 1868–1938. Uruguayan novelist. Among his novels were *Primitivo* (1896), *El extraño* (1897), *La raza de Caín* (1900), *El terruño* (1916), *El embrujo de Sevilla* (1922), and *El gaucho florido* (1932).

Rey·mont \ˈrā-mȯnt\ *or* **Rej·ment** \ˈrā-mentʸ\, Władysław Stanisław. 1867–1925. Polish novelist. Awarded Nobel prize for literature (1924) for *Chłopi* (*The Peasants,* 1902–09). Other works included *Komediantka* (1896), *Fermenty* (1897), *Sprawiedliwie* (1899), *Ziemia obiecana* (1899), *Wampir* (1911), *Rok 1794* (1914–19); also stories, etc.

Rey·naud \rā-nō\, Paul. 1878–1966. French politician. Minister of finance (1930), for colonies (1931–32), of justice (1932 and 1938), of finance (1938–40); prime minister (March–June 1940) at the period of France's surrender to Germany, resigned rather than conclude armistice; interned by Pétain government (1940); imprisoned by Germans (1942–45); member, Chamber of Deputies (1946–62); presided over drafting of constitution of Fifth Republic. Author of *Au coeur de la mêlée, 1930–45* (1951) and *Mémoires* (1960–63).

Reyn·olds \ˈren-ᵊl(d)z\, Sir Joshua. 1723–1792. English portrait painter. Pupil of Thomas Hudson (1740–43). Gained attention with portrait of Captain the Hon. John Hamilton (1746); studied in Italy (1750–52). On return to London became foremost fashionable portrait painter. Suggested founding (1764) of Literary Club, of which Dr. Johnson, Garrick, Goldsmith, Burke, Boswell, and Sheridan were members. First president of Royal Academy (1768) and delivered annual *Discourses on Art* (1769–90). Painter to king (1784). Executed portraits of Lord Heathfield, Johnson, Sterne, Goldsmith, Gibbon, Burke, Fox, Garrick, and of Mrs. Siddons as the Tragic Muse (1784); admired for his studies of women and children, including *Countess of Spencer and Her Daughter* (1761), *Nelly O'Brien* (1762), *Master Crewe as Henry VIII* (1776), *Lady Caroline Scott as "Winter"* (1778), *Duchess of Devonshire and Her Daughter* (1786), and *The Age of Innocence* (1788).

Reynolds, Osborne. 1842–1912. British engineer and physicist. Made researches in condensation and heat transfer between solids and liquids, on pumps and turbines, on wave and tidal motions in rivers, on group velocity, on the radiometer, and on mechanical equivalent of heat; known particularly for formulations of law of resistance in parallel channels (1883), of theory of lubrication (1886), and of the standard mathematical framework used in turbulence work (1889).

Reynolds, Walter. d. 1327. English prelate. Bishop of Worcester and (1310) chancellor of England; appointed (1313) archbishop of Canterbury by Pope Clement V on urging of Edward II despite previous election of Thomas de Cobham by Canterbury monks; carried on struggle for precedence between archbishops of York and Canterbury; introduced ecclesiastical reform; supported Edward II until 1324, when he took part of Adam of Orlton, bishop of Hereford; declared for Edward III, whom he crowned (1327).

Re·zā ʽAb·bā·sī \ri-ˈzä-ab-ˈbäs-ē\. 1575?–?1635. Persian painter. Employed at royal court at Isfahan; designed and executed decorative paintings for walls of palaces and public buildings; noted for miniatures, realistic portraits, and paintings of lovers.

Re·za·nov \ryi-ˈzá-nəf\, Nikolay Petrovich. 1764–1807. Russian entrepreneur in Alaska. An organizer of a fur-trading company, Russian-American Co. (1799); granted administration of, and a monopoly in, the coast of northwest America and the chain of islands off this coast.

Re·za Shah Pah·la·vi \ri-ˈzä-ˈshä-ˈpal-ə-vē\. *Orig. name* Reza Khan \-ˈk͟hän\. *First name also spelled* Ri·za \ri-ˈzä\. 1878–1944. Shah of Iran (1925–41). Rose from private to general in Iranian army; led successful coup d'état (1921); minister of war (1921–23); prime minister (1923–25). Elected shah by parliament after deposition (1925) of Aḥmad Shāh. Modernized country; strengthened finances and improved transportation and communications; emancipated women (1935); abdicated when country occupied by British and Russian troops (1941); succeeded by his son MOHAMMAD REZA PAHLAVI.

Rez·ni·ček \'rez-ni-chek\, Emil Nikolaus von. 1860–1945. Austrian composer. Composer chiefly of operas, including *Donna Diana* (1894), *Till Eulenspiegel* (1901), *Ritter Blaubart* (1920), and *Der Gondoliere des Dogen* (1931); also of 5 symphonies, 3 symphonic poems, variations for orchestra, a violin concerto (1925), overtures, string quartets, piano pieces, choral works, a requiem (1894), a mass (1898), songs, etc.

Rhä·ti·cus \'re-ti-,kus\ *or* **Rhe·ti·cus** \'rā-\. *Orig.* Georg Joachim Ise·rin \'ē-zə-rən\; *later used surname* von Lau·chen \fōn-'lau̇-kən\. 1514–1576. German astronomer and mathematician. Pupil and associate of Copernicus at Frauenburg (1539–40); instrumental in publishing Copernicus's *De revolutionibus orbium coelestium* to disseminate the Copernican theory; wrote *Opus Palatinum de triangulis* (1596).

Rhazes. See RĀZĪ.

Rhee \'rē\, Syngman. 1875–1965. Korean politician. Foremost leader of Korean independence movement (from 1911); president of provisional government in exile (1919–41); chairman of Korean Commission in Washington, D.C. (1941–45); returned to Korea (1945). First president of Republic of Korea (1948–60); assumed dictatorial powers; resigned (1960) in face of heavy opposition and fled to Hawaii.

Rhein·ber·ger \'rīn-,ber-gər\, Joseph Gabriel. 1839–1901. German composer, organist, conductor, and teacher, b. Liechtenstein. Professor at Munich Conservatory (1859–65, 1867–1901); teacher of Humperdinck, Wolf-Ferrari, Chadwick, and Parker (*qq.v.*); composer of organ pieces (esp. 20 sonatas), operas, symphonies, overtures, chamber music, piano pieces, choruses, songs, etc.

Rhenanus, Beatus. See BILD AUS RHEINAU.

Rheticus. See RHÄTICUS.

Rhett \'ret\, Robert Barnwell. *Orig. surname* Smith \'smith\. 1800–1876. American politician, b. Beaufort, S.C. Adopted surname Rhett (1837); member, U.S. House of Representatives (1837–49) and U.S. Senate (1850–52); a leader of secessionist movement (from 1850); chairman of Confederate constitution committee (1861).

Rhi·a·nus \rī-'ā-nəs\. b. c.275 B.C. Greek scholar and poet of Crete. Long resident in Alexandria; prepared edition of Homer; wrote epics as the *Messeniaca,* and epigrams.

Rhine \'rīn\, Joseph Banks. 1895–1980. American psychologist, b. Waterloo, Pa. Professor at Duke U. (1928–65); founder and director (1964–68), Institute of Parapsychology, Durham, N.C.; associate of William McDougall; known for investigations in parapsychology.

Rhins, Dutreuil de. See DUTREUIL DE RHINS.

Rhin·thon \'rin-,thän\. fl. c.300 B.C. Greek playwright. Invented the comic burlesque of tragedy known as hilaro-tragedy. Only the titles of a few of his plays are extant.

Rhodes \rȯd\, Alexandre de. 1591–1660. French Jesuit missionary. Missionary in Indochina (1619–46); introduced Christianity into Vietnam; persuaded Vietnamese to adopt a Latin script.

Rhodes \'rōdz\, Cecil John. 1853–1902. British colonial administrator and financier. Sent to Natal for his health (1870); moved to Orange Free State on discovery of diamonds and acquired fortune in Kimberley diamond fields. Entered Cape House of Assembly (1881); energetic in establishing cordial relations between British and Dutch in colony and in bringing about annexation of Bechuanaland (1884); obtained (1888) by cession from Lobengula, king of the Matabeles, territory north of Bechuanaland, named Rhodesia, and made sole manager (till 1896) of company incorporated with rights of sovereignty over the territory. Amalgamated diamond mines about Kimberley under the De Beers Consolidated Mines (1888). Prime minister of Cape Colony (1890–96); aimed at establishment of a Federal South African dominion under British flag; advanced project for Cape-to-Cairo railway; directed suppression of Matabeles (1893–94); plotted overthrow of South African Republic by encouraging Uitlander population in Transvaal to armed insurrection; on failure of Jameson Raid (1895) into Transvaal was disclosed as instigator of attack and forced to resign premiership (1896). Devoted himself to development of Rhodesia; through personal influence established permanent peace with Matabeles after outbreak (1896); reentered Cape Parliament (1898). By will endowed scholarships for education at Oxford of youth of British Empire, U.S., and Germany.

Rhodes, James Ford. 1848–1927. American historian, b. Cleveland. In coal and iron business (1874–85). Author of *History of the United States from the Compromise of 1850* (1893–1906), *History of the Civil War, 1861–1865* (1917), *History of the United States from Hayes to McKinley, 1877–1896* (1919), etc.

Rhondda, Viscount. See David Alfred THOMAS.

Rhyn, Otto Henne am. See HENNE AM RHYN.

Rhys \'rēs\, Ernest Percival. 1859–1946. English editor and writer. Editor of *The Camelot Series* (1886–91), *The Lyric Poets* (1894–99), *Everyman's Library.* Author of verse as *Welsh Ballads* (1898), *Lays of the Round Table* (1908), *Song of the Sun* (1937), the novels *The Fiddler of Carne* (1896), *Black Horse Pit* (1925), autobiographical works *Everyman Remembers* (1931) and *Wales England Wed* (1940), etc.

Rhys, Jean. 1894–1979. British writer, b. Dominica, West Indies. Author of novels as *Postures* (1928), *After Leaving Mr. Mackenzie* (1931), *Voyage in the Dark* (1934), *Good Morning, Midnight* (1939), *Wide Sargasso Sea* (1966), and collections of short stories as *The Left Bank* (1927), *Tigers Are Better-Looking* (1968), *Sleep It Off, Lady* (1976).

Rhys \'rēs\, Sir John. 1840–1915. Welsh scholar. First professor of Celtic at Oxford (1877); principal of Jesus Coll. (1895–1915). Author of numerous works on Celtic philology, inscriptions, history, religion; editor of Welsh texts.

Rhys \'(h)rēs\, Siôn Dafydd *or* John David. *Also known as* John Da·vies \'dā-vis\. 1534–c.1609. Welsh physician and grammarian. His *Cambrobrytannicae Cymraecaeve linguae institutiones et rudimenta* (1592) contained a grammar of Welsh language, a discussion of poetic art, and a collection of Welsh poetry.

Ri·ba·de·ney·ra \rē-bäth-ā-'nā-ē-rä\, Pedro de. 1527–1611. Spanish hagiologist. Follower of St. Ignatius of Loyola; joined Society of Jesus, Rome (1540); active in promulgation of Jesuit order. Author of *Vita Ignatii Loiolae* (1572), *Historia eclesiástica del cisma del reino de Inglaterra* (1588), *Flos sanctorum* (1599), etc.

Ri·bal·ta \rē-'bäl-tä\, Francisco. 1565–1628. Spanish painter. Studio at Valencia (1598 ff.); known for *tenebroso* style which emphasized darkness rather than light. His canvases included *Nailing to the Cross* (1582), *The Singer,* and *Christ Embracing St. Bernard* (both after 1612).

Ri·bault \rē-bō\, Jean. 1520?–1565. French naval officer and colonizer in America. Under patronage of Admiral Coligny, established French colony (1562) at what is now Port Royal, S.C.; colony abandoned two years later. Sent to reinforce Fort Caroline, Fla. (1565); left to attack St. Augustine; in his absence, Spaniards marched overland and destroyed the colony; Ribault's fleet was wrecked in storm; he was captured by Spaniards and killed.

Rib·ben·trop \'rib-ən-,trōp\, Joachim von. 1893–1946. German diplomat. Served in World War I; in business as wine merchant after the war. Conducted negotiations between Adolf Hitler and the German government (1930); identified himself with Hitler movement, and aided in organizing Nazi government (1933); ambassador at large (1935), to Great Britain (1936–38); minister of foreign affairs (1938–45); negotiated Anglo-German naval agreement (1935), German-Japanese anti-Comintern agreement (1936), Russo-German Nonaggression Pact (1939), and Italo-German-Japanese alliance (1940). Hanged as war criminal.

Ri·bei·ro \rē-'bā-rü\, Bernardim. 1482–1552. Portuguese writer. Secretary to King John III (1524); introduced pastoral mode to Portugal by writing five eclogues and the pastoral romance *Livro das Saudades* (1554–57), better known by its opening words *Menina e Moça.*

Ri·be·ra \rē-'bā-rä\, José, *Ital.* Giuseppe, *whence Span.* Jusepe, de. *Called in Italy* Lo Spa·gno·let·to \'lō-,spän-yō-'lāt-tō\. 1588–1652. Spanish painter and etcher. One of leading painters of the Neapolitan school; known esp. as a colorist and representative of the *tenebrosi.* Among his works were *Martyrdom of St. Bartholomew* (1630), *Archimedes* (1630), *Portrait of a Bearded Woman* (1631), *Immaculate Conception* (1635), *The Trinity* (1636–37), *Clubfooted Boy* (1642), *St. Jerome* (1644), *The Holy Family With St. Catherine* (1648).

Ri·bot \rē-bō\, Théodule-Armand. 1839–1916. French psychologist. Professor, Sorbonne (1885), Collège de France (1888); known for studies of memory loss as symptom of brain disease. Wrote *Les Maladies de la mémoire* (1881), *Les Maladies de la volonté* (1883), etc.

Ri·car·do \rik-'ärd-(,)ō\, David. 1772–1823. English economist. Founder of classical school of economics. Son of a Dutch Jew; followed his father in stock exchange; renounced by father on his entry into Church of England; succeeded as a broker. Having read *Wealth of Nations,* devoted himself to economic studies; created stir by pamphlet *The High Price of Bullion a Proof of the Depreciation of Bank-notes* (1810), which influenced report of Bullion Committee (1811); attempted systematic exposition of his theories in *Principles of Political Economy and Taxation* (1817), developing his theory of rent, profit, and wages, and presenting clear statement of the quantity theory of money. M.P. (1819–23); accepted as authority on financial matters.

Ri·ca·so·li \rē-'käs-ō-lē\, Bettino. Baron of Bro·lio \'brōl-yō\. 1809–1880. Italian politician. Assumed leadership in Tuscan liberal movements (1859); made dictator of Tuscany (1859–60); secured union of Tuscany and Sardinia

(1860); governor general of Tuscany (1860–61); prime minister of Italy (1861–62, 1866–67).

Ric·ca·ti \rēk-'kä-tē\, Jacopo Francesco. 1676–1754. Italian mathematician. Concerned chiefly with integration of differential equations, proposing (1724) the equation which bears his name.

Ric·ci \'rēt-chē\, Matteo. *Known in China as* Li Ma-tou \'lē-'mä-'tō\. 1552–1610. Italian missionary. Joined Jesuit order (1571); missionary to India (1578); settled in China (1583); permitted to found mission at Peking (1601); as a favorite of the emperor, succeeded in introducing Christianity into Chinese cities. Author of a work on Chinese geography and history and of several works in Chinese, as *On the Nature of God,* now a Chinese classic.

Ricci-Cur·bas·tro \-kůr-'bäs-trō\, Gregorio. 1853–1925. Italian mathematician. Professor at Padua (1880–1925). Instrumental in development of absolute differential calculus, now known as tensor analysis.

Ric·cio \'rēt-chō\, Andrea. *Orig. surname* Bri·o·sco \brē-'ōs-kō\. 1470?–1532. Italian sculptor and goldsmith. Known for his bronze statuettes, mainly of mythological subjects as *Warrior on Horseback* and *Arion;* executed paschal candlestick for S. Antonio at Padua (1507–16) and monument of Girolamo della Torre in S. Fermo, Verona (1516–21).

Riccio, David. See RIZZIO.

Riccio, Domenico. *Called* Il Bru·sa·sor·ci \ēl-,brü-zä-'sȯr-chē\. c.1516–1567. Italian painter of Veronese school. Among his works were *Vision of the Madonna, Entry of Charles V and Clement VII into Bologna, Annunciation,* and *Fable of Phaëthon.*

Ric·cio·li \rēt-'chȯ-lē\, Giambattista. 1598–1671. Italian Jesuit astronomer. Rejected Copernican theory; made (with P. Grimaldi) a detailed telescopic study of the moon, introducing nomenclature for lunar features still used. Author of *Almagestum novum* (1651).

Rice \'rīs\, Alice Caldwell, *nee* He·gan \'hē-gən\. 1870–1942. American novelist, b. Shelbyville, Ky. m. (1902) Cale Young Rice (1872–1943), poet. Author of *Mrs. Wiggs of the Cabbage Patch* (1901), *Lovey Mary* (1903), *Mr. Opp* (1909), *A Romance of Billy Goat Hill* (1912), *The Buffer* (1929), *Mr. Pete & Co.* (1933), *My Pillow Book* (1937), etc.

Rice, Dan. *Orig.* Daniel Mc·Lar·en \mə-'klar-ən\. 1823–1900. American circus clown, b. New York City. Made debut as clown (1844); most famous clown of his day with act consisting of singing, dancing, feats of strength, trick riding, and witty badinage with audience.

Rice, Edmund Ignatius. 1762–1844. Irish philanthropist. Abandoned provision merchant business on death of wife, joined (1808) seven others in taking religious vows, assumed a habit, and, as Christian Brothers (order sanctioned by pope, 1820), established schools in Cork, Dublin, Thurles, Limerick, and in England and Australia; as Brother Ignatius was first superior general of the order (1821–38).

Rice, Elmer Leopold. *Orig.* Rei·zen·stein \'rī-zən-,stīn\. 1892–1967. American playwright, b. New York City. Author of plays *On Trial* (1914), *Home of the Free* (1917), *The Adding Machine* (1923), *Close Harmony* (1924, with Dorothy Parker), *Street Scene* (1929, Pulitzer prize), *Left Bank* (1931), *Counsellor-at-Law* (1931), *We, the People* (1933), *Judgement Day* (1934), *Between Two Worlds* (1934), *American Landscape* (1939), *Dream Girl* (1946), etc.; novels *A Voyage to Purilia* (1930), *Imperial City* (1937), *The Winner* (1954), etc.; essays *The Living Theatre* (1939). A founder (1938) of, and director for, the Playwrights Company.

Rice, Grantland, *in full* Henry Grantland. 1880–1954. American sportswriter, b. Murfreesboro, Tenn. Considered dean of sportswriters; wrote (from 1901) for newspapers, esp. *New York Herald Tribune* (1914–30); wrote syndicated column "The Sportlight" (from 1930); selected All-America college football teams for *Collier's* magazine (1925–47); nicknamed Notre Dame's backfield of 1924 the "Four Horsemen."

Rice, James. 1843–1882. English novelist. Collaborator with Sir Walter Besant in *Ready-Money Mortiboy* (1872), *The Golden Butterfly* (1876), *The Seamy Side* (1881), etc.

Rice, Thomas Dartmouth. 1808–1860. American minstrel, b. New York City. Introduced "Jim Crow," a song and dance number (1828) with sensational success and toured U.S. and England with it; wrote plays as *Long Island Juba* (1833) and *Jim Crow in London* (1837), and a burlesque of *Othello;* known as "Father of American Minstrelsy."

Rice, William Marsh. 1816–1900. American merchant and philanthropist, b. Springfield, Mass. Opened store in Houston, Tex. (1838); developed large exporting, importing, and retail business; bequeathed his fortune for educational institution at Houston, Tex. Rice Institute was opened in 1912.

Rich \'rich\, Barnabe. 1542–1617. English soldier and writer. Served in Low Countries and Ireland (1562–1574); author of euphuistic tales *The Strange and Wonderful Adventures of Don Simonides* (1581) and *The Adventures of Brusanus* (1592). His story *Apolonius and Silla* (in *Riche His Farewell to Militarie Profession,* 1581) was Shakespeare's source for *Twelfth Night;* also wrote pamphlets, military works, reports on Ireland, and commentaries on manners and morals.

Rich, Claudius James. 1787–1820. English administrator and archaeologist. Business agent in Baghdad for East India Co. (1808–20). His survey of Babylon (1811) is considered beginning of Mesopotamian archaeology; findings published as *Memoir on the Ruins of Babylon* (1815) and *Second Memoir on Babylon* (1818); also wrote *Narrative of a Residence in Koordistan* (1836).

Rich, Edmund. See Saint EDMUND.

Rich, Sir Henry. 1st Baron Ken·sing·ton \'ken-ziŋ-tən, 'ken(t)-siŋ-\ *and* 1st Earl of Hol·land \'häl-ənd\. 1590–1649. English courtier. Son of Robert Rich, 1st Earl of Warwick, and Penelope Rich (Sir Philip Sidney's Stella: see at DEVEREUX family); brother of Robert Rich, 2d Earl of Warwick (*q.v.*). M.P. (1610); courtier favored by James I; sent to Paris (1624) to negotiate marriage of Prince Charles and Henrietta Maria, again (1625) to arrange treaty between Louis XIII and Huguenots. Deserted cause of Charles I (1641), joined Parliamentary party; member of committee of safety; shifted allegiance three times; captured by Parliamentarians and beheaded.

Rich, John. *Stage name* Lun \'lən\. 1692–1761. English theater manager and actor. Inherited (1714) from father Lincoln's Inn Field Theatre and managed it (to 1732); introduced the pantomime, playing part of Harlequin (1717); produced a pantomime annually (till 1760); produced John Gay's *The Beggar's Opera* (1728); opened Covent Garden (1732); considered father of English pantomime.

Rich, Lady Penelope. See under DEVEREUX.

Rich, Sir Richard. 1st Baron Rich. c.1496–1567. English chancery officer. Solicitor general (1533); as prosecutor acted basely in trial of Bishop Fisher and perjured himself in trial of Sir Thomas More (both 1535); profited by suppression of monasteries and disposal of their revenues; created baron (1547); lord chancellor of England (1547–51); supported Protector Somerset (1548–49); deserted to Warwick and effected overthrow of Somerset; signed proclamation in favor of Lady Jane Grey (1553) and immediately after declared for Mary, during whose reign he was active in persecution of Protestants.

Rich, Richard. fl. 1610. English soldier and adventurer. Sailed for Virginia with Captain Christopher Newport (1609); on return published *Newes from Virginia,* narrating shipwreck on Bermudas, probably suggesting scenes in Shakespeare's *Tempest.*

Rich, Robert. 2d Earl of Warwick. 1587–1658. English admiral and colonial administrator. Son of Robert Rich, 1st Earl of Warwick, and Penelope Rich (Sir Philip Sidney's Stella; see at DEVEREUX family). Managed New England, Bermudas, and Providence companies, member of Guinea, Amazon River, and Virginia companies; procured patent for Massachusetts Bay Colony (1628); granted (1632) patent for settlement (1635) of Saybrook, Conn. Estranged from court for Puritan sympathies; as admiral of the fleet (1642–49) fought on Parliamentarian side; intercepted king's ships and relieved ports. As head of commission for government of colonies aided in incorporation (1644) of Providence Plantations (later Rhode Island); advocated religious tolerance in colonies. Warwick, R.I., is named in his honor.

Rich·ard \'rich-ərd\. Name of three kings of England:

Richard I. *Surnamed* Coeur de Li·on \kœr-dəl-yōⁿ, *Angl* ,kər-dᵊl-'ī-ən\ *or* Lion-Hearted. 1157–1199. King (1189–99), of house of Anjou or Plantagenet. Third son of Henry II. Leagued against his father (1173–74, 1188–89); succeeded to throne of England, the duchy of Normandy, and county of Anjou (1189). Started on Third Crusade (1189), joining Philip II of France (1190); conquered Cyprus (1191); aided in capture of Acre (1191); recaptured Jaffa from Saladin (1192). On return captured in Austria (1192); ransomed and returned to England (1194). In France warring against Philip II (1194–99); mortally wounded by an arrow near Limoges. Wrote lyrics in French; hero of many romantic legends.

Richard II. 1367–1400. King (1377–99), of house of Anjou or Plantagenet. Son of Edward the Black Prince and grandson of Edward III. Succeeded Edward III as king (1377); during his minority, government administered by dukes of Lancaster and Gloucester. Pacified (1381) rebellion of peasants under Wat Tyler. Assumed control of government (1389); banished Henry of Bolingbroke, Duke of Hereford, and confiscated his Lancastrian estates (1398–99); defeated by Henry of Bolingbroke (later Henry IV), captured, deposed by Parliament (1399); imprisoned in Pontefract castle; died, possibly from self-starvation.

Richard III. 1452–1485. King (1483–85), of house of York. Duke of Gloucester; son of Richard Plantagenet, 3d Duke of York, and younger brother of Edward IV. Helped restore Edward IV to throne by defeating Lancastrians at Barnet and Tewkesbury (1471); rewarded with high offices and land grants; as lieutenant general for northern England pacified region (1480). On death of Edward IV, became protector of the young successor, Edward V, and soon took custody of him; assumed the crown (June 26, 1483) after Edward V had been declared illegitimate by an assembly of lords and commoners. Often accused by historians of the presumed murders of Edward V and Edward's younger brother Richard (disappeared, Aug. 1483). Suppressed rebellion led by Duke of Buckingham (1483), but was defeated and killed in the battle of Bosworth Field (Aug. 22, 1485) by the Earl of Richmond, who became Henry VII, first of the Tudor family.

Richard. Earl of Corn·wall \korn-wəl, *esp US* -ˌwol\ and king of the Romans. 1209–1272. Second son of King John of England. Commanded expedition that recovered Gascony (1225–26); frequently opposed (1227–38) his brother Henry III; went on crusade (1240–42); having married (1243) Sancha, sister of Queen Eleanor, became for a time peacemaker between barons and king, then ally of his brother against Simon de Montfort. Elected king of the Romans during interregnum of Holy Roman Empire; crowned at Aachen (1257); established authority in Rhine Valley until funds exhausted. Helped Henry overthrow Provisions of Oxford and also aided him against rebel barons (1263–64); taken prisoner at battle of Lewes (1264); released after Evesham (1265); helped obtain Dictum of Kenilworth (1266).

Richard. 3d Duke of York \'yȯ(ə)rk\. *Took (1460) surname* Plan·tag·e·net \plan-'taj-(ə-)nət\. 1411–1460. English statesman. Grandson of Edmund of Langley. Inherited possessions of maternal uncle Edmund Mortimer, 5th Earl of March. Had stronger claim to English throne but faithfully served Henry VI; king's lieutenant in France and Normandy (1436–37, 1440–45) and in Ireland (1447–50); strove against Queen Margaret of Anjou and Edmund Beaufort for place in king's counsels; protector during Henry VI's illnesses (1454–55, 1455–56). Killed Beaufort in battle at St. Albans (1455); marched on London and was declared heir apparent and protector by Parliament (1460). On expedition to quell rebellion in north, hemmed in by Lancastrians at Wakefield, gave battle and was killed. Three of his sons were Edmund IV, Richard III, and George, Duke of Clarence.

Richard of Aversa. d. 1078. Norman leader. Nephew of Rainulf of Aversa and brother-in-law of Robert Guiscard. To southern Italy (1045); became count of Aversa (1047); captured Capua (1057); with Robert Guiscard concluded Norman alliance with Pope Nicholas II and made prince of Capua (1059); supported Pope Alexander II against antipope Honorius II (1061); excommunicated by Pope Gregory VII for invading church lands in the Abruzzi, but reconciled before death.

Richard of Chichester. Saint. *Orig. surname* Wyche \'wich\, Wych \'wich\, *or* de Wi·cio \də-'wich(-ē)-(ˌ)ō\. c.1198–1253. English prelate. Chancellor of Oxford (1235–38); chancellor to St. Edmund of Abingdon (1236–40); bishop of Chichester (1244); at first prevented by Henry III from entering Chichester, later (1246) admitted.

Richard of De·vi·zes \di-'vī-zəz\. fl. 1189–1192. English chronicler. Benedictine monk at Winchester; known for *Chronicon de rebus gestis Ricardi Primi,* an account of events in England and Holy Land during Third Crusade.

Richard of Ely. See Richard FITZNEALE.

Richard I of Normandy. *Surnamed* sans Peur \sän-pœr\, *i.e.* the Fearless. c.932–996. Duke of Normandy (942–966). Warred against the last of the Carolingians; supported Hugh Capet and the Capetian dynasty. His son¶Richard II, *surnamed* le Bon \lə-bōn\, *i.e.* the Good (d. 1027), succeeded his father (996), remained loyal to the Capetian dynasty, waged successful war against the English and Swedes, and brought Normandy to its apex.

Richard of Saint-Victor. d. 1173. Scottish theologian. Entered Abbey of Saint-Victor, Paris, at early age and became (1162) its prior; his writings, as *Benjamin major* and *Benjamin minor,* became standard manuals on practice of mystical spirituality and influenced medieval and modern mysticism.

Richard de Bury. See Richard AUNGERVILLE.

Richard le Grant \-lə-'grant, -'grȧnt\. *Also known as* Richard Grant, Richard le Grand \-'grand, -'grȧnd\, *or* Richard of Weth·er·shed \'weth-ərz-ˌhed\. d. 1231. English prelate. Chancellor of Lincoln cathedral (1221–29); archbishop of Canterbury (1229–31); quarrelled with Henry III, asserting independence of clergy and his see from royal control; excommunicated Hubert de Burgh for taking possession of Tunbridge Castle and was upheld by Pope Gregory IX.

Richard Strongbow. 2d Earl of Pembroke. See under family de CLARE.

Rich·ards \'rich-ərdz\, Dickinson Woodruff. 1895–1973. American physician, b. Orange, N.J. At Columbia U. (1928–61). With André F. Cournand adapted Werner Forssmann's technique and perfected cardiac catheterization, permitting measurements of blood pressure, etc. inside the heart; awarded Nobel prize in physiology or medicine (1956) with Forssmann and Cournand.

Richards, Ellen Henrietta, *nee* Swal·low \'swäl-(ˌ)ō\. 1842–1911. American chemist, b. Dunstable, Mass. m. Robert H. Richards (1875). Instructor in sanitary chemistry, M.I.T. (1884–1911). First president of American Home Economics Association (1908). Author of *Chemistry of Cooking and Cleaning* (1882), *The Cost of Food* (1901), *Sanitation in Daily Life* (1907), etc.

Richards, Henry Brinley. 1817–1885. Welsh pianist and composer. Wrote a symphony, piano concerto, overtures, the song "God Bless the Prince of Wales" (1862).

Richards, Ivor Armstrong. 1893–1979. English literary critic. Professor at Cambridge (1922–29) and Harvard (1939–63). Originated New Criticism movement; developed C.K. Ogden's Basic English, an international language of 850 words. Author of *Foundations of Aesthetics* (with Ogden and James Wood, 1921), *The Meaning of Meaning* (with Ogden, 1923), *Principles of Literary Criticism* (1924), *Science and Poetry* (1925), *Practical Criticism* (1929), *Basic Rules of Reason* (1933), *Speculative Instruments* (1955), *Design for Escape* (1968), *Poetries and Sciences* (1970), *Internal Colloquies* (1972, collected verse), etc.

Richards, Laura Elizabeth, *nee* Howe \'hau̇\. 1850–1943. American writer, b. Boston. Daughter of Samuel Gridley Howe and Julia Ward Howe; m. Henry Richards (1871). Author of many juveniles as *Five Mice in a Mouse-Trap* (1881), *Queen Hildegarde* (1889), *Captain January* (1890), *Three Margarets* (1897), *Star Bright* (1927), and of biographies of Julia Ward Howe (with her sister Maud Howe Elliott, 1915, Pulitzer prize), Abigail Adams (1917), Joan of Arc (1919), Laura Bridgman (1928), Samuel Gridley Howe (1935).

Richards, Theodore William. 1868–1928. American chemist, b. Germantown, Pa. Teacher of chemistry, Harvard (1889–1928, professor from 1901). Best known for his determination of the atomic weights of about 60 elements, indicating existence of isotopes. Also conducted important investigations in thermochemistry, thermodynamics, thermometry, etc. Awarded the 1914 Nobel prize for chemistry.

Richards, Thomas Addison. 1820–1900. American painter and illustrator, b. London, England. To U.S. as a boy. Member of Hudson River school; professor of art, N.Y.U. (1867–87). Author and illustrator of *American Scenery* (1854) and *Appletons' Illustrated Hand-book of American Travel* (1857).

Richards, William. 1793–1847. American clergyman, b. Plainfield, Mass. In Hawaiian Islands as Congregational missionary (1822–38). In service of native Hawaiian government (from 1838); mainly responsible for progressive reforms in Hawaii's bill of rights (1839) and first constitution (1840); secured recognition of Hawaiian independence by U.S., Great Britain, and France (1842).

Richards, Sir William Buell. 1815–1889. Canadian jurist, b. Brockville, Upper Canada. Puisne judge (from 1853), chief justice (1873), Common Pleas Court of Upper Canada; first chief justice of Supreme Court of Canada (1875–79).

Rich·ard·son \'rich-ərd-sən\, Sir Benjamin Ward. 1828–1896. English physician. Contributed to advancement of pharmacology, esp. by studies of physiological effects of organic compounds; discovered some therapeutic drugs, as amyl nitrite and methylene bichloride.

Richardson, Charles. 1775–1865. English lexicographer. Developed his lexicon published in *The Encyclopaedia Metropolitana* (1818) into *A New Dictionary of the English Language* (1835–37), presenting etymologies designed to explain the basic, radical meaning of each word and illustrative passages to show how derived meanings developed.

Richardson, Dorothy Miller. 1872–1957. English novelist. Introduced stream-of-consciousness technique into English fiction with 12 novels, from *Pointed Roofs* (1915) to *Dimple Hill* (1938), known collectively as *Pilgrimage.*

Richardson, Ethel Florence Lindesay. *Pen name* Henry Handel Richardson. 1870–1946. Australian novelist. Author of *Maurice Guest* (1908), *The Getting of Wisdom* (1910), *The Fortunes of Richard Mahony* (1930; a trilogy), *The End of Childhood* (1934, short stories), *The Young Cosima* (1939).

Richardson, Henry Hobson. 1838–1886. American architect, b. Priestley Plantation, La. Initiator of Romanesque revival in U.S.; pioneer in development of indigenous American style of architecture. Works included Church of the Unity, Springfield, Mass. (1866), Episcopal church, West Medford, Mass. (1866), Brattle Street Church (1870) and Trinity Church (1872), Boston, Sever Hall (1878) and Austin Hall (1881) at Harvard, Marshall Field building, Chicago (1885), Allegheny Co. Buildings, Pittsburgh (1884–87), and many private residences.

Richardson, James. 1806–1851. English explorer. Led expedition in north central Africa to Lake Chad and western Sudan (1850).

Richardson, Sir John. 1787–1865. Scottish naturalist and explorer. In service of Royal navy (1807–55); surgeon and naturalist to Sir John Franklin's polar expeditions (1819–22, 1825–27); separating from Franklin, explored coast to the Coppermine River and Great Slave Lake (1826); conducted search expedition for Franklin (1848–49), exploring region between estuary of Mackenzie River and Cape Kendall. Author of *Fauna Boreali-Americana* (1829–37) and works on ichthyology and polar exploration.

Richardson, John. 1796–1852. Canadian writer, b. Queenston, Ont. Author of historical novels *Écarte* (1829), *Wacousta* (1832), *The Canadian Brothers* (1840); also historical account *War of 1812* (1842), etc.

Richardson, Lewis Fry. 1881–1953. English physicist and psychologist. First to apply (1913–22) mathematical techniques to meteorology, work published in *Weather Prediction by Numerical Process* (1922). Used mathematics to study causes of war in *Generalized Foreign Politics* (1939), *Arms and Insecurity* (1949), *Statistics of Deadly Quarrels* (1950); contributed to theory of calculus and study of diffusion.

Richardson, Sir Owen Willans. 1879–1959. English physicist. Professor, Princeton (1906–13), King's College, London (1914–24; director of research, 1924–44). Proved that electrons are emitted from hot metals and formulated Richardson's law relating rate of electron emission to absolute temperature of the metal (1911). Awarded 1928 Nobel prize for physics. Author of *The Electron Theory of Matter* (1914), *The Emission of Electricity from Hot Bodies* (1916), *Molecular Hydrogen and Its Spectrum* (1934).

Richardson, Sir Ralph David. 1902–1983. British actor. One of the preeminent actors of his time, both in classical and modern parts. Made London debut in *Yellow Sands* (1926); associated with the Old Vic (1930s ff.); celebrated in roles as Othello, Peer Gynt, Uncle Vanya, Falstaff, and Cyrano. Other stage appearances included *Flowering Cherry* (1958) and *Six Characters in Search of an Author* (1963) and with Sir John Gielgud *Home* (1970) and *No Man's Land* (1975). Among his films were *Four Feathers* (1939), *The Heiress* (1949), *The Sound Barrier* (1952), *Richard III* (1956), *Long Day's Journey Into Night* (1962), *Doctor Zhivago* (1965), *The Wrong Box* (1966), and *Greystoke* (1984).

Richardson, Samuel. 1689–1761. English novelist. Set up (1721) printing establishment in London; prospered and became printer of journals of the House of Commons; purchased moiety of patent of king's printer (1760). Author of *Pamela: or Virtue Rewarded* (1740), a novel of a maidservant's defense of her virtue told in form of correspondence, which attained phenomenal popularity; *Clarissa; or the History of a Young Lady,* usually called *Clarissa Harlowe,* which won him European fame (1747–48); embodied his ideal of a Christian gentleman in *Sir Charles Grandison* (1753); left seven folio volumes of correspondence, chiefly with women friends.

Riche \rēsh\, Gaspard-Clair-François-Marie. Baron de Prony \də-prō-nē\. 1755–1839. French mathematician and engineer. Director of cadastral survey (1791); as inspector general of bridges and roads (1805–39), responsible for all civil engineering projects, as harbor improvements, drainage of Pontine marshes, and straightening course of Po River; invented a friction brake (1821).

Richelieu, Duc de. See (1) Armand-Emmanuel du PLESSIS; (2) Armand-Jean du PLESSIS (Cardinal Richelieu); (3) Louis de VIGNEROT DU PLESSIS.

Richemont, Comte *or* Constable de. See ARTHUR.

Ri·che·pin \rēsh-pa^{n}\, Jean. 1849–1926. French writer, b. Algeria. In Paris contributed to various journals; imprisoned for month for coarse language and nihilism of *Chanson des gueux* (verse, 1876); followed this with other verse, *Les Caresses* (a verse drama, 1877), *Les Blasphèmes* (1884), *La Mer* (1886), etc. For the stage he wrote *Nana Sahib* (1883), *Le Flibustier* (1888), *Le Mage* (opera, 1891), *Par le glaive* (1894), etc. Also wrote Naturalist novels as *La Glu* (1881), *Le Pavé* (1883), *Les Braves Gens* (1886), *Flamboche* (1895), etc.

Ri·cher \rē-shā\ of Saint-Ré·my \sa^{n}-rā-mē\. 10th century. French chronicler. Author of a biography of Gerbert and a continuation of Hincmar's *Annales.*

Richer, Edmond. 1559–1631. French theologian. Opposed Jesuit policies and influence; forced to resign his various offices and to retract his Gallican doctrines; claimed superiority of councils over popes and other ideas later adopted by Jansenists.

Richer, Jean. 1630–1696. French astronomer. His observations at Cayenne, French Guiana (1672–73), were bases for determining the distance of Earth from the sun and the shape of the Earth.

Ri·chet \rē-she\, Charles-Robert. 1850–1935. French physiologist. Professor, U. of Paris (1887–1927). Conducted researches in serum therapy, physiology of respiration and digestion, epilepsy, regulation of body heat; discovered the phenomenon of anaphylaxis; awarded the 1913 Nobel prize for physiology or medicine; studied psychical phenomena.

Ri·chier \rēsh-yā\, Ligier. 1500?–1567. French sculptor. Among his notable works were the sepulcher of the Church of Saint-Étienne, the *Virgin and Saint John* at Saint-Mihiel, the mausoleum of René de Châlon.

Rich·mond \'rich-mənd\. *Duke of Richmond:* English title borne (1623–72) by members of Stewart family (*q.v.*) and (1675 to present) by members of Lennox family (*q.v.*). *Duchess of Richmond:* title borne by Frances Teresa Stuart (see STEWART family). *Earl of Richmond:* English title borne by Peter of Savoy (*q.v.*) and (from 1453) by Edmund Tudor (see TUDOR) and by his son Henry VII (*q.v.*) until his accession. *Countess of Richmond and Derby:* title borne by wife of Edmund Tudor, Margaret Beaufort (*q.v.*).

Richmond, Mary Ellen. 1861–1928. American social worker, b. Belleville, Ill. Director, Charity Organization Department of Russell Sage Foundation (1909–28). One of first to propose (1897) professional training for social workers; championed case work approach in *Social Diagnosis* (1917) and *What Is Social Case Work?* (1922).

Rich·ter \'rik-tər\, Charles Francis. 1900–1985. American seismologist, b. near Hamilton, Ohio. Spent entire professional career at Calif. Inst. Tech. (1927–70). With Beno Gutenberg created (1927) and perfected (1935) scale of earthquake magnitude now known as Richter scale, a measure of the earth's movement as recorded on seismographs. With Gutenberg wrote *Seismicity of the Earth* (1941; revised 1954).

Rich·ter \'rik-tər\, Ernst Friedrich Eduard. 1808–1879. German music theorist and composer. Wrote *Lehrbuch der Harmonie* (1853); composed an oratorio (1849), church vocal music, organ pieces, chamber music, sonatas, and songs.

Richter, Franz Xaver. 1709–1789. German composer. Representative of the Mannheim school; composed many symphonies, string quartets, sonata trios, and other chamber music, piano concertos, an oratorio, masses, requiems, motets, Psalms, passions, and other church music; introduced (with Stamitz) a new instrumental style represented by Haydn, Mozart, and Beethoven.

Richter, Hans. *First name also spelled* János. 1843–1916. German conductor, b. Hungary. Court opera conductor (1875–97), Vienna; conducted first complete performance of his friend Wagner's *Ring des Nibelungen,* Bayreuth (1876), and was one of chief conductors of Bayreuth Festspiele. Conducted Orchestra Festival Concerts, London (1879–97), and Hallé concerts, Manchester (1897–1911); directed German opera, London (from 1904); premiered many works of Brahms and Elgar; returned to Bayreuth (1912).

Richter, Hans. 1888–1976. American painter and film maker, b. Berlin, Germany. To U.S. (1941); director, Inst. of Film Techniques, C.C.N.Y. (1943–56). Known for films *Rhythm 21* (1921, first abstract animation) and *Dreams That Money Can Buy* (1947). Also executed abstract Dadaist paintings and wrote *Dada: Art and Anti-art* (1964).

Richter, Jean Paul Friedrich. *Pseudonym* Jean Paul \'paůl\. 1763–1825. German writer. His novels and romances included *Die unsichtbare Loge* (1793), *Hesperus* (1795), *Leben des Quintus Fixleins* (1796), *Siebenkäs* (1796–97), *Titan* (1800–03), *Die Flegeljahre* (1804–05), *Des Feldpredigers schmelzle Reise nach Flätz* (1809), and *Der Komet* (1820–22; incomplete); author also of *Levana* (on pedagogy, 1807), *Vorschule der Ästhetik* (reflections on art, 1804), and patriotic, philosophical, and political writings.

Richter, Jeremias Benjamin. 1762–1807. German chemist. Pioneer in stoichiometry; discovered Richter's law of neutrality, that acids and alkalies unite in constant proportions to form salts.

Richter, Theodor, *in full* Hieronymus Theodor. 1824–1898. German chemist. Codiscoverer, with Ferdinand Reich, of the element indium (1863).

Richt·ho·fen \'rikt-ˌhō-fən\, Ferdinand Paul Wilhelm von. Freiherr. 1833–1905. German geographer and geologist. Made reputation with geological investigations in Dolomite Alps and Transylvania. With Prussian mission to eastern Asia (1860–62); worked as geologist in California (1863–68); traveled in China and Japan (1868–72); professor at Berlin (1886–1905). Contributed to geographical methodology and geomorphology. Chief work *China, Ergebnisse eigener Reisen und darauf gegründeter Studien* (1877–1912).

Richthofen, Manfred von. Freiherr. *Known as* the Red Baron *or* Red Knight (*from color of his plane*). 1892–1918. German aviator. Top German aviator in World War I; shot down 80 enemy planes; killed in action.

Richt·my·er \'rikt-ˌmī-ər\, Floyd Karker. 1881–1939. American physicist, b. Ithaca, N.Y. Professor, Cornell U. (1910–39); known for work in X-ray spectroscopy; wrote *Introduction to Modern Physics* (1928).

Ric·i·mer \'ris-ə-mər\, Flavius. d. 472. Roman general, of Suevian birth. Destroyed the fleet of the Vandals (456); deposed Emperor Avitus and elevated Majorian to the throne (456); remained thereafter real sovereign of the Western Roman Empire, deposing and elevating emperors at his will.

Rick·ard \'rik-ərd\, George Lewis, *known as* Tex \'teks\. 1871–1929. American boxing promoter, b. Kansas City, Mo. Cattleman and town marshal in Texas, gold miner and gambler in Yukon; promoted prizefights (from 1906), esp. of Jack Dempsey, and first million-dollar gate (Dempsey–Carpentier, 1921).

Rick·en·back·er \'rik-ən-ˌbak-ər\, Edward Vernon. *Orig.* Rickenbacher. 1890–1973. American aviator and industrialist, b. Columbus, Ohio. Engaged in automobile racing (to 1917). Served in U.S. army air corps (1917–19); commanded 94th Aero Pursuit Squadron; credited with 26 air victories; awarded Medal of Honor. Author of *Fighting the Flying Circus* (1919). After World War I, organizer and vice president of Rickenbacker Motor Co., Detroit (to 1926); on staff of General Motors Corp., Fokker Aircraft Corp., American Airways, Inc., Aviation Corp., and North American Aviation, Inc.; president and general manager, Eastern Air Lines (1938–63). Rescued after 23 days on raft in Pacific Ocean (Nov. 1942) following special flight for U.S. government; described experience in *Seven Came Through* (1943).

Rick·ert \'rik-ərt\, Edith, *in full* Martha Edith. 1871–1938. American educator, b. Dover, Ohio. At U. of Chicago (1924–38). Wrote novels *Out of the Cypress Swamp* (1902), *Folly* (1906), *The Golden Hawk* (1907), *Severn Woods* (1930), etc. Collaborator with John M. Manly (*q.v.*) in *The Writing of English* (1919), *Contemporary British Literature* (1921), *Contemporary American Literature* (1922), *The Text of the Canterbury Tales* (1940), etc.

Rickert, Heinrich. 1863–1936. German philosopher. Disciple of Windelband; leader of Baden school of neo-Kantian philosophy; professor at Freiburg (1894), Heidelberg (1916). Author of *Zur Lehre von der Definition* (1888), *Der Gegenstand der Erkenntnis* (1892), *Die Philosophie des Lebens* (1920), *Die Logik des Prädikats und das Problem der Ontologie* (1930), etc.

Rick•etts \'rik-əts\, Howard Taylor. 1871–1910. American pathologist, b. Findlay, Ohio. Professor, U. of Chicago (1902–10); discovered that ticks transmit Rocky Mountain spotted fever and that body lice transmit tabardillo; causative organisms of both diseases named *Rickettsia* in his memory.

Ricketts, John Bill. d. 1799. English circus owner. Equestrian star at Royal Circus, London; to U.S. (1792); established (1793) first circus in U.S. and built amphitheaters in Philadelphia and New York City; toured with circus.

Rick•ey \'rik-ē\, Branch Wesley. *Nicknamed* the Ma·hat•ma \mə-'hät-mə, -'hat-\. 1881–1965. American baseball executive, b. Stockdale, Ohio. With professional baseball clubs St. Louis Browns (manager, 1913–15), St. Louis Cardinals (president, 1917–19; manager, 1919–25; general manager, 1925–42), Brooklyn Dodgers (president and general manager, 1943–50), Pittsburgh Pirates (vice president and general manager, 1950–55; board chairman, 1955–59). Devised farm system (1919); signed (1945) Jackie Robinson, first Negro to play (1947) in major leagues. Elected to Baseball Hall of Fame (1967).

Rick•man \'rik-mən\, Thomas. 1776–1841. English architect. Designed churches and country houses in Gothic style; chief work, New Court of St. John's College, Cambridge (1826–31). Author of *Attempt to Discriminate the Styles of Architecture in England* (1817), which was of influence in revival of medievalism.

Rick•o•ver \'rik-,ō-vər\, Hyman George. 1900–1986. American admiral, b. Makov, Russia (now Maków Mazowiecki, Poland). Commissioned ensign (1922); advanced to rank of rear admiral (1953) and vice admiral (1959); presided over buildup of U.S. nuclear-powered navy, beginning with first nuclear submarine *Nautilus* (1954).

Ri•cor•di \rē-'kȯr-dē\. Family of Italian music publishers, including: Giovanni (1785–1853), founder of publishing house in Milan (1808). His son ¶Tito (1811–1888) succeeded to business; friend and publisher of Verdi; founded *Gazetta Musicale* (1845). His son ¶Giulio (1840–1912) composed salon music under the pseudonym J. Burg•mein \'bu̇rk-,mīn\; discovered Puccini. His son ¶Tito (1865–1933), pianist; succeeded as head of business.

Rid•dell \'rid-əl, ri-'del\, Walter Alexander. 1881–1963. Canadian clergyman, diplomat, and labor specialist, b. Stratford, Ont. Deputy minister of labor (1919); with International Labor Office, Geneva (1920–25); represented Canada in League of Nations and international conferences (from 1925); high commissioner to New Zealand (1940–46); founder and director, International Relations Dept., U. of Toronto (1946–52). Authored Mothers' Allowance Act and Minimum Wage Act (both 1920).

Rid•der \'rid-ər\, Alfons De. *Pseudonym* Willem Els•schot \'els-kȯt\. 1882–1960. Dutch novelist. Known for ironic and naturalistic tales of ordinary life in Flanders, including *Villa des roses* (1913), *Lijmen* (1924), *Kaas* (1933), *Tsjip* (1934), *Het Dwaalicht* (1946).

Ri•der \'rīd-ər\, Fremont, *in full* Arthur Fremont. 1885–1962. American editor and publisher, b. Trenton, N.J. Editor of *Monthly Book Review* (1909–17), *Publishers' Weekly* (1910–17), *American Library Annual* (1912–17), *Library Journal* (1914–17). President of The Rider Press, magazine publishers (1914–33), and Cumulative Digest Corp. (1915–31). Librarian, Wesleyan U. (1933–53). Inventor of microcards, book truck, stack shelving, etc.

Ridg•way \'rij-,wā\, Robert. 1850–1929. American ornithologist, b. Mount Carmel, Ill. On staff of Smithsonian Institution, in charge of bird collections (1869–80); curator of birds, U.S. National Museum (1880–1929). Devised Ridgway color system to aid in describing bird coloration. Author of *A History of North American Birds* (with S. F. Baird and T. M. Brewer, 1874, 1884), *Color Standards and Nomenclature* (1886), *The Birds of North and Middle America* (1901–19), etc.

Rid•ley \'rid-lē\, Henry Nicholas. 1855–1956. English botanist. Forest administrator (1888–1912) of Straits Settlements and Singapore Botanic Gardens; largely responsible for establishment of rubber industry in Malay Peninsula; wrote *Flora of the Malay Peninsula* (1925).

Ridley, Nicholas. c.1503–1555. English reformer and Protestant martyr. Chaplain to Henry VIII and canon of Canterbury (1541); bishop of Rochester (1547). Pronounced in favor of reformed opinions; appointed as one of visitors to establish Protestantism in Cambridge U.; helped Cranmer with compilation of English prayer book and Thirty-nine Articles; succeeded Bonner as bishop of London on latter's deprivation (1550). Denounced queens Mary and Elizabeth as illegitimate and espoused cause of Lady Jane Grey; on Mary's accession declared a heretic and excommunicated; condemned and burned alive, with Latimer.

Ri•dol•fi \rē-'dȯl-fē\ *or* **Ri•dol•fo** \-fō\, Roberto di. 1531–1612. Florentine conspirator in England. Business agent in London (c.1555); plotted (from c.1569) to marry Mary, Queen of Scots, to Duke of Norfolk and set her on English throne; sought cooperation of Duke of Alba, Pius V, and Philip II to overthrow Elizabeth; failed when his emissary Charles Baillie was seized (1571) and Norfolk and Leslie were arrested.

Rie•beeck \'rē-,bāk\, Jan van. 1619–1677. Dutch surgeon and pioneer. Surgeon and administrator with Dutch East India Co. (from 1837); founded Cape Town (1652) and remained in South Africa (to 1662). Later, governor of Malacca and secretary (1665–77) to Council of India.

Riecke \'rē-kə\, Carl Viktor Eduard. 1845–1915. German physicist. Professor at Göttingen (from 1873); worked on the physics of crystals and on electrical conduction in metals and the electron theory.

Rie•ger \'rē-gər\, František Ladislav. 1818–1903. Czech politician. Leader of Czech movement in Prague revolution (1848); leader of Czech National party of conservative Old Czechs (1860); took part in Bohemian Declaration demanding Czech rights and Bohemian autonomy (1868); lost seat in Reichsrat after rise of radical Young Czechs (1891). Founded newspaper *Národní listy* and brought out first encyclopedia in Czech (both 1861).

Rieg•ger \'rē-gər\, Wallinford. 1885–1961. American composer, b. Albany, Ga. Composer of orchestral and choral works, many in 12-tone technique, including *La Belle dame sans merci* (1924), *Study in Sonority* (1927), *Dichotomy* (1932), *Variations* for violin and orchestra (1959), *Quintuple Jazz* (1959), and symphonies (esp. the *Third,* 1948); also dance and film scores.

Rie•go y Nú•ñez \'ryā-gō-ē-'nün-yāth\, Rafael del. 1785–1823. Spanish soldier. Active in Peninsular War against Napoléon; military leader of Revolution of 1820; president of the Cortes (1822–23); captured while resisting intervention of Holy Alliance, Málaga (1823); executed as traitor.

Riehl \'rēl\, Alois. 1844–1924. German philosopher. Professor at Graz (1878), Freiburg (1882), Kiel (1895), Halle (1898), Berlin (1905–19). Author of neo-Kantian works as *Der philosophische Kritizismus* (1876–87), *Friedrich Nietzsche* (1897), *Zur Einführung in die Philosophie der Gegenwart* (1903).

Riehl, Wilhelm Heinrich von. 1823–1897. German historian. Professor of political economy (1854) and history of culture (from 1859), Munich, and (1885) director of Bavarian National Museum. Author of works on history of culture, esp. *Die Naturgeschichte des deutschen Volkes als Grundlage einer deutschen Social Politik* (1851–69) and *Kulturstudien* (1873), and the stories *Geschichten aus alter Zeit* (1863–65), *Neues Novellenbuch* (1867), etc.

Riel \ryel\, Louis. 1844–1885. Canadian insurgent leader, b. St. Boniface, Manitoba. Succeeded father as leader of Métis opposed to incorporation of Northwest Territories into Canadian Dominion; headed rebels who captured Ft. Garry (Winnipeg) and set up provisional government in valley of Red River with Riel as president (1869); fled on capture of Ft. Garry by Col. Garnet Wolseley (1870). In U.S. (1879–84), organizing American Métis. Established (1885) second rebel government in Manitoba, bent on redressing wrongs of Métis; began active warfare; surrendered after fall of Batoche; found guilty of treason and hanged.

Rie•mann \'rē-,män\, Georg Friedrich Bernhard. 1826–1866. German mathematician. Taught at Göttingen (from 1854); originated a general non-Euclidean system of geometry; contributed to the development of the theory of functions; applied theory of potential to pure mathematics; his ideas on geometry provided foundations of relativity theory; many mathematical theorems and concepts are named after him.

Riemann, Hugo, *in full* Karl Wilhelm Julius Hugo. 1849–1919. German musical historian and critic. Teacher and (from 1901) professor, Leipzig. Composed technical studies and exercises for piano, chamber music, songs, and choruses. Author of musical textbooks, reference books, and historical studies, including *Musik-Lexikon* (1882).

Rie•men•schnei•der \'rē-mən-,shnī-dər\, Tilman. c.1460–1531. German sculptor and woodcarver. Settled in Würzburg (1483); councilman (1504–20), burgomaster (1520–25); imprisoned (1525) and tortured for siding against bishop in Peasants' War. His works in Late Gothic style included Altar of St. Jakob, Rothenburg (1501–05), Altar of the Virgin, Creglingen (c.1505), and tomb of Henry II and his wife.

Rien•zo \'ryent-sō\, Cola di. *Full prename* Niccolò. 1313–1354. Italian leader. Led revolution in Rome (1347), overthrew the aristocratic government, and promulgated a new constitution. Became head of the Roman state with title of tribune; attempted to restore ancient glory of Rome; antagonized the people by his arbitrary policies and the pope by his territorial ambitions; expelled from Rome (1348). Returned (1354) and again assumed dictatorial attitude and powers; murdered in a riot. Hero of an opera by Wagner and a novel by Bulwer-Lytton.

Ries \'rēs\. A family of German musicians, including: Ferdinand (1784–1838), pianist and composer; pupil of Beethoven (1801–05); resident in London (1813–24); author of *Biographische Notizen über Ludwig van Beethoven* (1838); composer of operas, oratorios, symphonies, overtures, piano concertos, and much piano and chamber music. His brother ¶Hubert, *in full* Pieter Hubert (1802–1886), violinist and composer of violin studies, was imperial concertmeister, Berlin (1836–72). Hubert's son ¶Franz (1846–1932), violinist, composer, and music publisher, was cofounder and director (1882–1924) of Ries and Erler, music publishers in Berlin; composed orchestral and chamber music, songs, and piano pieces.

Rie·se \'rē-zə\ *or* **Ries** \'rēs\, Adam. 1492–1559. German arithmetician. Pioneer in use of Indian numerals; his books did much to spread knowledge of arithmetic.

Rie·se·ner \rēz-ner\, Jean-Henri. 1734–1806. French cabinetmaker, b. Prussia. Master of marquetry. With workshop of Jean-François Oeben (from 1754) and ran it on Oeben's death (1763); completed Oeben's "bureau du roi"; royal cabinetmaker (1774).

Riesz \'rē-es\, Frigyes. 1880–1956. Hungarian mathematician. Professor, Kolozsvár (1911–20), Szeged (1920–46), Budapest (1946–56); did pioneer work in functional analysis, esp. with formulation (1907) of Riesz-Fischer theorem; contributed also to ergodic theory, orthonormal series, topology, and theory of partially ordered vector spaces; editor (1922) *Acta scientiarum mathematicarum;* author of *Leçons d'analyse fonctionnelle* (1952).

Riet·veld \'rēt-ˌvelt\, Gerrit Thomas. 1888–1964. Dutch architect and furniture designer. Associated (1918–31) with de Stijl movement; applied its principles in his famous red-and-blue armchair (c.1918) and designs of jewelry shop, Amsterdam (1921), and Schroeder House, Utrecht (1924); other designs included a housing development, Hoograven (1954–56), De Ploeg Textile Works, Bergeik (1956), Arnhem Art Academy (1962).

Rietz \'rētz\, Julius, *in full* August Wilhelm Julius. 1812–1877. German composer and conductor. Succeeded Mendelssohn as chief conductor, Düsseldorf opera (1835); Kapellmeister in Leipzig (1847–54) and Dresden (from 1860). Composed operas, symphonies, overtures, incidental music to works of Goethe and others, choruses, chamber music, piano pieces, and songs; edited chief operas of Mozart and complete works of Mendelssohn (1874–77).

RIF. See ALFASI.

Rifā'ah Rāfi' aṭ-Ṭahṭāwī. See ṬAHṬĀWĪ.

Ri·gaud \rē-gō\, André. 1761–1811. Haitian general. Opposed Toussaint L'Ouverture; was defeated and withdrew to France; returned to Haiti with Leclerc; imprisoned with Toussaint L'Ouverture; escaped and aroused Haitians in rebellion against Pétion (1810) but was defeated.

Rigaud, Hyacinthe. *Orig. name* Hyacinthe-François-Honoré-Mathias-Pierre-Martyr-André-Jean Ri·gau y Ros \rē-gau̇-ē-rōs\. 1659–1743. French painter. Most successful portrait painter at French court (from 1688); excelled in the great formal portrait, as of Louis XIV in robes of state (1701); also executed portraits of the bourgeoisie and personal friends.

Ri·gault de Gen·ouil·ly \rē-gō-də-zhə-nü-yē\, Charles. 1807–1873. French admiral. Initiated French invasion of Vietnam by capturing (1858) Tourane (now Da Nang); captured Saigon (1859). Senator (1860); minister of marine (1867–70).

Rig·don \'rig-dən\, Sidney. 1793–1876. American religious leader, b. Piny Fork, Pa. In Baptist ministry (1819); identified with Campbellite movement (1828–30) and with Mormons (from 1830). Became first counselor to Joseph Smith, founder of Mormonism, and official spokesman for Smith and the Mormon church. After Smith's assassination (1844), was excommunicated from Mormon church by Brigham Young. To Pittsburgh and declared (1845) prophet and leader by small group of Mormons, later (1862) known as Church of Jesus Christ. Sometimes credited (instead of Smith) with writing the *Book of Mormon.*

Ri·ghi \'rē-gē\, Augusto. 1850–1920. Italian physicist. Professor at Padua (1885–89) and Bologna (1889–1920); known for researches on electricity; designed an electrical oscillator.

Ri·gord \rē-gȯr\. c.1150–1207. French chronicler. Left medical profession to join (1189) monastery of Saint-Denis; known for detailed biography of King Philip II of France, *Gesta Philippi Augusti* (1196, 1207), continued to 1215 by Guillaume le Breton.

Riis \'rēs\, Jacob August. 1849–1914. American journalist and reformer, b. Ribe, Denmark. To U.S. (1870). Police reporter on staff of New York *Tribune* (1877–88) and New York *Evening Sun* (1888–99). Active in improving slum conditions in schools and tenements of lower New York; introduced parks and playgrounds in congested districts; established Jacob A. Riis Neighborhood House for social work (1888–89). Author of *How the Other Half Lives* (1890), *The Children of the Poor* (1892), *The Making of an American* (1901, autobiography), *Children of the Tenements* (1903), *Neighbors: Life Stories of the Other Half* (1914), etc.

Ri·ley \'rī-lē\, James Whitcomb. 1849–1916. American poet, b. Greenfield, Ind. On staff of *Indianapolis Journal* (1877–85); by contributions of verse to this paper established his fame. Wrote dialect poems dealing with scenes of simple life and marked by kindly humor, pathos, sincerity, and naturalness; gained sobriquet of "Hoosier poet." Among his works were *The Old Swimmin' Hole and 'Leven More Poems* (under pseudonym "Benj. F. Johnson, of Boone," 1883), *Old Fashioned Roses* (1888), *Rhymes of Childhood* (1890), *The Flying Islands of the Night* (1891), *Green Fields and Running Brooks* (1892), *A Child-World* (1896), *Home Folks* (1900), *The Raggedy Man* (1907), *The Little Orfant Annie Book* (1908), *When the Frost is on the Punkin* (1911), *Old Times* (1915), etc.

Ril·ke \'ril-kə\, Rainer Maria. 1875–1926. German poet, b. Prague. Traveled and lived throughout Europe, esp. Paris (where he associated with Auguste Rodin), Rome, Munich, and Switzerland. Published first volume of lyrical verse *Leben und Lieder* (1894); developed style of lyrical poetry, called "Ding-Gedicht," used in *Neue Gedichte* (1907–08); *Duineser Elegien* and *Die Sonette an Orpheus* (both 1923) considered culmination of his poetry; other books of verse included *Das Buch der Bilder* (1902), *Das Stunden-Buch* (1905), *Requiem* (1909), *Das Marienleben* (1913) and *Poèmes français* (1935). His prose works included *Vom lieben Gott und Anderes* (1900), *Die Weise von Liebe und Tod des Cornets Christoph Rilke* (1906), and *Die Aufzeichnungen des Malte Laurids Brigge* (1910).

Rim·baud \ra^{n}-bō, *Angl* ra^{n}(m)-'bō, ram-, 'ram-ˌ\, Arthur, *in full* Jean-Nicolas-Arthur. 1854–1891. French poet. Leading influence on Symbolist movement. Wrote his verse chiefly before the age of 20; conducted homosexual affair with Paul Verlaine (1871–73); led vagabond life (1873–80); merchant and trader in North Africa (1880–91). Author of "Le Bateau ivre" (1871), "La Chasse spirituelle" (1871–72), *Une Saison en Enfer* (1873), *Illuminations* (published by Verlaine, 1886, and containing "Sonnet des Voyelles").

Rimini, Francesca da. See under POLENTA.

Rim·mer \'rim-ər\, William. 1816–1879. American painter and sculptor, b. Liverpool, England. To America (c.1824). Stonecutter, sculptor, and painter, East Milton, Mass., where a patron brought his work to public attention. Among his best-known sculptures were *Alexander Hamilton, Chaldean Shepherd, Endymion, Osiris, St. Stephen, The Falling Gladiator, Fighting Lions,* and *The Dying Centaur;* wrote *Elements of Design* (1864), *Art Anatomy* (1877).

Rim·sky-Kor·sa·kov \'ryēm-skəi-kər-(ˌ)sə-'kȯf, *Angl* ˌrim(p)-skē-'kȯr-sə-ˌkȯf, -ˌkȯv, -ˌkȯr-sə-'\, Nikolay Andreyevich. 1844–1908. Russian composer. Professor, St. Petersburg Conservatory of Music (1871–1908); inspector of naval bands (1873–84); director, St. Petersburg Free Music School (1874–81); conductor of concerts at court chapel (1883–94); edited works of Mussorgsky and Borodin. Composed 16 operas, esp. *Snegurochka* (Snow Maiden, 1882), *Sadko* (1898), *Skazka o Tsare Saltane* (Tale of Tsar Saltan, 1900; includes "Flight of the Bumble Bee"), *Le Coq d'or* (1909); 3 symphonies; piano concerto (1882–83); *Fantasy on Russian Themes* (1886); *Capriccio espagnol* (1887); symphonic suite *Sheherazade* (1888); *Svetlry prazdnik* or *Russian Easter Festival* overture (1888); chamber music; over 80 songs.

Rin·cón \rēŋ-'kȯn\, Emanuele Gioacchino Cesare. Barone d'As·tor·ga \dä-'stȯr-gä\. 1680–?1757. Italian composer. Led wandering life in Italy, Spain, etc. Wrote chamber cantatas, of which c.170 survive, operas including *La moglie nemica* (1698), *Dafni* (1709); known esp. for *Stabat mater* (c.1707).

Rine·hart \'rīn-ˌhärt\, Mary, *nee* Roberts. 1876–1958. American novelist and playwright, b. Pittsburgh. m. Stanley M. Rinehart (1896; d. 1932). Her mysteries and romances included *The Circular Staircase* (1908), *Amazing Adventures of Letitia Carberry* (1911), *Tish* (1916), *The Amazing Interlude* (1917), *The Breaking Point* (1922), *Lost Ecstasy* (1927), *The Romantics* (1929), *The Door* (1930), *Haunted Lady* (1942), *The Yellow Room* (1945), *A Light in the Window* (1948), *The Frightened Wife* (1953); also plays mainly in collaboration with Avery Hopwood, as *The Bat* (1920).

Rinehart, Stanley Marshall, Jr. 1897–1969. American publisher, b. Pittsburgh. Son of Mary Roberts Rinehart. Pres., Rinehart & Co. (1929–60); vice president and director, Holt, Rinehart and Winston (1929–69).

Ring·er \'riŋ-ər\, Sydney. 1835–1910. English physician. On staff of U. Coll. Hospital, London (from 1863); known for work in clinical medicine and for physiological researches, esp. on the influence of organic salts on the circulation and heart beat; wrote *Handbook of Therapeutics* (1869).

Ring·ling \'riŋ-liŋ\. *Orig.* Rüng·e·ling *Ger* 'rɶŋ-ə-liŋ\. Name of five brothers, American circus owners: Albert C. (1852–1916), ¶Otto (1858–1911), ¶Alfred T. (1861–1919), ¶Charles (1863–1926), and ¶John (1866–1936). Organized their first circus at Baraboo, Wis. (1884); acquired Forepaugh-Sells circus (1906), Barnum and Bailey circus (1907), and American Circus Corp. (1929), final name of their circus being Ringling Bros. and Barnum & Bailey Circus.

Ringuet. See Philippe PANNETON.

Rin·te·len \'rin-tə-lən\, Anton. 1876–1946. Austrian jurist and politician. Governor of Styria (1919–26, 1928–33); minister of public instruction (1926,

1932–33); involved in Nazi putsch in Austria (1934); imprisoned (1935) and amnestied (1936).

Ri·nuc·ci·ni \ˌrē-nüt-ˈchē-nē\, Giovambattista. 1592–1653. Italian prelate. Archbishop of Fermo (1625). As papal nuncio to Ireland (1645–49) furnished supplies to Irish general Owen Roe O'Neill to rebel against England; denounced peace treaty between Irish and Charles I (1646).

Rinuccini, Ottavio. 1562–1621. Italian poet. Author of first Italian melodrama, *Dafne* (1594; music by Jacopo Peri); also wrote melodramas *Euridice* (1600) and *Arianna* (1607).

Rio·ja \ˈryō-k̲ä\, Francisco de. 1583–1659. Spanish poet. Follower of Herrera; known esp. for lyric poems, including sonnets, canciones, and silvas (verse of peculiar metrical arrangement).

Rí·os \ˈrē-ōs\, Juan Antonio. 1888–1946. Chilean politician. Minister of the interior (1932), of justice (1932); president of Chile (1942–46).

Rip·ley \ˈrip-lē\, George. 1802–1880. American critic and reformer, b. Greenfield, Mass. Ordained in Unitarian ministry (1826); pastor, Purchase Street Church, Boston (1826–41); withdrew from Unitarian ministry (1841). Associated with Emerson, Alcott, Margaret Fuller, and others in the Transcendental movement (from 1836); founded the *Dial* (1840) and aided Margaret Fuller in editing it. Organized and headed communal Brook Farm (1841–47); made it a phalanx of Fourier socialism by new constitution (1844). Edited the *Harbinger,* a Fourierite magazine (1845–49). Literary critic, *New York Tribune* (1849–80). Founder (1850) and literary editor (to 1854), *Harper's New Monthly Magazine.* With Charles A. Dana, edited *New American Cyclopaedia* (1858–63).

Ripley, Robert LeRoy. *Added prename* Robert *c.1914.* 1893–1949. American cartoonist, b. Santa Rosa, Cal. Sports cartoonist for several newspapers (from 1910); known for "Believe It or Not!" illustrated columns (created 1918) syndicated in many newspapers.

Ripley, William Zebina. 1867–1941. American anthropologist and economist, b. Medford, Mass. Professor, M.I.T. (1895–1901), Harvard (1901–33). In *Races of Europe* (1899) divided Europeans by race as Nordics, Alpines, or Mediterraneans; drew up plan for Interstate Commerce Commission for regional consolidation of railways (1920–23); also wrote *Trusts, Pools and Corporations* (1905), *Railway Problems* (1907), *Main Street and Wall Street* (1927).

Ripon, Earls and marquis of. See Frederick John and George Frederick ROBINSON.

Rip·per·da \ˈrip-ər-ˌdä\, Jan Willem. 1680–1737. Dutch adventurer. Dutch ambassador to Spain (1715); became a Roman Catholic and entered Spanish diplomatic service (1718); represented Spain at Vienna (1724–25) and concluded treaty of alliance between Spain and Emperor Charles VI; created duke and prime minister of Spain (1725–26). On failure of the alliance, imprisoned (1726–28); escaped to Holland and again became a Protestant. Served (from 1731) under the sultan of Morocco; became a Muslim; adopted name Os·man Pa·sha \ùs-ˈmän-ˈpä-shä\; commanded army defeated at Ceuta (1733); spent last years in exile at Tetuán.

Rippl-Ró·nai \ˈrip-əl-ˈrō-nä-ē\, József. 1861–1927. Hungarian painter and graphic artist. Exponent of modern Hungarian art; works included portraits, pastels, etchings, lithographs, and designs for glass paintings, tapestries, and bookbindings.

Ri·quet de Bon·re·pos \rē-ke-də-bōⁿ-re-pōs\, Pierre-Paul de. 1604–1680. French engineer. Planned Languedoc Canal (also called Canal du Midi) to connect Atlantic Ocean and Mediterranean; plan received approval (1662) of Colbert and Louis XIV; spent rest of his life and his personal fortune building the canal which was completed six months after his death; first to use explosive for blasting rock.

Ri·que·ti \rē-ke-tē\, Honoré-Gabriel. Comte de Mi·ra·beau \mē-rä-bō\. 1749–1791. French politician and orator. Son of Victor Riqueti. Joined cavalry regiment (1767); imprisoned several times for intrigues and wild conduct (1774–80); traveled throughout Europe, esp. London and Germany (1784–89); wrote pamphlets attacking Necker (1787–89). Sent by the Third Estate as deputy for Aix and Marseilles to Estates-General (1789); most important figure in first two years of French Revolution. Influenced National Assembly by personality and oratory; advocated a constitutional monarchy; broke with Necker and Lafayette; distrusted by both Louis XVI and the revolutionaries for his moderate stands; elected president of the Assembly (1791) but died soon after. Author of *Des lettres de cachet et des prisons d'état* (1782), *De la monarchie prussienne sous Frédéric le Grand* (1788), *Histoire secrète de la cour de Berlin* (1789), etc. His brother ¶André-Boniface-Louis (1754–1792), vicomte de Mirabeau; served in American army (1780–85); member of Estates-General (1789); royalist in sympathy; an emigré (from c.1790).

Riqueti, Victor. Marquis de Mirabeau. 1715–1789. French soldier and political economist. Associated with François Quesnay and the Physiocrats; author of *Mémoire concernant l'utilité des états provinciaux* (1750), *Ami des hommes, ou traité de la population* (1756–58), *Théorie de l'impôt* (1760), etc.

Riqueti de Mi·ra·beau \-də-mē-rä-bō\, Sibylle-Gabrielle-Marie-Antoinette de. Comtesse de Mar·tel de Jan·ville \də-mär-tel-də-zhäⁿ-vēl\. *Pseudonym* Gyp \zhēp\. 1850–1932. French writer. Contributed sketches to *Revue des Deux Mondes* and *Vie Parisienne.* Author of humorous novels of manners as *Petit Bob* (1882), *Autour du mariage* (1883), *Autour du divorce* (1886), *Ohé! la grande vie* (1891), *Le Baron Sinaï* (1897), *Les Profitards* (1918).

Ri Sam·pei \ˈrē-ˈsäm-ˈpā\. d. 1653. Korean ceramist. Taken to Japan by Lord Naoshige of Saga and naturalized as Japanese citizen; originator of Arita-ware pottery.

Ri·sen·burgh \ˈrē-sə(n)-bœrḡ, -səm-\, Bernard van. *Surname also spelled* Vanrisemburgh *or* Van Risen Burgh. c.1700–c.1765. French furniture maker of Dutch origin. Established workship in Paris (1730); worked in Rococo style; probably first to decorate work with porcelain plaques; used wood marquetry and lacquer veneers. His son ¶Bernard (d. 1799) continued his father's business; also known as a sculptor.

Ri·sing \ˈrē-siŋ\, Johan Classon. 1617–1672. Swedish colonial governor in America. Governor of New Sweden colony on Delaware River (1654–55); colony conquered by Dutch under Stuyvesant (1655).

Ris·ley \ˈriz-lē\, Sir Herbert Hope. 1851–1911. English civil servant and anthropologist. Served in India (1873–1910). Author of *Anthropometric Data* (1891), *Tribes and Castes of Bengal* (1891–92), *Ethnographical Glossary* (1892), and *The People of India* (1908).

Ris·so \ˈrēs-sō\, Giovanni Antonio. 1777–1845. Italian naturalist. Known for work on the mollusks of the Mediterranean; the Rissoidae family of marine snails named after him.

Rist \ˈrist\, Johann. 1607–1667. German poet. Wrote words and some of the music for many sacred and secular songs, including the hymn "O Ewigkeit, du Donnerwort"; also allegorical musical plays.

Ris·tić \ˈrē-stētʸ\, Jovan. 1831–1899. Serbian politician. Second regent for Milan Obrenović (1868–72); mainly responsible for promulgation of new constitution (1869). Foreign minister (1872–73, 1875, 1876–78); premier of Serbia (1873, 1878–80, 1887); chief of council of regency (1889–93).

Ri·sto·ri \rē-ˈstō-rē\, Adelaide. 1822–1906. Italian actress. One of leading tragediennes of European stage; played principally in Paris. Among her notable roles were Francesca da Rimini, Maria Stuart, Medea, Phaedra, Lady Macbeth, and Pia dei Tolomei.

Ritch·ey \ˈrich-ē\, George Willis. 1864–1945. American astronomer, b. Tupper's Plains, Ohio. On staff of Yerkes Observatory (1896–1904), solar observatory in Carnegie Institution (1905–09), Mt. Wilson Observatory; director of astrophotographic laboratory at Observatoire de Paris (1924–30). Coinventor of an aplanatic reflecting telescope; inventor of fixed vertical universal type of reflecting telescope, and of cellular type of optical mirrors; designer (1931) and constructor of a 40-in. reflecting telescope at the U.S. Naval Observatory in Washington, D.C.

Ritch·ie \ˈrich-ē\, Thomas. 1778–1854. American journalist, b. Tappahannock, Va. Founded (1804) and edited (1804–45) Richmond *Enquirer,* establishing it as one of leading papers in U.S.; edited *Union,* Washington, D.C. (1845–51).

Ritchie, Sir William Johnstone. 1813–1892. Canadian jurist, b. Annapolis, N.S. On New Brunswick council (1854–55); puisne judge (1855–65), chief justice (1865–75) of New Brunswick; puisne judge (1875–79), chief justice of Canada (1879–92).

Rit·schl \ˈrich-əl\, Albrecht. 1822–1889. German theologian. Professor at Bonn (1846–64) and Göttingen (1864–89). Founded Ritschlian school, emphasizing the ethical-social content of theology and holding that Christian theology should rest mainly on an appreciation of the inner life of Christ. Chief works *Die Entstehung der altkatholischen Kirche* (1850) and *Die christliche Lehre von der Rechtfertigung und Versöhnung* (1870–74).

Ritschl, Friedrich Wilhelm. 1806–1876. German classical philologist. Cousin of Albrecht Ritschl. Professor at Halle (1832–33), Breslau (1833–39), Bonn (1839–65), Leipzig (1865–76). Edited (with Theodor Mommsen) *Priscae Latinitalis Monumenta Epigraphica* (1862); author of works on Plautus, esp. an edition of his comedies (1848–54, 1871–74), and studies on linguistic history, metrics, and epigraphy, collected in *Opuscula Philologica* (1867–79).

Rit·son \ˈrit-sən\, Joseph. 1752–1803. English antiquary. Savagely criticized Warton's *History of English Poetry,* Johnson and Steevens for their texts of Shakespeare, Percy's *Reliques;* detected antiquary John Pinkerton's forgeries in *Select Scottish Ballads* (1784) and the Ireland forgeries (1795).

Rit·ten·house \ˈrit-ən-ˌhaùs\, David. 1732–1796. American astronomer, b. Germantown, Pa. Great-grandson of William Rittenhouse. Gained reputation by building two orreries, one for Princeton U. (c.1767) and one for the U. of Pennsylvania. Built observatory and a transit telescope, believed to be first telescope made in America, to observe the transit of Venus (1769). Inventor of a collimating telescope (1785); one of earliest to use spider webs as reticle in the eyepiece of a telescope. During Revolutionary War, served as member of Pennsylvania assembly (1776) and president of the council of safety (1777); treasurer of Pennsylvania (1777–89). First director, U.S. Mint (1792–95).

President, succeeding Benjamin Franklin, of American Philosophical Society (1791–96).

Rittenhouse, William. 1644–1708. American clergyman and industrialist, b. Mülheim an der Ruhr, Prussia. To America (1688) and settled in Germantown, Pa.; chosen first pastor of the Mennonite group there; elected bishop (1703) of first Mennonite church in America. Organized paper-manufacturing company and built (1690) first paper mill in America.

Rit·ter \'rit-ər\, Alexander. 1833–1896. German composer. Influenced Richard Strauss. Composed operas *Der faule Hans* (1885) and *Wem die Krone?* (1890), symphonic poems, piano pieces, songs, etc.

Ritter, Carl. 1779–1859. German geographer. Cofounder (with Alexander von Humboldt) of modern geographical science. Professor at Berlin (1820–59). Author of geographical interpretations of history; chief work *Die Erdkunde im Verhältniss zur Natur und zur Geschichte des Menschen* (incomplete; 1817 ff.).

Ritter, Johann Wilhelm. 1776–1810. German physicist. Discovered process of electroplating (1800); discovered existence of ultraviolet rays through their photochemical action (1801); observed thermoelectric currents (1801) and made other researches in electricity, anticipating subsequent discoveries; invented the dry voltaic cell (1802) and an electrical storage battery (1803).

Ritt·ner \'rit-nər\, Tadeusz. *Pseudonym* Tomasz Cza·szka \'chäsh-kä\. 1873–1921. Polish playwright and novelist. Author of plays as *W małym domku* (1904), *Głupi Jakób* (1910), *Wilki w nocy* (1916), and novels as *Drzwi zamknięte* (1922), *Most* (1926).

Ritz \'rits\, César. 1850–1918. Swiss hotelkeeper. Owner of fashionable hotels in London, Paris, New York, etc.; the opulence of his hotels made his name synonymous with social elegance accompanied by great wealth.

Rit·ze \'rit-sə\, Heinrich. *Known as* Euricius Cor·dus \'kȯr-du̇s\. 1484–1535. German physician and Humanist. Professor, Marburg (1527); city physician, Bremen (1534). Wrote Latin epigrams, satirical medical work *Liber de urinis* (1543), eclogues *Bucolicon* (1514); established scientific botany in Germany with *Botanologicon* (1534). His son ¶Valerius Cordus (1515–1544), physician and naturalist; compiled first German pharmacopoeia (pub. 1546); first to describe ethyl ether.

Ri·va Agüe·ro \'rē-vä-ä-'gwā-rō\, José Mariano de la. 1783–1858. Peruvian soldier and politician. One of early leaders for independence of Peru; joined army of San Martín (1822) and was twice imprisoned; first president of Peru republic (Feb. to Aug. 1823) but compelled by Bolívar and Sucre to resign.

Ri·va·da·via \rē-bä-'thäv-yä\, Bernardino. 1780–1845. Argentine politician. Active in struggle for independence (1811–14); Argentine envoy in London, Paris, and Madrid (1814–20); governor of Buenos Aires (1820–23). President of the Argentine Confederation (1826–27); organized a parliament and a court system; supported freedom of the press and individual and property rights; founded U. of Buenos Aires; resigned to avert civil war. Spent most of his later years in exile.

Ri·va·ro·la \rē-bä-'rō-lä\, Cirilo Antonio. d. 1871. Paraguayan politician. Fought in war against Argentina (1865–70); first president of republic of Paraguay (1870–71; retired); assassinated.

Ri·va·ro·li \rē-vä-rȯl-ē\, Antoine. *Called himself* Comte de Ri·va·rol \də-rē-vȯ-rȯl\. 1753–1801. French journalist. Royalist during French Revolution; an émigré (from 1792) in Brussels, London, and Hamburg. Best known for his epigrams, collected under the title *L'Esprit de Rivarol* (1802); wrote *De l'universalité de la langue française* (1784) and satirized contemporary authors in *Le Petit Almanach de nos grands-hommes* (1788).

Rivas, Duque de. See Ángel de SAAVEDRA.

Ri·ve·ra \rē-'bā-rä\, Diego. *In full* Diego María Concepción Juan Nepomuceno Estanislao de la Rivera y Barrientos Acosta y Rodríguez. 1886–1957. Mexican painter. A leader (with Orozco and Siqueiros) of Mexican politico-social school of painting. His leftist-oriented murals, often on native historical themes, are in the National Preparatory School, Mexico City (1922), National School of Agriculture, Chapingo (1926–27), National Palace, Mexico City (1929–35, 1944–57), Detroit Institute of Arts (1932), Hotel del Prado, Mexico City (1947–48). His *Man at the Crossroads* for Rockefeller Center, New York City (1933) was removed to the Palace of Fine Arts, Mexico City, because a figure resembled Lenin.

Rivera, José Eustacio. 1889–1928. Colombian writer. Lawyer by profession. Published collection of sonnets *Tierra de promisión* (1921); best known for psychological novel *La vorágine* (1924), protesting exploitation of rubber gatherers in the upper Amazon jungle.

Rivera, José Fructuoso. c.1788–1854. Uruguayan general and politician. Served under Artigas and was one of "the Thirty-three Immortals" who freed Uruguay (after 1825); led revolution (1830) and became first president of Uruguay (1830–35); at first supported Oribe, but later (1838) led revolt that deposed him; again president (1838–42); participated in Civil War (1842–51), leader of Colorados, besieged in Montevideo; defeated by Urquiza at the battle of India Muerta (1845) and fled to Brazil; chosen as one of three to administer provisional government of Uruguay (1853) but died the next year.

Rivers, Earl. See Richard and Anthony WOODVILLE.

Riv·ers \'riv-ərz\, Thomas Milton. 1888–1962. American virologist, b. Jonesboro, Ga. As chairman of virus research committee of National Foundation for Infantile Paralysis (1938–55) credited with planning and recruiting support for the long-range research program that led to development of Salk and Sabin polio vaccines.

Rivers, William Halse Rivers. 1864–1922. English physiologist and anthropologist. Director of Britain's first experimental psychology laboratory (1897; U. of London); founder of Cambridge school of experimental psychology; on anthropological expedition to Torres Straits (1898), to Melanesia (1908); neurological consultant to British army during World War I. Author of *The Todas* (1906), *Kinship and Social Organisation* (1914), *History of Melanesian Society* (1914), *Instinct and the Unconscious* (1920), etc.

Ri·vet \rē-ve\, Paul. 1876–1958. French ethnologist. Authority on South American Indian cultures. Director, Muséum National d'Histoire Naturelle, Paris (from 1928); published *Ethnographie ancienne de l'Équateur* (with René Verneau, 1912–22); founder of Musée de l'Homme, Paris (1937); suggested Australian and Melanesian origins for South American Indians in *Les Origenes de l'homme américain* (1943).

Ri·vière \rēv-yer\, Jacques. 1886–1925. French writer. Cofounder and editor of *Nouvelle Revue Française* (1919–25); championed Proust. His works included essays on the arts *Études* (1912) and *Nouvelles études* (1947), psychological novels *Aimée* (1922) and *Florence* (1935; unfinished), war memoirs *L'Allemand* (1918), and correspondence with his brother-in-law Alain-Fournier and Claudel.

Riv·ing·ton \'riv-iŋ-tən\, James. 1724–1803. American publisher, b. London, England. Succeeded (1742) to his father's publishing business; emigrated to Philadelphia (1760); set up bookshops in Philadelphia, New York, and Boston; Tory journalist; publisher of *Rivington's New York Gazetteer* (1773–75); bitterly attacked American Revolutionary movement; deprived of press by Sons of Liberty (1775), returned to England for new press, and set up *Rivington's New York Loyal Gazette* (later called *Royal Gazette,* 1777–83); turned spy for Washington (1781).

Ri·vi·nus \rē-'vē-nu̇s, *Lat* ri-'vī-nəs\, Augustus Quirinus. *Orig. surname* Bachmann \'bäk-,män\. 1652–1723. German botanist. Author of *Ordo Plantarum* (1690–99), in which he set forth a new system of plant classification based on the number and regularity of petals of a flower.

Rivoli, Duc de. See André MASSÉNA.

Ri·zal \rē-'säl\, José Protasio. 1861–1896. Philippine patriot and writer. National hero of the Philippines. Advocated reformation of Spanish rule. His political novels *Noli me tangere* (1886) and *El filibusterismo* (1891) caused his exile (1892–96) and provided the main stimulus to the Philippine revolution of 1896–98. On return from exile was arrested, charged with instigating native insurrection, condemned and shot. On eve of his execution wrote poem "Último Adiós."

Riza Shah Pahlavi. See REZA SHAH PAHLAVI.

Riz·zio \'rēt-tsyō, *Angl* 'rit-sē-,ō\ *or* **Ric·cio** \'rēt-chō, *Angl* 'rich-ē-,ō\, David. c.1533–1566. Italian musician and favorite of Mary, Queen of Scots. Accompanied Piedmontese ambassador to Scotland (1561); entered Mary's service as musician and bass singer, became valet de chambre and (1564) private foreign secretary; arranged marriage with Darnley; became virtual secretary of state, haughty and overbearing, excluding Darnley from political power; was dragged from Mary's supper chamber at Holyrood Palace by armed band, including Darnley, Morton, and Lindsay, and hacked to death with daggers.

Riz·zo \'rēt-tsō\, Antonio. 1430?–?1499. Italian sculptor. Employed at Vicenza and Venice (1467–98); known esp. for his tomb of Doge Niccolò Trono in Venice.

Roach \'rōch\, John. *Orig. surname* Roche \'rōch\. 1813–1887. American ironmaster and shipbuilder, b. Mitchelstown, Ireland. To U.S. (1830, naturalized 1842); built marine engines and iron steamships, including several war vessels; sometimes called "father of iron shipbuilding in America."

Robbia. See DELLA ROBBIA.

Ro·bec·chi-Bric·chet·ti \rō-'bek-kē-brēk-'ket-tē\, Luigi. 1855–1926. Italian explorer. Discovered vast necropolis at oasis of Siwa in western Egypt (1886); first European to cross the entire Somali peninsula (1890–91).

Rob·ert \'räb-ərt\. Name of two dukes of Burgundy:

Robert I. d. 1076. 3d son of King Robert II of France; on father's death (1031), waged civil war for throne against his older brother King Henry I; made duke of Burgundy (1032).

Robert II. d. 1306. Duke (1272–1306). Son of Duke Hugh IV of Burgundy; maternal grandfather of King John II the Good of France.

Robert. Name of three counts of Flanders:

Robert I. *Called* the Frisian. 1013?–1093. Count (1071–93). Made expeditions against Moors in Galicia and against Byzantines; regent of Flanders (1070) but forced to leave; made pilgrimage to Palestine (1085–91).

Robert II of Jerusalem. d. 1111. Count (1093–1111). Son of Robert I; took part in First Crusade (1096–99); fought with Louis VI against Henry I of England.

Robert III of Bé·thune \bā-tüēn\. 1240–1322. Count (1305–22). Son of Guy de Dampierre. Fought against King Philip IV of France (1297); held as prisoner at Chinon (1304–05); refused to grant lands to Philip; defeated (1319) by Philip.

Robert. Name of two kings of France:

Robert I. c.865–923. Count of Paris and as elected king of Frankish lords (922–923) often considered king of France. Son of Robert the Strong and brother of Eudes. Did not claim crown of France on death of Eudes (898); recognized by Charles III as duke of the Franks; defeated Normans at Chartres (911); led Neustrian lords in revolt against Charles (919); elected king by nobles (922); killed in battle in which his army routed Charles's.

Robert II. *Called* le Pieux \lə-pyœ\, *i.e.* the Pious. c.970–1031. King (996–1031). Son of Hugh Capet; m. (996) as second wife, his cousin Bertha; excommunicated (998) by Pope Gregory V because of marriage; conquered duchy of Burgundy after long struggle (1002–15). Last year of reign troubled by revolt of sons by his third marriage, incited by their mother, Constance of Arles \ȧrl\ (d. 1032).

Robert. *Called* the Wise. 1278–1343. King of Naples (1309–1343). Succeeded his father Charles II as king and as duke of Anjou; also duke of Calabria (1295). A leader of the Guelf (papal) faction in Italy; broke with Pope John XII (1330); helped drive King John of Luxembourg from Italy (1336); final years of reign marked by defections of his northern Italian towns and failure to regain Sicily. A man of learning and patron of literary men, esp. Petrarch and Boccaccio.

Robert. Name of two dukes of Normandy:

Robert I. *Called* le Dia·ble \lə-dyäblᵊ\, *i.e.* the Devil; *also called* le Ma·gni·fique \lə-män-yē-fēk\, *i.e.* the Magnificent. d. 1035. Duke (1027–35). Son of Duke Richard II; father of William the Conqueror. An unscrupulous and cruel ruler, but energetic and bold; aided nephews in England against Canute; supported claim of Henry I to French throne; made pilgrimage to Palestine; died at Nicaea on his return.

Robert II. *Called* Courte·heuse \kür-tœz\. 1054?–1134. Duke (1087–1134). Eldest son of William the Conqueror. Rebelled against his father (1077, 1080, 1082). Disputed Normandy with his brother William II of England (1089, 1091, 1094); incompetent as ruler, failed to control rebellious vassals or establish a central authority. Took important part in First Crusade (1096–99), distinguishing himself at battles of Dorylaeum (1097), Jerusalem (1099), and Ascalon (1099); delayed in Italy on his return (1100). Invaded England (1101) in attempt to take throne from his younger brother, Henry I; retired to Normandy; at war again with Henry (1105–06); defeated at Tinchebrai (1106); imprisoned at Cardiff (1106–34).

Robert. Count of Paris. See ROBERT I, king of France.

Robert. Name of three kings of Scotland:

Robert I. *Called* the Bruce. 1274–1329. King (1306–1329). Son of Robert VII de Bruce, and received his title of earl of Carrick (1292). Little known of his career to 1306, but in general supported Edward I of England. Killed, or had killed, John Comyn, nephew of John de Balliol (1306); crowned at Scone (1306). Defeated by English army at Methven and at Dalry and took refuge on Rathlin, Ireland (1306). Returned (1307); captured Perth (1313); gradually drove English out of Scotland, taking Edinburgh and gaining victory at Bannockburn (both 1314). Subdued Hebrides (1316); captured Berwick (1318); fought the English until Treaty of Northampton (1328) by which Edward III recognized independence of Scotland and Robert's right to throne. Succeeded by his son David II.

Robert II. 1316–1390. King (1371–1390). Founder of Stuart dynasty (see STEWART family). Succeeded to father's office as high steward and to estates (1326); confirmed by Scottish Parliament as heir apparent to David II (1326); led second division of Scottish army at Halidon Hill (1333); regent during David II's absence in France (1334–35, 1338–41) and after David II's capture at Neville's Cross (1346–57). Took no active part in war with England (1378–88); kingdom administered by sons John (1384–88; see ROBERT III) and Robert, Duke of Albany (1388–90).

Robert III. *Orig.* John Stewart. c.1337–1406. King (1390–1406). Created Earl of Ath·oll \'ath-əl\ (1367) and Earl of Car·rick \'kar-ik\ (1368). Ruled Scotland in name of his father Robert II (1384–88); lost position to brother Robert, Duke of Albany (see under STEWART family), after suffering disabling injury (1388). During reign country ruled by Albany; gave over guardianship of his elder son, David Stewart (1378?–1402), Duke of Rothe·say \'räth-sē, -ˌsā\, to Albany, who presumably starved him to death at Falkland; succumbed to grief on receipt of news of capture by English of his younger son, James, en route to France.

Robert. Earl of Glouces·ter \'gläs-tər, 'glós-\. d. 1147. English soldier. Illegitimate son of Henry I of England and half-brother of Matilda. Received by marriage large possessions in Normandy, Wales, and England; quarreled with his cousin Stephen (king of England), who confiscated his Welsh and English lands (1137); supported (from 1139) Matilda's claim to throne; conquered most of western England and southern Wales; captured Stephen at Lincoln (1141); was captured at Stockbridge and exchanged for Stephen (1141).

Robert of Be·lesme *or* Bel·lême \bā-lem\. Seigneur de Bellême, 3d Earl of Shrews·bury \'shrōz-b(ə-)rē\. c.1052–after 1130. Norman soldier. Originally supported Robert II Curthose; changed allegiance (1097) to William II Rufus, for whom he captured Helias, Count of Maine; rebelled against Henry I (1101–02) and was deprived of English holdings; returned to England as ambassador of King Louis VI of France (1112), immediately arrested and imprisoned for life. Noted for his cruelty; built castle of Gisors.

Robert of Cour·te·nay \ˌkür-tə-'nā\. d. 1228. Emperor of the Eastern Roman Empire (1221–28). Younger son of Emperor Peter of Courtenay (*q.v.*). A weak sovereign, lost most of his empire, esp. eastern lands in Asia Minor to John III Vatatzes (1225) and Thessalonica to Theodore Angelus (1228); died while fleeing a revolt of his barons.

Robert of Geneva. See antipope CLEMENT VII.

Robert of Glouces·ter \'gläs-tər, 'glós-\. fl. 1260–1300. English chronicler. Reputed author of last 3000 lines (covering period 1256–1270) of "The Chronicle of Robert of Gloucester," vernacular history of England from days of legendary Brut to 1270, written in rhymed couplets.

Robert of Ju·mièges \zhüēm-yezh\. d. c.1055. Norman prelate. Abbot of Jumièges (1037); crossed to England with Edward the Confessor (1042); bishop of London (1044). Became Edward's chief adviser; head of Norman party hostile to Earl Godwin; archbishop of Canterbury (1051), drove Earl Godwin into exile; fled to Normandy on Godwin's return (1052).

Robert of Mo·lesmes \mò-lem\. Saint. c.1027–1110. French Benedictine ecclesiastic. Abbot of Saint-Michel-de-Tonerre; became leader of hermitage at Molesmes (1075); in order to observe austere life founded (1098) Cîteaux Abbey, which developed into Cistercian Order. See Saint Stephen HARDING.

Robert the Bruce. See ROBERT I, king of Scotland.

Robert the Strong. d. 866. French warrior. Count of various regions, esp. Anjou and Blois. Ancestor of Capetian kings of France; father of Frankish kings Eudes and Robert I. Most trusted warrior of Charles II the Bald; revolted (856) against Charles but was reconciled (861); suppressed (from 862) raids of Norman brigands of the Loire, winning great victory at Neustria (865); killed in battle.

Robert the Wise. See ROBERT, king of Naples.

Rob·ert \'räb-ərt\, Henry Martyn. 1837–1923. American army officer, b. Robertville, S.C. Military engineer; during Civil War constructed defenses for Washington, D.C., and Philadelphia; retired as bridgadier general (1901). Author of *Robert's Rules of Order* (1876; revised 1915).

Ro·bert \rò-ber\, Hubert. 1733–1808. French painter. In Rome (1754–65); associate of Piranesi; traveled through southern Italy and Sicily with Fragonard (1859). Known for his French and Italian landscapes and for romantic representations of Roman ruins set in idealized surroundings.

Robert, Nicholas-Louis. 1761–1828. French inventor. With his brother ¶Anne-Jean (1758–1820) and Jacques Charles launched first hydrogen balloon (Paris; Aug. 27, 1783); with Charles ascended in a gondola carried by a hydrogen balloon (1783); invented first machine to produce paper in continuous sheets (1798).

Robert de Bor·ron \-də-bò-rōⁿ\. fl. c.1200. French writer. Author of two Grail romances now known as *Joseph d'Arimanthie* and *Merlin*.

Robert de France. Comte de Clermont. See BOURBON.

Robert de To·ri·gni \-tò-rēn-yē\. c.1110–1186. French chronicler. Joined Benedictine abbey at Bec (1128); abbot of Mont-Saint-Michel (from 1154); visited England (1157, 1175). His *Appendix* to chronicle of Sigebert de Gembloux covers England under Henry II from 1154 to 1186 and is important source.

Robert Guis·card \-gēs-kȧr\. *Also called* Robert de Hauteville \-d(ə-)ōt-vēl\. c.1015–1085. Norman military leader. Brother of Roger I of Sicily. To Italy (c.1047); conquered Apulia and Calabria and created (1059) duke of those regions by Pope Nicholas II; drove Byzantines from southern Italy (by 1071). With help of Roger conquered part of Sicily from the Saracens, capturing Palermo (1071) and Salerno (1076). Captured Rome (1084) and delivered Pope Gregory VII from Emperor Henry IV. Died during siege of Cephalonia.

Robert-Hou·din \-ü-daⁿ\, Jean-Eugène. 1805–1871. French magician. Considered father of modern conjuring. Exposed "fakes" and magicians who relied on supernatural explanations; contrived mechanisms to produce more remarkable illusions, but always explaining technical procedures; first magician to use electricity; in Algeria on government mission to successfully combat influence of dervishes by duplicating their feats (1856). Author of *Confidences d'un prestidigitateur* (autobiography, 1859), *Les Secrets de la prestidigitation et de la magique* (1868), etc.

Rob·erts \'räb-ərts\, Sir Charles George Douglas. 1860–1943. Canadian writer, b. Douglas, N.B. Considered father of Canadian literature. Best known for descriptive lyrics about New Brunswick and Nova Scotia landscapes. Among his books of verse were *Orion and Other Poems* (1880), *In Divers Tones* (1887), *Songs of the Common Day* (1893), *New York Nocturnes* (1898), *The Book of the Rose* (1903), *The Vagrant of Time* (1927), and *The Iceberg, and Other Poems* (1934). Also wrote volumes of nature and animal short stories, as *Earth's Enigmas* (1896), *The Kindred of the Wild* (1902), *Red Fox* (1905), and *Neighbours Unknown* (1911); several novels about the Maritime Provinces; and *History of Canada* (1897).

Roberts, Elizabeth Madox. 1886–1941. American poet and novelist, b. Perryville, Ky. Author of *Under the Tree* (verse, 1922), *The Time of Man* (1926), *My Heart and My Flesh* (1927), *Jingling in the Wind* (1928), *The Great Meadow* (1930), *A Buried Treasure* (1931), *The Haunted Mirror* (short stories, 1932), *He Sent Forth a Raven* (1935), *Black is my Truelove's Hair* (1938), *Song in the Meadow* (verse, 1940), *Not by Strange Gods* (short stories, 1941).

Roberts, Frederick Sleigh. 1st Earl Roberts. 1832–1914. British soldier, b. India. Served in Sepoy Mutiny (1857–58), winning Victoria Cross for heroism at Khudaganj. In Second Afghan War, forced Afghan position at Peiwar Kotal, took Kabul, and reentered Afghan capital (1879); performed memorable march from Kabul to relief of Qandahār, defeating Ayub Khan's Afghan army and achieving pacification of Afghanistan (1880). Commander in chief in India (1885–93); field marshal (1895); commander in chief in Ireland (1895–99). Held supreme command in South Africa (1899–1900); relieved Kimberley, compelled Boers under Cronjé to surrender at Paardeberg (1900); annexed Orange Free State; captured Johannesburg and Pretoria; annexed Transvaal. Devoted himself after retiring (1904) to creation of a citizen army. Author of *The Rise of Wellington* (1895) and *Forty-One Years in India* (1897).

Roberts, Sir Gilbert. 1899–1978. English civil engineer. Developed all-welded ships in World War II. Pioneered new designs and construction methods in bridge-building; designed bridges at Firth of Forth, Scotland; Severn River, England; Auckland, N.Z.; Volta River, Ghana; and across the Bosporus in Turkey.

Roberts, Glenn. *Nicknamed* Fireball. 1927–1964. American stock-car racer, b. Tavares, Fla. Won 32 races and set many records (from 1950); invented "drafting" technique in stock-car racing; died in crash during World 600-Mile race at Charlotte, N.C.

Roberts, Isaac. 1829–1904. British astronomer, b. Wales. Pioneer in nebular photography; known esp. for studies of the Pleiades; demonstrated that Andromeda nebula has a spiral structure.

Roberts, Kenneth Lewis. 1885–1957. American novelist, b. Kennebunk, Me. Author of historical novels *Arundel* (1930), *Rabble in Arms* (1933), *Captain Caution* (1934), *Northwest Passage* (1937), *Oliver Wiswell* (1940), *Lydia Bailey* (1947), etc.

Roberts, Owen Josephus. 1875–1955. American jurist, b. Philadelphia. Professor (1898–1918), U. of Penn.; special counsel for U.S. in prosecuting "oil cases" of Teapot Dome scandal (1924); associate justice, U.S. Supreme Court (1930–1945); dean, U. of Penn. Law School (1948–51).

Roberts, Tom, *in full* Thomas William. 1856–1931. Australian painter, b. England. To Australia (1869). Introduced Impressionism to Australia; a leader of Heidelberg school. Best known for paintings of rural life as *Shearing the Rams* (1889–90), and for *Opening of the First Commonwealth Parliament* (c.1901).

Roberts-Aus·ten \-'ós-tən, -'äs-\, Sir William Chandler. 1843–1902. English metallurgist. Added Austen to surname (1885). Employed by Royal Treasury (from 1869). Known for researches on alloys; invented automatic recording pyrometer (1891).

Rob·ert·son \'räb-ərt-sən\, Frederick William. 1816–1853. English Anglican clergyman. Gained reputation as earnest preacher and Broad Churchman, emphasizing not theology but principles of spiritual life; his sermons (pub. 1855–74) deeply influenced Anglican devotion.

Robertson, James. 1742–1814. American pioneer, b. Brunswick Co., Va. Led settlers to present site of Nashville, Tenn. (1870).

Robertson, Margaret. See Dame Madge KENDAL.

Robertson, Thomas William. 1829–1871. English dramatist. Brother of Dame Madge Kendal (*q.v.*). Actor, prompter, stage manager in London (from 1848); retired from stage and scored first writing success with *David Garrick* (1864). Gained fame with realistic social comedies as *Society* (1865), *Ours* (1866), *Caste* (1867), *Play* (1868), *School* (1869), *M.P.* (1870).

Robertson, William. 1721–1793. Scottish historian. Principal, U. of Edinburgh (1762); king's historiographer (1763); author of *History of Scotland 1542–1603* (1759), *History of the Reign of Emperor Charles V* (1769), which was praised by Voltaire and Gibbon and established his reputation on the Continent, and *History of America* (1777).

Robertson, Sir William Robert. 1860–1933. British soldier. Entered army (1877) and advanced through grades to field marshal (1920). During World War I, quartermaster general of British Expeditionary Force (1914), chief of the general staff of B.E.F. (1915), chief of Imperial General Staff (1915–18), commander in chief of British army on the Rhine (1919–20). Author of *From Private to Field-Marshal* (1921) and *Soldiers and Statesmen, 1914–18* (1926).

Ro·ber·val \rò-ber-vàl\, Gilles Per·sonne \per-sòn\ de *or* Per·so·nier \per-sòn-yā\ de. 1602–1675. French mathematician. Professor at Collège de France, Paris (1632–75); originated methods for constructing tangents and for determining the area of a cycloid; invented the balance which bears his name (1669).

Roberval, Jean-François de La Rocque \-là-ròk\ de. Sieur de Roberval. 1500–1561. French soldier. Named viceroy and lieutenant general of New France (1541) with Jacques Cartier (*q.v.*) as subaltern; attempted (1542–43) but failed to establish colony on lands discovered by Cartier.

Robe·son \'rōb-sən\, Paul Bustill. 1898–1976. American actor and singer, b. Princeton, N.J. Son of a former slave; All-America football player at Rutgers (1917, 1918). On stage in *Emperor Jones* (1923), *All God's Chillun* (1923), *Show Boat* (1926), *Black Boy* (1926), *Porgy* (1928), *The Hairy Ape* (1931), *Othello* (1943–44). Made first concert appearance, singing Negro spirituals, in New York City (1925); on concert tours in Europe (1926–28, 1931, 1938), America (1929), and Russia (1936). Starred or featured in films, including *Emperor Jones* (1933), *Sanders of the River* (1935), *Show Boat* (1936), and *The Proud Valley* (1940).

Ro·bes·pierre \rò-bes-pyer; *Angl* 'rōbz-,pi(ə)r, -,pye(ə)r\, Maximilien-François-Marie-Isidore de. 1758–1794. French revolutionist. Advocate at Arras (1781–89). Elected to Estates-General (1789). Acquired notoriety as a radical in Constituent Assembly (1789–91); opposed Girondists; leader in Jacobin Club (1791–92); with Pétion de Villeneuve, crowned by people of Paris as "incorruptible patriots" (1791). Not active in mob instigation and prison massacres (1792); elected first deputy from Paris to National Convention; became recognized leader of radical popular party (Montagnards). Demanded death of king (1793). Chosen member of second Committee of Public Safety (1793). For one year (1793–94) virtually prime minister of the committee. Responsible for much of the Reign of Terror; attacked Hébert; sent his friends, Desmoulins and Danton, to guillotine (1794). Inaugurated deistic worship of the Supreme Being (May–June 1794). Overthrown by Revolution of 9th Thermidor (July 27); arrested and guillotined the next day by Revolutionary Tribunal. Death ended Reign of Terror.

Ro·bey \'rō-bē\, Sir George. *Orig.* George Edward Wade \'wād\. 1869–1954. English comedian. Created many comic roles on stage, esp. in music-hall performances (from 1891); during World War I relieved London with musical comedy *The Bing Boys Are Here;* also in films, including *Don Quixote, Chu Chin Chow, Southern Roses.*

Rob·ins \'räb-ənz, 'rō-bənz\, Benjamin. 1707–1751. English mathematician and military engineer. Invented ballistic pendulum, first described in his *New Principles of Gunnery* (1742), which work laid groundwork for modern ordnance theory; made discoveries regarding rifling of gun barrels.

Rob·in·son \'räb-ən-sən\, Bill, *orig.* Luther. *Called* Bo·jan·gles \'bō-jaŋ-gəlz\. 1878–1949. American tap dancer, b. Richmond, Va. Successful dancer in nightclubs and on musical stage in New York City (1906–30, 1939 ff.); featured in films, mainly with Shirley Temple, as *The Little Colonel* (1935), *The Littlest Rebel* (1935), and *Rebecca of Sunnybrook Farm* (1937).

Robinson, Boardman. 1876–1952. American painter and illustrator, b. Somerset, N.S. Settled in New York; published political cartoons in newspapers and periodicals. Instructor in Art Students' League (1918–30); founder and director of Colorado Springs Fine Arts Center (1936–47). Painted murals in Radio City, New York City, and U.S. Department of Justice building, Washington, D.C. Coauthor with John Reed, whom he accompanied (1915) to Russia and the Balkans, of *The War in Eastern Europe* (1916).

Robinson, Charles. 1818–1894. American pioneer and politician, b. Hardwick, Mass. Leader of Free State faction in Kansas (from 1855); elected governor of the territory by this faction (1856). First governor of the state of Kansas (1861–63).

Robinson, Edward. 1794–1863. American scholar, b. Southington, Conn. Considered father of biblical geography. Professor, Andover (1830–33), Union Theol. Sem. (1837–63). Explored Palestine and Syria (1838) and published findings in *Biblical Researches in Palestine, Mount Sinai, and Arabia Petraea* (1841). Founded (1831) and edited (1831–35) *American Biblical Repository;* founded (1843) *Bibliotheca Sacra.* Compiled *A Hebrew and English Lexicon of the Old Testament* (1836), *A Greek and English Lexicon of the New Testament* (1836); also wrote *Harmony of the Four Gospels in Greek* (1845) and *Physical Geography of the Holy Land* (1865).

Robinson, Edwin Arlington. 1869–1935. American poet, b. Head Tide, Me. Best known for short dramatic poems set in a fictional New England village, Tilbury Town. His books included *The Children of the Night* (1897), *Captain Craig* (1902), *The Town Down the River* (1910), *The Man Against the Sky* (1916), *Merlin* (1917), *The Three Taverns* (1920), *Lancelot* (1920), *Avon's Harvest* (1921), *Collected Poems* (1921, Pulitzer prize), *Roman Bartholomew* (1923), *The Man Who Died Twice* (1924, Pulitzer prize), *Dionysus in Doubt* (1925), *Tristram* (1927, Pulitzer prize), *Sonnets* (1928), *Cavender's House* (1929), *The Glory of the Nightingales* (1930), *Matthias at the Door* (1931), *Nicodemus* (1932), *Talifer* (1933), *Amaranth* (1934), *King Jasper* (1935), and two plays (*Van Zorn,* 1914; *The Porcupine,* 1915).

Robinson, Frederick John. Viscount Gode·rich \ˈgōd-(ˌ)rich\ *and* 1st Earl of Rip·on \ˈrip-ən\. 1782–1859. English politician. M.P. (1806–27); president of Board of Trade (1818–23); chancellor of exchequer (1823–27); created viscount (1827); secretary for war, commissioner for Indian affairs, leader of House of Lords (1827); prime minister (1827–28); secretary for war and colonies (1830); lord privy seal (1833); created earl (1833); president of Board of Trade (1841) and of board of control for Indian affairs (1843–46).

Robinson, George Frederick Samuel. 1st Marquis and 2d Earl of Ripon. 1827–1909. English politician. Son of Frederick John Robinson. Liberal M.P. (1852–59); succeeded father as earl of Ripon and uncle as earl de Grey (1859); secretary for war (1863) and for India (1866); lord president of council in Gladstone's administration (1868–73); chairman of joint high commission on *Alabama* claims (1871); resigned as grand master of Freemasons, became a convert to Roman Catholicism (1874); governor general of India (1880–84); reversed Afghan policy of Lord Lytton; repealed restrictions on vernacular press; encouraged development of self-government; first lord of admiralty (1886); colonial secretary (1892–95); lord privy seal and Liberal leader in House of Lords (1905–08).

Robinson, Henry Crabb. 1775–1867. English journalist and diarist. Friend of Lamb, Blake, Coleridge, Wordsworth, Southey; kept a diary (35 vols.), journals (30 vols.), and letters and reminiscences (36 vols.), valuable sources of information for life of the period.

Robinson, Henry Peach. 1830–1901. English photographer. A leader of "high art" photography; known for composite photographs, or photomontages, as "Juliet with the Poison Bottle" (1857), "Fading Away" (1858), and "Autumn" (1863); his handbook *Pictorial Effect in Photography* (1869) was for many years the most influential work in English on photographic practice and aesthetics.

Robinson, Henry Wheeler. 1872–1945. English Baptist theologian and scholar. Principal of Regent's Park College (1920–42). Author of *The Christian Doctrine of Man* (1911), *The Religious Ideas of the Old Testament* (1913), *Redemption and Revelation* (1942), *Inspiration and Revelation in the Old Testament* (1946), etc.

Robinson, Sir Hercules George Robert. 1st Baron Ros·mead \ˈräz-ˌmēd\. 1824–1897. British colonial governor. Administrator in Ireland during famine (1848); governor of Hong Kong (1859–65), Ceylon (1865–72), New South Wales (1872–79), New Zealand (1879–80), Cape of Good Hope (1880–89, 1895–97); negotiated terms of peace with Boers (1881); annexed Bechuanaland (1885); gained control of Mashonaland (1888–89); negotiated release of Jameson raiders (1896).

Robinson, Jackie, *in full* John Roosevelt. 1919–1972. American baseball player, b. Cairo, Ga. First black baseball player in major leagues. Joined Brooklyn Dodgers (1947); rookie of the year (1947), most valuable player award (1949); lifetime batting average .311. Retired from baseball (1956) and entered business. Elected to Baseball Hall of Fame (1962).

Robinson, James Harvey. 1863–1936. American historian and educator, b. Bloomington, Ill. Professor, Columbia (1895–1919). Organizer of, and lecturer in, New School for Social Research, New York City (1919–21). A pioneer in new methods and content of history teaching, supplementing narratives of politics and war with a story of social, scientific, intellectual, and artistic progress. His books included *Introduction to the History of Western Europe* (1903), *The Development of Modern Europe* (with C.A. Beard, 1907), *The New History* (1911), *The Mind in the Making* (1921), *The Ordeal of Civilization* (1926), *The Human Comedy* (1937).

Robinson, John. c.1575–1625. English clergyman. Joined Separatist congregation at Scrooby, Nottinghamshire (1606 or 1607); moved with section of the exiled community to Leiden and was ordained pastor (1609); with Brewster, Bradford, and Cushman, organized Pilgrims' emigration to America and effected their removal to Plymouth, England (1620), whence they sailed in the *Mayflower;* intended to follow but died in Leiden. Author of religious tracts as *A Justification of Separation from the Church of England* (1610).

Robinson, Joseph Taylor. 1872–1937. American politician, b. Lonoke, Ark. Member, U.S. House of Representatives (1903–13); U.S. senator (1913–37) and Democratic leader in Senate (1923–37). Cosponsor of Robinson-Patman Act or Fair-Trade Agreement (1936).

Robinson, Lennox, *in full* Esmé Stuart Lennox. 1886–1958. Irish playwright and theater manager. Manager of Abbey Theatre in Dublin (1910–14, 1919–23), and director (from 1923). Author of many plays, most produced originally at Abbey Theatre, including *The Clancy Name* (1908), *Patriots* (1912), *The Whiteheaded Boy* (1916), *The Lost Leader* (1918), *The Big House* (1926), *Drama at Inish* (1933), *Church Street* (1934), and *Killycreggs in Twilight* (1937), and of autobiography *Curtain Up* (1942).

Robinson, Sir Robert. 1886–1975. English chemist. Professor at Oxford (1930–55); awarded Nobel prize for chemistry (1947) for studies in plant biology, esp. in alkaloid molecular structures.

Robinson, William. 1838–1935. British landscape designer. With Royal Botanic Society, London; exponent of the wild, or natural, garden. Author of *Wild Garden* (1870), *Alpine Flowers for English Gardens* (1870), *The English Flower Garden* (1883), etc.

Robinson, William Heath. 1872–1944. English cartoonist and illustrator. Best known for humorous cartoons featuring fantastic machinery, published in U.S. and English periodicals and collected in *Absurdities* (1934).

Ro·bi·quet \rō-bē-ke\, Pierre-Jean. 1780–1840. French chemist. Professor, École de Pharmacie (1811–24). With Vauquelin, discovered asparagine (1806); discovered narcotine (1817) and codeine in opium (1832); discovered caffeine (1821, independently of Pelletier and others); with Boutron-Charlard discovered amygdalin (1830).

Rob Roy. See (1) Robert MacGregor; (2) John MacGregor.

Robson, Eleanor Elise. See Eleanor Belmont.

Rob·son \ˈrōb-sən, ˈräb-\, May. *Orig.* Mary Jeanette Rob·i·son \ˈräb-ə-sən\. 1858–1942. American actress, b. Wagga Wagga, Australia. To U.S. (c.1874). Successful in comic roles on New York stage (from 1883); in films (from 1911), esp. *Dinner at Eight* (1933), *Lady for a Day* (1933), and *Bringing Up Baby* (1938).

Ro·bus·ti \rō-ˈbü-stē\, Jacopo. *Known as* Tin·to·ret·to \ˌtēn-tō-ˈrāt-tō\. c.1518–1594. Italian painter. One of greatest Mannerist painters of the Venetian school. Influenced by Michelangelo's design and Titian's coloring, later by Veronese. His religious, mythological, and historical paintings included *Christ and the Adulteress* (c.1547), *S. Rocco Among the Plague-Stricken* (1549), *Susanna Bathing* (c.1550), *St. George and the Dragon* (c.1550), *The Finding of Moses* (1555), wall and ceiling paintings for Scuola Grande di S. Rocco, Venice (1564–81), *Crucifixion* (1565), allegorical paintings for Doges' Palace, Venice (1581), *Last Supper* (1594); also portaits, as *Self-Portrait* (c.1546), *Woman in Black* (c.1553), *Jacopo Sansovino* (c.1556). His daughter ¶Marietta (1560–1590), *called* La Tintoretta, and his son ¶Domenico (1565–1637), *called* Tintoretto the Younger, were also painters.

Ro·ca \ˈrō-kä\, Julio Argentino. 1843–1914. Argentine general and politician. President of Argentina (1880–86, 1898–1904).

Ro·ca·fuer·te \rō-kä-ˈfwer-tā\, Vicente. 1783–1847. Ecuadorian politician. President of Ecuador (1835–39).

Roch \rōk\. Saint. *Lat.* Ro·chus \ˈrōk-əs\. c.1350–c.1379. French healer. Devoted himself to tending the sick and plague-stricken; known for gift of healing.

Rochambeau, Comte de. See Jean de Vimeur.

Rochas, Alphonse-Eugène Beau de. See Beau de Rochas.

Roche, Mazo de la. See de la Roche.

Roche·chou·art de Mor·te·mart \rōsh-wär-də-mȯr-tə-mär\, Françoise-Athénaïs. Marquise de Mon·tes·pan \mōⁿ-tes-päⁿ\. 1641–1707. French courtier. Daughter of marquis de Mortemart; m. (1663) marquis de Montespan; lady-in-waiting to Marie-Thérèse (1664); mistress of Louis XIV (1667–80), bearing him 6 children later legitimated; not implicated in but her position weakened by Affair of the Poisons (1679); retired to convent of Saint-Joseph (1691).

Roche·fort \rōsh-fȯr\, Henri, *in full* Victor-Henri. Marquis de Rochefort-Lu·cay \-lüē-sā\. 1830–1913. French journalist. Founded and edited *La Lanterne* (1868), *L'Intransigeant* (1880–1907), and *La Patrie* (1907 ff.). In politics, attacked empire of Napoléon III; supported Paris Commune (1871) and was banished (1873); returned after amnesty (1880). Turned to support extreme right causes, as Boulangism (1889) and against Dreyfus.

Rochefoucauld, François de la. See La Rochefoucauld.

Rochemont, Charles Pictet de. See Pictet de Rochemont.

Rochester, Earl of. See (1) Lawrence Hyde; (2) John Wilmot.

Rochester, Viscount. See Robert Carr.

Roch·es·ter \'räch-ə-stər, -ˌes-ter\, Nathaniel. 1752–1831. American pioneer, b. Westmoreland Co., Va. Purchased land (1800) in Genesee region of upper New York state and founded the city of Rochester (1811).

Rochus, Saint. See ROCH.

Rock \'räk\, John. 1890–1984. American obstetrician-gynecologist, b. Marlboro, Mass. Founder and director (1926–56) of fertility clinic, Brookline, Mass.; clinical professor of gynecology, Harvard U. (1947–56); director of Rock Reproductive Clinic, Brookline (1956 ff.). With Miriam Menkin achieved (1944) first successful fertilization of a human ovum in vitro; with Gregory Pincus and M.C. Chang developed first effective oral contraceptive ("the Pill"), which once marketed (1960) revolutionized sexual mores, population control, and status of women; a devout Roman Catholic, he failed to persuade the Church to reverse its stand on birth control. Author of *The Time Has Come* (1963).

Rocke·fel·ler \'räk-(i-)ˌfel-ər\, John Davison. 1839–1937. American industrialist and philanthropist, b. Richford, N.Y. Moved to Cleveland, Ohio (1853). In oil refining business (from 1863). Organized Standard Oil Co. (1870) and became its president; gained monopoly of oil business. Organized Standard Oil trust (1881), dissolved by court decree (1892); organized Standard Oil Co. of New Jersey (1899; dissolved by Supreme Court order, 1911). Remained dominant in oil business until his retirement (1911). Established Rockefeller Institute for Medical Research (1901), General Education Board (1902), Rockefeller Foundation (1913), Laura Spelman Rockefeller Memorial Foundation (1918), each of which he endowed with large amounts; principal benefactor of U. of Chicago (1891 ff.). His son ¶John Davison, Jr. (1874–1960) became associated with his father's business interests (1897) and later philanthropic corporations; planned and built Rockefeller Center in New York City; restored colonial Williamsburg, Va. His son ¶John Davison III (1906–1978) also associated with Rockefeller interests.

Rockefeller, Nelson Aldrich. 1908–1979. American politician, b. Bar Harbor, Me. Son of John D. Rockefeller, Jr. U.S. assistant secretary of state (1944–45); chairman, International Development Advisory Board of Point Four program (1950–51); undersecretary of Health, Education, and Welfare (1953–54). Governor of New York (1958–73). U.S. vice president (1974–77).

Rock·hill \'räk-ˌhil\, William Woodville. 1854–1914. American diplomat, b. Philadelphia. U.S. secretary of legation, Peking, China (1884–86); chargé d'affaires, Seoul, Korea (1886–87). Made two expeditions into Mongolia and Tibet under auspices of Smithsonian Institution (1888–89, 1891–92). Assistant secretary of state (1894–97); minister to Greece, Romania, and Serbia (1897–99); special agent in China after Boxer rebellion (1900); minister to China (1905–09); ambassador to Russia (1909–11) and Turkey (1911–13).

Rockingham, 2d Marquis of. See Charles WATSON-WENTWORTH.

Rock·ne \'räk-nē\, Knute Kenneth. 1888–1931. American football coach, b. Voss, Norway. To U.S. (1893) and settled in Chicago. Captain, Notre Dome football team (1913); assistant coach (1914–18); head coach (1918–31). Built Notre Dame into a national collegiate football power; instituted substitution of entire teams during games; coaching record 105 wins, 12 losses, 5 ties.

Rock·well \'räk-ˌwel, -wəl\, Norman. 1894–1978. American painter and illustrator, b. New York City. Known for his American genre paintings, as the *Four Freedoms* (1943), many appearing as *Saturday Evening Post* covers.

Rod \ròd\, Édouard. 1857–1910. Swiss novelist. Resident many years in Paris; Author of pessimistic, psychological novels, including *La Course à la mort* (1885), *Le Sens de la vie* (1889), *Le Ménage de pasteur Nandié* (1898), *Nouvelles romandes* (1890), *La Vie privée de Michel Teissier* (1893), *Le Silence* (1894), *L'Inutile effort* (1903); also critical works as *De la littérature comparée* (1886) and *Reflets d'Amérique* (1905).

Rod·ber·tus \rōt-'ber-tu̇s\, Johann Karl. 1805–1875. German economist and politician. Leader of Left Center in Prussian assembly (1848); a founder of German Socialism; advocated government regulation of wages so that they might rise in proportion to increases in national productivity.

Ro·de \'rō-thə\, Helge. 1870–1937. Danish poet, dramatist, novelist, and literary critic. Leader of an anti-rationalist movement opposing materialism and Darwinism, and championing a modern mysticism; chief critical works *Regenerationem i vort aandsliv* (1923) and *Det sjaelelige gennembrud* (1928).

Rode \ròd\, Pierre, *in full* Jacques-Pierre-Joseph. 1774–1830. French violinist. Professor, Paris Conservatory (1795–1803); violinist to Czar Alexander I (1804–08); Beethoven wrote expressly for him Opus 50 for violin and orchestra. Composer of many violin pieces, including a series of 24 caprices.

Ro·den·bach \'rō-dən-ˌbäk\, Albrecht. 1856–1880. Flemish writer. A leader of the Flemish literary revival movement *Blauwvoeterie.* Author of a romantic nationalistic drama *Gudrun* (1882) and poems *Eerste Gedichten* (1878).

Rod·er·ick \'räd-ər-ik, 'räd-rik\. *Span.* Ro·dri·go \rōth-'rē-gō\. d. 711 A.D. Last king of the Visigoths in Spain (710–711). Defeated, and probably slain, by the Muslims under Ṭāriq ibn Ziyād in the battle of Río Barbate.

Roderic O'Connor. See O'CONNOR.

Rod·gers \'räj-ərz\. Name of a family celebrated in American naval history, including: John Rodgers (1773–1838), captain (1799); in Mediterranean, engaged with Barbary pirates (1802–06); ranking officer in active service in War of 1812; head, Board of Naval Commissioners (1815–24, 1827–37); secretary of the navy (1823). His brother ¶George Washington (1787–1832) served through War of 1812; in Mediterranean (1816–19) and New York navy yard (1819–25). John's son ¶John (1812–1882), with North Pacific Exploring and Surveying Expedition (1852–56); aide to Admiral Du Pont at battle of Port Royal (1861); commanded flagship of fleet operating on James River (1862); engaged in attack on Fort Sumter (1863) and later captured Confederate ironclad *Atlanta;* rear admiral commanding Asiatic squadron (1870–72). ¶William Ledyard (1860–1944), son of John (1812–1882), held command in Atlantic fleet in World War I (1916–18); commanded Asiatic fleet (1918–19); retired as rear admiral (1924). A great-grandson of John (1773–1838) ¶John (1881–1926) served in World War I; commanded naval air station, Pearl Harbor, Hawaii (1922–25). George's son ¶Christopher Raymond Perry (1819–1892) served in Seminole War (1839–42) and Mexican War (1846–48); commanded flagship of Admiral Du Pont in attack on Port Royal (1861); fleet captain, South Atlantic blockading squadron (1862–63); engaged in attack on Charleston (1863); rear admiral (1874); superintendent, U.S. Naval Academy (1874–78); commander in chief, Pacific squadron (1878–80). Christopher's brother ¶George Washington (1822–1863) served in Mexican War (1846–48).

Rodgers, Jimmie, *in full* James Charles. *Nicknamed* the Singing Brakeman. 1897–1933. American singer and composer, b. Meridian, Miss. One of greatest country and western singers. Retired as railroad brakeman (1924) because of tuberculosis; recorded (1927–33) over 100 songs, including "In the Jailhouse Now," "Waiting for a Train," "The Brakeman's Blues," and 13 "Blue Yodels," esp. Nos. 1 ("T for Texas") and 8 ("Mule Skinner Blues").

Rodgers, Richard. 1902–1979. American composer, b. New York City. Collaborated with lyricist Lorenz Hart in writing musical comedies as *The Garrick Gaieties* (1925, including songs "Manhattan" and "Sentimental Me"), *On Your Toes* (1936), *Babes in Arms* (1937, "Where or When," "The Lady Is a Tramp," "My Funny Valentine"), *The Boys from Syracuse* (1938, "Falling in Love with Love"), *Pal Joey* (1940, "Bewitched, Bothered, and Bewildered"); with lyricist Oscar Hammerstein II on *Oklahoma!* (1943, Pulitzer prize; "Oh, What a Beautiful Morning," "The Surrey with the Fringe on Top," "People Will Say We're in Love"), *Carousel* (1945, "You'll Never Walk Alone"), *South Pacific* (1949, Pulitzer prize; "Younger Than Springtime," "Some Enchanted Evening," "I'm Gonna Wash That Man Right Outa My Hair"), *The King and I* (1951, "Getting to Know You," "Hello, Young Lovers"), *The Flower Drum Song* (1958), *The Sound of Music* (1959, " My Favorite Things," "Climb Every Mountain"); wrote music for documentary film *Victory at Sea* (1952).

Ro·din \rò-daⁿ, *Angl* 'rō-ˌdaⁿ(n)\, Auguste, *in full* François-Auguste-René. 1840–1917. French sculptor. First exhibited at the Paris Salon (1877) *L'Âge d'Airain,* which raised a storm of criticism for its realism. Commissioned (1880) to make *La Porte de l'Enfer,* bronze door for Musée des Arts Decoratif, Paris; never finished *La Porte* but it provided designs for *Le Penseur* (1880), *Le Baiser* (1886), etc. Other works included *St. Jean-Baptiste prêchant* (1878), *Les Bourgeois de Calais* (1884–86), monuments to Balzac (1893) and Victor Hugo (1897), portrait busts of Carrier-Belleuse, Victor Hugo, Proust, Bernard Shaw, Mahler, Clemenceau, and others.

Rod·man \'räd-mən\, Thomas Jackson. 1815–1871. American army officer, b. near Salem, Ind. Served in ordnance department (from 1841); invented (by 1847) Rodman gun, made by casting successive layers of metal around a hollow core; invented prismatic and perforated-cake gunpowder that burned evenly.

Rod·ney \'räd-nē\, Caesar. 1728–1784. American Revolutionary patriot, b. Dover, Del. Delegate to Stamp Act Congress (1765). Member of Continental Congress (1774–76, 1777, 1778), and signer of Declaration of Independence. Major general in Delaware militia in American Revolution. President of Delaware (1778–82). His brother ¶Thomas (1744–1811) was colonel in Delaware militia in Revolution, engaged at Trenton and Princeton; member, Continental Congress (1781–83, 1785–87); U.S. judge, Territory of Mississippi (1803–11). Thomas's son ¶Caesar Augustus (1772–1824) was member of U.S. House of Representatives (1803–05) and supporter of Jefferson; U.S. attorney general (1807–11); first U.S. minister to Argentina (1823–24).

Rodney, George Brydges. 1st Baron Rodney. 1718–1792. English admiral. Governor of Newfoundland (1749–52); M.P. (1751); reduced Martinique and took St. Lucia, Grenada, St. Vincent (1762); commander in chief at Jamaica (1771–74) and Leeward Islands (1779); admiral (1778); captured Spanish convoy off Cape Finisterre (1780), and off Cape St. Vincent took seven ships out of eleven (1780); seized Dutch settlements in West Indies (1781); captured seven ships and de Grasse himself in brilliant victory off Dominica (Apr. 12, 1782); raised to peerage, pensioned, lived in retirement.

Ro·dó \rō-'t͟hō\, José Enrique. 1872–1917. Uruguayan philosopher and essayist. Professor, Montevideo (from 1898). Advocated a unified Spanish America; warned against materialism. His books of essays included *Ariel* (1900), *Motivos de Proteo* (1908), and *El mirador de Próspero* (1913).

Rodolphe. See RUDOLF.

Ro·dri·gues Al·ves \rü-'t͟hrē-gēs-'äl-vēs\, Francisco de Paula. 1848–1919. Brazilian politician. President of São Paulo (1900–02, 1912–16). President of Brazil (1902–06); extensively rebuilt Rio de Janeiro and eliminated yellow fever there; settled border disputes. Elected president again (1918) but did not serve because of sickness.

Rodrigues Lo·bo \-'lō-bü\, Francisco. *Called* the Portuguese Theocritus. 1580–1622. Portuguese writer. Author of *Romances* (1596, ballads), *Églogas* (1605, pastoral eclogues), *O condestabre de Portugal* (1609, epic on Álvares Pereira), *Côrte na aldeia* (1619, prose dialogues), *La Jornada* (1623, verse), and a trilogy of pastoral novels *Primavera* (1601), *O pastor peregrino* (1608), and *O desencantado* (1614).

Ro·drí·guez \rōt͟h-'rē-gās\, Abelardo Luis. 1889–1967. Mexican general and politician. Provisional president of Mexico (1932–34) on Ortiz Rubio's resignation; governor of Sonora (1943–47).

Ro·drí·guez \rōth-'rē-gāth\, Lorenzo. c.1704–1774. Spanish architect. Designed in late Baroque or Churriqueresque style the Sagrario of the cathedral of Mexico (1749) and the Balvanera chapel of the church of San Francisco (c.1770), both in Mexico City.

Rodríguez, Ventura. 1717–1785. Spanish architect. His earlier works, as church of San Marcos in Madrid (1749–53), were in late Baroque style; later designs, as the facade for cathedral of Pamplona (1783), were Neoclassical.

Rodríguez Cam·po·ma·nes y Pe·rez \-käm-pō-'män-ā-sē-'pā-rāth\, Pedro. Conde de Campomanes. 1723–1802. Spanish politician and economist. Director, Royal Acad. of History (1764–91, 1798–1803). Adviser to government of Charles III, esp. on economic affairs; author of economic works, esp. *Discurso sobre el fomento de la industria popular* (1774).

Rodríguez de Fon·se·ca \-t͟hā-fōn-'sā-kä\, Juan. 1451–1524. Spanish prelate. Principal chaplain to Isabella I, later to Ferdinand. Head of department of affairs in the Indies (1493 ff.); enemy of Columbus; sent Bobadilla to New World to investigate Columbus's administration; later opposed Cortés; organized Council of the Indies with himself as chief (1511).

Rodríguez de Mon·tal·vo \-mōn-'täl-b͟ō\, Garci. *Sometimes erroneously called* Garci Ordoñez de Montalvo. 16th century. Spanish novelist. Author of chivalric romance *Amadís de Gaula* (1508) and sequel *Las sergas de Esplandián* (1510).

Ro·drí·guez Gal·ván \rōt͟h-'rē-gas-gäl-'b͟än\, Ignacio. 1816–1842. Mexican poet. Author of Romantic works as poem "La Profecía de Guatimoc" and historical plays *La capilla, Muñoz,* and *El privado del virrey.*

Ro·drí·guez Ma·rín \rōt͟h-'rē-gāth-mä-'rēn\, Francisco. 1855–1943. Spanish scholar. Known esp. as a Cervantes scholar; author of numerous lexicographic and critical works and of several editions of *Don Quixote.*

Rodríguez Sán·chez \-'sän-chāth\, Manuel Laureano. *Known as* Ma·no·le·te \män-ō-'lā-tā\. 1917–1947. Spanish bullfighter. One of the greatest bullfighters in Spain; noted for extreme economy of movement and dispassionate demeanor; gored to death in ring.

Roe \'rō\, Sir Edwin Alliott Verdon. 1877–1958. English aircraft manufacturer. First Englishman to build and fly an airplane (June 8, 1908); with brother ¶Humphrey Verdon (1878–1949) founded (1910) A.V. Roe and Co., manufacturer of Avro aircraft; founder and president (from 1928), Sanders-Roe, Ltd., flying boat manufacturer.

Roe, Sir Thomas. 1581?–1644. English diplomat. Won reputation by successful mission to court of Mughal emperor Jāhāngir at Agra to gain commercial treaty (1615–18); secured further privileges for English merchants as ambassador to Ottoman Empire (1621–28); took part in peace conferences at Hamburg (1638), Ratisbon (1641), and Vienna (1642); privy councilor (1640); M.P. (1640–43); left diplomatic memoirs.

Roeb·ling \'rō-bliŋ, *Ger* 'rœb-liŋ\, John Augustus. 1806–1869. American engineer and industrialist, b. Mühlhausen, Germany. To U.S. (1831, naturalized 1837). Established factory manufacturing first wire rope made in America (1841). Designed suspension bridges, including one over Niagara River at Niagara Falls (opened 1855), over Ohio River between Cincinnati and Covington (opened 1867); suggested and made preliminary plans for Brooklyn Bridge (plans approved, 1869). His son ¶Washington Augustus (1837–1926) associated with him (from 1857); served in Union army through Civil War; succeeded father as chief engineer in construction of Brooklyn Bridge (1869) and carried it to completion (1883).

Roe·buck \'rō-bək\, John. 1718–1794. English physician and inventor. Introduced leaden condensing chambers in manufacture of sulfuric acid (1746); set up vitriol works at Prestonpans (1749) and ironworks at Carron (1759), later famous for production of ordnance; patented (1762) process of converting cast iron into malleable iron by use of pit coal with artificial blast; subsidized steam engine experiments of James Watt (from 1765).

Roe·mer \'rœ-mər\, Friedrich Adolf. 1809–1869. German geologist. Teacher and director (1862–67), school of mining at Clausthal; authority on paleontology of the mountains of northwestern Germany. His brother ¶Ferdinand (1818–1891) was professor at Breslau (1855–91); investigated and wrote on the geology of Texas, Tennessee, and Silesia.

Roent·gen \'rœnt-gən\, Abraham. 1711–1793. German cabinetmaker. Learned marquetry, joinery, etc. in London (1731–38); opened workshop at Neuwied (1750) that became famous for Rococo furniture, clocks, music boxes, and mechanical toys. His son ¶David (1743–1807) succeeded him as head of workshop (1772); opened salon in Paris (1774); cabinetmaker to Marie-Antoinette (1780); also sold furniture to Catherine the Great and Frederick William II of Prussia; salon and workshop destroyed by French armies (1795). Expert in marquetry, metal mountings, and hidden mechanical devices.

Roentgen, Wilhelm Conrad. See RÖNTGEN.

Roe·rich \'rœ-rik, *Angl* 'rər-ik, 're(ə)r-\, Nikolay Konstantinovich. 1874–1947. Russian painter. Made several archaeological expeditions to Far East; landscape painter; known esp. for designing monumental historical sets for Diaghilev's Ballets Russes.

Roeth·ke \'ret(h)-kē\, Theodore. 1908–1963. American poet, b. Saginaw, Mich. Taught at Lafayette Coll. (1931–35), Penn. State U. (1936–43), Bennington Coll. (1943–47), U. of Washington (1947–63). Author of volumes of lyrical poems *Open House* (1941), *The Lost Son* (1948), *Praise to the End* (1951), *The Waking* (1953, Pulitzer prize), *Words for the Wind* (1957), *I Am! Says the Lamb* (1961), and *The Far Field* (1964); essays and lectures collected in *On the Poet and His Craft* (1965).

Rog·er \'räj-ər, *Fr* rō-zhā\. d. 1119. Prince of Antioch (1112–1119). Norman crusader; succeeded his uncle Tancred as prince; forestalled Turkish attempt to reconquer Syria by victory at Battle of Danith (1115); defeated and killed at Battle of the Field of Blood at Aleppo.

Roger. *Also known as* Roger Bor·sa \-'bōr-sä\. c.1060–1111. Duke of Apulia (1085–1111). Son of Robert Guiscard, half-brother of Bohemond I, and nephew of Roger I of Sicily and Gisulf II of Salerno. Aided his father in capture of Corfu (1083); at instigation of his mother Sichelgaita, sister of Gisulf, named heir to father's lands and title; quarrelled with Bohemund, who seized part of father's territory; a weak ruler who lost most of his duchy.

Roger. Name of two Norman rulers of Sicily:

Roger I. 1031–1101. To Italy (1057). Aided his brother Robert Guiscard, capturing Calabria (1060), Messina (1061), Palermo (1072), Catania, Girgenti, etc.; assumed title count of Sicily (1072); captured island of Malta from the Saracens (1090).

Roger II. 1095–1154. Son of Roger I. Succeeded elder brother Simon as count of Sicily (1105–30); acquired duchies of Calabria (1122) and Apulia (1127). King of Sicily (1130–54); waged successful war upon the Byzantine emperor Manuel Comnenus, pillaging cities on the Greek peninsula and capturing territory along the North African coast; established a civil service; made his court at Palermo a center of learning.

Roger of Helmarshausen. See THEOPHILUS (12th century).

Roger of Hove·den \'hǎv-dən\ *or* How·den \'hau̇d-ᵊn\. d. c.1201. English chronicler. Administered forest law and collected royal revenue for Henry II (1174–89); accompanied Richard I on crusade to Holy Land. Compiled *Chronica* covering period 649 to 1201 (1192–1201 is original, rest based on other chronicles), a valuable source of information, esp. on quarrel between Henry II and Thomas Becket.

Roger of Pont l'É·vêque \pōⁿ-lā-vek\. d. 1181. Norman-born prelate in England. Archdeacon of Canterbury (1148); chaplain to King Stephen; archbishop of York (1154). Supported Henry II in quarrel with Thomas Becket; defied papal prohibition to crown (1170) Henry II's son Henry and was suspended by Becket; accused but absolved of urging Becket's assassination.

Roger of Salis·bury \'sȯlz-ˌber-ē, -b(ə-)rē\. d. 1139. English prelate and politician. Chancellor under Henry I (1100–35); bishop of Salisbury (1101); remodeled administrative system of secular government; created exchequer system, the management of which was kept in his family for over a century; justiciar of England, next in power to king; ruled in Henry I's absence. Went over to Stephen, taking royal treasure and administrative system (1135); excited enmity of barons by avarice and acquisition of castles; forced to surrender castles and power (1139).

Roger of Wen·do·ver \'wen-ˌdō-vər\. d. 1236. English chronicler. Benedictine monk, St. Albans; in scriptorium at St. Albans compiled *Flores historiarum,* extending from creation to 1235, valuable from 1202 as firsthand authority.

Roger-Bernard I. Comte de Foix. See FOIX.

Ro·ger de Bul·ly \rō-zhā-də-bü̅e-lē\, Édouard. *Pseudonym* Roger de Beau·voir \bōv-wår\. 1809–1866. French writer. Author of verse *La Cape et l'épée,* novels *Écolier de Cluny, ou le sophisme* (1832; probably inspired Dumas père's

La Tour de Nesle), Le Chevalier de Saint-Georges (1840), dramas *Un Dieu du jour* (1850), *Les Enfers de Paris* (1853); etc.

Roger de Flor. See FLOR.

Ro·ger-Du·casse \rō-zhä-dæ-käs\, Jean-Jules-Aimable. 1873–1954. French composer. Known esp. for symphonic works as *Au Jardin de Marguerite* (1901–05), *Sarabande* (1911), *Nocturne de printemps* (1920); also a comic opera *Cantegril* (1931), motets, piano and string quartets, and piano pieces.

Rog·ers \'räj-ərz\, Bruce. 1870–1957. American printer and book designer, b. Lafayette, Ind. On staff, Riverside Press, Cambridge, Mass. (1895–1912). Printing adviser, Cambridge University Press (1917–19) and Harvard U. Press (1920–34). Designed Montaigne (1901) and Centaur (1915) typefaces.

Rogers, Carl Ransom. 1902–1987. American psychologist, b. Oak Park, Ill. Professor of psychology at various universities (1940–63). Resident fellow at Western Behavioral Science Inst. (1964–68) and Center for Studies of the Person (1968–87), La Jolla, Calif. Founded humanistic psychology; originated the non-directive, or client-centered, approach to psychotherapy; stressed importance of a personal relationship between therapist and client; pioneered encounter group technique. Writings included *Counseling and Psychotherapy* (1942), *Client-Centered Therapy* (1951), *Psychotherapy and Personality Change* (1954), and *On Becoming a Person* (1961).

Rogers, Edith, *nee* Nourse \'nərs\. 1881–1960. American politician, b. Saco, Me. m. (1907) John J. Rogers (d. 1925). Presidential representative to visit military and veterans' hospitals (1922–23, 1929). Member from Mass., U.S. House of Representatives (1925–60); first congresswoman from New England; introduced legislation that created Women's Army Corps (1942).

Rogers, Henry Darwin. 1808–1866. American geologist, b. Philadelphia. Foremost structural geologist of his time. Director, Geological Survey of New Jersey (1835–38) and Pennsylvania (1836–42); published findings of latter survey in *Report on Pennsylvania* (1858), an important contribution to theory of mountain building; professor at Glasgow, Scotland (1857–66). His brother ¶William Barton (1804–1882) also a geologist; aided Henry in geographical surveys and with him wrote *On the Physical Structure of the Appalachian Chain* (1842); instrumental in establishment of Massachusetts Inst. of Technology and its first president (1862–70, 1878–81); charter member (1863) and president (1878–82), National Academy of Sciences. Their brothers ¶James Blythe (1802–1852) and ¶Robert Empie (1813–1884) were chemists and educators and published *A Text Book on Chemistry* (1846).

Rogers, Henry Huttleston. 1840–1909. American financier, b. Mattapoisett, Mass. In oil business in Pennsylvania (1861); devised and patented (1871) machinery for separating naphtha from crude oil. Joined Standard Oil Co. (1874); originated idea of pipeline transportation; chief executive officer of Standard Oil interests. Friend and later financial manager of Mark Twain.

Rogers, James Blythe. See under Henry D. ROGERS.

Rogers, John. c.1500–1555. English Protestant reformer. In Antwerp and Wittenberg (1534–48); combined English translations of Old Testament by Tyndale and Coverdale, added Tyndale's New Testament and published complete Bible under pseudonym Thomas Mat·thew \'math-ˌyü\ (1537). Prebendary of St. Pauls (1551). Preached, on accession of Mary, an anti-Catholic sermon; imprisoned in Newgate by order of bishop of London; sentenced to death as heretic by Gardiner for denying Christian character of Roman Catholic church and the doctrine of transubstantiation.

Rogers, John. 1648–1721. American religious leader, b. Milford, Conn. Founder of the Rogerenes, a sect advocating pacifism and total separation of church and state and opposing a salaried clergy, formal prayers, and use of medicine; often persecuted and imprisoned for his beliefs.

Rogers, John. 1829–1904. American sculptor, b. Salem, Mass. Successful with *The Slave Auction,* exhibited in New York (1859–60). Best known for statuette groups illustrating Civil War scenes, literary and dramatic figures, and scenes from country life, as *Charity Patient, Coming to the Parson, Fetching the Doctor;* sculpted statue of Abraham Lincoln in Manchester, N.H.

Rogers, Mary Joseph, *orig.* Mary Josephine. 1882–1955. American religious, b. Boston. Founded (1912) at Hawthorne, N.Y., a lay group which developed into the Maryknoll Sisters of St. Dominic (approved by pope as diocesan religious congregation, 1920); superior general (1920–46); established many centers for training Maryknoll sisters for foreign missionary work.

Rogers, Moses. 1779–1821. American mariner, b. New London, Conn. Commanded steamer *Phoenix* on its initial trip around Sandy Hook and Cape May to the Delaware River (1809), first ocean voyage of a steamship; commanded steamer *Savannah* on first transatlantic voyage (1819).

Rogers, Robert. 1731–1795. American frontier soldier, b. Methuen, Mass. Headed Roger's Rangers, who adopted Indian fighting techniques in French and Indian War and Pontiac's War. At outbreak of Revolutionary War, negotiated with both British and Continentals; imprisoned by Washington on suspicion of espionage (1776); escaped and organized royalist force, the Queen's Rangers; defeated near White Plains, N.Y. Fled to England (1780).

Rogers, Robert Empie. See under Henry D. ROGERS.

Rogers, Samuel. 1763–1855. English poet. Published (1792) *The Pleasures of Memory,* on which his poetical reputation is based. Patron of artists and men of letters; friend of Edmund Burke, Wordsworth, Scott, and Byron; kept notebook of conversations, published as *Recollections of the Table-Talk of Samuel Rogers* (1856). Declined laureateship on Wordsworth's death.

Rogers, Will, *in full* William Penn Adair. 1879–1935. American actor and humorist, b. Oologah, Indian Territory (now Oklahoma). Rope artist with various Wild West and vaudeville shows (from 1902); developed successful accompanying monologue employing homespun humor and delivered in offhand manner; made New York appearance (1905). Associated with Ziegfeld Follies (from 1915). Starred in motion pictures as *A Connecticut Yankee* (1931), *State Fair* (1933), *David Harum* (1934). Wrote syndicated newspaper column in *New York Times* (weekly from 1922, daily from 1926). Killed in airplane crash with Wiley Post (*q.v.*). Author of *The Cowboy Philosopher on Prohibition* (1919), *Will Rogers's Political Follies* (1929), etc.

Rogers, William. *Called* Hang-Theology Rogers. 1819–1896. English educational reformer. Curate of St. Thomas', Charterhouse, London (1845–63); founded schools for poor children; rector of St. Botolph's, Bishopsgate (from 1863); advocated secular education; to accusations of promoting "godless education," replied "Hang theology; let us begin," thus earning nickname.

Rogers, William Barton. See under Henry D. ROGERS.

Rogers, Woodes. 1679?–1732. English seaman and colonial governor. Commander of privateering expedition against Spaniards in South Seas (1708–11); rescued Alexander Selkirk from Más a Tierra Island off coast of Chile (1709); published *A Cruising Voyage round the World* (1712). Rented Bahama Islands from lords proprietors and was commissioned governor (1718–21, 1729–32); suppressed piracy.

Ro·get \rō-'zhā, 'rō-ˌ\, Peter Mark. 1779–1869. English physician and scholar. Member of Royal Society (from 1815); instrumental in establishing U. of London; author of *Thesaurus of English Words and Phrases* (1852), which reached 28th edition during his lifetime.

Ro·gier \rōzh-yā\, Charles Latour. 1800–1885. Belgian politician. Helped found journal *Mathieu Laensbergh* which advocated Belgian patriotism (1824); a leader of Belgian Revolution of 1830; a principal member of the provisional government; arranged armistice with Dutch government. Foremost Liberal leader; minister of the interior (1832–34); sponsored national railway bill. Prime minister (1847–52, 1857–67); responsible for electoral reform law (1848), creation of secular school system (1850), and settling Scheldt Question, freeing Antwerp's maritime commerce (1863).

Ro·han \rō-äⁿ\. Name of a noble family of France derived from that of a small town in Morbihan, Brittany. The family claimed connection with early kings of Brittany and after the 15th century developed many branches, esp. the seigneurs of Gié, the princes of Soubise and Guéménée, and the dukes of Rohan-Chabot and Montbazon. The Rohan family included: Pierre de Rohan (1451–1513), seigneur de Gié \zhā\; marshal of France (1475); prevented Queen Anne from reoccupying her duchy of Brittany during illness of King Louis XII (1503); acquitted of criminal charges (1504–06) but had to retire from public life. His descendant ¶René (1550–1586) led a Calvinist army (1570) and defended Lusignan against Catholics (1574–75). His son ¶Henri (1579–1638), duc de Rohan (from 1603), led Huguenots in Bearnese revolts (1622, 1625–26, 1627–29); commanded French expedition against Habsburg forces at Valtellina (1635–36) and later served against Habsburgs in Germany; wrote *Mémoires* and a military treatise *Le Parfait Capitaine* (1636). Henri's brother ¶Benjamin (1583–1642), seigneur de Sou·bise \-də-sü-bēz\; Protestant leader in Huguenot wars (1621–29); unsuccessfully defended La Rochelle against Richelieu (1627–28); died in England.

¶Hercule (1568–1654), duc de Mont·ba·zon \-mōⁿ-bä-zōⁿ\, fought under Henry III and Henry IV against the Holy League; made governor of Paris. His daughter ¶Marie de Rohan-Montbazon (1600–1679), duchesse de Chev·reuse \-shəv-rœz\, m. duc de Lynes (1617; d. 1621), then Claude de Lorraine, duc de Chevreuse (1625); household superintendent of Louis XIII's queen, Anne of Austria (1618); unsuccessfully attempted to provoke a liaison between Anne and George Villiers, Duke of Buckingham (1625); exiled to Poitou and Lorraine for plot against Richelieu (1626–28); twice exiled for betraying French secrets to Spain (1633, 1637–43); intrigued against Mazarin (from 1643) but reconciled to him after breaking with the prince de Condé (1651); retired to Dampierre (1652).

¶Charles (1715–1787), prince de Soubise; in command during Seven Years' War; defeated at Rossbach (1757); won battles of Sondershausen and Lutterberg (1758); marshal of France (1758); retired (1763); prominent in court of Louis XVI. ¶Louis-René-Édouard (1734–1803), prince de Rohan; cardinal (1778); bishop of Strasbourg (1779–1801). Involved in the Affair of the Diamond Necklace (1785), in which he was duped into purchasing a necklace for Marie-Antoinette without her authority; tried and acquitted of fraud; exiled from court (1786), thus becoming a martyr of queen's enemies.

Roh·de \'rō-thə\, Ruth, *nee* Bry·an \'brī-ən\. 1885–1954. American diplomat, b. Jacksonville, Ill. Daughter of William Jennings Bryan; m. 1st Reginald Owen (1910; d. 1927), 2d Börge Rohde (1936). Member from Florida, U.S. House of Representatives (1929–33), first congresswoman from Deep South. U.S. minister to Denmark (1933–36), first U.S. woman diplomat.

Ró·he·im \'rō-he-im\, Géza. 1891–1953. Hungarian psychoanalyst. Professor at Budapest (1932–38); joined Worcester, Mass., State Hospital as analyst (1938); in private practice and lecturer at New York Psychoanalytic Inst. (from 1940). First to apply psychoanalytic approach in interpreting culture, esp. to tribes of Australia, New Guinea, and southwestern U.S. Works included *Australian Totemism* (1925), *Animism, Magic, and the Divine King* (1930), *The Origin and Function of Culture* (1943), *Psychoanalysis and Anthropology* (1950), *The Gates of the Dream* (1952), and *Magic and Schizophrenia* (1955).

Rohlfs \'rōlfs\, Charles. 1853–1936. American designer, b. New York City. m. (1884) Anna K. Green (*q.v.*). Originally an actor; began (c.1889) designing and making furniture in style influenced by Arts and Crafts and Art Nouveau movements.

Rohlfs, Christian. 1849–1938. German painter and printmaker. Painted landscapes in academic realist manner; later influenced by Monet and Van Gogh and developed an Expressionistic style (after 1900); known for landscapes, religious paintings as *St. Patroculus in Soest* (1905–06), and woodcuts as *Death and a Child* (1912–13).

Rohlfs, Friedrich Gerhard. 1831–1896. German explorer. Explored Morocco disguised as an Arab (1862); first European to cross Africa from Tripoli to Lagos (1865–66); visited Abyssinia and the oases between Tripoli and Egypt (1868), the Libyan desert (1873–74), etc.

Röhm \'rœm\, Ernst. 1887–1934. German soldier. Organized (1921) his private force into the Sturmabteilung (Brown Shirts); became supporter of Hitler in National Socialist Workers' party; took part in putsch in Munich (1923) and was imprisoned briefly as a ringleader. Military instructor in Bolivia (1925–30). As chief of staff, took over organization and command of the Brown Shirts and Black Shirts in Germany (1931); led national revolution in Bavaria (1933) and became state commissar and secretary of state in Bavaria. Charged with conspiracy to overthrow Hitler as chancellor; executed without trial.

Rohmer, Sax. See Arthur S. WARD.

Roi Adam. See ADENET LE ROI.

Ro·jas \'rō-kä̱s\, Fernando de. c.1465–1541. Spanish writer. Author of dramatic prose romance *Tragicomedia de Calisto y Melibea* (1499), better known as *La Celestina,* chief contribution to development of the national drama in the 15th century.

Rojas Pi·nil·la \-pē-'nē(l)-yä\, Gustavo. 1900–1975. Colombian soldier and politician. Overthrew Laureano Gómez and became president of Colombia (1953); regime noted for corrupt and authoritarian practices; forced into exile (1957); returned to Colombia (1958), impeached, and lost civil rights (1959; rights restored 1967); defeated for presidency (1962, 1970).

Rojas Vil·lan·dran·do \-vē(l)-yän-'drän-dō\, Augustin de. 1572–c.1635. Spanish dramatist and actor. Served as soldier in France, captured and ransomed; member of touring acting company. Author of play *El natural desdichado,* several *loas* (laudatory dramatic prologues), and *El viaje entretenido* (1603), a picaresque dialogue-novel about traveling actors.

Rojas Zor·ril·la \-thȯr-'rē(l)-yä\, Francisco de. 1607–1648. Spanish dramatist. Author of tragedies and a new kind of play (*comedia de figurón*) featuring an eccentric as main character; plays included *Entre bobos anda el juego, Cada cual lo que le toca, Donde ay agravios no ay celos,* and *Del rey abajo, ninguno.*

Rokeaḥ, Eleazar. See ELEAZAR BEN JUDAH.

Ro·ki·tan·sky \ˌrō-kē-'tän-skē\, Karl von. Freiherr. 1804–1878. Austrian pathologist. Professor of pathological anatomy, Vienna General Hospital (1844–74); one of the founders of modern pathological anatomy. First to detect bacteria in lesions of malignant endocarditis; established micropathology of pulmonary emphysema; first to describe spondylolisthesis (1839); made fundamental study of acute yellow atrophy of the liver (now known as Rokitansky's disease, 1843). Author of *Handbuch der pathologischen Anatomie* (1842–46).

Rok·ka·ku \rōk-kä-kü\ Shisui. *Orig. personal name* Chūtarō. 1867–1950. Japanese artist and art critic. Authority on Japanese lacquer ware. With Okakura Kakuzō toured provinces in search of old art works (1893); made study trips to art museums of Boston, New York, and Europe; helped excavate Chinese artifacts in Korea.

Ro·kos·sov·sky \rə-(ˌ)kə-'sȯf-skəi\, Konstantin Konstantinovich. 1896–1968. Russian army officer. Major in World War I; lieutenant general in command of defense of Moscow in World War II; as commander of the Don front, launched (1943) attack resulting in crushing of German resistance before Stalingrad; led Soviet armies through Poland; minister of defense in Poland (1949–56); U.S.S.R. deputy minister of defense (1956–58).

Rokycan, Jan z. See JAN Z ROKYCAN.

Ro·land de La Pla·tière \rō-läⁿ-də-lá-plá-tyər\, Jean-Marie. 1734–1793. French revolutionary. Became leader among the Girondists (1791); minister of interior (1792, 1793). Attacked Robespierre and Danton and attempted to save life of Louis XVI; forced to flee Paris into Normandy; committed suicide when he learned of execution of his wife ¶Jeanne-Marie *or* -Manon, *nee* Phli·pon \flē-pōⁿ\ (1754–1793), *commonly known as* Mme Roland; m. (1780) Roland; her salon in Paris was headquarters for Republicans and Girondists (1791–93); broke with Robespierre (1791) and became bitter enemy of Danton; directed activities of her husband while he was minister of interior; after fall of Girondists, she was arrested, condemned, and guillotined; her last words were "O Liberty, what crimes are committed in thy name!"

Ro·land Holst-van der Schalk \'rō-länt-'hōlst-vän-dər-'skälk\, Henriëtte Goverdina Anna. 1869–1952. Dutch Socialist and poet. Married (1896) Richard N. Roland Holst (1868–1938), a prose writer. Involved in international politics, advocating Socialism, pacifism, and anticolonialism. Her political ideals reflected in her writings, as play *Thomas More* (1912), volumes of poetry *De nieuwe geboort* (1902), *Opwaartsche wegen* (1907), *Heldensage* (1927), and biographies of Rousseau (1912), Tolstoy (1930), Romain Rolland (1946), and Gandhi (1947).

Rol·dán \rōl-'dän\, Pedro. c.1624–c.1700. Spanish sculptor, painter, and architect. Director of sculpture at Seville Academy (1664–72). Best known for Baroque altarpieces for churchs of Sagrario (1666) and La Caridad (1670–75) in Seville. His daughter ¶Luisa (1656–1704), *called* La Roldana, was only woman appointed as a Spanish royal sculptor; trained by her father; known for religious sculptures as *San Miguel* and polychromed figurines depicting religious scenes.

Rolfe \'rälf\, Frederick William Serafino Austin Lewis Mary. *Pseudonym* Bar·on Cor·vo \'bar-ən-'kȯr-(ˌ)vō\. 1860–1913. English writer. Led an itinerant life as schoolmaster, painter, journalist, photographer, etc.; converted to Catholicism (1886) and twice unsuccessful candidate for priesthood; lived in Venice (from 1908). His writings, mainly novels, included *Stories Toto Told Me* (1898), *In His Own Image* (1901, short stories), *Hadrian the Seventh* (1904), *Don Tarquino* (1905), *The Desire and Pursuit of the Whole* (1934), *Hubert's Arthur* (1935), *Nicholas Crabbe* (1958), and *Don Renato* (1963).

Rolfe, John. 1585–1622. English colonist. To Jamestown, Va. (1610). Discovered method of curing tobacco, thus making it an article of export and laying basis of Virginia's trade and prosperity during colonial period. Married (1614) Pocahontas (*q.v.*); probably killed by Indians in his Virginia home.

Rol·land \rō-läⁿ\, Romain. 1866–1944. French man of letters. Received 1915 Nobel prize for literature for novel cycle *Jean Christophe* (1904–12) and pacifist manifestos collected in *Au-dessus de la mêlée* (1915). Other works included a second novel cycle *L'Âme-enchantée* (1922–33); historical and philosophical plays collected in *Le Théâtre de la révolution* (1904; included *Les Loups,* 1898, and *Danton,* 1900) and *Les Tragédies de la foi* (1913; included *Aërt,* 1898); biographies *Beethoven* (1903), *Michel-Ange* (1905), *Tolstoi* (1911), and *Mahatma Gandhi* (1924); correspondence with Einstein, Schweitzer, Bertrand Russell, etc., published in *Cahiers Romain Rolland* (1948); and *Mémoires* (1956). Considered an apostle of heroic idealism; helped found international review *Europe* (1923).

Rolle \rōl\, Michel. 1652–1719. French mathematician. Member of Académie des Sciences (from 1685); expert on Diophantine equations; chief work, *Traité d'algèbre* (1690).

Rolle de Ham·pole \'rōl-də-'ham-ˌpōl\, Richard. c.1300–1349. English hermit, mystic, and writer. At Dalton, later at Hampole, led contemplative life. Author of mystical and ascetic treatises in Latin and English, including *De incendio amoris, Melos amoris, Ego dormio, The Commandment,* and *The Form of Perfect Living.*

Rolle·ston \'rōl-stən\, Thomas William. 1857–1920. Irish journalist and writer. Editor of *Treasury of Irish Poetry* (with Stopford Brooke, 1900); author of *Sea Spray* (verse, 1909), *Myths and Legends of the Celtic Race* (1911), etc.

Rol·li \'rōl-lē\, Paolo Antonio. 1687–1765. Italian poet and librettist. In London in service of English royal household (1715–44); influential in creating taste in London for Italian poetry and opera; translated Italian literature into English and *Paradise Lost* (1735) into Italian; wrote operatic librettos for Handel, Scarlatti, Giovanni Bononcini, and others; published lyrical odes and songs in *Le rime* (1717).

Rol·lins \'räl-ənz\, Hyder Edward. 1889–1958. American educator, b. Abilene, Tex. Professor of English, Harvard (from 1921). Editor of *Old English Ballads* (1920), *The Pepys Ballads* (1929–32), *England's Helicon* (1935), *Shakespeare's Poems* (in *New Variorum Shakespeare,* 1938), *The Letters of John Keats* (1957), etc.

Rolls \'rōlz\, Charles Stewart. 1877–1910. English manufacturer and aviator. Pioneer maker of automobiles in England; organized (1902) C.S. Rolls & Co., automobile manufacturers, which merged with Royce, Ltd. to form Rolls-Royce, Ltd. (1906). First to fly across the English Channel and back nonstop (June 1910); killed in plane crash, first English victim of aviation.

Röl·vaag \ˈrōl-ˌväg\, Ole Edvart. 1876–1931. American educator and novelist, b. Dönna I., Norway. To America (1869, naturalized 1908). Professor of Norwegian, St. Olaf College (1906–31). Achieved fame with *Giants in the Earth* (1927; English translation of his two Norwegian novels *I de Dage* and *Riket Grundlaegges*); also wrote *Peder Seir* (Eng. *Peder Victorious,* 1929) and *Den Signede Dag* (Eng. *Their Fathers' God,* 1931). A founder (1925) and first secretary of Norwegian-American Historical Association.

Romains, Jules. See Louis FARIGOULE.

Ro·man \ˈrü-ˌmän\, Johan Helmich. 1694–1758. Swedish violinist and composer. Master of the royal chapel (1727–45); produced first public concerts in Stockholm (1731). First significant Swedish composer; composed symphonies, suites, festival and church music, violin concertos, sonatas, cantatas, etc.

Ro·ma·nes \rō-ˈmän-ēz\, George John. 1848–1894. British biologist, b. Kingston, Ont. Intimate friend of Charles Darwin; at University College, London, made researches on nervous and locomotor systems of medusae and echinoderms; showed parallelism in development of mental faculties of animals and man in *Animal Intelligence* (1881) and *Mental Evolution in Animals* (1883), and further applied Darwin's theory of evolution to development of mind in *Mental Evolution in Man* (1888); argued for role of isolation in evolution in *Darwin and after Darwin* (1892–97).

Romano, Enotrio. See Giosuè CARDUCCI.

Romano, Giulio. c.1499–1546. See Giulio PIPPI DE' GIANUZZI.

Romano, Giulio. c.1545–1618. See Giulio CACCINI.

Ro·ma·noff \rə-ˈmän-ˌóf, -əf; ˈrō-mə-ˌnóf\, Michael. *Orig.* Harry F. Ger·gu·son \ˈg(y)ər-gə-sən\; *nicknamed* Prince Mike. 1892?–1971. American impostor and restaurateur, b. Vilna, Lithuania. Posed (from 1919) as Prince Michael Alexandrovich Dmitri Obolensky Romanoff, member of Romanov dynasty; opened (late 1930s) Romanoff's restaurant in Beverly Hills, Cal., and made fortune with subsequent restaurant chain; friend and confidant of Hollywood celebrities.

Ro·ma·nov \(ˌ)rə-ˈmá-nəf, *Angl* rō-ˈmän-əf, ˈrō-mə-ˌnäf\. Name of a Russian dynasty (1613–1917) which began with Michael Romanov, grandnephew of Ivan IV and son of Patriarch Philaret. The family originated with a German nobleman, Andrew Kobyla, who emigrated (14th century) from Prussia to Moscow; his descendants became prominent at Russian court, one member, Roman Yurev (d. 1543) taking the name Romanov; his daughter Anastasiya Romanovna married (1547) Czar Ivan IV as his first wife; their son Fyodor I (*q.v.*), last of Rurik (*q.v.*) dynasty. Nikita, brother of Anastasiya, chosen chairman of council acting as regent during reign of Fyodor I (1584–98); Nikita's son Fyodor, better known by his monastic name Philaret (*q.v.*) became metropolitan of Rostov after Boris Godunov's death (1605); his son Michael Romanov was chosen czar (1613). Michael was succeeded by his son Alexis (1645–76), whose three sons were in turn czars: Fyodor III (1676–82), Ivan V (1682–89), and Peter I the Great (1689–1725). Peter was followed by his wife Catherine I (1725–27), his grandson by his first wife, Peter II (last representative of direct male line, 1727–30), then by Anna (1730–40), daughter of Ivan V, then Ivan VI (1740–41), a descendant of Ivan V through Anton Ulrich of Brunswick, who married Anna Leopoldovna (*q.v.*). Line of succession returned (1741) to female side of house in Elizabeth (1741–62), daughter of Peter I and Catherine I. Elizabeth's sister Anna (d. 1728) married Charles Frederick of Holstein-Gottorp (see OLDENBURG, 3) and their son Peter III succeeded (1762) his aunt, establishing the so-called Hol·stein-Got·torp-Romanov \ˈhōl-ˌshtīn-ˈgó-tórp-\ line (1762–1917). Peter III was followed by his wife Catherine II the Great (1762–96) and their son Paul I (1796–1801). Later rulers were: Alexander I (1801–25), eldest son of Paul; Nicholas I (1825–55), brother of Alexander I; Alexander II (1855–81), son of Nicholas I; Alexander III (1881–94), son of Alexander II; and Nicholas II (1894–1917), son of Alexander III. Nicholas II abdicated (Mar. 1917) in favor of his brother Michael, who resigned the next day in favor of the provisional government. See individual biographies.

Romanov, Panteleymon Sergeyevich. 1884–1936. Russian novelist. Author of the prose epic *Rus'* (1924–36), short stories, and dramas.

Ro·ma·nus \rō-ˈmā-nəs\. d. 897. Pope (Aug.–Nov. 897). Pope during strife caused by Pope Stephen VI's Cadaver Synod and subsequent murder; reburied Formosus's body; deposed, probably by followers of Stephen.

Romanus. Name of four rulers of the Eastern Roman Empire:

Romanus I Lec·a·pe·nus \ˌlek-ə-ˈpē-nəs\. c.870–948. Emperor (920–944). A common soldier of Armenian birth, rose to grand admiral of the fleets. Married his daughter Helen to Emperor Constantine VII (919); crowned himself co-emperor (920) and held actual power; ignorant, but an able administrator; tried to establish a new dynasty but deposed by two of his sons; exiled to island of Prote.

Romanus II. 939–963. Emperor (959–963). Son of Constantine VII. Inept ruler; left state affairs to Joseph Bringas and military affairs to Nicephorus Phocas; after death, his widow Theophano helped Nicephorus become emperor.

Romanus III Ar·gy·rus \ˈär-jər-əs\. 968?–1034. Emperor (1028–34). Married Zoë, daughter of Constantine VIII; supposed to have been murdered by Zoë and Michael IV.

Romanus IV Di·og·e·nes \dī-ˈäj-ə-ˌnēz\. d. 1071. Married (1068) Eudocia Macrembolitissa, widow of Constantine X; emperor and coregent with her (1068–71), during minority of Michael VII Ducas. An able general, won many victories against Seljuq Turks (1067–71), but completely defeated by them under Alp-Arslan (1071) at Manzikert, Armenia; taken prisoner, but released and exiled to Prote.

Rom·berg \ˈróm-ˌberk\, Bernhard Heinrich. 1767–1841. German cellist and composer. Composer of operas as *Ulisse und Circe* (1807), chamber music, and esp. cello compositions. His cousin ¶Andreas Jakob (1767–1821), violinist, conductor, and composer of sacred music, operas, symphonies, violin concertos, chamber music, and esp. of music for Schiller's *Lied von der Glocke.*

Rom·berg \ˈróm-ˌberg, *Angl* ˈräm-ˌbərg\, Sigmund. 1887–1951. American composer, b. Nagykanizsa, Hungary. To U.S. (1909). Composed music for operettas, including *Maytime* (1917), *Blossom Time* (1921), *The Student Prince* (1924; included songs "Deep in My Heart," "Serenade," and "Drinking Song"), *The Desert Song* (1926; "One Alone"), *The New Moon* (1928; "Lover, Come Back to Me" and "Stout Hearted Men"), *May Wine* (1938), and *Up in Central Park* (1945). Also wrote songs (from 1929) for films, as "When I Grow Too Old to Dream" (1935).

Ro·mer \ˈrō-mər\, Alfred Sherwood. 1894–1973. American paleontologist, b. White Plains, N.Y. Authority on evolutionary history of vertebrates. Professor, U. of Chicago (1923–34) and Harvard (1934–65); director, Harvard Museum of Comparative Zoology (1946–61). Author of *Vertebrate Paleontology* (1933), *The Vertebrate Body* (1949), *The Osteology of the Reptiles* (1956), etc.

Rø·mer \ˈrœ̄-mər\, Ole *or* Olaus. 1644–1710. Danish astronomer. At Royal Observatory, Paris (1672–81); appointed royal mathematician and professor of astronomy at U. of Copenhagen (1781); mayor of Copenhagen (1705). Discovered that light travels at a finite speed and estimated its speed at 140,000 m.p.s. (announced 1676); perhaps first to use a telescope attached to a transit circle; met Fahrenheit (1708) and imparted to him many ideas later used in Fahrenheit thermometer.

Ro·me·ro \rō-ˈmā-rō\, Francisco. 1698–1763. Spanish matador. Introduced the *estoque* (matador's sword) and *muleta* to bullfighting.

Romero, José Rubén. 1890–1952. Mexican diplomat and writer. Held several diplomatic posts, esp. ambassadorships to Brazil and Cuba. Author of verse as *Fantasías* (1908), *La musa heroica* (1912), *Versos viejos* (1930), and esp. of novels set in rural Mexico as *Apuntes de un lugareño* (1932), *Desbandada* (1934), *La vida inútil de Pito Pérez* (1938), *Anticipación de la muerte* (1939), *Algunas cosillas de Pito Pérez* (1945), and *Rosenda* (1946).

Romero, Matías. 1837–1899. Mexican economist and diplomat. Minister to U.S. (1863–68, 1882–98); chief architect of economic development under Juárez.

Rom·il·ly \ˈräm-ə-lē\, Sir Samuel. 1757–1818. English lawyer and law reformer. Chancery lawyer (from 1783); chancellor of Durham (1805–15); M.P. (1806); early adopted Rousseauistic views. Made labor of his life (from 1807) reform of the criminal law of England, esp. abolishing capital punishment for many minor felonies and misdemeanors.

Rom·mel \ˈrō-məl\, Erwin Johannes Eugen. *Called* the Desert Fox. 1891–1944. German general. Served in World War I. Commanded a Panzer division in invasion of France (1940); commander of German forces in Africa (1941–43); recaptured Tobruk (1942) and drove British back to el-Alamein, Egypt; promoted to rank of general field marshal; defeated by British at el-Alamein (Nov. 1942) and withdrew to Tunis; recalled (Mar. 1943). In command of defense of French coast (1944). Took poison to avoid public trial after discovery of his contacts with anti-Hitler conspirators.

Romney, Earl of. See Henry Sidney (1641–1704) under SIDNEY family.

Rom·ney \ˈräm-nē, ˈrəm-\, George. 1734–1802. English portrait painter. Set up as portrait painter in London (1762); gained attention with *Death of General Wolfe* (1763); rival of Reynolds for patronage of aristocracy; met (c.1781–82) Emma Hart (later Lady Hamilton), who appeared in over 50 of his paintings. His portraits included *Sir George and Lady Warren and their Daughter* (1769), *Mrs. Yates as the Tragic Muse* (1771), *Mrs. Carwardine and Son* (1775), and *Sir Christopher and Lady Sykes* (1786).

Rom·u·ald \ˈräm-yə-wəld\. Saint. c.950–1027. Italian religious. Became Benedictine monk (c.970); abbot of San Apollinare (998–999); wandered thereafter founding monasteries and hermitages, esp. (1023–27) a monastery at Camaldoli, near Arezzo, which became motherhouse of ascetic order known as Camaldolese Benedictines.

Romuald. d. 687. Duke of Benevento (671–687). Son of Grimoald I. Ruled Benevento in father's absence (662–671) and succeeded him as duke (671). With father's aid repelled invasion of Constans II (663); retook Tarentum and Brindisi from Byzantines and extended his domain into Apulia, Campania, and Calabria; helped conversion of Lombards from Arianism to Catholicism.

Rom·u·lo \'räm-yə-lō\, Carlos Peña. 1899–1985. Philippine general, diplomat, and journalist. Became (1931) editor in chief of three Philippine newspapers; served during World War II as press aide to U.S. Gen. Douglas MacArthur and made broadcasts as the "Voice of Freedom"; after fall of Corregidor, joined Philippine government-in-exile in Washington, D.C.; returned to Philippines after the war. President of U.N. General Assembly (1949–50). Philippine secretary of foreign affairs (1950–52; 1968–78), minister of foreign affairs (1978–84), and ambassador to U.S. (1952–53; 1955–62). Last survivor of the 51 founding fathers of U.N.

Rom·u·lus Au·gus·tu·lus \'räm-yə-ləs-ȯ-'gəs-chə-ləs\. 5th century A.D. Last Roman emperor of the West (475–476). Son of Orestes; crowned by his father, but a puppet ruler only; deposed by Odoacer; retired to Campania.

Ron·de·let \rōⁿd-le\, Guillaume. 1507–1566. French naturalist and physician. Professor (from 1545) and chancellor (from 1556), U. of Montpellier; author of *Libri de piscibus marinis* (1554–55), descriptions of marine animals.

Ron·ne \'rō-nə, 'rän-ə\, Finn. 1899–1980. American explorer, b. Horten, Norway. To U.S. (1923). With Richard Byrd in Antarctica (1933–35, 1939–41); led Antarctic expeditions (1947–48, 1958–59, 1962–69); commander of Weddell Sea Station with IGY (1956–58); Ronne Ice Shelf named for him.

Ron·sard \rōⁿ-sȧr\, Pierre de. 1524–1585. French poet. Page at court (1536–42); turned to literature and scholarship after becoming partially deaf (1542); took minor orders (1543) but never ordained; chief member of the Pléiade, a group devoted to uplifting French language by using classical and Italian models; patronized by Charles IX. One of greatest poets of French Renaissance; perfected the alexandrine and helped fix French sonnet form. Among works were *Odes* (1550), *Bocages* (1550, 1554), *Amours* (1552, 1553, 1559), *Meslanges* (1554, 1559), *Hymnes* (1555–56), *Discours des misères de ce temps* (1562), *La Franciade* (1572; 4 vols. of unfinished epic), and *Sonnets pour Hélène* (1578).

Rönt·gen or **Roent·gen** \'rœnt-gən; *Angl* 'rent-gən, 'rənt-, -jən; 'ren-chən, 'rən-\, Wilhelm Conrad. 1845–1923. German physicist. Professor, Strassburg (1876), Giessen (1879), Würzburg (1888), Munich (1900–20). Awarded first Nobel prize for physics (1901) for his discovery (1895) of X-rays. Also made researches on elasticity, capillary action of fluids, specific heats of gases, conduction of heat in crystals, absorption of heat by gases, and piezoelectricity.

Rood \'rüd\, Ogden Nicholas. 1831–1902. American physicist, b. Danbury, Conn. Conducted researches in mechanics, electricity, acoustics, and optics; developed a flicker photometer for comparing brightness of different colors; wrote *Modern Chromatics* (1879), widely read by Impressionist painters.

Rooke \'ru̇k\, Sir George. 1650–1709. English admiral. Commanded unsuccessful expedition against Cádiz (1702) but destroyed French and Spanish fleet at Vigo; commander in chief of grand fleet (1703); captured Gibraltar (1704).

Roon \'rōn\, Albrecht Theodor Emil von. Graf. 1803–1879. Prussian soldier and politician. Helped suppress insurrection in Baden (1848); minister of war (1859–73), of marine (1861–71); field marshal (1873); president of Prussian ministry (1873). Effectively organized Prussian army which made possible its speedy mobilization leading to decisive victories in wars of 1866 and 1870–71.

Roos \'rōs\, Sjoerd Hendrik de. 1877–1962. Dutch book and type designer. Founded (c.1928) Heuvel Press at Hilversum, second Dutch private press, and designed Meidoorn type for it. Typeface designs included Holland Medieval (1912), Zilvertype (1915), Egmont (1933), and De Roos Roman (1947).

Roo·se·velt \'rō-zə-vəlt (*Roosevelts' usual pronunciation*), -ˌvelt, *also* 'rü-\, Eleanor, *in full* Anna Eleanor, *nee* Roosevelt. 1884–1962. American author, diplomat, and humanitarian, b. New York City. Niece of Theodore Roosevelt; m. (1905) distant cousin Franklin D. Roosevelt. Widely admired for support of liberal causes and humanitarian concerns; active in Democratic party. Delegate to United Nations (1945, 1949–52, 1961); chairman of UN Commission on Human Rights (1946–51), helped draft and secured adoption of Universal Declaration of Human Rights (1948). Author of syndicated column "My Day" (from 1936) and of books as *This Is My Story* (1937), *The Moral Basis of Democracy* (1940), and *On My Own* (1958).

Roosevelt, Franklin Delano. 1882–1945. Thirty-second president of the United States, b. Hyde Park, N.Y. 5th cousin of Theodore Roosevelt; m. (1905) Eleanor Roosevelt. Practiced law in New York (1907–10); member, New York State Senate (1910–13); assistant secretary of the navy (1913–20); Democratic nominee for vice president (1920); stricken with polio (1921). Governor of New York (1929–33); established nation's first state relief agency (1931). President of the United States (1933–45), only president to be elected for 3d and 4th terms. Assembled group of advisers known as the "brain trust" and developed administrative and legislative reforms known collectively as the New Deal; secured passage of legislation establishing during the "Hundred Days" (Mar.–June 1933) the Civilian Conservation Corps, Agricultural Adjustment Administration, Tennessee Valley Authority, National Recovery Administration, Public Works Administration, etc., reforming credit and banking laws, amending Volstead Act, etc.; subsequently secured establishment of Securities and Exchange Commission (1934), National Youth Administration (1935), Social Security system (1935). Secured passage of Lend-Lease Act (1941); met with Winston Churchill (Aug. 1941) to draw up Atlantic Charter; called for declaration of war on Japan (Dec. 8, 1941). Under emergency powers delegated by Congress established (1942–45) agencies to supervise military production and regulate civilian economy. Conferred on war strategy and international affairs with heads of state, esp. with Churchill and Stalin at Teheran (Dec. 1943) and again at Yalta, Crimea (Feb. 1945).

Roosevelt, Theodore. 1858–1919. Twenty-sixth president of the United States, b. New York City. Member, New York State legislature (1882–84). Lived outdoor life on North Dakota ranch (1884–86). Unsuccessful candidate for mayor of New York (1886). Member, U.S. Civil Service Commission (1889–95); president, New York City Board of Police Commissioners (1895–97). U.S. assistant secretary of the navy (1897–98). With Leonard Wood, organized first volunteer cavalry regiment, popularly known as Rough Riders, and as its lieutenant colonel, served with it in Cuba (1898). Governor of New York (1899–1900). Vice president of the United States (1901), succeeding to the presidency on death of McKinley (Sept. 14, 1901); elected to the presidency (1904) and served altogether 1901–09. Notable during his administration were the acquisition (1903) of Panama Canal Zone and the beginning of construction of Panama Canal; bringing representatives of Russia and Japan together at Portsmouth, N.H., with the resulting Treaty of Portsmouth (Sept. 5, 1905) ending Russo–Japanese War, for which he received Nobel prize for peace (1906); aggressive policies in regulating business and curbing trusts, esp. dissolution (1911) of Standard Oil Co. of New Jersey; efforts to conserve national resources, esp. passage of Newlands Reclamation Act (1902); announced (1904) Roosevelt Corollary, making U.S. defender of Western Hemisphere. Successfully maneuvered nomination of Taft for president (1908). Traveled in Africa and Europe (1909–10). Organized Progressive party, was its candidate for president, and defeated (1912). Author of *The Naval War of 1812* (1882), *Ranch Life and the Hunting-Trail* (1888), *Essays on Practical Politics* (1888), *The Winning of the West* (1889–96), *The Rough Riders* (1899), *The Strenuous Life* (1900), *Hunting the Grizzly* (1905), *Progressive Principles* (1913), *History as Literature* (1913), *Through the Brazilian Wilderness* (1914), *America and the World War* (1915), etc.

Roosevelt, Theodore, Jr. 1887–1944. American writer, soldier, explorer, and politician, b. Oyster Bay, N.Y. Son of Theodore Roosevelt. Served in both World Wars; an organizer of American Legion (1919). Assistant secretary of the navy (1921–24). Led expeditions to Asia (1925, 1928–29). Governor of Puerto Rico (1929–32); governor general of the Philippines (1932–33). Editor, Doubleday Doran & Co. (from 1935). Author of *Average Americans* (1919), *All in the Family* (1929), *Colonial Policies of the United States* (1937), etc.

Root \'rüt\, Elihu. 1845–1937. American lawyer and diplomat, b. Clinton, N.Y. Practiced law, New York City (from 1867). U.S. secretary of war (1899–1904); secured passage of Foraker Act (1900) to establish civil government in Puerto Rico; established governing policies for Cuba and the Philippines; reorganized army; created Army War College (1901). U.S. secretary of state (1905–09); negotiated Root-Takahira Agreement (1908) with Japan; strengthened friendly relations between U.S. and South American countries. U.S. senator from New York (1909–15). Counsel for U.S. in North Atlantic Fisheries arbitration (1910); member, Hague Tribunal (1910); president, Carnegie Endowment for International Peace (1910–25). Awarded Nobel prize for peace (1912). Strong supporter of League of Nations; helped frame statute for World Court (1920). Author of *Experiment in Government and the Essentials of the Constitution* (1913), *Military and Colonial Policy of the United States* (1916), etc.

Root, George Frederick. 1820–1895. American composer and teacher, b. Sheffield, Mass. Founded (1853) New York Normal Institute. Wrote cantatas, sacred music, and popular songs, esp. "Rosalie, the Prairie Flower" (1858) and Civil War songs "Battle Cry of Freedom" (1862), "Just Before the Battle, Mother" (1863), "Tramp, Tramp, Tramp, the Boys are Marching" (1865).

Root, John Wellborn. 1850–1891. American architect, b. Lumpkin, Ga. In partnership (Chicago) with Daniel H. Burnham, Burnham & Root (1873–91). Designer of the Montauk Building (1882), The Rookery (1884–86), and Monadnock Building (1889–91), Chicago. Consulting architect, World's Columbian Exposition (1890–91).

Roo·ze·boom \'rō-zə-ˌbōm\, Hendrik Willem Bakhuis. 1854–1907. Dutch physical chemist. Professor, Amsterdam (1896–1907); known for application of the phase rule to the study of heterogeneous equilibriums.

Ro·partz \rȯ-pȧr\, Joseph-Guy-Marie. 1864–1955. French composer. His compositions included an opera *Le Pays* (1910), symphonic poems *La Cloche des morts* (1887), *Les Landes* (1888), *La Chasse du Prince Arthur* (1912), symphonies, chamber music, sonatas, songs, and choral music.

Ro·per \ˈrō-pər\, William. 1496–1578. English biographer. Son-in-law of Sir Thomas More; wrote (c.1535; pub. 1626) *Mirrour of Vertue in Worldly Greatness or the life of Syr Thomas More,* one of first biographies in English.

Rops \rȯps\, Félicien. 1833–1898. Belgian painter, engraver, and lithographer. Known for licentious subjects; illustrated books in Paris (after 1874); published sketches in *Cent croquis pour réjouir les honnêtes gens;* executed *Buveuse d'absinthe* (1865) and *Dame au pantin* (1871); member of revolutionary art society XX in Brussels (from 1884).

Ropshin, V. See Boris SAVINKOV.

Rør·dam \ˈrœr-ˌdȧm\, Valdemar. 1872–1946. Danish poet. Author of verse narratives *Bjovulf* (1899), *Gudrun Dyre* (1902), and *Jens Hvas til Ulvborg* (1922–23), and idylls, lyrics, and dramas.

Ro·re \ˈrō-rə\, Cipriano de. 1516–1565. Flemish composer in Italy. Composed several books of 4-part and 5-part madrigals; also motets, masses, psalms, a Passion (1557), etc.

Rorik. See RURIK.

Rory O'Connor. See O'CONNOR family.

Ror·schach \ˈrōr-ˌshäk, *Angl* ˈrȯ(ə)r-ˌshäk\, Hermann. 1884–1922. Swiss psychiatrist. Influenced by his teachers Eugen Bleuler and Carl Jung; developed and introduced (1921) the inkblot test (known by his name) used for diagnosing psychopathology; chief work *Psychodiagnostik* (1921).

Ro·sa \ˈrȯ-zä\, Salvator. 1615–1673. Italian painter and poet. Leading painter of Neapolitan school; known chiefly for wildly romantic landscapes, marine paintings, and battle scenes. As a poet, wrote satires in terza rima as *La musica, La poesia, La guerra,* and *L'invidia.*

Ro·sa·li·a \ˌrō-zä-ˈlē-ä\. Saint. d. 1160. Italian religious. Niece of King William II of Sicily; patron saint of Palermo; lived as hermit in grotto on Monte Pellegrino.

Rosamund, Fair. See Rosamund Clifford under CLIFFORD family.

Rosa of Lima, Saint. See ROSE of Lima.

Ro·sas \ˈrȯ-säs\, Juan Manuel de. 1793–1877. Argentine dictator. Chief of Federalist party (from 1828); governor of Buenos Aires (1829–31, 1835–52). After other Argentine provinces joined Buenos Aires in a loose union, wielded supreme power over them all, though continuing nominally as merely governor of Buenos Aires. Waged war in alliance with Oribe, exiled president of Uruguay, to subjugate all Uruguay (1842–51), but was unable to capture Montevideo. Defeated (1852) by coalition of Brazilians, Uruguayans, French, and Argentines; fled to England and lived there in exile (1852–77).

Ros·ce·lin de Com·piègne \rȯs-la^{n}-də-kō^{n}-pyen^{y}\. *Lat.* Ros·cel·li·nus Com·p-en·di·en·sis \ˌräs-ə-ˈlī-nəs-kəm-ˌpen-dē-ˈen-səs\; *also* Ru·ce·li·nus \ˌrü-sə-ˈlī-nəs\. c.1050–c.1125. French Scholastic philosopher. Canon at Loches where Abelard was his pupil; founder of nominalism; forced by a council at Soissons (1092) to abjure his doctrine of the Trinity, by which he taught that the three persons of the godhead were three gods.

Ros·ci·us \ˈräsh-(ē-)əs\. *In full* Quintus Roscius Gallus. 126?–?62 B.C. Roman actor. Regarded as greatest of Roman comic actors. Friend of Cicero; his name became an honorary epithet for any successful actor.

Ros·coe \ˈräs-(ˌ)kō\, William. 1753–1831. English historian. Attorney and banker by profession. Author of *Life of Lorenzo de' Medici* (1795), *Life and Pontificate of Leo the Tenth* (1805), and a children's classic *The Butterfly's Ball and the Grasshopper's Feast* (1807). His grandson ¶Sir Henry Enfield Roscoe (1833–1915), chemist, with Bunsen laid foundations of photochemistry and formulated the reciprocity law; made elaborate investigation of vanadium compounds and devised process for preparing pure vanadium.

Roscommon, 4th Earl of. See Wentworth DILLON.

Rose \ˈrōz\ of Lima. Saint. *Orig.* Isabel de Flo·res \dā-ˈflō-rās\. 1586–1617. Peruvian religious. Born into wealthy family; led life of extreme austerity; took veil as sister of Third Order of St. Dominic (1606). Canonized (1671), first saint born in Western Hemisphere; patron saint of South America.

Rose, Billy. *Orig.* William Samuel Ro·sen·berg \ˈrōz-^{ə}n-ˌbərg\. 1899–1966. American theatrical impresario and composer, b. New York City. Married several times, esp. (1929; div. 1938) to Fanny Brice (*q.v.*). Chief stenographer for Bernard Baruch during World War I; owned several nightclubs in New York; produced shows, esp. *Crazy Quilt* (1931), *Jumbo* (1935), *Carmen Jones* (1943). Composed (from 1920s) over 400 songs, including "Barney Google," "That Old Gang of Mine," "It's Only a Paper Moon," "K-K-K-Katy," "Me and My Shadow," and "Without a Song."

Rose, Gustav and Heinrich. See under Valentin ROSE.

Rose, Hugh Henry. Baron Strath·nairn \strath-ˈne(ə)rn, -ˈna(ə)rn\. 1801–1885. British soldier. Consul general in Syria (1841–48). In Indian Mutiny (1857–58), gained victory over Tantia Topi, captured fortress of Jhānsi, captured Gwalior, and virtually reconquered Central India; commander in chief in India (1860). Commander in Ireland, kept Fenians under control (1865–70); general (1867) and field marshal (1877).

Ro·se \ˈrō-zə\, Valentin. 1736–1771. German apothecary. Discoverer of a fusible alloy (Rose's alloy). His son ¶Valentin (1762–1807), also an apothecary, first prepared inulin and sodium bicarbonate. ¶Heinrich (1795–1864), son of the younger Valentin, apothecary and chemist, rediscovered columbium which he called niobium (1844); wrote *Handbuch der analytischen Chemie* (1829). ¶Gustav (1798–1873), mineralogist, brother of Heinrich, was explorer of southern Asia, Vesuvius, Etna, and the extinct volcanoes of the Auvergne; pioneer in petrography; originator of a system of crystallography published in *Mineralsystem* (1852).

Rosebery, Earls of. See PRIMROSE family.

Rose·crans \ˈrō-zə-ˌkranz, ˈrōz-ˌkran(t)s\, William Starke. 1819–1898. American soldier, b. Kingston, Ohio. In U.S. army (1842–54). Volunteered at outbreak of Civil War; commissioned brigadier general (1861). Succeeded McClellan in command of Department of the Ohio (1861); commanding Department of West Virginia, expelled Confederates, thus making possible formation of state of West Virginia (1861). Succeeded Pope in command of army of the Mississippi (1862); engaged successfully at Iuka and Corinth (1862). Promoted major general of volunteers (1862). Commanded army of the Cumberland; defeated Confederates at Murfreesboro (1863) but was defeated at Chickamauga (1863) and relieved of his command. Commanded Department of the Missouri (1864). U.S. minister to Mexico (1868–69); member of U.S. House of Representatives from California (1881–85); U.S. register of the treasury (1885–93).

Ro·seg·ger \ˈrō-ˌzeg-ər, ˈrō-ˌseg-ər\, Peter, *known until 1894 as* P.K. *for* Petri Kettenfeier. 1843–1918. Austrian poet and novelist. Author of Styrian dialect verse *Zither und Hackbrett* (1870), of novels descriptive of provincial life as *Die Schriften des Waldschulmeisters* (1875) and *Waldheimat* (1877), and of philosophical and autobiographical works as *Der Gottsucher* (1883) and *Mein Weltleben* (1898).

Ro·sen·bach \ˈrōz-^{ə}n-ˌbak\, Abraham Simon Wolf. 1876–1952. American bibliophile, b. Philadelphia. With his brother Philip established (1902) the Rosenbach Co., which became one of the world's greatest rare-book concerns; his checklist *Early American Children's Books* (1933) is a standard reference. Author also of *The Unpublishable Memoirs* (1917), *Books and Bidders* (1927), *A Book Hunter's Holiday* (1936), etc.

Ro·sen·berg \ˈrō-zən-ˌberk\, Alfred. 1893–1946. German Nazi leader and writer. Considered the ideologist of Nazism. Joined Hitler in Nazi party (1919); editor in chief of *Völkischer Beobachter* (1921 ff.) and editor of *Nationalsozialistische Monatshefte* (1930); entered Reichstag (1930); director of newly established foreign policy office of Nazi party (1933); founder and leader of Kampfbund for German culture; Reichsminister for occupied eastern territories (from 1941); author of *Der Zukunftsweg einer deutschen Aussenpolitik* (1927), *Der Mythus des 20. Jahrhunderts* (1930), *Das Wesensgefüge des Nationalsozialismus* (1932), *Blut und Ehre* (1934), etc; hanged as war criminal.

Ro·sen·berg \ˈrōz-^{ə}n-ˌbərg\, Isaac. 1890–1918. English poet and painter. Trained as painter; killed in World War I. Known for "trench poems" (1916–18) published in *Collected Works* (1937).

Rosenberg, Julius (1918–1953) and his wife Ethel (1915–53), *nee* Green·glass \ˈgrēn-ˌglas\. American spies, both b. New York City. Members of Communist party. Both arrested (1950) for receiving nuclear weapons data from her brother David Greenglass (a U.S. army sergeant stationed at Los Alamos, N.M.) and passing it on to Harry Gold, a courier, and subsequently to ring-leader Anatoly A. Yakovlev, Soviet vice consul in New York. Convicted on basis of David's testimony and became first American civilians executed for espionage; case was an international cause célèbre.

Ro·sen·busch \ˈrō-zən-ˌbu̇sh\, Harry, *in full* Karl Heinrich Ferdinand. 1836–1914. German geologist. Professor at Strasbourg (1873) and Heidelberg (1878); director of Baden geological survey (1888–1907). Laid foundations of microscopic petrography. Author of *Mikroskopische Physiographie der petrographische wichtigen Mineralien* (1873), *Die mikroskopische Physiographie der massigen Gesteine* (1877), and *Elementen der Gesteinslehre* (1898).

Ro·se·ni·us \rō-ˈsen-ē-əs\, Karl Olaf. 1816–1868. Swedish religious leader. Influenced by Methodist leader George Scott; formed a Lutheran community in Stockholm that rejected the Scandinavian Pietist movement; launched (from 1850) a Lutheran evangelical movement in Sweden, Norway, and Denmark that also affected American Missouri Synod.

Ro·sen·mül·ler \ˈrō-zən-ˌmu̇el-ər\, Johann. c.1619–1684. German composer. Master at Thomasschule (from 1642) and organist of Nicolaikirche (1651), Leipzig; imprisoned on moral charges but escaped (1655); employed in Venice (1658–82); ducal Kapellmeister at Wolfenbüttel (1682–84). Compositions included *12 Sonate da camera a 5 stromenti* (1667), 2 Magnificats, and other sacred vocal music.

Ro·sen·wald \'rōz-ᵊn-ˌwȯld\, Julius. 1862–1932. American merchant and philanthropist, b. Springfield, Ill. Vice president and treasurer, Sears, Roebuck & Co. (1895–1910) and president (1910–25). Creator (1917) of Julius Rosenwald Fund for the "well-being of mankind." Did much to aid Negro education in the South and to alleviate Jewish distress in the Near East. Presented Chicago (1929) with Museum of Science and Industry.

Ro·senz·weig \'rō-zəns-ˌvīk\, Franz. 1886–1929. German theologian. Espoused an existentialist religious philosophy; devoted his life to study and teaching of Judaism; afflicted with paralysis (1922); with Martin Buber undertook a German translation of Hebrew Bible (1925). Author of *Hegel und der Staat* (1920), *Der Stern de Erlösung* (1921), etc.

Ro·set \rō-ze\, Michel. 1534–1613. Genevese politician. With Theodore Beza maintained Calvinist legacy in Geneva (from 1564). Elected municipal magistrate 14 times (between 1568–1612); secured French support with Treaty of Soleure (1579); negotiated perpetual alliance with Zürich and Bern (1584); negotiated peace treaty (2d Treaty of St. Julien) with Savoy (1603).

Rosh. See ASHER BEN JEHIEL.

Ros·lin \rȯ-'slēn\, Alexander. 1718–1793. Swedish painter. At courts of Bayreuth and Parma (until 1752); settled in Paris (1752). Did portraits of European royal families; known esp. for portrait of his wife, *The Lady with the Veil* (1768).

Rosmead, Baron. See Sir Hercules G. R. ROBINSON.

Ros·mi·ni-Ser·ba·ti \rōz-'mē-nē-sär-'bä-tē\, Antonio. 1797–1855. Italian priest and philosopher. Devoted life to reconciling Roman Catholicism with modern political and scientific thought. Founded religious order Institute of Charity (1828); adviser to Pius IX; worked in interest of Italian confederation (1848); fell into pope's disfavor and retired to Stresa after condemnation of his works by Congregation of the Index (1849). Author of *Nuovo saggio sull'origine delle idee* (1830), *Massime di perfezione Cristiana* (1830), *Il rinnovamento della filosofia in Italia* (1836), *Delle cinque piaghe della santa Chiesa* (1848), and *La costituzione secondo la giustizia sociale* (1848).

Ross, Barnaby. See Manfred LEE.

Ross \'rȯs\, Betsy, *in full* Elizabeth, *nee* Gris·com \'gris-kəm\. 1752–1836. American patriot, b. Philadelphia. m. John Ross (1773) and took over his upholstering business after his death (1776). Reputed to have made (June 1776) the first American flag at request of George Washington, Robert Morris, and George Ross. The stars-and-stripes flag was voted the national emblem by Continental Congress (June 14, 1777).

Ross, Edward Alsworth. 1866–1951. American sociologist, b. Virden, Ill. Professor, Stanford (1893–1900), Nebraska (1901–06), Wisconsin (1906–37). One of first to attempt to create a comprehensive sociological theory. Author of *Social Control* (1901), *The Foundations of Sociology* (1905), *Sin and Society* (1907), *Social Psychology* (1908), *Principles of Sociology* (1920), *Civic Sociology* (1925), etc.

Ross, George. 1730–1779. American jurist, b. New Castle, Del. Member, Continental Congress (1774–77), and a signer of Declaration of Independence.

Ross, Harold Wallace. 1892–1951. American editor, b. Aspen, Colo. Founder and editor (1925–51) of *The New Yorker* magazine; encouraged writers as Thurber, John O'Hara, etc.; initiated the one-line cartoon.

Ross, Sir James Clark. 1800–1862. Scottish explorer. Made four Arctic expeditions under Parry (1819–27) and led one with his uncle (1829–33); determined position of North Magnetic Pole (1831); commanded Antarctic expedition (1839–43), discovering Ross Sea and Victoria Land (1841); published *Voyage of Discovery* (1847); made voyage to Baffin Bay in search of Sir John Franklin (1848–49). For him are named Ross Sea, Ross Island, and other parts of Antarctica. His uncle ¶Sir John Ross (1777–1856) made expeditions in search of the Northwest Passage (1818, 1829–33), discovering and surveying Boothia Peninsula, King William Land, and Gulf of Boothia; published narratives of the two voyages; British consul at Stockholm (1839–46); undertook third voyage in search of Franklin (1850); rear admiral (1851).

Ross, John. *Indian name* Coowescoowe *or* Kooweskoowe. 1790–1866. American Indian chief, b. near Lookout Mountain, Tenn. Son of Scotch father and part-Cherokee mother. Served with Andrew Jackson against the Creeks (1812). President, National Council of Cherokees (1819–26); chief of Cherokee Nation (1828–39); resisted policy of moving Cherokee Nation from Georgia, but finally forced to lead it (1838–39) to Oklahoma Territory on journey known as "Trail of Tears." Chief, United Cherokee Nation (1839–66) and helped draft its constitution (1839).

Ross, Martin. See Violet Florence MARTIN.

Ross, Nellie, *nee* Tay·loe \'tā-(ˌ)lō\. 1876–1977. American politician, b. St. Joseph, Mo. m. William Bradford Ross (1902; d. 1924); elected governor of Wyoming to complete deceased husband's term (1925–27), first woman governor of a state; first woman director of U.S. Mint (1933–53).

Ross, Robert. 1766–1814. English soldier. Commanded expeditionary force in cooperation with Adm. Sir Alexander Cochrane against coasts of U.S. (1814); won battle of Bladensburg and burned Washington (1814); killed at North Point, Md.

Ross, Sir Ronald. 1857–1932. British physician, b. India. With Indian Medical Service (1881–99); began study of malaria (1892); discovered life history of the malarial parasite in mosquitoes (1897–98); found malarial mosquito in West Africa (1899); awarded 1902 Nobel prize for physiology or medicine. Professor, U. of Liverpool and Liverpool School of Tropical Medicine (1902–12); physician, King's College Hospital, London (from 1912); director in chief, Ross Institute and Hospital for Tropical Diseases, London. Author of *The Prevention of Malaria* (1910).

Ross, Sir William David. 1877–1971. Scottish philosopher. Critic of Utilitarianism; proposed a rationalist form of "situation ethics" based on intuitional knowledge; wrote *The Right and the Good* (1930), *Foundations of Ethics* (1939), etc.

Ross·by \'rȯs-bē\, Carl-Gustaf Arvid. 1898–1957. American meteorologist, b. Stockholm, Sweden. To U.S. (1926, naturalized 1938). Professor, M.I.T. (1931–39) and U. of Chicago (from 1941); assistant chief, U.S. Weather Bureau (1931–41). Made researches in heat exchange in air masses and atmospheric turbulence; developed Rossby diagram for plotting behavior of air masses (1932); identified the long sinusoidal waves of air in upper westerlies (Rossby waves) and developed theory of their movement (1935–40); identified the jet stream and developed theories of its behavior; introduced Rossby equations for weather prediction (1950); founded Inst. of Meteorology at U. of Stockholm (1947). Also contributed to rotating fluid mechanics, including Rossby number (1939).

Rosse, Earls of. See William PARSONS.

Ros·sel·li·ni \ˌrōs-säl-'lē-nē\, Roberto. 1906–1977. Italian film director. Directed first feature *La nave bianca* (1941). Gained international fame as a leader of Italian Neorealist movement with films *Roma città aperta* (1945) and *Paisà* (1947); other films included *Germania, anno zero* (1947), *Stromboli, terra di Dio* (1949), *Viaggio in Italia* (1952), *India* (1958), *Il Generale della Rovere* (1959), *Viva l'Italia* (1960), *Era notte a Roma* (1960), and *Vanina Vanini* (1960).

Ros·sel·li·no \ˌrōs-säl-'lē-nō\, Bernardo. 1409–1464. Florentine sculptor and architect. Among his works were tomb of Leonardo Bruni, tomb of Beata Villana (in Florence), tomb of Filippo Lazzari (in Pistoia); built Palazzo Ruccellai (at Florence), façade of church of the Misericordia (at Arezzo), the Palazzo Piccolomini (at Pienza), the Pienza cathedral, and was employed at the Vatican. His brother and pupil ¶Antonio (1427–1479) was also a sculptor; his works included the sarcophagus of St. Marcolinus (in the Forlì museum), the tomb of the cardinal of Portugal (in church of San Miniato, Florence), the group *Nativity,* bust of Matteo Palmieri (1468).

Ros·set·ti \rō-'zet-ē, -'set-\, Dante Gabriel, *orig.* Gabriel Charles Dante. 1828–1882. English painter and poet. With Holman Hunt, Millais, and others, founded Pre-Raphaelite school of painting (1848). Expressed the Pre-Raphaelite motive in *Ecce Ancilla Domini* (1850) and *Found* (1854); with patronage of Ruskin and friendship of William Morris, Swinburne, and Burne-Jones, executed paintings including the triptych *The Seed of David* for Llandaff cathedral; took part in revival of stained-glass painting. Executed a triptych of Paolo and Francesca (1855), *Beata Beatrix* (c.1863), *Monna Vanna* (1866), *Dante's Dream* (1871), *The Blessed Damozel* (1871–79), *Proserpina in Hades* (1874), and *Astarte Syriaca* (1877). As poet contributed "The Blessed Damozel," six sonnets, and four lyrics to *The Germ,* organ of the Pre-Raphaelite Brotherhood (1850); translated early Italian poetry (1861), later revised as *Dante and his Circle* (1874); published *Ballads and Sonnets* (1881), containing the sonnet sequence *House of Life,* and "Rose Mary," "The White Ship," "The King's Tragedy."

His brother ¶William Michael (1829–1919), art critic; financial supporter of Rossetti family; assistant secretary to Board of Inland Revenue (1869–94); a founder of Pre-Raphaelite Brotherhood and editor of its organ *The Germ;* art critic of *The Spectator* (from 1850); biographer of Shelley and Keats; editor of poetical works of Coleridge, Milton, Campbell, Blake, Whitman; edited collected works of his brother and sister.

Their sister ¶Christina Georgina (1830–1894), poet; contributed seven lyric poems to *The Germ* under pseudonym of Ellen Al·leyne \'al-ən; 'al-ˌēn, -ˌān, al-'\ (1850); model to her brother, also to Holman Hunt, Ford Madox Brown, and Millais; published her best verse in *Goblin Market* (1862); author of *Sing-Song* (children's poems, 1872), *Time Flies* (homilies, 1885), *The Face of the Deep* (1892), besides further poetical works *The Prince's Progress* (1866), *A Pageant* (1881), *New Poems* (1896).

Their father ¶Gabriele Pasquale Giuseppe (1783–1854), Italian poet and political refugee from Naples; as member of secret society of Carbonari took part in Napoleonic revolution of 1820 and saluted it with patriotic odes; fled on return to power of King Ferdinand (1824); professor of Italian, King's Coll.,

London (1831–47); eccentric commentator on Dante, showing the *Inferno* chiefly political and antipapal.

Rossi, Francesco de'. See Cecchino SALVIATI.

Ros·si \'rōs-sē\, Giovanni Battista de'. 1822–1894. Italian archaeologist. Known chiefly as discoverer (1849) of the catacombs of St. Callistus; regarded as founder of Christian archaeology; mapped Roman catacombs.

Rossi, Salomone. 1570?–?1630. Italian composer and instrumentalist. Composer at Mantuan court. Published books of sonatas, madrigals, canzonettas, and synagogal music as *Hashirim asher lish'lomo* (1622–23).

Ros·si·ni \rōs-'sē-nē\, Gioacchino Antonio. 1792–1868. Italian composer. Leading representative of bel canto school of opera; one of the last masters of opera buffa; resided in Paris (from 1823). Among his 39 operas were *La cambiale di matrimonio* (1810), *L'equivoca stravagante* (1811), *La pietra del paragone* (1812), *L'Italiana in Algeri* (1813), *Tancredi* (1813), *Elisabetta, regina d'Inghilterra* (1815), *Il barbiere di Siviglia* (1816), *Otello* (1816), *La cenerentola* (1817), *La gazza ladra* (1817), *La donna del lago* (1819), *Semiramide* (1823), *Le siège de Corinthe* (1827), *Moïse* (1827), *Le Comte Ory* (1828), and *Guillaume Tell* (1829). Nonoperatic compositions included sacred music as *Stabat Mater* (1832, rev. 1842) and *Petite Messe solennelle* (1864), cantatas as *La morte di Didone* (1811) and *Il viaggio a Reims* (1825), 5 string quartets (1808), songs, and many pieces for piano.

Rosslyn, Earl of. See Alexander WEDDERBURN.

Ros·so \'rōs-sō\, Giovanni Battista di Jacopo. *Called* Il Rosso *and* Il Rosso Fio·ren·ti·no \-ˌfyō-rān-'tē-nō\. 1494–1540. Florentine painter. Pupil of Andrea del Sarto. Painted in Mannerist style such works as *Assumption* (fresco, 1517), *Deposition* (1521), *Moses Defending the Daughters of Jethro* (c.1523). While in Rome (1523–27) developed more subdued style, as in *Dead Christ with Angels* (c.1526). Called to Fontainebleau as chief artist by Francis I (1530); developed ornamental style that exerted international influence; chief work was allegorical fresco cycle in Galerie François I at Fontainebleau (c.1534–37).

Rosso, Medardo. 1858–1928. Italian sculptor. An originator of Impressionist sculpture; his formless wax and plaster figures were shocking departure from academic art; influenced Rodin, Brancusi, and the Futurists; works included *Impression of an Omnibus* (1883–84), *Conversation in a Garden* (1893), *Sick Child* (1895), and *Boulevard Impression, Paris at Night* (1895).

Ros·tand \rȯ-stä^n\, Edmond-Eugène-Alexis. 1868–1918. French playwright. Author of many plays as *Les Romanesques* (1894), *La Princesse lointaine* (1895), *La Samaritaine* (1897), and his great successes *Cyrano de Bergerac* (1897), *L'Aiglon* (1900), and *Chantecler* (1910).

Ro·stop·chin \rə-(ˌ)stəp-'chēn\, Fyodor Vasilyevich. Count. 1763–1826. Russian soldier and politician. Aide-de-camp to Czar Paul I; promoted general and grand marshal of the court; minister of foreign affairs (1898–1801). Governor of Moscow (1812); organized its defense against Napoléon; believed to have ordered the burning of the city when its fall became inevitable. His daughter ¶Sophie (1799–1874) married Comte Eugène de Ségur and became comtesse de Sé·gur \də-sā-gœr\; lived in France; author of children's books whose central character was usually "Sophie," as *Les Malheurs de Sophie* (1859); wrote several volumes for children's book series *Bibliothèque Rose*.

Ro·stov·tzeff \(ˌ)rə-'stȯf-tsif\, Michael Ivanovitch. 1870–1952. American archaeologist, b. near Kiev, Russia. Authority on ancient Greek and Roman history. Professor of Latin, St. Petersburg (1898–1918); professor of ancient history, U. of Wisconsin (1920–25), Yale (1925–44). Directed excavation of a Hellenistic city in Syria (1928–37); also wrote on art and archaeology of southern Russia. Among his works were *History of the Ancient World* (1926–28), *Social and Economic History of the Roman Empire* (1926), *Dura-Europos and Its Art* (1938), and *Social and Economic History of the Hellenistic World* (1941).

Roswitha. See HROSVITHA.

Ro·szak \'rȯsh-ˌäk\, Theodore. 1907–1981. American sculptor, b. Poznań, Poland. To U.S. (1909, naturalized 1921). Known for his Abstract Expressionist sculptures in welded steel, including *Specter of Kitty Hawk, The Whaler of Nantucket, Mandrake,* and eagle for façade of U.S. Embassy, London (1960).

Ro·tha·ri \rō-'tär-ē\. d. 652. Lombard king of Italy (636–652). Waged war against the Byzantines, capturing Genoa (c.641); issued a code of civil and criminal law based on Germanic principles (643); last Lombard king to profess Arianism.

Ro·the \'rō-tə\, Richard. 1799–1867. German theologian. Member of German Idealist school; pupil of Hegel; professor at Heidelberg (from 1837). Author of *Die Anfänge der christlichen Kirche und ihrer Verfassung* (1837), *Theologische Ethick* (1845–48), *Stille Stunden* (1886), etc.

Ro·then·stein \'rō-thən-ˌstīn\, Sir William. 1872–1945. English painter. An official artist with English and Canadian armies during both World Wars; principal of Royal Coll. of Art (1920–35); known esp. for portrait drawings of contemporaries.

Rothermere, Viscount. See Harold Sidney HARMSWORTH.

Rothesay, Duke of. See David Stewart under ROBERT III of Scotland.

Roth·ko \'räth-(ˌ)kō\, Mark. *Orig.* Marcus Roth·ko·vitch \'rȯt-kəv-ˌyich\. 1903–1970. American painter, b. Dvinsk, Russia. To U.S. (1913). Painted in realistic style, as in *Subway* series of late 1930s, and in semi-abstract biomorphic forms, as *Baptismal Scene* (1945). Became (from 1948) a leading figure in Abstract Expressionism and introduced contemplative introspection into that school; used color as sole means of expression. His works included *No. 2, 1948* (1948), *Light, Earth, and Blue* (1954), *The Black and the Red* (1956), *Black on Grey* (1970), and a series of 14 canvases for a Houston, Texas, chapel (1958–66).

Rothmaler, Karl von. See Karl von EINEM.

Roth·schild *Ger* 'rōt-ˌshilt; *Angl* 'rȯth(s)-ˌchīld, 'rȯs-; *Fr* rȯt-shēld\. Family of Jewish financiers, including: Mayer Amschel (1744–1812), founder, a moneylender at Frankfurt am Main; financial adviser (1801) to the landgrave of Hesse-Kassel; agent of the British government in subsidizing European sovereigns in wars against Napoléon. His five sons: ¶Amschel Mayer (1773–1855), who succeeded his father as head of the Frankfurt establishment. ¶Salomon Mayer (1774–1855), who founded a branch at Vienna. ¶Nathan Mayer (1777–1836), who founded a branch at London. ¶Karl Mayer (1788–1855), who founded a branch at Naples. ¶James *or* Jakob (1792–1868), who founded a branch at Paris.

Nathan Mayer was succeeded by his son ¶Lionel Nathan (1808–1879), elected to Parliament (1847, 1849, 1852, 1857) but not allowed to take his seat because of his Jewish faith; instrumental in securing removal of ban on Jews (1858) and sat in Parliament (1858–68, 1869–74). Lionel Nathan was succeeded as head of the London banking house by his son ¶Sir Nathan Mayer, 1st Baron Rothschild (1840–1915), member of Parliament (1865–85) and of the House of Lords (from 1885), first Jew admitted to the House of Lords. Nathan Mayer's son ¶Lionel Walter, 2nd Baron Rothschild (1868–1937), M.P. (1899–1910), wrote zoological treatises; founded Rothschild Natural History Museum (1892); received the Balfour Declaration (1917).

Rothschild, Louis-Georges. See Georges MANDEL.

Ro·trou \rȯ-trü\, Jean de. 1609–1650. French playwright. Patronized by Cardinal de Richelieu; chief competitor of Corneille; house dramatist for Hôtel de Bourgogne, Paris. Author of comedies as *Les Ménechmes* (1632), *Les Sosies* (1636), *Les Captifs* (1638), tragicomedies as *Don Bertrand de Cabrère* (1647), and tragedies as *Le Véritable Saint Genest* (1647), *Venceslas* (1648), *Cosroès* (1649).

Rou·ault \rwō\, Georges, *in full* Georges-Henri. 1871–1958. French painter, printmaker, ceramist, and stained glass maker. Apprentice church glazier (1885–90); studied with Matisse and Marquet under Gustave Moreau (1891–98); loosely associated with Fauves. Noted for Expressionistic style and religious orientation; subjects included landscapes, religious themes, clowns, prostitutes, and judges. Among his canvases were *Judges* (1908), *Three Clowns* (1917), *Christ Mocked by Soldiers* (1932), *The Holy Face* (1933), *Christ and the High Priest* (1937), *The Three Judges* (1937), *Head of a Clown* (1948), and *Christian Nocturne* (1952).

Rou·bil·lac \rü-bē-yäk\ *or* **Rou·bi·liac** \rü-bēl-yäk\, Louis-François. c.1695 or 1705–1762. French sculptor. To London (c.1732); first independent commission was statue of Handel for Vauxhall Gardens (1737); opened own studio (1738). Works included portrait busts as of Hogarth and Alexander Pope, full length portrait statues, and monuments, esp. of Duke of Argyll (1746) and of Lady Elizabeth Nightingale (1761), both in Westminster Abbey.

Rou·get de Lisle \rü-zhe-də-lēl\, Claude-Joseph. 1760–1836. French army officer and composer. Known as composer of words and music of "La Marseillaise" (1792), originally published under title "Chant de guerre pour l'armée du Rhin."

Rou·her \rwer\, Eugène. 1814–1884. French politician. Member of Constituent Assembly (1848) and Legislative Assembly (1849). Premier of France and minister of justice (1849–51); minister of justice (1851–52), and of agriculture, commerce, and public works (1855); signed trade treaties with England (1860), Belgium (1861), and Italy (1863). Again premier (minister of state, 1863–69); attempted to suppress liberal movement. President of Senate (1869–70) and a leader of Bonapartists (1871).

Rou·main \rü-ma^n\, Jacques. 1907–1944. Haitian writer and politician. Co-editor of *La Revue indigène* (1927); stressed value of native Haitian culture. Author of poems and esp. of novels, including *La Proie et l'ombre* (1930), *La Montagne ensorcelée* (1931), and *Gouverneurs de la rosée* (1944).

Rou·ma·nille \rü-má-nēy\, Joseph. 1818–1891. French Provençal writer. Leader of the Félibrige ; a founder and editor of the Félibrige journal *Armana prouvençau* (1854). Among his works were *Li Margarideto* (1847), *Lis Oubreto* *en vers* (1862), *Lis Oubreto en prose* (1859), *Li Conte prouvençau* (1883), *Li Cascareleto* (1883), etc.

Rourke \ˈrů(ə)rk\, Constance Mayfield. 1885–1941. American historian, b. Cleveland. Author of *Trumpets of Jubilee* (1927), *American Humor* (1931), *Davy Crockett* (1934), *Audubon* (1936), *Charles Sheeler* (1938), etc.

Rous \ˈraůs\, Francis. 1579–1659. English Puritan and hymnologist. Author of *The Arte of Happiness* (1619) and *Testis Veritatis* (1626); known esp. for his metrical version of *Psalms* (1643).

Rous, Francis Peyton. 1879–1970. American pathologist, b. Baltimore. At Rockefeller Inst. (1910–45; emeritus 1945); awarded Nobel prize for physiology or medicine (1966) with C. B. Huggins for discovery (1910) of tumor-inducing viruses.

Rous·seau \rü-sō, *Angl* rů-ˈsō, ˈrü-ˌ\, Henri, *in full* Henri-Julien-Félix. *Known as* Le Dou·a·nier \lə-dwȧn-yā\. 1844–1910. French painter. Tax collector (whence nickname) in Paris toll office (1871–93); exhibited first with *Carnival Evening* (1886). Known for richly colored primitive paintings, esp. of jungles and wild beasts. His canvases included *Myself: Portrait-Landscape* (1890), *War* (1894), *The Sleeping Gypsy* (1897), *The Hungry Lion* (1905), *The Snake-Charmer* (1907), *Yadivigha's Dream* (1910), and *Tropical Forest with Monkeys* (1910).

Rousseau, Jean-Baptiste. 1671–1741. French poet and dramatist. Banished from France (c.1712) because of satirical couplets ascribed to him, attacking certain prominent men of letters. Best known for his *Cantates, Psaumes,* and *Ode à la Fortune.*

Rousseau, Jean-Jacques. 1712–1778. French philosopher and author, b. Geneva. Ran away to Italy and Savoy (1728); lived with Mme de Warens (1731–41), but with several periods of wandering during these years. Lived chiefly in Paris (from 1741); associated with Diderot; wrote an opera *Les Muses galantes* (1745) and articles on music and political economy for the *Encyclopédie;* took as mistress (1745) Thérèse Levasseur, an illiterate inn servant by whom he had five children, all placed in a foundling hospital. Acquired fame as a writer by his essay *Discours sur les arts et sciences* (1750), developing the paradox that the savage state is superior to the civilized; produced an operetta *Le Devin du village* (1752). Attacked private property in *Discours sur l'origine et les fondements de l'inégalité parmi les hommes* (1755); in *Lettre à d'Alembert sur les spectacles* (1758) argued against Voltaire's ideas on the theater, esp. in Geneva; broke with Diderot. Wrote *Julie, ou la Nouvelle Héloïse* (1761), a sentimental and moralizing romance written in the form of letters. Published *Du contrat social* (1762), a discussion of the principles of political right, upholding that the rightful authority is the general will, and *Émile, ou Traité de l'éducation* (1762), the simple romance of a child reared apart from other children by methods of experimentation, a book that influenced modern pedagogical movements; both books condemned by Parlement of Paris (1762). Fled to Switzerland (1762), then to London (1766); invited by David Hume to live at Wootton, Derbyshire; quarreled with Hume and fled to France (1767); undoubtedly partly insane during last 10 or 15 years of his life; in Paris (1770–78) writing *Confessions* (pub. 1781 and 1788), *Dialogues,* and *Rêveries du promeneur solitaire* (1782).

Rousseau, Théodore, *in full* Pierre-Étienne-Théodore. 1812–1867. French painter. Began painting landscapes directly from nature, a novel procedure at that time (1820s); settled in Barbizon (1840s) and became leader of Barbizon school of painting. His works included *Descent of the Cattle* (c.1834), *Under the Birches, Evening* (1842–44), and *The Marsh in the Landes* (1844–53).

Rous·sel \rü-sel\, Albert-Charles-Paul-Marie. 1869–1937. French composer. Pupil of d'Indy; taught (1902–14) at Schola Cantorum, Paris; pupils included Satie and Varèse. Works noted for lyrical fervor, austere technique, and harmonic audacity. Compositions included orchestral works as 4 symphonies (esp. No. 3, 1930), *Évocations* (1912), *Pour une fête de printemps* (1921), *Suite in F* (1927), *Piano Concerto* (1928), *Sinfonietta for Strings* (1934); operas *Padmâvatî* (1918), *La Naissance de la lyre* (1925); ballets *Le Festin de l'araignée* (1912), *Bacchus et Ariane* (1931); chamber music, esp. string quartet (1932), string trio (1937); piano pieces; and vocal music, esp. setting of Psalm 80 for chorus and orchestra (1928).

Rous·se·lot \rü-slō\, Jean-Pierre. 1846–1924. French phonetician. Pioneer in experimental phonetics and in study of dialect as related to geography and genealogy; at Collège de France (from 1897). Author of *Principes de phonétique expérimentale* (1897–1909) and *Précis de prononciation française* (1902, with F. Laclotte).

Routh \ˈraůth\, Edward John. 1831–1907. British mathematician, b. Quebec. Fellow of Peterhouse, Cambridge (from 1855); remembered as outstanding teacher. Author of classic works on dynamics and statics, including *Rigid Dynamics* (1860), *Treatise on the Stability of a Given State of Motion* (1877), *Analytical Statics* (1891).

Rou·vier \rüv-yā\, Maurice, *in full* Pierre-Maurice. 1842–1911. French politician. Member of National Assembly (1871), of Chamber of Deputies (1876–1902), and of Senate (1903–05). Minister of commerce and colonies (1881–82, 1884–85); premier of France (1887); minister of finance (1887, 1889–92, 1902–05); again premier (1905–06).

Rouv·roy \rüv-rwä\, Claude-Henri de. Comte de Saint-Si·mon \-də-saⁿ-sē-mōⁿ\. 1760–1825. French social reformer. Grandnephew of Louis de Rouvroy. Volunteer in French troops fighting with Americans in American Revolution (1777–83); on return to France (1783) made fortune in land speculation but lost it (by 1805), lived thereafter in poverty. Founded a religion of socialism combining teachings of Jesus with ideas of science and industrialism; his disciples spread his system, known as Saint-Simonianism, throughout Europe. His treatises included *Lettres d'un habitant de Genève à ses contemporains* (1803), *De la réorganisation de la societé européenne* (1814), *Du système industriel* (1820–21), and *Nouveau Christianisme* (1825).

Rouvroy, Louis de. Duc de Saint-Simon. 1675–1755. French soldier and writer. Served in army (1691–1702); member of council of regency during minority of Louis XV (1715–23); ambassador to Spain (1721–22). Best known for his *Mémoires* which covers 1694–1723 and is extremely valuable for information on affairs of the court.

Roux \rü\, Jacques. d. 1794. French priest and revolutionary. Leader of Enragés during French Revolution. Elected to Paris Commune (1791); led food riots and sans-culotte crowds that forced expulsion of Girondins from National Convention (1793); denounced the Convention for failure to curb hoarders and war profiteers; attacked by Robespierre and expelled from Commune (1793); arrested (1793) and committed suicide in prison.

Roux, Pierre-Paul-Émile. 1853–1933. French physician and bacteriologist. With Pasteur Institute (from 1888), director (1904–33). Worked with Pasteur on the etiology and treatment of various infectious diseases, including anthrax, tetanus, and hydrophobia; conducted researches (with Nocard) leading to the discovery of the pneumococcus; demonstrated (with Yersin, 1889) that the diphtheria bacillus produces a toxin, a discovery which led to the development of a diphtheria antitoxin by Emil von Behring.

Roux, Wilhelm. 1850–1924. German zoologist. Founder of modern experimental embryology; known for researches on the early development of the fertilized egg. Professor at Breslau (1886–89), Innsbruck (1889–95), Halle (1895–1921); founded *Archiv für Entwicklungsmechanik der Organismen* (1894).

Rovigo, Duc de. See Anne SAVARY.

Rowe \ˈrō\, Nicholas. 1674–1718. English poet and dramatist. Produced (1700–15) eight plays, including *The Ambitious Stepmother* (1700), *Tamerlane* (1702), *The Fair Penitent,* an adaptation in which appears Lothario, said to have suggested Lovelace to Samuel Richardson (1703), *The Biter* (1704, his only comedy), *The Tragedy of Jane Shore* (1714), *The Tragedy of Lady Jane Grey* (1715). First modern editor of Shakespeare; published edition of plays from fourth folio with biography containing collection of Shakespearean traditions made at Stratford by Thomas Betterton (1709); divided and numbered acts and scenes, noted entrances and exits, modernized grammar, spelling, and punctuation, prefixed the *dramatis personae.* Praised by Dr. Johnson for his translation of Lucan; poet laureate (1715).

Row·ell \ˈraů(-ə)l\, Newton Wesley. 1867–1941. Canadian lawyer and politician, b. Middlesex Co., Ont. Member of Dominion Parliament (1917–21); member of Imperial War Cabinet and Imperial War Conference (1918); Canadian delegate at first Assembly of League of Nations (1920); chief justice of Ontario (1936–37). Author of *Canada a Nation* (1923), etc.

Row·land \ˈrō-lənd\, Henry Augustus. 1848–1901. American physicist, b. Honesdale, Pa. First professor of physics, Johns Hopkins (1875–1901). Invented the concave diffraction grating for the spectroscope. Proved similarity in magnetic effect of an electric current and a high-speed electrostatic charge (1876); determined mechanical equivalent of heat and of the ohm (1879). Published *Photographic Map of the Normal Solar Spectrum* (1888) and a table of solar spectrum wavelengths (1895–97). First president of American Physical Society (1899–1901).

Row·land·son \ˈrō-lən(d)-sən\, Thomas. 1756–1827. English caricaturist. Settled in London as portrait painter (1777), soon turning to caricature and illustration; designed and engraved a series of plates entitled *Tours of Dr. Syntax* (1812, 1820, 1821), with verses by Dr. William Combe, also *The English Dance of Death* (1815–16), *The Dance of Life* (1816). Illustrated works of Smollett, Goldsmith, and Sterne, and *Baron Munchausen.*

Row·ley \ˈrō-lē, ˈraů-\, Samuel. d. 1633? English dramatist. Author of two extant plays, *When you see me, You known me. Or the famous Chronicle Historie of King Henry VIII* (1605) and *The Noble Souldier* (1634).

Rowley, Thomas. See Thomas CHATTERTON.

Rowley, William. 1585?–?1642. English actor and dramatist. Actor with Prince Charles' Men and King's Men (c.1610–c.1627). Published pamphlet "A Search for Money" (1609). Sole author of *A New Wonder, A Woman Never Vext* (1632), *A Match at Midnight* (1633), *All's Lost by Lust* (1633), *A Shoomaker a Gentleman* (1638). Collaborated with Dekker and Ford in *The Witch of Edmonton* (pub. 1658); with Middleton in *A Faire Quarrel* (1617), *The Spanish Gipsie* (pub. 1653), and *The Changeling* (performed 1621, pub.

1653); with Thomas Heywood in *Fortune by Land and Sea* (1655); with Fletcher in *The Maid in the Mill* (1622) and in *The Birth of Merlin* (1662).

Rown·tree \'raủn-trē\, Benjamin Seebohm. 1871–1954. English sociologist and philanthropist. Joined (1889) family cocoa business and improved factory conditions, as with pension plan, five-day week, and employee profit-sharing plan. Served in government positions. Known for studies of poverty and welfare, including *Poverty: A Study of Town Life* (1901), *Poverty and Progress* (1941), *English Life and Leisure* (1951), *Poverty and the Welfare State* (1951).

Row·son \'raủz-ᵊn\, Susanna, *nee* Has·well \'haz-wəl, -ˌwel\. 1762–1824. American author, actress, and educator, b. Portsmouth, England. m. William Rowson (1787). On English stage (1792) and American stage (1793–97). Ran a boarding school for young ladies near Boston, Mass. (1797–1824). Author of novels, including *Charlotte, a Tale of Truth,* better known as *Charlotte Temple* (1791), *Rebecca* (1792), *Reuben and Rachel* (1798), *Charlotte's Daughter,* better known as *Lucy Temple* (1828).

Rowton, Baron. See Montagu CORRY.

Rox·ana \räk-'san-ə, -'sä-nə\ *or* **Rox·ane** \-'san-ē, -'sä-nē\. d. c.310 B.C. Wife (m. 327) of Alexander the Great. Daughter of a Bactrian prince; with her son Alexander IV, placed under regency of Perdiccas after Alexander's death (323); had Stateira (Alexander's second wife) killed (323); later went to Macedonia; with her son, imprisoned at Amphipolis and murdered by order of Cassander.

Ro·xas y Acu·ña \'rō-käs-ē-ä-'kün-yä\, Manuel. 1892–1948. Philippine politician. Speaker, Philippine House of Representatives (1922–34); member of National Assembly (1935–38); secretary of finance (1938–40); first president of Republic of Philippines (1946–48).

Roxburgh, Earls and dukes of. See KERR family.

Roy \rwä\, Joseph Camille. 1870–1943. Canadian literary critic, b. Berthier-en-Bas, Que. Ordained Roman Catholic priest (1894); professor at Laval U., Quebec (from 1900). Authority on development of French-Canadian literature; author of *Nos origines littéraires* (1909), *Manuel d'histoire de la littérature canadienne-française* (1918), *Poètes de chez nous* (1934), etc.

Roy \'rȯi\, Manabendra Nath. *Orig.* Narendranath Bhat·ta·char·ya \bət-tə-'chär-yə\. 1887–1954. Indian Communist leader. Involved with Indian independence groups (to 1915); in Moscow on executive committee of Comintern; broke with Comintern (1929); returned to India and led Communist party; abandoned Communism after Indian independence (1947).

Roy·all \'rȯi(-ə)l\, Anne, *nee* New·port \'n(y)ü-ˌpō(ə)rt, -ˌpȯ(ə)rt\. 1769–1854. American author and journalist, b. Maryland. m. (1797) William Royall. Traveled throughout U.S. (from 1824) and published (1826–31) her observations, esp. *Sketches of History, Life and Manners in the United States by a Traveler* (1826); published muckraking papers *Paul Pry* (1831–36) and *The Huntress* (1836–54); also wrote novel *The Tennessean* (1827).

Royce \'rȯis\, Sir Henry, *in full* Frederick Henry. 1863–1933. English engineer and automobile manufacturer. Founded (1884) engineering firm Royce, Ltd., in Manchester; designed and built three experimental cars (1904); joined with C. S. Rolls (1906) in founding Rolls-Royce, Ltd.; made baronet (1930).

Royce, Josiah. 1855–1916. American philosopher, b. Grass Valley, Calif. Pupil of William James and Charles S. Peirce. Taught philosophy, Harvard (1882–1916; professor from 1892). Wrote on mathematical logic, psychology, metaphysics, religion, and social ethics; developed philosophy of Idealism emphasizing individuality and will rather than intellect. His writings included *The Religious Aspect of Philosophy* (1885), *The Spirit of Modern Philosophy* (1892), *The Conception of God* (1897), *Studies of Good and Evil* (1898), *The World and the Individual* (1900–01), *The Philosophy of Loyalty* (1908), *Sources of Religious Insight* (1912), *The Problem of Christianity* (1913), *The Hope of the Great Community* (1916).

Royen, Snellius van. See Willebrord SNELL.

Roy·er-Col·lard \rwä-yä-kō-lår\, Pierre-Paul. 1763–1845. French philosopher and politician. Secretary of Paris Commune (1790–92); elected to Council of Five Hundred (1797); after the Restoration, a leader of the Doctrinaires, advocates of constitutional monarchy; member (1815–42; president, 1828) of Chamber of Deputies. Developed a realist "philosophy of perception."

Ro·za·nov \(ˌ)rə-'zä-nəf, 'rȯz-ə-\, Vasily Vasilyevich. 1856–1919. Russian essayist. Published (1890) *Legend of the Grand Inquisitor,* first detailed study of Dostoyevsky; on staff of conservative paper *Novoye Vremya* (from 1899); books of essays included *Solitaria* (1912) and *Fallen Leaves* (1913, 1915).

Ruaidh, Máiri Nighean Alasdair. See Mary MACLEOD.

Ru·bens \'rü-bənz, *Angl* 'rü-bənz\, Peter Paul. 1577–1640. Flemish painter, b. Westphalia. Influenced by Renaissance paintings while in service of Vincenzo I Gonzaga of Mantua (1600–08); settled in Antwerp (1609). Called to Paris (1622) to decorate the Luxembourg for Marie de Médicis; on diplomatic missions for the Habsburgs (1621–30), esp. to Madrid (1628) and London (1629). Painted in Baroque style landscapes, portraits, and esp. historical and sacred subjects; renowned for excellence of his coloring. Among his works were *Elevation of the Cross* (1610), *The Last Judgment* (c.1616), *Marie de Médicis* (c.1622–25), *Rape of the Sabines* (1635), *Venus and Adonis* (c.1635), *The Kermesse* (c.1636–38), *The Judgment of Paris* (1638–39), and *Hélèna Fourment with Fur Cloak* (c.1638–40).

Ru·bey \'rü-bē\, William Walden. 1898–1974. American geologist, b. Moberly, Mo. Member of U.S. Geological Survey (1924–60); professor at U.C.L.A. (1960–69). Known for his theory (proposed 1951) of the origin of the Earth's atmosphere, oceans, and crust by fractional melting of the upper mantle.

Rubianus, Crotus. See Johann JÄGER.

Ru·bin·stein \rüb-yin-'shtīn, *Angl* 'rü-bən-ˌstīn\, Anton Grigoryevich. 1829–1894. Russian pianist and composer. Made many concert tours in Europe and (1872–73) U.S.; settled in St. Petersburg (1848); founded Russian Music Society (1859); founded and directed (1862–67, 1887–91) St. Petersburg Conservatory of Music; spent last years principally in Berlin (1890–92) and Dresden. Compositions included operas as *Dmitry Donskoy* (1852), *Sibirskiye okhotniki* (Siberian Huntsmen, 1854), *Demon* (1875), *Die Makkabäer* (1875), *Kupets Kalashnikov* (1880); 6 symphonies, esp. *Ocean* (No.2); concertos for piano (5), for cello (2), for violin; oratorios as *Der Thurm zu Babel* (1870) and *Moses* (1892); piano pieces, songs, and much chamber music.

Rubinstein \'rü-bən-ˌstīn\, Arthur. 1887–1982. American pianist, b. Lodz, Poland. A child prodigy; studied at Warsaw Conservatory from age of eight; made European debut at 13; debuted in U.S. with Philadelphia Orchestra at Carnegie Hall (1906); created sensation in Spain by introducing works by Manuel de Falla and Enrique Grandas (1916); rest of career an unbroken series of triumphs; huge repertoire included Beethoven, Mozart, Ravel, Stravinsky, and esp. Chopin; more than 200 recordings, selling over 10 million copies, ranked him as best-selling classical pianist ever. Considered one of the greatest concert pianists of 20th century for his lyricism, dashing technique, and distinctive "golden tone."

Rub·lyov \(ˌ)rəb-'lyȯf\, Andrey. 1360 to 1370–c.1430. Russian painter. Assistant to Theophanes the Greek; became a monk. Painted in Byzantine style; presumed painter of *The Old Testament Trinity* icon and also (1408) of panels of Saints John the Baptist, Paul, and Peter in cathedral of Vladimir.

Rubruquis *or* **Rubrouck** *or* **Rubruck,** William of. See WILLEM VAN RUYSBROECK.

Rucelinus. See ROSCELIN DE COMPIÈGNE.

Ru·cel·lai \ˌrü-chäl-'lä-ē\, Giovanni. 1475–1525. Italian poet and dramatist. Nephew of Lorenzo de' Medici. Became a churchman; served both Medici popes. One of first to use blank verse (*versi sciolti*), as in poem *Le api* (1524), in imitation of Virgil's *Georgics* (Book IV); known esp. as an initiator of Italian classic tragedy with plays *Rosmunda* (1515) and *Oreste* (1525).

Ruck·ers \'rœk-ərs\. Flemish family of harpsichord and virginal makers. Their instruments provided an important model for later north European builders. Its members included: Hans (c.1540 or 1550–1598), *surnamed* the Elder; founded the business in Antwerp; earliest known instrument dated 1581. His son ¶Hans (1578–1643), *also known as* Jan *or* Joannes, *surnamed* the Younger, succeeded him as head of the firm (1598). Another son of Hans the Elder, ¶Andreas (1579–after 1645) was also with the firm until bought out (1608) by Hans the Younger; afterwards made harpsichords on his own.

Rück·ert \'rœk-ərt\, Friedrich. 1788–1866. German poet. Professor of Oriental languages, Erlangen (1826–41) and Berlin (1841–48). Works included *Deutsche Gedichte* (containing anti-Napoleonic *Geharnischte Sonette* under pseudonym Freimund Rai·mar \'rī-ˌmär\, 1814), *Kranz der Zeit* (1817), *Liebesfrühling* (love poems, 1823), *Die Weisheit des Brahmanen* (1836–39), historical dramas, and translations and imitations of literature of the East.

Rū·da·kī \ˌrü-da-'gē\. *Orig.* Abū 'Abdollāh Ja'far ebn Moḥammad. c.859–940 or 941. Persian poet. Court poet at Sāmānid court of Naṣr II (to 937); author of a reported 100,000 couplets, of which some 1,000 are extant; translated *Kalilah wa Dimnah* from Arabic to New Persian. Father of Persian poetry.

Rud·beck \'rüd-bek\, Olof. 1630–1702. Swedish scientist. Professor, Uppsala (1655–91); discovered the lymphatic system (1650); attempted to prove that the cradle of human culture and Plato's Atlantis were in Sweden. The botanical genus *Rudbeckia* is named for him.

Rudd, Steele. See Arthur H. DAVIS.

Rud·di·man \'rəd-ə-mən\, Thomas. 1674–1757. Scottish classical scholar. Editor of Livy (1751); author of a Latin grammar that superseded all others (1714) and a philological work, *Grammaticae Latinae Institutiones* (1725–31).

Rude \rüed\, François. 1784–1855. French sculptor. Studio in Brussels (1815–27) and Paris (from 1827); best known for public monuments in Paris. Among his works were *Mercure rattachant ses talonnières* (1828), *Petit pêcheur napolitain jouant avec une tortue* (1834), *Départ des volontaires en 1792* (high relief on Arc de Triomphe; 1833–35), *Jeanne d'Arc écoutant ses voix* (1845–52), *Napoléon s'éveillant à l'immortalité* (1847), and various portrait busts and statues.

Rudini, Marchese di. See Antonio STARABBA.

Ru·dolf \'rü-ˌdȯlf, *Angl also* -ˌdälf\. 1858–1889. Archduke and crown prince of Austria. Only son of Emperor Francis Joseph. Excluded from participation in government because of his reformist and liberal views; developed romantic attachment for Baroness Marie Ve·tse·ra \'vech-er-ä\; resulted in tragedy when their bodies were found in Rudolf's hunting lodge of Mayerling. It was officially announced that the two had committed suicide; all investigation and further information were suppressed.

Rudolf. *Fr.* Ro·dolphe \rō-dȯlf\. Name of three kings of Burgundy:

Rudolf I. d. 912. Son of Conrad, Count of Auxerre; first king of Jurane Burgundy (888–912); vassal of Emperor Arnulf.

Rudolf II. d. 937. Son of Rudolf I and father of Empress Adelaide; king of Burgundy (912–937); king of Italy (922–926); defeated Berengar I near Piacenza (923); resigned Italian throne to Hugh of Arles; received Provence (933) from Hugh in return for renunciation of claims to Italy.

Rudolf III. d. 1032. Last independent king of Burgundy (993–1032); at his death lands bequeathed to Emperor Conrad II.

Rudolf *or* **Ra·oul** \rá-ül\. d. 936. King of France (923–936) and Duke of Burgundy. Son of Richard, Duke of Burgundy. Succeeded his father in the dukedom (921); m. Emma, daughter of Robert, Count of Paris. Leagued with Robert, drove Charles III the Simple from his throne; supported Robert as king of France until his death (923) and succeeded Robert on the throne.

Rudolf. *Called* Rudolf of Rhein·fel·den \'rīn-ˌfel-dən\. d. 1080. German king (1077–80) and Duke of Swabia. Given duchy of Swabia by Agnes of Poitou (1057); m. (1059) Matilda, daughter of Agnes and sister of Henry IV. Chosen king of Germany (1077) in opposition to Henry IV, who had been excommunicated; at first successful in conflict with Henry, but slain in battle (1080).

Rudolf. Name of two Holy Roman emperors:

Rudolf I. 1218–1291. Emperor (1273–91). Son of Albert IV, Count of Habsburg. Landgrave of Alsace (1239–91); elected king of Germany and Holy Roman emperor (1273), first of the Habsburg line (*q.v.*); recognized (1274) by Pope Gregory X on his promise to renounce imperial rights in Rome, the papal territories, and Sicily, and to lead a new crusade. Consolidated his power in Austria; invested his sons Albert and Rudolf with the duchies of Austria and Styria; defeated and killed Otakar II of Bohemia at Marchfeld (1278).

Rudolf II. 1552–1612. Emperor (1576–1612). Son of Maximilian II; crowned king of Hungary (1572) and of Bohemia (1575). Scholarly, but an impractical ruler and intolerant toward Protestants. Successful insurrection in Hungary forced him (1608) to make his brother Matthias king of Hungary and governor of Austria and Moravia; in *Majestätsbrief (Letter of Majesty),* granted Bohemians religious freedom (1609); transferred Bohemia to Matthias (1611).

Rudolf. King of Italy. See RUDOLF II of Burgundy.

Rudolf von Ems \'äms, 'ems\. c.1200–c.1254. Middle High German epic poet of Swiss descent. Successively in service of Simon de Montfort and Conrad IV. Author of legendary epics *Der gute Gerhard* and *Barlaam und Josaphat,* historical dramatic epics *Willehalm von Orlens* and *Alexander,* and *Weltchronik,* based on Old Testament.

Rue, Warren de la. See DE LA RUE.

Rue·da \'rwā-thä\, Lope de. 1510?–1565. Spanish dramatist. Goldbeater by trade; author-manager of a traveling theater company. Author of four comedies adapted from the Italian *Medora, Armelina, Eufemia,* and *Los engañados;* also of bucolic dialogues and esp. *pasos,* prose interludes in natural language.

Ruf·fin \'rəf-ən\, Edmund. 1794–1865. American agriculturist, b. Prince George Co., Va. Conducted experiments for restoring fertility of Virginia soil; wrote *An Essay on Calcareous Manures* (1832); founded and edited *Farmer's Register* (1833–42), a journal promoting scientific agriculture. Ardent advocate of Southern secession and was granted honor of firing (Apr. 12, 1861) first shot on Fort Sumter.

Ruf·fi·ni \rüf-'fē-nē\, Giovanni. 1807–1881. Italian writer. Follower of Mazzini; went into exile (1833); lived in England (1836–42, 1849 ff.). Author of several English novels including *Lorenzo Benoni* (1853), *Doctor Antonio* (1855); wrote libretto for Donizetti's *Don Pasquale* (1843).

Ruffini, Paolo. 1765–1822. Italian mathematician and physician. Professor (from 1788), rector (1814), U. of Modena; made studies of equations that anticipated the algebraic theory of groups; regarded as first to make significant attempt to prove there is no algebraic solution of the general quintic equation (1799).

Ruf·fo \'rüf-fō\, Fabrizio. 1744–1827. Italian prelate and soldier. Cardinal (1794); royal vicar of Naples (1799); as general in Neapolitan army led (1799) royalists against invading French forces under Championnet; his lenient peace terms with the French repudiated by his ally Lord Nelson.

Ru·fi·nus \rü-'fī-nəs\, Flavius. d. 395 A.D. Roman politician, b. Gaul. Praetorian prefect of the East under Theodosius the Great (392) and under Arcadius (395); became known for persecutions and other cruel practices; engaged in disloyal intrigue with the Visigoth Alaric and was murdered in Constantinople on instigation of Gainas, friend of his rival Stilicho.

Rufinus. *Sometimes called* Tyrannius Rufinus. 345–410. Italian theologian and presbyter. Lived as monk in Egypt, on Mount of Olives near Jerusalem, and in Aquileia; opposed former friend St. Jerome in bitter controversy over doctrines of Origen; translated into Latin the Greek Christian writers, Eusebius, the *Clementine Recognitions,* Origen's *Principia* and *Homilies,* and *Historia monachorum in Aegypto.*

Ru·fus \'rü-fəs\ of Eph·e·sus \'ef-ə-səs\. 1st century B.C.–1st century A.D. Greek anatomist and physician. Author of a treatise on the nomenclature of parts of the human body, which indicates the state of anatomical knowledge preceding Galen, and of several works on diseases.

Rufus, Lucius Verginius. See VERGINIUS RUFUS.

Rufus, Marcus Caelius. See CAELIUS.

Rufus, Publius Sulpicius. See Publius SULPICIUS RUFUS.

Rufus, Servius Sulpicius. See Servius SULPICIUS RUFUS.

Ru·ge \'rü-gə\, Arnold. 1803–1880. German writer. Edited various radical journals; with Ernst Echtermeyer founded (1838) *Hallesche Jahrbücher für Deutsche Wissenschaft und Kunst,* organ of Young German Hegelians; with Karl Marx issued (1844) *Deutsch-französische Jahrbücher* in Paris. Extreme leftist member of Frankfurt National Assembly (1848); fled to London (1849), where he helped Mazzini found European Democratic Committee. Settled in Brighton as teacher and writer (from 1850).

Rugg \'rəg\, Harold Ordway. 1886–1960. American educator, b. Fitchburg, Mass. Professor of education, Teachers College, Columbia (1920–51); editor, *Journal of Educational Psychology* (1920–31) and *Frontiers of Democracy* (1939–43); founder and editor of New World Education Series (1950–60). Author of *Culture and Education in America* (1931), *Foundations for American Education* (1947), and the *Man and His Changing Society* textbook series (1929–45).

Rug·gles \'rəg-əlz\, Carl. 1876–1971. American composer, b. Marion, Mass. Founder and conductor of Winona (Minn.) Symphony Orch. (1912–17); active in composers' organizations in New York (1923–33); taught composition at U. of Miami (1938–43); in later years turned to painting. Composed atonal, polyphonic works for orchestra, including *Vox clamans in deserto* (1923), *Men and Mountains* (1924; rev. 1936), *Portals* (1925; rev. 1952–53), *The Sun-treader* (1926–31); also *Toys* (1919; voice and piano), *Men and Angels* (1920, rev. 1938; brass), and hymn *Exaltation* (1958).

Ruggles-Brise \-'brīs\, Sir Evelyn John. 1857–1935. English penologist. Chairman of Prison Commission (1895–1921); originator of Borstal system whereby juvenile delinquents are dealt with in a special institution under supervision of Borstal Association established (1908) by act of Parliament.

Ruijsdael *or* **Ruisdael,** Salomon van. See RUYSDAEL.

Ruis·dael *or* **Ruys·dael** \'rȯis-ˌdäl\, Jacob van. 1628 or 1629–1682. Dutch painter and etcher. Nephew of Salomon van Ruysdael. Often considered greatest Dutch landscape painter; painted in Baroque style. Lived mainly in Amsterdam (from c.1655); traveled in Holland and Germany in search of material (1650–53). Works represented chiefly forest scenery, waterfalls, and shore and mountain scenes, with figures sometimes added by others. His canvases included *Dunes* (c.1647), *Bentheim Castle* (1653), *Jewish Cemetery* (c.1660), *Marsh in the Woods* (c.1665), *Windmill at Wijk bij Duurstede* (c.1665), and *Wheatfields* (c.1670).

Ruiz, José Martínez. See MARTÍNEZ RUIZ.

Ru·iz \rü-'ēth\, Juan. *Called* Archpriest of Hita. 1283?–?1351. Spanish poet. Known particularly for *Libro de buen amor* (1330; expanded 1343), a miscellany of fables, legends, amorous stories, satire, devotion, attacks on the church, etc.

Ruiz Agui·le·ra \-äg-ē-'lā-rä\, Ventura. 1820–1881. Spanish poet. Director of National Museum of Archaeology; author of *Ecos nacionales* (1849), *Elegías* (1862), *La Arcadia moderna* (1867), *Leyendas de Nochebuena* (1867), *Las estaciones del año* (1879), also political and religious works and a novel, *El beso de Judas* (1860).

Ru·iz Ca·mi·no \rü-'ē-skä-'mē-nō\, Carlos. *Known as* Carlos Ar·ru·za \ä-'rü-sä\. 1920–1966. Mexican bullfighter. In long career (1934–53) became one of highest-paid matadors; performed in Spain and Portugal (1944–46), and in South America.

Ru·iz de Alar·cón y Men·do·za \rü-'ēs-thā-äl-är-'kȯn-ē-män-'dō-sä, rü-'ēth-, -män-'dō-thä\, Juan. c.1581–1639. Spanish dramatist, b. Mexico. A leading playwright of the Golden Age. To Spain (1600–08, 1611 ff.); lawyer at Seville (1606); in Madrid (1614 ff.); member of Council for the Indies (1626 ff.). Published 24 plays (between 1628–34), including *Las paredes oyen, La prueba de las promesas, El examen de maridos, Ganar amigos, Los empeños de un engaño,* and *La verdad sospechosa* (source of Corneille's *La Menteur).*

Rul·hière \rūel-yer\, Claude-Carloman de. 1734–1791. French historian and poet. Author of verse, stories, and esp. historical studies as *Histoire de la* *révolution de Russie en 1762* (1768, 1773) and *Histoire de l'anarchie de Pologne* (1807).

Rullianus, Quintus Fabius Maximus. See FABIUS.

Rumford, Count. See Benjamin THOMPSON.

Rūmī, ar-. See JALĀL AD-DĪN AR-RŪMĪ.

Rumpf *or* **Rumph** \'rəm(p)f\, Georg Eberhard. 1627–1702. German naturalist. Sent (1653) by Dutch East India Co. to Amboina, Dutch East Indies, to study plant life; author of *Herbarium Amboinense* (1741–55), an extensive study of the East Indies flora.

Rum·sey \'rəm-sē\, James. 1743–1792. American inventor, b. Cecil Co., Md. Known for experiments in building a steamboat (from 1785); demonstrated on the Potomac (Dec. 1787) a boat driven by streams of water forced through the stern by a steam pump; also invented improved steam boiler. Received patents in England and U.S. (1791) on his steamboat and steam boiler. Died before his second demonstration steamboat was finished.

Ru·myan·tsev \(,)rəm-'yänt-sif\, Nikolay Petrovich. Count. 1754–1826. Russian politician. Son of Pyotr Rumyantsev. Envoy to Rhenish Palatinate (1781–95) and German Diet (1799). Director of water communications (1801–09); minister of commerce (1802–11); president of state council (1810–14); as foreign minister (1808–14) worked for closer relations with France. Also a patron of historiography and voyages of exploration.

Rumyantsev, Pyotr Aleksandrovich. Count. *Styled* Count Za·du·nay·sky \zə-(,)də-'nī-skəi\. 1725–1796. Russian general. Distinguished himself in Seven Years' War against Prussia (1756–63) and in Russo–Turkish War (1768–74), esp. in his victory at Kozludzha (1774) which forced Turks to sue for peace.

Rund·stedt \'rünt-,shtet\, Karl Rudolf Gerd von. 1875–1953. German field marshal. Chief of staff of army corps in World War I; commanded armies in Poland (1939), France (1940), and Russia (1941–42); general field marshal (1940); commander in chief on western front (1942–45).

Ru·ne·berg \'rü-nə-,berʸ\, Johan Ludvig. 1804–1877. Finnish poet writing in Swedish. Considered the greatest Finnish poet. Lecturer in classics at Porvoo (1837–57). Author of 3 volumes of lyric poems (1830, 1833, 1843), idylls *Elgskyttarne* (1832) and *Hanna* (1836), romantic Norse epic *Kung Fjalar* (1844), *Fänrik Ståls Sägner* (a series of ballads, romances, and tales dealing with war of independence of 1808 and containing national hymn of Finland "Vårt Land"; 1848, 1860), prose tales, and dramatic works.

Runge \'ruŋ-ə\, Friedlieb Ferdinand. 1795–1867. German chemist. Professor, Breslau (1828–31); worked thereafter in industry. Considered father of paper chromatography; discovered several components of coal-tar oil, including phenol and aniline.

Run·yon \'rən-yən\, Damon, *in full* Alfred Damon. 1884–1946. American journalist and writer, b. Manhattan, Kans. Sportswriter for *New York American* (1911 ff.); wrote syndicated columns "Both Barrels" (1918–36) and "The Brighter Side" (1937 ff.). Known esp. for stories about New York City nightlife, collected in *Guys and Dolls* (1931), *Blue Plate Special* (1934), *Money from Home* (1935), and *The Best of Runyon* (1938). Also wrote movie scripts as *Little Miss Marker* and *Lemon Drop Kid.*

Ru·pert \'rü-,pərt, *Angl* -pərt\. Saint. d. 718? Patron saint of Bavaria, of royal Frankish descent. Did missionary work in Bavaria (after 695) on invitation of Duke Theodor II; founded (c.700) St. Peter's abbey in Salzburg and became its first abbot bishop.

Rupert. *Ger.* Ru·precht Klem \'rü-,prekt-,klām\. 1352–1410. King of Germany (1400–10). Member of Wittelsbach dynasty; elector palatine of the Rhine (1398–1410); elected king of Germany after deposition of Wenceslas; campaigned unsuccessfully in Italy (1401–02); during reign struggled against adherents of Wenceslas.

Rupert. Prince. Count Palatine of Rhine *and* Duke of Bavaria. Duke of Cum·ber·land \'kəm-bər-lənd\ *and* Earl of Hol·der·ness \,hōl-dər-'nes\. 1619–1682. Son of Elector Palatine Frederick V and Elizabeth, daughter of James I of England; nephew of Charles I. Served against Imperialists in Thirty Years' War (1637–38); captured and imprisoned (1638–41). Appointed general of horse by Charles I (1642), became dominant figure of Royalist forces in English Civil War; took Bristol (1643) and most of Lancashire (June 1644), but defeated by Cromwell at Marston Moor, Yorkshire (July 2, 1644). Appointed commander in chief of king's army (1644); distinguished himself in defeat at Naseby; recognizing Charles's cause as both bad and lost, surrendered Bristol to Fairfax (1645); was dismissed from all offices; cleared by court-martial; on surrender of Oxford, ordered to leave England (1646). Commanded Royalist fleet (1648–50) in unprofitable campaign; escaped to West Indies after breaking up of squadron by Blake in mouth of Tagus (1650); retired to Germany (1654–60). At Restoration, privy councilor; given naval commands in Dutch wars (1665–67, 1672–74); admiral of fleet (1673); first lord of admiralty (1673–79). A founder and first governor of Hudson's Bay Co. (1670–82). Introduced mezzotint printmaking into England; experimented with making of gunpowder, boring of guns; invented a brasslike alloy, Prince Rupert's metal or Prince's metal.

Rupp \'rəp\, Adolph Frederick. *Nicknamed* the Baron. 1901–1977. American coach, b. Halstead, Kans. While basketball coach at U. of Kentucky (1930–72) won 4 national titles and record number of college basketball games (879).

Rüp·pell \rue-'pel\, Wilhelm Peter Eduard Simon. 1794–1884. German naturalist and explorer. Traversed The Sudan from the Nubian Desert south to Kordofan (1822–27) and Ethiopia (1830–34) from east to west, mapping Lake Tana for first time; amassed zoological and ethnographical collections from trips.

Rup·pert \'rü-pərt\, Jacob. 1867–1939. American brewer, b. New York City. Entered his father's brewing business and became (1915) its president. Co-owner (1914–23) and sole owner (1923–39), New York Yankees baseball team; built Yankee Stadium (dedicated 1923).

Ru·rik \'ryür-yik, *Angl* 'rür-ik\. *Also spelled* Ryu·rik, Ro·rik \'rōr-ik\ *or* Hro·rekr \'hrōr-ik(-ər)\. d. c.879 A.D. Founder of the Rurik dynasty that ruled Russia until the death (1598) of Fyodor I. A Scandinavian Varangian prince; said to have been invited (862) by Novgorod to rule that city; apparently the father of Igor, grand prince of Kiev.

Rush \'rəsh\, Benjamin. 1745–1813. American physician, educator, and patriot, b. near Philadelphia. Practiced in Philadelphia (from 1769). Professor of chemistry, College of Philadelphia (1769–91) and at U. of Pennsylvania (1791). Member, Continental Congress (1776, 1777) and signer of Declaration of Independence. Surgeon general of Continental army (1777–78). Established first free dispensary in U.S. (1786). Member, Pennsylvania constitutional ratification convention (1787). Treasurer, U.S. Mint (1797–1813). Author of *Syllabus of a Course of Lectures on Chemistry* (1770; first chemistry textbook in U.S.), *Medical Inquiries and Observations* (1789–98), *Medical Inquiries and Observations upon the Diseases of the Mind* (1812; first psychiatric treatise in U.S.), etc.

Rush, Richard. 1780–1859. American public official and diplomat, b. Philadelphia. Son of Benjamin Rush. Comptroller, U.S. Treasury (1811); attorney general of the United States (1814–17). As U.S. secretary of state (1817) negotiated Rush-Bagot Convention with Great Britain. Minister to Great Britain (1817–25); had a part in persuading Monroe and John Q. Adams to proclaim the Monroe Doctrine; secretary of the treasury (1825–28); minister to France (1847–49).

Rush, William. 1756–1833. American sculptor and woodcarver, b. Philadelphia. Renowned esp. for his figureheads carved to adorn the prows of ships; his life-sized statue of Washington is in Independence Hall, Philadelphia; a founder of Penn. Academy of the Fine Arts (1805); considered first native-born American sculptor.

Rush·worth \'rəsh-(,)wərth\, John. 1612?–1690. English historian. Sat in five parliaments for Berwick; secretary to council of state (1660); secretary to lord keeper (1667). Author of *Historical Collections of Private Passages of State* covering period 1618 to 1648 (1659–1701).

Ru·si·ñol \rü-sēn-'yōl\, Santiago. 1861–1931. Spanish painter and writer. Wrote in Catalan; a Modernist; chief work *L'auca del senyor Esteve* (as novel, 1907; as play, 1917).

Rusk \'rəsk\, Thomas Jefferson. 1803–1857. American jurist and legislator, b. Pendleton District, S.C. To Texas (1835); secretary of war, provisional government of Texas (1836). Fought in battle of San Jacinto (1836); commanded Houston's army after Houston was wounded. First chief justice, Texas Supreme Court (1840). Active in furthering annexation of Texas by U.S.; president of Texas convention which confirmed annexation and drew up constitution (1845). U.S. senator from Texas (1846–57).

Rus·kin \'rəs-kən\, John. 1819–1900. English art critic and writer. Visited Italy several times (from 1840). Set out to establish superiority of modern landscape painters, esp. Turner, over the old masters, in first volume of *Modern Painters* (1843), which in four later volumes (1846–60) expanded into discursive treatment of his views of the principles of true art. Published *Seven Lamps of Architecture* (1849) and *Stones of Venice* (1851–53), both arguing that Gothic style was supreme for its truth in nature and moral force. Defended Pre-Raphaelites; lectured on architecture, painting, political economy of art; issued treatises on drawing (1857) and perspective (1859). Influenced by Carlyle, attempted to inspire radical change in attitude to art, religion, and economics, developing heterodox views and urging social reform in *Unto this Last* (in *Cornhill Magazine,* 1860), *Munera Pulveris* (in *Fraser's Magazine,* 1862), *Sesame and Lilies* (1865), *The Crown of Wild Olive* (1866), *Time and Tide, by Weare and Tyne* (1867); advocated national system of education in countrywide lectures (1855–70). First Slade professor of fine arts, Oxford (1869–79, 1883–84). Issued at irregular intervals (1871–84) *Fors Clavigera,* 96 essays in form of letters to workmen on remedies for poverty and misery, one of practical applications of which was his founding (1871) of Company of St.

George, each member to give a tithe to philanthropy; dispersed whole of large fortune in philanthropy, living himself on income from his books. Brought out (1885–89) autobiography (up to 1864) *Praeterita*. Other works included *The King of the Golden River* (1851), *Ethics of the Dust* (1866), *The Queen of the Air* (1869), *Val d'Arno* (1874), *Proserpina* (1875–86), *The Art of England* (1884).

Rus·sell \'rəs-əl\. English family holding the earldom of Bed·ford \'bed-fərd\ (from 1550), dukedom of Bedford (from 1694), and barony of Ampt·hill \'am(p)-(,)til, 'am(p)t-,hil\ (from 1881), and tracing descent from Henry Russell, Weymouth wine merchant, probably of Gascon origin, who sat in four parliaments (1425–42).

John Russell (1486?–1555), 1st Earl of Beford. Great-grandson of Henry; saw military service in France; one of Henry VIII's executors; lord privy seal (1542, 1547, 1553); for his part in suppressing western rebellion, created earl (1550); joint ambassador to Philip of Spain (1554); left to descendants abbey lands of Tavistock, and in Bedfordshire the Cistercian house of Woburn, chief seat of family. His son ¶Francis (1527?–1585), 2d earl, took part in Wyatt's insurrection but escaped to Geneva (1554); warden of east marches; governor of Berwick; lord lieutenant of northern counties under Queen Elizabeth. ¶Sir William (1558?–1613), 1st Baron Russell of Thorn·haugh \'thórn-,hó\, 4th son of 2d earl. Fought beside Sir Philip Sidney at Zutphen; governor of Flushing (1587–88); lord deputy of Ireland (1594–97); with Sir John Norris reduced Tyrone (1597).

¶William (1613–1700), 5th Earl and 1st Duke of Bedford; son of 4th earl. As general of horse in Parliamentary army, fought at Edge Hill and Newbury; continued his father's work of draining the Fens (1649); created duke of Bedford and marquis of Tav·is·tock \'tav-ə-,stäk\ (1649).

¶William (1639–1683); Lord Russell (courtesy title); 3d son of 1st duke. Whig Parliamentary leader. M.P. (1660); as active member of the "country party" (1673), attacked Buckingham and Danby; proposed address to king to remove Duke of York from his councils (1678); attacked Lauderdale in full council (1680); presented Duke of York as popish recusant; again seconded motion for exclusion of Duke of York (1681); accused by informers along with Algernon Sidney of complicity in Rye House Plot; charged with high treason, and through perjury by Lord Howard and a packed jury, found guilty and beheaded; his attainder reversed on accession of William and Mary.

¶Edward (1653–1727), Earl of Or·ford \'ór-fərd\; naval commander; nephew of 1st Duke of Bedford. Served as agent of Prince of Orange (before 1688); later, a correspondent of exiled James; admiral of the blue under Torrington, whom he succeeded (1690); held chief command of English and Dutch fleets in victory of La Hogue over French off Point Barfleur (1692); first lord of admiralty (1694–99, 1709–10, 1714–17).

¶John (1710–1771), 4th duke; great-grandson of 1st duke. Whig leader; opposed Sir Robert Walpole; first lord of the admiralty in Pelham's administration; secretary for southern department on Chesterfield's resignation (1748–51); lord lieutenant of Ireland (1756–57); ambassador for negotiating treaty of peace with France (1762–63); president of council (1763–67). His grandson ¶John (1766–1839), 6th duke; lord lieutenant of Ireland (1806–07); rebuilt Covent Garden market, London (1830). For the earls Russell, descendants of 6th Duke of Bedford, see John RUSSELL and Bertrand RUSSELL at own entries.

Russell, Bertrand Arthur William. 3d Earl Russell. 1872–1970. English mathematician and philosopher. Grandson of John Russell (1792–1878). Influenced by G.E. Moore, became a physical Realist (from 1898); imprisoned for pacifist views (1918); in later years involved in protesting nuclear weapons and Vietnam War. Awarded Nobel prize for literature (1950). Known esp. for work in mathematical logic. Among his books were *Principles of Mathematics* (1903), *Principia Mathematica* (1910–13, with A.N. Whitehead), *Introduction to Mathematical Philosophy* (1919), *The Analysis of Mind* (1921), *The A B C of Relativity* (1925), *The Analysis of Matter* (1927), *Education and the Social Order* (1932), *In Praise of Idleness* (1935), *History of Western Philosophy* (1945), *Human Knowledge, Its Scope and Limits* (1948), *Political Ideals* (1963), *Autobiography* (1967–69).

Russell, Charles. 1st Baron Russell of Kil·low·en \kil-'ō-ən\. 1832–1900. British judge, b. Ireland. Liberal M.P. (1880–94); attorney general (1886, 1892–94); sought establishment of a subordinate parliament in Ireland; leading counsel for Parnell in Parnell Commission (1888–90); with Sir Richard Webster, represented Great Britain in Bering Sea arbitration (1893). Lord chief justice of England (1894–1900); presided at trial of leaders of Jameson Raid (1896); one of arbitrators of British Guiana–Venezuela boundary (1899).

Russell, Charles Marion. 1865–1926. American artist, b. St. Louis, Mo. To Montana (1880); known as painter of Western scenes of cowboy and Indian life, landscapes, etc.

Russell, Charles Taze. *Called* Pastor Russell. 1852–1916. American religious leader, b. Pittsburgh. Originally Congregationalist; organized International Bible Students' Association in Pittsburgh (1872). Founded Bible journal *The Watchtower* (1879) and the Watchtower Bible and Tract Society (1884). Preached (from 1877) doctrine that second coming of Christ occurred invisibly in 1874, that since then the world has been in the "Millennial Age," that the end of this age would come in 1914 to be followed by social revolution, chaos, resurrection of the dead, and finally establishment of Christ's kingdom on earth. See Joseph Franklin RUTHERFORD.

Russell, George William. *Pseudonym* Æ\'ā-'ē\. 1867–1935. Irish man of letters. A leader of the Irish literary renaissance. Editor of *The Irish Homestead* (1904–23) and *The Irish Statesman* (1923–30). His poetical works included *Homeward: Songs by the Way* (1894), *The Earth Breath* (1897), *The Nuts of Knowledge* (1903), *The Divine Vision* (1904), *Vale and Other Poems* (1931), *House of the Titans and Other Poems* (1934); also *Deirdre* (1907, play), *The Candle of Vision* (1918), *The Interpreters* (1922), etc.

Russell, Henry Norris. 1877–1957. American astronomer, b. Oyster Bay, N.Y. Professor and observatory director, Princeton (1911–47). Made lifelong study of binary stars, esp. methods to calculate their masses and distances; showed relationship between stars' brightnesses and spectral types (1913; known as Hertzsprung-Russell diagram); one of first to demonstrate predominance of hydrogen in stars. Author of *The Solar System and Its Origins* (1935), *The Masses of the Stars* (1940), etc.

Russell, John. 1745–1806. English painter. Painter to George III; noted for brilliantly colored chalk portraits; described his methods in *The Elements of Painting in Crayon* (1772). Also an amateur astronomer.

Russell, John. 1st Earl Russell of King·ston Russell \'kiŋ-stən-\. 1792–1878. British politician. 3d son of 6th Duke of Bedford (see RUSSELL family). Whig M.P. (1813–61); strenuous advocate of parliamentary reform, of repeal of Test and Corporation acts; supported Catholic Emancipaton Act (passed 1829). One of four framers of Reform Act of 1832; championed it till passage (1832). Leader of Whigs in House of Commons (1834); home secretary (1835); colonial secretary (1839) under Melbourne; committed himself to repeal of corn laws, helping protectionists to force Peel out of office. Prime minister and first lord of treasury (1846–52); quieted Ireland by combination of coercive and relief measures; sought to adapt free-trade policy to British commerce; founded national board of public health (1848); dismissed Lord Palmerston from post of foreign secretary for recognizing Napoléon's coup d'état (1851); defeated by Palmerston, resigned (1852). In Lord Aberdeen's coalition ministry as foreign secretary (1852–53), president of council (1854–55); lost popularity and was out of office (till 1859). Foreign secretary in Palmerston's ministry (1859–65). Created earl (1861). Influential in maintaining British neutrality during Civil War in U.S. Again prime minister (1865–66) on death of Palmerston; on defeat of his new reform bill, retired. Author of a *Life of William Lord Russell* (1819), *Memoirs of Affairs of Europe* (1824–29), *Recollections and Suggestions* (1875).

Russell, Lillian. *Orig.* Helen Louise Leon·ard \'len-ərd\. 1861–1922. American singer and actress, b. Clinton, Iowa. Sang in Tony Pastor's Bowery variety theater (1880). Rose to stardom in Edmond Audran's *The Great Mogul* (1881); excelled in comic-opera roles. With Weber and Fields burlesque company (1899–1904), sang in popular pieces as *Fiddle-dee-dee* and *Whoop-dee-doo;* acted in straight comic roles (1906–12).

Russell, Morgan. 1886–1953. American painter, b. New York City. Lived in Paris (1906–46). With Stanton Macdonald-Wright founded (1912) abstract art movement called Synchromism; known for his "Synchromies," paintings relying on color for spatial and emotional depth, as *Synchromy in Orange: To Form* (1913–14).

Russell, Richard Joel. 1895–1971. American geologist, b. Hayward, Calif. Professor at Louisiana State U. (1928–71); director of Coastal Studies Inst. (1953–66). Known for studies of coastal morphology; author of *Culture Worlds* (1951) and *River Plains and Sea Coasts* (1967).

Russell, Thomas. 1762–1788. English poet. Ordained (1786). Author of *Sonnets and Miscellaneous Poems* (1789), containing best poem "Sonnet Suppos'd to Be Written at Lemnos."

Russell, Thomas. 1767–1803. Irish revolutionist. Organized with Wolfe Tone and Napper Tandy the United Irish Society in Dublin (1791); arrested with other United Irishmen (1796) and imprisoned (till 1798); with Robert Emmet attempted to incite rising in Ireland (1803); executed for high treason.

Russell, Lord William. 1639–1683. See under RUSSELL family.

Russell, William Hepburn. 1812–1872. American freighter, b. Burlington, Vt. Founded Pony Express, between St. Joseph, Mo., and Sacramento, Calif. (1860), carrying mail across the West in ten days.

Russell, Sir William Howard. 1820–1907. British war correspondent. Reported for *The Times* (from 1841); published *The War from the Landing at Gallipoli to the Death of Lord Raglan* (1855–56); exposed mismanagement of Crimean War; inspired Florence Nightingale's work; applied phrase "thin red line" to infantry at Balaklava. Founder of *Army and Navy Gazette* (1860).

Russ·wurm \'rəs-,wərm\, John Brown. 1799–1851. American journalist and public official, b. Port Antonio, Jamaica. Son of a white American father and a black Jamaican mother. With John Cornish published in New York first black newspaper, *Freedom's Journal* (1827). Emigrated to Liberia (1828 or 1829); edited *Liberia Herald;* colonial secretary (1830–34); governor of Maryland Colony in Liberia (1836–51).

Ru·te·beuf \rüet-bœf\. *Also spelled* Ru·te·buef *or* Rus·te·beuf \rœs-tə-\. fl. 1245–1285. French trouvère. Author of various lyrics and didactic poems, many barbed with satire; author also of elegies, fabliaux, and a miracle play *Le Miracle de Théophile.*

Rut·gers \'rət-gərz\, Henry. 1745–1830. American philanthropist, b. New York City. Benefactor of Queen's College, New Brunswick, N.J., which changed its name (1825) to Rutgers College in his honor.

Ruth \'rüth\, George Herman. *Called* Babe \'bāb\. *Nicknamed* the Bam·bi·no \bam-'bē-nō\ *and* the Sultan of Swat. 1895–1948. American baseball player, b. Baltimore. Member of Boston Red Sox (1915–19), New York Yankees (1920–35), Boston Braves (1935). Hit 60 home runs in 1927 (record for 156-game season) and record (to 1974) 714 in career. Elected to Baseball Hall of Fame (1936).

Ruth·er·ford \'rəth-ə(r)-fərd, 'rəth-\, Ernest. 1st Baron Rutherford of Nel·son \'nel-sən\. 1871–1937. British physicist, b. New Zealand. Professor at McGill U., Montreal (1898–1907) and at U. of Manchester (1907–19); professor and director of Cavendish Laboratory, Cambridge (from 1919); professor of natural philosophy, Royal Institution (from 1921). Investigated and named alpha and beta rays; with Frederick Soddy formulated the transformation theory of radioactivity (1902); identified the alpha particle as a helium nucleus (1908); proposed the nuclear structure of the atom (1911); first to artificially disintegrate an element (1919). Awarded 1908 Nobel prize for chemistry. Member (from 1903), president (1925–30) of Royal Society. Author of *Radio-activity* (1904), *Radio-active Substances and Their Radiations* (1912), *The Newer Alchemy* (1937), etc.

Rutherford, Joseph Franklin. *Called* Judge Rutherford. 1869–1942. American religious leader, b. near Boonville, Mo. Joined Watch Tower Bible and Tract Society (1906) and became its legal adviser; succeeded Charles Taze Russell (*q.v.*) as its head (1916). Imprisoned (1918–19) because of his stand against military service and his encouragement to conscientious objectors. The society under his guidance changed name to Jehovah's Witnesses (1931).

Rutherford, Dame Margaret. 1892–1972. English actress. On London stage (from early 1930s), gaining fame in *Spring Meeting* (1938) and as Miss Prism in *The Importance of Being Earnest* (1939). In films (from 1936), esp. in *Passport to Pimlico* (1949) and as Miss Marple in a series of films based on Agatha Christie stories, as *Murder She Said* (1961); won Academy Award for best supporting actress in *The VIPs* (1963). Specialized in roles as a lovable English eccentric.

Rutherford, Mark. See William Hale WHITE.

Ruth·er·furd \'rəth-ə(r)-fərd, 'rəth-\, Lewis Morris. 1816–1892. American astrophysicist, b. Morrisania, N.Y. Set up small observatory at his home in New York (1856) and started photographing celestial bodies. Interested himself also in spectroscopy (from 1862); published first attempt to classify stellar spectra (1863). Designed ruling engine (1870) enabling him to construct finest interference gratings made up to that time for use in spectroscopic work.

Ruth·ven \'riv-ən, 'rüth-vən\. Name of a noble Scottish family bearing titles Baron Ruthven, Baron Gow·rie \'gaù(ə)r-ē\, and Earl of Gowrie, and including:

Patrick Ruthven (1520?–1566), 3d Baron Ruthven, was annually elected provost of Perth (1553–66); Protestant privy councilor of Mary, Queen of Scots; advocate of Darnley marriage; assistant in Rizzio murder (1566). His son ¶William (1541?–1584), 4th Baron Ruthven and 1st Earl of Gowrie, joined conspiracy against Rizzio; took active part, with his father, in intrigues on side of the kirk; custodian of Mary, Queen of Scots, at Lochleven; lord high treasurer for life (1571); chief conspirator in "Raid of Ruthven," for carrying off the boy king James VI and keeping him virtual prisoner (1582); pardoned, continued to plot with Angus, Mar, and others; beheaded for high treason. His son ¶John (1577?–1600), 3d Earl of Gowrie, continued family practices of intrigue and treason, first by joining Atholl and Montrose in offer to serve Queen Elizabeth; headed opposition to James VI; killed in his own house at Perth in the so-called Gowrie conspiracy, whether as result of the foiling of a kidnaping plot to make away with James VI or to obtain from him a settlement of his debt to Gowrie, or by veiled assassination by James VI and retainers, there is still doubt.

Ruthven, Patrick. Earl of Forth \'fō(ə)rth, 'fó(ə)rth\ *and* of Brent·ford \'brent-fərd\. 1573?–1651. Scottish soldier in English Royalist army. Descended from collateral line of Ruthven family *(q.v.)*. Gathered Royalist forces in Scotland (1638); surrendered Berwick to Covenanters (1640); general in chief of Charles I's army; declared traitor by Scottish Parliament (1644); forced surrender of Essex's army at Lostwithiel (1644); superseded by Prince Rupert (1644).

Ru·til·i·us Na·ma·ti·a·nus \rü-'til-ē-əs-nə-,mā-shē-'ā-nəs\, Claudius. fl. c.417 A.D. Roman poet. Prefect of Rome (414); author of *De reditu suo,* long poem in two books, describing a coastal voyage (made 417) from Rome to his ravaged estates in Gaul.

Rutilius Ru·fus \-'rü-fəs\, Publius. b. c.150 B.C. Roman jurist and general. With Scipio Aemilianus in siege of Numantia (133); praetor (118); consul (105); incurred hostility of equestrian order and was tried and condemned on trumped-up charge of corruption in office (92). Withdrew to Smyrna and devoted himself to writing his memoirs.

Rutland, Earls and dukes of. See MANNERS family.

Rut·ledge \'rət-lij\, Ann. 1813–1835. American woman. Daughter of Abraham Lincoln's landlord at New Salem, Ill.; long believed, incorrectly, to have been engaged to Lincoln.

Rutledge, John. 1739–1800. American politician, b. Charleston, S.C. Practiced law, Charleston, S.C. (from 1761); member of Continental Congress (1774–76, 1782–83); president of South Carolina (1776–78); governor (1779–82). Member of Constitutional Convention (1787), supporting slavery and concept of strong central government; member, state ratification convention (1788). Associate justice, U.S. Supreme Court (1789–91); appointed chief justice (1795) and served one term, but not confirmed by U.S. Senate. His brother ¶Edward (1749–1800), lawyer; member of Continental Congress (1774–77) and a signer of Declaration of Independence; member, South Carolina legislature (1782–96); governor of South Carolina (1798–1800).

Rutledge, Wiley Blount, Jr. 1894–1949. American jurist, b. Cloverport, Ky. Professor of law, Colorado (1924–26), Washington U. (1926–35; dean 1931–35); dean of law, Iowa (1935–39); associate justice, U.S. Court of Appeals for D.C. (1939–43); associate justice, U.S. Supreme Court (1943–49).

Ruvigny, Marquis de. See Henri de MASSUE.

Ruy López. See LÓPEZ DE SEGURA.

Ruys·broeck \'róis-,brük\ *or* **Ruus·broec** \'rües-,brük\, Jan van. 1293–1381. Flemish mystical theologian. Vicar of St. Gudule, Brussels (1317–43); founded (1349) Augustinian monastery of Groenendaal and became its prior; influenced Tauler, Gerhard Groote, and other mystics; beatified (1908). Author of mystic works in Flemish and Latin, esp. *Van den Rike der Ghelieven* and *Die Chierheit der gheesteliker Brulocht* (1350).

Ruysbroeck, William of. See WILLEM VAN RUYSBROECK.

Ruysch \'róis\, Rachel. 1664–1750. Dutch painter. Appointed court painter to elector palatine (1708); noted as painter of flowers, fruits, insects, and reptiles.

Ruysdael, Jacob van. See RUISDAEL.

Ruys·dael *or* **Ruis·dael** *or* **Ruijs·dael** \'róis-,dál\, Salomon van. *Orig. surname* de Goy·er \də-'gói-ər\. c.1602–1670. Dutch painter. Uncle of Jacob van Ruisdael. Member of Haarlem Guild of St. Luke (from 1628). Painted (from 1627) landscapes in Baroque style, chiefly village, river, canal, and winter scenes.

Ruy·ter \'rói-tər\, Michiel Adriaanszoon de. 1607–1676. Dutch admiral. Rear admiral in expedition to aid Portugal against Spain (1641); in merchant service (1641–51); distinguished himself under Tromp in First Dutch–English War (1652–53); commanded Dutch squadron in support of Denmark against Sweden (1659). Defeated English fleet under Monck in Four Days' Battle off Dunkirk (1666) during Second Dutch–English War (1665–67), but suffered subsequent defeat at North Foreland (1666); sailed up the Thames, and helped in concluding Peace of Breda (1667). During Third Dutch–English War commanded and won against combined English and French fleets off Solebay (1672) and Ostend and Kijkduin (1673), preventing a sea invasion of Dutch Republic; named general lieutenant admiral. Commanded Dutch-Spanish squadron in Mediterranean against French and Sicilians (1675–76) and was mortally wounded in battle off coast of Sicily.

Ru·žič·ka \'rü-,zhēch-kà, *Angl* rü-'zēch-kə, -'zhit-skə\, Leopold Stephen. 1887–1976. Swiss chemist, b. Croatia. Professor at Federal Inst. of Tech., Zürich (1923–26, 1929 ff.) and Utrecht (1926–29). Investigated (from 1916) natural odoriferous compounds; discovered ringed molecular structure of muscone and civetone; discovered molecular structure of testosterone and other male sex hormones and synthesized them (mid-1930s). With Adolf Butenandt awarded 1939 Nobel prize for chemistry.

Ruzzante, Il. See Angelo BEOLCO.

Ry·an \'rī-ən\, Abram Joseph. 1838–1886. American clergyman and poet, b. Hagerstown, Md. Became Vincentian Father (1856); chaplain in Confederate army (1862–65); pastor at Mobile, Ala. (1870–83). His lyrics celebrating the Confederate cause endeared him to the South and caused him to be called "the Poet of the Confederacy." His collected poems (pub. 1879) included such favorites as "The Conquered Banner," "The Sword of Robert E. Lee," "The Lost Cause," "In Memoriam."

Ryan, Elizabeth. 1892–1979. American tennis player, b. Los Angeles. Won 12 women's doubles and 7 mixed doubles titles at Wimbledon (1914–34); also won 659 tournaments.

Ryan, Thomas Fortune. 1851–1928. American financier, b. Lovingston, Va. Organized brokerage firm (1873); acquired New York City street-railway franchise and extended properties until (by 1900) his group controlled transportation lines in the city; consolidated his interests with August Belmont's subway interests (1905); withdrew from traction field (1906). Helped organize (early 1890s) American Tobacco Co., later (1911) ordered dissolved by the government as a monopoly. Also acquired extensive interests in New York banks, Seaboard Air Line Railroad, Equitable Life Assurance Society, rubber and mining properties in Belgian Congo, and coal deposits in Ohio and West Virginia.

Ryd·berg \'rœd-ˌberʸ\, Abraham Viktor. 1828–1895. Swedish writer. Member of Romantic school; champion of liberalism and tolerance. On staff of liberal newspaper *Göteborgs handelstidning* (1855–76). Professor at Stockholm (1884–95). His works included historical novels *Den siste atenaren* (1859) and *Vapensmeden* (1891), lyrical tale *Singoalla* (1857), religious criticism *Bibelns Lära om Kristus* (1862), art history *Romerska dagar* (1877), translation of Goethe's *Faust* (1876), lyrical verse *Dikter* (1882), and mythological study *Undersökningar i germanisk mytologi* (1886–89).

Rydberg, Johannes Robert. 1854–1919. Swedish physicist. Lecturer (1880), professor (1897–1919) at Lund; made contributions to spectroscopy, esp. discovery (1890) of the Rydberg constant, mathematically describing spectral series.

Ry·der \'rīd-ər\, Albert Pinkham. 1847–1917. American painter, b. New Bedford, Mass. Excelled in landscapes, marines, and figure paintings. His Romantic or allegorical canvases, generally in heavy impasto, included *Toilers of the Sea, The Race Track, The Flying Dutchman, Macbeth and the Witches, Siegfried and the Rhine Maidens,* and *Moonlight at Sea.*

Rydz-Śmig·ły \'rits-'shmēg-li\, Edward. 1886–1941. Polish general. Served with Piłsudski in World War I. Inspector general of Polish army, succeeding Piłsudski (1935); marshal of Poland and one of most powerful men in country (1936–39); fled to Romania after German occupation of Poland (1939).

Ry·kov \'rik-əf\, Aleksey Ivanovich. 1881–1938. Russian politician. Involved in revolutionary activities (from c.1898). Associated with Lenin (1917) in and after the Russian Revolution; chairman of Supreme Council of National Economy (1918–21); member of Politburo (after 1922). After Lenin's death (1924), served as chairman of the Council of People's Commissars (1924–30); opposed Stalin's policies and was dismissed from office; reinstated as commissar for posts and telegraph after publicly recanting his opposition (1931–36). Implicated in fabricated conspiracies and executed for treason.

Ryle \'rī(ə)l\, Gilbert. 1900–1976. English philosopher. A leader of the Oxford philosophy or "ordinary language" movement. Professor at Oxford (1945–68); editor of journal *Mind* (1948–71). Author of *The Concept of Mind* (1949), *Dilemmas* (1954), *A Rational Animal* (1962), *The Thinking of Thoughts* (1968), etc.

Ryle, Sir Martin. 1918–1984. British astronomer. Professor of radio astronomy, Cambridge U. (1959–82); director of Mullard Radio Astronomy Observatory, Cambridge (1957–82); Great Britain's Astronomer Royal (1972–82). Shared with Antony Hewish 1974 Nobel prize for physics for development of aperture synthesis technique, combining sensitive radio telescopes with elaborate computers to permit surveying and mapping of cosmic regions beyond range of optical telescopes. Champion of "big bang" theory of explosive origin of universe and of development of alternate sources of energy.

Ry·ley·ev \ril-'yā-yif\, Kondraty Fyodorovich. 1795–1826. Russian poet and revolutionary. Associate of Pushkin; author of narrative poems, esp. on revolutionary themes; a leader in Decembrist plot (1825), executed.

Ry·mer \'rī-mər\, Thomas. 1643?–1713. English critic. Succeeded Shadwell as court historiographer (1692); published collection of documents concerning treaties and alliances of Great Britain with other powers (from 1101–1654), under title *Foedera* (1704–13). Introduced into England principles of French Neoclassical criticism with translation of Rapin's *Réflexions sur la poétique d'Aristote* (1674). Author of play in rhymed verse *Edgar, or the English Monarch* (1678), of poems in memory of Waller; in *Tragedies of the Last Age Considered* passed unfavorable judgments on Beaumont and Fletcher's plays (1678); in *Short View of Tragedy* condemned Shakespeare's *Othello* as a "bloody farce" and rejected modern drama in favor of return to Greek tragedy (1692).

Ryō·nin \ryō-nēn\. 1072–1132. Japanese Buddhist priest. Founder of the Yūzū Nembutsu sect of the True Pure Land school of Amida Buddhism; initiated a revival of Buddhist thought.

Rys·brack \'reis-bräk, *Angl* 'rēs-ˌbrak\, John Michael. c.1693 or 1694–1770. Belgian sculptor in England. Settled in London (1720); rival of Roubillac. Works included 16 monuments in Westminster Abbey, equestrian statue in Bristol of William III, portrait busts, and tombs in several parish churches.

Ry·ti \'rue-tē\, Risto Heikki. 1889–1956. Finnish politician. Minister of finance (1921–24); governor of Bank of Finland (1923–45); president of Finland (1940–44); imprisoned as war criminal (1946–49).

Ryurik. See RURICK.

Rze·wu·ski \zhe-'vü-skē\, Henryk. 1791–1866. Polish novelist. Best known for a series of historical novels as *Listopad* (1845–46), *Adam Smigielski* (1850), *Zaporoże* (1854), etc.

S

Sá \'sȧ\, Mem de. 1500–1572. Portuguese colonial official. Governor general of Brazil (1557–72). Founder (1566–67) of city of Rio de Janeiro, in collaboration with his nephew ¶Estácio (1520?–1567), who died of wounds received in action against French and Indians besieging the city.

Sa·ada \sä-'äd-ə\, Antun. 1904–1949. Syrian political agitator, b. Brazil. Founded (1932) at Beirut a secret society, later called Syrian National party, that sought to unify Syria with neighboring areas it considered to be really Syrian; party clashed in Beirut with another Syrian nationalist group; arrested and convicted of treason; executed.

Saadī. See SA'DĪ.

Sa·'ad·ia ben Jo·seph \'sȧ-dē-ȧ-ben-'jō-zəf\. *Arab.* Sa'īd ibn Yūsuf al-Fayyūmī. 882–942. Jewish commentator and scholar. Left Egypt and settled (c.920) in Babylonia; as *gaon* of Sura (928–935, 937–942) brought school to peak of its reputation among Jewish communities. Translated most of the Bible into Arabic and wrote extensive commentaries on it; also author of treatises on Talmudic law, the first dictionary and grammar in Hebrew, religious poetry, *Book of Beliefs and Convictions,* works on the liturgy, and anti-Karaite polemical works.

Saa·ri·nen \'sär-i-nen, *Angl* 'sär-ə-nən\, Eero. 1910–1961. American architect, b. Kirkkonummi, Finland. Son of Eliel Saarinen; to U.S. with father (1923); naturalized (1940). Worked with his father (1938–50). Designs included Memorial Arch, St. Louis (1948), General Motors Tech. Center, Warren, Mich. (1948–56), M.I.T. auditorium and chapel (1953), U.S. Embassy, London (1955–60), Yale hockey rink (1958), and furniture designs.

Saarinen, Eliel, *in full* Gottlieb Eliel. 1873–1950. American architect, b. Rantasalmi, Finland. Foremost architect of his day in Finland; designed Helsinki railway station (1904–14). To U.S. (1923). Designed (1925–41) buildings of Cranbrook Foundation, Bloomfield Hills, Mich., and was president (1932–48) and architecture dept. head (1948–50) of its Academy of Art. Also designed Tabernacle Church of Christ in Columbus, Ind. (1940–42) and Christ Lutheran Church, Minneapolis (1949–50). Author of *The City, Its Growth, Its Decay, Its Future* (1943), *Search for Form* (1948), etc.

Sa·a·ve·dra \sä-ä-'bā-thrä\, Juan Bautista. 1870–1939. Bolivian jurist. President of Bolivia (1921–25).

Saavedra Fa·jar·do \-fä-'kär-thō\, Diego. 1584–1648. Spanish diplomat and writer. In diplomatic service, esp. ambassador to Rome (1631) and to Germany (1632). Author of an anti-Machiavellian emblem book *Idea de un príncipe político cristiano* (1640); also *Corona gótica* (1646) and *La república literaria* (1655).

Saavedra La·mas \-'läm-äs\, Carlos. 1878–1959. Argentine jurist. Minister of foreign affairs (1932–38); president, Assembly of the League of Nations (1936); rector of U. of Buenos Aires (1941–43). Presided over conference in Buenos Aires (1935) which ended the long Chaco war. Awarded Nobel peace prize (1936).

Saavedra Ra·mí·rez de Ba·quen·da·no \-rä-'mē-räth-thā-bäk-än-'thän-ō\, Ángel de. Duque de Ri·vas \-thā-'rē-bäs\. 1791–1865. Spanish politician and writer. Fought in war of independence; condemned to death for extreme liberal views (1823) but escaped; in exile until amnesty of 1834. Minister of interior (1836); exiled for conservative views (1837–38). Entered senate (1838); president of the government (1854); ambassador in Naples (1846) and Paris (1859). Championed Romanticism in Spain. His works included *El faro de Malta* (verse, 1828), *El moro expósito* (epic, 1834), *Don Álvaro* (play, 1835; source for Verdi's *La forza del destino*), and *Romances históricos* (verse, 1841).

Sa·ba \sä-'bä\ *or* **Sa·bas** \-'bäs\. Saint. 439–532. Turkish Christian monk. To Palestine (457); founded (483) near Jerusalem the Great Laura of Mar Saba; later founded 14 other monasteries and 4 hospices throughout southern Palestine. Known as a champion of orthodoxy, esp. against Origenism and Monophysitism.

Sabacon. See SHABAKA.

Sabas, Saint. Serbian prelate. See SAVA.

Sa·ba·tier \sȧ-bȧt-yā\, Auguste, *in full* Louis-Auguste. 1839–1901. French Protestant theologian. Professor, Strasbourg (1868–73), Paris (from 1877); known as representative of liberalism in theology; applied historical critical methods to biblical interpretation. Author of *Esquisse d'une philosophie de la religion* (1897), *Les Religions d'autorité et la religion de l'esprit* (1903), etc.

Sabatier, Paul. 1854–1941. French chemist. Professor, Toulouse (1884–1941), dean of science faculty (1905–29); engaged in researches on catalytic action; originated method of hydrogenating organic compounds in presence of finely divided metals. With Victor Grignard, awarded the 1912 Nobel prize for chemistry.

Sa·ba·ti·ni \,sä-bä-'tē-nē, *Angl* ,sab-ə-'tē-ne\, Rafael. 1875–1950. Italian novelist. Writer in English, chiefly of historical romances as *The Sea Hawk* (1915), *The Snare* (1917), *Scaramouche* (1921), *Captain Blood* (1922).

Ṣabbāḥ, Ḥasan-e. See ḤASAN-E.

Sabbatai Zebi. See SHABBETAI.

Sab·ba·ti·ni \säb-bä-'tē-nē\, Nicola. 1574–1654. Italian architect. Designed Teatro del Sole in Pesaro (1637); author of *Pratica di fabricar scene e macchine ne' teatri* (1638), a handbook on theater equipment and techniques, esp. for stage lighting.

Sa·bel·li·us \sə-'bel-ē-əs\. fl. c.220 A.D. Roman Christian prelate and theologian. Became a leader of Modalistic Monarchians; excommunicated (c.220) by Pope Calixtus. His followers were known as Sabellians.

Sab·ine \'sab-,īn, -in; 'sā-,bīn\, Sir Edward. 1788–1883. British soldier and astronomer. Astronomer to expeditions of John Ross (1818) and William Parry in search of the Northwest Passage (1819–20); at Spitsbergen and in tropical Africa conducted pendulum experiments for determining shape of earth; devoted most of life to researches on terrestrial magnetism; discovered (1852) interrelation between periodic variation of sunspots and magnetic disturbances on the earth; president of Royal Society (1861–71); general (1870).

Sa·bine \'sā-,bīn, -bən\, Wallace Clement Ware. 1868–1919. American physicist, b. Richwood, Ohio. Considered founder of science of architectural acoustics. Taught at Harvard (from 1890); a founder and dean of Harvard Graduate School of Applied Science (1906–15). Adviser in construction of Boston Symphony Hall (1898–1900). The unit of sound-absorbing power is named sabin in his honor.

Sa·bin·i·an \sə-'bin-ē-ən\. *Lat.* Sa·bin·i·a·nus \sə-,bin-ē-'ā-nəs\. d. 606. Pope (604–606). Under Pope Gregory I was papal ambassador at Constantinople to reconcile Roman church with Patriarch John IV. Pontificate marked by famines and Lombard attacks.

Sable \sȧblᵊ, *Angl* 'sā-bəl\, Jean Baptist Point. *Also known as* Point du Sable \pwaⁿ-dü̅-sȧblᵊ\. 1750?–1818. American pioneer trader, b. Haiti. Son of French father and black Haitian mother. To Great Lakes area (1770s). Founded (1779) a trading settlement at site of present-day Chicago, thereby earning him title Father of Chicago; moved to Missouri as farmer and trader (1800).

Sabunde, Raimundo. See RAYMOND of Sabunde.

Sa·bu·tai \'säb-ə-,tī\ *or* **Su·bo·tai** \'sə-bə-,tī\. c.1172–1245. Mongol general. A master strategist; chief general of Genghis Khan; led Mongol armies under Genghis and Ögödei in many campaigns in Asia; planned and aided Batu Khan's conquests in Europe (1237–41).

Sab·ze·vā·rī \säb-zä-'vär-ē\, Hājī Hādī. 1797 or 1798–1878. Persian philosopher and poet. Exponent of the *ḥikmah* (wisdom) school of Islāmic philosophy. Founded a school of philosophy at Sabzevār; author of *Asrār al-ḥikmah* ("Secrets of Wisdom") and *Sharḥ manzumah* ("Treatise on Logic in Verse"), basic texts of *ḥikmah* doctrine. Wrote poetry under name of As·rar \'äs-rär\.

Sac·a·ga·wea \,sak-ə-jə-'wē-ə, -'wā-ə; -'jä-wē-ə, -'gä-\, *i.e.* Bird Woman. Also Sac·a·ja·wea \-jə-'wē-ə, -'wā-ə; -'jä-wē-ə\. 1786?–1812. American Indian interpreter, b. probably near present Lemhi, Idaho. Member of Shoshone tribe; captured (1800) by Hidatsas and sold to a Canadian trapper, Toussaint Charbonneau, whom she married (1804) by Indian rites and later accompanied as guide to Lewis and Clark expedition (1805).

Sá-Car·nei·ro \'sá-kär-'nā-rü\, Mário de. 1890–1916. Portuguese writer. With Fernando Pessoa founded review *Orpheu* (1915). Works included *Dispersão* (1914, verse), *A confissão de Lúcio* (1914, novel), and *Céu em fogo* (1915, short stories).

Sa·ca·sa \sä-'kä-sä\, Juan Bautista. 1874–1946. Nicaraguan politician. Vice president of Nicaragua (1924–25); president of Nicaragua (1933–36); attempted reconciliation with Sandino forces (1933) that resulted in assassination of Sandino (1934) by National Guard; ousted by his nephew Anastasio Somoza and took refuge in U.S.

Sac·chet·ti \säk-'kāt-tē\, Franco. c.1330–1400. Italian poet and writer of novelle. Author of *Trecento novelle* in style of Boccaccio, *Le sposizioni di Vangeli,* burlesque and serious poetry, and letters.

Sac·chi \'säk-kē\, Andrea. 1599–1661. Italian painter. Pupil of Albani; influenced by Raphael; studio in Rome (1621 ff.). Painted chiefly religious subjects in Classical style, as *Miracle of St. Gregory* (1625–27), decorations of Sacchetti villa at Castel Fusano (1627–29, with Pietro da Cortona), *Allegory of Divine Wisdom* (1629–33, fresco in Palazzo Barberini at Rome), 2 altarpieces in Sta. Maria della Concezione, Rome (1631–38), 8 canvases of life of St. John the Baptist in Baptistery of St. John, Rome (1639–45).

Sacchi, Bartolomeo. *Called in Latin* Pla·ti·na \plə-'tī-nə\. 1421–1481. Italian Humanist and historian. Appointed Vatican librarian by Sixtus IV (1475). Wrote *Liber de vita Christi ac omnium pontificum* (1479) and treatises on politics, philosophy, and rhetoric.

Sac·chis \'säk-kēs\, Giovanni Antonio de'. *Called* Por·de·no·ne \ˌpōr-dā-'nō-nā\ *after his birthplace.* c.1483–1539. Venetian painter. Pupil of Pellegrino da S. Daniele; worked throughout northern Italy. Among his works were series of frescoes from the New Testament in Church of Castel Colalto near Conegliano, frescoes in cathedrals at Treviso and Cremona, frescoes from the lives of Virgin Mary and St. Catherine in Church of Madonna di Campagna at Piacenza, and portraits.

Sac·co \'säk-kō, *Angl* 'sak-(ˌ)ō, 'säk-\, Nicola (1891–1927) and ¶Bartolomeo Van·zet·ti \vänd-'zāt-tē, *Angl* van-'zet-ē, vän-\ (1888–1927). American political radicals, b. Italy. To U.S. (1908); arrested on charge of murder of a shoe-factory paymaster and guard at South Braintree, Mass. (1920) and theft of $16,000 payroll; tried and convicted (1921); on appeal of their case, doubt of their guilt led to widespread support and worldwide protests; electrocuted (1927) after special committee appointed by governor to review case had found trial fair.

Sacharissa. See Lady Dorothy Sidney under SIDNEY family.

Sa·cher-Ma·soch \'zäk-ər-'mäz-ōk\, Leopold von. Ritter. 1836–1895. German novelist. Author of *Venus im Pelz* (1870), *Das Vermächtnis Kains* (1870–77), *Die Schlange im Paradies* (1890), etc. The term *masochism* has become used for a form of abnormality depicted in some of his novels.

Sa·chev·er·ell \sə-'shev-ər-əl\, Henry. 1674?–1724. English clergyman. Preached two sermons (1709) attacking Whig ministry for neglect of the interests of the church and condemning toleration and occasional conformity, becoming thereby idol of Tory party; impeached at instigation of Godolphin and suspended from preaching for three years; on fall of Godolphin ministry, selected to preach Restoration sermon and presented to rich rectory by new Tory ministry (1713).

Sacheverell, William. 1638–1691. English politician. Opponent of court party; Whig M.P. (1670–91); member of committee preparing Test Act (1673); a manager of impeachment of five Catholic peers and impeachment of Thomas Osborne, 1st Earl of Danby; took prominent part in investigation of Oates's pretended Popish Plot; made first suggestion of excluding James, Duke of York, from the succession (1678) and promoted Exclusion Bill. Helped draw up Bill of Rights.

Sachs \'zäks, *Angl* 'saks\, Curt. 1881–1959. American musicologist, b. Berlin, Germany. Curator of state musical instrument collection (1919–33) and professor (1928–33), Berlin; in Paris (1933–37) produced recordings of early music *L'Anthologie Sonore;* professor, N.Y.U. (1937–53). A founder of modern organology; author of *Real-Lexikon der Musikinstrumente* (1913), *Die Musik der Antike* (1923), *The History of Musical Instruments* (1940), *The Commonwealth of Art* (1946), etc.

Sachs, Hans. 1494–1576. German poet and Meistersinger. Shoemaker by trade. Joined Nürnberg Meistersinger Guild (1509–11); head of Meistersinger group in Nürnberg (1554). Began writing (1514) and composed altogether over 6000 works, including tragedies, comedies, songs, fables, allegories, and narratives. Champion of Luther; wrote verse allegory *Die Wittembergisch Nachtigalle* (1523) to further the Reformation. Depicted as central figure in Wagner's opera *Die Meistersinger von Nürnberg* (1868).

Sachs, Julius von. 1832–1897. German botanist. Professor at Würzburg (1868–97). Known for investigations of metabolism of plants, influence of heat and light on growth of plants, mechanics of growth, formation of flowers, etc.; proved that starch in chloroplasts results from absorption of carbon dioxide (1862). Author of *Lehrbuch der Botanik* (1868), *Geschichte der Botanik vom 16. Jahrhundert bis 1860* (1875), etc.

Sachs, Nelly Leonie. 1891–1970. German poet and dramatist. Fled from Nazis to Sweden (1940). Shared Nobel prize for literature (1966) with S. Y. Agnon. Author of plays as *Eli: Ein Mysterienspiel vom Leiden Israels* (1951), and esp. books of lyrical verse as *In den Wohnungen des Todes* (1946), *Und niemand weiss weiter* (1957), *Flucht und Verwandlung* (1959).

Sack·ville \'sak-ˌvil\. Name of an English family possessing earldom and dukedom of Dor·set \'dȯr-sət\, and including: Sir Richard (d.1566), first cousin of Anne Boleyn; barrister; M.P. (1529); induced Roger Ascham to write *The Scholemaster;* father of Thomas Sackville (*q.v.*). ¶Sir Edward (1591–1652), 4th Earl of Dorset; grandson of Thomas Sackville; M.P. (1614); ambassador to Louis XIII (1621); privy councilor (1626); joined Charles I at outbreak of Civil War; commissioner of treasury (1643); lord chamberlain to king and lord president of council (1644). His grandson ¶Charles (1638–1706), 6th Earl of Dorset and 1st Earl of Mid·dle·sex \'mid-əl-ˌseks\; poet and courtier; M.P. (1660); notorious for riotous and dissipated life; served as volunteer in fleet against Dutch (1665); retired from court during James II's reign; made privy councilor and lord chamberlain (1689–97) by William of Orange; thrice regent during William III's absences; generous patron of men of letters, including Prior, Wycherley, Dryden; author of satirical and occasional verse. His son ¶Lionel Cranfield Sackville (1688–1765), 1st Duke of Dorset (cr. 1720); lord warden of Cinque Ports (1708–17, 1728, 1757–65); twice lord lieutenant of Ireland; lord president of the council (1745–51); often acting lord justice of Great Britain.

¶George Sackville Ger·main \'jər-ˌmān, -mən\ (1716–1785), 1st Viscount Sackville (cr.1782). Son of 1st duke; known as Lord George Sackville (till 1770). Second in command of St.-Malo expedition (1758); failed to lead cavalry charge needed to complete victory at Minden (1759); dismissed from service; assumed name Germain (1770); as secretary of state for colonies (1775–82), virtually directed war in America. With his son ¶Charles (1767–1843), 5th duke, the titles became extinct.

Sackville, Thomas. 1st Earl of Dorset *and* Baron Buck·hurst \'bək-ˌhərst\. 1536–1608. English poet and diplomat. Son of Sir Richard Sackville. Wrote *Induction* and *Buckingham's Complaint* for *A Myrroure for Magistrates,* elevated and allegoric poetry (1563); collaborated with Thomas Norton (*q.v.*) in blank verse *Tragedy of Gorboduc,* the earliest English tragedy (1561), probably writing last two acts. Grand master of freemasons (1561–67); raised to peerage as Baron Buckhurst (1567); announced her death sentence to Mary, Queen of Scots (1586); diplomat in France and Low Countries (1587–98); lord treasurer (1599–1608); presided at Essex's trial (1601); created earl (1604).

Sackville-West \-'west\, Victoria Mary. 1892–1962. English poet and novelist. m. (1913) Harold Nicolson (*q.v.*). Author of biographies of Aphra Behn and Andrew Marvell; of novels, including *The Edwardians* (1930), *All Passion Spent* (1931), *The Dark Island* (1934), *Pepita* (1937), *Grand Canyon* (1942); of poetry, including *The Land* (1926), *King's Daughter* (1930), *Collected Poems* (1933), *Solitude* (1938); of *Country Notes* (essays, 1939).

Sac·ro·bos·co \ˌsak-rō-'bäs-(ˌ)kō\, Johannes de. *Also* John of Hol·y·wood \'häl-i-ˌwu̇d\ *or* of Hal·i·fax \'hal-ə-ˌfaks\. d. 1244 or 1256. English mathematician. Professor, Paris (1221 ff.); one of first to use mathematical writings of Arabs; author of treatises on astronomy, as *De sphaera,* and on mathematics, as *De algorismo.*

Sá da Ban·dei·ra \'sá-thə-bən(n)-'dā-rə\, Bernardo de. 1795–1876. Portuguese politician. Premier of Portugal (1865, 1868–69, 1870–71).

Sa·dat \sä-'dät; *Angl* sə-'dat, -'dät\, Anwar as-, *in full* Muhammad Anwar. *Also* el-Sadat \el-\. 1918–1981. Egyptian soldier and statesman. Commissioned in army (1938); active (from c.1938) with Gamal Nasser (*q.v.*) in movement to overthrow British-backed monarchy; imprisoned (1942–44) and later expelled from army for plotting with Germans against British in Egypt. Reinstated in army (1950) and joined Nasser's Free Officers Committee which ousted (1952) King Farouk; held several prominent posts under Nasser, including (1964–67, 1969–70) vice president. Succeeded Nasser as president of Egypt (1970–81); expelled Soviet advisers and technicians (1972); assumed premiership and became military governor (1973); worked for Arab economic and military solidarity; with Syria instigated Arab–Israeli war of Oct. 1973; made dramatic journey to Jerusalem (Nov. 19–21, 1977), which resulted in peace treaty with Israel (signed March 1979); joint winner with Israeli Prime Minister Menachem Begin of 1978 Nobel peace prize; assassinated.

Sade \såd; *Angl* 'säd, 'sād, 'sad\, Donatien-Alphonse-François de. Comte. *Better known as* Marquis de Sade. 1740–1814. French writer. Army officer (1754–63); confined much of his life in various prisons for sexual perversions; died in an insane asylum. Author of erotic novels *Justine* (1791) and *Juliette*

(1798), collection of stories *Les Crimes de l'amour* (1788), plays, and *Les 120 Journées de Sodome* (1784). Sadism was described by him and received its name from him.

Sa·ded·din \sä-ded-'dēn\, Hoca. 1536–1599. Turkish historian. Tutor and trusted servant of Murad III; accompanied Murad's son Mehmed III on campaign to Hungary, contributing to victory at Erlau (1596). Author of *Tac üttevarih,* history covering period from origins of Ottoman Empire to end of Selim I's reign.

Sá de Mi·ran·da \'sá-t͟hə-mē-'rä^{n}(n)-də\, Francisco de. 1481–1558. Portuguese poet and playwright. Lived in Italy (1521–26); introduced Italian poetical styles into Portuguese poetry. His *Os estrangeiros* (c.1527) was Portugal's first prose comedy, and *Cleopatra* (c.1550) Portugal's first classical tragedy; other works included *Os vilhalpandos* (c.1538, comedy), eclogues *Alexo* and *Basto, Fábula do Mondego* (canzone), and *Cartas* (verse epistles). Credited with introducing Renaissance into Portugal.

Sa·'dī \sä-'dē\. *In full* Mosharref od-Dīn ibn Moṣleḥ od-Dīn Sa'dī. c.1213–1292. Persian poet. Traveled throughout the Islāmic world for 30 years; settled in birthplace of Shīrāz. Author of 2 great Persian classics, *Būstān* (1257, The Orchard), didactic stories in verse illustrating Muslim virtues, and *Golestān* (1258, The Rose Garden), stories and personal anecdotes mainly in prose; also known for his lyrics, panegyrics, odes, epigrams, elegies, etc.

Sad·ler \'sad-lər\, Michael Thomas. 1780–1835. English politician and reformer. Linen importer by profession; Tory M.P. (1829–32); a leader of the factory reform movement; introduced and secured passage of Factory Act of 1833 which restricted working hours in textile mills; argued against Malthus's theories in *Law of Population* (1830).

Sadler *or* **Sad·leir** *or* **Sad·leyer** \'sad-lər\, Sir Ralph. 1507–1587. English diplomat. One of Henry VIII's principal secretaries of state (c.1537); sent to Edinburgh to restrain influence of Cardinal Beaton (1542); helped arrange treaty of Leith (1560); one of commissioners to treat with Scots on flight of Mary, Queen of Scots (1568); guardian of Mary, Queen of Scots (1580–84).

Sad·li·er \'sad-lē-ər\, Denis. 1817–1885. American book publisher, b. County Tipperary, Ireland. To U.S. (1830); with his brother ¶James (d. 1869), founded a bookbinding and publishing business, D. & J. Sadlier & Co., New York City (1837); became principal publisher of Catholic books in America.

Sa·do·le·to \,sä-dō-'lā-tō\, Jacopo. 1477–1547. Italian prelate. Bishop of Carpentras (1527); cardinal (1536); papal secretary; early proponent of the Catholic Reformation.

Sa·do·vea·nu \,sä-dō-'vyän-ü\, Mihail. 1880–1961. Romanian politician and writer. Director of National Theater in Iași (1910–19); elected to parliament (1926); president of the senate (1930–31). Author of novels and tales depicting the place of the peasant in society, as *Mitrea Cocor* (1924), *Dumbrava minunată* (1926), *Baltagul* (1930).

Sae·mund Sig·fús·son \'sī-mœnd-'sik̲-fús-sȯn\. *Also* Sae·mundr Sigfússon \'sī-mœn-dœr-\. *Called* Saemund the Wise. 1056–1133. Icelandic chieftain-priest and scholar. First chronicler of Iceland; first Icelander to write in Latin; founded the School of Oddi, a center of learning; his Latin *History of the Kings of Norway* now lost. Bishop Brynjólfur Sveinsson, discoverer (1643) of the *Elder,* or *Poetic, Edda,* erroneously attributed it to Saemund, and it became also known as the *Edda of Saemund the Wise.*

Saen·re·dam \'sán-red-äm\, Pieter Jansz. 1597–1665. Dutch painter. Pioneer in "church portraits"; first Dutch artist to abandon traditional fanciful architectural depictions in favor of a new realism; canvases included *View in the Nieuwe Kerk at Haarlem* (1652) and *Interior of the St. Cunera Church at Rhenem* (1655).

Sá·enz \'sä-äns\, Manuela. *Called* La Sáenz. 1797–1856. Ecuadorian mistress of Simón Bolívar. m. (1815) James Thorne, a British merchant; became (1822) mistress of Bolívar and aided him in his cause until his death (1830); exiled from Bogotá (1834) and lived thereafter in Paita as a confectionery vendor.

Sá·enz Pe·ña \'sä-än-'spän-yä\, Luis. 1823–1907. Argentine politician. President of Argentina (1892–95). His son ¶Roque (1851–1914) was foreign minister (1890); ambassador to Spain (1901), to Italy (1907); president of Argentina (1910–14); author of electoral reform bill (passed 1912).

Ša·fa·řík \'sá-fár-zhēk\, Pavel Josef. 1795–1861. Czech scholar. Director of Serbian Orthodox school in Novi Sad (1819–33); thereafter a private scholar in Prague. A leading figure of Czech national revival; a pioneer of Slavonic philology and archaeology. Author of *Geschichte der slawischen Sprache und Literatur nach allen Mundarten* (1826), *Über den Ursprung und die Heimat des Glagolitismus* (1858), etc.

Ṣa·fa·vid \sä-'fá-vəd\. A Shī'ī Islāmic Persian dynasty (1501–1736) founded by Shāh Esmā'īl I ebn Ḥeydar and named after Ṣafī od-Dīn (*q.v.*). Its last ruler was Tahmāsp II, who was deposed by Nāder Shāh.

Ṣaf·fār·id \sä-'fár-əd\. A Muslim dynasty of Persia (c.866–903), established in the eastern part (Seistan); named from its founder Ya'qūb ebn Leys, nicknamed aṣ-Ṣaf·fār \ás-sáf-fár\, *i.e.* the Coppersmith. It was nominally dependent on the caliphs of Baghdad; became subordinate to the Sāmānids.

Ṣa·fī od-Dīn \sá-'fē-əd-'dēn\. 1252–1334. Persian mystic. Founder of the mystic Ṣūfī order of Ṣafavīyeh (also known as the Ṣafavids), which (c.1399) exchanged its Sunnī affiliation for Shī'ī. The Ṣafavid dynasty was named after his order.

Sa·fi·ye Sul·tan \sä-fē-'yes-ůl-'tän\. d. c.1605 to 1619. Ottoman consort. Favorite consort of Sultan Murad III and mother of his son Mehmed III; exercised strong influence on Ottoman affairs during their reigns.

Sa·gas·ta \sä-'g̅äs-tä\, Práxedes Mateo. 1825–1903. Spanish politician. Editor of progressist journal and member of Cortes (1858–63); took part against reactionary government of Isabella II (1859–68); became member of provisional government attached to Prim (1869–70); prime minister (1872–74); leader of Liberals in Cortes (1875–83); again prime minister (1885–90 and 1893–95); resigned because of trouble in Cuba but during critical period (war with United States) again conducted government (1897–99); prime minister (1901–02).

Sagaunash. See SAUGANASH.

Sage \'sāj\, Russell. 1816–1906. American financier and politician, b. Shenandoah, N.Y. Grocery clerk, Troy, N.Y. (1828–37); acquired interest in wholesale grocery firm (1839–57). Member of U.S. House of Representatives (1852–57). Moved to New York (1863); bought New York Stock Exchange seat (1874). Associated with Jay Gould in extensive stock market operations and security promotion. His 2d wife (m. 1869) ¶Margaret Olivia, *nee* Slo·cum \'slō-kəm\ (1828–1918), inherited unconditionally his $70,000,000 fortune and became known for her philanthropies; established Russell Sage Foundation for improving social and living conditions in the United States, with gift of $10,000,000 (1907); gave liberally to Emma Willard School, Rensselaer Polytechnic Institute, Cornell, Princeton, and Russell Sage Institute of Pathology.

Sagittarius, Henricus. See Heinrich SCHÜTZ.

Sa·gra \'säg̅-rä\, Ramón de la. 1798–1871. Spanish naturalist, sociologist, and anarchist. Associate of Proudhon; founded (1845) world's first anarchist journal *El Porvenir,* which was quickly suppressed.

Sa·ha \'sä-hä\, Meghnad N. 1893–1956. Indian astrophysicist. Professor, Allahabad U. (1923–39), Calcutta U. (from 1939); known for work on radiation and ionization, esp. development (1920) of the thermal ionization equation (Saha equation), later perfected by E. A. Milne and fundamental to stellar atmospheric studies. Founded journal *Science and Culture* (1935); coauthor of *A Treatise on Modern Physics* (1934).

Sa·ha·gún \sä-ä-'g̅ün\, Bernardino de. 1499–1590. Spanish Franciscan missionary and historian. To Mexico (1529). Author of *Historia general de las cosas de Nueva España,* principal source on Mexican culture at time of the Spanish conquest.

Sā·hib·dīn \'sä-(h)əb-'dēn\. 17th century. Indian painter. Leading member of the Mewār school of Rajasthani painting; painted in abstract style full of brilliant color several series illustrating Hindu epics, as on the *Bhāgavata-Purāṇa* (1648) and the *Rāmāyaṇa* (1652).

Sah·le Se·las·sie \'sä-le-sə-'läs-ē\. 1795 or 1801–1847. King of Shewa, Ethiopia (1813–47). Grandfather of Menelik II and great-grandfather of Haile Selassie. Expanded and consolidated Shewa; attempted to extend rule south to Galla; signed trade and friendship treaties with France and Great Britain.

Ṣā'·ib \'sá-ēb\. *Also called* Ṣā'ib of Tabriz *or* of Isfahan. d. 1677. Persian poet. Lived for a time in Mughal India; on return made poet laureate by 'Abbas II. Main exponent of Indian style in Persian poetry; wrote over 300,000 couplets; called King of the Poets.

Sai·chō \sī-chō\. *Known also by posthumous name* Den·gyō Dai·shi \den-gyō-dī-shē\. 767–822. Japanese religious. Became bonze at 13; to China for study (804); after return (805) to Japan, established Tendai sect; built his monastery on Hiei-zan near Kyōto; did much to spread Buddhism in Japan.

Sa·id Ha·lim Pa·şa \sä-'ēd-hä-'lim-pä-'shä\. 1863–1921. Turkish politician. President of the Council of State (1911); foreign minister (1911); grand vizier of Ottoman Empire (1913–16). Signed secret treaty of alliance with Germany (1914) but opposed Ottoman entry into World War I. Imprisoned by British in Malta (1918–21); assassinated in Rome.

Sa·'īd ibn Sul·ṭān \sä-'ēd-ib-ən-sůl-'tän\. *In full* Sa'īd ibn Sulṭān ibn Aḥmad ibn Sa'īd al-Būsa 'Īdī. *Also known as* Sa'īd Imām \-im-'äm\ *or* Sa'īd Say·yid \-'sī-(y)əd\. 1791–1856. Ruler of Muscat and Oman and of Zanzibar (1804, 1806–56). Regained throne (1806) from his cousin Badr who had usurped it; strengthened Omani control over the East African coast and encouraged its commercial development; made Zanzibar principal power in its region and the commercial capital of western Indian Ocean.

Sa'īd ibn Yūsuf al-Fayyūmī. See SA'ADIA BEN JOSEPH.

Sa·'īd Pa·sha \sa-'ēd-'pá-shä\. 1822–1863. Ottoman viceroy of Egypt (1854–63). Fourth son of Muḥammad 'Alī Pasha and uncle of 'Abbās I; passed laws that fostered development of individual land ownership and reduced influence of village headsmen (1855, 1858); attempted unsuccessfully to end slave trade; granted (1854) concession to de Lesseps for construction of Suez Canal (work begun 1859).

Sai·gō \sī-gō\ Takamori. 1828–1877. Japanese general and patriot. Led Imperial loyalist troops in the overthrow of the Tokugawa shogunate and restoration (Meiji Restoration) of the emperor (1868); member of the government (1871–73); killed while leading the unsuccessful Satsuma rebellion.

Saig·yō \sī-gyō\. *Orig.* Sa·to \sä-tō\ Norikiyo. 1118–1190. Japanese Buddhist priest-poet. Originally a soldier, later (1141) a priest. One of greatest masters of poetic form called *tanka;* poetic themes chiefly love of nature and devotion to Buddhism. Works included the anthology *Sankashū* and *Mimosusogawa utaawase* (Poetry Contest at Mimosusu River). Subject of many narratives and dramas.

Saikaku. See IHARA.

St. Albans, 1st Earl of. See Henry JERMYN.

Saint-Amant, Marc-Antoine Girard, sieur de. See Marc-Antoine GIRARD.

Saint-An·dré \sa^{n}-tä^{n}-drā\, André Jeanbon. *Orig. surname* Jean·bon \zhä^{n}-bō^{n}\. 1749–1813. French clergyman. Huguenot pastor at Montauban (1788); elected to National Convention (1792) and to Committee of Public Safety (1793–94); reorganized and strengthened the French navy (1793–94); consul to Algiers (1798); imprisoned by Turks (1799–1802); appointed prefect of Mainz by Napoléon (1802).

Saint-Ar·naud \sa^{n}-tår-nō\, Armand-Jacques Le·roy de \lər-wå-də-, -wä-\. 1798–1854. French soldier. Minister of war (1851–54), played decisive part in coup d'état of Napoléon III (Dec. 2, 1851); marshal of France (1852) and (1854) commander in chief of the French army in the Crimean War. Cooperated with Lord Raglan of the British army in winning the battle of Alma (1854).

Saint Clair. See SINCLAIR family.

St. Clair \sänt-'kla(ə)r, -'kle(ə)r, 'siŋ-,, 'sin-,\, Arthur. 1736–1818. American soldier, b. Thurso, Scotland. Bought estate in western Pennsylvania (1762); served in Continental army as brigadier general; at battles of Trenton and Princeton; major general (1777); evacuated Fort Ticonderoga before Burgoyne's advance. Member of Continental Congress (1785–87) and president (1787). First governor of Northwest Territory (1787–1802). As major general of federal troops, suffered defeat by Indians near Fort Wayne (Nov. 4, 1791) and resigned from his army command (1792). Removed from his governorship by Jefferson (1802) for criticism of congressional legislation creating the State of Ohio.

Saint-Cyran, Abbé de. See Jean DUVERGIER DE HAURANNE.

Saint-De·nis *or* **Saint-De·nys** \sa^{n}d(-ə)-nē\, Louis Ju·che·reau de \zhǖsh(-ə)-rō-də-\. 1676–1744. French-Canadian explorer. Prominent in French effort to establish trade relations with Spanish-American settlements; led expedition from Natchitoches, La., to San Juan Baptista, Mex. (1714); his presence in Texas caused Spanish to establish permanent settlements in San Antonio, Goliad, and Nacogdoches.

St. Den·is \sānt-'den-əs\, Ruth. 1879–1968. *Orig. surname* Den·nis \'den-əs\. American dancer and teacher, b. Newark, N.J. Initially a vaudeville and musical comedy dancer and actress. Influenced almost every phase of American dance, esp. with introduction of philosophical themes and Oriental dance forms and costumes; m. Ted Shawn (1914; separated 1931); with Shawn organized (1915) Denishawn School of Dancing in Los Angeles, later (1921) in New York, and the Denishawn Dancers, with whom she toured U.S. and England (1922–25) and the Orient (1925–26). Founded (1931) Society of Spiritual Arts and promoted use of dance in religion. Her choreographed works included *Radha* (1906), *Egypta* (1910), *O-mika* (1913), *Tragica* (1925). See Ted SHAWN.

Sainte-Beuve \sa^{n}t-bœv\, Charles-Augustin. 1804–1869. French man of letters. Studied medicine (1823) but gave it up for writing. Lifelong contributor to newspapers; considered leading literary critic of his time. His works included *Tableau historique et critique de la poésie française et du théâtre française au XVIe siècle* (1828), *Vie, poésies et pensées de Joseph Delorme* (verse, 1829), *Les Consolations* (verse, 1830), *Volupté* (novel, 1834), *Critiques et portraits littéraires* (1836–39), *Histoire de Port-Royal* (1840–48), and the famous series *Causeries du lundi* (1851–62) and *Nouveaux lundis* (1863–70), made up from his newspaper and periodical articles.

Sainte-Claire De·ville \sa^{n}t-kler-də-vēl\, Henri-Étienne. 1818–1881. French chemist. Professor, Besançon (1845), Paris (1853); devised method for commercial production of aluminum (1854); discovered nitrogen pentoxide (1849); studied metallurgy of platinum and platinum metals; investigated thermal dissociation; devised method of analyzing minerals.

Sainte-Maure, Benoît de. See BENOÎT DE SAINTE-MAURE.

Sainte-Pa·laye \sa^{n}t-på-le\, Jean-Baptiste de La Curne de \də-lå-kǖrn-də-\. 1697–1781. French medievalist and lexicographer. Elected member (1724) and director (1754) of Académie des Inscriptions. His research on troubadours was basis of Abbot Millot's *Histoire des troubadours* (1774). Famed for planning a comprehensive glossary of Old French, finally published (1875–92) as *Dictionnaire historique de l'ancien langage français.*

Saint-Évremond, Seigneur de. See Charles de MARGUETEL DE SAINT-DENIS.

Saint-Ex·u·pé·ry \sa^{n}-tāg-zǖ-pā-rē\, Antoine-Marie-Roger de. 1900–1944. French aviator and writer. Worked (from 1926) as a commercial and test pilot, publicity attaché for Air-France, and reporter for *Paris-Soir;* killed during a reconnaissance flight over North Africa in World War II. Author of novels, essays, and autobiographical works, most with aviation themes or settings, as *Courrier-Sud* (1929), *Vol de nuit* (1931), *Terre des hommes* (1939), *Pilote de guerre* (1942), *Lettre à un otage* (1943), *Le Petit Prince* (1943), and *Citadelle* (1948).

Saint-Gau·dens \sānt-'gȯd-ənz\, Augustus. 1848–1907. American sculptor, b. Dublin, Ireland. To U.S. in infancy; studio in New York (1873–85) and Cornish, N.H. (1885–1907). Often considered foremost American sculptor of late 19th century. His works included *Lincoln* in Lincoln Park, Chicago; *Farragut* in Madison Square, New York City; *Shaw Memorial* on Boston Common; *Deacon Chapin,* also called *The Puritan,* in Springfield, Mass.; Mrs. Henry Adams Memorial in Rock Creek Cemetery, Washington, D.C.; equestrian statues of *General Sherman* in New York and *General Logan* in Chicago; *Amor Caritas;* coins (as $20 gold piece of 1907) and portraits.

Saint-Ge·lais \sa^{n}zh(-ə)-le\, Mellin de. 1491–1558. French poet. Court poet of Francis I; identified with the school of Clément Marot; author of lyrics, rondeaux, epigrams, and other short pieces; said to have introduced the sonnet from Italy into France.

Saint-Ger·main \sa^{n}-zher-ma^{n}\, Comte de. 1707?–1784. Adventurer in Paris (from c.1750) of unknown origin. Claimed to possess philosophers' stone and elixir of life; employed by Louis XV as a diplomat on confidential missions; involved in many political intrigues of the day; retired to Schleswig-Holstein (c.1775) and studied occult sciences in association with Landgrave Charles of Hesse.

Saint-Hilaire, Étienne Geoffroy and Isidore Geoffroy. See GEOFFROY SAINT-HILAIRE.

Saint-Hilaire, Jules Barthélemy. See BARTHÉLEMY-SAINT-HILAIRE.

St. John \'sin-jən\, Henry. 1st Viscount Bol·ling·broke \'bäl-iŋ-,brůk, 'bůl-; *US also* 'bō-liŋ-,brōk\. 1678–1751. English politician and writer. Noted as brilliant conversationalist and notorious libertine; Tory M.P. (1701); secretary of war (1704–08); northern secretary of state (1710–15) in Robert Harley's ministry and his rival for control of the Tory party; created viscount (1712); dismissed from office by George I. Fled to Paris (1715) and supported the Jacobite cause, becoming secretary of state (1715–16) of James III, the Old Pretender. Attainted (1715); pardoned (1723), but excluded from peerage and House of Lords. Returned to England (1725); associated with Pope, Swift, Gay; unsuccessful in attempts to create a united "patriot" party and defeat Walpole; retired to France (1735). Author of historical, philosophical, and political works as *The Idea of a Patriot King* (1749), *Letters on the Study and Use of History* (1752), *Reflections Concerning Innate Moral Principles* (1752).

St. John, J. Hector. See Michel de CRÈVECOEUR.

St. John, Oliver. 1598?–1673. English judge. Consul for Lord Saye and John Hampden in resistance to payment of ship money (1637); married cousin of Oliver Cromwell (1638) and thereafter associated with him; member of Short and Long parliaments; solicitor general (1641–43); supported bill for Strafford's attainder; drew up Root and Branch and Militia bills; performed duties of attorney general (1644); chief justice, Court of Common Pleas (1648–60); upon Restoration excluded from public offices; spent last years on Continent. Published *Case of Oliver St. John* (1660) to disclaim any share in Charles I's execution and explain relations with Cromwells.

Saint-Just, Baron de. See Charles de BIENCOURT.

Saint-Just \sa^{n}-zhǖst\, Louis-Antoine-Léon de. 1767–1794. French revolutionary leader. In support of French Revolution wrote *Esprit de la Révolution et de la Constitution de France* (1791); member of the National Convention (1792) and intimate associate of Robespierre. Member of Committee of Public Safety (1793–94); oversaw military forces; led victory over Austrians at Fleurus (June 26, 1794); sponsored Ventôse Decrees redistributing confiscated property to the poor; active in overthrow of the Girondists and in bringing on the Reign of Terror. Arrested with Robespierre and guillotined.

St. Lau·rent \sa^{n}-lō-rä^{n}\, Louis Stephen. 1882–1973. Canadian lawyer and politician, b. Compton, Que. Professor of law at Laval U., Quebec (1914); Liberal member of House of Commons (1942–58); minister of justice and attorney general (1941–46, 1948); minister of external affairs (1945–48). As prime minister of Canada (1948–57) equalized provincial revenues, led Newfoundland into dominion, expanded social security and university education, and established a council for arts and letters.

St. Leg·er \sənt-'lej-ər, sānt-\ *or* **Sent·leg·er** \sənt-'lej-ər\, Sir Anthony. 1496?–1559. English administrator. Lord deputy of Ireland (1540–46, 1550–51, 1553–56); maintained peace by policy of persuading chieftains to renounce the pope and submit to Henry VIII in return for titles of nobility.

St. Leg·er \ˈsel-ən-jər, sənt-ˈlej-ər, sānt-\, Barry. 1737–1789. British officer in American Revolution. Took part under Gen. Abercrombie in siege of Louisbourg (1758); with Wolfe at Quebec; commanded expedition intended to join General Burgoyne in Hudson Valley but was stopped by Gen. Nicholas Herkimer at battle of Oriskany (1777). Founded (1776) the St. Leger, a horse race at Doncaster, England.

Saint-Lé·on \sa^{n}-lā-ō^{n}\, Arthur, *in full* Charles-Victor-Arthur-Michel. 1821–1870. French violinist, dancer, and choreographer. Made reputation as dancer on European tour (1838–59); m. (1845; separated 1851) dance partner Fanny Cerrito (*q.v.*); ballet master with St. Petersburg Imperial Theater (1859–69) and Paris Opéra (1863–70). First to choreograph a ballet based on Russian folklore, *The Humpbacked Horse* (1864); other choreographed ballets included *Le Fille de marbre* (1847, for Cerrito's debut), *Le Violon du diable* (1849), *La Source* (1866), and esp. *Coppélia* (1870). Published his system of dance notation as *La Sténochorégraphie* (1852).

St.-Leu, Comte de. See Louis BONAPARTE.

Saint-Mar·tin \sa^{n}-mȧr-ta^{n}\, Louis-Claude de. *Signed works* Le Phi·lo·sophe In·con·nu \lə-fē-lȯ-zȯ-fa^{n}-kȯ-nue̅\, *i.e.* the Unknown Philosopher. 1743–1803. French mystic philosopher. One of the Illuminati; at first under influence of Martínez Pasqualis; later influenced by writings of Jakob Boehme and subsequently by Emmanuel Swedenborg. Works included *Des erreurs et de la vérité* (1775), *L'Homme de désir* (1790), *Le Crocodile* (1798, allegorical poem), *Le Ministère de l'homme-espirit* (1802).

Saint-Maure \sa^{n}-mȯr\, Charles de. Duc de Mon·tau·sier \mō^{n}-tōz-yā\. 1610–1690. French soldier and man of letters. Distinguished himself in defense of Casale (1630–31); served on German front (1634–39); lieutenant general (1644); governor of Normandy (1663); created duc (1664); chief tutor of the dauphin Louis, son of Louis XIV (1668–79). His poems included in *Guirlande de Julie* (1641); compiled the "Delphin" edition of classical texts for the dauphin's use.

Saint-Pierre, Abbé de. See Charles-Irénée CASTEL.

Saint-Pierre, Jacques-Henri Bernardin de. See Jacques-Henri BERNARDIN DE SAINT-PIERRE.

Saint-Réal, Abbé de. See César VICHARD.

Saint-Rémy de Valois, Jeanne de. See under Marc-Antoine de LA MOTTE.

Saint-Saëns \sa^{n}-sä^{n}s\, Camille, *in full* Charles-Camille. 1835–1921. French composer. Organist at the Madeleine (1857–76); professor of piano at École Niedermeyer, Paris (1861–65). Composer of operas as *La Princesse jaune* (1872), *Samson et Dalila* (1877); symphonies, esp. No. 3 (*Organ*, 1886); symphonic poems, esp. *Le Rouet d'Omphale* (1871), *Danse Macabre* (1874); concertos for piano (5), for violin (3), for cello (2); *Carnaval des Animaux* for small orchestra (1886); much chamber, piano, and church music; songs and choral works. A gifted pianist and organist; also wrote criticism, poetry, essays, and plays.

Saints·bury \ˈsānts-ˌber-ē, -b(ə)rē\, George Edward Bateman. 1845–1933. English critic, journalist, and educator. Journalist in London (1876–95); professor of English, Edinburgh (1895–1915). Among his books were *The History of Elizabethan Literature* (1877), *The Flourishing of Romance and the Rise of Allegory* (1897), *A History of Criticism* (1900–04), *Minor Caroline Poets* (1905–21), *History of English Prosody* (1906–10), *The Later Nineteenth Century* (1908), *History of English Criticism* (1911), *History of English Prose Rhythm* (1912), *The English Novel* (1913), *History of the French Novel* (1917, 1919), etc.

Saint-Simon. (1) Duc de. See Louis de ROUVROY. (2) Comte de. See Claude de ROUVROY.

St. Victor, Hugh of. See HUGH of St. Victor.

Saint-Victor, Niepce de. See NIEPCE.

St. Vincent, Earl of. See John JERVIS.

St. Vrain \sa^{n}-vra^{n}\, Ceran de Hault de Las·sus de \dō-də-lȧ-sue̅s-də-\. 1802–1870. American fur trader, b. near St. Louis. Opened a supply store in Taos, N.M. (1825); with Charles and William Bent (*qq.v.*) formed (1831) Bent & St. Vrain Co., which became second largest fur trading company in Southwest; U.S. consul at Santa Fe (1834).

Sai Ong Hue \ˈsī-ˈȯŋ-ˈhwā\. *Reign title* Phra Sa·ya-Se·tha·ti·rath II \ˈprä-ˈsä-yə-se-tä-ˈtir-ät\. *Also known as* Se·tha·thi·rath II \se-tä-ˈtir-ät\. d. 1735. Ruler of Laotian kingdom of Lan Xang (1700–35). Grandson of Souligna-Vongsa; expelled (1698) from Vien Chang the usurper of the throne and declared himself king (1700); lost Luang Prabang to rival Kingkitsarat (1707); became vassal to king of Annam in return for protection; an ineffective leader.

Sai·on·ji \sī-ōn-jē\ Kimmochi. Prince. 1849–1940. Japanese politician. Founded (1881) newspaper *Tōyō Jiyū Shimbun* to promote democratic ideas; began official career as vice senator and senator (1881–84); minister to Austria (1885–87), to Germany (1887–91); privy councilor, minister of education, and acting prime minister for various periods (1892–1906); leader of the Rikken Seiyūkai party (1903); twice prime minister (1906–08, 1911–12); attempted to curtail military expenditures and effect party control of the cabinet; retired from politics (1914); represented Japan at Paris Peace Conference (1919); granted title of prince (1922); last surviving member of the *genro.*

Sais·set \ses-e\, Bernard. c.1232–?1311. French prelate. Protégé of Boniface VIII; abbot of Saint-Antonin at Pamiers (1267); first bishop of Pamiers (1295); denounced as traitor and blasphemer and his possessions impounded by King Philip IV the Fair (1301); set free and goods released on Boniface's order; exiled to Rome (1302) but apparently returned (1305).

Sa·it Fa·ik Aba·si·ya·nik \sä-ˈēt-fä-ˈē-kä-bä-sē-yä-ˈnēk\. 1907–1954. Turkish writer. Introduced into Turkish literature a new form of short story without a definite plot; published several volumes of such stories, mainly about lives of humble people, as *Semaver* (1936).

Sai·tō \sī-tō\ Makoto. 1858–1936. Japanese admiral and administrator. Naval aide-de-camp to the emperor in the Chinese–Japanese War (1894–95); served in Russo–Japanese War (1904–05); minister for the navy (1913–14); governor general of Korea (1919–27, 1929–31); prime minister of Japan (1932–34); assassinated in February mutiny.

Sa·kai \sä-kī\ Hōitsu. *Orig.* Ta·da·nao \tä-dä-nä-ō\. 1761–1828. Japanese painter and poet. Became a monk of the Nishihongan-ji (1797); retired to Negishi and led life of a gifted dilettante (1809). Revived and painted in style of Ogata Kōrin; published *Kōrin hyakuzu* ("One Hundred Designs of Kōrin") and *Ogata-ryū ryakuin-fu* ("Album of Simplified Seals in the Ogata Style"). A successful painter and haiku poet; chief painting *Kashū sōzu byōbu* ("Summer and Autumn Flowers").

Sakai Toshihiko. *Pseudonym* Ko·sen \kō-sen\; *also called* Shi·bu·ro·ku \shē-bu̇r-ō-ku̇\ Kaizuka. 1870–1933. Japanese Socialist. Originally a schoolteacher; started weekly paper *Heimin shimbun* (1903); helped organize Japanese Socialist party (1906); imprisoned (1923) for helping found (1922) Japanese Communist party; in later years opened an agricultural school.

Sa·kai·da \sä-kī-dä\ Kakiemon. *Orig.* Sakaida Kizaemon. *Also known as* Ka·ki·em·on \kä-kē-em-ōn\. d. 1666. Japanese potter. Originated (1643) the *aka-e* (red decoration) style in porcelain; made pottery in categories of *nigoshi-de* (white surface with delicate patterns painted in colored glazes) and *some-nishiki-de* (semi-transparent ground with brocaded patterns).

Sa·ka·mo·to \sä-kä-mō-tō\ Ryōma. 1835–1867. Japanese samurai and revolutionary. Forged an alliance (1866) between fiefs of Satsuma and Chōshū which was critical in setting stage for 1868 restoration to power of the emperor; began to develop an imperial navy; killed before he could institute plot to overthrow the shogun.

Sa·ker \ˈsā-kər\, Alfred. 1814–1880. English missionary. In Africa (1844–76); established first British mission in the Cameroons (1845); founded Victoria, Cameroon (1858); translated and printed the Bible into Douala (1872). David Livingston considered him most important English missionary in West Africa.

Saki. See Hector Hugh MUNRO.

Sa·ku·ma \sä-ku̇m-ä\ Shōzan. *Also known as* Sakuma Zōzen. 1811–1864. Japanese scholar. Supported the 1858 U.S.–Japan commercial treaty and policy of opening the country to Westernization; his slogan "Eastern ethics and Western science" became basis of Japanese modernization effort in late 19th century; his ideas spread by disciple Yoshida Shōin and helped inspire the Meiji Restoration of 1868; assassinated by group of nationalistic samurai.

Śākyamuni. See SIDDHĀRTHA GAUTAMA.

Sala \ˈsal-ə\, George Augustus Henry. 1828–1895. English writer. Correspondent of London *Daily Telegraph;* author of books of travel, social satire, novels, including *Strange Adventures of Captain Dangerous* (1863) and *Quite Alone* (1864), and an autobiography *Life and Adventures* (1895).

Sal·a·din \ˈsal-əd-ən, -ə-ˌdin\. *Arab.* Ṣalāḥ ad-Dīn Yūsuf ibn Ayyūb. *Also* al-Malik an-Nāṣir Ṣalāḥ ad-Dīn Yūsuf I. 1137 or 1138–1193. Muslim sultan and hero, b. Mesopotamia. Commander of Syrian forces and vizier in Egypt (1169); suppressed Fāṭimid dynasty (1171) and was proclaimed sultan of Egypt and Syria (1174). United Muslim territories of Syria, northern Mesopotamia, Palestine, and Egypt (1174–86). Campaigned to drive the Christians from Palestine and defeated them in a battle at Ḥaṭṭin (1187); went on to capture Acre, Nazareth, Ascalon, and other towns, esp. Jersualem (Oct. 2, 1187). Stalemated an army of crusaders (Third Crusade, 1189–92) under Richard I of England and Philip II of France; retired to Damascus (1192). Considered founder of the Ayyūbid dynasty and the greatest Muslim hero of all time.

Sa·la·man·ca \sä-lä-ˈmäŋ-kä\, Daniel. 1869–1935. Bolivian politician. President of Bolivia (1931–34); broke off diplomatic relations with Paraguay (1931); declared war (1933); forced to resign (1934).

Sa·lan·dra \sä-ˈlän-drä\, Antonio. 1853–1931. Italian politician. Minister of agriculture (1899–1900) and finance (1906, 1909–10); premier (1914–16); declared neutrality of Italy (1914) and eventually (1915) entered World War

I on Allied side; representative at Paris Peace Conference (1919). At first a supporter of Mussolini, later tempered his support; senator (1928 ff.).

Salanter, Israel. See Israel LIPKIN.

Sa·las Bar·ba·dil·lo \'sä-läs-bär-bä-'thē(l)-yō\, Alonso Jerónimo de. 1581–1635. Spanish writer. Friend of Cervantes; known esp. for picaresque novels and short stories as *El caballero puntual* (1614, 1619), *Corrección de vicios* (1615), *La casa del placer honesto* (1620), and *Don Diego de Noche* (1624).

Salatis. See SALITIS.

Sa·la·zar \sə-lə-'zär\, Antonio de Oli·vei·ra \thē-ō-lē-'vā-rə\. 1889–1970. Portuguese politician. Minister of finance (1926, 1928–40), war (1936–44), and foreign affairs (1936–47); premier (1932–68); chief author of 1933 constitution that established his authoritarian "New State"; virtual dictator of Portugal; rehabilitated public finances; modernized railways and carried out public works projects; suppressed opposition.

Sa·la·zar y Tor·res \sä-lä-'thär-ē-'tòr-rās\, Agustín de. 1642–1675. Spanish poet and playwright. Influenced by Góngora; published works as *Cítara de Apolo* (1681); known for poem *Eurídice y Orfeo* and comedies *El encanto es hermosura, Tetis y Peleo,* and *Elegir enemigo.*

Sal·chow \'säl-shōv\, Ulrich, *in full* Karl Emil Julius Ulrich. 1877–1949. Swedish figure skater. Won 10 world championships for men (1901–05, 1907–11) and first Olympic gold medal awarded for men's figure skating (1908); president of Internationale Eislauf-Vereinigung (1925–37); originator of the Salchow jump used in free-skating.

Şalcillo, Francisco. See SALZILLO.

Šal·da \'shäl-dä\, František Xaver. 1867–1937. Czech critic, poet, and novelist. Known for his influential books of literary criticism, esp. *Duše a dílo* (1913).

Sal·da·nha Oli·vei·ra e Daun \säl-'dän-yə-ō-lē-'vā-rə-ē-'thaün\, João Carlos de. Duque de Saldanha. 1790–1876. Portuguese general and politician. Grandson of Pombal; held military and diplomatic posts in Brazil (c.1810–22); minister of foreign affairs (1825); governor of Oporto (1826–27); supported Dom Pedro against usurper Dom Miguel; appointed marshal (1834); minister of war and president of the council (1835); exiled (1837–46) after instigating counterrevolution against Septembrists. Premier (1846–49, 1851–56, 1870); undertook political and economic reforms; ambassador to Rome (1862–64, 1866–69), Paris (1869), and London (1870).

Sales·bury \'sā(ə)lz-,ber-ē, -b(ə-)rē\ *or* **Salis·bury** \'sòlz-\, William. c.1520–c.1584. Welsh scholar. Edited collection of Welsh proverbs *Oll Synnwyr Pen Kembero Ygyd,* probably first book printed in Welsh (c.1546); compiler of *Dictionary in Englyshe and Welshe* (1547), first work of its kind. Translated New Testament into Welsh, with assistance of Richard Davies, bishop of St. Davids (printed 1567).

Sa·li·an \'sā-lē-ən\ house. *Sometimes called* Fran·co·ni·an \fraŋ-'kō-nē-ən\ house. Name of a German royal dynasty founded by a Salian Frank, Conrad II (ruled 1024–39) and ruling from 1024 to 1125. Conrad's successors were Henry III (1039–56), Henry IV (1056–1106), and Henry V (1106–25; died without heir).

Saliceto, Guglielmo da. See GUGLIELMO DA SALICETO.

Sa·lie·ri \säl-'yer-ē\, Antonio. 1750–1825. Italian composer. Court Kapellmeister in Vienna (1788–1824); friend of Haydn and Beethoven. Composer of operas as *Armida* (1771), *Tarare* (1787), and *Palmira* (1795), and sacred, choral, and chamber music. There was no foundation for Mozart's belief that Salieri had tried to poison him, a legend which formed basis of Rimsky-Korsakov's opera *Motzart et Salieri* (1898).

Ṣā·liḥ Ay·yūb \'säl-ik-ī-'yüb\, aṣ-. *In full* al-Malik aṣ-Ṣāliḥ Najm ad-Dīn Ayyūb. d. 1249. Ruler of Egypt (1239, 1245–49). Last effective ruler of Ayyūbid dynasty; in alliance with the Khwārezmians launched (1244) campaign against Jerusalem that provoked the 7th Crusade of Louis IV of France; killed during Louis's invasion; his dynasty overthrown by Mamlūk mercenaries (1250).

Sa·lim \'sä-lim\, Hadji Agus. 1884–1954. Indonesian nationalist and Islāmic leader. Joined nationalist group Sarekat Islām (1915) and became a leader; opposed messianic cult of its leader Omar Said Tjokroaminoto (*q.v.*); expelled Communists from group (1921) and directed it (from 1923) away from politics and toward pan-Islāmic movement.

Sa·lim·be·ne di Adam \säl-ēm-'ben-ā-dē-ä-'däm\. *Also* Ogni·be·ne de Adamo \,ōn-yē-'ben-ā-dā-ä-'dä-mō\. 1221–c.1290. Italian monk and chronicler. Entered Franciscan order (1238); never held a monastic office; traveled widely, esp. in France and Italy. Known chiefly for valuable *Cronica* (written 1282–90) dealing with period 1168–1288; also wrote *XII scelera Friderici imperatoris* (c.1248).

Sa·li·nas y Ser·ra·no \sä-'lē-näs-ē-ser-'rän-ō\, Pedro. 1891–1951. Spanish writer. Member of group of Spanish poets called "Generation of 1927"; taught at the Sorbonne (1914–17) and Cambridge (1922–23); to U.S. (1936) and taught at Wellesley Coll. and Johns Hopkins. His volumes of poetry included *Presagios* (1923), *Seguro azar* (1929), *La voz a ti debida* (1934), *Todo más claro* (1949); also known for studies on Jorge Manrique and Rubén Dario and a modern verse rendition of *Poema del Cid.*

Salisbury. See also SALESBURY.

Salisbury. (1) Earls of. See WILLIAM LONGESPÉE; MONTAGU family; NEVILLE family. (2) Earls and marquises of. See CECIL family. (3) Countess of. See Margaret Pole under POLE family.

Salisbury, John of. See JOHN of Salisbury.

Salisbury, Roger of. See ROGER of Salisbury.

Salis·bury \'sòlz-,ber-ē, -b(ə-)rē\, Rollin Daniel. 1858–1922. American geologist, b. Spring Prairie, Wis. Professor, Chicago (1892–1922); authority on glacial and Pleistocene deposits. Author of *Geology* (with Thomas C. Chamberlin, 1904–06).

Sa·lis-See·wis \'zä-lis-'zā-vis\, Johann Gaudenz. Freiherr. 1762–1834. Swiss soldier and poet. Officer in Swiss guards in Paris (1779); supported French Revolution; chief of staff of Swiss militia (1799); served in public offices. Known chiefly for lyrical elegies on friendship and nature, as "Lied eines Landmanns in der Fremde."

Sal·it·is *or* **Sal·at·is** \'sal-ət-əs\. *Also called* May·e·bre Sheshi \mī-'(y)eb-rā-shesh-ē\. fl. c.1670 B.C. King of Egypt. A leader of the Hyksos, Palestinian invaders; first Hyksos king of Egypt and founder of 15th dynasty; according to tradition overran all of Egypt, but probably ruled only Middle Egypt while rest of country was his vassalage; said to have made Avaris in Nile Delta the chief Hyksos garrison in Egypt.

Sal·lé \sà-lā\, Marie. c.1707–1756. French dancer and choreographer. With Paris Opéra (1721–40); rival of Marie Camargo; often danced in London (from 1725), esp. in Handel's operas. First woman to choreograph the ballets in which she appeared; introduced many dance innovations, as discarding traditional mask (in *Les Caractères de la danse,* 1729) and employing a Grecian-style muslin dress and loose hair instead of elaborate, restrictive costume (in *Pygmalion,* London, 1734). Her successes included solo *Les Caractères de l'amour* and ballet *Bacchus and Ariadne* (both in London, 1734) and as Hébé in *Castor et Pollux* (1737). A friend of Voltaire, Garrick, Noverre.

Sal·lust \'sal-əst\. *Full Latin name* Gaius Sal·lus·ti·us Cris·pus \sə-'ləs-ch(ē-)əs-'kris-pəs, -'ləs-tē-əs-\. c.86–35 or 34 B.C. Roman historian and politician. Tribune of the people (52 B.C.); expelled from Senate for alleged immorality (50); partisan of Julius Caesar; quaestor (49); praetor (46); accompanied Caesar to Africa and was present at defeat of Pompeian army at Thapsus (46). Governor of Numidia (46–45 or 44), where he amassed great fortune. On return to Rome, devoted himself to historical writing; credited with development of the monograph; his *History of the Jugurthine War* (41–40) and *Conspiracy of Catiline* (43–42) are extant; only fragments of his *History of the Roman Republic* have survived.

Sal·luste \sà-lüest\, Guillaume de. Seigneur du Bar·tas \bàr-täs\. 1544–1590. French poet. A Huguenot; trusted counsellor of Henry of Navarre. Attempted to employ La Pléiade's poetic techniques to present Protestant views. Author of epics *La Semaine* (1578, on the Creation) and *La Seconde semaine* (unfinished; a history from birth of Christ); also of biblical epic *Judith* (1574). His works translated into English by Josuah Sylvester (*q.v.*) and influenced Sidney, Spenser, Milton, et al.

Sal·mān al-Fā·ri·sī \säl-'män-əl-fä-rē-'sē\. 7th century. Persian national hero. Became a Christian as a boy; traveled to Syria and central Arabia on a religious quest; in Medina met the Prophet Muḥammad, with whose aid he purchased his freedom from slavery (622); helped Muḥammad repell a Meccan attack on Medina by suggesting a ditch be built across the city's approaches (Battle of the Ditch, 627).

Salmasius, Claudius. See Claude de SAUMAISE.

Sa·lo·me \sə-'lō-mə\. 1st century A.D. Judaean princess. Daughter of Herodias and Herod Philip, granddaughter of Herod the Great; instructed by her mother, asked Herod Antipas for the head of John the Baptist as a reward for her dancing. Married 1st Philip the Tetrarch, and 2d Aristobulus, son of Herod of Chalcis and king of Lesser Armenia.

Salome Alex·an·dra \-,al-ig-'zan-drə, -,el-ig-\. d. 67 B.C. Queen of Judea (76–67), of the Hasmonean dynasty. Succeeded her husband Alexander Jannaeus; reversed his policy and supported the Pharisees; bitter strife continued between them and the Sadducees; kingdom threatened by foreign powers.

Sa·lo·mon \'zäl-ō-mōn\, Alice. 1872–1948. German social worker. Founder and director of first German school of social work (1908–28; school named for her, 1932); helped found International Congress of Women (1904; vice president 1920); active in public health field; exiled by Nazis and went to U.S. (1937); an internationally prominent feminist.

Salomon, Erich. 1886–c.1944. German photographer. A founder of photojournalism; freelance photographer (from 1928); best known for candid photographs of statesmen and celebrities, many published in his *Berühmte Zeitgenossen in unbewachten Augenblicken* (1931). Fled from Nazis to Netherlands during World War II; apparently died in concentration camp at Auschwitz.

Sal·o·mon \'sal-ə-mən\, Haym. 1740–1785. American merchant and financier, b. Lissa, Poland. To America (1772); founded mercantile and brokerage business in New York City; imprisoned by British in New York as a spy (1776, again 1778); condemned to death (1778) but escaped to American lines. Opened brokerage business, Philadelphia; paymaster general of French forces in America; handled war subsidies advanced by French and Dutch governments; aided in maintaining American credit by extending large cash advances to American treasury; also gave financial aid to many patriot leaders, including Jefferson, Madison, and Randolph.

Sa·lo·mon \sá-lò-mō^{n}\, Louis-Étienne-Félicité. 1815–1888. Haitian general and politician. Minister of finance (1847–59); in exile (1859–79); president of Haiti (1879–88).

Salt \'sòlt\, Sir Titus. 1803–1876. English manufacturer. Wool stapler; started wool spinning (1834), devising machinery for using coarse Russian wool; discovered method of manufacturing alpaca (1836); opened model manufacturing town of Saltaire (1853); Liberal M.P. (1859).

Salten, Felix. See Siegmund SALZMANN.

Sal·ton·stall \'sòlt-ᵊn-,stòl\, Gurdon. 1666–1724. American clergyman, b. Haverhill, Mass. Governor of Connecticut (1707–24); established system of ecclesiastical discipline embodied by the Saybrook Synod in the Saybrook Platform (1708). Influenced chartering of Yale College and its removal from Saybrook to New Haven. His grandfather ¶Richard (1610?–1694) came to America (1630) and was one of original settlers of Watertown, Mass. A descendant ¶Leverett Saltonstall (1892–1979), b. Chestnut Hill, Mass.; lawyer; governor of Massachusetts (1939–44); U.S. senator (1944–67).

Sal·tus \'sòl-təs\, Edgar Evertson. 1855–1921. American author, b. New York City. Author of novels employing mannerisms of European school of Decadents, as *Mr. Incoul's Misadventure* (1887), *Vanity Square* (1906), *Daughters of the Rich* (1912); also studies of Balzac (1884), Schopenhauer (1885), antitheistic philosophies as *The Anatomy of Negation* (1886), and histories of Roman emperors *Imperial Purple* (1893) and Russian tsars *Imperial Orgy* (1920).

Sal·ty·kov \səl-ti-'kòf\, Mikhail Yevgrafovich. *Pseudonym* N. Shched·rin \'shched-ryin\. 1826–1889. Russian novelist. One of greatest Russian satirists; exiled (1848–55) from St. Petersburg to Vyatka for story *Zaputannoye delo;* provincial vice governor of Ryazen (1858–60) and Tver (1860–64); retired from civil service (1868) and devoted himself to literature; editor of radical periodicals. Author of satirical works, esp. against bureaucrats and the gentry, including *Gubernskiye ocherki* (1856–57), a comedy *Smert Pazukhina* (1857), *Pompadury i pompadurshi* (written 1863–74), *Istoriya odnoga goroda* (written 1869–70), his masterpiece *Gospoda Golovlyovy* (1876, The Golovlyov Family), *Skazki* (1880–85), and *Poshekhonskaya starina* (1887–89).

Saltykov, Pyotr Semyonovich. 1698?–1772. Russian field marshal. Commanded Russian army in the Seven Years' War (1756–63) and notably in the victory at Kunersdorf (1759).

Sa·lu·ta·ti \,säl-ü-'tä-tē\, Lino Coluccio di Piero. 1331–1406. Italian Humanist. Chancellor of Todi (1367), Lucco (1371), and the Florentine *signorie* (1375–1406). Author of Latin verse, epigrams, moral and political treatises, and of much private correspondence.

Sal·va·tier·ra \,säl-vä-'tyer-rä\, Juan María. 1648–1717. Italian Jesuit missionary. To Mexico (1675); founded (1697) Loreto, first settlement in Baja California.

Sal·vi \'säl-vē\, Niccolò *or* Nicola. 1697–1751. Italian sculptor. Designed (1732) and began construction of Fontana di Trevi Rome, which was finished (1762) by Giuseppe Pannini.

Sal·vi·a·nus \sal-vē-ā-nəs\. *Also known as* Salvianus of Marseilles. c.400–c.480. Germanic ecclesiastic. Ordained priest (c.428); author of *De gubernatione Dei* (c.450).

Sal·via·ti \säl-'vyä-tē\, Antonio. 1816–1900. Italian mosaicist. His mosaic works are in Westminster Abbey, St. Paul's Cathedral (London), cathedrals at Erfurt, Aachen, etc.

Salviati, Cecchino. *Orig.* Francesco de' Ros·si \dā-'rōs-sē\. 1510–1563. Italian painter. Studied and worked with Andrea del Sarto; protégé of Cardinal Giovanni Salviati from whom he took his surname; worked for several patrons throughout Italy, finally settled (1555) in Rome. A leading Mannerist fresco painter of Florentine-Roman school. Executed frescoes in Palazzo Vecchio, Florence (1544–48), and Palazzo Farnese, Rome (1555).

Salviati, Leonardo. *Academic name* In·fa·ri·na·to \,ēn-fä-rē-'nä-tō\. 1540–1589. Italian Humanist. Attacked work of Tasso; known chiefly for *Avvertimenti della lingua sopra il Decamerone* (1584, 1586).

Sal·vi·us Ju·li·a·nus \'sal-vē-əs-,jü-lē-'ā-nəs\. 2d century A.D. Roman jurist. Twice elected consul; drew up the *Perpetual Edict* (edictum perpetuum), or *Praetor's Edict* (131 A.D.).

Sal·zi·llo y Al·ca·raz \säl-'thē(l)-yō-ē-äl-kä-'räth\, Francisco. *Surname also spelled* Sal·ci·llo \säl-'thē(l)-yō\, Sal·si·llo \säl-'sē(l)-yō\, *or* Zar·ci·llo \thär-thē(l)-yō\. 1707–1783. Spanish sculptor. Studio in Murcia (from 1727); with assistance of brothers and sister produced many polychromed religious figures for the Holy Week procession; work highly humanized and detailed but flawed by his fondness for the spectacular.

Salz·mann \'shälz-män\, Siegmund. *Pen name* Felix Sal·ten \'shäl-tən\. 1869–1945. Hungarian novelist and journalist. As a Jew forced to flee Vienna (1939), settled in Switzerland. Known esp. for children's books as *Bambi* (1923) and *Florian, the Emperor's Stallion* (1934).

Sa·main \sá-ma^{n}\, Albert-Victor. 1858–1900. French poet. One of founders of *Mercure de France* (1890) and contributor to *La Revue des Deux Mondes.* His verse collected in *Au jardin de l'Infante* (1893), *Aux flancs du vase* (1898), and *Le Chariot d'or* (1901).

Sā·mān·id \sá-'mán-əd\. A Persian native dynasty ruling from Bukhara (819–999), founded by Sāmān-khodā \sá-'mán-k̲ò-'dá\, a Persian noble of Balkh. It overthrew the Saffārids; fostered Persian literature and art; nominally subject to caliphs of Baghdad; conquered by Ghaznavids.

Sa·ma·nie·go \sä-män-'yā-gō\, Félix María. 1745–1801. Spanish Basque poet. Influenced by French Encyclopédistes; joined Basque Society and taught at its seminary. Author of books of fables for schoolchildren, esp. *Fábulas morales* (1781).

Sam·bhā·jī \'səm-bä-jē\. d. 1689. Hindu raja of Marāthā (1680–89). Son and successor of Śivajī; captured by Aurangzeb and executed.

Sam·bourne \'sam-(,)bərn, -,bō(ə)rn, -,bò(ə)rn, -,bù(ə)rn\, Edward Linley. 1844–1910. English draftsman and illustrator. On staff (1871) and cartoonist in chief (1900–10), *Punch;* illustrator of Kingsley's *Water Babies* (1885).

Sam·bu·cuc·cio d'·Alan·do \,säm-bü-'küt-chō-dä-'län-dō\. d. c.1370. Corsican rebel. Led a successful revolt against the Cinarca family and their overlord James IV of Aragon (1356); obtained Genoese governorship of Corsica (1360); again sought Genoese aid after a revolt (1362); perhaps died of the Black Death.

Sam·mar·ti·ni \,säm-mär-'tē-nē\ *or* **San Mar·ti·ni** \,sän-mär-'tē-nē\, Giovanni Battista. *Orig. surname* Saint-Mar·tin \sa^{n}-mår-ta^{n}\. *Called* Il Mi·la·ne·se \,ēl-mē-lä-'nā-sā\. 1700 or 1701–1775. Italian composer. Maestro di capella at several Milanese churches; teacher of Gluck (1737–41). A leading figure in development of the Classical style; composed earliest known dated symphonies (1732) and some of earliest string quartets (1763–67) and string quintets (1773); considered first great master of the symphony. A prolific composer of symphonies, operas, sacred and secular vocal music, and chamber and solo works. His brother ¶Giuseppe Francesco Gaspare Melchiorre Baldassare (1695–1750), *called* Il Lon·do·ne·se \,ēl-lòn-dō-'nā-sā\; an esteemed composer, oboist and teacher of oboe in London (from 1728); in service of Frederick Louis, Prince of Wales (1736–50); composed in late Baroque style concerti grossi, trio sonatas, oboe and flute sonatas, overtures, cantatas, and a setting of Congreve's *Judgment of Paris* (1740).

Sam·mu·ra·mat \'säm-,ü-rä-'mät\. *Gr.* Se·mir·a·mis \sə-'mi(ə)r-ə-məs\. 9th century B.C. Assyrian queen. Wife of Shamshi-Adad V and mother of Adad-nirari III. Under name Semiramis became subject of a legend by the historian Diodorus Siculus that made her the wife of King Ninus, the ruler of Assyria after his death, and the builder of Babylon.

Sa·mo \'säm-ō\. d. c.660 A.D. Frankish merchant. Led the Slavic resistance to the Avars (624 ff.); controlled a large territory in what is now Austria and Bohemia.

Sa·mo·ry \sä-'mōr-ē, -'mòr-\. *In full* Samory Tou·ré \-tü-'rā\. c.1830–1900. West African ruler. Member of Mandingo tribe; established a kingdom in Kankan region of Guinea (1868); extended his rule from the Upper Volta region to Fouta Djallon; resisted French colonial expansion in West Africa (from 1883); captured by the French (1898); died in exile.

Sam·o·set \'sam-ə-,set, sə-'mäs-ət\. d. 1653? American Indian leader. Sachem of the Pemaquid; became (from 1621) a firm friend of the Pilgrims settled at Plymouth; signed first deed of land transfer between Indian and Englishman (1625).

Samp·son \'sam(p)-sən\, William Thomas. 1840–1902. American naval officer, b. Palmyra, N.Y. Commander in chief, North Atlantic Squadron, in Spanish–American War; destroyed Spanish fleet under Cervera when it tried to escape from harbor of Santiago de Cuba (July 3, 1898). Rear admiral (1899).

Sam Sene Thai \'säm-'sen-ə-'tī\, Phya. *Also spelled* Sam Sen Thai \-'sen-'tī\. *Orig.* Oun Hueun \'ōn-'hwā-'ün\. 1356–1417. Ruler of Lan Xang kingdom of Laos (1373–1417). Son and successor of Fa Ngum; continued his father's administrative policies; built pagodas and religious compounds; reign noted for peace, prosperity, and stability.

Sam·son \'sam(p)-sən\ of Tot·ting·ton \'tät-iŋ-tən\. c.1135–1212. English ecclesiastic. Abbot of abbey of Bury St. Edmunds (1182–1212); member of Royal Council; frustrated efforts of William de Longchamp to curtail rights of English Benedictines; built up abbey materially and morally. The original of Carlyle's essay on Abbot Samson in *Past and Present.* See JOCELIN DE BRAKELOND.

Sam·so·nov \(ˌ)səm-ˈsȯ-nəf\, Aleksandr Vasiliyevich. 1859–1914. Russian general. Commanded the army which invaded East Prussia (Aug. 1914); decisively defeated in Battle of Tannenberg (Aug. 26–31, 1914); committed suicide.

Sa·mu·dra Gup·ta \sə-ˈmu̇-drə-ˈgu̇p-tə\. d. c.380 A.D. Second emperor (c.330–c.380) of Gupta dynasty in India. Son of Candra Gupta I; brought all Ganges valley and northern part of Deccan under his control; greater part of his reign marked by prosperity, flourishing of literature and art, and religious tolerance. Considered an ideal king and hero.

Sam·u·el \ˈsam-yə(-wə)l\. *Hebrew* Shmu'el \shmü-ˈel\. c.11th century B.C. Hebrew judge and first of the great prophets. Brought up under the high priest Eli, whom he succeeded as judge; played major role in establishing monarchy in Israel by anointing Saul.

Samuel. d. 1014. Czar of Bulgaria (980–1014). Originally ruled in Macedonia; extended empire to Serbia, northern Bulgaria, Albania, and northern Greece; established his capital at Ochrida; revived the Bulgarian patriarchate. Waged war against Basil II Bulgaroctonus of Byzantium; defeated Basil near Sofia (early 980s); finally crushed by Basil in Battle of Belasitsa (July 29, 1014) and died soon after.

Samuel of **Ne·har·dea** \nə-ˈhärd-ē-ə\. *Also called* Mar Samuel \ˈmär-\. c.177–257. Babylonian scholar and rabbi. Disciple of Judah ha-Nasi; friend of King Shāpūr I of Persia; head of yeshiva of Nehardea; authority on civil law; an expert astronomer and physician.

Samuel, Sir Herbert Louis. 1st Viscount Samuel. 1870–1963. English politician. Liberal M.P. (1902–18, 1929–35) and leader of Liberal party (1929–35); parliamentary undersecretary to Home Office (1905–09); responsible for legislation (1908) that established juvenile courts and Borstal system. Chancellor of duchy of Lancaster, with seat in Cabinet (1909–10, 1915–16); postmaster general (1910–14, 1915–16); nationalized telephone services; home secretary (1916, 1931–32); first high commissioner to Palestine (1920–25); created viscount (1937); leader of Liberals in House of Lords (1944–55). Author of *Practical Ethics* (1935), *Belief and Action* (1937).

Samuel, Marcus. 1st Viscount Bear·sted \ˈbər-ˌsted, ˈba(ə)r-, ˈbe(ə)r-\ 1853–1927. English financier. Founded Shell Transport and Trading Co. (1897), amalgamated with Royal Dutch Petroleum Co. (1907), an oil producing and distributing firm. Lord mayor of London (1902–03).

Samuel ha-Na·gid \-hä-ˈnäg-ēd\. *In full* Abu Ibrahim Samuel ben Joseph Halevi ibn Nagrela. 993–1055 or 1056. Spanish Talmudic scholar, warrior, and politician. Vizier to caliph of Granada (1027 ff.); actual power behind throne, conducted all diplomatic and military affairs. As *nagid* (chief) of Granadian Jewry, appointed all judges and headed the Talmudic academy; patron of arts and learning. Wrote a concordance to the Bible; considered author of a long-lived Talmudic manual *Mevo ha-Talmud;* also wrote didactic poems and works on grammar.

Sanā'ī. See ABŪ AL-MAJD.

Să·nă·tes·cu \sən-ə-ˈtes-kü\, Constantin. 1885–1947. Romanian soldier and politician. General (1935); deputy chief of general staff (1937); headed Romanian delegation to Moscow (1940). Prime minister (Aug.–Dec. 1944); anti-Communist; forced to resign under pressure from Soviet Union.

San·a·tru·ces \ˌsan-ə-ˈtrü-ˌsēz\. *Also known as* Ar·sha·kan \ˈär-shə-ˌkan\. d. 70 or 69 B.C. King of Parthia (76 or 75–70 or 69 B.C.). Perhaps a son of Mithradates I; sought refuge with the Sacaraucase, a Scythian tribe, during dynastic struggles; restored unity to his kingdom and cleared up the problem of succession.

San·born \ˈsan-bərn, -ˌbȯ(ə)rn\, Franklin Benjamin. 1831–1917. American journalist, b. Hampton Falls, N.H. Associated with John Brown; editor, Boston *Commonwealth* (1863–67), Springfield *Republican* (1868–72); associated with William T. Harris in establishing Concord School of Philosophy (1879–88). Wrote biographies or recollections of Thoreau (1882), John Brown (1885), A. Bronson Alcott (with W. T. Harris, 1893), Ralph Waldo Emerson (1901), Hawthorne (1908).

Sanborn, James S. 1835–1903. American businessman, b. Wales, Me. Joined spice firm in Boston (1868); organized firm of Chase & Sanborn (1878).

San·ches \ˈsän-ches\ *or* **Sán·chez** \ˈsän-chāth\, Francisco. c.1550–1623. Portuguese or Spanish physician and philosopher. Professor of philosophy (from 1585) and medicine (from 1612) at Toulouse; in chief work *Quod nihil scitur* (1581) rejected Aristotelian theory of knowledge for a "constructive Skepticism."

Sán·chez Cer·ro \ˈsän-chās-ˈser-rō\, Luis M. 1889–1933. Peruvian soldier and politician. Led revolt in Arequipa against Leguía y Salcedo (1930) and forced his resignation; provisional president of Peru (1930–31); forced to resign by naval junta; elected president (1931–33).

Sán·chez Co·e·llo \ˈsän-chāth-kō-ˈā(l)-yō\, Alonso. 1531 or 1532–1588. Spanish painter. Studied under Anthonis Mor in Flanders; court painter to John III of Portugal (1550–55) and Philip II of Spain (1555–88). Executed religious paintings and esp. portraits, as of Philip II (c.1575) and Infanta Isabel Clara Eugenia (1579).

Sánchez Co·tán \-kō-ˈtän\, Juan. 1561–1627. Spanish painter. A pioneer of Baroque realism in Spain; student of Blas del Prado; entered Carthusian monastery in Segovia (1603); lived in Granada (1612 ff.). Known for still lifes marked by detailed realism, sense of volume and depth, and a mood of mystic harmony, esp. *Quince, Cabbage, Melon, and Cucumber* (1602).

Sánchez de Bustamante y Sirvén, Antonio. See BUSTAMANTE Y SIRVÉN.

Sancho I. King of Aragon. See SANCHO V of Navarre.

San·cho \ˈsän-chō\. Name of three kings of Castile:

Sancho II. c.1038–1072. King (1065–72). Eldest son of Ferdinand I; named El Cid commander of royal troops (1065); attempted to reunite his father's possessions; dispossessed his brothers García (of Galicia, 1071) and Alfonso VI (of León, 1072); assassinated while besieging Zamora.

Sancho III. c.1134–1158. King (1157–58). Eldest son of Alfonso VII and brother of Ferdinand II.

Sancho IV. 1258–1295. King (1284–95). Second son of Alfonso X; usurped throne from nephew Alfonso de La Cerda; repelled a Marinīd invasion of Andalusia (1290); married his daughter to James II of Aragon to secure support (1291).

Sancho I. *Called* el Cra·so \el-ˈkrä-sō\, *i.e.* the Fat. d. 965 or 966. King of León (956–58, 960–965 or 966). Son of Ramiro II; overthrown by his nobles and replaced by his cousin Ordoño IV (958); regained throne with aid of ʻAbd ar-Raḥmān III (960).

Sancho. Name of seven kings of Navarre (Pamplona):

Sancho I Gar·cés \gär-ˈthās\. d. 925. King (905–25). Expanded his kingdom south of Ebro River and maintained its independence despite sacking of his capital (924) by ʻAbd ar-Raḥmān III.

Sancho II Garcés. *Also called* Sancho Abar·ca \-ä-ˈb̠är-kä\. d. 994. King (970–94). Son of García II and grandson of Sancho I Garcés; count of Aragon (970–94). Defeated by the Moors (973, 981) and submitted to the caliphate; visited Córdoba (992) to pay homage to Almanzor, who had married a daughter of Sancho.

Sancho III Garcés. *Called* el Ma·yor \el-mä-ˈyȯr\, *i.e.* the Great. c.992–1035. King (1000–35). Son of García III and grandson of Sancho II Garcés; count of Aragon (1000–35) and of Castile (1029–35). Established hegemony over all the Christian states of Spain; divided his kingdom among his four sons (Ramiro I, García IV, Ferdinand I, Gonzalo), thus making fratricidal wars inevitable after his death.

Sancho IV. c.1039–1076. King (1054–76). Son of García IV, grandson of Sancho III Garcés, and cousin of Sancho V Ramírez. Persuaded the Moorish king of Saragossa to become his vassal; invaded by Alfonso VI (1076); assassinated, apparently by his brothers.

Sancho V Ra·mí·rez \rä-ˈmē-rāth\. 1043–1094. King of Aragon as Sancho I Ramírez (1063–94) and of Navarre as Sancho V Ramírez (1074–94). Son of Ramiro I; became king of Navarre after murder of his cousin Sancho IV, thus forestalling ambition of Alfonso VI to annex Navarre; conquered territory from Moors in regions of Huesca and Monzón; placed kingdom under feudal protection of the pope (1089).

Sancho VI. *Called* el Sa·bio \el-ˈsäb̠-yō\, *i.e.* the Wise. d. 1194. King (1150–94). Son of García V; first to use title king of Navarre instead of Pamplona; instituted administrative reforms; to avoid partition of Navarre by Castile and Aragon accepted Alfonso VII of Castile as his suzerain and married his daughter (1153); his daughter Berenguela married Richard the Lion-Heart.

Sancho VII. *Called* el Fuer·te \el-ˈfwār-tā\, *i.e.* the Strong. 1154–1234. King (1194–1234). Son of Sancho VI; a swashbuckling but enigmatic personality; offended the pope by his friendship with the Saracens; took burgesses of Bayonne under his protection (1204); helped defeat the Almohads at Las Navas de Tolosa (1212); last Spanish-descended king for 200 years.

San·cho \ˈsän-chü\. Name of two kings of Portugal of the house of Burgundy:

Sancho I. 1154–1211. King (1185–1211). Son of Afonso I; resettled depopulated areas; built towns, frontier castles, and roads; encouraged foreign settlers; gave vast territories to the military orders.

Sancho II. 1207–1248. King (1223–45). Son of Afonso II and grandson of Sancho I; defeated Moors at Tavira and Cacela (1238–39); reign marked by internal disorders; inability to govern led to deposition by Pope Innocent IV (1245); administration entrusted to his brother Afonso (later Afonso III).

San·chu·ni·a·thon \ˌsän-chu̇-ˈnī-ə-ˌthän\. 14th–13th century B.C.? Phoenician writer. According to Philo of Byblos, the author of a non-extant text on Phoenician culture translated by Philo as *Phoenicica;* Philo's claim has been questioned but much of Sanchuniathon's information has been supported by excavated Phoenician documents.

San·croft \'san(g)-kroft\, William. 1617–1693. English prelate. Dean of St. Paul's, London (1664–77); archbishop of Canterbury (1678); crowned James II (1685). Refused to read James II's Declaration of Indulgence (1688) exempting Catholics and dissenters from penal statutes and with six bishops, Ken, Lake, White, Turner, Lloyd, and Trelawny, petitioned against it; acquitted, with the bishops, of seditious libel; opposed William of Orange's claim to throne and deprived of his see (1690).

Sanctis, Francesco De. See DE SANCTIS.

Sanctorius. See SANTORIO.

Sand, George. See DUDEVANT.

San·day \'san-(ˌ)dā, -dē\, William. 1843–1920. English New Testament scholar. Professor at Oxford (1882–1919). A pioneer in introducing to English students the biblical criticism of continental scholars, esp. through *Commentary on Romans* (1895, with Arthur C. Headlam) and *Outlines of the Life of Christ* (1905).

Sand·burg \'san(d)-ˌbərg\, Carl. 1878–1967. American writer, b. Galesburg, Ill. On staff of the magazine *System* (Chicago, 1913), Chicago *Daily News* (1917); devoted himself to writing, lecturing, reading from his own works, singing folk songs, and collecting old ballads. His poetry, mostly in free verse, included *Chicago Poems* (1915), *Corn Huskers* (1918), *Smoke and Steel* (1920), *Slabs of the Sunburnt West* (1922), *Good Morning, America* (1928), *Early Moon* (1930), *The People, Yes* (1936), *Harvest Poems* (1960), *Honey and Salt* (1963); awarded Pulitzer prize for *Complete Poems* (1950). Author also of books for children, including *Rootabaga Stories* (1922), *Rootabaga Pigeons* (1923), and *Potato Face* (1930); biographies *Abraham Lincoln—The Prairie Years* (1926), *Steichen the Photographer* (1929), *Abraham Lincoln—The War Years* (1939, Pulitzer prize); songs collected in *The American Songbag* (1927), *New American Songbag* (1950); a novel *Remembrance Rock* (1948) and an autobiography *Always the Young Stranger* (1953). Considered the poet of America's common people.

Sand·by \'san(d)-bē\, Paul. 1725–1809. English engraver and painter. One of first English landscape watercolorists; an original member of Royal Academy (1768); introduced aquatint process of engraving into England.

San·deau \sän-dō\, Léonard-Sylvain-Julien, *known as* Jules. 1811–1883. French novelist and playwright. Intimate of George Sand (1831–33), with whom he collaborated in contributions to *Figaro,* including the novel *Rose et Blanche* (1831); collaborator with Émile Augier in the play *Le Gendre de Monsieur Poirier* (1854); alone wrote novels *Madame de Sommerville* (1834), *Le Docteur Herbeau* (1841), *Mademoiselle de la Seiglière* (1848), etc.

San·de·man \'san-də-mən\, Robert. 1718–1771. Scottish religious leader. Linen manufacturer in Scotland (1736–44); associated with John Glas, founder (c.1730) of Glasites, a Scottish sect teaching a strict primitive Christianity; m. Glas's daughter Catherine (1737, d. 1746); served as elder in Glasite churches in Scotland and in London (1744–64). To America (1764) and organized congregations of Glasites or Sandemanians in New England towns, esp. in Danbury, Conn.

San·de·mo·se \'sän-də-ˌmō-sə\, Aksel. *Orig. surname (to 1921)* Niel·sen \'nēl-sən\. 1899–1965. Norwegian novelist, b. Denmark. Ran away to sea at 15, later a lumberjack in Newfoundland; settled in Norway (1929). Author of psychological, partly autobiographical novels dealing mostly with social repressions and violence, including *En sjømann går iland* (1931), *En flyktning krysser sitt spor* (1933), *Der stod en benk i haven* (1937), *Der svudne er en drøm* (1946), *Varulven* (1958), *Mytteriet på barken Zuidersee* (1963).

San·ders \'san-dərz\, Harland. *Known as* Colonel Sanders. 1890–1980. American food franchiser, b. near Henryville, Ind. Operated (1929–56) Sanders' Cafe, Corbin, Ky., specializing in fried chicken; made honorary colonel by governor of Kentucky (1936); founder and owner (1956–64) of Kentucky Fried Chicken Corp., a franchising firm.

San·ders \'san-dərz, 'sän-\ *or* **San·der** \-dər\, Nicholas. 1530?–1581. English controversialist and historian. Ordained priest in Rome (1561); employed by Cardinal Hosius in checking spread of heresy; in Madrid, strove to effect Roman Catholic conquest of England (1573); sent to Ireland (1579) as papal agent to stir up rebellion; after annihilation of his Spanish and Italian supporters by Lord Grey (1580), died of cold and starvation in woods. Author of *De origine ac progressu schismatis anglicani* (completed by Edward Rishton), basis of Roman Catholic accounts of English Reformation.

Sanders, Otto Liman von. See LIMAN VON SANDERS.

San·der·son \'san-dər-sən\, Frederick William. 1857–1922. English educator. Headmaster (1892 ff.) of Oundle School for boys, near Peterborough, Northamptonshire; greatly expanded school facilities, including laboratories, workshops, a foundry, etc.; his ideas strongly influenced the *Hadrow Report on the Education of the Adolescent* (1926).

Sanderson, Thomas James Cobden-. See COBDEN-SANDERSON.

San·di·no \sän-'dē-nō\, Augusto César *or* César Augusto. 1893–1934. Nicaraguan guerrilla leader. Supported a liberal insurrection (1926) in Nicaragua and seized American property; proclaimed an outlaw by U.S. (1927); waged guerrilla warfare (1927–32) against U.S. Marines, declaring that attacks were motivated solely by his patriotic aim to end U.S. intervention in Nicaragua. U.S. withdrew last of its Marines from Nicaragua (1933) and Sandino agreed to amnesty terms. Assassinated in Managua.

San·do·val y Ro·jas \sän-dō-'b̲äl-ē-'rō-k̲äs\, Francisco Gómez de. Duque de Ler·ma \'ler-mä\. 1553–1623. Spanish politician. As prime minister (1598–1618), had complete control of Spanish government and ascendancy over Philip III; made peace with England (1604) and a truce with the Netherlands (1609); drove Moriscos from Spain (1609–14); greatly weakened finances of kingdom; made cardinal (1618).

San·dow \'zän-(ˌ)dō, *Angl* 'san-\, Eugene. 1867–1925. American strongman and exponent of physical culture, b. Königsberg, Germany. Gained fame under management of Florenz Ziegfeld at Chicago World's Fair (1893).

San·drart \'zän-ˌdrärt\, Joachim von. 1606–1688. German painter, engraver, and art scholar. Known esp. for portraits, but painted also altarpieces, biblical scenes, etc.

Sandwich, Earls of. See MONTAGU.

Sandys \'san(d)z\, Edwin. 1516?–1588. English prelate. Anglican bishop of Worcester (1559–70) and London (1570–76); archbishop of York (1576–88); one of translators of the Bishops' Bible (1565). His second son ¶Sir Edwin (1561–1629), colonial organizer; M.P. (1586–93, 1604–26); a leader of the opposition; assailed great monopolies, served on East India Co. committee (1619–23, 1625–29); member of council for Virginia (1607); joint manager of Virginia colony (1617), treasurer (1619–20), organized government of colony (1619); assisted in obtaining charter for the *Mayflower;* accused of attempt to establish republican, Puritan state in America, and imprisoned (1621); author of *A Relation of the State of Religion* (1605). Sir Edwin's youngest brother ¶George (1578–1644), colonist and poet; published account of his travels in the Middle East *Relation of a Journey* (1615); treasurer and director of industry and agriculture of Virginia Co. (1621–25); resident in Virginia (1621–28); member of governor's council (1624, 1626, 1628); after return to England (1628?), represented Virginia (1640) when its assembly petitioned for restoration of its charter rights; also wrote *Ovid's Metamorphoses Englished* (1626), *A Paraphrase Upon the Psalmes of David and Upon the Hymns Dispersed throughout the Old and New Testaments* (1636), etc.

Sandys, Frederick, *in full* Anthony Frederick Augustus. 1829–1904. English artist. Associate of Pre-Raphaelites; known chiefly for crayon portraits of Tennyson, Matthew Arnold, Browning, John Morely, and others.

Sandys, Sir John Edwin. 1844–1922. English scholar. Taught at Cambridge (1867–1907); author of *History of Classical Scholarship* (1908); editor of many Greek classics.

San·ford \'san-fərd\, Edward Terry. 1865–1930. American jurist, b. Knoxville, Tenn. Practiced law, Knoxville (1890–1907); justice of U.S. District Court in Tenn. (1908–22); associate justice, U.S. Supreme Court (1923–30).

San·fuen·tes An·do·na·e·gui \sän-'fwān-täs-än-dō-nä-'ā-g̅ē\, Juan Luis. 1858–1930. Chilean politician. Minister of interior (1901); president of Chile (1915–20).

San·gal·lo \säŋ-'gäl-lō\, Antonio Giamberti da. *Called* the Younger. 1483–1546. Florentine architect. Nephew of Antonio and Giuliano da Sangallo. Pupil and assistant of Bramante; worked on St. Peter's throughout career (chief architect, 1520 ff.); in Rome designed Palazzos Baldassini (1503), Farnese (1513; enlarged 1534–46), Leroy (c.1523), del Banco di S. Spirito (1523–24); also designed in the Vatican the Sala Regia, Chapelle Paoline, and altar to Leo X in church of Sta. Maria sopra Minerva. Most influential architect of the day.

Sangallo, Giuliano da. 1445?–1516. Florentine architect, sculptor, and military engineer. Assisted Raphael in designing and building Saint Peter's; distinguished himself as military engineer in Florentine army against Naples (1478); chief designer, Sta. Maria delle Carceri church in Prato (1485–91); also designed facade projects for S. Lorenzo, Florence (1515–16). His brother ¶Antonio (1455–1535), *called* the Elder, also an architect and military engineer; built a number of churches and palaces, esp. the Palazzo Tarugi (1515–30) and the pilgrimage church of Madonna di San Biago (1518 ff.), both in Montepulciano. A son of Giuliano ¶Francesco (1494–1576), *known as* Il Mar·got·ta \ˌēl-mär-'gȯt-tä\, sculptor; style characterized by minute detail; sculpted tombs in Florence of bishops Marzi-Medici (1546) and Bonofede (1550).

Säng·er \'zeŋ-ər\, Eugen. 1905–1964. Austrian rocket propulsion engineer. Directed Trauen rocket program in Germany (1936–45); worked for French armament ministry (1946–54); head of Jet Propulsion Physics Inst., Stuttgart (1954–63). Designed a stratosphere rocket plane (1933) and a rocket "antipodal bomber" (c.1942).

Sang·er \'saŋ-ər\, John (1816–1889) and his brother George (1825–1911). *Latterly known as* Lord John *and* Lord George. English circus proprietors (from 1853). Leased (1871) Astley's Amphitheater and exhibited an equestrian pantomime each winter, touring summers; ended partnership (late 1870s) and formed separate shows.

Sanger, Margaret Louise, *nee* Hig·gins \'hig-ənz\. 1879–1966. American founder of birth control movement, b. Corning, N.Y. m. William Sanger (1902), J. Noah H. Slee (1922). A trained nurse by profession; founded magazine on birth control *The Woman Rebel* (1914); indicted (1915) for sending birth control information through the mails. Founded (1916) in Brooklyn first birth control clinic in U.S.; organized first American Birth Control Conference, New York (1921); made world tour on behalf of movement (1922); founder and first president, American Birth Control League (1921–28); organized first World Population Conference, Geneva (1927); first president of International Planned Parenthood Federation (1953 ff.). Author of *What Every Mother Should Know* (1917), *My Fight for Birth Control* (1931), *Margaret Sanger: An Autobiography* (1938), etc.

San·jar \sän-'jär\. *In full* Mu'izz ad-Dīn Sanjar. 1084 or 1086–1157. Prince of Khorāsān (c.1096–1157). Member and head (from 1118) of Seljuq dynasty; gained power and victories in first half of reign; established suzerainty over Qarakhanid princes of Transoxania and Ghaznavids of India. Suffered setbacks in second half of reign; defeated near Samarkand by the Turkish Qarlugs and the Karakitai and lost Transoxania; barely suppressed rebellion of Atsiz in Khwārezm; captured and imprisoned by the Oğuz tribes in his realm (1153–55).

San·jō II \sän-jō\. *Jp.* Go·san·jō \gō-sän-jō\. *Personal name* Takahito. 1034–1073. 71st emperor of Japan (1168–72). One of few rulers of the period not born of a Fujiwara mother; attempted to reform court procedures and expenditures but frustrated by the Fujiwara clan; abdicated in favor of his son Shirakawa (1072); established precedent of government by retired emperor, thus contributing to the decline of the Fujiwara.

Sanjō Sanetomi. 1837–1891. Japanese politician. Political leader of nobles at court of emperor; helped restore power (1868) to Meiji emperor after a coup d'état; as chief minister of Council of State (throughout most of period 1871–85) was spokesman for government; made lord keeper of the privy seal at institution of modern cabinet system of government (1885).

Śan·ka·ra \'shən-kə-rə\ *or* **Śan·ka·rā·cār·ya** \ˌshən-kə-rä-'kär-yə\. 700?–?750. Indian philosopher and theologian. Most famous exponent of the Advaita Vedānta school of philosophy; preached that there is only one true reality (Brahman) which is the source of everything and all differentiations and pluralities are illusory. Founded four monasteries at the four extremities of India; author of many books in Sanskrit, esp. commentaries on the *Brahma-sūtra* and on the principal *Upaniṣads.*

San·ka·ran Na·ir \'səŋ-kə-rən-'nä-yər\, Sir Chettur. 1857–1934. Indian jurist and politician. Judge, Madras high court (1908). Founder and editor, *Madras Review* and *The Madras Law Journal;* delegate to Indian National Congress; member for education in viceroy's council (1915–19); member of Council of State of India (1925 ff.). In *Gandhi and Anarchy* (1922) attacked Gandhi's national movement and British actions under martial law.

San·key \'saŋ-kē\, Ira David. 1840–1908. American evangelist and hymn writer, b. Edinburg, Pa. Associated with Dwight L. Moody in evangelistic work (from 1870); toured U.S., England, Scotland, and Ireland (from 1873). Compiled collections of popular hymns used in evangelistic meetings, including *Sacred Songs and Solos* (1873), *Gospel Hymns* (a series, 1875–91).

Sankey, John. 1st Viscount Sankey. 1866–1948. English jurist. King's counsel (1909); judge, King's Bench Division of High Court of Justice (1914–28); lord chancellor of England (1929–35); British representative on Hague Tribunal (from 1930).

San Mar·tín \sän-mär-'tēn\, José Francisco de. 1778–1850. Argentinian soldier and statesman. National hero of Argentina. Officer in Spanish army (1789–1812); offered his services to Buenos Aires in its fight for independence (1812); defeated Spaniards (1813) and succeeded Belgrano as commander in chief (1814). Organized army in Cuyo province, Argentina (1814–16), crossed the Andes, and, with Gen. O'Higgins, defeated the Spanish at Chacabuco (1817) and Maipo (1818) in Chile; established independence of Chile; with aid of Lord Cochrane, developed a Chilean fleet and left with it for Peru (1820). Won over Peruvians and entered Lima (July 1821) as Spanish withdrew; proclaimed independence of Peru; assumed title of "Protector of Peru." Resigned (1822) and retired to France, refusing to oppose Bolívar's ambition, but his work had made possible Bolívar's later victories over the Spanish at Junín and Ayacucho (1824).

San Martini, Giovanni and Giuseppe. See SAMMARTINI.

San·mi·che·li \säm-mē-'kel-ē\, Michele. 1484–1559. Italian architect and military engineer. Studied under Bramante and Giuliano da Sangallo; chief architect for cathedral of Orvieto (1509–28); built Duomo of Montefiascone (1519), Cappella Pellegrini in church of S. Bernardino at Verona, church of Madonna di Campagna near Verona (1559), many palaces in Verona; worked on fortifications of Verona, Venice, Cyprus, Crete; reputedly first to employ bastionary system of fortification and inventor of pentagonal bastion.

San·na·za·ro \ˌsän-näd-'zä-rō\, Jacopo. *Academic name* Ac·ti·us Sin·ce·rus \'ak-sh(ē-)ə(s)-sin-'si(ə)r-əs\. 1458–1530. Italian writer. Court poet to House of Aragon (c.1475–1501). Author of *Arcadia* (1504), prototype of modern prose pastoral; also of Latin elegies, eclogues, epigrams, *Piscatoriae* (1526), and the religious poem *De partu Virginis* (1526); and, in Italian, *Rime, Farse,* and monologues.

San·som \'san-səm\, William. 1912–1976. English writer. Author of novels, including *The Body* (1949), *A Bed of Roses* (1954), *The Loving Eye* (1956), *Goodbye* (1966); collections of short stories *Fireman Flower* (1944), *Something Terrible, Something Lovely* (1948), *A Touch of the Sun* (1952), *Blue Skies, Brown Studies* (1960), *The Marmalade Bird* (1973); travel books on Europe, and *Proust and his World* (1973).

Sansovino, Andrea. See Andrea CONTUCCI.

San·so·vi·no \ˌsän-sō-'vē-nō\, Jacopo. *Orig. surname* Tat·ti \'tät-tē\. 1486–1570. Italian sculptor and architect. Pupil of Andrea Sansovino, whose surname he assumed; employed at Florence, Rome (to 1527), and Venice; Venetian state architect (1529); introduced High Renaissance style into Venice. Among his Venetian architectural works were Palazzo Corner della Ca' Grande, library of St. Mark, churches of San Giorgio dei Grechi, San Francesco della Vigna, and San Martino, and the Zecca (mint); sculptural works included *St. James the Elder* (1511–18), *Bacchus* (c.1514), *Madonna del Parto* (c.1519), *St. John the Baptist* (1554), *Mars and Neptune* (1554–56), and the monument to Doge Venier (1556–61).

San·ta An·na \'sän-tä-'ä-nä\, Antonio López de. 1794–1876. Mexican general and politician. Led revolts against Iturbide (1822), against Guerrero (1828), and against Bustamante (1832). President of Mexico (1833–36); attempted to crush Texan Revolution, seized the Alamo and won at Goliad (both 1836) but was defeated and captured by Sam Houston at San Jacinto (Apr. 21, 1836). Practically in control (1839–42), made dictator (1844) by the constitution of 1843; deposed and exiled (1845); recalled and made provisional president (1847); commanded army against U.S. (1846–47), defeated at Buena Vista, Cerro Gordo, and Puebla, and driven out of Mexico City by Gen. Scott. Exiled (1848) but recalled and made president (1853–55); again exiled (1855; revolution of Ayutla). Lived in Cuba, Venezuela, St. Thomas, and U.S. (1855–74); returned to Mexico City (1874) and died in poverty and neglect.

Santa Cruz, Marqués de. See Álvaro de BAZÁN.

Santa Cruz \-'krüth\, Alonso de. 1505–1567. Spanish cartographer and chronicler. Royal cartographer and astronomer to Charles V; wrote *Crónica de los Reyes Católicos,* a continuation of Hernando del Pulgar's chronicle; noted for *Isolario general* (1541) that included charts of all parts of the then-known world.

Santa Cruz \-'krüs\, Andrés. 1792–1865. Bolivian general and politician. Active in revolution of Peru against Spain (1820–23); president of Bolivia (1829–39); head (1836–39) of Peru-Bolivian Confederation, a union he had long planned; overthrown (1839) at battle of Yungay by Gen. Manuel Bulnes of Chile; exile in Europe.

Santa Ma·ría \-mä-'rē-ä\, Domingo. 1825–1889. Chilean politician. Minister of foreign affairs (1879) and of interior (1879–80); president of Chile (1881–86); brought war with Peru and Bolivia to successful conclusion (1883).

San·ta·na \sän-'tä-nä\, Pedro. 1801–1864. Dominican military and political leader. Leader of revolution by which Santo Domingo separated from Haiti (1844); president, Republic of Santo Domingo (1844–48, 1853–56, 1858–61).

San·tan·der \sän-tän-'der\, Francisco de Paula. 1792–1840. Colombian general and politician. Served in the revolutionary war and was promoted general of division at the battle of Boyacá (1819). Vice president (1821–28) and acting president in Bolívar's absence (1821–26, 1827); political activities led to banishment (1829–32). President of New Granada (1832–37); administration noted for its economy, firmness, and orderliness. Regarded as founder of New Granada (Colombia).

San·ta·ya·na \sän-tä-'yä-nä, *Angl* ˌsant-ə-'yän-ə, ˌsant-ē-'än-ə, ˌsänt-\, George[1]. 1863–1952. Spanish-American poet and philosopher, b. Madrid, Spain. To U.S. (1872) but retained Spanish citizenship. Teacher of philosophy, Harvard (1889–1912, professor 1907–12); resident in Europe (from 1912), chiefly in Italy (from 1912). Author of several volumes of verse and of *The Sense of Beauty* (1896), *The Life of Reason* (1905–06), *Winds of Doctrine* (1913), *Character and Opinion in the United States* (1920), *Scepticism and Animal Faith* (1923), *Dialogues in Limbo* (1925), *Platonism and the Spiritual Life* (1927), *The Realm of Essence* (1928), *The Realm of Matter* (1930), *The Genteel Tradition at Bay* (1931), *The Last Puritan* (1935, novel), *The Realm of Truth* (1937), *The Realm of Spirit* (1940), and the autobiographical *Persons and Places* (1944–53).

Sant'·Elia \sän-'tāl-yä\, Antonio. 1888–1916. Italian architect. Practiced in Milan (from 1912); associated with Futurist movement and wrote (1914) its manifesto; killed in World War I. Executed (1912–14) a series of visionary drawings of the city of the future, a group of them displayed (1914) under title *Città Nuova*.

San·terre \sänⁿ-ter\, Antoine-Joseph. 1752–1809. French revolutionary politician and general. Took part in storming of the Bastille (1789); commander in chief of the Parisian Garde Nationale (1792), protected royal family from the mob; appointed field marshal, guarded the royal prisoners up to the moment of their execution; a general of division, commanded a volunteer army against the Vendeans (1793) but without success; arrested and imprisoned (1793–94); released after fall of Robespierre.

Santerre, Jean-Baptiste. 1658–1717. French painter. Known for portraits and historical and religious paintings, esp. *Suzanne au bain* (1704).

Santi, Giovanni. See GIOVANNI.

Santillana, Marqués de. See Iñigo López de MENDOZA.

Šān·ti·rak·ṣi·ta \ˌshän-tir-ək-ˈshē-tə\. 8th century. Indian Buddhist teacher. Invited to Tibet by King Thī-srong-detsan; for 13 years abbot of monastery at Samye where he taught with Padmasambhava; taught doctrines of the Buddhist Yogā-cāra sect and Tantric philosophy; ordained first seven Tibetan Buddhist monks; credited with incorporating several elements of Bon into lowest level of Tantric Buddhism and with instituting symbolic worship instead of Bon animal sacrifices.

San·to·ri·ni \ˌsän-tō-ˈrē-nē\, Giovanni Domenico. 1681–1737. Italian physician. Foremost anatomist of his time; demonstrator in anatomy at Venice (1706–28); city physician in Spedaletto (1728 ff.); chief work *Observationes anatomicae* (1724). Santorini's duct and Santorini's cartilage were named for him.

San·to·rio \sän-ˈtȯr-yō\, Santorio. *Known by Lat. name* Sanc·to·ri·us \saŋk-ˈtȯr-ē-əs, -ˈtȯr-\. 1561–1636. Italian physician. In Balkan region (1587–99); professor at Padua (1611–24). First to employ instruments of precision in practice of medicine; adapted some inventions of his friend Galileo and developed a pulse clock (1602) and a clinical thermometer (1612); investigated insensible perspiration, published results in *De statica medicina* (1614), first systematic study of basal metabolism.

San·tos \ˈsän-tōs\, Eduardo. 1888–1974. Colombian politician. Journalist, owner of *El Tiempo;* served as member and president of the House of Representatives, later as senator and president (1935) of the Senate; president of Colombia (1938–42).

Santos, Máximo. 1847–1887. Uruguayan politician. President of Uruguay (1882–86).

San·tos-Du·mont \ˈsaⁿ(n)-tüz-dūē-ˈmōⁿ\, Alberto². 1873–1932. Brazilian aviation pioneer in France. Built and flew (1898) cylindrical balloon with gasoline engine and (1901) airship that won prize for making first flight from St.-Cloud around Eiffel Tower and return; erected (1903) at Neuilly first airship station, where he kept his dirigibles; made first officially observed powered flight in Europe in a box-kitelike airplane (1906); produced (1909) "Demoiselle" or "Grasshopper" monoplanes, forerunners of the modern light plane.

Sa·nu·do \sä-ˈnü-dō\, Marino. 1466–1536. Venetian chronicler. Senator (1498). Wrote *Vite dei dogi* and *La spedizione di Carlo VIII;* known chiefly for *I diarii* (58 vols., pub. 1879–1902), a chronicle of period 1496–1533, invaluable as historical source material.

Sa·nū·sī, as- \əs-sä-ˈnü-sē\. *In full* Sīdī Muḥammad ibn ʿAlī as-Sanūsī al-Mujāhirī al-Ḥasanī al-Indrīsī. c.1787–1859. Libyan theologian. Founded (1837) in the Hejaz a militant mystical movement, the Sanūsīyah; expelled (1841) from the Hejaz; moved (1843) order to Cyrenaica (now Libya), where it spread among local tribes and became instrumental in Libya's 20th-century independence movement.

Sanzio, Raffaello. See RAPHAEL.

Sa·pie·ha \sȧ-ˈpyā-ka̱\. *Orig.* So·pi·ha \sȯ-ˈpē-ka̱\. Princely family important in Polish history, descended from Ukrainian boyars subject to Lithuania. Members included: Lew (1557–1633), chancellor of Lithuania (1589–1623); encouraged Polish intervention in Russia during Time of Troubles. ¶Paweł Jan (c.1610–1665), active in wars against Muscovites, Cossacks, and Swedes; opposed John II Casimir Vasa's centralizing policies. ¶Leon (1803–1878), participated in November Insurrection of 1830 against Russia; chairman of the Austrian Galician Sejm (1861–75). ¶Eustachy (1881–1963), Polish envoy to London (1919–20); foreign minister of Poland (1920–21); a leader of the monarchist movement.

Sa·pir \sə-ˈpi(ə)r\, Edward. 1884–1939. American anthropologist and linguist, b. Lauenburg, Pomerania. To U.S. (1889); chief of anthropology for Canadian National Museum, Ottawa (1910–25); professor, Chicago (1925–31), Yale (1931–39). A founder of ethnolinguistics; principal developer of the American (descriptive) school of structural linguistics; known esp. for studies of North American Indian languages, including classification of those languages into 6 divisions. Author of *Language, an Introduction to the Study of Speech* (1921), etc.

Sapor *or* **Sapores.** See SHĀPŪR.

Sapper. See Herman MCNEILE.

Sap·pho \ˈsaf-(ˌ)ō\. *By herself spelled* Psappho. fl. c.610–c.580 B.C. Greek lyric poet, of Lesbos. Apparently a member of the upper class; may have been exiled to Sicily. Author of lyric poems composed in the local Lesbian-Aeolic dialect on themes of love and personal relationships, often with other women. Of her 9 books of lyrical verse and 1 of elegiac collected c.200 B.C., only one poem and a few fragments are extant. Highly esteemed by the ancients and ranked with Archilochus, Alcaeus, and Homer; called the "tenth Muse" by Plato in *Phaedrus.*

Sa·pron·ov \(ˌ)sə-ˈprȯn-əf\, Timofey Vladimirovich. 1887–?1939. Russian politician. Participated in Bolshevik Revolution; Soviet government and Communist party official; leader of the Democratic Centralist movement that agitated against mounting centralization and for more democracy in the Communist party (1920); arrested and disappeared (1930s).

Sap·ru \ˈsäp-rü\, Sir Tej Bahadur. 1875–1949. Indian jurist and politician. Member of Imperial Legislative Council (1916–20); law member of viceroy's council (1920–23); delegate to Round Table Conferences (1930–32); helped mediate Gandhi-Irwin Pact (1931); privy councilor (1934).

Sa·rac·o·ğlu \sä-ˌräj-ō-glūē\, Şükrü. 1887–1953. Turkish politician. Joined resistance movement of Atatürk (1918); elected to Grand National Assembly (1923); minister of education (1925), finance (1927–30), justice (1933–38), and foreign affairs (1938–42); prime minister (1942–46); maintained Turkish neutrality in World War II until Feb. 1945; responsible for capital tax and land reform laws; president of National Assembly (1948–50).

Sarapion. See SERAPION.

Sa·ra·sin *or* **Sar·ra·sin** \sȧ-rȧ-saⁿ\ *or* **Sar·ra·zin** \-zaⁿ\, Jean-François. 1614–1654. French poet. In service of the prince de Conti (1648–54). Author of witty and satiric verse which became the fashion of Parisian high society (c.1640); best known for *La Pompe funèbre de Voiture,* mock epic *Dulot vaincu,* epic fragments *Rollon conquérant* and *La Guerre espagnole;* also wrote historical works as *Histoire du siège de Dunkerque* (1649), *La Conspiration de Wallenstein* (unfinished).

Sarasvati, Dayananda. See DAYANANDA.

Sarawak, Raja of. See Sir James BROOKE.

Sar·biew·ski \sȧr-ˈbyef-skē\, Maciej Kazimierz. 1595–1640. Polish Jesuit and poet. Court poet and preacher to King Władysław IV; taught at Jesuit schools; his Latin epigrams and lyrics gained him title of the Christian, or Polish, Horace.

Sar·da·na·pa·lus *or* **Sar·da·na·pal·lus** \ˌsärd-ᵊn-ˈap-(ə-)ləs, -ᵊn-ə-ˈpā-ləs\. 7th century B.C.? According to Diodorus Sicullus, a king of Assyria known for his sybaritic way of life. He is apparently an amalgamation of Ashurbanipal and his brother Shamash-shum-ukin (*qq.v.*).

Sar·dou \sȧr-dü\, Victorien. 1831–1908. French playwright. Known as a craftsman of bourgeois drama, very popular in its day, as *Les Pattes de mouche* (1860), *Les Diables noirs* (1863), *La Famille Benoîton* (1865), *Divorçons* (1880), *La Tosca* (1887), *Madame Sans-Gêne* (1893, with Émile Moreau), *Robespierre* (1899), *La Sorcière* (1903); his work and influence belittled by G. B. Shaw as "Sardoodledom."

Sar·duri \sär-ˈdu̇(ə)r-ē\. Name of three kings of Urartu:

Sarduri I. 9th century B.C. King (c.840–830 B.C.). Founder of a dynasty that ruled Urartu until 609 B.C.

Sarduri II. 8th century B.C. King (c.755–735 B.C.). Extended rule north into Militene and west into Syria; defeated Ashur-nirari V of Assyria (c.753) and Kushtashpi of Commagene (c.745); routed near Halfeti by Tiglath-pileser III (743); may have been overthrown by a palace revolt.

Sarduri III. 7th century B.C. King (c.644–640 B.C.). Co-regent during later years of his father Rusas II; under suzerainty of Ashurbanipal.

Sarg \ˈsärg\, Tony, *in full* Anthony Frederick. 1882–1942. American illustrator and marionette maker, b. Guatemala, of a German father and English mother. Illustrator in London (1905); to U.S. (1915, naturalized 1921); creator of "Tony Sarg's Marionettes" (1915) and proprietor of marionette shows. Author and illustrator of *Tony Sarg's Animal Book* (1925), *Tony Sarg's Wonder Zoo* (1927), *Tony Sarg's Wonder Book* (1941), etc.

Sar·gent \ˈsär-jənt\, Charles Sprague. 1841–1927. American dendrologist, b. Boston. Professor at Harvard (1872–1927); first director, Arnold Arboretum, Harvard (1873–1927). Edited *Garden and Forest* (1888–97); author of *The Silva of North America* (1891–1902), *Manual of the Trees of North America* (1905), etc.

Sargent, John Singer. 1856–1925. American painter, b. Florence, Italy, of American parentage. Painted mainly in Paris and (from 1885) in London, with constant visits to U.S.; caused scandal at Paris Salon of 1884 with a portrait of Madame Gautreau entitled *Madame X;* executed (1890–1910) murals for

Boston Public Library and Boston Museum of Fine Arts; as an official war artist in World War I painted *Gassed* (1918) and *General Officers of the Great War* (1918–22). Known chiefly for elegant portraits of the Edwardian gentry as *The Boit Children* (1882), *Carnation, Lily, Lily, Rose* (1885–86), *Lady Meyer and Her Children* (1896), *The Wyndham Sisters* (1900), *Lord Ribblesdale* (1902); gave up painting portraits (c.1910) and thereafter painted murals and Alpine and Italian landscapes in watercolor.

Sargent, Winthrop. 1753–1820. American soldier and administrator, b. Gloucester, Mass. In Continental army through American Revolution; active in affairs of Ohio Company (1786 ff.); aided in founding Marietta, Ohio (1788). Appointed by Congress secretary of "Territory Northwest of the River Ohio" (1787–98). First governor, Mississippi Territory (1798–1801).

Sar·gon \'sär-gän\. *Assyrian* Sharru-kin, *i.e.* the Righteous King. Name of two kings:

Sargon of Ak·kad \'ak-,ad, 'äk-,äd\. 24th–23th century B.C. Mesopotamian ruler (c.2334–2279 B.C.). Founder of Semitic dynasty of Akkad; unified Sumerian territory with capital at Agade; conquered cities along the middle Euphrates to northern Syria, the mountains of southern Anatolia, and Elam; established trade contacts with the Indus Valley, coast of Oman, islands and shores of Persian Gulf, Badakhshān, Lebanon, Crete, and possibly Greece; considered founder of the Mesopotamian military tradition; favorite subject of later legends.

Sargon II. d. 705 B.C. King of Assyria (721–705 B.C.). Succeeded Shalmaneser V, who was probably his brother; presumed son of Tiglath-pileser III. Consolidated the empire, putting down rebellions that continually broke out in various parts; defeated Hamma and Damascus (720); ravaged Armenia; seized Carchemish (717); carried out successful expeditions against Urartu, Philistia, etc.; received homage of Cyprus (709); separated Elam from Babylon; engaged in great war against Merodach-baladan of Babylon, whom he completely defeated; built, as royal residence, Dur-Sharrukin (modern Khorsabad); killed in expedition against Cimmerians in Asia Minor. Succeeded by his son Sennacherib.

Şarino. See CHO Sok-chin.

Sā·ri·pu·tra \,shär-ē-'pü-trə\. *Pāli form* Sā·ri·put·ta \,sär-ē-'püt-ə\. c.6th century B.C. Indian Buddhist. One of two chief disciples of Buddha. Author of *Dharma-skandha,* a Buddhist sacred text.

Sar·is \'sar-əs\, John. d. 1646. English merchant and sea captain. Made first voyage of Englishmen to Japan (1613–14) and obtained emperor's commission to settle and trade in Japan.

Sa·rit Tha·na·rat \sär-it-tä-nä-'rät\. 1908–1963. Thai soldier and politician. Army officer (from 1929); served (1947–57) in regime of Pibul Songgram as minister of defense and commander of armed forces; deposed Pibul (1957); again deposed the government (1958) and made himself prime minister (1959–63) but was virtual dictator; regime highly authoritarian; launched campaigns against corruption, organized crime, and Chinese control of the economy.

Sar·kar \'sär-,kär\, Sir Jadunath. 1870–1958. Indian historian. Professor at Patna (1899–1917, 1923–26), Benares (1917–19), Cuttack (1919–23); on Bengal legislative council (1929–32). Foremost Indian historian of the Mughal dynasty; author of *India of Aurangzib* (1901), *Chaitanya* (1913), *Shivaji and His Times* (1919), *History of Aurangzib* (1924), and *Fall of the Mughal Empire* (1950).

Sar·mien·to \särm-'yān-tō\, Domingo Faustino. 1811–1888. Argentine educator, politician, and writer. Exiled by Rosas to Chile (1840–52), where he was a journalist and (1842) founding director of first normal school in South America; helped Urquiza defeat Rosas. President of Argentina (1868–74); terminated war against Paraguay; fostered public education, growth of commerce and agriculture, and development of transportation and communications. As author, best known for *Facundo* (1845), first serious study of the gaucho culture.

Sarmiento de Acu·ña \-thā-ä-'kün-yä\, Diego. Conde de Gon·do·mar \gōn-dō-'mär\. 1567–1626. Spanish diplomat. Ambassador to London (1613–18, 1620–22); gained great influence over James II, persuading him to abandon French and Protestant alliances with promise of marriage between James's son Charles and Infanta María.

Sarmiento de Gam·bo·a \-thā-gäm-'bō-ä\, Pedro. 1532–?1592. Spanish explorer. Led expeditions to Peru (1557), Pacific regions (1567–69), and Straits of Magellan (1579–80, 1581–86). Author of *Historia de los incas.*

Sar·noff \'sär-nóf\, David. 1891–1971. American communications executive, b. Minsk, Russia. To U.S. (1900); while a telegraph operator (from 1906) was first to pick up distress signal from the *Titanic* (1912); rose from commercial manager (1919) to president, Radio Corporation of America (1930–47), chairman of the board (1947–70). A pioneer in radio and television broadcasting; first proposed a commercially marketed radio receiver (1915); formed National Broadcasting Co. (1926) as subsidiary of RCA; established an experimental television station (1928); gave demonstration of television at New York World's Fair (1939).

Sa·ro·yan \sə-'ròi-ən\, William. 1908–1981. American writer, b. Fresno, Calif. Author of short stories as in *The Daring Young Man on the Flying Trapeze* (1934), *Inhale and Exhale* (1936), *Little Children* (1937), *Love, Here is My Hat* (1938), *The Trouble with Tigers* (1938), *My Name is Aram* (1940), *The Whole Voyald* (1956); of plays as *My Heart's in the Highlands* (1939), *The Time of Your Life* (1939; rejected 1940 Pulitzer prize), *Love's Old Sweet Song* (1939), *The Beautiful People* (1941), *Razzle Dazzle* (1942, short plays); of novels as *The Human Comedy* (1943), *Rock Wagram* (1951), *The Laughing Matter* (1953), *Mama, I Love You* (1956), *Papa You're Crazy* (1956); and of memoirs as *Here Comes, There Goes, You Know Who* (1961), *Not Dying* (1963), *Places Where I've Done Time* (1972).

Sar·pi \'sär-pē\, Paolo, *orig.* Pietro. *Also called* Fra Paolo *or* Pau·lus Ven·e·tus \'pò-ləs-'ven-ət-əs\. *Pseudonym* Pietro Soave Po·la·no \pō-'län-ō\. 1552–1623. Italian prelate, historian, scientist, and theologian. Entered Servite order (1565), of which he became provincial (1579) and vicar-general (1599–1604). State theologian of Venice (1606–22); opposed temporal power of pope; wrote against Paul V's interdict of Venice; counseled banishment of Jesuits from Venice. As anatomist (1582–85) credited with discovering the function of the venous valves, the circulation of blood, and the dilation of the iris. Known for his *Istoria del concilio Tridentino* (pub. 1619 under pseudonym).

Sar·rail \sá-ráy\, Maurice-Paul-Emmanuel. 1856–1929. French general. In World War I defended Verdun (1914); commanded French army at Salonika (1915–18), captured Monastir (1916), dethroned Constantine I of Greece (1917). French high commissioner in Syria (1924).

Sar·raut \sá-rō\, Albert-Pierre. 1872–1962. French colonial administrator and politician. Member of Chamber of Deputies (1902–24); minister of education (1914–15). As governor general of Indochina (1911–14, 1916–19) encouraged native participation in civil service and use of local laws and language. Minister of colonies (1920–24, 1932–33); senator (1926–40); minister of interior (1926–28, 1934, 1937–40) and of navy (1930–31); premier (1933, 1936). Member (1947), president (1949–58) of advisory assembly of French Union; editor of family newspaper *Dépêche de Toulouse* (from 1943).

Sarrasin *or* **Sarrazin,** Jean-François. See SARASIN.

Sar·rette \sá-ret\, Bernard. 1765–1858. French musical administrator. Founder (1795) and director (to 1816), Paris Conservatoire.

Sars \'särs\, Michael. 1805–1869. Norwegian marine biologist. Professor, U. of Christiania (now Oslo, 1854–69); a pioneer in marine zoology; made important studies of life cycles of marine invertebrates, esp. on alternation of generations in coelenterates.

Sars·field \'särs-,fēld\, Patrick. Titular Earl of Lu·can \'lü-kən\. d. 1693. Irish Jacobite and soldier. Served against Monmouth at Sedgemoor (1685); assisted in James II's reorganization of Irish forces into a Roman Catholic army; fled with James II to France and returned with him to Ireland (1689); present at battle of the Boyne (1690) and caused William III to raise siege of Limerick (1690); negotiated final Jacobite surrender at Limerick (1691); with Louis XIV's army in Spanish Netherlands (1691–93); killed in battle.

Sar·tain \'sär-,tān\, John. 1808–1897. American engraver, b. London, England. To U.S. (1830); on staff of *Graham's Magazine* (1841); introduced pictorial illustration as a characteristic feature in American periodicals. A founder and proprietor of *Sartain's Union Magazine of Literature and Art* (1849–52), to which the leading literary figures of the day contributed. His children included ¶Samuel (1830–1906), engraver; best known for his plates of biblical subjects. ¶Emily (1841–1927), engraver and painter. ¶William (1843–1924), painter; excelled in landscapes and genre paintings.

Sar·ti \'särt-ē\, Giuseppe. 1729–1802. Italian composer. Court musician at Copenhagen (1755–65, 1768–75) and St. Petersburg (1784–1801). Composed chiefly operas as *Il re pastore* (1753), *Le gelosie villane* (1776), *Fra i due litiganti* (1782), *Armida e Rinaldo* (1786), and sacred music.

Sarto, Andrea del. See ANDREA D'AGNOLO.

Sar·ton \'särt-ᵊn\, George Alfred Leon. 1884–1956. American scholar, b. Ghent, Belgium. To U.S. (1915, naturalized 1924); lecturer on history of science, Harvard (1916–18, 1920–40), professor (1940–51); associate of Carnegie Inst., Washington, D.C. (1918–48). One of greatest historians of science of his time; founder and editor of journals *Isis* (1912–52) and *Osiris* (1936–56). Author of *Introduction to the History of Science* (1927–47), *Ancient Science Through the Golden Age of Greece* (1952), *Hellenistic Science and Culture in the Last Three Centuries* B.C. (1959).

Sar·tre \sártrᵊ\, Jean-Paul. 1905–1980. French writer and philosopher. Taught (1931–45) in Le Havre, Laon, and Paris lycées; after World War II supported leftist political causes; developed a "Sartrian Socialism" in *Critique de la raison dialectique* (1960); awarded but refused 1964 Nobel prize for literature. Expounded his philosophy of Existentialism in novels *La Nausée* (1938) and *Les Chemins de la liberté* (trilogy, 1945–49); plays as *Les Mouches* (1943), *Huis-clos* (1944), *Les Mains sales* (1948), *Le Diable et le bon dieu* (1951), *Les*

Séquestrés d'Altona (1959); and philosophical works as *L'Imagination* (1936), *L'Imaginaire* (1940), *L'Être et le néant* (1943), *L'Existentialisme est un humanisme* (1946); also wrote *Les Mots* (1963, autobiography) and *Flaubert* (1971, literary study). With Simone de Beauvoir founded and edited review *Les Temps Modernes* (1946 ff.).

Sar·zec \sär-zek\, Gustave-Charles-Ernest Choc·quin de \shò-kaⁿ-də-\. 1832–1901. French diplomat and archaeologist. While French vice consul at Basra excavated (1877–1901) the mound of Tello (in present-day southern Iraq) and uncovered the Sumerian capital of Lagash; published findings in *Découvertes en Chaldée* (1884–1912, with Léon Heuzey).

Sā·sān \sä-'sän\. 1st century A.D.? Persian noble. Life history uncertain but apparently a prince in vassalage to Gochihr, the chief petty king in Persia; according to tradition married a daughter of Gochihr and fathered Papak, the father of Ardashīr I who founded the Sāsānian dynasty; another tradition makes him the son-in-law of Papak and the father of Ardashīr I.

Sā·sā·ni·ans *or* **Sās·sā·ni·ans** \sa-'sā-nē-ənz\ *or* **Sā·sā·nids** \'sas-ə-(,)nidz\. Name of last native dynasty (224–651 A.D.) of Persian kings, successors of the Arsacids. Founded by Ardashīr I, descendant of Sāsān (hence the name); it numbered about 25 kings, chief among them after Ardashīr I being Shāpūr I and II, Yazdegerd I, Kavadh I, Khosrow I and II; last sovereign was Yazdegerd III. See individual biographies for the kings; see also BAHRĀM, HORMIZD, and NARSES.

Sassetta. See STEFANO DI GIOVANNI.

Sas·soon \sə-'sün, sa-\, Siegfried Lorraine. 1886–1967. English writer. Served in World War I; befriended and influenced Wilfred Owen and published his works. Author of antiwar and devotional verse, including *The Old Huntsman* (1917), *Counter-Attack* (1918), *Satirical Poems* (1926), *The Heart's Journey* (1928), *Vigils* (1935), *Rhymed Ruminations* (1940), *The Path to Peace* (1960), and of autobiographical prose works *Memoirs of George Sherston* (originally published separately as *Memoirs of a Fox-Hunting Man*, 1928; *Memoirs of an Infantry Officer*, 1930; *Sherston's Progress*, 1936), *The Old Century and Seven More Years* (1938), *The Weald of Youth* (1942), *Siegfried's Journey* (1945).

Sas·tri \'shäs-trē, 'säs-\, Valangiman Sankarana-Rayana Srinivasa. 1869–1946. Indian politician. Member (1907), president (1915) of Servants of India Society; member, viceroy's legislative council (1916–20), council of state (1920). Founded Indian Liberal Federation (1922); Indian agent general in South Africa (1927); member of Round Table Constitutional Conference in London (1930–31); vice chancellor of Annamalai U. in Madras (1935–40).

Sas·tro·am·i·djo·jo \,säs-trō-äm-ē-'jō-zhō\, Ali. 1903–1975. Indonesian politician. With Sukarno and others founded Gerindo party (1937); negotiated a treaty whereby the Netherlands relinquished all claims to Indonesia (1949); prime minister (1953–55, 1956–57); delegate to United Nations (1957–60).

Sa·tie \sà-tē\, Erik-Alfred-Leslie. 1866–1925. French composer. Associated (early 1890s) with Rosicrucian movement and under its influence wrote several works, esp. *Messe des pauvres* (1895); led (from 1898) an eccentric and reclusive life in Arcueil, working mainly as a cafe pianist; adopted as patron saint by "Les Six" (1917) and "L'École d'Arcueil" (1923), groups of young composers. Composed spare, unconventional, often witty avant-garde music that influenced later composers, esp. Debussy, Ravel, Poulenc, and Milhaud. Works included ballets *Parade* (1917), *Mercure* (1924), and *Relâche* (1924), his masterpiece *Socrate* (1918, for voice and chamber orchestra), songs, "furniture music" for concert intervals, and esp. piano pieces as *Trois Sarabandes* (1887), *Trois Gymnopédies* (1888), *Trois Gnossiennes* (1890), *Trois Morceaux en forme de poire* (1890–1903), and *Nocturnes* (1919).

Sa·tō \sä-tō\ Eisaku. 1901–1975. Japanese politician. Brother of Kishi Nobusuke. Liberal-Democratic member of Diet (1949 ff.); minister of construction (1952–53), finance (1958–60), international trade and industry (1961–62). As prime minister (1964–72) guided Japan's reemergence as a major world power, esp. in economic affairs. For his policies on nuclear weapons was awarded (with Sean MacBride) Nobel prize for peace (1974).

Satō Haruo. 1892–1964. Japanese writer. Gained fame with fantasy short story "Supeinu ken-no-ie" (1916); author of lyrical and romantic verse as *Junjō shishū* (1921) and prose poems *Den'en-no-yūutsu* (1919) and *Tokai-no-yūutsu* (1922); in later years wrote criticism, esp. *Akiko mandara* (1955).

Satō Nobuhiro. 1769–1850. Japanese scientist. Wrote some of first Japanese studies of Western geography, history, science, and artillery; advised government leaders on coastal defense matters; advocated the development of an authoritarian type of government based on Western science and political institutions.

Sato Norikiyo. See SAIGYŌ.

Sat·ter·lee \'sat-ər-lē\, Francis Le Roy. 1881–1935. American roentgenologist, b. New York City. Took first X-ray photograph in America (Feb. 4, 1896); invented protective shield for X-ray operators; first to X-ray mouth and teeth.

Sat·ur·ni·nus \,sat-ər-'nī-nəs\, Lucius Appuleius. d. 100 B.C. Roman politician. Quaestor (104 B.C.); tribune (103, 100). With Glauca and Marius often opposed the Senate; sponsored laws assigning land in Africa to veterans of Jugurthine War, establishing permanent courts to try cases of treason, distributing land among veterans who served with Marius, and founding colonies to which Italians should be admitted. During year-end elections his partisans clubbed the senatorial candidate to death; with Glauca seized the Capitoline Hill but surrendered to Marius; stoned to death by members of opposition party.

Sa·ud \sà-'üd\. 1902–1969. King of Saudi Arabia (1953–64). Son and successor of Ibn Sa'ūd; with his brother Faisal led a successful campaign against Yemen (1934). As king continued his father's program of modernization; his mismanagement of financial affairs forced him to establish a council of ministers with Faisal as president (early 1950s); lost power to Faisal who eventually (1964) deposed him.

Sau·er \'saù(-ə)r\, Carl Ortwin. 1889–1975. American geographer, b. Warrenton, Mo. Chairman of geography dept., U. of Cal., Berkeley (1923–54). Authority on desert studies, tropical areas, human geography of American Indians, and agriculture and native crops of the New World.

Sau·ga·nash \'sò-gə-,nash\ *or* **Sa·gau·nash** \sə-'gòn-,ash\. 1780–1841. American Potawatomi Indian leader, b. Canada, partly of English or Irish descent. Interpreter to Tecumseh (to 1813); settled (1820) in Ft. Dearborn (now Chicago); justice of the peace (1826); instrumental in maintaining peace between white settlers and Indians in the Chicago area. Sauganash, an area of Chicago, is named for him.

Saul \'sòl\. *Heb.* Sha·'ul \shä-'ül\. 11th century B.C. First king of Israel (c.1020–1000). According to Bible, a Benjamite, son of Kish; anointed as king by Samuel; defended Israel against many enemies, esp. the Philistines; protector, later rival, of David; defeated and killed by the Philistines in battle of Mount Gilboa; succeeded by David.

Saul of Tarsus. See Saint PAUL.

Sau·maise \sō-mez\, Claude de. *Known by Lat. form* Claudius Sal·ma·sius \sal-'mā-sh(ē-)əs\. 1588–1653. French scholar. While studying at Heidelberg (1606–09) discovered Palatine manuscript of the Greek Anthology; *avocat* of Dijon parlement (1610); professor at Leiden (from 1631). Author of a commentary of Solinus's *Polyhistor* (1629), an edition of two antipapal tracts *De primatu papae* (1645), and defenses of usury *De usuris liber* (1638) and *De modo usurarum* (1639). Chiefly remembered for his *Defensio regia pro Carolo I* (1649) which occasioned Milton's *Defensio pro populo anglicano* (1651) in rebuttal.

Sau·ma·rez \'säm-ə-rəz, 'sō-mər-ē\, James. Baron de Saumarez. 1757–1836. British naval commander. Made commander for gallantry against the Dutch off Dogger Bank (1781); distinguished himself in French Revolutionary and Napoleonic Wars at battles of Lorient (1795), Cape St. Vincent (1797), and blockade of Cádiz (1797–98); wounded at battle of the Nile (1798); routed a Franco-Spanish fleet at Algeciras (1801). Commanded the Baltic Fleet in war with Russia (1809–14); admiral (1814); general of marines (1832–36).

Saunders, Richard. See Benjamin FRANKLIN.

Sau·ser \sō-zā\, Frédéric. *Pseudonym* Blaise Cen·drars \säⁿ-dràrs, -dràr\. 1887–1961. Swiss writer. Led life of adventure, losing an arm while serving in Foreign Legion. Author of verse *Le légende de Novgorode* (1909), *Pâques à New-York* (1912), *Prose du Transsibérien et de la petite Jeanne de France* (1913), *J'ai tué* (1918), etc., which influenced Apollinaire and the Symbolists; novels and stories *La Vénus noire* (1923), *Moravagine* (1926), *La Confession de Dan Yack* (1929), *Rhum* (1930), *Histoires vrais* (1938), *La Vie dangereuse* (1938), *La Main coupée* (1946), *Bourlinguer* (1948); essays *Aujourd'hui* (1931), *L'Homme foudroyé* (autobiography, 1945), *À l'aventure* (1958).

Saus·sier \sōs-yā\, Félix-Gustave. 1828–1905. French general. Engaged (1870) at Metz in Franco-Prussian War; was captured, escaped, and commanded a brigade in the army of the Loire (1871); commanded expeditionary force in Tunis (1881); military governor of Paris (1884–86).

Saus·sure, de \də-sō-sü̅r\. Name of a distinguished Swiss family including: Nicolas (1709–1790), agriculturist. His son ¶Horace-Bénédict (1740–1799), professor of philosophy and physics at Geneva (1762–86); made many researches in geology, physics, meteorology; developed what was probably the first electrometer (1766); built first hygrometer utilizing a human hair (1783); published his Alpine geological findings in *Voyages dans les Alpes* (1779–96), in which he introduced the term geology.

¶Nicolas-Théodore (1767–1845), son of Horace; chemist and naturalist; known for work on nutrition and respiration in plants, on fermentation, germination, composition of alcohol, transformation of starch into sugar, etc. His *Recherches chimiques sur la végétation* (1804) laid foundations of phytochemistry. Horaces's grandson ¶Henri (1829–1905), entomologist, authority on Orthoptera and Hymenoptera.

¶Ferdinand (1857–1913), son of Henri; linguist; professor at Geneva (1901–13). Author of *Mémoire sur le système primitif des voyelles dans les langues indo-européennes* (1879); his *Cours de linguistique générale* (1916), posthumously edited from his students' lecture notes, is one of the foremost works giving stimulus and direction to modern linguistics.

Sau·sta·tar \ˌsós-tä-ˈtär\ *or* **Shaush·sha·tar** \ˌshó-shə-ˈtär\. 16th–15th century B.C. King of Mitanni. Considered founder (c.1500 B.C.) of Mitanni empire; said to have looted the Assyrian palace in Ashur.

Sau·tuo·la \saù-ˈtwō-lä\, Marcellino de. d. 1888. Spanish amateur archaeologist. Excavated (1875, 1879) Altamira Cave, near Santillana, Spain, discovering the earliest known examples of Stone Age painting; published a book on his findings (1880).

Sau·veur \sō-vœr\, Albert. 1863–1939. American metallurgist, b. Louvain, Belgium. To U.S. (1887); taught at Harvard (1899–1939). A founder of physical metallurgy; made pioneering microscopic and photomicroscopic studies of metal structures, esp. in heat treatments of metals; wrote influential *The Metallography and Heat Treatment of Iron and Steel* (1912).

Sau·veur \sō-vœr\, Joseph. 1653–1716. French physicist. Professor, Collège de France (1686); engaged at siege of Mons to apply his principles of fortification (1691); credited with first calculation of absolute vibration numbers and with first scientific explanation of overtones.

Sa·va \ˈsä-vä\. Saint. *Lat.* Sa·bas \ˈsäb-əs\. c.1176–c.1236. Serbian prelate. Patronal founder of the Serbian church (1219); superior of the monastery at Studenista (c.1208); crowned (c.1216) his brother Stephen II; first bishop of Serbia (1219); responsible for a cultural and ecclesiastical renaissance that included the beginnings of a medieval Serbian literature.

Sav·age \ˈsav-ij\, Arthur William. 1857–1938. American arms manufacturer, b. Kingston, Jamaica. To U.S. (1886, naturalized 1895). Founder, Savage Arms Co., Utica, N.Y. (1893); inventor of a dirigible torpedo and improvements in magazine rifles.

Savage, Edward. 1761–1817. American painter and engraver, b. Princeton, Mass. Noted for portraits of George and Martha Washington, Jefferson, Benjamin Rush, etc.

Savage, Henry Wilson. 1859–1927. American theatrical producer, b. New Durham, N.H. Organized Castle Square Opera Company, Boston (1895), to present opera in English at moderate prices; expanded to New York and Chicago and toured the country; presented Wagner's *Parsifal* (1904) and Puccini's *Madame Butterfly* (1906) for the first time in English; made great success in producing Lehár's *The Merry Widow* (1907).

Savage, James. 1784–1873. American antiquary, b. Boston. Secured legislative incorporation of the Provident Institution for Savings, Boston (1816), one of first savings banks incorporated in U.S., of which he became president. A founder of Boston Athenaeum; published *Genealogical Dictionary of the First Settlers of New England* (1860–62).

Savage, Michael Joseph. 1872–1940. New Zealand politician, b. Australia. To New Zealand (1907); active in labor movement; Labour party parliamentary leader (1933). First Labour prime minister (1935–40); secured passage of anti-depression economic measures and educational and social security reform measures.

Savage, Richard. 1697?–1743. English poet. Put forward, but did not substantiate, claim that he was son of Richard Savage, 4th Earl Rivers, by Countess of Macclesfield. Friend of Dr. Johnson, who shared poverty with him and wrote his biography (1744; later included in *The Lives of the Poets*). Had plays acted at Drury Lane, including *Love in a Veil* (1718, comedy) and *Sir Thomas Overbury* (1723), in which he played title role. Barely escaped death penalty for killing a gentleman in tavern brawl (1727); alienated friends who aided him, of whom Pope was the most persevering; died in prison for debt. Author of poems *The Bastard* (1728) and, his masterpiece, *The Wanderer* (1729) and a prose satire on Grub Street, *An Author to Let* (1729).

Savage, Thomas Staughton. 1804–1880. American clergyman and naturalist, b. Cromwell, Conn. First missionary sent to Africa by Protestant Episcopal church; established mission station in Liberia (1836–46); on return to U.S. (1847), wrote papers on the gorilla, previously unknown to scientists, on the habits of the chimpanzee, and on the termites of western Africa.

Sa·var·kar \ˌsəv-ər-ˈkär\, Vir Vinayak Damodar. 1883–1966. Indian nationalist. Imprisoned (1911–37) for alleged complicity in assassination of an Indian official in London; president of the Hindu Mahasabha (1937–43); one of eight men charged with assassination of Gandhi but acquitted (1948).

Sa·vart \sá-vár\, Félix. 1791–1841. French physician and physicist. Professor, Collège de France (from 1828); invented a rotating toothed wheel for determining number of vibrations per second corresponding to a tone; made investigations on resonance, esp. in stringed instruments.

Sa·va·ry \sá-vá-rē\, Anne-Jean-Marie-René. Duc de Ro·vi·go \rò-vē-gō\. 1774–1833. French soldier and politician. Aide-de-camp to Napoléon (1800); appointed head of secret service when Napoléon was first consul (1802); supervised kidnapping and execution of duc d'Enghien (1804). General of division (1805); distinguished himself at battles of Jena (1806) and Ostrołęka (1807). Minister of police (1810–14); loyal to Napoléon during Hundred Days and appointed first inspector general of constabulary. Condemned to death after Waterloo but sentence reversed (1819); thereafter active in army.

Sa·vel·li \sä-ˈvel-le\, Luca. d. 1266. Roman politician. Nephew of Pope Honorius III and father of Honorius IV; senator (1234); declared Tuscany, Campania, and many cities in church territory to be under Roman jurisdiction and demanded tribute from Pope Gregory IX; revolt crushed by Frederick II and Savelli removed from office (1235).

Sa·very \ˈsāv(-ə)-rē\, Thomas. 1650?–1715. English military engineer. Patented first commercially successful steam engine, an atmospheric engine for pumping water (1698); invented a ship odometer and other devices.

Savery, William. 1721–1787. American cabinetmaker. Resident of Philadelphia; produced in Chippendale style highboys, lowboys, tables, armchairs, etc.

Sa·vi·gny \ˈzäv-in-yē\, Friedrich Karl von. 1779–1861. German jurist. Most influential 19th-century German jurist; professor at Berlin (1810–42); member of Prussian Privy Council (1817); head of department for revision of Prussian statutes (1842–48). A founder of the historical school of jurisprudence with pamphlet "Vom Beruf unserer Zeit für Gesetzgebung und Rechtswissenschaft" (1814); laid foundation of modern study of medieval law with *Geschichte des römischen Rechts im Mittelalter* (1815–31). Founder of a modern system of German civil law, embodied in *System des heutigen römischen Rechts* (1840–49), which also contained a system of international private law; also published *Vermischte Schriften* (1850) and *Das Obligationenrecht* (1851–53).

Sav·ile \ˈsav-ēl\, Sir George. Marquis of Hal·i·fax \ˈhal-ə-ˌfaks\. *Called* the Trimmer. 1633–1695. English politician and essayist. Member of Privy Council (1672–76, 1679–82); opposed test acts; brought about rejection of bill for exclusion of James from succession (1679–81); lord privy seal (1682–85, 1689–90); president of Council (1685), dismissed for opposition to repeal of test and habeas corpus acts. Attempted to arrange a compromise between James II and William of Orange (1688) but eventually sided with William; instrumental in persuading the Convention Parliament of 1689 to accept William and Mary as regents. Lord privy seal and chief minister of the crown (1689–90). One of first writers of political pamphlets, esp. *Character of King Charles the Second* and *Character of a Trimmer* (1688).

Savile, Sir Henry. 1549–1622. English scholar. Tutor in Greek to Queen Elizabeth; warden of Merton Coll., Oxford (1585–1622); translated four books of the *Historiae* of Tacitus (1591). One of scholars appointed to prepare Authorized Version of the Bible, assigned parts of Gospels, Acts, and Book of Revelation (1604 ff.). Published editions of St. Chrysostom (1610–13) and Xenophon's *Cyropaedia* (1613). Founded and endowed Savile professorships of geometry and astronomy, Oxford (1619).

Sa·vin·kov \ˈsá-vyin-kóf\, Boris Viktorovich. *Pseudonym* V. Rop·shin \ˈròp-shin\. 1879–1925. Russian revolutionary. Joined (1903) Socialist-Revolutionary party and became a leader in terrorist activities; organized assassinations of V. K. Plehve (1904) and Grand Duke Sergey Aleksandrovich (1905); arrested and condemned to death, but escaped to Switzerland (1906). To Russia (1917) and became vice minister of war in the Kerensky government. Opposed Bolsheviks (1918–21), first in Russia, then in Poland, and later in Paris. Returned to Russia (1924); arrested and sentenced to life imprisonment; committed suicide in prison. Author of terrorist novels *The Pale Horse* (1909) and *That Which Never Happened* (1913).

Sav·old \ˈsav-(ˌ)ōld, -əld\, Lee. *Orig. surname* Hul·ver \ˈhəl-vər\. 1914?–1972. American boxer, b. Canby, Minn. Professional fighter (early 1930s–52); recognized as world heavyweight champion in Great Britain and parts of continental Europe after defeating Bruce Woodcock (June 1950); his title claim ignored after defeat of Joe Louis by Ezzard Charles (Sept. 1950).

Sa·vo·na·ro·la \ˌsä-vō-nä-rò-lä, *Angl* ˌsav-ə-nə-ˈrō-lə, sə-ˌvän-ə-ˈrō-\, Girolamo. 1452–1498. Italian reformer. Joined Dominican order (1475); to Florence (1482); prior of San Marco, Florence (1491); denounced in vehement sermons corruption of secular life, licentiousness of ruling class, and worldliness of clergy. With aid of Charles VIII drove Piero de' Medici from power (1494); exercised virtual dictatorship in Florence, preaching crusade for establishment of an ideal Christian state; denounced Pope Alexander VI, whose enmity he incurred. Lost hold on Florentine republic as the Arrabbiati (aristocratic party) regained power; excommunicated (1497); openly rebelled against pope; captured by the Arrabbiati and tried for sedition and heresy (1498); tortured, hanged with two other Dominicans, and burned.

Sa·voy \sə-ˈvòi\. *Fr.* Sa·voie \sá-vwá\. *Ital.* Sa·vo·ia \sä-ˈvò-yä\. The oldest reigning family in Europe and the ruling house (1861–1946) of Italy. Founded by Umberto I the Whitehanded (d. c.1048; *q.v.*), constable of Emperor Conrad II and Count of Savoy. Possessions increased in 11th century; made duchy (1416) by Emperor Sigismund. For the more important counts and dukes of Savoy of the main line see AMADEUS, CHARLES EMMANUEL,

EMMANUEL PHILIBERT, PHILIBERT, and PHILIP.
Charles Emmanuel I, *called* the Great (reigned 1580–1630), m. Catherine of Spain; from them descended the two chief modern houses of Savoy: (1) Main line (1630–1831) included: Victor Amadeus I; Charles Emmanuel II; Victor Amadeus II (d. 1732), by Treaty of Utrecht (1713) made king of Sicily (1713–20), and king of Sardinia (1720) when Sicily was ceded to Emperor Charles VI. Subsequent Savoy kings of Sardinia were: Charles Emmanuel III, Victor Amadeus III, Charles Emmanuel IV, Victor Emmanuel I, and Charles Felix (see separate biogs). Succession to throne of Sardinia passed (1831) to Charles Albert of the Savoy-Carignan (Carignano) line (see 2).
(2) Cadet branch (Savoy-Carignan) originated with Thomas (1596–1656), Prince of Ca·ri·gnan \kȧ-rē-nyäⁿ\ (ancient Yvois, town in Ardennes, near Mézières), 4th son of Charles Emmanuel I. Seventh prince was Charles Albert, king of Sardinia, whose son was Victor Emmanuel II, first king of modern Italy, succeeded by Umberto I and Victor Emmanuel III. (See separate biogs; see also AMADEO, king of Spain).
There were two collateral branches of the Savoy-Carignan line, descended from Thomas: (a) Counts of Soissons, from Thomas's son Eugène Maurice de Savoie-Carignan (1633–1673), who acquired title from his maternal uncle Louis (1604–1641; *q.v.*) of the house of Bourbon, extinct (1736) in his son Prince Eugène of Savoy (*q.v.*); (b) Counts of Villafranca, who later (1888) took the title Villafranca-Soissons.
An early branch of house of Savoy acquired the duchy of Ne·mours \nə-mür\; granted to Louise of Savoy (*q.v.*, 1524) and transferred (1528) to her half-brother ¶Philippe de Savoie (1490–1533), comte de Ge·ne·vois \zhen-əv-wȧ\. His son ¶Jacques (1531–1585), duc de Nemours, was a soldier in royal service against Huguenots; renowned for chivalry; for a time considered a possible match for Elizabeth I of England; m. (1566) Anne d'Este, widow of the duc de Guise. His son ¶Charles-Emmanuel (1567–1595), duc, supported Holy League; arrested in Henry III's coup against the Guises (1588); later captured Vienne for League; prisoner (1593–94) of archbishop of Lyon. His brother ¶Henri I (1572–1632) succeeded as duc de Nemours; as marquis de Saint-Sor·lin \saⁿ-sȯr-laⁿ\ took part in capture of Saluzzo (1588) and other League campaigns. Title passed to his son ¶Louis (d. 1641); thence to second son ¶Charles-Amedée (1624–1652), who took part in third war of the Fronde but caused much dissension by quarrels and affairs; and thence to third son ¶Henri II (1625–1659), with whom male line ended.

Savoy, Peter of. See PETER of Savoy.

Saw \'sȯ\, U. *Also called* Ga·lon U Saw \'gäl-ȯn-\. 1900–1948. Burmese politician. Served in Burmese legislative council; owner and editor of nationalist newspaper *Thuriya;* founded Myochit party and a private army (1938); helped overthrow Ba Maw (1939); prime minister (1940–42); interned by British for negotiating with Japanese (1942–45). Rival of Aung San (*q.v.*); with Aung went to London to negotiate independence of Burma but refused to sign resulting treaty of Jan. 27, 1947; after adoption of treaty ordered assassination of Aung San (1947); convicted of conspiracy to murder and executed.

Sax \sȧks\, Antoine-Joseph, *known as* Adolphe. 1814–1894. Belgian maker of musical instruments. To Paris (1842); instructor at Paris Conservatoire (1857); with his father evolved the saxhorn (patented 1845) and invented the saxotromba (pat. 1845), the saxophone (pat. 1846), and other brass instruments; ruined by lawsuits brought against his patents by competing instrument makers. His father ¶Charles-Joseph (1791–1865) made wind and brass instruments in Dinant (to 1815) and Brussels.

Saxe \sȧks, *Angl* 'saks\. French name of Saxony, used in English chiefly in names of former duchies in Thuringia, which (1485–1547) was in electorate of Saxony. See WETTIN, ERNESTINE LINE, ALBERTINE LINE.

Saxe, Maurice, comte de. See MAURICE, comte de Saxe.

Saxe-Al·ten·burg \'säks-'äl-tən-bu̇rk\. A former German duchy (now part of Thuringia) and its ruling house, which formed a branch of the Ernestine line (*q.v.*) of Saxony. A part of the Wettin lands (from 1250), fell at their division (1485) to Ernestine line, then passed to Albertine line (1547–54); family branch founded 1603, became extinct 1672; land then made part of Saxe-Gotha. ¶Saxe-Go·tha-Altenburg \-'gō-tä-\ (1672–1825); made a duchy (1826) under Duke of Hildburghausen, who became Duke Frederick (1763–1834) of the new line of Saxe-Altenburg; Gotha exchanged for Saalfeld (1826; see SAXE-COBURG-GOTHA).

Saxe-Co·burg \-'kō-,bu̇rk\. (1) A German duchy, early (1247–1485) a possession of the Wettin family (*q.v.*), later (1485) fell to Ernestine line (*q.v.*). See SAXE-COBURG-GOTHA. (2) A royal house (1901–10) of Great Britain whose sole representative as ruler was Edward VII.

Saxe-Coburg-Gotha. A former German duchy (now a part of Thuringia) and its ruling house, which formed a branch of the Ernestine line (*q.v.*) of Saxony. The elder line (a branch of the Ernestine line) became extinct (1633). New line founded (1680) by Duke Albert, second son of Ernest the Pious; by acquisition of Saalfeld (1735) duchy became Saxe-Coburg-Saal·feld \-'zäl-,felt\; on extinction of Saxe-Gotha-Altenburg line (1825) Duke Ernest I exchanged Saalfeld for Gotha (1826). For important dukes of Saxe-Coburg-Gotha see Prince ALFRED and ERNEST I and II.
Connections with other ruling houses, through Duke Francis Frederick (1750–1806) of Saxe-Coburg-Saalfeld, father of Duke Ernest I of Saxe-Coburg-Gotha: (1) Princess Victoria Mary Louisa, daughter of Duke Francis, m. (1818) as second husband, Duke of Kent; their daughter was Queen Victoria of England. (2) Leopold (*q.v.*), youngest son of Duke Francis, became king of Belgium. (3) Ferdinand, eldest son of Duke Ferdinand (second son of Duke Francis), m. (1836) Queen Maria II of Portugal and became king consort. (4) Albert (*q.v.*), second son of Duke Ernest I and brother of Duke Ernest II, m. (1840) Queen Victoria of England. (5) Ferdinand (*q.v.*), king of Bulgaria, son of Prince Augustus of Saxe-Coburg, who was a brother of Ferdinand (3) and second son of Duke Ferdinand.

Saxe-Gotha. Early name (before acquisition of Coburg, 1672) of ducal house of Saxe-Coburg-Gotha (*q.v.*).

Saxe-Hild·burg·hau·sen \-'hilt-,bu̇rk-'hau̇-zən\. District around city of Hildburghausen; established (1683) as minor duchy by Ernest, sixth son of Ernest the Pious of Saxe-Gotha; became part of Saxe-Altenburg (1826) when its ruler Duke Frederick (1763–1834) founded new line of Saxe-Altenburg (*q.v.*).

Saxe-Mei·ning·en \-'mī-niŋ-ən\. A former German duchy (now a part of Thuringia) and its ruling house, which formed a branch of the Ernestine line (*q.v.*) of Saxony. It was founded (1680) by Bernhard (*q.v.*), third son of Ernest the Pious of Saxe-Gotha; duchy increased (1826) by addition of part of lands (including Saalfeld) of Saxe-Gotha-Altenburg on its extinction (see SAXE-ALTENBURG). See also GEORGE II, Duke of Saxe-Meiningen.

Saxe-Wei·mar-Ei·se·nach \-'vī-,mär-'ī-zə-,näk\. A former German duchy (now a part of Thuringia) and its ruling house. District came (1373) into possession of Wettin family (*q.v.*), from them (1485) to the Ernestine line (*q.v.*); formed (1547) one of the small duchies in Thuringia and (1640) a principality, Saxe-Weimar, which added Eisenach (1644); became grand duchy (1815). See BERNHARD (1604–1639) and CHARLES AUGUSTUS.

Saxe-Wittenberg. See WETTIN.

Saxo Gram·mat·i·cus \'sak-sō-grə-'ma-tə-kəs\. c.1150–after 1216. Danish historian. Probably secretary to Archbishop Absalon of Lund. Author of *Gesta Danorum,* a Latin history of legendary and historic Danish kings down to 1186, and containing the Amleth (Hamlet) legend; considered first Danish contribution to world literature.

Saxony, House of. See ALBERTINE LINE.

Sax·ton \'saks-tən\, Joseph. 1799–1873. American inventor, b. Huntington, Pa. Built a highly regarded electric generator and electric motor (c.1830). Curator, standard weighing machinery, U.S. Mint (1837–43); designed and built balances used to check standard weights of U.S. government's assay and coining offices. Superintendent of weights and measures, U.S. Coast Survey (1843–73); invented a deep-sea thermometer, a self-registering tide gauge, an immersed hydrometer, an ever-pointed pencil, etc.

Say \se\, Jean-Baptiste. 1767–1832. French economist. Became magazine editor (1794); member of the Tribunate (1799–1804); operated a cotton mill (1807–13); taught at Conservatoire des Arts et Métiers (1817–30) and Collège de France (1830–32). Known for his law of markets which postulates that supply creates its own demand, a central tenet of orthodox economics until the Great Depression. Author of *Traité d'économie politique* (1803), *Lettres à Malthus* (1820), and *Cours complet d'économie politique pratique* (1828–30). His grandson ¶Léon, *in full* Jean-Baptiste-Léon (1826–1896), active opponent of socialism; finance minister (1872–73, 1875–76, 1876–79, 1882). Author of *Le Socialisme d'état* (1884), *Les Solutions démocratiques de la question des impôts* (1886), etc.

Say \'sā\, Thomas. 1787–1834. American entomologist, b. Philadelphia. Zoologist on expeditions to the Rocky Mountains, upper Midwest, Florida, Georgia, Mexico (1818–29); curator of American Philosophical Society (1821–27); professor at U. of Penn. (1822–28); member of Robert Owen's utopian colony at New Harmony, Ind. (1825–34). Called the father of descriptive entomology in America, as author of *American Entomology* (1824–28); also wrote *American Conchology* (1830–34).

Sa·ya·di·an \sä-'yäd-ē-ən\, Aruthin. *Pseudonym* Sa·yat-Nova \'sä-yät-'nō-və\. 1712–1795. Armenian troubadour. A weaver, later (1750–65) court minstrel of Irakli II of Georgia; entered monastery (1770); martyred by Persian invaders. Famous for love songs, most in Azeri Turkish and rest in Armenian and Georgian.

Sā·ya·na \'sä-yə-nə\. 1320–1387. Hindu scholar. Brother of Mādhavācārya; minister of four kings of Vijayanagar. Author of famous commentaries on the Vedas.

Sa·ya San \'sī-ə-'sän\. d. 1931. Burmese nationalist. Buddhist monk, physician, and astrologer in Siam and Lower Burma; organized a peasant army, crowned himself king, and led a revolt against the British in Lower Burma (1930–31); revolt crushed and he was hanged.

Saya-Sethathirath III. See CHAO ANOU.

Sayce \'sās\, Archibald Henry. 1845–1933. English philologist. Authority on Near Eastern languages; tutor (1870–90), professor (1891–1919) at Oxford. Author of *Assyrian Grammar for Comparative Purposes* (1872), *Introduction to the Science of Language* (1879), *The Monuments of the Hittites* (1881), *The Early History of the Hebrews* (1897), *Early Israel and the Surrounding Nations* (1898), *The Archaeology of the Cuneiform Inscriptions* (1907), *Reminiscences* (1923), etc.

Saye and Sele, Viscount. See FIENNES.

Say·ers \'sa(ə)rz, 'se(ə)rz, 'sā-ərz\, Dorothy Leigh. 1893–1957. English writer. Author of mystery stories featuring detectives Lord Peter Wimsey or Montague Egg, including *Whose Body?* (1923), *Strong Poison* (1930), *Murder Must Advertise* (1933), *Gaudy Night* (1935), *Busman's Honeymoon* (1937), *In the Teeth of the Evidence* (1939); of religious plays as *The Devil to Pay* (1939), *The Man Born to be King* (1943); of translations of Dante; and of essays as *Begin Here* (1940), *The Mind of the Maker* (1941).

Sayers, Tom. *Called* the Little Wonder *and* Napoleon of the Prize Ring. 1826–1865. English boxer. Although weighing only 155 lbs., became boxing champion of England by defeating Bill Perry (1857); at Farnborough participated in first international heavyweight championship match against the American John C. Heenan and after 42 rounds fought him to a draw (1860); retired thereafter.

Sayf ad-Daw·lah \,sī-fůd-'daů-lä\. *In full* Sayf ad-Dawlah Abū al-Ḥasan ibn Ḥamdān. 916–967. Arab ruler of northern Syria. Established himself in Aleppo (946); captured Damascus (947); fought constantly against Byzantine Empire. A poet; patron of learning. During his reign Aleppo reached its peak of culture and prosperity.

Sayre \'sa(ə)r, 'se(ə)r, 'sā(-ə)r\, Lewis Albert. 1820–1900. American surgeon, b. Bottle Hill, N.J. Aided in organizing Bellevue Hospital Med. Coll. (1861), and professor of orthopedic surgery there (1861–98), the first such professor in U.S. Renowned as orthopedic surgeon; first American surgeon to perform a resection of the hip for hip-joint disease (1854); developed original treatment of lateral curvature of the spine.

Sayyid Ahmad Khan, Sir. See AHMAD KHAN.

Say·yids \'sī-(y)ədz\. *Arabic, literally,* princes *or* lords. A weak dynasty (1414–1451) of Muslim rulers of a small territory around Delhi, after the invasions of Tamerlane; driven out by the Afghan Lodīs.

Sa·zo·nov \(,)sə-'zȯ-nəf\, Sergey Dmitriyevich. 1861–1927. Russian diplomat. Minister of foreign affairs (1910–16); promoted close relations with France and Great Britain; supported Balkan League against Turkey (1912); made claim for annexation of Constantinople. Escaped from Russia after the Bolsheviks seized power (1917); became minister of foreign affairs for Kolchak, who was fighting the Bolsheviks; retired to private life (1920).

Scae·vo·la \'sē-və-lə, 'sev-ə-\, Gaius Mucius. 6th century B.C. Roman hero. According to legend, volunteered to assassinate Lars Porsena when he was besieging Rome (509 B.C.); penetrated to Porsena's camp, but mistook Porsena's secretary for Porsena and killed him. Threatened with being burnt alive if he refused to divulge details of plot, he thrust right hand into fire nearby and held it there until it was burned off. Porsena, impressed with his courage, released him and negotiated peace with Rome.

Scaevola, Publius Mucius. d. before 115 B.C. Roman jurist and orator. Consul (133 B.C.); advised Tiberius Gracchus on his agrarian reforms but later expressed approval of his murder; opposed Scipio Africanus the Younger; pontifex maximus (130); published a digest (80 books) of annals of the office of pontifex maximus, a landmark of Roman historiography; often mentioned by Cicero as a lawyer of repute.

His son ¶Quintus Mucius (d. 82 B.C.), *called* Pon·ti·fex \'pänt-ə-,feks\; consul (95 B.C.); with his colleague, Lucius Licinius Crassus, sponsored law denying Roman citizenship to allies in the future, legislation which caused the Social War; governor of Asia; pontifex maximus (c.89); proscribed by Marian party in civil turmoil and murdered. As author of an 80-volume systematic treatise on civil law is considered the founder of the scientific study of Roman law.

Scaevola, Quintus Mucius. *Called* Au·gur \'ȯ-gər\. d. 88 B.C. Roman jurist. Cousin of Quintus M. Scaevola Pontifex. Aedile (125); governor of Asia (c.120); consul (117); admirer of Marius and voted against Sulla's proposed censure of Marius (88); law teacher to Cicero, who mentions him in several treatises.

Sca·la, del·la \,dāl-läs-'käl-ä\. Italian noble family; ruled Verona (1260–1387). Its members included:

Mastino I della Scala (d. 1277), Ghibelline leader; podesta of Verona (1260 ff.); later appointed perpetual captain of Verona; suppressed revolts of Count of San Bonifacio (1263, 1272); supported Conradin against Charles of Anjou (1267); killed by an armed band, perhaps of Guelfs.

¶Cangrande I (1291–1329); nephew of Mastino I; appointed imperial vicar of Verona by Emperor Henry VII of Germany (1311); waged successful wars against Vicenza (1312–14) and Padua (1317–18); elected captain general of the Ghibelline League (1318); extended rule to Feltre and Belluno; excommunicated (1320) for recognizing Louis IV the Bavarian as Holy Roman emperor; named imperial vicar of Mantua by Louis (1328); known as patron of the arts, and as patron of Dante during latter's exile from Florence.

¶Mastino II (1308–1351), nephew of Cangrande; extended his power over Brescia (1332), Parma (1335), and Lucca (1335); invaded by a coalition of his enemies and lost all his territories save Verona and Vicenza (1339); spent last years struggling against the Gonzaga and Visconti families. His grandson ¶Antonio (1362–1388) was the last della Scala ruler of Verona; driven from power by Gian Galeazzo Visconti (1387).

Scales, Baron. See Anthony WOODVILLE.

Scal·i·ger \'skal-ə-jər\, Julius Caesar. *Orig. surname* Bor·don \bȯr-'dōn\. 1484–1558. Italian physician and scholar. Claimed descent from della Scala family and changed name to Scaliger. Practiced medicine in Agen, France (from 1524); naturalized (1528). Established fame with orations against Erasmus's *Ciceronianus* (1531, 1536). Writings, all in Latin, included verse; a Latin grammar on scientific principles *De causis linguae latinae* (1540); *De plantis* (1556); and *Poetice* (1561), a treatise on poetics which helped foster Classicism. Best known for his philosophical and scientific writings, including commentaries on works of Aristotle, Hippocrates, Theophrastus, and esp. his *Exercitationes exotericae de subtilitate* (1557) on Cardano's *De subtilitate.* His son ¶Joseph Justus (1540–1609) was one of the most renowned scholars of his time; became a Protestant (1562); professor, Geneva (1572–74), Leiden (from 1593). He laid down and applied in his editions of *Catalecta,* of Festus, Catullus, Tibullus, and Propertius, rules of criticism and of textual emendation that laid the foundation for modern textual criticism. His edition of Manilius (1579) and his *Opus de emendatione temporum* (1583) revolutionized accepted ideas on ancient chronology and laid the foundation of the modern study of the subject; in his *Thesaurus temporum* (1606) he collected, often restoring defective texts, all available extant chronological writings of classic Greek and Latin; established numismatics as a tool of historical research.

Sca·moz·zi \skä-'mȯt-tsē\, Vincenzo. 1552–1616. Italian architect. Considered the intellectual father of Neoclassicism. Worked mainly in Venice and Padua; designed palaces, villas, theaters, churches (esp. for Salzburg cathedral), and the fortress town of Palmanova. Completed (1585) Palladio's Teatro Olimpico; his writings, esp. *L'idea dell'architettura universale* (1615), caused Palladianism to influence English Neoclassical architecture.

Scanderbeg. See George KASTRIOTI.

Scar·lat·ti \skär-'lät-tē, *Angl* skär-'lät-ē\, Alessandro, *in full* Pietro Alessandro Gaspare. 1660–1725. Italian composer. Maestro di capella at court of Naples (1684–1702, 1709–18). Noted for thematic development and chromatic harmony; established form of Italian opera overture; contributed to development of the opera orchestra. Composed 115 operas, esp. *Gli equivoci nel sembiante* (1679), *Il Mitridate Eupatore* (1707), *La principessa fedele* (1710), *Il Tigrane* (1715), and his first opera buffa *Il trionfo dell'onore* (1718); also wrote masses, oratorios, serenades, concerti grossi, and over 600 chamber cantatas.

Scarlatti, Giuseppe Domenico. 1685–1757. Italian composer. Son of Alessandro Scarlatti. Wrote operas in Naples, Venice, Rome (1703–19); maestro di cappella at St. Peter's (1714–19); in service of courts of Portugal (1719–28) and Spain (1728–57). Composed over 500 sonatas for harpsichord featuring innovations of harmony and form; also cantatas and church music.

Scar·lett \'skär-lət\, Sir James Yorke. 1799–1871. English general. Held regimental command (1840–54); commanded heavy brigade in successful charge against Russian cavalry at Balaklava (Oct. 25, 1854); commanded entire British cavalry in Crimea (1855–56); adjutant general (1860–65).

Scar·pa \'skär-pä\, Antonio. 1752–1832. Italian anatomist and surgeon. Professor at Pavia (1783–1803); known esp. for work on the anatomy of the ear, nerve ganglia, and bones. Scarpa's triangle and Scarpa's foramen were named for him.

Scar·ron \skä-rōⁿ, skȧ-\, Paul. 1610–1660. French comic poet, novelist, and dramatist. Became an abbé (1629); entered service of bishop of Le Mans (1633); a paralytic last part of his life (1638–60); m. (1652) Françoise d'Aubigné, who later was Mme de Maintenon. Foremost French exponent of the burlesque. Among his works were *Le Typhon* (burlesque poem, 1664), the plays *Jodelet* (1645), *Don Japhet d'Arménie* (1647), and *Le Marquis ridicule* (1655), the burlesque epic *Virgile travesti* (1648–53), and esp. the picaresque novel *Le Roman comique* (1651–57).

Scau·rus \'skȯr-əs, 'skȯr-\, Marcus Aemilius. c.162–c.89 B.C. Roman politician. Consul (115, 107); headed embassy to Jugurtha (112–111); accused by opponents of accepting bribes from Jugurtha for a peace treaty unfavorable to Rome; censor (109); directed construction of the Via Aemilia; grain commissioner at Ostia (104); helped suppress Saturninus's reforms (100); supported Livius Drusus's attempt to enfranchise Rome's Italian allies (91). His son ¶Marcus Aemilius (d. after 52 B.C.) served during Third Mithradatic War (74–64 B.C.) as quaestor to Pompey; governor of Sardinia (55); accused of extortion in his province (54), defended by Cicero, Quintus Hortensius, and others, and acquitted; went into exile after being charged with electoral fraud (52).

Scève \sev\, Maurice. c.1501–c.1560 to 1564. French poet. Leader of Lyons poets; earliest and most accomplished French exponent of Petrarchism. Claimed to have discovered tomb of Petrarch's Laura at Avignon (1533). Author of *Les Blasons du corps féminin* (1537), *Saulsaye, églogue de la vie solitaire* (1547), epic *Le Microcosme* (1562), and his masterpiece, the poem cycle *Délie, objet de plus haute vertu* (1544).

Schacht \'shäkt\, Hjalmar³, *in full* Horace Greeley Hjalmar. 1877–1970. German financier. Director, Nationalbank für Deutschland (1916 ff.) and partner in Darmstädter und Nationalbank. Commissioner of currency for Germany (1923); halted inflation and stabilized the mark. President of the Reichsbank (1923–30, 1933–39); minister of economics (1934–37). Took part in Dawes Committee discussions (1924) and Reparations Commission deliberations (1929). Acquitted (1946) as war criminal.

Schack \'shäk\, Adolf Friedrich. 1815–1894. German man of letters. Accumulated art collection (Schack-Galerie, now part of the Bayerische Staatsgemäldesammlungen of Munich). Author of translations and literary criticism.

Scha·dow \'shäd-ō\, Johann Gottfried. 1764–1850. German sculptor. Prussian court sculptor (1788); rector (1805) and director (1816–50), Acad. of Art, Berlin. Regarded as founder of the modern Berlin school of sculptors. Among his works were a tombstone for Count Alexander von der Mark (1790), a group entitled *Quadriga of Victory* for the Brandenburger Tor in Berlin (1793), a group *The Princesses Luise and Frederike* (1797), and many portrait busts. His son ¶Rudolf (1786–1822) was also a sculptor; works included *The Spinner* (1816) and *The Girl Binding on Her Sandals* (1817). Another son ¶Wilhelm (1788–1862) was a painter; professor, Acad. of Art, Berlin (1819); director, Acad. of Art, Düsseldorf (1826); founder of the Düsseldorf school of anecdotal, religiously determined realism. Chief works were a portrait of Gabriele von Humboldt (1818), *Adoration of the Shepherds* (1824), and fresco of *The Wise and Foolish Virgins* (1842).

Schaep·man \'shäp-mən\, Hermanus Johannes Aloysius Maria. 1844–1903. Dutch politician and writer. Ordained Roman Catholic priest (1867); editor of newpapers *Tijd* (1872) and *De Katholiek* (1895); founded Catholic political clubs, forerunners of the Roman Catholic State party. Elected to Dutch Second Chamber (1880); became leader of Catholic legislators; established a coalition (1888–1905) with Calvinist legislators to obtain state aid for parochial schools; served in Kuyper's cabinet (1901–03). Poems included "De Paus" (1866) and "Aya Sofia" (1886); his political and religious articles collected in *Menschen en Boeken* (1893–1902).

Schäfer, Sir Edward Albert. See SHARPEY-SCHAFER.

Schäf·er \'shef-ər\, Wilhelm. 1868–1952. German writer. Author of collections of *Anekdoten* (1908, 1911, 1929, 1938), novels including *Karl Stauffers Lebensgang* (1913), *Der Hauptmann von Küpenick* (1930).

Schaff \'shaf\, Phillip. 1819–1893. American theologian and church historian, b. Chur, Switzerland. To U.S. (1844); professor in Mercersburg Theological Seminary (1844–65); with John W. Nevin formulated the Mercersburg Theology stressing the institutional church instead of the individual. Affiliated with Presbyterian church (from 1870); professor, Union Theological Seminary (1870–93). President of American Committee in work of revising the English Bible (1881–85); founder and first president of American Society of Church History (1888). His works included *History of the Christian Church* (1858–90), *The Creeds of Christendom* (1877). Edited American translation of Johann J. Herzog's *Realenzyklopädie* (1882–84; now known as *The Schaff-Herzog Encyclopedia of Religious Knowledge*).

Schäff·le \'shef-lə\, Albert. 1831–1903. German economist and sociologist. Member of Württemberg Landtag (1862–65) and of German Zollparlament (1868). Austrian minister of commerce and agriculture (1871); his plan for the imperial federalization of Bohemia was defeated. Author of *Kapitalismus und Sozialismus* (1870), *Bau und Leben des Sozialen Körpers* (1875–78), *Abriss der Soziologie* (1906).

Schaff·ner \'shäf-nər\, Jakob. 1875–1944. Swiss writer. Influenced by Nietzsche, Dostoyevsky and later by Nazism. Author of novels *Konrad Pilater* (1910), *Der Dechant von Gottesbüren* (1917), *Johannes* (1922), *Die Glücksfischer* (1925), *Eine deutsche Wanderschaft* (1931), *Kampf und Reife* (1939); poems *Bekenntnisse* (1940); essays *Die Predigt der Marienburg* (1931) and *Berge, Ströme und Städte* (1938).

Schall von Bell \'shäl-fön-'bel\, Johann Adam. *Chin. name* T'ang Jo-wang \'täŋ-'zhō-'wäŋ\. 1591–1666. German Jesuit missionary and astronomer. In China (from 1619); revised Chinese calendar and translated Western astronomical books; head of Imperial Board of Astronomy (1644–64); trusted adviser (1644–61) to Emperor Shun-chih, who made him a mandarin. Lost power after Shun-chih's death (1661); tried (1664) for plotting against the emperor and state; convicted but sentence commuted.

Scha·per \'shäp-ər\, Johann. 1621–1670. German ceramist. First to apply Schwarzlot painting on pottery (c.1660); known for delicate architectural and landscape painted enamelware.

Scharn·horst \'shärn-,hȯrst\, Gerhard Johann David von. 1755–1813. Prussian general. Distinguished himself in Belgium against French forces (1790s); chief of staff in war against Napoléon (1806–07). As head of Army Reform Commission (from 1807) developed the modern general staff system and (with Gneisenau) the "shrinkage system" of army training. Forced by Napoléon to leave Prussian service (1810), but on French defeat in Russia (1812) became chief of staff to Blücher; fought in War of Liberation; badly wounded at Lützen, died at Prague a month later.

Scha·roun \'shär-,ōn\, Hans Bernhard. 1893–1972. German architect. Follower of Bruno Taut; joined (1925) modernist group Der Ring; after World War II served in government and academic posts for town planning. Designs included houses of Siemensstadt Housing Estate, Berlin (1930), Schminke House, Löbau (1932), Geschwister Scholl Schule, Lünen (1955–62), Romeo and Juliet apartment buildings, Stuttgart (1963), and esp. the Berlin Philharmonic Orchestra hall (1963).

Schar·wen·ka \shär-'veŋ-kä\, Ludwig Philipp. 1847–1917. German composer. Wrote orchestral, choral, and chamber music, piano and violin pieces, and songs. His brother ¶Franz Xaver (1850–1924) was a piano virtuoso and composer; founded (1881) Scharwenka Conservatory of Music, Berlin; directed (1891–98) Scharwenka Music School in New York; composer of piano concertos, an opera, a symphony, chamber music, and piano pieces.

Schau·dinn \'shaů-dən\, Fritz Richard. 1871–1906. German zoologist. Director, Inst. for Protozoology at Imperial Ministry of Health (1904–06). With Erich Hoffmann discovered the organism (*Spirochaeta pallida*) causing syphilis (1905); proved that tropical dysentery is caused by a certain amoeba (*Endamoeba histolytica*); confirmed that hookworm infection occurs through the skin (1904); made researches on human and bird malaria.

Schaum·burg-Lip·pe \'shaům-,bůrk-'lip-ə\. A former German principality and its ruling family, founded (1643) by a younger member (Count Philip, 1601–1681) of the Lippe-Alverdissen branch, who inherited the county of Schaumburg (see LIPPE); became a principality (1807).

Schech·ter \'shek-tər\, Solomon. 1850–1915. American Talmudist and educator, b. Focşani, Romania. In England (1882–1901); reader in Talmudic studies, Cambridge (1890–1901); professor of Hebrew, U. of London (1899–1901). President, Jewish Theological Seminary, New York City (1902–15). Founded United Synagogue of America (1913); leader of U.S. Conservative Judaism. An editor, *Jewish Quarterly Review* and *The Jewish Encyclopedia.* Collected (1896) from the Geniza of Cairo, Egypt, store of about 50,000 manuscripts and fragments, chiefly in Hebrew and Arabic, which he contributed to Cambridge U. Discovered among the manuscripts lost chapters of Ecclesiasticus, which he published (1899) as *The Wisdom of Ben Sira;* also wrote *Studies in Judaism* (1908), *Some Aspects of Rabbinic Theology* (1909), etc.

Schee·le \'shā-lə\, Carl Wilhelm. *First name also spelled* Karl. 1742–1786. Swedish pharmacist and chemist. Discovered oxygen (c.1772) before Priestley; also discovered chlorine, baryta, glycerine, hydrogen sulfide, arsine, Scheele's green (copper arsenite), and citric, gallic, lactic, malic, molybdic, oxalic, prussic, and tartic acids.

Schee·ma·kers \'shā-,mäk-ərs\, Peter. 1691–1770. Belgian sculptor. In London (1735–69); considered a founder of modern sculpture in England; executed many statues and monuments, esp. (1741) the monument to Shakespeare in Westminster Abbey.

Scheer \'shār\, Reinhard. 1863–1928. German admiral. Chief of staff of high seas fleet under von Holtzendorff (1910); commanded a battle squadron (1913); famed submarine strategist; commander of German high seas fleet (Jan. 1916); led fleet in indecisive Battle of Jutland (May 31, 1916); chief of the admiralty staff (1918).

Schef·fel \'shef-əl\, Josef Victor von. 1826–1886. German poet and novelist. Among his works were the lyric-epic poem *Der Trompeter von Säkkingen* (1854), the historical novel *Ekkehard* (1857), and a collection of drinking songs *Gaudeamus* (1868).

Schef·fler \'shef-lər\, Johannes. *Pseudonym* An·gel·us Si·le·si·us \'an-jə-lə(s)-sī-'lē-zh(ē-)əs\. 1624–1677. Polish mystic, polemicist, and poet. Trained as physician; ordained Catholic priest (1661); became vigorous spokesman of Counter-Reformation. Published *Heiligen Seelenlust* (hymns, 1657), *Geistreiche Sinn- und Schlussreime* (1657, later called *Cherubinischer Wandersmann;* mystical poems), *Ecclesiologia* (1677, polemic).

Schei·bler \'shī-blər\, Johann Heinrich. 1777–1837. German silk manufacturer and amateur musician. Invented the "Aura," the first mouth harmonica (1816); devised a standard of musical pitch (known as Stuttgart, or Scheibler's, pitch, with a' at 440 vibrations) adopted by Stuttgart congress of physicists (1834).

Schei·de·mann \'shī-də-ˌmän\, Philipp. 1865–1939. German politician. Editor of Socialist newspaper (1895); member of Reichstag (1903–18); minister without portfolio in last imperial cabinet (Oct. 1918). Without party or government authorization proclaimed establishment of the Weimar Republic (Nov. 9, 1918); member of ruling council of interim government (Nov. 1918–Feb. 1919); first chancellor of the republic (Feb.–June 1919); resigned when National Assembly accepted terms of Treaty of Versailles. Mayor of Kassel (1920–25); fled when Nazis came to power; died in Copenhagen.

Scheidt \'shīt\, Samuel. 1587–1654. German organist and composer. Organist (1609) and Kapellmeister (1619–25, 1638–54) at court of Halle. Published keyboard and sacred vocal music which combined traditional counterpoint with the new Italian concerto style, including *Cantiones sacrae* (1620), *Tabulatura nova* (1624, first German organ music to use staff notation instead of alphabetical tablature), *Geistliche Concerten* (1631–40), and *Tablatur-Buch* (1650). Major influence on Baroque organ style of northern Germany.

Schein \'shīn\, Johann Hermann. 1586–1630. German composer. One of first to introduce the Italian Baroque style into German music; Kapellmeister at Weimar (1615); cantor at Thomasschule, Leipzig (from 1616). His publications of sacred and secular vocal music included *Cymbalum Sionium* (1615), *Opella nova* (1618), *Diletti pastorali* (1624), and *Cantional* (1627).

Schei·ner \'shī-nər\, Christoph. 1573–1650. German astronomer. Member of Jesuit order; discovered existence of sunspots independently of Galileo (1611); adhered to theory of a stable earth with a moving sun; invented a pantograph.

Sche·ler \'shā-lər\, Max. 1874–1928. German philosopher. Professor, Munich (1907–10), Cologne (1919), Frankfurt (1928). A leading exponent of Husserl's Phenomenological philosophy. Became a pacifist and Roman Catholic (by 1920); adopted a more pantheistic view of the world (c.1924). Works included *Der Formalismus in der Ethik und die materiale Wertethik* (1921), *Wesen und Formen der Sympathie* (1923), *Die Wissensformen und die Gesellschaft* (1926), and *Die Stellung des Menschen im Kosmos* (1928).

Schel·ling \'shel-iŋ\, Felix Emanuel. 1858–1945. American educator, b. New Albany, Ind. Professor, U. of Pennsylvania (1893–1934); editor of Elizabethan plays and author of books on Elizabethan literature, including *History of Elizabethan Drama* (1908), *English Literature During the Lifetime of Shakespeare* (1910), *The English Lyric* (1913), *Foreign Influences in Elizabethan Plays* (1923), *Elizabethan Playwrights* (1925).

Schelling, Friedrich Wilhelm Joseph von. 1775–1854. German philosopher. A leading figure of German Idealism. Professor, Jena (1798), Würzburg (1803), Munich (1827), Berlin (1841–46). Clashed with Fichte in article "Darstellung meines Systems der Philosophie" (1801) and later (c.1807) with Hegel. His works included *Ideen zu einer Philosophie der Natur* (1797), *System des transzendentalen Idealismus* (1800), *Philosophische Untersuchungen über das Wesen der menschlichen Freiheit* (1809), *Die Weltalter* (1811).

Schen·del \'shen-dəl\, Arthur François Émile van. 1874–1946. Dutch novelist. His works included *Een zwerver verliefd* (1904), *Een zwerver verdwaald* (1907), *Het fregatschip Johanna Maria* (1930), *Een hollandsch drama* (1935), *De grauwe Vogels* (1937), *De wereld een dansfeest* (1938).

Schen·ker \'sheŋ-kər\, Heinrich. 1868–1935. Austrian music theorist, b. Poland. Edited works of Bach, Handel, Beethoven; edited periodicals *Der Tonwille* (1921–24) and *Das Meisterwerk in der Musik* (1925–30). Known for his studies of harmony and counterpoint in 18th and 19th century composers, published in *Neue musikalische Theorien und Phantasien* (1906–35).

Scher·chen \'sher-kən\, Herman. 1891–1966. German composer. Founded the Neue Musikgesellschaft in Berlin (1918); edited music journal *Melos* (1920–21); fled to Brussels from Nazis (1933) and edited *Musica viva* (1933–36). Conducted (from 1911) various European orchestras; made U.S. debut with Philadelphia Orchestra (1964); known as champion of contemporary composers. Author of *Lehrbuch des Dirigierens* (1929), *Vom Wesen der Musik* (1946), *Musik für Jedermann* (1950), etc.

Sché·rer \shā-rer\, Barthélemy-Louis-Joseph. 1747–1804. French Revolutionary general. Distinguished himself at Valmy (1791); commanded army of Italy and won battle of Loano (Nov. 24, 1795); minister of war (1797–99); was defeated by the Austrians in Italy (1799) and resigned.

Sche·rer \'shā-rər\, Wilhelm. 1841–1886. German philologist. Professor, Vienna (1868), Strassburg (1872), Berlin (1877). Among his works were *Zur Geschichte der deutschen Sprache* (1868) and *Geschichte der deutschen Literatur* (1883).

Scher·rer \'sher-ər\, Paul Hermann. 1890–1969. Swiss physicist. Professor and director, Physics Inst. of U. of Zürich (from 1920). With Peter Debye developed the Debye-Scherrer method of X-ray diffraction analysis (c.1916); also contributed to solid-state, quantum, and nuclear physics.

Schia·pa·rel·li \ˌskyä-pä-'rel-lē\, Elsa. 1896–1973. French dress designer, b. Rome. Opened a couturier shop in Paris (c.1927) and expanded into jewelry, cosmetics, etc.; established a branch in New York (1949). A leader of the fashion scene; designed the padded shoulder (1932), fur bed jackets and rhinestone-trimmed lingerie (in 1940s), "shortie" coats (1950s).

Schiaparelli, Giovanni Virginio. 1835–1910. Italian astronomer. Observer (1860), director (1862–1900), Milan observatory; discovered asteroid Hesperia (1861); showed that meteor swarms travel in cometary orbits (1865); observed numerous double stars; observed markings on Mars which he called *canali* (1877); believed that Mercury and Venus rotate on their axes in the same time as they revolve around the sun.

Schiavone, Lo. See Andrea MELDOLLA.

Schi·chau \'shik-ˌau̇\, Ferdinand. 1814–1896. German engineer and shipbuilder. Constructed first screw-driven vessel in Germany, the *Borussia* (1855) and (with son-in-law Carl H. Ziese) the German navy's first gunboats with compound engines (1879).

Schick \'shik\, Béla. 1877–1967. American physician, b. Boglár, Hungary. Taught at Vienna (1902–23); to U.S. (1923, naturalized 1929); chief pediatrician, Mt. Sinai Hospital, N.Y.C. (1923–42); clinical professor of diseases of children, Columbia U. (1923–42). Discovered Schick test for determining susceptibility to diphtheria (1913). Known also for writings on scarlet fever, tuberculosis, nutrition of newborn children, etc.

Schick·e·le \'shik-ə-lə\, René. 1883–1940. German writer. Journalist in Paris and Berlin; published (1915–19) antiwar periodical *Weissen Blätter* in Zürich; fled Germany (1933) and became French citizen. One of foremost Expressionist writers in Germany; often wrote on his divided loyalty between Germany and France. Author of verse as *Der Ritt ins Leben* (1905), *Mein Herz, mein Land* (1915); plays *Hans im Schnakenloch* (1916), *Am Glockenturm* (1919); and novels as *Der Fremde* (1907), *Die Flaschenpost* (1937), and esp. the trilogy *Das Erbe am Rhein* comprising *Maria Capponi* (1925), *Blick auf die Vogesen* (1927), *Der Wolf in der Hürde* (1931).

Schick Gu·tiér·rez \'shik-gü-'tyer-rās\, René. 1910–1966. Nicaraguan politician. Minister of foreign affairs (1961–62); president of Nicaragua (1963–66).

Schiff \'shif\, Jacob Henry. 1847–1920. American banker and philanthropist, b. Frankfurt am Main, Germany. To U.S. (1865, naturalized 1870); partner in Kuhn, Loeb & Co. (from 1875) and head of firm (1885–1920). Associated with E. H. Harriman against J.J. Hill and J.P. Morgan & Co. in struggle for control of Northern Pacific Railroad, bringing on stock market panic of May 9, 1901; active in floating Japanese bonds in U.S. during Russo–Japanese War (1904) and in marketing Chinese loan (1911). Recipients of his philanthropies included the Montefiore Hospital; Henry Street Settlement; Columbia U.; Harvard U., where he established a Semitic Museum; Cornell, where he founded a chair for study of German culture; Tuskegee Institute; Jewish Theological Seminary in New York; the American Red Cross.

Schie·le \'shē-lə\, Egon. 1890–1918. Austrian painter. Strongly influenced by Jugendstil movement, the German art nouveau; met Gustav Klimt, leader of the Vienna Sezession group; developed expressionist style that candidly and erotically portrayed the human figure; used color and line to achieve a feverish tension. A founder of Vienna's Neukunstgruppe (1909).

Schiff, Moritz. 1823–1896. German physiologist. Professor at Bern (1859–63), Florence (1863–76), Geneva (1876–96). Studied functions of the thyroid gland and developed (1884) a thyroid-extract therapy for treatment of exophthalmos and myxedema; first to notice influence of the cerebral cortex on blood circulation; recognized role of the vagus nerve in regulating heart function; discovered the restoration of bile salts to the liver; studied the effects of the removal of the cerebellum and partial section of the spinal cord.

Schi·ka·ne·der \ˌshē-kä-'nād-ər\, Emanuel Johann Joseph. 1751–1812. German theater manager and librettist. Built the Theater an der Wien (1801); among his librettos was that of *Die Zauberflöte,* with music by Mozart (1791).

Schild·kraut \'shilt-ˌkrau̇t\, Rudolph. 1862–1930. German actor. Debut in Vienna (1893); acted in Hamburg and Berlin, with special success in Shakespearean roles; to U.S., associated with motion pictures in Hollywood (from 1926). Especially notable for his interpretations of Shylock and Mephistopheles; interpreted also plays of Hauptmann, Sudermann, Pinero, Shaw, and other moderns. His son ¶Joseph (1895–1964), also an actor; played in Berlin and Vienna (1913–20); on U.S. stage (from 1920); played in *Liliom, Peer Gynt, An American Tragedy* (1926), *Clash by Night* (1941), *Diary of Anne Frank* (1955); appeared in films *Orphans of the Storm* (1922), *King of Kings* (1927), *Show Boat* (1929), *Life of Emile Zola* (1938, Academy Award), *The Tell-Tale Heart* (1942, Academy Award), *Gallant Legion* (1948), etc.

Schil·ler \'shil-ər\, Ferdinand Canning Scott. 1864–1937. English philosopher. A Pragmatist; befriended and influenced by William James; tutor, Oxford (1903–26); professor, U. of Southern California (from 1929). Among his books were *Riddles of the Sphinx* (1891), *Studies in Humanism* (1907), *Formal Logic* (1912), and *Logic for Use* (1929).

Schiller, Johann Christoph Friedrich von. 1759–1805. German poet, playwright, and critic. Surgeon in a Württemberg regiment (1780); went absent without leave to witness performance of his first play, *Die Räuber* (1781); arrested by Duke of Württemberg and condemned to publish nothing except medical treatises. Left for Mannheim (1783–85), where his drama *Kabale und Liebe* was successfully produced (1784). In Weimar (1787); wrote blank verse *Don Carlos* (1787), historical work *Geschichte des Abfalls der vereinigten Niederlande* (1788), and the hymn "An die Freude," later used by Beethoven in his 9th Symphony. Professor of history, Jena (1789), where he completed his *Geschichte des dreissigjährigen Krieges* (1791–93) and published essays on aesthetics, as "Über Anmut und Würde," "Über das Erhabene," and "Über naive und sentimentalische Dichtung"; formed friendship with Goethe and was inspired thereby to produce more poetry; with Johann Friedrich Cotta, founded (1795) literary journal *Die Horen;* founded (1796) *Musenalmanach* and contributed poems "Das Ideal und des Leben," "Die Macht des Gesanges," "Würde der Frauen," "Der Spaziergang," "Der Ring des Polykrates," "Der Handschuh," "Der Taucher," "Das Lied von der Glocke"; also completed his trilogy *Wallenstein* (1800). Settled in Weimar (1799–1805) to be near Goethe and to devote himself completely to writing; wrote the dramas *Maria Stuart* (1800), *Die Jungfrau von Orleans* (1801), *Die Braut von Messina* (1803), *Wilhelm Tell* (1804), and translated *Macbeth,* Gozzi's *Turandot,* and Racine's *Phèdre.* During later years worked under the handicap of continuous ill health. Regarded as second only to Goethe in German literature, and as first among German dramatists.

Schil·lings \'shil-iŋz\, Max von. 1868–1933. German conductor and composer. Known for his operas, esp. *Moloch* (1906) and *Mona Lisa* (1915); also composed orchestral works, chamber and choral music, and songs.

Schilt·berg·er \'shilt-ˌber-gər\, Johann, *better known as* Hans. 1380–c.1440. German noble and traveler. Known for his *Reisebuch* (c.1460) describing travels in Egypt, Asia Minor, Armenia, Georgia, Siberia, the middle Volga, and southeastern Russia, while enslaved to the Turks (1396–1402) and to Tamerlane (1402–27).

Schim·mel \'sk̲im-əl\, Hendrik Jan. 1823–1906. Dutch journalist and writer. Editor of the newspaper *De Gids* (1851–67) and the monthly magazine *Nederland* (from 1854). Among his dramas were *Joan Woutersz* (1847), *Struensee* (1868); among his novels, *Mary Hollis* (1860), *Mylady Carlisle* (1864), *De Kaptein van de lijfgarde* (1888).

Schim·mel·pen·ninck \'sk̲im-əl-ˌpen-iŋk\, Rutger Jan. 1761–1825. Dutch politician. Leader of the Patriot party in its deposition of Prince William V of Orange (1795); president of Amsterdam city government (1796); delegate to Batavian National Assemblies (1796–98). Ambassador to France (1798–1802) and to Great Britain (1802–03). Appointed grand pensionary (1805–06) of the Batavian Commonwealth by Napoléon; reformed the tax and educational systems. Created baron of the French Empire and appointed to French Senate by Napoléon (1811); member of Dutch First Chamber (1815–21).

Schim·per \'shim-pər\. Family of German scientists including: Karl Friedrich (1803–1867), pioneer in modern plant morphology; formulated theory of phyllotaxis; made contributions in hydrology, meteorology, and geology. His cousin ¶Wilhelm Philipp (1808–1880), botanist; on staff (from 1835), latterly director of Natural History Museum, Strasbourg; authority on mosses; also wrote on zoology, geology, and paleobotany; author of *Bryologia Europaea* (1836–55). Wilhelm's son ¶Andreas Franz Wilhelm (1856–1901), botanist; assistant to Eduard Strasburger in Bonn (1882–98); professor at Basel (1898–1901); proved (1880) that starch is a source of stored energy for plants and a product of photosynthesis; named chloroplasts and demonstrated they arise from preexisting ones (1883); one of first to divide successfully the continents into floral regions, published findings (with other botanists) in *Pflanzen-Geographie auf physiologischer Grundlage* (1898).

Schin·de·wolf \'shin-də-ˌvȯlf\, Otto Heinrich. 1896–1971. German paleontologist. Professor at Marburg (1919–27) and Tübingen (1948–64); director, Geological Survey of Berlin (1927–48). Known for studies on corals and cephalopods; advocated a cataclysmic theory of evolution to explain the origin of the higher taxonomic categories. Author of *Grundlagen und Methoden der paläontologischen Chronologie* (1944), *Grundfragen der Paläontologie* (1950), and *Studien zur Stammesgeschichte der Ammoniten* (1961–68).

Schin·dler \'shin-dlər\, Anton Felix. 1795–1864. German conductor. Secretary (from 1820), close friend of Beethoven; wrote *Biographie von L. van Beethoven* (1840).

Schi·ner \'shē-nər\, Matthäus. *Also spelled* Mathias Schin·ner \'shin-ər\. c.1465–1522. Swiss prelate. Consecrated bishop of Sion (1499); made cardinal and bishop of Novara (1511); instrumental in accession of Massimiliano Sforza to ducal throne of Milan (1512) and of Leo X to papacy (1513); worked to preserve freedom of Papal States from French domination; intimate counsellor of Emperor Charles V (from 1519).

Schin·kel \'shiŋ-kəl\, Karl Friedrich. 1781–1841. German architect and painter. The leading arbiter of national aesthetic taste in his lifetime. State architect of Prussia (from 1815); his Romantic-Classical designs included a mausoleum for Queen Louise (1810), Königschauspelhaus (1818), Werdersche Kirche (1821–30), Altes Museum (1822–30), all in Berlin. Appointed director of Prussian office of public works (1830); decorated royal apartments; designed boulevards and squares in Berlin. Also noted for ironwork and stage designs, including scenery for Goethe's plays.

Schi·rach \'shē-räk̲\, Baldur von. 1907–1974. German politician. Joined Nazi party (1927); formed Nazi Students' League (1928); national director of Hitler Youth movement (from 1933); gauleiter in Vienna (1940–45); sentenced (1946) as war criminal to 20 years imprisonment.

Schir·mer \'shir-mər, *Angl* 'shər-\, Gustave. 1829–1893. American music publisher, b. Königsee, Saxony. To U.S. (1840); head of G. Schirmer, music publishers (from 1866). His son ¶Rudolph Edward (1859–1919) was associated with him in the music publishing house (from 1885) and became president of the firm as reorganized after Gustave's death.

Schjel·de·rup \'shel-dru̇p\, Gerhard Rosenkrone. 1859–1933. Norwegian composer. Wrote operas as *Sonntagsmorgen* (1893), *En hellig aften* (1895), *Vaarnat* (1906–07), 2 symphonies, tone poems, chamber music, and songs.

Schlaf \'shläf\, Johannes. 1862–1941. German writer. Collaborated with Arno Holz in naturalistic sketches as *Papa Hamlet* (1889) and *Neue Gleise* (1892), and is regarded therefore as a joint founder of the Naturalistic school in Germany. Later wrote novels, plays, philosophical essays, some poetry, and studies on and translations of Whitman, Verhaeren, Maeterlinck, Novalis.

Schläf·li \'shlef-lē\, Ludwig. 1814–1895. Swiss mathematician. Professor at Bern (from 1853). Founder of multidimensional geometry; wrote *Theorie der vielfachen Kontinuität* (1901).

Schle·gel \'shlā-gəl\, August Wilhelm von. 1767–1845. German man of letters. Professor, Bonn (1818–45). With his brother Friedrich, founded the literary journal *Athenäum* (1798), which became the organ of German Romanticism; closely associated (from 1804) with Madame de Staël; made special study (1818 ff.) of Oriental languages and literature; published (1820–30) the journal *Indische Bibliothek;* founded Sanskrit studies in Germany. Other works included translations of Shakespeare (1797–1810), *Gedichte* (1800, verse), a tragedy *Ion* (1803), *Spanisches Theater* (1803–09), *Über dramatische Kunst und Literatur* (1809–11).

Schlegel, Friedrich von. 1772–1829. German writer and critic. Brother of August von Schlegel. His philosophical ideas inspired much of the German Romantic movement. Studied Oriental languages in Paris (1802–04); published *Über die Sprache und Weisheit der Inder* (1808), first attempt at comparative Indo-Germanic linguistics and starting point of study of Indian languages and comparative philology. Adopted Roman Catholic faith (1808); secretary to the state chancery in Vienna (1809), and Austrian counselor of legation at Frankfurt am Main (1815–18); became editor (1820) of right-wing Catholic paper *Concordia* and published in it repudiations of his earlier beliefs. Works included lyric poems, the novel *Lucinde* (1799), the drama *Alarcos* (1802), *Über die neuere Geschichte* (1811), *Geschichte der alten und neuen Literatur* (1815), *Philosophie des Lebens* (1828), *Philosophie der Geschichte* (1829). His wife ¶Dorothea, *nee* Mendelssohn (1763–1839), was the daughter of Moses Mendelssohn *(q.v.);* m. 1st Simon Veit (1783), by whom she had a son, the painter Philipp Veit, and 2d Friedrich von Schlegel (1804); noted as a spirited letter-writer.

Schlegel, Johann Elias. 1719–1749. German playwright. Uncle of August and Friedrich von Schlegel. Became private secretary to Saxon ambassador in Copenhagen (1743); taught at Sorø Academy (1748–49). One of first in Germany to appreciate Shakespeare in *Vergleichung Shakespears und Andreas Gryphs* (1741). Author of tragedies as *Canut* (1743), and comedies as *Der geschäftige Müssiggänger* (1741), *Die stumme Schönheit* (1747), *Der Triumph der guten Frauen* (1748).

Schlei·cher \'shlī-k̲ər\, August. 1821–1868. German philologist. Professor at Prague (1850–57) and Jena (1857–68); applied Darwin's theory of natural selection to linguistics and devised the *Stammbaumtheorie* (family tree theory) of language; in chief work *Compendium der vergleichenden Grammatik der indogermanischen Sprachen* (1861–62) studied common characteristics of languages and attempted to reconstruct the proto-Indo-European parent language. Also wrote *Handbuch der litauischen Sprache* (1856–57), first scientific description and analysis of Lithuanian.

Schleicher, Kurt von. 1882–1934. German soldier and politician. Joined army (1900); with Reichswehr (from 1919); lieutenant general (1931). Appointed minister of defense (1932) and chancellor of Germany (Dec. 1932–Jan. 1933) until succeeded by Adolf Hitler and the Nazi regime. Murdered by Hitler's SS during the "night of the long knives."

Schlei·den \'shlī-dən\, Matthias Jakob. 1804–1881. German botanist. Professor at Jena (1839–62) and Dorpat (1863). Cofounder (with Theodor Schwann) of the cell theory, which he proposed in "Beiträge zur Phytogenesis" (1838); recognized importance of the cell nucleus and its connection with cell division; one of first German biologists to accept Darwin's theory of evolution; a successful popularizer of science.

Schlei·er·ma·cher \'shlī-ər-,mäk-ər\, Friedrich Ernst Daniel. 1768–1834. German theologian and philosopher. Considered founder of modern Protestant theology. Professor at Halle (1804–07) and Berlin (1810–34). Among his works were *Reden über die Religion* (1799), *Kurze Darstellung des theologischen Studiums* (1811), *Der christliche Glaube* (1821–22; 2d ed., revised 1830–31), and a translation of Plato's works (1804–28).

Schlemihl, Peter. See Ludwig THOMA.

Schlem·mer \'shlem-ər\, Oskar. 1888–1943. German painter. Instructor at the Bauhaus (1919–33); known for his costume and stage designs for ballet and modern dance.

Schlesinger. See also Bruno WALTER.

Schle·sing·er \'shlā-ziŋ-ər\, Arthur Meier. 1888–1965. American historian, b. Xenia, Ohio. Professor at Ohio St. (1912–19), U. of Iowa (1919–24), Harvard (1924–54). Wrote on American social and urban developments, including *The Colonial Merchants and the American Revolution, 1763–1776* (1918), *New Viewpoints in American History* (1922), *The Rise of the City, 1878–1898* (1933), *The American Reformer* (1950), etc.; with Dixon R. Fox edited *A History of American Life* (1928–43).

Schles·in·ger \'sles-iŋ-(g)ər\, Frank. 1871–1943. American astronomer, b. New York City. At Yerkes Observatory, U. of Chicago (1903–05); director, Allegheny Observatory, U. of Pittsburgh (1905–20) and Yale observatory (1920–41). Pioneered use of photography to map stellar positions and to measure stellar parallaxes; published *General Catalogue of Parallaxes* (1924).

Schlesinger, Hermann Irving. 1882–1960. American chemist, b. Minneapolis. Professor at U. of Chicago (1908–58); with Anton Burg developed a method of producing diborane (1931); made advancements in the chemistry of borohydrides and related compounds.

Schleswig-Holstein-Sönderborg-Glücksburg. See OLDENBURG, 4.

Schley \'slī\, Winfield Scott. 1839–1909. American naval officer, b. Frederick Co., Md. Commanded rescue expedition in Arctic (1884) searching for Lieut. Greely; second to Adm. William T. Sampson in commanding naval force blockading Santiago de Cuba (1898); because of Sampson's absence from the spot at time of emergence of Spanish fleet, directed action resulting in destruction of that fleet (July 3, 1898); central figure in controversy over assignment of credit for American victory. Rear admiral (1899).

Schley·er \'shlī-ər\, Johann Martin. 1831–1912. German clergyman and linguistic scholar. Inventor of Volapük (first published 1880).

Schlich \'shlik\, Sir William. 1840–1925. British forester, b. Germany. Naturalized in England (1886); organized first school of forestry in England (1885), transferred to Oxford U. (1905); professor, Oxford (1905–19). Author of *A Manual of Forestry* (1889–96), *Forestry in the United Kingdom* (1904), etc.

Schlick \'shlik\, Moritz, *in full* Friedrich Albert Moritz. 1882–1936. German philosopher. Professor at Vienna (1922–36); a Logical Empirist; a leader of group of Positivist philosophers known as the Vienna Circle; insisted on an individual's private experience as the ultimate test of the truth of any assertion of fact. Author of *Raum und Zeit in der gegenwärtigen Physik* (1917), *Allgemeine Erkenntnislehre* (1918), *Fragen der Ethik* (1930), *Grundzüge der Naturphilosophie* (1948), *Natur und Kultur* (1952).

Schlief·fen \'shlē-fən\, Alfred von. Graf. 1833–1913. German soldier. Chief of general staff (1891–1905); field marshal (1911); drew up what was known as the "swinging door" plan (Schlieffen plan) for a war against France, by which a northern army and a southern army were to swing around a central "hinge" and crush French resistance.

Schlie·mann \'shlē-,män\, Heinrich. 1822–1890. German archaeologist. Often considered modern discoverer of prehistoric Greece. Amassed fortune in trading business in St. Petersburg (1846–58); devoted himself thereafter to archaeology. Conducted excavations (1871) at Hisarlik in Turkey, which he believed to be ruins of ancient Troy; excavated and explored remains in Boeotia (1874–76), Mycenae (1876), Tiryns (1884). Among his works were *Ithaka, der Peloponnes und Troja* (1869), *Trojanische Altertümer* (1874), *Troja und seine Ruinen* (1875), *Mykenä* (1878), *Ilios* (1881), *Orchomenos* (1881), *Troja* (1883), *Tiryns* (1886).

Schlos·ser \'shlȯs-ər\, Friedrich Christoph. 1776–1861. German historian. Professor at Heidelberg (1817–61). Author of *Geschichte des 18. Jahrhunderts und des 19. bis zum Sturz des französischen Kaiser Reichs* (1836–48), *Weltgeschichte für das deutsche Volk* (1843–57).

Schlö·zer \'shlœt-sər\, August Ludwig von. 1735–1809. German historian. Tutor and lecturer in Stockholm, St. Petersburg, Göttingen. Chief works *Vorstellung seiner Universalhistorie* (1772), *Vorbereitung zur Weltgeschichte für Kinder* (1779).

Schlum·ber·ger \shlœⁿ-ber-zhā\, François-Conrad (1878–1936) and his brother Marcel (1884–1953). French geophysicists and petroleum geologists. Developed first geophysical method of detecting nonmagnetic ore deposits (1913); conducted first large-scale petroleum survey in Romania (1923); invented a method of continuous electric logging of boreholes (1928). Also developed an oil well recording thermometer and began the Schlumberger Well Surveying Corp.

Schlü·ter \'shlü-tər\, Andreas. 1664–1714. German sculptor and architect. Greatest native master of the late Baroque style in Germany. Court sculptor to Elector Frederick III (from 1694). Chief architect (1699–1706) of the royal palace in Berlin; among his sculptures were the bronze statue of Frederick III (1696–97) and the equestrian statue of the great Elector Frederick William in Berlin (completed 1703).

Schmer·ling \'shmer-liŋ\, Anton von. Ritter. 1805–1893. Austrian jurist and politician. Imperial minister of justice (1849–51) and of the interior (1860–65); chief author of the "February Patent" (1861) that established the Reichsrat; first president of Austrian Supreme Court (1865–91).

Schmid \'shmit\, Eduard. *Pseudonym* Kasimir Ed·schmid \'ed-,shmit\. 1890–1966. German writer. A leader of Expressionist movement; novels included *Die achatnen Kugeln* (1920), *Die Engel mit dem Spleen* (1923), *Sport um Gagaly* (1928), *Lord Byron* (1929), *Deutsches Schicksal* (1932), *Das Südreich* (1933), *Das gute Recht* (1946), *Der Zauberfaden* (1949), *Drei Kronen für Rico* (1954), *Whisky für Algerien?* (1964).

Schmidt \'shmit\, Bernhard Voldemar. 1879–1935. German optical instrument maker, b. Estonia. Telegraph operator, photographer, designer (to 1898); established an observatory and optical workshop in Mittweida (to 1926); on staff of Hamburg observatory, Bergedorf (from 1926). Designed (1929) a telescope without a coma (Schmidt camera) used to photograph large sections of the sky.

Schmidt, Johann Kaspar. *Pseudonym* Max Stir·ner \'shtir-nər\. 1806–1856. German philosopher. Made living as a translator, esp. of Adam Smith's *Wealth of Nations;* author of *Der Einzige und sein Eigentum* (1845) and other works which inspired many 19th- and 20th-century anarchists.

Schmidt, Johannes. 1843–1901. German philologist. Professor at Graz and (from 1876) Berlin. In *Die Verwandtschaftsverhältnisse der indogermanische Sprachen* (1872) criticized Schleicher's "family-tree" theory of linguistic change and proposed a "wave" theory (Wellentheorie).

Schmidt, Otto Ernst. *Pseudonym* Otto Ernst \'ernst\. 1862–1926. German writer. His plays included *Die grösste Sünde* (1895), *Jugend von Heute* (1899), *Bannermann* (1904); his fiction, *Kartäusergeschichten* (1895), *Semper der Jüngling* (1907), *Semper der Mann* (1916); his essays, *Nietzsche, der falsche Prophet* (1914), etc.

Schmidt, Wilhelm. 1868–1954. German anthropologist. Ordained Roman Catholic priest (1892); member of Society of the Divine Word missionary order; founded journal *Anthropos* (1906). Leader of the cultural-historical European school of ethnology; studied evolution of the family; applied Fritz Graebner's culture diffusion principle on a worldwide basis. Chief works *Der Ursprung der Gottesidee* (1912–55), *Ursprung und Werden der Religion* (1930).

Schmidt-Rott·luff \-'rȯt-lůf\, Karl. *Also called* Karl Schmidt. 1884–1976. German painter. With Ernst Kirchner and Erich Heckel formed Expressionist group Die Brücke in Dresden (1905); moved to Berlin (1911); influenced by Cubism and African sculpture (after 1912); forbidden to paint when Nazis gained power; resumed painting and teaching after World War II. Known esp. for his landscapes and nudes employing harsh colors and jagged forms. His canvases included *Self-Portrait* (1906), *Windy Day* (1907), *Self-Portrait with Monocle* (1910), *Rising Moon* (1912), *Dahlias in a Vase* (1912), *Self-Portrait with a Hat* (1919); woodcuts included *Woman with Hat* (1905), *Head of Christ* (1918), *Two Heads* (1918).

Schmitt \shmēt\, Florent. 1870–1958. French composer. Pupil of Massenet and Fauré; won Prix de Rome with lyric scene *Sémiramis* (1900); gained fame with *Psaume XLVI* for chorus and orchestra (1904), ballet *La Tragédie de Salomé* (1907), and a piano quintet (1908). Also known for orchestral works *Antoine et Cléopâtre* (1920), *Mirages* (1920–21), *Salammbô* (1925), piano duet *Reflets d'Allemagne* (1905), quartets for woodwinds and brass, and choral works.

Schmitz \'shmits\, Ettore. *Pseudonym* Italo Sve·vo \'svā-vō\. 1861–1928. Italian novelist. A pioneer of the psychological novel in Italy; befriended and encouraged by James Joyce (from 1907), also championed by Eugenio Montale. His novels included *Una vita* (1892), *Senilità* (1898), and *La coscienza di Zeno* (1923); also short-story collections *La novella del buon e la bella fanciulla* (1930) and *Corto viaggio sentimentale* (1949) and plays.

Schmol·ler \'shmōl-ər\, Gustav von. 1838–1917. German economist. Leader of a school of economic history which described the triumphs of the Bismarckian state; professor, Halle (1864), Strassburg (1872), Berlin (1882); member of Prussian upper house (1899). Among his works were *Grundriss der allgemeinen Volkswirtschaftslehre* (1900–04), *Die soziale Frage* (1918).

Schmuck·er \'shmək-ər\, Samuel Simon. 1799–1873. American theologian and educator, b. Hagerstown, Md. Helped establish General Synod of Lutheran churches (1820); ordained (1821); a founder of, and first professor in, Gettysburg Theol. Sem. (1826–64); a founder and first president of Gettysburg College (1832–34); leader of the low-church Lutheran party in America. Unsuccessfully attempted to revise the Augsburg Confession with *Definite Synodical Platform* (1855); also wrote *Elements of Popular Theology* (1834) and *The Unity of Christ's Church* (1870).

Schna·bel \'shnäb-əl\, Artur. 1882–1951. American pianist, b. Lipnik, Austria. Made debut in Vienna (1890), in U.S. (1921); specialized in Beethoven, Brahms, Schubert; to U.S. (1939, naturalized 1944). Composed numerous works for piano, orchestra, voice; edited and recorded Beethoven's piano sonatas. Wrote *Reflections on Music* (1933), *Music and the Line of Most Resistance* (1942).

Schnabel, Johann Gottfried. *Pseudonym* Gi·san·der \gē-'zän-dər\. 1692–?1750. German writer. Known esp. for his imitations of *Robinson Crusoe,* as in *Die Insel Felsenburg* (1731–43).

Schnei·der \'shnī-dər\, *later* **Schnit·ter** \'shnit-ər\, Johann. *Lat.* Johann Agri·co·la \ə-'grik-ə-lə\. *Also called* Magister Is·le·bi·us \is-'lē-bē-əs\. 1494–1566. German Protestant reformer. Disciple of Luther at Wittenberg; later a proponent of Antinomianism, opposing Melanchthon and Luther; court preacher to Joachim II of Brandenburg (1540); helped draft Augsburg Interim (1548) settlement between Protestants and Catholics; published collections of German proverbs (1528, 1529, 1548).

Schneider, Johann Christian Friedrich. 1786–1853. German composer and conductor. Composer of 7 operas, 15 oratorios, 25 cantatas, 13 Psalms, 5 hymns, 23 symphonies, many overtures, piano sonatas, choral works, and songs.

Schnei·der \shnā-der, *Angl* 'shnīd-ər\, Joseph-Eugène. 1805–1875. French industrialist. With his brother ¶Adolphe (1802–1845) organized company and bought (1836) ironworks at Le Creusot, which he later developed into largest steel-manufacturing and munitions plant in the world; his firm built first steam locomotive (1838) and first river steamboat (1840) in France. Elected deputy (1845); president of Corps Législatif (1867–70). His grandson ¶Charles-Prosper-Eugène (1868–1942) directed the firm during World War I.

Schneir·la \'shnī(ə)r-lə\, Theodore Christian. 1902–1968. American animal psychologist, b. Bay City, Mich. Taught at N.Y.U. (1928–68); associate curator (1942–47), curator (1947–68) of animal behavior, American Museum of Natural History. Made pioneering studies on behavior patterns of army ants; author of "Studies on Army Ants in Panama" (1933), *Principles of Animal Psychology* (1935), *Recent Experiments in Psychology* (1938).

Schnit·ger \'shnit-gər\, Arp. 1648–1719. German organ builder. Worked in Neuenfelde (from 1679); built c.150 organs in the northern Lutheran style characterized by a clear and transparent sound; among best was organ at St. Jakobi's Church, Hamburg (1688–93), often played by Bach.

Schnitter, Johann. See Johann SCHNEIDER.

Schnitzer, Eduard. See EMIN PAŞA.

Schnitz·ler \'shnits-lər\, Arthur. 1862–1931. Austrian physician, playwright, and novelist. Practiced in Vienna (from 1885). Known for psychological dramas that dissected turn-of-the-century Viennese bourgeois life, including *Anatol* (1893), *Liebelei* (1896), *Freiwild* (1896), *Reigen* (1897), *Professor Bernhardi* (1912); also wrote novels as *Leutnant Gustl* (1901), *Der Weg ins Freie* (1908), *Flucht in die Finsternis* (1931), and collections of short stories as *Doktor Gräsler, Badearzt* (1916), *Casanovas Heimfahrt* (1918), *Fräulein Else* (1924), *Traumnovelle* (1926).

Schnorr von Ca·rols·feld \'shnōr-fōn-'kär-ōls-,felt\, Julius. 1794–1872. German painter. In Rome (1818–25) associated with the Nazarenes; helped decorate Villa Massimo in Rome with frescoes after Ariosto. In service of Ludwig I in Munich (from 1825); continued painting frescoes in Germany; designed windows for Glasgow cathedral and St. Paul's in London; published *Picture Bible* (1852–60) with 200 woodcuts.

Scho·ber \'shō-bər\, Johann. 1874–1932. Austrian politician. In Austrian imperial police service (from 1898; president 1918–21, 1922–29). Chancellor of Austria (1921–22, 1929–30); signed Treaty of Lány with Czechoslovakia (1921); vice chancellor and minister of foreign affairs (1930–1932).

Scho·bert \'shō-bərt\, Johann. c.1735–1767. German harpsichordist and composer. Wrote sonatas, concertos, and chamber symphonies.

Schoeck \'shœk\, Othmar. 1886–1957. Swiss composer. Conductor of symphony concerts at Sankt Gallen (1917–44). Composer of operas, orchestral and choral works, chamber music, and esp. song cycles, including *Elegie* (1922–23, on poems of Lenau and Eichendorff), *Gaselen* (1923, on poems of G. Keller), and *Wandersprüche* (1928, on poems of Eichendorff).

Schoen·berg \'shœ̄n-,berk, *Angl* 'shə(r)n-,bərg\, Arnold Franz Walter. *Orig.* Schön·berg. 1874–1951. American composer, b. Vienna. Pupil and friend of Alexander von Zemlinsky, whose sister Mathilde he married (1901; d. 1923); befriended and encouraged by Mahler (from 1903); taught in Vienna (esp. Berg and Webern) and in Berlin at Prussian Academy of Arts (1925–33); dismissed for Jewish faith and moved to U.S. (1933, naturalized 1941); taught at U.C.L.A. (1936–44). One of the foremost composers of the 20th century. First to use atonal method of composition (1908); invented (1921) a 12-tone method which he often employed thereafter. His compositions included operas *Von Heute auf Morgen* (1924), *Moses und Aron* (1930–32, unfinished); orchestral works as *Pelleas und Melisande* (1902–03), 2 *Chamber Symphonies* (1906, 1939), *Five Orchestral Pieces* (1909), *Variations for Orchestra* (1928), concertos for violin (1934–36) and piano (1942); vocal music as *Gurrelieder* (1900–11), *Pierrot Lunaire* (1912), *Die Jakobsleiter* (1917, unfinished), *Ode to Napoleon Buonaparte* (1942), *A Survivor from Warsaw* (1947); songs; and chamber music, esp. the string sextet *Verklärte Nacht* (1899; orchestrated 1917, 1943).

Schoen·hei·mer \'shœ̄n-,hī-mər\, Rudolf. 1898–1941. German biochemist. Taught at Freiburg (1926–33) and Columbia U. (1933–41). With David Rittenberg developed (from 1934) technique of "tagging" molecules with radioactive isotopes to trace paths of organic substances through plants and animals, thus revolutionizing metabolic studies; also studied relation of cholesterol to atherosclerosis.

Schöf·fer *or* **Schoef·fer** \'shœf-ər\, Peter. 1425?–1502. German printer. With father-in-law Johann Fust founded first commercially successful printing firm (1456); probably first to use a title page (1463) and one of first to cast metal type; signed an early *Psalter* (1457; sometimes attributed to Gutenberg) which included paragraphs beginning with ornamental capital letters printed in two colors.

Scho·field \'skō-,fēld\, John McAllister. 1831–1906. American army officer, b. Gerry, N.Y. Brigadier general of volunteers (1861); major general (1863); army commander in Sherman's Atlanta campaign (1864); defeated Hood in battles of Franklin and Nashville; commander, department of North Carolina (1865). U.S. secretary of war (1868–69). Major general, U.S. army, commanding department of the Missouri (1869), division of the Pacific (1870–76, 1882–83), division of the Missouri (1883–86), division of the Atlantic (1886–88). Superintendent, U.S.M.A., West Point (1876–81). General in chief, U.S. army (1888–95). Lieutenant general (1895); retired (1895).

Scholarios. See GENNADIUS II SCHOLARIOS.

Schol·laert \'sk̲ōl-ärt\, François. 1851–1917. Belgian politician. Prime minister (1908–11); took over Congo Free State and made it a province of Belgium under name of Belgian Congo.

Schom·berg \'shōm-,berk, *Angl* 'shäm-,bərg\ *or* **Schön·berg** \'shœ̄n-,berk\, Friedrich Hermann. Duke of Schomberg (*cr. 1689, in English peerage*). 1615–1690. German soldier of fortune. Served under Prince of Orange (1633), in Swedish army in Germany (1634), in Dutch army (1639–50), in French army (from 1650), in Portuguese service (1660–68); executed a palace coup that made Dom Pedro regent of Portugal (1668). Naturalized in France (1668); French marshal (1675); left France after revocation of Edict of Nantes (1685); general in chief of Brandenburg army (1687). Accompanied William of Orange to England (1688) as second in command; naturalized in England (1689); commanded expedition to Ireland against James II (1689–90); killed at Battle of the Boyne.

Schom·berg \shōm-berg\, Gaspard de. Comte de Nan·teuil \naⁿ-tœy\. 1540–1599. French soldier, b. Germany. Naturalized in France (1570); distinguished himself at Moncontour (1569) and Dormans (1575); honored by Henry III and Henry IV; councilor in charge of administration of finance under Henry IV. His son ¶Henri, marquis d'Es·pi·nay \dā-pē-ne\ (1575–1632), marshal of France (1625), aided in siege of La Rochelle (1628) and fought in Lorraine (1631). Henri's son ¶Charles, duc d'Hal·lu·in \dȧ-lu̅e̅-aⁿ\ (1601–1656), was governor of Languedoc (1632–44), marshal of France (1637), viceroy of Catalonia (1648).

Schom·burgk \'shäm-,bərk, *Ger* 'shōm-,bu̇rk\, Sir Robert Hermann. 1804–1865. British explorer. Surveyed Anegada in British Virgin Islands (1831); made geographical and botanical exploration of British Guiana, on which he discovered the victoria regia lily (1835); surveyed boundaries of British Guiana, establishing Schomburgk line (1841–43); consul to Santo Domingo (1848) and Bangkok (1857–64); published *Description of British Guiana* (1840).

Schön·bein \'shœ̄n-,bīn\, Christian Friedrich. 1799–1868. German chemist. Professor at Basel (1835–68); discovered ozone (1839); first to produce guncotton (1845) and from it collodion; also made researches on passivity of iron, properties of hydrogen peroxide, and catalysis.

Schönberg. See (1) Friedrich SCHOMBERG; (2) Arnold SCHOENBERG.

Schön·born \'shœn-ˌbȯrn\, Friedrich Karl von. Graf. 1674–1746. German prince-prelate. Vice chancellor of Holy Roman Empire (1705–34); supported interests of small German states; successfully opposed attempted intrusions of Prussia into southern Germany; sided with Joseph I against papal Curia. Bishop of Bamberg and Würzburg (1729–46); made administrative and financial reforms; raised academy at Bamberg to university status (1735).

Schönborn, Johann Philipp von. 1605–1673. German prince-prelate. Bishop of Würzburg (1642) and Worms (1663); imperial elector and archbishop of Mainz (1647); organized German Protestant and Catholic princes into a Rheinbund (Confederation of the Rhine) to preserve the Peace of Westphalia (1648) and to assist Leopold I against France and Sweden; appointed Leibniz as his resident adviser (1669–72).

Schö·ne·mann \'shœ-nə-ˌmän\, Anna Elisabeth, *known as* Lili. 1758–1817. German woman. Beloved by Goethe (c.1774) and central figure, under name Lili, in Goethe's lyrics of this period; later married the Strasbourg banker Bernhard von Türckheim (d. 1831).

Schö·ner \'shœ-nər\, Johannes. 1477–1547. German astronomer and geographer. Author of numerous mathematical, astronomical, and geographical works; made terrestrial globes, including the first (1515) using the name "America."

Schö·ner·er \'shœ-nə-rər\, Georg von. Ritter. 1842–1921. Austrian politician. Elected to Reichsrat (1873, 1897); founded Pan-German party (1885); popularly credited with driving Prime Minister Badeni from office (1897); associated with anti-Catholic Los von Rom movement (from 1898); a virulent anti-Semite and nationalist.

Schön·feld \'shœn-ˌfelt\, Eduard. 1828–1891. German astronomer. Director of observatory of Mannheim (1859–75), Bonn (1875–91). Assisted Argelander (*q.v.*) in the preparation of *Bonner Durchmusterung,* a catalogue of stars of the Northern Hemisphere to the 9th magnitude, and later extended the catalogue to 23° south declination; also observed nebulae, variable stars, and comets.

Schon·gau·er \'shōn-ˌgau̇-ər\, Martin. *Also known as* Martin Schön \'shœn\ *and* Hipsch *or* Hübsch Mar·tin \'mär-(ˌ)tēn\. 1445 or 1450–1491. German engraver and painter. Worked mainly in Colmar; influenced by Rogier van der Weyden; chief painting, *Madonna in a Rose Garden* (1473), altarpiece of Church of Saint-Martin in Colmar; also executed two wings of the Orliac altar and murals of *Last Judgment* in Breisach cathedral. As an engraver, reputed the greatest of 15th-century northern Europe; brought art of engraving to its maturity by expanding its range of contrasts and textures; his c.115 plates included *Death of the Virgin, Madonna in a Courtyard, St. Sebastian.*

Schön·herr \'shœn-ˌher\, Karl. 1867–1943. Austrian playwright. Influenced by Ibsen; author of plays about problems of the medical profession, the middle class, and esp. peasant life, including *Judas von Tirol* (1897), *Die Bildschnitzer* (1900), *Erde* (1908), *Glaube und Heimat* (1910), *Volk in Not* (1916), *Vivat academia* (1922), *Es* (1923), *Die Hungerblockade* (1925).

Schön·lein \'shœn-ˌlīn\, Johann Lukas. 1793–1864. German physician. Professor at Würzburg (1824–33), Zürich (1833–40), Berlin (1840–59). First to use the microscope in conjunction with urine and blood analyses to diagnose disease; pioneer in clinical method of teaching medicine; coined term hemophilia (1828); first to describe purpura rheumatica (1837, hence called Schönlein's disease); discovered fungus causing favus (1839).

School·craft \'skül-ˌkraft\, Henry Rowe. 1793–1864. American explorer and ethnologist, b. Albany Co., N.Y. Explored mineral deposits of southern Missouri and Arkansas (1817–18); with Cass exploring expedition to Lake Superior region (1820). Indian agent in Lake Superior region (1822–36); superintendent of Indian affairs for Michigan (1836–41). Discovered source of Mississippi River at Lake Itasca, Minn. (1832); concluded treaty in which Ojibwa tribe ceded much of northern Michigan to U.S. (1836). Author of ethnological works *Algic Researches* (1839, basis of Longfellow's *Hiawatha*) and *Historical and Statistical Information Respecting the History, Condition, and Prospects of the Indian Tribes of the United States* (1851–57).

Scho·pen·hau·er \'shō-pən-ˌhau̇(-ə)r\, Arthur. 1788–1860. German philosopher. Resident in Frankfurt (from 1831); chief expounder of pessimism and of the irrational impulses of life arising from the will. His works included *Über die vierfache Wurzel des Satzes vom zureichenden Grunde* (1813), *Die Welt als Wille und Vorstellung* (1819), *Über den Willen in der Natur* (1836), *Die beiden Grundprobleme der Ethik* (1841), *Paregra und Paralipomena* (1851). His mother ¶Johanna, *nee* Tro·sie·ner \'trō-ˌzē-nər\ (1766–1838), was a writer of short stories, novels, and books of travel.

Schott \'shät\, Charles Anthony. 1826–1901. American geodesist, b. Mannheim, Germany. To U.S. (1848, naturalized 1853); on staff of U.S. Coast Survey (1848–1900); known esp. for researches in geodesy and terrestrial magnetism.

Schott·ky \'shȯt-kē\, Walter Hans. 1886–1976. German physicist. Professor at Rostock; made researches into the theory of electrons and ions, and the problem of electroacoustics; invented the screen-grid tube (1915); discovered an irregularity in the emission of thermions in a vacuum tube, the Schottky effect.

Schou·ten \'skau̇-tən\, Willem Corneliszoon. c.1580–1625. Dutch mariner. In service of East India Co.; first to traverse the Drake Passage (1615); discovered Cape Horn (1616); first European to sight the Schouten Islands.

Schrei·ber \'shrī-bər\, Moses ben Samuel. *Also known as* Moses So·fer \'zō-fər\. 1763–1839. German rabbi. A leading Orthodox rabbi and Halakist of his day; founded (c.1803) at Pressburg a prestigious yeshiva that became the center of vigorous opposition to Reform Judaism. His many works included *Hatam Sofer* (1855–64) and *Torat Mosheh* (1879–93).

Schrei·ner \'shrī-nər\, Olive Emilie Albertina. *Pseudonym* Ralph Iron \'ī(-ə)rn\. 1855–1920. South African novelist and feminist. Governess (1874–81); scored success with *The Story of an African Farm* (1883); other novels *Trooper Halket of Mashonaland* (1897), *From Man to Man* (1926, unfinished), *Undine* (1928); author also of works on politics and emancipation of women, esp. *Woman and Labour* (1911); correspondent of Havelock Ellis (1884–1917). Her brother ¶William Philip (1857–1919) was prime minister of Cape Colony (1898–1900); unsuccessfully tried to prevent South African War; later a champion of African civil rights.

Schre·ker \'shrā-kər\, Franz. 1878–1934. Austrian composer. Known for operas *Der ferne Klang* (1912), *Die Gezeichneten* (1918), and *Der Schatzgräber* (1920).

Schrie·ke \'skrē-kə\, Bertram. 1890–1945. Dutch social anthropologist. Professor at Batavia, Java (1924–29), and adviser to Netherlands Indies government on Indonesian and Arab affairs; professor at Amsterdam (1936–45) and head of ethnology for Royal Colonial Institute. Known for studies of early Indonesian economic and social history, cultural change, and foreign relations.

Schrö·der \'shrœ-dər\, Carl. 1848–1935. German composer and conductor. Court Kapellmeister, Sondershausen (1881), and founder of a conservatory of music there; instructor in Stern Conservatory of Music, Berlin (1911–21); composer of operas, symphonies, and vocal, piano, and violoncello pieces.

Schröder, Friedrich Ludwig. 1744–1816. German actor, theater manager, and playwright. Began as child actor in the company of his stepfather Konrad Ackermann (*q.v.*); manager of Hamburg National Theater (1771–80, 1785–98) and of Vienna Burgtheater (1780–84); first to bring Shakespeare to the German stage; also staged his own plays and those of Goethe, Klinger, Lillo, etc.; one of leading actors of his day.

Schrö·ding·er \'shrœ-diŋ-ər\, Erwin. 1887–1961. Austrian physicist. Professor at Zürich (1921–27) and Berlin (1927–33); with Dublin Inst. for Advanced Studies (1940–56). Developed (1926) the Schrödinger equation that describes wavelike behavior of subatomic particles and is the basic equation of quantum mechanics; with Paul Dirac won Nobel prize for physics (1933). Wrote *What Is Life?* (1944), *Nature and the Greeks* (1954), *Meine Weltansicht* (1961).

Schu·bart \'shü-ˌbärt\, Christian Friedrich Daniel. 1739–1791. German musician and poet. Founded *Deutsche Chronik,* Augsburg (1774); imprisoned by Duke of Württemberg (1777–87); under patronage of Frederick the Great (1787); music director of the court and theater in Stuttgart. Among his best poems were "Die Fürstengruft," "Kaplied," "Friedrich der Grosse."

Schu·bert \'shü-bərt, -ˌbert\, Franz Peter. 1797–1828. Austrian composer. Music teacher in Vienna (1814–18); set (1814) Goethe's poem "Gretchen am Spinnrade" to music, thus creating the German lied; noted for the melody and harmony in his songs and chamber music. His compositions included operas and operettas as *Die Zwillingsbrüder* (1818–19), *Der häusliche Krieg* (1823); 9 symphonies, esp. the *Unfinished* (1822), the *Great* (1828); choral music, including 7 masses and 3 cantatas; chamber music, including 22 string quartets, *String Quintet in C Major* (1828), *Piano Quintet in A Major* ("The Trout", 1819); piano works as 21 sonatas and 6 *Moments musicaux;* and over 500 songs, including song cycles *Die schöne Müllerin* (1823), *Winterreise* (1827), *Schwanengesang* (1828), and individual songs "Erlkönig," "Die junge Nonne," "Die Allmacht," "Das Heimweh," and "Der Tod und das Mädchen."

Schu·chardt \'shu̇k-ˌärt\, Hugo. 1842–1927. German philologist. Professor at Graz (1876–1900); author of *Romanisches und Keltisches* (1886), *Baskisch und Romanische* (1906), etc.

Schuch·ert \'shu̇k-ərt\, Charles. 1858–1942. American paleontologist, b. Cincinnati. A leader in development of paleogeography. Curator of U.S. National Museum (1894–1904); professor, Yale (1904–23). Author of *Textbook of Historical Geological Paleogeography of North America* (1910), *The Earth and Its Rhythms* (1927).

Schück \'shuek\, Johan Henrik Emil. 1855–1947. Swedish historian of literature. Professor, Lund (1890–98), Uppsala (1898–1920); president, Nobel Foundation (from 1918). Chief works *Illustrerad svensk litteraturhistoria* (1896–97), *Svenska folkets historia* (1914–15).

Schück·ing \'shuek-iŋ\, Levin. 1814–1883. German journalist and novelist. On editorial staff of *Allgemeine Zeitung,* Augsburg (1843–45), and *Kölnischen Zeitung* (1845–52). Influenced by Sir Walter Scott; author of popular novels with Westphalian settings, including *Die Ritterbürtigen* (1846), *Ein Sohn des Volks* (1849), *Der Bauernfürst* (1851), *Die Herberge der Gerechtigkeit* (1879).

Schul·te \'shu̇l-tə\, Johann Friedrich von. 1827–1914. German scholar. Professor, Prague (1854–73), Bonn (1873–1914); opposed doctrine of papal infallibility and became (from 1870) a leader among Old Catholics; regarded as an authority on canon law.

Schultheiss, Michael. See PRAETORIUS.

Schult·hess \'shu̇lt-ˌhes\, Edmund. 1868–1944. Swiss politician. President of Swiss Confederation for regular one-year terms (1917, 1921, 1928, 1933).

Schultz, Dutch. See FLEGENHEIMER.

Schult·ze \'shu̇lt-sē\, Carl Emil. *Pseudonym* Bun·ny \'bən-ē\. 1866–1939. American cartoonist, b. Lexington, Ky. Originated "Foxy Grandpa" comic strip, which appeared in New York *Herald* (1900–02) and in New York *American* (from 1902).

Schult·ze \'shu̇lt-sə\, Max Johann Sigismund. 1825–1874. German zoologist and cytologist. Professor (1859–74) at Bonn and director (1872–74) of the Anatomical Institute there; founder and editor (1865–74) of *Archiv für mikroskopische Anatomie.* Known esp. for researches in microscopic anatomy; altered the conception of the cell, emphasizing the living protoplasm and not the membrane (1861); recognized the protoplasm with its nucleus as the fundamental substance of both plants and animals; demonstrated minute nerve endings in the ear (1858), nose (1863), and retina (1866); introduced new techniques in histology, esp. use of osmic acid for staining fine details of cells.

Schul·ze \'shu̇lt-sə\, Alfred Otto Wolfgang. *Pseudonym* Wols \'vȯls\. 1913–1951. French painter, b. Berlin. Settled in Paris (1932); known for *art informel* or *art autre,* abstract improvisations of blots and fine lines, often in watercolors.

Schulze, Gottlob Ernst. *Pen name* Schulze-Ae·ne·si·de·mus \-ˌen-ä-zē-'dā-məs\. 1761–1833. German philosopher. A Skeptic and critic of Kant; professor at Wittenberg, Helmstadt (1788–1810), Göttingen (1810–33). Author of *Grundriss der philosophischen Wissenschaften* (1788–90), *Über die menschliche Erkenntnis* (1832), etc.

Schu·ma·cher \'shü-ˌmäk-ər, *Angl* -ˌmäk-, -ˌmāk-\, Ernst Friedrich. 1911–1977. British economist, b. Bonn, Germany. To England (1937); adviser to National Coal Board (1950–70); founder and chairman, Intermediate Technology Development Group (1965–77). In *Small Is Beautiful* (1973) argued for an "intermediate technology" that would result in a lessened economic growth but provide for basic needs; also wrote *Roots of Economic Growth* (1962), *A Guide for the Perplexed* (1977).

Schu·ma·cher \'shü-ˌmäk-ər\, Heinrich Christian. 1780–1850. Danish astronomer. Professor and director, Copenhagen observatory (1815); founded journal *Astronomische Nachrichten* (1823); directed a triangulation of Holstein and a geodetic survey of Denmark.

Schumacher, Peder. Count Grif·fen·feld \'grif-ən-ˌfelt\. 1635–1699. Danish politician. Royal librarian (1662); gained favor of Frederick III and became secretary of the king's chamber; drafted 1665 Kongeloven, a justification of absolutism; rose to high chancellor under Christian V (1674); in foreign policy sought a neutral course; attempted to maintain good relations with France without consulting the king; on Christian V's orders arrested for bribery (1676), tried, and imprisoned for life.

Schu·man \shü-män\, Robert. 1886–1963. French politician. Member of National Assembly (from 1919); a founder of Mouvement Républicain Populaire (1944); minister of finance (1946), foreign affairs (1948–52), justice (1955–56); prime minister (1947–48). Developed (1950) the Schuman Plan to promote European economic and military unity and a Franco-German rapprochement; plan resulted in creation (1952) of European Coal and Steel Community; first president (1958–60) and member (1958–63) of European Parliamentary Assembly.

Schu·mann \'shü-ˌmän\, Clara Josephine, *nee* Wieck \'vēk\. 1819–1896. German pianist and composer. Made concert debut (1828); toured throughout Europe often; m. (1840) Robert Schumann; intimate with Johannes Brahms (from 1853) and influenced his music; taught at Hoch Conservatory, Frankfurt (1878–92); renowned as interpreter of Chopin, Brahms, and her husband; composed songs and works for piano, including a concerto (1836).

Schu·mann \'shü-ˌmän, *Angl* -mən\, Elisabeth. 1885–1952. American soprano, b. Merseburg, Germany. Known for interpretations of lieder and music of Mozart and Richard Strauss. Made debut at Hamburg Opera (1909); took part of Sophie in *Der Rosenkavalier* at Metropolitan Opera, New York (1914); toured U.S. with Strauss (1921); settled in U.S. (1938, naturalized 1944); published *German Song* (1948).

Schumann, Georg Alfred. 1866–1952. German composer and conductor. Director of Berlin Singakademie (from 1900); composer of symphonies, symphonic poems, overtures, choral works, chamber music, organ and piano pieces, and songs.

Schumann, Robert Alexander. 1810–1856. German composer. One of greatest Romantic composers; renowned esp. for piano music and songs. Studied law in Leipzig; founded and edited (1834–44) the musical journal *Die Neue Zeitschrift für Musik;* settled in Dresden (1844); director of music, Düsseldorf (1850–53); committed to an asylum suffering from hallucinations (1854). Composer of opera *Genoveva* (1847–50); 4 symphonies; *Manfred* overture (1849); piano (1841–45) and cello (1850) concertos; choral works, esp. *Das Paradies und die Peri* (1841–43); chamber music, including a quintet and a quartet for piano (both 1842); piano music, esp. *Carnaval* (1834–35), *Phantasiestücke* (1837), *Fantasy in C Major* (1838); and songs, including song-cycles *Dichterliebe, Frauenliebe und Leben,* and 2 *Liederkreis* (all 1840).

Schumann, Victor. 1841–1913. German physicist. Technical director of an engineering firm, Leipzig (1865–93); known for development of photographic plates capable of registering ultraviolet light.

Schu·mann-Heink \'shü-ˌmän-'hīŋk, *Angl* -mən-\, Ernestine[2], *nee* Röss·ler \'rœs-lər\. 1861–1936. American contralto, b. Liben, near Prague, then in Austria. m. Ernst Heink (1882), Paul Schumann (1893). Known for interpretations of operas of Wagner and Richard Strauss and of German lieder. Made debut at Dresden (1879); sang in Wagnerian operas at Bayreuth (1896–1906); with New York Metropolitan Opera (1899–1904); naturalized U.S. citizen (1905); created role of Klytemnestra in *Elektra* (1909); in later years known for radio broadcasts.

Schum·pe·ter \'shu̇m-ˌpāt-ər\, Joseph Alois. 1883–1950. American economist, b. Triesch, Moravia. Austrian finance minister (1919); professor at Bonn (1925–32) and Harvard (1932–50). Known for theories of capitalist development and business cycles. Author of *Theorie der wirtschaftlichen Entwicklung* (1912), *Business Cycles* (1939), *Capitalism, Socialism, and Democracy* (1942), *History of Economic Analysis* (1954).

Schur \'shür\, Friedrich Heinrich. 1856–1932. German mathematician. Professor at Leipzig, Dorpat, Breslau; noted for contributions to analytical geometry. Works included *Lehrbuch der analytischen Geometrie* (1898), *Grundlagen der Geometrie* (1909).

Schur·man \'shu̇(ə)r-mən, 'shər-\, Jacob Gould. 1854–1942. American educator and diplomat, b. Freetown, Prince Edward Island. Professor of philosophy, Cornell (1886–92); president, Cornell (1892–1920). President, first U.S. Philippine commission (1899). U.S. minister to Greece and Montenegro (1912–13); ambassador to China (1921–25) and to Germany (1925–30). Author of *Kantian Ethics and the Ethics of Evolution* (1881), *Agnosticism and Religion* (1886), *The Ethical Import of Darwinism* (1888).

Schurz \'shu̇(ə)rts, 'shərts, 'shərz\, Carl. 1829–1906. American army officer, politician and reformer, b. near Cologne, Germany. Involved in revolutionary movement (1848–49); forced to flee Germany; to U.S. (1852); adm. to bar (1859); practiced in Milwaukee; campaigned for Lincoln (1860); U.S. minister to Spain (1861–62). Brigadier general of volunteers (1862); engaged at Second Bull Run, Chancellorsville, Gettysburg; major general (1863). Journalist (1865–68). U.S. senator from Missouri (1869–75); organized Liberal Republican party (1872) but rejoined Republicans (1876); U.S. secretary of the interior (1877–81). Editor, New York *Evening Post* (1881–83); editorial writer for *Harper's Weekly* (1892–98). President of National Civil Service Reform League (1892–1901). A supporter of high moral standards in government, civil rights, civil service reform, etc. Author of lives of Henry Clay (1887) and Lincoln (1889).

Schusch·nigg \'shu̇sh-(ˌ)nik, -(ˌ)nig\, Kurt von. 1897–1977. Austrian politician. Entered parliament (1927); minister of justice (1932–34) and education (1933–34); federal chancellor (1934–38); disbanded the Heimwehr (1936) and attempted to prevent takeover of Austria by Nazi Germany. Imprisoned by Nazis (1938–45). To U.S. and taught at St. Louis U. (1948–67). Returned to Austria (1967); published *Im Kampf gegen Hitler* (1969).

Schus·ter \'shü-stər\, Sir Arthur. 1851–1934. British physicist. Professor at Manchester (1888–1907); made researches in spectroscopy, esp. relating to the spectra of the solar corona and of the stars; also in calorimetry, radiometry, seismology, and terrestrial magnetism. Author of *A Theory of Optics* (1904), *The Progress of Physics* (1911), etc.

Schu·ster \'shü-stər\, Max Lincoln. 1897–1970. American publisher, b. Kalusz, Austria, of American parents. Cofounder (1924, with Richard Leo Simon, *q.v.*) and partner, Simon and Schuster, book publishers, N.Y. City.

Schütz \'shu̇ets\, Heinrich. *Lat.* Henricus Sa·git·ta·ri·us \zä-gə-'tä-rē-u̇s\. 1585–1672. German composer. Regarded as greatest German composer before Bach. Pupil of Gabrieli in Venice (1609–12); first known work a set of Italian madrigals (1611); Kapellmeister in Dresden to Elector Johann Georg I of Saxony (from 1617), except for visits to Danish court (esp. 1633–35, 1642–44). Introduced the Italian monody style into Germany; wrote first German opera *Daphne* (1627, text by Opitz; nonextant). Composed over 500 works, mainly vocal settings of sacred texts with or without instruments, including *Psalmen Davids* (1619), *Cantiones sacrae* (1625), *Symphoniae sacrae* (1629, 1647,

1650), Requiem *Musikalische Exequien* (1636), *Kleine geistliche Konzerte* (1636, 1639), *Geistliche Chormusik* (1648), *Christmas Oratorio* (1664), and a cappella Passions on texts of Matthew, Luke, and John (1665–66).

Schuy·ler \'skī-lər\, Philip John. 1733–1804. American politician, b. Albany, N.Y. Served (1755–60) in French and Indian War; delegate to Continental Congress (1775); major general, Continental army, commanding northern department; organized expedition (1775–76) to attack Canada; after disagreements with Gen. David Wooster and Gen. Horatio Gates, superseded in his command by Gates (1777); resigned (1779). Member, Continental Congress (1778–81); one of first two U.S. senators from New York (1789–91, 1797–98); strong supporter of financial program of Alexander Hamilton, his son-in-law.

Schwab \'shwäb\, Charles Michael. 1862–1939. American industrialist, b. Williamsburg, Pa. In employ of Carnegie Steel Co., beginning as stake driver in engineering gang; president, Carnegie Steel Co. (1897–1901), U.S. Steel Corp. (1901–03), Bethlehem Steel Corp. (1903–13) and chairman of the board (from 1913). During World War I served as director-general of shipbuilding for U.S. Shipping Board Emergency Fleet Corp. (1918).

Schwab \'shväp\, Gustav Benjamin. 1792–1850. German writer. Published *Der Bodensee* (verse, 1827), a life of Schiller (1840), anthologies of German prose and lyric poetry, and *Schönste Sagen des klassischen Altertums* (1838–40), *Deutsche Volksbücher* (1836–37).

Schwa·be \'shvä-bə\, Samuel Heinrich. 1789–1875. German astronomer. Discovered the periodicity of sunspots (1843); also made (1831) first known detailed drawing of the Great Red Spot on Jupiter.

Schwand·hardt \'shvänd-,härt\, Georg. 1611–1667. German glass engraver. Founder (1622) and leader of the Nürnberg school of glass engraving; work characterized by delicate, tiny landscapes, often with bold formal scrollwork.

Schwann \'shvän\, Theodor Ambrose Hubert. 1810–1882. German physiologist. Professor at Louvain and Liège (1848–79). Founded modern histology by defining the cell in *Mikroskopische Untersuchungen* (1839) as the basic unit of animal structure. Discovered pepsin (1836); investigated muscular contraction and nerve structure; discovered the striated muscle in the upper esophagus and the Schwann sheath; identified role of microorganisms in putrefaction; formulated basic principles of embryology by observing that the egg is a single cell that develops into a complete organism; coined term metabolism.

Schwartz \'shwȯ(ə)rts\, Arthur. 1900–1984. American composer, b. New York City. Collaborated (1928 ff.) with lyricist Howard Dietz (*q.v.*) to bring new sophistication to Broadway songwriting; their Broadway shows included *The Little Show* (1929), *The Bandwagon* (1931), *Flying Colors* (1932), and *Between the Devil* (1935). With Dietz collaborated on film musicals *Thank Your Lucky Stars* (1943), and *The Bandwagon* (1953). Songs included "Dancing in the Dark," "You and the Night and the Music," "Something to Remember You By," and "That's Entertainment."

Schwartz, Delmore. 1913–1966. American writer, b. Brooklyn, N.Y. Taught at Harvard (1940–47); editor for *Partisan Review* (1943–55) and *The New Republic* (1955–57). Called a poet of the city; author of cerebral and difficult books of verse as *In Dreams Begin Responsibilities* (1939), *Shenandoah* (1941, verse play), *Genesis, Book I* (1943), *Vaudeville for a Princess* (1950), *Summer Knowledge* (1959); also short-story collections *The World Is a Wedding* (1948) and *Successful Love* (1961) and literary criticism.

Schwarz \'shvärts\, Berthold. 14th century. German monk and alchemist. Possibly legendary; reputed inventor of gunpowder (c.1313), although now generally accepted that it was already well known in Europe; sometimes credited with being first European to cast bronze cannon.

Schwarz, Hermann Amandus. 1843–1921. German mathematician. Professor, Halle (1867–69), Zürich (1869–75), Göttingen (1875–92), Berlin (1892–1917); worked on the theory of minimal surfaces and of functions.

Schwarzburg-Blankenburg, Graf von. See GÜNTHER.

Schwar·zen·berg \'shvärt-sən-,berk\, Felix zu. Fürst. 1800–1852. Austrian statesman. Entered army (1818) and diplomatic service (1824); minister to Sardinia (1838) and Two Sicilies (1844); protégé of Metternich. Joined Radetzky's army at outbreak of 1848 revolution; prime minister and foreign minister (1848–52). Secured replacement of Ferdinand I by Francis Joseph I (1848); drew up a constitution transforming the Habsburg Empire into a centralized, absolutist state (enacted 1849); crushed insurrections in Hungary and Italy; revived the German Confederation in its old form (1850); caused Francis Joseph to abolish the 1849 constitution (1851), introducing new era of absolutism. Restored Habsburg Empire as a great European power.

Schwarzenberg, Karl Philipp zu. Fürst. 1771–1820. Austrian field marshal and diplomat. Entered army (1787); distinguished himself during War of the Second Coalition (1798–1802), esp. at Hohenlinden (1800). Instituted army reforms; persuaded Alexander I to delay support of France (1809). In command of Austrian contingent in Russia (1812); urged war against Napoléon; made field marshal and commander in chief of Allied forces opposing Napoléon (1813); defeated Napoléon near Leipzig (1813), pushed the French across the Rhine, and directed operations in France that led to final collapse of Napoléon's forces (1814). Head of Hofkriegsrat (1814–17); argued for more easily defensible frontiers for Habsburg Empire.

Schwarzert, Philipp. See MELANCHTHON.

Schwarz·schild \'shvärt-,shilt\, Karl. 1873–1916. German astronomer. Professor and observatory director at Göttingen (1901–09); director of Astrophysical Observatory at Potsdam (1909–14). First to introduce and apply precise methods in photographic photometry; pioneered in use of coarse grating in front of telescope objective; enunciated principle of radiative equilibrium and first to recognize clearly role of radiative processes in transport of heat in stellar atmospheres; developed the ellipsoidal hypothesis of stellar motion. In physics a pioneer in development of atomic spectra theory; independent of Sommerfeld, developed general rules of quantization, gave complete theory of Stark effect, and initiated quantum theory of molecular spectra; gave first exact solution of Einstein's general gravitational equations; developed theories known as Schwarzschild's radius and Schwarzschild singularities.

Schwei·gaard \'shvā-gȯr\, Anton Martin. 1808–1870. Norwegian jurist and economic reformer. Member of the Storting (1842–69); a leader in Norway's transition from a mercantilist-agricultural economy to one of free enterprise; with Frederik Stang responsible for economic reforms as free trade, freedom of choice of occupation, and road and railway development.

Schweig·ger \'shvī-gər\, Johann Salomo Christoph. 1779–1857. German physicist. Professor at Erlangen (1817) and Halle (1819–57); founder and editor (1811–28) of *Journal für Chemie und Physik;* invented the needle galvanometer (1820).

Schwein·furth \'shvīn-,fu̇rt\, Georg August. 1836–1925. German botanist and traveler. Explored (from 1866) the Bahr el Ghazal region; discovered Uele River (1870); proved existence of pygmies in Africa by discovery of Akka dwarfs; lived in Cairo and made scientific studies of Egypt (1875–88).

Schweit·zer \'shvīt-sər, *Angl* 's(h)wīt-sər\, Albert. 1875–1965. French theologian, philosopher, physician, and music scholar, b. Alsace of German descent. Missionary physician and founder of Lambaréné Hospital in French Equatorial Africa (1913). Author of *Von Reimarus zu Wrede* (1906), *Kulturphilosophie* (1923), *Die Mystik des Apostels Paulus* (1930), *Aus meinem Leben und Denken* (1931), *Das Problem des Friedens in der heutigen Welt* (1954), *Friede oder Atomkrieg* (1958), etc. In the field of music, wrote a monograph on J.S. Bach (1905) and (with Widor) published a critical edition of Bach's organ works (1912–14); known as a fine interpreter of Bach's works. Received Nobel prize for peace (1952).

Schwen·de·ner \'shven-də-nər\, Simon. 1829–1919. Swiss botanist. Professor, Basel (1867), Tübingen (1877), Berlin (1878–1919); maintained that lichens are a composite of algae and fungi (1869); set forth a mechanical theory of the development and arrangement of plant tissues and leaves.

Schwenck·feld von Os·sig \'shveŋk-,felt-fȯn-'ō-sik\, Kaspar. 1489–1561. German nobleman and mystic. Experienced a spiritual awakening (1518) and became leader of the Protestant Reformation in Silesia; disagreed (1523) with Luther's views on the Eucharist and founded the Reformation by the Middle Way movement, a course between Catholic and Lutheran theologies; quarrelled with Zwingli (1529); defended his doctrines against Bucer at Strassburg (1533); anathematized by Schmalkaldic League (1534) and became a religious fugitive thereafter. His followers, known as Schwenckfeldians, formed societies that survive in U.S. as Schwenckfeld church.

Schwim·mer \'shvim-mer, *Angl* 'shwim-ər\, Rosika. 1877–1948. Hungarian feminist, pacificist, and author. Organized several women's groups in Hungary, including Hungarian Feminist Assn. (1904); to U.S. (1914) and became a leader of the pacifist movement; instrumental in organization of International Congress of Women at The Hague (1915); to Hungary (1918) but deprived of civil rights and fled (1920); settled in U.S. (from 1921) but was refused citizenship because of pacifist views; formed Campaign for World Government (1937); author of fictive, pacifist, and political works.

Schwind \'shvint\, Moritz von. 1804–1871. German painter. Friend and roommate of Schubert in Vienna; settled in Munich (1826); professor at Munich Academy (1847). Best known for Romantic, lyrical, and detailed pictures of honeymooners, leave-takers, musing wanderers, etc.; also painted a set of historical cartoons for Wartburg castle, a triptych for Church of Our Lady in Munich, and windows of Glasgow cathedral.

Schwit·ters \'shvit-ərs\, Kurt. 1887–1948. German artist and writer. Known for Dadaist collages and relief constructions (which he called *Merzbilden*), esp. *Picture with Light Center* (1919); composed poems from newspaper headlines and other printed ephemera; also built 3 *Merzbau* assemblages, only last (1947–48, unfinished) of which survives.

Scip·io \'sip-ē-,ō\, Gnaeus Cornelius. d. 211 B.C. Roman general. Brother of Publius Cornelius Scipio. Consul (222 B.C.) and cooperated with Marcus Claudius Marcellus in subduing Cisalpine Gaul; campaigned with his brother in Spain against the Carthaginians (from 218); was defeated and slain.

Scipio, Publius Cornelius. d. 211 B.C. Roman general. Father of Scipio Africanus. Consul (218 B.C.) with Sempronius Longus; defeated by Hannibal at the Ticino and the Trebbia. Campaigned in Spain (from 218) with brother Gnaeus Cornelius Scipio; defeated by Carthaginians and killed.

Scipio Ae·mil·i·a·nus Af·ri·ca·nus Nu·man·ti·nus \-i-ˌmil-ē-ˈā-nə-ˌsaf-rə-ˈkā-nəs-ˌn(y)ü-mən-ˈtē-nəs\, Publius Cornelius. *Called* Scipio the Younger. 185 or 184–129 B.C. Roman general. Grandson by adoption of Scipio Africanus the Elder; son of Lucius Aemilius Paulus Macedonicus. Close friend of Polybius. Served in Spain as military tribune (151 B.C.) and in Africa at outbreak of Third Punic War (149); consul (147); commanded army against Carthage (147) and captured Carthage (146); censor (142); consul, with governorship of Spain (134); seized Numantia (133). Headed aristocratic party in Rome (132) in opposition to popular reforms.

Scipio Af·ri·ca·nus \-ˌaf-ri-ˈkā-nəs\, Publius Cornelius. *Called* Scipio the Elder. 236–184 or 183 B.C. Roman general. Father of Cornelia. Military tribune at Battle of Cannae (216); aedile (213); commanded forces in Spain (210–206); defeated the Carthaginians several times, esp. at Battle of Ilipa (206). Consul (205) and commanded Roman invasion of Carthage, his successes there causing Carthage to recall Hannibal from Italy; crushed Hannibal in great battle of Zama (202). Titular head of Senate and censor (199); went to Syria as legate with his brother Lucius Cornelius Scipio Asiaticus, who was consul and commander of expedition against Antiochus III; cooperated with brother in winning battle of Magnesia (190); lost power (184) and retired to Liternum. Regarded as Rome's greatest general up to time of Julius Caesar.

Scipio Na·si·ca Se·ra·pio \nə-ˈsī-kə-sə-ˈrā-pē-(ˌ)ō\, Publius Cornelius. 2nd century B.C. Roman politician. Consul (138 B.C.); pontifex maximus. Violently opposed to reforms of Tiberius Gracchus; with his partisans, attacked and murdered Gracchus (133).

Sci·pi·o·ne \shē-pē-ˈō-nā\, Francesco. Marchese di Maf·fei \mä-ˈfā\. 1675–1755. Italian dramatist, archaeologist, and scholar. Fought in War of Spanish Succession (1703–04); with Apostolo Zeno founded (1710) *Giornale dei letterati* to promote reformation of Italian drama; founded *Osservazioni letterarie* (1737–40). Attempted to introduce Greek and French classical simplicity into Italian drama with verse tragedy *Merope* (1713) and other plays; also wrote scholarly works, libretti, translations, and esp. *Verona illustrata* (1731–32).

Scog·an \ˈskäg-ən\, Henry. 1361?–1407. English poet. Tutor to Henry IV's sons; generally regarded as subject of Chaucer's humorous *Envoy to Scogan*.

Scogan, John. fl. 1480–1500. Jester at court of Edward IV of England. Alleged author of *The Geystes of Skoggan* (1565–66), said to have been compiled by Andrew Boorde.

Sco·pas \ˈskō-pəs\. 4th century B.C. Greek sculptor and architect. Native of Paros; long resident in Athens. Recognized pain and excitement as artistic themes. Carved decorations for Mausoleum of Halicarnassus and for temples of Artemis at Ephesus and of Athena Alea at Tegea.

Scopes \ˈskōps\, John Thomas. 1900–1970. American educator, b. Salem, Ill. As teacher in Rhea County High School, Dayton, Tenn., taught theory of evolution in defiance of a state law, thus precipitating famous Scopes (or "Monkey") trial (July 1925) in which the state's case was upheld by William Jennings Bryan and the defense by Clarence Darrow; convicted and fined a nominal sum ($100), but conviction was reversed on technical grounds by the Tennessee supreme court.

Scores·by \ˈskȯrz-bē\, William. 1789–1857. English clergyman, scientist, and explorer. Pioneered in scientific study of the Arctic. Demonstrated that polar ocean is warmer at great depths than at surface (1813); surveyed and charted 400 miles of east coast of Greenland (1822); entered church (1825); carried on investigations in natural history, meteorology, magnetism; while crossing Atlantic made observations on height of waves (1848); made voyage to Australia to gather data on terrestrial magnetism (1856). Author of *Account of the Arctic Regions with a History and Description of the Northern Whale-Fishery* (1820).

Scot \ˈskät\, Michael. 1175?–?1235. Scottish translator and astrologer with posthumous fame as a magician. Learned Arabic at Toledo (c.1217); at court of Emperor Frederick II worked with other scholars on translation of Aristotle's works and Averroës's commentaries from Arabic into Latin. Through his original works dealing with astrology, alchemy, and occult sciences, became known as a wizard; credited with magical exploits and, in popular legend, possessor of a demon horse and a demon ship and foreteller of own death.

Scott \ˈskät\, Alexander. 1525?–?1585. Scottish poet. Regarded as one of last of *makaris* of 16th century; author of short poems (1545–68) preserved only in Bannatyne MS. and brought forward by Allan Ramsay; known for love lyrics, burlesque "The Justing and Debait up at the Drum betuix William Adamsone and Johine Sym," and ceremonial alliterative poem "Ane New Yeir Gift to Quene Mary."

Scott, Charles. 1739?–1813. American Revolutionary officer, b. Goochland Co., Va. Commanded Virginia regiment (1775–77); brigadier general, Continental army (1777); brevetted major general (1783). Moved to Kentucky (1785); served under Gen. St. Clair in Indian fighting (1791) and under Gen. Wayne at battle of Fallen Timbers (1794). Governor of Kentucky (1808–12).

Scott, Cyril Meir. 1879–1970. English pianist and composer. Known chiefly for orchestral and piano compositions, esp. *Second Symphony* (1903); also for chamber music and several operas, including *Alchemist* (1917) and *Maureen O'Mara* (1946). Author of *My Years of Indiscretion* (1924), translations of Baudelaire, two volumes of poems, etc.

Scott, Dred. 1795?–1858. American slave, b. Southampton Co., Va. Central figure in the Dred Scott Case, inaugurated by his suit (1848) to obtain his freedom on ground that he had resided in free territory; lost suit in famous Supreme Court decision (1857) but soon emancipated; thereafter a hotel porter in St. Louis.

Scott, Dukinfield Henry. 1854–1934. English paleobotanist. Lecturer at Royal Coll. of Science (1885–92); assistant to William C. Williamson (1890–95) and with him published "Further Observations on the Organization of the Fossil Plants of the Coal Measures" (1894, 1895); author of *Studies in Fossil Botany* (1900) and many articles; did more than any other scientist to establish paleobotany on a firm scientific basis.

Scott, Duncan Campbell. 1862–1947. Canadian poet, b. Ottawa. With Department of Indian Affairs (1879–1932). Known for lyrics inspired by wild nature and life in Indian territories. Author of *The Magic House and Other Poems* (1893), *Labor and the Angel* (1898), *New World Lyrics and Ballads* (1905), *The Circle of Affection* (1947), and collections of stories *In the Village of Viger* (1896), *The Witching of Elspie* (1923).

Scott, Sir George Gilbert. 1811–1878. English architect. Stimulated by study of Pugin's works on medieval architecture, led Gothic revival, notably in England; built or restored cathedrals (esp. those at Ely, Salisbury, Lichfield, and Westminster Abbey), churches, schools, monuments, college and public buildings, esp. Albert Memorial (1863–72) and Midland Hotel (1867–74) at St. Pancras (both in London). His grandson ¶Sir Giles Gilbert Scott (1880–1960), architect, designed Liverpool cathedral (consecrated 1924), many public buildings and churches, Cambridge U. Library (1933), Bodleian Library (1941), and Waterloo Bridge in London (completed 1945).

Scott, George Herbert. 1888–1930. English airship commander. Took on patrol first British rigid airship (1917); navigated rigid airship *R34* on first transatlantic airship flight (1919).

Scott, Hugh Lenox. 1853–1934. American army officer, b. Danville, Ky. Commissioned (1876); served in Indian campaigns; studied Indian sign language and became a negotiator with various Indian tribes; in military administration of Cuba (1899–1902), Philippines (1903–06); superintendent, U.S.M.A., West Point (1906–10); chief of staff, U.S. army (1914–17); retired (1917) but kept on active duty (to 1919).

Scott, Hugh Stowell. *Pseudonym* Henry Seton Mer·ri·man \ˈmer-i-mən\. 1862–1903. English novelist. Author of *Young Mistley* (1888), *The Slave of the Lamp* (1892), *The Sowers* (1896), *The Velvet Glove* (1901), *Barlasch of the Guard* (1903), *The Last Hope* (1904).

Scott, James. Duke of Mon·mouth \ˈmän-məth\. 1649–1685. Claimant to English throne and leader of rebellion, b. Rotterdam, Holland. Natural son of Charles II and Lucy Walter. Reared a Protestant in Paris; installed at his father's court as a favorite (1662); m. (1663) Scottish heiress Anne Scott, Countess of Buccleuch, took her surname, and was created duke of Buccleuch; created duke of Monmouth (1663). Captain of the king's guard (1668); commanded English troops on the Continent in Anglo-Dutch War of 1672–74. Captain general of all English armed forces (1678); defeated Scottish Presbyterian rebels at Bothwell Bridge, Lanark (1679), winning popularity by his clemency. Championed for the throne by Earl of Shaftesbury; exiled by Charles II (Sept. 1679); soon returned and became candidate of exclusionists; involved in Rye House Plot (1682–83) but pardoned; banished from court and fled to Holland (1684). Returned at death of Charles II, landing at Lyme Regis, Dorset, with 82 followers and claiming throne in place of James II (June 1685); defeated by Feversham at Sedgemoor (July 6, 1685); captured and beheaded.

Scott, James Brown. 1866–1943. American jurist and educator, b. Kincardine, Ont. One of principal early advocates of international arbitration. Solicitor, U.S. Department of State (1906–10); secretary, Carnegie Endowment for International Peace (1910–40). Founder and secretary (1906–24), American Society of International Law; founder and editor, *American Journal of International Law* (1907–24). Delegate to peace conferences at The Hague (1907) and Paris (1919); helped establish Academy of International Law (1914) and Permanent Court of International Justice (1921), both at The Hague.

Scott, John. 1st Earl of El·don \ˈel-dən\. 1751–1838. English jurist. Called to bar (1776); M.P. (1783–99); solicitor general (1788–93); attorney general (1793–99); responsible for vigorous prosecutions for libel and constructive treason and suspension of habeas corpus during French revolutionary period; chief justice, court of common pleas (1799–1801); lord chancellor (1801–06, 1807–27); provided judicial support for extreme measures against Napoléon; dominant member of cabinet; resisted judicial reform and Catholic emancipation; helped formulate trademark law. Created baron (1799), earl (1821).

Scott, Orange. 1800–1847. American clergyman and abolitionist, b. Brookfield, Vt. Because of church opposition to his abolitionist views, withdrew (1841) from Methodist Episcopal church and with his supporters founded (1843) Wesleyan Methodist church of America.

Scott, Paul Mark. 1920–1978. English novelist. Served in India during World War II; author of novels mainly set in India, including *Johnnie Sahib* (1952), *The Alien Sky* (1953), *The Birds of Paradise* (1962), and a tetralogy *The Raj Quartet* (1976), consisting of *The Jewel in the Crown* (1966), *The Day of the Scorpion* (1968), *The Towers of Silence* (1971), and *A Division of the Spoils* (1975).

Scott *or* **Scot** \ˈskät\, Reginald *or* Reynold. 1538?–1599. English writer. Author of first practical treatise on hop culture in England (1574) and of *The Discouerie of Witchcraft* (1584), a brillant attack upon witch superstition.

Scott, Robert Falcon. 1868–1912. English explorer. Entered navy (1882); commander of Antarctic expedition (1901–04); surveyed South Victoria Land and interior of Antarctic continent, discovered King Edward VII Land, sounded Ross Sea. Commanded second Antarctic expedition (1910); with four companions reached South Pole (Jan. 17, 1912) shortly after Roald Amundsen's expedition; with companions, perished on return trip as result of bad weather and insufficient food; his records and diaries found by searching party (Nov. 1912).

Scott, Sir Walter. *At first used various pseudonyms, including* Jedediah Cleish·both·am \ˈklēsh-ˌbäth-əm\, Chrystal Croft·an·gry \ˈkräft-ˌaŋ-grē, ˈkrȯft-\, Captain Cuthbert Clut·ter·buck \ˈklət-ər-ˌbək\, Peter Pat·tie·son \ˈpat-i-sən\. *Known as* the Border Minstrel, the Wizard of the North, *and* the Great Magician. 1771–1832. Scottish poet, novelist, historian, and biographer. Called to bar (1792), sheriff of Selkirk (1799); a principal clerk to court of session (1812). Published anonymously (1796) translations of Bürger's *Lenore* and *Der wilde Jäger* and of Goethe's *Götz von Berlichingen* (1799); contributed ballads to Matthew Lewis's *Tales of Wonder* (1801). Published first important work *Minstrelsy of the Scottish Border* (1802–03) and first considerable original work *The Lay of the Last Minstrel* (narrative poem, 1805); increased reputation with *Marmion* (1808); started *Quarterly Review* (1809); edited Dryden's works, with a *Life* (1808); published poems *Lady of the Lake* (1810), *Vision of Don Roderick* (1811), *Rokeby* (1812), and *The Bridal of Triermain* (1813); declined laureateship in favor of Southey (1813); published *Life and Works of Swift* (19 vols., 1814). Invented the historical novel with *Waverley* (1814), enormously popular; published *Lord of the Isles* (1815), *Harold the Dauntless* (poem, 1817), and novels *Guy Mannering* and *The Antiquary* (1815), *The Black Dwarf* and *Old Mortality* (1816), and *Rob Roy* (1817), *The Heart of Midlothian* and *The Bride of Lammermoor* (1818), *The Legend of Montrose* and *Ivanhoe* (1819), *The Monastery* (1820). Made baronet (1820). Continued novels with *The Abbot* (1820), *Kenilworth* and *The Pirate* (1821), *The Fortunes of Nigel* (1822), *Peveril of the Peak, Quentin Durward,* and *St. Ronan's Well* (1824), *Redgauntlet* (1824), *Tales of the Crusaders, The Betrothed,* and *The Talisman* (1825). At pinnacle of fame as man of letters, but failing in health, found himself with liabilities of £130,000 when Constable and Co. and Ballantyne and Co. (publishing and printing firms in which he was partner) failed (1826). Set to work to pay off indebtedness, producing *Woodstock* (1826), *The Two Drovers, The Highland Widow, The Surgeon's Daughter,* and nine-volume *Life of Napoleon* (1827), *Fair Maid of Perth* (1828), *Tales of a Grandfather* (1828, 1829, 1830, 1831), *Anne of Geierstein* (1829), *History of Scotland* (1830), and his best play, *Auchindrane, or the Ayrshire Tragedy* (1830). Suffered apoplectic strokes (1830) from which he never recovered; produced two more novels, *Count Robert of Paris* and *Castle Dangerous* (1831).

Scott, Walter. 1867–1938. Canadian politician, b. London, Ont. Newspaper publisher (from 1892); member of House of Commons for Assiniboia West (1900, 1904); instrumental in creation of provinces of Saskatchewan and Alberta (1905); first premier of Saskatchewan (1905–16).

Scott, Walter Edward. *Known as* Death Valley Scotty. 1872–1954. American adventurer. Claiming to own a secret gold mine, became famous for his lavish and eccentric style of living, including a Moorish castle at Stovepipe Wells in Death Valley; his activities actually financed by Chicago businessman Albert Mussey Johnson (1872–1948) as a hobby.

Scott, William. Baron Stow·ell \ˈstō-əl\. 1745–1836. English jurist. Brother of John Scott, 1st Earl of Eldon. Intimate of Dr. Johnson; advocate general for lord high admiral (1782); judge of consistory court (1788–1821); privy councilor (1798); judge of high court of admiralty (1798–1828). Highest English authority on maritime and international law.

Scott, William Berryman. 1858–1947. American geologist, b. Cincinnati. Professor, Princeton (1884–1930); known for work on vertebrate paleontology and on extinct mammals of North and South America.

Scott, Winfield. *Nicknamed* Old Fuss and Feathers. 1786–1866. American army officer, b. near Petersburg, Va. Commissioned captain of artillery (1808); fought in War of 1812; brigadier general (1814); engaged at battles of Chippewa and Lundy's Lane (1814); brevetted major general (1814). On duty in South Carolina (1832), pacifying the nullifiers, and on Canadian border (1838–39), preventing conflict with Canada over boundary line. General in chief, U.S. army (1841–61); commander in Mexican War; captured Vera Cruz (Mar. 1847); defeated Mexicans at Cerro Gordo (Apr. 1847), Contreras and Churubusco (Aug. 1847), Molino del Rey and Chapultepec (Sept. 1847), and occupied Mexico City (Sept. 14, 1847); promoted lieutenant general (1852). Whig candidate for presidency (1852); defeated by Franklin Pierce; retired (1861).

Scottigena, John. See ERIGENA.

Scott-Mon·crieff \ˈskät-ˌmän-ˈkrēf, -mən-\, Charles Kenneth Michael. 1889–1930. Scottish translator. Captain in Scottish Borderers (1914); translator of *Song of Roland* (1919), *Beowulf* (1921), Stendhal's works; authorized translator of Proust's *Remembrance of Things Past* (1922–31) and works of Pirandello.

Scott-Paine \ˌskät-ˈpān\, Hubert. 1891–1954. English aircraft and marine engineer. Built first circular flying-boat hull (1913), first quadruplane and first plane with cabins for pilot and passengers (1915); opened first international flying boat service (1920; Le Havre–Southampton); designed gunboats, torpedo boats, etc.

Scotus, Duns. See John DUNS SCOTUS.

Scotus, John. See John Scotus ERIGENA.

Scria·bin *or* **Skrya·bin** \ˈskryȧb-yin, *Angl* skrē-ˈäb-ən\, Aleksandr Nikolayevich. 1872–1915. Russian composer. Piano instructor, Moscow Conservatory (1898–1903); settled in Switzerland (1904); toured U.S. (1906–07). Among his orchestral works were three symphonies, esp. No. 3 *Le Divin Poème* (1904), tone poems *Le Poème de l'extase* (1908) and *Prométhée, le poème du feu* (1910), and a piano concerto (1896); among his piano works were ten sonatas, études, preludes, and a number of dances.

Scribe \skrēb\, Augustin-Eugène. 1791–1861. French playwright. Master of the neatly plotted, tightly constructed "well-made" play; wrote or cowrote over 350 dramas of every kind, most extremely successful, including *Une Nuit de la garde nationale* (1815), *Bertrand et Raton* (1833), *La Camaraderie* (1836), *Le Verre d'eau* (1840), *Une Chaîne* (1841), *Le Puff* (1848), *Adrienne Lecouvreur* (with Legouvé, 1849), *Bataille des Dames* (1851); author also of opera librettos for Auber, Bellini, Donizetti, Meyerbeer, Rossini, Verdi, etc.

Scri·ble·rus \skri-ˈbli(ə)r-əs\, Martinus. Joint pseudonym of Pope, Swift, and Arbuthnot in *Memoirs of Martinus Scriblerus,* published with Pope's works (1751).

Scrib·ner \ˈskrib-nər\, Charles. *Surname orig.* Scriv·e·ner \ˈskriv(-ə)-nər\. 1821–1871. American publisher, b. New York City. A founder with Isaac D. Baker of Baker & Scribner, publishers (1846), the beginning of Charles Scribner's Sons (incorporated 1878). Founder and publisher, *Scribner's Monthly* (1870–81). His three sons ¶John Blair (1850–1879), ¶Charles (1854–1930), and ¶Arthur Hawley (1859–1932), continued the business; published *St. Nicholas* (1873–81) and a new *Scribner's Magazine* (1887–1939). A son of Charles (1854–1930), ¶Charles (1890–1952), succeeded to the presidency of the company in 1933. See Roswell SMITH.

Scri·bo·nia \skri-ˈbō-nē-ə\. 1st century B.C. Roman matron. Second wife (m. 40 B.C.) of Emperor Augustus; mother of Julia (*q.v.*); divorced (39 B.C.).

Scripps \ˈskrips\. Name of a family of American newspaper publishers, including: James Edmund (1835–1906), b. London, England; to U.S. (1844); founded and edited *Evening News,* Detroit (from 1873); associated with his half-brother Edward in founding or acquiring newspapers in Cleveland, St. Louis, and Cincinnati; purchased *Detroit Tribune* (1891). His sister ¶Ellen Browning (1836–1932), b. London, England; to U.S. (1844); on staff of *Detroit Evening News* (from 1873), *Cleveland Penny Press* (from 1878), Cincinnati *Post* (from 1882); founded (1926) Scripps College, Claremont, Calif. Their half-brother ¶Edward Wyllis (1854–1926), b. near Rushville, Ill.; on staff of *Detroit Evening News* (1872); with financial aid from family, founded (1878) and edited *Cleveland Penny Press,* purchased *Evening Chronicle,* St. Louis (1880), and *Penny Post,* Cincinnati (1882); in partnership (from 1889) with his half-brother George H. Scripps and Milton Alexander McRae, organized Scripps-McRae League of Newspapers (1894) and Scripps-McRae Press Association (1897); purchased Publishers' Press (1904) and merged it with Scripps-McRae Press into United Press (1907); organized (1902) Newspaper Enterprise Association to supply cartoons and feature articles to papers of his chain and to other papers, origin of modern syndicated matter; bought interest in *San Diego Sun* (1893) and added other newspapers to form a West Coast chain; with Ellen founded (1912) Scripps Inst. of Oceanography, La Jolla, Calif. ¶Robert Paine (1895–1938), b. San Diego; son of Edward Wyllis; editorial director of the Scripps-McRae newspapers (from 1917); entered (1922) into partnership with Roy W. Howard (*q.v.*) to form Scripps-Howard Newspapers.

Scroggs \'skrägz\, Sir William. 1623?–1683. English judge. Fought on Royalist side in Civil War; justice of common pleas (1676); lord chief justice of England (1678). Presiding in trial of victims of Titus Oates's alleged Popish Plot, intimidated defense witnesses but disparaged evidence of accusers to save George Wakeman, queen's physician, and adjourned grand jury to forestall indictment of Duke of York (later James II); impeached but never tried; removed from office (1681).

Scrope, le \lə-'skrüp\. Distinguished English family, including: Richard (1327?–1403), 1st Baron Scrope of Bol·ton \'bōlt-ən\, lawyer and soldier; served with John of Gaunt; warden of West March (1375); chancellor of England (1378–80, 1381–82). His son ¶William (1351?–1399), Earl of Wilt·shire \'wilt-ˌshi(ə)r, 'wil-chər, 'wilt-shər\; served under John of Gaunt in France; captain of Cherbourg and Brest; chamberlain of Richard II's household; ambassador to Scotland (1398); treasurer of England (1398); executed by Henry IV. His cousin ¶Richard (1350?–1405), prelate; bishop of Coventry and Lichfield (1386) and archbishop of York (1398–1405); supporter of revolution of 1399; leader, with Northumberland and Bardolf, of rebellion beyond Tyne (1404); executed at York. His nephew ¶Henry (1376?–1415), 3d Baron Scrope of Mash·am \'mas-əm\; treasurer of kingdom (1410–11); entrusted by Henry IV and Henry V with foreign negotiations; executed for complicity in plot to dethrone Henry V.

Scrope, George Julius Poulett. *Orig. surname* Thomson. 1797–1876. English geologist. Brother of Charles Poulett Thomson (*q.v.*); m. (1821) daughter and heiress of the artist and sportsman William Scrope and assumed her name. Studied volcanoes in Italy, France, Germany (1819–23); with Sir Charles Lyell sought to replace Wernerian theory of Neptunism with Uniformitarianism; his *Considerations on Volcanoes* (1825) regarded as earliest systematic treatise on volcanology; also wrote *On the Geology and Extinct Volcanoes of Central France* (1827). Liberal M.P. (1833–68); published many pamphlets advocating free trade and social and economic reforms, esp. of the poor law.

Scud·der \'skəd-ər\, Samuel Hubbard. 1837–1911. American entomologist, b. Boston. Best known for studies of butterflies and Orthoptera. Author of *Butterflies of the Eastern United States and Canada* (1888–89). His brother ¶Horace Elisha (1838–1902), b. Boston; editor of *Atlantic Monthly* (1890–98). Author of *Dream Children* (1864), *A History of the United States* (1884), and biographies *Noah Webster* (1882), *George Washington* (1890), and *James Russell Lowell* (1901).

Scu·dé·ry \skue-dā-rē\, Georges de. 1601–1667. French writer. Wrote a critical work directed against Corneille (1637), many plays, esp. the tragicomedy *L'Amour tyrannique* (1638), *Poésies diverses* (1649), and the epic *Alaric ou Rome vaincue* (1654). His sister ¶Madeleine (1607–1701), *often known as* Sa·pho \sȧ-fō\, was a poet, novelist, and lady of fashion whose Saturday salons were frequented by notable persons of the day; best known works were *Artamène ou le Grand Cyrus* (1649–53) and *Clélie* (1654–60).

Scul·lin \'skəl-ən\, James Henry. 1876–1953. Australian politician. M.P. (1910–13, 1922–49); leader of Labour party (1928–35); prime minister of Australia (1929–31).

Scurlock, Mary. See under Sir Richard STEELE.

Scy·lax \'sī-ˌlaks\ of Ca·ria \'kar-ē-ə, 'ker-\. 6th century B.C. Greek historian and geographer. Sent (c.515 B.C.) by Darius I to explore course of Indus River; sailed down it to sea and westward through Indian Ocean to Red Sea; wrote account (now lost) of journey.

Scylitzes, John. See JOHN SCYLITZES.

Scyl·lis \'sil-əs\ and **Di·poe·nus** \dī-'pē-nəs\. 6th century B.C. Greek sculptors (collaborators). Worked in wood, ebony, ivory, and, probably, marble; Scyllis sometimes credited with inventing art of carving in marble; their studio, according to Pliny, was in Sicyon.

Sea·bury \'sē-bər-ē, -ˌber-ē\, Samuel. 1729–1796. American clergyman, b. Groton, Conn. Ordained priest in Church of England (1753); loyalist during American Revolution; chosen bishop by Protestant Episcopal clergy of Connecticut (1783) and consecrated in Scotland by nonjuring Scottish prelates (1784); first bishop of the Protestant Episcopal church in America.

Seals·field \'sēlz-ˌfēld, *Ger also* 'zēls-ˌfēlt\, Charles. *Orig.* Karl Anton Postl \'pȯs-təl\. 1793–1864. American novelist, b. Poppitz, Moravia. Educated for priesthood but fled from monastery; to U.S. (1823) and naturalized; resident in Switzerland (after 1832) but retained his American citizenship. Author of *Tokeah* (1828), *Der Virey und die Aristokraten* (1834), *Die deutsch-amerikanischen Wahlverwandtschaften* (1839), *Das Kajütenbuch* (1841), *Lebensbilder aus der westlichen Hemisphäre* (1846), etc.

Sea·man \'sē-mən\, Elizabeth, *nee* Coch·rane \'käk-rən\. *Pseudonym* Nellie Bly \'blī\. 1867–1922. American journalist; b. Cochrane Mills, Pa. m. (1895) Robert L. Seaman (d. 1904). On staff, *Pittsburgh Dispatch, New York World,* and at the close of her life, *New York Journal.* Wrote muckraking articles and books, esp. *Ten Days in a Mad House* (1887) on insane asylum on Welfare Island; made trip around world in the then record time of 72 days, 6 hours, and 11 minutes and scored great success in resulting account, *Nellie Bly's Book: Around the World in Seventy-Two Days* (1890).

Searle \'sər(-ə)l\, Frederick Moore. *Pseudonym* Eric Par·ker \'pär-kər\. 1870–1955. English journalist and writer. Editor of *The Country Gentleman* (1902–07); editor in chief of *Fields* (1929–37). Author of books on field sports, cricket, dogs, natural history, and gardens, including *A Book of Zoo* (1909), *Promise of Arden* (1912, novel), *Eton in the Eighties* (1914), *Playing Fields* (1922), *The History of Cricket* (1950), *Surrey Gardens* (1954).

Sears \'si(ə)rz\, Edmund Hamilton. 1810–1876. American clergyman, b. Sandisfield, Mass. Unitarian minister at Wayland (1848–66) and Weston (from 1866; both in Mass.). Author of religious books and a number of hymns, including "Calm on the Listening Ear of Night" and "It Came Upon a Midnight Clear."

Sears, Isaac. 1730–1786. American merchant and Revolutionary patriot, b. W. Brewster, Mass. Leader of radical elements in New York City opposing British policy (from 1765); on receiving news of Lexington and Concord, seized New York arsenal and customhouse and controlled city until arrival of Washington's army (1775). Resident in Boston (1777–83), esp. engaged in sending out privateers to prey on British commerce.

Sears, Richard Dudley. 1862–1943. American tennis player, b. Boston. First American amateur champion at lawn tennis (1881–87) and court tennis (1892); U.S. men's doubles champion (1882–87); charter member of National Lawn Tennis Hall of Fame.

Sears, Richard Warren. 1863–1914. American merchant, b. Stewartville, Minn. Established mail-order business in Minneapolis (1886); moved to Chicago (1887); sold business (1889). Again opened mail-order business, with A. C. Roebuck, in Minneapolis; moved to Chicago (1893) and firm became Sears, Roebuck & Co., with Sears as president (to 1909; retired). Roebuck's interest purchased by Julius Rosenwald (1895).

Seastrom, Victor. See SJÖSTRÖM.

Seaton, 1st Baron. See Sir John COLBORNE.

Sea·ton \'sēt-ᵊn\, William Winston. 1785–1866. American journalist, b. King William Co., Va. Co-owner and co-editor, with Joseph Gales, of the *National Intelligencer,* Washington, D.C. (1812–64). With Gales, made shorthand reports of congressional debates (1812–29), afterwards published by authority of Congress, together with earlier reports, as *The Debates and Proceedings in the Congress of the United States* (1834–56). Gales and Seaton also published *Register of Debates in Congress* covering years 1824–37 (1825–37), and *American State Papers* (1832–61).

Seatoun. See SETON.

Se·at·tle *or* **Se·atlh** \se-'at-ᵊl\. 1786?–1866. American Suquamish Indian chief, b. near Seattle, Washington. Friendly to early white settlers; signed treaty (1855) ceding land to the whites. The city of Seattle is named after him.

Se·bas·tian \si-'bas-chən\. Saint. d. c.288. Christian martyr. Soldier by profession; served (from c.283) under emperors Carinus and Diocletian; made many converts to Christianity. Ordered by Diocletian to desist from proselyting; refused and was executed; his martyrdom a favorite subject of Renaissance artists.

Sebastian. *Port.* Se·bas·tião \sə-bəsh-'tyau̇ⁿ\. 1554–1578. King of Portugal (1557–78). Son of Dom John (1537–1554), only son of John III; during his minority (1557–68), government under his grandmother Catherine of Austria, and later his uncle Cardinal Henry (see HENRY, king of Portugal); led expedition to Morocco; defeated and slain at the battle of Alcázarquivir; last important ruler of House of Aviz (*q.v.*); subject of later legends and symbol of freedom from Spanish oppression.

Sebastiano del Piombo. See Sebastiano LUCIANI.

Se·bek·nef·ru *or* **So·bek·nef·ru** \sə-bek-'nef-(ˌ)rü\. d. 1786 B.C. Egyptian ruler. Daughter of Amenemhet III; on death of her brother and absence of male heir, took royal titles and ruled as king of Egypt (1789–1786 B.C.); last ruler of the 12th dynasty.

Se·be·twa·ne \ˌsā-bā-'twän-ā\. d. 1851. African king. Driven from his native Orange Free State (c.1820); led his Kololo people to Barotseland (in present-day western Zambia, 1838), conquered the Lozi natives, and established a kingdom; repelled two attacks by Mzilikazi; an able and humane ruler; met David Livingstone (1851), whose notes of Sebetwane's experiences are primary source of Kololo history.

Se·bük·ti·gin \sā-ˌbük-tē-'gin\. *In full* Abū Manṣūr Sebüktigin. c.942–997. Afghan ruler. Became governor of Ghazna (977); threw off Sāmānid rule, expanded territory; founder of Ghaznavid dynasty; father of Maḥmūd of Ghazna.

\ə\ abut \ᵊ\ kitten, *Fr.* **table \ər\ further \a\ ash \ā\ ace \ä\ cot, cart \au̇\ out \ch\ chin \e\ bet \ē\ easy \g\ go \i\ hit \ī\ ice \j\ job \ŋ\ sing \ō\ go \ȯ\ law \ȯi\ boy \th\ both \t͟h\ the \ü\ loot \u̇\ foot \y\ yet \zh\ vision \ȧ, ḵ, g̅, k̲, ⁿ, œ, œ̄, ue, ue̅, ʸ** *see* **Guide to Pronunciation**

Sec·chi \'sāk-kē\, Pietro Angelo. 1818–1878. Italian astronomer. Joined Jesuit order (1833); professor and director of observatory, Collegio Romano, Rome (1849 ff.). Made researches in solar and stellar spectroscopy, terrestrial magnetism, and meteorology; made first survey of the spectra of stars and suggested that stars be classified according to their spectral type; proved that prominences seen during solar eclipses are features of the Sun itself.

Séchelles, Marie-Jean Hérault de. See HÉRAULT DE SÉCHELLES.

Se·che·nov \'syā-chə-nəf\, Ivan Mikhaylovich. 1829–1905. Russian psychologist. Professor at St. Petersburg (1860–70, 1876–88), Odessa (1871–76), Moscow (1891–1901). Founder of Russian physiology and scientific psychology; discovered evidence of localized inhibitory function in the brain (Sechenov's center, 1863); developed theory that all acts of conscious or unconscious life are reflexes; teacher of Pavlov.

Sechten, Von. See Ludwig von SIEGEN.

Seck·en·dorff \'zek-ən-,dȯrf\, Veit Ludwig von. 1626–1691. German politician and historian. Credited with developing for Germany the public-health philosophy later systematized by Johann Frank and enacted into law by Bismarck. Chief work *Teutscher Fürstenstaat* (1656).

Se·con·dat \sə-gōⁿ-dä\, Charles-Louis de. Baron de La Brède et de Mon·tes·quieu \də-lá-bred-ā-də-mōⁿ-tes-kyœ\. 1689–1755. French political philosopher. Became advocate (1708); deputy president of Bordeaux Parlement (1716–26). Published *Lettres persanes* (1721), a satirical portrait of Parisian society; made grand tour, esp. (1729–31) in England; published chief work *L'Esprit des lois* (1748), a seminal contribution to political theory which profoundly influenced political thought in Europe and America; other works included *Considérations sur les causes de la grandeur des Romaines et de leur décadence* (1734) and *Défense de l'Esprit des lois* (1750).

Secydianus. See SOGDIANUS.

Se·daine \sə-den\, Michel-Jean. 1719–1797. French playwright. Author of *Épître à mon habit* (1745), *Le Diable à quatre* (1756), *Philosophe sans le savoir* (1765), *Gageure imprévue* (1768), and librettos for several of Monsigny's operas.

Sed·don \'sed-ᵊn\, Richard John. *Commonly called* King Dick. 1845–1906. New Zealand politician, b. Lancashire, England. To Australia (1863), New Zealand (1866); member of New Zealand Parliament (1879); minister of mines and public works (1891–93). Premier (1893–1906); carried through old-age pensions (1898); arranged universal penny postage (1901); annexed the Cook Islands (1901) but failed to incorporate Fiji; nationalized coal mines and fire insurance; in late years known as a British imperialist.

Sed·er·holm \'sed-er-,hȯlm\, Jakob Johannes. 1863–1934. Finnish geologist. Geologist (1888), director (1893–1933) of Geological Commission of Finland; pioneered in investigation of Precambrian rocks of Finland. Author of *Om granit och gneis* (1907), *On Migmatites and Associated Pre-Cambrian Rocks of Southwestern Finland* (1923–24), etc.

Sedg·wick \'sej-(,)wik\, Adam. 1785–1873. English geologist. Professor at Cambridge (from 1818). Studied geology of Cornwall and Devon, red sandstone of northern half of England, geology of Lake District and of Wales; named the Cambrian Period; with Murchison, introduced term Devonian for slates, etc., in West Somerset, Devon, and Cornwall. Chief work *A Synopsis of the Classification of the British Palaeozoic Rocks* (1855).

Sedgwick, Adam. 1854–1913. English zoologist. Grandnephew of Adam Sedgwick. Lecturer (1878), director (1882) of F.M. Balfour's zoological school; professor at Cambridge (1899) and Imperial College, South Kensington (1909); best known for researches on the wormlike organism *Peripatus.* Author of *A Student's Text-Book of Zoology* (1898–1909).

Sedgwick, John. 1813–1864. American army officer, b. Cornwall Hollow, Conn. Entered army (1837); brigadier general of volunteers (1861); served in Peninsular campaign; major general (1862); engaged at Antietam, Chancellorsville, Fredericksburg, Gettysburg, the Wilderness. Killed in action at Spotsylvania.

Sedgwick, Theodore. 1746–1813. American jurist, b. West Hartford, Conn. Military secretary to Gen. John Thomas (1776); member, Continental Congress (1785–88). Member, U.S. House of Representatives (1789–96, 1799–1801), speaker (1799–1801); U.S. senator (1796–99); justice, Massachusetts Supreme Court (1802–13).

Sed·ley \'sed-lē\, Sir Charles. 1639–1701. English wit and dramatist. A member of the Restoration "court wits"; notorious man of fashion and profligate; known for his bons mots; M.P. (from 1668); in later life reformed and became a serious legislator. Wrote tragedies *Antony and Cleopatra* (1677) and *The Tyrant King of Crete* (1702); comedies *The Mulberry Garden* (1668), *Bellamira* (1687), and *The Grumbler* (1719); verse translations and lyrics, including "Phillis is my only Joy."

Se·du·li·us \si-'jü-lē-əs\, Coelius *or* Caelius. 5th century. Roman poet. Chief work *Carmen Paschale,* a poetic version of the Gospels.

Sedulius Scot·tus \-'skät-əs\. fl. c.848–860 or 874? Irish poet and scholar. Leader of a colony of Irish scholars at Liège under protection of Bishop Hartgar (from 848). Author of poems, mostly in classical Latin meters, addressed to leading figures of the period, esp. Hartgar; wrote a verse and prose *De rectoribus Christianis,* one of earliest medieval mirrors for princes; also wrote biblical commentaries.

See \'sē\, Thomas Jefferson Jackson. 1866–1962. American astronomer, b. near Montgomery City, Mo. Astronomer at Lowell Observatory, Flagstaff, Ariz. (1896–98); professor of mathematics, U.S. navy (from 1899), in charge of U.S. Naval Observatory (1899–1902) and of naval observatory of Mare Island, Calif. (1903–30). Known esp. for investigations of double stars, the ether, the cause of universal gravitation and magnetism, cosmic evolution, and earthquakes; formulated wave theory of gravitation.

See·beck \'zā-,bek\, Thomas Johann. 1770–1831. German physicist. Worked with Goethe on theory of color; credited with discovery of thermoelectricity, whose laws he studied; discovered (1821) that an electric current flows between different conductive materials that are kept at different temperatures (Seebeck effect).

See·bohm \'sē-,bōm, -,bȯm\, Frederic. 1833–1912. English economic historian. Author of works upsetting prevailing view of Anglo-Saxon communal groups of freemen, *The English Village Community* (1883), *The Tribal System in Wales* (1895), *Tribal Custom in Anglo-Saxon Law* (1902); traced English open-field manorial system of farming to an amalgamation of the Roman villa with the Celtic tribal system.

Seeckt \'zākt\, Hans von. 1866–1936. German general. Entered army (1885); chief of staff of 11th army (1915–17); principal architect of breakthrough at Russian front at Gorlice-Tarnów (May 1915) and conquests of Serbia (1915) and Romania (1916–17); chief of staff of Turkish army (1917–18). Head of Truppenamt (1919); head of Reichswehr (1920–26) and successfully remodelled it; advocated cooperation with Russia. Member of Reichstag (1930–32); adviser to Chinese Nationalist army (1934–35). Wrote memoirs *Aus meinem Leben* (1938), *Aus seinem Leben* (1940).

See·ger \'sē-gər\, Alan. 1888–1916. American poet, b. New York City. To Paris (1912); enlisted in French Foreign Legion at outbreak of World War I. Author of poems "Ode in Memory of the American Volunteers Fallen for France," "I Have a Rendezvous with Death."

See·ley \'sē-lē\, Sir John Robert. 1834–1895. English historian. Caused storm of religious controversy by essay *Ecce Homo* (1865); in *Natural Religion* (1882) contended that supernaturalism is not essential to religion; professor, Cambridge (1869–95). Author of *Life and Times of Stein* (1878), *The Expansion of England* (1883), and *The Growth of British Policy* (1895).

Seers \'ser\, Eugène. *Pseudonym* Louis Dan·tin \däⁿ-taⁿ\. 1865–1945. French-Canadian writer and critic, b. Beauharnois, Que. Regarded as first major literary critic of French America; criticism collected as *Poètes de l'Amérique française* (1928) and *Gloses critiques* (1931, 1935); also wrote *Le Coffret de Crusoé* (1932, poems) and *Les Enfances de Fanny* (1951, novel).

Se·fe·ria·des \,sef-er-'yä-thēs\, Giorgos Stylianou. *Pseudonym* George Se·fe·ris \se-'fer-ēs\. 1900–1971. Greek poet and diplomat. With Greek diplomatic service (1926–62), esp. as ambassador to Great Britain (1957–62). Most distinguished Greek poet of "the generation of the '30s"; awarded Nobel prize for literature (1963). Author of collections of poems *Strophe* (1931), *Sterna* (1932), *Mythistorema* (1935), *Himerologion katastromatos 1* (1940), *Tetradio gymnasmaton* (1940), *Poiïmata* (1940), *Himerologion katastromatos 2* (1944), long poem *Kichle* (1942), and *Himerologion katastromatos 3* (1945); essays *Dokimes* (1944) and *Erotokritos* (1946); and translations.

Sef·ström \'sev-strœm\, Nils Gabriel. 1787–1854. Swedish chemist and mineralogist. Rediscovered and named the element vanadium (1830).

Se·gan·ti·ni \'sā-gän-'tē-nē\, Giovanni. 1858–1899. Italian painter. Settled in Engadin region of Swiss Alps (1894). Developed own pointillist technique; known for Alpine landscapes and allegorical pictures which blended Symbolist content with Neo-Impressionistic technique, including *The Punishment of Luxury* (1891), *The Unnatural Mothers* (1894), *Love at the Fountain of Life* (1896), and an unfinished triptych *Life, Nature, and Death.*

Se·gar \'sē-,gär\, Elzie Crisler. 1894–1938. American cartoonist, b. Chester, Ill. Originator (1919) of "Thimble Theater," a comic strip which eventually (Jan. 1929) featured Popeye the Sailor, whose name the strip adopted.

Se·ghers \sā-gərs\, Charles Jean. *Called* Apostle of Alaska. 1839–1886. Belgian prelate and missionary. Ordained (1863); bishop of Vancouver Island, Canada (1873–78); made missionary journeys in Alaska; archbishop of Oregon City, Ore. (1876–85); again bishop of Vancouver Island (1885–86); established permanent missions at Juneau and Sitka.

Seghers, Hercules Pietersz. 1589 or 1590–c.1638. Dutch painter and etcher. Known for stark, fantastic landscapes usually representing forbidding mountain scenes with scant traces of human habitation, as *Mountainous Landscape with a Distant Panorama;* also made original and impressive etchings.

Seg·ner \'zāg-nər\, Johann Andreas von. 1704–1777. German physicist and mathematician. Professor at Jena (1732–35), Göttingen (1735–55), Halle (1755–77). Developed (1750) a simple reaction waterwheel, later developed by

Leonhard Euler into a crude turbine; introduced (1751) concept of surface tension of liquids; studied theory of the spinning top.

Segonzac, Dunoyer de. See DUNOYER DE SEGONZAC.

Se·grais \sə-gre\, Jean Re·gnault de \rən-yō-də-\. 1624–1701. French poet. Secretary to duchesse de Montpensier (1648–72). Among works were *Bérénice* (novel, 1648–51), *Athis* (verse, 1653), *Poésies diverses* (1658), and verse translations of Virgil's *Aeneid* and *Georgics.*

Sé·guier \sāg-yā\, Pierre. Duc de Ville·mor \də-vēl-mȯr\. 1588–1672. French politician. Counsellor (1612), president (1624) in parlement of Paris; keeper of the seals (1633). Chancellor of France (1635–50, 1651, 1656–72); adhered to policies of Richelieu and Mazarin; suppressed rebellion in Normandy (1639); active in securing recognition of Anne of Austria as regent after death of Louis XIII; during the Fronde aligned with rebel princes until Aug. 1652; presided over Council of Justice for reform of legal system (from 1665). Patron of the arts; succeeded Richelieu as protector of Académie Française.

Sé·guin \sā-gaⁿ, *Angl* 'sā-gwən\, Édouard. 1812–1880. American physician, b. Clamecy, France. To U.S. (1850); specialist in mental disease, esp. in education of retarded children.

Sé·guin \sā-gaⁿ\, Marc. 1786–1875. French engineer. Nephew of Joseph Montgolfier. With his brother ¶Camille (d. 1852) erected first wire-cable suspension bridge (1824, over Rhône River at Tournon) and played leading role in construction of first French railroad (1824–33); invented (1827) the multiple fire-tube steam-engine boiler, used (1829) by George Stephenson in his "Rocket" locomotive; made contributions to theoretical physics; wrote treatises on the suspension bridge, the railroad, steam navigation, and steam power.

Ségur, Comtesse de. See under ROSTOPCHIN.

Se·hes·ted \'sā-hes-təth\, Hannibal. 1609–1666. Danish politician. Attached to court of Christian IV (from 1632); member of state council (1640–51); stadholder of Norway (1642); during Christian IV's 2d war with Sweden (1643–45) invaded Sweden several times and ably defended Norway; won for Norway partial control of its finances (1646–47); ceded estates to crown after being accused of embezzlement (1648) and lost power. Negotiated Treaty of Copenhagen with Swedes (1600) and regained royal favor; became lord high treasurer and again a state councilor; modernized Danish state administration.

Sehul, Mikael. See MIKAEL SEHUL.

Sei \'sā\ Shōnagon. 966 or 967–1013. Japanese diarist. Entered service of Empress Sakado (991); known for her *Makura no sōshi* (Pillow-Book), a miscellany or diary covering court life during years 991–1000.

Seidl \'zī-dəl\, Johann Gabriel. 1804–1875. Austrian journalist and poet. Wrote *Bifolien* (1836), *Gedichte in niederösterreichischer Mundart* (1844), and *Natur und Herz* (1853). His text "Gott erhalte Franz den Kaiser," to music by Haydn, became Austria's national anthem.

Sei·fert \'zī-fərt\, Jaroslav. 1901–1986. Czech poet and journalist. Supported himself (until 1950) as a journalist. Early poetry reflected his Communist sympathies; his poetry became more lyrical as disenchantment with Soviet Communism grew; broke with Communist party (1929); later poetry concerned with Czech nationalism and contemporary events; silenced for condemning Soviet invasion (1968); awarded 1984 Nobel prize for literature. Published about 30 volumes of poetry, including *Město v slzách* (1920), *Slavík zpívá špatně* (1926), *Světlena oděná* (1940), and *Přílba hlíny* (1945).

Sei·pel \'zī-pəl\, Ignaz. 1876–1932. Austrian prelate and politician. Minister for social welfare in last imperial cabinet (1918); head of Christian Socialist party (from 1921); in Karl Renner's coalition government (1919–21); formed alliance with Pan-German party (1921). Chancellor of Austria (1922–24, 1926–29); his use (1927) of the Heimwehr against Austria's Social Democrats strengthened the Fascist movement; minister of foreign affairs (1930).

Seitz \'zīts\, Karl. 1869–1950. Austrian politician. President of Provisional National Assembly and member of the State Council (1918–19); member of the Constituent National Assembly and the Nationalrat (1920). President of Nationalrat and acting president of Republic of Austria (1919–20); burgomaster and governor of Vienna (1923–34); under arrest after the rebellion (Feb. 1934) and again after German occupation of Austria (1938).

Se·ja·nus \si-'jā-nəs\, Lucius Aelius. d. 31 A.D. Roman politician and conspirator. Favorite of Emperor Tiberius, who made him (c.15) commander of praetorian guard. Allegedly poisoned emperor's son Drusus Caesar (23 A.D.) and persuaded (29) emperor to banish Agrippina, widow of Germanicus Caesar; the death, under suspicious circumstances, of Agrippina followed; consul (31). On discovery of his intrigues, he was executed by order of Tiberius.

Se·jong \'sā-'zhōŋ\. 1397–1450. King of Korea (1419–50). Member of Yi dynasty; during reign Korea reached height of cultural achievements; best known for his development of phonetic alphabet called Han'gŭl; banned Buddhist monks from Seoul, thus reducing power of Buddhist church.

Se·ki \sek-ē\ Takakazu. *Also* Seki Kōwa. *Commonly called* Shin·suke \shin-su̇k-e\. *Pseudonym* Kō·sai \kō-sī\. 1642–1708. Japanese mathematician. Generally considered founder of Japanese mathematics. Developed a mathematical theory of determinants that was more general than Leibniz's and predated it; credited with major discoveries in calculus.

Selborne, Earls of. See Roundell PALMER.

Sel·by \'sel-bē\, Norman. *Known as* Kid Mc·Coy \mə-'kȯi\. 1873–1940. American boxer, b. Rush Co., Ind. Known for trickery and cruelty in the ring; deceived Tommy Ryan into a welterweight championship match and won (1896); lost to Jack Root in first light-heavyweight championship bout (1903).

Sel·den \'sel-dən\, George Baldwin. 1846–1922. American lawyer and inventor, b. Clarkson, N.Y. Specialized in patent law; applied for patent on gasoline motor-propelled vehicle (1879) and was granted patent (Nov. 1895) for a "road engine," the first American patent for a gasoline-driven car (cf. C.E. DURYEA). Sold rights to his patent on royalty basis; protracted litigation followed, the Ford Motor Company refusing to pay royalties and finally gaining decision (1911) that its engine was of a different fundamental type.

Selden, John. 1584–1654. English jurist, antiquary, Orientalist, and politician. Acquired European reputation as scholar by the reference book *Titles of Honour* (1614) and *Analecton Anglo-Britannicon* (1615), a history of civil government of Britain before Norman conquest. Won fame as Orientalist by a Latin treatise inquiring into polytheism, *De diis Syris Syntagmata* (1617), and expositions of rabbinical law; collected Oriental manuscripts. Incurred indignation of clergy by his *History of Tythes* (1618), denying tithes as divine institution; imprisoned (1621) for part in repudiation by Parliament of king's doctrine that privileges of Parliament were originally royal grants. M.P. (1623); helped to draw up Petition of Right (1628); imprisoned with Eliot and Holles after discussion of tonnage and poundage (1629). Briefly became Royalist, writing *Mare clausum* (1635) in rebuttal to Grotius's *Mare liberum.* Member of Long Parliament; aided in drawing articles of impeachment of Laud (1641); lay member of Westminster Assembly (1643), sought to moderate fanaticism of his colleagues; disapproved execution of Charles I and took no further part in public affairs. His conversation published later as *Table Talk* (1689).

Sel·des \'sel-dəs\, Gilbert Vivian. 1893–1970. American journalist and writer, b. Alliance, N.J. On staff of *Collier's* (1919–20); editor of *The Dial* (1920–23); columnist for *New York Journal* (1931–37); program director for Columbia Broadcasting System (1937–45); professor and dean of School of Communications, U. of Penn. (1959–63). Author of criticism *The Seven Lively Arts* (1924), *The Movies Come from America* (1937), *The Public Arts* (1956), etc., also *The Wise-Crackers* (play, 1925), *Lysistrata* (play, 1930), etc.

Se·leu·cid \sə-'lü-səd\. A dynasty (312–64 B.C.) which, at height of its power, ruled over Bactria, Persia, Babylonia, Syria, and part of Asia Minor. Founded by Seleucus I Nicator; included 26 sovereigns; gave its name to Seleucidan Era; last remaining region (Syria) of empire made a Roman province by Pompey (64 B.C.). See individual biographies under SELEUCUS, ANTIOCHUS, DEMETRIUS.

Se·leu·cus \sə-'lü-kəs\. Name of six kings of the Seleucid Empire:

Seleucus I. *Surnamed* Ni·ca·tor \nī-'kāt-ər, -'kā-,tȯ(ə)r\. between 358 and 354–281 B.C. Macedonian general under Alexander the Great and founder of Seleucid dynasty. Satrap of Babylon (321–312), king of Babylon (312–281), and ruler of Seleucid empire (306–281). Fought in Alexander's campaigns (333–323); commander under Perdiccas (323) and, later (321), one of those responsible for his death; given satrapy of Babylon (321); founded Seleucia on the Tigris; joined coalition of Ptolemy, Lysimachus, and Cassander against Antigonus; after defeat of Antigonus at Gaza (312), made Babylon independent; conquered eastern regions as far as the Indus (311–302); with Lysimachus won decisive victory (301) at Ipsus over Antigonus I; received Syria and Asia Minor as parts of new empire (301); made Antioch his capital; m. (298) Stratonice (*q.v.*); took prisoner (285) Demetrius I of Macedonia; defeated Lysimachus (281); proclaimed himself king of Macedon; assassinated by Ptolemy Ceraunus. Succeeded by his son Antiochus I Soter.

Seleucus II. *Surnamed* Cal·li·ni·cus \,kal-ə-'nī-kəs\. d. 226 B.C. King (246–226 B.C.). Son of Antiochus II and father of Seleucus III and Antiochus III; raised to throne by his mother Laodice; at war (246–241) with Ptolemy III of Egypt; defeated in a war (241?–236) by his brother Antiochus Hierax, to whom he gave Asia Minor as independent kingdom; lost Parthia to rising Arsacid dynasty (227?).

Seleucus III. *Surnamed* So·ter \'sōt-ər\. d. 223 B.C. King (226–223 B.C.). Son of Seleucus II; failed in attempt to recover Asia Minor from Attalus.

Seleucus IV. *Surnamed* Phi·lop·a·tor \fi-'läp-ət-ər, -ə-,tȯ(ə)r\. 218?–175 B.C. King (187–175 B.C.). Son of Antiochus III; left helpless by Roman defeat of his father; assassinated; throne seized by his brother Antiochus IV.

Seleucus V. d. 125 B.C. King (125 B.C.). Son of Demetrius II and brother of Antiochus VIII; killed by his mother Cleopatra Thea.

Seleucus VI. *Surnamed* Epiph·a·nes Nicator \i-'pif-ə-,nēz-\. d. 95 B.C. King

(96–95 B.C.). Son of Antiochus VIII; brother of Antiochus XI, Antiochus XII, and Demetrius III.

Sel·fridge \'sel-frij\, Harry Gordon. 1864?–1947. British merchant, b. Ripon, Wis. On staff of Marshall Field & Co., Chicago (to 1904). To London, England (1906) and organized (1908) Selfridge & Co., Ltd., and developed it into one of the largest department stores in Europe; became naturalized British subject (1937).

Sel·ig·man \'sel-əg-mən\, Charles Gabriel. 1873–1940. English ethnologist. Professor at U. of London (1913–34). A pioneer in British anthropology; conducted significant field researches in Melanesia (1898, 1904), Ceylon (1907–08), and the Nilotic Sudan (1909–10, 1911–12, 1921–22). His *The Melanesians of British New Guinea* (1910) formed basis of later work by Bronisław Malinowski; also wrote *The Veddas* (1911), *Races of Africa* (1930), *Pagan Tribes of the Nilotic Sudan* (1932), *Egypt and Negro Africa* (1934).

Seligman, Gerald. 1886–1973. English glaciologist. Taught at Innsbruck, Austria (from 1963); known for researches on glacier flow and structure; wrote *Snow Structure and Ski Fields* (1936).

Seligman, Joseph. 1819–1880. American financier, b. Baiersdorf, Bavaria. To U.S. (1837); established J. & W. Seligman & Co., New York, international banking house (1862), with branches later at San Francisco, New Orleans, London, Paris, and Frankfurt; aided Union cause during Civil War by marketing bonds abroad; cooperated with U.S. treasury in handling conversion operations of U.S. bonds and resumption of specie payments (1874–79). Member, Committee of Seventy, which exposed the Tweed Ring in New York; chairman, New York City Rapid Transit Commission. A brother ¶Jesse (1827–1894), b. Baiersdorf, was also a financier, associated with Joseph in banking firm of J. & W. Seligman & Co. (from 1862) and its president (1880–94). A son of Joseph ¶Isaac Newton (1855–1917), b. New York City, was also a banker; associated with J. & W. Seligman & Co. (from 1876) and president of the firm (1894–1917). Another son of Joseph ¶Edwin Robert Anderson (1861–1939), b. New York City, was an economist; taught at Columbia (1885–1931), professor (from 1891); a national expert on public finance and taxation; helped formulate personal income tax base and banking system later enacted as Federal Reserve System. Author of *Essays in Taxation* (1895), *Economic Interpretation of History* (1902), *Principles of Economics* (1905), *Studies in Public Finance* (1925), etc.

Se·lim \sel-'ēm\. Name of three Ottoman sultans:

Selim I. *Called* Ya·vuz \yä-'vüz\, *i.e.* the Grim. 1467–1520. Sultan (1512–20). Son of Bayezid II, whom he dethroned in order to seize power; crushed the Shīʿite threat of Esmāʿīl I by defeating him at Battle of Chāldirān (1514); annexed the Anatolian Kurdish and Turkmen principalities; conquered sections of Persia (1514) and annexed Syria (1516) and Egypt (1517).

Selim II. *Called* Sa·ri \sä-'rē\ *or* the Blonde *or* the Sot. 1524–1574. Sultan (1566–74). Son of Süleyman I the Magnificent; entrusted state affairs to his grand vizier and son-in-law, Mehmed Sokullu; signed (1568) peace treaty with Austria, strengthening rule in Moldavia and Walachia; captured Cyprus (1570–71); lost Battle of Lepanto (1571); recaptured Tunisia (1574). Ottoman Empire dominated the Mediterranean during his reign.

Selim III. 1761–1808. Sultan (1789–1807). Son of Mustafa III; succeeded his uncle Abdülhamid I; undertook a program of administrative, taxation, land, and military reforms on Western models; concluded treaties with Austria (1791) and Russia (1792); at first (1798) allied against Napoléon but recognized him as emperor (1804); declared war on Russia and Great Britain (1806); revolts by the Janissaries (1805) and the Yamaks (1807) forced cancellation of reforms; deposed; murdered on orders of his successor Mustafa IV.

Sél·in·court \'sel-ən-,kō(ə)rt, -,kō(ə)rt\, Ernest de. 1870–1943. English educator. Professor of English, Birmingham (1908–35); edited critical editions of a number of English classics; published *Oxford Lectures on Poetry* (1934) and *Letters of William and Dorothy Wordsworth* (1935–39).

Sel·juq *or* **Sel·juk** \'sel-jük, sel-'\. Name of Turkish dynasty which ruled over large sections of western Asia during 11th–14th centuries; founded by Toghrïl Beg (*q.v.*); name derived from Seljuq, of Turkish tribe of the Oğuz (Ghuzz).

Selkirk, Earls of. See DOUGLAS family.

Sel·kirk \'sel-,kərk\ *or* **Sel·craig** \-,krāg\, Alexander. 1676–1721. Scottish sailor. The original of Defoe's hero Robinson Crusoe. Ran away to sea (1695); joined William Dampier in privateering expedition to South Seas; quarreled with his captain; set ashore (1704) at his own request on Más a Tierra, one of Juan Fernández islets, and remained there alone until taken off (Feb. 1709) by Thomas Dover, captain of one of prizes of a privateering expedition under Woodes Rogers and Dampier.

Sel·la \'sel-lä\, Quintino. 1827–1884. Italian politician. Elected to Piedmontese Chamber of Deputies (1860); minister of finance (1862, 1864–65, 1869–73); erased a critical budget deficit by tax on milling of grain; persuaded Victor Emmanuel II to seize Rome as national capital after withdrawal of French.

Sel·lers \'sel-ərz\, Isaiah. 1802?–1864. American Mississippi River steamboat pilot, b. Iredell Co., N.C. Under pseudonym of Mark Twain (later used by Samuel L. Clemens), contributor to New Orleans *Daily Picayune;* for 25 years held record for run from New Orleans to St. Louis (set 1844).

Sellers, Peter Richard Henry. 1925–1980. English actor. On BBC radio "Goon Show" (1952–59); starred in films *The Mouse that Roared* (1959), *I'm All Right, Jack* (1959), *World of Henry Orient* (1964), *Pink Panther* (1964), *A Shot in the Dark* (1964), *Dr. Strangelove* (1964), *Return of the Pink Panther* (1975), *Pink Panther Strikes Again* (1976), *Being There* (1979).

Sel·mi \'sāl-mē\, Francesco. 1817–1881. Italian toxicologist. Published (1845–50) first systematic study of inorganic colloids, esp. silver chloride, Prussian blue, and sulfur; coined term ptomaine poisoning (1870).

Se·lous \sə-'lüs\, Frederick Courteney. 1851–1917. English hunter and explorer. Hunted and explored in south central Africa, mainly in what is now Rhodesia (from 1872); collected natural history specimens for museums and private collections; made valuable ethnological investigations.

Sel·wyn \'sel-wən\, George Augustus. 1809–1878. English prelate. First Anglican bishop of New Zealand (1841–67); studied Maori and gained confidence of natives. Bishop of Lichfield (1868–78); Selwyn Coll., Cambridge, erected in his honor.

Selz·nick \'selz-nik\, David Oliver. 1902–1965. American motion-picture producer, b. Pittsburgh. On staff of Metro-Goldwyn-Mayer Corp. (1926–27), Paramount Pictures Corp. (1927–31), RKO Radio Pictures, Inc. (1931–33), and Metro-Goldwyn-Mayer (1933–35). Organized Selznick International Pictures, Inc. (1935–40); produced *Little Women* (1933), *Dinner at Eight* (1933), *King Kong* (1933), *Anna Karenina* (1935), *A Star Is Born* (1937), *Prisoner of Zenda* (1937), *Tom Sawyer* (1937), *Gone with the Wind* (1939), *Rebecca* (1940), *Duel in the Sun* (1946), *A Farewell to Arms* (1958), etc.

Se·me·nov \sə-'myȯn-əf\, Nikolay Nikolayevich. 1896–1986. Soviet chemist. Director of Institute of Chemical Physics, Academy of Sciences of U.S.S.R. (1931 ff.); director of Institute of Chemical Physics, Moscow (1944 ff.). Shared with Sir Cyril Hinshelwood 1956 Nobel prize for chemistry for research in chemical kinetics, notably mechanisms of chain and branched-chain chemical reactions. Published *Chemical Kinetics and Chain Reactions* (1935).

Semiramis. See SAMMU-RAMAT.

Sem·ler \'zem-lər\, Johann Salomo. 1725–1791. German Lutheran theologian. Professor, Halle (1753–91); pioneer in scientific biblical textual criticism; disciple and assistant of Siegmund Baumgarten. Chief work *Abhandlung von der freien Untersuchung des Kanons* (1771–76).

Sem·mel·weis \'zem-əl-,vīs\, Ignaz Phillipp. 1818–1865. Hungarian obstetrician. Assistant in obstetric clinic in Vienna (1844–49); professor at Pest (1855–65). Proved that puerperal fever is contagious (1847–49); became pioneer of antisepsis in obstetrics. Published *Die Ätiologie, der Begriff und die Prophylaxis des Kindbetfiebers* (1861).

Semmes \'semz\, Raphael. 1809–1877. American naval officer, b. Charles Co., Md. Resigned from U.S. navy to enter Confederate navy (1861); commanded Confederate commerce destroyers *Sumter* (1861–62) and *Alabama* (1862–64), which under his command became one of most famous of commerce destroyers; *Alabama* sunk by U.S. ship *Kearsarge* off Cherbourg (1864). Commissioned rear admiral and put in command of James River squadron (1865). Practiced law, Mobile, Ala. (from 1867).

Sem·per \'zem-pər\, Gottfried. 1803–1879. German architect. A principal practitioner of Neo-Renaissance style. Practiced in Dresden (1834–49); headed architecture dept. at Zürich Polytechnikum (1855–71); helped rebuild Vienna (1871–76). Works included Opera House (1837–41, rebuilt 1871–78), Dresden; Polytechnikum, railroad station, and observatory, Zürich; imperial palace, imperial museums, and theaters, Vienna. Wrote influential *Der Stil in den technischen und tektonischen Kunsten* (1860–63).

Sem·pill \'sem-pəl\ of Bel·trees \bel-'trēz\. Family of Scottish poets, including: Sir James (1566–1625), educated with young James VI and assisted him in preparing *Basilicon Doron* (1599); Scottish ambassador to England (1599) and France (1601); best known for antipapal poem in couplets *A picktooth for the Pope, or the packman's paternoster* (1630?). His son ¶Robert (1595?–?1665) wrote elegy on Habbie Simson, "The Life and Death of the Piper of Kilbarchan" (1640). His son ¶Francis (1616?–1682), ballad writer and wit, wrote "Maggie Lauder," "Hallow Fair," and "The Blythsome Bridal."

Sempronius Gracchus. See GRACCHUS.

Sem·pro·ni·us Lon·gus \sem-'prō-nē-ə-'slȯŋ-gəs\, Tiberius. d. c.210 B.C. Roman general and politician. Consul (218 B.C.); with his colleague Publius Cornelius Scipio (*q.v.*), defeated (218) by Hannibal at the River Trebbia.

Sen \sen\ Rikyū. *Orig.* Sen Sōeki. 1521–1591. Japanese tea master. Perfected the tea ceremony and raised it to level of a national art; redefined rules of procedure, utensils, teahouse architecture, etc.; established concepts of *wabi* (deliberate simplicity in daily living) and *sabi* (tranquility); exerted great influence on Japanese artistic standards and social etiquette.

Se·na·na·yake \,sā-nän-ä-'yä-kā\, Don Stephen. 1884–1952. Ceylonese politician. Member of Legislative Council (from 1922); founder of cooperative-society movement (1923); member (from 1931), leader (1942–47), State

Council; minister for agriculture and lands (1931–47). First prime minister of independent Ceylon (1947–52); also minister of defense and external affairs (1947–52) and of health and local government (1951–52). Considered father of the nation.

Sé·nan·cour \sā-na^{n}-kür\, Étienne Pi·vert de \pē-ver-də-\. 1770–1846. French writer. Journalist in Paris; admirer of Jean-Jacques Rousseau. Author of several works marked by deep pessimism, as *Rêveries sur la nature primitive de l'homme* (1799), *Obermann* (novel, 1804), *Observations sur le génie du Christianisme* (1816), *Résumé de l'histoire des traditions morales et religieuses* (1825), etc.

Se·na·pa·ti \ˌsā-nä-'pä-tē\. *Later known as* Adi·wi·jo·yo \ˌä-dē-wē-'jòi-ō\. d. 1601. King of Mataram. Court official at Jogjakarta; usurped throne of Pajang (1582) and founded Javanese empire of Mataram; attempted to unite eastern and central Java.

Se·ne·bier \sā-nā-byā\, Jean. 1742–1809. Swiss botanist. Ordained minister (1765); city librarian of Geneva (from 1773); published *Histoire littéraire de Genève* (1786). Made researches esp. in photosynthesis; demonstrated that green plants convert carbon dioxide to oxygen under the influence of light. Author of *Mémoires physicochimiques sur l'influence de la lumière* (1782), *Recherches sur l'influence de la lumière solaire* (1783), *Expériences sur l'action de la lumière solaire dans la végétation* (1788), *Physiologie végétale* (1800), etc.

Sen·e·ca \'sen-i-kə\, Lucius Annaeus. *Called* Seneca the Elder. c.55 B.C.–c.39 A.D. Roman rhetorician, b. Spain. Father of Seneca the Younger and grandfather of Lucan. Author of a work on declamation, *Oratorum sententiae divisiones colores,* and a historical work (now lost).

Seneca, Lucius Annaeus. *Called* Seneca the Younger. 4 B.C.?–65 A.D. Roman statesman and philosopher, b. Spain. Son of Lucius Annaeus Seneca and uncle of Lucan. Studied in Rome; began political career as quaestor (c.31); banished to Corsica for alleged adultery with emperor's niece (41). Summoned (49) to tutor Domitius, who later became emperor under name Nero; praetor (50); influential councilor of Nero in early years of his power; with Burrus introduced fiscal and judicial reforms in Senate. In later years, Nero turned against him; finally accused him of complicity in conspiracy of Piso; by order of Nero, took own life. Most important works were philosophic essays, including *Ad Marciam de consolatione, De ira, Ad Helviam de consolatione, De brevitate vitae, De constantia sapientis, De clementia, De vita beata, De beneficiis, De tranquillitate animi, De otio, De providentia.* Known also as author of nine tragedies, *Hercules Furens, Thyestes, Phoenissae, Phaedra, Oedipus, Troades, Medea, Agamemnon, Hercules Oetaeus* (perhaps spurious), and a satire *Apocolocyntosis divi Claudii.*

Se·ne·fel·der \'zā-nə-ˌfel-dər\, Aloys. 1771–1834. German lithographer, b. Prague. Invented lithography (1796); director of royal printing office, Munich (1809); published *Vollständiges Lehrbuch der Steindruckerey* (1818); established a school at Offenbach to train lithographers; invented process of lithographing in colors (1826).

Senfl \'zen-fəl\, Ludwig. c.1486–1542 or 1543. Swiss composer. Most important German-speaking master of his time. Pupil of Heinrich Isaac; composer to court of Maximilian I (1497–1519); with Duke William of Bavaria's Hofkapelle in Munich (from 1523). Edited (1520) *Liber selectarum cantionum,* first German printed anthology of motets; completed Isaac's *Choralis constantinus* (pub. 1550, 1555); composed 7 masses, a *Magnificat* cycle (1537), motets, and about 150 German lieder.

Sen·ior \'sē-nyər\, Nassau William. 1790–1864. English economist. First professor of political economy, Oxford (1825–30, 1847–52). Author of *An Outline of the Science of Political Economy* (1836), etc.

Sen·nach·er·ib \sə-'nak-ə-rəb\. *Akkadian* Sin-akhkhe-eriba. d. 681 B.C. King of Assyria (704–681 B.C.). Son of Sargon II; continued wars of his father against Merodach-baladan (*q.v.*) and alliance of Babylon and Elam; drove Merodach-baladan out of Babylon (703) and installed Bel-ibni as its king. Made campaign in West (701); captured Sidon and secured submission of Ashdod, Ammon, Moab, and Edom; failed to take Tyre; defied by Hezekiah; invaded Palestine and captured many cities of Judah; had fleet built by Phoenician captives and with it destroyed Babylonian colony in Elam (694); fought a great indecisive battle with Elamites (691) at Khalule; destroyed Babylon (689). A second campaign against Jerusalem and conflict with Taharka of Egypt (c.683) uncertain and unconfirmed by Assyrian records. Active in building, esp. in restoring Nineveh to great splendor. Killed by one (or more) of his sons; succeeded by Esarhaddon.

Sen·nett \'sen-ət\, Mack. *Orig.* Michael Sin·nott \'sin-ət\. 1880–1960. American motion-picture producer and director, b. Richmond, Que. Father of American slapstick comedy and creator of the Keystone Kops. Worked under D.W. Griffith at Biograph Studios (1909–11); owner (1911–33), Keystone Co., Los Angeles. Director or producer of over 1000 comedy shorts, usually featuring bathing beauties, custard pies, and the Keystone Kops; films included *Tillie's Punctured Romance* (1914; first American feature-length comedy), *His Bitter Pill* (1916), *A Small Town Idol* (1921), *The Shriek of Araby* (1923).

Še·no·a \shen-'ò-ä\, August. 1838–1881. Croatian writer. Father of modern Croatian literature. Contributed to Croatian national identity; led transition of Croatian from romanticism to realism. Artistic director of Croatian National Theater; editor of critical journal *Vijenac* (1869–81). Introduced the historical novel to Croatian literature, as with *Zlatarovo zlato* (1871), *Seljačka buna* (1877), *Diogenes* (1878); also wrote poems, plays, short stories, and essays.

Sentleger, Sir Anthony. See SAINT LEGER.

Septimius Severus, Lucius. See SEVERUS.

Se·púl·ve·da \sā-'pül-vā-t͟hä\, Juan Gi·nés de \k̲ē-'nās-t͟hā-\. 1490?–1572 or 1573. Spanish theologian and historian. Royal historiographer (from 1535); wrote (in Latin) theological treatises and histories of Charles V and Philip II; his *Democrates II,* in defense of Indian slavery, provoked a long controversy with Las Casas.

Se·qen·en·re II \ˌsā-ken-'en-rā\. *Also called* Seqenenre Tao II \-'taù\. 16th century B.C. King of Egypt (c.1575 B.C.). Member of 17th dynasty; quarrelled with Hyksos king Apopi; died violently, either by assassination or in battle.

Se·quoya *or* **Se·quoy·ah** *or* **Se·quoia** \si-'kwòi-ə\. *More correctly spelled* Si·kwayi \si-'kwòi-ə, -'kwī-\. *Took name* George Guess \'ges\ *at maturity, from American trader named Nathaniel Gist he believed to be his father.* between 1760 and 1770–1843. American Indian scholar, b. Taskigi, Tenn. Silversmith, painter, and warrior; served with U.S. army in Creek War (1813–14). Made study of his own Cherokee language and succeeded in forming syllabary (1809–21) approved by Cherokee council (1821) and effective in teaching thousands of his people to read and write. Name perpetuated in giant redwoods *Sequoia* and in Sequoia National Park.

Se·ra·fi·no·wicz \ser-ä-'fē-nō-vēch\, Leszek. *Pseudonym* Jan Le·choń \'lä-k̲ōn^{y}\. 1899–1956. Polish poet. Became editor in Warsaw of satirical weekly *Cyrulik Warszawski* (1926); cultural attaché in Paris (1932–40); to New York (1941); on staff of Radio Free Europe (1952–56). Author of *Karmazynowy poemat* (1920), *Srebrne i czarne* (1924), *Lutnia po Bekwarku* (1942), *Aria z kurantem* (1945).

Se·rao \sä-'rä-ō\, Matilda. 1856–1927. Italian novelist, b. Greece. Founded several periodicals, esp. *Corriere di Roma* (1885) and *Il Giorno* of Naples (1904). Author of about 40 novels dealing with lower middle class Neapolitan life, including *Il romanzo della fanciulla* (1886), *Il paese di cuccagna* (1890), *La ballerina* (1899), *Suor Giovanna della Croce* (1901).

Se·ra·phim \'syer-əf-yim\ of Sa·rov \'sár-əf\. Saint. *Orig.* Prokhor Mosh·nin \'mòsh-nyin\. 1759–1833. Russian monk and mystic. Entered Sarov monastery (1777); ordained priest (1793); hermit (1793–1815); extended to lay persons his system of meditation and ecstatic prayers; proclaimed saint (1913) by Russian Orthodox church.

Se·ra·pi·on *or* **Sa·ra·pi·on** \sə-'rā-pē-ən\. Saint. 4th century. Egyptian Christian theologian and prelate. Bishop of Thmuis in the Nile delta (before 339–c.359); supported Athanasius in his attacks on Arian heresy; with St. Anthony, a key figure in early monasticism. Wrote treatise *Against the Manichees;* compiled the *Euchologion,* a service book for eucharistic worship.

Serbati. See ROSMINI-SERBATI.

Ser·geant \'sär-jənt\, John. 1622–1707. English clergyman. Ordained Roman Catholic priest (1650); engaged most of his life in theological and philosophical controversies, esp. against Jeremy Taylor, Archbishop Peter Talbot, and John Locke, whom he attacked in *Solid Philosophy Asserted, Against the Fancies of the Ideists* (1697).

Ser·ge·yev \syir-'gyā-yif\ *or* **Ser·gue·eff** \syir-gü-'ā-yif\, Nicholas Grigorievich. 1876–1951. Russian dancer and ballet master. With St. Petersburg Imperial Ballet (1894–1918; *régisseur-général* 1914–18); left Russia (1918) with choreography for 21 ballets recorded in Stepanoff dance notation; recreated ballets for Western companies, thus preserving such classics as *Swan Lake, The Sleeping Beauty, The Nutcracker;* with Diaghilev's Ballets Russes, Metropolitan Opera Ballet, Sadler's Wells Ballet, International Ballet, etc. (from 1921).

Ser·gi·us \'sər-jē-əs\ and **Bac·chus** \'bak-əs\. Saints. d. c.303. Christian martyrs. Officers in Roman army on Syrian frontier; supposedly favorites of Emperor Maximian, who ordered them tortured and executed for refusing to sacrifice to Jupiter; commemorated in Eastern and Western churches.

Sergius. Name of four popes:

Sergius I. Saint. d. 701. Pope (687–701). Served under St. Leo and Conon; elected over antipope Paschal; rejected provisions of the Quinisext Council (692); protected by Roman soldiers from arrest by Byzantine emperor Justinian II; interested in Anglo-Saxons and Franks; baptized King Caedwalla of Wessex in Rome (689); ordered Bishop St. Wilfrid of York restored to see (c.691); consecrated St. Willibrord as bishop of the Frisians (695); with aid of King Cunipert of the Lombards ended the Aquileian controversy, unifying the church in Italy; credited with introducing the Agnus Dei to the mass and with instituting the procession for Candlemas.

Sergius II. d. 847. Pope (844–847). Imprisoned antipope John, the candidate of the populace (844); crowned Louis II king of the Lombards; made Drogo legate to Frankish kingdoms (844); delegated most papal business to his brother Bishop Benedict of Albano; during reign Rome plundered by the Saracens (846).

Sergius III. d. 911. Pope (904–911). Supported Stephen VI's annulment of Formosus; attempted to seize papacy on election of Pope John IX but expelled from Rome (898); deposed antipope Christopher (904); apparently ordered murders of Christopher and Pope Leo V (904); his pontificate dominated by Count Theophylactus; invalidated Formosus's ordinations; reputed to have been lover of Theophylactus's daughter Marozia and father of her son, the future Pope John XI; restored the Lateran basilica; considered one of worst pontiffs in history.

Sergius IV. *Orig.* Peter Buc·ca·por·ci \ˌbük-kä-ˈpȯr-kē\. *Nicknamed* Bucca Porci. d. 1012. Pope (1009–1012). Bishop of Albano (c.1004); pontificate dominated by Roman nobles and John II Crescentius; noted for aid to the poor and granting privileges to several monasteries.

Sergius. Name of two patriarchs of Constantinople:

Sergius I. d. 638. Patriarch (610–638). Strong supporter of Emperor Heraclius and regent (622–628) during his campaigns; repulsed attack of Avars on Constantinople (626); in attempts to solve Christological controversy formulated theory of monoenergism (c.621) and doctrine of monothelitism (638), both promulgated throughout Byzantine Empire by Heraclius and both rejected by Eastern and Western churches.

Sergius II. d. 1019. Patriarch (c.1001–1019). Claimed title Ecumenical Patriarch against papal objections; temporarily supported the Photian movement; supported Byzantine landowners against tax claims of Emperor Basil II.

Sergius IV. d. c.1034. Duke of Naples. Ruled jointly with his father (from 1002) and alone shortly thereafter; at war (from 1026) with Pandulph, who seized Naples; recovered Naples from Pandulph with aid of Norman soldier Ranulph Drengo; rewarded Ranulph by giving him Aversa, first Norman fief in Italy; entered monastery after transference of Norman allegiance to Pandulph (1032).

Sergius. *Orig.* Ivan Nikolayevich Stra·go·rod·sky \strə-(ˌ)gə-ˈrȯd-skəi\. 1867–1944. Russian prelate. Archbishop of Finland (1905); member of Holy Synod (1911); metropolitan of Novgorod (1917); supported (1922–23) the "Living Church" but later (1923) publicly repudiated it. Acting head of Russian Orthodox church (1927); issued declaration of solidarity with Soviet regime; metropolitan of Moscow (1934); aided Soviet army to repel German invasion of 1941; obtained from Stalin recognition of the Orthodox church as a religious bureau within the Socialist system (1943); elected patriarch of Moscow and all Russia (1943). Author of theological works, esp. *The Orthodox Doctrine of Salvation* (1895).

Sergius of Ra·do·nezh \ˈrä-dən-yizh\. Saint. *Orig.* Bartholomew Ki·ril·lo·vich \kyir-yil-ȯv-ˌyich\. 1314–1392. Russian monk. Took name Sergius when consecrated a monk (1337); founded the Sergian monastery of the Trinity in forest of Radonezh; monastery became the Russian center and symbol of religious renewal and national identity; famed for his ascetic life and compassion for the poor; carried out diplomatic missions to unite the scattered Russian principalities under Grand Prince Dmitry Donskoy of Moscow. Considered saint protector of Russia.

Sergius of Re·sai·na \rā-ˈsī-nə\. d. 536. Syrian scholar. Practiced medicine; later may have been a priest or monk; theologically, at first a Monophysite, then a Nestorian, finally held orthodox views on nature of Christ; legate to Rome for Ephraem of Antioch (c.535). One of fathers of Syriac literature; translated over 20 Greek writings, esp. Aristotle and Pseudo-Dionysius; wrote commentaries on Greek philosophers.

Ser·lio \ˈserl-yō\, Sebastiano. 1475–1554. Italian architect, painter, and theorist. In Rome (1514–27); studied under Baldassare Peruzzi; in Venice (1527–40); appointed consultant in building of palace at Fountainebleau (1540); introduced principles of ancient Roman architecture into France. Author of *Tutte l'opere d'architettura* (1537–75) which exerted immense influence throughout Europe; also contributed to scenography.

Ser·mis·sy \ser-mē-sē\, Claudin *or* Claude de. c.1490–1562. French composer. Member (from 1515), assistant director (from 1532) of royal chapel; canon of Sainte-Chapelle (1533–62). One of leading composers of chansons of his time; also published 12 masses and about 70 motets.

Se·rov \syi-ˈrȯf\, Aleksandr Nikolayevich. 1820–1871. Russian composer. Known for operas *Judith* (1863) and *Rogneda* (1865), symphonies, religious music, etc.

Ser·pa Pin·to \ˈser-pə-ˈpē^{n}(n)-tü\, Alexandre Alberto da Ro·cha \t͟hə-ˈrō-shə\. 1846–1900. Portuguese explorer and colonial administrator. Explored Zambezi River in East Africa (1869); crossed southern and central Africa from west to east (1877–79); governor of Mozambique (1889).

Ser·pot·ta \ser-ˈpȯt-tä\, Giacomo. 1656–1732. Italian sculptor and stuccoworker. His style employing illusions of perspective and asymmetrical arrangements of two or more independent decorations greatly influenced German Rococo artists. Decorations in Palermo included oratories of S. Lorenze (1690/98–1706), S. Zita (1668–1718), Rosario di S. Domenico (1710–17); also Palermo hospital chapel, archbishop's palace in Santa Chiara, Badio Nuovo at Alcomo, and statues (1723) in S. Francesco d'Assisi. Credited with raising Sicilian stuccowork to an art.

Ser·ra \ˈser-rä\, Junípero, *orig.* Miguel José. *Called* Apostle of California. 1713–1784. Spanish missionary. Entered Franciscan order (1730); to Mexico City (1749); missionary to Indians in Sierra Gorda missions (1750–58) and in south central Mexico (1758–67). Sent to Lower California (1767); cooperated with government in plans to establish missions in Upper California; founded mission at San Diego (July 16, 1769), first European settlement in Upper California; continued as leader in white occupation of California, establishing missions of San Carlos de Monterey (1770), San Antonio de Padua and San Gabriel (1771), San Luis Obispo (1772), San Francisco de Assisi and San Juan Capistrano (1776), Santa Clara (1777), and San Buenaventura (1782). A strenuous defender of Indians.

Ser·ra·no y Do·mín·guez \ser-ˈrä-nō-ē-t͟hō-ˈmēŋ-gāth\, Francisco. Duque de la Tor·re \t͟hā-lä-ˈtȯr-rā\. 1810–1885. Spanish general and politician. Served in Carlist wars under Queen Isabella (1834–39); field marshal (1840); captain general of Granada (1848); took part in the O'Donnell uprising (1854); governor of Cuba (1859–62). After death of O'Donnell (1867), became leader of Union Liberal party; with Prim dethroned the queen (1868) and later became regent (1869–71); military leader under King Amadeo; after coup of January 1874 headed government; in exile upon accession of Alfonso XII (1874–1881); ambassador to Paris (1884).

Ser·ra·to \ser-ˈrä-tō\, José. 1868–1960. Uruguayan politician. President of Uruguay (1923–27); minister of foreign affairs (1934–35, 1945).

Ser·to·ri·us \(ˌ)sər-ˈtōr-ē-əs, -ˈtȯr-\, Quintus. c.123–72 B.C. Roman general and politician. Served in Gaul against the Cimbri and Teutons (105, 102); quaestor in Cisalpine Gaul (90); served under, and remained a partisan of, Marius; praetor (83). Became independent ruler of most of Spain (from 80); allied with Mediterranean pirates and Mithradates VI of Pontus against Rome; pursued by troops under Metallus and Pompey (from 77); murdered by conspiracy headed by Marcus Perperna.

Sert y Ba·dia \ˈser-tē-ˈb͟ät͟h-yä\, José María. 1874–1945. Spanish painter. Known for his modern Baroque murals decorating buildings throughout the world, including the cathedral of Vich, the assembly hall of the League of Nations (Geneva), the RCA Building in Rockefeller Center and the Waldorf-Astoria Hotel (both New York City).

Sé·ru·sier \sā-rüēs-yā\, Louis-Paul-Henri. 1865–1927. French painter and theorist. Studied with Paul Gauguin (1888–90); painted in Cloisonnist manner, esp. *Bois d'amour* (1888); a founding member (1889) and theorist of the Nabis movement; influenced by visits (1897, 1903) to school of religious art at Benedictine abbey of Beuron, Germany; retired (1914) to Brittany and became a mystic. Published works on art theory, esp. *ABC de la peinture* (1921).

Ser·van·do·ni \ˌser-vän-ˈdō-nē\, Giovanni Nicolo, *Fr.* Jean-Nicolas. 1695–1766. Italian architect and painter. To Paris (1724); architect to the king (1732). Among his works were the façade of the Church of Saint-Sulpice (Paris), altar of the Church of the Chartreux (Lyon), and the altar of the cathedral at Sens; also known for Baroque stage sets.

Ser·ve·to \ser-ˈvā-tō\, Miguel. *Known as* Michael Ser·ve·tus \(ˌ)sər-ˈvēt-əs\. *Also used pseudonyms* Michel de Vil·le·neuve \vēl(-ə)-nœv\ *and* Vil·la·no·va·nus \vil-ˌā-nō-ˈvā-nəs\. 1511–1553. Spanish theologian and physician. Opposed doctrine of the Trinity in *De Trinitatis erroribus* (1531); in Lyon edited scientific works, esp. Ptolemy's *Geographia* (1535, 1541), and the Santis Pagnini Bible (1542). Lectured on geography and astronomy; practiced medicine at Charlieu and Vienne (1538–53). Opponent of Trinitarianism and infant baptism; publish *Christianismi restitutio* (1553) which contained his discovery of the pulmonary circulation of blood and for which he was arrested and brought to trial before Inquisition at Lyon; escaped, but was apprehended at Geneva; imprisoned at Calvin's request and burned at the stake as a heretic.

Ser·vice \ˈsər-vəs\, Robert William. 1874–1958. Canadian writer, b. Preston, England. To Canada (1894); worked for a bank, including 8 years in the Yukon; newspaper correspondent during the Balkan Wars (1912–13); lived in Europe (from 1912). Called "the Canadian Kipling" for rollicking ballads of the "Frozen North," as "The Shooting of Dan McGrew." Verse collections included *Songs of a Sourdough* (1907), *Ballads of a Cheechako* (1909), *Rhymes of a Red Cross Man* (1916), *Bar Room Ballads* (1940); also wrote novels as *The Trail of '98* (1910) and *The House of Fear* (1927), and autobiographical works *Ploughman of the Moon* (1945) and *Harper of Heaven* (1948).

Ser·vi·us \ˈsər-vē-əs\. *In full* Marius (*or* Maurus) Servius Hon·o·ra·tus \ˌ(h)än-ə-ˈrāt-əs\. 4th century A.D. Latin grammarian and scholar. Author of commentary on Virgil extant in long and short versions.

Servius Tul·li·us \-'təl-ē-əs\. 6th century B.C. Sixth legendary king (578–534 B.C.) of Rome. Either an Etruscan or Latin; founded shrine of Diana on Aventine Hill; credited with Servian Constitution. According to legend, born a slave of Tarquinius Priscus and became his son-in-law; slain by his daughter and her husband Tarquinius Superbus.

Se·sos·tris \sə-'säs-trəs\. Name of three kings of Egypt of 12th dynasty:

Sesostris I. d. 1928 B.C. Second king of the dynasty (1971–1928 B.C.). Son of Amenemhet I and father of Amenemhet II. Ruled as coregent with his father (1971–1962); led expeditions against Nubia and the Libyans; sole ruler (1962); completed conquest of Nubia and penetrated into Cush; did much building; built Karnak at Thebes; kept peace with Palestine and Syria; built his pyramid at Lisht; made his son coregent (1929). Brought Egypt to a peak of prosperity.

Sesostris II. d. 1878 B.C. Fourth king of the dynasty (1897–1878 B.C.). Son of Amenemhet II; ruled as coregent with father (1897–1895); continued mineral exploitation of Nubia; built town and pyramid near the Fayyūm; made his son Sesostris III coregent (1878).

Sesostris III. d. 1843 B.C. Fifth king of the dynasty (1878–1843 B.C.). Son of Sesostris II and father of Amenemhet III; reorganized the government into 3 districts, each with a vizier; had canal dug through first cataract of the Nile; conducted campaigns in Nubia, reaching second cataract; invaded Syria; built pyramid at Dashur; raised Egypt to state of great power.

Name Sesostris also given to a mythical king of Ptolemaic Egypt, whose exploits are founded on deeds of Ramses II and others.

Ses·shū \ses-shü\. *Family name* Oda \'ōd-ə\. *Earlier used name* Tō·yō \'tō-yō\. 1420–1506. Japanese Zen priest and artist. Greatest master of ink painting (*sumi-e*). Entered Zen temple and received name Tōyō (1431); lived in Kyōto (c.1440–60); studied painting under Shūbun and Buddhism under Shurin Suto; took (c.1466) name Sesshū (i.e. Snow Boat); traveled and studied in China (1468–69); studio at Yamaguchi. Adapted Chinese models to Japanese artistic ideals and aesthetic sensibilities; known for landscape scrolls, including *Four Seasons Landscape* (c.1470–90), *Winter Landscape* (c.1470–90), *Sansui Chōkan* scroll (c.1486), and *Ama-no-Hashidate* scroll (c.1502–05); also painted Zen Buddhist pictures and screens decorated with birds, flowers, and animals.

Ses·sions \'sesh-ənz\, Roger Huntington. 1896–1985. American composer, b. New York City. Taught at Princeton U. (1935–45; 1953–65) and at Juilliard School of Music (1965 ff.). Early adopted neoclassical style of Stravinsky but later incorporated serialism of Arnold Schoenberg; composed complex, difficult works. Important works included symphonic suite *The Black Maskers* (1928), eight symphonies (1927–68), operas *The Trial of Lucullus* (1947) and *Montezuma* (1941–63), cantata *When Lilacs Last in the Dooryard Bloom'd* (1970). Awarded 1974 Pulitzer prize for body of work and 1981 Pulitzer for *Concerto for Orchestra.*

Ses·son \ses-ōn\ Shūkei. *Orig.* Sa·ta·ke \sä-tä-ke\ Heizo. 1504–c.1589. Japanese artist. Most distinguished painter working in the style of Sesshū, therefore sometimes called the second Sesshū. A Buddhist monk of the Sōtō sect; lived in northern Honshu; took name Sesson Shūkei in tribute to his masters, Sesshū and Shūbun. Excelled in landscapes as *The Wind and the Waves* and *Eight Views;* figure drawings as *Li Po Gazing at the Waterfall;* animal pictures as *The Tiger;* and studies of flowers and birds as *Landscape with Hawks.*

Se·tha·thi·rath I \,se-tä-'tir-ät\. *Also known as* Set'·at'·ir·at Set·thau·ang·so \,se-tä-'tir-ät-,set-taù-'äŋ-sō\ *and* Sa·ya-set·tha·ti·rath \'sī-ə-,set-tä-'tir-ät\. 1534–1571. King of Laotian kingdom of Lan Xang (1547–1571). Son and successor of Photisarath; made Vien Chang (now Vientiane) his capital (1560); built a majestic temple for sacred statue Phra Kaeo; furthered Buddhism; formed alliance with Siamese against the Burmese; repulsed a Burmese invasion (1563). Still revered by Laotians; central figure in spiritual cult of the Kha.

Seti \'set-ē\. *Also spelled* Sethi *and* Seth·os \'set-,ōs\. Name of two kings of 19th dynasty of ancient Egypt:

Seti I. d. 1304 B.C. King (1318–1304 B.C.). Son of Ramses I and father of Ramses II; coregent with his father (c.1320–18); reorganized government of kingdom; overran Palestine; fought successful war with Libyans west of Nile delta; engaged in indecisive conflict with Hittites in Syria, made peace. Completed great temple of Amon at Karnak begun by his father; built splendid mortuary temple at Abydos and finest burial place in Valley of the Tombs of Kings at Thebes. Often considered greatest king of 19th dynasty.

Seti II. d. 1210 B.C. Last king (1216–1210) of 19th dynasty.

Se·ton *or* **Sey·ton** *or* **Sea·toun** \'sēt-ᵊn\. Name of an old Scottish family holding the earldoms of Win·ton \'wint-ᵊn\ (cr. 1600), of Dun·ferm·line \dən-'fərm-lən\ (cr.1606), and Eg·lin·ton \'eg-lin-tən\. Members included: George (1530?–1585), 5th Baron Seton; Roman Catholic, master of household of Mary, Queen of Scots (1561); assisted her in escape from Loch Leven (1568); entrusted with mission to Duke of Alba, seeking military aid (c.1571); one of Morton's (James Douglas) judges (1581). His son ¶Sir Alexander (1555?–1622), 1st Earl of Dunfermline; prior of Pluscarden (1565); lord president of court of session (1593); chief of the Octavians (1596); guardian of Prince Charles (who became Charles I of England); commissioner for union with England (1604); member of English privy council (1609). His son ¶Charles (d. 1673), 2d Earl of Dunfermline; one of leaders of Scottish Covenanting army opposing Charles I (1639); privy councilor in England (1640); supported attempted rescue of the king (1647); privy councilor (1660); extraordinary lord of session (1667); lord privy seal (1671).

Seton, Elizabeth Ann, *nee* Bay·ley \'bā-lē\. Saint. 1774–1821. American religious, b. New York City. m. William M. Seton (1794). A founder (1797) of Society for Relief of Poor Widows with Small Children, first charitable organization in New York. After death of husband (1803), joined Roman Catholic church (1805); opened (1809) Catholic elementary school in Baltimore and laid foundation of U.S. parochial school system; founded order (1809) which became known as Sisters of Charity of St. Joseph, or briefly, Sisters of Charity, and served as first superior of the order (1809–21); first native-born American canonized (1975). Seton Hall U. named in her honor.

Seton, Ernest Thompson. *Orig. surname* Thompson. 1860–1946. American naturalist and writer, b. South Shields, England. Founder of modern school of animal fiction writing. To Canada (1866); lived in Manitoba (1881–86); naturalized U.S. citizen (1930). Founder, Woodcraft Indians (1902); instrumental in founding of Boy Scouts of America (1910). Author of many nature stories, usually illustrated by himself, including *Wild Animals I Have Known* (1898), *The Biography of a Grizzly* (1900), *Lobo, Rag and Vixen* (1900), *Lives of the Hunted* (1901), *Biography of an Arctic Fox* (1937).

Set·tem·bri·ni \,sāt-tām-'brē-nē\, Luigi. 1813–1877. Italian writer and patriot. Imprisoned because of political activities (1839–42, 1849–58); escaped to England (1858); returned to Naples (1860); known esp. for *Lezioni di letteratura italiana* (1866–72).

Set·tle \'set-ᵊl\, Elkanah. 1648–1724. English playwright. Memorable chiefly through ridicule of Dryden and Pope. Author of the tragedy *Cambyses* (1671), first of series of bombastic dramas that annoyed Dryden; pilloried as Doeg by Dryden in second part of *Absalom and Achitophel* (1682).

Seu·rat \sǖ-rà\, Georges, *in full* Georges-Pierre. 1859–1891. French painter. Founder of Neo-Impressionism; originator (with Paul Signac) of Pointillism. A founder of Groupe des Artistes Indépendants (1884); influenced by Chevreul's chroma theory. His canvases included *Une Baignade, Asnières* (1883–84), *Un Dimanche d'été à la Grande Jatte* (1884–86), *Les Poseuses* (1887–88), *La Parade* (1887–88), *Le Chahut* (1889–90).

Seuse, Heinrich. See Heinrich SÜSE.

Se·ve·ri·an \sə-'vir-ē-ən\ of Gab·a·la \'gab-ə-lə\. d. after 408. Syrian prelate and theologian. Bishop of Gabala; to Constantinople (c.401); became protégé of John Chrysostom; famed orator; became hostile to Chrysostom and was his prosecutor and judge of Synod of the Oak (403); fled Constantinople after popular reaction to Chrysostom's exile; arranged second trial and exiled Chrysostom permanently (404); returned to Gabala (407). Noted as biblical exegete of the literal-historical school of Antioch; wrote commentaries on letters of St. Paul and homilies on first six books of Old Testament.

Se·ve·rin \'sā-və-ren\, Christian. *Known as* Lon·go·mon·ta·nus \,lòŋ-gō-män-'tā-nəs\ *(Lat. form of his birthplace Longberg).* 1562–1647. Danish astronomer. Assistant to Tycho Brahe (1588–97); systematized Brahe's program for the restoration of astronomy and published it as *Astronomia Danica* (1622). Professor (1607–47) at Copenhagen, where he initiated (1632) construction of its observatory.

Sé·ve·rin \sāv(-ə)-raⁿ\, Fernand. 1867–1931. Belgian poet. Author of *Le Lys* (1888), *La Solitude heureuse* (1904), *La Source au fond des bois* (1924), etc.

Se·ve·ring \'zā-və-riŋ\, Carl. 1875–1952. German politician. Socialist Democratic member of Reichstag (1907–12); member of Reichstag (1920–33) and Prussian Landtag (1921–33); Prussian minister of interior (1920–26, 1930–32); reformed state police force; German minister of interior (1928–30).

Se·ve·ri·ni \,sā-vā-'rē-nē\, Gino. 1883–1966. Italian painter. Worked in Pointillist manner (1900–1910); joined Futurist movement (1910); turned to Cubism (1916) and then to Neo-Classicism (1921). Author of *Du Cubisme au Classicisme* (1921). His canvases included *Pam Pam al Monico* (1909–11), *Dynamic Hieroglyph of the Bal Tabarin* (1912), *Red Cross Train* (1914), and *Spherical Expansion of Light (Centrifugal)* (1914).

Sev·er·i·nus \,sev-ə-'rī-nəs\. d. 640. Pope (640). Elected (638), but unable for more than a year to secure imperial confirmation because of his refusal to acknowledge Heraclius's *Ecthesis* (638).

Sev·ern \'sev-ərn\, Joseph. 1793–1879. English painter. Friend of Keats; known for portraits (including Keats, 1821) and historical subjects.

Seversky, Alexander de. See DE SEVERSKY.

Se·ve·rus \sə-'vir-əs\. Name of four Roman emperors:

Severus, Flavius Valerius. d. 307. Emperor (306–307). Army officer in

Pannonia; created caesar (305) to Constantius I Chlorus and given control of Pannonia, Italy, and Africa; made augustus of the West (306) by Galerius; sent against Maxentius, but unsuccessful.

Severus, Libius. d. 465. Emperor (461–465). Made emperor of the West by Ricimer on death of Majorian; a puppet ruler; reign marked by inroads of Vandals, Goths, and other barbarians in the empire.

Severus, Lucius Septimius. 146–211. Emperor (193–211), b. Africa. m. (187) Julia Domna. Entered Senate (c.173); consul (190); commander in chief of army in Pannonia and Illyria; proclaimed emperor by the soldiers; overcame his rivals Didius Julianus at Rome (193), Pescennius Niger in northern Syria (194), and Albinus in Gaul (197); named his son Caracalla co-emperor (197); waged successful war against the Parthians (197–202); annexed Mesopotamia (199); restructured government on military basis and reformed judicial system; spent last years (208–211) in Britain; died at Eburacum (York); succeeded by his sons Caracalla and Geta; his reign the golden age of jurists, esp. Papinian, Ulpian, and Paulus.

Severus Al·ex·an·der \\-ˌal-ig-ˈzan-dər, -ˌel-\\. *In full* Marcus Aurelius Severus Alexander. 208–235 A.D. Emperor (222–235). Native of Phoenicia; grandson of Julia Maesa and cousin of Elagabalus, who adopted him as heir (221); succeeded to throne on murder of Elagabalus (222); nominal ruler, real power being wielded by grandmother and mother, along with regency council of 16 senators; defeated by Persians in Mesopotamia (232); ended campaign against Alemanni tribe by buying peace (234); murdered by indignant soldiers.

Severus of An·ti·och \\ˈant-ē-ˌäk\\. c.465–538. Greek monk-theologian and prelate. Lived as monk in Palestine; became a leading exponent of Monophysitism; wrote (c.510) *Philalethes* in response to charges of heresy; in Christological dispute attempted to formulate a doctrine between extreme Monophysitism of Eutychian faction and orthodox view; became confidant of Emperor Anastasius who made him patriarch of Antioch (512); fled to Egypt on accession of Justin I (518); formulator and head of Monophysite movement in Egypt and Syria. Wrote vast amount of sermons, letters, and polemical tracts; considered a saint and martyr by Coptic church.

Severus, Gabriel. See GABRIEL SEVERUS.

Severus, Sulpicius. See SULPICIUS SEVERUS.

Se·vier \\sə-ˈvi(ə)r\\, John. 1745–1815. American soldier and politician, b. near New Market, Va. Emigrated to Tennessee (1772); member, local Committee of Safety (Knoxville, Tenn., 1776); led force across Smoky Mountains to win victory over British at battle of King's Mountain (Oct. 7, 1780). Governor of the temporary State of Franklin (1785–88); member, U.S. House of Representatives (1789–91); first governor of Tennessee (1796–1801, 1803–09); again member of U.S. House of Representatives (1811–15).

Sé·vi·gné \\sā-vēn-yā\\, Marie de, *nee* Ra·bu·tin-Chan·tal \\rȧ-büē-taⁿ-shäⁿ-tȧl\\. Marquise. 1626–1696. French writer and lady of fashion. m. Marquis Henri de Sévigné (1644; killed in a duel 1651); famed for her *Lettres de Mme de Sévigné,* written to her daughter Françoise-Marguerite, comtesse de Gri·gnan \\də-grēn-yäⁿ\\, who lived in Provence, where her husband was lieutenant governor. The letters recorded in faultless French events of daily interest in her life in Paris or at her country seat in Brittany.

Şev·ket Pa·şa \\shev-ˈket-pə-ˈshä\\, Mahmud. 1858–1913. Ottoman general and politician. Entered army as staff captain (1882); commander of 3d army of Salonika (1908); crushed a religious uprising against the government (31st of March Incident) and deposed Sultan Abdülhamid II (1909); became inspector general of first three army corps and minister of war (1909); grand vizier (1913); assassinated.

Sew·all \\ˈs(y)ü-əl\\, Samuel. 1652–1730. American merchant and jurist, b. Bishopstoke, England. To America (1661) and settled in Boston; member, governor's council (1684–86, 1689–1725); presiding judge at Salem over witchcraft cases, condemning 19 persons to be executed (1692); later (1697), publicly confessed error and guilt for his part in the trials. Justice, Massachusetts superior court (1692–1728) and chief justice (1718–28). Author of an antislavery tract *The Selling of Joseph* (1700), an argument for humane treatment of Indians *A Memorial Relating to the Kennebeck Indians* (1721), and a *Diary,* covering period 1674–77 and 1685–1729 (pub. 1878–82).

Se·ward \\ˈsē-wərd\\, Anna. *Called* the Swan of Lich·field \\ˈlich-ˌfēld\\. 1747–1809. English poet. Supplied Boswell with particulars about Dr. Johnson, whom she imitated in her letters (pub. 1811–13); published poetical novel *Louisa* (1782); bequeathed her poetical works, including elegies and sonnets, to Sir Walter Scott, who published them with a memoir (1810).

Sew·ard \\ˈs(y)ü-ərd\\, William Henry. 1801–1872. American politician, b. Florida, N.Y. Practiced law in Auburn, N.Y. (from 1823); governor of New York (1839–43); leader of the antislavery wing of Whig party, which he led (1855) into Republican party; U.S. senator (1849–61); famous for declaration in speech at Rochester (1858) that the antagonism between freedom and slavery was an "irrepressible conflict" between opposing and enduring forces. U.S. secretary of state (1861–69); prevented European official recognition of Confederacy; secured from Great Britain right of search of vessels on high seas; negotiated purchase of Alaska from Russia (1867).

Sew·ell \\ˈs(y)ü-əl\\, Anna. 1820–1878. English writer. Author of *Black Beauty; The Autobiography of a Horse* (1877).

Sex·ton \\ˈsek-stən\\, Anne, *nee* Har·vey \\ˈhär-vē\\. 1928–1974. American poet, b. Newton, Mass. m. (1948) Alfred M. Sexton; pupil of Robert Lowell; taught at Boston U. (1970–71) and Colgate (1971–72). Author of confessional poems published in *To Bedlam and Part Way Back* (1960), *All My Pretty Ones* (1962), *Live or Die* (1966, Pulitzer prize), *Love Poems* (1969), *Transformations* (1971), *The Book of Folly* (1972), *The Awful Rowing Toward God* (1975), *45 Mercy Street* (1976).

Sex·tus Em·pir·i·cus \\ˈsek-stə-sem-ˈpir-ə-kəs\\. 3d century A.D. Greek physician and philosopher. Headed a Skeptical school; major exponent of Pyrrhonistic "suspension of judgment." Author of *Outlines of Pyrrhonism,* which contained the Skeptical position and greatly influenced 17th- and 18th-century philosophy, and *Against the Dogmatists.*

Sey·dlitz \\ˈzīd-(ˌ)lits\\, Friedrich Wilhelm von. Freiherr. 1721–1773. Prussian cavalry commander. Distinguished himself under Frederick the Great in Seven Years' War (1756–63), esp. at Rossbach (1757) and Zorndorf (1758); major general (1757); gained reputation as one of greatest cavalry commanders in history; appointed general of cavalry (1767).

Sey·fed·din \\sā-fed-ˈdēn\\ *or* **Sey·fet·tin** \\-fet-ˈtēn\\, Omer. 1884–1920. Turkish writer. Author of short stories employing colloquial language and covering a wide range of themes, including "Bomba," "Bahar ve Kelebekler," "Eleğimsağma," "Gizli Mâbet," and "Beyaz Lâle."

Sey·fried \\ˈzī-ˌfrēt\\, Ignaz Xaver von. Ritter. 1776–1841. Austrian composer. Pupil of Albrechtsberger and Haydn; highly successful conductor-producer of operas in Vienna (1797–1828). Composed over 100 stage works and much instrumental and church music extremely popular in his day; a music theorist of considerable reputation; edited Albrechtsberger's works on harmony (1826) and Beethoven's studies in technique and composition (1832).

Şeyh Gâlib. See MEHMED ES'AD.

Şey·hi *or* **Shey·ki** \\shā-ˈkē\\, Sinan. d. 1428. Turkish poet. A skilled physician and man of great learning. Known for lyric poems, satirical narrative *Harname* (Book of the Ass), and esp. his version in *māsnavi* (rhymed couplets) of *Hüsrev ü Şirin* (Khosrow and Shirin); introduced the classical Persian *māsnavi* style into Ottoman literature.

Sey·mour \\ˈsē-ˌmō(ə)r, -ˌmȯ(ə)r, -mər\\. Name of English family originally from St. Maur, Normandy, in which were created earldom and marquisate of Hert·ford \\ˈhär(t)-fərd\\ and dukedom of Som·er·set \\ˈsəm-ər-ˌset\\.

DUKES OF SOMERSET: Edward Seymour (c.1500–1552), 1st Earl of Hertford (second creation 1537) and Duke of Somerset (created 1547). *Known as* the Protector. Accompanied Wolsey (1527) and Henry VIII (1532) to meetings with Francis I; with Cranmer and Audley, managed affairs in Henry's absence (1541); warden of Scottish marches (1542); lord high admiral (1542); led English forces into Scotland and sacked Edinburgh (1544); commanded army in France, winning great victory at Boulogne (1545). Named (1547) protector of Edward VI and became king in all but name; crushed Scottish resistance in Battle of Pinkie (1547); provoked Catholic uprisings by religious innovations and Protestant reforms; lost power by attempts at forbidding enclosures; indicted by Warwick and deposed from protectorate (1550); pardoned and readmitted to privy council; condemned on charge of conspiring with Arundel and Paget to murder Warwick and, despite flimsy evidence, beheaded on charge of felony.

His brother ¶Thomas (1508?–1549), Baron Seymour of Sude·ley \\ˈs(y)üd-lē\\; employed on diplomatic missions to European courts; marshal of English army in Netherlands (1543); admiral of fleet guarding Channel (1544); lord high admiral (1547); m. (1547) queen dowager Catherine Parr; schemed to displace his brother the protector as guardian of young king, Edward VI, and to marry Edward VI to Lady Jane Grey; bargained with pirates on west coast for their support; renewed attempts to marry Princess Elizabeth; for fomenting opposition to brother's authority, executed on charge of treason.

Their sister ¶Jane (1509?–1537); lady in waiting to Catherine of Aragon and Anne Boleyn; m. (1536) Henry VIII (as 3d wife); restored Mary to Henry's favor; died 12 days after giving birth to Edward VI.

¶Edward Seymour (1539?–1621), Earl of Hertford; son of Protector Somerset by his 2d marriage; *de jure* Duke of Somerset (1552), but deprived of title and estates by father's attainder; created (1559) baron Beau·champ \\ˈbē-chəm\\ and earl of Hertford by Queen Elizabeth; secretly m. (1560) Lady Catherine Grey, sister of Lady Jane Grey, for which he was imprisoned (1561–71) and fined £15,000; lord lieutenant of Somerset and Wiltshire (1602, 1608); high steward of revenue to Queen Anne (1612–19). His son ¶Edward (1561–1612), Baron Beauchamp, was supported by Cecil, Raleigh, Lord Howard of Effingham, and others in attempts to establish his legitimacy through his mother, Catherine Grey Seymour, as heir to throne on death of Queen Elizabeth.

The latter Edward's son ¶William (1588–1660), 2d Earl and 1st Marquis of

Hertford, and 2d Duke of Somerset, fell into disgrace for privately marrying (1610) Arabella Stuart, daughter of Earl of Lennox and heir to English throne after James I; escaped to Paris (until 1616); entered House of Lords as Baron Beauchamp (1621); succeeded his grandfather as earl of Hertford (1621); created marquis of Hertford (1640); took conspicuous part in Royalist cause in Civil War (1642–43), taking Hereford, reducing Cirencester, defeating Sir William Waller at Lansdown, and capturing Bristol; took seat in House of Peers (1660) as Baron Seymour and Duke of Somerset. On death of 4th duke (1675), the marquisate of Hertford became extinct.

¶Charles Seymour (1662–1748), 6th Duke of Somerset; great-grandson of Edward, Baron Beauchamp; m. Elizabeth Percy, daughter of last Earl of Northumberland (1682); refused to introduce papal nuncio at St. James's (1687); fought on side of Prince of Orange (1688); speaker of House of Lords (1690); joint regent (1701); enjoyed confidence of Queen Anne, as did his wife, who replaced Duchess of Marlborough (1711).

MARQUISES OF HERTFORD (2d creation): Francis Seymour-Con·way \-'kän-ˌwā\ (1719–1794), 1st Marquis of Hertford (2d creation); son of Francis Seymour, 1st Lord Conway; nephew of Sir Robert Walpole and 1st cousin of 8th Duke of Somerset; created viscount Beauchamp and earl of Hertford (1750), marquis of Hertford (1793); lord lieutenant of Ireland (1765–66); lord chamberlain (1766–82).

His son ¶Francis Ingram Seymour (1743–1822), 2d Marquis of Hertford; member of Irish House of Commons (1761–68); English M.P. (1766); opponent of repeal of American tea duty (1774) and advocate of union of Great Britain and Ireland; ambassador extraordinary to Berlin and Vienna (1793–94); lord chamberlain of household (1812–21).

¶Frederick Beauchamp Paget Seymour (1821–1895), 1st Baron Alces·ter \'ȯl-stər\; naval commander; great-grandson of 1st Marquis of Hertford; took *Meteor* floating battery out to Crimea and back to Portsmouth (1855–56); commanded naval brigade in New Zealand during Maori War (1860–61); rear admiral (1870) and vice admiral (1876); commander in chief in Mediterranean (1880–83), commanding bombardment of Alexandria (1882).

Seymour, David. 1911–1956. American photojournalist, b. Warsaw, Poland. Covered (from late 1930s) political events, esp. Spanish Civil War; to U.S. (1939); founded Magnum photographic cooperative (1947); known esp. for photographs for UNESCO of children damaged by World War II (1948); killed while covering Arab–Israeli war. His photographs collected in *Children of Europe* (1949), *The Vatican* (1950), *David Seymour* (1966).

Seymour, Horatio. 1810–1886. American politician, b. Onondaga Co., N.Y. Member of New York assembly (1842, 1844, 1845); instrumental in obtaining legislative sanction for construction of Erie Canal. Governor of New York (1853–55); again governor (1863–65). Democratic candidate for president of the United States (1868). Aided Governor Tilden in driving Boss Tweed from power (after 1868).

Seymour, Sir Michael. 1802–1887. British naval commander. Entered navy (1813); rear admiral (1854); commander on China station, captured Canton and forced passage of Pei (1856–58); admiral (1864) and vice admiral of United Kingdom (1875). His nephew ¶Sir Edward Hobart Seymour (1840–1929); naval commander; served in Black Sea in Crimean War (1854–56) and in capture of Canton and Taku forts (1857–63); guarded Suez Canal (1882); vice admiral (1895); commander in chief on China station through Boxer Rebellion (1897–1901); admiral of fleet (1905).

Seymour, Robert. 1800?–1836. English caricaturist and illustrator. Produced plates for first part of *Pickwick Papers* (1836–37).

Seyss-In·quart \'zī-'siŋk-ˌvärt\, Arthur. 1892–1946. Austrian politician. A leader of moderate Austrian Nazis; appointed to Staatsrat (1937); proponent of German–Austrian unification; Austrian minister of interior and of security in Schuschnigg cabinet (Feb.–Mar. 1938); chancellor and minister of defense in Austria after German occupation (1938); appointed by Hitler governor of Austrian territory (1938); admitted to German cabinet as minister without portfolio (1939); deputy governor of occupied German territory in Poland (1939–40); German high commissioner of the Netherlands (1940–45); hanged as war criminal.

Seyton. See SETON.

Sfor·za \'sfȯrt-sä\. Name of Italian family that ruled Milan (1450–1535), including: Muzio, *orig. surname* At·ten·do·lo \ät-'ten-dō-lō\ (1369–1424); founder of family; peasant from Romagna; joined a mercenary band (1384); leader of condottieri; made grand constable of Naples by King Ladislas (1412); took nickname Sforza (*Ital.* Force) as surname. His illegitimate son ¶Francesco Sforza (1401–1466), condottiere; accompanied his father to Naples (1412) and later served in his company (to 1424); condottiere of Florence (1434); captured Verona (1438) and defeated Milanese at Anghiari (1440); m. (1441) Bianca Marie (1423–1468), natural daughter of Filippo Maria Visconti, Duke of Milan; obtained dukedom of Milan by force and strategy (1450); ruled Lombardy and other parts of north Italy (1450–66); patron of the arts and enriched Milan architecturally.

His son ¶Galeazzo Maria (1444–1476), Duke of Milan (1466–76); a capable ruler but traditionally depicted as despotic and dissolute; built canals and encouraged commerce; patron of arts; his indecisive foreign policy led to Milan's isolation; assassinated. His son ¶Gian Galeazzo (1469–1494); Duke of Milan (1476–81) under regency of mother and uncle; expelled by Ludovico (1481).

¶Ludovico (1452–1508), *called* Il Mo·ro \ēl-'mȯr-ō\, *i.e.* the Moor; son of Francesco; Duke of Milan (1481–99); regent for Gian Galeazzo (1476–81); usurped government (1481); forged alliances with Lorenzo de' Medici of Florence and other Italian rulers; made court of Milan most splendid in Europe; purchased legitimate title to Milan from Maximilian I (1494); helped expel Charles VIII of France from Italy (1495); defeated by Louis XII (1499); imprisoned (1500); died in France; patron of Leonardo da Vinci.

¶Massimiliano (1493–1530); son of Ludovico; with aid of the Swiss restored as Duke of Milan (1512–15); defeated by Francis I of France at Marignano (1515); yielded duchy to Francis and retired to Paris on a pension.

His brother ¶Francesco Maria (1495–1535); Duke of Milan (1522–35); last of main line; duchy passed to Emperor Charles V.

Sgam·ba·ti \zgäm-'bä-tē\, Giovanni. 1841–1914. Italian pianist, conductor, and composer. Pupil and friend of Liszt; internationally known pianist; a leading figure in revival of instrumental and symphonic music in Italy in latter half of 19th century; helped establish Società Romana del Quartetto (1867); helped found (1877) and taught at Conservatorio di S. Cecilia, first public music school in Rome. Composed a Requiem Mass, two symphonies, a piano concerto, chamber music, songs, and piano pieces.

Sha·ab·an \shä-'äb-än\, Robert. 1911–1962. Swahili writer, b. Tanzania. Official with East African Railways and Harbours (to 1961). His works included verse as *Marudi Mema* (1952), *Almasi za Afrika* (1960), *Utenzi wa Vita vya Uhuru* (1967); novels as *Kusadikika* (1951), *Siku ya Watenzi Wote* (1968); essays *Insha ya mashairi* (1959); an autobiography *Maisha yangu* (1949); and a life of Siti Binti Saad (1958).

Shab·a·ka \'shab-ə-kə\. *Greek* Sab·a·con \'sab-ə-ˌkän\. d. 695 B.C. King of Egypt (716–695 B.C.). Succeeded his brother Piankhi (*q.v.*) as king of Kush (716); invaded Egypt and executed Bocchoris, 2d king of 24th dynasty; founded 25th (Ethiopian) dynasty of Egypt; made Memphis his capital; fostered religious orthodoxy in cult of Amon; revived practice of pyramid burials.

Shab·be·tai Tze·vi \'shäb-be-ˌtīt-'sä-vē\. *Also spelled* Sab·ba·tai Ze·bi \'säb-bä-ˌtīt-'sä-bē\. 1626–1676. Jewish mystic, b. Smyrna. Proclaimed himself the Messiah (1648); with a large retinue of followers, esp. Nathan of Gaza who assumed the role of a modern Elijah, traveled throughout Middle East; went to Constantinople and was immediately imprisoned (1666); converted to Islām to save his life and lost most of his followers. Considered most important of false messiahs of Judaism, he had adherents throughout Europe, Middle East, and North Africa.

Sha·bes·ta·rī \shä-bes-'tä-rē\, Sa'd od-Din Maḥmud. c.1250–c.1320. Persian mystic. Details of life obscure; lived in Tabriz. Known for *Golshan-e rāz* (1311 or 1317; The Mystic Rose Garden), a classic document of Ṣūfism that became popular in Europe (from c.1700).

Shab·o·nee \'shab-ə-(ˌ)nē\ *or* **Shab·bo·na** \'shab-ə-nə\. c.1775–1859. American Potawatomi Indian chief, b. near Maumee River, Ohio. Credited with saving many white settlers in Indian massacre at Chicago (1812) and in Winnebago uprising (1827); also saved white lives by making a Paul Revere-style ride through northern Illinois to warn of a Black Hawk raid (1832).

Shack·le·ton \'shak-əl-tən\, Sir Ernest Henry. 1874–1922. British explorer, b. Ireland. Junior officer on Antarctic expedition under Robert F. Scott (1901–04); accompanied Scott on sledge journey over Ross Shelf Ice. Sailed (1908) in *Nimrod* in command of expedition which reached point about 97 miles from South Pole (1909) and which sent parties to summit of Mt. Erebus and South Magnetic Pole. Commanded trans-Antarctic expedition in the *Endurance* (set out in 1914); when ship was crushed in ice, made trip of 800 miles with five companions to north coast of South Georgia to get help (1916); organized winter equipment of British North Russian expeditionary force (1918–19); died at South Georgia Island while on expedition to the Antarctic. Author of *Heart of the Antarctic* (1909) and *South* (1919).

Shā·dhi·lī, ash- \ash-ˌshäd-hē-'lē\. *In full* Abū al-Ḥasan 'Alī ibn 'Abd Allāh ash-Shādhilī. 1196 or 1197–1258. Moroccan theologian. Said to have been direct descendant of Prophet Muḥammad and to have gone blind from excessive study; to Tunisia (1218 or 1219) but expelled for his Ṣūfī teachings; in exile in Egypt, where he founded the Ṣūfī Muslim order of the Shādhilīyah, one of most popular mystical brotherhoods of Middle East and North Africa.

Shad·well \'shad-wəl, -ˌwel\, Thomas. 1642?–1692. English dramatist and poet. Became one of "court wits" after the Restoration; scored hit with comedy *The*

Sullen Lovers (1668); became champion of the Whigs and true-blue Protestants, attacking, in *The Lancashire Witches* (1682) and *The Medal of John Bayes* (1682), Dryden and the court party; immortalized in Dryden's retort *Mac Flecknoe* (1682); superseded Dryden as poet laureate and historiographer royal (1688). Other works included an opera *The Tempest* (1674, after Shakespeare), tragedies *Psyche* (1675) and *The Libertine* (1675), pastoral *The Royal Shepherdess* (1669), and comedies of manners *The Humourists* (1670), *The Miser* (1672), *Epsom-Wells* (1672), *The Virtuoso* (1676), *The Squire of Alsatia* (1688), *Bury-Fair* (1689), and *The Scowrers* (1690).

Shā·fi'ī, ash- \əsh-ˌshä-fē-'ē\, Abū 'Abd Allāh. *In full* Abū 'Abd Allāh Muḥammad ibn Idrīs ash-Shāfi'ī. 767–820. Muslim theologian and jurist. Studied Islāmic law with Mālik ibn Anas in Medina, later under Ḥanafī and other scholars; while residing in Cairo (815–820) composed *Risālah,* great synthesis of Islāmic legal thought; considered father of Muslim jurisprudence.

Shaf·ter \'shaf-tər\, William Rufus. 1835–1906. American army officer, b. Kalamazoo Co., Mich. Served in Civil War; on frontier duty (1867–97); major general of volunteers (1898) commanding expeditionary force to Santiago de Cuba; received surrender of the city (July 17, 1898). Retired (1899).

Shaftesbury, Earls of. See Anthony Ashley COOPER.

Shah. For many names beginning with *Shah* (a title of ruler in eastern countries, esp. Persia), see the first element following *Shah.*

Shāh 'Ālam II \'shä-'äl-äm\. *Orig.* 'Alī Gau·har \'gō-här\. 1728–1806. Mughal emperor of India (1759–1806). Son of 'Ālamgīr II; forced to flee Delhi (1758); proclaimed himself emperor after father's death (1759); became pensioner of the East India Company (1764); titular emperor only; became prisoner and tool of Marāthās (1771).

Shāh Ja·hān \-jə-'hän\. *Known in youth as* Prince Khur·ram \'ku̇r-əm\. 1592–1666. Mughal emperor of India (1628–1658). Son of Jahāngīr; m. (1612) ¶Ar·jū·mand Bā·nū Bay·gam \ˌär-ju̇-'mänd-bä-'nü-bī-'gäm\ (1592–1631), his favorite wife, better known as Mum·tāz Ma·ḥal \mu̇m-'täz-mȧ-'hȧl\. Rebelled against his father (1622–26). In his reign Mughal power reached its highest point; lost Afghan province of Kandahār (1653) but added parts of the Deccan (1636, 1655). His age the golden period of Muslim architecture in India; famous especially were the Tāj Mahal at Āgra erected (1632–49) as a mausoleum for his favorite wife, the Pearl Mosque in the Āgra fort, the palace and Great Mosque at Delhi, and the celebrated Peacock Throne. Founded (1638–48) modern city of Delhi (Hindu name, Shāhjahānābād). Deposed by his son Aurangzeb (1658); kept prisoner in the fort at Āgra (1658–66).

Shahn \'shän\, Ben, *in full* Benjamin. 1898–1969. American painter and graphic artist, b. Kaunas, Lithuania. To U.S. (1906, naturalized 1918); devoted his art to social and political causes; executed series of paintings on trials of Sacco and Vanzetti (1931–32) and Tom Mooney (1932–33); assisted Diego Rivera on murals at Rockefeller Center (1933); worked (1933–43) for Federal Arts Project, esp. on murals for Bronx, N.Y., post office and Social Security building in Washington, D.C.; published Harvard lectures as *The Shape of Content* (1957). His canvases included *Seurat's Lunch, Handball, Vacant Lot* (all 1939), *The Red Stairway* (1944), *Death of a Miner* (1947); also known for posters and book and magazine illustrations.

Shāh Rokh \'shä-'ro̅k\. *Also known as* Shāh Rokh Mīr·zā \-'mir-zä\. 1377–1447. Central Asian ruler. Son of Tamerlane; at father's death (1405) gained control of most of empire, including Persia and present-day Soviet Central Asia; known esp. as patron of the arts; his capital at Herāt, Afghanistan, an intellectual and cultural center.

Shāh Sho·jā' \-shō-'jä\ *or* **Shāh Shu·ja** \-shu̇-'jä\. 1780–1842. King of Afghanistan (1803–10). Grandson of Aḥmad Shāh; deposed his brother Maḥmūd (1803); his rule unpopular, himself deposed by Maḥmūd (1810); became pensioner of Indian government; defeated in battle by Dōst Moḥammed (1834); put forward by Lord Auckland (1838–39) during First Afghan War (1838–42) as ruler of Afghanistan in place of Dōst Moḥammed; escorted to Kabul (1839); killed by followers of Dōst Moḥammed.

Shāh Sul·tan Hu·sayn \-'su̇l-tȧn-hu̇-'sīn\. 1668–1726. Safavid emperor of Persia (1694–1722). A weak and ineffectual ruler; overwhelmed by Afghan invasion (from 1720) and forced to abdicate (1722); assassinated; succeeded by his son Ṭahmāsp II.

Sha·ka \'shäk-ə\. *Also spelled* Cha·ka *and* Tsha·ka \'chäk-ə\. c.1787–1828. Founder of the Zulu Empire. Became chief of Zulu clan (1816); reorganized army and introduced new tactics; exterminated many clans and conquered most of southern Africa; ruled with an iron hand; became insane (1827); murdered by his half-brothers.

Shake·speare \'shāk-ˌspi(ə)r\, William. *Family records show 44 different spellings of the surname.* 1564–1616. English dramatist and poet. Often considered greatest writer of all time. Born and spent early life in Stratford-upon-Avon; m. (1582) Anne Hathaway (c.1556–1623). Established in London as actor-playwright (by 1592); member of Lord Chamberlain's Company (formed 1594; became King's Men, 1603). Prospered financially, purchasing property in London and Stratford and a share in the Globe Theatre; grant of family arms made to his father (1596); continued to live chiefly in London (till 1610); moved to Stratford, but continued occasional playwriting and visits to London. Twenty plays published first in quarto form (from 1594); first collected edition (known as First Folio; pub. 1623) contained 36 plays. Plays (dates for the most part conjectural): comedies *The Comedy of Errors* (1592/93), *The Taming of the Shrew* (1593/94), *The Two Gentlemen of Verona* (1594/95), *Love's Labour's Lost* (1594/95), *Midsummer Night's Dream* (1595/96), *The Merchant of Venice* (1596/97), *Much Ado About Nothing* (1598/99), *As You Like It* (1599/1600), *The Merry Wives of Windsor* (1600/01), *Twelfth Night* (1601/02), *Troilus and Cressida* (1601/02), *All's Well That Ends Well* (1602/03), *Measure for Measure* (1604/05), *The Two Noble Kinsmen* (1612/13; probably with John Fletcher); histories *Henry VI* (3 parts, 1589–92), *Richard III* (1592/93), *Richard II* (1595/96), *King John* (1596/97), *Henry IV* (2 parts, 1597/98), *Henry V* (1598/99), *Henry VIII* (1612/13; perhaps with Fletcher); tragedies *Titus Andronicus* (1593/94), *Romeo and Juliet* (1594/95), *Julius Caesar* (1599/1600), *Hamlet* (1600/01), *Othello* (1604/05), *King Lear* (1605/06), *Macbeth* (1605/06), *Antony and Cleopatra* (1606/07), *Coriolanus* (1607/08), *Timon of Athens* (1607/08); romances *Pericles* (1608/09), *Cymbeline* (1609/10), *The Winter's Tale* (1610/11), *The Tempest* (1611/12). Poems: *Venus and Adonis* (1593), *The Rape of Lucrece* (1594), "The Phoenix and the Turtle" (1601), *Sonnets* (pub. 1609).

Sha·ler \'shā-lər\, Nathaniel Southgate. 1841–1906. American geologist, b. Newport, Ky. Professor, Harvard (1869–1906); head of Atlantic Coast division of U.S. Geological Survey (1884–1900); known for studies of crustal tectonics and Earth history. Author of *Aspects of the Earth* (1889), *Nature and Man in America* (1891), *Sea and Land* (1892), *The Interpretation of Nature* (1893), *Man and the Earth* (1905), etc.

Shal·ma·ne·ser \ˌshal-mə-'nē-zər\. *Assyrian* Shulmanu-asharidu. Name of five kings of Assyria:

Shalmaneser I. 13th century B.C. King (1274–1245 B.C.). Son of Adad-nirari I; conquered northern Mesopotamia; invaded northern Syria; removed capital from Ashur (Assyria) to Calah; succeeded by his son Tukulti-Ninurta I.

Shalmaneser II. 11th century B.C. King (1030–19 B.C. or 1019–08 B.C.). Little known of his reign.

Shalmaneser III. 9th century B.C. King (858–824 B.C.). Son of Ashurnasirpal II; embarked on campaign of conquest west of Euphrates, esp. against Damascus and Urartu; defeated Hittites; opposed by Damascus and Ahab of Israel; fought inconclusive battle of Karkar (854); again opposed by league (851); plundered Hama; broke power of alliance and received submission (841) of Damascus, Tyre and Sidon, and of Jehu of Israel.

Shalmaneser IV. 8th century B.C. King (782–772 B.C.). Fought against Urartu; successfully defended eastern Mesopotamia against Armenian attacks; lost most of Syria after campaign against Damascus (773).

Shalmaneser V. 8th century B.C. King (726–722 B.C.). Overran Phoenicia (725); defeated in naval battle by Tyrians; subjugated Israel; marched against rebellion of Hoshea, king of Israel (724); besieged and caused capture of Samaria (724–722), but probably city actually surrendered to his successor, Sargon II.

Shalom Aleichem. See Sholem RABINOWITZ.

Shalyapin, Fyodor Ivanovich. See CHALIAPIN.

Sha·mash-shum-u·kin \'shä-ˌmäsh-shu̇m-'ü-ˌkēn\. d. 648 B.C. Ruler of Babylon (668–648 B.C.). Vassal of his younger brother, Ashurbanipal, king of Assyria. Led revolt (654–648); according to legend committed suicide by making a pyre of his palace, treasury, and concubines.

Shā·mil \'shä-ˌmēl\. 1798?–1871. Caucasian leader. Joined (1830) the Murīdīs, a Ṣūfī brotherhood; elected (1834) imām of Dagestan and established an independent state; reorganized and led his Chechen and Dagestan forces against Russian troops in Caucasus region; defeated and captured (1859), effectively ending Caucasian resistance to Russian subjugation; lived in exile at Kaluga.

Sham·mai \'shäm-ˌmī\. 1st century A.D. Jewish sage in Palestine. A master of Jewish oral law; member of the Pharisees; presiding justice of the Sanhedrin while Rabbi Hillel was its president; his school (Bet Shammai) emphasized strict religious views and competed with Hillel's until the Jabneh assembly (90 A.D.) ruled in favor of Hillel.

Sham·shi-Adad \'shäm-shē-'äd-ˌäd\. Name of five kings of Assyria, about whom little more than names and dates of reign are known. Shamshi-Adad I (reigned c.1813–1781 B.C.). ¶II (c.1716–1687 B.C.). ¶III (1661–36 B.C.). ¶IV (d. 1039 B.C.), restored temple of Ishtar at Nineveh. ¶V (824–811 B.C.), had long wars with Urartu to the north and Babylon to the south; his queen was Sammu-ramat (*q.v.*).

Shang \'shäŋ\ *or* **Yin** \'yin\. Earliest historically verifiable dynasty of China; traditionally dated 1766–1122 B.C. but these dates now considered highly approximate; founded by T'ang (*q.v.*); had 38 rulers, at first capable, but dynasty degenerated until its last member, Chou Hsin (*q.v.*), was overthrown and the Chou dynasty established.

Shang K'o-hsi \'shäŋ-'kō-'shē\. d. 1676. Chinese general. Originally a Ming dynasty general; transferred loyalty to Manchu tribes of Manchuria (1633), which established (1644) Ch'ing dynasty; conquered Kwangtung province and was made its governor; his retirement (1673) triggered the Revolt of the Three Feudatories although he remained loyal.

Shang Yang \'shäŋ-'yäŋ\. *Orig.* Kung-sun Yang \'ku̇ŋ-su̇n-'yäŋ\. d. 338 B.C. Chinese politician. In service of Duke Hsiao, head of state of Ch'in; instituted land, military, taxation, and administrative reforms; insisted on strict and uniform administration of the law. The *Shang Chün shu,* a major work of Chinese Legalist school of philosophy, probably contains his ideas and writings.

Shan·kar \shäŋ-'kär, 'shäŋ-ˌ\, Uday. 1900–1977. Indian dancer and choreographer. Danced with Anna Pavlova and created for her dances *Hindu Wedding* and *Radha and Krishna* (1920s); formed dance company in India (1929); toured regularly in Europe and U.S.; founded (1938) at Almora, Uttar Pradesh, a school for dance, drama, and music; popularized traditional Hindu dance in India, Europe, and U.S. by adapting Western techniques.

Shao Yung \'shau̇-'yu̇ŋ\. *Also known as* Shao K'ang-chieh \-'käŋ-jē-'e\ *or* Shao Yao-fu \-'yau̇-'fü\. 1011–1077. Chinese philosopher. Through study of *I Ching* developed theories that numbers (esp. number 4) were the basis of all existence; theories greatly influenced development of Idealist school of Neo-Confucianism; brought into Confucianism the Buddhist theory of cyclical nature of history; his mathematical formulations influenced Leibniz in development of binary arithmetical system.

Shap·ley \'shap-lē\, Harlow. 1885–1972. American astronomer, b. Nashville, Mo. At Mt. Wilson Observatory, Calif. (1914–21); professor (1921–56), Harvard, and director of Harvard Observatory (1921–52). Using studies of Henry N. Russell determined dimensions of stars in binary systems (1913); first to propose that Cepheid variables are pulsating stars; his studies placed the Sun in the outer regions of the Galaxy; showed that galaxies tend to occur in clusters which he called metagalaxies. Works included *Star Clusters* (1930), *Flights from Chaos* (1930), *The Inner Metagalaxy* (1957), *Of Stars and Men* (1958).

Sha·posh·ni·kov \'shä-pəsh-nyik-əf\, Boris Mikhaylovich. 1882–1945. Russian army officer. Colonel during World War I; credited with devising most of Bolshevik military strategy during Civil War; chief of general staff of Red army (1928–31, 1937–43); made marshal of Red army following successful attack on Mannerheim line (Finland, 1940); commander in chief of Russian army and air force (1942–43).

Shā·pūr \shä-'pür\. *Pahlavi* Shah·puhr \shä-'pür\, *i.e.* Son of the King. *Lat.* Sa·por \'sā-ˌpȯ(ə)r\. *Greek* Sa·po·res \sä-'pȯr-ˌēz\. Name of three kings of the Sāsānian dynasty of Persia:

Shāpūr I. d. 272 A.D. King (241–272). Son and successor of Ardashīr I and father of Narses; resumed contest of his father with Rome; conquered Nisibis and Carrhae; invaded Syria; defeated and driven back by Roman general Timesitheus at Resaina (243); concluded peace with Emperor Philip (244); renewed war against Rome (256), invading Syria, Anatolia, and Armenia; sacked Antioch; defeated and took prisoner Emperor Valerian in battle near Edessa (260); held emperor captive until his death; overcome by Odenathus, Prince of Palmyra (262); lost Ctesiphon and Armenia. Built Gondēshāpūr, a center of learning, and the Band-e Qeyṣar, a dam at Shūshtar. Supported Manichaeism and Zoroastrianism.

Shāpūr II. 309–379 A.D. King (309–379). Posthumous son of Hormizd II; during regency (309–25) country governed by nobles; waged war against Arabs; at first only partially successful in long war (337–363) against Romans; forced Christians to convert to Zoroastrianism (337); after Emperor Constantius II's rejection of his claim to Mesopotamia, invaded Tigris valley (358); attacked (363) by great Roman army under Emperor Julian; near Ctesiphon, repulsed Julian; made peace (363) with Jovian, acquiring five Roman provinces; conquered Armenia; rebuilt Susa and founded Nīshāpūr. A brilliant military and diplomatic strategist; raised the Sāsānian Empire to its zenith of power.

Shāpūr III. d. 388. King (383–388). Son of Shāpūr II, brother of Bahrām IV, and uncle of Yazdegerd I.

Sha·raf ad-Dīn ʿAlī Yaz·dī \'shä-räf-əd-dēn-ä-'lē-yäz-'dē\. d. 1454. Persian historian. Lived mainly in Yazd; became adviser of Mīrza Sulṭān Muḥammad, governor of Iraq (1442 or 1443); best known for *Ẓafer-nāmeh* (1424 or 1425), a history of Timur probably based on one of same title by Nizam ad-Dīn Shami.

Sha ʿrā·nī, ash-l \'ash-əl-'sha-rä-'nē\. *Orig.* ʿAbd al-Wahhāb ibn Aḥmad. 1492–1565. Egyptian mystic. Founded a Ṣūfī order known as ash-Shaʿrawīyah that attempted to achieve a synthesis of the judicio-canonical structure of Islām and principles of Ṣūfism. Wrote a biographical dictionary of mystics *ṭabaqāt* and an autobiography *Laṭāʾ if al-Mīnan.*

Shar·ett \'shar-(ˌ)et\, Moshe. *Orig. surname (to 1948)* Sher·tock *or* Sher·tok \'sher-tȯk\. 1894–1965. Israeli politician, b. Ukraine. To Palestine (1906); Zionist pioneer and a leader in the establishment of Israel; head of political department of Jewish Agency for Palestine (1935–48); member of Knesset (1948–65); foreign minister (1948–56) and prime minister (1953–55) of Israel; chairman of executive of the Zionist Organization (1960–65).

Shar·ka·li·shar·ri \ˌshär-ˌkäl-ē-'shär-ē\. 23d–22d century B.C. King (c.2217–c.2193 B.C.) of the Semitic dynasty of Akkad.

Sharp \'shärp\, Cecil James. 1859–1924. English musician, music teacher, and anthologist. Music master at Ludgrove School (1893–1910); principal of Hampstead Conservatory (1896–1905). Collected (from 1903) and published many native English folk songs and dances in *Folk Songs from Somerset* (1904–09), *The Morris Book* (1907–13), *The Country Dance Book* (1909–22), *English Folk Songs* (1932), etc.; founded English Folk Dance Society (1911); initiated the teaching of folk song and dance in English schools.

Sharp, Granville. 1735–1813. English philanthropist and scholar. Zealous in cause of liberating slaves in England; through lawsuits, obtained formulation of principle that as soon as a slave set foot on English soil he was free (1772); founded society for abolition of slavery (1787); advocated cause of American colonies; agitated against press gangs.

Sharp, James. 1613–1679. Scottish prelate. Leader of Resolutioners against the Protesters, chosen to plead cause of moderate party before Cromwell (1657); sent to London again (1660); corrupted by Charles and Clarendon, betrayed interests of the Kirk and served interests of English bishops in reestablishment of episcopacy in Scotland; rewarded with archbishopric of St. Andrews (1661); severe in repression of covenanting principles; became tool of Lauderdale; murdered on Magus Moor in revenge by Covenanters.

Sharp, William. *Pseudonym* Fiona Mac·leod \mə-'klau̇d\. 1856–1905. Scottish writer. Author under his own name of several volumes of poems, biographies of D. G. Rossetti, Shelley, Heine, Browning, Sainte-Beuve, romances, and novels. Under pseudonym published series of mystical stories and poetical prose works about the primitive Celtic world, including *Pharais* (1894), *The Sin-eater* (1895), *Green Fire* (1896), *Drostan and Iseult* (1902), and the dramas *The Immortal Hour* (1900), *Deirdre* (1903), *The Winged Destiny* (1904). Played important part in the Celtic revival.

Sharpe, Alexander John. See A. J. ELLIS.

Sharpe \'shärp\, Sir Alfred. 1853–1935. English adventurer and colonial administrator. To Lake Nyasa region, Africa, on hunting and trading expedition (1887); helped secure African acquiescence in British colonization of Nyasaland, esp. in present Zambia; explored and mapped Lake Mweru and other parts of Zambia and Katanga (1889–95); vice consul (1891), governor (1897–1910) of Nyasaland Protectorate.

Sharpe, Richard Bowdler. 1847–1909. English ornithologist. On staff, British Museum (1872–1909); prepared its *Catalogue of Birds* (27 vols., 1874–98), of which he wrote thirteen volumes; contributed *Birds of Great Britain* (1894–97) to Allen's *Naturalists' Library;* proposed (1877) a passerine classification system used by many European ornithologists.

Shar·pey-Sha·fer \'shär-pē-'shā-fər\, Sir Edward Albert. *Orig. surname* Schäfer \'shef-ər, 'shā-fər\. 1850–1935. English physiologist. Professor at Edinburgh (1899–1933); pupil of William Sharpey, whose name he added (1918) in memory of his help; made contributions in endocrinology, esp. demonstration of existence of adrenalin (1894, with George Oliver); devised prone pressure method (Schafer method) of artificial respiration (1903). Founded and edited (1908–33) *Quarterly Journal of Experimental Physiology.*

Shar·ples \'shär-pəlz, -pləs\, James. c.1751–1811. American painter and inventor, b. England. To U.S. (1793); known for portraits of notables of the day, including George and Martha Washington; designed a steam carriage.

Sharru-kin. See SARGON.

Shas·tri \'shäs-trē\, Lal Bahadur. *Orig. surname* Ba·ha·dur \ˌbä-hə-'du̇r\. 1904–1966. Indian politician. Joined Gandhi's noncooperation movement (1921); graduated from the Kashi Vidyapith with title of *shastri* (learned in the scriptures); elected to central Indian legislature (1952); union minister for railways and transport (1952–56, 1957–61); minister for home affairs (1961–63); minister without portfolio (1964); prime minister of India (1964–66).

Shat·tuck \'shat-ək\, George Cheyne. 1813–1893. American physician, b. Boston. Practiced in Boston (from 1840); professor (1855), dean (from 1864), Harvard Medical School; founded St. Paul's School, Concord, N.H. (1855).

Shaugh·nes·sy \'shȯ-nə-sē, 'shän-ə-\, Clark Daniel. 1892–1970. American football coach, b. St. Cloud, Minn. Head coach at several colleges, including Tulane (1915–20, 1922–25), U. of Chicago (1933–39), and Stanford (1940–41), and of Los Angeles Rams (1948–49); advisory coach of Chicago Bears (1951–61); developed the T formation so proficiently that it became predominant offensive system of football teams in 1930s and '40s; also developed defensive systems.

Shauqi, Aḥmad. See SHAWQĪ.

Shaushshatar. See SAUSTATAR.

Shaw \'shȯ\, Albert. 1857–1947. American editor, b. Shandon, O. Founded (1891) and edited (1891–1937) *American Review of Reviews;* editor, *Literary Digest* (1937–39). Author of *Abraham Lincoln* (1929), etc.

Shaw, Anna Howard. 1847–1919. American preacher, physician, and suffragist, b. Newcastle upon Tyne, England. To U.S. (1851); licensed in Methodist ministry (1871); received M.D. degree (1886). Prominent as lecturer advocating woman suffrage (from 1885); president of National American Woman Suffrage Association (1904–15).

Shaw, George Bernard. 1856–1950. British playwright and critic, b. Dublin. To London to devote himself to writing (1876); art, music, and drama critic on London journals; a founding member of Fabian Society (1884) and edited its *Fabian Essays in Socialism* (1889). Wrote (1892) *Widowers' Houses,* first of many plays on social problems; first popular success was *John Bull's Other Island* (1904); later plays established him as leading British playwright since the 17th century. Among his plays were *Arms and the Man, Candida, You Never Can Tell, The Philanderer, Mrs. Warren's Profession,* and *The Man of Destiny* (contained in *Plays: Pleasant and Unpleasant,* 1898), *Captain Brassbound's Conversion, The Devil's Disciple,* and *Caesar and Cleopatra* (contained in *Three Plays for Puritans,* 1900), *Man and Superman* (1903), *Major Barbara* (1905), *The Doctor's Dilemma* (1906), *Getting Married* (1908), *The Shewing-up of Blanco Posnet* (1909), *Misalliance* (1910), *Fanny's First Play* (1911), *Androcles and the Lion* (1912), *Pygmalion* (1912), *Heartbreak House* (1919), *Back to Methuselah* (cycle of 5 plays, 1921), *Saint Joan* (1923), *The Apple Cart* (1929), *Too True to be Good* (1932), *Geneva* (1938), and *In Good King Charles's Golden Days* (1939). Among other works were novels *The Irrational Knot, Love among the Artists, Cashel Byron's Profession,* and *An Unsocial Socialist* (all written between 1879 and 1883); tracts and books on Socialism, including *Fabianism and the Empire* (1900) and *The Intelligent Woman's Guide to Socialism and Capitalism* (1928); and collections of music and dramatic criticism as *The Quintessence of Ibsen* (1891), *The Perfect Wagnerite* (1898), and *Our Theatres in the Nineties* (1932). Awarded Nobel prize for literature (1925).

Shaw, Henry Wheeler. *Pseudonyms* Josh Bil·lings \'bil-iŋz\ *and* Uncle Esek \'ē-sək, -ˌsek\. 1818–1885. American humorist, b. Lanesboro, Mass. Settled in Poughkeepsie, N.Y., as auctioneer and real-estate dealer (1858); first humorous sketches appeared in local newspapers; attracted wider notice by *An Essa on the Muel, bi Josh Billings,* published in a New York paper (1860). His books included *Josh Billings, His Sayings* (1865), *Josh Billings' Farmers' Allminax* (pub. annually 1869–80), *Josh Billings Struggling With Things* (1881); contributed to *Century* magazine as Uncle Esek.

Shaw, Lemuel. 1781–1861. American jurist, b. Barnstable, Mass. Father-in-law of Herman Melville. Practiced in Boston (from 1804); drafted first charter of Boston (1822), which remained in effect until 1913; chief justice, Massachusetts supreme court (1830–60).

Shaw, Martin Fallas. 1875–1958. English organist, composer, and editor. Organist in London at St. Mary's, Primrose Hill (1908–20), and St. Martin-in-the-Fields (1920–24); with Gordon Craig founded Purcell Operatic Society (1899); edited collections of native songs. Composed ballad opera *Mr. Pepys* (1926), church music, and over 100 songs. His brother ¶Geoffrey Turton Shaw (1879–1943) succeeded Martin as organist at St. Mary's (1920–42); inspector of music to Board of Education (1928–42); composed ballad opera *All at Sea* (performed 1952), church music, and music for children.

Shaw, Richard Norman. 1831–1912. British architect, b. Edinburgh. Started practice as partner of William Eden Nesfield (1862–68); worked in styles ranging from Gothic Revival (as church at Bingley, Yorkshire, 1864–68) to Neo-Baroque (as Piccadilly Hotel, London, 1905–08). His residential designs played important role in the English Domestic Revival and influenced the American Shingle style; town houses in London included Lowther Lodge, Kensington (1873), own house in Hampstead (1875), Old Swan House, Chelsea (1876); country houses included Glen Andred (1866–67), Wispers (1876), both in Sussex, and Adcote in Shropshire (1877). His garden suburb at Bedford Park, London (1876), was first of its kind and became a model.

Shaw, Robert Gould. 1837–1863. American soldier, b. Boston. Commissioned (Apr. 1863) colonel of 54th Massachusetts Regiment, first regiment of black troops from a free state mustered into federal service; killed at head of his troops in assault on Fort Wagner, S.C. (July 18, 1863). A monument by Augustus Saint-Gaudens stands in his memory on Boston Common.

Shaw, Thomas Edward. See Thomas Edward LAWRENCE.

Shaw, Warren Wilbur. 1902–1954. American automobile racing driver, b. near Indianapolis. Raced in the Indianapolis 500 (from 1927), winning in 1937, 1939, 1940 and placing second in 1933, 1935, 1938; retired (1941).

Shaw, Sir William Napier. 1854–1945. English meteorologist. Taught at Cambridge (1877–1906); member of Royal Society (1891); director, Meteorological Office (1905–20); professor, Royal Coll. of Science (1920–24); introduced the millibar and the tephigram. Chief work *Manual of Meteorology* (1926–31).

Shaw-Le·fe·vre \-lə-'fē-vər\, George John. 1st Baron Ev·ers·ley \'ev-ərz-lē\. 1831–1928. English politician. Liberal M.P. (1863–85, 1886–95); in maiden speech, urged stopping in port of Confederate privateer *Alabama;* commissioner of works (1880–83, 1892–94); postmaster general (1883); member of London County Council (1897–1901); raised to peerage (1906).

Shawn \'shȯn\, Ted, *orig.* Edwin Myers. 1891–1972. American dancer, b. Kansas City, Mo. m. (1914; separated 1931) Ruth St. Denis (*q.v.*); with St. Denis organized (1915) Denishawn Dancers, for whom he choreographed ballets and dances based on American Indian themes as *Invocation to the Thunderbird* (1918), *Osage-Pawnee* (1930), and *Zuni Indian* (1931); organized and directed (1933–40) a group of male dancers, for whom he choreographed *Labor Symphony, Olympiad, Kinetic Molpai,* etc.; founded (1933) Jacob's Pillow Dance Festival near Lee, Mass.; created a vigorous, masculine dance technique; lectured extensively. Wrote *The American Ballet* (1925), *Dance We Must* (1940), etc.

Shaw·qī \shȯ-'kē\, Aḥmad. *Sometimes spelled* Shau·qi. 1868–1932. Egyptian writer. Spent most of life in government service; exiled in Spain (1914–19); leading literary figure of his day (from 1921); was proclaimed (1927) the *amīr ash-shu'arā'* (prince of poets) of modern Arabic poetry. Pioneer in Arabic poetical drama; adapted traditional poetic meters to dramatic dialogue in such plays as *Masra' Kulyubatarah* (1929; The Fall of Cleopatra); also wrote verse and historical novels.

Shay \'shā\, Ephraim. 1839–1916. American inventor, b. Huron Co., O. Proprietor of a sawmill in Wexford Co., Mich.; invented (c.1877) the Shay geared steam locomotive, used on logging and mining railroads.

Shaykh, the. See USMAN DAN FODIO.

Shaykh al-Akbar, ash-. See IBN AL-'ARABĪ.

Shaykh Bahā'ī. See al-'ĀMILĪ.

Shays \'shāz\, Daniel. 1747?–1825. American Revolutionary officer and insurrectionary leader, b. prob. in Hopkinton, Mass. In the Revolution, engaged at Bunker Hill, Ticonderoga, Saratoga, and Stony Point; commissioned captain (1777). Prominent in the insurrection in western Massachusetts (1786–87), commonly called Shays' Rebellion; attacked U.S. government arsenal at Springfield, Mass., and was repulsed by militia (Jan. 1787); routed at Petersham (Feb. 1787); fled to Vermont. Condemned to death by Massachusetts supreme court, but pardoned (1788).

Shchedrin, N. See Mikhail SALTYKOV.

Shchek. See under KIY.

Shcher·bat·skoy \shir-(ˌ)bət-'skȯi\, Fyodor Ippolitovich. 1866–1942. Russian scholar. Educated in comparative linguistics, Sanskrit literature, Indian philosophy; one of foremost Western authorities on Buddhist philosophy; professor at St. Petersburg (from 1904). Works included *The Central Conception of Buddhism and the Meaning of the Word "Dharma"* (1923), *Conception of Buddhist Nirvana* (1927), and *Buddhist Logic* (1930–32).

Shean \'shēn\, Al, *in full* Albert. *Orig. surname* Schoen·berg \'shœn-ˌberk\. 1868–1949. American comedian and actor, b. Dornum, Germany. To U.S. (c.1876); organized (1884) Manhattan Comedy Four, familiar in vaudeville for 15 years; best known in vaudeville as partner (1910–14, 1920–25) of ¶Ed Gal·la·gher \'gal-ə-gər\ (1872?–1929) in comedy team of "Gallagher and Shean," for which he wrote theme song "Absolutely, Mr. Gallagher? Positively, Mr. Shean!" (1922). On legitimate stage and in films, including *Prisoner of Zenda* (1937) and *Ziegfeld Girl* (1941).

Shear·er \'shi(ə)r-ər\, Norma, *orig.* Edith Norma. 1900?–1983. American actress, b. Montreal. Known for her motion-picture portrayals of beautiful, sophisticated women; successfully went from silents to talkies. Films included *He Who Gets Slapped* (1924), *The Divorcee* (1930, Academy Award), *A Free Soul* (1931), *The Barretts of Wimpole Street* (1934), and *The Women* (1939).

Shearing, Joseph. See Gabrielle LONG.

Sheed \'shēd\, Francis Joseph, *called* Frank. 1897–1981. British publisher, b. Australia. To London (1922); joined (c.1923) Catholic Evidence Guild and became widely known for street lectures on Catholicism; with his wife, founded (1926) London firm of Sheed & Ward, which became a major publisher of books on Catholic topics; opened branch in New York City (1933). Author of works on Catholic theology, esp. *Theology and Sanity* (1947) and *Society and Sanity* (1953). His wife (m. 1926) ¶Mary Josephine Ward, *called* Maisie (1889–1975), was charter member of Catholic Evidence Guild in London (1919); cofounder and vice president of Sheed & Ward; known for lectures and for biographies of G.K. Chesterton (1943) and Cardinal Newman (1948).

Shee·ler \'shē-lər\, Charles. 1883–1965. American photographer and painter, b. Philadelphia. As photographer (from c.1912), known esp. for industrial-commercial assignments, as series of photographs of Ford Motor Co. plant at River Rouge, Mich. (1927); with Paul Strand produced *Mannahatta* (1920), a film study of New York buildings. Contributed six Cubist paintings to New York Armory Show of 1913; best known for Precisionist paintings of industrial subjects as *Upper Deck* (1929), *Rolling Power* (1939); also painted architectural subjects in abstract-realist style as *Bucks County Barn* (1923) and *American Interior* (1934).

Sheen \'shēn\, Fulton John. 1895–1979. American prelate, b. El Paso, Ill. Ordained Roman Catholic priest (1919); on faculty of Catholic U. of America (1926–50); consecrated auxiliary bishop of New York (1951); bishop of Rochester (1966–69); made titular archbishop of Newport, Wales (1969). Nationally known as spokesman for Roman Catholicism in U.S., esp. with radio program "The Catholic Hour" (1930–52) and television series "Life Is Worth Living" (1952–65). Author of *Peace of Soul* (1949), *Three to Get Married* (1951), *Life Is Worth Living* (1953–57), etc.

Shef·field \'shef-,ēld\, John. 3d Earl of Mul·grave \'məl-,grāv\, Marquis of Nor·man·by \'nȯr-mən-bē\, *and* 1st Duke of Buck·ing·ham and Normanby \'bək-iŋ-əm-\. 1648–1721. English politician and poet. Patron and friend of Dryden and Pope. Served against Dutch (1666–67, 1672–74); privy councilor (1685); joined opposition to William III, dismissed (1696); on accession of Queen Anne, lord of privy seal (1702), deprived of office by Whigs (1705); created duke (1703); lord president of council (1710–14). Author of *Essay on Poetry* (1682), *Essay on Satire* (1689, verse), and a recast of Shakespeare's *Julius Caesar* in two plays.

She·hu \she-'hü\, Mehmet. 1913–1981. Albanian politician. Volunteer in Spanish Civil War; led anti-Fascist guerilla bands in Albania; chief of staff of partisan army; member of Albanian Politburo (from 1948); prime minister (1954–81); noted for harshly ideological rule, frequent purges.

She·hu Ah·ma·du Lob·bo \'shā-,hü-äk-'mäd-ü-'lōb-bō\. 1775–1844. Fulani Muslim leader in West Africa. Influenced by teachings of Usman dan Fodio; began (1818) a holy war and founded a theocratic state in Macina region of present Mali; succeeded by Ahmadu II.

Sheil \'shē(ə)l\, Richard Lalor. 1791–1851. Irish dramatist and politician. Author of *Adelaide* (produced 1814 at Dublin), *Apostate* (1817, London), etc. Joined Catholic Assoc. (1823) and aided O'Connell with impassioned speeches until granting of Catholic emancipation (1829); M.P. (1829), aided O'Connell in agitation for repeal of union of Great Britain and Ireland; after defeat of repeal, took office under Melbourne ministry (1838–41), first Roman Catholic to be privy councilor; master of mint (1846–50); ambassador at Florence (1850).

She-kuei \'shā-'kwā\. 7th century. Turkish ruler. With support of Chinese emperor Yang Ti, overthrew Ch'u-lo Khan as ruler of western Turks (610); gained control of Turk states of the Tarim Basin.

Shelburne, 2d Earl of. See William PETTY (1737–1805).

Shel·by \'shel-bē\, Evan. 1719–1794. American militia officer, b. Tregaron, Wales. To America (c.1734). Served in Braddock's campaign (1755); in force under Gen. Forbes that captured Fort Duquesne (1758). Moved to southwest Virginia (1773); colonel of militia in Washington County; led expedition against Chickamauga Indian towns on lower Tennessee River (1779). Brigadier general of militia in North Carolina (1786); resigned (1787). His son ¶Isaac (1750–1826) was also a soldier; served in Revolutionary War, mostly against Indian tribes in Kentucky and Tennessee; colonel of militia in North Carolina (1780). Organized a colonial force after fall of Charleston (1780) and defeated British at Kings Mountain (Oct. 7, 1780); served in North Carolina legislature (1781, 1782); settled in Kentucky region (1783); first governor of State of Kentucky (1792–96, 1812–16); led Kentucky volunteers who joined General Harrison and defeated British at battle of the Thames (1813).

Shel·don \'shel-dən\, Charles Monroe. 1857–1946. American clergyman and author, b. Wellsville, N.Y. Ordained in Congregational ministry (1886); pastorates, Waterbury, Vt. (1886–88), Topeka, Kans. (1889–1912). Editor, *Christian Herald,* New York City (1920–25). Author of *Richard Bruce* (1891), *In His Steps* (1896, dramatized 1923), *The Narrow Gate* (1902), *The Heart of the World* (1905), *In His Steps Today* (1921), *He Is Here* (1931), etc.

Sheldon, Gilbert. 1598–1677. English prelate. Warden of All Souls Coll., Oxford (1626–48), ejected by Parliament for Royalist activities; bishop of London (1660) and, during Juxon's old age, virtual primate; archbishop of Canterbury (1663–77), severe against Dissenters; built Sheldonian Theatre at Oxford (1669).

She·le·khov *or* **She·li·kof** \'shāl-yi-kəf\, Grigory Ivanovich. 1747–1795. Russian merchant and fur trader. Organized (1783) trading and exploring expedition to Alaska; founded (Aug. 1784) first Russian colony in Alaska on Kodiak Island; expanded trade and influence to Alaskan mainland. His company became nucleus after his death of Russian-American Company (1799).

Shel·ford \'shel-fərd\, Victor Ernest. 1877–1968. American zoologist, b. Chemung, N.Y. Taught at U. of Illinois (1914–46, professor from 1927); first president of Ecological Society of America. His pioneering studies of animal communities, esp. *Animal Communities in Temperate America* (1913), helped establish ecology as a distinct discipline; developed biome concept in *Bio-ecology* (1939, with Frederic E. Clements) and *The Ecology of North America* (1963); also known for researches on insects.

Shel·ley \'shel-ē\, Mary Wollstonecraft, *nee* God·win \'gäd-wən, -(,)win\. 1797–1851. English novelist. Only child of William Godwin and Mary Wollstonecraft Godwin (*qq.v.*). Accompanied P. B. Shelley to Continent (1814) and married him (1816); much in company of Byron, Trelawny, and Leigh Hunt. Author of novels *Frankenstein* (1818), *Valperga* (1823), *The Last Man* (1826), *The Fortunes of Perkin Warbeck* (1830), *Lodore* (1835), *Falkner* (1837); travel books *History of a Six Weeks' Tour* (1817), *Rambles in Germany and Italy in 1840, 1842, and 1843* (1844); and a *Journal;* also edited her husband's literary remains.

Shelley, Percy Bysshe. 1792–1822. English poet. One of greatest English Romantic poets. Expelled, with his friend Thomas Jefferson Hogg, from Oxford for circulating pamphlet *The Necessity of Atheism* (1811); m. Harriet Westbrook (1811); became (1812) disciple of William Godwin and eloped to Switzerland with Godwin's daughter Mary (see Mary Wollstonecraft SHELLEY), whom he married (1816) after Harriet's suicide; visited Byron in Switzerland (1816). After pulmonary attack, left England permanently for Italy (1818); settled in Pisa (1820); worked on last poems at Lerici on Gulf of Spezia (1822); visited Leigh Hunt at Pisa and was lost in a storm while sailing back with Edward Williams; his body, washed ashore, was burnt on a pyre. Works included philosophical poem *Queen Mab* (1813), *Alastor, or the Spirit of Solitude,* "Hymn to Intellectual Beauty," and *Mont Blanc* (all written in 1816), *Revolt of Islam* (1817), *Rosalind and Helen* (1819), *Julian and Maddalo* (1824), lyrical drama *Prometheus Unbound* (1820), tragedy *The Cenci* (1819), *The Masque of Anarchy* (1819), the satire on Wordsworth *Peter Bell the Third* (1819), "Ode to the West Wind" (1819), the fantasy *The Witch of Atlas* (1820), satirical drama *Oedipus Tyrannus* (1820), lyrics, including "The Skylark" (1820), *Epipsychidion* (1821, written after meeting in Pisa a young Italian noblewoman, Emilia Viviani), the prose *Defence of Poetry* (written 1821) in answer to Peacock, the elegy "Adonais" (1821, on death of Keats), lyric drama *Hellas* (1822), and *The Triumph of Life* (1824).

Shel·ton \'shelt-ᵊn\, Thomas. fl. 1612–1620. English translator. First English translator of *Don Quixote* (part i, 1612; part ii, 1620).

Shen Chou \'shən-'jō\. *Also known as* Shen Shih-t'ien \'shən-'shi(ə)r-tē-'en\. 1427–1509. Chinese painter. Leading member of the Wu school of painting; painted chiefly nature scenes; teacher of Wen Cheng-ming.

Sheng Hsüan-huai \'shəŋ-shūē-'an-'hwī\. 1844–1916. Chinese government official and entrepreneur. Joined (1870) staff of Li Hung-chang and soon became his chief economic deputy; responsible for much of China's early industrialization; gained control of China Merchants' Steam Navigation Co. and established Imperial Telegraph Administration (by 1893); head of Board of Posts and Communications (1911); his attempt (1911) to nationalize the railway system led to a revolt that overthrew the Ch'ing dynasty.

Sheng-tsu. See HSÜAN-YEH.

Shen Kua \'shən-'kwä\. 1030–1093. Chinese government official, engineer, and astronomer. Entered imperial government service (1063); appointed commissioner for prefectural civil and military affairs in Yen-chou province (1077); banished from office after defeat of his troops by the Khitan tribes (1081). In later years wrote *Meng ch'i pi t'an* (Dream Pool Essays) which contained first reference to the magnetic compass, first account of relief maps, a rather accurate explanation of the origin of fossils, and other valuable scientific contributions.

Shenshin, Afanasy. See FET.

Shen·stone \'shen-,stōn, 'shen(t)-stən\, William. 1714–1763. English poet. Devoted (from 1745) much of his time to cultivating a garden at his estate; wrote "Unconnected Thoughts on Gardening" (1764). Author of *The Schoolmistress* (1742, a poem describing in Spenserian stanzas his own teacher), *Pastoral Ballad* (1755), etc.; influential in revival of the ballad; advised and assisted Bishop Percy with his *Reliques* (1765).

Shen Tsung. See (1) Chao Hsü under CHAO family; (2) Chu I-chün under CHU family.

She·nu·te \shi-'n(y)üt-ā\. *Also called* She·nould \shi-'nüld\ *or* She·nou·te \-nüt-ā\. 5th century. Egyptian Coptic religious. Abbot of the White Monastery in northern Egyptian desert; instituted austere monastic reforms and stabilized community life.

Shen Yen-ping \'shən-'yən-'piŋ\. *Pen name* Mao Tun \'mau̇-'dün\. 1896–1981. Chinese writer. Editor (1920–23) of *Hsiao-shuo yüeh-pao* (Short-Story Magazine); joined (1926) Northern Expedition as secretary to propaganda department of Kuomintang Central Executive Committee; helped found League of Left-wing Writers (1930); minister of culture (1949–64). Considered greatest Realist novelist of Republican China; novels included trilogy *Shih* (1930; Eclipse), *Tzu-yeh* (1933; Midnight); also wrote short stories and plays.

Shen-yüeh \'shən-yüē-'e\. 6th century A.D. Chinese courtier. Invented a system of determining the four tones of the Chinese language.

Shepard. See also SHEPHERD, SHEPPARD.

Shep•ard \'shep-ərd\, Ernest Howard. 1879–1976. English artist and cartoonist. Best known for illustrations for children's books, esp. A.A. Milne's *Winnie-the-Pooh* and Kenneth Grahame's *The Wind in the Willows.*

Shepard, Helen Miller, *nee* Gould. 1868–1938. American philanthropist, b. New York City. Daughter of Jay Gould; m. (1913) Finley J. Shepard. Among her gifts were a library building and Hall of Fame building to New York U.

Shepard, Thomas. 1605–1649. American clergyman, b. Towcester, England. To America (1635) and became pastor at Cambridge, Mass. Friend of John Harvard and influential in establishing Harvard College at Cambridge (1636). His diary (pub. 1747) recorded vividly life in the colony during his time.

Shepherd. See also SHEPARD, SHEPPARD.

Shep•herd \'shep-ərd\, William Robert. 1871–1934. American historian, b. Charleston, N.C. Professor at Columbia U. (1926–34); delegate to many pan-American conferences (from 1908); authority on Latin America and European overseas expansion. Wrote *Central and South America* (1914), *Latin America* (1914), *The Hispanic Nations of the New World* (1919), etc.

Shepherd Kings. See HYKSOS.

Sheppard. See also SHEPARD, SHEPHERD.

Shep•pard \'shep-ərd\, John. *Also spelled* Shep•herd. c.1519–1559 or 1560. English composer. Employed at courts of Edward VI and Queen Mary; wrote music for both Catholic and Protestant rites; his surviving compositions include five complete masses, two Magnificats, motets, and anthems.

Sheppard, John, *known as* Jack. 1702–1724. English robber. Committed almost daily robberies in or near London; captured through Jonathan Wild, whose enmity he had aroused; famous for daring escapes from Newgate Prison; hanged. Subject of painting by Sir James Thornhill, a narrative by Defoe, and a novel, *Jack Sheppard,* by Ainsworth.

Shep•stone \'shep-stən -,stōn\, Sir Theophilus. 1817–1893. South African politician, b. England. To Cape Colony (1820); secretary for native affairs of Natal (1856–77); secured recognition of Cetewayo as king of Zulus (1872), but on his failure to keep peace (1876) received discretionary powers from Lord Carnarvon and annexed Transvaal (1877); administrator of Transvaal (1877–79) and Zululand (1884).

Shep•toon La-Pha \'shep-,tün-lä-'pä\. 17th century. Tibetan lama. Became the first king of Bhutan; later became the spiritual head of Bhutan.

Sher•a•ton \'sher-ət-ən\, Thomas. 1751–1806. English furniture maker and designer. Known for his refined Neoclassical designs. In London (c.1790); never had shop of his own; gave drawing lessons; published *The Cabinet-Maker and Upholsterer's Drawing Book* (1791) and *The Cabinet Dictionary,* with engravings, advocating a severe style (1803). Showed tendency to the tortured and bizarre in later designs and in *The Cabinet Maker, Upholsterer and General Artists' Encyclopaedia,* with plates in color (1805).

Sherbrooke, Viscount. See Robert LOWE.

Sher•brooke \'shər-,brůk\, Sir John Coape. 1764–1830. English soldier. Second in command to Wellesley (afterward Duke of Wellington) in Peninsular War (1809); governor general of Canada (1816–18).

Sher•i•dan \'sher-əd-ən\, Philip Henry. 1831–1888. American army commander, b. Albany, N.Y.? Entered army (1853); served mainly on frontier duty. Ranked as captain at outbreak of Civil War; appointed colonel of 2d Michigan cavalry (1862); brigadier general (June 1862); major general (Dec. 1862). Engaged at Battle of Stones River (Dec. 1862–Jan. 1863) and Chickamauga (Sept. 1863); commanded cavalry of the army of the Potomac; engaged in the Wilderness, Spotsylvania, Cold Harbor; raided (May 1864) Confederate communication lines around Richmond; commanded army of the Shenandoah in drive through the Shenandoah Valley (1864); drove Gen. J.A. Early out of Winchester, Va. (Sept. 1864); made famous ride from Winchester to rally his troops after their repulse at Cedar Creek (Oct. 19, 1864); engaged in cavalry raids from Winchester to Petersburg (Feb.–Mar. 1865); deployed his army across Confederate line of retreat from Appomattox and thus forced Lee's surrender to Grant. Commanded military division of the Gulf (1865–67); military governor of 5th military district (Louisiana and Texas, 1867); severity of his administration led to his transfer to department of the Missouri; lieutenant general (1869). Succeeded Sherman as commander in chief, U.S. army (1883); general (1888). Author of *Personal Memoirs of P. H. Sheridan* (1888).

Sheridan, Richard Brinsley. 1751–1816. Irish dramatist and politician. Son of Thomas and Frances Sheridan. Collaborated with N. B. Halhed, student in Oxford, in metrical translation of Aristaenetus (1771) and in a farce, *Jupiter,* which foreshadowed *The Critic.* Eloped (1772) to France with Elizabeth Ann Linley (1754–1792), a concert singer and daughter of Thomas Linley (*q.v.*), and married her (1773). Settled in London (1773) and turned to dramatic composition; rose to first place among writers of comedies of manners by his three great comedies *The Rivals* (1775), *The School for Scandal* (1777), and *The Critic* (1779). Brought Garrick's share in Drury Lane Theatre, London, and became manager (1776); besides a farce *St. Patrick's Day* (1775), a comic opera *The Duenna* (1775), and a comedy *A Trip to Scarborough* (1777), produced only one other play, a patriotic melodrama adapted from Kotzebue, *Pizarro* (1799); lost his new theatre (opened 1794) by fire (1809). Whig M.P. (1780–1812); undersecretary for foreign affairs (1782); secretary to treasury (1783); confidential adviser to George, Prince of Wales; made two great speeches in impeachment of Warren Hastings, one moving adoption of Oudh charge (1787) and one as manager of impeachment (1788); electrified House of Commons with reply to Mornington's speech against French republic (1794); opposed Irish union (1799); treasurer of navy (1806–07).

Sheridan, Thomas. 1687–1738. Irish schoolmaster. At his home, Quilcagh House, his friend Jonathan Swift planned *The Drapier's Letters,* wrote part of *Gulliver's Travels,* and edited the *Intelligencer;* through Swift's influence obtained a chaplaincy to the lord lieutenant of Ireland, near Cork (1725); translated Sophocles's *Philoctetes* (1725) and the satires of Persius (1728) and Juvenal (1739). His son ¶Thomas (1719–1788) was an actor and theatrical manager; while an undergraduate wrote a farce *The Brave Irishman, or Captain O'Blunder;* scored success as Richard III at Smock Alley Theatre, Dublin (1743), and became its manager (1747–57); also played leading roles at Covent Garden, London (from 1744); gained pensions for Samuel Johnson and himself; published *A Plan of Education for the Young Nobility and Gentry* (1769) and *A general dictionary of the English language* (1780). His wife (m. 1747) ¶Frances, *nee* Cham•ber•laine \'chām-bər-lən\ (1724–1766), wrote novels as *Memoirs of Miss Sidney Bidulph* (1761), and plays as comedy *The Discovery* (1763). Their third son was Richard Brinsley Sheridan (*q.v.*).

Sher•ley *or* **Shir•ley** \'shər-lē\, Sir Thomas. 1564?–?1630. English soldier. Served in Netherlands and Ireland; tried to retrieve family fortunes by privateering expeditions in the Levant (1598–1602); captured by Turks (1603) and imprisoned two years. His brother ¶Sir Anthony (1565?–1635) served in Netherlands (1586) and Normandy (1591); commanded expedition against Caribbean settlements (1596); sent as ambassador to seek alliance between England and Shāh 'Abbās I of Persia (1599); having failed, sent by shāh to arrange military alliances in Europe against Turks; failed, incurred debts, got involved in intrigue; went off to squander Emperor Rudolf II's money in Morocco on pretext of setting Arabs against Turks (1605–06); general in Mediterranean under Philip of Spain (1609). His brother ¶Sir Robert (1581?–1628) accompanied Sir Anthony to Persia; became military adviser to 'Abbās I; distinguished himself in wars against Turks; sent twice by 'Abbās to negotiate European alliances against Turks but failed.

Sher•man \'shər-mən\, James Schoolcraft. 1855–1912. American politician, b. Utica, N.Y. Practiced law in Utica (from 1880); member of U.S. House of Representatives (1887–91, 1893–1909); vice president of the U.S. (1909–12).

Sherman, John. 1823–1900. American politician, b. Lancaster, O. Brother of William T. Sherman; practiced law in Mansfield, Ohio (1844–53) and Cleveland (from 1853). Member, U.S. House of Representatives (1855–61) and U.S. Senate (1861–77); chairman, U.S. Senate Finance Committee (1867–77); vigorously supported measures for prosecution of Civil War and for reconstruction of the South; defended protective tariff; prominent in securing passage of legislation for restoring specie payments and for refunding the national debt. U.S. secretary of the treasury (1877–81); again U.S. senator (1881–97); author of the Sherman Anti-Trust Act (1890) and Sherman Silver Purchase Act (1890); U.S. secretary of state (1897–98).

Sherman, Roger. 1721–1793. American jurist and politician, b. Newton, Mass. Member of Connecticut legislature (1755, 1756, 1758–61, 1764–66), Connecticut senate (1766–85); judge, Connecticut superior court (1766, 1767, 1773–88). Member of Continental Congress (1774–81, 1783, 1784); with Oliver Ellsworth introduced the Connecticut Compromise; signed the Declaration of Independence, Articles of Association (1774), Articles of Confederation (which he helped draft), and the Federal Constitution, only person to sign all four state papers. Mayor of New Haven (1784–93). Member, Constitutional Convention in Philadelphia (1787), U.S. House of Representatives (1789–91), U.S. Senate (1791–93).

Sherman, William Tecumseh. 1820–1891. American army commander, b. Lancaster, O. Brother of John Sherman. Served in army (1840–53); superintendent of military college in Alexandria, La. (1859–61). Colonel of 13th infantry (May 1861); after first battle of Bull Run made brigadier general of volunteers (Aug. 1861); served under Grant at Shiloh and Corinth; promoted major general (May 1862); took part in capture of Vicksburg (July 4, 1863). Commanded army of the Tennessee (1863) and the military division of the Mississippi (1864). Started from Chattanooga (May 1864) on his famous march through Georgia and reached Atlanta after a series of engagements (Sept. 1864); left Atlanta on the "March to the Sea" (Nov. 1864) and entered Savannah (Dec. 1864); marched northward through South Carolina and North Carolina (1865) and received the surrender of Johnston's army (April 26, 1865). Commanded military division of the Mississippi (1865) and the division of the Missouri (1866); lieutenant general (1866) and succeeded Grant as general and commander of the army (1869); retired (1884). Often quoted as author of saying "War is hell."

Sher·mar·ke \'sher-,märk-ə\, Abdi Rashid Ali. 1919–1969. Somalian politician. First prime minister of independent Somalia (1960–64); president of Somalia (1967–69); assassinated.

Sher·riff \'sher-əf\, Robert Cedric. 1896–1975. English writer. Scored great success with play *Journey's End* (1929), based on experiences in World War I; other plays included *Windfall* (1933), *Home at Seven* (1950); wrote novels as *The Hopkins Manuscript* (1939) and film scripts including *The Invisible Man* (1933), *Goodbye, Mr. Chips* (1936), *Odd Man Out* (1945), *The Dam Busters* (1955).

Sher·ring·ton \'sher-iŋ-tən\, Sir Charles Scott. 1857–1952. English physiologist. Professor at Liverpool (1895–1913) and Oxford (1913–35). Known for demonstration (1895–98) that reflexes in higher animals are integrated activities of the total organism; made lifelong study of the mammalian nervous function; coined terms neuron and synapse; shared, with Edgar Douglas Adrian, 1932 Nobel prize for physiology or medicine. Author of *The Integrative Action of the Nervous System* (1906), *Mammalian Physiology* (1916), *The Reflex Activity of the Spinal Cord* (1932), *Man on His Nature* (1941), etc.

Shēr Shāh \'shār-'shä\ of Sūr. *Full royal title* Farīd-ud-Dīn Shēr Shāh. *Orig.* Farīd Khān. 1486?–1545. Islāmic Sūr (Afghan) emperor of North India (1540–45). Enlisted as private in service of Jamāl Khān, governor of Jaunpur; later worked for Mughal king of Bihār, who awarded him title Shēr Khān. Conquered Bengal (1539); defeated Mughal emperor Humāyūn at Battle of Chausa (1539) and again at Kanauj (1540); drove enemies from Bengal, Bihār, Hindustān, and the Punjab; suppressed Baluchi chiefs of northwestern frontier; captured Gwalior and Mālwa; killed during seige of Kālinjar. One of great Muslim rulers of India; efficiently administered the army and tax collections; built roads, rest houses, wells. Buried in magnificient tomb at Sasarām.

Shertok *or* **Shertock,** Moshe. See SHARETT.

Sher·wood \'shər-,wůd, *also* ,she(ə)r-\, Mary Martha, *nee* Butt \'bət\. 1775–1851. English writer. m. (1803) Henry Sherwood and accompanied him to India (1805–16). Author of juveniles *Little Henry and his Bearer* (1815), *The History of the Fairchild Family* (1818–47), etc.

Sherwood, Robert Emmet. 1896–1955. American playwright, b. New Rochelle, N.Y. Drama editor of *Vanity Fair* (1919–20); associate editor (1920–24), editor (1924–28) of *Life*; member of Algonquin Round Table; helped form Playwrights' Company (1938); speechwriter and adviser to Pres. Franklin Roosevelt; secretary of the navy (1945). His plays included *The Road to Rome* (1927), *The Petrified Forest* (1935), *Idiot's Delight* (1936, Pulitzer prize), *Abe Lincoln in Illinois* (1938, Pulitzer prize), *There Shall Be No Night* (1940, Pulitzer prize); also won Pulitzer prize for biography *Roosevelt and Hopkins* (1949) and Academy Award for screenplay *The Best Years of Our Lives* (1946).

She·shonk \'shē-,shäŋk\ *or* **Sho·sheng** \'shō-,sheŋk\ *or* **Shi·shak** \'shī-,shak\. Name of four kings of 22d dynasty of ancient Egypt, especially Sheshonk I (10th century B.C.); founder of the dynasty; reigned c.935–914 B.C.; member of Libyan family settled in Heracleopolis in Middle Egypt or in Bubastis in eastern Delta; usurped throne and established new capital at Bubastis; invaded Palestine (c.930 B.C.) in support of Jeroboam against Rehoboam: plundered many towns, including Jerusalem; built temples and halls, esp. at Bubastis and Thebes.

Shev·chen·ko *or* **Šev·čen·ko** \shef-'chān-kō\, Taras Hryhorovych. 1814–1861. Ukrainian poet. Born a serf; freed (1838); professor, U. of Kiev (1845); arrested and exiled (1847–57) for participation in the Brotherhood of Cyril and Methodius. Published collection of poetry in Ukrainian language, *Kobzar* (1840), and many popular poems as "The Caucasus," "The Dream," "The Epistle," which gained him fame as the father of Ukrainian national literature and the foremost Ukrainian poet of the 19th century.

Sheykhi, Sinan. See ŞEYHI.

Shi·ba \shē-bä\ Kōkan. *Orig.* An·dō \än-dō\ Shun. *Also called* Yo·shi·ji·rō \yō-shē-jē-rō\ Ando. 1738–1818. Japanese painter. Studied under *Ukiyo-e* painter Suzuki Harunobi and imitated his style; changed to landscape paintings; influenced (from 1760) by Western art, esp. through Hiraga Gennai; produced first copperplate landscape in Japan (1783); landscapes included *Shi-chiri-ga-hama Beach at Kamakura.*

Shi·ba·ta \shē-bä-tä\ Zeshin. 1807–1891. Japanese lacquer artist and painter. Known for excellence of his technique and design.

Shi·bu·sa·wa \shē-bůs-ä-wä\ Eiichi. 1840–1931. Japanese businessman and government official. Founded (1868) banking and trading concern Shibusawa Company, first Japanese company to be incorporated; official in tax ministry (1869–73); helped institute tax, currency, weights and measures, and administrative reforms. Founder of First National Bank of Japan (1873; present Daiichi Bank), Ōji Paper Manufacturing Co. (1873), Ōsaka Spinning Co. (1883); also founded railways, steamship companies, fisheries, printing companies, steel plants, gas and electric industries, oil and mining concerns; leading Japanese industrialist of his day; retired (1916) to devote himself to social welfare causes.

Shi·de·ha·ra \shē-de-hä-rä\ Kijuro. Baron. 1872–1951. Japanese statesman. Entered diplomatic service (1899); ambassador to U.S. (1919–22); foreign minister (1924–27, 1929–31); advocated a peaceful foreign policy (called Shidehara diplomacy); premier (1945–46); speaker of the Diet (1946–51).

Shield \'shē(ə)ld\, William. 1748–1829. English composer. Viola player at King's Theatre, London (c.1773–91); composer of many operas staged at Covent Garden, including *The Flitch of Bacon* (1778), *The Poor Soldier* (1783), *The Woodman* (1791).

Shields \'shē(ə)ldz\, James. 1806?–1879. American politician, b. Altmore, Ireland. To U.S. (1823). Governor of Oregon Territory (1849); U.S. senator from Illinois (1849–55). Moved to Minnesota Territory (1855); U.S. senator from Minnesota (1858–59); moved to California (1859). Served in Civil War. Moved to Carrollton, Mo.; U.S. senator from Missouri (1879).

Shi·ga \shē-gä\ Kiyoshi. 1870–1957. Japanese bacteriologist. Collaborator with Paul Ehrlich in his experiments; discovered cause of endemic dysentery (1897; bacillus *Shigella* named after him); developed dysentery antiserum (1900); carried on experiments in leprosy, beriberi, and tuberculosis. Professor (1920–31) and president (1929–31) of U. of Seoul; appointed official of Imperial household (1936).

Shiga Naoya. 1883–1971. Japanese writer. Helped found literary journal *Shirakaba* (1910); known for objective, concise style and themes of difficult family relationships. Works included novels as *Wakai* (1917) and masterpiece *Anya Kōrō* (1922, 1937), and short stories as "Kinosaki Nite" (1917).

Shi·ge·mi·tsu \shē-gem-ēt-sü\ Mamoru. 1887–1957. Japanese diplomat. Member, Paris Peace Conference (1919); minister to China (1931–33); ambassador to Russia (1936–38), Britain (1938–41), Nanking government (1941–43); foreign minister (1943–45); signed Japanese surrender to the Allies (Sept. 2, 1945).

Shihāb ad-Dīn Aḥmad ibn Faḍl Allāh al-ʿUmarī. See ʿUMARĪ.

Shi·hāb-ud-Dīn Aḥ·mad I \shē-'häb-ůd-'dēn-'ak-mad\. 15th century. Indian Bahmanī sultan of the Deccan (1422–36). Engaged in territorial expansionist wars with Mālwa and Gujarāt.

Shihāb-ud-Dīn Maḥ·mūd \-mak-'müd\. 15th–16th century. Indian Bahmanī sultan of the Deccan (1482–1518). Presided over the rise of the power of the governors and provincial nobles of the expense of the Bahmanī dynasty.

Shihāb-ud-Dīn Muḥammad Ghūrī. See MU'IZZ-UD-DĪN MUḤAMMAD.

Shih-an. See CH'EN TU-HSIU.

Shih-che. See HSÜ CHIH-MO.

Shih Huang Ti. See CHENG.

Shih Ta-k'ai \'shi(ə)r-'dä-'kī\. 1821 or 1831–1863. Chinese rebel. One of five original leaders of the Taiping Rebellion (1850); assumed title i-wang (assistant king); split from the Taiping movement with a large following (1856); attempted to establish an independent kingdom in Szechwan but was unable to win a popular base; caught and executed by government forces.

Shih-t'ao \'shi(ə)r-'taů\. *Also known as* Tao-chi \'daů-'jē\. 1641–c.1720. Chinese painter. One of most famous of Individualist painters of early Ch'ing period. Buddhist monk; traveled widely; frequenter of Manchu court. Employed diverse painting styles; known also for theoretical writings, as "Hua-yü lu" (Comments on Painting).

Shih Tsu. See FU-LIN.

Shih Tsung. See (1) Chu Hou-tsung under CHU family; (2) YIN-CHEN.

Shil·la·ber \'shil-,ā-bər\, Benjamin Penhallow. 1814–1890. American humorist, b. Portsmouth, N.H. Best known as author of *Life and Sayings of Mrs. Partington* (1854).

Shi·ma·za·ki \shē-mä-zä-kē\ Tōson. *Orig.* Shimazaki Haruki. 1872–1943. Japanese novelist. Schoolteacher by profession; began (early 1890s) to write poetry but soon turned to novels. His novels, some in Naturalistic style, included *Hakai* (1906), *Haru* (1908), *Ie* (1910), *Shinsei* (1918), his masterpiece *Yoakemae* (1935; Before the Dawn), and *Tōhō no Mon* (unfinished).

Shi·ma·zu \shē-mä-zü\. Name of a powerful Japanese warrior family that controlled the southern tip of the island of Kyushu and was influential in Japanese history until the late 19th century; their Satsuma fief was one of largest in Japan. Members included:

¶Shimazu Tadahisa (1179–1227), founder of the clan; adopted surname Shimazu after being appointed governor of southern provinces of Kyushu by the Kamakura shogunate.

¶Shimazu Shigehide (1745–1833), head of the Satsuma fief (1755–87); learned Dutch and patronized specialists in Western studies; founded (1774) a medical school; established institutes for astronomy and mathematics; made Satsuma one of most technically advanced areas of Japan; married his daughter to the shogun and thereafter exercised great influence over the central government; at first lived extravagantly but later instituted financial reforms that greatly strengthened the Satsuma economy.

¶Shimazu Nariakira (1809–1858) succeeded to head of the clan (1851); introduced Western military techniques and armaments, including a cavalry force and a navy; built docks and blast furnaces for production of modern firearms; established nonmilitary industries; became a major adviser to Tokugawa government during crisis brought on by arrival of Matthew C. Perry (1853); advised temporary concessions to Perry until Japan could strengthen its armaments; ordered into retirement after criticism of government for excessive concessions to Perry.

¶Shimazu Hisamitsu (1817–1887) succeeded to head of Satsuma clan upon death of his elder brother Nariakira (1858); advocated granting more power to the emperor and feudal lords like himself; precipitated a major crisis when his retinue attacked four Britons for failure to pay proper respect (Sept. 1862), his capital of Kagoshima partly levelled by British when he refused to pay indemnity; symbolic leader of the 1868 overthrow of the shogunate; helped organize the new Imperial government.

Shimjon. See AN CHUNG-SHIK.

Shi·mo·mu·ra \shē-mō-mủr-ä\ Kanzan. *Orig. personal name* Harusaburō. 1873–1930. Japanese painter. Taught at Tokyo Fine Arts School and at Japan Fine Arts Academy; known for mastery of traditional Japanese and Chinese painting and his sense of coloring; contributed to modernization of traditional Japanese painting. Works included *Ōhara Gokō* (1908) and *The Weak Monk* (1915).

Shimshelevich, Isaac. See Itzhak BEN-ZVI.

Shingei. See under NŌAMI.

Shinn \'shin\, Everett. 1876–1953. American painter, b. Woodstown, N.J. To New York (1896) as a newspaper and magazine illustrator; exhibited as member of "The Eight" at Macbeth Galleries (1908). Executed Impressionistic paintings, chiefly of city scenes as *The Docks, New York City* (1901) and *London Hippodrome* (1903); also painted realistic murals of contemporary subjects, esp. for Trenton, N.J., City Hall (1911).

Shinnō. See NŌAMI.

Shin·ran \shin-rän\. *Childhood name* Wa·ka·ma·tsu-Ma·ru \wä-kä-mät-sủm-är-ü\. *First called himself* Han-en \hän-en\, *later* Sha·ka·kū \shä-kä-kü\, *and later* Gu·to·ku Shinran \gủt-ō-kủsh-in-rän\. 1173–1262. Japanese Buddhist philosopher and religious reformer. Received monastic training in Tendai sect at Mt. Hiei (1181–1201); studied under Buddhist saint Hōnen (1201–07) and adopted Amida pietism; exiled to Echigo for religious beliefs (1207); missionary in Kantō (1212–1235 or 1236); moved to Kyōto to assist his oppressed fellow believers. Founded (1224) the Jōdo Shinshū (Tree Pure Land School) sect of Buddhism, the largest school of Buddhism in Japan today. Compiled (c.1224) a monumental anthology *Kyōgyōshinshō* and wrote several theological works.

Shinsō. See Sōami under NŌAMI.

Ship·pard \'ship-ərd, -(,)ärd\, Sir Sidney Godolphin Alexander. 1837–1902. British colonial administrator. Practiced law in Cape Colony (from 1868); attorney general (1873) and high court recorder (1877) of Griqualand West; judge on Cape Supreme Court (1880–85); chief magistrate and administrator of Bechuanaland Protectorate (1885–95); supporter of Cecil Rhodes; preserved peace between British and Boers after Jameson Raid (1895); a director of the British South Africa Company (1898–1902).

Ship·pen \'ship-ən\, Edward. 1639–1712. American politician, b. Methley, Yorkshire, England. To America (1668); joined Society of Friends (1671); settled in Philadelphia (c.1694). Mayor of Philadelphia (1701–03) and city treasurer (1705–12). His great-grandson ¶Edward (1729–1806), b. Philadelphia, was a jurist; associate justice (1791–99) and chief justice (1799–1805), Pennsylvania supreme court. His daughter ¶Margaret, *known as* Peggy (1760–1804), married Benedict Arnold (1779). Edward's cousin ¶William (1736–1808), b. Philadelphia, was a physician; taught anatomy and midwifery, Philadelphia (from 1762); chief of medical department, Continental army (1777–81); a founder and president (1805–08) of Coll. of Physicians of Philadelphia; first professor of anatomy, surgery, and midwifery, U. of Pennsylvania (1791).

Shīr 'Alī Khān \'shir-al-'ē-'kän\. 1825–1879. Amīr of Afghanistan (1863–79). Son of Dōst Moḥammad Khān; secured hold on throne after struggles with brothers and nephew; attempted to maintain neutrality in power struggle between Russia and England; gained enmity of British after they concluded he was coming under Russian influence; action led to Second Afghan War (1878–81); unsuccessfully tried to repulse British invasion; placed his son Ya'qūb Khān on throne (1879) and died during flight to Turkistan.

Shi·ra·ka·wa \shē-rä-kä-wä\. Name of two emperors of Japan:

Shirakawa. 1053–1129. Emperor (1072–86). Abdicated (1086); established system whereby retired emperors continued to exercise power by means of a cloistered government; converted large tracts of public domain into Imperial estates; patronized Buddhism; failed to strengthen government, leading to rise of provincial warrior gentry.

Shirakawa II. 1127–1192. 77th emperor (1155–58). Succeeded his brother Konoe; fought Hōgen War against his brother Sutoku to secure the throne; after abdication (1158) attempted to retain control of government, but real power exercised by warrior Taira Kiyomori; constantly involved in plots to regain power; confined to quarters by Kiyomori (1179); never regained full power.

Shi·ras \'shī-rəs\, George. 1832–1924. American jurist, b. Pittsburgh, Pa. Admitted to bar (1855); practiced law chiefly in Pittsburgh; associate justice, U.S. Supreme Court (1892–1903).

Shīr·kūh \shir-'kü\, Asad ad-Dīn. d. 1169. Kurdish general. In command of Syrian armies in campaigns against the Egyptians and the Crusaders (c.1163–69); in last few months of life became vizier to Fāṭimid caliph of Cairo; succeeded in office by his nephew Saladin (*q.v.*).

Shirley. See also SHERLEY.

Shir·ley \'shər-lē\, James. 1596–1666. English dramatist. Settled in London (c.1624); first play *The Schoole of Complement* performed at the Phoenix, Drury Lane (1625); wrote for St. Werburgh's Theatre in Dublin (1636–40); succeeded Massinger as dramatist for King's Men at Blackfriars Theatre (1640); after Civil War became a teacher. Author of tragedies including *The Traytor* (1631), *The Maides Revenge* (1639), and *The Cardinal* (1641), comedies including *Changes, or Love in a Maze* (1632), *The Wittie Faire One* (1633), *Hyde Park* (1637), *The Gamester* (1637), *The Lady of Pleasure* (1637), and *The Constant Maid* (1640), and masques second only to those of Jonson, including *The Triumph of Peace* (1634) and *The Contention of Ajax and Ulysses* (1659).

Shirley, Laurence. 4th Earl Fer·rers \'fer-ərz\. 1720–1760. English nobleman. Last nobleman in England to suffer a felon's death; murdered a receiver of rents; tried by his peers; hanged, allegedly with a silk rope in deference to his rank.

Shirley, William. 1694–1771. American colonial governor, b. Preston, Sussex, England. Practiced law in London (1720–31); to America (1731) and settled in Boston; appointed admiralty judge (1733), king's advocate general (1734); governor of Massachusetts (1741–49); planned the successful expedition against Louisbourg (1745). In England (1749–53), member of commission in Paris to determine boundary between New England and French North America. Again governor (1753–56); appointed major general (1755) at outbreak of French and Indian War and became commander in chief of British forces in America upon Braddock's death; planned attack on Niagara (1755); criticized for failure of expedition; relieved of governorship (1756). Governor of the Bahama Islands (1761–67); returned to Massachusetts (1769).

Shir·reff \'shir-əf, 'sher-\, Emily Anne Eliza (1814–1897) and her sister Maria Georgina (1816–1906). English educators. In collaboration published *Thoughts on Self-Culture, Addressed to Women* (1850) and formed (1872) National Union for the Higher Education of Women, from which grew (1872) Girls' Public Day School Company. Emily was a member of the executive committee of Girton College, Cambridge (1870–97). Maria married (1841) William Grey \'grā\ and thereafter bore his surname; founded (1878) a training college for women teachers in secondary schools, later known as Maria Grey Training College.

Shishak. See SHESHONK.

Shi·shak·li \,shē-shak-'lē\, Adib ash-. 1909–1964. Syrian army officer. Overthrew the Syrian government (1949); did not hold civilian office but was real power in government; instituted land reforms; refused American aid. Formed (1952) Arab Liberation Movement party but did not gain political support; overthrown (1954) by military coup and exiled.

Shish·kov \shish-'kȯf\, Aleksandr Semyonovich. 1754–1841. Russian politician. Naval officer, rising to vice admiral; devoted himself to nationalistic causes; founded a literary society and wrote tracts in attempt to purge Russian language of foreign words; president of Russian Academy (1813–41). Made secretary of state by Alexander I; member of State Council (1814); minister of education and director of non-Orthodox religious affairs (1824–28); opposed mass education, instituted strict censorship, persecuted biblical societies for spreading revolutionary books. His ideas considered a precursor of Slavophile movement of 1830s and '40s.

Shivaji. See ŚIVAJĪ.

Shlo·mo Yit·zḥaqi \shlō-'mō-yis-'häk-ī\. Rabbi. *Known as* Ra·shi \'rä-shē\, *an acronym for his name.* 1040–1105. French Talmudist. Known esp. for commentaries on the Old Testament and the Talmud which greatly influenced later commentators; also wrote liturgical poems and discussions of law cases.

Shlon·sky \'shlȯn-skē\, Abraham. 1900–1973. Israeli poet, b. Ukraine. To Palestine (1921); literary editor of various periodicals; translated Western authors into Hebrew. Founder of Symbolist school in Israel; innovator in use of colloquial speech in Hebrew verse; often wrote of the Israeli pioneer's rejection of urban Western values and Israel's emergence as a modern country; verse included *Shire ha-mapolet ve-ha-piyyus* (1938) and *Al Milait* (1957).

Shlyap·ni·kov \'shlyȧp-nyi-kəf\, Aleksandr Gavrilovich. 1884–1943. Soviet government official. People's commissar of labor in first Soviet government (1917); head of Metalworkers' Union (1917, 1919–22); leader (1920–21) of Workers' Opposition which advocated trade union control of industry; expelled from Communist party (1933); imprisoned (1937–43).

Shmidt \'shmit\, Otto Yulyevich. 1891–1956. Soviet scientist and explorer. Professor at U. of Moscow (1926–56); director of Arctic Institute and head of administration of Northern Sea Route (1930–36); director of Institute of Theoretical Geophysics (1938–48). Responsible for Soviet program of exploration and exploitation of Arctic resources; made first crossing from Barents Sea to the Pacific in a single season (1932); established a scientific station on drifting ice near North Pole (1937); chief editor (1924–41) of *Great Soviet Encyclopedia* and science journal *Priroda*.

Shoen·berg \'shœ̄-byirk, *Angl* 'shə(r)n-ˌbərg\, Sir Isaac. 1880–1963. British electrical engineer, b. Russia. Installed first radio stations in Russia; to England (1914); as head (1931–35) of a research group for Electrical and Musical Industries (EMI), was principal inventor of first high-definition television system; director of EMI (from 1955).

Shōga. See TAKUMA.

Sho·ghi Ef·fen·di Rab·bā·nī \'shau̇-ē-ef-'fen-dē-räb-'bän-ē\. 1896–1957. Persian religious leader. Head of Bahā'ī faith (from 1921) with title of Guardian of the Cause of God; grandson of 'Abd ol-Bahā'.

Shōjirō. See TORII Kiyomasu.

Shōjō Gyōsai. See KAWANABE Gyōsai.

Shō·ka·dō \shō-käd-ō\ Shōjō. *Orig.* Na·ka·nu·ma \nä-kä-nu̇m-ä\ Shikibu. 1584–1639. Japanese calligrapher and painter. Priest and theologian of Shingon sect of Buddhism; retired to devote himself to calligraphy, painting, poetry, tea ceremony; moved (1637) to mountain retreat Shōkadō (Pine Flower Temple), whence his name. In calligraphy revived the traditional *sō* (grass) writing style; as painter worked in *Yamato-e* style and in monochromatic ink; his followers called the Shōkadō school.

Sholem Aleichem. See Sholem RABINOWITZ.

Sholes \'shōlz\, Christopher Latham. 1819–1890. American inventor, b. Mooresburg, Pa. Served in Wisconsin legislature (in 1850s); to Milwaukee (1860) as newspaper editor and later as collector of the port. Experimented with numbering machines and letter-writing machines (from 1864); concentrated on invention of typewriter (from 1867), including use of John Pratt's plans for a writing machine; with Carlos Glidden and Samuel W. Soulé received patent for a typewriter (1868); after Glidden and Soulé relinquished their rights, sold his own rights to Remington Arms Co. for $12,000 (1873), the Remington typewriter being later perfected on basis of this patent.

Sho·lo·khov \'shȯl-ə-ˌkȯf, -ˌkȯv\, Mikhail Aleksandrovich. 1905–1984. Soviet novelist. Best known for novels *Tikhiy Don* (1928–40, 4 vol.) and *Podnyataya tselina* (1932–60); the first of these was translated into English in two parts as *And Quiet Flows the Don* (1934) and *The Don Flows Home to the Sea* (1940); the parts of the second known in U.S. as *Seeds of Tomorrow* (1935) and *Harvest on the Don* (1960). Won 1965 Nobel prize for literature, but the authorship esp. of *Tikhiy Don* was called into question by Aleksandr Solzhenitsyn and others.

Shō·mu \shō-mu̇\. *Also* Shōmu Tennō. 701–756. 45th emperor of Japan (715–749). His consort declared (729) empress, first consort not of royal blood; vigorous promoter of Buddhism; erected temples; ordered (741) branch monasteries and nunneries built in each province; built (743–752) great Tōdai Temple at Nara. Succeeded by his daughter Kōken (*q.v.*).

Shore \'shōr\, Jane. d. 1527. Mistress of Edward IV of England. Daughter of London mercer; m. William Shore, Lombard Street goldsmith. Exercised influence over Edward (1470–83) by wit and beauty. Mistress of Marquis of Dorset and concubine to William, Lord Hastings; probably helped unite the Hastings and Woodville factions against Richard of Gloucester; accused of sorcery by Richard III, and made to do penance (1483); died a beggar.

Sho·rey \'shō-rē\, Paul. 1857–1934. American scholar, b. Davenport, Iowa. Professor, U. of Chicago (1892–1933); authority on Greek art, poetry, philosophy; managing editor of *Classical Philology* (1908–34); edited Plato's *Republic* (1930–35). Among his works were *The Idea of Good in Plato's Republic* (1895), *The Unity of Plato's Thought* (1903), *The Assault on Humanism* (1917), *What Plato Said* (1933).

Short \'shȯ(ə)rt\, James. 1710–1768. Scottish optician and instrument maker. Settled in London (1738); produced the first truly parabolic and elliptic mirrors for reflecting telescopes, considered among best available.

Short, Walter Campbell. 1880–1949. American army officer, b. Fillmore, Ill. Commissioned (1902); major general (1940); commander of Hawaiian department at the time of the Japanese attack (Dec. 7, 1941); retired (1942).

Short·house \'shȯ(ə)rt-ˌhau̇s\, Joseph Henry. 1834–1903. English novelist. Known for novel of ideas *John Inglesant* (1880).

Shoshenq. See SHESHONK.

Sho·sta·ko·vich \shəs-(ˌ)tə-'kȯv-ˌyich, *Angl* ˌshäs-tə-'kō-vich, ˌshȯs-, -'kȯ-\, Dmitry Dmitriyevich. 1906–1975. Russian composer. Established reputation with *First Symphony* (1924–25); condemned by government (1936) for avant-garde opera *Lady Macbeth of the Mtsensk District* (1930–32; later retitled *Katerina Izmaylova*); regained reputation and government favor with *Fifth Symphony* (1937); composed *Seventh Symphony* about and during German siege of Leningrad (1941); again attacked by government (1948); gained freedom to employ personal style after death of Stalin (1953). Professor at conservatories at Leningrad (1937–41, 1945–48) and Moscow (1943–48). Works included 15 symphonies; opera *Nos* (1927–28); ballets *Zolotoy vek* (1930), *Bolt* (1931), *Svetliy ruchey* (1935); concertos for violin (2), for cello (2), for piano (2); chamber music, including 13 string quartets; choral works including *Kazn' Stepana Razina* (1964); piano pieces; songs; film scores. Widely regarded as greatest symphonist of the mid-20th century.

Shōtoku. See KŌKEN.

Shō·to·ku \shō-tō-ku̇\ Taishi. 573–621. Regent of Japan. Son of Emperor Yōmei; named (593) crown prince and regent for his aunt Empress Suiko; de facto ruler of Japan. Sent envoys to China; imported Chinese artists, craftsmen, clerks; adopted Chinese calendar; built system of highways; erected Buddhist temples, including oldest extant wooden structure in the world, Hōryū-ji at Ikaruga (607). Instituted (603) system of 12 court ranks, changing hereditary government posts to bureaucracy of merit based on Chinese model; issued (604) "Seventeen Article Constitution" giving central government exclusive right to tax and instructing ruling class in Confucian ethics. Compiled (620) chronicles of government, first Japanese history book. Also known for land reclamation, social welfare programs, promotion of Buddhism; after death considered a Buddhist saint.

Shot·well \'shät-ˌwel, -wəl\, James Thomson. 1874–1965. American diplomat and historian, b. Strathroy, Ont. Professor, Columbia (1908–42). Adviser to Pres. Woodrow Wilson; delegate to Versailles peace conference; outlined terms of Pact of Locarno (1925) and Kellogg-Briand Pact (1928); director of Institute of Pacific Relations (1927–30) and Social Science Research Council (1931–33); assistant to Pres. F. D. Roosevelt on United Nations affairs (1943–45); president of Carnegie Endowment (1948–50). Edited *Economic and Social History of the World War* (1919–29); author of *An Introduction to the History of History* (1922), *War as an Instrument of National Policy* (1929), *Lessons on Security and Disarmament* (1947), etc.

Shoup \'shüp\, George Laird. 1836–1904. American merchant and politician, b. Kittanning, Pa. Governor of Idaho Territory (1889); first governor of State of Idaho (Oct.–Dec. 1890) and first U.S senator from Idaho (1890–1901).

Shrap·nel \'shrap-nᵊl\, Henry. 1761–1842. English artillery officer. Commissioned in Royal Artillery (1779); served in Newfoundland, Gibraltar, West Indies; made inspector of artillery (1804). Inventor of shrapnel shell, successfully used at Surinam (1804); improved howitzers and mortars.

Shreve \'shrēv\, Henry Miller. 1785–1851. American steamboat captain, b. Burlington Co., N.J. Inaugurated fur trade between St. Louis and Philadelphia, via Pittsburgh (1807); became stockholder and skipper of second steamboat on Mississippi River (1814); established practicability of steam navigation on Mississippi and Ohio rivers; devised shallow-draft boats with high-pressure engines mounted on deck for river traffic. Superintendent of western river improvements (1827–41); designed first snagboat to clear river debris; founded (1835) work-camp later (1839) known as Shreveport, La.

Shrewsbury, Earls and duke of. See (1) ROBERT of Belesme; (2) TALBOT family.

Shrewsbury, Countess of. See Elizabeth TALBOT.

Shu \'shü\. Name of two Chinese dynasties: (1) See under HAN dynasty; (2) a dynasty, divided into the Earlier Shu (907–925) and Later Shu (934–965), of the Ten Kingdoms of the Yangtze River Valley.

Shu·bert \'shü-bərt\. *Orig.* Sze·man·ski \shi-'mȧn-skəi\. Name of three brothers, American theatrical managers and producers: Lee, *orig.* Levi (1873?–1953), Samuel S. (1876–1905), and Jacob J. (1880–1963), all b. Shirvinta, Russia. To U.S. (1882); leased (1900) Herald Square Theatre in New York and built up a theatrical empire with theaters in most major American cities; waged long struggle with Klaw and Erlanger's Theatrical Syndicate; other family enterprises were a company controlling production rights to many plays, music-publishing company, and stage costume purveying firm. Jacob staged vast open-air operettas and was backer of Florenz Ziegfeld.

Shu·brick \'shü-(ˌ)brik\, William Branford. 1790–1874. American naval officer, b. Bull's Island, S.C. Commanded Pacific squadron in Mexican War (1847–48); commanded fleet (1858–59) sent to Paraguay to obtain satisfaction after a U.S. steamer had been fired on, and succeeded in obtaining a treaty settling all disputes. Retired (1861); rear admiral (1862).

Shū·bun \shu̇b-u̇n\. *Also known as* Ten·shō \ten-shō\ Shūbun. d. 1444–48? Japanese priest-painter. Key figure in development of monochromatic ink painting; became professional painter (c.1403); pupil of Josetsu and teacher of Sesshū; director of the Ashikaga court painting bureau (from 1404).

Shu·di \'shü-dē\, Burkat. *Orig.* Burkhardt Tschu·di *or* Tshu·di \'chü-dē\. 1702–1773. English harpsichord maker, b. Switzerland. To England (1718); established instrument factory in London (1728); rival of Jacob Kirkman (*q.v.*) as leading English harpsichord maker; took into partnership (1770) his son-in-law John Broadwood (*q.v.*). Succeeded in the partnership by his son ¶Burkat (c.1738–1803); ownership of firm passed to Broadwood after death of the younger Burkat.

Shu·jā-'ud-Daw·lah \shü-ˌjä-u̇d-dau̇-'lä\. 1754–1775. Indian governor of Oudh. Vassal of Mughal emperor; failed to eject British from Bengal and was defeated at Baksar (1764); later regained Oudh and with British aid conquered Rohilla country.

Shul·gi \'shu̇l-ˌgē\. 21st century B.C. Second king (2094–2047 B.C.) of Sumerian dynasty of Ur. Son of Ur-Nammu. His capital at Ur; consolidated empire; built many temples, ruins of some of which still exist.

Shull \'shəl\, George Harrison. 1874–1954. American botanist and geneticist, b. Clark Co., Ohio. Professor, Princeton (1915–42); known as father of hybrid corn (maize); founder (1916), managing editor (1916–25), associate editor (from 1925), of journal *Genetics.*

Shulmanu-asharidu. See SHALMANESER.

Shun-chih. See FU-LIN.

Shuppiluliumash I. See SUPPILULIUMAS.

Shurt·leff \'shərt-lef, -ləf\, Nathaniel Bradstreet. 1810–1874. American antiquary, b. Boston. Practiced medicine in Boston; mayor of Boston (1868–70). Edited *Records of the Governor and Company of the Massachusetts Bay in New England* (1853–54), *Records of the Colony of New Plymouth in New England* (1855–57).

Shu She-yü \'shü-'shə-'yü̅\. *Also called* Shu Ch'ing-ch'un \-'chiŋ-'chu̇n\. *Pen name* Lao She \'lau̇-'shə\. 1899–1966. Chinese novelist. Taught Chinese in England (1924–29); president of All-China Anti-Japanese Writers Federation during Sino–Japanese War; lectured in U.S. (1946–47); involved in cultural movements in China. His masterpiece *Lo-t'o Hsiang-tzu* (1936) became U.S. best-seller in a bowdlerized and unauthorized translation, *Rickshaw Boy* (1945), under anglicized name Lau Shaw. Other novels included *Niu T'ien-tz'u chuan* (1934), *The Yellow Storm* (1951), *The Drum Singers* (1952); also wrote short stories and much propagandistic literature, including plays *Lung-hsü kou* (1951) and *Ch'a-kuan* (1957).

Shu·ster \'shü-stər\, William Morgan. 1877–1960. American lawyer, financier, and publisher, b. Washington, D.C. Collector of customs at Manila (1901–06); secretary of public instruction in Philippines and member of Philippine Commission (1906–09); treasurer general and financial adviser, Persia (1911–12); president, The Century Co. (1915–33), Appleton-Century-Crofts Inc. (1933–52).

Shute \'shüt\, Henry Augustus. 1856–1943. American humorist, b. Exeter, N.H. Author of *The Real Diary of a Real Boy* (1902) and other books about boys, in most of which the hero is autobiographical character "Plupy Shute."

Shute, Nevil. See Nevil Shute NORWAY.

Shute, Samuel. 1662–1742. British colonial administrator in America. Governor of Massachusetts Bay and New Hampshire (1716–27); engaged in continuous dispute with the assembly over his rights and policies.

Shu·truk-Nah·hun·te \'shü-tru̇k-nä-'hu̇n-tə\. fl. c.1160 B.C. King of Elam. Invaded Mesopotamia and overthrew Zababa-Shum-iddina of Babylonia.

Shu·va·lov \shu̇-'vá-ləf\, Pyotr Andreyevich. Count. 1827–1889. Russian diplomat and police director. In Russian army (1845–56); director of political police in Ministry of Interior (1861–64); chief of staff of gendarmerie corps and head of political police ("3d section") of imperial chancery (from 1866); soon became close adviser to Alexander II; opposed liberal reforms and appointed reactionaries to important positions; ambassador to London (1874–79).

Shuysky, Vasily. See VASILY SHUYSKY.

Shver·nik \'shvyär-nyik\, Nikolay Mikhaylovich. 1888–1970. Soviet politician. Head of Soviet trade unions (1930–44); realigned labor unions to subordinate their interests to interests of state; chairman of Presidium of Supreme Soviet of the Soviet Union (1946–54).

Sibawayh. See ABŪ BISHR.

Si·be·li·us \sə-'bā-lē-u̇s\, Jean, *orig.* Johan, *in full* Jean Julius Christian. 1865–1957. Finnish composer. Established himself as leading Finnish composer of his generation with *Kullervo* Symphony (1892); influenced by Tchaikovsky and other Romantics, by early 1900s adopted a more Classical style; gained international reputation by 1900; virtually ceased composing by 1926. Compositions included 7 symphonies, esp. nos. 2 (1901), 4 (1911), 7 (1924); symphonic works including *Finlandia* (1899), *Pohjolan tytär* (1906), *Barden* (1913), *Tapiola* (1926); incidential music, esp. *Pelléas et Mélisande* (1905), *The Tempest* (1926); violin concerto (1903, rev. 1905); chamber music; piano music; and about 100 songs.

Sib·ley \'sib-lē\, Henry Hastings. 1811–1891. American pioneer and politician, b. Detroit. Agent of American Fur Co. in trading with the Sioux; established himself at Mendota, near Fort Snelling, Minn. (1835); first governor of State of Minnesota (1858); led militia in suppressing Indian uprisings (1862, 1863, 1864).

Sibley, Hiram. 1807–1888. American businessman, b. North Adams, Mass. Helped Samuel Morse obtain congressional backing to build nation's first telegraph line (1844); with Ezra Cornell, organized (1851) New York and Mississippi Valley Printing Telegraph Co., later (1856) renamed Western Union Telegraph Co.; president of the company (1856–69); projected and carried through first transcontinental line (1861). After retirement built railroads in Middle West and South, bought farm holdings and other businesses. An incorporator (with Ezra Cornell) and benefactor of Cornell U.; established Sibley College of Mechanical Engineering at Cornell; presented Sibley Hall to U. of Rochester.

Sib·yl \'sib-əl\. 1160–1190. Queen of crusader state of Jerusalem. Daughter of Almaric I and sister of Baldwin IV; on death of Baldwin (1185), conspired with her husband Guy of Lusignan to seize throne for themselves instead of their son Baldwin V; action led to disastrous war with Saladin.

Sick·el \'zik-əl\, Theodor von. 1826–1908. German historian. Professor, Vienna (1867); directed (1881–1901) Austrian Historical Inst. in Rome; considered founder of modern diplomatics. Author of *Beiträge zur Diplomatik* (1861–62), *Acta regum et imperatorum Karolinorum* (1867), etc.

Sick·ert \'sik-ərt\, Walter Richard. 1860–1942. British painter and etcher, b. Germany. To England (1868); pupil of Whistler (1882); greatly influenced by Degas; later (c.1905) influenced by Neo-Impressionists; founder of Camden Town (1911) and London (1913) groups. Known esp. for pictures of London music-hall interiors; canvases included *Ennui* (c.1913), *Baccarat at Dieppe, Echoes;* criticism published as *A Free House!* (1947). His brother ¶Bernhard (1862–1932) and grandfather ¶Johann Jürgen Sickert (1803–1864) were also painters.

Sick·ing·en \'zik-iŋ-ən\, Franz von. 1481–1523. German knight. Inherited estates on the Rhine; aided in election of Charles V as emperor (1519) and was made imperial chamberlain and councilor. Favored Reformation and headed a league (1522–23) for spreading Reformation throughout the German states and overthrowing hostile princes and ecclesiastical rulers; was defeated by alliance of Richard of Greiffendau, archbishop of Trier, Landgrave Philip of Hesse, and others.

Sick·les \'sik-əlz\, Daniel Edgar. 1825–1914. American army officer and politician, b. New York City. Member, U.S. House of Representatives (1857–61, 1893–95). Shot and killed (1859) Philip Barton Key, son of Francis Scott Key, because of Key's attentions to Mrs. Sickles; tried and acquitted on then-novel plea of temporary mental aberration. At outbreak of Civil War, organized brigade in New York and commanded it in the Peninsular Campaign. Promoted major general (1863); engaged at Chancellorsville and Gettysburg, where he lost his right leg in defense of his position on the famous Peach Orchard salient (July 2, 1863). Military governor of the Carolinas (1865–67). Retired as major general (1869). U.S. minister to Spain (1869–75). Instrumental in obtaining Central Park for New York City.

Siculus. See CALPURNIUS SICULUS.

Sid·dhār·tha Gau·ta·ma \sid-'där-tə-'gau̇-tə-mə\. *Pali* Sid·dhat·tha Go·ta·ma \sid-'dät-tə-'gō-tə-mə\. *Known as* the Bud·dha \'bu̇d-də, *Angl* 'büd-ə, 'bu̇d-ə\, *i.e.* Enlightened One. *Called* Śāk·ya·mu·ni \'shäk-yə-mu̇n-ē\, *i.e.* Sage of the Śākyas. c.563–c.483 B.C. Founder of Buddhism. Son of Śuddhodana, king of the Śākyas; b. Kapilavastu, site of present-day Rummindei, Nepal. At age 16 married his cousin Yasodharā; had one son, Rāhula. Became weary of luxuries of palace life; at 29 resolved on his great renunciation, giving up princely life and becoming a wandering ascetic; traveled south to the Magadha kingdom in search of truth and enlightenment; attained two forms of high mystical state but still dissatisfied; at village of Senānigama, near Uruvelā, practiced severe austerity and extreme self-mortification for six years, finally rejecting the ascetic way of life. Meditated under a banyan tree at Buddha Gayā (or Bodh Gayā), achieving enlightenment at age 35 (c.528 B.C.); thereafter taught his doctrine of the "four noble truths" and the "chain of causation" throughout Ganges valley and at his monastery at Jetavana; died at Kusinārā (modern Kasia or Kuśinagara).

Sid·dons \'sid-ᵊnz\, Sarah, *nee* Kem·ble \'kem-bəl\. 1755–1831. English tragic actress. Member of her father's traveling theatrical company (see KEMBLE family); m. (1773) actor William Siddons; appeared first at Drury Lane as Portia (1775); after success in provinces returned to Drury Lane (1782) as Isabella in Garrick's version of Southerne's *Fatal Marriage,* scoring a triumph and becoming acknowledged queen of the stage; played Shakespearean parts, including Lady Macbeth, her greatest role (from 1785), Volumnia in *Coriolanus,* Desdemona, Rosalind, Ophelia, Katherine in *Henry VIII;* gave her farewell performance as Lady Macbeth (1812). Painted by Reynolds as the Tragic Muse, and by Gainsborough, among others.

Sidetes. See ANTIOCHUS VII of Syria.

Sidg·wick \'sij-ˌwik\, Henry. 1838–1900. English philosopher. Taught at Cambridge (1859–1900; professor from 1883). One of founders and first president (1882–85, 1888–93) of Society for Psychical Research and member of Metaphysical Society. A follower of John Stuart Mill; made his chief contribution in ethics. Proponent of higher education for women; founded (1871) a house for women students which became (1880) Newnham College, Cambridge. Author of *Methods of Ethics* (1874), *Principles of Political Economy* (1883), *Practical Ethics* (1898), etc. His wife (m. 1876) ¶Eleanor Mildred, *nee* Balfour (1845–1936), sister of A. J. Balfour, actively supported movement for higher education for women and emancipation of women; principal of Newnham Coll. (1892–1910).

Sidgwick, Nevil Vincent. 1873–1952. English chemist. Nephew of Henry Sidgwick. Taught at Oxford (1900–52); made researches in chemical bonding; proposed idea of hydrogen bond to explain behavior of some organic molecules (c.1920); using concepts of Gilbert N. Lewis, showed efficacy of dative bonding (1927). Works included *Organic Chemistry of Nitrogen* (1910) and *Chemical Elements and Their Compounds* (1950).

Sidi Muḥammad ben Yūsuf. See MUḤAMMAD V.

Sidmouth, 1st Viscount. See Henry ADDINGTON.

Sid·ney \'sid-nē\. Name of a distinguished English family including: Sir William (1482?–1554); commanded English right at Flodden (1513); attended Henry VIII at Field of Cloth of Gold (1520); received manor of Penshurst in Kent (1552).

His son ¶Sir Henry (1529–1586), administrator in Ireland; brought up at court as companion of Prince Edward; vice treasurer of Ireland (1556–59) under his brother-in-law, lord deputy Thomas Radcliffe; president of Welsh marches (1559–86); lord deputy of Ireland (1565–71, 1575–78); restored Calvagh O'Donnell and crushed Shane O'Neill in Ulster; reduced rebellious Butlers in Munster (1569); returned to Ireland (1575) and once more pacified Ulster and southern Ireland; effected shire divisions on English model; suppressed rebellion of Earl of Clanricarde and his sons (1576) and hunted Rory O'More to his death (1578); recalled because of popular discontent with his arbitrary taxation. His eldest son was Sir Philip Sidney (*q.v.*); a daughter, Mary, m. Henry Herbert (see under HERBERT family).

Sir Henry's second son ¶Robert (1563–1626), Viscount Lisle \'lī(ə)l, 'lē(ə)l\ *and* 1st Earl of Leices·ter \'les-tər\ (fifth creation, 1618); entered Parliament (1585); accompanied his brother Sir Philip to Flushing and fought at Zutphen and Arnhem (1586); appointed governor of Flushing (1588); wounded at Steenwijck (1592), distinguished himself at Turnhout (1598); created Baron Sidney of Penshurst and appointed chamberlain to the queen consort (1603); member of Virginia, East India, and Northwest Passage companies; wrote words for Dowland's songs. His son ¶Robert (1595–1677), 2d earl; ambassador to Denmark and to France; m. (1616) Dorothy Percy; father of Algernon Sidney (*q.v.*) and the following:

¶Lady Dorothy (1617–1684), *later (1643)* Countess of Sun·der·land \'sən-dər-lənd\, celebrated as Sach·a·ris·sa \ˌsak-ə-'ris-ə\ in poems of Edmund Waller (*q.v.*), who paid literary court to her; m. (1639) Henry Spencer (see SPENCER family); benefactress of distressed clergy and Royalists.

¶Philip (1619–1698), 3d Earl of Leicester, styled Lord Lisle (till 1677); member of Short and Long parliaments; lord lieutenant of Ireland (1646–47); member of republican councils of state and of two Protectorate councils.

¶Henry (1641–1704), Earl of Rom·ney \'räm-nē, 'rəm-\; entered Parliament (1679); supported exclusion of Duke of York from succession; envoy to France (1672), to The Hague (1679–81); commander in Dutch service (1681–85); accompanied William of Orange to England and Ireland; lord lieutenant of Ireland (1692–93); a lord justice (1697).

Sid·ney *or* **Syd·ney** \'sid-nē\, Algernon. 1622–1683. English republican leader and martyr. Son of Robert Sidney (1595–1677; see SIDNEY family). In Civil War, cavalry officer on Parliamentary side; wounded at Marston Moor (1644); governor of Colchester (1645), of Dover (1648–50). M.P. (1646); as commissioner for trial of Charles I, took no part in trial; a severe republican, retired (1653–59) on account of Cromwell's usurpation of power; member of Council of State (1659), dispatched to Denmark and Sweden as mediator (1659–60). Pardoned by Charles II, returned to England (1677); as a republican, favored Duke of Monmouth as successor to Charles II; negotiated with Louis XIV to secure aid for support of Monmouth, received moneys from French ambassador; discussed insurrection with Whig leaders (1683); arrested on discovery of Rye House Plot, convicted of treason, executed. Author of *Discourses Concerning Government* (1698).

Sidney, Sir Philip. 1554–1586. English poet, politician, and soldier. Eldest son of Sir Henry Sidney (see SIDNEY family); nephew of Robert Dudley, Earl of Leicester. On grand tour of Europe (1572–75); appointed cupbearer to Queen Elizabeth (1576); ambassador to Emperor Rudolf and to Prince of Orange (1577). Saw much of Spenser (from 1578) and received dedication of *The Shepheardes Calender* (1579); wrote masque *Lady of May,* with which his uncle Leicester entertained the queen (1578). Fell out of favor of Queen Elizabeth after remonstrating against her proposed marriage with the duc d'Alençon; retired to Wilton, home of his sister Mary, Countess of Pembroke (see under HERBERT family). For amusement of Mary wrote (c.1580) pastoral romance *The Arcadia,* most important prose fiction of 16th-century England; began (1584) revision of *Arcadia* but left it incomplete. Addressed (1582) to Penelope Devereux (see DEVEREUX family) impassioned sonnets later published (1591) as *Astrophel and Stella;* wrote (c.1582; pub. 1595) *The Defence of Poesie* (also pub. 1595 as *An Apologie for Poetrie*), greatest example of Elizabethan literary criticism. M.P. (1581, 1584–85); m. (1583) Frances, daughter of Sir Francis Walsingham. With uncle Earl of Warwick appointed joint master of the ordnance (1585); sent with Leicester to support the Dutch against Spain (1585); made governor of Flushing (1585); with Prince Maurice made successful raid on Axel (1586); in attack at Zutphen (1586) wounded in thigh and died 26 days after at Arnhem. Considered ideal gentleman of his age and finest English prose writer of his generation.

Sidonius Apollinaris. See APOLLINARIS SIDONIUS.

Sie·be \'zē-bə\, Augustus. 1788–1872. German inventor in England. Invented (1819) the modern diving suit.

Sie·bold \'zē-ˌbȯlt\, Carl Theodor Ernst von. 1804–1885. German zoologist. Professor at Erlangen (1841–45), Freiburg (1845–50), Breslau (1850–52), Munich (1853–83). Specialized in invertebrate research; made studies of parthenogenesis and life cycles of parasites; founded (with Rudolf von Kölliker) *Zeitschrift für wissenschaftliche Zoologie* (1848); collaborated with Friedrich H. Stannius on *Lehrbuch der vergleichenden Anatomie* (1846), one of first important texts on comparative anatomy.

Sie·den·topf \'zē-dən-ˌtȯpf\, Henry Friedrich Wilhelm. 1872–1940. German physicist. Employed by Zeiss optical works (1899–1938); professor at Jena (from 1918). With Richard Zsigmondy invented the ultramicroscope (1903); developed a photomicroscope with a "Phoku" eyepiece and attached miniature camera (1922).

Sieg \'zēk\, Emil. 1866–1951. German Sanskritist and scholar. Professor at Kiel (1909), Göttingen (1920); with Wilhelm Siegling made first successful attempt at grammatical analysis and translation of manuscripts in Tocharian language (1908).

Sieg·bahn \'sēg-bän\, Karl Manne Georg. 1886–1978. Swedish physicist. Professor, U. of Lund (1920–23), Uppsala (1923–26), and at Nobel Inst. of Physics, Stockholm (from 1937); member of International Committee on Weights and Measures (1939–64); known for investigations in X-ray spectroscopy; discovered the M series in the X-ray spectrum (1916); awarded 1924 Nobel prize for physics.

Sie·gen \'zē-gən\ *or* **Sech·ten** \'zek-tən\, Ludwig von. 1609–c.1680. German painter and engraver. Spent early life in service of Landgravine Amelia Elizabeth and Landgrave William of Hesse-Kassel; supposedly influenced by Rembrandt while in Amsterdam (1641–c.44); later in service of Elector of Mainz and Duke of Brunswick in Wolfenbüttel. Invented the mezzotint; earliest dated mezzotint a portrait of Amelia Elizabeth (1642).

Sieg·wart-Mül·ler \'zēk-värt-mue-lər\, Konstantin. 1801–1869. Swiss politician. State secretary of Luzern (1834–39); joined (1839) and became head of clericalist Ultramontane party; elected to Luzern state council (1841); mayor and president of the Confederation Diet (1844); organizer (1845) and head of war council of the Sonderbund; fled country after league was defeated in Sonderbund War (1847); returned (1857).

Sie·mens \'zē-məns, *Angl* 'sē-mənz\. Name of four German brothers, electrical engineers and industrialists: Ernst Werner von Siemens (1816–1892); invented an electroplating process (1842); invented the dial telegraph (1846); laid an underground electric telegraph for the army (1847); first to suggest use of gutta-percha for insulation of conductors; with J.G. Halske founded at Berlin firm of Siemens & Halske for manufacture of telegraphic equipment (1847), subsequent expansion embracing manufacture of electrical apparatus and handling of electrical engineering projects; with brother Karl established subsidiary factories in London, St. Petersburg, Vienna, Paris; laid cables across the Mediterranean and from Europe to India; invented the self-excited generator (1866); Liberal member of Prussian Chamber of Deputies (from 1866).

¶Karl Wilhelm, *later* Sir Charles William (1823–1883); to England (1844, naturalized 1859); invented a regenerative steam engine (1847) and a water meter (1851); improved the regenerative furnace applied in Siemens process of making steel (1861); established a cable factory at Charlton, Kent (1863); laid first cable from Rio de Janeiro to Montevideo (1874) and first cable between Britain and U.S. (1875); laid electric tramway at Portrush, Ireland, one of first in United Kingdom (opened 1883).

¶Friedrich Siemens (1826–1904); worked at Wilhelm's firm in England; invented (1856) a regenerative smelting oven widely used in the glass- and steelmaking industries. ¶Karl von Siemens (1829–1906); organized (1853–67) and was director (1880–94) of Russian branch of Siemens & Halske.

Sie·me·ring \'zē-mə-riŋ\, Rudolf. 1835–1905. German sculptor. Executed monuments to Frederick the Great in Marienburg, Luther in Eisleben, and Emperor Frederick William I in Berlin, and the equestrian statue of George Washington in Philadelphia.

Sie·mie·no·wicz \shem-'yen-ō-vēch\, Kazimierz *or* Casimirus. d. after 1651. Polish artillerist. While serving in Low Countries published at Amsterdam *Artis magnae artilleriae pars prima* (1650).

Sien·kie·wicz \shen-'kyev-ēch\, Henryk Adam Aleksandr Pius. *Pseudonym* Lit·wos \lyēt-vōs\. 1846–1916. Polish novelist. Published first novel *Na marne* (1872; In Vain); in U.S. as special correspondent of *Gazeta polska* (1876–78); co-editor of daily *Słowo* (1882–87); promoted Polish independence during World War I. Author of short stories as "Janko Muzykant" (1879), "Latarnik" (1882), "Bartek Zwyciezca" (1882), and esp. colorful and action-filled novels, as *Quo Vadis?* (1896) and historical trilogy consisting of *Ogniem i mieczem* (1884; With Fire and Sword), *Potop* (1886; The Deluge), *Pan Wołodyjowski* (1887–88; Pan Michael). Awarded Nobel prize for literature (1905).

Sierra, Gregorio Martínez. See MARTÍNEZ SIERRA.

Siete Iglesias, Marqués de. See Rodrigo CALDERÓN.

Sie·vers \'sē-vərz\, Frederick William. 1872–1966. American sculptor, b. Fort Wayne, Ind. Among his works were portrait busts of James Madison and Zachary Taylor in the Capitol, Richmond, Va.; portrait bust of Matthew Fontaine Maury in American Hall of Fame; an equestrian statue of Gen. Robert E. Lee with group of Confederate soldiers at Gettysburg, Pa.

Sie·yès \syā-yes\, Emmanuel-Joseph. 1748–1836. French Revolutionary leader. Canon of Tréguier (1775); vicar general (1780), chancellor (1788) of Chartres diocese. Sympathized with reform movement preceding French Revolution and became prominent with publication of pamphlet on the third estate, *Qu'est-ce que la tiers état?* (1789). Member of the Estates-General (1789), National Assembly, National Convention (1792–95), Council of Five Hundred (1795–99), and the Directory (1799); one of chief organizers of coup d'état (1799) which raised Napoléon to first consul. Appointed senator and count of the empire by Napoléon. Exiled at the Restoration; returned to France (1830).

Si·ge·bert *Ger* 'zē-gə-,bert, *Fr* sēzh-ber\. Name of three Frankish kings of the Merovingian dynasty:

Sigebert I. d. 575. Youngest son of Chlotar I and Queen Ingund; king of Austrasia (561–575); on death (567) of eldest brother Charibert secured lands south of Garonne River and large area in west, including Touraine and Poitou; defeated Avars (562, c.568); moved capital from Reims to Metz; m. (567) Brunhilde (*q.v.*); spent last part of reign successfully conducting a civil war against half-brother Chilperic; assassinated.

Sigebert II. 601–613. Eldest son of Theuderic II; great-grandson of Sigebert I and Brunhilde; a pawn of Brunhilde, who caused him to be named king of whole Frankish kingdom (613); never actually acclaimed king; apparently killed by Chlotar II.

Sigebert III. 630 or 631–656. King of Austrasia (633 or 634–656). Son of Dagobert I and father of Dagobert II; real power exercised by mayors of the palace Pépin the Old (639–643) and Pépin's son Grimoald (from 643).

Si·ge·bert \sēzh-ber\ of Gem·bloux \zhäⁿ-blü\. c.1030–1112. Belgian chronicler. Entered Benedictine monastery of Gembloux as a child; taught at monastery of Metz (1050–70); returned to Gembloux to teach and write (1070). Known for universal history *Chronicon ab anno 381 ad 1113* and survey of ecclesiastical historians *De viris illustribus* (c.1105); wrote treatises supporting Holy Roman Emperor Henry IV in Investiture Controversy (1075) and also supporting imperial investiture against Pope Paschal II (1103); his hagiographies included *Vita Wicberti, Gesta abbatum Gemblacensium,* and *Vita Sigiberti III.*

Si·gel \'zē-gəl, *Angl* 'sē-gəl\, Franz. 1824–1902. American soldier and editor, b. Sinsheim, Germany. To U.S. (1852); served through Civil War on Union side; major general (1862). Publisher and editor, *Neu Yorker Deutsches Volksblatt.*

Si·ger de Bra·bant \sē-zhā-də-bra-bäⁿ\. c.1240–between 1281 and 1284. French philosopher. Professor at U. of Paris; a leading representative of school of radical Aristotelianism; engaged in disputes, esp. against Bonaventure and Thomas Aquinas (1266–72); condemned by Bishop Tempier of Paris (1270, 1277); summoned by French inquisitor but fled to Italy (1276); apparently restricted at papal curia to company of a cleric. Works on Aristotle included *Quaestiones in metaphysicam, Impossibilia,* and *Tractatus de anima intellectiva.* Immortalized by Dante in *Il Paradiso* (canto X).

Sig·e·rist \'zē-gə-rist, *Angl* 'sig-ə-\, Henry Ernest. 1891–1957. Swiss medical historian. Professor at Leipzig (1925–32), Johns Hopkins (1932–47); emphasized effect of social conditions on practice of medicine. Works included *Antike Heilkunde* (1927), *Man and Medicine* (1932), *American Medicine* (1934), *Socialized Medicine in the Soviet Union* (1937), *Medicine and Human Welfare* (1941), and first two volumes (1951, 1961) of projected 8-vol. *History of Medicine.*

Si·ghi·bul·di \,sē-gē-'bu̇l-dē\, Cino dei. *Known as* Cino da Pis·toia \dä-pē-'stȯi-ä\. c.1270–1336 or 1337. Italian jurist and poet, b. Pistoia. Exiled from Pistoia for Ghibelline politics (1303–06); ambassador to Florence; supported Henry VII; wrote legal commentary *Lectura in Codicem* (1314); taught law (1314–34) at Siena, Bologna, Florence, Perugia, Naples. One of most prolific of *dolce stil nuovo* poets; his love lyrics praised by his friend Dante and by Petrarch, who called him his master.

Sig·is·mund \'zē-gis-,mu̇nt, *Angl* 'sij-əs-mənd, 'sig-\. Saint. *Fr.* Si·gis·mond \sē-zhēs-mōⁿ\. d. 524. King of Burgundy (516–524). Succeeded his father Gundobad; converted to Catholicism; founded monastery of Saint-Maurice d'Agaune; defeated and made prisoner (523) by Chlodomer, king of the Franks.

Sigismund. 1368–1437. King of Hungary (1387–1437), of the Romans (1410–37), of Bohemia (1419–37), and of the Lombards (1431–37); Holy Roman emperor (1433–37) of the house of Luxembourg. Son of Charles IV; m. (1387) Mary, daughter of King Louis I of Hungary and Poland; intervened in struggles between his half-brother Wenceslas IV and Bohemian nobility; undertook crusade against the Turks (1396) but was badly defeated at Nicopolis by Bayezid I; campaigned against Venetians in Italy (1412–13); inaugurated Council of Constance (1414); implicated in the death of Jan Hus (1415); unsuccessfully fought the Hussites in Bohemia (1420s); again defeated by Turks during crusade (1428).

Sigismund. *Pol.* Zyg·munt \'zig-münt\. Name of three kings of Poland:

Sigismund I. *Called* Sta·ry \'stȧ-rē\, *i.e.* the Old. 1467–1548. Grand prince of Lithuania (1506–48) and king of Poland (1506–48). Son of Casimir IV. Encouraged reform of currency; concluded war with Teutonic Order and established suzerainty over Ducal Prussia (1525); annexed duchy of Mazovia (1529); defended eastern front against Moldavians (1531) and Russians (1535); patron of the arts; promoted development of Renaissance in Poland.

Sigismund II Au·gus·tus \ȯ-'gəs-təs\. 1520–1572. King (1548–72). Son of Sigismund I. Elected and crowned co-ruler with father (1530); supported Teutonic Knights against Russian attacks (1559); united Livonia with duchy of Lithuania (1561); constitutionally united all lands under Polish crown; incorporated Ukrainian provinces into Poland (1569). Last of Jagiellon line.

Sigismund III Va·sa \'vȧ-sȧ\. 1566–1632. King of Poland (1587–1632) and king of Sweden (1592–1599; crowned 1594). Son of John III Vasa of Sweden. Defeated (1598) at Stångebro by his uncle (later Charles IX of Sweden) and deposed (1599); waged intermittent war with Sweden in futile attempt to regain crown (from 1600); suppressed civil war in Poland (1606–08); laid claim to Russian throne, invading and holding Moscow (1610–12) and Smolensk (from 1611); fought in Moldavia against Ottoman forces (1617–21); lost most of Livonia to Gustav II Adolphus.

Sigismund. King of Sweden. See SIGISMUND III, king of Poland.

Sigismund, John. See JOHN, king of Hungary; JOHN SIGISMUND.

Si·gnac \sē-nyȧk\, Paul. 1863–1935. French painter. Introduced to Impressionism by Armand Guillaumin (c.1883); helped found Salon des Indépendants (1884); with Georges Seurat developed Pointillism; principal theorist of Neo-Impressionist movement; traveled widely on European coast. Known for watercolor landscapes, seascapes, and in later years, French city scenes; critical writings included *D'Eugène Delacroix au néo-impressionnisme* (1889) and *Jongkind* (1927).

Si·gno·rel·li \,sēn-yō-'rel-lē\, Luca. *In full* Luca d'E·gi·dio di Ven·tu·ra de' Signorelli \dā-'jēd-yō-dē-vān-'tü-räd-ā-\. *Also called* Luca da Cor·to·na \kȯr-'tō-nä\. 1445 to 1450–1523. Italian painter. Probably pupil of Piero della Francesca (1460s); influenced by scientific naturalism of Florentine brothers Pollaiuoli (1470s); elected (1479) to Council of 18 in Cortona and thereafter active in politics. Known esp. for nudes and compositional devices. Works included *Testament of Moses* fresco in Sistine Chapel (c.1483), S. Onofrio altarpiece for Perugia cathedral (1484), fresco cycle of scenes from life of St. Benedict in Monteoliveto Maggiore monastery (1497–98), frescoes *The End of the World* and *Last Judgment* in Orvieto cathedral (1499–1502), and *Deposition* at Sta. Croce, Umbertide (1515–16).

Si·go·nio \sē-'gōn-yō\, Carlo. *Lat.* Si·go·ni·us \si-'gō-nē-əs\. 1524–1584. Italian Humanist. Wrote (1574) *De regno Italiae,* a history of Italy from 570 to 1200.

Sig·our·ney \'sig-ər-nē\, Lydia Howard, *nee* Hunt·ley \'hənt-lē\. 1791–1865. American author, b. Norwich, Conn. m. Charles Sigourney (1819; d. 1854). Contributed verse and miscellaneous articles to current periodicals (from c.1820); immensely popular in her day; produced more than sixty volumes as *Moral Pieces in Prose and Verse* (1815), *How to be Happy* (1833), *Pocahontas and Other Poems* (1841), *The Faded Hope* (1853).

Sigs·bee \'sigz-bē\, Charles Dwight. 1845–1923. American naval officer, b. Albany, N.Y. Commissioned in navy (1863); cooperated with Alexander

Agassiz in deep-sea exploration in Gulf of Mexico (1875–78). Commanded U.S. battleship *Maine* at time it was blown up in Havana harbor (Feb. 15, 1898); commanded the *St. Paul* in Spanish–American War; defeated Spanish destroyer *Terror* and Spanish cruiser *Isabella II* off San Juan, Puerto Rico; rear admiral (1903); retired (1907).

Si·gurd \ˈsig-gu̇rd\. Name of two rulers of Norway:

Sigurd I. *Called* Jor·sa·la·fa·rer \ˈjór-sə-lə-ˌfär-ər\, *i.e.* Jerusalemfarer. c.1090–1130. King (1103–30). One of the three sons of Magnus III; ruled jointly with Eystein (1103–22) and Olaf Magnusson (1103–15) and alone after their deaths; made expedition to Holy Land (1107–11), having many adventures in Spain, Sicily, and at Constantinople; first Scandinavian king to participate in Crusades; strengthened Norwegian church by building cathedrals and monasteries and imposing tithes.

Sigurd II. *Called* Munnr \ˈmu̇n(-ər)\, *i.e.* Mouth. 1134–1155. King (1136–55). Natural son of Harold IV Gille; joint ruler with half-brothers Ingi (1137–55) and Eystein (1142–55); killed by supporters of Ingi. Supposed father of Sverrir.

Sigurdsson. See SVERRIR.

Si·gurds·son \ˈsi-gœrths-sȯn\, Jón. 1811–1879. Icelandic man of letters and politician. Archivist and librarian of Royal Norse Archaeological Society (1847–65). Published *Íslendinga sögur* (1843–47), *Edda Snorra Sturlusonar* (1848–52), *Lovsamling for Island* (1853–57). In political field, leader in long struggle to gain liberal reforms from Danish government, esp. freedom of trade (1854); helped persuade King Christian IX to restore Icelandic Althing (1843) and was elected to it (1845); regarded as chiefly responsible for Denmark's grant of a constitution to Iceland (1874).

Si·gur·jóns·son \ˈsi-gœr-ˌyōns-sȯn\, Jóhann. 1880–1919. Icelandic poet and playwright. His plays included *Dr. Rung* (1905), *Bóndinn á Hrauni* (1908), masterpiece *Fjalla-Eyvindur* (1911; Eyvind of the Hills), *Galdra-Loftur* (1915), *Løgneren* (1917).

Si·ji·stā·nī \ˌsē-jis-ˈtä-nē\, Abū Dā'ūd as-. 817–859. Muslim theologian. Compiled *Kitāb as-Sunan,* a collection of 4,800 traditions of the Prophet Muḥammad relating to matters of jurisprudence.

Si·kan·dar Lo·dī \sik-ˈən-dər-ˈlōd-ē\. d. 1517. Second Lodī sultan of Delhi (1489–1517). Conquered Bihar (1492); ruled extensive but weakly governed kingdom.

Si·kel·i·a·nós \ˌsē-kel-ē-ä-ˈnōs\, Angelos. 1884–1951. Greek poet. One of leading modern Greek lyrical poets; verse included *Alafroískiotos* (1909), *Prólogos tés zoí* (1917), *Pascha ton Hellenon* (1922), *Delphikós Lógos* (1927); also wrote plays as *Sibylla, Daedalus in Crete, Christ in Rome, The Death of Digenis, Asklepius.*

Siki, Battling. See Louis PHAL.

Si·klós \ˈsē-klōs\, Albert. *Orig. surname* Schön·wald \ˈshœn-väld\. 1878–1942. Hungarian cellist, composer, and musicologist. Taught at Academy of Music, Budapest (1910–42); wrote textbooks, essays, criticism on music. Composed operas, ballets, symphonic works, chamber music, choral works, and piano pieces.

Si·kor·ski \shē-ˈkȯr-skē\, Józef. 1813–1896. Polish composer and music critic. Founded (1857) first significant Polish musical periodical, *Ruch muzyczny;* exerted influence as music critic; author of musical publications, esp. on piano theory; composed cantatas, church music, piano works, etc.

Sikorski, Władysław Eugeniusz. 1881–1943. Polish general and politician. Founded a secret military organization of Polish nationalists (1908); a leader of Piłsudski's Polish legions (1914–18); commanded an army against Russia (1920); chief of general staff (1921). Prime minister of Poland (Dec. 1922–May 1923); minister of war (1924–25); guided modernization of army; opposed Piłsudski (1928); after German conquest of Poland (1939), became commander in chief of the Polish army in France and prime minister of Polish government in exile.

Si·kor·sky \syi-ˈkȯr-skəi, *Angl* sə-ˈkȯr-skē\, Igor Ivan. 1889–1972. American aeronautical engineer, b. Kiev, Russia. Designed and built his first aircraft, a helicopter (1909); tested S-1 biplane (1910); in S-5 set records by flying 30 miles at 70 m.p.h. (1911); built and flew world's first successful multimotor plane (1913). To U.S. (1919; naturalized 1928); founded (1923) Sikorsky Aero Engineering Corp., later a division of United Aircraft Corp. (1929), which he headed until retirement (1957). Built (1931) amphibian *American Clipper* that pioneered in transoceanic commerical flights; developed first practical American helicopter (1939).

Si·las \ˈsī-ləs\. Saint. fl. 50 A.D. Christian prophet and missionary. Worker in the early Christian church at Jerusalem, companion of Paul on his second missionary journey; generally regarded as the Sil·va·nus \sil-ˈvā-nəs\ of the Pauline epistles.

Sil·ber·man \ˈzil-bər-ˌmän\. German family of musical instrument builders, known esp. for organs and clavichords. Members included: Andreas (1678–1734), worked chiefly in Strasbourg; influenced by Parisian organ builders. His brother ¶Gottfried (1683–1753) was a pupil, later partner of Andreas in Strasbourg; to Freiburg (1710); court organ builder (from 1736); visited by J.S. Bach (1736); a pioneer of German piano building. Andreas's sons: ¶Johann Andreas (1712–1783) built organs at Strasbourg; ¶Johann Daniel (1717–1766), pupil of Gottfried and succeeded to head of business upon his death; ¶Johann Heinrich (1727–1799) made pianos at Strasbourg; gained wide reputation, receiving orders from as far away as India.

Si·les \ˈsē-lās\, Hernando. 1882–1942. Bolivian politician. President of Bolivia (1926–30).

Sil·hou·ette \sēl-wet, *Angl* ˌsil-ə-ˈwet\, Étienne de. 1709–1767. French politician. Controller general of finances (1759); introduced reforms but incurred ridicule and hostility on the part of the nobility by economies and attempts to reduce pensions and privileges. It was by way of ridicule that the nobles applied his name to a mere outline profile drawing, "silhouette."

Sil·i·us Ital·i·cus \ˈsil-ē-ə-sə-ˈtal-i-kəs\, Tiberius Catius Asconius. 25 or 26–101 A.D. Latin epic poet and politician. Consul (68 A.D.); proconsul in Asia (77); withdrew to private life; acquired Cicero's villa at Tusculum; became patron of letters, esp. of Martial, Epictetus, Cornutus. Author of epic *Punica* (17 books, about 12,000 lines) on the Second Punic War.

Sil·lan·pää \ˈsil-án-ˌpä\, Frans Eemil. 1888–1964. Finnish writer. Author of novels *Elämä ja aurinko* (1916), *Hurskas kurjuus* (1919; Meek Heritage), *Nuorena nukkunut* (1931; pub. in U.S. as *The Maid Silja*), *Miehen tie* (1932), *Ihmiset suviyössä* (1934); reminiscences *Poika eli elämäänsa* (1953), *Päivä korkeimmillaan* (1956); and collections of short stories; awarded Nobel prize for literature (1939).

Sil·li·man \ˈsil-ə-mən\, Benjamin. 1779–1864. American chemist and geologist, b. North Stratford, Conn. Professor, Yale (1802–53). Founded (1818) and edited *The American Journal of Science and Arts,* usually called *Silliman's Journal;* active in foundation of Sheffield Scientific School, Trumbull Gallery, and Yale medical school. Author of *A Journal of Travels in England, Holland and Scotland* (1810), *Elements of Chemistry* (1830), etc. His son ¶Benjamin (1816–1885), b. New Haven, Conn., chemist, became his father's teaching assistant (1837); associate editor (1838) and later editor, *American Journal of Science;* helped his father establish (1842) a chemical laboratory, which later became the Sheffield Scientific School; professor of chemistry, Yale (from 1853); his "Silliman Report" (1855) on potential uses of crude-oil products was important in establishment of American oil industry. Author of *First Principles of Chemistry* (1847), *First Principles of Physics* (1858), etc. Both father and son were original members of National Acad. of Sciences (1863).

Si·loé \sē-lō-ˈā\, Gil de. *Also called* Gil Siloé, Gil de Ur·li·o·nes \ür-lē-ˈō-nās\ *or* Ur·li·e·nes \ür-lē-ˈā-nās\, *and* Gil de Em·ber·res \äm-ˈber-rās\ *or* Am·be·res \äm-ˈbā-rās\. d. c.1501. Spanish sculptor. Origins unknown; perhaps the Abraham de Nürnberg brought to Spain by Alonso de Cartagena. Greatest Spanish sculptor of 15th century; worked in Burgos school of Gothic sculpture; works known for rich ornamentation, elaborate detail, and heightened naturalism of figures. Extant pieces include funerary statues of King John and his wife Isabella of Portugal (1489–93) and altarpiece (1496–99) in Miraflores monastery, and tombs of infante Alonso and Juan de Padilla. His son ¶Diego (c.1495–1563), sculptor and architect; greatest sculptor of Burgos Plateresque; designed the Escalera Dorada in Burgos cathedral (1519–26), Granada cathedral (1528–43), Salvador church at Ubeda (1536), and Guadix cathedral (1549).

Silone, Ignazio. See Secondo TRANQUILLI.

Sil·va \ˈsil-və\, Antônio José da. *Called* O Ju·deu \ü-zhü-ˈthā-ü\. 1705–1739. Portuguese playwright. Imprisoned by Inquisition (1726, 1737–39); charged with heresy; strangled and his body burned. Author of comedies interspersing prose dialogue with songs, written for *ópera dos bonecos* (puppet theater) in Lisbon; titles included *A vida do grande D. Quixote de la Mancha* (1733), *Esopaida* (1734), *Os encantos de Medeia* (1735), *Anfitrião* (1736), *Labirinto de Creta* (1736), *As guerras do Alecrim e da Mangerona* (1737), *As variedades de Proteu* (1737), *Precipicio de Faetonte* (1738).

Sil·va \ˈsēl-vä\, José Asunción. 1865–1896. Colombian poet. His metrical experimentation, melancholy lyricism, and highly personal style greatly influenced development of Modernist poetry in Spanish America; known esp. for *Crepúsculos* and *Nocturnos* (1894).

Silva Guimarães, Bernardo da. See GUIMARÃES.

Silvanus. See SILAS.

Sil·va Xa·vier \ˈsil-və-shəv-ˈyär\, Joaquim José da. *Called* Ti·ra·den·tes \tē-rá-ˈdān-tish\, *i.e.* Tooth-puller, *for skill in dentistry.* 1748–1792. Brazilian patriot. In state of Minas Gerais led first major uprising against Portuguese rule in Brazil (1789); captured and beheaded; considered a national hero.

Sil·ve·la \sēl-ˈvā-lä\, Francisco. 1843–1905. Spanish politician. Premier of Spain (1899–1900, 1902–03).

Sil·ve·ri·us \sil-'vir-ē-əs\. Saint. d. 537? Pope (536–537). Son of Pope St. Hormisdas; elected through influence of Theodahad, king of the Ostrogoths; on order of Byzantine empress Theodora, deposed by Belisarius and replaced with Vigilius; exiled to Anatolia; appealed to Justinian I the Great but unsuccessful in attempt to regain papacy; exiled to Palmaria; died by murder or starvation.

Sil·ver·man \'sil-vər-mən\, Sime. 1873–1933. American newspaper publisher, b. Cortland, N.Y. Founder (1905), publisher, and editor of New York show-business weekly paper *Variety;* started a daily *Variety* in Hollywood, Calif. (1933).

Silvester. See also SYLVESTER.

Sil·ves·ter Guz·zo·li·ni \sēl-'väs-tār-ˌgüd-dzō-'lē-nē\. Saint. 1177–1267. Italian religious. Resigned from parish work to become a hermit (1227); built a monastery at Montefano (1231), thereby founding the religious order of Silvestrines (also called Sylvestrine Benedictines); canonized by Pope Clement VIII (1598).

Sil·ves·tre \sēl-vestrᵊ\, Paul-Armand. 1837–1901. French writer. Wrote humorous and somewhat Rabelaisian tales as *Les Farces de mon ami Jacques* (1881), *Les Bêtises de mon oncle* (1883), *Fabliaux gaillards* (1888); also composed librettos for several operas, including Saint-Saëns's *Henry VIII* and Godard's *Jocelyn.*

Sim·coe \'sim-(ˌ)kō\, John Graves. 1752–1806. English soldier and colonial administrator. Entered army (1771); served in U.S. War of Independence, including command of Queen's Rangers (1777–81). M.P. (1790); first lieutenant governor of Upper Canada (1792–94); encouraged immigration and agriculture, worked on defense and road building; virtual founder of Toronto as capital. Governor of Santo Domingo (1797); lieutenant general (1797); appointed commander in chief of India (1806).

Sim·e·on \sim-ā-'ōn, *Angl* 'sim-ē-ən\ *or* **Sym·e·on** \sùm-ā-'ōn, *Angl* 'sim-ē-ən\. *Called* the Great. d. 927 A.D. Bulgarian sovereign. Succeeded his father Boris as prince of Bulgaria (893); at war with Byzantine Empire (894–897); secured a peace (897) by which Constantinople paid tribute; defeated Magyars; after death of Leo VI (912) again waged war with Byzantines (913–914, 919–924); assumed title (925) of czar of the Romans and Bulgars; educated as a monk, made his court a cultural center.

Sim·e·on \'sim-ē-ən\ of Dur·ham \'dər-əm\. *Also spelled* Sym·e·on \'sim-ē-ən\. d. 1130 to 1138. English chronicler. Entered Benedictine monastery at Jarrow, Durham (c.1071); made religious vows (1085 or 1086); became choirmaster of Durham; wrote (1104–08) *Historia ecclesiae Dunelmensis,* a history of the Durham church; also wrote part of *Historia regum,* history of kings of Northumbria.

Simeon the New Theologian, Saint. See SYMEON.

Sim·e·on \'sim-ē-ən\, Charles. 1759–1836. English clergyman. Perpetual curate of Trinity Church, Cambridge (1783–1836); leader of Evangelical (or Low Church) movement in Church of England; renowned as preacher; helped found Church Missionary Society (1797); wrote biblical commentary *Horae Homileticae* (1819–28).

Simeon bar Koziba. See KOKHBA.

Simeon ben Ga·ma·li·el II \-ˌben-gə-'mā-lē-əl\. 2d century A.D. High priest of Palestinian Jewish community (reigned c.135–175). Organized a high court to pass on disputed questions of Jewish law and dogma; concentrated all communal authority in his office; succeeded by his son Judah ha-Nasi.

Simeon ben Yo·ḥai \-yō-'kī\. 2d century A.D. Galilean rabbi. Some details of life recorded in Talmud but enmeshed with legend; disciple of Rabbi Akiba ben Joseph; forced into hiding for opposing Roman rule; according to legend, hid in a cave with his son Eleazar for 13 years; established a Jewish academy, pupils included Judah ha-Nasi; many of his aphorisms recorded by Judah in the Mishna. Advocated an ascetic ideal of total devotion to study of the Torah. Author or editor of legal commentaries (Midrashim) *Sifre* on Numbers and Deuteronomy and *Mekhilta de Rabbi Shim'on ben Yoḥai* on Exodus; considered by some scholars author of Jewish mystical work *Zohar,* which is normally ascribed to Moses de León.

Simeon Meta·phras·tes \-ˌmet-ə-'fras-ˌtēz\. c.900–after 984. Byzantine hagiographer. Held administrative post in Byzantine civil service; in later life became a monk. Author of *Menologion,* a 10-volume hagiography of early Eastern saints.

Simeon Sty·li·tes \-stī-'līt-(ˌ)ēz\. Saint. *Also called* Stylites, *i.e.* Pillar Dweller *or* Simeon the Elder. c.390–459. Syrian ascetic. First and most widely known pillar saint, or stylite; passed the last 30 years of his life on top of a pillar about 50 feet high. From this perch he preached, made many converts, and exercised through his disciples a considerable influence.

Sim·mel \'zim-əl\, Georg. 1858–1918. German philosopher and sociologist. Taught at Berlin (1885–1914) and Strassburg (1914–18); instrumental in establishment in Germany of sociology as a basic social science. Wrote chiefly on sociological methodology, including *Philosophie des Geldes* (1900); his works influential in U.S., esp. through translations by Albion Small (*q.v.*).

Sim·mons \'sim-ənz\, Edward Emerson. 1852–1931. American painter, b. Concord, Mass. Best known for his murals as in the Library of Congress in Washington and the Massachusetts State House in Boston.

Simmons, Furnifold McLendell. 1854–1940. American politician, b. near Polloksville, N.C. Member from N.C. of U.S. House of Representatives (1887–89) and Senate (1901–31); chairman, Senate Finance Committee (1913–19); cosponsor of Underwood-Simmons Tariff Act (1913).

Simms \'simz\, William Gilmore. 1806–1870. American writer, b. Charleston, S.C. Admitted to bar (1827); state legislator; editor of proslavery *Southern Quarterly Review* (1849–56). Often considered the outstanding Southern man of letters in 19th century. Known esp. for historical novels, often set in frontier of lower South, including *Martin Faber* (1833), *Guy Rivers* (1834), *The Yemassee* (1835), *Mellichampe* (1836), *Richard Hurdis* (1838), *The Kinsmen* (1841), *The Forayers* (1855), *Joscelyn* (1867); also wrote 19 volumes of poetry, esp. *Poems* (1853); *History of South Carolina* (1840); short story collection *The Wigwam and the Cabin* (1845); literary criticism *Views and Reviews of American Literature* (1845); and biographies, esp. *The Life of Francis Marion* (1844) and *The Life of Chevalier Bayard* (1847).

Sim·nel \'sim-nᵊl\, Lambert. c.1475–1535. English impostor. Educated and put forward by young Oxford priest as personator of the Duke of Clarence's son Edward (1475–1499), Earl of Warwick, who was imprisoned in Tower; taken to Ireland (1487), backed by his pretended aunt, Margaret, Duchess of Burgundy, sister of Edward IV; gained powerful following, crowned as King Edward VI in Dublin cathedral (1487); landed in Lancashire with force of Germans and ill-armed Irish levies; defeated at Stoke (1487); pardoned and became royal falconer.

Simon. See Saint PETER.

Si·mon \'sī-mən\. *Called* the Apostle. Saint. 1st century A.D. One of the 12 Christian Apostles. In Gospel of Luke given title Kananaios, Greek transliteration of Aramaic word meaning "the Zealot"; supposedly preached in Egypt and joined Apostle St. Judas in Persia; according to apocryphal Acts of Simon and Judas, martyred by being cut in half with a saw, but according to St. Basil the Great, died peacefully at Edessa.

Simon of St. Quen·tin \saⁿ-käⁿ-taⁿ\. 13th century. French Dominican friar. Accompanied a diplomatic and proselytizing mission sent by Pope Innocent IV to the Mongols of Persia and Armenia (1247); his account of the journey is preserved in *Speculum historiale* of Vincent of Beauvais.

Simon of Sud·bury \'səd-b(ə-)rē\. *Orig. surname* Tyb·ald \'tib-əld\ *or* The·baud \tā-'bō\ *or* Theob·ald \'tib-əld\. d. 1381. English prelate. Auditor at papal curia; nuncio to Edward III of England (1359); bishop of London (1361); archbishop of Canterbury (1375); crowned Richard II (1377); tried John Wycliffe at Lambeth (1378); chancellor of England (from 1380); during Peasants' Revolt of 1381 held accountable by peasants for instituting oppressive poll tax; dragged from Tower of London by Wat Tyler's insurgents and beheaded.

Simon, Sir John. 1816–1904. English physician. First medical officer of health to City of London (1848–55) and to central government (1855–76); instrumental in establishment of modern standards of public health service; created a state medical department to administer public health, supervise medical profession, etc.; his annual reports resulted in Sanitary Act of 1866 and Public Health Act of 1875.

Simon, Sir John Allsebrook. Viscount Simon. 1873–1954. British politician. Called to bar (1899); M.P. (1906–18, 1922–40); solicitor general (1910); attorney general (1913); home secretary (1915–16); chairman of Indian statutory commission (1927–30). Foreign secretary (1931–35); home secretary and deputy leader of House of Commons (1935–37); leader of Liberal National party (in 1930s); favored rapprochement between Britain and Nazi Germany; considered member of "Cliveden set" (from 1936); chancellor of the exchequer (1937–40); lord chancellor (1940–45). Created viscount (1940).

Si·mon \sē-mōⁿ\, Jules. *Orig.* Jules-François-Simon Suisse \swʸēs\. 1814–1896. French philosopher and politician. Professor at the Sorbonne, Paris (1839); member of the National Assembly (1848–50); lost his professorship because of refusal to take oath required by the emperor (1852). Member of Corps Législatif (1863–70) and steadily opposed the government; published (1868) *La Politique radicale,* which became a basis of Radical party program; minister of public instruction in the Government of National Defense (1870–71, 1871–73); senator for life (1875); premier of France (1876–77); his resignation at the instance of President Mac-Mahon caused constitutional crisis of May 16.

Simon, Richard. 1638–1712. French theologian. Member of the Congregation of the Oratory (1662–78); pioneer of modern historical method of biblical study. Among his works were *Histoire critique du Vieux Testament* (1678) which brought violent criticism from both Roman Catholics and Protestants, *Histoire critique du texte du Nouveau Testament* (1683), etc.; some of his books placed on Catholic Index.

Si·mon \'sī-mən\, Richard Leo. 1899–1960. American publisher, b. New York City. Cofounder (1924, with Max L. Schuster) and partner, Simon and Schuster, book publishers.

Simon de Montfort. See MONTFORT.

Si·mon·i·des \sī-'män-ə-,dēz\ of Amor·gos \ə-'mȯr-gəs\. fl. c.660 B.C. Greek poet. Founder of a colony on island of Amorgos; wrote esp. in iambics; only fragments of his work extant.

Simonides of Ce·os \'sē-,äs\. c.556–c.468 B.C. Greek poet. Resident at court of Hipparchus at Athens (to 514 B.C.), in Thessaly, and later in life at court of Hiero of Syracuse. Author especially of lyric verse, including odes, elegies, dirges, epigrams, and hymns to the gods; only fragments of his works extant; first known Greek poet to have written on commission for fees; wrote (520) earliest recorded epinician ode in honor of victors in Olympic Games.

Si·mon Ma·gus \'sī-mən-'mā-gəs\. *Also called* Simon the Magician *and* Simon the Sorcerer. 1st century A.D. Samaritan sorcerer. In the Bible, converted by Philip and severely rebuked by Peter for offering money to purchase the power of giving the Holy Ghost—hence the term simony; according to Justin Martyr, visited Rome at time of Emperor Claudius and deified by followers fascinated with his miracle working.

Simons, Menno. See MENNO SIMONS.

Si·mon·son \'sī-mən-sən\, Lee. 1888–1967. American designer, b. New York City. A founder (1919) and member of board of directors (1919–40) of Theatre Guild; his designs (from 1915) helped movement away from realistic sets to those suited to the meaning and action of each play. Published *The Stage Is Set* (1932), *The Art of Scenic Design* (1950), and *Part of a Lifetime* (1943); also an art critic, painter, magazine editor, theater consultant.

Si·mon Thas·si \'sī-mən-'thas-ē\. d. 135 B.C. Jewish high priest. Son of Mattathias; member of the Maccabee family which led a resistance against King Antiochus's suppression of Judaism.

Si·mo·vić \'sē-mȯ-vētʸ\, Dušan. 1882–1962. Yugoslav general and politician. Helped depose Prince Paul (1941); premier of Yugoslavia (1941–1942); cabinet official in Yugoslav government in exile.

Sim·pli·ci·us \sim-'plish(-ē)-əs\. Saint. d. 483. Pope (468–483). During his pontificate Western Empire fell before barbarians; upheld Chalcedonian orthodoxy against Zeno's pro-Monophysitic policy.

Simplicius of Ci·li·cia \sə-'lish-(ē-)ə\. fl. c.530 A.D. Greek Neoplatonic philosopher. Disciple of Ammonius and Damascius; author of commentaries on some of Aristotle's works and on the *Encheiridion* of Epictetus.

Simp·son \'sim(p)-sən\, Sir George. 1792–1860. Canadian explorer, b. Scotland. Administrator (1821–56) of Hudson's Bay Company's territory; crossed North American continent (1828); Simpson's Falls and Cape George Simpson named after him.

Simpson, Sir James Young. 1811–1870. Scottish physician. First to use ether as anesthetic in obstetric practice (1847); discovered anesthetic property of chloroform (1847), published *Account of a New Anaesthetic Agent,* and was first to use it in obstetric practice; appointed one of queen's physicians for Scotland (1847); introduced iron wire sutures and acupressure; developed the Simpson forceps; wrote on medical history, fetal pathology, hermaphroditism.

Simpson, Jeremiah. *Nicknamed* Sockless Jerry. 1842–1905. American politician, b. Westmoreland Co., N.B. To U.S. as a child; cattle rancher in Kansas (1884); entered politics as Populist; member of U.S. House of Representatives (1891–95, 1897–99); published journal *Jerry Simpson's Bayonet* (1899–1900) in Kansas City; noted for fiery campaign oratory.

Simpson, Sir John Hope. 1868–1961. English administrator in India. Held numerous government posts, rising to acting chief commander of Andaman and Nicobar Islands (1914–16); after retirement (1916), worked with refugee and relief services in China and Greece. Author of *The Refugee Problem* and *Refugees* (both 1939), two of earliest modern studies on refugees.

Simpson, Matthew. 1811–1884. American clergyman, b. Cadiz, O. Became Methodist minister (1836); president (1839–48) of Indiana Asbury U. (now DePauw); bishop (1852); opponent of slavery and strong supporter of Union cause during Civil War; delivered eulogy at Lincoln's burial in Springfield, Ill.

Simpson, Thomas. 1710–1761. English mathematician. School teacher; self-taught in mathematics, in which he became a leader in England. Author of *New Treatise on Fluxions* (1737) and several popular textbooks.

Simpson, Wallis, *nee* War·field \'wȯ(ə)r-,fēld\. Duchess of Windsor. 1896–1986. American socialite, b. Blue Ridge Summit, Penn. m. Ernest A. Simpson (1928). Her romantic liaison with King Edward VIII of England produced a constitutional crisis that resulted in his abdication (1936); m. (1937) Edward, newly created Duke of Windsor, in France; permanently estranged from British royal family, led with Edward an international social life.

Sim·rock \'zim-,rȯk\, Karl Joseph. 1802–1876. German writer and scholar. In Prussian government service (1823–30); professor, Bonn (from 1850); translated the *Nibelungenlied,* the *Edda,* and several poems of the Arthurian cycle; complied *Heldenbuch* (1843–49), *Deutsche Volksbücher* (1845–66), and *Handbuch der deutschen Mythologie* (1853–55).

Simrock, Nicolaus. 1751–1832. German music publisher. Established (1793) in Bonn famous music publishing firm, Simrock; published works of Beethoven, Haydn, Weber, etc.; promoted German folksong. His son ¶Peter Joseph (1792–1868) founded a branch in Cologne (1812); succeeded to head of firm on father's death (1832); published works of Mendelssohn, Schumann. His son ¶Friedrich August, *called* Fritz (1837–1901), succeeded as head of firm (1868); moved it to Berlin (1870); published works of Brahms and Dvořák.

Sims \'simz\, George Robert. 1847–1922. English journalist and playwright. Under pseudonym Dag·o·net \'dag-ə-nət, -(,)net\ wrote "Mustard and Cress" columns in the *Referee.* Among his books and plays were *The Dagonet Ballads, Rogues and Vagabonds, Anna of the Underworld, Puss in Boots,* etc.

Sims, James Marion. 1813–1883. American physician, b. Lancaster Co., S.C. Practiced in Alabama (1835–53), New York City (from 1853). With Ephraim McDowell considered originator of operative gynecology; developed technique to remove bladder fistula (1849); promoted founding (1855) of Woman's Hospital, New York City. Published *Clinical Notes on Uterine Surgery* (1866).

Sims, William Sowden. 1858–1936. American naval officer, b. Port Hope, Ont., of American parents. To U.S. (1872); entered navy (1880); wrote a much used textbook on navigation; instituted great improvements in naval gunnery; promoted adoption of convoy system in World War I; commissioned admiral (1918), reverting to permanent rank of rear admiral after World War I. Commanded American naval operations in European waters (1917–19); retired (1922). Coauthor, with Burton J. Hendrick, of *The Victory at Sea* (1920).

Si·nan \sə-'nän\. *Orig. Christian name* Joseph. 1489–1588. Turkish architect. Greatest Ottoman architect; his ideas served as basic themes of virtually all later Turkish architecture; designed more than 300 buildings, including the Şehzade Mosque (1548) and Mosque of Süleyman I the Magnificent (1550–57; both in Istanbul) and the Sultan Selim Mosque (1568–74; Edirne).

Si·nān \sə-'nän\, Rashīd ad-Dīn as-. *Known in West as* Old Man of the Mountain. d. 1192. Syrian warrior. Leader of Syrian branch of the Assassins, an Ismā'īlī Shī'ī Muslim sect; headquartered in a fortress in Maṣyāf; attempted several times to assassinate Saladin.

Şi·na·si \shin-ä-'si\, İbrahim. *Known also as* İbrahim Şinasi Efendi. 1826–1871. Turkish writer. Pioneered private journalism; started own newspaper *Tasvir-i efkâr* (1862). Founder of modern school of Ottoman literature; advocated reform of Turkish verse forms; introduced Western ideas; wrote first Turkish play; author of poetry, plays, prose works, and translations of French poems.

Sin·clair \'sin-,kla(ə)r, 'siŋ-, -,kle(ə)r, sin-', siŋ-'\. Name (variant of Saint Clair) of Scottish family, members of which have held the earldoms of Ork·ney \'ȯrk-nē\ (1379–1471) and of Caith·ness \'kāth-nes\ (from 1455), including: Sir William Sinclair *or* Saint Clair \'sin-,kla(ə)r, 'siŋ-, -kle(ə)r, sin-', siŋ-'\ (1240–?1303), Baron of Ross·lyn \'räs-lən\; partisan of Baliol and leader of Scots in revolt against Edward I of England. His grandson ¶Sir William Sinclair (d. 1330) accompanied Sir James Douglas to Palestine and was slain with him by Saracens in Andalusia. His son ¶Sir Henry (d. 1400?), Earl or Prince of Orkney (created by Haakon VI of Norway, 1379); aided by the Venetian navigators Niccolò and Antonio Zeno conquered (1391) Faeroe Islands (Frislanda) and Shetland.

Sir Henry's grandson ¶Sir William (1404?–1480), 3d Earl of Orkney *and* 1st Earl of Caithness (1455), assisted in repelling English invasion (1448); chancellor of Scotland (1454–56); one of regents and ambassador to England (1461); on cession of Orkney isles by Norway to King James III (1470), resigned his rights in favor of sovereign. Sir William's (1404?–1480) great-grandson ¶George (d. 1582), 4th Earl of Caithness; Roman Catholic supporter of Mary, Queen of Scots; implicated in Darnley murder; presided at trial of Bothwell; instigated acts of violence in northern Scotland.

¶Sir John Sinclair (1754–1835), writer on finance and agriculture; M.P. (1780–1811); first president of board of agriculture (1793–98), introduced improved methods of tillage and new breeds of livestock; gained reputation as financier with *History of the Public Revenue of British Empire* (1784); prevented extension of financial crisis by plan for issue of exchequer bills (1793); supervised compilation of *Statistical Account of Scotland* (21 vols., (1791–99). His daughter ¶Catherine (1800–1864) was author of tales, descriptive works, and children's books, esp. *Holiday House* (1839).

Sinclair, Harry Ford. 1876–1956. American businessman, b. Wheeling, W. Va. Entered petroleum business (1901); founder (1916) and president (to 1949), Sinclair Oil Corp. Indicted (1925) with Albert B. Fall and Edward L. Doheny (*qq.v.*) in Teapot Dome scandal; acquitted (1928) of charges of conspiracy with Fall to defraud the government.

Sinclair, Upton Beall. 1878–1968. American writer and social reformer, b. Baltimore, Md. Socialist candidate for U.S. Congress (1920, 1922) and for governor of California (1926, 1930); received Democratic nomination for governor (1934), running on a Socialist reform platform EPIC (End Poverty In California). Founded American Civil Liberties Union in California. Author of topical and polemical novels, including *The Jungle* (1906), *The Money Changers* (1908), *King Coal* (1917), *Oil!* (1927), *Boston* (1928), and an 11-volume series about a contemporary American, "Lanny Budd," beginning with *World's End* (1940) and including *Dragon's Teeth* (1942, Pulitzer prize), and *Presidential Mission* (1947); many political and social studies as *The Profits of Religion* (1918) and *The Goose-Step* (1923); and an autobiography (1932, revised 1962).

Sin·ding \'sin-diŋ\, Otto Ludwig. 1842–1909. Norwegian painter. Best known for religious, historical, and genre pictures. His brother ¶Christian August (1856–1941) was a composer of opera *Der heilige Berg* (1912), 4 symphonies, concertos, violin sonatas, piano pieces, and songs.

Sing·er \'siŋ-ər\, Isaac Merrit. 1811–1875. American inventor, b. Pittstown, N.Y. Patented a rock-drilling machine (1839) and a metal- and wood-carving machine (1849). Patented an improved sewing machine and organized (with Edward Clark) I.M. Singer & Co. to manufacture it (1851); patented twenty improvements in his machine (between 1851 and 1863). Sued by Elias Howe for patent infringement (1851–54) and lost case, but success of machine made penalty harmless; promoted installment credit plans; retired to England (1863).

Singer, Israel Joshua. 1893–1944. American writer, b. Bilgoraj, Poland. To U.S. (1933, naturalized 1939). Author of Yiddish short stories, plays, and esp. novels including *Shtool un aizn* (1927), *Yoshe Kalb* (1932), *Di brider Ashkenazi* (1936), *Khaver Nakhmen* (1938), *The Family Carnovsky* (1943).

Singh \'si^n-hə\, Rana Pratāp. 1545?–1597. Hindu maharaja of Mewar (1572–97). Son and successor of Rana Udai Singh; reorganized government; improved defenses; successfully resisted attacks of Mughal emperor Akbar; succeeded by his son Amar Singh. Honored as a hero in Rājasthān.

Sin·ha \'si^n-hə\, Sir Satyendra Prasanno. 1st Baron of Rai·pur \'rī-,pu̇r\. 1864–1928. Indian lawyer and statesman. First Indian appointed as advocate general of Bengal (1907–09, 1915–17) and as member of governor general's Executive Council (1909–10). Representative of India at Imperial War Conference in London (1917); undersecretary of state for India (1919–20); governor of Bihar and Orissa (1920–21); member of Judicial Committee of Privy Council (1926–28).

Sinjohn, John. See John GALSWORTHY.

Sin·le·qe·un·ni·ni *or* **Sin-le·qe-uni·ni** \,sin-,lā-kə-ü-'nē-nē\. 12th century B.C. Babylonian poet. Compiled an Akkadian version of traditions of Gilgamesh which was presumed original of fullest extant account.

Sin·mu·bal·lit \'sin-mu̇b-'äl-ēt\. 19th–18th century B.C. Fifth ruler of 1st dynasty of Babylon (reigned 1812–1793 B.C.). Succeeded by his son Hammurabi.

Sin·u·he \'sin-(y)ə-,hā\. 20th century B.C. Egyptian politician. Official in harem of Amenemhet I; after Amenemhet's assassination (1962 B.C.), fled to and settled in southern Syria; became a patriarch of the territory; returned to Egypt under patronage of Sesostris I.

Sion Cent \'shōn-'kent\. *Sometimes called* Siôn Gwent \-'gwent\, Siôn y Cent \-ə-'kent\, Siôn Kemp \-'kemp\, *or* Siôn Kempt \-'kem(p)t\. c.1367–c.1430. Welsh poet. Wrote a eulogy of Brecknockshire and several poems in *Cywydd* meter on religious and moral subjects.

Si Prat \'sē-'prät\. 17th century. Siamese poet. Member of court of King Narai at Ayutthaya; author of romantic poem *Aniruddha* and some love songs.

Si·quei·ros \sē-'kā-rōs\, David Alfaro. 1896–1974. Mexican painter. Involved in left-wing political activities from youth; collaborated with Diego Rivera on frescoes for National Preparatory School (1922); organized and led unions of artists and workers (from 1922); often jailed and exiled for political activities; established Experimental Workshop in New York City (1932) and Center of Realist Art in Mexico City (1944). His murals distinguished by sharp delineation, striking colors, and political ideology; best known murals *From Porfirio's Dictatorship to the Revolution* in National History Museum and *March of Humanity* in Parque de la Lama hotel (both Mexico City); also produced landscapes, portraits, and other canvases.

Si·rāj-ud-Daw·lah \sir-'äj-u̇d-'dau̇-lə\. *Orig.* Mīrzā Muḥammad. c.1732–1757. Nawab of Bengal (1756–57). Troubled by British fortification of Calcutta; with large force captured Calcutta (June 1756); responsible for tragedy of Black Hole; driven out of Calcutta by Robert Clive and Adm. Charles Watson (Jan. 1757); sided with the French in their contest with Clive; plotted against by his general Mīr Ja'far; his large army totally defeated by small force of Clive at Plassey (June 23, 1757); fled to Murshidābād but was captured and executed.

Sir·hin·dī \sir-'hin-dē\, Shaykh Aḥmad. *Posthumous title* Mujaddid-e Alf-e Sānī, *i.e.* Renovator of the Second Millennium. 1564–1624. Indian mystic and theologian. Joined orthodox mystic order Naqshbandīyah (1593–94); largely responsible for reintroduction of orthodox Islām into India; led movement against syncretistic beliefs that prevailed in Mughal Empire; chief work *Maktūbāt*, a compilation of letters containing his theology.

Siribunyasan *or* **Siribunyasarn.** See ONG BOUN.

Si·ri·ci·us \sə-'rish(-ē)-əs\. Saint. c.334–399. Pope (384–399). Issued papal decrees designating Easter and Pentecost as days of baptism, regulating consecrations, ordinations, and discipline of penance, and commanding celibacy for priests. Settled the Meletian Schism by recognizing Flavian I as bishop of Antioch (393); opposed Priscillianism; condemned several heretics, including Jovinian, Bishop Bonosus of Sardica, and Bishop Felix of Trier.

Si·sen·na \sə-'sen-ə\, Lucius Cornelius. 120?–67 B.C. Roman politician and historian. Quaestor in Sicily (77 B.C.); governor of Achaia; author of a history of Rome, of which only fragments are extant.

Sisines, Archelaus. See ARCHELAUS.

Si·sin·ni·us \sə-'sin-ē-əs\. d. 708. Pope (Jan.–Feb. 708). Ordered reinforcement of walls of Rome.

Sis·ler \'sis-lər\, George Harold. 1893–1973. American baseball player, b. Manchester, Ohio. First baseman, St. Louis Browns (1915–27; manager 1924–26) and Washington Senators (1928) of American League, Boston Braves of National League (1928–30). Hit .407 in 1920, .420 in 1922, career average .340; set major league record of 257 hits in a season (1920); elected to Baseball Hall of Fame (1939).

Sis·ley \sē-slā\, Alfred. 1839–1899. French painter, of English parents. A creator of French Impressionism; associated with Monet, Renoir, Bazille (from 1862); known esp. for landscapes as *Le Canal* (1872), *L'Écluse de Bougival* (1873), *La Barque pendant l'inondation* (1876).

Sis·mon·di \sē-smō^n-dē\, Jean-Charles-Léonard Si·monde de \sē-mō^{n}d-də-\. 1773–1842. Swiss historian and economist. A pioneer theorist on nature of economic crises and risks of limitless competition, overproduction, and underconsumption. Author of *Histoire des républiques italiennes au moyen âge* (1807–18), *Nouveaux principes d'économie politique* (1819), *Histoire des Français* (1821–44), etc.

Si·so·wath *or* **Si·so·vat** \'sē-sō-,vät\ *or* **Si Su·va·ta** \,sē-su̇-'vä-tä\. 1840–1927. King of Cambodia (1904–27). Son of Ang Duong, brother of Norodom, and half-brother of Si Votha; prevented Si Votha from seizing Cambodian throne (1861); succeeded Norodom (1904); a figurehead for the French colonial administration; succeeded by his son Monivong.

Sit·te \'sit-ə\, Camillo. 1843–1903. Austrian architect and town planner. Director of Vienna Staatsgewerbeschule; founded periodical *Der Städtebau* (1903); advocated building of garden cities. Chief work *Der Städtebau nach seinen kunstlerischen Grundsätzen* (1889).

Sit·ter \'sit-ər\, Willem de. 1872–1934. Dutch astronomer. Professor at U. of Leiden (from 1908) and director (from 1919) of its observatory. Studied distribution, motion, and parallax of stars; made researches on Galilean satellites of Jupiter; made cosmological deductions from Einstein's theory of relativity; studied recession of extragalactic nebulae from the sun; made calculation of radius of the universe; enunciated theory of an expanding universe.

Sittewald, Philander von. See Johann Michael MOSCHEROSCH.

Sit·ting Bull \,sit-iŋ-'bu̇l\. *Indian name* Tatanka Iyotake. c.1831–1890. American Indian leader, b. near Grand River, S.D. Member of Hunkpapa Sioux tribe; became leader of Strong Heart warrior society (c.1856); made head chief of entire Sioux nation (c.1867); a leader in Sioux war (1876–77), and with Gall and Crazy Horse at battle of the Little Big Horn, where Custer and all his men were slain (June 25, 1876); forced to retreat across Canadian border (1877). Returned to surrender at Fort Buford (1881); was located on Standing Rock Indian reservation; gained international fame as member of Buffalo Bill's Wild West Show (1885). Again active in Indian agitation (1890); arrested and shot by Indian guards. His prominence made him central figure in a number of legends.

Sit·well \'sit-,wel, -wəl\. English literary family, including: Sir George Reresby Sitwell, 4th Baronet Sitwell (1860–1943), author of *The First Whig* (1894), *Tales of My Native Village* (1934), *Idle Fancies in Prose and Verse* (1938). His daughter ¶ Dame Edith (1887–1964), poet, critic, and novelist; known for her formidable personality, Elizabethan dress, and eccentric opinions; with her brothers led a revolt against Georgian poetry. Author of collections of verse including *The Mother* (1915), *Clown's Houses* (1918), *Bucolic Comedies* (1923), *Façade* (1923; music by Sir William Walton), *The Sleeping Beauty* (1924), *Gold Coast Customs* (1929), *Street Songs* (1942), *Song of the Cold* (1945), *Gardeners and Astronomers* (1953), *The Outcasts* (1962); novel *I Live Under a Black Sun* (1937); and prose works *Alexander Pope* (1930), *Bath* (1932), *The English Eccentrics* (1933), *A Poet's Notebook* (1943), *A Notebook on William Shakespeare* (1948). Her brother ¶Sir Francis Osbert Sacheverell, 5th Baronet Sitwell (1892–1969); poet, playwright, and novelist; author of satirical and serious poetry as *Mrs. Kimber* (1937), *Wrack at Tidesend* (1952); novels including *Before the Bombardment* (1926), *The Man Who Lost Himself* (1929); short stories; and esp. prose memoirs *Left Hand! Right Hand!* (1944), *The Scarlet Tree* (1946), *Great Morning!* (1947), *Laughter in the Next Room* (1948), and *Noble Essences* (1950).

Si·va Day·al Sa·heb \'sē-və-'dī-äl-'sä-heb\. *Orig.* Tul·si Ram \'təl-sē-'räm\. 1818–1878. Indian religious. Founder of the Hindu sect Radha Soami Satsang (1861); wrote two books, one in prose and one in verse, both titled *Sār Bacan.*

Śi·va·ji *or* **Shi·va·ji** \'shiv-ä-jē\. *Known as* the Grand Rebel. 1627 or 1630–1680. Founder of the Marāthā kingdom of India. Organized (c.1655) bands of horsemen and carried on war with Bijāpur; seized Poona (1663) and declared himself independent (1664); at war with Aurangzeb; was captured and imprisoned but escaped (1666); sacked Surat (1670); crowned as independent king (1674); successfully extended his dominions to the south (1676); weakened rule of Mughals and greatly strengthened power of Marāthās; advocated religious tolerance.

Si·va·nan·da \sē-və-'nän-də\, Swami. 1887–1963. Indian Hindu religious. Founder of the Divine Life Society.

Sivertsen, Cort. See ADELAER.

Si Vo·tha \'sē-'vò-tä\ *or* **Si Vat·tha** \-'vät-tä\. 1841–1892. Cambodian prince. Son of Ang Duong and half-brother of Norodom and Sisowath; attempted unsuccessfully to seize throne from Norodom (1860–61); led unsuccessful insurrections against French forces (1876, 1885).

Si·ward \'syü-ərd\. *Called* the Strong. Earl of North·um·ber·land \nòr-'thəm-bər-lənd\. d. 1055. Danish warrior in England. Became earl of all Northumberland by murdering his wife's uncle (1041); supported Edward the Confessor against Godwine (1051); invaded Scotland in interests of his kinsman Malcolm Canmore, routed King Macbeth (1054), and established Malcolm III as king of Cumbria.

Six Dynasties. Name given to six successive Chinese dynasties following end of Han dynasty (220 A.D.) and all with capitals at Nanking: Wu (222–280), Eastern Chin (317–419), Liu-Sung (420–479), Southern Ch'i (479–502), Liang (502–557), and Ch'en (557–589).

Six·tus \'sik-stəs\. Name of five popes:

Sixtus I. Saint. *In earliest documents spelled* Xys·tus \'sis-təs, 'zis-\. d. c.125. Pope (c.115–c.125). Ruled during reign of Hadrian.

Sixtus II. Saint. *In earliest documents* Xystus. d. 258. Pope (257–258). Reconciled churches of North Africa and Rome; died a martyr under Valerian.

Sixtus III. *Also* Xystus. d. 440. Pope (432–440). Opposed Pelagianism; a conciliator; settled a christological dispute between patriarchs St. Cyril of Alexandria and John of Antioch (431–433); maintained peaceful relations with the East; sponsored building projects, including reconstruction of Liberian Basilica.

Sixtus IV. *Orig.* Francesco Del·la Ro·ve·re \dā-lä-'rō-vā-rā\. 1414–1484. Pope (1471–84). Minister general of Franciscan order (1464); cardinal (1467). Sent unsuccessful expedition against Muslim stronghold of Smyrna (1473); failed to reunite Russian church with Rome (1474, 1476); thereafter concentrated on Italian politics. Involved in a conspiracy against Lorenzo de' Medici which resulted in a war with Florence (1478–88); incited Venetians to attack Ferrara (1482) and then placed them under interdict (1483) for refusing to stop fighting. Annulled decrees of Council of Constance (1478); condemned abuses of Spanish Inquisition (1482); established first foundling hospital; built many churches, including Sta. Maria del Popolo, Sta. Maria della Pace, and the Sistine Chapel; became unpopular because of heavy taxations to finance buildings and for extreme nepotism.

Sixtus V. *Orig.* Felice Pe·ret·ti \pā-'rāt-tē\. 1520–1590. Pope (1585–90). Entered Franciscan order (1533); inquisitor general in Venice (1557–60); made bishop and vicar general of Franciscans (1566); cardinal (1570). As pope, instituted financial reforms to restore solvency of Papal States; sponsored a huge building program, including completion of St. Peter's dome, rebuilding of Lateran Palace and the Vatican, revision of street plans, and a general embellishment of Rome. Reformed central administration of the church; limited cardinals to 70 (1586); overhauled entire administrative system of the Curia (1588); encouraged missions in the Philippines and South America. Assisted Philip II of Spain against Huguenot King Henry III of Navarre.

Sjah·rir \'syä-ˌrir\, Sutan. 1909–1966. Indonesian politician. Helped found nationalist group Pendidikan Nasional Indonesia (1931); rival of Sukarno; exiled by Dutch authorities (1934–42); gained support of militant nationalists with pamphlet "Perdjuangan Kita" (1945). Prime minister (1945–47); favored adoption of Western constitutional democracy for Indonesia; negotiated Linggadjati Agreement securing Indonesian authority in Java and Sumatra from Dutch (1947); formed Socialist party Partai Sosialis Indonesia (1948); arrested on conspiracy charges and held without trial (1962–65).

Sjö·berg \'shœ̄-berʸ\, Birger. 1885–1929. Swedish poet. Journalist (1906–25); gained fame with collection of songs *Fridas bok* (1922); published novel *Kvartetten som sprängdes* (1924); created original poetic forms in *Kriser och Kransar* (1926) and *Minnen från jorden* (1940).

Sjöberg, Erik. *Pseudonym* Vi·ta·lis \vi-'tä-lis\. 1794–1828. Swedish poet. Wrote Romantic, idealist poems, satires, polemics.

Sjö·ström \'shœ̄-strœ̄m\, Victor. *Known in U.S. as* Victor Sea·strom \'sē-strəm\. 1879–1960. Swedish film actor and director. Directed and starred in his first film *Trädgårdsmästaren* (1912); also produced *Ingeborg Holm* (1913), *Terje vigen* (1916), *Berg ejvind och hans hustru* (1917), *Körkarlen* (1920); in Hollywood (1923–30) directing *He Who Gets Slapped* (1924), *The Scarlet Letter* (1926), *The Divine Woman* (1927), *The Wind* (1928); played aged hero of Ingmar Bergman's *Smultronstället* (1957; *Wild Strawberries*).

Skan·da Gup·ta \'skən-də-'gùp-tə\. d. 467 A.D. King of the Gupta dynasty of India (c.455–467). Son of Kumāra Gupta I; repulsed inroad of Huns from Central Asia (c.455); took title *Vikramaditya;* at time of his death Huns came again in great numbers and broke up Gupta empire (480–490).

Skanderbeg. See George KASTRIOTI.

Skar·bek \'skär-bek\, Fryderyk. 1792–1866. Polish writer. Leading Polish economist of his day; wrote comedies, historical works, and esp. humorous novels as *Damian Ruszczyc* (1827), *Życie* (1838).

Skar·ga \'skär-gä\, Piotr. *Orig.* Piotr Skarga Po·wes·ki \pò-'ves-kē\. 1536–1612. Polish preacher and writer. Joined Society of Jesus (1569); first rector of U. of Vilna (1579–84); court chaplain in Kraków to King Sigismund III Vasa (1588–1612). First Polish representative of the Counter-Reformation; famous as powerful critic of social and political abuses and apologist for the church. Works included hagiography *Żywoty świętych* (1579) and collections of sermons *Kazania na niedziele i święta* (1595), *Kazania sejmowe* (1597).

Skeat \'skēt\, Walter William. 1835–1912. English philologist. Professor, Cambridge (1878–1912). Edited *Piers Plowman* (1867–85) and Chaucer (1894–97); compiled *Etymological English Dictionary* (1879–82). Founded English Dialect Society (1873); wrote textbooks and prepared texts for Early English Text Society and Scottish Text Society; popularized philology.

Skel·ton \'skelt-ᵊn\, John. c.1460–1529. English poet. Court poet to Henry VII (from 1489); tutor to the future Henry VIII (1497–1502); took holy orders (1498); rector of Diss, Norfolk (1498–1529) though he lived in London from 1512; orator regius to Henry VIII (from c.1512). Developed an original style of caustic satire replete with slang, grotesque words, Latin quotations, and unrestrained jocularity, in short doggerel rhymed lines in a meter of his own invention; attacked abuses in church and state. Author of *The Bowge of Courte,* satire of life at court; *Speke Parrot* (1521), *Why come ye nat to Courte* (1522), *Colyn Cloute* (1522), all attacking the clergy and Wolsey; *The Tunnyng of Elynor Rummynge,* a coarse Hogarthian picture of low life; *The Boke of Phyllyp Sparowe,* lament for a pet bird but also a lampoon of liturgical office for the dead; and *Magnyfycence* (1516), first secular morality play in English.

Skene \'skēn\, William Forbes. 1809–1892. Scottish historian and antiquary. Historiographer royal for Scotland (1881). Author of *The Highlanders of Scotland* (1837) and *Celtic Scotland* (1876–80).

Skin·ner \'skin-ər\, Constance Lindsay, *orig.* Constance Annie. 1877–1939. American writer, b. Quesnel, British Columbia. To U.S. (1894); among her books were volumes of verse as *Songs of the Coast Dwellers* (1930); *Pioneers of the Old Southwest* (1919) and *Adventurers of Oregon* (1920) in Yale U. series of *Chronicles of America;* plays *David* (1910), *Good Morning, Rosamond!* (1917); a number of novels and juveniles.

Skinner, John. 1721–1807. Scottish song writer. Episcopalian minister at Longside, Aberdeenshire (1742–1807); author of "Tullochgorum," "Ewie wi' the Crookit Horn," and other songs.

Skinner, Otis. 1858–1942. American actor, b. Cambridge, Mass. Made stage debut in Philadelphia (1877); made debuts in New York (1879) and London (1886); played leading roles, esp. in Shakespearean plays and in *Kismet* (1911–14) and *Blood and Sand* (1921); active in theater until death. Author of *Footlights and Spotlights* (1924) and *Mad Folk of the Theatre* (1928). His daughter ¶Cornelia Otis (1901–1979), actress and writer; wrote, produced, and acted in series of "monodramas" as *The Wives of Henry VIII* (1931), *Edna, His Wife* (1937); played leading roles in *Candida* (1935), *Major Barbara* (1956), etc. Author of humorous travel book *Our Hearts Were Young and Gay* (1942, with Emily Kimbrough), play *The Pleasure of His Company* (1958, with Samuel Taylor), books of light verse and essays, etc.

Skinner, Stephen. 1623–1667. English physician and philologist. Author of *Etymologicon Linguae Anglicanae* (pub. 1671), which included botanical, forensic, and Old English words, also proper names, and which made a distinct contribution to etymology.

Sko·be·lev \'skòb-yil-yif\, Mikhail Dmitriyevich. 1843–1882. Russian soldier. Distinguished himself in Russian conquest of Turkistan and in Russo–Turkish War (1877–78) at Pleven, Shipka Pass, Edirne, and San Stefano; stormed Göktepe and conquered the Tekke Turkomans (1881); governor of Minsk (1881).

Ško·da \'shkò-dä\, Emil von. 1839–1900. Czech engineer and industrialist. Took over machine works in Pilsen and founded Skoda Works (1866), which he developed into famous factory for manufacture of military equipment, esp. large cannon and other artillery. His son ¶Karl (1879–1929) was director of firm (from 1909). His nephew ¶Josef Škoda (1805–1881), physician; known for diagnostic work, esp. in connection with percussion and auscultation.

Sko·lem \'skō-ləm\, Thoralf Albert. 1887–1963. Norwegian mathematician and logician. Professor at Oslo (1938–50); did important work in Diophantine equations; helped formulate axioms for set theory in logic.

Skou·ras \'skü-räs, *Angl* 'skůr-əs\, Spyros Panagiotes. 1893–1971. American motion-picture executive, b. Skourokhóri, Greece. To U.S. (1910, naturalized 1913). A founder (1935), president (1942–62), chairman (1962–69) of Twentieth Century-Fox movie company; made it one of dominant movie studios in Hollywood; produced first CinemaScope movie (*The Robe,* 1953).

Skram \'skrȧm\, Bertha Amalie, *nee* Al·ver \'äl-vər\. 1846–1908. Norwegian novelist. Author of Naturalist novels *Constance Ring* (1885), tetralogy *Hellemyrsfolket* (1887–98), *Professor Hieronimus* (1895), etc. Her 2d husband (m. 1884) ¶Erik Skram (1847–1923) was a Danish novelist; author of *Gertrude Colbjörnsen* (1897) and *Agnes Vittrup* (1897).

Skryabin. See SCRIABIN.

Skrzyń·ski \'skshinʸ-skē\, Aleksander. Count. 1882–1931. Polish politician. Prime minister (1925–26). Played important part in organization of League of Nations and in negotiations resulting in Locarno Pact (1925).

Slán·ský \'slän-skē\, Rudolf Salzmann. 1901–1952. Czechoslovakian politician. Joined Communist party (1921) and rose to secretary general (1945–51); played major role in Communist takeover of Czechoslovakia (1948); arrested (1951) on charge of leading a Jewish plot to overthrow Communism in Czechoslovakia; convicted in notorious "Slánský trial" (Nov. 1952) and hanged; posthumously absolved of charges.

Sla·ter \'slā-tər\, Samuel. 1768–1835. American industrialist, b. Belper, Derbyshire, England. Apprenticed to partner of Richard Arkwright, inventor of cotton-spinning machinery (1783). Familiarized himself with this machinery and machines invented by James Hargreaves and Samuel Crompton. To America (1789) and contracted with firm of Almy & Brown, Providence, R.I., to reproduce for them Arkwright's cotton machinery; this he did from memory. Established factory in Pawtucket under firm name of Almy, Brown & Slater (1793). Regarded as founder of American cotton industry.

Sla·tin \'slä-ˌtēn\, Rudolf Anton Karl von. Freiherr. *Known as* Slatin Pasha. 1857–1932. Austrian soldier. To the Sudan (1874); served in Egypt under General Gordon (1878 ff.); appointed governor of Darfur (1881). Captured by the Mahdīs and held prisoner (1884–95); escaped to Cairo and made pasha by the khedive (1895). British inspector general of the Sudan (1900–14). Author of *Feuer und Schwert im Sudan* (1896).

Slau·er·hoff \'slaů-ər-ˌhȯf\, Jan Jacob. 1898–1936. Dutch poet. His collections of Romantic, often pessimistic, poetry included *Archipel* (1923) and *Een eerlijk zeemansgraf* (1936); also wrote a play *Jan Pietersz Coen* (1931) and prose works.

Slave dynasty \'slāv\. Name of a dynasty of Muslim sultans of Delhi (1206–90) in northern India, founded by former slave Quṭb-ud-Dīn Aybak (*q.v.*). See also ILTUTMISH and BALBAN.

Sla·vey·kov \slȧ-'vā-kȯf\, Petko Rachev. 1827–1895. Bulgarian poet, journalist, and politician. Wrote patriotic lyrical poems *Smesena Kitka* and *Pesnopoyka* (both 1852); helped reestablish the vernacular as a literary language. Wrote pamphlets against Turkish oppression and for national church autonomy; in Istanbul (from 1863) contributed to Bulgarian émigré reviews, edited satirical and political periodicals; after Bulgarian liberation (1878) was president of constituent assembly and co-founded Democratic party; edited newspaper *Nezavisimost* in Plovdiv (1884). His son ¶Pencho Petkov (1866–1912), poet and critic; inspired by Goethe, Heine, Nietzsche; introduced contemporary European ideas into Bulgarian literature. Chief poems *Koledari* (1892) and *Kurvava Pesen* (1913, unfinished epic); collected Bulgarian folksongs in *Kniga za pesnite* (1917).

Sła·wek \'slȧ-vek\, Walery. 1879–1939. Polish politician. Assisted Piłsudski; prime minister of Poland (1930–31, 1935).

Sleidanus, Johannes. See Johannes PHILIPPI.

Sles·sor \'sles-ər\, Kenneth. 1901–1971. Australian poet and journalist. Newspaper editor and literary critic; collections of poetry included *Earth Visitors* (1926), *Cuckooz Country* (1932), *Five Bells* (1939); best known poem "Beach Burial," a tribute to Australian troops who fought in World War II.

Sle·vogt \'slā-ˌfōkt\, Max. 1868–1932. German painter. One of foremost German Impressionists; also known for book illustrations, lithographs, murals, stage designs.

Sle·zak \'slez-ȧk, *Angl* 'slā-ˌzak\, Leo. 1873–1946. Czechoslovakian singer. Established reputation in London and New York as operatic tenor (by 1909); best known for Wagnerian interpretations; in later years a film comedian in Austria.

Slick, Sam. See Thomas Chandler HALIBURTON.

Sli·dell \slī-'del, *by collateral descendants* 'slīd-ᵊl\, John. 1793–1871. American politician and diplomat, b. New York City. Brother of Alexander Slidell Mackenzie. Practiced law, New Orleans (1819–35); member, U.S. House of Representatives (1843–45) and U.S. Senate (1853–61); wielded great political influence in Buchanan's administration; withdrew from U.S. Senate and joined Confederacy (1861); appointed to represent the Confederacy in France (1861). With James M. Mason took passage on British steamer *Trent* en route to Paris; was arrested by Captain Wilkes of U.S.S. *San Jacinto* and taken to Boston (Nov. 1861); released after strong British protests and returned to British ship (Jan. 1862). Failed to gain recognition of Confederacy by France. Lived abroad (from 1862).

Slim \'slim\, William Joseph. 1st Viscount Slim. 1891–1970. English soldier. Served in World War I and in Indian army during interwar period. Led 10th Indian Division in the Middle East (1941); commander of 1st Burma Corps (1942–45); repelled Japanese invasion of India; defeated Japanese armies in Burma; supreme Allied commander of ground forces in Southeast Asia (1945–46). Commandant of Imperial Defense Coll. (1946–47); chief of Imperial General Staff (1948–52); field marshal (1948); governor general of Australia (1953–60).

Sling·e·land \'sliŋ-ə-länt\, Pietr Cornelisz van. 1640–1691. Dutch painter. Known for still lifes, portraits, and genre scenes.

Sli·pher \'slī-fər\, Vesto Melvin. 1875–1969. American astronomer, b. Mulberry, Ind. On staff (from 1901), director (1926–52) of Lowell Observatory, Flagstaff, Ariz. Known for investigations in astronomical spectroscopy, esp. planetary rotations and atmospheres; directed research leading to discovery of the planet Pluto; discovered rapid rotation and great velocities of spiral galaxies, first observational evidence supporting theory of expanding universe; discovered bright radiations of the night sky and their changes in intensity; proved sodium and calcium are scattered throughout interstellar space.

Sloan \'slōn\, Alfred Pritchard, Jr. 1875–1966. American industrialist, b. New Haven, Conn. President (1923–37), chairman (1937–56), honorary chairman (1956–66), General Motors Corp.

Sloan, James Forman, *known as* Tod. 1874–1933. American jockey, b. near Kokomo, Ind. Popularized the "monkey crouch" riding style now universal in flat racing.

Sloan, John French. 1871–1951. American painter, etcher, and illustrator, b. Lock Haven, Pa. Pupil of Robert Henri; with Henri and others gained fame as "The Eight" or "Ashcan School" in historic New York exhibition (1908); did illustrations for Socialist periodical *The Masses;* taught at Art Students' League, New York (1914–30, 1932–38); an organizer (1916) and president (1918–44) of Society of Independent Artists. Published *The Gist of Art* (1939). Known for dark, anecdotal, usually sympathetic portrayals of working people in mundane New York surroundings, including *Wake of the Ferry* (1907), *Sunday, Women Drying Their Hair* (1912), *McSorley's Bar* (1912), and *Backyards, Greenwich Village* (1914).

Sloane \'slōn\, Sir Hans. 1660–1753. British physician and naturalist. Physician to governor of Jamaica (1687–89), collected over 800 new species of plants; succeeded Sir Isaac Newton as president, Royal Society (1727–41); first physician to George II (1727–41); founded Botanic Garden (1721). Bequeathed to nation library of 50,000 volumes, several thousand manuscripts, pictures, coins, and curiosities, which formed nucleus of British Museum.

Sloat \'slōt\, John Drake. 1781–1867. American naval officer, b. Goshen, N.Y. Entered navy (1800); served in War of 1812; commanded Pacific squadron (1844); took over California from Mexico on outbreak of Mexican War (July 7, 1845); act commended by U.S. secretary of war; retired (1861); rear admiral (1866).

Slo·cum \'slō-kəm\, Henry Warner. 1827–1894. American army officer, b. Delphi, N.Y. Brigadier general of volunteers (1861); major general (1862); fought at 1st and 2d Bull Run, Maryland campaign, Chancellorsville. Commanded extreme right of Union line at Gettysburg (July 2–4, 1863); with Sherman on march to the sea and northward through the Carolinas (1864–65); member, U.S. House of Representatives (1869–73, 1883–85).

Sło·nim·ski \slȯn-'yim-skē\, Antoni. 1895–1976. Polish writer. One of most influential Polish writers of his time; associated with Skamander group (from c.1918). Works included verse *Sonety* (1918), *Alarm* (1940), *Popiol i wiatr* (1942); novels *Teatr w więzieniu* (1922), *Dwa końce świata* (1937); comedies *Rodzina* (1934), *Murzyn warszawski* (1935); and essays.

Sło·wac·ki \slȯv-'ät-skē\, Juliusz. 1809–1849. Polish poet and playwright. One of greatest Romantic poets in Poland; excelled in lyrics; émigré after 1831. Verse included love idyll *W Szwajcarii* (1839), travel narrative *Podróż do ziemi świętej* (pub. 1866), prose poem *Anhelli* (1838), and the mystical *Król-Duch* (1847); plays included *Lilla Weneda* (1840), *Fantazy* (1843), *Sen srebrny Salomei* (1844).

Sluij·ters \'slœi-tərs\, Jan. 1881–1957. Dutch painter. Evolved own form of Expressionism which he called "Colorism"; known for portraits, nudes, and paintings of children.

Slu·ter \'slü-tər\, Claus. c.1340 to 1350–1406. Dutch sculptor. In service (from 1385; chief sculptor from 1389) of Philip the Bold of Burgundy. Master of early Netherlandish sculpture; widely influenced northern European painters and sculptors of 15th century. Chief works were sculptures for dynastic mausoleum in Carthusian monastery of Champmol at Dijon (esp. group *Puits de Moïse*) and the tomb of Philip the Bold, now preserved in museum at Dijon.

Small \'smȯl\, Albion Woodbury. 1854–1926. American sociologist, b. Buckfield, Me. First sociology professor in U.S. and organized first sociology dept. in U.S., at U. of Chicago (1892–1924); published (1894) *An Introduction to the Study of Society,* considered world's first sociology textbook; founder (1895) and editor (1895–1926), *American Journal of Sociology;* also wrote *Between Eras from Capitalism to Democracy* (1913).

Smalls \'smȯlz\, Robert. 1839–1915. American naval hero and politician, b. Beaufort, S.C. Born a slave; impressed into Confederate navy (1861); while serving aboard frigate *Planter* commandeered it and delivered it into Union hands (May 13, 1862); appointed pilot in Union navy (1862); captain (1863–66), highest-ranking black officer in Union navy. Member of U.S. House of Representatives (1875–79, 1881–87); advocate of civil rights; port collector of Beaufort (1889–93, 1897–1913).

Small·wood \'smȯl-ˌwu̇d\, William. 1732–1792. American Revolutionary officer, b. Charles Co., Md. Commanded Maryland regiment (1776); engaged at battle of Long Island and covered Washington's retreat; engaged at White Plains; commissioned brigadier general (1776) and major general (1780); engaged in battle of Camden and received thanks of Congress. Governor of Maryland (1785–88).

Smart \'smärt\, Christopher. 1722–1771. English poet. Published *Poems on Several Occasions,* including "The Hop Garden" (1752), and replied to John Hill's criticism of it in his satire *Hilliad* (1753). After symptoms of mental aberration (1751) developed religious mania, confined to asylum; in confinement, produced his one original and powerful poem, *A Song to David* (1763); also wrote *Hymns for Amusement of Children* (1775), *Rejoice in the Lamb* (pub. 1939).

Smea·ton \'smēt-ᵊn\, John. 1724–1792. English civil engineer. Improved instruments used in navigation and astronomy; rediscovered (1756) hydraulic cement, unknown since fall of Rome; made improvements on windmills and watermills (1759); designed large atmospheric pumping engines; improved the diving bell; rebuilt Eddystone lighthouse (1759); constructed Ramsgate harbor (1774), Forth and Clyde Canal, and Perth, Banff, and Coldstream bridges. Founded Society of Engineers (1771); considered founder of the civil engineering profession in Britain.

Smec·tym·nu·us \smek-'tim-nyə-wəs\. A composite acrostic pseudonym of five English authors (Presbyterian clergymen) of a pamphlet (1641) assailing Bishop Joseph Hall's claim of divine right for the episcopacy: Stephen Marshall, Edmund Calamy, Thomas Young, Matthew Newcomen, William Spurstowe.

Smed·ley \'smed-lē\, Frank, *in full* Francis Edward. 1818–1864. English novelist. Author of *Frank Fairleigh* (1850), *Lewis Arundel* (1852), and *Harry Coverdale's Courtship* (1855), which were illustrated by Cruikshank and Phiz.

Smel·lie \'smel-ē\, William. 1697–1763. Scottish obstetrician. Lectured on obstetrics in London (from 1739); first to teach obstetrics and midwifery on scientific basis; invented an obstetric forceps; discovered and described how the infant's head adapts to pelvic canal changes during birth. Author of *Treatise on the Theory and Practice of Midwifery* (1752–64) and *A Sett of Anatomical Tables* (1754).

Smellie, William. 1740?–1795. Scottish printer and antiquary. Cofounder of Newtonian Society (1760) and Society of Antiquaries of Scotland (1780); master printer (1765); chief compiler and printer of 1st edition of *Encyclopaedia Britannica* (1768–71).

Smenkh·kare \smeŋ-'kär-ə\. 14th century B.C. King (1364–61 B.C.) of 18th dynasty of Egypt. Probably a son of Amenhotep III and brother of his successor Tutankhamen; probably ruled for a time in co-regency with his predecessor Akhenaton; moved to Thebes; restored cult of Amon.

Smerdis. See BARDIYA.

Smet, Pierre-Jean de. See DE SMET.

Sme·ta·na \'sme-tȧ-nȧ\, Bedřich. 1824–1884. Czech composer. Founder of Czech national school of music. Opened piano school in Prague (1848); conductor of philharmonic society, Göteborg, Sweden (1856–61) and of Prague Opera (1866–74); played leading part in establishment of national opera house, Prague (1862); became deaf (1874). Composer of 8 operas, esp. *Braniboři v Čechách* (1866), *Prodaná nevěsta* (1866, *The Bartered Bride*), *Dalibor* (1868), *Hubička* (1876), *Čertova stěna* (1882); symphonic poems, esp. cycle of six bearing title *Má vlast* (1874–79, *My Country*); chamber music, including string quartet *Z mého života* (1876); choral works, piano pieces, and songs.

Sme·to·na \ˌsma-tȯ-'nä\, Antanas. 1874–1944. Lithuanian statesman. Editor of first Lithuanian daily newspaper *Vilniaus Žinios* (1905); edited journal *Viltis* (1907–13); founded (1913) *Vairas,* later organ of Nationalist party. President of Council of Lithuania (1917–18); first president of Lithuania (1919–20); again president (1926–40); fled to U.S. from Soviet invasion (1940).

Smi·bert *or* **Smy·bert** \'smī-bərt\, John. 1688–1751. American painter, b. Edinburgh, Scotland. Portrait painter in London (1720–28); accompanied George Berkeley to America (1728); opened studio in Boston (1730) and painted portraits of the most eminent personages in the colony, the earliest of painters in America; best known for *Bishop Berkeley, Family and Friends* (1729); drew plans for Faneuil Hall, Boston (1742).

Śmigły-Rydz, Edward. See RYDZ-ŚMIGŁY.

Smiles \'smī(ə)lz\, Samuel. 1812–1904. Scottish author. Edited *Leeds Times* (1838–42); railway administrator (1845–66). Began series of biographies of leaders in industry with *Life of George Stephenson* (1857) and *Lives of the Engineers* (1861–62); scored popular success with *Self-Help* (1859); also wrote *Character* (1871), *Thrift* (1875), *Duty* (1880), *Life and Labour* (1887).

Smirke \'smərk\, Sir Robert. 1781–1867. English architect. Designed in Neoclassical style Covent Garden Theatre (1809), the British Museum (1823–47), General Post Office (1824–29), and College of Physicians (1825).

Smith. See also SMYTH, SMYTHE.

Smith \'smith\, Adam. 1723–1790. Scottish economist. Professor at Glasgow (1751–64), lecturing on theology, ethics, jurisprudence, political institutions; won reputation with his *Theory of Moral Sentiments* (1759); as tutor to the young Duke of Buccleuch (1763–65), traveled in France, conversed with Turgot and other physiocrats, saw Voltaire at Geneva. Retired to Kirkcaldy for study (1767–76), worked out theory of division of labor, money, prices, wages, and distribution, produced *Inquiry into the Nature and Causes of the Wealth of Nations* (1776), which laid foundation of science of political economy and which became authoritative in politics as well as economics, exerting influence throughout world equaled by few other books. In London, member of literary club of Garrick, Reynolds, Dr. Johnson; commissioner of customs, Edinburgh (1778); lord rector of Glasgow U. (1787).

Smith, Alexander. See John ADAMS (1760?–1829).

Smith, Alexander. 1830–1867. Scottish poet. One of chief representatives of the Spasmodic school; collaborated with Sidney Dobell in *War Sonnets* (1855); after publishing *City Poems* (1857), *Edwin of Deira* (1861), turned to prose with *Dreamthorp* (essays, 1863) and two novels.

Smith, Alfred Emanuel. 1873–1944. American politician, b. New York City. Member of New York State legislature (1903–15), and speaker (1913); sheriff of New York County (1915–17); president, New York Board of Aldermen (1917); governor of New York (1919–20, 1923–28). Democratic candidate for president of the United States (1928), first Roman Catholic to run for that office; president, Empire State, Inc., managing the Empire State Building in New York City.

Smith, Andrew Jackson. 1815–1897. American army officer, b. Bucks Co., Pa. Chief of cavalry under Halleck in Corinth campaign (1862); brigadier general of volunteers (1862); major general (1864). Defeated Forrest at Tupelo, Miss. (July 14, 1864); engaged at Nashville (Dec. 1864) and at Mobile (Mar.–Apr. 1865).

Smith, Ashbel. 1805–1886. American physician and politician, b. Hartford, Conn. Surgeon general, Republic of Texas (1837); Texas minister to England and France (1842–44); secretary of State of Texas (1845); negotiated treaty with Mexico by which Texan independence was acknowledged by Mexico (1845); served with Texas troops in Civil War. Author of *Reminiscences of the Texas Republic* (1876).

Smith, Bernard. *Orig.* Bernhard Schmidt \'shmit\. *Nicknamed* Father Smith. c.1630–1708. English organ builder, b. Germany. To England (1666); organist at St. Margaret's, Westminster (from 1675); appointed king's organ maker (1681); he and chief rival Renatus Harris were greatest English organ builders of their day.

Smith, Bessie, *in full* Elizabeth. 1894 or 1898–1937. American singer, b. Chattanooga, Tenn. One of greatest blues singers; protégé of "Ma" Rainey; known for emotional intensity, personal involvement, and earthy realism of her style; recorded (from 1923) almost 200 songs, often with great instrumentalists as Louis Armstrong and Benny Goodman; wrote songs, esp. "Back Water Blues" (1927).

Smith, Sir Charles E. Kingsford-. See KINGSFORD-SMITH.

Smith, Charles Henry. *Pseudonym* Bill Arp \'ärp\. 1826–1903. American humorist, b. Lawrenceville, Ga. Practiced law in Rome, Ga. (1851–77, except for service in Civil War). For 25 years contributed weekly letters to *Atlanta Constitution* from a humorous, rustic philosopher, "Bill Arp." Author of *Bill Arp, So Called* (1866), *Bill Arp's Peace Papers* (1873), *Bill Arp's Scrap Book* (1884), *Bill Arp: From the Uncivil War to Date* (1903), etc.

Smith, Charlotte, *nee* Turner. 1749–1806. English poet and novelist. m. (1765) Benjamin Smith; author of *Elegiac Sonnets and Other Essays* (1784) and successful novels, including *Emmeline* (1788), *Desmond* (1792), *The Old Manor House* (1793).

Smith, David Roland. 1906–1965. American sculptor, b. Decatur, Ind. Pupil of John F. Sloan and Jan Matulka; executed abstract metal sculptures, including *Medals of Dishonor* (1940), *Royal Bird* (1948), and the *Albany* (begun 1959), *Zig* (begun 1960), and *Cubi* (begun 1963) series.

Smith, David Stanley. 1877–1949. American composer and educator, b. Toledo, Ohio. Taught at Yale (from 1903), and dean of the school of music (1920–40). Composer of symphonic, chamber, and church music, and choral works with orchestra.

Smith, Donald Alexander. 1st Baron Strath·co·na and Mount Roy·al \strath-ˈkōn-ə-ən(d)-maủnt-ˈrȯi(-ə)l\. 1820–1914. Canadian fur trader, financier, and politician, b. Forres, Scotland. Head of Montreal department, Hudson's Bay Co. (1869); sent by Canadian government to negotiate with Louis Riel; member of dominion Parliament (1871–79, 1887–96); with his cousin George Stephen, completed greater part of Great Northern Railway (1879) and Canadian Pacific Railway (1885); governor of Hudson's Bay Co. (1889); high commissioner for Canada (1896).

Smith, Edmund Kirby. See KIRBY-SMITH.

Smith, Emily Sheila Kaye-. See KAYE-SMITH.

Smith, Ernest Bramah. *Pseudonym* Ernest Bra·mah \ˈbräm-ə\. 1869?–1942. English writer. Author of volumes of humorous tales set in China as *Wallet of Kai Lung* (1900), *Kai Lung's Golden Hours* (1922); creator of blind detective Max Carrados in *Max Carrados* (1914), *Eyes of Max Carrados* (1923), etc.

Smith, Florence Margaret. *Pseudonym* Stevie Smith. 1902–1971. English writer. Author of novels *Novel on Yellow Paper* (1936), *Over the Frontier* (1938), *The Holiday* (1949); verse *A Good Time Was Had by All* (1937), *Tender Only to One* (1938), *Mother, What Is Man?* (1942), *Harold's Leap* (1950), *Not Waving But Drowning* (1957), *The Frog Prince* (1966); and a book of drawings *Some Are More Human Than Others* (1958).

Smith, Francis Marion. 1846–1931. American prospector and financier, b. Richmond, Wis. With partner William T. Coleman discovered borax deposits in Nevada (1872); organized Pacific Coast Borax Co.; monopolized borax market; acquired additional deposits in Death Valley, Calif.

Smith, Sir Francis Pettit. 1808–1874. English inventor. Took out patent on a screw propeller (1836), six weeks ahead of John Ericsson; constructed screw steamer, the *Archimedes,* for British navy (1839), after success of which the first war screw steamer in British navy, the *Rattler,* was constructed (1841–43).

Smith, Frederick Edwin. 1st Earl of Bir·ken·head \ˈbər-kən-ˌhed\. 1872–1930. English politician. M.P. (1906–18); noted as orator, became Conservative leader; solicitor general (1915); attorney general (1915–18); supported Sir Edward Carson in opposing Irish home rule (1914); prosecuted Sir Roger Casement (1916). Created baron (1919); lord chancellor (1919–22); responsible for Law of Property Act (1922), County Courts Act (1924), Supreme Court of Judicature Act (1925) and other legal reforms. Helped negotiate Anglo-Irish treaty (1921). Created earl (1922). Secretary of state for India (1924–28).

Smith, George. 1789–1846. Scottish publisher. Founder of firm of Smith, Elder & Co., booksellers and stationers, and (from 1819) publishers. His son ¶George (1824–1901) joined firm (1838), became head (1846); published early works of John Ruskin, Charlotte Brontë's *Jane Eyre* (1848), Thackeray's *Henry Esmond* (1852); founded *Cornhill Magazine* (1859) with Thackeray as editor and, with Frederick Greenwood, *Pall Mall Gazette* (1865), a literary newspaper; published works of Browning, Arnold, Leslie Stephen, among others. Projected and published *Dictionary of National Biography* (63 vols., 1885–1900).

Smith, George. 1840–1876. English Assyriologist. Worked at British Museum (from 1867); deciphered (1872) from cuneiform tablets found by Sir Austen Layard the *Epic of Gilgamesh,* containing an account of a flood similar to the Deluge in Genesis; by excavations (1873) in Nineveh discovered further missing fragments of the tablets and fragments on duration of Babylonian dynasties; made two other expeditions in behalf of British Museum; wrote best-seller *Chaldean Account of Genesis* (1876).

Smith, Sir George Adam. 1856–1942. Scottish scholar and educator, b. Calcutta. Preacher at Aberdeen (1882–92); professor, Free Church Coll., Glasgow (1892–1909); principal of U. of Aberdeen (1909–35); helped win acceptance of higher criticism of the Old Testament. Author of *The Book of Isaiah* (1888–90), *The Twelve Prophets* (1896–98), *Modern Criticism and the Preaching of the Old Testament* (1901), *Jerusalem* (1907–08), *The Early Poetry of Israel* (1913), etc.

Smith, Gerrit. 1797–1874. American philanthropist, b. Utica, N.Y. Active in various movements as strict Sunday observance, antitobacco and prohibition agitation, dress reform and woman suffrage, prison reform. Associated with William Lloyd Garrison in abolitionist movement; aided John Brown and may have known about his plans against Harpers Ferry.

Smith, Giles Alexander. See Morgan Lewis SMITH.

Smith, Hannah, *nee* Whi·tall \ˈ(h)wīt-ᵊl\. 1832–1911. American religious leader, b. Philadelphia. m. (1851) Robert P. Smith (d. 1898). As a result of successive religious experiences, finally devoted herself to preaching a life of "absolute consecration, entire obedience, and simple trust"; a leader of "Higher Life" pentecostal movement (1873 ff.); a founder of Woman's Christian Temperance Union (1874); resident in England (from 1888). Author of *The Christian's Secret of a Happy Life* (1875), *Every-day Religion* (1893), *The Unselfishness of God* (1903), etc. Her son ¶Lloyd Logan Pearsall Smith (1865–1946), essayist, b. Millville, N.J.; author of *The Youth of Parnassus* (1895), *Trivia* (1902, 1918), *Life and Letters of Sir Henry Wotton* (1907), *Songs and Sonnets* (1909), *The English Language* (1912), *Words and Idioms* (1925), *On Reading Shakespeare* (1933), *Unforgotten Years* (1938), *Milton and His Modern Critics* (1940), etc.

Smith, Sir Harry George Wakelyn. Baronet Smith. 1787–1860. English soldier. Ensign (1805); served in South America (1807), Spain (1808–14), War of 1812, Cape Colony Frontier War (1834–35); took leading part in subduing Kaffirs (1836) and in Sikh campaigns (1842–46); by his strategy won battle of Aliwal against Sikhs (1846); major general (1847); governor of Cape Colony and high commissioner of South Africa (1847–52); routed Boers under Pretorius at Boomplaats (1848); put down Kaffir rebellion (1850).

Smith, Henry. *Called* Silver-Tongued Smith. 1550?–1591. English Puritan clergyman. Preached with great success in London (from c.1582); lecturer of St. Clement Danes, London (1587–90); wrote many religious tracts and sermons.

Smith, Henry John Stanley. 1826–1883. British mathematician, b. Ireland. Professor at Oxford (from 1860); leading authority of his day on theory of numbers; devoted himself (after 1864) to elliptic functions.

Smith, Henry Preserved. 1847–1927. American clergyman and scholar, b. Troy, Ohio. Ordained in Presbyterian ministry (1875); tried for heresy (1892–94) and suspended from ministry. Professor, Amherst (1898–1906), Meadville Theol. School (1907–13); librarian, Union Theol. Sem. (1913–25). A pioneer in modern biblical criticism in U.S. Works included *Samuel, Old Testament History* (1903) and *The Religion of Israel* (1914).

Smith, Henry Welles. See Henry Fowle DURANT.

Smith, Hoke. 1855–1931. American politician, b. Newton, N.C. Proprietor, *Atlanta Journal* (1887–1900); U.S. secretary of the interior (1893–96); governor of Georgia (1907–09, 1911); U.S. senator (1911–21); opposed U.S. entrance into League of Nations.

Smith, Holland McTyeire. *Nicknamed* Howlin' Mad. 1882–1967. American marine officer, b. Seale, Ala. Commissioned in Marine Corps (1905); served in World War I; director of Division of Operations and Training (1937–39); major general (1941); commanded Amphibious Force, Pacific Fleet (1942–44); helped plan assault operations in central Pacific; lieutenant general (1944); commander of Fleet Marine Force, Pacific (1944–45); made general and retired (1946).

Smith, Horace. 1808–1893. American inventor and manufacturer, b. Cheshire, Mass. Associated with Daniel Baird Wesson (from 1853); patented with Wesson a revolver (1854); began manufacture of Smith & Wesson revolvers in Springfield, Mass. (1857).

Smith, James. 1719?–1806. American lawyer and politician, b. Ireland. To America as a boy; member of Continental Congress (1776–78); a signer of the Declaration of Independence.

Smith, James (1775–1839) and his brother Horatio, *generally known as* Horace (1779–1849). English poets. Joint authors of *Rejected Addresses,* a classic of parody of leading contemporary poets, composed on occasion of reopening of Drury Lane Theatre (1812). James, a solicitor in government service, also wrote successful skits for Charles Mathews, *Country Cousins, A Trip to Paris, A Trip to America;* Horatio, a successful stockbroker, also wrote historical novels, including *Brambletye House* (1826) and *Gaieties and Gravities* (1826).

Smith, Jedediah Strong. 1799–1831. American fur trader and explorer, b. Jericho (now Bainbridge), N.Y. Made expeditions in Rocky Mountain areas (1822–26); with two partners operated fur-trading company in Salt Lake City (1826–30); made path-finding explorations in California, the Sierra Nevada, and the Oregon coast (1826–29). His explorations were exceeded in importance only by those of Lewis and Clark.

Smith, Jeremiah. 1759–1842. American jurist, b. Peterborough, N.H. Practiced law in Peterborough; governor of New Hampshire (1809–10); chief justice, New Hampshire supreme court (1802–09, 1813–16); associated with Daniel Webster and Jeremiah Mason as counsel for Dartmouth College trustees in famous Dartmouth College case (1816–20).

Smith *or* **Smyth** \ˈsmith\, John. *Called* the Se·bap·tist \ˈsē-ˌbap-təst\, *i.e.* Self-baptizer. d. 1612. English clergyman. Influenced by Brownists, left Anglican church and became pastor of independent congregation at Gainsborough (1606); migrated to Amsterdam to escape persecution (1608); became a Baptist under Mennonite influence. Works included *The Differences of the*

Church of the Separation. Founder of organized Baptists of England.

Smith, John. c.1580–1631. English colonist in America. Military adventurer in wars against the Turks (c.1600–04). To America and helped found Jamestown, Va. (May 14, 1607); on governing council of colony; made prisoner by Indians, condemned to death, and, according to his story, rescued by Pocahontas (1607). Led exploring expeditions up the Potomac and Rappahannock rivers and around Chesapeake Bay. President of the colony (1608–09); returned to England (1609). Explored New England coast (1614) and attempted a second voyage there but was captured by the French (1615). Author of *A True Relation of ... Virginia Since the First Planting of That Collony* (1608), *A Map of Virginia* (1612), *A Description of New England* (1616), *New England Trials* (1620), *The Generall Historie of Virginia, New-England, and the Summer Isles* (1624), *The True Travels, Adventures, and Observations of Captaine John Smith* (1630), etc.

Smith, John. 1616–1652. English writer. Member of the Cambridge Platonists; known for collection of sermons *Select Discourses* (1660).

Smith, John Stafford. 1750–1836. English composer and musicologist. Composer of anthems, glees, and songs, including "To Anacreon in Heaven," later used as tune of "The Star-Spangled Banner."

Smith, Joseph. 1805–1844. American religious leader, b. Sharon, Vt. According to his own account, began to have visions in 1820 telling him that the church of Christ had been withdrawn from the earth and that God had chosen him to restore it; received (1827) from an angel a book written in strange hieroglyphics on golden plates, telling the history of the true church in America; with miraculous aid translated the book and published it as *The Book of Mormon* (1830). Founded Church of Jesus Christ of Latter-day Saints at Fayette, N.Y. (1830). *The Book of Mormon,* with *A Book of Commandments* (1833) and *Doctrine and Covenants* (1835), provide the basis for the church's doctrine and organization. Moved his small congregation to Kirtland, Ohio (1831), then to Missouri (1838), and to Commerce, Ill., renamed Nauvoo; governed the Mormon colony despotically with aid of small group of advisers. When schism developed over practice of polygamy, put opponents to flight and destroyed their printing press. Arrested and jailed by non-Mormons in neighboring towns and villages; taken from jail at Carthage, Ill., by a mob and shot. See Brigham YOUNG. His son ¶Joseph (1832–1914), b. Kirtland, Ohio, accepted (1860) presidency of Reorganized Church of Jesus Christ of Latter-day Saints, an offshoot from the original Mormon church; opposed polygamy; moved to Lamoni, Iowa (1881); moved (1906) to Independence, Mo., still the headquarters of this sect. Author of *History of the Church* (with H. C. Smith, 1897 ff.). A nephew of Joseph Smith (1805–1844) ¶Joseph Fielding Smith (1838–1918) was taken to Utah with the Mormons under the leadership of Brigham Young (1848); made an apostle of the Mormon church (1866); president of the Mormon church (1901–18).

Smith, Joseph Lindon. 1863–1950. American painter, b. Pawtucket, R.I. Among his works were murals in the Boston Public Library and the Horticultural Hall in Philadelphia.

Smith, Kathryn Elizabeth. *Known as* Kate. 1909–1986. American singer, b. Greenville, Va. Reached height of popularity in 1930s and 1940s esp. on radio; introduced some 700 songs, of which 19 sold over a million copies, including theme "When the Moon Comes Over the Mountain" and "God Bless America"; starred in own television show (1950–54, 1960).

Smith, Sir Keith Macpherson. See under Sir Ross Macpherson SMITH.

Smith, Lloyd Logan Pearsall. See under Hannah Whitall SMITH.

Smith, Melancton. 1744–1798. American Revolutionary patriot, b. Jamaica, N.Y. Organized and captained first company of rangers organized in Dutchess County (1775); in business in New York City (from 1785). Member of Continental Congress (1785–88) and of constitutional ratification convention (1788). His grandson ¶Melancton (1810–1893), b. New York City, was a naval officer; served under Farragut at New Orleans (1862) and Port Hudson (1863); served under Porter at Fort Fisher (1864–65); rear admiral (1870).

Smith, Morgan Lewis. 1821–1874. American army officer, b. Mexico, N.Y. Organized and commanded Missouri infantry regiment (1861); engaged at Fort Donelson and in Shiloh and Corinth campaigns; brigadier general of volunteers (1862); engaged at Vicksburg, Missionary Ridge. His brother ¶Giles Alexander (1829–1876) served as officer in his brother's regiment and succeeded to colonelcy when brother became brigadier general (1862); engaged against Vicksburg; brigadier general (1863); served under Sherman in march through the Carolinas; major general (1865).

Smith, Nathan. 1762–1829. American physician, b. Rehoboth, Mass. Introduced teaching of anatomy, surgery, and medicine at Dartmouth (1797–1813); professor, Yale (1813–29); a founder of Yale Medical School. Author of *Practical Essay on Typhous Fever* (1824). His son ¶Nathan Ryno (1797–1877) was also a physician; first professor of anatomy at Jefferson Medical School, Philadelphia (1826–27); professor of anatomy (1827–29) and surgery (1829–77) at U. of Maryland.

Smith, Pauline. 1882–1959. South African writer. Among her books were a novel *The Beadle* (1926) and collections of short stories *The Little Karoo* (1925) and *Platkops Children* (1935).

Smith, Preserved. 1880–1941. American historian, b. Cincinnati, Ohio. Son of Henry Preserved Smith. Authority on the Protestant Reformation; professor, Cornell (1922–41). Author of *Life and Letters of Martin Luther* (1911), *The Age of the Reformation* (1920), *Erasmus* (1923).

Smith, Red. See Walter W. SMITH.

Smith, Richard. 1735–1803. American lawyer, b. Burlington, N.J. Adm. to bar (c.1760); member of Continental Congress (1774–76); writer of a detailed diary of proceedings of the Congress (Sept.–Oct. 1775 and Dec. 1775–Mar. 1776), valuable as historical source material.

Smith, Robert. 1689–1768. English mathematician. Professor of astronomy, Cambridge (1716–60). Author of *A Compleat System of Opticks in Four Books* (1738) and *Harmonics* (1749).

Smith, Robert. 1757–1842. See under Samuel SMITH.

Smith, Robert Angus. 1817–1884. Scottish chemist. Pioneer in sanitary engineering and chemistry of disinfection; published a series of analyses of air and water of large towns in Britain (from 1845); first inspector under the Alkali Act of 1863.

Smith, Robert Payne. See PAYNE SMITH.

Smith, Sir Ross Macpherson. 1892–1922. Australian aviator. Served in World War I (1914–18), in Royal Flying Corps (1916–18); made first flight from Cairo to Calcutta (1918). His brother ¶Sir Keith Macpherson Smith (1891–1955) served in Royal Flying Corps (1917–19). Together they made first flight from England to Australia (Nov. 12–Dec. 10, 1919).

Smith, Roswell. 1829–1892. American publisher, b. Lebanon, Conn. With Josiah Gilbert Holland, joined Charles Scribner in publishing business (1870). Purchased interests of Holland and Scribner (1881) and founded and headed The Century Co.; continued *Scribner's Monthly* under name of *Century Magazine;* published *The Century Dictionary and Cyclopedia* (1891).

Smith, Samuel. 1752–1839. American politician, b. Carlisle, Pa. Organized volunteer company (1775); engaged in battles of Long Island and Monmouth; commanded Maryland contingent sent to suppress Whiskey Insurrection (1791). Brigadier general of Maryland militia (1794); major general commanding defense of Baltimore (1812). Member of U.S. House of Representatives (1793–1803, 1816–22) and U.S. Senate (1803–15, 1835–38). His brother ¶Robert (1757–1842) was U.S. secretary of the navy (1801–09), U.S. secretary of state (1809–11).

Smith, Samuel Francis. 1808–1895. American clergyman and poet, b. Boston. Editorial secretary, American Baptist Missionary Union (from 1854). His poetry was published as *Poems of Home and Country* (1895); best known as author of national hymn "America" (first published in Mason's *The Choir,* 1832) and the missionary hymn "The Morning Light is Breaking."

Smith, Seba. *Pseudonym* Major Jack Dow·ning \'dau̇n-iŋ\. 1792–1868. American satirist, b. Buckfield, Me. Founded and edited first daily newspaper in Maine, the Portland *Courier* (1829), and contributed to it a series of letters written by a supposed Major Jack Downing and satirizing humorously politics of the Andrew Jackson period; wrote a second series (from 1847); also wrote *Way Down East* (1854).

Smith, Sir Sidney. 1764–1840. See Sir William Sidney SMITH.

Smith, Sidney, *in full* Robert Sidney. 1877–1935. American cartoonist, b. Bloomington, Ill. On staff of *Chicago Tribune* (1911–35); creator (1917) of "The Gumps."

Smith, Sophia. 1796–1870. American philanthropist, b. Hatfield, Mass. Inherited fortune from brother Austin Smith (d. 1861); on advice of her pastor, John Morton Greene, bequeathed fortune for founding a college for women, Smith College, Northampton, Mass., opened in 1875.

Smith, Stevie. See Florence SMITH.

Smith, Sydney. 1771–1845. English clergyman, essayist, and wit. Took orders (1794); with Jeffrey and Brougham, started *Edinburgh Review* (1802) and contributed articles to it; a favorite among Whigs at Holland House because of his wit and cogent political reasoning; parson in Foston-le-Clay, Yorkshire (1809–28); canon of St. Paul's, London (1831–45). Champion of parliamentary reform but opposed the ballot; produced *Letters of Peter Plymley* in defense of Catholic emancipation (1807). Originator of the character Mrs. Partington, later made famous by Shillaber.

Smith, Theobald. 1859–1934. American pathologist, b. Albany, N.Y. Professor, Harvard (1896–1915); director, Department of Animal Pathology, Rockefeller Institute for Medical Research (1915–29). Known for work in the cause and nature of infectious and parasitic diseases; developed a theory of immunization (1884–86); first to describe pleomorphism (1886); discovered (1889) the organism causing Texas fever, demonstrating (1889–93) that it is transmitted by a cattle tick; announced that there is distinction between human and bovine types of tubercle bacilli; first to demonstrate anaphylaxis from injection of an extract of diphtheria bacillus (1903); reported successful experiments on immunizing effects of neutral toxin-antitoxin mixtures in diphtheria (1909).

Smith, Sir Thomas. 1513–1577. English politician and scholar. Regius professor of civil law and vice chancellor, Cambridge (1544); one of two secretaries of state (1548–49, 1572–76). As diplomat for Elizabeth negotiated peace of Troyes (1564). Wrote legal tract *Commonwealth of England* (1586).

Smith, Sir Thomas. 1558?–1625. See Sir Thomas SMYTHE.

Smith, Thorne. 1892–1934. American humorist, b. Annapolis, Md. Author of a number of ribald and whimsical tales, including *Topper* (1926), *The Night Life of the Gods* (1931), *The Bishop's Jaegers* (1932), *Skin and Bones* (1933).

Smith, Walter Bedell. 1895–1961. American army officer, b. Indianapolis. Commissioned in U.S. army (1917); chief of staff to Gen. Eisenhower (1942–46); negotiated and accepted surrenders of Italy (1943) and Germany (1945); ambassador to Russia (1946–49); director of Central Intelligence Agency (1950–53); general (1951); undersecretary of state (1953–54).

Smith, Walter Wellesley, *called* Red. 1905–1982. American journalist, b. Green Bay, Wis. Sportswriter and columnist for *St. Louis Star* (1928–36), *Philadelphia Record* (1936–45), *New York Herald Tribune* (1945–67), *New York Times* (1971–82). Considered one of finest sportswriters; won Pulitzer prize for distinguished commentary (1976). His columns collected in *Out of the Red* (1950), *Views of Sports* (1954), *Strawberries in the Wintertime* (1974), etc.

Smith, William. 1697–1769. American jurist, b. Buckinghamshire, England. To America (1715); practiced law, New York City; a counsel for defense of John Peter Zenger (*q.v.*) when tried for seditious libel (1735). Associate justice, New York supreme court (1763–69). A son ¶William (1728–1793) was also a jurist; chief justice of New York (1780) and member of the provincial council (from 1767); refused (1777, 1778) to take oath of allegiance to the revolutionary state; to England (1783); chief justice of Canada (1786–93).

Smith, William. 1727–1803. American clergyman and educator, b. Aberdeen, Scotland. To New York (1751); teacher in the Academy and Charitable School in Philadelphia, which developed into U. of Pennsylvania (1754); first provost of the institution (1755–79, 1789–91). Edited *American Magazine and Monthly Chronicle* (1757–58).

Smith, William. 1769–1839. English geologist. Founder of stratigraphical geology. As mineral surveyor and civil engineer, noted regularity and inclination of strata; compiled a table of strata around Bath (1799); won fame with *A Delineation of the Strata of England and Wales* (1815), which formed basis for 21 separate county geological maps (1819–24).

Smith, Sir William. 1813–1893. English lexicographer. Editor of *Dictionary of Greek and Roman Antiquities* (1842), of which he himself wrote greater part, *Dictionary of Greek and Roman Biography* (1849), and *Greek and Roman Geography* (1857); edited Gibbon (1854); editor of dictionaries of the Bible (1860–65), of Christian antiquities (1875–80), of Christian biography (1877–87). Editor of *Quarterly Review* (1867–93).

Smith, William Robertson. 1846–1894. Scottish Semitic scholar. Professor of Oriental languages and Old Testament exegesis at Free Church College, Aberdeen (1870–81); dismissed (1881) because of heterodoxy of his biblical articles in ninth edition of *Encyclopaedia Britannica,* after trial that popularized his scholarly views and methods. Coeditor with T. S. Baynes of *Encyclopaedia Britannica* (from 1880), editor in chief (1887–88); professor of Arabic, Cambridge (1883–86, 1889–94). Author of *The Old Testament in the Jewish Church* (1881), *The Prophets of Israel* (1882), *Kinship and Marriage in Early Arabia* (1885), *Lectures on the Religion of the Semites* (1889).

Smith, Sir William Sidney. 1764–1840. English naval commander. While plenipotentiary at Constantinople, went to relief of Acre and compelled Napoléon to raise siege (1799); destroyed Turkish fleet off Abydos (1807); blockaded the Tagus River; vice admiral (1810), admiral (1821).

Smith, William Stephens. 1755–1816. American Revolutionary officer, b. New York City. Major, aide-de-camp to General Sullivan (1776); aide-de-camp to Washington (1781). A founder and president of Society of the Cincinnati.

Smith, Xanthus Russell. 1839–1929. American painter, b. Philadelphia. Painted Civil War battle scenes, landscapes, marines, and portraits as of Washington, Whitman, Lincoln.

Smith-Dor·ri·en \'smith-'dór-ē-ən, -'där-\, Sir Horace Lockwood. 1858–1930. British soldier. Served in Zulu War (1879), Egyptian War (1882), Nile expedition (1884), Sudan campaign (1885), in Bengal (1893–94) and the Punjab (1894–96), Boer War (1899–1901), again in India (1901–07); general (1912). In World War I, commanded 2d army corps, then 2d army, in British Expeditionary Force (1914–15); commanded East African forces (1915–16). Governor of Gibraltar (1918–23).

Smith·son \'smith-sən\, Harriet Constance. *Later* Madame Berlioz. 1800–1854. Irish actress. Made first appearance as Lady Teazle, Dublin (1815); engaged by Elliston; accompanied Macready to Paris (1828); again in Paris (1832) playing Shakespeare; m. (1833) Hector Berlioz (*q.v.*); separated (1840).

Smithson, Sir Hugh. See PERCY family.

Smithson, James. *Known until 1801 as* James Louis Ma·cie \'mā-sē\. 1765–1829. English chemist, b. Paris. Illegitimate son of Hugh Smithson Percy, 1st Duke of Northumberland, and Elizabeth Macie; took surname Smithson (1801); author of many scientific papers, including one on calamines, the mineral smithsonite (calamine) being named after him. Bequeathed over £100,000 to the United States to found at Washington, D.C., the Smithsonian Institution, which was established by act of Congress (1846).

Smo·hal·la \smə-'hal-ə\. *Many variants, including* Smowhola, Smoholler, Smokeholler, Smuxale, Snohallow, Somahallie. c.1815 to 1820–1895. American Indian religious leader, b. Washington. Chief of the Wanapum, a tribe living in Yakima County, Washington; famed as medicine man; wandered down Pacific coast to Mexico and back through Southwest; appeared among his own tribe as one miraculously returned from the dead. Gained wide following for his Dreamer religion; his teaching responsible for much of Indian hostility to the whites in period from 1870, esp. that culminating in the Nez Percé War (1877).

Smol·lett \'smäl-ət\, Tobias George. 1721–1771. Scottish novelist. Sailed as surgeon's mate on Cartagena expedition (1741–43); married a Jamaica heiress and settled (1743) as surgeon in London. After success of *The Adventures of Roderick Random,* a picaresque novel (1748), and *The Adventures of Peregrine Pickle* (1751), decided to live by his pen; published *Ferdinand Count Fathom* (1753); translated *Don Quixote* (1755); edited the Tory *Critical Review* (1756); broke his health producing *A Complete History of England* (1757–58); attempted a vast *Universal History;* translated Voltaire in 38 volumes; edited the unsuccessful *Briton* (1762–63). Ridiculed and imprisoned for political articles supporting Lord Bute; traveled abroad for his health and published *Travels through France and Italy* (1766); an invalid, retired to Italy (1768); launched Rabelaisian satire upon English public affairs in *The Adventures of an Atom* (1769); accomplished his best character drawing in his last novel *The Expedition of Humphry Clinker* (1771); died at Leghorn. Author also of a farce *The Reprisal, or the Tars of Old England* (produced 1757), a mediocre novel *Adventures of Sir Launcelot Greaves* (1760–61), and poems including "The Tears of Scotland" and "Ode to Independence."

Smoot \'smüt\, Reed. 1862–1941. American politician, b. Salt Lake City. U.S. senator (1903–33); co-sponsor of Smoot-Hawley Tariff Act (1930).

Smre·czyń·ski \smre-'chinʸ-skē\, Franciszek. *Pseudonym* Władysław Or·kan \'ór-kán\. 1876–1930. Polish writer. Works included novels *Wroztokach* (1903), *Pomór* (1910), *Komornicy* (1910), *Drzewicj* (1912); verse *Z tej smutnej ziemi* (1903); and plays.

Smuts \'smœts, *Angl* 'sməts\, Jan Christian. 1870–1950. South African soldier and politician. Practiced law at Cape Town and later at Johannesburg. A Boer leader in Boer War (1899–1902); commander in chief of Republican forces in Cape of Good Hope (1901–02). Largely instrumental in effecting the Union of South Africa. During World War I, organized South African forces and cooperated with General Botha in suppressing a rebellion in South Africa and in conquering Southwest Africa (1914–15); later (1916), commanded British troops in British East Africa. Representative of South Africa in Imperial War Cabinet (1917, 1918) and (with General Botha) at the Peace Conference in Paris; supported League of Nations. Prime minister of South Africa (1919–24, 1939–48); minister of justice (1933–39). Made field marshal (1941).

Smybert, John. See SMIBERT.

Smyth \'smith, 'smīth\, Dame Ethel Mary. 1858–1944. English composer, writer, suffragist. Composed "The March of the Women" (1911), battle song of the Women's Social and Political Union. Composer of operas as *The Wreckers* (1906) and *The Boatswain's Mate* (1916), a Mass in D (1891), symphonies, choral works, instrumental pieces, and songs.

Smyth, Henry Dewolf. 1898–1986. American physicist, b. Clinton, N.Y. Professor of physics, Princeton U. (1924 ff.); special consultant to Manhattan District of U.S. Army Corps of Engineers (1943–45); played key role in development of atomic bomb; wrote official government report *Atomic Energy for Military Purposes* (1945); served on Atomic Energy Commission (1949–54); U.S. representative to International Atomic Energy Agency (1961–70).

Smyth, John. See John SMITH.

Smyth, William Henry. 1788–1865. English naval officer and hydrographer. Surveyed coasts of Sicily and adjacent shores of Adriatic and Sardinia; published his results (1828); a founder of Royal Geographical Society (1830); admiral (1863). Author of *The Mediterranean* (1854) and *The Sailor's Word-book* (1867). His son ¶Charles Piazzi (1819–1900) was astronomer royal for Scotland (1845–88). Author of *Our Inheritance in the Great Pyramid* (1864) and *On the Antiquity of Intellectual Man* (1868).

Smythe \'smīth, 'smīth\ *or* **Smith** \'smith\, Sir Thomas. 1558?–1625. English merchant. Made fortune in commerce; organizer (1600) and governor (1600–21, except 1606–07) of East India Co.; governor of Muscovy and French companies; special ambassador to czar of Russia (1604–05). Obtained charter for Virginia Co., of which he was treasurer (1609–18) and for whose success he was mainly responsible; resigned because of charges of embezzlement (later proved false). Governor of Somers Island (Bermuda) Company; promoted other trade and exploratory expeditions.

Snee·vliet \'snā-vlēt\, Hendrik Josephus Franciscus Marie, *known as* Hendricus. 1883–1942. Dutch politician. To Dutch East Indies (1912); founded Social Democratic Association (1914); his revolutionary oratory a stimulus to the nationalist movement; deported (1917); employed by Communist International (from 1917); founded Revolutionary Socialist party in the Netherlands (1929); in parliament (1933–37); executed by the Germans.

Snef·ru \'snef-,rü\ *or* **Sne·fe·ru** \'snef-ə-,rü\. 27th–26th century B.C. First king (c.2613–c.2589 B.C.) of 4th dynasty of Egypt. Fostered evolution of a highly centralized administration; brought Egypt to high level of prosperity; built two pyramids, including the first true pyramid (at Dahshur); raided Nubia; conquered Sinai and developed copper mines; succeeded by his son Khufu.

Snel *or* **Snell** \'snel\, Willebrord. *Surname also given as* Snel van Roi·jen \'rȯi-yən\. *Lat.* Willebrordus Snel·li·us van Roy·en \'snel-ē-əs-vän-'rȯi-ən\. 1580–1626. Dutch astronomer and mathematician. Professor at Leiden (from 1613); his *Eratosthenes batavus* (1617) contained his method of measuring the Earth; discovered Snell's law of refraction (1621).

Snel·len \'snel-ən\, Herman. 1834–1908. Dutch ophthalmologist. Originated Snellen's test type for determining acuteness of vision.

Snell·man \'snel-män\, Johan Vilhelm. 1806–1881. Finnish philosopher and politician. Taught at Helsinski (from 1835); senator (1863–68). Prominent (from 1840s) in the establishment of Finnish as a national language; helped change monetary standard from rubles to marks (1865). Author of *Läran om staten* (1842) and *Maamiehen ystävä* (1844); with Elias Lönnrot edited *Litteraturblad för allmän medborgerlig bildning.*

Snoil·sky \'snȯil-skǖ\, Carl Johan Gustaf. Count. 1841–1903. Swedish lyric poet. Published *Italienska bilder* (1865) and *Dikter* (1869); in diplomatic corps (c.1870–79); returned to writing poetry, publishing *Nya dikter* (1881), *Svenska bilder* (1886), etc.

Snor·ri Stur·lu·son \'snȯr-ris-'tœ(r)d-lä-sȯn; *Angl* 'snȯr-ē-'stər-lə-sən, 'snär-\. 1179–1241. Icelandic politician and historian. A descendant of Egill Skallagrímsson; raised in home of Jón Loptsson; president of Icelandic high court (1215–18, 1222–32); involved in political intrigues with and against King Haakon IV of Norway (from 1218); assassinated on Haakon's order. Author of the *Heimskringla* (a poetic chronicle of Norse mythology and early history), the *Younger, or Prose, Edda* (a prose work treating of Norse mythology and the language and modes of composition of the scalds), and, probably, the *Egils Saga* (a poem about the life of Egill Skallagrímsson).

Snouck Hur·gron·je \'snōk-hœr-'grȯn-yə\, Christiaan. 1857–1936. Dutch colonial official and scholar. Professor at Leiden (1880–89, 1906–36) and Batavia, Java (1890–1906); as government adviser in Java developed a liberal policy toward Islām. Pioneer in scientific study of Islām; author of *Mekka* (1888–89), *De Atjèhers* (1893–94), etc.

Snow \'snō\, Charles Percy. Baron Snow. 1905–1980. English writer, physicist, and diplomat. Worked as physicist at Cambridge U. (1930–50); commissioner of Civil Service (1945–60); parliamentary secretary in Ministry of Technology (1964–66); created life peer (1964). Author of an 11-volume sequence of novels, collectively titled *Strangers and Brothers* (1940–70), centering on the life of Lewis Eliot and documenting contemporary English society, especially the corrupting influence of power; individual titles included *The Masters* (1951), *The New Men* (1954), *The Affair* (1960), *Corridors of Power* (1964), and *Last Things* (1970). Also wrote *The Two Cultures and the Scientific Revolution* (1959) and *Public Affairs* (1971). His wife (m. 1950) was Pamela Hansford Johnson (*q.v.*).

Snow, Edgar Parks. 1905–1972. American journalist, b. Kansas City, Mo. Far Eastern correspondent, London *Daily Herald* (1932–41); associate editor, *Saturday Evening Post* (1943–51). Author of *Red Star Over China* (1937), *The Battle for Asia* (1941), *The Other Side of the River* (1962), *The Long Revolution* (1972), etc.

Snow, John. 1813–1858. English physician. Discovered that cholera is transmitted by contaminated water (1854); introduced use of ether as anesthetic into English surgical practice (1846–47).

Snow, Lorenzo. 1814–1901. American religious leader, b. Mantua, Ohio. Went with Brigham Young to Salt Lake City (arriving 1848); made an apostle of the Mormon church (1849); founded Brigham City, Utah (1853); served in Utah territorial legislature (1852–82); imprisoned for polygamy (1886); fifth president of Church of Jesus Christ of Latter-day Saints (1898–1901).

Snow·den \'snōd-ᵊn\, Philip. 1st Viscount Snowden of Ick·orn·shaw \'ik-ȯrn-shȯ\. 1864–1937. English politician. Socialist (from 1893); chairman of Independent Labour party (1903–06, 1917–20); M.P. (1906–18, 1922–31); chancellor of the exchequer (1924, 1929–31); cut government expenditures and secured abandonment of gold standard; lord privy seal (1931–32).

Sny·ders \'snī-dərs\, Frans. 1579–1657. Dutch painter. Pupil of Pieter Brueghel the Younger and Hendrik van Balen; friend of and coworker with Rubens; principal painter to Archduke Albert, governor of Low Countries. Known for hunting scenes and animals in combat.

Sōami. See under NŌAMI.

Soane \'sōn\, Sir John. 1753–1837. English architect. Entered office of George Dance the Younger (1768); assistant to Henry Holland (1772–76); appointed architect to Bank of England (1788); professor at Royal Academy (from 1806). His Neoclassical style characterized by reduction of classical design elements to their structural essentials, linear ornamentation, use of shallow domes and top lighting; his many works included rebuilding of Bank of England, Dulwich College Picture Gallery, London (1811–14), and his house at 13 Lincoln's Inn Fields, London (1812–14).

Soardis, Johannes de. See JEAN DE PARIS.

Soa·res de Sou·sa \'swär-ish-t͟hə-'sō-sə\, Gabriel. c.1540–c.1592. Portuguese chronicler. Author of *Tratado descritivo do Brasil em 1587.*

Soa·ve \'swä-vā\, Francesco. 1743–1806. Swiss priest and writer in Italian. His *Novelle morali* (1782) was one of first literary works in Italian consciously written for children.

Sobeknefru. See SEBEKNEFRU.

So·bhu·za \sō-'bü-zə\. *Also spelled* So·phu·za \-'pü-\. Name of two Swazi rulers:

Sobhuza I. d. 1839. Founder of the Swazi nation. Forced by Zulu chiefs Shaka and Zwide to flee from home on Pongola River; led (from c.1815) his Ngwane and Dhlamini people and settled in present Swaziland; defeated Dingane (1839); succeeded by his son Mswati.

Sobhuza II. 1899–1982. King of Swaziland (1900–82). Son of King Ngwane V; under regency of father's favorite wife (1900–21); under British colonial rule (to 1969); overthrew constitutional system and assumed absolute sovereignty (1973); longest-reigning sovereign of his day.

Sobieski, John. See JOHN III SOBIESKI.

So·bre·ro \sō-'bre-rō\, Ascanio. 1812–1888. Italian chemist. Professor, Turin (1849–82); discovered nitroglycerin (1847).

Soch'i. See HO RYONG.

Socinus, Laelius and Faustus. See SOZZINI.

Soc·ra·tes \'säk-rə-,tēz\. c.470–399 B.C. Greek philosopher. Served as hoplite during Peloponnesian War; member of the Boule (406–405); married, apparently late in life, Xanthippe. Developed the Socratic method of inquiry and instruction, consisting of a series of questions designed to elicit a clear expression of something supposed to be implicitly known by all rational beings. Attacked by Aristophanes as a Sophist and innovator; accused of impiety and of corrupting youth, defended himself in a speech intentionally angering instead of conciliating the judges; condemned; drank hemlock in prison, with his disciples grouped about him. Left no writings of his own; his philosophy known through the writings of his disciple Plato. With Plato and Aristotle, laid the philosophical foundations of Western culture.

Socrates. *Surnamed* Scho·las·ti·cus \skō-'las-ti-kəs\. c.380–c.450. Byzantine church historian. A legal consultant; first known layman to write church history; his *Historia ecclesiastica* is invaluable documentary source for Christian history from 305 to 439.

Sod·dy \'säd-ē\, Frederick. 1877–1956. English chemist. Demonstrator at McGill U., Montreal (1900–02), where he did research in radioactivity with Rutherford; lecturer, U. of Glasgow (1904–14); professor, Aberdeen U. (1914–19), Oxford (1919–36). With Rutherford developed theory of atomic disintegration of radioactive elements; investigated origin and nature of isotopes; awarded 1921 Nobel prize for chemistry. Author of *Radioactivity* (1904), *The Interpretation of Radium* (1909), *Science and Life* (1920), *Interpretation of the Atom* (1932), etc.

So·den \'sō-dən\, Herman von. Freiherr. 1852–1914. German biblical scholar. Professor at Berlin (from 1893); in *Die Schriften des neuen Testament* (1902–13) theorized that all extant New Testament texts were derived from an original 2d century document and then altered by intrusion of Tatian's *Diatessaron* version.

Sö·der·berg \'sœ̄-dər-,berʸ\, Hjalmar Erik Fredrik. 1869–1941. Swedish writer. Author of novels *Förvillelser* (1895), *Martin Bircks ungdom* (1901), *Doktor Glas* (1905); collections of short stories, esp. *Historietter* (1898); and plays including *Gertrud* (1906). Often referred to as "the Anatole France of Sweden."

Sö·der·blom \'sœ̄-dər-,blu̇m\, Nathan. 1866–1931. Swedish Lutheran theologian. Professor, Uppsala (1901) and Leipzig (1912); archbishop of Uppsala and primate of Sweden (1914). Author of works on comparative religion, including *La Vie future d'après le Mazdéisme* (1901), *Gudstrons uppkomst* (1914),

Humor och melankoli och andra Lutherstudier (1919), *Christian Fellowship* (1923). Principal promoter of the Life and Work movement; awarded Nobel peace prize for ecumenical activities (1930).

Sö·der·gran \'sœ̄-dər-ˌgrån\, Edith Irene. 1892–1923. Swedish-Finnish poet, b. St. Petersburg, Russia. Her first book of Expressionist poems, *Dikter* (1916), inaugurated the Swedish-Finnish Modernist movement; later verse included *Septemberlyran* (1918), *Rosenaltaret* (1919), *Framtidens skugga* (1920).

Sodoma, Il. See Giovanni BAZZI.

Soem·mer·ring *or* **Söm·mer·ring** \'zœm-ə-riŋ\, Samuel Thomas von. 1755–1830. German anatomist. Professor, Kassel (1779–84), Mainz (1784–97). Established the number and names of the cranial nerves; made other neuroanatomical findings. Wrote *Vom Baue des menschlichen Körpers* (1791–96).

Soe·to·mo \sȯi-tō-mō\, Raden. 1888–1938. Javanese doctor and nationalist. Helped found (1908) Budi Utomo, one of first Western-style Indonesian nationalist organizations; prominent in the Indonesian independence movement in 1920s and early 1930s.

Sofer, Moses. See Moses SCHREIBER.

Sofya Alekseyevna. See SOPHIA.

So·ga \sō-gä\. Name of a Japanese family that held undisputed power in Japan from 592 to 643, and including:

¶Soga Umako. d. 626. Succeeded to head of the family (570); annihilated the dominant Mononobe clan and assumed supreme power for his family (587); installed his candidate Sushun as emperor (587); fell out with Sushun, had him murdered, and installed (592) his niece Suiko as empress, with his nephew Shōtoku Taishi as regent; instrumental in introducing Buddhism into Japan; supported Shōtoku's reforms.

¶Soga Emishi. d. 645. Succeeded his father Umako as head of family (626); gave his son a purple crown and assumed Imperial prerogatives, which provoked a coup d'état by Nakatomi Kamatari and Prince Nakano Ōe (later emperor Tenchi) that destroyed the power of the Soga family.

¶Soga Iruka. d. 645. Son of Emishi; named Imperial minister by his father; extremely high-handed in his office; assassinated probable heir Prince Yamashiro Ōe in plot to succeed to throne (643); himself assassinated by Nakatomi Kamatari and the future emperor Tenchi.

Soga Chokuan. d. 1614. Japanese painter. Known for brightly colored, realistic bird-and-flower screen paintings; also executed Chinese-style, or *suiboku* ("water-ink"), paintings.

Soga Shōhaku. *Name given at birth* Kōyū. 1730–1781. Japanese painter. Pupil of Takada Keiho of the Kanō school in Kyōto; became disillusioned with contemporary art and turned to the brush-style drawings of Soga Jasoku for inspiration; called himself Jasoku *ken* or Jasoku *jussei,* i.e. the tenth; excelled in ink monochrome portraits; also drew weird and demonic pictures.

So·ga \'sō-gä\, Tiyo. 1829–1871. South African Xosa journalist and clergyman. First African minister ordained in Great Britain (1856); his translation of *Pilgrim's Progress* (*U-Hambo lom-Hambi,* 1866) greatly influenced the Xosa language; contributed articles on many subjects to periodical *In-daba* (1860s); composed hymns; collected Bantu fables, legends, history, customs, etc.; exerted a notable influence on subsequent Xosa writers.

Sog·di·a·nus \ˌsäg-dē-'ā-nəs\ *or* **Se·cyd·i·a·nus** \sē-ˌsid-ē-'ā-nəs\. d. 424 B.C. King of Persia (424 B.C.). Natural son of Artaxerxes I of Persia; murdered his half-brother Xerxes II; after reign of few months, was killed by another brother, Darius II.

Sog·low \'säg-(ˌ)lō\, Otto. 1900–1975. American cartoonist, b. New York City. Cartoonist (from 1925) for magazines, esp. *The New Yorker,* and for King Features Syndicate (1933–75); creator of "The Little King."

Sohl·man \'sōl-mån\, August, *in full* Per August Ferdinand. 1824–1874. Swedish journalist. Editor of Stockholm daily *Aftonbladet* (1857–74); a leading supporter of the mid-19th century Pan-Scandanavian movement; championed Swedish culture and language in Finland.

Sohn \'zōn\. Name of family of German painters, including: Carl Ferdinand (1805–1867), known esp. for mythological scenes, portraits, and paintings of female figures. His son ¶Karl Rudolf (1845–1908), painter of portraits and genre scenes. Carl Ferdinand's nephew ¶Wilhelm (1830–1899), painter of biblical pictures and genre scenes.

Sohr \'zōr\ *or* **So·re** \'zō-rə\, Martin. *Lat.* Martin Agric·o·la \ə-'grik-ə-lə\. 1486–1556. German church musician and composer. One of first to write music for Reformed churches and to publish musical treatises in vernacular; invented much of German musical vocabulary. Writings included *Musica instrumentalis deudsch* (1529).

Sois·sons \swä-sōⁿ\, Comte de. Title held by members of Soissons branch of the Condé line of the house of Bourbon (*qq.v.*). On death of Comte Louis (1641; *q.v.*), title passed through his sister Marie (wife of Thomas, Prince of Carignan) to the Savoy-Carignan line of the house of Savoy (see SAVOY); title extinct on death of Prince Eugene of Savoy (1736).

So·kol·lu \sȯ-kȯl-'lü\, Mehmed Paşa. 1505–1579. Ottoman politician. High admiral of Ottoman fleet (1546); governor general of Rumelia; commanded forces of Selim II during conflict between Selim and Bayezid (1559–61); m. (1562) a daughter of Selim. Grand vizier (1565–79); opposed war with Venice (1570–73) and Persia (1578); lost power after Selim's death (1574); assassinated.

So·ko·low \'sȯ-kȯ-lȯv\, Nahum. 1861–1936. Polish writer and Zionist leader. Editor in Warsaw of periodicals *Ha-Asif* and *Sefer Ha-Shanah* (1885–1902); joined (1897) Zionist Organization and became (1906) its secretary general and editor of official organs *Die Welt* and *Ha-Olam;* traveled throughout world propagating Zionist ideas; to England at outbreak of World War I and later naturalized; took prominent part in Anglo-French negotiations leading to Balfour declaration (1917). Chairman of World Zionist Executive (1922–31); president of World Zionist Organization and of Jewish Agency (1931–35). His writings included *The History of Zionism, 1600–1918* (1919), *Hibbath Zion* (1934), *Yischim* (1911–35).

So·lan·der \sü-'lån-dər, *Angl* sō-'lan-dər\, Daniel Carl. 1733–1782. Swedish botanist. Pupil of and assistant to Linnaeus; to England (1760); instructed English botanists in Linnaean system; given charge of cataloguing natural history collections of British Museum (1763); accompanied Sir Joseph Banks on Cook's voyage in *Endeavour* (1768–71) and to Iceland (1772); curator of natural history, British Museum (1773 ff.).

So·la·ri \sō-'lä-rē\ *or* **So·la·rio** \-ryō\, Antonio. *Called* lo Zin·ga·ro \lōt-'sēŋ-gä-rō\, *i.e.* the Gypsy. fl. 1495–1514. Italian painter. Painted frescoes in the Benedictine monastery at Naples.

Solari *or* **Solario,** Cristoforo. *Known as* il Gob·bo \ēl-'gȯb-bō\, *i.e.* the Hunchback. 1460–1527. Italian sculptor and architect. Carved many statues for the cathedral of Milan; also employed at the Certosa di Pavia. His brother ¶Andrea, *also known as* Andrea del Gobbo (d. 1524) was a painter; trained by Cristoforo; influenced by Antonello da Messina and Leonardo da Vinci; visited France (1507) and probably Flanders. His canvases, known for their coloring, lush atmospheric effects, and animated composition, included *A Man With a Pink* (c.1492), *Madonna and Child with SS. Joseph and Jerome* (1495), *Madonna with the Green Cushion* (c.1507), *Flight into Egypt* (1515), and *Woman Playing a Guitar* (c.1515).

So·la·ro del·la Mar·ga·ri·ta \sō-'lär-ō-ˌdāl-lä-ˌmär-gä-'rē-tä\, Clemente. Conte. 1792–1869. Piedmontese politician. Entered diplomatic service (1816); foreign minister (1835–47); opposed constitutional reforms and advocated neutrality between France and Austria; member of Piedmontese parliament (1854–60); led opposition to the Risorgimento.

So·ler \sō-'lär\, Antonio Francisco Javier José. 1729–1783. Spanish composer. Chapelmaster at Lérida cathedral (c.1750) and at monastery at El Escorial (from 1752); joined Hieronymites (1752); pupil of Scarlatti; one of finest keyboard performers of his time; wrote *Llave de la modulación* (1762) on musical theory. Composed 120 keyboard sonatas, 9 masses, 6 quintets for organ and strings, 6 concerti for two organs, and incidental music for plays.

Solf \'zȯlf\, Wilhelm. 1862–1936. German diplomat. Governor of Samoa (1900–11); secretary for colonial affairs (1911–18); as foreign secretary (Oct.–Dec. 1918), negotiated the armistice with the Allies; ambassador to Tokyo (1920–28).

Solh Bey \'sȯl-'bā\, Riad. 1894–1951. Lebanese politician. Before World War II, often sentenced to death for pro-Arab activities against the French; first prime minister of Lebanon (1943–45); again prime minister (1947–51); assassinated.

Soliman. See SÜLEYMAN.

So·li·nus \sə-'lī-nəs\, Gaius Julius. 3d century A.D.? Latin grammarian and writer. Author of *Collectanea rerum memorabilium* (revised under title *Polyhistor*), a description of the world of his day with comments on historical, social, religious, and natural history topics.

Solís, Juan Díaz de. See DÍAZ DE SOLÍS.

So·lís y Ri·va·de·nei·ra \sō-'lē-sē-rē-b̲ä-t̲h̲ā-'nā-rä\, Antonio de. 1610–1686. Spanish historian, dramatist, and politician. Private secretary to Philip IV (1654); historiographer of the Indies (1665); ordained priest (1667); known esp. for his *Historia de la conquista de México* (1684); author also of the plays *Amor y obligación, El amor al uso, Un bobo hace ciento,* and *La gitanilla de Madrid.*

Solitario, El. See Serafín ESTÉBANEZ CALDERÓN.

Sol·lo·gub \sə-(ˌ)lə-'güp\, Vladimir Aleksandrovich. Count. 1813–1882. Russian writer. Author of novels, short stories, and plays, esp. *Tarantas* (1850) and *Chinovnik* (1856).

Solms \'zȯlms\, Heinrich Maastricht. Count of Solms-Braun·fels \-'braůn-fels\. 1636–1693. German soldier. General in Dutch army; accompanied William of Orange and led Dutch guards into Westminster (1689); distinguished himself at the Boyne (1690); censured after Steenkerke.

Sol·o·mon \'säl-ə-mən\. 10th century B.C. King of Israel. Son of David and Bathsheba. Under his rule Israel rose to the height of its greatness; established Palestine as a center of commerce; noted for his wealth and his wisdom; builder of Solomon's Temple in Jerusalem and many public buildings; made alliance with Hiram of Tyre. Reputed author of biblical books Proverbs, The Song of Solomon, Ecclesiastes, and Wisdom of Solomon.

Solomon ben Yehuda ibn Gabirol. See IBN GABIROL.

So·lo·mos \sȯ-lȯ-'mȯs\, Dhionísios. Count. 1798–1857. Greek poet. First great poet of modern Greece; established Demotic Greek as the poetic language. Author of some satires as *I Ginaíka tís Zakínthou,* and romantic poems including *Ímnos is tín elevtherían* (1823; "Hymn to Liberty"), *Lambros* (1833), *O kritikós* (1833), *Oi elévtheroi poliorkiménoi,* and *O pórfiras* (1849).

So·lon \'sō-lən, -ˌlän\. c.630–c.560 B.C. Athenian statesman. One of the Seven Wise Men of Greece. Distinguished himself first by publicly reciting a poem that inspired the Athenians to capture Salamis from the Megarians (c.600). In period of acute economic distress, elected archon (c.594) and given full powers to initiate economic and constitutional reforms: reorganized the Boule (senate), popular assembly, and council of the Areopagus, improved the lot of the debtors, divided the population into four income groups, strengthened trade by forbidding export of produce other than olive oil, minted new coinage on a more universal standard, reformed standard of weights and measures, and introduced a more humane law code. The reforms were bitterly opposed by some elements in the city and Solon, to escape the turmoil, left Athens for ten years, traveling in Egypt, Cyprus, and Lydia; shortly after his return, Peisistratus (*q.v.*) made himself tyrant of the city. Considered first great poet of Athens.

So·lov·yov \sə-(ˌ)ləv-'yȯf\, Sergey Mikhaylovich. 1820–1879. Russian historian. Professor, U. of Moscow (1847–79); author of *History of Russia* (1851–79), *Political and Diplomatic History of Alexander I* (1877). His son ¶Vladimir Sergeyevich (1853–1900) was philosopher and poet; attempted a synthesis of religious philosophy, ethics, and science in the context of a universal Christianity uniting the Orthodox and Roman Catholic churches under papal leadership. Author of poems and *The Crisis of Western Philosophy* (1875), *Godmanhood* (1880), *The Philosophical Principles of Integral Knowledge* (1877), *History and Future of Theocracy* (1887), *Russia and the Universal Church* (1889), *The Justification of the Good* (1898), *War, Progress, and the End of History* (1900).

Sol·vay \sȯl-'vā, *Angl* 'säl-ˌvā\, Ernest. 1838–1922. Belgian industrial chemist. Invented Solvay process for making soda ash (1861); erected (1863) at Couillet first plant for utilizing the process; improved the process and established plants in all parts of the world; used his wealth for philanthropic purposes and to establish (1894) a social science institute at Brussels.

Solway, Earl of. See 3d Duke of Queensberry, under DOUGLAS family.

Somacandra. See HEMACANDRA.

So·ma·de·va \'sō-mə-'dā-və\. fl. 1070 A.D. Sanskrit author. Native Brahman of Kashmir; court poet to King Ananta of Kashmir. Wrote *Kathā-saritsāgara* ("Ocean of Rivers of Stories"), a collection of tales and romances, mainly Brahmanistic, but containing much that is Buddhist in character.

Somers. See also SUMMERS.

Som·ers *or* **Sum·mers** \'səm-ərz\, Sir George. 1554–1610. English navigator. One of founders of South Virginia Company; commanded fleet carrying settlers which was wrecked on Bermudas or Somers Islands (1609); took possession of islands for king of England.

Somers, John. Baron Somers. 1651–1716. English lawyer and politician. Adm. to bar (1676); junior counsel for defense in trial of the Seven Bishops (1688; see William SANCROFT); chairman of committee that drew up Declaration of Rights; solicitor general (1689); attorney general (1692); lord keeper of great seal (1693); chief minister to William III (1696–1700); lord chancellor and Baron Somers of Evesham (1697). Leader of group of Whigs known as the Junto (1696–1716); one of council of regency during William III's absence in Holland. Compelled to resign the seal under repeated attacks by the Tories (1700); retired (1702) but active in settling terms of union with Scotland (1707); president of Privy Council (1708–10).

Somerset, Dukes of. See BEAUFORT and SEYMOUR families.

Somerset, Earls of. See (1) John Beaufort (1373?–1410), under BEAUFORT family; (2) Robert CARR.

Som·er·set \'səm-ər-ˌset, -sət\. An English family holding earldom, later marquisate, of Worces·ter \'wu̇s-tər\, merged (1682) with dukedom of Beau·fort \'bō-fərt\. Its founder, Charles Somerset (1460?–1520), Earl of Worcester, illegitimate son of Henry Beaufort, 3d Duke of Somerset (see BEAUFORT family), assumed name Somerset; m. daughter of William Herbert, Earl of Huntingdon; sent on diplomatic missions by Henry VII (1490–1505) and by Henry VIII (1515–18); created Baron Her·bert of Rag·lan \'hər-bərt-əv-'rag-lən\ (1506) and Earl of Worcester (1514), which titles descended in direct line to his great-great-grandson ¶Henry Somerset (1577–1646), 5th Earl and 1st Marquis of Worcester, provider of funds to Charles I at outbreak of Civil War.

Henry's son ¶Edward Somerset (1601–1667), 6th Earl and 2d Marquis of Worcester, and titular Earl of Gla·mor·gan \glə-'mȯr-gən\ (conferred 1644), inventor; began (1628) mechanical experimentation, including construction of a large wheel in attempt to create a perpetual motion machine (c.1638); at outbreak of Civil War defending South Wales for Charles I, defeated by Waller at Highnam (1643); succeeded father (1646), went into exile (1648); restored to portion of estates (1660). Author of *Century of Inventions* (1655, pub. 1663). His son ¶Henry (1629–1700), 3d Marquis of Worcester, 1st Duke of Beaufort (created 1682), renounced Catholicism and was member of Parliament; on Cromwell's death demanded free parliament and favored Restoration; defended Bristol against Monmouth's forces (1685) but surrendered it (1688) to William of Orange. His grandson ¶Henry (1684–1714), 2d Duke of Beaufort, was prominent Tory leader and member of Swift's Brothers' Club.

¶Fitzroy James Henry Somerset (1788–1855), Baron Raglan; 8th son of 5th Duke of Beaufort. Aide-de-camp to Duke of Wellington in Peninsular War (1808–12), military secretary (1812–14); lost his sword arm at Waterloo. Military secretary to Wellington (1827–52); succeeded Wellington as commander of forces and was created Baron Raglan of Raglan (1852). Commanded British troops in Crimean War; won battle of Alma (1854); his ambiguous order led to loss of Light Brigade at Balaklava (1854); made field marshal for victory at Inkerman (1854); made scapegoat for failure of commissariat during winter (1854–55); died ten days after repulse at Malakoff and Redan. The raglan overcoat was named for him.

Som·er·vell \'səm-ər-vəl, -(ˌ)vel\, Sir Arthur. 1863–1937. English composer. Known for operettas for children, the symphony in D minor *Thalassa* (1912), oratorio *The Passion of Christ* (1914), and the settings for lyrics of English poets.

Som·er·ville \'səm-ər-(ˌ)vil\, Edith Anna Oenone. 1858–1949. Irish novelist. Began (1886) long collaboration with her cousin Violet Florence Martin (*q.v.*), producing series of novels that wittily and sympathetically portrayed Irish society as *An Irish Cousin* (1889), *The Real Charlotte* (1894), and *Some Experiences of an Irish R.M.* (1899, short stories). After cousin's death (1915), published several works as products of collaboration, including *Stray-Aways* (1920); author also of *The Big House of Inver* (novel, 1925), *The States through Irish Eyes* (1930).

Somerville, Sir James Fownes. 1882–1949. British naval officer. In World War I (1914–18); commander in chief in East Indies (1938–39); vice admiral in Mediterranean (1940–42); commander in chief, Eastern Fleet (1942–44); admiral of the fleet (1945).

Somerville, Mary, *nee* Fair·fax \'fa(ə)r-ˌfaks, 'fe(ə)r-\. 1780–1872. Scottish writer on mathematics and physical science. m. (1812) her cousin Dr. William Somerville; on invitation of Lord Brougham, turned Laplace's *Mécanique céleste* into popularized English version *Celestial Mechanism of the Heavens* (1831). Author of *The Connection of the Physical Sciences* (1834), *Physical Geography* (1848). Somerville Coll., Oxford, is named after her.

Somerville *or* **Som·er·vile** \'səm-ər-(ˌ)vil\, William. 1675–1742. English poet. Author of *The Two Springs* (a fable, 1725), *The Chase* (four books of Miltonic blank verse on hunting, 1735), *Hobbinol* (a burlesque of rural games, 1740), and *Field Sports* (on hawking, 1742).

Som·meil·ler \sȯ-me-yā\, Germain. 1815–1871. French engineer. Built the Mont Cenis Tunnel between France and Switzerland (completed 1870) using a compressed-air drill which he developed.

Som·mer \'zȯm-ər\, Ferdinand. 1875–1962. German linguist. Professor at Basel (1902–09), Rostock (1909–13), Jena (1913–24), Bonn (1924–26), Munich (1926–51). His works on the Hittite and classical languages included *Handbuch der lateinischen Laut- und Formenlehre* (1902), *Hethiter und Hethitisch* (1947), *Zur Geschichte der griechischen Nominalkomposita* (1948).

Som·mer·feld \'zȯm-ər-ˌfelt\, Arnold Johannes Wilhelm. 1868–1951. German physicist. Professor at Aachen (1900–06), Munich (1906–31); with Felix Klein, developed a theory of the gyroscope; contributed to development of quantum theory, Bohr atomic theory, quantum theory of spectral lines, theory of metallic electrons, etc.

Som·mo \'sȯm-mō\, Judah Leone ben Isaac. *Also known as* Leone de Som·mi Por·ta·le·o·ne \'sȯm-mē-ˌpȯr-tä-lā-'ō-nā\. *Orig.* Yehuda Sommo. 1527–1592. Italian Jewish writer. Produced and wrote plays including first known Hebrew drama *Tzaḥut bediḥuta de-quiddushin* (1550); his *Dialoghi in materia di rappresentazioni sceniche* (c.1565) is valuable source on 16th-century Italian theatrical production.

So·mo·de·vil·la y Ben·go·e·chea \sō-mō-t͟hā-'vē(l)-yä-ē-b͟eŋ-gō-ā-'chā-ä\, Zenón de. Marqués de la En·se·na·da \en-sen-'ä-t͟hä\. 1702–1781. Spanish politician. Took part in naval expedition that captured Oran (1732); organized expedition against Naples that placed Charles IV (later III of Spain) on throne

(1736); prime minister (1743–54); carried out internal reforms, strengthened army and esp. navy, encouraged education; exiled to Granada (1754–59) for anti-British policy; restored to government service on accession of Charles III (1759); banished again (1766) for pro-Jesuit views.

So·mo·za \sō-'mō-sä\, Anastasio. *Nicknamed* Ta·cho \'tä-chō\. 1896–1956. Nicaraguan politician. Became head of army (1933); deposed the president, his uncle Juan Bautista Sacasa (1936); president of Nicaragua (1936–47) and, as commander in chief of army, virtual dictator until his death; fostered agriculture, mineral production, public works; amassed a large fortune and suppressed political opposition; assassinated. His son ¶Luis Anastasio Somoza De·bay·le \-thā-'bī-lā\ (1922–67) was president of Nicaragua (1957–63). His brother ¶Anastasio (1925–1980) continued the Somoza dynasty as president (from 1963); ruled despotically; overthrown (1979) by Sandinista movement and fled country; assassinated in Paraguay.

Sönderborg-Augustenburg. See OLDENBURG, 4.

Son·neck \'sən-,ek\, Oscar George Theodore. 1873–1928. American musician and librarian, b. Lafayette, N.J. First chief of the music division, Library of Congress (1902–17); on staff of G. Schirmer Co., music publishers, New York City (1917–28), and vice president (from 1921); edited *The Musical Quarterly* (1915–28); published treatises on American musical history.

Son·ni ʿAlī \sȯn-'ē-ä-'lē\. *Also* Sun·ni Ali \sün-'ē-\ *and* Sonni ʿAlī Ber \-'ber\, *i.e.* ʿAlī the Great. d. 1492. King of Songhai (c.1464–92). Expanded his kingdom by conquering Sudanese cities of Timbuktu (1468) and Jenné (1473); repulsed attacks from surrounding tribes; an effective strategist and tactician.

Son·ni·no \sōn-'nē-nō\, Giorgio Sidney. Baron. 1847–1922. Italian politician. Elected deputy (1880); minister of finance (1893–94), of treasury (1894–96); premier (1906, 1909–10); minister of foreign affairs (1914–19); promoted Italy's entrance into World War I; representative at Paris Peace Conference (1919).

Son \sȯn\ Pyong-hi. 1861–1922. Korean religious leader. Elected (1897) third leader of the apocalyptic anti-foreign Tonghak sect; renamed (1905) sect the Ch'ŏndogyo (Religion of the Heavenly Way); a leader of the 1919 movement for Korean independence.

Sonora, Marqués de la. See José GÁLVEZ.

Soong \'sůŋ\. *Also spelled* Sung. Influential Chinese family including: Charles Jones Soong. *Orig.* Soong Yao-ju \-'yaů-'zhü\. d. 1927. Merchant; to U.S. (c.1880); became a Christian and received at baptism name of Charles Jones after an American sea captain who befriended him; returned to China and became Bible manufacturer and salesman. His daughters, Ai-ling, Ch'ing-ling, and Mei-ling, married H. H. K'ung, Sun Yat-sen, and Chiang Kai-shek, respectively. His son ¶Tzu-wen \'dzü-'wən\, *also spelled* Tse-ven \'dzə-'vən\ *or* Tsu-ven \'dzü-'vən\, *better known by Anglicized name* T.V. Soong (1894–1971), began (1923) financing Sun Yat-sen's Kuomintang party; president, Central Bank, Canton (from 1924); minister of finance, Nationalist government (1925–33); reformed taxation and tariff systems, standardized the currency, centralized the banking system; member of the executive committee of Kuomintang; founded Bank of China (1936); foreign minister (1942–45); acting president, Executive Yuan (1932–33, 1944–47); to U.S. (1949) as banker and businessman.

So·phia \sō-'fī-ə, 'sō-fē-ə\. d. after 578. Byzantine empress. Niece of Empress Theodora; wife of Justin II (565–578); administered affairs of the empire (574–578) jointly with Tiberius II Constantinus.

So·phia \zō-'fē-ä\. d. 1284. German duchess, founder of the landgraviate of Hesse. Daughter of St. Elizabeth of Hungary and niece of Henry Raspe; m. Henry of Brabant; mother of Henry I, first male ruler of Hesse.

Sophia. 1630–1714. Electress of Hanover. See ERNEST AUGUSTUS.

Sophia. Russian empress. See under IVAN III.

Sophia. *Russ.* Sof·ya Ale·ksey·ev·na \'sȯf-yə-əl-(,)yəks-'yā-əv-nə\. 1657–1704. Regent of Russia. Daughter of Czar Alexis. Upon death of her brother Czar Fyodor III (1682), instigated an uprising among the *streltsy* (household troops), who murdered the supporters of her half-brother Peter (later Peter I); installed her brother Ivan V as co-ruler with Peter, took the regency for them, and ruled Russia (1682–89); encouraged industry; concluded peace treaties with Poland (1686) and China (1689); sponsored unsuccessful campaigns against the Crimean Tatars (1687, 1689). Forced by Peter into a convent at Moscow (1689) and later imprisoned (from 1698) on suspicion of again inciting rebellion among the *streltsy.*

So·phia Char·lotte \sō-'fī-ə-'shär-lət, 'sō-fē-ə-\. *Ger.* So·phie Char·lot·te \zō-'fē(ə)-shär-'lȯt-ə\. 1668–1705. Queen of Frederick I of Prussia. Daughter of Ernest Augustus, 1st Elector of Hanover, and sister of George I of England. Queen of Prussia (1701–05); spent early years in Paris; m. (1684), as 2d wife, Prince Frederick of Prussia (later King Frederick I); patron of arts and letters and special friend of Leibnitz; Charlottenburg named for her.

So·phia Dor·o·thea \sō-'fī-ə-,där-ə-'thē-ə\. *Ger.* So·phie Do·ro·thea \zō-'fē(-ə)-dō-rō-'tā-ä\. 1666–1726. German noblewoman. Daughter of Duke George William of the Brunswick-Lüneburg line; m. (1682) George Louis, Crown Prince of Hanover (later George I of England); accused of liaison with young Swedish nobleman, Count Philipp Christoph von Königsmark, colonel of the guards at Hanover; after his death (1694), arrested and tried; divorced by George and imprisoned for 32 years at Castle of Ahlden; known as Princess of Ahl·den \'äl-dən\. Her children were George II of England and Sophia Dorothea (1687–1757), wife (m. 1706) of Frederick William I of Prussia, by whom she was mother of Frederick the Great.

So·phie \zō-'fē(-ə), 'zȯ-fē\. 1805–1872. Archduchess of Austria. Daughter of King Maximilian I Joseph of Bavaria; m. (1824) Archduke Francis Charles of Austria. Mother of Emperor Francis Joseph, whom she was active in placing on throne at time of 1848 revolution.

Sophie. *In full* Sophie Dorothea Ulrike Alice. 1870–1932. Princess of Prussia and queen of Greece (1913–17, 1920–22). Daughter of Frederick III, Emperor of Germany, and sister of William II; m. (1889) Prince Constantine, who succeeded to throne of Greece (1913); left Greece (1917) at his abdication; after return (1920) left a second time when Constantine was forced to abdicate (1922); lived in Florence. Mother of Alexander I and George II, kings of Greece, and of Helen, who married Carol II of Romania.

Soph·o·cles \'säf-ə-,klēz\. c.496–406 B.C. Greek tragic playwright. Served as a treasurer of Athenian Empire (442); elected general under Pericles (440); appointed (413) one of 10 elder statesmen advising Athens on financial and domestic recovery after defeat at Syracuse (413). Ranked with Aeschylus and Euripides as greatest among Greek dramatists; defeated Aeschylus for the prize for tragedy (468); won altogether perhaps as many as 24 times. Wrote about 123 plays, of which 7 are extant, *Oedipus Tyrannus* (or *Oedipus Rex*), *Oedipus at Colonus, Antigone, Electra, Philoctetes, Ajax, The Trachiniae.*

Sophonias. See ZEPHANIAH.

Soph·o·nis·ba \,säf-ə-'niz-bə\. *Punic* Saphanbaʿal. d. c.204 B.C. Carthaginian noblewoman. Daughter of Hasdrubal of Carthage. Originally betrothed to the Numidian prince Masinissa, but married (for political reasons) to Masinissa's rival, Syphax. Masinissa defeated Syphax, captured Sophonisba, and married her, but was compelled by his Roman allies to discard her; sent her poison to commit suicide in order not to fall into the hands of the Romans. Her story is the theme of a number of tragedies.

So·phron \'sō-,frän\ of Syracuse. fl. c.430 B.C. Greek playwright. Best known as writer of rhythmical Doric prose mimes, a form of play apparently originated by him; depicted scenes of daily life; influenced Theocritus and Herodas; only fragments of his work have survived.

Sophronius. See also Saint JEROME.

So·phro·ni·us \sə-'frō-nē-əs\. c.560–638. Syrian prelate. Became monk in Egypt (c.580); entered monastery of St. Theodosius in Jerusalem (619); accompanied John Moschus on his travels. Patriarch of Jerusalem (634–638); sent (634) a synodical letter to Pope Honorius I and to Eastern patriarchs denouncing Monothelitism; chief proponent of orthodox tenet of Dyotheletism; works included sermons, doctrinal polemics, an encomium on Alexandrian martyrs Cyrus and John, and 23 anacreontic odes.

Sophuza. See SOBHUZA.

Sopiha. See SAPIEHA.

Sor \'sȯr\ *or* **Sors** \'sȯrs\, Fernando, *in full* José Fernando Macari. 1778–1839. Catalan composer and guitarist. His opera *Telemaco* staged in Barcelona (1797); left Spain (1813), resided thereafter in Paris, London, Moscow; his ballet *Cendrillon* achieved great success in London (1822) and Paris (1823). Famed as guitar virtuoso and teacher; known esp. for his fantasies, minuets, sonatas, studies, etc., for guitar; other compositions included ballets *L'Amante peintre* (1823) and *Le Sicilien* (1827), piano pieces, songs and duets. Wrote treatise *Méthode pour la guitare* (1830).

Sorak. See YI CHŎNG.

So·ra·nus \sȯr-'ā-nəs\ of Eph·e·sus \'ef-ə-səs\. 2d century A.D. Greek physician. Practiced in Alexandria and later in Rome; head of the "methodist school." His writings dominated medical opinion concerning women's diseases, pregnancy, and infant care for 15 centuries. Works included *On Midwifery and the Diseases of Women, On Acute and Chronic Diseases,* oldest known biography of Hippocrates, and a treatise on fractures.

Sor·bon \sȯr-bōⁿ\, Robert de. 1201–1274. French theologian. Chaplain and confessor of Louis IX; founded (1257) the Sorbonne.

Sor·by \'sȯr-bē\, Henry Clifton. 1826–1908. English geologist. Considered the father of microscopical petrology; devoted himself to independent investigation in spectroscopy, microscopy, marine biology, geology, archaeology; invented method of making thin slices of rock for microscopic inspection (1849); announced a new type of spectrum microscope for analyzing the light of organic pigments (1865); aided in founding of Sheffield U.

Sor·del·lo \sȯr-'del-lō, *Angl* sȯr-'del-(,)ō\. c.1200–before 1269. Italian troubadour. Left court of Richard of Bonifacio at Verona after abducting his wife for political reasons (1224); traveled as troubadour in Spain and southern France; settled at court of Raymond Berengar of Provence (1237); later a companion of Charles of Anjou; accompanied Charles to Italy when he became

Charles I of Naples and Sicily (1265). Among his works, written in Provençal, were love songs, satires, a lament on the death of his patron Blacatz, and a didactic poem *L'Ensenhamen d'onor;* made type of patriotic pride in Dante's *Purgatorio;* subject of Browning's *Sordello.*

Sore, Martin. See SOHR.

So·rel \sò-rel\, Agnès. *Sometimes known as* Dame de Beau·té \dȧm-də-bō-tā\. 1422?–1450. Mistress of King Charles VII of France (1444–50). Exerted great influence over Charles, who gave her an estate at Beauté-sur-Marne (whence her sobriquet); made many enemies; said to have died by poisoning.

Sorel, Charles. Sieur de Sou·vi·gny \sü-vēn-yē\. c.1600–1674. French writer. Historiographer of France (1635); best known for novels *La Vraie Histoire comique de Francion* (1623) and *Le Berger extravagant* (1627), both burlesquing the pastoral and chivalric romances so popular in his time.

Sorel, Georges-Eugène. 1847–1922. French Socialist. Retired from a civil service engineering post to devote himself to study (1892); became a Marxist (1893); passionate defender of Dreyfus; denounced the Socialist and Radical parties and preached revolutionary syndicalism (1902); developed theory on the creative role of myth and violence in the historical process; broke with syndicalists and joined the monarchist movement (1909); supported the Bolsheviks (1917). His works included *L'Avenir socialiste des syndicats* (1898), *Réflexions sur la violence* (1908), *Les Illusions du progrès* (1908), *La Révolution dreyfusienne* (1909), and *De l'utilité du pragmatisme* (1921).

Sø·ren·sen \'sœ̄-rən-sən\, Rasmus Møller. 1799–1865. Danish reformer. A leading agitator for agrarian reforms, equality of taxation, representative government; founded and edited journal *Almuevennen* (early 1840s; with J.A. Hansen); member of parliament (1849–52).

Sørensen, Søren Peter Lauritz. 1868–1939. Danish chemist. Director of chemical department, Carlsberg Laboratory, Copenhagen (1901–39). Suggested the symbol pH to denote the negative logarithm of the concentration of the hydrogen ion in a Sörensen scale to express acidity or alkalinity of a solution (1909); investigated protein solutions.

Sor·ge \'zȯr-gə\, Reinhard Johannes. 1892–1916. German playwright and poet. Wrote the first German Expressionist drama, *Bettler* (1912); also wrote *Guntwar* (dramatic poem, 1914), *Metanoeite* (Christmas mystery play, 1915), *König David* (play, 1916).

Sorge, Richard. 1895–1944. German journalist and spy. Sent (1929) by Comintern to China to organize a spy ring while serving as a journalist; joined Nazi party (1933); sent by Comintern to Tokyo, where he headed a successful Soviet spy ring during World War II; arrested (1941) and executed by the Japanese.

Soriano, Francesco. See Francesco SURIANO.

So·rin \sò-ra^n; *Angl* 'sōr-ən, 'sȯr-\, Edward Frederick. 1814–1893. American clergyman and educator, b. Ahuillé, France. Ordained priest (1838); joined Congregation of Holy Cross (1840); to Vincennes, Ind., as missionary (1841); founded Notre Dame U. (chartered 1844) and served as its first president (1844–65); founded *Ave Maria* magazine (1865); superior general, Congregation of Holy Cross (from 1868).

So·ro·kin \'sȯ-rə-kyin\, Pitirim Alexandrovitch. 1889–1968. American sociologist, b. Turya, Russia. Professor, St. Petersburg (1919–22); to U.S. (1923, naturalized 1930); professor, U. of Minnesota (1924–30), Harvard (1930–55); founded department of sociology at Harvard (1930) and the Harvard Research Center in Creative Altruism (1949). Developed theory dividing sociocultural systems into "sensate" and "ideational" types. Author of *Sociology of Revolution* (1925), *A Source Book in Rural Sociology* (1930–32), *Social and Cultural Dynamics* (1937–41), *Man and Society in Calamity* (1942), *Altruistic Love* (1950), *A Long Journey* (1963).

So·rol·la y Bas·ti·da \sō-'rō(l)-yä-ē-b̲äs-'tē-t̲h̲ä\, Joaquin. 1863–1923. Spanish painter. Gained success with historical and realist works as *Otra Margarita* (1892); turned to a conservative variant of Impressionism; known for genre paintings, landscapes, and beach scenes marked by sharp contrasts of light and shade, brilliant colors, vigorous brushstrokes, including *The Beach at Zarauz* (1910); painted series of murals of scenes of Spanish provinces for the Hispanic Society of America (1910–20).

Sors, Fernando. See SOR.

Sor·sky \'sȯr-skəi\, Nil. Saint. *Orig.* Nikolay May·kov \'mī-kəf\. c.1433–1508. Russian religious. One of great Russian *startsy* (holy men); founded monastery beside the Sora River (whence Sorsky); spoke against monastic ownership of property (1503); opposed involvement of monks in social welfare and political activity; first Russian mystic to write about the contemplative life and leave a guide for spiritual self-perfection.

So·san Dai·sa \sò-sän-dī-sä\. *Secular name* Hyu·jong \hyü-jōŋ\. 1520–1604. Korean Buddhist priest. Became Buddhist (1535); rose to highest post in Buddhist administration and to master priesthood at Bongunsa temple (1555); resigned (1556) to devote himself to study and practice Buddhism; led Buddhist opposition to invading Japanese (from 1592); played major part in fight to recapture Pyŏngyang and Seoul.

So·sig·e·nes \sō-'sij-ə-ˌnēz\ of Alexandria. 1st century B.C. Greek astronomer and mathematician. Commissioned by Julius Caesar (c.46 B.C.) to reform the Roman calendar; author of *Revolving Spheres,* only fragments of which are extant.

Sos·tra·tus \'säs-trət-əs\. 3d century B.C. Greek architect. Built (c.280 B.C.) for Ptolemy II at Alexandria the Pharos (lighthouse), which became one of the Seven Wonders of the World.

So·ta·des \'sōt-ə-ˌdēz\. 3d century B.C. Greek satirist. Known esp. as composer of scurrilous and licentious verse; lampooned Ptolemy II Philadelphus; was captured, sealed up in chest of lead, and cast into sea.

Sō·ta·tsu \sō-tät-sü\. *In full* Ta·wa·ra·va \tä-wä-rä-vä\ Sōtatsu. fl. 1600–1630s. Japanese painter. Developed an original decorative style from the Japanese *Yamato-e* (colorful decorative painting) tradition and the Chinese *sumi-e* (ink painting) technique; held rank of Hokkyō; works included pair of screens with scenes from the *Tale of Genji* and another pair of screens with scenes from the Matsushima isles.

So·ter \'sōt-ər\. Saint. d. c.174. Pope (166?–?174). Succeeded St. Anicetus.

Soter. See ANTIOCHUS I, ATTALUS I, DEMETRIUS I of Syria, PTOLEMY I and IX, SELEUCUS III.

Soth·e·by \'sət̲h̲-ə-bē, 'sät̲h̲-\. Family of English auctioneers and antiquaries, including: John (1740–1807), partner (from 1780) with George Leigh in a London auction house founded (1744) by John's uncle Samuel Baker (d. 1778). John's nephew ¶Samuel (1771–1842) joined the firm (1800) and became head on Leigh's death (1815). His son ¶Samuel Leigh (1805–1861) entered the business (c.1817) and succeeded as head on his father's death; specialist in cataloguing, author of works on early printing, block books, and on Milton's autograph.

Soth·ern \'sət̲h̲-ərn\, Edward Askew. 1826–1881. American actor, b. Liverpool, England. To U.S. (1852); success in role of Lord Dundreary in *Our American Cousin* (from 1858). His son ¶Edward Hugh (1859–1933), b. New Orleans, made debut in New York in his father's company (1879); leading man in Daniel Frohman's stock company at Lyceum Theater in New York (1886–1900), acting with success in romantic adventure plays; formed (1900) own company with wife (m. 1896, div. 1910) Virginia Harned, playing title roles in *Hamlet* (1900) and *Richard Lovelace* (1901) and Villon in *If I Were King* (1902–03); presented Shakespearean drama with Julia Marlowe (1904–07 and 1909–16); m. (1911) Marlowe (*q.v.*); retired (1927). Author of autobiography *The Melancholy Tale of Me* (1916).

So·to \'sō-tō\, Hernando de. 1496, 1499, or 1500–1542. Spanish explorer. Accompanied Pedro Arias Dávila to Central America (1516–20); participated in conquest of Nicaragua (1523) and served as its military commander for several years; with Pizarro in Peru (1531–36). Headed expedition to North America (1539); landed in Florida; explored territories in present Florida, Alabama, Tennessee, Mississippi, Arkansas, Oklahoma, and Louisiana in search of gold and treasure; in constant conflict with Indians; discovered (May 21, 1540) and crossed the Mississippi River; died of a fever near present Ferriday, La., and his body sunk in the Mississippi to prevent its being desecrated by Indians.

Soto, Marco Aurelio. 1846–1908. Honduran politician. President of Honduras (1876–83); administration marked by civil order and many progressive acts; new constitution promulgated (1880).

Sou·bei·ran \sü-bā-rä^n\, Eugène. 1797–1858. French apothecary. Professor in the school of pharmacy, Paris; one of the discoverers of chloroform (1831).

Soubirous, Bernadette. See BERNADETTE of Lourdes.

Soubise, Prince and seigneur de. See ROHAN family.

Sou·blette \sü-'blet\, Carlos. 1789–1870. Venezuelan politician. Took part in war of independence; minister of war and marine of Gran Colombia (1819–29); president of Venezuela (1843–47).

Souf·flot \sü-flō\, Jacques-Germain. 1713–1780. French architect. His style a transition between Classical Baroque and Neoclassical; best known as architect of the Panthéon, Paris; designed also Hôtel de Ville in Bordeaux and the cathedral in Rennes.

Sou·las \sü-läs\, Josias de. Sieur de Prime·fosse \prēm-fōs\. *Pseudonym* Flo·ri·dor \flō-rē-dȯr\. 1608?–1671 or 1672. French actor. Member (from c.1643) of the Hôtel de Bourgogne, Paris; succeeded Bellerose as head of Bourgogne; created roles in plays of Corneille and Racine.

Sou·lé \sü-lā\, Pierre. 1801–1870. American politician and diplomat, b. Castillon-en-Couserans, France. Involved in intrigues against King Charles X of France, escaped to England and thence to U.S. (1825). Settled in New Orleans and practiced law there; U.S. senator (1847, 1849–53); U.S. minister to Spain (1853–55); there engaged in intrigues to detach Cuba from Spain; associated with James Buchanan and John Y. Mason in framing the Ostend

Manifesto (1854) proposing the purchase of Cuba from Spain; manifesto repudiated by U.S. Secretary of State William L. Marcy and Soulé was made scapegoat for the administration.

Soulé, Samuel W. See Christopher SHOLES.

Sou·louque \sü-lük\ *or* **So·louque** \sö-\, Faustin-Élie. 1782?–1867. Haitian general and politician. Born a slave; participated in revolt expelling the French (1803); leader of the black majority against mulatto elite; elected president of Haiti (1847); proclaimed himself emperor of Haiti, under the title Faustin I (1849); made unsuccessful attempts to conquer Dominican Republic; deposed by mulattoes (1859) and thereafter lived in exile.

Soult \sült\, Nicolas-Jean de Dieu \də-dyœ\. Duc de Dal·ma·tie \dál-má-sē\. 1769–1851. French soldier and politician. Made general by Lefebvre for conduct at Battle of Fleurus (1794); replaced Lefebvre at Battle of Stokach (1799); in command of southern part of Kingdom of Naples (1800–02); created marshal by Napoléon (1804). Engaged at Austerlitz, Jena, Pułtusk, Preussisch-Eylau; created duc (1807). Served in Spain (1808–11) and French commander in chief there (1809–11); conquered Andalusia (1810); defeated at La Albuera (1811) and by Arthur Wellesley at Toulouse (1814). Minister of war under Louis XVIII (1814–15); rallied to Napoléon on his return from Elba. Lived in exile (1815–19); recalled to France (1819) and again appointed marshal (1820); minister of war (1830–34, 1840–44); president of the council (1832–34, 1839–40, 1840–47); responsible for conquest of Algeria; declared himself a republican on deposition of Louis-Philippe.

Sou·sa \'sü-zə, 'sü-sə\, John Philip. *Called* the March King. 1854–1932. American bandmaster and composer, b. Washington, D.C. Bandmaster of U.S. Marine Band (1880–92); organized his own band and toured U.S. and foreign countries with great success (from 1892). Composed about 140 military marches, including "Semper Fidelis" (1888), "Washington Post March" (1889), "Liberty Bell" (1893), "King Cotton" (1897), "Stars and Stripes Forever" (1897), "Hands Across the Sea" (1899). Among his comic operas were *El Capitan* (1896), *The Bride-Elect* (1897), *The Free Lance* (1906). Compiled *National, Patriotic and Typical Airs of All Lands* (1890); wrote three novels and the autobiography *Marching Along* (1928).

Sou·sa \'sō-zə\, Luís de. *Orig.* Manuel de Sousa Cou·ti·nho \-kō-'tēn-yü\. 1555–1632. Portuguese Dominican monk and writer. Took religious vows and changed name to Frei Luís de Sousa (1614); author of *História de São Domingos* (1623, 1662, 1678) and *Vida do Arcebispo D. Frei Bartolomeu dos Mártires* (1619).

Sousa, Martim Afonso de. 1500?–1564. Portuguese admiral. Commanded first colonizing expedition sent to Brazil (1530–33) and founded first Portuguese settlement there at São Vicente (1532); later, governor of colony in Goa, India.

Sousa, Tomé de. d. c.1573. Portuguese soldier. First governor general of the Portuguese colony of Brazil (1549–53).

Sousa Hol·stein \-'hól-stān\, Pedro de. Duque de Pal·me·la \päl-'mā-lə\. 1781–1850. Portuguese politician. Minister of foreign affairs (1817–20); after death of King John VI (1826), allied himself with Liberal party and supported accession of Maria II; prime minister (1842–46).

Sou·tar \'süt-ər\, William. 1898–1943. Scottish poet. Second to Hugh MacDiarmid among Scottish Renaissance writers. Author of verse in Scots, including *Seeds in the Wind* (1933, beast fables for children), *Poems in Scots* (1935), *Riddles in Scots* (1937), and in English as *Brief Words* (1935, epigrams) and *The Expectant Silence* (1944, nature lyrics).

South \'sau̇th\, Robert. 1634–1716. English preacher. Chaplain to Duke of York (1667); canon in Oxford (1670); chaplain to Charles II; supported doctrine of passive obedience and divine right of kings. Best known for his sermons, masterpieces of clearness in vigorous pithy English.

South·ack \'sət͟h-ək\, Cyprian. 1662–1745. American privateer and cartographer, b. London, England. To Boston, Mass. (1685); commissioned by Admiralty board to protect New England coast from pirates and privateers; in pursuance of duties, charted northeast coast of North America.

Southampton, Earls of. See WRIOTHESLEY.

South·cott \'sau̇th-kət\, Joanna. 1750–1814. English religious fanatic. Domestic servant, originally a Methodist; declared herself the woman of Revelation xii, announced that she was to be delivered of Shiloh, a second messiah, on Oct. 19, 1814; died of brain disease (Dec. 1814), leaving followers said to number 100,000. Author of several works of biblical interpretation and prophecy, including *The Book of Wonders* (1813–14).

South·erne \'sət͟h-ərn\, Thomas. 1660–1746. Irish dramatist. Known for two successful tragedies, *The Fatal Marriage* (1694), renamed by Garrick *Isabella, or the Fatal Marriage,* and *Oroonoko* (1696), both adapted from novels by Aphra Behn; also contributed prologues and epilogues to Dryden's plays.

Sou·they \'sau̇-t͟hē, 'sət͟h-ē\, Robert. 1774–1843. English poet and man of letters. With Coleridge and Robert Lovell, formed visionary socialistic scheme of a pantisocracy on banks of Susquehanna River in America (1794–95); visited (1800–01) Spain and Portugal; settled at Greta Hall, Keswick, in Lake District (1803). Became as strongly Tory as he had been Republican and received government pension. Contributed to *Quarterly Review* (1809–38); wrote *Life of Nelson* (1813); accepted poet laureateship (1813); revolutionary drama *Wat Tyler* (written 1794) published without authorization (1817); satirized by Byron in opening dedicatory stanzas of *Don Juan* (1819) and in *The Vision of Judgment* (1822). Remembered not for epic poems *Thalaba* (1801), *Madoc* (1805), *The Curse of Kehama* (1810), and *Roderick* (1821), as he hoped, but for shorter poems "The Holly Tree," "My days among the dead are past," "The Inchcape Rock," "The Battle of Blenheim," "Stanzas Written in My Library," and for his vigorous and graceful prose in *Letters of Espriella* (1807), *The Doctor* (1834–47), his *Commonplace Book* (1849–51), his biographical and historical works, and his *Letters* (1856).

South·well \'sau̇th-wəl, -(,)wel\, Robert. 1561–1595. English poet and Jesuit martyr. Ordained priest (1585); domestic chaplain to Countess of Arundel, in whose house he lived in hiding (from 1586); arrested, imprisoned, and tortured (1592–95); executed. Author of religious poetry including *St. Peter's Complaynt* (1595) and *The Burning Babe,* and prose religious works, esp. *An Epistle of Comfort* (1587).

South·worth \'sau̇th-(,)wərth\, Albert Sands (1811–1894), b. West Fairlee, Vt., and his partner ¶Josiah Johnson Hawes \'hȯz\ (1808–1901), b. East Sudbury, now Wayland, Mass. American photographers. Operated portrait studio in Boston (1841–61); known for portrait daguerreotypes that revealed the personalities of such sitters as Lemuel Shaw, John Q. Adams, Daniel Webster, Henry Clay, Harriet Beecher Stowe; also produced daguerreotypes of landscapes, cityscapes, and unconventional scenes; after end of partnership (1861), Hawes continued to photograph until his death.

Southworth, Emma Dorothy Eliza, *nee* Nev·itte \'nev-ət\. *Pen name* E.D.E.N. Southworth. 1819–1899. American novelist, b. Washington, D.C. m. Frederick H. Southworth (1840). Author of *Retribution* (1849), *The Missing Bride* (1855), *The Hidden Hand* (1859), *The Fatal Marriage* (1869), *The Maiden Widow* (1870), etc.

Sou·tine \sü-'tēn\, Chaim. 1893–1943. French painter, b. Lithuania. To Paris (1913); works characterized by thick impasto, agitated brushwork, convulsive compositional rhythms, disturbing psychological content; subjects included choirboys, cooks, and pageboys as *Page Boy at Maxim's* (1927), hung poultry as *Hanging Turkey* (c.1926), beef carcasses as *Side of Beef* (c.1925), and distorted portraits as *Woman in Red* (c.1923).

Soút·sos \'sōt-sȯs\, Aléxandros. 1803–1863. Greek poet. Founder of the Greek Romantic school of poetry. His verse satires inspired early development of modern Greek political liberalism; other works included poem *Periplanoménos* (1839), lyrics, dramas, and the novel *Exóristos* (1839).

So·va \'sȯ-vä\, Antonín. 1864–1928. Czech writer. Known for lyrical verses including *Květy intimních nálad* (1891) and *Zpěvy domova* (1918), and novels including *Tóma Bojar* (1910).

Sow·er \'sō-ər\, Christopher. 1695–1758. American printer and publisher, b. Ladenburg, Germany. To Germantown, Pa. (1724), and became (1738) first German printer and publisher in the colonies. Published a newspaper *Pensylvanische Berichte,* an almanac *Der Hoch-Deutsch Americanische Calender,* and many religious works in German, including first European-language colonial Bible (1743). A leader in German community; opposed slavery, Anglicization of Germans and German culture, mistreatment of immigrants and Indians. His son ¶Christopher (1721–1784) inherited the business (1758); published second (1763) and third (1776) editions of the Sower, or Germantown, Bible; arrested on supicion of treason, maltreated, and despoiled of all his property (1778). His son ¶Christopher (1754–1799) took over the publishing business (1774); was a Loyalist during the American Revolution; fled to England (c.1783); to New Brunswick (1785) and became deputy postmaster general and king's printer, also publisher of the *Royal Gazette and Weekly Advertiser.*

Sow·er·by \'sō-ər-bē\, James. 1757–1822. English artist. Compiled and illustrated *English Botany* (1790–1814) and *British Mineralogy* (1804–17); his *Mineral Conchology of Great Britain* (1812–46) completed by his son ¶James de Carle (1787–1871).

Sowerby, Leo. 1895–1968. American composer, b. Grand Rapids, Mich. Taught at American Conservatory of Music, Chicago (1925–62); organist at St. James Cathedral, Chicago (1927–62); founder and director (1962–68) of College of Church Musicians, Washington, D.C. Composed 5 symphonies, tone poems (esp. *Prairie,* 1929), *Canticle of the Sun* for chorus and orchestra (1944, Pulitzer prize), concerti for piano, cello, and organ, chamber music, organ and choral works.

Sōzen. See YAMANA Mochitoyo.

So·zo·me·nos \sō-'zȯm-ə-nȯs\, Salamanes Hermeios. *Known as* So·zo·men \'sō-zə-mən\. c.400–c.450. Greek historian. Christian lawyer in Constantinople; author of an ecclesiastical history modeled upon and closely paralleling that of Socrates Scholasticus (*q.v.*) and dealing with the period 324 to 425 A.D.

Soz·zi·ni \sōt-'tsē-nē\, Lelio Francesco Maria. *Also spelled* So·ci·ni \sō-'chē-nē\ *or* So·zi·ni \sōt-'sē-nē\. *Known by Lat. form* Laelius So·ci·nus \sə-'sī-nəs\.

1525–1562. Italian theologian. Trained in law but turned to biblical research; settled in Zürich (1548); corresponded with Calvin (1549) and met Melanchthon (1550). Author of an anti-Trinitarian doctrine developed into Socinianism by his nephew Fausto; composed an orthodox but ambiguous confession of faith (1555); in later years supported by courts of Vienna and Kraków. His nephew ¶Fausto Paolo Sozzini, *known by Lat. form* Faustus Socinus (1539–1604), was also a theologian; developed his uncle's anti-Trinitarian doctrine into Socinianism; denounced by the Inquisition (1559); took refuge in Zürich (1559–62); secretary to Duke Orsini in Florence (1563–75); settled in Kraków (1579) and became a leader of the Minor church; his property confiscated by the Inquisition (1590), left destitute. Among his works were *De sacrae scripturae auctoritate* (1570), *De Jesu Christo servatore* (1578), and *Christianae religionis institutio* (unfinished); his teachings exerted a strong influence on growth of Unitarianism.

Spaak \'spák\, Paul-Henri Charles. 1899–1972. Belgian statesman. Advocate of European unity; Socialist member of Chamber of Deputies (from 1932); minister of foreign affairs (1936–38, 1939–45, 1946–50, 1954–57, 1961–66); premier (1938–39, 1946, 1947–50); first president UN General Assembly (1946); secretary general of NATO (1957–61). Helped draft charters of Benelux (1944), UN (1945), NATO (1949), and the Common Market (1957).

Spaatz \'späts\, Carl. *Nicknamed* Too·ey \'tü-ē\. *Surname orig. (to 1937)* Spatz. 1891–1974. American air force officer, b. Boyertown, Pa. Entered U.S. army (1914); combat pilot in World War I; chief of air staff (1941), of U.S. air force in Europe (1941); initiated daylight bombing of German-occupied Europe (1942); chief, U.S. bombing force in Germany (1944) and Japan (1945); general (1945); first chief of staff of independent U.S. air force (1947); retired (1948).

Spa·da \'spä-dä\, Leonello. 1576–1622. Italian painter. Among his works were frescoes in Church of San Michele in Bosco (at Bologna), and in Church of Madonna della Chiara (at Reggio).

Spaeth \'spāth\, Sigmund. 1885–1965. American musician, lecturer, and writer, b. Philadelphia. Music editor for *McCalls* (1931–33), *Esquire* (1934), *Literary Digest* (1937–38); editor, *Music Journal* (1955–65). Author of *The Common Sense of Music* (1924), *The Art of Enjoying Music* (1933), *Great Symphonies* (1936), *Fun with Music* (1951), etc.

Spagnoletto, Lo. See José de RIBERA.

Spagnolo, Lo. See Giuseppe CRESPI.

Spagnuolo, Pietro. See Pedro BERRUGUETE.

Spalatin, Georg. See Georg BURCKHARDT.

Spal·ding \'spȯl-diŋ\, Albert. 1888–1953. American violinist, b. Chicago. Son of Albert G. Spalding. Concert debut, Paris (1905) and New York (1908); toured in Europe and U.S.; served in both World Wars. Composed suite for orchestra, two violin concerti, and other violin pieces; wrote autobiography *Rise to Follow* (1943) and novel *A Fiddle, a Sword, and a Lady* (1953).

Spalding, Albert Goodwill. 1850–1915. American sportsman and businessman, b. near Byron, Ill. Played professional baseball with Boston team (1871–75) and Chicago team (1876); was successively manager, secretary, and president (1882–91) of the Chicago club. Organized (1876) with his brother James Walter (1856–1931) a sporting-goods business in Chicopee, Mass.; edited *Spalding's Official Baseball Guide* (1878–80). Elected to Baseball Hall of Fame (1939).

Spalding, Henry Harmon. c.1801–1874. American Presbyterian missionary, b. near Bath, N.Y. Established (1836) near present Lewiston, Idaho, the Lapwai Mission for Nez Percé Indians, and first white home, church, and school in Idaho; founded first printing press in Pacific Northwest (1839).

Spal·lan·za·ni \ˌspäl-länt-'sän-ē\, Lazzaro. 1729–1799. Italian physiologist. Professor, Modena (1763–69) and Pavia (from 1769). Known for experiments on digestion, circulation of the blood, fertilization and regeneration in animals, the senses of bats; disproved the theory of spontaneous generation; pioneered in volcanology.

Spang·en·berg \'shpäŋ-ən-ˌberk, *Angl* 'spaŋ-ən-ˌbərg\, August Gottlieb. 1704–1792. German clergyman. Assistant to Nikolaus Zinzendorf at Herrnhut (1733) and allied himself with the Unitas Fratrum. To America (1735) and labored for Moravian church in Georgia and Pennsylvania. Bishop (1744); organized and directed Moravian settlement at Bethlehem, Pa. (1744–50) and on land grant in North Carolina (1752–62). Returned to Herrnhut (1762); dominating figure in his church (1762–92). Author of a life of Zinzendorf, a history of the Unitas Fratrum, and *Idea Fidei Fratrum,* a compendium of the Christian faith of the Unitas Fratrum (1779).

Sparks \'spärks\, Jared. 1789–1866. American historian, b. Willington, Conn. Bought and edited *North American Review* (1823–29). Published *The Diplomatic Correspondence of the American Revolution* (1829–30), *The Life of Gouverneur Morris* (1832), *The Writings of George Washington* (1834–37), *The Works of Benjamin Franklin* (1836–40), *The Library of American Biography* (1834–48). Professor at Harvard (1839–49); president of Harvard (1849–53).

Spar·ta·cus \'spärt-ə-kəs\. d. 71 B.C. Roman slave and gladiator, b. Thrace. Served in Roman army; deserted, caught, and sold as slave; leader of a slave insurrection (Gladiatorial War, 73–71 B.C.). After several times defeating Roman armies sent against him, he was finally beaten by Crassus and killed in action.

Spaul·ding \'spȯl-diŋ\, Gilbert R. 1811–1880. American circus impresario. Creator of "The Floating Palace," a steamboat that contained a regulation circus ring and a stage and toured the Mississippi and Ohio rivers during 1850s; introduced quarter poles for supporting tent roofs; one of first to transport his circus by railroad.

Spea·ker \'spē-kər\, Tristram E., *known as* Tris \'tris\. *Called* the Gray Eagle. 1888–1958. American baseball player, b. Hubbard, Texas. Center fielder in American League, with Boston (1909–15), Cleveland (1916–26), Washington (1927), Philadelphia (1928); lifetime batting average .344; one of greatest defensive and all-around players. Elected to Baseball Hall of Fame (1937).

Spear·man \'spi(ə)r-mən\, Charles Edward. 1863–1945. English psychologist. Professor at U. College, London (1911–31); known for studies determining correlations among human mental abilities. Author of "General Intelligence, Objectively Determined and Measured" (1904), *The Nature of 'Intelligence' and the Principles of Cognition* (1923), *The Abilities of Man* (1927), *Psychology Down the Ages* (1937), *Human Ability* (1950, with L. W. Jones).

Sped·ding \'sped-iŋ\, James. 1808–1881. English editor. Published *Works of Francis Bacon* (1857–59), *Life and Letters* (1861–74); author of *Life and Times of Bacon* (1878).

Spee \'shpā\, Maximilian Johannes Maria Hubert von. Graf. 1861–1914. German admiral. Entered navy (1878); chief of staff of German Ocean (North Sea) Command (1908–12); commander of Far Eastern Squadron (1912); surprised and defeated British squadron at Coronel off the Chilean coast (Nov. 1914); sank with his flagship *Scharnhorst* when his fleet was destroyed by the British under Adm. Sturdee near the Falkland Islands (Dec. 1914).

Speed \'spēd\, John. 1552–1629. English antiquarian and cartographer. Published a series of 54 maps of various parts of England and Wales (1608–10). Author of a *History of Great Britain* (1611).

Speel·man \'spāl-män\, Cornelis Janszoon. 1628–1684. Dutch colonial administrator. To Dutch East Indies (1645); appointed governor of Coromandel Coast (1663); conquered Macassar (1666); governor general of Dutch East Indies (1681–84); instrumental in Dutch expansion in the Indies.

Speer \'shpār\, Albert. 1905–1981. German architect and official. Joined Nazi party (1931); appointed head architect of Nazi government (1934); minister of armaments (1942–45) and war production (1943–45); imprisoned as war criminal (1946–66). Wrote memoirs *Inside the Third Reich* (1970), *Spandau* (1976), *Infiltration: The SS and German Armament* (1981).

Spei·cher \'spī-kər\, Eugene Edward. 1883–1962. American painter, b. Buffalo, N.Y. Known for portraits and landscapes, including *Katharine Cornell as Candida* (1926), *Farm News* (1944), *Consuela* (1947).

Speke \'spēk\, John Hanning. 1827–1864. English explorer. Accompanied Richard Burton in expedition into Somaliland (1854); in expedition under Burton, discovered lakes Tanganyika (1858, with Burton) and Victoria (1858, alone); confirmed his theory of the latter as source of the Nile (1862); published *Journal of the Discovery of the Source of the Nile* (1863); furnished information to Samuel Baker that enabled him to discover Lake Albert (1864).

Spell·man \'spel-mən\, Francis Joseph. 1889–1967. American prelate, b. Whitman, Mass. Consecrated bishop of Sila (1932), and archbishop of New York (1939); cardinal (1946); erected churches, schools, hospitals; wrote many newspaper and magazine articles and books.

Spel·man \'spel-mən\, Sir Henry. c.1564–1641. English antiquary. Prepared, as preliminary to his learned works on English law, a glossary of obsolete Latin and Old English terms (1626; completed by his son, 1664); author of *Concilia, Decreta, Leges, Constitutiones* (1639, 1664), an attempt to document ecclesiastical history. M.P.; sat on several royal commissions, including Council for New England (1620–35).

Spe·mann \'shpā-ˌmän\, Hans. 1869–1941. German embryologist. Professor at Rostock (1908–14); director, Kaiser Wilhelm Institute of Biology (1914–19); professor at Freiburg (1919–35). Worked esp. on the mechanics of embryologic development, discovering the directive function (embryonic induction) of certain tissues. Awarded 1935 Nobel prize for physiology or medicine.

Spence \'spen(t)s\, Sir Basil Urwin. 1907–1976. British architect. Best known for his design (1951) for new Coventry cathedral (completed 1962); professor at Royal Academy (1961–68); also designed British Embassy at Rome, British pavilion at Montreal Expo 67, buildings for U. of Sussex, churches, housing developments, theaters, factories, office buildings.

\ə\ abut \ᵊ\ kitten, *Fr.* **table \ər\ further \a\ ash \ā\ ace \ä\ cot, cart \au̇\ out \ch\ chin \e\ bet \ē\ easy \g\ go \i\ hit \ī\ ice \j\ job \ŋ\ sing \ō\ go \ȯ\ law \ȯi\ boy \th\ both \t͟h\ the \ü\ loot \u̇\ foot \y\ yet \zh\ vision \á, ḇ, ḡ, ḵ, ⁿ, œ, œ̄, ue, ue̅, ʸ** *see* **Guide to Pronunciation**

Spence, Joseph. 1699–1768. English anecdotist. His *Essay on Pope's Odyssey* (1727) won him a professorship of poetry at Oxford (1728) and the friendship of Pope. Recorded anecdotes from conversations of Pope and his friends (pub. 1820).

Spence, Thomas. 1750–1814. British pamphleteer. In *The Real Rights of Man* (1775) proposed public ownership of land rented out to individuals at moderate rates; active in reform movements in London (from 1792); author of pamphlets on the millennium, the natural state of man, and the like.

Spen·cer \'spen(t)-sər\. Name of English family descended from Hugh Despenser (*q.v.*) and holding earldom of Sunderland, earldom of Spencer, and dukedom of Marlborough, including among its members:

EARLS OF SUN·DER·LAND \'sən-dər-lənd\: Henry Spencer (1620–1643), 1st Earl of Sunderland, 3d Baron Spencer; grandson of Robert, 1st Baron Spencer; m. (1639) Lady Dorothy Sidney (see SIDNEY family); killed at battle of Newbury, fighting for Charles I.

His son ¶Robert (1641–1702), 2d earl; politician; ambassador at Madrid, Paris, and Cologne (1671–78); secretary of state for northern department (1679) and member of inner cabinet (1679–81); opposed Shaftsbury; worked to exclude Duke of York from succession and thereby lost his place in privy council (1681); reinstated as secretary of state (1683); architect of Charles II's pro-French foreign policy; influential under James II as lord president of council and principal secretary of state; effected dismissal of his rival, Rochester, after professing Roman Catholicism (1687); dismissed for disapproving James's plans (1688). On arrival of William of Orange in England fled to Holland; returned (1690); established himself as one of William's chief advisers; made lord chamberlain (1697) and one of lord justices; induced William to choose all his ministers from one party, the modern system; virtual head of government until forced by popular indignation to resign (1697).

His second son ¶Charles (1674–1722), 3d earl; m. (1700) Lady Anne Churchill, daughter of 1st Duke of Marlborough; secretary of state for southern department (1706–10), and one of five Whigs, called the Junto, who dominated government (1708–10). Joined cabinet as lord keeper of privy seal (1715); intrigued with Stanhope to secure dismissal of Townshend (1716) and Walpole (1717); became lord president of Privy Council and first lord of treasury (1718); having taken some part in promoting South Sea Bubble (1720), accused of taking bribe and forced to resign (1721); retained influence with George I. Collector of rare books; patron of Addison and other men of letters.

DUKES OF MARL·BOR·OUGH \'märl-,bər-ə, 'mȯl-, -,bə-rə, -brə\: ¶Charles Spencer (1706–1758), 3d Duke of Marlborough and 5th Earl of Sunderland; 3d son of 3d earl; succeeded his brother (1729) and succeeded (1733) to dukedom of Marlborough on death of maternal aunt, Marlborough's eldest daughter, duchess in her own right, thus merging two titles; commanded brigade at Dettingen (1743) and in expedition against St.-Malo (1758). His eldest son ¶George (1739–1817), 4th duke; lord privy seal in Grenville ministry (1763–65). George's eldest son ¶George (1766–1840), 5th duke; M.P. (1790); spent enormous sums on his gardens and library of early printing; took additional name of Church·ill \'chər-,chil, 'chərch-,hil\ by royal license (1817). George's (1766–1840) grandson ¶John Winston Spencer Churchill (1822–1883), 7th duke; prominent Conservative; as Marquis of Bland·ford \'blan(d)-fərd\, M.P. (1844), brought about carriage of Blandford Act (1856) for dividing parishes for purposes of church work; lord lieutenant of Ireland (1876–80); his 3d son was Lord Randolph Churchill (*q.v.,* at CHURCHILL).

EARLS SPENCER: ¶John Spencer (1734–1783), 1st Earl Spencer (created 1765), grandson of Charles Spencer, 3d Earl of Sunderland. ¶George John (1758–1834), 2d earl; by courtesy, Viscount Al·thorp \'ȯl-trəp, 'ȯl-,thȯrp\; son of 1st earl; Pitt's first lord of admiralty (1794–1801); singled out Nelson to command in Mediterranean; home secretary (1806–07); helped form Roxburghe Club (1812).

George's eldest son ¶John Charles (1782–1845), 3d earl, known as Viscount Althorp (to 1834); M.P. (1804–30), joined advanced Whig party; junior lord of treasury (1806–07); leader of Whig opposition (1830); chancellor of exchequer and leader in House of Commons (1830–34); industrious leader, played important part in preparing and carrying Reform Bill (1832); sponsored Factory Act of 1833 (Althorp's Act); retired after succession to earldom; first president of Royal Agricultural Society.

John Charles's nephew ¶John Poyntz Spencer (1835–1910), 5th earl, son of 4th earl; succeeded to earldom (1857); began long career as Liberal politician as lord lieutenant of Ireland under Gladstone (1868–74); lord president of council, with seat in cabinet (1880–82); reappointed lord lieutenant of Ireland (1882–85); again president of council (1886); first lord of admiralty (1892–95); Liberal leader in House of Lords (1902–05).

Spencer, Lady Diana. See under Topham BEAUCLERK.

Spencer, Dorothy. Countess of Sunderland. See under SIDNEY family.

Spencer, Herbert. 1820–1903. English philosopher. As subeditor of the *Economist* in London (1848–53), made acquaintance of Huxley, Tyndall, George Eliot, and John Stuart Mill, and developed the ethical and social views of his first important work, *Social Statics* (1851), advocating extreme individualism; thereafter absorbed in study of development of doctrine of evolution as applied to sociology; began to apply the doctrine of evolution in *Principles of Psychology* (1855); sought to develop the principle that all organic development is change from state of indefinite homogeneity to state of definite heterogeneity; provided by Darwin's *Origin of Species* (1859) with evidence of what had been speculation. Announced (1860) a *System of Synthetic Philosophy* covering metaphysics, biology, psychology, sociology, and ethics, of which he published *First Principles* (1862), *Principles of Biology* (1864, 1867), *Principles of Sociology* (1876, 1882, 1896), *Data of Ethics* (1879), *Principles of Ethics* (1892, 1893, of which *Data of Ethics* constitutes part one). Author also of *Education* (1861), *The Man versus the State* (1884), three volumes of essays, and *Autobiography* (1904). One of few modern thinkers to attempt systematic account of all cosmic phenomena, including mental and social principles.

Spencer, Platt Rogers. 1800–1864. American calligrapher, b. East Fishkill, N.Y. Originator of Spencerian style of handwriting; teacher of penmanship in schools and business colleges; author of copybooks and textbooks on penmanship.

Spencer, Sir Stanley. 1891–1959. English painter. Known esp. for religious paintings with Surrealistic overtones, often set in his native Cookham, including *Resurrection* (1928–29) and *The Resurrection: Port Glasgow* (1950); also executed landscapes and paintings of social satire as *The Nursery* (1936).

Spe·ner \'shpā-nər\, Philipp Jacob. 1635–1705. German theologian. Leader of Lutheran Pietism. President of Lutheran Church at Frankfurt am Main (1666); first court chaplain at Dresden (1686–91); provost of St. Nicholas' Church, Berlin (from 1691). Author of *Pia Desideria* (1675), *Das geistliche Priestertum* (1677), *Die allgemeine Gottesgelehrtheit* (1680), etc.

Speng·ler \'shpeŋ-lər, *Angl* 'speŋ-(g)lər\, Oswald. 1880–1936. German writer. Chief work *Der Utergang des Abendlandes* (1918–22; *The Decline of the West),* in which he predicted the eclipse of Western civilization; also wrote *Der Mensch und die Technik* (1931), *Jahre der Entscheidung* (1933).

Spenser. See also DESPENSER and SPENCER.

Spen·ser \'spen(t)-sər\, Edmund. 1552 or 1553–1599. English poet. Befriended by Gabriel Harvey while at Cambridge (1569–76); secured place in Earl of Leicester's household in London, and became acquainted with Sir Philip Sidney (1578); with Sidney, Dyer, and others formed a literary club, Areopagus. Launched first work of Elizabethan literature, *The Sheapheardes Calendar,* comprising 12 eclogues, dedicated to Sidney, friend and patron (1579). As secretary accompanied Arthur Lord Grey, lord deputy, to Ireland (1580); began writing *The Faerie Queene,* an imaginative allegory glorifying Protestant England and the English language; received grant of Kilcolman Castle, near Cork (1588/89); commemorated death of Sidney in a pastoral elegy *Astrophel* (1586); published three books of *Faerie Queene* (1590), which won him reputation of leading English poet of his day; published minor poems as *Complaints* (1591). Published (1595) sonnet cycle *Amoretti* and marriage ode *Epithalamion,* celebrating his courtship and marriage (1594) of Elizabeth Boyle. Published *Colin Clouts come home againe* (1595), written (1591) after he was presented to Queen Elizabeth by Sir Walter Raleigh; published second installment of three books of *Faerie Queene* (1596) and *Foure Hymnes* (on love and beauty and heavenly love) showing Platonic influence (1596); showed strong bias for relentless subjugation in his prose *View of the Present State of Ireland* (1596). Returned from second visit to England depressed in spirits and in health; sheriff of Cork (1598); in burning of Kilcolman castle by Irish insurrectionists (1598), lost his youngest child and perhaps additional books of *Faerie Queene;* died on mission to London with dispatches; buried in Westminster Abbey near Chaucer. Called "the Poet's Poet"; excelled in richness and beauty of imagination; enriched poetry with invention of Spenserian stanza.

Spe·ran·sky \spyi-'rán-skəi, *Angl* spə-'ran-skē\, Mikhail Mikhaylovich. 1772–1839. Russian politican. As administrative secretary and assistant (1807–12) to Czar Alexander I, promoted financial and administrative reforms and proposed (1809) a new constitution; unpopularity of reforms with nobility and high officials resulted in exile to Perm (1812); reentered state service (1816); governor general of Siberia (1819–21); member of State Council (from 1821). Published *Complete Collection of the Laws of the Russian Empire* (1830), first such collection; supervised preparation of *Digest of the Laws* (1832–39); made count (1839).

Sper·ry \'sper-ē\, Elmer Ambrose. 1860–1930. American electrical engineer and industrialist, b. Cortland, N.Y. Invented improved dynamo and new type of arc lamp (1879); organized Sperry Electric Company, Chicago (1880), Sperry Electric Mining Machine Company (1888), Sperry Electric Railway Company (1890), and National Battery Company. Founded (1900) electrochemical research laboratory in Washington, D.C., where (with his associate, C. P. Townsend) he developed process for making pure caustic soda from salt, a chlorine detinning process for recovering tin from old cans and scrap. Most notable inventions were gyroscopic compasses and stabilizers for ships and airplanes; organized Sperry Gyroscope Company (1910) for manufacturing these instruments and remained at its head until 1929. Also invented high-intensity arc searchlight (1918); founded total of eight manufacturing companies and took out over 400 patents.

Speu·sip·pus \spyü-'sip-əs\. d. 339 or 338 B.C. Greek philosopher. Nephew and disciple of Plato at Athens; accompanied Plato to Sicily (361 B.C.), and named by Plato his successor as head of the Academy (347). Only a fragment of one of his works, *On Pythagorean Numbers,* is extant.

Sphrantes, George. See GEORGE SPHRANTES.

Spie·ghel \'spē-gəl\, Henric Laurenszoon. 1549–1612. Dutch writer. Member of northern Dutch Renaissance; author of spiritual poetry, esp. the allegorical *Hertspiegel* (1614); plays including *Numa;* and prose works, esp. *Twe-spraack van de Nederduitsche Letterkunst* (1584), a Dutch grammar in which he advocated a purification and wider use of the Dutch language.

Spiel·ha·gen \'shpēl-ˌhä-gən\, Friedrich von. 1829–1911. German novelist. Editor of *Westermanns Monatshrefte* (1878–84); also an actor and active partisan in democratic movements. Author of social novels, including *Problematische Naturen* (1861), *Durch Nacht zum Licht* (1862), *In Reih und Glied* (1867), *Hammer und Amboss* (1869), and *Sturmflut* (1877); author also of plays, including *Hans und Grete* (1868) and *Liebe für Liebe* (1875).

Spier \'spi(ə)r\, Leslie. 1893–1961. American anthropologist, b. New York City. Professor at Yale (1932–39) and U. of New Mexico (1939–55); contributed to the ethnology of North American Indians using method of culture-historical analysis.

Spin·den \'spin-dən\, Herbert Joseph. 1879–1967. American anthropologist, b. Huron, S.D. Curator of American Indian art and primitive cultures, Brooklyn Museum (from 1929). Authority on ancient art and ancient American history; worked out chronology of Mayan inscriptions, the Mayan civil and Venus calendars, etc.

Spi·nel·li \spē-'nel-lē\, Spinello di Lu·ca \dē-'lü-kä\. *Called* Spinello Are·ti·no \ˌär-ā-'tē-nō\. c.1346–1410. Italian painter. Influenced by Orcagna and Nardo di Cione; noted for his Gothic style and vigorous narrative sense; painted frescoes for churches of S. Francesco at Arezzo, Antella (c.1387), S. Miniato al Monte at Florence (c.1387), for Campo Santo at Pisa (1391), and for Palazzo Pubblico at Siena (1407–10).

Spin·garn \'spin-ˌgärn\, Joel Elias. 1875–1939. American author, b. New York City. A founder and literary adviser of Harcourt, Brace & Co., publishers (1919–32); a founder (1909) and chairman of board of directors, National Association for the Advancement of Colored People (1913–19), treasurer (1919–30), president (1930–39); founded Spingarn medal (1914). Author of *A History of Literary Criticism in the Renaissance* (1899), *The New Criticism* (1911), *Creative Criticism* (1917), *The New Hesperides and Other Poems* (1911), *Poems* (1924), etc. His brother ¶Arthur Barnett (1878–1971) was president of the National Association for the Advancement of Colored People (1940–65).

Spi·no·la \'spē-nō-lä\, Ambrogio di Fi·lip·po \dē-fē-'lēp-pō\. *Span.* Ambrosio de Spí·no·la \thā-'spē-nō-lä\. Marqués de los Bal·ba·ses \thā-lōs-bäl-'bä-sās\. 1569–1630. Italian general in Spanish service. Led army to Netherlands against Maurice of Nassau (1602–09); commander of Spanish army there; captured Ostend (1604); conquered Palatinate (1620); resumed command of Spanish army in Netherlands (1621–28); dissolved Protestant Union (1621); captured Jülich (1622), Breda (1625); general and plenipotentiary in war with France over duchy of Mantua (1629–30).

Spi·no·za \spə-'nō-zə\, Baruch. *Surname also given as* de Spinoza *or* De·spi·no·za \thā-spē-'nō-zə\. *Lat.* Benedictus de Spinoza. 1632–1677. Dutch philosopher, of Portuguese-Jewish parentage. Excommunicated from the synagogue (1656); supported himself by grinding lenses; devoted himself chiefly to study of philosophy, esp. system expounded by Descartes; regarded as most eminent expounder of rational pantheism. Among his works were *Tractatus Theologico-Politicus* (1670), *Ethica Ordine Geometrico Demonstrata* (1677), and *Tractatus Politicus* (unfinished, 1677).

Spit·ta \'shpit-ä\, Julius August Philipp. 1841–1894. German music scholar. Helped found Bachverein in Leipzig (1874); professor at Berlin (1875–94); a chief founder of *Denkmäler deutscher Tonkunst* (1892). His *Johann Sebastian Bach* (1873–80) was first comprehensive work on Bach; edited works of Dietrich Buxtehude (1876–77) and Heinrich Schütz (1885–94).

Spit·te·ler \'shpit-ə-lər\, Carl. *Pseudonym* Carl Felix Tan·dem \'tän-dem\. 1845–1924. Swiss writer. Among his works were *Prometheus und Epimetheus* (epic in rhythmical prose, 1881), *Extramundana* (verse, 1883), *Schmetterlinge* (poems, 1889), *Conrad der Leutnant* (novel, 1898), *Lachende Wahrheiten* (essays, 1898), *Der Olympische Frühling* (epic, 1900–05), *Glockenlieder* (1906), *Imago* (novel, 1906), *Die Mädchenfeinde* (child's story, 1907), *Meine frühesten Erlebnisse* (story of his boyhood, 1914), and *Prometheus der Dulder* (epic, 1924). Awarded Nobel prize for literature (1919).

Spitz·weg \'shpits-vāk\, Carl. 1808–1885. German painter. Most representative of Biedermeier artists in Germany; known for humorous and detailed portrayals of small-town misfits, street musicians, postmen, lovers bidding farewell.

Spode \'spōd\, Josiah. 1754–1827. English potter. Founded a pottery factory at Stoke-on-Trent (1800); credited with introducing hybrid porcelain (made by adding bone ash to hardpaste porcelain ingredients) that became the standard English bone china (1800).

Spohr \'shpōr\, Louis, *orig.* Ludwig. 1784–1859. German violin virtuoso and composer. Orchestra director in Vienna at Theater an der Wien (1813–15); Kapellmeister at court of Kassel (1822–57). Made concert tours of Europe (from 1799), including 6 times to England; famed as violin teacher; published his violin method in *Violinschule* (1831). Composer of operas, including *Faust* (1816), *Zemire und Azor* (1819), *Jessonda* (1823), *Der Alchymist* (1830), *Die Kreuzfahrer* (1845); 10 symphonies, esp. No. 4 *Die Weihe der Töne;* 15 violin and 4 clarinet concerti; much chamber music, including 36 string quartets and a nonet; sacred and secular choral works, and songs.

Spon·ti·ni \spōn-'tē-nē\, Gaspare Luigi Pacifico. Conte di Sant' An·drea \dē-ˌsän-tän-'dre-ä\. 1774–1851. Italian composer. Composed operas in Paris (1803–20) as *La Vestale* (1807) and *Fernand Cortez* (1809; rev. 1817), and in Berlin (1820–42) as *Nurmahal* (1822) and *Agnes von Hohenstaufen* (1827); his German operas influenced the early works of Richard Wagner.

Spoo·ner \'spü-nər\, John Coit. 1843–1919. American politician, b. Lawrenceburg, Ind. Practiced law in Hudson, Wis. (from 1870); Republican member of U.S. Senate (1885–91, 1897–1907) and one of ablest members of Congress; opponent of Robert La Follette's Progressive movement in Wisconsin; practiced law in New York (from 1907).

Spooner, William Archibald. 1844–1930. English clergyman and educator. Dean (1876–89) and warden (1903–24) of New College, Oxford. An occasional lapse of speech, whereby he transposed sounds in two or more words (as *a blushing crow,* for *a crushing blow*), led to coinage of the word *spoonerism* in the English language.

Spots·wood \'späts-ˌwu̇d\, Alexander. 1676–1740. English colonial governor. Lieutenant governor of Virginia (1710–22); improved production of tobacco and favored making tobacco notes legal tender; encouraged better relations with Indians; urged construction of forts along the frontier; in conflict with his legislature over executive prerogatives. Deputy postmaster general of the American colonies (1730–39).

Spot·ted Tail \'spät-əd-ˌtāl\. *Indian name* Sinte-galeshka. 1833?–1881. American Sioux Indian chief, b. near Fort Laramie, Wyo. Advocated accommodation and compromise with whites; instrumental in causing surrender of his nephew Crazy Horse (1877); assassinated by fellow Sioux, Crow Dog.

Spot·tis·woode *or* **Spot·tis·wood** *or* **Spot·is·wood** \'spät(ə)-ˌswu̇d\ *or* **Spots·wood** \'spät-ˌswu̇d\, John. 1565–1639. Scottish prelate. Archbishop of Glasgow (1603) and member of Scots privy council (1605); James I's compliant agent in subjugating the kirk; archbishop of St. Andrews (1615); secured passage of Five Articles of Perth (1618) in interests of confirming episcopal government; chancellor of Scotland (1635–38); deposed and excommunicated by Glasgow General Assembly. Author of *History of Church of Scotland* (1655).

Sprague \'sprāg\, Frank Julian. 1857–1934. American electrical engineer and inventor, b. Milford, Conn. Assistant to Thomas Edison (1883–84); organized (1884) Sprague Electric Railway & Motor Co. to manufacture electric motors. Recognized as pioneer in modern electric trolley system as a result of his installation of first modern trolley at Richmond, Va. (1887); devised and installed high-speed and automatic electric elevators, making tall buildings practicable; invented multiple-unit system of electric train control (perfected 1895); developed high-tension direct-current electric railway system, automatic electric signal and train brake control. Considered the "father of electric traction."

Sprat \'sprat\, Thomas. 1635–1713. English prelate. A founding member and historian of the Royal Society; critic of "inkhorn terms" and advocate of a simpler style of speaking and writing. Author of *History of the Royal Society of London* (1667) and *An Account of the Life and Writings of Mr. Abraham Cowley* (1668); dean of Westminster (1683) and bishop of Rochester (1684).

Spreck·els \'sprek-əlz\, Claus. *Called* the Sugar King. 1828–1908. American sugar manufacturer, b. Lamstedt, Germany. To U.S. (1846), and San Francisco (1856); in sugar business (from 1863); secured virtual monopoly of manufacture and sale of sugar on Pacific coast; developed sugar plantations in Hawaiian Islands. His oldest son ¶John Diedrich (1853–1926) superintended family sugar properties in Hawaii (1876); founded J. D. Spreckels & Brothers Company, shipping and commission merchants (1880), operating Oceanic

Steamship Co. between Hawaii and U.S.; settled at San Diego (1887) and interested himself in its development. Associated in business with J. D. Spreckels were two of his brothers ¶Adolph Bernard (1857–1924) and ¶Rudolph (1872–1958).

Spreng·el \'shpreŋ-əl\, Christian Konrad. 1750–1816. German botanist. Discovered the part played by nectaries, insects, and the wind in the pollination of flowers; published discoveries in *Das entdeckte Geheimnis der Natur im Bau und in der Befruchtung der Blumen* (1793). His nephew ¶Kurt Polykarp Joachim Sprengel (1766–1833), physician and botanist; taught at Halle (from 1795); author of histories of medicine, esp. *Versuch einer pragmatischen Geschichte der Arzneikunde* (1792–99), works on surgery and botany, a handbook of pathology, etc.

Sprengel, Hermann Johann Philipp. 1834–1906. British chemist, b. Germany. His inventions included safety explosives and the Sprengel pump (1865), an air pump using mercury or other liquid.

Sprengt·por·ten \'spreŋ(k)t-,pȯr-tən\, Jakob Magnus. Baron. 1727–1786. Finnish soldier. Planned and led coup d'état that enabled King Gustav III to gain absolute power in Sweden (1772); promoted to lieutenant general and made director of fortification construction in Finland. His half-brother ¶Georg Magnus Sprengtporten (1740–1819), soldier and politician; involved in Jakob's coup d'état (1772); entered Russian service as a major general (1786); led Russian forces against Sweden (1788–90, 1808–09); instrumental in Russian annexation of Finland from Sweden (1809); made count (1809).

Sprigg \'sprig\, Sir John Gordon. 1830–1913. South African politician, b. Ipswich, England. Settled in Cape Colony (1861); prime minister of Cape Colony (1878–81, 1886–90, 1896–98, 1900–04).

Spring \'spriŋ\, Howard. 1889–1965. British novelist, b. Wales. Author of novels of provincial life and ambition, including *Shabby Tiger* (1934), *Rachel Rosing* (1935), *O Absalom!* (1938; American title *My Son, My Son*), *Fame is the Spur* (1940), *Hard Facts* (1944), and *The Houses in Between* (1951).

Springs \'spriŋz\, Elliot White. 1896–1959. American businessman and author, b. Lancaster, S.C. Ace pilot during World War I; succeeded his father as head of Springs Cotton Mills Co. (1931) and developed it into one of largest textile mills in U.S. Author of short stories and novels including *Warbirds* (1926), *Nocturne Militaire* (1927), *Warbirds and Ladybirds* (1931), and *Clothes Make the Man* (1948).

Sproul \'sprau̇(ə)l\, Robert Gordon. 1891–1975. American educator, b. San Francisco. President of U. of California (1930–1958) and responsible for building it up into one of world's greatest institutions.

Spru·ance \'sprü-ən(t)s\, Raymond Ames. 1886–1969. American admiral, b. Baltimore. Commissioned ensign in navy (1907); task force commander at Midway (June 1942); chief of staff to Admiral Nimitz; head of Central Pacific command (1943–44), in charge of conquest of Gilbert and Marshall Islands; admiral (1944); commander of U.S. 5th fleet (1944–45); commander in chief of U.S. Pacific fleet (1945–46); retired (1948); U.S. ambassador to the Philippines (1952–55).

Spur·geon \'spər-jən\, Caroline Frances Eleanor. 1869–1942. English educator. On staff of U. of London (lecturer, 1906–13; professor, 1913–29—first woman to hold a professorship in an English university); helped organize International Federation of University Women and was its first president (1920–24). Authority on Chaucer and Shakespeare; author of *Keats's Shakespeare* (1928), *Shakespeare's Imagery* (1935), etc.

Spurgeon, Charles Haddon. 1834–1892. English Baptist preacher. At New Park Street Chapel, London (1854); Metropolitan Tabernacle, seating 6000, built for him (1859–61), providing him a pulpit until his death. A decided Calvinist, distrusted modern biblical criticism, repudiated baptismal regeneration; published sermons weekly (collected into 50 volumes). Author of books of sayings *John Ploughman's Talks* (1869), *John Ploughman's Pictures* (1880).

Spurr \'spər\, Josiah Edward. 1870–1950. American geologist, b. Gloucester, Mass. On staff of U.S. Geological Survey (1894–1906), leading its first survey of Alaska (1895); made studies of lunar topography; developed a volcanic theory of lunar craters and was first to recognize the uniformity and extent of the overall structure in the Moon's crust in *Geology Applied to Selenology* (1944–49). Mt. Spurr in Alaska is named in his honor.

Spurstow, William. See SMECTYMNUUS.

Spurz·heim \'shpu̇rts-,hīm\, Johann Christoph. 1776–1832. German physician. Collaborated on neuroanatomical research with Franz Gall (1800–13; *q.v.*); developed Gall's theories into a complete system of phrenology and taught it widely.

Spy. See Sir Leslie WARD.

Spy·ri \'shpē-rē\, Johanna, *nee* Heus·ser \'hȯi-sər\. 1827–1901. Swiss writer. m. (1852) Bernhard Spyri; author of *Ein Blatt auf Vronys Grab* (1870), *Heidi* (1880–81), *Heimatlos* (1881), *Gritli* (1882), etc.

Squan·to \'skwän-(,)tō\. *Also called* Tis·quan·tum \tə-'skwänt-əm\. d. 1622. American Indian of the Pawtuxet tribe. Captured by expedition under John Smith (1615); sold as slave in Spain, escaped and eventually made way to England (1617) and America (1619); friendly to the whites of Plymouth colony; aided colonists by teaching them Indian methods of planting and fertilizing corn.

Squar·cio·ne \skwär-'chō-nā\, Francesco. 1394–c.1468. Italian painter. Founder of the Paduan school; works included panel paintings of a Madonna and a polyptych (1449–52), and a cycle of frescoes on exterior of S. Francesco at Padua (c.1452–66); notable chiefly as a teacher of painting; as such, exerted influence on northern Italian art; known particularly as the teacher of Andrea Mantegna.

Squibb \'skwib\, Edward Robinson. 1819–1900. American physician and manufacturer, b. Wilmington, Del. Founded Squibb chemical and pharmaceutical laboratory, Brooklyn, N.Y. (1858); admitted sons to partnership and changed firm name to E. R. Squibb & Sons (1892).

Squibob. See George Horatio DERBY.

Squier \'skwī(ə)r\, Ephraim George. 1821–1888. American diplomat and archaeologist, b. Bethlehem, N.Y. With Edwin H. Davis (*q.v.*) made first major exploration of earthworks of the Mound Builders in Ohio (1845–47), publishing findings in *Ancient Monuments of the Mississippi Valley* (1848); studied similar mounds in New York and published *Aboriginal Monuments of the State of New York* (1851); carried out expeditions in Central America, Peru, Bolivia in attempt to find origins of the Mound Builders; U.S. commissioner to Peru (1863–65); also published *Nicaragua* (1852), *The States of Central America* (1858), and *Peru* (1877).

Squire \'skwī(ə)r\, Sir John Collings. 1884–1958. English journalist and writer. Founder and editor (1919–34) of *London Mercury;* a leading poet of the Georgian school of pastoral poetry. Author of *Imaginary Speeches* (1912), *The Three Hills and Other Poems* (1913), *The Birds, and Other Poems* (1919), *Collected Parodies* (1921), *Essays on Poetry* (1924), *Apes and Parrots* (1928), *Sunday Mornings* (1930), *The Honeysuckle and the Bee* (1937), *Water Music* (1939), etc.

Squires \'skwī(ə)rz\, Sir Richard Anderson. 1880–1940. Canadian politician, b. Harbour Grace, Nfld. Elected to Newfoundland House of Assembly (1909); served on Legislative Council (1914–19); minister of justice and attorney general (1914–17); colonial secretary (1917–18); prime minister of Newfoundland (1919–23, 1928–32); promoted education and industrial development; gained reputation for extravagance and corruption.

Srong-brt-san-sgam-po \'srȯŋ-bərt-'sän-'skäm-'pō\. c.608–650. King of Tibet (629–650). Extended his rule to Nepal and parts of India and China; commissioned the creation of the Tibetan written language; credited with introducing Buddhism into Tibet; built the Gtsug-lag-khang temple in Lhasa; his reign marked the beginning of recorded history in Tibet.

Ssu of Ch'en, Prince. See Ts'ao Chih under TS'AO TS'AO.

Ssu-ma Ch'ien \'sü-'mä-chē-'(y)en\. c.145–c.185 B.C. Chinese historian. Succeeded his father Ssu-ma T'an as court historian (108); spent many years in compiling the *Shih-chi* ("Historical Memoirs"), a model for all later dynastic histories of China; also helped reform (105) the Chinese calendar, determining the system of chronology still in use.

Ssu-ma Hsiang-ju \-shē-'äŋ-'zhü\. 179–117 B.C. Chinese poet. Served at courts of Ching I (to 146), Prince Hsiao of Liang (146–144), and Wu (from 141); author of *fu* (a form of descriptive poetry), including "Tzu Hsü fu" ("Master Nil") and "Shang-lin fu" ("Supreme Park"), both on the joys of hunting.

Ssu-ma Kuang \-'gwäŋ\. 1019–1086. Chinese historian. Held high office in government; led opposition to radical reforms of Wang An-shih (1069–85); as leading minister of government, attempted to repeal all of Wang's measures (1085–86). Compiled (1066–84) the *Tzu-chih t'ung-chien* ("Comprehensive Mirror for Aid in Government"), a history of China from 403 B.C. to 959 A.D., considered one of greatest historical works in Chinese.

Ssu-ma T'an \-'tän\. d. 110 B.C. Chinese scholar. Grand historian at the Han court (140–110); collected much of the material used by his son Ssu-ma Ch'ien, the historian.

Ssu-ma Yen \-'yən\. *Posthumous title* Wu Ti \'wü-'tē\. 236–290. Founder and first emperor (265–290) of the Western Chin dynasty. Scion of the Ssu-ma clan; became most powerful general of the Wei dynasty; usurped the Wei throne and founded the Chin dynasty (265); conquered southern kingdom of Wu, thus reuniting China (280); disbanded his armies; attempted to reform government; unsuccessfully attempted to break power of great landowners; divided his domain into principalities for each of his 25 sons.

Ssu Tsung. See Chu Yu-chien under CHU family.

Sta·bi·li \stä-'bē-lē\, Francesco. *Known as* Cecco d'As·co·li \dä-'skō-lē\. 1269–1327. Italian poet and astrologer, b. Ascoli. Taught astrology at various Italian cities, finally at Bologna (1322–24); expelled for heresy (1324); became astrologer to Duke Carlo de Calabria of Florence; burned at stake by the Inquisition for heresy. Author of astrological works as *Tractus in sphaeram* and *De principiis astrologiae,* and of *L'acerba,* an encyclopedic poem attacking Dante's *Divina commedia.*

Sta·di·on-Wart·hau·sen \'shtä-dē-ōn-'värt-,haù-zən\, Johann Philipp Karl von. Graf. 1763–1824. Austrian politician. Served in imperial Privy Council (1783–87); to counter Napoléon, urged a union of Austria, Prussia, and Russia; minister of foreign affairs (1805–09); led Austria to join anti-French coalition (1813); president of the exchequer (1814); minister of finance (from 1816); established a national bank and introduced uniform land taxation.

Staël \stäl\, Anne-Louise-Germaine de, *nee* Nec·ker \ne-ker\. Baronne de Staël-Hols·tein \-öl-sten\. *Called* Madame de Staël. 1766–1817. French writer. Daughter of Jacques and Suzanne Necker (*qq.v.*); m. (1786) Baron Erik de Staël-Holstein, Swedish minister to Paris (d. 1802). Fled from France during the Revolution; on return to Paris (1794) maintained a salon for leading intellectuals of the day; had love affair with Benjamin Constant (1794–1808); exiled by Napoléon (1803); friend of Schlegel (from 1804) and Lord Byron (1816); returned to France (1815). Among her works were *Lettres sur le caractère et les écrits de J. J. Rousseau* (1788), *De l'influence des passions sur le bonheur des individus et des nations* (1796), *De la littérature* (1800), novels *Delphine* (1802) and *Corinne* (1807), memoirs *De l'Allemagne* (1810), *Dix années d'exil* (1821).

Stael \stäl\, Nicolas de. 1914–1955. French painter, b. Russia. Associated with the School of Paris; known for abstract, polychromatic still lifes and landscapes.

Staff \'stäf\, Leopold. 1878–1957. Polish poet and playwright. Associated with Young Poland movement; author of plays and over 30 volumes of poetry, including *Sny o potędze* (1901), *Dzień duszy* (1903), *Ucho igielne* (1927), *Wilkina* (1954).

Stafford, Marquis of. See LEVESON-GOWER.

Staf·ford \'staf-ərd\, Sir Edward William. 1819–1901. New Zealand politician, b. Scotland. To N.Z. (1843); prime minister and colonial secretary (1856–61); created three new provinces; established itinerant courts and native juries; again prime minister (1865–69, 1872); returned to England (1874).

Stafford, Humphrey. 1st Duke of Buck·ing·ham \'bək-iŋ-əm, *US also* -,ham\. 1402–1460. English soldier. Member of council of Henry VI (from 1424); campaigned in France (1430–32) and Flanders (1436); captain of Calais (1442); created duke (1444); warden of Cinque Ports (1450); killed at battle of Northampton. His grandson ¶Henry (c.1454–1483), 2d duke; as a Lancastrian, excluded from most public activities during Edward IV's reign; aided Duke of Gloucester usurp throne as Richard III (1483); publicly denied legitimacy of Edward IV's heirs and exhorted the people to accept Gloucester; raised force against Richard but was captured and executed at Salisbury. His son ¶Edward (1478–1521), 3d duke; privy councilor (1509); condemned and executed on trumped-up charges of disloyalty to Henry VIII.

Stafford, Humphrey. Earl of Dev·on \'dev-ən\. 1439–1469. English knight. Held several posts, including constable of Bristol (1461) and Bridgwater Castle (1465); privy councilor (1469); sent by Edward IV against the Yorkshire rebel known as Robin of Redesdale; after quarrel with Earl of Pembroke, withdrew with his troops; executed.

Stagg \'stag\, Amos Alonzo. 1862–1965. American football coach, b. West Orange, N.J. Member of Walter Camp's first All-America football team (1889); had longest coaching career (1889–1960), including head coach at U. of Chicago (1892–1932) and College of the Pacific (1933–46); developed the huddle (also credited to Bob Zuppke), end-around play, the shift, man in motion, tackling dummy for practice; his record of 314 career victories stood until 1981; called "the grand old man of football."

Stag·ne·li·us \stäŋ-'nā-lē-əs\, Erik Johan. 1793–1823. Swedish poet. Civil servant in Stockholm; his life and works marked by a conflict between strong erotic impulses and a radically ascetic religious position. Works included epic *Wladimir den store* (1817), religious lyrics *Liljor i Saron* (1821), dramas *Martyrerna* (1821) and *Backanterna* (1822).

Stahl \'shtäl\, Friedrich Julius. 1802–1861. German lawyer and Lutheran churchman. Defended connection between church and state; chief work *Die Philosophie des Rechts nach geschichtlicher Ansicht* (1830–37).

Stahl, George Ernst. 1660–1734. German physician and chemist. Professor at Halle (1694–1715); physician in Berlin to King Frederick William (1715–34); using Johann Becher's theories of combustion, originated phlogiston theory to explain combustion; enunciated in *Theoria medica vera* (1707) doctrine of vitalism.

Ståhl·berg \'stól-,berʸ\, Kaarlo Juho. 1865–1952. Finnish politician. Professor at Helsinki (1908–18); member of Finnish Diet (1908–17); drafted (1917) the basis of the constitution of 1919. After Finland gained its independence, elected (1919) first president of the republic; retired at end of presidential term (1925).

Stai·ner *or* **Stei·ner** \'shtī-nər\, Jakob. 1617?–1683. Austrian violin maker. Made violins based on German models and noted for their silvery tone.

Stai·ner \'stā-nər\, Sir John. 1840–1901. English organist and composer. Organist, St. Paul's Cathedral (1872–88); helped found Musical Association (1874); professor, Oxford (1889–99). Composer of oratorios, esp. *The Crucifixion* (1887), cantatas, anthems, church services, hymn tunes, madrigals, and songs. A pioneer of English musicology; published *Dufay and His Contemporaries* (1898) and *Early Bodleian Music* (1901).

Stair, Viscounts and earls of. See DALRYMPLE family.

Sta·kha·nov \(,)stə-'kä-nəf\, Aleksey Grigoriyevich. 1905–1977. Soviet coal miner. Initiated (1935) the Stakhanov movement for speeding up production by encouraging individual initiative and by increased pay for notable efficiency.

Sta·lin \'stäl-yin\, Joseph. *Orig.* Iosif Vissarionovich Dzhu·ga·shvi·li \jü-(,)gəsh-'vyēl-yi\. 1879–1953. Soviet political leader, b. Georgia. Joined Social Democratic party; sided with Bolsheviks after party split (1903); repeatedly exiled to Siberia for political activity (1904–17); became close associate of Lenin; took part in October revolution (1917). Member of revolutionary military council (1920–23); people's commissar for nationalities (1921–23); general secretary of Central Committee of Communist party (1922–53). After Lenin's death (1924), eliminated opposition of Trotsky, Zinovyev, Kamenev, Bukharin, Rykov, and others, and established himself as virtual dictator. Important events under his leadership included: development of Russian industry and agriculture under the "Five-Year plans" (from 1928); purges of Communist party and Russian army (1934–38); nonaggression pact with Germany (1939); annexation of eastern Poland after German invasion of Poland (1939); war with Finland (1939–40); annexation of Latvia, Estonia, Lithuania, and Bessarabia (1940). Following German invasion of Russia (June 1941), became commissar for defense and chairman of the Council of People's Commissars, thus taking over direction of military operations; conferred with Roosevelt and Churchill at Tehran (1943) and Yalta (1945) and with Truman, Churchill, and Attlee at Potsdam, Ger. (1945). After World War II, established Soviet hegemony in Eastern Europe, continued domestic repressive measures, and built up the Soviet Union as a rival to U.S. for world leadership.

Stal·lings \'stól-iŋz\, Laurence Tucker, Jr. 1894–1968. American playwright, b. Macon, Ga. Author of *Plumes* (novel, 1924), the plays *What Price Glory?* (with Maxwell Anderson, 1924), *The Buccaneer* (1925), *First Flight* (1925), *Deep River* (1926), and screenplays.

Stam·bo·liy·ski \,stäm-bó-'lē-skē\, Aleksandŭr. 1879–1923. Bulgarian politician. Became editor of Agrarian League's organ (1902); entered (1908) National Assembly as head of the Agrarian Union (Peasant party); during World War I supported Allies against King Ferdinand; imprisoned (1915–18); led insurrection which forced Ferdinand's abdication and proclaimed a republic (1918); monarchy later restored under Boris III. Prime minister of Bulgaria (1919–23); signed Treaty of Neuilly (1919); redistributed land to the peasants; reformed judicial system; favored universal suffrage and local self-government; attempted to found a South Slav federation in the Balkans and to initiate a "Green International" peasant alliance; overthrown and executed by a military coup.

Stam·bo·lov \,stäm-bó-'lóf\, Stefan Nikolov. 1854–1895. Bulgarian politician. Fought against Turkish rule; president of the Sobranye (1884–86); member of board of regency (1886–87); premier (1887–94); ruled despotically; opposed Russian influence and favored rapprochement with Turkey; assassinated.

Sta·mitz \'shtä-mits\, Johann Wenzel Anton, *orig.* Jan Václav Antonín. 1717–1757. Bohemian violinist and composer. Founder of Mannheim school; concertmaster of court orchestra at Mannheim (from 1745); contributed to development of sonata and symphony forms; composer of symphonies, concertos, sonatas, violin works, and harpsichord music. His son ¶Carl Philipp (1745–1801) played violin in the Mannheim court orchestra (1762–70); toured England and Russia; in service of Duke Louis of Noailles in Paris (1771–c.77); orchestra conductor at Jena (from 1794); composed symphonies, concertos and concertante works, quartets, trios, sonatas. His brother ¶Anton Thadäus Johann Nepomuk (1750–between 1789 and 1809) also played violin with the Mannheim orchestra (1764–70); moved to Paris with Carl and settled there (1770); composed symphonies, concertos, quartets, and sonatas.

Stamm·ler \'shtäm-lər\, Rudolf. 1856–1938. German legal philosopher. Professor at Halle (1885–1916), Berlin (1916–23); exerted wide influence in Germany, Spain, Latin America. Author of *Die Lehre von dem richtigen Rechte* (1902), *Theorie der Rechtswissenschaft* (1911), etc. His son ¶Wolfgang (1886–1965), philologist and literary historian; taught at Dorpat (1918–24), Greifswald (1924–36), Freiburg (1951–57); author of *Die deutsche Literatur des Mittelalterische Verfasserlexikon* (1933–55; with K. Langosch), etc.

Stämp·fli \'stemp-flē\, Jacob. 1820–1879. Swiss politician. Served in National Assembly (1848–54; president, 1851); elected to Bundesrat (1854); president of Swiss confederation (1856, 1859, 1862); headed departments of justice (1855), finance (1857, 1858), military (1860, 1861, 1863); led unsucessful attempt to nationalize railways (1862); prominent in Bernese politics (after 1863); again in National Assembly (from 1875).

Standaert. See Pieter van BLOEMEN.

Standish, Burt L. See Gilbert PATTEN.

Stan·dish \'stan-dish\, Myles *or* Miles. 1584?–1656. American colonist, b. Lancashire, England. Soldier of fortune in the Netherlands; accompanied Pilgrims to America on the *Mayflower* (1620); appointed captain, treated with the Indians, and superintended defenses of the colony. Served as agent in England for the colonists (1625–26), negotiating for ownership of their land and for supplies. Rose to place of leadership in colony; treasurer (1644–49); member of the governor's council for 29 years. With John Alden founded Duxbury, Mass. (1631) and resided there until his death. No historical basis exists for the tale of John Alden's proposal to Priscilla Mullens on behalf of Standish, as narrated in Longfellow's *The Courtship of Miles Standish.*

Stan·ford \'stan-fərd\, Sir Charles Villiers. 1852–1924. British composer, conductor, and teacher, b. Dublin. Conductor of Bach Choir (1885–1902), Leeds Philharmonic Society, and Leeds Music Festival (1901–10); professor at Royal College of Music, London (1883–1924) and at Cambridge (1887–1924); his pupils included Vaughn Williams, Bliss, Holst. Composer of operas, symphonies, orchestral works, esp. the 5 *Irish Rhapsodies,* oratorios, chamber music, cantatas, song cycles, etc.

Stanford, Leland, *in full* Amasa Leland. 1824–1893. American railroad builder and politician, b. Watervliet, N.Y. To California (1852); engaged in selling miners' supplies and other merchandise; governor of California (1861–63). Identified especially with promoting and financing Central Pacific Railroad (built 1863–69), western link in transcontinental line; president and director, Central Pacific Railroad (1863–93) and Southern Pacific (1885–90); U.S. senator (1885–93). In memory of his son Leland, Jr. (1869–1884), founded Leland Stanford Junior University, now Stanford Univ. (1885; opened 1891).

Stang \'stäŋ\, Frederick. 1808–1884. Norwegian jurist and politician. Appointed minister of interior (1845); with A.M. Schweigaard led transition of Norwegian economy into a capitalist system; favored continuance of Swedish–Norwegian union; first minister of state (1872–80).

Stan·hope \'stan-əp\. Name of English family descended from Philip Stanhope (1584–1656), 1st Earl of Chesterfield, and including among its members the earls Stanhope:

¶James (1673–1721), 1st earl; grandson of 1st Earl of Chesterfield; M.P. (1701–17); assisted Peterborough at Barcelona (1705); minister to Spain (1706); commander in chief in Spain (1708); won cavalry action at Almenar and victory at Saragossa (1710); forced to capitulate at Brihuega (1710). Leader of Whig opposition in House of Commons (1712); secretary of state for southern department (1714, 1718); directed suppression of Jacobite uprising (1715); first lord of treasury and chancellor of exchequer (1717); created Viscount Stanhope of Ma·hon \mə-'hün, -'hōn\ (1717) and Earl Stanhope (1718); negotiated quadruple alliance against Spain (1718) and compelled Spain to abandon plan of conquest (1719); partly responsible for South Sea Bubble, but did not profit from it.

His grandson ¶Charles (1753–1816), 3d earl, *called* Lord Mahon (1763–86); M.P. (1780), supported administration of 2d William Pitt, whose sister, Lady Hester Pitt, he married (1774); advocated discontinuance of war against American colonies and parliamentary reform (1781); broke with Pitt over French Revolution; chairman of Revolution Society, favoring French republicans; attacked suspension (1794) of Habeas Corpus Act, Anglo-Irish parliamentary unification (1800), and slave trade in British colonies. Spent great deal on scientific research and experimentation; constructed calculating machines (c.1777); perfected a process of stereotyping acquired by Clarendon Press, Oxford (1805); invented a monochord for tuning musical instruments, a steam carriage, first hand-operated iron printing press (1798), and a microscopic lens bearing his name. Author of *Principles of Electricity* (1779).

Charles's daughter ¶Lady Hester Lucy (1776–1839) left England forever (1810); settled among Druses on Mt. Lebanon (1814); adopted eastern manners, practiced astrology, held imperious ascendancy over tribes as a prophetess; intrigued against British consuls; deserted by followers and robbed, finished life in wretchedness.

¶Philip Henry (1805–1875), 5th earl, *better known by courtesy title* Lord Mahon; grandson of 3d earl; M.P. (1830); secured passage of bill amending copyright law (1842); obtained parliamentary grant for founding National Portrait Gallery, subsequently created by his executors; aided establishment of Historical Manuscripts Commission (1869); president of Society of Antiquaries (from 1846). Author of *History of War of Succession in Spain* (1832), *History of England from the Peace of Utrecht to the Peace of Versailles* (1836–54), *Life of William Pitt* (1861–62), and *Reign of Queen Anne* (1870). See Kaspar HAUSER.

Stanhope, Philip Dormer. 4th Earl of Ches·ter·field \'ches-tər-ˌfēld\. 1694–1773. English politician and letter-writer. Related to Stanhope family; Whig M.P. (1716–26); ambassador to Holland (1728–32, 1744); strong opponent of Walpole; as lord lieutenant of Ireland (1745–46), established schools, encouraged manufacturing, conciliated Orangemen and Catholics; secretary of state (1746–48); intimate of Pope, Swift, Voltaire; patron of letters, but repudiated by Samuel Johnson (1755). Author of political tracts and contributions to *The World* (1753–56); distinguished as wit, conversationalist, epigrammatist; best known as writer, to his natural son Philip Stanhope (1732–1768), of *Letters to His Son* (1774), shrewd, witty, exquisitely phrased guides to manners and arts of pleasing and of worldly success; also wrote similar *Letters to His Godson.*

Sta·ni·slav·sky \stən-yi-'släf-skəi; *Angl* ˌstan-ə-'slaf-skē, -'slav-\, Konstantin. *Orig.* Konstantin Sergeyevich Alek·se·yev \əl-yik-'syā-yəf\. 1863–1938. Russian actor, director, and producer. With Vladimir Nemirovich-Danchenko, founded (1897) Moscow Art Theater and produced plays, esp. Chekhov's *Seagull* (1898) and Gorky's *Lower Depths* (1902); also manager and leading actor of the company; headed Bolshoi Opera Studio (1918; later named for him); published autobiography *My Life in Art* (1924); founded Opera Drama Studio (1935); best known for his innovative "method" system of acting.

Sta·ni·sław \stá-'nē-slåf\. Saint. *Lat.* Stan·is·laus \'stan-ə-ˌslós\. 1030–1079. Polish prelate. Of noble birth; bishop of Kraków (1072); joined opposition against King Bolesław II of Poland; murdered by Bolesław; first Pole to be canonized (1253); patron saint of Poland.

Stanisław. Name of two kings of Poland:

Stanisław I Lesz·czyń·ski \lesh-'chinʸ-skē\. 1677–1766. King (1704–09, 1733–35). Opposed Augustus II of Saxony and Poland; secured support of Charles XII of Sweden, who had him chosen king (1704–09); defeated by Augustus after Charles lost battle of Poltava (1709); governor of Zweibrücken in Palatinate (1718–25). Daughter Maria became wife of Louis XV of France (1725); through this alliance restored to throne of Poland at death of Augustus II (1733); War of Polish Succession (1733–35) followed; driven out (1735–36) by Augustus III, supported by Russia; received duchies of Lorraine and Bar (1737) and received pension from France; maintained court at Lunéville and Nancy; promoted economic development and encouraged letters.

Stanisław II Augustus Po·nia·tow·ski \pón-yá-'tóf-skē\. 1732–1798. Last independent king of Poland (1764–95). Son of Stanisław Poniatowski; sent to Russian court at St. Petersburg (1757); became a romantic favorite of future Catherine II; through her influence made king (1764); unsuccessfully attempted to increase his royal power and effect government reforms; also unsuccessful in attempts to stop partitions of Poland by Russia, Prussia, and Austria (1772, 1793, 1795); resigned at third partition.

Stan·ley \'stan-lē\. English family holding earldom of Der·by \'där-bē, *chiefly US* 'dər-\. Founded by Sir John Stanley (1350?–1414), lieutenant in Ireland under Richard II, Henry IV, Henry V; granted Isle of Man (1405; held in family till 1736). His grandson ¶Thomas (1406?–1459), 1st Baron Stanley (cr. 1456), was lieutenant governor of Ireland (1431–37), lord chamberlain and privy councilor (1455).

¶Thomas Stanley (1435?–1504), 2d Baron Stanley and 1st Earl of Derby; son of 1st baron; m. Eleanor Neville, daughter of Yorkist leader; made chief justice of Cheshire and Flint by Edward IV (1461); held commands in France (1475) and Scotland (1482); m. (c.1482) Margaret Beaufort, Countess of Richmond and Derby; confirmed in all his offices and created earl of Derby (1485) by his wife's son Henry VII, despite his remaining neutral at Bosworth, where his brother ¶Sir William (d. 1495), justiciar of North Wales, saved the day for Richmond (Henry VII), later becoming lord chamberlain (1485).

¶James Stanley (1607–1651), 7th earl, *styled* Lord Strange \'strānj\ (till 1642), known as the "Great Earl of Derby"; fought on Royalist side through Civil War; joined Charles II at Worcester (1651); captured and executed.

¶Edward George Geoffrey Smith Stanley (1799–1869), 14th earl, *styled* Lord Stanley (till 1851); M.P. (1820); as chief secretary for Ireland (1830–33), supported Reform Bill and carried first national education bill; as colonial secretary (1833–34, 1841–44), carried act freeing slaves in West Indies; forced Whigs to modify proposals for Irish disendowment (1835); formed Protectionist ministry (Feb. 1852), but resigned after defeat on budget (Dec.); opposed Palmerston's foreign policy (1855–58); as prime minister again (1858–59), settled disputes with France and Naples and difficulties with America over right of search; refused crown of Greece (1863); as prime minister a third time (1866–68), carried parliamentary Reform Act of 1867; resigned in favor of Disraeli; made last speech in opposition to Irish disestablishment. One of greatest parliamentary orators; an accomplished classical scholar, translated the *Iliad* into blank verse (1864).

¶Edward Henry Smith Stanley (1826–1893), 15th earl; son of 14th earl; politician; Conservative M.P. (1848); as secretary for India (1858–59), carried measure transferring government of India to the crown; foreign secretary (1866–68, 1874–78); colonial secretary (1882–85); joined Liberal Unionist party (1886); its leader in House of Lords (1886–91). His brother ¶Frederick Arthur Stanley (1841–1908), 16th earl; secretary of state for war (1878–80); colonial secretary (1885–86); president of board of trade (1886–88); created Baron Stanley of Preston (1886); governor general of Canada (1888–93); first lord mayor of Liverpool (1895–96).

Stanley, Francis Edgar (1849–1918) and his twin brother Freelan O. (1849–1940). American inventors and manufacturers, b. Kingfield, Me. In collaboration, invented (1883) a photographic dry plate process and operated (1883–1905) a firm to manufacture the plates; built (1897) a steam-powered automobile; founded and directed (1902–17) Stanley Motor Co. to produce "Stanley Steamers"; broke world's record for fastest mile (28.2 seconds) in a steam car (1906).

Stanley, Sir Henry Morton. *Orig.* John Row·lands \'rō-lən(d)z\. 1841–1904. British journalist and explorer, b. Wales. Shipped as cabin boy from Liverpool to New Orleans (1858); adopted by New Orleans merchant Henry Morton Stanley and given his name (1859); served in Confederate army (1861–62); enlisted in U.S. navy (1864). Newspaper correspondent (from 1865) in Asia Minor (1866), Ethiopia and Crete (1868), Spain (1869). Commissioned (1869) by James Gordon Bennett of the New York *Herald* to lead expedition into central Africa to find David Livingstone (*q.v.*); after great difficulties reached Livingstone (Nov. 1871), greeting him with the famous remark "Dr. Livingstone, I presume?" Published *How I Found Livingstone* (1872). Led exploring expedition into Africa (1874–77); traced southern sources of the Nile River, circumnavigated Lake Victoria, discovered Lake Edward, surveyed Lake Tanganyika, and descended the Congo from Nyangwe to its mouth at Boma. Published *Through the Dark Continent* (1878). In service of King Leopold of Belgium, again went to Africa (1879–84) and opened up Congo region, establishing trading stations and building communication lines; on basis of his work Congo Free State was organized. Published *The Congo and the Founding of its Free State* (1885). Led final expedition to Africa (1887–89) to rescue Emin Paşa (*q.v.*); discovered the "Mountains of the Moon" (Ruwenzori) and traced the Semliki River to its source in Lake Edward. Published *In Darkest Africa* (1890). Became repatriated British subject (1892) and an M.P. (1895–1900). Additional works: *My Early Travels and Adventures in America and Asia* (1895), *Through South Africa* (1898).

Stanley, Thomas. 1625–1678. English scholar. Published translations of Tasso, Petrarch, Lope de Vega, and Greek and Latin poets; author of *History of Philosophy* (1655–62); edited Aeschylus with Latin translation and commentary (1663–64).

Stanley, Wendell Meredith. 1904–1971. American biochemist, b. Ridgeville, Ind. With Rockefeller Inst. for Med. Research (1932–48); professor at U. of Calif., Berkeley (1948–71); worked on purification and crystallization of viruses, thus demonstrating their molecular structure; crystallized tobacco mosaic virus (1935); also studied influenza viruses, for which he developed a preventive vaccine; corecipient (with John H. Northrop and James B. Sumner) of 1946 Nobel prize for chemistry.

Stanley, William. 1858–1916. American electrical engineer and inventor, b. Brooklyn, N.Y. Best known for his invention of the transformer (1885); first to install an alternating-current distribution system (1886, at Great Barrington, Mass.); also invented two-phase motors, generators, and a type of alternating-current watt-hour meter using magnetic suspension of its moving parts.

Stan·ton \'stant-ᵊn\, Edwin McMasters. 1814–1869. American lawyer and public official, b. Steubenville, Ohio. U.S. attorney general (1860–61); U.S. secretary of war (1862–68), guiding the war department through the Civil War. After death of Lincoln, opposed Johnson's policies and intrigued with Radical Republicans against him. Suspended by Johnson (Aug. 1867); restored by act of U.S. Senate (Jan. 1868); dismissed by Johnson (Feb. 1868); refused to leave office and was supported in his act by the Senate. Impeachment charges were brought against President Johnson because of his dismissal of Stanton; when these charges failed, Stanton resigned (May 1868). Appointed associate justice, U.S. Supreme Court (1869), but died before he could take his seat.

Stanton, Elizabeth, *nee* Ca·dy \'kād-ē\. 1815–1902. American woman suffrage leader, b. Johnstown, N.Y. m. (1840) Henry B. Stanton; organized (with Lucretia Mott) first woman's rights convention, Seneca Falls, N.Y. (July 1848), thus launching the woman suffrage movement. Associated with Susan B. Anthony in the movement (from 1851). First president, National Woman Suffrage Association (1869–90). Compiler, with Susan B. Anthony and Matilda Gage, of *History of Woman Suffrage* (1881–86). See Harriot BLATCH.

Stanton, Frank Lebby. 1857–1927. American journalist and poet, b. Charleston, S.C. On staff of *Atlanta Constitution* (from 1889); published *Songs of A Day and Songs of the Soil* (1892), *Songs from Dixie Land* (1900), *Up from Georgia* (1902), *Frank L. Stanton's Just from Georgia* (1927), etc.

Stan·y·hurst \'stan-ē-ˌhərst\, Richard. 1547–1618. Irish historian and translator. Contributed *Description of Ireland* and *History of Ireland* to Holinshed's *Chronicles* (1577); translated first four books of *Aeneid* into English hexameters (1582) in accordance with Gabriel Harvey's theory of quantitative verse.

Sta·ple·don \'stā-pəl-dən\, Sir Reginald George. 1882–1960. English agriculturalist. Professor at University Coll. of Wales and director of Welsh Plant Breeding Station (1919–42); pioneer in development of grassland science; did research on growing of grass, crop rotation; developed and improved strains of oats, clover, and other grasses.

Sta·ple·ton \'stā-pəl-tən\, Thomas. 1535–1598. English theologian and controversialist in Latin. Remembered for his English prose translations of Bede's works and for his life of Thomas More (in *Tres Thomae*, 1588).

Sta·rab·ba \stä-'räb-bä\, Antonio. Marchese di Ru·di·ni \rü-'dē-nē\. 1839–1908. Italian politician. Joined revolution against Bourbon kings of Naples (1859); appointed mayor of Palermo (1864) and prefect of Naples (1868); minister of interior (1869). Premier (1891–92, 1896–98); during 2d term concluded peace with Ethiopia and ceded Kassala to Great Britain.

Star·hem·berg \'shtär-əm-ˌberk\, Ernst Rüdiger von. Fürst. 1899–1956. Austrian politician. Became head of the Heimwehr (1930); vice chancellor under Dollfuss and Schuschnigg (1934–36) and minister for security (1934–35); became head of Vaterländische Front (1934); escaped after Nazi occupation of Austria (1938); served in British and Free French air forces; to Argentina (1942–55); returned to Austria.

Stark \'stärk\, Harold Raynsford. 1880–1972. American naval officer, b. Wilkes-Barre, Pa. Chief, Bureau of Ordnance (1934–37); commander, cruiser division of U.S. fleet (1937–39); admiral (1939); chief of naval operations (1939–42); commander in European waters (1942–45); retired (1946).

Stark \'shtark\, Johannes. 1874–1957. German physicist. Professor at Greifswald (1917–20) and Würzburg (1920–22); president of Reich Physical-Technical Inst. (1933–39); discovered Doppler effect in canal rays (1905) and Stark effect produced on spectrum lines by subjecting source of light to intense electric field (1913). Awarded 1919 Nobel prize for physics.

Stark \'stärk\, John. 1728–1822. American Revolutionary officer, b. Londonderry, N.H. Served in French and Indian War (1754–59); engaged at Bunker Hill (1775), in Canadian expedition (1776), at Trenton and Princeton; resigned commission (Mar. 1777); commissioned brigadier general of New Hampshire troops to aid Vermont in resisting Burgoyne; won battle of Bennington (Aug. 16, 1777); brigadier general in Continental army (Oct. 1777); commanded Northern Department; served in Rhode Island (1779) and at Battle of Springfield, N.J. (1780); member of court-martial that condemned Major André; brevetted major general (1783).

Star·key \'stär-kē\, James Sullivan. *Pseudonym* Seumas O'Sul·li·van \ō-'səl-ə-vən\. 1879–1958. Irish poet. Founder (1923) and editor of *Dublin Magazine*. Author of volumes of poems *The Twilight People* (1905), *The Lamplighter* (1929), *Dublin Poems* (1946), etc., and essays including *Mud and Purple* (1917), *The Rose and Bottle* (1946).

Star·ley \'stär-lē\, James. 1830–1881. English inventor. Engaged in manufacture of sewing machines and bicycles at Coventry (from 1857); invented several kinds of sewing machines; his bicycle improvements (from 1868) rendered the bicycle suitable for general use and included the tangentially spoked wheel (1874) and the differential gear used with chain drive (1877); his designs included the Coventry or "C" spring (c.1868), the Ariel, often considered the first true bicycle (1871), and the Coventry tricycle (1876); considered father of the bicycle industry.

Star·ling \'stär-liŋ\, Ernest Henry. 1866–1927. English physiologist. Professor, University Coll., London (1899–1923). Investigated lymph secretions; formulated (1896) Starling's equilibrium explaining balance in the capillary wall between intravascular pressure and osmotic forces; collaborated with William Bayliss on demonstration of the peristaltic wave in the digestive process (1899) and discovery of secretin (1912); coined term hormone (1905); formulated (1918) Starling's law of the heart which states that the force of muscular contraction is directly proportional to the extent to which the muscle is stretched; also studied kidney functions. Chief work *Principles of Human Physiology* (1912).

Starr \'stär\, Belle, *in full* Myra Belle, *nee* Shirley. 1848–1889. American outlaw, b. in or near Carthage, Mo. Bore a child by Cole Younger (c.1869); operated a livery stable in Dallas, often dealing in stolen horses; m. (1880) Sam Starr (d. 1887), a Cherokee Indian; settled near present Eufala, Okla., her cabin becoming a favorite hideout for outlaws, including Jesse James; her reputation as a mastermind of an outlaw gang is apparently apocryphal; shot and killed.

Starr, Ellen Gates. 1860–1940. American social worker, b. near Laona, Ill. Cofounder with Jane Addams of Hull-House in Chicago (1889); involved in trade union activities.

Star·rett \'star-ət\, Paul. 1866–1957. American building contractor, b. Lawrence, Kans. As president of George A. Fuller Co. (1903–22) responsible for erection in New York of the Flatiron Building, Pennsylvania Station, Plaza Hotel; as founder (1922) and president of Starrett Brothers, erected McGraw-Hill Building (1931) and the Empire State Building (1931), also in New York.

Stas \stäs\, Jean-Servais. 1813–1891. Belgian chemist. Professor at Brussels Military School (1840–68). Known for determinations of atomic weights; devised method for detection of vegetable alkaloids.

Sta·szic \'stä-zhēts\, Stanisław Wawrzyniec. 1755–1826. Polish writer. Foremost political writer of the Enlightenment period in Poland; worked as a geologist; in *Przestrogi dla Polski* (1790) advocated equal rights and free education for all citizens; also published philosophic poem *Rod ludzki* (1816–20) and a translation of the *Iliad*.

Sta·ti·us \'stā-sh(ē-)əs\, Publius Papinius. c.45–96 A.D. Roman poet. At court of Emperor Domitian; author of lyric verse collected under title *Silvae*, including elegies, odes, and poems in praise of the emperor, and of the epics *Thebaid* and *Achilleid* (cut short in 2d book by the poet's death).

Statius Caecilius. See CAECILIUS.

Stat·ler \'stat-lər\, Ellsworth Milton. 1863–1928. American hotel proprietor, b. Somerset Co., Pa. Started (1904) chain of Statler luxury hotels, with hotels in Buffalo, St. Louis, Cleveland, Detroit, Boston, and took over management of Hotel Pennsylvania in New York.

Stau·ding·er \'shtaü-diŋ-ər\, Hermann. 1881–1965. German chemist. Professor at Freiburg (1926–51); known for studies of polymers, including proof that they are formed by chemical interaction and not simply by physical aggregation. Awarded Nobel prize for chemistry (1953).

Staudt \'shtaüt\, Karl Georg Christian von. 1798–1867. German mathematician. Professor at Erlangen (1835–67); developed first complete theory of imaginary points, lines, and planes in projective geometry; also worked on properties of Bernoulli numbers; the Von Staudt-Clausen theorem is named in part for him. Published *Geometrie der Lage* (1847) and *Beiträge zur Geometrie der Lage* (1856–60).

Stauf·fen·berg \'shtaü-fən-,berk\, Claus Schenk von \'sheŋk-fön-\. Graf. 1907–1944. German soldier. Army colonel and chief of Panzer division in North Africa; assigned to Berlin reserve army staff (1943); leader of an unsuccessful attempt to assassinate Hitler at Rastenburg (July 20, 1944); executed that night.

Stau·ning \'staü-niŋ\, Thorvald. 1873–1942. Danish politician. Entered Folketing (1906); president, Socialist Democratic party (1910); premier of Denmark (1924–26, 1929–42); reformed criminal code; provided relief for farmers and the unemployed; secured passage of pioneering social welfare legislation.

Staun·ton \'stönt-ᵊn, 'stänt-\, Howard. 1810–1874. English chess player and scholar. World's chess champion (1843–51); designed (1849) chess pieces preferred for tournaments even today. Acted professionally; published edition of Shakespeare (1857–60).

Stau·pitz \'shtau-pəts\, Johann von. 1468 or 1469–1524. German clergyman. Helped found U. of Wittenberg and became its first dean of theological faculty (1502); vicar general of the German Augustinians (1503–20); unsuccessfully attempted to unite the two branches of the Augustinians; teacher and patron of Martin Luther before his break with the Roman Catholic church (from 1508); eventually condemned Luther as heretic; entered Benedictine order (1522) and later was abbot of St. Peter's Abbey.

Sta·vis·ky \stä-vē-skē\, Serge Alexandre. 1886–1934. French swindler, b. Russia. To Paris (1900); became French citizen (1914). Sold worthless bonds to workers of poorer classes; gigantic fraud discovered (Dec. 1933); fled to Chamonix; apparently committed suicide. Disclosure of frauds caused sensation in French politics, downfall of two ministries.

Stead \'sted\, William Thomas. 1849–1912. English journalist. Founded *Review of Reviews* (1890); as result of his exposure in *The Maiden Tribute of Modern Babylon* of outrages against women and children permitted by law, was imprisoned, but was instrumental in obtaining enactment of Criminal Law Amendment Act (1885). Author of *If Christ Came to Chicago* (1893) and *The Americanization of the World* (1902).

Stecchetti, Lorenzo. See Olindo GUERRINI.

Sted·man \'sted-mən\, Charles. 1753–1812. British military historian, b. Philadelphia. Served with British at Lexington and Bunker Hill; commissary to army of Sir William Howe; settled in England (1783). Author of *History of the Origin, Progress, and Termination of the American War* (1794), best contemporary British account.

Stedman, Edmund Clarence. 1833–1908. American poet and businessman, b. Hartford, Conn. Opened brokerage office in New York City (1865); member of New York Stock Exchange (1869–1900). Published *Poems Lyrical and Idyllic* (1860), *Hawthorne and Other Poems* (1877), *Mater Coronata* (1900), etc.; as critic, published *Victorian Poets* (1875) and *Poets of America* (1885), edited works of Poe and Landor, compiled anthologies.

Steeg \steg\, Théodore, *in full* Jules-Joseph-Théodore. 1868–1950. French politician. Member of Chamber of Deputies (1904–14) and the Senate (1914–40); minister of education (1911–13), of the interior (1912–20), of justice (1930), of state (1938); governor general of Algeria (1921–25) and resident general of France in Morocco (1925–29); premier of France (1930–31).

Steele \'stē(ə)l\, Sir Richard. 1672–1729. British essayist and dramatist, b. Dublin. Schoolfellow at Charterhouse of Joseph Addison (*q.v.*); in British army (1692–1705). Produced devotional manual *The Christian Hero* (1701) and three comedies, *The Funeral* (1701), *The Lying Lover* (1703), and *The Tender Husband* (1705). Held office of gazetteer (1707–10); m. (1707) Mary Scurlock, his "dear Prue." Started (1709) *The Tatler,* triweekly journal of politics and society into which, under name of Isaac Bick·er·staff \'bik-ər-,staf\, he inserted essays on manners and morality; received contributions by Addison; in conjunction with Addison, carried on *The Spectator,* in which appeared the *Sir Roger de Coverley* papers (1711–12); published other periodicals, including *The Guardian* (1713), *The Englishman* (1713–14, 1715), *The Lover* (1714), *The Reader* (1714), *Town-Talk* (1715–16), *The Theatre* (1720). Whig M.P. (1713–14, 1715–24); made governor of Drury Lane Theatre (1714); at odds with Addison (from 1719); illustrated views on dueling and respect for women in last play *Conscious Lovers* (1722).

Steele, Wilbur Daniel. 1886–1970. American writer, b. Greensboro, N.C. Author of short stories as *Land's End* (1918), *The Man Who Saw Through Heaven* (1927), *Tower of Sand* (1929); novels as *Isles of the Blest* (1924), *Diamond Wedding* (1956), and plays.

Steen \'stān\, Jan. c.1626–1679. Dutch painter. A founding member of Guild of St. Luke at Leiden (1648); pupil of Nicolaus Knupfer, Adriaen van Ostade, and Jan van Goyen. His paintings marked by humor, handling of color, and subtle capturing of facial expression; executed biblical and classical subjects, portraits, and esp. scenes of everyday life, including *Skittle Players Outside an Inn* (c.1660), *The Morning Toilet* (1663), *Merry Company* (c.1663), *The World Upside-down* (1663), *The Feast of St. Nicholas* (c.1667).

Steen \'stēn\, Marguerite. 1894–1975. English novelist. Author of *Gilt Cage* (1927), *Unicorn* (1931), *The Wise and the Foolish Virgins* (1932), *Matador* (1934), *The Lost One* (1937), *The Sun Is My Undoing* (1941), *Phoenix Rising* (1952), *A Candle in the Sun* (1964), etc.

Steensen, Niels. See STENSEN.

Steen·strup \'stin-strüp\, Johann Japetus Smith. 1813–1897. Danish zoologist. Professor at Copenhagen (1846–85); made researches on fossils, bogs, metagenesis, cephalopods.

Steen·wijk \'stān-,vīk\, Hendrik van. 1550?–1603. Dutch painter in Germany. Known esp. for paintings of interiors of Gothic churches. His son ¶Hendrik (1580?–1649) was also a painter; said to have been often employed by Vandyke to paint in architectural backgrounds of Vandyke's portraits.

Steer \'sti(ə)r\, Philip Wilson. 1860–1942. English painter. Founding member of New English Art Club (1886); painted, in Impressionistic style, beach scenes, landscapes, nudes, and esp. portraits as *Mrs. Cyprian Williams and Her Children* (1891).

Stee·vens \'stē-vənz\, George. 1736–1800. English Shakespearean commentator. Published reprint from original quartos, *Twenty of the Plays of Shakespeare* (1766); collaborated with Johnson in ten-volume edition (1773); prepared 15-volume edition (1793) in which he made reckless emendations, and which was reissued (1803) by Isaac Reed in 21 volumes, with additional notes by Steevens, as the "first variorum." Detected forgeries of Chatterton and Ireland.

Stefan. See also STEPHEN.

Ste·fan \'shtā-,fän\, Josef. 1835–1893. Austrian physicist. Professor (from 1863) at U. of Vienna and director of Physical Institute (from 1866); first stated Stefan-Boltzmann law that the total radiation from a black body is proportional to the fourth power of its absolute temperature (1879); investigated hydrodynamics, kinetic theory of gases, and theory of electricity.

Stefani, Alberto De. See DE STEFANI.

Ste·fa·no di Gio·van·ni \stā-'fän-ō-dē-jō-'vän-nē\. *Known as* Sas·set·ta \säs-'set-tä\. d. c.1450. Italian painter. Greatest Sienese painter of early 15th century; painted in International Gothic style. Works included altarpiece for Arte della Lana, Siena (1423–26), *Madonna of the Snow* altarpiece for Siena cathedral (1430–32), cycles of scenes from legend of St. Anthony the Abbot (c.1437) and from life of St. Francis (1437–44).

Ste·fáns·son \'stef-äns-sön\, Davíd. 1895–1964. Icelandic poet. Author of lyrical verse in a simple, personal style, including *Svartar fjadrir* (1919), *Ad nordan* (1936), *Ávarp fjallkonunnar* (1954), sociological novel *Sólon Islandus* (1940), and play *Gullna hlidid* (1941).

Ste·fans·son \'stef-ən-sən\, Vilhjalmur. 1879–1962. American ethnologist and explorer, b. Arnes, Man. Lived (1906–07) among the Eskimo, learning their language and culture; with Rudolph M. Anderson carried out ethnographical and zoological studies among the Mackenzie and Copper Eskimo (1908–12); in command of expedition to explore Canadian and Alaskan regions of the Arctic (1913–18); consultant to Northern Studies program at Dartmouth Coll. (from 1947). Author of *My Life with the Eskimo* (1913), *Friendly Arctic* (1921), *The Northward Course of Empire* (1922), *The Adventure of Wrangell*

Island (1925), *Unsolved Mysteries of the Arctic* (1939), *Greenland* (1942), *Northwest to Fortune* (1958), etc.

Stef·fa·ni \stef-'fä-nē\, Agostino. 1654–1728. Italian composer, diplomat, and cleric. In musical and diplomatic service of the electors of Hanover (1688–1703) and elector palatine of Düsseldorf (1703–09). Ordained priest (1680); papal prothonotary for northern Germany (1698); bishop of Spiga (1706). Composer of about 20 operas and over 100 chamber duets in cantata form.

Stef·fen \'shtef-ən\, Albert. 1884–1963. Swiss novelist and playwright. Joined Rudolf Steiner's anthroposophical movement (1907); succeeded Steiner as president of the Anthroposophical Society (1925). His novels included *Die Erneuerung des Bundes* (1913), *Aus Georg Archibalds Lebenslauf* (1950); plays *Hieram und Salomo* (1927), *Das Todeserlebnis des Manes* (1934), *Barrabas* (1949); essays *Der Künstler zwischen Westen und Osten* (1925); and autobiography *Buch der Rückschau* (1939).

Stef·fens \'shtef-əns\, Henrik. 1773–1845. German physicist and philosopher, b. Norway. Professor of mineralogy at Halle (1804–06, 1808–11) and of physics at Breslau (1811–32) and Berlin (1832–45); combined scientific ideas with German Idealist metaphysics. Wrote *Grundzüge der philosophischen Naturwissenschaft* (1806), *Anthropologie* (1824), autobiography *Was ich erlebte* (1840–44), etc.

Stef·fens \'stef-ənz\, Lincoln, *in full* Joseph Lincoln. 1866–1936. American journalist, b. San Francisco. City editor, New York *Commercial Advertiser* (1897–1902); managing editor, *McClure's Magazine* (1902–06); initiated and helped write series of muckraking articles; associate editor, *American Magazine* and *Everybody's Magazine* (1906–11); in later years supported revolutionary activities in Europe. Author of *The Shame of the Cities* (1904), *The Struggle for Self-Government* (1906), *Upbuilders* (1909), *The Least of These* (1910), and *Autobiography* (1931).

Stei·chen \'stī-kən\, Edward Jean, *orig.* Edouard Jean. 1879–1973. American photographer, b. Luxembourg. To U.S. (1882); pioneer in photography as art form. Helped Alfred Stieglitz found Photo-Secession Group (1902) and its 291 Gallery in New York (1905); in World War I, led photo division of air service; as fashion photographer (1923–38), known for portraits of Greta Garbo, Charlie Chaplin, etc.; in World War II, headed navy photo unit. Director, photo department, Museum of Modern Art, New York (1947–1962); organized "The Family of Man" exhibition (1955). Author of *A Life in Photography* (1968).

Stei·ger \'shtī-gər\, Schultheiss Niklaus Friedrich von. 1729–1799. Swiss politician. Chief magistrate (*avoyer*) of Bern canton (1787–98); most prominent political figure during last years of Swiss Confederation; fled to Bavaria after French defeat of the Bernese (1798); engaged in attempts to overthrow the French-supported Helvetian Republic.

Stein \'stīn\, Sir Aurel, *in full* Mark Aurel. 1862–1943. British archaeologist, b. Budapest. Principal of Oriental College, Lahore, India (1888–99); superintendent of Indian Archaeological Survey (1910–29). Made expeditions (1900–01, 1906–08, 1913–16, 1930) to central Asia, esp. Chinese Turkistan, tracing caravan routes between China and the West and discovering the Cave of the Thousand Buddhas near Tan Huang; traced Alexander the Great's eastern campaigns, identifying (1926) site of Alexander's storming of the Rock of Aornos; investigated relationship between Mesopotamian and Indus civilizations (1927–36). Author of *Chronicle of Kings of Kashmir* (1900), *Ancient Khotan* (1907), *Ruins of Desert Cathay* (1912), *The Thousand Buddhas* (1921), *Innermost Asia* (1928), *On Alexander's Track to the Indus* (1929), *Old Routes of Western Iran* (1940), etc.

Stein \'shtīn\, Charlotte Albertine Ernestine von, *nee* von Schardt \fôn-shärt\. 1742–1827. German writer. Lady in waiting in court of Duchess of Weimar (from 1758); m. Friedrich, Freiherr von Stein (1764). Beloved by Goethe (1775–89); recipient of many letters and poems from Goethe and served as inspiration for Iphigenie in *Iphigenie auf Tauris* and Natalie in *Wilhelm Meister;* her works included *Rino* (1776) and prose tragedy *Dido* (1792).

Stein, Edith. *Religious name* Teresa Benedicta of the Cross. 1891–1942. German philosopher and religious. Pupil of Edmund Husserl; baptized into Roman Catholic faith from Judaism (1922); joined Carmelites (1934); arrested by Gestapo because of her Jewish background; died in the gas chamber of Auschwitz. Attempted to synthesize Thomism and phenomenology in *Endliches und ewiges Sein;* also wrote *Studie über Joannes a Cruce* (pub. 1950).

Stein \'stīn\, Gertrude. 1874–1946. American writer, b. Allegheny, Pa. Resident in Paris (from 1903), where her home was a salon for leading writers and artists of the day; wrote experimental works paralleling theories of Cubism. Author of *Three Lives* (1908), *Tender Buttons* (1915), *Making of Americans* (1925), *Lucy Church Amiably* (1930), *How to Write* (1931), *The Autobiography of Alice B. Toklas* (1933), *Four Saints in Three Acts* (operetta, music by Virgil Thomson; 1934), *Everybody's Autobiography* (1937), *The World Is Round* (1939), *Brewsie and Willie* (1946), *Mother of Us All* (operetta, with Thomson; 1947), etc.

Stein \'shtīn\, Heinrich Friedrich Karl vom und zum \ˌfôm-ůnt-ˌtsům-, -ˌtsüm-\. Freiherr. 1757–1831. Prussian politician. Entered Prussian civil service (1780); minister of finance (1804–07); as minister of foreign affairs (1807–08), accomplished many reforms in administration, taxation, and civil service; abolished serfdom; assisted Scharnhorst and Gneisenau in army reorganization; forced to resign by Napoléon (1808). Fled to Austria (1809–12); summoned to Russia to act as counselor to czar (1812–13); head of the council of administration of reconquered German territory and leader in military diplomacy (1813–15); frustrated in plans for Germany by Metternich and Hardenberg at Congress of Vienna (1814–15); retired (1815).

Stein, Johann Georg Andreas. 1728–1792. German piano builder. Apprenticed to Johann Silbermann (1748–49); settled in Augsburg (1750); the action (key mechanism) of his pianos was widely copied in Germany and became the model of the Viennese action; also constructed organs and harpsichords. His business was continued by his children ¶Maria Anna, *known as* Nannette (1769–1833) and ¶Matthäus Andreas (1776–1842), who moved the firm to Vienna (c.1794). Matthäus established his own firm (1802) and was succeeded as its head by his son ¶Carl Andreas (1797–1863), who was also known as a pianist, teacher, composer.

Stei·nach \'shtī-ˌnäk\, Eugen. 1861–1944. Austrian physiologist and biologist. Professor, Prague (1907–12), Vienna (from 1912); known for experiments in rejuvenation of men and animals by grafting the sexual glands of young animals.

Stein·bach \'shtīn-ˌbäk\, Emil. 1846–1907. Austrian economist and jurist. Entered ministry of justice (1874); rose to department head (1887); developed programs benefiting workers; as minister of finance (1891–93) reformed personal tax system; his proposal for voting reform caused the downfall of the Taafe government (1893); president of Supreme Court of Justice (from 1904).

Stein·beck \'stīn-ˌbek\, John Ernst. 1902–1968. American novelist, b. Salinas, Calif. Known esp. for novels about agricultural workers as *Of Mice and Men* (1937) and *The Grapes of Wrath* (1939, Pulitzer prize); other works included *Cup of Gold* (1929), *Pastures of Heaven* (1932), *To a God Unknown* (1933), *Tortilla Flat* (1935), *In Dubious Battle* (1936), *The Moon Is Down* (1942), *Cannery Row* (1945), *The Wayward Bus* (1947), *Burning Bright* (1950), *East of Eden* (1952), *Sweet Thursday* (1954), *The Winter of Our Discontent* (1961), *Travels with Charlie* (1962). Awarded Nobel prize for literature (1962).

Steindl \'shtīn-dəl\, Emmerich von. 1839–1902. Hungarian architect. Designed the parliament building in Budapest (1885–1902).

Steiner, Jakob. 1617?–1683. See STAINER.

Stei·ner \'shtī-nər\, Jakob. 1796–1863. Swiss mathematician. A founder of synthetic (also called projective) geometry. Professor at Berlin (1834–63); discussed principle of duality in *Systematische Entwickelung der Abhängigkeit geometrischer Gestalten von Einander* (1832); discovered Steiner (or Roman) surface; developed Steiner and Poncelet-Steiner theorems; also worked on algebraic curves and surfaces and maxima and minima; considered greatest geometer since Apollonius of Perga.

Steiner, Rudolph. 1861–1925. Austrian social philosopher. Founder of the spiritualistic and mystical doctrine known as anthroposophy. Became associated with theosophy movement (from 1902); met Annie Besant and was strongly influenced by her; founded (1912) Der Anthroposophische Bund and a number of institutions for the teaching of his doctrines, as the Goetheanum at Dornach, near Basel ... der Freiheit (1894), *Vom Menschenrätsel* (1916) ...

Stein·heil \'shtīn-ˌhīl\, ... Professor, Munich (18... earth for a return cond... system (1849–52).

Stei·nitz \'shtī-nits\, ... Breslau (1910–20) a... positive rational num... mathematical fields.

Stei·nitz \'shtī-nits, ... chess master, b. Pra... of the world (186... matches (1894 an... *Modern Chess In*...

Stein·le \'shtīn-lə\, ... member of Nazar... (1828–33); paint...

\ə\ abut \ˈ\ kitte... \au̇\ out \ch\ chi... \ō\ go \ȯ\ law ... \zh\ vision \ȧ, ...

Stein·len \sta^{n}-len\, Théophile-Alexandre. 1859–1923. French artist, b. Switzerland. Settled in Paris (1878, naturalized 1901) and contributed drawings to the *Chat Noir, Gil Blas Illustré,* etc.; well known for his posters and lithographs; illustrated a number of books.

Stein·man \'stīn-mən\, David Barnard. 1886–1960. American civil engineer, b. New York City. In consulting practice (from 1923). Designer or consulting engineer for over 400 bridges, including suspension bridge at Florianópolis, Brazil, then largest bridge in South America (1922–26), Carquinez Strait Bridge in California (1923–27), St. John's Bridge, Portland, Oregon (1929–31), Harbor Bridge, Sydney, Australia (1932), Thousand Islands International Bridge (1938), Mackinac Bridge, Mich. (1954–57), and the George Washington (1931), Triborough (1936), and Henry Hudson bridges, New York City. Author of *Suspension Bridges* (1923), *Bridges and Their Builders* (1941), etc.

Stein·metz \'shtīn-ˌmets, *Angl* 'stīn-\, Charles Proteus, *orig.* Karl August Rudolf. 1865–1923. American electrical engineer, b. Breslau, Germany. Forced to leave Germany because of Socialist activities (1888); to U.S. (1889); consulting engineer, General Electric Co., Schenectady, N.Y. (from 1893); professor, Union Coll. (from 1902). Derived mathematically the law of hysteresis; worked on theory and calculation of alternating-current phenomena; investigated electrical phenomena duplicating those of lightning; developed lightning arresters for high-power transmission lines; patented over 200 inventions, including improvements on generators and motors. Author of *Engineering Mathematics* (1910), *Radiation, Light and Illumination* (1909), *America and the New Epoch* (1916), etc.

Stein·metz \'shtīn-ˌmets\, Karl Friedrich von. 1796–1877. Prussian soldier. Defeated Austrians at Náchod and Skalitz (1866); in Franco-Prussian War commanded 1st army in battles at Spichern, Colombey-Nouilly, and Gravelotte (1870); removed (1870) and appointed governor general of Posen and Silesia; field marshal (1871).

Stein·thal \'shtīn-ˌtäl\, Heymann. 1823–1899. German philologist. Professor, Berlin (1863–99); with Wilhelm Wundt and Moritz Lazarus, credited with founding comparative psychology; also with Lazarus founded (1859) journal *Zeitschrift für Völkerpsychologie und Sprachwissenschaft.*

Stein·way \'stīn-wā\, Henry Engelhard. *Orig.* Heinrich Engelhard Stein·weg \'shtīn-vāk̲\. 1797–1871. American piano manufacturer, b. Wolfshagen, Germany. Fought at Battle of Waterloo (1815); engaged in making of pianos (from 1836); to U.S. (1851); with several sons, founded piano factory in New York (1853); made numerous improvements in pianos, including overstrung scale and cast-iron frame. His son ¶Christian Friedrich Theodore (1825–1889) in piano manufacture in Germany (to 1865), joined American firm of Steinway & Sons (1865); returned to Germany (1870) but continued to give American firm benefit of his researches and experiments. Another son ¶William (1835–1896), president of Steinway & Sons (1876–96); first chairman of Rapid Transit Commission of New York City, which planned New York's first subway; founded Steinway, Long Island, and moved his factory there (1880).

Stella. Name associated in literature with (1) Lady Penelope DEVEREUX and (2) Esther JOHNSON.

Stel·la \'stäl-lä, *Angl* 'stel-ə\, Joseph, *orig.* Giuseppe. 1877–1946. American painter, b. near Naples, Italy. To U.S. (1869); associated with Futurist school; participated in New York Armory Show (1913); painted in abstract and, later, primitive styles; works included collages and canvases such as *Battle of Lights, Coney Island* (1913), *The Gas Tank* (1918), *Brooklyn Bridge* (1920), *New York Interpreted* (1922), *The Holy Manger* (1933).

Stella, Maria. See MARIA STELLA.

Stel·ler \'shtel-ər, *Angl* 'stel-\, Georg Wilhelm. *Surname orig.* Stoel·ler \'shtœl-ər\. 1709–1746. German naturalist. On expedition to north Asia led by Vitus Bering (1737); explored Kamchatka (1740–41, 1742–44); accompanied Bering to coast of Alaska, wintering on Bering Island (1741–42). Wrote accounts of his travels and described birds and animals, including Steller's sea cow (now extinct) and Steller's sea lion, both named after him.

Ste·mann \'stā-mån\, Poul Christian. 1764–1855. Danish politician. Premier of Denmark (1826–48); close adviser to Frederick VI and Christian VIII; [illegible]hampioned absolute monarchy and opposed liberal reforms, esp. agrarian and [illegible]litical demands of peasants; resigned during nationalistic demonstrations of [illegible] 1848.

[illegible] \'stān-bök\, Magnus Gustafsson. 1663 or 1664–1717. Swedish [illegible]guished himself at Narva (1700); defeated Danes at Hälsingborg [illegible]arshal (1712); invaded Holstein; defeated and forced to [illegible]g (1713).

[illegible]enri BEYLE.

[illegible] Dillon, *nicknamed* Casey. 1890 or 1891–1975. [illegible]manager, b. Kansas City, Mo. Outfielder with [illegible]1912–31); manager (from 1932), esp. of New [illegible]ork Mets (1962–65); led Yankees to ten [illegible]orld Series championships; known for showmanship and fractured use of language called "Stengelese." Elected to Baseball Hall of Fame (1966).

Sten·kil \'stān-ˌk̲ēl\. Name of early Swedish dynasty (1060–1125), founded by Stenkil Ragnvaldsson (d. 1066), Earl of West Götaland.

Sten·sen *or* **Steen·sen** \'stān-sən\, Niels. *Known as* Nicolaus Ste·no \'stā-(ˌ)nō\. 1638–1686. Danish geologist and anatomist. Made discoveries in functions of the heart, brain, procreative and glandular systems; discovered (1660) the parotid salivary duct (also called Stensen's duct). In *De solido intra solidum naturaliter contento dissertationis prodromus* (1669) laid foundations of crystallography and proposed revolutionary idea that fossils are remains of ancient living organisms and many rocks are result of sedimentation, thus also laying foundations of geology and paleontology. Royal anatomist at Copenhagen (1672–74); to Florence (1674); ordained Roman Catholic priest (1675); made apostolic vicar of northern Germany and Scandinavia and bishop of Titiopolis (1677).

Sten Stu·re \'stān-stü-rə\. Name of two regents of Sweden, members of the powerful Sture noble family:

Sten Sture. *Called* the Elder. c.1440–1503. Regent (1470–97, 1501–03). Son of half-sister of King Charles VIII; led Swedish forces against Danish rule, defeating Christian I in Battle of Brunkeberg (1471); helped Charles regain throne (1467) and appointed regent on his death (1470); reduced German influence in municipal governments; strengthened legal institutions; founded at Uppsala first Scandinavian university (1477); throughout reign contended with Oxenstierna family; reduced power of state council and increased his own; defeated (1497) by Danish forces and compelled to acknowledge King John of Denmark as king of Sweden; overthrew John (1501).

Sten Sture. *Called* the Younger. *Orig.* Sten Svan·tes·son \'svän-təs-sön\. c.1492–1520. Regent (1513–20). Son of Svante Nilsson Sture; seized power from regent Erik Trolle; gained control over the state council and the church; waged war against Archbishop Gustav Trolle; defeated Danish forces under Christian II (1517–20); killed in battle.

Sten·vall \'stān-väl\, Aleksis. *Pseudonym* Aleksis Ki·vi \'kē-vē\. 1834–1872. Finnish writer. Father of the Finnish novel and drama, creator of modern Finnish literary language, and first Finnish professional writer. Author of plays as tragedy *Kullervo* (1864) and rural comedies *Nummisuutarit* (1864) and *Kilaus* (1867); novels, esp. *Seitsemän veljestä* (1870), first novel in Finnish; and verse *Kanervala* (1866).

Ste·phan IV \'shtef-än\. *Called* the Great. 1435–1504. Prince of Moldavia (1457–1504). Secured throne with aid of Vlad IV the Impaler; repulsed Hungarian invasion (1467); conducted long resistance to invasions by Ottoman Turks, defeating them near Vaslui (1475) and at Valen Albă (1476); concluded (1503) treaty with Bayezid II preserving independence at cost of annual tribute; during his reign Moldavia reached peak of power and cultural development.

Steph·ans·son \'stef-ən-sən\, Stephan Gudmundson. 1853–1927. Canadian poet, b. Skagafjördur, Iceland. Emigrated to U.S. as farm and railroad laborer (1873); settled in Alberta, Canada, as a farmer (1889). Author of verse in Icelandic, including *Andvökur* (1909–38), *Heimleidis* (1917), and *Vígslódi* (1920).

Stephanus. See ESTIENNE family.

Ste·phen \'stē-vən\. Saint. d. c.36 A.D. Christian protomartyr. Traditionally the first defender of Christianity; a Hellenist; one of seven deacons chosen by the Apostles to dispense charity among early Christian community in Jerusalem; accused of blasphemy against the Temple and Jewish law; defended himself and Christianity before the Sanhedrin; stoned to death; first to proclaim Second Coming of Christ.

Stephen. Name of ten popes; see Stephen II (d. 752) for explanation of alternate numeration:

Stephen I. Saint. d. 257. Pope (254–257). Succeeded St. Lucius I; in controversies against St. Cyprian of Carthage, restored Spanish bishops Martial of Mérida and Basilides of León-Astorga, refused to depose Bishop Marcianus of Arles, and defended papal supremacy and validity of heretic baptism.

Stephen II. d. 752. Pope (752). Elected pope to succeed St. Zacharias but died before consecration. As consecration was considered (from 8th century) the official beginning of a pontificate, Stephen II was not listed among popes by his contemporaries or most medieval and modern historians; modern canon law now considers a pontificate as beginning with election, therefore subsequent Stephens are listed with traditional numbers first and alternate numbers in parentheses.

Stephen II (III). d. 757. Pope (752–757). Unsuccessful in negotiating an alliance with Lombard king Aistulf (753); crowned Aistulf's enemy, Frankish king Pepin the Short (753); received (756) from Pepin territories in exarchate of Ravenna, duchy of Rome, and districts of Venetia and Istria, thereby creating the Papal States; first temporal sovereign of Papal States.

Stephen III (IV). 720?–772. Pope (768–772). Elected after deposition of antipopes Constantine and Philip; summoned Lateran council to formally depose Constantine (769); made alliance with Lombard king Desiderius (771), antagonizing the Franks; approbated worship of icons for Eastern church; extended rights of cardinal bishops for Western church.

Stephen IV (V). d. 817. Pope (816–817). Of noble birth; ordered Romans to swear fidelity to Carolingian emperor Louis I the Pious (816); crowned Louis as Holy Roman emperor, thus solidifying papal-Frankish alliance and the right of popes to crown and anoint Holy Roman emperors.

Stephen V (VI). d. 891. Pope (885–891). Of noble birth; successfully urged Byzantine emperor Leo VI to depose Photius as patriarch of Constantinople; unsuccessfully petitioned Leo for aid against Saracens; used father's wealth to alleviate a famine; endorsed Pope John VIII's prohibition of the Moravian church's Slavic liturgy; unsuccessfully appealed to Arnulf to restore order in Italy from Saracen and Hungarian attacks and internal struggles for the throne; recognized Louis III the Blind as king of Provence (890); crowned Guy of Spoleto as Holy Roman emperor (891).

Stephen VI (VII). d. 897. Pope (896–897). Member of ruling family of Spoleto; succeeded Pope Formosus; supported by Lambert of Spoleto, implacable foe of Formosus; persuaded by Lambert to convene (897) "Cadaver Synod" (or Synodus Horrenda), in which Formosus's corpse was exhumed, convicted of various crimes, dumped into the Tiber River, and Formosus's pontificate annulled; deposed by an insurrection, imprisoned, and strangled.

Stephen VII (VIII). d. 931. Pope (929–931). While cardinal priest of St. Anastasia, Rome, active in Roman church administration; his election probably influenced by Marozia; extended privileges to Italian and French monasteries.

Stephen VIII (IX). d. 942. Pope (939–942). Educated in Germany; succeeded Leo VII; his pontificate dominated by Duke Alberic II of Spoleto; recognized King Louis IV of France; supported St. Odo's reform of monasticism.

Stephen IX (X). *Orig.* Frederick of Lorraine. c.1000–1058. Pope (1057–1058). Older brother of Godfrey II the Bearded; a prime papal adviser of his cousin Pope Leo IX; papal legate to Constantinople (1054); abbot of Monte Cassino, Italy (1057); as pope continued Leo's church reforms; denounced simony, enforced clerical celibacy; died before he could carry out plans to negotiate end of schism of Eastern and Western churches.

Stephen. c.1097–1154. King of England (1135–54). 3d son of Stephen Henry, Count of Blois and Chartres, and Adela, daughter of William the Conqueror. Brought up at court of uncle Henry I of England; regarded (to 1125) as heir to English throne; forced to swear, with lay barons, acknowledgment of Empress Matilda of Germany, Henry I's daughter, as future ruler and of ultimate claims of Matilda's son Henry of Anjou. On Henry I's death, claimed throne, declaring Matilda, daughter of a nun, illegitimate; enthroned by Londoners and crowned at Westminster (1135); granted two charters of liberties; drove back Scots (1138); opposed by Matilda's half-brother Robert, Earl of Gloucester; as result of quarrel with Bishop Roger of Salisbury, brought clergy against him. Taken prisoner (1141) by forces of Matilda (who had landed 1139) and Gloucester; released in exchange for Gloucester and again crowned (1141) after reign of six months by Matilda; lacked the resources and the will to suppress lawlessness and mediate between warring nobles; quarreled with papacy and failed to obtain papal sanction for coronation of son Eustace (1151); submitted on Eustace's death and acknowledged as his heir (1153) Henry of Anjou (later Henry II).

Stephen. *Hung.* Ist·ván \ˈist-vän\. Name of five kings of Hungary, especially:

Stephen I. Saint. 977–1038. First king of Arpád dynasty (997–1038). Considered founder of the state of Hungary; most renowned figure in Hungarian history. Son of Duke Géza; m. (996) Gisela, sister of Emperor Henry II; succeeded his father (997) as duke of Hungary; anointed king (1000); given title of "Apostolic King," held thereafter (to 1918) by sovereigns of Hungary; his reign generally peaceful; continued Christianizing policy of his father and suppressed paganism; called in foreign priests, endowed abbeys, and formed a council of nobles and high churchmen; encouraged agriculture and trade; became patron saint of Hungary; canonized (1083).

Stephen V. 1239–1272. King (1270–72). Son of Béla IV; as prince ruled duchy of Styria (1254–59) and invaded Bulgaria (1268); defeated Otakar II of Bohemia (1271).

Stephen. *Serb.* Stef·an \ˈstev-än\. Name of rulers of Serbia, including:

Stephen Ne·ma·nja \ˈne-män-yä\. d. 1200. Grand *župan* (clan leader) of Raška under Byzantine suzerainty (c.1167–1196). Founder of the Serbian state and the Nemanja dynasty; conquered Skopje, Prizren, Tetovo; defeated, but retained Kosovo, Peć, Prizren, Bar, Skadar, and Kotor; abdicated (1196) and joined his son St. Sava in a monastery.

Stephen II Nemanja. *Called* Stephen the First Crowned. d. 1228. King of Serbia (1196–1228). Son and successor of Stephen Nemanja; did much to solidify the unity of the Serbian state; obtained a royal crown from the papacy; received an independent archbishopric for Serbian church for his brother St. Sava from the Byzantine emperor.

Stephen Du·šan \ˈdü-shän\. 1308–1355. King (1331–55). Rebelled against father Stephen Uroš III and seized power (1331); seized Macedonia, Albania, and large parts of Greece from Byzantine Empire; had himself crowned emperor of the Serbs, Greeks, Bulgars, and Albanians (1346); drew up legal code (1349–54); conquered Bosnia (1350) and was marching on Constantinople at time of death.

Stephen, Sir James Fitzjames. Baronet Stephen. 1829–1894. English legal historian and judge. Brother of Sir Leslie Stephen; as legal member of council in India (1869–72), chiefly responsible for Indian Evidence Act (1872); professor of common law at Inns of Court (1875–79); judge of High Court of Justice (1879–91). Author of *General View of the Criminal Law of England* (1863), first attempt made since Blackstone to explain principles of English law, and *History of the Criminal Law of England* (1883); replied to J.S. Mill in *Liberty, Equality, Fraternity* (1873); his Indictable Offences Bill (late 1870s), though never enacted, greatly influenced reformations of criminal law in English-speaking nations.

Stephen, Sir Leslie. 1832–1904. English critic and biographer. Brother of Sir James Stephen and father of Virginia Woolf and Vanessa Bell. Cooperated in founding of *Pall Mall Gazette;* editor, *Cornhill Magazine* (1871–82); published *Hours in a Library* (1874, 1876, 1879), *History of English Thought in the Eighteenth Century* (1876), and *Science of Ethics* (1882). Inaugurated "English Men of Letters" series with biography of Samuel Johnson (1878); contributed biographies of Pope (1880), Swift (1882), George Eliot (1902), and Hobbes (1904). First editor (1882–91) of *Dictionary of National Biography.*

Stephen Bá·tho·ry \ˈbä-tȯr-ē\. *Hung.* István Báthory. *Pol.* Stefan Ba·to·ry \ˈbä-tȯ-rē\. 1533–1586. Prince of Transylvania (1571–76) and king of Poland (1575–86). Won renown as soldier with John Zápolya (from 1556); aided by Jan Zamoyski, overcame Habsburg objections and was elected king of Poland (1575) by nobility; overcame revolt of Gdánsk (1577); in war with Russia (1579–82) gained victory over Ivan the Terrible and annexed Polotsk and Livonia; attempted to promote the Counter-Reformation and strengthen royal power; died before achieving his goal of uniting Poland, Muscovy, and Transylvania under his rule. His son ¶Gabriel Báthory, *Hung.* Gábor (1589–1613), prince of Transylvania (1608–13); because of his cruelty, driven from country and murdered; last of the ruling members of the Báthory family. Stephen's niece ¶Elizabeth Báthory (d. 1614); known in legend and history for extreme cruelty; said to have killed more than 600 maidens and bathed in their blood; died in prison.

Ste·phens \ˈstē-vənz\, Alexander Hamilton. 1812–1883. American politician, b. Wilkes (now Taliaferro) Co., Ga. Member, U.S. House of Representatives (1843–59), allying himself first with the Whigs and later with the Democrats. Though disapproving immediate secession, remained loyal to his state when it voted to secede (1861). Vice president of the Confederacy (1861–65); head of Confederate mission at Hampton Roads Conference (Feb. 1865); at end of war, imprisoned (May–Oct. 1865) at Fort Warren, Boston. Elected U.S. senator (1866), but was refused a seat; member, U.S. House of Representatives (1873–82); governor of Georgia (1883). Author of *A Constitutional View of the Late War Between the States* (1868–70).

Stephens, Alfred George. 1865–1933. Australian literary critic and journalist. On staff of Sydney *Bulletin* (1894–1906); his "Red Page" book reviews (from 1896) promoted work of young Australian writers; as a literary agent arranged for publication of many important literary works; his writings included *Oblation* (1902, verse) and *The Red Pagan* (1904, selections from "Red Page" reviews).

Stephens, Frederic George. 1828–1907. English art critic. Member of Pre-Raphaelite Brotherhood; art critic to *Athenaeum* (1861–1901); author of *The Private Collections of England.*

Stephens, James. 1825–1901. Irish nationalist. Inaugurated Irish Republican Brotherhood (founded in New York as Fenian Brotherhood) on military basis (1858); founded *Irish People* as organ of party (1863); arrested in Dublin (1865), escaped to New York, where he was deposed by Fenians; expelled from France (1885).

Stephens, James. 1882–1950. Irish poet and novelist. While a solicitor's clerk discovered by George W. Russell; helped found *Irish Review* (1911). Author of pantheistic fairy tales set in Dublin slums and poems about animals, including *Insurrections* (verse, 1909), *The Hill of Vision* (verse, 1912), *The Charwoman's Daughter* (novel, 1912), *The Crock of Gold* (novel, 1912), *Here are Ladies* (1913), *The Demi-Gods* (novel, 1914), *The Rocky Road to Dublin* (1915), *Deirdre* (novel, 1923), *In the Land of Youth* (1924), *Etched in Moonlight* (1928), *Kings of the Moon* (1938).

Stephens, John Lloyd. 1805–1852. American traveler and archaeologist, b. Shrewsbury, N.J. Practiced law in New York (1826–34); made archaeological travels in eastern Mediterranean and eastern Europe (1834–36), in Central

America and Mexico (1839–40, 1841–42); his writings greatly stimulated archaeological interest in Central America. Author of *Incidents of Travel in Egypt, Arabia Petraea, and the Holy Land* (1837), *Incidents of Travel in Greece, Turkey, Russia, and Poland* (1838), *Incidents of Travel in Central America, Chiapas, and Yucatán* (1841), *Incidents of Travel in Yucatán* (1843).

Stephens, Uriah Smith. 1821–1882. American labor leader, b. Cape May, N.J. Tailor by trade; a founder (1869) of the Noble Order of the Knights of Labor; resigned (1879) his leadership of the Knights after conflict with Terence Powderly.

Ste·phen·son \'stē-vən-sən\, Benjamin Franklin. 1823–1871. American physician, b. Wayne Co., Ill. Served in Civil War as regimental surgeon; founder of Grand Army of the Republic (1866).

Stephenson, George. 1781–1848. English inventor and founder of railways. Devised miner's safety lamp, claiming priority over Sir Humphry Davy for its invention (1815); built locomotive tried successfully on Killingworth colliery railway (1814); patented locomotive engine with steam blast (1815); directed construction of railway eight miles long for Hetton colliery (opened 1822); with brother and cousin, established locomotive works at Newcastle (1823); construction engineer for Stockton and Darlington Ry. (opened 1825) and Liverpool and Manchester Ry. (opened 1830), winning contest to determine suitable engine for latter with his locomotive "Rocket," having tubular boiler (1829); engaged in building various other railways. His son ¶Robert (1803–1859) was also an engineer; manager of Newcastle locomotive works; made improvements in locomotives and assisted his father in construction of locomotive "Rocket" and of railways; chief engineer (from 1833) for Birmingham and London Ry., first railway into London (completed 1838); known for his bridges, including one over the Tyne at Newcastle, Victoria Bridge at Berwick, Menai tubular-girder bridge, and bridge over the St. Lawrence at Montreal. ¶George Robert Stephenson (1819–1905), civil engineer; employed by his uncle George Stephenson; directed construction of railways in Kent, Schleswig-Holstein, Jutland, and New Zealand; constructed fixed as well as swinging bridges in England and abroad; proprietor of Newcastle locomotive works (1859–86).

Stepnyak *or* **Stepniak,** S. See Sergey KRAVCHINSKY.

Ster·ling \'stər-liŋ\, George. 1869–1926. American poet, b. Sag Harbor, N.Y. Leader in artist colony at Carmel, Calif. (1908–15); influenced by Ambrose Bierce; his volumes of verse included *The Testimony of the Suns* (1903), *A Wine of Wizardry* (1909), *Thirty-five Sonnets* (1917).

Sterling, John. 1806–1844. British essayist and poet, b. Ireland. Author of *The Election* (humorous poem, 1841), *Strafford* (tragedy, 1843), and *Essays and Tales* (1848); rendered famous by Carlyle's biography *Life of Sterling* (1851).

Stern, Daniel. See Marie d'AGOULT.

Stern \'shtern\, Julius. 1820–1883. German musician. Cofounder (1850, with Adolf B. Marx and Theodor Kullak) of the Berlin (later Stern) Conservatory.

Stern \'shtern, *Angl* 'stərn\, Otto. 1888–1969. American physicist, b. Sohrau, Germany. Taught at Frankfurt (1914–21) and Hamburg (1923–33); professor, Carnegie Tech. (1933–45). Made theoretical studies of statistical thermodynamics (1912–18); verified the space quantization theory of atoms by the molecular beam method (1921); again using molecular beam, measured the magnetic moment of the proton (1933); awarded 1943 Nobel prize for physics.

Stern·berg \'stərn-ˌbərg\, George Miller. 1838–1915. American physician and bacteriologist, b. Otsego Co., N.Y. In Medical Corps, U.S. army (from 1861); detailed (1879) to duty with Havana Yellow Fever Commission; first to demonstrate the plasmodium of malaria (1885) and the bacilli of tuberculosis and of typhoid fever (1886); published *Manual of Bacteriology* (1892), first complete treatise of its kind in U.S. As U.S. surgeon general (1893–1902), established Army Medical School, Dental Corps, Nurse Corps, and founded Army Tuberculosis Hospital at Fort Bayard, N. Mex. Organized (1900) Yellow Fever Commission, headed by Major Reed, which discovered transmission of yellow fever; retired (1902).

Sternberg, Josef von. 1894–1969. American film director, b. Vienna. To U.S. as a boy. Established reputation with *Salvation Hunters* (1925), a realistic portrayal of waterfront life; made series of pictures about the criminal world as *Underworld* (1927), *The Dragnet* (1928), *Docks of New York* (1928); discovered Marlene Dietrich and directed her in *Der blaue Engel* (1930, *The Blue Angel*), *Morocco* (1930), *Dishonored* (1931), *Blonde Venus* (1932), *Shanghai Express* (1932), *The Scarlet Empress* (1934), *The Devil Is a Woman* (1935); also directed *The Last Command* (1928), *An American Tragedy* (1931), and *Crime and Punishment* (1935).

Stern·berg \'styirn-byirg\, Lev Yakovlevich. 1861–1927. Russian anthropologist. Known for ethnographic studies of the Gilyak and Oroki peoples of Sakhalin Island and the eastern Siberian mainland (pub. 1893, 1908, 1933); organized teaching of ethnography at U. of Leningrad after Revolution of 1917 (with V. G. Bogoraz); also wrote on the family and clan in northeastern Asia and on primitive religion.

Sterne \'stərn\, Laurence. 1713–1768. British novelist, b. Ireland. Vicar of Sutton-in-the-Forest (1738) and prebendary of York (1741). Created sensation with first two volumes of novel *The Life and Opinions of Tristram Shandy* (1760), partly because of its eccentric humor and whimsicality, partly because of its unconventionality and indecorum; after *Sermons of Mr. Yorick* (1760), published final seven volumes of *Tristram Shandy* (1761–67). Abroad for his health (1762–64); met in London Mrs. Elizabeth Draper, for whom he kept *The Bramine's Journal* (1767); published *A Sentimental Journey through France and Italy* (2 vols. of projected 4 vols., 1768), in which humor of *Tristram Shandy* was replaced by sentimental enjoyment of travels from Calais to Lyons; publication of his *Letters of Yorick to Eliza* (1766–67) authorized by Mrs. Draper (1773).

Sterne, Maurice. 1878–1957. American painter and sculptor, b. Libau, Latvia. To U.S. (1889); m. (1917; div. 1921) Mabel Dodge Luhan; influenced by Gauguin and culture of the East; his canvases included *Dance of the Elements* (1913) and *Girl in Blue Chair* (1928); also executed *Monument to Early Settlers* at Worcester, Mass. (1926–29) and murals for Dept. of Justice building, Washington, D.C. (1935–40).

Stern·heim \'shtərn-ˌhīm\, Carl. 1878–1942. German playwright. Author of plays satirizing the materialism and conformity of bourgeois society as *Die Hosen* (1910), *Die Kassette* (1911), *Der Snob* (1914), *Tabula Rasa* (1916), and *Das Fossil* (1922); sometimes called the German Molière.

Stern·hold \'stərn-ˌhōld\, Thomas. d. 1549. English versifier. Joint author with John Hopkins (d. 1570) of metrical versions of the Psalms formerly attached to the Prayer Book; designated as author of forty Psalms, to sixty by Hopkins, in the complete book of Psalms (1562), known (after 1696) as the Old Version.

Ste·sich·o·rus \stə-'sik-ə-rəs\. 632 or 629–556 or 553 B.C. Greek lyric poet. Active mainly at Himera, Sicily; wrote in Doric dialect mainly narrative poems dealing with myths; credited with originating bucolic poetry in his *Daphnis,* with writing forerunners of Hellenistic poetry *Calyce* and *Rhadine,* and with inventing the triadic stanza; only fragments of his works survive.

Stet·son \'stet-sən\, Augusta Emma, *nee* Sim·mons \'sim-ənz\. 1842–1928. American religious leader, b. Waldoboro, Me. m. Frederick J. Stetson (1864); joined (1884) Christian Science movement and began practice as a Christian Science healer; sent by Mrs. Eddy to New York City (1886) and there organized (1888) First Church of Christ, Scientist, and served as its pastor (1888–1909). Investigated by directors of the Mother Church in Boston (1909), found guilty of insubordination and false teaching, and offically excommunicated. Continued to proclaim her loyalty to Mrs. Eddy and preached her version of Christian Science.

Stetson, John Batterson. 1830–1906. American hat manufacturer, b. Orange, N.J. In family hat business as a boy; opened his own factory in Philadelphia (1865); known esp. for his western Stetson models; supported DeLand (Fla.) U., renamed Stetson U. in his honor (1889).

Stet·tin·i·us \stə-'tin-ē-əs, ste-\, Edward Reilly. 1865–1925. American industrialist and financier, b. St. Louis. Joined J.P. Morgan & Co. (1915), partner (1916–25); chief purchasing agent in U.S. for the allied governments during World War I. His son ¶Edward Reilly (1900–1949), chairman of finance committee, U.S. Steel Corp. (1935–39), and president (1939). Chairman, War Resources Board (1939–40); administrator of Lend-Lease (1941–43); undersecretary of state (1943–44); secretary of state (1944–1945) and chairman of U.S. delegation to United Nations conference at San Francisco; U.S. representative to UN Preparatory Commission and delegate (1945–46).

Steuart. See STEWART and STUART.

Steu·ben \'shtȯi-bən, *Angl* 'st(y)ü-bən\, Friedrich Wilhelm Ludolf Gerhard Augustin von. Baron. 1730–1794. American soldier, b. Magdeburg, Prussia. Entered Prussian army (1747), emerging as captain from service in the Seven Years' War (1756–63). To America (1777), recommended to Washington by Franklin; reported to Washington at Valley Forge (Feb. 1778); designated inspector general, Continental army, and given the task of training the army. Reorganized and drilled the army with marked success; commissioned major general in Continental army (1778); engaged at Monmouth and Yorktown; became trusted adviser to Washington. After the war, one of the organizers of the Society of the Cincinnati (1783). Honorably discharged from the army (1784). Naturalized American citizen (1783); made his home in New York (1784–94). Prepared *Regulations for the Order and Discipline of the Troops of the United States* (1778–79).

Steud·ner \'shtȯid-nər\, Hermann. 1832–1863. German physician and explorer. Traveled across Ethiopia from Mitsiwa on Red Sea to Lake Tana and north to Khartoum (1862); on expedition (1863) with Alexandrine Tinné up the Baḥr al-Ghazāl into the southwestern Sudan, where he died of fever.

Ste·vens \'stē-vənz\, Albert William. 1886–1949. American aerial photographer, b. Belfast, Md. In U.S. army (1914–42); made air maps of upper Amazon (1924); made first photograph showing laterally earth's curvature (1930) and first photographs of moon's shadow on earth during solar eclipse (1932); made balloon ascensions into stratosphere (60,600 ft., 1934; with Capt. O. A. Anderson, 72,395 feet, 1935).

Stevens, Alfred George. 1817–1875. English painter and sculptor. Designed vases and lions at British Museum; worked (from 1856) on monument of Duke of Wellington in St. Paul's Cathedral.

Stevens, Alfred. 1823–1906. Belgian painter. Best known for small canvases depicting Parisian ladies and genre scenes of Parisian society life. His brother ¶Joseph (1819–1892) painted animals, esp. dogs.

Stevens, Edwin Augustus. See under John STEVENS.

Stevens, George. 1905–1975. American film director, b. Oakland, Calif. Filmed many of early Laurel and Hardy comedies; gained fame as director with *Alice Adams* (1935), *Annie Oakley* (1935), and a series of comedies, including *Swing Time* (1936), *Vivacious Lady* (1938), *Woman of the Year* (1942), *The Talk of the Town* (1942), *The More the Merrier* (1943); won Academy Awards for best directing for *A Place in the Sun* (1951) and *Giant* (1956); also directed *I Remember Mama* (1948), *Shane* (1953), *The Diary of Anne Frank* (1959), *The Greatest Story Every Told* (1965), *The Only Game in Town* (1969); known for brilliant camerawork, careful integration of music and visuals, and skillful handling of sentimental themes.

Stevens, James Floyd. 1892–1971. American writer, b. Albia, Ia. Author of tales built around the legendary character "Paul Bunyan," as in *Paul Bunyan* (1925), *Saginaw Paul Bunyan* (1932), etc.

Stevens, John. 1749–1838. American inventor, b. New York City. Colonel in Revolutionary army; became interested in steamboat development by John Fitch and James Rumsey (1788); to protect inventors, secured federal legislation (1790) establishing first patent laws in U.S.; secured patents (1791) on a vertical steam boiler and an improved type of steam engine. Built (1802) a screw-driven steamboat, first example of a powered screw applied to ship propulsion; crossed the Hudson River with a twin-screw steamboat (1804); patented multitubular boiler (1803). Succeeded in building a practical steamship, the *Phoenix* (1808), and sent it from New York to Philadelphia (1809), thus making it the first seagoing steamboat in the world; inaugurated at Philadelphia world's first steam-ferry service (1811). Interested himself in rail transportation; received from New Jersey first railroad charter in U.S. (1815); built first American steam locomotive (1825); formed Camden and Amboy Railroad and Transportation Co. (1830). A son ¶Robert Livingston (1787–1856), b. Hoboken, N.J., was an engineer and inventor; served under Moses Rogers in handling the *Phoenix* on the sea trip from New York to Philadelphia (1809) and operated the *Phoenix* as a ferry between Philadelphia and Trenton; became naval architect; built ferryboat *Hoboken* along modern lines (1822); also interested himself in rail transportation; president and chief engineer of the Camden and Amboy Railroad and Transportation Company (1830). Invented the inverted-T rail (1830) and a hook-headed spike, developed the wooden-tie and gravel roadbed still in use. Imported locomotive from England and with it began (Nov. 1831) first steam railway service in New Jersey. Another son of John ¶Edwin Augustus (1795–1868), b. Hoboken, was also an engineer and inventor; participated in engineering projects of his father and brother; treasurer and manager, Camden & Amboy Railroad Transportation Company (1830); bequeathed land and money to found Stevens Institute of Technology, Hoboken, N.J.

Stevens, John Harrington. 1820–1900. American soldier and journalist, b. Brompton Falls, Que. To U.S. (1835); pioneer in Minnesota region; built (1849) first house in what became site of Minneapolis.

Stevens, Robert Livingston. See under John STEVENS.

Stevens, Thaddeus. 1792–1868. American lawyer and politician, b. Danville, Vt. Practiced at Gettysburg, Pa. (1816); member, U.S. House of Representatives (1849–53, 1859–68). Vigorously opposed slavery; supported financial measures but opposed many other administration policies. Leader of Radical Republicans in developing Congressional Reconstruction plan; insisted on stern requirements for readmission of Southern states into Union; strove for justice for freedmen; instrumental in preparation of 14th Amendment and military reconstruction acts of 1867; proposed impeachment of President Johnson and managed the trial.

Stevens, Wallace. 1879–1955. American poet, b. Reading, Pa. Trained as lawyer; with insurance firm in Hartford, Conn. (from 1916; vice president 1934–55). Author of poems exploring the relationship of reality and imagination, published in *Harmonium* (1923), *Ideas of Order* (1935), *The Man with the Blue Guitar* (1937), *Parts of a World* (1942), *Transport to Summer* (1947), *The Auroras of Autumn* (1950), *Collected Poems* (1954, Pulitzer prize); delineated his poetic theories in *The Necessary Angel* (1951).

Ste·ven·son \ˈstē-vən-sən\, Adlai Ewing. 1835–1914. American politician, b. Christian Co., Ky. Elected state's attorney of Illinois (1865); Democratic member, U.S. House of Representatives (1875–77, 1879–81); first assistant postmaster general (1885–89); vice president of the U.S. (1893–97). His grandson ¶Adlai Ewing Stevenson (1900–1965), b. Los Angeles; assistant to secretary of the navy (1941–44), to secretary of state (1945); U.S. delegate to UN General Assembly (1946–47); governor of Illinois (1949–53); Democratic candidate for U.S. president (1952, 1956); U.S. ambassador to UN (1961–65). Author of *Call to Greatness* (1954), *Friends and Enemies* (1958), *Looking Outward* (1963), etc., and speeches characterized by eloquence and wit.

Stevenson, Andrew. 1784–1857. American politician, b. Culpeper Co., Va. Democratic member, U.S. House of Representatives (1821–34) and speaker of the House (1827–34); staunch supporter of Andrew Jackson; U.S. minister to Great Britain (1836–41).

Stevenson, Robert. 1772–1850. Scottish civil engineer. Designed and built lighthouses (1797–1843), inventing intermittent and flashing lights; invented the hydrophore; author of *Account of the Bell Rock Lighthouse* (1824). Three of his sons were engineers: ¶Alan (1807–1865) designed ten lighthouses, introducing prismatic rings. ¶David (1815–1886) executed works for improvement of rivers in Scotland and northern England, and constructed beacons and lighthouses, introducing use of paraffin (1870) and aseismatic arrangement. ¶Thomas (1818–1887) invented azimuthal condensing system; devised Stevenson screen for thermometers (1864) and made other meteorological contributions.

Stevenson, Robert Louis Balfour. 1850–1894. Scottish essayist, novelist, and poet. Grandson of Robert Stevenson. Called to Scottish bar (1875) but never practiced; contributed essays to periodicals (from 1873); described canoe trip in France and Belgium (1876) in *An Inland Voyage* (1878) and foot journey in *Travels with a Donkey in the Cévennes* (1879). To California (1879) to follow and marry (1880) Fanny Van de Grift Osbourne. Produced *Virginibus Puerisque* (essays, 1881), *A Child's Garden of Verses* (poems, 1885), and a series of romantic adventure stories, including *New Arabian Nights* (1882), *Treasure Island* (1883), *Prince Otto* (1885), *Dr. Jekyll and Mr. Hyde* (1886), *Kidnapped* (1886), *The Merry Men* (1887), *The Black Arrow* (1888). Published lyric poems called *Underwoods* (1887) and left for America; wrote novel *Master of Ballantrae* (1889) and essays; set out (1888) on pleasure cruise to South Sea islands, settling permanently (1889) in Samoa; acknowledged by Samoans as chief with name Tu·si·ta·la \ˌtü-sə-ˈtäl-ä\, i.e. teller of tales. Published impressions of South Seas in *A Footnote to History* (1892) and *In the South Seas* (1896); wrote Pacific tales *Island Nights' Entertainments* (1893) and romances of Scottish life *Catriona* (1893) and *Weir of Hermiston* (unfinished). Collaborated with W. E. Henley in several unsuccessful dramas, with wife in *More New Arabian Nights* (1885), and with his stepson Lloyd Osbourne in *The Wrong Box* (1889), *The Wrecker* (1892), and *The Ebb Tide* (1894).

Stevenson, William. 1546–1575. English clergyman. Probable author of *Gammer Gurton's Needle,* early English comedy (acted 1566; pub. 1575); prebendary of Durham (1561).

Ste·vin \stə-ˈvīn\, Simon. *Lat.* Ste·vi·nus \stə-ˈvē-nəs\. 1548–1620. Dutch mathematician. Commissioner of public works and quartermaster general of the army under Maurice of Nassau; invented system of sluices as means of defense; in *De Beghinselen der Weeghconst* (1586) enunciated theorem of the triangle of forces; discovered that downward pressure of a liquid is independent of shape of its container; in *La Thiende* (1585) introduced decimal fractions into common use; showed that two lead spheres of differing weights fall at same rate of speed (1586); one of first to champion Copernican system, in *De Hemellop* (1608); also wrote on music theory, geography, navigation, engineering, civics, etc.

Stew·ard \ˈst(y)ü-ərd, ˈst(y)u̇(-ə)rd\, Julian H. 1902–1972. American anthropologist, b. Washington, D.C. With Smithsonian Institution (1935–46); professor at Columbia (1946–52) and U. of Illinois (from 1952). Authority on cultural evolution, peasant village structure, and New World civilization. Edited *Handbook of South American Indians* (1946–59); author of "Native Cultures of the Intermontane Area" (1940), *Theory of Culture Change* (1955), *Irrigation Civilizations* (1955), *Contemporary Change in Traditional Societies* (1967).

Stewart. See also STUART.

Stewart. Scottish and English royal house. See STUART.

Stew·art *or* **Stu·art** *or* **Steu·art** \ˈst(y)ü-ərt, ˈst(y)u̇(-ə)rt\. Surname of a family descended from a Breton immigrant to Norfolk, Alan Fitzflaald (d. 1114?), which inherited the Scottish and ultimately the English throne. Alan's elder son ¶William was ancestor of earls of Arundel (see FITZALAN family). ¶Walter Stewart (d. 1177), Alan's younger son, went to Scotland, where he received from David I lands in Renfrew and the hereditary dignity of high steward or seneschal of Scotland, whence the surname *Stewart* (modified by some branches to *Steuart* or to French form *Stuart*) took origin in reign (1153–65) of Malcolm IV.

¶Walter (1293–1326), 6th steward, was joint commander with Sir James

Douglas of left wing at battle of Bannockburn (1314); by marriage (1315) with Marjory, daughter of Robert the Bruce, brought Scottish crown to family, his son Robert ascending throne (1371) as Robert II (*q.v.*) and his grandson John succeeding as Robert III (*q.v.*).

DUKES OF AL·BA·NY \'ȯl-bə-nē\;

¶Robert Stewart (1340?–1420), 1st Duke of Albany; 3d son of Robert II; hereditary governor of Stirling (1373); chamberlain of Scotland (1382–1407); led invasion of England (1388); governor of Scotland because of physical disability of brother Robert III (1389–99); created duke (1398); plotted to gain throne of Scotland; defeated by English (1402); probably made away with David Stewart, Duke of Rothesay (see under ROBERT III of Scotland); regent of Scotland on capture of Prince James and death of Robert III (1406); prosecuted war with England; crushed revolt of Donald MacDonald, second lord of the isles (1411).

¶Alexander (1454?–1485), Duke of Albany (2d creation) and Earl of March \'märch\; 2d son of James II of Scotland; created duke (before 1458); received lordship of Isle of Man; high admiral of Scotland; warden of the marches; governor of Berwick; lieutenant of Scotland (1472); having pretensions to throne, intrigued with Edward IV of England, surrendered Berwick, and attempted to seize his brother James III (1482); after death of Edward IV, indicted and outlawed (1483).

¶John (c.1484–1536), Duke of Albany; only son of Alexander Stewart (1454?–1485) by his second wife; brought up in France; inaugurated regent of Scotland (1515); declared heir to throne (1516); negotiated at Rouen (1517) treaty with France against England; on return found disorder caused by rivalry between Angus and Arran; reconciled himself with Margaret Tudor, queen dowager, and aided her to obtain divorce from Angus (see under DOUGLAS family); accused by Henry VIII and Wolsey of ambition to marry queen dowager; attempted to invade England with large army, but on refusal of Scots to fight outside Scotland, returned to France (1522); made final fruitless attempt to storm Wark with French troops (1523); dismissed from regency on declaration of James V as king (1524); negotiated marriages of Henry, Duke of Orleans, with Catherine de Médicis (1533), and of James V.

¶Henry (1545–1565), *styled* Lord Darn·ley \'därn-lē\, son of 4th Earl of Lennox and, through his mother, great-grandson of Henry VII; educ. in England; with permission of Queen Elizabeth went to Scotland (1565); created earl of Ross \'rȯs\ and duke of Albany by his cousin Mary, Queen of Scots, and married her as her 2d husband (1565); became jealous of political influence of David Rozzio; joined conspiracy (1566) for Rizzio's murder but betrayed his accomplices to Mary; strangled at Kirk o'Field, Edinburgh, perhaps through Mary's complicity; father of James I of England and direct ancestor of all subsequent British sovereigns.

EARL OF AR·RAN \'ar-ən\:

¶James Stewart of Both·well·muir \'bäth-wəl-ˌmyu̇(ə)r, 'bäth-\ (d. 1596), son of 2d Baron Ochiltree; soldier of fortune in Netherlands; privy councilor (1581); claimed headship of Hamilton family and title earl of Arran on insanity of cousin James Hamilton, 3d earl (*q.v.*; 1581); driven from office by Ruthven raid (1582); lord chancellor (1584); alienated supporters by ruthlessness; accused by Queen Elizabeth of murder of Lord Russell (1585); banished (1585); assassinated by Sir James Douglas, nephew of regent Morton.

EARLS AND DUKES OF LEN·NOX \'len-əks\:

¶Sir John Stewart *or* Stuart (d. 1495), Lord Darnley, 1st Earl of Lennox (of Stewart line); joined conspiracy of 1482 against James III; headed rising in favor of James IV but surprised and defeated at Tallymoss (1488). ¶Matthew (1516–1571), 4th Earl of Lennox; heir male of Stuarts of Scotland at death of James V; keeper of Dumbarton Castle (1531); returned from France as rival claimant to James Hamilton, 2d Earl of Arran (1543); seized Mary of Guise, queen dowager, and Princess Mary at Edinburgh in fruitless attempt at marriage with Mary of Guise (1543); after treasonable negotiations with Henry VIII, joined English party, surrendered Dumbarton and Bute, won hand of Lady Margaret Douglas (*q.v.*), niece of Henry VIII, and became governor of Scotland (1544); outlawed in Scotland (1545); returned to Scotland, restored to title and lands (1564); arranged marriage (1565) between his eldest son, Henry Stewart, Lord Darnley (see above) and Mary, Queen of Scots; after Darnley's murder, took part in imprisonment of Mary at Loch Leven; provisional regent in behalf of his infant grandson, afterward James VI; confirmed in regency (1570) after assassination of Lord James Stewart, Earl of Moray; fought against queen's supporters, Huntly and the Hamiltons; captured at Stirling; mortally wounded in skirmish. His granddaughter ¶Arabella (1575–1615), first cousin of James VI of Scotland and next in succession to him to both Scottish and English thrones after Queen Elizabeth; center of intrigues aimed at eliminating James VI as Elizabeth's successor; closely guarded because of Elizabeth's suspicion, made ineffectual attempts to escape in order to marry successive suitors; secretly married (1610) William Seymour (see SEYMOUR family), also of royal descent; imprisoned, died insane in Tower. ¶Esmé Stuart *or* Stewart (1542?–1583), 6th Seigneur of Au·bi·gny \ō-bēn-yē\ and 1st Duke of Lennox; nephew of Matthew, 4th Earl of Lennox; sent to Scotland as agent of Guises to restore Roman Catholicism; became favorite of James VI, by whom he was made earl of Darnley and (1581) duke of Lennox; secured condemnation of James Douglas, 4th Earl of Morton, for murder of Darnley; expelled from Scotland for plotting invasion of England by a Spanish army (1582).

¶Charles Stuart (1639–1672), 6th Duke of Lennox, 3d Duke of Richmond, and 10th Seigneur of Aubigny; nephew of 4th Duke of Lennox; returned to England from France with Charles II. His wife (m. 1667) ¶Frances Teresa Stuart *or* Stewart (1647–1702), Duchess of Richmond and Lennox; remarkable beauty; known as La Belle \lə-'bel\ Stuart; maid of honor to Queen Catherine of Braganza; mistress of Charles II; the original of the figure of Brittannia on reverse side of the halfpenny (1672) and on medals.

EARLS OF MOR·AY OR MUR·RAY \'mər-ē\:

¶James Stewart *or* Stuart (1499?–1544), Earl of Moray; natural son of James IV; guardian of James V and lieutenant general of French forces in Scotland; suppressed insurrection of isles (1531); member of council of state (1543).

¶Lord James Stewart *or* Stuart (1531?–1570), Earl of Mar *and* Earl of Moray; natural son of James V; half-brother of Mary, Queen of Scots, whom he accompanied to France (1548) and whom he annoyed by joining the Reformers (1556); negotiated with Queen Elizabeth for help against French; with English help reoccupied Edinburgh (1560); dispatched (1561) by Scottish estates to France to invite Mary Stuart to return to her kingdom; on her arrival became virtually her home secretary, or prime minister, and tried to dissuade her from Romanizing Scotland; defeated Huntly for her; supported projected Spanish alliance for Mary; opposed Darnley match by appeal to arms and, lacking full Protestant support, had to seek asylum in England (1565); returned after assassination of Rizzio (1566), nominally reconciled to Mary; left for France immediately after Darnley's murder (1567); recalled as regent (1567) after Mary's abdication at Loch Leven; took no steps against principals in murder of Darnley; defeated Mary's forces at Langside (1568); proposed to Queen Elizabeth imprisonment of Mary in Scotland; secured peace in the realm; assassinated at Linlithgow by James Hamilton of Bothwellhaugh at instigation of Mary's adherents. ¶James Stewart *or* Stuart (d. 1592), 2d Earl of Moray; son-in-law of the preceding; called "the bonny earl"; slain by Huntly's men on James VI's warrant, perhaps because of his favor with the queen, and long left unburied, as related in popular ballads. 158 'half-brother

EARLS OF ORK·NEY \'ȯrk-nē\:

¶Lord Robert Stewart (d. 1592), Earl of Orkney; natural son of James V; half-brother of regent Moray. Abbot of Holyrood (1539); joined lords of the congregation; and knowledge of plot against Darnley and said to have warned him; imprisoned by Morton on charge of offering Orkney Islands to Denmark (1575); one of chief conspirers bringing about Morton's ruin (1580–81). His son ¶Patrick (d. 1614), 2d Earl of Orkney, virtual independent sovereign of the Orkneys and Zetland, was deprived of justiciarship and imprisoned on charge of tyranny and cruelty.

EARLS OF ATH·OLL \'ath-əl\:

¶Sir John Stewart of Balveny (1440–1512), 1st Earl of Atholl (of a new Stewart line); aided in subjugation of Angus of the Isles (1480); one of James III's generals (1488).

¶John (d. 1578), 4th Earl of Atholl; great-grandson of 1st earl; at first supported Protestant party in adhering to movement in favor of Queen Elizabeth's marriage to Arran, but soon after joined with Huntly in attempt to seize Edinburgh for papists; member of Queen Mary's first council (1561); leader of Scottish Catholic nobles after fall of Huntly; Mary's chief counselor after Darnley marriage, but not connected with Rizzio's or Darnley's murder; joined league against James VI's party and supported Mary's restoration (1570); joined (1578) Argyll against Morton and became chancellor; reconciled with Morton through English mediation; died under suspicion of poison.

EARL OF BUTE \'byüt\:

¶John Stuart (1713–1792), 3d Earl of Bute; gained favor of Frederick Louis, Prince of Wales (1747); became constant companion and confidant of Frederick's son George (later George III); after George III's accession, made secretary of state (1761); disliked by populace for Scottish heritage and for ousting William Pitt; prime minister (May 1762); aroused increased popular hostility by negotation for peace and Treaty of Paris (1763) and by cider tax; resigned (April 1763); failing in intrigue against Grenville, forced to withdraw from court (1765); devoted himself to scientific pursuits and patronage of arts; gave Dr. Johnson a pension of £300 a year.

Stewart, Alexander Turney. 1803–1876. American merchant, b. Lisburn, Ireland. To U.S. (c.1820) and settled in New York; opened small drygoods store (1823), which developed into great retail store of A. T. Stewart & Co.; contributed widely to charities; founded Garden City, Long Island, as planned community for families of moderate income (1869). See John WANAMAKER.

Stewart *or* **Steuart,** Archibald James Edward. See under DOUGLAS family.

Stewart, Balfour. 1828–1887. Scottish physicist and meteorologist. Director of Kew observatory (1859–71); professor at Owens Coll., Manchester (1870–87). His researches on radiant heat contributed to foundation of spectrum analysis; turned to meteorology, making special study of terrestrial magnetism; proposed (1882) that the variable part of the Earth's magnetic field could be ascribed to electric currents in the upper atmosphere, thus pioneering in ionospheric science; investigated sunspots. Author of *The Unseen Universe* (1875, with Peter G. Tait) and works on physics and sunspots.

Stewart, Charles. 1778–1869. American naval officer, b. Philadelphia. Grandfather of Charles S. Parnell. Commanded schooner *Experiment* (1800) and captured two French privateers; commanded brig *Siren* in war against Tripolitan pirates (1804). In War of 1812, commanded the *Constitution,* preying on British commerce (1813–14) and capturing two British warships, *Cyane* and *Levant* (1815). Created senior flag officer by act of Congress (1859); commissioned rear admiral on the retired list (1862).

Stewart, Sir Donald Martin. 1824–1900. British field marshal. Entered Bengal army (1840); commanded Abyssinian expedition (1867–68); commanded Kandahar field force in Afghan War (1878); sent Roberts on famous march from Kabul to Kandahar while he himself led rest of army through Khyber Pass to India; commander in chief in India (1880–85); field marshal (1894).

Stewart, Donald Ogden. 1894–1980. American writer, b. Columbus, Ohio. Member of Algonquin Round Table in New York (1920s); won Academy Award (with Dalton Trumbo) for screenplay for *The Philadelphia Story* (1940); blacklisted in Hollywood and settled in London (1951). Author of screenplays, including *Holiday, Prisoner of Zenda, The Barretts of Wimpole Street, Life with Father;* books of humor and plays.

Stewart, Dugald. 1753–1828. Scottish philosopher. Professor, Edinburgh (1785–1820; inactive from 1809). Major exponent of the Scottish "common sense" school of philosophy; held doctrine of natural realism, professed the Baconian empirical method, but disavowed its developments and retained intuitionism. Author of *Elements of the Philosophy of the Human Mind* (1792, 1814, 1827), *Outlines of Moral Philosophy* (1793), *Philosophical Essays* (1810), and *The Philosophy of the Active and Moral Powers* (1828).

Stewart, George Neil. 1860–1930. American physiologist, b. London, Ont. Head of laboratory of experimental medicine, Western Reserve U. (1907–30). Invented calorimetric method of measuring blood flow; investigated epinephrine output of adrenal glands; established efficacy of extracts of adrenal cortex. Author of *Manual of Physiology* (1895).

Stewart, James. 1843–1913. Scottish educator. Fellow of Trinity College, Cambridge; offered extension lectures on scientific subjects to workers thitherto denied an education (1867); persuaded Cambridge to provide extension courses (1873).

Stewart, Philo Penfield. 1798–1868. American clergyman, b. Sherman, Conn. Missionary to various Indian tribes; joined John J. Shipherd in Elyria, Ohio, and with him founded Oberlin College (1833).

Stewart, Potter. 1915–1985. American jurist, b. Jackson, Mich. Associate justice of U.S. Supreme Court (1958–81); a dissenter on liberal Warren Court; a centrist on conservative Burger Court; upheld many First Amendment claims, including 1971 Pentagon Papers case; concurred in 1973 *Roe v. Wade* case legalizing abortion but voted to disallow Medicaid funding for it; known for his 1964 opinion that he could not define pornography "but I know it when I see it."

Stewart, Robert. 2d Marquis of Lon·don·der·ry \ˌlən-dən-ˈder-ē, ˈlən-dən-ˌ\. *Known generally as* Viscount Cas·tle·reagh \ˈkas-əl-ˌrā\. 1769–1822. British politician, b. Dublin. Member of Irish Parliament (1790) and of English Parliament (1794–1805, 1806–22); chief secretary for Ireland (1798–1801), responsible for quelling the 1798 rebellion and for passage through Irish Parliament (1800) of Pitt's measure for immediate union; resigned on George III's refusal to allow introduction of Irish Catholic emancipation bill (1801). President of East India Board of Control (1802); appointed war secretary by Pitt (1805–06, 1807–09); responsible for Elbe expedition (1805); seized Danish fleet, extended war to Iberian Peninsula, selected Wellesley as general; made scapegoat of failure of Walcheren expedition; challenged his rival Canning to duel, wounded him slightly (1809). As foreign secretary and leader of House of Commons (1812–22), led coalition against Napoléon; prevented allies from treating separately with France; by threat of withdrawal of British subsidy, forced Bernadotte to send reinforcements to Blücher, whereupon battle of Laon was won (1814). As British representative at Congress of Vienna (1814), thwarted ambitions of Russia in Poland and Prussia in Saxony by secret treaties with France and Austria; after Waterloo, secured Napoléon's removal to St. Helena and settled terms of confinement; in opposition to Metternich, restrained allies from retaliation on France and minimized penalties exacted (1815). Defeated in House of Commons on income tax (1816); blamed for Six Acts (1819) impairing civil liberties; opposed Metternich's policy of intervention by Continental powers in revolutionary movement in Spain; in dread of Russian attack upon Turkey (1821), forced by Greek insurrection to cooperate with Metternich; wrote instructions to himself for conference at Verona (1822), which were carried out by Canning. Mentally disordered by overwork and responsibility; cut his own throat.

Stewart, William Morris. 1827–1909. American lawyer and politician, b. Galen, N.Y. To California (1850); admitted to bar (1852); attorney general of California (1854). To Nevada (1859) and practiced in Virginia City and Carson City; specialist in mining law; U.S. senator from Nevada (1864–75, 1887–1905); author (1869) of the 15th amendment to the Constitution in its final form; vigorous advocate of remonetization of silver (1888–1900).

Steyn \ˈstīn\, Marthinus Theunis. 1857–1916. South African lawyer and politician. Practiced in Bloemfontein (1883–89); on high court of Free State (1889–96). President of Orange Free State (1896–1900); advocated economic independence and purity of Dutch language; negotiated alliance of Orange Free State with the Transvaal (1897); guerrilla leader during South African War (1900–1902); after war became a behind-the-scenes power and resisted Louis Botha's program of conciliation.

Stick·ley \ˈstik-lē\, Gustave. 1858–1942. American furniture designer and manufacturer, b. Osceola, Pa. Designed and manufactured (from 1900) furniture in simple style later known as Mission Style; proprietor of Craftsman Workshops; founded (1901) *The Craftsman* magazine.

Stie·gel \ˈshtē-gəl, *Angl* ˈstē-\, Henry William, *orig.* Heinrich Wilhelm. 1729–1785. American ironmaster and glassmaker, b. near Cologne, Germany. To America (1750); employed in iron foundry in Lancaster Co., Pa. (1751); with partners, bought the foundry (1758); founded town of Manheim (1762) in Lancaster County. Brought glassmakers from England and established two glass factories at Manheim (1764, 1769); known for high quality of his blue, green, purple, and crystal-clear glassware. Went bankrupt (1774).

Stieg·litz \ˈstēg-ləts, -ˌlits\, Alfred. 1864–1946. American photographer and editor, b. Hoboken, N.J. Often called the father of modern photography; pioneer and passionate advocate in establishment of photography as a form of art. Founded the Photo-Secession Group (1902); with aid of Edward Steichen established the Photo-Secessionist 291 Gallery in New York (1905–17). Publisher and editor of photography magazines, esp. *Camera Work* (1903–17); promoted exhibitions of modern American and European painters, sculptors, and photographers, often in face of public derision. His worked marked by highest standards of quality, constant technical innovations, and realistic effects; known esp. for two series of 400 prints each consisting of portraits of his wife (m. 1924) Georgia O'Keeffe and of cloud patterns related to emotions. His brother ¶Julius Oscar (1867–1937), b. Hoboken; taught chemistry at U. of Chicago (1892–1933); studied molecular rearrangements, catalysis, theory of chemical indicators, structure of organo-nitrogen compounds; known for interpreting behavior and structure of organic compounds in light of valence theory and for applying methods of physical chemistry to organic chemistry. Author of *Elements of Qualitative Chemical Analysis* (1911).

Stie·ler \ˈshtē-lər\, Joseph Karl. 1781–1858. German painter. Known for portraits, including Goethe, Schelling, Humboldt, Beethoven, and family of King Maximilian II of Bavaria.

Stiel·tjes \ˈstēl-tyəs\, Thomas Jan. 1856–1894. French mathematician, b. Netherlands. To Paris (1886); naturalized French citizen. Professor at Toulouse (1886–94). Studied divergent and conditionally convergent series; made advances in theory of Riemann's function, number theory, and theory of spherical harmonics; proposed an important definition of integral now known as Stieltjes integral.

Stiern·hielm \ˈshern-ˌyelm\, Georg. *Orig. surname* Olofs·son \ˈü-lȯfs-sən\. 1598–1672. Swedish poet and scholar. Known as the father of Swedish poetry. Given official position in Dorpat (1630); raised to nobility with name Stiernhielm (1631); appointed councilor of war (1661) and director of college of antiquities (1667). Author of lyrics, sonnets, laudatory verse, court masques, esp. *Then Fångne Cupido* (1649), and an allegorical, didactic epic in hexameters *Hercules* (written c.1647, pub. 1658); poems collected in *Musae Suethizantes* (1668). As scholar, wrote on philology, history, philosophy; advocated purification of Swedish language.

Sti·fel \ˈshtē-fəl\, Michael. *Also* Sty·fel *or* Stif·fel \ˈshtē-fəl\. c.1487–1567. German mathematician. Augustinian monk converted to Protestantism (1523) through Luther's influence; professor, Jena (from 1559); regarded as first German authority on the theory of numbers.

Stif·ter \ˈshtif-tər\, Adalbert. 1805–1868. Austrian writer. Inspector of schools at Linz (1850–65). Author of simply structured works of fiction exalting the humble virtues of a simple life. Writings included novels *Der Nachsommer* (1857) and *Witiko* (1865–67); stories *Der Condor* (1840), *Feldblumen* (1841), *Die Mappe meines Urgrossvaters* (1841–42), and *Brigitta* (1844); collections of stories *Studien* (1844–50) and *Bunte Steine* (1853).

Stig·and \'stig-ənd\. d. 1072. English prelate. Chaplain to Canute; chief adviser to Queen Emma after death of Canute; bishop of Elmham (1038, consecrated 1043) and Winchester (1047); supported Earl Godwin against Edward the Confessor and arranged peace between them (1052); appointed archbishop of Canterbury (1052), but unrecognized by popes except briefly by Benedict X; submitted to William I (1066); deposed by papal legates and imprisoned till death for usurpation and plurality.

Stiles \'stī(ə)lz\, Charles Wardell. 1867–1941. American zoologist, b. Spring Valley, N.Y. Chief of zoology division, U.S. Public Health Service (1902–31); lecturer, Johns Hopkins (1897–1937); medical director, Rockefeller Commission for Eradication of Hookworm Disease (1909–14). Author of works on parasites; editor of *Index-catalogue of Medical and Veterinary Zoology* (with Albert Hassall; from 1908).

Stiles, Ezra. 1727–1795. American clergyman and scholar, b. North Haven, Conn. Pastor of Second Congregational Church, Newport, R.I. (1755–76 actively; 1776–86 in absentia); instrumental in founding of Brown U. (1764); staunch supporter of the Revolution; president, Yale (1778–95); also, professor of ecclesiastical history, and gave instruction in Hebrew, theology, and the sciences.

Stil·i·cho \'stil-i-ˌkō\, Flavius. c.365–408 A.D. Roman general and statesman. Son of Vandal chieftain in Roman service; m. a niece of Emperor Theodosius I; commander in chief of army (c.393–408); guardian and chief minister of Honorius; rival of Rufinus; de facto ruler of Western empire; repelled Alaric (403) and defeated Ostrogothic armies under Radagaisus (405–06); attempted to seize Illyricum (407). Suspected of being involved in conspiracy against Honorius; executed. Two of his daughters married Honorius.

Still \'stil\, Andrew Taylor. 1828–1917. American medical practitioner, b. Jonesboro, Va. Moved to Kansas (1853); busied with farming, doctoring Indians, and studying anatomy. Motivated by deaths of three of his children in epidemic of spinal meningitis, formulated (1874) principles of osteopathy. Moved to Kirksville, Mo. (1875), and developed large practice. Incorporated American School of Osteopathy, Kirksville, Mo. (1892); founded *Journal of Osteopathy* (1894).

Still, Clyfford. 1904–1980. American painter, b. Grandin, N.D. At first, painted realistic landscapes of the American West and a series of distorted figure studies (1930s); became an Abstract Expressionist (after 1943); rejected European tradition and created a personal painting idiom of jagged abstract forms covering huge canvases; exerted profound influence on modern American artists.

Still, William Grant. 1895–1978. American composer, b. Woodville, Miss. Worked as arranger for W.C. Handy and band leader Paul Whiteman (1920s); first Negro to conduct a professional symphony orchestra in U.S. (Los Angeles Philharmonic, 1936). His compositions marked by simple harmonies and orchestration and use of material from jazz, blues, and other folk idioms. Works included 5 symphonies, esp. No. 1 *Afro-American* (1930), No. 2 *Song of a New Race* (1937); 6 symphonic poems, esp. *Darker America* (1924), *Kaintuck* (1935); operas *Troubled Island* (1938), *A Bayou Legend* (1940), *Highway 1, U.S.A.* (1962); ballets *Sahdji* (1930), *Lenox Avenue* (1937); choral works *And They Lynched Him on a Tree* (1940), *Those Who Wait* (1942); instrumental music and songs.

Stil·ler \'stil-ər\, Mauritz. 1883–1928. Swedish motion picture director, b. Helsinki. Acted in and directed his first film *Mor och dotter* (1912); gained fame with pictorial beauty of *Herr Arnes pengar* (1919), cosmopolitan *Erotikon* (1920), lyrical nature scenes of *Gunnar Hedes saga* (1922); discovered Greta Garbo and starred her in his *Gösta Berlings saga* (1923); to Hollywood (1925) to direct *Hotel Imperial, Woman on Trial, The Street of Sin* (all 1927); returned to Sweden (1928).

Stilling, Heinrich. See Johann JUNG.

Stil·ling·fleet \'stil-iŋ-ˌflēt\, Edward. 1635–1699. English prelate. Chaplain to Charles II (1667); dean of St. Paul's, London (1678); bishop of Worcester (1689–99); engaged in ceaseless controversy with Nonconformists, Romanists, Deists, and Socinians; had controversy with Locke on the Trinity (1696–97).

Still·man \'stil-mən\, William James. 1828–1901. American artist and journalist, b. Schenectady, N.Y. As painter, influenced by Rossetti, Ruskin, Millais; U.S. consul at Rome, Italy (1862–65), and Crete (1865–68); as special correspondent of London *Times* in Italy (1875–98), induced British government to countenance Montenegrin aspirations during the Hercegovina insurrection (1875).

Sti·lo Prae·co·ni·nus \'stī-(ˌ)lō-ˌprē-kə-'nī-nəs\, Lucius Aelius. *Also called* Aelius Stilo. c.154–74 B.C. Roman philologist. Teacher of Varro and Cicero; dedicatee of works by friends Lucilius and Coelius Anorator. First systematic student, critic, and teacher of Latin philology and literature and of Roman and Italian antiquities; wrote commentaries on hymns of the Salii and on the Twelve Tables; drew up canon of 25 plays of Plautus; only fragments of his works are extant.

Stil·po \'stil-(ˌ)pō\ *or* **Stil·pōn** \-(ˌ)pōn, -ˌpän\. fl. c.380–300 B.C. Greek philosopher. Member of the Megarian school founded by Euclid; his philosophy valued dialectical skill, reflected doctrines of Eleatic monism and Cynic ethics, and rejected predication; teacher of Zeno of Citium, the founder of Stoicism; only fragments of his dialogues survive in quotations by other authors.

Stil·well \'stil-ˌwel, -wəl\, Joseph Warren. *Nicknamed* Uncle Joe *or* Vinegar Joe. 1883–1946. American army officer, b. Palatka, Fla. Commissioned in army (1904); served in World War I; became expert on China; military attaché in Peking (1935–39); appointed by Chiang Kai-shek chief of staff in China war theater; in command of all American forces in China-Burma-India theater (1942–44); conceived of idea of Ledo Road, later renamed Stilwell Road; general (1944); commander of U.S. army ground forces under MacArthur (1945); commander of U.S. 10th army in Pacific (1945–46).

Stim·son \'stim(p)-sən\, Henry Lewis. 1867–1950. American statesman, b. New York City. Practiced law in New York City (from 1891); U.S. secretary of war (1911–13); governor general, Philippine Islands (1927–29); U.S. secretary of state (1929–33); developed Stimson Doctrine against Japan; U.S. secretary of war (1940–45); guided expansion, training, and operation of U.S. army throughout World War II; chief adviser to Roosevelt and Truman on atomic policy; advised use of atomic bombs against Japan; author of books on U.S. foreign policy.

Stimson, Julia Catherine. 1881–1948. American nurse, b. Worcester, Mass. Cousin of Henry L. Stimson. Chief nurse of American Red Cross Hospital attached to British forces at Rouen, France (1917–18); chief nurse of American Red Cross in France (1918); director of nursing for American Expeditionary Forces (1918–19). Dean of U.S. Army School of Nursing (1919–33); superintendent of Army Nurse Corps (1919–37); major (1920); promoted to colonel on retired list (1948).

Stine \'stīn\, Charles Milton Altland. 1882–1954. American chemist, b. Norwich, Conn. With E. I. Du Pont de Nemours & Co. (from 1907); known for numerous patents including processes and products connected with propellant powder, high explosives, dyes, artificial leather, and paints.

Stin·nes \'shtin-əs, *Angl* 'stin-\, Hugo. 1870–1924. German industrialist. Founded (1893) Stinnes-Konzern, which included control of river and ocean barges and steamers, coal and iron mines, factories, power plants, etc. in Europe and South America; during World War I, served as head of industrial production in Germany and occupied Belgium; further expanded his interests to include timberlands, insurance companies, paper-manufacturing plants and newspapers, in order to extend political influence; member of the Reichstag (1920–24).

Stirling. (1) Earl of. See William ALEXANDER (1567–1640). (2) Lord. See William ALEXANDER (1726–1783).

Stir·ling \'stər-liŋ\, James. *Called* the Venetian. 1692–1770. Scottish mathematician. Studied mathematics at Venice (1715–25), where he discovered secret of Venetian glassmaking; friend of Newton; elected to Royal Society (1726); named manager of Scots Mining Co., Leadhills (1735); contributed to theory of infinite series and infinitesimal calculus. Author of *Lineae Tertii Ordines Newtonianae* (1717), *Methodus Differentialis* (1730), *On the Figure of the Earth* (1735), *A Description of a Machine to Blow Fire by Fall of Water* (1745).

Stirling, Robert. 1790–1878. Scottish clergyman and inventor. Pastor at Galston, Ayrshire (from 1824); inventor of the Stirling-cycle hot air engine (patented 1816).

Stirner, Max. See Johan Kasper SCHMIDT.

Sto·bai·os \stō-'bī-ōs\, Joannes. *Lat.* Sto·bae·us \stə-'bē-əs\. 5th century A.D.? Greek anthologist. Compiled an anthology of extracts from more than 500 Greek authors.

Sto·bo \'stō-(ˌ)bō\, Robert. 1727–?1772. Scottish soldier. Served with George Washington at Fort Necessity (1754); held as hostage by the French; escaped from Quebec down the St. Lawrence (1759); joined British at Louisbourg; assisted Wolfe in attack on Quebec (1759); captain in 15th regiment of foot (c.1760–70).

Stock \'shtȯk\, Alfred. 1876–1946. German chemist. Professor, Berlin (1900–09); organized and directed (1909–16) Inorganic Chemistry Inst., Breslau; with Kaiser Wilhelm Inst., Berlin (1916–36). Developed special high-vacuum methods whereby boron hydride mixtures could be separated (1912); directly produced compact beryllium by electrolysis (1921); also made researches on phosphorus and silicon hydrides, carbon compounds, mercury poisoning.

Stock, Thomas. See Robert RAIKES.

Stöcker, Adolf. See Adolf STOECKER.

Stock·mar \'shtȯk-ˌmär, *Angl* 'stäk-\, Christian Friedrich von. Baron. 1787–1863. Belgian statesman. Physician (from 1816), then secretary, adviser, and political agent to Duke Leopold of Saxe-Coburg and continued as his confidential adviser when he became king of Belgians (1831); Leopold's agent in England (1831–37); adviser (1837–57) to Leopold's niece Queen Victoria and arranged her marriage to Leopold's nephew Prince Albert (1840); attended German diets of Frankfurt (1848) and Erfurt (1850) and favored extension of Prussian influence.

Stock·ton \'stäk-tən\, Frank, *in full* Francis Richard. 1834–1902. American writer, b. Philadelphia. Wrote juvenile fiction while assistant editor of *St. Nicholas* (1873–81); scored success with whimsical novel *Rudder Grange* (1879); author of short story "The Lady or the Tiger?" (1882) and novels, mostly humorous, including *The Casting Away of Mrs. Lecks and Mrs. Aleshine* (1886) and its sequel *The Dusantes* (1888), *The Late Mrs. Null* (1886), *Rudder Grangers Abroad* (1891), *Pomona's Travels* (1894), *The Adventures of Captain Horn* (1895).

Stockton, Richard. 1730–1781. American lawyer, b. Princeton, N.J. Member of executive council of New Jersey (1768–76); associate justice, New Jersey supreme court (1774–76); member of Continental Congress (1776) and a signer of the Declaration of Independence. His son ¶Richard (1764–1828) was also a lawyer; U.S. senator (1796–99) and representative (1813–15). A son of this second Richard ¶Robert Field (1795–1866) was a naval officer; served in War of 1812; active in colonization movement to return freed slaves to Africa, including aiding in selection of territory for establishment of Liberia (1821); in command on Pacific coast of N. America (1845–47); took command of U.S. land and sea forces and conquered California; proclaimed California a territory of United States (Aug. 17, 1846) and assumed title of governor and commander in chief; forced to retake parts of territory with aid of army under Stephen W. Kearny (*q.v.*), with whom he later quarreled over questions of authority; resigned from navy (1850); U.S. senator from New Jersey (1851–53); president of Delaware and Raritan Canal Co. (1853–66). Stockton, Calif., is named in his honor.

Stod·dard \'städ-ərd\, Richard Henry. 1825–1903. American poet and literary critic, b. Hingham, Mass. Literary reviewer for New York *World* (1860–70); literary editor, New York *Mail and Express* (1880–1903). His home was a center of cultural life in New York for 30 years. His verse, unoriginal and now dated, included poem "Abraham Lincoln, An Horatian Ode" (1865) and collections *Songs of Summer* (1857) and *The Book of the East* (1867). His wife ¶Elizabeth Drew, *nee* Bar·stow \'bär-(,)stō\ (1823–1902), was a novelist and poet.

Stoddard, Solomon. 1643–1729. American clergyman, b. Boston. First librarian of Harvard (1667–74); pastor in Northampton, Mass. (1672–1729). Grandfather of Jonathan Edwards, who was his assistant pastor (1727–29); introduced doctrine of Stoddardeanism, in which a person's profession of faith, rather than an experience of grace, was sufficient for church admission and communion.

Stoddard, William Osborn. 1835–1925. American journalist, b. Homer, N.Y. Coeditor, *Central Illinois Gazette* (1858); private secretary to President Lincoln (1861–64); U.S. marshal of Arkansas (1864–66). Among his many books were *Abraham Lincoln* (1884), *Inside the White House in War Times* (1890), *The Table Talk of Lincoln* (1894), and more than 75 juveniles.

Stod·dert \'städ-ərt\, Benjamin. 1751–1813. American businessman and politician, b. Charles Co., Md. Served in Revolutionary War (1777–79); secretary to the Board of War (1779–81); acted as confidential agent for the government in securing tracts of land on which the federal capital city was to be established; first U.S. secretary of the navy (1798–1801); drafted bill organizing Marine Corps (1798); acquired properties for naval facilities on East Coast.

Stoeck·er \'shtœk-ər\, Adolf. *Also spelled* Stöck·er. 1835–1909. German clergyman and politician. Court and cathedral preacher in Berlin (1874–90); founder of Christian Social party (1878); originator of political anti-Semitism in Germany; member of Reichstag (1881–93, 1898–1908); founded (1890) Lutheran Social Congress and the United Lutheran Workers' League of Germany; instrumental in fashioning Tivoli program for Conservative party (1892).

Stoeller, Georg Wilhelm. See STELLER.

Sto·ja·di·no·vić \stò-yá-'dē-nò-vēt\, Milan. 1888–1961. Serbian banker and politician. Yugoslav minister of finance (1922–26). Prime minister and minister of foreign affairs of Yugoslavia (1935–39); negotiated alliances with Nazi Germany, Italy, Bulgaria; head of Yugoslav Radical Union; arrested (1940) but smuggled out of Yugoslavia (1941); in Argentina as editor and publisher of an economics magazine (from 1949).

Sto·ker \'stō-kər\, Abraham, *known as* Bram. 1847–1912. Irish writer. Business adviser and secretary to Sir Henry Irving (from 1878); published horror tale *Dracula* (1897) and other novels, including *The Mystery of the Sea* (1902), *The Jewel of Seven Stars* (1904), and *The Lady of the Shroud* (1909).

Stokes \'stōks\, Sir Frederick Wilfrid Scott. 1860–1927. English civil engineer and inventor. Received patents on improvements in breakdown cranes, railway, hydraulic, and refrigerating machinery, and ordnance; invented (1915) Stokes trench mortar.

Stokes, Sir George Gabriel. 1st Baronet Stokes. 1819–1903. British mathematician and physicist, b. Ireland. Professor of mathematics, Cambridge (from 1849); secretary (1854–85), president (1885–90) of Royal Society. Developed modern theory of motion of viscous fluids (1851); made investigations in optics, esp. on wave theory of light; published *The Dynamical Theory of Diffraction* (1849); pioneer in spectrum analysis; discovered nature of fluorescence; investigated ultraviolet spectrum; considered a founder of geodesy for his study of variations in gravity (1849).

Stokes, William. 1804–1878. Irish physician. Published one of earliest treatises in English on use of stethoscope (1825); edited *Dublin Journal of Medical Science;* founded Pathological Society (1838); author of treatises on typhus fever, cholera, and diseases of the heart and lungs.

Sto·kow·ski \stə-'kòf-skē, -'kòv-, *also* -'kaù-\, Leopold Antoni Stanislaw Boleslawowicz. 1882–1977. American conductor, b. London. Naturalized U.S. citizen (1915). Conductor of Cincinnati Symphony Orchestra (1909–12), Philadelphia Orchestra (1914–36), N.Y. Symphony Orchestra (1944–45), and Houston Symphony (1955–62); formed American Symphony Orchestra (1962). Known for lush interpretations of the classics, showmanship, and popularizing of classical music; made symphonic transcriptions of Bach, wrote *Music for All of Us* (1943), and was featured in films, esp. Walt Disney's *Fantasia* (1940).

Stol·berg \'shtōl-,berk\, Christian zu. Graf. 1748–1821. German poet. His poems and stage works were published jointly with those of his brother ¶Graf Friedrich Leopold (1750–1819), under the title *Der Brüder Christian und Friedrich Leopold Grafen zu Stolberg gesammelte Werke* (20 vols., 1820–25).

Sto·ly·pin \stə-'lip-yin\, Pyotr Arkadyevich. 1862–1911. Russian politician. Governor of Grodno (1902) and of Saratov (1903); minister of the interior (May 1906) and premier of Russia (July 1906); instituted liberal agrarian reforms granting freedoms to peasants; imposed harsh policies on Finland; gained enmity of most of political spectrum for his autocratic methods; assassinated.

Stone \'stōn\, Barton Warren. 1772–1844. American clergyman, b. near Port Tobacco, Md. Ordained Presbyterian minister (1798); preacher at Cane Ridge Church near Paris, Ky. (1801–03); leader of liberal "New Light" Presbyterian movement (1803); leader (from 1804) of movement promoting Christian unity by advocating autonomy of local churches and avoidance of use of any word except "Christian" in church titles; preached this doctrine in Ohio, Kentucky, Illinois, Missouri; founder and editor of *Christian Messenger* (1826–37, 1839–44); urged his followers to join Alexander Campbell's Disciples of Christ (1832).

Stone, Edward Durell. 1902–1978. American architect, b. Fayetteville, Ark. Head of architectural firm in New York City (from 1936); taught at New York U. (1935–40) and Yale (1946–52). His designs included El Panama Hotel, Panama City (1946), U.S. Embassy in New Delhi (1954), American Pavilion for Brussels World's Fair of 1958, New York Cultural Center (1959), John F. Kennedy Center for the Performing Arts (1964), General Motors Tower, New York (1964), and Standard Oil Tower, Chicago (1969). A leading exponent of International Style.

Stone, Edward James. 1831–1897. English astronomer. At Cape of Good Hope (1870–79); observer at Oxford (from 1879); produced *Cape Catalogue,* which lists 12,441 stars to 7th magnitude (1880), later extending catalogue to include stars from 25° S. declination to the equator.

Stone, Harlan Fiske. 1872–1946. American jurist, b. Chesterfield, N.H. Practiced in New York (1899–1924); professor of law (1902–05) and dean (1910–23), Columbia Law School; U.S. attorney general (1924–25); associate justice, U.S. Supreme Court (1925–41), chief justice (1941–46); reaffirmed many of New Deal reforms; advocate of judicial self-restraint.

Stone, Lucy. 1818–1893. American woman suffragist, b. West Brookfield, Mass. m. (1855) Henry B. Blackwell, but retained her maiden name as a protest against unequal laws applicable to married women and became known as Mrs. Stone. Lectured on women's rights and against slavery. Sent out call for first national women's-rights convention at Worcester, Mass. (1850); arranged for annual conventions thereafter. Aided in organizing New Jersey Woman Suffrage Association; became its president (1867); aided in forming American Woman Suffrage Association (1869). Raised money for founding *Woman's Journal* (1870); coeditor with her husband (1872–93).

Stone, Melville Elijah. 1848–1929. American journalist, b. Hudson, Ill. Founded the first Chicago penny daily newspaper, Chicago *Daily News* (1875); sold his interests in the paper (1888); organized and became president of Globe National Bank, Chicago (1892–98); general manager, Associated Press of Illinois (1893–1900) and Associated Press, incorporated in New York (1900–23); known for his promotion of objective journalism and securing legal rights for his profession.

Stone, Nicholas. 1587–1647. English sculptor and architect. Master mason to James I (1619) and Charles I (1626); executed designs of Inigo Jones in Renaissance architecture and rejuvenated art in England; executed tombs of Sir Thomas Bodley at Oxford (1615), Sir Charles Morrison at Watford (1619), John Donne at St. Paul's, London (1631), and the classical Lyttelton monument at Magdalen College, Oxford (1634).

Stone, Samuel. 1602–1663. American clergyman, b. Hertford, England. Emigrated with Thomas Hooker to New England (1633); pastor, Cambridge, Mass. (1633–36); purchased site of Hartford, Conn., from the Indians and settled there (1636); minister of the church in Hartford (1636–63).

Stone, William. 1603?–?1660. English colonial administrator. To Virginia (before 1628). Governor of Maryland (1648); had trouble with a Puritan parliamentary commission from England (1652 and 1654); forced by commission to resign (1654). Under orders from Lord Baltimore, rallied force but lost to his Puritan opponents at battle of Severn (Mar. 25, 1655); member of governor's council (1657). His great-great-grandson ¶Thomas Stone (1743–1787), b. Charles Co., Md., was a lawyer; began practice in Frederick, Md.; member of Continental Congress (1775–78) and a signer of the Declaration of Independence; member of the Congress of the Confederation (1784–85).

Stonehaven, Baron. See John Lawrence BAIRD.

Stone•man \'stōn-mən\, George. 1822–1894. American army officer and politician, b. Busti, N.Y. Brigadier general, chief of cavalry in the army of the Potomac under General McClellan (1861); served in Peninsular campaign (1861–62). Major general of volunteers (1862); engaged at Fredericksburg; under orders from General Hooker, led great raid (Apr. 13–May 2, 1863) toward Richmond; chief of cavalry bureau, Washington, D.C. (1863); engaged in Atlanta campaign under Sherman (1864); led raids in southwestern Virginia, eastern Tennessee, and the Carolinas (1864–65); retired (1871). Governor of California (1883–87).

Sto•ney \'stō-nē\, George Johnstone. 1826–1911. Irish physicist. Professor at Queen's Coll., Galway (1852–57); secretary, Queen's U. (1857–82). His work included investigations relating to physical optics, molecular physics, kinetic theory of gases, and the conditions limiting planetary atmospheres; introduced word *electron* to designate the elementary charge of electricity.

Stong \'stȯŋ\, Phil, *in full* Philip Duffield. 1899–1957. American writer, b. Keosauqua, Iowa. Author of many juvenile stories and of novels including *State Fair* (1932), *Village Tale* (1934), *The Rebellion of Lennie Barlow* (1937), *The Long Lane* (1939), *One Destiny* (1942), *Return in August* (1953).

Stopes \'stōps\, Marie Charlotte Carmichael. 1880–1958. English paleobotanist, birth-control advocate, and author. Investigated coal mines and fossil plants; lectured on paleobotany at University Coll. (London) and at U. of Manchester. After annulment (1916) of marriage with R.R. Gates, m. (1918) Humphrey V. Roe (*q.v.*), with whom she founded (1921) Mothers' Clinic for Constructive Birth Control, first instructional clinic for contraception in Britain; after World War II promoted birth control in Far Eastern countries. Author of *Married Love* (1918), *Wise Parenthood* (1918), *Contraception: its Theory, History and Practice* (1923), *Sex and the Young* (1926), *Enduring Passion* (1928), *Sex and Religion* (1929), etc.

Sto•race \'stȯr-əs, 'stär-\, Stephen John Seymour. 1762–1796. English composer. Studied under Mozart in Vienna, where he produced two operas; as composer to Drury Lane Theatre (from 1787), wrote comic operas, including *The Haunted Tower* (1789), *The Pirates* (1792), *The Cherokee* (1794), and *The Iron Chest* (1796), and afterpieces, esp. *No Song, No Supper* (1790); published chamber music, songs, and an anthology *Storace's Collection of Original Harpsichord Music* (1787–89). His sister ¶Ann Selina, *known professionally as* Anna *and commonly as* Nancy (1765–1817), coloratura singer, was the original Susanna in Mozart's *Nozze di Figaro*, Vienna (1786); sang with Drury Lane company (1789–96), being the original Margaretta in her brother's *No Song, No Supper* (1790) and Barbara in *Iron Chest* (1796); sang with John Braham on the Continent and in London (1797–1808).

Storm \'shtȯrm\, Theodor, *in full* Hans Theodor Woldsen. 1817–1888. German writer. Lawyer by profession; magistrate in Heiligenstadt (1856–64); to Husum (1864), where he held judicial posts until his retirement (1880). Representative of German poetic Realism; author of melancholy lyrics collected in *Gedichte* (1852) and *Tiefe Schatten* (1865), and over 50 novellas, including *Immensee* (1852), *Im Schloss* (1861), *Viola tricolor* (1874), *Pole Poppenspäler* (1874), *Aquis submersus* (1875), *Carsten Curator* (1877), *Renate* (1878), *Der Schimmelreiter* (1888).

Stør•mer \'stœr-mər\, Fredrik Carl Mülertz. 1874–1957. Norwegian mathematician and geophysicist. Professor at Oslo (1903–46). Made studies of series, function theory, and number theory; developed mathematical basis of polar aurora theory; invented an apparatus for photographing Aurora Borealis; organized network at Norwegian stations for study of auroras and special types of clouds; wrote *The Polar Aurora* (1955).

Stor•ni \'s(h)tȯr-nē\, Alfonsina. 1892–1938. Argentinian poet, b. Switzerland. Joined theatrical troupe at early age; later a schoolteacher. Author of verse, chiefly on love, including *La inquietud del rosal* (1916), *El dulce daño* (1918), *El mundo de siete pozos* (1934), and *Mascarilla y trébol* (1938).

Storr \'stȯ(ə)r\, Paul. 1771–1844. English goldsmith. Associated with firm of royal goldsmiths, Rundell and Bridge (1807–19); partner of John Mortimer (1822–38); known for outstanding workmanship of his richly ornamented works, esp. presentation silver such as the cup given to Lord Nelson for his victory at battle of the Nile (1798).

Storrs \'stȯ(ə)rz\, Sir Ronald Henry Amherst. 1881–1955. British colonial administrator. Military governor (1917–20), civil governor (1920–26) of Jerusalem; governor and commander in chief, Cyprus (1926–32) and Northern Rhodesia (1932–34). Author of memoirs *Orientations* (1937).

Sto•ry \'stōr-ē, 'stȯr-ē\, Isaac. *Pseudonym* Peter Quince \'kwin(t)s\. 1774–1803. American poet, b. Marblehead, Mass. Cousin of Joseph Story. Known for his political satire and wit in verses collected in *A Parnassian Shop, Opened in the Pindaric Stile; by Peter Quince, Esq.* (1801).

Story, John. 1510?–1571. English martyr. Lecturer on civil law, Oxford (1535), and first regius professor (1544). M.P. (1547), opposed Act of Uniformity (1548); returned from exile (1553) and served as Queen Mary's prosecutor of Protestant heretics; agent of Duke of Alba in establishing Inquisition in Netherlands (1565); kidnaped by English and executed for high treason.

Story, Joseph. 1779–1845. American jurist, b. Marblehead, Mass. Practiced in Salem, Mass. (1801–11). Member, U.S. House of Representatives (1808–09); associate justice, U.S. Supreme Court (1811–45); joined John Marshall in construing the Constitution in favor of expanding federal power; also, professor of law, Harvard (1829–45); a pioneer in organizing and directing teaching in Harvard Law School. Author of a famous series of commentaries, including *Commentaries on the Law of Bailments* (1832), *Commentaries on the Constitution of the United States* (1833), *The Conflict of Laws* (1834), *On Equity Jurisprudence* (1836), *Equity Pleading* (1838), *Law of Agency* (1839), *Law of Partnership* (1841), *Law of Bills of Exchange* (1843), *Law of Promissory Notes* (1845). With James Kent, considered a founder of equity jurisprudence in U.S. His son ¶William Wetmore (1819–1895), b. Salem, Mass., was a sculptor and man of letters; practiced law in Boston and wrote legal treatises; settled in Rome (1856) and thereafter devoted himself to sculpture; became intimate friend of the Brownings, Thackeray, Nathaniel Hawthorne, Charles Eliot Norton, Walter Savage Landor; his works included *Cleopatra* (described in Hawthorne's *Marble Fawn*), *Libyan Sibyl,* and *Medea.*

Stoss \'shtōs\, Viet. *Also* Wit Stosz \'stȯsh\ *or* Sto•wosz \'stȯ-vȯsh\. 1438 or 1439–1533. German sculptor and wood carver. Worked mainly in Poland, Bohemia, Hungary (1477–96); returned to Nürnberg (1496). Known for nervous, angular forms and realistic detail; carved high altar for the Marienkirche, Kraków (1477–89), tomb of Casimir IV (1492), tombstone of Archbishop Oleśnicki in Gniezno cathedral (1493), wood and stone sculpture in churches of St. Sebaldus (1499, 1520) and St. Lorenz (1513, 1518) in Nürnberg, and altar in Bamberg cathedral (1523). Regarded as master of wood carving in Germany.

Stös•sel \'shtœs-əl\, Anatoly Mikhaylovich. 1848–1915. Russian general. Commanded garrison at Port Arthur (1904); defeated and surrendered Port Arthur to Japanese (1905); court-martialed (1906), sentenced to 10 years' imprisonment; pardoned (1909).

Stoth•ard \'stath-ərd, -ärd\, Thomas. 1755–1834. English illustrator and painter. Elected full academician (1794), librarian (1812), of Royal Academy. Executed oil paintings of domestic or ideal subjects, esp. *The Canterbury Pilgrims* (1807); decorated many mansions with wall paintings; best known for graceful illustrations for works of Shakespeare, Milton, Byron, and other poets, and for *Pilgrim's Progress, Don Quixote, Robinson Crusoe, Peregrine Pickle, Tristram Shandy, The Vicar of Wakefield, Clarissa Harlow, Gulliver's Travels,* and other classics.

Stough•ton \'stōt-ᵊn\, Israel. d. 1645? British colonist in America. Founder of Dorchester, Mass. (1630); commander of Massachusetts troops in Pequot War (1637). His son ¶William (1630?–1701) was assistant on Massachusetts council (1671–86), lieutenant governor (1692–1701); presided at trial of Salem witches (1692).

Stout \'staůt\, George Frederick. 1860–1944. English philosopher and psychologist. Professor, St. Andrews U. (1903–36); advanced a system of psychology emphasizing mental acts; his textbooks greatly influenced development of psychology in Britain. Editor of *Mind* (1891–1920); author of *Analytic Psychology* (1896), *Manual of Psychology* (1898), *Mind and Matter* (1931), etc.

Stout, Rex Todhunter. 1886–1975. American writer, b. Noblesville, Ind. Author of detective stories centering around the detective "Nero Wolfe," including *Fer-de-Lance* (1934), *Black Orchids* (1942), *Gambit* (1962), *A Doorbell Rang* (1966), *A Family Affair* (1975).

Stout, Sir Robert. 1844–1930. New Zealand jurist and politician, b. Shetland Islands. To New Zealand (1863). Attorney general (1878–79); prime minister, attorney general, and minister of education (1884–87); reformed civil service and worked to expand opportunities for small farmers; chief justice of New Zealand (1899–1926); member of Legislative Council (1926–30).

Stout, William Bushnell. 1880–1956. American engineer, b. Quincy, Ill. Founder and president (from 1919) of Stout Engineering Laboratories; built first all-metal airplane in U.S. (1922); formed company to build metal commercial planes (1922–25), founded passenger airline (1926–29); engaged in research in airplane, railroad, and automotive fields; active in development of stainless-steel airplanes and welded-steel aircraft engines.

Stow \'stō\, John. 1525–1605. English historian and antiquary. A prosperous tailor; devoted himself (from c.1565) to collecting and transcribing manuscripts and producing histories. Published *The Workes of Geffrey Chaucer* (1561), *A Summarie of Englyshe Chronicles* (1565), *The Chronicles of England* (1580), and *A Survey of London* (1598, 1603), a standard authority on Old London.

Stowe \'stō\, Harriet Elizabeth, *nee* Bee·cher \'bē-chər\. 1811–1896. American author, b. Litchfield, Conn. Daughter of Lyman Beecher; sister of Henry Ward Beecher; m. Calvin Ellis Stowe (1836). During residence in Cincinnati (1833–50) became ardent abolitionist; encouraged by her brother and husband, wrote *Uncle Tom's Cabin, or Life Among the Lowly,* first published (as a serial, 1851–52) in an antislavery paper, the *National Era,* Washington, D.C., and in book form (1852). Book became important factor in solidifying sentiment in the North against slavery and making the issue a moral one; had much to do with bringing on the Civil War. Among her other novels were *Dred, A Tale of the Great Dismal Swamp* (1856), *The Minister's Wooing* (1859), *The Pearl of Orr's Island* (1862), *Oldtown Folks* (1869). Aroused storm of criticism by *Atlantic Monthly* article (Sept. 1869) entitled "The True Story of Lady Byron's Life" in which, on basis of information given her by Lady Byron, she charged Lord Byron with incest with his sister Augusta.

Stowell, Baron. See William SCOTT.

Strabane, Baron and viscount. See HAMILTON family.

Stra·bo \'strā-(,)bō\. 64 or 63 B.C.–after 23 A.D. Greek geographer, b. Amasya, Pontus. Lived in Rome (44–c.31 B.C.); became a Stoic; traveled to Greece (c.29) and up the Nile (25 or 24). Fragments of his *Historical Sketches* (47 vols, 20 B.C.) survive; wrote *Geographical Sketches* describing Europe, Asia, India, Syria, and other parts of the known world.

Strachan \'strȯn\, John. 1778–1867. Canadian clergyman, b. Aberdeen, Scotland. To Canada (1799); ordained Anglican deacon (1803) and archdeacon of Toronto (1825); as member of Executive Council (1815) and Legislative Council (1820), strove to establish ecclesiastical control of higher education; obtained royal charter for King's Coll. (1826–27); first bishop of Toronto (1839). Faced popular resentment over exclusive endowment of Episcopal education; energetically opposed division of Clergy Reserves; finally established King's Coll. (1843), with modifications of its charter; when King's Coll. reorganized as U. of Toronto, founded Trinity U. entirely under control of Episcopal church (1851). Created the Anglican synod of clergy and laity in British colonial empire (1851).

Stra·chey \'strā-chē\, Evelyn John St. Loe. 1901–1963. English Socialist writer and politician. M.P. (1929–31, 1945 ff.); undersecretary for air (1945–46); as minister of food (1946–50) began rationing of bread; war minister (1950–51). Author of *The Coming Struggle for Power* (1932), *The Nature of Capitalist Crisis* (1935), *The Theory and Practice of Socialism* (1936), *A Programme for Progress* (1940), *Contemporary Capitalism* (1956), *The End of Empire* (1959), and *On the Prevention of War* (1962).

Strachey, John. 1671–1743. English geologist. In *Observations on the Different Strata of Earths and Minerals* (1727), was first to suggest the theory of stratified rock formations.

Strachey, Lytton, *in full* Giles Lytton. 1880–1932. English writer. Member of the Bloomsbury group in London. With *Eminent Victorians* (1918) established a new style of biography marked by irony, elegance, wit, irreverence, and a concern for creating a work of art rather than a record of events; his works also included *Landmarks in French Literature* (1912), *Queen Victoria* (1921), *Books and Characters* (1922), *Pope* (1925), *Elizabeth and Essex* (1928), and *Portraits in Miniature* (1931).

Strachey, William. fl. 1606–1618. English colonist in Virginia. Secretary and recorder of Virginia under Lord De La Warr (1610–11); author of *The Historie of Travaile into Virginia Britannia* (pub. 1849).

Strach·witz \'shträk-vits\, Moritz Karl Wilhelm Anton von. Graf. 1822–1847. German poet. Member of Berlin literary club Tunnel über der Spree; competed with Theodor Fontane in writing ballads. Author of collections of lyric verse *Lieder eines Erwachenden* (1842) and esp. *Neue Gedichte* (1848) which contained "Der Himmel ist blau" and a national patriotic song "Germania."

Stra·del·la \strä-'del-lä\, Alessandro. 1644–1682. Italian singer and composer. In service (from 1658) of Queen Christina of Sweden and (from 1665) of Lorenzo Colonna in Rome; forced to leave Rome (1677); almost assassinated for involvement in amorous affair in Venice (1677); murdered for involvement in another amorous intrigue. Composer of operas, motets, oratorios, arias, and esp. over 200 chamber cantatas for religious observance; contributed to development of instrumental music by use of concerto grosso instrumentation first to accompany arias and finally for an independent instrumental composition. Subject of eight 18th-century operas and at least one novel.

Stra·di·va·ri \,strä-dē-'vär-ē\, Antonio. *Lat.* Antonius Strad·i·var·i·us \,strad-i-'var-ē-əs, -'ver-\. 1644?–1737. Italian violin maker. Lifelong resident of Cremona; pupil and associate of Nicolo Amati (to at least 1666). Considered greatest of all violin makers; began producing larger models with different varnishes and details in form (1684); created a new type of "long" model (1690); devised modern form of violin bridge and set proportions of modern violin; also produced cellos, violas, lutes, guitars, mandolins, etc. Assisted in later work by his sons ¶Francesco (1671–1743), who carried on father's art, and ¶Omobono (1679–1742), known esp. for skill in repairing stringed instruments.

Stradonitz, Kekule von. See KEKULE VON STRADONITZ.

Strafford, Earl of. See Sir Thomas WENTWORTH.

Strand \'strand\, Paul. 1890–1976. American photographer, b. New York City. Pupil of Lewis W. Hine (1907–09); associated with Alfred Stieglitz and other Photo-Secessionists; collaborated with Charles Sheeler on documentary film *Manhattan* (1921); photographed landscapes of Colorado (1926), Maine (1927–28), Gaspé Peninsula (1929), New Mexico (1930); as chief photographer and cinematographer to Mexican government (1933–34), produced still photographs and motion picture *Redes* (1935, *The Wave*); cameraman on Pare Lorentz's documentary *The Plow That Broke the Plains* (1936); head of Frontier Films (1937–42), producing documentaries. Known for his abstract and objective photographs as "Wall Street" (1915), "White Fence" (1916), "Lathe" (1923); published photographic books *Time in New England* (1950), *La France de profil* (1952), *Un Paese* (1954), *Living Egypt* (1969), etc.

Strand·berg \'stränd-,berʸ\, Carl Vilhelm August. *Pseudonym* Ta·lis Qua·lis \'täl-əsk-'väl-əs\. 1818–1877. Swedish poet and journalist. Known for rhetorical odes in support of "Scandinavianism"; published *Sånger i pansar* (1845), *Vilda rosor* (1848), etc.

Strang \'straŋ\, James Jesse *or* Jesse James. 1813–1845. American religious leader, b. Scipio, N.Y. Converted by Joseph Smith in Nauvoo, Ill., and ordained Mormon elder (1844); expelled from church for attempting to succeed Smith by fraudulent means (1844); led group of dissident Mormons to Voree, Wis., and organized Strangite sect; moved sect, 5000 strong, to Beaver Island, Mich. (1847); crowned himself King James I and purportedly translated *The Book of the Law of the Land* from golden plates from the ark of the Covenant (1850). Elected to Michigan legislature (1852, 1854) and became a local political power; assassinated by two former Strangites.

Stra·pa·ro·la \,strä-pä-'rȯ-lä\, Gianfrancesco. c.1480–after 1557. Italian writer. Known for his collection of 75 novelle and tales *Piacevoli notti* (1550–53), notable as source material for Shakespeare, Molière, et al., and containing such tales as *Beauty and the Beast* and *Puss in Boots.*

Stras·berg \'stras-,bərg\, Lee. *Orig.* Israel Strass·berg \'sträs-,berk\. 1901–1982. American theatrical director and teacher, b. Budzanow, Galicia (now in U.S.S.R.). To U.S. (1909); founding member (1931–37), Group Theater, N.Y.C.; artistic director (from 1948), Actors Studio, N.Y.C. Leading exponent in U.S. of Konstantin Stanislavsky's system of Method acting; his pupils included Marlon Brando, Paul Newman, Robert DeNiro, Joanne Woodward, Dustin Hoffman.

Stras·bur·ger \'shträs-,bu̇r-gər\, Eduard Adolf. 1844–1912. German botanist. Professor at Jena (1869–80) and Bonn (1880–1912). First to provide accurate description of embryonic sac in gymnosperms and angiosperms; laid down basic principles of mitosis in *Über Zellbildung und Zelltheilung* (1876); enunciated law of plant cytology that new nuclei of plants can arise only from division of other nuclei (1880); concluded that the nucleus is primary structure of heredity (1884); coauthor of *Lehrbuch der Botanik* (1894).

Stra·shi·mi·rov \,strásh-i-'mir-ôf\, Anton. 1872–1937. Bulgarian writer. Author of Realist works depicting contemporary society, including story "Kochalovskata kramola" (1895), novels *Yesenni dni* (1902), *Krŭstopŭt* (1904), *Sreshta* (1908), and plays *Vampir* (1902), *Svekŭrva* (1906), *Otvud* (1906), and *Robi* (1929).

Strassburg, Gottfried von. See GOTTFRIED VON STRASSBURG.

Stras·ser \'shträs-ər\, Otto Johan Maximilian. 1897–1974. German politician and writer. Served in World War I; edited newspapers in northern Germany; joined Nazi party (1925); broke with Hitler and organized Schwartze Front (1930); exiled (1933); lived in Vienna, Prague (where he edited *Die Deutsche Revolution,* 1934–39), Zürich, Paris; founder (1941) of Free German Movement; to Canada (1940); returned to Germany (1955). Wrote *Hitler and I* (1940), *Flight from Terror* (with Michael Stern, 1942), etc. His brother

¶Gregor (1892–1934) joined Nazi party (1920); participated in Munich Putsch (1923); as head of party in northern Germany (from 1924) built it up into a mass movement with aid from Otto and Joseph Goebbels; became (1932) head of Nazi political organization and second only to Hitler in power and authority; resigned (1932) after Hitler's refusal to join Schleicher's cabinet; lost all influence; murdered on Hitler's orders.

Strat·e·mey·er \'strat-ə-,mī-ər\, Edward. 1862–1930. American writer, b. Elizabeth, N.J. Author, under pseudonym Arthur M. Win·field \'win-,fēld\, of the *Bound to Win* and *Old Glory* series and the *Rover Boys* series (1899–1926); under pseudonym Capt. Ralph Bone·hill \'bōn-,hil\, of the *Flag of Freedom* (1899–1902), *Mexican War* (1900–02), *Frontier* (1903–07) series. Founded Stratemeyer Literary Syndicate (1906); using stable of hack writers and himself supplying characters and plot outlines, produced following series under pseudonyms: *Tom Swift* as Victor Appleton; *Motor Boys* as Clarence Young; *Bobbsey Twins* as Laura Lee Hope; *Hardy Boys* as Franklin W. Dixon; *The Boy Scouts* as Howard Payson; and *Nancy Drew* as Carolyn Keene. His daughter ¶Harriet Stratemeyer Adams (1893?–1982), m. Russell V. Adams (1915; d. 1966); joined syndicate and became senior partner (1930); wrote some 200 books for *Hardy Boys, Bobbsey Twins, Tom Swift, Jr.*, and esp. *Nancy Drew* series.

Strat·ford \'strat-fərd\, John de. d. 1348. English prelate. Made bishop of Winchester (1323) by pope against wishes of Edward II; sided with Queen Isabella, drew up six articles comprising reasons for deposition of Edward II, and obtained his abdication (1327). Member of royal council of Edward III; chancellor (1330–34, 1335–37, 1340) and chief adviser to Edward III (1330–40); archbishop of Canterbury (1333); president of council during Edward's absence (1345, 1346).

Stratford de Redcliffe, Viscount. See Stratford CANNING.

Strathcona and Mount Royal, Baron. See Donald Alexander SMITH.

Strathnairn, Baron. See Hugh Henry ROSE.

Stra·to \'strā-(,)tō\ *or* **Stra·ton** \-,tän\ of Lamp·sa·cus \'lam(p)-sə-kəs\. *Lat.* Strato Phy·si·cus \-'fiz-i-kəs\. d. c.270 B.C. Greek Peripatetic philosopher. Successor of Theophrastus as head of the Peripatos (c.287 B.C.); famous for his doctrine that all substances contain void; tempered Aristotle's interpretation of nature by insistence on causality and materialism and denial of supernatural forces at work in nature.

Strat·o·ni·ce \,strat-ō-'nī-sē\. fl. 300 B.C. Syrian queen. Daughter of Demetrius I Poliorcetes of Macedonia. When quite young, married (c.300) Seleucus I Nicator; given up by him (292) to become wife of his son (her stepson) Antiochus I, satrap of Bactria and later king of Syria; mother of Antiochus II.

Strat·ton \'strat-ᵊn\, Charles Sherwood. *Known as* General Tom Thumb \'thəm\. 1838–1883. American midget, b. Bridgeport, Conn. Joined P. T. Barnum's organization (1842) and was on exhibition in New York, England, and on the continent of Europe (1844–47). m. (1863) ¶Mercy Lavinia Warren Bum·pus \'bəm-pəs\, *known as* Lavinia Warren (1841–1919), a dwarf in Barnum's organization. Until he was in his teens, he was only 2'1" tall and weighed about fifteen pounds; at maturity, he was 3'4" tall and weighed about seventy pounds.

Stratton, Samuel Wesley. 1861–1931. American physicist, b. Litchfield, Ill. By request of U.S. secretary of the treasury, prepared report on a proposed Bureau of Standards, drafted bill establishing bureau (passed by Congress, 1901), and became first director of the bureau (1901–23). President, M.I.T. (1923–30).

Stratton Porter, Gene. See Gene PORTER.

Straus \'straůs\, Isidor. 1845–1912. American merchant, b. Otterberg, Bavaria. To U.S. (1854); with his father, Lazarus, organized crockery firm of L. Straus & Son in New York (1865); took over crockery and glassware department of R.H. Macy & Co. (1874); partner in Macy & Co. with his brother Nathan (1888), purchasing full ownership in 1896; developed Abraham & Straus, a department store in Brooklyn, N.Y.; member of U.S. House of Representatives (1894–95); lost in the *Titanic* disaster. His brother ¶Nathan (1848–1931) joined L. Straus & Son (1866); with Isidor became member (1888) and owner (1896) of R.H. Macy & Co.; New York City park commissioner (1889–93); president of board of health (1898); led campaign for pasteurized milk (from 1892) and established milk stations in New York and other large cities; retired from business (1914); in last 20 years of life largely devoted to public health work in Palestine; chosen by popular vote (1923) as the citizen who had done most for public welfare in the first quarter century of Greater New York history. Another brother ¶Oscar Solomon (1850–1926), lawyer and diplomat, joined L. Straus & Sons (1881); U.S. minister to Turkey (1887–89, 1898–1900); member of Permanent Court of Arbitration at The Hague (1902–26); U.S. secretary of commerce and labor (1906–09), first Jewish Cabinet member; first American ambassador to Turkey (1909–10); adviser to President Wilson at Versailles Treaty talks (1919); supported Zionist movement and rights of Jews in Palestine and European nations. Isidor's son ¶Jesse Isidor (1872–1936), merchant and diplomat; president of R.H. Macy & Co. (1919); minister to France (1933–36). Another son ¶Percy Selden (1876–1944) also became president of R.H. Macy & Co. (to 1940).

Straus \'shtraůs\, Oscar. 1870–1954. French composer, b. Vienna. Pupil of Max Bruch in Berlin (1891); theater conductor in Austria and Germany; naturalized French citizen (1939). Best known as composer of operettas, including *Ein Walzertraum* (1907), *Der tapfere Soldat* (1908; *The Chocolate Soldier;* adapted from Shaw's *Arms and the Man*), *Rund um die Liebe* (1914), *Der letzte Walzer* (1920), and *Die Musik kommt* (1948); also composed film scores as *La Ronde* (1950), ballets, orchestral works, chamber music, choruses, piano pieces, and about 500 cabaret songs.

Strauss \'shtraůs\, David Friedrich. 1808–1874. German theologian and philosopher. Developed a theory of biblical interpretation based on Hegelian dialectical philosophy; caused storm of controversy among German Protestants by describing the Gospels as "historical myth"; called to professorship in Zürich (1839), but strong opposition forced him to leave the city. Among his books were *Das Leben Jesu, kritisch bearbeitet* (1835–36), *Die christliche Glaubenslehre in ihrer geschichtlichen Entwicklung und im Kampfe mit der modernen Wissenschaft dargestellt* (1840–41), *Der alte und der neue Glaube* (1872), and a number of biographical studies.

Strauss, Johann Baptist. 1804–1849. Austrian composer. Formed (1825) own orchestra, playing at Viennese inns; established reputation as composer of waltzes by conducting (1830) at the "Sperl," a popular dance hall in Vienna; on tour in Germany (1833), in Paris and London (1837); appointed court dance music director (1835). Among his compositions were waltzes, polkas, galops, quadrilles, and marches. His son ¶Johann (1825–1899), *called* the Waltz King, conducted own dance band at a Viennese restaurant (1844); on father's death, combined his father's orchestra with his own and with it toured widely and successfully; court dance music director (1863–71); conducted concerts in New York and Boston (1872). Among his operettas were *Indigo* (1871), *Der Karneval in Rom* (1873), *Die Fledermaus* (1874), *Cagliostro* (1875), *Prinz Methusalem* (1877), *Eine Nacht in Venedig* (1883), *Der Zigeunerbaron* (1885), *Waldmeister* (1895); among his more than 150 waltzes were "Morgenblätter" (1864), "Künstlerleben" (1867), "An der schönen, blauen Donau" (1867, "The Blue Danube"), "Geschichten aus dem Wienerwald" (1868, "Tales from the Vienna Woods"), "Wein, Weib und Gesang" (1869), "Wiener Blut" (1871), and "Kaiserwaltzer" (1888). His brother ¶Josef (1827–1870) succeeded him as conductor of the family orchestra (1863); composed many dances. Another brother ¶Eduard (1835–1916) succeeded to leadership of the orchestra on Josef's death (1870); court dance music conductor (1872–1901); composed more than 200 dance pieces.

Strauss \'straůs\, Joseph Baermann. 1870–1938. American bridge engineer, b. Cincinnati. Founded (1904) own engineering firm with offices in Chicago and San Francisco; made improvements in bascule, lift, and suspension bridges; designed and built over 400 bridges, including Columbia River Bridge at Longview, Wash. (1930), George Washington Bridge across Hudson River from upper New York City (1931), the Golden Gate Bridge in San Francisco (1937).

Strauss, Levi. 1829?–1902. American manufacturer, b. Germany. Little known of early life; left New York City home for California (1850); sold pants made of tent canvas to gold miners; established (1850) Levi Strauss & Co., San Francisco, for manufacture of denim trousers which came to be known as "blue jeans" or "Levi's."

Strauss \'shtraůs\, Richard Georg. 1864–1949. German composer. Court conductor at Munich (1894–98); chief conductor of Berlin Court Opera (1898–1918); collaborator with Franz Schalk as head of the State Opera, Vienna (1919–24); president of the Reich's music bureau (1933–36). As composer, regarded as leader of the New Romantic school. Among his works were 15 operas, including *Salome* (1905), *Elektra* (1909), *Der Rosenkavalier* (1911), *Ariadne auf Naxos* (1912), *Die Frau ohne Schatten* (1919), *Die ägyptische Helena* (1928), *Arabella* (1933), *Die schweigsame Frau* (1935), *Daphne* (1938), *Die Liebe der Danae* (1940), *Capriccio* (1942); tone poems *Don Juan* (1889), *Macbeth* (1890), *Tod und Verklärung* (1891), *Till Eulenspiegels lustige Streiche* (1895), *Also sprach Zarathustra* (1896), *Don Quixote* (1897), *Ein Heldenleben* (1898), *Sinfonia Domestica* (1903), *Alpensinfonie* (1915); and ballets, symphonies, an oboe and two horn concertos, chamber music, choral works, and about 200 songs, esp. *Vier letzte Lieder* (1948).

Straussenburg, Arthur Arz von. See ARZ VON STRAUSSENBURG.

Stra·vin·sky \(,)strə-'vyēn-skəi, *Angl* strə-'vin(t)-skē\, Igor Fyodorovich. 1882–1971. American composer, b. Oranienbaum, Russia. One of greatest composers of the 20th century. Studied composition under Rimsky-Korsakov (1903–06); composed symphonic poem *Feu d'artifice* (1908); associated (1909–29) with Diaghilev's Ballets Russes, for which he composed ballets *L'Oiseau de feu* (1910), *Pétrouchka* (1911, rev. 1947), *Le Sacre du printemps* (1913), *Pulcinella* (1920), *Les Noces* (1923), *Apollon musagète* (1928); lived in Switzerland (1914–20), writing opera *Le Rossignol* (1914), burlesque *Renard* (1916), and

Histoire du soldat (1918, with Charles Ramuz); lived in France (1920–39, naturalized 1934). Abandoned Russian style of earlier years and adopted a Neoclassical idiom; composed *Symphonies of Wind Instruments* (1920, rev. 1947), *Concerto for Piano and Winds* (1924), vocal works *Oedipus Rex* (1927) and *Symphony of Psalms* (1930), *Capriccio* for piano and orchestra (1929), *Violin Concerto* (1931), ballets *Le Baiser de la fée* (1928), *Perséphone* (1934), *Jeu de cartes* (1937), and *Orpheus* (1947), *Dumbarton Oaks* concerto (1938), *Symphony in C Major* (1940), *Symphony in Three Movements* (1945), opera *The Rake's Progress* (1951). Settled in U.S. (1939, naturalized 1945); experimented with serial music in *Canticum Sacrum* (1955) and ballet *Agon* (1957); produced fully serial compositions including choral works *Threni* (1958), *Introitus* (1965), *Requiem Canticles* (1966), and orchestral works *Movements* (1959) and *Variations* (1964). Also composed chamber music, songs, and piano pieces.

Stray·horn \'strā-ˌhȯ(ə)rn\, William Thomas, *called* Billy. 1915–1967. American pianist and composer, b. Dayton, Ohio. Collaborator and amanuensis of bandleader Duke Ellington (1939–67); worked on most of Ellington's major concerts and exerted a strong influence on him; his compositions included "Lush Life," "Take the 'A' Train," "Chelsea Bridge," "Passion Flower," "Johnny-Come-Lately," "Midriff."

Street \'strēt\, George Edmund. 1824–1881. English architect. As assistant (1844–49) of Sir George Gilbert Scott, developed partiality for Gothic style and ability in restoring medieval monuments and cathedrals; opened own practice in London (1849); helped train many architects, as William Morris, Philip Webb, Richard Norman Shaw; president of Royal Institute of British Architects (1881). His publications *Brick and Marble in the Middle Ages* (1855) and *Some Account of Gothic Architecture in Spain* (1865) became widely used sourcebooks for Gothic Revival details. Designed about 260 buildings, chiefly for ecclesiastical use, including the Royal Courts of Justice, London (1874–82), and churches of St. James the Less, Oxford (1858–61), St. Georges, Oakengates (1861), St. John's, Torquay (1861–71), St. Mary Magdalene, London (1868–78), and Holmbury St. Mary (1879).

Street, Robert. 18th century. British inventor. Obtained patent (1794) describing an internal combustion engine employing a piston and a system of levers; used engine to raise water.

Stree·ter \'strēt-ər\, Burnett Hillman. 1874–1937. English theologian and biblical scholar. Ordained (1899); chaplain (1928), provost (1933), Queen's Coll., Oxford; member of Archbishop's Commission on Doctrine in the Church of England (1922–37). In *The Four Gospels* (1924) hypothesized a "four document" solution to the synoptic problem of the Gospels and developed theory of "local texts" in the manuscript transmission of the New Testament; in *The Primitive Church* (1929) argued there were three systems (not one) of church government in earliest churches; also wrote *The Chained Liberty* (1931), *The Buddha and the Christ* (1932), etc.

Strehlenau, Nikolaus Franz Niembsch von. See NIEMBSCH VON STREHLENAU.

Strei·cher \'shtrī-k̲ər\, Julius. 1885–1946. German journalist and politician. Became notorious for his anti-Semitic campaign (from 1919); joined Nazi movement and took part with Hitler in Munich Putsch (1923); arrested and imprisoned (1924); managing editor, *Der Stürmer* (1923–45); gauleiter of Franconia (1924–40); hanged as war criminal.

Streit·berg \'shtrīt-ˌberk\, Wilhelm August. 1864–1925. German philologist. Professor at Freiburg (1889–98), Münster (1899–09), Munich (1909–20), Leipzig (1920–25). Founder (1891, with Karl Brugmann) and editor (1892–1925) of journal *Indogermanische Forschungen;* chief works *Urgermanische Grammatik* (1896), *Gotisches Elementarbuch* (1897), *Die gotische Bibel* (1908–10).

Stre·se·mann \'shtrā-zə-ˌmän\, Gustav. 1878–1929. German politician. Member of Reichstag (1907–12, 1914–29); founded (1918) and led German People's party; chancellor of Germany (1923); minister of foreign affairs (1923–29). Chiefly responsible for restoration of Germany's international status after World War I; pursued conciliatory postwar policy; negotiated mutual security pact with France, the Locarno Pact, and secured Germany's admission to League of Nations; sponsored Germany's adoption of Dawes plan (1924) and Young plan (1929). Shared Nobel peace prize with Aristide Briand (1926).

Streuvels, Stijn. See Frank LATEUR.

Strib·ling \'strib-liŋ\, Thomas Sigismund. 1881–1965. American novelist, b. Clifton, Tenn. Author of *Birthright* (1921), *Fombombo* (1922), *Teeftallow* (1926), *Bright Metal* (1928), *Strange Moon* (1929), *Backwater* (1930), *The Forge* (1931), *The Store* (1932, Pulitzer prize), *Unfinished Cathedral* (1934), *These Bars of Flesh* (1938), etc.

Strick·er, Der \dər-'shtrik-ər\. fl. 1215–1250. German poet. Author of epics, fables, and tales as *Daniel vom dem blühenden Tal, Pfaffen Amis, Die Gauhühner,* etc.

Strick·land \'strik-lənd\, Agnes. 1796–1874. English biographer. Sister of Susanna S. Moodie and Catherine P.S. Traill. Collaborated with her older sister ¶Elizabeth (1794–1875) in *Lives of the Queens of England* (1840–48); sole author of *Lives of the Queens of Scotland and English Princesses* (1850–59), *Lives of the Last Four Stuart Princesses* (1872), novels including *How Will It End?* (1865), poetry, and books for children. Biographized (1887) by her sister ¶Jane Margaret (1800–1888), author of *Rome* (1854).

Strickland, William. 1787–1854. American architect and engineer, b. Philadelphia. In architecture, leader in the Greek Revival in America; designed the Masonic Temple (1810), Second Bank of the U.S. (1819–24), Naval Asylum (1826), U.S. Mint (1829), and the Merchants' Exchange (1834), all in Philadelphia; the Athenaeum, Providence, R.I. (1836–38); U.S. mints in Charlotte, N.C. (1835), and New Orleans (1835–36); the marble sarcophagus of Washington at Mount Vernon (1837); and the capitol of Tennessee at Nashville. Designed and built the Delaware Breakwater; encouraged construction of Pennsylvania Railroad Co. line; published works on engineering and architectural projects.

Strig·gio \'strēd-jō\, Alessandro. c.1540–1592. Italian composer and instrumentalist. Composer at Medici court at Florence (from early 1560s) and at Gonzaga court at Mantua (from 1584); composer of music for state occasions, intermezzi for Francesco d'Ambra's comedy *La cofanaria* (1565) and other court plays, *Il cicalamento delle donne al bucato* (1567), and esp. several books of madrigals. His son ¶Alessandro, *called* Alessandrino (1573?–1630), diplomat in service of Gonzaga family of Mantua; made chancellor of Gonzaga court (1628); wrote libretto of Monteverdi's opera *Orfeo* (1607) and probably of *Tirsi e Clori* (1615); also wrote (both 1608) *Il trionfo d'onore* and *Il sacrificio d'Ifigenia,* both set to music by Marco da Gagliano; published 3 books of madrigals by his father (1596–97).

Strij·dom \'strā-dəm\, Johannes Gerhardus. *Called* the Lion of Wa·ter·berg \'vät-ər-ˌberk̲\. 1893–1958. South African politician. Practiced law at Nylstroom, Transvaal; member of Parliament from Waterberg (1929–58); minister of lands and irrigation (1948–54); succeeded Daniel Malan as head of Purified Nationalist party (1954); prime minister of South Africa (1954–58); pursued policy of strict apartheid.

Strind·berg \'strin-ˌberʸ, *Angl* 'strin(d)-ˌbərg, 'strin-ˌber-ē\, August, *in full* Johan August. 1849–1912. Swedish playwright and novelist. Engaged variously as schoolteacher, private tutor, actor, and journalist; on staff of Royal Library, Stockholm (1874–82); gained national fame and caused public scandal with satirical, Naturalistic novel *Röda rummet* (1879); traveled about the Continent (1883–89); acquitted of charge of blasphemy for short-story collection *Giftas* (1884–85); underwent (during 1890s) a psychological crisis, emerging with a mystical religious faith that influenced subsequent works. Considered greatest writer of modern Sweden; profoundly influenced European and American dramatists. His writings, chiefly Naturalistic, included plays *Mäster Olof* (1872), *Lycko-Pers resa* (1881), *Fraden* (1887), *Fröken Julie* (1888), *Creditörer* (1888), *Till Damascus* (3 parts, 1898–1904), *Gustav Vasa* (1899), *Dödsdansen* (1901), *Drömspelet* (1902), *Spöksonaten* (1907), *Stora landsvägen* (1909); novels *Hemsöborna* (1887), *I havsbandet* (1890), *Götiska rummen* (1904); and autobiographical works *Le Plaidoyer d'un fou* (1888), *Inferno* (1897), and *Ensam* (1903).

String·er \'striŋ-ər\, Arthur John Arbuthnott. 1874–1950. American writer, b. Chatham, Ont. Author of adventure novels as *Gun Runner* (1912), *City of Peril* (1923), *The Wolf Woman* (1928), *Heather of the High Hand* (1937), etc., and several volumes of verse.

Strode \'strōd\, Ralph. fl. 1350–1400. English schoolman. Teacher of logic and philosophy, Oxford; opposed doctrines of his colleague John Wycliffe; dedicatee, with John Gower, of Chaucer's *Troilus and Criseyde.*

Strode, William. c.1599–1645. English Parliamentary leader. M.P. (1624–45); imprisoned (1629–40) for role in securing passage of resolutions condemning King Charles I's religious and financial policies; member of Short Parliament; in Long Parliament, proposed parliamentary control over ministerial appointments and the militia; supported Grand Remonstrance (1641); zealous in prosecution of Strafford and of Laud and bitter opponent of any compromise with Charles; one of five members impeached by Charles for high treason (1642).

Strode, William. 1602–1645. English poet. Canon of Christ Church, Oxford (1638). Author of *The Floating Island,* a tragicomedy acted before Charles I and his queen (1636), and of lyrics and elegies.

Stro·ga·nov \'strō-gə-nəf\. Family of wealthy Russian merchants, including: Anika *or* Ioanniki Stroganov (c.1498–1570), began (1515) a salt-mining enterprise at Solvychegodsk; expanded family holdings in salt mining, fishing, and furs throughout northeastern Russia. His three sons ¶Yakov, ¶Grigory, and ¶Semyon continued the business; Grigory received extensive land grants along the upper Kama and Chusovaya rivers from Ivan IV (1558); Semyon with

Cossack help conquered western Siberia and annexed it to Russia (1582); family received further land grants in Siberia from Ivan (1568, 1574) and was instrumental in bringing about accession of Michael Romanov to Russian throne (1613). ¶Grigory Dmitriyevich (1650–1715) became sole owner of family estates (1688); extended loans to the government; furnished two naval vessels to Peter the Great, who made him a baron. ¶Pavel Aleksandrovich (1772–1817), close adviser to Alexander I.

Stro·heim \'s(h)trō-ˌhīm\, Eric von. *Orig.* Erich Oswald Stroheim. 1885–1957. American motion picture actor and director, b. Vienna. Officer in Austrian cavalry (1902–09); to U.S. (1914, naturalized 1926); actor and assistant under D.W. Griffith; directed highly detailed and realistic films including *Blind Husbands* (1919), *The Devil's Passkey* (1920), *Foolish Wives* (1922), *Greed* (1924); scored commercial success with films *The Merry Widow* (1925), *The Wedding March* (1928), *Queen Kelly* (1928); as actor, famed for portraying sadistic, monocled Prussian officers, esp. in Jean Renoir's *La Grande Illusion* (1937).

Stroh·mey·er \'shtrō-ˌmī-ər\, Friedrich. 1776–1835. German chemist. Discovered the element cadmium (1817).

Ström·gren \'strœm-ˌgrān\, Svante Elis. 1870–1947. Swedish astronomer. Professor, Copenhagen (1907–40); studied orbits of comets and the three-body problem.

Strong \'strȯŋ\, Caleb. 1745–1819. American politician, b. Northampton, Mass. Member of Constitutional Convention of 1787; one of first two U.S. senators from Massachusetts (1789–96); governor of Massachusetts (1800–07, 1812–16).

Strong, Josiah. 1847–1916. American clergyman, b. Naperville, Ill. Published *Our Country* (1885), which attracted wide attention because it proposed religious solutions for social and industrial problems, followed by *The New Era* (1893), defining function of Christian church to extend the kingdom of Christ on earth through social work for the common good. Founded League for Social Service (1898), reorganized as American Institute for Social Service (1902), to carry on his Christian Socialism philosophy.

Strong, Leonard Alfred George. 1896–1958. Irish writer. Director of Methuen Ltd. (1938–58). Author of verse including *Dublin Days* (1921), *The Lowery Road* (1923), *The Body's Imperfection* (1957); novels including *Dewer Rides* (1929), *The Garden* (1931), *Sea Wall* (1933), *The Open Sky* (1939), *Deliverance* (1955); short-story collections *The English Captain* (1929), *Travellers* (1945), *Darling Tom* (1952), and other prose works.

Strong, William. 1808–1895. American jurist, b. Somers, Conn. Practiced law in Reading, Pa. (from 1833); member, U.S. House of Representatives (1847–51); on Pennsylvania Supreme Court (1857–68); associate justice, U.S. Supreme Court (1870–80); wrote majority opinion in the Supreme Court's reversal of its decision declaring the Legal Tender Act of 1862 unconstitutional (1871).

Strong, William Duncan. 1899–1962. American anthropologist, b. Portland, Ore. Professor at Columbia (1937–62); authority on culture of Indians of the Americas, esp. Peru; discovered (1946) 1000-year-old tomb of Peruvian warrior god Ai apaec. Writings included *An Introduction to Nebraska Archaeology* (1935) and *Cross Sections of New World Prehistory* (1943).

Strongbow, Richard. 2d Earl of Pembroke. See under de CLARE family.

Stross·maj·er \'shtrȯs-ˌmī-ər\, Josip Juraj. *Also spelled* Stross·may·er. 1815–1905. Croatian prelate and nationalist. Ordained Roman Catholic priest (1838); chaplain to Austrian emperor (1847–49); installed at Đakovo with title of bishop of Bosnia and Sirmium (1850). Became leader of Croatian national party, promoting autonomy and unification of all Croatian lands; principal founder of South Slav Academy (1867) and Zagreb U. (1874); helped reorganize educational systems of Dalmatia and Croatia-Slavonia; built a palace and cathedral at Đakovo; erected convents, seminaries, schools, libraries; published collections of national songs and tales; helped Augustin Theiner compile *Vetera Monumenta Slavorum Meridionalium Historiam Illustrantia* (1863); worked with Vladimir Solovyov on reunification of Roman Catholic and Russian Orthodox churches.

Stroud \'strau̇d\, Robert. *Called* the Bird-Man of Alcatraz. 1890–1963. American ornithologist, b. Seattle. Imprisoned (from 1909, including 1942–59 at Alcatraz Prison) for murdering a man in Juneau, Alaska (1909) and a guard in Leavenworth Prison (1916); became (by 1931) authority on canaries and diseases of birds; published *Stroud's Digest of the Diseases of Birds* (1942).

Stroud, William. 1860–1938. English inventor and industrialist. Professor of physics, Leeds (1885–1909); coinventor (see Archibald BARR) of range finders and other instruments; chairman of Barr & Stroud, Ltd. (from 1931).

Stroz·zi \'strȯt-tsē\. Noble Florentine family, including: Filippo (1426–1491), *known as* the Elder; a banker; commenced (1489) construction of Strozzi Palace (completed 1553). His son ¶Giovanni Battista (1488–1538), *known as* Filippo II; became involved in intrigues against the Medicis; led attacks of Florentine exiles against Florence; defeated and captured, committed suicide in prison. His son ¶Piero (1510–1558) also fought the Medicis; fled to France and, after suicide of his father, entered French service; campaigned in Italy (1544, 1551, 1554); created marshal of France (1556); mortally wounded in action before Thionville (1558). Piero's brother ¶Leone (1515–1554) entered Order of Malta; served in French navy against English and Spanish (1545–51); returned to command naval force of Order of Malta (1551); killed in battle of Sarlino.

Strozzi, Bernardo. *Sometimes called* Il Cap·puc·ci·no \ēl-ˌkä-püt-'chē-nō\. 1581–1644. Italian painter and engraver. A leading early Baroque painter of school of Genoa; Capuchin monk (1597–1610, hence nickname); settled in Venice (1631).

Strub·berg \'shtrüb-erk\, Friedrich Armand. *Pseudonym* Ar·mand \'är-ˌmänt\. 1806–1889. German novelist. In U.S. (1837–54), leading an itinerant life of adventure; wrote series of more than fifty novels based on his experiences in the United States, as *Sklaverei in Amerika* (1862) and *Der Krösus von Philadelphia* (1870).

Stru·be \'shtrü-bə\, Gustav. 1867–1953. American conductor and composer, b. Ballenstedt, Germany. To U.S. (1891, naturalized 1896); organizer and conductor of Baltimore Symphony Orchestra (1915–30). Composer of operas, symphonies, symphonic poems, concertos, and much chamber music.

Stru·en·see \'shtrü-ən-ˌzā\, Johann Friedrich. Graf. 1737–1772. German physician and politician. Appointed (1769) court physician to Christian VII of Denmark; gained dominance over Christian and wielded absolute power in Denmark (from 1770); abolished council of state and office of stadholder of Norway (1770); made privy cabinet member (1771); made many liberal reforms but gained enmity of officials; as lover of Queen Caroline Matilda, became victim of conspiracy of nobles; condemned to death, tortured, and beheaded.

Strutt \'strət\, John William. 3d Baron Ray·leigh \'rā-lē\. 1842–1919. English physicist. Professor at Cambridge (1879–84) and at Royal Institution (1887–1905); chancellor of Cambridge (1908–19). Published his first paper on J.C. Maxwell's electromagnetic theory (1869); published *The Theory of Sound* (1877–78); his work on the determination of densities of gases led to discovery (with Sir William Ramsay) of element argon (1895); proposed (1900) Rayleigh-Jeans law of black body radiation; did pioneer work in molecular acoustics; awarded Nobel prize for physics (1904).

Stru·ve \'shtrü-və\. Name of a family of astronomers including: Friedrich Georg Wilhelm von Struve (1793–1864), b. Germany; to Russia to avoid conscription by Napoleonic armies (1808); professor, U. of Dorpat (1813–39); director (1817–39), Dorpat observatory; director, Pulkovo observatory (1839–62); known for investigations of binary stars; made survey of some 122,000 stars from north celestial pole to 15° S declination; published *Stellarum duplicium mensurae micrometricae* (1837); one of the first to measure stellar parallax (1838). His son ¶Otto Wilhelm (1819–1905), b. Dorpat; director, Pulkovo observatory (1862–89); discovered about 500 new binary stars; made a new determination of the constant of precession; investigated rings of Saturn; made a determination of the mass of Neptune. Otto's son ¶Gustav Wilhelm Ludwig (1858–1920), professor and director of the observatory, U. of Kharkov (1894–1919), professor, Simferopol (1919–20); known for work on determination of the constant of precession and on proper motion of the solar system. Gustav's son ¶Otto Stru·ve *Angl* 'strü-vē\ (1897–1963), b. Kharkov, Russia; to U.S. (1921, naturalized 1927); teacher (from 1924) and professor (1932–47), U. of Chicago; director (1932–47) of both Yerkes Observatory and McDonald Observatory of U. of Texas; director of Leuschner Observatory of U. of Calif., Berkeley (1950–59) and of National Radio Astronomy Observatory, Green Bank, W. Va. (1959–62); made many contributions to stellar spectroscopy; proved presence of hydrogen in interstellar space (1938); demonstrated that many O and B stars rotate rapidly on their axes; made studies of stars with variable light and of spectra of double, multiple, and peculiar stars. Author of *Stellar Evolution* (1950), *The Universe* (1962), etc.

Strype \'strīp\, John. 1643–1737. English historian and biographer. Collected original documents, esp. of Tudor period. Author of *Ecclesiastical Memorials 1513–1558* (1721) and of biographies of Cranmer (1694), Sir John Cheke (1705), Matthew Parker (1710), Whitgift (1718).

Stuart. See also STEWART.

Stuart. For members of family other than Scottish and English sovereigns and royal pretenders see STEWART family.

Stu·art *or* **Stew·art** *or* **Steu·art** \'st(y)ü-ərt, 'st(y)u̇(-ə)rt\. Name of Scottish and English royal house tracing descent from a follower of William the Conqueror (see STEWART family), which provided several regents of Scotland, the sovereigns of Scotland from 1371 to 1688, the last four (from accession of James VI of Scotland as James I of England in 1603) being also sovereigns of England (see ROBERT II and III, JAMES I to V, and MARY, Queen of Scots; JAMES I, CHARLES I and II, JAMES II, MARY II, and ANNE, of England). After deposition of James II in 1688, the Jacobites long upheld the Stuart claim to British throne (for royal pretenders see CHARLES EDWARD, HENRY STUART, and JAMES EDWARD).

Stuart, Gilbert Charles. 1755–1828. American painter, b. North Kingstown, R.I. Studied under Benjamin West in London (1776–82); studio in London (1782–87) and Dublin (1787–93); gained distinction as portrait painter, ranked by contemporaries with Ramsay, Romney, Gainsborough, Reynolds. Studio in New York (1793), Philadelphia (1794–96), Germantown (1796–1803), Washington, D.C. (1803–05), and Boston (1805–28). Best known for his portraits of George Washington, including five full-length portrayals and the unfinished *Athenaeum Head* (1796); painted John Adams, John Quincy Adams, Jefferson, Madison, Joseph Story, Judge Stephen Jones, F. S. Richards of Boston. During his residence in England he painted George III, George IV (as Prince of Wales), Mrs. Siddons, Sir Joshua Reynolds, Benjamin West.

Stuart, James. 1713–1788. British painter and architect. After visits to Rome (1741) and Athens (1751), published with the architect Nicholas Revett *The Antiquities of Athens* (1762), which, as first accurate account of monuments of Athens, led to introduction of Greek architecture in London.

Stuart, Sir James. 1780–1853. Canadian jurist, b. Fort Hunter, N.Y. Solicitor general of Lower Canada (1801–09); member of House of Assembly (1808–17, 1825–31), leader of English party aiming at union of two provinces; chief justice of Lower Canada (1838–41), of Canada (from 1841); drafted Act of Union which became law (1841).

Stuart, James Ewell Brown, *known as* Jeb. 1833–1864. American army officer, b. Patrick Co., Va. In U.S. army (from 1854); resigned (1861) to join the Confederate service; brigadier general (Sept. 1861). Distinguished himself at First Bull Run (July 1861); made spectacular raid completely around McClellan's army (June 1862); engaged in Seven Days' Battles; promoted major general (Sept. 1862); engaged at Manassas. Led raid into Pennsylvania, reaching Chambersburg and again encircling Union army (Oct. 1862); commanded Confederate right at Fredericksburg; succeeded Jackson as 2d Corps commander at Chancellorsville (May 1863); criticized for absence at Gettysburg because he was off on a raid (July 1863); defeated and mortally wounded at Spotsylvania Courthouse.

Stuart, John McDouall. 1815–1866. Australian explorer, b. Scotland. Accompanied Captain Sturt's expedition (1844–45) as draftsman; made six expeditions (1858–62) into interior, the last bringing him to Van Diemen's Gulf on Indian Ocean.

Stuart, John Todd. 1807–1885. American lawyer, b. near Lexington, Ky. Practiced law in Springfield, Ill. (from 1828); in partnership with Abraham Lincoln in firm of Stuart and Lincoln (1837–41); member, U.S. House of Representatives (1839–43, 1863–65). He was a cousin of Mary Todd Lincoln.

Stuart, Mary. See Mary, Queen of Scots.

Stuart, Ruth, *orig.* Mary Routh, *nee* Mc·En·ery \mək-'en-ər-ē\. 1849–1917. American writer, b. Marksville, La. m. Alfred O. Stuart (1879; d. 1883). Her stories, chiefly of Southern life, included *A Golden Wedding and Other Tales* (1893), *Sonny* (1896), *In Simpkinsville* (1897), *The Second Wooing of Salina Sue* (1905), *The Unlived Life of Little Mary Ellen* (1910), *Daddy Do-Funny's Wisdom Jingles* (1913).

Stubbs \'stəbz\, George. 1724–1806. English painter. Published *The Anatomy of the Horse* (1766), for which he drew and engraved all plates; known chiefly for accurate paintings of horses.

Stubbs *or* **Stubbes** \'stəbz\, John. 1543?–1591. English Puritan. Author of pamphlet *The Discoverie of a Gaping Gulf* (1579), condemning Queen Elizabeth's proposed marriage with Henry, Duke of Anjou, for which he and his printer had their right hands struck off. His kinsman ¶Philip Stubbs *or* Stubbes (c.1555–c.1610), Puritan pamphleteer, denounced luxuries and evils of the times in *The Anatomie of Abuses* (1583), answered by Thomas Nash, and in *A Christal Glasse for Christian Women* (1591), a biographical account of his wife.

Stubbs, William. 1825–1901. English historian and prelate. Vicar of Navestock, Essex (1850–66); wrote *Registrum Sacrum Anglicanum* (1858). Oxford regius professor of modern history (1866–84); published chief work *The Constitutional History of England* (down to 1485; 1873–78), a standard authority. Canon of St. Paul's (1879); bishop of Chester (1884) and Oxford (1889); edited William of Malmesbury's works (1887–89). Considered founder of the systematic study of English medieval constitutional history.

Stuck \'shtu̇k\, Franz von. 1863–1928. German painter and sculptor. Painted (from 1889) religious and allegorical subjects and portraits; his sculptures included a bronze statue of an athlete and a bronze statue of an Amazon on horseback.

Stuc·ley *or* **Stuke·ly** \'st(y)ü-klē\, Thomas. 1525?–1578. English adventurer. Buccaneer (1558–65); engaged by Sir Henry Sidney in Ireland and by French ambassador in London; in service of Philip II of Spain, commanded three galleys at battle of Lepanto; concocted plots against England; joined expedition by King Sebastian of Portugal against Morocco; commanded center in battle of Alcázar, in which he was killed.

Stu·de·ba·ker \'st(y)üd-ə-,bā-kər\, Clement. 1831–1901. American wagon manufacturer, b. Pinetown, Pa. With older brother ¶Henry (1826–1895), founded firm of H. & C. Studebaker, South Bend, Ind. (1852). Other brothers John Mohler, Peter Everst, and Jacob Franklin also entered business; organized Studebaker Brothers Manufacturing Co. (1868), with Clement as president; developed largest wagon and carriage manufacturing company in the world; experimented with automobiles (from 1897). Manufacture of Studebaker automobiles begun after his death.

Stu·dent \shtü-'dent\, Karl. 1890–1978. German general. Commander in chief of airborne forces in World War II; his forces chiefly responsible for successful invasion of the Netherlands (1940).

Stu·dy \'shtü-dē\, Eduard. 1862–1930. German mathematician. Professor at Bonn (1904–27); pioneered in geometry of complex numbers; made first systematic studies of isotropic curves and introduced isotropic parameters (1909); chief work *Geometrie der Dynamen* (1903).

Stuke·ley \'st(y)ü-klē\, William. 1687–1765. English physician and antiquary. Made studies (1720s) of Stonehenge monuments, postulating extravagant theories relating them to the Druids; his antiquarian travels recorded in *Itinerarium Curiosum* (1724).

Stukely, Thomas. See Stucley.

Stü·ler \'shtǖ-lər\, Friedrich August. 1800–1865. German architect. Designer of the New Museum, several churches, and portions of the royal palace in Berlin, the Cologne Museum, the University of Königsberg, etc.

Stülp·na·gel \'shtu̇ēlp-,näg-əl\, Karl Heinrich von. 1886–1944. German general. Quartermaster general of the army (1938–40); chairman, German-French armistice commission (1940); commander of 17th army on eastern front (1940–41); commander of occupied France (1942–44); a chief conspirator in plot to assassinate Hitler (July 1944); executed.

Stumpf \'shtu̇mpf\, Carl. 1848–1936. German philosopher and psychologist. Professor at Würzburg (1873–79), Prague (1879–84), Halle (1884–89), Munich (1889–94), Berlin (1894–1921). Made researches on psychology of music and tone, esp. the fusion and sensation of tones. Wrote *Über den psychologischen Ursprung des Raumvorstellung* (1873), *Tonpsychologie* (1883–90); founded (1898) journal *Beiträge zur Akustik und Musikwissenschaft;* founded archives of phonograph records of primitive music (1900).

Stumpf, Johannes. 1500–1578. Swiss historian. Prior at Bubikon, Zürich (1522–62); friend of Zwingli and a leader of the Swiss Reformation. Wrote *Gemeiner loblicher Eydgnoschafft Stetten, Landen und Völckeren chronikwirdiger Thaaten Beschreybung* (1547–48).

Stur·dee \'stərd-ē\, Sir Doveton, *in full* Frederick Charles Doveton. 1859–1925. British naval commander. Rear admiral (1908), admiral (1917), and admiral of the fleet (1921). Commanded the *Invincible* in the naval action off Falkland Islands (Dec. 8, 1914) during which the German raiding squadron under Admiral von Spee was destroyed; commanded 4th battle squadron in battle of Jutland (May 31, 1916).

Stur·dza \'stürd-zä\. Romanian boyar family, including: Ion Sandu *or* Ioniţa (d. 1842), prince of Moldavia (1822–28); struggled against Russophile elements; drafted first Moldavian constitution; promoted public improvements but reduced peasantry to a state of greater servitude; captured by the Russians (1828); died in exile. ¶Michael *or* Mihai (1795–1884), prince of Moldavia (1834–49); headed Russophile opposition against Ion; helped prepare Organic Statute of 1832; established academy at Iaşi (1835); emancipated gypsies from serfdom (1844); inaugurated large-scale improvements in public works and administration; always subservient to Russia; suppressed Moldavian nationalist movement (1848); renounced throne (1849). His son ¶Gregory (1821–1901); rival candidate for Moldavian throne against his father (1859); resulting deadlock resolved by election of Alexandru Ion Cuza; after Romanian unification (1861), served as Russophile deputy in Romanian assembly. ¶Dimitrie Alexandru (1833–1914) helped depose Alexandru Cuza (1866); held several ministerial posts; chairman of Liberal party (from 1892); prime minister of Romania (1895–96, 1897–99, 1901–04, 1907–09); suppressed with great cruelty the 1907 peasant uprising; secretary general of Romanian Academy (from 1909).

Sture. See Sten Sture.

Sturge \'stərj\, Joseph. 1793–1859. English philanthropist, Quaker pacifist, and reformer. Prosperous grain dealer; instrumental in full abolition of slavery in British West Indies (1837); worked for worldwide abolition of slavery; toured U.S. slave states with John Greenleaf Whittier (1841); devoted himself (from 1842) to extension of suffrage, repeal of Corn Laws, and peace movements.

Stur·geon \'stər-jən\, William. 1783–1850. English electrical engineer. Devised first electromagnet capable of supporting more than its own weight (1825); described process of amalgamating zinc plate of battery with film of mercury (1830); constructed electromagnetic rotary engine (1832); invented the commutator; established *Annals of Electricity,* first electrical journal in

England (1836); invented first moving-coil galvanometer (1836); improved the voltaic battery and worked on theory of thermoelectricity.

Stur·ges \'stər-jəs\, Preston. *Orig.* Edmund Preston Bi·den \'bīd-ən\; *adopted (1901) by stepfather and thereafter known as Preston Sturges.* 1898–1959. American writer and motion picture director, b. Chicago. Wrote plays *Strictly Dishonorable* (1929), *Child of Manhattan* (1931); directed and won Academy Award for best original screenplay for *The Great McGinty* (1940). Known for directing series of satirical comedies, for which he also wrote screenplays, including *Christmas in July* (1940), *The Lady Eve* (1941), *Sullivan's Travels* (1942), *The Palm Beach Story* (1942), *The Miracle of Morgan's Creek* (1944), *Hail the Conquering Hero* (1944), and *Unfaithfully Yours* (1948).

Stürgkh \'shtūerk\, Karl von. Graf. 1859–1916. Austrian politician. Ultraconservative and clericalist member of the Reichsrat (from 1890); opposed suffrage reforms of 1907; minister of education (1908–11); prime minister (from 1911); secured passage of military program (1912–13); dissolved the Bohemian Landtag (1913) and the Reichstag (1914) and imposed own autocratic regime; assassinated.

Stur·la Thór·dar·son \'stue(r)d-lä-'thōr-där-sòn\. 13th century. Icelandic historian. Author of the *Íslendinga saga* about 12th-century Iceland.

Sturluson, Snorri. See SNORRI STURLUSON.

Sturm \stūerm\, Jacques-Charles-François. 1803–1855. French mathematician, b. Switzerland. Professor at Paris at École Polytechnique and Faculté des Sciences (from 1840); known for work on differential equations, projective geometry, optics, and mechanics; in *Mémoire sur la résolution des équations numériques* (1829) provided Sturm's theorem for determining the number and position of the real roots, between given limits, of an algebraic equation. Also wrote *Cours d'analyse de l'École Polytechnique* (1857–63) and *Cours de méchanique de l'École Polytechnique* (1861).

Sturm \'shtùrm\, Johannes. 1507–1589. German educator. Head of a school in Strassburg (1538 ff.) emphasizing maintenance of strict discipline and thorough mastery of the classics which became a model for secondary schools of Protestant countries during the Reformation. Author of treatises on educational organization and methods.

Stür·mer \'shtyürm-yər\, Boris Vladimirovich. 1848–1917. Russian politician. As premier, minister of the interior, and minister of foreign affairs (1916), mishandled Russia's war effort during World War I and aroused widespread opposition to the government; arrested (1917) and died in prison.

Sturm von Stur·meck \'shtùrm-fòn-'shtùr-mek\, Jakob. 1489–1553. German politician and Reformation leader. Represented Strassburg at Spires (1526) and later at second Diet of Spires (1529); signed the "protest" presented to the assembly and thus became one of the original "Protestants." Founded the Protestant Gymnasium in Strassburg (1538), which later developed into the University of Strassburg.

Štur·sa \'shtùr-sä\, Jan. 1880–1925. Czech sculptor. Influenced by Rodin and Bourdelle; regarded as a leader of the modern Czech school of sculpture.

Sturt \'stərt\, Charles. 1795–1869. English explorer. Secretary to Sir Ralph Darling, governor of New South Wales (1827); led several expeditions into interior of Australia; discovered Darling River (1828); led expedition down the Murrumbidgee River and discovered the Murray River (1829–30); surveyor general, South Australia (1833); returned from third expedition to the edge of Simpson Desert quite blind (1846); wrote narratives (1833, 1849) of his expeditions; colonial secretatry (1849–51); died in England.

Stur·te·vant \'stərt-ə-vənt\, Alfred Henry. 1891–1970. American geneticist, b. Jacksonville, Ill. Researcher at Carnegie Institution, Washington, D.C. (1915–28); professor at Calif. Inst. of Tech. (1928–70). Discovered technique for mapping genes (1913); published explanations of unequal crossing-over and of position effect (1925); also made researches in taxonomy.

Stur·zo \'stürt-sō\, Luigi. 1871–1959. Italian priest and political leader. Ordained priest (1894); politically organized miners and peasants of Sicily; as mayor of Caltagirone, Sicily (1905–20), built community housing and other public works; founded Partito Populare Italiano and became its political secretary (1919); exiled (1924) for refusal to support Mussolini; on return to Italy (1946), his movement revived as Democrazia Cristiana (Christian Democratic party); made senator for life (1952). Author of *Church and State* (1939), *The True Life* (1943), *The Inner Laws of Society* (1944), *Spiritual Problems of Our Times* (1945), *Italy and the Coming World* (1945), etc.

Stüs·si \'shtues-ē\, Rudolf. d. 1443. Swiss politician. Burgomeister of Zürich (1430–43); his claims to the estate of the Count of Toggenburg precipitated first civil war of the Swiss Confederation; withdrew economic sanctions against other cantons after defeats at Etzel (1439) and Pfäffikon (1440); concluded alliance with Austria (1442); again at war with other cantons (1443); slain in battle at Sankt Jacob an der Sihl.

Stutz \'stəts\, Harry Clayton. 1876–1930. American automobile manufacturer, b. near Ansonia, Ohio. Founder (1913) and president (1913–19), Stutz Motor Car Co., manufacturer of racing and sports cars, esp. the Stutz Bearcat; helped organize (1919) H.C.S. Motor Car Co., Indianapolis.

Stuy·ve·sant \'stœi-və-sänt, *Angl* 'stī-və-sənt\, Peter, *orig.* Petrus. c.1610–1672. Dutch administrator in America. Entered service of Dutch West India Company (c.1632); governor of Curaçao, Aruba, and Bonaire (1643); lost his right leg in campaign against island of St. Martin (1644). Appointed director general of New Netherland and adjacent regions (1645); arrived in New Amsterdam (May 1647). Conciliated the Indians; arranged a boundary line with Hartford settlers (1650); expelled the Swedes from Delaware (1655); aroused great discontent in colony by dictatorial measures. Forced to surrender New Netherland to the English (1664); defended himself in the Netherlands against charges (1665). Returned to New York and lived on his farm on the "Bouwerie" (Bowery).

Stylites, Saint Simeon. See SIMEON STYLITES.

Suá·rez \'swä-räth\, Francisco. 1548–1617. Spanish theologian and scholastic philosopher. Joined Society of Jesus (1564); ordained (1572). Taught philosophy at Ávila and Segovia (1571–74) and theology at Ávila, Segovia, and Valladolid (1574–80), Collegium Romanum at Rome (1580–85), and at Alcalá (1585–93), Salamanca (1593–97), and Coimbra (1597–1615). Considered foremost Jesuit theologian; adherent of Thomas Aquinas; opposed by strict Dominican Thomists for tending toward Molinism. Considered a founder of international law, esp. for doctrine that all countries are members of a worldwide community of nations. Author of a commentary on Thomas Aquinas's *Summa theologiae* (1590–1603), *Disputationes metaphysicae* (1597), *De virtute et statu religionis* (1608–25), *De legibus* (1612), *Defensio fidei catholicae* (1613), *De divina gratia* (1620), and *De vera intelligentia auxilii efficacis* (1655).

Šu·ba·šić \shü-'bàsh-ētʸ\, Ivan. 1892–1955. Yugoslav politician. A leader of Croatian Peasant party; governor of Croatia (1939–41); fled to U.S. from German invasion (1941); appointed by King Peter II premier of government in exile (1944); foreign minister in Tito's provisional government (1945); resigned because of Tito's intransigent Communism (1945).

Subbiluliuma I. See SUPPILULIUMAS.

Sub·lette \'səb-ˌlet, -lət\, William Lewis. 1799?–1845. American soldier and fur trader, b. Lincoln Co., Ky. Member of Ashley's expedition to the Rocky Mountains (1823); led his own expeditions to that region for trading (1828, 1832) and to Santa Fe (1831); part of Oregon Trail became known first as "Sublette's cut-off" and "Sublette's trace." Was first to drive wagons over the trail to the Rockies.

Subotai. See SABUTAI.

Su·chet \sūe-she, -shē\, Louis-Gabriel. Duc d'Al·bu·fe·ra \dàl-būe-fer-á\. 1772–1826. French soldier. Volunteered for service (1792); general in chief of the army of Italy (1800); commanded a division in the battles of Austerlitz (1805), Jena (1806), and Pułtusk (1806); served in Peninsular War (1808–14). Created marshal of France and duke (1811).

Suck·ert \'sùk-ərt\, Kurt Erich. *Pseudonym* Curzio Ma·la·par·te \ˌmäl-ä-'pär-tā\. 1898–1957. Italian journalist and writer. Founded literary magazines *900* (with Massimo Bontempelli, 1926) and *Prospettive* (1937); supported Fascist cause with *La Technique du coup d'état* (1931) and novels *Avventure di un capitano di Sventura* (1927), *Sodoma e Gomorra* (1931), *Sangue* (1937). Repudiated Fascism (early 1940s) and assisted Allies during World War II; published reports from Russian front as *Il Volga nasce in Europa* (1943). Other works included novels *Kaputt* (1944) and *La pelle* (1949), dramas *Du côté de chez Proust* (1948), *Das Kapital* (1949), and *Anche le donne hanno perso la guerra* (1954), screenplay *Il Cristo proibito* (1951), stories *Racconti italiani* (1957).

Suck·ling \'sək-liŋ\, Sir John. 1609–1642. English Cavalier poet. Inherited large estates from father (1627); traveled in France and Italy (1628–30); volunteered under Gustav Adolphus (1631–32). Became famous for wit and prodigality; inventor of game of cribbage; wrote *A Session of the Poets* (1637), poem descriptive of his contemporaries, and four plays valuable only for their good lyrics: *Aglaura* (1637), containing the lyric "Why so pale and wan, fond lover?," *The Goblins* (1638), *Brennoralt, or the Discontented Colonel* (1639), reflecting his own character, and *The Sad One* (unfinished). At outbreak of Civil War raised troop of one hundred horse, accompanied Charles on Scottish expedition (1639); was returned to Long Parliament; took part in plot to rescue Strafford from Tower (1641) and had to flee to France; said to have poisoned himself.

Su·cre \'sü-krā\, Antonio José de. 1795–1830. Venezuelan liberator and general. Bolívar's chief lieutenant in campaign (1821) against Spain in Quito (Ecuador); won battle of Pichincha (1822). Served under Bolívar in Peru (1823–25) and with him defeated Spanish at Junín; won battle of Ayacucho (1824). Convened deliberative assembly in Upper Peru, now Bolivia (1825). First president of new republic (1826–28); resigned because of opposition of native Bolivians. Defended Gran Colombia against Peru (1828–30); presided over "Admirable Congress" at Bogotá (1830); assassinated.

Sudbury, Simon of. See SIMON of Sudbury.

Su·der·mann \'züd-ər-,män\, Hermann. 1857–1928. German writer. A leading writer of the German Naturalist movement. Among his plays were *Die Ehre* (1889), *Sodoms Ende* (1891), *Heimat* (1893), *Schmetterlingsschlacht* (1895), *Glück im Winkel* (1895), *Morituri* (1896), *Drei Reiherfedern* (1899), *Es lebe das Leben!* (1902), *Der gute Ruf* (1913). Among his novels were *Frau Sorge* (1887), *Der Katzensteg* (1891), *Es war* (1894), *Das hohe Lied* (1908), *Der tolle Professor* (1926), *Die Frau des Steffen Tromholt* (1928).

Südfeld, Max Simon. See Max NORDAU.

Su·di·ro·hu·so·do \sü-,dir-ō-hü-'sōd-ō\, Mas Ngabehi Wahidin. 1852–1916. Indonesian physician and reformer. In attempt to improve educational opportunities for Indonesians, founded (1908) Budi Utomo (High Endeavor), the first Indonesian organization modeled after Western institutions.

Śū·dra·ka \'shü-drə-kə\. 4th century A.D. Indian writer. Author of the Sanskrit play *Mrcchakaṭikā* (The Little Clay Cart) describing the love of a noble Brahmin for the courtesan Vasantasena.

Sue \sū̅, *Angl* 'sü\, Eugène, *orig.* Marie-Joseph. 1804–1857. French novelist. Took name Eugène from his patron Prince Eugène de Beauharnais. Inherited fortune but dissipated it in life as dandy; served six years as naval surgeon; participated in 1848 revolution; elected Socialist deputy (1850); lived in exile in Savoy after Napoléon III's coup d'état (1851). At first published sea stories as *Plick et Plock* (1831), and novels of high society as *Arthur* (1838) and *Mathilde* (1841); later wrote novels championing Socialism and set in the underworld of Paris as *Les Mystères de Paris* (1842–43) and *Le Juif errant* (1844–45).

Suess \'zūs\, Eduard. 1831–1914. Austrian geologist, b. London. Professor at Vienna (1857–1901); Liberal member of Landtag of Lower Austria (1869–96) and of the Reichsrat (1872–96). Authority on structural geology; in *Die Entstehung der Alpen* (1875) argued that mountains and continents were formed not by vertical uplift but by thrusting movements that crumpled and broke outer portions of the Earth's crust; in *Das Antlitz der Erde* (1883–1909) postulated existence of Gondwana, a great southern continent that broke up to form Africa, Antarctica, Australia, India, and South America.

Sue·to·ni·us \swē-'tō-nē-əs, ,sü-ə-'tō-\. *In full* Gaius Suetonius Tran·quil·lus \tran-'kwil-əs, traŋ-\. c.69–after 122 A.D. Roman biographer and historian. Friend and protégé of Pliny the Younger, may have accompanied him on mission to Bithynia (c.110–113); in imperial service (from 117), holding posts of controller of Roman libraries, keeper of archives, and cultural adviser to Emperor Hadrian; secretary of imperial correspondence (c.121–c.122). Author of *De viris illustribus,* biographies of Roman literary figures, and *De vita Caesarum,* lives of first eleven emperors. Only fragments of his other works are extant.

Suffolk, Dukes of. See de la POLE family; Charles BRANDON; Henry Grey (d. 1554) under GREY family.

Suffolk, Earls of. See Robert and William de UFFORD; de la POLE family; HOWARD family.

Suf·fren de Saint-Tro·pez \sū̅-fren-də-saⁿ-trō-pā\, Pierre-André de. 1729–1788. French naval commander. Served under Adm. C.H. d'Estaing in America (from 1778); sent to Indian waters to fight the British (1781); in series of engagements against Sir Edward Hughes off coasts of India and Ceylon (1782–83), developed daring tactics consisting of isolating groups of enemy vessels, thus destroying a squadron piecemeal.

Su·ga·wa·ra \süg-ä-wä-rä\ Michizane. *Posthumous title* Ten-jin \ten-jēn\, *i.e.* Heavenly God. 845–903. Japanese politician. Scholar of Chinese literature; minister in government of Emperor Daigo; incurred enmity of powerful Fujiwara clan; exiled (901) as viceroy to Kyushu and died there. After death deified as patron god of learning and calligraphy.

Sug·den \'səg-dən\, Samuel. 1892–1950. English chemist. Professor at U. Coll., London (from 1937); did work in irradiation; introduced term parachor (1924). Author of *The Structure of Atoms* (1923), *The Parachor and Valency* (1929), etc.

Su·ger \sū̅-zher\ of Saint-De·nis \saⁿ-də-nē\. 1081–1151. French churchman and statesman. Became abbé of Saint-Denis (1122); principal adviser of Louis VI and Louis VII; regent of France (1147–49) while the king was away on the Second Crusade. An able administrator and author of several historical works. In rebuilding of his abbey church, introduced Gothic art and architecture to western Europe.

Su·gi·ya·ma \süg-ē-yä-mä\ Gen. 1880–1945. Japanese army officer. Minister of war (1937–38, 1944–45); commander in North China (1938–39); chief of general staff (1940–44); field marshal (1943); committed suicide.

Süh·baa·tar *or* **Sükh·ba·taar** \'sük-bä-tär\, Damdiny. 1894–1923. Mongolian nationalist. Cofounder and leader of Mongolian People's Revolutionary party, the leading force in the founding and development of the Mongolian People's Republic; considered the modern hero of his country.

Suh·ra·war·dī, as- \əs-sü-,rä-wär-'dē\. *In full* Shihāb ad-Dīn Yaḥyā ibn Ḥabash ibn Amīrak as-Suhrawardī. *Also known as* al-Maqtūl *and* Shaykh al-Ishrāq. c.1155–1191. Persian mystic theologian and philosopher. Favorably impressed Malik aẓ-Ẓāhir, ruler of Aleppo; gained enmity of the local leaders of learning, who persuaded Malik aẓ-Ẓāhir to execute as-Suhrawardī. A leading figure of the "illuminative" school of Islāmic philosophy; attempted to reconcile traditional philosophy and mysticism. Author of *Ḥikmat al-ishrāq* (The Wisdom of Illumination), other treatises on mysticism, commentaries on Aristotle and Plato; founded mystical order known as the Ishrāqīyah.

Sui \'swē\. A Chinese dynasty (581–618 A.D.), uniting China after several centuries of confusion; its two emperors were Yang Chien and Yang Kuang (*qq.v.*); followed by the T'ang dynasty.

Sui·ko \swē-kō\. *Also* Suiko Tennō. 554–628. Empress of Japan (592–628). Member of the powerful Soga clan; daughter of Emperor Kimmei; empress consort of Emperor Bidastu (572–585). Succeeded to throne upon murder (592) of her brother Emperor Sushun by her uncle Soga Umako; first reigning empress of Japan in recorded history; administration of government in hands of Crown Prince Shōtoku (regent 593–621).

Suk \'sük\, Josef. 1874–1935. Czech violinist and composer. Pupil and son-in-law of Antonín Dvořák; composer of symphonies, symphonic poems, choral works, chamber music, and piano pieces.

Su·kar·no \sü-'kär-nō\. *Orig.* Kus·na·sos·ro \,küs-nä-'sȯs-rō\. 1901–1970. Indonesian politician. Entered politics (by 1927); imprisoned (1929–31) and exiled (1933–42) by Dutch for nationalist activities; cooperated with Japanese during World War II; proclaimed independence of Indonesia (1945); led struggle against Dutch rule, obtaining formal independence from the Netherlands (1949). President of Indonesia (1949–67); achieved gains in health, education, and sense of national identity, but instituted an authoritarian "Guided Democracy"; regime marked by corruption and extravagance; his power drastically reduced after coup d'état led by General Suharto (1966); removed from office (1967) and spent rest of life under arrest.

Su·lay·mān \sül-ī-'man\. 674–717. Umayyad caliph (715–717). Brother and successor of al-Walīd; reformed government; appointed as his successor his cousin 'Umar II; besieged Constantinople (716–717); forced by Emperor Leo III to give up siege.

Sü·ley·man \sū̅-lā-'män\. *Also spelled* Sol·i·man \'säl-ə-mən\ *or* Su·lei·man \sū̅-lā-'man\. Name of two sultans of the Ottoman Empire:

Süleyman I. *Called* the Magnificent *by Westerners and* Ka·nu·ni \kä-nü-'nē\, *i.e.* Lawgiver, *by Turks.* 1494 or 1495–1566. Sultan (1520–1566). Son and successor of Selim I; conquered Belgrade (1521) and Rhodes (1522); defeated Hungarians at Mohács (1526) and later added south central Hungary to his empire; unsuccessfully laid siege to Vienna (1529); conquered Erzurum in Asia Minor and Iraq (1534–35); made Transylvania his vassal (early 1540s); conquered area around Lake Van (1548–49) and Tripoli (1551); built up naval strength and for a time was the dominant power in the Mediterranean. Reformed and improved administration of his country; built mosques, bridges, and other public works; made Istanbul into a great capital; encouraged arts and sciences. His reign considered a high point of Ottoman civilization.

Süleyman İbra·him II \-ib-rə-'him\. 1642–1691. Sultan (1687–1691). Succeeded his brother Mehmed IV; faced disturbed conditions within Turkey and an unsuccessful war with Austria; entrusted (from 1689) administration to his grand vizier Fazıl Mustafa Paşa, who reestablished order, drove Austrians out of Bulgaria and Transylvania, retook Belgrade and Niš (1690), and introduced numerous liberal reforms.

Süleyman. d. 1410. Ruler of Rumelia (1403–10). Son of Ottoman sultan Bayezid I; after Timur's defeat of Bayezid (1402), received Rumelia from Timur; made his capital at Edirne; defeated (1410) by his brother Mûsa under orders from another brother, Mehmed I.

Süleyman Çe·le·bi \-chä-lā-'bē\. *Also known as* Süleyman of Bur·sa \bůr-'sä\. d. 1429. Turkish poet and religious. Became a leader of the Khalwatiyah dervish order; *imām* at court of Bayezid I and (after 1402) at a mosque in Bursa. Author of the great religious poem *Mevlûd-i Nebi* or *Mevlûd-i Peygamberi* on the life and death of the Prophet Muḥammad.

Sul·la \'səl-ə\, Lucius Cornelius. *Surnamed* Fe·lix \'fē-liks\. 138–78 B.C. Roman general and politician. Served as quaestor in army of Marius against Jugurtha (107–106), and captured Jugurtha; served successfully against the Cimbri and Teutones (104–101). Praetor (94); propraetor in Cilicia (92); served in Social War (90–89); consul (88). Aspired to dictatorial power; opened civil war against Marius (88) and captured Rome. Led campaign against Mithradates IV of Pontus (from 88); captured Athens (86); imposed punitive treaty on Mithradates (85). During absence, declared public enemy by his opponents. Returned to Italy (83) and defeated the younger Marius (82). Dictator of Rome (82–79); reorganized the Senate and the judiciary and founded military colonies throughout Italy.

Sul·li·van \'səl-ə-vən\, Sir Arthur Seymour. 1842–1900. English composer. Organist and choirmaster, St. Michael's, London (1861–72); gained reputation by performance of his *Tempest* music at Crystal Palace (1862). Produced the cantata *Kenilworth* (1864); the ballet *L'Île enchantée* (1864); the comic opera *Cox and Box* (in collaboration with F. C. Burnand, 1867); overtures *In Memoriam* (1866), *Marmion* (1867), and *Overtura di Ballo* (1870); oratorios *The Prodigal Son* (1869) and *The Light of the World* (1873); *Te Deum* (1872). Conductor of a number of orchestras and festivals. Collaborated with W. S. Gilbert first in *Thespis* (1871), then in memorable series of comic operas (for which see William Schwenck GILBERT). First principal of National Training School of Music (1876–81); produced incidental music to *Henry VIII* (1877), cantatas *The Martyr of Antioch* (1880) and *The Golden Legend* (1886), and a serious opera *Ivanhoe* (1891). During disagreement with Gilbert produced opera *Haddon Hall* (1892); resumed collaboration with Gilbert in *Utopia Limited* (1893). In collaboration with others wrote operas *The Chieftain* (1895), *The Beauty Stone* (1898), *The Rose of Persia* (1899), and *The Emerald Isle* (unfinished). Also known for his songs, including "Orpheus with his Lute," "Thou'rt Passing Hence," "The Lost Chord," and tune for the hymn "Onward, Christian Soldiers."

Sullivan, Edward Vincent, *known as* Ed. 1902–1974. American journalist and entertainer, b. New York City. Gossip columnist for *New York Daily News* (1933–74); host of television variety show "The Ed Sullivan Show" (1948–71).

Sullivan, Francis John, *known as* Frank. 1892–1976. American humorist, b. Saratoga Springs, N.Y. Newspaper columnist, contributor to magazines; creator of "Mr. Arbuthnot," expert on clichés; contributed (1932–74) annual Christmas poem to *New Yorker* magazine. Author of *Life and Times of Martha Hepplethwaite* (1926), *Broccoli and Old Lace* (1931), *A Pearl in Every Oyster* (1938), *A Rock in Every Snowball* (1946), *The Night the Old Nostalgia Burned Down* (1953), *Moose in the Hoose* (1959), etc.

Sullivan, Harry Stack. 1892–1949. American psychiatrist, b. Norwich, N.Y. Clinical researcher at Sheppard and Enoch Pratt Hospital, Towson, Md. (1923–30); with Edward Sapir and others, helped establish (1936) Washington (D.C.) School of Psychiatry and taught there (to 1947); after World War II worked with UNESCO to lessen international tensions; helped found World Federation for Mental Health (1948). Influenced by William Alanson White and later by Adolf Meyer; known for his theory of interpersonal relations; developed techniques for treatment of schizophrenia. Author of *Conceptions of Modern Psychiatry* (1947), *The Interpersonal Theory of Psychiatry* (1953), *The Fusion of Psychiatry and Social Science* (1964), etc.

Sullivan, James Edward. 1860–1914. American publisher and sports promoter, b. New York City. Publisher of journal *Sporting Times* (from 1891); organized Amateur Athletic Union of the United States (1888); did much to revive Olympic games; served as American representative at the games; did much to maintain true standards of amateurism in sports.

Sullivan, John. 1740–1795. American Revolutionary officer, b. Somersworth, N.H. Practiced law in Durham, N.H. (from 1760); member of Continental Congress (1774, 1775, 1780, 1781); commissioned brigadier general (1775); served through siege of Boston (1775–76); major general (Aug. 1776); engaged and captured at battle of Long Island (Aug. 27, 1776) and exchanged. Led unsuccessful expedition against British on Staten Island (Aug. 1777); engaged at Germantown; spent winter at Valley Forge (1777–78). Commanded American forces besieging Newport (1778) but failed because of lack of cooperation by French fleet. With Gen. James Clinton defeated combined Indian-Loyalist contingent near Elmira, N.Y. (Aug. 1779) and ravaged the country. Resigned commission (Nov. 1779). Attorney general of New Hampshire (1782–86); president of New Hampshire (1786, 1787, 1789); U.S. district judge of New Hampshire (1789–95). His brother ¶James (1744–1808) was a lawyer; practiced at Limerick, Me. (to 1778), and Groton, Mass. (from 1778); member of Continental Congress (1782); governor of Massachusetts (1807, 1808).

Sullivan, John Lawrence. *Called* the Great John L. *and* the Boston Strong Boy. 1858–1918. American pugilist, b. Roxbury, Mass. Won heavyweight championship by defeat of Paddy Ryan at Mississippi City, Miss., fighting with bare knuckles and on the turf (Feb. 7, 1882); lost championship under Queensberry rules to James J. Corbett (Sept. 7, 1892); noted for blustering personality and fabled strength.

Sullivan, Louis Henry. 1856–1924. American architect, b. Boston. Partner of Dankmar Adler in Chicago and with him designed over 100 buildings (1881–95); in independent practice (from 1895). Notable among buildings designed by him were Auditorium Building, Chicago (1886–89); Transportation Building at World's Columbian Exposition (1893); Wainwright Building, St. Louis (1890–91); Guaranty (now Prudential) Building, Buffalo (1894–95); Carson Pirie Scott & Co. Building, Chicago (1899–1904); and seven banks in Midwestern towns. Regarded as the father of modern functionalism in architecture, esp. as adapting architecture to modern needs by his designs of the skyscraper.

Sullivan, Mark. 1874–1952. American journalist, b. Avondale, Pa. Columnist and commentator, New York *Herald-Tribune;* author of *Our Times—The United States* (1900–25), *The Education of an American* (1938), etc.

Sullivan, Timothy Daniel. 1862–1913. American politician, b. New York City. As member of Tammany organization (from 1890) was dominant political figure of New York's Lower East Side; member of state senate (1892–1902, 1908–12) and of U.S. House of Representatives (1903–07); supported liberal social legislation; responsible for New York's Sullivan Law on handguns.

Sul·li·vant \'səl-ə-vənt\, William Starling. 1803–1873. American botanist, b. Columbus, Ohio. Surveyor and civil engineer in Ohio; interest himself in botany (from c.1833); specialized in study of mosses. Author of *A Catalog of Plants, Native and Naturalized, in the Vicinity of Columbus, Ohio* (1840), *The Musci and Hepaticae East of the Mississippi River* (1856), *Icones Muscorum* (1864), etc.

Sully, Duc de. See Maximilien de BÉTHUNE.

Sul·ly \'səl-ē\, Thomas. 1783–1872. American painter, b. Horncastle, England. To U.S. (1792); studied with Gilbert Stuart in Boston (1807) and Benjamin West in London (1809); also influenced by Sir Thomas Lawrence; studio in Philadelphia (from 1808). One of leading portrait painters of his day; painted some 2000 portraits, including Marquis de Lafayette, Jefferson, Madison, Jackson, Col. Thomas Perkins (1831–32), Queen Victoria (1838), and over 500 historical subjects.

Sully Prudhomme. See René PRUDHOMME.

Sul·man \'səl-mən\, Henry Livingstone. 1861–1940. English metallurgist. In partnership with H. F. K. Picard in London as metallurgical consultants (from 1898); inventor or co-inventor of several processes for the extraction of gold, including treatment with bromocyanide; with Picard originated the froth flotation process for concentrating ores preliminary to the extraction of metals.

Sul·pi·ci·us Ru·fus \səl-'pish(-ē)-əs-'rü-fəs\, Publius. c.124–88 B.C. Roman orator and politician. Tribune of the plebs (88 B.C.); supported citizenship for Italians; his attempts to enact reforms against wishes of the Senate led to his downfall and to restrictions on powers of the tribunes. At outbreak of civil war between Sulla and Marius, declared in favor of Marius; captured by Sulla when Sulla seized Rome (88) and executed.

Sulpicius Rufus, Servius. c.106–43 B.C. Roman jurist. Studied rhetoric with Cicero; consul (51 B.C.); proconsul of Achaia (46). Two of his letters to Cicero survive; none of his nearly 180 law treatises is extant.

Sulpicius Se·ve·rus \sə-'vir-əs\. c.363–c.420. Christian ascetic and writer, b. Aquitania. In early life a lawyer; baptized with Paulinus of Nola (c.390); after early death of his wife, devoted himself to local church building and to life as literary recluse in Aquitania; associated with Martin of Tours. Author of a hagiography of Martin, a history of the world *Chronica* (c.402–404), valuable for contemporary history, and *Dialogi* (404) in which the merits of Martin's monastery are debated by an inmate and a traveler.

Sul·ṭān Mu·ḥam·mad \'sůl-tán-mů-'kám-ád\. 16th century. Persian painter. Pupil of Āqā Mīrak; patronized by Ṭahmāsp I. His miniature paintings, chiefly of happy romantic scenes, illustrated the manuscripts of Hāfez's *Dīvān* (1526), Ferdowsī's epic poem *Shāh-nāmeh* (1537), and Nezāmī's works (1539–43).

Sulz·ber·ger \'səlz-,bər-gər, 'sůlz-\, Arthur Hays. 1891–1968. American newspaper publisher, b. New York City. m. (1911) daughter of Adolph S. Ochs; on staff of *New York Times* (from 1919); president and director, New York Times Co. (1935–57); publisher of the *New York Times* (1935–61).

Sul·zer \'zůlt-sər\, Johann Georg. 1720–1779. Swiss philosopher and writer on aesthetics. Head of Berlin Ritterakademie (from 1763); chief work *Allgemeine Theorie der schönen Künste* (1771–74).

Sulzer, Salomon. *Orig. surname (to 1813)* Loe·wy \lœ̄-vē\. 1804–1890. Austrian cantor and composer. While cantor at Hohenems (1820–26), modernized the liturgy and introduced choral music to the service; chief cantor of Vienna (1826–81); reformed and reorganized musical parts of the liturgy; published collections of music for synagogue service, as *Shir Ẓion* (1840–66); also wrote secular pieces; as singer noted for performances of Schubert's songs. Called the "father of modern synagogue music."

Sul·zer \'sůlt-sər, 'zůlt-\, William. 1863–1941. American politician, b. Elizabeth, N.J. Member from N.Y. of U.S. House of Representatives (1895–1912); governor of New York (1913); impeached and removed from office as result of his quarrel with the Tammany Hall organization.

Su·man·gu·ru \,sü-mäŋ-'gü-rü\. 13th century. West African ruler. Originally ruler of Susu Kingdom of Kaniaga (in present Mali); captured (c.1203) Kumbi, capital of Ghana empire; also conquered several small western Sudanese states and molded them into an empire; unable to restore prosperity or political stability; defeated by Mandingo leader Sundiata at Kirina (c.1235).

Su·ma·ro·kov \sü-(,)mə-'rò-kəf\, Aleksandr Petrovich. 1718–1777. Russian writer. Director, first permanent theater in St. Petersburg (1756–61); later moved to Moscow and presented his plays there. Called the "Racine of the North" for adopting French theatrical conventions in his plays. Author of satiric comedies, tragedies including first Russian classical tragedy *Khorev*

(1747), an adaption of *Hamlet* (1748), lyric poems, and a journal *Trudolyubivaya pchela* (1759) exposing corrupt officials and abuses of serfdom.

Su·mi·yo·shi \sùm-ē-yō-shē\ Gukei, *orig.* Hirozumi. 1631–1705. Japanese painter. First official painter of the Tokugawa shogunate; painted in the *Yamato-e* style (use of Japanese subjects and techniques); established the Sumiyoshi school of painting and contributed to spread of *Yamato-e* style in Edo; known esp. for realistic and humorous *Rakuchū rakugai zumaki,* depicting daily life of Kyōto inhabitants.

Sum·mer·all \'səm-ə-,rȯl\, Charles Pelot. 1867–1955. American army officer, b. Lake City, Fla. Brigadier general (1919), major general (1920); served in France (1917–19) commanding 1st division (July–Oct. 1918) and later the 5th, 9th, and 4th army corps; chief of staff, U.S. army (1926–30); general (1929); retired (1931); president of The Citadel (1931–53).

Summerly, Felix. See Sir Henry COLE.

Summers. See also SOMERS.

Sum·mers \'səm-ərz\, Montague, *in full* Alphonsus Joseph-Mary Augustus Montague. 1880–1948. English man of letters. Authority on Restoration drama and on demonology; author of *History of Witchcraft and Demonology* (1926), *The Vampire, His Kith and Kin* (1928), *The Werewolf* (1933), *The Playhouse of Pepys* (1935), *A Popular History of Witchcraft* (1937), *The Gothic Achievement* (1939), *A Bibliography of the Gothic Novel* (1940), etc.

Sum·mer·skill \'səm-ər-,skil\, Edith Clara. Baroness Summerskill of Ken Wood \'ken-,wu̇d\. 1901–1980. English physician and politician. M.P. (1938–61); minister of national insurance (1950–51); chairman of Labour party (1954–55); created life peer (1961); championed women's rights, national health, and other social causes.

Sum·ner \'səm-nər\, Charles. 1811–1874. American politician, b. Boston. U.S. senator (1851–74); a leader in Congress among the opponents of slavery. His vitriolic attacks upon slavery and its defenders brought a physical assault on him by Representative Preston S. Brooks of South Carolina (1856), inflicting injuries from which he never fully recovered. Chairman of committee on foreign affairs, U.S. Senate (1861–71); persuaded President Lincoln to release Mason and Slidell in the *Trent* Affair (1861). Took prominent part in impeachment proceedings against President Johnson; opposed President Grant on question of annexing Santo Domingo (1871); opposed Grant's reelection (1872).

Sumner, James Batcheller. 1887–1955. American biochemist, b. Canton, Mass. Professor, Cornell (1929–55); first to crystallize an enzyme (urease, 1926); crystallized enzyme catalase (1937); corecipient (with John H. Northrop and Wendell M. Stanley) of 1946 Nobel prize for chemistry.

Sumner, William Graham. 1840–1910. American economist and sociologist, b. Paterson, N.J. Professor, Yale (1872–1910). Prolific publicist of Social Darwinism; prominent in advocating free trade, sound currency, civil service reform; strongly opposed Socialism, interference in business by the government, U.S. imperialistic policy. Author of *A History of American Currency* (1874), *The Financier and Finances of the American Revolution* (1891), *Folkways* (1907), *Science of Society* (completed and edited by A. G. Keller, 1927).

Sum·ter \'səm(p)-tər\, Thomas. *Called* the Carolina Gamecock. 1734–1832. American Revolutionary officer, b. near Charlottesville, Va. Served in French and Indian War; settled in South Carolina (1765); commissioned brigadier general (1780); raised troops and campaigned in South Carolina against the British; defeated Col. Banastre Tarleton at Blackstock (Nov. 1780). Member, U.S. House of Representatives (1789–93, 1797–1801), U.S. Senate (1801–10). Fort Sumter and Sumter, S.C., were named after him.

Sun Ch'üan \'sün-chu̅e̅-'an\. 181–251. Chinese emperor (222–251). Founder (222) and first emperor of the Wu dynasty; ruled in southeast China with capital at Chien-yeh.

Sun·day \'sən-dē\, William Ashley, *called* Billy. 1862–1935. American evangelist, b. Ames, Iowa. Professional baseball player (1883–91); engaged in Y.M.C.A. work (1891–95) and evangelistic work (from 1896); ordained in Presbyterian ministry (1903); preached a fundamentalist theology in a flamboyant style.

Sunderland, Earls of. See SPENCER family.

Sunderland, Countess of. See under SIDNEY family.

Sun·dia·ta *or* **Sun·dja·ta** \sùn-'jät-ä\. *Also known as* Mā·rī Diā·ṭa *or* Ma·ri Ja·ta \mä-'rē-'jät-ä\. d. 1255 A.D. Founder and ruler of Mali. A Mandingo from kingdom of Kangaba, near present Mali–Guinea border; organized army and defeated Sumanguru (*q.v.*) in Battle of Kirina (c.1235); destroyed (1240) Kumbi, former capital of Ghana; extended his empire north to the Sahara, east to Niger River, south to goldfields of Wangara, and west to Sénégal River; moved capital to Niana and made it a trading center in the Sudan.

Sung \'sùŋ\. Name of two Chinese dynasties: (1) A minor dynasty (420–479 A.D.) of the Six Dynasties period, with capital at Nanking, known (after its founder, Liu Yu) as Liu-Sung to distinguish it from the later and more famous dynasty. (2) A dynasty of eighteen sovereigns (960–1279), generally divided into the Sung dynasty proper (960–1126, founded by Chao K'uang-yin), called Northern Sung because its capital, K'ai-feng, was north of the Yangtze, and the Southern Sung (1126–1279), after K'ai-feng was captured (1126) by the Juchen tribes and the capital was relocated at Lin-an in South China. The dynasties were notable for progress in reforms, for high achievement in literature and arts, for development of the art of printing, and especially for painting and ceramics; dynasty fell (1279) to Kublai Khan, who established the Yüan dynasty. For its emperors see the CHAO family.

Sung Chiao-jen \'sùŋ-jē-'au̇-'zhən\. 1882–1913. Chinese politician. To Tokyo (1904) after expulsion from school for revolutionary activities; became a leading member of Sun Yat-sen's revolutionary party T'ung-meng-hui (1905); briefly in cabinet of Yüan Shih-k'ai (1912); founded the Kuomintang (Nationalist) party (1912); assassinated.

Sung Yang. See CH'Ü CH'IU-PAI.

Sun-tzu \'sünd-'zü\. 4th century B.C. Chinese writer. Reputed author of *Ping-fa* (The Art of War), one of earliest known treatises on war and strategy; his insistence on political aspects of war influenced modern strategists.

Sun Yat-sen \'sùn-'yät-'sən\. *Also transcribed as* Sun I-hsien \-'ē-shē-'ən\. *Orig.* Sun Wen \'sün-'wən\. *Also known as* Sun Chung-shan \-'jùŋ-'shäŋ\. 1866–1925. Chinese statesman and revolutionary leader. Lived in Hawaii (1879–83); first graduate (1894) of new Coll. of Medicine, Hong Kong. Founded (1894) Revive China Society, forerunner of his later secret revolutionary groups; failed in attempt to instigate uprising (1895) in Canton, forced to flee; during long exile (1895–1911) lived in Hawaii, U.S., England, and Japan; kidnaped for ten days by Chinese legation in London (1896). Planned revolution against the Manchus, which was finally brought about (1911); became leader of the Kuomintang (1912), establishing his three great principles (nationalism, democracy, people's livelihood); elected provisional president of new Chinese Republic (1911) but retired (1912) to allow Yüan Shih-k'ai to become provisional president of entire country. Appointed director of national railways (1912); unsuccessfully revolted against Yüan, fled to Japan (1913); elected generalissimo of separatist regime at Kwang-tung (1917); elected president of Southern Chinese Republic (1921); expelled by Gen. Ch'en Chiung-ming (1922); gained control of country, installing himself at Canton as generalissimo with Russian assistance (1923); reorganized Kuomintang on model of Soviet Communist party (1924); died of cancer. Known as the father of modern China. His second wife (m. 1914) ¶Soong Ch'ing-ling \'sùŋ-'chiŋ-'liŋ\ (1890–1981), second daughter of C. J. Soong (see SOONG family). Educ. in U.S.; on return to China (1913) became secretary to Sun Yat-sen, working with him until his death (1925). Supported left-wing group of Kuomintang at Hankow (1926–27); denounced the Kuomintang for purge of Communist members (1927); lived in Moscow (1927–31); supported National Salvation group (after 1931); organized (1937) China Defense League for welfare work; became important official in government of Chinese People's Republic, including appointment (1959) as one of two deputy chairmen; a symbol of revolutionary strength in China and a leading advocate of Communism.

Su·pan \'zü-,pän\, Alexander. 1847–1920. German geographer. Editor of *Petermanns geographische Mitteilungen* in Gotha (1884–1909); professor, Breslau (from 1909); author of *Grundzüge der physischen Erdkunde* (1884), etc.

Su·pa·ya·lat \,sü-pä-'yä-lät\. 19th century. Burmese queen. Wife of Thibaw (*q.v.*), last king of Burma (reigned 1878–85); exerted dominant influence on him; advised him to counteract British influence; deposed (1885) by British and exiled to India.

Su·per·vielle \su̅e̅-per-vyel\, Jules. 1884–1960. French writer, b. Montevideo, Uruguay. Divided his life between France and South America; wrote in French but in Spanish tradition. Author of verse as *Gravitations* (1925), *Les Amis inconnus* (1934), *La Fable du monde* (1938), *Naissance* (1951); novels, esp. *Le Voleur d'enfants* (1926) and *L'Enfant de la haute mer* (1931); fantasy plays as *La Belle au bois* (1932) and *Robinson* (1949); and a libretto (with Madeleine Milhaud) for Darius Milhaud's opera *Bolivar* (1950).

Su·pi·lo \'sü-pē-lȯ\, Fano. 1870–1917. Croatian nationalist. Founded (1900) Croatian journal *Novi List* at Rijeka; promoted Croatian-Serbian interests against Austro-Hungarian domination; drew up Rijeka Resolution to create a Croato-Serb coalition (1905); resigned as coalition president after attempt by Habsburg authorities to discredit him (1909); helped found Yugoslav Committee in London (1915); endorsed Declaration of Corfu (1917).

Sup·pé Dem·el·li \zü-'pā-,dem-el-'lē\, Francesco Ezechiele Ermenegildo. *Known as* Franz von Suppé. 1819–1895. Austrian composer, b. Dalmatia, of Belgian descent. Kapellmeister in Vienna at Theater an der Wien (1845–62), Kaitheater (1862–65), and Carltheater (1865–83). Composed over 200 stage works, including about 30 comic operas and operettas in the style of Offenbach such as *Gervinus* (1849), *Flotte Bursche* (1863), *Die schöne Galatea* (1865), *Die leichte Kavallerie* (1866), *Fatinitza* (1876), and *Boccaccio* (1879); also wrote overtures, esp. *Dichter und Bauer* (1845), choral works, symphonies, church music, string quartets, songs, etc.

Sup·pi·lu·liu·mas I \sə-ˌpil-ü-ˈlē-ü-ˌmäs\. *Also spelled* Shup·pi·lu·liu·mash \shə-ˌpil-ü-ˈlē-ü-ˌmäsh\ *and* Sub·bi·lu·liu·ma \sə-ˌbil-ü-ˈlē-ü-ˌmä\. d. c.1335 B.C. Hittite king (c.1375–c.1335 B.C.). Son and successor of Tudhaliyas III; raised Hittite kingdom to imperial power; rebuilt capital of Hattusas; instituted centralized system of government; conquered kingdom of Mitanni; gained suzerainty over Syria; installed his sons Telipinus and Piyassilis as kings of Halap and Carchemish; aided Mattiwaza, king of Mitanni, against Assyrian threats.

Sūr·dās \sür-ˈdäs\. 1483–1563. Indian Hindu poet. Lived at Mathura; wrote some 75,000 verses in Hindi; best known work *Sūrsāgar.*

Su·re·nas \s(y)ü-ˈrē-nəs\, *i.e.* the Suren. d. c.53 B.C. Parthian general. Personal name unknown; member of the noble Suren family; commanding a force of mounted archers and heavy cavalry, inflicted severe defeat on Romans under Crassus at Carrhae (53 B.C.).

Su·ria·no \sür-ˈyä-nō\ *or* **So·ria·no** \sōr-\, Francesco. 1548 or 1549–1621. Italian composer. Director of music at Gonzaga court at Mantua (1581–86); maestro di capella in Rome at S. Maria Maggiore (1587–99, 1601–03), St. John Lateran (1599–1601), St. Peter's (1603–20). With Felice Anerio revised chant books, published as *Editio Medicaea* (1614–15); composed 3 books of madrigals, 4 passions, masses, motets, Magnificats, and other sacred music.

Sur·ratt \sə-ˈrat\, Mary Eugenia, *nee* Jenkins. 1820?–1865. American alleged conspirator, b. Waterloo, Md. m. (1835) John H. Surratt; keeper of boardinghouse in Washington, D.C., which served as meeting place of John Wilkes Booth and his conspirators; hanged, probably on insufficient evidence, for complicity in assassination of President Lincoln. Her son ¶John H. (b. 1844), became secret dispatch rider for the Confederacy; as friend of Booth, took active part in his plot; after Lincoln's assassination, arrested (1866) and tried (1867), but released (1868) on failure of government to secure indictment.

Sur·rey \ˈsər-ē, ˈsə-rē\, Earl of. *Called commonly* Earl Warenne. English title held first (1088?–1148) by members of WARENNE family, next (till 1347) by a family descended from the daughter and heiress of Earl William, Isabel de Warenne, and her husband, Hamelin Plantagenet; then (from 1353), united with the earldom of Arundel, by the FITZALAN family; by John Mowbray (1451–1476); finally (from 1483) by the HOWARD family.

Sur·tees \ˈsərt-(ˌ)ēz\, Robert Smith. 1803–1864. English novelist. Cofounder with Rudolph Ackermann of the *New Sporting Magazine* (1831), to which he contributed sketches of the humorous character Mr. John Jorrocks, a fox-hunting cockney grocer, later collected as *Jorrock's Jaunts and Jollities* (1838) and followed by sequels *Handley Cross* (1843) and *Hillingdon Hall* (1845). Author also of *Hawbuck Grange* (1847), *Mr. Sponge's Sporting Tour* (1853), *Ask Mamma* (1858), *Plain or Ringlets?* (1860), *Mr. Romford's Hounds* (1865), etc.

Sur·ya·var·man \ˌsür-yə-ˈvär-mən\. Name of two rulers of the Khmer Kingdom in Cambodia:

Suryavarman I. *Posthumous title* Nir·vā·ṇa·pa·da \nir-ˈvän-ə-ˈpäd-ə\. d. c.1050 A.D. King (c.1010–c.1050). A foreigner, probably of Malay origin; defeated King Udayadityavarman (by 1002) and his would-be successor Jayaviravarman (by 1010); extended his rule into surrounding regions; built city of Angkor, founded monasteries, promoted public works; a Buddhist but tolerant of Hinduism of his subjects; his reign a peaceful and prosperous one.

Suryavarman II. d. 1150 A.D. King (c.1113–50). Established sole rule over Cambodia (by 1113); formally crowned by his guru Divākarapandita (1119); extended his kingdom into parts of Thailand, Burma, Vietnam, and Malay Peninsula; established relations with China (1116), recognized their suzerainty over him (1126); waged unsuccessful campaign against Vietnamese kingdom of Dai Vet (1123–36); annexed kingdom of Champa (1145) but his army later expelled. A religious reformer, promulgated Vaiṣṇavism as official religion; erected many temples, esp. the Angkor Wat, world's largest religious structure.

Sü·se \ˈzūē-zə\, Heinrich. *Mod. Ger.* Seu·se \ˈzòi-zə\. *Lat.* Su·so \ˈsü-(ˌ)sō\. *Orig.* Heinrich von Berg \ˈberk\. c.1295–1366. German mystic. Joined Dominicans (c.1308); took mother's family name; studied under Meister Eckehart in Cologne (c.1322–c.1325); taught at Constance (c.1326). Wrote *Büchlein der Wahrheit* (c.1327, Little Book of Truth) in defense of Eckehart and *Büchlein der ewigen Weisheit* (c.1328, Little Book of Eternal Wisdom), an extremely popular religious treatise; for his defense of Eckehart dismissed from professorship (1327/30) and condemned by the pope (1329). Preached a milder form of Eckehart's mysticism, esp. in Switzerland and the Upper Rhine; translated into Latin his *Ewigen Weisheit* as *Horologium sapientie* (c.1334/48); prior of the Friends of God in Constance (1343–44); suffered hardships and persecutions in later years; beatified (1831).

Su Shih \ˈsü-ˈshi(ə)r\. *Pen name* Su Tung-p'o \ˈsü-ˈdùŋ-ˈpō\. 1036–1101. Chinese poet and public official. Held public office during reigns of Sung emperors Shen Tsung and Che Tsung; banished (1079–84) to Hupeh province for opposition to reforms of Wang An-shih; exiled (1094) to Kwang-tung, returning shortly before death. Leader among poets attempting to loosen restrictions on classical poetic forms and meters; also essayist, painter, calligrapher.

Süss \ˈzūēs\, Hans. *Known as* Hans von Kulm·bach \ˈkülm-ˌbäk\. c.1480–1522. German painter. Worked under Dürer; court painter at Kraków (1514–18). Painted chiefly religious subjects as *Adoration of the Magi* (1511), *Tucheraltar* in St. Sebald, Nürnberg (1513); also designs for stained glass.

Sutherland. (1) Duke of. See George Granville LEVESON-GOWER. (2) Earls of. See GORDON family.

Suth·er·land \ˈsəth-ər-lənd\, Earl Wilbur, Jr. 1915–1974. American pharmacologist and physiologist, b. Burlingame, Kans. Professor at Case Western Reserve U. (1953–63) and Vanderbilt U. (1963–73); awarded Nobel prize for physiology or medicine (1971) for his discovery (1956) of cyclic adenosine monophosphate (cyclic AMP) and demonstration of its role in metabolic processes in animals.

Sutherland, George. 1862–1942. American jurist, b. Buckinghamshire, England. To U.S. (1864); member, U.S. House of Representatives (1901–03) and U.S. Senate (1905–17) from Utah; associate justice, U.S. Supreme Court (1922–38); wrote many opinions opposing Franklin Roosevelt's programs.

Sutherland, Graham Vivian. 1903–1980. English painter, etcher, and engraver. Taught at Chelsea School of Art (1926–40); official war artist (1941–44). Best known for Surrealistic landscapes and paintings incorporating anthropomorphic insect and plant forms, esp. thorns, as in *Crucifixion* (1946) and *Origins of the Land* (1951); also known for Expressionistic portraits, including Somerset Maugham (1949) and Sir Winston Churchill (1954); designed tapestry for Coventry cathedral (1954–57).

Su·to·ku \sü-tō-kü\. 1119–1164. Japanese emperor (1123–41). Ascended throne after abdication of his father Toba I (1123); father real power during reign; abdicated in favor of his brother Konoe (1141); attempted to overthrow his brother Shirakawa II (1156), resulting in Hōgen War; coup defeated by Taira Kiyomari; exiled from capital.

Su·tro \ˈsü-(ˌ)trō\, Adolph Heinrich Joseph. 1830–1898. American mining engineer, b. Aachen, Prussia. To U.S. (1850); to California (1851) and Nevada (1860). Planned Sutro Tunnel (over 20,000 feet long) into Mount Davidson to reach the rich Comstock lode and superintended its construction (1869–78); sold his interest in Sutro Tunnel (1879) and invested in San Francisco real estate. Mayor of San Francisco (1894–96).

Sut·ter \ˈsət-ər, ˈsüt-\, John Augustus. *Orig.* Johann August Su·ter \ˈzüt-ər\. 1803–1880. American pioneer, b. Kandern, Baden. To U.S. (1834); with trading parties to Santa Fe (1835, 1836) and to Oregon region (1838). Landed in San Francisco Bay (1839); founded colony of Nueva Helvetia on site of what is now Sacramento; became Mexican citizen (1841) and received from Governor Alvarado a grant of land; built (1841) Sutter's Fort, a frontier trading post. Gold was discovered on his property (Jan. 24, 1848); in the subsequent rush, his workmen deserted, his sheep and cattle were stolen, and his land was occupied by squatters; became bankrupt (1852). Given pension of $250 a month by state of California (1864–78). See James W. MARSHALL.

Sutt·ner \ˈzùt-nər\, Bertha Félice Sophie von, *nee* Kin·sky von Chi·nic und Tet·tau \ˈkin-skē-fòn-ˈshē-nē-kùnt-ˈte-ˌtaù\. 1843–1914. Austrian novelist. m. (1876) the novelist Baron Arthur Gundaccar von Suttner (1850–1902). Took active part in movement for international peace; founded (1891) Austrian Society of Friends of Peace; edited pacifist journal *Die Waffen nieder!* (1892–99); credited with influencing Bernhard Nobel in establishment of Nobel peace prize; awarded the Nobel peace prize (1905). Among her works were *Inventarium einer Seele* (1883), *Die Waffen nieder!* (1889), *Trente et Quarante* (1893), *Einsam und arm* (1896).

Sut·ton \ˈsət-ᵊn\, Walter Stanborough. 1877–1916. American physician and geneticist, b. Utica, N.Y. Studied under Clarence E. McClung (1897–1901); in private surgical practice in Kansas City, Kan., and Kansas City, Mo. (from 1909). Provided first conclusive evidence that chromosomes carry units of inheritance and occur in distinct pairs (1902–03); his work formed basis for chromosomal theory of heredity.

Sutton, Willie, *in full* William Francis, Jr. *Nicknamed* Willie the Actor. 1901–1980. American bank robber, b. Brooklyn, N.Y. Gained national notoriety for robbing banks (from 1927) employing series of ingenious disguises (hence nickname); also famous for spectacular attempts, usually unsuccessful, at escaping from prisons.

Su Tung-p'o. See SU SHIH.

Su·vo·rin \sü-ˈvò-ryin\, Aleksey Sergeyevich. 1834–1912. Russian journalist. Founder (1876) of Russian daily newspaper *Novoye Vremya;* published reference works and "libraries" of Russian and foreign classics; promoted Moscow Little Theater and wrote plays for it; helped Chekhov and other writers.

Su·vo·rov \sü-ˈvö-rəf\, Aleksandr Vasilyevich. 1729–1800. Russian field marshal. Served in Seven Years' War (1756–63); gained reputation as successful and unorthodox tactician in Russo-Polish War (1768–72); joined (1773) war against Turks on Danube, defending Hirsov and winning Battle of Kozludji (1774); made general (1787); commanded Russian army against the Turks (1787–92), winning the battle of Kinburn (1787) but earning official displeasure for conduct at siege of Ochakov (1788). Suppressed Polish revolt (1794). Created field marshal (1794); defeated the French at Cassano d'Adda, the Trebbia River, and Novi (1799). Commander in chief (1800).

Su·yū·ṭī, as- \ˌás-sü-ˈyü-tē\. *In full* Abū al-Faḍl ʿAbd ar-Raḥmān ibn Abī Bakr Jalāl ad-Dīn as-Suyūṭī. 1445–1505. Egyptian writer. Precocious student; became a Ṣūfī teacher (by 1462); promoted to chair in the mosque of Baybars in Cairo (1486–1501); revolt resulted from his attempt to reduce stipends of Ṣūfī scholars at mosque (1501); thereafter under house arrest at Rawda. Prolific writer; wrote on nearly every branch of Islāmic science and literature, including *Itqān fī ʿulūm al-Qurʾān* on exegesis, *Taʾrīkh al-khulafāʾ* (translated as *History of the Caliphs,* 1881), and linguistic encyclopedia *al-Muzhir fī ʿulūm al-lughah.*

Su·zu·ki \sü̇z-ü̇k-ē\ Bunji. 1885–1946. Japanese labor leader. Christian convert; early labor organizer in Japan (from 1911); formed Japanese Federation of Labor (1919); worked for passage of manhood suffrage act (1925); helped organize Social Democratic party; elected to Diet several times (from 1928).

Suzuki Daisetsu Teitarō. 1870–1966. Japanese Buddhist scholar. Disciple of Zen master Sōen; in U.S. (1897–1909), collaborating with Paul Carus as magazine editor; considered chief interpreter of Zen Buddhism to the West. Published *The Discourse on the Awakening of Faith in the Mahayana* (1900; translation) and *Outline of Mahayana Buddhism* (1907).

Suzuki Harunobi. *Orig.* Ho·zu·mi \hō-zü-mē\ Jihē. *Also known by personal name* Ji·rō·bei \jē-rō-bā\. 1725–1770. Japanese artist. Exponent of the *Ukiyo-e* style; established art of *nishiki-e* (polychrome prints); began designing *nishiki-e* for haiku poems (1765), creating fashion for pictures of lyrical scenes.

Suzuki Kantarō. 1867–1948. Japanese naval officer and politician. Served in wars against China (1894–95) and Russia (1904–05); promoted to full admiral (1923); prime minister of Japan (Apr.–Aug. 1945).

Suzuki Shōsan. 1579–1655. Japanese religious. Served as samurai under shogun Tokugawa Ieyasu; entered Zen priesthood (1620); in Shimabara (1638–48), erecting 32 Buddhist temples and endeavoring to remove Christian influences.

Svāmin. See KUMĀRILA.

Sva·to·pluk \ˈsvá-tö-plü̇k\. d. 894. Prince of Moravia (870–894). United Moravia, Slovakia, and Bohemia under name of Great Moravia against emperor of Germany; finally overcome by Magyars under Árpád. During his reign western Slavs converted by saints Cyril and Methodius (*qq.v.*).

Sved·berg \ˈsvād-ˌbarʸ\, The, *in full* Theodor. 1884–1971. Swedish chemist. Professor (1912–49), U. of Uppsala; director, Physikalisch-chemieches Institut (1931–49) and of Gustaf Werners Institut für Kernchemie (1949–67). Known for research in colloid chemistry, especially for development of the ultracentrifuge; also worked with Arne Tiselius in developing electrophoretic methods for separating proteins. Awarded 1926 Nobel prize for chemistry.

Šveh·la \ˈshvek-lá\, Antonín. 1873–1933. Czech politician. Leader of Agrarian party in the legislature; first minister of interior in new Czechoslovak state (1919–20); premier of Czechoslovakia (1922–29).

Svein. See SWEYN.

Svend·sen \ˈsven-sən\, Johan Severin. 1840–1911. Norwegian composer, violinist, and conductor. Composed symphonies, Norwegian rhapsodies, tone poems, overtures, chamber music, choral works, and songs.

Svens·son \ˈsvens-sön\, Jón Stefán. 1857–1944. Icelandic writer. Known for series of *Nonni* adventure books for juveniles.

Sverd·lov \ˈsvyerd-ləf, svyird-ˈlöf\, Yakov Mikhaylovich. 1885–1919. Russian revolutionary and politician. Secretary of Bolshevik party's Central Committee and chairman of Central Executive Committee (from 1917); titular chief of state; in virtual control of party organization and the state bureaucracy.

Sver·drup \ˈsvar-drü̇p\, Harald Ulrik. 1888–1957. Norwegian meteorologist and oceanographer. Head of scientific work on Maud expedition in Arctic (1917–25); research associate, Carnegie Institution, Washington, D.C. (1928–39); professor at and director of Scripps Institution of Oceanography (1936–48). Explained equatorial countercurrents; helped develop method of predicting surf and breakers. Wrote *Oceanography for Meteorologists* (1942); coauthor of *The Oceans* (1942) and *Breakers and Surf* (1944).

Sverdrup, Johan. 1816–1892. Norwegian politician. President of the Odelsting (1862–69) and of the Storting (1871–81); prime minister (1884–89).

Sverdrup, Otto Neumann. 1855–1930. Norwegian explorer. On Nansen's expedition to Greenland (1888) and polar expedition (1893–96); leader of expedition that unsuccessfully attempted to circumnavigate Greenland (1898–1902); leader of Arctic expeditions in 1914 and 1920 to search for lost Russian explorers and in 1928 to search for crew of Italian dirigible *Italia.*

Sver·ker \ˈsver-kər\. d. c.1156. King of Sweden (1130–50). Established several cloisters; deposed.

Sver·rir \ˈsver-ər\. *Also called* Sverrir Si·gurds·son \ˈsig-ürts-sön\. c.1149–1202. King of Norway (1184–1202). Supposed son of Sigurd II; became leader of the Birkebeiner, rivals of Magnus V (by 1177); claimed throne of Norway; proclaimed king in Trondheim region (1179); fought and often defeated Magnus (1179–84), finally at Norefjord, where Magnus was killed; weakened the aristocracy; built strong monarchy with support of peasantry; strong advocate of royal supremacy over the church; suppressed the Crosiers' rebellion (by 1202); one of Norway's greatest kings.

Světlá, Karolina. See Johanna MUŽÁKOVÁ.

Svevo, Italo. See Ettore SCHMITZ.

Svin·huf·vud \ˈsvēn-hüv-üd\, Pehr Evind. 1861–1944. Finnish politician. Entered parliament (1894), speaker (1907–12); banished to Siberia by Russian government (1914–17). Head of Finnish government (1917–18); led "White" government to victory during Civil War of 1918; secured Finland's independence from Russia; premier (1930–31); president (1931–37); suppressed Communist party in Finland and maintained rightist regime.

Svo·bo·da \ˈsvö-bö-dá\, Ludvík. 1895–1979. Czech soldier and politician. In World War I fought in Czechoslovak Legions in Russia (1915–20); in Czech army (1922–39); in Soviet Union as head of Czechoslovak army corps (1939–45); minister of defense (1945–50); head of Klement Gottwald Military Academy (1955–59). President of Czechoslovakia (1968–75); resisted Soviet demands during and after Soviet Union's invasion of Czechoslovakia in Aug. 1968; helped secure release of Alexander Dubček and aides from Soviets.

Svya·to·slav I \ˈsvyá-tə-sləf\. *In full* Svyatoslav Igor·e·vich \-i-ˈgör(-yəv)-ˌyich\. d. 972. Grand prince of Kiev (945–972). Son of Grand Prince Igor; probably grandson of Rurik. Last non-Christian ruler of Kiev; defeated Khazars on lower Don and Ossetes and Circassians in northern Caucasus (963–965); conquered Balkan Bulgars at behest of Byzantines (967); after declaring intention of establishing a Russo-Bulgarian empire, defeated (971) by John I Tzimisces and compelled to abandon claim to Balkan territory; greatest of Varangian princes of early Russian history.

Swam·mer·dam \ˈsväm-ər-ˌdäm\, Jan. 1637–1680. Dutch naturalist. Known for his biological researches with the microscope; first to describe the red blood cells (1658); discovered the valves of the lymph vessels (1664); studied the anatomy of insects, which he classified on the basis of development; devised improved techniques for injecting wax and dyes into cadavers; described ovarian follicles of mammals independently of Reiner de Graaf (1672). Chief works *Historia insectorum generalis* (1669) and *Bybel der Natuure* (1737–38).

Swan \ˈswän\, Sir Joseph Wilson. 1828–1914. English chemist and electrician. Developed a primitive electric light (1860); invented the dry photographic plate (by 1871); patented bromide photographic paper (1879); produced carbon-filament incandescent electric lamp, independently of Thomas A. Edison (1880); patented process for squeezing nitrocellulose through holes to form fibers (1883); invented cellular-surfaced lead-plate storage battery.

Swann \ˈswän\, William Francis Gray. 1884–1962. American physicist, b. Ironbridge, England. To U.S. (1913); professor, U. of Minn. (1918–23), Chicago (1923–24), Yale (1924–27); director, Bartol Research Foundation, Franklin Institute (1927–59). Known esp. for work on cosmic rays, also on thermal measurements, electroconductivity, relativity, atmospheric electricity, and atomic structure.

Swan·son \ˈswän-sən\, Gloria. *Orig.* Gloria May Josephine Svensson. 1899–1983. American actress, b. Chicago. Reigned as Hollywood glamour queen during golden age of silent motion pictures. Launched career with Essanay Studios, Chicago (1914–16). To Hollywood (1916); made comedies for Max Sennett; under Cecil B. De Mille starred in *Male and Female* (1919); later starred in *Manhandled* (1924), *Stage Struck* (1925), *Sadie Thomson* (1928), *Queen Kelly* (1928), etc.; her career waned but she made spectacular comeback with *Sunset Boulevard* (1950), delivering the self-descriptive line, "I *am* big — it's the pictures that got small."

Swan·ton \ˈswänt-ᵊn\, John Reed. 1873–1958. American anthropologist, b. Gardiner, Me. On staff, Smithsonian Inst. (1900–44); authority on culture of Indians of southeastern U.S. Author of *Contributions to the Ethnography of the Haida* (1905), *Indians of the Southeastern United States* (1946), *The Indian Tribes of North America* (1952), etc.

Swayne \ˈswān\, Noah Haynes. 1804–1884. American jurist, b. Frederick Co., Va. Practiced in Columbus, Ohio (1831–61); associate justice, U.S. Supreme Court (1862–81). His son ¶Wager (1834–1901) was a lawyer and army officer; served in Union army through Civil War; practiced law (from 1870).

Swaythling, Baron. See Samuel MONTAGU.

Swe·den·borg \ˈsvā-dən-ˌbörʸ, *Angl* ˈswēd-ᵊn-ˌbörg\, Emanuel. *Surname orig.* Swed·berg \ˈsvād-ˌberʸ\. 1688–1772. Swedish scientist, philosopher, and religious writer. Published (1716–18) *Daedalus Hyperboreus,* first Swedish scientific journal; assessor on Swedish Board of Mines (1716); ennobled (1719) and took seat in House of Peers. Devoted himself to scientific research, and published *Opera philosophica et mineralia* (1734; included *Principia rerum naturalium*), *Oeconomia regni animalis* (1740–41), and *Regnum animale* (1744–45). Began having visions (c.1743); resigned position as assessor of mines (1747) and devoted himself thereafter to psychical and spiritual research; wrote voluminous works on interpretation of the Bible, including *Arcana coelestia* (1749–56) and *Vera christiana religio* (1771). Although he himself never tried to preach or to found a religious sect, his followers, Swedenborgians, constitute a considerable society with a regular ecclesiastical organization, known as Church of the New Jerusalem.

Swee·linck \'svā-liŋk\, Jan Pieterszoon. 1562–1621. Dutch organist and composer. Organist of the Old Church, Amsterdam (c.1580–1621); famous as organ teacher, pupils included Samuel Scheidt, Heinrich Scheidermann, and others of the northern German school. Composed much sacred and secular vocal music in the French and Dutch polyphonic tradition as *Chansons* (1594), *Cantiones sacrae* (1619, motets), madrigals, psalm settings; his keyboard music included chorale variations, toccatas, fantasias, and sets of variations on secular tunes.

Sweet \'swēt\, Henry. 1845–1912. English phonetician. Published *History of English Sounds from the Earliest Period* (1874), *Anglo-Saxon Reader* (1876), *Handbook of Phonetics* (1877); chief founder of modern phonetics; applied phonetic method in *A New English Grammar* (1892, 1898) and *The History of Language* (1900); also wrote *The Sounds of English* (1908), Old and Middle English texts, primers of speech, an Anglo-Saxon dictionary, a historical English grammar.

Swet·ten·ham \'swet-nəm\, Sir Frank Athelstane. 1850–1946. English colonial administrator. Sent to Singapore as cadet in Straits Settlements civil service (1871); resident in Selangor (1882–84, 1887–89); constructed railway from Kuala Lumpur to port of Klang; resident in Perak (1889–95); resident general in Federated Malay States (1896–1901); governor and commander in chief, Straits Settlements (1901–04); highly influential in shaping British policy and structure of British administration in Malay Peninsula.

Sweyn *or* **Svein** \'sve(-i)n, 'svān\. Name of two kings of Denmark:

Sweyn I. d. 1014. King (c.987–1014). Son of Harold II Bluetooth and father of Canute II the Great. Rebelled against his father, who fled to Wendland (987); attacked Norway but was defeated by Haakon the Great (c.987); m. Gunnhild, widow of King Erik the Victorious of Sweden; led large fleet to England which did great damage (994) but assaulted London unsuccessfully; at war with Olaf Tryggvason of Norway (1000), who was defeated and killed; after massacre of Danes in England (1002), led or sent plundering expeditions annually (1003–14) that ravaged the land and exacted tribute; led successful campaign to England (1013–14); accepted as king, forcing Ethelred II into exile; died suddenly at Gainsborough.

Sweyn II. d. 1075. King (1047–75). Son of Earl Ulf and of Estrid, daughter of Sweyn I. Born in England; lived in Sweden after murder of his father (1027); made a viceroy by King Magnus I; became king (1047); at war with Harold III of Norway (1047–64); usually defeated, but finally won peace; successfully attacked England, aiding Anglo-Saxon rebels against William the Conqueror (1069); withdrew troops after agreement with William (1070); worked to establish independence of Danish church; succeeded by five of his sons as kings of Denmark.

Swift \'swift\, Gustavus Franklin. 1839–1903. American meat packer, b. Sagamore, Mass. Partner in a Boston meat market (1872); established himself at Chicago (1875). Commissioned development of refrigerator car; made first shipment of dressed beef to eastern market (1877); profited by utilization of by-products to make oleomargarine, soap, glue, fertilizer, etc. Incorporated business as Swift & Co. (1885). Developed overseas markets for American beef; established additional packing houses in other cities. His son ¶Louis Franklin (1861–1937) was president of Swift & Co. (1903–31) and chairman of its board of directors (1931–32).

Swift, Homer Fordyce. 1881–1953. American physician, b. Paines Hollow, N.Y. Specialized in treatment of syphilis, rheumatic fever, streptococcus infections, trench fever; developed (with Arthur W. M. Ellis) the Swift-Ellis treatment for cerebrospinal syphilis; a contributor to report *Trench Fever* (1918) and author of many medical articles.

Swift, Jonathan. 1667–1745. English churchman and writer, b. Dublin. Cousin of John Dryden; to England (1688) and became secretary to Sir William Temple; returned to Ireland, took orders (1694), and was appointed vicar of Kilroot, near Belfast. Returned to Sir William Temple in Surrey (1696–99), where he wrote *A Tale of a Tub* on corruption in religion and learning, and "The Battle of the Books," a travesty on the controversy over ancient and modern learning (pub. together, 1704); supervised education of Esther Johnson (*q.v.*), the Stella of his correspondence and journal. After Temple's death (1699), returned to Ireland and received some small preferments (1702–10); on frequent visits to London, became friend of Addison, Steele, Halifax, Congreve, and other Whig writers; wrote ecclesiastical and political pamphlets, verse, and, under pseudonym Isaac Bick·er·staff \'bik-ər-ˌstaf\, squibs on John Partridge the almanac maker (1708–09). Again in London (1710–14); grew disenchanted with Whig policies and administration; turned to Tory party (1710) and became its leading writer; edited (1710–11) Tory journal *The Examiner* and wrote political pamphlets including "The Conduct of the Allies" (1711); began (1710) *Journal to Stella* (pub. 1766–68); contributed to *Tatler, Spectator,* and *Intelligencer;* aided Pope and Arbuthnot in forming Scriblerus Club and contributed to *Memoirs of Martinus Scriblerus.* Made dean of St. Patrick's, Dublin (1713); on return of Whigs to office, retired to Ireland an embittered man (1715); devoted himself to exposing unfair treatment of Ireland and the English in Ireland by Whigs; successfully urged cancellation of "Wood's halfpence" in Ireland by his *Drapier's Letters* (1724); published most famous work *Gulliver's Travels* (1726), a keen satire upon cant and sham of courts, parties, statesmen; paid last visit to England (1727). A popular idol in Ireland as champion of people's grievances in ironical tracts such as "A Modest Proposal" (1729); continued writing poetry as "Cadenus and Vanessa" (1726) and "Verses on the Death of Dr. Swift" (1739); declared (1742) incapable of caring for himself after suffering a stroke. Considered Ireland's great patriot dean and the greatest satirist in the English language.

Swin·burne \'swin-(ˌ)bərn\, Algernon Charles. 1837–1909. English poet. Associated with Dante Gabriel Rossetti and William Morris (from 1857); recognized as lyric poet of high order on publication of *Atalanta in Calydon* (1865); not so successful in a trilogy relating to Mary, Queen of Scots, *Chastelard* (1865), *Bothwell* (1874), *Mary Stuart* (1881); evoked censure by paganism and sensuality in *Poems and Ballads* (first series, 1866). Met (1867) and influenced by Mazzini; issued republican *Songs before Sunrise* (1871) and a more subdued *Poems and Ballads* (second series, 1878); in alarming state of health, spent rest of life (from 1879) in house at Putney of W.T. Watts-Dunton. Published more verse, including *Tristram of Lyonesse* (1882), a third series of *Poems and Ballads* (1889), *Astrophel* (1894), *A Channel Passage* (1899), and several plays. Also noted as literary critic, esp. for *Essays and Studies* (1875) and monographs on Shakespeare (1880), Jonson (1889), etc.

Swing \'swiŋ\, Raymond Gram. 1887–1968. American journalist, b. Cortland, N.Y. War correspondent in Berlin for Chicago *Daily News* (1914–17), New York *Herald* (1919–22); later, foreign correspondent for Philadelphia *Public Ledger* and New York *Evening Post.* News commentator on American affairs for British Broadcasting Corporation (1935–45), on foreign and political affairs for Mutual Broadcasting System (1936–45), American Broadcasting System (1942–48), Voice of America (1951–53, 1959–64).

Swith·un *or* **Swith·in** \'swith-ən, 'swith-\. Saint. c.800–862. Anglo-Saxon ecclesiastic. Bishop of Winchester (852–862); counsellor to kings Ecgberht and Aethelwulf. Buried outside north wall of Winchester Minster; on being moved inside cathedral (July 15, 971), accomplished miracles, according to contemporary writers. Popularly associated with myth that if it rains on July 15, it will rain the forty succeeding days.

Swope \'swōp\, Gerard. 1872–1957. American electrical engineer and executive, b. St. Louis, Mo. Entered employ of General Electric Co. as helper (1893); rose to presidency of the corporation (1922–39, 1942–44); member of many governmental regulatory and advisory boards. His daughter ¶Henrietta Hill (1902–1980), b. St. Louis, was an astronomer; on staff of Harvard Coll. Observatory (1928–42) and of Mount Wilson and Palomar observatories (1952–68); discovered and measured numerous variable stars; as mathematician for U.S. Navy Hydrographic Office (1943–47), helped develop loran.

Swope, Herbert Bayard. 1882–1958. American journalist, b. St. Louis, Mo. Brother of Gerard Swope. War correspondent of *New York World* with German armies (1914–16); awarded Pulitzer prize for his reports (1917); newspaper correspondent at Paris Peace Conference (1919); executive editor, *New York World* (1920–29); chairman of N.Y. State Racing Commission (1934–45); often served government in advisory roles. Author of *Inside the German Empire* (1917), etc.

Sy·ag·ri·us \sī-'ag-rē-əs\. 430?–486. Last Roman governor in Gaul. Defeated by Clovis (486).

Sy·bel \'zē-bəl\, Heinrich von. 1817–1895. German historian. Pupil of Leopold von Ranke; founded *Historische Zeitschrift* (1859); broke with Ranke's method and became leading spokesman of political Prussianism; supported Bismarck (after 1866); director of Prussian archives (from 1875). His works included *Geschichte der Revolutionszeit 1789–95* (1853–60), *Die Begründung des deutschen Reichs durch Wilhelm I* (1889–94).

Sydenham, Baron. See Charles Edward Poulett THOMSON.

Syd·en·ham \'sid-ᵊn-əm, 'sid-nəm\, Thomas. 1624–1689. English physician. A founder of clinical medicine and epidemiology. Served in parliamentary forces in Civil War. Described scarlet fever, St. Vitus' dance (Sydenham's chorea), hysteria, malaria, smallpox, and gout; introduced opium into medical practice; one of first to use iron in treating anemia; studied epidemics in relation to different seasons, years, and ages; insisted on clinical observation instead of theory; friend of John Locke and Robert Boyle; chief works *Observationes medicae* (1676) and a treatise on gout (1683); often called "the English Hippocrates."

Sydney, Viscount. See Thomas Townshend under TOWNSHEND family.

Sykes \'sīks\, Sir Mark. 6th Baronet Sykes. 1879–1919. English diplomat. In World War I sent on missions to Near East; as chief British representative, negotiated Sykes-Picot Agreement (1916), assigning spheres of interest in Near East to Russia, France, and Britain. Author of travel books *Through Five Turkish Provinces* (1900) and *The Caliph's Last Heritage* (1915).

Sylva, Carmen. See ELIZABETH, Queen of Romania.

Sylvanus. See SILAS.

Syl·ves·ter \sil-'ves-tər\. Name of two popes and two antipopes:

Sylvester I. Saint. d. 335. Pope (314–335). Sent two legates to the Council of Nicea; story of his baptizing Constantine the Great a pure legend.

Sylvester II. *Orig.* Ger·bert \zher-ber\ of Au·ril·lac \ō-rē-yák\. c.945–1003. Pope (999–1003), b. France. An eminent scholar, esp. in mathematics and natural science; teacher at Reims; archbishop of Reims (991); befriended by emperors Otto II and III; as tutor, influenced the youth Otto III by his ideas of a restored empire; made archbishop of Ravenna (998). Took interest in affairs in all parts of central Europe; refused to crown Duke Bolesław king of Poland but agreed to kingship of Stephen; made Prague archbishopric for Slavs. Wrote textbooks and advanced learning, esp. music and the sciences; wrote letters, theological works, and two works on mathematics.

Sylvester III. *Orig.* Gio·van·ni \jō-'vän-nē\. d. 1046? Antipope (1045). Bishop of Sabrina; elevated on expulsion from Rome of Benedict IX; resigned papal claims and recognized Gregory VI as pope.

Sylvester IV. *Orig.* Ma·gi·nul·fo \ˌmäj-ē-'nül-fō\. d. 1111. Antipope (1105–1111). In opposition to Paschal II; never widely supported.

Sylvester, James Joseph. *Orig. surname* Joseph. 1814–1897. English mathematician. Professor, U. of Virginia (1841–42); in actuarial work in London (1844–56); professor, Royal Military Academy, Woolwich (1855–70), Johns Hopkins U. (1876–83), and Oxford (1883–97). First editor, *American Journal of Mathematics* (1878–84). Did original work in the theory of numbers, esp. in partitions and diophantine analysis; founded theory of algebraic invariants (with Arthur Cayley). Wrote *Treatise on Elliptic Functions* (1876). Also a poet; published *Laws of Verse* (1870).

Sylvester, János. c.1504–c.1552. Hungarian Humanist. Disciple of Erasmus; author of the first Hungarian poetry and the first Hungarian grammar; also translated the New Testament (1541).

Sylvester, Josuah. 1563–1618. English poet. Translated scriptural epics of Guillaume de Salluste as *The Divine Weekes and Workes* (1592–1608).

Syl·vis \'sil-vəs\, William H. 1828–1869. American labor leader, b. Armagh, Pa. Ironfounder by trade; involved in union activities (from 1857); called convention of workingmen to oppose impending Civil War (1861); helped found National Labor Union and was elected its president (1868); became part owner of *Workingman's Advocate* in Philadelphia (1869); one of most articulate labor spokesmen of his time.

Sylvius, Franciscus. See Franz DELEBOE.

Symeon. See also SIMEON.

Sym·e·on \'sim-ē-ən\. Saint. *Called* the New Theologian. c.949–1022. Byzantine monk and mystic. Became abbot of St. Mamas monastery, near Constantinople (980); forced to resign (1009) because of his austere monastic policy and dispute with patriarch of Constantinople; retired to Chrysopolis; preached a charismatic mysticism. Author of catecheses, sermons, series of short rules, and *Hymns of the Divine Loves* describing his spiritual experiences.

Sy·ming·ton \'sī-miŋ-tən, 'sim-iŋ-\, William. 1763–1831. Scottish engineer. With brother built working model of steam road carriage (1786); patented steam engine (1787), later used to propel a boat on Dalswinton loch (1788); developed (1801) a successful steam-driven paddle wheel, used (1802) to propel the *Charlotte Dundas,* one of first practical steamboats.

Sym·ma·chus \'sim-ə-kəs\. Saint. d. 514. Pope (498–514). Opposed by antipope Laurentius; favored by Theodoric the Great; expelled Manichaeans from Rome; erected and restored several Roman churches.

Symmachus, Quintus Aurelius. c.345–c.402. Roman orator and politician. Champion of paganism; proconsul of Africa (373); pontifex maximus; prefect of Rome (384); consul (391). Protested (382) against removal of statue and altar of Victory from senate building, and later (384) wrote to Emperor Valentinian II asking that these be restored. Ten books of letters and fragments of his speeches survive.

Symmachus, Quintus Aurelius Memmius. d. 524 A.D. Roman senator and patrician. Consul (485); defended his son-in-law Boethius against charge of treason; arrested and, with Boethius, executed by Theodoric.

Symmachus ben Jo·seph \-ben-'jō-zəf, *also* -səf\. fl. 200 A.D. Hebrew sage. Lived in Samaria; wrote treatises on diverse subjects, as nature of God and uses of money; said to have translated the Bible into Greek.

Symmes \'simz\, John Cleves. 1742–1814. American Revolutionary soldier, b. Southold, N.Y. Colonel of militia (1775); engaged at Monmouth and Short Hills; member of Continental Congress (1785, 1786); received (1788) grant of land between Miami and Little Miami rivers; founded colony centered around present Cincinnati, Ohio.

Sym·onds \'sim-ən(d)z\, John Addington. 1840–1893. English poet, essayist, and literary historian. Published his *Renaissance in Italy* (1875–86), a classic authority on subject; interrupted by illness, settled for rest of life at Davos Platz, Switzerland; published excellent translations of *Autobiography of Benvenuto Cellini* (1887) and of sonnets of Michelangelo and Campanella; biographer of Shelley (1878), Sir Philip Sidney (1886), Ben Jonson (1886), Walt Whitman (1893); also wrote *A Problem in Modern Ethics* (1881) and *A Problem in Greek Ethics* (1883), pioneering works on study of homosexuality.

Sy·mons \'sī-mənz, 'sim-ənz\, Arthur William. 1865–1945. English poet and critic. First English champion of French Symbolist poets; member of the Rhymers' Club; editor of *The Savoy* (1896). Published Impressionistic *fin de siècle* lyrics in *Silhouettes* (1892), *London Nights* (1895), *Images of Good and Evil* (1900), *The Fool of the World, and Other Poems* (1906), *Knave of Hearts* (1913); prose works included *The Symbolist Movement in Literature* (1899), *Spiritual Adventures* (1905), *Studies in Elizabethan Drama* (1920), *Confessions* (1930); author also of translations of Verlaine and travel pieces.

Symons, George James. 1838–1900. English meteorologist. Elected to Royal Meteorological Society (1856); established (1860) British Rainfall Organization; issued annual rainfall reports (1860–98); increased rainfall reporting stations from 168 to over 3,500; established standards of accuracy and uniformity on meteorological instruments and measurements.

Sy·ne·si·us \si-'nē-zh(ē-)əs\ of Cy·re·ne \sī-'rē-(ˌ)nē\. c.370–413. Greek prelate and Neoplatonic philosopher. Bishop of Ptolemais (from 410). Among his extant works are *Dio sive de suo ipsius Instituto, Aegyptus sive de Providentia, De insomniis,* and *Epistolae.*

Synge \'siŋ\, John Millington. 1871–1909. Irish dramatist. Promoter of Celtic revival of 1890s; settled in Paris (1895); visited Aran Isles annually (1898–1902) and, following suggestion of W. B. Yeats, abandoned literary criticism in order to portray primitive life of Aran islanders. Wrote plays *The Shadow of the Glen* and *Riders to the Sea* (performed 1903, 1904). Took up residence in Ireland (1903) and devoted himself to interests of the Abbey Theatre, Dublin, contributing to its fame by *The Well of the Saints* (1905) and his masterpiece *The Playboy of the Western World* (1907); author of descriptive essays *The Aran Islands* (1907) and *In Wicklow and In West Kerry* (1908); all but finished his tragedy *Deirdre of the Sorrows* (produced 1910).

Syntax, Doctor. See William COMBE.

Sy·phax \'sī-ˌfaks\. d. c.201 B.C. Numidian king. Rival of Masinissa and husband of Sophonisba; allied with Hannibal; defeated and captured by the Romans under Gaius Laelius at the Battle of the Great Plains, near Utica (203).

Szá·la·si \'sá-lä-sē\, Ferenc. 1897–1946. Hungarian politician. Founded the nationalistic and anti-Semitic Party of National Will (1935); often imprisoned by government; became head of the Fascist Arrow Cross party; made head of government (Oct. 1944); cooperated completely with German occupation forces; left Hungary with Germans (Apr. 1945); arrested and executed.

Szent–Györ·gyi \sänt-'jörj(-e)\, Albert von Nagyrapolt. 1893–1986. American biochemist, b. Budapest. Researcher at U. of Szeged, Hung. (1931–45). To U.S. (1947); director of Institute for Muscle Research, Woods Hole, Mass. (from 1947). Authority on muscular physiology; discovered actin, a protein in muscle that is partly responsible for muscular contraction; showed that adenosine triphosphate (ATP) is the immediate source of energy for contraction. Awarded 1937 Nobel prize for physiology or medicine for discoveries about the roles of organic compounds, esp. vitamin C, in the oxidation of nutrients by the cell.

Szápolyai, John. See JOHN, king of Hungary.

Szé·che·nyi \'sā-chen-yi\, István. Count. 1791–1860. Hungarian reformer and writer. Fought against Napoléon I; founded Hungarian National Academy of Sciences (1825); in *Hitel* (1830), *Vilag* (1831), *Stadium* (1833), etc., urged involvement of the nobility in modernizing reforms for Hungary; took initiative in projects to open the Danube from Buda to the Black Sea; introduced steamboats on the Danube, the Tisza, and Lake Balaton; built roads and first suspension bridge in Budapest; in 1840s lost many followers to Kossuth; minister of ways and communications (1848).

Szell \'sel\, George, *orig.* Georg. 1897–1970. American conductor, b. Budapest, Hungary. Conductor (from 1917) of various European orchestras, esp. German Opera and Philharmonic in Prague (1929–37); to U.S. (1939, naturalized 1946); conductor of the Cleveland Orchestra (1946–70).

Szi·lard \'sil-ˌärd, *Angl* 'zil-ˌärd, zə-'lärd\, Leo. 1898–1964. American physicist,

b. Budapest, Hungary. With Institute of Theoretical Physics, U. of Berlin (1922–33); on physics staff of St. Bartholomew's Hospital, London (1934–37); to U.S. (1938, naturalized 1943); on staff of Metallurgical Lab., U. of Chicago (1942–46); professor, U. of Chicago (from 1946). Established relation between entropy and transfer of information (1929); with T. A. Chalmers, developed first method of separating isotopes of artificial radioactive elements (1934); instrumental in establishing the Manhattan Project by persuading Alfred Einstein to write famous letter to President Roosevelt advocating development of an atomic bomb (1939); with Enrico Fermi, created the first sustained nuclear chain reaction (1942). After World War II, turned to biology and peaceful uses of atomic energy; developed the chemostat (with Aaron Novick); developed theories of aging and of memory and recall.

Szmu·ness \'shmü-nəs\, Wolf. 1919–1982. American epidemiologist, b. Warsaw, Poland. Spent 10 years in Siberian labor camp; earned M.D. and other advanced scientific degrees from Soviet universities. To U.S. (1968); medical technician (from 1968) and head of laboratory of epidemiology (1973–82) at New York Blood Center. Began (1978) classic field studies that determined effectiveness of the first hepatitis B vaccine (released in 1980).

Szold \'zōld\, Henrietta. 1860–1945. American Zionist leader, b. Baltimore, Md. With Jewish Publishing Society of America (1893–1916); founder and president (1912–26) of Hadassah; organized a large medical unit for Palestine (1916); first woman elected to World Zionist Organization (1927); became director (1933) of Youth Aliyah and founded (1940) Lemaan ha-Yeled (later Szold Foundation), both specializing in child welfare.

Szy·ma·now·ski \,shi-mä-'nóf-skē\, Karol Maciej. 1882–1937. Polish composer. Composed the operas *Hagith* (1922) and *Król Roger* (1926), ballet *Harnasie* (1935), chorales *Agave* (1917) and *Stabat Mater* (1929), piano cycles *Metopy* (1915) and *Maski* (1916), four symphonies, orchestral works, chamber music, and songs.

Szy·mo·no·wicz \,shi-mò-'nò-vēch\, Szymon. 1558–1629. Polish poet. Author of plays *Castus Joseph* (1587) and *Penthesilea* (1618); with *Sielanki* (1614), introduced the idyll into Polish literature.

T

Taaf·fe \'täf-ə\, Eduard von. Graf. 1833–1895. Austrian politician, of Irish descent. Entered civil service (1852); minister of interior (1867, 1870–71, 1879), of defense and public security (1867); premier of Austria (1868–70, 1879–93); forged a conservative coalition; guided Austria-Hungary to recovery of its former position of power; restored domestic order.

Ṭa·ba·rī, aṭ- \,at-ta-'bar-ē\. *In full* Abū Ja'far Muḥammad ibn Jarīr aṭ-Ṭabarī. c.839–923. Arab historian and theologian, b. northern Persia. Spent most of life in Baghdad; best known work *History of the Prophets and Kings* (*Ta'rīkh ar-Rusūl wa al-Mulūk*), a history of the world from the creation to 915 A.D.; also wrote Qur'ānic compendiums, esp. the *Qur'ān Commentary.*

Ta·ba·ta·ba'i \,tab-a-ta-'bī\, Sayyid Zia od-Din. c.1888–1969. Iranian politician. Created coalition of anti-Communist politicians; led coup d'état (Feb. 1921); prime minister (Feb.–May 1921); forced into exile by Reza Khan (1921); returned to Iran (1941); elected to parliament (1942); founded (1943) pro-British, anti-Communist party Iradah-yi milli (The National Will); in politics until 1951.

Ta·bin·shweh·ti \,täb-in-'shwä-tē\. 1512–1550. King of Burma (1531–50), of the Toungoo dynasty. Succeeded his father Minkyinyo; began unification of Burma by conquering Mon kingdom of Pegu (1539); seized Prome (1542) and most of Lower Burma; adopted Mon customs; made city of Pegu his capital (1546); unsuccessfully beseiged Ayutthaya, capital of Siam (1548); assassinated; succeeded by his brother-in-law Bayinnaung.

Tabley, Baron de. See John Byrne Leicester WARREN.

Ta·bou·rot \tá-bü-rō\, Jehan. *Pseudonym* Thoinot Ar·beau \ár-bō\. 1519–1595. French scholar. Priest, canon at Langres (from 1571); wrote *Orchésographie* (1588), history of early dance with detailed descriptions and illustrations.

Tac·chi·ni \täk-'kē-nē\, Pietro. 1838–1905. Italian astronomer. Director of Collegio Romano observatory (from 1879); known for observations of total solar eclipses and of solar prominences.

Ta·ché \tá-shā\, Sir Étienne Pascal. 1795–1865. Canadian politician, b. St. Thomas, Lower Canada. Practiced as physician; member of legislative assembly, Quebec (1841), speaker (1856); premier in Taché-Macdonald ministries (1856–57, 1864–65); presided over intercolonial conference held at Ottawa to discuss federation (1864).

Ta·chos \'täk-,ōs\. *Also called* Ta·khor \'täk-,ór\, Te·os \'tā-,äs, -,ōs\, *or* Zed·hor \'zed-,ór\. 4th century B.C. Egyptian king (362–361 B.C.), second of the 30th dynasty. Aided by Spartan king Agesilaus II and Athenian admiral Chabrias, led unsuccessful attack on the Persians in Phoenicia; deposed by Agesilaus, who placed Nectanebo II on throne; died an exile in Persia.

Tac·i·tus \'tas-ət-əs\, Cornelius. c.56–c.120 A.D. Roman orator, politician, and historian. Son-in-law of Gnaeus Julius Agricola; began career as a vigintivir and a military tribune; quaestor (81); praetor (88); consul (97); proconsul of Asia (112–113); famed as orator. Chief work *Historiae,* covering reigns from Galba to Domitian; other works, *Dialogus de oratoribus, De vita Julii Agricolae, De origine et situ Germanorum,* and *Annales* (history of the Julian emperors from the death of Augustus).

Tacitus, Marcus Claudius. c.200–276. Roman emperor (275–276). Elected by the Senate after death of Aurelian; ruled only about half a year; instituted reforms and favored restoration of power to the Senate; won victory over Goths in Asia Minor; killed by his soldiers; succeeded by his half-brother Florianus.

Tad. See Thomas Aloysius DORGAN.

Tadema. See ALMA-TADEMA.

Tae·wŏn–gun \ta-wən-gün\. *Also called* Yi Ha-ŭng \yē-hä-úŋ\. 1821–1898. Korean ruler. Regent (1864–73) for his son King Kojong; instituted reforms to strengthen central administration; modernized and increased armies; opposed concessions to Japan and the West; organized an anti-Japanese uprising (1882); kidnapped and taken to China (1882–85); on return, lost power.

Tafari. See HAILE SELASSIE.

Taft \'taft\, Alphonso. 1810–1891. American jurist and politician, b. Townshend, Vt. Began practice in Cincinnati, Ohio; judge, Cincinnati superior court (1865–72). U.S. secretary of war (1876); U.S. attorney general (1876–77); U.S. minister to Austria-Hungary (1882–84) and to Russia (1884–85). A son ¶Charles Phelps (1843–1929), lawyer and publisher, was proprietor and editor of Cincinnati *Times-Star* (from 1880). Another son ¶Horace Dutton (1861–1943), educator, was founder (1890) and headmaster (1890–1936) of The Taft School, Watertown, Conn.

Taft, Lorado Zadoc. 1860–1936. American sculptor, b. Elmwood, Ill. Studio in Chicago (from 1886); taught at Art Institute of Chicago (1886–1929); exercised important influence on development of sculpture in the Middle West. In addition to many portrait busts, executed *Solitude of the Soul* (1901), *Black Hawk,* a heroic statue in Oregon, Ill. (1911), *Columbus Memorial Fountain* in Washington, D.C. (1912), *Fountain of the Great Lakes* (1913), the colossal *Fountain of Time* (1922) in Chicago, and *Thatcher Memorial Fountain* in Denver (1917). Published *The History of American Sculpture* (1903) and *Modern Tendencies in Sculpture* (1921).

Taft, William Howard. 1857–1930. Twenty-seventh president of the United States, b. Cincinnati, Ohio. Son of Alphonso Taft. Practiced law in Cincinnati (from 1880); judge, Ohio superior court (1887–90); U.S. solicitor general (1890–92); U.S. circuit court judge (1892–1900). President, U.S. Philippine Commission (1900–01) and first civil governor of the Philippine Islands under American control (1901–04). U.S. secretary of war (1904–08). President of the United States (1909–13). Lost popularity by his defense of the Payne-Aldrich Tariff Act (1909) and his dismissal of Gifford Pinchot (1910); established post-savings system; enforced antitrust legislation. Lost political support of Theodore Roosevelt and was defeated for second term (1912). Professor of law, Yale (1913–21). Chief justice, U.S. Supreme Court (1921–30); secured passage of Judges Act of 1925. His son ¶Robert Alphonso (1889–1953), b. Cincinnati, practiced law in Cincinnati; U.S. senator from Ohio (1939–53); anti-interventionist; his espousal of traditional conservatism won him sobriquet "Mr. Republican"; sponsored Taft-Hartley Labor Relations Act (1947).

Ta·glia·coz·zi \,täl-yäk-'ōt-tsē\, Gaspare. 1545–1599. Italian surgeon. Developed a method of grafting flesh from one part of a body to repair an injury of another part, esp. of the nose, ears, or lips.

Ta·glio·ni \täl-'yō-nē\. Italian family of ballet dancers including: Filippo (1777–1871), ballet master at Stockholm, Kassel, Vienna (1805–10, 1819–27), Warsaw, etc.; choreographed many ballets, as *La Sylphide* (1832) and *La Fille du Danube* (1836). His daughter ¶Marie (1804–1884), trained by her father; made debut in Vienna (1822); among first women to dance on points of the toes; achieved European success in *La Sylphide* (from 1832), in which she created a new style marked by floating leaps, balanced poses, and delicate use of the points; her dancing typified the early 19th-century Romantic style. Her brother ¶Paul, *also* Paolo (1808–1884), ballet master at Berlin Court Opera (1856–83); choreographed many ballets, as *Les Metamorphoses* (1850) and *Flick und Flocks Abenteuer* (1858). His daughter ¶Marie (1833–1891), particularly successful at London (1847) and at Berlin Court Opera; created many roles in her father's ballets.

Ta·gore \'tä-gór; *Angl* tə-'gō(ə)r, -'gó(ə)r\, Debendranath. 1817–1905. Indian Hindu philosopher and religious reformer. Born into a wealthy princely family; with his friend Keshab Chunder Sen, attempted to bring education to the masses; active in the Brahmo Samaj; opposed Hindu idolatry; founded retreat Santiniketan (1886). Works included *Vedantic Doctrines Vindicated* (1845) and *Brahmo-Dharma* (1854).

Tagore, Sir Rabindranath. 1861–1941. Indian Bengali poet. Son of Debendranath Tagore. Established (1901) school at Santiniketan, Bolpur, Bengal, which developed (1924) into Visva-Bharati University; awarded Nobel prize for literature (1913); resigned his knighthood (1919) in protest against repressive measures in Punjab. Author of volumes of lyric verse in Bengali, often using settings and themes of the Bengali countryside, including *Mānasī* (1890),

Sonār Tari (1893), *Chitra* (1896), *Chaitālī* (1896), *Kalpanā* (1900), *Kṣaṇikā* (1900), *Naivedya* (1901), *Gitāñjalī* (1910), *Bālāka* (1914); also wrote novels as *Gorā* (1910), and plays as *Chitrāngadā* (1892), *Mālinī* (1895), and *Mukta Dhāra* (1922). Also a gifted composer, setting hundreds of poems to music, and one of India's foremost painters.

Ta·ha Hus·sein \'tä-hä-hùs-'ān\. 1889–1973. Egyptian writer. Blinded by illness at age two; professor at Cairo (1925–32, 1936–40); often caused controversy by application of critical methods to traditional Islāmic literature, as in *Fi sh-Shi'al-Jahili* (1926); minister of education (1950–52). Outstanding figure of Modernist movement in Egyptian literature; best known for autobiography *Al-Ayyam* (1929–32) and memoirs *Mudhakkirat* (1967); also wrote novels, short stories, and political and social essays as *Mustaquabal ath-Thaqafah fi Misr* (1938) on Egyptian culture.

Ta·har·qa \tə-'här-kə\. *Also* Tar·ku \'tär-ˌkü\ *or* Tir·ha·ka \ti(ə)r-'hā-kə\. 7th century B.C. Third king (reigned 689–664 B.C.) of the 25th dynasty of Egypt. Succeeded his cousin Shebitku; early in reign supported Palestinian resistance to Sennacherib; ruled in peace (689–675); defeated Esarhaddon of Assyria in great battle (675), but later (671) overwhelmed; regained control of Egypt but later completely routed by Ashurbanipal (667); fled to Nubia and died there.

Tah–gah–jute. See James LOGAN.

Ṭah·māsp \ta-'mäsp\. Name of two kings of Persia:

Ṭahmāsp I. 1514–1576. King (1524–76). Son and successor of Esmā'īl I; for long time after accession, a pawn of tribal leaders; lost large amounts of territory to Turkey (1534, 1538, 1543); annexed Shirvan (1538); made peace with Turkey (1555); in later years secluded himself in palace and paid little attention to public affairs; left Persia weaker than he found it.

Ṭahmāsp II. d. 1739. King (1722–32). Son and successor of Ḥoseyn; at first aided by Nāder Shāh (*q.v.*), but later deposed by him.

Ṭahmāsp Qolī Khān. See NĀDER SHĀH.

Ṭah·tā·wī \täk-'tä-wē\, Rifā'ah Rāfi' aṭ-. 1801–1873. Egyptian educator and scholar. In Paris as religious teacher to Egyptian students (1826–31); head of School of Languages in Cairo (1836); head of a translation bureau (1841); taught school in Khartoum (1848–54); returned to scholarly work in Cairo (1854). Influenced by Western thought; translated Western books; urged use of Western technology.

Ta·hue·reau \tá-wer-ō\, Jacques. c.1527–1555. French poet. Much influenced by Ronsard and Joachim du Bellay. Author of Petrarchan love lyrics as in *Premières poésies* (1554) and *Sonnets, odes et mignardises de l'admirée* (1554), and the satirical *Dialogues* (1595).

T'ai–ch'ang. See Chu Ch'ang-lo under CHU family.

Tai Chen \'dī-'jən\. *Literary name* Tai Tung-yüan \-'dùŋ-yüe-'än\. 1724–1777. Chinese philosopher. Born into poverty; appointed court compiler in Imperial Manuscript Library (1773); made (1775) *chin-shih* (advanced scholar) by royal decree after failing exam six times. Often considered greatest philosopher of Ch'ing period; attacked dualism of Sung philosophers, stressing need for close empirical investigation; wrote, edited, and compiled works on mathematics (including logarithmic theories of John Napier), philology, geography, and Confucian Classics.

Tai Chin \'dī-'jin\ *or* **Tai Wen-chin** \-'wən-'jin\. 1388–1462. Chinese painter. One of the foremost of the Ming dynasty; a leader in developing the Che, or academic, school of landscape technique in ink.

T'ai·go Wang·sa \tī-gó-wäŋ-sä\. 1301–1382. Korean monk. Entered Buddhism (1314); passed national Buddhist service exam (1326); practiced Buddhism at temple named T'aigoam (whence his name); studied in China under Shih-wu (1346–48); founded the T'aigo sect of Korean Buddhism; not very successful in attempts to reform Korean Buddhism.

Tai·kō \tī-kō\ Josetsu. 14th–15th century. Japanese Zen Buddhist priest and painter. Teacher of Tenshō Shūbun; painted in the Chinese *suiboku* (monochromatic ink painting) style; best known for landscape *Catching a Catfish with a Gourd;* may have painted *The Three Teachers,* a group portrait of Buddha, Lao-tzu, and Confucius.

Tail·le·fer \tá-yə-fer, tī-fer\. d. 1066. Norman trouvère. Said to have preceded the Norman army invading England (1066), singing of Charlemagne and Roland at Roncesvalles; permitted by William to strike first blow; killed at Hastings; depicted in Bayeux tapestry.

Taine \ten\, Hippolyte-Adolphe. 1828–1893. French philosopher, historian, and critic. Contributor to *Journal des Débats* and *Revue des Deux Mondes;* professor, École des Beaux-Arts, Paris (1864–84). One of leading exponents of French Positivism; applied the scientific method to study of the humanities. Among his works were *La Fontaine et ses fables* (1853), *Voyage aux eaux des Pyrénées* (1855), *Essai sur Tite-Live* (1856), *Essais de critique et d'histoire* (1858), *Histoire de la littérature anglaise* (1863–64), *Philosophie de l'art* (1865), *Vie et opinions de M. Frédéric-Thomas Graindorge* (1867), *De l'intelligence* (1870), *Origines de la France contemporaine* (in three parts, *L'Ancien Régime, La Révolution, Le Régime moderne,* 1876–99).

Tain·ter \'tānt-ər\, Charles Sumner. 1854–1940. American inventor, b. Watertown, Mass. Inventor of various sound-recording instruments, including the photophone (1880, with Alexander Graham Bell), the Graphophone (1881, patented 1886; with Chichester A. Bell), and the Dictaphone.

Ta·i·ra \tī-rä, tä-ē-rä\. *Also known, esp. contemporaneously, by its Chinese name* Hei·ke \'hā-'ke\. Japanese samurai clan or family; originated when name Taira was given (825) to Prince Takamune, grandson of Emperor Kammu; reached height of its power in 11th and 12th centuries; rivals of the Minamoto; monopolized high positions at the Imperial court (c.1156–85); totally defeated by Minamoto Yoshitsune (1185) at Dannoura. Its members included:

¶Taira Masakado. d. 940. Rebel leader. Great-great-grandnephew of Prince Takamune; gained control of southern part of Kantō; proclaimed himself *shinnō* ("New Emperor") in opposition to Emperor at Kyōto (939); organized a court, appointed governors for eight northern provinces; eliminated many blood relatives; defeated by two local rivals in the War in the Tengyō Era.

¶Taira Masamori. 12th century. Samurai. Held power in the Ise district; hired (1108) by the emperor to eliminate the Minamoto warriors occupying western Japan, along the Inland Sea; lavishly rewarded for accomplishing this task; allowed to settled his clan in western Japan, where they profited from trade with China; responsible for rise to power of the Taira clan.

¶Taira Tadamori. 1096–1153. Samurai. Son of Masamori; received titles, grants, and other rewards from Imperial court for suppressing pirates of the Inland Sea; grew rich from the China trade; supported the court against rival clans, esp. the Minamoto; highly cultivated and learned; personal bodyguard and confidant to the emperor; greatly raised influence and prestige of his clan.

¶Taira Kiyomori. 1118–1181. Samurai-ruler. Son of Tadamori; in Hōgen War (1156), supported Emperor Shirakawa II and, with help of the defector Minamoto Yoshitomo, defeated forces of Minamoto Tameyoshi; defeated Yoshitomo in Heiji War (1159–60), placing Taira clan in control and making himself most powerful figure in Japan; appointed prime minister (1167); married his daughters into the imperial family; de facto ruler of Japan; placed (1180) his grandson Antoku on throne but retained ruling power; four years after his death, Taira clan annihilated by Minamoto Yoshitsune.

Ta·i·rov \(ˌ)tə-'yir-əf\, Aleksandr Yakovlevich. *Surname orig.* Korn·blit \'kòrn-blyit\. 1885–1950. Russian theatrical producer. Founder and producer-director (1914–49) of Kamerny Theater, Moscow; unlike Stanislavsky, advocated a non-individualistic treatment of the actor; invented a nonrealistic or constructivistic setting employing a scaffolding supporting bare platforms on different levels.

Taishō. See YOSHIHITO.

Tait \'tāt\, Archibald Campbell. 1811–1882. Scottish prelate. Reared a Presbyterian; entered (1836) ministry of Church of England; opposed Oxford Movement. Headmaster of Rugby (1842); dean of Carlisle (1849); bishop of London (1856). Made archbishop of Canterbury (1868) to quiet strife over Irish disestablishment; withdrew opposition to Irish Church bill, by forbearance aided settlement; aroused resentment by trying to solve problems of ritualism by Public Worship Regulation Act (1874) and by support of the Burials Act (1880); esteemed as spokesman for Anglican church. Writings included *The Dangers and Safeguards of Modern Theology* (1861), *Harmony of Revelation and the Sciences* (1864).

Tait, Peter Guthrie. 1831–1901. Scottish physicist and mathematician. Professor, Edinburgh (from 1860). Instrumental in development of modern mathematical physics; helped develop quaternions. Investigated properties of ozone, the foundations of the kinetic theory of gases, thermoelectricity and thermal conductivity, etc. His publications included *Elementary Treatise on Quaternions* (1867), *Introduction to Quaternions* (with Philip Kelland, 1873), *Natural Philosophy* (vol. 1 with Lord Kelvin, 1867), *The Unseen Universe* (with Balfour Stewart, 1875), and *Paradoxical Philosophy* (also with Stewart, 1878).

T'ai Tsu. See (1) A-KU-TA; (2) Chu Yüan-chang under CHU family.

T'ai Tsung. See (1) Chu Ti under CHU family; (2) Li Shih-min under LI family; (3) Chao Kuei under CHAO family.

Tai Tung–yüan. See TAI CHEN.

Tai Wen–chin. See TAI CHIN.

Ta·ka·ha·shi \täk-ä-hä-shē\ Korekiyo. *Original surname* Ka·wa·mu·ra \kä-wäm-ùr-ä\. 1854–1936. Japanese financier. Adopted into Takahashi family and assumed that name; governor of Bank of Japan (1911 ff.); minister of finance (1913–14, 1918); premier of Japan (1921–22); again minister of finance (1927, 1931–34, 1934–36); assassinated.

Ta·ka·mu·ra \tä-kä-mùr-ä\ Kōun. *Orig.* Na·ka·ji·ma \nä-kä-jē-mä\ Kōzō. 1852–1934. Japanese sculptor. Studied under Takamura Tōun and took his surname; worked to preserve art of wood carving; became head of wood carving department of Tokyo Fine Arts School (1887). Although working within the Buddhist tradition, stressed a more realistic approach; works included *Aged Monkey* (1893) and bronze statues *Nankō dōzō* and *Saigō Takamori dōzō.*

Ta·ka·su·gi \tä-kä-sůg-ē\ Shinsaku. 1839–1867. Japanese politician. An Imperial loyalist; organized in Chōshū province several peasant militia units trained in Western-style military discipline, armed with Western arms, and led by extremist samurai; units defeated (1865) shogunate forces in Chōshū, resulting in shifting of power from the shōgun to imperial forces.

Takauji. See ASHIKAGA.

Ta·ke·da \tä-ked-ä\ Shingen. 1521–1573. Japanese warrior. Entered priesthood (1551); forced his father to retire as head of Takeda clan and assumed his position; fought series of battles with Uesugi Kenshin for control of Kantō Plain in central Japan, battles later celebrated in drama and folklore; began to wage war on Oda Nobunaga, but soon died in battle.

Ta·ke·mo·to \tä-kem-ō-tō\ Gidayū. *Also called* Ri·hē \rē-he\ Shimizu. 1651–1714. Japanese actor. Established a puppet theater in Ōsaka; originator of *gidayū-bushi* (Gidayū music), a style of chanting, in *jorūri* or puppet theater; began (1686) collaborating with playwright Chikamatsu Monzaemon.

Ta·ke·u·chi \tä-ke-ůch-ē\ Kōkichi. *Known as* Takeuchi Seihō. 1864–1942. Japanese painter. Became pupil of Kōno Bairei (1881); appointed teacher at Kyōto School of Arts and Crafts (1889); in Europe (1900–01). His style, based on Shijō style, also influenced by European Impressionism and Chinese painting; works included *Autumn in the Ancient Capital, Rain and Hail, Moonlight in Venice,* and *Oh, It Has Started Raining.*

Takhor. See TACHOS.

Ta·ki·za·wa \tä-kē-zä-wä\ Bakin, *orig.* Okikuni. 1767–1848. Japanese writer. Author of over 260 works, including over 30 long historical novels, esp. *Gepyō Kien, Nansō Satomi Hakkenden* (1814–42) considered a classic, and *Kinsei Bishōnenroku.*

Tak·sin \'täk-sin\. *Also called* Phra·ya Taksin \'prī-ə-\, Pa·ya Tak \'pī-ə-'täk\, *and* Phya Taksin \'pyä-\. 1734–1782. King of Siam (1767–82). Provincial governor with administrative title *phraya* (1764); lifted Burmese siege of Thai capital Ayutthaya (1768); united the five feudal Thai principalities into one kingdom; established new capital, Thon Buri; reconquered western provinces from Cambodia; alienated his subjects by demanding worship of him; deposed, executed, and succeeded by Chao Phraya Chakki.

Ta·ku·an \täk-ů-än\. 1573–1645. Japanese Zen Buddhist priest. Appointed chief priest at Daitoku temple (1607); during exile in northern Japan (1620–38) wrote *Fudō chishin myoroku* showing essential unity of Zen doctrines, and *Taia-ki* on swordsmanship; gained favor of shogun Tokugawa Iemitsu; responsible for construction of the Tōkai-ji.

Ta·ku·ma \tä-kům-ä\ Tamemoto. *Known as* Takuma Shōga. 12th century A.D. Japanese painter. High-ranking priest of Shingon sect of Buddhism; specialized in *butsuga* (Buddhist iconographical paintings); created a new style of religious painting incorporating features of Southern Sung art; chief work, a group of *Twelve Gods* painted on screens (1191).

Ta·lât Pa·şa \tä-'lät-pä-'shä\, Mehmed. 1872–1921. Turkish politician. Imprisoned for subversive political activity (1893–95); chief secretary of posts and telegraphs in Salonika (1895–1908); a leader of Young Turks; after Turkish revolution (1908), became successively minister of the interior, postmaster general, again minister of the interior; succeeded Said Halim Paşa as grand vizier of Turkey (Feb. 1917) but was forced into retirement (Oct. 1918); assassinated by an Armenian.

Ta·la·ve·ra \tä-lä-'b̲ā-rä\, Hernando de. 1428–1507. Spanish prelate. Bishop of Ávila (1485); archbishop of Granada (1492). Chaired royal commission that investigated Christopher Columbus's plan of exploration and ruled unfavorably (1490); after conquest of Granada (1492), advocated intellectual persuasion instead of force for conversion of Jews and Moors.

Tal·bot \'tȯl-bət\. Name of noble English family of Norman descent, holding earldom of Shrewsbury; prominent members included:

Gilbert (1277?–1346), 1st Baron Talbot; head of house under Edward II; took part in invasion of Scotland (1319); later took side of Thomas of Lancaster against king; pardoned by Edward III, confirmed in manor of Linton; summoned to Parliament as baron (1331).

¶John (c.1384–1453), 1st Earl of Shrews·bury \'shrōz-b(ə-)rē, 'sh(r)üz-, -ˌber-ē\ (cr. 1442); 2d son of 4th Baron Talbot; summoned to Parliament (1409–21); served in Welsh wars (1404–13); lord lieutenant of Ireland (1414–19); hero of forty fights in France during Henry VI's reign before he was checked at Orléans by Joan of Arc and at Patay taken prisoner (1429); on release (1433) was for five years mainstay of English cause in France, reconquering lost territory, capturing Clermont (1434), suppressing revolt of Pays de Caux (1436), defeating Burgundians (1437), and recovering Harfleur (1440); made marshal of France by Henry; sent again to govern Ireland (1445) and created earl of Wa·ter·ford \'wȯt-ər-fərd, 'wät-\ (1446); returned to France (1448); held hostage by French (1449–50); sent to aid of Gascons (1452), took Bordeaux but was defeated and killed at Castillon. His younger brother ¶Richard (d. 1449) was archbishop of Dublin (1417), lord chancellor of Ireland (1423), and deputy in viceroy's absences. ¶John (1413–1460), 2d Earl of Shrewsbury, son of 1st earl, was chancellor of Ireland (1446) and treasurer of England (1456); fell at Northampton fighting on king's side.

¶George (1468–1538), 4th Earl of Shrewsbury and Earl of Waterford; grandson of 2d earl; ambassador to Pope Julius II (1511) and to Ferdinand of Aragon (1512) in interests of alliance against France; present at Field of Cloth of Gold (1520); sent by Henry VIII against rebels in the Pilgrimage of Grace (1536). His grandson ¶George (1528?–1590), 6th earl; took part in Somerset's invasion of Scotland and was entrusted by Queen Elizabeth with custody of Mary, Queen of Scots (1569–84), chiefly at Sheffield Manor, a task made difficult by the machinations of his wife (see Elizabeth TALBOT).

¶Charles (1660–1718), 12th Earl and only Duke of Shrewsbury; became a Protestant (1679); one of seven signatories to letter of invitation to William of Orange (1688); secured Bristol and Gloucester for William (1688); a secretary of state (1689–90, 1694–98); one of regents during king's absences (1695, 1696); lived abroad (1700–07); became lord chamberlain (1710) in Tory administration; lord lieutenant of Ireland (1713); as lord high treasurer (1714) at great crisis on death of Queen Anne courageously promoted peaceful accession of George I and assured Hanoverian succession; lord chamberlain (1714–15).

Talbot, Arthur Newell. 1857–1942. American engineer and educator, b. Cortland, Ill. Taught at U. of Illinois (1885–1926), where he helped establish (1904) an engineering experiment station, first of its kind in world; made studies on stresses in railroad tracks, problems of water purification and municipal sanitary works.

Talbot, Elizabeth. Countess of Shrews·bury \'shrōz-b(ə-)rē, 'sh(r)üz-, -ˌber-ē\. *Known as* Bess of Hard·wick \'här-(ˌ)dwik\. 1518–1608. English noblewoman. Daughter and coheiress of John Hardwick of Hardwick, Derbyshire; inherited estates of her four husbands: the second, Sir William Cavendish; the fourth, George Talbot, 6th Earl of Shrewsbury; built Chatsworth on the Cavendish estates; entrusted with care of Mary, Queen of Scots (1569–84) at Tutbury.

Talbot, Mary Anne. 1778–1808. English soldier. Served in British army (1792–93) and navy (1793–96) disguised as a man; domestic servant (1804–07) to London publisher Robert S. Kirby, who published her adventures in his *Wonderful and Scientific Museum* (1804) and *Life and Surprising Adventures of Mary Anne Talbot* (1809).

Talbot, Richard. Earl and titular Duke of Tyr·con·nel \ti(ə)r-'kän-^{ə}l\. 1630–1691. Irish Jacobite. Served in Royalist forces in Civil War; plotted in London for upset of Commonwealth. At Restoration employed in household of Duke of York (James II); accused of complicity in Popish Plot (1678), went into exile. Made commander in chief in Ireland and earl of Tyrconnel by James II (1685); lord deputy in Ireland (1687); foreseeing revolution in England, endeavored to turn over Ireland to France; after battle of the Boyne fled to France; created duke of Tyrconnel (1689) by James II.

Talbot, Silas. 1751–1813. American naval officer, b. Dighton, Mass. Commissioned captain in Continental navy (Sept. 1779); captured by British and held as prisoner of war (1779–81); commanded the *Constitution* during the war with France.

Talbot, William Henry Fox. 1800–1877. English physicist. Pioneer in photography; produced (1839) photographic prints on paper treated with silver chloride, contemporaneously with invention of the daguerreotype; process later improved and known as the calotype or Talbotype (patented 1841); discovered method of instantaneous photography (1851); his *Pencil of Nature* (1844–46) was first photographically illustrated book. One of earliest to decipher cuneiform inscriptions of Nineveh.

Tal·fourd \'tal-fərd, 'tȯl-\, Sir Thomas Noon. 1795–1854. English judge. Editor of the letters (1837) and memorials (1848) of Charles Lamb. M.P. (1835); introduced and championed international copyright bill (1837); made famous speech as advocate of Edward Moxon, prosecuted for publishing Shelley's *Queen Mab.* Known for his tragedy *Ion* (1835).

Taliedo, Conte di. See Giovanni CAPRONI.

Ta·lie·sin \tål-'yes-ən, *Angl* ˌtal-ē-'es-\. 6th century. Welsh poet. Composed eulogies and elegies on rulers in northern Wales and northern Britain, esp. Urien, king of Rheged. In later medieval period he was identified with the mythical Taliesin about whom a number of poems and tales survive.

Talis Qualis. See Carl STRANDBERG.

Talle·mant des Ré·aux \tål-mä^{n}-dā-rā-ō\, Gédéon. 1619–1692. French writer. Abandoned position as counsel to parlement to devote himself to literary interests; wrote (c.1657–c.1659) series of *Historiettes,* short biographies of leading public figures of the day (pub. 1834–35).

Tal·ley·rand-Pé·ri·gord \tål-rä^{n}-pā-rē-gȯr, tå-le-rä^{n}-\, Charles-Maurice de. Prince de Bé·né·vent \də-bā-nā-vä^{n}\. 1754–1838. French statesman. Took orders (1775); became abbé of Saint-Denis (1775); appointed agent general of French clergy (1780); bishop of Autun (1788). Member of Estates-General and

\ə\ abut \$^{ə}$\ kitten, *Fr.* **table \ər\ further \a\ ash \ā\ ace \ä\ cot, cart \aů\ out \ch\ chin \e\ bet \ē\ easy \g\ go \i\ hit \ī\ ice \j\ job \ŋ\ sing \ō\ go \ȯ\ law \ȯi\ boy \th\ both \th̲\ the \ü\ loot \ů\ foot \y\ yet \zh\ vision \å, b̲, g̅, k̲, ^{n}, œ, œ̄, ue, ue̅, ^{y}** *see* **Guide to Pronunciation**

of National Assembly (1789); proposed confiscation of church property for raising funds to meet expenses of government; became a leader in financial discussions. Excommunicated by the pope (1791). Envoy to England (1792); minister of foreign affairs (1797–1807); created grand chamberlain by Napoléon (1804) and prince de Bénévent (1806). Quarreled with Napoléon (1809) and opposed the emperor's Russian and Spanish policy. At Napoléon's fall, was instrumental in securing restoration of the Bourbons; minister of foreign affairs (1814) and president of the Council (1815); French representative at Congress of Vienna (1814–15); forced by nobles at court to resign (Sept. 1815). Involved in Revolution of 1830; ambassador to Great Britain (1830–34); instrumental in organizing Quadruple Alliance (1834).

Tal·lien \tál-yaⁿ\, Jean-Lambert. 1767–1820. French revolutionary. Secretary of Commune of Paris (1792); member of National Convention (1792) and of Committee of Public Safety; sent by convention to Bordeaux, he increased the convictions and executions there during Reign of Terror (1793). Leader in the overthrow of Robespierre (1794) and thereafter a leader of the moderates (Thermidorians); suppressed Jacobins and the Revolutionary Tribunal; member of the Council of Five Hundred (1795–98). On Egyptian expedition with Napoléon; later served as consul at Alicante.

Tal·lis *or* **Tal·lys** *or* **Tal·les** \'tal-əs\, Thomas. c.1505–1585. English organist and composer. Organist at Dover Priory (1532) and at St. Mary-at-Hill, London (1537); gentleman of the Chapel Royal (from c.1543); with William Byrd granted monopoly for printing music and music paper in England (1575). Most important English composer of sacred music before Byrd; one of first to compose settings for Anglican liturgy; largely responsible for introducing styles of simple Reformation service music and of Continental polyphonic schools. His Latin sacred music included motets, esp. the 40-part *Spem in alium,* two settings each of the Magnificat and *Lamentations of Jeremiah,* 5 anthems, 7-part *Miserere nostri;* also wrote secular vocal music and keyboard pieces.

Tal·ma \tál-má\, François-Joseph. 1763–1826. French tragedian. Debut at Comédie-Française (1787); triumphed in Chénier's *Charles IX* (1789). One of founders of the Théâtre Français de la Rue Richelieu (1791), where he played some of his greatest roles, as Henry VIII, Nero, Aegisthus in *Agamemnon,* Othello, Macbeth, Hamlet; introduced realistic forms of acting, stage costuming, scenery; a favorite with Napoléon and later with Louis XVIII.

Ta·lon \tá-lōⁿ\, Jean-Baptiste. Comte d'·Or·sain·ville \dȯr-saⁿ-vēl\. c.1625–1694. French colonial administrator. Intendant (1665–68, 1670–72) of New France (Canada); encouraged immigration and exploration but unsuccessful in attempts to develop its economy. Created comte (1675); secretary of king's privy chamber (1681).

Tam \täⁿ, *Angl* 'tam\, Jacob ben Meir. 1100–1171. French Talmudist. A leading participant (from c.1160) in rabbinical synods of Troyes that established rules governing relations between Christians and Jews. Author of commentaries on the Talmud, esp. *Sefer ha-yashar* (pub. 1811), and religious poetry, some of which was incorporated into the Hebrew prayer book.

Ta·ma·ra \tə-'mä-rə\ *or* **Tha·mar** \'täm-är\. before 1160–1212. Queen of Georgia, in Asia (1184–1212). By her statesmanship raised Georgia to peak of its political power.

Ta·ma·yo y Baus \tä-'mä-yō-ē-'baùs\, Manuel. 1829–1898. Spanish dramatist. Key figure in transition from Romanticism to Realism in Spanish literature; with Lopez de Ayala, dominated Spanish stage of the day; stopped writing to become director of Biblioteca Nacional and secretary to Spanish Academy (1870). At first, under influence of Schiller, wrote romantic historical plays as *La ricahembra* (1854) and *Locura de amor* (1855); later wrote realistic dramas denouncing evils of society as *Lo positivo* (1862), *Lances de honor* (1863), *Un drama nuevo* (his masterpiece, 1867), and *Los hombres de bien* (1870).

Tamerlane *or* **Tamburlaine.** See TIMUR.

Ta·mir·is \tə-'mir-əs\, Helen. *Orig. surname* Beck·er \'bek-ər\. 1905–1966. American dancer, choreographer, and teacher, b. New York City. Concert debut in New York (1927); founder and director (1930–45) of own dance company and school in New York; director, Dance Repertory Theatre (1930–32); choreographed (1945–57) Broadway musicals, including *Annie Get Your Gun* (1946), *Touch and Go* (1949), *Plain and Fancy* (1955); formed (1960) Tamiris-Nagrin Dance Company with husband (m. 1946) Daniel Nagrin. One of first to use jazz, black spirituals, and social protest themes in dance, as in *How Long Brethren* (1937), *Adelante* (1939), and *Dance for Walt Whitman* (1958).

Tamm \'tȧm\, Igor Yevgenyevich. 1895–1971. Soviet physicist. Professor at Moscow (from 1930); studied quantum theory of diffused light in solid bodies; with Ilya M. Frank, developed theory of the Cherenkov radiation (1937). Awarded Nobel prize for physics (1958) with Pavel A. Cherenkov and I.M. Frank.

Tam·mām ibn Ghā·lib Abū Fi·rās \tam-'äm-ˌib-ən-'gä-lēb-ab-'ü-fē-'räs\. *Nicknamed* al-Fa·raz·daq \ùl-far-az-'dak\, *i.e.* the Lump of Dough. c.641–c.730. Arab poet. One of great poets of Umayyad period; maintained constant rivalry with Jarīr; official poet to caliphs al-Walīd and Sulaymān; also received patronage from Yazīd II; noted as eccentric; wrote satires, panegyrics, lampoons, laments, collected in *Dīwān.*

Tam·ma·ny \'tam-ə-nē\ *or* **Tam·a·nend** \'tam-ə-ˌnend\. fl. 1685. American Indian chief of the Delaware tribe. Invested by legend with many noble characteristics; adopted after American Revolution as patron saint of various political organizations, as the Society of Tammany in New York.

Tammen, Harry Heye. See under Frederick BONFILS.

Tammsaare, Anton H. See Anton HANSEN.

Ta-Mo. See BODHIDHARMA.

Tan. See Vladimir BOGORAZ.

Ta·na·be \tä-nä-be\ Hajime. 1885–1962. Japanese philosopher. Professor at Kyōto (1918–45); developed philosophy of "logic of the species"; attempted to synthesize Buddhism, Christianity, Marxism, and scientific thought. Works included *Suri tetsugaku* (1925) on mathematics, *Shu no ronri no benshōhō* (1947) on logic of species, and, on Christianity, *Jitsuzon to ai to jissen* (1946) and *Kirisutokyō no benshōhō* (1948).

Ta·na·ka \tän-äk-ä\ Giichi. Baron. 1863–1929. Japanese soldier and politician. Distinguished himself in Russo-Japanese War; minister of war (1918); created baron (1920); general (1921); elected president of Rikken Seiyūkai party (1925); prime minister of Japan and minister of foreign affairs (1927–29); author of Japan's aggressive policy toward China in 1920s.

Tan·a·quil \'tan-ə-ˌkwil\. 7th–6th century B.C. Roman queen. According to legend, married Lucumo in Etruscan city of Tarquinii; reputedly changed name to Gaia Caecilia when Lucumo became King Tarquinius Priscus of Rome; on death of Tarquinius (578 B.C.), won crown for son-in-law Servius Tullius. Many scholars believe Tanaquil and Gaia Caecilia were distinct personages.

Tan·chelm \'tän-kelm\. d. 1115? Flemish heretic. Denounced the sacraments of the church, and gained many followers known as Tanchelmians.

Tan·cred \'taŋ-krəd\. d. 1194. King of Sicily. Natural son of Roger, Duke of Apulia; imprisoned (1155–60), exiled (1161–74) for rebellions against his uncle William I of Sicily; crowned king of Sicily (1190); right to throne challenged by Emperor Henry VI of Germany; reign marked by prolonged struggle to maintain power.

Tancred. 1078?–1112. Norman crusader. Nephew of Bohemond; joined First Crusade (1096–99) and distinguished himself at capture of Nicaea and Tarsus, siege of Antioch, capture of Jerusalem, and battle of Ashkelon; became prince of Galilee (1099); as regent of Antioch (1101–12) and of Edessa (1104–08), was chief Latin magnate of northern Syria; engaged in continual warfare with Turks and Byzantines. His portrayal in Tasso's *Gerusalemme liberata* is largely imaginary.

Tandem, Carl Felix. See Carl SPITTELER.

Tan·dy \'tan-dē\, James Napper. 1740–1803. Irish revolutionary. Cofounder, with Wolfe Tone and Thomas Russell, and first secretary of Society of United Irishmen (1791); raised two battalions of a national guard and on its failure fled to America. Given command by French government of a corvette and soldiers, ineffectually invaded Donegal (1798); later taken by British and convicted, but released on intercession by Napoléon. Remembered as hero of "The Wearing of the Green."

Ta·ney \'tȯ-nē\, Roger Brooke. 1777–1864. American jurist, b. Calvert Co., Md. Adm. to bar (1799); practiced in Frederick, Md. (from 1801); served in Md. House of Delegates (1800, 1816–21). U.S. attorney general (1831–33); persuaded President Jackson to veto charter of the Bank of the United States. U.S. secretary of the treasury (1833–34); removed government deposits from Bank of the United States; appointment as secretary of the treasury not confirmed by U.S. Senate (June 1834). Nominated for associate justice, U.S. Supreme Court (1835), but rejected by U.S. Senate. Chief justice (1836–64), U.S. Supreme Court, succeeding John Marshall. Name always associated with the decision in the Dred Scott (*q.v.*) case (1857); in general, upheld federal supremacy over state authorities.

Ta·ne·yev \'tán-yi-yəf\, Sergey Ivanovich. 1856–1915. Russian composer. Studied under Tchaikovsky and Nikolay Rubinstein; professor (1878–1905), director (1885–89) at Moscow conservatory; concert pianist; principal practitioner of counterpoint in 19th-century Russian music; published *Invertible Counterpoint in the Strict Style* (1909). Composer of operatic trilogy *Oresteia* (1895), 4 symphonies, chamber music, including 6 string quartets, choral works, including setting of Khomyakov's "At the Reading of the Psalm" (1914), piano pieces, and songs.

T'ang \'täŋ\. Name of three Chinese dynasties: (1) A dynasty (618–907 A.D.), one of the most glorious in history of China; followed the Sui dynasty; founded by Li Yüan. Foreign commerce was encouraged, and suzerainty re-extended over much of Central Asia and Korea; Neo-Confucianism was state religion, but Buddhism flourished; under its prosperity China attained its golden age of literature and arts; for its rulers, see LI family and Empress WU CHAO. (2) One of the Five Dynasties (*q.v.*), known as the Later T'ang (923–936). (3) Southern T'ang dynasty (937–975), situated south of the Yangtze River; see LI YÜ.

T'ang. *Known as* Ch'eng T'ang \'chəŋ-'täŋ\. fl. c.1766–c.1754 B.C. Chinese emperor. Apparently a scion of a noble family; overthrew the Hsia dynasty and founded the Shang dynasty (c.1766); according to legend, a descendant of Huang Ti; revered as a humane and generous ruler.

T'ang, Prince of. See Chu Yü-chien under CHU family.

T'ang Chi-yao \-'jē-'yaü\. 1881–1927. Chinese soldier. Military governor of Yunnan Province (1913–27); provided crucial military support to rebels opposing Yüan Shih-k'ai (1915); lukewarm supporter of Sun Yat-sen; after Sun's death (1925), made unsuccessful attempt at leadership of national government.

Tan·guay \taŋ-'gā, 'taŋ-(,)gā\, Eva. 1878–1947. American entertainer, b. Marbleton, Que. To U.S. (1881); in stock troupes, musical comedies, and vaudeville, shocking audiences with scanty costumes and risqué songs such as "I Don't Care" and "It's All Been Done Before but Not the Way I Do It"; billed as the "Girl Who Made Vaudeville Famous."

Tan·guy \tän-gē, *Angl* taŋ-'gē\, Yves. 1900–1955. American painter, b. Paris, France. Friend of Jacques Prévert and André Breton; to U.S. (1939, naturalized 1948). Surrealist; known esp. for landscapes with familiar forms in bizarre environments; works included *Mama, Papa Is Wounded* (1927), *Chess Set* (1950), *Rose of the Four Winds* (1950).

T'ang Yin \'täŋ-'yin\. 1470–1523. Chinese painter. Pupil of Shen Chou; friend of Wen Cheng-ming; because of linkage with cheating scandal, excluded from government service; devoted himself to sybaritic life. Known for landscapes and paintings of women.

Tan·ḥum ben Jo·seph \'tän-kùm-ben-'jō-zəf, *also* -səf\ of Jerusalem. 13th century. Jewish rabbinic scholar. Lived in Palestine; noted for biblical commentaries in Arabic and for a lexicon to Moses Maimonides's *Mishne Torah.*

Ta·ni \tä-nē\ Bunchō. *Orig.* Sei-an \sä-än\ Bungorō. 1763–1840. Japanese painter. Founder of the *Nanboku gōitsu* or South and East school of painting; introduced use of Western perspective; painted landscapes and portraits, often noted for realism; teacher of Watanabe Kazan; also produced several art history books.

Ta·ni·za·ki \tä-nē-zäk-ē\ Jun-ichirō. 1886–1965. Japanese novelist. His novels, characterized by eroticism and traditionalism, included *Tade kuu mushi* (1929), *Sasame-yuki* (1943–48), *Kagi* (1956), *Fūten rōjin nikki* (1961–62); also wrote plays and criticism, esp. *Bunsho no dokuhon* (1934).

Tan Ma·la·ka \'tän-mä-'lä-kä\, Ibrahim Datuk. 1894–1949. Indonesian Communist leader. Appointed Comintern agent for Southeast Asia and Australia (1922); competed with Sukarno for control of Indonesian national movement (from 1944); imprisoned (1946–48) for unsuccessful coup d'état; proclaimed (1948) himself head of Indonesia, but his forces routed by the Dutch; captured and executed by supporters of Sukarno.

Tan·ner \'tan-ər\, Henry Ossawa. 1859–1937. American painter, b. Pittsburgh, Pa. Chief works were of a religious nature in a naturalistic style as *Resurrection of Lazarus* (1896), *Disciples at the Tomb* (1906), and *Destruction of Sodom and Gomorrah.*

Tan·ner \'tän-ner\, Väinö Alfred. 1881–1966. Finnish politician. Elected to parliament (1907); instrumental in rebuilding Social Democratic party after 1918 civil war; prime minister (1926–27); minister of finance (1937–39, 1942–44), of foreign affairs (1939–40), of commerce and industry (1941–43); lifelong opponent of Soviet expansion into Finland.

Tann·häu·ser \'tän-,hòi-zər, *Angl* 'tan-\. German lyric poet. c.1200–c.1270. A professional Minnesinger; traveled widely; apparently took part in Crusade of 1228–29. Extant works include six lyric lays, a group of gnomic poems, and some dance and love songs. Central figure of a legend used by Richard Wagner in his opera of the same name.

Ta·no·mu·ra \tä-nō-mùr-ä\ Chikuden. *Given name* Takanori. 1777–1835. Japanese painter. Pupil of Tani Bunchō; influenced by *bunjin-ga* (literati painting) style, but developed own style; painted gentle, melancholic renditions of flowers, birds, landscapes.

Tan·sil·lo \tän-'sēl-lō\, Luigi. 1510–1568. Italian poet. Among his works were didactic poems as *La balia* and *Il podere,* the religious epic *Le lagrime di san Pietro* (1560), lyrics, etc.

Tantia Topi. See Ramchandra PANDURANGA.

Ta·nuc·ci \tä-'nüt-chē\, Bernardo. Marchese. 1698–1783. Italian politician. Adviser (from 1732) to Don Carlos, ruler of Naples-Sicily; first secretary of state for justice (from 1734) and foreign minister (from 1755) of Naples-Sicily; regent during minority (1759–67) of Ferdinand I, King of Naples. Appointed premier secretary of state (1768); antagonized Queen Maria Carolina and lost influence; dismissed (1776).

Ta·nu·ma \tä-nüm-ä\ Okitsugu. 1719–1788. Japanese politician. Highest minister (1772–86) under shogun Tokugawa Ieharu; exerted complete authority over central government; restored financial basis of government by promoting industry, foreign and domestic trade, mineral production, establishment of banks, etc.; headed large fief in Kazusa; gained many enemies, blamed for corruption, and entered Japanese history as one of most unpopular officials; on death of Ieharu (1786), stripped of all offices and lost most of fief.

Tanwŏn. See KIM Hong-do.

Tanyū. See KANŌ.

T'ao Ch'ien \'taù-chē-'en\. *Also called* T'ao Yüan-ming \-yüe-'än-'miŋ\. 365–427. Chinese poet. Government official; retired (405) from post of county magistrate to a farming village south of the Yangtze. Master of the five-word line; wrote of country matters in a simple, straightforward style; also wrote prose pieces.

T'ao Hung–ching \-'hùŋ-'jiŋ\. 451–536. Chinese poet and calligrapher. Tutor in youth to Imperial court; retired (492) to Mao Shan to devote himself to Taoism; became most eminent Taoist of his time; adviser and friend of Liang emperor Hsiao Yen. Edited and annotated religious writings of Yang Hsi, Hsü Mi, and Hsü Hui, producing compendiums *Chen Kao* and *Teng-chen yin-chüeh;* also wrote major pharmacological work *T'u ching yen i pen ts'ao.*

Tao–kuang. See MIN-NING.

Ta·pa·rel·li \,tä-pä-'räl-lē\, Massimo. Marchese d'·Aze·glio \dä-'zäl-yō\. 1798–1866. Italian author and politician. Studied painting in Rome (1820–30); author of political novels *Ettore Fieramosca* (1833), *Niccolò de'Lapi* (1841), and of *Gli ultimi casi de Romagna* (1846), criticism of papal government and call for Italian federation; a leader of Risorgimento. Fought against Austria (1848); prime minister of Sardinia (1849–52) under Victor Emmanuel II; by Siccardi laws (1851) abolished ecclesiastical courts and immunities. Wrote memoirs *I miei ricordi* (1867).

Tap·pan \'tap-ən\, Arthur. 1786–1865. American merchant and philanthropist, b. Northampton, Mass. Prominent in abolitionist movement; at first associated with William Lloyd Garrison; cofounder and first president (1833–40) of American Anti-Slavery Society; organized (1840) and headed new American and Foreign Anti-Slavery Society. His brother ¶Benjamin (1773–1857) was a lawyer; U.S. senator from Ohio (1839–45); opposed to Bank of the United States, zealous antislavery member, sound-money advocate. Another brother ¶Lewis (1788–1873) was partner with Arthur in silk business in New York (1828–37); founded The Mercantile Agency (1841), first commercial credit-rating agency in U.S.; one of founders of American Anti-Slavery Society (1833); at first associated with William Lloyd Garrison but later associated with brother Arthur in organizing American and Foreign Anti-Slavery Society (1840) and became its treasurer.

Ṭa·ra·fah \tar-a-'fa\. *In full* Ṭarafah ʻAmr ibn al-ʻAbd ibn Sufyān ibn Mālik ibn Ḍubayʻah al-Bakrī ibn Wāʼil. 6th century. Arab poet. At court (554–568) of ʻAmr ibn Hind, king of al-Ḥīrah; executed by order of the king for his satires on royalty. Author of the longest of the seven odes in the anthology *al-Muʻallaqāt* which are still regarded as classic models of Arabic poetry.

Ta·ra·ka·no·va \tə-(,)rə-'kä-nə-və\, Yelizaveta Alekseyevna. *Also called* Princess Tarakanova. 1752?–1775. Pretender to Russian throne. Claimed to be daughter of Empress Elizabeth of Russia; sponsored by two Polish émigrés in Italy; seduced (1775) by Aleksey G. Orlov (*q.v.*), taken to St. Petersburg, and imprisoned.

Ta·ra Singh \'tä-rə-'sin(-hə)\. *Called* Master Tara Singh. 1885–1967. Indian Sikh leader. Became (1907) "master," or high school teacher (hence title); involved in civil disobedience movement (from 1930); leader of the Akālī Dal and the Central Gurdwārā Management Committee; prominent advocate for Sikh rights and for an autonomous Punjabi-speaking Sikh nation in the Punjab; vowed (1961) to fast until establishment of Sikh state or death, lost leadership to Sant Fateh Singh (see FATEH SINGH) by breaking off fast.

Tar·bell \'tär-bəl\, Ida Minerva. 1857–1944. American author, b. Erie County, Pa. On editorial staff of *McClure's Magazine* (1894–1906) and *American Magazine* (1906–15). Author of *The Life of Abraham Lincoln* (1900), *History of the Standard Oil Company* (1904), *The Business of Being a Woman* (1912), *New Ideals in Business* (1916), *The Rising of the Tide* (1919), *Owen D. Young* (1932), the autobiographical *All in the Day's Work* (1939), etc.

Tarde \tärd\, Jean-Gabriel de. 1843–1904. French sociologist and criminologist. Magistrate in Dordogne; director of criminal statistics bureau at Ministry of Justice, Paris (1894–1900); professor, Collège de France (from 1900). His theory of social interaction, in opposition to Émile Durkheim, emphasized the individual; developed a theory of imitation, holding that the inferior copy the superior, the lower class the upper class. His *Psychologie économique* (1902) influenced John Hobson and Thorstein Veblen; also author of *La Criminalité comparée* (1886), *Les Lois de l'imitation* (1890), *Les Lois sociales* (1898), etc.

Tar·dieu \tär-dyœ\, André-Pierre-Gabriel-Amédée. 1876–1945. French politician. Member of Chamber of Deputies (1914–24, 1926–36); delegate to the Paris Peace Conference (1918–19) and supporter of Clemenceau; minister of the liberated regions (1919–20); minister of public works and the liberated regions (1926–28); minister of the interior (1928); premier of France (1929–30); minister of agriculture (1931–32); again premier (1932).

Tar·di·vaux \tȧr-dē-vō\, René-Marie-Auguste. *Pseudonym* René Boy·lesve \bwȧ-lev\. 1867–1926. French novelist. Author of series of novels known as *romans tourangeaux,* including *Mademoiselle Cloque* (1899), *La Becquée* (1901), *L'Enfant à la balustrade* (1903), *La Jeune Fille bien élevée* (1909), social histories of Touraine region; also wrote *Le Médecin des dames de Néan* (1896), *La Leçon d'amour dans un parc* (1902), *Le Bel Avenir* (1905).

Tarente, Duc de. See Jacques MACDONALD.

Ṭā·riq ibn Zi·yād \'tär-ə-ˌkib-ən-zē-'ad\. d. c.720. Muslim general. Led first Muslim (Berber) invasion of Spain, landing (711) with army of 7000 at Gibraltar; defeated Visigoths under King Roderick (*q.v.*) near Rio Barbate (711); conquered Córdoba, Toledo, and other parts of Iberian Peninsula.

Tar·king·ton \'tär-kiŋ-tən\, Booth, *in full* Newton Booth. 1869–1946. American novelist, b. Indianapolis. Best known for satirical, sometimes romanticized depictions of Midwesterners; novels included *The Gentleman from Indiana* (1899), *Monsieur Beaucaire* (1900), *The Conquest of Canaan* (1905), *Penrod* (1914) and sequels centering about this boy character, *The Turmoil* (1915), *Seventeen* (1917), *The Magnificent Ambersons* (1918, Pulitzer prize), *Alice Adams* (1921, Pulitzer prize), *Women* (1925), *The Plutocrat* (1927), *Claire Ambler* (1928), *Mirthful Haven* (1930), *Presenting Lily Mars* (1933), *The Heritage of Hatcher Ide* (1940), *Kate Fennigate* (1943), etc. Author or co-author of a number of plays, including *The Man from Home* (1908), *Beauty and the Jacobin* (1912), *Mister Antonio* (1916), *Up from Nowhere* (1919).

Tar·kov·sky \tär-'kȯf-skē\, Andrey Arsenyevich. 1932–1986. Soviet film director and writer. Film director with Mosfilm Studios, Moscow (1960 ff.). Films included *Ivan's Childhood* (1962), *Andrei Rublev* (1969), *Solaris* (1971), *The Stalker* (1980), *The Sacrifice* (1986).

Tarku. See TAHARQA.

Tarle·ton \'tärl-tən\, Sir Banastre. 1754–1833. English soldier. Accompanied Cornwallis to America (1776); aided Clinton in capture of Charleston (1780); defeated Colonel Abraham Buford at Waxhaw Creek (1780); routed part of General Gates's force at Camden; defeated General Sumter at Catawba Fords; was defeated by General Morgan at Cowpens; with Cornwallis at surrender. Acquired reputation for barbaric cruelty; general (1812).

Tarl·ton \'tärl-tən\, Richard. d. 1588. English comedian. One of original company of Queen Elizabeth's players (1583–88), for whom he wrote *The Seven Deadly Sins* (1585); Elizabeth's favorite clown; creator of the stage yokel; known for his improvisations of doggerel verse; reputed author of anecdotes collected as *Tarltons Newes out of Purgatorie* (c.1590) and *Tarlton's Jests* (1611). Probable original of Spenser's Pleasant Willy and Shakespeare's Yorick.

Tarn \tȧrn\, Pauline. *Pseudonym* Renée Vi·vien \vēv-yaⁿ\. 1877–1909. French poet of Anglo-American origin. Known for craftsmanship, mastery of the sonnet form and hendecasyllabic line, exoticism influenced by Swinburne, Baudelaire, Keats. Works included *Études et préludes* (1901), *Cendres et poussières* (1902), *Brumes de fjords* (1902), *Evocations* (1903), *La Venus des aveugles* (1904), *Flambeaux éteints* (1907), *Sillages* (1908), *Dans un coin de violettes* (1908), *Le Vent des vaisseaux* (1909); translated works of Sappho.

Tar·now·ski \tȧr-'nȯf-skē\, Jan. Count. 1488–1561. Polish soldier. Took leading part in victories over Tatars at Wiśniowiec (1512) and Muscovites at Orsza (1514); appointed commander in chief of army (1527); halted Tatar raids; defeated Moldavians at Obertyn (1531); directed campaign against Muscovites (1535). Appointed governor of Kraków province (1535); member of senate; supported Sigismund I during Poultry War (1536); opposed restoration of independent Roman Catholic ecclesiastical courts (1553). Wrote *De bello cum...Turcis gerendo* (1552) and treatise on warfare *Consilium rationis bellica* (1558).

Tar·quin·i·us \tär-'kwin-ē-əs\. *Eng.* Tar·quin \'tär-kwin\. Name of two kings, perhaps legendary, of Rome:

Tarquinius Pris·cus \'pris-kəs\, Lucius. *Orig.* Lu·cu·mo \lü-'kü-mō\. d. 578 B.C. Fifth king (616–578 B.C.). On advice of his wife Tanaquil (*q.v.*), moved to Rome from Tarquinii, Etruria, changed name to Lucius Tarquinius; guardian to sons of Ancus Marcius; on Ancus's death, assumed throne; carried out building program, including Circus Maximus; probably instituted Roman Games; waged successful war against Sabines, Latins, and Etruscans; murdered by sons of Ancus Marcius.

Tarquinius Su·per·bus \s(y)ü-'pər-bəs\, Lucius. d. after 510 B.C. Seventh and last king (534–510 B.C.). Son of Tarquinius Priscus and son-in-law of Servius Tullius. By tradition a cruel despot; abolished certain rights of Romans but made city powerful among neighbors; driven into exile by people aroused and led by L. Junius Brutus because of crime of his son Tarquinius Sextus; failed in attempt to recover Rome with aid of Lars Porsena of Clusium through heroic defense of Horatius Cocles; with his exile Roman monarchy abolished (510 B.C.).

Tarquinius Col·la·ti·nus \ˌkäl-ȧ-'tī-nəs\, Lucius. 6th century B.C. Roman politician. Cousin of sons of King Tarquinius Superbus; m. Lucretia (*q.v.*); one of the first two consuls of Rome (509 B.C.).

Tarquinius Sex·tus \'seks-təs\. d. 496? B.C. Roman nobleman. Son of Tarquinius Superbus; raped Lucretia, wife of Tarquinius Collatinus, which caused her suicide; driven from Rome with his father.

Tar·rasch \'tär-äsh\, Siegbert. 1862–1934. German chess master. Practicing physician; wrote 9 books on chess; unsuccessfully challenged Emanuel Lasker for world championship (1908).

Tar·ta·glia \tär-'täl-yä\ *or* **Tar·ta·lea** \-'täl-ā-ä\, Niccolò. *Orig. surname* Fon·ta·na \fōn-'tä-nä\. 1499–1557. Italian mathematician. Adopted nickname Tartaglia, i.e. Stammerer, as surname; mathematics teacher at Venice (1534–48, 1550–57) and Brescia (1548–49); credited with discovery (1535) of the solution of the cubic equation, later published by G. Cardano (*q.v.*) as his own (1545). Wrote *Nova scientia* (1537) on gunnery; *Quesiti et inventioni diverse* (1546) on ballistics and algebraic problems; *Trattato di numeri et misure* (1556–60) on elementary mathematics; translations of Euclid and Archimedes, etc.

Tar·ti·ni \tär-'tē-nē\, Giuseppe. 1692–1770. Italian violinist and composer. Concertmaster at St. Anthony's, Padua (from 1721); composer of many violin concertos and sonatas, and of religious music, including a *Miserere* and a *Salve Regina;* discovered the "difference tone."

Ta·sche·reau \tȧsh-rō\, Elzéar Alexandre. 1820–1898. Canadian prelate, b. Sainte Marie, Que. Archbishop of Quebec (1871–98); first Canadian cardinal (1886). His nephew ¶Sir Henri Elzéar Taschereau (1836–1911), Canadian jurist, judge of Supreme Court (1878–1906), chief justice (1902–06); member, imperial privy council (1904); author of works on Canadian law.

Ta·shi·ro \tä-shē-rō\, Shiro. 1883–1963. American biochemist, b. Kagoshima, Japan. To U.S. (1901); taught at Cincinnati U. (1919–52); inventor of the biometer.

Taskin, Pascal. See BLANCHET family.

Tas·man \'täs-män\, Abel Janszoon. 1603?–?1659. Dutch navigator and explorer. Entered service of Dutch East India Co. (1632 or 1633); sent by Anthony van Diemen, governor general of Dutch East Indies, on expedition to Indian and Australian waters (Aug. 1642); discovered Tasmania (which he named Van Diemen's Land), New Zealand (Nov. 1642), and Tonga and the Fiji Islands (1643); on second voyage (1644) discovered Gulf of Carpentaria.

Tas·saert \'täs-ȧrt\, Jean Pierre Antoine. 1729–1788. Dutch sculptor. Court sculptor of Frederick the Great (from 1775).

Tas·saert \tȧ-sȧ-er, *Du* 'täs-ȧrt\, Nicolas-François-Octave. 1807–1874. French painter. Known for historical works and genre scenes as *Ma Chambre en 1825* and *Suicide.*

Tas·sie \'tas-ē\, James. 1735–1799. Scottish gem engraver and modeler. With Henry Quin developed a white enamel composition for gemstone replicas; in London (from 1766) produced reproductions of gems of richest cabinets in Europe, esp. collection of Catherine the Great (1780s); executed large profile medallion portraits of contemporaries; supplied molds for many Wedgwood factory pieces. His nephew ¶William Tassie (1777–1860), also a modeler; worked with his uncle; also known for gem reproductions and portrait medallions; gathered collection of over 20,000 pieces.

Tas·si·lo III \'täs-ē-ˌlō\. 742–794. Last Agilolfing duke of Bavaria (749–788). Forced by Charlemagne to relinquish his duchy.

Tas·sis Pe·ral·ta \'tä-sē-spä-'räl-tä\, Juan de. Conde de Vil·la·me·dia·na \'bē(l)-yä-mā-thē-'yä-nä\. 1582–1622. Spanish poet. Dissolute courtier, soldier in Naples and Lombardy; murdered mysteriously, according to one tradition on order of Philip IV. Author of *Fábula de Faéton, Fábula de Apolo y Dafne,* and *Fábula de Venus y Adonis* in imitation of Góngora; love poetry, political and personal lampoons, etc.

Tas·so \'täs-sō, *Angl* 'tas-(ˌ)ō\, Torquato. 1544–1595. Italian poet. Studied law at Padua and Bologna (1560–65); at Ferrara entered (1565) service of Cardinal Luigi d'Este; to Paris (1570); met French Pléiade; in retinue of Alfonso II d'Este, Duke of Ferrara (1572 ff.); beset by delusory fears of persecution (c.1575); began series of mad wanderings (1557 ff.); committed to insane asylum of Sant' Anna, Ferrara (1579–86). Known esp. for his *Gerusalemme liberata* (1581; revised as *Gerusalemme conquistata,* 1593), an heroic epic poem dealing with the capture of Jerusalem during First Crusade; his other works included Carolingian epic *Rinaldo* (1562), pastoral drama *Aminta* (1573), tragedy *Re Torrismondo* (1587), religious poems *Monte Oliveto* (1605) and *Sette giornate del mondo creato* (1607), and the prose *Discorsi del'arte poetica* (1587; revised as *Discorsi del poema eroico,* 1594). His father ¶Bernardo Tasso (1493–1569) was also a poet; in service of Ferrante Sanseverino, prince of Salerno, and later (1563 ff.) of Guglielmo Gonzaga, Duke of Mantua; known particularly for his *Amadigi di Gaula* (1560), a romantic epic in 100 cantos; his other works included the chivalric epic *Il floridante* (completed by Torquato Tasso, 1587) and *Rime, odi, e salmi* (1560).

Tas·so·ni \täs-'sō-nē\, Alessandro. 1565–1635. Italian poet and writer. Spent most of life in service of cardinals in Rome. Known particularly for his mock heroic poem *La secchia rapita* (12 cantos, 1622); also wrote literary criticism *Considerazioni sopra le rime del Petrarca* (1609) and political and philosophical collection *Dieci libri di pensieri diversi di Alessandro Tassoni* (1620).

Tas·tu \tås-tue\, Sabine-Casimire-Amable, *nee* Vo·ïart \vò-yår\. 1795–1885. French poet. m. Joseph Tastu (1816; d. 1849); achieved success with her *Oiseaux du sacre* (1825).

Ta·ta \'tä-,tä\, Jamsetji Nasarwanji. 1839–1904. Indian industrialist. Joined (1858) father's export trading firm and helped establish branches in Japan, China, Europe, U.S.; established cotton mills at Nagpur (1877) and at Bombay (1887); introduced production of raw silk to India; began (1901) organizing India's first large-scale ironworks; endowed scholarships. Under his son and successor ¶Sir Dorabji Jamsetji (1859–1932), business was organized under firm name Tata and Sons and expanded into a vast industrial complex; endowed a cancer research hospital in Bombay. His brother ¶Sir Ratanji (1871–1918), also associated with the business; endowed social science departments at London U. and London School of Economics.

Tă·tă·res·cu \tə-tə-'res-kü\, Gheorghe. 1892–1957. Romanian politician. Prime minister (1934–37, Nov. 1939); controlled by King Carol II; unable to stem Fascism; ambassador to France (1940); foreign minister (1945–47).

Tate \'tāt\, Allen, *in full* John Orley Allen. 1899–1979. American poet, critic, and biographer, b. Winchester, Ky. Member of poetic group the "Fugitives"; a founder of and contributor to literary magazine *The Fugitive* (1922–25); contributed to Southern manifesto *I'll Take My Stand* (1930); edited *The Sewanee Review* (1944–46); taught at U. of Minnesota (1951–68). A leading exponent of the "New Criticism." Author of biographies *Stonewall Jackson* (1928), *Jefferson Davis* (1929), and *Robert E. Lee* (1932); volumes of verse, including *Mr. Pope and Other Poems* (1928), *Three Poems* (1930), *The Mediterranean and Other Poems* (1936), *Winter Sea* (1944), *Poems* (1960); novel *The Fathers* (1938); critical essays *Reactionary Essays on Poetry and Ideas* (1936), *Reason in Madness* (1941), *Essays of Four Decades* (1968).

Tate, Sir Henry. 1819–1899. English sugar refiner and philanthropist. Gave to the nation his collection of modern paintings and the Tate Gallery to house the collection (opened 1897).

Tate, Nahum. 1652–1715. British poet and playwright, b. Dublin. Settled in London (1672). Wrote plays, mostly adaptations from Shakespeare (esp. *King Lear,* 1687) and other Elizabethan dramatists; commissioned by Dryden to write second part of *Absalom and Achitophel* (1682); poet laureate (1692); collaborated with Nicholas Brady in *A New Version of the Psalms of David* (1696); credited with hymns "While shepherds watched" and "As pants the hart"; author of the libretto of Purcell's opera *Dido and Aeneas* (c.1689); best poem "Panacea: a Poem upon Tea" (1700). Pilloried in the *Dunciad.*

Ta·tian \'tā-shən\. *Gr.* Ta·tia·nos \tä-'tyän-òs\. c.120–173. Syrian Christian writer. To Rome (c.152); studied under Justin Martyr, after whose death (c.165) he broke with Roman church; returned to Syria (c.172) and established a school and religious community of Encratites. Among his many writings only two are extant, *Oratio ad Graecos* and *Diatessaron.*

Tatius, Achilles. See ACHILLES TATIUS.

Tat·lin \'tåt-lyin\, Vladimir. 1885–1953. Soviet painter, sculptor, and architect. In Paris (1913–14), where he met Picasso and was influenced by him; created constructions called "painting reliefs"; theatrical designer (1934–52).

Tatti, Jacopo. See Jacopo SANSOVINO.

Ta·tum \'tāt-əm\, Arthur. 1910–1956. American musician, b. Toledo, Ohio. Considered one of greatest technical virtuosos in jazz on piano; played solo before forming (1943) a trio; extremely influential in setting jazz piano style.

Tatum, Edward Lawrie. 1909–1975. American biochemist, b. Boulder, Colo. At Stanford U. (1937–45, 1948–56), Yale U. (1945–48), Rockefeller U. (1957–75). Known for research in molecular genetics, esp. in demonstrating how mutations affect genetic chemical reactions; awarded Nobel prize for medicine or physiology (1958) with G. Beadle and J. Lederberg.

Tatya Tope. See PANDURANGA.

Tauch·nitz \'tauk-nits\, Karl Christoph Traugott. 1761–1836. German printer and publisher. Established printing house at Leipzig (1796); known esp. for editions of the classics. His nephew ¶Christian Bernhard Tauchnitz (1816–1895) founded (1837) a printing and publishing house in Leipzig; began publication (1841) of the highly successful "Tauchnitz Edition" of a *Collection of British and American Authors.*

Tau·ler \'taù-lər\, Johannes. c.1300–1361. German mystic and preacher. Member of Dominican Order; influenced by Eckehart; one of chief Rhineland mystics; stressed practical rather than speculative mysticism; associated for a time with the "Friends of God." His sermons, written in Middle High German, highly valued by Martin Luther.

Tau·ris·cus \tór-'is-kəs\ of Tral·les \'tral-,ēz\. 2d century B.C. Greek sculptor. Collaborated with his brother Apollonius of Tralles (*q.v.*) in carving the group of statuary known as the *Farnese Bull.*

Tau·sen \'taù-sən\, Hans. *Called* the Danish Luther. 1494–1561. Danish religious reformer. Originally a monk; studied under Luther in Wittenberg (1523–25) and thereafter preached the doctrines of the Reformation in Viborg and Copenhagen; became Lutheran bishop in Ribe (1542); translated the Pentateuch into Danish (1535); wrote sermons and hymns.

Taus·sig \'taù-sig\, Helen Brooke. 1898–1986. American pediatrician, physiologist, and embryologist, b. Cambridge, Mass. Professor of pediatrics, Johns Hopkins U. (1930–63); with Alfred Blalock developed surgical procedure for treating "blue baby" syndrome; procedure saved lives of tens of thousands of babies born since 1945 with heart defect affecting oxygen supply; warned against use of tranquilizer Thalidomide, thereby averting disaster in U.S.

Tav·er·ner \'tav-ə(r)-nər\, John. c.1490–1545. English composer. Choirmaster at Cardinal's College, Oxford (1526–30). Composer of polyphonic church music, including 8 masses, 3 Magnificats, a *Te Deum,* 28 motets; his setting of words *In nomine Domini* from his mass *Gloria tibi trinitas* became prototype for later similar compositions.

Taverner, Richard. 1505?–1575. English religious reformer. Wrote in support of Reformation; prepared revision of Matthew's Bible, known as Taverner's Bible (1539), and commentary on epistles and gospels (1540); translator of Erasmus.

Ta·ver·nier \tå-vern-yā\, Jean-Baptiste. 1605–1689. French traveler. Traveled in Turkey, Persia, central Asia, and the East Indies; wrote travel books.

Tavistock, Marquis of. See RUSSELL family.

Taw·fiq Pa·sha \taù-'fēk-'päsh-ä\, Muḥammed. *In full* Muḥammed Tawfīq Pasha ibn Ismā'īl ibn Ibrāhīm ibn Muḥammad 'Alī. 1852–1892. Khedive of Egypt (1879–92). Enjoyed little domestic support; in early part of reign lost much power and prestige to minister of war 'Urābī Pasha (*q.v.*); after British defeat of 'Urābī (1882), was controlled by occupation authorities.

Taw·ney \'tò-nē\, Richard Henry. 1880–1962. English economic historian. Member (1905–47), president (1928–44) of Workers' Educational Association; professor at London School of Economics (1931–49); served on many economic boards and committees and as adviser to governmental bodies; successful campaigner for social reforms. Author of *The Agrarian Problem in the Sixteenth Century* (1912), *The Acquisitive Society* (1920), the classic *Religion and the Rise of Capitalism* (1926), *Land and Labour in China* (1932), *Business and Politics Under James I* (1958), etc.

Ta·ya·ma \tä-yä-mä\ Rokuya. *Pen name* Tayama Katai. 1871–1930. Japanese novelist. A central figure in development of Japanese Naturalist school of writing. Made reputation with *Futon* (1907); fixed distinguishing form of Japanese Naturalism with trilogy of autobiographical novels *Sei* (1908), *Tsuma* (1908–09), *Enishi* (1910); other works included novels *Inaka Kyōshi* (1909) and *Zansetsu* (1917–18) and essay "Katai bunwa" (1911) on his literary theories.

Tay·lor \'tā-lər\, Ann (1782–1866) and her sister Jane (1783–1824). English writers of children's verse. Known as authors of *Original Poems for Infant Minds* (1804), *Rhymes for the Nursery* (1806; including Jane's poem "Twinkle, twinkle, little star"), and *Hymns for Infant Minds* (1810).

Taylor, Bayard, *in full* James Bayard. 1825–1878. American writer, b. Kennett Square, Pa. Commissioned by *Saturday Evening Post, United States Gazette,* and New York *Tribune* to travel in Europe, sending back letters (1844–46); published *Views Afoot* (1846). On staff of New York *Tribune* (1848); to California during the gold rush (1849–50); published *Eldorado* (1850). Traveled in Egypt, Asia Minor, Syria, and Europe (1851–52), and in India, China, and Japan (1852–53); published *A Journey to Central Africa* (1854), *The Lands of the Saracen* (1855), *A Visit to India, China, and Japan* (1855), and lectured widely on his travels. Published translation of Goethe's *Faust* (1870–71). U.S. minister to Germany (1878). Also published three novels and a number of volumes of verse.

Taylor, Bert Leston. 1866–1921. American journalist, b. Goshen, Mass. Wrote column called "A Line o' Type or Two," over his initials B.L.T., in Chicago *Daily Tribune* (1901–03, 1909–21); also published two novels, short stories, and collections from his column, including *Line-o'-Type Lyrics* (1902), *Motley Measures* (1913), etc.

Taylor, Brook. 1685–1731. English mathematician. Obtained solution of problem of center of oscillation (1708, published 1714); became founder of the calculus of finite differences through his *Methodus incrementorum directa et inversa* (1715) in which he also set forth Taylor's theorem, a fundamental theorem concerning functions; set forth principles of perspective in *Linear Perspective* (1715) and *New Principles of Linear Perspective* (1719). Elected to Royal Society (1712).

Taylor, David Watson. 1864–1940. American naval officer and marine architect, b. Louisa Co., Va. In U.S. navy (1885–1923); rear admiral (1917). Established and headed (1899–1914) Experimental Model Basin at Washington (D.C.) Navy Yard, first ship-model testing facility in U.S.; published *Speed and Power of Ships* (1910), expounding Taylor Standard Series Method which determines water resistance characteristics of a ship's hull. Responsible (1914–22) for design and construction of U.S. navy ships and aircraft, including the NC-4, first plane to fly the Atlantic (1919).

Taylor, Deems, *in full* Joseph Deems. 1885–1966. American composer and music critic, b. New York City. Music critic, New York *World* (1921–25); editor, *Musical America* (1927–29); music critic, New York *American* (1931–32); music consultant for Columbia Broadcasting System (from 1936). Composer of *The Siren Song* (symphonic poem, 1912), *The Chambered Nautilus* (cantata, 1914), *Through the Looking Glass* (suite for orchestra, 1918), *The King's Henchman* (opera with libretto by Edna St. Vincent Millay, 1927), *Peter Ibbetson* (opera, 1931), *Christmas Overture* (1943), *Restoration* (suite for orchestra, 1950), etc.; author of *The Well-Tempered Listener* (1940) and other books.

Taylor, Edward. 1645?–1729. American poet, b. in or near Coventry, England. Schoolteacher in England; to America (1668); Puritan minister at Westfield, Mass. (1671–1729). Left to his grandson Ezra Stiles (*q.v.*) a manuscript of religious metaphysical poems, divided into sequence "God's Determination Touching His Elect" and about 200 "Sacramental Meditations"; selection of poems finally published as *The Poetical Works of Edward Taylor* (1939); collection of sermons (delivered 1701–03) published as *Christographia* (1962). Considered foremost poet of colonial America.

Taylor, Edward Thompson. *Called* Father Taylor. 1793–1871. American clergyman, b. Richmond, Va. Cabin boy during youth; became Methodist preacher (c.1813); as chaplain (from 1829) of Seamen's Bethel Chapel, Boston, became one of most renowned preachers of his time, esp. among sailors. The original for Melville's "Father Mapple" in *Moby Dick*.

Taylor, Elizabeth, *nee* Coles \ˈkōlz\. 1912–1975. English novelist. m. (1936) manufacturer John W.K. Taylor. Her novels, marked by precise language and understated style, included *At Mrs. Lippincote's* (1945), *A Wreath of Roses* (1950), *A Game of Hide and Seek* (1951), *The Sleeping Beauty* (1953), *The Wedding Group* (1968); her short stories collected in *A Dedicated Man* (1965), *The Devastating Boys* (1972), etc.

Taylor, Frederick Winslow. 1856–1915. American efficiency engineer, b. Germantown, Pa. Employed by Midvale Steel Co., Philadelphia (1878–90, chief engineer from 1884); introduced (1881) there time study, intended to systematize shop management and reduce manufacturing costs; made remarkable success in applying his ideas of scientific management as consultant to various firms (from 1890). Developed (1899), with Maunsel White, Taylor-White process for heat-treating high-speed tool steels, increasing cutting capacities up to 300 per cent. From 1901, devoted himself to expounding the Taylor system of scientific management. Author of *The Principles of Scientific Management* (1911), etc.

Taylor, George. 1716–1781. American iron manufacturer, b. Ireland. To America (c.1736); operated furnace in Bucks County, Pa.; member of Committee of Correspondence (1774–76) and of Continental Congress (1776–77); a signer of the Declaration of Independence.

Taylor, Sir Henry. 1800–1886. English poet. Held appointments in Colonial Office (1824–72); author of verse dramas, including *Philip van Artevelde* (1834), a great success, and of lyrical poetry and prose essays.

Tay·lor \tā-lȯr\, Isidore-Justin-Séverin. Baron. 1789–1879. French writer. Royal administrator of the Théâtre Français; best known for his *Voyages pittoresques et romantiques de l'ancienne France* (1820–63).

Taylor, Jane. See Ann TAYLOR.

Tay·lor \ˈtā-lər\, Jeremy. 1613–1667. English prelate and author. Ordained Anglican minister (1633); chaplain to Laud and Charles I. After downfall of Royalist cause took refuge (1645) in Wales, kept a school, and produced *Liberty of Prophesying* (1646), *Holy Living* (1650), *Holy Dying* (1651), *Worthy Communicant* (1660). As bishop of Down and Connor (1661) and administrator of Dromore diocese, involved in conflicts with Presbyterian clergy; built cathedral of Dromore; served on Irish privy council; helped reconstitute U. of Dublin; wrote his last great work, *Dissuasive from Popery* (1664).

Taylor, John. *Called* the Water-poet. 1580–1653. English pamphleteer. A Thames waterman and collector of perquisites for lieutenant of Tower; published odd-titled booklets describing harebrained journeys, as a journey from London to Edinburgh on foot in *The Pennyles Pilgrimage* (1618), a voyage in a brown-paper boat from London to Queensborough in *Praise of Hempseed* (1620). Journeyed to Prague, where he was entertained by queen of Bohemia (1620). Kept public house at Oxford (1642); wrote Royalist pamphlets; returned (1645) to London and took over Crown public house in Phoenix Alley, Longacre.

Taylor, John. *Known as* John Taylor of Car·o·line \ˈkar-ə-ˌlīn\. 1753–1824. American politician and agriculturist, b. in either Orange or Caroline Co., Va. Served in Continental army (1775–79, 1781); U.S. senator from Virginia (1792–94, 1803, 1822–24); strong advocate of states' rights. Author of *An Inquiry into the Principles of Policy of the Government of the United States* (1814), *Tyranny Unmasked* (1822), etc.

Taylor, John. 1808–1887. American religious leader, b. Milnthorpe, England. To Canada (1832); baptized in Mormon church (1836); created apostle (1838). After death of Joseph Smith (1844), sided with Brigham Young in struggle for succession; accompanied Young to Utah and settled there; member of legislature of Territory of Utah (1857–76). After Brigham Young's death (1877) was acting head of the church; chosen president (1880); forced into exile (1884) to escape arrest by U.S. government; managed affairs of church from his retreat (1884–87).

Taylor, John Edward. 1791–1844. English liberal journalist. Founded the Manchester *Guardian* (1821).

Taylor, John Henry. 1871–1963. English golfer. Winner of British Open (1894, 1895, 1900, 1909, 1913), first Englishman to win it; a founder (1901) and first chairman of British Professional Golfers' Association; club professional (1899–1946); successful as golf equipment manufacturer and writer on golf.

Taylor, John W. 1784–1854. American politician, b. Charlton, N.Y. Member from N.Y. of U.S. House of Representatives (1813–33; speaker 1820–21, 1825–27); vigorously opposed slavery; instrumental in the realization of the Missouri Compromise (1820).

Taylor, Joseph. 1586?–1652. English actor. Member of Lady Elizabeth's Men (1611–16), of Prince's Men (1616–19), and, as principal actor succeeding Richard Burbage, of King's Men (1619–42). Mentioned in First Folio (1623) of Shakespeare as one of 26 who took principal parts in all of its plays; a signer of dedication of first folio (1647) of Beaumont and Fletcher. Acted in plays of most leading playwrights of his time.

Taylor, Laurette. *Orig.* Loretta Coo·ney \ˈkü-nē\. 1884–1946. American actress, b. New York City. Vaudeville debut (1896); m. (1901; div. 1909) Charles A. Taylor, in whose play *Child Wife* she toured; New York debut (1903); appeared on Broadway in *The Great John Ganton* (1909) by J. Hartley Manners; m. Manners (1912; d. 1928); great success in his *Peg o' My Heart* (1912; record 604 performances on Broadway); also played in Manners's *Harp of Life* (1916), *Wooing of Eve* (1917), *One Night in Rome* (1919), etc.; critical success in *Humoresque* (1923), *In a Garden* (1925). After long period of eclipse triumphed in *The Glass Menagerie* (1944).

Taylor, Nathaniel William. 1786–1858. American theologian, b. New Milford, Conn. Ordained in Congregational ministry (1812); professor, Yale Divinity School (1822–58). Developed system of theology involving freedom of will which divided New England churches into Taylorites and Tylerites (adherents of Bennet Tyler).

Taylor, Richard. 1826–1879. American army officer, b. near Louisville, Ky. Son of Zachary Taylor. Brigadier general, Confederate army (1861); served under Stonewall Jackson in Shenandoah Valley campaign; major general (1862); commanded district of West Louisiana; checked Banks at Pleasant Hill and Sabine Crossroads (Apr. 1864). Promoted lieutenant general (Aug. 1864); succeeded to command of Gen. J. B. Hood's army (Nov. 1864); surrendered to Gen. Canby at Citronelle, Ala. (May 4, 1865).

Taylor, Rowland. d. 1555. English Protestant martyr. Chaplain to Cranmer (1540); archdeacon of Exeter (1552); advocated cause of Lady Jane Grey; resisted restoration of the Mass under Mary; burnt for heresy near Hadleigh.

Taylor, Samuel Coleridge. See Samuel COLERIDGE-TAYLOR.

Taylor, Thomas. *Called* the Platonist. 1758–1835. English scholar. Published translations and expositions of Plato, Aristotle, and Neo-Platonists and Pythagoreans; influenced William Blake, Emerson and the Transcendentalists, W.B. Yeats, etc.

Taylor, Tom. 1817–1880. English dramatist. Made his first hit with *To Parents and Guardians* (1845); wrote or adapted over one hundred dramatic pieces, including *Our American Cousin* (1858), *Still Waters Run Deep* (1855), *The Overland Route* (1860), *The Ticket of Leave Man* (1863).

Taylor, William. 1821–1902. American clergyman, b. Rockbridge Co., Va. In Methodist evangelistic and missionary work in California (1849–56), cities of the U.S. and Canada (1856–61), Australia, Tasmania, and New Zealand (1861–64), South Africa (1866), England and Scotland (1867), India (1870–77), Peru and Chile (1877–78). Elected missionary bishop for Africa (1884) and served to 1896.

Taylor, Zachary. *Nicknamed* Old Rough-and-Ready. 1784–1850. Twelfth president of the United States, b. Orange Co., Va. Entered U.S. army as 1st lieutenant (1808); served in Northwest Indian campaigns, War of 1812, 2d Seminole War (1835–42); took command of the army in Texas (1845); defeated Mexicans at Palo Alto (May 8, 1846), Resaca de la Palma (May 9, 1846); occupied Matamoros (May 18, 1846); brevetted major general and named commander of the army of the Rio Grande. Captured Monterrey (Sept. 24, 1846); defeated Santa Anna at Buena Vista (Feb. 22–23, 1847), ending the war in northern Mexico. President of the United States (1849–50).

Tay Son brothers. See NGUYEN HUE.

Tch-, Tsch-. For some Russian names beginning Tch-, Tsch-, see also CH-.

Tchai·kov·sky \chī-'kȯf-skəi; *Angl* chī-'kȯf-skē, chə-, -'kȯv-\, Pyotr Ilich. *Also transcribed* Tschaikovsky *or* Chaykovsky. 1840–1893. Russian composer. Studied law in St. Petersburg; clerk in Ministry of Justice (1859–63); professor at Moscow Observatory (1866–77); on receiving annuity from Nadezhda von Meck, a wealthy widow, retired from teaching to devote all his time to composition; successfully toured London and the Continent (1888, 1889) and the U.S. (1891). His compositions included operas *Kuznets Vakula* (*Vakula the Smith,* 1876), *Evgeny Onegin* (1879), *Orleanskaya deva* (*The Maid of Orleans,* 1881), *Mazepa* (1883), *Pikovaya dama* (*Queen of Spades,* 1890), *Iolanta* (1892); ballets *Lebedinoye ozero* (*Swan Lake,* 1877), *Spyashchaya Krasavitsa* (*Sleeping Beauty,* 1889), *Shchelkunchik* (*The Nutcracker,* 1892); choral works; chamber music, including 3 string quartets, a piano trio, and sextet *Souvenir de Florence* (1890–92); songs and duets; and much orchestral music, including 6 symphonies, esp. No. 6 in B minor, *Pathétique* (1893), *Manfred* symphony (1885), fantasy overtures *Romeo and Juliet* (1869), *Francesca da Rimini* (1876), and *Hamlet* (1888), *Violin Concerto* (1878), *Serenade for Strings* (1880), *Capriccio italien* (1880), *1812 Overture* (1880), and 3 piano concertos.

Tche·rep·nin *or* **Che·rep·nin** \chir-yip-'nyēn\, Nikolay Nikolayevich. 1873–1945. Russian composer. Pupil of Rimsky-Korsakov; appointed conductor of Imperial Opera (1908); conducted Diaghilev's opera and ballet productions in western Europe (1908–14); director of Tiflis Conservatory (1918–21); settled (1921) in Paris and assumed directorship of Russian Conservatory there. His compositions, mainly in Russian nationalist style, included ballets *Le Pavillon d'Armide* (1908), *Narcisse et Echo* (1911), and *Le Masque de la mort rouge* (1922), symphonic poems, choral music, piano pieces, and songs. His son ¶Alexander Nikolayevich (1899–1977), pianist and composer; composer at Tiflis (1918–21); to Paris (1921); visited China and Japan (1934–37), establishing firm in Tokyo for publication of Japanese and Chinese composers; taught at DePaul U., Chicago (1949–64); naturalized American citizen (1958); settled in New York (1964). Known for stylistic mixture of Romanticism and modern experimentation, as with a nine-note scale and complex rhythms; compositions included ballet *La Femme et son ombre* (1948), opera *The Farmer and the Nymph* (1952), four symphonies, six piano concertos, *Harmonica Concerto* (1953), vocal works, chamber music, and piano pieces.

Tcher·ni·chow·sky *or* **Cher·ni·kov·sky** \chir-nyi-'kȯf-skəi\, Saul Gutmanovich. 1875–1943. Hebrew poet, b. Crimea, Russia. Physician by profession; left Russia (1922) and wandered about, including in U.S. (1928–29); settled in Tel Aviv (1931). Wrote love lyrics, sonnet cycles, idylls of Jewish village life in Russia; produced translations of Shakespeare, Molière, Longfellow, *Iliad* and *Odyssey, Epic of Gilgamesh,* etc.

Teach \'tēch\ *or* **Thatch** \'thach\, Edward. *Known as* Black·beard \'blak-ˌbi(ə)rd\. d. 1718. English pirate. Privateer in West Indies during War of Spanish Succession; turned pirate after cessation of hostilities (1713). Cruised along Spanish Main, among Bahamas, and north to the Carolinas; captured (1717) large French merchantman, equipped her with 40 guns, renamed her *Queen Anne's Revenge,* and preyed on shipping off Carolina and Virginia coasts; protected by corrupt governor of North Carolina; killed in attack by two naval sloops sent by lieutenant governor of Virginia.

Tea·gar·den \'tē-ˌgärd-ᵊn\, Jack, *orig.* Weldon Leo. 1905–1964. American musician, b. Vernon, Tex. Developed a widely imitated trombone jazz style; led own band (1939–47, 1951–57); member of Louis Armstrong's "All Stars" (1947–51); also known as jazz singer; appeared in movie *Birth of the Blues* (1941).

Teague \'tēg\, Walter Dorwin. 1883–1960. American industrial designer, b. Decatur, Ind. Design consultant for Eastman Kodak Co. (from 1927) and other industrial firms; senior partner of own design group. With Henry Dreyfuss and Raymond Loewy, pioneered in establishment of industrial design as profession in U.S.; designed the Marmon 16 automobile (1930), interiors and furnishings for U.S. Air Force Academy, interiors of Boeing 707 jet airliner, railway coaches, office machines, service stations, cameras, several buildings and exhibits for New York World's Fair of 1939, etc.

Teale \'tē(ə)l\, Edwin Way, *orig.* Edwin Alfred. 1899–1980. American naturalist, photographer, and writer, b. Joliet, Ill. Author of many books on nature, including *Grassroot Jungles* (1937), *The Lost Woods* (1945), *North With the Spring* (1951), *Autumn Across America* (1956), *Journey Into Summer* (1960), *Wandering Through Winter* (1965, Pulitzer prize), *A Walk Through the Year* (1978), etc.

Teas·dale \'tēz-ˌdāl\, Sara, *orig.* Sara Trevor. 1884–1933. American poet, b. St. Louis, Mo. Author of numerous volumes of verse, including *Rivers to the Sea* (1915), *Love Songs* (1917), *Flame and Shadow* (1920), *Dark of the Moon* (1926), *Strange Victory* (1933).

Te·cum·seh \tə-'kəm(p)-sə, -sē\ *or* **Te·cum·tha** \-thə\ *or* **Te·cum·the** \-thə, -thē\ *or* **Ti·kam·the** \tə-'käm(p)-thə, -thē\. 1768–1813. American Indian chief of the Shawnee tribe, b. Old Piqua, Ohio. Gifted orator; became chief spokesman for Indians of Ohio Valley; attempted (from 1808) to form an Indian confederation to resist white encroachment; after Battle of Tippecanoe (1811), threw in his lot with the British in War of 1812; helped capture Detroit; joined Gen. Henry Procter's invasion of Ohio; killed in action by forces of William Henry Harrison at the battle of the Thames (Oct. 5, 1813). His brother ¶Ten·skwa·ta·wa \ten(t)-'skwät-ə-ˌwä\, *known as* the Prophet (c.1768–1834), claimed (1805) reception of message from the "Master of Life"; gained fame as religious mystic and revivalist; advocated return to Indian ways of life; helped Tecumseh work for Indian confederacy; during absence of Tecumseh, was defeated by William Henry Harrison in Battle of Tippecanoe (Nov. 1811) and lost all his prestige; lived on British pension (to 1826), and thereafter in U.S.

Ted·der \'ted-ər\, Arthur William. 1st Baron Tedder. 1890–1967. British air chief marshal. Served in World War I in France (1915–17) and Egypt (1918–19), in air service from 1916; R.A.F. commander in Far East (1936–38); director general of research in air ministry (1938–40); R.A.F. deputy commander (1940–41) and commander in chief in Middle East (1940–41); coordinated air force activities in campaign that drove Rommel from Egypt and Libya; air commander in chief in Mediterranean theater (Feb. 1943); deputy commander of Allied Expeditionary Force under Eisenhower (1943–45); chief of air staff (1946–50).

Tef·nakh·te \tef-'näk-tə\. d. c.720 B.C. Egyptian king (c.730–720 B.C.) and founder of the 24th dynasty. Originally a Libyan prince of Sais in northwest Nile Delta; in attempt to conquer Upper Egypt, conquered Memphis and Hermopolis; defeated and reduced to vassalage by Piankhi; after Piankhi's departure (c.730 B.C.), proclaimed himself king of Egypt and ruled at Sais; succeeded by his son Bocchoris.

Te·get·mei·er \'teg-ət-ˌmī(-ə)r, 'tā-gət-\, William Bernhard. 1816–1912. English naturalist. Co-worker with Darwin on variation in animals; editor and editorial writer for fifty years of *The Field.*

Te·gett·hoff \'tā-gət-ˌhȯf\, Wilhelm von. 1827–1871. Austrian admiral. Commanded Austrian squadron which took part in Austro-Prussian victory over Danish fleet off Helgoland (1864); defeated Italian fleet in battle of Vis (1866).

Teg·gart \'teg-ərt\, Frederick John. 1870–1946. American historian, b. Belfast, Ireland. To U.S. (1889); professor (1911–40) at U. of California, Berkeley, founding (1919) department of social institutions. Author of *Prolegomena to History* (1916), *The Processes of History* (1918), *Theory of History* (1925), *Rome and China* (1939).

Tegh Ba·hā·dur \'teg-bä-'häd-u̇r\. 1621?–1675. Ninth Sikh Gurū (1664–75). From village of Bakāla, India; arrested by Aurangzeb for aiding some Hindu holy men; became second Sikh martyr when executed for refusal to convert to Islām.

Teg·nér \teŋ-'nār\, Esaias. 1782–1846. Swedish poet. Professor of Greek, Lund (1812–26); bishop of Växjö (from 1824). Originally associated with Romantic movement, later turned to the Classical; recognized as one of greatest Swedish poets. Among his works were religious idyll *Nattvardsbarnen* (1820), the narrative *Axel* (1822), romance cycle *Fritiofs saga* (1825), love lyrics, etc.

Tei·as \'tā-(y)əs\. d. 553. Last Ostrogoth king of Italy (552–553). A general in Gothic army; elected king on death of Totila; defeated and killed by Eastern Roman army during attempt to captute Cumae.

Teil·hard de Char·din \tā-yär-də-shär-daⁿ\, Pierre, *in full,* Marie-Joseph-Pierre. 1881–1955. French paleontologist and philosopher. Entered Society of Jesus (1899); ordained priest (1911); in China (1923–46), making geological and paleontological expeditions to northern China, Central Asia, India, Burma; helped discover Peking Man (1929); fellow (from 1946) of Wenner-Gren Foundation for Anthropological Research, esp. in New York (1951–55). Known for theory that man is presently evolving, mentally and socially, toward a final spiritual unity. Author of *Le Phénomène humain* (1955), *L'Apparition de l'homme* (1956), *L'Avenir de l'homme* (1959), etc.

Teir·linck \'tir-liŋk\, Herman. 1879–1967. Flemish writer. Author of verse, plays, short stories, and esp. novels, including *Mijnheer Serjanszoon* (1908), *Het ivoren aapje* (1909), and *Zelfportret of het galgemaal* (1955).

Teis·pes \'tā-ˌspēz\. *Old Persian* Chish·pish \'chish-(ˌ)pish\. d. c.640 B.C. Persian king (c.675–c.640) of Achaemenian dynasty. Son of Achaemenes; father of Cyrus I and Ariaramnes; ruled district of Anshan in Elam; maintained neutral position between kingdoms of Elam and Assyria.

Teis·se·renc de Bort \tes-räⁿ-də-bȯr\, Léon-Philippe. 1855–1913. French meteorologist. With Centre Administratif de la Météorologie Nationale, Paris (1880–96); established own observatory at Trappes (1896); pioneered in use of unmanned, instrumented balloons to investigate atmosphere; discovered the stratosphere (1900).

Tei·xei·ra \tā-'shā-rə\, Pedro. 1575–1640. Portuguese soldier in Brazil. Governor of Pará (1620–21, 1640); commanded expedition (1637–39) which carefully explored the Amazon, ascending that river and the Napo and crossing the mountains to Quito, and returning by the same route.

Teixeira Go·mes \-'gō-mish\, Manuel. 1860–1941. Portuguese politician. Ambassador to Great Britain (1911–19) and Spain (1922); president of Portugal (1923–25).

Te·ja·da Sor·za·no \te-'kä-thä-sȯr-'sä-nō\, José Luis. 1881–1938. Bolivian politician. President of Bolivia (1934–36); concluded the war in Chaco by a peace treaty with Paraguay (signed June 12, 1935); deposed.

Tek·a·kwitha \ˌtek-ə-'kwith-ə\, Kateri. *Also spelled* Teg·a·kwitha \ˌteg-\ *or* Teg·a·kouita \ˌteg-ə-'kwit-ə\. *Known as* the Lily of the Mohawks. 1656–1680. American Indian religious, b. Ossernenon (now Auriesville), N.Y. Instructed by Jesuits and baptized (1676); lived a life of sanctity; first North American Indian proposed for canonization.

Te Koo·ti Ri·ki·ran·gi \'tā-'kü-tē-ˌrē-kē-'räŋ-(g)ē\. c.1830–1893. Maori religious leader. While imprisoned on Chatham Islands, founded (1867) the Ringatu religious movement; escaped (1868) to New Zealand and led a guerrilla band; granted amnesty (1883).

Te–kuang \'də-'gwäŋ\. 10th century. Mongol leader. Leader of the Mongol Khitan people of Manchuria; established (947) the Khitan dynasty, called Liao, in Manchuria, Mongolia, and northeastern China.

Te·le·ki \'tel-ek-i\, Pál. Count. 1879–1941. Hungarian geographer and politician. Entered parliament (1905); foreign minister (1920), minister of education (1938), premier of Hungary (1920–21, 1939–41); supported Nazi Germany in early stages of World War II.

Teleki, Samuel. Count. 1845–1916. Hungarian explorer. Traversed (1887–88) Kenya and southern Ethiopia, discovering (1888) and naming Lakes Rudolf and Stefanie.

Te·le·mann \'tā-lə-ˌmän\, Georg Philipp. 1681–1767. German composer. Kapellmeister at Sorau (1705–08) and Eisenach (1708–12); city music director of Frankfurt am Main (1712–21) and Hamburg (1721–67). His compositions included over 50 operas as *Der gedultige Socrates* (1721), *Der neu-modische Liebhaber Damon* (1724), and *Pimpinone* (1725); cantatas, esp. collection *Der harmonische Gottesdienst* (1725–26); concertos, oratorios, Passions, orchestral suites, songs, and much chamber music.

Te·le·sio \tel-'ez-yō\, Bernardino. 1509–1588. Italian philosopher. Known particularly for his *De rerum natura juxta propria principia* (first 2 books, 1565; complete 9 books, 1586); revolted against medieval Aristotelianism; advocated empirical method; called "first of the moderns" by Francis Bacon.

Te·les·pho·rus \ti-'les-fə-rəs\. Saint. d. c.136 A.D. Pope (c.125–c.136). Witnessed persecutions of Christians by Hadrian; considered first pope after St. Peter to be martyred.

Tel·ford \'tel-fərd\, Thomas. 1757–1834. Scottish civil engineer. His works included the Ellesmere Canal (1793), Caledonian Canal, 920 miles of roads and 20 bridges in northern Scotland, improvements in Scottish harbors, Göta Canal between Baltic Sea and North Sea (1808–10), and the Menai Strait suspension bridge (1819–26).

Tel·i·pi·nus *or* **Tel·e·pi·nus** \ˌtel-i-'pī-nəs, -'pē-\. 16th century B.C. Last king (c.1525–c.1500 B.C.) of Hittite Old Kingdom in Anatolia. Seized throne during dynastic power struggle; attempted to impose domestic order and regulate royal succession; issued Edict of Telipinus, one of best sources for history of the times.

Té·llez \'tā(l)-yāth\, Gabriel. *Pseudonym* Tir·so de Mo·li·na \'tēr-sō-thā-mō-'lē-nä\. c.1580–1648. Spanish dramatist. Entered Order of Mercy (1611); made superior of monasteries at Trujillo (1626) and Soria (1645); as official historian (from 1632), wrote (1639) *Historia general de la Orden de la Merced.* One of greatest dramatists of Spanish Golden Age; published (1621) *Cigarrales de Toledo,* set of verses, tales, and plays; introduced Don Juan into literature in tragedy *El burlador de Sevilla* (1634); his 80 or so extant dramas, published chiefly in five *Partes* (1627–36), included *El condenado por desconfiado, La prudencia en la mujer, La venganza de Tamar, El vergonzoso en palacio, Don Gil de las calzas verdes, Marta la piadosa, La villana de Vallecas.*

Téllez-Gi·ron \-'kē-rōn\, Pedro. Duque de Osu·na \ō-'sü-nä\. 1574–1624. Spanish soldier and politician. Served in Flanders (1602–08); viceroy of Sicily (1611–16), of Naples (1616–20); abetted Bedmar's conspiracy against Venice (1618); suspected of attempting to usurp kingdom of the Two Sicilies; recalled to Spain (1620) and imprisoned (1621–24).

Tel·lier \tel-yā\, Charles-Albert-Abel. 1828–1913. French engineer. Pioneer in the cold-storage industry; conceived refrigerating machines for preserving meats, etc. (1868–69); transported foods across the Atlantic Ocean in a ship equipped with a refrigerating plant (1876).

Temple, Earls of. See under Richard Temple GRENVILLE.

Tem·ple \'tem-pəl\, Frederick. 1821–1902. English prelate and primate. Ordained priest (1847); government inspector of schools (1855–57). As headmaster of Rugby (1857–69), enlarged school and modernized curriculum. Bishop of Exeter (1869); bishop of London (1885–96); archbishop of Canterbury (1896–1902). His son ¶William (1881–1944) was headmaster of Repton (1910–14); chaplain to king (1915–21); canon of Westminster (1919–21); bishop of Manchester (1921–29); archbishop of York (1929–42); archbishop of Canterbury (1942–44). President of Workers' Educational Association (1908–24); leader in ecumenical movement and in educational and labor reforms. Author of *Mens Creatrix* (1917), *Christianity and Social Order* (1942), *The Church Looks Forward* (1944), etc.

Temple, Henry John. 3d Viscount Palm·er·ston \'päm-ər-stən\. *Nicknamed* Pam \'pam\. 1784–1865. English politician. Tory M.P. (from 1807); secretary for war (1809–28); supported Canning. Committed himself to parliamentary reform, lent support to Catholic emancipation, and associated himself with Whig party (1830). Foreign minister (1830–34, 1835–41, 1846–51); effected independence of Belgium (1830–31) and Greece (1832); formed Quadruple Alliance (1834); rescued Turkey from Russia and maintained her integrity by treaty (1840); annexed Hong Kong and opened the five ports (1840–41); supported national movements when in British interests; noted for belligerent attitude in foreign policy. Prime minister (1855–58, 1859–65); approved advance of Italian independence by French invasion; supported policy of neutrality in American Civil War. One of most popular ministers in English history.

Temple, Sir William. 1628–1699. English diplomat and essayist. Envoy at Brussels (1666); effected Triple Alliance (1668) of England, Holland, and Sweden against France; ambassador at The Hague (1668–70). Recalled to negotiate Treaty of Westminster (1674); again ambassador at The Hague (1674–79); brought about marriage of William of Orange and Princess Mary (1677); took part in conference at Nijmegen (1679), which made treaty bringing about general pacification. Tried ineffectually to reform (1679) Privy Council and for a time was one of an inner council of four; retired (1681) to Sheen, then (1686) to Moor Park in Surrey, where Swift was his secretary (1689) and assisted with his *Memoirs.* Author of *Observations upon the United Provinces* (1673) and numerous essays, esp. "Upon Ancient and Modern Learning" (1692).

Temple, William. 1881–1944. See under Frederick TEMPLE.

Temüjin. See GENGHIS KHAN.

Te·mür Khan \tā-'mu̇r-'kän\. *Posthumous title* Ch'eng Tsung \'chəŋ-'zu̇ŋ\. 1267–1307. Chinese emperor (1295–1307) of the Yüan dynasty. Grandson and successor of Kublai Khan; also great khan of the Mongol Empire; last Yüan ruler to maintain firm control over China; suppressed rebellions in Korea and South China; attempted to eliminate corruption in government.

ten Brink. See BRINK.

Ten Broeck \ten-'bru̇k, tən-\, Abraham. 1734–1810. American Revolutionary leader, b. Albany, N.Y. Brigadier general of militia of Albany County; participated in battle of Bemis Heights (1777), forcing retreat of General Burgoyne. Mayor of Albany (1779–83, 1796–99).

Tench \'tench\, Watkin. c.1758–1833. British soldier and writer. Commissioned lieutenant in British army (1778); in Australia as captain lieutenant of marines (1788–91); lieutenant general (1821). Author of *A Narrative of the Expedition to Botany Bay* (1789), *Complete Account of the Settlement at Port Jackson* (1793), and *Letters Written in France to a Friend in London* (1796).

Ten·chi \ten-chē\. *Orig.* Amem·i·ko·to-Ha·ru·ki·wa·ke \ä-mem-ē-kō-tō-hä-ru̇k-ē-wä-ke\. *Later known as* Na·ka·no-Ōe \nä-kä-nō-ō-e\. 626–671. Japanese emperor (662–671). As prince, much interested in reforms; conspired with Nakatomi Kamatari to murder (645) Soga Iruka, ending domination of court by Soga clan; granted (669) Kamatari the name of Fujiwara (*q.v.*); as emperor, published code of laws (670); in his reign Japanese expedition withdrew from Korea.

Ten·cin \tän-san\, Claudine-Alexandrine Gué·rin de \gā-ran-də-\. 1685–1749. French writer and society leader. Mistress of several prominent figures, as Cardinal Dubois and the regent; mother of d'Alembert, through a liaison with Louis Camus, chevalier Destouches; hosted (after 1726) a salon frequented by leading writers of the day. Author of *Le Siège de Calais* (1739), *Les Mémoires du comte de Comminges* (1735), *Les Malheurs de l'amour* (1747).

Te·ne·ra·ni \ˌtā-nā-'rä-nē\, Pietro. 1789–1869. Italian sculptor. Among his works were *Deposition from the Cross,* Bolívar's monument for Colombia, tomb of Pius VIII in St. Peter's, Rome, and portrait busts.

Te·niers \tə-'nērs, *Angl* 'ten-yərz\, David, *known as* the Elder. 1582–1649. Flemish painter. Said to have studied under Elsheimer and Rubens; master in Antwerp guild (1606–07); painted chiefly religious subjects. His son ¶David, *known as* the Younger (1610–1690), studied under him and became renowned as a genre, landscape, and portrait painter; court painter in Brussels to regents Leopold William (1651) and Don John of Austria (1656); among his canvases were *The Prodigal Son, Archers of Antwerp, Village Festival, A Merry Repast, Flemish Tap-Room, Backgammon Players, The Barber Shop, Cow Stable.*

Ten·i·son \'ten-ə-sən\, Thomas. 1636–1715. English prelate and primate. Bishop of Lincoln (1691); archbishop of Canterbury (1694).

Tenjin. See SUGAWARA Michizane.

Ten·nant \'ten-ənt\, Frederick Robert. 1866–1957. English theologian. Lecturer at Cambridge (1913–31); essayed a harmony of science and religion within an empirical approach to theology, esp. in *Philosophical Theology* (1928–30).

Tennant, Smithson. 1761–1815. English chemist. Professor, Cambridge (1813–15); discovered elements osmium (1803) and iridium (1804).

Ten·nent \'ten-ənt\, William. 1673–1746. American clergyman, b. Ireland. Ordained (1706); to America (c.1717) and joined Presbyterian ministry; pastorates in Bedford, N.Y. (1720–26), and Neshaminy, Pa. (1726–46); built a "log college" (1728) where he lived and taught and trained many for the Presbyterian ministry; college ceased at his death, and its supporters joined with others in organizing Princeton. His son ¶Gilbert (1703–1764) was also a Presbyterian clergyman; by his fervor and zeal prepared the way for the Great Awakening under George Whitefield's leadership; affiliated with "New Side" of Presbyterianism; pastorate at Philadelphia (1743–64).

Ten·niel \'ten-yəl, 'ten-ē-əl\, Sir John. 1820–1914. English cartoonist and illustrator. Cartoonist on staff of *Punch* (1850–1901), notable for dignity, geniality of satire, and good taste; illustrator of Lewis Carroll's *Alice's Adventures in Wonderland* (1865) and *Through the Looking Glass* (1872).

Ten·ny·son \'ten-ə-sən\, Alfred. 1st Baron Tennyson. *Commonly known as* Alfred, Lord Tennyson. 1809–1892. English poet. Published with his brother Charles *Poems by Two Brothers* (1827); at Trinity College, Cambridge (1827–31), won chancellor's medal with poem *Timbuctoo* (1829); published *Poems, Chiefly Lyrical* (1830). Traveled with Arthur Henry Hallam in the Pyrenees and on the Rhine (1832); met scant success with *Poems* (1832), including "The Lady of Shalott," "The Palace of Art," "The Lotos-Eaters," "A Dream of Fair Women." On death (1833) of Hallam, wrote "Two Voices" and began *In Memoriam;* published *Poems* (1842; including "Morte d'Arthur," "Ulysses," "Locksley Hall," "The Vision of Sin"), which secured his place as a great poet; added to his reputation with *The Princess* (1847); published *In Memoriam,* one of the great English elegies, and was appointed poet laureate on the death of Wordsworth (1850). Wrote *Ode on the Death of the Duke of Wellington* (1852); moved to Farringford in Isle of Wight (1853), where he lived part of each year for rest of his life. Wrote "Charge of the Light Brigade" (1854); puzzled the public with *Maud* (1855); awakened public to enthusiasm by returning to Arthurian legend with *The Idylls of the King* (1859; added to, 1869, 1872; completed, 1885). After *Enoch Arden* (1864; including "Aylmer's Field" and "The Northern Farmer"), turned to a series of historical dramas, *Queen Mary* (1875), *Harold* (1876), *Becket* (1884), and lesser plays, of which *The Cup* (1881) met some success when acted; raised to peerage as Baron Tennyson of Fresh·wa·ter and Ald·worth \'fresh-,wȯt-ər-ən(d)-'äl-,dwərth, -,wät-, -'ȯl-\ (1884). Showed active imagination and mature art during his last years in *Ballads and Other Poems* (1880; including "The Revenge," "Defence of Lucknow," "Rizpah"), *Tiresias and Other Poems* (1885; including "To Virgil" and "The Ancient Sage"), *Locksley Hall Sixty Years After* (1886), and *Demeter and Other Poems* (1889, including "The Progress of Spring," "Merlin and the Gleam," and "Crossing the Bar"), and *Death of Oenone, Akbar's Dream, and Other Poems* (1892); his play *The Foresters* (1892) successfully produced in New York. Buried in Westminster Abbey.

His two elder brothers were poets: ¶Frederick (1807–1898) contributed to *Poems by Two Brothers* (1827); author of *Days and Hours* (lyrics, 1854), *The Isles of Greece* (1890), *Daphne* (1891), and *Poems of the Day and Year* (1895). ¶Charles Tennyson Tur·ner \'tər-nər\ (1808–1879) entered the church, took name Turner under will of a great-uncle (1830); besides contributing to *Poems by Two Brothers* (1827), published over 300 sonnets (1830–80).

Alfred's eldest son ¶Hallam (1852–1928), 2d baron, was governor and commander in chief of South Australia (1899–1902); governor general of Commonwealth of Australia (1902–04); author of *Alfred, Lord Tennyson: a Memoir* (1897); editor of his father's works, with notes (1908).

Tenskwatawa. See under TECUMSEH.

Ten·zing \'ten-,ziŋ\, Norkey. 1914–1986. Nepalese mountaineer. Sherpa guide; served as porter with British, French, and Swiss expeditions in Himalayas (1935–52); with Sir Edmund Hillary made the first summit ascent of Mount Everest, May 29, 1953; director (from 1954) of field training at Himalayan Mountaineering Institute, Darjeeling, India.

Te·ra·u·chi \ter-ä-üch-ē\ Hisaichi. Count. 1879–1946. Japanese army officer. Son of Terauchi Masatake. General (1935); minister of war (1936–37); commander in North China (1938); member of supreme war council (1938 ff.); commander of Japanese forces in Southwest Pacific (1942).

Terauchi Masatake. *Orig.* Ta·da \'tä-dä\ Jusaburō. 1852–1919. Japanese general and politician. Adopted into Terauchi family in youth; protégé of Yamagata Aritomo; minister of war (1902–10); general (1906); governor general of Korea (1910); annexed Korea (1910); premier of Japan (1916–18).

Ter·borch *or* **Ter Borch** \tər-'bȯrk\, Gerard. 1617–1681. Dutch painter. Studied under his father Gerard (1584–1662), and under Molijn; known for portraits and interior genre paintings, esp. of middle class life; his canvases included *Peace Congress of Münster* (1648), *The Reading Lesson, The Concert, Paternal Admonition, Guitar Lesson, The Letter, The Smoker, The Toilet, A Lady Playing the Theorbo.*

Ter·brug·ghen \tər-'brœg-ən\, Hendrik. 1588–1629. Dutch painter. Studied under Abraham Bloemaert; in Rome (c.1604–c.1614); lived in Utrecht. His paintings, influenced by Caravaggio's chiaroscuro style, included two versions of *Calling of St. Matthew* (c.1617, 1621), *The Flute Player* (1621), *Crucifixion with the Virgin and St. John* (c.1625), and his masterpiece *St. Sebastian Tended by Irene and Her Maid* (1625).

Ter·ence \'ter-ən(t)s\. *Full Latin name* Publius Te·ren·ti·us Afer \tə-'ren-ch(ē-)ə-'sā-fər\. 186 or 185–?159 B.C. Roman playwright, b. Carthage. Taken to Rome as slave of a Roman senator, Terentius Lucanus, whose name he adopted when freed. A master of Latin comedy; much of his work modeled upon Menander; his plays, noted for purity of language and realism, included *Andria, Hecyra, Heauton timoroumenos, Eunuchus, Phormio,* and *Adelphi.*

Te·ren·ti·a·nus Mau·rus \tə-,ren-chē-'ā-nə-'smȯr-əs, -'smär-\. 2d century A.D. Roman prosodist. Author of hexameter treatise on prosody.

Terentius. See TERENCE.

Terentius Varro. See VARRO.

Te·re·sa \ter-'es-ə; *Angl* tə-'rē-sə, -'rā-, -zə\. 1070?–1130. Countess (1095–1112) and regent (1112–28) of Portugal. Natural daughter of Alfonso VI of León and Castile; m. (1095) Henry of Burgundy, Count of Portugal; on Henry's death (1112), took charge of government; refused to cede power to her son (later Afonso I) on his maturity; driven into exile by Afonso's followers (1128).

Te·re·sa \tā-'rā-sä\ of Ávi·la \'ä-b̲ē-lä\. Saint. *Sometimes called* Saint Teresa of Jesus. *Orig.* Teresa de Ce·pe·da y Ahu·ma·da \-t̲h̲ā-thā-'pā-t̲h̲ä-ē-ä-k̲ü-'mä-t̲h̲ä\. 1515–1582. Spanish religious. Entered Carmelite Convent of the Incarnation, Ávila (1535); founded (1562) Carmelite Reform (Discalced) order; founded many convents and monasteries; famous for her mystical visions; canonized (1622); made doctor of the church (1970). Author of spiritual classics *Camino de perfección* (1583), *Castillo interior* (1588), *Relaciones espirituales* (1588), *Libro de las fundaciones* (1610), and *Libro de su vida* (1611).

Teresa Benedicta of the Cross. See Edith STEIN.

Ter·hune \(,)tər-'hyün\, Albert Payson. 1872–1942. American writer, b. Newark, N.J. On staff of *New York Evening World* (1894–1916); author of many novels and short stories, esp. about dogs, as *Lad, a Dog* (1919), *Bruce* (1920), *The Heart of a Dog* (1926), *Lad of Sunnybank* (1928), etc.

Ter·man \'tər-mən\, Lewis Madison. 1877–1956. American psychologist, b. Johnson, Co., Ind. At Stanford U. (1910–42); developed the Stanford-Binet intelligence test; introduced term intelligence quotient (IQ). Author of *The Measurement of Intelligence* (1916), *Genetic Studies of Genius* (1926–59, with others), *Sex and Personality* (1936), *Psychological Factors in Marital Happiness* (1938).

Ter·mier \ter-myā\, Pierre-Marie. 1859–1930. French geologist. Professor at École Nationale Supérieure des Mines, Paris (1894); director, Service de la Carte Géologique de la France (1911); considered founder of modern tectonics and geodynamics; known for studies of the Eastern Alps. Works included *Les Nappes des Alpes orientales et la syntheses des Alpes* (1903), *À la gloire de la Terre* (1922), etc.

Ter·pan·der \(,)tər-'pan-dər\. fl. c.647 B.C. Greek musician and poet. Native of Lesbos; long resident in Sparta; known as "Father of Greek music" and regarded by some as founder of Greek lyrical poetry; said to have improved the lyre by increasing the number of its strings from 4 to 7, thus inventing the heptachord. Of his hymns to the gods, only a few lines are extant.

Ter·ra \'ter-rä\, Gabriel. 1873–1942. Uruguayan lawyer and politician. President of Uruguay (1931–38); made himself dictator (1933).

Ter·ra·gni \ter-'rän-yē\, Giuseppe. 1904–1942. Italian architect. Member of "Gruppo 7," which attempted to create an Italian tradition in modern building; his works, all at Como, included Novecomum apartment building (1927), Casa del Fascio (1932–36), S. Elia kindergarten (1936–37), etc.

Ter·ray \ter-e, -ā\, Joseph-Marie. 1715–1778. French priest and politician. Ecclesiastical counsellor to Parlement of Paris (1736); controller general of finances (1769–74); with aid of Maupeou, instituted series of financial reforms that dramatically increased government revenues; dismissed by Louis XVI due to pressure from nobles.

Ter·riss \'ter-əs\, William. *Orig.* William Charles James Lew·in \'lü-ən\. 1847–1897. English actor. Made London debut (1868); scored first success as Doricourt in Hannah Cowley's *Belle's Stratagem* (1873); played opposite Ellen Terry's Olivia in W.G. Wills's adaptation of *Vicar of Wakefield* (1878); in Shakespearean roles for Sir Henry Irving's Lyceum Theatre (1880–85); became public idol as leading man of the Adelphi Theatre (from 1885), playing Shakespeare and originating many roles. His daughter ¶Mary Ellaline (1871–1971) was actress under name Ellaline Terriss; m. (1893) Sir Seymour Hicks; popular in theater and music hall productions from 1890s to 1920s, esp. in her husband's plays as *Sleeping Partners* and *The Man in Dress Clothes.*

Ter·ry \'ter-ē\, Alfred Howe. 1827–1890. American army officer, b. Hartford, Conn. Engaged at First Bull Run, capture of Port Royal, S.C. (1861), and Fort Pulaski, Ga. (1862). Brigadier general (1862); engaged against Richmond and Petersburg (1864); brevetted major general (1864). Commanded land forces assaulting and capturing Fort Fisher (Dec. 1864–Jan. 1865); major general of volunteers (1865). Remained in regular army after Civil War, chiefly in the Northwest; commander of expedition against Sioux during which Col. Custer met defeat at Little Bighorn (1876).

Terry, Eli. 1772–1852. American clock manufacturer, b. South Windsor, Conn. Established clock factory in Plymouth, Conn. (1793); devoted himself to making shelf clocks with wooden works, perfecting (1814) a short shelf clock with light pillars and a scrolled top, known as the "Terry clock"; sold these in large quantities.

Terry, Dame Ellen, *in full* Alice Ellen. 1847–1928. English actress. Professional debut in London (1856); m. George Frederic Watts (1864; sep. 1865; div. 1877). Acted Katharine to Sir Henry Irving's Petruchio (1867); lived in retirement (1868–74) with Edward W. Godwin (*q.v.*), who fathered her son Edward Gordon Craig (*q.v.*). Success on stage as Portia (1875), and again as Olivia in W.G. Wills's adaptation of *Vicar of Wakefield* (1878). Irving's leading lady in Shakespearean roles and in plays by Wills, Tennyson, Charles Reade, Sardou (1878–1902); carried on (from 1890s) famous "paper courtship" in series of letters with George Bernard Shaw, who wrote several parts for her; received public tribute in jubilee (1906). Lectured on Shakespearean subjects in U.S., England, and Austrialia (1910–15); last appearance at Hammersmith in Walter de la Mare's *Crossings* (1925).

Ter·tul·lian \(,)tər-'təl-yən\. *Full Latin name* Quintus Septimius Florens Ter·tul·li·a·nus \(,)tər-,təl-ē-'ā-nəs\. c.155 or 160–after 220 A.D. Latin ecclesiastical writer, b. Carthage. One of the Fathers of the Church. Worked as jurist in Rome; returned to Cathage and converted to Christianity (c.190 A.D.); devoted himself to mastery of the Scriptures and the Christian literature; became a teacher and leading member of the African church; withdrew (c.210) from the orthodox church and became head of a small Montanist group in Carthage; broke with Montanists and formed own sect. Among his works were *Apologeticum* (a defense of Christianity), polemical treatises *Adversus Marcionem, De anima,* and *De praescriptione heriticorum,* and treatises on morals and discipline as *De cultu feminarum, De oratione,* and *De monogamia.*

Ter·za·ghi \ter-'zä-kē\, Karl. 1883–1963. American civil engineer, b. Prague. Professor at Robert College, Istanbul (1918–25), M.I.T. (1925–29), Technische Hochschule, Vienna (1929–38), Harvard (1946–56); naturalized U.S. citizen (1943); served as consultant to many construction projects. Founder of soil mechanics; chief works *Erdbaumechanik* (1925), *Soil Mechanics in Engineering Practice* (1948).

Tesch·ner \'tesk-ner\, Richard. 1879–1948. Czech puppeteer. Established (1911) puppet theater Figuren Spiegel in Vienna, where he adapted Javanese rod puppets to Western traditions; exerted great influence on 20th-century puppet revival.

Tes·la \'tes-lə\, Nikola. 1856–1943. American electrician and inventor, b. Smiljan, Croatia, of Serbian parents. Discovered (1881) principle of rotating magnetic field, basis of practically all alternating-current machinery; engineer in Paris (1882–84); constructed his first induction motor (1883); to U.S. (1884, naturalized 1889). Worked for Thomas Edison (1884–85); sold patent rights to his system of alternating-current machinery to George Westinghouse (1885); established own laboratory. Invented the Tesla coil (1891); his system used by Westinghouse to light the World's Columbian Exposition at Chicago (1893); won contract to install electric power machinery at Niagara Falls (1893); successfully demonstrated a wireless communications system (1897) and a radio-controlled boat (1898); discovered terrestrial stationary waves, lighted 200 lamps without wires from distance of 25 miles, and created artificial lightning (1899–1900).

Tes·sin \tes-'ēn\, Nicodemus, *called* the Elder. 1615–1681. Swedish architect. Appointed architectural director for Stockholm (1661) and court architect (1676); principal designer of royal palace of Drottningholm near Stockholm (begun 1662). His son ¶Nicodemus, *called* the Younger (1654–1728), was also an architect; completed the royal palace after his father's death; court superintendent; made count (1714). His son ¶Count Carl Gustaf (1695–1770) was a politician; succeeded his father as court superintendent (1728); a founder of the anti-Russian Hat party; elected speaker of parliament (1738); unable to prevent war with Russia (1741); became influential adviser to King Adolph Frederick; tutor to the future Gustav III (1746–54); head of chancellery (1746–52); retired (1761) from public life after losing queen's favor; also an accomplished poet and writer of fables and letters.

Te·tens \'tā-təns\, Johannes Nikolaus. 1736–1807. German mathematician and philosopher. Professor at Bützow (1760) and Kiel (1776); entered (1789) Danish public service, becoming assessor, then councilor of state and deputy in ministry of finance. As empirical philosopher, strongly influenced Immanuel Kant; chief works *Über die allgemeine spekulativische Philosophie* (1775) and *Philosophische Versuche über die menschliche Natur und ihre Entwickelung* (1777).

Tet·ma·jer \tet-'mä-yer\, Kazimierz. *Also* Tet·ma·jer-Prze·wa \-'mä-yerp-'sher-vä\. 1865–1940. Polish writer. One of the most popular members of Young Poland movement; his works included lyric poems *Poezje* (1891–1924), sketches and tales *Na skalnym Podhalu* (1904–10), novels *Król Andrzej* (1909) and *Grafal* (1910), and plays *Rewolucja* (1906) and *Judasz* (1917).

Te·traz·zi·ni \,tā-trät-'tsē-nē\, Luisa. 1871–1940. Italian coloratura soprano. Operatic debut as Inez in Meyerbeer's *L'Africaine* at Florence (1895); appeared at Covent Garden, London (1907) and Metropolitan Opera House, New York (1908); toured U.S. (1910–13); member of Chicago Opera Company (1913–14); resident chiefly in Italy (after 1914); sang notably in *Rigoletto, Lucia di Lammermoor, La Traviata.* Chicken Tetrazzini was named in her honor.

Tet·ri·cus \'tet-ri-kəs\, Gaius Pius Esuvius. 3d century A.D. Roman politician. Governor of Aquitania; pretender to throne of Western Roman Empire (270–274); defeated by Aurelian at Châlons (274); pardoned by Aurelian and appointed governor of southern Italy.

Te Tsung. See (1) Li Kua under Li family; (2) Tsai-t'ien.

Tet·zel *or* **Te·zel** \'tet-səl\, Johann. c.1465–1519. German Dominican monk. Inquisitor for Poland (1509); appointed (1517) by Archbishop Albert of Mainz to sell indulgences. His preaching aroused Luther to publish his 95 theses at Wittenberg (1517); answered Luther with 122 theses (actually composed by Konrad Wimpina), but was disowned and rebuked by Catholics.

Tev·fik \täv-'fēk\, Mehmed. *Pseudonym* Tevfik Fik·ret \fē-'krät\. *Also known earlier as* Tevfik Naz·mi \näz-'mē\. 1867–1915. Turkish poet. Considered founder of modern school of Turkish poetry. Editor of avant-garde periodical *Servet-i Fünun* (1896–1901); influenced by French Symbolist poets; attempted to adapt Turkish poetry to Western themes and verse forms. Author of collections of poems *Rübbab-i Shikeste* (1896) and *Haluk'un Defteri* (1911), and of anti-government polemic *Sis* (1902).

Tevfik Pa·şa \-pä-'shä\, Ahmed. 1845–1936. Turkish politician. Minister of foreign affairs (1895–1908); grand vizier (1909, 1918–19, 1920–22); ambassador at London (1909–14); head of Turkish delegation at London Conference (1921); fled to Egypt (1922) on deposition of sultan.

Te·vis \'tē-vəs, 'tev-əs\, Lloyd. 1824–1899. American businessman, b. Shelbyville, Ky. In partnership (from 1850) with James Ben Ali Haggin in Sacramento and (from 1853) in San Francisco; a promoter and president (1869–70) of Southern Pacific Railroad; president of Wells, Fargo & Co. (1872–92); owned large interests in mining, communications, and transportation companies.

Tewfik Pasha, Mohammed. See Tawfīq Pasha.

Te·wod·ros II \tā-'wó-drós\. *Orig.* Kas·sa \'käs-ä\. c.1818–1868. Emperor of Ethiopia (1855–68). Reunified Ethiopian kingdoms into one empire; attempted to abolish feudal system, gain control over Ethiopian church, modernize army, all unsuccessful; committed suicide after Napier expedition (1867–68) rescued British missionaries and envoys whom he had imprisoned.

Texeira. See Teixeira.

Tey, Josephine. See Elizabeth Mackintosh.

Tezel, Johann. See Tetzel.

Thā·bit ibn Qur·rah \'tä-bēt-,ib-ən-'kür-ä\. c.836–901. Syrian mathematician, physician, and philosopher. Court astronomer in Baghdad; author of treatises on mathematics, astronomy, mechanics, medicine, philosophy, ethics, etc.; also translated Greek mathematicians.

Thack·er·ay \'thak(-ə)-rē\, William Makepeace. *Pseudonyms:* Michael Angelo Tit·marsh \'tit-,märsh\, Charles James Yel·low·plush \'yel-(,)ō-,pləsh\, George Savage Fitz·boo·dle \fits-'büd-ᵊl\, Jeames \'jēmz\, Mr. Brown, Théophile Wag·staff \'wag-,staf\. 1811–1863. English novelist. Entered Middle Temple but turned to journalism; contributed regularly (from 1837) to periodicals in London; contributed *The Yellowplush Papers* (1837–38), *Catherine* (1839–40), *The Great Hoggarty Diamond* (1841), *Barry Lyndon* (1844) to *Fraser's Magazine;* published his first book *Paris Sketch-Book* (1840), followed by *Irish Sketch-Book* (1843); as contributor to *Punch* (1842–54), with pen and pencil, proved master of burlesque and gained wide recognition with *Jeames's Diary* and *The Book of Snobs,* among nearly 400 contributions; parodied novels of Bulwer-Lytton, Lever, and Disraeli in a series *Mr. Punch's Prize Novelists* (1847). Reached turning point in career with publication of *Vanity Fair* (1847–48) and maintained reputation as novelist of first rank with *Pendennis* (1848–50). Lecturer in England and (1852–53, 1854–55) America, taking as subjects *The English Humorists of the Eighteenth Century* (1851) and the *Four Georges* (1855). Reached height of his powers in *Henry Esmond* (1852) and *The Newcomes* (1853–55), showing a falling off in *The Virginians*

(1857–59). As editor of *Cornhill Magazine* (1859–62) contributed *Lovel the Widower* (1860), *The Adventures of Philip* (1861–62), *Roundabout Papers* (1860–63, essays), and *Denis Duval* (left unfinished at his death). Author also of *The Fitzboodle Papers* (1842–43), *Notes of a Journey from Cornhill to Grand Cairo* (1846), *The Kickleburys on the Rhine* (1850), *Rebecca and Rowena* (1850), *The Rose and the Ring* (1855), and ballads.

Thaddaeus. See JUDAS.

Tha·is \'thā-əs\. 4th century B.C. Greek hetaera. Mistress of Alexander the Great; according to tradition, incited Alexander to burn down the Persian palace at Persepolis.

Thai Sra. See BHUMINDARAJA.

Thai Ton. See HIEN VUONG.

Thal·berg \'thȯl-,bərg, 'thäl-\, Irving Grant. 1899–1936. American motion picture executive, b. Brooklyn, N.Y. As production manager (from 1924) of Metro-Goldwyn-Mayer Studios, Hollywood, was responsible for high artistic quality of its films, including esp. *Grand Hotel* (1932), *Mutiny On the Bounty* (1935), *Naughty Marietta* (1935), *Romeo and Juliet* (1936); called the "boy wonder of Hollywood"; discovered and developed many MGM film stars.

Thal·berg \'täl-,berk\, Sigismund Fortuné François. 1812–1871. German or Austrian pianist and composer. Said to be natural son of Prince von Dietrichstein; one of greatest piano virtuosos of his day; composer of a concerto, a sonata, études, fantasies, and variations on opera themes.

Tha·les \'thā-,lēz\ of Mi·let·us \mī-'lēt-əs, mə-\. 625?–?547 B.C. Greek philosopher and scientist. One of the Seven Wise Men of Greece. Gained fame in his own day by predicting an eclipse of the sun for May 28, 585 B.C. In mathematics, credited with discovering five geometrical theorems; considered by Aristotle to be the father of Greek philosophy; taught that water, or moisture, was the one element from which the world was formed.

Thäl·mann \'tel-,män\, Ernst. 1886–1944. German Communist leader. Joined Communist party (1920); head (from 1925) of Kommunistische Partei Deutschlands and made it subservient to the Comintern; candidate for president (1925, 1932); arrested and imprisoned during National Socialist revolution (1933).

Thamar. See TAMARA.

Thanet, Octave. See Alice FRENCH.

Thant \'thant, 'thänt\, U. 1909–1974. Burmese official. Secretary of ministry of information (1949–57); permanent Burmese representative to UN (1957–61); secretary general of United Nations (1961–71).

Than Tun \'tän-'tün\. *Also called* Tha·kin Than Tun \'tä-kēn-\. 1911–1968. Burmese politician. Founder and leader (1946–68) of White Flag Communist party of Burma; unsuccessfully revolted against government (1948); assassinated.

Tha·raud \tá-rō\, Jérôme (1874–1953) and his brother Jean (1877–1952). French journalists and novelists. Collaborated in writing *Dingley* (1902, Goncourt prize), *La Fête arabe* (1912), *Rabat* (1918), *Quand Israël est roi* (1921), *La Randonné de Samba Diouf* (1922), *Notre cher Péguy* (1926), etc.

Thar·ra·wad·dy Min \,tär-ə-'wäd-ē-'mēn\. d. 1846. Burmese king (1837–46), eighth of Konbaung, or Alaungpaya dynasty. Deposed his brother Bagyidaw; revoked Treaty of Yandabo; succeeded by his son Pagan Min.

Thatch, Edward. See TEACH.

Thax·ter \'thaks-tər\, Celia, *nee* Laigh·ton \'lāt-ᵊn\. 1835–1894. American poet, b. Portsmouth, N.H. m. (1851) Levi L. Thaxter (d. 1884). Her volumes of verse included *Poems* (1872), *Driftweed* (1879), *Poems for Children* (1884), *Idyls and Pastorals* (1886).

Thayendanegea. See Joseph BRANT.

Thayer \'tha(ə)r, 'the(ə)r, 'thā-ər\, Abbott Handerson. 1849–1921. American painter, b. Boston. Known for paintings of ideal figures as *Caritas* and *Virgin Enthroned*, and landscapes as *Winter Sunrise, Monadnock*.

Thayer, Ernest Lawrence. 1863–1940. American writer, b. Lawrence, Mass. Author of the poem "Casey at the Bat" (1888).

Thayer, Sylvanus. 1785–1872. American army officer and educator, b. Braintree, Mass. In U.S. army Corps of Engineers (from 1808). Superintendent, U.S.M.A., West Point (1817–33); established military organization and academic standards and methods of instruction which in their essential principles have been maintained since his superintendency; known as "Father of the Military Academy." Served on harbor fortifications and improvements (1833–63). Founded (1867) and endowed Thayer School of Engineering at Dartmouth College.

The·ae·te·tus \thē-'ēt-ət-əs\. c.414–c.369 B.C. Greek mathematician. Disciple of Socrates; provided a geometric basis for irrational numbers; author of Books X and XIII of Euclid's *Elements*. Eponym of one of Plato's dialogues.

The·ag·e·nes \thē-'aj-ə-,nēz\. 7th century B.C. Greek tyrant of Megara (640–620 B.C.). Credited with construction of an aqueduct for the city.

Thebaud, Simon. See SIMON of Sudbury.

Thec·la \'thek-lə\. Saint. 1st century A.D. Christian saint of Asia Minor. Reputedly a disciple of Saint Paul; said to have been the first woman martyr; one of the most famous saints of the Greek church.

Theebaw. See THIBAW.

Thei·le \'tī-lə\, Johann. 1646–1724. German composer. Composer of operas as *Adam und Eva* (1678), and esp. sacred music, including a *St. Matthew Passion* (1673), masses, motets, and Psalms.

Thei·ler \'tī-lər\, Max. 1899–1972. American physician and bacteriologist, b. Pretoria, South Africa. To U.S. (1922); on staff of Harvard Medical School (1922–30) and Rockefeller Institute, New York (1930–64); professor at Yale Medical School (1964–67). Awarded Nobel prize for physiology or medicine (1951) for discoveries concerning yellow fever and the 17-D vaccine (1937) to combat it.

The·mis·ti·us \thə-'mis-chē-əs, -tē-əs\. c.317–c.388. Greek rhetorician and politician. Taught rhetoric in Constantinople (from c.345); appointed senator (355); prefect of Constantinople (383–384). Author of panegyrics addressed to successive emperors of the East, and of paraphrases of some of Aristotle's works.

The·mis·to·cles \thə-'mis-tə-,klēz\. c.524–c.460 B.C. Athenian statesman and general. Elected archon (493); led party opposed to Aristides (*q.v.*); began development of Piraeus, the port of Athens, and induced Athenians to increase their naval strength. Commanded Athenian fleet in the victory over Persians at Salamis (480 B.C.). Continued urging measures for Athens's safety, including expansion of the fleet and land fortifications, but was ostracized (c.470). Accused of complicity in the treason of Pausanias, he was exiled; finally went to Persia, was received and pensioned by Artaxerxes.

Thé·nard \tā-nár\, Louis-Jacques. Baron. 1777–1857. French chemist. Taught at Collège de France (from 1802) and the Sorbonne (from 1809); chancellor of U. of Paris (1845–52); made baron (1825); member of Chamber of Deputies (1828–32). Author of a textbook *Traité élémentaire de chimie théorique et practique* (1813–16), which was standard for 25 years; with his friend Gay-Lussac (*q.v.*), carried on many researches; credited with discovery of hydrogen peroxide (1818); first prepared (1799) Thénard's blue, a coloring matter used for porcelain.

The·o·bald \'thē-ə-,bȯld, 'tib-əld\. c.1090–1161. Anglo-Norman prelate. Abbot of abbey of Bec (1136); archbishop of Canterbury (1138); after brief allegiance to Empress Matilda, crowned Stephen king; effected reconciliation (1153) between Stephen and Henry, Duke of Normandy, who became Henry II (1154); crowned Henry II. Made his archdeacon Thomas Becket chancellor to succeed him (1155) but was disappointed when Becket switched to cooperate with Henry II's ecclesiastical policy. Resisted efforts of monasteries to throw off episcopal control; introduced study of civil law and established canonical jurisprudence in England.

Theobald, Lewis. 1688–1744. English playwright and Shakespearean critic. Translated from Plato, the Greek dramatists, and Homer; wrote essays, biographies, and poems. In a pamphlet *Shakespeare Restored* (1726), criticized Pope's edition; immortalized as hero of first version of Pope's *Dunciad* (1728). Published edition of Shakespeare (7 vols., 1734) that placed him in front rank of Shakespearean commentators.

Theobald, Simon. See SIMON of Sudbury.

The·oc·ri·tus \thē-'äk-rət-əs\. c.310–250 B.C. Greek poet, b. Syracuse. Regarded as creator of pastoral poetry; his extant poems include bucolics and mimes, set in the country, and epics, lyrics, and epigrams with urban settings.

The·o·da·had \'thē-ə-də-,had\. d. 536. King of the Ostrogoths (534–536). Nephew of Theodoric; co-ruler with his cousin Queen Amalasuntha; intrigued to have Amalasuntha assassinated (535); attacked by armies of Justinian under Belisarius and defeated; assassinated by an officer of his own army.

The·o·do·lin·da \,thē-əd-ə-'lin-də\. d. 628. Lombard queen. Daughter of Garibald, Duke of Bavaria; m. (c.590) Lombard king Authari; on Authari's death (c.590), chose Agilulf as king and married him; persuaded Agilulf to adopt Catholic, instead of Arian, policies; regent during minority of her son Adaloald; retired to private life after his assassination (c.626).

The·o·do·ra \,thē-ə-'dōr-ə, -'dȯr-\. Name of three empresses of the Eastern Roman Empire:

Theodora. c.500–548. In early life an actress noted for her beauty; married Justinian I (525); exerted for 20 years a great influence over him and over the political and religious events of the empire; at time of Nika riot (532) prevented emperor from fleeing; ended persecution of Monophysites (533).

Theodora. c.810–862. Second wife of Emperor Theophilus (829); on his death (842), made regent for their son Michael III; devoted iconodule, caused iconoclasts to be expelled from office and brought back image worship; forced to retire to a convent (858).

Theodora. 980–1056. Daughter of Constantine VIII and elder sister of Zoe; plotted against Zoe (1031); crowned coempress (1042); joint ruler with Zoe (1042–50) and Constantine IX (1042–55); on latter's death became sole empress (1055–56), last of Macedonian dynasty.

Theodora. 10th century. Roman noblewoman. Wife of Theophylactus; granted title of "Senatrix" because of her influence in Roman and papal affairs; much profligacy, probably exaggerated, attributed to her and her daughter Marozia (*q.v.*).

The·o·dore \'thē-ə-,dō(ə)r, -,dȯ(ə)r\. Saint. c.602–690. Greek prelate, b. Cilicia. Consecrated archbishop of Canterbury by Pope Vitalian (668); to England (669) and founded a Greek school at Canterbury; gained submission of heterogeneous churches of several English kingdoms and established ecclesiastical unity; held first synod of clergy at Hertford (673), and later synods; divided diocese of Wilfrid into four, appointed bishops to them, who were displaced by Pope Agatho for Wilfrid's appointees; divided Mercia into five dioceses; reconciled to Wilfred (686); supervised, and wrote in part, a penitential (still extant).

Theodore. Name of two popes and one antipope:

Theodore I. d. 649. Pope (642–649). A Greek of Jerusalem; opposed the Monotheletes; excommunicated Pyrrhus I (648) and deposed (649) Paul, patriarchs of Constantinople; condemned the Ecthesis of the emperor Heraclius.

Theodore II. d. 897. Pope (Nov. 897). Validated pontificate of Formosus and honorably buried his corpse; may have been murdered.

Theodore. 7th century. Antipope (Sept.–Dec. 687). A Roman archpriest; antipope with Paschal in opposition to Sergius I; after a second election, acknowledged Sergius.

Theodore I. King of Corsica. See Theodor von NEUHOF.

Theodore. Name of two Nicaean emperors of the Eastern Roman Empire:

Theodore I Las·ca·ris \'las-kə-rəs\. c.1175–1222. First Nicaean emperor (1208–22). Son-in-law of Alexius III; soldier, fought against Franks when Constantinople fell (1204); rallied Greeks and Byzantines and founded new empire at Nicaea, in Asia Minor; assumed title of emperor (1208); able general and administrator; defeated Latins, Trebizond emperor David Comnenus, Turkish sultan Kaikhosrau (1211); annexed much of Trebizond; strengthened ties with Latin empire by marrying daughter of Empress Yolande; negotiated settlement (1222) with Robert of Courtenay, to whom he bethrothed his daughter Eudocia.

Theodore II Lascaris. 1222–1258. Emperor (1254–58). Son of John III Ducas and grandson of Theodore I Lascaris; renewed alliance with Seljuq sultan of Rūm; repulsed Bulgarians (1255–56); able ruler and a good soldier; at death was waging war against Nicephorus of Epirus; well educated and an author of many works.

Theodore. Czars of Russia. See FYODOR.

Theodore of **Mop·su·es·tia** \,mäp-sü-'es-ch(ē)ə\. c.350–428 or 429. Greek theologian. Considered greatest exegete of his time; spiritual head of the school of Antioch. With his friend St. John Chrystostom, studied under Libanius; ordained (381); became bishop of Mopsuestia (c.392). Opposed Monophysite doctrines of the school of Alexandria; considered main authority on matters of faith by Nestorian church; wrote commentaries on biblical books, Nicene Creed, the Lord's Prayer, the sacraments, and on theological and practical problems.

Theodore of **Rhai·thu** \'rī-,thü\. 6th century. Greek theologian. Theologian-monk of monastery at Rhaithu (modern aṭ-Ṭūr); considered last of Neo-Chalcedonian authors; in *Proparaskeuē* (written c.580–620), attempted to harmonize Chalcedonian doctrine with terminology of St. Cyril of Alexandria. Thought to be identical with the semi-Monophysite Theodore, bishop of Pharan. Possible author of Aristotelian *Compendium of Logic.*

Theodore As·ci·das \-'as-kəd-əs\. *Also called* The·o·do·ros As·ki·das \tā-ō-'dȯr-ō-'säs-kēd-äs\. d. 558. Greek prelate and theologian. As monk, perhaps also abbot, of "New Laura" monastery near Jerusalem, became spokesman of Origenists; contended with Pelagius and Mennas; archbishop of Caesarea (537); at Council of Constantinople (553), submitted (with Leontius of Byzantium) the *enhypostasia* formula to conciliate the Christological controversy.

Theodore bar Ko·nai \-bär-'kō-,nī\. 9th century. Syrian scholar. Native of Kaškar; probably a monk in Nestorian church; author of *Liber scholiorum,* a vast collection of annotations on the entire Syriac Bible.

Theodore Pro·dro·mus \-'prō-drə-məs\. *Sometimes called* Pto·cho·pro·dro·mus \,tō-kō-'prō-drə-məs\, *i.e.* Poor Prodromus. d. c.1166. Byzantine writer. Frequented courts of John II Comnenus and Manuel I; author of satirical epigrams, dialogues, letters, and occasional prose and verse pieces; works provide information on contemporary history; became a monk in later life.

Theodore Stu·di·tes \-st(y)ü-'dīt-,ēz\. Saint. *Also called* Theodore of Stu·di·us \-'st(y)üd-ē-əs\. 759–826. Byzantine theologian. Abbot of monastery near Mt. Olympus in Bithynia (794); exiled (796–797) for opposing adulterous second marriage of Constantine VI; with his community, moved (799) to monastery of Studius in Constantinople, where he instituted a policy of asceticism and monastic reform; exiled (816–820) for leading opposition to Iconoclasm; advocate of church independence from imperial power.

The·od·o·ret \thē-'äd-ə-rət\ of Cyr·rhus \'sir-əs\. c.393–c.458. Greek theologian of the Antioch school. Bishop of Cyrrhus (423 A.D.); deposed (449) by Alexandrian "Robber Synod" at Ephesus; restored by Council of Chalcedon (451). Vigorous opponent of Monophysite doctrine of Alexandrian school; defender of Nestorius. Author of a church history, commentaries, exegeses, controversial treatises, biographies, etc.

The·od·o·ric \thē-'äd-ə-rik\. *Late Lat.* The·od·o·ri·cus \thē-,äd-ə-'rī-kəs, ,thē-ə-də-\. *Ger.* Die·trich \'dē-trik\. *Often called* Theodoric the Great. 454?–526. King of the Ostrogoths and founder of the Ostrogothic kingdom in Italy. Son of a chieftain of the Amalings, b. Pannonia. Succeeded father as king (474); engaged in series of wars, sometimes against Emperor Zeno, sometimes in his service (474–487); began invasion of Italy (488); defeated Odoacer at Aquileia and Verona (489); completed conquest (489–493); caused death of Odoacer in violation of treaty and became sole ruler of Italy (493); issued Edict of Theodoric (506); made Ravenna his capital; defeated Franks and Bulgarians in minor wars and consolidated empire to include Sicily, Dalmatia, and part of the German lands; promoted harmony between Goths and Romans; an Arian, but tolerated Catholicism. Father of Amalasuntha (*q.v.*). In Teutonic legends, esp. in the *Nibelungenlied,* known as Dietrich von Bern \fòn-'bern\, *i.e.* Theodoric of Verona.

Theodoric I. d. 451. King of the Visigoths (419–451). Son of Alaric; killed at battle of Châlons-sur-Marne while fighting with Romans against Huns under Attila. His son ¶Theodoric II (426–466), king of the Visigoths (453–466); assassinated his brother King Thorismond (*q.v.*); invaded Spain and made conquests on Iberian Peninsula; assassinated by his brother Euric.

The·o·do·rus Lec·tor \,thē-ə-'dōr-ə-'slek-tər, -'dȯr\. *Eng.* Theodore the Reader. 6th century. Byzantine historian. Reader (*anagnōstēs*) at basilica of Hagia Sophia, Constantinople (520–530); using works of Socrates Scholasticus, Sozomen, and Theodoret of Cyrrhus, compiled *Eklogē ek tōn ekklēsiastikōn historiōn,* better known as *Historia tripartita,* covering Byzantine history 313–439; wrote continuation of the *Eklogē,* covering 450–518.

The·o·do·sius I \,thē-ə-'dō-sh(ē-)əs\. *Called* the Great. 347–395. Roman general and emperor (379–395), b. Spain. Son of General Flavius Theodosius. Accompanied his father into Britain (368); defeated Sarmatians in Moesia (374); summoned by Gratian to share empire (378); made augustus at Sirmium (379); given Egypt and the East and entrusted with their protection against Goths; made peace with Visigoths and Ostrogoths along the Danube (379–386); allowed Goths to settle within the empire; established creed of Council of Nicaea as the orthodox religion; gave son Arcadius title of augustus (383); accepted Maximus as colleague in the West (383–388); finally overthrew him (388) at Aquileia; at Milan (388–391), with short visit to Rome (389); humiliated himself publicly before Bishop Ambrose (390) as penance for cruel vengeance upon Thessalonica; aroused by murder of coemperor Valentinian II, led army against Eugenius and Arbogast and defeated them at Frigidus near Aquileia (394); caused second son, Honorius, to be proclaimed emperor of the West under guardianship of Stilicho (395); died at Milan.

Theodosius. Name of two rulers of the Eastern Roman Empire (see also THEODOSIUS I, Roman emperor before the division):

Theodosius II. 401–450. Emperor (408–450). Son of Arcadius; during minority (408–421) empire ably ruled by praetorian prefect Anthemius (d. 414) and emperor's sister Pulcheria, who ruled jointly with him (414–450); married (421) Eudocia, daughter of an Athenian philosopher; government controlled by corrupt Chrysaphius (after c.440). During reign his generals fought two wars against Persia (422 and 447); sent great fleet that ended piracies of Vandals (431); repulsed Huns (408), but later paid large tributes to keep Attila and armies out of the Balkans; Council of Ephesus (431); publication (438) of the Theodosian Code, a collection of imperial constitutions.

Theodosius III. d. after 717. Emperor (715–717). An obscure and incapable tax official, raised to the throne; forced to retire in favor of Leo III.

Theodosius. 2d century B.C. Greek geometer and astronomer. Chief work *Sphaerica,* on the geometry of the sphere.

Theodosius of Alexandria. d. 566. Byzantine prelate. Patriarch of Alexandria (535–566); opposed extreme Monophysitism; detained (536–566) in Constantinople while Justinian attempted to impose Chalcedonian doctrine on Egyptian church; wrote Coptic sermons and expositions of his moderate Monophysite doctrine.

Theodosius of Palestine. Saint. c.423–529. Byzantine religious. Introduced (c.451) to ascetic life by Simeon the Stylite and others; headed an ascetic monastic community near Bethlehem; elected (493) archimandrite of all convents in Jerusalem area; vigorous opponent of Monophysitism.

Theodosius I Bo·ra·di·o·tes \,bȯr-ə-'dī-ə-,tēz\. d. after 1183. Byzantine prelate. Patriarch of Constantinople (1179–83); persuaded Manuel I Comnenus to uphold stringent wording of oath taken by Muslim converts to Christianity; opposed reunification of Greek and Latin churches; guardian of Greek Orthodox morality at Byzantine court; forced to abdicate for refusing sanction of marriage of Emperor Andronicus I Comnenus's daughter.

The·o·do·tion \ˌthē-ə-ˈdō-shən\. 2d century A.D. Jewish scholar. Probably from Ephesus; compiled (c.180–190) a Greek version of the Old Testament which is sole remaining source of the complete Greek text of certain Old Testament books.

The·od·o·tus \thē-ˈäd-ət-əs\. *Also called* Theodotus the Tanner. 2d century A.D. Byzantine theologian. A tanner by trade; to Rome (c.189); espoused a form of Adoptionism termed "Dynamic Monarchianism"; excommunicated by Pope Victor (190). His sect of Theodotians continued into the next century.

Theodotus of An·cy·ra \an-ˈsī-rə\. d. c.466. Byzantine prelate. Bishop of Ancyra; at Council of Ephesus (431), was principal opponent of Nestorius on the Christological issue; maintained orthodox position of St. Cyril of Alexandria; denounced by the Nestorian Synod of Tarsus (432); wrote sermons and "Explanation of the Creed of Nicaea."

Theodotus the Gnostic. 2d century A.D. Christian theologian. Followed teachings of Valentinus; a principal formulator of Eastern Gnosticism; taught in Asia Minor (c.160–170). His theology survives in *Excerpta ex Theodoto,* an appendix to Clement of Alexandria's *Stromata.*

The·o·dulf \ˈthē-ə-ˌdəlf\ of Orléans. *Also spelled* Theodulphe *or* The·o·dul·fus \ˌthē-ə-ˈdəl-fəs\. 750–821. Visigothic ecclesiastic and scholar. Renowned as one of cultural leaders in Carolingian renaissance. Bishop of Orléans (775); abbot of Fleury (781); succeeded Alcuin as Charlemagne's chief theological adviser (804); received the pallium from Pope Stephen IV (816); deposed (818) and imprisoned by Louis I the Pious for supposed participation in conspiracy of King Bernard of Italy. Patron of the arts; builder and restorer of churches; defended the *Filioque* clause in *De spiritu sancto;* also wrote treatise *De ordine Baptismi* and poem *Ad Carolum Regem.*

The·ō·dū·rus Abū Qur·rah \ˌtäō-ˈdü-rə-ab-ˈü-ˈkůr-rä\. *Also written* Theodore Abū Kurra. c.750–c.825. Syrian Greek Orthodox prelate and theologian. Became monk at monastery of St. Sabas near Jerusalem; Melchite bishop of Harran; engaged in dialogue with Islāmic and other non-Christian peoples of the area; deposed as bishop, possibly for his advocacy of the Christological doctrine of the Council of Chalcedon; returned to St. Sabas; journeyed (after 815) to Alexandria and Armenia to promote orthodox Christology. First known Christian writer to use Arabic; his writings, also in Syriac and Greek, included the "Letter to the Armenians" (813) against Iconoclasm and Monothelitism.

The·og·nis \thē-ˈäg-nəs\. 6th–5th century B.C. Greek elegiac poet. Active at Megara; one of the chief gnomic poets; about 1400 lines ascribed to him are extant.

The·og·nos·tos \ˌthē-əg-ˈnäs-təs\. 9th century. Byzantine religious. Supported Ignatius against Photius during the Photian schism; helped Ignatius compose his "Letter of Appeal"; delivered (c.861) letter to Pope Nicholas I at Rome and secured Nicholas's condemnation of Photius; appointed by Ignatius superior of Pēgē monastery and administrator of Hagia Sophia basilica of Constantinople.

The·og·nos·tus \ˌthē-əg-ˈnäs-təs\ of Alexandria. 3d century. Greek theologian. Head (from c.265) of the catechetical school at Alexandria; disciple of Origen; author of *Hypotypōseis,* a doctrinal compendium for use at his school.

The·o·lep·tus \ˌthē-ə-ˈlep-təs\ of Philadelphia. c.1250–c.1326. Byzantine prelate and theologian. A married deacon of the Eastern church in Bithynia; actively opposed reunification of Eastern and Western churches; excommunicated (1274) by Patriarch John XI Beccus; retired (c.1275), probably to Mount Athos in Greece, to write on and practice Hesychasm; named archbishop of Philadelphia (1285); wrote polemical treatises against Beccus's unionist movement and against teachings of Patriarch Gregory II Cyprius, causing his dismissal.

The·on \ˈthē-ˌän\ of Alexandria. 4th century A.D. Greek mathematician. His recension of Euclid's *Elements* was only known Greek text of that work until an early 19th-century discovery of an earlier version; also wrote commentaries on Euclid's *Optics* and Ptolemy's *Syntaxis.*

The·oph·a·nes \thē-ˈäf-ə-ˌnēz\. *Called* the Confessor. c.752–818. Greek monk and chronicler. Founded the monastery of the Great Field near Cyzicus; opposed iconoclastic policy of Leo V; banished to island of Samothrace, where he died. At invitation of his friend George Syncellus, wrote (810–814) *Chronographia,* leading source for Byzantine history of the period it covered, 284–813 A.D.

Theophanes. *Called* the Greek. c.1330 or 1340–1405. Byzantine painter. Worked in Constantinople, the Crimea, and (after c.1370) in Russia; his murals, icons, and miniatures influenced the Novgorod and Moscow schools; painted the frescoes in Church of the Transfiguration at Novgorod (1378).

The·oph·a·no \thē-ˈäf-ə-ˌnō\. Name of two empresses of the Eastern Roman Empire:

Theophano. Saint. 866–893. First wife (m. 880) of Emperor Leo VI; famed for virtues and miracles.

Theophano. d. after 976. Second wife (m. 956) of Emperor Romanus II; of lowly birth; mother of Basil II and Constantine VIII; regent alone (963); wife of regent-emperor Nicephorus (969); exiled (970).

Theophano. Holy Roman empress. See under Emperor OTTO II.

Théophile. See Théophile de VIAU.

The·oph·i·lus \thē-ˈäf-ə-ləs\. d. 842. Emperor of the Eastern Roman Empire (829–842). Son of Michael II; a strong Iconoclast; also a great builder and lover of pomp and display; principal promoter of the 9th-century Byzantine renaissance of learning; in long war with Saracens (829–838), at first victorious but later (838) suffered severe defeat at Amorium in Phrygia, his chief ancestral city; captured Melitene (841).

Theophilus. d. 412. Greek prelate. Patriarch of Alexandria (385–412); destroyed many pagan shrines of North Africa, including temples of Mithra, Dionysius, and Sarapis; zealous opponent of Origenism, persecuted Origenist monks; effected condemnation and exile of John Chrysostom by Synod of the Oak (403); succeeded as patriarch by his nephew Cyril of Alexandria. Honored as saint by Egyptian Coptic church.

Theophilus. *Orig. probably* Roger of Hel·mars·hau·sen \ˈhel-märs-ˌhaů-zən\. 12th century. German Benedictine monk. Wrote (c.1110–40) *De diversis artibus,* account of craft techniques of the day. Probably identical with Roger of Helmarshausen, a German monk and metalworker who made (1100) a portable altar in cathedral of Paderborn.

Theophilus of Antioch. d. 180. Syrian prelate. Bishop of Antioch (by 170); one of the Fathers of the church; author of a defense of Christian religion; first known writer to use term "Trinity" of the Godhead.

The·o·phras·tus \ˌthē-ə-ˈfras-təs\. c.372–c.287 B.C. Greek philosopher and scientist. Disciple of Aristotle, and his successor (322 or 321) as head of Peripatetic school; continued teachings of Aristotle; distinguished in field of natural science with *Peri phytōn historia* and *Peri phytōn aitiōn;* wrote 30 character sketches *(Charaktēres)* delineating moral types.

The·o·phy·lac·tus \ˌthē-ō-fə-ˈlak-təs\. fl. 911 A.D. Roman nobleman and politician. Father of Marozia and grandfather of Alberic II; consul and senator; with his wife Theodora (*q.v.*), ruled Rome and the Holy See; extremely unscrupulous; eventually acquired countship of Tusculum.

Theophylactus of Ochri·da \ō-ˈkrēd-ä\. *Also written* The·oph·y·lact \thē-ˈäf-ə-ˌlakt\ of Ohrid \ˈō-ˌkrēd\. c.1050–c.1109. Greek prelate and scholar. Studied in Constantinople under Michael Psellus; deacon of basilica of Hagia Sophia; archbishop of Ochrida (c.1078); instrumental in diffusing Byzantine culture among the Balkan Slavs; aided in development of a native Bulgarian Orthodox church and literature, esp. by use of Old Church Slavonic religious texts; author of *Paideia Basilikē, Life of Clement of Ochrida, Allocutio de iis quorum Latini incusantur* (c.1090), letters, etc.

Theophylactus Sim·o·cat·tes \-ˌsim-ə-ˈkat-əs\. *Also written* Theophylact Sim·o·cat·ta \-ˌsim-ə-ˈkat-ə\. d. after 640. Byzantine historian. Prefect and imperial secretary at Constantinople under Heraclius; best known for his 8-volume history of the reign (582–602) of Emperor Maurice (written 628–638); also wrote *Peri diaphorōn physikōn aporēmatōn kai epilyseōn autōn* and *Epistolai ethikai, agroichikai, hetairikai.*

The·o·pom·pus \ˌthē-ō-ˈpäm-pəs\ of Chi·os \ˈkī-ˌäs\. b. c.380 B.C. Greek historian and rhetorician. Twice exiled from Chios, where he was leader of aristocratic party; studied in Athens under Isocrates; chief works, extant only in fragments, *Hellenica* (a history of Greece from 411 to 394), *Philippica* (a history of Philip of Macedon), and several panegyrics and hortatory addresses.

The·o·rell \te-ů-ˈrel\, Hugo, *in full* Axel Hugo Teodor. 1903–1982. Swedish biochemist. Professor, Uppsala (1932–33, 1935–36), Kaiser Wilhelm Inst., Berlin (1933–35); director of biochemical dept., Nobel Medical Inst., Stockholm (1937–70); known for studies of enzymes and coenzymes and elucidation of their precise chemical activities; awarded 1955 Nobel prize for physiology or medicine.

Theos. See ANTIOCHUS II of Syria.

Theos Philopator. See PTOLEMY XIII and XIV.

Theos Philopator Philadelphus Neos Dionysos. See PTOLEMY XII.

The·o·to·kó·pou·los \ˌtā-ó-tó-ˈkó-pü-lós\, Doménikos. *Also used spelling* Domenico The·o·to·co·pu·li \ˌtā-ə-tō-ˈkäp-(y)ə-lē\. *Known as* El Gre·co \äl-ˈgrā-kō\, *i.e.* the Greek. 1541–1614. Spanish painter, b. Candia, Crete. Studied under Titian in Venice (c.1560–70); in Rome (c.1570–76); resident in Toledo (from 1577). One of greatest artists and leading exponent of Spanish mysticism in painting. His works, chiefly of religious subjects, known for Mannerist style, contrast of vivid colors and shadowy settings, and elongated figures; canvases included *Christ Healing the Blind* (c.1570), *Espolio* (1577–79), *Martyrdom of St. Maurice* (1580–82), his masterpiece *Burial of the Conde de Orgaz* (1586–88), *Holy Family with the Magdalen* (1590–95), *St.*

Francis and Brother Leo Meditating on Death (1600–05), two series of *Apostolados* (1605–10, 1612–14), *Adoration of the Shepherds* (1612–14); also landscapes *View of Toledo* (c.1595) and *View and Plan of Toledo* (1610–14) and portraits.

The·ram·e·nes \thē-'ram-ə-nēz\. d. 404 or 403 B.C. Athenian politician and general. A leader of the Council of Four Hundred (411); overthrew it and established Committee of the Five Thousand (411); participated in destruction of Spartan fleet near Cyzicus (410); negotiated surrender of Athens to Lysander (405); became one of the Thirty Tyrants (404); accused of treason by Critias and required to drink hemlock.

Theresa. See TERESA.

Thé·rèse de Li·sieux \tā-rez-də-lēz-yœ\. Saint. *Orig.* Marie-Françoise-Thérèse Mar·tin \mär-taⁿ\. *Known as* the Little Flower *or* St. Thérèse of the Child Jesus. 1873–1897. French Carmelite nun. Member of the Carmelite convent at Lisieux (from 1888); developed doctrine of the "Little Way"; author of autobiography *Historie d'une âme* (1898); canonized (1925).

Ther·on \'ther-,än\. 5th century B.C. Tyrant of Acragas (488–472). With Gelon of Syracuse, defeated an invading Carthaginian army at Himera (480).

Thes·i·ger \'thes-ə-jər\, Frederick. 1st Baron Chelms·ford \'che(l)mz-fərd\. 1794–1878. English jurist. Called to bar (1818); solicitor general (1844); attorney general (1845, 1852); lord chancellor (1858–59, 1866–68). His son ¶Frederic Augustus (1827–1905), 2d Baron Chelmsford, was a soldier; served through Crimean War, Sepoy Mutiny, and Abyssinian campaign (1868); commanded troops in Kaffir war (1878) and Zulu war (1879); general (1888); lieutenant of Tower of London (1884–89). His son ¶Frederic John Napier (1868–1933), 1st Viscount Chelmsford, was a colonial administrator; governor of Queensland (1905–09), of New South Wales (1909–13); as viceroy of India (1916–21), formulated, with Edwin S. Montagu (*q.v.*), and put into effect (1920–21) system of dyarchy and other reforms which were rejected by followers of Gandhi; first lord of the admiralty (1924); agent general for New South Wales (1926–28).

Thes·pis \'thes-pəs\. 6th century B.C. Greek poet. Reputed founder of the tragic drama (hence the word thespian, an actor); said to have introduced monologues, and perhaps dialogues, in the existing choruses of hymns to Bacchus and other deities; first to win a prize for tragedy at City Dionysia (c.534 B.C.).

Theu·de·bald \'tüe-də-,bält\. d. 555. Merovingian king of Austrasia (548–555). Son and successor of Theudebert I; unable to continue his father's dynamic policies.

Theu·de·bert \'tüe-də-,bert\. Name of two Merovingian kings of Austrasia:
Theudebert I. d. 548. King (534–548). Son and successor of Theuderic I; made many conquests in Germany and northern Italy.
Theudebert II. d. 611 or 612. King (595 or 596–c.611). Elder son of Childebert II; incurred hostility of his grandmother Brunhilda, who successfully incited his brother Theuderic II to overthrow him.

Theu·der·ic \'tüed-ə-rik\. *Fr.* Thier·ry \tyer-ē\. Name of four Merovingian kings of Austrasia:
Theuderic I. d. 534. King (511–534). Became king of Austrasia when the Frankish realm of his father Clovis was partitioned; annexed Thuringia.
Theuderic II. d. 613. Son of Childebert II; inherited (595 or 596) kingdoms of Orléans and Burgundy; with support from his grandmother Brunhilda, deposed (c.611) his brother Theudebert II and gained throne of Austrasia.
Theuderic III. d. 690 or 691. King (679–690 or 691). Succeeded his brother Chlotar III as king of Neustria and Burgundy (673); deposed in favor of brother Childeric II but restored (675); again deposed and restored (676); became king of Austrasia (679).
Theuderic IV. d. 737. King of Neustria, Burgundy, and Austrasia (721–737). Son of Dagobert III; penultimate ruler of Merovingian dynasty.

Theu·di·us \thā-'üd-ē-əs\. 4th century B.C. Greek mathematician and philosopher. Last compiler before Euclid of the geometric *Elements;* his version was one probably used in Greek Academy and quoted by Aristotle.

Thiard, Pontus de. See TYARD.

Thi·baud \tē-bō\, Jacques. 1880–1953. French violinist. Known for performances of Mozart, Beethoven, and 19th-century French works; soloist with orchestra of Édouard Colonne (1898–99); toured widely; formed (1905) trio with Alfred Cortot and Pablo Casals.

Thi·bau·deau \tē-bō-dō\, Antoine-Clair. Comte. 1765–1854. French politician. Member of the National Convention (1792); president of the Council of Five Hundred (1796); ennobled (1809); exiled (1816–30); appointed to the Senate (1852).

Thi·bault \tē-bō\, Jacques-Anatole-François. *Pseudonym* Anatole France \fräⁿs\. 1844–1924. French writer. Noted for the wit, urbanity, irony, skepticism, and literary style of his works. Published *Poèmes dorés* (1873), literary criticism *La Vie littéraire* (1888–92), and novels *Le Crime de Sylvestre Bonnard* (1881), *Thaïs* (1890), *La Rôtisserie de la Reine Pédauque* (1893), *Les Opinions de M. Jérôme Coignard* (1893), *Le Lys rouge* (1894). Influenced by his support of Alfred Dreyfus, introduced social and political concerns into his play *L'Affaire Crainquebille* (1901) and novels *Histoire contemporaine* (collective title for *L'Orme du mail,* 1897; *Le Mannequin d'osier,* 1897; *L'Anneau d'améthyste,* 1899; *Monsieur Bergeret à Paris,* 1900), *L'Île des pingouins* (1908), *Les Dieux ont soif* (1912), *La Petit Pierre* (1918), *La Vie en fleur* (1922). Awarded Nobel prize for literature (1921).

Thibaut. Counts of Blois. See BLOIS.

Thi·baut IV \tē-bō\. 1201–1253. Count of Champagne and Brie (1201–53) and king of Navarre (1234–53). Joined (1226) league of barons opposed to Blanche of Castile, but soon became reconciled with her; led crusade of 1239–40. Most famous of the aristocratic trouvères; some 60 lyrics and 9 religious poems are extant.

Thi·baut \'tē-bō\, Anton Friedrich Justus. 1772–1840. German jurist. Professor at Kiel (1798), Jena (1802), Heidelberg (1806); his demand for codification of German law vigorously opposed by F.K. von Savigny. Chief works *Theorie der logischen Auslegung des römischen Rechts* (1799), *System des Pandektenrechts* (1803).

Thi·baw *or* **Thee·baw** \'tē-,baù\. 1858–1916. Last king of Burma (1878–85). Son of Mindon Min; strongly influenced by his wife Supayalat and her mother; sought French aid against the British, concluding (1885) a commercial treaty with Paris; defied British ultimatum demanding reconsideration of cheating charge against British company; defeated in Third Burmese War and deposed (1885), Burma being annexed into province of British Burma; exiled to India.

Thiel·mann \'tēl-män\, Johann Adolf von. Freiherr. 1765–1824. German soldier. Commandant of fortress of Torgau (1813); commanded 3d Prussian army corps (1815) and was engaged at Ligny and Wavre, contributing to final allied victory at Waterloo.

Thier·ry \tyer-ē\. 1100–1168. Count of Alsace and Flanders. Nephew of Robert II; contested county of Flanders with William Clito on death (1127) of Charles the Good; claim secured on William's death (1128); marriage of his son Philip to Elizabeth of Vermandois won county international prestige and extended its boundaries south toward Paris.

Thierry. Merovingian kings. See THEUDERIC.

Thierry, Augustin, *in full* Jacques-Nicolas-Augustin. 1795–1856. French historian. A leading interpreter of the Middle Ages in spirit of Romanticism; renown rests on *Historie de la conquête de l'Angleterre par les Normands* (1825) and *Lettres sur l'histoire de France* (1827).

Thierry de Chartres \-də-shärtrᵊ\. *Also known as* Thierry the Breton. *Lat.* The·o·do·ri·cus Bri·to \,thē-ə-'dōr-ə-kəs-,brit-(,)ō, -'dòr-\ *or* Ter·ri·cus Car·no·ten·sis \'ter-i-kə-,skär-nə-'ten(t)-səs\. c.1100–c.1156. French educator and theologian. Brother of Bernard of Chartres; taught at Chartres and (after 1136) at Paris; became archbishop and chancellor of Chartres (1141); attended Diet of Frankfurt (1149); retired to monastic life (c.1155). One of foremost Scholastic philosophers of his day; his *Heptateuchon* contains classics of the seven liberal arts.

Thiers \tyer\, Louis-Adolphe. 1797–1877. French politician and historian. Formed lifelong friendship with Mignet (*q.v.*). To Paris (1821); identified himself with opposition. Under Louis-Philippe held ministries of interior (1832, 1834–36) and of trade and public works (1833–34); premier and minister of foreign affairs (1836, 1840). In Revolution of 1848 a moderate, friendly to Republic; banished (1851–52); leader of Liberal opposition (1863–70), attacking Napoléon III's imperial policies. After Franco–Prussian War, led in rehabilitation of France and negotiated peace treaty with Germany (1871); crushed Paris Commune (1871). First president of Third Republic (1871–73); resigned, defeated by Monarchists and Clericals; led republican opposition (from 1873). Wrote *Histoire de la révolution française* (1823–27) and *Historie du consulat et de l'empire* (1845–62).

Thiet·mar \'tēt-,mär\ *or* **Diet·mar** \'dēt-,mär\ *or* **Dith·mar** \'dit-,mär\. 975–1018. German chronicler. Prior of convent of Walbeck (1002); bishop of Merseburg (1009–18); author of history *(Chronicon)* of Saxon sovereigns.

Thi·mon·nier \tē-mòn-yā\, Barthélemy. 1793–1859. French tailor. Patented in France (1830) first sewing machine put to practical use.

Thir·kell \'thər-kəl\, Angela Margaret, *nee* Mac·kail \mə-'kāl\. 1890–1961. English novelist. Cousin of Rudyard Kipling; m. (1918) as 2d husband G.L. Thirkell. Author of over 30 novels about middle- and upper-class life in "Barsetshire" dealing with descendants of Trollope's Barsetshire characters, including *Coronation Summer* (1937), *Pomfret Towers* (1938), *The Brandons* (1939), *Northbridge Rectory* (1941), *Growing Up* (1943), *Headmistress* (1945), *Miss Bunting* (1946), *The Duke's Daughter* (1951), etc.

This·tle·wood \'this-əl-,wùd\, Arthur. 1770–1820. English conspirator. Plotted assassination of Castlereagh and other cabinet ministers at the Earl of Harrowby's house, but was captured and hanged.

Thö·köly \'tœ-kœlʸ\, Imre. Count. 1657–1705. Hungarian patriot. Led insurrections against Austria (from 1678) with Turkish aid; forced Leopold I to restore Hungarian liberties in Treaty of Sopron (1681) and recognize his own quasi-sovereignty in north Hungary; continued campaigns against Austria until

Treaty of Karlowitz (1699); created by sultan prince of Widdin; resided thereafter in Constantinople.

Tho·ma \'tō-mä\, Hans. 1839–1924. German painter. Painted landscapes, genre scenes, portraits, religious and allegorical subjects; also known as lithographer, etcher, and illustrator.

Thoma, Ludwig. *Pseudonym* Peter Schle·mihl \shlā-'mēl\. 1867–1921. German journalist and writer. Editor of *Simplizissimus* (1899); known esp. as author of humorous sketches of Bavarian life, dramas, and satires.

Tho·mas \'täm-əs\. Saint. *Aramaic* Te'·o·ma \tā-'ō-mə\. *Gr.* Did·y·mus \'did-ə-məs\. d. traditionally 53 A.D. One of the twelve Apostles. His character outlined in Gospel of John, which contains story of his doubt of Jesus's resurrection until he had physical proof; according to tradition, preached in Parthia and India.

Thomas. Duke of Clar·ence \'klar-ən(t)s, 'kler-\. 1388–1421. English prince. Second son of Henry IV; lord lieutenant of Ireland (1401–13); created duke of Clarence (1412); took part in siege of Harfleur (1415); regent for brother Henry V (1416); led assault of Caen (1417); killed at Baugé.

Thomas. Earl of Lancaster, Leicester, Derby, Lincoln, and Salisbury. c.1278–1322. English nobleman. Son of Edmund, Earl of Lancaster, and grandson of Henry III. Leader, chiefly from personal ambition, of baronial opposition to Edward II; effected banishment of Piers Gaveston (1308); obliged Edward to surrender power to 21 "ordainers"; brought about execution of Gaveston (1312); took advantage of English defeat at Bannockburn (1314) to wrest control from Edward, but himself equally feeble in administration because of quarrels with barons and private war against Earl Warenne; reconciled with Edward by Treaty of Leake (1318); renewed quarrel with Edward on rise to power of the Despensers; taken by royal forces at Boroughbridge and beheaded.

Thomas of Ba·yeux \bá-yœ̄\. d. 1100. Anglo-Norman prelate. To England with Bishop Odo of Bayeux (1066); royal chaplain under William the Conqueror; appointed archbishop of York (1070); forced by council of bishops to yield obedience to Canterbury (1072); began development of St. Peter's Cathedral, York.

Thomas of Cantelupe, Saint. See CANTELUPE.

Thomas of Ce·la·no \chā-'lä-nō\. c.1190–c.1260. Italian monk. Follower of St. Francis of Assisi (from c.1214); author of biographical sketches of St. Francis, as *Vita I* (1228–29), *Vita II* (1244–47), and *Tractus miraculorum* (c.1250); reputed author of hymn *Dies irae.*

Thomas of Er·cel·doune \'ər-səl-,dün\. *Called also* Thomas the Rhymer *and* Thomas Lear·mont \'le(ə)r-mənt, -,mänt\. fl. 1220–1297. Scottish poet and prophet. Probable author of metrical romance *Sir Tristrem* (known from manuscript of c.1300); in popular lore linked with Merlin and other seers; prophecies attributed to him first published in 15th century; subject of Sir Walter Scott's ballad "Thomas the Rhymer."

Thomas of London. See Thomas BECKET.

Thomas of Wood·stock \'wu̇d-,stäk\. Duke of Glouces·ter \'gläs-tər, 'glós-\. Earl of Buck·ing·ham \'bək-iŋ-əm, *esp US* -,ham\. 1355–1397. English nobleman. Seventh son of King Edward III; created duke (1385); head of lords appellant in opposition to his nephew Richard II; virtual ruler of England (1386–89); one of judges condemning Michael de la Pole, Earl of Suffolk (1386); defeated Robert de Vere at Radcot Bridge, London (1387); lost power to Richard (1389), but appointed (1392) lieutenant of Ireland; arrested by Richard after reported plot to seize king (1397); committed to charge of Thomas Mowbray at Calais; murdered, possibly on Richard's orders.

Thomas the Rhymer. See THOMAS of Erceldoune.

Tho·mas \tò-mä\, Albert. 1878–1932. French politician. Socialist member of Chamber of Deputies (1910–21); appointed to organize production of munitions of war (1914); minister of armaments (1916–17); director of the International Labor Organization of the League of Nations at Geneva (1920–32).

Thomas, Ambroise, *in full* Charles-Louis-Ambroise. 1811–1896. French composer. Known esp. for his operas *La Double échelle* (1837), *Le Songe d'une nuit d'été* (1850), *Mignon* (1866), *Hamlet* (1868), *Françoise de Rimini* (1882); author also of masses, cantatas, a Requiem, motets, and choral works.

Tho·mas \'täm-əs\, Augustus. 1857–1934. American dramatist, b. St. Louis, Mo. Made first successes with *A Man of the World* (1883) and *The Burglar* (1889); manager of Madison Square Theater, New York; wrote or adapted some 70 plays noted for use of native material, including *In Mizzoura* (1893), *The Hoosier Doctor* (1897), *Arizona* (1899), *The Earl of Pawtucket* (1903), *The Harvest Moon* (1909), *As a Man Thinks* (1911), *The Copperhead* (1918).

Thomas, David Alfred. 1st Viscount Rhon·dda \'(h)rän-t͟hə\. 1856–1918. Welsh colliery owner and government official. Liberal M.P. (1888–1910); president of Local Government Board (1916); as controller of ministry of food (1917–18), stabilized prices, regulated supplies, and set up system of compulsory food rationing.

Thomas, Dylan Marlais. 1914–1953. Welsh poet. Resident in London (1936–46); writer and broadcaster for British Broadcasting Corporation; made four reading tours of America (1950–53); died in New York of overdose of liquor. His works included verse collections *18 Poems* (1934), *Twenty-five Poems* (1936), *The Map of Love* (1939), *Deaths and Entrances* (1946), *In Country Sleep* (1952), *Collected Poems* (1952); prose *Portrait of the Artist as a Young Dog* (1940), *Adventures in the Skin Trade* (1955), *A Prospect of the Sea* (1955); and radio play *Under Milk Wood* (1954).

Thomas, Ebenezer. *Pseudonym* Eben Fardd \'várt͟h\. 1802–1863. Welsh poet. Schoolmaster at Clynnog (from 1827). Won *eisteddfodau* at Welshpool (1824, with *Dinystr Jerusalem*), Liverpool (1840, with *Job*), and Llangollen (1858, with *Maes Bosworth*); published collection of hymns (1862); complete works published as *Gweithiau Barddonol Eben Fardd* (1875).

Thomas, Edward, *in full* Phillip Edward. 1878–1917. English poet and critic. Published essays *Horae Solitariae* (1902), and twenty-odd naturalist studies and critical biographies. Began to write poetry after forming friendship with Robert Frost (1912); enlisted in Artists' Rifles (1915); killed in battle of Arras. Author of *The South County* (1909), *Light and Twilight* (1911), *In Pursuit of Spring* (1914), and a volume of short stories, *Four-and-Twenty Blackbirds* (1915). His first book of *Poems* (1917) published under pseudonym Edward Eas·ta·way \'ē-stə-,wā\.

Thomas, George Henry. 1816–1870. American army officer, b. Southampton Co., Va. Served in Seminole and Mexican Wars. Remained loyal to Union during the Civil War; brigadier general of volunteers (1861); major general (1862); engaged at Perryville, and gained fame and the nickname "the Rock of Chickamauga" by his defense of his position in the battle of Chickamauga (Sept. 19–20, 1863). Commanded army of the Cumberland in battle of Chattanooga (Nov. 24–25, 1863) and in Sherman's Atlanta campaign (1864). Sent to Tennessee to repel Hood's army (Sept. 1864) and won battle of Nashville (Dec. 15–16, 1864); promoted major general in the regular army. Commanded military division of the Pacific (1869–70).

Thomas, Isaiah. 1749–1831. American printer, b. Boston. Published (1770–1802) Whig paper *Massachusetts Spy;* set up printing business in Worcester; later established branches in other colonial cities. In addition to printing a number of the magazines of the day, he published many books notable for beauty of typography, including first Bible printed in English in U.S., Perry's dictionary (first dictionary printed in U.S.), Perry's speller, Blackstone's *Commentaries,* textbooks, lawbooks, music, children's books. Author of *The History of Printing in America* (1810). Founded and incorporated American Antiquarian Society (1812) and was its first president.

Thomas, James Henry. 1874–1949. English labor leader and politician. General secretary, National Union of Railwaymen (1918–24, 1925–31); president of Trades Union Congress (1920) and of International Federation of Trade Unions (1920–24). M.P. (1910–36); secretary of state for colonies (1924, 1931, 1935–36); lord privy seal and minister of employment (1929–30); secretary of state for the dominions (1930–35); resigned in budget scandal.

Thomas, John. 1724–1776. American physician and Revolutionary officer, b. Marshfield, Mass. In army medical service (1746–60). Commissioned brigadier general in Continental army (1775); in command at Roxbury (1775–76); seized Dorchester Heights (Mar. 4, 1776), thereby forcing British evacuation of Boston. Promoted major general (Mar. 1776) and commander of American army operating against Quebec.

Thomas, John. 1805–1871. American physician and religious leader, b. London, England. To U.S. (1832); founder of the Christadelphian sect (1847).

Thomas, Lowell Jackson. 1892–1981. American traveler, journalist, and author, b. Wooding, Ohio. Through life made travels (from 1915) to distant parts of the globe; gave lectures, made travelogues, wrote books about them; headed commission sent by Pres. Wilson to prepare historical record of World War I; met (1917) T.E. Lawrence and made him famous with book *With Lawrence of Arabia* (1924). Newscaster on radio (1930–76), voice of "Movietone News" (1935–52), and host of television series *High Adventure* (1957–59) and *Lowell Thomas Remembers* (1976–79). Author of over 50 books of travel, comment, and adventure.

Thomas, Martha Carey. 1857–1935. American educator, b. Baltimore, Md. Dean, professor of English (1884–94), and president (1894–1922), Bryn Mawr College. Cooperated with Mary Elizabeth Garrett in founding (1885) Bryn Mawr School for Girls, Baltimore; founded (1910) first graduate school of social economy and research connected with an American college; founded (1921) Summer School for Women Workers in Industry. Prominent women suffragist. Author of *The Higher Education of Women* (1900).

Thomas, Norman Mattoon. 1884–1968. American social reformer and politician, b. Marion, Ohio. Ordained in Presbyterian ministry (1911; resigned 1931); joined Socialist party (1918). Founder and editor, *World Tomorrow* (1918–21); helped found American Civil Liberties Union (1920); associate editor, *The Nation* (1921–22); co-director, League for Industrial Democracy (1922–37). Socialist candidate for president of the United States (1928–48); advocated many measures now in law, as unemployment insurance, minimum-wage laws, five-day work week, abolition of child labor. After World War II, as chairman of Postwar World Council, involved in nuclear disarmament and world peace. Author of *The Choice Before Us* (1934), *The Test of Freedom* (1954), *The Prerequisites for Peace* (1959), *Socialism Re-examined* (1963), etc.

Thomas, Robert Bailey. 1766–1846. American publisher, b. Grafton, Mass. Founded (1792), edited, and published *The Farmer's Almanac* (1792–1846).

Thomas, Seth. 1785–1859. American clock manufacturer, b. Wolcott, Conn. Associated with Eli Terry and Silas Hoadley in firm of Terry, Thomas & Hoadley to manufacture clocks by mass production methods (1807). Founded clock factory of his own at Plymouth Hollow, Conn. (1812); organized Seth Thomas Clock Co. (1853). His son ¶Seth (1816–1888) continued the business at Plymouth Hollow, renamed (c.1860) Thomaston, Conn.

Thomas, Sidney Gilchrist. 1850–1885. English metallurgist and inventor. Discovered method for eliminating phosphorus from iron in Bessemer converter (1875); the method, now known as the Thomas-Gilchrist process, Thomas process, or basic open-hearth process, was proved to be effective by his cousin ¶Percy Carlyle Gilchrist (1851–1935).

Thomas, Theodore, *in full* Christian Friedrich Theodore. 1835–1905. American conductor, b. Esens, Germany. To U.S. (1845) and settled in New York; organized orchestra (1862); conducted symphony concerts in New York City and on tour; conductor, New York Philharmonic Orchestra (1877–78, 1880–91) and Chicago Symphony Orchestra (1891–1905). Exercised great influence on development of a knowledge and appreciation of symphonic music.

Thomas, William. *Pseudonym* Is·lwyn \'is-ˌlu̇in\. 1832–1878. Welsh clergyman and poet. Ordained in Calvinistic Methodist ministry (1859). A master of strict Welsh meters; major work, the philosophical poem *Y Storm* (1856, unfinished).

Thomas, William Isaac. 1863–1947. American sociologist, b. Russell Co., Va. Taught at U. of Chicago (1895–1918), New School for Social Research, New York (1923–28), Harvard (1936–37); made studies in cultural change, personality development, ethnography. Works included *Source-Book for Social Origins* (1909), *The Polish Peasant in Europe and America* (1918–21, with Florian Znaniecki), *The Unadjusted Girl* (1923), *Primitive Behavior* (1937).

Thomas à Becket. See BECKET.

Thom·as à Kem·pis \-ə-'kem-pəs, -(ˌ)ä-'kem-\. *Orig.* Thomas Ham·mer·ken \'häm-ər-kən\ *or* He·mer·ken \'hā-mər-kən\. 1379 or 1380–1471. Dutch ecclesiastic and writer, b. Kempen. Studied in Netherlands under Florentius Radewyns (1393–98); entered Augustinian monastery near Zwolle (1399); ordained (1413); chosen subprior of monastery (1425, 1448). Famed as reputed author of the religious classic *De Imitatione Christi* (*Imitation of Christ*).

Thomas Aqui·nas \-ə-'kwī-nəs\. Saint. *Ital.* Tommaso d'Aqui·no \-dä-'kwē-nō\. *Called from 14th century* Doctor communis *and later* Doctor angelicus. 1225–1274. Italian religious and philosopher, b. Aquino. Entered Dominican order (1243 or 1244); studied under Albertus Magnus; taught at Cologne (1248–52), Paris (1252–59, 1269–72); theological adviser and lecturer to papal Curia (1259–68); director of Dominican studies at U. of Naples (1272–74). Outstanding figure of Scholastic philosophy; integrated scientific rationalism and naturalism of Aristotle with Christian revelation and faith; supplanted Averroës as principal interpreter of Aristotle. Works included major syntheses *Summa contra gentiles* (1259–64) and *Summa theologiae* or *theologica* (1266–73); commentaries on Bible, on Peter Lombard's *Sententiae,* on Aristotle, etc.; monographs and opusculae as *De ente et essentia* (1254–55), *De unitate intellectus* (1270), *De aeternitate mundi* (1270); recorded disputations as *De veritate* (1256–59), *De potentia Dei* (1265–67), *De malo* (1269–72); and hymns and liturgical works. Canonized by Pope John XXII (1323); proclaimed doctor of the church by Pius V (1567).

Thomas de Cantelupe. See CANTELUPE.

Tho·ma·si·us \tō-'mä-zē-u̇s\, Christian. 1655–1728. German jurist and philosopher. Taught at U. of Halle (from 1694), helping to establish its academic reputation; departed from Scholastic curriculum, sought independence of philosophy from theology, lectured in vernacular. His works included *Institutiones jurisprudentiae divinae* (1688) and *Fundamenta juris naturae et gentium* (1705).

Tho·mé \tō-mā\, Francis, *in full* François-Luc-Joseph. 1850–1909. French composer. Wrote ballets, operettas, songs, and piano pieces, including *Simple aveu* and *Gavotte-madrigal.*

Thomond, Earls and marquises of. See O'BRIEN family.

Thompson. See also THOMSON.

Thomp·son \'täm(p)-sən\, Benjamin. Count von Rum·ford \'rəm(p)-fərd\. 1753–1814. British physicist, b. Woburn, Mass. Loyalist during American Revolution; knighted (1784). In service of elector of Bavaria (1784–95); became war and police minister and grand chamberlain; created count of the Holy Roman Empire (1791). In England (1795), introduced improvements in heating and cooking equipment, including a double boiler, a kitchen range, a drip coffeepot. Returned to Bavaria (1796) and headed council of regency; appointed Bavarian minister to Great Britain, but not received as such in London because he was a British subject. Instrumental in organization of the Royal Institution (1799); resident chiefly in Paris and Anteuil (from 1802). Known for studies of heat and friction (from 1798); in "An Experimental Enquiry Concerning the Source of the Heat which is Excited by Friction" (1798), argued that heat is a form of motion. Developed a calorimeter and a photometer, devised improvements in lighting.

Thompson, Sir D'Arcy Wentworth. 1860–1948. Scottish zoologist and classical scholar. Professor in Dundee at Univ. College (1884–1917) and St. Andrew's (from 1917); on expeditions to Pribilof Islands (1896, 1897). Wrote *A Glossary of Greek Birds* (1895), *On Growth and Form* (1917), papers and reports on fishery statistics and oceanography, etc.

Thompson, David. 1770–1857. Canadian explorer and fur trader, b. London, England. With Hudson's Bay Co. (1784–97) and North West Co. (1797–1836); explored (1789–1812) western parts of Canada and U.S., keeping careful journals and field notes of his travels; discovered Turtle Lake (1807); first white man to explore Columbia River from source to mouth (1811); his maps served as basis for all subsequent ones; head of British commission for fixing and marking U.S.–Canadian boundary (1816–26).

Thompson, Dorothy. 1894–1961. American journalist, b. Lancaster, N.Y. m. as 2d husband Sinclair Lewis (1928; div. 1942); correspondent in Vienna (1920–24), Berlin (1924–28); columnist, syndicated through New York Herald-Tribune Syndicate (1936–41), Bell Syndicate (1941–57). Author of *New Russia* (1928), *Political Guide* (1938), *Let the Record Speak* (1939), *The Courage to Be Happy* (1957).

Thompson, Edward Herbert. 1860–1935. American archaeologist, b. Worcester, Mass. U.S. consul in Mérida, Mexico (1885–1909). Made study of Mayan remains at Chichén-Itzá, including Sacred Well, great pyramid, astronomical observatory, etc., and obtained many objects of archaeological significance; recounted explorations in *People of the Serpent* (1932).

Thompson, Elizabeth Southerden. See under Sir William Francis BUTLER.

Thompson, Ernest Seton. See Ernest T. SETON.

Thompson, Francis. 1859–1907. English poet. In London (1885); working in bootmaker's shop, wrote his first poems, which were published (1888) by Wilfrid Meynell in *Merry England;* hospitalized and cared for by the Meynells (1888–93). Gained acclaim of critics with *Poems* (1893, including "The Hound of Heaven"), *Sister Songs* (1895) and *New Poems* (1897); author also of literary criticism, a life of Loyola (1909), and *Essay on Shelley* (1909).

Thompson, Sir Henry. 1820–1904. English surgeon. Surgeon, U. Coll. Hospital, London (from 1853); specialist in surgery of the urogenital tract; his publications included *Stricture of the Urethra* (1854), *Practical Lithotomy and Lithotrity* (1863).

Thompson, James Walter. 1847–1928. American businessman, b. Pittsfield, Mass. Established (1878) an advertising firm in New York, developing it into one of most successful in U.S.; esp. effective in marketing advertisements in magazines; sold interest in company (1916).

Thompson, Sir John Sparrow David. 1844–1894. Canadian jurist and politician, b. Halifax, N.S. Called to bar (1865); premier of Nova Scotia (1882); minister of justice for Canada (1885), defended hanging of Louis Riel; negotiated fisheries treaty with U.S. (1888); prime minister (1892–94); one of arbitrators of Bering Sea controversy (1893).

Thompson, John Taliaferro. 1860–1940. American army officer and inventor, b. Newport, Ky. In U.S. army (1882–1914, 1917–19); private consultant on armaments; inventor of firearms and airplane devices; with John N. Blish, invented the Thompson submachine gun (pat. 1920).

Thompson, Reginald Campbell. 1876–1941. English archaeologist. Conducted excavations at Nineveh (1904, 1927, 1929–32) and other Mesopotamian sites. Author of *The Devils and Evil Spirits of Babylonia* (1903–04), *Assyrian Medical Texts* (1923), *The Epic of Gilgamish* (translation, 1928; text, 1930), etc.

Thompson, Silvanus Phillips. 1851–1916. English physicist. Professor at Bristol (1878–85); principal of Finsbury Tech. College, London (1885–1916); author of works on electricity and magnetism, and on lives of scientists.

Thompson, Smith. 1768–1843. American jurist, b. Amenia, N.Y. Adm. to bar (1792); associate (1802–14) and chief (1814–18) justice, N.Y. Supreme Court; U.S. secretary of the navy (1819–23); associate justice, U.S. Supreme Court (1823–43).

Thompson, William. *Known as* Ben·di·go \'ben-də-ˌgō\. 1811–1880. English pugilist. In boxing career (1832–50) lost only one match; English champion (1839, 1845–50); later tavern keeper and then widely known Methodist evangelist. City of Bendigo, Victoria, Australia, named for him.

Thompson, William Tappan. *Pseudonym* Major Jones \'jōnz\. 1812–1882. American journalist and humorist, b. Ravenna, Ohio. To Georgia (c.1835);

published (1838–43) literary journal *Augusta Mirror;* founder and editor (1850–82), *Savannah Morning News.* Under pseudonym, wrote series of amusing dialect letters sketching Georgia-Florida backwoodsmen; letters collected as *Major Jones's Courtship* (1843), *Major Jones's Chronicles of Pineville* (1843), etc.

Thoms \'tämz\, William John. 1803–1885. English antiquary. Clerk of House of Lords (from 1845) and its deputy librarian (1863–1882); founder (1849) and editor (till 1872) of *Notes and Queries.*

Thom·sen \'tòm-sən\, Christian Jürgensen. 1788–1865. Danish archaeologist. Curator (1816–65) of National Museum of Denmark, Copenhagen; developed (by 1818) the chronological system which divides prehistory into the Stone, Bronze, and Iron Ages; system published in *Ledetraad til nordisk Oldkyndighed* (1836).

Thomsen, Julius, *in full* Hans Peter Jörgen Julius. 1826–1909. Danish chemist. Professor at Copenhagen (1866–91); known esp. for research on the heat changes involved in chemical reactions; devised first table of relative strengths of acids; invented (c.1853) process for the manufacture of soda from cryolite.

Thomsen, Vilhelm Ludvig Peter. 1842–1927. Danish philologist. Professor at Copenhagen (1887–1913); author of *Den gotiske Sprogklasses Indflydelse paa den finske* (1869), etc.; decipherer of the Orkhon inscriptions (1893).

Thomson. See also THOMPSON.

Thom·son \'täm(p)-sən\, Charles Edward Poulett. Baron Syd·en·ham \'sid-ᵊn-əm, 'sid-nəm\. 1799–1841. English politician and colonial administrator. Brother of George J. P. Scrope. Liberal M.P. (1826); vice president of Board of Trade (1830), president (1834–39); effected tariff changes in direction of free trade; advocated legislation on usury, banking, and factory management; negotiated commercial treaties. Governor general of Canada (1839–41); achieved union of Upper and Lower Canada (1840); introduced municipal institutions in Upper Canada; encouraged public works; established responsible government.

Thomson, Sir Charles Wyville. 1830–1882. Scottish naturalist. Professor at Belfast (1854–68) and Edinburgh (1870–82); made special study of deep-sea life; described sounding and dredging expeditions in *The Depths of the Sea* (1873) and his circumnavigating expedition in *The Voyage of the Challenger* (1877).

Thomson, Elihu. 1853–1937. American electrical engineer and inventor, b. Manchester, England. To U.S. (1858). An organizer (1883) of the Thomson-Houston Electric Co., which was merged (1892) with Thomas Edison's company to form the General Electric Co., which manufactured and operated under his inventions, for which he obtained more than 700 patents; consultant to General Electric (from 1892). Inventor of electric welding, the standard three-phase alternating-current generator, the high-frequency transformer, the high-frequency generator (1890), the centrifugal cream separator, the common watt meter, the street arc lamp; did work in radiology, esp. pioneering in stereoscopic X-ray pictures; first to suggest a helium-oxygen mixture to prevent caisson disease.

Thomson, George. 1757–1851. Scottish folk song collector. Secretary (1780–1830) to Board of Trustees for Encouragement of Arts and Manufactures in Scotland; collected melodies of Scottish, Irish, Welsh folk songs; engaged leading authors (as Robert Burns, Sir Walter Scott, Peter Pindar) and composers (as Haydn, Beethoven, Pleyel) to supply texts and accompaniments; published collections (1793–1841).

Thomson, Sir George Paget. 1892–1975. English physicist. Son of Sir Joseph John Thomson; professor, U. of Aberdeen (1922–30) and Imperial College of Science, London (1930–52); master of Corpus Christi, Cambridge (1952–62). Shared 1937 Nobel prize for physics with Clinton J. Davisson for their discovery (independently and by different methods) of the diffraction of electrons by crystals (1927). Author of *Applied Aerodynamics* (1919), *Theory and Practice of Electron Diffraction* (1939), *J.J. Thomson and the Cavendish Laboratory in His Day* (1965), etc.

Thomson, James. 1700–1748. Scottish poet. To London (1725); published blank-verse poems *Winter* (1726), *Summer* (1727), *Spring* (1728), *Autumn* (1730), brought together as *The Seasons,* for first time giving description of nature the leading place, and paving the way for the emotional treatment of nature by the Romantic poets. Author of dramas, including *Sophonisba* (1730) and *Tancred and Sigismunda* (1745), poem *Liberty* (1735–36), *The Masque of Alfred* (1740; with David Mallet; containing song "Rule, Britannia"; music by T. A. Arne), and the allegorical poem *The Castle of Indolence* (1748) in Spenserian stanzas, generally considered his masterpiece.

Thomson, James. *Pseudonyms* B. V. *or* Bysshe Va·no·lis \və-'nō-ləs\. 1834–1882. Scottish poet. Army school master (1851–62); clerk in London. Contributed "To Our Ladies of Death" (1861) and "The City of Dreadful Night" (1874; pub. as book, 1880) to his friend Charles Bradlaugh's *National Reformer;* wrote long poem *Sunday up the River* (1869); wrote chiefly in despairing and atheistic mood; published *Vane's Story, Weddah and Om-el-Bonain, and Other Poems* (1881) and collected prose writings as *Essays and Phantasies* (1881).

Thomson, John. 1778–1840. Scottish painter. Greatest Scottish landscape painter of his time; first to depict ruggedness of Scottish scenery.

Thomson, John. 1837–1921. British photographer. Best known for series of documentary photographs of English lower class reproduced as woodcut illustrations for book *Street Life in London* (1877).

Thomson, John Arthur. 1861–1933. Scottish biologist. Professor, U. of Aberdeen (1899–1930); made researches on soft corals; attempted in lectures and writings to popularize biology and to correlate science and religion. Author of *Evolution* (1911, with Sir Patrick Geddes), *The Wonder of Life* (1914), *Biology* (1924, with Geddes), *Science Old and New* (1924), *Science and Religion* (1925), etc.

Thomson, Joseph. 1858–1895. Scottish geologist and explorer. Geologist of expedition under Alexander Keith Johnston to Central Africa, succeeding as leader on death of Johnston (1879); reached Lake Tanganyika, discovered Lake Rukwa. Headed expedition through the Masai country (1882); discovered Lake Baringo (1882); reached Lake Victoria (1883). By expedition for Royal Niger Co. to Sokoto gained part of central Sudan for Great Britain (1885); explored Atlas Mountains, Morocco (1888). Wrote *To the Central African Lakes and Back* (1881), *Through Masai Land* (1885).

Thomson, Sir Joseph John. 1856–1940. English physicist. Professor, Cambridge (1884–1918), Royal Institution, London (1905–18); master, Trinity College, Cambridge (1918–40). Investigated conduction of electricity through gases, subatomic particles, and radioactivity; discovered the electron (1897); also an outstanding teacher. Awarded 1906 Nobel prize for physics. Author of *The Application of Dynamics to Physics and Chemistry* (1888), *Conduction of Electricity Through Gases* (1903), *Rays of Positive Electricity and Their Application to Chemical Analysis* (1913), *The Electron in Chemistry* (1923).

Thomson, Mortimer Neal. *Pseudonym* Q.K. Philander Doe·sticks \'dō-ˌstiks\, P.B. 1831–1875. American humorist, b. Riga, N.Y. On staff of New York *Tribune* (1855); created "Doesticks," assumed writer of a series of letters later collected and published as *Doesticks: What He Says* (1855); wrote *Plu-ri-bus-tah, a Song That's-by-No-Author* (a mock-heroic parody of *Hiawatha,* 1856), *Nothing to Say* (1857), etc.

Thomson, Robert William. 1822–1873. Scottish engineer. Invented the pneumatic tire, the principle of which he patented in England (1845). See John Boyd DUNLOP.

Thomson, Roy Herbert. 1st Baron Thomson of Fleet \'flēt\. 1894–1976. British businessman, b. Toronto, Ont. Proprietor of newspaper chains in Canada, England, Scotland, U.S.; purchased *The Scotsman* of Edinburgh (1952) and *The Times* of London (1967); also owned television stations in Canada and Scotland.

Thomson, Thomas. 1773–1852. Scottish chemist. Published *A System of Chemistry* (1802), the third edition (1807) of which contained first detailed account of John Dalton's atomic theory; professor at Glasgow U. (1817–52); founded first chemical laboratory for students in Britain (1818).

Thomson, Tom. 1877–1917. Canadian painter, b. Claremont, Ont. Commercial designer in Toronto (1905–13); associated with and influenced several painters later known as the Group of Seven; spent part of each year in Algonquin Provincial Park as woodsman, guide, painter (1913–17). Known for landscapes in brilliant colors of the Canadian wilderness, including *Northern River* (1915), *Spring Ice* (1916), *Jack Pine* (1917).

Thomson, William. 1st Baron Kel·vin \'kel-vən\ of Largs \'lärgz\. 1824–1907. British mathematician and physicist, b. Belfast, Ireland. Professor at Glasgow (1846–99); chief consultant during laying of first Atlantic cable (1857–58); knighted (1866); created baron (1892). Proposed (1848) the absolute, or Kelvin, temperature scale; in "On the Dynamical Theory of Heat" (1851) synthesized ideas of Carnot and Joule on the convertibility of heat into mechanical energy into a version of the second law of thermodynamics; contributed to the dynamical theory of heat. Made mathematical analyses of magnetism and electricity, laying basic ideas for the electromagnetic theory of light; investigated electric currents in cables. Became wealthy by invention (pat. 1858) of a mirror galvanometer for receiving telegraph signals; improved the mariner's compass (1876); devised apparatus for taking soundings (1872); invented a tide predictor, a harmonic analyzer, a siphon recorder, and numerous other devices. Contributed to theory of elasticity in "On Vortex Motion" (1868); investigated geomagnetism, hydrodynamics, the shape of the Earth, the geophysical determination of the Earth's age. Published *Treatise on Natural Philosophy* (1867, with P.G. Tait) and over 600 scientific papers.

Tho·net \'tò-net\, Michael. 1796–1871. German furniture manufacturer. Established workshop in Boppard, Germany (1819); developed technique of making light and curvilinear bentwood furniture; moved firm to Vienna (1842); perfected process for bending solid beechwood by heat into curvilinear shapes (by 1856); his mass-produced bentwood furniture exported throughout Europe and the Americas, becoming standard items of furniture for many households.

Thor·a·ven·sen \'thór-äv-ˌen-sən\, Bjarni Vigfússon. 1786–1841. Icelandic jurist and poet. Deputy justice (1811–17) and justice (1817–33) of Supreme Court; appointed governor of North and East Iceland (1833). First Romantic nationalist poet of Iceland; reintroduced Eddaic meters and primitive traditions into Icelandic literature; his poems, such as "Thú nafnkunna Landid," published in *Kvaedi* (1847).

Thor·becke \'tór-ˌbek-ə\, Johan Rudolf. 1798–1872. Dutch politician. University lecturer on law; published his liberal ideas in *Aanteekening op de grondwet* (1839); chief author of constitution of 1848. Head of Liberal party. Premier (1849–53, 1862–66, 1871–72); sponsored electoral reforms; promoted free trade and construction of canals and waterways; favored nondenominational schools; abolished slavery in Dutch East Indian colonies.

Tho·reau \thə-'rō, thó-, 'thór-(ˌ)ō, 'thər-(ˌ)ō *(the last apparently his own pronunciation)*\, Henry David, *orig.* David Henry. 1817–1862. American writer, b. Concord, Mass. Schoolmaster in Concord (1838–41); lived in home of Ralph Waldo Emerson (1841–43), where he was associated with such Transcendentalists as Bronson Alcott, George Ripley, and Margaret Fuller; helped edit *The Dial* and published poems and essays in it (1842–44). Retired to a hut beside Walden Pond at Concord (July 4, 1845–Sept. 6, 1847), where he devoted himself to a study of nature and to writing. Published during his lifetime only two books, *A Week on the Concord and Merrimack Rivers* (1849) and *Walden, or Life in the Woods* (1854), and a few magazine articles, esp. "Civil Disobedience" (1849). His journals, manuscripts, letters, etc., published as *The Writings of Henry David Thoreau* (20 vols., 1906).

Tho·rek \'thór-ˌek, -ək\, Max. 1880–1960. American physician, b. Hungary. To U.S. (1900); established (1908, with Solomon Greenspahn) in Chicago the American Hospital (now Thorek Medical Center) and served (1910–60) as its chief surgeon; perfected (1933) surgical technique that greatly reduced mortality rate in gallbladder operations; also contributed to reconstructive surgical techniques; founded International College of Surgeons, Geneva (1935). Works included *Surgical Errors and Safeguards* (1932) and *Modern Surgical Technic* (1938).

Tho·rez \tó-rez\, Maurice. 1900–1964. French politician. Joined (c.1920) French Communist party and served as its secretary general (1930–64); member of chamber of Deputies (1932–39, 1945–60); helped form Popular Front of leftist groups (1934); minister of state (1945–46); deputy premier (1947). Published *Fils du peuple* (1937) and *Une Politique de grandeur française* (1945).

Thor·finn Karl·sef·ni \'thór-fin-'kärl-ˌsev-nē\. fl. 1002–1007. Icelandic explorer. Headed an expedition from Greenland which sailed along the northeastern coast of North America and attempted to plant colonies in what are now Newfoundland and Massachusetts (1004–05); project abandoned (1006).

Thorgilsson, Ari. See Ari Thorgilsson.

Tho·rild \'tü-rild\, Thomas. *Surname orig.* Thor·én \'thór-en\. 1759–1808. Swedish journalist and poet. Engaged in literary controversies with Kellgren and Leopold; banished for political libel after assassination (1792) of Gustav III; appointed (1795) professor and librarian at Greifswald, Germany. Published *Passionerna* (verse, 1781), *En critik öfver critiker* (prose, 1791–92), *Götamannasånger* (verse, 1793), etc.

Thor·is·mond *or* **Thor·is·mund** \'thór-əz-mand\. d. 453. King of the Visigoths (451–453). Son of Theodoric I; ruled in Provence; joined Romans in defeat of Attila (451); assassinated by his brother Theodoric II.

Thor·kell \'thór-ˌkel\. *Called* the Tall. 11th century. Danish ruler in England. Served under Aethelred II the Unready (1012–15); made ruler of East Anglia by Canute (1016); outlawed by Canute (1021).

Thor·láks·son \'thór-laüks-són\, Gudbrandur. 1541–1627. Icelandic ecclesiastic and scholar. Bishop of Hólar (from 1570); responsible for the successful implantation of Lutheranism into Iceland; introduced Lutheran catechism in schools and first Lutheran prayer and service books. Published 84 works, including a complete Bible in Icelandic *Gudbrandsbiblia* (1584), hymnbook *Sálmabók* (1589), verse anthology *Vísnabók* (1612). Determined geographic position of Iceland and made best map of Iceland then known.

Thorn·bury \'thó(ə)rn-b(ə-)rē, -ˌber-ē\, George Walter. 1828–1876. English writer. Author of art criticisms, historical and topographical sketches, several novels, poems, a biography of J.M.W. Turner, and *Old and New London* (1872–76).

Thorn·dike \'thó(ə)rn-ˌdīk\, Ashley Horace. 1871–1933. American educator, b. Houlton, Me. Professor of English, Columbia (1906–33); authority on Elizabethan drama. Author of *Tragedy* (1908), *The Fact About Shakespeare* (with William A. Neilson, 1913), *Shakespeare's Theatre* (1916), *English Comedy* (1929), etc. His brother ¶Edward Lee (1874–1949), b. Williamsburg, Mass., psychologist; professor, Teachers Coll., Columbia (1904–40). Founder of experimental animal psychology and a pioneer in study of animal intelligence. Author of *An Introduction to the Theory of Mental and Social Measurements* (1904), *The Principles of Teaching Based on Psychology* (1906), *Animal Intelligence* (1911), *Educational Psychology* (1913–14), *The Measurement of Intelligence* (1926), *The Psychology of Wants, Interests, and Attitudes* (1935), *Human Nature and the Social Order* (1940), etc. Another brother ¶Lynn (1882–1965), b. Lynn, Mass., historian; taught history at Western Reserve U. (1909–24); professor, Columbia (from 1924); author of *The History of Medieval Europe* (1917), *A History of Magic and Experimental Science* (1923–41), etc.

Thorndike, Dame Sybil, *in full* Agnes Sybil. 1882–1976. English actress. Played Shakespearean leads at Old Vic (1914–18); took over management of New Theatre (1922) and several subsequent theaters; created title role in Shaw's *Saint Joan* (1924) and scored great success with it; toured widely; made farewell appearance in *There Was an Old Woman* for opening of Sybil Thorndike Theatre, Leatherhead, Surrey (1969). Known esp. for versatility in great variety of parts.

Thorn·hill \'thó(ə)rn-ˌhil\, Sir James. 1676–1734. English painter. Known for historical subjects painted in Baroque style; designed series of paintings for interior of dome of St. Paul's, allegories in "Painted Hall" of Greenwich Hospital, window in Westminster Abbey; painted portraits of Sir Isaac Newton, Steele, Bentley.

Thorn-Prik·ker \'tórn-'prik-ər\, Jan, *Ger.* Johan. 1868–1932. Dutch painter. Taught and worked in Germany (from 1904); associated with Symbolist and Art Nouveau movements; painted *The Bride* (1893); designed stained-glass windows and mosaic murals.

Thorn·ton \'thórnt-ᵊn\, Matthew. 1714?–1803. American physician and patriot in American Revolution, b. Ireland. To America (c.1718); practiced medicine in Londonderry, N.H. (1740–79); active in pre-Revolutionary agitation; member of Continental Congress (1776) and a signer of the Declaration of Independence.

Thornton, William. 1759–1828. American architect, b. Jost Van Dyke, B.W.I. To U.S. (1787, naturalized 1788); settled in Philadelphia. Though not trained as an architect, won competition for design of building for the Library Company of Philadelphia (1789). Associated with John Fitch in his steamboat experiments (1788–90); published *Short Account of the Origin of Steamboats* (1814). Won competition for design of National Capitol at Washington, D.C. (1792); design revised by Étienne S. Hallet. Commissioner of the District of Columbia (1794–1802); supervised construction of Capitol until replaced by Benjamin H. Latrobe (1803); first superintendent of Patent Office (1802–28). Also designed a number of private residences in Washington, including the Octagon (1798–1800); patented (1802–27) eight inventions for improving firearms, stills, etc.

Thor·ny·croft \'thór-nē-ˌkróft\, Sir Hamo, *in full* William Hamo. 1850–1925. English sculptor. Won recognition with *Warrior Bearing a Wounded Youth* (1876); known esp. for *The Mower* (1884), *A Sower* (1886), and statues of General Gordon (1888), Oliver Cromwell (1899), and King Alfred (1901).

Thornycroft, Sir John Isaac. 1843–1928. English naval architect. Brother of Sir Hamo Thornycroft. Established shipbuilding works at Chiswick (1866); later constructed first torpedo boat for English navy (1877); patented (1877) a hull that could skim, rather than cut through, the water; designed water-tube boilers for torpedo boats and one of earliest ship stabilizers; during World War I, developed a coastal torpedo speedboat known as "scooter"; pioneered use of oil fuel for navy.

Thór·odd·sen \'thōr-ód-sen\, Jón Thórdarson. 1819–1868. Icelandic novelist and poet. District judge (from 1850). Regarded as master of Icelandic prose; his *Piltur og stúlka* (1850) earliest true novel produced in Iceland; other works included unfinished novel *Madur og kona* (pub. 1876), lyrics, and drinking songs.

Thorp \'thó(ə)rp\, John. 1784–1848. American inventor, b. probably Rehoboth, Mass. Machinist by trade; invented (1828) the ring spinning machine.

Thorpe \'thó(ə)rp\, Benjamin. 1782–1870. English philologist. Pioneer in Old English translation, philology, and history; published *Anglo-Saxon Poems of Beowulf* (1855), *The Anglo-Saxon Chronicle* (1861), and *A Collection of English Charters* (1865).

Thorpe, Sir Edward, *in full* Thomas Edward. 1845–1925. English chemist. Professor, Royal College of Science, London (1885–94, 1909–12); director of government laboratories (1894–1909). Cooperated in magnetic survey of British Isles (1884–88); determined specific volumes of numerous substances, studied phosphorus oxides, measured viscosities of organic substances. Author of *A Dictionary of Applied Chemistry* (1893), *A History of Chemistry* (1909–10, 1924), etc.

Thorpe, James Francis, *known as* Jim. 1886–1953. American athlete, b. near Prague, Okla. Predominantly of Sauk and Fox Indian descent; halfback on Glenn Warner's teams at Carlisle Indian School; chosen to Walter Camp's

All-American football teams (1911, 1912). Won decathlon and pentathlon in Olympic Games (1912; later disqualified for previous loss of amateur status, medals restored 1982); also played professional baseball (1913–19) and football (1919–26). First president (1920–21) of National Football League. Jim Thorpe, Pa., named in his honor.

Thorpe, Rose Alnora, *nee* Hart·wick \'härt-(,)wik\. 1850–1939. American writer, b. Mishawaka, Ind. m. (1871) E.C. Thorpe. Best known for poem "Curfew Must Not Ring Tonight" (1870); also wrote children's books, novels, etc.

Thorpe *or* **Thorp,** Thomas Bangs. 1815–1878. American writer, b. Westfield, Mass. Newspaper publisher (1836–53) in New Orleans and Baton Rouge; painter, customhouse employee, journalist in New York (from 1854 except for Civil War service). Author of humorous stories of frontier life and character, including "The Big Bear of Arkansas" (1841) and others collected in *Mysteries of the Backwoods* (1846), *The Hive of the Bee Hunter* (1854).

Thors \'thórs\, Ólafur. 1892–1964. Icelandic politician. Member of Althing (1925–63); held ministries of justice (1932), trade and industries (1939–42), foreign affairs (1942, 1944–46), industries and export trade (1950–53); prime minister of Iceland (1942, 1944–46, 1949–50, 1953–56, 1959–61, 1962–63).

Thor·steins·son \'thór-,stīns-són\, Steingrímur. 1831–1913. Icelandic poet. In Copenhagen (1852–72); teacher, later headmaster, of Latin School in Reykjavík (1872–1913). Did much to improve culture in Iceland, esp. by his translations of *King Lear, Robinson Crusoe, Arabian Nights,* Byron, Goethe, etc.; author of popular lyrics on nature, love, and esp. patriotism.

Thor·vald·sen *or* **Thor·wald·sen** \'tór-väl-sən\, Bertel. 1768 or 1770–1844. Danish sculptor. First internationally acclaimed Danish artist; resident in Rome (1797–1838). Executed statues of various figures of classical mythology, including Jason, Ganymede, Venus, Psyche, and the Graces, and bas-reliefs *Triumphal Entry of Alexander into Babylon* (1812) and *Christ and the Twelve Apostles* (1821–27). Regarded as a leader in the classical revival.

Thou \tü\, Jacques-Auguste de. *Lat.* Thu·a·nus \tü-'ā-nəs\. 1553–1617. French politician and historian. Succeeded his uncle as canon of Notre Dame (1573); entered Parlement (1578); councilor of state (1588); president of Parlement of Paris (1595); negotiated Edict of Nantes (1598); opposed Council of Trent due to his advocacy of Gallicanism; lost much effectiveness during regency of Marie de Médicis. Pioneered in scientific approach to history; noted for *Historia sui temporis* (1604–20), a 5-part history of period 1545–1607.

Thrale, Mrs. See Hester Lynch PIOZZI.

Thra·ne \'thrä-nə\, Marcus Møller. 1817–1890. Norwegian journalist and Socialist leader. Teacher and journalist (to 1848); initiator and a leader of the Thrane movement that sought to better the condition of laborers (1848–50); imprisoned for sedition (1851–55); to U.S. (1855); published a series of Norwegian-language Socialist newspapers in Chicago.

Thra·sea Pae·tus \thras-'ē-ə-'pēt-əs\, Publius Clodius. d. 66 A.D. Roman politician. Senator; consul (56); opposed Nero; retired from public life out of disgust with Nero's immoralities (63); executed on Nero's command.

Thras·y·bu·lus \,thras-ə-'byü-ləs\. d. 388 B.C. Athenian general and politician. Aided Alcibiades in victories over Spartans at sea, at Cynossema (411), and Cyzicus (410). Exiled from Athens by the Thirty Tyrants (404); instrumental in effecting a return of democratic government in Athens (403). Induced Athens to join Theban League against Sparta (395); commanded fleet against Spartans (389).

Three·fin Blen·ny \'thrā-fin-'bled-nᵫ\. fl. c.1122. Icelandic skeptic.

Three Kingdoms. Name given to Chinese kingdoms which succeeded the breakup of the Later Han dynasty: (1) Wei (220–264; *q.v.*); (2) Shu Han (221–263; see HAN); and (3) Wu (222–280; *q.v.*). The Wu dynasty is usually considered one of the Six Dynasties (*q.v.*).

Thring \'thriŋ\, Edward. English educator. 1821–1887. As headmaster (1853–87) of Uppingham School, transformed it into a large and important public school; opened (1859) first school gymnasium in England and introduced wood and metal workshops. Founded Headmasters' Conference (1868); exerted great influence on English public school education.

Throck·mor·ton \thräk-'mórt-ᵊn, 'thräk-,\ *or* **Throg·mor·ton** \thräg-'mórt-, 'thräg-,\, Sir Nicholas. 1515–1571. English diplomat. M.P. (1545–67); fought at battle of Pinkie (1547) and siege of Boulogne (1549–50); ambassador to France (1559–64); friend and supporter of Mary, Queen of Scots; ambassador to Scotland (1565, 1567); imprisoned (1569) on suspicion of participating in conspiracy in favor of Mary, Queen of Scots. His daughter Elizabeth married Sir Walter Raleigh. His nephew ¶Francis Throckmorton *or* Throgmorton (1554–1584) was a zealous Roman Catholic and engaged in plots against English government; central figure in Throckmorton Plot (1583) to overthrow Queen Elizabeth with French and Spanish aid; arrested, confessed, executed.

Thu·cyd·i·des \th(y)ü-'sid-ə-,dēz\. d. c.401 B.C. Greek historian. Elected (424 B.C.) a military magistrate of Athens; during Peloponnesian War, commanded expedition sent (424) to aid Amphipolis, but failed to prevent capture of city by Brasidas; exiled (423–404), during which he wrote *History of the Peloponnesian War* (an account which carries war down to 411). Regarded as first critical historian; ranked as greatest historian of antiquity.

Thucydides. d. after 426 B.C. Athenian politician. After death of Cimon (449 B.C.) became leader of aristocratic party in opposition to Pericles; ostracized (443); returned (433) but had no influence.

Thue \'tü-ə\, Axel. 1863–1922. Norwegian mathematician. Professor at Oslo (1903–22); discovered (1909) Thue's theorem in number theory.

Thuil·le \'twil-ə\, Ludwig. 1861–1907. Austrian composer. Known for operas *Theuerdank* (1897), *Lobetanz* (1898), chamber music, etc.

Thumb, General Tom. See Charles STRATTON.

Thun·berg \'tün-,bərʸ\, Carl Peter. 1743–1828. Swedish botanist. Studied under Linnaeus at Uppsala; professor, U. of Uppsala (1784–1828); author esp. of works on the flora of the Cape of Good Hope and of Japan.

Thü·nen \'tᵫ-nən\, Johan Heinrich von. 1783–1850. German agriculturalist. Known for work on relationship of the costs of commodity transportation to the location of production, published in *Der isolierte Staat* (1826).

Thun und Hoh·en·stein \'tü-nùnt-'hō-ən-,shtīn\, Friedrich von. Graf. 1810–1881. Austrian diplomat and politician. As president of German federal diet at Frankfurt and head of Austrian delegation (1850), opposed Bismarck's proposals for highly centralized state led by Prussia; minister to Prussia (1852–54) and to Russia (1859–63); active in Bohemian and Austrian internal politics (after 1863). His brother ¶Graf Leo (1811–1888), also a politician; governor of Bohemia (1848); as Austrian minister for religious affairs and education (1849–60) improved educational system; active in Bohemian politics (after 1861); favored greater rights for Czechs and federalization of the Habsburg empire. Friedrich's son ¶Franz Anton (1847–1916), also a politician; governor of Bohemia (1890–95); favored compromise with Czech nationalists but forced to resign by riots of Young Czechs; prime minister of Austria (1898–99); ousted by German nationalists; created prince (1911); again governor of Bohemia (1911–15).

Thur·ber \'thər-bər\, Charles. 1803–1886. American inventor, b. East Brookfield, Mass. In partnership with brother-in-law Ethan Allen, firm of Allen & Thurber, manufacturing firearms in Worcester, Mass. (1836–56). Patented a hand printing machine (1843) which bore a resemblance to a modern typewriter.

Thurber, James Grover. 1894–1961. American cartoonist and writer, b. Columbus, Ohio. Managing editor (1927–33) of *The New Yorker,* to which he contributed throughout his career humorous drawings, essays, and short stories, esp. "The Secret Life of Walter Mitty" (1939). Author of *Is Sex Necessary?* (with E. B. White, 1929), *The Owl in the Attic* (1931), *The Seal in the Bedroom* (1932), *My Life and Hard Times* (1933), *The Middle-aged Man on the Flying Trapeze* (1935), *Fables for Our Time* (1940), play *The Male Animal* (with Elliott Nugent, 1941), *The Thurber Carnival* (1945), *The 13 Clocks* (1950), *The Thurber Album* (1952), *The Wonderful O* (1957), *Credos and Curios* (1962), etc. Played himself in stage adaptation (1960) of *The Thurber Carnival.*

Thu·reau-Dan·gin \tᵫ-rō-dä"-zha"\, Paul. 1837–1913. French historian. Author of *Histoire de la monarchie de Juillet* (1884–92), *Histoire de la renaissance catholique en Angleterre* (1890–1906), etc.

Thu·ret \tᵫ-re, -rā\, Gustave-Adolphe. 1817–1875. French botanist. Authority on marine algae; with Joseph Decaisne discovered spermatozoids in brown alga *Fucus* (1844); provided first account of fertilization process in *Fucus* (1854); with Édouard Bornet determined life cycle of red alga *Floridae* (1867); wrote *Études phycologiques* (1878) and *Notes algologiques* (1876–80).

Thur·loe \'thər-(,)lō\, John. 1616–1668. English politician. Secretary of state under the Commonwealth (1652–60); M.P. (1654); member of Cromwell's second council (1657); efficient in direction of intelligence and postal department; kept Cromwell informed of plans of foreign powers and of royalist plots; at Restoration, liberated from charge of high treason on condition of counseling secretaries of state. His correspondence (7 vols., 1742) provides chief source of information on the Protectorate.

Thur·low \'thər-(,)lō\, Edward. 1st Baron Thurlow. 1731–1806. English judge. Barrister (1754); M.P. (1765); solicitor general (1770); attorney general (1771); favored coercion of American colonies; prosecuted publisher and printers of the "Junius" letters; noted more for great oratory than legal wisdom. Lord chancellor (1778–83, 1783–92); worked in opposition to Burke's proposals of reform and against Rockingham government; presided at trial of Warren Hastings (1788); dismissed (1792) on insistence of Pitt. Defender of royal prerogatives and interests of slave traders; patron of Dr. Johnson and Crabbe.

Thur·ney·sen \'túr-,nī-zən\, Rudolf. 1857–1940. Swiss philologist. Professor at Jena (1885), Freiburg (1887), Bonn (1913); often considered first to use principles of modern historical linguistics in Celtic studies. Published

Handbuch des Altirischen (1909), *Die irische Helden- und Königssage bis zum 17. Jahrhundert* (1921), *Das keltische Recht* (1935), etc.

Thurn·wald \'tůrn-vält\, Richard Christian. 1869–1954. German anthropologist and sociologist. Professor at Berlin (from 1924); made research expeditions to the Solomon Islands and Micronesia (1906–09, 1932), New Guinea (1912–15), and East Africa (1930); founder (1925) and long-time editor of *Zeitschrift für Völkerpsychologie und Soziologie.* Author of *Die Gemeinde der Bánaro* (1921), *Die menschliche Gesellschaft in ihren ethnosoziologischen Grundlagen* (1931–35), *Aufbau und Sinn der Völkerwissenschaft* (1948), etc.

Thurs·tan \'thərs-tən\ *or* **Turs·tin** \'tərs-tən\. d. 1140. English prelate. Native of Bayeux; secretary of Henry I; archbishop of York (1114), but was refused consecration by Archbishop Ralph de Turbine of Canterbury unless he professed obedience; crowned by Pope Calixtus at Reims (1119). Refused to acknowledge new archbishop of Canterbury, William of Corbeil, as primate (1123), and continued controversy; took active part in gathering army that defeated Scots at battle of the Standard (1138); entered order of Cluniacs (1140); founder of large number of monasteries in north of England.

Thur·ston \'thər-stən\, Howard. 1869–1936. American magician, b. Columbus, Ohio. Made tour of the world (1904–07); starred with Harry Kellar (1907–08); led (1908–31) largest magic show in history; famous for large stage illusions, as the "floating lady"; gave (1931–35) one-hour shows in movie theaters. Author of *My Life of Magic* (1929).

Thur·stone \'thər-,stōn\, Louis Leon. 1887–1955. American psychologist, b. Chicago. Professor at U. of Chicago (1927–52) and at U. of North Carolina, Chapel Hill (1952–55); improved methods for measuring intelligence; helped in development of multiple-factor analysis. Chief works *The Vectors of Mind* (1935) and *Multiple-Factor Analysis* (1947).

Thut·mo·se \thüt-'mō-sə\. Name of four kings of 18th dynasty of Egypt:

Thutmose I. King (c.1525–c.1512 B.C.). Of unknown, but not royal, birth; son-in-law and successor of Amenhotep I and perhaps co-regent with him; conquered Nubia; led successful expedition into Asia as far as the Euphrates; spent much of reign in building operations; built two pylons and hypostyle halls at Karnak and erected two obelisks; restored temple of Osiris at Abydos; had record of his deeds preserved in an inscription on rocks near third cataract of Nile; first king to erect his tomb in Valley of the Kings at Thebes.

Thutmose II. d. 1504 B.C. King (c.1512–1504 B.C.). Son of Thutmose I; married his half-sister Hatshepsut (*q.v.*); suppressed a revolt in Nubia; sent a punitive expedition to Palestine against some Bedouins.

Thutmose III. d. 1450 B.C. King (1504–1450 B.C.). Son of Thutmose II and a concubine, Isis; father of Amenhotep II. Dominated by regency (1504–1482) of his step-mother Hatshepsut (*q.v.*). One of the greatest of Egyptian kings; brought Egypt to the zenith of its power. Invaded Syria with great army; won battle of Megiddo (1479); came into conflict with powerful state of Mitanni; ravaged its territory, capturing several cities including Carchemish on the Euphrates; made seventeen campaigns into Asia, using booty and tribute to adorn Egyptian temples; devoted much time to building; enlarged great temple of Amon at Karnak and had his annals inscribed on its walls; built or restored many temples in Egyptian cities (Heliopolis, Memphis, Abydos, etc.) and in Nubia; erected many obelisks (including two known as Cleopatra's Needles, one now in New York, the other in London).

Thutmose IV. d. 1417 B.C. King (1425–1417 B.C.). Grandson of Thutmose III, son of Amenhotep II, and father of Amenhotep III; m. a Mitannian princess; contracted friendly alliances with Babylonia and the Mitanni; led military expedition into Lower Nubia and crushed a revolt; erected at Thebes large obelisk that now stands before St. John Lateran church in Rome; left memorials at Memphis.

Thwaites \'thwāts\, Reuben Gold. 1853–1913. American historian, b. Dorchester, Mass. Secretary, State Historical Society of Wisconsin (1887–1913); with assistants edited *Jesuit Relations and Allied Documents* (73 vols., 1896–1901), *Original Journals of the Lewis and Clark Expedition* (8 vols., 1904–05), Hennepin's *New Discovery* (1903), *Early Western Travels* (32 vols., 1904–07), etc.; author of *Father Marquette* (1902), *Daniel Boone* (1902), *France in America* (1905), etc.

Thynne \'thin\, Thomas. 3d Viscount Wey·mouth \'wā-məth\. 1st Marquis of Bath \'bath, båth\. 1734–1796. English politician. Viceroy of Ireland (1765); secretary of state (1768–70, 1775–79); gained favor of George III by vigor in repressing Wilkes riots (1768); opposed Lord North's Irish policy and attempt to suppress American Revolution; an outstanding orator but guilty of dissolute habits, indolence, and secretiveness concerning his official policies.

Thynne, William. *Alternative family surname* Boté·ville \'bät-(,)vil\. d. 1546. English scholar. First editor of Chaucer's works (1532). His son ¶Francis (1545–1608), writer; with others revised and continued Holinshed's *Chronicle* (1585–87); criticized Speght's 1st edition of Chaucer (in *Animadversions,* 1599) and assisted him with his 2d edition (1602); wrote *Emblemes and Epigrames* (verse, 1600).

Thys·sen \'tues-ən\, Fritz. 1873–1951. German industrialist. Inherited control of great iron- and steel-manufacturing combine, Vereinigte Stahlwerke (1926). Became (1923) a principal financial backer of Nazi party and aided in Hitler's rise to power; became economic dictator of the Ruhr industrial region (1933); disagreements with Hitler's policies (beginning 1936) caused his flight to Switzerland (1939); captured (1941) and imprisoned by Nazis; fined (1948) by German denazification court for being a "minor Nazi."

Ti·bal·di \tē-'bäl-dē\, Pellegrino. 1527–1596. Italian painter and architect. Municipal architect, Milan (1562); head architect, Milan cathedral (1567); to Spain (1586) in service of Phillip II. Works included frescoes in Palazzo Poggi and Church of San Giacomo Maggiore at Bologna and in the Escorial at Madrid; easel pictures as *Adoration of the Shepherds* (1549); and architectural works as churches of San Fedele and San Sebastiano at Milan and San Gaudenzio at Novara. His brother ¶Domenico (1541–1582) was painter, engraver, and architect.

Tib·bett \'tib-ət\, Lawrence Mervil. 1896–1960. American singer, b. Bakersfield, Cal. Concert debut (1917); debut at Metropolitan Opera, New York City (1923); regular member of Metropolitan company (1925–50), becoming principal baritone esp. in Italian roles; popular also in light opera, films, on radio, and on Broadway as in *The Barrier* (1950), *Fanny* (1956).

Ti·be·ri·us \tī-'bir-ē-əs\. *In full* Tiberius Claudius Nero Caesar Augustus. 42 B.C.–37 A.D. Second emperor of Rome (14–37 A.D.). Son of Tiberius Claudius Nero and Livia Drusilla; adopted by Emperor Augustus when the latter married his mother (38 B.C.); carefully educated. Commanded expedition to Armenia (20 B.C.) and with brother Nero Claudius Drusus against the Rhaetians (15 B.C.); consul (13 B.C.); on death of Drusus recalled to Germany (9 B.C.); again consul (7 B.C.); tribune (6 B.C.); forced by Augustus to divorce his wife Vipsania Agrippina (11 B.C.) and to marry Julia, daughter of Augustus; retired to Rhodes (6 B.C.–2 A.D.); made his heir by Augustus (4 A.D.); led Roman armies in many campaigns in Germany, Dalmatia, and Pannonia (4–14 A.D.). Became emperor (14 A.D.); at first wise and beneficent; later, esp. under influence of Sejanus, vicious, cruel and tyrannical; strengthened navy; increased wealth of treasury; prob. caused death of his nephew Germanicus Caesar (19 A.D.); had Sejanus killed (31 A.D.); spent last years of his life (27–37 A.D.) at Capri.

Tiberius. Name of two rulers of Eastern Roman Empire (see also TIBERIUS, Roman emperor before division):

Tiberius II Con·stan·ti·nus \,kän(t)-stən-'tī-nəs\. d. 582. Emperor (578–582). Soldier and court officer; adopted by Justin II (574) and named co-emperor (574); in control jointly with Sophia (574–578); reign troubled by conflicts with Persians and Avars; forced to surrender Sirmium to Avars (582).

Tiberius III Ap·si·mar \'ap-sə-,mär\. d. 705. Emperor (698–705). Commander of the fleet; overthrew Leontius (698); gained military successes over Saracens; seized when Justinian II was restored; beheaded.

Tiberius, Mauricius Flavius. See MAURICE.

Tiberius Claudius Drusus Nero Germanicus. See CLAUDIUS I.

Ti·bul·lus \tə-'bəl-əs\, Albius. c.55–c.19 B.C. Roman elegiac poet. Apparently of equestrian rank; enjoyed patronage of Marcus Valerius Messala Corvinus and may have accompanied him (c.30 B.C.) on his campaign to put down an insurrection in Aquitania; little of his life history known. Known for clear and unaffected style and exquisiteness of feeling and expression; two books of his verse are extant.

Tichborne Claimant. See Arthur ORTON.

Tick·ell \'tik-əl\, Thomas. 1686–1740. English poet. Published translation of first book of *Iliad* (1715), which because of Addison's praise Pope assumed to be Addison's, designed to eclipse his own version, thus occasioning the quarrel between Addison and Pope; undersecretary to Addison, secretary of state (1717); secretary to lords justices of Ireland (from 1724). Collected and edited Addison's works (1721); author of *Kensington Gardens* (1722) and other verse.

Tick·nor \'tik-nər, -,nȯ(ə)r\, George. 1791–1871. American educator and historian, b. Boston. Professor of French and Spanish and belles-lettres, Harvard (1819–35); a founder of Boston Public Library (1852). Among his works were *History of Spanish Literature* (1849), *Life of William Hickling Prescott* (1864).

Ticknor, William Davis. 1810–1864. American publisher, b. Lebanon, N.H. Cousin of George Ticknor. Established publishing house in Boston, Mass. (1832), which later, under firm name of Ticknor & Fields, became one of chief publishing houses in the U.S. Published the *Atlantic Monthly* and works by Hawthorne, Thoreau, Emerson, Longfellow, and other leading authors of the day.

Tieck \'tēk\, Ludwig, *in full* Johann Ludwig. 1773–1853. German writer. Settled in Dresden (1819) and became literary adviser to court theater there (1825); invited to Berlin (1841) by Frederick William IV of Prussia, and became center of literary society there. Among his works were the novels *Die Geschichte des Herrn William Lovell* (1795–96), *Franz Sternbalds Wanderungen* (1798), *Dichterleben* (1824–29), *Der junge Tischlermeister* (1836), *Vittoria Accorombona* (1840); several volumes of short stories, including

Volksmärchen (1797, containing "Der blonde Eckbert") under pseudonym Peter Le·be·recht \'lā-bə-,rekt\; series of plays based on fairy tales as *Ritter Blaubart* and *Der gestiefelte Kater;* dramas *Karl von Berneck* (1797), *Leben und Tod der heiligen Genoveva* (1800), and *Kaiser Octavianus* (1804); narrative collection *Phantasus* (1812–16), volumes of dramatic and literary criticism; translations of *The Tempest* (1799) and *Don Quixote* (1799–1801); and many lyric poems. His brother ¶Christian Friedrich (1776–1851) was a sculptor; lived in Weimar in association with Goethe and his circle (1801); modeled a number of portrait busts, including Goethe, Schelling, Humboldt.

Tie·de·mann \'tē-də-,män\, Dietrich. 1748–1803. German philosopher. Professor at Marburg (1786–1803); works included *Untersuchungen über den Menschen* (1777–78) and *Geist der spekulativen Philosophie* (1791–97). His son ¶Friedrich (1781–1861) was an anatomist and physiologist.

Tie·le \'tē-lə\, Cornelis Petrus. 1830–1902. Dutch theologian. Pastor at Moordrecht and Rotterdam; professor at Leiden (1877–1902); exerted great influence on comparative study of religion. Works included *Geschiedenis van den godsdienst* (1876) and *Inleiding tot de godsdienstwetenschap* (1897–99).

Tie·mann \'tē-,män\, Johann Carl Wilhelm Ferdinand. 1848–1899. German chemist. Taught at Berlin (from 1871); investigated terpenes and camphors; discovered commercial method of preparing vanilla from eugenol (1891); discovered ionone.

T'ien-ch'i. See CHU family.

T'ien–shun. See CHU family.

T'ien–ts'ung. See ABAHAI.

T'ien-wang. See HUNG HSIU-CH'ÜAN.

Tie·po·lo \'tye-pō-lō\, Giovanni Battista. 1696–1770. Italian painter. Master of Venetian school; employed at Venice, Würzburg (1750–53), and in Spain (1762–70). His style marked by use of chiaroscuro, masterly control, underlying melancholy; among his works were frescoes in Villa Valmerana at Vicenza, Palazzo Arcivescovile at Udine, Palazzo Labia and church of Santa Maria del Rosario at Venice, royal palace at Würzburg, and royal palace at Madrid; easel pictures as *Adoration of the Trinity by Pope Clement* (c.1735) and *Adoration of the Magi* (1753); portraits as *Procurator Giovanni Querini;* and etchings. His son and pupil ¶Giovanni Domenico, *also called* Gian·do·me·ni·co \,jän-dō-'mā-nē-kō\ (1727–1804) was a talented genre painter, esp. of scenes from contemporary life and the commedia dell'arte; his works included frescoes at church of S. Polo, Venice (1747–49), guest wing of Villa Valmarana, Vicenza (1757), royal palace, Würzburg (1750–53); also drawings and etchings. His brother ¶Lorenzo (1736–1776) was also a painter; aided his father with frescoes at royal palace, Würzburg (1750–53); specialized in genre scenes in pastel.

Tier·ney \'ti(ə)r-nē\, George. 1761–1830. English politician. M.P. (1788), leading opponent of Pitt's policy; treasurer of navy (1802); president of Board of Control (1806); leader of Whigs in opposition (1817–21); master of mint (1827–28).

Tiet·jens \'tē-jəns\, Eunice Strong, *nee* Ham·mond \'ham-ənd\. 1884–1944. American author, b. Chicago. Sister of Laurens Hammond; m. Paul Tietjens (1904; div. 1914); lived in China, Japan, Europe; on staff of magazine *Poetry,* Chicago (from 1913); lecturer, U. of Miami (1933–35). Author of textbooks on China and Japan, plays, a few novels and juveniles, books of verse, including *Profiles from China* (1917), *Body and Raiment* (1919), *Profiles from Home* (1925), *Leaves in Windy Weather* (1929), and the autobiographical *The World at My Shoulder* (1938).

Tietz \'tēts\, Johann Daniel. *Lat.* Ti·tius \'tish(-ē)-əs\. 1729–1796. German astronomer. Professor at Wittenberg (1756–96); first published (1766) the empirical expression of planetary distances from the sun, later popularized by J.E. Bode (*q.v.*) and called Bode's law or Titius-Bode rule.

Tif·fa·ny \'tif-ə-nē\, Charles Lewis. 1812–1902. American jeweler, b. Killingly, Conn. Opened store in New York City (1837, with John B. Young); began manufacturing own jewelry (1848); established branch in Paris (1850) and London (1868); adopted firm name, Tiffany & Co. (1853); incorporated (1868). His son ¶Louis Comfort (1848–1933), b. New York City, was a painter and stained-glass artist; among his paintings were *The Dock Scene; Study of Quimper, Brittany; Market Day at Nuremberg;* a founder of Society of American Artists (1877). Developed original process of making peculiarly beautiful opalescent glass called "favrile"; established (1878) factory at Cirona, N.Y., for manufacturing this glass; became a leader of Art Nouveau movement; designed chapel for World's Columbian Exposition, Chicago (1893) and high altar for Cathedral of St. John the Divine, New York; established and endowed Louis Comfort Tiffany Foundation, for art students (1919), at Oyster Bay, N.Y.

Tig·el·li·nus \,tij-ə-'lī-nəs\, Ofonius. d. 69 A.D. Roman politician. Chief adviser (62–68) of Nero, who made him prefect of praetorian guard (62); encouraged Nero's reign of terror after conspiracy of Piso (65); deserted Nero and carried praetorian guard with him (68); forced by Otho to commit suicide.

Tig·lath-pi·le·ser \'tig-,lath-pī-'lē-zər, -pə-\. *Hebrew form of Akkadian* Tu-kul·ti-apil-esh·ar·ra \tü-'kůl-tē-'äp-ə-'lesh-ə-rə\. Name of three kings of Assyria:

Tiglath-pileser I. Reigned (c.1115–c.1077 B.C.). Extended Assyrian dominions, esp. to northwest in regions of old Hittite empire on upper Euphrates; led campaign to seacoast of Mediterranean; defeated king of Babylonia, Marduk-nadin-ahhe; expelled Mushki invaders from Assyrian Armenia; renowned as mighty hunter.

Tiglath-pileser II. Reigned (c.964–934 B.C.).

Tiglath-pileser III. *Also known as* Pu·lu \'pəl-(,)ü\. Reigned (745–727 B.C.). Seized throne from his brother; consolidated control over existing territories by administrative reforms; subjugated tribes to the east and north; defeated Urartian ruler Sardur III (743); conquered Arpad (741); subjugated Israel and Samaria; defeated Philistines; captured many cities, including Gaza and Damascus (733–732); crushed revolt in Babylon (729 or 728) and made himself king in name as well as fact.

Ti·gra·nes I \tī-'grā-nēz\. *Also spelled* Di·kran \'dī-,kran\. *Called* the Great. c.140–c.55 B.C. King of Armenia (95 or 94–c.55 B.C.). Extended territories by conquest of northern Mesopotamia, Sophene, Syria, Cappadocia; gained suzerainty over kings of Atropatene, Gordyene, Adiabene, Osroene, Iberia, and Albania; founded new royal city, Tigranocerta; attacked and defeated by Romans under Lucullus (69 and 68); surrendered to Pompey (66) and ruled thereafter as vassal of Rome.

Tikamthe. See TECUMSEH.

Ti·kho·mi·rov \tyik-(,)əm-'yē-rəf\, Vasily Dimitrievich. 1876–1956. Russian dancer and teacher. Joined (1893) Bolshoi Ballet, Moscow, and soon became its *premier danseur;* created role of Soviet Captain in own version of *The Red Poppy* (1927); also successful in *Raymonda, Le Corsaire;* toured with Anna Pavlova (1914); often partnered his wife Yekaterina Geltzer (*q.v.*); member (from 1896), director (1924–37) of Bolshoi school staff.

Ti·khon \'tyē-kən\. *Orig.* Vasily Ivanovich Be·la·vin \byil-'yav-yin\. 1865–1925. Patriarch of Moscow and head of Russian Orthodox church. Bishop of Orthodox church in North America (1898–1907). Elected patriarch (1917); denounced Soviet government purge of church, nationalization of church schools, secularization of marriage, suppression of liberty and faith; imprisoned (1922–23); opposed "Living Church" movement.

Ti·lak \'tē-läk\, Bal Gangadhar. 1856–1920. Indian nationalist. Mathematics teacher, later owner and editor of two newpapers; imprisoned (1897, 1908–14) by British for nationalist activities; founder (1914) and president of Indian Home Rule League; concluded (1916) with Mohammed Ali Jinnah the Lucknow Pact for Hindu–Muslim accord. Laid foundation of India's independence; first to introduce methods of boycott of British goods (1905) and passive resistance (1906) into nationalist movement.

Til·den \'til-dən\, Samuel Jones. 1814–1886. American politician, b. New Lebanon, N.Y. Practiced law in New York City (from 1841); leader in the Free Soil element of the Democratic party (from 1848); leader in overthrow of Tweed Ring (1868–72). Governor of New York (1875–76). Democratic candidate for president of the United States (1876); received about 250,000 more votes than Rutherford B. Hayes, and 184 uncontested electoral votes against 163 for Hayes, with two sets of returns for Oregon, Louisiana, South Carolina, and Florida; an Electoral Commission, created to examine the contested returns, reported all the states in favor of Hayes, electing him president by one electoral vote. Tilden accepted the result to avoid civil war, but always maintained that he was wrongfully deprived of the election. Bequeathed his fortune to a Tilden Trust, to be used for establishing a free public library in New York City.

Tilden, William Tatem II. *Called* Big Bill. 1893–1953. American tennis player, b. Philadelphia. Won Wimbledon men's singles (1920, 1921, 1930) and doubles (1927), U.S. singles (1920, 1925, 1929) and doubles (1918, 1921, 1923, 1927), U.S. clay court singles (1918, 1922, 1927), etc.; member of U.S. Davis Cup team (1920–30); became professional tennis player (1931). Author of *The Art of Lawn Tennis* (1923), etc.

Til·dy \'til-dē\, Zoltán. 1889–1961. Hungarian politician. Protestant Reformed minister; joined Smallholders' party after World War I; elected to parliament (1936); premier of Hungary (1945); first president of Hungarian Republic (1946–48); forced to resign by Soviet pressure; minister of state (Oct.–Nov. 1956) in Imre Nagy's revolutionary government; imprisoned by Soviets (1956–59).

Tilgh·man \'til-mən\, Benjamin Chew. 1821–1901. American inventor, b. Philadelphia. Perfected the production of steel shot chilled to hardness; invented sulfite process for producing wood pulp for papermaking (1867); invented the sandblast (1871).

Tilghman, Tench. 1744–1786. American Revolutionary officer, b. Talbot Co., Md. Aide-de-camp and military secretary to General Washington (1776–83).

Til·le·mont \tēy-mōⁿ\, Louis-Sébastien Le Nain de \lə-naⁿ-də-\. 1637–1698. French historian. Chaplain at Port-Royal (1675); ordained (1676); settled at family estate at Tillemont after Jansenist persecutions of 1679. Collaborated in edition of writings of Church Fathers (1669); author of *Histoire des empereurs* (1690–1738) and *Mémoires pour servir à l'histoire ecclésiastique des six premiers siècles* (1693–1712).

Til·lett \'til-ət\, Benjamin. 1860–1943. English labor leader. General secretary of Dock, Wharf, Riverside, and General Workers' Union from its beginning (1887) to its amalgamation (1921) with Transport and General Workers' Union; a leader of dock strikes of 1889 and 1911; Labour M.P. (1917–24, 1929–31).

Til·ley \'til-ē\, Cecil Edgar. 1894–1973. British mineralogist, b. Australia. Professor, Cambridge U. (1931–61); known for investigations of mineral and rock synthesis; also studied tektites and their comparison to volcanic glasses.

Tilley, Sir Samuel Leonard. 1818–1896. Canadian politician, b. Gagetown, N.B. Became wealthy in pharmaceutical business; premier of New Brunswick (1861–65); powerful influence in cause of confederation; member of London conference that passed British North America Act (1867); member of Dominion Parliament; minister of customs and excise (1867–73), of finance (1873, 1878–85); lieutenant governor of New Brunswick (1873–78, 1885–93); formulator of national policy of protective tariff.

Tilley, Vesta. *Orig.* Matilda Alice Powles \'pōlz\. *Later in private life* Lady de Frece \də-'frēs\. 1864–1952. English entertainer. On stage from age 3; outstanding male impersonator in music hall history; appeared in pantomimes, musical comedies, burlesque, straight plays; retired (1920). Many of her songs, as "The Piccadilly Johnny with the Little Glass Eye" and "Following in Father's Footsteps," were written by her husband (m. 1890) Sir Walter de Frece (d. 1935).

Til·lich \'til-ik, *Angl* -ik\, Paul Johannes. 1886–1965. American theologian and philosopher, b. Starzeddel, Prussia. Ordained in Lutheran church (1912); chaplain in German army during World War I; taught (from 1919) in German universities until barred (1933) by Nazi government; to U.S. (1933, naturalized 1940); professor at Union Theological Seminary, New York (1933–55), Harvard (1955–62), U. of Chicago (1962–65). Attempted to synthesize traditional Christianity and modern culture in his major work, *Systematic Theology* (1951–63); also wrote *The Courage To Be* (1952) and *Dynamics of Faith* (1957).

Til·lier \tēl-yā\, Claude. 1801–1844. French journalist and novelist. Best known for his novel *Mon oncle Benjamin* (1841).

Till·man \'til-mən\, Benjamin Ryan. *Nicknamed* Pitchfork Ben. 1847–1918. American politician. b. Edgefield Co., S.C. Governor of South Carolina (1890–94); U.S. senator (1895–1918); advocate of Southern agrarianism and populist legislation.

Til·lot·son \'til-ət-sᵊn\, John. 1630–1694. English prelate. Preached against atheism, Puritanism, and Roman Catholicism; chaplain to Charles II. Dean of Canterbury (1670); canon of St. Paul's, London (1675), dean (1689); reluctantly accepted appointment as archbishop of Canterbury (1691), after deposition of nonjuror Sancroft; pursued relentlessly by nonjurors.

Tilly, Graf von. See TSERCLAES.

Tilpin. See TURPIN.

Til·you \'til-ˌyü\, George Cornelius. 1862–1914. American businessman, b. New York City. Opened (1897) Steeplechase Park, first amusement park on Coney Island; devised such attractions as the Human Roulette Wheel, Electric Seat, Barrel of Love, Aerial Thrill; said to have invented the hot dog; also operated amusement parks in New Jersey, Connecticut, Massachusetts, St. Louis, San Francisco.

Ti·mae·us \tī-'mē-əs\. fl. c.400 B.C. Greek astronomer. Native of Locri in Italy. His name is attached to one of Plato's dialogues, which embodies a theory of the universe.

Timaeus. c.356–c.260 B.C. Greek historian, b. Sicily. Exiled by Agathocles; lived in Athens for fifty years. His chief work, extant only in fragments, was a history of Italy and Sicily from earliest times to 264 B.C.

Ti·mag·e·nes \ti-'maj-ə-nēz, tī-\. 1st century B.C. Greek historian. Originally from Alexandria; captured and taken as slave to Rome; when freed, opened school of rhetoric in Rome; gained favor of Emperor Augustus. Author of *History of Augustus* and *History of the Diadochi.*

Ti·man·thes \ti-'man-ˌthēz, tī-\. fl. c.400 B.C. Greek painter, of Sicyon. His chief work *Sacrifice of Iphigenia,* regarded as one of the great paintings of antiquity.

Ti·me·sith·e·us \ˌtī-mə-'sith-ē-əs, ˌtim-ə-\, Gaius Furius Sabinus Aquila. d. 243 A.D. Roman general. Father-in-law of Emperor Gordianus III; able official in many provinces of empire; praetorian prefect (241–243); in Persian war defeated Shāpūr I (243).

Tim·ken \'tim-kən\, Henry. 1831–1909. American inventor and manufacturer, b. near Bremen, Germany. To U.S. (c.1838); established carriage manufacturing works, St. Louis (1855); invented special type of carriage spring (patented 1877) and a tapered roller bearing (patented 1898); organized Timken Roller Bearing Axle Co. (1898).

Tim·mer·mans \'tim-ər-mäns\, Felix. 1886–1947. Flemish writer. Known for idyllic regional novels *Pallieter* (1916), *De pastoor uit den bloeyenden wijngaerdt* (1924), *Boerenpsalm* (1935); also wrote short stories, plays, travel tales, autobiographical works, and romanticized biographies of Bruegel (1928) and St. Francis (1932).

Ti·mo·le·on \ti-'mō-lē-ən, tī-\ of Corinth. d. after 337 B.C. Greek statesman and general. Disapproved of his brother ¶**Ti·moph·a·nes** \ti-'mäf-ə-ˌnēz, tī-\ making himself tryant of Corinth and acquiesced in his execution (c.364). Sent to aid Greek cities in Sicily against tyrants (344); defeated and removed Hicetas, tyrant of Leontini, and Dionysius the Younger, tyrant of Syracuse; reorganized government; successfully defended Syracuse against attacks by Hicetas and a Carthaginian army (c.341); withdrew to private life (337 or 336).

Ti·mom·a·chus \ti-'mäm-ə-kəs, tī-\. 1st century B.C. Byzantine painter. Among known paintings were *Ajax, Medea, A Gorgon, Iphigenia in Tauris.*

Ti·mon \'tī-mən\. 5th century B.C. Athenian misanthrope. A wealthy nobleman; lost wealth and retired from society after being refused help from friends. Subject of Shakespeare's play *Timon of Athens.*

Timon of Phli·us \'flī-əs\. c.320–c.230 B.C. Greek skeptic. In youth earned living as dancer; pupil of Stilpo at Megara and Pyrrhon of Elis; acquired fame and fortune by lecturing; retired to Athens (c.275). Author of satirical poems (known as *silloi*) against dogmatic philosophers; also wrote prose, satyr plays, comedies, tragedies, and epic poems, only fragments of which are extant.

Timophanes. See TIMOLEON.

Ti·mo·shen·ko \tyim-(ˌ)ə-'shen-kə\, Semyon Konstantinovich. 1895–1970. Soviet army commander. Served in World War I; directed occupation of eastern Poland (1939) and part of operations against Finland (1939–40); created marshal and commissar for defense (1940); commanded defense of Smolensk and Moscow (1941); credited with halting German drive on Moscow; commander in chief on southwestern front, directing defense of Stalingrad and the Caucasus (1941–42), on northwestern front, directing winter offensive (1942–43).

Ti·moth·e·us \ti-'mäth-ē-əs, tī-\. c.450–c.360 B.C. Greek poet. Friend of Euripides; of his many lyrics, only fragments are extant.

Timotheus. d. 354 B.C. Athenian statesman and general. Son of Conon; elected strategus (378); captured Corcyra (375) and Samos (366–365) but failed to take Amphipolis. During Social War (357–355), held joint command of fleet with Chares and Iphicrates; with Iphicrates, refused to engage enemy fleet because of weather conditions, Chares leading his division of fleet into action with disastrous results; subsequently fined; unable to pay, withdrew to Chalcis.

Tim·o·thy \'tim-ə-thē\. Saint. d. traditionally 97 A.D. Christian religious, b. Lystra, Turkey. Converted (50) by St. Paul, whom he accompanied on missions to Corinth, Ephesus, Asia Minor; traditionally, first bishop of Ephesus and martyred under Nero. Recipient of two New Testament pastoral letters from Paul; according to St. John of Damascus, witnessed assumption of the Virgin Mary.

Tim·rod \'tim-ˌräd\, Henry. 1828–1867. American poet, b. Charleston, S.C. Gained fame as "laureate of the Confederacy" with a series of impassioned poems inspired by outbreak of the Civil War, including "Ethnogenesis" (1861), "Cotton Boll," "Charleston," "Katie," "A Cry to Arms," "Carolina," "Magnolia Cemetery."

Ti·mur \tē-'mür\. *Also called* Timur Lenk \-'leŋk\, *i.e.* Timur the Lame. *Known in English as* Tam·er·lane \'tam-ər-ˌlān\ *or* Tam·bur·laine \'tam-(b)ər-\. 1336–1405. Turkic conqueror, b. near Samarkand. Made himself lord of Transoxiana with capital at Samarkand (by 1370); conquered Khurasan and eastern Persia (1383–85); subjugated (1386–94) Iraq, Armenia, Mesopotamia, and Georgia; routed the Golden Horde; marched into Russia and occupied Moscow; invaded (1398) India, destroying Delhi; sacked (1401) Damascus and Baghdad; defeated Turks in great battle at Angora (1402), capturing Sultan Bayezid I and compelling him to raise siege of Constantinople; died during expedition to conquer China; his mausoleum, the Gūr-e Amīr, one of gems of Islāmic art. Remembered for the barbarity of his conquests and for transforming Samarkand into a center of culture.

Ti·nayre \tē-ner\, Marcelle, *nee* Chas·teau \shä-tō\. 1872–1948. French novelist. m. Julien Tinayre (1889; d. 1923); wrote *Avant l'amour* (1897), *Maison du péché* (1899), *La Rebelle* (1905), *Un Drame de famille* (1925), *L'Ennemi intime* (1931).

Tinc·to·ris \tiŋk-'tō-rəs\, Johannes. c.1435–1511. Belgian composer and music theorist. In service of King Ferdinand I of Naples (from c.1472); member of Papal Chapel (1484–1500); established a public music school in Naples. Composed chiefly sacred music as *Missa l'homme armé;* his musical treatises included *Proportionale musices* (c.1473), *Liber de arte contrapuncti* (1477), and the earliest music dictionary, *Terminorum musicae diffinitorium* (c.1472, pub. 1495).

Tin·dal \'tin-dᵊl\, Matthew. 1657–1733. English Deist. Raised storm with *The Rights of the Christian Church Asserted* (1706), disputing possession by priests of any independent power over the church and defending theory of state control, and with *Christianity as Old as the Creation* (1730), divesting religion of the miraculous element and setting up morality as alone giving religion its claim to reverence.

Tindal *or* **Tindale,** William. See TYNDALE.

Tindaro, Marchese del. See Mariano RAMPOLLA.

Ti·nel \tē-nel\, Edgar Pierre Joseph. 1854–1912. Belgian pianist and composer. Wrote two operas, oratorios including *Franciscus* (1890), a mass for five voices, cantatas, etc.

Ting·ley \'tiŋ-lē\, Katherine Augusta, *nee* West·cott \'wes-kət\. 1847–1929. American theosophist, b. Newbury, Mass. m. Philo B. Tingley, her third husband (1888); merged (1898) the Theosophical Society into a new organization, Universal Brotherhood, of which she was the head, with headquarters at Point Loma, Calif.

Tin·ker \'tiŋ-kər\, Chauncey Brewster. 1876–1963. American educator, b. Auburn, Me. Taught English at Yale (1903–45); authority on Samuel Johnson and his period in English literature.

Tin·né \'tin-ə\, Alexandrine-Pieternella-Françoise. 1835–1869. Dutch explorer. Explored course of the Nile to Gondokoro (1861–62); explored the Upper Nile into northeastern Congo; murdered by Tuaregs at beginning of another expedition.

Ti·no di Ca·ma·i·no \'tē-nō-dē-ˌkäm-ä-'ē-nō\. c.1285–1337. Sienese sculptor. Possibly a pupil of Giovanni Pisano; made head of works at Pisa cathedral (1315); commissioned to make tomb for Emperor Henry VII (1315); supervised (1319–21) works at Siena cathedral, esp. monument for Cardinal Petroni; later worked in Florence and Naples.

Tintoretto. See Jacopo ROBUSTI.

Tiom·kin \'tyòm-kyin, *Angl* tē-'äm(p)-kin\, Dimitri. 1894–1979. American composer, b. St. Petersburg, Russia. Concert pianist in Europe; to U.S. (1929, naturalized 1937), settling in Hollywood, Calif.; resident in London (1968–79). Composed musical scores for over 140 films, including *Lost Horizon* (1937), *Duel in the Sun* (1947), *The Thing* (1951), *High Noon* (1952, won Academy Awards), *The High and the Mighty* (1954, Academy Award), *Giant* (1955), *The Old Man and the Sea* (1958, Academy Award), *The Guns of Navarone* (1961); also composed for television, esp. theme for "Rawhide" show.

Tip·pu Tib \'tē-pü-'tib\. *Also called* Muhammed bin Hamid. 1837–1905. Arab trader. Made trading expeditions into interior of Africa (from later 1850s or early 1860s); established a loosely organized state in east and central Congo (by late 1860s); monopolized ivory trade of the region; accompanied Stanley part way down the Congo (1876–77); allied himself with Sultan Barghash of Zanzibar (early 1880s); forced to recognize Leopold II's claim to the Congo Basin (1887); retired to Zanzibar (1890).

Tip·toft \'tip-tòft\, John. Earl of Worces·ter \'wůs-tər\. 1427?–1470. English administrator. Created earl (1449); lifelong supporter of house of York; treasurer of exchequer (1452–54); lord high constable (1462–67, 1470); gained reputation for cruelty by executions; virtually Edward IV's prime minister (1470) until the latter's flight; captured and executed.

Ti·pu Sul·tan \'tē-pü-'sůl-tän\. *Also spelled* Tippu. *Orig.* Fa·teh Ali Tipu \fä-'te-ä-'lē-\. 1749 or 1753–1799. Sultan of Mysore (1782–99). Son of Hyder Ali; fought against the Marāthās (1767–79); defeated Col. John Brathwaite at the Coleroon River (1782); built up powerful court at Seringapatam; provoked British invasion by attacking protected state of Travancore (1789); opposed by alliance of British with the Marāthās and the Nizām in Third Mysore War (1790–92); defeated and forced by treaty of Seringapatam (1792) to cede half his domain; killed in action at storming of Seringapatam in Fourth Mysore War (1799); his dominions partitioned.

Ti·ra·bo·schi \ˌtē-rä-'bòs-kē\, Girolamo. 1731–1794. Italian scholar. Librarian to Duke of Modena (1770); chief work *Storia della letteratura italiana* (13 vols., 1772–82).

Tiradentes. See SILVA XAVIER.

Ti·rard \tē-rár\, Pierre-Emmanuel. 1827–1893. French politician. Prime minister (1887–88, 1889–90); had to deal with Boulangist movement.

Tirhaka. See TAHARQA.

Tir·i·da·tes \ˌtir-ə-'dāt-(ˌ)ēz\. *Parthian* Trdat \tər-'dät\. Name of three kings of Armenia:

Tiridates I. d. 73? A.D. King (51–60, 63–?73 A.D.). Brother of an Arsacid king of Parthia; driven out (60) by Corbulo, a Roman general; restored (63); went to Rome and received (66) Armenian crown from Nero.

Tiridates II. *Also called* Khosrow the Great. d. c.238 A.D. King (217–c.238). Recognized as king by Romans after they unsuccessfully tried to annex his country; resisted the Sāsānian Persians; assassinated by Persian agent.

Tiridates III. c.238–314. King (259–314). Driven out of Armenia by Persians (252); became king (259); after defeat by Persians, again secured throne (286) with aid of Diocletian; made wide conquests; baptized (303) by Saint Gregory and established Christianity in Armenia.

Tiridates. *Parthian* Trdat. Name of two Parthian princes:

Tiridates II. 1st century B.C. Revolted and drove Phraates IV into exile (32 B.C.); fled (33) to Syria on return of Phraates; unsuccessfully invaded Mesopotamia (26).

Tiridates III. 1st century A.D. Grandson of Phraates IV; captured by Romans; taken to Rome and educated there; placed on Parthian throne by Romans (35 A.D.); fled to Syria on return of Artabanus III (36).

Tir·mi·dhī, at- \ůt-tir-mē-'dē\. *In full* Abū ʿĪsā Muḥammad ibn ʿĪsā ibn Sawrah ibn Shaddād at-Tirmidhī. d. c.892. Arab scholar. Author of *al-Jāmiʿ aṣ-ṣaḥīḥ,* one of six canonical collections of traditions of the prophet Muḥammad.

Ti·ro \'tī-rō\, Marcus Tullius. 1st century B.C. Roman freedman. Private secretary to Cicero; invented the Tironian system of shorthand; edited many of Cicero's works.

Tiro, Prosper. See PROSPER of Aquitaine.

Tir·pitz \'tir-pits\, Alfred von. 1849–1930. German naval commander. Commissioned in Prussian navy (1869); cruiser squadron commander in East Asia (1896–97); selected Tsingtao as German naval base in China (1897). As secretary of state in Imperial Navy department (1897–1916) credited with creating the formidable German high-seas fleet. After fall of German Empire (1918), took refuge in Switzerland, where he published *Erinnerungen* (1919); later returned to Germany and became member of Reichstag (1924–28).

Tirso de Molina. See Gabriel TÉLLEZ.

Ti·ru·val·lu·var \ˌtir-ə-'vəl-ə-var\. c.2d century A.D. Indian Tamil poet. By tradition, a weaver of southern India; reputed author of the *Kural,* a collection of 1330 maxims treating of virtue, wealth, and pleasure.

Tisch·bein \'tish-ˌbīn\, Johann Heinrich. 1722–1789. German painter. Court painter to William VIII of Hesse-Kassel; known esp. for his mythological canvases and portraits of German princes and princesses. A nephew ¶Johann Friedrich August Tischbein (1750–1812) was also a painter; director of Leipzig Academy (from 1800); known esp. for his portraits. Another nephew ¶Johann Heinrich Wilhelm Tischbein (1751–1829) was also a painter; a friend of Goethe; resident in Italy (1779–99); director of Naples art academy (1789–99); court painter to the Duke of Oldenburg (1809); best known for painting *Goethe in the Campagna* (1787).

Ti·schen·dorf \'tish-ən-ˌdòrf\, Konstantin von, *in full* Lobegott Friedrich Konstantin von. 1815–1874. German biblical scholar. Worked throughout life on recensions of New Testament text; traveled in Palestine and Near East (1844, 1853, 1859); discovered many manuscripts, including, at Monastery of St. Catherine in the Sinai, *Codex Sinaiticus* (which he edited, 1862); his 8th edition (1869) of the Greek New Testament is a standard book of reference.

Ti·se·li·us \ti-'sā-lē-əs\, Arne Wilhelm Kaurin. 1902–1971. Swedish biochemist. Research associate at Inst. for Advanced Study, Princeton U. (1934–35); professor at Uppsala (1938–68); awarded Nobel prize for chemistry (1948) for his studies concerning the nature of serum proteins.

Ti·si \'tē-sē\ *or* **Ti·sio** \'tēs-yō\, Benvenuto. *Known as* Benvenuto da Ga·ro·fa·lo \dä-ˌgär-ō-'fäl-ō\. 1481–1559. Italian painter. Most prolific 16th-century painter of the Ferrarese school; apprenticed to Domenico Panetti; influenced by paintings of Raphael and Michelangelo; works included several nativity scenes, ceiling paintings in Seminario at Ferrara (1519), *Sacrifice to Ceres* (1526), *Baptist Taking Leave of His Father* (1542).

Ti·so \'tyis-ò\, Josef *or* Joseph. 1887–1947. Slovak clergyman and politician. Ordained priest (1909); member of Slovak People's party (from 1921), succeeded Hlinka as its leader (1938); minister of public health (1927); prime minister of Slovakia (1938); president of Slovakia (1939–45); signed pact of adherence to Axis (1940); hanged.

Tis·san·dier \tē-saⁿ-dyā\, Gaston. 1843–1899. French aeronaut. Made numerous balloon ascensions (from 1868); with his brother Albert, constructed and flew first model of a dirigible propelled by electricity (1883).

Tis·sa·pher·nes \ˌtis-ə-'fər-ˌnēz\. *Old Persian* Chith·ra·far·na \ki-trä-'fär-nä\. d. 395 B.C. Persian satrap in Asia Minor. Satrap of Lydia and Caria; at first (413) allied with Sparta to regain Ionia; replaced as satrap by Darius (407); opposed Cyrus the Younger and supported Artaxerxes II; engaged in battle of Cunaxa (401); pursued the Greek Ten Thousand on their return march; appointed by Artaxerxes chief ruler in western Asia; defeated by Agesilaus near Sardis (395) and executed by order of the king.

Tis·se·rand \tēs-räⁿ\, François-Félix. 1845–1896. French astronomer. Professor at the Sorbonne (1883); director, Paris observatory (1892); noted for his textbook *Traité de mécanique céleste* (1889–96) and for producing the *Catalogue photographique de la carte du ciel* (from 1892).

Tis·sot \tē-sō\, James, *orig.* Jacques-Joseph. 1836–1902. French painter, engraver, and enameler. Traveled in Palestine (1887) and made studies for a set of 300 watercolor paintings, exhibited (1894) under the title *Vie de Notre-Seigneur Jésus-Christ.*

Ti·sza \'tis-ä\, Kálmán. 1830–1902. Hungarian politician. Prime minister of Hungary (1875–90); leader of Freethinkers' party; instituted social, economic, and legal reforms. His son ¶István (1861–1918), count, was also a politician; entered parliament (1886); a leader of Liberal party; prime minister of Hungary (1903–05, 1913–17); prominent supporter of Austro-Hungarian dualist system of government; opponent of reform; supported alliance with Germany throughout World War I and held responsible for Hungary's suffering during that war; assassinated.

Titch·e·ner \'tich-ən-ər, 'tich-nər\, Edward Bradford. 1867–1927. American psychologist, b. Chichester, England. Pupil and follower of Wilhelm Wundt; instructor (1892–95), professor (1895–1927), Cornell; known as foremost exponent of structural psychology; associate editor (1895–1921), editor (1921–25) of *American Journal of Psychology;* founded Society of Experimental Psychologists (1904). Author of *Experimental Psychology* (1901–05), *A Textbook of Psychology* (1909–10), etc.

Titch·marsh \'tich-ˌmärsh\, Edward Charles. 1899–1963. English mathematician. Professor at Oxford (1931–63); made many contributions to various branches of mathematical analysis. Author of *The Zeta-Function of Riemann* (1930), *The Theory of Functions* (1932), *Introduction to the Theory of Fourier Integrals* (1937), *Eigenfunction Expansions Associated with Second-Order Differential Equations* (1946, 1958), and *The Theory of the Riemann Zeta-Function* (1951).

Titcomb, Timothy. See Josiah HOLLAND.

Tite·louze \tēt-lüz\, Jehan. 1562 or 1563–1633. French organist and composer. Organist (1588–1633) and canon (1610) at Rouen cathedral; as organist, known for improvisational skills. Composed organ church music in a contrapuntal and modal style, including *Hymnes de l'église pour toucher sur l'orgue* (1623), eight cycles of versets in *Le Magnificat* (1626), masses for choir, etc.

Titian. See Tiziano VECELLI.

Titius, Johann Daniel. See Johann TIETZ.

Titl \'tēt-əl\, Anton Emil. 1809–1882. Bohemian composer. Wrote operas *Die Burgfrau* (1832) and *Das Wolkenkind* (1845), Singspiels, sacred music, orchestral pieces, and songs.

Titmarsh, Michael Angelo. See William THACKERAY.

Ti·to \'tē-tō, *Angl* 'tēt-(ˌ)ō\. *Orig.* Josip Broz \'brȯz, 'brōz\. 1892–1980. Yugoslav statesman. Mechanic by trade; decorated for bravery during World War I; joined Communist party (early 1920s) and rose to secretary general (1937); effective leader of Yugoslav partisans during World War II; became head of Yugoslavia and given title of marshal (1943); established independence from Soviet Union (1948). First president of republic of Yugoslavia (1953–80); conducted policy of nonalignment with Soviet Union or the West; established ties with other nonaligned nations in Africa, Asia, Latin America.

Ti·tu·le·scu \ˌtē-tü-'les-kü\, Nicolae. 1883–1941. Romanian diplomat and politician. Professor of civil law; minister of finance (1917, 1920–21); Romanian representative at peace negotiations at St. Germain and Trianon (1919–20); Romanian minister in London (1922–26, 1928–32); minister of foreign affairs (1927, 1932–36); a leading advocate of European collective security.

Ti·tus \'tīt-əs\. Saint. 1st century A.D. Christian religious. Disciple of and secretary to St. Paul the Apostle; apparently replaced Timothy as Paul's commissioner at Corinth; superintendent of churches in Crete, where he received a New Testament epistle from Paul; traditionally, bishop of Crete.

Titus. *In full* Titus Flavius Ves·pa·si·a·nus \ˌves-ˌpā-zhē-'ā-nəs\. 39–81 A.D. Second of the Flavian emperors of Rome (79–81). Eldest son of Emperor Vespasian; brother of Domitian. Served in campaigns in Germany and Britain; later entrusted by his father with command of legion in Judea (69–70); besieged and captured Jerusalem (70); granted joint triumph with Vespasian at Rome (71); Arch of Titus erected by Domitian (81) to commemorate taking of Jerusalem. Received command of praetorian guard (71); his father's colleague in censorship of 73 and in several consulships. Reign marked by great beneficence and by solicitude for welfare of people; helped rebuild Rome after fire of 80; completed construction of the Colosseum.

Tiy \'tē\. fl. 1400 B.C. Queen of Egypt. Wife of Amenhotep III and mother of Akhenaton; a commoner, daughter of the commander of the chariotry; exerted considerable influence during her husband's reign.

Tjo·kro·ami·no·to \ˌchō-krō-ˌäm-ē-'nō-tō\, Omar Said. 1882–1935. Indonesian nationalist. Organized (1912) nationalist group Sarekat Islām and shaped it into influential popular force; tutor and father-in-law to Sukarno; lost influence by passive and conciliatory policies.

To·ba II \tō-bä\. *Jp.* Go-Toba \gō-\. 1180–1239. 82d emperor of Japan (1183–98). Placed on throne by Minamoto clan; abdicated (1198) in favor of his son but retained control by forming a cloister government; instigated uprising (1221) against regent Hōjō Yoshitoki in attempt to return power from Kamakura shogunate to the imperial house; defeated after a month and thereafter exiled.

To·ba Sō·jō \tō-bä-sō-jō\. *Also called* Ka·ku·yū \käk-ü-yü\. *Known as* Abbot of Toba. 1053–1140. Japanese painter. 47th head priest of the Enryaku-ji; traditionally regarded as artist of important series of narrative scrolls featuring humorous secular subjects, *Shigisan engi* and *Chōjū giga,* latter using animals to represent human activities, foibles, etc.

To·bey \'tō-bē\, Mark. 1890–1976. American painter, b. Centerville, Wis. Art teacher (from 1922); traveled in Far East (1934–36); known for his "white line" or "white writing" technique based on Oriental calligraphy; works included *Broadway* (1936), *Multiple Voyages* (1957).

Toch \'tȯk\, Ernst. 1887–1964. American composer, b. Vienna, Austria. Taught in Berlin (1929–33), New School for Social Research, New York (1934–36), U. of Southern California (1937–48), privately (from 1948); naturalized (1940). Composed mainly in Neoclassical style but sometimes in chromatic idiom; works included 7 symphonies, esp. the *Third* (1956, Pulitzer prize), *Piano Concerto* (1926), *Bunte Suite* (1929), chamber music, chamber operas, vocal works, esp. *Gesprochene Musik* (1930), music for films, and much piano music; wrote *Melodielehre* (1923) and *The Shaping Forces in Music* (1948).

Tocque·ville \tȯk-vēl\, Alexis-Charles-Henri Clé·rel de \klā-rel-də-\. 1805–1859. French writer and politician. With Gustave de Beaumont spent 9 months in U.S. (1831–32) and with him published *Du système pénitentiaire aux États-Unis et de son application en France* (1833); gained international fame with *De la démocratie en Amérique* (1835, 1840), giving perceptive analysis of the American political system and social structure of the early 19th century. Elected to Chamber of Deputies (1839); member of Constituent Assembly (1848) and Legislative Assembly (1849); minister of foreign affairs (1849); opposed Louis-Napoléon's coup d'état (1851) and was for a short time imprisoned. His *L'Ancien Régime et la Révolution* (vol. 1, 1856) was incomplete at his death.

Todd \'täd\, Henry John. 1763–1845. English clergyman and editor. Edited Milton and Spenser; improved Johnson's etymologies and brought number of dictionary entries up to about 58,000 words in his edition of *Johnson's Dictionary* (1818).

Todd, Thomas. 1765–1826. American jurist, b. King and Queen Co., Va. Adm. to bar (1786); chief justice of Kentucky court system (1806); associate justice, U.S. Supreme Court (1807–26).

Todt \'tōt\, Fritz. 1891–1942. German military engineer. As inspector general of roads in Hitler's cabinet (1933), responsible for building high-speed highways; major general (1938); builder of the line of defenses in the West (West Wall) and the Atlantic Wall along the French and Belgian coasts.

Toep·ler \'tœp-lər\, August Joseph Ignaz. 1836–1912. German physicist. Worked in acoustics; invented an air pump for producing a high vacuum.

Toft \'tȯft, 'täft\, Thomas. fl. 1660–80. English potter. Worked in Staffordshire; known for excellence of his slipware; first to add fireclay to the paste. Another Staffordshire potter ¶Ralph Toft (fl. 1670–80) may have been Thomas's brother.

Togh·rïl Beg \tōg-'rēl-'beg\. *Also* Ṭugh·ril Beg \təg-\. c.990–1063. Founder of the Turkish Seljuq dynasty. Grandson of Seljuq; with his brother Chaghrï conquered Khorāsān (1040), which he gave to Chaghrï to rule; extended his empire into Caspian areas of Khorāsān, Rayy, and Hamadan (1040–44), to Isfahan and Anatolia; assumed leadership of the Islāmic world by establishing mastery over the 'Abbāsid caliphate in Baghdad (1060).

To·gliat·ti \tōl-'yät-tē\, Palmiro. 1893–1964. Italian politician. Became (1924) member of Central Committee of Italian Communist party and its leader; member of secretariat of Comintern (1935); minister without portfolio (1944); vice premier under Alcide de Gasperi (1945); made his party most powerful Communist party in western Europe.

To·gō \tō-gō\ Heihachirō. Marquis. 1846–1934. Japanese admiral. Served in Sino–Japanese War (1894–95). Commanded Japanese fleet in Russo–Japanese War (1904–05); directed successful naval blockade of Russian base at Port Arthur (Feb. 1904–Jan. 1905); won great battle of Tsushima, annihilating Russian fleet with a brilliant tactical maneuver of own devising (May 27–28, 1905). Member of supreme military council (1909); created count (1907) and marquis (1934).

To·gon-tem·ür \'tō-'gōn-'təm-'ɯ̄r\. *Posthumous names* Hui Tsung \'hwēd-'zùŋ\ *and* Shun Ti \'shün-'dē\. 1320–1370. Chinese emperor (1333–68), last of Yüan dynasty. A weak ruler, spending most of his time in sybaritic pursuits; at first (1333–39) power held by minister Bayan, later by eunuchs and Buddhist priests; fled (1368) Peking on advance by rebel leader Chu Yüan-chang, thus ending the Yüan dynasty.

Tō·jō \tō-jō\ Hideki. 1884–1948. Japanese soldier and politician. Chief of staff of Kwangtung army in Manchuria (1937–38); vice minister of war (1938–39); minister of war (1940–41); prime minister (1941–44); hanged as war criminal.

To·ki·wa \tō-kē-wä\ Mitsunaga. fl. 1173 A.D. Japanese painter. Famous for his detailed scroll paintings of groups of courtiers, as *Nenjū-gyōji* (1173), of which 20 of the original 60 hand scrolls survive in copies.

To·ku·da \tō-ku̇d-ä\ Shūsei. *Orig.* Tokuda Sueo. 1871–1943. Japanese novelist. One of the "four pillars" of Japanese Naturalism; early disciple of Ozaki Kōyō. Works included *Shin-jotai* (1907), *Ashiato* (1910), *Kabi* (1911), *Tadare* (1914), *Kasō jimbutsu* (1935–38), *Shukuzu* (1941–46).

To·ku·ga·wa \tō-ku̇g-ä-wä\. Japanese noble family holding the shogunate of Japan (1603–1867) with its capital at Edo (Tokyo); its shoguns had control over emperors until the Meiji Restoration (1867). Its shoguns were:

Tokugawa Ieyasu. *Orig.* Ma·tsu·dai·ra \mat-su̇d-ˈī-rä\ Takechiyo. 1543–1616. Shogun (1603–05). Allied himself with Oda Nobunaga (from c.1560) and (from 1582) with Toyotomi Hideyoshi; continually expanded his domains; established his capital at Edo (modern Tokyo); on Hideyoshi's death (1598), engaged in power struggle with other *daimyos,* totally defeating them at battle of Sekigahara (1600). Appointed shogun (1603) by the emperor, thus assuming complete control of government and establishing Tokugawa shogunate; his many sons put in possession of large fiefs. Abdicated (1605) in favor of his son Hidetada but actually retained complete control of affairs; at first sponsored trade with West and introduction of Christian missionaries, later (after 1612) discouraged both; built huge castle at Edo; besieged the Toyotomi castle at Osaka (1614–15), destroying last supporters of Hideyoshi and causing suicide of Toyotomi Hideyori.

Tokugawa Hidetada. 1579–1632. Shogun (1605–23). Son of Ieyasu; wielded little power until death (1616) of father; completed consolidation of family's rule; began elimination of Christianity from Japan, including ordering first executions of missionaries (1617); severed relations with Spain (1624); closed all ports to foreign vessels except for Nagaski and Hirodi.

Tokugawa Iemitsu. 1604–1651. Shogun (1623–51). Son of Hidetada; completed his father's program of eliminating Christianity; forced entire population to register as parishioners of some Buddhist temple; ordered massacre of Christians at Shimabara Peninsula (1638); expelled the Portuguese (1639); ended all commerce with outside world except for limited, strictly regulated trade with the Dutch and Chinese at Nagasaki; brought Tokugawa shogunate to zenith of its power.

Tokugawa Ietsuna. 1641–1680. Shogun (1651–80). Son of Iemitsu; a weak ruler, much authority exercised by his prime minister.

Tokugawa Tsunayoshi. 1646–1709. Shogun (1680–1709). Brother of Ietsuna; his reign one of most prosperous and peaceful in Japanese history; promoted the Neo-Confucianism of Chu Hsi; in later part of reign ignored governmental duties for pleasure; known as the "Dog Shogun" because of decree ordering death penalty for anyone harming a dog and for keeping over 50,000 dogs at government expense.

Tokugawa Ineobu. 1662–1712. Shogun (1709–12). Nephew of Tsunayoshi and grandson of Iemitsu.

Tokugawa Ietsugu. 1709–1716. Shogun (1712–16). Son of Ienobu.

Tokugawa Yoshimune. 1684–1751. Shogun (1716–45). Member of a branch of the main Tokugawa line; became head of fief of Kii (1705); as shogun instituted many reforms that totally revamped the government; eliminated court luxuries and combated corruption; did much for agriculture, developing new land and encouraging planting of new crops; permitted interest in Western science; helped develop law code completed after his death as Kansei Code.

Tokugawa Ieshige. 1711–1761. Shogun (1745–60). Son of Yoshimune, who handled government affairs until his death (1651); his reign a period of decline.

Tokugawa Ieharu. 1737–1786. Shogun (1760–86). Son of Ieshige; led profligate life, ignoring official duties; decline of shogunate continued.

Tokugawa Ienari. 1773–1841. Shogun (1786–1837). Grandson of Yoshimune; government ably administered (1787–1801) by Matsudaira Sadanobu (*q.v.*); took charge after Matsudaira's retirement (1801) and ruled over an age of luxury.

Tokugawa Ieyoshi. 1793–1853. Shogun (1837–53). Son of Ienari; his reign a troubled one; government controlled (1837–43) by Mizuno Tadakuni (*q.v.*), who instituted the Tempō reforms; refused trade to James Biddle (1846).

Tokugawa Iesada. 1824–1858. Shogun (1853–58). Son of Ieyoshi; signed treaty (1854) with Matthew Perry, opening two ports; forced to grant similar concessions to England and Netherlands (1855); faced with growing power of Ii Naosuke and the emperor; being without issue, appointed Iemochi heir.

Tokugawa Iemochi. 1846–1866. Shogun (1858–66). Member of branch of family in Kii; at first (1858–60) government completely controlled by prime minister Ii Naosuke (*q.v.*); later (1862) under guardianship of Tokugawa Keiki, who attempted by bring shogunate and imperial court closer; twice paid homage to the emperor.

Tokugawa Keiki. *Also known as* Hi·to·tsu·ba·shi \hē-tōt-süb-äsh-ē\ Keiki *and by assumed name* Tokugawa Yoshinobu. 1837–1913. Last shogun of Japan (1866–1867). Son of Tokugawa Nariaki (see below); was adopted by, and became (1862) head of, the Hitotsubashi family, branch of the Tokugawa family; appointed (1862) guardian of Iemochi; attempted to move shogunate and imperial court closer; had little success in subduing rebelling rulers of Chōshū fief (1864–66); as shogun made vain effort to obtain French aid; on Meiji Restoration secured a peaceful transition of power to the emperor; lived in retirement at Shizuoka; created prince (1902).

Other members of the family were:

¶Tokugawa Mitsukuni. 1628–1700. Feudal lord of Mito and historian. Grandson of Ieyasu; influential member of government; began (1657) his monumental history of Japan, *Dai Nihon shi,* a work that helped establish Confucianism in Japan and revive loyalty to the emperor (history finally completed in 1906).

¶Tokugawa Nariaki. 1800–1860. Feudal lord of Mito (from 1829). Father of Keiko; leader in movement to restore power to the emperor; vigorous advocate of keeping foreigners out of Japan; made his fiefdom one of most powerful by carrying out financial and administrative reforms; built extensive public works, iron and shipbuilding industries; demanded no concessions be made to Matthew Perry (1853); unsuccessfully attempted to make his son Keiki the shogun (1858); ordered into retirement for attacking treaty with U.S. (1858).

To·ku·to·mi \tō-ku̇t-ō-mē\ Sohō. *Orig.* Tokutomi Ichirō. 1863–1957. Japanese writer. One of leading nationalist writers before World War II, esp. with *Shōrai no Nihon* (1886); founded periodical *Kokumin no tomo* (1887) and newspaper *Kokumin Shimbun* (1890); also wrote *Kinsei Nihon Kokuminshi* (1918–46), valuable history of Japan from 1534 to late 19th century. His brother ¶Tokutomi Rōka, *orig.* Tetsujirō (1868–1927), was a novelist; worked as writer for his brother's publications; author of novels *Hototogisu* (1900) and *Omoide no ki* (1901), nature sketches *Shizen to jinsei* (1900), and autobiographical *Mimizu-no-tawagoto* (1913).

To·land \ˈtō-lənd\, John, *orig.* Junius Janus. 1670–1722. Irish Deist. Brought up as Roman Catholic, but became Protestant at early age; launched warfare between Deists and the orthodox with *Christianity not Mysterious* (1696); wrote *Life of Milton* (1698), which led to charges of heresy, answered in his *Amyntor* (1699), debating comparative evidence for canonical and apocryphal scriptures. By pamphlet *Anglia Libera* (1701), on succession of Hanoverian house, won favorable reception at court of Electress Sophia, to whose daughter Sophia Charlotte he addressed *Letters to Serena* (1704); sent by Harley on missions to Holland and Germany (1707), defended Harley and Marlborough in pamphlets (until 1714); later wrote partisan pamphlets for Harley's enemies. Returned to theological works in *Nazarenus* (1718) and *Tetradymus* (1720), and parodied Anglican liturgy in *Pantheisticon* (1720).

Tol·bert \ˈtōl-bərt, ˈtȯl-\, William Richard, Jr. 1913–1980. Liberian politician. Vice president (1951–71), president (1971–80) of the Republic of Liberia; executed after coup led by Samuel Doe.

Tol·bu·khin \(ˌ)təl-ˈbük-yin\, Fyodor Ivanovich. 1894–1949. Russian general. Commanded the army that helped defeat the German Sixth army at Stalingrad (1942–43); personally accepted Marshal Paulus's surrender (Feb. 1, 1943); created marshal (1944).

To·le·do \tō-ˈlā-thō\, Francisco de. Conde de Oro·pe·sa \ō-rō-ˈpā-sä\. 1515–1582. Spanish administrator in Peru. Viceroy of Peru (1569–81); allowed execution of Tupac Amarú (*q.v.*); introduced the Inquisition into Peru; founded several towns; promulgated new code of laws.

Toledo, Juan Bautista de. d. 1567. Spanish architect. Helped design, then superintended the building of the Escorial near Madrid (1563–67).

Toledo, Pedro de. 1484–1553. Spanish general. Viceroy of Naples (1532–53) under Emperor Charles V; broke political power of disloyal feudatories; failed in attempt to introduce the Spanish Inquisition.

To·len·ti·no de Al·mei·da \tō-lāⁿ(n)-ˈtē-nü-thā-äl-ˈmā-thə\, Nicolau. 1740–1811. Portuguese poet. Schoolmaster, later made officer of Secretaria do Estado dos Negócios do Reino. Known for poems satirizing contemporary society as "A guerra," "Os amantes," "O bilhar," and "Memorial a sua alteza."

Tol·kien \ˈtäl-ˌkēn, ˈtȯl-, *US often* ˈtōl- *or* -(ˌ)kin\, John Ronald Reuel. 1892–1973. British writer, b. South Africa. At Oxford U. (1925–59); author of scholarly works as *Chaucer as a Philologist* (1936), *Beowulf: The Monsters and the Critics* (1937); esp. known as writer of fantasies, including *The Hobbit* (1937), trilogy *The Lord of the Rings* (1954–55), *The Silmarillion* (1977), etc.

Tol·lens \ˈtȯl-əns\, Hendrik Franciscus Caroluszoon. 1780–1856. Dutch poet. Among his works were the plays *De bruiloft* (1799) and *Konstantijn* (1800) and the verse *Proeve van minnezangen en idyllen* (1800–03), *Tafereel van de* *overwintering der Hollanders op Nova Zembla* (1819), etc. Author of the national anthem "Wein Neerlands Bloed."

Tol·ler \'tòl-ər\, Ernst. 1893–1939. German poet, playwright, and political activist. Leader of social revolutionary movements in Germany following World War I; sentenced to five years in prison (1919) for political activities; banished from Germany by Nazis and went to U.S. (1933). In addition to several volumes of verse, he wrote Expressionist plays as *Die Wandlung* (1919), *Masse Mensch* (1921), *Die Maschinenstürmer* (1922), *Feuer aus den Kesseln* (1930), *Die blinde Göttin* (1936), and his autobiography *Eine Jugend in Deutschland* (1933).

Tol·man \'tōl-mən\, Richard Chace. 1881–1948. American physicist, b. West Newton, Mass. Professor (1922–48), dean of the Graduate School (1935–48), Calif. Inst. Tech.; known for studies on the theory of colloids, theory of relativity, quantum theory, statistical mechanics, thermodynamics, etc.; demonstrated the electron to be the charge-carrying particle in flow of electricity in metals and determined its mass. His brother ¶Edward Chace Tolman (1886–1959), b. West Newton, Mass., was a psychologist; taught at U. of Calif., Berkeley (1918–54); developed a system of psychology known as purposive, or molar, behaviorism; chief work *Purposive Behavior in Animals and Men* (1932).

Tol·stoy \(ˌ)təl-'stòi; *Angl* tòl-'stòi, tōl-', täl-', 'tòl-ˌ, 'tōl-ˌ, 'täl-ˌ\, Aleksey Konstantinovich. Count. 1817–1875. Russian writer. Distant relative of Leo Tolstoy; held various honorary posts at court. Began literary career with prose romance *Upyr* (1841); his works included satirical verse *Son statskogo sovetnika Popova* (1878), narrative poems "Portret" (1874) and "Drakon" (1875), historical novel *Knyaz Serebryany* (1862), and dramatic trilogy *Smert Ioanna Groznogo* (1866), *Tsar Fyodor Ioannovich* (1868), *Tsar Boris* (1870).

Tolstoy, Aleksey Nikolayevich. Count. 1882–1945. Russian writer. Distant relative of Leo Tolstoy; White Russian émigré in Paris (1919–23); returned to Soviet Union to become an honored artist. His novels included *Chudaki* (1910), *Khromoy barin* (1912), *Detstvo Nikity* (1921), *Aelita* (1922–23), *Pyotr I* (1929–45), and trilogy *Khozhdeniye po mukam* composed of *Sestry* (1920–21), *Vosemnadtsaty god* (1927–28), *Khmurye utro* (1940–41); also wrote children's stories, thrillers, and stories of international intrigue.

Tolstoy, Dmitry Andreyevich. Count. 1823–1889. Russian official. Minister of public instruction (1866–80); minister of interior (1883 ff.).

Tolstoy, Lev (*Eng.* Leo) Nikolayevich. Count. 1828–1910. Russian novelist and moral philosopher. Entered army (1852) and served in the Caucasus and in Crimean War (1854–56), commanding battery at Sevastopol (1855); retired (1856) to his country estate, Yasnaya Polyana; visited France, Switzerland, Germany (1857); published his great novels *Voyna i mir* (*War and Peace,* 1865–69) and *Anna Karenina* (1875–77). Underwent spiritual transformation (after 1876) which led him to develop a form of Christian anarchism and to devote himself to social reform; recorded his conversion and new beliefs in works such as the autobiographical *Ispoved* (1882), plays *Vlast tmy* (1886) and *Zhivoy trup* (1902), novel *Voskreseniye* (1899), and esp. in *Chto takoye iskusstovo?* (1898, *What is Art?*). Besides other social and philosophical works, wrote many short stories, as "Dva gusara" (1856), "Smert Ivana Ilicha" (1886), "Kreytserova sonata" (1891), "Otets Sergy" (1911), and "Falshivy kupon" (1911).

Tolstoy, Pyotr Andreyevich. Count. 1645–1729. Russian diplomat and politician. Close adviser of Peter the Great; sent to Turkey by Peter as ambassador (1702); imprisoned by Turks (1711–13); on release, concluded Peace of Adrianopolis (1713); appointed senator, president of board of trade, and member of commission for foreign affairs; accompanied Peter to western Europe (1716–17); member of supreme privy council under Catherine I (1726–27); fell into disfavor and banished to Solovetsky monastery (1727).

Tombs \'tümz\, Sir Henry. 1824–1874. English soldier. Distinguished himself in both Sikh wars (1845–49); during Sepoy Mutiny, won Victoria Cross by gallantry at siege of Delhi (1857); commanded troop at Lucknow (1858); served as brigadier general in subsequent operations (1863, 1864); major general (1867).

To·mi·o·ka \tō-mē-ō-kä\ Tessai. *Orig. personal name* Yūsuke, *later* Dōsetsu, *again later* Hyakuren. 1836–1924. Japanese painter. Left priesthood (1881) to devote himself to painting; belonged to the *bunjin-ga,* or "literati painting" tradition; works included *Gunsen kōkaizu* and *Abe Nakamaro minshū bōgetsu.*

To·mi·slav \'tò-mē-slåv\. 10th century A.D.. First king of Croatia. One of earliest independent princes of Croatia; extended his domain by annexing territory on Dalmatian coast of Adriatic Sea; crowned king by Pope John X (925).

Tom·kins \'täm(p)-kənz\, Thomas. 1572–1656. English organist and composer. Organist at Chapel Royal, London (from 1620); known for his English madrigals and anthems, keyboard pieces, pavanes, etc.

Tom·kis *or* **Tom·kys** \'täm-kis\, Thomas. fl. 1604–1615. English dramatist. Author of comedy *Albumazar* (1615), about an Arabian astronomer, acted before James I on visit to Cambridge, revived by Dryden and by Garrick.

Tom·lin \'täm-lən\, Bradley Walker. 1899–1953. American painter, b. Syracuse, N.Y. Influenced by Adolph Gottlieb and by Japanese calligraphy; his abstract canvases included *Tension by Moonlight* (1948) and *Number 9: In Praise of Gertrude Stein* (1950).

Tom·line \'täm-lən\, Sir George Pretyman. *Orig. surname* Pret·y·man \'prit-ē-mən\. 1750–1827. English prelate. Dean of St. Paul's and bishop of Lincoln (1787); bishop of Winchester (1820); assumed additional surname Tomline (1803) on receipt of estate.

Tom·lin·son \'täm-lin-sən\, Ambrose Jessup. 1865–1943. American religious leader. General overseer of the Church of God (1907–23); his assumption of total power led to numerous schisms and to his impeachment (1923); founded (1923) and headed the Tomlinson Church of God.

Tomlinson, Henry Major. 1873–1958. English journalist and writer. Literary editor, *Nation* (1917–23). Author of *The Sea and the Jungle* (1912), *London River* (1921), *Tidemarks* (1924), *Gallions Reach* (1927), *All Our Yesterdays* (1930), *Mars His Idiot* (1935), *The Turn of the Tide* (1945), *Morning Light* (1946), *Malay Waters* (1950), etc.

Tom·ma·seo \ˌtōm-mä-'ze-ō\, Niccolò. 1802–1874. Italian writer, b. Dalmatia. Involved in the Risorgimento and in other politics of the day. Works included *Dell'Italia* (1835), *La Commedia di Dante* (1837), *Fede e bellezza* (novel, 1840), *Canti popolari corsi, toscani, greci, e illirici* (1841), and *Dizionario della lingua italiana* (with B. Bellini, 1861–79).

Tom·ma·si·ni \ˌtōm-mä-'zē-nē\, Vincenzo. 1878–1950. Italian composer. Works included operas, ballets as *Le donne di buon umore* (1916), symphonic poems as *Poema erotico* (1909), *Il beato regno* (1920), and *La tempesta* (1941), 4 string quartets, instrumental and vocal compositions.

Tom·ma·so di Gio·van·ni di Si·mo·ne Gui·di \tōm-'mäs-ō-dē-jō-'vän-nē-dē-sē-'mō-nā-'gwē-dē\. *Known as* Ma·sac·cio \mä-'zät-chō\. 1401–1428. Italian painter. Member of Florentine school; works marked advance from medieval to Renaissance Florentine painting; first to use a central light source in painting and credited with other innovations in perspective, as first use of linear perspective in fresco painting. Chief work, series of frescoes (c.1424–27) for Brancacci Chapel of Sta. Maria del Carmine, Florence, executed in collaboration with Masolino and Filippino Lippi; also painted triptych with Madonna enthroned (1422), *Madonna and Child with St. Anne* (c.1424, begun by Masolino), and altarpiece for Sta. Maria del Carmine, Pisa (1426).

To·mo·na·ga \tō-mə-nä-gä, -mō-\ Shin'ichirō. 1906–1979. Japanese physicist. Professor (from 1941), president (1956–62), Tokyo U. of Education; wrote *Quantum Mechanics* (1962). Awarded Nobel prize for physics (1965) with Richard P. Feynman and Julian S. Schwinger for their work on quantum electrodynamics.

Tom·pi·on \'täm-pē-ən\, Thomas. 1639–1713. English clockmaker. Admitted to Clockmakers' Company (1671), became master (1704); clockmaker for royal observatory (1676); with Robert Hooke made one of first English watches with balance spring (1675); with William Houghton and Edward Barlow patented cylinder escapement (1695); made other watchmaking improvements; maker of barometers and sundials for William III.

Tomp·kins \'täm(p)-kənz\, Daniel D. 1774–1825. American politician, b. Scarsdale, N.Y. Associate justice, New York State supreme court (1804–07); governor of New York (1807–17); vice president of the United States (1817–25).

Tompkins, Sally Louisa. *Known as* Captain Sally. 1833–1916. American hospital administrator, b. Mathews Co., Va. Outfitted and maintained at her own expense hospital in Richmond (1861–65); commissioned by Jefferson Davis a captain in Confederate army (Sept. 9, 1861), only woman commissioned in Confederate service.

Tone \'tōn\, Wolfe, *in full* Theobald Wolfe. 1763–1798. Irish republican and rebel. With Thomas Russell and Napper Tandy founded Society of United Irishmen (1791); organized (1792) a Catholic convention of elected delegates that secured passage in Parliament of Catholic Relief Act of 1793; to Paris to promote landing of a French force for invasion of Ireland (1796); adjutant general of expedition under Hoche, consisting of 43 sail and 14,000 men, which was dispersed by a storm (1796). Embarked in small French squadron under General Hardy and Admiral Bompard, which was captured by British after fight off Lough Swilly (1798).

Tö·nis·son \'tœ-nēs-sòn\, Jaan. 1868–?1941. Estonian lawyer, newspaper editor, and politician. Founded (1905) National Liberal party; sat in first Russian Duma (1906); took part in negotiations for Allied recognition of Estonian independence. Prime minister (1919–20), president (1927–28, 1933), and foreign minister (1931–32) of Estonia; opposed Russian domination of Estonia; arrested by Soviet occupation forces (1940) and apparently died in prison.

Tön·nies \'tœn-yəs\, Ferdinand Julius. 1855–1936. German sociologist. Taught at Kiel (from 1881); developed theory reconciling the organic and social-contract conceptions of society. Produced editions of Thomas Hobbes (1889); author of *Gemeinschaft und Gesellschaft* (1887), *Thomas Hobbes Leben und Lehre* (1896), *Die Sitte* (1909), *Kritik der öffentlichen Meinung* (1922).

Ton·son \'tän(t)-sən\, Jacob. 1656–1736. English publisher. Published works by Dryden, including plays, his translation of Virgil (1697), and *Fables Ancient and Modern* (1700), as well as works by Addison, Pope's *Pastorals* (1709), and Rowe's *Shakespeare* (1709); became (1712) co-publisher of *The Spectator*.

Tonstall, Cuthbert. See TUNSTALL.

Ton·ti \'tōn-tē\, Lorenzo. 17th century. French banker, b. Italy. Originated the tontine system of life insurance (1653). His son ¶Henry de Ton·ti *or* Ton·ty \də-tōⁿ-tē, *Angl* 'tänt-ē\ (1650–1704) was a companion of La Salle in his Mississippi Valley explorations (1678–83); built fort and trading post in Illinois region and lived there (until c.1699), bringing in colonists and missionaries from Canada; moved to French settlement near mouth of the Mississippi (1700) and aided the Louisiana colony in exploration and trade (1700–04).

Tooke \'tu̇k\, Horne, *in full* John Horne. *Orig.* John Horne \'hō(ə)rn, 'hȯ(ə)rn\. 1736–1812. English political radical and philologist. Ordained to a curacy (1760); helped John Wilkes found Bill of Rights Society (1769); broke with Wilkes and created the Constitutional Society to agitate for parliamentary reform and self-government for American colonies (1771); for promoting subscription for relief of relatives of Americans "murdered" at Lexington and Concord, fined and imprisoned for year (1778); added name of friend William Tooke of Purley to his own (1782). Wrote treatise on etymology of English words *The Diversions of Purley* (1786, expanded 1798) in which he was one of first to insist upon studying Gothic and Anglo-Saxon for philology. Supported Pitt (1782–90) in pamphlets; tried for high treason, but acquitted (1794); M.P. (1801) but excluded by special act rendering clergymen ineligible.

Toombs \'tümz\, Robert Augustus. 1810–1885. American politician, b. Wilkes Co., Ga. Member, U.S. House of Representatives (1845–53); known for aggressively defending Southern position on slavery question; U.S. senator (1853–61); withdrew (1861) to join Confederacy. Secretary of state of the Confederate States (1861); brigadier general (1861); escaped arrest by fleeing to London (1865–67). Resumed law practice in Washington, Ga. (1867), but never asked for pardon to regain U.S. citizenship under the Reconstruction laws.

Too·mer \'tü-mər\, Jean. 1894–1967. American writer, b. Washington, D.C. Taught in public schools at Sparta, Ga. (1920–22); turned to writing and lecturing; led Gurdjieff groups in Harlem (1925) and Chicago (1926–33). One of "Harlem Renaissance" writers; author of experimental plays, poems, and stories, esp. *Cane* (1923) which contained all three genres.

Too·rop \'tō-rȯp\, Jan, *in full* Johannes Theodoor. 1858–1928. Dutch painter, b. Java. Leader (from c.1900) of the Luminist movement in Netherlands; also made designs for posters, tile paintings, stained glass windows.

To·pe·li·us \tō-'pā-lē-əs\, Zachris. 1818–1898. Finnish writer. Became (1863) professor of Finnish history, president (1875–78), at Helsinki U. Father of the Finnish historical novel. His works, written in Swedish, included five collections of lyrics, plays, children's stories, and esp. *Fältskärns berättelser* (1853–67), series of six romanticized novels picturing life in 17th- and 18th-century Sweden and Finland.

To·pe·te y Car·bal·lo \tō-'pā-tā-ē-kär-'b̲äl-yō\, Juan Bautista. 1821–1885. Spanish admiral and politician. Took active part in revolution of 1868; joined by Prim y Prats and Sagasta in winning over Cádiz and in provisional government that followed; in ministries of Serrano y Domínguez (1872, 1874).

Töpf·fer \tœp-fer\, Rodolphe. 1799–1846. Swiss artist and writer. Professor of belles-lettres, Geneva (1832–46); among his short stories in *Nouvelles génevoises* (1841) was "La Bibliothèque de mon oncle" (written 1832); published series of humorous drawings, collected in *Histoires en estampes* (1846–47).

Top·la·dy \'täp-ˌlād-ē\, Augustus Montague. 1740–1778. English clergyman. Curate at Broad Hembury (1768–78); champion of the doctrinal Calvinism of the Church of England; bitter antagonist of Wesley and Methodism. Author of "Rock of Ages" (1775), "Deathless principle, arise," and other hymns.

Tö·re·ge·ne *or* **Tö·rä·gö·nä** \ˌter-e-'gen-e\. 13th century. Mongol ruler. Wife of Ögödei; ruled (1241–46) as regent for her son Güyük.

To·rel·li \tō-'rel-lē\, Giacomo. 1608–1678. Italian stage designer and engineer. Designed and built (1641) the Teatro Novissimo at Venice and furnished it with ingenious machines, including the revolving stage; called (1645) to France by Louis XIV; equipped Théâtre du Petit-Bourbon in Paris with first effective machinery for rapid changes of heavy sets; designed sets, winning acclaim for production of Pierre Corneille's *Andromède* (1650); returned to Italy (1661) and designed the Teatro della Fortuna, Fano (1677).

Torelli, Giuseppe. 1658–1709. Italian violinist and composer. Helped establish form of violin concerto; wrote many concertos for stringed instruments and sonatas and concertos for brass instruments and strings.

Torelli, Salinguerra. c.1160–c.1244. Italian ruler of Ferrara. Brother-in-law and chief supporter of Ezzelino III da Romano; a leader of Ghibelline party. Seized Ferrara from Este family (1215); removed by popular government (1227); elected chief magistrate (1230) but ousted (1231) by Lombard League; with aid of Ezzelino and Emperor Frederick II regained Ferrara (1236); surrendered (1240) to Guelf forces and died in prison.

To·rii \tō-rē-ē\. Family of Japanese painters of the *Ukiyo-e* school, including: Torii Kiyonobu, *surname also* Shō-bei \shō-bā\ (1664–1729); founder of the Torii school; to Edo (1687) and became signboard painter for the Kabuki theater; also illustrated books; known for designing portraits of actors to be reproduced as prints; *Shōgi gachō* and *Fūryū shihō byōbu* (both 1700) contain some of his works. ¶Kiyomasu, *orig. personal name* Shōjirō (c.1694–1763); said to have been a son of Kiyonobu; depicted women and actors, and illustrated books. ¶Kiyomitsu (1725–1785); son and pupil of Kiyomasu; painted theatrical posters and illustrated books; perfected a two-color process. ¶Kiyonaga, *orig.* Se·ki·gu·chi \sek-ē-gu̇ch-ē\ Shinsuke (1752–1815); pupil and son-in-law of Kiyomitsu; adopted into family; most brilliant representative of the school, esp. skillful in line and color; depicted famous beauties as in *Minami jūniko* and *Tōsei yūri bijin awase*.

Tör·ne·bohm \'tœr-nə-bōm\, Alfred Elis. 1838–1911. Swedish geologist. Member (1859–73), director (1897–1906) of Swedish Geological Survey; became (1878) professor at Royal Inst. of Technology, Stockholm. Presented (1888) his theory of the overthrust of the Caledonian Range onto a foreland to the southeast; also studied iron ores of Sweden and crystalline phases of portland cement.

Tor·que·ma·da \tȯr-kā-'mä-t̲h̲ä\, Juan de. 1388–1468. Spanish Dominican monk and prelate. Ably supported papal policies at the council of Basel (1431–35); created cardinal (1439); author of many theological works.

Torquemada, Juan de. c.1563–1624. Spanish Franciscan monk and historian. Provincial of the Franciscan order in Mexico (1614–17); chief work *Monarquía indiana* (1615).

Torquemada, Tomás de. 1420–1498. Spanish Dominican monk. Nephew of Cardinal Juan de Torquemada; prior of Santa Cruz monastery (1452–74); confessor and adviser to Isabella and Ferdinand (from 1474), whom he persuaded (1492) to expel the Jews; appointed first inquisitor general for all the Spanish possessions (1483); made grand inquisitor by Innocent VIII (1487); organized the Inquisition in Spain; became notorious for the severity of his judgments and the cruelty of his punishments.

Tor·quet \tȯr-ke\, Eugène. *Pseudonym* John-Antoine Nau \nau̇\. 1873–1918. French writer, b. San Francisco. Author of verse *Au seuil de l'espoir* (1897), novel *La Force ennemie* (1903), which won the first Goncourt prize.

Torre, Duque de la. See Francisco SERRANO Y DOMÍNGUEZ.

Tor·rence \'tȯr-ən(t)s, 'tär-\, Ridgely, *in full* Frederic Ridgely. 1875–1950. American author, b. Xenia, Ohio. Poetry editor, *The New Republic* (1920–34); poet in residence, Antioch Coll. (from 1938). Author of volumes of verse including *The House of a Hundred Lights* (1900), *Abelard and Heloise* (poetic drama, 1907), *Hesperides* (1925), the plays *El Dorado* (1903) and *The Undefended Line* (1938), and plays of Negro life, including *Granny Maumee, The Rider of Dreams, Simon the Cyrenian* (all 1917).

Tor·rens \'tȯr-ən(t)s, 'tär-\, Sir Robert. 1780–1864. English soldier and economist. Fought in Peninsula War; M.P. (1831); one of first economists to attribute production of wealth to joint action of land, labor, and capital, and to state law of diminishing return; advocate of colonization of South Australia and of repeal of corn laws. His son ¶Sir Robert Richard (1814–1884), politician, emigrated to Australia (1839); served in South Australian Legislative Council (1851–55); first premier and colonial treasurer of South Australia (1857); originated Torrens land-title system; returned to England (1863); M.P. (1868–74).

Tor·res \'tȯr-rās\, Luis Va·ez de \bä-'äth-t̲h̲ā-\. fl. 1606. Spanish navigator. Sailed around New Guinea and discovered (1606) the Torres Strait, as well as the Louisiade Archipelago.

Torres Na·har·ro \-nä-'är-rō\, Bartolomé de. 1484?–?1525. Spanish dramatist. To Rome (1513) and took holy orders; also lived at Naples. First dramatist to create truly Spanish characters; considered creator of Spanish comedy; first to designate acts as *jornadas*. Author of *Propalladia* (1517), a collection of dramatic works including *Comedia Ymenea* and *Comedia tinellaria*, and also containing first published Renaissance theory of drama.

Torres Vil·lar·ro·el \-b̲ē-är-rō-'el\, Diego de. c.1693–1770. Spanish mathematician and writer. Began career as dancer, musician, bullfighter, lockpicker, seller of patent medicines; wrote (1721) first of many almanacs; made professor at Salamanca (1726); took holy orders (1745). Author of lyric and burlesque poetry, sketches of Madrid life *Sueños* (1743), and esp. *Vida* (1743), picaresque memoirs providing valuable information on life of his time.

Tor·rey \'tór-ē\, Charles Cutler. 1863–1956. American Semitic scholar, b. East Hardwick, Vt. Professor, Yale (1900–32); founder and first director (1900–01) of American School of Oriental Research, Jerusalem. Author of *The Mohammedan Conquest of Egypt and North Africa* (1901), *Ezra Studies* (1910), *The Translations Made from the Original Aramaic Gospels* (1912), *The Pseudo-Ezekiel and the Original Prophecy* (1930), *The Chronicler's History of Israel* (1954), etc.

Torrey, John. 1796–1873. American botanist and chemist, b. New York City. Professor, Coll. of Physicians and Surgeons, New York (1827–55), and at Princeton (1830–54); chief assayer, U.S. Assay Office, New York (1854–73). Published *Flora of the Northern and Middle Sections of the United States* (1824), *A Flora of North America* (1838–43, with Asa Gray), and *Flora of the State of New York* (1843). His botanical library and herbarium were deposited with Columbia (1860) and transferred to New York Botanical Garden (1899).

Tor·ri·cel·li \ˌtōr-rē-'chel-lē\, Evangelista. 1608–1647. Italian mathematician and physicist. Served at Florence as amanuensis to Galileo (1641–42); succeeded Galileo as mathematician to grand duke of Tuscany and professor at Florentine Academy (1642). Made improvements on the telescope; discovered principle of the barometer and devised earliest form of the instrument (1643); worked on the cycloid; published *Opera Geometrica* (1644).

Tor·ri·gia·no \ˌtōr-rē-'jä-nō\, Pietro. 1472–1522. Florentine sculptor. Worked in Rome, Bologna, Siena, Antwerp; executed tomb for Henry VII and his queen in Westminster Abbey (1518) and tomb of Margaret, Countess of Richmond; died in prison of the Inquisition in Spain.

Tor·ri·jos Her·re·ra \tór-'rē-kō-ser-'rā-rä\, Omar. 1929–1981. Panamanian general and politician. A leader of coup that overthrew President Arnulfo Árias (1968); as commander of National Guard (from 1968) was virtual dictator of Panama until his death; concluded treaty (1977) with U.S. calling for transfer of Panama Canal to Panama.

Torrington. (1) Earl of. See Arthur Herbert under HERBERT family. (2) Viscount. See George BYNG.

Tor·ro·ja Mi·ret \tór-'rō-kä-mē-'ret\, Eduardo. 1899–1961. Spanish architect and engineer. Consulting engineer (from 1927); founder and director (1951–61), Instituto Técnico de la Construcción y del Cemento. Pioneered in design of concrete shell structures; works included racecourse grandstand and sports hall (both 1935, Madrid), Aldoz aqueduct (1939), Elsa bridge at Zamora (1940), Las Corts soccer stadium, Barcelona (1943), churches at Xerrallo and Pont de Suert (both 1952).

Tor·sten·son \'tór-stən-ˌsón\, Lennart. Count of Or·ta·la \'ür-ˌtä-lä\. 1603–1651. Swedish soldier. Served under Gustav II in Germany (1630–32); commander in chief of Swedish army in Germany (1641); won battles of Schweidnitz (1642), Breitenfeld (1642), Jüterbog (1644), Jankau (1645); joined György Rákóczi, conquered Moravia and invaded Austria (1645); resigned command because of ill health (1646); spent last years opposing policies of Oxenstierna and gaining confidence of Queen Christina.

Tors·van \'tórs-ˌvän\, Berwick Traven. *Pseudonym* B. Tra·ven \'träv-ən\. 1890–1969. German novelist, b. Chicago. Actor and pacifist in Germany; participated in Munich revolt of 1918–19; fled to Mexico (1923) and lived there until death. Author of *Das Totenschiff* (1926), *Der Schatz der Sierra Madre* (1927), *Die Baumwollpflücker* (1927), *Die weisse Rose* (1929), *Die Rebellion der Gehenkten* (1936), etc.

To·ry \tò-rē\, Geoffroy. c.1480–c.1533. French printer and typographer. Royal printer (1530); mainly responsible for French Renaissance style of book decoration; encouraged use of roman letters instead of gothic; introduced in French printing the accent, the apostrophe, and the cedilla; published *Champfleury* (1529) and a number of "Books of Hours."

To·sa \tō-sä\. Family of Japanese artists forming the Tosa school of painting which revived and preserved the *Yamato-e* tradition; school, rival of the Kanō school, noted for illustrating Japanese literary classics as the *Genji monogatari*, and for providing official painters to the court until 1867; its leading members included: Tosa Mitsunobu (1434–1525), regarded as founder of Tosa school; head of court painting bureau (1493–96); appointed (1518) chief artist to Ashikaga shogunate; extant works include portrait of Emperor En-yū II (1492) and narrative scrolls illustrating histories and legends of temples and shrines. His great-grandson ¶Mitsunori (1583–1638) specialized in miniatures. Mitsunori's son ¶Mitsuoki, *orig. personal name* Fujimitsu, *called* Tsu·ne·a·ki \tsün-e-ä-kē\ (1617–1691) settled in Kyōto (1634) and revived the Tosa school there; became court painter (1654); adopted some techniques and subject matter from rival Kanō school; works included *Kitano Tenjin engi emaki* and *Kiku jun zu.* His son ¶Mitsunari (1646–1710) succeeded him (1681) as court painter.

To·sca·nel·li dal Poz·zo \ˌtō-skä-'nel-lē-däl-'pōt-tsō\, Paolo. 1397–1482. Italian physician and cosmographer of Florence. Reputed to have given Columbus suggestions by letter and map for a westward voyage to the Far East.

To·sca·ni·ni \ˌtō-skä-'nē-nē, *Angl* ˌtäs-kə-\, Arturo. 1867–1957. Italian conductor. Conductor at La Scala, Milan (1898–1907, 1921–31), Metropolitan Opera (1908–21), N.Y. Philharmonic-Symphony Orchestra (1928–36), guest conductor at Bayreuth Festival (1930–32), Salzburg Festival (1934–36), and with orchestras all over world. Organizer and conductor, National Broadcasting Co. Symphony (1937–54). Known for his dynamic interpretations of Beethoven, Verdi, and Wagner.

Tō·shū·sai \tō-shù-ī\ Sharaku. *Orig.* Sai·tō \sī-tō\ Jūrōbei. *Also known as* Sha·ra·ku \shär-ä-kü\. fl. 1795. Japanese painter. Said to have been a Nō actor in Awa Province; painted in *Ukiyo-e* style; his extant works of some 160 prints, chiefly of actors, noted for their intensity and exaggeration verging on caricature.

Tos·tig \'täs-tig\. Earl of North·um·bria \nór-'thəm-brē-ə\. d. 1066. Anglo-Saxon ruler. Son of Earl Godwin and brother of Harold II; made earl of Northumbria, Northamptonshire, and Huntingdonshire by his brother-in-law King Edward the Confessor (1055); his severity caused revolt of Northumbrians and setting up of Morcar in his place (1065); outlawed and exiled; joined Harold III Hardraade of Norway in invasion (1066) of northern England, where they defeated Morcar at York, but were defeated by Harold II at Stamford Bridge and slain.

Tot·i·la \'tät-ᵊl-ə\. *Also known as* Bad·ui·la \'bad-wə-lə\. d. 552. King of the Ostrogoths in Italy (541–552). Waged successful war against forces of Eastern Roman Empire; overran southern Italy (541–545); captured Rome (546); ravaged Sicily, Sardinia, and Corsica, and attacked Greece (546–551); took Rome a second time (549); defeated and killed at Taginae by Byzantine general Narses.

Totius. See Jakob DU TOIT.

Totnes, Earl of. See George CAREW.

Tot·tel \'tät-ᵊl\, Richard. c.1525–1594. English printer. Compiled and published (1557) *Songs and Sonettes,* first English anthology of poetry, known as *Tottel's Miscellany,* including previously unpublished poems by Surrey, Wyatt, Grimald, Heywood, and others. Charter member of Stationers' Co. (1557); published mostly law books, but also More's *Dialogue of Comfort* (1553), Lydgate's *Falls of Princes* (1554), and Hawes's *Passetyme of Pleasure* (1555).

Tottington. See SAMSON of Tottington.

Tou·let \tü-le\, Paul-Jean. 1867–1920. French writer. Author of collection of short lyric poems in an unusual verse form, *Les Contrerimes* (1921), and of several novels.

Tou·louse-Lau·trec \tü-lüz-lō-trek\, Henri de. *In full* Henri-Marie-Raymond de Toulouse-Lautrec-Mon·fa \-mōⁿ-fä\. 1864–1901. French painter. Suffered from deformed legs as result of two accidents; studied under Fernan Corman; set up studio in Montmartre district of Paris; painted popular entertainers and scenes of Parisian night life as *At the Moulin Rouge* (1892), *Jane Avril dansant* (1892), *La Danse de la Goulue* (1895), but achieved fame with poster *La Goulue at the Moulin Rouge* (1891); also produced over 300 lithographs, esp. series on *Le Café concert* (1893), on singer Yvette Guilbert (1894), *Elles* on brothel life (1896), and illustrations for Jules Renard's *Histoires naturelles* (1899).

Touraine, Comtes de. See BLOIS.

Touraine, Dukes of. See earls of Douglas under DOUGLAS family.

Tour·jée \tür-'zhā\, Eben. 1834–1891. American musician, b. Warwick, R.I. With Robert Goldbeck founded (1867) New England Conservatory of Music in Boston.

Tour·na·chon \tür-nä-shōⁿ\, Gaspard-Félix. *Pseudonym* Na·dar \nä-där\. 1820–1910. French writer, caricaturist, and photographer. Settled in Paris (1842) and sold caricatures to humor magazines; interested himself in photography, opening (by 1853) a photographic portrait studio; published (1854) *Panthéon-Nadar,* lithographic caricatures of prominent Parisians; patented (1855) idea of using aerial photographs for mapmaking and surveying; made first aerial photograph (1856 or 1858). Wrote novels, essays, satires, and the autobiographical *Mémoires du Géant* (1864) and *Quand j'étais photographé* (1900).

Tour·ne·fort \tür-nə-fór\, Joseph Pit·ton de \pē-tōⁿ-də-\. 1656–1708. French botanist and physician. Professor at Jardin des Plantes, Paris (1688–1708); one of the founders of modern systematic botany; credited with being first to group plants into genera. Author of *Éléments de botanique* (1694).

Tour·ne·mire \tür-nə-mēr\, Charles-Arnould. 1870–1939. French organist and composer. Wrote sacred and lyric dramas, symphonies, chamber music, choral and solo vocal works, and organ music as *L'Orgue mystique* (1927–32).

Tour·neur \'tər-nər\, Cyril. c.1575–1626. English dramatist. Served as Sir Edward Cecil's secretary on disastrous expedition to Cádiz (1625); on return trip, put ashore among sick in Ireland and died there. Author of two tragedies, *The Revenger's Tragedy* (1607) and *The Atheist's Tragedy* (1611), poetical satire *The Transformed Metamorphosis* (1600), a prose *Character* of Robert Cecil (pub. 1930), and elegies.

Tour·non \'tür-nōn\, Charles Thomas Maillard de. 1668–1710. Italian clergyman. As papal plenipotentiary of Clement XI, arrived (1705) in Peking to settle the rites controversy; proved inflexible and discourteous; expelled to Macao (1707) where he died in confinement.

Tourte \türt\, François-Xavier. 1747–1835. French manufacturer of violin bows. Devised (c.1820) the Tourte bow.

Tour·ville \tür-vēl\, Anne-Hilarion de Co·ten·tin de \də-kō-tän-tan-də-\. Comte. 1642–1701. French naval officer. Chief of squadron (1676) and second in command under Duquesne in clearing the Mediterranean of Algerian and Tripolitan pirates (1683); broke English blockade of Brest (1689); vice admiral of Mediterranean fleet and naval commander in chief (1689); defeated Anglo-Dutch fleet off the Isle of Wight (1690), but was defeated at La Hogue (May 29, 1692); created marshal of France (1693); triumphed over Anglo-Dutch fleet off Cape St. Vincent (May 26–27, 1693).

Tou·sard \tü-zär\, Anne-Louis de. 1749–1817. French army officer. To America (1777); engaged at Brandywine and Germantown; colonel (1798); planned and supervised construction of defenses at Fort Mifflin, Pa., West Point, N.Y., and Newport, R.I. French agent at New Orleans (1805) and later vice consul at Philadelphia, Baltimore, and New Orleans (to 1816).

Tous·saint-Lou·ver·ture \tü-san-lü-ver-tuer\. *Orig.* François-Dominique Toussaint. c.1743–1803. Haitian general and liberator. Born of African slave parents, freed (1777). Took prominent part in slave insurrection (1791); after slaves were freed (1793), joined French republicans; became their recognized leader; forced British to evacuate island (1798); defeated Rigaud, leader of mulattoes, in civil war (1799); invaded Spanish Santo Domingo and freed the slaves (1801); master of entire island (1801); gave just and firm administration (1801–02); resisted Napoléon's attempt to reestablish slavery; overcome by French forces under Gen. Leclerc (1802); charged with conspiracy and sent as prisoner to France; died in prison.

Tout \'taùt\, Thomas Frederick. 1855–1929. English historian. Pupil of William Stubbs; specialized in medieval history; with James Tait, a founder of "Manchester school" of historiography, stressing importance of records and archives.

Tou·tin \tü-tan\, Jean. 1578–1644. French painter. Introduced technique of enamel portraiture (c.1620–30).

To·vey \'tō-vē, 'təv-ē\, Sir Donald Francis. 1875–1940. English composer and writer on music. Professor, Edinburgh (from 1914); founded Reid Symphony Orchestra at Edinburgh (1917); composer of *Symphony in D* (1913), concertos for piano (1903) and for cello (1934), opera *The Bride of Dionysus* (1929), choral works, and chamber music. Author of *Essays in Musical Analysis* (1935–39), *Musical Articles from the Encyclopaedia Britannica* (1944), and *Essays and Lectures on Music* (1949).

Tow·ers \'taù(-ə)rz\, John Henry. 1885–1955. American naval officer, b. Rome, Ga. In naval aviation service (from 1911); commander, Air Force, Pacific fleet (1942–44); deputy commander (1944–45), commander (1945–47), Pacific fleet and Pacific Ocean Areas; admiral (1945).

Town \'taùn\, Ithiel. 1784–1844. American architect, b. Thompson, Conn. Designed Center Church (1812) and Trinity Church (1814), both in New Haven, Conn.; U.S. Custom House in New York City; in partnership with Martin E. Thompson (1827–28) and with Alexander J. Davis (1829–43); patented design for truss bridge (1820) and received many commissions for building bridges.

Town·send \'taùn-zənd, *esp Brit* -()zend\. Family of America cabinetmakers working in Newport, R.I., and forming with the Goddard family the Goddard-Townsend group, known for case furniture characterized by block fronts and decorative carved shells; its members included: Job (1699–1765), father-in-law of John Goddard; a desk-bookcase bearing his label survives. His brother ¶Christopher (1701–1773) produced similar pieces. Job's sons ¶Job Edward, Jr. (1726–1818); ¶Edmund (1736–1811); ¶Thomas (1742–1822), a carpenter, in later years an innkeeper; ¶Robert M. (d. 1805); and ¶James (d. 1827), considered by some responsible for much of carving of the Goddard-Townsend pieces. Christopher's son ¶John (1732–1804), one of outstanding craftsmen of the group; several pieces survive, including tables, chest of drawers, clock case. His brother ¶Jonathan (1745–1772) was also a cabinetmaker.

Townsend, Francis Everett. 1867–1960. American physician, b. Fairbury, Ill. Originator (1934) and head of the Townsend Recovery Plan, officially Old-Age Revolving Pensions, Ltd., which helped organize popular support for a federally administered social security program.

Townsend, Sir John Sealy Edward. 1868–1957. Irish physicist. Professor, Oxford (1900–41); made (1897) first direct measurement of the unit electrical charge (*e*); discovered that gas molecules can be ionized by collisions with ions (1901); studied electron swarms; independently of Carl Ramsauer, discovered the Ramsauer-Townsend effect. Author of *Motion of Electrons in Gases* (1925), *Electromagnetic Waves* (1951), etc.

Townsend, Meredith White. 1831–1911. English journalist. With Richard H. Hutton, bought and edited *Spectator,* London (1861–97).

Town·shend \'taùn-zənd\. Name of English family including distinguished statesmen and soldiers:

Charles Townshend (1674–1738), 2d Viscount Townshend of Rayn·ham \'rā-nəm\; married Sir Robert Walpole's sister (1713); secretary of state for northern department (1714); prompt and severe in suppressing Jacobite rising (1715); promoted defensive alliances with emperor and with France; dismissed after conflict with Stanhope's pro-French policy (1716); again secretary of state for northern department (1721); overshadowed by Walpole's financial ability and superior influence in House of Commons; dissatisfied with working of Quadruple Alliance, forced separation of emperor from Spain in order to break up Austrian dominions; won Hanoverian League to side of Spain (1729); prepared way for alliance between Spain and France; on threat of Prussia to join emperor, urged campaign against empire; opposed by Walpole and Queen Caroline, resigned (1730) and devoted himself to agriculture, improving cultivation of turnips and crop rotation.

His grandson ¶Charles (1725–1767); M.P (from 1747); a lord of admiralty (1754–55); secretary at war (1761–62); paymaster general (1765–66); chancellor of exchequer (1766); assumed effective control of ministry after Pitt's illness; suspended activities of New York assembly; as last official act, passed through Parliament measure taxing glass, paper, and tea on importation into American colonies, which led toward separation of colonies.

Charles's brother ¶George (1724–1807), 4th Viscount and 1st Marquis Townshend; soldier; served in Netherlands and at Culloden Moor (1746) and Laufeld (1747); as brigadier general under Wolfe, commanded left wing on Heights of Abraham in Quebec expedition, and on death of Wolfe succeeded to chief command (1759); as lord lieutenant of Ireland (1767–72), sought to break down government by introduction of settlers called undertakers, obtained parliamentary majority by corruption; created marquis (1786) and field marshal (1796).

¶Thomas (1733–1800), 1st Viscount Syd·ney \'sid-nē\; grandson of 2d viscount; joint paymaster of the forces (1767–68); war secretary in Rockingham's administration (1782), and home secretary in Shelburne's and again in Pitt's; created Baron Sydney (1783). Sydney, Australia, was named for him.

¶Sir Charles Vere Ferrers Townshend (1861–1924), soldier; great-grandson of 1st marquis; served in Sudan expedition (1884–85); distinguished himself by holding Chitral fort, India (1895); served in Boer War; major general (1911); took Kūt al-'Amārah (1915) but failed to capture Bagdad, and finally surrendered Kūt (1916).

Toyn·bee \'tòin-bē\, Arnold. 1852–1883. English sociologist and economist. Pioneer in social settlement movement in district of Whitechapel, where Toynbee Hall, first social settlement in the world, was erected (1884) in his honor. His brother ¶Paget (1855–1932), philologist, published *Life of Dante* (1900); editor of *Oxford Dante* (1924).

Toynbee, Arnold Joseph. 1889–1975. English historian. Nephew of Arnold and Paget Toynbee. Delegate to Paris Peace Conference (1919); professor, U. of London (1919–55). Wrote *The Western Question in Greece and Turkey* (1922); in chief work *A Study of History* (1934–61) divided history into 21 developed and 5 "arrested" civilizations.

Toyokuni. See UTAGAWA.

To·yo·to·mi \tō-yō-tō-mē\ Hideyoshi, *orig.* Hiyoshimaru. 1537–1598. Japanese warrior and statesman. Son of a peasant; entered (c.1557) service of Oda Nobunaga as foot soldier; by military talents rose to be one of Nobunaga's chief lieutenants; made lord of Nagahama (1573); on Nobunaga's death (1582) became chief supporter of Nobunaga's infant grandson as head of Oda family; built large castle at Ōsaka (1583); concluded alliance with Tokugawa Ieyasu (1584). Appointed (1585) by emperor *kampaku* (chief minister) and awarded family name Toyotomi; conquered Shikoku and Kyushu islands; united all Japan (1590); instituted measures for peace and stability, demilitarized strongholds, facilitated transportation, developed mineral resources. Abdicated (1592) in favor of nephew Toyotomi Hidetsugu, taking title *taikō* and retaining actual power; unsuccessfully invaded Korea (1592, 1597). His nephew and adopted son ¶Toyotomi Hidetsugu (1568–1595) was a valiant warrior; made *kampaku* on Hideyoshi's retirement (1582); led dissolute life and unable to handle power; banished (1593) by Hideyoshi and forced to commit suicide. Hideyoshi's natural son ¶Toyotomi Hideyori (1593–1615) became nominal ruler on death of Hideyoshi (1598); under regency of council of five warriors, including Tokugawa Ieyasu; married granddaughter of Ieyasu; committed suicide after his castle at Ōsaka was taken by Ieyasu.

Toz·zer \'täz-ər\, Alfred Marston. 1877–1954. American anthropologist, b. Lynn, Mass. Taught at Harvard (1905–47); authority on culture and language of Maya Indians; led (1909–10) expedition to Guatemala, finding ruins at Holmul. Edited and translated Landa's *Relación de las cosas de Yucatán* (1941); author of *A Comparative Study of the Mayas and the Lacandones* (1907), *Maya Grammar* (1921), *Social Origins and Social Continuities* (1925), *Chichen Itza and Its Cenote of Sacrifice* (1957).

Tra·cy \trá-sē\, Alexandre de Prou·ville de \də-prü-vēl-də-\. Marquis. 1603–1670. French soldier. Appointed (1663) lieutenant general of French possessions in North America; led expedition against Mohawks (1666), forcing them to sue for peace; returned to France (1667).

Tra·cy \'trā-sē\, Spencer. 1900–1967. American actor, b. Milwaukee. Won Academy Awards for best actor in *Captains Courageous* (1937) and *Boys' Town* (1938); starred in over 60 films, including *Woman of the Year* (1942), *Adam's Rib* (1949), *Pat and Mike* (1952), *Guess Who's Coming to Dinner* (1967), all with Katherine Hepburn, as well as *Bad Day at Black Rock* (1955), *The Old Man and the Sea* (1958), *Inherit the Wind* (1960), etc.

Trade·scant \'trād-ˌskant\, John. 1570 or 1575–1638. English naturalist. Naturalist and gardener to Charles I; collected plants and other natural history objects. His son ¶John (1608–1662) succeeded to post of royal gardener (1638); added to his father's collection. The collection passed to Elias Ashmole and formed the basis of Oxford's Ashmolean Museum.

Tra·et·ta \trä-'ät-tä\, Tommaso Michele Francesco Saverio. 1727–1779. Italian composer. Music master to Don Felipe, Duke of Parma (1758–65); director, Conservatorio dell'Ospedaletto, Venice (1765–68); music director to Catherine the Great of Russia (1768–75). Made operatic reforms; composed some 50 operas, esp. *Sofonisba* (1762) and *Ifigenia in Tauride* (1763), a *Stabat Mater* (c.1750), oratorio *Salomone* (1768), etc.

Tragus. See Hieronymus BOCK.

Tra·herne \trə-'hərn\, Thomas. 1637–1674. English poet and religious writer. Ordained in Anglican church (1660); lived (1669–74) in London and Teddington as chaplain of Sir Orlando Bridgeman. Author of *Roman Forgeries* (1673), *Christian Ethicks* (1675), *A Serious and Patheticall Contemplation of the Mercies of God* (known as *Thanksgivings,* 1699), and manuscripts of mystical religious poems and prose writings published as *Poems* (1903), *Centuries of Meditations* (1908), and *Poems of Felicity* (1910).

Traill \'trā(ə)l\, Catherine Parr, *nee* Strick·land \'strik-lənd\. 1802–1899. Canadian writer, b. London, England. Sister of Susanna Moodie and of Agnes, Elizabeth, and Jane Strickland; m. (1832) Thomas Traill. To Upper Canada with her husband and Susanna (1832); wrote books describing frontier and natural life of Canada, including *The Backwoods of Canada* (1836), *The Female Emigrant's Guide* (1854), *Canadian Wild Flowers* (1869), *Pearls and Pebbles* (1895); introduced children's animal story in Canadian literature with *Afar in the Forest* (1869).

Traill, Thomas Stewart. 1781–1862. Scottish physician. Professor of medical jurisprudence, Edinburgh (1832–62); editor of 8th edition of *Encyclopaedia Britannica.*

Train \trān\, George Francis. 1829–1904. American merchant, b. Boston. Opened successful shipping firm in Australia (1853); built Atlantic and Great Western Railway in Ohio (1858); invested in streetcar lines in Europe and Asia. Gained notoriety by eccentric enthusiasms, involving trips around the world, running presidential campaign, being member of Paris Commune (1870), writing pamphlets and books, etc.

Tra·jan \'trā-jən\. *Lat.* Marcus Ulpius Tra·ia·nus \trə-'yā-nəs\. *Called* Ger·man·i·cus \(ˌ)jər-'man-i-kəs\. 53–117. Roman emperor (98–117), b. near Seville, Spain. Early began career of soldier; military tribune for ten years; served in Syria and Spain; consul (91, 98); adopted as successor by Nerva (97). On accession took title Imperator Caesar Divi Nervae Filius Nerva Traianus Augustus; completed fortifications on Rhine (98–99); conducted first Dacian campaign (101–103), in which Decebalus was defeated; in second campaign (104–106) completely defeated Dacians and made Dacia a Roman province; Trajan's Column erected (113) to commemorate event; period of peace (107–114); conducted successful wars against Armenians and Parthians (114–116), capturing Ctesiphon and conquering territory to the Persian Gulf; died on return in Selinus. Reorganized administration of provinces; sent Pliny the Younger to govern Asia Minor; improved and constructed many buildings (especially Trajan's Forum); also built many roads and bridges throughout the empire.

Trakl \'träk-əl\, Georg. 1887–1914. Austrian poet. Known as one of foremost Expressionist poets of death and decay; published *Gedichte* (1913).

Tran Hung Dao \'drän-'hůŋ-'daů\. *Orig.* Tran Quoc Tuan \-'kwȯk-'dwän\. *Later titled* Hung Dao Vuong \-'vwȯŋ\. d. 1300 A.D. Vietnamese general. Defeated invading armies of Kublai Khan (1284, 1288); became a cultural hero and object of worship in modern Vietnam.

Tran·quil·li \trän-'kwēl-lē\, Secondo. *Pseudonym* Ignazio Si·lo·ne \sē-'lō-nā\. 1900–1978. Italian writer and politician. Helped found (1921) Italian Communist party but left it (1930); settled in Switzerland (1930); gained fame with anti-Fascist novels stressing need for social reforms in Italy as *Fontamara* (1930), *Pane e vino* (1937), *Il seme sotto la neve* (1940), and satire *La scuola dei dittatori* (1938). To Italy after World War II and became a leader of Democratic Socialist party. Later works included novels *Una manciata di more* (1952), *Il segreto di Luca* (1956), play *L'avventura d' un povero cristiano* (1968), and autobiographical *Uscita di sicurezza* (1965).

Trapassi, Pietro. See METASTASIO.

Trau·be \'traů-bə\, Isidor. 1860–1943. German physical chemist. Taught at Technische Hochschule, Berlin (1882–1939), and Edinburgh (from 1939); founder of capillary chemistry; made studies of gastric juices, blood, urine, milk; developed Traube's rule; devised a viscometer and a capillarimeter.

Traube, Ludwig. 1818–1876. German clinician and pathologist. Introduced experimentation with animals into the study of pathology; promoted use of percussion and auscultation and of thermometry in physical diagnosis. His brother ¶Moritz (1826–1894) was a wine merchant and physiological chemist; known for work on ferments and for discoveries (1864, 1867) of the formation of precipitation membranes.

Trau·bel \'traů-bəl\, Helen. 1903–1972. American operatic soprano, b. St. Louis. Member of Metropolitan Opera Co. (1939–53); known esp. for Wagnerian roles.

Traubel, Horace Logo. 1858–1919. American author, b. Camden, N.J. Close friend and a literary executor of Walt Whitman; published *With Walt Whitman in Camden* (1906–14).

Traun \'traůn\, Otto Ferdinand. Graf von Abens·perg und Traun \'ab-en-sper-kůnt-'traůn\. 1677–1748. Austrian soldier. Entered Austrian army (1697); during War of Polish Succession (1733–38) successfully resisted superior Spanish forces; made commander in chief for Lombardy (1735); acting governor of Milan (1736–43). Field marshal (1741); in War of Austrian Succession (1740–48) defeated Spaniards in Italy (1742–43), forced Frederick II out of Bohemia (1744), expelled the French from southern Germany (1745), secured election of Francis I as Holy Roman emperor.

Trautt·mans·dorff \'traůt-mäns-ˌdȯrf\, Maximilian von. Graf. 1584–1650. Austrian diplomat and statesman. Instrumental in securing Bohemian and Hungarian crowns (1617–18) and imperial title (1619) for Ferdinand II; concluded Peace of Prague (1635); chief minister (1634) of Ferdinand II; exerted paramount influence over policies of Ferdinand III. Chief imperial plenipotentiary during negotiations leading to Treaty of Westphalia (1648); prime minister of Austria (1648–50).

Traven, B. See TORSVAN.

Trav·ers \'trav-ərz\, Ben. 1886–1980. English playwright. Famed for series of farces (1925–33) produced by Aldwych Theatre, as *A Cuckoo in the Nest* (1925), *Rookery Nook* (1926), *A Night Like This* (1930); later scored successes with comedies, including *The Bed Before Yesterday* (1975).

Travers, Jerome Dunstan. 1887–1951. American golfer, b. New York City. Winner of U.S. Amateur championship (1907, 1908, 1912, 1913) and the U.S. Open (1915).

Travers, Morris William. 1872–1961. English chemist. Professor, U. Coll., London (1898–1903), U. Coll., Bristol (1903–06); director of Indian Inst. of Science, Bangalore (1906–14). With Sir William Ramsay, discovered the elements neon, krypton, and xenon (1898); known also for researches relating to low temperatures.

Tra·viès de Vil·lers \trȧv-yes-də-vē-ler\, Charles-Joseph. 1804–1859. French painter and caricaturist. A founder of *Charivari* (1831) and of *Caricature* (1838), where most of his work appeared; one of the illustrators (1848–55) of Balzac's novels.

Trav·is \'trav-əs\, Walter Jeremiah. 1862–1927. American golfer, b. Maldon, Australia. To U.S. as a young man; U.S. Amateur champion (1900, 1901, 1903); first American to win British Amateur championship (1904).

Travis, William Barret. 1809–1836. American lawyer and soldier, b. near Red Banks, S.C. Went to Texas (1831); rose to leadership among Texans ready to resist Mexican authority; commanded Texas force at the Alamo, completely destroyed by Mexican army under Santa Anna (Mar. 6, 1836).

Tre·bo·ni·us \trə-'bō-nē-əs\, Gaius. d. 43 B.C. Roman general. Quaestor (c.60); participated in conquest of Gaul and in Roman Civil War; praetor (48); governor of Further Spain (47); consul (45); an accomplice in assassination of Caesar (44) and received governorship of Asia; killed at Smyrna by Dolabella.

Tre·dia·kov·sky \tryid-yi-(ˌ)ə-'kȯf-skəi\, Vasily Kirillovich. 1703–1769. Russian poet and literary theoretician. A progenitor of the French classical tradition in Russian literature; first to advocate replacing syllabic meter in Russian poetry by the tonic meter with regular accented feet (1735). Author of *View of the Origin of Poetry and of Verse* (1752) and works on prosody.

Tree, Ellen. See Charles John KEAN.

Tree \'trē\, Sir Herbert Draper Beerbohm. *Orig. surname* Beer·bohm \'bi(ə)r-ˌbōm\. 1853–1917. English actor-manager. Half-brother of Max Beerbohm. Made stage debut (1876) as Herbert Beerbohm Tree; won first success as curate in *The Private Secretary* (1884); lessee and manager, Haymarket Theatre (1887–97), playing in Shakespeare, Ibsen, Wilde, Maeterlinck; as manager of Her Majesty's Theatre (from 1897), played wide range of parts, attempted to revive poetic drama with Stephen Phillips's plays, lauded for stage versions of Dickens; staged overelaborate productions of Shakespeare; founded (1904) what became Royal Academy of Dramatic Art. Author of *Thoughts and Afterthoughts* (1913). His wife (m. 1882) ¶Helen Maud Holt \'hōlt\ (1863–1937), actress under name of Mrs. Beerbohm Tree, was well known in her chief parts, Ophelia and Lady Teazle.

Treece \'trēs\, Henry. 1912–1966. English writer. With J.F. Hendry a founder of the Apocalypse movement in poetry. Author of verse as *The Black Seasons* (1945), *The Exiles* (1952); historical novels as *The Eagles Have Flown* (1954), *Red Queen, White Queen* (1958), *The Green Man* (1966); and children's literature, esp. series of Vikings novels as *Swords From the North* (1967).

Treich-La·plène \tresh-lȧ-plen\, Marcel. 1860–1890. French explorer. To Africa (1883); made journey (1888–89) into interior of West Africa, establishing the eastern boundary of Ivory Coast.

Treil·hard \tre-yȧr\, Jean-Baptiste. Comte. 1742–1810. French politician. Member of the Estates-General (1789), National Convention (1792), Council of Five Hundred, Court of Cassation; represented France at congress of Rastatt (1798); member of the Directory; president of court of appeal in Paris (1802); member of Council of State; played important part in drafting various legal codes.

Treitsch·ke \'trīch-kə\, Heinrich von. 1834–1896. German historian and publicist. Professor, Kiel (1866), Heidelberg (1867), Berlin (1874); edited *Preussische Jahrbücher* (1866–89); member of Reichstag (1871–84); succeeded Ranke as historiographer of Prussia (1886); strong supporter of Hohenzollern dynasty; advocated authoritarian power politics, unity of Germany through Prussian might, and colonial expansion; largely responsible for growth of anti-British feeling in Germany. Chief work *Deutsche Geschichte im 19. Jahrhundert* (1879–94).

Tre·law·ny \tri-'lȯ-nē\, Edward John. 1792–1881. English writer and adventurer. In navy (1805–12); companion of Shelley and Byron in Italy (1822); present at Leghorn on occasion of Shelley and Williams's drowning, superintended recovery and cremation of bodies (1822); with Byron, aided in Greek struggle for independence; became social favorite in London; buried beside Shelley. Author of the autobiographical *Adventures of a Younger Son* (1831) and *Recollections of the Last Days of Shelley and Byron* (1858; recast as *Records of Shelley, Byron and the Author,* 1878).

Trelawny, Sir Jonathan. 1650–1721. English prelate. Bishop successively of Bristol (1685), Exeter (1689), and Winchester (1707); one of the Seven Bishops (see William SANCROFT) who petitioned against James II's Declaration of Indulgence (1688), but were acquitted of charge of seditious libel. His son ¶Edward (1699–1754) was governor of Jamaica (1738–52); ended (1739) a long-standing war between white planters and descendants of black slaves known as Maroons.

Trem·blay \trän-ble, -blā\, François-Joseph le Clerc du \lə-kler-dᵫ\. *Known as* Père Joseph, *i.e.* Father Joseph. 1577–1638. French religious and political figure. Entered Capuchin order (1599); provincial of Touraine (1613); preached crusade, against Protestants, etc. His ardor to convert Protestants recommended him to Richelieu, whose agent he became (c.1612), first in ecclesiastical and then in diplomatic matters; gained sobriquet Émi·nence Grise \ā-mē-näns-grēz\, *i.e.* gray eminence, in contrast to Richelieu, the Éminence Rouge; chief architect of policies that led to Thirty Years' War.

Trem·bley \trän-ble, -blā\, Abraham. 1700–1784. Swiss naturalist. His experiments on regeneration in freshwater hydras published as *Mémoires, pour servir à l'histoire d'un genre polypes d'eau douce, à bras en forme de cornes* (1744); first to witness multiplication of protozoans by division and cell division in algae.

Tren·chard \'tren-ˌchärd, -chərd\, Hugh Montague. 1st Viscount Trenchard. 1873–1956. English airman. Entered army (1893); served in Boer War (1899–1902), World War I (1914–18); major general (1916); principal organizer of Royal Air Force (1918); chief of air staff (1918–29); air marshal (1919), air chief marshal (1922), marshal of the R.A.F. (from 1927); founded colleges for air officer cadets and staff officers; introduced system of short-service commissions. Commissioner, London metropolitan police (1931–35).

Tren·de·len·burg \'tren-də-lən-ˌbu̇rk\, Friedrich Adolf. 1802–1872. German philosopher. Professor, Berlin (from 1833); adherent of Aristotelianism and opponent of Hegel and Kant. Author of *Elementa Logices Aristotelicae* (1836), *Logische Untersuchungen* (1840), *Naturrecht auf dem Grunde der Ethik* (1860), *Kleine Schriften* (1871), etc.

Tre·pov \'tryā-pəf\, Fyodor Fyodorovich. 1803–1889. Russian police official. Chief of St. Petersburg police (1860–78); shot and wounded by revolutionary Vera Zasulich (1878). His son ¶Dmitry Fyodorovich (1855–1906), chief of police in Moscow (1896–1905); as governor general of St. Petersburg (1905) partially responsible for Bloody Sunday Massacre that precipitated the Russian revolution of 1905. His brother ¶Aleksandr Fyodorovich (1862–1928) was Russian prime minister (Nov. 1916–Jan. 1917).

Tré·sa·guet \trā-sȧ-ge\, Pierre-Marie-Jérôme. 1716–1796. French engineer. Served many years with Corps des Ponts et Chaussées; appointed inspector general (1775); his road-building method used by Swedish and Central European engineers and by Thomas Telford.

Tres·ham \'tres-əm\, Francis. 1567?–1605. English conspirator. Initiated into Gunpowder Plot, disapproved of it and revealed it to his brother-in-law Lord Monteagle.

Treub \'trœp\, Melchior. 1851–1910. Dutch botanist. Director of botanical gardens at Buitenzorg (now Bogor), West Java (1880–1909); author of works on plant physiology.

Tre·vel·lick \trə-'vel-ək\, Richard F. 1830–1895. American labor leader, b. St. Mary's, Scilly Isles, England. To U.S. (1857); official in several unions; president of National Labor Union (1869, 1871–72); instrumental in formation (1878) of Greenback-Labor party; tireless worker and speaker on behalf of labor.

Tre·vel·yan \tri-'vel-yən, -'vil-\, Sir George Otto. 2d Baronet Trevelyan. 1838–1928. English politician and historian. Nephew of Lord Macaulay. M.P. (1865); secretary to admiralty (1880–82); chief secretary for Ireland (1882–84); at first opposed, then reluctantly supported, Gladstone's introduction of Irish home rule (1886); secretary for Scotland (1886, 1892–95). Author of *The Life and Letters of Lord Macaulay* (1876), *The American Revolution* (1899–1914). His son ¶George Macaulay (1876–1962), historian; professor, Cambridge (1927–40); master of Trinity College, Cambridge (1940–51). Author of a trilogy on Garibaldi (1907, 1909, 1911), *British History in the Nineteenth Century, 1782–1901* (1922), *History of England* (1926), *Must England's Beauty Perish?* (1929), *England under Queen Anne* (1930–34), *The English Revolution, 1688* (1938), *English Social History* (1942), *The Seven Years of William IV* (1952), biographies of Lord Grey, Sir George Otto Trevelyan, etc.

Trevet, Nicholas. See TRIVET.

Trevethin, Baron. See Sir Alfred Tristram LAWRENCE.

Tre·vi·ra·nus \ˌtrā-vē-'rā-nu̇s\, Gottfried Reinhold. 1776–1837. German naturalist. Known esp. for histological and anatomical studies on invertebrates; published *Biologie* (1802–22) and *Erscheinungen und Gesetze* (1831–32); introduced into Germany idea of biology as distinct discipline. His brother ¶Ludolph Christian (1779–1864), physician and botanist; chief work *Physiologie der Gewächse* (1835–38).

Tre·vi·sa \tri-'vē-sə\, John. d. 1402. English translator. Fellow at Oxford (c.1362–c.1379); vicar of Berkeley (from c.1387); translator of Higden's *Polychronicon* (1387), with added introduction and continuation, and of *De proprietatibus rerum* of Bartholomaeus Anglicus (1398).

Trévise, Duc de. See MORTIER.

Trev·i·thick \'trev-ə-thik\, Richard. 1771–1833. English engineer and inventor. Engineer in Cornish mines (from 1790); constructed (1797) high-pressure working models of stationary and locomotive engines; built high-pressure steam engine (1800); completed road carriage, first vehicle to convey passengers by steam (Christmas Eve, 1801); built world's first steam railway locomotive (1803); first to use exhaust steam to increase draft in chimney; proved that friction of smooth wheels on track is adequate traction for ordinary grades; applied high-pressure steam engines to rock boring, dredging, and agriculture; to South America (1816) to seek fortune but returned (1827) penniless.

Tribolo, Il. See Niccolò PERICOLI.

Tri·bo·ni·an \trə-'bō-nē-ən\. *Lat.* Tri·bo·ni·a·nus \trə-ˌbō-nē-'ā-nəs\. d. 545. Byzantine jurist. Chief legal minister of Justinian, who appointed him (528) one of ten commissioners to prepare the *Codex* of imperial constitutions; chief of various commissions (530–534) that prepared under Justinian's orders the *Institutes*, the *Digesta* (or *Pandects,* 533), and revised *Codex;* held office of *quaestor sacri palatii* (530–532, 534–545).

Tri·cli·ni·us \trə-'klī-nē-əs\, Demetrius. *Ital.* Demetrio Tri·cli·nio \trē-'klēn-yō\. 14th century A.D. Byzantine scholar. Known for his editions, with scholia, of Aeschylus, Hesiod, Sophocles, Euripides, Pindar, Aristophanes, and Theocritus.

Trignan, Saint. See NINIAN.

Tri·go \'trē-gō\, Felipe. 1864–1916. Spanish novelist. Author of *Las ingenuas* (1901), *La sed de amar* (1902), *Sor demonio* (1905), *El médico rural* (1912), etc.

Tri·koú·pis \trē-'kü-pēs\, Kharílaos. 1832–1896. Greek politician. Elected to Chamber of Deputies (1865); minister of foreign affairs (1866, 1877–78); prime minister (1875, 1878, 1880, 1882–85, 1886–90, 1892–95).

Tril·ling \'tril-iŋ\, Lionel. 1905–1975. American literary critic, b. New York City. Taught at Columbia U. (1931–75); author of novel *The Middle of the Journey* (1947), studies of Matthew Arnold (1939) and E.M. Forster (1943), and criticism *The Liberal Imagination* (1950), *Freud and the Crisis of Our Culture* (1955), *Beyond Culture* (1965), *Sincerity and Authenticity* (1972), *Mind in the Modern World* (1972), etc.

Trim·ble \'trim-bəl\, Robert. 1777–1828. American jurist, b. Augusta Co., Va. Associate justice, U.S. Supreme Court (1826–28).

Trin·da·de Co·e·lho \trēⁿ(n)-'dä-də-kü-'āl-yü\, José Francisco. 1861–1908. Portuguese writer. Magistrate in Lisbon (1890–1907); known for *Os meus amores* (1891), volume of short stories of village life in northern Portugal.

Trinqueau. See NEPVEU.

Trippe \'trip\, Juan. 1899–1981. American businessman, b. Sea Bright, N.J. Founder (1927), head (1927–68) of Pan American Airways (later Pan American World Airways); began with Key West–Havana route and built system of 80,000 air miles linking 85 countries.

Tris·si·no \'trēs-sē-nō\, Gian Giorgio. 1478–1550. Italian writer and scholar. Served papacy as nuncio; propounded formation of an "Italian language" by a synthesis of Italian dialects; ardent neo-Aristotelian; known esp. for *Sofonisba* (1514–15, pub. 1524), first regular tragedy of modern literature, and *L'Italia liberata dai Goti* (1547–48), epic poem; first to use the verso sciolto (unrhymed hendecasyllabic verse); also wrote verse comedy *I simillimi* (1548) and first Italian odes modeled on Pindar and Horace; patron of Palladio.

Trist \'trist\, Nicholas Philip. 1800–1874. American diplomat, b. Charlottesville, Va. U.S. consul in Havana (1833–41); sent (1847) to Mexico as special agent to negotiate peace; signed Treaty of Guadalupe Hidalgo (Feb. 2, 1848), which ceded to U.S. much of present Southwest and West.

Tristan L'Hermite. See François L'HERMITE.

Tritheim *or* **Trithemius,** Johannes. See HEIDENBERG.

Triv·et \'triv-ət\ *or* **Trev·et** \'trev-\, Nicholas. 1258?–?1328. English chronicler. Dominican friar; taught at Oxford; author of theological and philological works and of *Annales sex regum angliae* (covering period 1136–1307).

Tri·vul·zio \trē-'vült-syō\. *Fr.* Tri·vulce \trē-vüls\. Name of noble family of Milan, including: Gian Giacomo (1441–1518), soldier; in service of Louis XII of France, who made him marshal of France and governor of Milan (1499); defeated by Swiss at Novara (1513) but won at Marignano (1515). His nephew ¶Teodoro (1456?–1531) was also in service of Louis XII and also created (1526) marshal of France; made governor of Genoa (1527). ¶Gian Giacomo Teodoro (1597–1656), cardinal (from 1629); governor of Milan (1655–56).

Troel·stra \'trül-strä\, Pieter Jelles. 1860–1930. Dutch politician. Founder of Social Democratic Labor party (1894) and its leader in the national legislature (1896–1924); secured passage of universal male suffrage (1917) and old-age insurance laws (1919). Author of verse in Frisian as *Nij Frysk Lieteboek* (1886).

Troeltsch \'trœlch\, Ernst. 1865–1923. German scholar. Professor of theology at Heidelberg (1894–1914) and of philosophy at Berlin (1915–23); member of Prussian Landtag; undersecretary of state for religious affairs (1919–21). His works included *Die Absolutheit des Christentums und die Religionsgeschichte* (1902), *Die Bedeutung des Protestantismus* (1906), *Die Soziallehren der christlichen Kirchen und Gruppen* (1912), *Der Historismus und seine Probleme* (1922), and *Der Historismus und seine Überwindung* (1924).

Tro·gus \'trō-gəs\, Pompeius. 1st century B.C. Roman historian. Author of *De animalibus* and esp. of *Historiae Philippicae,* a general history.

Tro·land \'trō-lənd\, Leonard Thompson. 1889–1932. American psychologist, physicist, and inventor, b. Norwich, Conn. Taught psychology, Harvard (1916–29); chief engineer of Technicolor Motion Picture Corp.; invented and perfected multicolor process for motion pictures; conducted important experiments in the psychology and physiology of vision. Author of *The Mystery of Mind* (1926), *The Principles of Psychophysiology* (1929–30), etc.

Trol·le \'tröl-lə\, Gustav Eriksson. 1488–1535. Swedish prelate. Became archbishop of Sweden and head of council of state (1514); leader of party favoring election of Christian II of Denmark-Norway as Swedish king; deposed (1517) by Sten Sture the Younger, inaugurating civil war; reinstated (1518); persuaded Christian to execute 82 opponents in Stockholm Bloodbath of 1520; forced to flee to Denmark; captured at battle of Öxnebjerg (1535).

Trol·lope \'träl-əp\, Anthony. 1815–1882. English novelist. In service of post office (1834–67), including postal surveyor to Ireland (1841–59). Author of some 50 novels, including: the series of "Barsetshire Chronicles" *The Warden* (1855), *Barchester Towers* (1857), *Doctor Thorne* (1858), *Framley Parsonage* (1861), *The Small House at Allington* (1864), *The Last Chronicle of Barset* (1867), all dealing with the social life of a small cathedral city; the "Parliamentary series" of political novels including *Can You Forgive Her?* (1865), *Phineas Finn* (1869), *Phineas Redux* (1874), *The Prime Minister* (1876), and *The Duke's Children* (1880); *The Three Clerks* (1858), *Orley Farm* (1862), *He Knew He Was Right* (1869), *Sir Harry Hotspur of Humblethwaite* (1871), *The Eustace Diamonds* (1873), *The Way We Live Now* (1875), *Ayala's Angel* (1881), *Mr. Scarborough's Family* (1883). His mother ¶Frances Trollope, *nee* Milton (1780–1863), novelist; m. (1809) Thomas Anthony Trollope (1774–1835) and accompanied him (1827–30) to Cincinnati; on return published *Domestic Manners of the Americans* (1832), arousing considerable resentment in U.S.; supported family through her writings, including books of travel and many novels as *The Vicar of Wrexhill* (1837), *The Widow Barnaby* (1839), and *The Widow Married* (1840).

Tromp \'trömp\, Maarten Harpertszoon. 1598–1653. Dutch admiral. Defeated Spanish fleet off Gravelines (Feb. 1639) and combined Spanish-Portuguese fleet off English coast (Sept. 1639). Engaged British fleet off Dover (May 1652) and was defeated, but won victory over British fleet under Blake (Nov. 1652); killed in engagement against British under Monck off Terheijde. His son ¶Cornelis Maartenszoon (1629–1691) was also an admiral; defeated by British at Southwold Bay (1665); won victories over allied British-French fleet (June 7 and June 14, 1673); commander of Dutch fleet (1691).

Trots·ky \'tröts-kē, *Angl* 'trät-skē, 'tröt-\, Leon. *Orig.* Lev Davidovich Bronstein \(,)brən-'shtīn\. 1879–1940. Russian Communist leader. Became underground revolutionary (1897); exiled to Siberia (1898); escaped to England (1902) and became associated with Lenin; on return to Russia (1905) promptly exiled again to Siberia; escaped to Vienna. Continued revolutionary activities while traveling in Europe and U.S.; rejoined Lenin after February Revolution (1917) and organized Bolshevik seizure of power in October Revolution of 1917. Became commissar for foreign affairs in Soviet government (1917); transferred to commissariat of war (1918) and organized armies that repelled attacks on four fronts. After Lenin's death (1924), was defeated in contest with Stalin for control of the Communist party; relegated to minor governmental posts; expelled from party (1927) and banished from Russia (1929); found haven in Mexico (1937) where he was murdered. Author of *The Defense of Terrorism* (1921), *Literature and Revolution* (1925), *My Life* (1930), etc.

Trot·ter \'trät-ər\, Wilfred Batten Lewis. 1872–1939. English surgeon and sociologist. Surgeon (from 1906) and professor (1935–39) at University College Hospital, London; honorary surgeon to the king (1928–32); popularized phrase "herd instinct" with writings on herd behavior in man and other animals as *Instincts of the Herd in Peace and War* (1916).

Trotzendorf, Valentin. See Valentin FRIEDLAND.

Trow·bridge \'trō-,brij\, John. 1843–1923. American physicist, b. Boston. Professor at Harvard (1870–1910); investigated electrical phenomena. Author of *The New Physics* (1884), *What Is Electricity?* (1896), etc.

Trowbridge, John Townsend. *Early pseudonym* Paul Crey·ton \'krāt-ᵊn\. 1827–1916. American writer, b. Ogden, N.Y. Author of novels as *Neighbor Jackwood* (1857), books for boys including the Jack Hazard, the Tide Mill, the Toby Trafford, and the Start in Life series, plays, verse, and an autobiography.

Troy \trwä\, Jean-François de. *Also spelled* De·troy \də-trwä\. 1679–1752. French painter. Known for his Rococo *tableaux de mode* as *Luncheon with Oysters* (1735) and *Hunt Breakfast* (1737).

Troy·on \trwä-yōⁿ\, Constant. 1810–1865. French painter. Member of the Barbizon group; known for landscapes and animal paintings; works included *Boeufs allant au labour, Forêt de Fontainebleau, Marché d'animaux, Vache blanche, Le Retour à la ferme.*

True·ba y la Quin·ta·na \'trwā-bä-ē-lä-kēn-'tä-nä\, Antonio de. 1819–1889. Spanish poet and novelist. Author of *El libro de los cantares* (1852) and *El libro de las montañas* (1868), historical novels as *El Cid campeador* and *Las hijas del Cid,* and Basque tales.

Truf·faut \trœ-fō\, François. 1932–1984. French film director. A leading figure in French *nouvelle vague* (New Wave). Began (1953) writing film criticism for influential *Cahiers du Cinéma;* proponent of "auteur theory," which asserted that the director should exercise creative control over all aspects of a film. Began (1955) own film career as director, first achieving international success with *Les Quatre Cent Coups* (1959). Films included *Tirez sur le pianiste* (1960), *Jules et Jim* (1961), *La Peau douce* (1964), *Fahrenheit 451* (1966), *Baisers volés* (1968), *L'Enfant sauvage* (1969), *La Nuit américaine* (1973, *Academy Award*), *L'Histoire d'Adèle H.* (1975), *Le Dernier Métro* (1980); acted in *Close Encounters of the Third Kind* (1977); praised Hollywood studio directors, esp. Alfred Hitchcock.

Trui·net \trwʸē-ne\, Charles-Louis-Étienne. *Known by anagrammatic pseudonym* Nuit·ter \nwʸē-ter\. 1828–1899. French writer. Wrote librettos for stage works, esp. for Offenbach's *Les Bavards* and *La Princesse de Trébizonde,* Delibes's *Coppélia* and *La Source,* Lalo's *Namouna,* etc.

Tru·ji·llo \trü-'kē-yō\, Julián. 1829–1884. Colombian politician. President of Colombia (1878–80).

Trujillo Mo·li·na \-mō-'lē-nä\, Rafael Leónidas. 1891–1961. Dominican army officer and politician. General (1917); overthrew President Horacio Vásquez (1930); president of Dominican Republic (1930–38, 1942–52); ruled oppressively; assassinated.

Tru·man \'trü-mən\, Harry S. 1884–1972. Thirty-third president of the United States, b. Lamar, Mo. Artillery officer in World War I; presiding judge,

Jackson County Court, Mo. (1926–34); U.S. senator (1935–45); vice president of the U.S. (1945); became president at death of F.D. Roosevelt (April 1945); ordered atomic bombing of Hiroshima and Nagasaki (1945). Elected President of U.S. (1948–53); unable to put into law his liberal domestic program; established a "containment" policy against Soviet Union; promulgated Truman Doctrine (1947), Marshall Plan (1948), NATO (1949); established Central Intelligence Agency (1947); initiated Point Four Program (1949); ordered Berlin Airlift (1948–49) and U.S. direct engagement in Korean War (1950).

Trum·bić \'trüm-bēt͟y\, Ante. 1864–1938. Croatian politician. Member of Dalmatian Diet (from 1895) and of Reichsrat in Vienna (from 1897); became (1915) president of Yugoslav Committee in London; concluded Declaration of Corfu with Serbia (July 1917), which led to organization of Yugoslavia; foreign minister (1918–20); represented Yugoslavia at Paris Peace Conference (1919).

Trum·bull \'trəm-bəl\, Benjamin. 1735–1820. American Congregational clergyman and historian, b. Hebron, Conn. Author of *A Complete History of Connecticut* (1797) and vol. I of projected *A General History of the United States of America* (1810).

Trumbull, John. 1750–1831. American lawyer and poet, b. Watertown, Conn. First cousin of Jonathan Trumbull (1710–1785). Practiced in Boston (1773–74), New Haven (1774–77), and Hartford (from 1781); judge of Connecticut superior court (1801–19) and supreme court (1808–19). A leader of the Hartford Wits; satirized collegiate instruction of his day in poem *The Progress of Dulness* (1772–73); satirized British blunders of American Revolution in burlesque epic poem *M'Fingal* (1776–82), popular imitation of *Hudibras.*

Trumbull, John. 1756–1843. American painter, b. Lebanon, Conn. Son of Jonathan Trumbull (1710–85). Served in Revolutionary War. Studied painting in London under Benjamin West (1780, 1782–83, 1784–85); began (by 1786) his famous historical paintings with *Battle of Bunker's Hill, The Death of General Montgomery in the Attack of Quebec, Death of General Mercer at the Battle of Princeton,* and *Capture of the Hessians at Trenton.* Studio in New York (1789) and Philadelphia (1792); George Washington sat for him a number of times. In diplomatic service in London (1794–1804); again opened studio in New York (1804); painted portraits of notables of the day; commissioned by Congress (1817) to paint four large pictures for the rotunda of the Capitol at Washington (*Surrender of General Burgoyne at Saratoga, Surrender of Lord Cornwallis at Yorktown, Declaration of Independence, Resignation of Washington*). Turned over collection of his paintings to Yale College; Trumbull Gallery, first art museum in America connected with an educational institution, was built to hold his collection (opened 1832).

Trumbull, Jonathan. 1710–1785. American merchant and politician, b. Lebanon, Conn. Entered father's mercantile house (1731). Deputy governor of Connecticut (1766–69) and governor (1769–84). Vigorous supporter of colonial cause during the Revolution; guided and encouraged Connecticut industry in supplying Continental army with food and munitions. His son ¶Joseph (1737–1778) was a businessman; in father's mercantile firm (1756–67); member of Continental Congress (1774); commissary general of Continental army (1775–77); member of the Board of War (1777–78). Another son ¶Jonathan (1740–1809) was a soldier and politician; first comptroller of the U.S. Treasury (1778–79); secretary on George Washington's staff (1781–83); member of U.S. House of Representatives (1789–95) and speaker of the House (1791–93); U.S. senator (1795–96); governor of Connecticut (1797–1809).

Trum·pler \'trəm-plər\, Robert Julius. 1886–1956. American astronomer, b. Zürich, Switzerland. To U.S. (1915); on staff of Lick Observatory (1920–38); professor, U. of Calif., Berkeley (1938–51). Made extensive studies of galactic star clusters; confirmed Einstein's general theory of relativity during solar eclipse expedition in Australia (1922); demonstrated (1930) presence of light-absorbing interstellar material that had caused stellar distances to be overestimated; devised methods of classification of galactic clusters.

Trung Trac \'trüŋ-'träk\ and her younger sister Trung Nhi \-'nē\. both d. 43 A.D. Vietnamese nationalists. Led movement (from 39 A.D.) to oust Chinese from northern Vietnam; controlled area from southern China to present Hue, proclaimed themselves queens; defeated by Chinese, committed suicide.

Trunk \'trüⁿk\, Yeḥiel Yeshaia *or* Jehiel Isaiah. 1887–1961. Polish writer. Author in Yiddish of short stories and novels as *Khelemer Ḥakomin* (1951) and *Der freylekhster Yid in der velt* (1953), memoirs *Poyln* (1944–53), and a study (1937–44) of Sholem Aleichem's works.

Tru·ong Vinh Ky \trü-'öŋ-'vēn-'kē\. *Also known as* Pétrus Ky *and* Jean-Baptiste Ky. 1837–1898. Vietnamese scholar. Popularized French language and culture in Vietnam; educ. by Catholic missionaries; in Europe, esp. France, as diplomatic interpreter (1863–65), founder and editor of first Vietnamese newspaper, *Gia-Dinh Bao* (1867–74); urged French colonization of northern Vietnam (1876). Author of didactic, historical, and linguistic works in Vietnamese and French as *Grammaire de la langue annamite* (1867) and *Cours d'histoire annamite* (1875–77).

Truth \'trüth\, Sojourner. c.1797–1883. American evangelist and reformer, b. Ulster Co., N.Y. Born a slave with name Isabella; freed (1827), taking former master's surname Van Wagener; to New York (c.1829), becoming religious missionary; adopted name Sojourner Truth and took to road (1843); gained national fame as preacher for abolition and woman suffrage; appointed counselor with National Freedmen's Relief Association (1864).

Trux·tun \'trək-stən\, Thomas. 1755–1822. American naval officer, b. near Hempstead, N.Y. Privateer during American Revolution; in merchant marine (1783–94); commissioned captain, U.S. navy (1794); commanded a squadron in West Indian waters during the war with France; captured French frigate *Insurgente* (1799) and defeated *La Vengeance* in night battle (1800). Influential in maintaining discipline and high morale in new U.S. navy.

Try·on \'trī-ən\, William. 1729–1788. British colonial administrator. Governor (1765–71) of North Carolina, where he took measures to suppress the Regulators' revolt (1771); governor of New York (1771–78); commanded (1778–80) force of Loyalists raiding Connecticut.

Tsagadai. See CHAGATAI.

Tsai–ch'un \'dzī-'chün\. *Reign title* T'ung-chih \'tüŋ-'ji(ə)r\. *Temple name* Mu Tsung \'müd-'zùŋ\. *Posthumous name* I Huang-ti \'ē-'hwäŋ-'dē\. 1856–1875. Chinese emperor (1862–75), eighth of the Ch'ing dynasty. Son of I-chu and Tz'u-hsi; under regency (1862–73) of Tz'u-hsi and his uncle I-hsin; his reign saw suppression of Taiping (1864), Nien (1868), and Muslim (1873) rebellions; finances and fortunes of government restored; a weak ruler controlled by Tz'u-hsi.

Ts'ai Hsiang \'tsī-shē-'äŋ\. 11th century A.D. Chinese horticulturist. Wrote (1059) *Li-chih-p'u* on the lichi, earliest monograph on a fruit tree.

Ts'ai Lun \'tsī-'lùn\. 50?–?118 A.D. Chinese eunuch at the Later Han court. According to official history of Han dynasty, invented (105) paper from tree bark, hemp, rags, and fish nets.

Tsai–t'ien \'dzī-tē-'ən\. *Reign title* Kuang-hsü \'gwäŋ-'shue̅\. *Temple name* Te Tsung \'dəd-'zùŋ\. *Posthumous name* Ching Huang-ti \'jiŋ-'hwäŋ-dē\. 1871–1908. Chinese emperor (1875–1908), ninth of the Ch'ing dynasty. Nephew of I-chu; under regency (1875–89) of his aunt, the Empress Dowager Tz'u-hsi, who dominated the government; issued (1898) edicts reforming military, agriculture, and administrative procedures; reforms negated by generals; compelled to accept regency of Tz'u-hsi; for rest of reign (1898–1908) a mere puppet.

Ts'ai Yüan-pei \'tsī-yue̅-'än-'bā\. 1863–1940. Chinese educator and revolutionary. Joined revolutionary party of Sun Yat-sen (1905); minister of education (1912); chancellor of Peking U. (1916–26); member of central supervisory (1924) and political (1926) councils of Kuomintang; a founder (1928) and first president of Academia Sinica.

Tsan·kov \'tsän-kȯf\, Aleksandŭr. 1879–1959. Bulgarian politician. Became leader of conservative group Naroden Zgovor (1922); premier (1923–26); his regime marked by great domestic unrest and violence; formed (Sept. 1944) short-lived Bulgarian government in exile in Austria.

Ts'ao Chan \'tsaù-'jän\. *Better known by courtesy name* Ts'ao Hsüeh-ch'in \-shue̅-'ech-'in\. 1715?–1763. Chinese novelist. Author of the major part of *Hung lou meng* (*Dream of the Red Chamber*), considered greatest Chinese novel; novel completed by Kao Eh, about whom little is known.

Ts'ao K'un \'tsaù-kün\. 1862–1938. Chinese soldier and politician. Served in Sino–Japanese War (1894); took part in Revolution (1911) that overthrew Manchu dynasty; military governor of Chihli (1917–23); became marshal and gained control of Peking, deposing President Li Yüan-hung (1923); at war with southern forces under Sun Yat-sen (1923); president of China (1923–24); entered Japanese puppet government (1937).

Ts'ao P'ei \'tsaù-'pā\. 188–227. Chinese emperor (220–227), first of Wei dynasty. Son of Ts'ao Ts'ao; accepted abdication of Hsien Ti, last of Han emperors; made his capital at Lo-yang; also known for lyric poems and essays.

Ts'ao Ts'ao \'tsaùt-'saù\. 155–220 A.D. Chinese general. Minister of state (208); held real power over Hsien Ti, last emperor of the Later Han dynasty; suppressed the Yellow Turban Rebellion; set up the new Wei dynasty (220) of which his son Ts'ao P'ei was first ruler; subject of many legends and stories. His son ¶Ts'ao Chih \'tsaù-'ji(ə)r\, *also known as* Ch'en Ssu Wang \'chən-'sü-'wäŋ\ *or* Prince Ssu of Ch'en (192–232), was one of greatest lyric poets of China; bitter rival of his elder brother Ts'ao P'ei; also wrote prose pieces.

Tsch- *or* **Tch-.** For many Russian names beginning Tsch- or Tch-, see CH-.

Tschaikovsky. See TCHAIKOVSKY.

Tscher·mak von Sey·se·negg \'cher-ˌmäk-fȯn-'zī-zə-ˌnek\, Gustav. 1836–1927. Austrian mineralogist. Known esp. for work in petrography, crystallography, and the study of meteorites. His son ¶Erich (1871–1962), botanist; taught

\ə\ abut \ᵊ\ kitten, *Fr.* **table \ər\ further \a\ ash \ā\ ace \ä\ cot, cart \aù\ out \ch\ chin \e\ bet \ē\ easy \g\ go \i\ hit \ī\ ice \j\ job \ŋ\ sing \ō\ go \ȯ\ law \ȯi\ boy \th\ both \t͟h\ the \ü\ loot \ù\ foot \y\ yet \zh\ vision \á, b̲, g̅, k̲, ⁿ, œ, œ̅, ue, ue̅, ʸ** *see* **Guide to Pronunciation**

(from 1901) at Hochschule für Bodenkultur, Vienna; independently rediscovered Mendel's laws (1900).

Tscher·ning \'cher-niŋ\, Anton Frederik. 1795–1874. Danish politician. Founder (1846) and chairman (1846–56) of reform group Bondevennernes Selskab; minister of war (1848); reorganized army; member of parliament (1849–66) and State Council (1854–64); urged democratic reforms and opposed annexation of Schleswig.

Tschir·ky \'chi(ə)r-kē\, Oscar Michel. *Known as* Oscar of the Wal·dorf \'wȯl-ˌdȯ(ə)rf\. 1866–1950. American maître d'hôtel, b. Locle, Switzerland. To U.S. (1883, naturalized 1888); with Waldorf-Astoria Hotel (1893–1943); creator of the Waldorf salad and other dishes.

Tschirn·haus \'chi(ə)rn-ˌhau̇s\, Ehrenfried Walter von. 1651–1708. German mathematician, physicist, and philosopher. Made discoveries in the production of porcelain; introduced a general transformation for simplifying algebraic equations. Author of the philosophical works *Medicina corporis et mentis* (1686–87) and *Gründliche Anleitung zu den nützlichen Wissenschaften* (1700).

Tschu·di \'chü-dē\, Aegidius *or* Gilg. 1505–1572. Swiss historian. Pupil of Zwingli but remained a Catholic; chief magistrate of Glarus (1558); regarded as the "father of Swiss history"; chief work *Chronicon Helveticum,* a chronicle of Swiss history from 1000 to 1470 (pub. 1734–36).

Tschudi, Burkhardt. See SHUDI.

Tse·der·baum \'tsäd-yir-ˌbau̇m\, Yuly Osipovich. *Pseudonym* L. Mar·tov \'mär-təf\. 1873–1923. Russian revolutionary. With Lenin formed St. Petersburg Union of Struggle for the Liberation of the Working Class (1895); imprisoned in Siberia (1896–99); leader (1905–07) of Mensheviks; frequently opposed Lenin; after Bolshevik Revolution (1917) supported existence of government but opposed repressive measures; edited *Socialist Courier* in Berlin (1920–23).

Tseng Kuo–fan \'dzəŋ-'gwō-'fän\. *Posthumous title* Wen-cheng \'wən-'jəŋ\. 1811–1872. Chinese soldier and administrator. In government service (from 1839); in Taiping Rebellion (1850–64) led in defense of Changsha, the capture of Wuchang and Hanyang, and in final years (1861–64), with the aid of Ward and Gordon, in the concluding victories around Nanking; less successful against Nien Rebellion (1865–66); viceroy of Chihli (1870).

Tseng-tzu \'dzəŋd-'zü\. *Also known as* Tseng Ts'an \'dzəŋt-'sän\. 505–c.436 B.C. Chinese philosopher. Disciple of Confucius; reputed author of *Ta hsüeh,* one of the *Ssu shu* (Four Books) of Confucian texts.

Tser·claes \'tser-kläs\, Johann. Graf von Til·ly \'til-ē\. 1559–1632. Flemish general. Served at siege of Antwerp (1585); joined (1594) Rudolf II's campaign against Turks. Appointed (1610) by Duke Maximilian of Bavaria to reorganize his armies. On outbreak of Thirty Years' War (1618), made commander in chief of field forces of Catholic League; won Battle of White Mountain (1620); conquered the Upper and Rhenish Palatinates (1621–23). Defeated Swedes at Battle of Lutter (1626); replaced Wallenstein in command of Imperial forces (1630); took Magdeburg by storm (1631), but could not restrain his army from terrible atrocities; completely defeated by Gustav II at Breitenfeld (1631) and at Lech River (1632), where he was mortally wounded.

Tshaka. See SHAKA.

Tshom·be \'chȯm-be, -bā\, Moise-Kapenda. 1919–1969. Congolese politician. Elected to Congolese Parliament and made president of Katanga province (1960); declared Katanga an independent state and served as its president (1960–63); defeated by United Nations troops and fled to Spain (1963); premier (1964–65) of Congo Republic (now Zaire).

Tsiol·kov·sky \tsi-(ˌ)əl-'kȯf-skəi\, Konstantin Eduardovich. 1857–1935. Russian scientist. Taught school in Borovsk (1880–92) and Kaluga (1892); elected to Socialist Academy (1919). Pioneer in rocket and space research; built model of all-metal dirigible with a movable shell; proposed several models for rockets; published works on problems of space, communications with extraterrestrial beings, etc.

Tsi·ra·na·na \ˌtsē-rä-'nä-nä\, Philibert. 1910–1978. Malagasy politician. President of the Malagasy Republic (1960–72).

Tso-ch'iu Ming \'dzō-chē-'ü-'miŋ\. 5th or 4th century B.C. Chinese author. Probably disciple of Confucius; author of *Tso chuan,* a commentary on the *Ch'un Ch'iu* (one of the Five Classics) and an interesting detailed account of China's feudal age.

Tsong-kha-pa \'tsȯŋ-'kä-'pä\. 1357–1419. Tibetan lama. Founder of Tibetan Buddhist sect known as Dge-lugs-pa or Yellow Hat sect; insisted on the wearing of yellow robes and adherence to rigorous routine.

Tso Tsung-t'ang \'dzōd-'zu̇ŋ-'täŋ\. 1812–1885. Chinese general and official. One of top Imperial commanders in suppression of Taiping Rebellion (1850–64); governor general of Chekiang and Fukien (1863–66); governor general of Shensi and Kansu (1866–73), where he put down Muslim rebellion and captured Suchow in Kansu. In later campaign (1875–78) conquered regions north and south of the Tien Shan mountains and added them as one province (Sinkiang) to China; granted rank of marquis; took part in war with French (1884).

Tsou Yen \'dzō-'yən\. 340–?260 B.C. Chinese philosopher. Lived in Ch'i (present Shantung); leading exponent of Yin-Yang school; reputed to have associated the Five Agents theory with the Yin-Yang doctrine.

Tsu·bo·u·chi \tsu̇b-ō-u̇ch-ē\ Shōyō. *Orig.* Tsubouchi Yūzō. 1859–1935. Japanese writer. Taught at Waseda U. (1883–1915); founded (1891) and edited literary journal *Waseda bungaku;* a founder of the *shingeki* (new theater) movement which introduced Shaw and Ibsen to Japan and staged modern Japanese plays. Author of novels as *Tōsei shoseikatagi* (1885–86), plays, translations of Shakespeare, Scott, and Bulwer-Lytton, and *Shōsetsu shinzui* (1885–86), first major work of modern Japanese literary criticism.

Tsui-weng. See OU-YANG HSIU.

Tsunayoshi. See under TOKUGAWA family.

Tsu·shi·ma \tsu̇sh-ē-mä\ Shuji. *Pseudonym* Da·zai \dä-zi\ Osamu. 1909–1948. Japanese writer. Author of works by turns wry, gloomy, farcical; considered a chief spokesman of post-World War II Japan. Works included *Bannen* (stories, 1936), *Otogi zōshi* (tales, 1945), and novels *Tsugaru* (1944), *Shayō* (1947), *Biyon no Tsuma* (1947), *Ningen Shikkaku* (1948).

Tsve·ta·ye·va \tsvyi-'tá-yə-və\, Marina Ivanovna. 1892–1941. Russian poet. Published collection of verse *Vecherny albom* (1911) and long poem *Tsar-devitsa* (1922); in Paris (1925–39), where she wrote poetry praising Czarist forces in Civil War, verse dramas, prose.

Tuan Ch'i–jui \du̇-'än-'chē-zhu̇-'ā\. 1865–1936. Chinese soldier and politician. Largely responsible for reorganization of northern army (1911); minister of war (1912); acting premier (1913); minister of war (1914); premier (1916–17, 1918); succeeded Ts'ao K'un as provisional president (1924–26).

Tu·bières–Gri·moard \tüēb-yer-grēm-wår\, Anne-Claude-Philippe de Pes·tels de Lé·vis de \də-pes-tel-də-lā-vē-də-\. Comte de Cay·lus \key-lüēs\. 1692–1765. French archaeologist and writer. Served in War of the Spanish Succession (1704–14); traveled to Italy, Constantinople, Greece, studying and collecting antiquities; became noted engraver. Author of *Recueil d'antiquités égyptiennes, étrusques, grecques, romaines, et gauloises* (1752–67).

Tub·man \'təb-mən\, Harriet, *orig.* Araminta. c.1820–1913. American abolitionist, b. Dorchester Co., Md. Escaped from a Maryland slave plantation (1849); became a leading abolitionist; called the "Moses of her people" for helping over 300 slaves escape to North on the Underground Railroad; during Civil War served as nurse, laundress, and spy with Federal forces operating in South Carolina; later settled in Auburn, N.Y.

Tubman, William Vacanarat Shadrach. 1895–1971. Liberian politician. Served as trial judge, public prosecutor, arbitration referee; associate justice of Liberian Supreme Court (1937–44); president of the Republic of Liberia (1944–71); instituted government, education, and social reforms.

Tuck·er \'tək-ər\, Abraham. 1705–1774. English moralist. Author of *The Light of Nature Pursued* (1768–78) on metaphysics, theology, and morals.

Tucker, Benjamin Ricketson. 1854–1939. American anarchist and journalist, b. South Dartmouth, Mass. Published *The Radical Review* (1877) and *Liberty* (1881–1905); translated writings of European anarchists. Author of *Instead of a Book* (1893) and *State Socialism and Anarchism* (1899).

Tucker, Charlotte Maria. *Pseudonym* A.L.O.E., *i.e.* A Lady of England. 1821–1893. English writer. Missionary in India (from 1875); wrote books for children, allegories and parables.

Tucker, Josiah. 1712–1799. English economist. Dean of Gloucester (1758); author of pamphlets advising separation from American colonies; forerunner of Adam Smith in his arguments against monopolies.

Tucker, Nathaniel Beverley. 1784–1851. American novelist, b. Chesterfield Co., Va. Professor of law at William and Mary Coll. (1834–51). Author of novels *George Balcombe* (1836), *The Partisan Leader* (1836), *Gertrude* (1844–45), and many treatises on political economy and law.

Tucker, Richard. *Orig.* Reuben Tick·er \'tik-ər\. 1913–1975. American singer, b. Brooklyn, N.Y. One of finest operatic tenors of his day; with N.Y. Metropolitan Opera (1945–75); known esp. for singing Canio in *Pagliacci* and Rodolfo in *La Bohème.*

Tucker, Samuel. 1747–1833. American naval officer, b. Marblehead, Mass. As captain of the *Franklin* and *Hancock,* preyed on British ships (1775–76); commissioned captain in Continental navy (1777); continued attacks on British commerce (1778–80).

Tucker, Sophie. *Orig.* Sophie Abu·za \ə-'byü-zə\. 1884–1966. American singer, b. Russia. To U.S. as a child; sang (from 1906) on burlesque, vaudeville, nightclub, and English music hall circuits; known for brassy, flamboyant style and trademark song "Some of These Days"; billed as the "last of the red hot mamas."

Tuck·er·man \'tək-ər-mən\, Joseph. 1778–1840. American Unitarian clergyman, b. Boston. Founder (1812), Boston Society for the Religious and Moral Improvement of Seamen, first sailors' aid society in U.S.

Tuck·ey \ˈtək-ē\, James Kingston. 1776–1816. British naval officer and explorer. To Australia (1802–04); helped found colony of New South Wales and explored its interior; surveyed harbor of Port Philip. Led (1816) expedition up Congo River in futile attempt to find connection with the Niger; died of fever during expedition; his journal published as *Narrative of an Expedition to Explore the River Zaire* (1816).

Tudela, Benjamin of. See BENJAMIN of Tudela.

Tud·ha·li·yas IV \tüd-ˈhal-ē-əs\. *Also spelled* Tud·kha·li·ash \-ˈkäl-ē-äsh\. 13th century B.C. Hittite king (c.1250–c.1220 B.C.). Son and successor of Hattusilis III; interested mainly in religious matters; reign troubled by threat of Assyria from east and Sea Peoples from west.

Tu·dor \ˈt(y)üd-ər\. Name of an English house and of the dynasty occupying throne of England (1485–1603), founded by Owen Tudor (c.1400–1461), squire of an old Welsh family; had three sons and a daughter by Henry V's widow Catherine of Valois (*q.v.*), whom he secretly married (c.1429); had annuity from Henry VI; fought at Mortimer's Cross on side of Lancastrians; captured by Yorkists and beheaded. His eldest son ¶Edmund (c.1430–1456), Earl of Rich·mond \ˈrich-mənd\ (cr. 1453), married the heiress of John of Gaunt, Margaret Beaufort (*q.v.*), by whom he was father of Henry VII. Owen's second son ¶Jasper (c.1431–1495), Earl of Pem·broke \ˈpem-ˌbrük, *US also* -ˌbrōk\ and Duke of Bed·ford \ˈbed-fərd\, fought for Henry VI at first battle of St. Albans (1455); defeated by Edward IV at Mortimer's Cross (1461) and retired to Scotland (1462); made attack on Wales (1468) only to be driven off by William Herbert; returned with Warwick (1470) but after battle of Tewkesbury fled with his nephew Henry (later Henry VII) to Paris, till their return to victory at Bosworth over Richard III (1485); created duke of Bedford (1485), earl marshal (1492).

The Tudor monarchs were: Henry VII (1485–1509) and VIII (1509–47), Edward VI (1547–53), Mary I (1553–58), Elizabeth (1558–1603). See these entries. Other members of Tudor house included Henry VII's daughters Mary Tudor (1496–1533), queen of Louis XII of France (see MARY of France), and Margaret Tudor (1489–1541), queen of James IV of Scotland (see MARGARET TUDOR), through whom the Stuart dynasty derived its title to throne of England (1603).

Tudor, William. 1779–1830. American author, b. Boston, Mass. Founder (1815) and first editor, *North American Review;* helped found Boston Athenaeum (1807); first to suggest erection of Bunker Hill Monument.

Tu Duc \ˈtü-ˈdu̇k\. *Orig.* Nguy·en Phuoc Hoang Nham \ˈnī-en-ˈpwȯk-ˈhwäŋ-ˈnäm\. 1829–1883. Emperor (1847–83) of kingdom of Annam in central Vietnam. Son of Thieu Tri; maintained isolation from European nations; his executions of Christian missionaries led to invasion (1858) by French forces and cession (1862) of three provinces to France; forced (1873) to grant trade concessions and eventually lost more territory to France.

Tufts \ˈtəf(t)s\, Charles. 1781–1876. American farmer and brick manufacturer, b. Somerville, Mass. Deeded land for establishment (1852) of Tufts College, Medford, Mass.

Tufts, John. 1689–1752. American Congregational clergyman, b. Medford, Mass. Author of *A Very Plain and Easy Introduction to the Art of Singing Psalm Tunes* (1714 or 1715), which had considerable influence on development of church singing in New England.

Tu Fu \ˈdü-ˈfü\. 712–770. Chinese poet. Failures (736, 746) to pass imperial examinations resulted in his adopting an itinerant mode of life; met Li Po (744); secured court position (755) but lost it during An Lu-shan Rebellion (755); in later years a gentleman farmer and traveler. One of greatest poets of China; wrote anti-war poems as "The Army Carts," satires as "The Beautiful Woman," and lyrics.

Tugh·luq \ˌtəg-ˈlək\. A Muslim dynasty of kings of Delhi (1320–1413) founded by Ghiyās-ud-Dīn Tughluq (*q.v.*), who led a rebellion overthrowing the Khaljīs; dynasty overthrown by the Sayyids. See also MUḤAMMAD IBN TUGHLUQ and FĪRŪZ SHĀH TUGHLUQ.

Ṭughril Beg. See TOGHRĪL.

Ṭug·well \ˈtəg-wəl\, Rexford Guy. 1891–1979. American economist, b. Sinclairville, N.Y. Taught, Columbia U. (1920–37); adviser to F. D. Roosevelt (from 1933); undersecretary of agriculture (1934–37); chairman, N.Y. City Planning Commission (1938–41); governor of Puerto Rico (1941–46); professor, U. of Chicago (1946–57). Author of *Industry's Coming of Age* (1927), *The Stricken Land* (1946), *The Place of Planning in Society* (1954), etc.

Tu·kā·rām \ˈtük-ä-ˈräm\. 1607–1649. Marathi poet. Retired from worldly life and became a wandering ascetic; wrote over 4,000 *abhangas* (hymn-like poems of religious devotion).

Tuke \ˈt(y)ük\, Sir Samuel. c.1620–1674. English Royalist and playwright. In Royalist army; commanded at Lincoln, fought at Marston Moor (1644); defended Colchester (1648); under Restoration sent on missions to French court. Author of tragicomedy *The Adventures of Five Hours* (1663).

Tu·kha·chev·sky \tük-(ˌ)hə-ˈchäf-skəi, *Angl* ˌtu̇k-ə-ˈchef-skē\, Mikhail Nikolayevich. 1893–1937. Russian general and politician. Served in World War I (1914–18); leader of Russian offensive in Russo-Polish War (1919–20); chief of staff (1925–28); member of Union Central Executive Committee; created marshal of the Soviet Union (1935); convicted on charge of treason and executed.

Tu·kul·ti-Nin·ur·ta \tü-ˈku̇l-tē-nē-ˈnu̇r-tä\. Name of two kings of Assyria:

Tukulti-Ninurta I. d. c.1208 B.C. King (c.1294–c.1208 B.C.). Son of Shalmaneser I; made Assyria a great power; defeated Kashtiliash IV, king of the Kassites; subjugated Armenia and Babylonia; erected temple to goddess Ishtar-Dinitu; built new capital of Kar-Tukulti-Ninurta across Tigris River from Ashur; slain by his son.

Tukulti-Ninurta II. d. 884 B.C. King (890–884 B.C.). Son of Adad-nirari II; restored Assyrian prestige; increased prosperity of people.

Tu·lane \tü-ˈlān, t(y)ü-\, Paul. 1801–1887. American merchant, b. near Princeton, N.J. Established drygoods and clothing business, New Orleans, La. (from 1822); gave liberally (from 1882) to U. of Louisiana, founded at New Orleans (1834); its name changed to Tulane U. (1884) in his honor.

Tu·lasne \tūē-län\, Louis-René. 1815–1885. French botanist. A founder of modern mycology; made studies of rusts and smuts, lichens, cryptogams. Published *Fungi hypogaei* (1851) and *Selecta fungorum carpologia* (1857–65).

Tull \ˈtəl\, Jethro. 1674–1741. English agriculturist. Invented and perfected machine drill for sowing seed (c.1701); introduced system of sowing in drills; confirmed his theories of use of manure and importance of pulverizing soil. Published *The New Horse Houghing Husbandry* (1731).

Tullius, Servius. See SERVIUS TULLIUS.

Tul·loch \ˈtəl-ək, -ək\, John. 1823–1886. Scottish theologian. Principal and professor of theology, St. Mary's Coll., St. Andrews (1854); moderator of general assembly of Church of Scotland (1878), founder of liberal church party; active in reorganization of education in Scottish schools and universities.

Tul·lus Hos·til·i·us \ˈtəl-əs-häs-ˈtil-ē-əs\. 7th century B.C. Third legendary king (673–642 B.C.) of the early Romans. Probably a historical figure; said to have incorporated Alba into Roman state.

Tul·ly \ˈtəl-ē\. Anglicized form of Tullius, once commonly used in reference to Marcus Tullius CICERO.

Tully, Jim. 1891–1947. American writer, b. St. Marys, Ohio. Worked at odd jobs as laborer, tramp, circus roustabout, pugilist, publicist for Charlie Chaplin, writer for screen magazines, and often jailed for vagrancy. His books included *Beggars of Life* (1924), *Jarnegan* (1925), *Circus Parade* (1927), *Shanty Irish* (1928), *Blood on the Moon* (1931), *The Bruiser* (1936), *A Hollywood Decameron* (1937), *Biddy Brogan's Boy* (1942).

Tulp \ˈtœlp\, Nicolaes *or* Claes Pieterszoon. *Orig. name* Nicolaes Pie·ters·zoon \ˈpē-tər-sōn\, *the name* Tulp *being added because of the tulip* (*Dutch* tulp) *carved on the façade of his house.* 1593–1674. Dutch anatomist. Professor, Surgeons' Guild, Amsterdam (1628–53); commissioned Rembrandt to paint (1632) *The Anatomy Lesson,* which shows Tulp demonstrating the structure of the human body to a group of his contemporaries.

Tul·sī·dās \ˈtu̇l-sē-ˈdäs\. 1543?–1623. Hindu poet. Called the greatest poet of medieval Hindustan. Lived most of life at Benares; a devotee of Rama. Wrote (1574–76?) in Awadhi *Rāmcaritmānas* (Lake of the Acts of Rama), greatest achievement of medieval Hindi literature and an abiding influence on Hindu culture of northern India; also the author of six other long works consisting of history, hymns, prayers, etc., of the Rama legend, and a number of shorter works.

Ṭū·lū·nid \tu̇-ˈlü-nəd\. Muslim dynasty in Egypt (868–905), of Turkish origin, founded by Aḥmad ibn Ṭūlūn (*q.v.*). It made Egypt independent of Baghdad and conquered Syria, but was overcome (905) by forces of Caliph al-Muktafī.

Tum·ul·ty \ˈtəm-əl-tē\, Joseph Patrick. 1879–1954. American lawyer, b. Jersey City, N.J. Private secretary to Woodrow Wilson as governor (1910–13) and as president of the United States (1913–21). Author of *Woodrow Wilson as I Know Him* (1921).

Tung Ch'i–ch'ang \ˈdu̇ŋ-ˈchē-ˈchäŋ\. 1555–1636. Chinese painter, calligrapher, and theoretician. Held official positions in Ming government (from 1589). One of finest painters of late Ming period; most distinguished connoisseur of his day; exerted considerable influence with his writings on painting, as *Hua-yen* and *Hua-chih.*

T'ung-chih. See TSAI-CH'UN.

Tung Cho \ˈdu̇ŋ-ˈjō\. d. 192 A.D. Chinese general. Seized power in Han court; burned (190) capital of Lo-yang and removed himself and the emperor to ancient capital of Ch'ang-an; his despotic rule divided empire into satrapies ruled by rival generals; assassinated.

Tung Chung–shu \'dụŋ-'jụŋ-'shü\. c.179–c.104 B.C. Chinese scholar. Chief minister to Emperor Wu of the Han dynasty (from c.140); dismissed all non-Confucian scholars from government and established Confucianism as state cult and basis of official political philosophy (136); interpreted (in *Ch'un Ch'iu fan lu*) the Confucian Classic *Ch'un Ch'iu* in such a way as to merge Confucianist and Yin-Yang schools of thought.

Tun•ney \'tən-ē\, Gene, *orig.* James Joseph. 1898–1978. American pugilist, b. New York City. Won heavyweight championship of the world by defeating Jack Dempsey (Sept. 23, 1926); retained it by defeating Dempsey again (1927); retired (1928) undefeated as champion, with career record of 76 wins and 1 loss.

Tun Per•ak \'tən-'per-,ak\. d. 1498. Malaccan politician. *Bendahara* (chief minister) of Malacca (1456–98) and its effective ruler; led forces in defeat of Siamese invasion (1456); pursued aggressive foreign policy resulting in a loose empire of entire Malay Peninsula and part of Sumatra; elevated to sultanate his kinsmen Mansur Shah, Ala'ud'din, and Mahmud Shah.

Tun•stall *or* **Ton•stall** \'tən-stəl\, Cuthbert. 1474–1559. English prelate and scholar. Friend of Erasmus and More; employed by Henry VIII and Wolsey on diplomatic missions to emperor (1515–21); master of rolls (1516–22); bishop of London (1522–30); keeper of privy seal (1523); succeeded Wolsey as bishop of Durham (1530). Adhered to Roman Catholic dogma but acquiesced in royal supremacy; voted against first act of uniformity (1549); accused of inciting to rebellion and deprived (1552); restored under Mary (1553), refrained from persecution of Protestants. On accession of Elizabeth, refused oath of supremacy and declined to consecrate Matthew Parker as archbishop of Canterbury, and was deprived (1559).

Tu•pac Ama•rú \tü-'päk-äm-'är-ü\. d. 1572. Inca chieftain. Last of the male line; offered no opposition to Spaniards; ordered seized by viceroy Francisco de Toledo and beheaded.

Tupac Amarú. *Name assumed (1771) by* José Gabriel Con•dor•can•qui \kòn-dòr-'käŋ-kē\. 1742?–1781. Peruvian Indian revolutionary. Maternal descendant of Tupac Amarú; recognized by Spanish as legal heir of Incas; headed a rebellion of Indians against Spanish government (1780); controlled large areas of Peru, Bolivia, Argentina; captured (1781), tortured, and executed.

Tupac Yu•pan•qui \-yü-'päŋ-kē\. d. 1493. Inca ruler (1471–93). Father of Huayna Capac; noted for his wide conquests, which extended Inca kingdom north into modern Ecuador, south into Chile, and covered large sections of Amazon Valley.

Tu•po•lev \'tü-pəl-yif\, Andrey Nikolayevich. 1888–1972. Russian aeronautical engineer. Studied under Nikolay Zhukovsky (1909–18); with Zhukovsky organized (1918) Central Aerohydrodynamic Institute and became its assistant director (1918–35) and head of its design bureau (1922–35); organized and directed an independent design group (1936); lieutenant general in Soviet army; deputy to Supreme Soviet (1944–56). Responsible for design of over 100 types of military and passenger aircraft, including the Tu-20 bomber (1955), the Tu-104 (1955; world's first jet to provide regular civilian passenger service), and the Tu-144 (1969; world's first supersonic passenger plane).

Tup•per \'təp-ər\, Benjamin. 1738–1792. American soldier and pioneer, b. Stoughton, Mass. Served through American Revolution; defended Springfield, Mass., in time of Shays's Rebellion (1786); influential in organization of Ohio Company to settle the Northwest Territory; a pioneer in settling Marietta, Ohio.

Tupper, Sir Charles. 1821–1915. Canadian politician, b. Amherst, N.S. Premier of Nova Scotia (1864–67); strong advocate of Canadian federation; responsible for legislation making Nova Scotia a province of Canada. Held various ministries under Sir John A. Macdonald (1872–73, 1878–84, 1887–88); first minister of railways and canals (1879–84); chiefly responsible for completion of Canadian Pacific Railway; high commissioner in London (1884–87, 1888–96); created baronet (1888); prime minister of Canada (1896). His son ¶Sir Charles Hibbert (1855–1927), b. Amherst, N.S., was a lawyer and politician; member of House of Commons (1882–1904); minister of marine and fisheries (1888–94); minister of justice (1894–96).

Tupper, Martin Farquhar. 1810–1889. English writer. Gained worldwide success with *Proverbial Philosophy* (1838–76), a series of didactic and moralizing commonplaces in free verse; author also of ballads, novels, and a naïve autobiography.

Tu•ra \'tü-rä\, Cosmè. c.1430–1495. Italian painter. Founder of the Ferrarese school; court artist to Este dukes Borso and Ercole I; probably pupil of Francesco Squarcione in Padua. Master of allegory; noted for careful detail and brilliant color; works included *Primavera* (c.1460), *Annunciation* on organ doors of Ferrara cathedral (1469), fresco cycle in Palazzo Schifanoia, Ferrara (1469–71), *Pietà* (c.1472), *Lamentation* (c.1472).

Tū•rān-Shāh \tü-'rän-'shäh\. d. 1250. Sultan (1249–50) of Ayyūbid dynasty of Egypt. His murder by group of officers led by Baybars I led to establishment of the Mamlūk dynasty.

Tu•ra•ti \'tü-'rä-tē\, Filippo. 1857–1932. Italian Socialist leader. Founder and manager of Socialist periodicals *Critica Sociale* (1890 ff.) and *La Lotta di Classe* (1898 ff.); formed Socialist party (1892); as opponent of Fascism, forced into exile (1926).

Tur•ber•ville *or* **Tur•ber•vile** \'tər-bər-,vil\, George. 1540?–before 1597. English poet. In Russia as secretary to Thomas Randolph (1568–69); pioneer in use of blank verse; author of *Epitaphes, Epigrams, Songs and Sonets* (1567), translations of Ovid and Mantuanus (both 1567), and prose works *The Booke of Faulconrie or Hawking* (1575) and *The Noble Art of Venerie* (1575).

Turenne, Vicomte de. See Henri de LA TOUR D'AUVERGNE.

Tur•ge•nev \tür-'gyān-yəf\, Aleksandr Ivanovich. 1784?–1846. Russian historian. Published *Historica Russiae Monumenta* (1841–42). His brother ¶Nikolay Ivanovich (1789–1871), government official and economist; a co-founder of revolutionary Northern Society that staged Dekabrist uprising of 1825; took refuge in Paris; author of *Russia and the Russians* (1847).

Turgenev, Ivan Sergeyevich. 1818–1883. Russian writer. Formed (1843) life-long liaison, perhaps platonic, with French singer Pauline Viardot; quarrelled with Tolstoy and Dostoyevsky, generally estranged from Russian literary life; lived (from c.1862) in Germany, London, Paris. His works included long poems *Parasha* (1843) and *Pomeshchik* (1846); eleven plays, esp. *Mesyats v derevne* (1855; *A Month in the Country*); criticism, as essay "Gamlet i Don Kikhot" (1860); stories collected as *Zapiski okhotnika* (1852), *Povesti i razskazy* (1856), etc.; and novels *Rudin* (1856), *Dvoryanskoye gnezdo* (1859), *Nakanune* (1860), his masterpiece *Otsy i deti* (1862; *Fathers and Sons*), *Dym* (1867), and *Nov* (1877).

Tur•got \tūr-gō\, Anne-Robert-Jacques. Baron de l'Aulne \də-'lōn\. 1727–1781. French administrator and economist. Intendant of Limoges (1761–74); minister of marine (1774); controller general of finance (1774–76); removed because of opposition to his Six Edicts. Member of the Physiocrats. As intendant, abolished the corvée, constructed roads and bridges, reformed interest rates, and distributed the burden of taxation more justly. As finance minister, introduced a rigid economy, abolished certain feudal privileges, and attempted to restore free trade in grain between the provinces. Best known works were *Lettres sur la tolérance* (1754) and *Réflexions sur la formation et la distribution des richesses* (1766).

Tu•ri•na \tü-'rē-nä\, Joaquín. 1882–1949. Spanish composer. Pupil in Paris of Moszkowski and d'Indy; on advice of Albéniz adopted material from Spanish folk music; music critic for Madrid paper *El debate.* Compositions included symphonic poem *La procesión del rocío* (1912), operas *Margot* (1914) and *Jardín de oriente* (1923), *Sinfonía sevillana* (1920), *Danzas fantásticas* for orchestra (1920), albums of piano miniatures as *Rincones sevillanos* (1911) and *La leyenda de la Giralda* (1927), *Canto a Sevilla* for voice and orchestra (1927), songs, and chamber music as *La oración del torero* (1925).

Tur•ing \'tùr-iŋ\, Alan Mathison. 1912–1954. English mathematician and logician. On staff of National Physical Laboratory (1945–48); assistant director of Computing Laboratory at U. of Manchester (from 1948). Pioneered in computer theory; published (1937) paper "On Computable Numbers, with an Application to the Entscheidungs Problem," giving theoretical description of a universal computer (Turing machine); contributed to construction of early computers and to development of early programming techniques. Published theoretical study of morphogenesis (1952).

Tur•mair \'tùr-,mīr\, Johannes. *Known as* Aven•ti•nus \,ā-vən-'tī-nəs, ,av-ən-\. 1477–1534. German Humanist and historian. Referred to as the "Bavarian Herodotus." Tutor to brothers of Duke William IV of Bavaria (1509–17); state historiographer (1517). Published Latin grammar, history of Bavarian dukes, first map of Bavaria (1523), and esp. *Annales Boiorum* (1517–21), important chronicle.

Turn•bull \'tərn-,bùl\, Herbert Westren. 1885–1961. English mathematician. Professor at United College, St. Andrews (1921–50); made contributions to study of algebraic invariants and concomitants of quadratics. Works included *Theory of Equations* (1957), *The Theory of Determinants, Matrices, and Invariants* (1960), *An Introduction to the Theory of Canonical Matrices* (1961), etc.

Turner, Charles Tennyson. See under Alfred TENNYSON.

Tur•ner \'tər-nər\, Charles Yardley. 1850–1918. American painter, b. Baltimore, Md. Best known for his figure paintings as *The Bridal Procession* (1886), and murals.

Turner, Francis. 1638?–1700. English prelate. Bishop of Rochester (1683), of Ely (1684); one of the Seven Bishops (see William SANCROFT) who petitioned against James II's Declaration of Indulgence (1688) but were acquitted of seditious libel; refused to take oath of allegiance to William and Mary; deprived of his see (1690).

Turner, Frederick Jackson. 1861–1932. American historian, b. Portage, Wis. Professor at U. of Wisconsin (1892–1910) and Harvard (1910–24); research associate, Huntington Library, San Marino, Calif. (1924–32); influenced treatment of American history by emphasis on significance of the frontier in

American national development. Author of *Rise of the New West* (1906), *The Frontier in American History* (1920), *The Significance of Sections in American History* (1932, Pulitzer prize).

Turner, Herbert Hall. 1861–1930. English astronomer. Chief assistant, Royal Observatory, Greenwich (1884–93); professor and observatory director, Oxford (1893–1930); pioneered many procedures used to determine stellar positions from astronomical photographs. Author of *Modern Astronomy* (1901), *Astronomical Discovery* (1904), *The Great Star Map* (1912), and *A Voyage in Space* (1915).

Turner, Joseph Mallord William. 1775–1851. English painter. Perhaps greatest landscapist of 19th century. Traveled over Britain and (from 1802) Europe, making many landscape drawings; professor at Royal Academy (1807–38). In period of his first style (1800–20) introduced historical and mythological subjects and imitated van de Velde, Claude Lorrain, and Poussin; etched plates for his *Liber Studiorum* (1807–19); painted *Calais Pier* (1803), *The Shipwreck* (1805), *Sun Rising Through Vapour* (1807), *Snowstorm: Hannibal and His Army Crossing the Alps* (1812), *Frosty Morning* (1813), *Dido Building Carthage* (1815), *Crossing the Brook* (1815), *England: Richmond Hill* (1819). Began period of his second style (1820–35) with visit to Italy; ceased to imitate, idealized scenery, showed heightened scale of color; painted the *Bay of Baiae* (1823), *Harbours of England* (1824), *Dido Directing the Equipment of the Fleet* (1828), *Ulysses Deriding Polyphemus* (1829), *Childe Harold's Pilgrimage* (1832), and a collection of watercolors on Venetian subjects. In his third period (1835–45), sought to convey his impressions of nature, gained more poetic and dreamlike effects and even more brilliant color and light, as in *Burning of the Houses of Parliament* (1835), *The Parting of Hero and Leander* (1837), *The Fighting Téméraire* (1839), *The Slave Ship* (1840), *Peace: Burial at Sea* (1842), *The Sun of Venice Going to Sea* (1843), and *Rain, Steam, and Speed–the Great Western Railway* (1844). His reputation increased by praise in Ruskin's *Modern Painters* (1843); exhibited for last time (1850). Also produced engravings and thousands of watercolor sketches and drawings.

Turner, Nat. 1800–1831. American slave leader, b. Southampton Co., Va. Became religious fanatic; sought to convince his fellow slaves of his divine inspiration and leadership; led (Aug. 1831) uprising of some 75 slaves; murdered his master's entire family and about 50 other whites in the vicinity; captured, tried, convicted, and hanged.

Turner, Ralph Edmund. 1893–1964. American historian, b. Anthon, Ia. Professor, Yale (1944–61); a planner of UNESCO (1944); chairman of UNESCO editorial board preparing six-volume *Cultural History of Mankind* (Vol. 1, 1963).

Turner, William. 1510–1568. English clergyman, physician, and botanist. Published botanical essay *Libellus de re herbaria* (1538); became intimate of Konrad Gesner in Zürich, collected plants in Rhine country, and wrote his *Newe Herball,* first essay on scientific botany in England (pub. 1551). Dean of Wells (1550–53); restored (1560) after living abroad through reign of Mary.

Tur·pin \tu̅e̅r-pa^{n}, *Angl* 'tər-pən\ *or* **Til·pin** \tēl-pa^{n}, *Angl* 'til-pən\. d. 794. French ecclesiastic. Monk at Saint-Denis (748 or 749); archbishop of Reims (753). Identified with Turpin, one of the 12 peers in Charlemagne's entourage.

Tur·pin \'tər-pən\, Richard, *known as* Dick. 1706–1739. English robber. Deer and cattle thief; smuggler; convicted of horse stealing; hanged. Subject of legend and fiction.

Turstin. See THURSTAN.

Tush·rat·ta \tu̇sh-'rat-ə\. 14th century B.C. Last independent king of the Mitanni. Repelled Hittite invasion; during reign of Amenhotep III maintained friendly relations with Egypt.

Ṭū·sī \'tü-sē\, Naṣīr ad-Dīn aṭ-. 1201–1274. Persian philosopher, scientist, and mathematician. In service of Ismāʻīlī rulers (by 1232); scientific adviser to Hülegü Khan (1258–74). Author of many books in Arabic and Persian, as mathematical treatises, table of planetary movements *Zīj-i Ilkhani, Tajrīd al-'aqā'id* on Shīʻite dogmatics, *Akhlāq Naṣīrī* on ethics, and Ismāʻīlī dissertations as the *Tusavvurat.*

Tusitala. See Robert Louis STEVENSON.

Tus·saud \tu̅e̅-sō; *Angl* 'tü-(,)sō, tə-'sȯd, tə-'sōd\, Marie, *nee* Gros·holtz \'grōs-,hȯlts\. *Known as* Madame Tussaud. 1760–1850. Swiss modeler in wax. Founder of Madame Tussaud's Exhibition in London. Art tutor at Versailles to sister of Louis XVI (1780–94); modeled heads of leaders and victims of French Revolution; m. (1794) engineer François Tussaud; moved to London and transferred her collection of figures (1802); finally settled it in Baker Street (1833) and connected with it a Chamber of Horrors, containing relics of criminals and instruments of torture.

Tus·ser \'təs-ər\, Thomas. 1524–1580. English versifier on agriculture. Settled as farmer at Cattiwade in Suffolk. Author of *Hundredth Good Pointes of Husbandrie* (1557) in lively verse, furnishing instruction in farming and wise maxims giving rise to many proverbs.

Tut·ankh·a·men \,tü-,taŋ-'käm-ən, -,täŋ-\. *Orig.* Tut·ankh·a·ten \,tü-,täŋ-'kät-ᵊn\. c.1370–1352 B.C. King (1361–52 B.C.) of the 18th dynasty of Egypt. Son of Amenhotep III; probably brother of Smenkhkare; son-in-law of Akhenaton. During much of reign controlled by advisers Ay and Horemheb; returned to religion of Amon; resided at Memphis; restored his father's Theban palace; sent army to aid the Mitanni (1352). His tomb discovered (1922) in the Valley of the Kings by Howard Carter.

Tut·wi·ler \'tət-,wī-lər\, Julia Strudwick. 1841–1916. American educator, b. Tuscaloosa, Ala. President, Livingston Normal College (1890–1910); instrumental in securing state grant for founding Alabama Girls Industrial School (opened 1896); gained admission (1896) of women to U. of Alabama; also interested herself in prison reform in Alabama; her poem "Alabama" (1873) was adopted as the state song.

Tuve \'tüv\, Merle Antony. 1901–1982. American physicist, b. Canton, S.D. On staff of Carnegie Institution of Washington, D.C. (1926–66), director of department of terrestrial magnetism (1946–66); confirmed existence of neutron (1933); studied short-pulse ratio propagation and confirmed existence of ionosphere; during World War II developed radar and proximity fuse for navy; best known for studies of seismic wave propagation and their use in mapping Earth's crust.

Tu·wim \'tü-vēm\, Julian. 1894–1953. Polish poet. Leader of poetic group Skamander; created a poetic diction using colloquial language. Works included *Czychanie na Boga* (1918), *Tańczący Sokrates* (1920), *Słowa we Krwi* (1926), *Kwiaty polskie* (1949), and children's songs.

Tuyll, Isabella van. See Isabelle de CHARRIÈRE.

Tvrt·ko I \'tvərt-kȯ\. *Surnamed* Ko·tro·ma·nić \'kȯ-trȯ-mȧn-ēt^{y}\. c.1338–1391. King of the Serbs and Bosnia (1377–91). *Ban* (provincial lord) of Bosnia (from 1353); at first (1363) waged war against Louis I of Hungary but later reconciled; halted Ottoman Turkish invasion at Bileća (1388); extended (1390) his power into Croatia and Dalmatian islands in Adriatic Sea.

Twacht·man \'twäk(t)-mən\, John Henry. 1853–1902. American painter, b. Cincinnati. One of first American Impressionists. Studied in Munich (1875–77) and Paris (1883); taught at Art Students' League, New York (1889–1902); a member of group known as The Ten. Known for scenes of nature veiled in cool, shimmering light as *Venetian Landscape* (1878), *The White Bridge, February, Snowbound, Hemlock Pool* (1902), etc.

Twain, Mark. See Samuel L. CLEMENS; Isaiah SELLERS.

Tweed \'twēd\, William Marcy. *Known as* Boss Tweed. 1823–1878. American politician, b. New York City. New York City Democratic alderman (1852–56); member of U.S. House of Representatives (1853–55). New York City commissioner of schools (1856–57) and of public works (1870); New York State senator (1867–71). Gained absolute power of Tammany Hall (1868) and controlled nominations and patronage; became head of a group of New York City politicians known as the Tweed Ring, which gained control of New York City finances and swindled the treasury of between 30 and 200 million dollars; exposed (1870) by *Harper's Weekly* (with powerful cartoons by Thomas Nast), *The New York Times,* and Samuel J. Tilden; convicted (1873) and imprisoned; on release (1875) arrested in civil action but escaped and fled to Spain; extradited (1876) and died in a New York jail.

Tweedsmuir, Baron. See John BUCHAN.

Twen·ho·fel \twen-'hō-fəl\, William Henry. 1875–1957. American geologist, b. Covington, Ky. Taught at Univs. of Kansas (1910–16) and Wisconsin (1916–45); contributed to stratigraphy, sedimentation, paleontology. Author of *Treatise on Sedimentation* (1926), *Invertebrate Paleontology* (with R. R. Schrock, 1935), *Principles of Sedimentation* (1939), *Methods of Study of Sediments* (1941), etc.

Twich·ell \'twich-əl\, Joseph Hopkins. 1838–1918. American Congregational clergyman, b. Southington, Conn. Pastorate, Hartford, Conn. (1865–1918). Close friend of Samuel L. Clemens, Charles Dudley Warner, Harriet Beecher Stowe. Figures as Harris in Twain's *A Tramp Abroad.*

Twitcher, Jemmy. See John MONTAGU, 4th Earl of Sandwich.

Twor·kov \'twȯr-,kȯf, -,kȯv\, Jack. 1900–1982. American painter, b. Biała, Poland. To U.S. (1913, naturalized 1928); worked on W.P.A. Federal Art Project (1935–41), where he met and was influenced by Willem de Kooning; taught at various colleges, esp. Queens Coll. (1948–55) and Pratt Inst. (1955–60); chairman, art department of Yale School of Art and Architecture (1963–69). One of leading representatives of New York School of Abstract Expressionism; his paintings characterized by gestural brushwork, shimmering fields of color, controlled rhythms; works included *Watergame* (1955), *Queen* (1957), *Transverse* (1957–58), *Height* (1958–59), *Homage to Stefan Wolpe* (1960), *Variables* (1963), *Crossfield* series (begun 1968).

Twort \'twȯ(ə)rt\, Frederick William. 1877–1950. English bacteriologist. Superintendent of Brown Animal Sanatory Inst., London (1907–44). First to describe bacteriophage (1915).

Twys·den \'twīz-dən\, Sir Roger. 1597–1672. English political writer. M.P. (1625–26); county justice of the peace (1636); imprisoned for anti-parliamentary activities (1642, 1643–47); again justice of the peace after the Restoration (1660). Author of *The Laws of Henry I* (1645), *Historiae Anglicanae Scriptores X* (1652), *An Historical Vindication of the Church of England* (1657), *Certain Considerations upon the Government of England* on the historical roots of English constitutional law (completed 1655, pub. 1849), and *An Historical Narrative of the two Houses of Parliament* (pub. 1858–61).

Tyard \'tyår\, Pontus de. c.1522–1605. French poet. At first associated with Maurice Scève and other Lyonese poets; later a member of the Pléiade; translated León Hebreo's *Dialoghi di amore;* bishop of Chalon-sur-Saône (1578–94). Published lyrical *Erreurs amoureuses* (1549) and expounded on poetic diction in prose *Discours philosophiques* (1587); also a popularizer of Renaissance learning for the elite.

Tybald, Simon. See SIMON of Sudbury.

Tye \'tī\, Christopher. c.1500–c.1573. English composer. Choir master at Ely cathedral (1543–61); music tutor to Prince Edward (1544–50); ordained (1560); rector of Doddington (from 1561). Translated first half of Acts of Apostles into English verse set to music (1553); extant works include two Latin masses, 14 English anthems, Psalm settings, and music for instrumental ensembles.

Ty·ler \'tī-lər\, Bennet. 1783–1858. American theologian, b. Middlebury, Conn. Ordained in Congregational ministry (1808); president, Dartmouth (1822–28); leader (from 1828) of conservatively orthodox clergymen (Tylerites) opposed to doctrine of Nathaniel W. Taylor (*q.v.*). A founder, professor of Christian theology, and president, Theological Institute of Connecticut, now the Hartford Theological Seminary (1834–57).

Tyler, John. 1747–1813. American jurist, b. York Co., Va. Judge, Virginia general court (1789–1808), one of first judges to maintain the overruling power of the judiciary; governor of Virginia (1808–11).

Tyler, John. 1790–1862. Tenth president of the United States, b. Charles City Co., Va. Son of John Tyler (1747–1813). Adm. to bar and began practice in Charles City Co. (1809); member of U.S. House of Representatives (1817–21); governor of Virginia (1825–27); U.S. senator (1827–36). Vice president of the United States (1841), succeeding to the presidency on death of President William Henry Harrison (Apr. 4, 1841); administration (1841–45) marked by party conflict (Tyler acting with the Democratic party although elected as a Whig), establishment of Naval Observatory and U.S. Weather Bureau, end of Second Seminole War in Florida, suppression of Door Rebellion (1842), negotiation of Webster-Ashburton Treaty, and annexation of Texas to the Union. Presided over Washington Peace Conference (1861); remained loyal to Virginia when it seceded.

Tyler, Lyon Gardiner. 1853–1935. American educator, b. Charles City Co., Va. Son of President John Tyler; president, Coll. of William and Mary (1888–1919). Author of *Cradle of the Republic* (1900), *England in America* (1904), *Williamsburg, the Old Colonial Capital* (1907), etc.; editor, *Narratives of Early Virginia, 1606–1625* (1907), *Biographical Dictionary of Virginia* (1915).

Tyler, Moses Coit. 1835–1900. American educator, b. Griswold, Conn. Professor of English literature, U. of Michigan (1867–73, 1874–81); professor of American history, Cornell (1881–1900); a founder of American Historical Association (1884). Author of *A History of American Literature During the Colonial Time, 1607–1765* (1878), *Three Men of Letters* (1895), *The Literary History of the American Revolution 1763–1783* (1897), etc.

Tyler, Royall. 1757–1826. American jurist and author, b. Boston. Major on Gen. Benjamin Lincoln's staff in suppression of Shays's Rebellion (1786). Chief justice, Vermont supreme court (1807–13); professor of jurisprudence, U. of Vermont (1811–14). Author of *The Contrast,* first comedy written by a native American and professionally produced (in New York, Apr. 16, 1787); also wrote other plays and a novel, *The Algerine Captive* (1797).

Tyler, Wat, *in full* Walter. d. 1381. English leader of Peasants' Revolt. Perhaps a tiler of Essex; chosen leader of mob assembled (June, 1381) in protest against Statute of Laborers and imposition of poll tax, as well as economic distress, and led movement on London; presented to Richard II at Smithfield demands for abolition of serfdom, removal of restrictions upon freedom of labor and trade, and amnesty for rebels; on presenting fresh demands the following day (June 15, 1381) killed by Lord Mayor Walworth.

Ty·lor \'tī-lər\, Sir Edward Burnett. 1832–1917. English anthropologist. Often regarded as the founder of cultural anthropology. Visited Mexico (1856), recorded visit in *Anahuac; or, Mexico and the Mexicans Ancient and Modern* (1861); made reputation with *Researches into the Early History of Mankind and the Development of Civilization* (1865); first professor of anthropology, Oxford (1896–1909); chief work, *Primitive Culture* (1871).

Ty·nan \'tī-nən\, Katharine. *Later* Katharine Hink·son \'hiŋk-sən\. 1861–1931. Irish poet and novelist. m. H. A. Hinkson (1893; d. 1919). A leader of Irish literary renaissance. Author of *Collected Poems* (1930), autobiographical works as *Twenty-five Years* (1913) and *The Wandering Years* (1922), and over 100 romantic novels including *The House in the Forest* (1928).

Tynan, Kenneth Peacock. 1927–1980. English drama critic. Illegitimate son of Sir Peter Peacock and Letitia Tynan. Drama critic for London *Observer* (1954–58, 1960–63) and *New Yorker* magazine (1958–60); literary manager, British National Theatre (1963–73); championed modern dramatists and "new realism" on the stage. Author of *Persona Grata* (1953), *Curtains* (1961), *Show People* (1980), etc.

Tyn·dale *or* **Tin·dal** *or* **Tin·dale** \'tin-dᵊl\, William. c.1494–1536. English translator of New Testament and Pentateuch. Began printing translation of New Testament at Cologne (1525); completed printing at Worms (1526); escaped seizure ordered by Wolsey; published his version of the Pentateuch at Marburg (1530); issued version of Jonah with prologue (1531); issued revised version of New Testament (1534); his version of the Bible the chief basis, with admixture of Wycliffe version, of the Authorized Version of 1611. Swung over to Zwinglian position on Eucharist; published tracts advocating principles of English Reformation, including *The Parable of the Wicked Mammon* (1528) and *The Obedience of a Christian Man* (1528); at Antwerp conducted controversy with Sir Thomas More (1531); arrested at Antwerp and condemned for heresy; strangled and burned at stake.

Tyn·dall \'tin-dᵊl\, John. 1820–1893. Irish physicist and popularizer of science. Professor (1853–87), superintendent (1867–87), Royal Institution; colleague of Faraday; scientific adviser to Trinity House and Board of Trade (1866–84); with T.H. Huxley studied glaciers in Switzerland. Investigated transmission, radiation, and absorption of heat by vapors and gases; studied diffusion of light by large molecules and dust, known as Tyndall effect; studied the decomposition of vapors by light; showed that the blue of the sky is due to fine particles in the atmosphere; by experiments with pure air, verified fallacy of doctrine of spontaneous generation (1881); discovered that the transmission of sound is affected by variations in density of the atmosphere. Published *Heat Considered as a Mode of Motion* (1863), *On Sound* (1867), *Contributions to Molecular Physics in the Domain of Radiant Heat* (1872), *Six Lectures on Light* (1873), etc.

Typhoid Mary. See Mary MALLON.

Tyrconnel, Earl of. See (1) Rory O'DONNELL; (2) Richard TALBOT (1630–1691).

Tyrone, Earls of. See under O'NEILL family.

Tyr·rell \'tir-əl\, George. 1861–1909. Irish theologian. Joined Roman Catholic church (1879); entered Jesuit order (1880); ordained priest (1891). A leading advocate of Modernism; associated (from 1907) with Friedrich von Hügel. His *Letter to a Professor of Anthropology* (pub. without his knowledge, 1906) caused his dismissal from Society of Jesus; refused the sacraments for his reply to Pius X's encyclical *Pascendi* against Modernism (1907). Author of *The Faith of the Millions* (1901), *The Church and the Future* (1903), *Through Scylla and Charybdis* (1907), *Medievalism* (1908), *Christianity at the Cross-Roads* (1909), and *Autobiography* (1912).

Tyrrell, Sir James. d. 1502. English soldier and royal official. Fought on Yorkist side at Tewkesbury (1471); became servant of Richard of Gloucester; made (1482) knight banneret for service in Richard's wars in Scotland; appointed governor of Guisnes Castle of Calais by Henry VII (1486); executed for harboring a traitor. There is little evidence for Sir Thomas More's claim that Tyrrell was the instrument of Richard III in murder of Edward V and his brother Richard, Duke of York (1483).

Tyr·tae·us \tər-'tē-əs\. fl. c.650 B.C. Greek elegiac poet of Sparta. According to tradition, his martial verses inspired Spartans to victory over Messenians; only fragments of his works are extant.

Tyr·whitt \'tir-ət\, Thomas. 1730–1786. English scholar. Edited classical authors, of which Aristotle's *Poetics* was his chief work (pub. 1794). Author of *Observations upon Shakespeare* (1766); edited and exposed *Rowley Poems* as forgeries by Chatterton (1777–78); editor of Chaucer's *Canterbury Tales* (1775–78), contributing to elucidation of Chaucer's versification and fixing of the Chaucer canon.

Tyrwhitt-Wil·son \-'wil-sən\, Sir Gerald Hugh. 14th Baron Ber·ners \'bər-nərz\. 1883–1950. English composer and painter. Composer of *Trois petites marches funèbres* for piano (1914), *Fantaisie espagnole* for orchestra (1918), *Valses bourgeoises* for piano duet (1919), a comic operatic version of Mérimée's *Le Carrosse du Saint Sacrement* (1924), and ballets *Triumph of Neptune* (1926), *Luna Park* (1930), *A Wedding Bouquet* (text by Gertrude Stein, 1937), and *Cupid and Psyche* (1939). Author of *First Childhood* (1934), *The Camel* (1936), *Far from the Madding War* (1941), *The Romance of a Nose* (1941), etc.

Ty·son \'tīs-ᵊn\, Edward. 1650–1708. English physician. Practiced in London (from 1677). Pioneered in comparative anatomy; compared human and simian similarities and differences in *Orang-Outang* (1699).

Tyt·ler \'tīt-lər\, James. c.1747–1804. Scottish writer. Known as debt-ridden eccentric in Edinburgh; as editor, wrote large portions of second and third editions of *Encyclopaedia Britannica*. Constructed balloon in which he was first person in Great Britain to navigate the air (1784), hence known as "Balloon Tytler." Expressed advanced views on reform in *The Historical Register* (1792); fled to Salem, Mass., to avoid arrest, and there published newspaper.

Tytler, Patrick Fraser. 1791–1849. Scottish historian. Author of *Life of the Admirable Crichton* (1819), *Lives of Scottish Worthies* (1831–33), *History of Scotland* (1828–43), *England under Reigns of Edward VI and Mary* (1839).

Tyut·chev \'tyüt-chəf\, Fyodor Ivanovich. 1803–1873. Russian poet. Served as diplomat in Munich and Turin for 22 years; author of love lyrics and patriotic verse; published volume (1854) including poems translated later into English as "Nature," "Spring," "An Autumn Evening," "The Deserted Villa," "The Last Love."

Tza·ra \'tsä-rä\, Tristan. *Orig. name variously given as* Samuel Ro·sen·feld \'rō-zən-ˌfelt\, Sami Ro·sen·stock \-ˌstȯk\, *and* S. Ro·sen·stein \-ˌstīn\. 1896–1963. French poet and essayist, b. Romania. Principal founder in Zürich of the Dada movement (1916); wrote first Dada texts *La Première Aventure céleste de Monsieur Antipyrine* (1916) and *Vingtcinq poèmes* (1918) and its manifestos *Sept Manifestes Dada* (1924); settled in Paris (1919); associated with Surrealist group (1929–35); joined Communist party (1936); in later years abandoned experimental writing for a more engaged literature. Also author of verse *L'Homme approximatif* (1931), *Midis gagnés* (1939), *Parler seul* (1950), *La Face intérieure* (1953), *La Rose et le chien* (1958), etc.

Tze·tzes \'tset-ˌsēz\, John. c.1110–c.1180. Byzantine poet and scholar. Author of *Book of Histories* (usually known as *Chiliades*), *Allegoriai* on the *Iliad* and *Odyssey*, treatises on poetry and grammar, and commentaries on certain Greek authors.

Tzu-ang. See CHAO MENG-FU.

Tz'u-hsi \'tsü-'shē\. *Also known by titles* Hsiao-ch'in \shē-'au̇-'chin\ *and* Hsien Huang-hou \shē-'ən-'hwäŋ-'hō\. *Sometimes referred to in West as* the Empress Dowager *or* the Old Buddha. 1835–1908. Chinese empress dowager. Concubine of Emperor I-chu and mother of Tsai-ch'un. Coregent with Prince Kung and former senior consort Tz'u-an for Tsai-ch'un (1862–73); on Tsai-ch'un's death (1875) assumed regency for her nephew and adopted son Tsai-t'ien; virtual dictator of China; retired (1889) but when the emperor attempted reforms (1898), again resumed regency and control of country; reactionary in her policies; encouraged the Boxers, but on final success of treaty powers in capturing Tientsin and Peking, fled from the court to Sian (1900); remained in exile (1900–02); always hostile to foreign influence.

Tzu Ssu \'dzü-'sü\. 483–402 B.C. Chinese philosopher. Grandson of Confucius; author of the *Chung yung* (Doctrine of the Mean), now part of the *Li Chi* and one of the *Ssu shu* (Four Books).

U

Ubal·di·ni \ˌü-bäl-ˈdē-nē\, Petruccio. 1524?–?1600. Florentine illuminator and scholar. To England (1545); fought in Scottish wars (1549); wrote *Vita di Carlo Magno Imperatore* (first Italian book printed in England, 1581) and historical and biographical narratives.

ʽUbayd Al·lāh \üb-ˈīd-al-ˈlä\. *Reign title* al-Mah·dī \ül-mä-ˈdē\. d. 934 A.D. First caliph (909–34) of Fāṭimid dynasty of North Africa. Imām of Shīʽites of North Africa; installed (909) on throne by Abū ʽAbd Allāh; established his capital at Mahdīyah (920).

Uber·ti \ü-ˈber-tē\, Farinata degli. d. 1264. Florentine nobleman. Became leader of Florentine Ghibellines (1239); exiled (1250); allied himself with Manfred (1258); defeated Guelfs at Montaperti and captured Florence (1260); according to Dante (*Inferno,* canto X), dissuaded his Ghibelline cohorts from razing Florence. A later member of his family ¶Bonifazio *or* Fazio degli Uberti (c.1305–c.1367), poet and Ghibelline; wrote love poetry, political canzoni, and a geographical, allegorical epic *Dittamondo* (unfinished) in imitation of Dante.

Ubi·co Cas·ta·ñe·da \ü-ˈb̲ē-kō-käs-tän-ˈyä-t̲h̲ä\, Jorge. *Nicknamed* Ta·ta \ˈtä-tä\. 1878–1946. Guatemalan soldier and politician. Commissioned in army (1897); rose to brigadier general; member of National Assembly; minister of war (1922–26). President of Guatemala (1931–44); built roads and public works, ended peonage of Indians, eliminated wholesale corruption; oppressive measures led to resignation.

Uc·cel·lo \üt-ˈchel-lō\, Paolo. *Orig.* Paolo di Do·no \dē-ˈdō-nō\. 1397–1475. Florentine painter. Apprenticed to Lorenzo Ghiberti; worked in Venice as mosaicist (1425–31). Attempted to reconcile late Gothic and early Renaissance styles; known esp. for experimental studies in foreshortening and linear perspective; known also as a designer of stained-glass windows. His works included frescoes of Sir John Hawkwood in Florence cathedral (1436) and of *The Flood* in Sta. Maria Novella, Florence (1447–48), *The Battle of San Romano* (mid 1450s), *St. George and the Dragon* (c.1460), and *A Hunt in a Forest* (after 1460).

Ucha·ti·us \ü-ˈk̲ät-sē-üs\, Franz von. Freiherr. 1811–1881. Austrian general, inventor, and authority on artillery. Introduced an improved process of manufacturing steel (1856) and invented ballistic apparatus, a steel bronze (called Uchatius bronze) for cannon, ring grenades (1875), etc.

Uchi·mu·ra \üch-ē-mür-ä\ Kanzō. 1861–1930. Japanese theologian. Founded independent Japanese Christian church (1882); caused storm of controversy by questioning divinity of the emperor (1891); his religious freethinking influenced many writers and intellectuals. Author of religious works as *Kirisuto-shinto-no nagusame* (1893) and *Yo-wa ikanishite Kirisuto-shinto to narishi ya* (1895).

Udall \ˈyüd-əl; ˈyü-ˌdȯl, -ˌdal\ *or* **Uve·dale** \ˈyüv-ˌdāl\, John. 1560?–1592. English Puritan preacher. Suspected of complicity in *Martin Marprelate* tracts; imprisoned (1590) and sentended to death (1591) for pamphlets attacking the episcopacy; died soon after being pardoned.

Udall, Nicholas. 1505–1556. English schoolmaster, Latin scholar, and playwright. Headmaster of Eton (1534); dismissed for misconduct (1541). Translated Erasmus's *Apophthegms* (1542), Peter Martyr's works on the Eucharist, and the Great Bible (1551); had his play *Ralph Roister Doister* produced (probably 1553), the earliest extant English comedy, modeled on Plautus's *Miles Gloriosus.* Playwriter to Queen Mary (1554); headmaster, Westminster (1554–56).

Uda Ten·nō \üd-ä-ten-nō\. 867–931. Japanese emperor (887–897). Son of Emperor Kōkō; at first (887–891), power wielded by civil dictator Fujiwara Mototsune; abdicated (897) in favor of son Daigo but retained power; obtained appointment (899) of Sugawara Michizane as minister of the right in unsuccessful attempt to curtail influence of Fujiwara family; with minister of the left Fujiwara Tokihira introduced tax reforms.

Uda·ya·nā·cār·ya \ˌüd-ə-yə-nä-ˈkär-yə\. 10th century A.D. Hindu logician. Attempted to reconcile the Vaiśeṣika and Old Nyāya systems of logic; wrote *Kusumāñjali* and *Bauddhadhikkāra.*

Udet \ˈü-ˌdet\, Ernst. 1896–1941. German aviator and army officer. Served in air force in World War I (1914–18); credited with destroying 62 enemy planes; chief of technical bureau of German air force, with rank of lieutenant general (1938).

Udr·žal \ˈüd-ər-zhäl\, František. 1866–1938. Czech politician. Agrarian leader; premier of Czechoslovakia (1929–32).

Uech·tritz \ˈœk̲-trits\, Friedrich von. 1800–1875. German writer. Author of tragedies, a dramatic poem, and religious novels as *Albrecht Holm* (1851–53) and *Der Bruder der Braut* (1860).

Ue·da \ü-ed-ä\ Senjiro. *Pseudonym* Ueda Akinari. 1734–1809. Japanese writer. Known for his tales of the supernatural collected in *Ugetsu monogatari* (1776) and *Harusame monogatari* (1808).

Ue·land \ˈwā-lənd\, Ole Gabriel Gabrielson. 1799–1870. Norwegian politician. Schoolteacher; for 30 years chief spokesman of the Peasant party in the Storting (from 1833); championed local self-government, mass public education, improved living and working conditions for laboring class; succeeded (mid-1860s) as leader of peasantry by Sören Jaabaek.

Ue·su·gi \ü-es-üg-ē\. Japanese warrior clan important in Japanese history from the 15th century; its leaders were the *daimyos* of Yonezawa in northern Honshu during the Tokugawa shogunate (1603–1867); its members included: ¶Uesugi Norimasa. 1523–1579. Appointed governor general of Kantō region of Honshu (1530); led sybaritic life; lost many battles and much power and land to the Hōjō clan; after defeat (1552) by the Takeda clan, took refuge with Uesugi Kenshin and adopted him as his son.

¶Uesugi Kenshin. *Also known as* Uesugi Terutora. *Orig.* Na·gao \nä-gä-ō\ Torachiyo. 1530–1578. Son of the head of Echigo province; after father's death, restored order to area and gained control of neighboring provinces on Kantō Plain of central Honshu; gave shelter to, and adopted as son by, Uesugi Norimasa (1552), also taking Uesugi as surname; waged series of battles against Hōjō and Takeda families with no permanent gain for any side; succeeded Norimasa as head of Uesugi family and as governor general of Kantō (1561); died before he could undertake expedition against Oda Nobunaga to restore the Ashikaga shogunate.

¶Uesugi Kagekatsu. 1555–1623. Succeeded his father-in-law Kenshin as head of clan; allied himself with Toyotomi Hideyoshi, who appointed him one of five regents for his son Hideyori; unsuccessfully challenged power of Tokugawa Ieyasu (1600), who nevertheless allowed him to retain part of his former domain.

Uf·ford \ˈəf-ərd\, Robert de. 1st Earl of Suf·folk \ˈsəf-ək\. 1298–1369. English soldier. Chief counselor of Edward III; served in English campaigns in France (from 1338), esp. distinguishing himself at Poitiers (1356). His son ¶William (1339?–1382), 2d earl, accompanied John of Gaunt through France (1373); served in France and Brittany (1377–78) and in Scotland (1380); Richard II's chief commissioner of array for Norfolk and Suffolk (1377); played part in Peasants' Revolt under Wat Tyler (1381), at first sought as their leader, later active in suppressing revolt; a leader in opposition to John of Gaunt (1381).

Uga·ki \üg-ä-kē\ Kazushige. 1869–1956. Japanese soldier and politician. Commissioned in army (1891); general (1924). Minister of the army (1924–27, 1929–31); governor general of Korea (1936); asked to be prime minister but unable to form cabinet due to army opposition (1937); minister of foreign affairs and colonization (1938); elected to House of Councilors (1953). In years before World War II, headed Control Faction of the Japanese army which stressed development of new weapons and opposed the rightist Imperial Way faction.

Ugar·te \ü-ˈgär-tā\, Manuel. 1874–1951. Argentine writer. Regarded as one of initiators of Modernism in Argentine literature; constant critic of U.S. activities in South America, creating phrase "Colossus of the North" in reference to U.S. Author of short stories collected in *Cuentos de la pampa* (1903) and *Cuentos argentinos* (1908), political works as *El destino de un continente* (1923), and literary history *Escritores iberamericanos de 1900* (1943).

Ugedei. See ÖGÖDEI.

Uggione, Marco da. See OGGIONO.

Ugo·li·ni \ˌü-gō-ˈlē-nē\, Vincenzo. c.1580–1638. Italian composer. Maestro di cappella at S. Luigi dei Francesi, Rome (1616–20, 1631–38) and at Cappella Giulia, St. Peter's (1620–26); composer of motets, Psalms, secular madrigals, etc.

Uh·de \ˈü-də\, Fritz von. 1848–1911. German painter. His paintings included *Family Concert, The Sermon on the Mount, The Wise Men from the East, The Ascension, The Last Supper, Going Home,* and impressionistic portraits.

Uh·land \ˈü-länt\, Johann Ludwig. 1787–1862. German poet, philologist, and politician. Practiced law; supported democratic movement in Württemberg; represented Tübingen (1819–27) and Stuttgart (1826–29) in the Ständeversammlung; professor at Tübingen (1829–33); member of national assembly in Frankfurt (1848). Member of Swabian school of poetry, inspired by Romanticism; a founder of modern medieval studies. His works included poems, ballads, and songs published in *Vaterländische Gedichte* (1815) and some 50 subsequent editions; plays *Ernst, Herzog von Schwaben* (1818) and *Ludwig der Bayer* (1819); essays and treatises as *Über das altfranzösische Epos* (1812), *Walther von der Vogelweide* (1822), and *Der Mythus von Thor* (1836), and the collection *Alte hoch- und niederdeutsche Volkslieder* (1844–45).

Uh·len·beck \ˈü-lən-ˌbek\, Christianus Cornelius. 1866–1951. Dutch philologist. Professor, Leiden (1899–1926). Chief works *Etymologisches Wörterbuch der gotischen Sprache* (1896), *Etymologisches Wörterbuch der altindischen Sprache* (1898–99).

Uh·len·huth \ˈü-lən-ˌhüt\, Paul. 1870–1957. German bacteriologist and hygienist. Professor, Strassburg (1911), Marburg (1921), Freiburg (1923). Discoveries included serums against hog cholera and (with Löffler) foot-and-mouth disease, the cause of Weil's disease, and the treatment of syphilis with arsenicals.

Uich'on. See DAIGAK GUKSO.

Ui·sang Dai·sa \wē-säŋ-dī-sä\. 625–702. Korean Buddhist monk. Became monk (645); studied the Garland Sutra in China under Chih-yen (662–671); on return to Korean state of Silla, propagated teaching of the Garland Sutra; wrote *An Explanatory Diagram on the Garland World System.*

Ujej·ski \ü-ˈyā-skē\, Kornel. 1823–1897. Polish poet. Among his works were *Maraton* (1847), *Skargi Jeremiego* (1847), and *Tłumaczenia Szopena* (1866). His hymn *Z dymem pożarów* is known among Poles as the national anthem of Poland in mourning.

Ukrainka, Lesya. See KOSACH-KVITKA.

Ulász·ló \ù-ˈläs-lō\. *Pol.* Wła·dy·sław \vlȧ-ˈdis-lȧf\. Name of two kings of Hungary:

Ulászló I. King (1440–44). See WLADYSLAW III of Poland.

Ulászló II. 1456–1516. King of Bohemia (1471–1516) and of Hungary (1490–1516). Son of Casimir IV of Poland; weak and vacillating ruler, dominated by his advisers; by Treaty of Olomouc (1478) lost Moravia, Silesia, and Lusatia to Matthias Corvinus; lost territories to the Habsburgs by Peace of Pressburg (1491) and Treaty of Vienna (1515).

Ul·bricht \ˈül-(ˌ)brikt\, Walter. 1893–1973. East German politician. Joined (1919) German Communist party and was elected (1923) to its central committee; became member of Reichstag (1928); during exile (1933–45) persecuted Trotskyites and other Communist deviationists for Stalin and the Comintern. Helped establish (1946) Socialist Unity party, the Communist party in East Germany; as first secretary of Socialist Unity party (1953–71) and chairman of Council of State (1960–73) exercised complete control in East Germany and developed it into a leading industrial power and the most rigidly orthodox nation in the Soviet bloc; erected the Berlin Wall (1961); implacable foe of West Germany.

Ulenspegel, Till. See EULENSPIEGEL.

Ul·fi·las \ˈəl-fə-ˌlas, -ləs\. *Gothic* Wul·fi·la \ˈwúl-fə-lə\. c.311–c.382. Cappadocian prelate. Consecrated bishop of the Gothic Christians (341); served as missionary bishop among Visigoths beyond Danube (341–348); preached the homoean formula; led his congregation to Moesia (c.348); attended Council of Constantinople (360). From a Greek original translated Bible into Gothic, devising for purpose an alphabet based on Greek and Latin; extant fragments of his Bible constitute (with a few other scattered remains) earliest known specimen of Teutonic languages.

Ul·la·thorne \ˈəl-ə-ˌthó(ə)rn\, William Bernard. 1806–1889. English prelate. Descendant of Thomas More; joined Benedictines (1823); ordained Roman Catholic priest (1831); vicar general in Australia (1832–42), serving convicts there; his *Horrors of Transportation Briefly Unfolded* (1836) and his testimony secured abolition (1857) of system of transporting British convicts to Australia; first bishop of Birmingham, England (1850–88); cofounded Dominican convent at Stone (1853); titular archbishop of Cabasa, Egypt (1888–89).

Ul·loa \ü(l)-ˈyō-ä\, Antonio de. 1716–1795. Spanish naval officer and scientist. With French scientific expedition to South America (1736–45) to measure an arc of the meridian; published *Relación histórica del viaje a la América meridional* (1748, with Jorge Juan); collaborated in secret report on conditions in Peru (c.1749; pub. under title *Noticias secretas de América,* 1826); governor of Louisiana (1766–68); lieutenant general of Spanish naval forces (1779); pioneer in many branches of science in Spain.

Ul·ma·nis \ˈúl-män-is\, Kārlis. 1877–? Latvian statesman. A leader in Latvian independence movement; exile in U.S. (1905–13), teaching at U. of Nebraska; first prime minister of Latvian Republic (1918–21); again prime minister (1925–26, 1931–32); prime minister, minister of foreign affairs, and virtual dictator (from 1934), and president (1936–40) until his country was annexed to Russia; arrested (1940) by Soviets and deported to Russia; his fate unknown.

Ul·pi·an \ˈəl-pē-ən\. *Full Latin name* Domitius Ul·pi·a·nus \ˌəl-pē-ˈā-nəs\. d. 228 A.D. Roman jurist. Subordinate to Papinian and later edited his works; master of petitions under Caracalla; praetorian prefect under Servus Alexander (222–228); murdered by some of his officers. Author of many legal commentaries as *Libri ad Sabinum* (51 vols. on civil law) and *Libri ad edictum* (81 vols. on praetorian edicts); his writings supplied one-third of Justinian's *Digest* (533).

Ul·rich \ˈúl-rik\ *or* **Ul·ric** \-rik\. Saint. c.890–973. German prelate. Of noble birth; bishop of Augsburg (924–973); supported Otto I the Great; by fortifying Augsburg helped it resist a Magyar siege until Otto's defeat of the Magyars (955); granted by Otto unprecedented right to coin money. First person known to have been canonized by a pope (993); patron saint of Augsburg.

Ulrich. 1487–1550. Duke of Württemberg. Succeeded to duchy (1498); assumed personal control (1503); won new territory (1504). Aroused rebellion of peasants because of oppressions (1514) and opposition of nobility because of murder of Hans von Hutten; expelled by Swabian League (1519). With aid of Philip of Hesse, recovered his dukedom (1534) but only as a fief of Austria. Introduced Reformation into Württemberg; joined Schmalkaldic League and fought against Charles V (1546); forced to accept Augsburg Interim; again threatened with deposition at time of death.

Ulrich von Lich·ten·stein \-fón-ˈlik-tən-ˌshtīn\. c.1200–1275. Styrian noble and poet. Author of *Frauendienst* (1255), an autobiographical novel in verse containing minnesongs and dancing songs, and *Frauenbuch* (1257), descriptive of the customs and morals of his time.

Ulrich von Tür·heim \-fón-ˈtyər-ˌhīm\. fl. 1236–1285. German poet and noble. Continued Gottfried von Strassburg's *Tristan und Isolde* (c.1236) and completed (after 1243) Wolfram von Eschenbach's *Willehalm.*

Ul·ri·ci \úl-ˈrēt-sē\, Hermann. 1806–1884. German philosopher. Opponent of Hegel; professor, Halle (from 1834); author of *Über Shakespeares dramatische Kunst* (1839), *Über Prinzip und Methode de hegelschen Philosophie* (1841), *Glauben und Wissen* (1858), etc.

Ul·ri·ka Ele·o·no·ra \əl-ˈrē-kȧ-ˌel-e-ō-ˈnō-rȧ\. 1688–1741. Queen of Sweden. m. (1715) Frederick of Hesse-Kassel; chosen queen of Sweden (1718) after death of her brother Charles XII; abdicated (1720) in favor of her husband who became king as Frederick I (*q.v.*).

Ulster, Earl of. See MORTIMER family.

Ulūgh Beg \ˈü-lüg-ˈbeg, -ˈbā\. 1394–1449. Tatar prince. Son of Shāh Rokh and grandson of Timur; ruler of Turkestan (from 1447); made Samarkand a center of Muslim culture; wrote poetry and history; founded an observatory at Samarkand; compiled astronomical tables.

Ulyanov, Vladimir Ilyich. See LENIN.

ʿUmar \ˈü-mär\. Name of two caliphs:

ʿUmar I. *In full* ʿUmar ibn al-Khaṭṭāb. c.586–644. Second Muslim caliph (634–644). Succeeded Abū Bakr; opposed Muḥammad and followers (before 617), then converted to Islām and aided Abū Bakr in conquests of the new religion; greatly extended Muslim empire, defeating Persians at Kadisiya (637) and at Nehavend (641); conquered Syria and Palestine (635–640); sent (639) his general ʿAmr ibn al-ʿĀṣ to invade Egypt; assassinated at Medina by a Persian slave. Organizer of Muslim power; inaugurated system of dating Muslim events from the Hegira.

ʿUmar II. *In full* ʿUmar ibn ʿAbd al-ʿAzīz. 682 or 683–720. Umayyad caliph (717–720). Governor of Hejaz province (706–712); made caliph by will of predecessor Sulariman; attempted to strengthen caliphate by emphasizing religion and a return to original principles of Islām and by instituting domestic reforms, as dismissing unpopular governors, reforming tax system, and granting the Mawali same fiscal rights as Arab Muslims.

ʿUmarī, al- \úl-ˌü-mär-ˈē\. *In full* Shihāb ad-Dīn Aḥmad ibn Faḍl Allāh al-ʿUmarī. 1301–1349. Syrian scholar. Head of chancery of Mamlūk Empire (1339–42); wrote *at-Taʿrīf bial-muṣṭalaḥ ash-sharīf* and *Masālik al-abṣār fī mamālik al-amṣār,* both on Mamlūk administrative practices and both standard sources for Mamlūk history.

ʻUmar ibn Abī Ra·bī·ʻah \ˈü-mär-ˌib-ə-nab-ˈē-rab-ˈē-ä\. *In full* ʻUmar ibn ʻAbd Allāh ibn Abī Rabīʻah al-Makhzūmī. 644–712 or 719. Arab poet. Member of merchant aristocracy of Mecca; regarded as greatest amatory poet of early Arabic literature.

Umay·yad \ùm-ˈī-yəd\ *or* **Omay·yad** \ō̇m-\. First great Muslim dynasty to rule the Empire of the Caliphate (661–750); its name derived from an ancestor, Umayyah or Omayyah, and its capital was Damascus. Umayyad rule was divided between two branches of the family: (1) the Sufyānid (661–684), descendants of Mecca merchant Abū Sufyan, whose rulers included Muʻāwiyah I and II and Yazīd I (*qq.v.*); (2) the Marwānid (684–750), descendants of Marwān I and including ʻAbd al-Malik, al-Walīd I, ʻUmar II, Hishām, and Marwān II (*qq.v.*). The Umayyads were overthrown by the ʻAbbāsids. ʻAbd ar-Raḥmān I (*q.v.*), however, escaped and established an emirate (756–929), later a caliphate (929–1031), at Córdoba; this dynasty had eleven members, reaching its zenith of power in reigns of ʻAbd ar-Raḥmān III and Ḥakam II (*qq.v.*); overthrown by the Berbers.

Um·ber·to I \üm-ˈber-tō\. 1844–1900. King of Italy (1878–1900) and duke of Savoy. Son of Victor Emmanuel II; took part in wars for unification of Italy (1866–70); attempted to reconcile various political and regional factions; brought Italy into Triple Alliance with Germany and Austria-Hungary (1882); tariff war with France led to economic difficulties (1888); his colonial policy in Africa terminated by defeat of Italian forces by Ethiopians at Adowa (1896); increasing social unrest led to his condoning of imposition of martial law (1898); assassinated at Monza. Succeeded by his son Victor Emmanuel III.

Umberto. Name of three counts of Savoy:

Umberto I. *Called* the Whitehanded. d. c.1048. Perhaps of Saxon or Burgundian origin; held extensive territories including Little and Great St. Bernard passes, northern approach of Simplon Pass; rewarded with further territories for services to Emperor Conrad II. Founder of house of Savoy.

Umberto II. d. 1103. Count (1080–1103). Son of Amadeus II.

Umberto III. *Called* the Saint. d. 1189. Count (1148–89). Son of Amadeus III.

Um·fra·ville, de \dē-ˈəm(p)-frə-vil\. English family of Norman descent, prominent in English-Scottish history in 13th and 14th centuries, including: Gilbert (d. c.1245), m. (1243; d. c.1267) Matilda, Countess of An·gus \ˈaŋ-gəs\ in her own right and the last of the Celtic line earls. His son ¶Gilbert (1244?–1307), first Norman earl of Angus, fought for Edward I against Baliol and Wallace (1296–98). His son ¶Robert (1277–1325) and grandson ¶Gilbert (1310–1381) both held title of earl, but the title and estates were taken by Robert Bruce and vested in the Stewart family (1329).

Una·mu·no y Ju·go \ü-nä-ˈmü-nō-ē-ˈk̲ü-gō\, Miguel de. 1864–1936. Spanish philosopher and writer. Professor (1891 ff.), rector (1901–14, 1931–36), U. of Salamanca. Partisan of republican government in Spain; banished to Canary Islands (1924); in voluntary exile at Paris (1924–30); deputy in the Cortes (1931–33). An early exponent of Existentialism. His works included *Paz en la guerra* (1897), *Amor y pedagogía* (1902), *Vida de Don Quijote y Sancho Panza* (1905), *Mi religión* (1910), *Contra esto y aquello* (1912), *Del sentimiento trágico de la vida* (1913), *Niebla* (novel, 1914), *Ensayos* (7 vols., 1916–19), *El Cristo de Velázquez* (poem, 1920), *Tres novelas ejemplares* (1920), *De Fuerteventura a París* (sonnets, 1925), *San Manuel bueno, mártir* (novel, 1931), and plays as *Sombras de sueño* (1931) and *El otro* (1932).

Unas \ˈ(y)ü-nəs\. d. 2345 B.C. Egyptian king (?–2345 B.C.). Last king of the 5th dynasty; first to inscribe interior of his pyramid with the religio-magical Pyramid Texts; succeeded by son-in-law Teti.

Un·cas \ˈəŋ-kəs\. 1588?–?1683. American Indian sachem. Son of a Pequot sachem; rebelled against Sassacus and became leader (1637) of independent Mohegan tribe, western division of the Pequot tribe; engaged in series of wars with Narragansett tribe (1643–47); attacked Massasoit (1661) but English intervened to force surrender of his prisoners and plunder; required (1675) to leave sons in English hands as pledge of his neutrality or aid in King Philip's War.

Uncle Sam. See Samuel WILSON.

Un·dén \ün-ˈdān\, Bo Östen. 1886–1974. Swedish statesman. Professor of civil law (1913–37), rector (1929–32), U. of Uppsala; member of Riksdag (1917–65); delegate to League of Nations Assembly (1921–39); minister of foreign affairs (1924–26, 1945–62); minister without portfolio (1932–36); chancellor, Swedish universities (1937–51); delegate to UN (1946–61).

Un·der·hill \ˈən-dər-ˌhil\, Evelyn. 1875–1941. English writer. Became noted lecturer on mysticism and religious life; led regular retreats (from 1924). Author of prose and verse works on mystical religion, including *Mysticism* (1911), *The Mystic Way* (1913), *Life of the Spirit and Life of To-day* (1922), *Worship* (1936).

Underhill, John. 1597?–1672. American colonial soldier, b. England. To Massachusetts Bay to organize militia (1630); took part in expedition against Pequot Indians (1637); banished from Massachusetts for unorthodoxy (1638); governor of Dover (N.H.) colony (1638–40); entered Dutch service (1643); in English service in Dutch War (1652–53); helped secure English rule over New Amsterdam (1664–65).

Un·der·wood \ˈən-dər-ˌwu̇d\, John Thomas. 1857–1937. American industrialist, b. London, England. To U.S. (1873); succeeded to father's paper and ink business (1882); bought rights from Franz Wagner (1895) to first practical visible-writing typewriter, introduced as Underwood typewriter (1896); president of Underwood Typewriter Co. (1896–1927).

Underwood, Francis Henry. 1825–1894. American reformer and editor, b. Enfield, Mass. Lawyer in Kentucky; returned to Massachusetts and engaged in politics and abolitionist cause; entered publishing firm of Phillips, Sampson and Co. (1854), which he persuaded to undertake new magazine *Atlantic Monthly* (1857); assistant editor under James Russell Lowell (1857–59); U.S. consul at Glasgow (1886–89), Leith (1893–94). Author of stories, novels, biographies, and *Quabbin, the Story of a Small Town* (1893).

Underwood, Oscar Wilder. 1862–1929. American politician, b. Louisville, Ky. Member, U.S. House of Representatives (1895–96, 1897–1915) and U.S. Senate (1915–27); Democratic floor leader in the House (1911–15) and chairman of the Committee on Ways and Means; known for sponsorship of the Underwood Tariff act (1913).

Und·set \ˈün-set\, Sigrid. 1882–1949. Norwegian novelist. Author of novels typically portraying plight of women and (from 1924) reflecting her conversion to Roman Catholicism; works included *Fru Marta Oulie* (1907), *Den lykkelige alder* (1908), *Jenny* (1911), *Vaaren* (1914), *Splinten av trollspeilet* (1917), trilogy *Kristin Lavransdatter* (1920–22), *Olav Audunssøn* (1925–27), *Den braendende busk* (1930), *Den trofaste hustru* (1936); wrote autobiographical *Elleve aar* (1934) and, while in U.S. during Nazi occupation of Norway (1940–45), *Return to the Future* (1942), *Happy Days in Norway* (1943). Awarded 1928 Nobel prize for literature.

Un·ga·ret·ti \ˌüŋ-gä-ˈret-tē\, Giuseppe. 1888–1970. Italian poet. In Paris (1912–14) associated with Apollinaire, Péguy, Valéry, Picasso, Braque, etc.; influenced esp. by Symbolists, evolved free poetic style known as Hermeticism; professor, São Paulo (1936–42), Rome (1942–57). Volumes of verse included *Il porto sepolto* (1916), *Allegria di naufragi* (1919), *La guerra* (1919), *Sentimento del tempo* (1933), *Il dolore* (1947), *La terra promessa* (1950), *Un grido e paesaggi* (1952), *Il taccuino del vecchio* (1960), *Morte delle stagioni* (1967); published *Traduzioni* (1946–50), translations from Racine, Shakespeare, Góngora, Mallarmé, William Blake.

Un·kei \ün-kā\. 1148?–1223. Japanese sculptor. Probably a descendent of Jōchō; commissioned by Kamakura shogunate to execute statues for Kōfuku-ji and Tōdai-ji temples in Nara; best known for colossal figures of the Niō at Todai-ji.

Un·ko·ku \ün-kō-kü\ Tōgan. 1547–1618. Japanese painter. Abandoned orthodox Kanō style to adopt style of Sesshū, the *suiboku-ga* or "water-ink painting" style; in famous legal contest won right to call himself "fifth generation of Sesshū."

Un·ruh \ˈün-rü\, Fritz von. 1885–1970. German playwright, poet, and novelist. Became pacifist after service in World War I; lived in France (1932–40), U.S. (1940–52). Author of Expressionistic works as plays *Offiziere* (1911), *Von der Entscheidung* (1914), *Ein Geschlecht* (1916), *Rosengarten* (1921), *Stürme* (1922), *Bonaparte* (1927), *Berlin in Monte Carlo* (1931), *Zero* (1932); tales *Opfergang* (1919); novels *The End is not Yet* (1947), *The Saint* (1950), *Fürchte Nichts* (1952), *Im Hause des Prinzen* (1967), etc.

Un·ter·mey·er \ˈənt-ər-ˌmī(-ə)r\, Louis. 1885–1977. American author and editor, b. New York City. Poetry editor, *American Mercury* (1934–37); lecturer and poet-in-residence at numerous colleges. Author of verse and editor of many anthologies as *Treasury of Great Poems* (1955), *Lives of the Poets* (1959), *World's Great Stories* (1964), *Treasury of Great Humor* (1972).

Un·ter·my·er \ˈənt-ər-ˌmī(-ə)r\, Samuel. 1858–1940. American lawyer, b. Lynchburg, Va. Practiced in New York City (from 1879); noted trial and corporate lawyer; carried through merger of Utah Copper Co., Boston Consolidated Co., and Nevada Consolidated Co.; counsel for Pujo investigating committee on banking and currency of U.S. House of Representatives (1912–13); chairman of board that framed income tax law and excess profits laws during World War I.

Un·ver·dor·ben \ˌün-fer-ˈdȯr-bən\, Otto. 1806–1873. German chemist. Discovered aniline among the products obtained in the destructive distillation of indigo (1826).

Un·win \ˈən-wən\, Sir Stanley. 1884–1968. English publisher. Formed (1928) publishing firm of Allen & Unwin and built large business on works of Bertrand Russell, Edwin Muir, Croce, Strindberg, Sorel, Jules Romains, Arthur Waley, Sydney Webb, Freud, Harold Laski, Tolkien, etc. Author of *The Truth about Publishing* (1926).

Up·dike \ˈəp-ˌdīk\, Daniel Berkeley. 1860–1941. American printer and publisher, b. Providence, R.I. Designer for Houghton, Mifflin & Co. (1880–93); founded the Merrymount Press, Boston (1893); instrumental in improving typography in U.S. Author of *Printing Types—Their History, Forms and Use* (1922).

Up·field \'əp-ˌfēld\, Arthur William. 1888–1964. Australian novelist, b. England. To Australia (1911); author of over 30 popular novels featuring the half-Aboriginal detective Inspector Napoleon Bonaparte, as *The Barrakee Mystery* (1929), *Murder Down Under* (1943), *The Widows of Broome* (1949).

Up·john \'əp-ˌjän\, Richard. 1802–1878. American architect, b. Shaftesbury, England. To U.S. (1829); opened architect's office in Boston (1834), New York (1839). One of founders of American Institute of Architects, and its first president (1857–76). Among his notable works of Gothic Revival were Trinity Church in New York (consecrated 1846); Church of the Pilgrims in Brooklyn, N.Y.; Grace Church in Newark, N.J.; St. Paul's Church in Buffalo, N.Y.; Bowdoin College chapel; Trinity Chapel in New York City. Author of *Upjohn's Rural Architecture* (1852) intended for poorer parishes. His son ¶Richard Mitchell (1828–1903) was in partnership with father (from 1853); moved from Gothic toward eclectic picturesqueness in design; among notable buildings designed by him were State Capitol of Connecticut at Hartford, Central Congregational Church of Boston, Madison Square Presbyterian Church of New York.

Upp·dal \'üp-däl\, Kristofer. 1878–1961. Norwegian novelist. Author of proletarian novels as the 10-vol. *Dansen gjenom skuggeheimen* (1911–24); also wrote lyric verse as *Kvaede* (1905), *Snørim* (1915), *Altarelden* (1920), *Kulten* (1947).

Up·son \'əp-sən\, Ralph Hazlett. 1888–1968. American aeronautical engineer, b. New York City. Winner of International Balloon Race (1913) and American National Balloon Race (1913, 1919, 1921); chief aeronautical engineer, Goodyear Tire & Rubber Co. (1914–20); designed airships and dirigibles for navy; designed first successful metal-clad airship (1929); pioneer in streamline design for railroad locomotives; professor, U. of Minn. (1946–56); with aerospace division of Boeing Aircraft Co. (1956–64).

Up·ton \'əp-tən\, Emory. 1839–1881. American army officer, b. near Batavia, N.Y. Entered army (1861); brigadier general of volunteers (1864); commandant of cadets, West Point (1870–75). Author of important works on tactics as *A New System of Infantry Tactics* (1867), *Armies of Asia and Europe* (1878), *Military Policy of the United States* (1904).

Upton, George Putnam. *Pseudonym* Peregrine Pick·le \'pik-əl\. 1834–1919. American journalist and writer, b. Roxbury, Mass. On staff, Chicago *Evening Journal* (1856–62), Chicago *Daily Tribune* (1862–1919; music critic 1863–81). Author of *Letters of Peregrine Pickle* (1869), *Women in Music* (1880), *Standard Operas* (1886), *Standard Oratorios* (1887), *Standard Symphonies* (1889), *Musical Memories* (1908), etc.

ʽUq·bah ibn Nā·fiʽ \'ùk-bə-ˌib-ən-'na-fi(ə)\. *Also spelled* Okba. d. 683 A.D. Arab warrior. Nephew of ʽAmr ibn al-ʽĀṣ; sent by caliph Muʽāwiyah to conquer North Africa; founded (670) al-Qayrawān (Kairouan); continued conquests as far as Tangier; killed at Biskra on return; raised to sainthood by Arabs; great mosque in al-Qayrawān dedicated to him.

ʽUrā·bī Pa·sha \ù-'rä-bē-'päsh-ä\. *Sometimes* Arabi Pasha. *In full* Aḥmad ʽUrābī Pasha al-Miṣrī. 1839–1911. Egyptian nationalist. Entered army, served in Egyptian–Ethiopian War (1875–76); took part in officers' revolt against khedive Ismāʽīl Pasha (1879); led revolt against dominance of Turkish and Circassian officers in Egyptian army (1881); minister of war in nationalist government (1882); organized resistance to British and French intervention (1882) and proclaimed khedive Tawfīq a traitor; defeated by British under Gen. Sir Garret Wolseley at at-Tall al-Kabīr (1882); sentenced to death but exiled to Ceylon (1882–1901).

Ura·ga·mi \ùr-ä-gäm-ē\ Gyokudō. *Also called* Hyō·u·em·on \hyō-ü-em-ōn\ Gyokudō. 1745–1820. Japanese painter and musician. In service of Lord Ikeda of Okayama (to 1795); self-taught exponent of *Nan-ga* school of realistic landscape painting; a master of the 7-stringed zither, helped revive *gagaku*, or Imperial court music.

Ur·ban \'ər-bən\. Name of eight popes:

Urban I. Saint. d. 230. Pope (222–230). Succeeded St. Calixtus I; his reign, under Emperor Alexander Severus, one of peace for church.

Urban II. *Orig.* Odo \'ōd-(ˌ)ō\ of La·ge·ry \lȧzh-rē\ *or* Eudes de Châ·til·lon \œ̄d-də-shȧ-tē-yōⁿ\. c.1035–1099. Pope (1088–99), b. Châtillon-sur-Marne, France. Archdeacon of Reims (c.1055–67); entered monastery of Cluny, prior superior (c.1070–74); to Rome (1079), made cardinal (1079); papal legate to Germany (1084–85); opposed (1088–97) antipope Clement III; continued policy of Gregory VII in opposing Emperor Henry IV; excommunicated Henry IV and Philip I of France; convoked councils (1095) at Piacenza and Clermont; at latter preached First Crusade; died before news of capture of Jerusalem reached Italy.

Urban III. *Orig.* Uberto Cri·vel·li \krē-'vel-lē\. d. 1187. Pope (1185–87). Cardinal and archbishop of Milan (1182); succeeded Lucius III, from whom he inherited dispute with Emperor Frederick I; opposed marriage of Frederick's son Henry (later Henry VI) to daughter of Roger II of Sicily and his coronation as king of Italy; consecrated as archbishop of Trier a rival of the imperial candidate (1186), provoking Frederick to invade Italy; died en route to Venice to excommunicate Frederick.

Urban IV. *Orig.* Jacques Pan·ta·lé·on \päⁿ-tȧ-lā-ōⁿ\. c.1200–1264. Pope (1261–64). Priest at Lyons; professor, Paris (1251–53); bishop of Verdun (1253); patriarch of Jerusalem (1255); forced by Roman civil wars to reside in Viterbo and Orvieto; opposed Manfred of Naples and offered Sicilian crown to Charles of Anjou; sided with Henry III of England against his barons; appointed many French cardinals, later a cause of Western Schism; instituted feast of Corpus Christi (1264).

Urban V. *Orig.* Guillaume de Gri·mo·ard \də-grē-mō-ȧr\. 1310–1370. Pope (1362–70). Benedictine; abbot of Saint-Germaine, Auxerre (1352–61), Saint-Victor, Marseilles (1361–62); tried to return pontificate from Avignon to Rome (1367–70), but compelled to leave because of unsettled conditions; failed to capitalize on Byzantine emperor John V Palaeologus's offer to end Latin–Greek schism.

Urban VI. *Orig.* Bartolomeo Pri·gna·no \prēn-'yä-nō\. c.1318–1389. Pope (1378–89). Archbishop of Acerenza (1363), Bari (1377); by harsh actions alienated French cardinals, who began Great Western Schism by retiring to Fondi to elect antipope Clement VIII (1378); excommunicated Queen Joan I of Naples (1380); fought Neapolitan army at Nocera (1385); possibly poisoned.

Urban VII. *Orig.* Giambattista Cas·ta·gna \käs-'tän-yä\. 1521–1590. Pope (1590). Bishop of Rozzano (1553); governor of Fano (1555), of Perugia and Umbria (1559); papal nuncio to Spanish court (1565–72); cardinal priest (1583); legate at Bologna (1584–90); inquisitor general (1586); elected to succeed Sixtus V, reigned 12 days.

Urban VIII. *Orig.* Maffeo Bar·be·ri·ni \ˌbär-bā-'rē-nē\. 1568–1644. Pope (1623–44). Papal legate to France (1601); nuncio to France and archbishop of Nazareth (1604); cardinal (1606); bishop of Spoleto (1608); acquired duchy of Urbino for the papacy (1626); in Thirty Years' War, sided with France against emperor and Spain; greatly developed defenses of Papal States; founded Collegium Urbanum (1627); opened China and Japan to all missionary orders (1633); condemned Galileo (1633), Jansenism (1643); prohibited slavery in Latin America (1639); engaged in unsuccessful War of Castro (1642–44) against Parma; patron of Bernini; built Fort Urbano at Castelfranco, Castel Gandolfo, etc.

Urban, Joseph. 1872–1933. American architect and decorator, b. Vienna, Austria. To America (1911, naturalized 1917); art director for Boston Opera Company (1911–14); designed stage sets for the Ziegfeld *Follies* (1915), for the Metropolitan Opera, and for some of James K. Hackett's Shakespearean productions; designed Ziegfeld Theatre, New School for Social Research.

Urban, Sylvanus. See Edward CAVE.

Urbino, Dukes of. See Lorenzo de' Medici (1492–1519) under MEDICI family; MONTEFELTRO.

Urchard, Sir Thomas. See URQUHART.

Ur·da·ne·ta \ùr-t͟hä-'nā-tä\, Andrés de. 1498–1568. Spanish religious and navigator. In early years an adventurer, esp. in Moluccas; entered Augustinian order in Mexico City (1553); at request of King Philip II, sailed to Philippines (1565) and discovered best west-to-east return route to America, making possible colonization and commercial development of Philippines.

U'·Ren \ùr-'en\, William Simon. 1859–1949. American reformer, b. Lancaster, Wis. Practiced law in Colorado (1881–86), later in Oregon; member of Oregon legislature (1896–97); through such organizations as Direct Legislation League, People's Power League, Anti-Monopoly League, a leader in movements that secured initiative and referendum (1902), direct primaries (1904), popular election of U.S. senators (by constitutional amendment, 1913).

Urey \'yù(ə)r-ē\, Harold Clayton. 1893–1981. American chemist, b. Walkerton, Ind. On teaching staff, Columbia (from 1929), professor (1934–45); professor, U. of Chicago (1945–58), U. of California, La Jolla (1958 ff.); discovered (1931) heavy water and its component deuterium; studied radioactive isotopes and contributed to atomic bomb development; studied origin of planets. Awarded 1934 Nobel prize for chemistry for discovery of heavy hydrogen.

Ur·fé \ᵫ̄r-fā\, Honoré d'. 1568–1625. French writer. Known esp. as author of the chivalric pastoral romance *L'Astrée* (1607–27), whose characters (Céladon, Astrée, Silvandre, Hylas) became popular types in 17th-century romance.

Uri·bu·ru \ü-rē-'b̶ü-rü\, José Evaristo. 1831–1914. Argentine politician. Ambassador to Bolivia (1857–60); deputy (from 1861); vice president (1892–95); president of Argentina (1895–98); senator (1901–10).

Uriburu, José Félix. 1868–1932. Argentine soldier and politician. Nephew of José Evaristo Uriburu; army officer (to 1929); on behalf of landed oligarchy, led revolution that overthrew Irigoyen (1930); provisional president of Argentina (1930–32); largely dismantled liberal reforms of past decades.

Urliones, Gil de. See Gil de SILOÉ.

Ur-Nam·mu \ˈər-ˈnäm-ˌü, ˈu̇(ə)r-\. *Also called* Ur-En·gur \-ˈen-ˌgu̇(ə)r, -ˈeŋ-\. 22d–21st century B.C. King of Ur (c.2112–c.2095 B.C.). First king of the 3d (Sumerian) dynasty of Ur; author of the Sumerian legal code.

Ur·quhart \ˈər-kərt, -kärt\ *or* **Ur·chard** \ˈər-kərd, -ˌkärd\, Sir Thomas. 1611–1660. Scottish author. Fought on Royalist side in Civil War; wounded and taken prisoner at Worcester (1651); released on parole by Cromwell; died abroad. Author of *Epigrams* (1641), *Trissotetras,* a treatise on trigonometry (1645), several quaint tracts as *Pantochronocanon* (1652) and *Ekskubalauron* (1652, containing an account of James Crichton), and his masterpiece of free translation the *Works of Mr. Francis Rabelais* (books I and II, 1653; III, 1693; books IV and V being completed by Peter Anthony Motteux, *q.v.,* 1708).

Ur·qui·za \u̇r-ˈkē-sä\, Justo José de. 1801–1870. Argentine soldier and politician. Prominent in business and the army; confidant of Rosas; governor of Entre Ríos province (1841–54); defeated Rivera (1845); defeated Rosas at Monte Caseros (1852); provisional dictator, called constitutional congress at Santa Fe (1853); first constitutional president of Argentina (1854–60); commander in chief of national forces and again governor of Entre Ríos (after 1860); defeated (1861) by Mitre in war with Buenos Aires; commanded Argentine army against Paraguay (1865–68); assassinated.

Ur·ra·ca \u̇r-ˈrä-kä\. 1080 or 1081–1126. Queen of Castile and León (1109–26). Daughter of Alfonso VI; m. 1st Raymond of Burgundy; 2d (1109) Alfonso I of Aragon and Navarre (her third cousin); political implications of 2d marriage provoked long civil war; quarreled with Alfonso; defeated in battle of Sepúlveda (1111); succeeded by her son Alfonso VII.

Ur·sins \ue̅r-saⁿ\, Marie-Anne de La Tré·moille des \də-lȧ-trām-wȧy-dez-\. Princesse. 1642–1722. French noblewoman. Daughter of duc de Noirmoutier; m. 1st (1657) prince de Chalais, 2d (1675; d. 1698) Flavio Orsini (*Fr.* Ursins), Duke of Bracciano; helped arrange marriage of Philip V of Spain to María Luisa of Savoy and was sent by Louis XIV to be María Luisa's principal lady of the bedchamber (1701); ruled the queen, who in turn ruled Philip, and effectively controlled Spanish policy, latterly in concord with Jean Orry; almost caused breakdown of negotiation of peace of Utrecht (1713) by attempts to secure an independent principality; arranged 2d marriage of Philip, to Isabella Farnese, who, forewarned, banished her from Spain (1714).

Ur·si·nus \(ˌ)ər-ˈsī-nəs\. d. after 385? Antipope (366–367). Roman deacon; elected simultaneously with St. Damasus I to succeed Liberius; after battles between rival factions, exiled to Gaul; allowed to return by Emperor Valentinian I (367) but expelled from Rome following further violence (368) and with followers exiled again; settled in Milan (370); condemned by Roman synod and exiled to Cologne (378).

Ur·su·la \ˈər-syu̇-lə\. Saint. 4th? century. Legendary Christian martyr. Patroness and leader of virgins on a pilgrimage to Rome; with her 11,000 virgins, put to death near Cologne by Huns, according to the ancient legend which received increase of detail in twelfth century and was popularized by Geoffrey of Monmouth.

Uşak·lı·gil \ü-shäk-lə-ˈgēl\, Halid Ziya. 1866–1945. Turkish writer. Considered first true exponent of contemporary novel in Turkish; influenced esp. by Stendhal, Flaubert, Balzac. Works included *Bir Ölünün Defteri* (1889), *Ferdi ve Şürekâsı* (1894), *Mai ve Siyah* (1897), *Aşk-ı Memnu* (1900); also wrote stories, verse.

User·kaf \ˌü-sər-ˈkaf\. 25th century B.C. Egyptian king. Probably a descendant of Redjedef; m. royal heiress Khentkaues; considered first king of the 5th dynasty (established 2494 B.C.); raised cult of sun god Re to great importance and built many shrines.

Usk \ˈəsk\, Thomas. d. 1388. English writer. Author of allegorical prose work *The Testament of Love,* formerly ascribed to Chaucer.

Usmān ʿAlī Khān. See OSMAN ALI.

Us·man dan Fo·dio \ü-ˈsmän-dän-fō-ˈdē-ō\. *Arab.* ʿUth·mān ibn Fū·dī \u̇th-ˈmȧn-ˌib-ən-fü-ˈdē\. *Also called* She·hu \ˈshā-hü\ *or* the Shaykh \ˈshīk\. 1754–1817. Fulani religious and political leader. Student and later teacher of Islāmic and esp. Ṣūfī doctrine; gained large following among Fulani, Hausa, and other western Sudanese peoples; came into conflict with king of Gobir; at Gudu formally established (1804) new caliphate; conducted *jihād* (holy war) against king of Gobir (1804–08), ending with capture of capital at Alkalawa; reestablished caliphate at Sokoto (c.1809); went into virtual retirement (1812) and devoted himself to teaching and writing. His son ¶Muhammad Bello (d. 1837) was de facto ruler (from 1809); given eastern half of caliphate (1812); succeeded to title of caliph (1817) and brought Sokoto caliphate to its greatest influence.

Uspen·sky \üs-ˈpyän-skəi\, Gleb Ivanovich. 1843–1902. Russian writer. Published essays on proletarian life *Nravy Rasteryayevoy* (1866); best known for anti-Romantic realistic novels of peasant life as *Vlast zemli* (1882).

Ust·i·nov \ü-ˈstē-nəf\, Dmitry Fedorovich. 1908–1984. Soviet politician. Commissar of armaments (1941–46); minister of armaments (1946–53); minister of defense industries (1953–57). After German invasion (1941), removed Soviet arms industry beyond the Urals; after World War II, presided over huge buildup of Soviet military might. Minister of defense, member of Politburo, and a marshal of the Soviet Union (all from 1976).

Ussh·er \ˈəsh-ər\, James. 1581–1656. Irish prelate and scholar. Ordained (1601); professor, Trinity Coll., Dublin (1607–21); bishop of Meath (1621); archbishop of Armagh (1625); corresponded with Laud (1628–40); defeated attempt to make doctrinal standards of Irish church conform exactly to those of the English (1634); urged Charles I not to abandon Strafford; noted for Latin edition of St. Ignatius of Antioch; propounded a scheme of biblical chronology long accepted, according to which the creation took place 4004 B.C.

Ustād Manṣūr. See MANṢŪR.

Uta·ga·wa \üt-ä-gä-wä\ Kunisada. 1786–1864. Japanese painter and printmaker. Student of Utagawa Toyokuni; one of the most prolific producers of woodblock prints in *Ukiyo-e* manner, known esp. for decadent erotic portraits of women; illustrated Ryūtei Tanehiko's parody *Nise murasaki inaka genji.*

Utagawa Kuniyoshi. *Orig.* Igusa \ē-gu̇s-ä\ Magosaburō. 1797–1861. Japanese painter and printmaker. Student of Utagawa Toyokuni and rival of Utagawa Kunisada; known for print series *Tsūzoku Suikoden gōketsu hyakuhachinin* on warriors (c.1827) and landscape series *Tōto meisho* and *Tōto Fujimi sanjūrokkei.*

Utagawa Toyokuni. *Orig.* Ku·ra·ha·shi \ku̇r-ä-hä-shē\ Kumakichi. *Also known as* To·yo·ku·ni \tō-yō-ku̇n-ē\. 1769–1825. Japanese painter and printmaker. One of the most popular artists in *Ukiyo-e* manner, known for prints of actors and women executed in bold, vivid style.

Utamaro. See KITAGAWA.

ʿUth·mān ibn ʿAf·fān \u̇th-ˈmȧn-ˌib-ən-af-ˈfȧn\. d. 656. Third Muslim caliph. Member of Umayyad clan of Mecca; first of his social class to accept teachings of Muḥammad; married a daughter of Muḥammad; chosen to succeed ʿUmar as caliph (644); established official version of Qurʾān; strengthened caliphal administration but failed to assert full authority; killed during a rebellion; the question of succession provoked violent dispute in Muslim community.

Utril·lo \ue̅-trē-yō\, Maurice. 1883–1955. French painter. Known for his paintings of Parisian street scenes, esp. of the Montmartre district.

Uvedale. See UDALL.

Uz \ˈüts, ˈu̇ts\, Johann Peter. 1720–1796. German poet. Author of love and anacreontic lyrics *Lyrische Gedichte* (1749), *Ode an die Weisheit* (1757), the didactic *Versuch über die Kunst* (1760), etc.

Uzbek. See ÖZ BEG.

Uzun Ḥa·san \ü-ˈzün-kä-ˈsän\. c.1420–1478. Turkish ruler. Emerged from long civil war (1435–53) as ruler of Turkmen Ak Koyunlu dynasty, succeeding Kara Osman; m. (1458) Catherine, daughter of Kalo-Ioannes of Trebizond; campaigned against Kara Koyunlus (1461–69) and annexed all Azerbaijan and Iran; extended rule to Iraq, Armenia; defeated by Ottoman Turks at Terjan (1473).

Uz·zi·ah \ə-ˈzī-ə\ *or* **Az·a·ri·ah** \ˌaz-ə-ˈrī-ə\ *or* **Ozi·as** \ō-ˈzī-əs\ *or* **Az·a·ri·as** \ˌaz-ə-ˈrī-əs\. 8th century B.C. King of Judah (c.791–739 B.C.). Son of Amaziah; enjoyed long prosperous reign, in which Judah reached height of its power; finally subdued Philistines.

V

Vaca, Álvar Núñez Cabeza de. See CABEZA DE VACA.

Vă·că·re·scu \ˌvœ-kə-ˈre-skü\. Name of a Walachian boyar family of Greek origin, including: Ienăchiță (1740–1799), scholar and poet, author of first Romanian grammar written in the vernacular (1787) and a history of Turkey; poems included *Amărită turturea* and *Testamentul.* His sons ¶Alecu (1765–1799) and ¶Nicolae (1784–1825) were well known as poets. Alecu's son ¶Iancu (1792–1863) inaugurated modern Romanian poetry, aided in establishing the Romanian theater, and translated German and French works into Romanian. Alecu's niece ¶Elena (1866–1947), author of novels and poems in Romanian and in French, including *Chants d'aurore* (1886), *L'Âme sereine* (1896), *Lueurs et flammes* (1903), *Dans l'or du soir* (1928).

Va·car·i·us \və-ˈkar-ē-əs\. c.1115 or 1120–after 1198. Italian legal scholar. To England as counselor to Archbishop Theobold (c.1143); popular lecturer, first known teacher of Roman law at Oxford; in service of Roger de Pont l'Évêque, archbishop of York (1154 ff.). Author of *Liber pauperum,* treatise on Digest and Codex of Justinian designed for use by impoverished students.

Va·chell \ˈvā-chəl\, Horace Annesley. 1861–1955. English writer. Author of novels, including *Romance of Judge Ketchum* (1894), *John Charity* (1900), *The Hill* (1905), *Her Son* (1907, dramatized 1907), *Quinney's* (1914, dramatized 1915), *Whitewash* (1920), *Vicar's Walk* (1933), *Quinneys for Quality* (1938); plays, including *Jelf's* (1912), *Fishpingle* (1916), *Count X* (1921), *Plus Fours* (1923); essays as *My Vagabondage* (1936), *Little Tyrannies* (1940); autobiographical *Methuselah's Diary* (1949), *More from Methuselah* (1951).

Va·che·rot \vásh-rō\, Étienne. 1809–1897. French philosopher. Professor at the Sorbonne (1839–52), removed for refusing to sign the oath of allegiance to the empire; member of national assembly (1871). Among his works were *La Métaphysique et la Science* (1858), *La Démocratie,* for which he was imprisoned (1859), *La Religion* (1868), etc.

Václav. See WENCESLAS.

Va·dé \vá-dā\, Jean-Joseph. 1719–1757. French poet and dramatist. Author of verse, libretti, chansons, etc., in realistic vernacular *genre poissard* style; wrote many opéras comiques, esp. *La Fileuse* (1752), *Les Troqueures* (1753); best known verse the burlesque *La Pipe cassée* (1758).

Vadianus. See Joachim von WATT.

Vaez de Torres, Luis. See TORRES.

Vaga, Perino del. See Pietro BONACCORSI.

Va·ga·no·va \(ˌ)və-ˈgá-nə-və\, Agrippina Yakovlevna. 1879–1951. Russian dancer and teacher. With Mariinsky (now Kirov) Theater troupe (1897–1917), ballerina (1915–17); teacher with Leningrad Khorteknikum (1921–51), director (from 1934); also taught at Leningrad Ballet School (1934–41), Leningrad Conservatory (1946–51); developed a teaching system combining traditional Russian technique with modern Soviet acrobatic style. Author of *Fundamentals of the Classic Dance* (1934).

Vai·da-Voe·vod \ˈvī-dä-vói-ˈvȯd\, Alexandru. 1872–1950. Romanian politician. Romanian nationalist in Hungarian parliament (1906–18); after Austria's collapse (1918), selected to represent Romania at Paris Peace Conference. Prime minister of Romania (1919–20); gained recognition of incorporation of Bessarabia into Romania; minister of interior (1928–30); prime minister and minister of foreign affairs (1932); again prime minister (1933).

Vai·hing·er \ˈfī-iŋ-ər\, Hans. 1852–1933. German philosopher. Professor, Strassburg (1883–1906), Halle (1906–33); founder of the Kant Society (1904); cofounder (1919) and editor (1919–29) of *Annalen der Philosophie.* Developed his "as if" philosophy in *Die Philosophie des Als Ob* (1911), *Der Mythus und das Als Ob* (1927), etc.

Vail \ˈvā(ə)l\, Alfred Lewis. 1807–1859. American pioneer in telegraphy, b. Morristown, N.J. Financed Samuel F. B. Morse in later stages (1837–38) of development of the telegraph in return for interest in the American and foreign patents. Collaborated with Morse in demonstrating instrument in New York, Philadelphia, and Washington (1837–38); on receiving end of Morse's "What hath God wrought!" message (1844).

Vail, Theodore Newton. 1845–1920. American telephone and telegraph executive, b. near Minerva, Ohio. Cousin of A.L. Vail; telegraph operator for Western Union Co. in New York City (1864–66). General manager, Bell Telephone Co. (1878–87); incorporated American Telephone & Telegraph Co. (1885) to unify the telephone industry and provide long-distance system; president of A.T.&T. (1885–89, 1907–19); developed first transcontinental telephone line (1915), transatlantic radiotelephone (1915).

Vail·lant \vá-yäⁿ\, Édouard-Marie. 1840–1915. French politician. Member of the Commune of Paris (1871); condemned to death (1871) but escaped to England, where he associated with Karl Marx; returned (1880); active as Blanquist Socialist; member of Chamber of Deputies (from 1893) and collaborator with Jean Jaurès (from 1905).

Vair \ver\, Guillaume du. 1556–1621. French writer. Lawyer; held offices under Henry IV; celebrated as orator; known for treatise on Christian Stoicism *De la constance et consolation ès calamités publiques* (1593).

Vajiravudh. See RAMA VI.

Vakh·tan·gov \(ˌ)vək-ˈtán-gəf\, Yevgeny. 1883–1922. Russian theatrical director. Pupil of Stanislavsky; a leader in the Moscow Art Theater and director of its Third Workshop (1920–22); combined Stanislavsky's Naturalism with bold theatricality influenced by Meyerhold to produce striking and influential productions of *The Dybbuk* (1922), *Turandot* (1922), etc.

Va·lan·čius \vä-ˈlän-chu̇s\, Motiejus. 1801–1875. Lithuanian prelate and writer. Bishop of Samogitia (1850); author of didactic works as *Vaiku knygelė* (1868), *Paaugusiu žmoniu knygelė* (1868), tales as *Antano Tretininko pasakojimas* (1872), etc.; after Russian suppression of printing of Lithuanian books in Latin (1864), arranged for printing of such books in Prussia and smuggling them into Lithuania.

Va·lao·rí·tis \vä-lau̇-ˈrē-tis\, Aristotelís. 1824–1879. Greek poet and politician. Famed as Greek patriot; fought Turks, played role in union of Ionian Islands with Greece (1863); active in politics (1863–69). Author of fervently Romantic and patriotic verse as *Stichourgemata* (1847), *Mnemosyna* (1857), *Kyra Phrosini* (1859), *Athanases Diakos* (1867), *Astrapoyiannos* (1867), unfinished *Phōteinos* (1891).

Valbert, G. See Victor CHERBULIEZ.

Valdegamas, Marqués de. See DONOSO CORTÉS.

Val-de-Grâce \vál-də-grás\, Jean-Baptiste du. Baron de Cloots \klōts, klȯts\. *Known as* Anacharsis Cloots. 1755–1794. French revolutionist. Member of noble Prussian family; to Paris (1776), assisted Diderot in compiling *Encyclopédie;* member of Jacobin club at outbreak of Revolution (1789); assumed role of spokesman for democracy and title of "Orator of Mankind" under pseudonym Anacharsis; member of National Convention (1792); called for revolutionary crusade of liberation; became Hébertist and promoter of worship of goddess Reason; guillotined with other Hébertists.

Valdemar. See also WALDEMAR.

Val·de·mar \ˈvál-də-mär\. Name of four kings of Denmark:

Valdemar I. *Called* the Great. 1131–1182. King (1157–82). Son of Knud Lavard and descendant of Sweyn II; emerged as winner of 25-year civil war and claimed throne; ended Wend power in Denmark by capture of Rügen (1169); broke with Emperor Frederick I Barbarossa and recognized Pope Alexander III (c.1165), for which he secured canonization for his father and recognition of hereditary rule of his line (1170); greatly increased Danish defenses and army.

Valdemar II. 1170–1241. King (1202–41). Son of Valdemar I; made duke of Schleswig (1188); conquered Holstein and Hamburg (1200–01); succeeded brother Canute VI (1202); early supported Otto IV and Welf faction, later switched to Frederick II; campaigned in Estonia (1219) and conquered entire country, establishing bishoprics of Reval and Dorpat; captured and imprisoned (1223–25) by Count Heinrich of Schwerin, released on relinquishing most of eastern lands; attempted to regain territories but defeated at Bornhöved (1227).

Valdemar III. 1314–1364. King (1326–30). Duke of Schleswig; elected king in opposition to and subsequently deposed in favor of Christopher II.

Valdemar IV At·ter·dag \'ät-tər-ˌdäg\. c.1320–1375. King (1340–75). Son of Christopher II; lived at court of Emperor Louis IV the Bavarian (1328–38); recognized as king (1340); secured control of Jutland and other former Danish territories; sold Estonia (1346); controlled Zealand (1349); supported Margrave Louis of Brandenburg against Charles IV (1350) and reaffirmed Danish rule over Rügen and Rostock; completed reunification of Denmark with acquisition of Skåne (1360); conquered Gotland (1361); defeated by coalition of Hanseatic League, Sweden, Mecklenburg, Holstein (1368) and forced to cede commercial privileges to League in Treaty of Stralsund (1370).

Valdemar. c.1238–1302. King of Sweden (1250–75). Son of Birger Jarl; elected to succeed Erik Eriksson, becoming founder of Folkung dynasty; overthrown by brother Magnus Ladulås (1275) and accepted part of Götaland.

Val·dès \väl-des\. *Also called* Pierre Valdès *or* Val·do \väl-dō\. *Eng.* Peter Wal·do \'wäl-(ˌ)dō, 'wȯl-\. *Lat.* Petrus Val·de·si·us \val-'dē-zē-əs\ *or* Wal·den·ses \wȯl-'den-ˌsēz\. d. before 1218. French religious leader. Began preaching in Lyons (c.1170–76) from vernacular translations of the Gospels; practiced voluntary poverty; attended 3d Lateran Council (1179), where Pope Alexander III confirmed his vow of poverty but forbade him to preach; excommunicated and banished from Lyons (1184) along with his followers, known as Pauperes or Pauperes de Lugduno or Pauperes Spiritu. Movement subsequently influenced by other groups as the Humiliati, Arnoldists, Cathars, etc., and became known as Waldenses; suffered severe persecutions (from c.1197).

Val·dés \bäl-'dās\, Alfonso de (1490?–1532) and his twin brother Juan de (1490?–1541). Spanish Humanists. Both held posts at court of Emperor Charles V; Alfonso held post at diets of Worms and Regensburg; both were correspondents of Erasmus. Alfonso was author of *Diálogo de Mercurio y Carón* and *Diálogo de las cosas ocurridas en Roma;* Juan of *Diálogo de la doctrina cristiana* and *Diálogo de la lengua.*

Valdés, Armando Palacio. See PALACIO VALDÉS.

Valdés, Gabriel de la Concepción. *Pseudonym* Plá·ci·do \'plä-sē-t͟hō\. 1809–1844. Cuban poet. Known esp. for poems about the slave trade and apostrophes to liberty, published as *Poesías* (1838), *El Veguero* (1841), *El hijo de maldición* (1843); best known poem "Plegaria a Dios" written while in prison on charge of involvement in slave rebellion; executed.

Valdés, Juan de. See under Alfonso de VALDÉS.

Valdés, Juan Meléndez. See MELÉNDEZ VALDÉS.

Val·dés Le·al \bäl-'dā-slā-'äl\, Juan de. 1622–1690. Spanish painter and engraver. A founder (1660) and president (1663–66) of Seville Academy; succeeded Murillo as leading painter of Spain; known for dramatic, pessimistic, often violent paintings in Late Baroque manner as *San Andrés, Las lágrimas de san Pedro, Tentaciones de san Jerónimo, La Virgen de los plateros, El triunfo de la muerte, Finis Gloria mundi, Christo disputando con los doctores.*

Val·di·via \bäl-'dē-b͟yä\, Pedro de. c.1498–1553. Spanish soldier. To New World (1534); served under Pizarro in battle at Las Salinas, Peru (1538); led expedition into Chile (1540); founded Santiago (1541); aided in suppressing rebellion of Gonzalo Pizarro in Peru (1547–48); returned to Chile as governor (1549); resumed war against Araucanian Indians (1549); founded Concepción (1550) and Valdivia (1552); killed in battle.

Valdo, Pierre. See VALDÈS.

Va·lence \vá-läⁿs\, William de. Earl of Pem·broke \'pem-ˌbru̇k\. d. 1296. French soldier and diplomat. Son of English King John's widow, Isabella of Angoulême, by second marriage; m. (1247) heiress of Anselm Marshal, Earl of Pembroke, assuming title. Fought on side of half-brother Henry III against Simon de Montfort, and at Lewes and Evesham; to Holy Land with Prince Edward (1270–73). His son ¶Aymer (1265?–1324), Earl of Pembroke, English soldier and ambassador, led van of Edward II's army against Bruce (1306); defeated Scots at Ruthven (1306); defeated by Bruce at Loudon Hill (1307); shared in king's defeat at Bannockburn (1314); arranged temporary peace (1318) between Thomas of Lancaster and Edward II (later broken, and Lancaster beheaded); his 2d wife ¶Mary of St. Pol (d. 1377) founded Pembroke Hall at Cambridge.

Valencia, Duke of. See Ramón María NARVÁEZ.

Va·len·cia \bä-'lān-thyä\, Guillermo. 1873–1943. Colombian poet and politican. Conservative deputy (1896–98, 1903–04); minister of public instruction (1903–04); senator (1909 ff.); minister of war (1914–18); professor and rector, U. of Cauca (from 1928). A leader of Modernist movement in Colombia with verse *Ritos* (1898, rev. 1914); also made translations into Spanish; wrote essays as *Panegíricos, discursos y artículos* (1933).

Va·len·ciennes \vá-läⁿ-syen\, Achille. 1794–1865. French zoologist. On staff (from 1812), professor (from 1832), Muséum d'Histoire Naturelle, Paris. Author of *Histoire naturelle des poissons* (1828–49; the first 8 of 22 volumes in collaboration with Georges Cuvier), etc.

Va·lens \'vā-lənz, -ˌlenz\. 328?–378 A.D. Roman emperor of the East (364–378). Made emperor (364) by his brother Emperor Valentinian I of the West; defeated rival Procopius (366); waged successful war against Visigoths (367–369); made discreditable treaty of peace with Persia (376); allowed Visigoths, overwhelmed by the Huns, to settle south of the Danube in Thrace; his unwise treatment of them led to war (377–378); defeated and slain by Visigoths under Fritigern at Adrianople (worst rout of Romans since Cannae).

Val·en·tine \'val-ən-ˌtīn\. Saint. 3d century. Name of two Christian martyrs, one a Roman priest and physician killed in persecutions of Claudius II Gothicus, the other bishop of Turni; conceivably they were in fact one; commemorated Feb. 14. The custom of sending valentines on this day originated probably in Roman festival of Lupercalia; association of the custom with Saint Valentine is accidental.

Valentine. Pope. See VALENTINUS.

Val·en·tin·i·an \ˌval-ən-'tin-ē-ən, -'tin-yən\. *Lat.* Val·en·tin·i·a·nus \ˌval-ən-ˌtin-ē-'ā-nəs\. Name of three Roman emperors:

Valentinian I. *Orig.* Flavius Valentinianus. 321–375. Emperor (364–375). Entered army at early age; advanced rapidly, but supposedly degraded by Constantius (357) and banished by Julian (362); restored (363); fought in the East; on death of Jovian, chosen emperor by army; appointed his brother Valens as colleague; kept western lands for his own administration; forced to contend (365–370) with many barbarian invasions in Gaul, Illyricum, and Africa; brought about reforms in religion, legal practice, and education.

Valentinian II. *Orig.* Flavius Valentinianus. 371–392. Emperor (375–392), jointly with his half-brother Gratian (375–383). Son of Valentinian I; received Italy, Illyricum, and Africa; during minority, government administered by Empress Justina; gave promise of becoming wise ruler; driven out of Italy (387) by Magnus Maximus; murdered at Vienna, perhaps by agents of Arbogast, Frankish commander of his army.

Valentinian III. *Orig.* Flavius Valentinianus. 419–455. Emperor (425–455) in the West. Son of Constantius and Galla Placidia; grandnephew of Valentinian I. Raised to the throne by Theodosius II; under mother's regency (425–437), thereafter gave government over to Aetius and never actually ruled; during his reign much of Western Empire seized or ravaged by Vandals, Visigoths, and Suevi; murdered Aetius (454) and was killed in revenge by his followers.

Val·en·ti·no \ˌval-ən-'tē-nō\, Rudolph. *Orig.* Rodolfo Alfonzo Raffaelo Pierre Filibert Guglielmi di Valentina d'·An·ton·guol·la \ˌdän-təŋ-'gwȯl-lä\. 1895–1926. American actor, b. Castellaneta, Italy. To U.S. (1913); entered films (1918); attained stardom and became first great film lover and matinee idol in *Four Horsemen of the Apocalypse* (1921), *The Sheik* (1921), *Blood and Sand* (1922), *A Sainted Devil* (1924), *Cobra* (1925), *The Eagle* (1925), *Son of the Sheik* (1926).

Val·en·ti·nus \ˌval-ən-'tī-nəs\. d. 827. Pope (827). Archdeacon under Pope St. Paschal I, whom he was elected to succeed; reigned about 40 days.

Valentinus. 2d century A.D. Gnostic philosopher and teacher, b. Egypt. Went to Rome and taught (c.136–160 A.D.), his disciples including Origen, Clement of Alexandria, and Heracleon; passed over for bishop of Rome (c.140), abandoned orthodoxy; withdrew from Rome to Cyprus (c.160) in hope of finding a more favorable reception for his doctrines. His interpretation of Gnostic doctrines was known as Valentinian Gnosticism, or Valentinianism.

Valera, Eamon de. See DE VALERA.

Va·le·ra y Al·ca·lá Ga·lia·no \bä-'lā-rä-ē-äl-kä-'lä-gäl-'yä-no\, Juan. 1824–1905. Spanish writer and diplomat. Minister to Frankfurt (1865), Lisbon (1881–83), Washington (1883–86), Brussels (1886–88); ambassador to Vienna (1893–95). Works included novels as *Pepita Jiménez* (1874), *Las ilusiones del doctor Faustino* (1875), *El comendador Mendoza* (1877), *Doña Luz* (1879), and *Juanita la Larga* (1885); shorter prose works, critical works, and verse translations of Goethe's *Faust,* Uhland's ballads, Thomas Moore's *Paradise and the Peri,* Longus's *Dafnis y Cloe,* poems of Whittier, James Russell Lowell, etc.

Va·le·ri·an \və-'lir-ē-ən\. *Lat.* Publius Licinius Va·le·ri·a·nus \və-ˌlir-ē-'ā-nəs\. d. 260 A.D. Roman emperor (253–260). Consul under Alexander Severus; commander on upper Rhine; loyal to Gallus, but arrived with legions from Gaul too late to save him; chosen emperor by soldiers; renewed persecution of Christians, executed Sixtus II; took his son Gallienus as colleague; tried to stop Persian conquest of Syria and Armenia; at first successful but was surprised and defeated by Shāpūr I at Edessa (260); died in captivity.

Va·le·ri·us Flac·cus \və-'lir-ē-əs-'flak-əs\, Gaius. 1st century A.D. Roman poet. Author of epic *Argonautica* (more than half of which is extant) on legend of quest of the golden fleece, based in part on Apollonius Rhodius.

Valerius Max·i·mus \-'mak-sə-məs\. fl. c.20 A.D. Latin writer. Attached to retinue of Sextus Pompeius; prepared *Factorum et dictorum memorabilium libri ix,* a compilation of historical anecdotes, chiefly taken from Cicero, Livy,

Sallust, and Trogus, apparently intended for use as a textbook in rhetoric classes.

Va·lé·ry \vȧ-lā-rē\, Paul, *in full* Ambroise-Paul-Toussaint-Jules. 1871–1945. French man of letters. Known as a poet and a philosopher; as a poet, associated with the Symbolist group; among his books of verse were *La Jeune Parque* (1917), *L'Album de vers anciens* (1920), *Charmes* (1922), etc. Among his prose writings were *Introduction à la méthode de Léonard de Vinci* (1895), *Soirée avec M. Teste* (1895), *Eupalinos* (1923), *L'Âme et la danse* (1924), *Variété* (1924–44), *Analecta* (1927), *Choses tues* (1930), *Regards sur le monde actuel* (1931), *Degas. Danse. Dessin* (1938), *Mauvaises pensées* (1942).

Va·li·gna·no \ˌväl-ēn-ˈyä-nō\, Alessandro. 1539–1606. Italian missionary. Entered Society of Jesus (1566); to Portuguese India (1574); helped develop missionary work in Goa, Macau, and esp. Japan, where he supported mission with share of silk trade, developed native clergy, and saw Christianity grow to some 300,000 adherents.

Val·la \ˈväl-lä\, Lorenzo. *Lat.* Laurentius Val·len·sis \və-ˈlen(t)-səs\. 1407–1457. Italian Humanist. Protégé of Popes Nicholas V and Calixtus VI; papal secretary (1448 ff.). Among his works were philosophical dialogue *De voluptate* (1431), *Declamatio* (1440), *De Elegantiae linguae latinae* (1471), Latin translations of Homer, Herodotus, and Thucydides, and critical and theological treatises.

Val·la·bha \ˌvəl-ə-ˈbä\. *Also called* Val·la·bhā·cār·ya \ˌvəl-ə-bä-ˈkär-yə\. 1479–1531. Indian philosopher and religious leader. Founded devotional Hindu sect called Vallabhācārya, based on doctrine of *puṣṭimārga,* or "way of divine grace."

Val·lan·di·gham \və-ˈlan-də-gəm\, Clement Laird. 1820–1871. American politician, b. New Lisbon, Ohio. Member, U.S. House of Representatives (1858–63); strongly opposed policies leading to Civil War. Became leader of the Peace Democrats, or "Copperheads" (from 1862); defied Gen. Burnside's order in military district of Ohio against public statements against war or in sympathy with the enemy; arrested (May 1863), tried by military commission, convicted, and jailed; sentence commuted by President Lincoln to banishment to the Confederacy. Returned to Ohio (1864) and conducted speaking campaign against Lincoln and the prosecution of the war.

Val·le \ˈväl-ˌlā\, Pietro della. 1586–1652. Italian traveler. Traveled to Istanbul, Jerusalem, Damascus, Baghdad, Persia, India (1614–26); studied languages and customs; chief work *Viaggi in Turchia, Persia, ed India descritti in 54 lettere famigliari* (1650–63).

Val·le-In·clán \ˈbäl-yā-ēŋ-ˈklän\, Ramón María del. *Orig.* Ramón del Val·le y Pe·ña \thāl-ˈbä(l)-yä-ē-ˈpān-yä\. 1866–1936. Spanish writer. Early influenced by Symbolists, later developed genre of *esperpentos* to express bitter social criticisms. Works included novels as four *Sonatas* (1902–05), esp. *Sonata de otoño* (1902); *Flor de santidad* (1904); the *Comedias bárbaras* including *Aguila de blasón* (1907), *Romance de lobos* (1908), *Cara de plata* (1923); *Tirano Banderas* (1926); *El ruedo ibérico* series as *La corte de los milagros* (1927), *Viva mi dueño* (1928). Wrote poetry as *Aromas de leyenda* (1907), *La pipa de kif* (1919), *Claves líricas* (1930); plays as *El embrujado* (1913), *La marquesa Rosalinda* (1913).

Val·le·jo \bä-ˈyā-kō\, Mariano Guadalupe. 1808–1890. American soldier and politician, b. Monterey, Cal. In Mexican military service (from 1823); supported his nephew Juan Bautista Alvarado in rebellion (1836) resulting in proclamation of the "free state" of California; lived at Sonoma as semi-independent chief (1836–46). Aided in securing Californian submission to United States; state senator in California's first legislature.

Val·lès \vȧ-les\, Jules. 1832–1885. French Socialist and journalist. Member of Commune (1871); founded (1871) *Le Cri du Peuple,* which became France's leading Socialist newspaper; exile in London (1871–83). Author of *Jacques Vingtras,* trilogy of autobiographical novels comprising *L'Enfant* (1879), *Le Bachelier* (1881), *L'Insurgé* (1886).

Valnay, Raoul. See A.-M.-É. HERVÉ.

Va·lois \vȧl-wȧ\. Name of a royal house of France derived from an ancient district of Picardy, northeast of Paris, a county (10th to 12th century), united to crown by King Philip Augustus (1214), but soon detached. Granted by Philip III (1285) to his son Charles (see CHARLES, Count of Valois). On death of King Charles IV (last of main Capetian line), Charles de Valois's son Philip, Count of Valois and nephew of Philip IV, was called to throne as Philip VI (1328–50), first of house of Valois (1328–1589).

Three collateral branches of the house: (1) CAPETIAN (1328–1498)—Philip VI, John II, Charles V, VI, VII, Louis XI, Charles VIII. (2) ORLÉANS (1498–1515)—descended from Louis, duc d'Orléans and comte de Valois, a son of Charles V; represented by Louis XII. (3) ANGOULÊME (1515–1589)—descended from Jean, another son of Louis, duc d'Orléans, and from Charles, son of Jean, both counts of Angoulême; represented by Francis I, Henry II, Francis II, Charles IX, Henry III. On death of Henry III (1589), French crown passed to the house of Bourbon.

County of Valois granted (1344) to Philippe, duc d'Orléans, son of Philip VI; made a duchy (1406), remained generally as property of dukes of Orléans until the Revolution (1789).

Valois, Charles de. Duc d'An·gou·lême \däⁿ-gü-lem\. 1573–1650. French courtier and soldier. Natural son of Charles IX and Marie Touchet; colonel general of cavalry under Henry IV, served against Catholic League; pardoned for role in conspiracy of Marshal de Biron (1601); imprisoned (1605) for plotting with Spain; released by Louis XIII (1616) and created duc d'Angoulême (1619); given military commands against Protestants by Richelieu and Mazarin.

Val·sal·va \väl-ˈsäl-vä\, Antonio Maria. 1666–1723. Italian anatomist. Lecturer in Bologna (from 1705); known for his researches on the ear described in *De aure humana tractatus* (1704); invented technique known as Valsalva maneuver.

van. For many names containing *van,* see that part of the name following *van.*

Van·brugh \ˈvan-brə, van-ˈbrü\, Sir John. 1664–1726. English dramatist and architect, of Flemish descent. Wrote *The Provok'd Wife* (1690–92; produced 1697), *The Relapse* (1696), followed by adaptations from the French including *Aesop* (1697), *The Country House* (1703), and *The Confederacy* (1705). Turned to architecture; designed new Haymarket Theatre (1705); with Nicholas Hawksmoor designed Castle Howard (completed 1714) and other country mansions in English Baroque style; commissioned (1705) by Queen Anne to design and build Blenheim Palace, Woodstock (completed by Duchess of Marlborough); comptroller of queen's works (1702–13, 1715–26).

Van Bu·ren \van-ˈbyu̇r-ən, vən-\, Martin. 1782–1862. Eighth president of the United States, b. Kinderhook, N.Y. Practiced law (from 1803); attorney general of New York (1816–19). Leader of "Bucktail" faction of state Democratic party and member of influential group nicknamed the "Albany regency." U.S. senator (1821–28); governor of New York (1829); resigned to become U.S. secretary of state (1829–31); close ally of Andrew Jackson; nominated U.S. minister to Great Britain, but nomination not confirmed by U.S. Senate (1832); vice president of the United States (1833–37); president of the United States (1837–41); unsuccessful Democratic candidate for presidency (1840) and Free-Soil party candidate (1848).

Vance \ˈvan(t)s\, Louis Joseph. 1879–1933. American novelist, b. Washington, D.C. Author of *Terence O'Rourke, Gentleman Adventurer* (1905), *The Brass Bowl* (1907), *The Lone Wolf* (1914), *Linda Lee, Inc.* (1922), *They Call It Love* (1927), *The Lone Wolf's Son* (1931), etc.

Vance, Zebulon Baird. 1830–1894. American politician, b. Buncombe Co., N.C. Member, U.S. House of Representatives (1858–61); in Confederate army (1861–62); governor of North Carolina (1862–66, 1876–78); elected to U.S. Senate but denied seat (1870); U.S. senator (1879–94).

Van Ceulen. See Cornelius JANSSEN.

Van Cort·landt \vän-ˈkȯrt-länt, *Angl* van-ˈkȯrt-lənt, -lənd\, Oloff Stevenszen. 1600–1684. Dutch businessman. In New Amsterdam (from 1638); burgomaster (1655–60, 1662–63); one of commissioners treating with English to surrender city (1664); deputy mayor (1667); his name is perpetuated in Van Cortlandt Park, New York City, originally a part of his estate. His son ¶Stephanus (1643–1700), b. New Amsterdam, was a businessman and politician; first native-born mayor of New York City (1677, 1686, 1687); associate justice (1691–1700) and chief justice (1700), New York supreme court.

Van·cou·ver \van-ˈkü-vər\, George. 1757–1798. English navigator. Entered navy (1770); on Cook's 2d and 3d voyages (1772–75, 1776–80); commanded an expedition of exploration and discovery (1791–92) along coasts of Australia, New Zealand, Tahiti, Hawaiian Islands; circumnavigated Vancouver Island and explored Pacific coast of North America (1792–94).

Van·ču·ra \ˈvȧn-chü-rȧ\, Vladislav. 1891–1942. Czech physician and novelist. Communist activist and member of avant garde artistic group Devětsil. Author, in an idiosyncratic baroque style, of novels as *Pekař Jan Marhoul* (1924), *Pole orná a válečná* (1925), *Markéta Lazarová* (1931), *Útěk do Budína* (1932), *Tři řeky* (1936); wrote Czech history *Obrazy z dějin národa českého* (1939–40).

Van de Graaff \ˈvan-də-ˌgraf\, Robert Jemison. 1901–1967. American physicist, b. Tuscaloosa, Ala. Research associate (1931–34), professor (1934–60), M.I.T.; a founder (1946), chief physicist (1946–67), High Voltage Engineering Corp.; known for development of high-voltage electrostatic generator used as X-ray generator and as nuclear particle accelerator.

Van·de·grift \ˈvan-də-ˌgrift\, Alexander Archer. 1887–1973. American marine corps officer, b. Charlottesville, Va. Commissioned (1909); served in Nicaragua (1912), Veracruz, Mexico (1914), Haiti (1915–23 at various times), China (1927–29, 1935–37); brigadier general (1940), major general (1942); in charge of landing and subsequent operations on Guadalcanal (Aug.–Dec. 1942),

Bougainville (Nov. 1943); Medal of Honor, lieutenant general (1943); commandant of Marine Corps (1944–48); general (1945).

van den, van der. For many names containing one of these elements, see that part of the name following the element.

Van·den·berg \'van-dən-ˌbərg\, Arthur Hendrick. 1884–1951. American politician, b. Grand Rapids, Mich. Editor, *Grand Rapids Herald* (1906–28); U.S. senator (1928–51); led Republican opposition to Pres. Roosevelt's foreign policy; reversed himself and declared support of overseas political and military alliances (1945); delegate to United Nations conference (1945) and to UN General Assembly (1946); led Senate approval of Marshall Plan (1948), NATO (1949); chief Republican architect of bipartisan foreign policy.

Van De·poele \'van-də-ˌpül\, Charles Joseph. 1846–1892. American inventor, b. Lichtervelde, Belgium. To America (1869, naturalized 1878). Demonstrated practicability of electric traction (1874) and patented an electric railway (1883); sold patents to Thomson-Houston Electric Co. (1888) and entered their employ as electrician. Received patents also on an electric generator (1880), a carbon commutator brush (1888), an alternating-current electric reciprocating engine (1889), a telpher system (1890), a coal-mining machine (1891), a gearless electric locomotive (1894).

Van·der·bilt \'van-dər-ˌbilt\. Name of an American family prominent in transportation and finance, including: Cornelius (1794–1877), *known as* Commodore Vanderbilt, b. Port Richmond, Staten Island, N.Y.; founded (1810) freight and passenger ferry business between Staten Island and New York City; sold his vessels (1818) and became captain (1818–29) on ferry line between New Brunswick, N.J., and New York City; established his own shipping service on Hudson River (1829), running in successful competition with lines already there; financed and established a line to California via Nicaragua (1847), which he sold out (1858) to competitors; bought controlling interest in New York and Harlem Railroad (1862–63), the Hudson River Railroad, and the New York Central Railroad; engaged in bitter stock-market struggle with James Fisk and Daniel Drew for control of Erie Railroad (1867–68); consolidated railroads (1869) and with acquisition of Lake Shore & Michigan Southern (1873) extended the lines to Chicago; built Grand Central Terminal, N.Y.C. (1873). Left large bequest to Central U. of Nashville, Tenn., which was renamed Vanderbilt U. His son ¶William Henry (1821–1885), b. New Brunswick, N.J., inherited the bulk of his fortune; became (1877) president of New York Central Railroad; engaged in rate wars with other lines, fought public regulation; remembered for expostulation "The public be damned!" (1882).

William Henry left four sons: ¶Cornelius (1843–1899), president, New York & Harlem Railroad (1886–99); chairman of board of New York Central & Hudson River and of Michigan Central; regarded as head of the Vanderbilt family (from 1885). ¶William Kissam (1849–1920), chairman of Lake Shore & Michigan Southern Railroad (1883–1903); president of New York, Chicago & St. Louis Railway (1882–87); surrendered active management of Vanderbilt railroad interests to a Rockefeller-Morgan-Pennsylvania Railroad group (1903); enthusiastic yachtsman, owned and sailed the *Defender* in Americas Cup race (1895). ¶Frederick William (1856–1938), expert in railroad management; noted as a yachtsman. ¶George Washington (1862–1914) interested himself in agriculture and forestry; acquired vast landed estate near Asheville, N.C., where he built magnificent country home, "Biltmore"; there he directed experiments in agriculture, forestry, and stockbreeding.

A son of William Kissam ¶Harold Stirling (1884–1970) was associated with management of New York Central lines; won Americas Cup in yachts *Enterprise* (1930), *Rainbow* (1934), *Ranger* (1937); developed (1926) game of contract bridge and endowed Vanderbilt Cup.

Van der Donck \'vän-dər-'dȯŋk\, Adriaen. 1620–?1655. Dutch lawyer and colonist in America. To America (1641); established colony on site of what is now Yonkers (1645); author of a description of New Netherland (pub. 1655).

Van·der·lyn \'van-dər-lən\, John. 1775–1852. American painter, b. Kingston, N.Y. Attracted attention of Aaron Burr, who sponsored his studies in Paris (1796–1801); largely responsible for introducing Neoclassical style to U.S.; again in Europe (1803–15). Works included *Death of Jane McCrea* (1804), *Marius amid the Ruins of Carthage* (1807), *Ariadne Asleep on the Island of Naxos* (1812), *Landing of Columbus* (1842–44) for U.S. Capitol Rotunda; also portraits of Zachary Taylor, James Madison, Andrew Jackson, John C. Calhoun, Burr, etc.

Van·der·vel·de \'vän-dər-'vel-də\, Émile. 1866–1938. Belgian politician. Socialist deputy (from 1894); president of 2d International (1900); minister of state and member of the Belgian cabinet during World War I (1914–18); minister of justice (1919–21) and of foreign affairs (1925–27); helped negotiate Locarno Pact (1925); minister of public health (1936–37).

Van De·van·ter \'van-də-'van-tər\, Willis. 1859–1941. American jurist, b. Marion, Ind. Practiced law at Cheyenne, Wyo. (from 1884); chief justice, Wyo. Territory (1888–90); U.S. circuit judge, 8th circuit (1903–10); associate justice, U.S. Supreme Court (1910–37).

Van Dine, S. S. See Willard Huntington WRIGHT.

van Dongen, Kees. See Cornelis DONGEN.

Van Do·ren \van-'dōr-ən, vən-, -'dȯr-\, Carl Clinton. 1885–1950. American writer, b. Hope, Ill. Taught at Columbia U. (1911–30); managing editor, *Cambridge History of American Literature* (1917–21); literary editor, *The Nation* (1919–22), *Century Magazine* (1922–25); editor, The Literary Guild (1926–34). Author of *The American Novel* (1921), *Contemporary American Novelists* (1922), *James Branch Cabell* (1925), *Swift* (1930), *Sinclair Lewis* (1933), *Benjamin Franklin* (1938, Pulitzer prize), *Secret History of the American Revolution* (1941), *Mutiny in January* (1943), *The Great Rehearsal* (1948), etc. His brother ¶Mark (1894–1972), b. Hope, Ill., taught at Columbia U. (1920–59, professor from 1942); literary editor (1924–28), motion picture critic (1935–38), *The Nation*. Author of verse, including *Spring Thunder* (1924), *Collected Poems, 1922–1938* (1939, Pulitzer prize), *Selected Poems* (1954), *Narrative Poems* (1964), *That Shining Place* (1969), *Good Morning* (1973); novels as *The Transients* (1935), *Windless Cabins* (1940); studies of Thoreau (1916), Dryden (1920), Shakespeare (1939), Hawthorne (1949); plays, essays, etc.

Van Dorn \van-'dȯ(ə)rn\, Earl. 1820–1863. American army officer, b. near Port Gibson, Miss. Entered army (1842); resigned (1861) to enter Confederate army. Colonel of cavalry, stationed in Texas (1861); received surrender of Union troops there (Apr. 1861); promoted major general (Sept. 1861); commander of Trans-Mississippi Dept. (1862), army of West Tennessee (1862–63); attacked Rosecrans at Corinth, Miss. (Oct. 3, 1862); raided Holly Springs, Miss. (Dec. 1862); murdered.

Van Dru·ten \van-'drüt-ᵊn\, John William. 1901–1957. American playwright and novelist, b. London, England. Lawyer; lecturer, U. Coll. of Wales (1923–26); to U.S. (naturalized 1944). Author of *Young Woodley* (produced in N.Y. 1925; pub. as a novel 1929), *A Woman on Her Way* (novel, 1930), *There's Always Juliet* (1931), *The Distaff Side* (1933), *And Then You Wish* (novel, 1936), *Gertie Maude* (1937), *Old Acquaintance* (1939), *Leave Her to Heaven* (1940), *Voice of the Turtle* (1943), *I Remember Mama* (1944, from stories of Kathryn Forbes), *The Druid Circle* (1947), *Make Way for Lucia* (1948, from E. F. Benson's novels), *Bell, Book and Candle* (1950), *I Am A Camera* (1951, from Christopher Isherwood's stories); also wrote screenplays.

Van Dyck *or* **Van·dyke** \vän-'dīk, *Angl* van-, vən-\, Sir Anthony. 1599–1641. Flemish painter. Studied under Rubens and was his assistant on some of his great canvases; in England (1620–21, from 1632); knighted by Charles I of England (1632) and appointed court painter. Notable for color, for portrayal of delicate emotion, and esp. for facility in conveying idealized individuality in portraits, of which he produced over 500. Well known works included *Taking of Christ, Madonna of the Rosary, Samson and Delilah, Lamentation for Christ, Cupid and Psyche;* also did oil sketches, watercolors, engravings.

Van Dyke \van-'dīk, vən-\, Henry. 1852–1933. American clergyman and writer, b. Germantown, Pa. Pastor, Brick Presbyterian Church, New York (1883–99); professor, Princeton (1899–1913, 1919–23). U.S. minister to the Netherlands and Luxembourg (1913–16). Author of *The Reality of Religion* (1884), *Little Rivers* (1895), *The Story of the Other Wise Man* (1896), *The Builders, and Other Poems* (1897), *Fisherman's Luck* (1899), *The Ruling Passion* (1901), *The Blue Flower* (1902), *Music, and Other Poems* (1904), *The Unknown Quantity* (1912), *The Valley of Vision* (1919), *The Golden Key* (1926), *Gratitude* (1930), etc.

Vane \'vān\, Sir Henry. *Called* the Elder. 1589–1655. English politician. Rose in households of James I and Charles I (from 1611); M.P. (1614, 1621–26, 1628); undertook diplomatic missions; privy councilor (1630); secretary of state (1640); as king's agent in Short Parliament (1640), provoked deadlock that led to dissolution; again M.P. (Long Parliament, 1640–53); helped secure attainder and execution of Thomas Wentworth, Earl of Strafford (1641); dismissed by king (1641); joined Parliamentary side, served in Cromwell's Parliament (1653).

Vane, Sir Henry. *Called* the Younger. 1613–1662. English Puritan statesman. Son of Sir Henry Vane the Elder; to America (1635) and settled at Boston; governor of Massachusetts (1636–37); lost popularity by taking side of Anne Hutchinson in theological dispute; defeated for reelection and returned to England. Joint treasurer of royal navy (1639); member of Long Parliament (1640 ff.), leader of Commons (from 1643); one of commissioners who negotiated the Solemn League and Covenant with Scotland (1643); approved the Self-Denying Ordinance and the New Model (1645); condemned Pride's Purge (1648). Member of Council of State (1649–53); imprisoned (1656) for attack on Cromwell's Protectorate; arrested after the Restoration (1660); held for two years in prison; tried, convicted and executed for treason.

Vane, Sutton, *in full* Vane Sutton. 1888–1963. English playwright. Known for unconventional play *Outward Bound* (1923), which he was forced to produce himself and which was a great success in London and New York and made into a motion picture.

Van Gen·nep \vàn-zhə-nep, väⁿ-\, Arnold. 1873–1957. French ethnographer and folklorist. Best known for *Les Rites de passage* (1909); also published *Religions, moeurs et légendes* (1908–14), *Folklore de Dauphiné* (1933), *Folklore de la Bourgogne* (1936), *Manuel du folklore français contemporaine* (1943–58), etc.

Van Hise \van-'hīs\, Charles Richard. 1857–1918. American geologist, b. Fulton, Wis. Professor (1883–1903), president (1903–18), U. of Wisconsin. On U.S. Geological Survey staff (from 1883); prepared monographs on Wisconsin geology, esp. covering iron-producing sections in Lake Superior region.

Van Horne \van-'hō(ə)rn, -'hó(ə)rn\, Sir William Cornelius. 1843–1915. Canadian railroad executive, b. near Joliet, Ill. General manager (1881–84), vice president (1884–88), president (1888–99), chairman (1899–1910), Canadian Pacific Railway, superintending its construction (1881–86) and the first years of its operation. Projected and constructed railroad in Cuba (1900–02) and in Guatemala (1903–08).

Va·ni·ni \vä-'nē-nē\, Lucilio. *Pseudonym* Giulio Cesare Vanini. 1584–1619. Italian philosopher. Ordained priest; expounded a materialistic pantheism in *Amphytheatrum aeternae providentiae* (1615) and *De admirandis naturae reginae deaeque mortalium arcanis* (1616); condemned and burned at the stake.

Van Loo *or* **Van·loo** \väⁿ-lō, *Du* vän-'lō\. Family of French painters of Dutch origin, including: Jakob *or* Jacques (c.1614–1670), moved from Amsterdam to Paris (1662) and achieved success as portraitist. His son ¶Abraham Louis, *known as* Louis (c.1656–1712), was noted for decorative paintings as in the chapel of the marine hospital, Toulon. Louis's son ¶Jean-Baptiste (1684–1745) was a portraitist in Savoy, Geneva, Turin, Rome, and Paris; known for portraits of the prince de Carignan, prince de Piémont, and many of Louis XV; also executed religious and mythological works as *Sainte Famille, Diane et Endymion.* His brother ¶Charles-André, *called* Carle (1705–1765), was noted Rococo portraitist in Paris; professor (1737), director (1763) of Academy; first painter to the king (1762); patronized by Mme de Pompadour; also painted genre scenes; noted for technical virtuosity; works included *Mariage de la Vierge, Apollon écorchant Marsyas, Un déjeuner de chasse.*

Van Loon \van-'lōn\, Hendrik Willem. 1882–1944. American historian and writer, b. Rotterdam, Netherlands. To U.S. (1902, naturalized 1919); journalist and lecturer. Wrote and illustrated *The Story of Mankind* (1921, Newbery medal), *The Story of the Bible* (1923), *America* (1927), *R.v.R., Life and Times of Rembrandt van Rijn* (1931), *Van Loon's Geography* (1932), *Ships* (1935), *Christmas Carols* (1937), *The Arts* (1937), *Van Loon's Lives* (1942), etc.

Van Nos·trand \van-'nōs-trənd\, David. 1811–1886. American publisher, b. New York City. Founded (c.1848) publishing house of Van Nostrand & Co.; specialized in scientific, technical, and military works.

Van·nuc·ci \vän-'nüt-chē\, Pietro di Cristoforo. *Known as* Pe·ru·gi·no \ˌper-ü-'jē-nō\. c.1450–1523. Italian painter, b. Città della Pieve, near Perugia. A master of early Renaissance; employed at Florence, Rome, Perugia; master of Raphael; executed best work from 1490 to 1500. Among his paintings were *Vision of St. Bernard, Madonna and Saints, Pietà, Francesco delle Opere* (portrait); frescoes *Giving of the Keys To St. Peter* (Sistine Chapel, 1481–82), *Crucifixion* (in Florence), and a cycle for Sala dell'Udienza (Perugia).

Vanolis, Bysshe. See James THOMSON (1834–1882).

Van Rensselaer, Kiliaen. See RENSSELAER.

Van Rens·se·laer \ˌvan-ˌren(t)-sə-'li(ə)r, -ˌren-'sli(ə)r, vən-; -'ren(t)-s(ə-)lər\, Mariana Alley, *nee* Griswold. 1851–1934. American art critic, b. New York City. m. Schuyler Van Rensselaer (1873; d. 1884). Author of *Book of American Figure Painters* (1886), *American Etchers* (1886), *English Cathedrals* (illustrated by Joseph Pennell, 1892), *Art Out of Doors* (1893), *History of the City of New York in the Seventeenth Century* (1909), *Poems* (1910), *Many Children* (1921), etc.

Van Rensselaer, Martha. 1864–1932. American home economist, b. Randolph, N.Y. On Cornell U. staff as organizer and director of extension courses for farm women (from 1900); lecturer (1907), professor (1911) of home economics, Cornell. Director, New York State College of Home Economics (1925).

Van Rensselaer, Stephen. 1764–1839. American army officer and politician, b. New York City. Inherited great Van Rensselaer estate in New York (1769); lieutenant governor of New York (1795–1801); major general of New York militia; in command (1812) of New York's northern frontier; attacked Queenstown, Canada, across Niagara River (Oct. 13, 1812) and met with disaster. Member, U.S. House of Representatives (1822–29). Member of first Erie canal commission (1810), and of second canal commission (1816–39), president (1825–39). Founded (1824) Rensselaer School, now Rensselaer Polytechnic Institute.

Vanrisemburgh, Bernard. See RISENBURGH.

Van·sit·tart \van-'sit-ərt, vən-\, Henry. 1732–1770. British colonial administrator. Governor of Bengal (1760–64); waged war on Mīr Qāsim (1763).

Vansittart, Sir Robert Gilbert. 1st Baron Vansittart of Den·ham \'den-əm\. 1881–1957. British diplomat. Descendant of Henry Vansittart; secretary to foreign secretary Curzon (1920–24); permanent undersecretary of state for foreign affairs (1930–38); chief diplomatic adviser to foreign secretary (1938–41); advocate of total permanent disarmament of Germany; created baron (1941). Author of novels, verse, plays including *Les Pariahs* (1902), *Dead Heat* (1939), *Shy at the Moon,* autobiography *The Mist Procession* (1958).

Van Swe·ring·en \van-'swir-iŋ-ən, -'swer-\, Oris Paxton (1879–1936) and his brother Mantis James (1881–1935). American railroad executives, b. Wooster, Ohio. Entered real estate business in Cleveland; developed (from 1905) suburb of Shaker Heights; acquired New York, Chicago and St. Louis Railroad ("Nickel Plate" line, 1916), Toledo, St. Louis and Western (1922), Chesapeake and Ohio (1922), Erie (1923), Pere Marquette (1923), Missouri Pacific (1930); created efficient integrated system of some 21,000 miles of rail; system broken up within a year after their deaths.

van't Hoff \vänt-'hóf\, Jacobus Hendricus. 1852–1911. Dutch physical chemist. Professor, Amsterdam (1878), Berlin (from 1896). Advanced (1874) theory of asymmetric carbon atom, laying foundation for stereochemistry; studied rates of reaction, osmotic pressure; propounded theory that dissolved substances obey the laws of gases; investigated the formation and decomposition of double salts, esp. those occurring at Stassfurt, Saxony. With Wilhelm Ostwald founded (1887) *Zeitschrift für physikalische Chemie;* author of *Études de dynamique chimique* (1884), etc. Awarded 1901 Nobel prize for chemistry.

Van Twil·ler \vant-'vil-ər, *Angl* van-'twil-ər\, Wouter. 1580?–?1656. Dutch administrator in America. Nephew of Kiliaen van Rensselaer; governor of New Netherland (1633–37).

Van Vech·ten \van-'vek-tən\, Carl. 1880–1964. American writer, b. Cedar Rapids, Iowa. On staff of *New York Times* (1906–13); author of *Music After the Great War* (1915), *In the Garret* (1920), *Peter Whiffle, His Life and Works* (1922), *The Blind Bow-Boy* (1923), *The Tattooed Countess* (1924), *Nigger Heaven* (1926), *Spider Boy* (1928), autobiography *Sacred and Profane Memories* (1932), etc.

Van·vi·tel·li \ˌvän-vē-'tel-lē\, Luigi. 1700–1773. Italian architect. Worked with Nicolo Salvi on modifications of Bernini's Palazzo Chigi; master of Late Baroque; works included Chiesa del Gésu (1743–45), Lazzaretto in Ancona, Chiesa dell'Annunciata in Naples (1756 or 1761–82), Carolino aqueduct (1752–64), and esp. the great Palace at Caserta, summer residence of Bourbon kings of Naples (1752–74).

Van Vleck \van-'vlek\, John Hasbrouck. 1899–1980. American physicist, b. Middletown, Conn. At Harvard U. (1934–69); awarded (with Philip W. Anderson and Sir Nevill F. Mott) Nobel prize for physics (1977) for studies of atomic structure and magnetism.

Vanzetti, Bartolomeo. See under Nicola SACCO.

Va·rā·ha·mi·hi·ra \və-ˌrä-hə-mē-'hē-rə\. *Also called* Va·ra·ha \və-'rä-hə\ *or* Mi·hi·ra \mē-'hē-rə\. 505–587. Indian philosopher, astronomer, and mathematician. Author of astronomical compendium *Pañca-siddhāntikā,* which summarized Egyptian, Greek, Roman, Indian knowledge; also wrote treatises on astrology, etc.

Varahran. See BAHRĀM.

Var·chi \'vär-kē\, Benedetto. 1503–1565. Italian scholar. Known esp. for *Storia fiorentina* (pub. 1721), a history of Florence in the period 1527–38 written for Cosimo I de' Medici.

Var·dha·mā·na \ˌvär-də-'män-ə\. *Known as* Ma·hā·vī·ra \mə-hä-'vē-rə\, *i.e.* Great Hero. c.599–527 B.C. Indian religious leader. Last of the 24 Tīrthankaras (prophets) of Jainism. Reared in luxury; married; renounced the world (569) and practiced asceticism; attained (557) *kevala-jñāna,* the highest knowledge. Basing his teachings on doctrines of the 23d Tīrthankara, Pārśvanātha, systematized Jaina doctrine and established rules for the Jaina *sangha* (religious order); preached nonviolence, austerity, vegetarianism, and acceptance of the "five great vows" of renunciation. Considered historical founder of Jainism.

Var·don \'värd-ᵊn\, Harry. 1870–1937. English golfer. Professional (from 1903); won British Open championship six times (1896, 1898, 1899, 1903, 1911, 1914), the U.S. Open (1900), and the German Open (1911); popularized Vardon overlapping grip. Vardon Trophy named for him.

Va·rè \vä-'re\, Daniele. 1880–1956. Italian diplomat and author. Minister to China; author of *The Maker of Heavenly Trousers* (1936), *Gate of Happy Sparrows* (1938), *Laughing Diplomat* (1938), *Temple of Costly Experience* (1940), *Two Impostors* (1949), *Ghosts of the Rialto* (1956), etc.

Va·ren \'fär-ən\, Bernhard. *Lat.* Bernhardus Va·re·ni·us \və-'rē-nē-əs, *Ger* vä-'rā-nē-ůs\. 1622–1650 or 1651. German geographer. Author of *Descriptio Regni Japoniae* (1649) and *Geographia Generalis* (his chief work, 1650).

Va·rèse \və-ˈräz, -ˈrez\, Edgard, *orig.* Edgar Victor Achille Charles. 1883–1965. American composer, b. Paris, France. Studied in Paris and Berlin with d'Indy, Widor, Busoni, etc.; to U.S. (1915); founder and director, International Composers' Guild (1921–27). Composed works in atonal, arhythmic, nonthematic style and pioneered in electronic music; works included *Hyperprism* (1923), *Intégrales* (1925), *Arcana* (1927), *Ionisation* (1931), *Density 21.5* (1935), *Déserts* (1954), *Poème électronique* (1958), *Nocturnal* (1961).

Var·gas \ˈvȧr-gəs\, Getúlio Dornelles. 1883–1954. Brazilian politician. Member of congress (1922–26); governor of Rio Grande do Sul (1928–30); led successful revolution against President Washington Luiz (1930); provisional president of Brazil (1930–34); president (1934–37); directed coup that eliminated constitutional government and ruled as dictator of "New State" (1937–45); overthrown (1945); senator (1945–50); again president (1951–54); suicide. Wrote political history of Brazil (1938).

Var·gas \ˈbär-gäs\, José Maria. 1786–1854. Venezuelan politician. Vice president (1834) and president (1835–36), Venezuela; senator (1838–46); councilor of state (1847–51). Resident in U.S. (from 1853).

Vargas, Luis de. c.1505–1567 or 1568. Spanish painter. Among his works were *Nascimiento* (Seville cathedral), *Generación temporal de Cristo,* popularly known as *La gamba* (Seville cathedral), *Crucifixion* (Seville cathedral), *Juicio final, Purificación.*

Var·i·an \ˈvar-ē-ən\, Russell Harrison. 1898–1959. American physicist, b. Washington, D.C. Known for research in microwaves and electronics; inventor, with his brother ¶Sigurd (1901–61), of the klystron UHF resonator (1939); research associate, Stanford U. (1937–40, 1946–59); engineer, Sperry Gyroscope Co. (1940–46); president (1948–56), chairman (1956–59), Varian Associates.

Var·i·us Ru·fus \ˈvar-ē-əs-ˈrü-fəs\, Lucius. 1st century B.C. Roman poet. Friend of Horace, Virgil, and Maecenas; author of tragedy *Thyestes* and two epics; commissioned by Emperor Augustus to edit Virgil's *Aeneid.* Only fragments of works extant.

Var·ley \ˈvär-lē\, John. 1778–1842. English painter and teacher. Known as landscapist; one of founders of Royal Society of Painters in Water Colours, where he exhibited (1805–42).

Varn·ha·gen von En·se \ˈfärn-hä-gən-fȯn-ˈen-zə\, Karl August. 1785–1858. German diplomat and writer. Entered Austrian army (1809) and Russian army (1813), and took part in War of Liberation; in Prussian diplomatic service (1814); resident, Karlsruhe (1815–19). Author of *Geschichte der Hamburger Ereignisse* (1813), *Geschichte der Kriegzüge des Generals von Tettenborn* (1815), *Biographische Denkmale* (1824–30), biographies of General Seydlitz (1834), field marshals Schwerin (1841) and Keith (1844), Queen Sophia Charlotte (1837), and others. His wife (m. 1814) ¶Rahel, *nee* Le·vin \ˈlā-ˌvēn, lā-ˈ\ (1771–1833) presided over a notable literary salon in Berlin.

Var·num \ˈvär-nəm\, James Mitchell. 1748–1789. American lawyer and Revolutionary officer, b. Dracut, Mass. Brigadier general, Continental army (1777); commanded defense of Forts Mercer and Mifflin on the Delaware River; commanded department of Rhode Island (1779). Member, Continental Congress (1780–82, 1786, 1787). U.S. judge, Northwest Territory (1787); aided in framing code of territorial laws. His brother ¶Joseph Bradley (1751–1821), b. Dracut, served in Massachusetts legislature (1780–95, 1817–21), U.S. House of Representatives (1795–1811; speaker 1807–11), U.S. Senate (1811–17).

Va·ro·lio \vä-ˈrōl-yō\, Costanzo. 1543–1575. Italian surgeon and anatomist. Professor, Bologna (1569–72); author of *De nervis opticis* (1573), in which he described the pons Varolii on undersurface of the brain.

Va·ro·ta·ri \ˌvä-rō-ˈtä-rē\, Alessandro. *Called* il Pa·do·va·ni·no \ēl-ˌpä-dō-vä-ˈnē-nō\. 1588–1648. Italian painter. Among his works were *Diana and Calisto, Minerva,* and *The Marriage at Cana.*

Var·ro \ˈvar-(ˌ)ō\, Gaius Terentius. 3d century B.C. Roman general and politician. Consul with Lucius Aemilius Paulus (216 B.C.); impatient with Fabian strategy, gave battle to Hannibal; defeated in battle of Cannae (216).

Varro, Marcus Terentius. 116–27 B.C. Roman scholar. Served with Pompey in Spain (76 B.C.); in civil war, joined Pompey, but after Pharsalus (48), was reconciled with Caesar and appointed director of the library Caesar planned to found; after Caesar's assassination, was proscribed by Second Triumvirate but his life was saved by his friends. Wrote on languages, religion, law, customs, political institutions, philosophy, geography; works included *Saturae Menippeae* (satires), *Trikaranos* (on First Triumvirate), *Antiquitates rerum humanarum et divinarum, De re rustica, De lingua Latina, Hebdomades vel de imaginibus, De poematis.*

Varro, Publius Terentius. *Surnamed* At·a·ci·nus \ˌat-ə-ˈsī-nəs\. 1st century B.C. Roman poet. Wrote satires, didactic verse, and an epic *Argonautica* or *Argonautae* adapted from Apollonius of Rhodes.

Var·the·ma \ˈvär-tā-mä\ *or* **Bar·the·ma** \ˈbär-tā-mä\, Lodovico de. *Lat.* Var·to·ma·nus \ˌvärt-ə-ˈmā-nəs\ *or* Ver·to·man·nus \ˌvərt-ə-ˈman-əs\. c.1470–after 1510. Italian traveler and writer. Traveled through Egypt, Syria (becoming first Christian known to have visited Mecca), Arabia, Persia, India, islands of Malay Archipelago, and as far east as the Moluccas (1502–07), returning home via Cape of Good Hope. Author of *Itinerario de Lodovico de Varthema Bolognese* (1510; 1st Eng. trans. 1576–77).

Var·us \ˈvar-əs\, Publius Quintilius. d. 9 A.D. Roman general. Consul (13 B.C.); governor of Syria (6–4 B.C.); commanded Roman army in Germany (6–9 A.D.); committed suicide when his army was destroyed by Germans under Arminius in battle of Teutoburger Wald.

Va·sa \ˈvä-ˌsȧ\. Name of dynasty of Swedish kings (1523–1818) derived from that of family estate in Uppland, region around Uppsala. Taken by Gustav Eriksson, king (1523–60) as Gustav I Vasa and founder of dynasty; his successors were: Eric XIV, John III, Sigismund, Charles IX, Gustav II Adolphus, and Christina (ruled 1632–54). Next four sovereigns of dynasty are sometimes termed the Palatinate branch (1654–1720) because Charles X Gustav, its first member, was son of count palatine of Zweibrücken and Catherine, sister of Gustav Adolphus; his successors were Charles XI, Charles XII, and Ulrika Eleonora. The Holstein-Gottorp line (1751–1818), following the reign of Frederick I, included Adolf Frederick, Gustav III, Gustav IV, Charles XIII. See individual biographies.

Members of Vasa family also held (1587–1668) Polish throne; see Sigismund III Vasa, Władysław IV Vasa, John II Casimir Vasa.

Va·sa·ri \vä-ˈzä-rē\, Giorgio. 1511–1574. Italian painter, architect, and art historian. Studied painting under Andrea del Sarto and Michelangelo; protégé of the Medici; paintings included Mannerist frescoes in Palazzo Vecchio, Florence, and Cancellaria, Rome; as architect designed Uffizi palace, Florence, church, monastery, and palace for the Cavalieri di S. Stefano, Pisa. Best known for his series of biographies of Italian artists from Cimabue to Michelangelo, *Vite de' più eccelenti architetti, pittori ed scultori italiani* (1550), chief source book for history of Italian Renaissance artists.

Vasco da Gama. See GAMA.

Vasconcelos, Jorge Ferreira de. See FERREIRA DE VASCONCELOS.

Vas·con·ce·los \bäs-kōn-ˈsā-lōs\, José. 1882–1959. Mexican politician, philosopher, and writer. Rector, U. of Mexico (1920 ff.); minister of public education (1920–24); unsuccessful candidate for presidency (1929); director of national library (1940); president, Instituto Mexicano de Cultura Hispánica (1948). Author of works on history, philosophy, literature, etc., as *El monismo estético* (1918), *La caída de Carranza* (1920), *La raza cósmica* (1925), *Bolivarismo y Monroismo* (1934); best known for autobiographical series *Ulises Criollo* (1935), *La tormenta* (1936), *El desastre* (1938), *El proconsulado* (1939), *La flama* (1959).

Vas·con·ce·los e Sou·sa \vash-kōⁿ(n)-ˈsā-lü-shā-ˈsō-zə\, Luis de. Conde de Cas·te·lo Me·lhor \kȧs-ˈtā-lü-ˈmel-yȯr\. 1636–1720. Portuguese courtier and politician. Royal favorite of Afonso VI; effective governor of Portugal; successfully prosecuted war with Spain (1662–67) leading to Portuguese independence (1668).

Va·sek \ˈvȧ-sek\, Vladimir. *Pseudonym* Petr Bez·ruč \ˈbez-rüts\. 1867–1958. Czech poet. Postal official in Moravia; author of series of vivid verse portrayals of scenes and people of his native Silesia, published (1899–1903) in periodical *Čas* and later collected in *Slezske pisne.*

Va·si·le \vä-ˈsē-le\. *Called* Vasile Lu·pu \-ˈlü-pü\, *i.e.* Basil the Wolf. 1595–1661. Prince of Moldavia (1634–53). Of Albanian origin; attempted unsuccessfully to seize Walachian throne (1637, 1639); promoted Greek monasticism, first codification of Moldavian law (1646); introduced first printing press; defeated by Matei Basarab of Transylvania and deposed by boyars (1653); died in prison in Istanbul.

Va·si·ly \(ˌ)vəs-ˈyēl-yəi\. Name of four Russian rulers:

Vasily I. *Russ.* Vasily Dmitriyevich. 1371–1425. Grand prince of Moscow (1389–1425). Son of Dmitry Donskoy; visited Tatar khan Tokhtamysh (1383) to secure patent for father to rule Russian lands as prince of Vladimir; held hostage (1383–86); led Muscovite contingent in Tokhtamysh's campaign against Timur Lenk (1388); succeeded father as grand prince (1389); annexed Nizhni Novgorod and Murom; clashed frequently with Novgorod; raised large army, turned back invasion by Timur Lenk (1395), obtaining effective independence from Tatars; reduced again to vassalage by khan Edigü (1408).

Vasily II. *Called* Tyom·ny \ˈtyȯm-nyəi\, *i.e.* the Blind. 1415–1462. Grand prince of Moscow (1425–62). Son of Vasily I; fought civil war (1425–47) to secure rule against rivals including uncle Yury, who briefly seized power (1434), and cousin Dmitry Shemyaka, who seized power (1446–47) and blinded him; fostered development of Muscovy into integrated, powerful state; absorbed Ryazan (1447), Vyatka (1460); defeated siege by Tatars (1451).

Vasily III. *Russ.* Vasily Ivanovich. 1479–1533. Grand prince of Moscow (1505–33). Son and successor of Ivan III; annexed Pskov (1510), Ryazan (1517), Starodub and Novgorod-Seversk (1523); captured Smolensk from Lithuania (1514); suffered defeats by Lithuanians and Tatars, but left strengthened state to son Ivan IV.

Vasily Shuy·sky \-ˈshü-is-kəi\. 1552–1612. Czar of Russia (1606–10). A boyar; conducted investigation of death of Dmitry Ivanovich, heir of Czar Fyodor I (1591); later reversed himself and supported first False Dmitry, (1605); reversed himself again, declared Dmitry an impostor; exiled; instigated boyar plot against Dmitry, assassinated him (1606); declared czar; suppressed rebellion of Cossacks and peasants (1607); with Swedish aid drove court of second False Dmitry from Tushino (1610); faced with Polish war and renewed strength of second False Dmitry, was deposed by Muscovites (1610).

Va·sil·yev \(,)vəs-ˈyēl-yəf\, Sergey Dmitriyevich. 1900–1959. Russian film maker. Known for documentary films, most made with Georgy Vasilyev (no relation), on Russian Civil War and Communist party, notably *Chapayev* (1934).

Vassa, Gustavus. See Olaudah EQUIANO.

Vas·sar \ˈvas-ər\, Matthew. 1792–1868. American merchant, b. Norfolk, England. To America (1796) and settled in Dutchess County, N.Y.; operated brewery in Poughkeepsie, N.Y.; founded (1861) and endowed at Poughkeepsie a college for women, later named Vassar College in his honor.

Va·su·ban·dhu \və-sü-ˈbən-dü\. 4th century A.D. Indian philosopher. Author of works of Buddhist philosophy; best known for contributions to classic Indian syllogistic logic.

Vat·tel \ˈfät-əl\, Emmerich von. 1714–1767. Swiss jurist. Entered Saxon service in Dresden (1743). Known for treatise of international law *Le Droit des gens* (1758).

Va·tu·tin \(,)və-ˈtü-tyin\, Nikolay Fyodorovich. 1900–1944. Russian army officer. Major general, commander in Ukraine (1936); colonel general, commander of southwestern front forces in Stalingrad victory (1942); commander of 1st Ukrainian army; took part in capture of Kharkov and Kiev (1943), liberated Ukraine, advanced into Poland (1943–44); retired for ill health.

Vau·ban \vō-bä^n\, Sébastien Le Pres·tre de \lə-pret(rᵊ)-də\. 1633–1707. French military engineer. Entered regiment of prince de Condé (1651); joined engineer corps (1655); engineer in chief at successful siege of Gravelines (1658); in subsequent wars of Louis XIV gained fame for devising tactics that led to capture of Tournai, Douai, and Lille (1667), Maastricht (1673), Valenciennes (1677), Luxembourg (1684), Philippsburg (1688), Mons (1691), Namur (1692), Charleroi (1693), Ath (1697), Alt-Breisach (1703); designed fortifications for Strasbourg (1681), Landau (1687), Neuf-Brisach (1698–1701); marshal of France (1703). Invented socket bayonet. Author of important treatises on fortification and siegecraft as *De l'attaque et de la défense des places* (1737).

Vau·can·son \vō-kä^n-sō^n\, Jacques de. 1709–1782. French inventor. Built many automata as "The Flute Player" and "The Duck"; made (from 1741) many improvements in silk-weaving machinery, esp. the automated loom perfected by J.-M. Jacquard.

Vau·cher \vō-shā\, Jean Pierre Étienne. 1763–1841. Swiss botanist. Clergyman; honorary professor of botany (1798–1807), professor of ecclesiastical history (1807–39), Geneva; credited with discovery of conjugation and spore formation in algae.

Vau·dreuil \vō-drœy\, Philippe de Ri·gaud de \də-rē-gō-də-\. Marquis. 1643–1725. French soldier and colonialist. To Canada (1687); governor of New France (1703–25). His son ¶Pierre de Rigaud, *often surnamed* de Ca·va·gnal \kȧ-vȧn-yȧl\ (1698–1778), entered army in New France; governor of Trois Rivières (1733); governor of Louisiana (1742–53), of New France (1755–60); forced to capitulate to British (1760); imprisoned France (1760–62).

Vaugelas, Seigneur de. See Claude FAVRE.

Vaughan \ˈvȯn, ˈvän\, Henry. *Sometimes called* the Silurist *as native of South Wales.* 1621?–1695. British mystic poet. Practiced medicine in South Wales. Author of sacred poems *Silex Scintillans* (first part 1650, second 1655); secular verse *Poems, with the tenth Satyre of Juvenal Englished* (1646), *Olor Iscanus* (1651), *Thalia Rediviva* (1678); prose works *Mount of Olives* (1652), *Flores Solitudinis* (1654); translations. His twin brother ¶Thomas (1621?–1666) was ordained but later evicted from his living (1650) on sundry charges; conducted chemical experiments informed by his Neoplatonic and Theosophical inclinations and wrote treatises notorious for obscurity as *Anthroposophia theomagica* (1650), *Anima magica abscondita* (1650), *Lumen de lumine* (1651).

Vaughan, Herbert Alfred. 1832–1903. English prelate. Bishop of Salford (1872–92); archbishop of Westminster (1892–1903); cardinal (1893); active in social and educational programs; largely responsible for passage of Education Act (1902) whereby British denominational schools became state-supported; built Westminster cathedral. His brother ¶Roger William Bede (1834–1883) entered Benedictine order (1854); archbishop of Sydney, Australia (1877–83); biographer of Thomas Aquinas.

Vaughan Wil·liams \ˈvȯn-ˈwil-yəmz, ˈvän-\, Ralph. 1872–1958. English composer. Considered founder of nationalist school in England; collected English folk songs (from 1903); edited *The English Hymnal* (1906), to which he contributed "Sine Nomine"; principal conductor of Leith Hill Musical Festival (1905–53); professor, Royal College of Music (from 1919); conductor of the Bach Choir (1920–28). Works included theatrical works as *Shepherds of the Delectable Mountains* (1921), *Hugh the Drover* (1924), *Sir John in Love* (1929), *The Poisoned Kiss* (1936), *Riders to the Sea* (1937), *Pilgrim's Progress* (1951); orchestral works including 9 symphonies, esp. *Sea Symphony* (1910), *London Symphony* (1914), *Pastoral* (1922), *Sinfonia Antarctica* (7th, 1953), Ninth (1958), also 3 *Norfolk Rhapsodies* (1905–06), *Fantasia on a Theme by Thomas Tallis* (1910), *Lark Ascending* (1914), *Fantasia on Greensleeves* (1934), *Romance* for harmonica and orchestra (1952); vocal and choral works as *5 Mystical Songs* (1911), *On Wenlock Edge* (1923), *Flos campi* (1925), *Sancta Civitas* (oratorio, 1926), *Dona nobis pacem* (1936), *Oxford Elegy* (1947–49); many carols, hymns, songs, and arrangements of folk songs.

Vau·que·lin \vō-kla^n\, Louis-Nicolas. 1763–1829. French chemist. Assistant to Fourcroy (1783–91), and succeeded him on the faculty of medicine, Paris (1809); deputy (1827). Discovered chromium (1797), beryllium (1798); also discovered quinic acid, camphoric acid, and, with P. J. Robiquet, asparagine.

Vauquelin de La Fres·naye \-dlȧ-frā-ne, -fre-\, Jean. Sieur des Yve·teaux \dā-zēv-tō\. 1536–1606 to 1608. French poet. Admirer of Ronsard; promoted classicism and introduced the genre of satire into French literature. Works included *Foresteries* (1555), *Idillies et pastorales* (c.1560), five books of *Satires* (1581–85), *L'Art poétique* (1605).

Vau·tier \vōt-yā\, Benjamin. 1829–1898. Swiss painter and illustrator. Known for genre scenes of the life of the Swiss and Black Forest peasants.

Vau·ve·nargues \vōv-nȧrg\, Luc de Cla·piers de \də-klȧp-yā-də-\. Marquis. 1715–1747. French soldier and moralist. In army (1733–44), seeking fulfillment in heroic action. Remembered for his *Introduction à la connaissance de l'esprit humain,* with appended *Réflexions* and *Maximes* (1746), in which he anticipated both Rousseau and Stendhal in view of man.

Vaux \ˈvȯz, ˈväks, ˈvȯks, ˈvōks\, Calvert. 1824–1895. American landscape architect, b. London, England. To U.S. (1850); assisted Andrew Jackson Downing (1850–52) with U.S. Capitol grounds, and Frederick Law Olmsted with Central Park, Riverside Park in New York City, Prospect Park, Brooklyn, South Park, Chicago, etc.

Vaux, Thomas. 2d Baron Vaux of Har·row·den \ˈhar-ə-dən\. 1510–1556. English poet. Captain of Isle of Jersey (1533–36). Emulator of Wyatt and Surrey and contributor of 2 poems to *Tottel's Miscellany* (1557) and 13 poems of chivalric love and religious poems to popular anthology *The Paradyse of daynty deuises* (1576).

Va·vi·lov \(,)vəv-ˈyē-ləf\, Nikolay Ivanovich. 1887–1943. Russian geneticist. Professor, Saratov (1917–21); director, Bureau of Applied Botany, Petrograd (now Leningrad); collected thousands of wild plant specimens; propounded theory that geographical region of greatest diversity of a plant species is region of species's origin; denounced by T.D. Lysenko (1934–39); imprisoned (from 1940).

Va·zov \ˈvȧ-zȯf\, Ivan Minchov. 1850–1921. Bulgarian poet and novelist. Civil servant and district judge; contributed to and edited literary journals. Author of novels as *Pod igoto* (1894), *Nova zemya* (1896), *Kazalarskata tsaritsa* (1903); stories *Razkazi* (1891), *Draski i sharki* (1893–95); verse *Pryaporets i gusla* (1876), *Izbavlenie* (1878), *Slivnitsa* (1886), *Zvukove* (1893), *Legendi pri Tsarevets* (1910), *Novi ekove* (1917); plays *Ruska* (1883), *Hushove* (1894), *Borislav* (1909), *Kum propast* (1910); memoirs, travel books, etc.

Vázquez de Ayllón, Lucas. See AYLLÓN.

Veb·len \ˈveb-lən\, Oswald. 1880–1960. American mathematician, b. Decorah, Iowa. Nephew of Thorstein Veblen. Professor, Princeton U. (1905–32), Institute for Advanced Study (1932–50); made major contributions to projective geometry, differential geometry, relativity; laid foundation of modern topology. Author of *Projective Geometry* (1910–18, with J.W. Young), *Analysis Situs* (1922), *Invariants of Quadratic Differential Forms* (1927), *Foundations of Differential Geometry* (1932, with J.H.C. Whitehead).

Veblen, Thorstein Bunde. 1857–1929. American economist, b. Manitowoc Co., Wis. On teaching staff, U. of Chicago (1892–1906), Stanford (1906–09), U. of Missouri (1911–18), New School for Social Research, New York City (1919–26). Noted for trenchant social criticisms. Author of *The Theory of the Leisure Class* (1899), *The Theory of Business Enterprise* (1904), *The Instinct of Workmanship* (1914), *Imperial Germany and the Industrial Revolution* (1915), *The Higher Learning in America* (1918), *The Vested Interests and the State of the Industrial Arts* (1919), *Absentee Ownership and Business Enterprise in Recent Times* (1923), etc.

Vec·chi \ˈvek-kē\, Orazio Tiberio. 1550–1605. Italian composer. Maestro di capella, Modena (1593–1604); known for canzonets and madrigal-comedies, esp. *L'Amfiparnasso* (1594).

Vecchio, Palma. See Jacopo PALMA.

Ve·cel·li \vā-'chel-lē\ *or* **Ve·cel·lio** \-lyō\, Tiziano. *Known as* Ti·tian \'tish-ən\. 1488 or 1490–1576. Italian painter. Pupil of Giovanni Bellini in Venice; collaborated with and influenced by Giorgione (to 1510); gained international fame; received patronage from Pope Paul III, Emperor Charles V, Philip II of Spain, Alfonso I d'Este, Farnese family, etc.; met Michelangelo and other painters in Rome (1545–46); resided chiefly in Venice. One of greatest painters in history; chief master of Venetian school; known esp. for his handling of color and depiction of human character. His works included religious pictures as *Assumption* (1516–18), *Pesaro Madonna* (1519–26), *Entombment* (1526–32), *Christ Before Pilate* (1543), *Pietà* (1576); mythological pictures as *Bacchus and Ariadne* (1520–23), *Venus of Urbino* (1538–39), *Danae with Nursemaid* (1553–54), *Perseus and Andromeda* (1554–56), *The Rape of Europa* (1559–62); and portraits as *The Vendramin Family* (1543–47), *Paul III and His Grandsons Ottavio and Cardinal Alessandro Farnese* (1546), *Emperor Charles V at Mühlberg* (1548), *Philip II* (1550–51), *Triple Portrait Mask* (c.1570).

Ve·dān·ta·de·śi·ka \vā-'dän-tə-'dā-shi-kə\. *Also called* Ven·ka·ṭa·nā·tha \,ven-kə-tə-'nä-tə\. 1268–1370. Indian theologian. By his interpretation of surrender to divine grace, became founder of Vaḍakalai subsect of Śrivaiṣṇava Hinduism; prolific author in Sanskrit and Tamil of verse, devotional works, scriptural commentaries, philosophical treatises.

Ved·der \'ved-ər\, Elihu. 1836–1923. American painter and illustrator, b. New York City. Studio in Rome (from 1866); known esp. for paintings drawn from dreams and fantasy as *Lair of the Sea Serpent, The Lost Mind;* executed *Minerva* and accompanying murals for Library of Congress, Washington, D.C. (1896–97); illustrated edition (1884) of *Rubáiyát of Omar Khayyám.*

Ve·del \'vā-dəl\, Anders Sørensen. 1542–1616. Danish historian. Published Danish translation (1575) of *Gesta Danorum* of Saxo Grammaticus; collected 100 medieval Danish ballads in *Et Hundrede Udvalgte Danske Viser* (1591).

Veen \'vān\, Otto van. *Lat.* Octavius Vae·ni·us \'vā-nē-əs, 'vī-\ *or* Ve·ni·us \'vā-\. 1556–1629. Dutch painter. Teacher of Rubens; known for religious and historical works.

Vefik Paşa. See Ahmed Vefik Paşa.

Vega, Garcilaso de la. See Garcilaso de la Vega.

Ve·ga \'bā-gä\, Lope de. *In full* Lope Félix de Vega Car·pio \'kär-pyō\. *Called* el Fé·nix \el-'fā-niks\, *i.e.* the Phoenix. 1562–1635. Spanish dramatic poet and founder of the Spanish national drama. Led adventurous early life; banished from Castile (1588) for libel resulting from scandalous love affair; served in Spanish Armada (1588); secretary to Duke of Alba at Alba de Tormes (1590–95); returned to Madrid (1596); in service of various nobles, esp. as confidential secretary to Duke of Sessa (1605–35); lived in Toledo (1605–10), Madrid (from 1610). Entered Franciscan order (1611) and ordained priest (1614) after death of second wife; apostolic prothonotary (1616); doctor of theology (1627). Reputed author of about 1800 plays and several hundred *autos* and *entremeses,* of which 426 plays and 42 *autos* are extant; developed comic character called the *gracioso.* Works included plays *El castigo sin venganza, Porfiar hasta morir, La estrella de Sevilla, El mejor alcalde el rey, El acero de Madrid, La noche toledana, El perro del hortelano, El hermano honrado, Juana de Napoles, Si no vieran las mujeres, El príncipe perfecto, Los tellos de meneses, La boba para otros y discreta para sí, La fuente ovejuna;* poems as *La dragontea* (epic attacking Sir Francis Drake, 1598), *El Isidro* (1599), *La hermosura de Angélica* (1602), *Rimas* (sonnets, 1602), *Jerusalén conquistada* (epic after Tasso, 1609), *Arte nuevo de hacer comedias en este tiempo* (1609), *Corona trágica* (1627), *La gatomaquia* (1634); the prose-verse pastoral *Arcadia* (1598); prose romances as *El peregrino en su patria* (1604) and *La Dorotea* (1632); and prose tales as *Guzmán el bravo* and *La desdicha por la honra.*

Vega y Vargas, Sebastián Garcilasco de la. See under Garcilaso de la Vega (1539–1616).

Ve·ge·ti·us \və-'jē-sh(ē-)əs\. *In full* Flavius Vegetius Re·na·tus \rə-'nāt-əs\. 4th century A.D. Roman writer. Author of a treatise on military science *Epitoma rei militaris* or *Rei militaris instituta,* that was highly influential in Middle Ages and later.

Ve·gio \'vā-jō\, Maffeo. *Lat.* Mapheus Ve·gi·us \'vē-jē-əs, 'vā-\. 1407–1458. Italian Humanist. In papal service (from 1435); author of important pedagogical work *De educatione liberorum et eorum claris moribus* (pub. 1491); also wrote epics *Velleris aurei* (1431) and *Antoniados* (1437), the *De rebus antiquis memorabilibus Basilicae S. Petri* (1448), etc.

Vein·te·mil·la \be-ēn-tā-'mē-yä\, José Ignacio de. 1830–1909. Ecuadorian general. Minister of war (1865–67); exiled (1869–75); led revolt that overthrew Pres. Borrero; provisional president (1876–78); elected president (1878–83); abolished concordat with church of Rome (1878); deposed (1883) during a civil war and exiled.

Veit \'fīt\, Philipp. 1793–1877. German painter. Grandson of Moses Mendelssohn and son of Dorothea Schlegel; converted to Catholicism (1810). A founder and member of the Nazarenes, Rome (1815–30); director of the Städel Art Institute, Frankfurt am Main (1830–43). Works included *Triumph of Religion, Immaculate Conception, Two Marys at the Sepulcher,* murals for Mainz cathedral, portraits, etc.

Ve·la \'vā-lä\, Vincenzo. 1820–1891. Italian sculptor. Among his works were *Spartacus,* decorative figures for the tomb of Donizetti, *Primavera, Dying Napoleon,* and statues of Charles Albert and Cavour.

Ve·las·co \bā-'läs-kō\, Luis de. 1511–1564. Spanish administrator. Viceroy of Navarre (1547–48); viceroy of Mexico (1550–64); emancipated great numbers of native Indians; founded U. of Mexico (1553); equipped Legazpe's expedition to Philippines. His son ¶Luis, marqués de Sa·li·nas \sä-'lē-näs\ (1539–1616), was viceroy of Mexico (1590–95, 1607–11) and of Peru (1596–1604).

Ve·las·co Al·va·ra·do \bā-'läs-kō-äl-bä-'rä-thō\, Juan. 1910–1977. Peruvian soldier and politician. General of division (1965); led coup against Pres. Belaúnde Terry (1968); president (1968–75); nationalized utilities and instituted extensive agrarian reforms; overthrown by military coup.

Ve·láz·quez \bā-'läth-kāth, -'läs-käs\, Diego. *Full surname* Velázquez de Cuél·lar \-thā-'kwā(l)-yär\. 1465–1524. Spanish soldier and administrator. To Hispaniola with Columbus (1493); sent to conquer Cuba (1511); governor of Cuba (1511–24); founded Santiago and Havana (1514). Sent out expeditions under Córdoba (1517), Grijalba (1518), and Cortés (1519). Ordered Cortés to return (1520); on his refusal sent Narváez to arrest him.

Ve·láz·quez \bā-'läth-kāth\, Diego Ro·drí·guez de Sil·va \rō-'thrē-gāth-thā-'sēl-bä\. 1599–1660. Spanish painter. Student and later son-in-law of Francisco Pacheco; attained fame with religious works and genre works in new *bodegón* manner; to Madrid (1622); appointed court painter (1623); visited Italy (1629–31, 1649–51); chamberlain of king's household (1652 ff.). Early painted in highly naturalistic style; later developed mastery of color and brushwork and anticipated Impressionism in rendering of light. Paintings included *Almuerzos, Trio musical, El aguador de Sevilla, La cena en Emaús, Vieja friendo huevos, Cristo en casa de Marta y María, Los borrachos, La fragua de Vulcano, La túnica de José, Dama del abanico, La rendición de Breda, Venus del espejo* (or *Rokeby Venus*); portraits of Philip IV, Infanta Margarita, Infanta María, Olivares, Marianna of Austria, Duke of Modena, Innocent X, court jesters, dwarfs, idiots, and beggars; equestrian portraits of Philip IV, the queen, Prince Balthazar, and Olivares.

Vel·de, van de \vän-də-'vel-də\. A family of Dutch painters, including: Esaias (1591?–1630), painter of landscapes and of military and carnival scenes; a founder of 17th century realist school with simplified compositions and reduced palette. His brother ¶Willem (1611–1693), draftsman and painter, esp. of marines and naval battles, resident in London (from 1673) as court painter. Their cousin ¶Jan (1593–1641) painted portraits, landscapes, historical and genre scenes. Willem's son ¶Willem (1633–1707) painted marines and Anglo-Dutch sea battles; resident in London (from 1673) as court painter. A second son ¶Adriaen (1636–1672) painted landscapes with animals and figures and mythological and biblical scenes.

Vel·de \'vel-də\, Henry Clemens van de. 1863–1957. Belgian architect and craftsman. An originator of Art Nouveau style (Jugendstil); follower of Ruskin and William Morris in Arts and Crafts movement; a founder of Werkbund movement in Germany (from 1907); director of Kunstgewerbeschule, Weimar (1902–14); works included residences, design of Werkbund theater in Cologne (1914), Museum Kröller-Müller in Otterloo (1937–54), university library in Ghent (1935–40). Author of *Vom neuen Stil* (1907), *Amo* (1910), *Les Formules d'une esthétique moderne* (1925), *Le nouveau style* (1931), etc.

Veldeke, Heinrich von. See Heinrich von Veldeke.

Vé·lez de Gue·va·ra \'bā-läth-thā-gā-'bä-rä\, Luis. 1579–1644. Spanish writer. Soldier; held various posts in household of Philip IV. Author of reputed 400 plays in manner of Lope de Vega, including *Reinar después de morir, La serrana de la Vera, El diablo está en Cantillana, La niña de Gómez Arias, Los hijos de la Barbuda, El conde Don Sancho Niño;* best known for fantastic novel *El diablo cojuelo* (1641), source of Alain Lesage's *Le Diable boiteux* (1707).

Vel·le·ius Pa·ter·cu·lus \və-'lē-(y)əs-pə-'tər-kyə-ləs\, Marcus. c.19 B.C.–after 30 A.D. Roman soldier and historian. Wrote a compendium of Roman history down to 29 A.D.

Venantius Fortunatus. See Fortunatus.

Ven·dôme \vän-dōm\. Family of French nobility, holding countship of Vendôme from about 10th century. Vendôme made duchy (1515) by Francis I and bestowed on Charles de Bourbon; Charles's son Anthony de Bourbon married Jeanne of Navarre and was father of Henry IV of France, who granted duchy to his natural son César de Bourbon. See Bourbon.

Venette, Jean de. See Jean de Venette.

Veneziano, Domenico. See Domenico Veneziano.

Ven·ing Mei·nesz \'ven-iŋ-'mā-nəs\, Felix Andries. 1887–1966. Dutch geophysicist. Professor, Delft Technical U. (1938–57); devised mechanical and mathematical means for measuring precisely the strength of gravity at points on the earth; made numerous submarine cruises in North Sea, Atlantic, Pacific, in East Indies, to measure gravity; studied convection currents in the Earth, deformation of Earth's crust by solar movements.

Ve·ni·zé·los \ˌven-yə-ˈzel-ōs\, Eleuthérios. 1864–1936. Greek politician, b. Crete. Member of Cretan assembly (1887 ff.); led unsuccessful insurrection against Turkish rule (1897); minister of justice (1899–1901); led insurrection against Prince George (1905); alternately head of government and of opposition (1905–09). Called to Athens as political adviser (1909) and effected peaceable settlement between king and Military League; appointed premier of Greece (Oct. 1910). Instrumental in organizing Balkan League (1912) and after First Balkan War (1912) in forming alliance against Bulgaria which participated in Second Balkan War (1913); gained southern Macedonia, South Ipiros, Crete, Aegean Islands for Greece. During World War I, vigorously championed cause of Allied Powers; when opposed by the pro-German king resigned premiership (Mar. 1915). Aided Koundouriotes in establishing provisional government at Salonika (1916); forced abdication of King Constantine (1917); formed a ministry (June 1917) and took Greece into the war on the side of the Allies. Successful in safeguarding Greek interests at Peace Conference in Paris (1919). Defeated by royalist coalition in election (1920); held premiership again for short time (1924); after establishment of republic, again premier of Greece (1928–32, 1933). Leader of opposition (from 1933); instigated unsuccessful military and naval revolt (March 1935); forced into exile.

Venn \ˈven\, John. 1834–1923. English logician and man of letters. Teacher of logic at Cambridge (from 1862); author of *The Logic of Chance* (1866), *Symbolic Logic* (1881), and *The Principles of Empirical Logic* (1889).

Venosta, Emilio Visconti-. See VISCONTI-VENOSTA.

Ven·tid·i·us \ven-ˈtid-ē-əs\, Publius. c.91–after 38 B.C. Roman general and politician. Captured by Strabo during revolt of Rome's Italian allies (90–88); later freed; assisted Julius Caesar in civil war; entered Senate under Caesar's sponsorship, named praetor (44); joined Mark Antony, who made him consul; defeated Parthians (39 and 38). His rise from captive to general often cited by authors as example of change of fortune.

Ven·tris \ˈven-trəs\, Michael George Francis. 1922–1956. English architect and cryptographer. Known for success in deciphering Minoan Linear B script (1952) and demonstrating that it is Greek in oldest known form; author of *Documents in Mycenaean Greek* (1956, with John Chadwick).

Ven·tu·ri \vän-ˈtü-rē\, Adolfo. 1856–1941. Italian art historian. Director of Galleria Estense, Modena (1878–88); chief inspector of fine arts (1888–98) and professor (1898–1931), Rome. Author of *Storia dell'arte italiana* (25 vols., 1901–40; unfinished).

Venturi, Giovanni Battista. 1746–1822. Italian physicist. Credited with first observing the phenomenon upon which the operation of the Venturi tube (later invented by Clemens Herschel) depends.

Ve·ra·ci·ni \ˌvā-rä-ˈchē-nē\, Francesco Maria. 1690–1768. Italian violinist, and composer. In service of Dresden court (1716–22); mainly in London (1733–45); in Florence (from 1745). A celebrated virtuoso; composed 4 operas, 9 oratorios, 4 sets of 12 violin sonatas, concertos, etc.

Veragua, Duke of. See Luis Columbus under Christopher COLUMBUS.

Ver·biest \vər-ˈbēst\, Ferdinand. *Known in China as* Nan Huai-jen \ˈnän-ˈhwī-ˈzhən\. 1623–1688. Flemish missionary and astronomer. Entered Jesuit order (1641); to China, where he succeeded Adam Schall von Bell as head of imperial astronomical bureau, Peking (1669); instrumental in determining boundary between China and Russia.

Ver·cel \ver-sel\, Roger. 1894–1957. French novelist. Author of *Notre père Trajan* (1930), *Au large de l'Eden* (1932), *Capitaine Gonan* (1934, Goncourt prize), *Léna* (1936), *La Hourie* (1942), *Rafales* (1946), *Au bout du môle* (1960), etc.

Ver·cin·get·o·rix \ˌvər-sən-ˈjet-ə-riks\. d. 46 B.C. Gallic chief of the Arverni. Leader of rebellion which initiated Gallic War; after preliminary successes, was besieged by Caesar in Alesia and forced to surrender (52 B.C.); taken to Rome and exhibited in Caesar's triumph (46), then executed.

Ver·da·guer \ˌver-t͟hə-ˈger\, Mossèn Jacint. 1845–1902. Catalan poet. Author of epics *L'Atlàntida* (1877), *Canigó* (1886), lyrics drawing on folkloric or mystical inspiration as *Idillis i cants místics* (1879), *Lo somni de Sant Joan* (1887), *Roser de tot l'any* (1894), *Flors de Calvari* (1896), *Flors de Maria* (1902).

Ver·de \ˈver-dā\, Cesário, *in full* José Joaquim Cesário. 1855–1886. Portuguese poet. Author of colloquial, unsentimental lyrics of everyday life that rescued Portuguese poetry from pretentious rhetoric; works published posthumously as *O livro de Cesário Verde* (1887).

Ver·di \ˈvār-dē, *Angl* ˈve(ə)rd-ē\, Giuseppe Fortunino Francesco. 1813–1901. Italian composer. Made first impression with opera *Oberto,* produced at La Scala, Milan (1839); followed with *Nabucodonosor* (known as *Nabucco,* 1842), *I lombardi* (1843), *Ernani* (1844), *I due Foscari* (1844), *Giovanna d'Arco* (1845), *Macbeth* (1847), *I masnadieri* (1847), *Jérusalem* (1847), *Il corsaro* (1848), *La battaglia di Legnano* (1849), *Luisa Miller* (1849), *Stiffelio* (1850); began development of more unified dramatic presentation in *Rigoletto* (1851), *Il trovatore* (1852), *La traviata* (1853), *Les Vêpres siciliennes* (1855), *Simone Boccanegra* (1857), *Un ballo in maschera* (1859), *La forza del destino* (1862), *Don Carlos* (1867), *Aïda* (1871); aided by libretti by Arrigo Boito, produced his tragic and comic masterpieces *Otello* (1887) and *Falstaff* (1893). Credited, with Richard Wagner, with developing opera into a fully integrated art form, the *dramma per musica.* Other works included *Messa da requiem* (1874), *Ave Maria* (1889), *Te Deum* (1896), *Stabat Mater* (1897), etc.

Vere, de \də-ˈvi(ə)r\. Family name of the earls of Ox·ford \ˈäks-fərd\ (1st creation, 1142–1703), including: Robert (1170?–1221), 3d earl, one of the 25 executors of Magna Carta. ¶Robert (1362–1392), 9th earl, bosom friend of Richard II; created marquis of Dublin (1385) and duke of Ireland (1386) with viceregal powers; accused (1387) of treason by Thomas of Woodstock, Duke of Gloucester, at a time when the young king's authority had been suspended; escaped with Richard's connivance, fled northward, raised an army, and marched toward London; deserted by his troops and routed by enemy lords at Radcot Bridge; escaped to Continent; attainted (1388); killed in a boar hunt. ¶John (1442–1513), 13th earl, a Lancastrian; aided in restoration of Henry VI (1470); made constable of England; escaped from Barnet field to France (1471); after unsuccessful invasion was imprisoned (1473–84); fought for Henry Tudor (Henry VII) at Bosworth (1485) and was restored to his title, estates, and hereditary chamberlainship; led van of royal army at Stoke (1487); commanded expedition in Picardy (1492); defeated Cornish rebels (1497). ¶Edward (1550–1604), 17th earl, *known as* Lord Bul·beck \ˈbu̇l-ˌbek\ (until 1562); courtier and lyric poet; ward of Lord Burghley; angered Queen Elizabeth by dueling and by insulting Sir Philip Sidney (1579); ran through his estates; sat as judge in trial of Mary, Queen of Scots; fought against Spanish Armada (1588). Patron of writers and (from 1580) of dramatic company Oxford's Men (formerly patronized by Earl of Warwick); held by so-called Oxfordian school to have been author of Shakespeare's dramatic works.

Vere, Aubrey Thomas de. See DE VERE.

Vere \ˈvi(ə)r\, Sir Francis. 1560–1609. English soldier. Grandson of John de Vere, 15th Earl of Oxford. In command of English troops in Low Countries (1589); served in Cádiz expedition (1596); aided in victory at Turnhout (1598), Nieuport (1600), and defense of Ostend (1601–02). His brother ¶Sir Horace (1565–1635), Baron Vere of Tilbury, took over command from Sir Francis (1604); in Thirty Years' War was forced to surrender at Mannheim to Tilly (1622).

Ver·e·ker \ˈver-ə-kər\, John Standish Surtees Prendergast. 6th Viscount Gort \ˈgȯ(ə)rt\. 1886–1946. British soldier. Entered army (1905); in France and Netherlands (1914–18); chief of imperial general staff (1937–39); general (1937); commander in chief of British Expeditionary Force in France and Belgium (1939–40); relieved during evacuation of Dunkirk (1940); inspector general (1940–41); governor and commander in chief of Gibraltar (1941–42), Malta (1942–44); field marshal (1943); high commissioner of Palestine and Trans-Jordan (1944–45).

Vérendrye, Sieur de La. See LA VÉRENDRYE.

Ve·re·shcha·gin \vyir-yish-ˈchäg-yin\, Vasily Vasilyevich. 1842–1904. Russian painter. Served in the Caucasus and in Russo–Turkish War (1877–78). Among his paintings were cycles from history of India, from the Russian campaign in Turkestan, and from the Russo–Turkish War. Sailed with the Russian fleet (1904) against Japan and was killed in explosion of battleship *Petropavlovsk* in harbor of Port Arthur.

Ver·ga \ˈvār-gä\, Giovanni. 1840–1922. Italian novelist. With Capuana, leader of *verismo* school of realists; known particularly for portrayals of Sicilian life and customs. Among his works were novels *I carbonari della Montagna* (1861–62), *Eva* (1873), *Tigre reale* (1873), *Eros* (1875), *I malavoglia* (1881), *Mastro-don Gesualdo* (1889), *Pane Nero* (1902); short stories collected in *Vita dei campi* (1880), *Novelle rusticane* (1883); play *Cavalleria rusticana* (1884, based on one of his stories; source of Mascagni's opera).

Vergara, Prince of. See Baldomero ESPARTERO.

Ver·gennes \ver-zhen\, Charles Gra·vier de \gräv-yā-də-\. Comte. 1719–1787. French statesman. Ambassador to Turkey (1754–68), Sweden (1771–74), aiding Gustav III in his coup d'état (1772); minister of foreign affairs under Louis XVI (1774–87); advocated anti-British policies, esp. financial and ultimately military and naval support of American colonies in their War of Independence; formed offensive and defensive alliance with new republic (1778); negotiated Treaty of Paris (1783).

Vergil. See VIRGIL.

Ver·gi·lio \ver-ˈjēl-yō\, Polidoro. *Eng.* Polydore Ver·gil \ˈvər-jəl\. c.1470–1555. Italian ecclesiastic and Humanist. Sent by Pope Alexander VI to England as subcollector of Peter's pence (1502–15); archdeacon of Wells (1508); returned to Italy (1550). Edited Gildas (1525); author of *Proverbiorum libellus,* known as *Adagio* (1498), *De rerum inventoribus* (1499), and esp. *Anglicae historiae* *libri XXVI,* an accurate history in elegant Latin, esp. valuable for Henry VII's reign, but with strong bias against Wolsey (first ed. 1534; full text pub. 1651).

Ver·gin·i·us Ru·fus \(ˌ)vər-ˈjin-ē-əs-ˈrü-fəs\, Lucius. 15–97 A.D. Roman soldier. Several times consul; as military governor of Upper Germany, put down rebellion of Gallic governor Vindex (68); declined nomination by his troops to succeed Nero as emperor (68) and relieved of command by Galba; again offered throne by troops after suicide of Otho (69) and again declined.

Ver·gniaud \vern-yō\, Pierre-Victurnien. 1753–1793. French politician. Advocate in parlement of Bordeaux (1781); president of the Legislative Assembly (1791); member of the National Convention, a leader of the Girondists; renowned for his oratory; guillotined.

Ver·hae·ren \vər-ˈhä-rən\, Émile. 1855–1916. Belgian poet. One of the editors of *La Jeune Belgique;* considered leading Belgian poet in French for his lyrical Symbolist verse celebrating Flanders, domestic love, human energy. Author of *Les Flamandes* (1883), *Les Moines* (1886), *Les Soirs* (1887), *Les Débâcles* (1888), *Les Flambeaux noirs* (1890), *Au bord de la route* (1891), *Les Apparus dans mes chemins* (1891), *Les Campagnes hallucinées* (1893), *Les Heures claires* (1896), *Les Visages de la vie* (1899), *Les Forces tumultueuses* (1902), *Tendresses premières* (1904), *La Multiple Splendeur* (1906), *Les Rythmes souverains* (1910), *Les Blés mouvants* (1912); verse plays as *Les Aubes* (1898), *Le Cloître* (1900), *Philippe II* (1901), *Hélène de Sparte* (1912).

Ver·jus \ver-zhüe\, Louis. Comte de Cré·cy \də-krā-sē\. 1629–1709. French diplomat. Represented France at the signing of the Truce of Ratisbon (1684) and the Treaty of Rijswijk (1697).

Ver·laine \ver-len\, Paul. 1844–1896. French poet. At first associated with the Parnassians; later known as a leader among the Symbolists; led tempestuous, violent life of bohemianism, esp. as companion of Rimbaud. Author of some of the most musical verse in French as *Poèmes saturniens* (1866), *Fêtes galantes* (1869), *La Bonne Chanson* (1870), *Romances sans paroles* (1874), *Sagesse* (1881), *Les Poètes maudits* (1884), *Jadis et naguère* (1884), *Amour* (1888), *Femmes* (1890), *Bonheur* (1891), *Chansons pour elle* (1891), *Odes en son honneur* (1893), *Élégies* (1893), *Invectives* (1896).

Ver·meer \vər-ˈmär\, Jan. *Known also as* Jan van der Meer \vän-dər-ˈmär\ *and* Jan van Delft \vän-ˈdelft\. 1632–1675. Dutch painter. Little known of his life, passed entirely in Delft; displayed in his paintings a scientific interest in light, perspective, color, and attained unprecedented mastery in their artistic use. Some 30 to 35 paintings are attributed to him, including *The Procuress, Girl Asleep, Lady Reading a Letter, Kitchen Maid, Young Woman with Water Jug, Little Street, Music Lesson, View of Delft, Woman Weighing Gold, Allegory of Painting, Lacemaker, Girl with Red Hat, Girl with Flute, The Letter, The Astronomer, Allegory of the Faith.*

Vermeer van Haarlem, Jan. See Jan van der MEER.

Ver·mi·gli \vär-ˈmēl-yē\, Pietro Martire. *Eng.* Peter Mar·tyr \ˈmärt-ər\. 1500–1562. Florentine religious. Augustinian abbot of St. Peter ad Aram, Naples (1533); met Juan de Valdes and read works of Reformers; fled (1542) to Zürich after accepting Reformed faith; divinity professor, Strasbourg (1542–47, 1553–56). Brought to London by Cranmer; divinity professor, Oxford (1547–53); aided Cranmer in 1552 *Book of Common Prayer;* his Zwinglian doctrine of the Eucharist began a controversy at Oxford (1549); Hebrew professor, Zürich (1556 ff.).

Ver·muy·den \vər-ˈmœi-dən, *Angl* -ˈmīd-ᵊn\, Sir Cornelius. 1595–?1683. British engineer, b. Netherlands. To England (c.1621, naturalized 1633); employed in repairing Thames embankments (1621); employed by Charles I to drain Hatfield Chase, Yorkshire (1626); drained Great Fens, Cambridgeshire (1630–37), and reclaimed area (1649–52) after it was flooded in Civil War.

Ver·nad·sky \vyir-ˈnät-skəi\, Vladimir Ivanovich. 1863–1945. Russian geochemist and mineralogist. Professor, Moscow (1898–1911); director, State Radium Inst., Leningrad (1926–38); founder and director (from 1928), biogeochemical laboratory of Leningrad Academy of Sciences; considered a founder of geochemistry.

Verne \vern\, Jules. 1828–1905. French writer. Successful writer for the theater, as with *Les Pailles rompues* (1850); achieved great success with novels of technological adventure that helped create genre of science fiction, including *Cinq Semaines en ballon* (1863), *Voyage au centre de la terre* (1864), *De la Terre à la Lune* (1865), *Vingt Mille lieues sous les mers* (1870), *Le Tour du monde en quatre-vingts jours* (1873), *L'Île mystérieuse* (1874), *Michel Strogoff* (1876), *César Cascabel* (1890), *Le Sphinx des glaces* (1897).

Ver·ner \ˈver-nər\, Karl Adolph. 1846–1896. Danish philologist. Professor of Slavic philology, Copenhagen (from 1888); propounded (1875) Verner's law, a systematic explanation of apparent exceptions to Grimm's law of phonetic shifts in Indo-European languages.

Ver·net \ver-ne\. Family of French painters, including: Claude-Joseph, *known as* Joseph (1714–1789), painter of marines and landscapes, notably the series of 15 *Ports of France* (1754–65) for Louis XV. His son ¶Antoine-Charles-Horace, *known as* Carle (1758–1835), historical and animal painter, accompanied Napoléon to Italy and made many sketches later used in battle pictures as *Bataille de Marengo,* etc.; court painter to Louis XVIII, for whom he did sporting scenes. His son ¶Horace, *in full* Émile-Jean-Horace (1789–1863), painted battle and genre scenes, chiefly of Arab life (after 1833).

Verneuil, Marquise de. See Catherine-Henriette de Balzac d'ENTRAGUES.

Ver·nier \vern-yā, *Angl* ve(ə)rn-ˈyā, ˈvər-nē-ər\, Pierre. c.1580–1637. French mathematician. Held various government posts; invented (1631) Vernier caliper, or Vernier scale, for making accurate measurements of linear magnitudes, described in his *Construction, l'usage, et les propriétéz du quadrant nouveau de mathématiques* (1631).

Vernio, Conte del. See Giovanni BARDI.

Ver·non \ˈvər-nən\, Edward. *Called* Old Grog \ˈgräg\. 1684–1757. English admiral. Entered navy (1700); M.P. (1722 ff.); vice admiral (1739); stormed Porto Bello (1739); failed in Cartagena expedition (1741); first to issue rum diluted with water, which came to be known as grog (1740); cashiered (1746) for pamphlets attacking admiralty.

Veronese, Guarino. See GUARINO DA VERONA.

Veronese, Paolo. See Paolo CALIARI.

Ve·ron·i·ca \vər-ˈän-ə-kə\. Saint. 1st century A.D. Legendary woman of Jerusalem. Subject of various legends, principally that according to which as Christ bore the cross, she wiped his face with a cloth which miraculously retained the imprint of his countenance.

Ver·ra·za·no \ˌvär-rät-ˈsän-ō\ *or* **Ver·raz·za·no** \-rät-ˈtsä-\, Giovanni da. 1485?–?1528. Florentine navigator. Explored coast of North America (1524) from Cape Fear northward, probably as far as Cape Breton, discovering New York and Narragansett bays.

Ver·res \ˈver-ˌēz\, Gaius. c.115–43 B.C. Roman politician. Proquaestor in Cilicia under praetor Cornelius Dolabella (80 B.C.); praetor (74); governor of Sicily (73–71); made himself notorious by extortion, excessive taxation, pillage, and disregard of civil rights of Roman citizens; brought to trial (70) and prosecuted by Cicero; went into exile to escape conviction. Murdered by order of Mark Antony.

Ver·ri \ˈvär-rē\, Pietro. 1728–1797. Italian economist, journalist, and writer. Leader of Milanese Società dei Pugni, editor of its journal *Il Caffè* (1764–66); held various posts in city government. Author of *Riflessioni sulle legge vincolanti* (1769), *Meditazioni sull' economia politica* (1771), *Osservazione sulla tortura* (1777), *Storia di Milano* (1783–99), etc. His brother ¶Alessandro (1741–1816) was also member of Società dei Pugni and assisted on *Il Caffè;* translated *Iliad* and works of Shakespeare into Italian; known for Romantic novels as *Le avventure di Saffo poetessa di Mitilene* (1780) and *Le notti romane al sepolcro degli Scipioni* (1792–1804), and plays as *La congiura di Milano* (1779).

Ver·rill \ˈver-əl\, Addison Emery. 1839–1926. American zoologist, b. Greenwood, Me. Professor, Yale (1864–1907); curator of zoology, Peabody Museum of Natural History (1865–1910), where he built a great collection; outstanding taxonomist; in charge of scientific work of U.S. Commission of Fish and Fisheries in southern New England (1871–87). His son ¶Alpheus Hyatt (1871–1954), b. New Haven, Conn., made explorations in the West Indies, Guiana, Central America, and Panama (1889–1920); rediscovered supposedly extinct insectivorous mammal *Solenodon paradoxus* in Santo Domingo (1907); in Central America discovered remains of unknown prehistoric culture (1924–27); conducted explorations in Peru and Bolivia (1928–32); author of many adventure books for boys and books on natural history.

Ver·rio \ˈver-ē-ˌō\, Antonio. 1639?–1707. Italian painter. Employed by Charles II and James II of England to decorate Windsor Castle, by William III and Queen Anne to decorate Hampton Court.

Ver·ri·us Flac·cus \ˈver-e-əs-ˈflak-əs\, Marcus. 1st–2d century A.D. Roman grammarian and teacher. A freedman, called to court by Augustus to tutor his grandsons Gaius and Lucius. Chief work the long-used *De significata verborum,* now lost.

Ver·roc·chio \vär-ˈrȯk-kyō\, Andrea del. *Orig.* Andrea di Mi·che·le di Fran·ces·co Cio·ne \dē-mē-ˈkel-ā-dē-frän-ˈchā-skō-ˈchō-nā\. 1435–1488. Florentine sculptor and painter. After Donatello, leading sculptor of Tuscan school. Fellow pupil with Botticelli of Filippo Lippi; teacher of Leonardo da Vinci, Perugino. His sculptures included the bronze statue *David,* sarcophagus of Piero de' Medici and brother Giovanni, *Christ and St. Thomas,* reliefs, and an equestrian statue of Bartolomeo Colleoni (completed by A. Leopardi). His paintings included *Baptism of Christ, Madonna and Child,* and *Unknown Young Woman.*

Ver·schaf·felt \vərs-ˈkäf-əlt\, Peter Anton von. *Known also by Italian name* Pietro Fiam·min·go \fyäm-ˈmēŋ-gō\, *i.e.* Peter the Fleming. 1710–1793. Flemish sculptor. Executed marble statue of Pope Benedict XIV in Rome (c.1742); director and architect of Mannheim Academy (1756 ff.).

Vertomannus. See Lodovico di VARTHEMA.

Vertov, Dziga. See Denis KAUFMAN.

Ver·tue \ˈvər-(ˌ)chü, -(ˌ)tyü\, George. 1684–1756. English engraver and antiquary. His collected materials for history of art in England were purchased and used by Horace Walpole in *Anecdotes of Painting in England.*

Verulam, Baron. See Francis BACON.

Ve·rus \ˈvi(ə)r-əs\, Lucius Aurelius. *Orig.* Lucius Ceionius Com·mo·dus \ˈkäm-ə-dəs\. 130–169. Roman emperor (161–169) jointly with Marcus Aurelius. Adopted by Emperor Hadrian (136) and later (138) by Emperor Antoninus Pius along with Marcus Aurelius; after death of emperor (161), made coruler with tribunitian and proconsular powers; led expedition to Parthia (162); took part in wars in northern Italy and Pannonia (167–168).

Ver·wey \vər-ˈvī\, Albert. 1865–1937. Dutch poet and critic. A leader in "1880 movement" for revival of Dutch literature and co-founder (1885) of its organ *De Nieuwe Gids;* later reacted against movement to follow own mystical bent; edited *De Beweging* (1905–19); professor, Leiden (1925–35). Verse included *Van de liefde die vriendschap heet* (1885–86), *Cor Cordium* (1886), *Van het leven* (1888), *De Joden* (1892), *Aarde* (1896), *Dagen en Daden* (1901), *Het Levensfeest* (1912), *De Weg van het Licht* (1922), *Het lachende Raadsel* (1935); highly influential as critic.

Ver·woerd \fər-ˈvürt\, Hendrik Frensch. 1901–1966. South African politician. Professor, U. of Stellenbosch (1927–37); editor of Nationalist daily *Die Transvaler* (1937–48); senator (1948–58); minister of native affairs (1950–58); elected to House of Assembly (1958); prime minister (1958–66); applied rigorous policy of apartheid, established resettlement of blacks; led South Africa out of British Commonwealth (1961); assassinated.

Ve·ry \ˈver-ē, ˈvir-ē\, Jones. 1813–1880. American poet and essayist, b. Salem, Mass. During prolonged period of religious exaltation (1833–40) wrote mystical verse and prose pieces, collected and, under patronage of Ralph Waldo Emerson, published as *Essays and Poems* (1839), extravagantly praised by Channing, Bryant, and Emerson.

Ve·saas \ˈvā-sós\, Tarjei. 1897–1970. Norwegian novelist. Author of symbolic and allegorical works as *Menneskebonn* (1923), *Grindegård* (1925), *Dei svarte hestane* (1928), *Klokke i haugen* (stories, 1929), *Det store spelet* (1934), *Kvinnor ropar heim* (1935), *Kimen* (1940), *Huset i mørkret* (1945), *Tårnet* (1948), *Vindane* (stories, 1952), *Fuglane* (1957), *Brannen* (1961), *Is-slottet* (1963), *Bruene* (1966), *Båten om kvelden* (autobiography, 1968).

Ve·sa·li·us \və-ˈsā-lē-əs, -ˈsāl-yəs, və-ˈzā(l)-\, Andreas. 1514–1564. Belgian anatomist. Lectured at Padua, Basel, Pisa, and Bologna; on basis of his own dissections of human cadavers, which he was one of the first to perform, repudiated Galenic tradition and prepared drawings published as *De humani corporis fabrica* (1543); made physician to Emperor Charles V (1543) and a count (1556); physician to Philip II in Madrid (1559).

Ve·sey \ˈvē-zē\, Denmark. c.1767–1822. American insurrectionist, b. probably St. Thomas, Danish West Indies. Sold to a Bermuda slaver (1781), whose surname he took and with whom he settled in Charleston, S.C. (1783); purchased own freedom (1800); secretly planned uprising of slaves of Charleston and surrounding plantations, enlisting perhaps as many as 9000 followers; arrested following detection of conspiracy, tried, and hanged along with 36 other alleged plotters.

Ves·pa·sian \ve-ˈspā-zh(ē-)ən\. *Lat.* Titus Flavius Sabinus Ves·pa·si·a·nus \ves-ˌpā-zhē-ˈā-nəs\. 9–79 A.D. Roman emperor (69–79), founder of Flavian dynasty. Held various public offices (military tribune, quaestor, aedile, and praetor); sent by Claudius in command of legion in Germany and later (43) in Britain; conquered Isle of Wight; consul (51); proconsul of Africa (63) under Nero; sent to conduct war against Jews (67); won favor of soldiers, who, after Otho's suicide, chose him emperor at Alexandria (69); gained further support, including finally that of Senate, and entered Rome (70). Reign marked by suppression of revolt of Batavians (69–70), triumph with Titus (71), beginning of erection of Colosseum, and conquests in Britain by Agricola (78–79).

Ves·puc·ci \vā-ˈspüt-chē, *Angl* ve-ˈspü-chē\, Amerigo. *Lat.* Americus Ves·pu·ci·us \ve-ˈspyü-shəs\. 1454–1512. Italian navigator. Merchant in service of Medici; helped outfit ships for Columbus's 2d and 3d voyages; took part in several early voyages to New World (1497, 1499, 1501, 1503); navigator of expedition of Ojeda (1499–1500) that first discovered mainland; in Portuguese service, discovered Baía de Guanabara and Río de la Plata (1502); in last two voyages (1505, 1507), explored Darien region; appointed pilot major of Spain (1508); his accounts published (1507) by Martin Waldseemüller, who suggested new lands be named "America."

Vesque von Pütt·ling·en \ˈvesk-fón-ˈpœt-liŋ-ən\, Johann. *Pseudonym* J. Ho·ven \ˈhō-fən\. 1803–1883. Austrian composer. Known esp. for operas, including *Turandot* (1838), *Johanna d'Arc* (1840), *Liebeszauber* (1845), *Der lustige Rath* (1852).

Vest·dijk \ˈves-tāk\, Simon. 1898–1971. Dutch writer. Author of cerebral, often shocking anti-bourgeois works as verse *Vrouwendienst* (1934); novels *Meneer Vissers Hellevaart* (1936), *Het vijfde zegel* (1937), *Rumeiland* (1940), *Iersche nachten* (1944), *De vuuraanbidders* (1947), *Ivoren Wachters* (1951), *Het glinsterend pantser* (1956), and a multivolume "Anton Wachter cycle" including *Terug tot Ida Damman* (1934), *Sint Sebastiaan* (1939), *De andere school* (1954), *De beker van de min* (1957), *De laatste kans* (1960); also wrote criticism and essays.

Ves·tine \ˈves-ˌtīn\, Ernest Harry. 1906–1968. American geophysicist, b. Minneapolis, Minn. On staff of Carnegie Institution of Washington (1938–56), of Rand Corp. (1956–66); professor, U.C.L.A. (1966–68); known for studies of terrestrial magnetism and magnetic storms.

Ves·tris \ves-trēs\. Family of French dancers of Italian origin, including: Gaetano Appolino Baldassare, *Fr.* Gaëtan-Apolline-Balthasar (1729–1808); made debut at Paris Opéra (1748) and became premier danseur (1751–88); member (from 1749), ballet master and choreographer (1770–75), premier danseur (1776–81) of Ballets du Roi. His illegitimate son ¶Marie-Jean-Augustin, *called* Auguste, *known also as* Vestr'Allard (1760–1842), made debut at Opéra (1772), becoming primo ballerino (1778); noted for brilliant technique, prodigious leaps; said to have created "demi-caractère comique" style; retired (1816). His son ¶Auguste-Armand (1788–1825) made debut at Opéra (1800); ballet master of King's Theatre, London (1809–17).

Vestris, Lucia Elizabeth, *nee* Bar·to·loz·zi \ˌbär-tō-ˈlòt-tsē\. *Known as* Mme Vestris. 1797–1856. British actress, singer, and manager. Granddaughter of Francesco Bartolozzi; m. (1813) Auguste-Armand Vestris, 2d (1838) Charles James Mathews; debut in opera *Il ratto di Proserpina* at King's Theatre, London (1815); great favorite of English audiences (1820–54), esp. in breeches parts; lessee of Olympic Theatre (1831–38), Covent Garden (1839–42), Lyceum (1847–55), producing burlesques and extravaganzas.

Vetsera, Baroness Marie. See Archduke RUDOLF of Austria.

Veuil·lot \vœ-yō\, Louis-François. 1813–1883. French journalist. Editor of *L'Univers* (1843–60), organ of Ultramontanist sentiment in France. Author of *Çà et Là* (1859), *Le Pape et la diplomatie* (1861), *Satires* (1863), *Les Odeurs de Paris* (1866), *Oeuvres poétiques* (1878), novels, etc.

Via·da·na \vyä-ˈdä-nä\, Lodovico. *Orig.* Lodovico Gros·si \ˈgrós-sē\. c.1560–1627. Italian composer. Works included *Cento concerti ecclesiastici* (1602), a cappella masses, requiems, motets, canzonets, and madrigals.

Vian·ney \vyȧ-ne\, Jean-Baptiste-Marie. Saint. *Known as* le Cu·ré d'Ars \kü̅-rā-dȧrs\. 1786–1859. French cleric. Ordained (1815); priest at Ars (from 1818); famed for purity of life and intensity of faith, resulting in making Ars a place of pilgrimage during his life and after his death; beatified by Pius X (1905) and canonized by Pius XI (1925).

Viau \vyō\, Théophile de. *Known also as* Thé·o·phile \tā-ó-fēl\. 1590–1626. French poet. A Huguenot, later freethinker; condemned to death for participation in the writing and publication of *Parnasse satirique* (1622), but sentence commuted to banishment; author also of the tragedy *Pyrame et Thisbé* (1623).

Viaud \vyō\, Louis-Marie-Julien. *Pseudonym* Pierre Lo·ti \lò-tē\. 1850–1923. French naval officer and novelist. Entered navy (1869); served in Middle and Far East; captain (1906); retired (1910) but recalled to serve in World War I. Among his novels were *Aziyadé* (1879), *Le Mariage de Loti* (1882), *Pêcheur d'Islande* (1886), *Madame Chrysanthème* (1887), *Le Roman d'un enfant* (1890), *Fantôme d'Orient* (1891), *Ramuntcho* (1897), *Les Désenchantées* (1966), *Prime jeunesse* (1919), *Un Jeune Officier pauvre* (1923).

Vicence, Duc de. See Armand CAULAINCOURT.

Vi·cen·te \vē-ˈsäⁿn-tə\, Gil. c.1465–c.1536. Portuguese writer. Court dramatist to Manuel I and John III; regarded as a founder of Portuguese drama. Author of 44 extant plays, including *autos,* tragicomedies as *Amadís de Gaula* and *Templo de Apolo,* comedies, and farces.

Vi·cen·ti·no \vē-chān-ˈtē-nō\, Nicola. 1511–c.1576. Italian composer and theorist. Attempted to revive chromatic and enharmonic Greek modes; invented the archicembalo and archiorgano, musical instruments fitted with keyboards suitable for rendering Greek modes; composed madrigals, motets.

Vi·chard \vē-shȧr\, César. *Known as* Abbé de Saint-Réal \saⁿ-rā-ȧl\. 1639–1692. French historian. Author of *De l'usage de l'histoire* (1671) and *La Conjuration des Espagnols contre la république de Venise* (1674), latter inspiring Thomas Otway's play *Venice Preserv'd* (1682).

Vi·chy-Cham·rond \vē-shē-shäⁿ-rōⁿ\, Marie de. Marquise du Def·fand \dā-fäⁿ\. 1679–1780. French hostess. m. (1701; separated 1722) marquis du Deffand; mistress of duc d'Orléans; established brilliant salon frequented by Fontenelle, Houdar de la Motte, Voltaire, Hénault, D'Alembert, Turgot, and others; engaged Julie de Lespinasse (1754–64) to assist; remembered for her correspondence with Voltaire, Horace Walpole, the duchesse de Choiseul.

Vick \ˈvik\, James. 1818–1882. American horticulturist and publisher, b. Chichester, England. To U.S. (1833); succeeded A.J. Downing as publisher of *Horticulturist* (1852–55); editor of *Rural New Yorker* (1857–62); published

Vick's Monthly Magazine (from 1878); developed mail-order seed business that became largest in U.S.

Vick·ers \'vik-ərz\, Edward. 1804–1897. English steel manufacturer. Joint founder (1828) with his father-in-law George Naylor of steel-manufacturing company for making tools, files, etc., at Sheffield and Wadsley, which became (1867) Vickers' Sons & Co. and developed (1888) into armament factory; merged (1897) into Vickers' Sons and Maxim (see Sir Hiram S. MAXIM). His sons ¶Thomas Edward (1833–1915) and ¶Albert (1838–1919) entered firm and were each chairman in turn (1873–1909, 1909–18). Firm merged (1927) with Sir W. G. Armstrong, Whitworth and Co., Ltd., to form Vickers Armstrong, Ltd. See also William G. ARMSTRONG.

Vick·e·ry \'vik(-ə)-rē\, Howard Leroy. 1892–1946. American naval officer, b. Bellevue, Ohio. Commissioned (1915); member of U.S. Maritime Commission (1940–46), vice chairman (1942–46); deputy administrator of War Shipping Administration (1942–46); rear admiral (1942), vice admiral (1944); supervised building of over 5500 ships, aggregating some 40 million gross tons, during World War II.

Vi·co \'vē-kō\, Giambattista. 1668–1744. Italian philosopher. Professor, Naples (1699–1744); known esp. for his *Principi di una Scienza Nuova d'intorno alla comune natura delle nazioni* (1725, 1730, 1744), an attempt to discover and organize laws common to the evolution of all society; also wrote *De nostri temporis studiorum ratione* (1709), *De antiquissima Italorum sapientia* (1710).

Vic·tor \'vik-tər\. Name of three popes and two antipopes:

Victor I. Saint. d. 199. Pope (c.189–199). Disputed with bishops of Asia over Easter usage and succeeded in imposing Roman date; established Latin as church language.

Victor II. *Orig.* Geb·hard von Dolln·stein-Hirsch·berg \'gep-ˌhärt-fön-dôln-ˌshtīn-'hirsh-ˌberk\. c.1018–1057. Pope (1055–57). German noble; bishop of Eichstätt (1042); adviser of Emperor Henry III; during pontificate, reformed the clergy; guardian (1056–57) of infant Henry IV.

Victor III. *Orig.* Dau·fe·ri \dō-'fā-rē\. *Lat.* Dau·fe·ri·us \dȯ-'fir-ē-əs\. 1027–1087. Pope (1086–87). Abbot, under the name Des·i·de·ri·us \ˌdes-ə-'dir-ē-əs\, in charge of the cloister Monte Cassino (1058–86); cardinal priest (1059); elected pope against his will, driven from Rome by partisans of Emperor Henry IV and antipope Clement III; convened synod at Capua (1087); sent army to Tunis (1087) that defeated Saracens; excommunicated Clement III; esp. famous as abbot of Monte Cassino during its golden age, causing some 70 books to be copied.

ANTIPOPES:

Victor IV. *Orig.* Gregorio Con·ti \'kōn-tē\. 12th century. Antipope (1138). Elected by faction of Roger II of Sicily to succeed Anacletus II in opposition to Innocent II.

Victor IV. *Orig.* Oc·ta·vi·us \äk-'tā-vē-əs\. d. 1164. Antipope (1159–64). Cardinal (1138). Established by Emperor Frederick I Barbarossa in opposition to Alexander III.

Victor *or* **Victor-Perrin.** See Claude PERRIN.

Victor, Orville James. 1827–1910. American author and publisher, b. Sandusky, Ohio. For firm of Beadle & Adams (see Erastus F. BEADLE), originated (c.1860) idea of the "dime novel," a story of adventure intended to reach a wide market and to be sold for ten cents; organized, trained, and directed corps of writers to turn out such books rapidly. His wife (m. 1856) ¶Metta Victoria, *nee* Fuller (1831–1885), wrote verse, sentimental novels; contributed over 100 stories to Dime Novel series, including *Maum Guinea* (1862).

Victor, Sextus Aurelius. 4th century A.D. Roman historian, b. Africa. Governor of Pannonia Secunda (361), prefect of Rome (c.389). Author of *De Caesaribus,* history of imperial Rome.

Vic·tor Am·a·de·us \'vik-tər-ˌam-ə-'dē-əs\. *Ital.* Vit·to·rio A·me·de·o \vēt-'tȯr-yo-ˌä-mā-'de-ō\. Name of three Italian rulers:

Victor Amadeus I. 1587–1637. Duke of Savoy (1630–37). Son of Charles Emmanuel I.

Victor Amadeus II. 1666–1732. Duke of Savoy (1675–1730); king of Sicily (1713–20) and of Sardinia-Piedmont (1720–30). Son of Charles Emmanuel II; at first under control of Louis XIV; joined (1690) Habsburg alliance against France; in War of Spanish Succession sided first with France; defeated at Chiari (1701) by his cousin Prince Eugene of Savoy in command of army of alliance against France; joined the alliance (1704); aided Eugene, who gained great victory at Turin (1706); by Treaty of Utrecht (1713) made king of Sicily; ceded Sicily to Austria (1720) and received Sardinia in exchange. Abdicated (1730) in favor of son Charles Emmanuel III.

Victor Amadeus III. 1726–1796. Duke (1773–96); king of Sardinia (1773–96) as Victor Amadeus II. Son of Charles Emmanuel III; joined First Coalition against France (1792–93); lost Nice, Savoy, and part of Piedmont to Napoléon.

Victor Em·man·u·el \e-'man-yü-əl, ə-\. *Ital.* Vit·to·rio E·ma·nue·le \vēt-'tȯr-yō-ˌā-män-'wel-ā\. Name of three Italian rulers:

Victor Emmanuel I. 1759–1824. Duke of Aosta, duke of Savoy, and king of Sardinia (1802–21). Son of Victor Amadeus III; led Sardinian forces against French (1792–96); succeeded as king on abdication of brother Charles Emmanuel IV; all dominions except Sardinia in possession of French (1802–14); kingdom restored (1814–15). Abdicated (1821) in favor of brother Charles Felix.

Victor Emmanuel II. 1820–1878. King of Sardinia-Piedmont (1849–61) and of Italy (1861–78). Son of Charles Albert of Sardinia; took part in war against Austria (1848–49); after defeat at Novara (1849), became king on abdication of his father; chose d'Azeglio and Cavour as ministers to help in strengthening kingdom and bringing about unification of Italy; guided by Cavour, joined England and France in Crimean War (1854–56); formed closer alliance with France (1856–59); defeated Austria in brief war (1859–61), having personally commanded at Magenta and Solferino; Lombardy, Modena, Parma, Two Sicilies, and other states annexed (1860–61), but Nice and Savoy ceded to France (1861); secretly encouraged Garibaldi in conquest of Sicily and Naples; led invasion of Papal States (1861); assumed title of king of Italy; joined Prussia against Austria (1866) and, as a result, acquired Venetia; Rome freed of French troops (1870) and made capital.

Victor Emmanuel III. 1869–1947. King of Italy (1900–46). Son of Umberto I; active leader in World War I; acquiesced in Fascist seizure of power and in Mussolini's unconstitutional acts; reduced largely to figurehead sovereign; assumed titles of emperor of Ethiopia (1936) and king of Albania (1939); by concordat (1929) recognized full independent sovereignty of Vatican City; failed to secure Italian neutrality in World War II or to assert authority on failure of Mussolini; relinquished all power to son Umberto II (1944) and abdicated (1946).

Vic·to·ria \vik-'tōr-ē-ə, -'tȯr-\. *In full* Al·ex·an·dri·na Victoria \ˌal-eg-zan-'drē-nə-, ˌal-əg-\. 1819–1901. Queen of the United Kingdom of Great Britain and Ireland (1837–1901), and (from 1876) empress of India. Only child of George III's fourth son, Edward, Duke of Kent (*q.v.*), and Mary Louisa Victoria, daughter of Duke of Saxe-Coburg. Succeeded uncle King William IV (June 1837); first years as queen passed under guidance of Lord Melbourne, Whig prime minister. m. her cousin Prince Albert of Saxe-Coburg-Gotha (1840); accepted guidance in state policies of Albert and his adviser Baron Stockmar. Achieved measure of personal authority by requiring of Lord Palmerston that he inform her of every proposed course of action and that he modify in no way measures once sanctioned by her (1850); during Crimean War, founded Victoria Cross, first conferred in 1857. Conferred title of prince consort on her husband (1857). Approved abolition of East India Co. and reorganization of Indian government (1858); dissuaded Prussia from intervening in Franco-Sardinian war (1858). After death of prince consort (1861), endeavored to carry on political duties as she believed he would have had her do. Used personal influence in passage of Disraeli's Reform Act (1867); accepted Irish Disestablishment Act and aided in its passage through House of Lords (1869). Frequently at odds with Gladstone; welcomed Disraeli as prime minister (1874); accepted title of empress of India (1876). Celebrated golden jubilee (1887) and diamond jubilee (1897). Supported vigorous prosecution of Boer War (1899) and passage of Australian Commonwealth bill (1900). At time of her death, recognized as symbolizing a new conception of British monarchy and a unified empire. Author of *Leaves from the Journal of our Life in the Highlands* (1868), *More Leaves* (1883).

Vic·to·ria \bēk-'tōr-yä\, Guadalupe. *Orig.* Manuel Félix Fer·nán·dez \fer-'nän-dās\. 1789–1843. Mexican soldier and politician. Joined revolution under Hidalgo (1810); adhered to plan of Iguala (1821), but joined Santa Anna (1823) in revolt against Iturbide. First president of republic (1824–29).

Victoria, Tomás Luis de. *Ital.* Tommaso Lodovico de Vit·to·ria \dä-vēt-'tȯr-yä\. c.1548–1611. Spanish composer. Chorister in Ávila; chorister and organist at S. Maria di Monserrato, Rome (1569–74); maestro di cappella, Collegio Germanico (1573–77); ordained (1575); chaplain of S. Girolamo della Carità (1578–85); chaplain to dowager Empress María at monastery in Madrid (c.1587–1603) and organist there (1604–11). With his friend Palestrina and Orlando di Lasso, outstanding composer of 16th century; works included 21 masses, 44 motets, 18 Magnificats, hymns, Psalm settings, set of Holy Week music, Passions, etc.

Vic·to·ria Ad·e·laide Mary Lou·ise \vik-'tōr-ē-ə-'ad-əl-ˌād-'me(ə)r-ē-lə-'wēz, -'tȯr-, -'ma(ə)r-ē-, -'mā-rē-\. 1840–1901. Princess royal of Great Britain and German empress. Eldest child of Queen Victoria and Prince Albert; m. (1858) Prince Frederick William of Prussia, later Emperor Frederick III, and by him became mother of William, later Kaiser William II; consistently opposed policies of Bismarck; resided at her country place, Friedrichshof, near Kronberg (from 1888).

Victoria Eu·gé·nie Ju·lia Ena \-ōi-'gā-nē-ə-'jül-yə-'ā-nä\. *Earlier known as* Princess Ena of Bat·ten·berg \'bat-ən-ˌbərg\. 1887–1969. Queen of Alfonso XIII of Spain. Daughter of Prince Henry Maurice of Battenberg; m. (1906) Alfonso and was queen (1906–31).

Vic·to·ri·nus \ˌvik-tə-ˈrī-nəs\. *Also known as* Vic·to·ri·us \vik-ˈtō-rē-əs\ of Aq·ui·ta·nia \ˌak-wə-ˈtā-nē-ə, -nyə\. 5th century. Gallic? astronomer. Commissioned (c.465 A.D.) by Pope Hilarius to correct the calendar and fix the date of Easter; combined Metonic cycle with solar cycle and thus derived a period of 532 Julian years, at end of which the Easter moon would come in same month and on same day of week. Dionysius Exiguus made a few changes and gave his name to the new period (Dionysian period).

Victorinus of Pet·tau \ˈpet-ˌau̇\. Saint. d. c.303 A.D. Christian prelate and theologian. Bishop of Pettau in Styria; author of first Latin exegeses of biblical literature; martyred in Diocletian's persecution.

Victorinus, Gaius Marius. 4th century A.D. Latin writer, b. Africa. Taught rhetoric in Rome; in later life, converted to Christianity; author of works on grammar, philology, and esp. philosophy.

Vi·da \ˈvē-dä\, Marco Girolamo. c.1490–1566. Italian poet. Bishop of Alba (1532 ff.); known particularly for his Latin epic *Christias* (1535); also wrote *De arte poetica* (1527).

Vi·dal de la Blanche \vē-dȧl-də-lȧ-blä^{n}sh\, Paul. 1845–1918. French geographer. Professor, École Normale Supérieure (1877–98), Sorbonne (1898–1918); pioneer in close study of relationship of geographical environment and human activity; considered founder of French school of human geography. Founder and editor (1891–1918) of journal *Annales de Géographie*; author of *Tableau de la géographie de la France* (1903), *La France de l'Est* (1917), etc.

Ví·da·lín \ˈvē-däl-ēn\, Jón Thorkelsson. 1666–1720. Icelandic prelate. Grandson of Arngrímur Jónsson; Lutheran bishop (1697); known for vivid sermons collected in *Húspostilla* (1715–20), outstanding example of Icelandic prose.

Vi·docq \vē-dȯk\, François-Eugène. 1775–1857. French police officer and adventurer. Served in army; created and directed specialized detective force in Paris (1809–27, 1832), forerunner of the *police de sûreté*; dismissed for alleged role in a robbery; formed (1832) private police agency, forerunner of private detective agencies; associate of Lamartine in provisional government (1848). *Mémoires de Vidocq* (1828–29), *Les Voleurs* (1837), *Les Vrais Mystères de Paris* (1844), etc., published under his name but likely written by others.

Vi·dor \ˈvēd-(ˌ)ȯ(ə)r\, King Wallis. 1894–1982. American motion-picture director, b. Galveston, Tex. To Hollywood (1915) as extra, scenarist, newsreel cameraman; directed his first feature *The Turn in the Road* (1919); established his reputation with *The Big Parade* (1925) and *The Crowd* (1928). Directed some 50 films notable for their sensitive simplicity, serious themes, illuminating characterization, including *Hallelujah!* (1929, first film with all-black cast), *Street Scene* (1931), *The Champ* (1931), *Our Daily Bread* (1934), *The Wedding Night* (1935), *The Citadel* (1938), *H.M. Pulham, Esq.* (1941), *Duel in the Sun* (1947), *The Fountainhead* (1949), *Ruby Gentry* (1952), *War and Peace* (1956). Published autobiography *A Tree is a Tree* (1953).

Vid·ya·sa·gar \ˈvid-yä-sä-gȯr\, Isvar Chandra. *Also spelled* Isvarcandra Bidyasagar. 1820–1891. Bengali writer and reformer. Obtained (1839) title of *Vidyasagar* (i.e. "ocean of learning"); appointed (1850) head pandit of Fort William Coll.; principal of Sanskrit Coll. (1851); active in cause of female education and in establishing aided schools; secured legislation allowing remarriage of Hindu widows; simplified method of learning Sanskrit. Author of tales *Vetāl Pañcavimsati* (1847), *Shakuntalā* (1854), *Sitār Vanavās* (1860).

Vie·big \ˈfē-bik\, Clara. 1860–1952. German writer. Author of Naturalistic novels and stories as *Rheinlandstochter* (1897), *Kinder der Eifel* (1897), *Das tägliche Brot* (1900), *Das Weiberdorf* (1900), *Die Wacht am Rhein* (1902), *Eine Mutter Sohn* (1906), *Das Eisen im Feuer* (1913), *Töchter der Hekuba* (1917), *Das rote Meer* (1920), *Die mit den tausend Kindern* (1929), *Insel der Hoffnung* (1933), etc.

Vieille \vyey\, Paul-Marie-Eugène. 1854–1934. French engineer. Investigated shock waves; invented (1884) a smokeless powder (poudre B) adopted by the French army.

Viei·ra \ˈvyā-ē-rə\, António. 1608–1697. Portuguese missionary and writer. To Brazil (1614); entered Society of Jesus (1623); became influential preacher; active among Indians and Negro slaves; in Portugal (1641–52), where he undertook diplomatic missions for King John IV; returned to Brazil (1652) as director of missions in Maranhão; deported to Portugal by colonists (1661); imprisoned by the Inquisition; to Rome (1668–74) as preacher; retired to Brazil (1681); Jesuit provincial, Brazil (1688 ff.). His works, among the earliest of Portuguese prose, included sermons (15 vols., 1679–1748), *Esperanças de Portugal,* etc.

Vier·eck \ˈvi(ə)r-ək, -(ˌ)ek\, George Sylvester. 1884–1962. American writer, b. Munich, Germany. To U.S. (1895); associate editor, *Current Literature* (1906–15); editor, *International* (1912–18), *American Monthly* (1914–27); author of *Nineveh and Other Poems* (1907), *Confessions of a Barbarian* (1910), *The Candle and the Flame* (1912), *Glimpses of the Great* (1930), *The Kaiser on Trial* (1937), *The Temptation of Jonathan* (1938), etc. Imprisoned (1942–47) for pro-German propaganda.

Vier·kandt \ˈfēr-ˌkänt\, Alfred Ferdinand. 1867–1953. German sociologist. Professor, Berlin (1921–53); known for work in creating a philosophical foundation for sociology. Author of *Naturvölker und Kulturvölker* (1896), *Die Stelligkeit im Kulturwandel* (1908), *Staat und Gesellschaft in der Gegenwart* (1921), *Familie, Volk und Staat* (1936), *Triebleben und Kultur* (1949).

Viète \vyet\, François. *Lat.* Franciscus Vieta \vī-ˈēt-ə\. 1540–1603. French mathematician. Lawyer; in service of Henry IV (from 1577); decoded cipher used by Philip II of Spain in war against Huguenots. Developed methods for solution of plane and spherical triangles by all six trigonometric functions in *Canon mathematicus seu ad triangula* (1579); introduced systematic and essentially modern algebraic notation in *In artem analyticem isagoge* (1591); solved equations of 2d, 3d, and 4th degree in *De aequationum recognitione et emendatione* (1615).

Vieuzac, Bertrand Barère de. See BARÈRE DE VIEUZAC.

Vi·ga·nò \vē-ˈgän-ō\, Salvatore. 1769–1821. Italian dancer and choreographer. Active in Madrid, Paris, Vienna; ballet master of La Scala, Milan (1811–21); developed the dance-drama of J.-G. Noverre by blending dance and pantomime into highly dramatic works. Ballets included *Die Geschöpfe des Prometheus* (1801, music by Beethoven), *Gli strelizzi* (1809), *Otello* (1818), *I titani* (1819).

Vi·gée-Le·brun \ve-zhā-lə-brœ^{n}\, Élisabeth, *in full* Marie-Louise-Élisabeth, *nee* Vigée. 1755–1842. French painter. m. (1776) J.-B.-P. Lebrun; at outbreak of French Revolution, fled from France (1789). Best known for her portraits, including those of the English princesses Adelaide and Victoria, Lady Hamilton as a bacchante, Lord Byron, Mme de Staël, and more than twenty of Marie-Antoinette.

Vi·ge·land \ˈvē-gə-län\, Gustav, *in full* Adolf Gustav. 1869–1943. Norwegian sculptor. Known for the more than 100 massive symbolic figures in Frogner Park, Oslo; also a portraitist.

Vi·ger \vē-zhā\, Denis Benjamin. 1774–1861. Canadian politician, b. Montreal. Member of legislature of Lower Canada (1808–30); sent to England as exponent of French Canadian grievances (1828, 1831); cousin and supporter of L.J. Papineau; imprisoned in Canada for seditious articles (1838–40); member of Upper Canadian parliament (1841–47) and of Legislative Council (1848–58).

Vig·fús·son \ˈvig-füs-sȯn\, Gudbrandur. 1827–1889. Icelandic philologist and scholar. In Copenhagen (1849–64); called to London (1864) to complete Richard Cleasby's *Icelandic–English Dictionary* (1869–74); reader in Scandinavian language and literature, Oxford (from 1884). Published editions of the sagas and the *Corpus Poeticum Boreale* (1883).

Vig·i·lan·ti·us \ˌvij-ə-ˈlan-sh(e-)əs\. fl. c.403 A.D. Gallic Christian presbyter. Author of a book (now lost) against superstitious practices, which drew forth from Jerome a bitter attack, *Contra Vigilantium.*

Vi·gil·i·us \və-ˈjil-ē-əs\. d. 555. Pope (537–555). Papal representative at Constantinople (536–537); installed to succeed deposed Pope Silverius by Belisarius; summoned by Justinian to Constantinople (545); at first refused to condemn the Three Chapters, but finally (554) ratified action of Council of Constantinople in condemning them, provoking violent reaction in Western church and the Aquileian Schism.

Vigna, Pietro della. See PIETRO DELLA VIGNA.

Vi·gne·rot du Ples·sis \vēn-yer-ō-dūē-plā-sē\, Louis-François-Armand de. Duc de Ri·che·lieu \rē-shə-lyœ̄\. 1696–1788. French soldier and diplomat. Grandnephew of Cardinal Richelieu. Distinguished himself in War of Polish Succession, esp. at seige of Philippsburg (1733), and in War of Austrian Succession at Fontenoy, Ravenna, and Lawfeld; freed Genoa from Austrian siege (1748); created marshal of France (1748). Commanded campaign in Hanover, ending in capitulation of Closterseven (1757).

Vignerot du Plessis de Richelieu, Emmanuel-Armand de. Duc d'·Ai·guil·lon \deg-w^{y}ē-yō^{n}\. 1720–1788. French politician. Rose to lieutenant general during Seven Years' War; minister of foreign affairs (1771–74) and of war (1774) under Louis XV; with René-Nicolas de Maupeou and Joseph-Marie Terray, formed triumvirate that temporarily deprived *parlements* (high courts) of their political powers.

Vignola, Giacomo da. See Giacomo BAROZZI.

Vi·gny \vēn-yē\, Alfred-Victor de. Comte. 1797–1863. French man of letters. Officer in the French army (1814–26). A leader among French Romantics, produced verse influenced by Byron and Thomas Moore and novels influenced by Scott. Among his works were *Poèmes* (1822), *Poèmes antiques et modernes* (1826), *Cinq-Mars* (historical novel, 1826), a series of analytical "consultations" including *Stello* (1832) and *Servitude et grandeur militaires* (1835), *Chatterton* (romantic play, 1835), *Les Destinées* (verse, 1864), and translations into French verse of Shakespeare's *Othello* and *Merchant of Venice.*

Vi·la·ka·zi \ˌvē-lä-ˈkäz-ē\, Benedict Wallet. 1906–1947. Zulu writer and educator. Taught at U. of Witwatersrand, Johannesburg, S. Africa; known for

\ə\ abut \ᵊ\ kitten, *Fr.* table \ər\ further \a\ ash \ā\ ace \ä\ cot, cart \au̇\ out \ch\ chin \e\ bet \ē\ easy \g\ go \i\ hit \ī\ ice \j\ job \ŋ\ sing \ō\ go \ȯ\ law \ȯi\ boy \th\ both \t͟h\ the \ü\ loot \u̇\ foot \y\ yet \zh\ vision \ȧ, k̲, g̲, k̲, ^{n}, œ, œ̄, üe, ūē, ^{y}\ *see* Guide to Pronunciation

study and writing of Zulu verse; works included *Inkondlo KaZulu* (1935), *Amal' Ezulu* (1945).

Vi·lar \vē-lär\, Jean. 1912–1971. French actor and director. Founded (1943) Théâtre de Poche, Paris; directed annual festival of dramatic art at Avignon (from 1947); director of Théâtre National Populaire (1951–63), which he is credited with revitalizing.

Vildrac, Charles. See Charles MESSAGER.

Vile \'vī(ə)l\, William. c.1700–1767. English cabinetmaker. In partnership with John Cobb (from c.1750); royal cabinetmaker (1751); noted for outstanding quality of work, as inlaid mahogany jewel cabinet for Queen Charlotte (1761).

Vilhelm. See WILLIAM.

Vil·la \'bē(l)-yä\, Francisco, *known as* Pancho. *Orig.* Doroteo Aran·go \ä-'räŋ-gō\. 1878–1923. Mexican bandit and revolutionary leader. Active in Madero revolution (1909–10); imprisoned (1912), escaped to U.S.; raised "División del Norte" and joined revolt of Carranza (1913); governor of Chihuahua (1913); helped defeat Huerta (1914) but soon turned against Carranza (1914–15); driven into mountains of northern Mexico; crossed American border and raided Columbus, N.M., killing 16 persons and partly burning town (Mar. 1916); pursued by American troops under Pershing, who withdrew when President Carranza objected to their presence on Mexican soil; assassinated.

Villafranca, Counts of. See under house of SAVOY.

Vil·la-Lo·bos \,vē-lä-'lō-bȯsh\, Heitor. 1887–1959. Brazilian composer. Director of musical education in São Paulo (1930–32), for all Brazil (1932 ff.); founded (1942) a conservatory for popular singing and (1945) Brazilian Academy of Music (president, 1945–59). Known for applying classical forms and techniques to Afro-Brazilian themes; works included 12 symphonies (1920–58), a set of 14 *Chôros* (1920–29), set of 9 *Bachianas brasileiras* (1930–44), symphonic poems *Uirapuru* (1917), *Amazonas* (1929), *Dawn in a Tropical Forest* (1954), cello concertos, harmonica concerto, guitar concerto, chamber works, choral and piano works, etc.

Villamediana, Conde de. See TASSIS PERALTA.

Vil·la·ni \vēl-'lä-nē\, Giovanni. c.1275–1348. Italian historian. Known for his *Cronica,* or *Storia fiorentina,* history of the city of Florence (to 1348), written from a bourgeois and pre-Humanist point of view. His brother ¶Matteo (d. c.1363) extended the chronicle to 1363.

Villanova, Arnold of. See ARNAU DE VILLANOVA.

Vil·la·nue·va \bēl-yän-'wā-vä\, Juan de. 1739–1811. Spanish architect. Royal architect to Charles IV; his works included numerous royal residences, Prado Museum (1785–87), Madrid astronomical observatory, etc.

Vil·lard \və-'lär(d)\, Henry. *Orig.* Ferdinand Heinrich Gustav Hil·gard \'hil-,gärt\. 1835–1900. American journalist, railroad executive, and financier, b. Speyer, Bavaria, Germany. To U.S. (1853); on staff of New York *Staats-Zeitung* (1858), New York *Herald* and New York *Tribune* (1861–63). Became involved in finance as agent for German bondholders of Oregon & California Railroad (1874); president of Oregon Steamship Co. (1876); formed (1879) Oregon Railway and Navigation Co.; formed a pool and bought control of Northern Pacific Railroad; president (1881–84) and chairman (1889–93). Promoted formation (1890), president (1890–92) of Edison General Electric Co.; bought control of New York *Evening Post* (1881). His wife (m. 1866) ¶Helen Frances, *nee* Garrison (1844–1928), daughter of William Lloyd Garrison, interested herself in social reform; helped form (1910) National Association for the Advancement of Colored People; founded and headed Women's Peace Society (1919–28). Their son ¶Oswald Garrison (1872–1949), journalist; editor and president, New York *Evening Post* (1900–18); editor (1918–32) and owner (1918–35) of *The Nation;* author of *John Brown* (1910), *Germany Embattled* (1915), *Prophets True and False* (1928), *The German Phoenix* (1933), *Fighting Years* (1939, autobiographical), *Within Germany* (1940), etc.

Vil·lard de Hon·ne·court \vē-lär-də-ȯn-ə-kür\. c.1225–c.1250. French architect. Itinerant master mason; known for sketchbook in which he recorded and described architectural practices, theory, design of the period.

Vil·la·ret de Joy·euse \vē-lä-red-zhwä-yœz\, Louis-Thomas de. Comte. 1750–1812. French admiral. Fleet commander in battle with English under Lord Howe, off Brest (1794); commander of naval forces in the Santo Domingo expedition (1801–02); governor of Martinique and St. Lucia (1802–09); governor of Venice (1811).

Vil·lars \vē-lär\, Claude-Louis-Hector de. Duc. 1653–1734. Marshal of France. Served in Germany and Flanders (1672–83) under Turenne, Condé, and Luxembourg and in the wars of the League of Augsburg (1688–97); lieutenant general (1693); ambassador to Venice (1683, 1697–1701). In command of army during War of the Spanish Succession (1701–14); defeated Louis William I of Baden at Friedlingen (1702); made marshal of France (1702); won battle of Höchstädt (1703); suppressed Camisards (1704); conducted successful campaign in Germany (1705–08); inflicted heavy casualties on Marlborough at Malplaquet (1709), defeated Eugene of Savoy at Denain (1712); with Eugene concluded Treaty of Rastatt (1714). Member of council of regency under Louis XV. Named marshal general at outbreak of War of Polish Succession (1733).

Villedieu, Mme de. See Marie-Catherine DESJARDINS.

Vil·le·gas \bē(l)-'yā-gäs\, Esteban Manuel de. 1589–1669. Spanish poet. Early abandoned literary career to practice law; author of *Poesías eróticas y amatorias* (a volume of poems in imitation of Anacreon, Horace, and Catullus, 1617–18) and a translation of Boethius's *De consolatione philosophiae* (1665).

Ville·har·douin \vē-lə-är-dwaⁿ\, Geoffroi de. c.1150–c.1213. French nobleman. Served in the Fourth Crusade (1199–1207) under Thibaut III of Champagne and wrote its history in his *Chronique,* known also as *Conquête de Constantinople,* one of the oldest extant specimens of French prose.

Vil·lèle \vē-lel\, Joseph, *in full* Jean-Baptiste-Guillaume-Joseph de. Comte. 1773–1854. French politician. Ultraroyalist deputy (1815–16); minister without portfolio (1820–21); minister of finance (1821–28); made comte and premier (1822); identified with reactionary policies of Charles X.

Ville·mes·sant \vēl-mā-säⁿ, -me-\, Jean-Hippolyte-Auguste Car·tier de \kär-tyā-də-\. 1812–1879. French journalist. Founded *Le Figaro,* first (1854) as a weekly and later (1866) as a daily journal; director (1854–75).

Villena, Marqués de. See Juan PACHECO.

Vil·le·na \bē(l)-'yā-nä\, Enrique de. *Also* Enrique de Ara·gón \thā-är-ä-'gōn\. c.1384–1434. Spanish writer and scholar. Made first prose translations of Virgil's *Aeneid* and Dante's *Divina commedia;* author of *Arte de trobar, Arte cisoria, Libro del aojamiento,* and *Doce trabajos de Hércules.*

Villeneuve, Arnau de. See ARNAU DE VILLANOVA.

Ville·neuve \vēl-nœv\, Jean-Marie-Rodrigue. 1883–1947. Canadian prelate, b. Sacré-Coeur de Montreal, Que. Ordained (1907); professor, Ottawa (1907–20); bishop of Gravelbourg (1930); archbishop of Quebec (1931); cardinal (1933).

Villeneuve, Pierre-Charles-Jean-Baptiste-Silvestre de. 1763–1806. French admiral. Vice admiral (1804); commander of fleet designed to invade England (1805); defeated by Nelson in the battle of Trafalgar (Oct. 21, 1805).

Ville·roi \vē-lər-wä\, François de Neuf·ville de \nœ-vēl-də-\. Duc. 1644–1730. French soldier. Favorite of Louis XIV; general of brigade (1672), field marshal (1674), lieutenant general (1677), marshal of France (1693); commanded armies in the Low Countries (1695); defeated and captured by Prince Eugene of Savoy at Cremona (1702); defeated at Ramillies (1706).

Villiers, de. See DE VILLIERS.

Vil·liers \'vil-(y)ərz\, Barbara. Countess of Cas·tle·maine \'kas-əl-'mān\. Duchess of Cleve·land \'klēv-lənd\. 1641–1709. Mistress of Charles II of England. Daughter of 2d Viscount Grandison; m. (1659) Roger Palmer, later Earl of Castlemaine; mistress of Charles II (1660–74); became Roman Catholic (1663); carried on traffic in sale of offices; instrumental in dismissal of ministers; was created duchess of Cleveland (1670); lived in Paris (1677–84). Mother by Charles II (acknowledged paternity) of ¶Charles Fitz·roy \fits-'rȯi\ (1662–1730), Duke of Southampton and Earl of Chichester (cr. 1675); succeeded as earl of Southampton and duke of Cleveland (1709); Henry Fitzroy (1663–1690), Duke of Grafton (see under FITZROY); ¶George Fitzroy (1665–1716), Duke of Northumberland (cr. 1674); and two daughters.

Villiers, Charles Pelham. 1802–1898. English politician and reformer. M.P. (1835–98) as a free trader; repeated resolution against corn laws annually till their abolition (1846); president of Poor-Law Board (1859–66), holding cabinet rank.

Villiers, George. 1st Duke of Buck·ing·ham \'bək-iŋ-əm, *US also* -iŋ-,ham\. 1592–1628. English courtier and politician. Favorite of James I after fall of Earl of Somerset (1615); created earl of Buckingham (1617), marquis (1618), duke (1623). As lord high admiral (1619), urged English assistance for Bohemian Protestants; bungled schemes to marry Prince Charles (later Charles I) first to infanta Maria of Spain (1623), later to Henrietta Maria, sister of Louis XIII of France; sent futile expeditions under a German soldier, Count Mansfeld, against Palatinate (1625) and under his favorite, Sir Edward Cecil, against Cádiz (1625); saved from impeachment by Charles's dissolution of Parliament (1627, 1628); personally led expedition to relieve Rochelle, failed miserably; assassinated.

His son ¶George (1628–1687), 2d duke; reared with future Charles II and James II; joined Royalists (1643) and served under Prince Rupert; joined Lord Holland's rising in Surrey (1648); retained favor of Charles II and became privy councilor (1650); aided in advancement by cousin Barbara Villiers, the king's mistress; member of Cabal (1667–69); engaged in series of intrigues and caused much scandal by his personal immorality; attacked in Parliament as promoter of popery and arbitrary government; lost influence to Arlington; dismissed from offices (1674). Author of several comedies, including the burlesque *The Rehearsal* (1671).

Villiers, George William Frederick. 4th Earl of Clar·en·don \'klar-ən-dən\ of the Villiers line, and 4th Baron Hyde \'hīd\. 1800–1870. English statesman. As ambassador at Madrid (1833–39), conducted negotiations over question of

Spanish succession; inherited earldom from uncle (1838); lord privy seal in Melbourne's government (1839–41); lord lieutenant of Ireland (1847–52); foreign secretary (1853–58) through Crimean War, exerting much influence in drafting of Declaration of Paris (1856) laying down international rules of maritime warfare; foreign secretary (1865–66, 1868–70), responsible for basis adopted in later settlement of *Alabama* claims.

His grandson ¶George Herbert Hyde Villiers (1877–1955), 6th Earl of Clarendon, was chief government whip, House of Lords (1922–25); chairman, British Broadcasting Corp. (1927–30); governor general of Union of South Africa (1931–37); lord chamberlain of king's household (1938–52).

Vil·liers de L'Isle-Adam \vēl-yād-lē-lá-dä^n\, Auguste de, *in full* Jean-Marie-Mathias-Philippe-Auguste de. Comte. 1838–1889. French writer. Author of works marked by distaste for Naturalism and by Romantic interest in sensualism, cruelty, and the occult, including *Premières poésies* (1859); *Isis* (novel, 1862); short stories *Contes cruels* (1883, 1888), *Tribulat Bonhomet* (1887), *Histoires insolites* (1888); plays *Ellen* (1865), *Morgane* (1866), *La Révolte* (1870), *Le Nouveau Monde* (1875), *Axel* (1890).

Vil·lon \vē-yō^n, vē-lō^n\, François. *Orig.* François de Mont·cor·bier \də-mō^n-kȯrb-yā\ *or* des Loges \də-lōzh\. 1431–after 1463. French poet. Adopted by Guillaume de Villon, whose surname he assumed. Led irregular life; fatally stabbed a priest (1455); involved in robbery at the Collège de Navarre in Paris (1456); arrested for theft (1462) and for brawling (1462), and sentenced to death, the sentence being later commuted to banishment from Paris. His works, highly lyrical, technically accomplished, emotional and learned, included "Pour prier Nostre-Dame," *Le Petit Testament* or *Le Lais* (c.1456), "Épître à Marie d'Orléans," *Le Testament* (c.1461), "Ballade des pendus" or "L'Épitaphe Villon."

Villon, Jacques. See Gaston DUCHAMP.

Vi·meur \vē-mœr\, Jean-Baptiste-Donatien de. Comte de Ro·cham·beau \rō-shä^n-bō\. 1725–1807. French soldier. Served in War of Austrian Succession and Seven Years' War; lieutenant general (1780). Commanded French force sent (1780) to aid Americans in Revolutionary War; joined Washington's Continental army at White Plains, N.Y. (July 1781). The joint forces defeated Cornwallis at Yorktown, Va., with French fleet preventing an escape by sea (Oct. 19, 1781). Returned to France (1783); commanded army of the North during French Revolution (1791); created marshal of France (1803).

Vin·cent \'vin(t)-sənt\. Saint. d. 304. Spanish martyr. Deacon to Bishop Valerius of Saragossa; tortured and executed at Valencia under Diocletian.

Vincent of Beau·vais \bō-'vā\. *Lat.* Vincentius Bel·lov·a·cen·sis \bel-,äv-ə-'ken(t)-səs\. c.1190–1264. French scholar. Entered Dominican order (c.1220); labored (c.1220–44) on compendium of universal knowledge *Speculum majus,* the greatest encyclopedia before 18th century; lector and chaplain to court of Louis IX (c.1250); also wrote *De eruditione filiorum nobilium.*

Vincent of Lé·rins \lā-ra^{n}s\. *Lat.* Vincentius Le·ri·nen·sis \,ler-ə-'nen(t)-səs\. Saint. d. c.450. French religious. Entered (c.425) Abbey of Lérins, of which he became outstanding theologian. Author, under pseudonym Per·e·gri·nus \,per-ə-'grī-nəs\, of noted work of heresiography *Commonitoria,* upholding Semi-Pelagianism against Augustinian doctrine of predestination.

Vincent, Sir Howard, *in full* Charles Edward Howard. 1849–1908. English soldier and politician. First director of criminal investigation, Scotland Yard (1878–84); Conservative M.P. (1885–1908); advocated legislation on alien immigration and appointment of public trustee (passed 1905 and 1906). Author of *Police Code and Manual of Criminal Law* (1882).

Vincent, John Heyl. 1832–1920. American clergyman, b. Tuscaloosa, Ala. Ordained in Methodist Episcopal church (1855); founded Union Sunday School Institute for the Northwest and monthly *Sunday School Teacher* (1864); originator, with Lewis Miller, of Chautauqua movement, beginning (1874) in a Sunday-school teachers' assembly at Lake Chautauqua, N.Y. Elected bishop (1888), episcopal residence at Buffalo, N.Y. (1888–92), Topeka, Kans. (1892–1900), and Zürich, Switzerland (1900–04); retired (1904). Author of *The Chautauqua Movement* (1886), etc.

Vin·cent \va^n-sa^n\, Sténio Joseph. 1874–1959. Haitian politician. Lawyer, diplomat, educational official; founded newspapers *L'Effort* (1902) and *Haïti-Journal* (1930); president of Haiti (1930–41).

Vin·cent de Paul \va^n-sa^n-də-pȯl, *Angl* 'vin(t)-sənt-də-'pȯl\. Saint. 1581–1660. French clergyman. Renowned for his benevolence, zeal, and genius for practical organization; founded Congregation of the Mission (1625), known as Lazarists or Vincentians, and, with St. Louise de Marillac, Daughters of Charity (1633), also known as Vincentians. Canonized (1737).

Vin·cen·tel·lo d'·Is·tria \,vin-chen-'tel-lō-'dis-trē-ə\. 1380–1434. Istrian adventurer. With aid of Alfonso V of Aragon, invaded Corsica and raised insurrection against Genoese rule (c.1414); captured all of island but Bonifacio and ruled as Aragonese viceroy (1420–34); captured and executed by Genoese.

Vin·cent Fer·rer \'vin(t)-sənt-fə-'rer\. Saint. *Span.* San Vi·cen·te Fer·rer \vē-'thān-tā-fer-'rer\. c.1350–1419. Spanish religious. Entered Dominican order (1368); ordained (1379); renowned for piety, scholarship, preaching; confessor to antipope Benedict XIII (1394–99) but later helped turn Benedict's supporters to Roman pontiff, thus contributing to end of Great Western Schism; an elector of Ferdinand I of Aragon (1412). Canonized (1455).

Vin·ci \'vēn-chē\, Leonardo. c.1690–1730. Italian composer. A leader of Neapolitan school; composed comic operas as *Lo cecato fauzo* (1719), *Lo scagno* (1720), *La festa di Bacco* (1722), *La mogliera fedele* (1724), serious operas as *Silla dittatore* (1723), *Il trionfo di Camilla* (1725), *Didone abbandonata* (1726), *Artaserse* (1730); also oratorios, motets, masses.

Vinci, Leonardo da. See LEONARDO DA VINCI.

Vin·dex \'vin-deks\, Gaius Julius. d. 68 A.D. Roman politician. Senator and perhaps praetor; governor of Lugdunensis, or Gallia Celtica; first Roman governor to rebel against Nero; his revolt failed but sparked others in Spain, Africa, Egypt.

Vinea, Petrus de. See PIETRO DELLA VIGNA.

Vi·net \vē-ne\, Alexandre-Rodolphe. 1797–1847. Swiss theologian. Professor in Basel (1817–37), Lausanne (1837–45); ordained (1819); instrumental in introducing Protestantism into French-speaking Switzerland; devoted himself (1845–47) to organization of Free churches in Vaud. Among his works were *Essai sur la manifestation des convictions religieuses et sur la séparation de l'Église et de l'État* (1842), *Études sur Blaise Pascal* (1848), *Études sur la littérature française au 19e Siècle* (1849–51).

Vin·je \'vin-yə\, Aasmund Olafsson. 1818–1870. Norwegian poet, journalist, and reformer. Took active part in movement to establish Landsmål (Nynorsk) language (from 1851); published Landsmål newspaper *Dølen* (1858–60). Author of *Ferdaminni fraa sumaren 1860* (a description of Norwegian country life, 1861), *Storegut* (epic cycle, 1866).

Vi·no·gra·doff \,vē-nə-'gräd-əf\, Sir Paul Gavrilovitch. 1854–1925. British jurist and historian, b. Russia. To England (1902); professor of jurisprudence, Oxford (1903–25); authority on feudal England. Author of *Villeinage in England* (1892), *Growth of the Manor* (1905), *English Society in the Eleventh Century* (1908), *Historical Jurisprudence* (1920–22).

Vi·no·gra·dov \,vē-nə-'gräd-əf\, Ivan Matveyevich. 1891–1983. Soviet mathematician. Taught mathematics at Leningrad Polytechnic Institute (from 1920), Leningrad State University (from (1925), and Moscow State University (from 1934). Known esp. for contributions to the analytical theory of numbers, including a partial solution of the Goldbach conjecture concerning the possibility of expressing integers as the sum of a few primes. Author of *The Method of Trigonometrical Sums in the Theory of Numbers* (1954), *An Introduction to the Theory of Numbers* (1955), etc.

Vinogradsky. See WINOGRADSKY.

Vin·son \'vin(t)-sən\, Carl. 1883–1981. American politician, b. near Milledgeville, Ga. Member of U.S. House of Representatives (1914–64), a record.

Vinson, Frederick Moore. 1890–1953. American jurist, b. Louisa, Ky. Member, U.S. House of Representatives (1924–29, 1931–38); associate justice, U.S. Court of Appeals for D.C. (1938–43); director, Office of Economic Stabilization (1943–45); secretary of the treasury (1945–46); chief justice, U.S. Supreme Court (1946–53).

Vio \'vē-ō\, Tommaso de, *orig.* Jacopo de. *Known as* Caj·e·tan \'kaj-ə-,tan\, *Lat.* Caj·e·ta·nus \,kaj-ə-'tā-nəs\, *Ital.* Gaetano. 1469–1534. Italian prelate, b. Gaeta. Entered Dominican order (1484); taught at Padua (1493–94), Pavia (1497–99), Sapienza in Rome (1501–08); master general of Dominicans (1508–18); defended papal authority against Council of Pisa (1511); urged reform at Fifth Lateran Council (1512–17); cardinal (1517); as papal legate to Germany (1518) met Luther at Augsburg; bishop of Gaeta (1519); helped draft bull condemning Luther (1520); papal legate to Hungary, Poland, Bohemia (1523–24). Author of commentaries on Aristotle, Porphyry, Peter Lombard, and esp. on Aquinas's *Summa theologiae* (1507–20).

Violino, Carlo del. See Carlo CAPROLI.

Violle \vyȯl\, Jules-Louis-Gabriel. 1841–1923. French physicist. Professor at École Normale Supérieure (1884–92), Conservatoire des Arts et Métiers (1892 ff.); made first high-altitude determination of solar constant (1875); proposed a photometric unit (Violle's standard, or violle, 1881).

Viol·let-le-Duc \vyȯ-lel-dūēk\, Eugène-Emmanuel. 1814–1879. French architect. A leader in the Gothic revival in France; designed the restoration of many medieval buildings in France, including abbey church of La Madeleine at Vézelay (1840), Sainte-Chapelle, Paris (1840), Abbey of Saint-Denis, Paris (1846), Saint-Sernin, Toulouse (1862); did major work on the cathedrals of Amiens, Laon, and Notre Dame de Paris; restored the Cité de Carcassonne, the Château de Pierrefonds, Château d'Arragory. Compiler of the illustrated *Dictionnaire raisonné de l'architecture française du XIe au XVIe siècle*

(1854–68) and *Dictionnaire raisonné du mobilier française de l'époque carlovingienne à la Rénaissance* (1858–75).

Viot·ti \'vyȯt-tē\, Giovanni Battista. 1755–1824. Italian violinist. Lived at Paris (1782–92, 1819 ff.), London (1792–98, 1801–19, 1823–24); director of Italian opera, Paris (1819–22); last great representative of Italian school of violin playing; works included 29 violin concertos, sonatas, and duets, string trios and quartets, and compositions for piano.

Vir·chow \'fir-ḵō\, Rudolf. 1821–1902. German pathologist and political leader. Professor of pathological anatomy, Würzburg (1849); professor and director, Pathological Institute, Berlin (from 1856). Founded cellular pathology; carried on researches on blood, phlebitis, tuberculosis, rickets, tumors, trichinosis, etc. Made sanitary reforms in Berlin; established farms utilizing sewage for fertilizing the land. Worked also in archaeology and anthropology. A founder and leader of the Fortschrittspartei and later of the German Liberal party; member of Prussian National Assembly (from 1861) and of the German Reichstag (1880–93); opposed policies of Bismarck. Founded (1847, with Benno Reinhardt) *Archiv für pathologische Anatomie und Physiologie,* later known as *Virchows Archiv.* Author of *Die Cellularpathologie* (1858), *Handbuch der speziellen Pathologie und Therapie* (1854–76), etc.

Vi·ret \vē-re\, Pierre. 1511–1571. Swiss theologian. Associate of Farel (from 1531); converted Lausanne and Vaud to Protestant faith (1536); opposed by people of Bern, was deposed (1559); withdrew to Geneva.

Vir·gil \'vər-jəl\. *Also spelled* Vergil. *Full Lat. name* Publius Vergilius Ma·ro \'mär-(,)ō\. 70–19 B.C. Roman poet. Greatest of Roman poets; lived life of scholar, taking no part in events; friend of Horace and Gallus; enjoyed patronage of Maecenas and Augustus. Works included *Eclogae* or *Bucolica,* set of 10 poems (42–37 B.C.), *Georgica,* 4 books on rural topics (36–29), and the great epic of the founding of Rome *Aeneis* or *Aeneid* (30–19).

Vir·i·a·thus \,vir-ē-'ā-thəs\ *or* **Vir·i·a·tus** \-təs\. d. c.139 B.C. Lusitanian rebel. Shepherd of Lusitania (Portugal) who conducted war (147–139 B.C.) against Romans; assassinated.

Vir Singh \'vir-'sin(-hə)\, Bhai. 1872–1957. Indian writer and theologian. Founded weekly newspaper *Khālsā Samācār* in Amritsar (1899); became leading exponent of Sikh revival and of Punjabi literary language. Author of novels imbued with Sikh philosophy as *Bijai Singh* (1899), *Kalgīdlur Camathār* (1935), *Sundarī* (1943), *Bābā Noudh Singh* (1946) and of biography *Gurū Nānak Camathār* (1936).

Vir·ta·nen \'vir-tá-nen\, Artturi Ilmari. 1895–1973. Finnish biochemist. Professor, Finland Inst. of Technology (1931–39), U. of Helsinki (1939–48); director, Biochemical Inst., Helsinki (1931–73); awarded 1945 Nobel prize for chemistry for development of AIV method of protecting silage from destructive fermentation.

Vi·rués \bēr-'wās\, Cristóbal de. 1550–1609. Spanish poet. Captain in Spanish army; friend and early rival of Lope de Vega. Author of five tragedies and the epic *El Monserrate* (1588, rev. 1602).

Vi·scher \'fish-ər\. A family of Nürnberg sculptors and brass founders, including: Hermann, *called* the Elder (d. 1488), who established the foundry. His son ¶Peter, *called* the Elder (1460?–1529), whose works included the tomb of Archbishop Ernst of Saxony, the shrine of St. Sebald (1508–19), and bronze figures of Kings Arthur and Theodoric for the tomb of Emperor Maximilian. Peter's sons and assistants ¶Hermann, *called* the Younger (1486?–1517), ¶Peter, *called* the Younger (1487–1528), ¶Hans (1489?–1550), whose works included the double monument of Electors Joachim I and Johann Cicero of Brandenburg in Berlin cathedral and the fountain figure Apollo in Nürnberg, and ¶Paulus (d. 1531).

Vischer, Friedrich Theodor von. 1807–1887. German poet, critic, and aesthetician. Professor, Tübingen (1844–55, 1866–69), Zürich (1855–66), Stuttgart (1869–87); developed Hegelian aesthetics into theoretical foundation of Realism. Author of *Kritische Gänge* (1844, new series 1860–73), *Ästhetik oder Wissenschaft des Schönen* (1846–58), volumes of verse as *Lyrische Gänge* (1882), whimsical novel *Auch Einer* (1879), etc.

Vi·scon·ti \vēs-'kōn-tē\. Name of powerful Lombard family in Milan, of Ghibelline faction (c.1200–1447), furnishing ruling *signore,* or lords (1311–1447). Most important were: Ottone (1207?–1295), archbishop of Milan (1262–95); defeated Della Torre family at Desio (1277) and began family claim to authority. ¶Matteo I, *called* the Great (1250–1322), grandnephew of Ottone; captain of the people (1287); imperial vicar in Milan (1294); exiled by Della Torre resurgence (1302–10), recaptured city and firmly established family rule; lord of Milan until abdication (1322) in favor of son. His son ¶Galeazzo I (1277?–1328), lord (1322–28). ¶Azzo (1302–1339), son of Galeazzo I; lord (1328–39). Followed by his uncles ¶Giovanni (1290–1354) and ¶Luchino (1292–1349), sons of Matteo; ruled jointly; Giovanni was archbishop (from 1342) and sole ruler (from 1349) of Milan; annexed Genoa (1353); friend of Petrarch. Giovanni was succeeded by his two nephews ¶Galeazzo II (1321–1378) and ¶Bernabò (1323–1385), who held court at Pavia and ruled jointly; Galeazzo was a patron of Petrarch and founded U. of Pavia. His son ¶Gian Galeazzo, *called* Count of Valour (1351–1402), succeeded his father and held court at Pavia as joint ruler (1378–85) with uncle Bernabò, whom he imprisoned and possibly put to death (1385); became master of northern and central Italy; made prince of the empire and duke of Milan (1395) and count of Pavia (1396) by Emperor Wenceslas; began cathedral of Milan (1386) and monastery Certosa di Pavia (1396); bought Pisa and seized Siena (1399), Perugia (1400); annexed Bologna (1402); patron of literature and art. His son ¶Giovanni Maria (1388–1412), duke (1402–12); lost several Lombard cities and was assassinated. His brother ¶Filippo Maria (1392–1447), last Visconti to rule as duke (1412–47); died while awaiting aid against Venice from his son-in-law Francesco Sforza. ¶Valentina (1366–1408), daughter of Gian Galeazzo; m. (1387) Louis, duc d'Orléans; mother of Charles d'Orléans the poet and grandmother of Louis XII of France. Through her, Louis based his claims to Milan.

Visconti, Luchino. Duca di Mo·dro·ne \mȯ-'drō-nā\. 1906–1976. Italian motion-picture director. Known as father of Italian Neorealist film; films included *Ossessione* (1942), *La terra trema* (1948), *Bellissima* (1951), *Siamo donne* (1952), *Senso* (1954), *Rocco e i suio fratelli* (1960), *Il gattopardo* (1963), *Vaghe stelle dell'orsa* (1965), *Lo straniero* (1967), *La caduta degli dei* (1969), *Morte a Venezia* (1971), *L'innocente* (1976); known also as operatic producer.

Visconti-Ve·no·sta \-vā-'nȯs-tä\, Emilio. Marchese. 1829–1914. Italian politician and diplomat. Supporter of Mazzini (1848–49); as Piedmontese commissar, effected union of Parma and Modena with the new kingdom (1859–61); deputy (1860 ff.); minister of foreign affairs (1863–64, 1866–67, 1869–76, 1896–98, 1899–1901); senator (1886); Italian representative at Moroccan Conference at Algeciras (1906).

Vis·scher \'vis-ər\, Roemer. 1547–1620. Dutch poet and moralist. A leader of movement to standardize and purify Dutch language; author of miscellaneous verse published without his knowledge as *Brabbeling* (1612); also wrote moral essays *Sinnepoppen* (1614). His daughter ¶Ann Roemers (c.1583–1651) was also a poet; wrote sonnets and odes; translated Georgette Montenay's *Cent emblèmes Christiens* (pub. 1854); produced revised and improved version of father's *Sinnepoppen* (1640).

Vi·tal \vē-'täl\, Ḥayyim ben Joseph. 1542 or 1543–1620. Palestinian Kabbalist. Disciple of Isaac ben Solomon Luria; claimed to be sole exponent of Lurian school after master's death (1572); rabbi and head of a yeshiva in Jerusalem (1577–85). Author of *Etz Ḥayyim.*

Vi·ta·li \vē-'täl-ē\, Giovanni Battista. 1632–1692. Italian composer. In service of Este court at Modena (1674–92); composed chiefly trio sonatas, dance music, oratorios, cantatas; author of important pedagogical work *Artifici musicali* (1689). His son ¶Tomaso Antonio (1663–1745) also served Modena court (1675–1742); composed chamber works and violin pieces; possibly not composer of the violin *Ciacona* long attributed to him.

Vi·tal·ian \və-'tā(ə)l-yən, -'tā-lē-ən\. Saint. *Lat.* Vi·ta·li·a·nus \və-,tā-lē-'ā-nəs\. d. 672. Pope (657–672). Opposed Monothelitism; received Emperor Constans II in visit at Rome (663); consecrated St. Theodore of Tarsus as first archbishop of Canterbury (668).

Vitalis. See Erik SJÖBERG.

Vitalis, Ordericus. See ORDERICUS VITALIS.

Vi·tel·li·us \və-'tel-ē-əs\, Aulus. 15–69 A.D. Roman emperor (69). Consul (48); proconsul in Africa (c.61); given command (68) of legions in Germany by Galba; proclaimed emperor by his soldiers; entered Rome after suicide of Otho; opposed by Vespasian and his army under Antonius Primus; defeated by Primus and killed.

Vi·tet \vē-te\, Louis, *called* Ludovic. 1802–1873. French writer and politician. Member of Chamber of Deputies (1834–38), Legislative Assembly (1849), and National Assembly (1871). Author of *Les Barricades* (1826), *Les États de Blois* (1827), and *La Mort de Henri III* (1829), published together (1844) as a trilogy under the title *La Ligue.*

Vi·to·ria \vē-'tō-rē-ä\, Francisco de. 1486?–1546. Spanish theologian. Entered Dominican order; lectured at Valladolid (1523–26); professor at Salamanca (1526–46); outspoken critic of government policies, esp. war with France, conquest of New World and barbarous treatment of natives, whom he defended as rational creatures due Christian treatment; argued against just wars except in extreme cases; consulted by Charles V, Philip II; remembered as outstanding teacher; left no writings.

Vi·tru·vi·us \və-'trü-vē-əs\. *In full* Marcus Vitruvius Pol·lio \'päl-ē-,ō\. 1st century B.C. Roman architect and engineer. Little known of life history; author of *De architectura,* dedicated presumably to Augustus, and for many centuries accepted as final authority on classical architecture.

Vitry, Jacques de. See JACQUES DE VITRY.

Vi·try \vē-trē\, Philippe de. 1291–1361. French prelate. Bishop of Meaux (1351); known as a poet, composer, and authority on musical theory. Wrote treatise on musical notation *Ars nova* (c.1322–23).

Vit·to·ne \vēt-'tō-nā\, Bernardo Antonio. c.1705–1770. Italian architect. Outstanding exponent of Rococo design; designed 27 churches, including Sta.

Chiara, Bra (1742), Sta. Maria di Piazza, Turin (1751), S. Michele, Rivarolo Canavese (1759). Author of *Istruzione elementari* (1760), *Istruzione diverse* (1766).

Vittoria, Tommaso Lodovico da. See Tomás Luis de VICTORIA.

Vit·to·ri·ni \ˌvēt-tō-ˈrē-nē\, Elio. 1908–1966. Italian novelist and critic. A pioneer in translating English and U.S. authors into Italian, as Faulkner, Poe, Saroyan, Defoe, Hemingway, Auden, T.S. Eliot; a leader of Neorealist movement. Novels included *Conversazione in Sicilia* (1941), *Uomini e no* (1945), *Il sempione strizza l'occhio al frejus* (1947), *Il garofano rosso* (1948), *Le donne di messina* (1949). Edited journals *Il Politecnico* (1945–47) and *Il Menabò* (with Italo Calvino).

Vittorino da Feltre. See VITTORINO RAMBOLDINI.

Vit·to·ri·no Ram·bol·di·ni \ˌvēt-tō-ˈrē-nō-ˌräm-bōl-ˈdē-nē\ *or* **de' Ramboldini** *or* **de' Ram·bal·do·ni** \ˌräm-bäl-ˈdō-nē\. *Known as* Vittorino da Fel·tre \ˈfel-trā\. 1378–1446. Italian educator. Often called greatest Humanist schoolmaster of Renaissance. Taught at Padua; tutor to children of Gonzaga rulers of Mantua (1423 ff.); founded (1425) La Giocosa, school admitting noble and poor children and employing curriculum based on Roman and Greek texts.

Vittorio. See VICTOR.

Vi·val·di \vē-ˈväl-dē, *Angl* vi-ˈväl-dē, -ˈvȯl-\, Antonio Lucio. 1678–1741. Italian composer. Ordained priest (1703); violin teacher at Pio Ospedale della Pietà, Venice (1703–09, 1711–16), and maestro de' concerti there (1716–38). Considered most original and influential Italian composer of his day, an innovator in form, orchestration, and technique, and a highly inventive and prolific composer. Composed over 700 numbered works, including some 450 concertos, 73 sonatas, 43 operas, 33 cantatas; notable works included *L'estro armonico* (12 violin concertos, 1703), *La stravaganza* (12 violin concertos, 1714), *Il cemento dell'armonia e dell'inventione* (12 violin concertos including those known as "The Four Seasons," 1725), *La cetra* (12 violin concertos, 1728), operas *Armida al campo d'Egitto* (1718), *Giustino* (1724), *La fida ninfa* (1732), *L'Olympiade* (1734), oratorio *Juditha triumphans* (1716).

Vivaldi, Ugolino and his brother Vadino. 13th century. Genoese merchants. Perished apparently in first recorded attempt by Europeans to reach the Indies by sea (1291). Subject of legends, as that they succeeded in circumnavigating Africa and were held prisoner by Prester John in Ethiopia.

Vi·va·ri·ni \ˌvē-vä-ˈrē-nē\. Family of Venetian painters, including: Antonio, *orig. surname* da Mu·ra·no \dä-mü-ˈrä-nō\ (1415?–1476 or 1484), who collaborated with his brother-in-law Giovanni d'Alemagna (1440–47), and among whose joint works were altarpieces for S. Zaccaria, Venice (1443–44), frescoes in Eremitani, Padua (1447–50), *Madonna with Holy Fathers,* and *Coronation of the Virgin.* Antonio's brother ¶Bartolomeo da Murano, *later called* Vivarini (c.1432–c.1499), collaborated with Antonio (from 1450); produced altarpieces for SS. Giovanni e Paolo (1473), Sta. Maria dei Frari (1474), S. Giovanni in Bragora (1478). Antonio's son ¶Alvise Vivarini (c.1446–c.1505), pupil of his uncle Bartolomeo; a chief representative of late Gothic; collaborator with and rival of Giovanni Bellini; painter of *Virgin and Child, Enthroned Madonna, Madonna with Saints,* and *Santa Clara.*

Vi·ve·ke·nan·da \ˌvē-və-kə-ˈnän-də\. *Orig.* Na·ren·dra·nath Dat·ta \nə-ˈren-drə-nət-ˈdət-tə\; *also spelled* Dutt \ˈdət\. 1863–1902. Indian religious leader. Joined Hindu reform movement Brahmo Samaj; leading disciple of Ramakrishna; lectured throughout the world; founded (1898) Ramakrishna Mission near Calcutta.

Vi·ves \ˈbē-b̲ās\. Amadeo. 1871–1932. Spanish composer. Founded with Luis Millet (1891) choral society Orféo Català; composed over 100 operettas, operas, zarzuelas, including *Artus* (1895), *Euda d'Uriach* (1900), *Maruxa* (1914), *Balada de carnaval* (1919), *Doña Francisquita* (1923).

Vives, Juan Luis. 1492–1540. Spanish Humanist. Professor, Louvain (1519 ff.); friend of Erasmus. To England (1523) on invitation of Henry VIII; tutor to Princess Mary; lectured at Oxford; lost royal favor through opposition to divorce of Catherine of Aragon (1527); retired to Bruges (1529). Known esp. as a logician; opposed Scholasticism; one of first to emphasize induction as a philosophical and psychological method. Works included commentary on Augustine's *De civitate dei* (1522); pedagogical works *De ratione studii puerilis* (1523), *De disciplinis* (1531), *Introductio ad sapientiam* (1540); a major work on psychology and philosophical method *De anima et vita* (1538).

Vi·via·ni \vēv-yȧ-nē\, René. 1863–1925. French politician. Socialist deputy for Paris (1893–1902, 1906–10); minister of labor (1906–10); responsible for workmen's pensions law; minister of public instruction (1913–14); premier and minister of foreign affairs (1914–15); minister of justice in Briand's cabinet (1915–17); senator (1922).

Vi·via·ni \vēv-ˈyä-nē\, Vincenzo. 1622–1703. Italian mathematician. Assistant to Galileo (1639 ff.); helped Torricelli build barometer; with G.A. Borelli measured velocity of sound (1660); attempted to reconstruct lost mathematical treatises of Aristaeus and Apollonius; published (1690) Italian version of Euclid's *Elements.*

Vivien, Renée. See Pauline TARN.

Vi·vien de Saint-Mar·tin \vēv-yaⁿ-də-saⁿ-mȧr-taⁿ\, Louis. 1802–1897. French geographer. Author of *Histoire de la géographie et des découvertes géographiques* (1873); editor of *L'Année géographique* (1863–76), *Nouveau dictionnaire de géographie universelle* (completed by Louis Rousselet, 1876–95).

Vivonne de Savelli, Catherine de. See ANGENNES.

Viz·ca·í·no \bēth-kä-ˈē-nō, bēs-\, Sebastián. 1550?–1616. Spanish explorer. To Mexico (c.1586); led expeditions on western coast of Mexico north from Acapulco to Lower California (1596–97), and along Californian coast as far as 43° N (1602–03), entered San Diego and Monterey bays, anchored (1603) in bay at Point Reyes, north of San Francisco; made voyage of discovery (1611–14) from Mexico into Pacific, attempting unsuccessfully to establish trade with Japan.

Viz·e·tel·ly \viz-ə-ˈtel-ē\, Henry Richard. 1820–1894. English publisher. Correspondent of *Illustrated London News* in Paris (1865–72) and Berlin (1872); issued cheap reprints of English and European authors (later called the Mermaid Series); fined and jailed for publishing works of Zola (1889). His brother ¶Frank (1830–?1883) helped found (1857) *Le Monde illustré* in Paris; war correspondent of *Illustrated London News* from 1859 to his death in the Sudan. Two sons of Henry were journalists: ¶Edward Henry (1847–1903), correspondent of *New York Times* and London *Daily News* during Franco–Prussian War, and commander of New York *Herald* relief expedition (1889) to find Stanley; and ¶Ernest Alfred (1853–1922), correspondent during Franco–Prussian War, editor of bibliophilists' *Heptameron* (1894), author of three novels and of French biographies, esp. of Zola (1904). Another son ¶Frank (Francis) Horace (1864–1938) settled in New York (1891, naturalized 1926); member of Funk & Wagnalls Co.'s editorial staff (from 1891); associate editor of *Standard Dictionary* (from 1891), editor (1914–38); editor of *New Standard Encyclopaedia of Universal Knowledge* (1931, 1935), of *New International Year Book* (1932–38), and of numerous other reference books; conducted "Lexicographer's Easy Chair" column in *Literary Digest* (1904–10, 1912–37).

Vla·čic \ˈvlȧ-chēts\, Matija. *Surnamed* Il·ir \ˈil-ir\, *i.e.* the Illyrian. *Lat.* Matthias Flacius Il·lyr·i·cus \il-ˈir-i-kəs\. 1520–1575. Istrian theologian and historian. Pupil of Luther at Wittenberg; professor of Hebrew there (1544–49); championed strict interpretation of Luther's beliefs; professor of New Testament at Jena (1557); carried on bitter controversy with Melanchthon over adiaphorism which resulted in lasting rift with Lutheranism; dismissed from Jena (1561) for personal attacks on Melanchthon; subsequently in Regensburg, Antwerp, Frankfurt, Strassburg. Directed compilation (1559–74) of church history known as *Centuriae Magdeburgenses;* produced own version of Luther's works (1555) and wrote *Book of Confutation* (1559) on adiaphorism.

Vlacq \ˈvläk\, Adriaan. *Surname also spelled* Vlack. 1600–1666 or 1667. Dutch mathematician. Published (1628) tables of common logarithms between 20,000 and 90,000, filling a gap left by previous tables, and (1633) tables of trigonometric functions and their logs.

Vlad Țepeș. See BASARAB dynasty.

Vla·di·mir \(ˌ)vlə-ˈdyē-mir, *Angl* ˈvlad-ə-ˌmi(ə)r, vlə-ˈdē-ˌmi(ə)r\. Name of two Russian rulers:

Vladimir I. Saint. c.956–1015. Grand prince of Kiev (980–1015). Son of Svyatoslav of Kiev; made prince of Novgorod (970); on father's death (972) forced to flee to Scandinavia, whence he returned to seize Kiev from brother Yaropolk; consolidated rule over realm from Baltic to Ukraine; made pact (c.987) with Emperor Basil II of Constantinople, receiving Basil's sister in marriage and converting to Christianity; first Russian ruler to accept Christianity; forcibly converted Kiev and Novgorod.

Vladimir II. *Surnamed* Mo·no·makh \mə-(ˌ)nə-ˈmȧk̲\. 1053–1125. Grand prince of Kiev (1113–25). Son of Vsevolod I Yaroslavich and great-grandson of Vladimir I; grandson through mother of Byzantine emperor Constantine IX Monomachus; prince of Chernigov (1078–94); succeeded cousin Svyatopolk II in Kiev (1113); founded city of Vladimir; renowned as ruler, warrior, and writer of works on events and conditions in contemporary Russia that are earliest known works of Russian secular literature.

Vla·di·mi·res·cu \ˌvläd-ē-mē-ˈres-kü\, Tudor. c.1780–1821. Walachian leader. Officer in Russian army; joined Greek revolutionary society Philikí Etairía; following Etairist uprising of Ypsilantis, organized separate rising in Walachia (1821) against Greek-Turkish government; suspected of conspiracy with Turks, arrested and executed on order of Ypsilantis.

Vladislav. See (1) ULÁSZLÓ (kings of Hungary); (2) WŁADYSŁAW (kings of Poland).

Vla·minck \vlȧ-maⁿk\, Maurice de. 1876–1958. French painter. A member of Fauvist group with Derain, van Dongen, etc.; early landscapes and still lifes marked by bold color and brushwork; later influenced by Cezanne, developed a personal style of Expressionism.

Voet \'vüt\, Gijsbert. *Lat.* Gisbertus Voe·ti·us \'ve-shē-əs\. 1589–1676. Dutch theologian. Professor, Utrecht (from 1634); uncompromising Calvinist, opposed Arminianism, Cocceianism, and Cartesianism.

Vo·gau \'vò-gaù\, Boris Andreyevich. *Pseudonym* Boris Pil·nyak \pyil-'nyák\. 1894–?1938. Russian novelist. Author notably of tales dealing with transition from old czarist Russia to new Communist society; criticized for sympathizing with earlier era. Among his novels were *Goly god* (1922), *Mashiny i volki* (1924), *Volga vpadayet v Kaspiyskoye more* (1930), *Kamni i korni* (1935), *O.K.* (1935), *Sozrevarie plodov* (1936).

Vo·gel \vò-gel, vō-\, Charles-Louis-Adolphe. 1808–1892. French composer. Composed chiefly operas; known for song "Les trois couleurs" sung after the July revolution (1830).

Vo·gel \'fō-gəl\, Hermann Karl. 1842–1907. German astronomer. Director of private observatory in Bothkamp (1870–74); on staff of new Potsdam observatory (from 1874), director (from 1882); known for spectroscopic studies of planets and stars, discovery (1889) of spectroscopic binary stars, studies of stellar motions by spectroscopic Doppler shifts.

Vo·gel \'vō-gəl\, Sir Julius. 1835–1899. New Zealand politician, b. England. To Australia (1852), New Zealand (1861); in Parliament (1863–76); leader of opposition (1865–68); colonial treasurer (1869–72); prime minister (1873–75, 1876); agent general in London (1876–80); again M.P. (1880–89).

Vo·gel·sang \'fō-gəl-,zäŋ\, Karl von. Freiherr. 1818–1890. German reformer. In Prussian government service (to 1848); became Roman Catholic (1850) and evolved a program of corporative state socialism based on Christian ethic; in Vienna (from 1864) strongly influenced Austrian Christian Socialist party; founded (1879) *Monatsschrift für Christliche Sozialreform*. Author of *Die Konkurrenzfähigkeit der Industrie* (1883), *Die materielle Lage des Arbeiterstandes in Österreich* (1884), etc.

Vo·gel von Falck·en·stein \'fō-gəl-fòn-'fäl-kən-,shtīn\, Eduard. 1797–1885. German general. Chief of staff under Wrangel in Danish War (1864), and governor of Jutland; defeated Hanoverians at Langensalza (1866); defeated southern German troops and besieged Frankfurt am Main; governor general of Bohemia; governor general of German coast provinces (1870–71).

Vogelweide. See WALTHER VON DER VOGELWEIDE.

Vogl \'fō-gəl\, Johann Nepomuk. 1802–1866. Austrian poet. Author of *Balladen und Romanzen* (1835–41), *Lyrische Gedichte* (1844), *Soldatenlieder* (1849), etc.

Vo·gler \'fō-glər\, Georg Joseph. *Usually called* Abt \äpt\, *or* Ab·bé \'ä-bā\, Vogler. 1749–1814. German organist, composer, and writer. Chaplain (1772–75), assistant Kapellmeister (1775–83) at Mannheim court; founded Mannheim Tonschule; Kapellmeister in Munich (1784–86), in service of Swedish court at Stockholm (1786–99), at court of Darmstadt (1807–14). Composed operas, sacred and secular vocal music, orchestral works, etc. Best known for theoretical and pedagogic works as *Tonwissenschaft und Tonsetzkunst* (1776), *Kuhrpfälzische Tonschule* (1778).

Vogt \'fòkt\, Johan Herman Lie. 1858–1932. Norwegian geologist. Professor, Christiania (now Oslo, 1886–1912), Trondheim (1912–28); pioneer in use of physical-chemical methods in study of origin of igneous rocks and ores. Author of *Studier over slagger* (1884), *Die Silikatschmelzlösungen* (1903–04).

Vogt, Nils Collett. 1864–1937. Norwegian writer. Author of verse *Digte* (1887), *Fra Vaar til Høst* (1894), *Det dyre brød* (1900), *Septemberbrand* (1907), *Hjemkomst* (1917), *Ned fra bjerget* (1924), *Et liv i digt* (1937); novels *Familiens Sorg* (1889), *Harriet Blich* (1902), *Mennesker* (1903), *Levende og døde* (1922), *Fra gutt til mann* (1932), *Oplevelser* (1934); plays, etc.

Vo·güé \vòg-wʸā\, Eugène-Melchior de. Vicomte. 1848–1910. French writer and diplomat. In diplomatic service (1871–82) at Constantinople, Cairo, St. Petersburg; on staff of *Revue des Deux Mondes* and *Journal des Débats*. Among his books were *Le Roman russe* (1886), *Coeurs russes* (1894), *Histoire et poésie* (1898), *Les Morts qui parlent* (novel, 1899), *Le Maître de la mer* (novel, 1903), *Maxime Gorki* (1905).

Voigt \'fōkt\, Woldemar. 1850–1919. German physicist. Professor, Göttingen (1883–1919); known for work in crystallography; developed equations (1887) later known as Lorenz transformations, introduced term "tensor" into mathematical physics (1898).

Voi·sin \vwá-zaⁿ\, Gabriel. 1880–1973. French manufacturer of airplanes. Pioneer experimenter in aviation in France with brother ¶Charles (1882–1912), who made first manned free flight in Europe (1907); established first aircraft manufactory (1908) and constructed the biplanes used by Léon Delagrange and Henri Farman in their first successful flights; factory later (1918) turned to automobile production.

Voit \'fòit\, Carl von. 1831–1908. German physiologist. Professor, Munich (1863–1908); founder, with Ludwig von Buhl and Max von Pettenkofer, of *Zeitschrift für Biologie* (1864); with Pettenkofer conducted pioneering experiments in animal and human metabolism, making first measurements of energy requirements and determinations of oxygen and nutrient utilization.

Voi·ture \vwá-tü̅r\, Vincent. 1597–1648. French man of letters. Enjoyed patronage of duc d'Orléans; became a leader of the salon of the marquise de Rambouillet; wrote light verse, witty letters, and developed the style known as *la belle galanterie* based on wit, irony, and passion; answered Isaac de Benserade's sonnet "Job" with "L'Amour d'Uranie avec Philis," precipitating literary controversy that split the salon.

Vojtěch. See Saint ADALBERT.

Vol·kelt \'fòl-kəlt\, Johannes Immanuel. 1848–1930. German philosopher. Professor at Jena (1879), Basel (1883), Würzburg (1889), Leipzig (1894). Author of *Kants Erkenntnistheorie* (1879), *System der Ästhetik* (1905–14), *Das Problem der Individualität* (1928), etc.

Volk·mann \'fòlk-,män\, Richard von. 1830–1889. German surgeon. Professor at Halle (from 1867); pioneer in antiseptic methods and orthopedics. Author of medical works, fairy tales, and poems, including *Träumereien an französischen Kaminen* (1871), under the pen name Richard Le·an·der \lā-'än-dər\.

Vol·kov \'vòl-kəf\, Fyodor Grigoriyevich. 1729–1763. Russian actor. Organized (1755) first troupe of actors in Russia; called to St. Petersburg by Czarina Elizabeth; founded (1756) Moscow Theater by royal command.

Volkov, Vladislav Nikolayevich. 1935–1971. Soviet astronaut. Flight engineer on Soyuz 7 mission (Oct. 1969); killed in malfunction of Soyuz 11 capsule during landing.

Vol·lard \vò-lár\, Ambroise. 1865–1939. French art dealer and publisher. Opened gallery in Paris (1893); championed avant-garde works and sponsored first individual exhibits of Cézanne (1898), Picasso (1901), Matisse (1904); sponsored deluxe editions of literary masterpieces illustrated by leading avant-garde artists.

Volney, Comte de. See Constantin-François CHASSEBOEUF.

Vo·lo·ga·ses \,vō-lə-'gā-,sēz\. *Also spelled* Vologaeses. *Parthian* Wlgš. Name of five kings of Parthia:

Vologases I. d. 77 or 78 A.D. King (51–77 or 78). Son of Vonones II; gave Media Atropatene to brother Pacorus and Armenia to brother Tiridates; fought Romans (54–63) over Armenia.

Vologases II. d. 147? King (c.128–147). Claimed throne of Pacorus II and maintained claim to death of Osroes (c.128); overcame rival Mithradates IV and ruled much of Parthia.

Vologases III. d. 192. King (148–192). Invaded Cappadocia and Syria (161) and in consequence suffered heavy invasion by Romans (162–165).

Vologases IV. d. 208 or 209. King (192–208 or 209). Son of Vologases III; reasserted authority between invasions of Roman forces under Septimius Severus (195, 198–202).

Vologases V. d. c.220. King (c.209–c.220). Son of Vologases IV. Reign beset by rebellion.

Vol·stead \'väl-,sted, 'vòl-, 'vōl-, -stəd\, Andrew John. 1860–1947. American politician, b. near Kenyon, Minn. Member, U.S. House of Representatives (1903–23); author of the Volstead Act (passed Oct. 1919), to enforce prohibition of manufacture, sale, and transportation of intoxicating liquors under the 18th Amendment; author also of the Farmers' Cooperative Marketing Act (1922).

Vol·ta \'vòl-tä\, Alessandro Giuseppe Antonio Anastasio. Conte. 1745–1827. Italian physicist. Professor, Pavia (1779–1804); invented the electrophorus (1775) and the voltaic pile (1800); did research on the composition of marsh gas and isolated methane (1778); studied atmospheric electricity. Made count and senator of kingdom of Lombardy by Napoléon (1801); director of philosophical faculty at Padua (from 1815). The volt, an electrical unit, is named in his honor.

Volta, Ingo della. d. 1164. Genoese noble and financier. Last of an oligarchic line that ruled Genoa; negotiated alliance (1162) with Emperor Frederick I Barbarossa to invade Norman Sicily; failure of invasion, coupled with wars with Pisa and Sardinia, led to civil revolt; murdered.

Vol·taire \vòl-ter, *Angl* vōl-'ta(ə)r, väl-, vòl-, -'te(ə)r\. *Assumed name of* François-Marie Arou·et \àr-we\. 1694–1778. French writer. Began writing at early age, his expert satire getting him into trouble from the first; a leading wit of Paris during Regency; imprisoned in Bastille (1717–18), where he finished his first tragedy *Oedipe* (produced 1718) and began *Henriade,* an epic poem on Henry IV of France; again in Bastille (1726); released on condition of leaving France. To England (1726–29); returned with definitive edition of *Henriade* (printed secretly 1723; 2d ed. 1728). His observations on English social and political liberalism were contained in the *Lettres anglaises ou philosophiques* (1734), which caused an uproar making it necessary for him to seek seclusion; resided at Château de Cirey in Lorraine (1734–49) with Mme du Châtelet, a woman of learning who exerted on him an important intellectual influence; published *Éléments de la philosophie de Newton* (1738). After her death, accepted (1750) invitation to visit Frederick the Great at Prussian court, where he prepared and published (1751) his greatest historical work *Le Siècle* *de Louis XIV;* quarreled with Frederick and left Prussia (1753); spent last twenty years of life at Ferney, near Geneva. Gained fame as defender of victims of religious intolerance, but chiefly as master of satire. Among his works were the tragedies *Brutus* (1730), *Zaïre* (1732), *Alzire* (1736), *Mahomet* (1741), *Mérope* (1743); philosophical novels *Zadig* (1747), *Micromégas* (1752), and *Candide* (1759, a satire on the philosophical optimism of Pope and Leibnitz), *Le Blanc et noir* (1764), *Le Taureau blanc* (1774); philosophical poems *Le Mondain* (1736), *Discours sur l'homme* (1738), and *Le Désastre de Lisbonne* (1756); historical works *Charles XII* (1731), and *Essai sur les moeurs* (1756); and the *Dictionnaire philosophique* (1764).

Vol·ter·ra \vòl-'ter-rä\, Vito. 1860–1940. Italian mathematician and physicist. Professor, Pisa (1883–92), Turin (1892–1900), Rome (1900–31); senator (1905); contributed to theory of functionals, integral and integro-differential equations; helped develop improved airships, pioneered in use of helium.

Volterrano, Il. See Baldassare FRANCESCHINI.

von, von dem, von den, von der, von und zu. For many names containing one of these elements, see that part of the name following the element.

Vonck \'vōⁿk\, Jean-François. 1743–1792. Belgian political leader. Organized secret society Pro Aris et Focis to agitate for representative government (1781); joined forces of Henri Van der Noot in ejecting Austrians and establishing United Belgian States (1789); forced into exile (1790); organized Belgian legion that joined in French liberation of Belgium (1792).

Von·del \'vòn-dəl\, Joost van den. 1587–1679. Dutch poet and dramatist. Author of works reflecting his own classical studies and his journey of faith from Mennonite views to Roman Catholicism (1641). Works included translations from Seneca, Sophocles, Virgil, Euripides, etc.; poetry as *Roskam* (1630), *Altaargeheimenissen* (1645), *Poëzy* (1647), *Bespiegelingen van Godt en godtsdienst* (1662), *De Heerlyckheit der Kerke* (1663); 32 plays, including *Het Pascha* (1612), *Palamedes* (1625), *Gijsbrecht van Aemstel* (1637), *Gebroeders* (1639), *Joseph in Egypten* (1640), *Maria Stuart* (1646), *Salomon* (1648), *Lucifer* (1654), *Jeptha* (1659), *Adam in ballingschap* (1664), *Noah* (1667).

Vo·no·nes I \vō-'nō-ˌnēz\. d. 19 A.D. King of Parthia (7 or 8–11). Son of Phraates IV; held as hostage in Rome; on death of Orodes III (c.7 A.D.), sent by Tiberius to assume Parthian throne; driven out by Artabanus III (11), fled to Armenia and ruled there (to 15); in Roman custody in Antioch (15–19).

Voragine, Jacobus de. See JACOBUS DE VORAGINE.

Vo·ron·tsov \və-(ˌ)rənt-'sòf\. Distinguished Russian family, including: Mikhail Ilarionovich (1714–1767), aided Elizabeth in coup d'état (1742) by which she seized Russian throne; became vice chancellor (1744) and chancellor (1758); removed by Catherine (1762) for his continuing support of Peter III; restored (1763), retired (1763). His niece Yekaterina became Princess Dashkova (*q.v.*). His nephew ¶Aleksandr Romanovich (1741–1805) was minister to Great Britain and Dutch Netherlands and imperial chancellor (1802–04) under Czar Alexander I. Aleksandr's brother ¶Semyon Romanovich (1744–1832) was Russian minister at Vienna (1783–84) and London (1784–1806). Semyon's son ¶Mikhail Semyonovich (1782–1856) served against Napoléon (1805–07, 1812–14), against Turks (1806–11); commanded corps of occupation in France (1815–18); governor general of New Russia (south Russia, 1823–44), where he built up city of Odessa and was first to introduce steamboats on Black Sea; commander in chief and governor of the Caucasus (1844–53); conquered most of Dagestan (by 1848); created prince (1845) and field marshal (1856).

Vo·ro·shi·lov \və-(ˌ)rə-'shē-ləf\, Kliment Yefremovich. 1881–1969. Soviet soldier and politician. Joined Social Democratic Workers' party (1903); banished from Russia (1907–14); in World War I was notable military commander; carried on guerrilla warfare against Germans in Ukraine (1918), where he became associated with Stalin; commander of north Caucasian military district (1921) and Moscow district (1924–25); member of Politburo (from 1926); marshal of the Soviet Union (1935). As president of revolutionary military council and people's commissar for defense (1925–40), credited with reorganization of Russian general staff, mechanization of army, development of air force; removed as commissar following defeats on Finland front (1940); member of committee for state defense (1941–44); in command on Leningrad front at outbreak of war (1941); chairman of Presidium (1953–57).

Vö·rös·marty \'vœ-rœsh-märtʸ\, Mihály. 1800–1855. Hungarian poet and dramatist. Greatest of Hungarian nationalist writers. Editor of magazine *Tudományos Gyűjtemény* (1828 ff.); first member of new Hungarian Academy (1830); embraced Kossuth's revolution and became member of parliament (1848); forced into hiding in subsequent repression (1849–52). Chief works were epic on Árpád's conquest *Zalán futása* (1825), fairy drama *Csongor és Tünde* (1830); other verse included *Tündervölgy* (1826), *Két szomszédvár* (1831), dramatic works *Vérnász* (1833), *A fátyol titkai* (1834).

Vor·ster \'fòr-stər\, Balthazar Johannes. 1915–1983. South African politician. Member of extreme Nationalist organization Ossewabrandwag; as minister of justice (1961–66) drafted and enforced repressive measures against non-white peoples; prime minister (1966–78); sought to improve relations with other African countries; prepared for some power-sharing with Colored community; maintained commitment to apartheid; refused to support Rhodesia's last-ditch stand; resigned (1978) in midst of scandal involving information minister; held ceremonial post of president (1978–79).

Vorster, Pancratius. 1753–1829. Swiss prelate. Last prince-abbot of St. Gall (1796–1805); attempted to undo reforms of predecessor; forced to flee; restored by Austrian troops (1799) but again forced to flee by French (1799); monastery dissolved (1805); pensioned by Congress of Vienna (1815).

Vor·ti·gern \'vòr-tə-ˌgərn\. fl. 450. British ruler. Said by Gildas and Bede to have invited the Saxons to Britain to repel the Picts and Scots and to have married Rowena, daughter of Hengist.

Vos \'vòs\, Cornelis de. 1584–1651. Flemish painter. Known for portraits as *The Artist and his Family, Two Daughters of the Artist, Hutten Family.* His brother ¶Paul (c.1596–1678) was best known for his hunting scenes.

Vos, Gerrit Jansz. *Lat.* Gerardus Johannes Vos·si·us \'vò-sē-əs, -sh(ē-)əs\. 1577–1649. Dutch Humanist and theologian. Teacher of philology and theology (from 1600), director (1615–19), state theological college of Leiden; professor, U. of Leiden (1622–32), Athenaeum of Amsterdam (1632–49). Author of *Institutiones oratoriae* (1606), *Theses theologicae de variis doctrinae christianae capitibus* (1615), *Historiae de controversiis, quas Pelagius* (1618), *De historicis graecis* (1624), *De historicis latinis* (1627), etc. His son ¶Isaac (1618–1689) was also a noted scholar; tutor and librarian to Queen Christina of Sweden (1648–58); to England (1670); canon of Windsor (1673).

Vos, Maerten de. 1531–1603. Flemish painter. Leading Italianate painter of Antwerp; known for portraits and religious subjects.

Voss \'fòs\, Johann Heinrich. 1751–1826. German poet, translator, and philologist. Member of Göttinger Hainbund group of poets; professor at Jena (1805–26). Translated Homer, Virgil, Horace, Hesiod, Aristophanes, and with his sons Heinrich and Abraham, Shakespeare's plays (1818–29); author of verse collected as *Sämtliche Gedichte* (1802) and critical and controversial works.

Voss, Richard. 1851–1918. German writer. Author of historical dramas as *Savonarola* (1878), *Luigia Sanfelice* (1882), *Alexandra* (1886), *Eva* (1889), *Der König* (1896), novels as *Rolla* (1883), *Dahiel, der Konvertit* (1888), *Villa Falconieri* (1896), *Zwei Menschen* (1911), *Sphinx* (1914).

Vossius. See Gerrit VOS.

Vou·et \vwe\, Simon. 1590–1649. French painter. First painter of the court (1627); introduced Italian Baroque style into France; painted a portrait of Louis XIII; executed murals for Cardinal Richelieu, Marshal d'Effiat.

Vought \'vòt\, Chance Milton. 1890–1930. American aeronautical engineer and designer, b. New York City. With Birdseye B. Lewis, founded Lewis & Vought Corp. (1917), which later became the Chance Vought Corp., for manufacture of airplanes; merged with Pratt & Whitney Aircraft Co. and Boeing Airplane Co. to form United Aircraft & Transport Corp. (1929).

Voy·er \vwȧ-yā\. Name of notable French family of politicians and diplomats, comtes and marquises d'·Ar·gen·son \dȧr-zhäⁿ-sōⁿ\, including: René de Voyer (1596–1651), councilor to parlement of Paris (1620); undertook numerous missions for Richelieu; negotiated with Catalonian rebels (1640) and was named French administrator of Catalonia (1643); created comte d'Argenson (1643); ambassador to Venice (1651). His son ¶Marc-René, comte d'Argenson (1623–1700), was councilor to parlement of Rouen (1642); associated with father in various tasks and succeeded him as ambassador to Venice (1651–55). A second son ¶Pierre de Voyer, vicomte d'Argenson (1625–1709), was governor of New France (1657–61). Marc-René's son ¶Marc-Rene, marquis d'Argenson and marquis de Paul·my \pòl-mē\ (1652–1721), held various offices before being appointed lieutenant general of police of Paris (1697–1718); keeper of the seals (1718); as temporary president of council of finances (1718–20), went over to opposition to John Law's financial system. His son ¶René-Louis de Voyer de Paulmy, marquis d'Argenson, *known as* Argenson la Bête \lȧ-bet\ (1694–1757), was councilor to parlement of Paris (1716); intendant of Hainaut (1720–24); as foreign minister (1744–47) under Louis XV attempted unsuccessfully to restore French hegemony through a system of international arbitration aimed at Spain, Austria, and Russia. His brother ¶Marc-Pierre de Voyer, comte d'Argenson (1696–1764) was lieutenant general of police (1720); intendant of Paris (1740); secretary of state for war (1743–57); a friend of Voltaire, Diderot, d'Alembert, who dedicated the *Encyclopédie* to him. René-Louis's son ¶Antoine-René de Voyer, marquis de Paulmy d'Argenson (1722–1787), was councilor to parlement (1744), master of requests (1747), ambassador to Switzerland (1748–51), commissary general; succeeded his uncle as secretary for war (1757–58); later ambassador to Poland, Venice.

Voy·sey \'vòi-zē\, Charles Francis Annesley. 1857–1941. English architect and designer. Disciple of Ruskin and Pugin; established practice in London (c.1882); developed series of residential designs grounded in Arts and Crafts movement; designed furniture, fittings, decorations, and influenced Art Nouveau movement.

Vraz \'vráz\, Stanko. *Orig.* Jakob Fras \'fräs\. 1810–1851. Croatian poet, of Slovene origin. Author of sonnets, ballads, satires, romances, etc.; compiled anthology of national songs of both Slovenes and Croats.

Vrchlický, Jaroslav. See Emil FRÍDA.

Vriendt, Cornelis and Frans de. See FLORIS.

Vries, De. See also DE VRIES.

Vries \'vrēs\, Adriaan de. c.1560–1626. Dutch sculptor. Outstanding Mannerist sculptor; worked in Italy, Germany, Denmark, Bohemia; his works included bronze groups *Mercury and Psyche* and *Adonis and Venus; Mercury Fountain* and *Hercules Fountain* in Augsburg, busts of Rudolf II, *Triton, Neptune Fountain* for Frederiksburg Castle.

Vries, Hugo Marie de. 1848–1935. Dutch botanist and geneticist. Professor, Amsterdam (1878–1918); conducted lengthy experiments in plant breeding to study variation and heredity (c.1890 ff.); deduced laws of heredity similar to those of Mendel; discovered Mendel's work (1900); known also for studies of osmosis in plant cells. Author of *Die Mutationstheorie* (1901–03), *Arten und Varietäten* (1906), etc.

Vries, Matthijs de. 1820–1892. Dutch philologist. Professor at Groningen and (from 1853) Leiden; compiled *Groot Woordenboek der Nederlandsche Taal* (in part with L. A. te Winkel, 1864 ff.; continued by others) and other works on linguistic subjects. He introduced the modern system of Dutch orthography with L. A. te Winkel.

Vuil·lard \vwʸē-yȧr\, Édouard, *in full* Jean-Édouard. 1868–1940. French painter, printmaker, and decorator. Member of the Nabis group; later developed, with his friend Pierre Bonnard, Intimist manner in small domestic scenes rendered in subtle colors and composition; executed lithographs as *Paysages et intérieurs* series (1899); executed mural decorations for Théâtre des Champs-Élysées (1913), Palais de Chaillot (1937), League of Nations, Geneva (1939); later works included many portraits.

Vul·pi·us \'vu̇l-pē-u̇s\, Christian August. 1762–1827. German writer. Librarian in Weimar (from 1797). Author of many popular historical novels, esp. *Rinaldo Rinaldini* (1798); also wrote historical and antiquarian works as *Kuriositöten der physisch-literarisch, artistisch-historisch Vor- und Mitwelt* (1810–23); published periodical *Die Zeit* (1817–25). His sister ¶Christiane (1765–1816) was companion (from 1788) and wife (from 1806) of Goethe.

Vyā·sa \'vyä-sə\. *Also called* Kṛṣṇa Dvai·pa·yā·na \'krish-nəd-ˌvī-pə-'yän-ə\ *or* Bā·da·rā·ya·na \ˌbäd-ə-'rī-ə-nə\. 5th? century B.C. Indian sage. Credited with compiling the *Mahābhārata* collection of legendary and didactic poetry.

Vyc·pá·lek \vit-'späl-ek\, Ladislav. 1882–1969. Czech composer. On staff of national library, Prague (1907–42); composed in contrapuntal, polyphonic manner. Works included pieces for piano, for violin, for string quartet; songs, esp. settings of Moravian folk poetry and Czech and German Symbolist verse; cantatas *O posledních večech člověka* (*On the Last Things of Man,* 1920–22), *Blahoslavený ten člověk* (Psalm setting, 1933), *České requiem* (1940), and other choral works.

Vy·shin·sky \və-'shin-skəi\, Andrey Yanuaryevich. 1883–1954. Soviet diplomat and politician. Joined Menshevik faction of Social Democratic Workers' party (1903); public prosecutor (from 1920), deputy (1933) and chief prosecutor (1935) of Soviet Union; gained international attention as prosecutor in Great Purge trials (1934–38); member of Central Committee of Communist party; supervised annexation of Latvia (1940) and establishment of Soviet regime in Romania (1945); foreign minister (1949–53) and UN representative (1949–54).

Vy·tau·tas \vē-'tau̇-täs\. *Called* the Great. *Also known as* Wi·told \'vē-tōld\. 1350–1430. Lithuanian ruler. Son of Kęstutis; rival of cousin Jogaila (later Władysław II Jagiełło) for control of Lithuania; captured (1382) but escaped to refuge with Teutonic Knights; made temporary peace with Jogaila (1384); made formal treaty (1392) by which he acquired rule over Lithuania as vice regent for Jogaila (now king of Poland); defeated in attempt to subdue Tatars (1399); signed treaty of union with Poland (1401) and began long joint struggle against Teutonic Knights; defeated Knights at Grunwald, or Tannenberg (1410).

W

Waa·ge \'vō-gə\, Peter. 1833–1900. Norwegian chemist. Professor (from 1866), Christiania (now Oslo); with C. M. Guldberg, established the law of mass action (1864).

Waals \'väls\, Johannes Diderik van der. 1837–1923. Dutch physicist. Professor at Amsterdam (1877–1907); known for his work on the continuity of the liquid and gaseous states and formulation of the van der Waals equation and more complete equation of corresponding states to describe them; also studied electrolytic dissociation and the thermodynamic theory of capillarity; awarded 1910 Nobel prize for physics.

Wac·cho \'wäk-kō\. d. c.539. Lombard king (c.510–c.539). Murdered and usurped throne of uncle Tato (c.510); made treaty with Byzantine emperor Justinian I (536) and in observing it declined to aid Ostrogoths of Italy against Byzantines.

Wace \'wās, 'wäs\. c.1100–after 1174. Anglo-Norman poet. Author of two poetical chronicles written in Norman French, *Roman de Brut* (1155) and *Roman de Rou* (1160–74).

Wach \'väk\, Joachim. 1898–1955. American theologian, b. Chemnitz, Germany. Professor at Leipzig (1929–35); to U.S. (1935, naturalized 1946); professor, Brown U. (1937–45), Chicago (1945–55); a founder of "science of religion" method, known for studies of hermeneutics, sociology of religion. Author of *Religionswissenschaft* (1924), *Das Verstehen* (1926–33), *Sociology of Religion* (1944), *Types of Religious Experience* (1951), etc.

Wack·en·ro·der \'väk-ən-,rō-dər\, Wilhelm Heinrich. 1773–1798. German writer and critic. With Ludwig Tieck a leader of German Romanticism; wrote anecdotal biographies, some imaginary, and essays on art and music collected as *Herzensergiessungen eines kunstliebenden Klosterbruders* (1797), continued by Tieck in *Phantasien über die Kunst* (1799).

Wack·er·na·gel \'väk-ər-,nä-gəl\, Wilhelm. 1806–1869. German scholar. Professor (from 1833), Basel; leading Germanic scholar of the day; author of *Geschichte der deutschen Literatur* (1848–55), *Altdeutsches Wörterbuch* (1861), *Poetik, Rhetorik, Stilistik* (1873), etc. His son ¶Jacob (1853–1938), linguist; professor at Basel (1879), Göttingen (1902), Basel (1915); known for studies of Greek and Indic languages; author of *Altindische Grammatik* (1896–1905, 1930), etc.

Wad·del \wä-'del\, Moses. 1770–1840. American educator, b. present Iredell Co., N.C. Schoolmaster in various places, esp. in Willington, S.C., where his pupils included John C. Calhoun, W.H. Crawford, Hugh S. Legaré, A.B. Longstreet, George McDuffie, J.L. Petigru; president of Franklin Coll. (now U. of Georgia, 1819–29).

Wad·dell \wä-'del\, Hugh. 1734?–1773. American soldier, b. Lisburn, Ireland. To U.S. when young; settled in North Carolina. Major general and commander in chief of North Carolina troops under Gov. Tryon in campaign to pacify the Regulators (1771). His great-grandson ¶James Iredell Waddell (1824–1886) was a naval officer; commanded Confederate raider *Shenandoah* (1864–65), which harassed Union shipping in the Pacific and continued operations until Aug. 1865, in ignorance of collapse of Confederacy; only Confederate naval commander to sail around the world.

Wad·ding \'wäd-iŋ\, Luke. 1588–1657. Irish religious and historian. Entered Franciscan order (1604); developed college in Rome for Irish Franciscans (1625); compiled *Annales minorum,* history of Franciscan order (1625–54), and monumental edition of life and writings of Duns Scotus (1639).

Wad·ding·ton \'wäd-iŋ-tən\, William Henry. 1826–1894. French archaeologist and politician of English parentage. Traveled and explored in Asia Minor, Greece, and Syria, and published his *Voyage archéologique en Grèce et en Asie Mineure* (1866–77). Member of National Assembly (1871) and Senate (1876–94); minister of public instruction (1873, 1877) and foreign affairs (1877–79); premier (1879); French ambassador to Great Britain (1883–93).

Wade \'wād\, Benjamin Franklin. 1800–1878. American politician, b. Springfield, Mass. U.S. senator from Ohio (1851–69); a leader of Radical Republicans in Senate; vigorously supported prosecution of war against seceding states; joint author of Wade-Davis Manifesto (Aug. 1864), condemning Lincoln's usurpation of power and insisting that Congress was paramount in matters of Reconstruction in the South. Bitterly opposed Johnson and voted for Johnson's conviction in impeachment trial (preparing, as Senate president pro tem, to succeed him).

Wade, George. 1673–1748. British soldier, b. Ireland. Entered army (1690); in Scotland (1724–37) disarmed clans, built roads and bridges; field marshal (1743); commanded British forces in Flanders (1744–45); commander in chief in England (1745); failed to stop southward march of Prince Charles Edward; superseded by Duke of Cumberland.

Wade, Sir Thomas Francis. 1818–1895. English soldier, diplomat, and scholar. Ambassador at Peking (1871–83); Chinese professor, Cambridge (1888); introduced Wade (subsequently known as Wade-Giles) system of transliterating Chinese language. Cf. Herbert A. Giles.

Wag·nalls \'wag-nəlz\, Adam Willis. 1843–1924. American publisher, b. Lithopolis, Ohio. With I.K. Funk (*q.v.*) founded publishing firm Funk & Wagnalls (1877); vice president (1877–1912), president (1912–24).

Wag·ner \'wag-nər\, George Raymond. *Known as* Gorgeous George. 1915?–1963. American wrestler, b. Seward, Neb. Became professional wrestler at 19; with great showmanship helped build professional wrestling into lucrative business; established popularity of televised wrestling (1947–52).

Wagner, John Peter, *known as* Ho·nus \'hō-nəs\ *or sometimes* Hans. *Called* the Flying Dutchman. 1874–1955. American baseball player, b. Carnegie, Pa. Shortstop for Louisville Colonels (1897–99), Pittsburgh Pirates (1900–17); while at Pittsburgh led National League in batting 8 times, in stolen bases 5 times; batted over .300 in 17 consecutive seasons; lifetime batting average .327 or .329, total of 3415 or 3430 hits, including still-record 252 triples; considered perhaps greatest all-around player of all time; one of first elected to Baseball Hall of Fame (1936).

Wag·ner \'väg-nər\, Otto. 1841–1918. Austrian architect. Considered founder of modern movement in architecture; professor, Vienna Academy (1894–1912); a member of Wiener Sezession (1899–1905); influenced Art Nouveau; works included a general plan for Vienna (1893, never executed), metropolitan railway stations (1894–97), Postal Savings Bank (1905), churches, hospitals, etc.

Wagner, Richard, *in full* Wilhelm Richard. 1813–1883. German composer. Originator of the music drama and pioneer in the development of the leitmotiv. Music director of theaters at Magdeburg (1834–36), Königsberg (1836), and Riga (1837–39); in early years composed operas *Die Feer* (1833), *Das Liebesverbot* (1836). In Paris (1839–42) trying to gain foothold in theater; studied music, esp. that of Berlioz, and completed *Faust Overture* (1840) and operas *Rienzi* (1840) and *Der fliegende Holländer* (1841). To Dresden, where *Rienzi* and *Der fliegende Holländer* were successfully produced (1842, 1843); court Kapellmeister (1843–49); completed *Tannhäuser* (1845), *Lohengrin* (1848, produced 1850). Following participation in May Day uprising (1849), fled to Zürich, his chief residence until 1858; there wrote prose works *Die Kunst und die Revolution* (1849), *Das Kunstwerk der Zukunft* (1849), etc., and began writing and composing cycle of musical dramas on the Siegfried saga, called collectively *Der Ring des Nibelungen.* Completed *Tristan und Isolde* (1859, performed 1865). Returned to Germany following amnesty (1861) and lived in various cities; gained patronage of Louis II of Bavaria (1864) and completed *Die Meistersinger von Nürnberg* (1867); saw first performances of *Ring* dramas conducted by Hans von Bülow. Married (1870) Liszt's daughter Cosima (see below); settled in Bayreuth (1872), where his theater was founded (1872) and opened (1876) with first complete performance of the *Ring,* comprising *Das Rheingold* (1854, performed 1869), *Die Walküre* (1856, performed 1870), *Siegfried* (1871, performed 1876), *Gotterdämmerung* (1874, performed 1876). Composed last opera *Parsifal* (1882); other works included orchestral choral works as *An Webers Grabe* (performed 1844), several overtures, the *Siegfried Idyll* (1870), cantatas, choruses, songs, piano pieces, and arrangements. Wrote *Oper und Drama* (1851), *Über das Dirigieren* (1869), *Beethoven* (1870), *Religion und Kunst* (1880), *Mein Leben* (1911). His wife ¶Cosima (1837–1930), daughter of Franz Liszt, first married (1857) Hans von Bülow (divorced 1869); helped develop idea of Bayreuth Festival, and was art director of festival plays (until 1908). Their son ¶Siegfried Helferich Richard (1869–1930) was a composer and director; conductor and director (from 1896) and general director of Bayreuth Festival plays; compositions included symphonic poems, a violin concerto, operas as *Der Bärenhäuter* (1899), *An allem ist Hütchen Schuld* (1917). His son ¶Wieland Adolf Gottfried (1917–1966) revived (1951) the Bayreuth Festival after World War II and was co-director of the festival (1951–66) with his brother Wolfgang; known for stark, Symbolist stage designs and productions.

Wag·ner \ˈwag-nər\, Robert Ferdinand. 1877–1953. American politician, b. Hesse-Nassau, Germany. To U.S. (1885); member of N.Y. legislature (1904–19); supreme court justice, N.Y. (1919–26); as U.S. senator (1927–49) introduced social legislation, including National Industrial Recovery Act (1933), Social Security Act (1935), National Labor Relations Act (Wagner Act, 1935), Wagner-Steagall Housing Act (1937).

Wag·ner von Jau·regg \ˈväg-nər-fòn-ˈyaù-rek\, Julius. *Surname also* Wagner-Jauregg. 1857–1940. Austrian neurologist and psychiatrist. On psychiatric staff, U. of Vienna (1883–89); professor, Graz (1889–93), Vienna (1893–1928); introduced (1917) treatment of general paresis by infection of patient with malaria, earliest form of shock therapy; awarded 1927 Nobel prize for physiology or medicine.

Wagstaffe, Launcelot. See Washington IRVING.

Wahhāb, ʽAbd al-. See ʽABD AL-WAHHĀB.

Wai·bling·en \ˈvī-bliŋ-ən\. An alternate name of the Hohenstaufen family of Swabia, derived from that of a village estate in their possession; name later was applied to imperial faction in Italy in Italian form Ghibelline.

Wainfleet, William of. See WILLIAM of Waynflete.

Wain·wright \ˈwān-ˌrīt\, Jonathan Mayhew. 1883–1953. American army officer, b. Walla Walla, Wash. Commissioned (1906); served in Philippines (1908–10), France (1918); major general in command of Philippines division (1940); after Japanese invasion (Dec. 1941), commanded northern front until he succeeded MacArthur as commander in chief; defended Bataan and Corregidor against heavy attack until forced to surrender (May 1942); prisoner of war; rescued in Manchuria (1945); general (1945); commander, Fourth army (1946–47).

Wainwright, Richard. 1817–1862. American naval officer, b. Charlestown, Mass. Entered navy (1831); commanded the *Hartford,* Farragut's flagship (1861–62); in action running past forts Jackson and St. Phillip in lower Mississippi (Apr. 1862) and later at Vicksburg; engaged Confederate ram *Arkansas* below Vicksburg (July 1862). His son ¶Richard (1849–1926), b. Washington, D.C., entered navy (1868); executive officer, battleship *Maine* (1897–98), when the *Maine* was sunk in Havana harbor (Feb. 15, 1898); commanded the *Gloucester,* formerly J.P. Morgan's *Corsair,* in battle of Santiago Bay (July 3, 1898), attacking Spanish destroyers successfully; captain (1903) and rear admiral (1908).

Waite \ˈwāt\, Morrison Remick. 1816–1888. American jurist, b. Lyme, Conn. Practiced law in Connecticut and Ohio; one of American counsel in arbitration of *Alabama* claims (1871–72); chief justice, U.S. Supreme Court (1874–88); wrote over 1000 opinions, including several construing 14th Amendment.

Waitz \ˈvīts\, Georg. 1813–1886. German historian. Disciple of Ranke; professor, Kiel (1842), Göttingen (1849–75), where he founded a school of historians, and Berlin (1875), where he directed *Monumenta Germaniae Historica.* Author of *Deutsche Verfassungsgeschichte* (1844–78), *Schleswig-Holsteins Geschichte* (1851–54), etc.

Waitz, Theodor. 1821–1864. German philosopher and anthropologist. Professor, Marburg (1862–64); based his philosophy on that of Herbart; sought to make psychology the basis of philosophy. Author of *Grundlegung der Psychologie als Naturwissenschaft* (1846), *Anthropologie der Naturvölker* (1859–72).

Wake \ˈwāk\, William. 1657–1737. English prelate. Bishop of Lincoln (1705); archbishop of Canterbury (1716–37); negotiated with French Jansenists on proposed union with English church (1717–20).

Wake·field \ˈwāk-ˌfēld\, Edward Gibbon. 1796–1862. English colonialist. In *Letter from Sydney* (1829) proposed colonization by sale of smallholdings to ordinary citizens; influenced ending of transportation of criminals; organized and managed New Zealand Land Company (1839–49) from London; sent shipload of colonists to New Zealand in the *Tory* (1839), compelling British government to recognize it as a colony in time to forestall annexation to France; a founder of Church of England colony at Canterbury (1849). Also influenced Earl of Durham's report (1839) that led to union of Upper and Lower Canada. His brother ¶William Hayward (1803–1848) sailed in the *Tory* and directed colonial operations in New Zealand; founded Wellington (1840).

Wakefield, Gilbert. 1756–1801. English scholar. Ordained Anglican deacon (1778), left church and became a nonsectarian; tutor, Warrington Academy, a Unitarian school (1779–83); edited Bion and Moschus, the *Georgics,* Horace, Lucretius, and Greek plays; author of *Silva Critica* (1789–95), critical comments on the Scriptures, based on classical sources.

Wak·ley \ˈwāk-lē\, Thomas. 1795–1862. English surgeon. Founder (1823) of *The Lancet,* weekly medical paper in which he campaigned for various medical and public health reforms; M.P. (1835–52).

Waks·man \ˈwäk-smən, ˈwak-\, Selman Abraham. 1888–1973. American biochemist, b. Priluka, Ukraine (now U.S.S.R.). To U.S. (1910, naturalized 1916); at Rutgers U. (1918–58, professor from 1924); organized and directed division of marine microbiology at Woods Hole Inst. (1930–42); known for work with actinomycete bacteria; discovered (1943) antibiotic streptomycin. Awarded Nobel prize for physiology or medicine (1952).

Wa·la \ˈväl-ä\. d. 836. Frankish prelate. Cousin and adviser of Charlemagne; fled Aachen on accession of Louis I; later became tutor to Louis's son Lothair; abbot of Corbie (826); encouraged rebellions against Louis by Lothair (829) and Pepin I (830); exiled by Louis; to Italy with Lothair (834), becoming abbot of Bobbio.

Wa·la·frid Stra·bo \ˈväl-ə-ˌfrēd-ˈsträb-ō\. c.808–849. Swabian religious and poet. Benedictine; tutor to Charles the Bald (829 ff.); abbot of Reichenau (838); banished (839) for supporting Lothair I against Louis I, but reinstated (842). Author of theological works; wrote mystical poem *Visio Wettini* (c.826), *Liber de cultura hortorum,* panegyric *De imagine Tetrici;* revised Einhard's biography of Charlemagne.

Wal·bur·ga \väl-ˈbùr-gä\ *or* **Wal·pur·ga** \-ˈpùr-gä\ *or* **Wal·pur·gis** \-gəs\ *or* **Wald·burg** \ˈvält-ˌbùrk\. Saint. c.710–779. English religious. Benedictine nun; summoned to Hildesheim by brother Winebald; abbess (from 761).

Wal·cott \ˈwòl-kət\, Charles Doolittle. 1850–1927. American geologist and paleontologist, b. New York Mills, N.Y. Joined staff (1879), chief geologist (1893), director (1894–1907), U.S. Geological Survey; secretary, Smithsonian Institution (from 1907). Author of *Cambrian Faunas of North America* (1884), *Pre-Cambrian Fossiliferous Formations* (1899), *Evidences of Primitive Life* (1916), etc.

Wald \ˈwòld\, Lillian D. 1867–1940. American nurse and social worker, b. Cincinnati, Ohio. Founder (1893) and organizer of public-health nursing service known as Henry Street Settlement, New York City; pioneered in public-school nursing (1902) and insurance company nursing (1909; see Haley FISKE); suggested district nursing service of American Red Cross (1912) and federal Children's Bureau (established 1912); active in all branches of social work. Author of *The House on Henry Street* (1915), *Windows on Henry Street* (1934).

Wal·deck-Rous·seau \val-dek-rü-sō\, Pierre-Marie-René. 1846–1904. French politician. Deputy (1879–89); minister of interior (1881–82, 1883–85); responsible for legalization of trade unions (1884); senator (1894–1904); premier of France (1899–1902); pardoned Dreyfus (1899).

Waldemar. See also VALDEMAR.

Wal·de·mar *or* **Wol·de·mar** \ˈwòl-də-ˌmär, ˈväl-\. 1281?–1319. Margrave of Brandenburg (1308–19) of the Ascanian line. Fought successfully (1314–19) against league of German princes led by kings of Denmark and Sweden, against Slavs, etc.; extended boundaries of his margraviate; succeeded by his cousin Henry the Child, whose death (1320) ended Ascanian line.

Wal·den \ˈväl-dən\, Paul. 1863–1957. Latvian chemist. Professor, Riga Polytechnicum (1894–1919), Rostock (1919–34); discovered (1896) Walden inversion in reactions of optical isomers; also investigated electrical conductivity of solutions, dissociation constants, etc.

Wal·der·see \ˈväl-dər-ˌzā\, Alfred von. Graf. 1832–1904. German soldier. Chief of staff to grand duke of Mecklenburg-Schwerin and to governor of Paris (1871); chief of general staff (1888); field marshal (1900); commander of European forces in China during Boxer rebellion (1900–01).

Wal·dis \ˈväl-dəs\, Burkard. 1495–?1556. German poet and fabulist. Franciscan monk; embraced Lutheranism (1524); imprisoned during religious persecutions (1536–40). His works included a Shrovetide play in Low German *De Parabell vam verlorn Szohn* (1527) and *Esopus,* a translation and revision in verse of Aesop (1548).

Wald·mann \ˈvält-ˌmän\, Hans. c.1435–1489. Swiss soldier and political leader. Led Zürich contingent in defeat of Charles the Bold of Burgundy at Morat (1476); mayor of Zürich (1483); gained virtually dictatorial power and great wealth through sale of Swiss mercenary troops to various rulers; attempted to exert authority over other cantons; finally arrested and executed by Zürich opposition faction.

Wald·mül·ler \ˈvält-mɶl-ər\, Ferdinand Georg. 1793–1865. Austrian painter. Known for landscapes, genre works, portraits.

Waldo, Peter. See VALDÈS.

Wald·see·mül·ler \'vält-zā-ˌmuel-ər\ *or* **Walt·ze·mül·ler** \'vält-sā-\, Martin. *Lat.* Hy·la·com·y·lus \ˌhī-lə-'käm-ə-ləs\ *or* Ila·com·i·lus \ˌī-lə-'käm-ə-ləs\. c.1470–c.1518 or 1521. German cartographer. Credited with being first to call the New World *America,* applying the name to South America in his *Cosmographiae Introductio* (1507) containing a map of the world in 12 sheets.

Wald·teu·fel \vål-tœf-el\, Émile, *in full* Charles-Émile. *Orig. surname* Lé·vy \lā-vē\. 1837–1915. French composer. Best known for his waltzes, including "Manolo," "Bien aimés," "Dorlorès," "Je t'aime," "Sur la plage," "Tout Paris," "España," "Les Patineurs."

Wa·lew·ski \vä-'lef-skē\, Alexandre-Florian-Joseph Co·lon·na \kȯ-lȯ-nȧ\. Comte. 1810–1868. French diplomat. Natural son of Napoléon and Polish countess Maria Walewska; served in French army (to 1837); minister to Florence (1849), Naples (1850); ambassador to Spain (1851) and Great Britain (1851); senator (1855–65), deputy (1865–68); minister of foreign affairs (1855–60); president of the legislature (1865).

Wa·ley \'wā-lē\, Arthur David. *Orig. surname* Schloss \'shlȯs, 'shläs\. 1889–1966. English sinologist. Assistant keeper (1912–30), dept. of prints and drawings, British Museum; lectured at School of Oriental and African Studies, London (from 1930). Translator of Chinese and Japanese literary works as *170 Chinese Poems* (1919), *Japanese Poetry* (1919), *The No Plays of Japan* (1921), *Tale of Genji* (1925–32), *The Analects of Confucius* (1939), and Wu Ch'eng-en's *Monkey* (1942).

Wal·green \'wȯl-ˌgrēn\, Charles Rudolph. 1873–1939. American businessman, b. Knox Co., Ill. Worked as pharmacist; built chain of pharmacies (from 1902); helped popularize drugstore lunch counter; at his retirement (1934), the Walgreen Co. operated over 500 drugstores.

Wa·lī Al·lāh \wä-'lē-ä-'lä\, Shāh. 1702 or 1703–1762. Muslim theologian of India. To Mecca (1732); in period of disintegration of Indian Muslim empire, developed theology that dismissed fatalism and encouraged reinterpretation of Islāmic law and tradition to meet new circumstances. Author of *Asrār ad-dīn* and an annotated Persian translation of the Qur'ān.

Wa·līd, al- \ˌal-wä-'lēd\. d. 715. Islāmic caliph (705–715). Son of 'Abd al-Malik; reign one of greatest in history of Islām; his generals completed conquests in western Asia and India, and one of them, Ṭāriq ibn Ziyād, led (711) victorious army into Spain; noted for building schools, hospitals, and mosques, esp. the cathedral mosque at Damascus.

Walīd ibn Ya·zīd, al- \-ˌib-ən-yä-'zēd\. *More completely* Abū al-'Abbās al-Walīd ibn Yazīd ibn 'Abd al-Malik ibn Marwān. *Also called* al-Walīd II. c.707–744. Islāmic caliph (743–744). Largely abandoned public duties to cultivate artistic life; built a number of desert castles.

Walk·er \'wȯ-kər\, Amasa. 1799–1875. American economist, b. Woodstock, Conn. Farmer, store clerk, manufacturer's agent, shoe-shop proprietor (to 1840). On teaching staff, Oberlin (1842–49), Harvard (1853–60), Amherst (1860–69). Member, U.S. House of Representatives (1862–63). Author of *The Nature and Uses of Money* (1857), *The Science of Wealth* (1866). His son ¶Francis Amasa (1840–1897), b. Boston; economist and educator; served through Civil War, rising from private to brevet brigadier general; chief, U.S. Bureau of Statistics (1869–71); U.S. commissioner of Indian affairs (1871–72); superintendent of the 9th and 10th United States censuses (1870, 1880). Professor, Yale (1873–81); president, M.I.T. (1881–97). Widely known as advocate of international bimetallism. Author of *The Indian Question* (1874), *The Wages Question* (1876), *Money* (1878), *Land and Its Rent* (1883), *International Bimetallism* (1896).

Walker, David. 1785–1830. American abolitionist, b. Wilmington, N.C. Son of slave father; to Boston, where he owned used-clothing store; contributed to *Freedom's Journal* (from 1827); wrote *Appeal to the Colored Citizens of the World,* known also as *Walker's Appeal* (1829), calling on slaves to fight for freedom; pamphlet banned in South.

Walker, Edward Patrick, *known as* Mickey. *Called* the Toy Bulldog. 1901–1981. American boxer, b. Elizabeth, N.J. In career (1919–35) won 99, lost 11 bouts; won world welterweight title from Jack Britton (1922), lost it to Pete Latzo (1926); won middleweight title from Tiger Flowers (1926), relinquished it (1931); lost light-heavyweight title bouts; fought heavyweight Max Schmeling to draw (1931). Wrote autobiography *The Will to Conquer* (1953).

Walker, Sir Emery. 1851–1933. English engraver and printer. Founded engraving and printing firm (1886, with Walter Boutall); influenced William Morris to establish Kelmscott Press; helped found (1888) Arts and Crafts Exhibition Society; with T.J. Cobden-Sanderson founded (1900) Doves Press and produced Doves Bible (1903–05); designed type for Doves Press, later for Ashendene Press and for Cranach-Presse of Germany.

Walker, George. 1618–1690. Irish clergyman, of English parents. Joint governor of Derry during 150-day siege (April–July 1689) by troops of James II; nominated by William III to bishopric of Derry; killed at battle of the Boyne (1690).

Walker, James John. 1881–1946. American politician, b. New York City. Mayor of New York (1926–32); involved in state legislative investigation of corruption in municipal government; summoned before Gov. Franklin D. Roosevelt to answer charges; resigned.

Walker, John. 1732–1807. English actor, elocutionist, and lexicographer. Actor at Drury Lane and in Dublin (to 1768); professional lecturer on elocution (1771 ff.); compiler of *A Rhyming Dictionary* (1775), *A Critical Pronouncing Dictionary* (1791).

Walker, John. 1781?–1859. English druggist. Inventor of the friction match (1827).

Walker, John Brisben. 1847–1931. American journalist and publisher, b. near Pittsburgh, Pa. Managing editor, Washington (D.C.) *Chronicle* (1876–79); owner and editor, *Cosmopolitan Magazine* (1889–1905).

Walker, Joseph Reddeford. 1798–1876. American trapper and guide, b. Virginia. Became a trapper and mountain man with trading headquarters at Independence, Mo. (1820–32); member of Bonneville's expedition to Rocky Mountains (1833); guided Frémont's third expedition to California (1845–46); to California (1849), Arizona (1861–62). Walker Lake and Walker Pass are named after him.

Walker, Mary Edwards. 1832–1919. American physician and reformer, b. near Oswego, N.Y. Received physician's certificate from Syracuse (N.Y.) Medical College (1855); from youth an advocate of women's rights and dress reform; served as nurse (1861–63) and assistant surgeon (1863–65) with Union army; awarded Medal of Honor (1865; later rescinded but restored in 1977); noted for wearing of male attire.

Walker, Robert John (*or* James). 1801–1869. American politician, b. Northumberland, Pa. Practiced law in Pittsburgh, Pa. (1821–26) and Natchez, Miss. (from 1826); U.S. senator from Mississippi (1836–45); U.S. secretary of the treasury (1845–49); largely responsible for creation of U.S. Dept. of Interior (1849); governor of Kansas Territory (1857–58); financial agent of U.S. government in Europe (1863–64).

Walker, Sarah, *nee* Breed·love \'brĕd-ˌləv\. *Known as* Madame C.J. Walker. 1867–1919. American businesswoman, b. Delta, La. m. (1906) C.J. Walker; invented (1905) and successfully exploited a preparation for straightening kinky hair; established factory in Indianapolis (1910) and a corps of agents in U.S. and Caribbean who sold the "Walker System"; built business into largest Negro-owned firm in U.S.; bequeathed fortune to educational institutions and charities.

Walker, Thomas. 1715–1794. American land speculator and explorer, b. King and Queen Co., Va. Helped form (1748) Loyal Land Co. and secured land grant in the west; led exploring party to survey grant and discovered (1750) Cumberland Gap; began settlement of Clinch and Holston valleys.

Walker, William. 1824–1860. American filibuster, b. Nashville, Tenn. To California with gold rush (1850); organized band of "colonists" and invaded Lower California (1853); declared Lower California an independent republic with himself as president; proclaimed annexation (1854) of Mexican state of Sonora; forced out of Mexico; tried (1854) in San Francisco for violation of neutrality laws but acquitted. Led small band of adventurers to Nicaragua and joined a revolutionary faction there (1855); captured Granada (Sept. 1855); elected president (1856); recognized by U.S. Incurred hostility of Cornelius Vanderbilt by seizure of boats belonging to Vanderbilt interests; ousted by coalition of Central American powers inspired by Vanderbilt; fled (May 1857) to protection of U.S. warship. Tried repeatedly to return to Nicaragua; arrested at San Juan del Norte (Nov. 1857) by Commodore Paulding and returned to U.S.; arrested (1860) by British naval officer in Honduras and turned over to Honduran authorities; court-martialed, convicted, and shot.

Wal·lace \'wäl-əs\, Alfred Russel. 1823–1913. English naturalist. Trained as surveyor and architect; devoted himself to natural history (from 1845); on collecting expedition to the Amazon (1848–52); visited Malay Archipelago (1854–62); while there originated independently a theory of natural selection (1858), an account of which he sent to Darwin; the accounts of both were published in a joint paper by the Linnaean Society of London (1858). Investigated the geographical distribution of animals and noted the dissimilar forms in the Oriental and Australian regions of the archipelago separated by Wallace's line. Author of *Travels on the Amazon and Rio Negro* (1853), *On the Tendency of Varieties to Depart Indefinitely from the Original Type* (1858), *The Malay Archipelago* (1869), *Contributions to the Theory of Natural Selection* (1870), *The Geographical Distribution of Animals* (1876), *Darwinism* (1889), *The Wonderful Century* (1898), *Man's Place in the Universe* (1903), *My Life* (1905), *The World of Life* (1910).

Wallace, DeWitt, *in full* William Roy DeWitt. 1889–1981. American editor and publisher, b. St. Paul, Minn. With his wife (m. 1921) developed idea for magazine reprinting digests of articles from a variety of sources and founded (1922) *Reader's Digest;* launched British edition (1939) and first of many foreign-language editions (1940); became largest-circulation magazine in the world (30.5 million copies in 16 languages, 1981).

Wallace, Edgar, *in full* Richard Horatio Edgar. 1875–1932. English writer. Author of popular thrillers as *Four Just Men* (1905), *Sanders of the River* (1911), *The Crimson Circle* (1922), *The Green Archer* (1923), *The Ringer* (1926), *The Flying Squad* (1928), *The Terror* (1930); also wrote plays and film scripts.

Wallace, Henry. 1836–1916. American editor and author, b. near West Newton, Pa. To Iowa (1863); owner and editor (1895–1916), *Wallaces' Farm and Dairy,* later called *Wallaces' Farmer;* author of *Uncle Henry's Letters to the Farm Boy* (1897), *Letters to the Farm Folks* (1915), etc. His son ¶Henry Cantwell (1866–1924), b. Rock Island, Ill.; joined staff of and acquired part interest in *Farm and Dairy* journal (1894), which his father acquired (1895); associate editor (1895–1916), editor (1916–24); U.S. secretary of agriculture (1921–24). His son ¶Henry Agard (1888–1965), b. Adair Co., Iowa, was associate editor (1910–24) and editor (1924–29), *Wallaces' Farmer,* and editor of its successor *Wallaces' Farmer and Iowa Homestead* (1929–33); secretary of agriculture (1933–40); vice president of the U.S. (1941–45); secretary of commerce (1945–46); editor, *New Republic* (1946–47); Progressive party candidate for president (1948). Author of *Agricultural Prices* (1920), *Corn and Corn Growing* (1923), *America Must Choose* (1934), *Century of the Common Man* (1943), *Sixty Million Jobs* (1945), *Long Look Ahead* (1960), etc.

Wallace, Lewis. 1827–1905. American soldier and writer, b. Brookville, Ind. Served in Mexican War (1846–48); practiced law; in Civil War served at Fort Donelson, Shiloh, defended Cincinnati (1863) and Washington, D.C. (1864); major general of volunteers (1862); sat on military court that tried conspirators in Lincoln's assassination (1865); governor of New Mexico Terr. (1878–81); U.S. minister to Turkey (1881–85). Author of novels *The Fair God* (1873), *Ben Hur* (1880), *Boyhood of Christ* (1888), *Prince of India* (1893).

Wallace, Sir Richard. 1818–1890. English art connoisseur. Natural son of 4th Marquis of Hertford; British commissioner at Paris Exhibition (1878); M.P. (1873–85); inherited and augmented collection of paintings and art objects, which his widow bequeathed as Hertford-Wallace collection to British nation (1897).

Wallace, Vincent, *in full* William Vincent. 1812–1865. Irish composer. Pianist, violinist, and organist in Dublin, Thurles, etc.; gave concerts in Tasmania and Australia (1835–38); great success in New York City (1843–44); continued to appear in London, South America, U.S., Europe. Composed operas including *Maritana* (1845), *Matilda of Hungary* (1847), *Lurline* (1860); also wrote piano pieces.

Wallace, Sir William. *Also* Wal·ays \ˈwäl-əs\ *or* Wal·len·sis \wä-ˈlen(t)-səs\, *i.e.* Welshman. c.1270–1305. Scottish patriot, of Welsh extraction. Led Scottish insurgents, drove English out of Perth, Stirling, and Lanark (1297); defeated English at Stirling (1297) and ravaged Northumberland, Westmorland, and Cumberland (1297); proclaimed warden of Scotland; suffered rout at hands of Edward I of England at Falkirk (1298); waged guerrilla warfare (1299); outlawed by Edward I (1304); betrayed to English at Glasgow (1305); tried in Westminster Hall, London; found guilty and hanged, drawn, and quartered.

Wal·lach \ˈväl-ˌäk\, Otto. 1847–1931. German chemist. Professor, Göttingen (1889–1915); known for researches on chemical composition of camphors, perfumes, and essential oils. Awarded 1910 Nobel prize for chemistry.

Wal·lack \ˈwäl-ək\, Henry John. 1790–1870. American actor, b. London, England. On English stage (to 1819); American debut in Baltimore (1819). Leading man, Chatham Garden Theatre, New York City (1824); leading man and stage manager at Covent Garden, London (1834–36); stage manager and actor, National Theatre, New York (1837); at New Chatham Theatre, New York (1839–40); rented Covent Garden, London (1843); acted Sir Peter Teazle in opening performance, Broadway Theater, New York (1847). His brother ¶James William (1795–1864) was an actor of melodrama and light comedy; at Drury Lane (1808–18); New York debut (1818); stage manager and actor in alternate engagements in London and New York; settled in New York (1852); actor and manager, Wallack's (formerly Lyceum) Theatre, New York (1852–61); built and, with his son Lester (see below), opened new Wallack's Theatre (1861); among his notable Shakespearean roles were Iago, Macbeth, Richard III, Romeo, Hamlet. A son of Henry John ¶James William (1818–1873), b. London, was an actor on stage in U.S. and England from childhood; in America (from 1855), well known for Shakespearean roles Othello, Hotspur, Iago, Richard III; made great success (1867) as Fagin in *Oliver Twist.* A son of the elder James William ¶Lester, *orig.* John Johnstone (1820–1888), b. New York City, was an actor and dramatist; stage debut in New York (1847); stage manager (1852–61) and manager (1861–87) of Wallack's Theatre; became noted for elegant productions of British plays; made particular success in his own *Rosedale* (1863); also wrote *The Three Guardsmen* (1849), *The Four Musketeers* (1849), *Two to One* (1854), *The Veteran* (1856), and a volume of reminiscences, *Memories of Fifty Years* (1889).

Wal·las \ˈwäl-əs\, Graham. 1858–1932. English political scientist. Lecturer, London School of Economics (1895–1923); professor, U. of London (1914–23); member of Fabian Society (1886–1904); on London County Council (1904–07); known for contributions to development of empirical basis and scientific methods in social sciences. Author of *Life of Francis Place* (1898), *Human Nature in Politics* (1908), *The Great Society* (1914), *The Art of Thought* (1926).

Wal·len·berg \ˈväl-lən-ˌberʸ\, André Oscar. 1816–1886. Swedish financier. Founded (1856) and directed the Enskilda Bank of Stockholm until his death, when his sons ¶Knut Agaton (1853–1938) and ¶Marcus Laurentius (1864–1943) succeeded him. Knut was foreign minister (1914–17) and an architect of Swedish neutrality. Marcus was Swedish representative at Supreme Economic Council, Paris (1919), Amsterdam meeting (1919), and Brussels conference (1920); on finance committee, League of Nations (1924).
Marcus's sons ¶Jacob (1892–1980) and ¶Marcus (1899–1982) succeeded to directorship of the family's financial empire which eventually encompassed a third of Swedish industry and included the Enskilda (later Scandinaviska Enskilda) Bank, SKF ball-bearing company, Saab-Scania cars and aircraft, Electrolux home appliances, and L.M. Ericsson telephone equipment.

Wal·len·da \wə-ˈlen-də\, Karl. 1905–1978. American circus performer, b. Magdeburg, Germany. Founded family high-wire act the Great Wallendas; performed with Ringling Brothers Circus (1928–46); developed 4-man pyramid and 3-tiered 7-man pyramid; suffered losses of family members in accidents (1962, 1963, 1972); killed while performing an open-air high-wire routine.

Wal·len·stein \ˈväl-ən-ˌshtīn, *Angl* ˈwäl-ən-ˌstīn\, Albrecht Eusebius Wenzel von. Duke of Fried·land \ˈfrēt-ˌlänt\ and Meck·len·burg \ˈmek-lən-ˌbu̇rk, ˈmāk-\. Prince of Sa·gan \ˈzä-gän\. 1583–1634. Austrian general. Served in campaigns in Hungary and against Venice (1617); remained loyal to Emperor Ferdinand II during rebellion (1618–23) of other Bohemian nobles; acquired vast holdings in confiscated estates; created duke (1625). Given command of imperial armies (1625); won successes against Mansfeld and king of Denmark (1626–27); with Graf von Tilly, conquered Mecklenburg, Holstein, Schleswig, Denmark; given Sagan (1627) and Mecklenburg (1629); failed in siege of Stralsund (1628) and in scheme to monopolize commerce on Baltic and North seas; at insistence of Diet of Regensburg, dismissed by Ferdinand (1630); intrigued with Gustav II Adolphus; recalled to imperial command after defeat of Tilly at Breitenfeld (1631); drove Gustav from Bavaria and Franconia, but defeated by him at Lützen (Nov. 16, 1632); attempted to mount revolt with trusted generals (1634); dismissed by Ferdinand, assassinated by Irish and Scottish officers.

Wal·ler \ˈwäl-ər\, Augustus Volney. 1816–1870. English physiologist. Invented (1849) Wallerian method of identifying tracts of nerve fibers by observing the direction of degeneration after cutting.

Waller, Edmund. 1606–1687. English poet. Cousin of John Hampden; conducted (1641) impeachment of Sir Francis Crawley, judge in common pleas, for maintaining (1636) legality of ship money; detected in plot, known as "Waller's Plot," for seizing London for Charles I (1643); spared death on betrayal of associates; expelled from House of Commons, fined £10,000, and banished (1644). Permitted to return (1652); wrote panegyric of Cromwell (1655) and poem of rejoicing on his death (1659). On Restoration wrote eulogy of Charles II; M.P. (1661–87) and favorite at court. Author of verses addressed to "Sacharissa" (Lady Dorothy Sidney), of graceful and elegant *Poems,* including "Go, lovely Rose" (1645), *St. James's Park* (1661), and *Divine Poems* (1685); made the heroic couplet fashionable.

Wal·ler \ˈväl-ər, vȧ-ler\, Max. *Orig.* Maurice War·lo·mont \vȧr-lō-mōⁿ\. 1860–1889. Belgian poet. Founded (1881) and edited (1881–89) literary review *La Jeune Belgique;* author of novels as *Greta Friedmann* (1885) and *Daisy* (1892), and esp. of verse influenced by Parnassians collected in *La Flute à Siebel* (1892).

Wal·ler \ˈwäl-ər\, Thomas Wright, *called* Fats. 1904–1943. American musician, b. New York City. Professional pianist (from 1919), influenced esp. by James P. Johnson's "stride" style; led small band and made hundreds of recordings, achieving considerable commercial success by blend of jazz and comic manner; first jazz musician to master organ. Composed songs including "Honeysuckle Rose," "Ain't Misbehavin'," "Squeeze Me," "Blue Turning Grey Over You."

Waller, Willard Walter. 1899–1945. American sociologist, b. Murphysboro, Ill. Professor, U. of Nebraska (1929–31), Pennsylvania State Coll. (1931–37), Barnard Coll. (1937–45); a founder of sociology of knowledge and sociology of education. Author of *Sociology of Teaching* (1932), *The Family* (1938), *War in the Twentieth Century* (1940), *War and the Family* (1940), *The Veteran Comes Back* (1944), etc.

Waller, Sir William. c.1597–1668. English general. Member of Long Parliament (1640); a leader of Parliamentary army, won successes over Royalists in west of England (1642–43); major general (1643); captured Hereford (1643); defeated by Sir Ralph Hopton at Lansdown and by Earl of Rochester at Roundway Down (1643). Raised new troops in London; stopped Hopton's second advance at Cheriton (1644); defeated at Cropredy Bridge (1644); led expedition for relief of Taunton (1645); relieved from command by Self-denying Ordinance (1645). Suggested idea for army reform that led to the organization (1645) of the New Model army; became a leader of Presbyterian-Royalist opposition to Commonwealth; imprisoned (1648–51); plotted Royalist rising (1659); recovered seat in Parliament (1660).

Wal·lin \vǎl-ˈlēn\, Johan Olof. 1779–1839. Swedish prelate and hymnist. Archbishop of Uppsala (1837); published revised Swedish hymnal *Svenska psalmboken* (1819), to which he contributed 120 original hymns and about 200 translations and adaptations; best known hymn "Dödens ängel" (1634).

Wal·lis \ˈwäl-əs\, Hal Brent. 1899–1986. American film producer, b. Chicago. Joined (1923) Warner Brothers Pictures as a publicist; advanced to producer (1930); his production *Little Caesar* (1930) launched a vogue for gangster films; executive producer at Warner (1933 ff.); operated as independent producer for various studios (1944 ff.). His approximately 200 films included *The Maltese Falcon* (1941), *Casablanca* (1942), *Come Back, Little Sheba* (1952), *The Rose Tattoo* (1955), *Becket* (1964), and *True Grit* (1969).

Wallis, John. 1616–1703. English mathematician. Savilian professor of geometry, Oxford (1649–1703); in *Arithmetica Infinitorum* (1655) introduced the notation ∞ for infinity and reduced the idea of limit to arithmetic form and arrived at results from which the binomial theorem, the differential calculus, and the integral calculus were developed; in *Mathesis Universalis* (1657) introduced negative and fractional exponents; charter member of Royal Society (1662); in *Treatise on Algebra* (1685) treated conoids and anticipated notion of complex number. Also studied grammar, publishing (1652) a treatise on English grammar with an appendix describing the various means of producing articulate sounds.

Wallis, Samuel. 1728–1795. English naval officer. Circumnavigated the globe in *Dolphin* (1766–68); discovered Tahiti and Wallis Islands in Pacific (1767).

Wallis, Wilson Dallam. 1886–1970. American anthropologist, b. Forest Hill, Md. Known for studies of religion and science among American Indian tribes and for methodological contributions to cultural anthropology. Author of *Messiahs: Christian and Pagan* (1918), *Messiahs: Their Role in Civilization* (1943), *Canadian Dakota* (1947, with wife Ruth S. Wallis), *The Malecite Indians* (1957, with wife), *Culture Patterns in Christianity* (1964).

Wal·lon \vá-lōⁿ\, Henri-Alexandre. 1812–1904. French historian and politician. Professor, Sorbonne (1846 ff.); member of Legislative Assembly (1849–50) and National Assembly (1871–75); carried motion that led to establishment of French Republic (1875); minister of public instruction (1875–76); elected senator for life (1875). Author of *Du monothéisme chez les races sémitiques* (1859), *Saint Louis et son temps* (1875), etc.

Wal·pole \ˈwȯl-ˌpōl, ˈwäl-\, Horace, *baptized* Horatio. 4th Earl of Or·ford \ˈȯr-fərd\. 1717–1797. English man of letters. 4th son of Sir Robert Walpole. Made grand tour with poet Thomas Gray (1739–41); M.P. (1741–68); purchased (1747) Strawberry Hill, a villa outside Twickenham, converted it into a small Gothic castle, decorated it with curios and works of art; established there (1757–89) a printing press upon which first editions of many of his works were printed, also Gray's *Odes;* succeeded to earldom (1791). Author of *The Castle of Otranto* (1764), the forerunner of Gothic romances of Mrs. Radcliffe and Matthew Gregory Lewis, of *Mysterious Mother,* a tragedy in verse (1768), several antiquarian works including *Historic Doubts on Richard III* (1768) and *Anecdotes of Painting in England* (1762–71), and posthumously published records of his own time *Memoirs of the Last Ten Years of the Reign of George II* (1822), *Memoirs of the Reign of King George III* (1845). Owes literary reputation chiefly to his charming, vivacious, often brilliant letters (1732–97).

Walpole, Sir Hugh Seymour. 1884–1941. English novelist, b. New Zealand. Published *The Wooden Horse* (1909), *Maradick at Forty* (1910), *Mr. Perrin and Mr. Traill* (1911); won reputation with *Fortitude* (1913); followed with *The Dark Forest* (1916), *The Green Mirror* (1918), *The Secret City* (1919), *Jeremy,* first of a series on life of the English boy (1919), *The Cathedral* (1922), *The Old Ladies* (1924), a tetralogy comprising *Rogue Herries* (1930), *Judith Paris* (1931), *The Fortress* (1932), and *Vanessa* (1933), *The Bright Pavilions* (1940), *Katherine Christian* (1943), etc.

Walpole, Sir Robert. 1st Earl of Or·ford \ˈȯr-fərd\. 1676–1745. English statesman. Whig M.P. (1701–42); secretary at war (1708–10); treasurer of navy (1710–11); expelled from House of Commons on political charge of venality in navy office (1712). Advocated Hanoverian succession; paymaster of forces on accession of George I (1714); conducted impeachment of Bolingbroke and Harley; first lord of treasury (tantamount to prime minister) and chancellor of exchequer (1715–17; resigned); devised first general sinking fund for reducing national debt (1717). Helped accomplish reconciliation of George I and the Prince of Wales (1720); again paymaster (1720); profited through speculation in South Sea scheme; called by public demand after South Sea collapse to restore order in public affairs; first lord of treasury and chancellor of exchequer (1721–42), sharing power with Townshend, secretary of state; reduced import and export duties (1721) to encourage trade; crushed Jacobite plot and exiled Atterbury (1723); cultivated friendship of France and opposed Austrian alliance; quarreled with Townshend and forced his retirement (1730); managed transfer of power from House of Lords to House of Commons; controlled government and opposition through skill in debate and in use of royal patronage; first to unify cabinet government in person of prime minister; strove to establish sound finance at home; forced into hostilities with Spain (1739); defeated in House of Commons (Jan. 1742); created earl (1742).

Walpurga *or* **Walpurgis,** Saint. See WALBURGA.

Walram I and **II.** See NASSAU.

Wal·ras \vál-rá\, Léon, *in full* Marie-Esprit-Léon. 1834–1910. French economist. Professor, Lausanne (1870–92); considered founder of Lausanne school of economics; first to apply comprehensive mathematical analysis to general economic equilibrium in *Éléments d'économie politique pure* (1874–77); also wrote *Théorie mathématique de la richesse social* (1883), *Théorie de la monnaie* (1886), etc.

Walsh \ˈwȯlsh\, Raoul. 1887–1980. American film director, b. New York City. Led adventurous early life as cowboy; hired by D.W. Griffith (1912); assisted in filming and acted in *Life of Villa* (1914) and *Birth of a Nation* (1915); directed more than 100 films, notable for action, adventure, conflict, including *Regeneration* (1916), *Thief of Baghdad* (1924), *What Price Glory* (1926), *Sadie Thompson* (1927), *The Big Trail* (1929), *Strawberry Blonde* (1940), *High Sierra* (1941), *Objective Burma* (1945), *White Heat* (1949).

Walsh, Thomas James. 1859–1933. American politician, b. Two Rivers, Wis. Practiced law at Helena, Mont. (from 1890); U.S. senator from Montana (1913–33). In charge (1922–23) of investigation of leasing of naval oil reserves in Wyoming and California; uncovered Teapot Dome scandal (1923).

Wal·sing·ham \ˈwȯl-siŋ-əm\, Sir Francis. c.1532–1590. English statesman. M.P. (1563 ff.); ambassador at French court (1570–73); principal secretary of state to Elizabeth I (1573–90); frequently overruled by both Burghley and Elizabeth; failed to secure Anglo-French alliance against Spain (1581); organized, largely at his own expense, efficient system of secret intelligence, by which he detected plots against Elizabeth, among them Throckmorton's (1583) and Anthony Babington's (1586); secured conviction and execution of Mary, Queen of Scots (1587); forewarned Elizabeth (1587) of preparations of Spanish Armada and vainly urged defensive measures.

Walsingham, Thomas. d. 1422? English monk. Benedictine in abbey of St. Albans; compiled *Historia Anglicana* (continuing work of Matthew Paris), a chief authority for reigns of Richard II, Henry IV, and Henry V.

Wal·ta·ri \ˈvál-tär-ē\, Mika Toumi. 1908–1979. Finnish novelist. Author of historical novels as *Sinuhe, egyptiläinen* (1945, *The Egyptian*), *Mikael Hakim* (1949, *The Wanderer*), *Turms kuolematon* (1955, *The Etruscan*); also wrote detective novels, stories, travel books, plays.

Wal·ter \ˈwȯl-tər\ of Coventry. fl. 1290–1300. English monk. Compiled historical works and chronicles of Marianus Scotus, Florence of Worcester, Henry of Huntingdon, Roger Howden, etc., in *Memoriale Fratris Walteri de Coventria,* valuable for knowledge of King John's reign.

Walter the Penniless. See GAUTIER SANS AVOIR.

Wal·ter \ˈväl-tər, ˈwȯl-\, Bruno. *Orig.* Bruno Walter Schle·sing·er \ˈs(h)lā-ziŋ-ər\. 1876–1962. American conductor, b. Berlin, Germany. Conductor, Imperial Opera, Vienna (1901–13), Munich Opera House (1913–22), Municipal Opera, Berlin (1925–29), Leipzig Gewandhaus Orchestra (1929–33), Vienna State Opera (1935–38); to U.S. (1939); conducted regularly at Metropolitan Opera (from 1941); conductor of N.Y. Philharmonic-Symphony (1947–49); noted for interpretations of Mozart, Mahler, Bruckner.

Wal·ter \ˈwȯl-tər\, Hubert. d. 1205. English prelate and statesman. Entered household of Henry II (by 1182); dean of York (1186); bishop of Salisbury (1189); accompanied Richard I on Third Crusade, led army back to England; as archbishop of Canterbury and chief justiciar (1193), governed kingdom and raised Richard's ransom; papal legate (1195); levied land tax to be assessed by knights, or middle-class landowners, elected to represent townships and hundreds (1198); instituted reforms in administration; resigned as justiciar (1198); chancellor (1199–1205) under King John; instituted national customs system (1202).

Wal·ter *or* **Wal·ther** \ˈväl-tər\, Johann. *Surname orig.* Blan·ken·mül·ler \ˈbläŋ-kən-ˌmᵫl-ər\. 1496–1570. German composer and poet. Teacher of singing in Torgau and Dresden; friend of Martin Luther (from 1524), whom he advised on framing the German Mass and who wrote introduction to his *Geystliches gesangk Buchleyn* (1524), first Protestant hymnbook.

Wal·ter \ˈwȯl-tər\, John. 1739–1812. English newspaperman. Coal merchant (1755–81); underwriter (1781–83), bankrupt by loss of shipping (1782). Bought patent for printing from logotypes (1782); did logographic printing of books; started newspaper *The Daily Universal Register* (1785), which was renamed *The Times* (1788). Convicted several times for libel. His son ¶John (1776–1847) became sole manager of *The Times* (1803), editor (1803–17); converted scandal sheet into serious newspaper allied to rising commercial class; lost printing of government advertisements and customhouse papers by reason of opposition to Pitt; initiated sending of special foreign correspondents abroad (1805); organized fast news-gathering system including Channel steamers, pigeon post, couriers; among first to adopt electric telegraph; adopted steam printing press (1814); M.P. (1832–37, 1841). His son ¶John (1818–1894), barrister (1847), became sole manager of *The Times* (1847); to compete with new penny press, introduced the Walter press (1866), pioneer of modern newspaper printing presses; M.P. (1847–65, 1868–85). His son ¶Arthur Fraser (1846–1910) was chief proprietor of *The Times* (1894–1908) and under new ownership of Lord Northcliffe was chairman of board of directors (1908–10).

Wal·ter \ˈwȯl-tər, *orig* ˈwȯt-ər\, Lucy. *Known also as* Mrs. Bar·low \ˈbär-(ˌ)lō\. 1630–1658. British woman, b. Wales. Mistress of Charles II (1648–51) and by him mother of James, Duke of Monmouth (b. 1649).

Wal·ter \ˈwȯl-tər\, Thomas Ustick. 1804–1887. American architect, b. Philadelphia. Designed Girard College, Philadelphia (1833), often regarded as finest example of Classic architecture in U.S.; appointed architect of Capitol, Washington, D.C. (1851); designed and supervised construction of wings added to central building, and of the dome (1851–65).

Wal·theof \ˈwäl-ˌtha-əf\. *Lat.* Wal·de·vus \wȯl-ˈdē-vəs\ *or* Gual·le·vus \gwä-ˈlē-vəs\. d. 1076. English earl. Son of Siward the Strong; submitted to William the Conqueror after battle of Hastings (1066); joined Danish invaders in massacre of French at York (1069); pardoned by William and married William's niece Judith; earl of Northumberland (1072); convicted of complicity in plot for Danish invasion of England and beheaded. Ancestor of Scottish kings through marriage of his daughter Matilda to David I.

Wal·ther \ˈväl-tər\, Carl Ferdinand Wilhelm. 1811–1887. American clergyman, b. Langenschursdorf, Saxony. Ordained in Lutheran church (1837); to U.S. (1839) with religious colony of German settlers; founded (1839) theological school at Altenburg, which moved to St. Louis (1850) and was named Concordia Theological Seminary; professor of theology there (from 1850) and president (from 1854). An organizer (1847), German Evangelical Lutheran Synod of Missouri, Ohio, and other states.

Walther, Johann. See Johann WALTER.

Walther, Johannes. 1860–1937. German geologist. Professor, Jena (1892–1906), Halle (1906–29); known for studies of deserts of North Africa and Middle East. Author of *Das Gesetz der Wüstenbildung* (1900), etc.

Walther, Johann Gottfried. 1684–1748. German organist and composer. Organist at Thomaskirche, Erfurt (1702–07); town organist (1707–21), court organist (1721–48) at Weimar; friend of J.S. Bach. Composed chorale preludes and variations, toccatas, fugues, etc.; compiled *Musicalisches Lexicon* (1732), first such encyclopedic work on musical topics.

Walther von der Vo·gel·wei·de \fȯn-dər-ˈfō-gəl-ˌvī-də\. 1170?–?1230. Middle High German poet and Minnesinger. Educated in monastery school; learned music from Reinmar von Hagenau at Vienna court of Leopold V; at various times supported Hohenstaufen or Welf cause, frequently in opposition to the pope; lived life of a wandering singer (after 1198) chiefly in courts of Philip of Swabia, Landgrave Hermann of Thuringia, Otto IV, and Frederick II, from whom he received a fief (c.1215). His poems included love songs, notably "Unter den Linden," moral and didactic poems, and political and religious songs in which he championed German independence and unity.

Wal·ton \ˈwȯlt-ᵊn\, Brian *or* Bryan. c.1600–1661. English scholar. Issued, with others, the *London*, or *Walton's, Polyglot Bible* (1653–57) with all or parts in Greek, Latin, and seven Oriental languages; bishop of Chester (1660).

Walton, George. 1741–1804. American politician, b. near Farmville, Va. Member of Continental Congress (1776–79, 1781); a signer of the Declaration of Independence and the Articles of Confederation; governor of Georgia (1779–80, 1789); chief justice of Georgia (1783–89); judge, Georgia superior court (1790–92, 1793–95, 1799–1804); U.S. senator (1795–96).

Walton, Izaak. 1593–1683. English biographer and author. Carried on draper's business in London (from 1614); retired from London to Stafford (c.1650). Published biographies of John Donne (1640), Sir Henry Wotton (1651), Richard Hooker (1665), George Herbert (1670), and Bishop Robert Sanderson (1678). His masterpiece was *The Compleat Angler, or the Contemplative Man's Recreation* (1st ed. 1653; 5th ed. 1676), made up of dialogues between Piscator (angler), Venator (hunter), and Auceps (falconer), with anecdotes, quotations, country scenery, snatches of verse, enlarged by appending of part two by Charles Cotton on fly-fishing and making flies.

Walton, Sir William Turner. 1902–1983. British composer. Wrote in the manner of late-19th-century composers; first major success was witty and jazzy *Façade*, set to satiric poems by Edith Sitwell. Other works included overture *Portsmouth Point* (1926), choral work *Belshazzar's Feast* (1931), two symphonies (1935, 1960), ballet *The Quest* (1943), opera *Troilus and Cressida* (1954), and music for films as *First of the Few* (1942), *Henry V* (1944), *Hamlet* (1948), and *Richard III* (1955).

Waltz \ˈvälts\, Jean-Jacques. *Pseudonym* Han·si \äⁿ-sē\ *or* On·cle Han·si \ōⁿ-kläⁿ-sē\. 1873–1951. French caricaturist and satirist. Author of *Le Professeur Knatschke* (1912), *L'Alsace racontée* (1912), *Mon village* (1913), *L'Alsace heureuse* (1918), etc.

Waltzemüller, Martin. See Martin WALDSEEMÜLLER.

Wal·worth \ˈwȯl-(ˌ)wərth\, Sir William. d. 1385. English politician. Fish merchant; sheriff (1370) and lord mayor (1374, 1381) of London; lent money to Richard II; defended London Bridge against Kentish peasants (1381) and at Smithfield, in Richard II's presence, killed their leader, Wat Tyler.

Wan·a·ma·ker \ˈwän-ə-ˌmā-kər\, John. 1838–1922. American merchant, b. Philadelphia. With brother-in-law Nathan Brown (d. 1868), started men's clothing business (1861), which within ten years developed into largest retail men's clothing store in U.S.; expanded business into a department store (from 1877); U.S. postmaster general (1889–93).

Wang An-shih \ˈwäŋ-ˈän-ˈshi(ə)r\. 1021–1086. Chinese statesman and reformer. Provincial official (to 1060), then entered imperial service; appointed second privy councilor (1069), gained great influence with Emperor Shen Tsung; initiated broad "New Policies" consisting of fiscal reforms; established financial bureau that made loans to farmers, instituted pay for government labor, levied an income tax, reassessed property taxes more equitably, organized a conscript militia, revised educational system and Confucian examinations for civil service; retired (1076). A noted prose stylist.

Wang Chen \-ˈjən\. d. 1449. Chinese courtier. Eunuch of court of Emperor Cheng-t'ung, whom he dominated; persuaded emperor to ignore advice of generals and to attack Oyrat Mongols in northwest; killed with emperor and generals in Mongol ambush.

Wang Ching-wei \-ˈjiŋ-ˈwā\. *Orig.* Wang Chao-ming \-ˈjau̇-ˈmiŋ\. 1883–1944. Chinese politician. Joined revolutionary party and attempted (1910) to assassinate prince regent; sentenced to imprisonment for life but released (1911) after establishment of the republic; one of Sun Yat-sen's chief assistants (1911–25); chairman of national government (1925–27); head of left faction (1927) but lost influence after purging Communists; joined Chiang Kai-shek (1932); president of Kuomintang (1932–38); deserted Nationalist government (1938) and fled to Hong Kong; became strongly pro-Japanese; made puppet ruler of occupied China (1940–44).

Wang Ch'ung \-ˈchuŋ\. 27–?100 A.D. Chinese philosopher. Held official positions for a few years but retired to write *Lun-heng*, in which he ridiculed superstitions and criticized freely the teachings of Confucius and Mencius and Taoist doctrines from a strongly rationalist, naturalist viewpoint.

Wang Fu-chih \-ˈfü-ˈji(ə)r\. 1619–1692. Chinese historian. Raised army to resist Mongol overthrow of Ming dynasty (1644–50); devoted himself thereafter to study; one of first to write from a nationalistic viewpoint. Works included *Tu t'ung-chien lun* and *Sung lun;* also noted as a poet.

Wang Hsi-chih \-ˈshē-ˈji(ə)r\. 321–379. Chinese calligrapher. Most celebrated of Chinese calligraphers, ardently studied and imitated; best known work the *Lan-t'ing hsü* recording in *hsing shu* script a famous gathering of poets at Orchid Pavilion (353).

Wang Hui \-ˈhwē\. 1632–1717. Chinese painter. Chief among the Four Wangs, representative of orthodox school; commissioned (1691–98) to produce series of scrolls commemorating emperor's southern tour; known principally as landscapist.

Wang Mang \-ˈmäŋ\. *Known as* the Usurper. 45 B.C.–23 A.D. Chinese emperor (9–23 A.D.). Through his aunt, wife of Yüan Ti, Han emperor, he obtained influence and high position at court; regent for two child emperors (1–8 A.D.). Seized throne (9 A.D.), thus terminating Han dynasty; established Hsin dynasty; introduced many reforms, esp. with regard to taxes, usury, ownership of land, price levels, and business monopolies; faced with unrest following natural disasters; killed by rebels of Red Eyebrows faction.

Wang Meng \-ˈməŋ\. 1308–1385. Chinese painter. Grandson of Chao Meng-fu; with his friend Ni Tsan one of the Four Masters of the Yüan dynasty.

Wang Pi \-ˈbē\. 226–249. Chinese philosopher. Anticipated Neo-Confucians with metaphysical commentaries on *Tao-te Ching* and *I Ching.*

Wang Shih-fu \-ˈshi(ə)r-ˈfü\. *Orig.* Wang Te-hsin \-ˈdə-ˈshin\. c.1250–?1337. Chinese dramatist. Leading dramatist of Yüan dynasty; reputedly author of 14 plays of which 3 are extant, esp. the still popular *Hsi hsiang chi.*

Wang T'ao \-ˈtau̇\. 1828–?1897. Chinese journalist. Fled to Hong Kong (1860) because of sympathy with Taiping Rebellion; assisted James Legge on translation of Confucian Classics; founded one of earliest modern-style newspapers in China (1870); urged adoption of Western methods, technology, democracy.

Wang Wei \-'wā\. 699–759 A.D. Chinese poet and painter. Founder of Southern literati school of painter-poets; a pioneer in landscape art, best known for ink monochrome snowscapes; celebrated as lyric poet with Li Po and Tu Fu; an ardent Buddhist, spent latter part of life in a monastery.

Wang Yang-ming \-'yäŋ-'məŋ\. *Orig.* Wang Shou-jen \-'shō-'rən\. *Literary name* Pe-an \'bā-'än\. *Canonized as* Wen-ch'eng \'wən-'chəŋ\. *Known in Japan* as Ōyō-mei \ō-yō-mā\. 1472–1529. Chinese philosopher. Held various high posts in imperial government. At first a Taoist but later (c.1506) began to teach Confucianism in a new Idealist interpretation. As governor of Southern Kiangsi (1516–19) suppressed banditry; defeated and captured rebellious Prince of Ning (1519); governor of all Kiangsi (1519–21); war minister (1521–29). Revered as sage and honored by sacrificial offerings in Confucian temples (from 1584).

Wan-li. See Chu I-chün under CHU family.

Wā·qi·dī, al- \əl-'wä-kə-dē\. *In full* Abū 'Abd Allāh Muḥammad ibn 'Umar al-Wāqidī. 747–823. Arab historian. Chief work *Kitāb al-maghāzī,* a history of Muḥammad's military campaigns.

War·beck \'wȯr-ˌbek\, Perkin. 1474?–1499. Flemish impostor. Servant of Breton silk merchant in Ireland; professed (1492) to be Richard, Duke of York, second of Edward IV's sons, murdered in Tower; acknowledged as nephew by Margaret, dowager Duchess of Burgundy, sister of Edward IV of England; supported by earls of Desmond and Kildare; entertained as Richard IV by Charles VIII of France; supplied with money by Emperor Maximilian I for unsuccessful invasion of Kent, England, and Waterford, Ireland (1495); welcomed by James IV of Scotland and given Lady Catherine Gordon in marriage; landed in Cornwall, proclaiming himself king (1499); advanced to Exeter; taken prisoner, confessed imposture; imprisoned in Tower of London; hanged for endeavoring to escape.

War·burg \'vär-ˌbu̇rk, *Angl* 'wȯr-ˌbərg, 'vär-ˌbu̇(ə)rk\, Aby. 1866–1929. German art historian. Specialist in Renaissance studies; founded (1905) what became Warburg Inst., U. of London.

Warburg, Max. 1867–1946. German banker. Brother of Aby Warburg. Entered family bank (1893); adviser to German delegation at Paris Peace Conference (1919); adviser to the Reichsbank (from 1924); fled to U.S. (1938); author of works on finance. His brother ¶Paul Moritz (1868–1932), partner in M. M. Warburg & Co., Hamburg (1895); to U.S. (1902) and joined banking firm of Kuhn, Loeb & Co., New York; naturalized (1911); aided in planning national banking reorganization (1907–14); member of first Federal Reserve Board (1914–18); author of *The Federal Reserve System* (1930). Another brother ¶Felix Moritz (1871–1937), to U.S. (1894, naturalized 1900); member Kuhn, Loeb & Co., New York (from 1896); widely known for his philanthropies. A son of Paul Moritz ¶James Paul (1896–1969); to U.S. as a child; vice president, International Acceptance Bank, New York City (1921–29); financial adviser to World Economic Conference in London (1933); author of *Acceptance Financing* (1922), *The Money Muddle* (1934), *Hell Bent for Election* (1935), etc.

Warburg, Otto Heinrich. 1883–1970. German biochemist. Professor, Berlin (from 1915); member (from 1913), director (from 1930), Kaiser Wilhelm Institute for Biology; known for researches on respiratory ferments, on the physical chemistry and respiration of living cells, and on cancer; first to note action of coenzymes (1935); pioneer in manometric studies of respiration. Awarded 1931 Nobel prize for physiology or medicine.

War·bur·ton \'wȯr-bərt-ᵊn\, Bartholomew Elliot George, *usually known as* Eliot. 1810–1852. Irish novelist. Author of *The Crescent and the Cross* (1845), *Memoir of Prince Rupert* (1849), *Darien* (1851), etc.

Warburton, William. 1698–1779. English prelate, theologian, and controversialist. Gained court favor with *Alliance between Church and State* (1736); chaplain to king (1754); dean of Bristol (1757); bishop of Gloucester (1759). Gained friendship of Alexander Pope with a defense of his *Essay on Man* (1739); persuaded Pope to add a fourth book to *Dunciad;* Pope's literary executor (1744); brought out edition of Pope's works (1751). Published, after quarrel with Lewis Theobald, with whom he had formerly collaborated, edition of Shakespeare's works (1747) that was severely criticized. Engaged in controversies with Lord Bolingbroke, Methodists, Hume, Voltaire, etc. Author also of *Divine Legation of Moses* (1737–41), *Doctrine of Grace* (1762).

Ward \'wȯ(ə)rd\, Aaron Montgomery. 1843–1913. American merchant, b. Chatham, N.J. In Chicago established drygoods business (1872) which developed into great mail-order house of Montgomery Ward & Co.; retired (1901). His wife (m. 1872) ¶Elizabeth J., *nee* Cobb \'käb\ (1857–1926), established a medical and dental school (1923) at Northwestern U. in memory of her husband.

Ward, Artemas. 1727–1800. American Revolutionary commander, b. Shrewsbury, Mass. Organized resistance to General Gage as governor of Massachusetts (1774–75). On news of battle of Lexington, assumed command of American forces; commissioned general and commander in chief of Massachusetts troops (May 1775); directed siege of Boston until Gen. Washington's arrival. Named by Continental Congress as second in command (to Gen. Washington) in Continental army, and commissioned major general (June 1775). Under his orders, Gen. John Thomas (*q.v.*) seized Dorchester Heights (Mar. 4, 1776) and thus forced British evacuation of Boston. Resigned from army (Mar. 1776). Member of Massachusetts executive council (1777–79), Continental Congress (1780–82), and U.S. House of Representatives (1791–95).

Ward, Artemus. See Charles Farrar BROWNE.

Ward, Arthur Sarsfield. *Pen name* Sax Roh·mer \'rō-mər\. 1886–1959. English writer. Author of over 25 mystery novels featuring the fictional Chinese criminal genius Fu Manchu, as *Dr. Fu Manchu* (1913, first of series), *The Trail of Fu Manchu* (1934), *Re-enter Fu Manchu* (1957), and *The Return of Fu* (1959).

Ward, Barbara Mary. Baroness Jackson of Lods·worth \'lädz-(ˌ)wərth\. 1914–1981. English economist and writer. m. (1950) Sir Robert Jackson. On staff of *The Economist* (1939 ff.); visiting professor, Harvard U. (1957–68), Columbia U. (1968–73); influential adviser to the Vatican, the UN, the World Bank. Author of *The International Share-Out* (1938), *The West at Bay* (1948), *Faith and Freedom* (1954), *India and the West* (1961), *The Rich Nations and the Poor Nations* (1962), *Spaceship Earth* (1966), *Nationalism and Ideology* (1967), *Only One Earth* (1972, with René Dubos), *Home of Man* (1976), *Progress for a Small Planet* (1980).

Ward, Edward, *called* Ned. 1667–1731. English tavern keeper and humorist. Writer of coarse doggerel verse; author of *The London Spy* (1698–1709), a prose work containing sketches of social life and characters of Queen Anne's time, esp. in London, and *Hudibras Redivivus* (1705–07), vulgar satire upon Whigs and the Low Church party.

Ward, Elizabeth Stuart. *Nee* Mary Gray Phelps \'felps\. 1844–1911. American author, b. Boston. m. (1888) Herbert D. Ward. Author of *The Gates Ajar* (1868), *Poetic Studies* (1875), *Doctor Zay* (1882), *Beyond the Gates* (1883), *Songs of the Silent World* (1884), *The Madonna of the Tubs* (1887), *Jack, the Fisherman* (1887), *A Singular Life* (1895), *Within the Gates* (1901), etc.

Ward, Frederick Townsend. 1831–1862. American military adventurer, b. Salem, Mass. In China (1859–62); organized foreign mercenary troops to aid Chinese government forces in suppressing Taiping rebellion; his command, called "the Ever-Victorious Army," won a number of successes; mortally wounded in action and succeeded by Charles G. Gordon (*q.v.*).

Ward, Mrs. Humphry. See Mary Augusta WARD.

Ward, James. 1843–1925. English philosopher and psychologist. Fellow of Trinity Coll., Cambridge (from 1875); professor of mental philosophy (1897–1925). Author of *Naturalism and Agnosticism* (1899), *The Realm of Ends, or Pluralism and Theism* (1911), *Psychological Principles* (1918), *A Study of Kant* (1922).

Ward, John. 1571?–?1638. English composer. Known for sacred vocal music, many pieces for viol, and esp. *First Set of English Madrigals* (1613).

Ward, John Quincy Adams. 1830–1910. American sculptor, b. near Urbana, Ohio. Studio in Washington, D.C. (c.1857–59); sculptured busts of Alexander H. Stephens, Hannibal Hamlin, and others; studio in New York (from 1861). President, National Academy of Design (1874). Among his works were *Indian Hunter* and *Pilgrim* (Central Park, New York), *Good Samaritan* (Public Gardens, Boston), *The Freedman,* equestrian statues of General Sheridan (Albany, N.Y.), Gen. George H. Thomas (Washington, D.C.), and General Hancock (Philadelphia); statues of Gen. John F. Reynolds (Gettysburg, Pa.), Henry Ward Beecher (Brooklyn, N.Y.), and many portrait busts.

Ward, Sir Joseph George. 1856–1930. New Zealand politician, b. Australia. M.P. (1887–1919, 1925–30); postmaster general (1891); colonial treasurer (1893–94); pioneered loans to settlers (1894); minister of industries and commerce (1894–96); colonial secretary, postmaster general, and minister of industries and commerce (1899–1901); introduced inland penny postage (1901); world's first minister of public health (1901–06); introduced state fire insurance (1903); prime minister (1906–12); minister of finance and postmaster general (1915–19); with W.F. Massey represented N.Z. at Imperial war cabinets (1917, 1918) and Paris Peace Conference (1919); again prime minister (1928–30).

Ward, Sir Leslie. *Pseudonym* Spy \'spī\. 1851–1922. English caricaturist and portrait painter. Caricaturist on *Vanity Fair* (from 1873).

Ward, Lester Frank. 1841–1913. American sociologist, b. Joliet, Ill. On staff, U.S. Treasury Department (1865–81); geologist (1883–92), paleontologist (1892–1906), U.S. Geological Survey; professor of sociology, Brown U. (1906–13); pioneer in field of sociology in U.S. Author of *Dynamic Sociology*

(1883), *The Psychic Factors of Civilization* (1893), *Outlines of Sociology* (1898), *Glimpses of the Cosmos* (1913–18).

Ward, Maisie. See under Francis J. SHEED.

Ward, Mary Augusta, *nee* Ar·nold \'är-nəld\. *Known as* Mrs. Humphry Ward. 1851–1920. English novelist, b. Tasmania. Niece of Matthew Arnold; m. (1872) Thomas Humphry Ward. In her best known novel, the spiritual romance *Robert Elsmere* (1888), envisioned a vigorous Christianity, divested of the miraculous element and fulfilling the social gospel. Founded (1890) settlement in London which developed into Passmore Edwards Settlement (1897); opponent of woman suffrage. Author of other novels, including *David Grieve* (1892), *Marcella* (1894), *Lady Rose's Daughter* (1903), *The Case of Richard Meynell* (1911), *Missing* (1917), *Harvest* (1920).

Ward, Montgomery. See Aaron Montgomery WARD.

Ward, Nathaniel. 1578?–1652. English clergyman. Entered Anglican ministry, but was dismissed for nonconformity (1633); to America and became pastor at Agawam (now Ipswich), Mass. (1634–38). Prepared legal code for Massachusetts (enacted 1641), first code of laws to be established in New England. Over pseudonym Theodore de la Guard \ˌdel-ə-'gärd\ published *The Simple Cobler of Aggawam in America* (1645), the supposed reflections of a cobbler on contemporary political and religious issues.

Ward, Ned. See Edward WARD.

Ward, Robert DeCourcy. 1867–1931. American meteorologist, b. Boston. On Harvard teaching staff (from 1890); professor of climatology (from 1910), first such professor in U.S. Author of *Climate, Considered Especially in Relation to Man* (1908), *The Climates of the United States* (1925).

Ward, Seth. 1617–1689. English bishop and astronomer. Professor of astronomy, Oxford (1649–60); bishop of Exeter (1662–67), of Salisbury (1667); propounded alternative to Kepler's area law of planetary motion (1653); engaged in philosophical controversy with Thomas Hobbes.

Ward, William George. 1812–1882. English theologian and writer. Ordained in Anglican church (1840); joined Oxford Movement; condemned by Oxford U. and deprived of degree for *The Ideal of the Christian Church* (1844); joined Roman Catholic church (1845); taught at St. Edmund's Coll. (1851–58); editor of *Dublin Review* (1863–78); a founder (1869) of Metaphysical Society.

Ward·law \'wȯrd-ˌlȯ\, Henry. d. 1440. Scottish prelate. Bishop of St. Andrews (1403); tutor to James I of Scotland; founded St. Andrews U., the first in Scotland (1411); completed restoration of St. Andrews cathedral.

Ware \'wa(ə)r, 'we(ə)r\, Henry. 1764–1845. American clergyman, b. Sherborn Mass. Hollis professor of divinity, Harvard (1805–40); from his courses developed Harvard Divinity School (organized 1816), in which he was professor of systematic theology and evidences of Christianity (1816–45); associated with the liberal, or Unitarian branch of Congregationalists. His son ¶Henry (1794–1843), b. Hingham, Mass.; Unitarian clergyman; professor, Harvard Divinity School (1830–42); author of *The Life of the Saviour* (1833), and poems, addresses, and sermons. Another son ¶William (1797–1852), b. Hingham; Unitarian clergyman and writer; pastor, New York City (1821–36); author of *Zenobia* (1837), its sequel *Probus* (1838), *Julian* (1841), etc.

Ware, William Robert. 1832–1915. American architect, b. Cambridge, Mass. Son of Henry Ware (1794–1843). Worked in office of Richard M. Hunt; formed partnership with Henry Van Brunt (1863); executed Memorial Hall at Harvard U., First Church of Boston, etc.; appointed to establish and head school of architecture at Massachusetts Inst. of Technology (1865); organized architectural courses and taught at Columbia U. (1881–1903). Author of *Modern Perspective* (1883), *The American Vignola* (1902–06).

Wa·renne \wä-'ren, *Fr* vȧ-ren\ *or* **War·ren** \'wȯr-ən, 'wär-\, de. Name (derived from Varenne, Normandy) of an Anglo-Norman family holding large estates in Surrey, Sussex, Norfolk, and Yorkshire, founded in England by William de Warenne (1030?–1088), 1st Earl of Sur·rey \'sər-ē, 'sə-rē\ (more commonly styled, as were his successors, Earl Warenne); distant cousin of William the Conqueror; fought at Hastings; joint chief justiciar (1075); founder of Cluniac priories; fatally wounded at siege of Pevensey Castle. His son ¶William (1071?–1138), 2d earl, took part in Duke Robert's invasion of England (1101); pardoned by Henry II; fought in Normandy (1106, 1119, 1135). The latter's son ¶William (c.1119–1148), 3d earl, supported King Stephen; killed on Second Crusade. ¶Isabel (d. 1203), heiress of 3d earl; m. Hamelin Plantagenet (d. 1202), illegitimate son of Geoffrey Plantegenet and Henry II's half-brother, who took (from 1163) name de Warenne and title of Earl Warenne; denounced Thomas Becket, supported Henry II and Richard I, opposed Prince John (1191–99), and built great keep at Conisbrough. Their son ¶William (d. 1240), 6th Earl of Surrey, sided with John against pope and against barons; warden of Cinque Ports (1216); m. (1225) Matilda, coheiress of William Marshal, 1st Earl of Pembroke; a regent (1230); member of council to prevent king from squandering subsidy (1238).

William's (d. 1240) son ¶John (1231?–1304), 7th earl, took Henry III's side against barons (1258–59); fought under Prince Edward at Lewes, fled to France, and lost lands to barons (1264); pardoned (1268); took oaths to Edward I; served in Wales (1277, 1282–83); received earldom of Sussex on death of his sister (1282); led invasion of Scotland, took Dunbar Castle (1296); routed by Wallace (1297) at Stirling Bridge; commanded rear at Falkirk (1298). His grandson ¶John (1286–1347) succeeded him as 8th earl (1304); joined barons' party, but alienated by execution of Piers Gaveston, went over to Edward II (1312) and received pardon; stripped of many estates by Lancaster (1317–19); supported Edward II against Lancaster and against Queen Isabella; made commissioner to Scots (1327); sheriff of Surrey and Sussex (1339). At his death without issue, northern Warenne lands passed to Edmund of Langley (later Duke of York), southern lands to Richard Fitzalan, 3d Earl of Arundel.

Wa·rens \vȧ-rän, vȧ-'rans\, Louise-Éléanore de, *nee* de la Tour du Pil \tür-dü̅-pēl\. Baronne. 1700–1762. French aristocrat. Fled husband and business debts to protection of King Victor of Savoy; in Savoy met Jean-Jacques Rousseau (1728), whom she engaged in an idyllic liaison (1733–42).

Wa·re·ru \wä-'rā-rü\. *Also known as* Mo·ga·do \mō-'gäd-ō\ *or* Chao Fa Rua \'chau̇-'fä-rü-'ä\. fl. 1300. Mon ruler. Tai adventurer; joined (1287) Tarabya, Mon prince, in driving Burmese out of Irawaddy delta; killed Tarabya and made himself king, establishing Hanthawaddy dynasty seated at Martaban; compiled *Dharma-śāstra* or *Dhammathat,* first law code in Burma.

War·ham \'wȯr-əm\, William. c.1450–1532. English prelate. Master of the rolls (1494); keeper of the seal (1502); bishop of London (1503); lord chancellor (1504–15); archbishop of Canterbury (1504); crowned Henry VIII and Catherine of Aragon (1509); gradually withdrew in favor of Wolsey after controversy over legatine authority (1518); acquiesced in Henry VIII's being declared head of church (1531) but protested (1532) Reform measures.

War·hol \'wȯr-ˌhȯl, -ˌhōl\, Andy. *Orig.* Andrew Warhola. 1928?–1987. American artist, b. Pittsburgh. Founder and leading exponent of pop art. Achieved (1962) instant notoriety with exhibition of paintings of Campbell soup cans and sculptures that were replicas of Brillo soap pad boxes; advanced concept of the artist as an impersonal, passive agent; produced repetitive art by mechanical means in order to convey the banality and tawdriness of American pop culture; also noted for his series of silk-screened protraits of pop celebrities. Created underground films, as *The Chelsea Girls* (1966) and *Blue Movie* (1969), marked by bizarre eroticism, great length, and uneventfulness. A shrewd self-publicist, predicted that in the future everyone would be famous for 15 minutes.

War·ing \'war-iŋ, 'wer-\, Edward. 1734–1798. English mathematician. Practiced medicine; professor of mathematics, Cambridge (from 1760); first to set forth method of approximating values of imaginary roots; proposed Waring's problem on decomposition of natural numbers into cubes and biquadratics (1770, solved 1909), classified quartic curves. Author of *Miscellane analytica* (1762), *Meditationes algebraicae* (1770), *Meditationes analyticae* (1776), etc.

Wariston, Lord. See Archibald JOHNSTON.

Warlock, Peter. See Philip Arnold HESELTINE.

War·ming \'vär-mēŋ\, Johannes Eugenius Bülow. 1841–1924. Danish botanist. Professor, Royal Inst. of Technology, Stockholm (1882–85), U. of Copenhagen (1885–1911); credited with founding of plant ecology. Author of *Om Grønlands Vegetation* (1888), *Lagoa Santa* (1892), *Plantesamfund* (1895), etc.

Warne \'wȯ(ə)rn\, Frederick. 1825–1901. English publisher. In partnership with George Routledge (1851–65); formed own firm (1865); inaugurated *Chandos Classics* (1868); published Frances Hodgson Burnett's novels; introduced American *Century, St. Nicholas, Scribner's* to English public.

Warner brothers. See Harry Morris WARNER.

Warner, Anna Bartlett. See under Susan Bogert WARNER.

War·ner \'wȯr-nər\, Charles Dudley. 1829–1900. American man of letters, b. Plainfield, Mass. An editor (1867–1900), Hartford (Conn.) *Courant;* contributing editor, *Harper's New Monthly Magazine* (1884–98) and coeditor of *Library of the World's Best Literature* (30 vols., 1896–97). Collaborated with Mark Twain in writing *The Gilded Age* (1873). Known for books of familiar essays, including *My Summer in a Garden* (1871), *Backlog Studies* (1873), *Being a Boy* (1878), *On Horseback* (1888), *Fashions in Literature* (1902).

Warner, Glenn Scobey. *Called* Pop Warner. 1871–1954. American football coach, b. Springville, N.Y. Coach at U. of Georgia (1894–96), Cornell (1897–98, 1904–06), Carlisle (Pa.) Indian School (1898–1904, 1906–1915), U. of Pittsburgh (1915–23), Stanford (1924–32), Temple U. (1933–38); career record 312 wins, 104 losses, 32 ties; devised double-wing formation, etc.

Warner, Harry Morris. *Orig. surname* Ei·chel·baum \'ī-kəl-ˌbau̇m\. 1881–1958. American motion-picture executive, b. Krasnosielce, Poland. To U.S. (c.1887); with brothers ¶Albert (1884–1967), ¶Samuel Louis (1887–1927), and ¶Jack Leonard (1892–1978), b. London, Ont., entered film exhibition and distribution business (1903); opened nickelodeon in New Castle, Pa. (1905), first of a chain; abandoned distribution for production (1912); first notable production *My Four Years in Germany* (1917); established studios in Hollywood, Cal. (1918), and incorporated as Warner Brothers Pictures (1923), of which Harry was president (1923–56) followed by Jack (1956–66); firm produced *Don Juan* with synchronized musical score (1926), *The Jazz Singer,* first "talkie" (1927),

Lights of New York, first full-length all-talking picture (1928), *On With the Show,* first all-talking color picture (1929); later notable films included *Little Caesar* (1930), *Gold Diggers* series, *42nd Street* (1933), *Green Pastures* (1936), *Casablanca* (1942), *Watch on the Rhine* (1943), *Streetcar Named Desire* (1952); firm pioneered in television film production; merged with Seven Arts Productions (1966).

Warner, Seth. 1743–1784. American Revolutionary officer, b. Roxbury, Conn. With Ethan Allen and Benedict Arnold at capture of Ticonderoga (May 10, 1775); led force that seized Crown Point (May 12, 1775); lieutenant colonel of "Green Mountain Boys" (1775); led regiment in battle of Bennington (Aug. 16, 1777). Commissioned brigadier general by Vermont assembly (1778).

Warner, Susan Bogert. *Pseudonym* Elizabeth Weth·er·ell \'weth-ər-əl\. 1819–1885. American novelist, b. New York City. Made great success with her first two books *The Wide, Wide World* (1850) and *Queechy* (1852). Among her later novels were *Melbourne House* (1864), *Daisy* (1868), *Diana* (1877), *Nobody* (1882). Collaborated in many books with her sister ¶Anna Bartlett (1827–1915), including *Say and Seal* (1860), *Wych Hazel* (1876). Anna was author of *Stories of Vinegar Hill* (6 vols., 1872), *The Fourth Watch* (1872), a number of books on gardening, and hymns including "Jesus Loves Me, This I Know" and "Jesus Bids Us Shine."

Warner, Sylvia Townsend. 1893–1978. English writer. Author of verse as *The Espalier* (1925), *Time Importuned* (1928), *Opus 7* (novel in verse, 1931), *Whether a Dove or a Seagull* (with V. Ackland, 1934), of fiction including *Lolly Willowes* (1926), *Mr. Fortune's Maggot* (1927), *Elinor Barley* (1930), *The Salutation* (1932), *After the Death of Don Juan* (1938), *Garland of Straw* (1943), *The Corner That Held Them* (1948), *Flint Anchor* (1954), *Boxwood* (1960), *Stranger With a Bag* (1966), *Kingdoms of Elfin* (1977); wrote biography *T. H. White* (1967).

Warner, Sir Thomas. d. 1649. English colonizer. Founded colonies of St. Kitts (1624), Nevis (1628), Antigua (1632), Montserrat (1632).

Warner, William. c.1558–1609. English poet. Published *Pan his Syrinx,* consisting of 7 prose tales (1585), and his chief work *Albion's England* (1586), in 14-syllabled verse, consisting of history, mythical tales, theology.

Warnerius. See IRNERIUS.

War·ren \'wȯr-ən, 'wär-\, Sir Charles. 1840–1927. British soldier and archaeologist, b. Wales. Entered Royal Engineers (1857); excavated at Jerusalem (1867) and surveyed Palestine (1867–70); served in military operations in South Africa, Egypt, in Boer War (1899–1900); general (1904). Author of *Recovery of Jerusalem* (1871), *Underground Jerusalem* (1876), *Temple and Tomb* (1880), *Survey of Western Palestine* (1884), etc.

Warren, Earl. 1891–1974. American jurist, b. Los Angeles. Governor of California (1943–53); Republican candidate for vice president on Dewey ticket (1948); chief justice, U.S. Supreme Court (1953–69). Noted for opinions in *Brown* v. *Board of Education* outlawing segregated schools (1954), *Reynolds* v. *Sims* requiring state legislative reapportionment (1964), *Miranda* v. *Arizona* on rights of police suspects (1966).

Warren, Gouverneur Kemble. 1830–1882. American army officer, b. Cold Spring, N.Y. Entered army (1850); brigadier general of volunteers (1862); chief topographical engineer, army of the Potomac (from Feb. 1863). Major general of volunteers (1863) and chief engineer of army of the Potomac; at Gettysburg, by prompt action in seizing and holding Little Round Top, saved the day (July 2, 1863) for Union army. Commanded V corps (1864); engaged in the Wilderness, Spotsylvania, Cold Harbor, Five Forks; commanded department of Mississippi (May 1865). On military engineering duty (1865–82).

Warren, Harry. *Orig.* Salvatore Gua·ra·gna \g(w)är-'än-yə\. 1893–1981. American songwriter, b. Brooklyn, N.Y. Composed over 300 songs, chiefly for motion pictures, with lyricists Al Dubin, Johnny Mercer, Mack Gordon, Ira Gershwin, etc., including "I Love My Baby," "Forty-Second Street," "We're In the Money," "I Only Have Eyes for You," "Lullaby of Broadway" (Academy Award, 1935), "You Must Have Been a Beautiful Baby," "You'll Never Know" (Academy Award, 1943), "Chattanooga Choo-Choo," "September in the Rain," "On the Atchison, Topeka and the Santa Fe" (Academy Award, 1946), "Serenade in Blue," "That's Amore."

Warren, John Byrne Leicester. 3d Baron de Tab·ley \də-'tab-lē\. 1835–1895. English poet. Author of the tragedies *Philoctetes* (1866) and *Orestes* (1868), *Guide-book to Bookplates* (1880), and *Poems Dramatic and Lyrical* (1893, 1895).

Warren, Joseph. 1741–1775. American physician and Revolutionary officer, b. Roxbury, Mass. Practiced medicine in Boston; active in patriot agitation (from 1765); helped prepare Suffolk Resolves (1774); as member of Committee of Safety sent Paul Revere and William Dawes to Lexington to warn Hancock and Adams of their danger (Apr. 18, 1775); president pro tempore of provincial Congress (1775). Commissioned major general (June 1775); killed at Breed's Hill (battle of Bunker Hill, June 17, 1775).

His brother ¶John (1753–1815), physician, practiced in Salem, Mass.; active in Boston Tea Party (Dec. 18, 1773); joined army as surgeon; senior surgeon of hospital at Cambridge (1775–76) and later of that on Long Island (1776–77); with Benjamin Waterhouse drew up plans for Harvard Medical School (1782), and was its first professor of anatomy and surgery (from 1783). John's son ¶John Collins (1778–1856), surgeon, practiced with his father in Boston (from 1802); professor, Harvard Medical School (1809–47); first surgeon, Massachusetts General Hospital, Boston (1821); best known as surgeon who gave first public demonstration of ether anesthesia in surgical operation (Oct. 16, 1846, ether administered by W.T.G. Morton).

Warren, Josiah. 1798?–1874. American reformer, b. Boston. Joined Robert Owen's community at New Harmony, Ind. (1825); tried out theory of time value of labor in "equity store" in Cincinnati (1827–29). Established social community, known as "Modern Times," on Long Island, N.Y., which attracted a number of eccentrics. Regarded as founder of philosophical anarchism in America. Author of *Equitable Commerce* (1846), *True Civilization an Immediate Necessity* (1863).

Warren, Lavinia. See under Charles Sherwood STRATTON.

Warren, Mercy, *nee* Otis \'ō-təs\. 1728–1814. American woman of letters, b. Barnstable, Mass. Sister of James Otis; m. (1754) James Warren; friend and correspondent of leading political figures of her day, including John Adams, Samuel Adams, Thomas Jefferson, Elbridge Gerry. Author of political satires, notably *The Adulateur* (1773) and *The Group* (1775), several plays, *Poems Dramatic and Miscellaneous* (1790), and *History of the Rise, Progress, and Termination of the American Revolution* (1805).

Warren, Sir Peter. 1703–1752. British naval officer. Entered navy (1717); commanded British naval force that captured French fortress of Louisbourg (1745); rear admiral (1745); commanded squadron that defeated French squadron off Cape Finisterre (1747); knighted and promoted vice admiral (1747).

Warren, Samuel. 1807–1877. English lawyer and novelist. Author of many legal textbooks and of *Ten Thousand a Year* (1841), *Now and Then* (1847), *The Lily and the Bee* (1851).

Warrington, Earl of. See under George BOOTH.

Warriston, Lord. See Archibald JOHNSTON.

Wartenburg. See YORCK VON WARTENBURG.

War·ton \'wȯrt-ᵊn\, Joseph. 1722–1800. English literary critic. Headmaster (1766–93) of Winchester; revolted in *The Enthusiast* (1744) and *Odes* (1746) against critical rules of Pope and the "correct" school of poetry, and displayed an unfashionable love of nature and natural scenery; edited Virgil and translated *Eclogues* and *Georgics* (1753); known chiefly for *Essay on the Genius and Writings of Pope* (1756, 1782). Edited Pope (1797); friend of Dr. Johnson and member of Literary Club.

His brother ¶Thomas (1728–1790) was a literary historian and critic, and poet laureate; attracted attention with blank verse *Pleasures of Melancholy* (1747) and heroic poem in praise of Oxford *The Triumph of Isis* (1749); established reputation with *Observations on the Faerie Queene of Spenser* (1754); brought to bear vast stores of learning in *The History of English Poetry* (1774–81), extending to end of Elizabethan age; one of the first detect Chatterton forgeries (1782); poet laureate (1785–90).

Warville, de. See BRISSOT DE WARVILLE.

War·wick \'wär-ik, *US also* 'wȯr-ik, 'wȯr-(ˌ)wik\. English earldom, created in 1088, and held by various families, including the Beauchamps, Nevilles, Plantagenets, Dudleys, Riches, and (since 1759) Grevilles. The chief holders of the title were: Richard and Thomas BEAUCHAMP, Richard NEVILLE (1428–1471), EDWARD (1475–1499), John DUDLEY, Robert RICH.

Wa·ser \'väs-ər\, Johann Heinrich. 1600–1669. Swiss politician. Active as arbiter among Protestant cantons; mayor of Zürich (from 1652); proponent of stronger confederation.

Wash·a·kie \'wäsh-ə-kē, 'wȯsh-\. 1804?–1900. American Indian leader, b. Montana. Chief of Eastern Shoshone tribe (from early 1840s); counseled friendship to whites and acquiescence in settlement; aided U.S. army in Indian wars on Great Plains; signed Treaty of Fort Bridger (1868) allowing railroad right of way through Shoshone land.

Wash·burn \'wäsh-(ˌ)bərn\, Israel. 1813–1883. American politician, b. Livermore, Me. Member from Maine of U.S. House of Representatives (1851–61); helped form Republican party (1854); governor of Maine (1861–62). His brother ¶Elihu Benjamin, who spelled his name Washburne (1816–1887), member from Illinois of U.S. House of Representatives (1853–69); friend of U.S. Grant, who named him U.S. secretary of state (1869); U.S. minister to France (1869–77). Another brother ¶Cadwallader Colden (1818–1882) was member from Wisconsin of U.S. House of Representatives (1855–61, 1867–71); governor of Wisconsin (1872–74). Another brother ¶William Drew

(1831–1912) was member from Minnesota of U.S. House of Representatives (1879–85) and of U.S. Senate (1889–95).

Wash·ing·ton \'wösh-iŋ-tən, 'wäsh-\, Booker Taliaferro. 1856–1915. American educator, born a slave in Franklin Co., Va. After great hardships in his youth, gained an education at Hampton Institute, where he taught in a program for American Indians (1879–81). Chosen (1881) to establish and head Tuskegee Institute at Tuskegee, Ala., for practical training of Negroes in trades and professions, which at his death had over 100 buildings, a faculty of about 200, a student body of 1500, and an endowment of $2 million. Spokesman for conservative viewpoint among American Negroes opposed to agitation for social and political ends. Author of *Up From Slavery* (1901).

Washington, Bushrod. 1762–1829. American jurist, b. Westmoreland Co., Va. Nephew of George Washington; served in Continental army in American Revolution; practiced law in Alexandria, Va. (to 1790) and Richmond (from 1790); associate justice, U.S. Supreme Court (1798–1829). Resided (after 1802) at Mount Vernon, which his uncle had left him.

Washington, George. 1732–1799. First president of the United States, b. Westmoreland Co., Va. Privately educated, chiefly by his elder half-brother, Lawrence. Gained experience as surveyor by assisting in survey of certain Fairfax holdings in Shenandoah Valley (1748); county surveyor, Culpeper Co., Va. (1749). Inherited Mount Vernon after death of Lawrence (1752). Commissioned district adjutant by Gov. Dinwiddie (1752); sent to carry ultimatum (1753) to French who were encroaching on English territory in Ohio region; delivered message but received unconciliatory reply. Commissioned lieutenant colonel and sent with 150 men (1754) to establish outpost on site of present city of Pittsburgh; found French in possession of Fort Duquesne; entrenched himself at Great Meadows, Pa., in Fort Necessity; defeated first French force sent against him (May 28, 1754); gained honorable terms from French after resisting a ten-hour attack (July 3). Served on General Braddock's staff (1755) in British expedition against Fort Duquesne. Commissioned colonel and commander in chief of Virginia troops (1755), charged with defense of frontier from French and Indian attacks; engaged in fighting (1755–58) until French abandoned Fort Duquesne and British occupied it (Nov. 1758). Retired to Mount Vernon to live life of Virginia gentleman farmer. Member, Virginia House of Burgesses (1759–74); became one of leaders of Virginia and colonial opposition to British policies in America. Member of First and Second Continental Congresses (1774–75). Elected to command all Continental armies (June 1775); assumed command at Cambridge, Mass. (July 1775); forced British evacuation of Boston (Mar. 1776); engaged in New York and Long Island area (1776), and conducted masterly retreat southward through New Jersey; surprised and defeated Hessians at Trenton (Dec. 26, 1776), won battle of Princeton and forced British retirement to Brunswick, N.J.; established headquarters at Morristown, N.J. (1777). Engaged at Brandywine (Sept. 11, 1777), Germantown (Oct. 3–4, 1777), and held army together at Valley Forge through bitter winter (1777–78), where the troops were drilled by Baron von Steuben. Heartened by French alliance (1778), attacked British at Monmouth (June 28, 1778) and held the field while British retired to New York. Enabled by cooperation of French fleet under de Grasse and French army under Rochambeau to march against Cornwallis at Yorktown, Va., and force his surrender (Oct. 19, 1781). With great difficulty, held army together before New York until British evacuated city (Apr. 1783). Resigned commission (Dec. 1783) and again retired to Mount Vernon. Called from retirement to preside at federal convention in Philadelphia (1787). Unanimously chosen president of the United States under the new constitution; took oath of office in New York City (Apr. 30, 1789); unanimously reelected (1793); declined third term, and after a farewell address to the American people (Sept. 1796) retired from political life (Mar. 1797). On threat of war with France (1798) accepted commission as lieutenant general and commander in chief of army.

His wife (m. 1759) ¶Martha, *nee* Dan·dridge \'dan-ˌdrij\ (1732–1802), m. (1749) Daniel Parke Custis (d. 1757). Known as a gracious hostess in the first president's home. Through a son, John Parke Custis (d. 1781), by her first husband she had four grandchildren, the two younger of whom were adopted by Washington after the death of their father.

Washington, Henry Stephens. 1867–1934. American geologist, b. Newark, N.J. Associated with Whitman Cross, J. P. Iddings, L. V. Pirsson, in devising CIPW classification system of igneous rocks on basis of chemical composition; on staff of geophysical laboratory, Carnegie Institution, Washington, D.C. (from 1912).

Wā·ṣil ibn 'Aṭā' \'wä-shē-ˌlib-ə-nä-'tä\. *In full* Wāṣil ibn 'Aṭā' al-Ghazzāl. *Also known as* Abū Ḥudhayfah. c.700–748. Muslim theologian. Considered founder of Mu'tazilah sect; supported 'Abbāsid revolution against Umayyad dynasty.

Was·ser·mann \'väs-ər-ˌmän, *Angl* 'wäs-ər-mən, 'väs-\, August von. 1866–1925. German bacteriologist. Assistant (1890–1906), director (1906–13), department of experimental therapy and biochemistry, Koch Institute for Infectious Diseases; director of department of experimental therapy, Kaiser Wilhelm Institute in Berlin-Dahlem (1913–25); discovered (1906) Wassermann reaction, basis for universal blood-serum test for syphilis.

Wassermann, Jakob. 1873–1934. German novelist. Wrote *Die Juden von Zirndorf* (1897), *Der Moloch* (1903), *Caspar Hauser* (1909), *Das Gänsemännchen* (1915), *Christian Wahnschaffe* (1919), *Der Fall Maurizius* (1928), *Olivia* (1937); autobiography *Mein Weg als Deutscher und Jude* (1921); biographies, short stories, essays one-act plays.

Wast, Hugo. See Gustavo MARTÍNEZ ZUVIRÍA.

Wa·ta·na·be \wä-tä-nä-be\ Kazan. *Orig.* Watanabe Jōzei. 1793–1841. Japanese painter and scholar. Pioneer in adapting Western perspective to Japanese art; noted esp. for portraits of unsparing realism marked by deep insight.

Wa·ter·house \'wöt-ər-ˌhaùs, 'wät-\, Alfred. 1830–1905. English architect. Champion of Gothic Revival; won competitions (1859, 1868) for design of Manchester assize courts and town hall; at Cambridge designed Balliol (1867–69), Caius (1868), Pembroke (1871) colleges; designed Owens College, Manchester (1870–98), Natural History Museum, South Kensington (1873–81); used terra cotta and one of first to use structural ironwork freely.

Waterhouse, Benjamin. 1754–1846. American physician, b. Newport, R.I. First professor of theory and practice of physic, Harvard (1783–1812). Best known as pioneer in vaccination in America (from 1800); published report *A Prospect of Exterminating the Small Pox* (1800) and *Information Respecting the Origin, Progress, and Efficacy of the Kine Pock Inoculation* (1810). Also wrote *Shewing the Evil Tendency of the Use of Tobacco* (1805).

Wa·ter·man \'wöt-ər-mən, 'wät-\, Lewis Edson. 1837–1901. American inventor and manufacturer, b. Decatur, N.Y. Perfected and patented (1884) an improved fountain pen.

Wa·ters \'wöt-ərz, 'wät-\, Ethel. 1896–1977. American singer and actress, b. Chester, Pa. Appeared on Broadway in *Blackbirds* (1930), *As Thousands Cheer* (1933), *Mamba's Daughters* (1938), *Cabin in the Sky* (1940), *Member of the Wedding* (1950), in films *Cabin in the Sky* (1943), *Pinky* (1949), *The Sound and the Fury* (1959); as a singer, identified with songs "Heat Wave," "Dinah," "Stormy Weather." Wrote autobiography *His Eye Is on the Sparrow* (1951).

Waters, Muddy. *Orig.* McKinley Mor·gan·field \'mör-gən-ˌfēld\. 1915–1983. American musician, b. Rolling Fork, Miss. A seminal figure in development of blues; as guitarist, harmonica player, and singer became master of "Chicago sound" and influenced a generation of U.S. and British rock bands. To Chicago (1943), where he electrically amplified his blues and started recording; led (1950s) first electric blues-rock band. Songs included "Hoochie Coochie Man," "Got My Mojo Working," "Honey Bee," and "Rollin' Stone."

Wa·tie \'wät-ē\, Stand. *Orig.* Degataga Oowatie *or* Uwetie. 1806–1871. American Indian leader, b. near present Rome, Ga. Signed Treaty of New Echota (1835) and counseled acquiescence in removal of Cherokee tribe to Indian Territory; raised regiment of Cherokee mounted riflemen for Confederate service (1861); brigadier general (1864).

Wat·kins \'wät-kənz\, Vernon Phillips. 1906–1967. Welsh poet. Author of mystical and visionary verse as *Ballad of Mari Lwyd* (1941), *The Lamp and the Veil* (1945), *Lady with the Unicorn* (1948), *Death Bell* (1954), *Cypress and Acacia* (1959), *Affinities* (1962).

Wat·son \'wät-sən\, Elkanah. 1758–1842. American businessman and agriculturist, b. Plymouth, Mass. Promoted a cattle show (1810) and organized (1811) Berkshire Agricultural Society to continue such annual agricultural fairs; regarded as father of the county fair in U.S.

Watson, John. *Pseudonym* Ian Mac·lar·en \mə-'klar-ən\. 1850–1907. Scottish clergyman and author. Presbyterian minister, Liverpool (1880–1905); won reputation with *Beside the Bonnie Brier Bush* (1894), followed by other "kailyard school" portrayals of humble Scottish life as *Days of Auld Lang Syne* (1895), *Kate Carnegie* (1896); also wrote religious works, including *The Upper Room* (1896), *The Potter's Wheel* (1898), *Children of the Resurrection* (1912).

Watson, John Broadus. 1878–1958. American psychologist, b. Greenville, S.C. Professor, Johns Hopkins (1908–20); a leading exponent, codifier, and popularizer of behaviorism. Wrote *Animal Education* (1903), *Behavior* (1914), *Behaviorism* (1925), *Psychological Care of Infant and Child* (1928), etc.

Watson, John Christian. 1867–1941. Australian politician, b. Chile of English parents. To Australia (1886); Labour member of New South Wales assembly (1894–1901), Commonwealth House of Representatives (1901–09); prime minister (1904).

Watson, Richard. 1737–1816. English chemist and clergyman. Professor of chemistry (1764), regius professor of divinity (1771), Cambridge; bishop of Llandaff (1782). Made discovery (1772) leading to black-bulb thermometer; investigated volume and freezing rates of saline solutions; defended Christianity against Edward Gibbon and Bible against Tom Paine.

Watson, Sereno. 1826–1892. American botanist, b. East Windsor Hill, Conn. Joined Clarence King's exploring expedition surveying Great Basin (1867); became botanist of the expedition; classified collection and published *Botany* (1871), often called "Botany of the King Expedition." Curator of Gray

Herbarium in Cambridge, Mass. (1874–92). Collaborated with Asa Gray and W.H. Brewer in *Botany of California* (1876–80). Revised Gray's *Manual of Botany* (with J.M. Coulter, 1889).

Watson, Thomas. c.1557–1592. English poet. Wrote Latin poems; translated into Latin Sophocles's *Antigone* (1581) and Tasso's *Aminta* (1585); translated into English collection of Italian madrigals (1590); author of *Hecatompathia, or Passionate Centurie of Love,* a collection of 18-line Petrarchan love poems in English (1582), and of *Tears of Fancie,* sonnets (1593).

Watson, Thomas Augustus. 1854–1934. American telephone technician, b. Salem, Mass. Assistant to Bell in his experiments (1874–77); became research and technical head of the Bell Telephone Co. (to 1881). Opened machine shop and shipyard at East Braintree, Mass.; received contracts for warships for U.S. navy; incorporated business as Fore River Ship & Engine Co. (1901).

Watson, Thomas Edward. 1856–1922. American politician, b. Columbia Co., Ga. Political leader of agrarian sentiment in Georgia; elected to one term (1891–93) in U.S. House of Representatives on Farmers' Alliance ticket; introduced first resolution ever passed providing for free delivery of rural mail. Populist nominee for vice president of the United States (1896) and for president (1904); published violently segregationist and anti-Semitic newspaper *Weekly Jeffersonian;* U.S. senator (1921–22).

Watson, Thomas John. 1874–1956. American businessman, b. Campbell, N.Y. Executive of National Cash Register Co. (1899–1914); president (1914–49), chairman (1949–56), Computing-Tabulating-Recording Co., known (from 1924) as International Business Machines.

Watson, William. 1559?–1603. English clergyman. Ordained Roman Catholic priest in France (1586); missionary in England (1586–1603); frequently imprisoned and tortured; opposed Jesuits; instigator of "Bye Plot" to kidnap James I to force him to grant toleration to Catholics; plot revealed by Jesuits; executed for treason.

Watson, Sir William. 1715–1787. English physician. Influential in introducing Linnaean system of botanical classification into England; awarded Copley medal (1745) for electrical research; developed theory of electricity similar to Franklin's (1746, 1748).

Watson, Sir William, *in full* John William. 1858–1935. English poet. Author of lyrical, political, and esp. occasional verse; published *The Prince's Quest* (1880); gained recognition with *Wordsworth's Grave* (1890) and fine ode on death of Tennyson, *Lacrymae Musarum* (1892); published *Odes* (1894), *Father of the Forest* (1895), expressed political convictions in sonnets *The Purple East* (1896), *The Year of Shame* (1896); later volumes *For England* (1903), *Sable and Purple* (1910), *Muse in Exile* (1913), *The Man Who Saw* (1917), etc.

Wat·son-Went·worth \ˈwät-sən-ˈwent-ˌwərth\, Charles. 2d Marquis of Rock·ing·ham \ˈräk-iŋ-əm\. 1730–1782. English politician. Gentleman of the bedchamber (1751–62). Prime minister (1765–66); repealed Stamp Act. Leader of parliamentary group opposed to Lord North's American policy (1768–81); favored independence for American colonies. Again prime minister (March–July 1782); initiated peace negotiations with American colonists; secured legislative independence for Irish Parliament.

Wa·tsu·ji \wät-sủj-ē\ Tetsurō. 1889–1960. Japanese philosopher. Professor at Kyōto (1931–34), Tokyo (1934–49); known for studies of Western thought, publishing works on Nietzsche (1913) and Kierkegaard (1915), and on ethics, drawing on traditional Buddhist thought. Works included *Ethics* (1937–49), *A Climate* (1961).

Watt \ˈwät\, James. 1736–1819. Scottish engineer and inventor. Mathematical-instrument maker, U. of Glasgow (1757). Conceived numerous improvements to a model of the Newcomen steam engine given to him to repair; invented modern condensing steam engine (1765, patented 1769) in which the exhaust steam from cylinder is condensed in separate chamber (condenser); invented the double-acting engine (1782); effected other improvements on the steam engine, including sun-and-planet wheels and other means for converting reciprocal motion into rotary motion, and the centrifugal governor for regulating speed. Formed a partnership with Matthew Boulton and manufactured steam engines at Soho Engineering Works, Birmingham (1775–1800). Originated (with Boulton) the term *horsepower.* The watt, a unit of power, is named in his honor. His son ¶James (1769–1848), marine engineer, fitted with engines the *Caledonia,* first steamship to leave an English port (1817).

Watt \ˈvät\, Joachim von. *Pseudonym* Joachim Va·di·an \ˈväd-ē-ən\ *or* Va·di·a·nus \ˌväd-ē-ˈä-nủs\. 1484–1551. Swiss Humanist. Crowned poet laureate by Emperor Maximilian (1514); professor (1512), rector (1516), U. of Vienna; physician (from 1518), burgermeister (from 1526), St. Gallen; friend of Zwingli, promoted Reformation in St. Gallen; helped edit works of Ovid, Pliny the Elder, etc.

Wat·teau \vȧ-tō, *Angl* wä-ˈtō, vä-\, Antoine, *in full* Jean-Antoine. 1684–1721. French painter. Known esp. for his Rococo *fêtes galantes,* scenes of conventional shepherds and shepherdesses, *fêtes champêtres,* country dances.

Wat·ten·bach \ˈvät-ən-bäk\, Wilhelm. 1819–1897. German historian and paleographer. Professor, Heidelberg (1862), Berlin (1872); directed (1875–88) the *Monumenta Germaniae Historica.*

Wat·ter·son \ˈwät-ər-sən, ˈwȯt-\, Henry. *Nicknamed* Marse Henry. 1840–1921. American journalist and politician, b. Washington, D.C. Served with Confederate army through Civil War. Editor, Louisville (Ky.) *Courier-Journal* (1868–1918); rose to eminence as one of the great editors of the United States. Fought for restoration of home rule in southern states; supported Samuel J. Tilden for presidency; opposed Cleveland (in 1892) and Bryan (in 1896); bitterly attacked Theodore Roosevelt; supported Wilson but opposed entrance into League of Nations. Member, U.S. House of Representatives (1876–77). Awarded Pulitzer prize for journalism (1917) for his editorials welcoming U.S. declaration of war against Central Powers. Author of *The Compromises of Life* (1903), *"Marse Henry": An Autobiography* (1919), etc.

Watts \ˈwäts\, Alan Witson. 1915–1973. American philosopher, b. Chislehurst, England. Editor of *Middle Way* magazine (1934–38); to U.S. (1939); ordained in Protestant Episcopal church (1944); chaplain, Northwestern U. (1944–50); professor, Coll. of the Pacific (1951–57); known esp. as popularizer of Oriental thought. Author of *Spirit of Zen* (1936), *Wisdom of Insecurity* (1951), *Myth and Ritual in Christianity* (1954), *The Way of Zen* (1957), *Nature, Man, and Woman* (1958), *Two Hands of God* (1963), *Beyond Theology* (1964), etc.

Watts, George Frederic. 1817–1904. English painter and sculptor. Exhibited *A Wounded Heron* and two portraits (1837); won prize (1842) for cartoon *Caractacus;* won British competition in oils (1847) with *King Alfred;* commissioned to fresco *George and the Dragon* in Hall of Poets of the Houses of Parliament (1848–53). Painted series of about 300 portraits of distinguished contemporaries (1864–95), including Garibaldi, Thiers, Guizot; painted symbolical pictures and moral allegories including *Life's Illusions* (1849), *Watchman, What of the Night* (1880), *Hope* (1886), *Love and Death* (1877, 1896), *Sic Transit* (1892); as sculptor executed monuments including bronze equestrian statues of Hugo Lupus (1884) and *Physical Energy* (1904).

Watts, Isaac. 1674–1748. English theologian and hymn writer. Pastor of Mark Lane Independent Chapel, London (1702–12). Composed 600 hymns including "O God, Our Help in Ages Past," "When I Survey the Wondrous Cross," "There is a Land of Pure Delight," published in *Horae Lyricae* (1706), *Hymns and Spiritual Songs* (1707), *Psalms of David Imitated* (1719). Author also of philosophical and theological works showing Arian tendencies.

Watts, Sir Philip. 1846–1926. British naval architect. Director of naval construction of the Admiralty (1902–12); designed British warships used in World War I including the *Dreadnought* battleship class (1906) and *Indomitable* and *Indefatigable* battle cruiser classes (1907, 1909).

Watts-Dun·ton \ˈwäts-ˈdənt-ᵊn\, Walter Theodore. 1832–1914. English critic and poet. Added to his surname mother's name Dunton (1897). Contributed to *Examiner* and *Athenaeum* (from 1874); intimate friend of Rossetti; took A. C. Swinburne into his house, fostered his genius (1879–1909); from early life studied East Anglian and Welsh gypsies. Author of verse *The Coming of Love* (1897), *Aylwin* (novel, 1898), *The Renascence of Wonder* (criticism, 1903), sonnets, and essays.

Waugh \ˈwȯ\, Alec, *in full* Alexander Raban. 1898–1981. English writer. Brother of Evelyn Waugh. Author of *Loom of Youth* (1917), *Island in the Sun* (1956), *Mule on the Minaret* (1965), *Fatal Gift* (1973), etc.

Waugh, Edwin. 1817–1890. English poet. Author of *Poems and Songs* (1860), *Tufts of Heather* (1862), etc., in Lancashire dialect and of humorous *Besom Ben Stories* (1892).

Waugh, Evelyn Arthur St. John. 1903–1966. English novelist. Brother of Alec Waugh. Considered finest satirical novelist in English in his day; works included *Decline and Fall* (1928), *Vile Bodies* (1930), *Black Mischief* (1932), *Handful of Dust* (1934), *Scoop* (1938), *Brideshead Revisited* (1945), *The Loved One* (1948), *Helena* (1950), *Men at Arms* (1952), *Officers and Gentlemen* (1955), *Ordeal of Gilbert Pinfold* (1957), *Unconditional Surrender* (1961); also wrote travel books, biographies.

Wa·vell \ˈwā-vəl\, Archibald Percival. 1st Earl. 1883–1950. British army officer. Entered army (1901); served in South African War, on Indian frontier (1908), in World War I, with Egyptian Expeditionary Force (1917–20); major general (1933); lieutenant general (1938); commander in chief of British forces in the Middle East (1938–41); general (1940); destroyed Italian armies in North Africa and Middle East; defeated by Gen. Erwin Rommel; commander in chief in India (1941); supreme commander of Allied forces in Southwest Pacific (1942), of Allied forces in India and Burma (1942); field marshal and viscount (1943); viceroy of India (1943–47). Author of *The Palestine Campaigns* (1928), *Allenby* (1940), *Generals and Generalship* (1941), *Allenby in Egypt* (1943).

Way·land \'wā-lənd\, Francis. 1796–1865. American clergyman and educator, b. New York City. Ordained Baptist minister (1821); president, Brown U. (1827–55); effected during administration the liberalization of curriculum and enlargement of university equipment, faculty, and student body; contributed also to development of public schools and libraries in Rhode Island. His son ¶Francis (1826–1904) was dean, Yale Law School (1873–1903); reorganized and raised standards of Yale Law School during his administration; author of legal treatises.

Wayne \'wān\, Anthony. *Known as* Mad Anthony. 1745–1796. American Revolutionary officer, b. Waynesboro, Pa. Colonel of Pennsylvania regiment in Continental army (Jan. 1776); covered retreat of American force from Canada to Fort Ticonderoga (1776). Brigadier general (Feb. 1777); commanded center in battle of Brandywine (Sept. 11, 1777), distinguished himself at Germantown (Oct. 4, 1777), and led advance in battle of Monmouth (June 28, 1778). Led brilliant attack which surprised and captured British garrison at Stony Point on the Hudson (July 16, 1779). On news of Arnold's attempted treason, moved troops to reinforce West Point (Sept. 1780). Engaged in Yorktown campaign (1781); retired (1783) as brevet major general. Member from Georgia, U.S. House of Representatives (1791–92). Appointed major general (1792) by President Washington to pacify Indians of Ohio Valley; decisively defeated Indians at battle of Fallen Timbers near present Toledo, Ohio (Aug. 20, 1794), and thereafter negotiated satisfactory treaty with them (1795).

Wayne, James Moore. 1790–1867. American jurist, b. Savannah, Ga. Member, U.S. House of Representatives (1829–35); associate justice, U.S. Supreme Court (1835–67).

Wayne, John. *Called* Duke. *Orig.* Marion Michael Morrison. 1907–1979. American actor, b. Winterset, Iowa. Became embodiment of a type of American hero in motion pictures, chiefly Westerns and war films, including *The Big Trail* (1929), *Stagecoach* (1939), *Long Voyage Home* (1940), *Fort Apache* (1948), *Red River* (1948), *She Wore a Yellow Ribbon* (1949), *Sands of Iwo Jima* (1949), *Rio Grande* (1950), *The Quiet Man* (1952), *The Alamo* (1960), *Longest Day* (1962), *El Dorado* (1966), *Green Berets* (1968), *True Grit* (1969, Academy Award), *The Cowboys* (1972), *The Shootist* (1976).

Waynflete, William of. See WILLIAM of Waynflete.

Weare \'wa(ə)r, 'we(ə)r\, Meshech. 1713–1786. American jurist and politician, b. Hampton Falls, N.H. Justice of superior court (1747–75); chief justice (1776–82); first president, State of New Hampshire (1784–85) under constitution of 1784.

Weatherford, William. See RED EAGLE.

Weath·er·ly \'weth-ər-lē\, Frederic Edward. 1848–1929. English lawyer and songwriter. Composed popular songs as "Nancy Lee," "Darby and Joan," "London Bridge," "Ailsa Mine," "Danny Boy," "Roses of Picardy."

Wea·ver \'wē-vər\, James Baird. 1833–1912. American politician, b. Dayton, Ohio. Served through Civil War; brevet brigadier general (Mar. 1864). Member from Iowa, U.S. House of Representatives, elected as a Greenbacker (1879–81) and as a Democrat and Greenback-Labor candidate (1885–89). Candidate of Greenback-Labor party for president of the U.S. (1880) and of the People's party (1892), in the latter year winning 22 electoral votes and a popular vote of more than 1,000,000.

Weaver, John. 1673–1760. English dancer and ballet master. Produced and appeared in dance dramas at Drury Lane and Lincoln's Inn Fields theaters, London (1700–36); in *Tavern Bilkers* (1702) adopted *commedia dell'arte* style and characters and pioneered pantomime ballet; produced *Loves of Mars and Venus* (1717), considered first *ballet d'action.* Author of *Orchesography,* first English translation of Feuillet's *Chorégraphie* (1706), *Anatomical and Mechanical Lectures upon Dancing* (1721), etc.

Webb \'web\, Sir Aston. 1849–1930. English architect. Designed principal block of Victoria and Albert Museum (1891), Royal College of Science (1900–06), Admiralty Arch (1911), eastern façade of Buckingham Palace (1913), etc.

Webb, Beatrice Potter. See under Sidney James WEBB.

Webb, Clement Charles Julian. 1865–1954. English philosopher. Fellow and tutor, Magdalen Coll., Oxford (1889–1922); first Oriel professor of philosophy of Christian religion, Oriel Coll. (1920–30). Published editions of *Policraticus* (1909) and *Metalogicon* (1929) of John of Salisbury; author of *Group Theories of Religion and the Individual* (1916), *God and Personality* (1918), *Divine Personality and Human Life* (1920).

Webb *or* **Webbe** \'web\, John. 1611–1672. English architect. Pupil and executor of Inigo Jones and editor of his tract on Stonehenge.

Webb, Mary Gladys, *nee* Mer·e·dith \'mer-əd-əth\. 1881–1927. English novelist. m. Henry B. L. Webb (1912); author of *The Golden Arrow* (1916), *Gone to Earth* (1917), *House in Dormer Forest* (1920), *Seven for a Secret* (1922), *Precious Bane* (1924), and of essays, poems, and short stories.

Webb, Matthew. 1848–1883. English swimmer. Followed sea (from 1862); master mariner (1875); professional swimmer (from 1875); first to swim English Channel, from Dover to Calais (Aug. 24–25, 1875, in 21 3/4 hours); drowned in attempt to swim rapids below Niagara Falls.

Webb, Philip Speakman. 1831–1915. English architect and designer. With William Morris formed firm of Morris, Marshall, Faulkner & Co. (1861), to design domestic furnishings, and the Society for the Protection of Ancient Buildings (1877); designed Red House in Upton, Kent, for Morris (1859) and other country houses as Clouds, Wiltshire (1886), Standen, Sussex (1891); designed glassware, jewelry, stained glass, decorative accessories.

Webb, Sidney James. 1st Baron Pass·field \'pas-fēld\. 1859–1947. English economist, Socialist, and statesman. Civil service clerk in war office (1878), colonial office (1881–91). One of founders of Fabian Society (1885); author of Society's tract *Facts for Socialists* (1887) and *Socialism in England* (1890); taught economics, U. of London (1912–27). Member, London County Council (1892–1910); member, royal commission on trade-union law (1903–06); comember of royal poor-law commission (1905–09) with his wife ¶Beatrice, *nee* Pot·ter \'pät-ər\ (1858–1943; m. 1892), writer on economics and sociology; assisted her cousin Charles Booth on his *Life and Labour of the People in London;* author of *The Co-operative Movement in Great Britain* (1891), *Factory Acts* (1901), and *My Apprenticeship* (1926); submitted minority report in favor of the Poor Law (1909) that anticipated welfare state; jointly (from 1914) provided intellectual leadership to British Labour party, helped found *New Statesman* (1913), promoted London School of Economics and Political Science; proposed nationalization of coal mines (1919). Sidney was M.P. (1922–29); president of board of trade in first Labour cabinet (1924); secretary for colonies (1929–31) and dominions (1929–30); created Baron Passfield (1929). Joint authors of *History of Trade Unionism* (1894), *Industrial Democracy* (1897), *The State and the Doctor* (1910), *Consumers' Co-operative Movement* (1921), *Decay of Capitalist Civilisation* (1923), *English Poor Law History* (1927, 1929), *Soviet Communism: a New Civilisation?* (1935), *The Truth about Soviet Russia* (1942).

We·ber \'vā-bər\, Carl Maria Friedrich Ernst von. 1786–1826. German composer. Born into family musical and theatrical troupe; studied under Michael Haydn, Abbé Vogler; Kapellmeister at Breslau (1804–06); secretary at court of Frederick I of Württemberg (1806–10); conductor of Prague Opera (1813–16); director of German opera at Dresden (1817–26). In compositions, reviews, criticism, a leading creator of German Romanticism and nationalism in music; works included 9 operas as *Das Waldmädchen* (1800), *Abu Hassan* (1811), *Der Freishütz* (1821), *Euryanthe* (1823), *Oberon* (1826), orchestral works as *Konzertstück* (1821), piano, bassoon, and clarinet concertos, chamber music, much piano music, a mass, etc.

Weber, Ernst Heinrich. 1795–1878. German anatomist and physiologist. Professor, Leipzig (1818–78); known for studies of sensory response and esp. sense of touch; introduced concept of just-noticeable difference; considered a founder of experimental psychology. Author of *Der Tastsinn und das Gemeingefühl* (1851).

Weber, Friedrich Wilhelm. 1813–1894. German poet. Author of *Dreizehnlinden* (an epic, 1878), *Gedichte* (1881), *Marienblumen* (1885), etc.

Web·er \'web-ər\, Joseph Morris, *known as* Joe (1867–1942), and ¶Lewis Maurice Fields \'fē(ə)ldz\, *orig.* Schan·field \'shan-,fē(ə)ld\, *known as* Lew (1867–1941). American comedy team, both b. New York City. Appeared together in juvenile Dutch skits (1877). Organized theatrical company, Weber and Fields (1885), managers of theatrical enterprises, including Broadway Music Hall (1895–1904); produced such shows as *Helter Skelter* (1899), *Whirl-i-gig* (1899), *Fiddle-dee-dee* (1900), *Hoity-Toity* (1901), *Whoop-dee-doo* (1903). Fields opened Lew Fields Theater, New York City (1904) and acquired Herald Square Theater (1906). Weber was proprietor and manager of Weber's Theater (from 1904). Weber and Fields again teamed up for *Hokey Pokey* (1912), *Roly Poly* (1912).

We·ber \'vā-bər\, Karl Julius. 1767–1832. German writer. Author of critical works and satirical and humorous writings as *Deutschland oder Briefe eines in Deutschland reisenden Deutschen* (1826–28), *Demokritos* (1832–40).

Weber, Max. 1864–1920. German sociologist. Professor, Berlin (1893), Freiburg (1894), Heidelberg (1897–1903), Munich (1919); a chief theorist of liberal imperialism; best known for thesis linking Protestantism and capitalism. Author of *Die römische Agrargeschichte* (1891) and journal articles later published as *Die protestantische Ethik und der Geist des Kapitalismus* (1920), *Hinduismus und Buddhismus* (1920), *Das antike Judentum* (1920), *Wirtschaftsgeschichte* (1923), etc.

Web·er \'web-ər\, Max. 1881–1961. American painter, b. Bialystok, Russia. To U.S. (1891); teacher of painting; produced paintings influenced by Fauvism, Cubism, Hasidic Jewish themes. Author of *Cubist Poems* (1914), *Essays on Art* (1916), *Primitives* (1927).

We·ber \'vā-bər\, Wilhelm Eduard. 1804–1891. German physicist. Brother of Ernst H. Weber. Professor at Göttingen (from (1831); with Gauss, investigated terrestrial magnetism, and devised an electromagnetic telegraph (1833); introduced the absolute system of electrical units patterned after Gauss's system of magnetic units. The weber, formerly the coulomb, a magnetic unit, is named in his honor.

We·bern \'vā-bərn\, Anton Friedrich Wilhelm von. 1833–1945. Austrian composer. Student of Schoenberg and associate of Berg in developing theory of atonality and practice of 12-tone composition. Works included orchestral *Im Sommerwind* (1904), *Passacaglia* (1908), *Sechs Stücke* (1909), *Fünf Stücke* (1911–13), *Symphonie* (1928), *Konzert* (1934), *Variationen* (1940); chamber works *Langsamer Satz* (1905), *Rondo* (c.1906), *Sechs Bagatellen* (1913), string quartets, trios, etc.; piano pieces as *Satz* (c.1906), *Kinderstück* (1924), *Klavierstück* (1925); choral works *Enflicht auf leichten Kähnen* (1908), *Das Augenlicht* (1935), cantatas (1938–39, 1941–43); vocal pieces as songs, canons.

Web·ster \'web-stər\, Daniel. 1782–1852. American lawyer and statesman, b. Salisbury, N.H. Practiced law at Portsmouth, N.H. (from 1807). Member, U.S. House of Representatives from New Hampshire (1813–17), from Massachusetts (1823–27); achieved national recognition as lawyer for Dartmouth College trustees in Dartmouth College case (1818); appeared before Supreme Court in several other important cases. Member, U.S. Senate (1827–41). Gained fame as orator for his constitutional speeches in reply to Hayne (1830) and in opposition to Calhoun (1833); opposed President Jackson on U.S. Bank issue. U.S. secretary of state (1841–43); negotiated Webster-Ashburton treaty with Great Britain (1842). Again U.S. senator from Massachusetts (1845–50); opposed Mexican War and annexation of Texas; supported compromise measures on slavery proposed by Clay (1850). Again U.S. secretary of state (1850–52).

Webster, Jean, *orig.* Alice Jane Chandler. 1876–1916. American writer, b. Fredonia, N.Y. Author of series of stories about a fictional character, Patty, including *When Patty Went to College* (1903) and *Just Patty* (1911), and the very successful novel *Daddy-Long-Legs* (1912) and its sequel *Dear Enemy* (1914).

Webster, John. c.1580–c.1625. English dramatist. Collaborated (from 1602) with members of Philip Henslowe's company of dramatists; part author with Dekker of *Westward Hoe* and *Northward Hoe* (c.1604); altered, and wrote introduction to Marston's *Malcontent* (1604); also collaborated with Michael Drayton, Thomas Middleton, John Ford, etc.; approached tragic power and poetic genius of Shakespeare in two plays incontestably his, *The White Divel or Vittoria Corombona* (produced c.1612) and *The Duchess of Malfi* (c.1613); brought out involved tragicomedy *Devil's Law-case* (1619 or 1620).

Webster, Margaret. 1905–1972. British actress and director, b. New York City. Played with John Barrymore in *Hamlet* in her London debut (1925) and with Sybil Thorndike in *The Trojan Women;* directed Shakespearean presentations of Maurice Evans in New York (1937–39); also staged, directed, and acted in *Family Portrait* (1939), *Othello* (with Paul Robeson, 1943), etc.; formed Margaret Webster Shakespeare Co. (1948); first woman to direct at Metropolitan Opera, N.Y.C., with *Don Carlos* (1950), *Aïda* (1951). Author of *Shakespeare without Tears* (1942, 1955), *Same Only Different* (1969), *Don't Put Your Daughter on the Stage* (1972).

Webster, Noah. 1758–1843. American lexicographer and author, b. West Hartford, Conn. Served in Revolutionary War; taught school in various places (1779–83); wrote *Grammatical Institute of the English Language,* part I (1783) being a spelling book later known as *Webster's Spelling Book* or *Blue-Backed Speller,* which for more than 100 years had enormous sale; completed parts II (grammar, 1784) and III (reader, 1785) of the *Institute;* agitated for uniform copyright law. Became ardent Federalist; his *Sketches of American Policy* (1785) one of first publications advocating strong central government; in New York founded and edited *The American Magazine* (1787–88); published (1793–98) *The Minerva* (later *The Commercial Advertiser*) and *The Herald* (later *The Spectator*), Federalist papers. Published *A Compendious Dictionary of the English Language* (1806); began (1807) work on larger dictionary; visited England and France (1824–25) for study necessary to complete his dictionary; published *An American Dictionary of the English Language* (2 vols., 1828). Compiled brief *History of the United States* (1832), widely used as a schoolbook; published (1833) a revision of Authorized Version of English Bible. Rights to his dictionary sold by his heirs (1843) to firm of G. & C. Merriam of Springfield, Mass.

Weck·her·lin \'vek-ər-,lēn\, Georg Rudolph. 1584–1653. German poet. In London (from 1620); secretary for foreign tongues to Parliament (1644–49); assistant to John Milton (1652). Helped to introduce into German literature Renaissance verse forms and feeling, as in the ode and sonnet. Published *Oden und Gesänge* (1618–19), *Geistliche und weltliche Gedichte* (1641).

Weck·mann \'vek-,män\, Matthias. 1619?–1674. German organist and composer. Organist in electoral chapel, Dresden (1637–42), in Nykøbing, Denmark (1642–47), again in Dresden (1647–55), at Jacobikirche, Hamburg (1655–74); pupil, associate, and successor of Heinrich Schütz; composed organ works, cantatas, chamber works, etc.

Wed·dell \wə-'del, 'wed-ᵊl\, James. 1787–1834. British navigator, b. Netherlands. In command of brig *Jane* visited South Georgia I. (1822) and named South Orkney Is. (1822); on subsequent voyage (1822–24) reached 74° 15′ S latitude; gave name to Weddell Sea.

Wed·der·burn \'wed-ər-bərn\, Alexander. 1st Baron Lough·bor·ough \'ləf-,bər-ə, -b(ə-)rə\. 1st Earl of Ross·lyn \'räs-lən\. 1733–1805. British judge, b. Scotland. Member of Scottish bar (1754), of English bar (1757); M.P. (1761–80); solicitor general (1771–78), attorney general (1778–80); chief justice of common pleas (1780–92); lord chancellor (1793–1801); created baron (1780), earl (1801).

Wed·di·gen \'ved-i-gən\, Otto. 1882–1915. German naval officer. Commander of submarine U-9 in World War I; sank British cruisers *Aboukir, Hogue,* and *Cressy* (Sept. 22, 1914), and the *Hawke* (Oct. 15, 1914); killed in ramming of new command, U-29, by *Dreadnought.*

We·de·kind \'vā-də-,kint\, Frank. 1864–1918. German poet and playwright. On staff of satirical weekly *Simplicissimus* (1896 ff.); cabaret performer. Author of satirical, symbolical plays anticipating Expressionism and Theater of the Absurd, including *Frühlings Erwachen* (1891), the "Lulu" cycle *Erdgeist* (1895) and *Die Büchse der Pandora* (1904), *Der Marquis von Keith* (1900), *König Nicolo oder So ist das Leben* (1901), *Hidallah* (1904), *Totentanz* (1906), *Oaha* (1908), *Franziska* (1912), *Bismarck* (1916); also wrote novels as *Die Fürstin Russalka* (1897), *Mine-Haha* (1903), *Feuerwerk* (1906), verse, essays, songs.

We·del-Jarls·berg \'vād-ᵊl-'yärls-,bərg\, Herman, *in full* Johan Caspar Herman. Count. 1779–1840. Norwegian political leader, b. France. Advocate of Norwegian-Swedish union; member of Norwegian constituent assembly (1814), helped draft constitution; finance minister (1814–36); first Norwegian to hold office of *statholder* (governor) of Norway within the union (1836–40).

Wedg·wood \'wej-,wu̇d\, Josiah. 1730–1795. English potter. Partner (1754–59) of Thomas Whieldon; established own firm (1759); conducted exhaustive experiments in glazes, materials, etc.; developed (1765) a glazed cream-colored domestic earthenware, Queen's ware; improved vitreous black ware in form known as "basalt"; named new factory Etruria (1769). Improved marbled ware and invented jasper ware (1773–80); assisted by John Flaxman, who modeled delicate designs after remains of Pompeii and Greek vases from Campania; invented a pyrometer (c.1782). Developed firm into one of world's leading producers of domestic and decorative ceramics.

Weed \'wēd\, Thurlow. 1797–1882. American journalist and politician, b. Cairo, N.Y. Active in N.Y. state politics, esp. in Anti-Masonic party (1826 ff.); editor, *Albany Evening Journal* (1830–62); became leader of Whig, and later of Republican, party; instrumental in nomination of Harrison (1836, 1840), Clay (1844), Taylor (1848), Scott (1852); associate of Seward and Greeley in political domination of New York State. Vigorously supported Lincoln and his war policies; sent abroad on unofficial mission (1861–62). Editor, New York *Commercial Advertiser* (1867).

Weelkes \'wē(ə)lks\, Thomas. c.1576–1623. English composer. Organist, Chichester cathedral (1601?–23); known chiefly for madrigals (pub. 1598, 1600, 1608), of which about 100 are extant; also wrote anthems, 10 Anglican services, etc.

Weems \'wēmz\, Mason Locke. *Known as* Parson Weems. 1759–1825. American clergyman and author, b. Anne Arundel Co., Md. Ordained in Anglican church (1784); pastor in Maryland (1784–92); itinerant bookseller (1794–1825) for Mathew Carey, publisher. Author of *The Life and Memorable Actions of George Washington* (1800; enlarged in later editions), which is responsible for popular stories about Washington, including that of the hatchet and cherry tree (first inserted in edition of 1806). Author of biographies *Francis Marion* (1809), *Benjamin Franklin* (1815), and *William Penn* (1822), and moral tracts.

Wee·nix \'vā-niks\, Jan Baptist. 1621–1660. Dutch painter. Known for Italianate landscapes, seascapes, still lifes with game, portraits. His son and pupil ¶Jan (1640?–1719) was court painter in Düsseldorf (1702–12), later in Amsterdam; known chiefly for landscapes, still life, dead game, and hunting scenes.

We·ge·li·us \vā-'gā-lē-u̇s\, Martin. 1846–1906. Finnish educator and composer. Founder and director (1882–1906), Helsinki Music Coll. (now Sibelius Acad.); teacher of Sibelius, Melartin, Kuula, and Palmgren; composed orchestral works, cantatas, chamber music, and songs.

We·ge·ner \'vā-gə-nər\, Alfred Lothar. 1880–1930. German geophysicist and meteorologist. On expeditions to Greenland (1906–08, 1912–13, 1929, 1930); professor, Graz (1924); studied thermodynamics of the atmosphere; originated Wegener hypothesis of continental drift according to which the continents have drifted slowly apart from an original single land area that he called Pangaea. Author of *Thermodynamik der Atmosphäre* (1911), *Die Entstehung der Kontinente und Ozeane* (1915), etc.

Wei \ˈwā\. Name of several dynasties of China, esp.: (1) One ruling (220–264 A.D.) in the state of Wei, one of the Three Kingdoms north of the Yangtze. Its first ruler was Ts'ao P'ei (*q.v.*), with capital at Lo-yang, and it followed the Later Han dynasty. It absorbed Shu and in turn came (264) under the control of the Western Chin dynasty. (2) The Northern Wei, a dynasty (386–534 A.D.) in northern China of the Toba Tatars, with capital at Lo-yang (495–534), which divided (534) into two short-lived dynasties: the Eastern Wei (534–550) and the Western Wei (535–556). See HSIAO WEN TI.

Wei Chung-hsien \ˈwā-ˈjŭŋ-shē-ˈən\. *Also known as* Li Chin-chung \ˈlē-ˈjin-ˈjəŋ\. 1568–1627. Chinese courtier. Eunuch in service of mother of future emperor Chu Yu-chao; gained great influence over Chu, who relegated all government to him upon ascending to throne (1620); fostered corruption throughout government, persecuted Confucian scholars and reformers; fell from power on emperor's death (1627); took own life to avoid trial.

Wei·den·reich \ˈvī-dən-rīk\, Franz. 1873–1948. German anatomist and anthropologist. Professor, Strassburg (1904–18), Heidelberg (1922–24), Institute for Physical Anthropology, Frankfurt (1928), Peking Union Medical College (1935); with American Museum of Natural History, N.Y.C. (1941–48); best known for his studies of fossil man, esp. Peking man.

Weid·man \ˈwīd-mən\, Charles Edward, Jr. 1901–1975. American dancer and choreographer, b. Lincoln, Neb. Dancer with Denishawn group (1921–27); with Doris Humphrey formed Humphrey-Weidman School and Company (1927–45); interested principally in characterization and pantomime; choreographed *Happy Hypocrite* (1931), *Candide* (1933), *Kinetic Pantomime* (1934), *Opus 51* (c.1937), *On My Mother's Side* (1940), *Flickers* (1942), *And Daddy Was a Fireman* (1943), and Broadway shows as *As Thousands Cheer* (1933), *I'd Rather Be Right* (1937); formed Theatre Dance Co. (1948).

Wei·er·strass \ˈvī-ər-ˌshträs\, Karl Theodor Wilhelm. 1815–1897. German mathematician. Taught (from 1856) at Royal Polytechnic, Berlin; developed modern theory of analytical functions from work of Abel and Jacobi.

Wei·gl \ˈvī-gəl\, Joseph. 1766–1846. Austrian composer. Kapellmeister and composer to imperial court, Vienna (1792–1846). Composed operas as *Die unnützte Vorsicht* (for marionettes, 1783), *La Principessa d'Amalfi* (1794), *Das Petermännchen* (1794), *L'amor marinaro* (1797), *Das Dorf im Gebirge* (1798), *L'uniforme* (1800), *Cleopatra* (1807), *Das Waisenhaus* (1808), *Die Schweizerfamilie* (1809), *L'imboscata* (1815); ballets as *Pigmalione* (1794), *Riccardo cor di Leone* (1795), *Il ratto d'Elena* (1795), *Alonso e Cora* (1796), *Alcina* (1798), *I spagnoli nell'isola Cristina* (1802), *La ballerina d'Athene* (1802); also wrote much sacred music.

Wei·gle \ˈwī-gəl\, Luther Allan. 1880–1976. American scholar, b. Littlestown, Pa. Ordained Lutheran minister (1903); professor, Carleton Coll. (1905–16), Yale (1916–49); dean of Yale Divinity School (1928–49); helped organize National Council of Churches (1941); head (from 1929) of committee responsible for producing Revised Standard Version of the Bible (1946–52).

Weil \vey\, Simone. 1909–1943. French philosopher, mystic, and writer. Left France (1942) for U.S. and then England, where she worked for the Resistance. Author of paradoxical, mystical works on religion and philosophy as *La Pesanteur et la grâce* (1946), *L'Enracinement* (1949), *La Connaissance surnaturelle* (1950), *Attente de Dieu* (1951), *La Condition ouvrière* (1951), *Intuitions préchrétiennes* (1951), *La Source grecque* (1953).

Weill \ˈvīl\, Kurt Julian. 1900–1950. American composer, b. Dessau, Germany. Studied with Busoni; gained position in theater with operas *Der Protagonist* (with Georg Kaiser, 1926), *Na Und?* (1926), *Royal Palace* (1927), and *Mahagonny* (with Bertolt Brecht, 1927), a Singspiel expanded into 3-act opera (1930); with Brecht created *Die Dreigroschenoper* (1928), *Der Jasager* (1930), *Der Lindberghflug* (1930); wrote *Die Bürgschaft* (with Casper Naher, 1933); proscribed by Nazi regime (1933), fled to Paris; wrote *Die sieben Todstunden* for George Balanchine (1933); to U.S. (1935); composed Broadway shows *Knickerbocker Holiday* (with Maxwell Anderson, 1938), *Lady in the Dark* (1941), *One Touch of Venus* (with Ogden Nash, 1943), *Street Scene* (with Elmer Rice, 1947), *Lost in the Stars* (with Anderson, 1949).

Wein·ber·ger \ˈvīn-ˌber-gər, *Angl* ˈwīn-ˌbər-\, Jaromír. 1896–1967. American composer, b. Prague, Czechoslovakia. To U.S. (in 1930s); wrote operas *Švanda Dudák* (1927), *Valdštejn* (1937); also wrote nonoperatic works.

Wei·ner \ˈvā-ner\, Leó. 1885–1960. Hungarian composer and teacher. Teacher at High School of Musical Art, Budapest (from 1908). Composed in tradition of Brahms and Mendelssohn; wrote for the stage, esp. incidental music for Vörösmarty's *Csongor és Tünde* (1913) and a ballet from same source (1930), instrumental works *Farsang* (*Carnival*, 1907), *Pastorale, phantaisie et fugue* (1934), *Romanze* (1949), *Toldi* (1952), chamber and piano works, etc.

Wein·gart·ner \ˈvīn-gärt-nər\, Felix, *in full* Paul Felix. Edler von Münz·berg \ˈmu̇ents-ˌberk\. 1863–1942. Austrian composer, conductor, and writer on music, b. Dalmatia. Naturalized Swiss (1937). Conductor of symphony concerts, Berlin and Munich (until 1908); director, Vienna Court Opera (1908–11), Vienna Volksoper (1919–24), conservatory and music society, Basel (1927), Vienna Staatsoper (1935–36); known esp. as interpreter of Beethoven and Wagner. Composer of operas as *Sakuntala* (1884), *Genesius* (1892), *Kain und Abel* (1914), *Dame Kobold* (1916), and *Meister Andrea* (1920), orchestral works, including seven symphonies, symphonic poems, and chamber music, incidental stage music, songs, piano pieces, choruses.

Wein·he·ber \ˈvīn-ˌhā-bər\, Josef. 1892–1945. Austrian poet. Author of *Der einsame Mensch* (1920), *Von beiden Ufern* (1923), *Boot in der Bucht* (1926), *Adel und Untergang* (1934), *Wien wörtlich* (1935), *Späte Krone* (1936), *O Mensch, gib acht* (1937), *Zwischen Göttern und Dämonen* (1938), *Kammermusik* (1939), *Hier ist das Wort* (1947); also wrote novels *Das Waisenhaus* (autobiographical, 1925), *Der Nachwuchs* (1927), essays *Im Namen der Kunst* (1936), *Über die Dichtkunst* (1949).

Wein·hold \ˈvīn-ˌhȯlt\, Karl. 1823–1901. German philologist. Professor, Breslau (1849), Kraków (1850), Graz (1851), Kiel (1861), Breslau (1876), Berlin (1889); author of *Über deutsche Dialektforschung* (1853), grammars of German and Middle High German, works on literary history; collected Christmas plays and songs of southern Germany and Silesia (1853).

Wei·ning·er \ˈvī-niŋ-ər\, Otto. 1880–1903. Austrian philosopher. Converted from Judaism to Christianity (1902); published *Geschlecht und Charakter* (1903), containing controversial characterization of Judaism.

Wein·stein \ˈwīn-ˌstīn\, Nathan Wallenstein. *Pseudonym* Nathanael West \ˈwest\. 1903–1940. American novelist, b. New York City. Author of *Dream Life of Balso Snell* (1931), *Miss Lonelyhearts* (1933), *A Cool Million* (1934), *Day of the Locust* (1939).

Weir \ˈwi(ə)r\, Robert Stanley. 1856–1926. Canadian lawyer, b. Hamilton, Upper Canada (Ont.). Practiced in Montreal; judge of exchequer court (1926). Author of the words of the English version of "O Canada" (1908).

Weir, Robert Walter. 1803–1889. American painter, b. New Rochelle, N.Y. On teaching staff, U.S.M.A., West Point (1834–76); best known for *Embarkation of the Pilgrims* for U.S. Capitol Rotunda.

Weisengrund-Adorno, Theodor. See ADORNO.

Wei·ser \ˈvī-zər, *Angl* ˈwī-\, Conrad. 1696–1760. American Indian agent, b. near Herrenberg, Germany. To America (1710), settled in Hudson Valley; moved to Berks Co., Pa. (1729); interpreter in various negotiations with Iroquois Indians, helped form Iroquois-English alliance against French.

Weis·haupt \ˈvīs-ˌhau̇pt\, Adam. 1748–1830. German mystic, philosopher, and religious leader. Founder (1776) of the Illuminati, or Perfectibilists, a secret rationalistic anticlerical sect.

Weis·mann \ˈvīs-ˌmän\, August Friedrich Leopold. 1834–1914. German biologist. Professor of zoology, Freiburg (1866–1912); developed theory of germ plasm; denied that acquired characters are transmitted to offspring; contended that only variations of the germ plasm are inherited. Author of *Die Entwicklung der Dipteren* (1864), *Studien zur Deszendenztheorie* (1875–76), *Das Keimplasma, eine Theorie der Vererbung* (1892).

Weiss \ˈvīs\, Bernhard. 1827–1918. German theologian. Professor at Königsberg (1852–63), Kiel (1863–77), Berlin (1877–1908); an originator of two-source theory of the Gospels. Author of a life of Jesus (1882) and contributions to H.A.W. Meyer's New Testament commentaries.

Weiss, Peter Ulrich. 1916–1982. German playwright and novelist. Resident of Sweden (from 1939). Author of plays *Der Turm* (1963), *Nacht mit Gästen* (1963), *Die Verfolgung und Ermordung Jean Paul Marats dargestellt durch die Schauspielgruppe des Hospizes zu Charenton unter Anleitung des Herrn de Sade* (1964, known as *Marat/Sade*), *Die Ermittlung* (1965), *Gesang vom Lusitanischen Popanz* (1967), *Trotzki im Exil* (1970), *Hölderlin* (1971); novels including *Die Schatten des Körpers des Kutschers* (1960), *Abschied von den Eltern* (1961), *Fluchtpunkt* (1962), *Duelle* (1972).

Weiss \ves\, Pierre. 1865–1940. French physicist. Professor in Zürich (1902), U. of Strasbourg (1919); investigated magnetism, determining a unit of magnetic moment known as the Weiss magneton and developing a theory of molecular magnetic fields.

Weis·se \ˈvī-sə\, Christian Felix. 1726–1804. German poet and dramatist. Friend of Lessing. Author of verse *Scherzhafte Lieder* (1758), *Amazonenlieder* (1760), plays, operettas, etc.; editor of *Der Kinderfreund,* a weekly journal for children (24 vols., 1775–82). His grandson ¶Christian Hermann Weisse (1801–1866), philosopher; professor, Leipzig (from 1845); evolved a speculative theism which opposed the pantheistic philosophy of Hegel.

Weiss·mul·ler \ˈwīz-ˌməl-ər\, Johnny, *orig.* Peter John. 1904–1984. American swimmer and actor, b. Windber, Penn. Regarded as the greatest swimmer of the first half of the 20th century. Won three gold medals in 1924 Olympics, Paris; won two gold medals in 1928 Olympics, Amsterdam; broke 67 world records; won 52 national championships. Swimming glory led to his being chosen to assume role of Tarzan in the movies. Starred (1932–48) in 12 Tarzan movies, beginning with *Tarzan the Ape Man* (1932); became the most famous of the movie Tarzans; played (1948–55) role of Jungle Jim in a series of movies and then on television.

Weis·wei·ler \'vīs-,vī-lər, -,fī-\, Adam. c.1750–1810. German cabinetmaker. Established in Paris (c.1777); noted for architectural designs, superb mounts, inlays and veneers, and finishes.

Wei Yüan \'wā-'yüe-'än\. 1794–1856. Chinese historian and geographer. A leader of Statecraft school urging practical solutions to problems of government. Author of *Huang-ch'ao ching-shih wen-pien* on statecraft (1826) and *Hai-kuo t'u-chih* on geography of foreign nations (1844).

Weiz·mann \'vīt-smän\, Chaim Azriel. 1874–1952. Russian chemist and Zionist leader. Taught at Geneva (1900–04), Manchester (1904 ff.); noted for research on dyes; discovered means of mass producing acetone (1916). Active on behalf of Jewish interests, and in securing Balfour Declaration (1917) in favor of Jewish national home in Palestine; president, World Zionist Organization (1920–31) and Jewish Agency for Palestine (1929–31, 1935–46); president, Hebrew U., Jerusalem (from 1932); founded (1934) Daniel Sieff Research Inst.; secured U.S. support for formation of state of Israel (1948); provisional president of Israel (1948–49), first president (1949–52).

We·ker·le \'ve-ker-le\, Sándor. 1848–1921. Hungarian politician. Premier of Hungary (1892–95, 1906–10, 1917–18).

Welch \'welch, 'welsh\, Adam Cleghorn. 1864–1943. Scottish clergyman and scholar, b. Jamaica. Presbyterian clergyman (1887–1913); professor at New Coll., Edinburgh (1913–34); instrumental in effecting reunion of United Free church and Church of Scotland (1929). Author of *The Code of Deuteronomy* (1925), *Deuteronomy: The Framework to the Code* (1932), *Post-Exilic Judaism* (1935), *Prophet and Priest in Old Israel* (1936), etc.

Welch, Denton. 1917–1948. English novelist, b. Shanghai. Known for two novels of adolescence, *Maiden Voyage* (1943) and *In Youth Is Pleasure* (1944).

Welch, Joseph Nye. 1890–1960. American lawyer, b. Primghar, Iowa. Practiced in Boston (from 1918); noted trial lawyer; counsel for U.S. army before U.S. Senate subcommittee hearing directed by Sen. Joseph R. McCarthy (1954).

Welch, Robert Henry Winborne. 1899–1985. American political activist, b. Chowan County, N.C. Engaged in candy manufacturing (1922–56). Founded (1958) John Birch Society, ultraconservative, fiercely anti-Communist organization that reached its peak in 1960s; published books and two monthly magazines; produced a weekly radio program and operated some 400 bookstores; preached militant Americanism and isolationism.

Welch, William Henry. 1850–1934. American pathologist, b. Norfolk, Conn. Opened first pathology laboratory in U.S., Bellevue Hospital Medical College, N.Y.C. (1879); professor, Johns Hopkins (1884–1916), pathologist to Johns Hopkins Hospital (1889–1916), first dean of Johns Hopkins medical school (1893–98); director, Johns Hopkins School of Hygiene and Public Health (1916–26), and professor of history of medicine (1926–31). Discovered (1892) *Clostridium welchii,* agent of gas gangrene. Author of *General Pathology of Fever* (1888), *Bacteriology of Surgical Infections* (1895), etc.

Welck·er \'vel-kər\, Friedrich Gottlieb. 1784–1868. German philologist and archaeologist. Professor, Giessen (1809), Göttingen (1816), Bonn (1819), where he organized and directed (to 1854) the library. Author of works on Greek art and literature as *Die griechischen Tragödien* (1839–41), *Alte Denkmäler erklärt* (1849–64). His brother ¶Karl Theodor (1790–1869) was professor of law at Kiel (1814), Heidelberg (1817), Bonn (1819), Freiburg (1822); member (1831–49) and with F.G. Rotteck leader of liberal opposition in Baden assembly; coeditor with Rotteck of the *Staatslexikon* (1834–48).

Weld \'weld\, Sir Frederick Aloysius. 1823–1891. English colonial administrator. To New Zealand (1844); member of N.Z. House of Representatives (1853–65); minister for native affairs (1860–61); premier (1864–65); governor of Western Australia (1869–75), Tasmania (1875–80), Straits Settlements (1880–87); brought Malay Peninsula under British control.

Weld, Theodore Dwight. 1803–1895. American reformer, b. Hampton, Conn. Persuaded Arthur and Lewis Tappan to support Lane Theological Seminary (1832); organized antislavery debates at Lane (1834); dismissed, led much of Lane student body to Oberlin Coll. (1834); organizer for American and Foreign Anti-Slavery Society; m. (1838) Angelina Grimké (*q.v.*). Author of *The Bible Against Slavery* (1837), *Slavery As It Is* (1839), etc.

Welf \'velf\. A German princely family originating in Altdorf, Swabia, and taking its name from Duke Welf (d. before 825). Family gained control of much of southern Germany. Members included: ¶Welf II (d. 1030), Count of Lechrain. His son ¶Welf III (d. 1055) was Duke of Carinthia; his daughter Kunigunde married Azzo II, founder of the Este line of Ferrara; their son ¶Welf IV (1030 or 1040–1101) was adopted as heir by uncle Welf III and became Duke of Bavaria and Carinthia; first of family to support papal party against emperor. His son ¶Henry, *called* der Schwar·ze \der-shfärt-sə\, *i.e.* the Black (c.1074–1126), was Duke of Bavaria; his children included Henry the Proud (*q.v.*), Welf VI, and Judith, who married Frederick II, Duke of Swabia, thus uniting houses of Welf and Hohenstaufen. In 12th century, Welf VI, uncle of Henry the Lion, was defeated (1140) by Conrad III (first of the Hohenstaufen kings of Germany) at Weinsberg. Most famous Welf was Henry the Lion (*q.v.*), Duke of Saxony and Bavaria, who defied Emperor Frederick Barbarossa and lost his possessions (1180–81). In Italy, supporters of the Welfs were called Guelfs, a faction supporting papacy against the imperial (Ghibelline) faction.

Wel·ha·ven \'vel-,hä-vən\, Johan Sebastian Cammermeyer. 1807–1873. Norwegian poet and critic. Professor at Kristiania (now Oslo; from 1846); championed conservatism in literature; attacked ornate style of Henrik Wergeland; author of the satirical sonnet cycle *Norges daemering* (1834), patriotic and lyrical poems, ballads, and critical works.

Welles. See also WELLS.

Welles \'welz\, Gideon. 1802–1878. American politician, b. Glastonbury, Conn. Editor and part owner, *Hartford Times* (1826–36). Postmaster, Hartford (1836–41). Aided in organization of Republican party and in founding (1856) a Republican newspaper, *Hartford Evening Press.* U.S. secretary of the navy (1861–69); directed great increase in navy during Civil War. Articles which he contributed to the *Galaxy* (1871–77) and his *Diary of Gideon Welles* (1911) are important historical documents.

Welles, Orson, *in full* George Orson. American director, producer, screenwriter, and actor, b. Kenosha, Wis. Early acclaimed as a "boy wonder," he debuted on stage in Dublin (1931); debuted on Broadway as Tybalt in *Romeo and Juliet* (1934); with John Houseman founded (1937) Mercury Theatre, which became famous for its innovative productions; staged all-black "voodoo" version of *Macbeth;* staged (1937) leftist opera *The Cradle Will Rock,* which federal officials attempted to close down; presented modern-dress version of *Julius Caesar;* created (Oct. 30, 1938) a panic with vivid dramatization on radio of a fictional Martian invasion of New Jersey. Turning to film, created the monumental *Citizen Kane* (1941), of seminal influence in use of deep-focus photography, high-contrast black-and-white film, and imaginative editing and sound. Among his other American films were *The Magnificent Ambersons* (1942), *Journey into Fear* (1943), and *Touch of Evil* (1958); chronically pressed for funds, made in Europe films *The Trial* (1962), *Chimes at Midnight* (1966), etc. As actor appeared in *Jane Eyre* (1944), *The Third Man* (1949), *A Man for All Seasons* (1966), etc. Received life achievement award from American Film Institute (1975).

Welles, Sumner. 1892–1961. American diplomat, b. New York City. Entered Foreign Service (1914); assistant chief and chief, Latin American affairs division in Department of State (1920–22). In Dominican Republic (1922 and 1929) and in Honduras (1924) laid foundation for American "good-neighbor" policy. U.S. ambassador to Cuba (1933). Assistant secretary and undersecretary of state (1933–43); U.S. delegate to conferences of American republics in Panama (1939), Rio de Janeiro (1942). Author of *World of the Four Freedoms* (1943), *Seven Decisions that Shaped History* (1951).

Welles·ley \'welz-lē\, Arthur. *Surname orig.* Wes·ley \'wes-lē, 'wez-\. 1st Duke of Wel·ling·ton \'wel-iŋ-tən\. *Called* the Iron Duke. 1769–1852. British general and statesman, b. Ireland. Son of Garret Wesley, 1st Earl of Mornington; entered army (1787); Irish M.P. (1790–97); commanded a division in war with Tipu Sultan (1799); appointed by his brother (then governor general of India) to supreme military and political command in the Deccan (to 1805); defeated Marāthā chiefs (1803); returned to England (1805); M.P. (1806–09); Irish secretary (1807–09). Given command as lieutenant general in Peninsular War (1808); on death of Sir John Moore, given chief command; defeated forces of King Joseph (Bonaparte) under Victor at Talavera (1809); forced French under Masséna to retreat from Portugal (1810–11), defeated them at Salamanca, and entered Madrid (1812); given supreme command in Spain, defeated King Joseph at Vitoria (1813) and drove French across Pyrenees (1814), pursuing as far as Toulouse; promoted field marshal and created duke (1814). Ambassador to France (1814) and representative at Congress of Vienna (1814–15). Entrusted with command of army in Netherlands; with aid of Blücher, crushed Napoléon in Waterloo campaign (1815); spoke strongly against cession of French territory to Prussia; commanded army of occupation in France (1815–18). Master general of ordnance with seat in cabinet (1818–27); as English representative in Congress of Verona (1822), unsuccessfully argued against French armed intervention in Spain; failed in mission to Russia to induce czar not to threaten war with Turkey in behalf of Greek independence (1826); commander in chief (1827–28, 1842–52). Prime minister (1828–30); opposed Catholic emancipation but became convinced that only way to avoid civil war in Ireland was to force Catholic Emancipation Act through Parliament (1829); declared against any reform of parliamentary representation and caused ministry to be voted out of office (1830); stubbornly opposed Reform Bill (1831–32); foreign secretary under Peel (1834–35); member of Peel's second cabinet (1841–46); supported Peel in corn-law legislation; subordinated party spirit to national interest; organized the military in London during Chartist uprisings (1848).

Wellesley, Richard Colley. 2d Earl of **Mor·ning·ton** \'mȯr-niŋ-tən\ *and* Marquis of Wellesley. 1760–1842. British statesman, b. Ireland. Son of Garret Wesley, 1st earl, and brother of Arthur Wellesley, Duke of Wellington. Irish M.P. (1780–81); entered Irish House of Lords (1781); M.P. (1784–97); lord of the treasury (1786); privy councilor (1793); governor of Madras (1797); governor general of Bengal (1797–1805); defeated Tipu Sultan (1799), restored Hindu dynasty in Mysore, annexed much of Deccan after victory in Marāthā war (1803); forced concessions from Oudh and other Indian states; opposed French colonial power; recalled by directors of East India Co. (1805). Ambassador to Madrid (1809); foreign secretary (1809–12). Lord lieutenant of Ireland (1821–28, 1833–34); advocated Catholic emancipation.

Well·hau·sen \'vel-ˌhau̇-zən\, Julius. 1844–1918. German theologian and scholar. Professor at Greifswald (1872), Halle (1882), Marburg (1885), Göttingen (1892); originated Graf-Wellhausen theory that the basic document of the Pentateuch is the youngest element of the work, thus sparking great activity in biblical criticism. Author of *Geschichte Israels* (1878), *Die Komposition des Hexateuch* (1889), *Israelitische und jüdische Geschichte* (1894), *Einleitung in die drei ersten Evangelien* (1905), etc.

Wellington, Duke of. See Arthur WELLESLEY.

Well·man \'wel-mən\, Walter. 1858–1934. American journalist and explorer, b. Mentor, Ohio. Founded (1879) *Cincinnati Post;* Washington correspondent, *Chicago Herald* and *Record-Herald* (1884–1911). Led expedition to Spitsbergen (1894) and to Franz Josef Land (1898–99); also attempted flight in dirigible over North Pole, but failed (1907 and 1909); also attempted flight in dirigible across Atlantic and failed (1910), but broke existing world records for time and distance sailing by airship (1008 miles in 72 hours).

Wells. See also WELLES.

Wells \'welz\, Carolyn. 1862–1942. American writer, b. Rahway, N.J. Writer of some 170 volumes of humorous sketches, parodies, juveniles, short stories, novels, and detective fiction, including *The Jingle Book* (1899), *A Nonsense Anthology* (1902), *Fluffy Ruffles* (1907), *The Maxwell Mystery* (1913), *Vicky Van* (1918), *Spooky Hollow* (1923), *The Skeleton at the Feast* (1931), *Fleming Stone Omnibus* (1933), *The Killer* (1938).

Wells, Charles Jeremiah. *Pseudonym* H. L. **How·ard** \'hau̇-ərd\. 1800?–1879. English poet. Friend of Hazlitt and Keats. Author of a pseudo-Jacobean drama in verse *Joseph and His Brethren* (1823). Made popular by Swinburne (1875).

Wells, David Ames. 1828–1898. American economist, b. Springfield, Mass. His pamphlet *Our Burden and Our Strength* (1864) demonstrated economic strength of U.S. Special commissioner of U.S. revenue (1865–69). Leading advocate of free-trade policies (from 1868). Among his books were *The Silver Question* (1877), *Our Merchant Marine* (1882), *Practical Economics* (1885), *The Theory and Practice of Taxation* (1900).

Wells, Henry. 1805–1878. American express operator, b. Thetford, Vt. In express business (from 1841); founded American Express Co. (1850); organizer (with William G. Fargo) of Wells, Fargo & Co. (1852).

Wells, Herbert George. *Occasional pseudonym* Reginald **Bliss** \'blis\. 1866–1946. English novelist, sociologist, and historian. Taught science; journalist (1893). Wrote series of fantastic scientific romances *The Time Machine* (1895), *The Island of Doctor Moreau* (1896), *The Wheels of Chance* (1896), *The Invisible Man* (1897), *The War in the Air* (1908); developed in combination with scientific speculation, a strain of sociological idealism in *The War of the Worlds* (1898), *First Men in the Moon* (1901), *The Food of the Gods* (1904), *A Modern Utopia* (1905); stated his social creed in *New Worlds for Old* (1908), *First and Last Things* (1908). Wrote novels of character and humor including *Love and Mr. Lewisham* (1900), *Kipps* (1905), *The History of Mr. Polly* (1910), *Ann Veronica* (1909); novels of contemporary English life including *Tono-Bungay* (1909), *The New Machiavelli* (1911), *Marriage* (1912), *The Passionate Friends* (1913), *The Research Magnificent* (1915), *Mr. Britling Sees It Through* (1916), *Joan and Peter* (1918); novels of discussion as *Christina Alberta's Father* (1925), *The World of William Clissold* (1926), *Mr. Blettsworthy on Rampole Island* (1928). His *Outline of History* (1920) was paralleled by *The Science of Life* (1929, with his son George Philip and with Julian Huxley) and *The Work, Wealth, and Happiness of Mankind* (1932). Later works included several scenarios and *The Shape of Things to Come* (1933), *Experiment in Autobiography* (1934), *The Croquet Player* (1936), *World Brain* (1938), *The Holy Terror* (1939), *The New World Order* (1940), *Guide to the New World* (1941), *Phoenix* (1942), *Mind at the End of its Tether* (1945).

Wells, Horace. 1815–1848. American dentist, b. Hartford, Vt. Interested (from 1840) in anesthetic effects of nitrous oxide; learned how to administer the gas (1844); attempted demonstration in dental case before Harvard medical class (1845) but with unsatisfactory result because of extraction before patient was completely anesthetized. His claim (Dec. 7, 1846) to priority in discovery of anesthesia was made about two months after W.T.G. Morton's demonstration of use of ether.

Wells, Ida Bell. *Also known as* Ida **Wells-Bar·nett** \'welz-'bär-nət\. 1862–1931. American journalist, b. Holly Springs, Miss. Schoolteacher (1876–91); part owner and editor of *Memphis Free Speech* (1891–92), in which she launched an anti-lynching crusade; forced to flee Memphis by mob; m. (1895) Ferdinand L. Barnett; contributed to *New York Age* and *Chicago Conservator;* published *Red Record,* study of lynching (1895); secretary (1898–1902), National Afro-American Council; founder (1910) of Negro Fellowship League.

Wells, Sir Thomas Spencer. 1818–1897. English surgeon. Surgeon for Queen Victoria's household (1863–96); perfected the operation of ovariotomy.

Wells, William Charles. 1757–1817. American physician and scientist, b. Charleston, S.C. Practiced medicine in London, England (from 1788); studied vision, blood, etc.; credited by Darwin with anticipating idea of natural selection; demonstrated origin of dew in condensation (1814).

Welsbach, Carl Auer von. See Carl AUER.

Wel·ti \'vel-tē\, Emil, *in full* Friedrich Emil. 1825–1899. Swiss politician. Chief executive of Aargau canton (1858, 1862, 1866); member of federal council (1857–66), president (1860, 1866); member of Bundesrat (from 1866), president of Swiss Confederation (1869, 1872, 1876, 1880, 1884, 1891); urged federal centralization, railroad development, military reorganization.

Wen·ce·slas *or* **Wen·ce·slaus** \'wen(t)-sə-ˌslȯs, -sləs\. *Ger.* **Wen·zel** \'vent-səl\. *Czech.* **Vác·lav** \'vät-slȧv\. Saint. c.907–929. Prince-duke of Bohemia. Raised a Christian by grandmother St. Ludmila, who was regent when he acceded to throne (c.921); subsequently under regency of pagan mother Drahomíra (to 924 or 925); encouraged German missionaries; submitted to Henry I the Fowler (929); killed by brother Boleslav; remains interred (932) in St. Vitus Cathedral, Prague. Patron saint of Bohemia.

Wenceslas *or* **Wenceslaus.** *Ger.* Wenzel. *Czech.* Václav. Name of four kings of Bohemia of Přemyslid dynasty:

Wenceslas I. 1205–1253. King (1230–53). Son of Otakar I; usually supported Emperor Frederick II; opposed by nobility for encouragement of German immigration; succeeded by his son Otakar II.

Wenceslas II. 1271–1305. King (1278–1305). Son of Otakar II; under German regency (1278–83); assumed full control (1290); reduced power of nobles; annexed most of Upper Silesia, occupied Kraków (1291); elected king of Poland (1300), but resigned (1305); at war with Albert I (1304–05).

Wenceslas III. 1289–1306. King of Hungary (1301–04), of Bohemia (1305–06). Son of Wenceslas II; killed in Polish uprising against his attempt to secure throne.

Wenceslas IV. See WENCESLAS, Holy Roman emperor.

Wenceslas. *Ger.* Wenzel. 1361–1419. King of Germany and Holy Roman emperor (1378–1400). King of Bohemia (1378–1419) as Wenceslas IV. Son of Charles IV and brother of Sigismund; a weak ruler, failed to settle disputes of German towns and princes, to appoint an imperial governor, or at length to attend diets called by princes to end anarchy; deposed by German electors (1400); lost power in Bohemia to Jobst, Margrave of Moravia (1396); deposed (1402) by Sigismund but regained throne; gave up authority to council.

Wen Cheng-ming \'wən-'jəŋ-'miŋ\. *Orig.* Wen **Pi** \-'bē\. 1470–1559. Chinese printer, calligrapher, and scholar. Student of Shen Chou and with him a leader of Wu school of scholar-artists; noted also as connoisseur of calligraphy.

Wen·dell \'wen-dᵊl\, Barrett. 1855–1921. American man of letters and educator, b. Boston. Taught at Harvard (1880–1921). Among his books were *Cotton Mather, the Puritan Priest* (1891), *English Composition* (1891), *William Shakspere* (1894), *A Literary History of America* (1900), *The Privileged Classes* (1908), *The Mystery of Education* (1909), *The Traditions of European Literature, from Homer to Dante* (1920).

Wendover, Roger of. See ROGER of Wendover.

Wen-hsiang \'wən-shē-'äŋ\. 1818–1876. Chinese politician. Head of foreign office (1861–76); advocate of Westernization and promoter of Western studies; trained first company of Chinese soldiers to use modern firearms.

Wen·ner·berg \'ven-nər-ˌberʸ\, Gunnar. 1817–1901. Swedish poet, composer, and politician. Minster of education (1870–75, 1888–91); governor of Växjö (1875); composer of words and music for *Gluntarne,* duets for male voices descriptive of student life at Uppsala (1849–51), of patriotic songs as "Hör oss, Svea!," hymns, Psalms, oratorios, a *Stabat Mater.*

Wen·ner-Gren \'ven-nər-ˌgrān\, Axel Leonard. 1881–1961. Swedish industrialist. Salesman for Swedish electric-lamp company, gradually becoming majority stockholder; formed Electrolux Company to manufacture vacuum cleaners (1920) and, later, refrigerators; acquired large interests in many industries in Sweden; donated large sums to establish foundations for scientific research in Sweden and U.S. and (1937) the Axel Wenner-Gren Foundation for Nordic Cooperation and Research.

Went \'vent\, Friedrich August Ferdinand Christian. 1863–1935. Dutch botanist. Director of sugarcane experiment station, Java (1891–96); professor, Utrecht (1896–1934); pioneer in study of tropisms, auxins, hormones.

Wen Ti. See (1) Liu Heng under LIU family; (2) YANG CHIEN.

Wen T'ing-yün \'wən-'tiŋ-'yüen\. *Also called* Wen Ch'i \-'chē\ *or* Wen Fei-ch'ing \-'fä-'chiŋ\. 812 or 818–870. Chinese poet. Considered earliest popularizer of the *tz'u,* or song poem.

Wen Tsung. See (1) I-CHU; (2) Li Ang under LI family.

Went·worth \'went-(,)wərth\, Benning. 1696–1770. British colonial governor, b. Portsmouth, N.H. Active in movement to make New Hampshire independent of Massachusetts; first royal governor of New Hampshire (1741–67). Made (1761) extensive grants of land, known as New Hampshire grants, in area west and east of Connecticut River claimed by both New York and New Hampshire, causing long dispute between the two provinces settled only by creation of State of Vermont. His nephew ¶Sir John Wentworth (1737–1820) succeeded to the governorship (1767); Loyalist on outbreak of American Revolution and forced to flee (1775); lieutenant governor of Nova Scotia (1792–1808); created baronet (1795).

Wentworth, Cecile de, *nee* Smith. d. 1933. American painter, b. New York City. m. (c.1888) J.W. Wentworth; exhibited at Paris Salon (from 1889); best known for her portraits, including Pope Leo XIII, Theodore Roosevelt, William H. Taft, Queen Alexandra.

Wentworth, Thomas. Earl of Straf·ford \'straf-ərd\. 1593–1641. English politician. m. (1611; d. 1622) Margaret Clifford, daughter of Earl of Cumberland; M.P. (1614 ff.); opposed war with Spain; imprisoned (1627) for refusing to subscribe forced loan to crown; supported Petition of Right in Parliament (1628), but won over to court party; made lord president of the north (1628), privy councilor (1629). As lord deputy for Ireland (1632–41) reformed administration and applied rigorous "thorough" policy in enforcing king's and his own authority; greatly increased crown revenues and enriched himself; created earl (1640); commanded king's army in disastrous Second Bishop's War against Scotland (1640); impeached by Commons led by John Pym (1640); convicted on bill of attainder, unwillingly assented to by Charles I, and executed.

Wentworth, William Charles. 1793–1872. Australian politician. Practiced law, Sydney, and started *The Australian,* a newspaper (1824) in which he advocated admission to politics of "emancipists" (ex-convicts) and discouraged the "exclusivists" (officials) and "interlopers" (voluntary immigrants); his agitation largely responsible for Constitution Act (1842) which gave colonial self-government to New South Wales; led "pastoral" or "squatter" party in first legislature (1843); founder of Sydney University (1852); secured new colonial constitution (1854); settled in England (1862) but continued to work for a federal parliament for all Australia. Author of *Statistical, Historical, and Political Description of the Colony of New South Wales* (1819).

Wen Wang \'wən-'wäŋ\. 1231?–?1135 B.C. Chinese ruler. Ruler of state of Chou; imprisoned (1144) by Chou Hsin, last of the Shang dynasty; while in prison supposed to have written *I Ching,* one of the Five Classics; release secured by his son Wu Wang, who became first emperor of the Chou dynasty.

Wenzel. See WENCESLAS.

Wer·bő·czi \ver-'bœt-si\, István. c.1458–1542. Hungarian statesman and jurist. For King Ulászló II codified Hungarian law in *Tripartitum* (1514), fixing equality of all nobility and servile status of peasantry; palatine (1525–26) to King Louis; supported János Zápolya for throne and served as chancellor; served Turkish administration (from 1541) but was poisoned by pasha of Buda.

Werdt, Johann von. See WERTH.

We·ren·skiold \'ver-ən-shōl\, Erik. 1855–1938. Norwegian illustrator and painter. A leader of nationalist school; known for portraits and Norwegian landscapes and scenes of folk life.

Wer·fel \'ver-fəl\, Franz. 1890–1945. German poet, dramatist, and novelist, b. Prague of Jewish parents. Served in World War I; resident chiefly in Vienna (from 1918); to France (1938), U.S. (1940). Author of volumes of Expressionist verse, including *Der Weltfreund* (1911), *Der Gerichtstag* (1919), *Beschwörungen* (1922), *Schlaf und Erwachen* (1935); novels as *Nicht der Möder, der Ermordete ist schuldig* (1920), *Verdi* (1924), *Der Tod des Kleinbürgers* (1927), *Der Abituriententag* (1928), *Barbara oder die Frömmigkeit* (1929), *Die Geschwister von Neapel* (1931), *Die 40 Tage des Musa Dagh* (1933), *Das Lied von Bernadette* (1941); plays including *Die Versuchung* (1913), *Die Troerinnen des Euripides* (1915), *Bocksgesang* (1921), *Schweiger* (1922), *Juarez und Maximilian* (1924), *Das Reich Gottes in Böhmen* (1930), *Jacobowski und der Oberst* (1944).

Werff \'verf\, Adriaen van der. 1659–1722. Dutch painter. Court painter in Palatinate (from 1696); known for biblical, mythological, and genre scenes.

Wer·ge·land \'ver-gə-län\, Henrik Arnold. 1808–1845. Norwegian poet, dramatist, and patriot. Championed Norwegian nationalism in literature, in opposition to Welhaven. Author of verse including *Digte* (1829), philosophical poem *Skabelsen, mennesket og messias* (1830), *Spaniolen* (1833), *Jan van Huysums blomsterstykke* (1840), *Jøden* (1842), *Jødinden* (1844), and *Den engelske Lods* (1844).

Wer·ner \'ver-nər\. *Ital.* Guer·nie·ri \gern-'yä-rē\. Duke of Ur·sling·en \'ür-,sliŋ-ən\. d. c.1354. German soldier of fortune. Served Pisa against Florence (1340–43); formed (c.1343) mercenary band that became infamous as Grand Company; ravaged Italian cities and countryside; joined expedition of Louis I of Hungary against Naples (1348); ravaged Papal States (1348–51).

Werner, Abraham Gottlob. 1750–1817. German geologist and mineralogist. Inspector and teacher, Freiberg School of Mining (from 1775); proponent of neptunism, the theory that all of the rocks of the earth's crust were formed by the agency of water; arranged geological formations into groups; classified minerals systematically.

Werner, Alfred. 1866–1919. Swiss chemist. Professor, Zürich (from 1893). Announced (1891) the coordination theory of chemical constitution, which led to discovery of many cases of isomerism. Awarded 1913 Nobel prize for chemistry. Author of *Lehrbuch der Stereochemie* (1904).

Werner, Zacharias, *in full* Friedrich Ludwig Zacharias. 1768–1823. German poet and dramatist. In Rome (1809–13), where he embraced Catholicism (1810); became priest (1814) and preached mainly in Vienna. Author of the dramas *Die Söhne des Thales* (1803), *Das Kreuz an der Ostsee* (1806), *Martin Luther oder die Weihe der Kraft* (1807), *Attila* (1808), and *Wanda* (1810), of the one-act *Der vierundzwanzigste Februar* (1810, one of the first "fate tragedies"), and of poems, hymns, sermons, etc.

Wern·her \'vern-her\, Bruder, *i.e.* Brother Wernher. 13th century. Middle High German poet. Possibly a member of a brotherhood of pilgrims to the Holy Sepulcher; one of the 12 founders of the Meistersinger guild.

Wer·nicke \'ver-nik-ə\, Carl. 1848–1905. German neurologist. Professor, Breslau (1885–1904), Halle (1904–05); known for studies of aphasia and encephalopathy.

Wer·nicke *or* **Wer·nig·ke** \'ver-nik-ə\, Christian. 1661–1725. German poet and epigrammatist. Resident minister of king of Denmark at French court (1708–23); author of *Überschriften oder Epigrammata* (1697, 1701, 1704) and the heroic poem *Hans Sachs* (1701).

Wert \'vert\, Giaches *or* Jaches de. *Surname also spelled* Vuert, Werth. 1535–1596. Flemish composer. In Italy from childhood; *maestro di capella* to Duke of Mantua (1565–85) and of Sta. Barbara, Mantua (1565–92); a master of counterpoint, composed madrigals published in 12 books (1558–1608), motets, canzonets, etc.

Werth *or* **Werdt** \'vert\, Johann von. *Also* Jean de Weert \də-värt\. c.1600–1652. German general. Served in the Thirty Years' War, at first (1622) in Imperialist, later (1630) in Bavarian service; distinguished himself at Nördlingen (1634).

Wert·hei·mer \'vert-hī-mər\, Max. 1880–1943. German psychologist and philosopher. Professor, Berlin (1918), Frankfurt (1929), New School for Social Research, N.Y.C. (1933–43); founder, with Köhler and Koffka, of Gestalt psychology. Author of *Über Schlussprozesse im produktiven Denken* (1920), *Productive Thinking* (1945), etc.

Wes·ley \'wes-lē, 'wez-\, John. 1703–1791. English religious leader. Ordained priest (1728); became leader of his brother Charles's Methodist society at Oxford (1729–34). Accompanied Governor Oglethorpe to Georgia as missionary among colonists and Indians (1735–37); on voyage, met and was influenced by German Moravian colonists; compiled *Collection of Psalms and Hymns* (1737); in London met Peter Böhler, by whom he was considerably influenced (1738). Prompted by experience at a prayer meeting in Aldersgate Street, London (1738), accepted principle of justification by faith and abandoned ecclesiastical and High Church views; encouraged by George Whitefield, preached to crowds in open air (1739); bought deserted gun foundry near London for preaching (1739); gained following of societies in London, Bristol, etc.; organized class meetings under lay leadership, with membership signaled by tickets; published *Rules* (1743) governing societies and encouraged expulsion of insincere and undesirable members; held first conference of Methodists (1744); preached rejection of doctrine of election and caused temporary breach with Whitefield (1741) and later secession of Welsh Calvinistic Methodists (1743); journeyed on horseback organizing societies through England (1742), Ireland on 42 trips (from 1747), Scotland on 22 trips (from 1751); appointed Francis Asbury (*q.v.*) general superintendent in America (1772); founded (1778) *Methodist Magazine.* Prepared declaration (1784) providing regulation of Methodist chapels and preachers; ordained preachers for colonies and presbyters to administer sacraments (1784). Author of educational treatises, translations from Greek, Latin, and Hebrew, histories of Rome and England, an ecclesiastical history, biblical commentaries; compiled an English dictionary; with his brother published 23 collections of hymns; recorded his itineraries and spiritual life in his *Journal* (1735–90).

His brother ¶Charles (1707–1788) gathered together at Oxford (1729) a group of fellow students, including his brother John, James Hervey, and George Whitefield, who shared religious zeal for regularity of living and strict observance of weekly sacrament; group called derisively "methodists" and later the Holy Club; resigned leadership to John; accompanied his brother to Georgia as secretary to Governor Oglethorpe (1735) but returned in failing health (1736); experienced evangelical conversion (1738); active itinerant Methodist preacher (1739–56); opposed separation from Anglican church (1755) and disagreed with his brother John's advocacy of doctrine of perfection (1762) and his ordination of presbyters (1784). Author of several thousand hymns, comprising most of those published jointly with John, including "Love Divine, all Loves excelling," "Hark, the Herald Angels sing," "Christ the Lord is ris'n today," "Soldiers of Christ, arise," "Jesu, Lover of my Soul."

Wesley, Samuel. 1766–1837. English organist and composer. Son of Charles Wesley; outstanding English organist of the day, noted esp. for improvisations; a leader of revival of interest in music of J.S. Bach; with K.F. Horn published English edition of *Das wohltemperierte Klavier* (*The Well-Tempered Clavier,* 1810–13). Composed symphonies, concerti, services, anthems, motets, hymns. His natural son ¶Samuel Sebastian (1810–1876) was also an organist; chorister of Chapel Royal and St. Paul's; organist at numerous churches and cathedrals, latter including Hereford (1832–35), Exeter (1835–41), Winchester (1849–65), Gloucester (1865–76); a masterly organist and extemporizer; as composer known for anthems as *Blessed be the God and Father, The Wilderness, Wash me thoroughly, Cast me not away, Let us lift up our heart,* and services, etc.

Wes·sel \'ves-əl\, Caspar. 1745–1818. Norwegian mathematician. First to develop (1797) graphical means of representing complex numbers, later known as Argand diagrams.

Wessel, Horst. 1907–1930. German student. Member of Nazi party (1926–30); author of the "Horst Wessel song," sung as the official Nazi rallying song.

Wessel, Johan Herman. 1742–1785. Norwegian writer. A founder of Norske Selskab at U. of Copenhagen (1772); led bohemian life; known for satiric epigrams and light verse and mock-tragic *Kiaerlighed uden Strømper* (1772).

Wes·son \'wes-ᵊn\, Daniel Baird. 1825–1906. American inventor and manufacturer, b. Worcester, Mass. In partnership with Horace Smith, invented new type of repeating action for pistols and rifles (1854); organized Smith & Wesson Co., Springfield, Mass. (1857) to manufacture the new firearm.

West \'west\, Benjamin. 1738–1820. American painter, b. near Springfield, Pa. Self-taught; studio in Philadelphia (to 1759) and New York (1759–60). In Italy (1760–63) and London (1763–1820). Established studio in London and gained fame by his historical paintings; close friend of Sir Joshua Reynolds; appointed by George III a charter member of the Royal Academy (1768) and historical painter to the king (from 1772). Succeeded Reynolds as president of the Royal Academy (1792–1820). Among his paintings were *The Death of Wolfe, Battle of La Hogue, Christ Healing the Sick, Death on the Pale Horse, Alexander the Great and his Physicians, Penn's Treaty with the Indians,* and many portraits, esp. of George III and members of the royal family.

West, Joseph. fl. 1669–1685. American colonial governor, b. England. Designated by the English proprietors commander of an expedition of three vessels to settle Carolina (1669); made settlement at Albemarle Point, under governorship of William Sayle; succeeded Sayle (d. 1671) and served as governor (1671–72, 1674–82, 1684–85); left the settlement (1685).

West, Mae. 1893?–1980. American entertainer, b. Brooklyn, N.Y. On stage (from c.1901); played in repertory, vaudeville; starred on Broadway in *A la Broadway and Hello Paris* (1911); perfected stage persona of sultry, nonchalant sensuality, with languid delivery of sexually-charged dialogue; wrote and performed in plays *Sex* (1926), *The Pleasure Man* (1928), *Diamond Lil* (1928), *Constant Sinner* (1931); appeared in films *She Done Him Wrong* (1932), *I'm No Angel* (1933), *Klondike Annie* (1934), *My Little Chickadee* (1940, written with W.C. Fields), *Myra Breckinridge* (1970). Wrote autobiography *Goodness Had Nothing to Do With It* (1959).

West, Nathanael. See Nathan WEINSTEIN.

West, Dame Rebecca. *Orig.* Cicily Isabel Fair·field \'fe(ə)r-ˌfēld\. 1892–1983. British journalist. Trained as actress, but joined woman suffrage movement, writing for feminist paper *Freewoman* and assuming name of heroine of Ibsen's *Rosmersholm.* Interviewed H.G. Wells, later becoming his common-law wife; published first novel *The Return of the Soldier* (1918); m. Henry Maxwell Andrews (1930); preoccupied (from 1930s) with reporting; journey to Serbia produced study of Balkan politics, culture, and history *Black Lamb and Grey Falcon* (1942); reported (1945–46) treason trial of Nazi propagandist William Joyce; collected reports published as *The Meaning of Treason* (1949); later published *The New Meaning of Treason* (1964). Also wrote novels *The Fountain Overflows* (1957) and *The Birds Fall Down* (1966), short stories, essays, criticism, etc.

West, Thomas. 12th Baron De La Warre \ˌdel-ə-'wo(ə)r, -ˌwär\. 1577–1618. English soldier and colonialist. Served under Earl of Essex in Netherlands and Ireland; briefly imprisoned (1601) for complicity in Essex's revolt; succeeded to barony (1602); on council of Virginia Company (1609); made governor and captain general of Virginia (1610); halted colonists' adandonment of Jamestown, restored order (1610–11); returned to England; died on way back again. Author of *Relation* on Virginia (1611). Delaware named for him.

Westbury, 1st Baron. See Richard BETHELL.

West·cott \'wes(t)-kət\, Brooke Foss. 1825–1901. English prelate and scholar. Regius professor of divinity, Cambridge (1870–90). One of revisionists of New Testament (1870–81); brought out, in conjunction with F.J.A. Hort, a new critical text of New Testament in Greek (1881). Canon of Westminster (1883–90); bishop of Durham (1890–1901).

Westcott, Edward Noyes. 1846–1898. American banker and novelist, b. Syracuse, N.Y. In banking business (from 1862); author of *David Harum, A Story of American Life* (1898), which achieved wide popularity.

Wes·ter·mann \'ves-tər-ˌmän\, Diedrich. 1875–1956. German scholar. Missionary in Togo; studied African languages; professor, Berlin (1921–50); director, International African Institute, London (1926–56). Author of *Grammatik der Ewe-Sprache* (1907), *Die Sudansprache* (1911), *The Shilluk People* (1912), *Die Kpelle* (1921), *Geschichte Afrikas* (1952).

Wes·ter·marck \'ves-tər-ˌmärk, *Angl* 'wes-tər-ˌmärk\, Edward Alexander. 1862–1939. Finnish philosopher and anthropologist. Lecturer, U. of Helsinki (1890–1906); professor, Åbo (1906–30) and London (1890–1930). His works included *The History of Human Marriage* (1891), *The Origin and Development of the Moral Ideas* (1906–08), *Early Beliefs and Their Social Influence* (1932), *Ethical Relativity* (1932), *Christianity and Morals* (1939), etc.

West·hei·mer \'west-ˌhī-mər\, Irvin Ferdinand. 1879–1980. American banker and philanthropist, b. Newark, N.J. Founded (1903) Big Brother movement.

Wes·ting·house \'wes-tiŋ-ˌhau̇s\, George. 1846–1914. American inventor and manufacturer, b. Central Bridge, N.Y. Invented (1869) railroad air brake and organized (1869) Westinghouse Air Brake Co. to manufacture it. Also invented automatic railroad signal devices and was one of organizers of Union Switch & Signal Co. (1882). Interested himself in use of electricity; became pioneer in introducing in America the high-voltage alternating-current single-phase system for transmission of electricity, and organized (1886) Westinghouse Electric Co. for manufacturing and marketing purposes. Also patented a number of devices for practicable and economical transmission of natural gas. Took out altogether more than 400 patents during his lifetime.

West·lake \'wes(t)-ˌlāk\, John. 1828–1913. English lawyer and reformer. Helped found (1854) Working Men's Coll., London; a founder of Institut de Droit International (1873); M.P. (1885–86); Whewell professor of international law, Cambridge (1888–1908). Author of *Treatise on Private International Law* (1858), *International Law,* comprising *Peace* (1904), *War* (1907).

Westmorland. (1) Barons of. See CLIFFORD family. (2) Earls of. See NEVILLE family; John FANE.

Wes·ton \'wes-tən\, Edward. 1850–1936. American electrical engineer, b. near Wolverhampton, England. To U.S. (1870, naturalized 1923); built first successful dynamo for electroplating (1872); established first factory in U.S. devoted to manufacture of dynamo machinery (1875); turned to incandescent lighting equipment; formed (1888) Weston Electrical Instrument Co.

Weston, Edward. 1886–1958. American photographer, b. Highland Park, Ill. Became professional photographer with studio in Glendale, Cal. (1904); pioneer in modern photographic aesthetics emphasizing sharp realism, form, full tonal range, and eschewing darkroom manipulation of images. Published works in *Art of Edward Weston* (1932), *California and the West* (1940), *Cats of Wildcat Hill* (1942), *My Camera on Point Lobos* (1950).

Weston, Edward Paycon. 1839–1929. American walker, b. Providence, R.I. Walked from Boston to Washington, D.C., in 10 days (1861); from Portland, Me., to Chicago (1867); New York City to San Francisco and back (1909–10); New York City to Minneapolis at age 75 (1913).

Weston, Richard. 1st Earl of Port·land \'pōrt-lənd, 'pȯrt-\. 1577–1635. English politician. M.P. (1601–28); chancellor of exchequer (1621); lord high treasurer (1628–33); created baron (1628), earl (1633).

Wet \'vät\, Christiaan Rudolf de. 1854–1922. Boer soldier and politician. Served in Basuto wars (1860s); in South African (Boer) War, succeeded Cronjé as commander in chief of Orange Free State forces (1900); became legendary as guerilla leader against British. As acting president of Orange Free State for one day, signed peace treaty of Vereeniging (May 1902). Sat in union convention (1908–09). Supporter of Hertzog's separatist policy; helped found Nationalist party (1914); organized Afrikaner rebellion but was defeated in the field by L. Botha (1914); convicted of treason and imprisoned (1915).

Wetherell, Elizabeth. See Susan Bogert WARNER.

Wet·tach \'vet-äk\, Charles Adrien. *Pseudonym* Grock \'grȯk\. 1880–1959. Swiss circus clown. One of best-loved clowns in Europe (1903–54).

Wet·ter·bergh \'vet-tər-ˌberʸ\, Carl Anton. *Pseudonym* On·kel Adam \'ȯŋ-kəl-'ä-dȧm\. 1804–1889. Swedish writer. Author of humorous stories and sketches of everyday life collected in *Genremålninger* (1842), *De fura signaturerna* (1843), *Guvernanten* (1843), *Pastorsadjunkten* (1845), *Ett namn* (1845), etc.

Wet·tin \ve-'tēn\. A German family of nobility, originated in the 10th century; later (c.1104) took name from castle on the Saale near Halle; Conrad I

(1098–1157) gained margraviate of Meissen (1123) and lower Lusatia (1136); Margrave Henry the Illustrious (*q.v.*) gained Thuringia (1247); electoral duchy of Saxony (around Wittenberg; hence, Saxe-Wittenberg) granted by emperor to Frederick of Wettin (1423); divided (1485) into Ernestine line and Albertine line (*qq.v.*). It had in later times in its various branches many members of European ruling houses.

Wett·stein \ˈvet-ˌshtīn\, Johann Rudolf. 1594–1666. Swiss politician. Burgomaster of Basel (1645); represented Swiss Confederation at Peace of Westphalia (1647–48) and won recognition of Swiss independence and Habsburg renunciation of all claims.

Wet·zel \ˈwet-səl\, Lewis. 1764–?1808. American scout, b. Lancaster Co., Pa. Scout and Indian fighter in Virginia and Ohio (from 1777); noted for remorselessness and cruelty toward Indians.

Wetz·stein \ˈvet-ˌshtīn\, Johann Gottfried. 1815–1905. German Orientalist. Prussian consul in Damascus (1848–62); proposed (1873) literal reading of the Song of Solomon as anthology of love songs of no religious significance.

Wex·ler \ˈwek-slər\, Harry. 1911–1962. American meteorologist, b. Fall River, Mass. With U.S. Weather Bureau (from 1939), chief of meteorological research (from 1955); known for studies of heat balance and dynamics of atmosphere, ozone circulation, etc.

Wey·den \ˈvī-dən\, Rogier van der. *Also known as* Roger de La Pas·ture \də-lá-pä-tu̅e̅r\. 1399?–1464. Flemish painter. Painter to town of Brussels (1435–64); patronized by Medici, Este, and other courts; most influential painter of the day, noted esp. for realistic clarity, color. Works included *Annuciation, St. Luke Painting the Portrait of the Virgin, Virgin and St. John, Christ on the Cross, Entombment, Last Judgment,* and portraits.

Wey·er·haeu·ser \ˈwī-ər-ˌhau̇-zər\, Frederick. 1834–1914. American businessman, b. Niedersaulheim, Germany. To U.S. (1852); acquired vast timber holdings in Minnesota region, extending eventually to Pacific Northwest and amounting to over 2 million acres; known as "the Lumber King."

Wey·gand \ve-gä^{n}\, Maxime. 1867–1965. French soldier, b. Brussels. Chief of Foch's general staff (1914–23); general (1916); reorganized Polish army to resist Bolshevik attack (1920); French high commissioner in Syria (1923); chief of army general staff (1930); commander in chief in Near East (1939); took over command in France during retreat (1940) but was unable to prevent German victory; under Vichy regime, minister of national defense (1940); military commander in North Africa (1940–41); German prisoner (1942–45).

Weyl \ˈvīl\, Hermann. 1885–1955. German mathematician. Professor, Zürich (1913–30), Göttingen (1930–33), Inst. for Advanced Study, Princeton, N.J. (1933–51); contributed particularly to development of differential geometry, theory of continuous groups; known also for work on differential equations, relativity, quantum mechanics, philosophy of mathematics. Author of *Die Idee der Riemannschen Fläche* (1913), *Raum, Zeit, Materie* (1918), *Gruppentheorie und Quantenmechanik* (1928), *Symmetry* (1952), etc.

Wey·ler y Ni·co·lau \ˈwā-ler-ē-nē-kō-ˈlä-ü\, Valeriano. Marqués de Te·ne·ri·fe \tā-nā-ˈrē-fā, *Angl* ˌten-ər-ˈif, -ˈēf\. 1838–1930. Spanish soldier. Captain general of Canary Is. (1878–83), Balearic Is. (1883), Philippines (1888), Cuba (1896–97); recalled in response to American protest to his ruthless policy in Cuba. Minister of war (1901–05, 1907); captain general of Catalonia (1909); president, supreme war council (1910).

Wey·man \ˈwā-mən\, Stanley John. 1855–1928. English novelist. Author of popular cloak-and-sword romances with French historical background, including *A Gentleman of France* (1893), *The Red Cockade* (1895), *Under the Red Robe* (1896), *The Long Night* (1903), and of period novels with English setting, including *Chippinge* (1906), *Ovington's Bank* (1922), *The Lively Peggy* (1928).

Weymouth, 3d Viscount. See Thomas THYNNE.

Wey·precht \ˈvī-prekt\, Carl. 1838–1881. German explorer. On expedition with Payer to Spitsbergen and Novaya Zemlya (1871); with Payer, leader of Austro-Hungarian expedition (1872–74) which discovered Franz Josef Land; proposed International Polar Commission.

Whal·ley \ˈhwā-lē, ˈwā-; ˈhwȯ-lē, ˈwȯ-\, Edward. d. 1674 or 1675. English regicide. Served in Puritan army in the English Civil War, and engaged at Marston Moor and at Naseby; entrusted with care of King Charles I (1647); member of court that tried Charles I and a signer of the king's death warrant; major general (1655); at Restoration, fled to New England and remained in hiding the rest of his life.

Whar·ton \ˈhwȯrt-^{ə}n, ˈwȯrt-\, Edith Newbold, *nee* Jones. 1862–1937. American novelist, b. New York City. m. Edward Wharton (1885). Author of *The Valley of Decision* (1902), *The House of Mirth* (1905), *Ethan Frome* (1911), *The Age of Innocence* (1920, Pulitzer prize), *A Son at the Front* (1923), *Twilight Sleep* (1927), *The Children* (1928), *Hudson River Bracketed* (1929), *Certain People* (1930); also wrote *The Writing of Fiction* (1925) and autobiography *A Backward Glance* (1934).

Wharton, Joseph. 1826–1909. American industrialist, b. Philadelphia. Developed first commercially successful production of spelter in U.S. Bought a nickel mine in Pennsylvania (1864); for many years, only U.S. producer of refined nickel; developed process (1875) for making pure malleable nickel. A founder of Swarthmore College; benefactor of U. of Pennsylvania, which with his gifts established Wharton School of Finance and Commerce.

Wharton, Thomas. 1st Marquis of Wharton. 1648–1715. English politician. Author of *Lilliburlero* (1687), a doggerel ballad ridiculing Irish papists; controller of William of Orange's household (1689–1702); created earl (1706); lord lieutenant of Ireland (1708–10), with Addison as secretary; received dedication of Addison's *Spectator* (vol. 5); joined Whigs in proclaiming George I (1714); created marquis (1714). His son ¶Philip (1698–1731), Duke of Wharton, supported government in Irish House of Peers; created duke (1718); in London published opposition newspaper *True Briton* (1723–24); supported cause of Old Pretender; served with Spaniards against English at Gibraltar (1727); outlawed and shorn of title and estates (1729).

Whate·ly \ˈhwāt-lē, ˈwāt-\, Richard. 1787–1863. English logician and theologian. Satirized skepticism by reducing to absurdity the application of logic to the Scriptures in *Historic Doubts Relative to Napoleon Bonaparte* (1819); professor of logic, Oxford (1829–31); archbishop of Dublin (1831–63). Opposed Tractarian movement, supported Roman Catholic emancipation, advocated state endowment of Catholic clergy; a founder of Broad-Church policy; exerted himself in favor of common unsectarian religious education for Protestant and Roman Catholic schools (1831–53), and wrote manuals suited to the purpose. Author of *Logic* (1826), *Rhetoric* (1828), *Christian Evidences* (1837), etc.; edited Bacon's *Essays* and Paley's *Evidences* and *Moral Philosophy.*

Wheat·ley \ˈhwēt-lē, ˈwēt-\, Phillis. 1753?–1784. American poet, b. probably Senegal. Kidnaped and taken as slave to Boston (1761); maid-servant to wife of John Wheatley, Boston; m. John Peters, a free Negro (1778). At age of 13 began writing poetry in English; regarded as a prodigy in Boston; to England (1773), where she achieved great popularity; published *Poems on Various Subjects, Religious and Moral* (1773).

Whea·ton \ˈhwēt-ən, ˈwēt-\, Henry. 1785–1848. American jurist and diplomat, b. Providence, R.I. Practiced law in Providence (1806–12); edited Jeffersonian *National Advocate* in New York City (1812–15); reporter of U.S. Supreme Court (1816–27); U.S. chargé d'affaires in Denmark (1827–35); U.S. minister to Prussia (1837–46). Author of *History of the Northmen* (1831) and most notably of *Elements of International Law* (1836, with succeeding editions published for nearly a century after).

Wheat·stone \ˈhwēt-ˌstōn, ˈwēt-, *chiefly Brit* -stən\, Sir Charles. 1802–1875. English physicist and inventor. Professor, King's Coll., London (from 1834); invented the concertina (1829); carried on researches in electricity, light, and sound; demonstrated velocity of electricity in a conductor (1834); with William F. Cooke, devised an electric telegraph for transmitting messages (patented 1837) and a single-needle apparatus (patented 1845); suggested the stereoscope (1838); made improvements on the dynamo; invented (1843) the Wheatstone bridge for measuring electrical resistances.

Whe·don \ˈhwēd-^{ə}n, ˈwēd-\, Daniel Denison. 1808–1885. American clergyman, b. Onondaga, N.Y. Professor, Wesleyan Coll. (1833–43), U. of Michigan (1845–51); editor, *Methodist Quarterly Review* (1856–84); known for his *Commentaries on the New Testament* (5 vols., 1860–80) and *Commentaries on the Old Testament* (9 vols., of which he supervised preparation of first four).

Whee·ler \ˈhwē-lər, ˈwē-\, Burton Kendall. 1882–1975. American politician, b. Hudson, Mass. U.S. senator from Montana (1923–47); Progressive party candidate for vice president on ticket headed by Robert M. La Follette (1924).

Wheeler, Joseph. 1836–1906. American army officer and politician, b. near Augusta, Ga. Resigned from U.S. army to join Confederate service (1861); commander of the cavalry of the army of Mississippi (1862), almost continuously in the field; lieutenant general (Feb. 1865). Member, U.S. House of Representatives (1881–82, 1883, 1885–1900). Widely known for his efforts to promote reconciliation between the North and the South. Commissioned major general of volunteers at outbreak of Spanish–American War; commanded cavalry division in Shafter's corps; fought at Las Guásimas (June 24, 1898) and San Juan Hill (July 1, 1898). Commanded brigade in the Philippines (1899). Retired (1900).

Wheeler, Wayne Bidwell. 1869–1927. American lawyer and reformer, b. Trumbull Co., Ohio. Attorney, general superintendent (1898–1915), national superintendent (1915–27), Anti-Saloon League of America; leading figure in prohibition movement, reaching success in passage and ratification of the Eighteenth Amendment to the U.S. Constitution (1919). Claimed authorship of what is known as the Volstead Act.

Wheeler, William Almon. 1819–1887. American politician, b. Malone, N.Y. Member, U.S. House of Representatives (1861–63, 1869–77); author of

Wheeler Compromise, by which a disputed election in Louisiana (1874) was satisfactorily settled; vice president of the U.S. under Hayes (1877–81).

Whee·lock \'hwē-,läk, 'wē-\, Eleazar. 1711–1779. American clergyman and educator, b. Windham, Conn. Congregational minister (from 1735); tutored American Indians (from 1743) and founded (1754) Moor's Charity School, Lebanon, Conn.; obtained charter (1769) for new college, Dartmouth Coll., which he established in Hanover, N.H.; first president of Dartmouth (1770–79). His son ¶John (1754–1817) graduated in first Dartmouth class (1771); succeeded his father as president of Dartmouth (1779–1817); last twelve years of administration marked by dispute with trustees of the college, bringing legislative interference, the legislature passing a bill changing name of Dartmouth College to Dartmouth University and enlarging number of trustees to give Wheelock adherents control of the university; result was court action brought by trustees of the college to maintain their rights under the original charter, the famous Dartmouth College Case argued by Daniel Webster and decided (1818) in favor of the college by U.S. Supreme Court.

Wheel·wright \'hwē(ə)l-,rīt, 'we(ə)l-\, John. 1592?–1679. American clergyman, b. England. To America (1636); involved in Antinomian controversy, defending his sister-in-law Anne Hutchinson; arrested, tried, and found guilty of sedition and contempt of the civil authority (1637); disfranchised and banished from Massachusetts. Settled and became pastor at Exeter, N.H., later at Wells, Me. (to 1646). On his repentance, sentence was reversed (1644).

Wheelwright, William. 1798–1873. American businessman and promoter, b. Newburyport, Mass. Formed (1840) Pacific Steam Navigation Co. connecting Panama, Chile, and England; built (1851) first railway in Chile; introduced telegraph, gas lighting, water sanitation in Chile and Peru; built Grand Central Argentine Railway (opened 1870) and planned the trans-Andean railway.

Whet·stone \'hwet-,stōn, 'wet-\, George. 1551?–1587. English playwright and author. His *Promos and Cassandra* (1578), a tale in prose from Giambattista Giraldi's *Ecatommiti,* was used by Shakespeare in *Measure for Measure.*

Whew·ell \'(h)yü-əl\, William. 1794–1866. English philosopher and mathematician. Professor, Cambridge (1828–55), master of Trinity Coll. (1841–66), vice chancellor of university (1843, 1856); instituted tripos of moral science and of natural science (1848); known for studies in natural sciences and of philosophy of Kant. Author of *Astronomy and General Physics* (1833), *History of the Inductive Sciences* (1837), *Philosophy of the Inductive Sciences* (1840), *History of Scientific Ideas* (1858), *Novum Organon Renovatum* (1858), and *On the Philosophy of Discovery* (1860).

Which·cote *or* **Whitch·cote** \'hwich-kət, 'wich-\, Benjamin. 1609–1683. English theologian. Member, probably founder, of Cambridge Platonists.

Whip·ple \'hwip-əl, 'wip-\, Abraham. 1733–1819. American naval officer, b. Providence, R.I. Served in French and Indian War; commodore of Rhode Island fleet (1775); commissioned captain in the Continental navy (1775); captured eight East Indiamen, with cargoes worth over $1,000,000 (1779).

Whipple, George Hoyt. 1878–1976. American pathologist, b. Ashland, N.H. Resident pathologist, Johns Hopkins Hospital (1910–14); professor, U. of California (1914–21); professor of pathology, U. of Rochester (1921–55; dean, 1921–53). Shared Nobel prize for physiology or medicine (1934) with George Minot and William P. Murphy for experiments proving that liver was therapeutic in cases of anemia in animals.

Whipple, Henry Benjamin. 1822–1901. American clergyman, b. Adams, N.Y. Ordained Episcopal priest (1850); consecrated first bishop of Minnesota (1859). Worked for better treatment of Indians by government.

Whipple, Squire. 1804–1888. American civil engineer, b. Hardwick, Mass. Known esp. as bridge builder; inventor of the Whipple truss of trapezoidal form used in bridge construction. Author of *Work on Bridge Building* (1847), first scientifically based guide to bridge engineering.

Whipple, William. 1730–1785. American Revolutionary leader, b. Kittery, Me. Member from New Hampshire of Continental Congress (1776–79) and a signer of Declaration of Independence; commanded militia contingents in the Saratoga campaign (1777) and the Rhode Island campaign (1778). Associate justice of the superior court in New Hampshire (1782–85).

Whis·tler \'hwis-lər, 'wis-\, James Abbott McNeill. 1834–1903. American painter and etcher, b. Lowell, Mass. To Paris (1855) to study painting, never thereafter returned to U.S.; painted in studios in Paris and in London alternately. Published his first group of etchings in Paris (1858) and a second set, views of the Thames (1860). Achieved recognition by series of paintings, many with musical titles as "symphony," "nocturne," "caprice," including *The White Girl* (rejected at the Royal Academy, a sensation in the Salon des Refusés, 1863), *Valparaiso* (1866), *Artist in his Studio* (1867–68), *Arrangement in Grey and Black, No.1: Portrait of the Artist's Mother* (1872), *The Lagoon, Venice* (1880), *The Life Boat* (c.1884), portraits of Carlyle, Miss Alexander, Rosa Corder, etc. Gained great notoriety by suing John Ruskin (1878) for slander because of criticisms by Ruskin of *Nocturne in Black and Gold: the Falling Rocket;* won verdict and one farthing damages. Recognition of his genius came slowly, somewhat retarded by his pugnacity and personal idiosyncrasies; acknowledged one of most influential artists of the day. Excelled also as an etcher; his *Thames Series* (1871) placed him in first rank; later published *First Venice Series* (1880) and *Second Venice Series* (1881). Author of *The Gentle Art of Making Enemies* (1890).

Whistler, Rex John. 1905–1944. English painter and illustrator. Known for murals in the Tate Gallery and in Haddon Hall in Derbyshire, and for book illustrations for *Gulliver's Travels* (1930), etc.

Whis·ton \'hwis-tən, 'wis-\, William. 1667–1752. English theologian and mathematician. Succeeded Newton as Lucasian professor of mathematics, Cambridge (1703); expelled (1710) from university on account of his Arian views, later promulgated in *Primitive Christianity Revived* (1711–12); known for his translation of Josephus (1737).

Whit·a·ker \'hwit-ə-kər, 'wit-\, Joseph. 1820–1895. English publisher. Edited *Gentleman's Magazine* (1856–59); founded the *Bookseller* (1858); started (1868) *Whitaker's Almanack,* annual book of reference.

Whitchchote, Benjamin. See WHICHCOTE.

White \'hwīt, 'wīt\, Alma, *in full* Mollie Alma, *nee* Brid·well \'brid-,wel, -wəl\. 1862–1946. American religious leader, b. Kinniconick, Ky. m. (1887) Kent White, Methodist clergyman, and became herself a Methodist evangelist. Founded (1901) Methodist Pentecostal Union church, known (from 1917) as the Pillar of Fire church, incorporated in Colorado (1902), headquarters in Zarephath, N.J. (from 1907); senior bishop (from 1918).

White, Andrew Dickson. 1832–1918. American educator and diplomat, b. Homer, N.Y. Professor, U. of Michigan (1857–62); with Ezra Cornell, organized Cornell U. (chartered 1865; opened 1868); president of Cornell (1868–85); U.S. minister to Germany (1879–81), to Russia (1892–94); U.S. ambassador to Germany (1897–1902). Chairman of United States delegation to the Hague Peace Conference (1899). Author of *History of the Warfare of Science with Theology* (1896), etc.

White, Canvass. 1790–1834. American engineer, b. Whitesboro, N.Y. Employed on Erie Canal construction (1816–25); inspected canal construction in England (1817–18); designed locks, discovered means of making concrete from local limestone; worked on Delaware and Raritan, Lehigh canals (1825–34).

White, David, *in full* Charles David. 1862–1935. American paleobotanist and geologist, b. near Palmyra, N.Y. On staff of U.S. Geological Survey (from 1886), chief geologist (1912–22); curator of paleobotany, U.S. National Museum (1903–35); developed (1915) carbon-ratio method of classifying coal deposits. Author of *Fossil Flora of the Lower Coal Measures of Missouri* (1899), *Flora of the Hermit Shale* (1929), etc.

White, Edward Douglass. 1845–1921. American jurist, b. Lafourche Parish, La. In Confederate army (1861–63). U.S. senator (1891–94); associate justice, U.S. Supreme Court (1894–1910), chief justice (1910–21). Known for enunciation of the "rule of reason" for interpretation and application of antitrust laws.

White, Edward Higgins II. 1930–1967. American astronaut, b. San Antonio, Tex. Air force pilot; entered astronaut corps (1962); on Gemini 4 flight (June 1965) became first U.S. astronaut to maneuver in space outside spacecraft; killed in flash fire in Apollo 1 capsule.

White, Elijah. 1806–1879. American physician and pioneer. Appointed (1842) government Indian agent for the Northwest. Gathered party of about 120 emigrants and (1842) led them to Oregon country, the first considerable overland migration to this region.

White, Ellen Gould, *nee* Har·mon \'här-mən\. 1827–1915. American religious leader, b. Gorham, Me. Follower of William Miller (from 1842); became Adventist preacher (1844); m. (1846) James S. White, Adventist minister; experienced numerous visions that guided formation (1860) and doctrine of Seventh-Day Adventists. Author of *Testimonies for the Church* (1855 and many enlarged editions).

White, Elwyn Brooks. 1899–1985. American writer, b. Mount Vernon, N.Y. Staff writer for magazines *The New Yorker* (from 1927) and *Harper's* (1938–43). A highly versatile writer; his works included the children's books *Stuart Little* (1945), *Charlotte's Web* (1952), and *The Trumpet of the Swan* (1970), the revision of William Strunk Jr.'s classic *The Elements of Style* (1935), the spoof (written with James Thurber) *Is Sex Necessary?* (1929), and collections of verse and essays as *The Second Tree From the Corner* (1954), *Points of My Compass* (1962), and *Poems and Sketches of E.B. White* (1981). Awarded special Pulitzer Prize (1978).

White, Francis. d. 1711. English publican. Proprietor of White's Chocolate House in St. James's St., London, famous for meetings of White's Club (originated c.1697).

White, George Leonard. 1838–1895. American music teacher and choral director, b. Cadiz, N.Y. Organized (1871) and conducted (1871–85) Jubilee Singers of Fisk U., who successfully toured U.S. and Great Britain.

White, Sir George Stuart. 1835–1912. British soldier. Entered army (1853); served in second Afghan war (1878–80); brought end to third Burmese war (1885–86); commander in chief in India (1893–97); commanded in Natal,

South Africa, and defended Ladysmith through siege of 119 days (1899–1900); governor of Gibraltar (1900–04); field marshal (1903).

White, Gilbert. 1720–1793. English clergyman and naturalist. Curate at Selborne; author of classic *Natural History and Antiquities of Selborne* (1789).

White, Henry Kirke. 1785–1806. English poet. Attracted approval of Southey with *Clifton Grove* (1803); chief poem *The Christiad,* a fragment; known for hymn "Oft in danger, oft in woe."

White, Hugh Lawson. 1773–1840. American lawyer and politician, b. Iredell Co., N.C. Presiding judge, Tennessee supreme court of errors and appeals (1809–15). U.S. senator from Tennessee (1825–40); independent candidate for president in opposition to Van Buren (1836); joined Whigs (1838).

White, Israel Charles. 1848–1927. American geologist, b. Monongalia Co., Va. (now W.Va.). State geologist of W.Va. (1897–1927); formulated (1885) anticlinal theory for location of petroleum and gas deposits.

White, John. d. 1593? English painter and cartographer. Member of Raleigh's expedition to Virginia (1585); executed several paintings of Indian life, flora and fauna; prepared maps of coastal region from Florida to Virginia; governor of second expedition, which founded colony of Roanoke (1587); returned to England for supplies (1587); on return (1590), found no trace of colony. Virginia Dare (*q.v.*) was his granddaughter.

White, Joseph Blanco. *Orig.* José María Blan•co y Cres•po \ˈb̲läŋ-kō-ē-ˈkrā-spō\. 1775–1841. British writer, b. Spain, of Irish father and Andalusian mother. Ordained priest (1800); abandoned priesthood (1810); conducted, from England, Spanish patriotic newspaper *Español* (1810–14); took orders in English church but later became Unitarian; tutor in Whately's family, Dublin (1832–35). Author of *Letters from Spain* (1822) and an autobiography; best known in literature for sonnet "Night and Death," praised by Coleridge.

White, Leslie Alvin. 1900–1975. American anthropologist, b. Salida, Colo. Professor, U. of Michigan (1932–75); known for studies of culture and cultural evolution. Author of *Science of Culture* (1949), *Evolution of Culture* (1959).

White, Minor. 1908–1976. American photographer, b. Minneapolis. Teacher at California School of Fine Arts (1947–52), Rochester Inst. of Technology (1955–64); professor, M.I.T. (1965–76); founder and editor of *Aperture* (1952–76); editor of *Image* (1953–57); a leading theoretician of photographic aesthetics, noted as meticulous technician in producing works of abstract art.

White, Pearl Fay. 1889–1938. American actress, b. Green Ridge, Mo. Star of film serials *The Perils of Pauline* (1914), *Exploits of Elaine* (1914–15), *Iron Claw* (1916), *Pearl of the Army* (1916–17), *Fatal Ring* (1917), *House of Hate* (1918), *Black Secret* (1919–20), *Plunder* (1923), etc.

White, Peregrine. 1620–1704. American colonist. Born on the *Mayflower,* in Cape Cod harbor, thus the first child of English parents born in New England.

White, Richard Grant. 1821–1885. American essayist and critic, b. New York City. Musical critic (1846–59), editor (1851–59), *Morning Courier and New-York Enquirer;* clerk on staff of New York Custom House (1861–78). Editor of a twelve-volume edition of *The Works of William Shakespeare* (1857–66). Among his books were *Handbook of Christian Art* (1853), *Shakespeare's Scholar* (1854, reprinting his 1853 criticism of J. P. Collier's emendations), *Words and Their Uses* (1870), *Every-day English* (1880), *England Without and Within* (1881), *Studies in Shakespeare* (1886).

White, Stanford. 1853–1906. American architect, b. New York City. Son of Richard Grant White. Trained by H. H. Richardson; formed firm of McKim, Mead & White (1879) with C. F. McKim and W. R. Mead. Among buildings designed by him were the Casino at Newport, R.I. (1881), the Villard Houses (1885), Madison Square Garden (1889), Madison Square Presbyterian Church (demolished 1919), Century Club, Players Club, and Metropolitan Club, and Washington Arch, all in New York; several buildings for U. of Virginia; Battle Monument at U.S.M.A., West Point. Murdered by Harry K. Thaw.

White, Stewart Edward. 1873–1946. American writer, b. Grand Rapids, Mich. Author chiefly of adventure stories against a western U.S. background, as *The Claim Jumpers* (1901), *The Blazed Trail* (1902), *The Forest* (1903), *The Rules of the Game* (1909), *The Forty Niners* (1918), *Back of Beyond* (1927), *Ranchero* (1933), *Stampede* (1942).

White, Terence Hanbury. 1906–1964. English writer, b. India. Author of brilliant adaptation of Arthurian legend in tetralogy *The Once and Future King,* comprising *The Sword in the Stone* (1939), *The Witch in the Wood* (1940, later called *Queen of Air and Darkness*), *The Ill-Made Knight* (1941), *The Candle in the Wind* (1958); also wrote *England Have My Bones* (1936), *The Age of Scandal* (1950), *The Scandalmonger* (1951), *The Goshawk* (1951).

White, Theodore Harold. 1915–1986. American journalist, b. Boston. Best known for carefully detailed accounts of American presidential campaigns; published *The Making of a President 1960* (1961, Pulitzer Prize) and succeeding volumes devoted to campaigns of 1964, 1968, and 1972; also wrote Watergate book *Breach of Faith: The Fall of Richard Nixon* (1975) and autobiographical *In Search of History* (1978), etc.

White, Thomas. 1628–1698. English prelate. Chaplain (1683) to Anne (later Queen Anne); bishop of Peterborough (1685); one of the "seven bishops" (see William SANCROFT) who petitioned against James II's Declaration of Indulgence (1688) but were acquitted of charge of seditious libel; refused to take oath of allegiance to William and Mary (1689); deprived of his see (1690).

White, Walter Francis. 1893–1955. American author, b. Atlanta, Ga. Assistant secretary (1918–29), secretary (1931–55), National Association for the Advancement of Colored People; leader of campaign against lynching; recipient of Spingarn Medal (1937). Author of *Fire in the Flint* (novel, 1924), *Flight* (novel, 1926), *Rope and Faggot: A Biography of Judge Lynch* (1929), *A Rising Wind* (1945), autobiography *A Man Called White* (1948).

White, William. 1748–1836. American clergyman, b. Philadelphia. Ordained in Anglican ministry, London (1772); rector of Christ Church, Philadelphia (1776–1836); consecrated in England first bishop of Pennsylvania (1787); instrumental in organization of Protestant Episcopal church in the United States (1789); drafted original constitution of the church and secured its adoption; collaborated with William Smith in preparing American revision of Book of Common Prayer; presiding bishop of the church (1796–1836).

White, William Alanson. 1870–1937. American neurologist and psychiatrist, b. Brooklyn, N.Y. Superintendent (from 1903), Government Hospital for the Insane (later St. Elizabeth's), Washington, D.C., which he made a center of research and reform in mental care; professor, Georgetown U. (from 1903), George Washington U. (from 1904). Author of *Outlines of Psychiatry* (1907), *Principles of Mental Hygiene* (1917), *Foundations of Psychiatry* (1921), *The Major Psychoses* (1928), *Crimes and Criminals* (1933), etc.

White, William Allen. *Known as* the Sage of Emporia. 1868–1944. American writer and journalist, b. Emporia, Kans. Editor and proprietor, Emporia *Gazette* (from 1895), which he developed into one of the most notable small papers of the United States, distinguished for its editorials and its policies; won Pulitzer prize (1923) for editorials. Author of *The Real Issue and Other Stories* (1896), *In Our Town* (1906), *A Certain Rich Man* (1909), *In the Heart of a Fool* (1918), *The Editor and His People* (1924), *Forty Years on Main Street* (1937), *A Puritan in Babylon* (1938), *The Changing West* (1939), *Autobiography* (1946, Pulitzer prize), etc. His son ¶William Lindsay (1900–1973), b. Emporia; on staff of Emporia *Gazette* (from 1914; editor and publisher, 1944–73), Washington *Post* (1935), *Fortune* (1937); war correspondent in Europe (1939–40), England (1940–41). Author of *What People Said* (novel, 1938), *Journey for Margaret* (1941), *They Were Expendable* (1942), *Report on the Russians* (1945), *Land of Milk and Honey* (1949), etc.

White, William Hale. *Pseudonym* Mark Ruth•er•ford \ˈrət̲h-ə(r)-fərd, ˈrəth-\. 1831–1913. English novelist. Author of novels on village religion and nonconformity including a trilogy *Autobiography of Mark Rutherford* (1881), *Mark Rutherford's Deliverance* (1885), and *The Revolution in Tanner's Lane* (1887); also *Miriam's Schooling* (1890), *Catherine Furze* (1893), *Clara Hopgood* (1896); translated Spinoza's *Ethica* (1883).

White•field \ˈhwit-ˌfēld, ˈhwit-, ˈwit-, ˈwīt-\, George. 1714–1770. English evangelist. Succeeded Wesleys as leader of Methodists in Oxford; ordained in Church of England (deacon 1736, priest 1739); followed Wesleys on missionary journey to Georgia (1738), appointed minister at Savannah. Returning to England to raise funds, began open-air preaching at Bristol (1739), winning audiences of all classes by oratorical and histrionic gifts; returned to Georgia (1739); made evangelical tour through Virginia, Pennsylvania, New York, to Boston (1740); parted with Wesley over predestination, became leader of rigid Calvinists (1741); soon reconciled personally with Wesley; presented by his supporters with Moorfields Tabernacle in London (1741). Toured America (1744–48); made evangelizing tours of Great Britain, Ireland, and America; compiled hymnbook (1753); returned to America for seventh time (1769). Credited with inspiring foundation of some 50 colleges and universities in U.S.

White•head \ˈhwīt-ˌhed, ˈwīt-\, Alfred North. 1861–1947. English mathematician and philosopher. Lecturer on mathematics, Trinity College, Cambridge (1885–1911), University College, London (1911–14); professor, Imperial College of Science and Technology, U. of London (1914–24); professor of philosophy, Harvard (1924–36). Author of *Treatise on Universal Algebra* (1898), *Principia Mathematica* (with Bertrand Russell, 1910–13), *The Principles of Natural Knowledge* (1919), *The Concept of Nature* (1920), *Principle of Relativity* (1922), *Science and the Modern World* (1925), *Religion in the Making* (1926), *Aims of Education* (1928), *Process and Reality* (1929), *Adventures of Ideas* (1933), *Nature and Life* (1934), etc.

Whitehead, Charles. 1804–1862. English poet and novelist. Published *The Solitary* (poem, 1831) and novels *Autobiography of Jack Ketch* (1834) and *Richard Savage* (1842); also wrote plays as *The Cavalier* (1836) in blank verse.

\ə\ abut \ᵊ\ kitten, *Fr.* table \ər\ further \a\ ash \ā\ ace \ä\ cot, cart \au̇\ out \ch\ chin \e\ bet \ē\ easy \g\ go \i\ hit \ī\ ice \j\ job \ŋ\ sing \ō\ go \ȯ\ law \ȯi\ boy \th\ both \t̲h\ the \ü\ loot \u̇\ foot \y\ yet \zh\ vision \á, b̲, g̲, k̲, ⁿ, œ, œ̄, ue, ue̅, ʸ\ *see* Guide to Pronunciation

Whitehead, Henry, *in full* John Henry Constantine. 1904–1960. British mathematician, b. India. Fellow of Balliol Coll., Oxford (1932–41); Waynflete professor (1947–60); known for contributions to topology, esp. to homotopy theory. Author of *Foundations of Differential Geometry* (with Oswald Veblen, 1932) and many papers.

Whitehead, Robert. 1823–1905. English inventor. Invented a self-propelled underwater torpedo (1866); established (1872) firm in Fiume to manufacture torpedoes.

Whitehead, William. 1715–1785. English poet. Wrote tragedies for Drury Lane, *The Roman Father* (1750) and *Creusa* (1754); succeeded Colley Cibber as poet laureate (1757); replied to attacks on his productions with *A Charge to the Poets* (1762); produced (1762) his most successful play, the comedy *School for Lovers.*

White·ing \'hwīt-iŋ, 'wīt-\, Richard. 1840–1928. English journalist and novelist. Contributed to London *Evening Star* satirical sketches later collected in book form as *Mr. Sprouts —His Opinions* (1867); known for *The Island* (1888), *No. 5 John Street* (1899), and *All Moonshine* (1907).

White·ley \'hwīt-lē, 'wīt-\, William. 1831–1907. English merchant. Founder of London's first department store (1863); known by self-applied epithet "Universal Provider," his boast being that there was nothing his stores could not supply.

White·locke \'hwīt-,läk, 'wīt-\, Bulstrode. 1605–1675. English lawyer and politician. Member of Long Parliament (1640); chairman of committee that prosecuted Strafford (1641); one of four commissioners of Great Seal under Commonwealth (1648), one of three (1649, 1654–55), but dismissed on opposing Cromwell's changes in courts of chancery (1655); negotiated treaty with Sweden (1654); president of council of state in fall of Richard Cromwell, and member of the superseding committee of safety. Lived in retirement after Restoration.

White·man \'hwīt-mən, 'wīt-\, Paul. 1890–1967. American orchestra conductor, b. Denver, Colo. Toured U.S., England, and the Continent (from 1920) with large band, noted for ensemble and arrangements, that helped popularize jazz; remembered esp. for commissioning and giving premiere performance of Gershwin's *Rhapsody in Blue* (1924).

Whit·gift \'hwit-,gift, 'wit-\, John. c.1530–1604. English prelate. Regius professor of divinity, Cambridge (1567); chaplain to the queen (1567); vice chancellor of Cambridge (1570, 1573); bishop of Worcester (1577); archbishop of Canterbury (1583–1604). Carried out Queen Elizabeth's policy of enforcing religious uniformity, giving rise to Marprelate tracts; first bishop appointed to privy council by Elizabeth (1586); one of drafters (1595) of Lambeth Articles; crowned James I.

Whi·ting \'hwīt-iŋ, 'wīt-\, John Robert. 1917–1963. English playwright. Author of intense, intellectually demanding dramas as *A Penny for a Song* (1951), *Saints' Day* (1951), *Marching Song* (1954), *Gates of Summer* (1956), *The Devils* (1961, based on Aldous Huxley's *Devils of Loudun*); also translated plays of Jean Anouilh.

Whit·ley \'hwit-lē, 'wit-\, John Henry. 1866–1935. English politician. Liberal M.P. (1900–28); deputy speaker of House of Commons (1911–21), speaker (1921–28); declined peerage (1928). Chairman of parliamentary committee (1916–19) proposing "Whitley councils" for employer-employee negotiations; chairman of royal commission on labor in India (1929–31); chairman, British Broadcasting Corporation (1930–35).

Whit·lock \'hwit-,läk, 'wit-\, Brand. 1869–1934. American journalist, politician, and diplomat, b. Urbana, Ohio. Mayor of Toledo, Ohio (1905–11), succeeding Samuel Jones; U.S. minister to Belgium (1913–22); after outbreak of World War I (1914), gained international fame by his tact, vigor, and efficiency in handling difficult problems, and greatly aided work of Belgian relief. Author of *The 13th District* (novel, 1902), *Forty Years of It* (autobiography, 1914), *Belgium: A Personal Narrative* (1919), *J. Hardin and Son* (novel, 1923), *Uprooted* (novel, 1926), *La Fayette* (1929), etc.

Whitlock, Mrs. Elizabeth. See Elizabeth KEMBLE.

Whit·man \'hwit-mən, 'wit-\, Charles Otis. 1842–1910. American zoologist, b. North Woodstock, Me. Professor, Imperial U., Tokyo (1879–81); assistant to Agassiz at Harvard Museum of Comparative Anatomy (1882–86); professor, Clark U. (1889–92), U. of Chicago (1892–1910); a founder and first director (1893–1908) of Marine Biological Laboratory, Woods Hole, Mass.; known for studies of genetics and behavior in leeches, pigeons, etc.

Whitman, Marcus. 1802–1847. American missionary and pioneer, b. Rushville, N.Y. Went to Oregon region as missionary (1835, 1836–47); established Waiilatpu mission to Cayuse, Walla Walla, and Umatilla tribes; returned to the East (1842–43), conferred with the secretary of war; returning to the West, accompanied emigrants to the valley of the Columbia, Oregon (1843) and continued his work; regarded as instrumental in securing the Oregon country for U.S. He, his wife, and twelve other persons were massacred by Cayuse Indians.

Whitman, Sarah Helen, *nee* Pow·er \'pau̇(-ə)r\. 1803–1878. American poet, b. Providence, R.I. m. John W. Whitman (1828; d. 1833). Fiancée of Edgar Allen Poe (1848), to whom Poe wrote the second of his poems entitled "To Helen"; published *Edgar Poe and His Critics* (1860) in defense of Poe. Her collected poems (1879) contained many associated with Poe and many closely imitating Poe's verse forms and cadences.

Whitman, Walt, *in full* Walter. 1819–1892. American poet, b. West Hills, Long Island, N.Y. Variously, office boy, printer's devil, schoolteacher, typesetter, and journalist (1830–46). Editor, *Brooklyn Eagle* (1846–48); on staff of New Orleans *Crescent* (1848); again journalist in Brooklyn (1848–54). Published volume of verse *Leaves of Grass* (1855), received unfavorably by American reviewers, revised and enlarged in later editions (1856, 1860, 1867, 1871, 1876, 1881–82, 1882, 1888–89, 1892). Served as hospital nurse in Washington, D.C. (1862–64). Clerk in U.S. Department of the Interior (1865), dismissed by the secretary of the interior because of the nature of his poetry in *Leaves of Grass;* given position as clerk in office of attorney general of the United States (1865–73). Stricken with paralysis (1873); lived thereafter in Camden, N.J. Appreciation of his genius came slowly, first abroad and later in U.S. Conceived of himself as the great poet of democracy. Other of his books were war poems *Drum-Taps* (1865, subsequently incorporated in *Leaves of Grass*), prose *Democratic Vistas* (1871) and *Specimen Days* (1882). Well known poems included "Song of Myself," "I Sing the Body Electric," "By Blue Ontario's Shore," "Out of the Cradle Endlessly Rocking," "Song of the Open Road," "When Lilacs Last in the Dooryard Bloom'd," "O Captain! My Captain!"

Whit·ney \'hwit-nē, 'wit-\, Anne. 1821–1915. American sculptor, b. Watertown, Mass. Among her works were the statue of Samuel Adams in Statuary Hall in the U.S. Capitol, Charles Sumner in Harvard Square, Cambridge, Mass., *Lady Godiva, Africa, Roma,* and portrait busts of Harriet Beecher Stowe, Frances Willard, Lucy Stone, etc.

Whitney, Asa. 1791–1874. American inventor, b. Townsend, Mass. Employed on Mohawk and Hudson Railroad (1830–39); New York State canal commissioner (1839–42); in partnership with Matthias W. Baldwin (1842–46) in manufacture of locomotives; formed Asa Whitney and Sons Co. (1849) to manufacture improved cast-iron railroad car wheel of his own invention.

Whitney, Eli. 1765–1825. American inventor, b. Westboro, Mass. Guest on plantation of Mrs. Nathanael Greene, in Georgia (1792–93), where a chance suggestion led him to experiment with machine for cleaning seed from cotton fibers; invented cotton gin (1793, patented 1794); entered partnership with Phineas Miller, manager of Mrs. Greene's plantation, to manufacture cotton gins, but failed to profit because of infringements and long litigation. Importance of invention immediately manifest in enormous increase of cotton production. Obtained government contract for 10,000 stand of muskets; devised system of manufacturing interchangeable parts in production of guns, probably first instance of this system; secured other firearms contracts and operated factory at Whitneyville, near New Haven, Conn.

Whitney, Gertrude Vanderbilt. See under William Collins WHITNEY.

Whitney, Harry Payne. See under William Collins WHITNEY.

Whitney, Josiah Dwight. 1819–1896. American geologist, b. Northampton, Mass. On geological survey work in Michigan (1847–49); geological consultant (1850–55); professor, U. of Iowa (1855–58); state geologist of California (1860–74); measured highest peak in California (1864), subsequently named Mt. Whitney after him; professor, Lawrence Scientific School, Harvard (1875–96). Author of *Metallic Wealth of the United States* (1854), *Climatic Changes of Later Geological Times* (1882), etc. His brother ¶William Dwight (1827–1894) was a philologist; professor, Yale (1854–94); noted as a scholar in Sanskrit and in linguistic science, as a teacher of modern languages, and as a lexicographer. Author of *Sanskrit Grammar* (1879) and a number of Sanskrit texts, *Language and the Study of Language* (1867), *Oriental and Linguistic Studies* (1873–74), *The Life and Growth of Language* (1875), *Essentials of English Grammar* (1877); editor of the 1864 edition of *Webster's Dictionary;* editor in chief of *The Century Dictionary and Cyclopedia* (1889–91).

Whitney, Mary Watson. 1847–1920. American astronomer, b. Waltham, Mass. Professor of astronomy and director of observatory (1888–1910), Vassar. Published observations on positions of comets and asteroids, on variable stars, and on the measurement of photographic plates.

Whitney, William Collins. 1841–1904. American financier and politician, b. Conway, Mass. Practiced law in New York City (from 1865); corporation counsel, New York City (1875–82). Prominent in affairs of New York's street-railway system (1883–1902). U.S. secretary of the navy (1885–89). Widely known as a sportsman, owner of a stud farm and a racing stable. His son ¶Harry Payne (1872–1930) was trained to take over his father's large financial interests; associated with Guggenheim interests in ownership of mining properties in western U.S. and Mexico; noted polo player, captain of American team which won international cup from England (1909) and defended it (1911, 1913); continued his father's interest in horse breeding and racing; financed expedition to the South Sea (1921–22), under sponsorship of American Museum of Natural History, to collect birds of Polynesia. His wife (m. 1896) ¶Gertrude, *nee* Van·der·bilt \'van-dər-,bilt\ (1875–1942), daughter of Cornelius Vanderbilt; carved *Aztec* fountain in Pan-American building and the *Titanic* memorial in Washington, D.C.; equestrian statue of Col. William F. Cody; Columbus monument for Palos, Spain; war memorial at St.-Nazaire, France; *Spirit of Flight* for 1939 World's Fair, N.Y.C., etc.; opened Whitney Museum of American Art in New York City (1931).

Whitney, William Dwight. See under Josiah Dwight WHITNEY.

Whit·ta·ker \'hwit-i-kər, 'wit-\, Charles Evans. 1901–1973. American jurist, b. near Troy, Kans. Associate justice, U.S. Supreme Court (1957–62).

Whittaker, Edmund Taylor. 1873–1956. English mathematician. Professor at Dublin and astronomer royal of Ireland (1906–12); professor, Edinburgh (1912–46); known for contributions to study of functions of complex variables, special functions; discovered (1902) general solution to Laplace's equation; originated (1903) confluent hypergeometric function. Author of *Course of Modern Analysis* (1902), *Treatise on the Analytical Dynamics of Particles and Rigid Bodies* (1904), *History of the Theories of Aether and Electricity* (1910, rev. 1951).

Whit·ti·er \'hwit-ē-ər, 'wit-\, John Greenleaf. 1807–1892. American poet, b. near Haverhill, Mass. Largely self-educated; vigorous abolitionist and deeply religious Quaker. Worked as journalist; editor, *New England Weekly Review* (1830–32). Among his books were *Legends of New England in Prose and Verse* (1831), *Moll Pitcher* (1832), *Mogg Megone* (1836), *Lays of My Home* (1843), *The Voices of Freedom* (1846), *Songs of Labor* (1850), *The Panorama* (1856), *Home Ballads* (1860), *In War Time* (1864), *Snow-Bound* (1866), *Miriam* (1871), *Hazel Blossoms* (1875), *The Vision of Echard* (1878), *At Sundown* (1890). Among widely known poems were "Massachusetts to Virginia," "Maud Muller," "Barefoot Boy," "Telling the Bees," "Barbara Frietchie," "Ichabod," "Laus Deo"; one of the "Household Poets."

Whit·ting·ton \'hwit-iŋ-tən, 'wit-\, Richard. c.1358–1423. English mercer and philanthropist. Alderman of London (1393) and lord mayor (1397–99, 1406–07, 1419–20); M.P. (1416); made loans to Henry IV and Henry V; left legacies for rebuilding Newgate Prison, founding an almshouse, organizing Whittington College (suppressed, 1548). Became the subject of several legends.

Whit·tle·sey *or* **Wit·tle·sey** \'hwit-ᵊl-zē, 'wit-, -sē\, William. d. 1374. English prelate. Nephew of Simon Islip; archbishop of Canterbury (1368–74).

Whit·tredge \'hwit-(,)rij, 'wit-\, Worthington, *in full* Thomas Worthington. 1820–1910. American painter, b. Springfield, Ohio. Painter of Romantic landscapes in Hudson River School manner, but noted as exponent of Luminist style learned in Düsseldorf; executed huge canvases of Western scenes (1865 ff.). Posed as Washington for Leutze's *Washington Crossing the Delaware.*

Whit·worth \'hwit-,wərth, 'wit-\, Sir Joseph. Baronet. 1803–1887. English mechanical engineer and inventor. Discovered method of producing an absolutely plane surface of metal; secured (1841) standardization of screw threads (Whitworth thread); devised new, highly accurate measuring machine and system of master gauges; widely known for screw-cutting lathes, drilling, planing, slotting, shaping machines; devised hexagonal bore for rifles, improving their accuracy and range; discovered new way of making ductile steel for guns.

Whorf \'hwȯ(ə)rf, 'wȯ(ə)rf\, Benjamin Lee. 1897–1941. American linguist, b. Winthrop, Mass. Fire prevention authority for Hartford Fire Insurance Co. (1918–41); pioneered in comparative linguistics in studies of Hebrew, Maya, Aztec, Hopi; developed hypothesis that language conditions culture by influencing cognition through preexisting categories.

Whym·per \'hwim-pər, 'wim-\, Edward. 1840–1911. English wood engraver and alpinist. First to ascend Les Écrins (1864) and other peaks in Mont Blanc group; found route up the Matterhorn (1865); visited Greenland (1867, 1872); first to reach summit of Chimborazo (1880). Wrote and illustrated *Scrambles Amongst the Alps* (1871), *Travels Amongst the Great Andes* (1892).

Whyte-Mel·ville \'hwīt-'mel-,vil, 'wīt-\, George John. 1821–1878. British novelist, b. Scotland. Captain, Coldstream Guards (1846–49); served in Turkish cavalry in Crimean War (1854). Author of novels of fox hunting and steeplechasing, including *Digby Grand* (1853) and *Tilbury Nogo* (1861), and of historical novels, the best known being *The Gladiators* (1863).

Wiart, Henri Carton de. See CARTON DE WIART.

Wick·er·sham \'wik-ər-shəm\, George Woodward. 1858–1936. American lawyer, b. Pittsburgh. Practiced law in Philadelphia and New York City (from 1880); as U.S. attorney general (1909–13) pursued vigorous antitrust policy, initiating suits against Standard Oil, U.S. Steel, International Harvester, etc.; supporter of World Court and League of Nations; head of Wickersham Committee appointed (1929) by Pres. Hoover to study federal law enforcement; president of International Arbitral Tribunal under the Young-plan treaties (1932–36).

Wick·ham \'wik-əm\, Sir Henry. 1846–1928. English explorer. Smuggled (1872) from Brazil seeds of rubber trees from which developed rubber industry in the Far East.

Wickham, William of. See WILLIAM of Wykeham.

Wick·sell \'vik-səl\, Knut, *in full* Johan Gustaf Knut. 1851–1926. Swedish economist. Professor, Lund (1900–16); originated theory of marginal productivity. Author of *Über Wert, Kapital und Rente* (1893), *Geldzins und Güterpreise* (1898), *Vorlesungen über Nationalökonomie auf der Grundlage des Marginalprinzipes* (1913–22).

Wiclif *or* **Wickliffe.** See WYCLIFFE.

Wi·dal \vē-dȧl\, Fernand, *in full* Georges-Fernand-Isidore. 1862–1929. French physician. Professor, U. of Paris (1911–29); known esp. for work on bacterial agglutination and its application (in Widal reaction) to the diagnosis of typhoid fever (1896); recognized (1906) value of salt deprivation in nephritis and cardiac edema; with Georges Hayem described (1907) Hayem-Widal (acquired) jaundice. See Max von GRUBER.

Wide·ner \'wīd-nər\, Peter Arrell Brown. 1834–1915. American businessman, b. Philadelphia. Engaged in meat business; became financially interested in street railways in Philadelphia, New York, and Chicago, and in other enterprises; collected paintings, Chinese porcelains, tapestries, antiques, and other objets d'art which he bequeathed to city of Philadelphia; built and endowed Widener Memorial Industrial Training School for Crippled Children (1906). His grandson ¶Harry Elkins (1885–1912), bibliophile; lost on the *Titanic;* the Harry Elkins Widener Memorial Library at Harvard (opened 1915) was given to the university in his honor by his mother.

Wid·man \'vēt-,män\, Johannes. *Surname also spelled* Wei·de·man \'vīd-ə-,män\ *or* Wi·de·man \'vēd-ə-\. c.1462–after 1498. German mathematician. Lectured at Leipzig (1485 ff.); gave first course on algebra in Germany (1486). Author of *Behend und hüpsch Rechnung uff allen Kauffmanschafften* (1489), one of the earliest printed arithmetic textbooks in German and first to employ plus and minus signs.

Wid·mann \'vēt-,män\, Joseph Viktor. 1842–1911. Swiss writer, b. Moravia. Editor of daily *Der Bund* in Bern (1880–1910). Author of verse "Buddha" (1869), "Mose und Zipora" (1874), *Der Heilige und die Tiere* (1905), dramatic works *Iphigenie in Delphi* (1865), *Orgetorix* (1867), *Oenone* (1880), *Die Muse des Aretin* (1902), novels *Aus dem Fasse der Danaiden* (1884), *Die Patrizierin* (1888), travel books *Spaziergänge in den Alpen* (1885), *Sommerwanderungen und Winterfahrten* (1896), *Du schöne Welt* (1907).

Wi·dor \vē-dȯr\, Charles-Marie-Jean-Albert. 1844–1937. French organist and composer. Organist at Saint Sulpice, Paris (from 1870); succeeded César Franck at Paris conservatory of music (1890). Composed ballets *La Korrigane* (1880), *Jeanne d'Arc* (1890), operas as *Maître Ambros* (1886), *Les Pêcheurs de Saint-Jean* (1905), 10 organ symphonies as *Symphonie gothique* (1895), *Symphonie romaine* (1900), chamber and orchestral works, sacred and secular vocal works.

Widukind. See WITTEKIND.

Wied, Count of. See HERMANN V.

Wied, Princess of. See ELIZABETH, Queen of Romania.

Wied \'vēd\, Gustav Johannes. 1858–1914. Danish writer. Author of "satyr dramas" as *Fire Satyrspiel* (1897), *Det svage køn* (1900), *Skaermydsler* (1901), *Dansemus* (1905), *Ranke Viljer* (1906); novels as *Slaegten* (1898), *Livsens Ondskab* (1899), *Knagsted* (1902), *Faedrene aede Druer* (1908); stories *Barnlige Sjaele* (1893), *Menneskenes Børn* (1894), *En "Bohéme"* (1894).

Wied, Maximilian, Prinz zu. See MAXIMILIAN.

Wie·de·mann \'vē-də-,män\, Gustav Heinrich. 1826–1899. German physicist and chemist. Professor, Basel (1854), Brunswick (1863), Karlsruhe (1866), Leipzig (1871); with Rudolph Franz discovered (1853) Wiedemann-Franz ratio of thermal and electrical conductivity; enunciated (c.1863) Wiedemann's rule for magnetism of compounds. Edited *Annalen der Physik und Chemie* (1877–99); author of *Die Lehre vom Galvanismus* (1861–63).

Wie·land \'vē-,länt\, Christoph Martin. 1733–1813. German poet, prose writer, and translator. Brought up a Pietist; professor, Erfurt (1769–72); lived chiefly in Weimar (from 1772); friend of Goethe, Schiller, and Herder. Founded and edited *Der Teutsche Merkur,* a monthly literary magazine (1773–89); founded and edited (1796–1809) *Das Attische Museum.* His works, chief representatives of the Rococo in German literature, included dramas, and epics and narratives in verse, as *Lady Johanna Gray,* earliest German blank-verse drama (1758), *Idris und Zenide,* which introduced the Italian stanza into German literature (1768), *Musarion* (1768), *Der neue Amodis* (1771), *Das Wintermärchen* (1776), *Das Sommermärchen* (1777), and *Oberon* (1780); novels and romances as *Don Sylvio von Rosalva* (1764), *Geschichte des Agathon,* which established the genre of *Bildungsroman*

(1766–67), the satire *Die Abderiten* (1774), and *Aristipp* (1800–01); a fantastic tale *Dschinnistan* (1786–89), on which Mozart based his *Magic Flute;* and the first German prose translations of Shakespeare's plays (22 plays, 1762–66), as well as translations of Horace, Lucian, and Cicero.

Wieland, Heinrich Otto. 1877–1957. German chemist. Professor, Freiburg (1921), Munich (1925); known for research on bile acids, chlorophyll, and hemoglobin. Awarded 1927 Nobel prize for chemistry.

Wie·lo·pol·ski \vyel-ô-'pôl-skē\, Aleksander. Marquis. 1803–1877. Polish politician. Publicly called for Polish submission to Russian rule (1846); entered government and successfully introduced various reforms; made head of civil government (1861–63) to curb popular revolt; introduced major reforms but failed to pacify revolutionaries, who considered him traitor; retired and later emigrated to Saxony.

Wien \'vēn\, Wilhelm. 1864–1928. German physicist. Professor, Giessen (1899), Würzburg (1900), Munich (1920); awarded 1911 Nobel prize for physics for research on the radiation of energy from black bodies and enunciation of Wien's law (1893); worked also on X-rays, hydrodynamics, etc. His cousin ¶Max Wien (1866–1938), also a physicist, is credited with discovery of impulse excitation (1906), of importance in the development of wireless telegraphy; constructed acoustical device for measuring strength of tones.

Wien·barg \'vēn-,bärk\, Ludolf. 1802–1872. German writer. Lecturer on aesthetics and literature, Kiel (1833); became a leading exponent, with Gutzkow and others, in the Young Germany group, which he named. Works included *Holland in den Jahren 1831 und 1832* (1834), *Ästhetische Feldzüge* (1834), *Literarishe und kritische Blätter der Börsenhalle* (1842–46).

Wie·ner \'wē-nər, 'vē-\, Leo. 1862–1939. American scholar, b. Bialystok, Poland. To U.S. (1882); taught Slavic languages and literature at U. of Missouri (1892–95), Harvard (1896–1930; professor from 1911). Author of *An Interpretation of the Russian People* (1915), etc.

Wiener, Norbert. 1894–1964. American mathematician, b. Columbia, Mo. Son of Leo Wiener; professor, M.I.T. (1919–60); contributed greatly to study of stochastic processes and harmonic analysis; best known as founder of cybernetics (a term he coined), study of information processing and control. Author of *Cybernetics* (1948), *Human Use of Human Beings* (1950), *God and Golem, Inc.* (1964), and autobiographical *Ex-Prodigy* (1953) and *I Am a Mathematician* (1956).

Wie·niaw·ski \vyen-'yäf-skē\, Henryk. 1835–1880. Polish violinist and composer. Toured widely as virtuoso (from 1850); professor, St. Petersburg Conservatory (1862–68), Brussels Conservatory (1875–80). Composed brilliant Romantic concertos, études, and genre pieces for the violin.

Wier·zyń·ski \vyer-'zinʸ-skē\, Kazimierz. 1894–1969. Polish poet. A leader of the Skamander group (1928). Works included *Wiosna i wino* (1919), *Wielka Niedźwiedzica* (1923), *Laur Olimpijski* (1927), *Barbakan warszawski* (1940), *Korzec maku* (1950), *Sen mara* (1969), etc.

Wig·gin \'wig-ən\, Kate Douglas, *nee* Smith. 1856–1923. American writer and educator, b. Philadelphia. m. Samuel B. Wiggin (1881; d. 1889). Studied kindergarten training methods (1877); organized in San Francisco first free kindergarten on Pacific coast (1878); founded, with her sister, California Kindergarten Training School (1880). First literary success was *The Birds' Christmas Carol* (1887); also wrote *Timothy's Quest* (1890), *Polly Oliver's Problem* (1893), *Penelope's Progress* (1898), the enormously popular *Rebecca of Sunnybrook Farm* (1903), autobiography *My Garden of Memory* (1923).

Wig·gles·worth \'wig-əlz-,wərth\, Michael. 1631–1705. American clergyman and poet, b. Yorkshire?, England. To America (1638); pastor at Malden, Mass. (from 1656). Author of *The Day of Doom,* a long poem written in ballad meter (1662), *Meat Out of the Eater or Meditations Concerning the Necessity, End, and Usefulness of Afflictions Unto God's Children* (1669), etc.; shorter theological poems as "Short Discourse on Eternity," "Vanity of Vanities."

Wight·man \'wīt-mən\, Hazel, *nee* Hotch·kiss \'häch-(,)kis\. 1886–1974. American tennis player, b. Healdsburg, Cal. m. George W. Wightman. U.S. amateur women's champion (1909, 1910, 1911, 1919); with Helen Wills won Wimbledon doubles title (1924); 6 times U.S. doubles champion; won 45 national titles, the last at age 68. Gave Wightman Cup (1923) for annual U.S.–Great Britain tournament.

Wig·more \'wig-,mō(ə)r, -,mȯ(ə)r\, John Henry. 1863–1943. American legal scholar, b. San Francisco. Practiced law in Boston (1887–89); professor at Keio U., Tokyo (1889–92), and at Northwestern U. (1893–1929) and dean of its faculty of law (1901–29). Author of *Treatise on the Anglo-American System of Evidence* (1904–05), *Principles of Judicial Proof* (1913), etc.

Wiht·red \'wikt-,rād\. d. 725. King of Kent (690–725). Drew up code of laws (695?).

Wi·la·mo·witz-Moel·len·dorff \,vē-lä-'mō-vits-'mœl-ən-,dȯrf\, Ulrich von, *in full* Emmo Friedrich Richard Ulrich von. 1848–1931. German scholar. Professor, Greifswald (1876), Göttingen (1883), Berlin (1897); editor of *Philologische Untersuchungen* (1880–1925); editorial director of *Inscriptiones Graecae* (from 1902). Author of *Zukunftsphilologie,* an attack on Nietzsche's *Geburt der Tragödie* (1872–73), and of critical works on Greek history, literature, and writers.

Wil·ber·force \'wil-bər-,fō(ə)rs, -,fȯ(ə)rs\, William. 1759–1833. English philanthropist and politician. M.P. (1780–1825); converted to evangelical Christianity (1785) through Isaac Milner, his former schoolmaster, then dean of Carlisle; led agitation in House of Commons against slave trade (1787); through support of Thomas Clarkson, Pitt, and Quakers, won abolition of slave trade (1807); a founder of Anti-slavery Society (1823), urging extinction of slavery itself. Leader of the "Clapham Sect" of evangelical Christians and a founder of its organ *Christian Observer* (1801); supported extension of missionary teaching in India, and Catholic emancipation; expended most of fortune in philanthropy; heard on deathbed of second reading of bill abolishing slavery, which became law a month later. Author of *Practical View of Christianity* (1797). His son ¶Samuel (1805–1873), *called* Soapy Sam because of his oratorical facility, was an Anglican prelate; bishop of Oxford (1845), of Winchester (1869); diverged from Tractarians, took a leading part in several controversies, notably with T. H. Huxley over evolution (1860); secured restoration to convocations of Canterbury and York of some of ancient authority as synodical asssembly. Author of *Agathos* (1840) and *History of Protestant Episcopal Church in America* (1844).

Wil·brandt \'vil-,bränt\, Adolf von. 1837–1911. German writer. Author of historic iambic tragedies in the manner of Schiller, including *Gracchus* (1872), *Arria und Messalina* (1874), *Nero* (1876), *Kriemhild* (1877), *König Teja* (1908); of novels and stories as *Geister und Menschen* (1864), *Meister Amor* (1880), *Adams Söhne* (1890), *Der Dornenweg* (1894), *Der Sänger* (1899), *Franz* (1900), *Fesseln* (1904), *Am Strom der Zeit* (1908), *Die Tochter* (1911); and of poems, literary histories, and biographies.

Wilbrord *or* **Wilbrod,** Saint. See WILLIBRORD.

Wil·bye \'wil-bē\, John. 1574?–1638. English composer. One of finest madrigalists of his time, composer of 66 madrigals (most pub. 1598, 1609), setting verses by Sidney and Spenser and translations from Italian.

Wil·cox \'wil-,käks\, Ella, *nee* Wheeler. 1850–1919. American journalist and poet, b. Johnstown Center, Wis. m. Robert M. Wilcox (1884; d. 1916); for many years wrote a daily poem for a syndicate of newspapers; published over twenty volumes of verse, including *Drops of Water* (1872), *Poems of Passion* (1883), *Poems of Pleasure* (1888), *Poems of Sentiment* (1906), *Pastels* (1909), *Gems* (1912), *Cameos* (1914); also wrote fiction, essays, and works on spiritualism.

Wilcox, Stephen. 1830–1893. American inventor, b. Westerly, R.I. Invented safety water-tube boiler with inclined tubes (patented 1856), steam generator of similar type (patented 1867); with George Herman Babcock, organized firm Babcock, Wilcox & Co. (1867) to manufacture his boilers and steam engines.

Wil·czyn·ski \wəl-'zin-skē\, Ernest Julius. 1876–1932. American mathematician, b. Hamburg, Germany. To U.S. as a child; professor, U. of California (1898–1907), U. of Illinois (1907–10), U. of Chicago (1910 ff.); considered founder of projective differential geometry.

Wild \'wī(ə)ld\, Jonathan. 1682?–1725. English criminal. During a term in a debtors' prison, became acquainted with thieves and their ways; built criminal organization for thieving and for disposal of stolen goods; arranged for apprehension and conviction of disobedient members and nonmember criminals; hanged at Tyburn. Inspired story by Defoe (1725) and Fielding's satire *Jonathan Wild* (1743).

Wilde \'wī(ə)ld\, Oscar Fingal O'Flahertie Wills. 1854–1900. Irish poet, wit, and dramatist. At Oxford won Newdigate prize and became apostle of a cult of art for art's sake; burlesqued in Gilbert and Sullivan's comic opera *Patience* (1881). Lectured in U.S. (1882) on aesthetic philosophy, gaining notoriety by eccentricities. A noted conversationalist and epigrammatist. Wrote essays and reviews; published *Poems* (1881), collections of fairy tales *The Happy Prince* (1888) and *House of Pomegranates* (1891), novel *The Picture of Dorian Gray* (1891), *Collected Poems* (1892); followed up *The Duchess of Padua,* a tragedy in blank verse (1891), with a series of light comedies with dexterously conceived situations and sparkling dialogue, including *Lady Windermere's Fan* (1892), *A Woman of No Importance* (1893), *An Ideal Husband* (1895), *The Importance of Being Earnest* (1895); produced drama *Salomé* in French, staged in Paris by Sarah Bernhardt (1894), later made into libretto of an opera by Richard Strauss. On failure of his libel suit against the Marquis of Queensbury, was tried on charge of sodomy, convicted, and imprisoned (1895–97); wrote in prison a prose apologia *De Profundis* (1905); lived in Paris under name of Sebastian Mel·moth \'mel-məth\; wrote anonymously *Ballad of Reading Gaol* (1898), reflecting his tragic experiences.

Wil·den·bruch \'vil-dən-bru̇k\, Ernst von. 1845–1909. German writer. Author of dramatic works as *Spartacus* (1875), *Harold* (1882), *Das neue Gebot* (1886), *Die Haubenlerche* (1890), *Der neue Herr* (1891), *Die Rabensteinerin* (1907), novels as *Der Meister von Tanagra* (1880), *Eifernde Liebe* (1893), *Das schwarze Holz* (1905), *Lukrezia* (1907), verse *Lieder und Gesänge* (1877), *Dichtungen und Balladen* (1884), etc.

Wildenvey, Herman. See Herman PORTAAS.

Wil·der \ˈwīl-dər\, Alexander Lafayette Chew, *known as* Alec. 1907–1980. American composer, b. Rochester, N.Y. Wrote popular songs as "I'll Be Around," "While We're Young," "It's So Peaceful in the Country"; composed ballets as *Juke Box* (1942), operas as *Ellen* (1955), orchestral works as *Child's Introduction to the Orchestra* (1954), *Carl Sandburg Suite* (1960), jazz pieces and arrangements, art songs, etc. Author of *American Popular Song* (with J.T. Maher, 1972).

Wilder, Burt Green. 1841–1925. American zoologist, b. Boston. Professor, Cornell (1867–1910); successfully collected and wove spider silk (1860s); built up large collection of brains of vertebrates for comparative study, including human brains as those of E.B. Titchener, Rosika Schwimmer, Alice Chenoweth, Theobald Smith, and himself. Author of *What Young People Should Know* (1874), *The Brain of the Sheep* (1903), etc.

Wilder, Laura, *nee* In·galls \ˈiŋ-gəlz\. 1867–1957. American writer, b. Pepin, Wis. m. (1885) Almanzo J. Wilder. Author of novels for children based on her own life on the frontier, including *Little House in the Big Woods* (1932), *Little House on the Prairie* (1935), *On the Banks of Plum Creek* (1937), *By the Shores of Silver Lake* (1939), *The Long Winter* (1940), *Little Town on the Prairie* (1941), *Those Happy Golden Years* (1943).

Wilder, Thornton Niven. 1897–1975. American novelist and playwright, b. Madison, Wis. Instructor in English, Lawrenceville Acad. (1921–28), U. of Chicago (1930–37). Author of novels *The Cabala* (1926), *The Bridge of San Luis Rey* (1927, Pulitzer prize), *The Woman of Andros* (1930), *Heaven's My Destination* (1934), *The Ides of March* (1948), *The Eighth Day* (1967), and plays *The Angel That Troubled the Waters* (1928), *Our Town* (1938, Pulitzer prize), *The Skin of Our Teeth* (1942, Pulitzer prize), *The Matchmaker* (1954, later a musical as *Hello, Dolly!*, 1964), *Plays for Bleecker Street* (1962), etc.

Wild·gans \ˈvilt-gäns\, Anton. 1881–1932. Austrian poet and dramatist. Author of collections of lyrics as *Herbstfrühling* (1909), *Österreichische Gedichte* (1915), *Mittag* (1917), *Wiener Gedichte* (1926), the satirical epic poem *Kirbisch* (1927), and of Expressionist plays including the trilogy *Armut* (1914), *Liebe* (1916), *Dies Irae* (1918), and the biblical tragedy *Kain* (1920).

Wi·ley \ˈwī-lē\, Harvey Washington. 1844–1930. American chemist and reformer, b. Kent, Ind. Professor of chemistry, Purdue (1874–83); Indiana state chemist and investigator of food adulteration (1881–83). Chief chemist, U.S. Department of Agriculture (1883–1912); performed great public service in leading campaign against food adulteration; instrumental in securing passage of the Food and Drugs Act by U.S. Congress (1906), and in its effective administration. Director of bureau of foods, sanitation, and health for *Good Housekeeping* magazine (1912–30). Professor of agricultural chemistry, George Washington U. (1899–1914). Wrote *Principles and Practice of Agricultural Analysis* (1894–97), *Foods and Their Adulteration* (1907), *Not by Bread Alone* (1915), *History of a Crime Against the Food Law* (1929), etc.

Wil·frid \ˈwil-frəd\ *or* **Wil·frith** \ˈwil-frəth\. Saint. 634–709. English prelate. Entered monastery at Lindisfarne (648); abbot at Ripon (c.658); determined by his argument at Whitby (664) overthrow of the Celtic or Columbite party by the Roman discipline in England. Bishop of York, taking over his see in 668 or 669; built churches of architectural splendor (669–678); journeyed to Rome (679) to recover his divided bishopric, thus establishing a precedent; engaged in lengthy dispute over his rights, bowing at length to synodal decision (705) and becoming bishop of Hexham.

Wil·gus \ˈwil-gəs\, William John. 1865–1949. American engineer, b. Buffalo, N.Y. Worked for various railroads (1885–1908); directed building of new Grand Central Terminal, N.Y.C. (1903–07); consulting engineer (1908–30); chairman of board of consulting engineers for building vehicular tunnel under Hudson River connecting New York and New Jersey (1919–22).

Wilhelm. See also WILLIAM.

Wil·helm \ˈvil-ˌhelm\, Carl. 1815–1873. German conductor and composer. Director of the choral society, Krefeld (1840–65); composed the music to Max Schneckenburger's *Die Wacht am Rhein* (1854).

Wil·hel·mi·na \ˌvil-hel-ˈmē-nä, *Angl* ˌwil-(ˌ)hel-ˈmē-nə, ˌwil-ə-ˈmē-\. *In full* Wilhelmina Helena Pauline Maria. 1880–1962. Queen of the Netherlands (1890–1948). Daughter of William III and Emma of Waldeck-Pyrmont; under regency of her mother (1890–98); declared of age (1898); m. (1901) Duke Henry of Mecklenburg-Schwerin; inspired Dutch resistance to German occupation in radio broadcasts from London during World War II; abdicated in favor of daughter Juliana (1948).

Wil·hel·mj \vil-ˈhel-mē\, August. 1845–1908. German violinist. One of great virtuosos of the day; toured frequently, including world tour (1878–82).

Wil·helm von Hir·sau \ˈvil-ˌhelm-fòn-ˈhir-ˌzaù\. *Lat.* Wil·hel·mus Hir·saugien·sis \vil-ˈhel-mùs-ˌhir-zaù-ˈgyen-səs\. d. 1091. Bavarian religious. Benedictine monk at St. Emmeram; abbot of Hirsau (1069); instituted reforms and promoted liberal studies; won support of Pope Gregory VII, whose reforms he promoted in Germany; adopted Cluniac rule (1079), adding to it his own innovation of external, or lay, brothers. Author of *Constitutiones Hirsaugienses* as well as *Dialogi de musica, De astronomia,* etc.

Wilkes \ˈwilks\, Charles. 1798–1877. American naval officer, b. New York City. Entered navy (1818); commanded exploring expedition (1838–42) to the Antarctic islands of the Pacific and northwest coast of America; established that Antarctica is a continent; Wilkes Land is named in his honor; published *Narrative of the United States Exploring Expedition* (5 vols., 1844). Commanded *San Jacinto* (1861), halted British mail steamer *Trent* near the Bahamas and took off by force two Confederate commissioners, James M. Mason and John Slidell (Nov. 1861); after vigorous British protest, the "Trent affair" was settled by return of the Confederate commissioners to the British. Rear admiral (1866).

Wilkes, John. 1725–1797. English politician. Joined the "Mad Monks of Medmenham Abbey" (see Sir Francis DASHWOOD); M.P. (1757); led profligate life. Founded *The North Briton* (1762), in which he attacked Lord Bute and charged George III with falsehood (issue No. 45, 1763); prosecuted for libel but obtained verdict, with damages for illegal arrest, against the secretary of state (1769). Expelled from House of Commons (1764) for seditious libel; outlawed for failing to stand trial. Returned from Continent (1768) and elected M.P.; stood trial on the old libel charge and was fined and imprisoned. Expelled from house on taking his seat (1769) and immediately reelected and reexpelled, a third election being declared by the house in favor of his opponent, who had polled fewer votes. Became idol of mob rioting for "Wilkes and liberty," and supported by London merchants; championed program of parliamentary reform, including suppression of rotten boroughs, and safeguarding of individual liberty against ministerial autocracy; lord mayor of London (1774). Admitted to House of Commons (1774–90); championed colonial rights in American Revolution; chamberlain of city of London (1779–97); lost popularity by his part in suppressing Gordon Riots (1780). Secured to Britons abolition of general warrants, freedom of press in reporting debates in House of Commons, enfranchisement of artisans and middle class.

Wil·kie \ˈwil-kē\, Sir David. 1785–1841. Scottish painter. Known for genre works and portraits; achieved great popularity with *Pitlessie Fair* (1804), *Village Politicians* (1806); painter in ordinary to king (1830); turned to historical paintings, two of best known being *Preaching of Knox* (1832) and *Columbus* (1835).

Wil·kins \ˈwil-kənz\, Sir George Hubert. 1888–1958. Australian explorer and aviator. On Stefansson's Arctic expedition (1913–16); navigator, England–Australia flight (1919); second in command, British Imperial Antarctic expedition (1920–21); naturalist, Shackleton's Antarctic expedition (1921–22); leader, Wilkins Australia and Islands expedition for British Museum (1923–25); led expeditions to Arctic (1926–27, 1928, 1931), Antarctic (1928–29, 1933–39); flew from Point Barrow to Spitsbergen over polar regions (1928). Author of *Flying the Arctic* (1928), *Undiscovered Australia* (1928), *Under the North Pole* (1931), *Thoughts Through Space* (with H.M. Sherman, 1942).

Wilkins, John. 1614–1672. English prelate and scientist. Warden of Wadham Coll., Oxford (1648); m. (1656) Robina, sister of Oliver Cromwell; master of Trinity Coll. (1659); one of the founders of the Royal Society (1662); bishop of Chester (1668). Author of *The Discovery of a World in the Moone* (1638), *A Discourse Tending to Prove That 'Tis Probable Our Earth Is One of The Planets* (1640), *On the Principles and Duties of Natural Religion* (1678), etc.

Wilkins, Mary Eleanor. See Mary Eleanor Wilkins FREEMAN.

Wilkins, Roy. 1901–1981. American civil rights leader, b. St. Louis, Mo. Editor of weekly *Call* in Kansas City, Mo. (1923–31). Joined National Association for the Advancement of Colored People (1931), editor of organ *Crisis* (1934–49), executive secretary (1955–64), executive director (1965–77). Awarded Spingarn Medal (1964).

Wil·kin·son \ˈwil-kən-sən\, Ellen Cicely. 1891–1947. English feminist and politician. Active in woman suffrage and labor movements; M.P. (1924–31, 1935–47); parliamentary secretary to ministry of home security (1940–45); minister of education (1945–47).

Wilkinson, James. 1757–1825. American army officer and adventurer, b. Calvert Co., Md. Commissioned captain in Continental army (1776); with Arnold in retreat from Montreal to Albany (1776); engaged at Trenton and Princeton; promoted lieutenant colonel (1777) and brevetted brigadier general. Secretary of board of war (1778). Involved in Conway cabal and forced to resign commission (1778); clothier general of Continental army (1779–81). Engaged in trade in Mississippi Valley region (1784); conspired with Esteban Miró, Spanish governor of Louisiana, to gain trade monopolies for himself in return for efforts to separate Kentucky region from U.S. and turn it over to Spain. In military service against Indians (1791); lieutenant colonel, U.S. army (1791), brigadier general (1792); took over Detroit from British (1796) and, on

General Wayne's death (1796), became ranking officer of U.S. army. With Gov. William C.C. Claiborne, represented U.S. in taking over Louisiana Purchase (1803) from French; governor of Louisiana (1805–06). Implicated in Aaron Burr's conspiracy and chief witness at Burr's trial; acquitted by court of inquiry and later (1811) by court-martial. Commissioned major general (1813) and commanded American forces on Canadian frontier; failed in campaign against Montreal (1813–14); again brought before court of inquiry and acquitted (1814); honorably discharged (1815).

Wilkinson, Jemima. 1752–1819. American religious leader, b. Cumberland, R.I. Emerged from a trance suffered in course of a fever convinced that she was resurrected from death and commissioned by God to warn the world to flee from the wrath to come (1776); took name "Publick Universal Friend." Her preaching led to establishment of churches in Rhode Island and Connecticut, and founding of a colony near Seneca Lake in western New York (1788; dissolved 1819).

Wilkinson, John. 1728–1808. English ironmaster. Invented machine for accurate boring of cylinders (1775); designed and cast first iron bridge in England (1779); built first iron barge (1787); patented process of making lead pipe (1790).

Wilkinson, John. 1821–1891. American naval officer, b. Norfolk, Va. Entered navy (1837); resigned (1861) to enter Confederate service. Famed as commander of blockade runner *Robert E. Lee* (1863). Led unsuccessful attempt to capture a steamer on Lake Erie and free Confederate prisoners held on Johnson's Island in the lake (1863).

Wilkinson, Sir John Gardner. 1797–1875. English traveler and Egyptologist. In Egypt and Nubia (1821–33); author of *Materia Hieroglyphica* (1828), *Survey of Thebes* (1830), *Manners and Customs of the Ancient Egyptians* (1837), etc.

Wilkinson, Richard James. 1867–1941. British colonial administrator. To Straits Settlements (1889) as civil servant; rose to colonial secretary in Singapore (1911–16); encouraged Malay literature, published Malay writings, established libraries, compiled Malay–English dictionary; attempted to foster general education and took lead in founding (1905) Malay Coll.; governor of Sierra Leone (1916–22).

Wil·la·ding \'vil-ə-diŋ\, Johann Friedrich. 1641–1718. Swiss politician. Leader of anti-French party in Bern; instrumental in securing transfer of principality of Neuchâtel to House of Hohenzollern (1707); chief magistrate of Bern (1708–18).

Wil·laert \'vil-ärt\, Adriaan. c.1490–1562. Flemish composer. In service of Este family in Ferrara (c.1515–27); maestro di capella of St. Mark's, Venice (1527–62), where his school attracted pupils from all Europe. Originated style of writing music for two choirs; composed masses, Magnificats, motets, Psalms, hymns; contributed greatly to development of Italian madrigal and the chanson; one of earliest composers of purely instrumental music.

Wil·lard \'wil-ərd\, Archibald MacNeal. 1836–1918. American painter, b. Bedford, Ohio. Known for genre paintings as *Pluck, Jim Bludso, The Drummer's Latest Yarn,* and esp. *Yankee Doodle, or the Spirit of '76,* exhibited at Centennial Exposition, Philadelphia (1876).

Willard, Emma, *nee* Hart \'härt\. 1787–1870. American educator, b. Berlin, Conn. m. John Willard (1809; d. 1825). Established and directed Middlebury Female Sem. (1814–19), Waterford (N.Y.) Acad. (1819–21), Troy (N.Y.) Female Sem., now known as Emma Willard School (1821–38); retired (1838). Pioneer in field of higher education for women; published textbooks in history and a volume of poems including notably "Rocked in the Cradle of the Deep."

Willard, Frances Elizabeth Caroline. 1839–1898. American educator and reformer, b. Churchville, N.Y. President, Evanston (Ill.) Coll. for Ladies (1871–73); dean of women and professor, Northwestern U. (1873–74); devoted herself to temperance movement (from 1874), appearing on lecture platform and for a time conducting prayer groups on streets and in saloons; president, National W.C.T.U. (1879–98) and World's W.C.T.U. (1891–98); aided in organizing Prohibition party (1882). First president of National Council of Women (1888–90). Author of *Woman and Temperance* (1883), autobiography *Glimpses of Fifty Years* (1889); edited *Woman of the Century* (1893, with Mary A. Livermore).

Willard, Jess. 1881–1968. American boxer, b. Pottawatomie Co., Kan. Won heavyweight championship from Jack Johnson (Apr. 5, 1915); lost championship to Jack Dempsey (July 4, 1919).

Willard, Simon. 1753–1848. American clockmaker, b. Grafton, Mass. Settled in Roxbury (c.1780) and manufactured clocks, specializing in church, hall, and gallery clocks. Patented (1802) the Willard Patent Timepiece, which came to be known as the banjo clock. His brother ¶Benjamin (1743–1803) also manufactured clocks (from c.1765); noted esp. for tall-case (grandfather) clocks. Another brother ¶Aaron (1757–1844) manufactured clocks in Roxbury and (from 1790) in Boston.

Will·cocks \'wil-ˌkäks\, Sir William. 1852–1932. British engineer, b. India. With irrigation department, Indian public works (1872–83) and Egyptian public works (1883–97); designed the dam at Aswān, Egypt (1898–1902); undertook irrigation work in South Africa (1901), Mesopotamia (1911).

Wil·le \'vil-ə\, Ulrich. 1848–1925. Swiss military leader. Artillery officer (1867); reformed cavalry (1881–92); head of army and chief instructor (1892–95); resigned (1895); resumed active duty (1900); general and commander in chief of Swiss army (from 1914); remade traditional citizens' army into trained disciplined corps.

Willem. See also WILLIAM.

Wil·le·mer \'vil-ə-mər\, Marianne von, *nee* Jung \'yůŋ\. 1784–1860. German dancer and actress. m. (1814) Frankfurt banker Johann Jakob von Willemer. Renowned for her friendship with Goethe, who wrote of her (under poetic name "Zuleika") in a number of his poems.

Wil·lems \'vil-əms\, Jan Frans. 1793–1846. Flemish scholar and poet. Assistant archivist (1815–21), registrar (1821–30) at Antwerp; archivist at Ghent (1835–46); founded and edited journal *Belgisch Museum* (1837–40); a leader of Flemish national school; translated medieval tales as *Van den vos Reinaerde* (1834, 1836).

Wil·lem van Ruys·broeck \'vil-əm-vän-'rœis-brük\. *Lat.* Wilhelmus Ru·bruquis \rü-'brü-kəs\. *Eng.* William of Ru·brouck \'rü-ˌbrük\. c.1215–c.1295. French Franciscan friar and traveler. Sent by Louis IX of France on mission to Mongol Empire (1253); traversed the Crimea and steppes between Don and Volga rivers and country eastward to Mongolia; returned (1255). Wrote account of trip, considered best written of any medieval Christian traveler; account published in part by Hakluyt (1598–99) and complete in 1839.

William. See also GUILLAUME, WILHELM.

Wil·liam \'wil-yəm\. *Fr.* Guil·laume \gē-yōm\. Name of ten dukes of Aquitaine, including:

William I. *Called* le Pieux \lə-pyœ\, *i.e.* the Pious. d. 918. Duke (898 or 909–918). Comte de Tou·louse \tü-lüz\ as William II (885 or 886–918). Founded (910) abbey of Cluny.

William V. *Called* le Grand \lə-gräⁿ\, *i.e.* the Great. c.960–1030. Comte de Poi·tiers \pwá-tyā\ and duc d'Aqui·taine \á-kē-ten\ (994–1030). Strengthened duchy and made it virtually independent; declined offer (1024) of Italian crown; patron of arts and literature.

William IX. 1071–1127. Comte de Poitiers, duc d'Aquitaine and de Gas·cogne \gás-kônʸ\ (1086–1127); twice excommunicated for licentiousness; led crusade but was defeated at Heraclea (1101); a poet of renown, accounted first of the troubadours; 11 of his poems are extant.

William X. 1099–1137. Duc (1127–37). Son of William IX; at death betrothed his daughter to Louis VII of France, thus uniting France and Aquitaine.

William. Name of four kings of England:

William I. *Called* William the Conqueror. c.1028–1087. King of England (1066–87). Bastard son of Robert I the Devil, Duke of Normandy; accepted by nobles as William II, Duke of Normandy (1035); with help of Henry I of France, suppressed rebellion of nobles (1047); defeated Geoffrey Martel, Count of Anjou, and conquered Anjou (1051); probably received promise that he should succeed Edward the Confessor as king of England; married (c.1053) Matilda, daughter of Baldwin V of Flanders and a descendant of King Alfred, in defiance of a prohibition by the church on ground of consanguinity, but received papal dispensation (1059); repulsed two invasions (1054, 1058) by Henry I and annexed county of Maine (1062); exacted promise (1064) from Harold, Earl of Wessex, to support his claim to English throne. Invaded England on death of Edward and accession of Harold (1066); aided by invasion of northern England by Tostig, Harold's banished brother; encamped at Hastings; defeated Harold (Oct. 14) at a place called by a chronicler Senlac, later called Battle; crowned at Westminster on Christmas Day. Quelled insurrections in west and north (1068); repelled Danish invasion; completed conquest of England (1070); appointed Lanfranc archbishop of Canterbury (1070); compelled Malcolm III of Scotland to do him homage (1072). Conquered Maine (1073); returned to England (1075) to settle punishment of rebels under earls of Hereford and Norfolk, who had been defeated by Lanfranc. Strengthened power of the crown by building castles; gave confiscated land of rebels to his followers; caused all titles to land to be derived from his grant; established feudal system; ordered Domesday Book to be compiled (1086); organized church as department of government; separated spiritual from temporal courts; asserted supremacy of his own authority and refused homage to the pope. Engaged in wars in France; quelled uprisings led by his son Robert, Duke of Normandy (1080, 1082); in war with Philip I of France (1087), received fatal injury when his horse stumbled entering the captured town of Mantes; buried in abbey that he had built at Caen.

William II. *Called* William Ru·fus \'rü-fəs\. c.1056–1100. King of England (1087–1100). Second surviving son of William the Conqueror. Bore arms with father against brother Robert (1079); designated king of England by the witan, according to father's dying request; crowned at Westminster (1087). By ruthless, shortsighted, rapacious rule provoked barons under his uncle Odo, bishop of Bayeux, to insurrection in favor of Robert; quelled insurrection by promises, never fulfilled, of good laws, reduction of taxes, redress for losses from William I's afforestments (1088). Appointed Anselm archbishop of Canterbury (1093); quarreled with him for maintaining church liberties (1097). Invaded Normandy (1089, 1091, 1094); received mortgage upon Normandy when brother Robert required funds for a crusade (1096); recovered Maine and failed to recover Vexin; invaded Wales three times without success. Slain by an arrow from an unknown hand (traditionally, that of Walter Tirel, a Norman) while hunting in New Forest; his body refused religious rites by clergy of Winchester.

William III. 1650–1702. King of England, Scotland, and Ireland (1689–1702). See WILLIAM III, Count of Nassau.

William IV. 1765–1837. *Called* the Sailor-King *and* Silly Billy. King of Great Britain and Ireland (1830–37) and of Hanover (1830–37). 3d son of George III. As midshipman served in action off Cape St. Vincent (1780); captain of frigate (1785) and stationed in West Indies; rear admiral (1790). Duke of Clarence (1789); sat in House of Lords and opposed emancipation of slaves; sustained a connection with Dorothea Jordan, the actress (1791?–1811), which produced 10 children, surnamed FitzClarence; m. (1818) Adelaide of Saxe-Meiningen; became heir to throne and lord high admiral (1827). Succeeded brother George IV as king (1830); by declining to accept resignation of Tory ministry and to create new peers, caused long political crisis and obstructed passage of second Reform Bill; brought about its passage (1832) by appeal in circular letter to peers, one hundred of whom absented themselves. As king of Hanover gave new constitution to that country (1833). Last English sovereign to attempt to force a ministry (the ministry of Sir Robert Peel, 1834) upon an unwilling majority in Parliament.

William. *Called* William of Holland. *Ger.* Wil·helm von Hol·land \ˈvil-ˌhelm-fȯn-ˈhȯl-änt\. 1228–1256. King of Germany (1247–56). Son of Floris IV, Count of Holland, whom he succeeded as count (1234); elected king of Germany (1247) as papal candidate in opposition to Conrad IV; remained an antiking until Conrad's departure for Italy and subsequent recognition by Saxony, Brandenburg (1252), and the Rhenish League (1254).

William. *Ger.* Wil·helm \ˈvil-ˌhelm\. Name of two German emperors and kings of Prussia:

William I. *In full* Wilhelm Friedrich Ludwig. 1797–1888. King of Prussia (1861–88) and German emperor (1871–88). Second son of Frederick William III of Prussia. Fought against Napoléon (1814–15); m. (1829) Augusta (1811–1890), daughter of Charles Frederick, Duke of Saxe-Weimar; on accession of his brother Friedrich Wilhelm IV (1840), became prince of Prussia and heir presumptive; unpopular because of absolutist ideas and suppression of insurrections; fled to England (1848); made regent (1858–61) when king became insane. His reign a continuous struggle with liberals; aided by Bismarck (from 1862), esp. in bringing about war with Austria (1866); commanded at Sadowa (1866); head of the North German Confederation (1867); led German armies in Franco-Prussian War (1870–71), personally commanding at Gravelotte and Sedan; proclaimed German emperor at Versailles (Jan. 18, 1871); in general acceded to policies of Bismarck, although he disagreed with the Kulturkampf and certain others; supported Bismarck and his generals in strengthening control of Germany by Prussia.

William II. *In full* Friedrich Wilhelm Viktor Albert. 1859–1941. Emperor of Germany and king of Prussia (1888–1918). Grandson of William I; son of Frederick III and Victoria; m. (1881) Princess Augusta Victoria (1858–1921) of Schleswig-Holstein-Sonderburg-Augustenburg. On accession (1888), asserted divine mission of house of Hohenzollern to rule; dismissed Bismarck (1890); encouraged Adm. von Tirpitz to begin development of strong German fleet; unsuccessfully opposed growth of Socialism (1893–1912); expressed friendship to President Kruger of the South African Republic (1896); directed policy of seizing territory for indemnity in China (1897); continually undercut efforts of Caprivi, Hohenlohe, von Bülow, and other ministers to construct balanced domestic and foreign policies; provoked controversy with France over Morocco (1904–11); severely criticized at home for impetuous speech on friendship for Great Britain (1908). Sided with Austria-Hungary in crisis with Serbia (1914); dominant force of Central Powers at beginning of World War I (1914); prestige gradually declined as Germany failed to win a decision; frequently visited battle fronts, but his control over army greatly reduced; toward the end (1918) saw inevitable defeat but refused to surrender; was denied support of army and navy; fled to Holland; abdicated (Nov. 28, 1918). Resident at Doorn, near Utrecht (from 1920); after Kaiserin Augusta Victoria's death (1921), m. (1922) Princess Hermine of Schönaich-Carolath; granted payment (1926) by Prussian government for confiscated property.

William. *In full* Friedrich Wilhelm Viktor August Ernst. 1882–1951. Crown prince of Germany (1888–1918). Son Emperor William II of Germany; m. (1905) Cecilie Auguste Marie of Mecklenburg-Schwerin; traveled in Orient and Italy (1903) and in India (1910–11); in World War I commanded 5th army (1914); commanded army group in unsuccessful attack on Verdun (1916); fled to Holland with kaiser (1918); renounced rights to crowns of Prussia and German Empire (1918); returned to Germany (1923); supported Nazi party (1932 ff.); interned by French (1945).

William. Name of six landgraves and two electors of Hesse-Kassel, esp.:

William IV. *Called* der Wei·se \der-ˈvī-zə\, *i.e.* the Wise. 1532–1592. Founder of the elder line of the house of Hesse (see HESSE-KASSEL). Son of Philip the Magnanimous. Administered government (1547–52) during imprisonment of father; with brother Maurice of Saxony fought Emperor Charles V and secured father's release (1552); landgrave (1567–92), receiving Hesse and Kassel on division of landgraviate (1567); a Protestant, and wise ruler; a pioneer astronomer and patron of Tycho Brahe; at Kassel built first observatory with revolving dome (1561).

William IX. 1743–1821. Landgrave (1785–1803); elector as William I (1803–21). Son of Frederick II; furnished the Hessian mercenary troops to Great Britain for use in the American Revolution; joined coalition against France (1792); lost his lands to the French (1806–13); restored by Congress of Vienna (1814–15).

William II. 1777–1847. Elector (1821–47). Son of William I. Served in Prussian army against Napoléon (1813); caused unrest by his conservatism (1830–31); forced to grant a new constitution (1831).

William IV. 1852–1912. Grand duke of Luxembourg (1905–12). Son of Adolf of Nassau; made family statute (1907) enabling daughters to succeed to the throne; succeeded by his daughter Marie Adélaïde.

William. *Dutch* Wil·lem \ˈvil-əm\. Name of eight rulers of the Netherlands, five as stadholders and three as kings:

William I. *Known as* William the Silent. 1533–1584. Stadholder (1579–84). Son of William, Count of Nassau, and Juliana of Stolberg; succeeded to principality of Orange (1544); page to Emperor Charles V (1548); m. (1551) Anna van Buren (d. 1558), of the Egmont family; appointed to Council of State and made stadholder of Holland, Zeeland, and Utrecht by Philip II (1559); succeeded as count of Nassau (1559); opposed Philip II (1559–67) in his persecution of Protestants in Orange and Holland; m. (1561), as second wife, Anna of Saxony; forced to flee to Germany (1567); refused to appear before Council of Blood (1566); led revolt (1568–76), the "War of Liberation," against Duke of Alba and Spanish armies; lost help of French Huguenots (after 1572); joined revolt of Calvinists in northern provinces (1572); Leiden relieved (1574); suffered several defeats, expecially at Gembloux (1578); by Pacification of Ghent (1576) united southern provinces against Spain, and by Union of Utrecht (1579) seven northern provinces, which formally declared their independence of Spain; became first stadholder (1579–84); made hereditary (1581); m. (1583), as fourth wife, Louise de Coligny, daughter of Gaspard II de Coligny; assassinated at Delft by Balthazar Gérard. His eldest son Philip William (d. 1618) was held as prisoner in Spain. Other sons were Maurice of Nassau (see MAURICE) and Frederick Henry (*q.v.*).

William II. 1626–1650. Stadholder (1647–50). Son of Frederick Henry and grandson of William the Silent; m. (1641) Mary, daughter of Charles I of England. Succeeded father as prince of Orange and stadholder of all provinces but Friesland (1647); established peace with Spain (1648) which recognized independence of United Provinces; negotiated treaty with France (1650); planned war to regain Spanish Netherlands and opposed reduction of army; secured additional powers from Estates-General but failed to subdue Holland; died of smallpox. After his death, stadholdership temporarily suspended (1650–72). See Johan de WITT.

William III. 1650–1702. Stadholder (1672–1702) and king of England (1689–1702). Posthumous son of William II. Prince of Orange; despite Act of Seclusion (1654), trained for stadholder; accepted at length by Johan de Witt as future ruler; appointed captain general (1672) for war with France and England; despite Perpetual Edict (1667), also named stadholder in response to popular outcry (1672); defeated France (1674) and achieved general peace in Treaty of Nijmegen (1673). m. (1677) Mary, daughter of Duke of York, later James II of England; after Glorious Revolution in England (1688) appealed to by both Whigs and Tories to be English king; landed at Torbay, Devonshire, with Dutch army (1688); invited by Parliament to accept throne; crowned (1689) as joint sovereign with Mary; accepted Declaration of Rights (1689); Act of Toleration passed (1689); went to Ireland, defeated James at battle of the Boyne (1690); reigned as sole sovereign after death of Mary (1694); plot to assassinate him (1696) discovered and conspirators executed. Joined first Grand Alliance against France (1689) which led to war (1689–97), concluded by Treaty of Rijswijk (1697); issued Act of Settlement (1701); formed second Grand Alliance (1701); died as a result of a fall from his horse.

William IV. *Orig.* Charles Henry Fri·so \ˈfrē-sō\. 1711–1751. First general stadholder of Dutch Republic (1747–51). Son of John William Friso;

succeeded father as prince of Orange and stadholder of Friesland (1711), subsequently becoming stadholder of Groningen and Gelderland; m. (1734) Anne, daughter of George II of England; on French invasion (1747), proclaimed stadholder of all provinces, captain general and admiral general.

William V. 1748–1806. Stadholder (1751–95). Son of William IV, whom he succeeded as prince of Orange and as stadholder; affairs of state controlled during his minority by queen mother (1751–59) and by regents (1759–66), Holland remaining neutral during Seven Years' War (1756–63); m. Wilhelmina of Prussia, who dominated him; under his weak rule, country weakened by taking part in European conflicts (1780, 1792–93), by party strife (1787), and finally by the general revolutionary spirit, which (1795) overthrew the stadholdership; fled to England.

William I. *In full* Willem Frederik. 1772–1843. King (1815–40). Son of William V, whom he succeeded (1806) as prince of Orange; commanded Dutch army against France (1793–95); joined army of Prussia; captured at Jena (1806); lost (1806) hereditary lands in Germany; fought at Wagram in Austrian army (1809); recovered German territories (1813); accepted invitation to be sovereign prince of the Netherlands (1813); proclaimed himself king of new United Netherlands erected out of Belgium and Holland by the Congress of Vienna (1815); relinquished German duchy for Luxembourg (1815); sparked commercial revival, but alienated many by autocratic methods, subjection of church to state control, imposition of Dutch as official language; unable to prevent separate establishment of Belgium as kingdom (1830); abdicated (1840) in favor of his son.

William II. *In full* Willem Frederik George Lodewijk. 1792–1849. King (1840–49). Son of William I. Fought in Spain under Wellington and commanded Dutch forces at Waterloo (1815); named prince of Orange (1815); attempted to appease Belgian revolutionaries (1830); commanded Dutch army that defeated Leopold I and occupied Belgium (1831) but was defeated (1832) by the French; made king on abdication of his father (1840); aided financial improvements; against a conservative Estates-General secured (1848) a new constitution with many liberal features.

William III. *In full* Willem Alexander Paul Frederik Lodewijk. 1817–1890. King (1849–90). Son of William II. Abolished slavery in Dutch West Indies (1862); fought long against establishment of government by parliamentary ministries (1853–62), but finally forced to yield; m. (1879), as second wife, Emma (*q.v.*) of Waldeck-Pyrmont; succeeded by their daughter Wilhelmina.

William. *Fr.* Guillaume. Name of several dukes of Normandy:

William I. *Called* Longue-Épée \lōⁿ-gā-pā\, *i.e.* Longsword. d. 942. Duke (c.930–942). Son of Robert I; secured control of Rennes and Vannes; treacherously assassinated by Arnoul II, count of Flanders.

William II. See WILLIAM I of England.

William III. *Surnamed* Cli·ton \klē-tōⁿ\. 1101–1128. Titular duke. Son of Robert II Curthose; aided by Louis VI of France and Fulk of Anjou, attempted several times in vain to recover Normandy from Henry I of England, who had imprisoned Robert (1106); made count of Flanders by Louis (1127); killed by rival for Flanders, Thierry d'Alsace, at siege of Alost.

William. *Called* the Aeth·e·ling \'ath-ə-liŋ, 'at͟h-\. 1103–1120. Duke (1120). Only legitimate son of Henry I of England; received homage of Norman barons (1115); m. (1119) Matilda, daughter of Fulk V of Anjou; invested with duchy by father (1120); drowned returning to England in the "White Ship."

William. *Called* the Lion. 1143–1214. King of Scotland (1165–1214). Son of Henry, Earl of Northumberland; succeeded as earl (1152); forced to relinquish earldom to Henry II of England (1157); succeeded brother Malcolm IV as king (1165); joined in revolt of Henry's sons (1173); captured at Alnwick (1174), released on submitting to Henry's overlordship and supremacy of English church; bought release from subjection from Richard I (1189); continued to agitate for restoration of Northumberland until forced to renounce claim (1209) by King John. Extended feudal administration of Scotland, created many burghs and sheriffdoms; founded (1178) Arbroath Abbey.

William. Name of two kings of Sicily:

William I. *Called* the Bad. 1120–1166. King (1154–66). Son of Roger II; defeated rebellious barons and an invasion by Byzantine forces of Manuel I Comnenus at Brindisi (1155); secured acknowledgment from Pope Adrian IV of his sovereignty over all Norman lands in the East; lost African possessions (1158–60); suppressed new baronial revolt (1160); patron of scholars and artists, including many Muslims.

William II. *Called* the Good. 1154–1189. King (1166–89). Son of William I; under mother's regency (1166–71); m. (1177) Joan, daughter of Henry II of England; formed alliance with Frederick I Barbarossa (1177); undertook major campaign against Byzantine empire (1185) but was heavily defeated.

William of Au·vergne \ō-vernʸ, ō-\. *Fr.* Guillaume d'Auvergne. *Also called* William of Paris. after 1180–1249. French philosopher and theologian. Professor at Paris (1225 ff.); bishop of Paris (1228); defended mendicant orders and supported clerical reform. Drew from Aristotle and Avicenna and from Neoplatonism those elements consistent with orthodox Christianity and constructed a theology based on God as essential being. Chief work *Magisterium divinale* (written 1223–40).

William of Au·xerre \ō-ser\. *Fr.* Guillaume d'Auxerre. c.1150–1231. French philosopher and theologian. Master and administrator at U. of Paris; French envoy to Gregory IX to plead cause of students against King Louis IX (1230); named by Gregory to council ordered to censor works of Aristotle; argued against suppression of any works. Chief work *Summa super quattuor libros sententiarum,* called the *Summa aurea* (Golden Compendium), setting forth an Idealist theology; also wrote *Summa de officiis ecclesiasticis* on liturgy, worship, etc.

William of Champeaux. See GUILLAUME DE CHAMPEAUX.

William of Conches \kōⁿsh\. *Fr.* Guillaume de Conches. c.1100–1154. French philosopher. Pupil of Bernard of Chartres; taught at Chartres and Paris; tutor to future Henry II of England; a philosophical Realist leaning to pantheism. Author of commentaries on Plato and Boethius, of *Philosophia mundi* and *Dragmaticon philosophiae;* believed to be author of *Summa moralium philosophorum.*

William of Cor·beil \kȯr-bey\. *Also spelled* Corbail, Corbeuil, Curbuil. d. 1136. British prelate, b. Corbeil, France. Entered order of St. Augustine; prior of St. Osyth, Essex; archbishop of Canterbury (1123–36); made papal legate in England and Scotland (1126); completed and dedicated (1130) cathedral of Canterbury; crowned King Stephen (1135).

William of Hirsau. See WILHELM VON HIRSAU.

William of Holland. See WILLIAM, king of Germany.

William of Malmes·bury \'mämz-ˌber-ē, 'mälmz-, -b(ə-)rē\. c.1090–c.1143. English historian. Monk at Malmesbury; helped assemble library there. Wrote *Gesta regum Anglorum* (c.1125), modeled on Bede, *Gesta pontificum Anglorum* (c.1126), and *Historia novella,* bringing his English history down to 1142.

William of Moer·beke \'mür-ˌbek-ə\. c.1215–c.1286. French prelate and scholar, b. Brabant. Entered Dominican order; papal chaplain and confessor (1265–78); consultant to Gregory X at Council of Lyons (1274); archbishop of Corinth (1278). Translated into Latin works of Aristotle, of various Greek commentators on Aristotle, of Neoplatonists as Proclus, of Hippocrates and Ptolemy, making them available for the first time to medieval scholars and philosophers.

William of New·burgh \'n(y)ü-ˌbərg\. 1136–c.1198. English chronicler. Augustinian monk at Newburgh; for Abbot Ernald of Rievaux wrote *Historia rerum Anglicarum,* history of the period 1066–1198, one of the most valuable sources for the period.

William of Nor·wich \'nȯ(ə)r-(ˌ)wich; 'nȯr-ich, 'när-\. Saint. 1132?–?1144. English martyr. Found dead (Easter 1144 or perhaps 1145); first of several boys held in popular rumor to have been victims of Jewish ritual murder. Cf. HUGH of Lincoln.

William of Ockham. See OCKHAM.

William of Orange. See WILLIAM, stadholders and kings of Netherlands.

William of Paris. See WILLIAM of Auvergne.

William of Rubrouck *or* Ruysbroeck. See WILLEM VAN RUYSBROECK.

William of Saint-Amour \saⁿ-tá-mür\. *Fr.* Guillaume de Saint-Amour. c.1200–1272. French philosopher and theologian. Dean of theology masters at U. of Paris (c.1250); led university's attack on mendicant orders; secured suspension of Dominican masters (1254) and action by Pope Innocent IV against orders (1254); resisted restoration of privileges by Pope Alexander V; suspended by Alexander (1256) for violently anti-Dominican *Liber de Antichristo et ejusdem ministris;* secured collaboration of other Parisian masters in *De periculis novissimorum temporum* (1256) which was also condemned; exiled from France (1257); permitted to return (1266).

William of Saint-Thier·ry \saⁿ-tyer-ē\. *Fr.* Guillaume de Saint-Thierry. c.1085–1148. French theologian and mystic. Entered Benedictine monastery at Reims (1113); abbot of Saint-Thierry (1119); withdrew (1135) to contemplative life in Cistercian monastery of Signy. Author of theological works and biblical commentaries as *De natura et dignitate amoris, De contemplando Deo, De sacramento altaris,* and of works on spirituality and the contemplative life, many attempting to synthesize Eastern and Western theology and mysticism, as *Meditativae orationes, Speculum fidei* (1140), *Aenigma fidei* (1144), *Epistola ad fratres de Monte Dei* (1144, known as the Golden Epistle).

William of Saliceto. See GUGLIELMO DA SALICETO.

William of Tyre \'tī(ə)r\. c.1130–1185. Latin prelate, b. Syria, probably of French parents. Archdeacon of Tyre (1167); tutor to future Baldwin IV (1170); chancellor of kingdom of Jerusalem and archdeacon of Nazareth (1174); archbishop of Tyre (1175); attended Third Lateran Council in Rome (1179); failed to secure election as patriarch of Jerusalem (1180), retired to Rome (1183). Author of lost history of the Arab East *Gesta orientalium principum* and a history of the Latin East *Historia rerum in partibus transmarinis gestarum.*

William of Wayn·flete *or* Wain·fleet \'wān-ˌflēt\. *Orig.* William Pat·yn \'pat-ᵊn\. 1395?–1486. English prelate. Bishop of Winchester (1447–86); founded Magdalen Coll., Oxford (1448); lord chancellor (1456–60).

William of Wyke·ham *or* Wick·ham \'wik-əm\. 1324–1404. English prelate and politician. Entered service of Edward III (c.1356); lord chancellor of England (1367–71), bishop of Winchester (from 1367); persecuted by John of Gaunt but later pardoned by Richard II; again chancellor (1389–91). Founded New College, Oxford (1380), and Winchester College (1382).

William the Aetheling. See WILLIAM, Duke of Normandy.

William the Bad. See WILLIAM I, king of Sicily.

William the Conqueror. See WILLIAM I, king of England.

William the Good. See WILLIAM II, king of Sicily.

William the Lion. See WILLIAM, king of Scotland.

William the Silent. See WILLIAM I, stadholder of Netherlands.

William the Wise. See WILLIAM IV, landgrave of Hesse-Kassel.

William Aetheling. See WILLIAM, Duke of Normandy.

William Au·gus·tus \ó-'gəs-təs\. Duke of Cum·ber·land \'kəm-bər-lənd\. 1721–1765. English military commander. Third son of George II and Queen Caroline; created duke (1726); privy councilor (1742); served on Main at Dettingen (1743); commander in chief of British, Hanoverian, Austrian, and Dutch forces, unsuccessfully engaged Marshal Saxe at Fontenoy (1745); quelled Jacobite uprising headed by Prince Charles Edward in victory of Culloden Moor (1746); suppressed Jacobitism with utmost severity, acquiring nickname of "the Butcher"; again in Flanders, defeated by Saxe at Lauffeld or Val (1747); defeated by d'Estrées at Hastenbeck (1757); capitulated and evacuated Hanover; retired to private life (1757).

William Cliton. See WILLIAM III, Duke of Normandy.

William de la Mare \-ˌdel-ə-'ma(ə)r, -'me(ə)r\. d. c.1290. English philosopher and theologian. Entered Franciscan order; master at U. of Paris (c.1275); an early and chief critic of Aquinas in *Correctorium fratris Thomae* (1278).

William de Valence. See VALENCE.

William Fitzosbern. See FITZOSBERN.

William Long·es·pée \ˌlōⁿ-gā-'pā\, *i.e.* Longsword. 3d Earl of Salis·bury \'sólz-ˌber-ē, -b(ə-)rē\. d. 1226. English soldier. Illegitimate son of Henry II of England and, according to tradition, "Fair Rosamund" Clifford (see under CLIFFORD family); granted by Richard I hand of heiress of William, Earl of Salisbury, and the title (1198). Warden of Cinque Ports (1204–06), of Welsh marches (1208); organized King John's Flemish allies (1213–14), leading right wing of allied army at Bouvines (July 1214). In John's war against barons, deserted him after landing of Louis of France (1216); returned to royal allegiance (by March 1217) and faithfully supported his nephew Henry III. Served against the Welsh (1223) and in Gascony (1225). Benefactor, with his wife, of Salisbury cathedral.

William Louis. *Du.* Willem Lodewijk. 1560–1620. Count of Nassau. Son of Count John; defeated Georges de Lalaing, pro-Spanish stadholder of Friesland and Groningen (1579); captain general and stadholder of Friesland (1584); chief military adviser to cousin Maurice of Nassau; led successful campaign that drove out Spanish (1590–97); stadholder of Groningen and Drenthe (1594); with Maurice and Oldenbarnevelt ruled Dutch Republic (1588–1618).

William Rufus. See WILLIAM II, king of England.

Wil·liams \'wil-yəmz\, Ben Ames. 1889–1953. American writer, b. Macon, Miss. Author of novels *Splendor* (1927), *Great Oaks* (1930), *Hostile Valley* (1934), *The Strumpet Sea* (1938), *The Strange Woman* (1941), *Time of Peace* (1942), *Leave Her to Heaven* (1944), *House Divided* (1947), etc.

Williams, Bert, *in full* Egbert Austin. 1876?–1922. American comedian and songwriter, b. New Providence, Bahama Islands. To U.S. as a child. Partner with George Walker in vaudeville (1895–1903) and musical comedy (1903–09); leading comedian in Ziegfeld *Follies* (1909–19); appeared in *In Dahomey* (1903), *Bandana Land* (1908), etc. Songs included "Nobody."

Williams, Daniel Hale. 1858–1931. American surgeon, b. Hollidaysburg, Pa. Practiced in Chicago. Organizer (1891) of Provident Hospital, Chicago, affording facilities for training Negroes as interns and nurses; surgeon on staff of this hospital (1891–1912). Credited with performing (1893) first successful surgical closure of a wound of the heart and pericardium.

Williams, Eleazar. 1789?–1858. American missionary, b. Caughnawaga, Que. Descendant of a St. Regis Indian chief and an American girl, Eunice Williams, one of the captives made in the French and Indian raid on Deerfield, Mass. (1704). Began missionary work among Indians of northern New York (c.1813). Asserted himself (from 1839) to be the lost dauphin of France, son of Louis XVI. Author of books on Indian subjects, some written in Iroquois; credited with simplifying the writing of the Mohawk language.

Williams, Ephraim. 1714–1755. American army officer, b. Newton, Mass. Captain of Massachusetts militia (1745); commanded troops along northern Massachusetts border; ambushed and killed. Bequeathed funds for founding of school that later (1793) became Williams College.

Williams, Sir Frederic Calland. 1911–1977. English electrical engineer. Professor, Manchester (from 1946); invented radar aircraft identification system, first fully automatic radar system for fighter aircraft; best known for development (1946) of Williams tube store, earliest computer memory system.

Williams, Sir George. 1821–1905. English merchant and philanthropist. Founder (1844) of Young Men's Christian Association, treasurer (1863–85), president (1886).

Williams, George Washington. 1849–1891. American politician and historian, b. Bedford Springs, Pa. Served in Negro regiment in Civil War; ordained Baptist minister (1874); admitted to Ohio bar (1878); in Ohio legislature (1879–81); U.S. minister to Haiti (1885–86); later interested in securing employment of American Negroes by Belgian government in the Congo. Author of *History of the Negro Race in America* (1883), *History of the Negro Troops in the War of the Rebellion* (1888).

Williams, Gluyas. 1888–1982. American cartoonist, b. San Francisco. Contributor of cartoons to *Collier's, The New Yorker,* and daily newspapers; illustrator of works of Robert Benchley.

Williams, Hank, *in full* Hiram Hank. 1923–1953. American singer and songwriter, b. near Georgiana, Ala. Performed on radio and in traveling country music shows; wrote over 100 songs rooted in blues, traditional country music, and hymns, most popular among them including "Lovesick Blues," "Your Cheatin' Heart," "Jambalaya," "Cold, Cold Heart," "Kaw-liga," "Half as Much," "Hey, Good Lookin'."

Williams, Isaac. 1802–1865. Welsh clergyman and author. Associated with Keble and Richard Hurrell Froude in Tractarian movement; known chiefly for his Tract No. 80 on *Reserve in Communicating Religious Knowledge;* wrote and translated many hymns.

Williams, James Robert. 1888–1957. American cartoonist, b. Halifax, N.S. Produced "Out Our Way," a daily syndicated cartoon.

Williams, John. 1796–1839. English missionary. Labored in Society Is. (1817), Raratonga (1823), Samoa, etc.; eaten by natives of New Hebrides.

Williams, Mary Lou. *Orig.* Mary Elfrieda Winn \'win\. 1910–1981. American musician, b. Pittsburgh. m. John Williams (c.1925); pianist with Andy Kirk band (1929–42), later led own groups and performed solo; one of most influential jazz performers and arrangers of the day; wrote and arranged "Froggy Bottom," "Twinklin'," "Walkin' and Struttin'," "Mary's Idea," "Cloudy," "Roll 'Em" and "Camel Hop" for Benny Goodman, "Trumpets No End" for Duke Ellington, "In the Land of Oo-bla-dee" for Dizzy Gillespie; later composed larger works as *Zodiac Suite* (1946), *Black Christ of the Andes* (1963), three masses including *Mary Lou's Mass* (1971).

Williams, Sir Monier Monier-. See MONIER-WILLIAMS.

Williams, Ralph Vaughan. See VAUGHAN WILLIAMS.

Williams, Roger. 1603?–1683. American clergyman and founder of Rhode Island, b. London, England. To America (1630); pastor in Plymouth, Mass. (1632–33); incurred hostility of civil authorities by his doctrines and outspoken criticisms of what he deemed their abuse of their powers; banished by Massachusetts General Court (1635). With a few faithful adherents, founded Providence (1636), earliest settlement in Rhode Island. Maintained good relations with the Indians and, by his friendship with the Narragansetts, aided in colonial success in the Pequot War. Withdrew from all church connections (1639), accepting no creed but maintaining a fundamental belief in Christianity. To England (1643) and secured a charter for the Providence Plantations in Narragansett Bay (Mar. 1644). President of the colony (1654–57). Famous as apostle of religious toleration and an advocate of democracy and liberal government. Author of *A Key into the Language of America* (1643), *Bloudy Tenent of Persecution* (1644), *The Hireling Ministry None of Christ's* (1652).

Williams, Tennessee, *orig.* Thomas Lanier. 1911–1983. American playwright, b. Columbus, Miss. Introduced to the American theater such previously taboo subjects as homosexuality, nymphomania, castration, and cannibalism. Established reputation with highly autobiographical *The Glass Menagerie* (1944); confirmed his place in American drama with *A Streetcar Named Desire* (1947, Pulitzer Prize). Among his other plays were *Summer and Smoke* (1948), *The Rose Tattoo* (1951), *Camino Real* (1953), *Cat on a Hot Tin Roof* (1955, Pulitzer Prize), *Sweet Bird of Youth* (1959), *Suddenly Last Summer* (1958), and *The Night of the Iguana* (1961); later plays were unsuccessful. Wrote screenplays for several of his theater works and for *Baby Doll* (1956), *The Fugitive Kind* (1960), and *Boom!* (1968). Also wrote novel *The Roman Spring of Mrs. Stone* (1950), short stories, essays, verse, and *Memoirs* (1975). Regarded by many as greatest American dramatist after Eugene O'Neill.

Williams, William. *Known as* Williams Pant·y·cel·yn \ˌpän-tə-'kel-in\. 1717–1791. Welsh clergyman and hymn writer. Itinerant Methodist preacher (from c.1843); author of over 800 hymns, including the one translated as "Guide Me, O Thou Great Jehovah."

Williams, William. 1731–1811. American merchant and politician, b. Lebanon, Conn. Member, Continental Congress (1776–78, 1783, 1784) and a signer of the Declaration of Independence.

Williams, William Carlos. 1883–1963. American physician and writer, b. Rutherford, N.J. Author of verse *Poems* (1909), *The Tempers* (1913), *Al Que Quiere!* (1917), *Kora in Hell* (1920), *Sour Grapes* (1921), *Spring and All* (1922), *An Early Martyr* (1935), *Adam and Eve in the City* (1936), *The Wedge* (1944), the epic *Paterson* (1946–58), *Pictures from Breughel* (1962, Pulitzer prize); essays *In the American Grain* (1925); novels *A Voyage to Pagany* (1928) and trilogy *White Mule* (1937), *In the Money* (1940), and *The Build-Up* (1952); stories collected as *Knife of the Times* (1932), *Life Along the Passaic River* (1938), *Make Light of It* (1950), *Farmers' Daughters* (1961).

Williams, Sir William Fenwick. 1800–1883. British army officer. As commander of Turkish force in Crimean War, hero of defense of Kars against Russians (1855).

Wil·liam·son \ˈwil-yəm-sən\, Alexander William. 1824–1904. English chemist. Professor, U. Coll., London (1849–87); known for work on etherification and the constitution of ether; demonstrated relation of ethers and alcohols (1850), elucidated reversible reactions, dynamic equilibrium, catalysis.

Williamson, Edward Nagle, *called* Ned. 1857–1895. American baseball player, b. Philadelphia. Professional major-league infielder (1878–90), chiefly for Chicago White Stockings (National League); set record for single-season home runs (27 in 1884) that stood until broken by Babe Ruth (1919).

Williamson, Henry. 1895–1977. English novelist. Author of autobiographical tetralogy *The Flax of Dream,* comprising *The Beautiful Years* (1921), *Dandelion Days* (1922), *The Dream of Fair Women* (1924), *The Pathway* (1928); also wrote *Tarka the Otter* (1927, Hawthornden prize), *Salar the Salmon* (1935), *The Phasian Bird* (1948), and a 15-novel cycle titled *Chronicle of Ancient Sunlight* (1951–69).

Williamson, John Lee, *called* Sonny Boy. 1914–1948. American musician, b. Jackson, Tenn. To Chicago (1932), where he became a shaping force in blues idiom; introduced widely influential harmonica and vocal styles in such recordings as "Good Morning School Girl," "Big Apple Blues," "Bad Luck Blues," "War Time Blues."

Williamson, William Crawford. 1816–1895. English naturalist. First professor of natural history, anatomy, and physiology, Owens College, Manchester (1851–92); carried on researches on development of the teeth and bones of fishes; considered a founder of paleobotany for his work on submarine deposits, coal fossils, etc.

Wil·li·bald \ˈwil-ə-ˌbȯld\. Saint. 700–786. English missionary. Nephew and associate of Saint Boniface and brother of St. Walburga; bishop of Eichstätt (741).

Wil·li·brord \ˈwil-ə-ˌbrȯrd\ *or* **Wil·brord** \ˈwil-ˌbrȯrd\ *or* **Wil·brod** \ˈwil-ˌbräd\. Saint. 658?–739. English missionary. Entered Benedictine monastery at Ripon; ordained (688); sent by St. Egbert to Friesland (690); archbishop of the Frisians (695), residing at Utrecht; extended work into Denmark, founding (698) monastery at Echternach; baptized Pepin III the Short (714); later assisted by St. Boniface.

Willingdon, Marquis of. See FREEMAN-THOMAS.

Wil·lis \ˈwil-əs\, Bailey. 1857–1949. American geologist, b. Idlewild-on-Hudson, N.Y. Son of Nathaniel P. Willis. On staff of U.S. Geological Survey (1882–1910, 1914–15); helped organize Argentine geological survey (1910–14); professor, Stanford (1915–22); known for studies of earthquakes, erosion, and esp. of mountain-building; conducted pioneering model studies of folding and deformation; instrumental in securing establishment (1899) of Mount Rainier National Park.

Willis, Henry. 1821–1901. English organ builder. Established firm in London (1848); built or restored some 1000 organs in Great Britain, including those in Gloucester cathedral, Crystal Palace of Great Exhibition of 1851, King's Coll., London (1856), Royal Albert Hall (1871), St. Paul's Cathedral (1872); organs noted for balance, voicing, brilliant reed stops.

Willis, Nathaniel Parker. 1806–1867. American editor and writer, b. Portland, Me. Founded and edited *American Monthly* in Boston (1829–31). Traveled in Europe as correspondent of New York *Mirror* (1831–36); associate editor of the *Evening Mirror* (1844–46) and the *Home Journal* (1846–67). Author of *Poetical Scripture Sketches* (1827), *Fugitive Poetry* (1829), *Inklings of Adventure* (1836), *À l'Abri; or, the Tent Pitch'd* (1839), *Loiterings of Travel* (1840), *American Scenery* (1840), *Pencillings by the Way* (1844), *Dashes at Life with a Free Pencil* (1845), *Rural Letters* (1849), *Famous Persons and Places* (1854), *Paul Fane* (1856), *The Convalescent* (1859), and the play *Tortesa, or the Usurer Matched* (1839).

Willis, Thomas. 1621–1675. English anatomist and physician. Professor at Oxford (1660–75); a founder of the Royal Society (1662); first to describe myasthenia gravis (1671) and puerperal fever; distinguished diabetes mellitus from other forms of diabetes; discovered system of connecting arteries at base of brain known as circle of Willis; published *Cerebri anatomi* (1664) on the brain and nervous system.

Wil·lis·ton \ˈwil-ə-stən\, Samuel Wendell. 1852–1918. American paleontologist, b. Roxbury, Mass. Assistant to O.C. Marsh at Yale (1876–85); professor of anatomy, Yale (1886–90); professor of geology and paleontology, U. of Kansas (1890–1902); founder and first dean (1898–1902) of medical school of U. of Kansas; head of department of vertebrate paleontology, Univ. of Chicago (from 1902); known for studies of dinosaurs, esp. of Permian era; known also as entomologist for studies of Diptera.

Will·kie \ˈwil-kē\, Wendell Lewis. 1892–1944. American politician, b. Elwood, Ind. Practiced law in Indiana and Ohio (1916–29); in New York as attorney (1929–33), president (1933–40), Commonwealth and Southern Corp.; Republican nominee for president of the United States (1940); practiced law in New York (1941 ff.); made tour of Egypt, Middle East, Russia, and China (1942), recording experiences and conclusions in *One World* (1943).

Wil·lough·by \ˈwil-ə-bē\, Francis William. 5th Baron Willoughby of Par·ham \ˈpar-əm\. c.1613–1666. English colonialist. Parliamentary commander in the field (1642–45); speaker of House of Lords (1647); fled impeachment to Holland and joined Royalists (1648); governor of Barbados (1650–52); driven out by Parliamentary forces; sent expedition that established (1651) first settlement in Surinam; restored to Barbados (1663) and given joint proprietorship of Surinam with Lawrence Hyde.

Willoughby, Sir Hugh. d. 1554. English navigator. Commander of a fleet of three vessels, one captained by Richard Chancellor, sent out by Sebastian Cabot to search for northeastern passage to Cathay (China) and India (1553); ships dispersed in a storm, Willoughby's ship and another landing in a harbor in Lapland. During the winter all perished.

Wills \ˈwilz\, William Gorman. 1828–1891. Irish playwright and poet. Made great success with *Man o'Airlie* (1866) and esp. with *Charles I* (1872), played by Henry Irving; other plays included *Medea in Corinth* (1872), *Olivia* (1873), *Jane Shore* (1876). Author of ballads, including "I'll Sing Thee Songs of Araby."

Wills, William John. 1834–1861. Australian explorer, b. Devonshire, England. Emigrated to Victoria (1852); second in command to Robert O'Hara Burke (*q.v.*) in ill-fated expedition to discover northward route across Australia (1860); died of starvation.

Will·stät·ter \ˈvil-ˌstet-ər\, Richard. 1872–1942. German chemist. Professor, Zürich (1905–12); director, Kaiser Wilhelm Inst., Berlin (1912–16); professor, Munich (1916–24); known for researches on complex organic substances, esp. on the coloring matter (anthocyanins and chlorophyll) in plants and on enzymes. Awarded 1915 Nobel prize for chemistry.

Wil·lugh·by \ˈwil-ə-bē\, Francis. 1635–1672. English naturalist. Student and associate of John Ray; toured Britain, Low Countries, Germany, Italy, Spain (1660–64), collecting botanical and zoological specimens; began work of classification completed by Ray (*q.v.*).

Wil·lum·sen \ˈvē-lu̇m-sən\, Jens Ferdinand. 1863–1958. Danish painter and sculptor. Created works showing influence of Symbolists, Gauguin, Redon, and latterly the Mannerism of El Greco.

Wil·lys \ˈwil-əs\, John North. 1873–1935. American industrialist, b. Canandaigua, N.Y. Started in bicyle business (1890); bought Overland Automobile Co. plant in Indianapolis (1907), moved it to Toledo, and manufactured Willys-Overland and other automobiles; president (1907–29, 1935), chairman (1929–35). U.S. ambassador to Poland (1930–32).

Wilmington, Earl of. See Spencer COMPTON.

Wil·mot \ˈwil-mət, -ˌmät\, David. 1814–1868. American politician, b. Bethany, Pa. Member, U.S. House of Representatives (1845–51); introduced Wilmot Proviso (1846) attached to a bill for purchasing territory from Mexico, the amendment providing that slavery should be prohibited in any such territory thus acquired; the proviso was adopted in the House but defeated in the Senate. One of the founders of the Republican party; U.S. senator (1861–63).

Wilmot, Frank Leslie Thomson. *Pseudonym* Furn·ley Mau·rice \ˈfərn-lē-ˈmȯr-əs, -ˈmär-\. 1881–1942. Australian poet. Worked in Melbourne bookshop (1895–1929); manager of Melbourne University Press (1932–42). Best known for antiwar poem "To God: From the Warring Nations" (1917); his books of verse included *Some Verses* (1903), *Unconditioned Songs* (1913), *The Bay and Padie Book* (children's verse, 1917), *Eyes of Vigilance* (1920), *The Gully* (1929), *Melbourne Odes* (1934).

Wilmot, John. 2d Earl of Roch·es·ter \ˈräch-ə-stər, -ˌes-tər\. 1647–1680. English poet. Companion of Charles II; a leader of the "court wits"; notorious for debaucheries and escapades; patron and lover of Elizabeth Barry; supposedly repented on deathbed, according to Bishop Burnet. Author of the tragedy *Valentinian* (1685), graceful amorous lyrics, and esp. verse satires as *A Satyr against Mankind* (1675).

Wil·son \ˈwil-sən\, Alexander. 1766–1813. American ornithologist, b. Paisley, Scotland. To U.S. (1794); schoolmaster in rural schools in New Jersey and eastern Pennsylvania. Encouraged by William Bartram, began serious ornithological work (c.1802). Aided by Alexander Lawson, who prepared plates of the birds described, began publication of *American Ornithology* (1808–14), recognized as a classic in its field. Author also of a volume of verse (1790) and a poetical account of a walking trip from Philadelphia to Niagara Falls and back, under the title of *The Foresters* (1805).

Wilson, Sir Arthur Knyvet. 1842–1921. British naval officer. Entered navy (1855); served in Crimean War, in operations against Alexandria (1880); rear admiral (1895); vice admiral (1901); commander in chief of home and channel fleets (1903–07); admiral of the fleet (1907); first sea lord (1910–12).

Wilson, Charles Edward. 1886–1972. American industrialist, b. New York City. With General Electric Co. (from 1899), president (1940–42, 1944–50); vice chairman (1942), executive vice chairman (1943–44), War Production Board; director, Office of Defense Mobilization (1950–52).

Wilson, Charles Erwin. 1890–1961. American engineer and industrialist, b. Minerva, Ohio. With General Motors Corp. (from 1919), vice president (1929–40), president (1941–53); U.S. secretary of defense (1953–57).

Wilson, Charles Thomson Rees. 1869–1959. Scottish physicist. Professor, Cambridge (1925–34); known for research on atmospheric electricity and development (1895–1911) of the Wilson cloud chamber, which made possible direct and photographic observation of ionizing radiation. Awarded (jointly with A.H. Compton) 1927 Nobel prize for physics.

Wilson, Dover, *in full* John Dover. 1881–1969. British scholar, b. Scotland. Professor, King's Coll., London (1924–35), Edinburgh (1935–45); noted Shakespearian scholar; editor of New Cambridge edition of Shakespeare (1921 ff.). Author of *Life in Shakespeare's England* (1911), *The Essential Shakespeare* (1932), *What Happens in Hamlet* (1934), *The Fortunes of Falstaff* (1943), *Shakespeare's Happy Comedies* (1962), *Shakespeare's Sonnets* (1963).

Wilson, Edmund. 1895–1972. American critic and writer, b. Red Bank, N.J. Author of influential criticism of contemporary literature and politics in *Axel's Castle* (1931), *Travels in Two Democracies* (1936), *The Triple Thinkers* (1938), *To the Finland Station* (1940), *The Wound and the Bow* (1941), *The Boys in the Back Room* (1941), etc.; miscellaneous essays as *Europe Without Baedecker* (1947), *Classics and Commercials* (1950), *American Earthquake* (1958), *Apologies to the Iroquois* (1960), *Patriotic Gore* (1962), *O Canada* (1965), *The Bit Between My Teeth* (1965), *Fruits of the MLA* (1968), *Upstate* (1972); novel *I Thought of Daisy* (1929) and stories *Memoirs of Hecate County* (1946); edited anthology *The Shock of Recognition* (1943) and late works and papers of F. Scott Fitzgerald.

Wilson, Edmund Beecher. 1856–1939. American biologist, b. Geneva, Ill. Professor, Bryn Mawr (1885–91), Columbia U. (1891–1928); known for work in morphology, embryology, cytology, heredity; showed chromosomal basis of sex determination in the embryo (1905). Author of *The Cell in Development and Inheritance* (1896), revised for 3d edition as *The Cell in Development and Heredity* (1928).

Wilson, Edward Adrian. 1872–1912. English physician and explorer. On Robert F. Scott's last Antarctic expedition as chief of scientific staff; with party of five which reached South Pole (Jan. 1912) and perished on return journey.

Wilson, Halsey William. 1868–1954. American publisher, b. Wilmington, Vt. Compiled (1898) *Cumulative Book Index;* inaugurated *United States Catalog* (1899), *Readers' Guide to Periodical Literature* (1901); formed (1903) H.W. Wilson Co., president (1903–52); published *Book Review Digest* (from 1905), *Wilson Library Bulletin* (from 1914), *Union List of Serials* (1927), *Educational Film Guide* (1936), etc.

Wilson, Harry Leon. 1867–1939. American writer, b. Oregon, Ill. m. (1902) Rose C. O'Neill. Editor, *Puck* (1896–1902); author of *Zig Zag Tales* (1896), *Bunker Bean* (1912), *Ruggles of Red Gap* (1915), *Merton of the Movies* (1922), *Cousin Jane* (1925), *Two Black Sheep* (1931), etc.; collaborated with Booth Tarkington on play *The Man From Home* (1907).

Wilson, Henry. *Orig.* Jeremiah Jones Col·bath \ˈkōl-ˌbath\. 1812–1875. American politician, b. Farmington, N.H. Engaged in manufacture of shoes (from c.1833). Ardent antislavery advocate; headed group that bolted Whig convention (1848) and founded the Free-Soil party; edited Free-Soil party journal *Boston Republican* (1848–51); chairman, Free-Soil convention (1852). Joined the American (Know-Nothing) party (1854) but soon withdrew. U.S. senator from Massachusetts (1855–73); one of founders of Republican party; chairman of Senate committee on military affairs through the Civil War. Vice president of the United States (1873–75).

Wilson, Henry Braid. 1861–1954. American naval officer, b. Camden, N.J. Entered navy (1881); rear admiral (1917); commanded patrol force of the Atlantic fleet (1917–18) and U.S. naval forces in France (1918–19); admiral (1919) and commander in chief of the Atlantic fleet (1919–21); superintendent, U.S. Naval Academy (1921–25).

Wilson, Sir Henry Hughes. Baronet. 1864–1922. British army officer, b. Ireland. Entered army (1882); served in Burma, Boer War; brigadier general (1907); commandant of Staff Coll. (1907–10); advocated cooperation with France in event of Continental war; as director of military operations (1910–14), instrumental in landing expeditionary force in France without loss of a man or horse (1914); principal liaison officer with French headquarters (1914–15); lieutenant general (1915). Commander of Eastern Command (1917–18); chief of imperial general staff (1918–22); field marshal (1919). M.P. for North Down, Ireland (1922); advocate of drastic coercion against Sinn Féin; murdered by two Sinn Féiners.

Wilson, Henry Maitland. 1st Baron. 1881–1964. British army officer. Entered army (1900); served in Boer War, World War I; major general (1935), lieutenant general (1939); commander, forces in Egypt (1939); military governor of Cyrenaica (1941); commander in Greece (1941), in Palestine and Trans-Jordan (1941), in Persia-Iraq (1942–43); British commander in chief in Middle East (1943–44); supreme Allied commander in Mediterranean (1944); field marshal (1944); chief of British joint staff mission in Washington (1945–47); created baron (1946).

Wilson, Horace Hayman. 1786–1860. English Orientalist. Professor of Sanskrit, Oxford (1832–60); librarian, East India House (1836–60). Published edition of the *Meghadūta* (1813); compiled *Sanskrit–English Dictionary* (1819) and Sanskrit grammar (1841); translated *Vishnupurāna* (1840), part of *Rig-Veda* (1850 ff.).

Wilson, Jack. See WOVOKA.

Wilson, James. 1742–1798. American lawyer and politician, b. Carskerdy, Scotland. To U.S. (1765) and settled in Philadelphia. Member of Continental Congress (1774, 1775–77); prepared and published for distribution to his fellow members *Considerations on the Nature and Extent of the Legislative Authority of the British Parliament,* in which he adopted the extreme position that Parliament had no authority over the colonies; signer of Declaration of Independence. Member of Continental Congress again (1782, 1783, 1785–87); delegate from Pennsylvania to the Constitutional Convention (1787) and to the Pennsylvania ratification convention (1788); largely drafted constitution of Pennsylvania (1790). Associate justice, U.S. Supreme Court (1789–98); first professor of law, U. of Pennsylvania (from 1790).

Wilson, James. 1805–1860. British economist. Founded *The Economist* (1843); M.P. (1847–59); financial secretary to treasury (1853–58); in India as financial member of council of India (from 1859); established paper currency in India.

Wilson, James Harrison. 1837–1925. American army officer, b. near Shawneetown, Ill. Entered army (1860); brigadier general of volunteers (Oct. 1863); commanded 3d division in Sheridan's cavalry corps, army of the Potomac; chief of cavalry, military division of the Mississippi, and brevet major general (Oct. 1864); defeated Forrest at Franklin (Nov. 30, 1864) and at Ebenezer Church (Apr. 1, 1865), captured Montgomery, Ala., and Columbus, Ga., and reached Macon when hostilities ended. Resigned from army (1870); volunteered in Spanish–American War; second in command to Gen. Adna R. Chaffee of contingent sent to China at time of Boxer uprising (1900).

Wilson, John. 1595–1674. English composer and lute virtuoso. Musician to Charles I (1635) and to Charles II (1661); professor, Oxford (1656–61); set to music Shakespeare's *Take, O Take Those Lips Away* and composed airs and glees, including *In the Merry Month of May.* Probably the Jack Willson of stage direction in *Much Ado about Nothing* in the folio edition of 1623.

Wilson, John. *Pseudonym* Christopher North \ˈnȯ(ə)rth\. 1785–1854. Scottish poet, essayist, and critic. Friend of Wordsworth, Southey, Coleridge, and De Quincey; published two volumes of graceful poetry, *The Isle of Palms* (1812), *The City of the Plague* (1816). Joined (1817) J. G. Lockhart in *Blackwood's Magazine;* professor of moral philosophy, Edinburgh (1820–51); turned to prose fiction in *Lights and Shadows of Scottish Life* (1822), *Trials of Margaret Lyndsay* (1823), *The Foresters* (1825); contributed to *Blackwood's* critical essays on Homer and Spenser and greater number of *Noctes Ambrosianae* (1822–35), a symposium on literature, politics, philosophy, and topics of the day.

Wilson, John Dover. See Dover WILSON.

Wilson, John Mackay. 1804–1835. English writer. Originator of the *Tales of the Borders,* realistic narratives of stirring incident or sentiment, in weekly numbers (1834–35), continued by Alexander Leighton.

Wilson, Richard. 1714–1782. Welsh painter. Influenced by Poussin, Claude Lorrain, etc., became one of first important British landscapists; blended classicism with picturesque effects. Works included *View of Rome from the Villa Madama, Lake Nemi, Snowdon, Minchenden House.*

Wilson, Robert. d. 1600. English actor and playwright. Original member of Earl of Leicester's company (1572); author of several morality plays including *Three Ladies of London* (1584), containing the incident of the Jew seeking to recover his debt, later used by Shakespeare in his *Merchant of Venice.*

Wilson, Sir Robert Thomas. 1777–1849. English army officer. Commanded brigade under Wellington in Peninsular War; British commissioner attached to Russian army (1811); commanded Prussian reserve at Lützen (1813); M.P. (1818–31); general (1841); governor of Gibraltar (1842–49). Author of accounts of expeditions to Egypt (1802) and campaigns in Poland (1811), and of a *Sketch of the Military and Political Power of Russia* (1817).

Wilson, Rose O'Neill. See Rose O'NEILL.

Wilson, Samuel. 1766–1854. American meat packer, b. Arlington, Mass. Resident of Troy, N.Y. (from 1789), where he was known as "Uncle Sam"; during War of 1812, acted as inspector for a government contractor and stamped barrels of meat with initials U.S. (for United States), from which came the use of "Uncle Sam" for the U.S. government.

Wilson, Thomas. 1525?–1581. English scholar and politician. M.P. (1563–67, 1572–81); secretary of state (1577–80); dean of Durham (1580); undertook many diplomatic and other missions for Elizabeth I. Author of highly influential *Arte of Rhetorique* (1553); also wrote *Rule of Reason,* a handbook of logic (1551).

Wilson, William Bauchop. 1862–1934. American labor leader, b. Blantyre, Scotland. To U.S. (1870); employed in Pennsylvania coal mines (from 1871); one of organizers of United Mine Workers of America (1890) and its secretary-treasurer (1900–08); prominent in coal strikes (1899, 1902). Member, U.S. House of Representatives (1907–13). First U.S. secretary of labor (1913–21); organized new department and established U.S. Employment Service (1914); did important work in promoting mediation in labor disputes and advocating collective bargaining.

Wilson, William Lyne. 1843–1900. American politician, b. Middleway, Va. (now W.Va.). Served in Confederate army through Civil War; professor, Columbian Coll. (1865–71); president, U. of West Virginia (1882–83). Member, U.S. House of Representatives (1883–95); associated with tariff legislation, esp. with Wilson-Gorman Tariff (1894). U.S. postmaster general (1895–97). President, Washington and Lee U. (1897–1900).

Wilson, Woodrow, *in full* Thomas Woodrow. 1856–1924. Twenty-eighth president of the United States, b. Staunton, Va. Instructor in history, Bryn Mawr (1885–88), Wesleyan (1888–90); professor of jurisprudence and political economy, Princeton (1890–1902); president of Princeton (1902–10); developed preceptorial system and advocated a house system based on the English universities with their component colleges. Governor of New Jersey (1911–13); attracted national attention by pushing through legislature important reform measures, including a primary election law, a corrupt practices act, an employers' liability act. President of the United States (1913–21); his "New Freedom" domestic policies produced legislation as three constitutional amendments (17th, 1913, providing for direct popular election of senators; 18th, 1919, providing for prohibition; 19th, 1920, extending suffrage to women), Underwood Tariff Act (1913), Clayton Antitrust Act (1914), establishment of Federal Reserve banking system (1914), creation of Federal Trade Commission (1914), Child Labor Law (1916), etc. In foreign affairs, sent U.S. troops to occupy Veracruz, Mexico (1914), and to pursue Pancho Villa into Mexico (1916); in Europe maintained neutrality in World War I with great difficulty until Germany, contrary to pledges previously given, announced (Jan. 1917) unrestricted submarine warfare in waters around Great Britain; sinking of American ships following the change in German policy led to declaration of war (Apr. 6, 1917); proposed war as crusade to "make the world safe for democracy"; formulated (Jan. 1918) Fourteen Points plan for peace; plan accepted by Germany (Oct. 1918) and reluctantly by Allies, leading to Armistice (Nov. 11, 1918). Personally participated in Versailles Peace Conference and forced acceptance of League of Nations covenant as an integral part of the treaty of peace. Awarded Nobel peace prize for 1919. In U.S., found a strong opposition in the Senate to ratification of the treaty of peace; refused to compromise on the terms; attempted country-wide speech-making campaign to put the issue before the people but suffered nervous collapse (Sept. 1919); an invalid through remainder of his term of office. Lived in retirement in Washington (from 1921). Among his books were *Congressional Government* (1885), *The State* (1889), *A History of the American People* (1902), *Constitutional Government in the United States* (1908).

Wiltshire, Earl of. See James Butler (1420–1461) under BUTLER family; William le Scrope under SCROPE family.

Wi·man \ˈwē-ˈmän\. *Chin.* Wei Man \ˈwā-ˈmän\. fl. c.190 B.C. Chinese general. Possibly a Korean in Chinese service; usurped throne of Korean state of Chosŏn; established new capital on site of present P'yŏngyang.

Wimbledon, Viscount. See CECIL family.

Wim·phe·ling *or* **Wim·pfe·ling** *or* **Wym·pfe·ling** \ˈvimp-fə-liŋ\, Jacob. 1450–1528. German Humanist. Preacher at Speyer cathedral (1484); professor at Heidelberg (1498). Author of *Stylpho,* first German example of Italianate New Latin comedy (1470), *Germania* (1501), *Epitome rerum Germanicarum usque ad nostra tempora,* one of earliest histories of Germany (1505), *Catalogus episcoporum Argentinensium* (1507), etc.

Win·chell \ˈwin-chəl\, Alexander. 1824–1891. American geologist, b. Northeast, N.Y. Professor, Michigan (1853–73, from 1879). Author of *Sketches of Creation* (1870), *The Doctrine of Evolution* (1874), *World Life* (1883), *Geological Studies* (1886). His brother ¶Newton Horace (1839–1914), geologist and archaeologist, was state geologist of Minnesota (1872–1900); professor, U. of Minnesota (1874–1900); believed that man lived on American continent in latter part of Ice Age; founder and editor (1888–1905) of *American Geologist,* first American geological periodical. Newton's son ¶Horace Vaughn (1865–1923), b. Galesburg, Mich., was geologist for Anaconda Copper Co. (1898–1906), Northern Pacific Railroad (1906–08); consulting geologist (1908–21); authority on ore formation, mining law; helped found and edited (1905–10) *Economic Geology,* incorporating his father's *American Geologist.* Another son ¶Alexander Newton (1874–1958), b. Minneapolis; professor, Wisconsin (1907–44); author with his father of standard *Elements of Optical Mineralogy* (1909).

Winchell, Walter. 1897–1972. American journalist, b. New York City. In vaudeville (1909–20), for a time with George Jessel; columnist for *Vaudeville News* (1922–24), *New York Evening Graphic* (1924–29), *New York Daily Mirror* (1929–63); known for slangy, gossipy, opinionated reporting; on radio (1932–53) and later television.

Win·chel·sea *or* **Win·chel·sey** \ˈwin-chəl-sē\, Robert de. d. 1313. English prelate. Chancellor of Oxford (1288); archbishop of Canterbury (1293); strenuously upheld privileges of clergy; bore papal mandate (1300) forbidding Edward I's attack on Scots, and otherwise upheld papal authority; exiled (1306–07); aided barons in struggle against Edward II.

Winchester, Marquises of. See PAULET.

Win·ches·ter \ˈwin-ˌches-tər, -chə-stər\, Oliver Fisher. 1810–1880. American industrialist, b. Boston. Bought control of an arms-manufacturing company in New Haven, Conn. (1857), and acquired repeating-rifle inventions of various inventors; introduced Henry repeating rifle (1860) and later various improved models, notably the Winchester 73; reorganized company under name of Winchester Repeating Arms Co. (1867).

Winchilsea, Earls and countess of. See FINCH family.

Winck·el·mann \ˈviŋ-kəl-ˌmän\, Johann Joachim. 1717–1768. German archaeologist and art critic. Librarian to Count von Bünau (1748–54); Roman Catholic convert (1754); to Rome (1755), where he studied art and classical antiquities; visited Florence, Pompeii, Naples, etc.; in charge of antiquities (from 1763) and scriptor of the Vatican; murdered (1768). Author of *Gedanken über die Nachahmung der griechischen Werke,* which defined Greek aesthetic and essentially created Neoclassical movement in the arts (1755), *Geschichte der Kunst des Altertums* (1764), *Monumenti antichi inediti* (1767), etc.

Winck·ler \ˈviŋ-klər\, Hugo. 1863–1913. German archaeologist. Professor, Berlin (1904); took part in excavations of ancient Sidon (1903–04); in Boğazköy (1906–12) uncovered the ancient Hittite capital and discovered tablets in Hittite and other languages. Author of works on cuneiform inscriptions and the culture and history of ancient Babylonia and Assyria.

Win·daus \ˈvin-ˌdau̇s\, Adolf Otto Reinhold. 1876–1959. German chemist. Professor, Freiburg (1905–13), Innsbruck (1913–15); professor and head of chemical institute, U. of Göttingen (1915–44); known for researches on sterols, esp. cholesterol, whose structure he established (1932), and for experiments proving that ultraviolet light activates ergosterol, producing vitamin D; discovered histamine. Awarded 1928 Nobel prize for chemistry.

Win·del·band \ˈvin-dəl-ˌbänt\, Wilhelm. 1848–1915. German philosopher. Professor, Zürich (1876), Freiburg (1877), Strassburg (1882), Heidelberg (1903); a founder of Neo-Kantian philosophy. Author of *Die Geschichte der neueren Philosophie* (1878–80), *Geschichte der alten Philosophie* (1888), *Über Willensfreiheit* (1904), etc.

Wind·ham \ˈwin-dəm\, William. 1750–1810. English politician. Friend of Dr. Johnson and Burke; M.P. (1784–1810); on outbreak of French Revolution turned reactionary with Burke and joined cabinet under Pitt as secretary at war (1794–1801); held secretaryships of war and of colonial office in Grenville's government (1806–07); carried measures for pensions and shorter terms of service for army; advocated protection of England with large navy.

Win·disch·grätz \ˈvin-dish-ˌgrets\, Alfred Candidus Ferdinand zu. Fürst. 1787–1862. Austrian field marshal. Entered army (1804); commander in Bohemia (1840–48); suppressed Czech uprising in Prague (1848), defeated Hungarians at Schwechat, made field marshal (1848); suppressed insurrection in Vienna; with Schwarzenberg, helped elevate Francis Joseph I to the throne (1848); occupied Budapest, defeated Hungarians at Kápolna, but was defeated at Gödöllö and removed from command (1849); member, Austrian upper house (1861).

Wind·sor \ˈwin-zər\. Official name of royal family of Great Britain since 1917, superseding family name of Wettin (*q.v.*) and dynastic designation of Saxe-Coburg-Gotha (*q.v.*). Its ruling members have been: George V (from 1917), Edward VIII, George VI, and Elizabeth II.

Windsor, Duchess of. See Wallis SIMPSON.

Windsor, Duke of. See EDWARD VIII of Great Britain.

Windsor, Alice de. See Alice PERRERS.

Windt·horst \'vint-ˌhȯrst\, Ludwig. 1812–1891. German politician. Justice minister of Hanover (1851–53, 1862–65); member of Reichstag (1867) and Prussian Chamber of Deputies; became leader (1871) of newly organized Catholic Center party; during Kulturkampf, champion of ultramontane cause; leading opponent of Bismarck government, but a supporter of its economic policy.

Winfield, Arthur M. See Edward STRATEMEYER.

Win·gate \'win-ˌgāt, -gət\, Orde Charles. 1903–1944. British soldier, b. India. Entered army (1923); served in Sudan (1928–33), Palestine (1936–38); organized and led Ethiopian-Sudanese force that recaptured Addis Ababa (May 1941); recognized as expert in irregular mobile tactics; to China; organized irregular "Chindit" brigade and helped train U.S. Merrill's Marauders; harassed Japanese in Burma (1943); major general (1944); in command of airborne troops invading central Burma (1944).

Wingate, Sir Reginald, *in full* Francis Reginald. Baronet. 1861–1953. British army officer and administrator. Entered army (1880); served on Sudan frontier (1889, 1891), in reconquest of Sudan (1896–98); succeeded Kitchener as governor general of Sudan (1899–1916); general (1913); high commissioner for Egypt (1917–19); baronet (1920). Author of *Mahdiism and the Egyptian Sudan* (1891).

Wing·field \'wiŋ-fēld\, Edward Maria. 1560?–?1613. English colonist. One of those to whom Virginia charter was issued (Apr. 10, 1606); accompanied first settlers and was chosen first president of Virginia colony (Apr. 1607); deposed (Sept. 1607); sent to England (1608) and published his defense *A Discourse of Virginia* (1608).

Wingfield, Walter Clopton. *Known as* Major Wingfield. 1833–1912. English soldier and sportsman. Credited with central role in invention of modern lawn tennis; published rulebook *Sphairistikè, or Lawn Tennis* (1873) and patented game and equipment (1874).

Win·kel \'viŋ-kəl\, Dietrich Nikolaus. c.1780–1826. German inventor. Invented (c.1812) the metronome, which was patented and commercialized by J.N. Maelzel.

Winkel, Lambert Allard te. 1806–1868. Dutch philologist. Founder of modern Dutch grammar and, with Matthijs de Vries (see VRIES) of modern Dutch orthography. Coeditor with de Vries of *Groot Woordenboek der Nederlandsche Taal* (1864); author of *De Grondbeginselen der Nederlandsche Spelling* (1863), *Leerboek der Nederlandsche Spelling* (1865), *Woordenlijst voor de Spelling der Nederlandsche Taal* (with de Vries, 1866), etc.

Win·kel·man \'viŋ-kəl-män\, Henri Gerard. 1876–1952. Dutch general. Entered army (1896); retired as general (1934); recalled as commander in chief of army and navy (1939); directed defense against German invasion (May 10–15, 1940); surrendered; interned by Germans (1940–45).

Wink·ler \'viŋ-klər\, Clemens Alexander. 1838–1904. German chemist. Professor, Freiberg School of Mining (1873–1902); discovered germanium (1886).

Win·ner \'win-ər\, Septimus. 1827–1902. American songwriter, b. Philadelphia. Wrote under various pseudonyms popular songs as "What Is Home Without a Mother?" (1854), "Listen to the Mocking Bird" (1855), "Oh Where, Oh Where Is My Little Dog Gone?," originally "The Deutcher's Dog" (1864), "Ten Little Injuns" (1868), "Whispering Hope" (1868).

Wi·no·grad·sky *or* **Vi·no·grad·sky** \vyin-(ˌ)ə-'grät-skəi\, Sergei Nikolaevitch. 1856–1953. Russian microbiologist. Member of Pasteur Inst., Paris (1890–91); director of microbiology (1891–1902), general director (1902–05), Inst. of Experimental Medicine, St. Petersburg; director of agricultural microbiology, Pasteur Inst. (1922–40); elucidated metabolism of sulfur bacteria; discovered (1889–90) bacteria responsible for nitrification; discovered nitrogen-fixing bacterium *Clostridium pastorianum* (1893–95).

Wins·low \'winz-ˌlō\, Edward. 1595–1655. American colonist, b. Droitwich, England. Arrived at Plymouth on the *Mayflower* (Dec. 21, 1620); wrote *A Relation or Iournall of the Beginning and Proceedings of the English Plantation Setled at Plimoth in New England* (printed in London, 1622), and *Good News from New England* (1624). Engaged in trading and exploring along New England coast. Served as member of the governor's council (1624–47) and as governor (1633, 1636, 1644). In England (from 1646); appointed by Cromwell a commissioner on expedition to capture the Spanish West India colonies, and seized Jamaica (1655); died at sea on return trip. Also wrote *Glorious Progress of the Gospel among the Indians in New England* (1649). His son ¶Josiah (1629?–1680), b. Plymouth, was member of the governor's council (1657–73) and governor of New Plymouth Colony (1673–80), first native-born governor in America; commanded forces of United Colonies in King Philip's War (1675–76).

Winslow, John Ancrum. 1811–1873. American naval officer, b. Wilmington, N.C. Entered navy (1827); served in Mexican War; captain (1862); commanded *Kearsarge* in victory over Raphael Semmes in Confederate raider *Alabama* off Cherbourg (June 19, 1864).

Win·sor \'win-zər\, Justin. 1831–1897. American librarian and historian, b. Boston. Librarian of Boston Public Library (1868–77) and of Harvard College (1877–97). A founder of American Library Association (1876) and its president (1876–85, 1897); a founder of the *Library Journal.* Author of *The Reader's Handbook of the American Revolution* (1879), *Christopher Columbus* (1891), *Cartier to Frontenac* (1894), *The Mississippi Basin* (1895), *The Westward Movement* (1897). Assembled a group of workers and coordinated their writing in producing *The Memorial History of Boston* (1880–81) and *Narrative and Critical History of America* (1884–89).

Win·stan·ley \'win-stən-lē\, Gerrard. 1609?–after 1660. English reformer. Leader of the Diggers (1649–50), a group upholding right of common people to land rent free for cultivation and dwelling; alleged (by Thomas Comber, dean of Durham) to have been real founder of the Quaker sect. Outlined a communistic society in *Law of Freedom in a Platform* (1652), dedicated to Oliver Cromwell.

Win·stedt \'win-stət, -ˌstet\, Sir Richard Olof. 1878–1966. English educator and scholar. School inspector (1902–16), assistant director (1916–21), director (1921–35) of education, Malay Federated States. Author of *Malay Grammar* (1913), *Colloquial Malay* (1916), *English–Malay Dictionary* (1914–17), *Shaman, Saiva and Sufi* (1925), *History of Malaya* (1935), *History of Malay Literature* (1939), *The Malays—A Cultural History* (1947), etc.

Wint, Peter de. See DE WINT.

Win·ter \'vin-tər\, Jan Willem de. 1761–1812. Dutch admiral. A leader of Patriot party (1785); fled to France (1787); entered French army at outbreak of Revolution (1789), rising to brigadier general; took part in invasion of Dutch Republic (1795); assigned by Estates-General to reorganize Dutch fleet and made admiral and commander in chief (1796); defeated by British fleet off Camperdown (Oct. 11, 1797). Ambassador to France (1798–1802). Commanded Dutch fleet that defeated Tripoli pirates (1802).

Winter, Peter von. 1754–1825. German composer. Orchestra director (1778–87), assistant Kapellmeister (1787–98), Kapellmeister (1798–1825) at electoral court, Munich. Composed operas as *Helena und Paris* (1782), *Das unterbrochene Opferfest* (1796), *Der Sturm* (1798), *Marie von Montalban* (1800), *Colmal* (1809), ballets, chamber and orchestral music, masses, etc.

Win·ter·hal·ter \'vin-tər-ˌhäl-tər\, Franz Xaver. 1805–1873. German painter. Court painter, Karlsruhe (1828); lived in Paris (1834–70); became one of most fashionable portraitists in Europe.

Win·ters \'wint-ərz\, Yvor, *in full* Arthur Yvor. 1900–1968. American poet and critic, b. Chicago. Taught at Stanford U. (1928–68, professor from 1949). Author of verse *The Immobile Wind* (1921), *The Magpie's Shadow* (1922), *The Bare Hills* (1927), *The Proof* (1930), *Before Disaster* (1934), *Collected Poems* (1952, 1960, Bollingen prize); criticism *Primitivism and Decadence* (1937), *Maule's Curse* (1938), *Anatomy of Nonsense* (1943), *In Defense of Reason* (1947), *Function of Criticism* (1957).

Win·ther \'vin-tər\, Christian, *in full* Rasmus Villads Christian Ferdinand. 1796–1876. Danish poet. Author of love lyrics *Til Een* (1848), the epic poem *Hjortens Flugt* (1855), prose tales and sketches of Danish life, etc.

Win·throp \'win(t)-thrəp\, John. 1588–1649. American colonist, b. Edwardstone, England. Practiced law in London; associated himself (c.1629) with group obtaining charter from Charles I for settlement on a land grant in eastern Massachusetts; elected governor (1629) before the group set sail for America. Sailed in the *Arbella* and reached Salem (June 1630); total community of about 1800 conveyed in the *Arbella* and in other ships arriving about the same time. Reelected governor (1631, 1632, 1633, 1637–40, 1642–44, 1646–49); opposed Henry Vane; in period of Antinomian controversy, opposed Anne Hutchinson and presided at the court that found her guilty and sentenced her to banishment. Influential in organizing United Colonies of New England (1643), and first president of the confederation. Two volumes of his *Journal* were published in 1790 and, with another volume, appeared in 1825–26 as *The History of New England from 1630 to 1649.*

His son ¶John (1606–1676), b. Groton, England, was also a colonial governor; landed at Boston (1631); leader of group that settled Ipswich (1633); in England (1634–35), where he was commissioned (July 1635) governor of a new "plantation" in Connecticut sponsored by Lord Saye and Sele and Lord Brooke; acted as governor (1636) and then returned to Massachusetts; later took up permanent abode in Connecticut and was governor (1657, 1659–76); obtained new liberal charter for Connecticut (1662). His son ¶John, *often known as* Fitz-John (1638–1707), b. Ipswich, Mass., was also a colonial governor; served as officer in the Parliamentary army in England and Scotland (1660); settled at New London, Conn. (1663); commander of Connecticut troops against the Dutch (1673), the Indians (1675–76), the French (1690); governor of Connecticut (1698–1707).

Winthrop, John. 1714–1779. American astronomer and physicist, b. Boston. Descendant of John Winthrop (1588–1649). Professor, Harvard (1738–79). Did important research work in astronomy, observing sunspots (1739), transits of Mercury (1740, 1743, 1769) and of Venus (1761, 1769); established (1746) first laboratory of experimental physics in America; introduced (1751) study of differential and integral calculus in the Harvard curriculum.

Winthrop, Robert Charles. 1809–1894. American politician, b. Boston. Descendant of John Winthrop (1588–1649). Member, U.S. House of Representatives (1840–50), speaker of the House (1847–49); U.S. senator from Massachusetts (1850–51).

Winthrop, Theodore. 1828–1861. American writer, b. New Haven, Conn. Descendant of John Winthrop (1588–1649). Volunteered at outbreak of Civil War; engaged in defense of Washington; killed at Great Bethel. Author of novels, published posthumously, *Cecil Dreeme* (1861), *John Brent* (1862), *Edwin Brothertoft* (1862), *The Canoe and the Saddle* (1863), *Life in the Open Air* (1863).

Winton, Earl of. See SETON family.

Win·ton \'wint-ᵊn\, Alexander. 1860–1932. American manufacturer, b. Grangemouth, Scotland. To U.S. (1880); in bicycle business, Cleveland (1884 ff.); built experimental automobile (1896) and formed Winton Motor Carriage Co. (1897); pioneered in opening chain of service stations, in sponsoring long-distance and speed competition, in building 8-cylinder engines; retired (1924).

Win·wood \'win-wu̇d\, Sir Ralph. 1563?–1617. English diplomat. Ambassador to France (1601–03); agent to Estates-General of Holland (1603–14); secretary of state for life (1614); defended in Parliament king's right to levy impositions; urged Sir Walter Raleigh to pillage Spanish settlements in South America.

Wireker, Nigel. See NIGEL.

Wirnt von Gra·fen·berg \'virnt-fōn-'grä-fən-berk\. 13th century. Middle High German poet. Authur of the epic romance in verse *Wigalois* (c.1204 or 1230), after a French source.

Wirt \'wərt\, William. 1772–1834. American lawyer, b. Bladensburg, Md. Practiced in Virginia. One of counsel for the prosecution in case against Aaron Burr (1807). U.S. attorney general (1817–29), appeared in famous law cases, including *McCulloch* v. *Maryland, Gibbons* v. *Ogden,* and the Dartmouth College case. Anti-Masonic candidate for president of the United States (1832).

Wirth \'virt\, Joseph, *in full* Karl Joseph. 1879–1956. German politician. Joined Catholic Center party; member of Reichstag (1914, 1920–33), and Weimar National Assembly (1919); minister of finance (1920–21) and chancellor (1921); accepted reparations terms of Allies (London ultimatum) and announced a policy of fulfillment (*Erfüllungspolitik*), but withdrew following disagreement over partition of Upper Silesia; formed second cabinet (1921) and acted as part-time foreign minister; represented Germany at Genoa Conference (1922); resigned as chancellor (1922) and was subsequently a leader of the left group of the Center party, Reichstag; minister of occupied provinces (1929–30) and minister of interior in Brüning's cabinet (1930–31).

Wirth \'vi(ə)rt\, Louis. 1897–1952. American sociologist, b. Gemünden, Germany. Professor, U. of Chicago (1926–52); known for studies of urbanism. Author of *The Ghetto* (1928), *Community Life and Social Policy* (1956), etc.; chief author of *Our Cities* by U.S. National Resources Committee (1937).

Wise \'wīz\, Isaac Mayer. *Orig. surname* Weis \'vīs\. 1819–1900. American clergyman, b. Steingrub, Bohemia. Rabbi at Radnice (1844–46); to U.S. (1846); rabbi of congregations in Albany, N.Y. (1846–54), and Cincinnati (1854–1900); a chief advocate of Reform Judaism and the adaptation of Jewish usages to American customs. Prominent in organization of Union of American Hebrew Congregations (1873), Hebrew Union College (1875; president 1875–1900), Central Conference of American Rabbis (1899); published newspapers *American Israelite* and *Die Deborah.* Wrote prayer book *Minhag America* (1857).

Wise, John. 1652–1725. American clergyman, b. Roxbury, Mass. Congregational pastor in Ipswich, Mass. (1680–1725); known for his zeal in maintaining democratic rights. Author of *Vindication of Government of New England Churches* (1717).

Wise, John. 1808–1879. American balloonist, b. Lancaster, Pa. Made first balloon ascent (1835); contributed several improvements to ballooning, notably the rip panel for making rapid descents; set distance record of 804 miles (St. Louis to Henderson, N.Y., 1859) that stood until 1900.

Wise, Stephen Samuel. 1874–1949. American clergyman, b. Budapest, Hungary. To U.S. (1875); rabbi in N.Y.C. (1893–1900), Portland, Ore. (1900–06); founded Free Synagogue, N.Y.C. (1907), rabbi there (1907–49); a leader in democratization of Reform Judaism, in civic reform, and in Zionist movement; a founder of Zionist Organization of America (1898; president 1917, 1936–38); founded (1922) Jewish Inst. of Religion; founder and editor of magazine *Opinion.* Author of *The Improvement of Moral Qualities* (1902), *How to Face Life* (1917), etc.

Wise·man \'wīz-mən\, Nicholas Patrick Stephen. 1802–1865. English prelate. Rector of English College, Rome (1828–40); founded (1836) *Dublin Review;* bishop (1840); influenced Oxford Movement and confirmed Newman; vicar apostolic of London district (1848); cardinal (1850) and first archbishop of Westminster. Wrote *Appeal to the Reason and Good Feeling of the English People* (1850) to allay storm of indignation at the papal establishment of hierarchy with territorial titles in England; author also of *Horae Syriacae* (1827), novel *Fabiola* (1854).

Wish·art \'wish-ərt\, George. c.1513–1546. Scottish reformer and martyr. Met Hugh Latimer at Cambridge (1538); visited Continent; tutor at Cambridge (1542–43); influenced John Knox; arrested, handed over to Cardinal Beaton, convicted of heresy by convocation of bishops, and burned.

Wis·li·ce·nus \ˌvis-lēt-'sā-nu̇s\, Johannes Adolph. 1835–1902. German chemist. Professor, Zürich (1861–72), Würzburg (1872–85), Leipzig (1885–1902); performed research on lactic acid, etc., of importance in development of stereochemistry.

Wiss·ler \'wis-lər\, Clark. 1870–1947. American anthropologist, b. Wayne Co., Ind. Curator, American Museum of Natural History (1906–41); professor, Yale (1924–40). Author of *North American Indians of the Plains* (1912), *The American Indian* (1917), *Man and Culture* (1923), *Social Anthropology* (1929), *Indian Cavalcade* (1938), *Indians of the United States* (1940), etc.

Wiss·mann \'vis-män\, Hermann von. 1853–1905. German army officer and explorer. Accompanied Pogge to Angola and Nyangwe (1881) and continued alone across continent to Zanzibar; discovered Sankuru River; made other journeys in equatorial Africa; proved navigability of Kasai River (1885); as commissioner (1888–91), suppressed Arab uprising in German East Africa (1888); founded Langenburg on Lake Nyasa; governor of German East Africa (1895–96).

Wis·so·wa \vi-'sō-vä\, Georg. 1859–1931. German philologist. Professor, Marburg (1886), Halle (1895). His works included *Religion und Kultus der Römer* (1902) and revised editions of August Pauly's *Real-Encyclopädie der Classischen Altertumswissenschaft* (1894–1909) and Friedländer's *Darstellungen aus der Sittengeschichte Roms* (1919–23).

Wis·tar \'wis-tər, 'vis-tär\, Caspar. 1696–1752. American glass manufacturer, b. near Heidelberg, Germany. To America (1717) and settled in Philadelphia; began manufacturing glass and glassware (1739) at Wistarberg, N.J., first glass factory of note in America.

Wis·ter \'wis-tər\, Owen. 1860–1938. American novelist, b. Philadelphia. Author of *Red Men and White* (1898), *Lin McLean* (1898), *The Virginian* (1902), *Members of the Family* (1911), *The Pentecost of Calamity* (1915), *Roosevelt—The Story of a Friendship* (1930), and short stories and verse.

Wit, Pieter de. See Pieter CANDID.

Wi·te·lo \vē-'tā-lō\ *or* **Vi·tel·lio** \vē-'tel-yō\. c.1230 or 1235–after 1275. Polish scientist. Known esp. for studies in optics. Author of *Perspectiva* (c.1274; printed 1535), which together with Ibn al-Haytham's works on optics formed *Opticae Thesaurus* (1572, edited by F. Risner), most influential work on optics until 17th century.

With·er \'with-ər\, George. 1588–1667. English poet and pamphleteer. Imprisoned in Marshalsea for satire *Abuses Stript and Whipt* (1613), said to be libelous; during imprisonment wrote pastoral *Shepherd's Hunting* (1615), containing famous passage in praise of poetry; after a love elegy *Fidelia* (1615), including song "Shall I, wasting in despair," returned to satire in *Wither's motto* (1621); after the fanciful lyric *Faire-Virtue, The Mistresse of Phil' Arete* (1622), became Puritan and devoted himself to religious poetry, the best of which was hymnbook *Hallelujah* (1641), and controversial, often scurrilous, pamphlets. Raised troop of horse on Parliamentary side (1642); imprisoned (1660–63) for a verse pamphlet *Vox Vulgi,* satirizing Parliament of 1661. His best verse collected in *Juvenilia* (1622).

With·er·spoon \'with-ər-ˌspün\, John. 1723–1794. American clergyman, b. Gifford, Scotland. Ordained Presbyterian minister (1745); to America to become president, College of New Jersey (1768–94; now Princeton U.). Member of Continental Congress (1776–79, 1780–81, 1782) and a signer of the Declaration of Independence; member of New Jersey constitutional ratification convention (1787). One of organizers of Presbyterian church along national lines (1785–89) and moderator of the church's first General Assembly (1789).

Wi·ti·gis \'vēt-ə-ˌgēs\. fl. 536–540. King of Italy (536–540). Ostrogoth; elected king to succeed Theodahad; besieged Belisarius in Rome (537–538); retreated from Belisarius until shut up in Ravenna, last Gothic stronghold (540); agreed to abdicate; seized by Belisarius and taken to Constantinople; fate unknown.

Witkowski. See Maximilian HARDEN.

Witold. See VYTAUTAS.

Wi·tos \'vē-tȯs\, Wincenty. 1874–1945. Polish politician. Member of Galician Diet (1908–14) and Austrian Reichsrat (1911–18); member of Polish Sejm

(1919–33); leader of Peasant party; prime minister of Poland (1920–21, 1923, 1926); overthrown in Piłsudski's coup; imprisoned (1930, 1939–45).

Witt \'vit\, Friedrich. 1770–1836. German cellist and composer. Kapellmeister to prince-bishop of Würzburg (from 1802). Wrote oratorio *Der leidende Heiland* (1802), other theatrical works, symphonies, chamber works, etc.; remembered as composer of *Jena* symphony, discovered (1909) and long attributed by many to Beethoven.

Witt, Johan de. 1625–1672. Dutch statesman. As pensionary of Dordrecht (1650) opposed William III on question of Spanish campaign. Grand pensionary of Holland (1653–72); concluded Treaty of Westminster (1654) ending First Dutch War with England and including secret Seclusion clause excluding prince of Orange from post of stadholder; rebuilt Dutch navy, restored finances, extended Dutch commerce in Far East; sent fleet to help Denmark in First Northern War with Sweden (1658–59); conducted successful Second Anglo-Dutch War (1665–67), ending in favorable Treaty of Breda; formed Triple Alliance with England and Sweden against France (1668); secured passage of Perpetual Edict abolishing office of stadholder (1667); forced to resign as grand pensionary following French invasion and Orangist riots (1672); with brother Cornelis, killed by mob in The Hague.

Wit·te \'vit-ə\, Emanuel de. 1617–1692. Dutch painter. Chief master of Dutch architectural painting, esp. of church interiors; known also for genre scenes.

Witte, Karl. 1800–1883. German jurist and scholar. Published (1862) a critical edition of original text of Dante's *Divinia commedia,* and translations of Dante and Boccaccio.

Witte, Pieter de. See Pieter CANDID.

Wit·te \'vyēt-tyi\, Sergey Yulyevich. 1849–1915. Russian politician. Minister of finance (1892–1903); president, council of ministers (1903). Negotiated Treaty of Portsmouth (1905) ending Russo-Japanese War. First constitutional Russian premier (1905–06); resigned premiership (1906) and was appointed member of council of the empire.

Wit·te·kind \'vit-ə-,kint\ *or* **Wi·du·kind** \'vēd-ə-,kint\. d. c.807. Westphalian chieftain. Leader of the Saxons against Charlemagne; raided the Rhineland (778) and may have taken part in annihilation of Frankish army at Süntelberg (782); again led war until 785, when he submitted to Charlemagne and was baptized at Attigny; said to have been appointed duke of the Saxons and to have died in battle (807).

Wit·tels·bach \'vit-əls-,bäk\. A German family that ruled in Bavaria (12th century–1918) and in Rhenish Palatinate for part of that time. Count Otto VI became Duke Otto I of Bavaria (1180); family several times divided and reunited, but by 1559 some of branches were extinct; duchy became an electorate (1623) and Duke Maximilian was made elector. The following were electors: Maximilian the Great, Ferdinand Maria, Maximilian II Emanuel, Charles Albert, and Maximilian III Joseph, last of direct line. Duchy of Bavaria then (1777) passed to Palatinate branch, Elector Charles Theodore and Maximilian IV Joseph; electorate made a kingdom (1806) by Napoléon, Elector Maximilian continuing as King Maximilian I Joseph; succeeding kings: Louis I, Maximilian II Joseph, Louis II, Otto, Louis III. Three of the kings of Germany were members of Wittelsbach family: Louis IV of Bavaria, Rupert of the Palatinate, and Charles VII of Bavaria. See individual biographies.

Wittenberg line. See ALBERTINE line.

Witt·gen·stein \'vit-gən-,shtīn, *Angl also* -,stīn\, Ludwig Josef Johan. 1889–1951. British philosopher, b. Vienna. To Cambridge (1929); fellow of Trinity Coll. (1930–36), professor (1939–47); naturalized (1938). Exerted great influence on logical positivism, linguistic analysis, and semantics. Works included *Tractatus logico-philosophicus* (1921), *Philosophische Untersuchungen* (1953), *Bemerkungen über die Grundlagen der Mathematik* (1956).

Witz \'vits\, Konrad. c.1400–c.1445. German painter. Active in Basel (from 1434); worked in late Gothic manner; one of first to introduce realistic landscapes into religious paintings. Works included Heilsspiegal altarpiece for St. Leonhard, Basel (c.1435); *Augustinus, Bartholomäus und Christophorus, Antipater vor Caesar, Esther vor Ahasverus, Fischzug Petri, Befreiung Petri.*

Wi·val·lius \vē-'väl-yůs\, Lars. 1605–1669. Swedish poet and adventurer. Traveled across Europe posing as a nobleman (1625–29); imprisoned for marrying under false name; deported to Finland (1634–41). Author of lyrics on freedom and nature, including "Ack libertas du ädle ting" and "Klagevisa över denna torra och kalla vår."

Władysław. Kings of Hungary. See WŁADYSŁAW III of Poland; ULÁSZLÓ II.

Wła·dys·ław \vlä-'dis-läf\. Name of four kings of Poland:

Władysław I. *Called* **Ło·kie·łek** \lók-'yel-ek\, *i.e.* the Short. 1260 or 1261–1333. King (1320–33). Son of Casimir I, Prince of Kujawy; succeeded as prince (1275); acquired other territories; elected prince of Great Poland (1296) but subsequently lost allegiance of Polish princes to Wenceslas II, who became king (1300); made war on Wenceslas (1305) with Hungarian support; conquered Little Poland (1305), Great Poland (1314), Pomerania (later lost to Teutonic Knights), Gdańsk; crowned at Kraków (1320); again fought Teutonic Knights and defeated them at Płowce (1331).

Władysław II Ja·giel·ło \yäg-'yel-lō\. *Orig.* Jo·gai·la \yō-'gī-lä\. 1351–1434. King (1386–1434). Son of Algirdas, whom he succeeded as grand duke of Lithuania (1377); defeated rival and uncle Kęstutis and at length won support of cousin Vytautas; offered throne of Poland by marriage to queen Jadwiga (*q.v.*); accepted in treaty of Krewo (1385); m. Jadwiga (1386), converted to Christianity, and began conversion of Lithuania; recognized Vytautas as duke of Lithuania in Polish-Lithuanian union (1401); with Vytautas defeated Teutonic Knights in series of wars (1409–11, 1414, 1422, 1431–32); checked Tatar expansion; recovered Ruthenia (1387) and effected alliance with Hungary (1412).

Władysław III. 1424–1444. King (1434–44). Son of Władysław II; largely dominated by Zbigniew Oleśnicki; through Oleśnicki's efforts, elected king of Hungary as Ulászló I (1440); with János Hunyadi led army into Balkans and forced Sultan Murad II to sign Peace of Szeged (1444), agreeing to evacuate Serbia and Albania and pay large indemnity to Hungary; resumed invasion; killed in battle of Varna.

Władysław IV Va·sa \'vä-sä\. 1595–1648. King (1632–48). Son of Sigismund III Vasa; at father's instance, elected czar of Russia while Polish forces occupied Moscow (1610) but never took throne; took part in military campaigns of Chodkiewicz against Muscovy (1617–18) and Ottomans (1621); elected to succeed father (1632); broke Russian siege of Smolensk (1633) and forced Czar Michael to sign Peace of Polyanov (1634); moved army south to Lwów and forced Ottomans to come to terms on rule over Tatars, Cossacks, joint sovereignty over Moldavia and Walachia; made advantageous peace with Sweden (1635) but failed in plan to capture Swedish crown; opposed by Sejm in efforts to strengthen monarchy.

Wode·house \'wůd-,haůs\, Sir Pelham Grenville. 1881–1975. English novelist. Conducted column in London *Globe* (1903–09). Began as writer of stories for boys, including *The Pothunters* (1902), *A Prefect's Uncle* (1903), followed by humorous novels, many of which center about the following characters or groups: Psmith, as *Psmith in the City* (1910), which gained him wide reputation, Bertie Wooster and his valet Jeeves, as in *The Inimitable Jeeves* (1924), *The Code of the Woosters* (1938), *Much Obliged, Jeeves* (1971), Stanley Featherstonehaugh Ukridge in *Ukridge* (1924), Mr. Mulliner in *Meet Mr. Mulliner* (1927), *Mulliner Omnibus* (1935), Lord Emsworth and the family at Blandings Castle in *Blandings Castle* (1935), *Lord Emsworth and Others* (1937). Collaborator with Guy Bolton in musical comedies including *The Cabaret Girl* (1922), and with Ian Hay in plays including *Leave it to Psmith* (1930). Captured by Germans (1939) and interned in Germany; became U.S. citizen (1955).

Woes·tij·ne \vü-'stā-nə\, Karel van de. 1878–1929. Belgian poet. Government official (1907–20); professor, Ghent (1920–29). Author of highly subjective, Symbolist, often world-weary lyrics in Flemish, including *Het vaderhuis* (1903), *De boomgaard der vogelen en der vruchten* (1905), *De gulden schaduw* (1910), *De modderen man* (1920), *God aan zee* (1926), *Het bergmeer* (1928); also wrote essays, tales.

Wof·fing·ton \'wäf-iŋ-tən\, Margaret, *known as* Peg. c.1714–1760. Irish actress. Debut in London (1740) as Silvia in *The Recruiting Officer;* became a favorite as Sir Harry Wildair in *The Constant Couple* (1741) and in other "breeches parts." At Drury Lane (1740–46), Covent Garden (1747–50, 1754–57), Dublin (1750–54), played chief roles in comedy and tragedy, probably best as elegant women of fashion, Lady Betty Modish and Lady Townly.

Wöh·ler \'vœ-lər\, Friedrich. 1800–1882. German chemist. Teacher in Berlin and Kassel (1825–36); professor, Göttingen (1836–82); first to obtain metallic aluminum (1827) and beryllium (1828); with Liebig, pioneer in study of isomerism; discovered calcium carbide and used it to prepare acetylene; discovered quinone, hydroquinone, etc.; first to synthesize an organic compound (urea, 1828). Author of *Grundriss der unorganischen Chemie* (1831), *Grundriss der organischen Chemie* (1840).

Wohl·ge·muth *or* **Wohl·ge·mut** *or* **Wol·ge·mut** \'vōl-gə-,müt\, Michel *or* Michael. 1434–1519. German painter. Teacher of Albrecht Dürer. His works included many carved altarpieces with painted wings (executed with others), the Hofer altar (now in Munich), high altars of churches at Zwickau, Nürnberg, Feuchtwangen, and Schwabach. Noted also as designer of woodcuts.

Woj·cie·chow·ski \,vói-che-'kóf-skē\, Stanisław. 1869–1953. Polish economist and politician. Joined Socialist party; political activities forced him to leave Poland (1892); in London published Socialist periodical *Przedswit;* returned to Poland (1906). During World War I headed Polish group favoring Allies. Minister of interior (1919–20); elected to Sejm (1922) as member of Peasant party; president of Poland (1922–26); deposed by coup d'état effected by Marshal Piłsudski.

Wol·cot \'wůl-kət\, John. *Pseudonym* Peter Pin·dar \'pin-dər, -ˌdär\. 1738–1819. English satirist and poet. Physician (1767–73) to Sir William Trelawny, governor of Jamaica; abandoned practice of medicine in England (1778) for writing pungent poetical satires, witty but coarse, on George III (the *Lousiad,* 1785–95), Boswell and Mrs. Piozzi, Pitt, and many others.

Wol·cott \'wůl-kət\, Roger. 1679–1767. American colonial administrator, b. Windsor, Conn. Deputy governor of Connecticut (1741–50); major general, second in command of troops that captured Louisbourg from the French (1745); governor of Connecticut (1751–54); author of *Poetical Meditations* (1725), first volume of verse published in Connecticut. His son ¶Oliver (1726–1797) was member of Continental Congress (1775–78, 1780–84) and a signer of the Declaration of Independence; commander of Connecticut militia reinforcing Gen. Putnam on the Hudson River (1776); commanded volunteer contingent joining Gates's army against Burgoyne, and as major general (1779) provided for defense of Connecticut coast against Tryon's raids; lieutenant governor of Connecticut (1787–96) and governor (1796–97). His son ¶Oliver (1760–1833) was a lawyer and politician; auditor of U.S. Treasury (1789–91); comptroller of U.S. Treasury (1791–95); U.S. secretary of the treasury, succeeding Hamilton (1795–1800); governor of Connecticut (1817–27).

Wolf. See also WOLFE, WOLFF.

Wolf \vòlf\, Charles-Joseph-Étienne. 1827–1918. French astronomer. At Paris observatory (from 1862); professor, Paris (1875–1901); with Georges Rayet discovered spectroscopically (1867) Wolf-Rayet stars.

Wolf \'vòlf\, Friedrich August. 1759–1824. German philologist. Friend of Goethe and Wilhelm von Humboldt. Professor, Halle (1783–1806), Berlin (1810–24). Author of *Prolegomena ad Homerum* (1795), in which he argued that the *Iliad* and *Odyssey* are the work not of one but of several authors, and of *Darstellung der Altertumswissenschaft* (1807), in which he championed the study of classical antiquity; edited Homor, Plato, Cicero, and others.

Wolf, Hugo Philipp Jakob. 1860–1903. Austrian composer. Music critic for *Wiener Salonblatt* (1883 ff.); strongly influenced by Liszt and Wagner. Composed over 300 German lieder, including musical settings for poems of Mörike, Eichendorff, Goethe, Ibsen, Michelangelo, and other poets and for translations by Heyse and Geibel; opera *Corregidor* (1895) after Alarcón; instrumental works including a string quartet (1880), the symphonic poem *Penthesilea* (1883), *Italienische Serenade* (1892).

Wolf, Maximilian Franz Joseph Cornelius. 1863–1932. German astronomer. Director, Königstuhl observatory (1893); professor, Heidelberg (1893); discovered comet (1884); established existence of dark clouds of interstellar matter; discovered 228 asteroids, including Achilles (1906); pioneered use of stereocomparator in celestial photography.

Wolf, Rudolf. 1816–1893. Swiss astronomer. Director, Bern observatory (1847), Zürich observatory (1855); professor, Zürich (1885); confirmed Schwabe's sunspot cycle; correlated sunspots and magnetic variations on Earth (1852).

Wolfe \'wůlf\, Charles. 1791–1823. Irish clergyman and poet. Author of short stirring elegy "The Burial of Sir John Moore at Corunna," appearing anonymously (1817).

Wolfe, Humbert. *Orig.* Umberto Wolff \'vòlf\. 1886–1940. British poet, b. Italy. Attracted notice with satires *Lampoons* (1925), *News of the Devil* (1926); gained recognition with *Requiem* (1927), *The Silver Cat* (1928), *This Blind Rose* (1928), *Snow* (1931), *Kensington Gardens in Wartime* (1940); also wrote critical works on Tennyson, Herrick, Shelley, etc.

Wolfe, James. 1727–1759. British army officer. Entered army (1741); served in Flanders and Germany and against Young Pretender (1742–47); present at Dettingen, Falkirk, and Culloden Moor; under Amherst played a brilliant part in siege of Louisbourg (1758); commanded with rank of major general expedition against Quebec (1759); scaled heights to Plains of Abraham, routed French under Montcalm and thus completed British conquest of North America; fell mortally wounded on field.

Wolfe, Thomas Clayton. 1900–1938. American novelist, b. Asheville, N.C. Author of *Look Homeward, Angel* (1929), *Of Time and the River* (1935), *From Death to Morning* (stories, 1935), *The Story of a Novel* (memoir, 1936), and posthumously edited and published works *The Web and the Rock* (1939), *You Can't Go Home Again* (1940), *The Hills Beyond* (1941), *Letters to His Mother* (1943).

Wolfe-Barry, Sir John Wolfe. See under Sir Charles BARRY.

Wolff. See also WOLF.

Wolff *or* **Wolf** \'vòlf\, Christian von. Freiherr. 1679–1754. German philosopher and mathematician. Professor, Halle (1707–23), Marburg (1723–40); science adviser to Peter the Great (1716–25); professor, chancellor of U. of Halle (1741–54). Chief German spokesman of the Enlightenment; developed and popularized philosophy of Leibnitz; championed deductive rationalistic system of philosophy. Author of numerous works, in Latin and German, on all branches of philosophy, and in mathematics and physics.

Wolff \vòlf\, Pierre. 1865–1944. French playwright. Author of *Jacques Bouchard* (1890), *Leurs filles* (1891), *Le Béguin* (1900), *Le Secret de Polichinelle* (1903), *Le Ruisseau* (1907), *Les Ailes brisées* (1920), *La Belle de nuit* (1932).

Wolff-Bek·ker \vòlf-'bek-ər\, Elisabeth, *nee* Bekker. *Called* Betje. 1738–1804. Dutch writer. m. Adriaan Wolff (1759; d. 1777). Collaborated with Aagje Deken on first Dutch novels *Sara Burgerhart* (1782), *Willem Leevend* (1784–85), etc.

Wolf-Fer·ra·ri \'vōlf-fär-'rä-rē\, Ermanno. *Surname orig.* Wolf. 1876–1948. Italian composer. Added mother's maiden name to his own (c.1895). Composer of comic operas as *Cenerentola* (1900), *I quattro rusteghi* (1906), *Il segreto di Susanna* (1909), *Gli amanti sposi* (1925), *Sly* (1927), tragic opera *I gioielli della Madonna* (1911); also choral, chamber, instrumental works.

Wölff·lin \'vœlf-lin\, Eduard. 1831–1908. Swiss scholar. Professor, Munich (1880–1905); helped found and organize the *Thesaurus Linguae Latinae,* for which he prepared the *Archiv für Lateinische Lexikographie und Grammatik* (1884–1909); author of many philological works, esp. on colloquial Latin and the history of Latin.

Wölfflin, Heinrich. 1864–1945. Swiss art historian. Professor, Basel (1893–1901), Berlin (1901–12), Munich (1912–24), Zürich (1924–34); strongly influenced by Jacob Burckhardt; evolved theory of intuitive forms expressing psychological aspects of period and culture in art. Author of *Renaissance und Barock* (1888), *Die klassische Kunst* (1899), *Die Kunst Albrecht Dürers* (1905), *Das Problem des Stils* (1912), *Kunstgeschichtliche Grundbegriffe* (1915), *Das Erklären von Kunstwerken* (1922), etc.

Wol·fram von Eschen·bach \'vòl-främ-fòn-'esh-ən-ˌbäk\. c.1170–c.1220. Middle High German poet and Minnesinger. Lived (1202–17) at court of Hermann of Thuringia, where he met Walther von der Vogelweide. Author of eight lyric poems called *Tagelieder,* of the epic *Parzival,* a metrical romance of the Holy Grail based in part on Chrétien de Troyes's *Perceval* and from which Wagner derived the libretto of his *Parsifal,* of the *Titurel* fragments, and of an incomplete historical epic *Willehalm.*

Wolgemut, Michel. See WOHLGEMUTH.

Wolkenstein, Oswald von. See OSWALD VON WOLKENSTEIN.

Woll \'wōl\, Matthew. 1880–1956. American labor leader, b. Luxembourg. To U.S. (1891); photoengraver by trade; president of International Photo-Engravers' Union of North America (1906–29); vice president of American Federation of Labor (1919–56); active esp. in international labor affairs.

Wol·las·ton \'wůl-ə-stən\, William. 1659–1724. English philosopher. Lived and wrote mainly in seclusion, destroying many manuscripts out of literary fastidiousness. Known for *The Religion of Nature Delineated* (1722), expounding theory of ethical conduct as conformity to truth.

Wollaston, William Hyde. 1766–1828. English chemist and physicist. Practiced medicine; showed identity of frictional and voltaic electricity (1801); first to observe (1802) Fraunhofer lines in spectrum; discovered palladium (1802) and rhodium (1804); devised method of making platinum malleable; invented camera lucida (1807), reflecting goniometer (1809), Wollaston's doublet (a form of magnifying glass for correcting spherical aberrations). Member (from 1793), secretary (1804–16), Royal Society; for Geological Society founded the Wollaston medal, awarded annually for mineralogical research.

Wollstonecraft, Mary. See Mary Wollstonecraft GODWIN.

Wols. See Alfred SCHULZE.

Wolse·ley \'wůlz-lē\, Garnet Joseph. 1st Viscount Wolseley. 1833–1913. British army officer. Entered army (1852); served in Second Burmese War, Crimean War, Sepoy Mutiny; accompanied Anglo-French expedition into China (1860); in Canada (1861–71), commanded expedition to quell Riel uprising in Red River (1870); as energetic reformer, put into effect Cardwell's short-service system and abolished the purchase of commissions; commanded Ashanti expedition (1873–74); major general (1874); held high command in Natal (1875), Cyprus (1878), southeast Africa (1879–80); suppressed 'Urābī Pasha's rebellion in Egypt with victory at Tall al-Kabīr (1882); commanded Nile expedition (1884) that arrived too late to relieve General Gordon at Khartoum; viscount (1885); field marshal (1894); commander in chief of British army (1895–1901).

Wol·sey \'wůl-zē\, Thomas. c.1475–1530. English prelate and statesman. Ordained (1498); became favorite of Henry VII; rose rapidly under Henry VIII to royal almoner and dean of Lincoln (1509); privy councilor in control of public and foreign affairs (1511); directed war preparations and campaign in northern France (1512–13); bishop of Tournai and of Lincoln, and archbishop of York (1514); cardinal (1515); lord chancellor (1515–29); papal legate a latere (1518), an office whose practical permanence he secured; affected extravagant pomp and arrogated to himself royal privileges. Reversed England's foreign policy of alliance with France on election of Charles V as emperor; concluded secret defensive and offensive alliance with Charles against France (1521); negotiated marriage of Princess Mary (later Mary I of England) and Charles (1522); endeavored to hold balance so that Francis I and Charles would by turns support England; aided Charles, according to his detractors, in order to obtain Charles's furtherance of his candidacy for papacy, but both in 1521 and 1524 failed to receive Charles's support; dealt England's prestige heavy blow by permitting emperor to defeat Francis at Pavia (1525) and before Naples (1528); aroused detestation of all classes by attempts to raise forced loans and benevolences (1526–28); concluded treaties with Francis I at Amiens (1527). Conducted negotiations with Pope Clement VII for consent to Henry VIII's divorce from Queen Catherine (1527); sat in judgment, along with Cardinal Campeggio, papal legate on divorce (1529); forced, partly by Catherine's intransigence, to appeal to Rome; lost appeal because Emperor Charles, victorious in Italy over French, obliged papal refusal of appeal; deprived of king's support, stripped of all offices and honors except archbishopric of York (1529); arrested on charge of high treason, on ground that he had invoked aid of Francis (1530); died on way to London.

Wol·zo·gen \ˈvōlt-sō-gən\, Ernst Ludwig von. Freiherr. 1855–1934. German writer. Founded paper *Überbrettl* in Berlin (1901). Author of humorous novels as *Die Kinder der Exzellenz* (1888), *Die tolle Komtess* (1889), *Blau Blut* (1892), *Ecce Ego* (1896), *Der Kraft-Mayr* (1897), *Der Erzketzer* (1911), comedies as *Das Lumpengesindel* (1892), *Ein unbeschriebenes Blatt* (1902), etc.

Wolzogen, Karoline von, *nee* von Leng·e·feld \fōn-ˈleŋ-ə-ˌfelt\. Freifrau. 1763–1847. German writer. m. Wilhelm von Wolzogen (1794; d. 1809). Friend of Schiller, who married her sister Charlotte. Author of novels *Agnes von Lilien* (1798, published anonymously and taken by many as the work of Goethe or Schiller) and *Cordelia* (1840), and a life of Schiller (1830).

Won·hyo \wŏn-hyō\. *Also called* Wonhyo Dai·sa \dī-sä\. 617–686. Korean religious leader. Considered one of the Ten Sages of ancient Korean kingdom; first to systematize Korean Buddhism; propounded a humanistic approach to ethical striving after the ideal.

Wood, Aaron. See under Ralph WOOD.

Wood \ˈwu̇d\, Anthony *or* Anthony à. 1632–1695. English antiquary and historian. Author of *Historia et Antiquitates Universitatis Oxoniensis,* a history of Oxford U. (1674); of *Athenae Oxonienses* (1691–92), a biographical dictionary of notable Oxford graduates (from 1500).

Wood, Edward Frederick Lindley. Earl of Hal·i·fax \ˈhal-ə-ˌfaks\. 1881–1959. English politician. Descendant of Charles Montagu, 1st Earl of Halifax (1st creation); M.P. (1910–25); undersecretary for colonies (1921–22); minister of agriculture (1924–25); created Baron Ir·win \ˈər-wən\ (1925); viceroy of India (1925–31); attempted to compromise with Gandhi and other nationalist leaders but was unable to persuade Conservative leaders in England to grant measure of self-rule; secretary for war (1935); lord privy seal (1935–37); lord president of the Council (1937–38); foreign secretary (1938–40); ambassador to U.S. (1941–46); created earl (1944).

Wood, Enoch. See under Ralph WOOD.

Wood, Fernando. 1812–1881. American politician, b. Philadelphia. Associated with Tammany Hall (from 1834); member, U.S. House of Representatives (1841–43); mayor of New York (1855–58, 1861, 1862); proposed that New York declare itself a free city (1861); associated with Vallandigham in organizing Peace Democrats (1863); again member of U.S. House of Representatives (1863–65, 1867–81).

Wood, Garfield Arthur. 1880–1971. American boat builder and racer, b. Mapleton, Iowa. Designed *Miss America* series of hydroplanes and in them won Harmsworth Trophy 8 times (1920–21, 1926, 1928–30, 1932–33); won Gold Cup races (1917, 1919–21); chairman of Gar Wood Industries, Inc., and a backer of Chris-Craft Corp.; credited with numerous inventions, including a hydraulic hoist; devised for the navy the PT boat used in World War II.

Wood, George Bacon. 1797–1879. American physician, b. Greenwich, N.J. Compiler, with Franklin Bache, of *The Dispensatory of the United States of America* (1833); author of *Treatise on the Practice of Medicine* (1847), etc. Bequeathed valuable collection of medicinal plants to U. of Pennsylvania for establishment of botanical garden.

Wood, Grant De Volsen. 1892–1942. American painter, b. near Anamosa, Iowa. Taught art in Cedar Rapids, Iowa, public schools (1919–24); professor and artist in residence, School of Fine Arts, U. of Iowa (1934 ff.). Evolved a cold, sharply realistic style that contrasted with others of Regionalist school. Among his paintings were *John B. Turner* (1929), *Woman with Plants* (1929), *American Gothic* (1930), *Midnight Ride of Paul Revere* (1931), *Arbor Day* (1932), *Daughters of Revolution* (1932), *Dinner for Threshers* (1934), *Death on Ridge Road* (1934), *Parson Weems' Fable* (1939).

Wood, Mrs. Henry, *nee* Ellen Price \ˈprīs\. 1814–1887. English novelist. m. Henry Wood (1836; d. 1866). Achieved great success with *East Lynne* (1861), a melodramatic novel, several times dramatized; editor of the *Argosy* (from 1867), for which she wrote the *Johnny Ludlow* stories; author of over 30 other novels including *The Channings* (1862), *The Shadow of Ashlydyat* (1863), *Within the Maze* (1872), *Edina* (1876).

Wood, Sir Henry Joseph. 1869–1944. English conductor and composer. Won international reputation as conductor of symphony and Promenade concerts at Queen's Hall (1895–1940) and Royal Albert Hall (1941–44); known as popularizer of contemporary works. Composed a mass, songs, arrangements of works of Purcell, Handel, J.S. Bach. Author of *The Gentle Art of Singing* (1927–28), *My Life of Music* (1938), *About Conducting* (1945).

Wood, James Rushmore. 1813–1882. American surgeon, b. Mamaroneck, N.Y. With associates, developed Bellevue Hospital, New York City (1847), and became its chief surgeon; introduced first hospital ambulance service (1869) and first training school for nurses (1873); one of organizers of Bellevue Hospital Medical College (1856).

Wood, John. *Called* the Elder *and* Wood of Bath. c.1704–1754. English architect. In Bath (from 1727), largely fixed physical plan and character of the city with groups and blocks of buildings as North and South Palisades (1728), Queen Square (1735), Prior Park (1735–48), Royal Mineral Water Hospital (1738), the Circus (completed 1764), the Royal Crescent (1767–69); other works included exchanges in Bristol (1740–43) and Liverpool (1748–55), Bath–Bristol Canal, and Llandaff cathedral restoration. His son ¶John, *called* the Younger (d. 1782), brought to fruition many of his father's plans, as the Circus and Royal Crescent in Bath; noted also as a landscape architect, as at Prior Park.

Wood, John George. 1827–1889. English clergyman and writer. Author of *Illustrated Natural History* (1853), *My Feathered Friends* (1856), *Man and Beast* (1874), books on sports, etc.

Wood, Sir Kingsley, *in full* Howard Kingsley. 1881–1943. English politician. M.P. (1918–43); parliamentary secretary to ministry of health (1924–29); privy councilor (1928); postmaster general (1931–35); minister of health (1935–38); secretary of state for air (1938–40); lord privy seal (1940); chancellor of exchequer (1940–44); introduced "pay as you earn" income tax (1944).

Wood, Leonard. 1860–1927. American physician and army officer, b. Winchester, N.H. Commissioned in U.S. army medical corps (1886). Close friend of Theodore Roosevelt (from 1897); cooperated with Roosevelt in raising and organizing the Rough Riders, and commanded the regiment in battle of Las Guásimas, Cuba (June 24, 1898); brigadier general (1898). Appointed military governor of Santiago and did notable work in cleaning it up and establishing order; military governor of Cuba (1899–1902). Major general (1903); governor of Mindanao and nearby islands in the Philippines (1903); commanded U.S. forces in the Philippines (1906–08). Chief of staff, U.S. army (1910–14). In command, department of the East (1914). Prominent candidate for Republican nomination for president of the United States (1916 and 1920). Governor general of the Philippines (1921–27).

Wood, Ralph. 1715–1772. English potter. Apprenticed (1730) to John Astbury; later worked for Thomas Whieldon; m. (1738) Mary Wedgwood; produced salt-glazed wares and gradually developed distinctive type of earthenware figures with colored glazes; employed as modeler by Josiah Wedgwood (sporadically, 1758–72), for whom he developed block-cutting process that made possible mass production of wares and the popular Toby mug (1762). His sons ¶Ralph (1748–1795) and ¶John (1746–1797) continued association with Wedgwood at Burslem for a time; Ralph entered into partnership (1797) with his cousin Enoch (see below) and continued to produce family's distinctive wares. A cousin of the elder Ralph ¶Aaron Wood (1717–1785) was noted as a modeler and innovator in glazing; works included "St. George and the Dragon," "Vicar and Moses," "Apollo and Diana," and animal groups. His son ¶Enoch (1759–1840) modeled busts of Shakespeare, Handel, Milton, Homer, Rousseau, etc., which proved popular line for his partnership with cousin Ralph Wood; later in partnership with James Caldwell and later still operated Enoch Wood and Sons (1818–46); called the "father of the Potteries."

Wood, Robert Elkington. 1879–1969. American army officer and businessman, b. Kansas City, Mo. Officer in U.S. army (1900–15) and again during World War I; vice president of Montgomery Ward & Co., Chicago (1919–24); vice president (1924–28), president (1928–39), chairman (1939–54), Sears Roebuck & Co., Chicago; chairman, America First Committee (1940–41).

Wood, Robert Williams. 1868–1955. American physicist, b. Concord, Mass. Professor, Johns Hopkins (1901–53); first to observe field emission (1897); improved diffraction gratings for spectroscopy; developed a color-photography process; carried on researches in optics, radiation, and on the biological and physiological effects of high-frequency sound waves. Author of *Physical Optics* (1905) and *Supersonics, the Science of Inaudible Sounds* (1939), and of fiction including *The Man Who Rocked the Earth* (with Arthur Train, 1915) and illustrated nonsense verse *How to Tell the Birds from the Flowers* (1907).

Wood, William. 1671–1730. English ironmaster. Obtained (1722) patent to coin halfpence and farthings for circulation in Ireland (Wood's halfpence), sharing difference between bullion value and nominal value with George I's mistress, the Duchess of Kendal. Also granted patent (1722) to strike halfpence, pence, and twopences for the American colonies, these coins, dated 1722 and 1723, of "Wood's metal," being known as the Rosa Americana coinage. Forced to surrender both patents before popular indignation, which was increased by *The Drapier's Letters* (1724) of Jonathan Swift.

Wood·ard \'wu̇d-ərd\, Nathaniel. 1811–1891. English clergyman and educator. Ordained Anglican priest (1842); founded series of public schools available to children of the middle class, including St. Nicolas at Lansing, St. John's at Hurstpierpoint, St. Saviour's at Ardingly; there were eventually 18 Woodard Schools throughout the country.

Wood·ber·ry \'wu̇d-ˌber-ē, -b(ə-)rē\, George Edward. 1855–1930. American man of letters, b. Beverly, Mass. Frequent contributor to the *Atlantic Monthly* and *The Nation* (1876–91); literary editor, Boston *Post* (1888); professor of literature, Columbia U. (1891–1904). Remainder of life passed in traveling and in retirement. Author of *The North Shore Watch and Other Poems* (1890), *Wild Eden* (verse, 1899), *Heart of Man* (essays, 1899), *Makers of Literature* (essays, 1900), *The Torch* (1905), *The Appreciation of Literature* (1907), *Great Writers* (1907), *Ideal Passion* (verse, 1917), *The Roamer and Other Poems* (1920), etc.

Wood·bridge \'wu̇d-brij\, Frederick James Eugene. 1867–1940. American educator, b. Windsor, Ont. To U.S. (1868); professor of philosophy, Columbia U. (1902–39) and dean of graduate faculties (1912–29); specialist in thought of Aristotle and Spinoza. Author of *The Purpose of History* (1916), *The Realm of Mind* (1926), *Nature and Mind* (1937), etc.

Wood·bury \'wu̇d-ˌber-ē, -b(ə-)rē\, Levi. 1789–1851. American jurist, b. Francestown, N.H. Governor of New Hampshire (1823–24); U.S. senator (1825–31); U.S. secretary of the navy (1831–34); U.S. secretary of the treasury (1834–41); again U.S. senator (1841–45); associate justice, U.S. Supreme Court (1845–51).

Wood·fall \'wu̇d-fȯl\, Henry Sampson. 1739–1805. English printer and journalist. Took over from his father and conducted (1758?–93) the *Public Advertiser,* in which he printed (1769–72) the *Letters of Junius* (see Sir Philip FRANCIS) without having acquaintance with their author.

Wood·hull \'wu̇d-həl\, Victoria, *nee* Claf·lin \'klaf-lən\. 1838–1927. American reformer, b. Homer, Ohio. With sister ¶Tennessee Celeste Claflin (1845–1923) developed spiritualist act as child; toured widely with family medicine show; m. Dr. Canning Woodhull (1853; div. 1864); to New York City (1868), where they impressed Cornelius Vanderbilt and with his backing opened successful brokerage firm (1870); Victoria published (1870–72) *Woodhull and Claflin's Weekly,* promoting single moral standard, legalized prostitution, dress reform, etc.; campaigned for woman suffrage and ran for president on "Equal Rights" ballot (1872); published charges of adultery against Henry Ward Beecher in *Weekly* (1872) and was jailed by Anthony Comstock for violation of obscenity laws; moved to England (1877). Author of *Stirpiculture* (1888), *Garden of Eden* (1889), *Humanitarian Money* (1892).

Wood·ruff \'wu̇d-rəf\, Wilford. 1807–1898. American religious leader, b. Avon, Conn. In first group of Mormons to enter valley of Great Salt Lake (1847); official church historian (1875); president of the quorum of the Twelve Apostles (1880–89); succeeded John Taylor as president of the Mormon church (1889–98); issued proclamation ending practice of polygamy (1890).

Woods \'wu̇dz\, Margaret Louisa, *nee* Brad·ley \'brad-lē\. 1856–1945. English writer. m. (1879) Rev. H. G. Woods. Author of *A Village Tragedy* (1887), *The Invader* (1907), *Pastels under the Southern Cross* (1911), *The Spanish Lady* (1927).

Woods, William Burnham. 1824–1887. American jurist, b. Newark, Ohio. Judge, U.S. 5th circuit (1869–80); associate justice, U.S. Supreme Court (1880–87).

Wood·son \'wu̇d-sən\, Carter Godwin. 1875–1950. American historian, b. New Canton, Va. Taught school in Washington, D.C. (1909–18); dean at Howard U. (1919–20), W. Va. State Coll. (1920–22). Founded (1915) Association for the Study of Negro Life and History and its *Journal of Negro History* (1916 ff.); founded (1922) Associated Publishers, Inc., to publish works on Negro life and culture. Author of *A Century of Negro Migration* (1915), *The Negro in Our History* (1922), *African Myths* (1928), *The Rural Negro* (1930), *The African Background Outlined* (1936), *African Heroes and Heroines* (1939), etc. Awarded Spingarn Medal (1926).

Woodstock, Edward of. See EDWARD, Prince of Wales (1330–1376).

Woodstock, Thomas of. See THOMAS of Woodstock.

Wood·ville \'wu̇d-vəl, -ˌvil\ *or* **Wyde·ville** \'wid-\, Richard. 1st Earl Riv·ers \'riv-ərz\. d. 1469. English soldier. m. (1436?) secretly Jacquetta, widow of John of Lancaster, Duke of Bedford; accompanied Duke of York to France (1441); helped to put down Jack Cade's Rebellion (1450); privy councilor (1450); fought for Lancastrians at Towton (1461), but quitted Henry VI after the battle and tendered allegiance to Edward IV; treasurer (1466) and constable of England (1467); so powerful at court as to arouse enmity of Richard Neville, Earl of Warwick; after Edward's defeat at Edgecot, executed, along with his son Sir John Woodville. Another son ¶Anthony Woodville *or* Wyd·ville \'wid-vəl, -ˌvil\ (c.1440–1483), Baron Scales \'skā(ə)lz\ and 2d Earl Rivers, tendered allegiance to Edward IV after Towton (1461); fought famous tournament with Anthony, Bastard of Burgundy (1467); lieutenant of Calais (1470); aided Edward IV in victorious return from exile (1471); guardian and governor to Edward, Prince of Wales (1473); made pilgrimage to Rome (1475–76); protected and encouraged Caxton; his translations from French brought out by Caxton, one being *Dictes or Sayengs of the Philosophres* (1477); beheaded without trial at Pontefract by Richard III. For Elizabeth Woodville (1437?–1492) and her daughter Elizabeth, wife of Henry VII, see ELIZABETH, queen of Edward IV of England.

Wood·ward \'wu̇d-wərd, -ərd\, Sir Arthur Smith. 1864–1944. English paleontologist. With British Museum (1882); keeper, department of geology (1901–24); known for research on extinct vertebrates, esp. fishes; by firm conviction of the genuineness of the Piltdown skull, ensured success of Charles Dawson's hoax (1912–14).

Woodward, Robert Burns. 1917–1979. American chemist, b. Boston, Mass. At Harvard U. (1937–79); known esp. for work in determining structure of complex organic substances as penicillin (1945), strychnine (1947), oleandomycin (1960), and synthesis of organic molecules as quinine (1944), cholesterol and cortisone (1951), strychnine and lysergic acid (1954), reserpine (1956), chlorophyll (1960), tetracycline (1962), vitamin B_{12} (1971); awarded Nobel prize for chemistry (1965).

Wool \'wu̇l\, John Ellis. 1784–1869. American army officer, b. Newburgh, N.Y. Entered army (1812); colonel and inspector general, U.S. army (1816–41); brigadier general (1841). Organized (1846) and led volunteers in Mexican War; second in command at battle of Buena Vista, and brevetted major general for his service there. Commanded Eastern military division (1848–53), department of the Pacific (1854–57), department of the East (1857–61); sent reinforcements in time to save Fortress Monroe for the Union (1861); major general (1862); retired (1863).

Wool·dridge \'wu̇l-ˌdrij\, Harry Ellis. 1845–1917. English painter and writer. Slade professor of fine art, Oxford (1895–1904); contributed first two volumes (1901, 1905) of *Oxford History of Music.* Lifelong friend of Robert Bridges, with whom he collaborated in the *Yattendon Hymnal* (1895–99).

Woolf \'wu̇lf\, Leonard Sidney. 1880–1969. English writer. Civil servant in Ceylon (1904–11); m. (1912) Virginia Stephen; joined Fabian Society (1913); with his wife founded (1917) the Hogarth Press; literary editor of *The Nation* (1923–30); joint editor of *Political Quarterly* (1931–59). Author of novels *The Village in the Jungle* (1913) and *The Wise Virgins* (1914) and *International Government* (1916), *Co-operation and the Future of Industry* (1919), *Socialism and Co-operation* (1921), *Imperialism and Civilization* (1928), *After the Deluge* (1931, 1939), *Barbarians at the Gate* (1939), and volumes of autobiography *Sowing* (1960), *Growing* (1961), *Beginning Again* (1964), *Downhill All the Way* (1967), *The Journey not the Arrival Matters* (1969).

Woolf, Virginia, *in full* Adeline Virginia, *nee* Stephen. 1882–1941. English novelist. Daughter of Sir Leslie Stephen; m. (1912) Leonard Woolf; a central figure in the "Bloomsbury group." Author of *The Voyage Out* (1915), *Night and Day* (1919), *Monday or Tuesday* (stories, 1921), in which she launched a new method of revealing thoughts of characters by their effects on their surroundings, developed in *Jacob's Room* (1922), *Mrs. Dalloway* (1925), in which she initiated bolder experimentation in the stream-of-consciousness technique, perfected in *To the Lighthouse* (1927), *Orlando* (1928), *The Waves* (1931), *The Years* (1937), *Between the Acts* (1941); also wrote miscellaneous prose including *A Room of One's Own* (1930), *The Common Reader* (critical essays; 1925, 1932), *Flush* (1933), *Roger Fry* (biography, 1940), *The Death of the Moth* (1942). For her sister Vanessa, see under Clive BELL.

Wooll·cott \'wu̇l-kət\, Alexander Humphreys. 1887–1943. American journalist and writer, b. Phalanx, N.J. Dramatic critic, *New York Times* (1914–22), New York *Herald* (1922–24), New York *World* (1925–28); radio broadcaster (1929–43); appeared on Broadway in *The Man Who Came To Dinner* (1939). Author of *The Command is Forward* (1919), *Shouts and Murmurs* (1923), *Mr. Dickens Goes to the Play* (1923), *The Story of Irving Berlin* (1925), *Going to Pieces* (1928), *While Rome Burns* (1934); compiler of anthologies *The Woollcott Reader* (1935), *Woollcott's Second Reader* (1937), *As You Were* (1943).

Wool·lett \'wu̇l-ət\, William. 1735–1785. English draftsman and line engraver. Established reputation with engravings *Temple of Apollo* (1760), after Claude Lorrain, and *Niobe* (1761), after Richard Wilson; gained with his most famous work, *Death of General Wolfe* (1776), after Benjamin West, appointment as historical engraver to the king.

Wool·ley \'wu̇l-ē\, Sir Leonard, *in full* Charles Leonard. 1880–1960. English archaeologist. Conducted excavations in Corbridge (1906–07), in Nubia

(1907–11, 1912), Carchemish (1912–14, 1919), Sinai (1914), Tell el-Amarna (1921–22), Ur (1922–34), near Antioch, Syria (1937–39, 1946–49). Author of *The Sumerians* (1928), *Ur of the Chaldees* (1929), *Digging Up the Past* (1930), *The Royal Cemetery* (1934), *Abraham* (1936), *The Ziggurat* (1939), *Excavations at Ur* (1954), *Alalakh* (1955), etc.

Woolley, Mary Emma. 1863–1947. American educator, b. South Norwalk, Conn. Professor, Wellesley Coll. (1896–1900); president, Mount Holyoke College (1900–37); active in movements for world peace.

Wool·man \ˈwu̇l-mən\, John. 1720–1772. American clergyman and reformer, b. Rancocas, N.J. Tailor by trade; itinerant Quaker preacher (1743–72), traveling through the colonies both northern and southern and inveighing against slavery; also advocated just Indian policy, curtailment of rum trade. Best known for his *Journal* (first published in 1774).

Wool·ner \ˈwu̇l-nər\, Thomas. 1825–1892. English sculptor and poet. Member of Pre-Raphaelite Brotherhood (1848), contributing the poem "My Beautiful Lady" to first number of their magazine *The Germ.* Began with bust of Tennyson (1857) success with portrait busts and medallions of eminent men; executed statues of Macaulay, John Stuart Mill, Captain Cook; professor at Royal Academy (1877–79).

Wool·nough \ˈwu̇l-nəf\, Walter George. 1876–1958. Australian geologist. Professor, U. of Sydney (1898–1913), U. of Western Australia (1913–19); geologist for mining firm (1919–27), for Australian government (1927–42); officer in ministry of national development (1942–51); known for studies of geology of Australia and New Guinea. Author of *Direction Finding by Sun, Moon, and Stars* (1943).

Wool·sey \ˈwu̇l-sē\, Theodore Dwight. 1801–1889. American educator, b. New York City. Professor of Greek language and literature, Yale (1831–46); president of Yale (1846–71). Chairman, New Testament company of the American committee for revision of the English version of the Bible (1871–81). Author of editions of Greek classics and *Political Science* (1878), *Communism and Socialism* (1880), etc.

Woolsey, Sarah Chauncey. *Pseudonym* Susan Coo·lidge \ˈkü-lij\. 1835–1905. American writer, b. Cleveland, Ohio. Niece of Theodore D. Woolsey. Author of popular books for girls as *What Katy Did* (1872), *What Katy Did at School* (1873), *Cross Patch* (1881), *What Katy Did Next* (1886), *Clover* (1888), *Just Sixteen* (1889), *Not Quite Eighteen* (1894), etc.

Wool·son \ˈwu̇l-sən\, Constance Fenimore. 1840–1894. American writer, b. Claremont, N.H. Grandniece of James Fenimore Cooper. Author of *The Old Stone House* (1873), *Castle Nowhere: Lake Country Sketches* (1875), *Rodman the Keeper: Southern Sketches* (1886), and the novels *Anne* (1882), *For the Major* (1883), *East Angels* (1886), *Jupiter Lights* (1889), *Horace Chase* (1894), *Dorothy* (1896).

Wool·ston \ˈwu̇l-stən\, Thomas. 1670–1733. English deist. Author of skeptical works *The Old Apology for the Truth of the Christian Religion Against the Jews and Gentiles Revived* (1705), *The Moderator Between an Infidel and an Apostate* (1725), *Discourse on our Saviour's Miraculous Power of Healing* (1730); imprisoned (1729–33).

Wool·worth \ˈwu̇l-(ˌ)wərth\, Frank Winfield. 1852–1919. American merchant, b. Rodman, N.Y. Opened first successful five-cent store, in Lancaster, Pa. (1879); soon added ten-cent goods; expanded until the Woolworth five-and-ten-cent stores became famous in all large cities of U.S.; merged four chains of such stores in F. W. Woolworth Co. (1912). Erected Woolworth Building, New York City (1913), at the time the world's tallest building.

Woos·ter \ˈwu̇s-tər\, David. 1711–1777. American Revolutionary officer, b. Stratford, Conn. Brigadier general in Continental army (June 1775); succeeded Montgomery as commander in Canada, but was recalled and put on inactive status (1776). Major general of Connecticut militia (1776); mortally wounded fighting Col. Tryon's invasion at Ridgefield, Conn. His grandson ¶Charles Whiting Wooster (1780–1848) commanded American privateer *Saratoga* preying on British commerce in War of 1812; entered service of Chile as naval captain (1817–19) and commander of Chilean naval forces (1822–35); cooperated with land forces in successful attack on last stronghold of the Spaniards in Chile, the island of Chiloé (Jan. 1826); rear admiral (1829).

Worcester. (1) Earl of. See Thomas Percy (1344?–1403) under PERCY family; John TIPTOFT. (2) Earls and marquises of. See SOMERSET family.

Worces·ter \ˈwu̇s-tər\, Joseph Emerson. 1784–1865. American lexicographer, b. Bedford, N.H. First of his series of dictionaries was an edition of *Johnson's English Dictionary...with Walker's Pronouncing Dictionary, Combined* (1828). His *Comprehensive Pronouncing and Explanatory Dictionary of the English Language* (1830) brought charges of plagiarism from Noah Webster and initiated what was known as "the War of the Dictionaries." Compiled *A Universal and Critical Dictionary of the English Language* (1846), *A Pronouncing, Explanatory, and Synonymous Dictionary of the English Language,* containing discrimination of synonyms (1855), *A Dictionary of the English Language,* an illustrated quarto (1860).

Worcester, William. *Also known as* William Bot·o·ner \ˈbät-nər, -ən-ər\. 1415–c.1482. English topographer and antiquary. In service of Sir John Fastolf (from 1438); known for *Itinerarium,* including a survey of Bristol and record of his journey (1478) from Norwich to St. Michael's Mount, Cornwall.

Worde \ˈwȯ(ə)rd\, Wynkyn de. *Orig.* Jan van Wyn·kyn \ˈwiŋ-kin\. d. 1534? British printer and stationer, b. Alsace. Became assistant to Caxton in Westminster (1477) and succeeded him (1491); removed to Fleet Street (1500); made improvements in the art of type cutting; issued over 600 distinct works; first printer in England to use italic type (1524).

Wor·den \ˈwərd-ən\, John Lorimer. 1818–1897. American naval officer, b. Westchester Co., N.Y. Entered navy (1834); commanded *Monitor* in passage from Greenpoint, Long Island, to Hampton Roads, Va., and in battle with Confederate *Merrimack* (Mar. 9, 1862); commanded monitor *Montauk* in attack on Fort McAllister (Jan. 27, 1863), in sinking Confederate cruiser *Nashville* (Feb. 1863), and in attack on Charleston (Apr. 1863). Rear admiral (1872).

Words·worth \ˈwərdz-(ˌ)wərth\, Christopher. 1774–1846. English clergyman and biographer. Youngest brother of William Wordsworth. Chaplain to archbishop of Canterbury (1805); master of Trinity College, Cambridge (1820–41). Author of *Ecclesiastical Biography* (6 vols., 1810) and *Who Wrote Eikon Basilike* (1824), supporting authorship of Charles I. His son ¶Charles (1806–1892) was a noted scholar and cricketer; Warden of Trinity Coll., Glenalmond (1847); bishop of St. Andrews (1853); advocate of reunion of churches of England and Scotland; one of the New Testament revisers (1870); author of *Shakespeare's Knowledge and Use of the Bible* (1864). Another son ¶Christopher (1807–1885) was headmaster of Harrow (1836–44); bishop of Lincoln (1869); author of *Athens and Attica* (1836) and other works of classical scholarship, of a commentary on the whole Bible (1856–70), and a church history to 451 A.D. (1881–83).

Wordsworth, Dorothy. 1771–1855. English writer. Sister of William Wordsworth. Constant companion to William (1795–1802) and continued to live with him after his marriage (1802); by testimony of brother, of S.T. Coleridge, De Quincey, and others a remarkable observer and interpreter of nature and the inspiration or source of many of William's lyrics. Best known for her poetic, intimate descriptions of their lives, thoughts, and work in *Alfoxden Journal* (written 1798) and *Grasmere Journal* (written 1800–03).

Wordsworth, William. 1770–1850. English poet. Orphaned at 13, reared by uncle; educated at Cambridge; traveled in France (1792); sympathized with French revolutionary spirit. Published (1793) first works, *The Evening Walk* and *Descriptive Sketches,* the latter an account of a walking tour in the Alps; began (1793) *Guilt and Sorrow,* showing Godwinian rationalistic influence; in a period of pessimism wrote (1795–96) a tragedy, *The Borderers.* On receipt of a £900 legacy settled with his sister Dorothy at Racedown, Dorsetshire; moved to Alfoxden, Somerset, to be near Samuel Taylor Coleridge, with whom he wrote *Lyrical Ballads* (1798, 1800, 1802, 1805), a collection of poems representing revolt against the artificial style and language, including notably "Lines composed a few miles above Tintern Abbey"; the volume is generally considered the first and one of the greatest works of English Romantic movement. Lived (1798–99) in Germany, where he wrote "Ruth" and "Lucy Gray" and other similar poems, and began *The Prelude* (completed 1805, pub. after his death), a spiritual autobiography. Settled (1799) at Grasmere with Dorothy; m. (1802) Mary Hutchinson. Became an opponent of liberalism; made tours in Scotland (1801, 1803) and began friendship with Walter Scott (1803); published two volumes of poems, including "Ode to Duty," "Intimations of Immortality," "Yarrow Unvisited," "Solitary Reaper" (1807). Made Rydal Mount, Grasmere, his home (from 1813) for rest of his life, which was marked by few events of note beyond publishing of his works. Published *The Excursion* (1814), intended as part of a projected poem, never completed, to be entitled *The Recluse.* Published "Laodamia" (1814) and other poems on classical subjects (1816, 1817); collected his poems (1815) and published (1815–19) *The White Doe of Rylstone* (a tragedy, written 1807), *Peter Bell* (written 1798), *The Waggoner* (written 1805); created in *Ecclesiastical Sonnets* (1822) some of his most perfect sonnets. Succeeded Southey as poet laureate (1843).

Work \ˈwərk\, Henry Clay. 1832–1884. American songwriter, b. Middletown, Conn. Among his songs were "We Are Coming, Sister Mary" for Christy Minstrels (1854), "Kingdom Coming" (1861), "Babylon Is Fallen" (1863), "Come Home, Father" (1864, often sung in temperance play *Ten Nights in a Barroom*), "Marching Through Georgia" (1865), "Grandfather's Clock" (1876).

Work·man \ˈwərk-mən\, William Hunter. 1847–1937. American physician and explorer, b. Worcester, Mass. With his wife (m. 1881) ¶Fanny, *nee*

Bul·lock \'bu̇l-ək\ (1859–1925), traveled and explored widely thoughout the world, esp. among the Himalayas; Mrs. Bullock Workman set climbing record for women on Nun Kun (23,300 feet, 1906). Collaborated in writing *Algerian Memories* (1895), *In the Ice World of Himálaya* (1900), *Through Town and Jungle* (1904), *Peaks and Glaciers of Nun Kun* (1909), *The Call of the Snowy Hispar* (1910), etc.

Worm \'vȯrm\, Ole. *Lat.* Olaus Wor·mi·us \'vȯr-mē-əs\. 1588–1654. Danish physician. Known for studies of runes; published collection of Danish and Norwegian runic inscriptions as *Monumenta danica* (1643).

Wor·rell \'wər-əl, 'wə-rəl, 'wär-əl\, Sir Frank Mortimer Maglinne. 1924–1967. West Indian cricketer, b. Barbados. Captain (1960–63) of West Indian team that dominated world competition; member of Jamaican Senate (1962–64); dean of students, U. of West Indies, Trinidad (1964–67).

Wor·saae \'vōr-sȯ\, Jens Jacob Asmussen. 1821–1885. Danish historian and archaeologist. Inspector of Danish historic and prehistoric monuments (1847); lectured at U. of Copenhagen (from 1855); director of Museum of Northern Antiquities (from 1865); discovered (1851) ancient kitchen middens and thereby established Paleolithic Age; a chief founder of prehistoric archaeology. Author of *Danmarks Oldtid* (1843).

Worth \'wərth\, Charles Frederick. 1825–1895. English dressmaker. As designer of women's clothes (from 1858) in Paris, gained notice of Princess Metternich and Empress Eugénie; first man to gain prominence in haute couture; pioneered in advance showing of collections, in designing dresses to be copied and widely distributed; arbiter of Paris fashions for 30 years.

Worth, Nicholas. See Walter Hines PAGE.

Worth, William Jenkins. 1794–1849. American army officer, b. Hudson, N.Y. Entered army (1813); colonel of infantry (1838); in command at victory of Palatka (1842) against the Seminole Indians in Florida. In Mexican War, engaged at Palo Alto, Resaca de la Palma, and Monterrey; brevetted major general; also engaged at Cerro Gordo, Churubusco, Chapultepec, and Mexico City. Commanded department of Texas (1848–49).

Wot·ton \'wu̇t-ᵊn, 'wät-\, Sir Henry. 1568–1639. English diplomat and poet. Friend of John Donne. Traveled on Continent (1589–95); confidential agent of Robert Devereux, Earl of Essex, supplying foreign intelligence (1595) until Essex's downfall (1601); sent from Italy by way of Norway to warn James VI of Scotland, afterwards James I of England, of a murder plot. Employed by James as ambassador (1604–23), mostly in Venice, whence he forwarded to James installments of Paolo Sarpi's history of the Council of Trent as fast as written. M.P. (1614, 1625). Financially ruined, made provost of Eton (1624); pensioned on agreement to write history of England; associated with Izaak Walton and John Hales. Author of oft-quoted poems "On his Mistris, the Queen of Bohemia" and "The Character of a Happy Life," and of the famous description of an ambassador as an honest man sent abroad to lie for the good of his country.

Wou·wer·man \'vō-vər-ˌmän\, Philips. 1619–1668. Dutch painter. Known esp. for studies of horses, battle and hunting scenes, and landscapes.

Wo·vo·ka \wō-'vō-kə\. *Known also as* Jack Wil·son \'wil-sən\. 1858?–1932. American Paiute Indian mystic, b. Esmeralda Co., Nev. Following mystical experience (1888 or 1889) began preaching a millennial message to Indians that gave rise to the Ghost Dance frenzy, esp. among Sioux (1890–91); accepted by his Indian followers as a messiah.

Wran·gel \'vrän-gyil, *Angl* 'raŋ-gəl\, Ferdinand Petrovich von. Baron. 1796–1870. Russian explorer. On expeditions around world (1817–19, 1825–27); commanded expedition to polar regions north of Asiatic Russia (1820–24); governor general of Russian America (Alaska, 1829–35); opposed sale of Alaska to U.S. Wrangel Island sought for but not found by Wrangel (1823) after being first reported by native Siberians; it was sighted by Capt. (later Sir Henry) Kellett (1849) and named for Wrangel by T. Long, an American whaler who discovered it in 1867.

Wrang·el \'vräŋ-əl\, Friedrich Heinrich Ernst von. Graf. 1784–1877. Prussian field marshal general. Commanded allied and Prussian troops in Schleswig-Holstein (1848) and suppressed uprising in Berlin (1848); field marshal (1856); commanded Prussian and Austrian forces against Denmark (1864).

Wrang·el \'vräŋ-əl\, Karl Gustav. Count of Sal·mis \'säl-mis\ and Söl·ves·borg \ˌsœl-vəs-'bȯrʸ\. 1613–1676. Swedish admiral and marshal. Distinguished himself in army and in navy during Thirty Years' War; major general (1638); distinguished himself at Wolfenbüttel (1641), Leipzig (1642); commanded fleet in victory over Denmark at Fehmarn (1644); field marshal (1646); succeeded Torstenson (1646) as commander in chief of Swedish army in Germany; with Turenne defeated Imperialists and Bavarians at Zusmarshausen (1648); created count (1651); vice admiral (1653); took part in Charles X's wars against Poland, Brandenburg, and Denmark (1655–58); grand admiral (1657); member (1660–72) of regency council during minority of Charles XI; grand marshal (1664); commanded Swedish army against Brandenburg (1674); defeated at Fehrbellin (1675).

Wran·gel \'vrän-gyil\, Pyotr Nikolayevich. Baron. 1878–1928. Russian general. Served in Russo-Japanese War (1904–05) and World War I (1914–17). After Bolshevik coup d'état (Nov. 1917), allied himself with Denikin; after Denikin's retreat (Apr. 1920), succeeded as commander in chief of volunteer White army. Took command in the Crimea; reorganized his army; after a few initial successes, lost Sevastopol (Nov. 1920) and was forced to evacuate with such troops as he could save; retired to Yugoslavia, later (1926) to Belgium.

Wray, John. See John RAY.

Wre·de \'vrā-də\, Karl Philipp. Fürst. 1767–1838. Bavarian field marshal. Major general at Hohenlinden (1800); commanded Bavarian division against Austria (1805); as cavalry general, in alliance with the French, led Bavarians in invasion of Russia (1812); negotiated alliance with Austria at Ried (1813) and commanded an Austro-Bavarian army against French at Hanau; defeated (1813); made field marshal and prince (1814); represented Bavaria in Congress of Vienna (1814–15); led Bavarian forces in France (1815); generalissimo of Bavarian army (1822).

Wren \'ren\, Sir Christopher. 1632–1723. English architect. Professor of astronomy, Gresham Coll. (1657–61), Oxford (1661–73); a charter member of Royal Society; devoted himself to architecture (c.1663). Proposed plans for rebuilding city of London after Great Fire (1666); surveyor general (1669); designed and built 53 churches in London in a variety of styles and plans; best known for design of new St. Paul's Cathedral (1675–1711). Other works included the Sheldonian Theatre, Oxford (1662–69), chapel of Pembroke Coll., Cambridge (1663–65), Custom House (1668), Temple Bar (1670–72), monument commemorating the Great Fire (1671–78), library of Trinity College, Cambridge (1676–84), chapel of Queen's College, Oxford (1682), Chelsea Hospital (1682–85), and additions to Hampton Court Palace (1696–1704).

Wright \'rīt\, Sir Almroth Edward. 1861–1947. British physician and pathologist. Professor, Army Medical School (1892–1902), St. Mary's Hospital, London (1902–46); known for bacteriological and immunological research; developed typhoid vaccine.

Wright, Benjamin. 1770–1842. American engineer, b. Wethersfield, Conn. Engaged (1811) by N.Y. State Canal Commission to determine route for canal from Rome, N.Y., to Waterford, N.Y.; chief engineer for construction of resulting Erie Canal (1817–25); chief engineer of Chesapeake and Ohio Canal (1828–31), St. Lawrence Canal (1833), and consulting engineer to many others.

Wright, Carroll Davidson. 1840–1909. American statistician, b. Dunbarton, N.H. First commissioner, U.S. Bureau of Labor, Department of the Interior (1885–1905); professor, Columbian U. (now George Washington U.; 1900–02); first president, Clark College (1902–09). Author of *Industrial Evolution of the United States* (1895), *Outline of Practical Sociology* (1899).

Wright, Chauncey. 1830–1875. American philosopher and mathematician, b. Northampton, Mass. Employed on *American Ephemeris and Nautical Almanac* (1852–70); professor, Harvard (1874–75); author of many articles on mathematics, physics, evolution, philosophy; a pioneer in philosophy of science and a major influence on colleagues William James and C.S. Peirce.

Wright, Elizur. 1804–1885. American reformer and actuary, b. South Canaan, Conn. Professor of mathematics, Western Reserve Coll. (1829–33); participated in the antislavery movement and edited antislavery journals; to Boston (1838). Began lobbying (1853) in Massachusetts legislature for reform of life-insurance practices; state commissioner of insurance (1858–66); secured legislation requiring life-insurance companies to maintain adequate reserves against their policies, and demonstrated how such reserves are computed; later (1861) secured legislation preventing companies from appropriating reserves for their own use, and finally (1880) secured legislation requiring companies to pay in cash the value of lapsed policies.

Wright, Frances *or* Fanny. 1795–1852. American reformer, b. Dundee, Scotland. First toured U.S. (1818–20) and wrote *Views of Society and Manners in America* (1821); again toured U.S., accompanying Lafayette (1824); founded short-lived community Nashoba in western Tennessee for freed slaves (1825); settled in New York City (1829); with Robert Dale Owen published *Free Enquirer* (1829 ff.); scandalized contemporary America by appearing on the lecture platform (from 1830) attacking religion and the existing system of education, and defending equal rights for women, marriage based on moral obligation only, birth control, emancipation of women, more equal distribution of wealth, emancipation of slaves and their colonization outside U.S.

Wright, Frank Lloyd. 1867–1959. American architect, b. Richland Center, Wis. Assistant to Louis Sullivan (1889–93); practiced in Chicago (from 1893), producing from the beginning of his practice strikingly original designs, both in private dwellings and public buildings; chief theorist and practitioner of "Prairie school" of architecture. Later worked in other styles, all showing mastery of space, form, and human-centered design. Major works included many residences as Winslow House, River Forest, Ill. (1893), Bradley House and Hickox House, Kankakee, Ill. (1900), Willits House, Highland Park, Ill. (1902), Heurtley House (1902) and Cheney House (1904) in Oak Park, Ill., Conley House, Riverside, Ill. (1908), his own Taliesin, Spring Green, Wis. (1911), Fallingwater, Mill Run, Pa. (1936), Taliesin West, Scottsdale, Ariz. (1938); other works included Larkin Building, Buffalo, N.Y. (1904), Unity Temple, Oak Park (1906), Imperial Hotel, Tokyo (1915–22), S.C. Johnson & Son, Inc., Racine, Wis. (1936–49), Florida Southern Coll. (1940–49), Guggenheim Museum, N.Y.C. (1943–59), Price Tower, Bartlesville, Okla. (1956). Author of *Autobiography* (1932), *An Organic Architecture* (1939), *An American Architecture* (1955), *A Testament* (1957), etc.

Wright, Harold Bell. 1872–1944. American novelist, b. Rome, N.Y. In ministry of the Christian church (1897–1908). Author of many popular novels, including *That Printer of Udell's* (1903), *The Shepherd of the Hills* (1907), *The Calling of Dan Matthews* (1909), *The Winning of Barbara Worth* (1911), *The Mine with the Iron Door* (1923), *God and the Groceryman* (1927), *Ma Cinderella* (1932), *The Man Who Went Away* (1942).

Wright, Henry. 1835–1895. American baseball manager, b. Sheffield, England. To U.S. (1836); professional cricket player in New York (1856–66); to Cincinnati (1866), where he organized (1868) Cincinnati Red Stockings baseball team, which became first to tour professionally (1869); later managed teams in Boston (1876–82), Providence (1882–83), Philadelphia (1884–93); head umpire, National League (1894–95).

Wright, Henry. 1878–1936. American architect and town planner, b. Lawrence, Kans. In practice in Kansas City, Mo. (1909–23), New York City (1923–36); known for planning of integrated communities as Sunnyside Gardens, Queens, N.Y., Radburn in Fair Lawn, N.J., Chatham Village in Pittsburgh, and several suburbs of St. Louis. Author of *Rehousing Urban America* (1935).

Wright, Horatio Gouverneur. 1820–1899. American army officer, b. Clinton, Conn. Entered army (1841); brigadier general of volunteers (1861); commanded force capturing Florida coastal cities (Feb. 1862); commanded department of the Ohio (1862–63). Major general (May 1864); repulsed Jubal A. Early in his raid toward Washington (July 1864); served under Sheridan in Shenandoah Valley. Commanded first troops to enter Confederate works at Petersburg (Apr. 2, 1865). Chief of engineers (1879); retired (1884).

Wright, John. 1770?–1844. English bookseller. Operated shop in Piccadilly, London, that became the rallying place of friends of the Pitt ministry, as was Debrett's of the opposition; published the *Anti-Jacobin* (1797); through debt forced to become William Cobbett's hack, editing Cobbett's *Parliamentary History, Parliamentary Debates,* etc.; edited 36 vols. of *Debates* (1812–30) for new proprietor Hansard; edited *Debates of the House of Commons* (1839–43) from 48 vols. of shorthand notes of the parliamentary reporter Sir Henry Cavendish.

Wright, John Joseph. 1909–1979. American prelate, b. Boston, Mass. Ordained (1935); auxiliary bishop of Boston (1947); bishop of Pittsburgh (1958); cardinal and prefect of Congregation for the Clergy, Vatican (1969).

Wright, Joseph. *Called* Wright of Der·by \ˈdär-bē\. 1734–1797. English painter. Known for candlelight or fireside scenes and as a pioneer in depiction of industrial scenes; also a portraitist.

Wright, Orville. See under Wilbur WRIGHT.

Wright, Patience, *nee* Lov·ell \ˈləv-əl\. 1725–1786. American sculptor, b. Bordentown, N.J. m. Joseph Wright (1748; d. 1769); made wax models of well known persons and exhibited them in a traveling show; to London (1772) and opened a wax museum; known also for her blunt, eccentric personality. Her son ¶Joseph (1756–1793) executed portraits of the Founding Fathers, including Washington; also wax modeler and diemaker; the first official American coins and medals were probably his work.

Wright, Quincy, *in full* Philip Quincy. 1890–1970. American political scientist, b. Medford, Mass. Taught at Harvard (1916–19) and U. of Minnesota (1919–23); professor, U. of Chicago (1923–56); adviser to State Department (1943–45) and to Nürnberg Tribunal (1945). Author of *The Enforcement of International Law Through Municipal Law in the United States* (1916), *The Control of American Foreign Relations* (1922), *The Causes of War and the Conditions of Peace* (1935), *A Study of War* (1942), *Problems of Stability and Progress in International Relations* (1954), *The Study of International Relations* (1955), *The Role of International Law in the Prevention of War* (1961).

Wright, Richard Nathaniel. 1908–1960. American novelist, b. Roxie, Miss. To Chicago (1927) and worked in menial jobs; joined Communist party (1932); member of Federal Writers' Project (1935–37); to New York (1937) as Harlem editor of *Daily Worker;* left Communist party (1944); settled in Paris (1946). His fiction dealt with the prejudice, alienation, and suffering of his fellow urban American blacks. His novels were *Native Son* (1940), *The Outsider* (1953), *Savage Holiday* (1954), *The Long Dream* (1958), and *Lawd Today* (1963); also wrote collections of stories *Uncle Tom's Children* (1938) and *Eight Men* (1961), autobiography *Black Boy* (1945), and non-fiction *Twelve Million Black Voices* (1941), *Black Power* (1954), *The Color Curtain* (1956), *Pagan Spain* (1957), *White Man, Listen!* (1957).

Wright, Thomas. 1810–1877. English antiquary and historian. A founder of Camden (1838) and Percy (1841) societies; edited early English texts, *Piers Plowman,* and the *Canterbury Tales;* published *History of Domestic Manners and Sentiments in England during the Middle Ages* (1862) and works on literary subjects.

Wright, Wilbur (1867–1912) and his brother Orville (1871–1948). American pioneers in aviation, Wilbur b. near Millville, Ind., and Orville at Dayton, Ohio. Brothers formed Wright Cycle Co. (1892), manufacturing bicycles. Interested in aviation (from c.1896); first experimented with kites and gliders (1896–1903). First successful flight in a motor-powered airplane made at Kill Devil Hills, near Kitty Hawk, N.C., when the machine piloted by Orville stayed in the air 12 seconds and traveled 120 ft. (Dec. 17, 1903); later in same day Wilbur flew for 59 seconds, covering 852 ft. Continued experiments and improvements; made successful circular flight of 24¼ miles in 38 minutes and 3 seconds at Dayton, Ohio (Oct. 5, 1905); received patent for their flying machine (1906). Made exhibition flights in France (1908) and won Michelin trophy (Dec. 31, 1908) by a flight of 124 kilometers in 2 hours and 20 minutes. Completed airplane for U.S. army (1908), successfully tested (June 1909). Organized American Wright Company (1909) to manufacture airplanes under their patents. After Wilbur's death from typhoid fever (1912), Orville sold his interest in the airplane manufacturing company (1915); director of Wright Aeronautical Laboratory, Dayton, Ohio.

Wright, Willard Huntington. *Pseudonym* S.S. Van Dine \van-ˈdīn\. 1888–1939. American novelist, b. Charlottesville, Va. Creator of the detective Philo Vance in various novels, including *The Canary Murder Case* (1927), *The Greene Murder Case* (1928), *The Bishop Murder Case* (1929), *The Casino Murder Case* (1934), *The Gracie Allen Murder Case* (1938).

Wright, William Aldis. 1836?–1914. English scholar. Edited Bacon's *Essays* (1862); joint editor, with William George Clark, of *Cambridge Shakespeare* (1863–66) and sole editor of second edition (1891–93); edited, with Clark, the *Globe Shakespeare* (1864); carried on editing of Clarendon Press series (1874–97); secretary to (British) Old Testament Revision Company (1870–85).

Wrig·ley \ˈrig-lē\, William, Jr. 1861–1932. American businessman, b. Philadelphia. Founded William Wrigley, Jr., & Co., manufacturers of chewing gum, Chicago (1891), and served as president until 1921; held interests in hotels, mines, and the Chicago Cubs baseball team. His son ¶Philip Knight (1894–1977), b. Chicago, succeeded as president (1925–61) and board chairman (1961–77) of the Wrigley Co.; also president and owner of Chicago Cubs.

Wriothes·ley \ˈrī-əth-slē, ˈrät(-ə)-slē, ˈrith-le, ˈriz-lē\. Name of English family holding title of earl of South·amp·ton \sau̇th-ˈ(h)am(p)-tən\. Members included: Thomas (1505–1550), politician; personal secretary to Thomas Cromwell (from c.1532); succeeded Cromwell as one of two joint principal secretaries of state to Henry VIII (1540); lord chancellor of England (1544–47); created 1st earl of Southampton (1547); supported overthrow of Edward Seymour, Duke of Somerset.

His grandson ¶Henry (1573–1624), 3d earl, soldier; gained favor of Queen Elizabeth and friendship of Earl of Essex; liberal patron of poets, esp. Shakespeare, who dedicated *Venus and Adonis* (1593) and *The Rape of Lucrece* (1594) to him; may have been addressee of Shakespeare's sonnets. Accompanied Essex on expeditions to Cádiz and the Azores (1596, 1597) and to Ireland (1599); took part in Essex's rebellion, attempting to incite public feeling by effecting revival of Shakespeare's *Richard II* (1601); sentenced to death (1601); sentence commuted to life imprisonment; released (1603) by James I; regained court favor; made captain of Isle of Wight (1603); entertained Queen Anne with performance of *Love's Labor's Lost* (1603). Active member of Virginia and East India companies; made privy councilor (1619) but lost favor by opposing Duke of Buckingham; volunteered, with his eldest son, for service of United Provinces of Netherlands against Spain but succumbed to fever after landing at Bergen op Zoom. His second son ¶Thomas (1607–1667), 4th earl, was adviser to Charles I and II; lord high treasurer of England (1660–67).

Wró·blew·ski \vrü-ˈblef-skē\, Zygmunt Florenty von. 1845–1888. Polish physicist. Professor, Kraków (1882); known for work on the liquefaction of gases, esp. oxygen, nitrogen, and carbon monoxide.

Wu \ˈwü\. Name of two Chinese dynasties: (1) Dynasty (222–280 A.D.), founded by Sun Ch'üan (*q.v.*), ruling in state of Wu; one of the Three Kingdoms in central part along the lower Yangtze and in the south; capital was Nanking;

finally absorbed by the Western Chin. (2) Dynasty (907–937) in the Yangtze Valley, one of the Ten Kingdoms.

Wu Chao \'wü-'jaů\. *Known as* Wu Hou \-'hō\ *or* Wu Tse-t'ien \'wüd-'zə-tē-'en\. 625–705. Empress of China. Concubine to emperors T'ai Tsung (638–649) and Kao Tsung; by means of intrigue, had herself appointed Kao Tsung's empress (655) and eliminated all rivals for power; gained control of Kao Tsung (by 660); after his death (683) was real ruler of China. An effective administrator; directed conquest of Korea (655–675); placed her son by Kao Tsung, Chung Tsung, on throne (683) and quickly replaced him with another son, Jui Tsung; deposed Jui Tsung and usurped throne (690); only woman sovereign in Chinese history; made Chung Tsung crown prince but retained power (698); forced by her ministers and generals to cede throne to Chung Tsung (705).

Wu Chen \'wü-'jən\. 1280–1354. Chinese painter. One of the Four Masters of the Yüan dynasty; led reclusive life; known for his landscapes, esp. scenes of fishermen.

Wu Ch'eng-en \'wü-'chəŋ-'ən\. c.1500–c.1582. Chinese novelist. Author of folk novel *Hsi-yu chi* (1592; English title *Monkey*), based on the pilgrimage of Hsüan-tsang (*q.v.*).

Wu Ching-tzu \'wü-'jiŋ-dzü\. 1701–1754. Chinese novelist. Failed higher official examinations; moved to Nanking (1733), where he lived in poverty. Author of first and best Chinese satirical novel, *Ju-lin wai-shih* (Eng. title *The Scholars*), an attack on corruption of contemporary official society.

Wulf·he·re \'wůlf-,her-ə\. d. 674. King of the Mercians (from 657). First Mercian king to be baptized; spread Christianity; controlled much of England south of the Humber; waged war against West Saxons; defeated in attempt to invade Northumbria (674).

Wulfila. See ULFILAS.

Wulf·stan \'wůlf-stən, -,stan\. d. 1023. English prelate. Bishop of London (996–1002); archbishop of York (1002–23); bishop of Worcester (1003–16). Adviser (from 1008) to kings Aethelred and Canute and drafted their laws; involved in church reform. Author of *The Canons of Edgar, Institutes of Polity* on the organization of society, two *Chronicle* poems, and many homilies, esp. *Sermo Lupi ad Anglos* describing desperate conditions after Danish raids.

Wulfstan *or* **Wul·stan** \'wůl-stən, -,stan\. Saint. c.1008–1095. English prelate. Benedictine monk; bishop of Worcester (1062); submitted to William the Conqueror and left in his see; adviser to William the Conqueror and William II Rufus; noted for administrative ability, preaching, personal asceticism; helped compile the Domesday Book; put end to slave trade practiced at Bristol upon English men and women; canonized (1203).

Wu Li \'wü-'lē\. 1632–1718. Chinese painter and priest. Converted to Roman Catholicism, baptized Simon Xavier (1676); entered Jesuit order (1682); ordained priest, adopting surname A Cunha (1688); missionary in Kiangsu. Member of the orthodox school of "literati painting" (*wen-jen-hua*); author of poems published as *Mo-ching shi-ch'ao* (1719).

Wul·len·we·ver \'vůl-ən-'vā-vər\, Jürgen. c.1492–1537. Hanseatic politician. Elected burgomaster of Lübeck (1533); aimed to restore supremacy of Lübeck on Baltic, chiefly by subjection of Denmark and Sweden, and to spread Protestantism; his policies greatly weakened the city; imprisoned, tortured into self-accusations, and executed.

Wüll·ner \'vuel-nər\, Franz. 1832–1902. German conductor and composer. Composer of choral works with and without orchestra (including the cantata *Heinrich der Finkler,* a Miserere, a Stabat Mater, the 125th Psalm), chamber music, songs, piano pieces, etc.

Wundt \'vůnt\, Wilhelm. 1832–1920. German physiologist and psychologist. Founder of experimental psychology. Studied under Johannes Müller; taught at Heidelberg (1857–71) and Zürich (1874–75); professor at Leipzig (1875–1917); founded first psychological laboratory (1879); founded journal *Philosophische Studien* (1881); believed that psychology must be based directly on experience; prescribed methodology of introspection. Author of *Beiträge zur Theorie der Sinneswahrnehmung* (1862), *Vorlesungen über die Menschen und Thierseele* (1863), *Grundzüge der physiologischen Psychologie* (1873–74), *Logik* (1880–83), *Ethik* (1886), *Grundriss der Psychologie* (1896), *Völkerpsychologie* (1900–20), *Erlebtes und Erkanntes* (autobiography, 1920), etc.

Wu P'ei-fu \'wü-'pā-'fü\. 1874–1939. Chinese general. Served under Ts'ao K'un; made commander of third division army (1916); conducted successful campaigns in northern and central China (1917–20), becoming leader of Peking government against Sun Yat-sen forces in the south and Chang Tso-lin in Manchuria; defeated Chang Tso-lin (1922); lost much popularity by his stern attitude and his brutal suppression (1923) of railroad strike; defeated by Chang Tso-lin in great battle near Tientsin (1924), fled Peking; regained control temporarily (1926–27); opposed to Chiang Kai-shek; defeated by him and retired to Yochow (1927); refused to aid Japanese (1937–39).

Wurm·ser \'vůrm-zər\, Dagobert Siegmund von. Graf. 1724–1797. Austrian field marshal. Distinguished himself at Habelschwerdt (1779) in War of Bavarian Succession; led an army corps in French Revolution (1793), defeated at Weissenburg, and forced to recross Rhine; defeated French and took Mannheim (1795); commander in Italy against Napoléon and was defeated (1796) at Castiglione, Rovereto, and Bassano; besieged in Mantua and surrendered (1797).

Würt·tem·berg \'vuer-təm-,berk\. German county and duchy, later (1806) a kingdom, and its ruling family, which originated in late 11th century. County was a part of Swabia, ruled by Hohenstaufens (*q.v.*); first counts Ulrich (1241–65), Eberhard I (1279–1325; *q.v.*), and successors ruled in valley of the Neckar and adjacent lands; divided into several lines (15th century); Count Eberhard V became duke (1495) as Eberhard I (*q.v.*); succeeded by Duke Ulrich (1498–1550; *q.v.*) and ten other dukes (1550–1797), most of them Protestant; lands suffered severely in Thirty Years' War and later conflicts; Duke Frederick II made king as Frederick I (1805; *q.v.*); succeeded as king by William I (1781–1864; king from 1816), Charles I (1823–1891; king from 1864), and William II (1848–1921; king 1891–1918, abdicated). See also ALBERT, Duke of Württemberg.

Wurtz \'vuerts\, Charles-Adolphe. 1817–1884. French chemist. Assistant to J.-B.-A. Dumas at the Sorbonne (1845); professor there (from 1853). Known for researches on organo-nitrogen compounds, hydrocarbons, and glycols; discovered phosphorus oxychloride; synthesized ethylamine (1849); studied reaction of sodium with organic halogen compounds (now known as Wurtz-Fittig reaction), esp. in preparation (1856) of ethylene glycol, the first dihydroxy alcohol; also synthesized phenol (with August Kekule, 1867), choline, aldol, neurine, etc.

Wu San-kuei \'wü-'sän-'gwā\. 1612–1678. Chinese general. Commanded imperial army in last days of Ming dynasty; called Manchus to his assistance and defeated (1644) rebel leader Li Tzu-ch'eng; helped establish Manchu (Ch'ing) dynasty (1644); served new rulers in subduing western and southwestern provinces; governor of Yunnan and Szechwan; led revolt against Manchus (from 1673) but overcome and killed.

Wu Tao-tzu \'wü-'daů-'dzü\ *or* **Wu Tao-hsüan** \-shue-'än\. c.700–760 A.D. Chinese painter. Generally regarded as greatest of all Chinese figure painters; known for his landscapes and Buddhist religious pictures, nearly all now lost; his influence on painters of China and Japan very great.

Wu Ti. See (1) HSIAO YEN; (2) Liu Ch'e under LIU family; (3) SSU-MA YEN.

Wu Tse-t'ien. See WU CHAO.

Wu Tsung. See Chu Hou-chao under CHU family.

Wutt·ke \'vůt-kə\, Heinrich. 1818–1876. German historian and politician. Professor, Leipzig (from 1848); member, National Assembly, Frankfurt (1848) and cofounder of the "Great German" party. Author of *Polen und Deutsche* (1847), *Entstehung der Schrift und des Schrifttums* (1872), etc.

Wu Wang \'wü-'wäŋ\. d. 1115 B.C. Founder and first ruler (c.1122–1115 B.C.) of the Chou dynasty of China. Son of Wen Wang; succeeded his father as head of semibarbaric state of Chou; formed coalition with eight other border states and overthrew (c.1122) the Shang dynasty; established a feudal form of government.

Wy·ant \'wī-ənt\, Alexander Helwig. 1836–1892. American painter, b. Evans Creek, Ohio. One of painters of the Hudson River school; known for landscapes as *The Mohawk Valley* (1866), *An Old Clearing* (1881), *In the Adirondacks, Passing Clouds, Moonlight and Frost.*

Wy·att \'wī-ət\, Sir Francis. 1575?–1644. English colonial administrator. Great-grandson of poet Sir Thomas Wyatt; named governor of Virginia colony (1620); arrived in Virginia (1621) and remained as governor for Virginia Company until company's dissolution (1624) and thereafter as first royal governor of the colony (1624–26); again governor (1639–41); credited with promoting cause of representative government in the colony.

Wyatt, James. 1746–1813. English architect. Made reputation with Neoclassical design of London Pantheon (opened 1772); succeeded Sir William Chambers as surveyor to Board of Works (1796); restored Westminster Abbey, Windsor Castle, and cathedrals of Durham, Hereford, Lichfield, Salisbury; built Neoclassical Heaton Hall, Lancashire (1772), and Heveningham Hall, Suffolk (c.1788–99); best known for his Gothic Revival country house for William Beckford, Fonthill Abbey in Wiltshire (1796–1807). His son ¶Benjamin Dean (1775–?1850), architect, designed Drury Lane theater (1811) and Crockford's clubhouse (1827), London.
James's nephew ¶Sir Jeffry (1766–1840); adopted (1824) surname Wy·at·ville \'wī-ət-,vil\; practiced architecture with his uncle (1792–99); built additions to Sidney Sussex Coll., Cambridge (1821–32); remodeled Windsor Castle (1824–28).

Wyatt, Sir Matthew Digby. 1820–1877. English architect. Published *Geometric Mosaics of the Middle Ages* (1848); surveyor to East India Company (1855); first Slade professor of Fine Arts, Cambridge (1869); author of books on metalwork and fine art.

Wy·att *or* **Wy·at** \'wī-ət\, Sir Thomas. 1503–1542. English poet and diplomat. Privy councilor (1533); a lover of Anne Boleyn; courtier in favor of Henry VIII, who sent him on diplomatic missions, esp. to Spain (1537–39). Translator of

Petrarchan sonnets; introduced the sonnet (with his creation of a rhymed couplet as a conclusion), *ottava rima,* and *terza rima* verse forms, and the French rondeau into English literature; contributed three satires in heroic couplets and *Songes and Sonettes* to Tottel's *Miscellany* (1557); author of *Certayne Psalmes* (1549).

His son ¶Sir Thomas, *called* the Younger (1521?–1554), soldier, joined volunteers raised by Henry Howard, Earl of Surrey, and was active at Landrecies and Boulogne (1543–50); joined Edward Courtenay, Earl of Devonshire, in a general insurrection to prevent the marriage of Queen Mary with Philip of Spain (1554); led forces from Kent into Southwark; executed for high treason.

Wyatville, Sir Jeffry. See under James WYATT.

Wyche, Richard. See RICHARD of Chichester.

Wych·er·ley \ˈwich-ər-lē\, William. 1640–1716. English dramatist. Gained fame and court favor with his comedy *Love in a Wood, or St. James's Park* (1671); produced *The Gentleman Dancing-Master* (1672), comedy of intrigue; best known for *The Country Wife* (1675) and *The Plain Dealer* (1676), comedies satirizing manners and society as well as human foibles.

Wyc·liffe \ˈwik-ˌlif, -ləf, *also* ˈwīk-\, John. *Also* Wyc·lif, Wic·lif, Wick·liffe, *etc.* c.1330–1384. English religious reformer and theologian. Master of Balliol (1360–61); vicar of Fillingham (1361) and of Ludgershall (1368); rector of Lutterworth (1374), continuing to teach and write at Oxford (till 1381). Developed systematic attack upon the hierarchical system; won favor (1376) of John of Gaunt, Duke of Lancaster, by justifying limitation of the church's lordship over temporal affairs; presented in Latin pamphlets arguments for national refusal of certain tribute demanded by Rome. Expounded (c.1376) doctrine of "dominion as founded in grace," by which all authority, both ecclesiastical and secular, is derived from God and is forfeited when its possessor falls into mortal sin; attacked friars and the worldliness of the medieval church; accused of heresy by Pope Gregory XI (1377) and summoned before bishop of London to answer this charge (1377); escaped trial as court session was terminated by general rioting before he could be interrogated; protected by queen mother and by public opinion at second hearing at Lambeth (1378) and was not sentenced. Denied (after 1378) priestly power of absolution, and power to enforce confession; rejected penances and indulgences, insisting upon inward and practical religion as against formalism; denied doctrine of transubstantiation (1380); forbidden to teach at Oxford and permitted to retire (1381); his works condemned by a London synod (1382). Initiated the first complete translation of the Bible into English, his contribution to the text still uncertain. Considered a forerunner of the Protestant Reformation.

Wy·eth \ˈwī-əth\, Newell Convers. 1882–1945. American illustrator and painter, b. Needham, Mass. Very successful as illustrator of Stevenson's novels (*Treasure Island, Kidnapped, The Black Arrow*) and an edition of *Robin Hood.* Among his mural paintings were panels in the Missouri State Capitol, Federal Reserve Bank at Boston, Metropolitan Life Insurance Building at New York City, National Cathedral at Washington, D.C., etc.

Wykeham *or* **Wickham,** William of. See WILLIAM of Wykeham.

Wy·ler \ˈwī-lər\, William. 1902–1981. American motion-picture director, b. Mulhouse, Germany (now in France). To U.S. (1920, naturalized 1928); directed some 50 westerns for Universal Studios, Hollywood (1925–27); established his reputation with *Counsellor-at-Law* (1933) and *These Three* (1936); won Academy Awards for best director for *Mrs. Miniver* (1942), *The Best Years of Our Lives* (1946), and *Ben Hur* (1959); other films included *Dodsworth* (1936), *Dead End* (1937), *Jezebel* (1938), *Wuthering Heights* (1939), *The Westerner* (1940), *The Letter* (1940), *The Little Foxes* (1941), *The Memphis Belle* (war documentary, 1944), *The Heiress* (1949), *Roman Holiday* (1953), *Friendly Persuasion* (1956), *The Big Country* (1958), *The Children's Hour* (1962), *The Collector* (1965), *Funny Girl* (1968).

Wy·lie \ˈwī-lē\, Elinor Morton, *nee* Hoyt \ˈhȯit\. 1885–1928. American poet and novelist, b. Somerville, N.J. m. 2d Horace Wylie (1915; div. 1923), 3d William Rose Benét (1923). Author of verse as *Nets to Catch the Wind* (1921), *Black Armour* (1923), *Trivial Breath* (1928), *Angels and Earthly Creatures* (1929), *Last Poems* (1943), and the novels *Jennifer Lorn* (1923), *The Venetian Glass Nephew* (1925), *The Orphan Angel* (1926), *Mr. Hodge and Mr. Hazard* (1928).

Wylie, Philip Gordon. 1902–1971. American author, b. Beverly, Mass. Best known for nonfiction *Generation of Vipers* (1942), a critical survey of American institutions; also wrote novels and nonfiction as *Finnley Wren* (1934), *Essay on Morals* (1947), *Opus 21* (1949), *The Disappearance* (1951), *The Answer* (1956), *The Spy Who Spoke Porpoise* (1969), *The End of the Dream* (1971), and popular series of "Crunch and Des" stories in *Saturday Evening Post.*

Wynd·ham \ˈwin-dəm\, George. 1863–1913. English politician and man of letters. Conservative M.P. (1889–1913); chief secretary for Ireland (1900–05); adopted conciliatory program to maintain union and carry out economic development; made bold use of imperial credit in Irish Land Purchase Act (1903). Friend of W.E. Henley; edited North's version of Plutarch's *Lives* (1895–96) and Shakespeare's poems (1898).

Wyndham, John. See John HARRIS.

Wyndham, Sir William. 3d Baronet Wyndham. 1687–1740. English politician. Tory M.P. (1710–40); close associate of Viscount Bolingbroke and privy to his Jacobite intrigues; secretary of war (1712); chancellor of the exchequer (1713); head of the treasury (1714); fell into disgrace (1715) but returned (1726) as leader of the opposition to Sir Robert Walpole.

Wyndham-Quin \-ˈkwin\, Windham Thomas. 4th Earl of Dun·ra·ven and Mount-Earl \ˌdən-ˈrā-və-nən(d)-maůnt-ˈər(-ə)l\, 2d Baron Ken·ry \ˈken-rē\. 1841–1926. Irish politician. Succeeded to titles and seat in House of Lords (1871); undersecretary of state for colonies (1885–86, 1886–87); chairman of House of Lords committee on sweated labor (1888–90); as chairman of Irish Land Conference (1902–03) devised policy that Irish landlords should be bought out by tenants, embodied in Wyndham Land Act (1903); supported devolution; urged federal solution to Irish home rule question at Irish Convention (1917); senator of Irish Free State (1921). Noted yachtsman. Author of *The Great Divide* (1876), *The Irish Question* (pamphlet, 1880), *Past Times and Pastimes* (1922).

Wynfrid *or* **Wynfrith.** See Saint BONIFACE.

Wynn \ˈwin\, Ed. *Orig.* Isaiah Edwin Le·o·pold \ˈlē-ə-ˌpōld\. 1886–1966. American comedian, b. Philadelphia. Early on vaudeville stage; joined Ziegfeld *Follies* (1914); wrote lyrics and music for and starred in stage comedies *Ed Wynn's Carnival* (1920), *The Perfect Fool* (1921), *The Grab Bag* (1924), *Boys and Girls Together* (1940); starred in radio show "Texaco's Fire Chief" (1932–39). Also starred on television, winning Emmy Award for his dramatic role in *Requiem for a Heavyweight* (1956), and in motion pictures as *The Great Man* (1957), *Marjorie Morningstar* (1958), *The Diary of Anne Frank* (1959), *Mary Poppins* (1964).

Wynne \ˈwin\, Ellis. 1671–1734. Welsh author. Published (1703) the Welsh allegorical prose classic *Gweledigaethau y Bardd Cwsc* (Visions of the Sleeping Bard); took orders; rector of Llandanwg (1704) and Llanfairjuxta-Harlech (1711); edited Welsh prayer book (1710).

Wyn·toun \ˈwint-ᵊn\, Andrew of. c.1350–c.1423. Scottish chronicler. Canon of St. Andrews; prior of St. Serf's in Loch Leven (c.1393–1421). Wrote *Orygynale Cronykil,* a metrical account of world history (esp. in Scotland) from the creation to 1408, philologically important as an example of old Scots vernacular.

Wys·piań·ski \vis-ˈpyänʸ-skē\, Stanisław Mateusz Ignacy. 1869–1907. Polish painter, poet, and playwright. Creator of modern Polish drama. His plays, on themes from Greek mythology and Polish history, included *Legenda* (1897), *Meleager* (1898), *Warszawianka* (1898), *Klątwa* (1899), *Wesele* (1900), *Wyzwolenie* (1903), *Akropolis* (1904), *Noc Listopadowa* (1904), *Sedziowie* (1907); verse included *Bolesław Śmiały* (1900), *Kazimierz Wielki* (1900), *Henryk Pobożny* (1903). Also known for his designs for stained-glass windows.

Wyss \ˈvēs\, Johann Rudolf. 1781–1830. Swiss writer and philosopher. Professor of philosophy at Bern Academy (1805 ff.); edited the *Alpenrosen* almanac (1811–30); author of the Swiss national anthem "Rufst du mein Vaterland?" (1811); collector of Swiss tales and folklore published in *Idyllen, Volkssagen, Legenden und Erzählungen aus der Schweiz* (1815). Completed and edited novel *Der Schweizerische Robinson* (*The Swiss Family Robinson,* 1812–13), begun by his father Johann David Wyss (1743–1818).

Wy·szyń·ski \vish-ˈinʸ-skē\, Stefan. 1901–1981. Polish prelate. Ordained Roman Catholic priest (1924); professor at Higher Seminary, Włocławek (1930–39); founded Catholic Workers University at Włocławek (1935); resistance leader during German occupation of Poland in World War II. Bishop of Lublin (1946). Archbishop of Gniezno and Warsaw and primate of Poland (from 1949); cardinal (1952); imprisoned (1953–56) for refusal to denounce Bishop Kaczmarek; maintained strength and unity of the church in constant struggle against Communist government.

Wythe \ˈwith\, George. 1726–1806. American jurist and statesman, b. Elizabeth City Co., Va. Admitted to bar (1746); practiced in Williamsburg, where he taught law (1762–67) to Thomas Jefferson. Member (1754–55, 1758–68) and clerk (1769–75), Virginia House of Burgesses; member of Continental Congress (1775–77) and a signer of the Declaration of Independence. Judge, Virginia high court of chancery (1778–1806; sole chancellor, 1788–1801); in *Commonwealth* v. *Caton* asserted the power of courts to annul unconstitutional laws. First professor of law in U.S., at College of William and Mary (1779–89), where John Marshall was his student. Member of Constitutional Convention (1787) and Virginia ratifying convention (1788). Opened

Wys·piań·ski \vis-ˈpyän^y-skē\, Stanisław Mateusz Ignacy. 1869–1907. Polish painter, poet, and playwright. Creator of modern Polish drama. His plays, on themes from Greek mythology and Polish history, included *Legenda* (1897), *Meleager* (1898), *Warszawianka* (1898), *Klątwa* (1899), *Wesele* (1900), *Wyzwolenie* (1903), *Akropolis* (1904), *Noc Listopadowa* (1904), *Sedziowie* (1907); verse included *Bolesław Śmiały* (1900), *Kazimierz Wielki* (1900), *Henryk Pobożny* (1903). Also known for his designs for stained-glass windows.

Wyss \ˈvēs\, Johann Rudolf. 1781–1830. Swiss writer and philosopher. Professor of philosophy at Bern Academy (1805 ff.); edited the *Alpenrosen* almanac (1811–30); author of the Swiss national anthem "Rufst du mein Vaterland?" (1811); collector of Swiss tales and folklore published in *Idyllen, Volkssagen, Legenden und Erzählungen aus der Schweiz* (1815). Completed and edited novel *Der Schweizerische Robinson* (*The Swiss Family Robinson,* 1812–13), begun by his father Johann David Wyss (1743–1818).

Wy·szyń·ski \vish-ˈin^y-skē\, Stefan. 1901–1981. Polish prelate. Ordained Roman Catholic priest (1924); professor at Higher Seminary, Włocławek (1930–39); founded Catholic Workers University at Włocławek (1935); resistance leader during German occupation of Poland in World War II. Bishop of Lublin (1946). Archbishop of Gniezno and Warsaw and primate of Poland (from 1949); cardinal (1952); imprisoned (1953–56) for refusal to denounce Bishop Kaczmarek; maintained strength and unity of the church in constant struggle against Communist government.

Wythe \ˈwith\, George. 1726–1806. American jurist and statesman, b. Elizabeth City Co., Va. Admitted to bar (1746); practiced in Williamsburg, where he taught law (1762–67) to Thomas Jefferson. Member (1754–55, 1758–68) and clerk (1769–75), Virginia House of Burgesses; member of Continental Congress (1775–77) and a signer of the Declaration of Independence. Judge, Virginia high court of chancery (1778–1806; sole chancellor, 1788–1801); in *Commonwealth* v. *Caton* asserted the power of courts to annul unconstitutional laws. First professor of law in U.S., at College of William and Mary (1779–89), where John Marshall was his student. Member of Constitutional Convention (1787) and Virginia ratifying convention (1788). Opened school of law in Richmond, where Henry Clay was a pupil and also clerk of his court.

X

Xan·thip·pe \zan-ˈt(h)ip-ē\. 5th century B.C. Greek woman. Wife of Socrates (*q.v.*). Her peevish scolding and quarrelsome temper have become proverbial.

Xan·thip·pus \zan-ˈt(h)ip-əs\. 5th century B.C. Athenian commander. Father of Pericles; commanded Athenian fleet in victory at Mycale (479 B.C.).

Xanthippus. 3d century B.C. Spartan general. Reorganized Carthaginian army in First Punic War; defeated Regulus (255 B.C.).

Xa·vi·er \ˈzā-vē-ər, ig-ˈzā-\, Francis. Saint. *Span.* Francisco Ja·vier \kä<u>b</u>-ˈyer\. *Orig.* Francisco de Ya·su y Javier \thā-ˈyä-sü-ē-\. 1506–1552. Spanish missionary. Youngest son of noble Basque family; studied in Paris (1525–34), where he made acquaintance of Ignatius of Loyola, whom he aided in founding Jesuit order (1534); ordained priest at Venice (1537); in service of order at Rome (1538–40). Sent by John III of Portugal to Goa as missionary (1541–42); preached at Goa and on southwest coast of India with great success (1542–45); continued missionary work in Malacca and the Moluccas (1545–48), where he converted many. Sailed for Kagoshima, Japan (1549); worked in Japan with some success for two years; returned to India (1551) where he was made superior of Jesuit Province of the Indies; died of fever in Sancian Island while attempting to secure entrance into China. Pioneered idea that the missionary must adapt to local customs and language; advocated education of a native clergy. Canonized (1622).

Xe·noc·ra·tes \zi-ˈnäk-rə-ˌtēz\. 396–314 B.C. Greek philosopher. Pupil of Plato; left Athens with Aristotle on death of Plato; returned and succeeded Speusippus as head of the Academy (339–314); the classical distinction between mind, soul, and body has often been attributed to him.

Xe·noph·a·nes \zi-ˈnäf-ə-ˌnēz\. c.560–c.478 B.C. Greek philosopher, b. Colophon, Asia Minor. Banished from Greece (c.546), wandered throughout Mediterranean, finally settled at Elea in southern Italy. Wrote poems attacking anthropomorphism in religion and the immorality of Olympian gods. Precursor of Eleatic school of philosophy.

Xen·o·phon \ˈzen-ə-fən\. c.431–c.352 B.C. Greek historian. Disciple of Socrates; joined expedition of Cyrus the Younger against his brother Artaxerxes II of Persia (401); after death of Cyrus in battle of Cunaxa (401) and murder by Persians of the Greek commanders, rose to leadership among the 10,000 Greek soldiers and guided them back to Black Sea. Served with Spartans at Coronea (394); banished to his estate in Elis (to 370); returned to Athens (c.365). Chief works *Anabasis* (an account of Cyrus's expedition and the Greek retreat), *Memorabilia* (account of the life and teachings of Socrates), *Hellenica* (history of Greece from 411 to 362), *Symposium* (a dialogue representing Socrates as the chief figure), *Cyropaedia* (political romance based on life of Cyrus), and essays on horsemanship and hunting.

Xer·xes \ˈzərk-ˌsēz\. *Greek name for Persian* Khsha·yār·shā \<u>k</u>shá-ˈyár-shá\. Name of two kings of the Achaemenidae of Persia:

Xerxes I. *Called* the Great. c.519–465 B.C. King (486–465 B.C.). Son of Darius I and Atossa. Suppressed revolts in Egypt and Babylonia (485–484); carried on task of Darius of punishing Greeks; prepared great expedition (483–481); bridged the Hellespont; marched through Thrace, Macedonia, and Thessaly; his fleet checked by Greek navy at Artemisium and his army by small force of Leonidas at Thermopylae; won at Thermopylae (480); burned Athens; his fleet defeated at Salamis (480); returned to Asia Minor, but left army in Greece under Mardonius; his army beaten by Greeks at Plataea (479) and his fleet at Mycale on same day; continued his father's vast construction project at Persepolis; passed his later years at Susa in dissolute living; murdered by Artabanus, captain of the guards, who was in turn killed (464) by Xerxes's son Artaxerxes I.

Xerxes II. d. 424 B.C. King for few weeks only (424 B.C.). Son of Artaxerxes I; murdered by his half-brother Sogdianus.

Xerxes III. Name given in some sources to Arses (*q.v.*).

Xiph·i·li·nus \ˌzif-ə-ˈlī-nəs\, John VIII. c.1010–1075. Byzantine jurist and prelate. Head of faculty of law at U. of Constantinople (1045); entered monastery of Holy Spirit on Mt. Olympus (1054), later its abbot. Patriarch of Constantinople (1063–75); much revered in his time; left an encomium on Eugenius of Trabzon and some legal work but his philosophical writings not extant.

Xystus. See SIXTUS.

Y

Ya·bloch·kov \'yä-bləch-kəf\, Pavel Nikolayevich. *Also spelled* Paul Ja·bloch·kov. 1847–1894. Russian electrical engineer. Director of telegraph lines between Moscow and Kursk (1871–75); settled in Paris (1876); invented (1876) the Yablochkov candle, first practical arc lamp.

Ya·din \yä-'dēn\, Yigael. 1917–1984. Israeli army officer, politician, and archaeologist. Member of Haganah military organization (1932–48); chief of the general staff of Israel Defense Forces (1949–52); formed political party (1977); deputy prime minister (1977–81). Professor of archaeology at Hebrew U. (from 1959); a leader of major archaeological expeditions in Israel, including those at Hazor (1955–58; 1968), the Dead Sea Caves (1960–61), and Masada (1963–65). Author of *The Message of the Scrolls* (1957), *Hazor* (1958–62), and *Masada* (1966), etc.

Yaḥ·ya \'yäk-,yä\. *In full* Yaḥyā Maḥmūd al-Mutawakkil. 1867–1948. Imām of Yemen (1904–48). Waged sporadic warfare against Ottoman Empire (1904–11) until it recognized his autonomy; after World War I recognized as independent ruler of Yemen; decisively defeated by Saudi Arabia (1934) and thereafter isolated his country from outside world; assassinated.

Yaḥ·yā ibn Maḥ·mūd al-Wā·si·ṭī \'yäk-,yä-,ib-ən-mäk-'müd-al-,wä-sē-'tē\. 13th century. Mesopotamian illustrator. Created 96 illustrations for al-Ḥarīrī's *Maqāmāt* (c.1237) and 99 illustrations for Ferdowsī's *Shāh-nāmeh*.

Ya·kub Beg \'yä-kůb-'beg\. 1820–1877. Kokand soldier. To northwest China (1864); through series of military and political maneuvers, took advantage of Muslim uprisings and established himself as head of kingdom of Kashgaria with capital at Turfan; expanded northward; recognized by Ottoman sultan, who made him amir of Kashgaria; gained international recognition by signing commercial treaties with Russia (1872) and Great Britain (1873); defeated by Chinese forces under Tso Tsung-t'ang (1877) and committed suicide.

Yale \'yā(ə)l\, Caroline Ardelia. 1848–1933. American educator, b. Charlotte, Vt. Teacher (1870 ff.), associate principal (1873–86), and principal (1886–1922) of Clarke School for the Deaf, Northampton, Mass.; founded and directed (1889–1933) a highly effective teacher training department at Clarke; pioneered in introduction of manual skills classes and athletic programs; championed oral method of teaching the deaf; developed a phonetic system expounded in *Formation and Development of Elementary English Sounds* (1892); published autobiography *Years of Building* (1931).

Yale, Elihu. 1649–1721. English colonial administrator, b. Boston, Mass. To England (1652); in employ of East India Company (from 1671); on duty in Madras, where he became president and governor of Fort Saint George (1687–92); resident in England (from 1699). Made gift of books and goods to the Collegiate School, then located at Saybrook, Connecticut (1714 and 1718), and the school changed its name to Yale College (1718).

Yale, Linus. 1821–1868. American inventor and manufacturer, b. Salisbury, N.Y. Set up lock business at Shelburne Falls, Mass. (early 1840s); at first produced bank locks, as his Yale Infallible Bank Lock (1851); patented a pin tumbler cylinder lock for doors (1861) and an improved cylinder lock (1865), basis of Yale lock still in use; introduced the combination lock (c.1862). With partners founded Yale Lock Manufacturing Co. at Stamford, Conn. (1868).

Ya·ma·be \yä-mä-be\ Akahito. 8th century. Japanese poet. Master of the *hanka* form; known from verses anthologized in *Manyō-shū*.

Ya·ma·ga \yä-mä-gä\ Sokō, *orig.* Takasuke. *Also called* Jin·go·za·em·on \jiŋ-gō-zä-em-ōn\. 1622–1685. Japanese military strategist and philosopher. A *rōnin* (masterless samurai); studied Confucianism under Hayashi Razan; military instructor to lord of fief of Akō (1652–60); moved to Edo, where he was a popular teacher of military science; banished to Akō for 10 years for offending the shogun. Emphasizing duty, developed a neo-Confucian code of honor for the samurai class expounded in *Yamaga-gorui* (1665); his thought became core of *Bushido* (Way of the Warrior), the guiding ethos of Japanese military down to end of World War II. Also wrote *Chūchō-jijitsu* in which he argued superiority of Japanese civilization to that of China.

Ya·ma·ga·ta \yä-mä-gä-tä\ Aritomo. Prince. 1838–1922. Japanese army commander and politician. Commanding officer of the Kiheitai, anti-shogunate irregular troops (1863); advocated adoption of Western military weapons and techniques; minister of war (1873); chiefly responsible for modernization of army; chief of general staff (1878, 1904–05); minister of home affairs (1885–89); premier (1889–91, 1898–1900); minister of justice (1892–93); president of privy council (intermittently, 1903–09); wielded great political power from 1909 until publicly censured (1921).

Ya·ma·mo·to \yä-mä-mō-tō\ Gombē *or* Gonnohyōe. 1852–1933. Japanese admiral and politician. Minister of the navy (1898–1906); admiral (1904); premier of Japan (1913–14, 1923–24).

Yamamoto Isoroku. *Surname orig.* Ta·ka·no \tä-kä-nō\. 1884–1943. Japanese admiral. Served in Russo-Japanese War (1904–05); chief of aviation department of navy (1935); commander in chief of combined fleet (1939 ff.); devised Japanese naval strategy in the Pacific including attack on Pearl Harbor.

Ya·ma·na \yä-mä-nä\ Mochitoyo. *Monastic name* Sō·zen \sō-zen\. 1404–1473. Japanese clan lord. Head of a powerful warrior clan in western Japan; Buddhist monk; engaged in power struggle with shogunal prime minister Hosokawa Katsumoto (*q.v.*) which resulted in Ōnin War (1467–77).

Ya·ma·no·u·chi \yä-mä-nō-ůch-ē\. Name of Japanese family of feudal lords ruling fief of Tosa in southeastern Japan (1600–1868) and powerful in Japanese politics. Members included: Yamanouchi Kazutoyo (1545–1605), founder of the family; awarded (1590) small fief in Kakegawa for his military services to Toyotomi Hideyoshi; after death of Hideyoshi (1598), switched allegiance to Tokugawa Ieyasu and aided him at battle of Sakigahara (1600); rewarded with fief of Tosa. His wife (m. 1573) ¶Yamanouchi Kazutoyo-no-Tsuma (1557–1617) greatly aided her husband in his rise to power. ¶Yamanouchi Toyoshige (1827–1872) succeeded as head of clan (1848); helped overthrow Tokugawa shogunate (1868); Tosa made into Kōchi Prefecture and Toyoshige given hereditary title of prince, but his feudal prerogatives eliminated (1868).

Ya·ma·no·ue \yä-mä-nō-ů-ē\ Okura. c.660–c.733. Japanese poet. Governor of Chikuzen province in Kyushu (726–732). His poems, characterized by a Confucian-inspired didacticism and moral emphasis, were published in 8th-century anthology *Manyō-shū*.

Ya·ma·shi·ta \yä-mä-shē-tä\ Tomoyuki. 1885–1946. Japanese general. Lieutenant general (1937); commanded division in northern China (1939); commanded Malayan campaign, received surrender of Singapore (Feb. 1942); took command of campaign in Philippines (1944); tried and executed for atrocities.

Yamato-Hime-Mikoto. See HIMIKO.

Ya·ma·za·ki \yä-mä-zä-kē\ Ansai. 1618–1682. Japanese philosopher. A Buddhist monk before his embracing of Confucianism; renowned as teacher of Confucianism; reduced Chu Hsi's Neo-Confucian philosophy to simple moral code and amalgamated it with Shintō religious values to produce Suika Shintō.

Yan·cey \'yan(t)-sē\, William Lowndes. 1814–1863. American politician, b. Warren Co., Ga. Admitted to bar (1834); practiced in Alabama. Member, U.S. House of Representatives (1844–46); a leader in secession movement; bolted Democratic National Convention (1860) and organized Constitutional Democratic party, nominating Breckinridge for presidency; prepared ordinance of secession for Alabama convention (1861). Confederate commissioner to England and France (1861–62); member of Confederate Senate (1862–63).

Yang Chien \'yäŋ-jē-'en\. *Reign title* Wen Ti \'wən-'dē\. 541–604. Emperor of China (581–604) and founder of the Sui dynasty. Entered military service of the Northern Chou dynasty at age 14; married a daughter of the Chou crown prince; on emperor's death, prevailed over rival claimants and seized the throne (581), thus founding Sui dynasty. Established a strong centralized government; abolished inheritance of office; introduced a civil service system; promulgated law code (583); erected a new capital city; conquered southern China and reunified China under his rule; broke power of the Mongols and Turks in northern part of China (by 603); perhaps assassinated by his son and successor Yang Ti. His reign one of greatest in Chinese history.

Yang Chu \ˈyäŋ-ˈjü\. 440–?360 B.C. Chinese philosopher. Advocated naturalism but his thought distorted by Meng-tzu as representing extreme hedonism; his teachings resembled those of Epicurus.

Yang Hsiu-ch'ing \ˈyäŋ-shē-ˈü-ˈchiŋ\. d. 1856. Chinese rebel. A dealer in firewood; joined (c.1849) Taiping band and quickly rose to high position; made commander in chief of Taiping forces by Hung Hsiu-ch'üan (1851); organized the army and an extensive spy system; won several victories in Taiping Rebellion, esp. capture of Nanking (1853); made Taiping prime minister; attempted to usurp Hung's position and was executed on Hung's orders.

Yang Hsiung \ˈyäŋ-shē-ˈuŋ\. 53 B.C.–18 A.D. Chinese poet and philosopher. Court poet under three emperors (from c.13 B.C.). Excelled in writing poetry in *fu* form; in later years turned to philosophy, his thought a synthesis of Confucianism, Taoism, and naturalistic speculation. His chief philosophic works were *Fa-yen* on history, ethics, etc., and *T'ai-hsüan ching* in imitation of *I Ching*.

Yang Kuang \ˈyäŋ-ˈgwäŋ\. *Reign title* Yang Ti \-ˈdē\. 580–618. Second and last emperor (604–618) of the Sui dynasty of China. Succeeded, and perhaps assassinated, his father Yang Chien (604); built an extensive system of canals throughout China; erected palaces; founded a second capital city at Lo-yang; extended his rule south to Vietnam and north into Central Asia; his disastrous campaigns against Korea (612–614) resulted in revolt of the people; fled to South China; assassinated.

Yang Kuei-fei \ˈyäŋ-ˈgwā-ˈfā\. d. 756 A.D. Chinese concubine. Daughter of a high official; one of few obese women in Chinese history considered beautiful; became concubine to son of T'ang emperor Hsüan Tsung; soon beloved by the emperor himself, who made her and her two sisters his concubines; wielded great influence at court; her brother Yang Kuo-chung made first minister of the empire. Made An Lu-shan (*q.v.*) her protégé, adopted son, and, according to many, her lover; killed by Imperial guards after An Lu-shan's rebellion.

Yang Ti. See YANG KUANG.

Yang Yen \ˈyäŋ-ˈyən\. 727–781. Chinese politician. Chief minister to T'ang emperor Te Tsung; greatly reduced power of aristocratic classes by abolishing land, labor, produce, and other taxes on the peasants and instituting a double tax on the land; committed suicide after being accused of bribery and corruption.

Yap Ah Loy \ˈyäp-ˈä-ˈlȯi\. 1837–1885. Chinese leader in Malaya. To Selangor (1856); trusted aide to Liu Ngim Kong (1862–69). As Capitan China of Kuala Lumpur (from 1869), leader of Chinese community and important in Malay political system; largely responsible for development of Kuala Lumpur as a commercial and mining center; amassed large fortune; lost much power with appointment (1879) of first British resident to city.

Ya·ʿqūb ebn Leys aṣ-Ṣaf·fār \yȧ-ˈkü-ˌbeb-ən-ˈlā-sȧ-sȧf-ˈfär\. 840–879. Founder of the Ṣaffarid Empire. A coppersmith (*ṣaffār*, whence name of dynasty); raised army and conquered parts of Afghanistan; acted as independent ruler (from c.866); seized control of much of Persia and parts of Pakistan; unsucccessful in attempt to capture Baghdad (878); fostered revitalization of Persian language.

Ya·ʿqū·bī, al- \al-ya-ˈkü-bē\. *In full* Aḥmad ibn Abū Yaʿqūb ibn Jaʿfar ibn Wahb ibn Wāḍiḥ al-Yaʿqūbī. d. 897. Arab historian and geographer. Lived in Armenia and Khorāsān under Ṭāhirid patronage (to 873); traveled to India and the Maghrib, died in Egypt. Author of *Tāʾrīkh ibn Wāḍiḥ*, a universal history (to 872), and of *Kitāb al-buldān*, a treatise on historical geography, first of its kind in Arabic literature.

Yarmouth, Earls of. See PASTON family.

Ya·ro·slav \yə-(ˌ)rə-ˈsläf\. *Called* the Wise. 980–1054. Grand prince of Kiev (1019–54). Promoted Christianity and civilization in Russia; built Cathedral of St. Sophia and the "Golden Gate" of Kiev fortress; began codification of law; expanded his rule into Baltic regions; maintained commercial and diplomatic relations with the West; married his daughters to Harold III of Norway, Henry I of France, and Andrew I of Hungary.

Ya·su·da \yä-ˈsüd-ä\ Zenjirō. 1838–1921. Japanese businessman. Rose from shop assistant to founder of a giant banking empire; expanded into other businesses; his *zaibatsu* (industrial and financial combine) was fourth largest in pre-World War II Japan; also known as philanthropist.

Ya·sui \yä-sü-ē\ Sōtarō. 1888–1959. Japanese painter. Studied in France (1907–14); influenced by Courbet and Cézanne. Painted in Western style; excelled in drawing, esp. portraits. Works included *Nude Washing Her Feet* (1913), *Panlownia Blossoms* (1924), *Woman With a Fan* (1929), *Seoul* (1938), *At the Studio* (1951).

Yates, Dornford. See Cecil W. MERCER.

Yates \ˈyāts\, Richard. 1815–1873. American politician, b. Warsaw, Ky. Practiced law in Jacksonville, Ill. Member, U.S. House of Representatives (1851–55); governor of Illinois (1861–64), strongly supporting Lincoln's policies throughout Civil War; U.S. senator from Illinois (1865–71).

Yates, Robert. 1738–1801. American jurist, b. Schenectady, N.Y. Practiced in Albany, N.Y. Member of provincial congresses (1775–77) and Committee of Safety (1776). Justice, New York Supreme Court (1777–98) and chief justice (1790–98). Leader of Antifederalists (from c.1785); in Constitutional Convention (1787) opposed framing of a federal constitution; attacked Constitution in campaign against its ratification (1787–88).

Yavoro, Peyo. See Peyo KRACHOLOV.

Yavuz. See SELIM I.

Yaz·de·gerd \yȧz-de-ˈgerd\. *Middle Persian* Yzdkrt. Name of three Sāsānid kings of Persia:

Yazdegerd I. d. 420. King (339–420). Son of Bahrām IV; kept peace with Roman Empire; tried to free country of domination by nobles and Magian priests; at first halted persecution of Christians but later resumed it.

Yazdegerd II. d. 457. King (438–457). Grandson of Yazdegerd I and son of Bahrām V; zealous Zoroastrian; persecuted Christians and Jews; at war with Rome (442); also fought in the east against the Kushans and Kidarites; succeeded in turn by sons Hormizd III and Fīrūz.

Yazdegerd III. d. 651. King (632–651). Last of the Sāsānian dynasty. Son of Shahryār and grandson of Khosrow II; too young actually to rule; country torn by civil war; Arab invasions began (633); overwhelmed by Arabs in battles of al-Qādisīya (636 or 637) and Nahāvand (642); fled to Media; slain at Merv. His accession date (June 16, 632 A.D.) marked beginning of Jalalaean Era, still used in calendar of Parsis.

Ya·zīd \yȧ-ˈzēd\. Name of three Umayyad caliphs:

Yazīd I. *In full* Yazīd ibn Muʿāwiyah ibn Abī Sufyān. c.645–683. Caliph (680–683). Son of Muʿāwiyah I; engaged successfully in civil war with Ḥusayn (*q.v.*), son of ʿAlī; faced with revolt of Meccans; reformed financial and tax systems; strengthened administrative structure; improved military defenses and agricultural methods.

Yazīd II. d. 724. Caliph (720–724). Son of ʿAbd al-Malik ibn Marwān.

Yazīd III. d. 744. Caliph for a few months (744).

Ya·zīd ibn al-Mu·hal·lab \yȧ-ˈzē-ˌdib-ə-nül-mü-ˈhȧl-lȧb\. 672–720. Persian politician. Served under several Umayyad caliphs, esp. as governor of Iraq (715) under Sulaymān; persecuted followers of his enemy al-Hajjāj, former governor of Iraq; later also named governor of Khorāsān; his administration cruel and corrupt; died leading a rebellion against the caliphate.

Yā·zi·ji \ˈyä-zē-jē\, Nāṣīf. 1800–1871. Lebanese scholar. In service (to 1840) of Bashīr Shihāb II, emir of Lebanon; moved to Beirut (1840). As a Christian helped American missionaries prepare Arabic textbooks for mission schools; did much to revitalize classical Arabic language and literary traditions.

Yeard·ley \ˈyärd-lē\, Sir George. 1587?–1627. English colonial administrator. Landed in Virginia (1609); acting governor of Virginia (1616–17); governor (1619–21, 1626–27); during first administration summoned first representative assembly in American colonies.

Years·ley \ˈyi(ə)rz-lē\, James. 1805–1869. English surgeon. Established (1837) London practice, first to practice as ear, nose, and throat specialist; founded Ear, Nose and Throat Hospital, London (1840), first of its kind; wrote classic *Deafness Practically Illustrated* (1840); invented an artificial eardrum (c.1843); cofounder of British annual *Medical Directory* (1845).

Yeats \ˈyāts\, William Butler. 1865–1939. Irish poet and dramatist. Began literary work with translations of Gaelic tales and compilations of Irish folklore; his early lyric verse included *The Wanderings of Oisin* (1889), *The Wind among the Reeds* (1899), and *In the Seven Woods* (1904); later work in austere style included *Responsibilities* (1914), *The Wild Swans at Coole* (1917), *Michael Robartes and the Dancer* (1921; included "Easter 1916"), *The Tower* (1927). Fell in love with Maud Gonne (1889); friend of William Morris, W. E. Henley, and Arthur Symons; a founder of Rhymer's Club. Wrote first poetic plays *The Countess Kathleen* (1892) and *The Land of Heart's Desire* (1894), folk stories collected in *The Celtic Twilight* (1893), and *The Secret Rose* (1897), and critical essays *Ideas of Good and Evil* (1903), *The Cutting of an Agate* (1912), and *Per Amica Silentia Lunae* (1918). Assumed leadership (1901) of Irish literary revival (see also George MOORE); began dramatic activities by writing plays according to his mystical theories of drama; with aid of Lady Gregory and Edward Martyn, staged first performance of Irish Literary Theatre (1899), which became established (1904) as the Abbey Theatre; brought J. M. Synge from Paris to write plays; produced three plays in prose *Cathleen ni Houlihan* (1902), *The Pot of Broth* (1902), and *The Hour-Glass* (1903); wrote verse plays, including *The Shadowy Waters* (1900), *The King's Threshold* (1904), *Deirdre* (1907), and later prose plays as *The Player Queen* (1919), *The Cat and the Moon* (1924), *The Resurrection* (1927), and *The Words upon the Window-Pane* (1934). Set out his personal mythology and theories of art and poetry in prose work *A Vision* (1925). One of first senators of Irish Free State (1922–28); awarded Nobel prize for literature (1923). Later verse included *The Winding Stair* (1929), *Wheels and Butterflies* (1934), and

Dramatis Personae (1936). Author also of the autobiographical *Reveries over Childhood* (1915) and *The Trembling of the Veil* (1922).

His father ¶John Butler (1839–1922) was a distinguished artist, member of Royal Hibernian Academy. William's younger brother ¶Jack Butler (1871–1957); writer and landscape and genre painter; author of *Sligo* (1930), *Apparitions* (1933), *The Amaranthers* (1936), *Harlequin's Positions* (play, 1939), *Ah Well* (novel, 1942), etc.

Yeats-Brown \'yāts-'braůn\, Francis. 1886–1944. British army officer and writer. Served in India (1906–13), France and Mesopotamia (1914–15); prisoner of war in Turkey (1925–18); retired (1925). Author of *Bengal Lancer* (1930), *Dogs of War* (1934), *Lancer at Large* (1936), *The Confessions of a Thug* (1938), *European Jungle* (1939).

Yeh-lü Ch'u-ts'ai \'yel-'ūē-'chüt-'sī\. 1190–1244. Chinese politician. Originally a Chin state official; chief minister and trusted adviser to Genghis Khan and Ögödei; mainly responsible for establishment of Chinese-style administrative and taxation systems for Yüan dynasty.

Yeh-lü Ta-shih \-'dä-'shi(ə)r\. *Posthumous title* Te Tsung \'dād-'zůŋ\. 1098–1135. Chinese ruler. Member of ruling family of Liao dynasty; on dynasty's overthrow (1125), fled to Turkistan and founded the Western Liao dynasty of Central Asia; controlled oases east and west of Pamir Mountains; dynasty overthrown (1211) by the Mongols.

Yeh T'ing \'ye-'tiŋ\. *Also called* Yeh Hsi-p'ing \'yesh-'ē-'piŋ\. 1897–1946. Chinese soldier. Joined Communist party (1925); quickly rose to commander of a vanguard unit on Northern Expedition; key figure in Nan-ch'ang Uprising (Aug. 1, 1927) and in Canton Commune after coup of Dec. 11, 1927; in Soviet Union (1928) and western Europe (1929–34). Appointed commander of New 4th army at outbreak of Sino-Japanese War (Oct. 1937); arrested by Nationalists and many of his army slain (Jan. 1941); imprisoned (1941–46).

Yehuda. See JUDAH.

Yekaterina. See CATHERINE.

Yelizaveta. See ELIZABETH.

Yellowplush, Charles James. See William Makepeace THACKERAY.

Yendys, Sydney. See Sydney DOBELL.

Yen Fu \'yən-'fü\. 1853–1921. Chinese scholar. Studied in England; after China's defeat by Japan (1895), advocated liberal social and political reforms; translated T.H. Huxley, J.S. Mill, Herbert Spencer, Adam Smith, et al., in attempt to show that Western institutions rather than techniques were basis of Western wealth and power.

Yen Hsi-chai. See YEN YÜAN.

Yen Hsi-shan \'yən-'shē-'shän\. 1883–1960. Chinese general. Military governor of "model province" of Shansi (1912–28); supported Gen. Chiang Kai-shek (1927–30); commander in chief, Peking and Tientsin garrisons (1928–30); member, Central Executive Committee, Kuomintang (1930); joined Feng Yu-hsiang in revolt (1930); fled to Dairen, but sent back to Shansi by Japanese (1931) and reinstated in Kuomintang; successfully opposed Japanese in northern China (1935–37).

Yen Jo-chü \-'jō-'jūē\. 1636–1704. Chinese scholar. Published *Shang shu ku-wen shu-cheng,* which proved that the first 25 chapters of the *Shu Ching* were forged.

Yen La Wang. See AN LU-SHAN.

Yen Li-pen \-'lē-'bən\. c.600–673. Chinese painter. High official at T'ang court; painted Buddhist and Taoist subjects; known for hand scroll *Portraits of the Emperors* depicting selected emperors from previous 800 years.

Yen Yüan \-yūē-'än\. *Literary name* Yen Hsi-chai \-'shē-'jī\. 1635–1704. Chinese scholar. With his pupil Li Kung, founded Yen-Li school of Confucianism, a pragmatic empirical system opposed to Neo-Confucianism; advocated study of original Confucian Classics instead of Neo-Confucian interpretations; proponent of Meng-tzu's "well-field" plan of communal living; director of Chang-nan Academy (1696).

Yer·kes \'yər-kēz\, Charles Tyson. 1837–1905. American financier, b. Philadelphia. Opened brokerage firm (1859) and banking house (1862); lost fortune (1871) but regained it by investments in railroads and Philadelphia transit systems. To Chicago (1882); gained control of Chicago streetcar system; accused of political manipulation to secure transit franchises (1897); thwarted by public protests; sold out his interests (1899). To England (1900) and headed syndicate building London subway system. Made gift to U. of Chicago for construction of Yerkes Observatory, Lake Geneva, Wis.

Yerkes, Robert Mearns. 1876–1956. American psychologist, b. Breadysville, Pa. Taught at Harvard (1902–17); professor, Minnesota (1917–19), Yale (1924–44). Known for studies of intelligence in man, primates, and lower animals. During World War I directed Army Alpha, first mass-scale psychological testing program; founder (1929) and director (1929–41) of Yale Laboratories of Primate Biology (renamed Yerkes Laboratories, 1942), Orange Park, Fla. Author of *The Dancing Mouse* (1907), *Introduction to Psychology* (1911), *The Mental Life of Monkeys and Apes* (1916), *The Mind of a Gorilla* (1927), *The Great Apes* (with his wife Ada Watterson Yerkes, 1929), *Chimpanzees* (1943), etc.

Yer·mak Ti·mo·fe·ye·vich \yir-'mák-tyim-(,)ə-'fyā(-yəv)-,yich\. d. 1584. Cossack leader. In employ of merchant Stroganov family, led small army of Cossacks in expedition to conquer Siberia (1581–84); occupied Tatar capital Kashlyk (1582); subject of many songs, tales, literary works.

Yer·sin \yer-saⁿ\, Alexandre-Émile-John. 1863–1943. Swiss bacteriologist. With Pierre Roux discovered diphtheria toxin (1889); discovered the plague bacillus in Hong Kong simultaneously with Kitasato (1894); developed a protective serum against the plague (1895); founder and director of Pasteur Institute branch at Nha Trang, Vietnam.

Ye·se·nin \yis-'yān-yin\, Sergey Aleksandrovich. *Also spelled* Ese·nin. 1895–1925. Russian poet. Published lyrical verse *Radunista* (1916) and *Inoniya* (1918) celebrating the traditions of "wooden Russia" against the modern world of steel and stone; founded (1919) Imagists, group of Russian poets; took up dissolute and bohemian life in Moscow; m. (1922) as 2d wife Isadora Duncan (*q.v.*) and accompanied her on tour to Europe and U.S. Published cynical, swaggering tavern poetry as *Ispoved khuligana* (1924) and *Moskva kabatskaya* (1924); his increasing self-deprecation and despair recorded in confessional poem "Cherny chelovek" (1925); committed suicide.

Ye·zhov \yi-'zhóf\, Nikolay Ivanovich. 1895–?1939. Soviet politician. People's commissar of internal defense (1936–37); commissar of state security (1937–38), of internal affairs (1938); administered most severe stage of great purges, known as *Yezhovshchina;* disappeared in 1939.

Ye·zier·ska \yi-'zyir-skə\, Anzia. 1885–1970. American writer, b. Sukovoly, Russia. To U.S. (1901, naturalized 1912); factory worker and domestic servant in New York City. Known for novels and short-story collections dealing with Russian immigrant Jews living in New York City ghetto, including *Hungry Hearts* (1920), *Salome of the Tenements* (1922), *Children of Loneliness* (1923), *Arrogant Beggar* (1927), *All I Could Never Be* (1932), etc.

Yi \yē\. Name of last and longest-lived Korean dynasty (1392–1910) and also of its ruling family; founded by Yi Sŏng-gye, a general who overthrew the Koryŏ dynasty (1392), named his kingdom Chosŏn, and established his capital at Hanyang (now Seoul); modeled government after Chinese bureaucracy and adopted Neo-Confucianism as state ideology; dynasty ended when Korea was annexed by Japan (1910). Its 26 rulers included Sejong, perhaps the greatest, and Kojong (*qq.v.*).

Yi Chŏng. *Known also as* Nae-ong \na-ôŋ\ *or* So·rak \sò-räk\. 1578–1607. Korean painter. Employed academic Northern Sung style; precocious as child, gaining fame as gifted painter by his 11th birthday; said to have been commissioned at 13 to paint great murals at Chang-an-sa temple.

Yi Chŏng. *Known also as* Ta·nŭm \tä-nům\, *i.e.* Ocean Hermit. 1541–? Korean artist. Great-great-grandson of King Sejong; personification of the ideal Korean aristocrat; famous as poet, painter, calligrapher, and for his regal and generous disposition. As painter, master of traditional styles and of monochromatic paintings of bamboo.

Yi In-mun. *Known also as* Yu-ch'un \yü-chün\, *i.e.* Exist Spring. 1745–1821. Korean painter. Follower of traditional Northern school of Chinese painting; known for subtlety of design and confidence of brushstroke; excelled in landscapes as *River in Spring;* his use of watercolor started new trend in Korean art.

Yi Sang-cha. *Known also as* Hak-p'o \häk-pó\, *i.e.* Study Garden. 16th century. Korean painter. Originally a slave; made official court painter and member of court officialdom (1546). Painted portraits of royal family and landscapes as *Moon Viewing.*

Yildirim. See BAYEZID I.

Yin. See SHANG.

Yin-chen \'yin-'jən\. *Reign title* Yung-cheng \'yůŋ-'jəŋ\. *Temple name* Shih Tsung \'shi(ə)rd-'zůŋ\. *Posthumous name* Hsien Huan Ti \shē-'en-'hwän-'dē\. 1678–1735. Chinese emperor (1723–35), third of the Ch'ing dynasty. Son of Hsüan-yeh; spent early part of reign consolidating his power; removed imperial princes from control of military units; reorganized administrative system, replacing Grand Secretariat with Grand Council as highest ministerial body (1729); checked corruption; increased state revenues.

Ying Tsung. See Chu Ch'i-chen under CHU family.

Yitzhaqi, Shlomo. See SHLOMO YITZHAQI.

Yo Fei \'yō-'fā\ *or* **Yüeh Fei** \yūē-'ef-'ā\. 1103–1141. Chinese general. After capture of Sung capital by Juchen warriors (1126), retreated to south with future emperor Kao Tsung; took command of Sung forces; checked advance of the Juchen and recovered some territory in central China; prevented from pushing northward by minister Ch'in Kuei, who had him imprisoned and executed; revered as national hero.

Yohannes. See JOHN.

Yo·ko·mi·tsu \yō-kō-mēt-sü\ Riichi. *Also called* Yokomitsu Toshikazu. 1898–1947. Japanese novelist and critic. With Kawabata Yasunari, a leader of Neo-sensualist school of Japanese writing; joined Kawabata in publication of journal *Bungei jidai* (1923). His works included *Atama narabi-ni hara* (1924), *Haru wa basha ni notte* (1926, *Spring Comes in a Horse-Drawn Cart*), *Kikai* (1930, *Machine*), *Junsui shō-setsu ron* (1935).

Yo·ko·ya·ma \yō-kō-yä-mä\ Taikan. *Orig.* Sa·kai \säk-ī\ Hidemaro. 1868–1958. Japanese painter. With his friend Hishida Shunsō contributed to revitalization of traditional Japanese painting; studied under Okakura Kakuzo; reestablished Okakura's Japan Fine Arts Academy (1914). Developed a new style of painting (nicknamed *mōrōtai*), which eliminated lines and concentrated on color combinations; works included *Mountain Path, Vicissitudes, Cherry Blossoms at Night.*

Yo·lande \yȯ-lä^{n}d\. d. 1219. Empress of Eastern Empire (1217–19). Sister of Baldwin I and Henry, first two Latin emperors of Eastern Empire; m. Peter of Courtenay; after his death (1217) succeeded to throne; followed by her son Robert of Courtenay.

Yolande. d. 1227. Queen of Jerusalem (1212–27). Daughter of John of Brienne; m. (1225) as second wife, Frederick II, Holy Roman emperor.

Yo·nai \yō-nī\ Mitsumasa. 1880–1948. Japanese naval officer and politician. Commander in chief, Imperial fleet (1936); minister of navy (1937–39, 1944–45); prime minister (1940); deputy prime minister (1944–45).

Yonge \'yəŋ\, Charlotte Mary. 1823–1901. English novelist. Edited girls' magazine *The Monthly Packet* (1851–90). Influenced by her friend John Keble to convey morality and High Church teachings in fiction; gained popular success with *The Heir of Redclyffe* (1853), *Heartsease* (1854), *The Daisy Chain* (1856), and *The Young Stepmother* (1861). Wrote historical romances including *The Dove in the Eagle's Nest* (1866), and biographical and historical works.

Yorck von War·ten·burg \'yȯrk-fȯn-'vär-tən-ˌbu̇rk\, Johann Hans David Ludwig. Graf. *Also spelled* York. 1759–1830. Prussian field marshal. Entered Prussian army (1772); cashiered (1779) but reinstated (1787); took part in Polish campaign (1794) and war against France (1806); major general (1807); an excellent tactician, developed the infantry scout and line of skirmishers; opposed Gen. von Gneisenau's liberal army reforms. Governor general of East and West Prussia (1811); commanded Prussian contingent of Napoléon's army in Russian campaign (1812) and entered into neutrality convention of Tauroggen with the Russians (1812); corps commander in campaign of 1813–14; defeated Beauharnais at Möckern and fought at Bautzen, on the Katzbach, and at Leipzig (1813); served in French campaign at Montmirail, Laon, and Paris (1814). Withdrew from army (1815); field marshal (1821).

Yoritomo. See under MINAMOTO family.

York \'yȯ(ə)rk\, House of. English royal house, one branch of the Plantagenets, which was given prominence by Richard, 3d Duke of York (see RICHARD), who was paternal grandson of the fifth son of King Edward III, Edmund of Langley (see EDMUND), but who derived claim to throne from descent through his mother from Lionel of Antwerp, 1st Duke of Clarence, who was third son of King Edward III. Symbol of house in Wars of the Roses was the white rose. Reigning York kings were Edward IV, Edward V, and Richard III (*qq.v.*).

York, Duke of. Title frequently conferred by British sovereign upon his second son. Conferred (1385) by Edward III of the house of Plantagenet upon his fifth son, Edmund of Langley, progenitor of house of York, and borne by latter's son Edmund of Langley (see EDMUND) and grandson Edward (*q.v.*). Conferred (1474) by Edward IV upon son Richard Plantagenet (see PLANTAGENET). Borne by James Stuart until his accession (1685) as James II of England. Conferred (1784) by George III on second son, Frederick Augustus (*q.v.*). Borne (1892) by George (later George V) as second son of Prince of Wales. Conferred (1920) upon George V's second son, who became George VI.

York, Cardinal. See HENRY STUART.

York, Alvin Cullum. 1887–1964. American soldier, b. Pall Mall, Tenn. Applied for conscientious objector status (1917) but entered army after petition was denied; as a private first class in battle of Argonne (Oct. 8, 1918), led detachment in attack on German machine-gun nest; after his detachment was pinned down by enemy fire, charged second machine-gun nest alone and captured 90 men; marched his prisoners ahead of him toward a third machine-gun position and captured it with 42 more prisoners; promoted to sergeant (Nov. 1, 1918); later awarded Medal of Honor and French Croix de Guerre. On return to America, received gift of a farm in Tennessee; published autobiography (1928); donated money to York Foundation for support of an industrial school and a Bible school in Tennessee.

York and Albany, Duke of. See FREDERICK AUGUSTUS.

Yorke \'yȯ(ə)rk\, Henry Vincent. *Pseudonym* Henry Green. 1905–1973. English novelist. While employed in family engineering firm published novels of sophisticated social satire, *Blindness* (1926), *Living* (1929), *Party Going* (1939), *Caught* (1943), *Loving* (1945), *Back* (1946), *Concluding* (1948), *Nothing* (1950), *Doting* (1952).

Yorke, Philip. 1st Earl of Hard·wicke \'härd-ˌwik\. 1690–1764. English judge. Solicitor general (1720); attorney general (1724); chief justice and privy councilor (1733); lord chancellor (1737). His son ¶Philip (1720–1790), 2d earl; privy councilor (1760); high steward of Cambridge U. (1764–90); edited *Walpoliana* (1783).

Yosa Buson. See BUSON.

Yo·sa·no \yō-sän-ō\ Akiko. *Nee* Ōto·ri \ō-tō-rē\ Akiko. *Known also as* Ho Sho \hō-shō\. 1878–1942. Japanese poet. Joined (1900) Shinshisha (New Poetry Association) of Yosano Hiroshi and began contributing poems to his magazine *Myōjō;* m. (1901) Yosano Hiroshi. Freshness and unconventionality of her poetic style caused sensation in Japanese literary circles; gained fame with *Midaregami* (1901, *Tangled Hair*) and *Yume no hana* (1906); founded (1921) and taught at Bunka Gakuin School for Girls, Tokyo. Other poetic books included *Natsu yori aki e* (1914) and *Hakuōshū* (1942).

Yo·shi·da \yō-shē-dä\ Isoya. 1894–1974. Japanese architect. His works included Tsuruya Restaurant in Kyōto, Botan Restaurant in Tokyo, Gotō Art Museum in Tokyo, and Yamato Bunkaku Museum in Nara.

Yoshida Kenkō. *Orig.* Ura·be \u̇r-äb-e\ Kaneyoshi. 1283–1350. Japanese poet and essayist. In service of Emperor Uda II; became Buddhist priest (1324). His fame rests on *Tsurezure-gusa* (c.1330), a collection of essays on wide range of subjects, esp. religion and philosophy.

Yoshida Kanetomo. *Surname orig.* Ura·be \u̇r-äb-e\. 1435–1511. Japanese religious. Founder of the Yoshida Shintō religious school (also called Yui-itsu Shintō).

Yoshida Shigeru. *Surname orig.* Ta·ke·u·chi \tä-ke-u̇ch-ē\. 1878–1967. Japanese politician. Entered foreign ministry (1906); ambassador to Sweden, Norway, and Denmark (1928) and to Great Britain (1936–39); foreign minister (1945–46). Prime minister, forming five separate cabinets (1946–47, 1948–54); gave Japan political stability, guided her to economic prosperity, and established close relations with U.S. and western Europe.

Yoshida Tetsurō. 1894–1956. Japanese architect. Met German architects Hugo Häring and Ludwig Hilberseimer while visiting Europe (1930–31); at their urging wrote *The Japanese House* (1935), explaining Japanese architecture to the West. Introduced Western motifs in his designs, including town hall at Beppu (1928), bank at Niigata (1951), and post offices at Kyotō (1922), Tokyo (1931), and Ōsaka (1939).

Yo·shi·hi·to \yō-shē-hē-tō\. *Reign name* Tai·shō \tī-shō\. 1879–1926. Emperor of Japan (1912–26), 123d in direct lineage. Son of Mutsuhito; proclaimed crown prince (1889). During reign, Japan joined Allies in World War I and became world power of first rank; use of parliamentary procedures increased. Mentally deranged in later years; succeeded by son Hirohito, who had acted as regent (1921–26).

Yoshiie. See under MINAMOTO family.

Yo·shi·ka·wa \yō-shē-kä-wä\ Hidetsugu. *Pseudonym* Yoshikawa Eiji. 1892–1962. Japanese novelist. Established reputation with *Ken nan jo nan* (1925) and *Naruto hicho* (1926–27); best known for popular historical novels as *Miyamoto Musashi* (1935–39), *Shin Heike monogatari* (1950–57), and *Shihon taihei-ki* (1958–61). First popular author to receive Cultural Merit Award (1960).

Yoshimasa. See under ASHIKAGA family.

Yoshimitsu. See under ASHIKAGA family.

Yoshimune. See under TOKUGAWA family.

Yo·shi·no \yō-shē-nō\ Sakuzō. 1878–1933. Japanese politician and educator. Early converted to Christianity; professor at Tokyo U. (1913–24). Prominent in Christian Socialist movement; forceful advocate of parliamentary government, universal suffrage, civilian control of army, gradual establishment of socialist state; founded (1918) Reimeikai party to promote his goals.

Yoshinobu. See under TOKUGAWA family.

Yoshitomo. See under MINAMOTO family.

Yoshitsune. See under MINAMOTO family.

Yost \'yōst\, Fielding Harris. *Nicknamed* Hurry-up Yost. 1871–1946. American football coach, b. Fairview, W. Va. Head football coach (1901–23, 1925–27) and director of intercollegiate athletics (1921–41), U. of Michigan; known esp. for his "point-a-minute" teams of 1901–05.

You·lou \'yü-ˌlü, yü-'lü\, Fulbert. 1917–1972. Congolese politician. Prominent in independence movement as leader of Union Démocratique de Défense des Intérêts Africains; first premier and president (1959–63) of the Congo (Brazzaville).

You·mans \'yü-mənz\, Vincent Millie. 1898–1946. American composer, b. New York City. Composed scores for Broadway musicals, including *Two Little Girls in Blue* (1921), *Wildflower* (1923), *No, No, Nanette* (1925, including songs "Tea for Two" and "I Want to Be Happy"), *Oh, Please!* (1926), *Hit the Deck* (1927), *Rainbow* (1928), *Smiles* (1930), *Through the Years* (1932); also wrote film score for *Flying Down to Rio* (1933).

Young \'yəŋ\, Art, *in full* Arthur Henry. 1866–1943. American cartoonist, b. near Orangeville, Ill. Settled in New York City (c.1903); became Socialist;

actively campaigned for woman suffrage, labor organization, racial equality, abolition of child labor. Known esp. for satiric cartoons in *The Masses* (1911–17); cartoons collected in *The Best of Art Young* (1936); wrote autobiography *Art Young: His Life and Times* (1939).

Young, Arthur. 1741–1820. English agriculturist and writer. Edited *Annals of Agriculture* (1784–1809); reported political and social observations in *Six Months' Tour through the North of England* (1770), *Farmer's Tour through the East of England* (1771), *Political Arithmetic* (1774), *Tour in Ireland* (1780); reported pre-Revolutionary conditions in French provinces in *Travels in France* (1792).

Young *or* **Yong** \ˈyəŋ\, Bartholomew. fl. 1577–1598. English translator. Known for his translation (1598) of the *Diana* of Jorge de Montemayor (*q.v.*).

Young, Brigham. 1801–1877. American religious leader, b. Whitingham, Vt. Journeyman painter and glazier by trade; settled in Mendon, N.Y. (1829), near where Joseph Smith published *The Book of Mormon* (1830). Was converted and baptized in Mormon faith (1832); successful itinerant missionary (from 1833); member of the Quorum of the Twelve Apostles (1835); directed Mormon settlement in Nauvoo, Ill. (1838). Missionary in England (1839–41). Succeeded Joseph Smith as head of the Mormon church (1844; elected president, Dec. 1847); directed and superintended mass migration of Mormons to Great Salt Lake Valley in Utah; organized and directed the settlement there, assuming dictatorial powers; contributed stability and cohesion to his church. First governor of Territory of Utah (1849–57); proclaimed and practiced polygamy; at odds with U.S. government and removed from governorship by President Buchanan, but remained dominant in community.

Young, Charles Augustus. 1834–1908. American astronomer, b. Hanover, N.H. Professor, Dartmouth (1866–77), Princeton (1877–1905); first to observe spectrum of solar corona (1869); discovered the reversing layer in solar atmosphere (1870); measured rotational velocity of the Sun (1876) and the diameter of Mars (1879). Author of *The Sun* (1881), *General Astronomy* (1888), *Manual of Astronomy* (1902), etc.

Young, Charles Mayne. 1777–1856. English actor. Played largely Shakespearian roles with John Philip Kemble (from 1808), with Kean (from 1822).

Young, Chic. See Murat B. YOUNG.

Young, Clarence. See Edward STRATEMEYER.

Young, Denton True, *known as* Cy \ˈsī\. 1867–1955. American baseball player, b. Gilmore, Ohio. Pitcher, in National League with Cleveland (1890–98), St. Louis (1899–1900), and Boston (1911), and in American League with Boston (1901–08) and Cleveland (1909–11). Pitched 3 no-hit games (including perfect game, May 5, 1904); established major league records: 509 or 511 victories, 313 or 315 or 316 defeats, 816 or 818 starts, 750 or 751 complete games, 7,356 or 7,377 innings pitched. Elected to Baseball Hall of Fame (1937).

Young, Edward. 1683–1765. English poet. Had two tragedies of ungoverned passion produced, *Busiris* (1719) and *Revenge* (1721); published seven satires under title of *The Universal Passion* (1725–28). Became rector of Welwyn (1730); gained popularity with series of nine poems *The Complaint; or, Night-Thoughts on Life, Death and Immortality,* commonly referred to as *Night Thoughts* (1742–45), which gave rise to a school of "graveyard poets." Had his tragedy *The Brothers* (written 1726) produced (1753); wrote prose *Conjectures on Original Composition* (1759); published last important poem *Resignation* (1762).

Young, Edward. 1831–1896. English explorer. Commanded expedition in search for Livingstone (1867); explored Lake Nyasa region (1875) and wrote *Nyassa* (1878).

Young, Ella, *nee* Flagg \ˈflag\. 1845–1918. American educator, b. Buffalo, N.Y. m. (1868) William Young (d. 1869). District superintendent of schools in Chicago (1887–99); professor of education, U. of Chicago (1899–1904); principal, Chicago Normal School (1905–09); superintendent of Chicago public schools (1909–15). Associated with Jane Addams in Chicago social settlement work.

Young, Francis Brett. 1884–1954. English novelist. Author of *Dark Tower* (1914), *The Tragic Bride* (1920), *Woodsmoke* (1924), *Portrait of Clare* (1927), *My Brother Jonathan* (1928), *Jim Redlake* (1930), *They Seek a Country* (1937), *Dr. Bradley Remembers* (1938), *The City of Gold* (1939), *A Man About the House* (1942), etc., and of several volumes of poems and the plays *Captain Swing* (1919) and *The Furnace* (1928).

Young, Sir John. Baron Lis·gar \ˈlis-ˌgär\. 1807–1876. English administrator. Chief secretary for Ireland (1852–55); commissioner of Ionian Islands (1855–59); governor general of New South Wales (1861–67); governor general of Canada (1869–72).

Young, John Russell. 1840–1899. American journalist, b. County Tyrone, Ireland. To U.S. in infancy. Civil War correspondent of Philadelphia *Press* (1861); famous for graphic account of Federal defeat and retreat after battle of Bull Run. U.S. minister to China (1882–85). Foreign correspondent of New York *Herald* (1885 ff.), chiefly in London and Paris. Librarian of Congress (1897–99). Author of *Around the World with General Grant* (1879) and reminiscences.

Young, John Wesley. 1879–1932. American mathematician, b. Columbus, Ohio. Professor, Dartmouth (1911 ff.); author of *Lectures on the Fundamental Concepts of Algebra and Geometry* (1911) and, with Oswald Veblen, of *Projective Geometry* (1910–18).

Young, Lester Willis. *Nicknamed* Pres \ˈprez\. 1909–1959. American musician, b. Woodville, Miss. Developed new style of playing the tenor saxophone, characterized by a metallic, honking sound and spare, melodic solos; played with jazz bands of King Oliver, Count Basie (1935–40, 1943–44), and others; soloist for last 15 years of life with Norman Granz's Jazz and other groups. Long associated with Billie Holiday, whom he often accompanied on records; best known recordings "Lady Be Good" (1936), "One O'clock Jump" (1937), "Lester Leaps In" (1939).

Young, Mahonri Mackintosh. 1877–1957. American sculptor, painter, and etcher, b. Salt Lake City. Grandson of Brigham Young. Known for statuettes of workmen, cowboys, etc., the bronzes *Stevedore* and *Man with Pick,* and *Sea Gull Monument* in Salt Lake City (1913).

Young, Murat Bernard, *known as* Chic \ˈchik\. 1901–1973. American cartoonist, b. Chicago. With King Features Syndicate (1923–73); created and drew comic strips "Dumb Dora" (1924–30) and "Blondie" (from 1930).

Young, Owen D. 1874–1962. American lawyer and corporation executive, b. Hornesville, N.Y. Practiced law in Boston (1896–1913); counsel for General Electric Co. (from 1913); chairman of board, General Electric Co. (1922–39, 1942–44). Associated with Charles G. Dawes as American representative to the Reparations Conference (1924); agent general for German reparations during inauguration of Dawes plan. Chairman of Reparations Conference (1929); cooperated in preparation of the Young plan for German reparations payments.

Young, Stark. 1881–1963. American writer and critic, b. Como, Miss. On editorial staff, *New Republic* (1921–57); associate editor, *Theatre Arts Monthly* (1921–40); drama critic, *New York Times* (1924–25). Author of plays *The Saint, The Colonnade,* etc., a volume of poetry, books of dramatic criticism, and novels *The Torches Flare* (1927), *River House* (1929), *So Red the Rose* (1934).

Young, Thomas. 1587–1655. Scottish clergyman. Tutor of John Milton; a leader in opposition to introduction of episcopacy into Scotland. See SMECTYMNUUS.

Young, Thomas. 1773–1829. English physician, physicist, and Egyptologist. Set up medical practice in London (1800); physician to St. George's Hospital, London (1811–29); superintendent of *Nautical Almanac* (1818–29), secretary of Board of Longitude (1818–1828). First to describe and measure astigmatism (1800–01); first to explain color sensation as due to presence in retina of structures corresponding to colors red, green, and violet, respectively (1801; theory later modified by Hermann von Helmholtz as the Young-Helmholtz three-color theory); discovered (1801) interference of light, thus contributing to establishment of wave theory of light; explained theory of capillarity (which was set forth independently by Laplace); assisted in translating the demotic text of the Rosetta stone (1813–14).

Young, Whitney Moore, Jr. 1921–1971. American civil rights leader, b. Lincoln Ridge, Ky. Executive secretary, Omaha Urban League (1950–54); dean of School of Social Work, Atlanta U. (1954–61). Executive director, National Urban League (1961–71); advocated a "domestic Marshall Plan" to raise social and educational levels of American blacks; many of his proposals incorporated into Pres. Lyndon Johnson's antipoverty program. Author of *To Be Equal* (1964) and *Beyond Racism* (1969).

Youn·ger \ˈyəŋ-gər\, Cole, *in full* Thomas Coleman. 1844–1916. American desperado, b. Jackson Co., Mo. In Civil War served with Confederate guerrilla bands of William Quantrill and "Bloody Bill" Anderson. Prominent member of Jesse James gang (from 1866); captured and sentenced to life imprisonment after bank robbery at Northfield, Minn. (Sept. 7, 1876); pardoned (1903).

Young·hus·band \ˈyəŋ-ˌhəz-bənd\, Sir Francis Edward. 1863–1942. British explorer, b. India. Entered army (1882); explored mountain barrier between China and Kashmir (1886); transferred from army to political department (1890); explored Pamir mountains (1890–91); commissioner to Tibet (1902–04); led British expedition into forbidden city of Lhasa (1904); forced conclusion of Anglo-Tibetan trade treaty (Sept. 1904); resident, Kashmir (1906–09). Author of *Heart of a Continent* (1898), *India and Tibet* (1910), *Life in the Stars* (1927), *Everest: The Challenge* (1936), *A Venture of Faith* (1937), *The Sum of Things* (1939).

Young Pretender. See CHARLES EDWARD.

Yov·kov \ˈyȯf-kȯf\, Yordan Stefanovich. 1880–1937. Bulgarian writer. Officer in First Balkan War and World War I; teacher in the Dobruja; later in government service. Known esp. for stories of Balkan peasant life and military experiences; works included novels *Jetvaryat* (1920) and *Chiflikut krai granitsata* (1933), story collections *Zemlyatsi* (1915) and *Staroplaninski legendi* (1927), and plays *Albena* (1930), *Milionerut* (1930), and *Boryana* (1932).

Ypres, Earl of. See John Denton Pinkstone FRENCH.

Yp·si·lan·tis \ˌip-sə-ˈlant-ēz\ *or* **Hy·pse·lan·tes** *or* **Hy·psi·lan·tis** \ˌēp-sə-ˈlän-ˌdēs\. Distinguished Greek Phanariot family, including: Alexander Alexandros (c.1725–1806), hospodar of Walachia (1774–82, 1796–97) and Moldavia (1786–88); executed at Constantinople for conspiracy. His son ¶Konstantinos (1760–1816), hospodar of Moldavia (1799–1801) and Walachia (1802–06); encouraged Serbians in rebellion against Turkey and had to take refuge in Russia. His son ¶Alexandros (1792–1828); officer in Russian Imperial Guard (1809–20); took command of secret Greek organization Philiki Extairía (1820); promoted cause of Greek freedom; defeated by Turks (June 19, 1821); fled to Austria, where he was imprisoned (1821–27). His brother ¶Demetrios (1793–1832); fought in war for Greek independence (1821 ff.); successfully defended Argos (1823) and Napoli (1825); commander in chief of Greek forces (1828–30).

Yriarte, Tomás de. See Tomás de IRIARTE.

Yr·jö-Kos·kin·en \ˈüer-yœ-ˈkös-kin-en\, Sakari. *Orig.* Georg Zacharias Forsman \ˈförs-mån\. 1830–1903. Finnish historian and politician. Leader (from 1870s) of Fennoman party advocating supremacy of Finnish language over Swedish; member of Diet (1872–82) and Senate (1882–99); guided (from 1898) Old Finn party to compliance with russification program in Finland. Author of *Suomen kansan historia* (1869–72), first history of Finland in Finnish.

Ysa·ÿe \ē-zä-ē\, Eugène-Auguste. 1858–1931. Belgian violinist, conductor, and composer. Professor at Brussels Conservatory (1886–98); made extensive tours in Europe and America and established himself as one of greatest virtuosos of his time; conductor of Cincinnati Symphony (1918–22). Composed opera in Walloon *Piére li houïeu* (1931), works for violin as 8 concertos and 6 sonatas, and chamber music.

Yü \ˈyüe\ *or* **Ta Yü** \ˈdä-ˈyüe\. 23d–22d century B.C. Chinese emperor. Of undetermined historicity, but traditionally the founder (c.2205 B.C.) of the Hsia dynasty, the first Chinese dynasty.

Yüan \yüe-ˈän\ *or* **Mon·gol** \ˈmäŋ-gəl; ˈmän-ˌgōl, ˈmäŋ-\. A Chinese dynasty (1279–1368) of Mongol origin, founded by Kublai Khan; capital established at Peking, Chinese-style administration adopted, and extensive foreign trade and relations carried out; it had eleven rulers and was superseded by the Ming dynasty. See BUYANTU, TEMÜR KHAN, and TOGON-TEMÜR.

Yüan-chang. See MI FEI.

Yüan Chen \yüe-ˈän-ˈjən\. 779–831 A.D. Chinese poet. For many years an official of the T'ang state. Close friend of Po Chü-i, with whom he exchanged many poems and letters; reputed author of story *Ying-ying chuan* (or *Hui-chen chi),* a favorite theme for drama.

Yüan Chi \yüe-ˈän-ˈjē\. 210–263. Chinese poet. Most prominent member of the Seven Sages of the Bamboo Grove; led hedonistic life at Wei dynasty court which enabled him to freely write satirical poems and essays against ruling class; finally retired to the country. Best known collection of poems *Yung huai shih.*

Yüan Hui. See CHU HSI.

Yüan-hui. See MI YU-JEN.

Yüan Shih-k'ai \yüe-ˈän-ˈshi(ə)r-ˈkī\. 1859–1916. Chinese soldier and politician. Served in army (1882–85); Chinese resident at Seoul, Korea (1885–94); adviser to the emperor Kuang Hsü (1898); governor of Shantung (1900); remained neutral during Boxer uprising (1901); viceroy of Pechili (Pohai) province (1901–07); made grand councilor (1907) but banished on death of emperor (1908). On overthrow of the Manchus (1911) became commander in chief of northern forces and (Feb. 1912) by last imperial edict was made premier and authorized to organize a republican form of government; became provisional president of all China (1912–13) by resignation of Sun Yat-sen in the south; president (1913–16); sought to be dictator, suppressing Sun and followers, dismissing parliament (1914), and appointing an advisory council; restored Confucianism; attempted to reestablish monarchy (1915–16) but prevented by opposition of southern provinces and foreign powers.

Yüan Ti. See Liu Shih under LIU family.

Yüan-tsang. See HSÜAN-TSANG.

Yu Ch'ien \ˈyü-chē-ˈen\. 1398–1457. Chinese politician. Defense minister under Ming emperor Cheng-t'ung; after capture (1449) of emperor by Mongol invader Esen, saved China by preparing a cannon defense of Peking and installing Ching-t'ai on the throne, thus negating Cheng-t'ung's value as a hostage; siege soon abandoned by Esen; executed as traitor upon return to throne of Cheng-t'ung.

Yu·de·nich \yüd-ˈyān-yich\, Nikolay Nikolayevich. 1862–1933. Russian soldier. Served on general staff (1887–1902) and in Russo–Japanese War (1904–05); major general (1907) and lieutenant general (1913); during World War I, commanded Russian forces in Caucasus (1914–15, 1917). After Russian Revolution (1917) took command of an anti-Bolshevik army operating from Estonia (1919); twice defeated near Petrograd (May and Oct. 1919) and forced to retreat to Estonia; disbanded his army (1920); fled to France.

Yüeh Fei. See YO FEI.

Yui \yü-ē\ Shōsetsu. d. 1651. Japanese rebel. Famed military teacher in Edo; gathered army of *rōnin* (masterless samurai) and concocted plot to overthrow the Tokugawa shogunate; committed suicide after plot was discovered before its commencement; to placate *rōnin,* government retrained them for administrative rather than military positions.

Yu·ka·wa \yü-kä-wä\ Hideki. 1907–1981. Japanese physicist. Professor, Kyotō (1939–48), Institute for Advanced Study at Princeton, N.J. (1948–49), Columbia (1951–53); professor and director of Research Institute for Fundamental Physics, Kyotō U. (1953–70). Postulated the existence of the meson (1935; confirmed by C.F. Powell and others, 1947). Awarded Nobel prize for physics (1949) for his work on nuclear forces.

Yung-cheng. See YIN-CHEN.

Yung-li. See Chu Yu-leng under CHU family.

Yung-lo. See Chu Ti under CHU family.

Yung-shu. See OU-YANG HSIU.

Yung-yen \ˈyüŋ-ˈyən\. *Reign title* Chia-ch'ing \jē-ˈä-ˈchiŋ\. *Temple name* Jen Tsung \ˈzhənd-ˈzüŋ\. *Posthumous name* Jui Huang-ti \zhü-ˈē-ˈhwäŋ-ˈdē\. 1760–1820. Chinese emperor (1796–1820), fifth of the Ch'ing dynasty. Ascended throne on abdication of his father Hung-li (1796); arrested powerful and corrupt minister Ho-shen (1799); suppressed White Lotus Rebellion (1796–1804) and pirates preying on south coast (1800–10); unsuccessful in attempts to stop corruption, restore treasury and power of the dynasty; one of most unpopular Ch'ing emperors.

Yün Ku Lao-jen. See CHU HSI.

Yün Shou-p'ing \ˈyüen-ˈshō-ˈpiŋ\. *Known also as* Yün Nan-t'ien \-ˈnän-tē-ˈen\. 1633–1690. Chinese painter. Continued orthodox tradition of painting; close friend and admirer of Wang Hui; known for landscapes and esp. for flower paintings executed in a *mo-ku* (boneless) manner that emphasized washes instead of lines.

Yush·ke·vich \yüsh-ˈkyāv-ˌyich\, Semyon Solomonovich. 1868–1927. Russian novelist and playwright. Author of works chiefly on Jewish themes, including *Golod* (1905), *Dina Glan* (1906), *Leon Drey* (1922), *Golubinoe tsarstvo* (1923), *Sen' dney* (1933).

Yust \ˈyüst\, Walter. 1894–1960. American editor, b. Philadelphia. Journalist, chiefly in N.Y. and Philadelphia (1917–30); advertising manager (1930–32), associate editor (1932–38), editor in chief (1938–60), *Encyclopaedia Britannica* publications.

Yū·suf ibn Tā·shu·fīn \ˈyü-süf-ˌib-ən-ˌtä-shü-ˈfēn\ *or* **Tāsh·fīn** \-täsh-ˈfēn\. d. 1106. King of the Almoravids (1061–1106). Given Morocco by his cousin Abū Bakr; founded (1062) Marrakesh as his capital; conquered western Algeria; invaded Spain (1086), defeating Alfonso VI of León and Castile and subjugating all Muslim Spain as far as Toledo; established his regional capital at Seville.

Yü Wen \ˈyüe-ˈwən\. *Courtesy name* Yü Ta-fu \-ˈdä-ˈfü\. 1896–1945. Chinese writer. Studied in Japan, where he helped Kuo Mojo and others found (1921) Ch'uang-tsao shë (Creation Society); pioneer of autobiographical confessional fiction in China with publication of short-story collection *Ch'en-lun* (1921); turned from personal themes to treatment of the masses (1923). Other works included *Kuo-ch'ü* (1927), *Jih-chi chiu-chung* (1927), *Ch'u-pen* (1935).

Yves de Chartres \ēv-də-shärtrᵊ\. c.1040–1116. French prelate. Bishop of Chartres (1090); upheld rights of church against royal encroachment and maintained high standards of conduct among his clergy; compiled a collection of canon law.

Yveteaux, Sieur des. See VAUQUELIN DE LA FRESNAYE.

Yvon \ē-vōⁿ\, Adolphe. 1817–1893. French painter. Best known for his historical canvases as *La Bataille de Koulikowo, L'Assaut de Malakof, Solferino, Magenta, Les États Unis d'Amérique;* also painted a number of portraits.

Z

Za·bło·cki \zä-ˈblo̅t-skē\, Franciszek. 1750 or 1751–1821. Polish writer. Author of 54 satirical comedies, odes, fables, pastorals, lampoons, etc.

Zac·ca·ria \dzäk-kä-ˈrē-ä\, Antonio Maria. Saint. 1502–1539. Italian religious. Ordained priest (1528); founded Clerks Regular of St. Paul, known as Barnabites (1530); its provost general (to 1536); also founded similar order for women, Angelicals of St. Paul (1535); canonized (1897).

Zaccaria, Benedetto. d. c.1307. Genoese merchant, diplomat, and admiral. Made (1264) ambassador to Byzantine emperor Michael VIII Palaeologus, who gave him fief of Phocaea; built up a huge commercial empire trading in Mediterranean countries. Commanded fleet that defeated Pisan navy in battle of Meloria (1284); grand admiral of fleet of Sancho IV of Castile (1290); commanded navy of Philip IV of France against England (1294–1300).

Zac·co·ni \dzäk-ˈkō-nē\, Ludovico. 1555–1627. Italian music theorist and composer. Ordained priest (1575); entered Augustinian order (1577); in service of Archduke Charles of Austria (1585–90) and Duke William V of Bavaria (1590–96); returned to Italy (1596) as preacher and administrator of his order. Known esp. for his *Prattica di musica* (1592, 1622), a standard encyclopedic summary of Renaissance musical theory and practice; his compositions included a set of ricercari for organ and four books of canons.

Zach \ˈtsäk\, Franz Xaver von. 1754–1832. German astronomer. Director of observatory near Gotha (1787–1806); editor, *Monatliche Korrespondenz zur Beförderung der Erd- und Himmelskunde* (28 vols., 1800–13). In last years of 18th century formed group of 24 astronomers that discovered the asteroids.

Zacharias. See ZECHARIAH.

Zach·a·ri·as \ˌzak-ə-ˈrī-əs\ *or* **Zach·a·ry** \ˈzak(-ə)-rē\. Saint. d. 752. Pope (741–752), b. Calabria, of Greek parentage. Had great personal influence over kings of the Lombards; prevented exarchate of Ravenna from becoming part of Lombard kingdom; encouraged missionary work of St. Boniface and confirmed his anointing of Pépin at Soissons (751) as king of the Franks, the first of the Carolingians.

Za·chow \ˈtsä-ˌkō\ *or* **Za·chau** \ˈtsä-ˌkau̇\, Friedrich Wilhelm. 1663–1712. German musician and composer. Teacher of Handel; organist, Halle (1684–1712); composer esp. of church cantatas, organ works, and choral arrangements.

Zadkiel. See Richard James MORRISON.

Zad·kine \zȧd-ˈkēn\, Ossip. 1890–1967. Russian sculptor. Worked chiefly in Paris; in U.S. during World War II. At first a Cubist; later influenced by ancient Greek sculpture and developed own style. Known esp. for Rotterdam monument *The Destroyed City* (1951); other sculptures included *Musicians* (1924), *Christ* (1939), *Birth of Forms* (1947).

Zaeh·ner \ˈzā-nər\, Robert Charles. 1913–1974. English historian. Professor of eastern religions and ethics, Oxford (from 1952); authority on evolution of ethical systems and forms of mysticism. His books included *Mysticism Sacred and Profane* (1957), *Hindu and Muslim Mysticism* (1960), *The Dawn and Twilight of Zoroastrianism* (1961), *Evolution in Religion* (1971), and *Dialectical Christianity and Christian Materialism* (1971).

Zaffanii, John. See John ZOFFANY.

Zagh·lūl \zag-ˈlül\, Sa'd. *More completely* Sa'd Zaghlūl Pasha ibn Ibrāhīm. 1857–1927. Egyptian politician. Lawyer and journalist in Cairo; judge of Court of Appeal (1892); minister of education (1906–10), of justice (1910–12). After World War I, became head of Nationalist party which demanded breaking of ties binding Egypt to Great Britain and achievement of complete Egyptian independence. Deported to Malta (1919) and then to Ceylon; returned to Egypt (1921) as national hero and most powerful figure in Egyptian politics. Premier of Egypt (1924); failed to conclude satisfactory negotiations with British prime minister MacDonald.

Za·go·skin \(ˌ)zə-ˈgȯ-skyin\, Lavrenty Alekseyevich. 1807–1890. Russian explorer. Made expeditions along the Koyukuk, Yukon, and Kuskokwim rivers in Alaska (1842–44); claimed discovery of Yukon River (1842); published (1847–48) account of his discovery.

Zagoskin, Mikhail Nikolayevich. 1789–1852. Russian novelist and playwright. Theater director in St. Petersburg and later in Moscow. Known esp. for historical novel *Yury Miloslavsky* (1829).

Za·har·i·as \zə-ˈhar-ē-əs\, Mildred Ella, *known as* Babe. *Nee* Di·drik·son \ˈdē-drik-sən\. 1914–1956. American athlete, b. Port Arthur, Tex. One of the greatest woman athletes; on women's All-America basketball team (1930–32); won 8 events and tied for a 9th in women's national track and field championships (1930–32); at 1932 Olympic Games in Los Angeles won gold medals in 80-meter hurdles and javelin throw, disqualified from victory in high jump for use of Western roll technique; m. (1938) George Zaharias. Took up golf and soon became leading U.S. woman golfer; as amateur won 1946 National Women's Amateur title and 17 consecutive tournaments during 1947 (including British Ladies' Amateur); as professional, won U.S. Women's Open (1948, 1950, 1954) and was leading money winner on women's golf tour (1948–51).

Za·ha·roff \(ˌ)zə-ˈkä-rəf\, Sir Basil. *Orig.* Basileios Za·cha·ri·as \ˌzäk-ä-ˈrē-äs\. 1849–1936. French armament contractor, b. Turkey, of Greek parents. Agent in Balkans area for T.V. Nordenfelt (early 1880s) and in eastern Europe and Russia for Maxim-Nordenfelt firm (1888–95); agent for Vickers Company (from 1895); amassed fortune from gun sales; became French citizen (1913). Allied intelligence agent during World War I; knighted by British government (1918); also engaged in banking and oil enterprises; retired to Monte Carlo (1926).

Ẓa·hīr-ud-Dīn Mu·ḥam·mad \zä-ˈhē-ru̇d-ˈdēn-mu̇-ˈkäm-mäd\. *Known as* Bā·bur \ˈbä-bu̇r\, *i.e.* Lion, Tiger, *or* Panther. 1483–1530. Emperor of India, founder of Mughal dynasty. Descendant of Timur and Genghis Khan; son of ruler of Fergana, to which he succeeded. Attempted to regain Timur's capital, Samarkand (1494–1504), occupying it twice (1497, 1501); lost Fergana to Uzbek leader Muḥammad Shaybānī Khān (1504); seized Kābul (1504); conquered Qandahār (1522) to open way to Sind; made several raids into Punjab; defeated Sultan Ibrāhīm Lodī at Pānīpat (1526) and occupied Delhi and Āgra; defeated large Rājput army under Rāna Sāngā at Khānua (1527) to consolidate power; drove Afghans from Lucknow and defeated Maḥmūd Lodī at Ghāghara (1529); passed empire to son Humāyūn. Author of classic autobiography *Bābur-nāmeh* and verses in Turki.

Zah·le \ˈsȧ-lə\, Carl Theodor. 1866–1946. Danish politician. Radical Liberal deputy (1895–1928); member of Landsting (1928 ff.). Prime minister and minister of justice (1909–10); again prime minister (1913–20); minister of justice (1929–35).

Zahn \ˈtsän\, Ernst. 1867–1952. Swiss writer. Member of Heimatkunst movement; known for realistic depictions of daily life of Alpine people. Among his novels were *Albin Indergand* (1901), *Herrgottsfäden* (1901), *Die Frauen von Tannò* (1911), *Frau Sixta* (1926), *Der Weg hinauf* (1935), *Die grosse Lehre* (1943), *Welt im Spiegel* (1951); his short-story collections included *Bergvolk* (1896), *Helden des Alltags* (1906), *Ernte des Lebens* (1950).

Zahn-Har·nack \ˈtsän-ˈhär-ˌnäk\, Agnes von. 1884–1950. German writer. Daughter of Adolf K.G. von Harnack; leader in German feminist movement; author of *Die arbeitende Frau* (1924), *Die Frauenbewegung* (1928), etc.

Za·ï·mis \zä-ˈē-mēs\, Alexandros. 1855–1936. Greek politician. Minister of justice (1890–92); premier (1897–99, 1901–02, 1904–06); as high commissioner of the powers in Crete (1906–11) helped bring about its subsequent annexation by Greece (1913); governor of the Greek National Bank (1913 ff.); premier (briefly, 1915, 1916, 1917) and head of an ecumenical government and two succeeding coalition cabinets (1926–28); president of the Republic of Greece (1929–35).

Zajc \ˈzīts\, Ivan. *Often used form* Giovanni von Zaytz \fȯnt-ˈzīts\. 1832–1914. Croatian composer. His compositions included orchestral works, masses, oratorios, cantatas, songs, chamber works, Italian and German operas and operettas, and the first Croatian operas as *Ban Leget* (1872), *Nikola Šubić Zrinjski* (1876), and *Prvi grijeh* (1912).

Za·krzew·ska \zäk-ˈshef-skä\, Marie Elizabeth. 1829–1902. American physician, b. Berlin, Germany, of Polish parents. To U.S. (1853); founder (1862), attending physician (1863–87), advisory physician (from 1887), New England Hospital for Women and Children.

Za·les·ki \zä-ˈles-kē\, Józef Bogdan. 1802–1886. Polish poet. Took part in Polish rebellion (1830–31) and lived thereafter in exile, chiefly in Paris. A founder of "Ukrainian school" of poetry that idealized the Cossacks and the Ukraine; author of *Rusałki* (1829), *Przenajświętsza Rodzina* (1841), *Dumy i dumki* (1841), etc.

Zalman, Elijah ben Solomon. See ELIJAH BEN SOLOMON.

Za·makh·sha·rī \zä-ˌmäk-shä-ˈrē\, Abū al-Qāsim Maḥmud ibn ʿUmar az-. 1075–1144. Persian Arabic scholar, theologian, and philologist. As theologician, a member of the Muʿtazilite school and author (1134) of *al-Kashshāf ʿan Ḥaqāʾiq at-Tanzīl,* a commentary on the Qurʾān; author also of three collections of apothegms, a series of moral discourses, poems, and grammatical works as *al-Mufaṣṣal* (1119–21).

Za·men·hof \ˈzä-men-ˌkȯf\, Ludwik Lejzer. *Pseudonym* Dr. Es·pe·ran·to \ˌes-pə-ˈrant-(ˌ)ō, -ˈrän-(ˌ)tō\, *i.e.* One Who Hopes. 1859–1917. Polish oculist and philologist. Practiced as oculist in Warsaw. Known esp. for advocacy of an international language designed to promote international understanding and peace; inventor of Esperanto, explained in *Lingvo Internacia* (1887) and *Fundamento de Esperanto* (1905); translated many works into Esperanto.

Za·moj·ski \zä-ˈmȯi-skē\. Distinguished Polish family, including: Jan (1542–1605), secretary to King Sigismund II (1565–72); after death of Sigismund (1572) worked to exclude Austrian Habsburgs from throne; secured election of Stephen Báthory as king; chancellor (1578 ff.); commander in chief of Polish armies (1581–1602); successful in defending Poland against Turks, Cossacks, and Swedes. ¶Andrzej (1716–1792); after service in Saxon army, returned to Poland (1754) and became chancellor (1764–68); drew up new code of laws (1776). His son ¶Stanisław Kostka (1775–1856) received Austrian title of count (1820). His son ¶Andrzej (1800–1874) was president of an agricultural society (1858–61); worked for abolition of serfdom; called for Polish autonomy during uprising (1861–63) against Russian rule and was exiled (1863). His brother ¶Władysław (1803–1868) took part in 1830–31 insurrection; emigrated to England and there represented interests of Polish prince Adam Czartorski; organized Polish contingents serving in Sardinian army against Austria (1848–49); commanded (1855) a Polish cavalry division in Turkish army during Crimean War.

Za·mo·ra \thä-ˈmō-rä\, Antonio de. c.1664–1728. Spanish dramatist. Court poet (1694 ff.); author of comedies as *Mazariegos y Monsalves* and the farce *El hechizado por fuerza,* and dramas as *Judas Iscariote* and *No hay plazo que no se cumpla,* a version of the Don Juan story.

Zampieri, Domenico. See DOMENICHINO.

Zam·ya·tin \(ˌ)zəm-ˈyät-yin\, Yevgeny Ivanovich. 1884–1937. Russian novelist and playwright. Naval engineer by profession; wrote satirical stories *Uyezdnoye* (1913, on provincial life) and *Na Kulichkakh* (1914, on military life); in England during World War I supervising construction of Russian ships; wrote *Ostrovityane* (1918) satirizing English society; best known for *My* (1924, *We*), an anti-utopian novel commenting on the Soviet state; his works banned in Soviet Union; allowed (1931) to emigrate to Paris.

Za·nar·del·li \ˌdzä-när-ˈdel-lē\, Giuseppe. 1826–1903. Italian politician. Active in national movement (1848–49); minister of public works (1876–77), interior (1878), justice (1881–83, 1887–91, 1897–98). Premier (1901–03); advocated parliamentary rights, decreased taxes on the poor, ended strike-breaking by army.

Zan·chi \ˈtsäŋ-kē\, Girolamo. *Lat.* Hieronymus Zan·chi·us \ˈ(t)zäŋ-ke-əs\. 1516–1590. Italian theologian. An Augustinian canon; embraced Calvinism and was forced (1551) to leave Italy; professor at Strasbourg (1553–68), Heidelberg (1568–76), Neustadt an der Haardt (1576–90); wrote several theological and philosophical works; developed the classic formulation of the Reformed Orthodox doctrine of the perseverance of the elect.

Zand \ˈzänd\. Persian dynasty (1750–94) with capital at Shīrāz. Its chief ruler was Karīm Khān Zand Moḥammad (*q.v.*); its last ruler, Loṭf ʿAlī Khān Zand (*q.v.*), was overthrown by the Qājārs.

Zan·do·nai \ˌdzän-dō-ˈnä-ē\, Riccardo. 1883–1944. Italian composer. His works included operas as *Il grillo del focolare* (1908), *Conchita* (1911), *Francesca da Rimini* (1914), and *I cavalieri di Ekebù* (1925), choral works, a *Messa da Requiem,* and orchestral pieces.

Zane \ˈzān\, Ebenezer. 1747–1812. American pioneer, b. near Moorefield, W. Va. Established claim to land at junction of Wheeling Creek and Ohio River (1770) and there made first Ohio River permanent settlement; acquired additional lands in that region, including tracts on site of present Zanesville (laid out 1799) and Lancaster, Ohio (laid out 1800). His sister ¶Betty (c.1766–c.1831) was heroine of an attack by Indians on Fort Henry, near Wheeling, when she ran through enemy fire to a hut nearby and brought back a keg of powder.

Zan·gī \zaŋ-ˈgē\. *Also transliterated* Zen·gi \zeŋ-ˈgē\. *More completely* ʿImād ad-Dīn Zangī ibn Aq Sonqur. 1084–1146. Seljuq governor of Mosul (1127–46). Governor of Basra (1126); supported Sultan Maḥmūd II against ʿAbbasid caliph al-Mustarshid and was given governorship of Mosul as reward (1127); successful in his battles with Crusaders; extended his rule over northern Syria; founded Zan·gid \ˈzaŋ-gəd\ dynasty ruling over Mesopotamia and Syria (1127–1222). Succeeded by his son Nureddin (*q.v.*).

Zan·gwill \ˈzaŋ-ˌ(g)wil\, Israel. 1864–1926. English playwright and novelist. Edited *Ariel,* a comic journal, in which he published witty stories, including *The Bachelors' Club* (1891) and *The Old Maids' Club* (1892). Established reputation with *The Children of the Ghetto* (1892), a novel depicting Jewish immigrant life in the East London ghetto; followed with other novels on Jewish themes, including *Ghetto Tragedies* (1893), *The King of Schnorrers* (1894), and *Dreamers of the Ghetto* (1898). Joined in Zionist cause of Theodor Herzl (1896); founder and president (1905–25) of Jewish Territorial Organization for the Settlement of the Jews Within the British Empire. Scored immense American success with *The Melting Pot* (1908), a drama of race fusion in America; appealed for international amity in *The War God* (1911); produced tragicomedies including *The Grey Wig* (1903), *The Next Religion* (1912), *Plaster Saints* (1914), *The Cockpit* (1921), *The Forcing House* (1922). Returned to novel writing with *Jinny the Carrier* (1919), set in rural Essex. Produced his last play *We Moderns* (1924) in New York.

Zan·uck \ˈzan-ək\, Darryl Francis. 1902–1979. American motion-picture producer, b. Wahoo, Neb. With Warner Bros. Pictures, Inc. (1924–33), supervisor of production (1929–33); produced *The Jazz Singer,* which introduced sound to motion pictures (1927), *Little Caesar* (1930), *The Public Enemy* (1931). With Joseph Schenck organized (1933) 20th Century Pictures, which merged (1935) with Fox Films. Vice president in charge of production (1935–52), president (1962–69), chairman (1969–71), 20th Century-Fox. Pioneered in use of foreign locations for films; produced first CinemaScope film, *The Robe* (1953). Produced *The Grapes of Wrath* (1940), *How Green Was My Valley* (1941), *The Ox-Bow Incident* (1943), *Winged Victory* (1944), *Gentleman's Agreement* (1947), *Viva Zapatá!* (1952), *The Man in the Gray Flannel Suit* (1956), *The Longest Day* (1962), *The Sound of Music* (1965), *Patton* (1970), etc.

Za·pa·ta \sä-ˈpä-tä\, Emiliano. 1879–1919. Mexican revolutionist. Champion of agrarianism; began revolutionary activities in native village of Anenecuilco, Morelos (1897); gained prominence as guerrilla leader by helping Francisco Madero overthrow Porfirio Díaz (1911); pressed Madero for program of distributing hacienda lands to the peasants; broke (1911) with Madero upon refusal, helped draft agrarian Plan of Ayala, and renewed the revolution. Refused to aid Victoriano Huerta (1913); joined Pancho Villa in struggle for control of country against Venustiano Carranza (1914–19); continued agrarian reforms in areas under his control; won several battles against Carranza's army but was finally ambushed and assassinated in Morelos. Chiefly responsible for making the Mexican Revolution an agrarian revolution.

Zapolska, Gabriela. See Maria KORWIN-PIOTROWSKA.

Zápolya, John. See JOHN, king of Hungary.

Zá·po·toc·ký \ˌzäp-ō-ˈtȯt-skē\, Antonín. 1884–1957. Czech politician. Member of Social Democratic party for 20 years; cofounder of Czech Communist party (1921); elected to parliament (1925); secretary general of Communist Trade Unions (1929–39); chairman of Revolutionary Trade Union Movement (1945–48). Played major role in Communist government takeover (1948); prime minister (1948–53); president of Czechoslovakia (1953–57).

Zarathushtra. See ZOROASTER.

Zarcillo y Alcaraz, Francisco. See SALZILLO Y ALCARAZ.

Zar·co \ˈzär-kü\, João Gon·cal·ves \gōⁿ-ˈsäl-vēzh\. 15th century. Portuguese navigator. Discoverer of Madeira; founded Funchal (1421).

Zar·li·no \dzär-ˈlē-nō\, Gioseffo. 1517–1590. Italian composer and music theorist. Franciscan monk (1537 ff.); studied under Adriaan Willaert; maestro di cappella, St. Mark's, Venice (1565–1590). Best known for his treatises on counterpoint *Istitutioni harmoniche* (1558), *Dimostrationi harmoniche* (1571), and *Sopplimenti musicali* (1588).

Zau·di·tu *or* **Zaw·di·tu** \zau̇-ˈdē-ˌtü\. *Eng.* Judith. 1876–1930. Empress of Ethiopia (1917–30). Daughter of Menelik II; succeeded to throne (1916) on deposition of her nephew Lij Iyasu; crowned (1917); reign much disturbed; Ethiopia admitted (1923) to League of Nations; rule merely nominal after coronation as king (1928) of Regent Ras Tafari (Haile Selassie, *q.v.*), a distant cousin.

Zauffely, John. See ZOFFANY.

Za·yas y Al·fon·so \'sä-yäs-ē-äl-'fōn-sō\, Alfredo. 1861–1934. Cuban politician. Took part in Liberal revolution against Estrada Palma (1906); vice president of Cuba (1909–13); president (1921–25).

Za·yas y So·to·ma·yor \'sä-yäs-ē-sō-tō-mä-'yōr\, María de. 1590–?1661. Spanish novelist. Author of erotic and melodramatic novels of the complications of married life, collected in *Novelas ejemplares y amorosas* (1637) and *Novelas y saraos* (1647–49).

Zayd ibn Thā·bit \'zīd-,ib-ən-'tä-bēt\. 7th century. Muslim scribe. Companion of Muḥammad; official compiler of the Qur'ān.

Zaytz, Giovanni von. See Ivan ZAJC.

Ze·a·mi \zā-äm-ē\ Motokiyo. 1363–1443. Japanese playwright and drama theorist. Creator, with his father Kan-ami (*q.v.*), of present Nō theater; wrote series of manuals (as *Kadensho,* 1440–42) setting down rules for acting, staging, and writing of Nō drama; author of almost half of the 250 or so Nō plays still performed.

Zebi, Sabbatai. See SHABBETAI TZEVI.

Zech·a·ri·ah \,zek-ə-'rī-ə\ *or* **Zach·a·ri·as** \,zak-ə-'rī-əs\. fl. 520–518 B.C. Jewish prophet. With Haggai, persuaded the Jews to rebuild the Temple. The Old Testament book of Zechariah contains his exhortations to the returned exiles and prophecy of Messianic deliverance.

Zé·dé \ze-dā\, Gustave-Alexandre. 1825–1891. French naval engineer. Designer of first successful French naval submarine the *Gymnote,* launched 1888.

Zed·e·ki·ah \,zed-ə-'kī-ə\. 6th century B.C. Last king of Judah. Uncle of Jehoiachin; placed by Nebuchadrezzar II on the throne in Jerusalem (597 B.C.); revolted against Nebuchadrezzar (588); defeated (586) and taken in chains to Babylon.

Ze·dlitz \'tsād-,lits\, Joseph Christian von. 1790–1862. Austrian poet and dramatist. Author of *Totenkränze* (1828), dramatic works, a translation of Byron's *Childe Harold's Pilgrimage* (1836), the epic poems *Waldfräulein* (1843) and *Altnordische Bilder* (1850), *Soldatenbüchlein* (1848–50), etc.

Zee·land \'zā-,länt\, Paul van. 1893–1973. Belgian economist and politician. Delegate to various economic conferences (1922–33); prime minister of Belgium (1935–37).

Zee·man \'zā-,män\, Pieter. 1865–1943. Dutch physicist. Professor, U. of Amsterdam (1900–35), and director (from 1908) of its Physical Institute. Discovered (based on suggestion of Hendrik A. Lorentz) the Zeeman effect, the resolution of single spectral lines into several components in a magnetic field (1896). Awarded (jointly with Lorentz) 1902 Nobel prize for physics.

Zeiss \'tsīs, *Angl* 'zīs\, Carl. 1816–1888. German manufacturer of optical instruments. Founded at Jena (1846) optical factory, taken over at his death by his partner, Ernst Abbe (*q.v.*).

Zeit·blom \'tsīt-,blōm\, Bartholomäus. c.1455–1518. German painter. Chief master of the Swabian school of Ulm. Among his works were the Eschach altarpiece and the Heerberg altarpiece (in Stuttgart).

Ze·la·ya \sā-'lä-yä\, José Santos. 1853–1919. Nicaraguan politican. President of Nicaragua (1893–1910); invaded Honduras and tried to foment revolution in El Salvador in attempt to unify Central American (1907); his policy hostile to U.S.

Że·leń·ski \zhe-'lenʸ-skē\, Tadeusz. *Pseudonym* Boy \'bȯi\. 1874–1941. Polish writer. Author of verse *Słowka* (1913), humorous works as *Plotki, plotki* (1927) and *Znaszli ten kraj?* (1931), essays, and literary criticism as *Ludzie żywi* (1929), *Brązownicy* (1930), and *Perfumy i krew* (1936); translator of French classics, as Molière, Rabelais, Montaigne.

Zélide. See Isabelle de CHARRIÈRE.

Zell \'tsel\, Matthäus. 1477–1548. German religious reformer. Lecturer (1511) and rector (1517) at Freiburg-im-Breisgau; minister of Roman Catholic cathedral at Strassburg (1518); embraced doctrines of Martin Luther and instigated the Reformation in Strassburg (1521); replied to attacks by his bishop with *Christlichen Verantwortung* (1523); wrote catechism *Frag und Antwort* (1536).

Zel·ler \'tsel-ər\, Eduard. 1814–1908. German philosopher and theologian. Professor at Heidelberg (1862–72) and Berlin (1872–95); author of *Platonische Studien* (1839), *Die Philosophie der Griechen* (1845–52), *Geschichte der deutschen Philosophie seit Leibniz* (1873), *Grundriss der Geschichte der griechischen Philosophie* (1883), etc.

Zeller, Carl Johann Adam. 1842–1898. Austrian composer . Official in ministry of education and culture (1873–95). Composer of the operettas *Der Vogelhändler* (1891) and *Der Obersteiger* (1894), choruses, songs, etc.

Zel·ter \'tsel-tər\, Carl Friedrich. 1758–1832. German composer and conductor. Directed Berlin Singakademie (1800–29); teacher of Felix Mendelssohn; did much to revive interest in J.S. Bach's music; composed solos and choruses, music for poems by Goethe and Schiller, cantatas, etc.

Zem·lin·sky \zem-'lēn-ski\, Alexander von. 1871–1942. Austrian composer and conductor, of Polish Jewish parents. Friend and brother-in-law of Arnold Schoenberg; Kapellmeister at Vienna Volksoper (1906–11); opera conductor at Deutsches Landestheater, Prague (1911–27) and at Kroll Opera, Berlin (1927–32); fled to Vienna (1933) and U.S. (1938). Composer of operas as *Sarema* (1895), *Es war einmal* (1900), *Eine florentinische Tragödie* (1917), and *Der Zwerg* (1922), three symphonies, *Lyrische Symphonie* (1923), choral works, songs, and chamber music including a string quintet and four string quartets.

Ze·mur·ray \zə-'mər-ē\, Samuel. *Surname orig.* Zmu·ri \'zmür-yi\. 1877–1961. American businessman, b. Shargorod, Ukraine. To U.S. (1892); banana stevedore at Mobile, Ala. (1896); established a banana-importing company (1903), a shipping line (1905), and Cuyamel Fruit Co. of Honduras (1910); Cuyamel purchased (1929) by United Fruit Co., of which he became managing director (1933–38) and president (1938–51); preeminent developer of agriculture in 13 nations of American tropics, introduced some 30 crops; also known as philanthropist.

Zeng·er \'zeŋ-(g)ər\, John Peter. 1697–1746. America printer and journalist, b. Germany. To America (1710); established printing shop in New York City (1726). Central figure in seditious libel trial (1734–35), resulting from censures of the government published in his antiadministration newspaper *New York Weekly Journal* (founded 1733); defended by Andrew Hamilton of Philadelphia; acquitted by a jury, the decision being regarded as fundamental in establishing freedom of the press in America. Public printer for New York (from 1737) and for New Jersey (from 1738).

Zengi. See ZANGI.

Ze·no \'zē-(,)nō\. *Orig.* Ta·ra·si·co·dis·sa \,tar-ə-si-'kōd-ə-sə\. d. 491. Emperor of the Eastern Roman Empire (474–491), b. Isauria. m. (466 or 467) Ariadne, daughter of Emperor Leo I. Had to put down revolts; yielded to usurper Basiliscus (475–476); Western Roman Empire overthrown (476); issued letter *Henotikon* (482) in unsuccessful attempt to settle diffences between Eastern and Western churches (Monophysite controversy); conflicts with Ostrogoths in Balkan Peninsula; finally persuaded (488) Theodoric to invade Italy.

Zeno of Ci·tium \'sish(-ē)-əm\. c.335–c.263 B.C. Greek philosopher, b. Citium, Cyprus. To Athens (313); studied under Cynic philosophers Crates of Thebes and Stilpon of Megara and at the Academy; founded Stoic school of philosophy; taught in Athens for some fifty years.

Zeno of Elea \'ē-lē-ə\. c.495–c.430 B.C. Greek philosopher, b. Elea (Velia), Italy. Disciple of Parmenides, whom he accompanied to Athens; called inventor of dialectic by Aristotle; famed for his paradoxes based on difficulties of analysis of the continuum.

Zeno of Si·don \'sīd-ᵊn\. c.150–c.70 B.C. Greek philosopher, b. Sidon, Phoenicia. Teacher of Cicero; head of Epicurean school in Athens.

Ze·no \'dzen-ō\, Apostolo. 1668–1750. Italian poet and scholar. A founder of *Giornale dei letterati d'Italia,* first Italian critical journal (1710); court poet and historiographer to Emperor Charles VI at Vienna (1718–29); notable for his melodramatic librettos and oratorios.

Zeno, Carlo. 1334–1418. Venetian admiral. Helped Vettore Pisani defeat the Genoese at Chioggia (June 1380); succeeded Pisani as grand admiral of Venetian fleet (1380); later retired to civilian life and served in embassies to France and England; recalled to military service (1403), fighting French fleet off Genoa and on land against Francesco I Carrara, lord of Padua; later, in command of Cyprian army, expelled the Genoese from Cyprus; returned to Venice (1410).

Ze·no·bia \zə-'nō-bē-ə\. *In full* Septimia Zenobia. *Lat. form of Aramaic* Bat Zab·bai \'bät-'zäb-,bī\. d. after 274 A.D. Queen of Palmyra (267 or 268–272). Wife of Odaenathus, king of Palmyra, at whose death (267 or 268) she succeeded to throne as regent for her son Wahballat (*Lat.* Vaballathus); ambitious to extend power of Palymra over all the Roman empire in the East; occupied Egypt (269) and fixed garrisons in Asia Minor, all supposedly in close alliance with Rome; shortly after Aurelian's accession (270), discarded all pretexts of allegiance; defeated (271–272) and captured by Emperor Aurelian, who took her to Rome.

Ze·nod·o·tus \zə-'näd-ə-təs\. c.325–260 B.C. Greek grammarian. Pupil of Philetas of Cos; first superintendent of the library in Alexandria (from c.284); first critical editor of Homer's *Iliad* and *Odyssey;* complied a Homeric glossary; edited Hesiod's *Theogony;* said to have written epic poetry.

Zenshōbō Renchō. See NICHIREN.

Zeph·a·ni·ah \,zef-ə-'nī-ə\ *or* **Soph·o·ni·as** \,säf-ə-'nī-əs\. 7th century B.C. Jewish prophet. Lived in time of Josiah, king of Judah; his prophetic warnings to Judah are recorded in the Old Testament book of Zephaniah.

Zeph·y·ri·nus \,zef-ə-'rī-nəs\. Saint. d. 217. Pope (199–217). Pontificate marked by many controversies on doctrine; dominated by his deacon Calixtus.

Zep·pe·lin \,tsep-ə-'lēn, 'tsep-ə-,lēn, *Angl* 'zep-(ə-)lən\, Ferdinand Adolf August Heinrich von. Graf. 1838–1917. German soldier, aeronaut, and airship designer. Served in American Civil War (with Union army, 1863), Austro–Prussian War (1866), and Franco–Prussian War (1870–71). Founded manufactory for airships at Friedrichshafen; constructed (1900) first airship of rigid type known as *Zeppelin;* active in building and flying airships (from 1906).

Zer·ni·ke \'zer-nik-ə\, Frits. 1888–1966. Dutch physicist. Lecturer (1915), professor (1920–58), Groningen. Awarded Nobel prize for physics (1953) for invention of the phase contrast microscope (1932).

Że·rom·ski \zhe-'rôm-skē\, Stefan. 1864–1925. Polish novelist, poet, and playwright. Librarian in Rapperswil (1892–96) and Warsaw (1897–1903); arrested (1908) for advocating education for the masses; lived in Paris (1909–12). Noted for his naturalistic and lyrical style; best known for novels as *Syzyfowe Prace* (1897), *Popioły* (1904), *Dzieje grzechu* (1908), *Uroda życia* (1912), *Wierna rzeka* (1912), and *Przedwiośnie* (1925).

Ze·rub·ba·bel \zə-'rəb-ə-bəl\. 6th century B.C. Governor of Judaea. In direct line of house of David; led returning exiles from Babylon (c.538 B.C.) and took charge of rebuilding the Temple at Jerusalem; contemporary of Haggai and Zechariah.

Ze·sen \'tsā-zən\, Philipp von. 1619–1689. German rhetorician and author. Founded at Hamburg (1643) Deutschgesinnte Genossenschaft, literary society which aimed to purify German language. Author of lyric verse and of the novels *Die adriatische Rosemund* (1645) and *Assenat* (1670).

Zet·kin \'tset-kən\, Clara, *nee* Eiss·ner \'ī-snər\. 1857–1933. German feminist and politician. Joined Socialist party (1881); m. Ossip Zetkin (d. 1889); participated in founding congress of Second Socialist International (1889); edited Socialist women's paper *Die Gleichheit* in Stuttgart (1892–1917); crusaded for women's rights and child labor laws; cofounder of International Socialist Women's Congress (1907). Longtime friend of Lenin and Rosa Luxemburg; helped organize international women's conference against World War I (Bern, 1915); a founder of Spartakusbund (1916). Joined (1919) German Communist party and was member of its central committee; member of Reichstag (1920–33); elected (1921) to presidium of Third International (Comintern).

Zeu·ner \'(t)sȯi-nər\, Frederick Everard. 1905–1963. British geologist, b. Berlin, Germany. Professor of environmental archaeology, U. of London (1946–63); known for theories of climatic change and application of radioactive-carbon dating methods to prehistory and paleobotany. Wrote *Dating the Past* (1946).

Zeu·ner \'tsȯi-nər\, Gustav Anton. 1828–1907. German physicist and engineer. Specialist in mechanics, hydraulics, and thermodynamics; director, Polytechnic Institute, Dresden (1873–97). Chief work *Grundzüge der mechanischen Wärmetheorie* (1860).

Zeuss \'tsȯis\, Johann Kaspar. 1806–1856. German historian and philologist. Pioneered in modern Celtic philology; edited *Grammatica Celtica* (1853); wrote *Die Deutschen und die Nachbarstämme* (1837), *Die Herkunft der Baiern von den Markomannen* (1839), etc.

Zeux·is \'zük-səs\. 5th century B.C. Greek painter. Studied in Athens; studio in Ephesus; excelled in coloring and expression; works not extant, but painted chiefly genre and mythological scenes and still lifes; decorated palace at Pella for Archelaus of Macedonia (413–399 B.C.). In legend his painting of a bunch of grapes was so realistic that birds tried to eat the fruit.

Ze·vin \'zev-ən\, Israel Joseph. *Pseudonym* Tash·rak \,tash-'rak\. 1872–1926. American journalist and writer, b. Gorki, Belorussia, Russia. To U.S. (1889) and settled in New York. On staff of *Jewish Daily News* (from c.1892), contributing humorous stories in Yiddish based on life in New York's crowded East Side, later collected in *Tashrak's beste Erzeilungen* (1910), *Maaselech far Kinder* (1919), etc.; also wrote novel *Fun Achzen dis Dreisig* (1929).

Zhda·nov \'zhdä-nəf\, Andrey Aleksandrovich. 1896–1948. Soviet politician. Secretary, Central Committee of the All-Union Communist party (Bolsheviks); member, Politburo (1935) and Presidium of the Supreme Soviet of the U.S.S.R.; chairman, Presidium of the Supreme Soviet of the Russian Socialist Federated Soviet Republic; president, foreign affairs committee of the U.S.S.R. (1938); after World War II severely restricted cultural activities.

Zhu·kov \'zhü-kəf\, Georgy Konstantinovich. 1896–1974. Soviet soldier and politician. Entered army (1915); served in Bolshevik forces (1917–18); commanded against Japanese in Mongolia (1938–39); chief of staff (Jan. 1941); conducted defense of Moscow against Germans; commander in chief on central front (Oct. 1941); as representative of the supreme command on southwestern front, then on northern front, responsible for Russian offensives breaking sieges of Stalingrad and Leningrad (Oct. 1942–Jan. 1943); marshal of the Soviet Union (Jan. 1943); commanded final assault on Berlin (Apr. 1945); commander of Soviet occupation force (1945–46). Minister of defense (1955–57); attempted to make army more autonomous; alternate (1955) and full (June 1957) member of Presidium; dismissed from all posts (Oct. 1957).

Zhu·kov·sky \zhü-'kȯf-skəi\, Vasily Andreyevich. 1783–1852. Russian poet. Reader to Maria Fyodorovna (1815); tutor to Alexander II (from 1818); friend of Pushkin. Known for innovations in poetical language (in the manner of Karamzin) and translations, esp. of German and English poetry. Wrote words of the Russian national anthem "God Save the Czar" (see Aleksey F. LVOV).

Zia·ni \tsē-'än-ē\, Sebastiano. c.1102–c.1180. Venetian judge, financier, and politician. One of wealthiest men in Venice; member of consortium that collected Rialto market revenues (1164–75). Doge of Venice (1172–78); built first bridge across Grand Canal; increased oligarchic nature of government; aided Pope Alexander III against Emperor Frederick I; after defeat of Frederick (1176) by Lombard League, mediated peace treaty.

Zieg·feld \'zig-,feld, 'zēg-, *also* -,fēld, -fəld\, Florenz. 1869–1932. American theatrical producer, b. Chicago. Entered entertainment field as agent during World's Columbian Exposition in Chicago (1893); turned (1896) to theatrical management by introducing Anna Held to American audiences. Introduced new type of production, the "revue," with *The Follies of 1907,* followed by annual "follies," popularly known as *Ziegfeld's Follies* (to 1931, except for 1926, 1928–29). m. Anna Held (1897; div. 1913) and Billie Burke (1914). Managed production of *Sally* (1920), *Rio Rita* (1927), *Show Boat* (1927), etc.

Zie·gler \'tsē-glər\, Karl Waldemar. 1898–1973. German chemist. Professor at Heidelberg (1928), Halle (1936), Aachen (1947); director, Kaiser Wilhelm (later Max Planck) Institute for Coal Research at Mülheim an der Ruhr (1943). Explained reactions in synthesis of rubber (c.1928); made researches in organometallic and organoaluminum compounds; converted ethylene into 1-butene (1953). Awarded Nobel prize for chemistry (1963) with Giulio Natta for studies in the field of chemistry and technology of high polymers.

Zie·ten *or* **Zie·then** \'tsē-tən\, Hans Joachim von. 1699–1786. Prussian general. Distinguished in first two Silesian Wars; commander, Brandenburg regiment of hussars (1741); marched through enemy's territory to Jägerndorf to join Margrave Charles (1745) and won victory at Hohenfriedeberg (1745). Served in Seven Years' War; decided the victory of Torgau (1760).

Zi·ga·be·nus \,zē-gə-'bā-nəs\, Euthymius. *Also spelled* Zi·ga·de·nus *or* Zy·ga·de·nus \,zē-gə-'dā-nəs\. d. after 1118. Byzantine theologian. Polemicist for Emperor Alexius I's repression of Bogomil sect; best known for *Panoplia dogmatikē tēs orthodoxou pisteōs,* an encyclopedic history of Christian heresies valuable as source for medieval and early theological disputes.

Zil·cher \'tsil-k̲ər\, Hermann Karl Josef. 1881–1948. German composer. Principal of Würzburg Conservatory (1920–44). Composed operas as *Fitzebutze* (1903) and *Dr. Eisenbart* (1922), 5 symphonies, 3 violin and 2 piano concertos, song cycles, choral works, chamber music, etc.

Zil·li·a·cus \zēl-lē-'ä-küs\, Konni. *Swed.* Konrad Viktor Zilliacus. 1855–1924. Finnish nationalist. Journalist in Chicago (1890s); returned to Finland and became involved in nationalist and anti-Russian activities; a founder (1904) of underground revolutionary Activist Opposition party and editor of its organ *Fria Ord;* prominent in affair of gunrunning ship *John Grafton* (1905–06); active against Russian rule during World War I.

Zim·ba·list \'zim-bə-ləst\, Efrem Alexandrovich. 1890–1985. American violinist and composer, b. Rostov-na-Donu, Russia. As a violin virtuoso made debuts in Berlin and London (both 1907) and U.S. debut in Boston (1911); settled in U.S.; toured extensively; began recording (1915); known for understated, highly polished performances. Director of Philadelphia's Curtis Institute (1941–68). Compositions included symphonic poem *Portrait of an Artist* (1945), opera *Landara* (1956), concertos, chamber music, and solo violin music.

Zim·mer·mann \'tsim-ər-,män\, Arthur. 1864–1940. German politician. Undersecretary of state for foreign affairs (1911–1916); foreign minister (1916–1917); sent (Jan. 1917) "Zimmerman telegram" which directed German ambassador to Mexico to offer Mexico alliance with Germany and support in reconquering lost territory in Texas, New Mexico, and Arizona; telegram was intercepted and decoded by British naval intelligence and published in U.S. and became one of determining factors leading U.S. into World War I.

Zimmermann, Bernd Alois. 1918–1970. German composer. Professor at Cologne Musikhochschule (1957–70). His compositions included opera *Die Soldaten* (1958–64); orchestral works including concertos for violin (1950), oboe (1952), trumpet (1954), and cello (1954), *Musique pour les soupers du roi Ubu* (1966), *Requiem für einen jungen Dichter* (with choruses, 1967–69), *Stille und Umkehr* (1970); chamber and vocal works; radio and theater scores.

Zimmermann, Robert von. 1824–1898. Austrian philosopher and aesthetician. Professor, Prague (1852), Vienna (1861); follower of Herbart; opponent of Hegel and Vischer. Author of *Ästhetik* (1858–65), *Anthroposophie* (1882), etc.

Zin·ga·rel·li \,tsēŋ-gä-'rel-lē\, Niccolò Antonio. 1752–1837. Italian composer. Maestro di cappella, Milan cathedral (1793–94), Santa Casa at Loreto (1794–1804), St. Peter's at Rome (1804–11), Naples cathedral (1816 ff.); director of Naples Conservatory (1813 ff.). Best known as composer of some 40 operas, including *Montezuma* (1781), *Alsinda* (1785), *Antigono* (1786), *La morte de Cesare* (1790), *Il mercato di Monfregoso* (1792), *Giulietta e Romeo* (1796), *Carolina e Mexicow* (1798), *Il brevitore fortunato* (1803), and *Berenice* (1811); also composed symphonies, chamber music, Magnificats, masses, oratorios, requiems, motets, and hymns.

Zinn \'tsin\, Johann Gottfried. 1727–1759. German physician and botanist. Author of *Descriptio Anatomica Oculi Humani Iconibus Illustrata* (1755), reputed to be the first book on the anatomy of the eye. Linnaeus named in his honor the plant genus *Zinnia.*

Zi·nov·yev *or* **Zi·nov·iev** \zyi-'nȯf-yif\, Grigory Yevseyevich. *Orig.* Ovsel Gershon Aronov Ra·do·mysl·sky \rə-(,)də-'mü-səl-skəi\. 1883–1936. Russian Communist leader. Joined Social Democratic party (1901); associated with Lenin in forming Bolshevik group (1903); elected to party's Central Committee (1907). Imprisoned and exiled (1908); with Lenin in Switzerland during early years of World War I (1914 ff.). Returned to Russia (1917); president of Leningrad Soviet of Workers and member of Politburo (1918); president of Third International (1919); an alleged letter from him to British Communists was used in British political campaign to defeat Ramsay MacDonald's first Labour government (1924). After Lenin's death (1924), for a time allied with Kamenev and Stalin as a ruling triumvirate, but soon conspired with Kamenev and Trotsky against Stalin and was expelled from his various offices (1926–27). Recanted his opposition (1928) and was readmitted to Communist party. Accused of complicity in murder of Sergey Kirov (1934), confessed and was executed.

Zins·ser \'zin(t)-sər\, Hans. 1878–1940. American bacteriologist, b. New York City. Professor, Columbia (1913–23), Harvard Medical School (from 1923). Member of American Red Cross commission to Serbia to investigate typhus (1915); sanitary commissioner in Russia for League of Nations to study cholera (1923). With associates demonstrated method of producing immunization against certain varieties of typhus fever (1930). Author of *Textbook of Bacteriology* (with Philip H. Hiss, Jr., 1910), *Infection and Resistance* (1914), *Rats, Lice, and History* (1935), *As I Remember Him* (autobiography, 1940), etc.

Zin·zen·dorf \'tsint-sən-,dȯrf\, Nikolaus Ludwig von. Graf. 1700–1760. German religious leader. Interested himself in the fate of the Unitas Fratrum, or Bohemian Brethren, a sect so severely persecuted as almost to have lost its identity; invited members of this sect to settle on his estate at Herrnhut; reorganized the church as the Moravian Brethren, or more exactly, the Renewed Church of the United Brethren; ordained (1737) a bishop of the Moravian Brethren. Expelled from Saxony; went to London (1737); established Moravian settlements in the Netherlands, Baltic states, and England. To America (1741); established Moravian congregations in several towns in Pennsylvania; returned to England (1743). His banishment from Saxony repealed (1748); his church recognized in Saxony and England (1749); resident of Herrnhut until his death.

Zir·kel \'tsir-kəl\, Ferdinand. 1838–1912. German mineralogist. Professor at Lemberg (1865–68), Kiel (1868–70), Leipzig (1870–1909); visited Henry C. Sorby in England (1868); pioneered in microscopic petrography. Author of *Lehrbuch der Petrographie* (1866), *Untersuchungen über die mikroskopische Zusammensetzung und Struktur der Basaltgesteine* (1870), *Die mikroskopische Beschaffenheit der Mineralien und Gesteine* (1873), etc. The mineral zirkelite is named after him.

Zí·tek \'zē-tek\, Josef. 1832–1909. Czech architect. Designed the museum at Weimar (1863–68), the National Theater at Prague (1868–81), etc.

Zit·tel \'tsit-əl\, Karl Alfred von. Ritter. 1839–1904. German paleontologist and geologist. Professor at Karlsruhe Polytechnic (1863) and Munich (1866); from evidence gathered as geologist on F.G. Rohlf's expedition to Libya (1873–74) proved that the Sahara had not been under water during the Pleistocene Ice Age; known for work on fossils, esp. fossil sponges. His books included *Handbuch der Paläontologie* (1876–93), *Grundzüge der Paläontologie* (1895), and *Geschichte der Geologie und Paläontologie* (1899).

Živ·ko·vić \'zhēv-kȯ-,vētʸ, *Angl* 'zhiv-kə-,vich\, Petar. 1879–1947. Yugoslav soldier and politician. Involved in assassination of King Alexander Obrenović and installation of Peter I on throne (1903). Commanded cavalry division in Balkan War (1912–13) and World War I (1914–18); commander of palace guards (1921); supported Alexander I in antiparliamentary coup d'état (1929); premier (1929–32); dissolved political parties and elective local governments and persecuted his opponents.

Zi·ya \zē-'yä\, Mehmed. *Pseudonym* Ziya Gö·kalp \gœ-'kälp\. 1875 or 1876–1924. Turkish scholar and writer. Active in revolutionary and nationalist movements; intellectual spokesman for Pan-Turkism and for Westernization; professor of sociology, Ankara (1912–18); exiled (1918–22); member of Turkish parliament (1923–24). Author of verse *Kızıl elma* (1914), fables *Altın ışık* (1918), *Türkleşmek, Islamlaşmak, Muasırlaşmak* (1918), etc.

Žiž·ka \'zhish-kä\, Jan. Count. c.1376–1424. Bohemian general and Hussite leader. Spent much of life as mercenary for Polish army; became a leader of the Taborites (1420); instituted innovative military methods as mobile artillery; built stronghold of Tabor; repulsed Imperial armies near Prague (1420); continued victorious campaign against Sigismund's armies (1421–22); headed the Orebites during the Hussite civil wars (1423–24).

Zmaj. See Jovan Jovanović.

Zna·nie·cki \znän-'yet-skē\, Florian Witold. 1882–1958. American sociologist, b. Świętniki, Poland. To U.S. (1914) as collaborator of William I. Thomas (*q.v.*), with whom he published *The Polish Peasant in Europe and America* (1918–20), a work pioneering in empirical methodology and analysis of immigrant social disorganization; lectured at U. of Chicago (1917–19); professor, Poznań (1920–39, except for visiting professorship at Columbia 1932–34); professor, U. of Illinois (1941–50). Other works included *The Laws of Social Psychology* (1925), *Socjologia wychowania* (1928–30), *The Method of Sociology* (1934), *Social Actions* (1936), *The Social Role of the Man of Knowledge* (1940), *Modern Nationalities* (1952), *Cultural Sciences, Their Origin and Development* (1952), *Social Relations and Social Roles* (1965).

Zoë *or* **Zoe** \'zō-ē\. Name of three empresses of the Eastern Roman Empire:

Zoë Za·üt·za \zä-'üt-sə\. d. 896. 2d wife of Emperor Leo VI.

Zoë Car·bo·nop·si·na \,kär-bə-näp-'sī-nə\, *i.e.* Black-eyed. d. 919. Mistress and later (906) wife of Leo VI; mother of Constantine VII; on Leo's death (912) driven out but returned as regent for son (913–919).

Zoë. 980–1050. Daughter of Constantine VIII; married (1028) Romanus III Argyrus; empress (1028–34); conspired with Michael IV to have Romanus murdered (1034); married Michael IV and adopted Michael V (1040); after revolution had deposed Michael V (1042), became coempress with sister Theodora (1042); married as third husband Constantine IX (1042); joint ruler with Theodora and Constantine (1042–50).

Zoë. Russian empress. See under Ivan III Vasilyevich.

Zof·fa·ny *or* **Zof·fa·nji** *or* **Zaf·fa·nii** \'zäf-ə-nē\, John *or* Johann. *Perhaps orig.* Zauf·fe·ly \'tsau̇-fə-lē\. c.1733–1810. British painter, b. Germany. To England (c.1761); under royal patronage became success as painter of portraits and dramatic conversation pieces, esp. of David Garrick's London successes as *The Farmer's Return* (1762); a founder-member of Royal Academy (1768); in Italy (1772–79), where he painted *The Tribuna of the Uffizi;* portraitist in India (1783–89); returned to England and continued painting, as *Charles Towneley Among His Marbles* (1790).

Zog I \'zōg\. *Personal name* Ah·med Bey Zogu \äk-'med-'bā-'zōg(w)\. 1895–1961. King of Albania (1928–39). During World War I (1914–18) served in Austrian army; minister of interior (1920, 1921–22); minister of war (1921); premier of Albania (1922–24); elected president of Albanian Republic (1925); proclaimed king (1928); pursued policy of close collaboration with Italy; driven from Albania by Italian invasion (1939).

Zo·ï·lus \'zō-ə-ləs\. 4th century B.C. Greek rhetorician and critic. Known for severity of his criticisms of Homer's poems; also criticized Isocrates and Plato.

Zo·la \zȯ-lä, *Angl* 'zō-lə, 'zō-,lä, zō-'lä\, Émile-Édouard-Charles-Antoine. 1840–1902. French novelist. Founder of Naturalism in literature. Employee in the Hachette bookstore, Paris (1862–66); thereafter a full-time writer. Among his works were *Contes à Ninon* (short stories, 1864), *La Confession de Claude* (1865), *Thérèse Raquin* (1867), *Madeleine Férat* (1868); the series of 20 novels published under the collective title *Les Rougon-Macquart* and consisting of *La Fortune des Rougon* (1871), *La Curée* (1872), *Le Ventre de Paris* (1873), *La Conquête de Plassans* (1874), *La Faute de l'abbé Mouret* (1875), *Son Excellence Eugène Rougon* (1876), *L'Assommoir* (1877), *Un Page d'amour* (1878), *Nana* (1880), *Pot-bouille* (1882), *Au bonheur des dames* (1883), *La Joie de vivre* (1884), *Germinal* (1885), *L'Oeuvre* (1886), *La Terre* (1887), *La Rêve* (1888), *La Bête humaine* (1890), *L'Argent* (1891), *La Débâcle* (1892), *Le Docteur Pascal* (1893); the trilogy *Les Trois Villes* (*Lourdes,* 1894; *Rome,* 1896; *Paris,* 1898). Vigorous defender of Alfred Dreyfus; published letter (beginning "J'accuse") in newspaper *L'Aurore* (Jan. 13, 1898) denouncing the French general staff; forced to flee to England (1898–99). Author also of a number of works of criticism as *Mes Haines* (1866), *La République française et la littérature* (1879), *Le Naturalisme au théâtre* (1881), *Les Romanciers naturalistes* (1881).

Zol·lin·ger \'tsȯ-liŋ-ər\, Albin. 1895–1941. Swiss novelist and poet. Primary school teacher in Zürich. Influenced by Impressionists; master of landscape description. His works included verse *Gedichte* (1933), *Sternfrühe* (1936), *Stille des Herbstes* (1939), *Haus des Lebens* (1939); novels *Der halbe Mensch* (1929), *Die grosse Unruhe* (1939), *Pfannenstiel* (1940), *Bohnenblust* (1942); and novella *Das Gewitter* (1943).

Zöll·ner \'tsœl-nər\, Carl Friedrich. 1800–1860. German composer. Founded and directed several choral groups in Leipzig; composer of songs for male and mixed choruses, including 6-song cycle *Des Müllers Lust und Leid* (1844). His son ¶Heinrich (1854–1941), composer, conductor, and writer; composer of 10 operas including *Faust* (1887), *Matteo Falcone* (1894), *Der Überfall* (1895), and *Die versunkene Glocke* (1899), choruses, cantata *Die neue Welt* (1892), 5 symphonies, orchestral pieces, chamber music, songs, etc.

Zöllner, Johann Karl Friedrich. 1834–1882. German astrophysicist. Professor, Leipzig (from 1872); known for photometric work, esp. invention of the astrophotometer and the reversion spectroscope, for study of theoretical questions, esp. of solar phenomena, for researches on mental delusions, esp. optical illusions, and for expansion of the electrodynamical theory of W. Weber.

Zon·a·ras \'zän-ə-rəs\, John. 12th century. Byzantine historian. Author of *Epitome historiarum,* a world history from the creation to 1118, valued chiefly for work of Dio Cassius (*q.v.*) which he incorporated in his own book.

Zopyrion. See under PAMPHILUS.

Zo·rach \'zō-ˌräk\, William. 1887–1966. American sculptor, b. Eurburg, Lithuania. To U.S. (1891); Fauvist and later Cubist painter; gave up painting for sculpture (1922); taught at Art Students League, New York (1929–60). Known for monumental, simple statues executed in direct carving method. Works included *Mother and Child* (1930), *Spirit of the Dance* at Radio City Music Hall, New York (1932), *Benjamin Franklin* (1937), *Builders of the Future* (1939), *Man and Work* relief at Mayo Clinic, Rochester, Minn. (1953), *The Family* (1957), *Spirit of the Sea* at Bath, Me. (1962).

Zorn \'sȯrn\, Anders Leonard. 1860–1920. Swedish painter, etcher, and sculptor. His paintings were esp. of Swedish subjects, female nudes, figures, landscapes, and portraits; his etchings included nudes, portraits of Renan, Anatole France, Paul Verlaine, Proust, Rodin, Strindberg, and the *Portrait of the Artist and his Wife;* his sculptures included *Alma,* a bronze statue of Gustav Vasa (in Mora), *Faun and Nymph* (1896), etc.

Zo·ro·as·ter \'zōr-ə-ˌwas-tər, 'zȯr-\. *Old Iranian* Za·ra·thush·tra \zá-rá-'thu̇sh-trá\. c.628–c.551 B.C. Persian religious leader. Founder of Zoroastrianism (known as Parsiism in India); little known with certainty about his life; said to have converted Vishtāspa, king of Chorasmia, in 588 B.C.; reputed author of the *Gāthās,* five hymns forming the oldest and holiest part of the Avesta, the sacred book of Zoroastrianism.

Zor·ril·la de San Mar·tín \sȯr-'rē-(l)yä-t͟hā-sän-mär-'tēn\, Juan. 1855–1931. Uruguayan poet. Published lyrical verse *Notas de un himno* (1876) and patriotic ode *La leyenda patria* (1879); founded Catholic periodical *El bien publico* (1878); held various diplomatic posts; chief work the epic poem *Tabaré* (1886).

Zor·ril·la y Mo·ral \thȯr-'rē-(l)yä-ē-mō-'räl\, José. 1817–1893. Spanish poet and dramatist. Gained immediate success with recitation of an elegy at funeral of Mariano José de Larra (1837); in Mexico (1855–66) as head of national theater; crowned national poet of Granada (1889). Major figure of the nationalist wing of the Spanish Romantic movement. Author esp. of lyrical, historical *leyendas* as *Cantos del trovador* (1841), *Vigilias del estío* (1842), *Flores perdidas* (1843), and *Un testigo de bronce* (1845), the uncompleted narrative poem *Granada* (1852), and plays as *El zapatero del rey* (1840), *El molino de Guadalajara* (1843), *El puñal del godo* (1843), *Don Juan Tenorio* (1844), and *Traidor, inconfeso y mártir* (1849).

Zoser. See DJOSER.

Zo·shchen·ko \'zȯsh-chin-kə\, Mikhail Mikhailovich. 1895–1958. Soviet writer. Joined Serapion Brothers literary group in Petrograd (1921); produced humorous satires on Soviet everyday life, including *Rasskazy Nazara Ilyitcha gospodina Sinebryukhova* (1923), *Sobranie sochineniy* (1931), *Izbrannye rasskazy* (1935); under pressure from authorities, began (in 1930s) to write in Social Realist style, as *Istoriya odnoy zhizhni* (1935); his first series of episodes and reminiscences, *Pored voskhodom solntsa,* published in *Oktyabr* magazine (1943); condemned by government and expelled from Union of Soviet Writers after publication (1946) of his short story "Priklyucheniya obezyany."

Zo·si·mus \'zō-sə-məs, 'zäs-ə-\. Saint. d. 418. Pope (417–418). Touched off dissatisfaction in Gaul by appointing Patroclus, bishop of Arles, as papal vicar; condemned Pelagius and his doctrines.

Zosimus. 5th century A.D. Byzantine historian. Author of *Historia nova,* a history of Rome from Augustus to capture of Rome by Alaric (410).

Zot·to \'tsȯt-tō\. d. 591. Founder and first ruler of duchy of Benevento. A Lombard general in army of Alboin which invaded Italy (568); marched southward (570) and established duchy of Benevento; defeated army of Justin II near Naples (576); destroyed many churches and abbeys; attacked Naples but was defeated (581).

Zouche \'züsh\, Richard. 1590–1661. English jurist. Regius professor of civil law, Oxford (1620–61); M.P. (1621, 1624); judge of Court of Admiralty (1641), deprived because of Royalist adherence (1649); restored (1661); author of *Elementa Jurisprudentiae,* mapping whole field of law in departments (1629), and *Juris et Judicii Fecialis,* first treatise to exhibit law of nations as an orderly system (1650).

Zrí·nyi \'zrēn-yi\, Miklós. 1508–1566. Hungarian army commander. Ban of Croatia (1542–61); famed for defense of Szigetvár against Turks (1566), and killed in final sally from castle of the city. His great-grandson ¶Miklós (1620–1664), ban of Croatia (from 1647); outstanding military leader; campaigned with success against Turks; opposed Habsburg rule; author of first and finest epic in Hungarian literature, *Szigeti Veszedelem* (1645–46), dealing with his great-grandfather's defense of Szigetvár.

Zschok·ke \'chō-kə\, Johann Heinrich Daniel. 1771–1848. Swiss writer. Author of historical novels as *Abällino der grosse Bandit* (1794, dramatized 1795), *Alamontade der Galeerensklave* (1803), *Das Goldmacherdorf* (1817), and *Die Branntweinpest* (1837), of short stories as *Bilder aus der Schweiz* (1825–26), of *Stunden der Andacht* (a religious work, 1809–16), of studies in Bavarian and Swiss history, etc.

Zsig·mon·dy \'shig-mȯn-dē\, Richard Adolf. 1865–1929. German chemist. Professor, Göttingen (from 1908); made researches on the nature of colloids; invented the ultra-microscope (with H.F.W. Siedentopf, 1903); awarded 1925 Nobel prize for chemistry.

Zuc·ca·rel·li \tsük-kä-'rel-lē\, Francesco. 1702–1788. Italian painter. Employed in Venice (from c.1732) and London (1752–62, 1765–71); founding member of British Royal Academy (1768); known esp. for his landscapes.

Zu·car·ri \'tsü-kär-rē\ *or* **Zuc·ca·ro** \'tsük-kä-rō\ *or* **Zuc·che·ri** \'tsük-ker-ē\, Taddeo. 1529–1566. Italian painter. Self-trained at Rome; known esp. for decorative frescoes in the manner of the school of Raphael; painted (1559–66) frescoes in Palazzo Farnese at Caprarola. His brother and pupil ¶Federico (c.1540–1609) was also a Mannerist painter; employed at Rome, northern Italy, England (1575), and Spain (1585–89); codified theory of Mannerism in *L'idea de' scultori, pittori e architetti* (1607); among his works were the fresco *Last Judgment* (in dome of Florence cathedral; begun by Vasari), frescoes in the Pauline Chapel (Vatican), in the Doge's Palace (Venice), and in the church of the Escorial (Spain), and portraits, as of Queen Elizabeth and the Earl of Leicester.

Zuck·may·er \'tsu̇k-ˌmī-ər\, Carl. 1896–1977. German playwright. Associated with Bertolt Brecht and Max Reinhardt at the Deutsches Theater (1924); scored dramatic success with *Der fröhliche Weinberg* (1925) and *Der Hauptmann von Köpenick* (1930); plays banned in Germany; fled to Austria (1933); to U.S. (1939) and naturalized; resident in Switzerland (from 1946). Other plays included *Der Schelm von Bergen* (1934), *Des Teufels General* (1946), *Barbara Blomberg* (1949), *Der Gesang im Feuerofen* (1950), *Das kalte Licht* (1955); author also of novels *Salwàre oder Die Magdalena von Bozen* (1936) and *Die Fastnachtsbeichte* (1959), short stories in collections *Die Affenhochzeit* (1932), *Ein Sommer in Österreich* (1937), and *Die Erzählungen* (1952), lyric poetry, essays, motion-picture scenarios as *Der blaue Engel* (1930), and autobiographies *Second Wind* (1940) and *Als wär's ein Stück von mir* (1966).

Zu·hayr \zü-'hīr\. *More completely* Zuhayr ibn Abī Sulmā Rabī'ah ibn Riyāḥ al-Muzanī. c.520–c.609. Arab poet. Best known for his poem in anthology *al-Mu'allaqāt* praising the peacemakers between the 'Abs and Dhubyān clans; also wrote satires and other poems of praise.

Zu·kor \'zü-kər\, Adolph. 1873–1976. American motion-picture producer and executive, b. Ricse, Hungary. To U.S. (1888); founded (1912) Famous Players Film Co. which merged (1916) with J.L. Lasky's Feature Play Co., resulting in firm later known as Paramount Pictures, Inc.; board chairman (1935–66).

Zu·lo·a·ga \sü-lō-'ä-gä\, Félix. 1814–1876. Mexican soldier and politician. Supported Comonfort in presidency (1855–58); seized Mexico City and was proclaimed president of Mexico (1858–59, 1861–62).

Zu·lo·a·ga y Za·ba·le·ta \thü-lō-'ä-gä-ē-thä-b̲ä-'lā-tä\, Ignacio. 1870–1945. Spanish painter. Known esp. for his landscapes, portrayals of popular Spanish types as gypsies, bullfighters, beggars, etc., and portraits of women. Among his works were *Daniel Zuloaga and his Daughters, Doña Mercedes, Market Scene, Promenade After the Bull Fight, Gypsy Bull Fighter's Family,* and *Mlle Lucienne Bréval as Carmen.*

Zu·ma·la·cár·re·gui y de Imaz \thü-mä-lä-'kär-reg-ē-ē-t͟ha-'ē-mäth\, Tomás de. 1788–1835. Spanish general. Served against Napoléon; military governor of El Ferrol (1823); dismissed from army as Carlist (1832); assumed leadership of Carlist forces in Biscay (1833); waged successful campaigns and guerrilla wars against the Cristinos.

Zu·már·ra·ga \thü-'mär-rä-gä, sü-\, Juan de. 1468–1548. Spanish prelate. Member of Franciscan order; first bishop of Mexico (1527); burned collections of Aztec manuscripts as heretical books; championed rights of Indians; extended missionary stations to Spanish conquests in Mexico and Central America; first archbishop of Mexico (1547).

Zum·pe \'tsu̇m-pə\, Johann Christoph. 1735–1800. German pianoforte maker. Apprenticed to Gottfried Silbermann; to London (1750s) and worked for Burkat Shudi; set up own shop (1761); built earliest known British piano (1766); known for quality of his products; returned to Germany (1784).

Zumpt \'tsu̇mpt\, Karl Gottlob. 1792–1849. German scholar. Author of a Latin grammar (1818), *Annales Veterum Regnorum et Populorum* (1819), *Die Religion der Römer* (1845), and other works on classical antiquities.

Zum·steeg \'tsu̇m-shtāk\, Johann Rudolf. 1760–1802. German composer. Court concertmaster at Stuttgart (from 1793); pioneer of the ballad and exerted strong influence on Franz Schubert; composed songs and ballads, operas as *Die Geisterinsel* (1798) and *Das Pfauenfest* (1801), cello concertos and other instrumental works, music for *Die Räuber* of his friend and schoolmate Schiller, church cantatas, etc.

Zunz \'tsu̇nts\, Leopold. *Heb. name* Yom-Tob Lipp•mann \'lip-,män\. 1794–1886. German scholar. Founder (1819) of Wissenschaft des Judentums, the scientific study of Jewish culture and literature; a founder (1819) and leader (to 1824) of Verein für Kultur und Wissenschaft der Juden; newspaper editor (1822–31); teacher and principal at Jewish teachers' seminary in Berlin (1840–50). Author of *Etwas über die rabbinische Litteratur* (1818), *Gottesdienstlichen Vorträge der Juden* (1832), *Die Namen der Juden* (1836), *Zur Geschichte und Literatur* (1845), *Die synagogale Poesie des Mittelalters* (1853), *Die Ritus des synagogalen Gottesdienstes* (1859), *Literaturgeschichte der synagogalen Poesie* (1865), etc.

Zupp•ke \'zəp-kē\, Robert Carl, *known as* Bob. 1879–1957. American football coach, b. Berlin, Germany. To U.S. (1881); head football coach at U. of Illinois (1913–41); his 1914, 1919, 1923, and 1927 teams recognized as national champions; introduced the huddle (early 1920s) and helped develop other offensive innovations.

Zu•ra•ra \zü-'rá-rə\, Gomes Eanes de. c.1410–1474. Portuguese chronicler. Keeper of royal archives (1454); author of *Crónica da tomada de Ceuta, Crónica do descobrimento e conquista da Guiné,* etc.

Zur•ba•rán \,thür-bä-'rän\, Francisco de. 1598–1664. Spanish painter. Apprenticed to Pedro Díaz de Villanueva (1614–16); worked chiefly in Seville; court painter to Philip IV (1638). Known for religious paintings and for monastic portraiture; works characterized by a Caravaggesque naturalism and tenebrism, later by more idealized figures and shadowed forms. Among his works were *Immaculate Conception, Crucifixion, St. Francis of Assisi, St. Anselm, Labors of Hercules* (ten canvases) and *Defense of Cádiz* for Buen Retiro palace, *Holy Family, Ecstasy of the Beatified Alonso Rodriguez, Life of St. Buenaventura* (four panels), *Life of St. Peter.*

Zu•ri•ta y Cas•tro \thü-'rē-tä-ē-'käs-trō\, Jerónimo de. 1512–1580. Spanish historian. Held several offices under Charles I and Philip II of Spain; historiographer of Aragon (1548). Author of *Anales de la corona de Aragón* (1562–80).

Zūzānī, az-. See Ḥamzah ibn 'Alī.

Zvo•ni•mir \'zvȯ-nē-mēr\. *In full* Zvonimir-Dmi•tar \'zvȯ-nē-mērd-'mē-tär\. d. 1089. King of Croatia (1076–89). His support of the Croatian Latin faction against the strict nationalists resulted in his assassination, civil war, and Hungarian domination.

Zwaar•de•croon \'zvär-də-,krōn\, Hendrick. 1667–1728. Dutch colonial administrator. Governor general of Dutch East Indies (1718–25); imported the coffee tree, improved cultivation of crops, expanded trade with China, suppressed (1721) conspiracy of Pieter Erberfelt.

Zwan•gen•da•ba \,zwäŋ-(g)ən-'däb-ə\. c.1785–c.1845. King of the Jere in Africa (from c.1815). Expelled from eastern part of southern Africa by the Mfecane (1818); led his Jere people on 20-year, 1000-mile migration to southern end of Lake Tanganyika in present Tanzania; founded city of Mapupo.

Zweig \'tsvīk\, Arnold. 1887–1968. German novelist, playwright, and essayist. Served in World War I; exiled from Germany (1933); to Palestine (1934); lived in East Germany (from 1948). Author of plays as *Ritualmord in Ungarn* (1914), *Die Umkehr* (1925), and *Bonaparte in Jaffa* (1939); novels *Die Novellen um Claudia* (1912), *Der Streit um den Sergeanten Grischa* (1927), *Junge Frau von 1914* (1931), *De Vriendt kehrt heim* (1932), *Erziehung vor Verdun* (1935), *Einsetzung eines Königs* (1937), *Das Beil von Wandsbek* (1948), *Die Feuerpause* (1954), *Die Zeit ist reif* (1958), etc.

Zweig, Stefan. 1881–1942. Austrian writer. Resident in Salzburg (1913), London (1934–40, naturalized), and (from 1940) Brazil. Best known for his psychoanalytical biographies, including *Drei Meister* (1920), *Der Kampf mit dem Dämon* (1925), *Drei Dichter ihres Leben* (1928), *Sternstunden der Menschheit* (1928), *Joseph Fouché* (1929), *Marie Antoinette* (1932), *Maria Stuart* (1935), and *Magellan* (1938); author also of novel *Ungedud des Herzens* (1938), stories as *Angst* (1920), *Amok* (1922), *Verwirrung der Gefühle* (1925), and *Schachnovelle* (1943), plays as *Jeremias* (1917) and *Volpone* (adapted from Ben Jonson, 1927), and the autobiographical *Die Welt von Gestern* (1942).

Zwicky \'tsvik-ē\, Fritz. 1898–1974. Swiss astronomer and physicist. Taught at Calif. Inst. of Technology (1927–68, professor from 1942); director of research (1943–49), technical adviser and chief research consultant (from 1949), Aerojet Engineering Corp. Published papers arguing that supernovae are completely different from ordinary novae (with Walter Baade, 1934); discovered 18 supernovae (1937–41); also made researches in thermodynamics and cosmic rays; pioneered in development of jet engines and rocket propellants, including JATO units.

Zwing•li \'tsviŋ-lē\, Huldrych. 1484–1531. Swiss religious reformer. Pastor at Glarus (1506–16); served as chaplain to Glarus troops in Italy, at the battles of Novara (1513) and Marignano (1515). Pastor at Einsiedeln (1516); appointed people's priest at the Grossmünster in Zürich (1518) where he was rector and teacher of religion. By his preaching, established Reformation in Switzerland (1522); became a leader in political and religious affairs throughout Switzerland; conferred at Marburg with Saxon reformers, including Luther (1529), but was at variance with Luther on some doctrinal points; accompanied Zürich troops as chaplain in their campaign against Catholic cantons; killed at the battle of Kappel (Oct. 11, 1531). Chief work *De vera et falsa religione* (1525).

Zwor•y•kin \'zvȯrʸ-kyin, *Angl* 'zwȯr-i-kən\, Vladimir Kosma. 1889–1982. American engineer and inventor, b. Murom, Russia. To U.S. (1919, naturalized 1924); employed by Westinghouse Electric Co. (1920–29), Radio Corporation of America (1929–54, vice president from 1947); director, medical electronics laboratory, Rockefeller Inst. for Medical Research (now Rockefeller U.; 1959–62). Invented many electronic devices, notably the iconoscope (1923) and kinescope (1929) that together constituted the first all-electronic television system; also contributed to development of the electron microscope, infrared detection and imaging devices, electronic controls. Author of *Television* (1940), *Electron Optics and the Electron Microscope* (1945), *Television in Science and Industry* (1958), etc.

Zygadenus, Euthymius. See Zigabenus.

Zygmunt. See Sigismund.

Zy•go•ma•las \,zē-gō-'mä-läs\, Theodore. 1544–after 1581. Byzantine theologian. First secretary (prothonotary) to Patriarch Jeremias II; engaged in theological correspondence (1574–81) with Martin Crusius of Tübingen comparing Greek Orthodox and Lutheran dogmas; defended Orthodox position and unable to reconcile differences in faiths; sent Crusius material that enabled him to write *Turco-Graecia* (1584).

Pronouncing Lists of Name Elements, Titles, and Prenames

The following lists indicate the end-of-line division and pronunciation for those name elements, titles, and prenames that are not given pronunciations in the entries themselves. In these lists pronunciation transcriptions are preceded by the appropriate language label or labels. English pronunciations are not labelled except as noted below. An English prename derived from a surname is not included in the list of prenames if the surname occurs at least twice as a main entry. Thus, the pronunciation of the prenames Addision, Fowler, Johnson, and Thornton, for example, may be found at the main entries for the surnames. If an entry in these lists has different pronunciations in various languages the transcriptions are numbered and labelled. English pronunciations are given first and an *Eng.* label is included only if the same pronunciation is shared by one or more additional languages:

Au·gus·tus 1\ȯ-ˈgəs-təs\ 2 *Ger.* \au̇-ˈgu̇s-tu̇s\

Mark 1 *Eng., Du.* \ˈmärk\ 2 *Russ.* \ˈmȧrk\

End-of-line divisions and minor orthographic variations, such as the presence of accent marks, apply to all variants following the boldface form. For example, the division **Si·me·on** in the entry below applies to both the Russian and the Spanish form:

Sim·e·on 1 \ˈsim-ē-ən\ 2 **Si·me·on** *Russ.* \syim-yi-ˈȯn\ 3 *Span.* \sē-mā-ˈōn\ 4 *Fr.* **Si·mé·on** \sē-mā-ō^{n}\

In a few cases the pronunciation of the prename of someone entered in the book may be ambiguous. When this occurs a small superscript number following the name in the text corresponds to the number of the appropriate pronunciation in the list of prenames. For instance, at the entry for **Kimbangu** ..., Simon[2], the superscript refers to the second listed variant in the prenames list:

Si·mon. . . 2 *Fr.* \sē-mō^{n}\

Name Elements

a, à \ə, (ˌ)ä\
af *Norw., Swed.* \ˈäv\
ap 1 \(ˌ)ap\ 2 *Welsh* \(ˌ)ȧp\
bar *Heb.* \(ˌ)bär\
ben *Heb.* \(ˌ)ben\
bin *Arab.* \(ˌ)bin\
d' 1 *Fr., Ger., Ital.* \d\ 2 *Port.* \t͟h, d\
da 1 \də\ 2 *Ital.* \dä\ 3 *Port.* \t͟hə, də; t͟hȧ, dȧ\
dal *Ital.* \däl\
dal·l' *Ital.* \(ˌ)däl-l\
de 1 \də, (ˌ)dē\ 2 *Du., Fr., Ger.* \də\ 3 *Ital.* \dā\ 4 *Lat.* \(ˌ)dē\ 5 *Port.* \t͟hə, də, *before vowels* t͟hē, dē; t͟hā, dā\ 6 *Russ.* \dyə\ 7 *Span.* \t͟hā, dā\
de' *Ital.* \dā\
de·gli *Ital.* \ˈdāl-yē\
dei *Ital.* \(ˌ)dā(-ē)\
del 1 *Ital.* \dāl\ 2 *Span.* \t͟hel, del\
del·l' *Ital.* \(ˌ)dāl-l\
del·la *Ital.* \ˌdāl-lä\
del·le *Ital.* \ˌdāl-lā\
dem *Ger.* \dām, dem, dəm\
den 1 *Du.* \dən, də\ 2 *Ger.* \dān, den, dən\
der 1 *Du.* \der\ 2 *Ger.* \dār, der, dər\
des *Fr.* \dā, *before vowels and sometimes h* dāz\
di *Ital.* \dē\
do *Port.* \t͟hü, dü\
du *Fr.* \dᵫ\
e *Port.* \ē, ä\
ebn *Pers.* \ˌeb-ən, ˌib-\
el *Span.* \el\
et *Fr.* \ā\
ha *Heb.* \(ˌ)hä\
ibn *Arab* \ˌib-ən\
il *Ital.* \ēl\
l' *Fr.* \l\
la 1 \lə\ 2 *Fr.* \lȧ\ 3 *Ital., Span.* \lä\
las *Span.* \läs\
le *Eng., Fr.* \lə\
lo *Ital.* \lō\
los *Span.* \lōs\
met *Du.* \met\
og·lu *Turk.* \ō-ˈglü\
te *Du.* \tə\
ten *Du.* \tən\
ter *Du.* \tər\
til *Swed.* \til\
und *Ger.* \(ˌ)u̇nt\
van 1 \(ˌ)van\ 2 *Du.* \(ˌ)vän\ 3 *Ger.* \(ˌ)vän, (ˌ)fän\
van·der *Du.* \ˌvän-dər\
van't *Du.* \vänt\
vom *Ger.* \ˈfȯm\
von 1 *Dan.* \vȯn\ 2 *Finn., Ger., Hung., Pol., Russ., Swed.* \fȯn\
y *Span.* \ē\
zu *Ger.* \(ˌ)tsü\
zum *Ger.* \tsu̇m, tsüm\
zur *Ger.* \tsu̇r, tsür\

Titles

ab·bé *Fr.* \ȧ-bā\
amir *Arab.* \ȧ-ˈmēr\
ba·ha·dur *Hind.* \bə-ˈhäd-u̇r\
bar·on 1 \ˈbar-ən\ 2 *Fr.* **ba·ron** \bȧ-rō^{n}\
ba·ro·ne *Ital.* \bä-ˈrō-nā\
bar·on·ess \ˈbar-ə-nəs\
bar·on·et \ˈbar-ə-nət, *US also* ˌbar-ə-ˈnet\
ba·ronne *Fr.* \bȧ-rȯn\
Bru·der *Ger.* \ˈbrüd-ər\
cap·tal *Fr.* \kȧp-tȧl\
ca·va·lie·re *Ital.* \ˌkäv-äl-ˈye-rā\
châte·lain *Fr.* \shät-la^{n}\
che·va·lier 1 \ˌshev-ə-ˈli(ə)r, shə-ˈval-ˌyā\ 2 *Fr.* \shə-vȧl-yā\
comte *Fr.* \kō^{n}t\
com·tesse *Fr.* \kō^{n}-tes\
con·de 1 *Port.* \ˈkō^{n}(n)-də; -dā\ 2 *Span.* \ˈkȯn-dā\
con·te *Ital.* \ˈkōn-tā\
con·tes·sa *Ital.* \kōn-ˈtās-sä\
count \ˈkau̇nt\
count·ess \ˈkau̇nt-əs\
cu·ré 1 \kyu̇-ˈrā, ˈkyu̇(ə)r-ˌā\ 2 *Fr.* \kᵫ-rā\
czar \ˈzär, ˈ(t)sär\
cza·ri·na \zä-ˈrē-nə, (t)sä-\
dame \ˈdām\
dan \ˈdan\
dom 1 \ˈdäm\ 2 *Fr.* \dō^{n}\ 3 *Port.* \ˈdō^{n}, ˈt͟hō^{n}\
don 1 \ˈdän\ 2 *Ital.* \ˈdȯn, ˈdōn\ 3 *Span.* \ˈdȯn, ˈt͟hȯn\
do·ña *Span.* \ˈdȯn-yä, ˈt͟hȯn-\
duc *Fr.* \dᵫk\
du·ca *Ital.* \ˈdü-kä\
du·ce *Ital.* \ˈdü-chā\
duch·ess \ˈdəch-əs\
du·chesse *Fr.* \dᵫ-shes\
duke \ˈd(y)ük\

\ə\ abut \ə\ kitten, *Fr.* table \ər\ further \a\ ash \ā\ ace \ä\ cot, cart \au̇\ out \ch\ chin \e\ bet \ē\ easy \g\ go \i\ hit \ī\ ice \j\ job \ŋ\ sing \ō\ go \ȯ\ la[w] \ȯi\ boy \th\ both \t͟h\ the \ü\ loot \u̇\ fo[ot] \y\ yet \zh\ vision \ȧ, ḇ, g̱, ḵ, ^{n}, [...] œ, ue, ᵫ, ^{y}\ *see* Guide to Pronunciation

du·que 1 *Port.* \'dü-kē, -kä\ 2 *Span.* \'dü-kä\

earl \'ər(-ə)l\

ed·ler *Ger.* \'äd-lər\

efen·di, ef·fen·di 1 *Eng.* \e-'fen-dē, ə-\ 2 *Pers.* \e-'fen-dē\ 3 *Turk.* \ef-en-'di\

emir *Arab.* \á-'mēr\

em·per·or \'em-pər-ər, -prər\

em·press \'em-prəs\

fra *Ital.* \'frä\

frá·ter *Hung.* \'frá-ter\

Frau *Ger.* \'frau̇\

fray *Span.* \'frä-ē, 'frī\

frei *Port.* \'frā-ē, 'frī\

Frei·frau *Ger.* \'frī-,frau̇\

Frei·herr *Ger.* \'frī-,her\

Fürst *Ger.* \'fuērst\

Fürst·in *Ger.* \'fuēr-stən\

gaek·war *Gujarati* \'gī-,kwär\

graaf *Du.* \'gräf\

Graf *Ger.* \'gräf\

Gräf·in *Ger.* \'gref-in\

ha·ci *Turk.* \hä-'jē\

had·ji *Arab.* \'häj-ē\

hai *Heb.* \'hī\

ḥāj·jī *Pers.* \kä-'jē\

jam *Hind.* \'jäm\

jarl 1 *Dan., Norw.* \'yärl\ 2 *Swed.* \'yárl\

jon·ker *Du.* \'yȯŋ-kər\

jonk·heer *Du.* \'yȯŋk-här\

khan, khān 1 \'kän, 'kan\ 2 *Afghan, Arab., Turk.* \'k̲än\ 3 *Pers.* \'k̲án\

king \'kiŋ\

la·dy \'lād-ē\

laird \'la(ə)rd, 'le(ə)rd\

land·grave \'land-,grāv\

land·gra·vine \'land-grə-,vēn\

ma·dame 1 \'mad-əm; mə-'dam, ma-\ 2 *Fr.* \má-dám\

ma·de·moi·selle 1 \,mad-(ə-)m(w)ə-'zel, mam-'zel\ 2 *Fr.* \mád(-ə)-mwá-zel, mán-mwá-\

ma·gis·ter *Lat.* \mə-'jis-tər, 'maj-ə-stər\

ma·ha·ri·shi *Hind.* \,mə-hə-'rē-shē\

ma·lik *Hind.* \'mäl-ik\

ma·na·ben·dra *Bengali* \,mə-nə-'ben-drə\

mar·che·sa *Ital.* \mär-'kā-zä\

mar·che·se *Ital.* \mär-'kā-zā\

mar·chio·ness \'mär-sh(ə-)nəs\

ma·ré·chal *Fr.* \má-rā-shál\

mar·grave \'mär-,grāv\

mar·quês 1 *Port.* \mər-'kāsh; -'kās\ 2 *Span.* **mar·qués** \mär-'kās\

mar·quis 1 \'mär-kwəs, mär-'kē\ 2 *Fr.* \már-kē\

mar·quise 1 \mär-'kēz\ 2 *Fr.* \már-kēz\

mir·za *Pers.* \mēr-'zá\

Mlle *Fr.* \mád(-ə)-mwá-zel, mán-mwá-\

Mme 1 \'mad-əm; mə-'dam, ma-\ 2 *Fr.* \má-dám\

mou·la·na *Arab.* \mau̇-'lä-nä\

mu·lai *Arab.* \mu̇-'lī\

nath *Bengali* \'nät\

pa·dre *Ital.* \'pä-drā\

pan·dit *Hind.* \'pən-dət, 'pän-\

pa·şa *Turk.* \pä-'shä\

pa·sha 1 *Arab.* \'päsh-ä\ 2 *Turk.* \pä-'shä\

père *Fr.* \per\

pha·raoh \'fe(ə)r-(')ō, 'fa(ə)r-(,)ō, 'fā-(,)rō\

pope \'pōp\

prince 1 \'prin(t)s\ 2 *Fr.* \pra^{n}s\

prin·ce·sa *Span.* \prēn-'thā-sä; prēn-'sä-\

prin·cess \'prin(t)-səs, 'prin-,ses, *Brit often* prin-'ses\

prin·cesse *Fr.* \pra^{n}-ses\

prin·ci·pe *Span.* \'prēn-thē-pā; 'prēn-sē\

prin·ci·pes·sa *Ital.* \,prēn-chē-'päs-sä\

Prinz *Ger.* \'prints\

pun·dit *Hind.* \'pən-dət\

queen \'kwēn\

rab 1 \'rab\ 2 *Heb.* \'räv\

ra·ja *Hind.* \'räj-ə\

Rit·ter *Ger.* \'rit-ər\

sa·hib *Arab., Hind.* \'sä-hib\

saint, St. 1 \'sānt, *before a name* (,)sānt, sənt\ 2 *Fr.* \sa^{n}, *before vowels and sometimes h* sa^{n}t\

san *Ital., Span.* \'sän\

sant' *Ital.* \'sänt\

sa·yid, say·yid *Arab.* \'sī-yid\

sei·gneur *Fr.* \sen-yœr\

ser *Ital.* \'ser\

se·yid *Turk.* \sä-'yēd\

sey·yid *Arab.* \'sī-yid\

shaykh *Arab.* \'shīk̲\

shri *Skt.* \'shrē\

sieur *Fr.* \syœr\

si·gno·re *Ital.* \sēn-'yō-rä\

sir \'sər\

sir·dar *Hind.* \sir-'där\

sire *Fr.* \sēr\

sor *Span.* \'sȯr\

sri *Skt.* \'shrē, 'srē\

sul·tan *Arab.* \su̇l-'tän\

swa·mi *Hind.* \'swäm-ē\

sy·ed *Arab.* \'sī-yid\

tej *Hind.* \'tāj\

Ten·nō *Jp.* \ten-nō\

U *Burmese* \'ü\

vi·comte *Fr.* \vē-kō^{n}t\

vi·com·tesse *Fr.* \vē-kō^{n}-tes\

vis·con·de *Port.* \vēsh-'kō^{n}(n)-də; vēs-\

vis·count \'vī-,kau̇nt\

vis·count·ess \'vī-,kau̇nt-əs\

Prenames

Aa·bye *Dan.* \'ȯb-ue̅\

Aa·ge *Dan.* \'ō-g̲ə\

Aag·je *Du.* \'äk̲-yə\

Aall *Norw.* \'ȯl\

Aar·on 1 \'ar-ən, 'er-\ 2 **Aa·ron** *Dan., Ger.* \'är-,ȯn\ 3 *Fr.* \ä-rō^{n}\

Aa·ro·no·vich *Russ.* \(,)ə-'rȯn(-əv)-,yich\

Aar·re *Finn.* \'är-re\

Aart *Du.* \'ärt\

Aas·mund *Norw.* \'ȯs-mu̇n\

Aba·día *Span.* \ab̲-ä-'th̲ē-ä\

Ab·a·ste·nia \,ab-ə-'stē-nyə, -nē-ə\

Ab·ba 1 \'ab-ə\ 2 *Heb.* \'áb-bä\

Ab·by \'ab-ē\

Abd·al·lah *Pers.* \,ábd-ál-'lá\

Ab·dank *Lith.* \'äb-,dänk\

Ab·del *Arab.* \'äb-du̇l\

Ab·di *Arab.* \əb-'dē\

Abd·ul *Arab.* \'äb-du̇l\

Ab·dul·lah 1 \ab-'dəl-ə\ 2 *Arab.* **Abd·ul·lah** \əb-du̇l-'lä\

Ab·dy \'ab-dē\

Abe \'āb\

Abel 1 \'ā-bəl\ 2 *Dan., Du.* \'áb-əl\ 3 *Fr.* \á-bel\

Abe·lar·do *Span.* \äb̲-ā-'lär-th̲ō\

Abels \'ā-bəlz\

Ab·er·dour \,ab-ər-'dau̇r\

Abi·a·thar \ə-'bī-ə-thər\

Abi·el \'ā-bē-əl, ə-'bī-\

Ab·i·gail \'ab-ə-,gāl\

Abi·jah \ə-'bī-jə\

Abi·lio *Port.* \ə-'bēl-yü; á-\

Ab·ner \'ab-nər\

Ab·ney \'ab-nē\

Aboyne \ə-'bȯin\

Abra·ham 1 \'ā-brə-,ham\ 2 *Dan.* \'á-brä-,hám\ 3 *Du.* \'á-brá-,häm\ 4 *Fr.* \á-brá-ám\ 5 *Ger.* \'äb-rä-,häm\ 6 *Span.* \äb̲-'rän, -rä-'än\ 7 *Swed.* \'ä-brä-hám\

Abra·hán *Span.* \äb̲-'rän, -rä-'än\

Abram 1 \'ā-brəm\ 2 *Russ.* \(,)ə-'brám\

Abra·mo·vich *Russ.* \(,)ə-'brám(-əv)-,yich\

Ab·sa·lon *Norw.* \'äp-sə-lón\

Ab·thorpe \'ab-,thȯ(ə)rp\

Abū \'áb-ü\

Abu·ba·kar *Arab.* \,áb-ü-'bäk-ər\

Ab·ul·fa·tah *Arab.* \,áb-u̇l-'fä-tä\

Aby *Ger.* \'äb-ē\

Ac·cep·ted \ik-'sep-təd, ak-\

Acha·tes 1 \ə-'kāt-ēz\ 2 *Swed.* \á-'kät-əs\

Achille 1 *Fr.* \á-shēl\ 2 *Ital.* **Achil·le** \ä-'kēl-lā\

Achil·les 1 \ə-'kil-ēz\ 2 *Ger.* \ä-'kil-es\

Achim *Ger.* \'äk̲-im\

Acis·clo *Span.* \ä-'thēs-klō; -'sēs-\

Acis·lo *Span.* \ä-'thēs-lō; -'sēs-\

Ac·land \'ak-lənd\

Ad \'ad\

Ada 1 \'ād-ə\ 2 *Fr.* \á-dá\ 3 *Ital.* \'ä-dä\

Adah \'ād-ə\

Adair \ə-'da(ə)r, -'de(ə)r\

Adal·bert 1 *Dan.* \'ád-ál-,bert\ 2 *Ger.* \'äd-äl-,bert\

Ad·am 1 \'ad-əm\ 2 **Adam** *Dan., Pol., Serb.-Cr.* \'ád-ám\ 3 *Du.* \'ád-äm\ 4 *Fr.* \á-dä^{n}\ 5 *Ger.* \'äd-äm\ 6 *Russ.* \(,)ə-'dám\ 7 *Swed.* \'ä-dám\

Ada·man·tios *Mod. Gk.* \,ä-th̲ä-'män-(,)dyȯs\

Ada·mon·ti *Ital.* \,äd-ä-'mōn-tē\

Ada·mo·vich *Russ.* \(,)ə-'dám(-əv)-,yich\

Adán *Span.* \ä-'th̲än\

Adare \ə-'da(ə)r, -'de(ə)r\

ad-Dín *Arab.* \u̇d-'dēn\

Ad·dis \'ad-əs\

Ad·e·la 1 \'ad-^{ə}l-ə\ 2 *Span.* **Ade·la** \ä-'th̲ā-lä\

Ad·e·laide 1 \'ad-^{ə}l-,äd\ 2 *Ital.* **Ade·la·ide** \,äd-ā-'lä-ē-(,)dā\ 3 *Fr.* **Adé·la·ïde** \á-dā-lá-ēd\

Adé·lard *Fr.* \á-dā-lár\

Ade·lar·do *Span.* \äth̲-ā-'lär-th̲ō\

Adel·bert 1 \'ad-^{ə}l-(,)bərt, ə-'del-\ 2 *Ger.* \'äd-əl-,bert\

Adele 1 \ə-'del\ 2 *Ger.* **Ade·le** \ä-'dā-lə\

Adèle \ə-'del\ 2 *Fr.* \á-del\

Adel·heid *Ger.* \'äd-əl-,hīt\

Ad·e·li·na 1 \,ad-^{ə}l-'ī-nə, ,ad-ə-'lī-\ 2 *Ital.* **Ade·li·na** \,äd-ā-'lē-nä\

Ad·e·line 1 \'ad-^{ə}l-,īn, -,ēn, -ən\ 2 *Dan.* **Ade·line** \,ád-ə-'lē-nə\

Adelle \ə-'del\

Adel·steen *Norw.* \'äd-^{ə}l-,stān\

Ade·o·da·to *Ital.* \,äd-,ā-ō-'dä-tō\

Ad·ger \'aj-ər\

Ad·hé·mar *Fr.* \á-dā-már\

Ad·ib *Arab.* \a-'dēb\

Adin \'äd-^{ə}n\

Ad·jai \'aj-,ī\

Adjeng *Javanese* \'äj-eŋ\

Ad·lai \'ad-(,)lā, -lē, -,lī\

Ad·na \'ad-nə\

Adolf 1 \'ad-,älf, 'ā-,dälf, ə-'dälf\ 2 *Czech, Dan.* \'á-,dȯlf\ 3 *Du., Ger., Norw., Pol., Swed.* \'äd-,ȯlf\ 4 *Russ.* \(,)ə-'dȯl^{y}f\

Adol·fi·ne *Norw.* \,äd-ȯl-'fē-nə\

Adol·fo 1 *Ital.* \ä-'dȯl-fō\ 2 *Span.* \äth̲-'ȯl-fō\

Adolph 1 \'ad-,älf, 'ād-,älf, ə-'dälf\ 2 *Dan., Ger.* \'ád-,ȯlf\

Adolphe 1 \'ad-,älf, 'ād-,älf, ə-'dälf\ 2 *Fr.* \á-dȯlf\

Adol·pho *Port.* \ə-'th̲ȯl-fü; á-\

Adol·phus \ə-'dȯl-fəs, -'däl-\

Ad·o·ni·jah \,ad-ə-'nī-jə, ,ad-^{ə}n-'ī-\

Ad·o·ni·ram \ˌad-ə-ˈnī-rəm, ˌad-ən-ˈī-\
Adri·aan *Du.* \ˈá-drē-ˌán\
Adri·aans·zoon *Du.* \ˌá-drē-ˈán(t)-sən, -ˌsón, -ˌsōn\
Adri·aen *Du.* \ˈá-drē-ˌán\
Adri·aensz *Du.* \ˈá-drē-ˌán(t)s\
Adri·an 1 \ˈā-drē-ən\ 2 *Du.* \ˈá-drē-ˌán\ 3 *Ger.* \ˈäd-rē-ˌän\
Adri·a·no *Ital.* \ˌäd-rē-ˈän-ō\
Adri·a·nus *Lat.* \ˌā-drē-ˈā-nəs, ˌad-rē-\
Adri·en 1 \ˈā-drē-ən\ 2 *Fr.* \á-drē-a^{n}\
Adri·enne \ˈā-drē-ˌen, -ən, ˌā-drē-ˈen\ 2 *Fr.* \á-drē-en\
Aedh *Ir. Gael.* \ˈā\
Ae·gi·di·us *Ger.* \e-ˈgēd-yu̇s, -ˈgēd-ē-u̇s\
Ae·lia *Lat.* \ˈē-lē-ə\
Ae·li·us *Lat.* \ˈē-lē-əs\
Ae·mil·i·a·nus *Lat.* \i-ˌmil-ē-ˈā-nəs\
Ae·mil·i·us *Lat.* \i-ˈmil-ē-əs, -ˈmil-yəs\
Ae·ne·as *Lat.* \ə-ˈnē-əs\
Aer·nout *Du.* \ˈär-ˌnau̇t\
Aert *Du.* \ˈärt\
Afa·na·sy *Russ.* \ə-(ˌ)fə-ˈnás-yəi\
Afa·na·sye·vich *Russ.* \ə-(ˌ)fə-ˈnás(-yiv)-ˌyich\
Af·fon·so, A·fon·so *Port.* \ə-ˈfō^{n}-sü; á-\
Afra·nio *Port.* \ə-ˈfrán-yü; á-\
Afra·ni·us *Lat.* \ə-ˈfrā-nē-əs\
Af·ri·ca·nus \ˌaf-ri-ˈkā-nəs\
Agard \ˈā-ˌgärd\
Ag·a·tha \ˈag-ə-thə\
Agathe 1 *Fr.* \á-gát\ 2 *Ger.* **Aga·the** \ä-ˈgä-tə\
Aga·thon *Fr.* \á-gá-tō^{n}\
Age·nor 1 *Ger.* \ä-ˈgā-ˌnȯr\ 2 *Fr.* **Agé·nor** \á-zhā-nȯr\
Agi·de *Ital.* \ˈäj-ē-(ˌ)dā\
Agi·di·us *Ger.* \e-ˈgēd-yu̇s, -ˈgēd-ē-u̇s\
Agnel·lo *Ital.* \än-ˈyel-lō\
Ag·nes 1 \ˈag-nəs\ 2 *Ger.* \ˈäg-nes\ 3 *Norw.* \ˈäŋ-nəs\ 4 *Fr.* **Agnès** \án-yes\
Ag·new \ˈag-ˌn(y)ü\
Agno·lo *Ital.* \ˈän-yō-(ˌ)lō\
Ag·nus \ˈag-nəs\
Agost *Hung.* \ˈá-ˌgȯsht\
Agos·ti·nho *Port.* \ə-güsh-ˈtēn-yü; á-güs-\
Ago·sti·no *Ital.* \ˌäg-ō-ˈstē-nō\
Agos·ton *Hung.* \ˈá-ˌgȯsh-ˌtȯn\
Agrip·pa 1 \ə-ˈgrip-ə\ 2 *Fr.* \á-grē(p)-pá\
Agrip·pi·na *Russ.* \ə-gryip-ˈyē-nə\
Agui·lar *Span.* \ˌäg-ē-ˈlär\
Agus *Indonesian* \ˈäg-u̇s\
Ah·mad *Arab.* \ˈám-ád, ˈák-mád\
Ah·med *Alb.* \äk-ˈmed\
Ah·met *Turk.* \ä-ˈmet\
Ai·dan \ˈād-^{ə}n\
Aik·man \ˈāk-mən\
Ai·ma·ble *Fr.* \e-mábl^{ə}\
Ai·mé 1 \ā-ˈmā\ 2 *Fr.* \e-mā\
Ai·mee 1 \em-ˈā\ 2 *Fr.* **Ai·mée** \e-mā\
Ai·no *Finn.* \ˈī-ˌnō\
Aitch·e·son \ˈā-chə-sən\
Aka·hi·to *Jp.* \äk-ä-hē-tō\
Akhil·lefs *Mod. Gk.* \ä-ˈkē-lēfs\
Aki·ba *Pol.* \ä-ˈkē-bá\
Aki·ko *Jp.* \äk-ē-kō\
Akim 1 *Pol.* \ˈá-kēm\ 2 *Russ.* \(ˌ)ək-ˈyēm\
Akin \ˈā-kən\
Aki·na·ri *Jp.* \ä-kē-när-ē\
Akin·i·fy *Russ.* \(ˌ)ək-ˈyēn-yif-yəi\
Aki·tsu·ne *Jp.* \ä-kēt-su̇n-e\
Ak·sel *Finn.* \ˈäk-ˌsel\
Al \ˈal\
Al·ain 1 \ˈal-ən\ 2 *Fr.* **Alain** \á-la^{n}\
Al·an \ˈal-ən\
Al·an·son \ˈal-ən-sən\
Al·a·ric 1 \ˈal-ə-rik\ 2 *Fr.* **Ala·ric** \á-lá-rēk\
Ala·rik *Swed.* \ˈäl-á-ˌrik\
Al·as·dair *Sc. Gael.* \ˈal-ə-stər\
Al·as·tair \ˈal-ə-ˌsta(ə)r, -ˌste(ə)r, ˌal-ə-ˈ; ˈal-ə-stər\
Al·ban 1 \ˈȯl-bən, ˈal-\ 2 *Fr.* \ál-bä^{n}\ 3 *Ger.* \äl-ˈbän, ˈäl-ˌ\
Al·bans *Fr.* \ál-bä^{n}\
Al·ba·ny \ˈȯl-bə-nē\
Al·ben \ˈal-bən\
Al·be·rich *Ger.* \ˈäl-bə-ˌrik\
Al·be·ri·co *Ital.* \ˌäl-bā-ˈrē-kō\
Al·be·ri·cus *Lat.* \ˌal-bə-ˈrī-kəs\
Al·be·rik *Ger.* \ˈäl-bə-ˌrik\
Al·bert 1 \ˈal-bərt\ 2 *Dan., Finn., Hung.* \ˈäl-ˌbert\ 3 *Du., Ger.* \ˈäl-ˌbert\ 4 *Fr.* \ál-ber\ 5 *Norw.* \ˈäl-bərt, -ˌbert\ 6 *Swed.* \ˈál-bərt\
Al·ber·ti·na \ˌal-bər-ˈtē-nə\
Al·ber·tine 1 \ˈal-bər-ˌtēn\ 2 *Fr.* \ál-ber-tēn\ 3 *Ger.* **Al·ber·ti·ne** \ˌäl-ber-ˈtē-nə\
Al·ber·to 1 *Ital.* \äl-ˈber-tō\ 2 *Port.* \äl-ˈber-tü\ 3 *Span.* \ä-ˈber-tō\
Al·berts *Latvian* \ˈäl-berts\
Al·ber·tus 1 \al-ˈbərt-əs\ 2 *Du.* \äl-ˈber-tœs\
Al·bi·cius *Lat.* \al-ˈbish(-ē)-əs\
Al·bin 1 \ˈal-bən\ 2 *Fr.* \ál-ba^{n}\ 3 *Ger.* \äl-ˈbēn, ˈäl-ˌ\
Al·bine *Fr.* \ál-bēn\
Al·bi·no 1 *Ital.* \äl-ˈbē-nō\ 2 *Span.* \äl-ˈbē-nō\
Al·bi·on \ˈal-bē-ən\
Al·bi·us *Lat.* \ˈal-bē-əs\
Al·brecht 1 *Dan.* \ˈäl-(ˌ)brekt\ 2 *Ger.* \ˈäl-(ˌ)brekt\
Al·bree \ˈȯl-brē\
Al·can \ˈal-kən\
Al·cán·ta·ra *Span.* \äl-ˈkän-tär-ä\
Al·cée *Fr.* \ál-sā\
Al·cide 1 *Fr.* \ál-sēd\ 2 *Ital.* **Al·ci·de** \äl-ˈsē-dā\
Al·ci·mus *Lat.* \ˈal-sə-məs\
Al·ci·phron \ˈal-si-ˌfrän\
Al·de·gonde *Fr.* \ál-də-gō^{n}d\
Al·den \ˈȯl-dən\
Al·der·man \ˈȯl-dər-mən\
Al·dert *Du.* \ˈäl-dərt\
Al·dis \ˈȯl-dəs, -dis\
Al·do *Ital.* \ˈäl-dō\
Al·donce *Fr.* \ál-dō^{n}s\
Al·dous \ˈȯl-dəs\
Al·dred \ˈȯl-drəd, ˈal-, -ˌdred\
Al·dro \ˈal-(ˌ)drō\
Al·dus *Lat.* \ˈȯl-dəs, ˈal-\
Ald·worth \ˈȯl-(ˌ)dwərth\
Ale·ar·do *Ital.* \ˌä-lā-ˈär-dō\
Al·ec, Al·eck \ˈal-ək\
Ale·cu *Rom.* \ä-ˈlek-ü\
Ale·jan·dro *Span.* \äl-ā-ˈkän-drō\
Alek·san·dar *Serb.-Cr.* \ˌá-ˌlek-ˈsán-där\
Alek·san·der *Pol.* \ˌá-lek-ˈsán-der\
Alek·san·dr *Russ.* \əl-yik-ˈsán-dər\
Alek·san·dra *Russ.* \əl-yik-ˈsán-drə\
Alek·san·dro·vich *Russ.* \əl-yik-ˈsán-drəv-ˌyich, -ˌdryich\
Ale·ksan·dŭr *Bulg.* \äl-ek-ˈsán-dər\
Alek·sey *Russ.* \əl-yik-ˈsyā(-ē)\
Alek·se·ye·vich *Russ.* \əl-yik-ˈsyā(-yiv)-ˌyich\
Alek·se·yev·na *Russ.* \əl-yik-ˈsyā(-yi)v-nə\
Al·ers \ˈal-ərz\
Aleš *Czech* \ˈá-ˌlesh\
Ales·san·dro *Ital.* \ˌä-lās-ˈsän-drō\
Ales·sio *Ital.* \ä-ˈles-syō\
Alet·ta *Du.* \á-ˈlet-á\
Al·ex 1 \ˈal-iks, ˈel-\ 2 **Alex** *Fr.* \á-leks\ 3 *Ger.* \ˈäl-eks\
Alexa \ə-ˈlek-sə\
Al·ex·an·der 1 \ˌal-ig-ˈzan-dər, ˌel-, *Brit also* -ˈzän-\ 2 **Alex·an·der** *Du.* \ˌá-lek-ˈsän-dər\ 3 *Finn., Pol.* \ˌá-lek-ˈsán-ˌder\ 4 *Ger.* \ˌäl-ek-ˈsän-dər\ 5 *Norw.* \ˌäl-ək-ˈsän-dər\ 6 *Russ.* \əl-yik-ˈsán-dər\ 7 *Swed.* \ˌál-ək-ˈsán-dər\
Al·ex·an·dra \ˌal-ig-ˈzan-drə, ˌel-, *Brit also* -ˈzän-\ 2 *Dan.* **Alex·an·dra** \ˌá-lek-ˈsán-drä\
Al·ex·an·dre 1 \ˌal-ig-ˈzan-dər, ˌel-, *Brit also* -ˈzän-\ 2 *Fr.* **Alex·an·dre** \á-lek-sä^{n}dr^{ə}\ 3 *Port.* **Ale·xan·dre** \ə-lē-ˈshá^{n}(n)-drə; ä-lē-ˈshá^{n}(n)-drā\
Al·ex·an·dri·na \ˌal-ig-ˌzan-ˈdrē-nə, ˌel-, *Brit also* -ˌzän-\
Alex·an·dri·ne 1 *Du.* \ˌá-ˌlek-sän-ˈdrē-nə\ 2 *Fr.* \á-lek-sä^{n}-drēn\
Alex·an·dros *Mod. Gk.* \ä-ˈlek-sän-ˌthrȯs\
Alex·an·dru *Rom.* \ˌäl-ek-ˈsän-drü\
Alex·i·ne *Du.* \ˌá-lek-ˈsē-nə\
Alex·is 1 \ə-ˈlek-səs\ 2 *Finn.* \ˈá-ˌlek-sis\ 3 *Fr.* \á-lek-sē\ 4 *Ger.* \ä-ˈlek-sis\
Alex·i·us 1 \ə-ˈlek-sē-əs\ 2 *Ger.* \ä-ˈleks-yu̇s, -ˈlek-sē-u̇s\
Alf 1 \ˈalf\ 2 *Norw.* \ˈälf\
Al·fa·ro *Span.* \äl-ˈfär-ō\
Al·fons *Ger.* \ˈäl-ˌfȯn(t)s\
Al·fonse \ˈal-ˌfän(t)s, -ˌfänz, ˌal-ˈ\
Al·fon·si·na *Swed* \äl-fȯn-ˈsē-nä\
Al·fon·so 1 \al-ˈfän(t)-(ˌ)sō, -ˈfän-(ˌ)zō\ 2 *Ger.* \äl-ˈfȯn-zō\ 3 *Ital., Span.* \äl-ˈfȯn-sō\
Al·ford \ˈȯl-fərd, ˈal-, -ˌfō(ə)rd\
Al·fred 1 \ˈal-frəd, -fərd\ 2 *Du.* \ˈäl-ˌfret\ 3 *Finn., Swed.* \ˈál-ˌfred\ 4 *Fr.* \ál-fred\ 5 *Ger.* \ˈäl-ˌfrāt\ 6 *Norw.* \ˈäl-ˌfred\ 7 *Pol.* \ˈál-ˌfret\
Al·fré·dine *Fr.* \ál-frā-dēn\
Al·fre·do 1 *Ital.* \äl-ˈfrā-dō\ 2 *Span.* \äl-ˈfrā-thō\
Al·fried *Ger.* \ˈäl-frēt\
Al·ger·non 1 \ˈal-jər-nən, *US usu* -ˌnän\ 2 *Fr.* \ál-zher-nō^{n}\
Ali, ʿAlī 1 \ä-ˈlē, ˈal-ē, ˈäl-ē\ 2 *Arab., Pers.* \á-ˈlē\ 3 *Turk.* \ä-ˈlē\
Al·ice 1 \ˈal-əs\ 2 *Fr.* **Alice** \á-lēs\ 3 **Ali·ce** *Ger.* \ä-ˈlē-sə\ 4 *Ital.* \ä-ˈlē-chā\
Ali·cia 1 \ə-ˈlish(-ē)-ə\ 2 *Ital.* \ä-ˈlē-chä\ 3 *Span.* \ä-ˈlēth-yä; -ˈlēs-\
Ali·di·us *Du.* \á-ˈlēd-ē-œs\
Alin·da *Ital.* \ä-ˈlēn-dä\
Aline \ə-ˈlēn, a-; ˈal-ˌēn\
Al·i·son \ˈal-ə-sən\
Al·is·ter \ˈal-əs-tər\
Ali·tza *Ger.* \ä-ˈlēt-sä\
Al·ix 1 \ˈal-iks\ 2 **Alix** *Fr.* \á-lēks\ 3 *Ger.* \ˈäl-iks\
Al·la *Russ.* \ˈäl-lə\
Al·lan \ˈal-ən\
Al·lard 1 *Du.* \ˈäl-ˌärt\ 2 *Fr.* \á-lár\
Al·lar·dice, -dyce \ˈal-ər-ˌdīs\
Al·lart *Du.* \ˈäl-ˌärt\
Al·le·mand *Fr.* \ál-mä^{n}\
Al·len \ˈal-ən\
Al·ler·ton \ˈal-ər-tən, -ərt-^{ə}n\
Al·li·ott \ˈal-ē-ət, ˈal-yət\
Al·li·son \ˈal-ə-sən\
Al·lis·ton \ˈȯl-əs-tən\
Allse·brook \ˈȯls-ˌbru̇k\
All·son \ˈȯl-sən\
All·ston \ˈȯl-stən\
All·var *Swed.* \ˈál-vár\
Al·lyn \ˈal-ən\
Al·ma 1 \ˈal-mə\ 2 *Ger.* \ˈäl-mä\
Al·man·za \al-ˈman-zə\
Al·ma·rin \ˈal-mə-rən\
Al·mer \ˈal-mər, ˈȯl-\
Al·me·rin \ˈal-mə-rən\
Al·mi·ra \al-ˈmī-rə\
Al·mon \ˈal-mən, ˈȯl-\

\ə\ **abut** \ᵊ\ **kitten**, *Fr.* **table** \ər\ **further** \a\ **ash** \ā\ **ace** \ä\ **cot, cart** \au̇\ **out** \ch\ **chin** \e\ **bet** \ē\ **easy** \g\ **go** \i\ **hit** \ī\ **ice** \j\ **job** \ŋ\ **sing** \ō\ **go** \ȯ\ **law** \ȯi\ **boy** \th\ **both** \t͟h\ **the** \ü\ **loot** \u̇\ **foot** \y\ **yet** \zh\ **vision** \á, b̲, g̲, k̲, ^{n}, œ, œ̄, ue, ue̅, ^{y}\ *see* Guide to Pronunciation

Alm·roth \ˈalm-ˌrōth\
Al·my \ˈal-mē\
Al·no·ra \al-ˈnōr-ə, -ˈnȯr-\
Alois 1 \ə-ˈlȯis\ 2 *Czech* \ˈä-ˌlȯis\ 3 *Ger.* **Alo·is** \ˈäl-ō-ˌēs, ˈäl-ˌȯis\
Alo·isio *Ital.* \ˌäl-ō-ˈēz-yō\
Al·o·i·sius 1 \ˌal-ə-ˈwish-əs\ 2 *Ger.* **Al·o·i·si·us** \ˌäl-ō-ˈēz-yu̇s, -ˈē-zē-u̇s\
Alon·so 1 \ə-ˈlän-zō\ 2 *Ital., Span.* \ä-ˈlȯn-sō\
Alon·zo \ə-ˈlän-(ˌ)zō\
Alo·ys 1 *Fr.* \ȧ-lȯ-ēs\ 2 *Ger.* \ˈäl-ō-œs, ˈäl-ȯis\
Al·o·y·sia \ˌal-ə-ˈwish-ə\
Alo·y·sio *Ital.* \ˌäl-ō-ˈēz-yō\
Al·o·y·sius 1 \ˌal-ə-ˈwish-əs\ 2 **Al·o·y·si·us** *Du.* \ˌȧl-ō-ˈē-sē-œs\ 3 *Ger.* \ˌäl-ō-ˈu̅e̅z-yu̇s, -ˈu̅e̅-zē-u̇s\
Al·phe·us 1 \ˈal-fē-əs, al-ˈfē-\ 2 *Ger.* \äl-ˈfā-u̇s\
Al·phon·sa \al-ˈfän(t)-sə\
Al·phonse 1 \ˈal-ˌfän(t)s, -ˌfänz, ˌal-ˈ\ 2 *Fr.* \ȧl-fō^{n}s\
Al·phon·so \al-ˈfän(t)-(ˌ)sō, -ˈfän-(ˌ)zō\
Al·phon·sus \al-ˈfän(t)-səs\
Al·pi·nien *Fr.* \ȧl-pēn-ya^{n}\
Als·worth \ˈalz-(ˌ)wərth, ˈȯlz-\
Al·ter \ˈäl-tər, ˈȯl-\
Al·ton \ˈȯlt-^{ə}n, ˈalt-\
Al·un *Welsh* \ˈȧl-in, ˈal-ən\
Al·u·red \ˈal-yə-ˌred\
Al·va 1 \ˈal-və\ 2 *Span.* \ˈäl-vä\
Al·vah \ˈal-və\
Al·van \ˈal-vən\
Al·var 1 *Finn.* \ˈȧl-ˌvȧr\ 2 *Sp.* **Ál·var** \ˈäl-b̲är\
Ál·va·res *Port.* \ˈäl-və-rish; -vär-is\
Ál·va·rez *Span.* \ˈäl-vär-äth; -äs\
Ál·va·ro 1 *Port.* \ˈäl-və-rü; -vär-ü\ 2 *Span.* \ˈäl-b̲är-ō\
Al·ver·son \ˈal-vər-sən\
Al·ves *Port.* \ˈäl-vish; -vis\
Al·vil·de *Norw.* \äl-ˈvil-də\
Al·vin \ˈal-vən\
Al·vi·se *Ital.* \äl-ˈvē-zä\
Al·vord \ˈȯl-ˌvō(ə)rd, ˈal-, -ˌvȯ(ə)rd, -vərd\
Al·win 1 \ˈal-wən\ 2 *Ger.* \ˈäl-ˌvēn\
Am·a·bel \ˈam-ə-ˌbel\
Ama·ble *Fr.* \ȧ-mȧbl^{ə}\
Ama·deo 1 *Ital.* \ˌäm-ä-ˈde-ō\ 2 *Span.* \äm-ä-ˈt̲h̲ā-ō\
Am·a·de·us 1 \ˌam-ə-ˈdē-əs, ˌäm-, -ˈdā-\ 2 **Ama·de·us** *Ger.* \ˌä-mä-ˈdā-u̇s\ 3 *Swed.* \ˌä-mȧ-ˈdā-əs\
Ama·dieu *Fr.* \ȧ-mȧd-yœ̄\
Am·a·dis 1 \ˈam-ə-dəs\ 2 *Fr.* **Ama·dis** \ȧ-mȧ-dēs\
Ama·do *Span.* \ä-ˈmät̲h̲-ō\
Ama·lia 1 *Ger.* \ä-ˈmäl-yä, -ˈmäl-ē-ä\ 2 *Ital.* \ä-ˈmäl-yä\
Ama·lie 1 *Dan.* \ȧ-ˈmȧ-lē-ə\ 2 *Ger.* \ä-ˈmäl-yə, -ˈmäl-ē-ə\
Amand *Fr.* \ȧ-mä^{n}\
Aman·da 1 \ə-ˈman-də\ 2 *Ger.* \ä-ˈmän-dä\
Aman·dine *Fr.* \ȧ-mä^{n}-dēn\
Aman·dus 1 \ə-ˈman-dəs\ 2 *Ger.* \ä-ˈmän-du̇s\
Ama·ne *Jp.* \ä-mä-ne\
Ama·ra *Ger.* \ä-ˈmär-ä\
Am·a·ri·ah \ˌam-ə-ˈrī-ə\
Ama·sa \ˈam-ə-sə, ə-ˈmā-sə\
Amau·ry *Fr.* \ȧ-mȯ-rē\
Am·bro·gio *Ital.* \äm-ˈbrō-jō\
Am·broise *Fr.* \ä^{n}-brwȧz\
Am·brose 1 \ˈam-ˌbrōz, -ˈbrōs\ 2 *Du.* \ˈäm-ˌbrōs\
Am·bro·sio *Span.* \äm-ˈbrō-syō\
Am·bro·si·us 1 \am-ˈbrō-zhəs, -zē-əs\ 2 *Du.* \äm-ˈbrō-sē-œs\ 3 *Ger.* \äm-ˈbrōz-yu̇s, -ˈbrō-zē-u̇s\
Amé·dée *Fr.* \ȧ-mā-dā\
Ame·deo *Ital.* \ˌäm-ā-ˈde-ō\
Ameen *Arab.* \ȧ-ˈmēn\
Ame·lia 1 \ə-ˈmēl-yə\ 2 *Ital.* \ä-ˈmel-yä\ 3 *Span.* \ä-ˈmāl-yä\
Ame·lie 1 *Ger.* \ä-ˈmāl-yə, -ˈmā-lē-ə; ˈäm-ā-lē\ 2 *Fr.* **Amé·lie** \ȧ-mā-lē\
Ame·li·ta *Ital.* \ˌäm-ā-ˈlē-tä\
Amé·ri·co *Span.* \ä-ˈmā-rē-kō\
Amer·i·cus 1 \ə-ˈmer-ə-kəs\ 2 *Du.* **Ame·ri·cus** \ȧ-ˈmā-rē-kœs\
Ame·ri·go *Ital.* \ˌäm-ā-ˈrē-gō\
Ames \ˈāmz\
Ami *Fr.* \ȧ-mē\
Ami·as \ˈā-mē-əs, ˈam-ē-\
Ami·co *Ital.* \ä-ˈmē-kō\
Ami·el \ˈam-ē-əl, ˈā-mē-\
Amil·ca·re *Ital.* \ä-ˈmēl-kä-(ˌ)rā\
Ami·li·us *Ger.* \e-ˈmēl-yu̇s, -ˈmē-lē-u̇s\
Amin *Arab.* \ȧ-ˈmēn\
Am·mi \ˈam-ˌī\
Amos 1 \ˈā-məs\ 2 *Czech* **Ámos, Amos** \ˈä-mȯs\
Amour *Fr.* \ȧ-mür\
Am·schel 1 \ˈam-shəl\ 2 *Ger.* \ˈäm-shəl\
Amy 1 \ˈā-mē\ 2 *Fr.* \ȧ-mē\
Am·zi \ˈam-ˌzī\
Ana *Span.* \ˈän-ä\
Ana·char·sis *Fr.* \ȧ-nȧ-kȧr-sēs\
Ana·ïs \ə-ˈnī-əs\
Anan·da *Bengali* \ˌä-nən-ˈdə\
Ana·stas *Russ.* \ə-(ˌ)nə-ˈstȧs\
Anas·tase *Fr.* \ȧ-nȧ-stäz\
An·as·ta·sia 1 \ˌan-ə-ˈstā-zh(ē-)ə, -sh(ē-)ə\ 2 *Ger.* **Ana·sta·sia** \ˌän-ä-ˈstäz-yə, -ˈstäz-ē-ə\
Anas·ta·sio 1 *Ital.* \ˌän-äs-ˈtäz-yō\ 2 *Span.* \ˌän-äs-ˈtäs-yō\
An·as·ta·si·us 1 \ˌan-ə-ˈstā-zh(ē-)əs, -sh(ē-)əs\ 2 *Ger.* **Ana·sta·si·us** \ˌän-ä-ˈstäz-yu̇s, -ˈstäz-ē-u̇s\
Anas·ta·si·ya *Russ.* \ə-(ˌ)nə-ˈstȧ-sē-(ˌ)yə\
Ana·tole *Fr.* \ȧ-nȧ-tȯl\
Ana·to·ly *Russ.* \ə-(ˌ)nə-ˈtȯl-yəi\
An·crum \ˈaŋ-krəm\
An·ders 1 *Dan.* \ˈȧn-ərs\ 2 *Swed.* \ˈȧn-dərs\
An·der·sen *Dan.* \ˈȧn-ər-sən\
An·der·son \ˈan-dər-sən\
An·do *Jp.* \än-dō\
An·doche *Fr.* \ä^{n}-dȯsh\
An·drás *Hung.* \ˈän-ˌdrȧsh\
An·drault *Fr.* \ä^{n}-drō\
An·dré 1 *Fr.* \ä^{n}-drā\ 2 *Swed.* \ȧn-ˈdrā\
An·drea *Ital.* \än-ˈdre-ä\
An·dre·as 1 \ˈan-drē-əs\ 2 *Dan.* \ȧn-ˈdri-ȧs\ 3 *Du., Ger., Norw.* \än-ˈdrā-äs\ 4 *Lat.* \ˈan-drē-əs, an-ˈdrē-\ 5 *Mod. Gk.* \än-ˈt̲h̲re-äs\ 6 *Swed.* \ȧn-ˈdrā-ȧs\
An·drée *Fr.* \ä^{n}-drā\
An·drei *Bulg.* \ȧn-ˈdre-ē\
An·drej *Slovak* \ˈȧn-drā\
An·drés *Span.* \än-ˈdrās\
An·dreu *Span.* \än-ˈdrāu̇\
An·drew \ˈan-(ˌ)drü\
An·drey *Russ.* \(ˌ)ən-ˈdrā-(ē)\
An·dre·ye·vich *Russ.* \(ˌ)ən-ˈdryā(-yiv)-ˌyich\
An·dries *Du.* \ˈän-drēs\
An·dri·eu \ˈan-dr(ē-)ü\
An·dri·ja *Serb.-Cr.* \ȧn-ˈdrē-yȧ\
An·dri·ya *Lith.* \ˈȧn-drē-yȧ\
An·drus \ˈan-drəs\
An·drzej, -drzei *Pol.* \ˈȧn-(ˌ)jā\
An·dy \ˈand-ē\
Anet *Fr.* \ȧ-ne\
Aneu·rin \ə-ˈnī-rən\
Ange *Fr.* \ä^{n}zh\
An·gel 1 \ˈān-jəl\ 2 *Span.* **Án·gel** \ˈäŋ-k̲äl\
An·ge·la 1 \ˈan-jə-lə\ 2 *Ital.* \ˈän-jä-(ˌ)lä\
An·gel·i·ca 1 \an-ˈjel-i-kə\ 2 **An·ge·li·ca** *Ger.* \äŋ-ˈgā-lē-kä\ 3 *Ital.* \än-ˈjel-ē-(ˌ)kä\
An·ge·li·co *Ital.* \än-ˈjel-ē-(ˌ)kō\
An·gel·i·cus \an-ˈjel-i-kəs\
An·ge·li·na \ˌan-jə-ˈlē-nə\
An·gé·lique *Fr.* \ä^{n}-zhā-lēk\
An·ge·lo 1 \ˈan-jə-(ˌ)lō\ 2 *Ger., Ital.* \ˈän-jā-(ˌ)lō\
An·ge·lus \ˈan-jə-ləs\
An·gier \ˈan-ˌji(ə)r\
An·gio·lo *Ital.* \ˈän-jō-(ˌ)lō\
An·gus \ˈaŋ-gəs\
Aní·bal *Span.* \ä-ˈnē-b̲äl\
An·ice \ˈan-əs\
Ani·ce·to 1 *Ital.* \ˌän-ē-ˈche-tō\ 2 *Span.* \ˌän-ē-ˈthā-tō; -ˈsā-\
Ani·cius *Lat.* \ə-ˈnish-(ē-)əs\
Aniel·lo *Ital.* \än-ˈyel-lō\
Ani·ka *Russ.* \(ˌ)ən-ˈyē-kə\
Ani·ki·ta *Russ.* \ən-yik-ˈyē-tə\
Ani·ta 1 \ə-ˈnēt-ə\ 2 *Dan., Ger., Span.* \ä-ˈnē-tä\
Ann \ˈan\
An·na 1 \ˈan-ə\ 2 *Du.* \ˈän-ȧ\ 3 *Fr.* \ȧn-nȧ\ 4 *Ger.* \ˈän-ä\ 5 *Ital., Latvian* \ˈän-nä\ 6 *Pol., Swed.* \ˈän-nȧ\ 7 *Russ.* \ȧn-nə\
An·na·bel·la \ˌan-ə-ˈbel-ə\
An·nae·us *Lat.* \ə-ˈnē-əs\
Anne 1 \ˈan\ 2 *Fr.* \än, ȧn\ 3 *Swed.* \ˈȧn\ 4 *Ger.* **An·ne** \ˈän-ə\
An·ne·ma·rie *Ger.* \ˌän-ə-mä-ˈrē\
Annes·ley \ˈanz-lē\
An·net·ta 1 \ə-ˈnet-ə\ 2 *Ital.* \än-ˈnāt-tä\
An·nette 1 \a-ˈnet, ə-\ 2 *Fr.* \ȧ-net\ 3 *Ger.* **An·net·te** \ä-ˈnet-ə\
An·nia *Lat.* \ˈan-ē-ə\
An·ni·bal *Fr.* \ȧ-nē-bȧl\
An·ni·ba·le *Ital.* \än-ˈnē-bä-(ˌ)lā\
An·nie 1 \ˈan-ē\ 2 *Swed.* \ˈȧn-nē\
An·ni·us *Lat.* \ˈan-ē-əs\
An·non·ciade *Fr.* \ȧ-nō^{n}-syȧd\
An·sai *Jp.* \än-sī\
An·sa·no *Ital.* \än-ˈsän-ō\
An·sel \ˈan(t)-səl\
An·selm 1 \ˈan-ˌselm\ 2 *Ger.* \ˈän-ˌzelm\ 3 *Swed.* \ˈȧn-selm, -səlm\
An·selme *Fr.* \ä^{n}-selm\
An·sel·mo *Ital.* \än-ˈsel-mō\
An·son \ˈan(t)-sən\
An·stey \ˈan-stē\
An·tal *Hung.* \ˈän-ˌtäl\
An·ta·nas *Lith.* \än-ˈtän-äs\
An·te *Serb.-Cr.* \ˈȧn-te\
An·te·ro 1 *Finn.* \ˈȧn-ˌter-ˌō\ 2 *Port.* \ä^{n}(n)-ˈter-ü\
An·thelme *Fr.* \ä^{n}-telm\
An·tho·nie *Du.* \än-ˈtō-nē\
An·tho·nis, -nisz *Du.* \än-ˈtō-nəs\
An·tho·ny 1 \ˈan(t)-thə-nē, *chiefly Brit* ˈan-tə-\ 2 *Du.* \än-ˈtō-nē\
An·tim *Rom.* \än-ˈtēm\
An·ti·och, -okh *Russ.* \ən-tyi-ˈōk̲\
An·tioche *Fr.* \ä^{n}-tyȯsh\
An·ti·po·vich *Russ.* \ən-tyi-ˈpȯv-ˌyich\
An·tis·ti·us *Lat.* \an-ˈtis-tē-əs, -ch(ē)əs\
An·to *Du.* \ˈän-ˌtō\
An·toine 1 \ˈan-ˌtwän, an-ˈ\ 2 *Fr.* \ä^{n}-twȧn\
An·toi·nette 1 \ˌan-t(w)ə-ˈnet\ 2 *Fr.* \ä^{n}-twȧ-net\ 3 *Ger.* **An·toi·net·te** \ˌän-tō-ä-ˈnet-ə\
An·ton 1 \ˈant-^{ə}n, ˈan-ˌtän, -ˌtōn\ 2 *Czech, Swed.* \ˈȧn-ˌtȯn\ 3 *Du., Est., Norw.* \ˈän-ˌtȯn\ 4 *Ger.* \ˈȧn-tōn\ 5 *Ital.* \än-ˈtȯn\ 6 *Russ.* \(ˌ)ən-ˈtȯn\ 7 *Sp.* **An·tón** \än-ˈtȯn\
An·to·ni *Pol.* \ȧn-ˈtȯ-nē\
An·to·nia 1 \an-ˈtō-nē-ə, -ˈtōn-yə\ 2 *Fr.* \ä^{n}-tȯn-yȧ\ 3 *Ital.* \än-ˈtȯn-yä\ 4 *Span.* \än-ˈtōn-yä\
An·to·nie *Ger.* \än-ˈtōn-yə, -ˈtō-nē-ə\
An·to·nin 1 *Fr.* \ä^{n}-tȯ-na^{n}\ 2 *Czech* **An·to·nín, -nin** \ˈȧn-tȯn-ˌyēn\
An·to·ni·na *Russ.* \ən-(ˌ)tən-ˈyē-nə\
An·to·ni·nus *Lat.* \ˌan-tə-ˈnī-nəs\

An·to·nio 1 \anˈtō-nē-ˌō, -ˈtōn-(ˌ)yō\ 2 *Fr.* \ä^{n}-tȯn-yō\ 3 *Ger.* \än-ˈtōn-yō, -ˈtō-nē-ˌō\ 4 *Ital.* \än-ˈtȯn-yō\ 5 *Port.* \ä^{n}(n)-ˈtȯn-yü\ 6 *Span.* \än-ˈtōn-yō\ 7 *Port.* **An·tô·nio** \ä^{n}(n)-ˈtȯn-yü\
An·to·nios *Mod. Gk.* \än-ˈdȯn-(ˌ)yȯs\
An·to·nisz *Du.* \än-ˈtō-nəs\
An·to·ni·ta \ˌan-tə-ˈnēt-ə\
An·to·ni·us 1 \an-ˈtō-nē-əs, -ˈtōn-yəs\ 2 *Du.* \än-ˈtō-nē-ue̅s\
An·to·no·vich *Russ.* \(ˌ)ən-ˈtȯn(-əv)-ˌyich\
An·to·ny 1 \ˈan-tə-nē\ 2 *Du.* \än-ˈtō-nē\ 3 *Fr.* \ä^{n}-tȯ-nē\
An·toon *Du.* \ˈän-ˌtōn\
An·trim \ˈan-trəm\
Ant·ti *Finn.* \ˈȧnt-tē\
An·tun *Arab.* \ˈän-tün\ 2 *Serb.-Cr.* \ˈȧn-tün\
Ant·werp \ˈant-ˌwərp, ˈan-ˌtwərp\
An·zhe·li·ka *Russ.* \ən-zhil-ˈyē-kə\
An·zia *Russ.* \(ˌ)ənz-ˈyȧ\
Ao·nio *Ital.* \ä-ˈȯn-yō\
Ao·ni·us *Lat.* \ā-ˈō-nē-əs\
Aph·ra \ˈaf-rə\
Api·ra·na *Maori* \ä-pē-ˈrä-nä\
Apo·li·na·rio *Span.* \ä-pō-lē-ˈnär-yō\
Apo·li·na·ry *Pol.* \ȧ-ˌpȯl-ē-ˈnȧ-ri\
Apol·li·naire *Fr.* \ȧ-pȯ-lē-ner\
Apol·li·ni *Fr.* \ȧ-pȯ-lē-nē\
Apol·lon *Russ.* \ə-(ˌ)pəl-ˈlȯn\
Ap·ol·lo·ni·us 1 \ˌap-ə-ˈlō-nē-əs\ 2 *Ger.* **Apol·lo·ni·us** \ˌäp-ō-ˈlōn-yu̇s, -ˈlō-nē-u̇s\
Apo·lo *Luganda* \ä-ˈpō-lō\
Apos·to·lo *Ital.* \ä-ˈpȯs-tō-(ˌ)lō\
Ap·pia·no *Ital.* \äp-ˈpyä-nō\
Ap·pi·us *Lat.* \ˈap-ē-əs\
Ap·po·lo·nia *Pol.* \ˌap-pȯ-ˈlȯn-yȧ\
Ap·pu·le·ius *Lat.* \ˌap-yə-ˈlē-(y)əs\
Ap·thorp \ˈap-ˌthȯ(ə)rp\
Aq·ui·la *Lat.* \ˈak-wə-lə\
Ar·a·bel·la \ˌar-ə-ˈbel-ə\
Aram *Arm.* \är-ˈäm\
Ara·min·ta \ˌar-ə-ˈmint-ə\
Ar·bo·gast *Ger.* \ˈär-bō-ˌgäst\
Ar·buth·not, Ar·buth·nott \är-ˈbəth-nət, ˈär-bəth-ˌnät\
Ar·can·ge·lo *Ital.* \är-ˈkän-jä-(ˌ)lō\
Arch·dale \ˈärch-ˌdāl\
Ar·chey \ˈär-chē\
Ar·chi·bald \ˈär-chə-ˌbȯld, -bəld\
Ar·chie \ˈär-chē\
Ar·chi·mède *Fr.* \ȧr-shē-med\
Ar·chi·me·des \ˌär-kə-ˈmēd-ēz\
Ar·cisse *Fr.* \ȧr-sēs\
Ar·co *Ital.* \ˈär-kō\
Ar·da·bur·i·us *Lat.* \ˌärd-ə-ˈb(y)u̇r-ē-əs\
Ar·de·lia \är-ˈdē-lē-ə, -ˈdēl-yə\
Ar·den \ˈärd-^{ə}n\
Arendt, Arent *Du.* \ˈär-ənt\
Ar·e·tas \ˈar-ət-əs\
Arey *Ger.* \ˈär-ˌī\
Ar·gen·ti·no *Span.* \är-k̲än-ˈtē-nō\
Arias *Span.* \ˈär-yäs\
Arie \ˈa(ə)r-ē, ˈe(ə)r-ē\
Arild *Dan.* \ˈä-ˌrēl\
Ari·no·ri *Jp.* \är-ē-nō-rē\
Ar·io \ˈar-ē-ō, ˈer-\
Ari·star·co *Ital.* \ˌär-ē-ˈstär-kō\
Aris·tide 1 *Fr.* \ȧ-rē-stēd\ 2 *Ital.* **Ari·sti·de** \ä-ˈrēs-tē-(ˌ)dā\
Ar·is·ti·des 1 \ˌar-ə-ˈstīd-ēz\ 2 *Span.* **Aris·ti·des** \ä-rēs-ˈtē-t̲h̲äs\
Aris·to·te·lís *Gk.* \ˌär-ē-ˌstȯ-tə-ˈlēs\
Ari·to·mo *Jp.* \ä-rē-tō-mō\
Ar·ka·dy *Russ.* \(ˌ)ər-ˈkȧd-yəi\
Ar·kad·ye·vich *Russ.* \(ˌ)ər-ˈkȧd(-yəv)-ˌyich\
Ar·kle \ˈär-kəl\
Ar·koll \ˈär-käl, -kȯl\
Ark·wright \ˈärk-ˌrīt\
Ar·la·ni·bä·us *Ger.* \ˌär-lä-nē-ˈbe-u̇s\
Ar·ling·ton \ˈär-liŋ-tən\
Ar·lo \ˈär-(ˌ)lō\
Ar·man 1 \ˈär-mən\ 2 *Fr.* \ȧr-mä^{n}\
Ar·mand 1 \ˈär-mənd, -ˌmänd\ 2 *Fr.* \ȧr-mä^{n}\ 3 *Ger.* \ˈär-ˌmänt\ 4 *Rom.* \är-ˈmänd\
Ar·man·do *Ital., Span.* \är-ˈmän-dō\
Ar·mar \ˈär-mər\
Ar·mas *Finn.* \ˈȧr-ˌmȧs\
Ar·mau·er *Norw.* \ˈär-ˌmau̇-ər\
Ar·mi *Finn.* \ˈȧr-mē\
Ar·min 1 *Ger.* \är-ˈmēn\ 2 *Hung.* **Ár·min** \ˈȧr-min\
Ar·min·da \är-ˈmin-də\
Ar·mos *Finn.* \ˈȧr-ˌmȯs\
Arms \ˈärmz\
Ar·nail *Fr.* \ȧr-nȧy\
Ar·nal·dus *Lat.* \är-ˈnal-dəs, -ˈnäl-\
Ar·naud *Fr.* \ȧr-nō\
Ar·nault *Fr.* \ȧr-nō\
Ar·naut *Fr.* \ȧr-nō\
Arndt *Ger.* \ˈärnt\
Ar·ne *Norw.* \ˈär-nə\
A̧rn·grí·mur *Icel.* \ˈäd-^{ə}n-ˌgrē-mu̇r\
Ár·ni *Icel.* \ˈau̇d-ni\
Ar·no *Ger.* \ˈär-(ˌ)nō\
Ar·nold 1 \ˈärn-^{ə}ld\ 2 *Dan., Norw.* \ˈär-ˌnȯl\ 3 *Du., Ger.* \ˈär-ˌnȯlt\ 4 *Fr.* \ȧr-nȯld\
Ar·nol·do·vich *Russ.* \(ˌ)ər-ˈnȯl^{y}-dəv-ˌyich, -ˌdyich\
Ar·nol·dus *Du.* \är-ˈnäl-dœs\
Ar·nolt *Ger.* \ˈär-ˌnȯlt\
Ar·not, Ar·nott \ˈär-nət, -ˌnät\
Ar·nould *Fr.* \ȧr-nü\
Ar·noux \ˈär-ˌnü\
Ar·nulf *Ger., Norw.* \ˈär-(ˌ)nu̇lf\
Ar·nul·fo *Span.* \är-ˈnül-fō\
Aron 1 \ˈar-ən, ˈer-\ 2 *Latvian* \ˈär-wȯn\
Arp *Ger.* \ˈärp\
Ar·rell \ar-ˈel\
Ar·ri·go *Ital.* \är-ˈrē-gō\
Ar·sène *Fr.* \ȧr-sen\
Ar·se·nio 1 *Ital.* \är-ˈsen-yō\ 2 *Span.* \är-ˈsān-yō\
Ar·senne *Fr.* \ȧr-sen\
Ar·shi·le *Arm.* \är-ˈshē-lə\
Ar·ta·mon *Russ.* \ər-(ˌ)tə-ˈmȯn\
Ar·te·mas \ˈärt-ə-məs\
Ar·te·mis·ia \ˌärt-ə-ˈmiz-ē-ə, -ˈmizh(-ē)-ə, -ˈmish(-ē)-ə\
Ar·te·mus \ˈärt-ə-məs\
Ar·tha *Ger.* \ˈär-tä\
Ar·thur 1 \ˈär-thər\ 2 *Fr.* \ȧr-tue̅r\ 3 *Ger., Hung.* \ˈär-tu̇r\ 4 *Port.* \ər-ˈtür; ȧr-\
Art·tu·ri *Finn.* \ˈärt-tu̇r-ē\
Ar·tur 1 *Ger.* \ˈär-tu̇r\ 2 *Pol.* \ˈȧr-tür\ 3 *Port.* \ər-ˈtür; ȧr-\ 4 *Russ.* \(ˌ)ər-ˈtür\ 5 *Swed.* \ˈȧr-tər\
Ar·tu·ro 1 *Ital., Span.* \är-ˈtü-rō\ 2 *Port.* \ər-ˈtü-rü; ȧr-\
Ar·tus 1 *Du.* \ˈär-tœs\ 2 *Fr.* \ȧr-tœs\
Aru·nah \ə-ˈrü-nə\
Aru·thin *Arm.* \ˈär-ü-thēn\
Ar·vid *Swed.* \ˈȧr-vid\
Ary *Fr.* \ȧ-rē\
Asa \ˈā-sə\
As·ad *Arab.* \as-ˈad\
Asad·ul·lāh *Per.* \ȧ-sȧd-ül-ˈlȧ\
Asa·hel \ˈā-sə-ˌhel, ˈas-ə-, -həl, ˈā-səl\
Asa·ji·rō *Jp.* \ä-sä-jē-rō\
Asaph \ˈā-səf, ˈas-əf\
Asca·nio *Ital.* \äs-ˈkän-yō\
Asco·ni·us \as-ˈkō-nē-əs, əs-\
As·ger *Dan.* \ˈȧs-kər\
Ash \ˈash\
Ash·bel \ˈash-ˌbel\
Ash·bur·ton \ˈash-ˌbərt-^{ə}n\
Ash·bury \ˈash-ˌber-ē, -b(ə-)rē\
Ash·down \ˈash-ˌdau̇n\
Ash·er \ˈash-ər\
Ashe·ton \ˈash-tən\
Ashi·hei *Jp.* \ä-shē-hā\
Ash·ley \ˈash-lē\
Ash·man \ˈash-mən\
Ash·raf *Arab.* \ash-ˈraf\
Ash·ur \ˈash-ər\
Ash·ville \ˈash-ˌvil, -vəl\
Asin·i·us *Lat.* \ə-ˈsin-ē-əs\
As·kew \ˈas-ˌkyü\
As·mus 1 *Dan.* \ˈȧs-ˌmu̇s\ 2 *Ger.* \ˈäs-ˌmu̇s\
As·mus·sen *Dan.* \ˈȧs-ˌmu̇s-ən\
Asshe·ton \ˈash-tən\
Ass·mann *Ger.* \ˈäs-ˌmän\
A̱s·trid 1 *Dan.* \ˈȧs-trēt̲h̲\ 2 *Swed.* \ˈȧs-trid\
ʻAṭā *Pers.* \ˈȧ-tȧ\
Ata·na·sio 1 *Ital.* \ˌä-tä-ˈnäz-yō\ 2 *Span.* \ä-tä-ˈnäs-yō\
Atha·nase *Fr.* \ȧ-tȧ-näz\
Atha·na·sios *Mod. Gk.* \ˌä-thä-ˈnäs-(ˌ)yȯs\
Ath·a·na·si·us 1 \ˌath-ə-ˈnā-sh(ē-)əs, -sē-əs\ 2 *Ger.* **Atha·na·si·us** \ˌä-tä-ˈnäz-yu̇s, -ˈnäz-ē-u̇s\
Ath·el·stane \ˈath-əl-ˌstān\
Athé·na·ïs *Fr.* \ȧ-tā-nȧ-ēs\
Ath·ole \ˈath-əl\
Athon *Fr.* \ȧ-tō^{n}\
Atil·i·us *Lat.* \ə-ˈtil-ē-əs\
At·kins \ˈat-kənz\
At·lee \ˈat-lē\
Atsu·no·bu *Jp.* \ät-su̇n-ō-bu̇\
Atsu·ta·ne *Jp.* \ät-su̇-tä-ne\
At·ti·la *Hung.* \ä-ˈtil-ä\
At·ti·lio *Ital.* \ät-ˈtēl-yō\
At·ti·us *Lat.* \ˈat-ē-əs\
At·tus *Lat.* \ˈat-əs\
Au·bert *Fr.* \ō-ber\
Au·brey \ˈȯ-brē\
Auck·land \ˈȯk-lənd\
Au·drey \ˈȯ-drē\
Auge *Fr.* \ōzh\
Au·gier *Fr.* \ōzh-yā\
Au·gur \ˈȯ-gər\
Au·gust 1 \ˈȯ-gəst\ 2 *Dan., Finn., Ger.* \ˈau̇-gu̇st\ 3 *Pol.* \ˈau̇-(ˌ)güst\ 4 *Swed.* \ˈau̇-(ˌ)gəst\
Au·gus·ta 1 \ȯ-ˈgəs-tə, ə-\ 2 *Fr.* \ȯ-gue̅s-tȧ, ō-\ 3 *Ger.* \au̇-ˈgu̇s-tä\ 4 *Ital.* \au̇-ˈgü-stä\ 5 *Span.* \au̇-ˈg̅ü-stä\
Au·guste 1 *Fr.* \ȯ-gue̅st, ō-\ 2 *Ger.* **Au·gus·te** \au̇-ˈgu̇s-tə\
Au·gus·tin 1 \ȯ-ˈgəs-tən, ə-\ 2 *Czech* \ˈau̇-gu̇s-ˌtyin\ 3 *Du.* \ˈau̇-gue̅-ˌstĭn\ 4 *Fr.* \ȯ-gue̅s-ta^{n}, ō-\ 5 *Ger.* \ˌau̇-gu̇s-ˈtēn\ 6 *Swed.* \ˌau̇-gə-ˈstēn\
Au·gus·ti·nas *Lith.* \ˌau̇-gu̇s-ˈtī-näs\
Au·gus·tine 1 \ˈȯ-gəs-ˌtēn; ȯ-ˈgəs-tən, ə-\ 2 *Fr.* \ȯ-gue̅s-tēn, ō-\
Au·gus·ti·no *Ital.* \ˌau̇-gü-ˈstē-nō\
Au·gus·ti·nus *Lat.* \ˌȯ-gə-ˈstī-nəs\
Au·gus·to 1 *Ital.* \au̇-ˈgü-stō\ 2 *Port.* \au̇-ˈgüsh-tü; -ˈgüs-\ 3 *Span.* \au̇-ˈg̅ü-stō\
Au·gus·tus 1 \ȯ-ˈgəs-təs, ə-\ 2 *Ger.* \au̇-ˈgu̇s-tu̇s\
Au·lus *Lat.* \ˈȯ-ləs\
Au·rel 1 \ˈo(ə)r-(ˌ)el\ 2 *Ger.* \au̇-ˈrāl\
Au·rèle *Fr.* \ȯ-rel, ō-\
Au·re·lia·no *Span.* \au̇-rāl-ˈyän-ō\

Au·re·lio 1 *Ital.* \aù-ˈrel-yō\ 2 *Span.* \aù-ˈrāl-yō\
Au·re·lius 1 \ȯ-ˈrē-lē-əs, -ˈrē(ə)l-yəs\ 2 *Ger.* \aù-ˈrāl-yùs, -ˈrā-lē-ùs\
Au·re·o·lus *Lat.* \ȯ-ˈrē-ə-ləs\
Au·ro·bin·do \ˈȯr-ō-ˈbin-(ˌ)dō\
Au·ro·ra 1 \ə-ˈrōr-ə, ȯ-, -ˈrȯr-\ 2 *Ger., Span.* \aù-ˈrō-rä\
Au·rore *Fr.* \ȯ-rȯr, ō-\
Au·si·às *Catalan* \aù-zē-ˈäs\
Au·sone *Fr.* \ō-zȯn\
Au·so·nio *Ital.* \aù-ˈzȯn-yō\
Ave·li·no *Span.* \äb̲-ā-ˈlē-nō\
Av·gou·sti·nos *Mod. Gk.* \ˌäv-gü-ˈstē-(ˌ)nȯs\
Av·gust *Serb.-Cr.* \ˈȧv-güst\
Avid·i·us *Lat.* \ə-ˈvid-ē-əs\
Ávi·la *Span.* \ˈäb̲-ē-lä\
Av·i·tus *Lat.* \ˈav-ə-təs\
Avra·am *Russ.* \əv-(ˌ)rə-ˈȧm\
Awa *Jp.* \ä-wä\
Ax·el 1 \ˈak-səl\ 2 *Dan., Swed.* \ˈȧk-səl\ 3 *Ger., Norw.* \ˈäk-səl\
Ax·ton \ˈak-stən\
Ayer \ˈa(ə)r, ˈe(ə)r\
Ay·fa·ra \ˈā-fə-rə\
Ayl·mer \ˈā(ə)l-mər\
Ay·lott \ˈā-ˌlät, -lət\
Ayl·ward \ˈā(ə)l-wərd\
Ayn \ˈīn\
Ayns·ley \ˈānz-lē\
Ayr·ton \ˈa(ə)r-tən, ˈe(ə)r-; ˈa(ə)rt-^{ə}n, ˈe(ə)rt-\
Ays·cough \ˈas-ˌkyü, -kə; ˈās-kəf; -ˌkō\
Az·a·ri·ah \ˌaz-ə-ˈrī-ə\

Bab·bitt \ˈbab-ət\
Bac·chus \ˈbak-əs, ˈbäk-\
Bac·cio *Ital.* \ˈbät-chō\
Bache \ˈbāch\
Back·house \ˈbak-ˌ(h)aùs, -əs\
Back·us \ˈbak-əs\
Ba·con \ˈbā-kən\
Bad·de·ley \ˈbad-lē, -^{ə}l-ē\
Bad·ger \ˈbaj-ər\
Baer·mann \ˈba(ə)r-mən, ˈbe(ə)r-\
Bag·nall \ˈbag-nəl\
Bag·nell \ˈbag-nəl\
Bag·ot \ˈbag-ət\
Bag·shaw, Bag·shawe \ˈbag-ˌshȯ\
Bai·gan *Jp.* \bī-gän\
Bail·lie \ˈbā-lē\
Bain·bridge \ˈbān-(ˌ)brij\
Baines \ˈbānz\
Baird \ˈba(ə)rd, ˈbe(ə)rd\
Ba·ker \ˈbā-kər\
Bak·huis *Du.* \ˈbäk-ˌhœis\
Ba·kin *Jp.* \bä-kēn\
Bal *Marathi* \ˈbäl\
Balch \ˈbȯlch, ˈbȯlsh\
Bal·com \ˈbal-kəm\
Bal·das·sa·re *Ital.* \ˌbäl-däs-ˈsär-ā\
Bal·do·me·ro *Span.* \bäl-dō-ˈmā-rō\
Bal·duc·ci *Ital.* \bäl-ˈdüt-chē\
Bal·du·in *Ger.* \ˈbäl-dü-(ˌ)ēn\
Bal·dur *Ger.* \ˈbäl-dùr\
Ba·lil·la *Ital.* \bä-ˈlēl-lä\
Bá·lint *Hung.* \ˈbȧ-lint\
Bal·lard \ˈbal-ərd\
Bal·lin·ger \ˈbal-ən-jər\
Bal·ling·ton \ˈbal-iŋ-tən\
Bal·loch \ˈbal-ək̲, -ək\
Bal·ta·sar *Span.* \bäl-tä-ˈsär\
Bal·ta·za·ri·ni *Ital.* \bäl-ˌtä-zä-ˈrē-nē\
Bal·tha·sar 1 \ˈbal-thə-ˌzär; bal-ˈthā-zər, -ˈthaz-\ 2 *Du.* \ˈbäl-tä-ˌsär\ 3 *Fr.* \bȧl-tȧ-zȧr\ 4 *Ger.* \ˈbäl-tä-ˌzär\
Bal·tha·zar 1 \ˈbal-thə-ˌzär; bal-ˈthā-zər, -ˈthaz-\ 2 *Fr.* \bȧl-tȧ-zȧr\
Bal·zac *Fr.* \bȧl-zȧk\
Bam·fylde \ˈbam-ˌfēld\
Ban \ˈban\
Ban·as·tre \ˈban-ə-stər\
Ban·is·ter \ˈban-ə-stər\
Bank·head \ˈbaŋk-ˌhed\
Ban·kim *Bengali* \ˈbȯŋ-kim\
Banks \ˈbaŋ(k)s\
Ban·na·tyne \ˈban-ə-ˌtīn\
Ban·ner·man \ˈban-ər-mən\
Ban·nis·ter \ˈban-ə-stər\
Ban·zan *Jp.* \bän-zän\
Bap·tist 1 \ˈbap-təst\ 2 *Du., Ger.* \bäp-ˈtist\
Bap·tis·ta 1 \bap-ˈtis-tə\ 2 *Flem.* \bäp-ˈtis-tä\ 3 *Port.* \bə-ˈtēsh-tə; bȧ-ˈtēs-tȧ\
Bap·tiste *Fr.* \bȧ-tēst\
Bar *Heb.* \ˈbär\
Bar·ba·ra 1 \ˈbär-b(ə-)rə\ 2 *Ger., Ital.* \ˈbär-bär-ä\ 3 *Russ.* \(ˌ)bər-ˈbȧ-rə\
Bar·bee \ˈbär-(ˌ)bē\
Bar·ber \ˈbär-bər\
Bar·bra *Norw.* \ˈbär-brä\
Bar·bu *Rom.* \ˈbär-bü\
Bar·by \ˈbär-bē\
Ba·rend *Du.* \ˈbȧr-ənt\
Bar·ing \ˈba(ə)r-iŋ, ˈbe(ə)r-\
Bar·na·ba *Ital.* \ˈbär-näb-ä\
Bar·na·be 1 \ˈbar-nə-(ˌ)bē\ 2 *Fr.* **Bar·na·bé** \bȧr-nȧ-bā\
Bar·na·by \ˈbär-nə-ˌbē\
Bar·nas \ˈbär-nəs\
Bar·net \ˈbär-ˌnet, -nət\
Bar·nett \ˈbär-ˌnet, -nət; bär-ˈnet\
Bar·ney \ˈbär-nē\
Barn·well \ˈbärn-ˌwel, -wəl\
Bar·on \ˈbar-ən\
Bar·ret, Bar·rett \ˈbar-ət\
Bar·stow \ˈbär-ˌstō\
Bart \ˈbärt\
Bar·tel *Serb.-Cr.* \ˈbȧr-tel\
Barth *Du.* \ˈbärt\
Bar·thel *Ger.* \ˈbär-təl\
Bar·thé·le·mi *Fr.* \bȧr-tāl-(ə-)mē, -tel-mē\
Bar·thé·le·my *Fr.* \bȧr-tāl-(ə-)mē, -tel-mē\
Bar·thold *Du., Ger.* \ˈbär-ˌtȯlt\
Bar·thol·o·mae·us *Lat.* \bär-ˌtäl-ə-ˈmē-əs, -ˌthäl-\
Bar·tho·lo·mä·us 1 *Du.* \ˌbär-ˌtō-lō-ˈmā-œs\ 2 *Ger.* \ˌbär-ˌtō-lō-ˈme-ùs\
Bar·tho·lo·meu *Port.* \ˌbȧr-tü-lü-ˈmāù\
Bar·tho·lo·me·us *Du.* \ˌbär-ˌtō-lō-ˈmā-œs\
Bar·thol·o·mew \bär-ˈthäl-ə-ˌmyü\
Bar·tle \ˈbärt-^{ə}l\
Bart·lett, Bart·lette \ˈbärt-lət\
Bart·ley \ˈbärt-lē\
Bart·lit \ˈbärt-lət\
Bar·to·lo·mé *Span.* \bär-tō-lō-ˈmā\
Bar·to·lo·meo *Ital.* \ˌbär-tō-lō-ˈme-ō\
Bar·to·lo·meu *Port.* \ˌbȧr-tü-lü-ˈmāù\
Bar·to·lom·meo *Ital.* \ˌbär-tō-lōm-ˈme-ō\
Ba·ruch 1 *Du.* \ˈbȧr-ˌük̲\ 2 *Ger.* \ˈbär-ùk̲\
Bar·wick \ˈbar-ək\
Bar·zil·lai \bär-ˈzil(-ā)-ˌī\
Bas·com \ˈbas-kəm\
Bash·ford \ˈbash-fərd\
Ba·sile *Fr.* \bȧ-zēl\
Ba·si·lei·os *Gk.* \ˌbä-sē-ˈlā-ȯs\
Ba·si·lio 1 *Ital.* \bä-ˈzēl-yō\ 2 *Port.* **Ba·sí·lio** \bə-ˈzēl-yü; bȧ-\
Ba·si·li·us 1 *Ger.* \bä-ˈzēl-yùs, -ˈzē-lē-ùs; ˌbäz-i-ˈlē-ùs\ 2 *Lat.* **Ba·sil·i·us** \bə-ˈsil-ē-əs, -ˈzil-\
Bas·tia·no *Ital.* \bäs-ˈtyän-ō\
Bas·tien *Fr.* \bȧ-styaⁿ\
Bat \ˈbat\
Bate \ˈbāt\
Bat·tey \ˈbat-ē\
Bat·tis·ta *Ital.* \bät-ˈtēs-tä\
Bau·chop \ˈbȯ-kəp\
Bau·tis·ta *Span.* \baù-ˈtē-stä\
Bay·ard \ˈbī-ərd, ˈbā-\
Bayle \ˈbā(ə)l\
Bayles \ˈbā(ə)lz\
Bay·nard \ˈbā-nərd\
Baz·ley \ˈbäz-lē\
Beall \ˈbel\
Bé·at *Fr.* \bā-ȧ\
Be·a·trice 1 \ˈbē-(ə-)trəs, bē-ˈa-trəs\ 2 **Be·a·tri·ce** *Ger.* \ˌbā-ä-ˈtrē-sə\ 3 *Ital.* \ˌbā-ä-ˈtrē-chā\
Be·a·trix 1 \ˈbē-(ə-)triks, bē-ˈa-triks\ 2 *Ger.* \bā-ˈä-triks\ 3 *Lat.* \bē-ˈā-triks\
Be·a·tus 1 *Ger.* \bā-ˈä-tùs\ 2 *Lat.* \bē-ˈāt-əs\
Beau·champ \ˈbē-chəm\
Beau·fort \ˈbō-fərt, ˈbyü-\
Beau·mont \ˈbō-ˌmänt, -mənt\
Beau·voir \ˈbē-vər, bōv-ˈwär\
Beck·les \ˈbek-əlz\
Bede \ˈbēd\
Be·dell \bə-ˈdel\
Bed·ford \ˈbed-fərd\
Be·dřich *Czech* \ˈbed-rzhik̲\
Bee·be, Bee·bee \ˈbē-bē\
Beer *Ger.* \ˈbār\
Beete \ˈbēt\
Bee·ver \ˈbē-vər\
Beh·ram·ji *Parsi* \bā-ˈräm-jē\
Beil·by \ˈbē(ə)l-bē\
Bei·san·jin *Jp.* \bā-sän-jēn\
Bel \ˈbel\
Be·la 1 \ˈbē-lə, ˈbā-; ˈbel-ə\ 2 *Hung.* **Bé·la** \ˈbā-lä\
Bel·ding \ˈbel-diŋ\
Bel·fort \ˈbel-fərt\
Be·li·sa·rio 1 *Ital.* \ˌbā-lē-ˈzär-yō\ 2 *Span.* \bā-lē-ˈsär-yō\
Bel·knap \ˈbel-ˌnap\
Bell \ˈbel\
Bel·la 1 \ˈbel-ə\ 2 *Ger.* \ˈbel-ä\ 3 *Ital.* \ˈbel-lä\
Bel·la·my \ˈbel-ə-mē\
Bel·las \ˈbel-əs\
Belle \ˈbel\
Bel·lew \ˈbel-ˌ(y)ü, bə-ˈl(y)ü\
Bel·lo·ni *Fr.* \be-lȯ-nē\
Bel·ton \ˈbelt-^{ə}n\
Bel·trán *Span.* \bel-ˈträn\
Bel·va \ˈbel-və\
Ben \ˈben\
Be·ne·det·to *Ital.* \ˌbā-nā-ˈdāt-tō\
Ben·e·dict 1 \ˈben-ə-ˌdikt, *Brit also* ˈben-ət\ 2 **Be·ne·dict** *Du.* \ˈbā-nə-(ˌ)dikt\ 3 *Ger.* \ˈbā-nā-(ˌ)dikt\ 4 *Fr.* **Bé·né·dict** \bā-nā-dēkt\
Be·ne·dic·ta *Ger.* \ˌbā-nā-ˈdik-tä\
Ben·e·dic·tus *Lat.* \ˌben-i-ˈdik-təs\
Be·ne·dikt *Ger.* \ˈbā-nā-(ˌ)dikt\
Be·ne·dik·tus *Ger.* \ˌbā-nā-ˈdik-tùs\
Benge \ˈbenj\
Bengt *Swed.* \ˈbeŋt\
Bé·ni *Hung.* \ˈbā-nē\
Be·nia·mi·no *Ital.* \ˌbān-yä-ˈmē-nō\
Be·nigne *Fr.* \bā-nēnʸ\
Be·nig·no *Span.* \bā-ˈnēg-nō\
Be·nig·nus 1 \bi-ˈnig-nəs\ 2 *Dan.* \be-ˈnēg-nùs\ 3 *Ger.* \bā-ˈnig-nùs\
Be·ni·to *Ital., Span.* \be-ˈnē-tō\
Ben·ja·mim *Port.* \ˌbāⁿ-zhə-ˈmēⁿ; -zhȧ-\
Ben·ja·min 1 \ˈbenj-(ə-)mən\ 2 *Du.* \ˈben-yȧ-mən\ 3 *Fr.* \baⁿ-zhȧ-maⁿ\ 4 *Ger.* \ˈben-yä-(ˌ)mēn\ 5 *Hung.* \ˈben-yȧ-(ˌ)min\

Benn \ˈben\
Ben·net, Ben·nett \ˈben-ət\
Ben·ning \ˈben-iŋ\
Ben·ning·ton \ˈben-iŋ-tən\
Ben·no 1 *Ger.* \ˈben-ō\ 2 *Russ.* \ˈben-nə\
Ben·ny \ˈben-ē\
Be·noist \bən-ˈwä\
Be·noît *Fr.* \bən-wȧ\
Be·noîte *Fr.* \bən-wȧt\
Ben·oni \ben-ˈō-ˌnī, bə-ˈnō-\
Be·noz·zo *Ital.* \bā-ˈnȯt-tsō\
Ben·theim *Dan.* \ˈbin-ˌtām\
Ben·to *Port.* \ˈbā^{n}(n)-tü\
Ben·ve·nu·to *Ital.* \ˌbān-vā-ˈnü-tō\
Be·rend *Ger.* \ˈbā-rənt\
Be·ri·ah \bə-ˈrī-ə\
Berke·ley \ˈbərk-lē, *Brit usu* ˈbärk-\
Ber·na \ˈbər-nə\
Ber·na·bé *Span.* \ber-nä-ˈb̲ā\
Ber·na·bò *Ital.* \ˌbār-nä-ˈbȯ\
Ber·na·dotte \ˈbər-nə-ˌdät\
Ber·nal *Span.* \ber-ˈnäl\
Ber·nard 1 \bər-ˈnärd, ˈbər-ˌnärd, ˈbər-nərd\ 2 *Du.* \ˈber-ˌnärt\ 3 *Fr.* \ber-nȧr\ 4 *Pol.* \ˈber-nȧrt\
Ber·nar·dim *Port.* \bər-nər-ˈdē^{n}; ber-nȧr-\
Ber·nar·dine *Fr.* \ber-nȧr-dēn\
Ber·nar·di·no 1 *Ital.* \ˌbār-när-ˈdē-nō\ 2 *Port.* \bər-nər-ˈdē-nü; ber-nar-\ 3 *Span.* \ber-när-ˈt͟hē-nō\
Ber·nar·do 1 *Ital.* \ber-ˈnär-dō\ 2 *Port.* \bər-ˈnȧr-dü; ber-\ 3 *Span.* \ber-ˈnär-t͟hō\
Ber·nar·do·vich *Russ.* \byir-ˈnȧrd(-əv)-ˌyich\
Ber·narr \(ˌ)bər-ˈnär\
Ber·nat *Catalan* \ber-ˈnät\
Ber·nay \ˈbər-(ˌ)nā, bər-ˈnā\
Bern·hard 1 \ˈbər-ˌnärd, ˈbərn-ˌhärd\ 2 *Dan., Du., Ger.* \ˈbern-ˌhärt\ 3 *Swed.* \ˈber-nȧrd\
Bern·hardt \ˈbərn-ˌhärt\
Bern·har·dus 1 *Ger.* \bern-ˈhär-du̇s\ 2 *Lat.* \ˌbərn-ˈhär-dəs\
Ber·nice \(ˌ)bər-ˈnēs, ˈbər-nəs\
Bernt *Ger., Norw.* \ˈbernt\
Ber·nulf \ˈbər-nəlf\
Ber·rie·dale \ˈber-ə-ˌdāl\
Ber·ri·en \ˈber-ē-ən\
Ber·ry \ˈber-ē\
Bert 1 \ˈbərt\ 2 *Ger.* \ˈbert\
Ber·ta 1 \ˈbərt-ə\ 2 *Ger.* \ˈber-tä\
Ber·tel *Dan., Swed.* \ˈber-təl\
Ber·tha 1 \ˈbər-thə\ 2 *Ger.* \ˈber-tä\
Berthe *Fr.* \bert\
Ber·thel *Dan.* \ˈbert-əl\
Ber·thold 1 *Fr.* \ber-tȯld\ 2 *Ger.* \ˈber-ˌtȯlt\
Ber·tho·let *Fr.* \ber-tȯ-le\
Ber·tie \ˈbərt-ē\
Ber·ti·ta \bər-ˈtēt-ə\
Ber·told, Ber·tolt *Ger.* \ˈber-ˌtȯlt\
Ber·ton 1 \bərt-^{ə}n\ 2 *Fr.* \ber-tō^{n}\
Ber·tram \ˈbər-trəm\
Ber·trand 1 \ˈbər-trənd\ 2 *Fr.* \ber-trä^{n}\
Ber·wick \ˈber-ik\
Bess \ˈbes\
Bes·sie \ˈbes-ē\
Be·thune \ˈbēt-^{ə}n\
Bet·je *Du.* \ˈbech-ə\
Bet·sy \ˈbet-sē\
Bet·ti·na 1 \bə-ˈtē-nə, be-\ 2 *Ger.* \be-ˈtē-nä\
Bet·ti·no *Ital.* \bāt-ˈtē-nō\
Bet·ton \ˈbet-^{ə}n\
Betts \ˈbets\
Bet·ty \ˈbet-ē\
Beu·lah \ˈbyü-lə\
Bev·er·ley, Bev·er·ly \ˈbev-ər-lē\
Bev·il \ˈbev-əl\
Bey·non \ˈbī-nən\
Bhai *Punjabi* \ˈbī\
Bhim·rao *Marathi* \ˈbēm-ˌrau̇\
Bhu·la·bhai *Gujarati* \ˈbu̇l-ə-ˌbī\
Bian·ca *Ital.* \ˈbyäŋ-kä\
Bibb \ˈbib\
Bib·bins \ˈbib-ənz\
Bi·che·no \bə-ˈshē-(ˌ)nō\
Bick·er·ton \ˈbik-ərt-^{ə}n, -ər-tən\
Bick·ford \ˈbik-fərd\
Bick·nell \ˈbik-nəl\
Bid·dulph \ˈbid-əlf\
Bien·ai·mé *Fr.* \bya^{n}-ne-mā\
Bien·ve·nu *Fr.* \byä^{n}v-(ə-)nue̅\
Big·e·low \ˈbig-ə-ˌlō\
Big·ham \ˈbig-əm\
Bill \ˈbil\
Bil·lie \ˈbil-ē\
Bil·ly \ˈbil-ē\
Bin·ning \ˈbin-iŋ\
Bi·on \ˈbī-ən\
Bip·in *Bengali* \ˈbip-in\
Birch \ˈbərch\
Bir·chard \ˈbər-chərd\
Bird·wood \ˈbərd-ˌwu̇d\
Birge \ˈbərj\
Bir·ger *Swed.* \ˈbir-yər\
Birk·beck \ˈbər(k)-ˌbek\
Bir·ket \ˈbər-ˌket, -ˌkit, -kət\
Bir·ney \ˈbər-nē\
Bi·ró *Hung.* \ˈbi(ə)r-(ˌ)ō\
Bi·sha·ra *Arab.* \bē-ˈshär-ä\
Bis·marck \ˈbiz-ˌmärk\
Bis·sett \ˈbis-ˌet, -ət\
Bis·sot *Fr.* \bē-sō\
Bjar·ni *Icel.* \ˈbyäd-nē\
Björn *Norw.* \ˈbyœ̅rn\
Björns·son *Swed.* \ˈbyœrn-sȯn\
Björn·stjer·ne *Norw.* \ˈbyœ̅rn-ˌstyer-nə\
Black·er \ˈblak-ər\
Black·ford \ˈblak-fərd\
Black·ie \ˈblak-ē\
Black·man \ˈblak-mən\
Black·wood \ˈblak-ˌwu̇d\
Blaine \ˈblān\
Blair \ˈbla(ə)r, ˈble(ə)r\
Blaise *Fr.* \blez\
Blake \ˈblāk\
Blan·chard \ˈblan-chərd, -shərd\
Blanche 1 \ˈblanch\ 2 *Fr.* \blä^{n}sh\
Bland·ford \ˈblan(d)-fərd\
Blan·ford \ˈblan-fərd\
Blas *Span.* \ˈbläs\
Bled·soe \ˈbled-ˌsō\
Bleeck·er \ˈblēk-ər\
Bliss \ˈblis\
Blood \ˈbləd\
Blos·si·us *Lat.* \ˈbläs-ē-əs\
Blount \ˈblənt\
Blythe \ˈblīt͟h\
Bo *Swed.* \ˈbü\
Bo·ak·ye *Twi* \bō-ˈäk-yē\
Board·man \ˈbō(ə)rd-mən, ˈbȯ(ə)rd-\
Bob \ˈbäb\
Bob·by \ˈbäb-ē\
Boc·cac·cio *Ital.* \bōk-ˈkät-chō\
Bo·dae·us *Du.* \bō-ˈdā-ues\
Bod·ham \ˈbäd-əm\
Bo·do *Ger.* \ˈbō-(ˌ)dō\
Bo·e·ti·us *Du.* \bō-ˈā-tē-ues\
Bog·dan 1 *Bulg., Pol.* \ˈbȯg-ˌdȧn\ 2 *Rom.* \bȯg-ˈdän\ 3 *Russ.* \(ˌ)bəg-ˈdȧn\
Bo·gert \ˈbō-gərt\
Bo·gis·law *Ger.* \ˈbō-gis-ˌläf\
Bo·gu·mil *Ger.* \ˈbō-gu̇m-ˌēl\
Bo·gu·mił *Pol.* \bȯ-ˈgü-mēl\
Boh·dan *Ukrain.* \ˈbȯg-dȧn\
Bohn \ˈbōn\
Bo·ho·mi·el \bō-ˈhō-mē-əl\
Bo·hu·slav *Czech* \ˈbȯ-hu̇-slȧf\
Boies \ˈbȯiz\
Bo·le·sław *Pol.* \bȯ-ˈles-lȧf\
Bo·le·sław·o·wicz *Pol.* \bȯ-les-ˈlȧv-ȯ-vēch\
Bol·i·var \ˈbäl-ə-vər\
Bol·ler \ˈbäl-ər\
Bol·ling \ˈbō-liŋ\
Bom·bas·tus *Ger.* \bȯm-ˈbäs-tu̇s\
Bon *Fr.* \bō^{n}\
Bo·na *Ger.* \ˈbō-nä\
Bon·a·my \ˈbän-ə-mē\
Bon·ar \ˈbän-ər\
Bo·na·ven·tu·ra 1 *Ger.* \ˌbō-nä-ven-ˈtü-rä\ 2 *Ital.* \ˌbȯ-näv-ān-ˈtü-rä\
Bon·a·ven·ture 1 \ˌbän-ə-ˈven-chər, ˈbän-ə-ˌ\ 2 *Fr.* **Bo·na·ven·ture** \bȯ-nȧ-vä^{n}-tue̅r\
Bo·na·wen·tu·ra *Pol.* \ˌbȯ-nȧ-ven-ˈtü-rȧ\
Bon·i·face 1 \ˈbän-ə-fəs, -ˌfās\ 2 *Fr.* **Bo·ni·face** \bȯ-nē-fȧs\
Bo·ni·fa·cio 1 *Ital.* \ˌbē-nē-ˈfäch-ō\ 2 *Port.* **Bo·ni·fá·cio** \bü-nē-ˈfȧs-yü\
Bon·i·fa·cius 1 \ˌbän-ə-ˈfā-sh(ē-)əs\ 2 *Ger.* **Bo·ni·fa·ci·us** \ˌbō-nē-ˈfäts-yu̇s, -ˈfät-sē-u̇s\
Bon·nell \bə-ˈnel\
Bon·ne·vie *Norw.* \ˈbȯn-nə-(ˌ)vē\
Bon·not *Fr.* \bȯ-nō\
Boog \ˈbōg\
Book·er \ˈbu̇k-ər\
Boor·man \ˈbu̇(ə)r-mən\
Boott \ˈbüt\
Bo·ris 1 \ˈbōr-əs, ˈbȯr-, ˈbär-\ 2 *Bulg.* \ˈbȯr-(ˌ)ēs, bȯ-ˈrēs\ 3 *Russ.* \(ˌ)bər-ˈyēs\
Bo·ri·so·vich *Russ.* \(ˌ)bər-ˈyēs(-əv)-ˌyich\
Bor·lase \ˈbȯr-ləs\
Bor·ne·mann *Norw.* \ˈbȯr-nə-ˌmän\
Bör·ri·es *Ger.* \ˈbœr-yəs, -ē-əs\
Borth·wick \ˈbȯrth-ˌwik\
Bos·well \ˈbäz-ˌwel, -wəl\
Bos·wood \ˈbäz-ˌwu̇d\
Bo·tho *Ger.* \ˈbō-(ˌ)tō\
Bots·ford \ˈbäts-fərd\
Bou·chard *Fr.* \bü-shȧr\
Bou·det *Fr.* \bü-de\
Bou·ver·ie \ˈbü-vər-ē\
Bowd·ler \ˈbau̇d-lər\
Bow·en \ˈbō-ən\
Bow·ers \ˈbau̇-ərz\
Bowes \ˈbōz\
Bowles \ˈbōlz\
Bow·ling \ˈbō-liŋ\
Bowne \ˈbau̇n\
Boy \ˈbȯi\
Boyd \ˈbȯid\
Boyn·ton \ˈbȯin-tən\
Bo·že·na *Czech* \ˈbȯ-zhen-ȧ\
Brace \ˈbrās\
Brack·en \ˈbrak-ən\
Brack·ett \ˈbrak-ət\
Brad·ley \ˈbrad-lē\
Brad·street \ˈbrad-ˌstrēt\
Brad·war·dine \ˈbrad-wər-ˌdēn\
Brai·nard \ˈbrā-nərd\
Brai·nerd \ˈbrā-nərd\
Braith·waite \ˈbrāth-ˌwāt\
Bram \ˈbram\
Bram·well \ˈbram-ˌwel, -wəl\

\ə\ **abut** \$^{ə}$\ **kitten,** *Fr.* **table** \ər\ **further** \a\ **ash** \ā\ **ace** \ä\ **cot, cart** \au̇\ **out** \ch\ **chin** \e\ **bet** \ē\ **easy** \g\ **go** \i\ **hit** \ī\ **ice** \j\ **job** \ŋ\ **sing** \ō\ **go** \ȯ\ **law** \ȯi\ **boy** \th\ **both** \t͟h\ **the** \ü\ **loot** \u̇\ **foot** \y\ **yet** \zh\ **vision** \ȧ, b̲, g̲, k̲, ^{n}, œ, œ̅, ue, ue̅, ^{y}\ *see* Guide to Pronunciation

Bran·a·mour 1 \'bran-ə-ˌmu̇(ə)r\ 2 *Fr.* \brȧ-nȧ-mür\
Branch \'branch\
Bran·der \'bran-dər\
Bran·dreth \'bran-drəth\
Bran·ford \'bran-fərd\
Bran·ko *Serb.-Cr.* \'brȧŋ-kȯ\
Bran·ston \'bran(t)-stən\
Brant·ley \'brant-lē\
Bran·well \'bran-ˌwel, -wəl\
Bran·white \'bran-ˌ(h)wīt\
Bras·sey \'bras-ē\
Brau·lio *Span.* \'brau̇l-yō\
Brax·ton \'brak-stən\
Braz *Port.* \'brȧsh; 'brȧs\
Braz·il \'braz-əl\
Breck \'brek\
Bre·da *Norw.* \'brā-dä\
Breese \'brēz\
Brem·ner \'brem-nər\
Bren·da \'bren-də\
Bren·dan \'bren-dən\
Brere·ton \'bri(ə)rt-ᵊn, 'bra(ə)rt-, 'bre(ə)rt-\
Bret \'bret\
Bret·land \'bret-lənd\
Brett \'bret\
Bret·ting·ham \'bret-iŋ-əm\
Bre·vard \bre-'värd\
Bre·voort \brə-'vō(ə)rt, -'vȯ(ə)rt\
Brew·er·ton \'brü-ərt-ᵊn, 'bru̇(-ə)rt-ᵊn\
Brew·ing·ton \'brü-iŋ-tən\
Bri·an \'brī-ən\
Brice \'brīs\
Bri·cie \'brī-sē\
Bridg·er \'brij-ər\
Bridg·es \'brij-əs\
Bri·dle \'brīd-ᵊl\
Brig·ham \'brig-əm\
Brigh·ty \'brīt-ē\
Bri·git·ta 1 *Ital.* \brē-'jēt-tä\ 2 *Swed.* \bri-'git-tȧ\
Brin·dly \'brin(d)-lē\
Brin·ker·hoff \'briŋ-kər-ˌhȯf\
Brin·ley \'brin-lē\
Brins·ley \'brinz-lē\
Brin·ton \'brint-ᵊn\
Bris·ben \'briz-bən\
Bris·bin \'briz-bən\
Bri·tes *Port.* \'brē-tish; -tis\
Brit·on \'brit-ᵊn\
Brit·ten \'brit-ᵊn\
Broa·dus \'brȯd-əs\
Brock·den \'bräk-dən\
Brock·holst \'bräk-ˌhōlst\
Brock·man \'bräk-mən\
Brod·head \'bräd-ˌhed\
Bro·die \'brōd-ē\
Brom·ley \'bräm-lē, 'brəm-\
Bro·ni·slaw *Pol.* \brȯ-'nē-slȧf\
Bro·ni·sła·wa *Pol.* \brȯ-nē-'slȧ-və\
Brön·num *Dan.* \'brœn-u̇m\
Bron·son \'brän-sən\
Bron·terre \brän-'ta(ə)r, -'te(ə)r\
Bron·wyn \'brän-wən\
Brook \'bru̇k\
Brooke \'bru̇k\
Bror *Swed.* \'brür\
Bros·trup *Norw.* \'brȯ-stru̇p\
Brougham \'brü(-ə)m\
Broun \'brün\
Brow·nell \brau̇-'nel; 'brau̇-ˌnel, -nəl\
Brown·son \'brau̇n-sən\
Bruce \'brüs\
Bru·ines \'brü-ənz\
Brun *Norw.* \'brün\
Brune \'brün\
Bru·net·to *Ital.* \brü-'nāt-tō\
Brun·lees \'brən-ˌlēz\
Bru·no 1 \'brü-(ˌ)nō\ 2 *Fr.* \brᵫ-nō\ 3 *Ger., Ital., Swed.* \'brü-(ˌ)nō\ 4 *Lith.* \'bru̇n-ȯ\
Bru·yn \'brü-ən\
Bry·an \'brī-ən\
Bry·ant \'brī-ənt\
Bry·die \'brīd-ē\
Bryn·jolf 1 *Icel.* \'brin-ˌyȯlv\ 2 *Norw.* \'brᵫ̄n-ˌyȯlf\
Bry·son \'brī-sən\
Bubb \'bəb\
Bu·ben·heim \'bü-bən-ˌhīm\
Buck \'bək\
Buck·hout \'bək-ˌau̇t\
Buck·ley \'bək-lē\
Buck·lin \'bək-lən\
Buck·min·ster \'bək-ˌmin-stər\
Buck·ner \'bək-nər\
Budes *Fr.* \bᵫ̄d\
Bud·ing·ton \'bəd-iŋ-tən\
Bu·el, Bu·ell \'byü(-ə)l\
Bugge \'bəg\
Bui·dhe *Ir. Gael., Sc. Gael.* \'bü-ə(-t͟hə)\
Bulk·ley \'bəlk-lē\
Bul·lock \'bu̇l-ək\
Bü·low *Dan.* \'bᵫ̄-ˌlau̇\
Bul·strode \'bu̇l-ˌstrōd\
Bunce \'bun(t)s\
Bun·chō *Jp.* \bu̇n-chō\
Bun·go·rō *Jp.* \bu̇n-gō-rō\
Bun·ji *Jp.* \bu̇n-jē\
Bun·ker \'bəŋ-kər\
Bun·so·do *Jp.* \bu̇n-sō-dō\
Buon·ac·cor·so *Ital.* \ˌbwȯn-äk-'kōr-sō\
Buo·na·parte \'bō-nə-ˌpärt\
Bur·bank \'bər-ˌbaŋk\
Bur·chard \'bər-chərd\
Bur·dett \bər-'det\
Bur·don \'bərd-ᵊn\
Bu·reau *Fr.* \bᵫ̄-rō\
Bur·ford \'bər-fərd\
Bur·ges, Bur·gess \'bər-jəs\
Burg·hardt \'bərg-ˌhärd\
Burk·hard *Ger.* \'bu̇rk-ˌhärt\
Bur·kard *Ger.* \'bu̇r-ˌkärt\
Bur·kitt \'bər-kət\
Bur·ley \'bər-lē\
Bur·lin·game \'bər-liŋ-ˌgām, -lən-\
Bur·man \'bər-mən\
Burr \'bər\
Bur·rage \'bər-ij, 'bə-rij\
Bur·rill \'bər-əl, 'bə-rəl, 'bu̇r-əl\
Bur·ris \'bər-əs, 'bə-rəs, 'bu̇r-əs\
Bur·ritt \'bər-ət, 'bə-rət, 'bu̇r-ət\
Burt \'bərt\
Bur·ten·shaw \'bərt-ᵊn-ˌshȯ\
Bur·tis \'bərt-əs\
Bur·ton \'bərt-ᵊn\
Bush \'bu̇sh\
Bush·rod \'bu̇sh-ˌräd\
Bus·ter \'bəs-tər\
Bus·till \'bəs-təl\
But·ter·worth \'bət-ər-ˌwərth\
Bux·ton \'bək-stən\
Bu·yo *Jp.* \bu̇-yō\
By·am \'bī-əm\
By·ford \'bī-fərd\
Byles \'bī(ə)lz\
Bysshe \'bish\

Cab·ell \'kab-əl\
Cä·ci·lia *Ger.* \tset-'sēl-yä, -'sē-lē-ä\
Cad·mus \'kad-məs\
Ca·dog·an \kə-'dəg-ən\
Cad·wal·la·der \kad-'wȯl-ə-dər\
Ca·dy \'kā-dē\
Cae·cil·ius *Lat.* \si-'sil-ē-əs, -'sil-yəs\
Cae·li·us *Lat.* \'sē-lē-əs\
Cae·pio *Lat.* \'sē-pē-(ˌ)ō\
Cae·sar \'sē-zər\
Cae·so *Lat.* \'sē-zō, -sō\
Ca·ius \'kā-əs, 'kī-\
Cal·braith \'kal-ˌbreth\
Cal·der \'kȯl-dər\
Cald·well \'kȯl-ˌdwel, -dwəl, 'käl-\
Cale \'kā(ə)l\
Ca·leb \'kā-ləb\
Cal·houn \kal-'hün, kə-\
Ca·lix·to *Span.* \kä-'lē(k)s-tō\
Cal·kins \'kȯ-kənz\
Call \'kȯl\
Cal·la·han \'kal-ə-ˌhan, -hən\
Call·cott \'kȯl-kət\
Cal·ly·han \'kal-ə-ˌhan, -hən\
Ca·louste *Arm.* \kä-'lüst\
Cal·pur·ni·us *Lat.* \kal-'pər-nē-əs\
Cal·vagh *Ir. Gael.* \'kal-vək̲\
Cal·ver·ley \'kal-vər-lē\
Cal·vert \'kal-vərt\
Cal·vin \'kal-vən\
Cam \'kam\
Cam·el \'kam-əl\
Ca·mil·la 1 \kə-'mil-ə\ 2 *Ital.* \kä-'mēl-lä\ 3 *Norw.* \kä-'mil-lä\
Ca·mille 1 \kə-'mē(ə)l\ 2 *Fr.* \kȧ-mēy\
Ca·mil·lo 1 *Ger.* \kä-'mil-ō\ 2 *Ital.* \kä-'mēl-lō\ 3 *Port.* \kə-'mē-lü; kȧ-\
Ca·mi·lo 1 *Port.* \kə-'mēlü; kȧ-\ 2 *Span.* \kä-'mē-lō\
Cam·mer·mey·er *Norw.* \'käm-mər-ˌmā-ər\
Camp \'kamp\
Camp·bell \'kam-bəl, *US also* 'kam-əl\
Ca·na·let·to *Ital.* \ˌkän-ä-'let-tō\
Can·di·do 1 *Ital.* \'kän-dē-dō\ 2 **Cán·di·do** *Port.* \'kȧn-dē-t͟hō\ 3 *Span.* \'kän-dē-t͟hō\
Can·di·dus *Ger.* \'kän-dē-du̇s\
Can·field \'kan-ˌfēld\
Cant·well \'kant-ˌwel, -wəl\
Can·vass \'kan-vəs\
Ca·pell \'kā-pəl\
Ca·rad·oc \kȧ-'rȧd-ȯg, kə-'rad-ək\
Car·dale \'kär-ˌdāl\
Car·di·nal *Fr.* \kȧr-dē-nȧl\
Car·do·sa *Port.* \kər-'dȯ-zə; kȧr-'dȯ-zȧ\
Car·do·zo *Port.* \kər-'dō-zü; kȧr-\
Card·well \'kär-(ˌ)dwel, -dwəl\
Ca·rel 1 *Du.* \'kär-əl\ 2 *Fr.* \kȧ-rel\
Car·ey \'ka(ə)r-ē, 'ke(ə)r-\
Ca·ril·lo *Span.* \kä-'rē(l)-yō\
Ca·rit *Dan.* \'kär-(ˌ)ēt\
Carl 1 \'kär(-ə)l\ 2 *Dan., Ger., Norw., Swed.* \'kärl\ 3 *Finn.* \'kȧrl\
Car·la \'kär-lə\
Carle 1 \'kär(-ə)l\ 2 *Fr.* \kȧrl\
Car·less \'kär-ləs\
Carle·ton \'kär(-ə)l-tən, 'kärlt-ᵊn\
Car·let·to *Ital.* \kär-'lāt-tō\
Carl·in \'kär-lən\
Car·li·no *Ital.* \kär-'lē-nō\
Carll \'kär(-ə)l\
Car·lo 1 *Eng., Ital.* \'kär-(ˌ)lō\ 2 *Swed.* \'kȧr-lō\
Car·lo·man *Fr.* \kȧr-lȯ-mäⁿ\
Car·los 1 \'kär-(ˌ)lōs, -ləs\ 2 *Ger.* \'kär-ˌlȯs\ 3 *Port.* \'kȧr-lüsh; -lüs\ 4 *Span.* \'kär-lōs\
Car·lot·ta 1 \kär-'lät-ə\ 2 *Ital.* \kär-'lȯt-tä\
Carl·ton \'kär(-ə)l-tən, 'kärlt-ᵊn\
Car·lyle \kär-'lī(ə)l, 'kär-ˌ\
Car·mel·a \kär-'mel-ə\
Car·mi \'kär-ˌmī\

Car·mi·chael \'kär-ˌmī-kəl, kär-'\
Car·nac \'kär-ˌnak\
Car·ol 1 \'kar-əl\ 2 *Rom.* **Ca·rol** \'kär-ȯl\
Car·o·li·na 1 \ˌkar-ə-'k-nə\ 2 **Ca·ro·li·na** *Ital.* \ˌkär-ō-'lē-nä\ 3 *Span.* \kär-ō-'lē-nä\
Car·o·line 1 \'kar-ə-ˌlīn, -lən\ 2 *Fr.* **Ca·ro·line** \ká-rȯ-lēn, kä-\
Ca·ro·lus 1 *Fr.* \ká-rȯ-lūēs\ 2 *Lat.* **Car·o·lus** \'kar-ə-ləs\
Ca·ro·lus·zoon *Du.* \'kär-ə-lœs-ˌōn\
Car·o·lyn \'kar-ə-lən\
Car·rie \'ka(ə)r-ē, 'ke(ə)r-ē\
Car·roll \'kar-əl\
Car·ruth·ers \kə-'rəth-ərz\
Car·ry \'ka(ə)r-ē, 'ke(ə)r-ē\
Car·sten *Dan., Ger., Norw.* \'kär-stən\
Car·ty \'kärt-ē\
Ca·ruth·ers \kə-'rəth-ərz\
Car·va·lho *Port.* \kər-'vál-yü\
Car·vell \'kär-vəl\
Car·vill \'kär-vəl\
Cary \'ka(ə)r-ē, 'ke(ə)r-ē\
Car·yl \'kar-əl\
Cä·sar *Ger.* \'tsez-ˌär\
Ca·sey \'kā-sē\
Cash \'kash\
Cas·i·mir 1 \'kaz-ə-ˌmi(ə)r\ 2 *Fr.* **Ca·si·mir** \ká-zē-mēr\
Ca·si·mire *Fr.* \ká-zē-mēr\
Cas·par 1 \'kas-pər\ 2 *Dan.* \'kás-ˌpär\ 3 *Du., Ger., Norw.* \'käs-ˌpär\
Cas·pa·rus *Lat.* \'kas-pə-rəs\
Cas·per 1 \'kas-pər\ 2 *Ger.* \'käs-pər\
Cass \'kas\
Cas·sa·day \'kas-ə-ˌdā\
Cas·si·a·ni·us \ˌkash(-ē)-'ā-nē-əs, ˌkas-ē-'ā-\
Cas·sin \'kas-ən\
Cas·si·us \'kash(-ē)-əs, 'kas-ē-əs\
Cas·tel·lain \'kas-tə-ˌlān\
Cas·wall \'kaz-ˌwȯl, -wəl\
Cas·well \'kaz-ˌwel, -wəl\
Ca·ta·ri·na *Ital.* \ˌkä-tä-'rē-nä\
Ca·te·ri·na *Ital.* \ˌkä-tā-'rē-nä\
Cate·ri·no *Ital.* \ˌkä-tā-'rē-nō\
Ca·thal *Ir. Gael.* \'ka-həl\
Cath·a·rine \'kath-(ə-)rən\
Cath·er·ine 1 \'kath-(ə-)rən\ 2 *Fr.* **Ca·the·rine** \ká-t(ə-)rēn\
Ca·tius *Lat.* \'kā-sh(ē-)əs\
Cat·lett \'kat-ˌlet, -lət\
Ca·to *Norw.* \'kä-(ˌ)tō\
Cat·te·ri·no *Ital.* \ˌkät-tä-'rē-nō\
Ca·tulle *Fr.* \ká-tūēl\
Cec·co *Ital.* \'chāk-kō\
Ce·cil \'sē-səl; 'ses-əl, 'sis-\
Ce·cile 1 \sə-'sē(ə)l; 'ses-əl, 'sis-\ 2 *Fr.* **Cé·cile** \sā-sēl, *Can* -sil\
Ce·ci·lia 1 \si-'sil-ē-ə, -'sil-yə, -'sēl-\ 2 *Port.* \sā-'sēl-yə; -yá\ 3 *Span.* \thā-'thēl-yä; sā-'sēl-\
Ce·ci·lio *Span.* \thā-'thēl-yō; sā-'sēl-\
Ce·cil·i·us \sə-'sil-ē-əs, -'sil-yəs\
Çe·dar \'sēd-ər\
Če·do·milj *Serb.-Cr.* \'ched-ȯ-ˌmēl^{y}\
Ced·ric \'sed-rik, 'sē-drik\
Ce·io·ni·us *Lat.* \sē-'(y)ō-nē-əs\
Cei·riog *Welsh* \'kār-yȯg\
Çe·le·bi *Turk.* \chel-eb-'ē\
Ce·leste 1 \sə-'lest\ 2 *Fr.* **Cé·leste** \sā-lest\
Cé·les·tin *Fr.* \sā-les-ta^{n}\
Ce·le·sti·no *Ital.* \ˌchā-lā-'stē-nō\
Cel·ia \'sēl-yə\
Cel·so *Span.* \'thel-sō; 'sel-\
Cen·cio *Ital.* \'chen-chō\
Cen·ni·no *Ital.* \chān-'nē-nō\
Ce·nón *Span.* \thā-'nȯn; sā-\
Cen·zio *Ital.* \'chent-syō\
Ce·phas \'sē-fəs\
Ce·ran *Fr.* \sā-rä^{n}\
Cer·tain *Fr.* \ser-ta^{n}\
Cé·saire *Fr.* \sā-zer\
Cé·sar 1 *Fr.* \sā-zár\ 2 *Span.* \'thā-sär; 'sā-\
Ce·sa·re *Ital.* \'chā-zär-(ˌ)ā\
Ce·sá·reo *Span.* \thā-'sär-ā-ō; sā-\
Ce·sar·io *Port.* \sā-'zär-yü\
Cha·bot *Fr.* \shá-bō\
Chace \'chās\
Cha·im 1 *Heb.* \kī-'(y)im, 'kī-(y)im\ 2 *Yiddish* \'kī-(y)im\
Champ \'champ\
Champ·lin \'cham-plən\
Chance \'chan(t)s\
Chan·cel·lor \'chan(t)-s(ə-)lər\
Chan·dra 1 *Bengali* \'chȯn-(ˌ)drō\ 2 *Skt.* \'chən-drə\
Chap·lin \'chap-lən\
Char·le·magne 1 \'shär-lə-ˌmān\ 2 *Fr.* \shár-lə-mán^{y}\
Charles 1 \'chär(-ə)lz\ 2 *Du.* \'shärl\ 3 *Fr.* \shárl\
Char·lie \'chär-lē\
Char·lot·ta *Swed.* \shár-'lȯt-tá\
Char·lotte 1 \'shär-lət\ 2 *Fr.* \shár-lȯt\ 3 *Swed.* \shár-'lȯt\ 4 *Ger.* **Char·lot·te** \shär-'lȯ-tə\
Charl·ton \'chär(-ə)l-tən, 'chärlt-^{ə}n\
Chat·ham \'chat-əm\
Chat·man \'chat-mən\
Chaun·cey \'chȯn-sē, 'chän-\
Chav·e·li·ta \ˌchav-ə-'lēt-ə\
Cha·yim 1 *Heb.* \kī-'(y)im, 'kī-(y)im\ 2 *Yiddish* \'kī-(y)im\
Che *Span.* \'chā\
Chee·ver \'chē-vər\
Che·ri 1 \she(ə)r-'ē\ 2 *Fr.* **Ché·ri** \shā-rē\
Ches·ter \'ches-tər\
Chet·wynd \'chet-ˌwind\
Che·u *Kor.* \che-ü\
Chew \'chü\
Chich·es·ter \'chich-is-tər\
Chi·ka·fu·sa *Jp.* \chē-kä-fu̇s-ä\
Chi·ku·den *Jp.* \chē-ku̇d-en\
Childe \'chī(ə)ld\
Childs \'chī(ə)ldz\
Chip·man \'chip-mən\
Chip·pen·dall \'chip-ən-ˌdȯl\
Chit·ta *Bengali* \'chit-tə\
Chit·ten·den \'chit-^{ə}n-dən\
Chlod·wig *Ger.* \'klōt-(ˌ)vik\
Chō·fū *Jp.* \chō-fü\
Cho·ku·an *Jp.* \chō-ku̇-än\
Chō·mei *Jp.* \chō-mā\
Chō·min *Jp.* \chō-mēn\
Chŏng *Kor.* \chəŋ\
Chŏng-hi *Kor.* \chəŋ-hē\
Chō·shun *Jp.* \chō-shu̇n\
Chre·stos *Mod. Gk.* \'krēs-(ˌ)tȯs\
Chré·tien *Fr.* \krā-tya^{n}\
Chris·ta·bel \'kris-tə-ˌbel, -bəl\
Chris·ten 1 *Dan.* \'kris-tən\ 2 *Norw.* \'kris-t^{ə}n\
Chris·tence *Dan.* \'krēs-təns\
Chris·ten·sen *Dan.* \'kris-tən-sən\
Chris·ti·aan *Du.* \'kris-tē-ˌán\
Chris·ti·aan·szoon *Du.* \'kris-tē-ˌán(t)-sən, -ˌsȯn, -ˌsōn\
Chris·tian 1 \'kris(h)-chən\ 2 *Dan.* \'krē-styán\ 3 *Fr.* \krē-styä^{n}\ 4 *Ger.* \'kris-tyän, -tē-ˌän\ 5 *Norw.* \'kris-tyán\ 6 *Swed.* \'kris-tē-án, 'krish-án\ 7 *Du.* **Chris·ti·an** \'kris-tē-ˌän\
Chris·ti·a·na *Ger.* \ˌkris-'tyän-ä, -tē-'än-ä\
Chris·ti·a·ne *Ger.* \ˌkris-'tyän-ə, -tē-'än-ə\
Chris·ti·a·nus *Du.* \ˌkris-tē-'án-ues\
Chris·tie \'kris-tē\
Chris·tiern *Dan.* \'krēs-tye(ə)rn\
Chris·ti·na \kris-'tē-nə\
Chris·tine 1 \kris-'tēn, 'kris-(ˌ)tēn\ 2 *Fr.* \krē-stēn\ 3 *Swed.* \kri-'stēn\ 4 *Ger.* **Chris·ti·ne** \kris-'tē-nə\
Christ·lop *Ger.* \'krist-(ˌ)lōp\
Christ·mas \'kris-məs\
Chris·to·fer *Norw., Swed.* \kris-'tȯ-fər\
Chris·toff *Ger.* \'kris-ˌtȯf\
Chris·tof·fel *Ger.* \kris-'tȯ-fəl\
Chris·tof·fer *Swed.* \kris-'tȯf-fər\
Chri·sto·fo·ro *Ital.* \krē-'stȯ-fō-(ˌ)rō\
Chris·toph 1 *Du., Ger., Swed.* \'kris-ˌtȯf\ 2 *Hung.* \'kris-tōf\
Chris·tophe *Fr.* \krē-stȯf\
Chris·to·pher 1 \kris-tə-fər\ 2 *Swed.* \kris-'tȯ-fər\
Chris·ty \'kris-tē\
Chrow·der \'krau̇d-ər\
Chry·sos·tome *Fr.* \krē-zȯ-stōm\
Chry·sos·to·mus *Ger.* \krūē-'zȯs-tō-mu̇s\
Chrys·tal \'kris-t^{ə}l\
Chry·zos·tom *Pol.* \kriz-'ȯs-tȯm\
Chu·ang *Thai* \'jü-'äŋ\
Chung Hee *Kor.* \chüŋ-hē\
Chur·ton \'chərt-^{ə}n\
Cic·e·ly \'sis(-ə)-lē\
Ci·cé·ron *Fr.* \sē-sā-rō^{n}\
Cic·i·ly \'sis(-ə)-lē\
Cil·ni·us *Lat.* \'sil-nē-əs\
Cin·cin·na·tus \ˌsin(t)-sə-'nat-əs, -'nāt-\
Ci·no *Ital.* \'chē-nō\
Ci·pri·a·no 1 *Ital.* \ˌchē-prē-'än-ō\ 2 *Span.* \thē-prē-'än-ō; sē-\
Ci·ri·lo *Span.* \thē-'rē-lō; sē-\
Ci·ro *Ital.* \'chē-rō\
Cis·sie \'sis-ē\
Claes *Du.* \'klás\
Claesz *Du.* \'klás\
Clag·gett \'klag-ət\
Clair 1 \'kla(ə)r, 'kle(ə)r\ 2 *Fr.* \kler\
Claire 1 \'kla(ə)r, 'kle(ə)r\ 2 *Fr.* \kler\ 3 *Ger.* \'kler\
Clapp \'klap\
Clara 1 \'klar-ə\ 2 **Cla·ra** *Fr.* \klá-rá\ 3 *Ger., Span.* \'klär-ä\
Clare \'kla(ə)r, 'kle(ə)r\
Clar·ence 1 \'klar-ən(t)s\ 2 *Fr.* **Cla·rence** \klá-rä^{n}s\
Cla·ret *Fr.* \klá-re\
Cla·ri·na \klə-'rē-nə\
Cla·ris *Fr.* \klá-rēs\
Cla·ris·sa \klə-'ris-ə\
Clark, Clarke \'klärk\
Clark·son \'klärk-sən\
Cla·ro *Span.* \'klär-(ˌ)ō\
Clary \'kla(ə)r-ē, 'kle(ə)r-\
Clas·son *Swed.* \'klás-ȯn\
Claud \'klȯd\
Claude 1 \'klȯd\ 2 *Fr.* \klōd\
Clau·dia 1 \'klȯd-ē-ə\ 2 *Ital.* \'klau̇d-yä\
Clau·di·a·nus *Lat.* \ˌklȯd-ē-'ā-nəs\
Clau·din *Fr.* \klō-da^{n}\
Clau·dine *Fr.* \klō-dēn\
Clau·dio 1 *Ital.* \'klau̇d-yō\ 2 *Span.* \'klau̇th-yō\
Cláu·dio *Port.* \'klau̇th-yü\
Clau·di·us 1 \'klȯd-ē-əs\ 2 *Ger.* \'klau̇-dyu̇s, -dē-u̇s\
Claus *Du., Norw.* \'klau̇s\
Cla·ver·house \'klā-vər-ˌhau̇s\

\ə\ abut \$^{ə}$\ kitten, *Fr.* table \ər\ further \a\ ash \ā\ ace \ä\ cot, cart \au̇\ out \ch\ chin \e\ bet \ē\ easy \g\ go \i\ hit \ī\ ice \j\ job \ŋ\ sing \ō\ go \ȯ\ law \ȯi\ boy \th\ both \th\ the \ü\ loot \u̇\ foot \y\ yet \zh\ vision \á, b, g, k, ^{n}, œ, œ̄, ue, ūē, ^{y}\ *see* Guide to Pronunciation

Clav·er·ing \ˈklav-(ə-)riŋ, ˈkläv-\
Clay \ˈklā\
Clay·poole \ˈklā-ˌpül\
Clay·ton \ˈklāt-^{ə}n\
Clegg \ˈkleg, ˈklāg\
Cleg·horn \ˈkleg-ˌ(h)ȯ(ə)rn, ˈkleg-ərn\
Clem·ence 1 \ˈklem-ən(t)s\ 2 *Fr.* **Clé·mence** \klā-mä^{n}s\
Clem·ens 1 \ˈklem-ənz\ 2 **Cle·mens** *Ger.* \ˈklā-men(t)s\ 3 *Lat.* \ˈklem-enz, ˈklē-menz\
Clem·ent 1 \ˈklem-ənt\ 2 *Fr.* **Clé·ment** \klā-mä^{n}\
Cle·men·te 1 *Ital.* \klā-ˈmen-tā\ 2 *Span.* \klā-ˈmān-tā\
Cle·men·ti·a·nus *Lat.* \kli-ˌmen-shē-ˈā-nəs\
Clé·men·tine *Fr.* \klā-mä^{n}-tēn\
Clem·ents \ˈklem-ən(t)s\
Clem·son \ˈklem(p)-sən\
Cle·o·fon·te *Ital.* \ˌklā-ō-ˈfōn-tā\
Clé·o·phas *Fr.* \klā-ȯ-fäs\
Cler·i·hew \ˈkler-i-ˌhyü\
Clerk \ˈklərk, *esp Brit.* ˈklärk\
Cle·to *Span.* \ˈklā-tō\
Cleves \ˈklēvz\
Cliffe \ˈklif\
Clif·ford \ˈklif-ərd\
Clif·ton \ˈklif-tən\
Clinch \ˈklinch\
Clin·ton \ˈklint-^{ə}n\
Clip·ston \ˈklip-stən\
Clive \ˈklīve\
Clo·di·us *Lat.* \ˈklōd-ē-əs\
Clop·ton \ˈkläp-tən\
Clo·rinne *Fr.* \klȯ-rēn\
Clo·tilde 1 *Fr.* \klȯ-tēld\ 2 *Ital.* **Clo·til·de** \klō-ˈtēl-dā\
Cloudes·ley \ˈklau̇dz-lē\
Clo·vis *Fr.* \klȯ-vēs\
Clowdis·ley \ˈklau̇dz-lē\
Cloyd \ˈklȯid\
Cloyne \ˈklȯin\
Clyde \ˈklīd\
Clyf·ford \ˈklif-ərd\
Cnae·us *Lat.* \ˈnē-əs\
Cne·ius *Lat.* \ˈnē-(y)əs\
Coal·ter \ˈkōl-tər\
Coape \ˈkōp\
Cob·ham \ˈkäb-əm\
Coc·ce·ius *Lat.* \käk-ˈsē-(y)əs\
Coch·ran \ˈkäk-rən\
Coch·rane \ˈkäk-rən\
Cock·ayne \kä-ˈkān\
Cod·man \ˈkäd-mən\
Coe \ˈkō\
Coe·li·us *Lat.* \ˈsē-lē-əs\
Cof·fay \ˈkȯf-ē\
Cof·fee \ˈkȯ-fē, ˈkäf-ē\
Coff·man \ˈkȯf-mən\
Cogs·well \ˈkägz-ˌwel, -wəl\
Coit \ˈkȯit\
Co·la *Ital.* \ˈkȯ-lä\
Col·burn \ˈkōl-(ˌ)bərn\
Col·by \ˈkōl-bē\
Col·den \ˈkōl-dən\
Col·ding·ham \ˈkōl-diŋ-əm\
Cole \ˈkōl\
Cole·brooke \ˈkōl-(ˌ)bru̇k\
Cole·man \ˈkōl-mən\
Cole·ridge \ˈkōl-rij, ˈkō-lə-rij\
Coles \ˈkōlz\
Co·lette *Fr.* \kȯ-let\
Co·ley \ˈkō-lē\
Co·lin 1 \ˈkäl-ən, ˈkō-lən\ 2 *Fr.* \kȯ-la^{n}\ 3 *Ger.* \ˈkō-lin, -(ˌ)lēn\
Col·leer \kə-ˈli(ə)r\
Col·let \ˈkäl-ət\
Col·lett *Norw.* \ˈkȯl-lət\
Col·ley \ˈkäl-ē\
Col·ling·ham \ˈkäl-iŋ-əm\
Col·lings \ˈkäl-iŋz\
Col·lis \ˈkäl-əs\
Co·lón *Span.* \kō-ˈlȯn\
Co·lon·na *Fr.* \kȯ-lȯ-nȧ\
Colt \ˈkōlt\
Col·ton \ˈkōlt-^{ə}n\
Col·trin \ˈkōl-trən\
Co·luc·cio *Ital.* \kȯ-ˈlüt-chō\
Co·lum·bus \kə-ˈləm-bəs\
Col·ville \ˈkōl-(ˌ)vil, ˈkäl-, -vəl\
Com·fort \ˈkəm(p)-fərt\
Com·mer·ford \ˈkəm-ər-fərd\
Com·yn \ˈkəm-ən\
Com·yns \ˈkəm-ənz\
Con \ˈkän\
Con·al \ˈkän-^{ə}l\
Co·nan \ˈkȯ-nən, ˈkō-\
Co·nant \ˈkō-nənt\
Con·cep·ción *Span.* \kȯn-thep-ˈthyȯn; -seps-ˈyȯn\
Con·cha *Span.* \ˈkȯn-chä\
Con·ci·no *Ital.* \kȯn-ˈchē-nō\
Con·dé 1 \ˈkän-(ˌ)dā, kän-ˈ, kōn-ˈ\ 2 *Fr.* \kō^{n}-dā\
Con·ings·by \ˈkän-iŋz-bē, ˈkən-\
Con·ley \ˈkän-lē\
Con·nie \ˈkän-ē\
Con·nop \ˈkän-əp\
Con·nor, Con·or \ˈkän-ər\
Con·o·ver \ˈkän-ə-vər\
Con·rad 1 \ˈkän-ˌrad, -rəd\ 2 *Dan.* \ˈkȯn-ˌrät͟h\ 3 *Du., Ger.* \ˈkȯn-ˌrät\
Con·ra·do *Span.* \kȯn-ˈrät͟h-ō\
Con·stance 1 \ˈkän(t)-stən(t)s\ 2 *Fr.* \kō^{n}-stä^{n}s\
Con·stant 1 \kän(t)-stənt\ 2 *Fr.* \kō^{n}-stä^{n}\ 3 *Ger.* \kȯn-ˈstänt\
Con·stan·tijn *Du.* \ˈkȯn-stän-ˌtīn\
Con·stan·tin 1 \ˈkän(t)-stən-(ˌ)tin\ 2 *Fr.* \kō^{n}-stä^{n}-ta^{n}\ 3 *Ger., Rom.* \ˌkȯn-stän-ˈtēn\
Con·stan·tine \ˈkän(t)-stən-ˌtēn, -ˌtīn\
Con·stan·ti·no *Ital.* \ˌkōn-stän-ˈtē-nō\
Con·stan·ze *Ger.* \kȯn-ˈstänt-sə\
Con·tee \ˈkän-tē\
Con·vers \ˈkän-vərz\
Con·way \ˈkän-(ˌ)wā\
Con·wy \ˈkän-wē\
Con·yers \ˈkän-yərz\
Con·yng·ham \ˈkən-iŋ-əm, *US usu* -ˌham\
Coo·ley \ˈkü-lē\
Coombs \ˈkümz\
Coote \ˈküt\
Cope \ˈkōp\
Cope·land \ˈkō-plənd\
Cop·ley \ˈkäp-lē, ˈkōp-\
Co·ra 1 \ˈkōr-ə, ˈkȯr-\ 2 *Norw.* \ˈkō-(ˌ)rä\
Cor·dell \ˈkȯ(ə)r-ˌdel, kȯr-ˈ\
Cor·dy \ˈkȯrd-ē\
Co·ren·tin *Fr.* \kȯ-rä^{n}-ta^{n}\
Co·rin·na \kə-ˈrin-ə, -ˈrē-nə\
Co·rinne \kə-ˈrin, -ˈrēn\
Cor·less \ˈkȯr-ləs\
Cor·ne·lia \kȯr-ˈnēl-yə, -ˈnē-lē-ə\
Cor·ne·lis, Cor·ne·lisz *Du.* \kȯr-ˈnā-ləs\
Cor·ne·lio *Ital.* \kȯr-ˈnel-yō\
Cor·ne·lis·zoon *Du.* \kȯr-ˈnā-lə-sən, -ˌsȯn, -ˌsōn\
Cor·ne·liu *Rom.* \kȯr-ˈnel-yü\
Cor·ne·lius 1 \kȯr-ˈnēl-yəs, -ˈnē-lē-əs\ 2 **Cor·ne·li·us** *Dan.* \kȯr-ˈnil-ē-u̇s\ 3 *Du.* \kȯr-ˈnā-lē-œs\ 4 *Ger.* \kȯr-ˈnāl-yu̇s, -ˈnā-lē-u̇s\
Corne·wall \ˈkȯrn-wəl, *esp US* -ˌwȯl\
Cor·ra \ˈkȯr-ə, ˈkär-\
Cor·ra·do *Ital.* \kōr-ˈräd-ō\
Cor·reia *Port.* \kȯr-ˈrā-ə; -ȧ\
Cor·rowr \kə-ˈrau̇(ə)r\
Cor·so *Ital.* \ˈkȯr-sō\
Cort 1 \ˈkō(ə)rt, ˈkȯ(ə)rt\ 2 *Dan.* \ˈkȯ(ə)rt\
Cor·tés \kȯr-ˈtās\
Cor·y·ton \ˈkȯr-ə-tən, ˈkär-\
Co·si·ma *Ger.* \ˈkō-zē-mä\
Co·si·mo *Ital.* \ˈkȯ-zē-(ˌ)mō\
Cos·mas *Ger.* \ˈkȯs-ˌmäs\
Cos·mè *Ital.* \ˈkȯz-mā\
Cos·mo 1 \ˈkäz-(ˌ)mō\ 2 *Ital.* \ˈkȯz-mō\
Cos·sar \ˈkäs-ər\
Cos·ta, da \də-ˈkȯst-ə\
Cos·ta·che *Rom.* \kȯs-ˈtäk-e\
Co·stan·zo *Ital.* \kō-ˈstänt-sō\
Cotes·worth \ˈkōts-(ˌ)wərth\
Cot·ter \ˈkät-ər\
Cot·ton \ˈkät-^{ə}n\
Couch \ˈküch\
Coul·son \ˈkōl-sən, ˈkül-\
Coun·sel·man \ˈkau̇n(t)-səl-mən\
Coun·tee \kau̇n-ˈtā\
Court \ˈkō(ə)rt, ˈkȯ(ə)rt\
Courte·nay \kō(ə)rt-nē, ˈkȯ(ə)rt-, -^{ə}n-(ˌ)ā\
Courte·ney \ˈkō(ə)rt-nē, ˈkȯ(ə)rt-\
Court·land \ˈkō(ə)rt-lənd, ˈkȯ(ə)rt-\
Coutts \ˈküts\
Cow·an \ˈkau̇-ən\
Cow·den \ˈkau̇d-^{ə}n\
Coy \ˈkȯi\
Crabb \ˈkrab\
Crace \ˈkrās\
Craig \ˈkrāg\
Cranch \ˈkranch\
Cran·field \ˈkran-ˌfēld\
Cran·nell \ˈkran-^{ə}l\
Cran·stoun \ˈkran(t)-stən\
Cran·will \ˈkran-ˌwil, -wəl\
Crapo \ˈkrap-(ˌ)ō\
Crary \ˈkra(ə)r-ē, ˈkre(ə)r-ē\
Crau·furd, Craw·ford \ˈkrȯ-fərd\
Craw·shay \ˈkrȯ-ˌshā\
Cre·mu·ti·us *Lat.* \kri-ˈmyü-sh(ē-)əs\
Cres·ap \ˈkres-əp\
Cres·co·ni·us *Lat.* \kres-ˈkō-nē-əs\
Cres·son \ˈkres-^{ə}n\
Cres·wicke \ˈkrez-ik\
Cris·ler \ˈkrī-slər\
Cri·sós·to·mo *Span.* \krē-ˈsōs-tō-mō\
Cris·pus \ˈkris-pəs\
Cris·ti·na *Ital.* \krē-ˈstē-nä\
Cris·tó·bal *Span.* \krēs-ˈtō-b͟äl\
Cris·to·fa·no *Ital.* \krē-ˈstȯ-fän-(ˌ)ō\
Cris·to·fo·ro *Ital.* \krē-ˈstȯ-fō-rō\
Cris·well \ˈkris-ˌwel, ˈkriz-, -wəl\
Crom·bie \ˈkräm-bē, ˈkrəm-\
Cromme·lin \ˈkrəm-lən, ˈkräm-\
Cro·nyn \ˈkrō-nən\
Croom \ˈkrüm\
Cros·well \ˈkrȯz-ˌwel, -wəl\
Crum \ˈkrəm\
Crun·dall \ˈkrən-d^{ə}l\
Cruz *Span.* \ˈkrüth; ˈkrüs\
Cu·bitt \ˈkyü-bət\
Cul·lem \ˈkəl-əm\
Cul·ling \ˈkəl-iŋ\
Cul·ross \kəl-ˈrȯs\
Cum·ming \ˈkəm-iŋ\
Cun·liffe \ˈkən-(ˌ)lif\
Cur·bas·tro *Ital.* \kür-ˈbäs-trō\
Cu·ri·us *Lat.* \ˈkyu̇r-ē-əs\
Cur·rer \ˈkər-ər\
Cur·son \ˈkərs-^{ə}n\
Cur·zio *Ital.* \ˈkürt-syō\
Cus·tance \ˈkəs-tən(t)s\
Cus·to·dio 1 *Port.* \küsh-ˈtȯt͟h-yü; küs-\ 2 *Span.* \kü-ˈstōt͟h-yō\
Cut·cliffe \ˈkət-ˌklif\

Cuy·ler \'kī-lər\
Cy \'sī\
Cyn·thia \'sin(t)-thē-ə\
Cyp·ri·an 1 \'sip-rē-ən\ 2 *Pol.* \'tsip-ryán\
Cy·pri·en *Fr.* \sē-prē-a^{n}\
Cyp·rjan *Pol.* \'tsip-ryán\
Cy·riel *Du.* \si-'rēl\
Cyr·il \'sir-əl\
Cy·rus 1 \'sī-rəs\ 2 *Fr.* \sē-rues\
Cy·via *Pol.* \'tsēv-yá\

Dab·ney \'dab-nē\
Da·comb \'dā-kəm\
da Cos·ta \də-'kó-stə\
Da·cre \'dā-kər\
Da·da·bhai *Parsi* \'dä-dä-'bī\
Dae-gon *Kor.* \da-gón\
Da·fydd *Welsh* \'däv-ith\
Dag·mar 1 \'dag-ˌmär\ 2 *Dan.* \'dág-mär\
Da·go·bert 1 *Fr.* \dá-gó-ber\ 2 *Ger.* \'däg-ō-ˌbert\
Daines \'dānz\
Dai·se·tsu *Jp.* \dī-set-sü\
Dai·shi *Jp.* \dī-shē\
Dai·sy \'dā-zē\
Dale \'dā(ə)l\
Dal·lam \'dal-əm\
Dal·zell \dal-'zel, 'dal-ˌ; dē-'el\
Da·mi·an 1 *Ger.* \ˌdäm-'yän, -ē-'än\ 2 *Span.* Da·mián \däm-'yän, thäm-\
Da·mia·no *Ital.* \däm-'yän-ō\
Da·mião *Port.* \dəm-'yau^{n}, thəm-; dám-, thám-\
Da·mo·dar *Hind.* \ˌdəm-ə-'där\
Da·mon \'dā-mən\
Dan \'dan\
Da·na \'dā-nə\
Dan·dridge \'dan-(ˌ)drij\
Dan·forth \'dan-ˌfō(ə)rth, -ˌfó(ə)rth\
Dan·iel 1 \'dan-yəl\ 2 Da·ni·el *Du.* \'dá-nē-ˌel\ 3 *Ger.* \'dän-yel, -ē-el\ 4 *Swed.* \'dä-nē-əl\ 5 Da·niel *Fr.* \dán-yel\ 6 *Span.* \thän-'yel; dän-\
Dá·ni·el *Hung.* \'dá-ni-(ˌ)el\
Da·nie·le *Ital.* \dän-'yel-ā\
Da·niel·lo *Ital.* \dän-'yel-lō\
Dan·jū·ro *Jp.* \dän-jür-ō\
Dank·mar \'daŋk-ˌmär\
Dan·te 1 \'dän-(ˌ)tā, 'dan-, -(ˌ)tē; 'dant-ē, 'dänt-\ 2 *Ital.* \'dän-tā\
Daph·ne \'daf-nē\
Darch \'därch\
Da·rio *Ital.* \'där-yō\
Da·ri·us 1 \də-'rī-əs\ 2 *Fr.* Da·rius \dár-yues\
Dar·ling \'där-liŋ\
Dar·ling·ton \'där-liŋ-tən\
Dar·rah \'dar-ə\
Dar·rell \'dar-əl\
Dar·ryl \'dar-əl\
Dart·mouth \'därt-məth\
Da·shiell \də-'shē(ə)l\
da Sil·va 1 \də-'sil-və\ 2 *Port.* \thə-'sil-və, də-; thá-'sil-vá, dá-\
Da·to *Malay* \dä-tō\
Da·tuk *Indonesian* \'dä-ˌtük\
Dau·mont *Fr.* \dō-mō^{n}\
Da·vey \'dā-vē\
Da·vid 1 \'dā-vəd\ 2 *Du.* \'dá-vət\ 3 *Fr.* \dä-vēd\ 4 *Ger.* \'däv-ēt, 'däf-, -it\ 5 *Ital.* \'däv-ēd\ 6 *Russ.* \(ˌ)dəv-'yēd\
Da·vi·do·vich *Russ.* \(ˌ)dəv-'yēd(-əv)-ˌyich\
Da·vidsz *Du.* \'dá-vits\
Da·vy 1 \'dā-vē\ 2 *Fr.* \dá-vē\
Da·vy·do·vich *Russ.* \(ˌ)də-'vid(-əv)-ˌyich\
Da·vys \'dā-vəs\

Dawn \'dón, 'dän\
Day·don \'dād-ən\
Day·yan \dī-'(y)än\
De·al·try \'dē-əl-trē, 'dól-trē\
Dear·ing \'di(ə)r-iŋ\
De·bau·fre \də-(ˌ)bō-'frā\
De·ben·dra·nath *Bengali* \də-'ben-drə-'nät\
de Bow \də-'bō\
Dec·i·mus \'des-ə-məs\
De·ci·us \'dē-sh(ē-)əs\
De Cour·cy \də-'kúr-sē\
De·de *Turk.* \dā-'dā\
Deer·ing \'dir-iŋ\
De·for·est \di-'fór-əst, -'fär-\
De·hon \də-'hän\
De·hone \də-'hōn\
Del·a·haye \'del-ə-ˌhā\
De La·mar \'del-ə-ˌmär\
de la Mer \'del-ə-mər, -ˌmi(ə)r\
Del·a·mere \'del-ə-ˌmi(ə)r\
de la Mothe \'del-ə-ˌmät\
De Land \də-'land\
de La·tour \ˌdel-ə-'tú(ə)r\
Del·a·van \'del-ə-vən, -ˌvan\
Del·e·van \'del-ə-vən, -ˌvan\
Del·fim *Port.* \del-'fē^{n}, thel-\
Del·fi·na *Span.* \del-'fē-nä; thel-\
Del·ia \'dēl-yə, 'dē-lē-ə\
Del·mi·ra *Span.* \del-'mē-rä\
Del·phin *Fr.* \del-fa^{n}\
Del·phine *Fr.* \del-fēn\
Del·ta \'del-tə\
Del·u·cen·na \ˌdel-yü-'sen-ə\
Dem·a·rest \'dem-ə-rəst, -ˌrest\
Dem·bitz \'dem-bəts\
De·me·trio *Ital.* \dā-'mā-trē-ō\
De·me·tri·os *Mod. Gk.* \thē-'mē-trē-ˌós\
De·me·tri·us \də-'mē-trē-əs\
Dem·ing \'dem-iŋ\
De·mós·te·nes *Span.* \dā-'mōs-tā-nās; thā-\
Dene \'dēn\
Den·is 1 \'den-əs\ 2 De·nis *Du.* \də-'nēs\ 3 *Fr.* \də-nē\ 4 *Russ.* \dyin-'yēs\
Den·mark \'den-ˌmärk\
Den·son \'den(t)-sən\
Den·ton \'dent-ən\
Den·zil \'den-zəl\
De·nys *Fr.* \də-nē\
Dé·o·dat *Fr.* \dā-ó-dá(t)\
De·o·do·ro *Port.* \dē-ü-'thō-rü, thē-\
Der·mot \'dər-mət\
Derr \'de(ə)r\
Der·rick \'der-ik\
Der·went \'dər-wənt\
De·si·de·ri·us 1 *Ger.* \ˌdā-zē-'där-yüs, -'dā-rē-üs\ 2 *Lat.* Des·i·de·ri·us \ˌdes-i-'dir-ē-əs\
Dé·si·ré *Fr.* \dā-zē-rā\
Dé·si·rée *Fr.* \dā-zē-rā\
Des·mond \'dez-mənd\
de So·la \də-'sō-lə\
Det·lev 1 \'det-ləf\ 2 *Ger.* \'det-lef\
de Vane \də-'vān\
de Wa·ter \də-'wót-ər, -'wät-\
de Witt, De Witt, De·witt \di-'wit\
de Wiv·eles·lie \də-'wiv-əlz-lē\
De Wolf, De Wolfe \də-'wúlf\
Dex·ter \'dek-stər\
De·zső *Hung.* \'dezh-(ˌ)œ\
Dhan *Bengali* \'dón(-ˌó)\
Dhan·pat *Bengali* \'dón-ˌpät\
Dhio·ní·sios *Gk.* \thyó-'nēs-yós\
Dhir·en·da *Hindi* \'dir-ən-də\
Dhon·do *Hindi* \'dón-dō\
Di·ana \dī-'an-ə\
Diar·maid \'dər-məd, -mət\
Diar·mid \'dər-məd, -mət\

Dick \'dik\
Dick·er·man \'dik-ər-mən\
Di·de·rich *Dan.* \'dē-də-rēk\
Di·de·ri·cus *Du.* \ˌdēd-ə-'rē-kues\
Di·de·rik *Du.* \'dēd-ə-rək\
Di·dier *Fr.* \dēd-yā\
Die·de·rich *Ger.* \'dē-də-ˌrik\
Die·de·rik *Du.* \'dēd-ə-rik\
Die·drich \'dē-drik\
Die·go *Span.* \'dyā-gō; 'thyā-\
Diehl \'dē(ə)l\
Die·rik *Du.* \'dē-rək\
Die·trich 1 *Fr.* \dē-trēk\ 2 Ger. \'dē-(ˌ)trik\
Dieu *Fr.* \dyœ\
Dieu·don·né *Fr.* \dyœ-dó-nā\
Diez *Fr.* \dēts\
Dig·by \'dig-bē\
Digh·ton \'dīt-ən\
Dike·man \'dīk-mən\
Di·kran \də-'krän\
Dill \'dil\
Dil·ler \'dil-ər\
Dill·man \'dil-mən\
Dil·lon \'dil-ən\
Dil·worth \'dil-ˌwərth\
Di·mi·tri 1 \di-'mē-trē\ 2 *Mod. Gk.* \thē-'mē-trē\ 3 *Russ.* \dyim-'yē-tryəi\
Di·mi·trie *Rom.* \dē-'mē-trē-(y)e\
Di·mi·tri·je *Serb.-Cr.* \dē-'mē-trē-ye\
Di·mi·try 1 *Rom.* \di-'mē-tri\ 2 *Russ.* \dyim-'mē-tryəi\
Di·mond \'dī-mənd\
Di·nah \'dī-nə\
Di·nes *Dan.* \'dē-nes\
Din·ham \'din-əm\
Di·nís *Port.* \dē-'nēsh\
Di·no *Ital.* \'dē-nō\
Dio \'dī-ˌō\
Dio·go *Port.* \'dyō-gü, 'thyō-\
Di·o·me·de *Ital.* \ˌdē-ō-'med-ā\
Di·on \'dī-ˌän, 'dē-, -ən\
Di·o·ni·sio 1 *Ital.* \ˌdē-ō-'nēz-yō\ 2 *Span.* Dio·ni·sio \dyō-'nēs-yō; thyō-\
Dio·ny·sios *Mod. Gk.* \thyón-'yēs-ˌyós\
Di·o·ny·sius \ˌdī-ə-'nis(h)-ē-əs, -'nish-əs, -'nī-sē-əs\
Dirck *Du.* \'dirk\
Dirk 1 \'dərk\ 2 *Du.* \'dirk\
Dit·lev *Dan.* \'dēt-(ˌ)lev\
Djan·go 1 \'jaŋ-(ˌ)gō\ 2 *Fr.* \jáŋ-gō\
Dju·na \'jü-nə\
Dmi·tri \di-'mē-trē\
Dmi·tri·ye·vich *Russ.* \'dmyē-tryi(-yiv)-ˌyich\
Dmi·try *Russ.* \'dmyē-trəi\
Dobbs \'däbz\
Dob·in·son \'däb-ən-sən\
Do·bry·nia *Russ.* \(ˌ)də-'brin-yə\
Do·cia \'dō-sh(ē-)ə\
Do·die \'dō-dē\
Dod·son \'däd-sən\
Do·kai *Jp.* \dō-kī\
Dol·i·ver \'däl-ə-vər\
Dol·ly \'däl-ē\
Do·lo·res 1 \də-'lōr-əs, -'lór-\ 2 *Span.* \dō-'lō-rās; thō-\
Dol·son \'dōl-sən\
Do·me·la *Du.* \'dó-mə-lá\
Do·me·ni·co *Ital.* \dō-'mā-nē-(ˌ)kō\
Do·min·go 1 *Port.* \dü-'mē^{n}(ŋ)-gü, thü-\ 2 *Span.* \dō-'mēŋ-gō, thō-\

\ə\ abut \ᵊ\ kitten, *Fr.* table \ər\ further \a\ ash \ā\ ace \ä\ cot, cart \aü\ out \ch\ chin \e\ bet \ē\ easy \g\ go \i\ hit \ī\ ice \j\ job \ŋ\ sing \ō\ go \ó\ law \ói\ boy \th\ both \th\ the \ü\ loot \ú\ foot \y\ yet \zh\ vision \á, b, g, k, ^{n}, œ, œ̄, ue, ue̅, ʸ\ *see* Guide to Pronunciation

Do·min·gos *Port.* \dü-'mē^{n}(ŋ)-güsh, thü-; -güs\
Dom·i·nic, -nick \'däm-ə-(,)nik\
Do·mi·nik *Ger.* \'dō-mē-,nik\
Do·mi·ni·kus *Ger.* \dō-'mē-nē-kůs\
Do·mi·nique *Fr.* \dȯ-mē-nēk\
Do·mi·ti·us *Lat.* \dō-'mish(-ē)-əs\
Don \'dän\
Do·nal *Ir. Gael.* \'thyü-nəl\
Don·ald \'dän-^{ə}ld\
Do·na·tien *Fr.* \dȯ-nás-ya^{n}\
Do·na·to *Ital.* \dō-'nä-tō\
Do·na·tus *Ger.* \dō-'nä-tůs\
Don·is·thorpe \'dän-əs-,thȯrp\
Donn \'dän\
Don·na \'dän-ə\
Don·ough 1 \'dän-ō\ 2 *Ir. Gael.* \'thən-(,)ō\
Dop·po *Jp.* \dōp-pō\
Do·ra \'dōr-ə, 'dȯr-\
Do·rab·ji *Bengali* \dä-'räb-jē\
Do·reen \dȯ-'rēn, də-; 'dōr-ēn, 'dȯr-\
Do·re·mus \də-'rē-məs\
Dor·is \'dȯr-əs, 'där-\
Do·ri·us *Ger.* \'dōr-yůs, 'dō-rē-ůs\
Dor·man \'dȯr-mən\
Dor·mer \'dȯr-mər\
Dor·mont *Fr.* \dȯr-mō^{n}\
Dorn \'dȯ(ə)rn\
Dor·nel·les *Port.* \dür-'nel-ish, thür-; -is\
Dorn·ford \'dȯ(ə)rn-fərd\
Do·ro·teo *Span.* \dō-rō-'tā-ō; thō-\
Dor·o·thea 1 \,dȯr-ə-'thē-ə, ,där-\ 2 *Ger.* **Do·ro·thea** \,dō-rō-'tā-ä\
Do·ro·thée *Fr.* \dȯ-rȯ-tā\
Dor·o·thy \'dȯr-ə-thē, 'där-\
Dor·the *Norw.* \'dȯr-tə\
Dor·win \'dȯr-wən\
Dō·se·tsu *Jp.* \dō-set-sů\
Dos·i·tej *Serb.-Cr.* \'dȯ-sē-tey\
Doud \'daůd\
Dou·gal \'düg-əl\
Doug·las, -lass \'dəg-ləs\
Doust \'daůst\
Dou·ville \'dü-,vil, -vəl\
Dou·wes *Du.* \'daů-əs\
Dove·ton \'dəv-tən\
Dow·ner \'daů-nər\
Dow·nie \'daů-nē\
Dra·gan *Bulg.* \'drá-,gán\
Dra·gol·jub *Serb.-Cr.* \drá-'gȯl-yüb\
Dra·gu·tin *Serb.-Cr.* \'drá-gü-,tēn\
Drax \'draks\
Dra·ža *Serb.-Cr.* \'drá-zhá\
Dred \'dred\
Drew \'drü\
Drink·er \'driŋ-kər\
Dru \'drü\
Druc·ki *Pol.* \'drüt-skē\
Drum·mond \'drəm-ənd\
Dru·ry \'drů(ə)r-ē\
Dru·sus *Lat.* \'drü-səs\
Drys·dale \'drīz-,dā(ə)l\
Duar·te *Port.* \'dwár-tə, 'thwár-; -tā\
Du·Bi·gnon \dü̅e-bēn-yō^{n}\
Du Bose \də-'bōz, d(y)ů-\
Du·clos *Fr.* \dü̅e-klō\
Dud \'dəd\
Dud·ley \'dəd-lē\
Duer \'d(y)ü-ər\
Duff \'dəf\
Duf·field \'dəf-,ēld\
Duf·fle \'dəf-əl\
Du·gald \'d(y)ü-gəld\
Du·i·liu *Rom.* \dü-'ēl-yü\
Du·mas 1 \d(y)ü-'mä, 'd(y)ü-,\ 2 *Fr.* \dü̅e-má\
Du·mi·tra·şcu *Rom.* \,dü-mē-'träsh-kü\
Du·mi·tru *Rom.* \dü-'mē-trü\
Du·mont *Fr.* \dü̅e-mō^{n}\
Dun·bar \'dən-,bär, ,dən-'\
Dun·can \'dəŋ-kən\
Dun·glas \dən-'glás, -'glas\
Dun·kin·field \'dəŋ-kən-,fēld\
Dunn \'dən\
Dun·na·chie \'dən-ə-kē\
Duns·more \'dənz-,mō(ə)r, -,mȯ(ə)r\
Dun·stan \'dən-stən\
Dun·wo·dy \'dən-,wůd-ē\
Dun·woody \'dən-,wůd-ē\
du Pre 1 \dü-'prā\ 2 *Fr.* \dü̅e-prā\
Du·Rant \d(y)ů-'rant\
Du·rell \d(y)ů-'rel\
Du·šan *Serb.-Cr.* \'dü-shán\
Du·shan *Serb.-Cr.* \'dü-shán\
Dus·tin \'dəs-tən\
Dwight \'dwīt\
Dwy·er \'dwī-ər\
Dy·er \'dī(-ə)r\
Dyke \'dīk\
Dyl·an \'dil-ən\
Dyne·ley \'dīn-lē\
Dy·o·ni·zy *Pol.* \,di-ȯ-'nē-zi\

Ead·weard \'ed-wərd\
Ea·ger \'ē-gər\
Ea·gle \'ē-gəl\
Ea·mon *Ir. Gael.* \'ā-mən\
Ea·nes *Port.* \'ā-nəsh\
Eard·ley \'ərd-lē\
Earl, Earle \'ər(-ə)l\
Ear·nest \'ər-nəst\
Ea·son \'ēs-^{ə}n\
Eb·ba *Swed.* \'eb-,bá\
Eb·be·sen \'eb-ə-sən\
Eb·en \'eb-ən\
Eb·en·e·zer 1 \,eb-ə-'nē-zər\ 2 *Fr.* **Ebe·ne·zer** \ā-bā-nā-zer\
Eber·hard, -hardt *Ger.* \'ā-bər-,härt\
Ec·cle·stone \'ek-əl-stən\
Ec·di·ci·us *Lat.* \ek-'dish(-ē)-əs\
Eck·ert \'ek-ərt\
Eck·hard *Ger.* \'ek-,härt\
Écou·chard *Fr.* \ā-kü-shár\
Ec·tor \'ek-tər\
Ed \'ed\
Ed·da *Ital.* \'ed-dä\
Ed·die, Ed·dy \'ed-ē\
Ede *Hung.* \'ed-e\
Ede·les·tand *Fr.* \ed-les-tä^{n}\
Ed·gar 1 \'ed-gər\ 2 *Fr.* \ed-gár\ 3 *Ger.* \'et-,gär\
Ed·gard *Fr.* \ed-gár\
Edg·cumbe \'ej-kəm, -,küm\
Edith 1 \'ēd-əth\ 2 *Fr.* \ā-dēt\ 3 *Ger.* \'ā-(,)dit\
Ed·mands \'ed-məndz\
Ed·me *Fr.* \edm^{ə}\
Ed·mée *Fr.* \ed-mā\
Ed·mond 1 \'ed-mənd\ 2 *Fr.* \ed-mō^{n}\
Ed·mon·do *Ital.* \ād-'mōn-dō\
Ed·mon·stone \'ed-mən-stən\
Ed·mond·stoune \'ed-mən-stən\
Ed·mund 1 \'ed-mənt\ 2 *Ger.* \'et-,můnt\
Ed·mun·do·vich *Russ.* \id-'münd(-əv)-,yich\
Ed·munds \'ed-mən(d)z\
Ed·mund·son \'ed-mən(d)-sən\
Ed·na \'ed-nə\
Edo·ar·do *Ital.* \,ā-dō-'är-dō\
Édou·ard *Fr.* \ā-dwár\
Ed·ric \'ed-rik\
Ed·sel \'ed-səl\
Ed·son \'ed-sən\
Edu·ard 1 *Czech* \'ed-ů-árt\ 2 *Du.* \'ā-dü̅e-ärt\ 3 *Ger.* \'ā-dü-ärt\ 4 *Russ.* \id-ü-'árt\ 5 *Dan.* **Ed·uard** \'id-,värd\
Eduar·do 1 *Ital.* \ād-'wär-dō\ 2 *Port.* \ē-'thwár-dü\ 3 *Span.* \ā-'thwär-thō\
Edu·ard·o·vich *Russ.* \id-ü-'árt(-əv)-,yich\
Ed·vard 1 *Dan.* \'id-,värd\ 2 *Czech* \'ed-várt\ 3 *Norw.* \'ed-,värt, 'ād-\ 4 *Swed.* \'ād-,várd\
Ed·vart *Norw.* \'ed-,värt, 'ād-\
Ed·ward 1 \'ed-wərd\ 2 *Dan.* \'id-,värd\ 3 *Ger.* \'et-,värt\ 4 *Pol.* \'ed-,várt\
Ed·win 1 \'ed-wən\ 2 *Ger.* \'et-,vēn\
Ed·wi·na \ed-'wē-nə, -'win-ə\
Ed·wyn \'ed-wən\
Eel·co *Du.* \'āl-(,)kō\
Ee·lis *Finn.* \'ā-lis\
Ee·mil *Finn.* \'em-il\
Ee·ro 1 \'e(ə)r-(,)ō\ 2 *Finn.* \'er-,ȯ\
Ef·fie \'ef-ē\
Ef·rem \'ef-rəm\
Eg·bert 1 \'eg-bərt\ 2 *Du.* \'ek-bərt\
Eg·ber·tus *Du.* \ek-'ber-tœs\
Ege·berg *Norw.* \'ā-kə-,ber\
Eg·gert *Icel.* \'eg-gert\
Eg·gle·ston \'eg-əl-stən\
Egid *Ger.* \ā-'gēt\
Égide *Fr.* \ā-zhēd\
Egi·dio *Ital.* \ā-'jēd-yō\
Eg·le·ston \'eg-əl-stən\
Eg·lin·ton \'eg-lən-tən\
Eglon *Du.* \'ā-,glȯn\
Eg·mont *Ger.* \'eg-,mȯnt\
Eg·na·ti·us *Lat.* \ig-'nā-sh(ē-)əs\
Egon *Ger.* \'ā-,gȯn\
Egron *Swed.* \'ā-grȯn\
Eh·ren·fried 1 *Ger.* \'ā-rən-,frēt\ 2 *Swed.* \'ā-rən-,frēd\
Eh·ren·gard *Ger.* \'ā-rən-,gärt\
Eh·rich \'ā-,rik\
Ei·fu *Jp.* \ā-fů\
Ei·ichi *Jp.* \ā-ē-chē\
Ei·ji *Jp.* \ā-jē\
Ei·ki *Jp.* \ā-kē\
Ei·leen \ī-'lēn, ā-; 'ī-,, 'ā-,\
Ei·lert *Norw.* \'ā-lərt\
Eil·hardt *Ger.* \'īl-,härt\
Ei·lif *Norw.* \'ā-lēf\
Ei·nar 1 *Dan.* \'ī-,när\ 2 *Icel.* \'ā-,när\ 3 *Swed.* \'ā-,nár\
Ei·no *Finn.* \'ā-nō\
Ei·rik *Norw.* \'ā-rēk\
Ei·ríkr *Icel.* \'ā-,rē-kər\
Ei·tel *Ger.* \'ī-təl\
Ei·to·ku *Jp.* \ā-tō-kü\
Ei·vind *Norw.* \'ā-vin\
Ej·ler *Dan.* \'ī-lər\
Ej·nar *Dan.* \'ī-,när\
Ek·i·ken *Jp.* \ek-ē-ken\
Elaine \i-'lān\
El·bert \'el-bərt\
El·bridge \'el-brij\
El·da \'el-də\
El·don \'el-dən\
El·dredge \'el-drij\
El·dridge \'el-drij\
El·ea·nor \'el-ə-nər, -nȯ(ə)r, -nō(ə)r\
El·e·a·zar 1 \,el-ē-'ā-zər\ 2 **Ele·á·zar** *Span.* \ā-lā-'ä-thär; -sär\
Elec·tus \i-'lek-təs\
Elek *Hung.* \'el-ek\
Élé·mir *Fr.* \ā-lā-mēr\
El·e·na 1 \'el-ə-nə, ə-'lē-nə\ 2 **Ele·na** *Ger.* \'ā-lā-,nä\ 3 *Ital.* \'el-ā-(,)nä\ 4 *Rom.* \e-'len-ä\
El·e·o·no·ra 1 \,el-ə-'nȯ(ə)r-ə, -'nō(ə)r-\ 2 *Ital.* **Ele·o·no·ra** \,ā-lā-ō-'nȯr-ä\

Ele·o·no·re 1 *Ger.* \ˌā-lā-ō-ˈnō-rə\ 2 *Fr.* **Élé·o·nore** \ā-lā-ò-nòr\
Elert *Ger.* \ˈā-lərt\
Eleu·te·rio *Span.* \ā-leů-ˈtār-yō\
Éleu·thère *Fr.* \ā-lœ̄-ter\
Eleu·the·rios *Mod. Gk.* \ˌel-yef-ˈther-(ˌ)yȯs\
El·ford \ˈel-fərd\
El·ger·us *Swed.* \el-ˈyā-rus\
El·ha·nan \el-ˈhā-nən\
Eli \ˈē-ˌlī\
Eli·a·kim \i-ˈlī-ə-ˌkim\
Eli·as 1 \i-ˈlī-əs\ 2 *Finn.* \ˈel-ˌyas\ 3 *Ger.* \ā-ˈlē-äs\ 4 *Swed.* \el-ˈē-ás\ 5 *Span.* **Elí·as** \ā-ˈlē-äs\
Élie *Fr.* \ā-lē\
Elié·cer *Span.* \āl-ˈyā-thār\
Eli·el *Finn.* \ˈel-ēəl\
Eli·e·ser *Ger.* \ˌā-lē-ˈā-zər\
Eli·gio *Span.* \ā-ˈlē<u>k</u>-yō\
Eli·gi·us *Ger.* \ā-ˈlēg-yůs, -ˈlē-gē-ůs\
El·i·hu \ˈel-ə-ˌhyü, i-ˈlī-hyü\
Eli·ja \i-ˈlī-jə\
Eli·jah \i-ˈlī-jə\
El·i·nor \ˈel-ə-nər, -ˌnȯ(ə)r\
Elio *Ital., Span.* \ˈāl-yō\
El·i·ot \ˈel-ē-ət, ˈel-yət\
Eliph·a·let \i-ˈlif-ə-lət, -ˌlet\
Eli·sa 1 *Ger., Ital.* \ā-ˈlē-zä\ 2 *Fr.* **Éli·sa** \ā-lē-zá\
Eli·sa·bet *Ger.* \ā-ˈlē-zä-(ˌ)bet\
Elis·a·beth 1 \i-ˈliz-ə-bəth\ 2 **Eli·sa·beth** *Ger.* \ā-ˈlē-zä-(ˌ)bet\ 3 *Swed.* \el-ˈē-sá-ˌbet\ 4 *Fr.* **Éli·sa·beth** \ā-lē-zá-bet\
Eli·sä·us *Norw.* \ˌel-i-ˈsā-ůs\
Elise 1 \ə-ˈlēs\ 2 *Fr.* **Élise** \ā-lēz\
Éli·sée *Fr.* \ā-lē-zā\
Eli·sha \i-ˈlī-shə\
Eli·za 1 \i-ˈlī-zə\ 2 *Pol.* \ā-ˈlē-zá\
Eliz·a·beth 1 \i-ˈliz-ə-bəth\ 2 *Du.* **Eli·za·beth** \ā-ˈlē-zá-ˌbet\
Eli·zur \i-ˈlī-zər\
El·kan \ˈel-kən\
El·ka·nah \el-ˈkā-nə, -ˈkä-\
El·king·ton \ˈel-kiŋ-tən\
El·kins \ˈel-kinz\
El·la \ˈel-ə\
El·len 1 \ˈel-ən\ 2 *Swed.* \ˈel-lən\
El·ler·ker \ˈel-ər-kər\
El·lery \ˈel-ər-ē\
El·lett \ˈel-ət\
El·lice \ˈel-əs\
El·li·cott \ˈel-i-kət\
El·lies *Fr.* \ā-lē\
El·ling *Norw.* \ˈel-liŋ\
El·ling·ton \ˈel-iŋ-tən\
El·ling·wood \ˈel-iŋ-ˌwůd\
El·lin·wood \ˈel-ən-ˌwůd\
El·li·ot \ˈel-ē-ət, ˈel-yət\
El·li·ott \ˈel-ē-ət, ˈel-yət\
El·lis \ˈel-əs\
El·li·son \ˈel-ə-sən\
El·ly \ˈel-ē\
El·ma·no *Port.* \el-ˈmán-ü\
Elme *Fr.* \elm\
El·mer \ˈel-mər\
El·more \ˈel-ˌmō(ə)r, -ˌmȯ(ə)r\
Éloi *Fr.* \āl-wá\
Elon \ˈe-lən\
Eloy *Span.* \ā-ˈlȯi\
El·pi·dio *Span.* \el-ˈpe<u>th</u>-yō\
El·ring·ton \ˈel-riŋ-tən\
El·roy \ˈel-ˌrȯi\
El·sa 1 \ˈel-sə\ 2 *Fr.* \el-sá\ 3 *Ger.* \ˈel-zä\ 4 *Swed.* \ˈel-sá\
Els·beth *Ger.* \ˈels-bet\
El·se *Ger.* \ˈel-zə\
El·se·us *Norw.* \el-ˈsā-ůs\
El·sie \ˈel-sē\
El·speth \ˈel-ˌspeth, -spəth\
Els·wyth \ˈelz-(ˌ)with\
El·ton \ˈelt-ᵊn\
El·vi·ra \el-ˈvī-rə, -vi(ə)r-ə\
El·well \ˈel-ˌwel, -wəl\
El·win *Ger.* \ˈel-(ˌ)vēn\
El·wood \ˈel-ˌwůd\
El·wyn \ˈel-wən\
Ely \ˈē-lē\
El·ye·sa *Alb.* \el-ˈyā-sä\
El·zé·ar *Fr.* \el-zā-ár\
El·zie \ˈel-zē\
Ema \ˈem-ə\
Eman·u·el 1 \i-ˈman-yə(-wə)l\ 2 **Ema·nu·el** *Czech* \ˈem-ˌá-nə-ˌwel\ 3 *Dan.* \i-ˈmá-nə-wəl\ 4 *Du.* \ā-ˈmá-nœ̄-ˌel\ 5 *Finn.* \e-ˈmá-nə-ˌwel\ 6 *Fr.* \ā-má-nwʸel, e-\ 7 *Ger.* \ā-ˈmän-ü-ˌel\ 8 *Swed.* \e-ˈmä-nə-wəl\
Ema·nue·le *Ital.* \ˌā-män-ˈwel-ā\
Éme·ric *Fr.* \ā-mə-rēk, em-rēk\
Em·er·ich 1 \ˈem-ər-ik\ 2 *Ger.* **Eme·rich** \ˈā-mə-ˌri<u>k</u>\
Em·ery \ˈem-(ə-)rē\
Emil 1 \ˈē-məl, ˈā-; ˈem-əl\ 2 *Czech, Finn., Hung.* \ˈem-il\ 3 *Dan.* \i-ˈmēl\ 4 *Ger.* \ˈā-mēl\ 5 *Pol.* \ˈem-ēl\ 6 *Swed.* \ˈā-mil\ 7 *Fr.* **Émil** \ā-mēl\
Emi·laud *Fr.* \ā-mē-lō\
Emile 1 \ā-ˈmē(ə)l, -məl\ 2 **Émile** *Du.* \ā-ˈmēl\ 3 *Fr.* \ā-mēl\
Emil·ia 1 \ə-ˈmil-ē-ə, -ˈmil-yə\ 2 *Span.* **Emi·lia** \ā-ˈmēl-yä\
Emi·lia·no 1 *Ital.* \ˌā-mēl-ˈyän-ō\ 2 *Span.* \ā-mēl-ˈyän-ō\
Em·i·lie 1 \ˈem-(ə-)lē\ 2 **Emi·lie** *Ger.* \ā-ˈmē-lē-ə\ 3 *Swed.* \e-ˈmil-ē\ 4 *Fr.* **Émi·lie** \ā-mē-lē\
Émi·lien *Fr.* \ā-mē-lyaⁿ\
Emi·lio *Ital., Span.* \ā-ˈmēl-yō\
Emi·li·us *Dan.* \im-ˈē-lē-ůs\
Em·i·ly \ˈem-(ə-)-lē\
Emin *Turk.* \e-ˈmēn\
Emi·shi *Jp.* \em-ē-shē\
Em·lin \ˈem-lən\
Em·lyn \ˈem-lən\
Em·ma 1 \ˈem-ə\ 2 *Du.* \ˈem-á\ 3 *Fr.* \em-má\ 4 *Ger.* \ˈem-ä\ 5 *Ital.* \ˈem-mä\
Em·man·uel 1 \i-ˈman-yə(-wə)l\ 2 **Em·ma·nu·el** *Fr.* \ā-má-nwʸel, e-\ 3 *Ger.* \e-ˈmän-ü-ˌel\ 4 *Mod. Gk.* **Em·ma·nuel** \ˌem-än-ˈwēl\
Em·ma·nue·le *Ital.* \ˌäm-män-ˈwel-ā\
Em·me·line \ˈem-ə-ˌlīn, -ˌlēn\
Em·me·rich *Ger.* \ˈem-ə-ˌri<u>k</u>\
Em·mi *Ger.* \ˈem-ē\
Em·mons \ˈem-ənz\
Em·mus·ka *Hung.* \ˈem-ˌmůsh-ˌkä\
Em·my *Eng., Ger.* \ˈem-ē\
Em·o·ry \ˈem-(ə-)rē\
Em·pie \ˈem-pē\
Em·roy \ˈem-ˌrȯi\
Ems·ley \ˈemz-lē\
En·di·cott \ˈen-di-kət, -də-ˌkät\
En·dre *Hung.* \ˈen-dre\
End·sor \ˈen-zər\
En·dym·i·on \en-ˈdim-ē-ən\
Enea *Ital.* \ā-ˈne-ä\
En·field \ˈen-ˌfēld\
Eng·el·bert 1 *Finn.* \ˈeŋ-el-ˌbert\ 2 *Ger.* \ˈeŋ-əl-ˌbert\
Eng·el·hard *Ger.* \ˈeŋ-əl-ˌhärt\
En·gle \ˈeŋ-(g)əl\
En·guer·rand *Fr.* \äⁿ-ge-räⁿ\
Enid \ˈē-nəd\
En·ne·mond *Fr.* \en-mōⁿ\
En·nio *Ital.* \ˈen -nyō\
En·nis \ˈen-əs\
En·no *Ger.* \ˈen-(ˌ)ō\
Enoch \ˈē-nək, -nik\
Enos \ˈē-nəs\
En·ri·co *Ital.* \än-ˈrē-kō\
En·ri·ka *Ger.* \en-ˈrē-kä\
En·ri·que *Span.* \än-ˈrē-kā\
En·ryo *Jp.* \en-rē-ō\
En·shū *Jp.* \en-shů\
En·sor \ˈen-zər\
Eo·ba·nus *Ger.* \ˌā-ō-ˈbän-ůs\
Eo·ghan *Ir. Gael.* \ˈō-ən\
Eoin *Ir. Gael.* \ˈyōn, ˈō-ən\
Epa·mei·non·das *Mod. Gr.* \ˌep-ä-mē-ˈnȯn-(ˌ)<u>th</u>äs\
Epar·chi·us *Lat.* \ə-ˈpär-kē-əs\
Epes \ˈeps\
Ephra·im 1 \ˈē-frā-əm, -frē-\ 2 *Ger.* \ˈā-frä-ˌim, ā-ˈfrä-im\
Epi·ta·cio *Port.* \ē-pē-ˈtás-yü\
Ep·per·son \ˈep-ər-sən\
Erasme *Fr.* \ā-rásmᵊ\
Eras·mo *Ital.* \ā-ˈräz-mō\
Eras·mus 1 \i-ˈraz-məs\ 2 *Dan.* \i-ˈräs-můs\ 3 *Ger.* \ā-ˈräs-můs\
Eras·tus \i-ˈras-təs\
Erazm *Pol.* \ˈer-áz-ᵊm\
Er·co·le *Ital.* \ˈer-kō-(ˌ)lā\
Erd·mann *Ger.* \ˈārt-ˌmän\
Er·hard *Ger.* \ˈār-ˌhärt\
Er·ic 1 \ˈer-ik\ 2 **Eric** *Dan.* \ˈir-ēk\ 3 *Norw.* \ˈā-rēk\ 4 *Swed.* \ˈā-rik\
Erich *Ger.* \ˈā-ri<u>k</u>\
Eri·co *Port.* \ē-ˈrē-kü\
Erig·e·na \i-ˈrij-ə-nə\
Erik 1 *Dan.* \ˈir-ēk\ 2 *Fr.* \ā-rēk\ 3 *Ger., Swed.* \ˈā-rik\ 4 *Norw.* \ˈā-rēk\
Eri·ka *Ger.* \ˈā-rē-ˌkä\
Eri·kit *Fr.* \ā-rē-kēt\
Eris *Ger.* \ˈā-rik\
Er·ken·bald \ˈər-kən-ˌbȯld\
Erk·ki *Finn.* \ˈerk-kē\
Er·land *Swed.* \ˈer-lánd\
Erle \ˈər(ə)l\
Er·man·no *Ital.* \ār-ˈmän-nō\
Er·men·gil·do *Ger.* \ˌer-män-ˈgil-dō\
Er·me·te *Ital.* \ār-ˈme-tā\
Er·mi·nia *Ital.* \ār-ˈmēn-yä\
Er·mi·nie, Er·min·nie \ˈər-mə-nē\
Er·nald \ˈər-nəld\
Er·nest 1 \ˈər-nəst\ 2 *Fr.* \er-nest\ 3 *Ger.* \er-ˈnest\ 4 *Swed.* \ˈer-nəst\
Er·nes·tas *Lith.* \er-ˈnes-täs\
Er·nes·tine 1 \ˈər-nə-ˌstēn\ 2 *Ger.* **Er·nes·ti·ne** \ˌer-nes-ˈtē-nə\
Er·nes·to 1 *Ital.* \ār-ˈnes-tō\ 2 *Port.* \ēr-ˈnesh-tü; -ˈnes-\ 3 *Span.* \er-ˈnā-stō\
Er·nes·tus *Ger.* \er-ˈnes-tůs\
Er·nie \ˈər-nē\
Ern·le \ˈərn-ᵊl\
Er·nő *Hung.* \ˈer-(ˌ)nœ̄\
Ernst 1 \ˈərn(t)st, ˈe(ə)rn(t)st\ 2 *Du., Ger., Norw., Swed.* \ˈernst\
Er·rett \ˈer-ət\
Er·ri·co *Ital.* \ār-ˈrē-kō\
Er·ro *Finn.* \ˈer-ˌrō\
Er·si·lio *Ital.* \ār-ˈsēl-yō\
Ert·skin \ˈərt-skən\

\ə\ **abut** \ᵊ\ **kitten,** *Fr.* **table** \ər\ **further** \a\ **ash** \ā\ **ace** \ä\ **cot, cart** \aů\ **out** \ch\ **chin** \e\ **bet** \ē\ **easy** \g\ **go** \i\ **hit** \ī\ **ice** \j\ **job** \ŋ\ **sing** \ō\ **go** \ȯ\ **law** \ȯi\ **boy** \th\ **both** \<u>th</u>\ **the** \ü\ **loot** \ů\ **foot** \y\ **yet** \zh\ **vision** \á, <u>b</u>, <u>g</u>, <u>k</u>, ⁿ, œ, œ̄, ue, ue̅, ʸ\ *see* Guide to Pronunciation

Er·vin \'ər-vən\
Er·win 1 \'ər-wən\ 2 *Ger.* \'er-(,)vēn\
Esa·ias 1 *Du.* \ā-'sä-,yäs, -'sī-,(y)äs\ 2 *Swed.* \e-'sī-äs\
Esek \'ē-,sek\
Es·mé \'ez-mē\
Es·mond \'ez-mənd\
Es·prit *Fr.* \es-prē\
Es·ta·brook \'es-tə-,brůk\
Es·ta·cio *Port.* \ēsh-'tás-yü; ēs-\
Es·ta·nis·lao *Span.* \ā-stän-ē-'slä-ō\
Es·te·ban *Span.* \ā-'stā-b̲än\
Es·tell \'es-t^{ə}l\
Es·telle \es-'tel, es-t^{ə}l\
Es·ten \'es-tən\
Es·tes \'es-təs\
Es·ther \'es-tər\
Es·tienne *Fr.* \ā-tyen, es-\
Est·lin \'est-lən\
Es·tra·da *Span.* \ā-'strä-t̲h̲-ä\
Esu·vi·us *Lat.* \i-'s(y)ü-vē-əs\
Ethan \'ē-thən\
Eth·el \'eth-əl\
Eth·el·bert \'eth-əl-(,)bərt\
Eth·e·lin·da \,eth-ə-'lin-də\
Eth·el·re·da \,eth-əl-'rē-də\
Eth·el·reid \'eth-əl-,rēd\
Étienne *Fr.* \ā-tyen\
Étien·nette *Fr.* \ā-tyen-et\
Et·to·re *Ital.* \'et-tō-(,)rā\
Eu·bie \'yü-bē\
Eudes *Fr.* \œ̄d\
Eu·gen *Ger.* \ȯi-'gān\
Eu·gene 1 \yü-'jēn, 'yü-,\ 2 *Fr.* **Eu·gène** \œ̄-zhan\
Eu·ge·nia \yů-'jē-nē-ə, -'jēn-yə\
Eu·gé·nie 1 *Fr.* \œ̄-zhā-nē\ 2 *Ger.* **Eu·ge·nie** \ȯi-'gā-nē-ə, -nyə\
Eu·ge·nio 1 *Ital.* \āů-'jen-yō\ 2 *Span.* \ā-ü-'k̲än-yō\ 3 *Port.* **Eu·gé·nio** \āů-'zhān-yü\
Eu·ge·ni·us 1 *Dan.* \eů-'gin-ē-ůs\ 2 *Gk.* \ev-'gēn-ēfs\
Eu·ge·niusz *Pol.* \eů-'gān-yüsh\
Eu·la·lie \'yü-lə-lē\
Eu·las \'yü-ləs\
Eu·nice 1 \'yü-nəs\ 2 *Lat.* **Eu·ni·ce** \yů-'nī-sē\
Eu·phra·sie *Fr.* \œ̄-frá-zē\
Eu·phros·y·ne \yů-'fräs-^{ə}n-(,)ē\
Eu·ret·ta \yů-'ret-ə\
Eu·ri·cius *Lat.* \yů-'rish(-ē)-əs\
Eu·ri·co *Port.* \āů-'rē-kü\
Eu·sa·pia *Ital.* \āů-'zäp-yä\
Eu·se·bio 1 *Ital.* \āů-'zeb-yō\ 2 *Span.* \āů-'sā-b̲-yō\
Eu·se·bi·us *Ger.* \ȯi-'zāb-yůs, -'zā-bē-ůs\
Eus·tace \'yü-stəs\
Eus·tache *Fr.* \œ̄-stásh\
Eu·trope *Fr.* \œ̄-trȯp\
Eu·tych *Ger.* \ȯi-'tæk̲\
Eva 1 \'ē-və\ 2 *Ger., Norw.* \'ā-vä\
Ev·an \'ev-ən\
Evan·der \i-'van-dər\
Evan·ge·line \i-'van-jə-,lēn, -,līn, -lən\
Evan·ge·lis·ta 1 *Ger.* \,ā-väŋ-gā-'lis-tä\ 2 *Ital.* \,ā-vän-jā-'lēs-tä\
Ev·ans \'ev-ənz\
Éva·riste *Fr.* \ā-vá-rēst\
Eva·ris·to 1 *Port.* \ē-və-'rēsh-tü; ē-vá-'rēs-\ 2 *Span.* \ā-b̲ä-'rēs-tō\
Ev·arts \'ev-ərts\
Eve·li·na *Ital.* \,ā-vā-'lē-nä\
Ev·e·lyn \'ev-(ə-)lən, *chiefly Brit* 'ēv-\
Ev·er·ard \'ev-ər-,ärd\
Ev·er·end \'ev-(ə-)rənd\
Ev·er·ett, -ette \'ev-(ə-)rət\
Ever·har·dus *Du.* \,ā-vər-'här-dœs\
Ev·er·ley, -ly \'ev-ər-lē\
Ev·ers \'ev-ərz\
Ev·er·shed \'ev-ər-shed\
Ev·ert 1 \'ev-ərt\ 2 *Du.* **Evert** \'ā-vərt\
Ev·ert·son \'ev-ərt-sən\
Ev·ge·nios *Mod. Gk.* \ev-'yen-(,)yȯs\
Evind *Finn.* \'ā-,vind\
Évrard *Fr.* \āv-rár\
Ewald *Ger.* \'ā-,vält\
Ew·art \'yü-ərt\
Ew·banke \'yü-,baŋk\
Ew·ell \'yü-əl\
Ew·en \'yü-ən\
Ew·ing \'yü-iŋ\
Eyre \'a(ə)r, 'e(ə)r\
Ey·steinn *Icel.* \'ā-stād-^{ə}n\
Ey·ster \'ī-stər\
Ey·ton \'īt-^{ə}n\
Ey·vind *Norw.* \'ā-vin\
Ezech·iel *Ger.* \āt-'sek̲-yel, -'sēk̲-ē-el\
Eze·chiele *Ger.* \āt-'säk̲-yā-lə\
Ezek·iel \i-'zē-kyəl, -kē-əl\
Eze·quiel *Span.* \ā-thāk-'yel; ā-sāk-\
Ez·ra \'ez-rə\

Fa·bi·an 1 \'fā-bē-ən\ 2 *Ger.* \'fäb-yän, -ē-än\
Fa·bio *Ital.* \'fäb-yō\
Fa·bi·us *Lat.* \'fā-bē-əs\
Fa·bre *Fr.* \fábr^{ə}\
Fa·bri *Fr.* \fá-brē\
Fa·brice *Fr.* \fá-brēs\
Fa·bri·ci·us 1 *Ger.* \fä-'brēt-sē-ůs\ 2 *Lat.* \fə-'brish(-ē)-əs\
Fa·bri·zio *Ital.* \fäb-'rēts-yō\
Fa·cun·do *Ital.* \fä-'kün-dō\
Fad·dey *Russ.* \(,)fəd-'yä(-ē)\
Fad·de·ye·vich *Russ.* \(,)fəd-'yä(-yiv)-,yich\
Fair \'fa(ə)r, 'fe(ə)r\
Fair·child \'fa(ə)r-,chīld, 'fe(ə)r-\
Fair·fax \'fa(ə)r-,faks, 'fe(ə)r-\
Fair·field \'fa(ə)r-,fēld, 'fe(ə)r-\
Fair·ly \'fa(ə)r-lē, 'fe(ə)r-\
Fait *Turk.* \'fīt\
Faith·ful \'fāth-fəl\
Fal·con \'fal-kən *also* 'fȯl- *sometimes* 'fȯ-kən\
Fales \'fā(ə)lz\
Fal·las \'fal-əs\
Fal·low \'fal-(,)ō\
Fan·nie \'fan-ē\
Fan·ning \'fan-iŋ\
Fan·ny 1 \'fan-ē\ 2 *Fr.* \fá-nē\ 3 *Ger.* \'fän-ē\
Fa·no *Serb.-Cr.* \'fä-nȯ\
Fan·shaw, -shawe \'fan-,shȯ\
Far·a·day \'far-ə-,dā, -əd-ē\
Fa·ri·na·ta *Ital.* \,fär-ē-'nä-tä\
Far·kas *Hung.* \'fär-,käsh\
Farn·ham \'fär-nəm\
Farns·worth \'färnz-(,)wərth\
Far·quhar \'fär-k(w)ər\
Far·quhar·son \'fär-k(w)ər-sən\
Far·thing \'fär-t̲h̲iŋ\
Faulk·land \'fȯ(l)-klənd\
Faus·tin *Fr.* \fō-sta^{n}\
Faus·ti·na *Ital.* \faů-'stē-nä\
Faus·tino \faů-'stē-nō\
Faus·to *Ital., Span.* \'faů-stō\
Faus·tus *Lat.* \'fȯs-təs\
Fa·vre *Fr.* \fávr^{ə}\
Faw·cett \'fȯs-ət\
Fay \'fā\
Fay·ette \fā-'et\
Fa·zil *Turk.* \fä-'zœl\
Fear·gus \'fər-gəs\
Fear·on \'fi(ə)r-ən\
Fé·dé·ric *Fr.* \fā-dā-rēk\
Fe·de·ri·co 1 *Ital.* \,fā-dā-'rē-kō\ 2 *Span.* \fā-t̲h̲ā-'rē-kō\
Fe·de·ri·go 1 *Ital.* \,fā-dā-'rē-gō\ 2 *Span.* \fā-t̲h̲ā-'rē-g̲ō\
Fe·dor *Ger.* \'fā-,dōr, -,dȯr\
Fe·lix 1 \'fē-liks\ 2 *Du.* \'fā-ləks\ 3 *Ger.* \'fā-liks\ 4 *Hung.* \'fel-iks\ 5 **Fé·lix** *Fr.* \fā-lēks\ 6 *Span.* \'fā-lēks\
Fel·ia *Russ.* \'fyil-yə, 'fyäl-yi-yə\
Fe·li·ber·to *Port.* \fə-lē-'ber-tü; fā-\
Fe·li·cia·no 1 *Port.* \fə-lēs-'yá-nü; fā-\ 2 *Span.* \fā-lēth-'yän-ō; -lēs-\
Fe·li·ce *Ital.* \fā-'lē-chā\
Fe·li·cia 1 \fə-'lish-(ē-)ə, -'lis-\ 2 *Span.* \fā-'lēth-yä; -'lēs-\
Fé·li·cien *Fr.* \fā-lēs-yan\
Fé·li·ci·té *Fr.* \fā-lē-sē-tā\
Fe·liks 1 *Pol.* \'fel-ēks\ 2 *Russ.* \'fyäl-yiks\
Fe·lim *Ir. Gael.* \'fā-lim\
Fe·li·pe *Span.* \fā-'lē-pā\
Fel·lows \'fel-(,)ōz\
Fen·e·lon \'fen-^{ə}l-ən\
Fen·i·more \'fen-ə-,mō(ə)r, -,mȯ(ə)r\
Fen·no \'fen-ō\
Fen·tress \'fen-trəs\
Fen·wick \'fen-,wik, *esp Brit* -ik\
Fe·o·dor 1 *Ger.* \'fā-ō-,dōr, -,dȯr\ 2 *Russ.* \fyi-'ȯ-dər\
Fe·o·do·ra \,fē-ō-'dōr-ə, -'dȯr-\
Fe·o·fan *Russ.* \fyi-(,)ə-'fán\
Fe·o·fi·lak·to·vich *Russ.* \fyi-əf-yi-'lákt(-əv)-,yich\
Fer·ber \'fər-bər\
Fer·chault *Fr.* \fer-shō\
Fer·de \'fərd-ē\
Fer·di·nand 1 \'fərd-^{ə}n-,and\ 2 *Dan.* \'fer-di-,nȧn\ 3 *Du., Ger.* \'fer-dē-,nänt\ 4 *Fr.* \fer-dē-nä^{n}\ 5 *Russ.* \fyir-dyi-'nánt, 'fyer-dyi-nənt\ 6 *Swed.* \'fer-di-,nȧnd\
Fer·di·nande *Fr.* \fer-dē-nä^{n}d\
Fer·di·nan·do 1 \,fərd- ^{ə}n-'an-dō\ 2 *Ital.* \,fär-dē-'nän-dō\
Fer·dy·nand *Pol.* \fer-'di-nánt\
Fe·renc, Fe·rencz *Hung.* \'fer-ents\
Fé·ré·ol *Fr.* \fā-rā-ȯl\
Fer·gus \'fər-gəs\
Fer·min *Fr.* \fer-ma^{n}\
Fern \'fərn\
Fer·nam *Port.* \fər-'naů^{n}; fer-\
Fer·nan 1 *Fr.* \fer-nä^{n}\ 2 **Fer·nán** *Span.* \fer-'nän\
Fer·nand *Fr.* \fer-nä^{n}\
Fer·nan·des *Port.* \fər-'ná^{n}(n)-dish; fer-'ná^{n}(n)-dis\
Fer·nan·dez 1 \fər-'nan-,dez\ 2 *Port.* \fər-'ná^{n}-(n)-dish; fer-'ná^{n}(n)-dis\ 3 **Fer·nán·dez** *Span.* \fer-'nän-dāth; -dās\
Fer·nan·do 1 \fər-'nan-dō\ 2 *Ital.* \fär-'nän-dō\ 3 *Port.* \fər-'ná^{n}(n)-dü; fer-\ 4 *Span.* \fer-'nän-dō\
Fer·não *Port.* \fər-'naů^{n}; fer-\
Fer·ran·te *Ital.* \fär-'rän-tā\
Fer·ris \'fer-əs\
Fer·ruc·cio *Ital.* \fär-'rüt-chō\
Fes·tus *Lat.* \'fes-təs\
Fet·tes \'fet-əs\
Fèvre, Le *Fr.* \lə-fevr^{ə}\
Fev·zi *Turk.* \fev-'zē\
Fiacre *Fr.* \fyákr^{ə}\
Fid·di·an \'fid-ē-ən\
Fi·del *Span.* \fē-'t̲h̲el\
Fi·de·lio *Ger.* \fē-'dāl-yō, -'dā-lē-(,)ō\
Fi·de·lis *Ger.* \fē-'dā-lis\
Fiennes \'fīnz\
Fife \'fīf\

Fi·li·ber·to *Ital.* \ˌfē-lē-ˈber-tō\
Fi·lin·to *Port.* \fē-ˈlē^n(n)-tü\
Fi·lipp *Russ.* \fyil-ˈyēp\
Fi·lip·pi·no *Ital.* \ˌfē-lēp-ˈpē-nō\
Fi·lip·po *Ital.* \fē-ˈlēp-pō\
Fil·ley \ˈfil-ē\
Find·lay \ˈfin(d)-lā, -lē\
Find·ley \ˈfin(d)-lē\
Fin·gal \ˈfiŋ-gəl, ˈfin-\
Fin·ley \ˈfin-lē\
Finn 1 *Eng., Swed.* \ˈfin\ 2 *Icel.* \ˈfid-ᵊn\
Fin·ne *Swed.* \ˈfin-ne\
Fin·nur *Icel.* \ˈfin-nœr\
Fi·o·na \fi-ˈō-nə, fē-\
Fi·o·rel·lo \ˌfē-ə-ˈrel-(ˌ)ō\
Fio·ren·zo *Ital.* \fyō-ˈrent-sō\
Fir·min *Fr.* \fēr-ma^n\
Fi·roz *Urdu* \fi-ˈrōz\
Fish \ˈfish\
Fish·el *Russ.* \ˈfyish-yil\
Fitts \ˈfits\
Fitz \ˈfits\
Fitz·ed·ward \fits-ˈed-wərd\
Fitz-Greene \ˈfits-ˌgrēn, ˌfits-ˈgrēn\
Fitz·hugh \ˈfits-ˌhyü, fits-ˈhyü\
Fitz·james, -James \ˈfits-ˌjāmz, fits-ˈjāmz\
Fitz-John, Fitz·John \ˈfits-ˌjän, fits-ˈjän\
Fitz·mau·rice \fits-ˈmȯr-əs, -ˈmär-\
Fitz·ran·dolph \fits-ˈran-ˌdälf\
Fitz-Roy, Fitz·roy \ˈfits-ˌrȯi, fits-ˈrȯi\
Fitz·si·mons \fit(s)-ˈsī-mənz\
Fitz·wil·liam \fits-ˈwil-yəm\
Fla·ci·us *Lat.* \ˈflā-kē-əs\
Flack \ˈflak\
Fla·mi·nio *Ital.* \flä-ˈmēn-yō\
Fla·vel \ˈflā-vəl\
Fla·via *Lat.* \ˈflā-vē-ə\
Fla·vio *Ital.* \ˈfläv-yō\
Fla·vi·us \ˈflā-vē-əs\
Fleem·ing \ˈflem-iŋ\
Flex·ner \ˈfleks-nər\
Flin·ders \ˈflin-dərz\
Flood \ˈfləd\
Flo·ra \ˈflōr-ə, ˈflȯr-\
Flor·ance \ˈflȯr-ən(t)s, ˈflär-\
Flor·ence 1 \ˈflȯr-ən(t)s, ˈflär-\ 2 *Fr.* **Flo·rence** \flȯ-ra^{n}s\
Flo·ren·cio *Span.* \flō-ˈrān-thyō; -syō\
Flo·rens 1 *Ger.* \ˈflōr-en(t)s\ 2 *Lat.* \ˈflōr-enz\
Flo·rensz *Du* \ˈflōr-əns\
Flo·rent 1 *Du.* \flō-ˈrent\ 2 *Fr.* \flȯ-rä^n\
Flo·ren·tin *Fr.* \flȯr-a^n-ta^n\
Flo·ren·ti·us *Du.* \flō-ˈren-tē-œs\
Flo·ren·ty *Pol.* \flȯr-ˈen-ti\
Flo·renz \ˈflōr-ənz, ˈflȯr-, -ən(t)s\
Flo·res·tan *Fr.* \flȯr-es-tä^n\
Flo·re·sta·no *Ital.* \ˌflō-rās-ˈtän-ō\
Flo·ri·an 1 \ˈflō-rē-ən\ 2 *Ger.* \ˈflōr-yän, -rē-än\ 3 *Fr.* **Flo·rian** \flȯr-yä^n\ 4 **Flo·rián** *Span.* \flōr-ˈyän\
Flo·ria·no *Port.* \flür-ˈyȧ-nü\
Flo·ri·mond 1 *Flem.* \ˈflōr-ē-ˌmȯnt\ 2 *Fr.* \flȯr-ē-mō^n\
Flo·ri·mund *Ger.* \ˈflō-rē-ˌmu̇nt\
Floyd \ˈflȯid\
Flynt \ˈflint\
Fogg \ˈfȯg, ˈfäg\
Fol·co *Ital.* \ˈfōl-kō\
Fol·ger \ˈfōl-jər\
Fol·ke *Swed.* \ˈfōl-kə\
Folkes \ˈfōks\
Fol·len \ˈfäl-ən\
Fol·lett \ˈfäl-ət\
Fo·mich *Russ.* \ˈfōm-yich\
Fo·mi·nit·shna *Pol.* \fō-mē-ˈnēch-nə\
Fon·taine \fän-ˈtān, ˈfän-tān\
Forbes *Fr.* \fȯrb\
Force \ˈfō(ə)rs, ˈfȯ(ə)rs\
For·dyce \ˈfȯr-ˌdīs\
For·est \ˈfȯr-əst, ˈfär-\
For·es·ter \ˈfȯr-əs-tər, ˈfär-\
For·man \ˈfōr-mən, ˈfȯr-\
For·rest \ˈfȯr-əst, ˈfär-\
For·res·ter \ˈfȯr-əs-tər, ˈfär-\
For·sha \ˈfȯr-shə\
Fort \ˈfō(ə)rt, ˈfȯ(ə)rt\
For·tu·nat *Fr.* \fȯr-tue̅-nȧ\
For·tu·na·to *Ital.* \ˌfōr-tü-ˈnä-tō\
For·tu·na·tus \ˌfȯr-chə-ˈnāt-əs\
For·tune 1 \ˈfȯr-chən\ 2 *Fr.* **For·tu·né** \fȯr-tue̅-nā\
Foss \ˈfȯs\
Fos·ter \ˈfȯs-tər, ˈfäs-\
Foth·er·gill \ˈfät͟h-ər-ˌgil\
Foun·tain \ˈfau̇nt-ᵊn\
Fow·ell \ˈfau̇(-ə)l\
Fowle \ˈfau̇(ə)l\
Fowles \ˈfau̇(ə)lz\
Fownes \ˈfau̇nz\
Fox·croft \ˈfäks-ˌkräft\
Fox·well \ˈfäks-ˌwel, -wəl\
Fran·ce *Slovene* \ˈfrȧnt-sə\
Fran·ces \ˈfran(t)-səs\
Fran·ces·ca *Ital.* \frän-ˈchās-kä\
Fran·ces·co *Ital.* \frän-ˈchās-kō\
Fran·chi·no *Ital.* \fräŋ-ˈkē-nō\
Fran·cis 1 \ˈfran(t)-səs\ 2 *Du.* \ˈfrän(t)-səs\ 3 *Fr.* \fra^n-sēs\ 4 *Ger.* \ˈfränt-sis\ 5 *Norw.* \ˈfrän(t)-sis\
Fran·cis·ca 1 \fran-ˈsis-kə\ 2 *Port.* \frȧ^n-ˈsēsh-kə; -ˈsēs-kȧ\ 3 *Span.* \frän-ˈthēs-kä; -ˈsēs-\
Fran·cis·co 1 \fran-ˈsis-kō\ 2 *Port.* \frȧ^n-ˈsēsh-kü; -ˈsēs-\ 3 *Span.* \frän-ˈthēs-kō; -ˈsēs-\
Fran·cis·cus 1 *Du.* \frän-ˈsis-kœs\ 2 *Lat.* \fran-ˈsis-kəs\
Fran·cisque *Fr.* \frä^n-sēsk\
Fran·ci·szek *Pol.* \frȧn-ˈchē-shek\
Franck, Francke \ˈfraŋk, ˈfräŋk\
Fran·co *Ital.* \ˈfräŋ-kō\
Fran·çois *Fr.* \frä^n-swȧ\
Fran·çoise *Fr.* \fra^n-swȧz\
Frands *Dan.* \ˈfrän(t)s\
Frank 1 \ˈfraŋk\ 2 *Du., Ger.* \ˈfräŋk\ 3 *Fr.* \frä^{n}k\
Frank·fort \ˈfraŋk-fərt\
Frank·lin, -lyn \ˈfraŋ-klən\
Fra·nov *Serb.-Cr.* \ˈfrȧ-nȯv\
Frans 1 *Dan., Du.* \ˈfrän(t)s\ 2 *Finn., Swed.* \ˈfrȧn(t)s\
Fran·sen *Du.* \ˈfrän-sən\
Fran·ti·šek *Czech* \ˈfrȧn-chi-ˌshek\
Frants *Norw.* \ˈfränts\
Fran·tse·vich *Russ.* \ˈfrȧnts(-yiv)-ˌyich\
Frantz *Fr.* \frä^n(t)s\
Franz 1 \ˈfrants, ˈfranz, ˈfränts\ 2 *Fr.* \frä^{n}s\ 3 *Ger.* \ˈfränts\ 4 *Russ.* \ˈfrȧnts\
Fran·zis·ka *Ger.* \fränt-ˈsis-kä\
Fra·zer \ˈfrā-zər, -zhər\
Fra·zier \ˈfrā-zhər\
Fred \ˈfred\
Freda \ˈfred-ə\
Fred·er·ic 1 \ˈfred(-ə)-rik\ 2 *Norw.* **Fre·de·ric** \ˈfred-rik\ 3 *Fr.* **Fré·dé·ric** \frā-dā-rēk\
Fre·de·ri·ca *Ger.* \ˌfrā-dā-ˈrē-kä
Fred·er·ick \ˈfred(-ə)-rik\ 2 *Dan.* **Fre·de·rick** \ˈfrit͟h-rik\ 3 *Fr.* **Fré·dé·rick** \frā-dā-rēk\
Fred·er·icka \ˌfred-ə-ˈrik-ə\
Fre·de·rik 1 *Dan.* \ˈfrit͟h-rik\ 2 *Du.* \ˈfrā-də-rək\ 3 *Swed.* \ˈfrā-də-rik\
Fre·de·ri·ka *Dan.* \ˌfrit͟h-ə-ˈrē-kȧ\
Fred·ric 1 \ˈfred-rik\ 2 *Swed.* **Fre·dric** \ˈfrā-drik\
Fred·ri·ca \fred-ˈrē-kə\
Fred·rik 1 *Dan.* \ˈfrit͟h-rik\ 2 *Norw.* \ˈfred-rik\ 3 **Fre·drik** *Du.* \ˈfrā-drək\ 4 *Finn., Swed.* \ˈfrā-drik\
Fred·ri·ka *Swed.* \fred-ˈrē-kȧ\
Free·land \ˈfrē-lənd\
Free·man \ˈfrē-mən\
Free·mont \ˈfrē-ˌmänt\
Freer \ˈfrir\
Frei·mund *Ger.* \ˈfrī-ˌmu̇nt\
Fre·ling·huy·sen \ˈfrē-liŋ-ˌhīz-ᵊn\
Fre·man·tle \ˈfrē-man-təl\
Fre·mont \ˈfrē-ˌmänt\
Frend \ˈfrend\
Frensch *Afrik.* \ˈfre^{n}s\
Fres·nin *Fr.* \frā-na^n\
Fri·da *Ger.* \ˈfrē-(ˌ)dä\
Fri·do·lin *Du.* \ˈfrē-dō-lən\
Fridt·jof *Norw.* \ˈfrit-yȯf\
Frie·da *Ger.* \ˈfrē-(ˌ)dä\
Frie·de·mann *Ger.* \ˈfrē-də-ˌmän\
Frie·de·ri·ke *Ger.* \ˌfrē-də-ˈrē-kə\
Fried·lieb *Ger.* \ˈfrēt-(ˌ)lēp\
Frie·drich 1 \ˈfrē-drik\ 2 *Ger.* \ˈfrē-(ˌ)drik̲\
Fries \ˈfrēs\
Frig·yes *Hung.* \ˈfrig-yes\
Frin·i·wyd \ˈfrin-ə-(ˌ)wid, -wəd\
Frink \ˈfriŋk\
Fris·bie \ˈfriz-bē\
Frit·hiof *Swed.* \ˈfrit-yȯf\
Frits *Dan.* \ˈfrēts\
Fritz \ˈfrits\
Fro·men·tal *Fr.* \frȯ-mä^n-tȧl\
Fruc·tuo·so *Span.* \frük-ˈtwō-sō\
Fry \ˈfrī\
Fry·de·ryk *Pol.* \fri-ˈder-ik\
Fryn·i·wyd \ˈfrin-ə-wəd\
Fu·ad *Arab.* \ˈfü-ad\
Fuch *Fr.* \ˈfük\
Fu·fi·us *Lat.* \ˈfyü-fē-əs\
Fu·hi·to *Jp.* \fu̇-hē-tō\
Fu·ji·mi·tsu *Jp.* \fu̇j-ē-mēt-su̇\
Ful·cran *Fr.* \fue̅l-krä^n\
Ful·gence *Fr.* \fue̅l-zhä^{n}s\
Ful·gen·cio *Span.* \fül-k̲än-thyō; -syō\
Fulke \ˈfu̇lk\
Ful·ler·ton \ˈfu̇l-ər-tən\
Fü·löp *Hung.* \ˈfuel-(ˌ)œp\
Ful·ton \ˈfu̇lt-ᵊn\
Ful·via *Ital.* \ˈfül-vyä\
Ful·vi·us *Lat.* \ˈfəl-vē-əs\
Fum·i·ko *Jp.* \fu̇m-ē-kō\
Fu·mi·ma·ro *Jp.* \fu̇-mē-mä-rō\
Funk \ˈfəŋk\
Fürch·te·gott *Ger.* \ˈfuerk̲-tə-ˌgȯt\
Fu·rio *Ital.* \ˈfür-yō\
Fu·ri·us *Lat.* \ˈfyu̇r-ē-əs\
Fur·man \ˈfər-mən\
Fur·neaux \ˈfər-nō\
Fur·ni·fold \ˈfər-nə-ˌfōld\
Fu·sée *Fr.* \fue̅-zā\
Fynes \ˈfīnz\
Fyo·dor *Russ.* \ˈfyȯd-ər\
Fyo·do·ro·vich *Russ.* \ˈfyȯd-ər(-əv)-ˌyich\
Fyo·do·rov·na *Russ.* \ˈfyȯd-ər(-ə)v-nə\

\ə\ **abut** \ᵊ\ **kitten**, *Fr.* **table** \ər\ **further** \a\ **ash** \ā\ **ace** \ä\ **cot, cart** \au̇\ **out** \ch\ **chin** \e\ **bet** \ē\ **easy** \g\ **go** \i\ **hit** \ī\ **ice** \j\ **job** \ŋ\ **sing** \ō\ **go** \ȯ\ **law** \ȯi\ **boy** \th\ **both** \t͟h\ **the** \ü\ **loot** \u̇\ **foot** \y\ **yet** \zh\ **vision** \ȧ, b̲, g̲, k̲, ^{n}, œ, œ̄, ue, ue̅, ^{y}\ *see* Guide to Pronunciation

Gab·bert \'gab-ərt\
Gá·bor *Hung.* \'gä-(ˌ)bȯr\
Ga·bri·el 1 \'gā-brē-əl\ 2 *Du.* \'gäb-rē-(ˌ)el\ 3 *Fr.* \gȧ-brē-el\ 4 *Ger.* \'gäb-rē-(ˌ)el\ 5 *Norw., Swed.* \'gäb-rē-əl\ 6 *Pol.* \'gȧb-ryel\ 7 *Port.* \gə-brē-'el; gȧ-\ 8 *Span.* \gäb-rē-'el\
Ga·bri·e·la 1 *Pol.* \gȧb-rē-'ā-lȧ\ 2 *Span.* \gäb-rē-'ā-lä\
Ga·bri·e·le 1 *Ger.* \ˌgäb-rē-'ā-lə\ 2 *Ital.* \ˌgäb-rē-'el-ā\
Ga·bri·el·la \ˌgā-brē-'el-ə, ˌgab-rē-\
Ga·bri·elle 1 \ˌgā-brē-'el, ˌgab-rē-\ 2 *Fr.* \gȧ-brē-el\
Ga·bri·el·lo *Ital.* \ˌgäb-rē-'el-lō\
Ga·bri·el·son *Norw.* \'gäb-rē-əl-sȯn\
Ga·bri·els·son *Swed.* \'gä-brē-əl-ˌsȯn\
Ga·brjel *Pol.* \'gȧb-ryel\
Ga·bry·e·la *Pol.* \ˌgȧ-bri-'el-ȧ\
Gad·do *Ital.* \'gäd-dō\
Gads·by \'gadz-bē\
Ga·é·tan *Fr.* \gȧ-ā-tä^{n}\
Ga·e·ta·na *Ital.* \ˌgä-ā-'tän-ä\
Ga·e·ta·no *Ital.* \ˌgä-ā-'tän-ō\
Gail \'gā(ə)l\
Gaines \'gānz\
Gaird·ner \'ga(ə)rd-nər, 'ge(ə)rd-, 'gärd-\
Ga·ius *Lat.* \'gā-(y)əs, 'gī-\
Ga·lak·ti·o·no·vich *Russ.* \gə-lək-tyi-'ȯn(-əv)-ˌyich\
Gal·bert *Fr.* \gȧl-ber\
Gal·braith \'gal-ˌbrāth\
Gale \'gā(ə)l\
Ga·le·az·zo *Ital.* \ˌgäl-ā-'ät-tsō\
Ga·le·ria *Lat.* \gə-'lir-ē-ə\
Ga·le·ri·us *Lat.* \gə-'lir-ē-əs\
Gal·i·leo 1 \ˌgal-ə-'lē-ō\ 2 *Ital.* **Ga·li·leo** \ˌgäl-ē-'le-ō\
Ga·lis·sard *Fr.* \gȧ-lē-sȧr\
Gal·la \'gal-ə, 'gäl-ə\
Gal·la·tin \'gal-ət-^{ə}n\
Gal·lo·way \'gal-ə-ˌwā\
Ga·lon *Burmese* \'gäl-ȯn\
Gal·ton \'gȯlt-^{ə}n\
Gal·lus *Ger.* \'gäl-ůs\
Ga·lu·sha \gə-'lü-shə\
Gam·age \'gam-ij\
Ga·mal *Arab.* \jə-'mäl\
Ga·ma·li·el \gə-'mā-lē-əl, -'māl-yəl\
Gam·ble \'gam-bəl\
Gan·ga·dhar *Marathi* \'gäŋ-gəd-ər\
Gan·na·way \'gan-ə-ˌwā\
Gan·nett \'gan-ət\
Gans *Ger.* \'gän(t)s\
Ga·on *Heb.* \'gä-ōn, gä-'ōn\
Gar·cia 1 *Port.* \gər-'sē-ə; gȧr-'sē-ȧ\ 2 *Span.* **Gar·cía** \gär-'thē-ä; -'sē-\
Gard \'gärd\
Gar·et \'gar-ət\
Gar·field \'gär-ˌfēld\
Gari \'ga(ə)r-ē, 'ge(ə)r-\
Gar·i·bal·di \ˌgar-ə-'bȯl-dē\
Gar·ret, -rett \'gar-ət\
Gar·rick \'gar-ik\
Gar·rigue *Czech* \gə-'rēg\
Gar·ri·gues \'gar-ig-ˌyüz\
Gar·ri·son \'gar-ə-sən\
Garth \'gärth\
Garv \'gärv\
Gar·ver \'gär-vər\
Gary \'ga(ə)r-ē, 'ge(ə)r-ē\
Gas·par 1 \'gas-pər\ 2 *Lat.* \'gas-(ˌ)pär\ 3 *Port.* \gəsh-'pȧr; gȧs-\ 4 *Span.* \gäs-'pär\
Gas·pard *Fr.* \gȧs-pȧr\
Gas·pa·ro *Ital.* \'gäs-pär-(ˌ)ō\
Gas·sa·way \'gas-ə-ˌwā\
Gas·sett \'gas-ət\
Gas·ton 1 \'gas-tən\ 2 *Fr.* \gȧ-stō^{n}\
Gas·tone *Ital.* \gäs-'tō-nā\
Ga·thorne \'gā-ˌthȯ(ə)rn\
Gau·denz *Ger.* \'gaů-(ˌ)dents\
Gau·den·zio *Ital.* \gaů-'dent-syō\
Gau·tier *Fr.* \gō-tyā\
Gav·an \'gav-ən\
Gav·in \'gav-ən\
Ga·vi·us *Lat.* \'gā-vē-əs\
Gav·ri·il *Russ.* \gəv-ryi-'ēl\
Gav·ril *Russ.* \(ˌ)gəv-'ryil\
Gav·ri·la *Russ.* \(ˌ)gəv-'ryē-lə\
Ga·vri·lo *Serb.-Cr.* \'gȧv-rē-lȯ\
Gav·ri·lo·vich *Russ.* \gəv-ryi-'lȯv-ˌyich\
Ga·win \'gä-(w)ən\
Gay·lord \'gā-ˌlȯ(ə)rd\
Geat·ing \'gēt-iŋ\
Geb·hard *Ger.* \'gep-ˌhärt\
Gé·dé·on *Fr.* \zhā-dā-ō^{n}\
Ged·ney \'ged-nē\
Geer \'gi(ə)r\
Geer·har·dus *Du.* \gē(ə)r-'här-dœs\
Geert *Du.* \'gē(ə)rt\
Geer·trui·da *Du.* \gē(ə)r-'trœi-dȧ\
Ge·la·sio *Ital.* \jā-'läz-yō\
Ge·lett \jə-'let\
Gem·ma *Ital.* \'jem-mä\
Gen *Jp.* \gen\
Ge·na \'jē-nə\
Gene \'jēn\
Gen·e·vieve 1 \'jen-ə-ˌvēv\ 2 *Fr.* **Gene·viève** \zhən-vyev\
Gen·na·di·yev·ich *Russ.* \gyin-'nȧd-yiv-ˌyich\
Gen·na·ro *Ital.* \jän-'när-ō\
Gen·shi·chi *Jp.* \gen-shē-chē\
Gen·ta·ro *Jp.* \gen-tä-rō\
Gen·ti·le *Ital.* \jän-'tē-lā\
Geof·frey \'jef-rē\
Geof·froi, Geof·froy *Fr.* \zhȯ-frwä\
Ge·org 1 *Dan.* \gi-'ȯr(g)\ 2 *Finn.* \'ye-ˌȯrg\ 3 *Ger.* \gā-'ȯrk\ 4 *Norw.* \'gā-ˌȯrg\ 5 *Swed.* \'yā-ȯr^{y}\
George 1 \'jȯ(ə)rj\ 2 *Fr.* \zhȯrzh\ 3 *Ger.* \'zhȯrsh\ 4 *Rom.* \'zhůrzh, 'jȯr-je\ 5 *Du.* **Geor·ge** \'zhȯr-zhə\
Georges *Fr.* \zhȯrzh\
Geor·gette \jȯr-'jet\
Ge·or·gi 1 *Bulg.* \gā-'ȯr-gē\ 2 *Russ.* \gyi-'ȯr-gyəi\
Geor·gia \'jȯr-jə\
Geor·gi·ana \ˌjȯr-jē-'an-ə, -'än-ə\
Geor·gie \'jȯr-jē\
Geor·gi·na \jȯr-'jē-nə\
Ge·or·gi·os *Mod. Gk.* \ye-'ȯr-yē-ˌȯs\
Geor·gi·us 1 *Lat.* \'jȯr-jē-əs, jē-'ȯr-\ 2 *Swed.* **Ge·or·gi·us** \ye-'ȯr-yi-əs\
Ge·or·gi·ye·vich *Russ.* \gyi-'ȯrg-yi(-yiv)-ˌyich\
Ge·or·gy *Russ.* \gyi-'ȯrg-yəi\
Ge·raert *Du.* \'gā-ˌrȧrt\
Ger·ald 1 \'jer-əld\ 2 *Fr.* \zhā-rȧld\
Ger·al·dine \'jer-əl-ˌdēn\
Ge·rard 1 \jə-'rärd\ 2 *Du.* \'gā-ˌrärt\ 3 *Ger.* \'gā-ˌrärt\ 4 *Fr.* **Gé·rard** \zhā-rȧr\
Ge·rar·do *Span.* \kā-'rär-thō\
Ge·rar·dus 1 *Du.* \gā-'rär-dœs\ 2 *Lat.* \jə-'rär-dəs\
Ge·ra·si·mo·vich *Russ.* \gyi-'rȧs-yim(-əv)-ˌyich\
Gé·raud *Fr.* \zhā-rō\
Ger·bert *Fr.* \zher-ber\
Ger·brand *Du.* \'ger-ˌbränt\
Gerd *Ger.* \'gert\
Ger·gely *Hung.* \'ger-(ˌ)gel^{y}\
Ger·hard 1 *Du.* \'gā-ˌrärt\ 2 *Ger.* \'gār-ˌhärt\ 3 *Norw.* \'ger-ˌhärt\ 4 *Swed.* \'yār-ˌhärd\
Ger·hardt \'ger-ˌhärt\
Ger·har·dus *Lat.* \(ˌ)jər-'här-dəs\
Ger·hart *Ger.* \'gār-ˌhärt\
Ger·main *Fr.* \zher-ma^{n}\
Ger·maine 1 \(ˌ)jər-'mān\ 2 *Fr.* \zher-me^{n}\
Ger·man 1 \'jər-mən\ 2 *Span.* **Ger·mán** \ker-'män\
Ger·ma·no·vich *Russ.* \'gyer-mən(-əv)-ˌyich\
Ge·ro·la·mo *Ital.* \jā-'rō-läm-(ˌ)ō\
Ge·rold *Ger.* \'gā-ˌrōlt\
Ge·ro·ni·mo 1 *Ital.* \jā-'rō-nē-(ˌ)mō\ 2 *Span.* **Ge·ró·ni·mo** \kā-'rō-nē-mō\
Ger·rard \jə-'rärd, *chiefly Brit* 'jər-ärd\
Ger·rish \'ger-ish\
Ger·rit 1 \'ger-ət\ 2 *Du.* \'ger-ət\
Ger·rits, -ritsz *Du.* \'ger-əts\
Ger·ry \'ger-ē\
Ger·schon \'gər-shən\
Ger·shom \'gər-shəm\
Ger·son *Ger.* \'ger-ˌzōn\
Ger·trud 1 *Dan.* \'ger-(ˌ)trůth\ 2 *Ger.* \'ger-ˌtrüt\
Ger·trude \'gər-ˌtrüd\
Ger·tru·dis *Span.* \ther-'trü-thēs\
Ger·ty \'gərt-ē\
Ger·vais *Fr.* \zher-ve\
Ger·va·sio *Span.* \ker-'väs-yō\
Ge·si·nus *Du.* \gā-'sē-nœs\
Ge·tu·lio \zhə-'tül-yü\
Gé·za *Hung.* \'gā-zä\
Ghee·raert *Du.* \'gā-ˌrärt\
Ghee·rardt *Du.* \'gā-ˌrärt\
Gheor·ghe *Rum.* \'gyȯr-ge\
Ghe·rar·do *Ital.* \gā-'rär-dō\
Ghis·lain *Fr.* \gē-la^{n}\
Ghi·yās *Pers.* \gē-'yäs\
Ghol·son \'gōl-sən\
Giaches *Fr.* \zhȧsh\
Gia·cin·to *Ital.* \jä-'chēn-tō\
Gia·co·mo *Ital.* \'jäk-ō-(ˌ)mō\
Gia·co·muz·zo *Ital.* \ˌjäk-ō-'müt-tsō\
Gia·co·po *Ital.* \'jäk-ō-(ˌ)pō\
Giam·bat·tis·ta *Ital.* \ˌjäm-bät-'tēs-tä\
Giam·berti *Ital.* \jäm-'ber-tē\
Giam·ma·ria *Ital.* \ˌjäm-mä-'rē-ä\
Gian *Ital.* \'jän\
Gian·an·to·nio *Ital.* \ˌjän-an-'tōn-yō\
Gian·fran·ces·co *Ital.* \ˌjän-frän-'chās-kō\
Gian·ga·le·az·zo *Ital.* \ˌjäŋ-ˌgäl-ā-'ät-tsō\
Gian·gior·gio *Ital.* \jän-'jōr-jō, -'jȯr-\
Gian·ma·ria *Ital.* \ˌjäm-mä-'rē-ä\
Gian·ni *Ital.* \'jän-nē\
Gia·no *Ital.* \'jän-ō\
Gi·da·yū *Jp.* \gē-dä-yů\
Gid·e·on 1 \'gid-ē-ən\ 2 *Ger.* \'gē-dā-ˌȯn\
Gif·fard \'gif-ərd\
Gif·ford \'gif-ərd, 'jif-\
Gi·ichi *Jp.* \gē-ē-chē\
Gijs·bert *Du.* \'gīs-bərt\
Gil 1 *Port.* \'zhil\ 2 *Span.* \'hēl\
Gi·lar·mi *Ital.* \jē-'lär-mē\
Gil·bert 1 \'gil-bərt\ 2 *Fr.* \zhēl-ber\
Gil·ber·tus *Lat.* \gil-'bər-təs\
Gil·christ \'gil-krist\
Gil·der·sleeve \'gil-dər-ˌslēv\
Giles \'jī(ə)lz\
Gilg *Ger.* \'gilk\
Gill \'gil\
Gil·les 1 *Du.* \'gil-əs\ 2 *Fr.* **Gilles** \zhēl\
Gil·lies \'gil-əs, -əz, -(ˌ)ēz\
Gil·lis *Du.* \'gil-əs\
Gil·more \'gil-ˌmō(ə)r, -ˌmȯ(ə)r\
Gil·pin \'gil-pən\
Gi·nés *Span.* \kē-'näs\
Gi·no *Ital.* \'jē-nō\
Gio·ac·chi·no *Ital.* \jō-äk-'kē-nō\
Gior·da·no *Ital.* \jōr-'dän-ō\

Gior·gio 1 *Ital.* \'jȯr-jō, 'jȯr-\ 2 *Hung.* Gi·ör·gio \'dyœrd-yō\
Gio·suè *Ital.* \jōz-'we\
Gio·van *Ital.* \jō-'vän\
Gio·van·na \jō-'vän-ə\
Gio·van·ni *Ital.* \jō-'vän-nē\
Gio·via·no *Ital.* \jōv-'yän-ō\
Gip·sy \'jip-sē\
Gi·raud *Fr.* \zhē-rō\
Gir·ja *Hind.* \'gir-jä\
Gir·ling \'gər-liŋ\
Gi·ro·la·mo *Ital.* \jē-'rȯ-läm-(,)ō\
Gi·rón *Span.* \k̲ē-'rȯn\
Gis·bert 1 *Du.* \'g̅is-bərt\ 2 *Ger.* \'gis-,bert\
Gis·le *Norw.* \'gis-lə\
Gi·tha \'gē-thə\
Giu·dit·ta *Ital.* \jü-'dēt-tä\
Giu·lia *Ital.* \'jül-yä\
Giu·lia·no *Ital.* \jül-'yän-ō\
Giu·lio *Ital.* \'jül-yō\
Giu·sep·pe *Ital.* \jü-'zep-pā\
Giu·sep·pi·na *Ital.* \,jü-zāp-'pē-nä\
Giu·sto *Ital.* \'jü-stō\
Glad·heim \'glad-hīm\
Glad·stone \'glad-,stōn, *chiefly Brit.* -stən\
Glad·ys \'glad-əs\
Glas·gow \'glas-(,)kō, -(,)gō, 'glaz-(,)gō\
Glass \'glas\
Glass·ford \'glas-fərd\
Glea·son \'glē-sən\
Gleb *Russ.* \'glyāp\
Glen, Glenn \'glen\
Glen·ville \'glen-,vil, vəl\
Glen·way \'glen-,wā\
Glo·ria \'glōr-ē-ə, 'glȯr-\
Glov·er \'gləv-ər\
Glu·yas \'glü-yəs\
Glyn \'glin\
Gnae·us *Lat.* \'nē-əs\
Gnei·se·nau \gə-'nī-zə-,nau̇\
God·dard \'gäd-ərd\
Go·de·fried *Du.* \'g̅ō-də-(,)frēt\
Gode·froi *Fr.* \gȯd-frwä\
Go·de·froid 1 *Flem.* \'gōd-ə-,frwä\ 2 *Fr.* \gȯd-frwä\
Gode·froy *Fr.* \gȯd-frwä\
Go·dert *Du.* \'g̅ō-dərt\
God·frey \'gäd-frē\
God·fried *Du.* \'g̅ȯt-(,)frēt\
Go·dol·phin \gə-'dȯl-fən, -'däl-\
God·ske *Dan.* \'gȯt̲h̲-skə\
God·win \'gäd-wən\
Goff \'gäf\
Gof·fre·do *Ital.* \gōf-'frā-dō\
Gold \'gōld\
Gol·da *Heb.* \'gōl-də\
Gol·den \'gōl-dən\
Gol·die \'gōl-dē\
Golds·bor·ough \'gōldz-,bər-ə, *esp Brit.* -brə\
Gold·smith \'gōld-smith\
Golds·wor·thy \'gōldz-,wər-t̲h̲ē\
Gold·win \'gōl-dwən\
Gom·baud *Fr.* \gō^{n}-bō\
Gom·bē *Jp.* \gōm-be\
Gom·bei *Jp.* \gōm-bā\
Go·mes *Port.* \'gō-mish; -mis\
Gó·mez *Span.* \'gō-māth; -mās\
Gon·ça·lo *Port.* \gō^{n}-'sȧ-lü\
Gon·su·ke *Jp.* \gōn-su̇k-e\
Gon·za·les 1 *Du.* \gȯn-'zäl-əs\ 2 *Span.* \gȯn-'thäl-äs; -'säl-\
Gon·zá·lez *Span.* \gȯn-'thäl-äth; -'säl-läs\
Gon·za·lo *Span.* \gȯn-'thäl-ō; -'säl-\
Gon·zalve *Fr.* \gō^{n}-zȧlv\
Good·all \'gu̇d-ȯl\
Good·hue \'gu̇d-(,)(h)yü\
Good·loe \'gu̇d-(,)lō\
Good·man \'gu̇d-mən\
Good·rich \'gu̇d-(,)rich\
Good·will \'gu̇d-wəl\
Good·win \'gu̇d-wən\
Good·year \'gu̇d-,yi(ə)r, 'gu̇j-,i(ə)r\
Goold \'güld\
Go·pal 1 *Bengali* \gō-'pȯl(-ȯ)\ 2 *Marathi* \gō-'päl(-ə)\
Gö·ran *Swed.* \'yœ-,rȧn\
Gorch *Ger.* \'gȯrk̲\
Gor·don \'gȯrd-^{ə}n\
Gore \'gō(ə)r, 'gȯ(ə)r\
Gor·ham \'gōr-əm, 'gȯr-\
Gor·ing \'gō(ə)r-iŋ, 'gȯ(ə)r-\
Gor·man \'gȯr-mən\
Go·ro *Jp.* \gō-rō\
Go·ron·wy *Welsh* \gȯ-'rȯn-wē, gə-'rän-\
Gor·ton \'gȯrt-^{ə}n\
Gos·combe \'gäs-kəm\
Gö·sta *Norw., Swed.* \'yœ-stä\
Got·hard *Dan.* \'gȯt-,härd\
Go·ti·fre·do *Ital.* \,gō-tē-'frā-dō\
Gott·fried 1 *Ger.* \'gȯt-,frēt\ 2 *Swed.* \'gȯt-,frēd\
Gott·hard 1 *Ger.* \'gȯt-,härd\ 2 *Swed.* \'gȯt-,(h)ärd\
Gott·hardt *Ger.* \'gȯt-,härt\
Gott·helf *Ger.* \'gȯt-,helf\
Gott·hilf *Ger.* \'gȯt-,hilf\
Gott·hold *Ger.* \'gȯt-,hȯlt\
Gott·lieb 1 \'gät-lēb\ 2 *Finn., Swed.* \'gȯt-,lēb\ 3 *Ger.* \'gȯt-,lēp\
Gott·lob 1 *Dan.* \'gȯt-,lȯb\ 2 *Ger.* \'gȯt-,lōp\
Götz *Ger.* \'gœts\
Gou·ver·neur \,gəv-ə(r)-'nu̇r, ,gu̇v-, -'nər\
Go·vaert *Du.* \'g̅ō-(,)värt\
Gove \'gōv\
Go·ver·di·na *Du.* \,gō-vər-'dē-nä\
Go·vind *Punjabi* \gō-'vind\
Go·vin·da *Skt.* \gō-'vin-də\
Gow·en \'gau̇-ən\
Go·win \'gō-ən\
Gow·land \'gau̇-lənd\
Grac·chus *Fr.* \grȧ-kües\
Grace \'grās\
Gra·cie \'grā-sē\
Gra·cil·ia·no *Span.* \gräs-ē(l)-'yän-ō\
Gra·dy \'grā-dē\
Graeme \'grām\
Gram \'gram\
Gran·ber·ry \'gran-,ber-e, -bər-\
Gran·di·son \'gran-də-sən\
Gra·ni·us \'grā-nē-əs\
Grant \'grant\
Grant·ly \'grant-lē\
Gra·ta *Lat.* \'grät-ə\
Gra·tien *Fr.* \grȧ-sya^{n}\
Grat·tan \'grat-^{ə}n\
Gratz \'grats\
Gra·zia *Ital.* \'grät-syä\
Gra·zia·dio *Ital.* \,grät-syä-'dē-ō\
Gree·ley \'grē-lē\
Green·field \'grēn-lē\
Green·leaf \'grēn-,lēf\
Gree·nough \'grē-,nō\
Greer \'gri(ə)r\
Gregg \'greg\
Gré·goire *Fr.* \grā-gwȧr\
Greg·or 1 \'greg-ər\ 2 *Ger.* Gre·gor \'grā-,gōr, grā-'gōr\
Gre·go·rio 1 *Ital.* \grā-'gȯr-yō\ 2 *Span.* \grā-'g̅ōr-yō\
Gre·go·ri·us *Lat.* \grē-'gōr-ē-əs\
Greg·o·ry \'greg-(ə-)rē\
Gren·fill \'gren-,fel, -fəl\
Gres·ham \'gres-əm\
Gré·sinde *Fr.* \grā-za^{n}d\
Gre·ta 1 \'grē-tə, 'gret-ə\ 2 *Swed.* \'grā-tȧ\
Gre·the *Ger.* \'grā-tə\
Grey \'grā\
Grey·so·lon *Fr.* \gre-sȯ-lō^{n}\
Grier \'gri(ə)r\
Griggs \'grigz\
Gri·go·ry, -ri *Russ.* \gryi-'gȯr-yəi\
Gri·gor·ye·vich *Russ.* \gryi-'gȯr(-yiv)-,yich\
Grimes \'grīmz\
Grin·ling \'grin-liŋ\
Gris·wold \'griz-wəld, -wōld, -wȯld\
Gri·zel \grə-'zel, 'griz-^{ə}l\
Gros·ve·nor \'grōv-nər, 'grō-vən-ər\
Grote \'grōt\
Gro·ver \'grō-vər\
Groves \'grōvz\
Grubb \'grəb\
Grze·gorz *Pol.* \'gzheg-ȯsh\
Gua·da·lu·pe *Span.* \gwät̲h̲-ä-'lü-pā\
Gua·ri·no *Ital.* \gwä-'rē-nō\
Gud·bran·dur *Icel.* \'gvœt̲h̲-brän-dœr\
Gud·mund *Swed.* \'güd-,mənd\
Gud·mund·son *Icel.* \'gvœt̲h̲-mœnd-,sȯn\
Guđ·mun·dur *Icel.* \'gvœt̲h̲-,mœn-dœr\
Guern·sey \'gərn-zē\
Guer·ra *Port.* \'ger-rə; -rȧ\
Gu·gliel·mo *Ital.* \gül-'yel-mō\
Gu·gli·el·mus *Lat.* \,gü-glē-'el-məs\
Gui *Fr.* \gē\
Gui·chard *Fr.* \gē-shȧr\
Gui·do 1 \'gēd-(,)ō, 'gwēd-\ 2 *Du.* \'g̅ē-,dō\ 3 *Ital.* \'gwē-dō\ 4 *Ger.* Gu·i·do \gü-'ē-dō, 'gē-(,)dō\
Gui·du·bal·do *Ital.* \,gwē-dü-'bäl-dō\
Guild·ford \'gil-fərd\
Gui·lher·me *Port.* \gēl-'yer-mə; -mā\
Guil·laume *Fr.* \gē-yōm\
Guil·lén *Span.* \gē(l)-'yān\
Guil·ler·mo *Span.* \gē(l)-'yer-mō\
Guit·ton·ci·no *Ital.* \,gwēt-tōn-'chē-nō\
Gu·kei *Jp.* \gu̇k-ā\
Gu·li·el·mus *Lat.* \,gyü-lē-'el-məs\
Gun·nar 1 *Icel.* \'gœn-när\ 2 *Norw.* \'gu̇n-när\ 3 *Swed.* \'gən-nȧr\
Gun·ning \'gən-iŋ\
Gun·no *Swed.* \'gən-nō\
Gün·ther *Ger.* \'gœn-tər\
Gur·don \'gər-dən\
Gur·ney \'gər-nē\
Gus \'gəs\
Gus·taaf *Du.* \'g̅œs-tȧf\
Gus·taf 1 *Finn.* \'gu̇s-,tȧf\ 2 *Ger.* \'gu̇s-,täf\ 3 *Swed.* \'gəs-,täv\
Gus·tafs·son *Swed.* \'gəs-täv-,sȯn\
Gus·tav 1 *Dan.* \'gu̇s-,täv\ 2 *Ger.* \'gu̇s-,täf\ 3 *Swed.* \'gəs-,täv\
Gus·tave 1 \'gu̇s-,täv\ 2 *Fr.* \gu̅e̅-stȧv\ 3 *Ger.* Gus·ta·ve \'gu̇s-,täv-ə\
Gus·ta·vo 1 *Port.* \gush-'tȧ-vü; güs-\ 2 *Span.* \gü-'stäv-ō\
Gus·taw *Pol.* \'güs-tȧf\
Gusz·tav *Hung.* \'gu̇s-täv\
Guthe \'güth\
Gu·tier·re *Span.* \gü-'tyer-rā\
Gut·man·o·vich *Russ.* \güt-'mȧn(-əv)-,yich\
Gut·zon \'gət-sən\
Guy 1 \'gī\ 2 *Fr.* \gē\

\ə\ abut \$^{ə}$\ kitten, *Fr.* table \ər\ further \a\ ash \ā\ ace \ä\ cot, cart \au̇\ out \ch\ chin \e\ bet \ē\ easy \g\ go \i\ hit \ī\ ice \j\ job \ŋ\ sing \ō\ go \ȯ\ law \ȯi\ boy \th\ both \t̲h̲\ the \ü\ loot \u̇\ foot \y\ yet \zh\ vision \ȧ, k̲, g̅, k̲, ^{n}, œ, œ̅, ue, ue̅, ^{y}\ *see* Guide to Pronunciation

Gwen \'gwen\
Gwen·do·line \'gwen-də-lən\
Gwi·nett \gwin-'et\
Gwlad·ys \'glad-əs\
Gwynne \'gwin\
Gyo·ku·dō *Jp.* \gyō-ku̇d-ō\
György *Hung.* \'dyœrdʸ\
Gyō·sai *Jp.* \gyō-sī\
Gyp·sy \'jip-sē\
Gyu·la *Hung.* \'dyu̇l-ä\

Ha·bak·kuk *Ger.* \'hä-bä-ˌkük, -ˌku̇k\
Hab·dank *Pol.* \'häb-ˌdäŋk\
Hab·lot \'hab-(ˌ)lō\
Ha·chi·ro *Jp.* \hä-chē-rō\
Ha·chi·ro·e·mon *Jp.* \hä-chē-rō-(y)e-mōn\
Hack \'hak\
Hack·ett \'hak-ət\
Had·don \'had-ᵊn\
Ha·den \'hād-ᵊn\
Had·jar *Indonesian* \'häj-ˌär\
Ha·gar \'hā-gər, -ˌgär\
Ha·ge·rup *Norw.* \'hä-gə-ru̇p\
Hahn \'han\
Haigh \'hāg, hā\
Ha·im *Heb.* \k̲ī-'(y)im, 'k̲ī-(y)im\
Haines \'hānz\
Ha·ji·me *Jp.* \häj-ē-me\
Ha·ku·chō *Jp.* \hä-ku̇ch-ō\
Ha·ku·se·ki *Jp.* \hä-ku̇s-ek-ē\
Hal \'hal\
Hal·bert \'hal-bərt\
Hal·cott \'hȯl-kət\
Hal·cy·on \'hal-sē-ən\
Hal·den \'hȯl-dən\
Ha·ley \'hā-lē\
Half·dan 1 *Dan.* \'hälv-ˌdän\ 2 *Norw.* \'hälv-ˌdän\
Ha·lid *Turk.* \hä-'lēd\
Hal·lam \'hal-əm\
Hal·lett \'hal-ət\
Hall·grí·mur *Icel.* \'häl-grē-mœr\
Hal·li·day \'hal-ə-dā\
Hal·lie \'hal-ē\
Hal·lock \'hal-ək\
Hal·lo·well \'hal-ə-wel, -wəl\
Hal·lowes \'hal-(ˌ)ōz\
Hal·per \'hal-pər\
Halse \'hȯls, 'häls\
Hal·sey \'hȯl-sē, -zē\
Hal·stead, -sted \'hȯl-stəd, -ˌsted\
Halv·dan *Norw.* \'hälv-ˌdän\
Hal·vor *Norw.* \'häl-vȯr\
Ha·mar \'hā-mər\
Hame·lin \'ham(-ə)-lən\
Ha·mer \'hā-mər\
Ha·mish \'hā-mish\
Ha·mo \'hā-(ˌ)mō\
Hand \'hand\
Han·da·syd \'han-də-ˌsīd\
Han·der·son \'han-dər-sən\
Hand·ley \'hand-lē\
Han·dy \'han-dē\
Han·dy·side \'han-dē-ˌsīd\
Han·ford \'han-fərd\
Han·kins \'haŋ-kənz\
Han·ley \'han-lē\
Han·na, -nah \'han-ə\
Han·nes *Icel.* \'hän-nes\
Han·ni·bal 1 \'han-ə-bəl\ 2 *Dan.* \'hän-i-bäl\
Han·ning \'han-iŋ\
Han·nis \'han-əs\
Hanns *Ger.* \'hän(t)s\
Hans 1 \'hanz, 'hän(t)s\ 2 *Dan., Swed.* \'hän(t)s\ 3 *Du., Ger., Norw.* \'hän(t)s\
Han·sen *Dan.* \'hän(t)-sən\
Hans·ford \'han(t)s-fərd\
Ha·nuš *Czech* \'hä-ˌnu̇sh\
Ha·rald 1 *Dan., Norw.* \'här-ˌäl\ 2 *Ger.* \'hä-rält\ 3 *Swed.* \'hä-ˌräld\
Har·butt \'här-bət\
Har·de·man \'här-də-mən\
Har·die \'härd-ē\
Hard·wicke \'här-ˌdwik\
Har·ford \'har-fərd\
Har·i·ett \'har-ē-ət\
Har·lan 1 \'här-lən\ 2 *Span.* \'är-län\
Har·land \'här-lənd\
Har·lean \här-'lēn\
Har·ley \'här-lē\
Har·low, -lowe \'här-ˌlō\
Har·man \'här-mən\
Har·mar \'här-mər\
Har·men *Du.* \'här-mən\
Har·mensz *Du.* \'här-məns\
Har·mens·zoon *Du.* \'här-mən-sən, -ˌsȯn, -ˌsōn\
Har·mo·dio *Span.* \är-'mōt͟h-yō\
Har·mon \'här-mən\
Har·nam \'här-nəm\
Har·old \'har-əld\
Har·perts·zoon *Du.* \'här-pərt-sən, -ˌsȯn, -ˌsōn\
Har·rell \'har-əl\
Har·ri·et \'har-ē-ət\
Har·ring·ton \'har-iŋ-tən\
Har·ri·ot, -ott \'har-ē-ət\
Har·ris \'har-əs\
Har·ri·son \'har-ə-sən\
Har·ry 1 \'har-ē\ 2 *Dan., Ger.* \'här-ē\
Hart·man \'härt-mən\
Hart·mann *Ger.* \'härt-ˌmän\
Hart·pole \'härt-pōl\
Harts·horne \'härts-ˌhȯ(ə)rn\
Hart·well \'härt-ˌwel, -wəl\
Hart·wick \'härt-ˌwik\
Hart·wig *Ger.* \'härt-vik̲\
Hart·zell \'härt-səl\
Ha·ru·ki *Jp.* \hä-ru̇k-ē\
Ha·ru·no·bi *Jp.* \här-u̇n-ō-bē\
Ha·ruo *Jp.* \hä-ru̇-ō\
Ha·ru·sa·bu·ro *Jp.* \hä-ru̇s-ä-bu̇r-ō\
Har·vey \'här-vē\
Har·wood \'här-wu̇d\
ha-Sal·lah *Heb.* \hä-säl-'läk̲\
Has·dai *Arab.* \'häs-ˌdī\
Has·kell \'has-kəl\
Has·kins \'has-kinz\
Has·ty \'hā-stē\
Has·well \'haz-ˌwel, -wəl\
Hatch·er \'hach-ər\
Hat·field \'hat-fēld\
Hat·to *Fr.* \ä-tō\
Ha·vel *Czech* \'hä-vel\
Have·lock \'hav-ˌläk, -lək\
Ha·ven \'hā-vən\
Hav·er·gal \'hav-ər-gəl\
Hav·er·sham \'hav-ər-shəm, 'här-shəm\
Haw·ley \'hȯ-lē\
Haw·thorne \'hȯ-ˌthȯ(ə)rn\
Ha·ya·to *Jp.* \hä-yä-tō\
Hay·ley \'hā-lē\
Haym *Pol.* \'hīm\
Hay·man \'hā-mən\
Haynes \'hānz\
Ḥay·yim *Heb.* \k̲ī-'(y)im, 'k̲ī-(y)im\
Ḥa·zan *Jp.* \hä-zän\
Haz·ard \'haz-ərd\
Ha·zle·hurst \'hā-zəl-hərst\
Haz·lett \'haz-lət, 'hāz-\
Haz·litt \'haz-lət, 'hāz-\
Head·land \'hed-lənd\
Hea·ley \'hē-lē\
Heard \'hərd\
Heas·lip \'hē-sləp\
Heath·cote \'heth-kət, 'hēth-kōt\
He·ber \'hē-bər\
Heck \'hek\
Hec·tor 1 \'hek-tər\ 2 *Fr.* \ek-tȯr\ 3 *Span.* **Héc·tor** \'ek-tȯr\
Hedg·es \'hej-əz\
Hed·vig *Swed.* \'hed-vig\
Hed·wig *Ger.* \'hāt-vik̲\
Hed·worth \'hed-wərth\
Hef·ner *Ger.* \'hāf-nər\
Hei·ha·chi·ro *Jp.* \hā-hä-chē-rō\
Hei·ke *Du.* \'hī-kə\
Heik·ki *Finn.* \'hāk-kē\
Hein *Du.* \'hīn\
Hei·ne \'hī-nə\
Hei·no \'hī-ˌnō\
Hein·rich 1 *Dan.* \'hīn-rēk̲\ 2 *Ger.* \'hīn-rik̲\
Heinz *Ger.* \'hīnts\
Heiss \'hīs\
Hei·tor *Port.* \'ā-tȯr\
Hel·en \'hel-ən\
Hel·e·na 1 \'hel-ə-nə, həl-'ē-nə, hel-'ā-nə\ 2 **He·le·na** *Du.* \hā-'lā-nä\ 3 *Ger.* \'hā-lā-ˌnä\
He·le·ne 1 *Ger.* \hā-'lā-nə\ 2 *Fr.* **Hé·lène** \ā-len\
He·le·nus *Swed.* \he-'lā-nəs\
Hel·ga *Swed.* \'hel-gä\
Hel·ge *Dan.* \'hel-gə\
He·lia·de *Rom.* \hel-'yä-de\
Hé·li·dore *Fr.* \ā-lē-dȯr\
Hé·lio·dore *Fr.* \āl-yō-dȯr\
He·li·us *Ger.* \'hā-lē-u̇s\
Hell·muth *Ger.* \'hel-ˌmüt\
Helm \'helm\
Hel·mich *Swed.* \'hel-mik\
Hel·mi·ne *Ger.* \hel-'mē-nə\
Hel·mut, -muth *Ger.* \'hel-ˌmüt\
Hel·ve·ti·us *Du.* \hel-'vā(t)-sē-œs\
Hel·vi·us *Lat.* \'hel-vē-əs\
Hel·wig \'hel-ˌwig\
He·man \'hē-mən\
Hem·ing \'hem-iŋ\
Hemp·stead \'hem(p)-sted, -ˌstəd\
Hen·dric \'hen-ˌdrik\
Hen·drick *Du.* \'hen-drək\
Hen·drick·je *Du.* \'hen-drək-yə\
Hen·dricks \'hen-ˌdriks\
Hen·dricksz *Du.* \'hen-drəks\
Hen·dri·cus *Du.* \hen-'drē-kœs\
Hen·drik \'hen-ˌdrik\
Hen·dry \'hen-drē\
Hen·eage \'hen-ij\
Hen·gist \'heŋ-gəst, -ˌgist\
Hen·ley \'hen-lē\
Henn \'hen\
Hen·ney \'hen-ē\
Hen·nig *Ger.* \'hen-ik̲\
Hen·ni·ker \'hen-ə-ker\
Hen·ning 1 *Ger.* \'hen-iŋ\ 2 *Swed.* \'hen-niŋ\
Hen·ri 1 *Flem.* \'häⁿ-rē\ 2 *Fr.* \äⁿ-rē\
Hen·rick 1 *Dan.* \'hen-rēk\ 2 *Du.* \'hen-rək\
Hen·ri·cus 1 *Du.* \hen-'rē-kœs\ 2 *Lat.* \hen-'rī-kəs\
Hen·ri·et·ta \ˌhen-rē-'et-ə\
Hen·ri·ette 1 *Fr.* \äⁿr-yet\ 2 *Ger.* **Hen·ri·et·te** \ˌhen-rē-'et-ə\ 3 *Du.* **Hen·ri·ët·te** \ˌhen-rē-'et-ə\
Hen·rik 1 *Eng., Finn., Ger., Hung., Norw., Swed.* \'hen-rik\ 2 *Dan.* \'hen-rēk\
Hen·ri·que 1 *Port.* \äⁿ-'rē-kə; -kä\ 2 *Span.* \än-'rē-kä\
Hen·ri·ques *Port.* \äⁿ-'rē-kish; -kis\

Hen·ry 1 Eng., Ger. \'hen-rē\ 2 Flem. \'hä^{n}-rē\ 3 Fr. \ä^{n}-rē\
Hen·ryk Pol. \'hen-rik\
Hens·leigh \'henz-lē\
Hens·ley \'henz-lē\
Hep·burn \'hep-(,)bərn, Brit also 'heb-ərn\
Hep·ple \'hep-əl\
Hep·worth \'hep-(,)wərth\
He·rac·li·us 1 Lat. \hi-'rak-lē-əs\ 2 Fr. Hé·ra·cli·us \ā-rá-klē-ūēs\
Her·bert 1 \'hər-bərt\ 2 Ger. \'her-,bert\ 3 Swed. \'her-bərt\
Her·cule Fr. \er-kūēl\
Her·cu·les 1 \'hər-kyə-,lēz\ 2 Du. \'he(ə)r-kūē-ləs\
He·ren·ni·us Lat. \hə-'ren-ē-əs\
Her·e·ward \'her-ə-wərd\
Her·holdt Dan. \'her-,hólt\
He·ri·bert Du., Ger. \'hā-rē-,bert\
He·ri·ber·to Span. \ā-rē-'ber-tō\
Her·man 1 \'hər-mən\ 2 Dan., Finn. \'her-,mán\ 3 Du., Ger., Norw. \'her-,män\
Her·mann 1 \'hər-mən\ 2 Dan. \'her-,mán\ 3 Du., Ger., Icel. \'her-,män\ 4 Fr. \er-mán\
Her·ma·nus Du. \he(ə)r-'mán-ues\
Her·me·ne·gild Czech \'he(ə)r-men-e-,gilt\
Her·me·ne·gil·do 1 Port. \,er-mə-nə-'zhil-dü; ,er-mā-nā-\ 2 Span. \er-mā-nā-'hēl-dō\
Her·mei·os Gk. \her-'mā-ós\
Her·mes Port. \'er-mish; -mis\
Her·me·to Port. \ĕr-'mā-tü\
Her·mi·ne Ger. \her-'mē-nə\
Her·mione Fr. \erm-yón\
Her·mog·e·nes \hər-'mäj-ə-nēz\
Her·mon \'hər-mən\
Her·nán Span. \er-'nän\
Her·nán·dez Span. \er-'nän-dāth; -dās\
Her·nan·do Span. \er-'nän-dō\
Hern·don \'hərn-dən\
Her·ries \'her-əs\
Her·ron \'her-ən\
Her·sey \'hər-sē\
Hers·leb 1 Dan. \'her-slib\ 2 Norw. \'hesh-leb, 'hers-\
Her·tha \'hər-thə\
Hertz·berg \'hərts-,bərg\
Her·vé Fr. \er-vā\
Her·vey \'hər-vē, esp Brit 'här-vē\
Her·warth Ger. \'her-,värt\
Hes·ba \'hez-bə\
He·si·od \'hē-sē-əd, 'hes-ē-\
Hes·keth \'hes-kəth\
Hes·sels Du. \'hes-əls\
Hes·sin \'hes-ən\
Hes·ter \'hes-tər\
Heth \'heth\
Heth·er·ing·ton \heth(-ə)-riŋ-tən\
Het·ty \'het-ē\
Hew \'hyü\
Hew·ard \'hyü-ərd\
Hew·lett \'hyü-lət\
Hew·son \'hyü-sən\
Hey·gate \'hā-,gāt, -gət\
Heyl \'hī(ə)l\
Hey·man Dan. \'hī-mán\
Hey·mann Ger. \'hī-,män\
Hey·worth \'hā-wərth\
Hez·e·ki·ah \,hez-ə-'kī-ə\
Hib·bard \'hib-ərd\
Hib·bert \'hib-ərt\
Hice \'hīs\
Hick·ey \'hik-ē\
Hick·ling \'hik-liŋ\
Hick·man \'hik-mən\
Hicky \'hik-ē\
Hic·ok \'hik-,äk\
Hid·den \'hid-^{ə}n\
Hi·de·ki Jp. \hē-dek-ē\
Hi·de·ma·ro Jp. \hē-dem-är-ō\
Hi·de·ta·da Jp. \hē-dā-täd-ä\
Hi·de·tsu·gu Jp. \hē-det-sùg-ù\
Hi·de·yo Jp. \hē-de-yō\
Hi·de·yo·ri Jp. \hē-de-yō-rē\
Hi·de·yo·shi Jp. \hē-de-yō-shē\
Hi·er·on·y·mus 1 \,hī(-ə)-'rän-ə-məs\ 2 Hi·e·ro·ny·mus Du. \,hē-ə-'rō-nē-mues\ 3 Ger. \,hē-ā-'rō-nūē-mùs\
Hig·gins \'hig-ənz\
Hig·gin·son \'hig-ən-sən\
High·am \'hī-əm\
High·land \'hī-lənd\
Hi·gi·nio Span. \ē-'kēn-yō\
Hi·ko·i·chi Jp. \hē-kō-ē-chē\
Hi·ko·no·jo Jp. \hē-kō-nō-jō\
Hi·laire 1 \hil-'a(ə)r, -'e(ə)r, Brit also 'hil-,\ 2 Fr. \ē-ler\
Hi·la·rio Span. \ē-'lär-yō\
Hi·la·rion 1 Fr. \ē-lär-yō^{n}\ 2 Span. Hi·la·rión \ē-lär-'yón\
Hi·la·ri·us Ger. \hē-'lä-rē-ùs\
Hil·a·ry \'hil-ə-rē\
Hil·borne \'hil-bərn, -,bó(ə)rn\
Hil·da \'hil-də\
Hil·de·bert Ger. \'hil-də-,bert\
Hil·de·brand 1 \'hil-də-,brand\ 2 Du., Ger. \'hil-də-,bränt\
Hil·de·garde \'hil-də-,gärd\
Hil·dreth \'hil-drəth\
Hil·lard \'hil-ərd\
Hil·ler \'hil-ər\
Hil·lier \'hil-yər\
Hill·man \'hil-mən\
Hil·ton \'hilt-^{ə}n\
Hinck·ley \'hiŋk-lē\
Hi·ner \'hī-nər\
Hin·rich Ger. \'hin-rik\
Hin·ton \'hint-^{ə}n\
Hi·ob Ger. \'hē-,óp\
Hi·pó·li·to Span. \ē-'pō-lē-tō\
Hip·po·lyte Fr. \ē(p)-pó-lēt\
Hipsch Ger. \'hipsh\
Hi·ram \'hī-rəm\
Hi·ra·o·ka Jp. \hē-rä-ō-kä\
Hi·ra·ya·ma Jp. \hē-rä-yä-mä\
Hi·ro·bu·mi Jp. \hē-rō-bùm-ē\
Hi·ro·shi Jp. \hē-rō-shē\
Hi·ro·yu·ki Jp. \hē-rō-yùk-ē\
Hi·ro·zu·mi Jp. \hē-rō-zùm-ē\
Hi·sa·mi·tsu Jp. \hē-sä-mēt-sù\
Hi·sa·ya Jp. \hē-sä-yä\
His·lop \'hiz-,läp, -ləp\
Hi·to·ma·ro Jp. \he-tō-mär-ō\
Hitz \'hits\
Hi·yo·shi·ma·ru Jp. \hē-yō-shē-mä-rù\
Hjal·mar 1 Dan. \'yál-,mär\ 2 Finn., Swed. \'yäl-,már\ 3 Icel., Norw. \'yäl-,mär\
Hjör·leifs·son Icel. \'yœr-lāfs-són\
Hjorth Norw. \'yórt\
Hoad·ley \'hōd-lē\
Hob·son \'häb-sən\
Ho·ca Turk. \hō-'jä\
Hod·ding \'häd-iŋ\
Hodg·don \'häj-dən\
Hodg·es \'häj-əz\
Hodg·son \'häj-sən\
Hoey \'hói, 'hō-ē\
Ho·i·tsu Jp. \hō-ēt-sù\
Ho·jo Jp. \hō-jō\
Hoke \'hōk\
Hol·brook \'hōl-brùk, 'häl-\
Hol·burt \'häl-bərt\
Holds·worth \'hōldz-,wərth\
Hol·ger Dan. \'hól-gər\
Hol·la·day \'häl-ə-dā\
Hol·land \'häl-ənd\
Hol·ley \'häl-ē\
Hol·li·day \'häl-ə-da\
Hol·lings·worth \'häl-iŋz-,wərth\
Hol·lis \'häl-əs\
Hol·lis·ter \'häl-əs-tər\
Holl·way \'häl-(,)wā\
Hol·ly \'häl-ē\
Holm Norw. \'hólm\
Hol·man \'hōl-mən\
Ho·mans \'hō-mənz\
Ho·mer \'hō-mər\
Hom·mel Dan. \'hóm-əl\
Hon-Ami Jp. \hōn-ä-mē\
Hon·ey·wood \'hən-ē-,wùd\
Hong-do Kor. \hóŋ-dó\
Ho·no·rat Fr. \ó-nó-rá\
Hon·o·ré 1 \,än-ə-'rā, 'än-ə-,rā\ 2 Fr. Ho·no·ré \ó-nó-rā\
Ho·no·rio Port. \ü-'nór-yü\
Ho·no·ri·us Lat. \hō-'nōr-ē-əs\
Hook \'hùk\
Hook·ham \'hùk-əm\
Hope \'hōp\
Hop·kin \'häp-kən\
Hop·wood \'häp-,wùd\
Hor·ace 1 \'hór-əs, 'här-\ 2 Fr. Ho·race \ó-rás\
Ho·ra·cio Span. \ó-'räth-yō; -'räs-\
Ho·ra·tio \hə-'rā-sh(ē-)ō\
Ho·ra·tius \hə-'rā-sh(ē-)əs\
Hor·muzd \här-'mùzd\
Hor·nell \hór-'nel, 'hór-nel\
Hors·ley \'hórz-lē, 'hór-slē\
Horst Ger. \'hórst\
Hor·tense 1 \,hór-'tens, 'hór-,tens\ 2 Fr. \ór-tä^{n}s\
Hor·ton \'hórt-^{ə}n\
Ho·sea \hō-'zā-ə, -'zē-\
Hos·mer \'häz-mər\
Hotch·kin \'häch-kən\
Hotch·kiss \'häch-kəs\
Hoth·am \'häth-əm\
Hou·a·ri Arab. \hü-'är-ē\
Hough \'həf, 'häf\
Hough·wout \'haù-ət\
Hous·ton \'(h)yü-stən\
Hov·ey \'həv-ē\
How·ard \'haù(-ə)rd\
How·arth \'haù-ərth, -,ärth\
How·land \'haù-lənd\
Hox·ie \'häk-sē\
Hoyt \'hóit\
Hry·ho·ro·vych Ukrainian \grē-'gór-ó-,vēch\
Hu·bert 1 \'hyü-bərt\ 2 Du. \'hūē-bərt\ 3 Fr. \ūē-ber\ 4 Ger. \'hü-,bert\
Hu·ber·tus 1 Du. \hūē-'be(ə)r-tues\ 2 Ger. \hü-'ber-tùs \
Hübsch Ger. \'huepsh\
Hucks \'həks\
Hud·die \'həd-ē\
Hud·dle·ston \'həd-^{ə}l-stən\
Hu·ey \'hyü-ē\
Huff \'həf\
Huf·fam \'həf-^{ə}m\
Hu·gei·a·nus Lat. \,(h)yü-gā-'ā-nəs\
Hu·ger \'hjü-gər\
Hugh \'hyü\
Hugh·lings \'hyü-liŋz\

\ə\ abut \$^{ə}$\ kitten, Fr. table \ər\ further \a\ ash \ā\ ace \ä\ cot, cart \aù\ out \ch\ chin \e\ bet \ē\ easy \g\ go \i\ hit \ī\ ice \j\ job \ŋ\ sing \ō\ go \ó\ law \ói\ boy \th\ both \th\ the \ü\ loot \ù\ foot \y\ yet \zh\ vision \á, b, g, k, ^{n}, œ, œ̄, ue, ūē, ^{y}\ see Guide to Pronunciation

Hu·go 1 \'hyü-(,)gō\ 2 *Du.* \'hue-(,)gō\ 3 *Finn.* \'hü-gö\ 4 *Ger., Swed.* \'hü-(,)gō\ 5 *Pol.* \'hü-gō\
Hugues *Fr.* \ueg\
Hui·bert *Du.* \'hœi-bərt\
Hui·dong *Kor.* \hwē-dōŋ\
Huig, Huigh *Du.* \'hœik\
Hul·beart, -bert \'həl-bərt\
Hul·drych *Ger.* \'hül-drik\
Hulse \'həls\
Hultz \'həlts\
Hum·bert \'həm-bərt\
Hum·ber·to *Port.* \ü(^{n})m-'ber-tü\
Hum·mell \'həm-əl\
Hum·phrey \'həm(p)-frē\
Hum·phry \'həm(p)-frē\
Hun·ger·ford \'həŋ-gər-fərd\
Hun·ter \'hənt-ər\
Hun·ting·ton \'hənt-iŋ-tən\
Hunt·ley, -ly \'hənt-lē\
Hu·ot *Fr.* \ue-ō\
Hurd \'hərd\
Hur·rell \'hər-əl\
Hur·ta·do *Span.* \ür-'tä-thō\
Hus·band \'həz-bənd\
Hus·sein *Turk.* \hue-'sān\
Hus·ton \'(h)yü-stən\
Hutch·e·son \'həch-ə-sən\
Hutch·ings \'həch-iŋz\
Hutch·ins \'həch-ənz\
Hutch·i·son \'həch-ə-sən\
Hu·tin \'(h)yüt-^{ə}n\
Hut·tle·ston \'hət-^{ə}l-stən\
Hut·ton \'hət-^{ə}n\
Huw *Welsh* \'hyü\
Huy·brecht *Du.* \'hœi-(,)brekt\
Huy·ghen *Du.* \'hœi-gən\
Hya·cinthe *Fr.* \yá-sa^{n}t\
Hya·ku·ren *Jp.* \hyä-kür-en\
Hy·men \'hī-mən\
Hy·nek *Czech.* \'hin-,ek\
Hy·po·lite *Fr.* \ē-pō-lēt\

Ia·co·po *Ital.* \'yäk-ō-(,)pō\
Ian \'ē-ən\
Ian·cu *Rom.* \'yäŋ-kü\
I'An·son \'ī-ən-sən\
İbra·him *Turk.* \,ib-rä-'him\
Ich·a·bod \'ik-ə-,bäd\
Ichi·no·jo *Jp.* \ē-chē-nō-jō\
Ichi·ro *Jp.* \ē-chē-rō\
Ichi·ta·ro *Jp.* \ē-chē-tär-ō\
Ichi·yō *Jp.* \ē-chē-(y)ō\
Ici·lius *Fr.* \ē-sēl-yues\
Ida 1 \'ī-də\ 2 *Ger.* \'ē-,dä\ 3 *Pol.* \'ē-dá\
Ide \'īd\
Ide·mil *Norw.* \'ē-də-mēl\
Ie·ha·ru *Jp.* \ē-e-här-ü\
Iem·i·tsu *Jp.* \ē-em-ēt-sü\
Ie·mo·chi *Jp.* \ē-em-ō-chē\
Ie·na·ri *Jp.* \ē-en-är-ē\
Ien·o·bu *Jp.* \ē-en-ō-bü\
Ie·sa·da *Jp.* \ē-es-ä-dä\
Ie·shi·ge *Jp.* \ē-esh-ē-ge\
Ie·tsu·gu *Jp.* \ē-et-süg-ü\
Ie·tsu·na *Jp.* \ē-et-sün-ä\
Ie·ya·su *Jp.* \ē-e-yäs-ü\
Ie·yo·shi *Jp.* \ē-ē-yō-shē\
Ignace *Fr.* \ēn-yás\
Ig·na·cio 1 *Port.* \ēg-'nás-yü\ 2 *Span.* \ēg-'näth-yō; -'näs-\
Ig·na·cy *Pol.* \ēg-'nát-si\
Ig·na·ti·us \ig-'nā-sh(ē)-əs\
Ig·naz *Ger.* \'ig-,näts, ig-'näts\
Igna·zio *Ital.* \ēn-'yät-syō\
Igor *Russ.* \'ē-gər^{y}\
Ih·no *Ger.* \'ē-(,)nō\
Ii·sak·ki *Finn.* \'ē-sák-ki\
Ik \'ik\
Il·de·bran·do *Ital.* \,ēl-dā-'brän-dō\
Il·ich 1 *Arm.* \il-'ich\ 2 *Russ.* \il-'yēch\
Ili·ja *Serb.-Cr.* \'ē-lē-yä\
Ili·ya *Arab.* \'il-ē-(y)ä\
Il·lar·ion·o·vich *Russ.* \il-(,)ər-'yōn(-əv)-,yich\
Il·ma·ri *Finn.* \'il-má-rē\
Ilo·na *Hung.* \'il-ō-(,)nä\
Il·se *Ger.* \'il-zə\
Il·ya *Russ.* \il-'yä\
Il·yich *Russ.* \il-'yēch\
İma·ded·din *Turk.* \ē-mä-ded-'dēn\
Im·bault *Fr.* \a^{n}-bō\
Imo·ko *Jp.* \ē-mō-kō\
Im·man·u·el 1 \i-'man-yə(-wə)l\ 2 **Im·ma·nu·el** *Dan.* \ē-'mán-ə-wəl\ 3 *Ger.* \i-'män-ü-,el\
Im·o·gen \'im-ə-jən\
Im·pey \'im-pē\
Im·re *Hung.* \'im-re\
Ina \'ē-nə\
Ina·zo *Jp.* \ē-nä-zō\
In·crease \'in-,krēs, in-'\
In·da·le·cio *Span.* \ēn-dä-'lāth-yō; -'lās-\
In·dira \in-'dir-ə\
Inés *Span.* \ē-'nās\
Inez 1 \'ē-,nez, 'ī-\ 2 *Span.* \ē-'nāth; -'nās\
Ing·e·borg 1 *Dan.* \'ēŋ-ə-,bōrg\ 2 *Ger.* \'iŋ-ə-,bōrk\
Ing·e·bret·sen *Norw.* \'iŋ-ə-,bret-sən\
Ing·ham \'iŋ-əm\
In·go *Ital.* \'iŋ-gō\
In·gram \'iŋ-grəm\
Ing·rid *Eng., Swed.* \'iŋ-grəd\
In·i·go 1 \'in-ə-gō\ 2 *Span.* **Íñi·go** \'ēn-yē-gō\
In·mun *Kor.* \in-mün\
In·nes, In·ness \'in-əs\
In·no·cen·zo *Ital.* \,ēn-nō-'chent-sō\
Ino·cên·cio *Port.* \,ē-nü-'sā^{n}-syü\
Ioan *Rom.* \'ywän\
Io·ann *Russ.* \(,)yə-'án\
Io·an·nes, -nis *Mod. Gk.* \yō-'än-yēs\
Io·an·ní·dis *Mod. Gk.* \yō-än-'nē-thēs\
Io·an·ni·ki *Russ.* \(,)yə-'án-yik-yi\
Ion *Rom.* \'yōn\
Io·na·che *Rom.* \yō-'näk-e\
Io·niţa *Rom.* \yō-'nēt-sä\
Io·sif *Russ.* \i-'ōs-yif, 'yōs-yif\
Io·si·fo·vich *Russ.* \i-'ōs-yif(-əv)-,yich, 'yōs-yif-\
Ip·po·lit *Russ.* \ip-(,)pəl-'yēt\
Ip·po·li·to *Ital.* \ēp-'pō-lē-(,)tō\
Ip·po·li·to·vich *Russ.* \yip-(,)pəl-'yēt(-əv)-,yich\
Ira \'ī-rə\
Ire·dell \'ī(ə)r-,del\
Ire·nae·us \ī-rə-'nē-əs\
Ire·nä·us *Ger.* \,ē-rā-'ne-üs\
Irene 1 \ī-'rēn, *esp. Brit.* ī-'rē-nē\ 2 **Ire·ne** *Ger.* \ē-'rā-nē\ 3 *Lat.* \ī-'rē-nē\ 4 *Fr.* **Irène** \ē-ren\
Iré·née *Fr.* \ē-rā-nā\
Iru·ka *Jp.* \ē-rük-ä\
Ir·vin, Ir·vine \'ər-vən\
Ir·ving \'ər-viŋ\
Ir·win \'ər-wən\
İsa *Turk.* \ə-'sä\
Isaac 1 \'ī-zik, -zək\ 2 *Fr.* \ē-zák\ 3 *Pol.* \'ē-sák\ 4 *Russ.* \i-'sák\ 5 **Isa·ac** *Ger.* \'ē-zä-,äk\ 6 *Span.* \ē-sä-'äk\ 7 *Du.* **Isaäc** \'ē-säk\
Isaacs \'ī-ziks, -zəks\
Isaak 1 *Du.* \'ē-,säk\ 2 *Ger.* **Isa·ak** \'ē-zä-,äk, 'ē-zäk\
Is·a·bel 1 \'iz-ə-,bel\ 2 *Span.* **Isa·bel** \ē-sä-'bel\
Is·a·bel·la 1 \,iz-ə-'bel-ə\ 2 **Isa·bel·la** *Du.* \,ē-sá-'bel-á\ 3 *Ital.* \,ē-zä-'bel-lä\
Isa·belle 1 *Fr.* \ē-zá-bel\ 2 *Ger.* **Isa·bel·le** \,ē-zä-'bel-ə\
Isack *Du.* \'ē-,säk\
Is·a·dor, Is·a·dore \'iz-ə-,dō(ə)r, -,dō(ə)r\
Is·a·do·ra \,iz-ə-'dō-rə\
Isa·ia *Ital.* \,ē-zä-'ē-ä\
Isa·iah \ī-'zā-ə, *chiefly Brit* -'zī-\
Isa·i·as *Span.* \ē-sä-'ē-äs\
Isak *Dan.* \'ē-,sák\
Is·am·bard \'iz-əm-,bärd\
Isa·mu *Jp.* \ē-sä-mü\
Isham \'ī-shəm\
Ish·bel \'ish-bel\
Is·i·dor 1 \'iz-ə-,dō(ə)r, -,dō(ə)r\ 2 *Ger.* **Isi·dor** \'ē-zē-,dōr, ,ē-zē-'dōr\
Is·i·dore 1 \'iz-ə-,dō(ə)r, -,dō(ə)r\ 2 *Fr.* **Isi·dore** \ē-zē-dōr\
Isi·do·ro 1 *Ital.* \ē-sē-'dō-rō\ 2 *Span.* \ē-sē-'thō-rō\
Isi·dro *Span.* \ē-'sē-thrō\
Is·ma·el 1 *Ger.* \'is-mä-,el\ 2 *Span.* \ēz-mä-'äl\
Is·ma·il *Russ.* \yis-'mä-(y)il\
Is·ma·'īl *Arab.* \is-mä-'ēl\
Is·mar *Ger.* \'ē-,smär\
İs·met *Turk.* \is-'met\
Iso, Isoh *Jp.* \ē-sō\
Isol·de *Ger.* \ē-'zōl-də\
Iso·ro·ku *Jp.* \ē-sō-rō-kü\
Iso·ya *Jp.* \ē-sō-yä\
Is·ra·el 1 \'iz-rē-əl\ 2 *Du.* \'is-rá-,el\ 3 *Fr.* \ēs-rá-el\ 4 *Swed.* \'ēs-rá-əl\
Is·ra·hel *Du.* \'is-rá-,el\
Is·sa *Jp.* \es-sä\
Is·sa·char \'is-ə-kär\
Is·sei *Jp.* \ēs-sī\
Ist·ván *Hung.* \'isht-(,)ván\
Ital *Ger.* \'ē-,täl\
Ita·lo *Ital.* \'ē-täl-(,)ō\
It·chō *Jp.* \ē-chō\
Ith·i·el \'ith-ē-əl\
Ito \ē-tō\
Itu·ri *Span.* \ē-'tü-rē\
Iu·lia *Russ.* \'yül-yə\
Iu·liu *Rom.* \'yül-yü\
Ivah \'ī-və\
Ivan 1 \ē-'vän, 'ī-vən\ 2 *Bulg.* \ē-'ván\ 3 *Russ.* \i-'ván\ 4 *Serb.-Cr.* \'ē-ván\ 5 *Swed.* \'ē-ván\
Iva·noe *Ital.* \ē-'vän-ō-,ā\
Iva·nov *Bulg.* \ē-'vá-nōf\
Iva·no·vich, -vitch *Russ.* \i-'ván(-əv)-,yich\
Ivar 1 *Norw.* \'ē-vär\ 2 *Swed.* \'ē-vár\
Ives \'īvz\
Ivey \'ī-vē\
Ivor \'ē-vər, 'ī-\
Ivy \'ī-vē\
Iwan 1 *Fr.* \ē-vä^{n}\ 2 *Ger.* \ē-'vän, 'ē-,\
Iwao *Jp.* \ē-wä-ō\
Iye·sa·to *Jp.* \ē-ye-sä-tō\
Izaak 1 \'ī-zik, -zək\ 2 *Du.* \'ē-,zäk\

Jaak·ko *Finn.* \'yäk-,kō\
Jaan *Est.* \'yän\
Ja·bez \'jā-bəz\
Ja·cek *Pol.* \'yät-sek\
Jaches *Fr.* \yásh\
Ja·cint *Catalan* \zhá-'sēnt\
Ja·cin·to *Span.* \kä-'thēn-tō; -'sēn-\
Jack \'jak\
Ja·cob 1 \'jā-kəb\ 2 *Afrik., Ger., Norw., Swed.* \'yä-,kōp\ 3 *Dan., Du.* \'yá-,kōp\ 4 *Fr.* \zhá-kōb\

Ja·co·bi·na *Ger.* \ˌyä-kȯ-ˈbē-nä\
Ja·co·bus 1 \jə-ˈkō-bəs\ 2 *Du.* \yä-ˈkō-bœs\ 3 *Ger.* \yä-ˈkō-bu̇s\
Ja·comb \ˈjā-kəm\
Ja·co·po *Ital.* \ˈyäk-ō-(ˌ)pō\
Jac·que·line 1 \ˈjak-(w)ə-lən, -ˌlēn\ 2 *Fr.* \zhä-klēn\
Jacques 1 *Du., Ger.* \ˈzhäk\ 2 *Fr.* \zhäk\
Ja·dun·ath *Bengali* \ˈjəd-ə-ˌnät\
Jad·wi·ga *Pol.* \yäd-ˈvē-gä\
Jaf·fray \ˈjaf-ˌrā, -rē\
Ja·gad·gu·ru *Skt.* \ˈjəg-əd-ˈgu̇r-ü\
Ja·ga·dis *Bengali* \ˌjəg-ə-ˈdēs\
Jah·ver·bhai *Gujarati* \jə-ˈvär-ˌbä-ē\
Jai *Tamil* \ˈjī\
Jai·me *Span.* \ˈk̲ī-mā\
Ja·kob 1 *Dan., Du.* \ˈyä-ˌkȯp\ 2 *Ger., Swed.,* \ˈyä-ˌkȯp\ 3 *Pol.* **Ja·kób** \ˈyä-küp\
Ja·ku·chū *Jp.* \jä-ku̇ch-ü\
James 1 *Eng., Ger.* \ˈjāmz\ 2 *Fr.* \jem(p)s, zhäm\
Jam·set·jee, -ji *Bengali* \jəm-ˈset-jē\
Jan 1 \ˈjan\ 2 *Czech., Pol.* \ˈyän\ 3 *Du., Ger., Latvian* \ˈyän\
Jane 1 \ˈjān\ 2 *Fr.* \zhän\
Janes \ˈjānz\
Ja·net 1 \ˈjan-ət, jə-ˈnet\ 2 *Fr.* \zhä-ne\
Jane·way \ˈjān-ˌwā\
Jan·is 1 \ˈjan-əs\ 2 *Latvian* **Jā·nis** \ˈyän-is\
Jan·kiew *Pol.* \ˈyän-kyef, ˈyäŋ-\
Jan·ko *Slovak* \ˈyäŋ-kō\
Já·nos *Hung.* \ˈyä-(ˌ)nōsh\
Jan·sen *Du.* \ˈyän(t)-sən\
Jansz *Du.* \ˈyäns\
Jans·zoon *Du.* \ˈyän(t)-sən, -ˌsȯn, -ˌsōn\
Ja·nuá·rio *Port.* \zhən-ˈwär-yü; zhän-\
Jan·u·ar·i·us 1 \ˌjan-yə-ˈwer-ē-əs\ 2 *Ger.* **Ja·nu·a·ri·us** \ˌyän-ü-ˈär-yu̇s, -ˈär-ē-u̇s\
Ja·nus \ˈjā-nəs\
Ja·nusz *Pol.* \ˈyä-nüsh\
Ja·pe·tus *Dan.* \yä-ˈpi-tu̇s\
Jar·ed \ˈjar-əd\
Jarl 1 *Finn.* \ˈyärl\ 2 *Norw.* \ˈyärl\
Jar·mi·la *Czech* \ˈyär-mil-ä\
Ja·ro·mír *Czech* \ˈyä-rȯ-ˌmē(ə)r\
Ja·ro·slav *Czech* \ˈyä-rȯ-ˌsläf\
Ja·ro·slaw *Ger.* \ˈyär-ō-ˌsläf\
Ja·son \ˈjās-^{ə}n\
Jas·par, Jas·per \ˈjas-pər\
Jas·want *Marathi* \ˈjəs-vənt\
Ja·vier *Span.* \k̲äv-ˈyer\
Ja·wa·har·lal *Kashmiri* \jə-ˈwä-hər-ˌläl\
Jay \ˈjā\
Ja·ya *Tamil* \ˈjī-ə\
Jayne \ˈjān\
Jaynes \ˈjānz\
Jean 1 \ˈjēn\ 2 *Finn.* \ˈzhän\ 3 *Flem., Ger.* \ˈzhä^n\ 4 *Fr.* \zhä^n\
Jeanne 1 \ˈjēn\ 2 *Fr.* \zhän, zhän\
Jean·nette \jə-ˈnet\
Jean·not *Fr.* \zhä-nō\
Jeb \ˈjeb\
Je·bu·sa \jə-ˈbyü-sə, ˈjeb-yü-sə\
Jed·e·di·ah, Jed·i·di·ah \ˌjed-də-ˈdī-ə\
Jef 1 *Du.* \ˈzhef\ 2 *Fr.* \zhef\
Jeff \ˈjef\
Jef·fery \ˈjef-(ə-)rē\
Jef·fer·ys \ˈjef-(ə-)rēz\
Jef·frey \ˈjef-rē\
Jef·freys, Jef·fries \ˈjef-rēz\
Jef·fry \ˈjef-rē\
Je·han *Fr.* \zhə-än, zhän\
Je·han·net *Fr.* \zh(ə-)ä-ne\
Je·hiel *Heb.* \yəˈk̲ēl\
Je·hosh·a·phat \ji-ˈhäs(h)-ə-ˌfat\
Je·hu·da \jə-ˈhü-də\
Je·hu·di \jə-ˈhüd-ē\
Jel·les *Du.* \ˈyel-əs\
Jelly *Hung.* \ˈyel^y\
Jem \ˈjem\
Je·mi·ma \jə-ˈmī-mə\
Jem·i·son \ˈjem-ə-sən\
Jem·my \ˈjem-ē\
Jen·ings \ˈjen-iŋz\
Jen·kin \ˈjeŋ-kən\
Jen·kins \ˈjeŋ-kənz\
Jen·kin·son \ˈjeŋ-kən-sən\
Jen·ners \ˈjen-ərz\
Jen·nette \jə-ˈnet\
Jen·ni *Du.* \ˈyen-ē\
Jen·nie \ˈjen-ē, *Brit also* ˈjin-ē\
Jen·nings \ˈjen-iŋz\
Jen·ny \ˈjen-ē, *Brit also* ˈjin-ē\
Je·nő *Hung.* \ˈyen-(ˌ)œ̄\
Jens *Dan., Ger., Norw.* \ˈyen(t)s\
Jeph·son \ˈjef-sən\
Jep·pe *Dan.* \ˈyā-bə\
Jep·tha \ˈjep-thə\
Jer·e·mi·ah \ˌjer-ə-ˈmī-ə\
Je·re·mi·as *Du., Ger.* \ˌyā-rā-ˈmē-äs\
Jé·ré·mie *Fr.* \zhā-rā-mē\
Jer·e·my \ˈjer-ə-mē\
Jer·myn \ˈjər-mən\
Jer·nej *Serb.-Cr.* \ˈyer-ney, -nā\
Jer·ning·ham \ˈjər-niŋ-ˌham, -əm\
Je·roen *Du.* \yə-ˈrün\
Jer·rold \ˈjer-əld\
Je·rom *Du.* \yə-ˈrōm\
Je·rome 1 \jə-ˈrōm, *Brit also* ˈjer-əm\ 2 *Fr.* **Jé·rôme** \zhā-rōm\
Je·rô·ni·mo 1 *Port.* \zhə-ˈrō-nē-mü; zhā-\ 2 *Span.* **Je·ró·ni·mo** \k̲ā-ˈrō-nē-mō\
Je·room *Du.* \yə-ˈrōm\
Jer·ry \ˈjer-ē\
Jer·vis \ˈjər-vəs, *Brit also* ˈjär-vəs\
Je·rzy *Pol.* \ˈyezh-i\
Jess \ˈjes\
Jes·se \ˈjes-ē\
Jes·sie \ˈjes-ē\
Jes·up \ˈjes-əp\
Je·sús *Span.* \k̲ā-ˈsüs\
Jeth·ro \ˈjeth-rō, ˈjē-thrō\
Jew·ett \ˈjü-ət\
Ji·hē *Jp.* \jē-he\
Jim \ˈjim\
Jim·my \ˈjim-ē\
Jin·sai *Jp.* \jin-sī\
Ji·ří *Czech* \ˈyir-zhē\
Ji·ro *Jp.* \jē-rō\
Jo 1 \ˈjō\ 2 *Du.* \ˈyō\
Jo·a·chim 1 \ˈjō-ə-ˌkim\ 2 *Dan.* \ˈyō-ä-kēm\ 3 *Du.* \yō-ä-k̲əm\ 4 *Fr.* \zhō-ä-kēm\ 5 *Ger.* \ˈyō-äk̲-im\ 6 *Norw.* \ˈyō-ä-kim\ 7 *Pol.* \yȯ-ˈä-k̲ēm\
Jo·a·kim *Serb.-Cr.* \ˈyȯ-ä-ˌkēm\
Joan 1 \ˈjō(-ə)n, jō-ˈan\ 2 *Catalan* \ˈzhwän\
Jo·an·na \jō-ˈan-ə\
Jo·an·nes 1 \jō-ˈan-ēz, -əs\ 2 *Du.* \yō-ˈän-əs\ 3 *Mod. Gk.* \yȯ-ˈän-yēs\
João *Port.* \ˈzhwau̇^{n}\
Joa·quim *Port.* \zhwə-ˈkē^n; zhwä-\
Joa·quin 1 \wä-ˈkēn\ 2 *Span.* **Joa·quín** \k̲wä-ˈkēn\
Joa·qui·na *Span.* \k̲wä-ˈkē-nä\
Job 1 \ˈjōb\ 2 *Du.* \ˈyȯp\
Jobst *Ger.* \ˈyȯpst, ˈyōpst\
Joce·lyn \ˈjäs-(ə-)lən\
Jo·do·cus 1 *Ger.* \yō-ˈdō-ku̇s\ 2 *Lat.* **Jod·o·cus** \ˈjäd-ō-kəs\
Joe \ˈjō\
Jo·el 1 \ˈjō-əl\ 2 *Finn.* \ˈyȯ-el\ 3 *Fr.* **Jo·ël** \zhȯ-el\
Joest *Du.* \ˈyüst\
Jo·han 1 *Dan.* \yu̇-ˈhän\ 2 *Du., Norw.* \yō-ˈhän\ 3 *Est.* \ˈyō-ˌhän\ 4 *Finn., Swed.* \ˈyü-ˌhän\
Jo·hann 1 *Dan.* \yu̇-ˈhän\ 2 *Du., Ger.* \yō-ˈhän\ 3 *Finn., Swed.* \ˈyü-ˌhän\ 4 *Icel.* **Jó·hann** \ˈyō-ˌhän\
Jo·han·na 1 \jō-ˈ(h)an-ə\ 2 *Du.* \yō-ˈhän-ä\ 3 *Ger.* \yō-ˈhän-ä\ 4 *Swed.* \yō-ˈhän-nä\
Jo·han·ne 1 *Dan.* \yu̇-ˈhän-ə\ 2 *Ger.* \yō-ˈhän-ə\
Jo·han·nes 1 \jō-ˈhan-əs\ 2 *Dan.* \yu̇-ˈhän-əs\ 3 *Du., Ger.* \yō-ˈhän-əs\ 4 *Finn.* \yu̇-ˈhän-nes\ 5 *Fr.* \zhȯ-ä-nes\ 6 *Swed.* \yō-ˈhän-nəs\
John 1 \ˈjän\ 2 *Fr.* \jȯn, zhȯn\
John·nie \ˈjän-ē\
Johns \ˈjänz\
John·ston, -stone \ˈjän(t)-stən, -sən\
Jo·ki·chi *Jp.* \jō-kē-chē\
Jo·lán *Hung.* \ˈyȯ-(ˌ)län\
Jo·mo *Kenyan* \ˈjō-mō\
Jon 1 \ˈjän\ 2 *Norw.* \ˈyōn, ˈyȯn\ 3 *Rom.* \ˈyȯn\ 4 *Icel.* **Jón** \ˈyōn\
Jo·nas 1 \ˈjō-nəs\ 2 *Du., Ger., Norw.* \ˈyō-näs\ 3 *Lith.* \ˈyȯ-näs\ 4 *Swed.* \ˈyü-näs\ 5 *Icel.* **Jó·nas** \ˈyō-ˌnäs\
Jon·a·than 1 \ˈjän-ə-thən\ 2 *Ger.* **Jo·na·than** \ˈyō-nä-ˌtän\
Jöns *Swed.* \ˈyœns\
Jons·son 1 *Norw.* \ˈjȯns-sȯn\ 2 *Swed.* **Jöns·son** \ˈyœn-sȯn\
Joos *Du.* \ˈyōs\
Jost *Du., Ger.* \ˈyōst\
Jor·dan \ˈjȯrd-^{ə}n\
Jörg *Ger.* \ˈyœrk̲\
Jor·ge 1 *Port.* \ˈzhȯr-zhə; -zhā\ 2 *Span.* \ˈhȯr-hā\
Jör·gen 1 *Dan.* \ˈyœr-g̅ən\ 2 *Norw.* \ˈyœr-gən\
Jo·ris *Du.* \ˈyōr-əs\
Jo·sa·phat *Ger.* \ˈyō-zäf-ˌät\
Josce·lyn \ˈjäs-(ə-)lən\
Jo·sé 1 *Port.* \zhü-ˈze\ 2 *Span.* \hō-ˈsā\
Jo·sef 1 \ˈjō-zəf *also* -səf\ 2 *Czech* \ˈyȯ-ˌsef\ 3 *Du.* \ˈyō-ˌsef\ 4 *Ger.* \ˈyō-ˌzef\ 5 *Swed.* \ˈyü-ˌsef\
Jo·se·fa *Span.* \k̲ō-ˈsā-fä\
Jo·seph 1 \ˈjō-zəf *also* -səf\ 2 *Du.* \ˈyō-ˌsef\ 3 *Fr.* \zhō-zef\ 4 *Ger.* \ˈyō-ˌzef\ 5 *Swed.* \ˈyü-ˌsef\
Jo·se·pha \jō-ˈsē-fə\
Jo·sèphe *Fr.* \zhō-zef\
Jo·sé·phin *Fr.* \zhō-zā-fa^n\
Jo·se·phine 1 \ˈjō-zə-fēn, ˌjō-zə-ˈfēn\ 2 **Jo·se·phi·ne** *Du.* \ˌyō-sə-ˈfē-nə\ 3 *Ger.* \ˌyō-ze-ˈfē-nə\ 4 *Fr.* **Jo·sé·phine** \zhō-zā-fēn\
Jo·se·phus 1 \jō-ˈsē-fəs\ 2 *Du.* \yō-ˈsā-fœs\
Jo·se·tu *Jp.* \jō-se-tu̇\
Josh \ˈjäsh\
Josh·ua \ˈjäsh-(ə-)wə\
Jo·si·ah \jō-ˈsī-ə, -ˈzī-\
Jo·si·as 1 \jō-ˈsī-əs, -zī-\ 2 *Ger.* \yō-ˈzē-äs\ 3 *Fr.* **Jo·sias** \zhōz-yäs\
Jo·sip *Serb.-Cr.* \ˈyȯ-sēp\
Jos·lin \ˈjäs-lən, ˈjäz-\
Jos·quin *Fr.* \zhȯs-ka^n\
Josse *Fr.* \zhȯs\
Jos·se·lin *Fr.* \zhȯs-la^n\
Josse·lyn \ˈjäs-(ə-)lən\
Joss·lyn \ˈjäs-lən\
Jost *Ger.* \ˈyōst\
Jo·sué *Fr.* \zhō-zw^{y}ā\
Jo·van *Serb.-Cr.* \ˈyȯ-vän\
Jo·vi·a·nus *Lat.* \ˌjō-vē-ˈā-nəs\

\ə\ **abut** \ə\ **kitten,** *Fr.* **table** \ər\ **further** \a\ **ash** \ā\ **ace** \ä\ **cot, cart** \au̇\ **out** \ch\ **chin** \e\ **bet** \ē\ **easy** \g\ **go** \i\ **hit** \ī\ **ice** \j\ **job** \ŋ\ **sing** \ō\ **go** \ȯ\ **law** \ȯi\ **boy** \th\ **both** \t̲h̲\ **the** \ü\ **loot** \u̇\ **foot** \y\ **yet** \zh\ **vision** \ä, b̲, g̅, k̲, ^{n}, œ, œ̄, u̇e, ūe, ^{y}\ *see* Guide to Pronunciation

Joy \'jȯi\
Joyce \'jȯis\
Jo·zef 1 *Du.* \'yō-ˌzef\ 2 *Pol.* **Jó·zef** \'yü-zef\
Jō·zei *Jp.* \jō-zä\
Jó·zsef *Hung.* \'yō-(ˌ)zhef\
Juan 1 *Fr.* \zhwyän\ 2 *Span.* \'k̲wän\
Jua·na *Span.* \'k̲wän-ä\
Ju·bal \'jü-bəl\
Ju·dah \'jüd-ē\
Ju·das *Fr.* \zhue̅-dä\
Judd \'jəd\
Ju·dith 1 \'jüd-əth\ 2 *Du.* \'yue̅-dət\ 3 *Fr.* \zhue̅-dēt\ 4 *Ger.* \'yü-dit\
Jud·son \'jəd-sən\
Ju·ha·ni *Finn.* \'yu̇-ˌhán-ē\
Ju·ho *Finn.* \'yü-ˌhȯ\
Ju·i·chi \ju̇-ē-chē\
Jules \'jülz\ 2 *Fr.* \zhue̅l\
Ju·lia 1 \'jül-yə\ 2 *Du.* \'yue̅-lē-á\ 3 *Finn.* \'yü-li-á\ 4 *Fr.* \zhue̅l-yá\
Jul·ian 1 \'jül-yən\ 2 *Pol.* \'yül-(ˌ)yán\ 3 *Ger.* **Ju·lian** \ˌyü-lē-'än, yül-'yän\ 4 *Span.* **Ju·lián** \k̲ül-'yän\
Ju·li·ana \ˌjü-lē-'an-ə\
Ju·lia·ne *Ger.* \ˌyü-lē-'än-ə, yül-'yän-\
Ju·li·a·nus *Lat.* \ˌjü-lē-'ā-nəs\
Ju·lie 1 \'jü-lē\ 2 *Fr.* \zhue̅-lē\ 3 *Ger.* \'yü-lē-ə, 'yül-yə\
Ju·lien 1 \'jül-yən\ 2 *Fr.* \zhue̅l-yan\
Ju·li·et \'jül-yət, ˌjü-lē-'et, 'jü-lē-ˌ\
Ju·li·ette \ˌjü-lē-'et\ 2 *Fr.* \zhue̅l-yet\
Ju·lio 1 *Span.* \'k̲ül-yō\ 2 *Port.* **Jú·lio** \'zhül-yü\
Jul·ius 1 \'jül-yəs\ 2 **Ju·li·us** *Czech* \'yu̇-li-u̇s\ 3 *Dan., Ger.* \'yü-lē-u̇s\ 4 *Du.* \'yue̅-lē-œs\ 5 *Swed.* \'yü-lē-(ˌ)əs\
Ju·liusz \'yül-(ˌ)yüsh\
Jump \'jəmp\
June \'jün\
Ju·ni·a·nus *Lat.* \ˌjü-nē-'ā-nəs\
Jun·ichi·rō *Jp.* \ju̇n-ē-chē-rō\
Ju·ní·pe·ro *Span.* \k̲ü-'nē-pā-rō\
Jun·ius \'jü-nyəs, -nē-əs\
Jun·no·su·ke *Jp.* \ju̇n-nō-su̇k-e\
Ju·raj *Serb.-Cr.* \'yü-ráy, -rī\
Jürg *Ger.* \'yu̇erk̲\
Jür·gen 1 *Dan.* \'yue̅r-gən\ 2 *Ger.* \'yu̇er-gən\
Ju·ri·aen *Du.* \'yue̅-rē-ˌán\
Ju·ri·an *Du.* \'yue̅-rē-ˌän\
Jū·rō·bei *Jp.* \ju̇r-ō-bā\
Ju·sa·bu·rō *Jp.* \ju̇s-ä-bu̇r-ō\
Ju·se·pe *Span.* \k̲ü-'sā-pā\
Jus·si *Swed.* \'yəs-sē\
Just *Fr.* \zhue̅st\
Jus·ta *Lat.* \'jəs-tə\
Juste *Fr.* \zhue̅st\
Jus·tice \'jəs-təs\
Jus·tin 1 \'jəs-tən\ 2 *Fr.* \zhue̅-stan\ 3 *Ger.* \yu̇s-'tēn\
Jus·tine *Fr.* \zhue̅-stēn\
Jus·tin·i·an \ˌjə-'stin-ē-ən\
Jus·ti·nia·no *Span.* \k̲ü-stēn-'yän-ō\
Jus·ti·nus 1 *Ger.* \yu̇s-'tē-nu̇s\ 2 *Lat.* \jəs-'tī-nəs\
Jus·to *Span.* \'k̲ü-stō\
Jus·tus 1 \'jəs-təs\ 2 *Du.* \'yœs-tœ̅s\ 3 *Ger.* \'yu̇s-tu̇s\
Ju·ta·ro *Jp.* \ju̇-tär-ō\
Ju·ven·ti·us *Lat.* \jü-'ven-sh(ē-)əs\

Kaa·re *Dan.* \'kȯr-ə\
Kaar·lo *Finn.* \'kär-ˌlȯ\
Ka·a·ru *Jp.* \kä-är-u̇\
Kae·so *Lat.* \'kē-sō\
Ka·fū *Jp.* \kä-fu̇\
Ka·ge·a·ki *Jp.* \kä-ge-ä-kē\
Ka·ge·ka·tsu *Jp.* \käg-ek-ät-su̇\
Kah·lil \kə-'lē(ə)l\
Kaj *Dan.* \'kī\
Ka·ki·chi *Jp.* \kä-kē-chē\
Ka·ki·em·on *Jp.* \kä-kē-em-ōn\
Ka·ku·zō *Jp.* \kä-kü-zō\
Kál·mán *Hung.* \'kál-(ˌ)mán\
Ka·ma·ta·ri *Jp.* \kä-mä-tä-rē\
Ka·ma·to *Jp.* \kä-mä-tō\
Ka·me·ki·chi *Jp.* \käm-e-kē-chē\
Ka·mil *Pol.* \'kám-yēl\
Ka·mon·no·ka·mi *Jp.* \kä-mōn-nō-kä-mē\
Kan *Jp.* \kän\
Ka·na·o·ka *Jp.* \kän-ä-ō-kä\
Ka·ne·ra *Jp.* \kä-ner-ä\
Ka·ne·to·mo *Jp.* \kän-e-tō-mō\
Ka·ne·yo·shi *Jp.* \kän-e-yō-shē\
Ka·nik *Turk.* \kä-'nēk\
Kan·ji *Jp.* \kän-jē\
Kan·ji·rō *Jp.* \kän-jē-rō\
Ka·no *Jp.* \kä-nō\
Kan·ta·ro *Jp.* \kän-tä-rō\
Kan·zan *Jp.* \kän-zän\
Kan·zō *Jp.* \kän-zō\
Ka·o·ru *Jp.* \kä-ō-ru̇\
Ka·pen·da *Bantu* \kä-'pen-də\
Ka·ram·chand *Gujarati* \'kə-rəm-ˌchənd\
Ka·rel 1 *Czech* \'ká-ˌrel\ 2 *Du.* \'kár-əl\
Ka·rell *Swed.* \'kä-rəl\
Ka·ren *Dan., Norw.* \'kär-ən\
Ka·ri *Jp.* \kä-rē\
Ka·rim *Arab.* \ká-'rēm\
Ka·rin *Dan.* \'kär-(ˌ)ēn\
Kar·ker \'kär-kər\
Karl 1 *Eng., Dan., Du., Ger., Norw., Swed.* \'kärl\ 2 *Finn., Russ.* \'kárl\ 3 *Fr.* \kárl\
Kār·lis *Latvian* \'kär-lis\
Kar·lo·vich *Russ.* \'kárl(-əv)-ˌyich\
Ka·rol *Pol.* \'kár-ȯl\
Ka·ro·li·na *Swed.* \ˌkä-rȯ-'lē-ná\
Ka·ro·li·ne *Ger.* \ˌkär-ō-'lē-nə\
Ká·roly *Hung.* \'ká-(ˌ)rōly\
Ka·sim *Pers.* \'kás-im\
Ka·si·mir *Ger.* \'käz-ē-ˌmēr\
Kas·par 1 *Dan.* \'kás-ˌpär\ 2 *Du., Ger.* \'käs-ˌpär\ 3 *Hung.* \'käsh-ˌpär\
Kaš·par *Czech* \'kásh-pár\
Kas·per *Pol.* \'kás-per\
Kas·sell \'kas-əl\
Ka·tai *Jp.* \kä-tī\
Kate \'kāt\
Ka·te·ri *Algonquian* \'kät-ə-rē\
Ka·tha·ri·na *Ger., Hung.* \ˌkät-ä-'rē-nä\
Kath·a·rine 1 \'kath-(ə-)rən\ 2 *Ger.* **Ka·tha·ri·ne** \ˌkät-ä-'rē-nə\
Kä·the *Ger.* \'ket-ə\
Kath·er·ine \'kath-(ə-)rən\
Kath·leen \kath-'lēn\
Kath·ryn \'kath-(ə-)rən\
Ka·tri·na \kə-'trē-nə\
Ka·tsu·gu·ma *Jp.* \kät-su̇g-u̇m-ä\
Kat·sumo·to *Jp.* \kät-su̇m-ō-tō\
Kat·su·no·ri *Jp.* \kät-su̇-nō-rē\
Kat·su·no·su·ke *Jp.* \kät-su̇-nō-su̇-ke\
Kauf·mann *Ger.* \'kau̇f-ˌmän\
Kay, Kaye \'kā\
Ka·zan *Jp.* \kä-zän\
Ka·zi·mie·ras *Lith.* \kä-zim-'yer-äs\
Ka·zi·mierz *Pol.* \ká-'zēm-yesh\
Ka·zi·mir *Russ.* \kəz-yim-'yēr\
Káz·mér *Hung.* \'káz-ˌmār\
Ka·zu·shi·ge *Jp.* \käz-u̇sh-ē-ge\
Ka·zu·to·yo *Jp.* \kä-zu̇-tō-yō\
Ka·zys *Lith.* \'kä-zēs\
Kean \'kēn\
Kears·ley \'kirz-lē\
Kea·tinge \'kē-tiŋ\
Ke·ble \'kē-bəl\
Ke·gan \'kē-gən\
Kei *Jp.* \kā\
Kei·ei *Jp.* \kā-ā\
Kei·ki *Jp.* \kā-kē\
Keir \'kir\
Kei·shi·ro *Jp.* \kā-shē-rō\
Kei·su·ke *Jp.* \kā-su̇k-e\
Keith \'kēth\
Kel·head \'kel-ˌhed\
Kells \'kelz\
Kel·ly \'kel-ē\
Kel·sea \'kel-sē\
Kel·sey \'kel-sē\
Kel·so \'kel-(ˌ)sō\
Kel·vey \'kel-vē\
Ken·drick \'ken-drik\
Ken·elm \'ken-ˌelm\
Ken·e·saw \'ken-ə-ˌsȯ\
Ken·ji *Jp.* \'ken-jē\
Ken·kō *Jp.* \ken-kō\
Ken·na·way \'ken-ə-ˌwā\
Ken·neth \'ken-əth\
Ken·nett \'ken-ət\
Ken·rick \'ken-rik\
Ken·shin *Jp.* \ken-shēn\
Ken·sing·ton \'ken-ziŋ-tən\
Ken·su·ke *Jp.* \ken-su̇k-e\
Ken·ta·ro *Jp.* \ken-tä-rō\
Ken·tish \'ken-təsh\
Ken·yon \'ken-yən\
Ken·zan *Jp.* \ken-zän\
Ken·zo *Jp.* \ken-zō\
Ker·che·ver \'kər-chə-vər\
Ker·mit \'kər-ˌmit\
Ker·sey \'kər-zē\
Ker·stin *Swed.* \'k̲esh-tin\
Kesh·av *Hind.* \'kesh-äv\
Ketch·um \'kech-əm\
Kev·in \'kev-ən\
Khan *Urdu* \'k̲än\
Kha·ri·la·os *Mod. Gk.* \k̲ä-'rē-lä-ȯs\
Kho·dā·ba·nah *Pers.* \ˌk̲ō-dä-'ban-ə\
Khri·sti·an *Russ.* \k̲ryis-tyi-'án\
Khris·ti·a·no·vich *Russ.* \k̲ryis-tyi-'án(-əv)-ˌyich\
Khris·to *Bulg.* \'k̲rēs-(ˌ)tō\
Khri·sto·do·lou *Gk.* \ˌk̲rē-stō-'th̲ō-lü\
Khris·to·fo·ro·vich *Russ.* \k̲ryis-(ˌ)tə-'fȯr(-əv)-ˌyich\
Khris·to·fo·rov·na *Russ.* \k̲ryis-(ˌ)tə-'fȯr(-ə)v-nə\
Khu·ri *Arab.* \'k̲ü-rē\
Khwā·ja *Pers.* \'k̲wáj-ə\
Ki 1 *Indonesian* \'kē\ 2 *Jp.* \kē\
Kib·ble \'kib-əl\
Ki·chi·bē *Jp.* \kē-chē-be\
Ki·chi·sa·bu·ro *Jp.* \kē-chē-sä-bu̇-rō\
Ki·chol *Kor.* \kē-chȯl\
Kid \'kid\
Kid·der \'kid-ər\
Kif·fin \'kif-in\
Ki·ha·chi·ro *Jp.* \kē-hä-chē-rō\
Ki·i·chi·ro *Jp.* \kē-ē-chē-rō\
Ki·jai *Arab.* \'kē-zhī\
Ki·ju·ro *Jp.* \kē-ju̇-rō\
Ki·ku·ji·ro *Jp.* \kē-ku̇j-ē-rō\
Kil·burn \'kil-bərn\
Ki·li·aen *Du.* \'kē-lē-ˌán\
Ki·lian *Ger.* \'kil-ˌyän\
Kil·jan *Icel.* \'kyil-ˌyän\
Kil·li·an *Du.* \'kē-lē-ˌán\
Kil·ling·worth \'kil-iŋ-ˌwərth\
Kim·ball \'kim-bəl\
Kim·ble \'kim-bəl\
Kim·brough \'kim-ˌbrō\

Kim·mo·chi *Jp.* \kēm-mō-chē\
Ki·mu·ra *Jp.* \kē-mu̇-rä\
King·dom \'kiŋ-dəm\
King·don \'kiŋ-dən\
Kin·go·ro *Jp.* \kēn-gō-rō\
King·ston \'kiŋ-stən\
Kin·naird \kə-'ne(ə)rd, -'na(ə)rd\
Kin·ney \'kin-ē\
Kin·ni·cut, -cutt \'kin-ə-kət\
Kin·nier \kə-'nir\
Ki·no·su·ke *Jp.* \kē-nō-su̇k-e\
Kin·zie \'kin-zē\
Ki·ril *Bulg.* \kē-'rē(ə)l\
Ki·rill *Russ.* \kyir-'yēl\
Ki·ril·lo·vich *Russ.* \kyir-'yēl(-əv)-ˌyich\
Ki·ril·lov·na *Russ.* \kyir-'yē-ləv-nə\
Kirk, Kirke \'kərk\
Kirk·man \'kərk-mən\
Kirk·pat·rick \kərk-'pat-rik\
Kir·sopp \'kər-səp\
Kir·sten *Norw.* \'k̲yisht-^{ə}n, 'k̲yirst-^{ə}n\
Kirt·land \'kərt-lənd\
Kirt·ley \'kərt-lē\
Ki·shi *Jp.* \kē-shē\
Kis·sam \'kis-əm\
Kit \'kit\
Ki·ta·ga·wa *Jp.* \kē-tä-gä-wä\
Ki·ta·ro *Jp.* \kē-tä-rō\
Kitch·ell \'kich-əl\
Kitch·en \'kich-ən\
Kit·til *Norw.* \'kit-til\
Kit·to \'kit-ō\
Kit·ty \'kit-ē\
Ki·yo·chi·ka *Jp.* \kē-yō-chē-kä\
Ki·yo·ka·ta *Jp.* \kē-yō-kä-tä\
Ki·yo·ma·sa *Jp.* \kē-yō-mäs-ä\
Ki·yo·ma·su *Jp.* \kē-yō-mäs-u̇\
Ki·yo·mo·ri *Jp.* \kē-yō-mō-rē\
Ki·yo·na·ga *Jp.* \kē-yō-näg-ä\
Ki·yo·no·bu *Jp.* \kē-yō-nō-bu̇\
Ki·yo·shi *Jp.* \kē-yō-shē\
Ki·yo·ski *Jp.* \kē-yō-skē\
Ki·yo·ta·ka *Jp.* \kē-ō-tä-kä\
Ki·za·em·on *Jp.* \kē-zä-em-ōn\
Kjeld *Dan.* \'kyeld\
Kjers·chow *Norw.* \'k̲yesh-ko̅v, 'k̲yers-\
Klap·ka \'klap-kə\
Kla·ra *Ger.* \'klär-ä\
Klas *Swed.* \'kläs\
Klaus *Ger.* \'klau̇s\
Klav·di·ya *Russ.* \'kläv-dyi-yə\
Kle·mens 1 *Ger.* \'klā-ˌmen(t)s\ 2 *Pol.* \'klem-en(t)s\
Klem·ent *Czech.* \'klem-ent\
Kle·o·fas *Pol.* \kle-'ȯ-fäs\
Kli·ment 1 *Bulg.* \'klē-(ˌ)mänt\ 2 *Russ.* \'klyēm-yint\
Knick·er·bock·er \'nik-ə(r)-ˌbäk-ər\
Knowles \'nō(ə)lz\
Knud 1 *Dan.* \'knüt̲h̲\ 2 *Norw.* \'knüt\
Knut *Norw., Swed.* \'knüt\
Knute \'nüt\
Knyv·et \'niv-ət\
Kō·e·tsu *Jp.* \kō-et-su̇\
Ko·go·rō *Jp.* \kō-gō-rō\
Ko·hen *Heb.* \'kō-ən\
Kō·in *Jp.* \kō-ēn\
Kō·kan *Jp.* \kō-kän\
Ko·kei *Jp.* \kō-kā\
Ko·ki *Jp.* \kō-kē\
Kō·ki·chi *Jp.* \kō-kē-chē\
Ko·ko·ro *Jp.* \kō-gō-rō\
Ko·lo·man *Ger.* \'kō-lō-ˌmän\
Kō·mei *Jp.* \kō-mā\
Kon·dra·ty *Russ.* \(ˌ)kən-'drät-yəi\
Kon·ni *Finn.* \'ko̅n-nē\
Kon·rad 1 *Dan.* \'ko̅n-ˌräd\ 2 *Ger.* \'ko̅n-ˌrät\ 3 *Pol.* \'ko̅n-ˌrät\ 4 *Rom.* \'ko̅n-räd\
Kon·ra·din *Ger.* \'kän-rä-ˌdēn\
Kon·stan·tin 1 *Czech* \'ko̅n-stän-ˌchin\ 2 *Dan.* \ˌko̅n-stän-'tēn\ 3 *Est.* \'ko̅n-stän-ˌtin\ 4 *Ger.* \ˌko̅n-stän-'tēn, 'ko̅n-stän-ˌ\ 5 *Russ.* \kən-(ˌ)stən-'tyēn\
Kon·stan·ti·nos *Mod. Gk.* \ˌko̅n-stän-'dē-(ˌ)no̅s\
Kon·stan·ti·no·vich *Russ.* \kən-(ˌ)stən-'tyēn(-əv)-ˌyich\
Kon·stan·ti·nov·na *Russ.* \kən-(ˌ)stən-'tyēn(-əv)-nə\
Kon·stan·ty *Pol.* \ko̅n-'stän-ti\
Kon·stanz *Ger.* \'ko̅n-ˌstänts\
Koos *Du.* \'kōs\
Ko·re·ki·yo *Jp.* \kō-re-kē-yō\
Kō·rin *Jp.* \kō-rēn\
Kor·nel *Pol.* \'ko̅r-nel\
Kor·ne·lis *Du.* \ko̅r-'nā-ləs\
Kor·y·but *Pol.* \'ko̅r-i-büt\
Kóstas *Gk.* \'ko̅s-täs\
Kos·tes *Gk.* \ko̅s-'tēs\
Kost·ka *Pol.* \'ko̅st-kä\
Kotzsch·mar \'käch-ˌmär\
Kō·un *Jp.* \kō-u̇n\
Kō·wa *Jp.* \kō-wä\
Ko·ya·ta *Jp.* \kō-yä-tä\
Kō·yō *Jp.* \kō-yō\
Kō·yū *Jp.* \kō-yu̇\
Kō·zō *Jp.* \kō-zō\
Kraft, Krafft *Ger.* \'kräft\
Krish·na *Marathi, Skt.* \'krish-nə\
Krish·nan *Marathi* \'krish-nən\
Kris·ten *Dan.* \'krē-stən\
Kris·tian 1 *Dan.* \'krēs-ˌtyän\ 2 **Kris·ti·an** *Du.* \'kris-tē-ˌän\ 3 *Finn.* \'kris-ti-ˌän\
Kris·ti·jo·nas *Lith.* \ˌkris-ti-'yo̅-näs, -tē-'ō-\
Krist·mann *Icel.* \'krist-ˌmän\
Kris·to·fer 1 *Norw., Swed.* \kris-'to̅-fər\
Kris·tof·fer 1 *Dan.* \krēs-'to̅f-ər\ 2 *Norw., Swed.* \kris-'to̅f-fər\
Krom \'kräm\
Kru·ne *Afrik.* \'krue̅-nə\
Ksa·ver *Serb.-Cr.* \'ksä-ver\
Ksa·we·ry *Pol.* \ksä-'ver-i\
Ku·ma·ki·chi *Jp.* \ku̇m-ä-kē-chē\
Ku·ni·a·ki *Jp.* \ku̇n-ē-ä-kē\
Ku·ni·ma·tsu *Jp.* \ku̇n-ē-mät-su̇\
Ku·ni·no·bu *Jp.* \ku̇n-ē-nō-bu̇\
Ku·ni·sa·da *Jp.* \ku̇n-ē-sä-dä\
Ku·ni·yo·shi *Jp.* \ku̇n-ē-yō-shē\
Ku·no *Ger.* \'kü-(ˌ)nō\
Ku·ra·hei *Jp.* \ku̇-rä-hā\
Kurd *Ger.* \'ku̇rt\
Kurt 1 *Ger.* \'ku̇rt\ 2 *Swed.* \'kərt\
Kus·ti *Finn.* \'ku̇s-tē\
Kuz·ma *Russ.* \küz^{y}-'mä\
Kuz·mich *Russ.* \küz^{y}-'myēch\
Kwa·me *Twi* \'kwäm-e, -ē\
Kwan·ichi *Jp.* \kwän-ē-chē\
Kye·re·twi *Twi* \'kyer-e-ˌtwē\
Kyle \'kīl\
Kyō·ka *Jp.* \kyō-kä\
Kyo·ku·tei *Jp.* \kyō-ku̇-tā\
Kyong *Kor.* \kyo̅ŋ\
Kyös·ti *Finn.* \'kue̅ə-stē\
Kyo·ta·ro *Jp.* \kyō-tär-ō\
Ky·ria·kos *Mod. Gk.* \ˌkyēr-yä-'ko̅s\
Ky·ril·los *Mod. Gk.* \'kyē-rē-ˌlo̅s\
Kyrle \'kərl\
Kyū·sō *Jp.* \kyu̇s-ō\
La·cher *Fr.* \lä-sher\
Lach·lan \'lak-lən, 'läk-\
La·con \'lā-kən\
La·cy \'lā-sē\
Lad·is·las 1 \'lad-əs-ləs, -ˌläs\ 2 *Fr.* **La·dis·las** \lä-dē-släs\
La·dis·laus *Ger.* \'läd-is-ˌlau̇s\
La·di·slav *Czech* \'läj-is-ˌläf\
Lae·li·us *Lat.* \'lē-lē-əs\
Lae·ti·tia \li-'tish-(ē-)ə, -'tish-yə\
La·Fay·ette, La·fay·ette \ˌläf-ē-'et, ˌlaf-\
Laf·cad·io \läf-'käd-ē-(ˌ)ō\
Lafe \'lāf\
Laird \'la(ə)rd, 'le(ə)rd\
La·jos *Hung.* \'lä-yo̅sh\
Lal *Hind.* \'läl\
La·la *Hind.* \'lä-lə\
La·lande *Fr.* \lä-lä^{n}d\
La·lor \'lā-lər\
La·man \'lā-mən\
Lam·ar·tine \'lam-ər-ˌtēn\
Lam·bert 1 \'lam-bərt\ 2 *Du.* \'läm-bərt\ 3 *Fr.* \lä^{n}-ber\
Lam·ber·to *Ital.* \läm-'ber-tō\
Lam·ber·tus *Du.* \läm-'be(ə)r-tœs\
La Menthe \lə-'mänt\
La·mine *Fr.* \lä-mēn\
La·mo·raal *Du.* \lä-mo̅-'räl\
La·mo·ral *Fr.* \lä-mo̅-ral\
Lam·son \'lam(p)-sən\
Lan·ce·lot \'lan(t)-sə-ˌlät, 'län(t)-, -s(ə-)lət\
Lan·cy \'lan(t)-sē\
Land \'land\
Lan·dey \'lan-dē\
Lan·dis \'lan-dəs\
Lan·do *Ital.* \'län-dō\
Lan·do·lin *Ger.* \'län-dō-ˌlēn\
Lan·don \'lan-dən\
Land·seer \'lan(d)-ˌsi(ə)r\
Lang·a·li·ba·le·le *Zulu* \ˌläŋ-ˌ(g)äl-ē-bä-'lā-ˌlā\
Lang·bridge \'laŋ-ˌbrij\
Lange *Norw.* \'läŋ-ə\
Lang·ford \'laŋ-fərd\
Lang·horne \'laŋ-ˌho̅(ə)rn, -ərn\
Lan·glois *Fr.* \lä^{n}g-lwä\
Lang·son \'laŋ-sən\
Lang·ston \'laŋ-stən\
Lang·ton \'laŋ(k)-tən\
Lan·neau \'lan-(ˌ)ō\
Lan·sing \'lan(t)-siŋ\
Lant \'lant\
La·o·ni·cus *Lat.* \ˌlā-ō-'nī-kəs\
Lar·com \'lär-kəm\
La·ri·sa *Ukrain.* \lä-'rē-sä\
Lar·kin \'lär-kən\
La·roy \lə-'ro̅i\
Lar·ry \'lar-ē\
Lars 1 *Eng., Lat.* \'lärz\ 2 *Swed.* \'läzh\
Larz \'lärz\
La·scăr *Rom.* \'läs-kər\
Las·celles \'las-əlz\
La·ska·ri·na *Mod. Gk.* \ˌläs-kä-'rē-nä\
Las·sa 1 \'las-ə\ 2 *Ger.* \'läs-ä\
Las·sen *Dan.* \'läs-^{ə}n\
Lász·ló *Hung.* \'läs-(ˌ)lō\
La·tham \'lā-thən, -t̲h̲ən\
La·throp \'lā-thrəp\
Lat·i·mer \'lat-ə-mər\
La·tin·i·us \lə-'tin-ē-əs, la-\

\ə\ abut \$^{ə}$\ kitten, *Fr.* table \ər\ further \a\ ash \ā\ ace \ä\ cot, cart \au̇\ out \ch\ chin \e\ bet \ē\ easy \g\ go \i\ hit \ī\ ice \j\ job \ŋ\ sing \ō\ go \o̅\ law \o̅i\ boy \th\ both \t̲h̲\ the \ü\ loot \u̇\ foot \y\ yet \zh\ vision \ä, b̲, g̲, k̲, ^{n}, œ, œ̄, ue, ue̅, ^{y}\ *see* Guide to Pronunciation

La·ti·nus *Lat.* \la-'tin-əs, lə-, -'tī-nəs\
La·tour *Fr.* \lá-tür\
Lat·ta \'lat-ə\
Lau·der \'lȯd-ər\
Lau·ge *Dan.* \'lau̇-gə\
Laugh·ton \'lȯt-ᵊn\
Laun·ce·lot \'lȯns-(ə-)lət, 'läns-, -(ə-),lät\
Launt \'lȯnt, 'länt\
Lau·ra 1 \'lȯr-ə\ 2 *Ital.* \'lau̇-rä\ 3 *Swed.* \'lau̇-rá\
Laure *Fr.* \lȯr\
Lau·re·a·no *Span.* \lau̇-rā-'ä-nō\
Lau·rel \'lȯr-əl, 'lär-\
Lau·rence \'lȯr-ən(t)s, 'lär-\
Lau·rens 1 \'lȯr-ənz, 'lär-, -ən(t)s\ 2 *Du.* \'lau̇-rəns\
Lau·rent *Fr.* \lȯ-rän\
Lau·ren·tine \'lȯ-rən-,tīn, -,tēn\
Lau·ren·ti·us 1 *Lat.* \lȯr-'en-sh(ē-)əs\ 2 *Swed.* \lau̇-'rent-sē-əs\
Lau·re·nus \lȯ-'rē-nəs\
Lau·rette \lȯ-'ret\
Lau·ri *Finn.* \'lau̇-rē\
Lau·rie \'lȯ-rē, 'lär-\
Lau·rits, -ritz 1 *Dan.* \'lau̇-(,)rēts\ 2 *Norw.* \'lau̇-rits\
Lau·ro *Ital.* \'lau̇-rō\
La·val \lə-'val\
La Verne \lə-'vərn\
Lav·ing·ton \'lav-iŋ-tən\
La·vin·ia 1 \lə-'vin-ē-ə\ 2 *Ital.* **La·vi·nia** \lä-'vēn-yä\
Lavr *Russ.* \'lá-vər\
Lav·ren·ty *Russ.* \(,)ləv-'ryen-tyəi\
Lav·rent·ye·vich *Russ.* \(,)ləv-'ryent(-yiv)-,yich\
Lav·ro·vich *Russ.* \'láv-rəv-,yich, -,ryich\
Lawes \'lȯz\
Law·rence \'lȯr-ən(t)s, 'lar-\
Law·ry \'lȯr-ē, 'lär-\
Law·ton \'lȯt-ᵊn\
Lay·ton \'lāt-ᵊn\
La·za *Serb.-Cr.* \'lá-zá\
La·zar 1 *Russ.* \'lá-zərʸ\ 2 *Hung.* **Lá·zár** \'lá-(,)zár\
La·zare *Fr.* \lá-zár\
Lá·za·ro *Span.* \'läth-är-ō; 'läs-\
Laz·a·rus 1 \'laz-ə-rəs\ 2 *Ger.* **La·za·rus** \'lät-sär-u̇s\
La·zelle \lə-'zel\
Laz·za·ro *Ital.* \'läd-dzär-(,)ō\
Lea·der \'lē-dər\
Leam·ing·ton \'lem-iŋ-tən\
Le·an·der 1 \lē-'an-dər\ 2 *Ger.* \lā-'än-dər\
Le·an·dro *Ital., Span.* \lā-'än-drō\
Lear·ie \'li(ə)r-ē\
Lear·ned \'lər-nəd\
Lea·tham \'lē-thəm\
Leav·itt \'lev-it\
Le Bar·on \lə-'bar-ən\
Leb·by \'leb-ē\
Le·be·recht *Ger.* \'lā-bə-,rekt\
Leb·recht 1 *Dan.* \'lib-(,)rekt\ 2 *Ger.* \'lā-(,)prekt, -(,)brekt\
Le Bret·on \lə-'bret-ᵊn\
Le·clerc *Fr.* \lə-kler\
Led·bet·ter \'led-,bet-ər\
Led·yard \'led-yərd\
Lee \'lē\
Leeds \'lēdz\
Leete \'lēt\
Lee·vi *Finn.* \'lev-ē\
Leg·att \'leg-ət\
Legh \'lē\
Le·grand *Fr.* \lə-grän\
Leh·man \'lā-mən, 'lē-\
Leib *Yiddish* \'lāb\
Leices·ter \'les-tər\
Leigh \'lē\
Lei·la \'lē-lə\
Lei·ning·er *Dan.* \'lā-niŋ-ər\
Leith \'lēth\
Le·jeune *Ger.* \lə-'zhœ̄n\
Le·lio *Ital.* \'lel-yō\
Lem·bert *Fr.* \län-ber\
Le Me·su·rier \lə-'mezh-ə-rər\
Lem·on \'lem-ən\
Lem·u·el \'lem-yə(-wə)l\
Le·na \'lē-nə\
Len·nart *Swed.* \'len-nárt\
Le·noir \lə-'nȯ(ə)r, -'nō(ə)r\
Lent \'lent\
Leo 1 \'lē-(,)ō\ 2 *Du., Ger.* \'lā-(,)ō\ 3 *Finn.* \'lā-(,)ȯ\ 4 *Ital.* \'le-(,)ō\ 5 *Fr.* **Léo** \lā-ō\ 6 *Hung.* **Lēó** \'le-ō\
Lé·o·ca·die *Fr.* \lā-ȯ-ká-dē\
Le·of·ric \lā-'äf-rik, -'ō-frik\
Le·o·line \'lē-ə-,līn\
Le·on 1 \'lē-,än, -ən\ 2 *Ital.* \lā-'ōn\ 3 *Fr.* **Lé·on** \lā-ōn\ 4 *Span.* **Le·ón** \lā-'ōn\
Le·o·na \lē-'ō-nə\
Leon·ard 1 \'len-ərd\ 2 **Le·o·nard** *Du., Ger.* \'lā-ō-,närt\ 3 *Pol.* \le-'ō-nárt\ 4 *Swed.* \'lā-ō-,nárd\ 5 *Fr.* **Lé·o·nard** \lā-ȯ-nár\
Le·o·nar·do 1 *Ital.* \,lā-ō-'när-dō\ 2 *Span.* \lā-ō-'när-thō\
Le·o·nar·dus *Du.* \,lā-ō-'när-dœs\
Lé·once *Fr.* \lā-ōns\
Le·o·ne *Ital.* \lā-'ō-nā\
Le·o·nel·lo *Ital.* \,lā-ō-'nel-lō\
Le·on·hard 1 *Ger.* \'lā-ȯn-,härt\ 2 *Swed.* \'lā-ō-,nárd\
Le·o·nid *Russ.* \lyi-(,)ən-'yēt\
Le·o·ni·da *Ital.* \lā-'ō-nē-(,)dä\
Le·on·i·das 1 \'lē-'än-əd-əs\ 2 *Span.* **Le·o·ni·das** \lā-ō-'nē-thäs\
Lé·o·nide *Fr.* \lā-ȯ-nēd\
Le·o·ni·do·vich *Russ.* \lyi-(,)ən-'yēd(-əv)-,yich\
Le·o·nor \'lē-ə-nōr, -nȯr\
Le·o·no·ra \,lē-ə-'nōr-ə, -'nȯr-\
Le·o·pold 1 \'lē-ə-,pōld\ 2 *Du., Ger.* \'lā-ō-,pōlt\ 3 *Finn.* \'le-ō-,pȯlt\ 4 *Pol.* \le-'ō-pȯlt\ 5 *Fr.* **Lé·o·pold** \lā-ō-pȯl(d)\
Le·o·pol·di·na *Ger.* \,lā-ō-pȯl-'dē-nä\
Le·o·pol·di·ne 1 *Ger.* \,lā-ō-pȯl-'dē-nə\ 2 *Fr.* **Lé·o·pol·dine** \lā-ō-pȯl-dēn\
Le·o·pol·do 1 *Ital.* \,lā-ō-'pȯl-dō\ 2 *Span.* \la-ō-'pȯl-dō\
Le·os *Czech* \'le-,ȯsh\
Le·roy, Le Roy \li-'rȯi, 'lē-,\
Les·ley, Les·lie \'les-lē *also* 'lez-\
Les·ter \'les-tər\
Les·ton \'les-tən\
L'Es·trange \lə-'strānj\
Les·ya *Ukrain.* \'lās-yä\
Le·szek *Pol.* \'lā-shek\
Leth·bridge \'leth-,brij\
Le·ti·tia \li-'tish(-ē)-ə\
Le·ti·zia *Ital.* \lā-'tēt-syä\
Let·tice \'let-əs\
Let·tie \'let-ē\
Lev *Russ.* \'lyef\
Lev·er·ett \'lev-(ə-)rət\
Leve·son \'lüs-ᵊn\
Le·vi \'lē-vī, -vē\
Lev·in 1 \'lev-ən\ 2 *Ger.* **Le·vin** \'lā-,vēn\
Lev·ing·ton \'lev-iŋ-tən\
Lew \'lü\
Lew·el·yn \lə-'wel-ən\
Lew·is \'lü-əs\
Lib·bie \'lib-ē\
Li·bé·ral *Fr.* \lē-bā-rál\
Li·be·ra·to *Span.* \lē-bā-'rä-tō\
Lib·er·ty \'lib-ərt-ē\
Li·cin·i·a·nus *Lat.* \lə-,sin-ē-'ā-nəs\
Li·cin·i·us *Lat.* \li-'sin-ē-əs\
Lieb·mann *Ger.* \'lēp-,män\
Light·foot \'līt-,fu̇t\
Light·ner \'light-nər\
Li·gier *Fr.* \lēzh-yā\
Li·li 1 *Fr.* \lē-lē\ 2 *Ger.* \'lil-ē\
Lil·i·an \'lil-yən, 'lil-ē-ən\
Li·lio *Ital.* \'lēl-yō\
Li·liu *Hawaiian* \li-'lē-(,)ü\
Lil·lah \'lil-ə\
Lill·burn \'lil-bərn\
Lil·li *Ger.* \'lil-ē\
Lil·li·an \'lil-yən, 'lil-ē-ən\
Lil·lie \'lil-ē\
Lil·lis \'lil-əs\
Lily 1 *Eng., Ger.* \'lil-ē\ 2 *Fr.* **Li·ly** \lē-lē\
Li·na *Ger., Ital.* \'lē-nä\
Lin·coln \'liŋ-kən\
Lin·da \'lin-də\
Lin·den·berg \'lin-dən-,bərg\
Lind·ley \'lin-(d)lē\
Lin·dol·fo *Span.* \lēn-'dȯl-fō\
Lin·don \'lin-dən\
Lind·say \'lin-zē\
Lin·ley \'lin-lē\
Linn \'lin\
Lin·nae·us \lə-'nē-əs\
Li·no *Ital.* \'lē-nō\
Lins·ly \'linz-lē\
Lin·thi·cum \'lin-thə-kəm\
Li·nus \'lī-nəs\
Li·on \'lī-ən\
Lio·nar·do *Ital.* \lyō-'när-dō\
Li·o·nel \'lī-ən-ᵊl, -ə-,nel\
Lip·ot *Hung.* \'lip-ōt\
Lip·pard \'lip-,ärd\
Lip·pin·cott \'lip-ən-kət, -əŋ-, -,kät\
Lip·pi·no \lēp-'pē-nō\
Lip·po *Ital.* \'lēp-pō\
Lip·trot \'lip-,trät\
Li·sa *Ital.* \'lē-zä\
Li·san·dro *Span.* \lē-'sän-drō\
Li·sar·do *Span.* \lē-'sär-thō\
Lis·beth *Ger.* \'lēs-bet\
Li·se *Ger.* \'lē-zə\
Li·set·te *Ger.* \lē-'zet-ə\
Lisle \'lī(ə)l\
Lis·ter \'lis-tər\
Li·tel·lus \lə-'tel-əs, lī-\
Live *Fr.* \lēv\
Liv·er·more \'liv-ər-,mō(ə)r\
Liv·ia *Lat.* \'liv-ē-ə\
Li·viu *Rom.* \'lēv-yü\
Liv·i·us *Lat.* \'liv-ē-əs\
Liv·sey \'liv-zē, -sē\
Li·za \'lī-zə\
Li·zar·do *Span.* \lē-'thär-thō; -'sär-\
Li·zette \lə-'zet\
Li·zin·ka *Fr.* \lē-zan-kä\
Liz·zie \'liz-ē\
Lju·bo·mir *Serb.-Cr.* \'lyü-bȯ-,mēr\
Lju·de·vit *Serb.-Cr.* \'lyü-de-,vēt\
Llew·el·lyn, Llew·el·yn \lə-'wel-ən\
Lloyd \'lȯid\
Lo·am·mi \lō-'am-ī\
Löb *Ger.* \'lœ̄p\
Lob·ban \'läb-ən\
Lock·hart \'läk-,härt, -ərt\
Lock·wood \'läk-wu̇d\
Lo·de·wijk, -wyck *Du.* \'lō-də-,vīk\
Lo·do·vi·co *Ital.* \,lō-dō-'vē-kō\
Lod·o·wick, -wicke \'läd-ə-wik, 'lō-də-\
Lof·tin \'lȯf-tən\
Lo·gan \'lō-gən\

Lo·gie \'lō-gē\
Lo·ie \'lō-ē\
Lo·la \'lō-lə\
Lo·mer *Fr.* \lȯ-mer\
Lon \'län\
Long·bourne \'lȯŋ-,bō(ə)rn, -,bȯ(ə)rn, -bərn\
Lon·gi·no·vich *Russ.* \'lȯn-gyin(-əv)-,yich\
Long·streth \'lȯŋ-,streth\
Longue·ville \'lȯŋ-,vil\
Lons·bury \'lanz-,ber-ē, -b(ə-)rē\
Loo·mis \'lü-mis\
Lo·pe *Span.* \'lō-pā\
Ló·pez *Span.* \'lō-pāth; -pās\
Lo·ra·do \lə-'räd-(,)ō\
Ló·ránt *Hung.* \'lō-(,)ránt\
Lord \'lȯ(ə)rd\
Lore \'lō(ə)r, 'lȯ(ə)r\
Lo·rentz 1 *Dan.* \'lȯr-ən(t)s\ 2 *Norw.* \'lōr-ən(t)s\
Lo·renz *Ger.* \'lō-(,)rents\
Lo·ren·zi·no *Ital.* \,lō-ränt-'sē-nō\
Lo·ren·zio *Ital.* \lō-'rent-syō\
Lo·ren·zo 1 \lə-'ren-zō\ 2 *Ital.* \lō-'rent-sō\ 3 *Span.* \lō-'ren-thō; -sō\ 4 *Swed.* \lȯ-'rent-sō\
Lo·ret·ta \lə-'ret-ə, lȯ-\
Lo·rine \lō-'rēn\
Lo·ring \'lō-riŋ\
Lor·na \'lȯr-nə\
Lor·rain, Lor·raine \lə-'rān, lȯ-\
Lor·rin \'lär-ən\
Lot \'lät\
Lo·ta·rio *Ital.* \lō-'tär-yō\
Lo·thar *Ger.* \lō-'tär, 'lō-,\
Lo·throp \'lō-thrəp\
Lott \'lät\
Lot·ta 1 \'lät-ə\ 2 *Finn.* \'lȯt-tá\
Lot·te *Ger.* \'lȯt-ə\
Lo·tus \'lōt-əs\
Lou \'lü\
Lo·uel·la \lə-'wel-ə\
Lough·bor·ough \'ləf-,bər-ə, -,bə-rə, -b(ə-)rə\
Lough·ton \'lau̇t-^{ə}n\
Louiche *Fr.* \lwēsh\
Lou·is 1 \'lü-əs, 'lü-ē\ 2 *Du.* \lü-'ē\ 3 *Fr.* \lwē\ 4 *Ger., Swed.* \'lü-ē\ 4 *Norw.* \'lü-ē, -is\
Lou·i·sa 1 \lü-'e-zə\ 2 *Du.* \lü-'ē-sá\
Lou·ise 1 \lə-'wēz\ 2 *Fr.* \lwēz\ 3 **Lou·i·se** *Dan.* \lu̇-'ē-sə\ 4 *Du.* \lü-'ē-sə\ 5 *Ger.* \lü-'ē-zə\
Lou·kas *Gk.* \lü-'käs\
Love \'ləv\
Love·good \'ləv-,gu̇d\
Lo·vis *Ger.* \'lō-vis\
Lo·vi·sa *Swed.* \'lü-vis-,á\
Low·ell \'lō-əl\
Lowes \'lōz\
Lowndes \'lau̇n(d)z\
Low·rie, Low·ry \'lau̇(ə)r-ē\
Low·ther \'lau̇-t͟hər\
Low·thi·an \'lō-t͟hē-ən, -t͟hyən\
Loy \'lȯi\
Loyd \'lȯid\
Loys *Fr.* \lwá\
Loy·set *Fr.* \lwá-ze\
Lu·ang *Thai* \lü-'äŋ\
Lub·bock \'ləb-ək\
Luc *Fr.* \lu̅e̅k\
Lu·ca *Ital., Rom.* \'lü-kä\
Lu·cas 1 \lü-kəs\ 2 *Du.* \'lu̅e̅-,käs\ 3 *Fr.* \lu̅e̅-kä\ 4 *Ger.* \'lü-,käs\ 5 *Span.* \'lü-käs\
Luc·chi·no, Lu·chi·no *Ital.* \lük-'kē-nō\
Luce 1 \'lüs\ 2 *Fr.* \lu̅e̅s\
Lu·cia 1 \'lu-shē-ə, -shə\ 2 *Ger.* \'lüt-sē-(,)ä\ 3 *Ital.* \lü-'chē-ä\
Lu·cian 1 \'lü-shən\ 2 *Ger.* \,lüt-sē-'än, lüts-'yän\ 3 *Pol.* \'lüts-yán\ 4 *Rom.* \lü-'chän\
Lu·cia·no 1 *Ital.* \lü-'chän-ō\ 2 *Port.* \lüs-'yá-nü\ 3 *Span.* \lüth-'yän-ō\
Lu·cie 1 \'lü-sē\ 2 *Fr.* \lu̅e̅-sē\
Lu·cien 1 \'lü-shən\ 2 *Fr.* \lu̅e̅s-ya^{n}\
Lu·cienne *Fr.* \lu̅e̅s-yen\
Lu·ci·la *Span.* \lü-'thē-lä; -'sē-\
Lu·cile 1 \lü-'sē(ə)l\ 2 *Fr.* \lu̅e̅-sēl\
Lu·ci·lio *Ital.* \lü-'chēl-yō\
Lu·cille \lü-'sē(ə)l\
Lu·cin·da \lü-'sin-də\
Lu·cinde *Fr.* \lu̅e̅-sa^{n}d\
Lu·ci·us \'lü-sh(ē-)əs\
Lu·cjan *Pol.* \'lüt-syán\
Lu·cre·tia \lü-'krē-sh(ē-)ə\
Lu·cre·zia *Ital.* \lü-'kret-syä\
Lu·cy \'lü-sē\
Lu·do *Ger.* \'lü-(,)dō\
Lu·dolf 1 *Dan., Ger.* \'lü-,dȯlf \ 2 *Du.* \'lu̅e̅-,dȯlf\
Lu·dolph 1 *Du.* \'lu̅e̅-,dȯlf\ 2 *Ger.* \'lü-,dȯlf\
Lu·do·vic 1 \'lü-dō-vik\ 2 *Fr.* \lu̅e̅-dȯ-vēk\
Lu·do·vi·ca *Ger., Ital.* \,lü-dō-'vē-kä\
Lu·do·vick \'lü-dō-vik\
Lu·do·vi·co *Ital.* \,lü-dō-'vē-kō\
Lu·do·vi·cus *Lat.* \,lü-dō-'vē-kəs\
Lud·vig 1 *Dan.* \'lüt͟h-vē\ 2 *Swed.* \'ləd-vig\
Lud·vík *Czech* \lu̇d-'vēk\
Lud·well \'ləd-,wel, -wəl\
Lud·wig 1 \'ləd-wig, 'lüd-\ 2 *Dan.* \'lüt͟h-vē\ 3 *Ger.* \'lüt-vik\ 4 *Swed.* \'ləd-vig\
Lud·wik *Pol.* \'lüd-vēk\
Luf·kin \'ləf-kən\
Lu·i·gi *Ital.* \lü-'ē-jē\
Luin·each *Ir. Gael.* \'lin-ək\
Lu·is 1 *Port.* \lü-'ēsh\ 2 *Span.* \lü-'ēs\
Lu·i·sa *Ital.* \lü-'ē-zä\
Lu·i·se 1 *Dan.* \lu̇-'ē-sə\ 2 *Ger.* \lü-'ē-zə\
Lu·it·pold *Ger.* \'lü-it-,pȯlt\
Lu·iz *Port.* \lü-'ēsh\
Lu·jo *Ger.* \'lü-(,)yō\
Lu·kas *Ger.* \'lü-,käs\
Lu·kasz *Pol.* \'lü-kásh\
Luke \'lük\
Lu·kens \'lü-kənz\
Lu·kich *Russ.* \'lük-yich\
Lu·la \'lü-lə\
Lu·lu *Ger.* \'lü-(,)lü\
Lum·ley \'ləm-lē\
Lum·mis \'ləm-əs\
Lu·nel \lu̇-'nel\
Luns·ford \'lənz-fərd\
Lu·per·cio *Span.* \lü-'per-thyō; -syō\
Lu·ta·ti·us *Lat.* \lü-'tā-sh(ē-)əs\
Lut·fi *Arab.* \'lu̇t-,fē\
Lu·ther \'lü-thər\
Lut·widge \'lət-wij\
Lvo·vich *Russ.* \'lyȯv-yich\
Lyd·ia 1 \'lid-ē-ə\ 2 *Ger.* **Ly·dia** \'lu̅e̅d-yä, 'lu̅e̅-dē-ä\
Ly·ell \'lī(ə)l\
Lyle \'lī(ə)l\
Ly·man \'lī-mən\
Lynde \'lind\
Lyn·don \'lin-dən\
Lyne 1 \'līn\ 2 *Dan.* **Ly·ne** \'lu̅e̅-nə\
Lynn \'lin\
Ly·on \'lī-ən\
Lys·ter \'lis-tər\
Lyt·tel·ton \'lit-^{ə}l-tən\
Lyt·ton \'lit-^{ə}n\
Lyu·ben *Bulg.* \'lyü-byən\
Ly·ulph \'lī-(,)əlf\
Maar·ten *Du.* \'mär-tən\
Maar·tens·zoon *Du.* \'mär-tənt-sōn\
Maas·tricht *Ger.* \'mäs-(,)trikt\
Ma·bel \'mā-bəl\
Ma·ben \'mā-bən\
Ma·bi *Jp.* \mä-bē\
Ma·bu·chi *Jp.* \mä-bu̇ch-ē\
Mac·al·lan \mə-'kal-ən\
Mc·Al·lis·ter \mə-'kal-əs-tər\
Ma·ca·ri *Catalan* \má-'kär-ē\
Ma·ca·rius *Russ.* \má-'kär-yüs\
Mac·beth \mək-'beth\
Mac·Bride \mək-'brīd\
Mc·Cal·mont \mə-'kal-mänt\
Mc·Car·rell \mə-'kar-əl\
McCau·ley \mə-'kȯl-ē\
Mc·Ches·ney \mək-'ches-nē\
Mc·Chord \mə-'kȯ(ə)rd\
Mac·ci·us *Lat.* \'mak-sē-əs\
Mc·Clel·lan \mə-'klel-ən\
Mc·Clel·land \mə-'klel-ənd\
Mc·Clurg \mə-'klərg\
Mc·Cul·lagh \mə-'kəl-ə\
Mc·Dou·all \mək-'dau̇-əl\
Mac·Dou·gal \mək-'dü-gəl\
Ma·ce·do·nio *Ital.* \,mäch-ā-'dȯn-yō\
Mc·El·der·ry \'mak-əl-,der-ē\
Ma·cer *Lat.* \'mā-sər\
Mc·Far·lan, -lane \mək-'fär-lən\
Mc·Gar·el \mə-'gar-əl\
Mc·Gav·ock \mə-'gav-ək\
Mc·Gil·li·vray \mə-'gil-ə-,vrā\
Ma·ciej *Pol.* \'má-chā\
Mc·In·tyre \'mak-ən-,tī(ə)r\
Mc·Kean \mə-'kēn\
Mc·Kee \mə-'kē\
Mc·Keen \mə-'kēn\
M'·Kel·lar \mə-'kel-ər\
Mc·Ken·dree \mə-'ken-drē\
Mac·Kin·lay \mə-'kin-lē\
Mc·Kin·ney \mə-'kin-ē\
Mac·Kin·non \mə-'kin-ən\
Mack·lin \'mak-lən\
Mac·Knight \mək-'nīt\
Mack·worth \'mak-(,)wərth\
Mc·Lain \mə-'klān\
Mc·Lane \mə-'klān\
Mc·Lar·en \mə-'klar-ən\
Mac·Lean, Mc·Lean \mə-'klān\
Mc·Lel·land \mə-'klel-ənd\
Mc·Len·dell \mə-'klen-dəl\
Mac·Len·nan, Mc·Len·nan \mə-'klen-ən\
Mac·Leod, Mc·Leod \mə-'klau̇d\
Mc·Ma·hon \mək-'mä(-ə)n\
Mc·Mas·ters \mək-'mas-tərz\
Mac·mil·lan \mək-'mil-ən\
Mc·Mur·trie \mək-'mər-trē\
M'·Nair \mək-'na(ə)r, -'ne(ə)r\
Mc·Nee·ly \mək-'nē-lē\
Mc·Neill \mək-'nē(ə)l\
Ma·con \'mā-kən\
Mc·Phail \mək-'fā(ə)l\
Mac·pher·son \mək-'fərs-^{ə}n\
Mac·quorn \mə-'kwȯ(ə)rn\
Ma·crae \mə-'krā\
M'·Tag·gart \mək-'tag-ərt\
Mc·Tag·gart \mək-'tag-ərt\
Mc·Tyeire \mək-'tyi(ə)r, -'tye(ə)r\
Mac·vey, Mac·Vey \mək-'vā\

Mad·den \ˈmad-^{ə}n\
Mad·dern \ˈmad-ərn\
Mad·dock \ˈmad-ək\
Mad·e·leine 1 \ˈmad-^{ə}l-ən\ 2 *Fr.* **Ma·de·leine** \mȧd-len\
Madge \ˈmaj\
Ma·dhu *Bengali* \ˈmȯ-dü, ˈmä-\
Ma·dhu·sud·an *Bengali* \ˌmȯ-dü-ˈsü-dȯn, ˌmä-\
Mad·i·son \ˈmad-ə-sən\
Mad·ox \ˈmad-əks\
Mae·cil·i·us *Lat.* \mē-ˈsil-ē-əs\
Máe·doc *Ir. Gael.* \ˈmȯi-dək\
Máel *Ir. Gael.* \ˈmȯil\
Maer·ten *Du.* \ˈmȧr-tən\
Maf·feo *Ital.* \mäf-ˈfe-ō\
Mag·da *Rom.* \ˈmäg-dä\
Mag·de·leine *Fr.* \mȧg-də-len\
Mag·gie \ˈmag-ē\
Ma·gill \mə-ˈgil\
Ma·glinne \mə-ˈglin\
Mag·nus 1 \ˈmag-nəs\ 2 *Dan.* \ˈmȧg-nu̇s\ 3 *Ger.* \ˈmäg-nu̇s\ 4 *Norw.* \ˈmaŋ-nu̇s\ 5 *Swed.* \ˈmȧŋ-nu̇s\
Ma·go·sa·bu·rō *Jp.* \mä-gō-sä-bu̇r-ō\
Ma·gou·e·mon *Jp.* \mä-gō-(w)em-ōn\
Ma·ha *Burmese* \mə-ˈhä\
Ma·ha·deo *Marathi* \ˈmə-hä-ˈdā-ō\
Ma·ha·dev *Marathi* \ˈmə-hə-ˈdev\
Ma·ha·lia \mə-ˈhāl-yə\
Ma·har·ban·ji *Parsi* \ˌmə-hər-ˈbän-jē\
Mah·lon \ˈmā-lən, ˈmä-\
Mah·mud *Turk.* \mä-ˈmüd\
Ma·ho·ney \mə-ˈhō-nē, ˈmä-(ə-)nē\
Ma·hon·ri \ˈmā-ən-rē\
Mail·lard *Ital.* \mī(l)-ˈyär(d)\
Main \ˈmān\
Main·wa·ring \ˈman-ə-riŋ, ˈmān-wə-riŋ\
Mair \ˈma(ə)r, ˈme(ə)r\
Màiri *Sc. Gael.* \ˈmär-ə\
Mai·sie \ˈmā-zē\
Mak·dou·gall \mək-ˈdü-gəl\
Make·peace \ˈmāk-ˌpēs\
Ma·ki·bi *Jp.* \mä-kē-bē\
Ma·ko·to *Jp.* \mä-kō-tō\
Mak·sim *Russ.* \(ˌ)mək-ˈsyēm\
Mak·si·mo·vich *Russ.* \(ˌ)mək-ˈsyēm(-əv)-ˌyich\
Mal·a·by \ˈmal-ə-bē\
Mal·colm \ˈmal-kəm\
Ma·lek *Pers.* \ˈmȧ-lek\
Males·herbes \ˌmal-ˈzərb\
Mal·har *Marathi* \məl-ˈhär\
Ma·lik *Arab.* \ˈmȧ-lik\
Ma·lin \ˈmā-lən\
Mal·la·han \ˈmal-ə-han\
Mal·lord \ˈmal-ərd\
Mal·lo·ry \ˈmal-(ə-)rē\
Ma·lo *Fr.* \mȧ-lō\
Ma·lone \mə-ˈlōn\
Mal·vin \ˈmal-vən\
Mal·vi·na \mal-ˈvē-nə\
Ma·mo·ru *Jp.* \mä-mō-ru̇\
Man \ˈman\
Ma·nas·seh \mə-ˈnas-ə\
Man·dé *Fr.* \mä^{n}-dā\
Man·dell \ˈman-d^{ə}l\
Man·ford \ˈman-fərd\
Man·fred 1 \ˈman-frəd\ 2 *Ger.* \ˈmän-ˌfrāt\
Man·fre·di *Ital.* \män-ˈfrā-dē\
Man·fre·do *Ital.* \män-ˈfrā-dō\
Ma·ni·us *Lat.* \ˈmā-nē-əs\
Man·key \ˈmaŋ-kē\
Man·ley \ˈman-lē\
Man·li·us \ˈman-lē-əs\
Man·ne *Swed.* \ˈmȧn-ne\
Man·nes \ˈman-əs\
Man·ning·ton \ˈman-iŋ-tən\
Ma·no·el *Port.* \mən-ˈwel; mȧn-\
Ma·no·el·lo *Ital.* \män-ˈwāl-lō\
Ma·non *Fr.* \mȧ-nō^{n}\
Man·suète *Fr.* \mä^{n}-sw^{y}et\
Man·sur *Pers.* \mȧn-ˈsür\
Man·tis \ˈmant-əs\
Man·u·el 1 \ˈman-yə(-wə)l\ 2 **Ma·nu·el** *Port.* \mən-ˈwel; mȧn-\ 3 *Span.* \män-ˈwel\
Ma·nu·ela *Span.* \män-ˈwā-lä\
Man·us \ˈman-əs, ˈmän-, ˈmā-nəs\
Man·ville \ˈman-ˌvil, -vəl\
Man·ya *Pol.* \ˈmȧn-yȧ\
Ma·phe·us *Lat.* \mə-ˈfē-əs\
Mara \ˈma(ə)r-ə\
Marc 1 \ˈmärk\ 2 *Fr.* \mȧrk\
Marc An·to·nio, Marc'·An·to·nio, Marc·an·to·nio *Ital.* \ˌmär-kän-ˈtȯn-yō\
Mar·cel *Fr.* \mȧr-sel\
Mar·ce·lin *Fr.* \mȧr-sə-la^{n}\
Mar·ce·line *Fr.* \mȧr-sə-lēn\
Mar·ce·li·no *Span.* \mär-thā-ˈlē-nō; mär-sē-\
Mar·celle *Fr.* \mȧr-sel\
Mar·cel·lin *Fr.* \mȧr-sə-la^{n}\
Mar·ce·lli·no *Span.* \mär-thā(l)-ˈyē-nō, -sā(l)-\
Mar·cel·lo *Ital.* \mär-ˈchel-lō\
Mar·cel·lus 1 \mär-ˈsel-əs\ 2 *Du.* \mär-ˈsel-œs\
Mar·ce·lo *Span.* \mär-ˈthā-lō; -ˈsā-\
March \ˈmärch\
Mar·cia \ˈmär-shə\
Mar·cial *Span.* \mär-ˈthyäl; -ˈsyäl\
Mar·cien *Fr.* \mȧrs-ya^{n}\
Mar·cin *Pol.* \ˈmȧr-chēn\
Mar·ci·us *Lat.* \ˈmär-sh(ē-)əs\
Mar·co 1 \ˈmär-(ˌ)kō\ 2 *Fr.* \mȧr-kō\ 3 *Ital., Span.* \ˈmär-kō\
Mar·cos 1 *Port.* \ˈmȧr-küsh\ 2 *Span.* \ˈmär-kōs\
Mar·cus 1 \ˈmär-kəs\ 2 *Du.* \ˈmär-kēs\ 3 *Ger., Norw.* \ˈmär-ku̇s\ 4 *Swed.* \ˈmȧr-kəs\
Mar·cy \ˈmär-sē\
Ma·re·su·ke *Jp.* \mä-re-su̇k-e\
Mar·fa *Russ.* \ˈmȧr-fə\
Mar·ga·ret \ˈmär-g(ə-)rət\
Mar·ga·re·ta *Swed.* \ˌmȧr-gȧ-ˈrā-tȧ\
Mar·ga·re·te *Ger.* \ˌmär-gä-ˈrā-tə\
Mar·ga·ret·ta \ˌmar-gə-ˈret-ə\
Mar·ga·ri·ta \ˌmar-gə-ˈrē-tə\
Mar·gery \ˈmärj-(ə-)rē\
Mar·ghe·ri·ta *Ital.* \ˌmär-gā-ˈrē-tä\
Mar·got \ˈmär-(ˌ)gō, -gət\
Mar·gre·te *Dan.* \mär-ˈgrē-tə\
Mar·gue·rite 1 \ˌmär-gə-ˈrēt\ 2 *Fr.* \mȧr-gə-rēt\
Ma·ria 1 \mə-ˈrī-ə, -ˈrē-ə\ 2 *Du., Finn.* \mȧ-ˈrē-ȧ\ 3 *Ger., Ital.* \mä-ˈrē-ä\ 4 *Pol.* \ˈmȧr-yȧ\ 5 *Port.* \mə-ˈrē-ə; mȧ-ˈrē-ȧ\ 6 *Russ.* \(ˌ)mər-ˈyē-yə\ 7 *Swed.* \mȧ-ˈrē-ȧ\ 8 *Span.* **Ma·ría** \mä-ˈrē-ä\
Mar·i·an \ˈmer-ē-ən, ˈmar-\
Mar·i·ana \ˌmer-ē-ˈan-ə, ˌmar-, -ˈä-nə\
Ma·ri·an·na *Port.* \mə-rē-ˈȧ-nə; mȧ-rē-ˈȧ-nȧ\
Mar·i·anne 1 \ˌmər-ē-ˈan, ˌmar-\ 2 *Ger.* **Ma·rian·ne** \ˌmär-ē-ˈän-ə, mär-ˈyän-\
Ma·ria·no *Ital., Span.* \mär-ˈyän-ō\
Ma·rie 1 \mə-ˈrē, *Brit also* ˈmär-ē, ˈmar-ē\ 2 *Dan., Ger.* \mä-ˈrē(-ə)\ 3 *Du., Swed.* \mȧ-ˈrē\ 4 *Fr.* \mȧ-rē\ 5 *Norw.* \mä-ˈrē-ə\
Mar·i·et·ta 1 \ˌmer-ē-ˈet-ə, ˌmar-\ 2 *Ital.* \ˌmär-ē-ˈāt-tä\
Ma·rin 1 *Fr.* \mȧ-ra^{n}\ 2 *Serb.-Cr.* **Ma·rīn** \ˈmȧ-rēn\
Ma·ri·na *Russ.* \(ˌ)mər-ˈyē-nə\
Ma·ri·no *Ital.* \mä-ˈrē-nō\
Ma·ri·nus 1 \mə-ˈrē-nəs, -ˈrī-\ 2 *Du.* \mȧ-ˈrē-nœs\
Ma·rio 1 *Fr.* \mȧr-yō\ 2 *Ital., Span.* \ˈmär-yō\
Mar·i·on \ˈmer-ē-ən, ˈmar-ē-\
Mar·i·us 1 \ˈmer-ē-əs, ˈmar-\ 2 **Ma·ri·us** *Du.* \ˈmȧ-rē-œs\ 3 *Ger.* \ˈmär-yu̇s, ˈmä-rē-u̇s\ 4 *Norw.* \ˈmä-rē-u̇s\ 5 *Fr.* **Ma·rius** \mȧr-yu̅e̅s\
Ma·ri·ya *Russ.* \(ˌ)mər-ˈyē-(y)ə\
Ma·rja *Pol.* \ˈmȧr-yȧ\
Ma·rjan *Pol.* \ˈmȧr-yȧn\
Mar·jo·rie, Mar·jo·ry \ˈmärj-(ə-)rē\
Mark 1 *Eng., Du.* \ˈmärk\ 2 *Russ.* \ˈmȧrk\
Mar·ko *Serb.-Cr.* \ˈmȧr-kō\
Mar·kos *Mod. Gk.* \ˈmär-(ˌ)kȯs\
Mar·ko·vich *Russ.* \ˈmȧrk(-əv)-ˌyich\
Marks \ˈmärks\
Mar·kus *Ger.* \ˈmär-ku̇s\
Mar·land \ˈmär-lənd\
Mar·ma·duke \ˈmär-mə-ˌd(y)ük\
Már·quez *Span.* \ˈmär-kāth; -kās\
Mar·quis \ˈmär-kwəs\
Marr \ˈmär\
Mar·ri·ner \ˈmar-ə-nər\
Mar·ri·ot, Mar·ri·ott \ˈmar-ē-ət\
Mars·den \ˈmärz-dən\
Marsh \ˈmärsh\
Mar·shall \ˈmär-shəl\
Marsh·man \ˈmärsh-mən\
Mar·si·lio *Ital.* \mär-ˈsēl-yō\
Mar·ston \ˈmär-stən\
Mar·ta *Russ.* \ˈmȧr-tə\
Mar·tha \ˈmär-thə\
Mar·thi·nus *Du.* \mär-ˈtē-nœs\
Mar·tial *Fr.* \mȧrs-yȧl\
Mar·ti·a·nus *Lat.* \ˌmär-shē-ˈā-nəs\
Mar·tim *Port.* \mər-ˈtē^{n}; mȧr-\
Mar·tin 1 \ˈmärt-^{ə}n\ 2 *Dan., Ger., Norw.* \ˈmär-tēn\ 3 *Du.* \ˈmär-tən, mär-ˈtīn\ 4 *Finn., Swed.* \ˈmȧr-tin\ 5 *Fr.* \mȧr-ta^{n}\ 6 *Span.* **Mar·tín** \mär-ˈtēn\
Mar·tine *Fr.* \mȧr-tēn\
Mar·tí·nez *Span.* \mär-ˈtē-nāth; -nās\
Mar·ti·nia·no *Port.* \mər-tēn-ˈyȧ-nü; mȧr-\
Mar·ti·ni·us *Norw.* \mär-ˈtē-nē-u̇s\
Mar·ti·no *Ital.* \mär-ˈtē-nō\
Mar·ti·nus 1 \mär-ˈtī-nəs\ 2 *Du.* \mär-ˈtē-nœs\
Mar·ti·re *Ital.* \mär-ˈtē-rā\
Mar·tyn \ˈmärt-^{ə}n\
Mar·tyr 1 \ˈmärt-ər\ 2 *Fr.* \mȧr-tēr\
Mar·vin \ˈmär-vən\
Mary \ˈme(ə)r-ē, ˈma(ə)r-ē\
Mar·ya 1 *Pol.* \ˈmȧr-yȧ\ 2 *Russ.* \ˈmȧr-yə\
Mar·zia·le *Ital.* \märt-ˈsyäl-ā\
Mas *Indonesian* \ˈmäs\
Ma·sa·ha·ru *Jp.* \mä-sä-hä-ru̇\
Ma·sa·hi·ro *Jp.* \mä-sä-hē-rō\
Ma·sa·ka·do *Jp.* \mä-sä-kä-dō\
Ma·sa·ka·zu *Jp.* \mä-sä-kä-zu̇\
Ma·sa·ko *Jp.* \mä-sä-kō\
Ma·sa·mo·ri *Jp.* \mä-sä-mō-rē\
Ma·sa·na *Jp.* \mä-sä-nä\
Ma·sa·nao *Jp.* \mä-sä-nä-ō\
Ma·sa·no·bu *Jp.* \mä-sä-nō-bu̇\
Ma·sao *Jp.* \mä-sä-ō\
Ma·sa·shi·ge *Jp.* \mäs-ä-shē-ge\
Ma·sa·ta·ka *Jp.* \mä-sä-tä-kä\
Ma·sa·to·shi *Jp.* \mä-sä-tō-shē\
Ma·sa·yo·shi *Jp.* \mä-sä-yō-shē\
Ma·sa·yu·ki *Jp.* \mä-sä-yu̇k-ē\
Mas·ke·lyne \ˈmas-kə-ˌlīn, -lən\
Ma·so *Ital.* \ˈmäz-ō\
Mas·sey \ˈmas-ē\
Mas·si·mi·lia·no *Ital.* \ˌmäs-sē-mēl-ˈyän-ō\
Mas·si·mo *Ital.* \ˈmäs-sē-(ˌ)mō\
Mas·su·ri·us *Lat.* \mə-ˈsu̇r-ē-əs\
Mas·sy \ˈmas-ē\
Mas·ter·man \ˈmas-tər-mən\
Mas·ters \ˈmas-tərz\
Ma·sti·no *Ital.* \mäs-ˈtē-nō\
Ma·su·ji·rō *Jp.* \mä-su̇j-ē-rō\

Ma·ta·bei *Jp.* \mä-täb-ā\
Ma·teo *Span.* \mä-'tā-ō\
Ma·thä·us *Ger.* \mä-'te-u̇s\
Math·e·son \'math-ə-sən\
Math·ew \'math-(,)yü\
Math·ew·son \'math-yu̇-sən\
Ma·thi·as 1 \mə-'thī-əs\ 2 *Ger., Norw.* \mä-'tē-äs\ 3 *Port.* \mə-'tē-əsh; mȧ-'tē-ȧs\ 4 *Fr.* **Ma·thias** \mȧt-yäs\
Ma·thieu *Fr.* \mȧt-yœ̄\
Ma·thilde 1 *Fr.* \mȧ-tēld\ 2 **Ma·thil·de** *Ger.* \mä-'til-də\ 3 *Russ.* \mə-'tyil-də\
Math·i·son \'math-ə-sən\
Ma·thu·rin *Fr.* \mȧ-tue̅-ra^{n}\
Ma·thys *Du.* \mä-'tīs\
Ma·tí·as *Span.* \mä-'tē-äs\
Ma·ti·ja *Serb.-Cr.* \'mȧ-tē-yȧ\
Ma·til·da 1 \mə-'til-də\ 2 *Ital.* \mä-'tēl-dä\
Ma·tilde *Fr.* \mȧ-tēld\
Matt \'mat\
Mat·teo *Ital.* \mät-'te-ō\
Mat·te·son \'mat-ə-sən\
Mat·thä·us *Du., Ger.* \mä-'te-u̇s\
Mat·thew \'math-(,)yü\
Mat·thi·as 1 \mə-'thī-əs\ 2 *Finn.* \mȧ-'tē-ȧs\ 3 *Ger., Norw.* \mä-'tē-äs\ 4 *Icel.* **Mat·thí·as** \'mät-,tē-äs\
Mat·thieu *Fr.* \mȧt-yœ̄\
Mat·thijs *Du.* \mä-'tīs\
Mat·tia *Ital.* \mät-'tē-ä\
Mat·toon \mə-'tün\
Mat·ty \'mat-ē\
Mat·vey *Russ.* \(,)mət-'vyā(-ē)\
Mat·ve·ye·vich *Russ.* \(,)mət-'vyā(-yiv)-,yich\
Má·tyás *Hung.* \'mȧ-(,)tyȧsh\
Maud, Maude \'mȯd\
Maui *Maori* \'mau̇-ē\
Maule \'mȯl\
Maunde \'mȯnd\
Maun·sel \'man-səl\
Maur \'mȯr\
Mau·rice 1 \'mȯr-əs, 'mär-; mȯ-'rēs\ 2 *Fr.* \mȯ-rēs\
Mau·ris \'mȯr-əs, 'mar-əs\
Mau·rits *Du.* \'mau̇-rits\
Mau·ritz *Du., Norw., Swed.* \'mau̇-rits\
Mau·ri·zio *Ital.* \mau̇-'rēt-syō\
Mau·rus 1 *Ger.* \'mau̇-ru̇s\ 2 *Lat.* \'mȯr-əs\
Mau·ry·cy *Pol.* \mau̇-'rich-i\
Max 1 \'maks\ 2 *Du., Ger.* \'mäks\ 3 *Fr.* \mȧks\
Max·ence *Fr.* \mȧk-sä^{n}s\
Max·field \'maks-fēld\
Max·im *Russ.* \(,)mək-'syēm\
Max·ime *Fr.* \mȧk-sēm\
Max·im·i·a·na *Lat.* \mak-,sim-ē-'ā-nə\
Max·i·mil·ian 1 \,mak-sə-'mil-yən\ 2 **Ma·xi·mi·lian** *Ger.* \,mäk-sē-'mēl-yän, -'mē-lē-än\ 3 *Norw.* \,mäk-sē-(,)mē-lē-'än\ 4 *Pol.* \,mȧk-si-'mēl-yȧn\
Ma·xi·mi·lia·na *Ger.* \,mäk-sē-,mē-lē-'än-ä, -mēl-'yän-\
Ma·xi·mi·lia·ne *Ger.* \,mäk-sē-,mē-lē-'än-ə, -mēl-'yän-\
Ma·xi·mi·lia·no *Span.* \mäk-sē-mēl-'yän-ō\
Max·i·mi·lien *Fr.* \mȧk-sē-mēl-ya^{n}\
Max·i·mil·i·enne \,mak-si-,mil-ē-'en\
Max·i·min *Fr.* \mȧk-sē-ma^{n}\
Má·xi·mo *Span.* \mäk-sē-mō\
Max·i·mus *Lat.* \'mak-sə-məs\
Max·ine \mak-'sēn\
Max·well \'mak-,swel, -swəl\
May \'mā\
May·er 1 \'mī-ər, 'mā-\ 2 *Ger.* \'mī-ər\
May·ers \'mā-ərz\
May·field \'mā-fēld\
May·nard \'mā-nərd -,närd\
Mayne \'mān\
Ma·zo \'mā-(,)zō\
Mead·ows \'med-ōz\
Mearns \'mərnz\
Mech·til·de *Ger.* \mek-'til-də\
Me·dar·do *Ital.* \mā-'där-dō\
Mé·dart *Fr.* \mā-dȧr\
Mé·dé·ric *Fr.* \mā-dā-rēk\
Me·dill \mə-'dil\
Mee·ker \'mē-kər\
Megh·nad \māg-'näd\
Me·he·met, Meh·med *Turk.* \me-'met\
Meh·met *Alb., Turk.* \me-'met\
Mei·er \'mī(-ə)r\
Mein·dert *Du.* \'mīn-dərt\
Mein·hard *Ger.* \'mīn-,härt\
Mein·rad *Ger.* \'mīn-,rät\
Meir 1 \'mi(ə)r\ 2 *Dan.* \'mīr\ 3 *Heb.* \me-'ir\
Mel \'mel\
Me·lanch·thon, Me·lanc·thon \mə-'laŋ(k)-t(h)ən\
Me·lanc·ton \mə-'laŋ(k)-tən\
Mel·ba \'mel-bə\
Mel·bourne \'mel-bərn, -,bȯrn\
Mel·chi·or 1 \'mel-kē-ȯr\ 2 *Ger.* \'melk-yȯr, 'mel-kē-ȯr\ 3 *Fr.* **Mel·chior** \mel-kyȯr\
Mel·chior·re *Ital.* \māl-'kyȯr-rā\
Mel·chis·sé·dech *Fr.* \mel-kē-sā-dek\
Mel·chor *Span.* \mel-'chȯr\
Mel·e·si·na \,mel-ə-'sē-nə\
Mel·len \'mel-ən\
Mel·lin *Fr.* \me-la^{n}\
Mel·ton \'melt-^{ə}n\
Me·lu·si·na *Ger.* \,mā-lü-'zē-nä\
Mel·vin \'mel-vən\
Mem, Men *Port.* \'mā^{n}\
Mem·mi·us *Lat.* \'mem-ē-əs\
Me·na·hem *Ger.* \'mā-nä-(,)hem, mā-'nä-hem\
Men·des *Port.* \'mā^{n}(n)-dish; -dis\
Men·no *Du.* \'men-(,)ō\
Me·not·ti *Ital.* \mā-'nȯt-tē\
Men·tor \'men-,tȯ(ə)r, 'ment-ər\
Mer·cer \'mər-sər\
Mer·chant \'mər-chənt\
Mer·cu·ri·us *Du.* \mer-'kue̅-rē-ues\
Mer·cy \'mər-sē\
Mer·e·dith \'mer-əd-əth\
Mé·ria·dec *Fr.* \mār-yȧ-dek\
Mer·i·am \'mer-ē-əm\
Mer·i·an \'mer-ē-ən\
Mé·ric *Fr.* \mā-rēk\
Mer·i·weth·er \'mer-i-,weth-ər\
Merle \'mər(-ə)l\
Mer·lin \'mər-lən\
Mer·li·no *Ital.* \mār-'lē-nō\
Mer·li·nus *Lat.* \(,)mər-'lī-nəs\
Me·ro·pi·us *Lat.* \mi-'rō-pē-əs\
Mer·rill \'mer-əl\
Mer·ri·ott \'mer-ē-ət\
Mer·ry \'mer-ē\
Mer·ven \'mər-vən\
Mer·vil \'mər-vəl\
Mer·vyn \'mər-vən\
Mer·wan *Parsi* \'mār-vän\
Mer·wan·gi, -ji *Parsi* \mār-'vän-jē\
Mer·win \'mər-wən\
Me·shech \'mē-,shek\
Mes·sin·ger \'mes-^{ə}n-jər\
Mes·si·us *Lat.* \'mes-ē-əs\
Me·ta \'mēt-ə\
Met·calfe \'met-,kaf, -kəf\
Met·tus *Lat.* \'met-əs\
Meux \'myüks\
Mey·er *Eng., Dan., Ger.* \'mī(-ə)r\
Mey·rick \'mer-ik; 'mā-,rik, 'mī-\
Me·zio *Ital.* \'met-syō\
Mi·cah \'mī-kə\
Mi·ca·jah \mī-'kā-yə\
Mi·chael 1 \'mī-kəl\ 2 *Dan.* \mi-'kȧl, 'mēk-kəl\ 3 *Norw.* \mē-'käl\ 4 **Mi·cha·el** *Du.* \'mē-kȧ-,el\ 5 *Finn.* \'mē-kȧ-,el\ 6 *Ger.* \'mik-ä-(,)el\ 7 *Serb.-Cr.* \'mē-kä-el\
Mi·chae·lov·na *Russ.* \myi-'kī-ləv-nə\
Mi·chał *Pol.* \'mē-kȧl\
Mi·cheál *Ir. Gael.* \mi-'kīl\
Mi·chel 1 \'mī-kəl\ 2 *Fr.* \mē-shel\ 3 *Ger.* \'mik-əl\
Mi·chel·an·ge·lo 1 \,mī-kə-'lan-jə-,lō, ,mik-ə-'lan-, ,mē-kə-'län-\ 2 *Ital.* \,mē-käl-'än-jā-(,)lō\
Mi·che·le *Ital.* \mē-'kel-ā\
Mi·chell \mə-'shel\
Mi·chelle *Fr.* \mē-shel\
Mi·chiel *Du.* \mi-'kē(ə)l\
Mi·chi·ki·yo *Jp.* \mē-chē-kē-yō\
Mi·chi·na·ga *Jp.* \mē-chē-nä-gä\
Mi·chit·su·ra *Jp.* \mē-chēt-su̇-rä\
Mi·chi·za·ne *Jp.* \mē-chē-zän-e\
Mich·ler \'mik-lər\
Mie·czy·sław *Pol.* \mye-'chis-lȧf\
Mien·se *Du.* \'mēn(t)-sə\
Mi·guel 1 *Port.* \mē-'gel\ 2 *Span.* \mē-'gel\
Mi·guez *Port.* \mē-'gāsh\
Mi·hai *Rom.* \mē-'hī\
Mi·ha·il *Rom.* \,mē-hä-'ēl\
Mi·hály *Hung.* \'mi-,hȧl^{y}\
Mi·ka *Finn.* \'mē-kȧ\
Mi·ka·el *Swed.* \'mē-kȧ-əl\
Mi·kal *Norw.* \mē-'käl\
Mi·kha·il 1 *Bulg.* \,mē-kȧ-'ēl\ 2 *Russ.* \myik-(,)ə-'ēl\
Mi·khai·lov·na *Russ.* \myi-'kīl(-ə)v-nə\
Mi·khay·lo *Ukrain.* \mē-'kī-lō\
Mi·khay·lo·vich, -khai·lo·vich *Russ.* \myi-'kīl(-əv)-,yich\
Mik·kel *Dan.* \'mēk-kəl\
Mik·kel·sen *Dan.* \'mēk-kəl-sən\
Mik·kjel *Norw.* \'mik-kyəl\
Mi·klós *Hung.* \'mik-,lōsh\
Mi·ko·łaj *Pol.* \mē-'kȯl-,ī\
Mi·lan 1 *Czech.* \'mil-ȧn\ 2 *Serb.-Cr.* \'mē-lȧn\
Mil·bry \'mil-brē\
Mil·burn, -burne \'mil-bərn\
Mil·dred \'mil-drəd\
Miles \'mī(ə)lz\
Mi·li·vo·je *Serb.-Cr.* \'mē-lē-vȯ-ye\
Mil·ka *Serb.-Cr.* \'mēl-kȧ\
Mil·lard \'mil-ərd\
Mil·ledge \'mil-ij\
Mil·li·cent \'mil-ə-sənt\
Mil·li·gan \'mil-ə-gən\
Mil·ling·ton \'mil-iŋ-tən\
Mil·more \'mil-,mō(ə)r\
Mil·nor \'mil-nər, -,nȯr\
Mi·lo·slav *Czech* \'mil-ȯ-,slȧf\
Mi·lo·van *Serb.-Cr.* \'mē-lȯ-vȧn\
Mil·ton \'milt-^{ə}n\
Mi·ly *Russ.* \'myēl-yəi\
Mi·mi *Fr.* \mē-mē\
Min·chō *Jp.* \min-chō\
Mi·nei·chi·ro *Jp.* \mē-nā-chē-rō\
Mi·ner \'mī-nər\
Mi·ner·va \mə-'nər-və\
Minge \'minj\
Min·na 1 *Finn.* \'min-nȧ\ 2 *Ger.* \'min-ä\
Min·ne·us *Lat.* \mi-'nā-əs\

\ə\ **abut** \$^{ə}$\ **kitten**, *Fr.* **table** \ər\ **further** \a\ **ash** \ā\ **ace** \ä\ **cot, cart** \au̇\ **out** \ch\ **chin** \e\ **bet** \ē\ **easy** \g\ **go** \i\ **hit** \ī\ **ice** \j\ **job** \ŋ\ **sing** \ō\ **go** \ȯ\ **law** \ȯi\ **boy** \th\ **both** \th\ **the** \ü\ **loot** \u̇\ **foot** \y\ **yet** \zh\ **vision** \ȧ, b, g, k, ^{n}, œ, œ̄, ue, ue̅, ^{y} *see* Guide to Pronunciation

Min·nie \'min-ē\
Mi·no *Ital.* \'mē-nō\
Mi·nor \'mī-nər, -,nȯr\
Min·turn \'min-tərn\
Mir *Turk.* \'mēr\
Mir·a·beau \'mir-ə-,bō\
Mi·ran·da \mə-'ran-də\
Mir·i·am \'mir-ē-əm\
Mi·ron 1 \'mī-rən\ 2 *Rom.* \mē-'rȯn\
Mi·ro·no·vich *Russ.* \myi-'rȯn(-əv)-,yich\
Mi·scha 1 \'mē-shə\ 2 *Russ.* \'myē-shə\
Mis·key \'mis-kē\
Mi·te *Ger.* \'mē-tə\
Mit·su·go·ro *Jp.* \mit-su̇-gō-rō\
Mi·tsu·ku·ni *Jp.* \mēt-su̇k-ün-ē\
Mit·su·ma·sa *Jp.* \mēt-su̇m-ä-sä\
Mi·tsu·na·ga *Jp.* \mēt-su̇n-äg-ä\
Mi·tsu·na·ri *Jp.* \mēt-su̇n-är-ē\
Mi·tsu·no·bu *Jp.* \mēt-su̇n-ō-bü\
Mi·tsu·no·ri *Jp.* \mēt-su̇n-ō-rē\
Mi·tsu·o·ki *Jp.* \mēt-su̇-ō-kē\
Mi·tsu·yo·ri *Jp.* \mit-su̇-yō-rē\
Mix \'miks\
Miz·zi *Czech* \'mit-sē\
Moa *Swed.* \'mü-ə\
Mo·ber·ly \'mō-bər-lē\
Mo·chi·to·yo *Jp.* \mō-chē-tō-yō\
Mod·er·a·tus *Lat.* \,mäd-ə-'rāt-əs\
Mo·dest *Russ.* \(,)məd-'yest\
Mo·deste *Fr.* \mȯ-dest\
Mo·des·to *Span.* \mō-'thā-stō\
Mo·di·bo *Mali* \mō-'dē-bō\
Mo·ham·med 1 \mō-'ham-əd, -'häm-\ 2 *Afghan* \mō-'həm-məd\ 3 *Arab.* \mu̇-'ham-mad\ 4 *Pers.* \mȯ-'ham-mad\
Mo·han·das *Gujarati* \'mō-hən-,däs\
Moi·ra \'mȯi-rə\
Moi·se 1 *Bantu* \'mȯi-shə\ 2 *Fr.* **Mo·ïse** \mȯ-ēz\
Moi·sey *Russ.* \mə-is-'yā(-ē)\
Moi·se·ye·vich *Russ.* \mə-is-'yā(-yiv)-,yich\
Mo·ko·pu *Sesotho* \mō-'kō-pü\
Moll \'mäl\
Møl·ler 1 *Dan.* \'mœl-ər\ 2 *Norw.* \'mœl-lər\
Mol·ly \'mäl-ē\
Molt·ke *Norw.* \'mȯlt-kə\
Mol·y·neux \'mäl-ən-,yü(ks), 'məl-\
Mom·či·lo *Serb.-Cr.* \'mȯm-chē-lȯ\
Mon·cure \män-'kyu̇(ə)r, mən-, 'män-,\
Mon·i·ca \'män-i-kə\
Mon·roe \mən-'rō, *Brit. also* 'mən-,\
Mon·son \'mən(t)-sən\
Mon·ta·cute \'män-tə-,kyüt, 'mən-\
Mon·tan *Fr.* \mō^{n}-tä^{n}\
Mon·teith \män-'tēth\
Mon·tes·quieu \,mänt-əs-'kyü\
Mont·fort \'mänt-fərt\
Mont·gom·er·ie \(,)mən(t)-'gəm-(ə-)rē, män(t)-, -'gäm-\
Mont·rose \'män-,trōz\
Mon·za·em·on *Jp.* \mōn-zä-em-ōn\
Moors \'mu̇(ə)rz, 'mō(ə)rz\
Mór *Hung.* \'mōr\
Mor·daunt \'mȯrd-^{ə}nt\
Mor·de·cai \'mȯrd-i-,kī\
Mor·dey \'mȯr-dē\
Mo·reau \'mōr-(,)ō, 'mȯr-\
Mo·rei·ra *Port.* \mō-'rā-rȧ\
Mo·rell \mō-'rel\
More·ton \'mȯrt-^{ə}n\
Mor·gan \'mȯr-gən\
Mo·ri *Jp.* \mō-rē\
Mo·ri·ka·ge *Jp.* \mō-rē-käg-e\
Mo·rin *Fr.* \mȯ-ra^{n}\
Mo·ri·no·bu *Jp.* \mō-rē-nō-bu̇\
Mo·ritz *Ger.* \'mō-rits\
Mo·riz *Ger.* \'mō-rits\
Mo·ro·no·bu *Jp.* \mō-rō-nō-bu̇\
Mor·rill \'mär-əl\
Mor·ris 1 \'mȯr-əs, 'mär-\ 2 *Dan.* \'mȯr-(,)ēs\
Mor·row \'mär-(,)ō, 'mȯr-, -ə(-w)\
Mor·te·mart *Fr.* \mȯr-tə-mȧr\
Mor·ten *Dan.* \'mȯr-dən\
Mor·ti·mer \'mȯrt-ə-mər\
Mor·ton \'mȯrt-^{ə}n\
Mo·sén *Span.* \mō-'sān\
Mo·ses 1 \'mō-zəz *also* -zəs\ 2 *Ger.* \'mō-(,)zes\
Mo·she *Heb., Yiddish* \'mō-shə\
Moss \'mȯs\
Mos·sèn *Catalan* \mȯ-'sān\
Moss·man \'mȯs-mən\
Mo·tie·jus *Lith.* \mȯ-'tyā-yu̇s\
Mo·tier *Fr.* \mȯt-yā\
Mo·ti·lal *Kashmiri* \'mō-ti-,läl\
Mo·to·ki·yo *Jp.* \mō-tō-kē-yō\
Mo·to·no·bu *Jp.* \mō-tō-nō-bu̇\
Mo·to·no·ri *Jp.* \mō-tō-nō-rē\
Mo·to·tsu·ne *Jp.* \mō-tōt-su̇n-e\
Mou·lay *Arab.* \mau̇-'lā\
Moun·tain \'mau̇nt-^{ə}n\
Mount·stu·art \mau̇nt-'st(y)ü-ərt\
Mow·bray \'mō-,brā, -brē\
Mu·ci·us *Lat.* \'m(y)ü-sh(ē-)əs\
Mu·ḥam·mad 1 *Arab.* \mu̇-'ham-mad\ 2 *Pers.* \mȯ-'ham-mad\
Muir·head \'myu̇(ə)r-hed\
Mu·ji·bur *Bengali* \'mü-yē-bür\
Mul·drup \'məl-drəp\
Mü·lertz *Norw.* \'mue̅-lərts\
Mul·ford \'məl-fərd\
Mum·ford \'məm-fərd\
Mu·na·ti·us *Lat.* \m(y)u̇-'nā-sh(ē-)əs\
Mu·ne·fu·sa *Jp.* \mu̇n-ef-ü̇s-ä\
Mu·ne·mit·su *Jp.* \mu̇-ne-mēt-su̇\
Mun·go \'məŋ-gō\
Mun·nik *Du.* \'mʊen-ək\
Mun·ro, Mun·roe \mən-'rō, 'mən-,\
Mu·rad *Ger.* \mü-'rät\
Mu·rat \m(y)ə-'rat\
Mur·do \'mər-dō\
Mur·doch \'mər-dək, -,däk\
Mu·ri·el \'myu̇r-ē-əl\
Mur·ray \'mər-ē, 'mə-rē\
Mur·rough \'mər-(,)ō, 'mə-(,)rō\
Mur·ry \'mər-ē, 'mə-rē\
Mur·ton \'mərt-^{ə}n\
Mu·sa 1 *Ital.* \'mü-zä\ 2 *Arab.* **Mū·sā** \'mü-sȧ\
Mu·sa·shi *Jp.* \mu̇s-ä-shē\
Mus·kett \'məs-kət\
Mus·ta·fā 1 *Arab.* \,mu̇s-'tä-fȧ\ 2 *Turk.* \mu̇s-tä-'fä\
Mu·ya·ka *Bantu* \mu̇-'yä-kä\
Mu·zio *Ital.* \'müt-syō\
Mvum·bi *Zulu* \$^{ə}$m-'vu̇m-bē, em-\
My·er \'mī-ər\
Myles \'mī(ə)lz\
My·nors \'mī-nərz, -,nȯrz\
My·ra \'mī-rə\
My·rick \'mī-rik\
Myr·na \'mər-nə\
My·ron \'mī-rən\
Myr·til·la \mər-'til-ə\
Myr·tle \'mərt-^{ə}l\

Nach·man *Heb.* \'nȧk̲-män\
Na·dezh·da *Russ.* \nəd-'yezh-də\
Na·dine \nā-'dēn\
Na·e·ra *Maori* \nä-'ā-rä\
Na·few \'nā-fyü\
Na·ga·ma·sa *Jp.* \näg-äm-ä-sä\
Na·ga·shi·ge *Jp.* \nä-gä-shē-ge\
Na·gel *Norw.* \'näg-əl\
Na·hum 1 \'nā-(h)əm, -,həm\ 2 *Ger.* \'nä-,hu̇m\
Na·mık *Turk.* \nä-'mək\
Nance \'nan(t)s\
Nan·cy \'nan(t)-sē\
Nan·nerl *Ger.* \'nän-ərl\
Nan·ni *Ital.* \'nän-nē\
Na·no \'nā-nō\
Na·o·mi \nā-'ō-mē\
Na·o·no·bu *Jp.* \nä-ō-nō-bu̇\
Na·o·su·ke *Jp.* \nä-ō-su̇k-e\
Na·o·ta·ke *Jp.* \nä-ō-tä-ke\
Na·o·ya *Jp.* \nä-ō-yä\
Naph·ta·li 1 \'naf-tə-,lī\ 2 *Russ.* \(,)nəf-'täl-yi\
Na·pi·er \'nā-pē-ər, -,pi(ə)r; nə-'pi(ə)r\
Na·po·le·on 1 \nə-'pōl-yən, -'pō-lē-ən\ 2 *Ger.* \nä-'pō-lā-ȯn, -lā-ō^{n}\ 3 *Fr.* **Na·po·lé·on** \nȧ-pȯ-lā-ō^{n}\
Na·po·le·o·ne *Ital.* \,näp-ō-lā-'ō-nā\
Nap·per \'nap-ər\
Nar·ci·so *Span.* \när-'thē-sō; -'sē-\
Nar·cisse *Fr.* \nȧr-sēs, *Can.* -sis\
Nar·don *Fr.* \nȧr-dō^{n}\
Na·ren·dra·nath *Bengali* \nə-'ren-drə-nət\
Na·ri·a·ki *Jp.* \nä-rē-äk-ē\
Na·ri·a·ki·ra *Jp.* \nä-rē-ä-kē-rä\
Nā·ṣif *Lebanese* \nä-'shēf\
Na·ṣir *Pers.* \nȧ-'sēr\
Nas·sau \'nas-(,)ȯ\
Nat \'nat\
Nat·a·lie \'nat-ə-lē\
Na·ta·lio *Span.* \nä-'täl-yō\
Na·tal·ya *Russ.* \(,)nə-'täl-yə\
Nath *Bengali* \'nət\
Na·than 1 \'nā-thən\ 2 *Ger.* \'nä-tän\ 3 *Swed.* \'nä-tȧn\
Na·than·a·el 1 \nə-'than-ā-əl\ 2 *Ger.* **Na·tha·na·el** \nä-'tä-nä-,el\
Na·than·iel \nə-'than-yəl\
Nat·suko *Jp.* \nät-su̇k-ō\
Na·um *Russ.* \nȧ-ü̇m\
Na·zaire *Fr.* \nȧ-zer\
Na·zım *Turk.* \nä-'zəm\
Neal, Neale \'nē(ə)l\
Ned \'ned\
Need·ham \'nēd-əm\
Ne·e·mia *Russ.* \nyi-'ām-yə\
Neeve \'nēv\
Neg·ley \'neg-lē\
Ne·he·mi·ah \,nē-(h)ə-'mī-ə\
Neil \'nē(ə)l\
Neil·son \'nē(ə)l-sən\
Neith \'nēth\
Né·lie *Fr.* \nā-lē\
Nell \'nel\
Nel·lie \'nel-ē\
Nel·son \'nel-sən\
Né·o·clès *Fr.* \nā-ȯ-kles\
Né·po·mu·cène *Fr.* \nā-pȯ-mue̅-sen\
Ne·po·mu·ce·no *Span.* \nā-pō-mü-'thā-nō; -'sā-\
Ne·po·muk *Czech, Ger.* \'nā-pō-,mu̇k\
Né·rée *Fr.* \nā-rā\
Ne·ri *Ital.* \'ner-ē\
Ne·ro \'nē-(,)rō, 'ni(ə)r-(,)ō\
Nes·ta \'nes-tə\
Nes·tor 1 \'nes-tər\ 2 *Finn.* \'nes-,tȯr\ 3 *Fr.* \nes-tȯr\ 4 *Span.* **Nés·tor** \'nā-stȯr\
Net·ty *Ger.* \'net-ē\
Neu·mann *Norw.* \'nœi-,män\
Nev·il, Nev·ile, Nev·ill, Nev·ille \'nev-əl\
Nev·ins \'nev-ənz\
New \'n(y)ü\
New·bold \'n(y)ü-,bōld\
New·en·ham \'n(y)ü-ən-əm\

New·ing·ton \ˈnyü-iŋ-tən\
New·zam \ˈn(y)ü-zəm\
Nga·be·hi *Indonesian* \eŋ-ä-ˈbā-hē\
Ngaio \ˈnī-(ˌ)ō\
Niall *Ir. Gael.* \ˈnē(ə)l\
Ni·caise *Fr.* \nē-kez\
Ni·ca·sio *Span.* \nē-ˈkäs-yō\
Nic·co·la *Ital.* \nēk-ˈkō-lä\
Nic·co·lò *Ital.* \ˌnēk-kō-ˈlō\
Nic·co·lo *Ital.* \ˈnēk-kō-(ˌ)lō\
Ni·cé·phore *Fr.* \nē-sā-fȯr\
Ni·ceph·o·rus *Lat.* \nī-ˈsef-(ə-)rəs\
Ni·ce·to *Span.* \nē-ˈthā-tō; -ˈsā-\
Nich·ol \ˈnik-əl\
Nich·o·las \ˈnik-(ə-)ləs\
Nich·olls, Nich·ols \ˈnik-əlz\
Nick \ˈnik\
Ni·co·de·mus *Swed.* \ni-kō-ˈdā-məs\
Nic·ol \ˈnik-əl\
Ni·co·la 1 *Ital.* \nē-ˈkō-lä\ 2 *Serb.-Cr.* \ˈnē-kō-lä\
Ni·co·laas *Du.* \ˈnē-kə-ˌläs\
Ni·co·lae *Rom.* \nē-kō-ˈlī\
Ni·co·laes *Du.* \ˈnē-kə-ˌläs\
Ni·co·lai 1 *Dan.* \ˌnē-kə-ˈlī\ 2 *Du.* \ˌnē-kō-ˈlä-ē\ 3 *Ger.* \ˌnē-kō-ˈlä-ē, ˈnē-kō-ˌlī\
Ni·co·láo *Port.* \nē-kü-ˈlaů\
Nic·o·las 1 \ˈnik-(ə-)ləs\ 2 **Ni·co·las** *Dan.* \ˈnē-kə-ˌläs\ 3 *Du.* \ˈnē-kə-läs\ 4 *Fr.* \nē-kō-lä\ 5 *Span.* **Ni·co·lás** \nē-kō-ˈläs\
Ni·co·lau *Port.* \nē-ˈkō-laů\
Ni·co·la·us 1 *Ger.* \ˌnē-kō-ˈlä-ůs, ˈnē-kō-ˌlaůs\ 2 *Lat.* **Nic·o·la·us** \ˌnik-ə-ˈlā-əs\
Ni·cole *Fr.* \nē-kȯl\
Nic·oll \ˈnik-əl\
Ni·co·lò *Ital.* \ˌnē-kō-ˈlō\
Nic·ol·son \ˈnik-əl-sən\
Ni·co·me·de *Ital.* \ˌnē-kō-ˈmed-ā\
Nie·cis·law *Pol.* \ˈnyā-chē-ˌsläv\
Niel \ˈnē(ə)l\
Niels 1 *Dan.* \ˈnils\ 2 *Norw.* \ˈnēls\
Niel·sen *Norw.* \ˈnēl-sən\
Ni·gid·i·us *Lat.* \nə-ˈgid-ē-əs\
Ni·ki·fo·ro·vich *Russ.* \nyik-ˈyē-fər(-əv)-ˌyich\
Ni·ki·ta *Russ.* \nyik-ˈyē-tə\
Ni·ki·tich *Russ.* \nyik-ˈyē-tyich\
Ni·klaas *Du.* \ˈnē-ˌkläs\
Ni·klas 1 *Ger.* \ˈnē-(ˌ)kläs\ 2 *Swed.* \ˈnik-läs\
Ni·ko·dem *Ger.* \ˌnē-kō-ˈdām\
Ni·ko·de·mus *Ger.* \ˌnē-kō-ˈdā-mus\
Ni·ko·laas *Du.* \ˈnē-kə-ˌläs\
Ni·ko·lai 1 *Dan.* \ˌnē-kə-ˈlī\ 2 *Russ.* \nyik-(ˌ)ə-ˈlī\
Ni·ko·laj *Dan.* \ˌnē-kə-ˈlī\
Ni·ko·la·os *Mod. Gk.* \nyē-ˈkō-lä-(ˌ)ōs\
Ni·ko·las *Ger.* \ˈnē-kō-ˌläs\
Ni·ko·la·us *Ger.* \ˌnē-kō-ˈlä-ůs, ˈnē-kō-ˌlaůs\
Ni·ko·lay *Russ.* \nyik-(ˌ)ə-ˈlī\
Ni·ko·la·ye·vich *Russ.* \nyik-(ˌ)ə-ˈlä(-yiv)-ˌyich\
Ni·ko·la·yev·na *Russ.* \nyik-(ˌ)ə-ˈlä(-i)v-nə\
Nil *Russ.* \ˈnyēl\
Niles \ˈnī(ə)lz\
Ni·lo \ˈnē-lü\
Nils 1 *Dan., Swed.* \ˈnils\ 2 *Norw.* \ˈnēls\
Nils·son *Swed.* \ˈnils-sōn\
Ni·lus *Gk.* \ˈnī-ləs\
Nim·mons \ˈnim-ənz\
Ni·na 1 \ˈnī-nə, ˈnē-nə\ 2 *Russ.* \ˈnyē-nə\
Nin·ga *Jp.* \nin-gä\
Nin·i·an \ˈnin-ē-ən\
Ni·no *Ital.* \ˈnē-nō\
Ni·non *Fr.* \nē-nō^{n}\
Nin·sei *Jp.* \nin-sā\
Nix·on \ˈnik-sən\
No·ah \ˈnō-ə\
No·bu·a·ki *Jp.* \nō-bů-ä-kē\
No·bu·hi·ro *Jp.* \nō-bů-hē-rō\
No·bu·ka *Jp.* \nō-bůk-ä\
No·buk·at·su *Jp.* \nō-bůk-ät-sů\
No·bu·ma·sa *Jp.* \nō-bům-ä-sä\
No·bum·o·ri *Jp.* \nō-bům-ō-rē\
No·bu·shi·ge *Jp.* \nō-bůsh-ē-ge\
No·bu·ta·ke *Jp.* \nō-bů-tä-ke\
No·bu·yu·ki *Jp.* \nō-bů-yůk-ē\
No·el \ˈnō-əl\
No·ël 1 \ˈnō-əl\ 2 *Fr.* \nō-el\
No·é·mi *Fr.* \nō-ā-mē\
No·guei·ra *Port.* \nō-gwā-rä\
No·land \ˈnō-lənd\
Nom·par *Fr.* \nō^{n}-pär\
Non·na *Rom.* \ˈnō-nä\
Noon \ˈnün\
No·ra \ˈnō-rə, ˈnȯr-\
Nor·bert 1 \ˈnȯ(ə)r-bərt\ 2 *Czech, Ger.* \ˈnȯr-bert\ 3 *Fr.* \nȯr-ber\
Nor·borne \ˈnȯ(ə)r-bərn\
Nor·cliffe \ˈnȯ(ə)r-ˌklif\
Nor·dahl, -dal *Norw.* \ˈnȯr-däl\
No·ri·ma·sa *Jp.* \nō-rē-mäs-ä\
No·ri·na·ga *Jp.* \nō-rē-nä-gä\
Nor·key \ˈnȯr-kē\
Nor·ma \ˈnȯr-mə\
Nor·man \ˈnȯr-mən\
Nor·reys \ˈnär-əs, -ēz\
North·more \ˈnȯ(ə)rth-ˌmō(ə)r, -ˌmȯ(ə)r\
Nor·throp \ˈnȯr-thrəp\
Nor·val \ˈnȯr-vəl\
Nor·vin \ˈnȯr-vən\
Nor·wood \ˈnȯr-wůd\
Nott \ˈnät\
Not·tidge \ˈnät-ij\
No·vel·lo 1 \nə-ˈvel-ō, nō-\ 2 *Ital.* \nō-ˈvel-lō\
Noyes \ˈnȯis\
No·za·ki *Jp.* \nō-zäk-ē\
Nuck·les \ˈnək-əlz\
Nu·ma 1 *Fr.* \nu̅e̅-mä\ 2 *Span.* \ˈnü-mä\
Nú·ñez *Span.* \ˈnün-yāth; -yās\
Nu·nho *Port.* \ˈnün-yü\
Nu·no 1 *Port.* \ˈnü-nü\ 2 *Span.* **Nu·ño** \ˈnün-yō\
Nu·ri *Turk.* \nü-ˈrē\

Oakes \ˈōks\
Oa·key \ˈō-kē\
Oba·di·ah \ˌō-bə-ˈdī-ə\
Ob·be *Du.* \ˈō-bə\
Obed \ˈō-bəd\
Ober·to *Ital.* \ō-ˈber-tō\
Obiz·zo *Ital.* \ˈō-bēt-(ˌ)tsō, ō-ˈbēt-\
Oc·tave 1 \ˈäk-ˌtāv, äk-ˈtāv\ 2 *Fr.* \ȯk-täv\
Oc·ta·via \ȯk-ˈtä-vē-ə\
Oc·ta·vian *Rom.* \ˌȯk-täv-ˈyän\
Oc·ta·vio 1 *Ger.* \ȯk-ˈtäv-yō, -ˈtäv-ē-ō\ 2 *Span.* \ȯk-ˈtäb-yō\
Oc·ta·vi·us \äk-ˈtā-vē-əs\
Oc·tav·us \äk-ˈtav-əs\
Od·do·ne *Ital.* \ȯd-ˈdō-nā\
Odet *Fr.* \ō-de\
Odi·lon *Fr.* \ō-dē-lō^{n}\
Odo \ˈō-dō\
Odo·ar·do *Ital.* \ˌō-dō-ˈär-dō\
Ödön *Hung.* \ˈœd-œn\
Oe·no·ne \ē-ˈnō-nē\
Off·ley \ˈȯf-lē\
O'·Fla·her·tie \ō-ˈflä-(h)ər-tē\
Ofo·ni·us *Lat.* \ə-ˈfō-nē-əs, ō-\
Ogai *Jp.* \ō-gī\
Oge \ˈōg\
Ogg \ˈäg\
Ohio \ō-ˈhī-(ˌ)ō\
Oki·ku·ni *Jp.* \ō-kē-kůn-ē\
Oki·tsu·gu *Jp.* \ō-kēt-sůg-ů\
Oku·ni *Jp.* \ō-kůn-ē\
Oku·ra *Jp.* \ō-kůr-ä\
Ola *Swed.* \ˈü-lä\
Olaf 1 \ˈō-ləf, -ləv\ 2 *Dan.* \ˈō-ˌläf\ 3 *Norw.* \ˈō-ˌläf\ 4. *Swed.* \ˈü-läf, -läv\
Olafs·son *Norw.* \ˈō-läf-ˌsȯn\
Olaf·ur *Icel.* \ˈō-läf-u̇r\
Olau·dah \ō-ˈlaů-də, -(ˌ)dä\
Ola·us 1 *Dan.* \ō-ˈlaůs\ 2 *Ger.* \ō-ˈlä-ůs, ˈō-ˌlaůs\ 3 *Lat.* \ə-ˈlā-əs, ō-\ 4 *Swed.* \ů-ˈlä-əs\
Olav *Norw.* \ˈō-ˌläv, -ˌläf\
Ole *Dan., Norw.* \ˈō-lə\
Oleg *Russ.* \ˈō-leg\
Oley \ˈō-lē\
Ol·ga 1 \ˈōl-gə, ˈäl-, ˈōl-\ 2 *Russ.* \ˈōl^{y}-gə\
Olim·pia *Ital.* \ō-ˈlēm-pyä\
Olin \ˈō-lən\
Olin·do *Ital.* \ō-ˈlēn-dō\
Olin·thus \ə-ˈlin-thəs, ō-\
Olin·to *Ital.* \ō-ˈlēn-tō\
Ol·ive \ˈäl-iv, -əv\
Ol·i·ver \ˈäl-ə-vər\
Oliv·ia \ə-ˈliv-ē-ə, ō-\
Oli·vier 1 *Du.* \ˈō-li-ˌvir\ 2 *Fr.* \ȯ-lēv-yā\
Ol·lie \ˈäl-ē\
Olof 1 \ˈō-ləf\ 2 *Swed.* \ˈü-lȯv, -lȯf\
Oloff *Du.* \ˈō-ˌlȯf\
Oluf *Dan., Ger., Norw.* \ˈō-(ˌ)lůf\
Olympe *Fr.* \ȯ-la^{n}p\
Olym·pia \ə-ˈlim-pē-ə, ō-\
Omar 1 \ˈō-ˌmär\ 2 *Fr.* \ō-mär\
Omo·bo·no *Ital.* \ˌō-mō-ˈbō-nō\
O'·Moore \ō-ˈmō(ə)r, -ˈmȯ(ə)r, -ˈmů(ə)r\
Onck·en \ˈäŋ-kən\
On·no *Ger.* \ˈōn-ō\
Ono·ra·to *Ital.* \ˌō-nō-ˈrät-ō\
Ons·low \ˈänz-lō\
Ope·li·us *Lat.* \ə-ˈpē-lē-əs, ō-, -ˈpēl-yəs\
Opid *Pol.* \ˈō-pēt\
Op·ta·ti·a·nus *Lat.* \äp-ˌtā-shē-ˈā-nəs\
Or·ace \ˈȯr-əs, ˈär-\
Ora·zio *Ital.* \ō-ˈrät-syō\
Orde \ˈō(ə)rd, ˈȯ(ə)rd\
Ord·way \ˈȯrd-wā\
Oren \ˈō-rən\
Orest *Russ.* \(ˌ)ər-ˈyāst\
Ore·ste *Ital.* \ō-ˈres-tā\
Ores·tes \ə-ˈres-(ˌ)tēz, ō-\
Ori·be *Jp.* \ō-rē-be\
Ori·el \ˈōr-ē-əl, ˈȯr-\
Oris \ˈōr-əs, ˈȯr-\
Or·i·son \ˈär-ə-zən\
Or·la *Dan.* \ˈȯr-(ˌ)lä\
Or·lande *Fr.* \ȯr-lä^{n}d\
Or·lan·do 1 \ȯr-ˈlan-(ˌ)dō, -ˈlän-\ 2 *Ital.* \ōr-ˈlän-dō\
Or·lan·dus *Lat.* \ȯr-ˈlan-dəs\
Or·ley \ˈȯr-lē\
Or·lo \ˈȯr-lō\
Orms·bee \ˈȯrmz-bē\
Orms·by \ˈȯrmz-bē\
Orne \ˈȯrn\
Oronce *Fr.* \ȯ-rō^{n}s\
Oron·ti·us *Lat.* \ə-ˈrän-shē-əs, -chē-\
Oron·zo *Ital.* \ō-ˈrȯnt-sō\
Oroz·co *Span.* \ō-ˈrȯth-kō; -ˈrōs-\
Or·pheus \ˈȯr-ˌfyüs, -fē-əs\

\ə\ abut \ᵊ\ kitten, *Fr.* table \ər\ further \a\ ash \ā\ ace \ä\ cot, cart \aů\ out \ch\ chin \e\ bet \ē\ easy \g\ go \i\ hit \ī\ ice \j\ job \ŋ\ sing \ō\ go \ȯ\ law \ȯi\ boy \th\ both \t͟h\ the \ü\ loot \ů\ foot \y\ yet \zh\ vision \á, b̲, g̅, k̲, ^{n}, œ, œ̅, u̇e, u̅e̅, ^{y}\ *see* Guide to Pronunciation

Or·ren \ˈȯr-ən, ˈär-\
Or·ridge \ˈȯr-ij, ˈär-\
Or·ris \ˈȯr-əs, ˈär-\
Or·son \ˈȯr-sən\
Or·ville \ˈȯr-vəl\
Osa \ˈō-sə\
Osa·chi *Jp.* \ō-sä-chē\
Osa·mi *Jp.* \ō-sä-mē\
Osa·mu *Jp.* \ō-säm-ü\
Os·bern \ˈäz-(ˌ)bərn\
Os·bert \ˈäz-bərt\
Os·car 1 \ˈäs-kər\ 2 *Fr.* \ȯs-kȧr\ 3 *Ger., Norw.* \ˈȯs-ˌkär\ 4 *Pol., Swed.* \ˈȯs-ˌkȧr\ 5 *Russ.* \ˈȯs-kər\ 6 *Span.* **Ós·car** \ˈōs-kär\
Osip *Russ.* \ˈȯs-yip\
Osi·po·vich *Russ.* \əs-(ˌ)yi-ˈpȯv-ˌyich\
Os·kar 1 \ˈäs-kər\ 2 *Finn., Swed.* \ˈȯs-ˌkȧr\ 3 *Ger., Norw.* \ˈȯs-ˌkär\
Os·man *Turk.* \ȯs-ˈmän\
Os·mond \ˈäz-mənd\
Os·sa·wa \ˈäs-ə-wə\
Os·sian 1 \ˈäsh-ən, ˈäs-ē-ən\ 2 *Fr.* \ȯs-yä^{n}\
Os·sip *Russ.* \ˈȯs-yip\
Östen *Swed.* \ˈœ̄-stən\
Os·vald *Swed.* \ˈȯs-ˌvȧld\
Os·wald 1 \ˈäz-wəld\ 2 *Ger.* \ˈȯs-ˌvält\
Os·wal·do *Port.* \ȯzh-ˈwäl-dü; ȯz-\
Ota·kar *Czech.* \ˈō-tȧ-ˌkȧr\
Ot·fried *Ger.* \ˈȯt-(ˌ)frēt\
Othe·nin *Fr.* \ȯt-na^{n}\
Oth·mar *Ger.* \ˈōt-ˌmär\
Oth·ni·el \ˈäth-nē-əl\
Otho \ˈō-thō\
Othon *Fr.* \ȯ-tō^{n}\
Otis \ˈōt-əs\
Ot·mar *Ger.* \ˈȯt-ˌmär\
Oto·ji·ro *Jp.* \ō-tō-jē-rō\
Oton *Serb.-Cr.* \ˈȯ-tȯn\
Otsu·zo *Jp.* \ōt-su̇z-ō\
Ot·ta·via·no *Ital.* \ˌōt-täv-ˈyän-ō\
Ot·ta·vio *Ital.* \ōt-ˈtäv-yō\
Ot·ti·li·a·na *Swed.* \ˌȯt-ti-lē-ˈän-ȧ\
Ot·ti·lie *Ger.* \ō-ˈtē-lē-ə, -ˈtēl-yə\
Ott·mar *Ger.* \ˈȯt-ˌmär\
Ott·mer \ˈät-mər\
Ot·to 1 \ˈät-(ˌ)ō\ 2 *Dan., Du., Ger.* \ˈȯ-(ˌ)tō\ 3 *Est., Norw.* \ˈȯt-(ˌ)tō\ 4 *Finn.* \ˈȯt-(ˌ)tȯ\ 5 *Swed.* \ˈȯt-tu̇\
Ot·to·bo·no *Ital.* \ˌōt-tō-ˈbō-nō\
Ot·to·kar *Ger.* \ˈȯ-tō-ˌkär\
Ot·to·line \ˈät-^{ə}l-(ˌ)ēn\
Ot·to·mar *Ger.* \ˈȯ-tō-ˌmär\
Ot·to·ne *Ital.* \ōt-ˈtō-nā\
Ot·to·ri·no *Ital.* \ˌōt-tō-ˈrē-nō\
Ours *Fr.* \ürs\
Ove *Dan.* \ˈō-və\
Ove·ta \ə-ˈvē-tə, ō-\
Ovide *Fr.* \ȯ-vēd\
Ovi·diu *Rom.* \ō-ˈvēd-yü\
Ov·sel *Russ.* \ˈȯf-syil\
Ow·ain *Welsh* \ˈō-ˌ(w)īn\
Ow·en 1 \ˈō-ən\ 2 *Welsh* \ˈō-en\
Ozi·as \ə-ˈzī-əs, ō-\

Paa·vo *Finn.* \ˈpä-ˌvȯ\
Pa·blo *Span.* \ˈpäb̲-lō\
Pa·cia·no *Sp.* \päth-ˈyän-ō, päs-\
Padh·raic, Pád·raic 1 \ˈpä-drig, ˈpät̲h̲-rig\ 2 *Ir. Gael.* \ˈpȯt̲h̲-rig\
Paf·nu·ti *Russ.* \(ˌ)pəf-ˈnü-tyəi\
Pa·ga·no *Ital.* \pä-ˈgä-nō\
Paige \ˈpāj\
Pál *Hung.* \ˈpȧl\
Pal·mel·la \pal-ˈmel-ə\
Palm·er \ˈpäm-ər, ˈpäl-mər\
Pal·mi·ro *Ital.* \päl-ˈmē-rō\
Pam·e·la \ˈpam-ə-lə\
Pam·fi·lo *Ital.* \ˈpäm-fē-(ˌ)lō\
Pam·phile *Fr.* \pä^{n}-fēl, *Can.* -fil\
Pa·na·ges, Pa·na·gis *Mod. Gk.* \ˌpä-nä-ˈyēs\
Pa·na·gi·o·tes *Gk.* \ˌpä-nä-yē-ˈō-tēs\
Pa·na·it *Rom.* \ˌpän-ä-ˈēt\
Pa·na·yo·tis *Mod. Gk.* \ˌpän-ä-ˈyȯ-tēs\
Pan·cho *Span.* \ˈpän-chō\
Pan·coast \ˈpan-ˌkōst, ˈpaŋ-\
Pan·cra·ti·us *Ger.* \pän-ˈkrät-sē-u̇s\
Pan·dol·fo *Ital.* \pän-ˈdȯl-fō\
Pán·fi·lo *Span.* \ˈpäm-fē-lō\
Pang·er·an *Javanese* \ˈpäŋ-(g)er-ˌän\
Pan·ta·lé·on *Fr.* \pä^{n}-tȧ-lō^{n}\
Pan·te·lei·mon *Russ.* \pən-tyil-ˈyä(-ē)-mən\
Pa·oa *Hawaiian* \pä-ˈō-ä\
Pa·o·lo *Ital.* \ˈpä-ō-(ˌ)lō\
Pa·pi·a·nus *Lat.* \ˌpā-pē-ˈā-nəs, ˌpap-ē-\
Pa·pin·i·us *Lat.* \pə-ˈpin-ē-əs\
Pa·pir·i·us *Lat.* \pə-ˈpir-ē-əs, pa-\
Par·fait *Fr.* \pȧr-fe\
Par·is 1 \ˈpar-əs\ 2 *Ital.* \pä-ˈrēs\
Par·ish \ˈpar-ish\
Parks \ˈpärks\
Par·ley \ˈpär-lē\
Par·me·le, -lee \ˈpär-mə-lə, -lē\
Par·mo *Dan.* \ˈpär-(ˌ)mō\
Pas·cal *Fr.* \pȧs-kȧl\
Pas·chal \ˈpas-kəl\
Pas·coe \ˈpas-kō\
Pas·cual *Span.* \päs-ˈkwäl\
Pa·squa·le *Ital.* \päs-ˈkwäl-ā\
Pas·quier *Fr.* \päk-yā\
Pass·more \ˈpas-ˌmō(ə)r, -ˌmȯ(ə)r\
Pas·tor 1 \ˈpas-tər\ 2 *Span.* \päs-ˈtȯr\
Pat \ˈpat\
Patch \ˈpach\
Pa·tience \ˈpā-shən(t)s\
Pa·ton \ˈpāt-^{ə}n\
Pa·trice *Fr.* \pȧ-trēs\
Pa·tri·cia \pə-ˈtrish-ə, -ˈtrē-shə\
Pa·tri·cio *Span.* \pä-ˈtrēth-yo; -ˈtrēs-\
Pat·rick \ˈpa-trik\
Pa·trik *Swed.* \ˈpä-trik\
Pat·yn \ˈpat-^{ə}n\
Paul 1 \ˈpȯl\ 2 *Afrik.* \ˈpō-u̇l\ 3 *Dan., Du., Ger., Norw., Swed.* \ˈpau̇(ə)l\ 4 *Fr.* \pȯl\
Pau·la 1 \ˈpȯ-lə\ 2 *Ger., Span.* \ˈpau̇-lä\ 3 *Port.* \ˈpau̇-lə; -lȧ\
Paule *Fr.* \pōl\
Pau·lin *Fr.* \pȯ-la^{n}\
Pau·li·na *Ital.* \pau̇-ˈlē-nä\
Pau·line 1 \pȯ-ˈlēn\ 2 *Fr.* \pȯ-lēn\ 3 **Pau·li·ne** *Du., Ger.* \pau̇-ˈlē-nə\
Pau·li·nus \pȯ-ˈlī-nəs\
Pau·lus 1 *Afrik.* \ˈpō-u̇l-œs\ 2 *Ger.* \ˈpau̇-lu̇s\ 3 *Lat.* \ˈpȯl-əs\
Pa·vel 1 *Czech* \ˈpȧ-ˌvel, ˈpȧvl\ 2 *Russ.* \ˈpȧv-yil\
Pav·los *Mod. Gk.* \ˈpäv-(ˌ)lȯs\
Pav·lo·vich *Russ.* \(ˌ)pəv-ˈlȯv-yich\
Pa·vol *Slovak* \ˈpȧ-vȯl\
Pay·con \ˈpās-^{ə}n\
Pay·son \ˈpās-^{ə}n\
Paz *Span.* \ˈpäth; ˈpäs\
Peace \ˈpēs\
Peach \ˈpēch\
Pea·cock \ˈpē-ˌkäk\
Pearl \ˈpər(-ə)l\
Pear·sall \ˈpi(ə)r-ˌsȯl, -səl\
Pearse \ˈpi(ə)rs\
Pe·da·ni·us *Lat.* \pi-ˈdā-nē-əs\
Pe·der *Dan.* \ˈpi-t̲h̲ar\
Pe·ders·søn *Norw.* \ˈpäd-ər-sœn\
Pe·do *Lat.* \ˈpē-dō\
Pe·dra·rias *Span.* \pā-ˈt̲h̲rär-yäs\
Pe·dro 1 *Port.* \ˈpā-t̲h̲rü\ 2 *Span.* \ˈpā-t̲h̲rō\
Pef·fer \ˈpef-ər\
Peg \ˈpeg\
Peg·gy \ˈpeg-ē\
Pehr *Finn., Swed.* \ˈper\
Pei·der *Romansh* \ˈpā-der\
Peire *Fr.* \per\
Pé·lage *Fr.* \pā-lȧzh\
Pel·a·ti·ah \ˌpel-ə-ˈtī-ə\
Pe·la·yo *Span.* \pā-ˈlä-yō\
Pe·leg \ˈpē-leg\
Pel·le·gri·no *Ital.* \ˌpāl-lā-ˈgrē-nō\
Pel·le·vé *Fr.* \pel-vā\
Pel·lio·ne \pāl-ˈlyō-nā\
Pe·lot \pə-ˈlōt\
Pem·ber \ˈpem-bər\
Pem·ell \ˈpem-əl\
Pen·al·ver \pen-ˈal-vər\
Pène *Fr.* \pen\
Pe·nel·o·pe \pə-ˈnel-ə-pē\
Pen·ne·fa·ther \ˈpen-i-ˌfät̲h̲-ər\
Pen·rhyn \ˈpen-rin, pen-ˈrin\
Pent·land \ˈpent-lənd\
Pent·ti *Finn.* \ˈpent-tē\
Pep·per·ell \ˈpep-ər-əl\
Pep·pi·no *Ital.* \pāp-ˈpē-nō\
Per *Swed.* \ˈper\
Per·ce·val \ˈpər-sə-vəl\
Per·cey \ˈpər-sē\
Per·ci·val, -vall \ˈpər-sə-vəl\
Per·e·grine \ˈper-ə-grən, -ˌgrēn, -ˌgrin\
Pe·re·gri·nus *Lat.* \ˌper-ə-ˈgrī-nəs, -ˈgrē-\
Pé·rez *Span.* \ˈpā-rāth; -rās\
Pe·ri·no *Ital.* \pā-ˈrē-nō\
Pe·ro *Port.* \ˈpā-rü\
Per·rin \ˈpər-ən\
Per·rott \ˈpər-ət\
Per·ry \ˈper-ē\
Per·si·for \ˈpər-sə-fər, -ˌfȯr\
Per·son \ˈpərs-^{ə}n\
Per·so·nier *Fr.* \per-sȯn-yā\
Per·sonne *Fr.* \per-sȯn\
Pers·son *Swed.* \ˈpers-sȯn\
Pes·cen·nius *Lat.* \pə-ˈsen-ē-əs\
Pe·tar *Serb.-Cr.* \ˈpe-tȧr\
Pe·ter 1 \ˈpēt-ər\ 2 *Dan.* \ˈpi-tər\ 3 *Du., Ger., Norw., Swed.* \ˈpā-tər\ 4 *Hung.* **Pé·ter** \ˈpā-(ˌ)ter\
Pe·ter·field \ˈpē-tər-ˌfēld\
Pe·til·li·us *Lat.* \pə-ˈtil-ē-əs\
Pet·ko *Bulg.* \ˈpet-(ˌ)kȯ\
Petr *Czech.* \ˈpet-ər\
Pe·tra·che *Rom.* \pe-ˈträk-e\
Pe·tre \ˈpē-tər\ 2 *Rom.* \ˈpe-tre\
Pe·tri *Ger.* \ˈpā-trē\
Pe·tri·cei·cu *Rom.* \ˌpe-trē-ˈchā-kü\
Pé·tro·nille *Fr.* \pā-trȯ-nēy\
Pe·tro·ni·us *Lat.* \pə-ˈtrō-nē-əs\
Pe·tros *Mod. Gk.* \ˈpe-(ˌ)trȯs\
Pe·trou *Gk.* \ˈpā-trü\
Pe·tro·vić *Serb.-Cr.* \ˈpe-trȯ-ˌvēt^{y}\
Pe·tro·vich *Russ.* \pyi-ˈtrȯv-yich\
Pe·trov·na *Russ.* \pyi-ˈtrȯv-nə\
Pe·truc·cio *Ital.* \pā-ˈtrüt-chō\
Pe·trus 1 *Du.* \ˈpā-trœs\ 2 *Lat.* \ˈpē-trəs\ 3 *Swed.* \ˈpā-(ˌ)trəs\ 4 *Fr.* **Pé·trus** \pā-trœs\
Pett \ˈpet\
Pet·ter *Norw.* \ˈpet-tər\
Pet·ti·bone \ˈpet-ə-ˌbōn\
Pet·tus \ˈpet-əs\
Pey *Fr.* \pey\
Pe·yo *Bulg.* \ˈpā-ō\
Pey·ton \ˈpāt-^{ə}n\
Phe·lim *Ir. Gael.* \ˈfā-lim\

Phé·lip·peaux *Fr.* \fā-lē-pō\
Phelps \ˈfelps\
Phil \ˈfil\
Phi·lan·der 1 \fə-ˈlan-dər\ 2 *Du., Ger.* \fē-ˈlän-dər\
Phi·la·rète *Fr.* \fē-lȧ-ret\
Phil·brook \ˈfil-bru̇k\
Phi·lé·as *Fr.* \fē-lā-äs\
Phi·le·mon \fə-ˈlē-mən, fī-\
Phi·li·bert *Fr.* \fē-lē-ber\
Phi·li·dor *Fr.* \fē-lē-dȯr\
Phil·ip 1 \ˈfil-əp\ 2 **Phi·lip** *Du.* \ˈfē-ləp\ 3 *Ger.* \ˈfē-lip, ˈfil-ip\ 4 *Swed.* \ˈfē-lip\
Phi·lipp 1 *Ger.* \ˈfē-lip, ˈfil-ip\ 2 *Russ.* \fyil-ˈyēp\ 3 *Swed.* \ˈfē-lip\
Phi·lippe *Fr.* \fē-lēp\
Phi·lip·pine *Fr.* \fē-lē-pēn\ 2 *Ger.* **Phi·lip·pi·ne** \ˌfē-lip-ˈē-nə\
Phi·lip·pus \fi-ˈlip-əs\
Phil·ips 1 \ˈfil-əps\ 2 *Du.* **Phi·lips** \ˈfē-ləps\
Phil·lis \ˈfil-əs\
Phi·lo \ˈfī-(ˌ)lō\
Phi·lo·the·os *Gk.* \fē-lō-ˈthē-ȯs\
Phil·pot \ˈfil-ˌpät\
Phim·is·ter \ˈfim-əs-tər\
Phin·e·as \ˈfin-ē-əs\
Phin·ney \ˈfin-ē\
Pho·cas *Lat.* \ˈfō-kəs\
Phoe·be \ˈfē-bē\
Phoe·bus \ˈfē-bəs\
Phya *Laotian* \ˈpyä\
Phyl·lis \ˈfil-əs\
Pic·co·ni *Ital.* \pēk-ˈkō-nē\
Pick·man \ˈpik-mən\
Pick·stone \ˈpik-ˌstōn\
Pier 1 *Dan.* \ˈpi(ə)r\ 2 *Ital.* \ˈpyer\
Pier·chon *Fr.* \pyer-shō^{n}\
Pier·fran·ces·co *Ital.* \ˌpyer-frän-ˈchās-kō\
Pier·i·na *Ital.* \pyer-ˈē-nä\
Pier·lu·i·gi *Ital.* \ˌpyer-lü-ˈē-jē\
Pie·ro *Ital.* \ˈpyā-rō\
Pier·pont \ˈpi(ə)r-ˌpänt\
Pierre 1 \pē-ˈe(ə)r, ˈpi(ə)r\ 2 *Flem.* \ˈpyer\ 3 *Fr.* \pyer\
Pierre·pont \ˈpi(ə)r-ˌpänt\
Piers \ˈpi(ə)rz\
Pier·son \ˈpi(ə)rs-^{ə}n\
Piet *Du.* \ˈpēt\
Pie·ta·ri *Finn.* \ˈpyet-ˌȧ-rē\
Pie·ter *Du.* \ˈpē-tər\
Pie·ters *Du.* \ˈpē-tərs\
Pie·ter·sen *Du.* \ˈpē-tər-sən\
Pie·tersz *Du.* \ˈpē-tərs\
Pie·ters·zoon *Du.* \ˈpē-tər-sən, -ˌsȯn, -ˌsōn\
Pietr *Du.* \ˈpē-tər\
Pie·tro *Ital.* \ˈpye-trō\
Pi·mi·ku *Jp.* \pē-mē-kü\
Pi·nel *Fr.* \pē-nel\
Pin·ḥas *Heb.* \ˈpēn-k̲əs\
Pink·stone \ˈpiŋk-ˌstōn, -stən\
Pi·no *Ital.* \ˈpē-nō\
Pi·not *Fr.* \pē-nō\
Pio 1 *Ital.* \ˈpē-ō\ 2 *Span.* **Pío** \ˈpē-ō\
Piotr *Pol., Russ.* \ˈpyȯ-tər\
Pi·raud *Fr.* \pē-rō\
Pir·ro *Ital.* \ˈpēr-rō\
Pi·sco·pia *Ital.* \pē-ˈskȯp-yä\
Pi·ta *Maori* \ˈpē-tä\
Pit·ton *Fr.* \pē-tō^{n}\
Pitts \ˈpits\
Pi·us *Lat.* \ˈpī-əs\
Pla·cide *Fr.* \plȧ-sēd\
Plá·ci·do *Span.* \ˈpläth-ē-t̲h̲ō; ˈpläs-\
Plan·ci·a·des *Lat.* \plan-ˈsī-ə-ˌdēz\
Pla·ton *Russ.* \(ˌ)plə-ˈtȯn\
Play·fair \ˈplā-ˌfa(ə)r, -ˌfe(ə)r\
Plea·ter \ˈplēt-ər\
Plim·mon \ˈplim-ən\
Pliny \ˈplin-ē\
Plump·ton \ˈpləm(p)-tən\
Plu·tar·co *Span.* \plü-ˈtär-kō\
Plytt *Norw.* \ˈplœt\
Poer, de la \ˌdel-ə-ˈpu̇r\
Point *Fr.* \pwa^{n}\
Pol 1 *Du.* \ˈpȯl\ 2 *Fr.* \pȯl\
Poles \ˈpōlz\
Po·li·car·po *Span.* \pō-lē-ˈkär-pō\
Po·li·do·ro *Ital.* \ˌpō-lē-ˈdȯr-ō\
Po·ly·carp *Ger.* \ˌpō-lue̅-ˈkärp\
Po·ly·carpe *Fr.* \pȯ-lē-kȧrp\
Pol·y·dore 1 \ˈpäl-i-ˌdō(ə)r\ 2 *Fr.* **Po·ly·dore** \pȯ-lē-dȯr\
Po·ly·karp *Ger.* \ˌpō-lue̅-ˈkärp\
Pom·er·oy \ˈpäm(-ə)-ˌrȯi, ˈpəm(-ə)-ˌrȯi\
Pom·pe·ia *Lat.* \päm-ˈpē-ə\
Pom·pe·ius *Lat.* \päm-ˈpē-əs\
Pom·peo *Ital.* \pōm-ˈpe-ō\
Pom·pi·lio *Span.* \pȯm-ˈpēl-yō\
Pom·po·nio *Ital.* \pōm-ˈpȯn-yō\
Pom·po·ni·us *Lat.* \päm-ˈpō-nē-əs\
Ponce *Fr.* \pō^{n}s\
Pon·cia·no *Span.* \pȯn-ˈthyän-ō; -ˈsyän-\
Pons *Fr.* \pō^{n}s\
Pon·tas *Fr.* \pȯn-täs\
Pon·ti·cus *Lat.* \ˈpänt-i-kəs\
Pon·tius *Lat.* \ˈpän-shəs, ˈpänt-ē-əs\
Pon·tus 1 *Fr.* \pȯ^{n}-tue̅s\ 2 *Swed.* \ˈpȯn-təs\
Pon·tus·son *Swed.* \ˈpän-tu̇s-sȯn\
Po·pil·i·us *Lat.* \pə-ˈpil-ē-əs\
Pó·po·lo *Span.* \ˈpō-pō-lō\
Por·ci·us *Lat.* \ˈpȯr-sh(ē-)əs\
Por·fi·rio *Span.* \pȯr-ˈfēr-yō\
Por·fir·ye·vich *Russ.* \(ˌ)pər-ˈfyēr(-yiv)-ˌyich\
Por·rett \ˈpär-ət\
Por·ter·field \ˈpōr-tər-ˌfēld\
Por·tus \ˈpōr-təs\
Post \ˈpōst\
Pos·tu·mi·us *Lat.* \päs-ˈt(y)ü-mē-əs\
Pot·ter \ˈpät-ər\
Potts \ˈpäts\
Poul *Dan.* \ˈpau̇(ə)l\
Pou·lett \ˈpȯl-ət\
Poult·ney \ˈpōlt-nē\
Pow·el, -ell \ˈpau̇(-ə)l, *Brit also* ˈpō-əl\
Pow·ha·tan \ˌpau̇-ə-ˈtan, pau̇-ˈhat-^{ə}n\
Pow·is \ˈpō-əs, ˈpau̇-\
Poyntz \ˈpȯints\
Prae·co·ni·nus *Lat.* \ˌprē-kə-ˈnī-nəs, ˌprek-ə-\
Pra·ger *Du.* \ˈprȧ-gər\
Praise-god \ˈprāz-ˌgäd\
Pra·kash *Tamil* \prä-ˈkäsh\
Pra·san·no *Bengali* \prȯ-ˈsȯn-nȯ\
Pra·tāp *Hind.* \prə-ˈtäp\
Pra·xe·de *Ital.* \präk-ˈsā-də\
Prá·xe·des *Span.* \ˈpräk-sā-t̲h̲äs\
Pre·serv·ed \prē-ˈzər-vəd\
Pri·mo *Span.* \ˈprē-mō\
Prin·dle \ˈprin-dəl\
Pris·cil·la \prə-ˈsil-ə\
Probe *Fr.* \prȯb\
Pro·by \ˈprō-bē\
Pro·cof·ieff *Russ.* \(ˌ)prə-ˈkȯf-yif\
Pro·co·pi·us *Ger.* \prō-ˈkōp-yu̇s, -ˈkō-pē-u̇s\
Pro·khor *Russ.* \ˈprȯ-k̲ər\
Pro·me·theus \prə-ˈmē-ˌth(y)üs, -thē-əs\
Pros·per 1 \ˈpräs-pər\ 2 *Fr.* \prȯs-per\ 3 *Ger.* \ˈprȯs-pər\
Pros·pe·ro 1 *Ital.* \ˈprȯs-pā-(ˌ)rō\ 2 *Span.* **Prós·pe·ro** \ˈprō-spā-rō\
Pro·teus \ˈprō-ˌt(y)üs, ˈprōt-ē-əs\
Prowse \ˈprau̇s\
Pru·dence \ˈprüd-^{ə}n(t)s\
Pru·den·cio *Span.* \prü-ˈt̲h̲ān-thyō; -syō\
Pru·dens *Du.* \ˈprue̅-dens\
Pru·den·te *Port.* \prü-ˈt̲h̲ā^{n}(n)-tə; -tā\
Pry·or \ˈprī-ər\
Pub·li·us *Lat.* \ˈpəb-lē-əs\
Pue \ˈpyü\
Pun·chard \ˈpən-chərd\
Pur·die \ˈpər-dē\
Pur·don \ˈpərd-^{ə}n\
Pur·dy \ˈpər-dē\
Pur·roy \ˈpər-ˌȯi, ˈpə-ˌrȯi\
Pur·ser \ˈpər-sər\
Pur·ves \ˈpər-vəs\
Pyke \ˈpīk\
Pyne \ˈpīn\
Pyong-hi *Kor.* \pyȯŋ-hē\
Pyotr *Russ.* \ˈpyȯ-tər\
Py·rame *Fr.* \pē-rȧm\

Quayle \ˈkwā(ə)l\
Quen·tin 1 \ˈkwent-^{ə}n\ 2 *Du.* \ˈkvin-tən, ˈkven-; kvin-ˈtin, kven-\ 3 *Fr.* \kä^{n}-ta^{n}\
Quil·ler \ˈkwil-ər\
Quinc·ti·us *Lat.* \ˈkwiŋ(k)-sh(ē-)əs\
Quin·cy \ˈkwin-zē, ˈkwin(t)-sē\
Quin·ten *Du.* \ˈkvin-tən\
Quin·til·i·a·nus \kwin-ˌtil-ē-ˈā-nəs\
Quin·til·ius *Lat.* \kwin-ˈtil-ē-əs, -ˈtil-yəs\
Quin·tin \ˈkwint-^{ə}n\
Quin·ti·no *Ital.* \kwēn-ˈtē-nō\
Quin·ti·us *Lat.* \ˈkwin-sh(ē-)əs, ˈkwint-ē-əs\
Quin·tus \ˈkwin-təs\
Qui·rijn *Du.* \kvē-ˈrīn\
Qui·rin 1 *Fr.* \kē-ra^{n}\ 2 *Ger.* \kvē-ˈrēn\
Qui·ri·no *Ital.* \kwē-ˈrē-nō\
Qui·ri·nus 1 *Du.* \kvē-ˈrē-nœs\ 2 *Ger.* \kvē-ˈrē-nu̇s\

Ra·ban \ˈrā-ˌban\
Rab·ban *Turk.* \räb-ˈbän\
Ra·bin·dra·nath *Bengali* \rə-ˈbēn-drə-ˌnät\
Ra·chel 1 \ˈrā-chəl\ 2 *Du.* \ˈrȧ-ˌk̲el\ 3 *Fr.* \rȧ-shel\
Ra·chev *Bulg.* \ˈrȧ-k̲ef\
Ra·den *Indonesian* \ˈrä-den\
Rad·ko *Bulg.* \ˈrȧt-(ˌ)kō\
Ra·dó *Hung.* \ˈrä-(ˌ)dō\
Ra·do·mir *Serb.-Cr.* \ˈrȧ-dȯ-ˌmēr\
Rae \ˈrā\
Ra·fa·el *Span.* \räf-ä-ˈel\
Ra·fael·szoon *Du.* \ˈräf-el-ˌsōn\
Rafe \ˈrāf\
Ra·felsz *Du.* \ˈrȧ-ˌfel(t)s\
Raf·fa·e·le *Ital.* \ˌräf-fä-ˈel-ā\
Raf·fa·el·lo *Ital.* \ˌräf-fä-ˈel-lō\
Rag·nar *Swed.* \ˈrȧŋ-när\
Ra·hel *Ger.* \ˈrä-(ˌ)hel, -əl\
Raikes \ˈrāks\
Rail·ton \ˈrā(ə)lt-^{ə}n\
Rai·mond *Fr.* \rā-mō^{n}\
Rai·mund *Ger.* \ˈrī-(ˌ)mu̇nt\
Rai·mun·do 1 *Port.* \rī-ˈmü^{n}(n)-dü\ 2 *Span.* \rī-ˈmün-dō\

Rai·mun·dus *Lat.* \rī-'mən-dəs\
Raine \'rān\
Rai·ner *Du., Ger.* \'rī-nər\
Rai·ney \'rā-nē\
Rains·ford \'rānz-fərd\
Ra·ïs·sa *Fr.* \rà-ē-sà\
Ra·jen·dra *Hind.* \rä-'jān-drə\
Ralls \'rȯlz\
Ralph 1 \'ralf, *Brit also* 'rāf\ 2 *Ger.* \'rälf\
Ra·ma·lho *Port.* \rà-'màl-yō\
Ram·chan·dra *Marathi* \rəm-'chən-drə\
Ra·mí·rez *Span.* \rä-'mē-rāth; -rēs\
Ram·ji *Marathi* \'räm-jē\
Ram·mo·han *Bengali* \'räm-mō-hän\
Ra·món *Span.* \rä-'mȯn\
Ram·say \'ram-zē\
Ran·ald \'ran-^{ə}ld\
Ran·dal, -dall, -dle \'ran-d^{ə}l\
Ran·dolph \'ran-ˌdälf\
Ran·don *Fr.* \rä^{n}-dō^{n}\
Ran·fur·ly \'ran-fər-lē\
Ra·nie·ro *Ital.* \rän-'yer-ō\
Ran·jan *Bengali* \'rən-jən\
Ran·ken \'raŋ-kən\
Ra·na *Hind.* \'rä-nä\
Rann \'ran\
Ran·nulf \'ran-əlf\
Rans·ford \'rans-fərd\
Ra·nuc·cio *Ital.* \rä-'nüt-chō\
Ra·nulf, -nulph \'rä-nəlf, 'ran-əlf\
Rao *Marathi* \'raù\
Ra·oul 1 *Fr.* \rà-ül\ 2 *Ger., Span.* \rä-'ül\
Ra·pha·el 1 \'raf-ē-əl, 'rā-fē-\ 2 *Fr.* \rà-fà-el\ 3 *Ger.* \'rä-fä-(ˌ)el\ 4 **Ra·phael** *Du.* \'rà-ˌfel\
Rash \'rash\
Ra·shīd *Arab.* \ra-'shēd\
Ras·mus *Dan., Norw.* \'räs-mùs\
Ra·tan·ji *Bengali* \'rə-tən-'jē\
Rat·cliffe \'rat-ˌklif\
Rath·bone \'rath-ˌbōn, -bən\
Rat·tray \'rat-rā\
Ra·úl *Span.* \rä-'ül\
Ra·ven \'rā-vən\
Raw·don \'rȯd-^{ə}n\
Raw·lins \'rȯ-lənz\
Raw·son \'rȯs-^{ə}n\
Ray \'rā\
Ray·mond 1 \'rā-mənd\ 2 *Fr.* \re-mō^{n}\
Ray·mund *Ger.* \'rī-(ˌ)mùnt\
Ray·ner \'rā-nər\
Raynes \'rānz\
Raynes·ford, Rayns·ford \'rānz-fərd\
Ra·zan *Jp.* \rä-zän\
Ready \'red-ē\
Reave·ley \'rēv-lē\
Re·ba \'rē-bə\
Re·bec·ca, Re·bek·ah \ri-'bek-ə\
Re·cai·za·de *Turk.* \ˌrā-kī-'zäd-ə\
Red·cliffe \'red-klif\
Redd \'red\
Red·de·ford \'red-(ə-)fərd\
Red·den \'red-^{ə}n\
Red·ding \'red-iŋ\
Rede \'rēd\
Red·fern \'red-(ˌ)fərn\
Red·man \'red-mən\
Red·vers \'red-vərz\
Rees \'rēs\
Re·gi·na \rā-'jē-nä\
Reg·i·nald \'rej-ən-^{ə}ld\
Reg·i·nal·do \ˌrej-i-'nal-(ˌ)dō\
Ré·gis *Fr.* \rā-zhēs\
Re·gnault *Fr.* \rən-yō\
Reg·nier *Du.* \rī-'nē(ə)r\
Rei·gnier \'rān-yā\
Rei·ji·ro *Jp.* \rā-jē-rō\
Reil·ly \'rī-lē\
Rei·na *Span.* \'rā-nä\
Rei·naud *Fr.* \rə-nō\
Rein·hard *Ger.* \'rīn-ˌhärt\
Rein·hart *Du.* \'rīn-ˌ, härt\
Rein·hold 1 \'rīn-ˌhōld\ 2 *Ger.* \'rīn-ˌhōlt\
Rei·nier *Du.* \rī-'nē(ə)r\
Rem·bert *Du., Ger.* \'rem-bərt\
Rem·ber·tus *Lat.* \rem-'bər-təs\
Rem·brandt \'rem-ˌbrant\
Re·mi *Fr.* \rā-mē\
Rem·ick \'rem-ik\
Re·mi·gio *Span.* \rā-'mēk-yō\
Re·mi·gi·us *Ger.* \rā-'mēg-yùs, -'mē-gē-ùs\
Rem·sen \'rem(p)-sən, 'rem-zən\
Re·mus *Ger.* \'rā-mùs\
Ré·my *Fr.* \rā-mē\
Re·na \'rē-nə\
Re·na·to \rā-'nä-tō\
Re·na·tus *Lat.* \rə-'nā-təs\
Re·naud *Fr.* \rə-nō\
Ren·del \'ren-d^{ə}l\
Re·né 1 *Eng., Ger.* \rə-'nā\ 2 *Fr.* \rə-nā\
Re·née *Fr.* \rə-nā\
Renn \'ren\
Ren·nie \'ren-ē\
Rens·se·laer \'ren(t)-sə-ˌli(ə)r\
Reres·by \'ri(ə)rz-bē\
Re·şat *Turk.* \rā-'shät\
Res·sam *Turk.* \res-'äm\
Reu·ben \'rü-bən\
Rev·er·dy \'rev-ərd-ē\
Re·wi \'rā-wē\
Rex \'reks\
Rex·ford \'reks-fərd\
Rey·nal·do *Span.* \rā-'näl-dō\
Rey·ner *Ger.* \'rī-nər\
Reyn·old \'ren-^{ə}ld\
Rhea \'rā, 'rē, 'rē-ə\
Rhijn·vis *Du.* \'rīn-vəs\
Rhine·land·er \'rīn-ˌlan-dər\
Rhoades \'rōdz\
Rho·da \'rōd-ə\
Rhys \'rēs\
Ri·ad *Arab.* \rē-'äd\
Ri·car·da *Ger.* \rē-'kär-dä\
Ri·car·do *Span.* \rē-'kär-thō\
Ric·car·do 1 \rik-'ärd-(ˌ)ō\ 2 *Ital.* \rēk-'kär-dō\
Ric·ciot·ti *Ital.* \rēt-'chȯt-tē\
Rich·ard 1 \'rich-ərd\ 2 **Ri·chard** *Du.* \'rē-ˌshärt\ 3 *Fr.* \rē-shàr\ 4 *Ger.* \'rik-ˌärt\
Rich·ard·son \'rich-ərd-sən\
Rich·ford \'rich-fərd\
Rich·mal \'rich-məl\
Rick·art *Swed.* \'rik-ˌárt\
Rick·et·son \'rik-ət-sən\
Rick·man \'rik-mən\
Ri·da \'rēd-ə\
Ridge·ly \'rij-lē\
Ridge·way, Ridg·way \'rij-ˌwā\
Ri·dol·fo *Ital.* \rē-'dȯl-fō\
Rig·nall \'rig-nəl\
Ri·i·chi *Jp.* \rē-ē-chē\
Ri·kard *Norw.* \'rik-ˌkärd, -ˌkärt\
Rik·yu *Jp.* \rik-yù\
Ri·nal·do 1 \rə-'nal-(ˌ)dō\ 2 *Ital.* \rē-'näl-dō\
Ring \'riŋ\
Ring·gold \'riŋ-ˌgōld\
Rin·ta·rō *Jp.* \rēn-tär-ō\
Ris·to *Finn.* \'ris-ˌtȯ\
Rit·ten·house \'rit-^{ə}n-ˌhaùs\
Rit·ter \'rit-ər\
Ri·vière *Fr.* \rēv-yer\
Ri·za·e·mon *Jp.* \rē-zä-em-ōn\
Ri·zos *Mod. Gk.* \'rē-(ˌ)zȯs\
Roach \'rōch\
Ro·ald *Norw.* \'rō-äl\
Roark \'rȯ(ə)rk, 'rō(ə)rk\
Ro·bard \'rō-ˌbärd\
Rob·bins \'räb-ənz\
Ro·be·na \rō-'bē-nə\
Rob·ert 1 \'räb-ərt\ 2 **Ro·bert** *Dan., Ger.* \'rō-ˌbert\ 3 *Du.* \'rȯb-ərt\ 4 *Finn.* \'rȯ-ˌbert\ 5 *Fr.* \rȯ-ber\ 6 *Russ.* \(ˌ)rəb-'yert, 'rȯb-yirt\ 7 *Swed.* \'rȯb-bərt\
Ro·ber·to 1 *Ital.* \rō-'ber-tō\ 2 *Span.* \rō-'ber-tō\
Rob·ert·son \'räb-ərt-sən\
Ro·bey, Ro·bie \'rō-bē\
Rob·ley \'räb-lē\
Rob·recht *Du.* \'rȯb-ˌrekt\
Ro·bun *Jp.* \rō-bùn\
Roch *Fr.* \rȯk\
Roche 1 \'rōch\ 2 *Fr.* \rȯsh\
Ro·che·gu·ne *Dan.* \'rō-kə-gü-nə\
Ro·chus *Ger.* \'rȯk-ùs\
Rock·hill \'räk-ˌhil\
Rock·ing·ham \'räk-iŋ-əm, *US also* -iŋ-ˌham\
Rock·wood \'räk-ˌwùd\
Rocky \'räk-ē\
Ro·den \'rōd-^{ə}n\
Rod·er·ic \'räd-ər-ik, 'räd-rik\
Ro·de·rich *Ger.* \'rō-də-(ˌ)rik\
Rod·er·i·go \räd-'rē-gō\
Ro·di·on *Russ.* \rəd-yi-'ȯn\
Rod·ney \'räd-nē\
Ro·dol·fo 1 *Ital.* \rō-'dȯl-fō\ 2 *Span.* \rō-'thȯl-fō\
Ro·dolphe *Fr.* \rȯ-dȯlf\
Ro·dol·pho *Ital.* \rō-'dȯl-fō\
Ro·dol·phus 1 *Du.* \rō-'dȯl-fœs\ 2 *Lat.* \rō-'däl-fəs\
Rod·ri·go 1 \räd-'rē-(ˌ)gō\ 2 **Ro·dri·go** *Ital.* \rō-'drē-gō\ 3 *Span.* \rō-'thrē-gō\
Ro·drigue *Fr.* \rȯ-drēg\
Ro·drí·guez *Span.* \rō-'thrē-gāth; -gās\
Rod·well \'räd-ˌwel, -wəl\
Roe·lof *Du.* \'rü-ˌlȯf\
Roe·mer *Du.* \'rü-mər\
Rof·fey \'räf-ē\
Rog·er 1 \'räj-ər\ 2 *Fr.* \rȯ-zhā\
Ro·gier *Du.* \rō-'gē(ə)r\
Ro·han *Jp.* \rō-hän\
Rō·ka *Jp.* \rō-kä\
Ro·ku·ya *Jp.* \rō-kù-yä\
Ro·land 1 \'rō-lənd\ 2 *Fr.* \rȯ-lä^{n}\ 3 *Ger.* \'rō-ˌlänt\
Rolf \'rälf\
Rol·lin \'räl-ən\
Ro·lin·da \rō-'lin-də\
Rol·lin·son \'räl-ən-sən\
Rol·lo \'räl-(ˌ)ō\
Ro·ma \'rō-mə\
Ro·main *Fr.* \rȯ-ma^{n}\
Ro·maine \rō-'mān\
Ro·man 1 *Pol.* \'rȯ-ˌmán\ 2 *Russ.* \(ˌ)rə-'mán\
Ro·ma·no·vich *Russ.* \(ˌ)rə-'mán(-əv)-ˌyich\
Ro·ma·nov·na *Russ.* \(ˌ)rə-'mán-əv-nə\
Ro·man·za \rō-'man-zə\
Ro·mer \'rō-mər\
Ro·me·ro *Span.* \rō-'mā-rō\
Ro·meyn \rō-'mān, -'mīn\
Rom·ney \'räm-nē, 'rəm-\
Ro·mo·al·do *Ital.* \ˌrō-mō-'äl-dō\
Ro·mo·lo *Ital.* \'rō-mō-(ˌ)lō\
Ro·mu·ald *Ger.* \'rō-mü-ˌält\
Ró·mu·lo *Span.* \'rō-mü-lō\
Rom·u·lus \'räm-yə-ləs\
Ron·ald 1 \'rän-^{ə}ld\ 2 **Ro·nald** *Norw.* \'rō-ˌnäl(d)\ 3 *Port.* \rü-'näld\
Ro·nayne \rō-'nān\
Rood \'rüd\
Rookes \'rùks\

Roo·ney \'rü-nē\
Root \'rüt\
Rootes \'rüts\
Ro·que *Span.* \'rō-kā\
Ro·ry \'rō(ə)r-ē, 'rȯ(ə)r-ē\
Ro·sa 1 \'rō-zə\ 2 *Fr.* \rō-zá\ 3 *Ger.* \'rō-zä\ 4 *Ital.* \'rȯ-zä\ 5 *Span.* \'rō-sä\
Ros·a·belle \'räz-ə-,bel, 'rō-zə-\
Ro·sal·ba *Ital.* \rō-'zäl-bä\
Ro·sa·lía *Span.* \rō-zä-'lē-ä\
Ro·sa·lie 1 \'räz-(ə-)lē, 'rōz-\ 2 *Fr.* \rō-zá-lē\
Ros·a·lind \'räz-(ə-)lind, 'rōz-, -,līnd\
Ros·a·mond, -mund \'räz-(ə-)mənd, 'rōz-\
Ro·san·na \rō-'zan-ə\
Ros·coe \'räs-(,)kō\
Rose 1 \'rōz\ 2 *Fr.* \rōz\
Rose·monde *Fr.* \rōz-mōⁿd\
Ro·sen·kro·ne *Norw.* \'rō-zən-,krō-nə\
Rose·well \'rōz-,wel, -wəl\
Ro·si·ka *Hung.* \'rȯ-si-kä\
Ro·si·na \rō-'zē-nə\
Ro·sine *Fr.* \rō-zēn\
Ro·si·ta \rō-'zēt-ə\
Ros·set·ter \'räs-ət-ər\
Ros·si·ter \'räs-ət-ər\
Ross·keen \'räs-,kēn\
Ross·lyn \'räs-lən\
Ros·so *Ital.* \'rȯs-sō\
Ros·trev·or \räs-'trev-ər\
Ros·well \'räz-,wel, -wəl\
Roun·dell \'raůn-dəl, raůn-'del\
Row·an \'rō-,an\
Rowe \'rō\
Row·land \'rō-lənd\
Row·ley \'raů-lē, 'rō-\
Rox·burgh \'räks-b(ə-)rə\
Rox·ey \'räk-sē\
Roy \'rȯi\
Roy·al, Roy·all \'rȯi(-ə)l\
Royds \'rȯidz\
Ru·adh *Scot.* \'rü-äth\
Ru·aidh·ri *Ir. Gael.* \'rü-ə-rē\
Ru·bén *Span.* \rü-'bān\
Ru·bens \'rü-bənz\
Ru·bert \'rü-bərt\
Ru·bin \'rü-bən\
Ru·by \'rü-bē\
Ruck·er \'rək-ər\
Rudd \'rəd\
Rü·di·ger *Ger.* \'rue-di-gər\
Rud·jer *Serb.-Cr.* \'rüd-yer\
Ru·dolf 1 \'rü-,dälf\ 2 *Czech., Finn.* \'rüd-,ȯlf\ 3 *Du.* \'rue-dȯlf\ 4 *Ger., Swed.* \'rü-,dȯlf\
Ru·dolph 1 \'rü-,dälf\ 2 *Du.* \'rue-,dȯlf\ 3 *Ger., Norw.* \'rü-,dȯlf\
Ru·dulph \'rü-dəlf\
Rud·yard \'rəd-yərd\
Ru·fi·no *Span.* \rü-'fē-nō\
Ru·fus \'rü-fəs\
Rug·ge·ro, Rug·gie·ro *Ital.* \rüd-'jer-ō\
Rug·gles \'rəg-əlz\
Rug·las \'rüg-ləs\
Ru·iz *Span.* \rü-'ēth; -'ēs\
Rulffs \'rulfs\
Run·ci·man \'rən-sə-mən\
Run·nell \'rən-ᵊl\
Ru·pert 1 \'rü-pərt\ 2 *Ger.* \'rü-,pert\ 3 *Swed.* \'rü-pərt\
Ru·per·to *Span.* \rü-'per-tō\
Ru·ry \'rů(ə)r-ē\
Rush \'rəsh\
Rush·di *Turk.* \ruesh-'tue\
Rush·more \'rəsh-,mō(ə)r, -,mȯ(ə)r\
Rush·ton \'rəsh-tən\
Rush·worth \'rəsh-,wərth\
Russ \'rəs\
Rus·sa \'rəs-ə\
Rus·sel, Rus·sell \'rəs-əl\
Rüş·tü *Turk.* \ruesh-'tue\
Rut·ger *Du.* \'rut-gər\
Ruth \'rüth\
Ru·til·i·us *Lat.* \rü-'til-ē-əs\
Rut·land \'rət-lənd\
Rut·sen \'rət-sən\
Rut·ter \'rət-ər\
Ruy 1 *Port.* \'rü-ē\ 2 *Span.* \rü-'ē\
Ry·ley \'rī-lē\
Ry·mer \'rī-mər\
Ryo·kei *Jp.* \ryō-kā\
Ry·ō·ma *Jp.* \rē-ō-mä\
Ry·ong *Kor.* \rē-ȯŋ\
Ryō·su·ke *Jp.* \rē-ō-sůk-e\
Rys·to *Finn.* \'rues-,tȯ\
Ry·szard *Pol.* \'rish-ärd\
Ryū·no·su·ke *Jp.* \rē-ůn-ō-sůk-e\

Sa·bato \sə-'bat-(,)ō\
Sab·ba·ti·us *Lat.* \sə-'bā-sh(ē-)əs\
Sa·bès *Fr.* \sá-bes\
Sa·bine 1 \'sab-ən\ 2 *Fr.* \sá-bēn\
Sa·bi·nus *Lat.* \sə-'bī-nəs\
Sa·bu·ro *Jp.* \sä-bů-rō\
Sa·cha *Fr.* \sá-shá\
Saʿd *Arab.* \'sád\
Sa·daie *Jp.* \sä-dī-e\
Sa·da·ki·chi *Jp.* \sä-dä-kē-chē\
Sa·da·na·ru *Jp.* \sä-dä-nä-rů\
Sa·da·no·bu *Jp.* \sä-dä-nō-bů\
Sa·dao *Jp.* \sä-dä-ō\
Ṣā·deq *Iran.* \'shä-dek\
Sa·di *Fr.* \sá-dē\
Saf·ford \'saf-ərd\
Sa·gesse *Fr.* \sá-zhes\
Sai·ka·ku *Jp.* \sī-kä-kü\
Saint Clair, St. Clair, StClair \sānt-'kla(ə)r, -'kle(ə)r, *esp Brit* 'siŋ-,, 'sin-,\
St. Hill \sānt-'hil\
Saint John \sānt-'jän, *esp Brit* 'sin-jən\
St. Leg·er \sānt-'lej-ər, *Brit also* 'sel-ən-jər\
St. Loe \sānt-'lü\
Sait *Turk.* \'sīt\
Sa·ka·ri *Finn.* \'sák-,á-rē\
Sa·ku·ta·rō *Jp.* \sä-ků-tä-rō\
Sa·ku·zō *Jp.* \sä-kůz-ō\
Ṣa·lāḥ *Arab.* \sá-'läk\
Sa·la·ma·nes *Gk.* \sä-lä-'mä-nēs\
Sal·bi·go·ton *Fr.* \sál-bē-gȯ-tōⁿ\
Sa·le·ius *Lat.* \sə-'lē-əs\
Sa·lem \'sā-ləm\
Ṣā·liḥ *Arab.* \'sä-lēk\
Sa·lin·guer·ra *Ital.* \,sä-lēŋ-'gwer-rä\
Sal·lie \'sal-ē\
Sal·ly 1 \'sal-ē\ 2 *Finn.* \'sál-lē\
Sal·mon 1 \'sal-mən\ 2 *Fr.* \sál-mōⁿ\
Sa·lo·me \sə-'lō-mē\
Sa·lo·mo *Ger.* \'zäl-ō-(,)mō\
Sa·lo·mon 1 *Du.* \'sá-lō-,mȯn\ 2 *Fr.* \sá-lȯ-mōⁿ\ 3 *Ger.* \'zä-lō-,mȯn\ 4 *Swed.* \'sä-lü-,mȯn\
Sa·lo·mo·ne *Ital.* \,säl-ō-'mō-nā\
Sal·ter \'sȯl-tər\
Sal·ton·stall \'sȯlt-ᵊn-,stȯl\
Sa·lud *Span.* \sä-'lüth\
Sa·lus·tia·no *Span.* \säl-üs-'tyän-ō\
Sal·va·dor *Span.* \säl-vä-'thȯr\
Sal·va·tor *Ital.* \,säl-vä-'tōr\
Salz·mann *Czech* \'sálz-mán\
Sam \'sam\
Sa·mi *Turk.* \sä-'mē\
Sa·moy·lo·vich *Russ.* \sə-(,)məi-'lȯv-,yich\
Samp·son \'sam(p)-sən\
Sam·son 1 \'sam(p)-sən\ 2 *Ger.* \'zäm-,zȯn\
Sam·u·el 1 \'sam-yə(-wə)l\ 2 **Sa·mu·el** *Du.* \'sá-mue-,el\ 3 *Fr.* \sá-mwʸel\ 4 *Ger.* \'zäm-ü-,el\ 5 *Pol.* \sá-'mü-el\ 6 *Span.* \säm-'wel\
Sa·mu·il *Russ.* \səm-ü-'ēl\
Sa·mu·i·lo·vich *Russ.* \sə-mü-'ēl(-əv)-,yich\
Sán·chez *Span.* \'sän-chāth; -chās\
Sand·field \'san(d)-fēld\
Sand·ford \'san(d)-fərd\
Sán·dor *Hung., Serb.-Cr.* \'shán-dȯr\
San·dro *Ital.* \'sän-drō\
Sands \'sandz\
San·du *Rom.* \'sän-dü\
Sa·ne·no·ri *Jp.* \sä-nen-ōr-ē\
Sa·ne·to·mi *Jp.* \sä-ne-tō-mē\
San·ford \'san-fərd\
Sang-cha *Kor.* \säŋ-jä\
San·ra·ku *Jp.* \sän-räk-ů\
Sant *Punjabi* \'sənt\
San·ta *Ital., Span.* \'sän-tä\
San·tes *Ital.* \'sän-tās\
San·tia·go *Span.* \sän-'tyäg-ō\
San·to·rio *Ital.* \sän-'tȯr-yō\
San·tos *Span.* \'sän-tōs\
Sap·ping·ton \'sap-iŋ-tən\
Sa·ra, Sa·rah 1 \'ser-ə, 'sar-ə, 'sā-rə\ 2 *Fr.* \sá-rá\
Sar·dar *Afghan* \'sär-,där\
Sar·kis *Armenian* \sär-'kēs\
Sar·mien·to *Span.* \särm-'yān-tō\
Sa·ro·ji·ni *Bengali* \sə-'rō-jin-ē\
Sars·field \'särs-fēld\
Sar·ve·pal·li *Hind.* \'sər-və-'pəl-lē\
Sas·kia *Du.* \'säs-kē-á\
Sa·tyen·dra *Bengali* \sȯ-'tyān-drȯ\
Saul \'sȯl\
Saun·ders \'sȯn-dərz, 'sän-\
Sau·ter *Fr.* \sō-ter\
Sa·va *Serb.-Cr.* \'sá-vá\
Sa·ve·rio *Ital.* \sä-'ver-yō\
Sa·vi·nien *Fr.* \sá-vēn-yaⁿ\
Sav·vich *Russ.* \'sáv-vyich\
Saw·don \'sȯd-ᵊn\
Saw·yer \'sȯ-yər, 'sȯi-ər\
Sax \'saks\
Sca·ra·muc·cia *Ital.* \,skär-ä-'müt-chä\
Scar·face \'skär-,fās\
Scar·pet·ta *Ital.* \skär-'pet-tä\
Sca·ve·ni·us *Dan.* \ská-'vi-nē-ůs\
Scaw·en \'skō-ən\
Schack *Dan.* \'shák\
Schaw \'shȯ\
Schel·te *Du.* \'skel-tə\
Schley \'s(h)lī\
School·craft \'skül-,kraft\
Schrö·der \'shrə(r)d-ər, 'shrōd-\
Schult·heiss *Ger.* \'shůlt-,hīs\
Schu·ma·cher *Dan.* \'shü-,mák-ər\
Schwenck \'shweŋk\
Sciar·ra *Ital.* \'shär-rä\
Sci·pion *Fr.* \sēp-yōⁿ\
Sci·pio·ne *Ital.* \shē-'pyō-nā\
Sco·bey \'skō-bē\
Scott \'skät\
Sco·tus *Lat.* \'skōt-əs\
Scri·bo·ni·us *Lat.* \skri-'bō-nē-əs\
Scull \'skəl\
Sea·ly \'sē-lē\

Sea·man \'sē-mən\
Sean, Seán *Ir. Gael.* \'shȯn, 'shän\
Sear·gent \'sär-jənt\
Sea·ton \'sēt-ᵊn\
Sea·ver \'sē-vər\
Sea·vey \'sē-vē\
Se·ba \'sē-bə\
Se·bald 1 *Du.* \'sā-ˌbält\ 2 *Ger.* \'zā-ˌbält\
Se·bas·tian 1 \sə-'bas-chən\ 2 **Se·bas·ti·an** *Du., Norw.* \sā-'bäs-tē-än\ 3 *Ger.* \zā-'bäs-tyän, -tē-än\ 4 *Pol.* \se-'bás-tyán\ 5 *Span.* **Se·bas·tián** \sā-b̲äs-'tyän\
Se·bas·tia·no *Ital.* \ˌsā-bäs-'tyän-ō\
Se·bas·ti·a·nus *Lat.* \sə-ˌbas-chē-'ā-nəs\
Se·bas·tião *Port.* \sə-bəsh-'tyau̇ⁿ; sā-bás-\
Sé·bas·tien *Fr.* \sā-bás-tyaⁿ\
Se·bas·tyan *Pol.* \se-'bás-tyán\
Sech·ler \'sek-lər\
Seck·el \'sek-əl\
See·bohm \'sē-ˌbōm\
Sef·ton \'sef-tən\
Se·gel·cke *Norw.* \'sā-gəl-kə\
Sei·hin *Jp.* \sā-hin\
Sei·hō *Jp.* \sā-hō\
Sei·i·chi *Jp.* \sā-ē-chē\
Sei·i·ti·ro *Jp.* \sā-ē-tē-rō\
Sei·ji *Jp.* \sā-jē\
Sei·ki *Jp.* \sā-kē\
Sei·sa·ku *Jp.* \sā-säk-ü\
Sei·shi·ro *Jp.* \sā-shē-rō\
Sei·shi·sai *Jp.* \sā-shē-sī\
Se·lah \'sē-lə\
Sel·by \'sel-bē\
Se·lim 1 \sē-ləm\ 2 *Finn.* \'sā-lim\
Se·li·na \sə-'lē-nə, -'lī-nə\
Sell \'sel\
Sel·lif *Swed.* \'sel-lif\
Sel·ma *Swed.* \'sel-má\
Sel·wyn \'sel-wən\
Sem *Ital.* \'sem\
Sem·pro·ni·us *Lat.* \sem-'prō-nē-əs\
Şem·sed·din *Turk.* \shem-sed-'dēn\
Se·myon *Russ.* \syim-'yȯn\
Se·myo·no·vich *Russ.* \syim-'yȯn(-əv)-ˌyich\
Seng·stacke \'seŋ-ˌstak\
Sen·ji·ro *Jp.* \sen-jē-rō\
Sen·ju·ro *Jp.* \sen-jü-rō\
Sep·ti·mia *Lat.* \sep-'tim-ē-ə\
Sep·tim·i·us \sep-'tim-ē-əs\
Sep·ti·mus \'sep-tə-məs\
Se·ra·fín *Span.* \sā-rä-'fēn\
Se·ra·fi·no *Ital.* \ˌsā-rä-'fē-nō\
Se·raph *Ger.* \'zā-ˌräf\
Sé·ra·phin *Fr.* \sā-rá-faⁿ\
Sé·ra·phine *Fr.* \sā-rá-fēn\
Şer·ban *Rom.* \sher-'bän\
Se·re·no \sə-'rē-nō\
Serge *Fr.* \serzh\
Ser·geant \'sär-jənt\
Ser·gey, -gei *Russ.* \syir-'gyā(-ē)\
Ser·ge·ye·vich *Russ.* \syir-'gyā(-yiv)-ˌyich\
Ser·gio *Span.* \'ser-k̲yō\
Ser·vais *Fr.* \ser-ve\
Ser·vil·ius *Lat.* \sər-'vil-ē-əs, -'vil-yəs\
Ser·vi·us *Lat.* \'sər-vē-əs\
Ses·sions \'sesh-ənz\
Seth 1 \'seth\ 2 *Ger.* \'zāt\
Se·thus *Lat.* \'sē-thəs\
Se·ton \'sēt-ᵊn\
Seu·mas *Ir. Gael.* \'shā-məs\
Seu·se *Ger.* \'zȯi-zə\
Se·ve·rin 1 *Norw.* \ˌsev-ə-'rēn\ 2 *Fr.* **Sé·ve·rin** \sāv-raⁿ\
Se·ve·ri·no·vich *Russ.* \syiv-yir-'yēn(-əv)-ˌyich\
Sev·er·i·nus *Lat.* \ˌsev-ə-'rī-nəs\
Se·ve·ro *Span.* \sā-'b̲ā-rō\
Sew·all \'sü-əl\
Sew·ard \'sü-ərd, 'su̇(ə)rd, *Brit also* 'sē-wərd\
Sew·ell \'sü-əl\
Se·we·ryn *Pol.* \se-'ver-in\
Sex·tus *Lat.* \'sek-stəs\
Sfor·za *Ital.* \'sfȯrt-sä\
Shack·er·ley \'shak-ər-lē\
Sha·drach \'shā-ˌdrak\
Shad·worth \'shad-(ˌ)wərth\
Shae·mas *Ir. Gael.* \'shā-məs\
Shai·ler \'shā-lər\
Shak·er·ley \'shak-ər-lē\
Shake·speare \'shāk-ˌspi(ə)r\
Sha·ler \'shā-lər\
Sha·lom *Heb.* \shä-'lōm\
Shane *Ir. Gael.* \'shān\
Shan·kar *Hind.* \'shəŋ-kər\
Shan·non \'shan-ən\
Sha·ra·ku *Jp.* \shär-ä-ku̇\
Shar·on \'shar-ən, 'sher-\
Shar·tle \shärt-ᵊl\
Shay \'shā\
Sheaf \'shēf\
Shed·den \'shed-ᵊn\
She·he·ri·ar·ji *Parsi* \shə-hā-rē-'är-jē\
Shei·la \'shē-lə\
Shel·by \'shel-bē\
Shel·don \'sheld-ᵊn\
Shel·ford \'shel-fərd\
Shel·ton \'shelt-ᵊn\
Shem·tob, Shem Tov *Heb.* \shem-'tōb̲, -'tōv\
Shep·ard \'shep-ərd\
Sher·ard \'sher-ərd, -ˌärd\
Sher·burne \'shər-bərn\
Sher·iff \'sher-əf\
Sher·man \'sher-mən\
Sher·ry \'sher-ē\
Sher·win \'sher-wən\
Sher·wood \'shər-wu̇d *also* 'she(ə)r-\
Shi·ba·sa·bu·ro *Jp.* \shē-bä-sä-bu̇-rō\
Shi·dō *Jp.* \shē-dō\
Shield \'shē(ə)ld\
Shields \'shē(ə)ldz\
Shi·ge·hi·de *Jp.* \shē-ge-hē-de\
Shi·gen·a·re *Jp.* \shē-gen-ä-rē\
Shi·ge·no·bu *Jp.* \shē-gen-ō-bu̇\
Shi·ge·no·ri *Jp.* \shē-gen-ō-rē\
Shi·ge·ru *Jp.* \shē-ger-ü\
Shi·ge·ta·ro *Jp.* \shē-ge-tä-rō\
Shi·ge·yu·ki *Jp.* \shē-ge-yu̇k-ē\
Shi·hei *Jp.* \shē-hā\
Shi·ki *Jp.* \shē-kē\
Shi·ki·bu *Jp.* \shē-kē-bu̇\
Shi·kō *Jp.* \shē-kō\
Shi·ma·zu *Jp.* \shē-mä-zu̇\
Shi·mei *Jp.* \shē-mā\
Shim·pei \shēm-pā\
Shin·gen *Jp.* \shēn-gen\
Shin·i·chi·ro *Jp.* \shēn-ē-chē-rō\
Shin·sa·ku *Jp.* \shin-sä-ku̇\
Shin·su·ke *Jp.* \shēn-su̇k-e\
Ship·ley \'ship-lē\
Shir *Turk.* \'shēr\
Shir·ley \'shər-lē\
Shi·ro *Jp.* \shē-rō\
Shive·ly \'shīv-lē\
Shlo·mo \'shlō-(ˌ)mō\
Sho·bal \'shō-bəl\
Sho·ē·ki *Jp.* \shō-ek-ē\
Shō·ga *Jp.* \shō-gä\
Shō·ha·ku *Jp.* \shō-hä-ku̇\
Shō·ji·rō *Jp.* \shō-jē-rō\
Shō·jō *Jp.* \shō-jō\
Sho·lem *Yiddish* \'shō-lem\
Sho·lom *Heb.* \'shȯ-ləm\
Shol·to \'shȯl-(ˌ)tō\
Shō·na·gon *Jp.* \shō-nä-gōn\
Shō·san *Jp.* \shō-sän\
Shō·se·tsu *Jp.* \shō-set-su̇\
Shō·yō *Jp.* \shō-yō\
Shō·zan *Jp.* \shō-zän\
Shu·ji *Jp.* \shu̇j-ē\
Shū·kei *Jp.* \shu̇k-ā\
Shuk·ri *Arab.* \'shu̇k-rē\
Shū·mei *Jp.* \shu̇-mā\
Shun·ro·ku *Jp.* \shu̇n-rō-ku̇\
Shun·shō *Jp.* \shu̇n-shō\
Shun·sō *Jp.* \shu̇n-sō\
Shū·sei *Jp.* \shu̇s-ā\
Shus·ter \'shüs-tər\
Shū·sui *Jp.* \shu̇-swē\
Shu·zo *Jp.* \shu̇z-ō\
Si·bert \'sī-bərt\
Sib·yl \'sib-ᵊl\
Si·byl·la *Ger.* \zē-'bu̇l-ä\
Si·bylle *Fr.* \sē-bēl\
Sid \'sid\
Sid·dons \'sid-ᵊnz\
Si·dey \'sī-dē\
Sid·ney \'sid-nē\
Si·do·nie 1 *Fr.* \sē-dȯ-nē\ 2 *Ger.* \zē-'dō-nē-ə\
Si·dô·nio *Port.* \sē-'t̲hōn-yü\
Sieg·bert *Ger.* \'zek̲-ˌbert\
Sieg·fried 1 \'sig-ˌfrēd, 'sēg-\ 2 *Ger.* \'zek̲-ˌfrēt\
Sieg·mund *Ger.* \'zēk̲-mu̇nt\
Sient·je *Du.* \'sēn-chə\
Sif·frein *Fr.* \sē-fraⁿ\
Si·ful *Norw.* \'sif-fu̇l\
Sig·björn, -bjørn *Norw.* \'sig-byœrn\
Sig·frid *Ger.* \'zēk̲-ˌfrēt\
Sig·fús *Icel.* \'sik̲-füs\
Si·gis·bert *Fr.* \sē-zhēz-ber\
Si·gis·mon·do *Ital.* \ˌsē-jēz-'mōn-dō\
Sig·is·mund 1 \'sig-ə-smənd, ˌsij-\ 2 **Si·gis·mund** *Ger.* \'zē-gis-ˌmu̇nt\ 3 *Swed.* \'sē-gis-(ˌ)mənd\
Sig·mund 1 \'sig-mənd\ 2 *Ger.* \'zēk̲-mu̇nt\
Sig·ni·us *Dan.* \'sēg-nē-ūs\
Si·grid 1 *Ger.* \'zē-grit, -ˌgrēt\ 2 *Norw.* \'sig-rē\ 3 *Swed.* \'sē-grid\
Si·gurd *Norw.* \'sig-gu̇rd\
Si-hyŏng *Kor.* \sē-hyəŋ\
Si·las \'sī-ləs\
Sil·frède *Fr.* \sēl-fred\
Silk \'silk\
Sil·li·man \'sil-ə-mən\
Sil·vain *Fr.* \sēl-vaⁿ\
Sil·van \'sil-vən\
Sil·va·nus \sil-'vā-nəs\
Sil·ves·tre 1 *Fr.* \sēl-vestrᵊ\ 2 *Span.* \sēl-'b̲ā-strā\
Sil·ves·tro *Ital.* \sēl-'ves-trō\
Sil·vio 1 *Ger.* \'zil-(ˌ)vyō, -vē-(ˌ)ō\ 2 *Ital.* \'sēl-vyō\
Sim \'sim\
Si·ma·nas *Lith.* \si-'män-äs\
Sime \'sīm\
Sim·e·on 1 \'sim-ē-ən\ 2 **Si·me·on** *Russ.* \syim-yi-'ȯn\ 3 *Span.* \sē-mā-'ōn\ 4 *Fr.* **Si·mé·on** \sē-mā-ōⁿ\
Si·mon 1 \'sī-mən\ 2 *Fr.* \sē-mōⁿ\ 3 *Ger.* \'zē-mȯn\ 4 *Russ.* \'syē-mən\ 5 *Serb.-Cr.* \'sē-mȯn\ 6 *Span.* **Si·món** \sē-'mȯn\
Si·monde *Fr.* \sē-mōⁿd\
Si·monds \'sī-mən(d)z, 'sim-ən(d)z\
Si·mo·ne *Ital.* \sē-'mō-nā\
Si·mos *Mod. Gk.* \'sē-(ˌ)mȯs\
Sim·plice *Fr.* \saⁿ-plēs\
Sin·gle·ton \'siŋ-gəl-tən\
Si·ni·bal·do *Ital.* \ˌsē-nē-'bäl-dō\
Sinks \'siŋks\
Siôn *Welsh* \'shän, 'shȯn\
Sis·ley \'siz-lē, 'sis-\

Sis·to *Ital.* \'sēs-tō\
Sit·ling·ton \'sit-liŋ-tən\
Si·vert·sen *Norw.* \'sē-vərt-sən\
Sjoerd *Du.* \'shü(ə)rt\
Sjoerds *Du.* \'shürts\
Skar·bek *Pol.* \'skär-bek\
Skeele \'skē(ə)l\
Skel·ton \'skelt-ᵊn\
Skene \'skēn\
Sla·ter \'slāt-ər\
Slee·per \'slē-pər\
Sli·dell \'slīd-ᵊl, slī-'del\
Slings·by \'sliŋz-bē\
Sloan, Sloane \'slōn\
Sloat \'slōt\
Slo·bo·dan *Serb.-Cr.* \slò-'bò-dàn\
Slo·cum \'slō-kəm\
Smed·ley \'smed-lē\
Smi·ley \'smī-lē\
Smith 1 \'smith\ 2 *Dan.* \'smēt\
Smythe \'smīth, smīth\
Snave·ly \'snāv-lē\
Snell *Du.* \'snel\
Snow·den \'snōd-ᵊn\
Sny·der \'snīd-ər\
Soame \'sōm\
So·bi·es·ki \,sō-bē-'es-kē\
Soc·ra·tes 1 \'säk-rə-,tēz\ 2 *Mod. Gk.* **So·cra·tes** \sòk-'rä-(,)tēs\
Sō·eki *Jp.* \sō-ek-ē\
So·fia *Swed.* \sù-'fē-à\
So·fo·nis·ba *Ital.* \,sō-fō-'nēz-bä\
So·fus *Dan., Norw.* \'sō-fùs\
Sof·ya *Russ.* \'sòf-yə\
Sō·gi *Jp.* \sō-gē\
So·hō *Jp.* \sō-hō\
Sō·i·chi·ro *Jp.* \sō-ē-chē-rō\
So·journ·er \'sō-,jər-nər, sō-'\
Sok *Kor.* \sòk\
Sok-chīn *Kor.* \sòk-chēn\
Sō·ki·chi *Jp.* \sō-kē-chē\
So·kō *Jp.* \sō-kō\
Sol \'säl\
So·la·no *Span.* \sō-'län-ō\
So·lis \'sō-ləs\
Sol·li·us *Lat.* \'säl-ē-əs\
Sol·o·mon \'säl-ə-mən\
So·lo·mo·no·vich *Russ.* \sə-(,)lə-'mòn(-əv)-,yich\
So·lon \'sō-lən, -,län\
Sol·y·man \'säl-i-mən\
So·mhair·le *Ir. Gael., Sc. Gael.* \'sò(-və)r-lə\
Sŏn *Kor.* \sən\
Son·to·ku *Jp.* \sōn-tō-kù\
So·nya *Russ.* \'sòn-yə\
So·phia 1 \sə-'fē-ə, -'fī-; 'sō-fē-ə\ 2 *Dan., Swed.* \sù-'fē-à\ 3 *Ger.* \zō-'fē-ä\ 4 *Russ.* \'sòf-yə\
So·phie 1 \'sō-fē\ 2 *Fr.* \sò-fē\ 3 *Ger.* \zō-'fē(-ə)\ 4 *Swed.* \sù-'fē\
So·phus 1 \'sō-fəs\ 2 *Dan., Norw.* \'sō-fùs\ 3 *Ger.* \'zō-fùs\
So·rai *Jp.* \sō-rī\
Sö·ren *Dan.* \'sœ-rən\
Sø·ren·sen *Dan.* \'sœ-rən-sən\
Sor·ley \'sòr-lē\
Sō·se·ki *Jp.* \sō-sek-ē\
Sos·the·nes \'säs-thə-,nēz\
Sō·ta·rō *Jp.* \sō-tä-rō\
So·to·ki·chi *Jp.* \sō-tō-kē-chē\
Sou·thall \'saù-,thòl\
South·cote \'saùth-kət, -,kōt\
South·er·den \'səth-ər-dən\
South·gate \'saùth-,gāt, -gət\
Sow·den \'saùd-ᵊn\
Spahr \'spär\
Spar·row \'spar-(,)ō\
Speak·man \'spēk-mən\
Spear \'spi(ə)r\
Spear·man \'spi(ə)r-mən\
Speed \'spēd\
Speirs \'spi(ə)rz\
Spence \'spen(t)s\
Spen·cer, Spen·ser \'spen(t)-sər\
Sper·ry \'sper-ē\
Sphere \'sfi(ə)r\
Spi·cer \'spī-sər\
Spi·nel·lo *Ital.* \spē-'nel-lō\
Sprague \'sprāg\
Sprang·er \'sprān-jər, 'spraŋ-ər\
Sprigg \'sprig\
Spring \'spriŋ\
Spur·geon \'spər-jən\
Spu·ri·us *Lat.* \'spyùr-ē-əs\
Spy·ri·don *Mod. Gr.* \spē-'rē-(,)thòn\
Spy·ros *Gk.* \'spē-rōs\
Squire \'skwī(ə)r\
Sta·cey, Sta·cy \'stā-sē\
Stan·bor·ough \'stan-,bər-ə, -,bə-rə, -brə\
Stan·bur·rough \'stan-,bər-ə, -,bə-rə, -brə\
Stan·dish \'stan-dish\
Sta·nis·lao *Ital.* \,stän-ēz-'lä-ō\
Stan·is·las 1 \'stan-ə-,slòs, -,släs\ 2 *Fr.* \stà-nē-släs\
Stan·is·laus 1 \'stan-ə-,slòs\ 2 *Ger.* \'shtän-is-,laùs, 'stän-\
Sta·ni·slav *Czech* \'stàn-yis-,làf\
Sta·ni·sław *Pol.* \stà-'nē-slàf\
Stan·ko *Serb.-Cr.* \'stàŋ-kò\
Stan·lake \'stan-,lāk\
Stan·ley \'stan-lē\
Stan·nard \'stan-ərd\
Stan·nus \'stan-əs\
Stans·bur·y \'stanz-,ber-ē, -b(ə-)rē\
Stan·ton \'stant-ᵊn, *Brit also* 'stän-\
Stan·wood \'stan-wùd\
Stan·yan \'stan-yən\
Sta·ples \'stā-pəlz\
Sta·ple·ton \'sta-pəl-tən\
Stapp \'stap\
Starck, Stark, Starke \'stärk\
Star·key \'stär-kē\
Star·ling \'stär-liŋ\
Star·rett \'star-ət\
Staugh·ton \'stòt-ᵊn\
Stearns \'stərnz\
Steb·bins \'steb-ənz\
Sted·man \'sted-mən\
Steel, Steele \'stē(ə)l\
Steen *Dan.* \'stin\
Steen·berg *Dan.* \'stin-,be(ə)rḡ\
Steen·sen *Dan.* \'stin-sən\
Ste·fan 1 *Bulg., Pol.* \'stef-(,)àn\ 2 *Ger.* \'shtef-än\ 3 *Rom.* **Şte·fan** \shte-'fän\
Ste·fa·no *Ital.* \'stā-fän-(,)ō, 'stef-än-\
Ste·fa·no·vić *Serb.-Cr.* \ste-'fà-nò-,vētʸ\
Ste·fa·no·vich *Bulg.* \ste-'fàn-ò-,vēch\
Stein 1 \'stīn\ 2 *Norw.* \'stān\
Stei·ner \'stī-nər\
Stein·grí·mur *Icel.* \'stīn-ḡrē-mœr\
Stel·la \'stel-ə\
Sten *Norw., Swed.* \'stān\
Sté·nio *Fr.* \stān-yō\
Sten·ka *Russ.* \'styen-kə\
Ste·pan 1 *Russ.* \styi-'pàn\ 2 *Serb.-Cr.* \'step-àn\
Ste·pa·no·vich *Russ.* \styi-'pàn(-əv)-,yich\
Ste·phan 1 *Ger.* \'shtef-än\ 2 *Norw.* \'stā-fän\
Sté·phane *Fr.* \stā-fàn\
Sté·pha·nie *Fr.* \stā-fà-nē\
Ste·pha·nos *Mod. Gk.* \'stef-ä-(,)nòs\
Ste·pha·nus *Du.* \stā-'fän-ŭes\
Ste·phen 1 \'stē-vən\ 2 *Fr.* \stā-fen\ 3 *Ger.* \'shtef-ən\
Stern·dale \'stərn-dāl\
Ster·ry \'ster-ē\
Steu·art \'st(y)ü-ərt, 'st(y)ù(-ə)rt\
Ste·van *Serb.-Cr.* \'stev-àn\
Ste·vens·zen *Du.* \'stā-vən-sən\
Ste·vens·zoon *Du.* \'stā-vən-sən, -,sòn, -,sōn\
Stew·art \'st(y)ü-ərt, 'st(y)ù(-ə)rt\
Stick·ney \'stik-nē\
Stig *Swed.* \'stē\
Stijn *Du.* \'stīn\
Stile \'stī(ə)l\
Stil·lé \'stil-(,)ā\
Stil·ling·fleet \'stil-iŋ-,flēt\
Still·man \'stil-mən\
Still·son \'stil-sən\
Still·well, Stil·well \'stil-,wel, -wəl\
Stje·pan *Serb.-Cr.* \'styep-àn\
Stock·man \'stäk-mən\
Stod·art \'städ-ərt\
Stod·dert \'städ-ərt\
Sto·jan *Serb.-Cr.* \'stò-yàn\
Stop·ford \'stäp-fərd\
Storm \'stò(ə)rm\
Stor·row \'stär-ō\
Storrs \'stō(ə)rz, 'stò(ə)rz\
Stow·ell \'stō-əl\
Sto·yan *Bulg.* \stò-'yàn\
Stoy·chev *Bulg.* \'stòi-chəf\
Strachan \'stròn, 'sträk-ən\
Strat·ford \'strat-fərd\
Stra·thern \strath-'ern, strə-'thərn\
Stree·ter \'strēt-ər\
Striery \'stri(ə)r-ē\
String·er \'striŋ-ər\
String·fel·low \'striŋ-fel-ō\
Strud·wick \'strəd-wik\
Struth·ers \'strəth-ərz\
Strutt \'strət\
Stu·art \'st(y)ü-ərt, 'st(y)ù(-ə)rt\
Stud·dert \'stəd-ərt\
Sturge \'stərj\
Stur·ges \'stər-jəs\
Styles \'stī(ə)lz\
Sub·has *Bengali* \s(h)ùb-'häsh\
Su·dan *Bengali* \'sü-dòn\
Sud·dards \'səd-ərdz\
Sudre *Fr.* \sǖdrᵊ\
Su·eo *Jp* \sù-e-ō\
Suk·e·ha·chi·ro *Jp.* \sùk-e-hä-chē-rō\
Su·ke·no·bu *Jp.* \sùk-e-nō-bù\
Su·ke·no·ri *Jp.* \sùk-en-ō-rē\
Şü·krü *Turk.* \shǖ-'krǖ\
Su·lei·man *Turk.* \sǖ-lā-'män\
Sul·pice *Fr.* \sǖl-pēs\
Sul·pi·ci·us \səl-'pish(-ē)-əs\
Su·mi·to·mo *Jp.* \sùm-ē-tō-mō\
Sum·mers \'səm-ərz\
Sun-chu *Kor.* \sün-chü\
Su·ren·dra·nath 1 *Bengali* \sù-'rān-drò-,nòt, -drə-,nät\ 2 *Hind.* \sə-'ren-drə-,nät\
Sur·ridge \'sər-ij\
Sur·tees \'sər-,tēz\
Su·san \'süz-ᵊn\
Su·san·na, -nah \sü-'zan-ə\
Su·san·ne *Ger.* \zü-'zän-ə\
Su·sette \sù-'zet\
Su·tan *Indonesian* \'sü-,tän\
Su·te·ji·ro *Jp.* \sù-tej-ē-rō\
Su·te·mi *Jp.* \sù-tem-ē\

\ə\ **abut** \ᵊ\ **kitten**, *Fr.* **table** \ər\ **further** \a\ **ash** \ā\ **ace** \ä\ **cot, cart** \aù\ **out** \ch\ **chin** \e\ **bet** \ē\ **easy** \g\ **go** \i\ **hit** \ī\ **ice** \j\ **job** \ŋ\ **sing** \ō\ **go** \ò\ **law** \òi\ **boy** \th\ **both** \th\ **the** \ü\ **loot** \ù\ **foot** \y\ **yet** \zh\ **vision** \à, b, ḡ, k, ⁿ, œ, ǣ, ue, ǖ, ʸ\ *see* Guide to Pronunciation

Su·war·di *Indonesian* \sə-'wär-dē\

Su·zanne 1 \sü-'zan\ 2 *Fr.* \sᵫ-zán\

Su·zor *Fr.* \sᵫ-zȯr\

Su·zu·ki *Jp.* \sùz-ùk-ē\

Sva·ne *Dan.* \'sfän-ə\

Svan·te *Swed.* \'svàn-te\

Sva·to·pluk *Czech.* \'svá-tȯ-ˌplùk\

Svein·björn *Icel.* \'svān-ˌbyœd-^{ə}n\

Sveinn *Icel.* \'svād-^{ə}n\

Sven *Dan., Norw., Swed.* \'sven\

Svend *Dan.* \'sven\

Sver·re *Norw.* \'sver-rə\

Sve·to·zar 1 *Slovak* \'svye-tȯ-zár\ 2 *Serb.-Cr.* \'sve-tȯ-zár\

Swain \'swān\

Swan, Swann \'swän\

Swan·wick \'swän-ik\

Swart·out \'swȯ(ə)rt-ˌau̇t\

Sweet \'swēt\

Sweet·ser \'swēt-sər\

Swett \'swet\

Swin·ner·ton \'swin-ərt-^{ə}n\

Swin·ton \'swint-^{ə}n\

Swyn·fen \'swin-fən\

Syb·il \'sib-əl\

Syd·en·ham \'sid-^{ə}n-əm, -nəm\

Syd·ney \'sid-nē\

Syd·nor \'sid-nər\

Syl·vain *Fr.* \sēl-va^{n}\

Syl·va·nie *Fr.* \sēl-vá-nē\

Syl·va·nus \sil-'vā-nəs\

Syl·vère *Fr.* \sēl-ver\

Syl·ves·ter \sil-'ves-tər\

Syl·ves·tre *Fr.* \sēl-vestr^{ə}\

Syl·via \'sil-vē-ə\

Syl·vio *Ital.* \'sēl-vyō\

Sy·mon *Ukrain.* \'syē-mȯn\

Sy·monds \'sim-ən(d)z, sīm-\

Syng, Synge \'siŋ\

Syng·man *Kor.* \'siŋ-mən, 'sig-\

Szczęs·ny *Pol.* \'shche^{n}s-ni\

Szy·mon *Pol.* \'shim-ȯn\

Ta·ber \'tā-bər\

Tac·ed·din *Turk.* \ˌtäj-ed-'dēn\

Ta·da·hi·ra *Jp.* \tä-dä-hē-rä\

Ta·da·hi·sa *Jp.* \tä-dä-hē-sä\

Ta·da·ku·ni *Jp.* \tä-dä-kùn-ē\

Ta·da·mo·ri *Jp.* \tä-dä-mō-rē\

Ta·dao *Jp.* \tä-dä-ō\

Ta·da·su *Jp.* \tä-dä-sù\

Ta·da·su·ke *Jp.* \tä-dä-sùk-e\

Tad·deo *Ital.* \täd-'de-ō\

Tá·dé *Hung.* \'tá-(ˌ)dā\

Ta·deo *Span.* \tä-'t͟hā-ō\

Ta·de·usz *Pol.* \tá-'de-üsh\

Tadhg *Ir. Gael.* \'thīg, 'thāg, 'tāg\

Ta·fa·wa *Nigerian* \tä-'fä-wä\

Tag·gart \'tag-ərt\

Ta·hu·po·ti·ki *Maori* \ˌtä-hü-pō-'tē-kē\

Tai·ga *Jp.* \tī-gä\

Tai·kan *Jp.* \tī-kän\

Tai·shi *Jp.* \tī-shē\

Tai·su·ke *Jp.* \tī-sùk-e\

Ta·ka·a·ki·ra *Jp.* \tä-kä-ä-kē-rä\

Ta·ka·hi·to *Jp.* \tä-kä-hē-tō\

Ta·ka·ka·zu *Jp.* \tä-kä-kä-zü\

Ta·ka·mi·ne *Jp.* \tä-kä-mē-ne\

Ta·ka·no·ri *Jp.* \täk-ä-nō-rē\

Ta·ka·shi *Jp.* \tä-kä-shē\

Ta·ka·su·ke *Jp.* \tä-kä-sùk-e\

Ta·ka·to·ri *Jp.* \tä-kä-tō-rē\

Ta·ka·to·shi *Jp.* \tä-kä-tō-shē\

Ta·kau·ji *Jp.* \tä-kau̇-jē\

Ta·ka·ya·su *Jp.* \tä-kä-yä-sù\

Ta·ka·yo·shi *Jp.* \tä-kä-yō-shē\

Ta·ke *Rom.* \'täk-e\

Ta·ke·chi·yo *Jp.* \tä-kech-ē-yō\

Ta·keo *Jp.* \tä-ke-ō\

Ta·ki·ji *Jp.* \tä-kē-jē\

Ta·ku·bo·ku *Jp.* \täk-ùb-ō-kù\

Ta·ku·ma *Jp.* \täk-ùm-ä\

Tal·bot, -but \'tȯl-bət, 'tal-\

Tal·cott \'tal-kət, 'tȯl-\

Tal·ia·ferro \'täl-ə-vər\

Tal·lu·lah \tə-'lü-lə\

Tal·madge \'tal-mij\

Ta·ma·ra *Russ.* \(ˌ)tə-'már-ə\

Ta·más *Hung.* \'tä-(ˌ)másh\

Ta·me·chi·ka *Jp.* \tä-mech-ē-kä\

Ta·me·mo·to *Jp.* \tä-mem-ō-tō\

Ta·me·sa·da *Jp.* \tä-mes-ä-dä\

Ta·me·yo·shi *Jp.* \täm-e-yō-shē\

Tan·a·quil·lus *Lat.* \ˌtan-ə-'kwil-əs\

Tan·cred *Finn.* \'tȧŋ-ˌkrād\

Tan·crède *Fr.* \tä^{n}-kred\

Tan·natt \'tan-ət\

Tan·ne·gui *Fr.* \tán-gē\

Tan·ner \'tan-ər\

Tan·worth \'tan-wərth\

Tan·yu *Jp.* \tän-yù\

Tap·pan \'tap-ən\

Tap·ping \'tap-iŋ\

Ta·ras *Russ.* \'tár-əs\

Tar·ie·lo·vich *Russ.* \(ˌ)tər-'yel(-əv)-ˌyich\

Tar·jei *Norw.* \'tär-yā\

Tarle·ton \'tärl-tən\

Ta·ro *Jp.* \tä-rō\

Tar·qui·nio *Port.* \tər-'kwēn-yü; tár-\

Tar·quin·i·us *Lat.* \tär-'kwin-ē-əs\

Tas·ker \'tas-kər\

Tas·si·lo *Ger.* \'täs-ē-(ˌ)lō\

Ta·tsu·ki·chi *Jp.* \tät-sùk-ē-chē\

Tat·sun·o·suke *Jp.* \tät-sùn-ō-sùk-e\

Tat·suo *Jp.* \tät-sù-ō\

Tat·ton \'tat-^{ə}n\

Tau·rus *Lat.* \'tȯr-əs\

Tax·ile *Fr.* \ták-sēl\

Tay·ler, Tay·lor \'tā-lər\

Taze \'tāz\

Ta·zio *Ital.* \'täd-zē-ō\

Te·cum·seh \tə-'kəm(p)-sə, -sē\

Ted \'ted\

Tei·ka *Jp.* \tā-kä\

Tei·ta·rō *Jp.* \tā-tä-rō\

Tei·to·ku *Jp.* \tā-tō-kù\

Te·ja·da *Span.* \tā-'k͟äth-ä\

Te·les·fo·ro *Span.* \tā-lās-'fōr-ō\

Té·les·phore *Fr.* \tā-les-fȯr\

Tell \'tel\

Tem·pler \'tem-plər\

Tench \'tench\

Ten·er \'ten-ər\

Ten·i·son \'ten-ə-sən\

Ten·nes·see \ˌten-ə-'sē, 'ten-ə-ˌ\

Ten·ney \'ten-ē\

Ten·ny·son \'ten-ə-sən\

Te·o·bal·do *Ital.* \ˌtā-ō-'bäl-dō\

Te·o·dor 1 *Pol.* \tē-'ó-dȯr\ 2 *Swed.* \'tā-ō-ˌdȯr\

Te·o·do·ro 1 *Ital.* \ˌtā-ō-'dȯr-ō\ 2 *Span.* \tā-ō-'t͟hōr-ō\

Te·ó·du·lo *Span.* \tā-'ō-t͟hü-lō\

Te·o·fil *Pol.* \te-'ó-fēl\

Te·o·fi·lo 1 *Ital.* \tā-'ó-fē-(ˌ)lō\ 2 *Port.* **Te·ó·fi·lo** \tē-'ó-fē-lü\

Ter·ence \'ter-ən(t)s\

Te·ren·ti·us *Lat.* \tə-'ren-sh(ē-)əs\

Te·ren·zio *Ital.* \tā-'rent-syō\

Te·re·sa 1 \tə-'rē-sə\ 2 *Ital.* \tā-'rez-ä\ 3 *Span.* \tā-'rā-sä\

Ter·rick \'ter-ik\

Ter·rot \'ter-ət\

Ter·ry \'ter-ē\

Te·ru·to·ra *Jp.* \ter-ù-tō-rä\

Ter·zi *Ital.* \'tert-sē\

Tess \'tes\

Tes·sai *Jp.* \tes-sī\

Tes·si·ma \'tes-ə-mə\

Tet·ley \'tet-lē\

Te·tsu·ji·rō *Jp.* \tet-sùj-ē-rō\

Te·tsuo *Jp.* \tet-sü-ō\

Te·tsu·rō *Jp.* \tet-sùr-ō\

Tev·fik, Tew·fik *Turk.* \tev-'fēk\

Thack·er \'thak-ər\

Thad·dä·us *Ger.* \tä-'de-ùs\

Thad·de·us, Thad·e·us \'thad-ē-əs\

Thas·ci·us *Lat.* \'thas-ē-əs\

Thax·ter \'thaks-tər\

The·da \'thād-ə\

Theo 1 \'thē-ō\ 2 *Du.* \'tā-ō\

The·o·bald 1 \'thē-ə-ˌbȯld, 'tib-əld\ 2 *Ger.* \'tā-ō-ˌbält\ 3 *Fr.* **Thé·o·bald** \tā-ó-báld\

Thé·o·de·linde *Fr.* \tā-ód-la^{n}d\

The·o·door *Du.* \'tā-ō-ˌdō(ə)r\

The·o·dor 1 \'thē-ə-ˌdō(ə)r, -ˌdȯ(ə)r, -əd-ər\ 2 *Dan.* \'ti-ō-ˌdȯr\ 3 *Du.* \'tā-ō-ˌdȯr\ 4 *Ger., Norw.* \'tā-ō-ˌdōr\ 5 *Swed.* \'tā-ó-ˌdȯr\ 6 *Fr.* **Thé·o·dor** \tā-ó-dȯr\

The·o·dore 1 \'thē-ə-ˌdō(ə)r, -ˌdȯ(ə)r, -əd-ər\ 2 *Fr.* **Thé·o·dore** \tā-ó-dȯr\

The·od·o·ric 1 \thē-'äd-ə-rik\ 2 *Fr.* **Thé·o·do·ric** \tā-ó-dȯ-rēk\

The·o·do·ros *Mod. Gk.* \the-'ōt͟h-ȯr-ˌȯs\

The·o·do·rus *Lat.* \ˌthē-ə-'dōr-əs\

The·o·do·sia \ˌthē-ə-'dō-sh(ē-)ə\

The·o·do·si·us *Ger.* \ˌtā-ō-'dōz-yùs, -'dō-zē-ùs\

The·od·ric \thē-'äd-rik\

Thé·o·dule *Fr.* \tā-ó-dᵫl\

The·o·phil 1 \'thē-ə-ˌfil\ 2 *Ger.* \'tā-ō-ˌfēl\

Thé·o·phile *Fr.* \tā-ó-fēl\

The·oph·i·lus 1 \thē-'äf-ə-ləs\ 2 **The·o·phi·lus** *Dan.* \tē-'ō-fē-lùs\ 3 *Ger.* \tā-'ō-fē-lùs\

Thé·o·phraste *Fr.* \tā-ó-fràst\

The·o·phra·stus *Ger.* \ˌtā-ō-'fräs-tùs\

The·re·sa 1 \tə-'rē-sə, -zə\ 2 *Fr.* **Thé·ré·sa** \tā-rā-zá\

The·re·se 1 *Ger.* \tā-'rā-zə\ 2 *Fr.* **Thé·rèse** \tā-rez\

Ther·kel *Dan.* \'te(ə)r-kəl\

Theu·nis *Du.* \'tœ-nəs\

Thier·ry *Fr.* \tye-rē\

Thies *Ger.* \'tēs\

Tho·by \'thō-bē\

Thoi·not *Fr.* \twá-nō\

Thom·as 1 \'täm-əs\ 2 **Tho·mas** *Dan.* \'tȯ-ˌmás\ 3 *Du., Ger.* \'tō-ˌmäs\ 4 *Fr.* \tȯ-mä\ 5 *Norw.* \'tȯm-ˌmäs\ 6 *Swed.* \'tü-ˌmás\

Tho·ma·si·ne *Dan.* \ˌtȯ-má-'sē-nə\

Thom·a·son \'täm-ə-sən\

Tho·ralf *Norw.* \'tōr-älf\

Thor·burn \'thȯr-bərn\

Thór·dar·son *Icel.* \'thōr-ˌdär-sȯn\

Thor·kels·son *Icel.* \'thȯr-kels-sōn\

Thor·kild *Dan.* \'tù(ə)r-ˌkē(ə)l\

Thorn·dike \'thȯrn-ˌdīk\

Thorne \'thȯ(ə)rn\

Thor·ney·croft \'thȯr-nə-ˌkrȯft\

Thorn·hill \'thȯrn-ˌhil\

Thorn·well \'thȯrn-ˌwel, -wəl\

Thor·old \'thər-əld\

Thor·stein \'thȯr-ˌstīn\

Thor·steinn *Icel.* \'thȯr-stān\

Thor·vald *Dan.* \'tù(ə)r-ˌvál\

Thor·val·dur *Icel.* \'thȯr-väl-dᵫr\

Thra·sy·bou·los *Mod. Gk.* \thrä-ˈsē-vü-ˌlȯs\
Thresh·ie \ˈthresh-ē\
Throck \ˈthräk\
Thros·by \ˈthräz-bē\
Thu·re *Swed.* \ˈtü-re\
Thur·low \ˈthər-lō\
Thur·man \ˈthər-mən\
Thurs·ton \ˈthərs-tən\
Thy·ra 1 \ˈthī-rə\ 2 *Swed.* \ˈtue̅-rȧ\
Tib·bitts \ˈtib-əts\
Ti·be·rio *Ital.* \tē-ˈber-yō\
Ti·be·ri·us 1 \tī-ˈbir-ē-əs\ 2 *Du.* \tē-ˈbā-rē-ues\
Ti·bur·cio *Span.* \tē-ˈb̲ür-thyō; -syō\
Tier·ney \ˈti(ə)r-nē\
Tif·fa·ny \ˈtif-ə-nē\
Tift \ˈtift\
Ti·kho·no·vich *Russ.* \ˈtyē-k̲ən(-əv)-ˌyich\
Til·ford \ˈtil-fərd\
Till *Ger.* \ˈtil\
Til·ling·hast \ˈtil-iŋ-ˌhast\
Til·loch \ˈtil-ək\
Til·man *Ger.* \ˈtil-(ˌ)män\
Til·ston, Til·stone \ˈtil-stən\
Ti·mo·fey *Russ.* \tyim-(ˌ)ə-ˈfyā\
Ti·mo·fe·ye·vich *Russ.* \tyi-(ˌ)mə-ˈfyā(-yəv)-ˌyich\
Ti·mo·lé·on *Fr.* \tē-mȯ-lā-ō^{n}\
Ti·mo·teo *Ital.* \tē-ˈmȯ-tā-(ˌ)ō\
Ti·mo·thée *Fr.* \tē-mȯ-tā\
Tim·o·thy \ˈtim-ə-thē\
Tim·son \ˈtim(p)-sən\
Ti·na *Ger.* \ˈtē-nä\
Tin·ney \ˈtin-ē\
Tip·la·dy \ˈtip-ˌlā-dē\
Tis·dale \ˈtiz-ˌdāl\
Ti·tian \ˈtish-ən\
Ti·to *Ital.* \ˈtē-tō\
Tits·worth \ˈtits-(ˌ)wərth\
Tit·ta *Ital.* \ˈtēt-tä\
Ti·tus \ˈtī-təs\
Ti·tusz *Hung.* \ˈtit-u̇s\
Ti·va·dar *Hung.* \ˈtiv-ä-ˌdär\
Ti·yo *Xosa* \ˈtē-(y)ō\
Ti·zia·no *Ital.* \tēt-ˈsyän-ō\
Tjal·ling \ˈtyäl-iŋ\
Tjip·to *Indonesian* \ˈchip-tō\
To·bi·as 1 \tə-ˈbī-əs\ 2 *Du., Ger.* \tō-ˈbē-äs\ 3 *Swed.* \tu̇-ˈbē-ȧs\
To·bie, To·by \ˈtō-bē\
Tod, Todd \ˈtäd\
To·de·schi·ni *Ital.* \ˌtō-dā-ˈskē-nē\
Tod·hun·ter \ˈtäd-ˌhən-tər, -ən-\
Tō·fū *Jp.* \tō-fü\
Tō·gan *Jp.* \tō-gän\
Tō·ha·ku *Jp.* \tō-hä-ku̇\
Toirdheal·bhach *Ir. Gael.* \ˈthər-lək̲\
Toi·vo *Finn.* \ˈtȯi-vȯ\
Tō·ju *Jp.* \tō-jü\
To·ki·ha·ra *Jp.* \tō-kē-hä-rä\
To·ki·ma·sa *Jp.* \tō-kē-mä-sä\
To·ki·mune *Jp.* \tō-kē-mu̇n-e\
To·ki·yo·ri *Jp.* \tō-kē-yō-rē\
Tō·ko *Jp.* \tō-kō\
To·ku·su·ke *Jp.* \tō-ku̇s-u̇k-e\
To·ku·ta·rō *Jp.* \tō-ku̇-tä-rō\
Tol·bert \ˈtäl-bərt\
Tom 1 \ˈtäm\ 2 *Dan.* \ˈtȯm\ 3 *Ger.* \ˈtōm\
To·ma *Rom.* \ˈtȯ-mä\
To·más 1 *Span.* \tō-ˈmäs\ 2 *Czech* **To·máš** \ˈtȯ-ˌmäsh\
To·masz *Pol.* \ˈtȯ-mȧsh\
To·maz *Port.* \tü-ˈmȧsh\
Tom·kyns \ˈtäm-kənz\
Tom·ma·so *Ital.* \tōm-ˈmäz-ō\
To·mo·mi *Jp.* \tō-mō-mē\
To·mo·sa·bu·ro *Jp.* \tō-mō-sä-bu̇-rō\
To·mo·yu·ki *Jp.* \tō-mō-yu̇k-ē\
To·ny 1 \ˈtō-nē\ 2 *Fr.* \tȯ-nē\
Top·ham \ˈtäp-əm\
Top·ping \ˈtäp-iŋ\
Tor *Swed.* \ˈtür\
To·ra·chi·yo *Jp.* \tō-rä-chē-yō\
Tor·bern *Swed.* \ˈtȯr-bərn\
Tor·cua·to *Span.* \tȯr-ˈkwä-tō\
To·re *Norw.* \ˈtōr-ə\
To·ri *Jp.* \tō-rē\
To·ri·bio *Span.* \tō-ˈrēb̲-yō\
Tor·nov \ˈtȯr-(ˌ)nȯf\
Tor·qua·to *Ital.* \tōr-ˈkwä-tō\
To·sa *Jp.* \tō-sä\
To·shi·a·ki *Jp.* \tō-shē-ä-kē\
To·shi·hi·ko *Jp.* \tō-shē-hē-kō\
To·shi·ka·zu *Jp.* \tō-shē-käz-u̇\
To·shi·mi·chi *Jp.* \tō-shē-mē-chē\
To·shio *Jp.* \tō-shē-ō\
To·shi·rō *Jp.* \tō-shē-rō\
Tō·son *Jp.* \tō-sōn\
Tou·mi *Finn.* \ˈtō-mē\
Tous·saint *Fr.* \tü-sa^{n}\
Tou·tant *Fr.* \tü-tä^{n}\
Tov *Yiddish* \ˈtȯv\
To·yo·hi·ko *Jp.* \tō-yō-hē-kō\
To·yo·ku·ni *Jp.* \tō-yō-ku̇n-ē\
To·yo·shi·ge *Jp.* \tō-yō-shē-ge\
To·yo·to·mi *Jp.* \tō-yō-tō-mē\
Tra·cey, Tra·cy \ˈtrā-sē\
Traf·ford \ˈtraf-ərd\
Tra·ia·no *Ital.* \trä-ˈyän-ō\
Trau·gott *Ger.* \ˈtrau̇-ˌgȯt\
Treat \ˈtrēt\
Tre·bo·ni·a·nus *Lat.* \trə-ˌbō-nē-ˈā-nəs\
Tre·law·ney \trē-ˈlȯ-nē\
Trem·bly \ˈtrem-blē\
Tre·me·heere \ˈtrē-mən-ˌhi(ə)r\
Tren·chard \ˈtren-chərd, -ˌchärd, -shərd, -ˌshärd\
Tre·vel·yan \tri-ˈvel-yən, -ˈvil-\
Trev·or \ˈtrev-ər\
Trick \ˈtrik\
Trigg \ˈtrig\
Trim·ble \ˈtrim-bəl\
Tri·stan 1 *Fr.* \trē-stä^{n}\ 2 *Rom.* \trē-ˈstän\ 3 *Span.* \trēs-ˈtän\
Tris·tão *Port.* \trēsh-ˈtau̇^{n}; trēs-\
Tris·tram \ˈtris-trəm\
Triv·ett \ˈtriv-ət\
Trix·ie \ˈtrik-sē\
Tro·phime *Fr.* \trȯ-fēm\
Trot·wood \ˈträt-wu̇d\
Troy \ˈtrȯi\
True \ˈtrü\
Tru·fant \ˈtrü-fənt\
Tru·man \ˈtrü-mən\
Trus·ler \ˈtrəs-lər\
Trus·low \ˈtrəs-ˌlō\
Tryg·gve *Norw.* \ˈtrueg-və\
Tryg·ve *Norw.* \ˈtrueg-və\
Tser·claes *Flem.* \tser-ˈklȧs\
Tshe·ki·so *Tswana* \chā-ˈkē-zō\
Tsug·u·ha·ru *Jp.* \tsu̇g-u̇-här-u̇\
Tsug·uji *Jp.* \tsu̇g-u̇j-ē\
Tsu·ma *Jp.* \tsu̇m-ä\
Tsu·na·yo·shi *Jp.* \tsu̇n-ä-yō-shē\
Tsu·nen·o·ri *Jp.* \tsu̇n-en-ō-rē\
Tsu·neo *Jp.* \tsu̇n-e-ō\
Tsun·e·to·ki *Jp.* \tsu̇n-e-tō-kē\
Tsu·ra·yu·ki *Jp.* \tsu̇r-ä-yu̇k-ē\
Tsu·yo·shi *Jp.* \tsu̇-yō-shē\
Tu·an·ku *Indonesian* \ˈtwäŋ-kü\
Tu·dor 1 \ˈt(y)üd-ər\ 2 *Rom.* \ˈtü-dȯr\
Tuf·nell \ˈtəf-nəl\
Tuf·ton \ˈtəf-tən\
Tu·ka·ji *Marathi* \ˈtu̇k-äj-ē\
Tul·lio *Ital.* \ˈtül-lyō\
Tul·li·us *Lat.* \ˈtəl-ē-əs\
Tul·ly \ˈtəl-ē\
Tun *Malay* \ˈtu̇n\
Tu·nis \ˈt(y)ü-nəs\
Tun·stall \ˈtən-st^{ə}l, -ˌstȯl\
Tur·ber·ville \ˈtər-bər-ˌvil, -vəl\
Tu·re *Swed.* \ˈtü-re\
Ture·man \ˈt(y)u̇r-mən\
Tur·lough *Ir. Gael.* \ˈthu̇r-(ˌ)lō\
Tur·ney \ˈtər-nē\
Tur·pin \ˈtər-pən\
Tu·ru·pa *Maori* \tü-ˈrü-pä\
Tut·tle \ˈtət-^{ə}l\
Tu·ve *Swed.* \ˈtü-ve\
Twi·ning \ˈtwī-niŋ\
Ty \ˈtī\
Ty·as \ˈtī-əs\
Ty·cho 1 *Dan.* \ˈtue̅-(ˌ)kō\ 2 *Ger.* \ˈtue̅-(ˌ)k̲ō\
Tyng \ˈtiŋ\
Ty·ran·ni·us *Lat.* \ti-ˈran-ē-əs\
Ty·ree \ti-ˈrē\
Ty·rone \ˈtī-ˌrōn, ti-ˈ; tir-ˈōn\
Ty·rus \ˈtī-rəs\
Tyr·whitt \ˈtir-ət\
Ty·son \ˈtīs-^{ə}n\
Tzevi *Heb.* \ˈtsev-ē\

Ubal·do *Ital.* \ü-ˈbäl-dō\
Ub·bo *Du.* \ˈueb-(ˌ)ō\
Uber·ti·no *Ital.* \ˌü-bär-ˈtē-nō\
Uber·to *Ital.* \ü-ˈber-tō\
Udal·ri·cus *Lat.* \ˌyüd-^{ə}l-ˈrī-kəs\
Uday *Bengali* \u̇-ˈdī\
Ugo *Ital.* \ˈü-gō\
Ugo·li·no *Ital.* \ˌü-gō-ˈlē-nō\
Uguc·cio·ne *Ital.* \ü-güt-ˈchō-nā\
Uh·ler \ˈyü-lər\
Ulf \ˈu̇lf\
Ulick \ˈyü-lik\
Uli·ses *Span.* \ü-ˈlē-säs\
Ulis·se *Ital.* \ü-ˈlēs-sā\
Ul·pi·us *Lat.* \ˈəl-pē-əs\
Ul·ric \ˈəl-rik\
Ul·rich 1 \ˈəl-rik\ 2 *Fr.* \ue̅l-rēk\ 3 *Ger.* \ˈu̇l-rik̲\
Ul·rik 1 *Norw.* \ˈu̇l-rik\ 2 *Swed.* \ˈəl-rik\
Ul·ri·ka 1 *Finn.* \ˈu̇l-ˌrē-kȧ\ 2 *Swed.* \əl-ˈrē-kȧ\
Ul·ri·ke *Ger.* \u̇l-ˈrē-kə\
Ulysse *Fr.* \ue̅-lēs\
Ulys·ses 1 \yu̇-ˈlis-(ˌ)ēz\ 2 *Ger.* \ü-ˈlues-es\
Uma·ko *Jp.* \u̇m-ä-kō\
Um·ber·to *Ital.* \üm-ˈber-tō\
Una \ˈyü-nə\
Un·win \ˈən-wən\
Up·ham \ˈəp-əm\
Ur·bain *Fr.* \ue̅r-ba^{n}\
Ur·ba·no *Ital.* \ür-ˈbän-ō\
Ur·ba·nus *Ger.* \u̇r-ˈbän-u̇s\
Ur·ho \ˈu̇r-hȯ\
Uri·ah \yə-ˈrī-ə\
Uri·an \ˈyu̇r-ē-ən\
Uri·el *Port.* \ür-ˈyel\
Ur·jö *Finn.* \ˈu̇r-ˌyœ\
Urs *Ger.* \ˈu̇rs\
Ur·su·la 1 \ˈər-sə-lə\ 2 *Ital.* \ˈür-sü-(ˌ)lä\
Ur·syn *Pol.* \ˈür-sin\

Ush·er \'əsh-ər\
Us·ta·zade *Fr.* \ᵫ-stá-zád\
Ustick \'yü-stik\
Uta·ga·wa *Jp.* \ü-tä-gä-wä\
Uve·dale \'yüv-ˌdāl\

Va·ca·nar·at \ˌvak-ə-'nar-ət\
Va·chel \'vā-chəl\
Vá·clav *Czech* \'vät-ˌsláf\
Va·di·no *Ital.* \vä-'dē-nō\
Vagn *Swed.* \'väŋn\
Vail \'vā(ə)l\
Väi·nö *Finn.* \'vā-nœ\
Va·lan·cy \və-'lan(t)-sē\
Val·de·mar 1 *Dan.* \'väl-də-ˌmär\ 2 *Swed.* \'väl-də-ˌmär\
Val·di·mer \'val-də-mər, 'vòl-\
Va·len·tin 1 *Fr.* \vá-lä^{n}-ta^{n}\ 2 *Ger.* \'väl-en-ˌtēn\ 3 *Serb.-Cr.* \'vál-en-ˌtēn\ 4 *Span.* **Va·len·tín** \bäl-ān-'tēn\
Va·len·ti·na *Ital* \ˌväl-ān-'tē-nä\
Val·en·tine 1 \'val-ən-ˌtīn\ 2 *Ger.* **Va·len·ti·ne** \ˌvä-len-'tē-nə\
Va·len·ti·no *Ital.* \ˌväl-ān-'tē-nō\
Va·len·ti·no·vich *Russ.* \vəl-yin-'tyēn(-əv)-ˌyich\
Va·lé·rand *Fr.* \vá-lā-rä^{n}\
Va·lère *Fr.* \vá-ler\
Va·le·ria \və-'lir-ē-ə\
Va·le·ria·no *Span.* \bäl-ār-'yän-ō\
Va·le·ri·a·nus *Lat.* \və-ˌlir-ē-'ā-nəs\
Va·lé·rie *Fr.* \vá-lā-rē\
Va·le·rio *Ital.* \vä-'ler-yō\
Va·le·ri·us 1 *Ger.* \vä-'lā-rē-ùs\ 2 *Lat.* \və-'lir-ē-əs\
Va·le·ry, -ri 1 *Russ.* \(ˌ)vəl-'yer-yəi\ 2 *Fr.* **Va·lé·ry** \vá-lā-rē\
Val·labh·bhai *Gujarati* \'vəl-ləb-'bä-ē\
Val·lance \'val-ən(t)s\
Val·py \'val-pē\
Van \'van\
Van Bu·ren \van-'byür-ən, vən-\
Vance \'van(t)s\
Van·cou·ver \van-'kü-vər\
Van·der·burg \'van-dər-ˌbərg\
Van·de·veer \'van-də-ˌvi(ə)r\
Van Do·ren \van-'dōr-ən, vən-, -'dòr-\
Van·dyke, Van Dyke \van-'dīk, vən-\
Van·es·sa \və-'nes-ə\
Van Ness \van-'(n)es\
Van Nest \van-'(n)est\
Van·ne·var \və-'nē-vär\
Van·ni *Ital.* \'vän-nē\
Van·noc·cio *Ital.* \vän-'nōt-chō\
Van Nos·trand \van-'nō-strənd\
Van·noy \və-'nòi\
Van Rens·se·laer \ˌvan-ˌren(t)-sə-'li(ə)r, -ˌren-'sli(ə)r, vən-; -'ren(t)-s(ə-)lər\
Van·sit·tart \van-'sit-ərt\
Van Wyck \van-'wīk\
Var·dis \'vär-dəs\
Va·ri·na \və-'rē-nə\
Var·i·us *Lat.* \'var-ē-əs\
Var·let *Fr.* \vár-le\
Var·num \'vär-nəm\
Va·sa \'vä-sə, -zə\
Vas·co 1 *Port.* \'vásh-kü; 'vás-\ 2 *Span.* \'väs-kō\
Va·sil *Bulg.* \vá-'sēl\
Va·si·le *Rom.* \vä-'sē-le\
Va·si·ly, Vas·si·ly, -li *Russ.* \(ˌ)vəs-'yēl-yəi\
Va·sil·ye·vich *Russ.* \(ˌ)vəs-'yēl(-yiv)-ˌyich\
Va·si·lyev·na *Russ.* \(ˌ)vəs-'yil-yəv-nə\
Vas·lav *Russ.* \(ˌ)vət-'sláf\
Vás·quez \'bäs-kāth; -kās\
Vas·sall \'vas-əl\
Va·tro·slav *Serb.-Cr.* \'vá-trò-ˌsláv\
Vaughan \'vòn, 'vän\
Vea·zey, Vea·zie \'vē-zē\
Veik·ko *Finn.* \'vāk-ˌkò\
Ve·le·mir *Russ.* \'vyel-yim-yir\
Ve·li *Turk.* \ve-'lē\
Ven·a·ble \'ven-ə-bəl\
Ven·a·bles \'ven-ə-bəlz\
Ve·nan·cio *Span.* \bā-'nän-thyō; -syō\
Ve·nan·ti·us *Lat.* \və-'nan-sh(ē-)əs\
Ve·ne·dik·to·vich *Russ.* \vyin-yi-'dyēk-təv-ˌyich, -'dyēk-ˌtyich\
Ven·ga·lil *Marathi* \'veŋ-gə-ˌlil\
Venn \'ven\
Ven·tu·ra *Span.* \bān-'tür-ä\
Ve·nus·tia·no *Span.* \bā-nüs-'tyän-ō\
Ve·ra 1 \'vir-ə\ 2 *Russ.* \'vyer-ə\
Ve·ra·nus \və-'rā-nəs\
Vere \'vi(ə)r\
Ver·gil·i·us *Lat.* \(ˌ)vər-'jil-ē-əs\
Ver·mil·ye \vər-'mil-yə\
Verne \'vərn\
Ver·ner 1 \'vər-nər\ 2 *Swed.* \'ver-nər\
Ver·ney \'vər-nē\
Ver·non \'vər-nən\
Ver·rall \'ve(ə)r-ˌòl\
Ver·ri·us *Lat.* \'ver-ē-əs\
Ver·tu *Fr.* \ver-tᵫ\
Ve·rus *Lat.* \'vir-əs\
Ve·sey \'vē-zē\
Ves·ta \'ves-tə\
Ves·to \'ves-tō\
Vet·ti·us *Lat.* \'vet-ē-əs\
Vet·to·re *Ital.* \vāt-'tō-rā\
Vian·na *Port.* \'vyá-nə; -ná\
Vib·i·us *Lat.* \'vib-ē-əs\
Vic·ars \'vik-ərz\
Vic·a·ry \'vik(-ə)-rē\
Vi·cen·te *Span.* \bē-'thān-tā; -'sān-\
Vi·cen·zo *Ital.* \vē-'chent-sō\
Vicki *Ger.* \'vik-ē\
Vic·toire *Fr.* \vēk-twár\
Vic·tor 1 \'vik-tər\ 2 *Dan.* \'vēk-ˌtòr\ 3 *Fr.* \vēk-tòr\ 4 *Ger.* \'vik-ˌtòr\ 5 *Rom.* \vēk-'tòr\ 6 *Span.* **Víc·tor** \'bēk-tòr\
Vic·to·ria 1 \vik-'tōr-ē-ə, -'tòr-\ 2 *Fr.* \vēk-tòr-yá\ 3 *Ger.* \vik-'tōr-ē-ä\ 4 *Swed.* \vik-'tü-rē-á\
Vic·to·ria·no *Span.* \bēk-tōr-'yän-ō\
Vic·to·rien *Fr.* \vēk-tòr-ya^{n}\
Vic·to·rine *Fr.* \vēk-tò-rēn\
Vic·to·ri·no *Span.* \bēk-tō-'rē-nō\
Vic·tur·nien *Fr.* \vēk-tᵫr-nya^{n}\
Vi·da \'vē-də, 'vī-\
Vid·kun *Norw.* \'vid-(ˌ)kùn\
Viel \'vē(ə)l\
Vie·ri *Ital.* \'vyā-rē\
Viets \'vēts\
Vig·fús·son *Icel.* \'vik-füs-sòn\
Vig·go *Dan.* \'vēg-(ˌ)ō\
Vih·to·ri *Finn.* \'vik-ˌtòr-ē\
Vik·tor 1 *Czech, Ger., Swed.* \'vik-ˌtòr\ 2 *Russ.* \'vyēk-tər\
Vik·to·ro·vich *Russ.* \'vyēk-tər(-əv)-ˌyich\
Vil·brun *Fr.* \vēl-brœ^{n}\
Vil·fre·do *Ital.* \vēl-'frā-dō\
Vil·helm 1 *Dan., Norw.* \'vil-ˌhelm\ 2 *Swed.* \'vil-(h)əlm\
Vil·hel·mi·na *Finn.* \'vil-hel-ˌmē-nä\
Vil·hel·mo·vich *Russ.* \vyil-'yelm(-əv)-ˌyich\
Vil·helms *Latvian* \'vil-helms\
Vil·hjal·mur \'vil-ˌhyaùl-mər\
Vil·jo *Finn.* \'vil-yō\
Vil·lads *Dan.* \'vēl-(ˌ)ás\
Vil·liers \'vil-(y)ərz\
Vil·mos *Hung.* \'vil-(ˌ)mòsh\
Vi·na·yak *Hind.* \vin-ī-'(y)äk\
Vin·cas *Lith.* \'vin-käs\
Vince \'vin(t)s\
Vin·cenc *Czech* \'vint-ˌsents\
Vin·cent 1 *Eng., Norw.* \'vin(t)-sənt\ 2 *Du.* \vin-'sent\ 3 *Fr.* \va^{n}-sä^{n}\
Vin·cente *Eng.* \'vin(t)-sənt\
Vin·cen·ti·us *Lat.* \vin-'sen-sh(ē-)əs\
Vin·cenz *Ger.* \'vint-(ˌ)sents\
Vin·cen·zo *Ital.* \vēn-'chent-sō\
Vin·nie \'vin-ē\
Vin·ti·lă *Rom.* \vēn-'tē-lə\
Vin·ton \'vint-^{ə}n\
Vin·zenz *Ger.* \'vint-(ˌ)sents\
Vi·o·la \vī-'ō-lə, vē-'ō-, 'vī-ə-, 'vē-ə-\
Vi·o·let \'vī(-ə)-lət\
Vip·sa·ni·us *Lat.* \vip-'sā-nē-əs, -'sān-yəs\
Vir *Hind.* \'vir\
Vir·gil \'vər-jəl\
Vir·gile *Fr.* \vēr-zhēl\
Vir·gin·ia 1 \vər-'jin-yə, -'jin-ē-ə\ 2 *Ital.* **Vir·gi·nia** \vēr-'jēn-yä\
Vir·gi·nie *Fr.* \vēr-zhē-nē\
Vir·gi·nio *Ital.* \vēr-'jēn-yō\
Vir·gin·i·us \vər-'jin-yəs, -'jin-ē-əs\
Vis·sa·ri·on *Russ.* \vyis-sər-yi-'òn\
Vis·sar·ri·o·no·vich *Russ.* \vyis-sər-yi-'òn(-əv)-ˌyich\
Vi·tal *Fr.* \vē-tál\
Vi·ta·le *Ital.* \vē-'täl-ā\
Ví·tě·slav *Czech* \'vē-ches-ˌláf\
Vith·thal·bhai *Gujarati* \'vit-təl-'bä-ē\
Vi·to *Ital.* \'vē-tō\
Vit·to·re *Ital.* \vēt-'tō-rā\
Vit·to·ria *Ital.* \vēt-'tòr-yä\
Vit·to·rio *Ital.* \vēt-'tòr-yō\
Vi·tus *Dan.* \'vē-tùs\
Vit·zént·zos *Gk.* \vēt-'sent-sòs\
Vi·vant *Fr.* \vē-vä^{n}\
Viv·i·an \'viv-ē-ən, 'viv-yən\
Vi·vi·gens *Ger.* \'vē-vē-ˌgen(t)s\
Vlad·i·mir 1 \'vlad-ə-ˌmi(ə)r, vlə-'dē-\ 2 **Vla·di·mir** *Russ.* \(ˌ)vlə-'dyēm-yir\ 3 *Serb.-Cr.* \'vlád-ē-ˌmēr\ 4 *Czech* **Vla·di·mír** \'vláj-im-ˌēr\
Vla·di·mi·ro·vich *Russ.* \(ˌ)vlə-'dyēm-yir(-əv)-ˌyich\
Vla·di·slav 1 *Czech* \'vláj-is-ˌláf\ 2 *Russ.* \vlə-dyi-'sláf\
Vla·di·sla·vo·vich *Russ.* \vlə-dyi-'sláv(-əv)-ˌyich\
Vlas·ti·mil *Czech* \'vlás-chim-ˌil\
Vo·ji·slav *Serb.-Cr.* \'vò-yē-ˌsláv\
Voj·těch *Czech* \'vòi-ˌchek\
Vo·kos *Mod. Gk.* \'vòk-(ˌ)òs\
Vol·cher *Du.* \'vòl-kər\
Volck·erts·zoon *Du.* \'vòl-kərt-sən, -ˌsòn, -ˌsōn\
Vol·de·mar *Ger.* \'vòl-də-ˌmär\
Vol·e·ro *Lat.* \'väl-ə-(ˌ)rō\
Volk·mar *Ger.* \'fòlk-ˌmär\
Vol·ko *Ger.* \'fòl-(ˌ)kō\
Vol·lam \'väl-əm\
Vol·ney \'väl-nē\
Vol·rath *Ger.* \'fòl-ˌrät\
Vol·ter *Finn.* \'vòl-ter\
Vos·dan·ig *Arm.* \vòs-'dän-əg\
Vose \'vōz\
Vse·vo·lod *Russ.* \'fsyev-ə-lət\
Vuk *Serb.-Cr.* \'vük\
Vya·che·slav *Russ.* \vyi-chis-'láf\
Vy·ell \'vī-əl\
Vy·ner \'vī-nər\
Vyv·yan \'viv-ē-ən, 'viv-yən\

Wa·cław *Pol.* \ˈväch-ˌläf\
Wad·dy \ˈwäd-ē\
Wad·leigh \ˈwäd-lē\
Wads·worth \ˈwädz-(ˌ)wərth\
Wa·ger \ˈwā-jər\
Wag·ga·man \ˈwag-ə-mən\
Wag·staff \ˈwag-ˌstaf\
Wa·hi·din *Indonesian* \wä-ˈhē-din\
Wait \ˈwāt\
Wake·ley \ˈwāk-lē\
Wake·lin \ˈwāk-lən\
Wake·ly \ˈwāk-lē\
Wake·lyn \ˈwāk-lən\
Wake·man \ˈwak-mən\
Wal·bridge \ˈwȯl-ˌbrij\
Wal·cott \ˈwȯl-kət\
Walde·grave \ˈwȯl-grāv\
Wal·de·mar 1 \ˈwȯl-də-ˌmär\ 2 *Ger., Norw.* \ˈväl-də-ˌmär\
Wal·do \ˈwȯl-(ˌ)dō, ˈwäl-\
Wal·dorf \ˈwȯl-dȯrf\
Wal·er·an \ˈwäl-ər-ən\
Wa·le·ry *Pol.* \vä-ˈler-i\
Wales \ˈwā(ə)lz\
Wal·ford \ˈwȯl-fərd\
Wal·frid *Swed.* \ˈväl-frid\
Wal·house \ˈwȯl-hau̇s\
Walk·er \ˈwȯk-ər\
Wall \ˈwȯl\
Wal·lace \ˈwäl-əs\
Wal·len·sis \wȯ-ˈlen-səs\
Wal·len·stein \ˈwäl-ən-ˌstīn\
Wal·let \ˈwäl-ət\
Wal·lin·ford \ˈwȯl-ən-fərd, -ˌfȯ(ə)rd, -ˌfō(ə)rd\
Wal·rod \ˈwȯl-räd\
Wal·sin *Fr.* \väl-sa^n\
Walt \ˈwȯlt\
Wal·ter 1 \ˈwȯl-tər\ 2 *Ger.* \ˈväl-tər\
Wal·ters \ˈwȯl-tərz\
Wal·ther 1 *Fr.* \väl-ter\ 2 *Ger.* \ˈväl-tər\
Wan·da 1 \ˈwän-də\ 2 *Pol.* \ˈvän-dä\
Ward \ˈwȯ(ə)rd\
War·dell \wȯr-ˈdel\
War·der \ˈwȯrd-ər\
Ware \ˈwa(ə)r, ˈwe(ə)r\
War·ing \ˈwa(ə)r-iŋ, ˈwe(ə)r-\
Wark \ˈwȯrk\
War·mol·dus *Du.* \vär-ˈmȯl-dœs\
Warne \ˈwȯrn\
War·ner \ˈwȯr-nər\
War·ren \ˈwȯr-ən, ˈwär-\
War·ren·der \ˈwär-ən-dər\
War·ring·ton \ˈwär-iŋ-tən\
War·wick \ˈwar-ik, *US also* ˈwȯr-ik, ˈwȯr-(ˌ)wik\
Wash·burn \ˈwäsh-(ˌ)bərn\
Wash·ing·ton \ˈwȯsh-iŋ-tən, ˈwäsh-\
Was·si·ly *Russ.* \(ˌ)vəs-ˈyēl-yəi\
Was·son \ˈwäs-ᵊn\
Wat \ˈwät\
Wat·cyn *Welsh* \ˈwät-kin\
Wa·ter·man \ˈwät-ər-mən, ˈwȯt-\
Wa·ters \ˈwȯt-ərz, ˈwät-\
Wat·kin \ˈwät-kən\
Wat·kins \ˈwät-kənz\
Wat·kiss \ˈwät-kəs\
Wat·ter·son \ˈwät-ər-sən, ˈwȯt-\
Watts \ˈwäts\
Waw·rzy·niec *Pol.* \väv-ˈzhin-yets\
Way \ˈwā\
Way·land \ˈwā-lənd\
Wayne \ˈwān\
Web·ley \ˈweb-lē\
Wed·der·burn \ˈwed-ər-bərn\
Wed·lake \ˈwed-ˌlāk\
Weeks \ˈwēks\
Weet·man \ˈwēt-mən\
Wei·by *Norw.* \ˈvī-bü̅e\
Weight·man \ˈwāt-mən\
Weik·hart *Ger.* \ˈvīk-ˌhärt\
Wel·bore \ˈwel-bō(ə)r\
Wel·burn \ˈwel-bərn\
Wel·by \ˈwel-bē\
Wel·don \ˈwel-dən\
Well·born \ˈwel-bərn\
Wel·ling·ton \ˈwel-iŋ-tən\
Well·man \ˈwel-mən\
Welsh \ˈwelsh\
Wel·tach *Ger.* \ˈvel-ˌtäk\
Wemyss \ˈwēmz\
Wen·ces·lao *Span.* \bān-thā-ˈslä-ō, wān-; bān-sā-, wān-\
Wen·ces·las *Du.* \ˈven-sə-ˌsläs\
Wen·ces·lau *Port.* \ˌvā^n-səzh-ˈlau̇; -säz-\
Wen·ces·laus *Ger.* \ˈvent-sə-ˌslau̇s\
Wen·del 1 \ˈwen-dᵊl\ 2 *Ger.* \ˈven-dəl\
Wen·de·lin *Ger.* \ˈven-də-ˌlēn\
Wen·dell \ˈwen-dᵊl\
Wend·ling *Ger.* \ˈvent-liŋ\
Wen·sel *Du.* \ˈven-səl\
Wen·zel *Ger.* \ˈvent-səl\
Wen·zes·laus *Ger.* \ˈvent-sə-ˌslau̇s\
Wer·ner 1 \ˈwər-nər, ˈvər-\ 2 *Ger., Swed.* \ˈvər-nər\
Wes·ley \ˈwes-lē, ˈwez-\
Wes·paz·jan *Pol.* \ves-ˈpäz-yän\
Wes·sels *Du.* \ˈves-əl(t)s\
West·brook \ˈwest-bru̇k\
Wes·tel \ˈwes-təl\
Wes·ter \ˈwes-tər\
West·land \ˈwest-lənd\
West·ley \ˈwest-lē\
Wes·tren \ˈwes-trən\
Weth·er·bee \ˈwe<u>th</u>-ər-bē\
Wet·more \ˈwet-mō(ə)r\
Wex·els *Norw.* \ˈvek-səls\
Wha·len \ˈhwā-lən\
Whee·lock \ˈhwē-ˌläk, ˈwē-\
Wheel·ton \ˈhwē(ə)lt-ᵊn, ˈwē(ə)lt-\
Whet·ten \ˈhwēt-ᵊn, ˈwēt-\
Whit \ˈhwit, ˈwit\
Whit·a·ker \ˈhwit-ə-kər, ˈwit-\
Whit·bread \ˈhwit-ˌbred, ˈwit-\
Whit·comb \ˈhwit-kəm, ˈwit-\
White·field \ˈhwit-fēld, ˈhwīt-, ˈwit-, ˈwīt-\
White·hill \ˈhwīt-ˌhil, ˈwīt-\
White·law \ˈhwīt-ˌlȯ, ˈwīt-\
Whit·field \ˈhwit-ˌfēld, ˈwit-\
Whit·ford \ˈhwit-fərd, ˈwit-\
Whit·ing \ˈhwīt-iŋ, ˈwīt-\
Whit·ley \ˈhwit-lē, ˈwit-\
Whi·ton \ˈhwīt-ᵊn, ˈwīt-\
Whit·ten \ˈhwit-ᵊn, ˈwit-\
Whit·ti·er \ˈhwit-ē-ər, ˈwit-\
Whit·ting·ham \ˈhwit-iŋ-əm, ˈwit-, -ᵊn-jəm\
Whit·well \ˈhwit-ˌwel, ˈwit-, -wəl\
Wi·chard *Ger.* \ˈvik-ˌärt\
Wickes \ˈwiks\
Wi·gand *Ger.* \ˈvē-ˌgänt\
Wig·gin·ton \ˈwig-ən-tən\
Wig·gles·worth \ˈwig-əlz-ˌwərth\
Wight \ˈwīt\
Wight·man \ˈwīt-mən\
Wil·ber \ˈwil-bər\
Wil·ber·force \ˈwil-bər-ˌfō(ə)rs, -ˌfȯ(ə)rs\
Wil·bert \ˈwil-bərt\
Wil·bor \ˈwil-bər\
Wil·bourne \ˈwil-bərn\
Wil·bur \ˈwil-bər\
Wilds \ˈwī(ə)lds\
Wiles \ˈwī(ə)lz\
Wi·ley \ˈwī-lē\
Wil·ford \ˈwil-fərd\
Wil·fred \wil-frəd\
Wil·frid 1 \ˈwil-frəd\ 2 *Fr.* \wēl-frēd\
Wil·fried *Ger.* \ˈvil-frēt\
Wil·helm 1 *Dan., Ger., Norw.* \ˈvil-ˌhelm\ 2 *Swed.* \ˈvil-(h)əlm\
Wil·hel·ma *Ger.* \vil-ˈhel-mä\
Wil·hel·mi·na 1 \ˌwil-hel-ˈmē-nə\ 2 *Du.* \ˌvil-hel-ˈmē-nä\ 3 *Ger.* \ˌvil-hel-ˈmē-nä\
Wil·hel·mine 1 *Fr.* \vē-lel-mēn\ 2 *Ger.* **Wil·hel·mi·ne** \ˌvil-hel-ˈmē-nə\
Wil·hel·mus *Du.* \vil-ˈhel-mœs\
Wi·li·bald *Ger.* \ˈvil-ē-ˌbält\
Wil·kie \ˈwil-kē\
Will \ˈwil\
Wil·la \ˈwil-ə\
Wil·lans \ˈwil-ənz\
Wil·lard \ˈwil-ərd\
Will·cox \ˈwil-ˌkäks\
Wil·le·brod *Du.* \ˈvil-ə-brȯ(ə)rt\
Wil·le·brord *Du.* \ˈvil-ə-ˌbrȯrd\
Wil·le·bror·dus *Lat.* \ˌwil-ə-ˈbrȯ(ə)r-dəs\
Wil·lem *Du.* \ˈvil-əm\
Wil·let \ˈwil-ət\
Wil·ley \ˈwil-ē\
Wil·li *Ger.* \ˈvil-ē\
Wil·liam 1 \ˈwil-yəm\ 2 *Fr.* \wēl-yäm\
Wil·lia·mi·na \ˌwil-yə-ˈmī-nə\
Wil·li·bald *Ger.* \ˈvil-ē-ˌbält\
Wil·lie \ˈwil-ē\
Wil·lis \ˈwil-əs\
Wil·lis·ton \ˈwil-əs-tən\
Wil·lock \ˈwil-ək\
Will·sie \ˈwil-sē\
Will·son \ˈwil-sən\
Wil·ly 1 \ˈwil-ē\ 2 *Ger.* \ˈvil-ē\
Wil·marth \ˈwil-ˌmärth\
Wil·mer \ˈwil-mər\
Wil·mot \ˈwil-mət\
Wil·shere \ˈwil-shər, -ˌshi(ə)r\
Wil·son \ˈwil-sən\
Wilt·ber·ger \ˈwilt-ˌbər-gər\
Wil·ton \ˈwilt-ᵊn\
Wilts \ˈwilts\
Win·cen·ty *Pol.* \vēnt-ˈsen-ti\
Winck·worth \ˈwiŋk-(ˌ)wərth\
Wind·ham \ˈwin-dəm\
Win·field \ˈwin-ˌfēld\
Win·ford \ˈwin-fərd\
Win·fred \ˈwin-frəd\
Wing \ˈwiŋ\
Win·i·fred \ˈwin-ə-ˌfred, -frəd\
Wink·worth \ˈwiŋk-(ˌ)wərth\
Win·ni·fred \ˈwin-ə-ˌfred, -frəd\
Win·ning·ton \ˈwin-iŋ-tən\
Wi·no·na \wə-ˈnō-nə\
Win·sor \ˈwin(d)-zər\
Win·ston \ˈwin(t)-stən\
Wi·re·mu *Maori* \wir-ˈā-ˌmü\
Wirt \ˈwərt\
Wis·tar, Wis·ter \ˈwis-tər\
Wit *Pol.* \ˈvēt\
With·er·ell \ˈwi<u>th</u>-ər-əl\
With·er·le \ˈwi<u>th</u>-ər-lē\
With·ers \ˈwi<u>th</u>-ərz\
Wit·lam \ˈwit-ləm\
Wit·mer \ˈwit-mər\
Wi·told *Pol.* \ˈvē-tȯld\
Wit·ter \ˈwit-ər\
Wix·om \ˈwik-səm\

\ə\ abut \ᵊ\ kitten, *Fr.* table \ər\ further \a\ ash \ā\ ace \ä\ cot, cart \au̇\ out \ch\ chin \e\ bet \ē\ easy \g\ go \i\ hit \ī\ ice \j\ job \ŋ\ sing \ō\ go \ȯ\ law \ȯi\ boy \th\ both \<u>th</u>\ the \ü\ loot \u̇\ foot \y\ yet \zh\ vision \ȧ, <u>b</u>, <u>g</u>, <u>k</u>, ^{n}, œ, ue̅, ue, ü̅e, ^{y}\ *see* Guide to Pronunciation

Wla·di·mir *Ger.* \vlä-ˈdē-mir\

Wła·dy·sław *Pol.* \vlȧ-ˈdis-lȧf\

Wło·dzi·mierz *Pol.* \vlȯ-ˈjēm-yesh\

Wode·house \ˈwu̇d-ˌhau̇s\

Woj·ciech *Pol.* \ˈvȯi-chek\

Wol·cott \ˈwu̇l-kət\

Wol·de·mar 1 *Finn.* \ˈwȯl-de-ˌmȧr\ 2 *Ger.* \ˈvȯl-de-ˌmär\

Wolf·gang *Ger.* \ˈvȯlf-ˌgäŋ\

Wolf·gang·us *Ger.* \vȯlf-ˈgäŋ-u̇s\

Wol·ter *Du., Ger.* \ˈvȯl-tər\

Wood·bine \ˈwu̇d-ˌbīn\

Wood·bridge \ˈwu̇d-(ˌ)brij\

Wood·burn \ˈwu̇d-bərn\

Wood·bury \ˈwu̇d-ˌber-ē, -b(ə-)rē\

Woodd \ˈwu̇d\

Woodes \ˈwu̇dz\

Wood·field \ˈwu̇d-ˌfēld\

Wood·fin \ˈwu̇d-fən\

Wood·hill \ˈwu̇d-hil\

Wood·ley \ˈwu̇d-lē\

Wood·row \ˈwu̇d-(ˌ)rō\

Wood·ruff \ˈwu̇d-rəf\

Wood·son \ˈwu̇d-sən\

Wood·ville \ˈwu̇d-ˌvil, -vəl\

Wood·worth \ˈwu̇d-(ˌ)wərth\

Woody \ˈwu̇d-ē\

Wooll·gar \ˈwu̇l-ˌgär\

Wool·ston \ˈwu̇l-stən\

Words·worth \ˈwərdz-(ˌ)wərth\

Work \ˈwərk\

Wor·rall \ˈwär-əl\

Wor·thing·ton \ˈwər-thiŋ-tən\

Wort·ley \ˈwərt-lē\

Wou·ter *Du.* \ˈvau̇-tər\

Wrig·ley \ˈrig-lē\

Wriothes·ley \ˈriz-lē, ˈräts-lē\

Wulf \ˈwu̇lf\

Wyc·liffe \ˈwik-ˌlif, -ləf\

Wyke \ˈwīk\

Wyke·ham \ˈwik-əm\

Wyl·lis \ˈwil-əs\

Wy·ly \ˈwī-lē\

Wy·man \ˈwī-mən\

Wy·mark \ˈwī-ˌmärk\

Wym·ber·ley \ˈwim-bər-lē\

Wynd·low \ˈwind-lō\

Wyn·kyn \ˈwiŋ-kən\

Wynne \ˈwin\

Wys·tan \ˈwis-tən\

Wythe \ˈwith\

Xan·thus \ˈzan-thəs\

Xa·ver 1 *Ger.* \ˈksäv-ər, ksä-ˈvär\ 2 *Czech* \ˈksȧ-vər\

Xa·vi·er 1 \ˈzā-vē-ər, ig-ˈzā-\ 2 **Xa·vier** *Fr.* \gzȧv-yā\ 3 *Port.* \shəv-ˈyär; shȧv-\ 4 *Span.* \häv-ˈyer\

Yak-jong *Kor.* \yäk-jȯŋ\

Ya·kov *Russ.* \ˈyȧ-kəf\

Ya·kov·le·vich 1 *Russ.* \ˈyȧ-kəv-lyiv-ˌyich, -kəv-ˌlyich\ 2 *Ukrain.* \ˌyȧ-kȯv-ˈlyev-yich\

Ya·kov·lev·na *Russ.* \(ˌ)yə-ˈkȯv-ləv-nə\

Yá·ñez *Span.* \ˈyän-yāth; -yās\

Yán·nis *Gk.* \ˈyȧn-ēs\

Ya·no·su·ke *Jp.* \yä-nō-su̇k-e\

Ya·nu·ar·ye·vich *Russ.* \yən-yü-ˈär(-yəv)-ˌyich\

Ya·ˈqūb *Arab.* \yȧ-ˈküb\

Yard·ley \ˈyärd-lē\

Ya·su·hi·to *Jp.* \yä-su̇-hē-tō\

Ya·su·ji·ro *Jp.* \yä-su̇j-ē-rō\

Ya·su·ka·ta *Jp.* \yä-su̇k-ä-tä\

Ya·su·ma·sa *Jp.* \yä-su̇m-ä-sä\

Ya·suo *Jp.* \yäs-ü-ō\

Ya·su·shi *Jp.* \yä-su̇-shē\

Ya·sut·o·ki *Jp.* \yä-su̇-tō-kē\

Ya·su·ya *Jp.* \yä-su̇-yä\

Ya·su·yo·shi *Jp.* \yä-su̇-yō-shē\

Ya·ta·rō *Jp.* \yä-tä-rō\

Yates, Yeates \ˈyāts\

Ye·fim *Russ.* \yif-ˈyēm\

Ye·fi·mo·vich *Russ.* \yif-ˈyēm(-əv)-ˌyich\

Ye·fre·mo·vich *Russ.* \yif-ˈryem(-əv)-ˌyich\

Ye·gor *Russ.* \yi-ˈgȯr\

Ye·ḥiel *Heb.* \yə-ˈkēl\

Ye·ka·te·ri·na *Russ.* \yik-ət-yir-ˈyē-nə\

Ye·li·za·ve·ta *Russ.* \yil-yiz-(ˌ)ə-ˈvyā-tə\

Yel·ver·ton \ˈyel-vər-tən\

Ye·mel·yan *Russ.* \yim-yil-ˈyȧn\

Ye·mel·ya·no·vich *Russ.* \yim-yil-ˈyän(-yəv)-ˌyich\

Ye·mil·ye·vich *Russ.* \(ˌ)yim-ˈyil(-yəv)-ˌyich\

Ye·shaia *Heb.* \yə-ˈshī-ə\

Yev·ge·ny *Russ.* \yiv-ˈgyā-nəi\

Yev·gen·ye·vich *Russ.* \yif-ˈgyān(-yiv)-ˌyich\

Yev·gra·fo·vich *Russ.* \yiv-ˈgräf(-əv)-ˌyich\

Yev·se·ye·vich *Russ.* \yif-ˈsyā(-yiv)-ˌyich\

Yig·a·el \ˈyig-ə-el\

Yip·sel \ˈyip-səl\

Yo·it·su *Jp.* \yō-ēt-su̇\

Yo·lande *Fr.* \yȯ-lä^{n}d\

Yom *Yiddish* \ˈyȯm\

Yo·ne *Jp.* \yō-ne\

Yonge \ˈyəŋ\

Yong-un *Kor.* \yȯŋ-ün\

Yor·dan *Bulg.* \ˈyȯr-dən\

Yo·ri·mi·chi *Jp.* \yō-rē-mē-chē\

Yo·ri·no·bu *Jp.* \yō-rē-nō-bu̇\

Yo·ri·to·mo *Jp.* \yō-rē-tō-mō\

Yo·ri·yo·shi *Jp.* \yō-rē-yō-shē\

Yo·sa *Jp.* \yō-sä\

Yo·shi·a·ki *Jp.* \yō-shē-ä-kē\

Yo·shi·fu·sa *Jp.* \yō-shē-fu̇s-ä\

Yo·shi·ie *Jp.* \yō-shē-ē-e\

Yo·shi·ma·sa *Jp.* \yō-shē-mä-sä\

Yo·shi·mi·chi *Jp.* \yō-shē-mē-chē\

Yo·shi·mit·su *Jp.* \yō-shē-mēt-su̇\

Yo·shi·mu·ne *Jp.* \yō-shē-mu̇n-e\

Yo·shi·na·ga *Jp.* \yō-shē-näg-ä\

Yo·shi·no·bu *Jp.* \yō-shē-nō-bu̇\

Yo·shi·no·ri *Jp.* \yō-shē-nō-rē\

Yo·shi·sa·bu·ro *Jp.* \yō-shē-sä-bu̇r-ō\

Yo·shi·sa·da *Jp.* \yō-shē-sä-dä\

Yo·shi·su·ke *Jp.* \yō-shē-su̇k-e\

Yo·shi·to·ki *Jp.* \yō-shē-tō-kē\

Yo·shi·to·mo *Jp.* \yō-shē-tō-mō\

Yo·shi·tsu·ne *Jp.* \yō-shēt-su̇n-e\

Yō·su·ke *Jp.* \yō-su̇k-e\

Youle \ˈyül\

Youngs \ˈyəŋz\

Ysi·dro \ə-ˈsē-drō\

Yu·do·vich *Russ.* \ˈyüd(-əv)-ˌyich\

Yu·ki·chi *Jp.* \yu̇k-ē-chē\

Yu·ki·na·ga *Jp.* \yu̇k-ē-näg-ä\

Yu·ki·na·ri *Jp.* \yu̇k-ē-nä-rē\

Yu·kio *Jp.* \yu̇k-ē-ō\

Yu·ko *Jp.* \yu̇k-ō\

Yu·nus *Turk.* \ˈyü-nu̇s\

Yu·ry *Russ.* \ˈyür-yəi\

Yur·ye·vich *Russ.* \ˈyür(-yiv)-ˌyich\

Yū·shō *Jp.* \yu̇sh-ō\

Yū·suf *Arab.* \ˈyü-su̇f\

Yū·su·ke *Jp.* \yu̇s-u̇k-e\

Yū·zen *Jp.* \yu̇z-en\

Yū·zen·sai *Jp.* \yu̇z-en-sī\

Yū·zō *Jp.* \yu̇z-ō\

Yv·do·ki·ya *Russ.* \yiv-(ˌ)dək-ˈyē-yə\

Yves *Fr.* \ēv\

Yvette *Fr.* \ē-vet\

Yvon *Fr.* \ē-vō^{n}\

Yvonne *Fr.* \ē-vȯn\

Yvor \ˈī-vər, ˈē-ˌvȯ(ə)r\

Zá·boj *Czech* \ˈzä-ˌbȯi\

Zach·a·ri·ah \ˌzak-ə-ˈrī-ə\

Za·cha·ri·as 1 *Du.* \ˌzȧ-kȧ-ˈrē-äs\ 2 *Ger.* \ˌtsäk-ä-ˈrē-äs\

Zach·a·ry \ˈzak-ə-rē\

Zach·ris *Swed.* \ˈsȧk-ris\

Za·de *Turk.* \zä-ˈde\

Za·dock \ˈzā-dək\

Za·kir *Bihari* \ˈzä-kir\

Zane \ˈzān\

Zbig·niew *Pol.* \ˈzbēg-nyev\

Zden·ko *Czech* \ˈzdeŋ-(ˌ)kȯ\

Zeal·ous \ˈzel-əs\

Ze·bi·na \zə-ˈbī-nə\

Zeb·u·lon \ˈzeb-yu̇-lən\

Zech·a·ri·ah \ˌzek-ə-ˈrī-ə\

Ze·lea *Rom.* \ˈzāl-yä\

Zel·ia \ˈzēl-yə, ˈzē-lē-ə\

Zé·lide *Fr.* \zā-lēd\

Ze·mah *Heb.* \ˈzā-ˌmä\

Zen·go *Jp.* \zeŋ-gō\

Ze·nith \ˈzē-nəth, *Can also & Brit usu* ˈzen-əth, -ith\

Zen·ji·rō *Jp.* \zen-jē-rō\

Zé·nobe *Fr.* \zā-nȯb\

Ze·no·bio *Ital.* \dzā-ˈnȯb-yō\

Ze·non 1 *Pol.* \ˈzen-ȯn\ 2 *Span.* **Ze·nón** \thā-ˈnȯn; sā-\

Ze·nus \ˈzē-nəs\

Zeph·a·ni·ah \ˌzef-ə-ˈnī-ə\

Ze·shin *Jp.* \zesh-ēn\

Ze·vi 1 *Heb.* \ˈtsvē\ 2 *Russ.* \ˈzyāv-yi\

Zig·frids *Latvian* \ˈzig-fridz\

Zi·na·i·da *Russ.* \zyi-(ˌ)nə-ˈē-də\

Ži·vo·jin *Serb.-Cr.* \ˈzhēv-ˌȯ-yēn\

Zi·ya *Turk.* \zē-ˈyä\

Zoë, Zoe 1 \ˈzō-ē\ 2 *Fr.* **Zoé** \zȯ-ā\

Zo·fia, Zo·fja *Pol.* \ˈzȯ-fyȧ\

Zoi·la *Span.* \ˈthȯi-lä; ˈsȯi-\

Zol·tán *Hung.* \ˈzȯl-(ˌ)tȧn\

Zo·na \ˈzō-nə\

Zo·ra \ˈzō-rə\

Zo·si·mo *Ital.* \ˈdzȯ-zē-(ˌ)mō\

Zō·zen *Jp.* \zō-zen\

Zsig·mond *Hung.* \ˈzhig-(ˌ)mȯnd\

Zsolt *Hung.* \ˈzhōlt\

Zul·fi·kar *Pakistani* \ˈzül-fi-kär\

Zwier *Du.* \ˈzvē(ə)r\

Zyg·munt *Pol.* \ˈzig-(ˌ)mu̇nt\